APPLETON'S
NEW SPANISH-ENGLISH
AND ENGLISH-SPANISH
DICTIONARY

NUEVO DICCIONARIO
Inglés-Español y Español-Inglés
DE ÁPPLETON

CONTIENE MÁS DE SEIS MIL VOCABLOS MODERNOS Y VEINTICINCO MIL
ACEPCIONES, VOCES TÉCNICAS Y MODISMOS QUE NO SE ENCUENTRAN
EN NINGÚN OTRO DICCIONARIO DE ESTA CLASE, CON LAS FOR-
MAS FUNDAMENTALES DE LOS VERBOS IRREGULARES Y
LA PRONUNCIACIÓN DE CADA PALABRA POR MEDIO
DE UN NUEVO Y SENCILLÍSIMO SISTEMA DE
REPRESENTACIÓN FONÉTICA

POR

ARTURO CUYÁS

Corregido y aumentado

POR

ANTONIO LLANO

TERCERA EDICIÓN, CON SUPLEMENTOS

D. APPLETON–CENTURY COMPANY
INCORPORATED

NEW YORK   LONDON

1942

APPLETON'S NEW

English-Spanish and Spanish-English

DICTIONARY

CONTAINING MORE THAN SIX THOUSAND MODERN WORDS AND TWENTY-
FIVE THOUSAND ACCEPTATIONS, IDIOMS AND TECHNICAL TERMS
NOT FOUND IN ANY OTHER SIMILAR WORK: WITH A PRO-
NOUNCING KEY AND THE FUNDAMENTAL TENSES
OF IRREGULAR VERBS

BY

ARTURO CUYÁS

Revised and enlarged

BY

ANTONIO LLANO

THIRD EDITION, WITH SUPPLEMENTS

D. APPLETON–CENTURY COMPANY

INCORPORATED

NEW YORK   LONDON

1942

PARTE I

INGLÉS–ESPAÑOL

———

PART I

ENGLISH–SPANISH

PREFACIO DE LA PRIMERA EDICIÓN

Los prodigiosos descubrimientos e invenciones que marcan el progreso realizado de medio siglo a esta parte en todos los ramos de la actividad humana, y sus múltiples aplicaciones a los usos de la vida, han enriquecido de tal modo el vocabulario de las lenguas modernas, y muy particularmente de la inglesa, que cada día se hace sentir más la necesidad de un diccionario que responda a las exigencias del creciente intercambio de ideas y productos entre los pueblos de la raza anglosajona y los que hablan la armoniosa lengua castellana.

A mediados del siglo XIX vió la luz el diccionario bilingüe de Velázquez, basado sobre el antiguo de Seoane, Neuman y Baretti, y aumentado con multitud de vocablos que lo ponían a la altura de aquella época.

Cuantos diccionarios se han publicado posteriormente, tanto en Europa como en América, han sido meras copias del famoso léxico de Velázquez, o, a lo sumo, revisiones más o menos concienzudas, con aditamento de algunas palabras modernas. Pero, por muy meritorias que sean algunas de esas revisiones, resultan deficientes en la práctica para los que tienen ocasión de consultar con frecuencia el diccionario.

Esa experiencia ha evidenciado la necesidad de compilar un diccionario bilingüe enteramente nuevo, trazado sobre un patrón más moderno y más exacto que el que ha servido para los publicados hasta hoy día.

El propósito a que se ha ajustado la presente obra ha sido reunir en un volumen manuable el más nutrido, completo y correcto vocabulario de los idiomas inglés y español que pueda hallarse en un diccionario bilingüe, descartando un sinnúmero de arcaísmos, vocablos desusados, provincialismos y palabras de incorrecta ortografía de que suelen estar plagados otros diccionarios y que sólo contribuyen a engrosar su tamaño.

Con este fin, y para que el diccionario resulte enteramente nuevo y contenga los más recientes y autorizados neologismos de uno y otro idioma, el autor ha adoptado como base y punto de partida, para la parte española-inglesa, la reciente edición del Diccionario de la Academia, transcribiendo palabra por palabra cuantos vocablos contiene aquel léxico, así como todos los más usuales modismos, con la sola excepción de las voces anticuadas y de las que han caído totalmente en desuso, y anotando los equivalentes ingleses de las diversas acepciones de cada palabra. Igual procedimiento se ha seguido para la parte inglesa-española, sirviendo de base el admirable *Standard Dictionary*, también de reciente publicación, cuyos vocablos, acepciones y modismos se han transcrito con sus equivalencias castellanas.

El convencimiento de que el oficio y la verdadera utilidad de todo diccionario bilingüe consisten en dar equivalencias en lugar de definiciones, que en nada auxilian al traductor y que éste puede buscar en el diccionario de su propio idioma, ha hecho necesaria una cuidadosa y ardua labor de investigación para hallar los equivalentes exactos en una y otra lengua, especialmente de las voces de tecnología científica y de los tecnicismos mercantiles e industriales que en gran número se han incluído en esta obra, por considerarlos de suma utilidad, dado el creciente desarrollo de las relaciones entre los Estados Unidos y los países hispanoamericanos.

Para tener una idea de lo nutrida que va esta obra en punto a tecnicismos, bastará cotejar las voces cuyas raíces son *electr-, hydr-, micro-, photo-,* con las de otros diccionarios bilingües, sin contar los innumerables términos que figuran entre las acepciones de muchos vocablos y cuyo carácter técnico se indica por medio de una abreviatura entre paréntesis, lo cual, sobre economizar espacio y hacer inútiles otras explicaciones, es de gran auxilio para el traductor.

En otro punto esencial difiere esta obra de todos los diccionarios bilingües publicados hasta la fecha, y es en el sistema de anotación fonética adoptado para representar la pronunciación inglesa. Tras un estudio detenido de este importantísimo punto y después de examinar cuidadosamente los sistemas adoptados en otros diccionarios, el autor ha formulado uno enteramente nuevo que se expone a continuación, en el cual ha procurado simplificar las dificultades que presenta la pronunciación inglesa, reduciéndolas a una clave breve, sencilla y de fácil aplicación.

Multum in parvo ha sido el ideal que ha perseguido el autor en la compilación de esta obra, y al logro de este empeño han coadyuvado eficazmente los editores produciendo un libro que contiene, en forma compacta y de esmerada tipografía, mayor suma de información que otros voluminosos diccionarios.

Arturo Cuyás.

Nueva York, *julio de 1903.*

PREFACIO DE LA NUEVA EDICIÓN

He aquí sucintamente los cambios principales que se han hecho en esta edición:

Autoridades. En cuanto al español, se ha tomado por norma, hasta donde ha sido posible, la última edición (la decimoquinta de 1925) del Diccionario de la Academia; pero se han consultado y a menudo seguido otros diccionarios, como los de Zerolo, Alemany, Toro y Gisbert (*Pequeño Larousse ilustrado*) y Salvat, las grandes Enciclopedias Espasa, Seguí y Montaner (*Diccionario enciclopédico hispanoamericano*), y muchas obras técnicas y científicas dignas de confianza en lo relativo a la corrección de su terminología. Aun cuando se han evitado neologismos, galicismos, anglicismos y provincialismos inútiles, no se ha vacilado en emplear términos que, si bien la Academia no los trae, están sancionados por otras autoridades competentes y por el uso general. Hoy es perogrullada decir que a quien se ciñe estrictamente al Diccionario de la Academia le es imposible escribir acerca de asuntos modernos con la concisión que tanto ellos mismos como las reglas fundamentales de la retórica exigen. Hay ciertos términos, como *garaje* (que no debe escribirse con *g*), *baseball*, *boxeo*, que son de uso común y corriente en el lenguaje ordinario, en diarios y revistas y en obras acerca de las especialidades respectivas. Su adopción general es prueba convincente de que satisfacen necesidades psicofilológicas que el gramático y el lexicógrafo no pueden despreciar, so pena de quedarse marcando el paso a la retaguardia del progreso. Deber ineludible del buen lexicógrafo es reconocer que el mundo marcha, y que, en esta edad de vertiginosa aceleración, no sólo marcha, sino que vuela. Cuando la humanidad anda en el veloz aeroplano, el idioma no puede ir al anca del buey medieval en que cabalgan los celosos custodios de su virginidad. No que debamos apresurarnos a abrazar cuanto neologismo surja en el oleaje de la arrolladora corriente, muchos de los cuales quedarán pronto en las playas del pasado; pero sí distinguir y aceptar los que se presenten con caracteres de vida perdurable. Bien podemos guiarnos por la máxima de Pope:

> "Be not the first by whom the new is tried,
> Nor yet the last to lay the old aside."

En cuanto al inglés, se ha tomado por norma la última edición del *New International Dictionary of the English Language,* de Wébster, obra monumental de autoridad universalmente reconocida, en vez del *Standard Dictionary,* que Cuyás siguió y es también de sumo mérito, aunque, en lo concerniente a pronunciación y escritura, no goza de la misma reputación que el Wébster. Como los dos diccionarios difieren mucho en este último respecto, ha sido necesario hacer un grandísimo número de cambios, según se explicará adelante. Naturalmente, se han consultado, fuera de estos dos léxicos admirables, el *Century,* el *Oxford* y muchas otras obras de primera categoría.

Aditamentos. Apenas si es preciso advertir que, por cuanto una de las principales razones de ser de esta edición ha sido poner al día la obra de Cuyás, en ella se han introducido todos los términos importantes que el progreso de los últimos años ha traído consigo. Son éstos numerosísimos, a causa de los grandes y rápidos adelantos efectuados en las ciencias, la industria y el comercio, de las condiciones que surgieron durante la guerra y que han surgido después como efectos de ella, y de la efervescencia social universal, que ha afectado profundamente la política, la economía, las costumbres, la sociología, la pedagogía, la psicología y aun la ética y la teología. Mas, fuera de estos términos, se han agregado varios millares de voces, frases y locuciones que Cuyás excluyó, sin duda para no abultar demasiado su libro, pero cuya grande importancia exige que se incluyan, a fin de que el diccionario no adolezca de deficiencias serias. Ejemplos de lo mucho que se ha agregado pueden verse comparando los artículos **absolute, after, air, angle, as, be, bear, blow, break, by, call, carry, cast, center, chain, clean, cross, cut** (sin mencionar más que tres letras) de esta edición con los correspondientes de la anterior.

La lista de nombres propios se ha hecho varias veces mayor que la de Cuyás, incluyendo en ella los más importantes que figuran en la historia.

Se han agregado muchísimas abreviaturas de valor práctico, y suprimido varias que escasamente son de utilidad alguna.

Supresión de palabras y corrección de equivalentes. Imposible hubiera sido hacer los aditamentos mencionados sin engrosar excesivamente la obra y sin quitar nada de lo que contenía. La dificultad se ha obviado suprimiendo muchas voces inglesas enteramente inusitadas y por ende inútiles, y, sobre todo, un diluvio de sinónimos y semisinónimos españoles dados como equivalentes de una misma palabra inglesa, los cuales, fuera de ocupar superfluamente valioso espacio, tienden más bien a confundir al traductor que a ayudarlo. Esto se comprenderá mejor por los dos ejemplos siguientes:

> *Primera edición:* "**elear,** *a.* claro, transparente, diáfano; perspicuo, evidente, indisputable, patente, manifiesto, palmario, paladino, visible; despejado; raso; abierto, franco, liberal; sereno, limpio, puro, inocente; expreso, explícito; neto, líquido; desempeñado, sin deudas; desenredado; claro, distinto, sonoro."
>
> *Nueva edición:* "**clear,** *a.* claro; despejado; raso; abierto; franco, libre; limpio, inocente; neto, líquido; desempeñado, sin deudas; puro, sin mezcla."
>
> *Primera edición:* "**conduit,** *s.* conducto, caz, cacera, atarjea, caño, encañado, tubo, tubería, cañería, arcaduz."
>
> *Nueva edición:* "**conduit,** *s.* conducto; (elec.) tubo o canal (para conductores eléctricos)."

Como se verá, las diez palabras de **conduit** se han reducido a una—*conducto*—que tiene en español los mismos significados, y se ha agregado un significado especial, que la edición anterior no trae. Esa multiplicación de sinónimos, si bien útil en uno que otro caso, es perjudicial y engañosa en la mayor parte de los casos. Cualquiera creería, por ejemplo, que cuando en inglés quiere decirse *atarjea, caño* o *tubo*, se dice siempre **conduit,** lo cual no es cierto, pues las voces usadas son respectivamente **culvert, pipe** y **tube: conduit** es el término general que los comprende a todos, como *conducto* es el término general español. Sin embargo, en la distribución eléctrica tiene el término un sentido restringido, y por eso en la nueva edición se ha llamado la atención a él.

Por lo dicho se verá que con la supresión de sinónimos y aplicaciones especiales superfluas se ha economizado mucho espacio, sin sacrificar en lo más mínimo la entereza de las traducciones.

De las palabras inglesas dadas por Cuyás, quizá hubieran podido suprimirse muchas más de las suprimidas; pero no se ha hecho así, por respeto al criterio y al gusto del autor, que tendría sus razones para escoger las que puso.

En la traducción de muchas palabras importantes se han corregido errores en que, como es de esperarse en una obra de este carácter, ardua y laboriosa en sumo grado, incurrió el autor. Esto ha ocurrido con especialidad en la traducción de términos técnicos, como **abarticulation, aclinic, boiler shell, surveying, commutator, hydrometer,** etc.

Arreglo y escritura de palabras compuestas y de frases. Como Cuyás se guió por el *Standard Dictionary,* y aquí se ha seguido el Wébster. ha sido necesario hacer numerosos cambios en la forma

y el orden de las palabras. El *Standard* da muchas palabras compuestas separando los dos elementos por un guión, las cuales, según el sistema (no uniforme) de Cuyás deben ir en el artículo correspondiente al primer elemento; al paso que el Wébster las da, ya como frases en que el primer elemento modifica al segundo, ya como palabras indivisas (sin guión). En el primer caso, ha habido que suprimir el guión, pero dejando la frase donde estaba la palabra dividida; en el segundo caso, ha habido que poner la palabra indivisa en el lugar que alfabéticamente le corresponde como término independiente. Sirvan de ejemplo las expresiones **coffee tree** (cafeto) y **coffeehouse** (café—establecimiento), que Wébster escribe como acaban de darse, mientras que Cuyás, siguiendo al *Standard*, escribe **coffee-tree, coffee-house:** la primera (**coffee tree**) se ha dejado en el artículo **coffee,** pero suprimiendo el guión; mientras que la segunda **(coffeehouse)** se ha puesto como palabra independiente en artículo aparte.

Un cambio importantísimo que se ha hecho es la adopción, como regla general, de dar toda frase en que entran dos o más términos, sea que éstos formen o no una palabra compuesta con sus elementos divididos por un guión, en el artículo correspondiente al primer elemento, con el cual principia la frase o palabra respectiva, haciendo caso omiso de cuál de dichos elementos sea el más importante— problema á veces imposible de resolver. Por ejemplo, **cast iron** se da en el artículo **cast,** y no en **iron; carbon steel,** en **carbon,** y no en **steel; broad-faced,** en **broad; folding bed,** en **folding; easy-chair,** en **easy.** Si el lector tiene presente esta regla fija, no perderá tiempo buscando frases donde no están. Hay unas pocas excepciones, como el substantivo **close-up,** provenientes de la dificultad de clasificación gramatical; mas ellas no causarán dificultad alguna, si el lector observa la regla adicional, también muy útil, de buscar toda expresión compuesta de dos palabras separadas primero como frase, bajo el primer elemento, y luego como voz independiente. Otras excepciones se deben a que el segundo elemento es el que casi seguramente buscará el lector.

Recíprocamente, si no encontrare como voz independiente una palabra compuesta que se le presente, puede hallarla como frase bajo el primer elemento. Si, por ejemplo, viere en alguna parte **waterwheel,** y no hallare esta voz en el lugar que le corresponde como palabra indivisa, puede buscar la frase **water wheel** en el artículo **water.** Por desgracia, en la escritura de muchas expresiones de esta índole no hay uniformidad, y en la práctica se hallan ya en una forma, ya en otra. Esto pone una vez más de manifiesto la ventaja de la regla aquí adoptada. A no ser por ella, quien viese la frase **coffee house** quizá fuese a buscar su significado en **house**; mas, si sigue nuestra regla, sabrá que se hallará en **coffee**, y si no, unas pocas líneas más abajo como palabra indivisa—**coffeehouse**.

A propósito de frases, inclusas las formadas por verbos modificados por partículas, se ha adoptado el orden alfabético para los elementos que siguen a la palabra principal; orden que, a pesar de ser el más racional y cómodo y economizar muchísimo tiempo, por rareza se sigue en la primera edición. Después de las frases que principian con la palabra principal, se dan, también en orden alfabético, los idiotismos en que ella entra, si los hay, que no empiecen con ella. Para ahorrar espacio, la palabra que encabeza el artículo no se repite en cada frase, poniendo solamente su inicial. Véanse, por ejemplo, los artículos **back** y **cat**.

En las frases formadas por un verbo seguido de una partícula modificante, se han separado las correspondientes al verbo usado transitivamente de las correspondientes al verbo usado intransitivamente, cuando el verbo se usa de ambos modos. Esto también ahorra mucho tiempo.

Cuando en un mismo párrafo se dan los equivalentes de una palabra que pertenece a dos o más partes de la oración, los correspondientes a cada una de éstas van encabezados por un número romano impreso en letra gruesa, que se destaca claramente, facilitando así el trabajo de buscar los equivalentes en la división del caso.

Términos técnicos. Salvo los diccionarios ingleses-españoles y españoles-ingleses puramente técnicos (de los cuales no puede decirse sin remordimiento que valgan juntos una milésima de ardite), ningún otro diccionario bilingüe de las dos lenguas contiene tantos términos técnicos como el de Cuyás. Las traducciones de muchos de los más importantes se han enmendado, por cuanto necesitaban enmienda, y se han agregado muchísimos nuevos, sobre todo relativos al automovilismo, la aeronáutica y la radiocomunicación.

En beneficio del traductor de catálogos, anuncios y otro material análogo, se han introducido términos, como **balloon tire, clamshell bucket, cushion tire, cement gun, pull box, fishing wire, extruded metal, knockout** (en planchas, etc.), **gilding (metal), Mazda lamp** y multitud de vocablos más que se usan frecuentemente en el comercio, en varios officios y aun en la vida ordinaria, si bien algunos de ellos no han ingresado todavía ni siquiera en los diccionarios ingleses más extensos y comprensivos.

Pero, no obstante su abundancia de voces técnicas, no se pretende que éste sea un diccionario técnico completo; ni podría serlo, sin perder su carácter de tomo manual para convertirse en cuatro o cinco volúmenes ponderosos. Ni aun los monumentales léxicos ingleses antes mencionados contienen todo el vocabulario técnico y científico de la lengua; y esperar hallar en ellos o en éste cuanto término ocurre en anuncios y catálogos fuera pedir peras al olmo. Una gran multitud de tales términos son nombres de fábrica, cuya vida no pasa a menudo de unos pocos meses, y cuyo significado no les es conocido sino a los fabricantes y sus parroquianos. No es raro el caso en que un fabricante invente y emplee términos que no entienden ni aun los demás fabricantes de productos de la misma clase. En vista de esto, el traductor no debe culparse a sí mismo por no comprender algunos de ellos, ni al lexicógrafo por no tenerlos, ni vacilar en pedir al fabricante que se los defina o explique. El buen traducir no es canonjía ni arte plebeyo, como que requiere conocimiento profundo de las lenguas respectivas, paciencia y escrupulosidad a toda prueba, habilidad en el decir, claro discernimiento, y (¡rarísima dote o condición creada por larga y penosa experiencia!) un ánimo humilde, convencido, como Socrates, de que infinitamente más es lo que le falta por aprender que lo que sabe.

Pronunciación. Con excepción de dos cambios, el sistema de pronunciación de Cuyás se ha dejado como estaba. Estos cambios consisten en la introducción de la ʊ mayúscula para representar el sonido de *u* en **fun,** que es muy distinto del de la misma letra en **fur;** y del símbolo ȳ para representar el sonido de la *j* francesa, que difiere mucho del de la *j* inglesa.

————

El corrector y los editores creen que, con los cambios mayores arriba descritos y muchos menores que ocurren en todo el libro y que aquí no es posible especificar, la nueva edición será aun más valiosa que la anterior, y abrigan la esperanza de que reciba la misma buena acogida que merecidamente se dió a la primera.

Antonio Llano.

Nueva York.

PRONUNCIACIÓN INGLESA

El alfabeto inglés consta de 26 letras, de las cuales cinco son vocales, veinte consonantes y una—la *y*—puede, como en español, hacer ambos oficios.

Pero, al paso que el alfabeto español tiene 28 letras para expresar los 25 sonidos que constituyen la fonética del idioma, las 26 letras del alfabeto inglés no bastan para representar los numerosos sonidos que se emplean en la complicada pronunciación de esa lengua. Ni siquiera están acordes los ortólogos ingleses respecto del número de sonidos de su fonética: mientras la Asociación Filológica Americana limita a 32 los sonidos fundamentales, hay gramáticos que reconocen 43 sonidos distintos (RICHARD MORRIS, *Historical Outlines of English Accidence*, pp. 61, 62), y otros los hacen ascender a 46 (EVAN DANIEL, *The Grammar, History and Derivation of the English Language*, p. 290). La segunda cifra parece ser la más aproximada, puesto que a las solas vocales hay que asignar 19 sonidos diferentes, quedando 27 para las consonantes.

No tan sólo respecto de los sonidos fundamentales, sino hasta en la pronunciación de numerosas palabras están en completo desacuerdo ortólogos y lexicógrafos ingleses de reconocida autoridad, por no haber reglas generales que determinen la recta pronunciación de los vocablos; de suerte que algunos de éstos, como *caricature, exemplary, expurgator, familiarity, cynosure, capillary, euthanasia,* etc., pueden pronunciarse de diez o doce modos distintos, según el diverso parecer de los peritos. (*V.* Webster's *New International Dictionary of the English Language*, 1924, pp. lx–lxxv.)

Son tantas las dificultades prosódicas que presenta el idioma, que los lexicógrafos ingleses se ven en la necesidad de representar en sus diccionarios la correcta pronunciación de cada vocablo por medio de una clave fonética. Pero tampoco en esto se encuentra concordancia en los varios léxicos. Basta leer en el prefacio de los principales, como el monumental del Dr. Murray que se publica en Oxford, el de Wébster, el *Century* y el *Standard* publicados en los Estados Unidos, la parte que dedican a explicar el sistema de representación fonética que cada uno de ellos ha adoptado, para comprender las dificultades que ofrece la representación exacta simbólica de los 43 sonidos distintos del idioma. Y si esto es así tratándose de diccionarios destinados a personas para quienes el inglés es idioma vernáculo, ¿qué no será cuando se intente explicar gráficamente esos sonidos a personas de habla distinta, para quienes muchos de ellos son desconocidos y de difícil pronunciación?

Siendo pues imposible representar fiel, exacta y sencillamente todas las diversas y finísimas graduaciones de los sonidos ingleses, creemos preferible evitar la confusión que pudiera producir una clave complicada, y nos limitaremos a dar una representación *aproximada* de la pronunciación de cada vocablo por medio de las letras de nuestro alfabeto que mejor la indiquen, con el auxilio de unos pocos caracteres especiales. A ese fin damos a continuación una sencillísima clave, cuyo uso no ofrecerá la menor dificultad después de leer las explicaciones que la acompañan. La comparación que en ellas se hace de ciertos sonidos ingleses con otros semejantes del francés, alemán, italiano y catalán, servirá a los que viven en países donde no se habla el inglés para consultar a personas que conozcan alguno de los citados idiomas y oír de viva voz dichos sonidos, único modo de aprenderlos correctamente.

CLAVE Y EXPLICACIÓN DE LOS SONIDOS QUE MÁS SE DIFERENCIAN DEL CASTELLANO

a *breve*
Signo
fonético

§ 1. Dos de los muchos sonidos que tiene la *a* son: uno indefinido entre la *a* y la *e*, parecido al que suelen dar a la *a* los catalanes y al de la *i* francesa nasal (como en *fin, chemin*); y el otro sordo e indistinto, semejante al anterior pero pronunciado ligera y casi imperceptiblemente. Ocurre el primero en muchas voces, sobre todo monosílabas, acabadas en consonante, en que la *a* es enfática, como en **fat, man, hat, have, cannon, attic;** y el segundo en sílabas en que la *a* no es enfática, sobre todo en sílabas finales, como en **machine, attire, filial, fiscal.** Representaremos estos dos sonidos con el mismo signo con que los anglosajones representan el primero . . . . **æ**

c = s = z

§ 2. En ciertos casos estas tres consonantes tienen un sonido suave igual al que tiene la *s* o la *z* francesa en las palabras *rose, maison, gazon,* la *s* italiana y catalana en *rosa, casa,* o la alemana en *rose, nase.* Ejemplos: **sacrifice, suffice, has, noise, rose, nose, ribs, zeal, prize.** Lo representaremos con el signo . . . . **ŝ**

c = s = sh = t = x

§ 3. Estas consonantes en ciertas palabras tienen un sonido igual al de la *ch* francesa en *chiffon, pêche,* la *sc* italiana en *scivolare, uscire, pesce,* la *sch* alemana en *schiff, fisch, kirsche,* o la *x* catalana en *xicot, caixal, peix.* Ejemplos: **ocean, social, precious; dimension, sure; ship, fish; action, partial; anxious.** Lo representaremos con . . **ŝh**

e = i = o = u = y

§ 4. Estas vocales tienen en un sinnúmero de voces inglesas un sonido medio entre *e* y *u*, casi igual al del diptongo francés *eu* en *peur*, *leur*, o la *ö* alemana en *schön*, *börse*, *Körper*. Ejemplos: **ermine, verge, proper, firm, Sir, director, cur, fur, burst, current, myrtle.** Lo representaremos con . . . . **œ**

o = u

§ 5. Estas dos letras tienen a menudo un sonido corto y abrupto intermedio entre los de la *e* y la *u*, semejante al de la *o* corta francesa en *homme*. Ejemplos: **done, love, oven, become, but, cutter, radium, custom.** Lo representaremos con la letra mayúscula . . **U**

g = j

§ 6. En algunos vocablos, como **giant, college, John, Joseph,** estas consonantes tienen un sonido parecido al descrito en el § 3 (**ŝh**) precedido del sonido de *t*. Es un sonido peculiar que no puede aprenderse sino oyéndolo. Lo representaremos con la letra mayúscula . . **Y**

g = j = s = z

§ 7. En algunas palabras, como **mirage, jeun, pleasure, vision, azure, seizure,** estas letras tienen el sonido de *j* francesa (como en *jour, ajouter*), que aquí se representa con el símbolo . . . . . . **ȳ**

th

Esta combinación tiene dos sonidos: uno suave y otro fuerte.

§ 8. El sonido suave, que tiene en vocablos como *the, this, that, them,* es casi el mismo que el la *d* castellana entre dos vocales, y se pronuncia tocando suavemente con la lengua el borde de los dientes superiores. Lo representaremos con la letra mayúscula . . . . **D**

§ 9. El sonido fuerte, que tiene en vocablos como *thick, throat, theatre, truth,* es igual al de la *z* castellana pronunciada como en Castilla colocando la punta de la lengua entre las dos hileras de los dientes. Lo representaremos con *z bastardilla* . . . . **z**

Si el consultor de este diccionario procura retener en la memoria el sonido que corresponde a cada uno de los nueve signos indicados, no tendrá la menor dificultad en pronunciar las palabras inglesas, *leyendo como si fuera en castellano la representación fonética que acompaña a cada vocablo y cuidando de cargar la inflexión de voz en la vocal marcada con acento.*

Los sonidos de los numerosos diptongos y de la vocales y consonantes inglesas no expresados arriba, se representarán aproximadamente como suenan en castellano.

En resumen: la correcta pronunciación del inglés sólo puede aprenderse de viva voz. Por muy detallada y comprensiva que sea una clave fonética, el estudiante que no tenga otro medio de aprender los sonidos sólo llegará a adquirir una pronunciación aproximada e imperfecta. Cuanto más sencilla y clara sea la clave, tanto más se le facilitará el estudio de la pronunciación en los principios, y después, cuando esté más avanzado en el conocimiento del idioma, podrá con más provecho perfeccionar su pronunciación consultando léxicos ingleses como el Wébster, el *Standard*, el *Century* o el *Oxford*.

ALFABETO INGLÉS

No obstante lo expuesto, sería incompleta nuestra labor si no apuntásemos a continuación, siquiera someramente y por vía de inventario, los diversos sonidos que tienen cada letra del alfabeto inglés, los diptongos y triptongos y algunas otras combinaciones. Entiéndase que lo dicho en cuanto a los casos en que las letras tienen los sonidos expresados son sólo generalidades, no *reglas*. En inglés no hay reglas de pronunciación.

I. LETRAS

Letra	Nombre	Sonidos	Ejemplos
a	éi	tiene ocho sonidos, prescindiendo de ciertas gradaciones difíciles de distinguir; a saber:	
		(1) sonido muy semejante al de la *a* española o la francesa en *pas*: suele tenerlo cuando va seguida de *r, lf, lm, lv, th*.	car, far, arm, barb, calf, palm, father.
”	”	(2) y (3) sonido entre *a* y *e*, descrito más arriba (§ 1): suele tenerlo en los monosílabos cuando no va seguida de las consonantes expresadas, y en muchos polisílabos.	man, has, and, hand, lamb, camp, cavalry, matrimony, machine, senate.
”	”	(4) sonido de *éi* española: lo tiene sobre todo antes de una consonante o de *bl* seguida de *e* muda y en los polisílabos cuya raíz es un monosílabo que tiene este sonido.	fate, fame, pale, case; table, fable; paleness, famous, lady, Cambridge.
”	”	(5) sonido de *e* española: lo tiene en muy pocas palabras.	many, any, Thames.
”	”	(6) sonido de *o* española en *sol*: lo tiene antes de *ll* o de *l* seguida de otra consonante que no sea una de las ya indicadas.	all, ball, call, tall, false, salt, paltry.
”	”	(7) sonido de *éa*, o *éœ* (§ 1): lo tiene cuando la *a* precede a una *r* seguida de *e* muda.	bare, care, dare, fare, farewell.
”	”	(8) sonido intermedio entre los definidos en (1) y (2): lo tiene en algunas palabras que se pronuncian de distinto modo según la localidad; es casi idéntico al de la *a* española.	ask, fast, dance, branch bath, pass.
b	bi	(1) tiene el sonido más fuerte que en castellano; se pronuncia apretando los labios.	babble, baby, booby, bobbin.
”	”	(2) es muda cuando va seguida de *t* o precedida de *m* al final de dicción.	debt, doubt, comb, dumb, lamb.
c	si	(1) sonido gutural de *k*, antes de *a, o, u, r, l, t*.	car, corn, cut, crib, clam, act.

Letra	Nombre	Sonidos	Ejemplos
C	,,	(2) sonido de *s* antes de *e, i, y,* y también de *e* muda.	cent, city, fancy, place.
,,	,,	(3) sonido de *s* o *z* francesa descrito en § **2:** lo tiene en algunas palabras que terminan en *-ice.*	sacrifice, suffice.
d	di	(1) tiene el sonido más fuerte que en castellano: se pronuncia colocando la punta de la lengua sobre la raíz de los dientes superiores.	doll, den, did, dude, added, cadet, cadmium.
,,	,,	(2) en algunos participios terminados en *ed,* la *d* suena como *t.*	puffed, dashed, passed, mixed.
,,	,,	(3) en ciertas palabras tiene el sonido descrito más arriba en § 6.	soldier, grandeur.
e	i	tiene cinco sonidos, a saber: (1) sonido muy breve como el de la *e* española: lo tiene cuando va seguida de una consonante al fin de sílaba, y en las voces que empiezan con *ec, ef, el, em, en, er, es, ex.*	let, men, pen, fell; effect, elegant, empire, excellence.
,,	,,	(2) sonido de *éi:* lo tiene en pocas palabras, sobre todo en las de origen francés o español.	crochet, sachet, café, eclair, eclat.
,,	^	(3) sonido de *i:* lo tiene cuando termina un monosílabo; cuando precede a una consonante seguida de *e* muda, en ciertas palabras en que recibe el acento y cuando es doble.	be, he, she; eve, scene, theme; adhesion, concede (primera *e*); knee, see.
,,	,,	(4) sonido parecido al diptongo francés *eu* descrito en § 4: lo tiene sobre todo cuando va seguida de *r* al final de sílaba.	her, lover, pert, expert, person, version, converter.
,,	,,	(5) sonido de *ía* o *íœ* (§ 1): lo tiene cuando precede a una *r* seguida de *e* muda.	ere, mere, hereto, adhere.
,,	,,	(6) la *e* es muda al final de dicción, excepto en algunos derivados del griego.	sense, face, table, native, importance.
f	ef	sonido igual al de la *f* española, aunque un poco más fuerte.	far, fell, fib, roof.
g	ɣi	(1) sonido gutural como el de la *g* española en las sílabas *ga, go, gu:* lo tiene antes de *a, e, i, o, u, l, n, r.*	game, get, begin, gone, gun, glass, grit, agnostic.
,,	,,	(2) sonido que se define en § 6: lo tiene antes de *e, i, y.*	gem, gin, 'gigantic, gymnast.
h	éich	(1) sonido de *j* española, aunque más suave: lo tiene cuando forma principio de sílaba.	hat, he, hot, hum, adhere.

Letra	Nombre	Sonidos	Ejemplos
i	ái	tiene cinco sonidos, a saber:	
		(1) sonido muy breve de *i* que se aproxima al de la *e*: lo tiene en muchos monosílabos y en la mayoría de los casos.	pin, milk, bridge, zinc, picture, principal.
"	"	(2) sonido de *ái*: lo tiene en algunos monosílabos y en ciertas palabras en que precede a una o más consonantes seguidas de *e* muda.	high, knife, price, twice, sublime.
"	"	(3) sonido de *eu* francesa descrito en § 4: lo tiene cuando va seguida de *r*.	sir, bird, flirt, virgin.
"	"	(4) sonido de *i* española: lo tiene en ciertas palabras tomadas de lenguas latinas.	machine, police, valise.
"	"	(5) sonido de *áia*, o *áiœ* (§ 1): lo tiene cuando va seguida de *r* y *e* muda.	fire, wire, tire.
j	yéi	sonido que se describe en § 6.	jam, joy, just.
k	kéi	(1) sonido gutural igual al de la *q*.	kill, oak.
"	"	(2) es muda cuando le sigue una *n*.	knot, knight.
l	el	sonido igual al que tiene en español.	lord, ale.
m	em	sonido igual al que tiene en español.	man, ham.
n	en	(1) sonido igual al de la *n* española.	no, nun.
"	"	(2) cuando va seguida de *g*, tiene un sonido nasal seguido de un sonido casi imperceptible de *j*.	singer, thinking.
"	"	(3) es muda al final de dicción cuando va precedida de *l* o *m*.	kiln, condemn.
o	óu	tiene seis sonidos, a saber:	
		(1) sonido de *o* española: lo tiene cuando forma por sí sola sílaba no acentuada; o antes de *r* no seguida de *e* muda.	obey, oracular, original, for, form, corn.
"	"	(2) sonido de *óu*: lo tiene cuando termina una sílaba acentuada, o cuando precede a una consonante seguida de *e* muda.	no, go, notice, local, motion, note, lonely, alone.
"	"	(3) sonido de *u*: lo tiene en algunos monosílabos y en ciertas voces sin regla fija.	to, do, who, tomb, prove, woman.
"	"	(4) sonido de *o* muy breve que tira un poco a *a*.	not, got, hot, lofty, modern, gone.
"	"	(5) sonido de *óa*, u *oœ*: lo tiene cuando va seguida de *r* y *e* muda.	more, sore, pore, before.
"	"	(6) sonido del diptongo francés *eu*, descrito en § 4: lo tiene generalmente cuando va seguida de *n* o *r* al final de sílaba.	director, orator, worm, worry.

Letra	Nombre	Sonidos	Ejemplos
o	"	(7) sonido descrito en § 5.	come, done, son, oven, love.
p	pi	(1) tiene igual sonido que en español.	people, map, pepper.
"	"	(2) es muda cuando precede a la *s* o la *t* al principio de dicción o cuando está entre *m* y *t*.	psalm, ptisan; temptation, contempt.
q	kiú	tiene el mismo sonido que en español y va siempre seguida de *u*, la cual se pronuncia, excepto en algunas voces francesas. (*V.* **u.**)	quality, queen, quit, question, request.
r	ar	tiene un sonido especial semejante al de la *r* española, aunque menos perceptible; cuando termina sílaba casi no se oye.	red, rat, rose, merry, marriage, carriage, irregular, car, more, north.
s	es	(1) sonido sibilante de la *s* española: lo tiene al principio de dicción, al final de muchos monosílabos, y en muchos casos sin regla fija.	so, say, sit, yes, us, ask, also, castle.
"	"	(2) sonido de *s* o *z* francesa (descrito en § 2): lo tiene en las terminaciones *bs*, *ds*, *gs*, *ves*, *ls*, *ms*, *ns*, *rs*, *ys*, y en muchos casos en que está entre vocales.	ribs, lads, hives, souls, forms, horrors, boys, days, praise, rose, easy.
"	"	(3) sonido descrito en § 7: lo tiene en algunas palabras que terminan en *sion* y en *sure*.	evasion, illusion, corrosion, pleasure, leisure.
"	"	(4) es muda en algunas voces.	island, viscount.
t	ti	(1) sonido parecido al de la *t* española, sólo que se pronuncia colocando la punta de la lengua sobre la raíz de los dientes superiores.	tea, cat, total.
"	"	(2) sonido descrito en § 3: lo tiene en las terminaciones -*tion*, -*tience* y otras.	action, patience, satiate.
"	"	(3) sonido de *ch* española: lo tiene en la terminación -*ture* y cuando precede a *i* o *u* seguida de vocal.	picture, furniture, christian, virtue, actual.
"	"	(4) es muda en ciertos vocablos en que le preceden *f* o *s* y le sigue la terminación *en*.	listen, hasten, often, soften.
u	iú	tiene cinco sonidos, a saber: (1) sonido de *iú*: lo tiene cuando es final de sílaba acentuada, y cuando precede a una consonante seguida de *e* muda.	music, stupid, pupil; mule, tube, confuse.
"	"	(2) sonido descrito en § 5: lo tiene cuando está entre dos consonantes, o cuando precede a una o más consonantes.	tub, nut, us, up, under, supper, butter.

Letra	Nombre	Sonidos	Ejemplos
u	"	(3) sonido de *u* española: lo tiene en monosílabos que empiezan con *b, p, f* y terminan con *l, s, t*.	bull, full, put, pull, puss.
"	"	(4) sonido de *úa* o *iúa*: cuando va seguida de *r* y *e* muda.	sure, pure, cure, endure.
"	"	(5) sonido descrito en § 4: lo tiene a fin de sílaba cuando va seguida de *r*.	burn, fur, occur, current.
"	"	(6) es muda en algunas palabras francesas cuando la precede la *q*.	coquette, antique.
v	vi	el sonido inglés es más marcadamente labiodental que en castellano.	velvet, vivisection.
w	dóbliu	(1) sonido semejante al de *hu* española en *huevo*, u *ou* francesa en *oui*.	woman, award, worm, awake, we.
"	"	(2) es muda cuando va seguida de *r* al principio de dicción, y en otras voces.	write, wrong; sword, answer.
x	ecs	(1) sonido fuerte de *cs*: lo tiene cuando termina una sílaba acentuada, o cuando precede a una consonante.	excellent, exile, tax, excuse, next.
"	"	(2) sonido suave de *gŝ*: lo tiene cuando precede a una vocal acentuada.	exact, exist, examine, example.
"	"	(3) sonido descrito en § 2: lo tiene cuando empieza una palabra.	xylograph.
y	uái	(1) tiene el sonido fricativo de la *y* española cuando empieza una palabra o precede a una vocal.	year, yard, yell, yes; halyard.
"	"	(2) sonido breve de *i* española cuando hace el oficio de vocal al fin de dicción.	truly, fancy, very, liberty.
"	"	(3) sonido de *ái* cuando es acentuada, en medio o al fin de dicción.	type, by, rye, why, defy.
z	ŝi	sonido descrito en § 2.	zeal, wizard; prize, dazzle.

II. DIPTONGOS

ae	tiene a veces el sonido de *e*	maelstrom.
ai	" " " " *éi*	train, claim.
"	" " " " *e*	said, again.
"	" " " " *ai*	aisle.
"	" " " " *éa*	chair, pair.
au	" " " " *a*	launch, flaunt.
"	" " " " *éi*	gauge.
"	" " " " *o*	fraud, daub.
aw	" " " " *o*	law, awl.
ay	" " " " *éi*	ray. say.

DIPTONGOS (continuación)

ea	"	"	"	"	*a* . . . . heart, hearth.
"	"	"	"	"	*éi* . . . . break, great.
"	"	"	"	"	*e* . . . . bread, instead.
"	"	"	"	"	*éa* . . . . . . pear, bear.
"	"	"	"	"	*i* . . . . leaf, clean.
"	"	"	"	"	*ía* . . . . . . rear, near.
"	"	"	"	"	*œ* (*V.* § 4) . . . earth, hearse.
ee	"	"	"	"	*i* . . . . feel, need.
"	"	"	"	"	*i* breve . . . . . been.
ei	"	"	"	"	*ái* . . . . . . height.
"	"	"	"	"	*e* . . . . heifer.
"	"	"	"	"	*éa* . . . . . . heir.
"	"	"	"	"	*éi* . . . . reign, eight.
"	"	"	"	"	*i* . . . . seize.
eo	"	"	"	"	*e* . . . . leopard.
"	"	"	"	"	*i* . . . . people.
"	"	"	"	"	*o* . . . . yeoman.
"	"	"	"	"	ʊ (*V.* § 5) . . . . surgeon, dungeon.
eu	"	"	"	"	*iú* . . . . . . feud, deuce.
ew	"	"	"	"	*iú* . . . . . . dew, clew, few.
"	"	"	"	"	*óu* . . . . . . sew.
"	"	"	"	"	*u* . . . . blew, flew.
ey	"	"	"	"	*ái* . . . . . . eye, geyser.
"	"	"	"	"	*éi* . . . . eyry, whey.
"	"	"	"	"	*i* . . . . key.
ie	"	"	"	"	*ái* . . . . . . tie, pie, die.
"	"	"	"	"	*e* . . . . friend.
"	"	"	"	"	*i* larga . . . . fiend, mien.
"	"	"	"	"	*i* breve . . . . sieve.
io	"	"	"	"	ʊ (*V.* § 5) . . . . question, million.
oa	"	"	"	"	*o* . . . . broad.
"	"	"	"	"	*óu* . . . . . . load, road.
oe	"	"	"	"	*óu* . . . . . . toe, foe, hoe.
"	"	"	"	"	ʊ (*V.* § 5) . . . . does.
"	"	"	"	"	*u* . . . . shoe.
oo	"	"	"	"	*o* . . . . floor, door.
"	"	"	"	"	*u* . . . . crook, wool.
"	"	"	"	"	ʊ (*V.* § 5) . . . . blood, flood.
ou	"	"	"	"	*áu* . . . . . . loud, count.
"	"	"	"	"	*o* . . . . court.
"	"	"	"	"	ʊ (*V.* § 5) . . . . touch, young.
"	"	"	"	"	*u* . . . . could, should.
ow	"	"	"	"	*áu* . . . . . . cow, down.
"	"	"	"	"	*óu* . . . . . . low, crow.
"	"	"	"	"	*o* . . . . knowledge.
ua	"	"	"	"	*uéi* . . . . . . suave, persuade.
ue	"	"	"	"	*iú* . . . . . . due, pursue.
"	"	"	"	"	*u* . . . . true, blue.
ui	"	"	"	"	*i* . . . . build, guilt.
"	"	"	"	"	*u* . . . . juice, bruise.
uy	"	"	"	"	*ái* . . . . . . buy, guy.

III. TRIPTONGOS

eau	tiene a veces el sonido de				*o* . . . . beau.
"	"	"	"	"	*iú* . . . . . . beautiful.
ieu	"	"	"	"	*iú* . . . . . . adieu.
iew	"	"	"	"	*iú* . . . . . . view.
uay	"	"	"	"	*i* . . . . quay.

IV. OTRAS COMBINACIONES

ch	tiene a veces el sonido de *ch*	church.
„	„ „ „ „ *k*	chaos.
„	„ „ „ „ *ch* francesa . . .	crochet.
ck	„ „ „ „ *k*	lock.
gh	„ „ „ „ *g*	ghost.
„	„ „ „ „ *f*	rough.
„	es a veces muda	high, night.
gu	tiene generalmente el sonido de *gu* en *guitarra* .	guitar, guest.
„	tiene a veces el sonido de *gu* en *lengua*	guitguit.
ph	tiene a veces el sonido de *f*	philosophy.
„	es a veces muda	phthisis.
qu	tiene a veces el sonido de *ku*	quantity, aqua.
„	„ „ „ „ *k*	antique, piquant.
rh	tiene a veces el sonido de *r*	rhetoric.
sh	tiene el sonido que se define más arriba en § 3 .	shall, cash.
th	tiene dos sonidos: uno fuerte como *z* española .	thick, truth.
„	otro suave parecido a la *d* castellana	this, that,
wh	tiene a veces el sonido de *j*	who, whom.
„	„ „ „ „ *ju*	what, when.

ADVERTENCIA

PARA LA MEJOR COMPRENSIÓN DEL PLAN DE LA OBRA

La tendencia a simplificar la ortografía ha hecho que en los Estados Unidos se elimine alguna letra innecesaria en ciertas palabras, como **clamor, honor, labor,** que en Inglaterra continúan escribiéndose en su integridad (**clamour, honour, labour**). Estas y otras supresiones parecidas, autorizadas por el uso y por los lexicógrafos, se indican encerrando entre paréntesis la letra que suele o puede suprimirse, v. gr.: **clamo(u)r, hono(u)r, labo(u)r, jewel(l)er, jewel-(le)ry, judg(e)ment, rat(t)an, gast(e)ropod.**

Asimismo, para economizar espacio, se marcan con un paréntesis algunos substantivos y los numerosos adjetivos que tienen dos terminaciones, v. gr.: **gelatin(e, presage(ment, knur(l, kurd(ish, labiate(d, grammatic(al, comic (al,** que pueden escribirse íntegramente o bien **gelatin, presage, knur, kurd, labiate, grammatic, comic.**

En la representación fonética de los vocablos que tienen dos terminaciones o de aquellos que pueden pronunciarse de dos maneras distintas, se suprimen las sílabas idénticas que ya sabrá suplir el buen sentido del lector, v. gr.: **precursive, precursory** [precŏrsiv, sori], pronúnciese [precŏrsiv, precŏrsori]; **predecessor** [pre- o(pri-) desésœr], quiere decir que esa palabra puede pronunciarse [predesésœr o pridesésœr]; **predominance, predominancy** [pridómi-nans, i], quiere decir que la primera se pronuncia [predóminans] y la segunda [predóminansi].

Análogamente, al dar palabras que tienen una misma parte común que se pronuncia de igual manera en todas ellas, la pronunciación completa no siempre se indica sino en la primera, y con las otras se da únicamente la de la parte no común precedida de un guión. Así, **censorious** (sensóriʋs), **censoriously** (-li), **censoriousness** (-nes), indica que las dos últimas deben pronunciarse (sensó-riʋsli), (sensóriʋsnes).

Los vocablos que no van acompañados de representación fonética, se pronuncian en inglés aproximadamente como se leen en español.

En cuanto a palabras compuestas y frases, téngase presente lo dicho en el *Prefacio de la nueva edición*, pág. ix.

En algunos casos en que las traducciones requieren pocas palabras, las derivadas y compuestas indivisas se dan bajo la primitiva o principal, si bien indicando su pronunciación y oficio gramatical; pues siendo los párrafos muy cortos, todas se destacan claramente, a causa del tipo grueso en que van impresas. Por ejemplo, **clownishly,** *adv.,* y **clownishness,** *s.* se dan en el artículo **clownish.**

ABREVIATURAS DE LA ·PARTE
INGLESA–ESPAÑOLA

Fuera de estas abreviaturas, se usan las bien conocidas del sistema métrico. A propósito de éstas bueno es advertir que, cuando se refieren a un número decimal, se escriben siempre después del número completo, y no hacia arriba de los enteros; así: 4,75 m., y no 4^m,75.

a	adjetivo.
adv.	adverbio.
aer	aeronáutica
agr.	agricultura.
alb.	albañilería.
álg.	álgebra.
Am.	América.
anat.	anatomía.
ant.	anticuado.
apl.	aplícase.
arit.	aritmética.
arq.	arquitectura.
art.	artículo.
arti.	artillería.
astr.	astronomía.
aut.	automovilismo.
aux.	auxiliar.
azú.	industria azucarera.
b. a.	bellas artes.
bact.	bacteriología.
bib.	bíblico, Biblia.
biol.	biología.
blas.	blasón.
bot.	botánica.
cant.	cantería.
carp.	carpintería.
carr.	carruajería.
caz.	caza.
cerá.	cerámica.
cir.	cirugía.
coc.	cocina.
com.	comercio.
comp.	comparativo.
conj.	conjunción.
constr.	construcciones.
contr.	contracción.
cost.	costura.
danz.	danza.
defect.	defectivo.
dep.	deportes.
der.	derecho.
despec.	despectivo.
dib.	dibujo.
dim.	diminutivo.
dipl.	diplomacia.
elec.	electricidad.
enc.	encuadernación.
ent.	entomología.
e. p.	economía política.
equit.	equitación.
esc.	escultura.
Esco.	Escocia.
esgr.	esgrima.
esp.	especialmente.
E. U.	Estados Unidos.
fam.	familiar.
farm.	farmacia.
f. c.	ferrocarriles.
fig.	figurado.
filos.	filosofía.
fís.	física.
fisiol.	fisiología.
for.	voz forense.
fort.	fortificación.
foto.	fotografía.
fr.	francés.
fund.	fundición.
gen.	generalmente.
geog.	geografía.
geol.	geología.
geom.	geometría.
ger.	gerundio.
gram.	gramática.
herr.	herraduría.
hidr.	hidráulica.
hist.	historia.
hist. n.	historia natural.
ict.	ictiología.
igl.	iglesia.
impers.	impersonal.
impr.	imprenta.
ind.	industria.
indef.	indefinido.
indic.	indicativo.
ing.	ingeniería.
Ingl.	Inglaterra.
interj.	interjección.
intern.	internacional.
irr.	irregular.
joy.	joyería.
lat.	latín.
leng. ord.	lenguaje ordinario
locom.	locomotora
lóg.	lógica.
ll.	llámase, llamado.
magn.	magnetismo
m. comb. int.	máquinas de combustión interna
maq.	maquinaria.
mar.	marina.
mat.	matemáticas.
mec.	mecánica.
med.	medicina.
metal.	metalurgia.
Méx.	México.
mil.	milicia.
min.	minería.
mit.	mitología.
mús.	música.
m. v.	máquinas de vapor.
obst.	obstetricia.
ópt.	óptica.
orn.	ornitología.
pa.	participio activo.
pal.	paleontología.
pat.	patología.
pers.	personal.
pint.	pintura.
piro.	pirotecnia.
pl.	plural.

poét. . . . . . . poética.
pol. . . . . . . política.
pos. . . . . . . posesivo.
pp. . . . . . . participio pasado.
prep. . . . . . . preposición.
pret. . . . . . . pretérito.
P. Rico . . . . . Puerto Rico.
pron. . . . . . . pronombre.
psic. . . . . . . psicología.
quím. . . . . . . química.
rad. . . . . . . radiocomunicación.
radtlf. . . . . . radiotelefonía.
radtlg. . . . . . radiotelegrafía.
relig. . . . . . . religión
ret. . . . . . . retórica.
s. . . . . substantivo.
S. A. . . . . . . Sud América.
sast. . . . . . . sastrería.
sing. . . . . . . singular.
somb. . . . . . . sombrerería.
subj. . . . . . . subjuntivo.
super. . . . . . superlativo.

t. . . . . también.
teat. . . . . . . teatro.
tec. . . . . . . tecnología.
tej. . . . . . . tejidos.
tlf. . . . . . . telefonía.
tlg. . . . . . . telegrafía.
ten. . . . . . . tenería.
teo. . . . . . . teología.
tint. . . . . . . tintorería.
top. . . . . . . topografía.
Ú., ú. . . . . . Úsase, úsase.
u. ref. . . . . . usado reflexivamente.
V., v. . . . . . Véa(n)se, véa(n)se.
va. . . . . verbo activo.
Venez. . . . . . Venezuela.
vet. . . . . . . veterinaria.
vn. . . . . verbo neutro.
vr. . . . . verbo reflexivo.
vulg. . . . . . . vulgarismo.
zap. . . . . . . zapatería.
zool. . . . . . . zoología.

NUEVO DICCIONARIO BILINGÜE

DE LAS

LENGUAS INGLESA Y ESPAÑOLA

PARTE INGLESA-ESPAÑOLA

Las abreviaturas y los nombres propios van al final.

a [éi], *n.* a (letra); (*mús.*, **A**) la, sexta nota de la gama.—**A 1, A number 1,** de primera calidad o categoría, de lo mejor.—**from A to Z,** desde el alfa hasta la omega, de pe a pa.

a [e; *o, si es enfático,* éi]. **I.** *art. indef.* un, una (antes de *sonido consonante;* v.g. *a man,* un hombre; *a woman,* una mujer; *a unit,* una unidad); por, cada; v.g. *ten dollars a pound,* diez dólares por libra. Se pospone a los adjetivos *many, such, what,* y a adjetivos precedidos de *as, how, so, too;* v.g. *many a man,* muchos hombres (*v.* MANY); *such a man,* un hombre tal, semejante hombre; *what a man!* ¡qué hombre! *as old a man,* un hombre tan viejo; *too old a man,* un hombre demasiado viejo.—**II.** *prep.* Se usaba, y aún se usa a veces, antes del gerundio para indicar acción o proceso, en casos en que hoy se emplea el gerundio solo o el infinitivo; v.g. *he went a hunting,* él fué a cazar; *she is a weeping,* ella está llorando.

A [éi], *a.* en A, en forma de A.

Aaronic(al [ærónic, -æl], *a.* aarónico, aaronita; levítico, pontifical.

Aaron's-beard [érunš bíard], *s.* (bot.) barba de Aarón; zumillo; también se da este nombre a varias otras plantas.

abaca [ábacá], *s.* abacá.

aback [æbǽk], *adv.* detrás, atrás; hacia atrás; a alguna distancia; (mar.) en facha.—**to take a.,** turbar, asombrar.

abacus [ǽbæcus], *s.* (arit.) abaco; (arq.) loseta rectangular; aparador; báculo.

abaft [æbǽft], *adv.* (mar.) a popa; más cerca de la popa que, entre la popa y (*abaft the mast,* entre la popa y el mástil).—**a. the beam,** entre (la dirección de) bao y proa.

abalienate [æbélieneit], *va.* enajenar.

abalienation [æbéilienéišun], *s.* enajenación, traspaso.

abalone [æbaloun], *s.* (zool.) oreja marina.

abandon [æbǽndun]. **I.** *va.* abandonar, dejar; entregar, ceder.—**to a. oneself,** entregarse (al vicio, etc.). **II.** *s.* indiferencia, naturalidad, desenfado.

abandoned [æbǽndund], *a.* abandonado; encenagado (en los vicios); malvado.

abandonment [æbǽndunmœnt], *s.* abandono, abandonamiento, desamparo.

abarticulation [æbartikiuléišun], *s.* diartrosis.

abase [æbéis], *va.* abatir, humillar, degradar.

abasement [abéismœnt], *s.* humillación, degradación.

abash [abǽsh], *va.* avergonzar, correr, confundir.

abashment [abǽshment], *s.* confusión, vergüenza, embarazo.

abate [æbéit]. **I.** *va.* disminuir, reducir, rebajar; humillar; (for.) suprimir, impedir; suspender; condonar; anular; (metal.) reducir el temple. **II.** *vn.* menguar, moderarse; (for.) frustrarse, no surtir efecto, fallar; ocupar sin derecho fincas tras la muerte de su último dueño.

abatement [æbéitment], *s.* extenuación, rebaja, diminución o supresión; (for.) anulación; cesación; cantidad rebajada o condonada; ocupación, sin derecho, de una finca tras la muerte de su último dueño.

abater [æbéitœr], *s.* = ABATOR; (for.) instancia de anulación o cesación (= PLEA IN ABATEMENT).

abatis, abattis [ǽbœtis], *s.* (mil.) valla defensiva de árboles enteros cortados.

abator [æbéitœr], *s.* (for.) el que suprime o mitiga (un estorbo, impedimento, etc.); intruso, usurpador.

abattoir [æbætuár], *s.* matadero, desolladero.

abb [æb], *s.* urdimbre; lana para la urdimbre; lana en borra.

abbacy [ǽbasi], *s.* abadía.

abbatial [abéshal], *a.* abacial, abadengo.

abbé [abé], *s.* abate.

abbess [ǽbes], *s.* abadesa, prelada.

abbey [ǽbe], *s.* abadía, monasterio.

abbot [ǽbot], *s.* abad.

abbotship [ǽbotship], *s.* abadía (dignidad).

abbreviate [abríveit], *va.* abreviar, reducir, compendiar.

abbreviation [abríviéišun], *s.* abreviación; abreviatura; cifra.

abbreviator [abríviéitœr], *s.* abreviador, compendiador; (igl.) abreviador.

abbreviatory [abríviétori], *a.* abreviatorio.

abbreviature [abríviachuœr], *s.* compendio, epítome.

A B C, a-b-c [éi bi si], *s.* abecedario, abecé; cartilla; rudimentos.

abdicant [ǽbdicant], *s. y a.* abdicante, que abdica.

abdicate [ǽbdikeit]. **I.** *va., vn.* abdicar, renunciar. **II.** *va.* (for.) desheredar.

abdication [æbdikéišun], *s.* abdicación, renuncia; dimisión; dejamiento, dejación.

abdicative [ǽbdiketiv], *a.* abdicativo, renunciativo.

abdomen [æbdómen], *s.* abdomen, vientre.

abdominal [æbdóminæl]. **I.** *a.* abdominal. **II.** *s. y a.* (zool.), abdominal, malacopterigio.

abducent [æbdiúsent], *a.* (anat.) abductor.

abduct [æbdúct], va. secuestrar (a alguien), robarse (a alguien).

abduction [æbdúkŝhʊn], s. robo, secuestración (de una persona); (anat. y lóg.) abducción.

abeam [æbím], adv. (mar.) por el través.

abecedarian [æbicidéiriæn], s. y a. que aprende o enseña el alfabeto; novicio, bisoño.

abed [æbéd], adv. en cama, acostado.

abelmosk [ébelmosk], s. abelmosco.

aberrance, aberrancy [æbœrrans, -ci], s. error, desvío, extravío.

aberrant [æbœrrant], a. extraviado; anormal, anómalo.

aberration [æberréiŝhʊn], s. error; extravío; desliz; (astr. y opt.) aberración.

abet [æbét], va. instigar, excitar, inducir.

abetment [æbétmœnt], s. instigación, excitación.

abetter, abettor [æbétœr], s. (for.) fautor, instigador; cómplice.

abeyance [æbéians], s. inacción transitoria, suspensión; estado latente.—**In a.**, en suspenso; latente; (for.) en espera de su dueño o reclamante legítimo (dícese de bienes monstrencos, cargos vacantes, etc.)

abeyant [æbéiant], a. = IN ABEYANCE.

abhor [æbjór], va. detestar, abominar, odiar.

abhorrence [æbjórrens], s. aborrecimiento, detestación, aversión, execración.

abhorrent [æbjórrent], a. repugnante, detestable, odioso; contrario, opuesto; que detesta.

abhorrently [æbjórrentli], adv. aborreciblemente, odiosamente.

abhorrer [æbjórrœr], s. aborrecedor.

abidance [æbáidans], s. permanencia, residencia.—**a. by**, adhesión a.

abide [æbáid] (pret. y pp. ABODE). I. va. esperar; soportar, sufrir. II. vn. morar; permanecer; perdurar.—**to a. by**, sostenerse en; estar con; sujetarse a, obrar de acuerdo con, cumplir con.

abiding [æbáiding]. I. s. permanencia; residencia. II. a. durable, perdurable.

abigail [ábiguell], s. doncella (criada).

ability [abíliti], s. poder, facultad, habilidad, capacidad, talento, ingenio.

abintestate [abintésteit], a. abintestato.

abiogenesis [æbioyénesis], s. abiogénesis, generación espontánea.

abiological [æbaiolóyical], a. abiológico, inorgánico.

abiology [æbaióloyi], s. abiología, ciencia de los seres inorgánicos.

abiosis [æbaiósis], s. abiosis, ausencia de vida.

abject [æbyéct], a. abyecto, servil; desanimado.

abjection [æbyékŝhʊn], n. abyección, servilismo.

abjectly [æbyéctli], adv. abyectamente.

abjectness [æbyéctnes], n. = ABJECTION.

abjuration [æbyuréiŝhʊn], s. abjuración, retractación; renuncia.

abjure [æbyúar]. I. va. abjurar, retractarse de; renunciar solemnemente a. II. vn. retractarse; hacer renuncia solemne (del reino, etc.).

ablation [æbléiŝhʊn], s. (cir.) ablación; (geol.) desgaste (de una roca); merma, reducción (de un helero por derretimiento).

ablative [æblativ], a. y s. (gram.) ablativo.

ablaut [áplaut], s. variación de la raíz de una palabra.

ablaze [æbléiŝ], a. en llamas, ardiendo.

able [éibel], a. capaz, apto, hábil, competente; (for.) capaz, competente, legalmente habilitado.—**a.-bodied**, robusto, sano, físicamente capaz.—**a.-minded**, de gran talento.—**to be a.**, poder.

ablegate [æbleguéit], s. (igl.) nuncio.

abloom [æblúm], a. en flor; floreciente.

abluent [æbluent], a. detersivo, detergente.

ablush [æblúŝh], a. y adv. avergonzado.

ablution [æblúŝhʊn], s. ablución; lavamiento.

ably [éibli], adv. hábilmente.

abnegate [æbneguéit], va. renunciar a; abjurar; negar.

abnegation [æbneguéiŝhʊn], s. abnegación; renuncia, repudiación.

abnormal [æbnórmal], a. anormal.

abnormality [æbnormáliti], s. irregularidad, anomalía.

abnormally [æbnórmali], adv. anormalmente.

abnormity [æbnórmiti], s. anomalía; deformidad, monstruosidad.

aboard [æbœrd], adv. (mar.) a bordo.—**to fall a.**, abordar, chocar.—**to go a.**, ir a bordo, embarcarse.—**all a.**, "pasajeros al tren," "listos."

abode [æbóud], s. domicilio, residencia, habitación, morada; estancia, permanencia.

abode, pret. y pp. de ABIDE.

abolish [æbóliŝh], va. abolir, suprimir, derogar.

abolishable [æbóliŝhabœl], a. abolible.

abolisher [æbóliŝhœr], s. derogador, anulador, revocador, destructor.

abolishment [æbóliŝhment], s. abolición.

abolition [æboliŝhʊn], s. abolición, derogación.

abolitionist [æboliŝhʊnist], s. abolicionista; (E. U.) abolicionista, enemigo de la esclavitud.

aboma [æbóuma], s. (zool.) aboma, especie de boa.

abomasum [æboméisʊm], s. (anat.) abomaso.

abominable [æbóminabœl], a. abominable, execrable, detestable; nefando.

abominableness [æbóminabœlnes], s. calidad de abominable.

abominably [æbóminabli], adv. abominablemente.

abominate [æbómineit], va. abominar, detestar.

abomination [æboméiŝhʊn], s. abominación, odio, detestación; enormidad, gran maldad.

aboriginal [æboríyinal], a. aborigen.

aborigines [æboríyinis], s. pl. aborígenes.

abort [æbórt], vn. abortar, malparir; (biol.) cesar prematuramente de crecer; atrofiarse prematuramente; perder la fecundidad, hacerse estéril.

aborted [æbórted], a. nacido prematuramente; (biol.) de desarrollo incompleto; que ha perdido la fecundidad.

aborticide [æbórtisaid], s. aborticidio, destrucción del feto; lo que destruye el feto y causa aborto.

abortifacient [æbórtiféiŝhent], s. y a. que causa aborto.

abortion [æbórŝhʊn], s. aborto, malparto; fiasco, fracaso.

abortive [æbórtiv]. I. s. y a. abortivo. II. a. infructuoso, malogrado; (biol.) imperfectamente desarrollado; estéril; (med.) que acorta la duración (de una enfermedad).

abortively [æbórtivli], adv. abortivamente; a destiempo; prematuramente.

abortiveness [æbórtivnes], s. abortamiento, fracaso.

abound [abáund], vn. abundar.—**to a. with**, abundar en.

about [æbáut]. I. adv. casi; poco más o menos, como (about six hours, como seis horas); alrededor, por todos lados, a la redonda; acá y acullá, de Ceca en Meca; por aquí, por ahí (en el lugar, edificio, etc.); en la dirección opuesta; por turnos, en rotación.—**a. face** (mil.), media vuelta.—**to be a.**, estar levantado y andando (dícese de un enfermo). II. prep. de, acerca de, con respecto a; alrededor de; por en (to walk about town, andar o pasear por el pueblo); cerca de; como de, poco más o menos de (the book is about this size, el libro es como de este tamaño); ocupado en, atendiendo a; a ocuparse en, a meterse en; a punto de, al; con (I have no money about me, no tengo dinero conmigo, o aquí).

above [æbúv]. I. a. dicho, susodicho; superior. II. adv. arriba.—**from a.**, de lo alto, del cielo. III. pre. arriba de, sobre; por encima de; superior a; más que.—**a. all**, sobre todo, ante todo.—**to be a.**, tener, ser incapaz de, estar por encima de.

aboveboard [-bord], a. y adv. franco, sincero; francamente, al descubierto.

aboveground [-graund]. I. a. y adv. sobre la superficie de la tierra o arriba de ella. II. a. vivo.

abracadabra [æbracadǽbra], *s.* abracadabra; palabra altisonante y misteriosa.

abrade [æbréid], *va.* raer, desgastar por rozamiento, raspar.

abrasion [æbréiɏυn], *s.* desgaste (esp. por rozamiento); raspadura; (geol. y med.) abrasión.

abrasive [-šiv]. **I.** *a.* rayente, raspante. **II.** *s.* substancia raspante. (Algunos dicen *abrasivo*, que es palabra bien formada.)

abreast [abrést], *adv.* de frente.—**four a.,** cuatro de frente.

abridge [abríɏ], *va.* abreviar, compendiar; privar, despojar.

abridgment [abríɏmœnt], *s.* compendio, resumen; abreviación; diminución.

abroad [æbród], *adv.* en el extranjero, fuera del país; fuera de su morada ordinaria (como los animales); en grande espacio; entre el público, del dominio público, en público. (A veces no se traduce, o se emplea otra forma: *there is a rumor abroad*, hay un rumor, se dice; *to set abroad*, hacer público, divulgar).—**to be a., to be all a.,** estar errado, extraviado o perplejo.

abrogate [æbroguéit], *va.* abrogar.

abrogation [æbroguéišhυn], *s.* abrogación.

abrogative [æbrogativ], *a.* revocatorio.

abrotanum [æbrótanυm], *s.* (bot.) abrótano.

abrupt [æbrúpt], *a.* brusco, repentino; quebrado, áspero, precipitoso.

abruption [æbrúpšhυn], *s.* separación violenta.

abruptly [æbrrúptli], *adv.* precipitadamente; de fondón; bruscamente, exabrupto.

abruptness [æbrrúptnes], *s.* precipitación, inconsideración; prontitud; brusquedad.

abscess [æbses], *s.* absceso, apostema.

abscissa [æbsísa], *s.* (mat.) abscisa.

abscission [æbsíɏυn], *s.* corte, abscisión.

abscond [æbscónd], *vn.* esconderse, evadirse.

absconder [æbscóndœr], *s.* desaparecido, prófugo.

absence [æbsens], *s.* ausencia; falta; distracción de ánimo.—**In the a. of,** a falta de.

absent [æbsent], *a.* ausente; no existente; distraído, abstraído.—**a.-minded,** distraído, absorto, encantado.—**a.-mindedness,** distracción, enajenamiento.

absent [æbsént], *vr.* ausentarse, retirarse, dejar de concurrir.

absentee [æbsentí], *s.* el que permanece o está ausente.

absenteeism [æbsentíism], *s.* absentismo.

absinthe [æbsinz], *s.* absenta, licor de ajenjo.

absinthian [æbsínzian], *a.* perteneciente al ajenjo.

absinthiate [æbsínzieit], *va.* mezclar con ajenjo.

absinthin [æbsínzin], *s.* (quím.) absintina.

absinthism [æbsínziâm], *s.* absintismo, enfermedad debida al abuso del ajenjo.

absinthium [æbsínziυm], *s.* (bot.) ajenjo.

absis [æbsis], *s.* = APSIS.

absolute [æbsoliut], *a.* absoluto; completo, perfecto; categórico, perentorio; (for.) absoluto, sin restricción; (quím.) puro.—**the a.,** lo absoluto.—**a. electrometer,** (elec.) electrómetro absoluto.—**a. pressure,** (fís.), presión absoluta, en que cero corresponde al vacío.—**a. temperature,** (fís.) temperatura absoluta.—**a. term,** (mat.) término absoluto o independiente (que no contiene la incógnita).—**a. unit,** (fís.) unidad absoluta.—**a. value,** (mat.) valor absoluto.—**a. weed,** (agr.) maleza perjudicial y sin valor intrínseco.—**a. zero,** (fís.) cero absoluto.

absolutely [æbsoliutli], *adv.* absolutamente; terminante o categóricamente.

absoluteness [æbsoliutnes], *s.* calidad de absoluto.

absolution [æbsoliúšhυn], *s.* absolución.

absolutism [æbsoliutiâm], *s.* absolutismo; doctrina de la predestinación.

absolutist [æbsoliutist], *s.* y *a.* absolutista.

absolutory [æbsóliutori], **absolvatory** [æbsólvatori], *a.* absolutorio.

absolve [æbsólv], *va.* absolver, justificar; desligar, exentar.

absolver [æbsólvœr], *s.* absolvedor, dispensador.

absolving [æbsólving], *a.* absolutorio.

absonant [æbsonant], *a.* discordante, contrario.

absorb [æbsórb], *va.* absorber; ocupar (el ánimo) intensamente, preocupar; incorporar; amortiguar.

absorbable [æbsórbæbœl], *a.* absorbible.

absorbability [æbsórbæbíliti], *s.* absorbibilidad.

absorbed [æbsórbt], *a.* absorbido; absorto.

absorbefacient [æbsórbiféišhent], *s.* y *a.* que causa absorción.

absorbent [æbsórbent], *a.* absorbente.—**a. cotton** (med.) algodón hidrófilo.—**a. gland,** glándula linfática.

absorber [æbsórbœr], *s.* absorbente; (mec.) amortiguador; economizador (de energía).

absorbing [æbsórbing], *a.* absorbente; interesante.

absorption [æbsórpšhυn], *s.* absorción; concentración, preocupación.—**a. lines,** (fís.) rayas oscuras (del espectro), rayas de Fraunhofer.—**a. spectrum** (fís.), espectro de absorción o de rayas oscuras.

absorptive [æbsórptiv], *a.* absorbente.

abstain [æbstéin], *vn.* abstenerse, privarse.

abstainer [æbstéinœr], *s.* el que se abstiene.

abstemious [æbstímiυs], *a.* sobrio.

abstemiously [æbstímiυsli], *adv.* sobriamente.

abstemiousness [æbstímiυsnes], *s.* sobriedad.

abstention [æbsténšhυn], *s.* abstención.

absterge [æbstœry], *va.* absterger.

abstergent [æbstœryent], *a.* abstergente.

abstersion [æbstœršhυn], *a.* abstersión.

abstersive [æbstœrsiv], *a.* abstergente.

abstinence, abstinency [æbstinens], *s.* abstinencia, sobriedad.—**total a.,** abstinencia absoluta de bebidas alcohólicas.

abstinent [æbstinent], *a.* abstinente, sobrio.

abstinently [æbstinentli], *adv.* abstinentemente.

abstract [æbstract]. **I.** *a.* sumario, resumen; término abstracto; abstracción.—**In the a.,** en abstracto. **II.** *a.* abstracto; distraído.

abstract [æbstráct], *va.* abstraer (t. *vn*); compendiar, resumir; quitar, sustraer; separar, alejar; distraer; hurtar; (quím.) extraer.

abstractedly [æbstréctedli], *adv.* abstractivamente; sencillamente.

abstractedness [æbstréctednes], *s.* calidad de abstraído.

abstracter, abstractor [æbstráctœr], *s.* compendiador; ratero, ladrón.

abstraction [æbstrécšhυn], *s.* abstracción; separación; retraimiento, recogimiento; desatención, descuido; ratería, hurto.

abstractive [æbstréctiv], *a.* abstractivo.

abstractly, abstractively [æbstréctli, -ivli], *adv.* en abstracto, abstractivamente.

abstruse [æbstrús], *a.* abstruso, recóndito.

abstrusely [æbstrúsli], *adv.* abstrusamente.

abstruseness [æbstrúsnes], *s.* obscuridad, dificultad, calidad de recóndito.

absurd [æbsœrd], *a.* absurdo, irracional, ridículo, disparatado, descabellado, prepóstero.

absurdity [æbsœrditi], *s.* absurdo, despropósito, disparate, dislate.

absurdly [æbsœrdli], *adv.* absurdamente.

abulia [æbúlia], *s.* (med.) abulia.

abundance [æbúndans], *s.* abundancia, copia, plenitud, exuberancia, afluencia; caudal.

abundant [æbúndant], *a.* abundante.

abundantly [æbúndantli], *adv.* abundantemente, copiosamente; asaz.

abuse [æbiús]. **I.** *v.* abusar de; engañar; profanar, violar; denostar, injuriar; ultrajar, maltratar. **II.** *s.* abuso; corruptela; seducción, engaño; injuria, denuesto; (quím.)e, maltrato; violación, estupro.

abuser [abiúsœr], *s.* abusador; ultrajador; denostador, denigrador; embaucador, engañador.

abusive [abiúsiv], *a.* abusivo, ofensivo, insultante.

acinus [æsinʊs], *s.* (anat.) acino.

acknowledge [æcnóley], *va.* reconocer; confesar, admitir; (for.) certificar, testificar, confirmar. —**to a. receipt**, acusar recibo.

acknowledgment [æcnóleyment], *s.* reconocimiento; confesión, admisión; acuse de recibo; confirmación; (for.) testificación, testificata.

aclinic [aclínic], *a.* aclínico.

acme [æcmi], *s.* cima, pináculo; auge, culminación, colmo.

acne [æcne], *s.* (pat.) acne, barro.

acock [æcóc], *a.* ladeado (el sombrero, etc.); avisado.

acolyte [ácolait], *s.* acólito; monacillo.

aconite [æconait], **aconitum** [æconaitʊm], *s.* (med. y bot.) acónito.

aconitine [æcónitin], *s.* (quím.) aconitina.

acorn [éicorn], *s.* (bot.) bellota.

acotyledon [acotilídon], *s.* acotiledón.

acotyledonous [acotilídonʊs], *a.* acotiledóneo.

acoustic [acústic], *a.* acústico.

acoustics [acústics], *s.* acústica.

acquaint [ækuéint], *va.* instruir, familiarizar; enterar, informar, hacer saber a.—**to a. oneself with**, familiarizarse con, ponerse al corriente de.

acquaintance [ækuéintans], *s.* conocimiento (a. **with**, conocimiento de); conocimiento mutuo (de dos personas), hecho de conocerse entre sí; conocido (persona a quien se conoce).

acquainted [ækuéinted], *a.* conocido (*are you two acquainted?* ¿se conocen Vds. dos?); impuesto, enterado.—**to be a. with**, conocer (un hecho), conocer a (una persona).—**to make a. with**, relacionar con; enterar de.

acquest [akuést], *s.* (for.) adquisición; propiedad comprada.

acquiesce [akuiés], *vn.* asentir; consentir.

acquiescence [akuiésens], *s.* aquiescencia, asenso, consentimiento, conformidad; sumisión, resignación.

acquiescent [akuiésent], *a.* condescendiente, acomodadizo, conforme, sumiso.

acquirable [akuáirabœl], *a.* adquirible, asequible.

acquire [akuáicœr], *va.* adquirir, obtener; contraer (hábitos, etc.).

acquirement [akuáicœrmœnt], *s.* adquisición.— *pl.* conocimientos, saber.

acquirer [akuáirʊr], *s.* adquirente.

acquisition [akuisíshʊn], *s.* adquisición.

acquisitive [ækuísitiv], *a.* capaz de adquirir; dispuesto a adquirir; (for.) adquisitivo.—**a. prescription** (for.) prescripción adquisitiva.

acquisitively [akuísitivli], *adv.* por adquisición.

acquisitiveness [akuísitivnes], *s.* calidad de adquisitivo; tendencia a adquirir.

acquit [ækuít], *va.* absolver, exculpar; exonerar; pagar.—**to a. oneself**, portarse, conducirse, desempeñar su trabajo, hacerlo (bien, mal).

acquittal [akuítal], **acquitment** [akuítmœnt], *s.* absolución; descargo; pago.

acquittance [akuítans], *s.* descargo de una deuda; recibo, quita, carta de pago.

acre [éikœr], *s.* acre (medida de superficie— 40,47 áreas); (Canadá) medida lineal como de 60 m.—**a. foot** (Ing.) acrepié, cantidad de agua suficiente para cubrir un acre hasta una altura de 1 pie.—**a. inch**, acrepulgada, cantidad de agua necesaria para cubrir un acre hasta una altura de 1 pulgada.—**God's a.**, camposanto.

acreage [éikœrey], *s.* número de acres.

acred [éikœrd], (*term.*) de acres, que posee tierras (*large-acred man*, hombre de muchos terrenos).

acrid [ácrid], *a.* acre, mordaz, picante.

acridity, acridness [acríditi, ácridnes], *s.* acritud, acrimonia.

acrimonious [æcrimóniʊs], *a.* acrimonioso, sarcástico, mordaz, picante.

acrimoniously [æcrimóniʊsli], *adv.* con acrimonia, con aspereza.

acrimoniousness [æcrimóniʊsnes], **acrimony** [ácrimoni], *s.* acrimonia, acritud, amargura, aspereza, mordacidad.

acritical [acrítical], *a.* (pat.) acrítico.

acrobat [æcrobat], *s.* acróbata, volatín.

acrobatic [æcrobǽtic], *a.* acrobático.

acrogen [æcroyen], *s.* acrógena.

acromial [æcrómial], *a.* (anat.) acromiano, acromial.

acromion [æcrómion], *s.* (anat.) acromio.

acronycal [æcrónical], *a.* (astr.) acrónico.

acronycally [æcrónicali], *adv.* acrónicamente.

acropolis [æcrópolis], *s.* acrópolis.

across [æcrós]. **I.** *adv.* de través, a través, transversalmente; de una parte a otra; al otro lado; en cruz. **II.** *prep.* a través de; al otro lado de; por.—**to come**, o **run, a.**, encontrarse (algo); encontrarse con.

acrostic [ácróstic], *s.* acróstico.

acroterium [æcrotíriʊm], *s.* acrotera.

act [æct], *vn.* obrar, actuar, funcionar; representar (en el teatro); fingir, simular; conducirse, portarse.—*va.* hacer o desempeñar el papel de (vg.: *to act the buffoon*, hacer de bufón.)—**to a. on**, o **upon**, influir en; obrar sobre.

act [æct], *s.* acción, acto, hecho, obra; (teat.) acto; (for.) ley, disposición, decreto; instrumento, documento.—**a. of honor**, (com.) acto o protesta de intervención.—**a. of indemnity**, bill de indemnidad.—**a. of settlement**, (Ing.) ley que ha fijado la sucesión en la casa de Hánover.—**Acts, Acts of the Apostles**, (bib.) Hechos de los Apóstoles.

acting [ǽcting]. **I.** *s.* acción; (teat.) representación, desempeño. **II.** *a.* interino, suplente.

actinic(al [æctínic(al], *a.* actínico.

actinism [ǽctinism], *s.* actinismo.

actinium [actíniʊm], *s.* (quím.) actinio.

actinolite [æctínolait], *s.* (min.) actinota.

actinometer [actinómitœr], *s.* actinómetro.

actinometric [actinométric], *a.* actinométrico.

actinometry [-nómetri], *s.* actinometría.

actinomycosis [æctinomaicósis], *s.* (med.) actinomicosis.

action [ǽcshʊn], *s.* acción, acto, obra; funcionamiento; actividad; actuación; movimiento; gesto; (teat.) argumento; (mil.) acción, batalla; (mec.) mecanismo; (for.) acción, demanda, proceso; expediente.—**to take a. on**, dar curso a, tomar medidas acerca de.

actionable [æcshʊnabœl], *a.* (for.) punible, criminal, procesable.

actionably [æcshʊnabli], *adv.* de un modo procesario.

activate [ǽctiveit], *va.* activar, hacer activo.

active [ǽctiv], *a.* activo; (gram.) activo, transitivo; (com.) que devenga interés; del haber (*the active side*, el lado del haber).—**a. capital** (com.) activo.—**a. component, a. current** (elec.) componente (de una corriente alterna) en fase con la fuerza electromotriz.—**a. list**, lista de oficiales militares en servicio.

actively [ǽctivli], *adv.* activamente, acuciosamente.

activity [æctíviti], *s.* actividad, diligencia, vigor. —*pl.* ocupaciones, actividades, unciones.

actor [ǽctœr], *s.* agente; (teat.) cómico, actor; (for.) actor, demandante; apoderado.

actress [ǽctres], *s.* (teat.) actriz.

actual [ǽkchual], *a.* real, verdadero; existente; actual. (Hoy apenas si se usa en este último sentido.)

actuality [ækchuǽliti], **actualness** [ækchualnes], *s.* realidad.

actually [ækchuali], *adv.* realmente, en realidad.

actuary [ækchueri], *s.* actuario (especialista en cálculos de seguros); actuario, escribano; notario.

actuate [ǽkchueit]. **I.** *va.* mover, impulsar, excitar. **II.** *vn.* obrar.—**actuated** [-ed], *a.* movido, animado.—**actuation** [-éishʊn], *s.* impulsión; puesta en acción.

acuity [akiúiti], *s.* agudeza.

acumen [ækiúmen], *s.* cacumen; (bot.) punta aguda.

acuminate [ækiúminate]. **I.** *a.* (bot.) acuminado, que termina en punta. **II.** *va.* aguzar. **III.** *vn.* rematar en punta.

acumination [ækiúminéishun], *s.* punta aguda.

acupuncture [ǽkiupúnkchur]. **I.** *s.* (cir.) acupuntura.—**II.** *va.* (cir.) acupunturar.

acute [akiút], *a.* agudo; ingenioso, perspicaz, vivo, fino, delgado, sutil, penetrante; (med.) agudo.—**a. angle**, ángulo agudo.—**a.-angle**, o **a.-angled**, acutángulo.

acutely [akiútli], *adv.* agudamente; despiertamente, vivamente.

acuteness [akiútnes], *s.* agudeza; delgadez, sutileza; perspicacia, viveza, penetración; violencia de una enfermedad.

acyclic [æsáiclic], *a.* (elec.) acíclico (se aplica a dínamos); (bot.) acíclico o no verticilado; (quím.) graso.

ad absurdum [ǽd absǽrdum], *adv.* (lóg. y mat.) al absurdo, por reducción al absurdo.—**reductio ad a.**, reducción al absurdo.

adage [ǽdey], *s.* adagio, refrán.

adagio [adáyo], *s.* (mús.) adagio.

Adam [ǽdam], *s.* Adán; pecado original, depravación humana.—**A.'s ale** (fam.) agua.—**A.'s apple**, nuez de la garganta, manzana de Adán.—**A.'s wine**=A.'S ALE.—**not to know from A.**, (fam.), no conocer absolutamente.

adamant [ǽdamant]. **I.** *s.* adamante; diamante; (poét.) dureza. **II.** *a.* firme, inexorable.

adamantine [ǽdamǽntin], *a.* diamantino; adamantino; indisoluble; inflexible, impregnable. —**a. spar**, corindón de la India.

Adamite [ǽdamait], *s.* adamita.

adapt [adǽpt], *va.* adaptar; tomar y compendiar (un escrito); (teat.) refundir, arreglar.

adaptable [adǽptabœl], **adaptive** [adǽptiv], *a.* adaptable, aplicable.

adaptability [adǽptabíliti], *s.* adaptabilidad.

adaptation [adǽptéshun], **adaption** [adǽpshun], *s.* adaptación; ajuste; (teat.) arreglo, refundición.

adapter [adǽptér], *s.* el o lo que adapta; (tec.) adaptador; (quím.) alargadera, tubo que comunica una retorta con otra vasija.

add [æd]. **I.** *va.* sumar; agregar, añadir.—**to a. up**, sumar. **II.** *vn.* sumar; agregar.—**to a. to**, aumentar.

addend [ǽdend], *s.* (arit.) sumando.

addenda [adénda], *s.* (mec.) círculo primitivo de una rueda dentada; (pl. de ADDENDUM) aditamentos; apéndice.

addendum [adéndum], *s.* adición, apéndice; (mec.) cabeza de un diente de engranaje.—**a. circle, a. line**, o **a.** simplemente, (mec.) periferia de una rueda dentada.

adder [ǽdœr], *s.* víbora; serpiente.—**puff a.**, víbora sudafricana.—**a.'s grass** [ǽdœrs gras], o **a.'s tongue**, (bot.) lengua de sierpe.—**a.'s wort**, (bot.) escorzonera.

addict [adíct], *vr.* entregarse a (algo); dedicarse.

addicted [adíct], *a.* adicto, dado, entregado.—**a. to**, apasionado por, partidario de.

addictedness [adíctednes], **addiction** [adícshun], *s.* inclinación, propensión.

additament [ǽdítæment], *s.* aditamento.

addition [adíshun], *s.* adición, añadidura; aditamento, adjunto; (arit.) adición, suma.—**in a. to**, además de, fuera de.

additional [adíshunal]. **I.** *a.* adicional. **II.** *s.* aditamento.

additionally [-i], *adv.* adicionalmente.

additive [ǽditiv], *a.* aditivo, que debe agregarse.

addle [ǽdœl]. **I.** *a.* huero; podrido; estéril, agotado, inservible. **II.** *va.* y *vn.* enhuerar(se), echar(se) a perder; decaer, debilitarse.—**a.-brain**, *s.*; **a.-head**, *[s.]*; **a.-pate**, *s.*; **a.-brained**, *a.*, etc. estúpido.

address [**I** y **II**, ædrés; **III**, ǽdres]. **I.** *va.* dirigir la palabra, hablar, arengar a; dirigirse a (de palabra o por escrito); dirigir, poner el sobrescrito a (una carta); aplicarse, consagrase (ú. refl.); dirigirse a (ú. refl.); enamorar, requebrar; (com.) consignar.—**to a. the ball**, prepararse para golpear la pelota, en el golf. **II.** *vn.* alistarse. **III.** *s.* dirección, señas; dirección, sobrescrito; discurso; trato; manera de hablar o conversar; petición, solicitud; proclama, alocución, mensaje; habilidad, destreza, maña; galanteo, requiebro (generalmente *pl.*); (com.) consignación.

addressee [adresí], *s.* destinatario (de una carta, mercancías, etc.).

addresser [adrésœr], *s.* peticionario, exponente.

addressograph [adrésograf], *s.* máquina para imprimir sobrescritos.

adduce [adiús], *va.* aducir.

adducent [-ent], *a.* (anat.) aductor.

adduction [adúcshun], *s.* presentación, exposición (de hechos, etc.); (anat.) aducción.

adductor [-tœr], *s.* (anat.) músculo aductor.

ademption [adémpshun], *s.* (for.) enajenación, en vida, de bienes testados.

adenitis [ædenáitis o ítis], *s.* (pat.) adenitis.

adenography [ædenógrafi], *s.* (anat.) adenografía.

adenoid, adenoidal [ǽdenoid, -al], *a.* glandiforme.

adenoid [por lo común en *pl.*], *s.* (med.) vegetación o tumor adenoideo.

adenopathy [ædenópazi], *s.* adenopatía.

adept [adépt], *s.* y *a.* adepto, perito.

adequate [ǽdekueit]. **I.** *va.* adecuar, asemejar, igualar. **II.** *a.* adecuado, proporcionado.

adequately [ǽdekuetli], *adv.* adecuadamente.

adequateness [ǽdekuetnes], **adequation** [ǽdekuéishun], *s.* adecuación.

adhere [adjícœr], *vn.* adherirse, unirse; allegarse; pegarse; aficionarse.

adherence [ædjírens], **adherency** [ædjírensi], *s.* adhesión.

adherent [adjírent], *a.* adherente, adicto; adhesivo, pegajoso.

adherent, adherer [ædjírœr], *s.* adherente, secuaz, partidario, parcial.

adherently [adjírentli], *adv.* con adhesión, parcialmente.

adhesion [ædjíʃun], *s.* adhesión, adherencia.

adhesive [ædjísiv], *a.* adhesivo, pegajoso; tenaz; engomado.—**a. plaster**, esparadrapo.

adhesively [ædjísivli], *adv.* tenazmente, en unión estrecha.

adhesiveness [ædjísivnes], *s.* calidad de adhesivo; adhesividad, propensidad a la amistad y a la sociabilidad.

adiabatic [ædiæbǽtic], *a.* (fís.) adiabático.

adieu [adiú]. **I.** *interj.* adiós. **II.** *s.* despedida; adiós.—**to bid a.**, despedirse.

adipocere [ædiposícer], *s.* adipocira.

adipose [ædipous], *a.* adiposo, seboso.

adiposis [ædipósis], *s.* gordura; (med.) adiposis.

adiposity [adipósiti], *s.* adiposidad.

adit [ǽdit], *s.* (min.) socavón.

adjacency [ædyásensi], *s.* contigüidad; cosa contigua.

adjacent [ædyásent], *a.* adyacente; limítrofe.

adject [adyéct], *va.* añadir, juntar.

adjection [ædyécshun], *s.* adición, añadidura.

adjectitious [ædyectíshus], *a.* añadido.

adjectival [ædyectival], *a.* (gram.) adjetival.

adjective [ædyéctiv], *s.* (gram.) adjetivo.

adjectively [-li], *adv.* adjetivadamente.

adjoin [ædyóin]. **I.** *va.* lindar con, estar contiguo a; agregar. **II.** *vn.* estar en contigüidad o proximidad; colindar.

adjoining [ædyóining], *a.* contiguo; siguiente.

adjourn [ædyǽrn]. **I.** *va.* diferir, aplazar; suspender o levantar la sesión de (un cuerpo deliberante). **II.** *vn.* levantarse la sesión; terminarse las sesiones (de un cuerpo deliberante).

adjournment [-mœnt], *s.* aplazamiento, traslación, suspensión.

adjudge [adɣúy]. **I.** *va.* adjudicar; conceder (premio); decidir, juzgar; sentenciar, condenar; decretar. **II.** *vn.* dictar sentencia.

adjudger [-œr], *s.* adjudicador.

adjudgment [-mœnt], **adjudication** [adɣudikéiʃʜun], *s.* adjudicación; (naut.) enjagüe.

adjudicate [adɣúdikeit]. **I.** *va.* determinar judicialmente; adjudicar. *V.* ADJUDGE. **II.** *vn.* ejercer las funciones de juez.

adjudicative [adɣúdiketiv], *a.* adjudicativo.

adjudicator [adɣudikéitœr], *s.* adjudicador.

adjunct [ǽdɣunct]. **I.** *s.* aditamento, adjunto; ayudante, subalterno; (gram.) modificante, modificativo. **II.** *a.* auxiliar, subordinado.

adjunction [ædɣúncʃʜun], *s.* unión, adición; (for.) adjunción.

adjunctive [ædɣúnctiv], *s.* y *a.* que junta o une; adjunto; adjetivado.

adjunctively [ædɣúnctivli], *adv.* juntamente.

adjunctly [-tli], *adv.* de un modo auxiliar.

adjuration [ædɣuréʃʜun], *s.* imprecación, conjuro.

adjure [ædɣúœr], *va.* implorar, impetrar, suplicar; mandar, ordenar solemnemente.

adjust [ædɣúst], *va.* ajustar, acomodar, adaptar; arreglar; finiquitar; regular, graduar; (top., etc.) verificar, corregir (un instrumento).

adjustable [ædɣústæbœl], *a.* arreglable, componible; regulable, graduable, adaptable.

adjuster [ædɣústœr], *s.* el o lo que arregla o adapta; mediador.

adjustment [ædɣústment], *s.* arreglo, adaptación; arreglo, ajuste, composición (de disputas, etc.); (com.) prorrateo (de pérdidas, ganancias, etc.); (top, etc.) arreglo; regulación; corrección, verificación (de un instrumento).

adjutancy [ædɣutansi], *s.* ayudantía.

adjutant [ædɣutant], *s.* ayudante; (orn.) grulla de la India.

adjuvant [ædɣuvant], *a.* y *s.* adjutor.

admeasurement [ædméƴœrmœnt], *s.* repartimiento; medición justa.

administer [ædmínistœr]. **I.** *va.* administrar, manejar; suministrar, proveer; dar, aplicar (remedios, un golpe, un castigo, etc.).—**to a. an oath**, tomar juramento. **II.** *vn.* contribuir; obrar en calidad de administrador.

administerial [ædmínistírial], *a.* administrativo.

administrable [ædmínistrabœl], *a.* que se puede administrar.

administrant [ædmínistrant], *a.* y *s.* director, jefe ejecutivo; administrador, ra.

administration [ædmínistréʃʜun], *s.* administración; ministerio, gobierno, dirección; intendencia, mayordomía; manejo; distribución.

administrative [ædmínistretiv], *a.* administrativo; gubernativo.

administrator [ædmínistréitœr], *s.* administrador, curador; albacea, testamentario; gobernante.—**public a.**, fideicomisario abintestato.

administratorship [-rʃhip], *s.* administración, empleo o dignidad de administrador.

administratrix [ædmínistréitrics], *s.* administradora; curadora, albacea; fideicomisaria abintestato.

admirable [ǽdmirabœl], *a.* admirable.

admirableness [ǽdmirabœlnes], **admirability** [ædmirabíliti], *s.* excelencia.

admirably [ǽdmirabli], *adv.* admirablemente.

admiral [ǽdmiral], *s.* almirante; almiranta (nave); jefe de una flota mercante.

admiralship [ǽdmiralʃhip], *s.* almirantazgo, título (grado).

admiralty [ǽdmiralti], *s.* almirantazgo (tribunal); departamento o ministerio de marina.—**a. law**, derecho marítimo; código marítimo.

admiration [ædmiréʃhun], *s.* admiración.

admire [ædmáiar]. **I.** *va.* admirar; contemplar. **II.** *vn.* admirarse.

admirer [ædmáirœr], *s.* admirador; enamorado.

admiring [ædmáiring], *a.* admirativo.

admiringly [ædmáiringli], *adv.* admirativamente.

admissibility [ædmisibíliti], *s.* admisibilidad.

admissible [ædmísibœl], *a.* admisible, aceptable; permitido, lícito.

admissibly [ædmísibli], *adv.* admisiblemente.

admission [ædmíʃhun], *s.* admisión, entrada; recepción, acceso; precio de entrada; concesión, asenso.—**a. ticket**, billete de entrada.

admissive [ædmísiv], **admissory** [ædmísori], *a.* que implica admisión.

admit [ædmít], *va.* admitir; recibir, dar entrada; permitir.

admittance [ædmítans], *s.* entrada; derecho de entrada; (elec.) admitancia.—**no a.**, se prohíbe la entrada.

admittedly [ædmítedli], *adv.* reconocidamente, concedidamente.

admitter [ædmítœr], *s.* el que admite.

admittible [ædmítibœl], *a.* admisible.

admix [ædmíx], *va.* mezclar.

admixtion [ædmíxcʜun], **admixture** [ædmíxchur o tiur], *s.* mixtura, mezcla.

admonish [ædmóniʃh], *va.* amonestar.

admonisher [ædmóniʃhœr], *s.* amonestador.

admonishment [ædmóniʃhmœnt], **admonition** [ædmoníʃhun], *s.* amonestación.

admonitor [ædmónitor], **admonitioner** [ædmoníʃhunœr], *s.* admonitor, censor.

admonitory, admonitive [ædmónitori, -iv], *a.* admonitorio, parenético.

adnascence [ædnǽsens], *s.* adhesión de partes entre sí por toda su superficie.

adnascent [ædnǽsent], **adnate** [ǽdnet], *a.* (bot.) adnato.

ado [ædú], *n.* alharaca; trabajo, dificultad.—**much a. about nothing**, nada entre dos platos, más es el ruido que las nueces.—**without more a.**, sin más ni menos, sin más rodeos.

adobe [adóbe], *s.* adobe.

adolescence [ædolésens] o **adolescency** [ædolésensi], *s.* adolescencia.

adolescent [ædolésent], *a.* y *s.* adolescente.

Adonic [ædónic], *a.* verso adónico.

adopt [adópt], *va.* adoptar, prohijar, ahijar; asumir; aceptar, tomar.

adoptedly [adóptedli], *adv.* adoptivamente.

adopter [adóptœr], *s.* adoptante.

adoption [adópʃhun], *s.* adopción, prohijamiento; aceptación.

adoptive [adóptiv], *a.* adoptivo.

adorable [adórabœl], *a.* adorable.

adorableness [adórabœlnes], *s.* cualidad de adorable.

adorably [adórabli], *adv.* adorablemente.

adoration [adoréʃhun], *s.* adoración, culto.

adore [adóœr], *va.* adorar, idolatrar.

adorer [adóœrœr], *s.* adorador.

adorn [ædórn], *va.* adornar, ornar.

adornment [ædórnment], *s.* adorno.

adrenal [ædrínœl], *a.* suprarrenal.

adrenalin(e [ædrínœlin], *s.* adrenalina.

adrift [adríft], *adv.* (mar.) al garete; a la ventura.

adrip [adríp], *a.* goteando.

adroit [adróit], *a.* diestro, hábil, listo, astuto.

adroitly [adróitli], *adv.* hábilmente, diestramente.

adroitness [adróitnes], *s.* destreza, habilidad, prontitud, ten con ten.

adry [adrái], *a.* sediento, seco.

adscititious [ædsitíʃhus], *a.* completivo, adicional, añadido.

adsorb [ædsórb], *va.* adsorber, condensar y retener por adhesión las partículas de un gas.

adsorption [ædsórpʃhun], *n.* adsorción, adherencia de las partículas de un gas u otro cuerpo disuelto a una superficie sólida; la acción de esta superficie.

adulate [ædiuleit], *va.* adular, lisonjear.

adulation [ædiuléʃhun], *s.* adulación, lisonja.

adulator [ædiuleitor], *s.* adulador.

adulatory [ædiulatori], *a.* adulatorio.

adult [adúlt], *a.* y *s.* adulto.

---

adultness [adúltnes], s. edad adulta.

adulterant [adúltœrant], s. y a. adulterante.

adulterate [adúltœret]. I. va. adulterar, impurificar, falsear, falsificar, viciar.—II. vn. cometer adulterio. III. a. adulterado, falso, espurio; adúltero.

adulterately [-li], adv. adulteradamente.

adulteration [adúltœréshʊn], **adulterateness** [adúlteratnes], s. adulteración, corrupción, impureza, falsificación; sofisticación.

adulterer [adúltœrœr], s. adúltero.

adulteress [adúltœres], s. adúltera.

adulterine [adúltœrin]. I. a. espurio. II. s. hijo adulterino.

adulterous [adúltœrʊs], a. adúltero; adulterino, espurio.

adultery [adúltœri], s. adulterio.

adumbrant [ædúmbrant], a. (pint.) bosquejado; ligeramente sombreado.

adumbrate [ædʊmbret], va. esquiciar; presagiar, anunciar.

adumbration [ædʊmbréshʊn], s. esquicio, esbozo; indicación, presagio; (pint.) adumbración.

aduncate [ædúnket]. I. vn. encorvarse como un garfio. II. a. adunco, combo, encorvado.

aduncity [adúnsiti], s. corvadura, comba.

aduncous [adúncʊs], a. adunco, encorvado.

adust [adúst]. I. a. cálido; adusto; tostado, requemado, moreno. II. adv. polvoriento.

ad valorem [æd valórem], (com.) ad valórem.

advance [ædváns]. I. va. avanzar, poner más adelante; adelantar, promover, ascender, mejorar; acelerar, apresurar; (com.) anticipar dinero, pagar adelantado; proponer, ofrecer, insinuar; encarecer. II. vn. avanzar, adelantarse; adelantar, progresar; subir (apl. a precios). III. s. avance; mejora, adelanto, progreso; vanguardia, cabeza; (pl.) propuestas, solicitudes, insinuaciones; (pl.) requerimientos amorosos; (com.) adelanto, anticipo, préstamo; alza; recargo de precio, precio adicional (=EXTRA); (mec.) avance a la admisión.—a. guard (mil.) avanzada.—in a., anticipadamente; antes; al frente; adelante; de antemano; (com.) por adelantado, anticipado.

advanced [ædvánst], a. avanzado, adelantado, desarrollado.—a. in years, entrado en años, de edad madura.

advancement [ædvánsmœnt], s. adelantamiento, progreso; promoción, ascenso; elevación, subida, prosperidad.

advancer [ædvánsœr], s. adelantador; promotor, impulsor.

advantage [ædvántey]. I. s. ventaja, superioridad, facilidad; ganancia, provecho, beneficio.—to take a. of, aprovecharse de, valerse de; engañar, embaucar.—to have the a. of, llevar ventaja a. II. va. adelantar, mejorar; remunerar; promover. III. vn. medrar, sacar ventaja.

advantaged [ædvánteyd], a. adelantado; ventajoso.

advantageous [ædvantéiyʊs], a. provechoso, ventajoso, conveniente.

advantageously [-li], adv. ventajosamente.

advantageousness [-nes], s. ventaja, conveniencia, calidad de ventajoso.

advent [ædvent], s. venida, advenimiento, llegada; adviento.

adventitious [ædventíshʊs], a. adventicio.

adventitiously [-li], adv. accidentalmente.

adventive [ædvéntiv], a. (biol.) advenedizo; accidental, casual.

adventure [ædvénchœr]. I. s. aventura; casualidad, contingencia; lance; (com.) ancheta, pacotilla. II. va. aventurar, arriesgar. III. vn. osar, atreverse, arriesgarse.

adventurer [ædvénchʊrœr], s. aventurero; pacotillero.

adventuresome [ædvénchʊrsʊm], **adventurous** [ædvénchʊrʊs], a. aventurero, audaz, emprendedor, arrojado, intrépido; arriesgado, aventurado, peligroso.

adventuress [ædvénchures], s. aventurera.

adventurously [ædvénchʊrʊsli], adv. arriesgadamente, arrojadamente.

adventurousness, adventuresomeness [-nes], s. intrepidez, arrojo, temeridad, osadía.

adverb [ædvœrb], s. (gram.) adverbio.

adverbial [ædvœrbial], a. adverbial.

adverbially [ædvœrbiali], adv. adverbialmente.

adversary [ædvœrseri], s. adversario.—the A., Santanás.

adversative [ædvœrsativ], a. adversativo.

adverse [ædvœrs], a. adverso; opuesto; hostil.

adversely [ædvœrsli], adv. adversamente.

adverseness [ædvœrsnes], s. oposición, contrariedad, resistencia.

adversity [ædvœrsiti], s. adversidad.

advert [ædvœrt], va. hacer referencia, advertir, notar.

advertence [ædvœrtens], **advertency** [ædvœrtensi], s. atención, consideración.

advertent [ædvœrtent], a. avisado, atento.

advertise [ædvœrtais], va. avisar, anunciar, poner anuncios.

advertisement [ædvœrtáismœnt o ædvœrtismœnt], s. aviso, anuncio, notificación.

advertiser [ædvœrtáisœr], s. anunciante.

advice [ædváis], s. consejo; aviso, noticia, informe, notificación.—a. boat, (mar.) aviso.—to take a., pedir o seguir consejo.

advisability [ædvaisabíliti], **advisableness** [ædváisabœlnes], s. prudencia, cordura; conveniencia, propiedad; ventaja.

advisable [ædváisabœl], a. aconsejable, prudente; deseable, conveniente.

advise [ædváis]. I. va. aconsejar; avisar, informar, notificar.—II. vn. consultar, aconsejarse, pedir o tomar consejo; aconsejar.

advised [ædváisd], a. premeditado, deliberado; avisado, aconsejado, advertido, orejeado.

advisedly [ædváisedli], adv. deliberadamente, advertidamente.—**advisedness** [-nes], s. juicio, reflexión, deliberación.

advisement [ædváismœnt], s. deliberación, consideración.—to take under a., someter a consideración, estudio o deliberación.

adviser [ædváisœr], s. consejero; asesor; informante.—legal a., abogado.

advisory [ædváisori], a. aconsejador; de carácter de consejo; consultivo.—a. board, junta consultiva.

advocacy [ædvokasi], s. defensa (de una doctrina, de un reo).

advocate [ædvokeit]. I. va. defender, abogar por. II. s. defensor; abogado (apl. al de cada parte en una causa); intercesor.

advowee [ædvaui], s. (igl.) colador.

advowson [ædváshʊn], s. (igl.) colación.

adynamia [ædinémia], s. adinamia.

adynamic [ædinámic], a. débil, adinámico.

adz, adze [ædš]. I. s. azuela.—cooper's a., doladera. II. va. azolar, desbastar.

æ [i o e], diptongo de origen latino, equivalente al griego ai; en muchos derivados se reemplaza æ por la e sola.

ædile [idail], s. edil.—**ædileship** [-ship], s. edilidad.

ægilops [íyilops], s. (med.) egílope; (bot.) egílope, rompesacos.

ægis [íyis], s. escudo, broquel, égida.

ægyptiacum [iyiptáiacʊm], s. (vet.) egipciaco.

Æolian [iólian], a. = EOLIAN.

aerate [écreit], va. airear, ventilar; (med.) producir aeración en el agua potable, o en la sangre.

aerated [écreited], a. dícese del pan hecho con anhídrido carbónico preparado separadamente, en vez de obtenerlo por la fermentación de la masa.

aeration [ecréshʊn], s. aeración.

aerator [ecréitœr], s. aparato para la aeración.

aerial [eírial]. I. a. aéreo.—a. sickness, mal de altura, enfermedad de los aviadores.—a. ladder, escalera alargable de bombero. II. s. (aer.) antena.

aerie [éœri], *s.* nido de águila.
aeriform [éœriform], *a.* aeriforme.
aerify [éœrifai], *va.* aerificar.
aerobia, aerobes [éœróubia, -oubŝ], *s. pl.* (biol.) aerobios.
aerobian [eœróubian]. **I.** *s.* (biol.) aerobio. **II.** *a.* aeróbico.
aerobic [eœróbic], *a.* (biol.) aeróbico.
aerobiosis [eœrobaiósis], *s.* aerobiosis, vida que se alimenta de aire u oxígeno.
aeroboat [éœrobout], *s.* hidroaeroplano.
aerobus [-bʊs], *s.* aeroplano de viajeros, aerobús.
aerocraft [-cræft], *s.* = AIRCRAFT.
aerocurve [-cœrv], *s.* (aer.) avión de superficies curvas.
aerodrome [-droum], *s.* = AIRDROME.
aerodynamics [éœrodainǽmics], *s.* aerodinámica.
aerofoil [-foil], *s.* (aer.) superficie de sustentación.
aerogram [éœrogram], *s.* radiotelegrama, aerograma.
aerography [eœrógrafi], *s.* aerografía.
aerolite [éœrolait], *s.* aerolito.
aerology [eœróloyi], *s.* aerología.
aeromancy [éœromǽnsi], *s.* aeromancia.
aeromechanics [éœromecǽnics], *s.* aeromecánica.
aerometer [eœrómetœr], *s.* aerómetro.
aerometric [eœrométric], *a.* aerométrico.
aerometry [eœrómetri], *s.* aerometría.
aeromotor [éœromótor], *s.* motor de aeroplano; aeroplano impulsado por motor.
aeronaut [éœronot], *s.* aeronauta.
aeronautic [éœronótik], *a.* aeronáutico.
aeronautics [éœronótics], *s.* aeronáutica, aerostación.
aeronef [éœronef], *s.* máquina de volar.
aeroplane [éœropléin], *s.* aeroplano, avión.
aerophone [-foun], *s.* aerófono.
aeroscopy [eœróscopi], *s.* aeroscopia.
aerostat [éœrostat], *s.* aeróstato, globo dirigible; globo aerostático.—**aerostatic** [-tátic], *a.* aerostático.—**aerostatics,** *s.* aerostática.—**aerostation** [-téiŝhʊn], *s.* aerostación, navegación aérea en globos dirigibles.
æruginous, *V.* ERUGINOUS.
æsthesia [eszíŝia], *s.* sensibilidad.
æsthete, æsthetic, æsthetically, æsthetics, *V.* ESTHETE, ESTHETIC, etc.
æstival, estival.
æther [ízœr], *s.* éter.
ætiology [itióloyi], *s.* (filos. y med.) etiología.
afar [afár], *adv.* lejos, distante, a gran distancia.—**from a.** de lejos, desde lejos, a distancia.—**a. off,** muy distante, remoto.
afeard [afíœrd], *a.* (fam.) miedoso, con miedo.
afebrile [afébril], *a.* sin fiebre.
Afer [éifœr], *s.* ábrego.
affability [æfabíliti], **affableness** [ǽfabœlnes], *s.* afabilidad, agrado, dulzura, amabilidad.
affable [ǽfabœl], *a.* afable, amable, atento.
affably [ǽfabli], *adv.* afablemente.
affair [æféar], *s.* asunto, negocio, cuestión, lance; (mil.) acción, encuentro.—**a. of honor,** lance de honor, duelo.
affect [æféct], *va.* afectar, influir en; afectar, conmover; tomar la forma o el carácter de; afectar, fingir; frecuentar; gustar de, tener afición a; (com.) hipotecar.
affectation [æfectéŝhʊn], *s.* afectación.
affected [æfécted], *a.* emocionado, conmovido; afectado, artificioso; inclinado, afecto; afectado, alterado; atacado (de enfermedad).—**a. quadratic,** (mat.) ecuación completa de segundo grado.
affectedly [æféctedli], *adv.* afectadamente.
affectedness [æféctednes], *s.* afectación.
affecter [æféctœr], *s.* afectador, fingidor.
affecting [æfécting], *a.* conmovedor.
affectingly [æféctingli], *adv.* conmovedoramente.
affection [æfékŝhʊn], *s.* afecto, cariño; emoción, sentimiento; inclinación, propensidad; estado transitorio; propiedad; (med.) afección.
affectionate [æfékshʊnet], *a.* afectuoso.
affectionately [-li], *adv.* afectuosamente.
affectionateness [-nes], *s.* cualidad de afectuoso.
affective [æféctiv], *a.* afectivo; commovedor.
affectively [æféctivli], *adv.* afectuosamente.
afferent [ǽfœrœnt], *a.* aferente.
affiance [æfáians]. **I.** *s.* palabra de casamiento, esponsales; confianza. **II.** *va.* dar palabra de casamiento; dar prenda.
affiant [æfáiant], *s.* (for.) deponente, declarante.
affidavit [æfidévit], *s.* (for.) declaración escrita.
affiliate [æfílieit]. **I.** *va.* afiliar; prohijar, adhijar, adoptar; (for.) legitimar.—**II.** *vn.* & *vr.* afiliarse.
affiliate(d [æfíliet(ed], *a.* prohijado, afiliado.
affiliation [æfíliéŝhʊn], *s.* afiliación; adopción (de un hijo); (for.) legitimación de un hijo.
affined [æfáind], *a.* afín, pariente por afinidad.
affinity [æfíniti], *s.* afinidad, atracción; afinidad, semejanza o analogía; amor; persona que inspira enamoramiento; afinidad, parentesco por matrimonio; (biol. y gram.) analogía que indica origen común.
affirm [afœ́rm]. **I.** *va.* afirmar, aseverar; confirmar. **II.** *vn.* afirmarse en alguna cosa; declarar formalmente ante un juez.
affirmable [-abœl], *a.* que se puede afirmar.
affirmably [afœ́rmabli], *adv.* afirmativamente.
affirmance [afœ́rmans], *s.* afirmación; confirmación, ratificación.
affirmant [afœ́rmant], *s.* afirmante.
affirmation [afœrméŝhʊn], *s.* afirmación, aserción; palabra que se da solemnemente en vez de juramento; confirmación, ratificación.
affirmative [afœ́rmativ]. **I.** *a.* afirmativo. **II.** *s.* aserción; afirmativa.
affirmatively [afœ́rmativli], *adv.* afirmativamente, aseveradamente, asertivamente.
affirmatory [afœ́rmatori], *a.* asertorio.
affirmer [afœ́rmœr], *s.* afirmante.
affix [afíx], *va.* añadir, pegar, unir; poner (firma, sello).
affix [ǽfix], *s.* añadidura; (gram.) afijo.
afflation [afléŝhʊn], *s.* resuello, inspiración.
afflatus [aflétʊs], *s.* estro, aflato, inspiración; (med.) golpe de aire.
afflict [aflíct], *va.* afligir, angustiar.—**to be afflicted with,** sufrir de.
afflicting [æflícting], *a.* aflictivo.
afflictingly [aflíctingli], **afflictively** [aflíctivli], *adv.* aflictivamente.
affliction [æflíkŝhʊn], *s.* aflición, tribulación; desgracia; mal, achaque.
afflictive [aflíctiv], *a.* aflictivo, penoso.
affluence [ǽfluens], **affluency** [ǽfluensi], *s.* abundancia, opulencia, riqueza; afluencia, aflujo.
affluent [ǽfluent]. **I.** *a.* opulento, afluente, abundante, copioso. **II.** *s.* afluente, tributario.
affluently [ǽfluentli], *adv.* copiosamente.
afflux [ǽflʊx], **affluxion** [æflʊ́cŝhʊn], *s.* afluencia; (med.) aflujo.
afford [æfórd], *va.* producir; proporcionar; deparar. [Con *can*, indica capacidad—generalmente financiera—de hacer algo sin perjuicio propio, v.g., *I cannot* **afford** *to buy that,* no me conviene (o no tengo con que) comprar eso; *he can* **afford** *a house,* tiene con que comprar (o mantener) una casa; *the candidate cannot* **afford** *to be frank,* al candidato no le conviene ser franco.]
afforestation [aforestéŝhʊn], *s.* plantación de un bosque.
affranchise, affranchisement, *V.* ENFRANCHISE, ENFRANCHISEMENT.
affray [afréi], *s.* riña, pendencia, refriega.
affreightment [afréitmœnt], *s.* (com.) fletamento.
affright [afráit]. **I.** *va.* (poét.) aterrar, espantar, asustar. **II.** *s.* terror repentino, susto.
affrighted [afráited], *a.* aterrorizado, asustado.
affrightedly [afráitedli], *adv.* con espanto.
affrighter [afráitœr], *s.* espantador.

affront [afrónt]. **I.** *va.* afrentar, insultar, ultrajar. **II.** *s.* afrenta, insulto, ultraje, agravio.
affronté [afronté], *a.* (blas.) afrontado, frente a frente.
affronter [afrúntœr], *s.* agresor, provocador.
affronting, affrontive [æfrʌnting, -tiv], *a.* insultante, injurioso.
affusion [afiúȝʊn], *s.* afusión.
afghan [ǽfgan], *s.* cubrecama de punto; (**A-**) afgano, de Afganistán.
afield [afíld], *adv.* en el campo.
afire [afáicœr], *adv.* ardiendo.
aflame [afléim], *adv.* en llamas.
afloat [aflóut], *a.* y *adv.* flotante; a bordo; sin rumbo; en circulación (apl. a rumores, etc.); inundado.
afoot [afút], *adv.* a pie; en movimiento; en preparación.
afore [afócer]. **I.** *prep.* antes de; delante. **II.** *adv.* (poco u.) en otro tiempo; (mar.) a proa.
aforegoing [afócergóing], *a.* antedicho, precedente.
aforehand [afócerjand], *adv.* de antemano; con preparación.
aforementioned [afócermênshʊnd], **aforenamed** [-néimd], **aforesaid** [-sed], *a.* dicho, susodicho, mencionado.
aforethought [afócerzót]. **I.** *a.* premeditado. **II.** *s.* premeditación.—**with malice a.**, con premeditación.
aforetime [afócertáim], *adv.* en otro tiempo, antiguamente.
afoul [afául], *adv.* y *a.* (mar.) en colisión; enredado.
afraid [afréid], *a.* amendrentado, atemorizado, temeroso, tímido.—**to be a.**, tener miedo, temer.
afresh [afrésh], *adv.* de nuevo, otra vez.
African [áfricæn], *s.* y *a.* africano; negro.
Africander [æfricándœr], *s.* el nacido en el África del Sur de raza europea.
afront [afrónt], *adv.* enfrente, al frente, de cara.
aft [aft], *adv.* (mar.) a popa o en popa.
after [áftœr]. **I.** *prep.* después de; detrás de; tras; por; respecto de; según. **II.** *adv.* después.—**a. all**, después de todo.—**day a. tomorrow** pasado mañana.—**the day a.**, el día siguiente.
NOTA.—After entra en la composición de muchas palabras y significa después de, nuevo, posterior, subsiguiente; los principales compuestos, fuera de los que se dan después como voces separadas, son: **a.-acceptation**, aceptación tardía.—**a.-account**, cuenta nueva.—**a.-act**, acto subsiguiente.—**a.-age**, posteridad.—**a.-attack**, (mil.) segundo ataque.—**a.-comer**, sucesor.—**a.-cost**, gasto extraordinario.—**a.-crop**, segunda cosecha.—**a.-damp**, mofeta.—**a. dinner**, sobremesa (**a.-dinner speech**, brindis, discurso de sobremesa).—**a.-game**, desquite.—**a.-gathering**, espigadura.—**a.-glow**, resplandor crepuscular.—**a.-hope**, esperanza renovada.—**a.-hours**, deshora, tarde.—**a.-law**, ley posterior.—**a.-image**, imagen accidental (que persiste como estado psicológico).—**a.-life**, vida futura.—**a.-love**, segunda pasión, nuevos amores.—**a.-pains**, (obst.) entuertos.—**a.-reckoning**, nueva cuenta.—**a.-repentance**, arrepentimiento tardío.—**a.-state**, estado o vida futura.—**a.-taste**, resabio, dejo, gustillo.—**a.-times**, tiempos venideros, porvenir.—**a.-tossing**, marejada.—**a.-touch**, (pint.) retoque.—**a.-wit**, entendimiento tardío.
afterbirth [áftœrbœrz], *s.* secundina, pares, placenta.
aftermath [áftœrmæz], *s.* segunda siega; resultados, consecuencias.
afternoon [áftœrnun], *s.* tarde.
afterpiece [áftœrpis], *s.* sainete, entremés; (mar.) talón del timón.
afterthought [áftœrzót], *s.* idea tardía; algo que se ocurrió más tarde.
afterward o **afterwards**, [áftœrucerd, -s] *adv.* después.—**long a.**, mucho tiempo después.
afterwise [áftœruais], *a.* discreto pasada la ocasión, o después de tiempo.

again [aguén], *adv.* otra vez, segunda vez, aun, de nuevo; por otra parte, además; asimismo. **a. and a.**, muchas veces.—**as much a.**, otro tanto más.—**now and a.**, a veces, de vez en cuando.—**once and a.**, repetidas veces.—**never a.**, nunca más.—**come a.**, vuelva Vd.
against [æguénst], *prep.* contra; enfrente de; en contraste con, comparado con, por; listo para.—**a. time**, dentro de tiempo limitado (apl. a carreras); para ganar tiempo.—**a. the fiber**, a contrapelo; de mal grado.
agamic [ægǽmic], *a.* (biol.) asexual; (bot.) criptógamo.
agape [agáp o aguép], *adv.* con la boca abierta.
agaric [ǽgaric], *s.* agárico, garzo.
agasp [agásp], *adv.* y *a.* jadeante; anhelante, ansioso.
agate [ǽguet], *s.* ágata; (imp.) tipo de 5½ puntos.—**a.-ware**, utensilios de imitación de ágata.
agaty [ǽgati], *a.* parecido al ágata.
agave [aguévi o agáve], *s.* (bot.) maguey, cabuya.
agaze [aguéish], *a.* y *adv.* en el acto de mirar.
age [éiȳ]. **I.** *s.* edad; época, período; vejez, ancianidad.—**ages** (fam.), larguísimo tiempo, una eternidad.—**full a.**, mayor edad.—**golden a.**, edad de oro; siglo de oro.—**of a.**, mayor de edad.—**under a.**, de menor edad.—**to become of a.**, llegar a mayor edad. **II.** *vn.* envejecerse; deteriorar (a veces mejorar) por envejecimiento. **III.** *va.* (tec.) acelerar artificialmente el desarrollo de ciertas propiedades; curar.
aged [éyed], *a.* viejo, anciano; de la edad de.
agency [éyensi], *s.* acción; agente, instrumento; agencia; diligencia, gestión, influencia, medio, órgano, fuerza; factoraje.—**a. office**, oficina de negocios.—**free a.**, libre albedrío.
agenda [æyénda], **agendum** [æȳéndʌm], *s.* agenda, memorándum; programa (de deliberaciones, etc.); (igl.) ritual. (La primera palabra, que es el plural de la segunda, es más usada.)
agent [éirent]. **I.** *a.* activo. **II.** *s.* agente, el que o lo que obra; agente, representante; (fís.) agente; (for.) mandatario, apoderado.
agentship [éyentship], *s.* agencia, factoría.
agglomerate [æglómœreit], *va.* aglomerar, amontonar.
agglomerate, agglomeration [-éishun], *s.* aglomeración, amontonamiento.
agglutinant [æglútinant], *a.* aglutinante.
agglutinate [æglútinet], *va.* aglutinar, pegar.
agglutination [æglútinéishun], *s.* aglutinación.
agglutinative [æglútinativ], *a.* aglutinante, adhesivo.—**a. language**, lengua aglutinante.
aggrandize [ǽgrandais], *va.* agrandar, engrandecer; elevar, exaltar.
aggrandizement [ǽgrandáishmœnt o agrándishmœnt], *s.* engrandecimiento; elevación, exaltación.
aggrandizer [ǽgrandaisœr], *s.* ensalzador.
aggravate [ǽgraveit], *va.* aumentar, agravar; irritar; exasperar.
aggravating [ǽgravéiting], *a.* agravante; irritante, provocativo.
aggravatingly [ǽgravéitingli], *adv.* agravantemente.
aggravation [ǽgravéishun], *s.* agravación, agravamiento; (for.) circunstancia agravante; (fam.) provocación, vejación; irritación.
aggregate [ǽgrigueit]. **I.** *a.* agregado, juntado, unido; aglomerado; mezclado. **II.** *s.* conjunto, totalidad; mezcla, materias mezcladas; (ing.) agregado, material duro (apl. al hormigón). **III.** *va.* agregar, juntar; ascender a.
aggregately [ǽgriguetli], *adv.* colectivamente, en junto.
aggregation [ægreguéishun], *s.* agregación; agregado, colección; masa, conjunto, total.
aggregative [ǽgreguetiv], *a.* colectivo.
aggregator [ǽgrigueitœr], *s.* colector, agregador.
aggress [ægrés], *vn.* agredir; invadir.
aggression [ægréshun], *s.* agresión.

Para la pronunciación de æ, œ, ᴅ, s, sh, ʊ, ȳ, ʏ, z, véase la clave al principio del libro.

aggressive [ægrésiv], *a*. agresivo.
aggressively [ægrésivli], *adv*. agresivamente.
aggressiveness [ægrésivnes], *s*. carácter agresivo.
aggressor [ægrésœr], *s*. agresor.
aggrieve [ægrív], *va*. afligir; vejar, oprimir.
aggroup [ægrúp], *va*. agrupar.
aghast [agást], *a*. horrorizado, despavorido, estupefacto.
agile [ǽyil], *a*. ágil, pronto, listo.
agility [aɣíliti], *s*. agilidad, ligereza, expedición, soltura, prontitud.
agio [ǽyio], *s*. (com.) agio, agiotaje.
agistor [aɤístœr], *s*. (for.) guardabosque.
agitable [ǽyitabœl], *a*. agitable.
agitate [ǽyiteit]. **I.** *va*. agitar, revolver, menear; inquietar, perturbar, alborotar; debatir con ahinco; tramar, urdir, maquinar. **II.** *vn*. excitar la opinión pública; alborotar.
agitation [æyitéshun], *s*. agitación; discusión, ventilación; perturbación.
agitator [ǽyitéitœr], *s*. agitador, revolvedor; perturbador, alborotador; demagogo, innovador.
agleam [aglím], *a*. (poét.) fulguroso.
aglet [ǽglet], *s*. herrete; (bot.)antera.
aglow [agló], *adv*. y *a*. fulgurante, en fulguración.
agnail [ǽgneil], *s*. panadizo, uñero.
agnate, agnatic [ægnét, ægnǽtic], *a*. agnaticio; (for.) agnado.
agnation [ægnéshun], *s*. agnación; parentesco.
agnomen [ægnómœn], *s*. sobrenombre.
agnomination [ægnominéshun], *s*. (ret.) paronomasia.
agnostic [ægnóstic], *a*. y *s*. agnóstico.
agnosticism [ægnóstisism], *s*. agnosticismo.
agnus [ǽgnus], **Agnus Dei** [-déi], *s*. agnusdéi.—**a. castus**, (bot.) agnocasto o sauzgatillo.
ago [agó], *adv*. (*contr*. de AGONE) hace, ha: *a long time ago*, hace mucho tiempo; *long ago*, tiempo ha; *how long ago*? ¿cuánto ha?
agog [agóg], *adv*. y *a*. ansioso, anhelante; ansiosamente, (Cuba) con embullo.
agoing [agóing], *adv*. en acción, en movimiento. —**to set a.**, poner en marcha.
agometer [ægómetœr], *s*. (elec.) una especie de reóstato.
agonic line [ægónic láin], (fís.) línea agónica.
agonistes [ægonístis], **agonist**, *s*. atleta o combatiente; competidor.
agonistic(al [ægonístic(al], *a*. agonístico.
agonistically [ægonísticali], *adv*. por modo agonístico.
agonize [ǽgonais]. **I.** *va*. causar gran pena, atormentar. **II.** *vn*. sufrir intensamente, retorcerse de dolor; luchar; hacer grandes esfuerzos.
agonizingly [ægonáisingli], *adv*. en agonías.
agony [ǽgoni], *s*. agonía; angustia, zozobra; intensa emoción.
agouti [agúti], *s*. (zool.) agutí.
agraffe [agráf], *s*. broche; grapita que sujeta cada cuerda del piano.
agrarian [agrérian], *a*. agrario.
agrarianism [agrérianism], *s*. (pol.) división y reparto igual de tierras.
agree [ægrí], *vn*. concordar, acordar, estar de acuerdo; entenderse, ponerse de acuerdo; consentir; convenir (*we agreed to go*, convinimos en ir; *we agreed on the price*, convinimos en el precio); sentar bien; hacer provecho (*this climate agrees with me*, este clima me sienta bien; *wine does not agree with me*, el vino me hace daño); (gram.) concordar.
agreeability [agríabíliti], *s*. afabilidad, agrado, complacencia.
agreeable [agríabœl], *a*. agradable; satisfactorio, aceptable; afable, simpático; condescendiente, complaciente.—**a. to**, de acuerdo con.
agreeableness [agríabœlnes], *s*. agrado, afabilidad, placibilidad, deleite.
agreeably [agríabli], *adv*. agradablemente; complacientemente; conformemente.
agreed [agríd], *a*. convenido, concedido; reconocido; ajustado, acordado; de acuerdo.

agreement [ægríment], *s*. acuerdo, convenio, pacto; consentimiento; armonía; conformidad; (gram.) concordancia.—**In a.**, de acuerdo.
agrestial, agrestic(al [agréstial, agréstic(al], *a*. agreste, rústico, tosco, campestre.
agricultural [ægricúlchural], *a*. agrícola.
agriculture [ǽgricúlchœr], *s*. agricultura; agronomía.
agriculturalist [ǽgricúlchœralist], **agriculturer** [-œr], **agriculturist** [-ist], *s*. agrónomo.
agrimony [ǽgrimoni], *s*. (bot.) agrimonia.
agronomics [ægronómics], *s*. agronomía (considerada como parte de la economía política).
agronomy [agrónomi], *s*. agronomía.
agrope [agróup], *adv*. a tientas.
aground [agráund], *adv*. (mar.) varado, encallado; (fig.) empantanado, en el atolladero.—**to run a.**, encallar, vararse.
ague [éiguiu], *s*. (med.) fiebre o calentura intermitente; calofrío, escalofrío.—**a. tree**, (bot.) sasafrás.
aguish [éiguiuish], *a*. palúdico.
aguishness [-nes], *s*. (med.) paludismo.
ah! [a], *interj*. ¡ah! ¡ay!
aha! [ajá], *interj*. ¡ajá!
ahead [ajéd], *adv*. delante, al frente, a la cabeza; adelante; hacia delante; (mar.) por la proa, avante.—**to be a.**, ir a la cabeza, ir delante.
aheap [ajíp], *adv*. en montón, al granel.
ahem! [ajém], *interj*. ¡oiga! ¡hola!
ahoy! [ajói], *interj*. ¡ah del barco! ¡ha!
aid [eid]. **I.** *va*. y *vn*. ayudar. **II.** *s*. ayuda, auxilio; subsidio; auxiliador; (mil.) ayudante.—**first a.**, primeros auxilios (en accidentes).
aide-de-camp [éi-de-cáng], *s*. (mil.) edecán, ayudante de campo.
aider [éidœr], *s*. auxiliador, auxiliante.
aidless [éidles], *a*. desvalido, desamparado.
aigret o **aigrette** [égret], *s*. (orn.) garzota; cresta, copete, penacho; plumero.
aiguillette o **aiguiet** [éguiulet], *s*. (mil.) herrete, agujeta.
ail [éil]. **I.** *va*. afligir, molestar, inquietar.—**what ails you?** ¿qué tiene Vd.? ¿qué le pasa a Vd.? **II.** *vn*. sufrir, estar enfermo, indispuesto.
ailanthus o **ailantus** [eilánzus, -tus], *s*. (bot.) ailanto.
aileron [éileron], *s*. (aer.) alerón.
ailing [éiling], *a*. doliente, achacoso, enfermizo.
ailment [éilmœnt], *s*. dolencia, achaque.
aim [éim]. **I.** *va*. apuntar (un arma); dirigir, largar, asestar, encarar. **II.** *vn*. (con *at*) hacer puntería; aspirar a, pretender, tratar de, proponerse. **III.** *s*. puntería, encaro; blanco; designio, mira, propósito.—**to miss one's a.**, errar el tiro.—**to take one's a. well**, tomar bien sus medidas.
aimless [éimles], *a*. sin objeto, sin designio, a la ventura.
ain't [éint], *contr*. *vulg*. de *am not*, *is not*, *are not*, *has not*, *have not*.
air [éar]. **I.** *va*. airear, ventilar; secar (al aire o por calor); ostentar; sacar a lucir, pregonar (opiniones propias). **II.** *s*. aire; atmósfera; brisa; semblante, ademán, talante; (mús.) aire, tonada; pl. ínfulas (*to put on airs*, darse ínfulas). **III.** *a*. de aire; neumático; para aire; aéreo; aeronáutico, de aviación.—**a. bladder**, vejiga natatoria.—**a.-borne**, llevado por el aire.—**a. box**, cámara de aire.—**a. brake**, freno neumático.—**a. brush**, pulverizador de aire comprimido.—**a.-built**, quimérico, vano, sin fundamento.—**a. castle**, castillo de naipes.—**a. chamber**, cámara de aire.—**a. cock**, llave de escape de aire.—**a. compressor**, compresor de aire.—**a. condenser**, condensador de enfriamiento por aire.—**a.-cooled**, enfriado por aire.—**a. cooling**, enfriamiento por aire.—**a. drain**, conducto de ventilación; conducto de escape de gases.—**a.-dried**, secado al aire.—**a. drill**, taladro neumático.—**a. fleet**, flotilla de aeroplanos, fuerzas militares aeronáuticas.—**a. force**, fuerzas aéreas militares; ejército aéreo; servicio militar de aviación.—**a. furnace**, horno

de tiro natural; horno de calentar aire.—**a. gap** (elec.) entrehierro.—**a. gun,** escopeta de viento. —**a. hole,** respiradero; (fund.) escarabajo, sopladura; (aer.) vacío, región de extrema rarefacción del aire.—**a. jacket,** camisa de natación.—**a. level,** nivel de burbuja.—**a. lift,** bomba de aire comprimido.—**a. line,** línea recta.—**A. Ministry,** (Ingl.) Ministerio de Aviación.—**a. motor,** motor de aire comprimido.—**a. proof,** hermético.—**a. pump,** (fís.) máquina neumática; (m. v.) bomba de aire, bomba de aspiración del condensador.—**a. shaft,** respiradero, pozo de ventilación.—**a.-slaked,** apagada al aire (apl. a la cal).—**a. speed,** (aer.) velocidad del aire, velocidad (de un avión) relativa al aire.—**a.-speed indicator, o meter,** (aer.) indicador de velocidad (con respecto al aire). —**a.-tight,** hermético, a prueba de aire.—**a. trap,** sifón obturador, tubo en U.—**a. valve,** válvula (de admisión o de salida) de aire.

aircraft [éarcræft], *s.* máquina o máquinas de volar (aeroplanos, dirigibles, etc.)

airdrome [éardroum], *s.* aeródromo, campo de aviación.

airily [éarili], *adv.* ligeramente, vivamente, alegremente, (fam.) pomposamente, con ínfulas.

airiness [éarines], *s.* ventilación, oreo; vivacidad, viveza; ligereza, actividad.

airing [éaring], *s.* caminata, paseata, paseo.

airless [éarles], *a.* falto de ventilación.

airlike [éarlaik], *a.* tenue o ligero como el aire.

airman [éarmæn], *s.* aviador, aeronauta.

airplane [éarplein], *s.* aeroplano.

airport [éarport], *s.* paradero o estación para aeroplanos.

airship [éarship], *s.* aeronave, dirigible.

airsickness [éarsicnes], *s.* = AERIAL SICKNESS.

airway [éaruéi], *s.* conducto para aire; pozo o galería de ventilación; (aer.) ruta de aviación.

airwoman [éarúman], *s.* aviadora.

airworthy [éaruerbi], *a.* (aer.) buen volador, seguro (apl. a aeroplanos y dirigibles).

airy [éari], *a.* aéreo; etéreo, vaporoso, tenue; ligero, trivial; vivaz, alegre; visionario; vanidoso, estirado.

aisle [áil], *s.* pasillo, pasadizo; (arq.) nave, ala.

aisled [áild], *a.* provisto de pasillos.

ait [éit], *s.* isleta (en un río).

ajar [ayár], *adv.* y *a.* entreabierto, entornado; en pugna.

akimbo [akímbo], *a.* en jarras.

akin [akín], *a.* consanguíneo, emparentado; análogo, semejante.

alabaster [élabástœr], *s.* alabastro.

alack! alackaday! [aléc, alécadei], *interj.* ¡ay! ¡ay de mí!

alacrity [alécriti], *s.* alacridad, presteza, celo.

alamode [alamóud], *adv.* (fam.) a la moda.

alar [élar], *a.* alado, alígero; axilar.

alarm [alárm]. **I.** *s.* alarma; despertador; mecanismo de alarma; señal de alarma; rebato.—**a. bell,** campana o timbre de alarma.—**a. clock,** despertador.—**to sound the a.,** dar la alarma. **II.** *va.* alarmar; dar la alarma a; asustar. **III.** *vn.* dar la alarma.

alarming [alárming], *a.* alarmante.

alarmingly [alármingli], *adv.* alarmantemente.

alarmist [alármist], *s.* alarmista.

alarum [alárum], *s.* rebato; despertador.

alas [alás], *interj.* ¡ay! V. ALACK!

alate, alated [éileit, -ed], *a.* (bot.) alado.

alaternus [alatœrnus], *s.* (bot.) ladierno.

alb [ælb], *s.* (igl.) alba.

albacore [élbæcor], *s.* (ict.) albacora, bonito.

Albanian [ælbénian], *a.* albanés.

albata [ælbéta], *s.* plata blanca de Alemania.

albatross [élbatros], *s.* (ornit.) albatros.

albeit [olbfit], *adv.* (ant.) aunque, bien que.

albescent [ælbésent], *a.* blanquecino, emblanqueciéndose.

albino [ælbíno], *s.* albino.

Albion [élbiun], *s.* Albion, Inglaterra.

albuginea [ælbiuyínia], *s.* (anat.) conjuntiva.

albugineous [ælbiuyíneus], *a.* albugíneo.

albugo [ælbiúgo], *s.* (med.) albugo.

album [élbum], *s.* album.

albumen, albumin [ælbiúmen], *s.* (quím.) albúmina; (bot.) albumen.

albumenize [ælbiúmenaiś], *va.* impregnar con albumen.

albuminoid [ælbiúminoid]. **I.** *a.* albuminoideo, albuminoide. **II.** *s.* albuminoide.

albuminous [ælbiúminus], *a.* albuminoso.

albuminuria [ælbiúminúria], *s.* (med.) albuminuria.

alburnum [albœrnum], *s.* (bot.) alburno, albura.—V. SAPWOOD.

alcaic [ælkéic]. **I.** *s.* verso alcaico. **II.** *a.* alcaico.

alcazar [ælcásar], *s.* alcázar.

alchemic(al [ælkémic(al], *a.* alquímico.

alchemically [ælkémicali], *adv.* alquímicamente.

alchemist [ælkemist], *s.* alquimista.

alchemistic(al [ælkemístic(al], *a.* alquímico.

alchemy [élkemi], *s.* alquimia.

alcohol [élcojol], *s.* alcohol.—**absolute a.,** alcohol absoluto o puro.—**denatured a.,** alcohol desnaturalizado, alcohol de arder.—**wood a.,** alcohol metílico.

alcoholic [ælcojólic]. **I.** *a.* alcohólico. **II.** *s.* (en *pl.*) líquidos alcohólicos.

alcoholimeter [ælcojolímetœr], **alcoholmeter** [ælcojolmítœr], **alcoholometer** [ælcojolómetœr], *s.* alcoholímetro.

alcoholism [élcojolism], *s.* alcoholismo.

alcoholization [ælcojoliśéshun], *s.* alcoholización.

alcoholize [élcojolaiś], *va.* alcoholar o alcoholizar.

Alcoran [ælcorán], *s.* Alcorán.

Alcoranish [ælcoránish], *a.* alcoránico.

alcove [élcov], *s.* alcoba, retrete.

alcyon [élcion], *a.* y *s.* V. HALCYON.

Aldebaran [ældébaran], *s.* (astr.) Aldebarán.

aldehyde [éldejaid], *s.* aldehido.

alder [óldœr], *s.* (bot.) aliso.

alderman [óldœrman], *s.* regidor.

aldermanate, aldermanship [óldœrmanet, -ship], *s.* regiduría.

aldermanic [-ménic], *a.* perteneciente al regidor.

aldern [óldœrn], *a.* hecho de aliso.

Aldine [éldin], *a.* aldino.

ale [éil], *s.* cerveza inglesa.—**a. conner,** inspector de cervecerías.

aleak [alík], *adv.* y *a.* que se sale o deja fugar (el agua, etc.); saliéndose.

aleatory [é- (o á-) leatori], *a.* (for.) aleatorio; de azar.

aleberry [éilberi], *s.* bebida de cerveza hervida con pan y especias.

alecost [éilcost], *s.* (bot.) atanasia.

alee [alí], *adv.* (mar.) a sotavento.

alehoof [éiljuf], *s.* hiedra terrestre.

alehouse [éiljaus], *s.* taberna.—**a. keeper,** tabernero.

alembic [alémbic], *s.* alambique.

alert [alœrt]. **I.** *a.* alerta, vigilante; vivo, activo. —**on the a.,** sobre aviso. **II.** *s.* (mil.) sorpresa.

alertness [alœrtnes], *s.* vigilancia, cuidado; viveza, actividad, prontitud.

alewife [éiluaif], *s.* tabernera; (ict.) especie de arenque norteamericano.

alexanders [ælegsǽndœrs], *s.* (bot.) esmirnio, o apio caballar.

Alexandrian [ælegsǽndriæn], *s.* y *a.* alejandrino.

Alexandrine [ælegsǽndrin], *s.* verso alejandrino.

alexia [ælécsia], *s.* alexia, pérdida de la facultad de leer, sin pérdida de la vista.

alexin [æléksin], *s.* (quím.) alexina.

alexipharmic, alexiteric(al [alecsifármic, alecsitéric (al], *a.* alexifármaco.

alfalfa [ælfalfa], *s.* alfalfa.

alga [élga], *pl.* **algae** [élyi], *s.* (bot.) alga.

algal [élgal], *a.* algáceo.

algaroth [élgaroz], *s.* régulo de antimonio.

algebra [élyebra], *s.* álgebra.

algebraic(al [ælyebréic(al], *a.* algebraico.

algebraist [ǽlɣebréist], *s.* algebrista.
Algerian [ælɣírian], **Algerine** [ælɣerín], *a.* y *s.* argelino.
algid [ǽlɣid], *a.* álgido.
algoid [ǽlgoid], *a.* algoide, semejante a las algas.
algology [ælgóloɣi], *s.* estudio de las algas.
Algonkin [ælgónkin], **Algonquian** (-kian), **Algonquin** (-kin), *s.* y *a.* algonquín.
algor [ǽlgœr], *s.* (med.) algidez.
algorithm [ǽlgorizm], *s.* algoritmo.
algous [ǽlgus], *a.* algoso; algoide.
alguazil [ælguaŝil], *s.* alguacil, corchete, esbirro.
alias [éilias], *adv.* alias, por otro nombre.
alibi [ǽlibai], *s.* (for.) coartada.—**to prove an a.**, probar la coartada.
alible [ǽlbœl], *a.* nutritivo.
alidade [ǽlided], *s.* alidada.
alien [élien]. **I.** *a.* ajeno, no pertinente, extraño; extranjero; de extranjeros; discorde, contrario. **II.** *s.* extranjero.
alienable [élienabœl], *a.* enajenable, traspasable.
alienage [élieney], **alienship** [élienŝhip], *s.* extranjía, extranjería.
alienate [élienet], *va.* enajenar, traspasar; quitar, robar (el amor, etc.); alejar, hacer indiferente.
alienation [elienéŝhun], *c.* enajenamiento, enajenación, desapropio, traspaso de dominio; extrañación, desapego, desunión, desvío; alienación, descarrío, enajenación mental.
alienee [elieni], *s.* aquel a quien pasa la propiedad de una cosa.
alienism [élienism], *s.* = ALIENAGE; (med.) frenopatía.
alienist [élienist], *s.* alienista, frenópata.
alienor [élienor], *s.* (for.) enajenante; enajenador.
aliform [ǽliform], *a.* aliforme.
alight [ælait]. **I.** *vn.* bajar, apearse, desmontarse; (con *on*) posarse (sobre); dar (con.). **II.** *a.* y *adv.* ardiendo; encendido; iluminado.
align [aláin], *va.* alinear. *V.* ALINE.
alignment [aláinmœnt], *s.* alineación.
alike [aláic]. **I.** *a.* igualmente, del mismo modo; a la par. **II.** *a.* semejante; igual.
aliment [ǽlimœnt], *s.* alimento.
alimental [æliméntal], **alimentary** [æliméntari], *a.* nutritivo, alimenticio.
alimentally [æliméntali], *adv.* nutritivamente.
alimentation [ælimentéŝhun], *s.* alimentación.
alimentiveness [æliméntivnes], *s.* instinto de la alimentación.
alimony [ǽlimoni], *s.* (for.) alimentos, asistencias de divorcio o separación.
aline [aláin], *va.* y *vn.* alinear(se).
alinement [aláinmœnt] =ALIGNMENT.
aliped [ǽliped], *a.* alípedo, quiróptero.
aliphatic [ælifǽtic], *a.* (quím.) alifático, graso.
aliquant [ǽlikuant], *a.* alicuanta.
aliquot [ǽlikuot], *a.* alícuota.—**a. parts** (arit.) partes alícuotas.
alish [éiliŝh], *a.* acervezado.
Alisma *s.* (bot.) alisma.
alive [aláiv], *a.* vivo, viviente; vivo, no apagado; activo, animado, concurrido; sensible.—**a. with,** lleno de.
alizarine [alíŝarin], *s.* alizarina.
alkalescent [ælcalésent], *a.* alcalescente.
alkalescence [ælcælésens], *s.* alcalescencia.
alkali [ǽlcalai], *s.* álcali; carbonato sódico calcinado; substancias minerales de las aguas y suelos, menos la sal común.—**a. soil** (agr.) suelo con gran cantidad de sales solubles eflorescentes.—**a. waste,** residuos de la fabricación de álcalis.
alkalify [ælcǽlifai o élcalifai], *va.* alcalizar.
alkaligenous [ælcalíɣenus], *a.* alcalígeno.
alkalimeter [ælcalímetœr], *s.* alcalímetro.
alkalimetry [ælcalímetri], *s.* alcalimetría.
alkaline [ǽlcalain], *a.* alcalino.
alkalinity [ælcalíniti], *s.* alcalinidad.
alkalization [ælcaliŝéŝhun], *s.* alcalización.
alkalize [ǽlcalaiŝ], *va.* alcalizar.
alkaloid [ǽlcaloid], *s.* alcaloide, base orgánica.

alkanet [ǽlcanet], *s.* (bot.) orcaneta, buglosa, onoquiles, melera; ancusa.
alkermes [ælkœrmiŝ], *s.* alquermes.
all [oll]. **I.** *a.* todo, todos; todo, lleno de (*he was all promises,* era todo promesas).—**a. of,** todo, todos; por lo menos.—**a. other,** los demás.—**a. that,** otras cosas por el estilo. **II.** *s.* todo; todos, todo el mundo; todo lo.—**a. and singular, a. and sundry,** (for.) todos y cada uno, colectiva e individualmente.—**a. hail!** ¡salud! ¡bienvenido!—**a. in a.,** todo, todas las cosas; (*adv.*) en conjunto; completamente.—**a. told,** en conjunto, por todo.—**after a.,** después de todo.—**above a.,** sobre todo, ante todo.—**for a.,** a pesar de.—**in a.,** por todo, en junto.—**once for a.,** una vez por todas, por última vez.—**the All,** el gran todo, el universo.—**III.** *adv.* completamente; muy, -ísimo.—**a. abroad,** defectuoso, equivocado; confundido, perplejo.—**a. along,** siempre, constantemente; de un extremo a otro de, por todo (el camino, etc.).—**a. around,** por todas partes; en todo respecto.—**a. but,** casi.—**a. in,** (fam.) agotado, postrado, medio muerto.—**a. in the wind,** (fam.) confundido, perplejo; (mar.) en facha.—**a. one,** igual, indiferente.—**a. over,** terminado, acabado (*it is all over,* ha terminado, ha pasado); por todas partes; (fam.) exactamente, como, copia de.—**a. right** (fam.) está bien, corriente, bueno.—**a. round,** completo; de idoneidad general; por todas partes.—**a. too,** perfectamente, evidentemente.—**a. the better** (worse), tanto mejor (peor).—**a. the same,** a pesar de eso, a pesar de todo.—**at a.,** absolutamente; de alguna (o ninguna) manera; en absoluto.—**for good and a.,** una vez por todas; definitivamente.—**not at a.,** de ninguna manera, nada de eso; no por cierto, no tal; no hay de qué.

NOTA.—**All** entra en la composición de numerosos vocablos, unas veces como adverbio en el sentido de "enteramente," y otras como nombre o adjetivo en el sentido de "todo" o "todos." En unos pocos compuestos, como **almighty,** todopoderoso, pierde una **l:** en los demás suele escribirse con un guión entre los dos elementos, como se ve en los siguientes, que son los más usados:—
a.-consuming, que todo lo consume.—**a.-embracing,** omnímodo.—**A.-fools' Day,** día de engañabobos (el primero de abril en varios países). *V.* APRIL.—**a.-fours,** los cuatro palos de naipes; cuatro patas.—**to go on a. fours,** gatear, andar a gatas.—**A.-hallowe'en,** víspera de Todos los Santos.—**A.-hallowmass, A.-hallowtide,** festividad de Todos los Santos.—**a.-powerful,** omnipotente, poderosísimo.—**a.-seeing,** omnividente, que todo lo ve.—**A.-souls' Day,** día de Difuntos.
Allah [ǽla], *s.* Alá.
alantois [ælǽntois], *s.* alantoides.
allay [aléi], *va.* aliviar, aquietar; apaciguar.
allayment [æléimœnt], *s.* alivio, desahogo.
allegation [æleguéŝhun], **allegement** [aléɣmœnt], *s.* alegación; (for.) alegato.
allegator [aleguétœr], **alleger** [aléɣœr], *s.* alegador, afirmante, declarante.
allege [aléɣ], *va.* alegar; declarar o afirmar; sostener; pretender.
allegeable [aléɣabœl], *a.* que se puede alegar.
allegiance [aléɣians], *s.* lealtad, homenaje (a un país o gobierno); fidelidad.—**to swear a.,** hacer pleito homenaje.
allegiant [aléɣiant]. **I.** *a.* leal. **II.** *s.* súbdito.
allegoric(al [ælegóric(al], *a.* alegórico.
allegorically [ælegóricali], *adv.* alegóricamente.
allegoricalness [ælegóricalnes], *s.* calidad de alegórico.
allegorist [ǽlegorist], **allegorizer** [ælegoráiŝer], *s.* el que alegoriza.
allegorize [ǽlegoraiŝ]. **I.** *va.* alegorizar. **II.** *vn.* usar alegorías.
allegory [ǽlegori], *s.* alegoría.
allegretto [ælegréto], *s.* (mús.) alegreto.
allegro [ælégro], *s.* (mús.) alegro.
allelujah [ælelúya], *s.* aleluya.
allemande [ælemánd], *s.* (danz.) alemana o alemanda.
alleviate [ælívieit], *va.* aliviar.—**alleviation** [-ieiŝhun], *s.* alivio, paliativo, calmante.

alleviative [ælíviativ], *a.* y *s.* paliativo.

alley [ǽle], **alley-way** [-uei], *s.* callejuela, callejón, caminillo; pasillo, pasadizo.

alliance [aláians], *s.* alianza, unión, asociación.

allied [aláid], *a.* aliado, unido; relacionado.

allies [aláis], *s.* (*pl.* de ALLY) aliados.

alligation [aliguéshun], *s.* (arit.) aligación.

alligator [æliguéitor], *s.* caimán; (Mex.) lagarto. —**a.-apple**, anona de los pantanos.—**a. pear**, aguacate.—**a.-tree**, árbol que de el liquidámbar.

alliteration [ælítœréshun], *s.* aliteración, paronomasia.

alliterative [ælítœrativ], *a.* voces que empiezan con una misma letra.

allocate [álokeit], *va.* colocar; señalar, asignar.

allocation [alokéshun], *s.* colocación; asignación, distribución.

allocatur [alokéitur], *s.* (for.) "cúmplase."

allocution [alokiúshun], *s.* alocución.

allodial [alódial], *a.* (for.) alodial.

allodium [alódium], *s.* (for.) alodio.

allopath [ǽlopaz], **allopathist** [ælópazist], *s.* alópata.

allopathic [ælopázic], *a.* alopático.

allopathy [ælópazi], *s.* alopatía.

allot [ælót], *va.* distribuir, partir, repartir, asignar.

allotment [ælótmœnt], *s.* lote, parte, porción; asignación, repartimiento.

allotropic [ælotrópic], *a.* alotrópico.

allotropism [ælótropism], **allotropy** [alótropi], *s.* (quím.) alotropía.

allottable [alótabœl], *a.* repartible.

allow [æláu]. **I.** *va.* permitir, dejar, conceder; dar, ceder; confesar, admitir; aprobar; (com.) rebajar, descontar, deducir. **II.** *vn.* (con **for**) tener en cuenta; dejar (espacio, etc.) para.

allowable [æláuabœl], *a.* admisible, permisible.

allowableness [æláuabœlnes], *s.* calidad de permisible.

allowably [æláuabli], *adv.* permisivamente.

allowance [æláuans], *s.* concesión; asignación; ración, gajes, pensión, abono, alimentos, mesada; permiso; indulgencia; (com.) descuento, rebaja; (tecn.) tolerancia, discrepancia permitida.—**to make a. for**, hacerse cargo de; tener en cuenta.

alloy [ælói]. **I.** *s.* mezcla; impureza; (fun.) aleación; liga.—**a. steel**, acero de aleación (que contiene otros elementos—níquel, cromo, etc.— que hierro y carbono). **II.** *va.* desvirtuar con elementos impuros o de inferior calidad (literal y figuradamente); (fun.) alear, ligar.

alloyage [alóiey], *s.* (fund.) aleación.

allspice [ólspais], *s.* V. PIMENTO.

allude [æliúd], *vn.* aludir.

allure [æliúcer], *va.* halagar, atraer, tentar, seducir; cebar.

allurement [æliúcermœnt], *s.* tentación, seducción; cebo, añagaza.

allurer [æliúcœrœr], *s.* seductor, engañador.

alluring [æliúcering], *a.* seductivo, tentador.

alluringly [æliúcœringli], *adv.* halagüeñamente, seductoramente.

alluringness [æliúcœringnes], *s.* calidad de atractivo o tentador.

allusion [æliúyun], *a.* alusión; insinuación, indirecta.

allusive [æliúsiv], *a.* alusivo.

allusively [æliúsivli], *adv.* alusivamente.

allusiveness [æliúsivnes], *s.* calidad de alusivo.

alluvial [æliúvial], *a.* aluvial.—**a. cone**, o **fan**, abanico aluvial (apl. al formado por un arroyo al entrar en un valle).

alluvion [æliúvion], *s.* avenida, inundación; (geol.) aluvión; erupción de lodo; (for.) derrubio.

alluvium [æliúvium], *s.* (geol.) aluvión.

ally [ælái]. **I.** *va.* unir. **II.** *vn.* aliarse. **III.** *n.* (ǽlai) aliado; confederado, compañero; auxiliador; cuerpo u organismo análogo.

Almagest [ǽlmœyest], *s.* Almagesto.

alma mater [ǽlma métœr], *s.* la universidad o colegio donde uno se ha educado.

almanac [ólmanac], *s.* almanaque, calendario.

almandite [ǽlmændait], *s.* (min.) almandina.

almightiness [olmáitines], *s.* omnipotencia.

almighty [olmáiti], *a.* todopoderoso.

almond [ámund o ǽlmund], *s.* (bot.) almendra, alloza; almendro, allozo; (anat.) amígdala.

almoner [ǽlmunœr], *s.* limosnero.

almonry [-ri], *s.* lugar donde se reparten limosnas.

almost [ólmoust], *adv.* casi.

alms [ams], *s.* limosna.—**a. basket**, bacinilla, plato o cesto para limosna; alcancía.

almsdeed [ámsdíd], *s.* obra de caridad.

almsgiver [-guívœr], *s.* limosnero; el que da limosna.

almsgiving [-guíving], *s.* acto de dar limosna.

almshouse [-jáus], *s.* hospicio, casa de caridad.

almug [ǽlmug], *s.* (bot.) sándalo.

alnagar, **alnager** [ǽlneigœr], *s.* el que anea.

alnage [ǽlney], *s.* aneaje.

aloe [ǽlo], *s.* (bot.) áloe, lináloe; azabara; palo de áloe.—**aloes**, (*sing.* y *pl.*) áloe o acíbar; zábida o zábila.

aloetic(al [aloético(al], *a.* aloético.

aloft [alóft], *adv.* arriba, en alto.—**lay a.**, (mar.) todo el mundo arriba.—**to set a.**, elevar, subir.

aloin [ǽloin], *s.* acíbar.

alomorph [ǽlomorf], *s.* alomorfo.

alone [alóun], *a.* y *adv.* solo; solamente, tan sólo; único.

aloneness [alóunnes], *s.* el estado de ser solo y sin igual (apl. a Dios).

along [ælóng]. **I.** *prep.* a lo largo de; en todo el largo de; al lado de. **II.** *adv.* a lo largo; adelante.—**a. with**, con, junto con.

alongshore [alóngshoar], *adv.* a lo largo de la costa, a la orilla.

alongside [ælóngsaid], *adv.* y *prep.* a lo largo de, al lado, costado con costado, junto a (*alongside a ship*, al costado de un buque).

aloof [alúf], *adv.* lejos, de lejos, apartado, a distancia.—**to stand a.**, mantenerse apartado, no mezclarse.

alopecia [ælopísia], *s.* (med.) alopecia; (vulg.) peladera.

aloud [aláud], *adv.* alto, en voz alta, recio.

alow [aló], *adv.* (mar. y poét.) abajo o bajo.

alpaca [ælpéca], *s.* alpaca, paco; género de alpaca.

alpenstock [ǽlpenstoc], *s.* (alem.) palo con punta de hierro que se emplea en la ascensión de los Alpes.

alpha [ǽlfa], *s.* alfa; (fig.) principio.—**a. and omega**, el primero y el último, el principio y el fin.—**a. rays**, rayos alfa.

alphabet, **alphabetize** [ǽlfabetais], *va.* colocar por orden alfabético.

alphabetarian [ælfabetérian], *s.* el que aprende el alfabeto.

alphabetic(al [ælfabétic(al], *a.* alfabético.

alphabetically [ælfabéticali], *adv.* alfabéticamente.

alphenic [ælfénic], *s.* alfeñique; azúcar candi.

alphonsin [ælfónsin], *s.* (cir.) sacabalas.

alpine [ǽlpin], *a.* alpestre; de las grandes alturas.

Alpini [olpini], *s. pl.* alpinos, soldados italianos de montaña.

Alpino [olpino], *s.* (Singular de ALPINI.)

alpinist [ǽlpinist], *s.* alpinista, aficionado a excursiones en las montañas.

alpist [ǽlpist], *s.* alpiste.

alquifou [ǽlkiful], *s.* alquifol.

already [olrédi], *adv.* ya, antes de ahora.

Alsatian [ælséishæn], *s.* y *a.*, alsaciano.

alsike [ǽlsic], *s.* trébol sueco.

also [ólso], *adv.* también, igualmente, además; (for.) otrosí.

alt [ælt], *a.* (mús.) alto; agudo.

altar [óltar], *s.* altar; ara; árula.—**a. cloth**, sabanilla, mantel, palia.—**a.-piece**, retablo.— **a. screen**, contrarretablo.—**a. slab**, ara.—**a. table**, mesa del altar.

altarage [óltarey], *s.* (igl.) pie de altar.

altarwise [óltaruaiś], *adv.* en forma de altar.
altazimuth [æltǽsĭmuᴅ], *s.* (astr.) altazimut.
alter [óltœr]. **I.** *va.* alterar, cambiar, modificar; (E. U.) castrar.—**to a. one's condition,** tomar estado, casarse. **II.** *vn.* alterarse, cambiar, variar.
alterability [óltœrabíliti], *s.* alterabilidad.
alterable [óltœrabœl], *a.* alterable; mudable.
alterableness [óltœrabœlnes], *s.* alterabilidad.
alterably [óltœrabli], *adv.* mudablemente.
alterant [óltœrant], *a.* alterante.
alteration [oltœréśʜʊn], *s.* alteración, cambio; corrección.
alterative [óltœretiv]. **I.** *a.* alterativo. **II.** *s.* alterante.
altercate [ǽltœrket], *vn.* altercar.
altercation [æltœrkéśʜʊn], *s.* alteración, altercado; agarrada.
alterer [óltœrœr], *s.* alterador.
altern [óltœrn], *a.* (mat.) alterno.
alternant [æltœrnant], *a.* (mat.) alternante.
alternate [ǽltœrneit]. **I.** *va.* alternar; revezar. **II.** *vn.* alternar, turnar; (elec.) alternar. **III.** [ǽltœrnet], *a.* alterno o alternativo. **IV.** *s.* suplente, substituto.
alternately [æltœrnetli], *adv.* alternadamente, por turno.
alternating [ǽltœrnéiting], alternante, alternativo.—**a. current,** (elec.) corriente alterna.
alternation [æltœrnéśʜʊn], **alternacy** [altœrnasi], **alternateness** [æltœrnetnes], *s.* alternación; turno, revezo.
alternative [æltœrnetiv]. **I.** *s.* alternativa. **II.** *a.* alternativo.
alternatively [æltœrnetivli], *adv.* alternativamente, por turno.
alternativeness [æltœrnativnes], **alternity** [æltœrniti], *s.* alternativa.
alternator [æltœrneitor], *s.* (elec.) alternador
althea [ælȝía], *s.* (bot.) malvavisco.
altho, although [olȝó], *conj.* aunque.
altimeter [æltímetœr], *s.* altímetro.
altimetry [æltímetri], *s.* altimetría.
altisonant [æltísonant], **altisonous** [æltísonʊs], *a.* altisonante, pomposo; altísono.
altitude [ǽltitiud], *s.* altura, altitud, elevación; cumbre, cima.
alto [ǽlto], *a.* y *s.* (mús.) contralto; viola.
altogether [óltuguéᴅœr]. **I.** *adv.* en junto; enteramente, del todo, para siempre. **II.** *s.* conjunto, totalidad.
alto-relievo [álto-rilívo], *s.* (b. a.) alto relieve.
altruism [ǽltruiśm], *s.* altruismo.
altruist [ǽltruist], *s.* altruísta.
altruistic [æltruístic], *a.* altruístico, perteneciente al altruísmo; benévolo, desinteresado.
aludel [ǽludel], *s.* (quím.) aludel.
alum [ǽlᴜm]. **I.** *s.* alumbre.—**a. flower,** alumbre calcinado en polvo.—**a. glass,** alumbre cristalizado.—**a. stone,** alunita.—**concentrated a.,** sulfato de aluminio. **II.** *va.* (tint.) alumbrar.
alumish [álᴜmiśh], *a.* alumbroso, alumbrado.
alumina [aliúmina], *s.* (quím.) alúmina.
aluminium [æluminiᴜm], **aluminum** [aliúminᴜm], *s.* (quím.) aluminio.—**a. bronze, a. gold,** bronce de aluminio (aleación de cobre y aluminio).
aluminous [aliúminᴜs], *a.* aluminoso, arcilloso; alumbroso, alumbrado.
alumna, alumnus [alúmnæ, -nᴜs], *s.* alumna, alumno; beca.
alumni [ælúmnai], *s. pl. de* ALUMNUS.
alumniate [alúmniet], *s.* tiempo que dura la enseñanza de un alumno.
alumnus [ælúmnᴜs], *s.* graduado de una universidad o escuela.
alundum [ælúndʊm], *s.* alundo, corindón artificial.
alunite [ǽliunait], *s.* (min.) alunita.
alveary [ǽlvieri], *s.* colmena; (anat.) alveario.
alveolar [ǽlveolar], *a.* alveolar.
alveolate [ǽlveolet], *a.* alveolado.
alveolus [ælvíolᴜs], *s.* alvéolo; celdilla, cavidad.
alveus [álveᴜs], *s.* álveo.

alvine [ǽlvin *o* ǽlvain], *a.* alvino.
alway [ólue], **always** [ólueś], *adv.* siempre.
alyssum [alísᴜm], *s.* (bot.) alhelí.
am [æm] (*1a pers. de indicat. del verbo* TO BE).—**I a.,** yo soy o estoy.
amadou [ǽmadu], *s.* yesca, hupe.
amain [améin], *adv.* con vehemencia, vigorosamente.
amalgam [amǽlgæm], **amalgama** [amǽlgama], *s.* amalgama; mezcla.—**a. arc,** (elec.) arco formado en un tubo de vació con electrodos de amalgama.
amalgamate [amǽlgamet], *va.* y *vn.* amalgamar; unir, incorporar.
amalgamation [amǽlgaméśʜʊn], *s.* amalgamación; mezcla.
amalgamator [amǽlgaméitœr], *s.* amalgamador; azoguero.
Amanita [ǽmænaitæ], *s.* (bot.) amanita.
amanuensis [amǽniuénsis], *s.* amanuense, escribiente, memorialista.
amaranth [ǽmaranz], *s.* (bot.) amaranto, moco de pavo; color carmesí.
amaranthine [æmaránzin], *a.* de amaranto; encarnado; inmarcesible.
Amaryllis [æmarílis], *s.* (bot.) familia de las amarilídeas; (**a-**) planta amarilídea.
amass [amás], *va.* acumular, amontonar.
amassment [amásmœnt], *s.* cúmulo, montón.
amateur [ǽmachúœr], *s.* aficionado.
amateurish [-iśh], *a.* como de aficionado, superficial.
amateurishly [-li], *adv.* chapuceramente.
amative [ǽmativ], *a.* amotorio.
amativeness [ǽmativnes], *s.* amatividad.
amatorial [æmatórial], **amatorious** [æmatórius], **amatory** [ǽmatori], *a.* amatorio, erótico.
amaurosis [æmorósis], *s.* amaurosis.
amaurotic [æmorótic], *a.* amaurótico.
amaze [améś], *va.* asombrar, pasmar, dejar atónito, sorprender.
amazed [améśt], *a.* atónito, pasmado.
amazedly [améśedli], *adv.* pasmadamente.
amazedness [améśednes], **amazement** [améśmœnt], *s.* asombro, pasmo, aturdimiento.
amazing [améśing], *a.* pasmoso, asombroso, sorprendente.
amazingly [améśingli], *adv.* pasmosamente, asombrosamente.
Amazon [ǽmæśon], *s.* amazona; (**a-**) marimacho; papagayo del Amazomas.—**A. stone,** (min.) amazonita.
Amazonian [-iæn], *a.* amazónico.
amazonite [æmǽśonait], *s.* (min.) amazonita.
ambage [æmbéy], *s.* camino tortuoso.
ambassador [æmbǽsador], *s.* embajador.
ambassadress [æmbǽsadres], *s.* embajadora.
amber [ǽmbœr]. **I.** *s.* ámbar; color de ámbar.—**a. seed,** ambarina, semilla del abelmosco.—**a. varnish,** barniz de succino.—**black a.,** azabache.—**yellow a.,** succino. **II.** *a.* ambarino. **III.** *va.* cubrir con ámbar; ambarar.
ambergris [ǽmbœrgris], *s.* ámbar gris.
ambidexter [æmbidéxtœr], *s.* persona ambidextra; (fig.) el que obra con doblez o come a dos carrillos.
ambidexterity [æmbidextériti], **ambidextrousness** [æmbidéxtrusnes], *s.* igual manejo de ambas manos; doblez, simulación.
ambidextrous [æmbidéxtrᴜs], *a.* ambidextro; falso, hipócrita.
ambient [ǽmbient], *a.* ambiente.
ambiguity [æmbiguíiti], **ambiguousness** [æmbiguiuᴜsnes], *s.* ambigüedad.
ambiguous [æmbíguiuᴜs], *s.* ambiguo, equívoco
ambiguously [-li], *adv.* ambiguamente.
ambit [ǽmbit], *s.* ámbito, circuito, contorno.
ambition [æmbíśʜʊn], *s.* ambición; aspiración.
ambitious [æmbíśʜᴜs], *a.* ambicioso; de aspiraciones; enérgico, emprendedor.
ambitiously [æmbíśʜusli], *adv.* ambiciosamente; anhelosamente.

---

ambitiousness [æmbíshusnes], *s.* calidad de ambicioso; energía.

ambitus [ámbitus], *s.* borde; ámbito; extensión.

amble [æmbœl]. **I.** *vn.* amblar. **II.** *s.* paso de andadura.

ambler [æmblœr], *s.* caballo que ambla.

amblingly [æmblingli], *adv.* a paso de andadura.

amblyopia [æmbliópia], *s.* (med.) ambliopía.

ambo [æmbo], *s.* (igl.) ambón.

ambroid [æmbroid], *s.* ámbar reconstruído, hecho de fragmentos de ámbar.

ambrosia [æmbrósia], *s.* ambrosía; (bot.) ambrosía.

ambrosial [æmbrósial], *a.* delicioso, deleitable; celestial, divino.

Ambrosian [æmbrósian], *a.* ambrosiano.

ambry [æmbri], *s.* despensa; aparador; armario; alacena.

ambulance [æmbiulans], *s.* hospital de sangre; ambulancia.

ambulant [æmbiulant], *a.* ambulante.

ambulation [æmbiuléshun], *s.* paseo.

ambulative [æmbiuletiv], *a.* ambulante, ambulativo, mudable.

ambulatory [æmbiulatori]. **I.** *s.* paseo, galería, corredor. **II.** *a.* =AMBULATIVE.—a. **automatism**, automatismo ambulatorio.

ambuscade [æmbuskeid]. **I.** emboscada. **II.** *va.* atacar desde una emboscada. **III.** *vn.* estar en o preparar una emboscada.

ambush [æmbush]. **I.** *va.* acechar, poner celada. **II.** *s.* (mil) emboscada, celada; sorpesa.—**to lie in a.**, estar emboscado.

ameba, *s.* = AMEBA.

ameer, amir [amíœr], amir, emir.

ameliorate, *va. V.* MELIORATE.

amelioration [amilioréshun], *s.* mejora, adelanto; mejoría, alivio.

ameliorator [amiliorétœr], *s.* mejorador, aumentador, perfeccionador.

amen [emén o (mús.) amén], *interj.* amén.

amenability [amínabíliti], **amenableness** [-bœlnes], *s.* responsabilidad.

amenable [amínabœl], *a.* responsable; sujeto a; tratable, dócil.

amend [aménd]. **I.** *va.* enmendar, corregir, reformar. **II.** *vn.* enmendarse, reformarse.

amendable [améndabœl], *a.* enmendable, reparable, reformable, corregible.

amendatory [améndatori], *a.* correctivo, reformatorio.

amender [améndœr], *s.* enmendador, reformador, corrector.

amending [aménding], *s.* la acción de enmendar.

amendment [améndment], *s.* enmienda, reforma; cambio, modificación; (agr.) substancia que mejora el suelo cambiando sus propiedades físicas no nutritivas.

amends [aménds], *s.* compensación, satisfacción, reparación.—**to make a.**, dar cumplida satisfacción; compensar.

amenity [améniti], *s.* amenidad; afabilidad.

amenorrhea [amenorría], *s.* (med.) amenorrea; menostasia, opilación.

ament [æment], **amentum** [améntum], *s.* (bot.) amento.

amentaceous [amentéshus], *a.* (bot.) amentáceo.

amentia [aménshia], *s.* demencia, locura.

amerce [amœrs], *va.* multar; despojar.

amerceable [amœrsabœl], *a.* digno de ser multado.—**amercement** [-mœnt], *s.* multa a discreción del juez.—**amercer** [-œr], *s.* multador.

American [æméricæn], *s.* y *a.* americano; norteamericano.—**A. plan**, sistema de piezas con alimento (apl. a hoteles en que no se alquilan los cuartos sin alimentación).—**A. Union**, Unión Norteamericana, Estados Unidos.

Americana [æmericána], *s.* colección de objetos o escritos americanos.

Americanism [æméricænism], *s.* americanismo; instituciones norteamericanas; fidelidad a estas instituciones.

Americanist [-ist], *s.* americanista.

Americanize [américanais], *va.* americanizar.

Amerind [æmœrind], *s.* amerindio, indígena americano.

Amerindian [æmœrindiæn], *a.* americoindio, amerindio, relativo a los indígenas americanos.

amethyst [æmezist], *s.* amatista; color de amatista.—**amethystine** [-zístin], *a.* parecido a la amatista.

amiability [emiabíliti], **amiableness** [émiabœlnes], *s.* amabilidad, afabilidad.

amiable [émiabœl], *a.* amable, afable.

amiably [émiabli], *adv.* amablemente.

amianth [émianz], **amianthus** [æmiénzus], *s.* (min.) amianto.

amicable [émicabœl], *a.* amigable, amistoso.

amicability [émicabíliti], **amicableness** [émicabœlnes], *s.* afecto, cariño, amistad, amigabilidad.

amicably [émicabli], *adv.* amigablemente.

amice [émis], *s.* (igl.) amito.

amid [amíd], **amidst** [amídst], *prep.* entre, en medio de; mezclado con; rodeado por.

amidships (mar.) en medio del navío.

amid(e [æmid], *s.* (quím.) amida.

amidol [-dol], *s.* (quím.) amidol.

amir [æmír], *s.* = AMEER.

amiss [amís]. **I.** *adv.* fuera de lugar o de sazón, mal, impropiamente, fuera del caso, de más.—**to take a.**, llevar a mal. **II.** *a.* inoportuno; impropio; malo, errado.

amity [émiti], *s.* amistad, bienquerencia, concordia, armonía.

ammeter [æmitœr], *s.* amperímetro.

ammonia [æmónia], *s.* (quím.) amoníaco.

ammoniac [æmóniac], *s.* amoníaco (goma.)

ammoniac(al [æmoníac(al], *a.* amoniacal.

ammonic [æmónic], *a.* amónico.

ammonification [æmónifikéishun], *s.* (agr.) saturar de amoníaco o sales amoniacales; formación de amoníaco por acción microbiana.

ammonify [-fai], *va.* tratar con amoníaco o sales amoniacales.

Ammonite [æmonait], *s.* y *a.* (hist.) amonita, descendiente de Amón.

ammonite, *s.* (pal.) amonita (molusco fósil); (quím.) amonita (explosivo); (agr.) abono obtenido de residuos animales de las fábricas de grasas.

ammonium [æmónium], *s.* (quím.) amonio.

ammunition [æmiuníshun], *s.* (mil.) munición, pertrechos.

amnesia [æmnísia o nísia], *s.* (med.) amnesia.

amnesty [æmnesti], *s.* amnistía, indulto.

amnion [æmnion], **amnios** [æmnios], *s.* amnios.

amniotic [amniótik], *a.* amniótico.

amœba [amíba], *s.* (biol.) amiba, ameba.

amomum [amómum], *s.* (bot.) amomo.

among [amúng], **amongst** [-st], *prep.* entre, mezclado con, en medio de.

amoral [æmóræl], *a.* amoral, sin moralidad.

amorist [æmorist], *s.* amante, galán.

Amorite [æmorait], *s.* amorreo, amorita.

amorous [æmorus], *a.* enamorado, amoroso, tierno, apasionado, cariñoso.

amorously [-li], *adv.* amorosamente.

amorousness [-nes], *s.* calidad de amoroso; enamoramiento.

amorphism [amórfism], *s.* amorfia; nihilismo.

amorphous [amórfus], *a.* amorfo, informe; anómalo, heterogéneo; (quím.) amorfo.

amort [amórt], *a.* exánime.

amortization [amortiséshun], **amortizement** [amórtismœnt], *s.* (for. y com.) amortización.

amortize [amórtais], *va.* (for. y com.) amortizar.

amount [amáunt]. **I.** *s.* cantidad, importe, suma; monto (capital más intereses). **II.** *vn.* montar, subir, ascender; (con **to**) valer.

amour [amúr], *s.* amores, amoríos.

amperage [ampéarey], *s.* (elec.) amperaje.

ampere [æmpéar], *s.* (elec.) amperio.—**a. centimeter,** amperio-centímetro.—**a. foot,** amperiopie.—**a. hour,** amperio-hora.—**a. turn,** amperiovuelta.—**back a. turn,** contra-amperio-vuelta.

amperemeter [-mítœr], *s.* amperímetro.

ampersand [æmpœrsænd], *s.* el signo &, que significa y.

Amphibia [amfíbia], *s. pl.* anfibios.

amphibian [-fibian]. **I.** *s.* y *a.* anfibio. **II.** *s.* (aer.) anfibio, aeroplano de tierra y agua.

amphibious [æmfíbius], *a.* anfibio.

amphibiousness [-nes], *s.* calidad de anfibio.

amphibole [æmfíbol], *s.* (min.) anfíbol.

amphibological [æmfibolóyical], *a.* anfibológico, dudoso, obscuro.

amphibologically [-i], *adv.* anfibológicamente.

amphibology [æmfibóloyi], *s.* anfibología, doble sentido.

amphiboly [æmfíboli], *s.* ambigüedad, equívoco.

amphibrach [æmfíbrac], *s.* (pros.) anfíbraco. (◡—◡).

amphictyon [ænfíction], *s.* anfictión.

amphictyonic [ænfictiónic], *a.* anfictiónico.

amphictyony [ænfíctioni], *s.* anfictionía.

amphimacer [æmfímascœr], *s.* (ros.) anfímacro.

amphioxus [ænfíoxus], *s.* anfioxo.

amphisbæna [æmfisbína], *s.* anfisbena.

amphiscians [æmfíshianz], **amphiscii** [æmfíshiai], *pl.* anfiscios.

amphitheater, amphitheatre [æmfíziatœr], *s.* anfiteatro, circo.—**amphitheatrical** [-ziátrical], *a.* de forma de anfiteatro.

Amphitryon [æmfítrion], *s.* anfitrión.

amphora [æmfora], *s.* ánfora.

amphoric [æmfóric], *a.* anfóreo.

ample [æmpœl], *a.* amplio; lato, liberal; bastante, suficiente; abundante.

ampleness [æmpœlnes], *s.* amplitud, anchura, holgura, abundancia, profusión.

ampliation [æmpliéshun], *s.* (for.) plazo, demora, prórroga, respiro; (med.) dilatación.

ampliative [æmpliativ], *a.* ampliativo.

amplification [æmplifikéshun], *s.* amplificación; (ópt.) aumento (del microscopio, etc.)

amplificative [æmplificativ], **amplificatory** [æmplificatori], *a.* amplificativo, amplificador.

amplificator [æmplifikétœr], *s.* amplificador.

amplifier [æmplifaier], *s.* amplificador, ampliador, aumentador.

amplify [æmplifai], *va.* (ret.) amplificar; ampliar, extender, dilatar, agrandar, aumentar.

amplitude [æmplitiud], *s.* amplitud.

amply [æmpli], *adv.* ampliamente; liberalmente, latamente; suficientemente; abundantemente.

ampulla [æmpúla], *s.* (anat.) ampolla; (igl.) vinajera.

ampullaceous [æmpuléshus], *a.* ampollar.

amputate [æmpiutet], *va.* amputar.

amputation [æmpiutéshun], *s.* (cir.) amputación; desmembración.

amuck [amúk], *adv.* furiosamente.—**to run a.,** atacar a ciegas, a troche y moche.

amulet [æmiulet], *s.* amuleto, talismán.

amuse [amiús], *va.* entretener, distraer, divertir; embobar, engañar.

amusement [amiúsmœnt], *s.* diversión, pasatiempo.

amuser [amiúscœr], *s.* entretenedor.

amusing [amiúsing], **amusive** [amiúsiv], *a.* divertido, entretenido; risible, gracioso.

amusingly [amiúsingli], **amusively** [amiúsivli], *adv.* divertidamente, entretenidamente.

amygdala [amígdala], *s.* (anat.) amígdala.

amygdalate [amígdalet], *a.* hecho de almendras.

amygdalin [amígdalin], *s.* (quím.) amigdalina.

amygdaline, amigdaloid [amígdalin, -loid], *a.* almendrado.

amygdaloid [amígdaloid], *s.* (geol.) roca amigdaloide.

amyl [æmil]. **I.** *s.* amilo. **II.** *a.* amílico.—**a. alcohol,** alcohol amílico.

amylaceous [æmiléshus], *a.* amiláceo.

amylene [æmilin], *s.* amileno.

amylic [æmílic], *a.* amílico.

an [æn], *art. indef.* un, uno, una (antes de *sonido vocal).*

ana [æna], *s.* (med.) ana.

ana [æna], *s. pl.* apuntes curiosos.

Anabaptism [ænabæptišm], *s.* anabaptismo.

Anabaptist [ænabæptist], *s.* anabaptista.

Anabaptistic [ænabæptístic], **Anabaptistical** [ænabæptístical], *a.* anabaptístico.

anabatic [ænæbætic], *a.* ascendente.

anabolism [ænæbolišm], *s.* (biol.) anabolismo, asimilación de los alimentos por las células.

anacamptic [ænæcæmptic], *a.* (fís.) referente a la reflexión, sobre todo del sonido.

anacardium [-cárdium], *s.* (bot.) anacardo.

anachronism [ænæcronišm], *s.* anacronismo.

anachronistic [ænæcronístic], *a.* anacronístico.

anaclastics, *s. V.* DIOPTRICS.

anaconda [ænæcónda], *s.* anaconda.

anacreontic [ænæcreóntic], *a.* anacreóntico.

anæmia [anímia], *s.* (med.) anemia.

anæmic [animic], *a.* anémico.

anæsthesia [æneszísia], *s.* (med.) anestesia.

anæsthetic [æneszétic], *a.* y *s.* anestésico.

anæsthetize [ænészetaiš], *va.* anestesiar.

anaglyph [ænaglif], *a.* (b. a.) anáglifo.

anagogical [ænagóyical], **anagogetical** [ænagoyética], *a.* anagógico, místico.

anagogics [ænagóyics], *s.* anagogía.

anagram [ænagræm], *s.* anagrama.

anagrammatical [ænagræmætical], *a.* que forma anagrama.

anagrammatist [ænagræmatist], *s.* el que hace anagramas.

anagrammatize [ænagræmataiš], *vn.* componer anagramas.

anal [énal], *a.* anal.

analecta [ænælécta], **analects** [ænalects], *s. pl.* analectas

analepsis [ænalépsis], *s.* (med.) analepsia.

analeptic [ænaléptic], *a.* (med.) analéptico, restaurativo.

analgesia [ænælyisia], *s.* analgesia.

analgesic [-yesic], *a.* analgésico.

analogical [ænalóyical], *a.* analógico.

analogically [-i], *adv.* anológicamente.

analogicalness [-nes], *s.* calidad de analógico.

analogize [ænalóyais], *va.* explicar por analogía.

analogous [ænálogus], *a.* análogo.

analogously [-li], *adv.* análogamente.

analogue [ænalog], *s.* término análogo.

analogy [ænáloyi], *s.* analogía, semejanza, correlación, afinidad.

analphabet [ænálfabet], *a.* analfabeto.

analysis [ænálisis], *s.* análisis.

analytics [ænalítiks], *s.* análisis; (filos.) analítica; (mat.) geometría analítica.

analyst [ænalist], *s.* analizador.

analytic(al [ænalític(al], *a.* analítico.—**a. geometry,** geometría analítica.

analytically [ænalíticali], *adv.* analíticamente.

analyze [ænalaiš], *va.* analizar.

analyzer [ænaláiscœr], *s.* analizador.

anamorphosis [ænamórfosis], *s.* anamorfosis.

ananas [ænánas], *s.* (bot.) ananás.

anapest [ænapest], *s.* (pros.) anapesto (◡◡—).

anaphora [ænáfora], *s.* (ret.) anáfora.

anaphrodisia [ænæfrodísia], *s.* anafrodisia.

anaphrodisiac [ænæfrodísiac], *s.* anafrodisíacc; antiafrodisíaco.

anarchic(al [ænárkic(al], *a.* anárquico.

anarchism [ænarkišm], *s.* anarquismo.

anarchist [-ist], *s.,* **anarchistic** [-ístic], *a.* anarquista.

anarchy [ænarki], *s.* anarquía.

anasarca [ænasárca], *s.* (med.) anasarca.

anasarcous [ænasárcus], *a.* hidrópico.

anastasis [ænæstasis], *s.* (med.) convalescencia.

anastatic [ænæstátic], *a.* grabado en relieve.

anastigmatic [ænǽstigmǽtic], *a.* anastigmático, sin astigmatismo.

anastomosis [-tomósis], *s.* (med.) anastomosis.

anastomotic [ænæstomótic], *a.* anastomótico.

anastrophe [anǽstrofe], *s.* (gram.) anástrofe.

anathema [anǽzema], *a.* anatema.

anathematical [-mǽtical], *a.* perteneciente al anatema.—**anathematically** [-mǽticali], *adv.* a modo de anatema.

anathematization [-matiŝéŝhun], *s.* anatema.

anathematize [-mataiŝ], *va.* anatematizar.

anathematizer [-matáiŝœr], *s.* anatematizador.

anatomical [anætómical], *a.* anatómico.

anatomically [anætómicali], *adv.* anatómicamente.

anatomist [anǽtomist], *s.* anatomista.

anatomize [anǽtomaiŝ], *va.* anatomizar; disecar, analizar minuciosamente.

anatomy [anǽtomi], *s.* anatomía; disección; disecación; esqueleto.

anbury [ǽnburi], *s.* (vet.) tumor blando y grumoso.

ancestor [ǽnsestœr], *s.* progenitor, antecesor, antepasado, ascendiente.

ancestral [ænséstral], *a.* de los antepasados.

ancestry [ǽnsestri], *s.* linaje, prosapia, abolengo, alcurnia.

anchor [ǽncœr]. **I.** *va.* (mar.) sujetar con el ancla, poner (el barco) sobre el ancla; (tec.) sujetar; asegurar, empotrar. **II.** *vn.* (mar.) anclar. **III.** *s.* (mar.) ancla; (tec.) artificio o pieza de sujeción.—**a. arms,** brazos del ancla.—**a. back,** galga del ancla.—**a. beam,** serviola.—**a. bill,** pico del ancla.—**a. bolt,** tornillo o perno de anclaje o de cimiento.—**a. chocks,** calzos de ancla.—**a. cross,** cruz del ancla.—**a. escapement,** escape de áncora.—**a. flukes,** uñas del ancla.—**a. forge,** ancorería.—**a. ground,** fondeadero.—**a light,** linterna de un buque anclado.—**a. ring,** arganes.—**a. shank,** caña del acla.—**a. stock,** cepo del ancla.—**a. stopper,** capón.—**a. tripper,** disparador.—**a. watch,** guardia de cubierta de un barco anclado.—**at a.,** al ancla, anclado.—**best bower a.,** ancla de ajuste.—**drag a.,** ancla de arrastre.—**foul a.,** ancla enredada.—**kedge a.,** anclote.—**sheet a.,** ancla mayor.—**small bower a.,** ancla sencilla.—**to drop a.,** dar fondo, anclar.—**to ride at a.,** estar anclado.—**to stock the a.,** encepar el ancla.—**to weigh a.,** levar el ancla.

anchorable [ǽngcorabœl], *a.* propio para anclaje.

anchorage [ǽngcorey], *s.* (mar.) ancladero, agarradero; anclaje, ancoraje.

anchored [ǽncœrd], *a.* de forma de ancla.

anchoress [ǽngcores], *s.* ermitaña.

anchoret [ǽngcoret], **anchorite** [ǽngcorait], *s.* ermitaño, anacoreta.

anchorless [áncorles], *a.* sin ancla; inseguro.

anchorsmith [áncorsmiz], *s.* ancorero.

anchovy [ænchóvi], *s.* anchova, anchoa.

ancient [énŝhent]. **I.** *a.* antigno. **II.** *s.* (en *pl.*) antepasados, mayores; la antigüedad.

anciently [énŝhentli], *adv.* antiguamente.

ancientry [énŝhentri], *s.* antigüedad.

ancillary [énsilari], *a.* ancilario; subordinado, dependiente, auxiliar, sucursal.

ancipital, ancipitous [ænsípital, -us], *a.* de dos caras; de doble filo.

ancoral [éncoral], *a.* perteneciente o semejante a un áncora; (zool.) encorvado.

and [ænd], *conj.* y, e; si:—**ifs and ands,** dimes y diretes. Se emplea a veces antes del infinitivo, sobre todo después de *to go, to come, to try,* para indicar acción o propósito, vg. *I must go and see,* debo ir a ver; *I shall try and speak to him,* trataré de hablarle.

Andalusian [ændalúyan], *a.* andaluz.

andalusite [ændaliúsait], *s.* (min.) andalusita.

andante [andánte], *a., adv.* y *s.* (mús.) andante.

andantino [andantíno], *a., adv.* y *s.* (mús.) andantino.

Andean [ændían], *a.* andino.

andirons [ændíaœrnŝ], *s. pl.* morillos.

andesite [ǽndiŝait], *s.* (min.) andesita.

androgynal [ændróyinal], **androgynous** [-us], *a.* andrógino.

androgyne [-yin], *s.* hermafrodita, andrógino.

android [ændroid], *s.* androide, autómata de forma humana.

anecdotal [ænécdotæl], **anecdotic(al** [ænecdóticæl], *a.* anecdótico.

anecdote [ǽnecdot], *s.* anécdota.

anemia [ænímia], *s.* anemia.

anemograph [ænémogræf], *s.* anemógrafo, anemómetro registrador.

anemography [ænemógrafi], *s.* anemografía.

anemographic [anemográfic], *a.* anemográfico.

anemometer [ænemómetœr], *s.* anemómetro.

anemometry [ænemómetri], *s.* anemometria.

anemone [anémone], *s.* (bot.) anémone, anémona.—**sea a.,** actinia, anémona de mar.

anemoscope [ænémoscoup], *s.* anemoscopio.

anent [anént], *prep.* tocante a, contra.

aneroid, [ǽncœroid], *a.* aneroide.—**a. barometer,** barómetro aneroide.

aneroidograph [ænœróidogræf], *s.* barómetro aneroide registrador.

aneurism [ǽniurism], *s.* (med.) aneurisma.

aneurismal [æniurísmal], *a.* aneurismal.

anew [aniú], *adv.* de nuevo, otra vez; nuevamente, de un modo nuevo, de refresco.

anfractuous [ænfrǽctiuos], **anfractuose** [anfrǽctiuos], *a.* anfractuoso, sinuoso, desigual.

anfractuosity [ænfrǽctiuósiti], *s.* anfractuosidad, sinuosidad.

angel [éinyel]. **I.** *s.* ángel; ángel, nombre de una antigua moneda.—**a. fish,** (ict.) angelote.—**a.-like,** angelical.—**a. shot,** (arti.) palanquetas. **II.** *a.* angelical.

angelhood [-jud], *s.* condición de angel.

angelic [ænyélic], **angelical** [-cal], *a.* angelical.

angelica [æyélica], *s.* vino dulce de California; (bot.) angélica.

angelically [ænyélicali], *va.* angélicamente, angelicalmente.

Angelus [ényelus], *s.* (igl.) ángelus.

anger [éngœr]. **I.** *s.* ira, cólera, enojo.—**to provoke to a.,** encolerizar, causar ira. **II.** *va.* enfadar, provocar, enfurecer, enojar, encolerizar.

angina [ænyína o ænyáina], *s.* (med.) angina.—**a. pectoris,** angina de pecho, esternalgia.

Angiospermæ [ényiospœrmi], *s.* (bot.) angiospermas.—**angiospermous** [-mus], *a.* angiospermo.

angle [ǽngœl]. **I.** *vn.* pescar con caña; intrigar, insinuarse; buscar solapadamente. **II.** *s.* ángulo; punta; filo; avíos de pescar; punto de vista; (tec.) codo; hierro en ángulo.—**a. bar** = A. IRON.—**a. block** (const.) bloque o zapata en la unión de dos piezas; polea de cambio de dirección.—**a. brace,** (const.) cuadral; (mec.) berbiquí de manivela para esquinas.—**a. bracket,** escuadra saliente de esquina; escuadra de unión.—**a. bulb,** hierro en ángulo con un borde ensanchado.—**a. gauge,** goniómetro.—**a. iron,** hierro en ángulo, escuadra.—**a. line,** (top.) poligonal, línea quebrada.—**a. of advance,** (m. v.) ángulo de avanee (de la excéntrica).—**a. of attack,** (aer.) ángulo de ataque.—**a. of bank,** (aer.) ángulo de balance o de escora lateral.—**a. of contact,** (mec.) ángulo o arco de contacto (de una correa).—**a. of depression,** ángulo de depresión.—**a. of draft** = ANGLE OF TRACTION.—**a. of elevation,** ángulo de elevación, ángulo con el horizonte.—**a. of entrance,** (m. v., hidr.) ángulo de entrada.—**a. of friction,** ángulo de rozamiento.—**a. of incidence,** ángulo de incidencia.—**a. of intersection,** (f. c.) ángulo de contingencia.—**a. of lag,** (elec.) ángulo de retraso.—**a. of lead,** (elec.) ángulo de avance.—**a. of reflection,** (fís.) ángulo de reflexión.—**a. of refraction,** (fís.) ángulo de refracción.—**a. of roll,** (aer.) = A. OF BANK.—**a. of torsion,** ángulo de torsión.—**a. of traction,** ángulo de tracción, ángulo entre la fuerza de tracción y la superficie de arrastre.—**a. of twist,** ángulo de torsión.—**a. of zero lift,** (aer.) ángulo de resistencia nula.—**a. rafter,** (arq.) lima (de un tejado).—**a. tie,** (const.) cuadral.—**a. valve,** válvula de conductos en ángulo recto;—**at an a.,** en ángulo, inclinado.—**at right angles,** en ángulo recto.

Angle, *s.* anglo.

angled [ǽngœld], *a.* anguloso, esquinado.

angler [ǽnglœr], *s.* pescador de caña; (ict.) pejesapo.

angleworm [-uœrm], *s.* lombriz de tierra.

Anglican [ǽnglican], *a.* y *s.* anglicano.

Anglicanism [ǽnglicanĭsm], *s.* anglicanismo.

Anglicism [ǽnglisĭsm], *s.* anglicismo.

Anglicize [ǽnglisaĭs], *va.* inglesar.

angling [ǽngling], *s.* pesca (con caña).

Anglo-American [ǽnglo-américan], *a.* y *s.* angloamericano.

Anglo-Indian [ǽnglo-índian], *a.* y *s.* angloindio.

Anglomania [ænglománia], *s.* anglomanía.

Anglomaniac [ængloméniac], *a.* y *s.* anglómano.

Anglo-Norman [ǽnglo-nórman], *s.* y *a.* anglonormando.

Anglo-Saxon [ǽnglo-sáxon], *s.* y *a.* anglosajón.

Angora [ængóra], *s.* angora.—**A. cat, goat,** gato, cabra de Angora o Angola.

angrily [ǽngrili], *adv.* coléricamente.

angry [ǽngri], *a.* enojado, encolerizado, bravo, airado; (med.) irritado, inflamado.

anguilliform [ængüíliform], *a.* en forma de anguila.

anguish [ǽngüĭsh], *s.* ansia, angustia, zozobra.

anguished [ǽngüĭsht], *a.* atormentado, angustiado, afligido, acongojado.

angular [ǽnguiular], *a.* angular, anguloso.

angularity [ænguiuláriti], **angularness** [ǽnguiularnes], **angulosity** [ænguiulósiti], *s.* cualidad de angular o anguloso.

angularly [ǽnguiularli], *adv.* angularmente.

angulate, angulated [ǽnguiulet, -ed], *a.* (bot.) anguloso, angular.

anhelation [ænjeléshun], *s.* (med.) anhélito.

anhydride [ænjáidrid *o* draid], *s.* (quím.) anhídrido.

anhydrite [ænjáidrait], *s.* (min.) anhidrita.

anhydrous [ænjáidrus], *a.* (quím.) anhidro.

anights [anáits], *adv.* de noche.

anil [ǽnil], *s.* (bot.) añil.

anile [ǽnil], *a.* vieja chocha.

anilin *o* **aniline** [ǽnilin], *s.* anilina.

animadversion [ǽnimadvérshun], *s.* animadversión, censura, reproche; castigo.

animadvert [ǽnimadvœrt], *vn.* censurar, reprochar; observar.

animadverter [-œr], *s.* censurador, criticastro.

animal [ǽnimal], *s.* y *a.* animal; bruto.—**a. spirits,** vivacidad, ardor.

animalcule [ænimǽlkiul], *s.* animálculo.

animalism [ǽnimalĭsm], *s.* estado animal; sensualidad.—**animality** [-méliti], *s.* animalidad.

animalization [-malĭséishun], *s.* animalización.

animalize [ǽnimalaĭs], *va.* animalizar.

animate, [ǽnimeit], *va.* animar; infundir ánimo o valor, excitar, alentar; vivificar.

animate *a.* viviente, animado.

animated [ǽniméited], *a.* vivo, vivaz, animado.

animating [ǽniméiting], *a.* animante, vivificante, excitante; alegre, divertido.

animation [ǽniméshun], *s.* animación; (fig.) movimiento, calor, fuego; viveza, espíritu.

animative [ǽnimetiv], *a.* animador.

animator [ǽniméitœr], *s.* animador, alentador.

anime [ǽnime], *s.* anime (resina).

animism [ǽnimĭsm], *s.* animismo.

animosity [animósiti], *s.* animosidad, rencor.

animus [ǽnimus], *s.* ánimo; mala voluntad, inquina, odio.

anion [ǽnion], *s.* (elec.) anión.

anise [ǽnis], *s.* (bot.) anís.

aniseed [ǽnisid], *s.* anís, grano de anís.

anisette [ænisét], *s.* (Fr.) aniseté.

ankle [ǽngkœl], *s.* tobillo.

ankled [ǽngkœld], *a.* de grueso tobillo.

anklet [ǽngklet], *s.* ajorca; (cir.) tobillera.

ankylosis [ængkilósis], *s.* (med.) anquilosis.

annalist [ǽnalist], *s.* analista, cronista.

annals [ǽnalŝ], *s. pl.* anales; misas de aniversario.

annats [ǽnnats], *s.* anata.

annatto [ænnǽto], *s.* achiote; bija, orellana.

anneal [æníl], *va.* (fund.) recocer; (ind.) fijar (colores, esmalte) por calor; (fig.) fortalecer.

annealing [ænníling], *s.* recocción; esmaltación. —**a. pot,** crisol de templar.

annelid [ænnélid], *a.* y *s.* anillado; anélido.

Annelida [ænélidæ], *s.* anélidos.

annex [ænnéx]. **I.** *va.* anexar, unir. **II.** *s.* adita-mento, anexo, adición, apéndice; dependencia. —*pl.* anexidades.

annexation [ænnexéshun], **annexment** [ænéxmœnt], *s.* anexión, adición, unión.

annexationist [-ist], *s.* anexionista.

annexed [ænnéxt], *a.* adjunto, anexo.

annexive [ænnéxiv], *a.* que une o anexa, o tiende a anexar.

annihilable [ænáijilabœl], *a.* destructible, aniquilable.

annihilate [-eit]. **I.** *va.* aniquilar, anonadar, destruir. **II.** *a.* aniquilado.

annihilation [-éishun], *s.* aniquilación, anonadamiento.

annihilator [-éitœr], *s.* aniquilador.

anniversary [ænivérsari]. **I.** *s.* aniversario. **II.** *a.* anual.

annotate [ǽnnoteit], *va.* anotar, comentar.

annotation [ænnotéshun], *s.* nota, notación; anotación, apunte, acotación, apostilla.

annotator [ǽnnotéitœr], *s.* anatador, comentador, postillador.

annotto, *V.* ANNATTO y ARNOTTO.

announce [ænnáuns], *va.* anunciar, notificar, declarar; pregonar.

announcement [ænnáunsmœnt], *s.* aviso o anuncio; declaración, proclama; prospecto.

announcer [ænnáunsœr], *s.* anunciador, publicador, avisador.

annoy [ænnói], *va.* molestar, incomodar, vejar, fastidiar, cargar, aburrir, encocorar.

annoyance [ænnóians], *s.* molestia, pena, incomodidad; disgusto, fastidio, aburrimiento; lata, engorro, pejiguera, chinchorrería.

annoyer [ænnóicœr], *s.* molestador, persona enojosa, chinchorrero.

annoying [ænnóying], *a.* fastidioso, molesto, incómodo, importuno, engorroso.

annual [ǽnyual]. **I.** *a.* anual, añal, cadañal. **II.** *s.* (igl.) añal, aniversario.

annually [ǽnyual], *adv.* anualmente.

annuary [ǽnyueri], *a.* anuario.

annuitant [ænníuitant], *s.* rentista, censualista.

annuity [ænníuiti], *s.* anualidad, renta vitalicia, pensión, censual.

annul [ænnŭl], *va.* anular, invalidar; revocar, abolir; destruir, anonadar.

annular [ǽnyular], **annulary** [ǽnyuleri], *a.* anular.

annulate(d [ǽnyulet(ed], *a.* anuloso, anillado.

annulet [ǽnyulet], *s.* anillejo, sortijilla.

annulment [ænnŭlmœnt], *s.* anulación, rescisión, cancelación, revocación, derogación.

annulose [ǽnyulos], *a.* anuloso, anillado.

annulus [ǽnyulus], *s.* anillo; (geom.) corona circular.

annunciate [ænnŭnŝhieit], *va.* V. ANNOUNCE.

annunciation [-éishun], *s.* anunciación, proclamación; promulgación: (igl.) Anunciación.

annunciator [-éitœr], *s.* anunciador, avisador; proclamador; indicador (en ho teles).

anodal [ænódal], **anodic** [anódic], *a.* perteneciente al ánodo.

anode [ænod], *s.* (elec.) ánodo.—**a. battery,** (rad.) batería de la lámpara termiónica.—**a. rays,** rayos anódicos de un tubo de vacío.

anodyne [ænodain], *a.* y *s.* anodino.

anoint [anóint], *va.* untar, pringar; (igl.) ungir, olear; signar con óleo.—**to a. a dying person,** administrar la extremaunción.—**to a. the palm,** (fam.) untar la mano.

anointer [anóintœr], *s.* untador; el que unge.

anointing [anóinting], **anointment** [anóintmœnt], s. unción; untadura, untamiento.

anomalism [anómalism], **anomalousness** [anómalusnes], **anomaly** [anómali], s. anomalía.

anomalistic(al [anomalístic(al], a. anomalístico. —**anomalistic year**, año anomalístico.

anomalous [anómalus], a. anómalo, irregular.

anomalously [-li], adv. anómalamente.

anon [anón], adv. pronto, a poco, luego, en seguida, inmediatamente.—**ever and a.**, una y otra vez, a menudo.

anonym [ǽnonim], s. persona o escritor anónimo; seudónimo.

anonymous [anónimus], a. anónimo.

anonymously [-li], adv. anónimamente.

anopheles [ænófiliš], s. anofeles, género de mosquitos que transmiten la malaria.

anopheline [-filin]. **I.** a. anofelino, perteneciente al anofeles. **II.** s. anofeles, mosquito de la malaria.

anorexia [ænoréxia], s. (med.) inapetencia.

anortite [ǽnortait], s. (min.) anortita.

another [ænúdœr], a. y pron. otro.—**one a.**, uno a otro, unos a otros; entre sí; unos . . . otros (bricks placed on one another, ladrillos puestos unos sobre otros).

ansated [ǽnseted], a. con asas.

anserine [ǽnsœrin], a. ansarino; como ganso; tonto, necio, mentecato.

answer [ǽnsœr], va. y vn. responder, contestar; refutar; corresponder, satisfacer; obedecer; llenar el objeto, servir, convenir; comparecer. —**to a for**, abonar, acreditar, salir fiador de, responder de; ser responsable de.

answer, s. respuesta, contestación; refutación, réplica, dúplica; defensa; (mat.) solución, resultado.

answerable [ǽnsœrabœl], a. responsable; correspondiente; equivalente; conforme; propio; discutible, refutable.

answerably [ǽnsœrabli], adv. correspondientemente; responsablemente.

answerableness [ǽnsœrabœlnes], s. responsabilidad; cuenta; correspondencia, correlación.

answerer [ǽnsœrœr], s. fiador; respondedor.

ant [ænt], s. hormiga.—**a. bear**, oso hormiguero.—**a. hill**, hormiguera en forma de montículo.—**a. lion**, hormiga león.

a'n't [éint], (= AIN'T).

anta [ǽnta], s. (arq.) anta, pilastra, parástade; (zool.) danta, tapir.

antagonism [æntǽgonism], s. antagonismo.

antagonist [æntǽgonist], s. antagonista.

antagonistic [æntægonístic], a. antagónico. contrario, opuesto, hostil.

antagonize [æntægonaíš]. **I.** va. contender con, oponerse a; contrariar. **II.** vn. ser antagónico.

antalgic [æntǽlyic], a. anodino.

antaphrodisiac [æntæfrodíšiæc], **antaphroditic** [æntafrodític], s. y a. antiafrodisíaco.

antapoplectic [æntæpopléctic], a. (med.) antiapopléctico.

antarctic [æntárctic], a. antártico.

antarthritic [æntarzrític], a. (med.) antiartrítico.

antasthmatic [æntasmǽtic], a. antiasmático.

ante [ǽnti]. **I.** prefijo, ante, antes, antes de.—**a. bellum**, antes de la guerra.—**a. meridiem** (A.M.), antes del mediodía.—**a. mortem**, antes de morir. **II.** vn. (generalmente con up), poner su tanto o apuesta (en el juego); pagar la apuesta. **III.** s. tanto, suma que se apuesta y se pone sobre la mesa.

anteater [ǽntitœr], s. mamífero hormiguero; oso hormiguero.

antecedaneous [æntesedéniŭs], a. precedente.

antecede [æntesíd], vn. anteceder, preceder.

antecedence [æntesídens], **antecedency** [æntesídensi], s. precedencia.

antecedent [æntesídent], a. y s. antecedente, precedente.

antecedently [æntesídentli], adv. anteriormente.

antecessor [æntesésœr], s. antecesor, precedesor.

---

antechamber [ǽntechéimbœr], s. antecámara, antesala.

antedate [ǽntedeit]. **I.** va. antedatar, retrotraer. **II.** s. anticipación; antedata.

antediluvian [æntedilúvian], a. y s. antediluviano.

antelope [ǽnteloup], s. antílope; gacela, gamuza.

antemeridian [æntemerídian], a. antemeridiano.

antemetic [æntemétic], s. y a. antiemético.

antemundane [æntemúndein], a. que antecedió a la creación del mundo.

antenna [ænténa], s. antena; (rad.) antena.

antennæ [-ni], s. pl. antenas.

antenuptial [æntenúpšhal], a. antenupcial.

antepaschal [æntepáscal], a. antepascual.

antepenult [æntepenúlt] o **antepenultimate** [-imet], a. y s. (gram.) antepenúltima.

antepileptic [æntepiléptic], a. (med.) antiepiléptico.

anterior [æntíriœr], a. anterior, delantero, de adelante, precedente.

anteriority [ænterióriti], s. anterioridad, precedencia, antelación.

anteriorly [æntíriorli], adv. anteriormente.

anteroom [ǽnterrúm], s. antecámara.

anteversion [æntevœršhŭn], s. anteroversión.

antevert [ǽntevœrt], va. volver hacia adelante.

anthelmintic [ænzelmíntic], a. antielmíntico.

anthem [ǽnzem], s. antífona, motete.

anther [ǽnzœr], s. (bot.) antera.

antheral [ǽnzœral], a. referente a anteras.

anthological [ænzolóyical], a. antológico.

anthology [ænzóloyi], s. antología, florilegio.

anthophagous [ænzófagus], a. antófago.

Anthozoa [ænzošóa], s. pl. (zool.) antozoarios.

anthracic [ænzrǽsic], a. referente al ántrax.

anthracite [ǽnzrasait], s. antracita.

anthrax [ǽnzrax], s. (med.) ántrax, carbunclo, avispero; fiebre espléncia.

anthropocentric [ænzroposéntric], a. antropocéntrico.

anthropogeny [-póyeni], s. antropogenia.

anthropography [ænzropógrafi], s. antropografía.

anthropoid [ǽnzropoid], s. y a. antropoide, antropoide.

anthropologic(al [ænzropolóyic(al], a. antropológico.

anthropologist [ænzropóloyist], s. antropólogo.

anthropology [ænzropóloyi], s. antropología.

anthropomorphism [ænzropomórfism], s. antropomorfismo.

anthropomorphite [-mórfait], s. antropomorfita.

anthropomorphous [ænzropomórfŭs], a. antropomorfo.

anthropophagi [ænzropófayai], s. antropófagos.

anthropophagous [-gus], a. antropófago.

anthropophagy [-yi], s. antropofagía.

anti [ǽnti], afijo, contra o contrario a.—NOTA. Con este afijo se forman muchos compuestos, cuyo significado es lo contrario de lo que expresa el segundo elemento.

antiacid, a. = ALKALI.

antiaircraft [æntieǽrcræft], a. (mil.) de defensa contra fuerzas aéreas, antiaéreo.

antiapostle [æntiapóscœl], s. antiapóstol.

antiarthritic [æntiarzrític], a. antiartrítico.

antibilious [æntibílyŭs], a. antibilioso.

antibody [æntibódi], s. (fisiol.) anticuerpo o antisubstancia, cualquier substancia de la sangre que neutraliza los agentes tóxicos o nocivos.

antic [ǽntic]. **I.** a. extraño, raro, ridículo, grotesco. **II.** s. zapateta, cabriola, travesura; adefesio, esperpento; bufón, saltimbanco.

anticathode [anticǽzoud], s. extremo opuesto al cátodo de un tubo de vacío.

antichamber, s. V. ANTECHAMBER.

Antichrist [ǽnticrast], s. anticristo.

antichristian [-críschan], s. y a. anticristiano.

anticipate [æntísipeit], va. esperar, prever; anticiparse, adelantarse a; frustrar, impedir.

anticipation [-péišhŭn], s. anticipación, adelantamiento; expectación.

---

anticipator [-péitœr], s. anticipador.
anticipatory [æntísipatori], a. que anticipa.
anticlimax [ænticláimax], s. (ret.) anticlímax.
anticlinal [ænticláinal], a. (geol.) anticlinal.
anticline [-clain], s. (geol.) anticlinal.
anticlinorium [-clinóriʊm], s. (geol.) sucesión de anticlinales paralelos superpuestos.
anticoherer [-co)fœrœr], s. (radtlg.) anticohesor.
anticorrosive [-corrósiv], a. anticorrosivo.
anticosmetic [ænticosmétic], a. anticosmético.
anticyclone [æntisáiclon], s. contraciclón.
antidotal [æntidotal], a. alexifármaco.
antidote [æntidot], s. antídoto.
antidysenteric [-disentéric], a. antidisentérico.
antiface [æntifeis], s. antifaz.
antifanatic [æntifanétic], s. antifanático.
antifebrile [æntifíbril], a. (med.) antifebril.
antifebrin [æntifíbrin], s. antifebrina.
antiforeignism [æntifóreniśm], s. xenofobia, odio o aversión a los extranjeros.
antifriction [-fricśhʊn], a. contra el rozamiento.
—a. compound, lubricante.—a. metal, metal antifricción.—a. wheels, rodillos de fricción.
antihysteric [æntijistéric], s. antihistérico.
anti-imperialism [-impírialiśm], s. antiimperialismo; (E. U.) oposición a la expansión territorial por la anexión de pueblos extraños; (Ingl.) oposición a la extensión del imperio y de la autoridad de Inglaterra sobre sus dominios.
anti-imperialist [-list], s. antiimperialista.
Antillean [æntíliæn], s. y a. antillano.
antilogarithm [æntilógærıᴅm], s. antilogaritmo, número correspondiente a un logaritmo.
antilogy [antíloyi], s. antilogía.
antimacassar [æntimacáesar], s. cubierta del respaldo de un sofá o sillón.
antimalarial [æntimalérial], a. antipalúdico.
antimonarchic(al [æntimonárkic(al], a., antimonarchist [-mónarkist], s. antimonárquico.
antimonial [æntimóniæl], a. antimonial.
antimoniate [-niet], s. antimoniato.
antimonic [-nic], a. antimónico.
antimonide [æntimonaid], a. antimoniuro.
antimonious [æntimóniʊs], a. antimonioso.
antimony [æntimoni], s. antimonio.
antimoralist [æntimóralist], s. enemigo de la moralidad.
antinational [æntinǽshʊnal], a. antinacional.
antinephritic [æntinefrític], a. antinefrítico.
antineuritic [æntiniurític], s. y a. antineurítico.
antinomy [æntínomi], s. antinomia; paradoja.
Antiochian [æntiókiæn], s. y a. antioquiano, antioquense, de Antioquía.
antipapal [æntipépal], antipapistical [æntipapístical], a. antipapista.
antipathetic(al [æntipazétic(al], a. contrario, opuesto; adverso.
antipathy [æntípazi], s. antipatía, antagonismo, tirria, repugnancia.
antiperistaltic [æntiperistéltic], a. antiperistáltico.
antipharmic [æntifármic], a. antidotal.
antiphlogistic [-floyístic], s. y a. antiflogístico.
antiphon [æntifon], antiphony [æntífoni], s. (igl.) antífona; eco.
antiphona [æntífonal], antiphonical [æntifónical], a. antífonal.
antiphonal [æntífonal], antiphonar [æntífonar], s. antifonal o antifonario.
antiphrasis [æntífrasis], s. (ret.) antífrasis.
antipodal [æntípodal], antipodean [æntipódean], a. antípoda; contrario; opuesto.
antipode [æntipod], s. antípoda.
antipodes [æntípodiś], s. pl. antípodas.
antipoison [-póiśʊn], s. antídoto, contraveneno.
antipope [æntipoup], s. antipapa.
antipyretic [æntipairétic], a. y s. antipirético, febrífugo.
antipyrin [æntipáirin], s. antipirina.
antiquarian [æntikuérian], s. y a. anticuario.

antiquarianism [æntikuérianiśm], s. afición a las antigüedades.
antiquary [æntikueri], s. anticuario.
antiquate [æntikuet], va. anticuar.
antiquated [æntikuéited], a. anticuado.
antique [æntíc]. I. a. antiguo. II. s. antigüedad, antigualla.
antiquity [æntíkuiti], s. antigsedad; ancianidad, vejez, vetustez.
antirevolutionary [æntirrevolúshʊnœri], a. antirrevolucionario.
antirevolutionist [-ist], s. antirrevolucionario.
antirheumatic [-rumætic], a. antirreumático.
antisabbatarian [-sæbætéiriæn], s. y a. que se opone a la obligación moral o legal de guardar el domingo.
anti-saloon [-salún], a. enemigo de las tabernas y de la venta de licor en general; prohibicionista.
antisacerdotal [æntisasœrdótal], a. hostil a los sacerdotes.
antiscians [æntíśhanś] o antiscii [æntíśhiai], s. pl. antecos.
antiscorbutic(al [æntiscorbiútic(al], a. antiescorbútico.
antiscrofulous [-scrófiulœs], a. antiescrofuloso.
anti-Semite [-sémait], s. antisemita.
anti-Semitic [-semític], a. antisemítico.
anti-Semitism [-sémitiśm], s. antifemitismo.
antisepsis [æntisépsis], s. antisepsia.
antiseptic [æntiséptic], a. y s. antiséptico.
antiseptical [æntiséptical], a. = ANTISEPTIC.
antiseptically [-i], adv. de un modo antiséptico.
antiserum [æntisirʊm], s. especie de antitoxina obtenida de animales inoculados.
antislavery [æntislévœri]. I. s. antiesclavismo, oposición a la esclavitud. II. a. antiesclavista.
antisocial [æntisóshal], a. antisocial.
antispasmodic [æntispaśmódic], a. antiespasmódico.
antispastic [æntispástic], a. antispástico.
antisplenetic [æntisplenétic], a. antiesplénico.
antistrophe [æntístrofe], s. antistrofa.
antisyphilitic [æntisifilític], a. y s. antisifilítico.
antithesis [æntízesis], s. (ret.) antítesis, retruécano; oposición, contraste.
antithetical [æntizétical], a. antitético.
antitoxin [æntitócsin], s. antitoxina.
antitrinitarian [-trinitérian], s. antitrinitario.
antitype [æntitaip], s. prototipo.
antivenereal [antivenírial], a. antivenéreo.
antler [æntlœr], s. asta del venado.
antlered [æntlœrd], a. que tiene astas.
antœci [æntísai], s. (geog.) antecos.
antonomasia [æntonoméiyia], s. antonomasia.
antonym [ǽtonim], s. antónimo, vocablo de significación opuesta a otro.
antrum [æntrʊm], s. antro, cueva; (anat.) antro.
Anura [æniúræ], s. pl. (zool.) anurios.
anuria [æniúria], s. anuria.
anus [éinʊs], s. ano.
anvil [ænvil]. I. s. yunque; (mec.) pico o boca de un instrumento de medir, como un calibre micrométrico; (tlg.) calvija inferior de contacto del manipulador; (anat.) yunque.—double-peak a., bigornia.—to be on the a., estar sobre el tapete (en discusión o preparación). II. va. formar o trabajar sobre el yunque; martillar.
anxiety [ænǽiti], s. ansia, ansiedad, inquietud, cuidado; anhelo.
anxious [ǽnśhʊs], a. inquieto, impaciente, ansioso; anheloso, deseoso; angustioso, aflictivo.
anxiously [-li], adv. ansiosa o impacientemente.
anxiousness [-nes], s. ansiedad, solicitud; anhelo.
any [éni]. I. a. y pron. cualquiera, cualesquiera; algún, alguno; alguien.—a. way, de cualquier modo.—In a. case, de todos modos, sea como fuere.—not a., ninguno.—[Cuando any se usa partitiva o negativamente, por lo común no se traduce; v.g. have you any money? ¿tiene Vd. dinero? I have not any money, no tengo dinero.] II. adv. Como adverbio, any es a menudo expletivo

o enfático, y no se traduce; v.g. *any farther*, más lejos.—**a. longer**, más tiempo, todavía; más. —**a. more**, más, aún; todavía.—**not a. longer, not a. more**, ya no.

anybody [énibódi], *pron.* alguno, alguien, cualquiera; todo el mundo, toda persona; nadie. —**not a.**, nadie, ninguno.

anyhow [énijau], *adv.* de cualquier modo; en cualquier caso; de todos modos.

anyone [éniuɒn], *s.* = ANYBODY.

anything [éniȝing], *pron.* algo, alguna cosa, cualquier cosa; todo, todo lo que; (con negación) nada.

anyway, anyways [éniuei, -ueiŝ], *adv.* salga lo que saliere; sin embargo, con todo; sea lo que se fuere.

anywhere [énijuear], *adv.* donde quiera, en todas partes; (con negación) en ninguna parte.

anywise [éniuaiŝ], *adv.* de cualquier manera.

aorist [éorist], *s.* y *a.* (gram.) aoristo.

aorta [eórta], *s.* (anat.) aorta.

aortic [eórtic], *a.* aórtico.

apace [apés], *adv.* aprisa, aceleradamente.

Apache [æpǽche], *s.* y *a.* apache.

apart [apárt], *adv.* aparte, a un lado; separadamente; además; dejando a un lado; en padazos, en partes.

apartment [apártmœnt], *s.* aposento; piso, apartamiento.

apathetic [æpazétic], *a.* apático, indiferente.

apathy [æpazi], *s.* apatía, flema.

apatite [æpatait], *s.* (min.) apatita.

ape [éip]. **I.** *s.* mono (aplícase con especialidad a los grandes antropoides); imitador. **II.** *va.* imitar, remedar.

apeak [apíc], *adv.* (mar.) en posición vertical.

aperient [apírient], **aperitive** [apéritiv], *a.* aperitivo.

aperture [æpœrchuœr], *s.* abertura, paso, rendija, buco, portillo.

apetalous [apétalʊs], *a.* (bot.) apétalo.

apex [éipecs], *s.* (*pl.* -XES o APICES) ápice, cúspide, punta, vértice; fastigio, cima.

aphæresis [aféresis], *s.* (gram.) aféresis.

aphasia [aféiȳia], *s.* (med.) afasia.

aphasic [aféŝic], *a.* afásico.

aphelion [affliuɒn], *s.* (astr.) afelio.

aphid [áefid], *s.* afidio.

Aphidiæ [æfídii], *s. pl.* afidios.

aphonia [afónia], *s.* afonía, ronquera crónica.

aphonic [afónic], *a.* sin sonido; afónico, afono; mudo.—**a. letter**, letra muda.

aphorism [æforiŝm], *s.* aforismo.

aphoristical [æforístical], *a.* aforístico.

aphoristically [-i], *adv.* sentenciosamente.

aphrodisiac [afrodíŝiac], **aphrodisiacal** [afrodiŝáiacal], *a.* afrodisíaco; lascivo, lujurioso.

aphtha [áefza], *s.* (med.) aftas.

aphthous [áefzʊs], *a.* aftoso.

aphyllous [afílʊs], *a.* (bot.) sin hojas.

apiary [épieri], *s.* colmenar, abejar.

apical [æpical], *a.* cimero.

apiculture [epicúlchœr], *s.* apicultura.

apiculturist [epicúlchœrist], *s.* apicultor.

apiece [apíŝ], *adv.* por persona; cada uno.

apiology [æpióloyi], *s.* estudio de las abejas.

Apis [éipis], *s.* Apis, el buey Apis.

apish [éipiŝh], *a.* gestero, monesco.

apishly [-li], *adv.* afectadamente, frívolamente.

apishness [-nes], *s.* monería, monada.

apivorous [apívorʊs], *a.* apívoro.

aplanatic [aplanǽtic], *a.* aplanático.

aplomb [aplóm], *s.* aplomo, seguridad; posición vertical.

apocalypse [apócalips], *s.* apocalipsis.

apocalyptic(al [apocalíptic(al], *a.* apocalíptico.

apochromatic [apocromǽtic], *a.* apocromático.

apocopate [apócopeit], *va.* (gram.) apocopar.

apocope [apócope], *s.* (gram.) apócope.

apocrypha [apócrifa], *s. pl.* libros apócrifos.

apocryphal [apócrifal], *a.* apócrifo.

apod [æpod], **apodal** [-al], **apodous** [-ʊs], *a.* ápodo.

apodictic(al [apodíctic(al], *a.* apodíctico.

apodosis [apódosis], *s.* (ret.) apódosis.

apogee [æpoȳi], *s.* (astr.) apogeo; auge.

apograph [æpograf], *s.* apógrafo.

Apollinarian [apolinérian], **Apollinarist** [apolinérist], *s.* apolinarista.

apologetic(al [apóloȳétic(al], *a.* apologético.

apologetically [-i], *adv.* apologéticamente.

apologetics [apoloȳétics], *s.* (teo.) apologética.

apologia [æpoloȳíæ], *s.* justificación.

apologist [apóloyist], *s.* apologista.

apologize [apóloyaiŝ]. **I.** *va.* excusar, disculpar. **II.** *vn.* disculparse, excusarse, dar satisfacción.

apologizer [-œr], *s.* defensor, apologista.

apologue [æpolog], *s.* apólogo, fábula.

apology [apóloyi], *s.* apología, defensa; excusa, justificación; satisfacción.

apomorphin(e [æpomórfin], *s.* apomorfina.

aponeurosis [-niurósis], *s.* (anat.) aponeurosis.

aponeurotic [æponiurótic], *a.* aponeurótico.

apophasis [æpófasis], *s.* (ret.) insinuación por pretendida omisión.

apophlegmatic [æpoflegmǽtic], *a.* apoflemático, expectorante.

apophthegm, *s. V.* APOTHEGM.

apophysis [apófisis], *s.* (anat.) apófisis.

apoplectic(al [æpopléctic(al], *a.* apoplético.

apoplexy [æpoplecsi], *s.* (med.) apoplejía.

aport [apórt], *adv.* (mar.) a babor (el timón).

aposiopesis [æposaiopísis], *s.* (ret.) reticencia.

apostasy [apóstasi], *s.* apostasía.

apostate [apósteit]. **I.** *s.* apóstata. **II.** *a.* falso, pérfido.

apostatical [æpostǽtical], *a.* apostático.

apostatize [apóstataiŝ], *va.* apostatar, renegar.

apostem [æpostem], o **aposteme** [apóstim], *s.* apostema, absceso.

apostemate [apóstimet], *vn.* apostemarse.

apostle [apóŝœl], *s.* apóstol.

apostleship [apóŝœlŝhip], **apostolate** [apóstolet], *s.* apostolado.

apostolic(al [apostólic(al], *a.* apostólico.

apostolically [-i], *adv.* apostólicamente.

apostolicalness [-nes], *s.* calidad de apostólico.

apostrophe [apóstrofe], *s.* (ret.) apóstrofe; (gram.) apóstrofo, virgulilla.

apostrophic(al [apostrófic(al], *a.* perteneciente al apóstrofe.

apostrophize [apóstrofaiŝ]. **I.** *va.* apostrofar. **II.** *vn.* (gram.) hacer una elisión; usar el apóstrofo.

apothecary [apózékeri], *s.* boticario, farmacéutico.—**a.'s measure**, sistema de medidas para líquidos usado en farmacia.—**a.'s shop**, botica, farmacia.—**a.'s weight**, sistema de pesos usado en farmacia.

apothecium [æpozíŝhium], *s.* (bot.) apotecia.

apothegm [æpozem], *s.* apotegma, proloquio.

apothegmatical [apozegmátical], *a.* sentencioso.

apothem [æpozem], *s.* (geom.) apotema; (farm.) sedimento de una pócima.

apotheosis [æpozíosis o apozeósis], *s.* apoteosis.

apotheosize [æpozíosaiŝ], *va.* deificar.

apozem [æposém], *s.* pócima.

Appalachian [æpælǽchiæn], *a.* apalache, de los montes Apalaches o Alleganys.

appall [æpól], *va.* espantar, aterrar; desmayar, desanimar.

appalling [æpóling], *a.* espantoso, aterrador.

appanage [æpaney], *s.* dependencia; infantado, infantazgo; don o condición natural o concomitante.

apparatus [æparétʊs o -rátʊs], *s.* (mec. y fisiol.), aparato.

apparel [æpǽrel]. **I.** *s.* ropa; vestiduras; (mar.) aparejo y demás accesorios (de un barco).—**wearing a.**, ropa. **II.** *va.* vestir; adornar; proveer.

apparency [æpérensi], *s.* calidad de evidente, lo evidente; calidad de presunto heredero.

apparent [-rent], *s.* aparente; claro, manifiesto. —**a. horizon**, horizonte sensible.—**a. time**, tiempo solar verdadero.

---

apparently [appérœntli], *adv.* evidentemente, claramente; al parecer, aparentemente.

apparition [aparíshʊn], *s.* aparición, aparecimiento; visión, fantasma, espectro.

apparitor [appéritœr], *s.* ministril, esbirro, muñidor; bedel.

appeal [appíl]. **I.** *vn.* (seguido de *to*) mover, desperatar, excitar, hacer llamamiento a; interesar a; llamar la atención de; atraer a; apelar o recurrir a; pedir a, suplicar a; poner por testigo a; exhortar a; (for.) apelar; (seguido de *from*, for.) apelar de.—**to a. to the country,** (pol.) apelar al pueblo disolviendo el parlamento para hacer nuevas elecciones. **II.** *va.* apelar de, llevar a un tribunal superior. **III.** *s.* súplica, instancia; llamamiento; exhortación; recurso a decisión ajena; (for.) apelación; citación, requerimiento.

appealable [-æbœl], *a.* apelable.—**appealer** [-œr], *s.* apelante.—**appealing** [-ing], *a.* suplicante; que despierta simpatía o aprobación.

appear [appíar], *vn.* aparecer, aparecerse; parecer, semejar; (for.) comparecer.

appearance [-ans], *s.* apariencia, cosa que parece; apariencia, aspecto; aparición; (for.) comparecencia.

appeasable [apísabœl], *a.* aplacable.

appeasableness [apísabœlnes], *s.* aplacabilidad.

appease [apís], *va.* aplacar, apaciguar; calmar, mitigar.

appeasement [apísmœnt], *s.* apaciguamiento; alivio.

appeaser [apísœr], *s.* apaciguador, reconciliador, pacificador.

appeasive [apísiv], *a.*, **appeasing** [apísing], *a.* apaciguador, pacificador; calmante.

appellancy [apélansi], *s.* apelación.

appellant [apélænt]. **I.** *s.* apelante; demandante. **II.** *a.* perteneciente al apelante o a la apelación.

appellate [apéleit], *a.* (for.) de apelación; que tiene jurisdicción en las apelaciones.

appellation [apeléshʊn], *s.* nombre; título.

appellative [apélativ]. **I.** *s.* (gram.) apelativo. **II.** *a.* apelativo, común.

appellatively [apélativli], *adv.* apelativamente.

appellee [apelí], *s.* (for.) apelado.

append [apénd], *va.* añadir, anexar; atar; colgar.

appendage [apéndex], *s.* pertenencia, dependencia, accesorio; colgajo; (biol.) apéndice.

appendant [apéndænt]. **I.** *a.* pendiente, colgante; anexo, adjunto; puesto, pegado; accesorio. **II.** *s.* accesorio; dependencia.

appendicitis [apéndisáitis], *s.* apendicitis.

appendicular [apendíkiulœr], *a.* apendicular; relativo al apéndice vermiforme.

appendiculate [-kiulet], *a.* apendiculado.

appendix [apéndix], *s.* apéndice, suplemento; aditamento; (bot. y zool.) apéndice; (anat.) apéndice vermiforme; (aer.) apéndice (de un dirigible).

apperceive [apœrsiv], *va.* (filos.) percibir y reconocer las relaciones del objeto percibido con percepciones o ideas anteriores, conocer por apercepción.

apperception [apœrsépshʊn], *s.* (filos.) apercepción, conciencia.

appertain [apœrtéin], *vn.* pertenecer, tocar, relacionarse (con).

appetence [apetens], **appetency** [apetensi], *s.* anhelo, avidez; apetencia, inclinación.

appetent [apetent], *a.* apetecedor, ávido, anhelante.

appetite [apetait], *s.* apetito; deseo, anhelo.

appetitive [apetaitiv], *a.* apetitivo; apetecedor.

appetize [apetaiś], *va.* abrir o excitar el apetito.

appetizer [apetaiśœr], *s.* aperitivo, apetitivo.

appetizing [apetaísing], *a.* apetitivo; apetitoso, aperitivo; tentador, excitante.

applaud [aplód], *va.* y *vn.* aplaudir.

applauder [aplódœr], *s.* aplaudidor.

applause [aplóś], *s.* aplauso; alabanza.

applausive [aplósiv], *a.* laudatorio.

apple [ǽpœl], *s.* (bot.) manzana; manzano; bola, pedazo más o menos redondo (como de mineral).—**a. of Cain,** madroño.—**a. of discord,** manzana de la discordia.—**a. of love,** tomate.—**a. of the eye,** niña del ojo.—**a. orchard,** manzanal.—**a.-pie order,** (fam.) orden perfecto.—**a. rot,** manchas podridas del manzano, causadas por un hongo del mismo nombre.—**a. tree,** manzano.

applejack [-ræc], *s.* aguardiente de manzana.

applesauce [-sos], *s.* compota de manzana.

appliance [apláians], *s.* herramienta, instrumento, utensilio, aparato, adminículo, artificio, artefacto; aplicación.

applicability [aplicabíliti], **applicableness** [aplicabœlnes], *s.* aplicabilidad.

applicable [aplicabœl], *a.* aplicable.

applicably [aplicabli], *adv.* aplicablemente.

applicant [aplicant], *s.* suplicante; aspirante, pretendiente, candidato.

application [aplikéshʊn], *s.* aplicación; consagración; medicamento aplicado; súplica; petición, solicitud, (Méx.) ocurso.—**to make a. to,** recurrir a; dirigirse a.

applicative [aplikætiv], **applicatory** [aplicatori], *a.* aplicable, aplicativo.

applied [apláid], *a.* aplicado; adaptado, utilizado.—**a. for,** pedido, encargado.—**patent a. for,** se ha solicitado patente.

applier [apláiœr], *s.* el que aplica o adapta.

apply [apláil]. **I.** *va.* aplicar; dar, administrar; poner; fijar; (refl.) darse, aplicarse o consagrarse. **II.** *vn.* dirigirse, acudir, ir.—**to a. for,** solicitar, pedir.

appoint [appóint], *va.* nombrar, designar, elegir; señalar, asignar; ordenar, prescribir, resolver; amueblar; equipar, proveer de lo necesario o de accesorios (en este sentido generalmente no se usa sino el participio **appointed,** v.g., *a well-appointed room,* un cuarto bien amueblado y provisto): establecer, sentar.

appointee [appointí], *s.* persona nombrada o electa; (for.) aquel a quien se asigna el derecho de disponer de bienes ajenos total o parcialmente.

appointer [appóintœr], *s.* el que nombra, ordena, designa.

appointment [appóintment], *s.* nombramiento; puesto, empleo, destino; cita, compromiso; acuerdo, convenio; orden, mandato, decreto; *pl.* equipo; mobiliario; accesorios.

apportion [appórshʊn], *va.* prorratear.

apportionment [appórshʊnmœnt], *s.* prorrateo; prorrata, rateo.

appose [appóś], *va.* poner delante, aplicar; yuxtaponer.

apposite [apósit], *a.* adaptado, propio, oportuno, a propósito; (gram.) apositivo.

appositely [apósitli], *adv.* convenientemente, a propósito.

appositeness [apósitnes], *s.* adaptación; propiedad.

apposition [aposíshʊn], *s.* (gram.) aposición; adición, añadidura, yuxtaposición.

appositive [apósitiv], *a.* (gram.) apositivo.

appraisable [appréiśabœl], *a.* tasable.

appraise [appréiś], *va.* avaluar, valuar, tasar; estimar, apreciar.

appraisal [appréiśal], **appraisement** [appréiśmœnt], *s.* tasación, avalúo, valuación.

appraiser [appréiśœr], *s.* tasador, avaluador.

appreciable [apríshiabœl], *a.* apreciable, estimable; perceptible, sensible, notable.

appreciate [apríshieit]. **I.** *va.* apreciar, estimar; valuar, tasar. **II.** *vn.* subir en valor.

appreciation [aprishiéshʊn], *s.* valuación, tasa, avalúo; alza, aumento de precio; aprecio, reconocimiento; susceptibilidad, sensibilidad estimativa.

appreciative, appreciatory [apríshiativ, -atóri], *a.* apreciativo.

appreciator [aprishiéitœr], *s.* avaluador, tasador; (ind.) medidor del gluten de la harina.

apprehend [æprejénd], *va.* comprender, entender, percibir; temer, sospechar, maliciar; aprehender, asir; prender, capturar.

apprehender [æprejéndœr], *s.* el que aprehende.

apprehensible [æprejénsibœl], *a.* comprensible.

apprehension [æprejénŝʜʊn], *s.* aprensión, cuidado; malicia; comprensión; aprehensión, estimación, idea; presa, prisión, captura; embargo.—**to be dull of a.**, tener la cabeza dura.

apprehensive [æprejénsiv], *a.* aprensivo, receloso, tímido; aprehensivo, agudo, penetrante, perspicaz; sensible, consciente.

apprehensively [-li], *adv.* aprehensivamente.

apprehensiveness [-nes], *s.* aprensión, recelo.

apprentice [æpréntis], *s.* aprendiz.

apprenticeship [-ŝhip], *s.* aprendizaje, noviciado.

apprise, apprize [æpráiŝ], *va.* informar, avisar, comunicar, dar parte; valuar, tasar.

apprizement [æpráiŝmœnt], *s.* avalúo, tasa.

apprizer [æpráiŝœr], *s.* valuador, tasador.

approach [æpróuch]. **I.** *va.* y *vn.* aproximar(se), acercar(se); allegar(se). **II.** *s.* acercamiento, acceso; proximidad; *pl.* maniobras, intrigas; *pl.* (fort.) aproches, ataques; *pl.* (const.) accesos, vía de entrada o de acceso.

approachable [æpróuchabœl], *a.* accesible, atracable; comunicativo.

approaching [-ing], *a.* próximo, cercano, venidero.

approbate [æprobeit], *va.* (E. U.) aprobar; licenciar, autorizar.

approbation [æprobéŝʜʊn], *s.* aprobación, aplauso, aceptación, beneplácito.

approbative [æprobetiv], **approbatory** [æprobéitori], *a.* aprobatorio.

appropriable [æprópriabœl], *a.* apropiable.

appropriate [æpróprieit]. **I.** *va.* apropiar, destinar; apropiarse; incautarse, adjudicarse; votar, asignar (una partida). **II.** *a.* apropiado, apto, a propósito, pertinente.

appropriately [-li], *adv.* propiamente, aptamente.

appropriateness [-nes], *s.* aptitud; propiedad.

appropriation [æpropriéŝʜʊn], *s.* apropiación; suma votada por el Congreso para algún objeto; (for.) enajenación de un beneficio.

appropriator [æpropriétœr], *s.* apropiador.

approvable [æprúvabœl], *a.* aprobable.

approval [-væl], *s.* aprobación; consentimiento.

approve [æprúv]. **I.** *va.* aprobar, sancionar, confirmar; probar, demostrar; ensayar; (for.) apropiarse.—**to a. one's self** (seguido de un adjetivo), demostrar que uno es (seguido del adjetivo correspondiente), v.g. *he approved himself worthy*, demostró que era digno. **II.** *vn.* (seguido de *of*), aprobar, sancionar.

approvement [-ment], *s.* (for.) confesión de un reo en que acusa a sus cómplices.

approver [æprúvœr], *s.* aprobador, aprobante.

approximate [æprócsimeit]. **I.** *a.* próximo, inmediato, cercano; aproximado. **II.** *va.* aproximar. **III.** *vn.* acercarse.

approximately [-li], *adv.* aproximadamente.

approximation [æprócsiméŝʜʊn], *s.* aproximación, acercamiento.

approximative [æpróximativ], *a.* aproximativo, aproximado.

approximatively [-li], *adv.* aproximadamente.

appulse [æpʊls], *s.* choque, encuentro; aproximación.

appurtenance [æpœrtenans], *s.* (for.) adjunto; pertenencia, dependencias.—*pl.* incidentes.

appurtenant [-ant], *a.* (for.) perteneciente.

apricot [épricot o épricot], *s.* (bot.) albaricoque, damasco.—**a. tree**, albarcoquero o albaricoquero.

April [éipril], *s.* abril.—**A.-fool day**, primer día de abril ("día de inocentes").—**A.-fool**, el que es burlado en ese día.

apron [éiprʊn o éipœrn], *s.* delantal, devantal, excusali; mandil; batiente de un dique; plancha de protección, plancha de guía; cubierta, manta; (art.) planchada o plomada de cañón; (mec.) cubierta protectora de palastro; portaherramienta; correa sin fin; plancha delantera de

un torno; (hidr.) entablado, empedrado u otra obra de protección al pie de una presa, muro de defensa, etc.—**a. of the stern** (mar.) albitana, contrabanque.—**a. strings**, cintas del delantal.

aproned [éprœnd], *a.* vestido con delantal.

apropos [apropó], *adv.* y *a.* a propósito, oportunamente, oportuno.

apse, apsis [æps, æpsis], *s.* (arq.) ábside, bóveda, nicho; (astr.) ápside.

apsidal [æpsidal], *a.* del ábside.

apt [æpt], *a.* apto, idóneo, capaz; propio, pertinente; propenso, listo, inclinado; fácil, dispuesto, pronto, vivo.

apterous [æptœrʊs], *a.* (ent.) áptero, sin alas.

aptitude [æptitiud], **aptness** [æptnes], *s.* aptitud, capacidad, idoneidad; tendencia, disposición, facilidad.

aptly [æptli], *adv.* aptamente; prontamente; perspicazmente.

apyretic [æpirétic], *a.* apirético, sin fiebre.

apyrexia [-rexia], *s.* apirexia, período sin fiebre.

aqua [éicua], *s.* agua.—**a. ammoniæ**, agua amoniacal.—**a. fontana**, agua de manantial.—**a. fortis**, agua fuerte.—**a. regia**, agua regia.—**a. tofana**, tofana.—**a. vitæ**, alcohol, licor.

aquamarine [éicuamarín], *s.* (min.) aguamarina.

aquarium [akuériʊm], *s.* acuario, pecera.

Aquarius [akuériʊs], *s.* (astr.) Acuario.

aquatint [ékuatint], *s.* acuatinta.

aquatic(al [akuátic(al], *a.* acuático, acuátil.

aqueduct [ékuedʊct], *s.* acueducto.

aqueous [éikuiʊs], **aquose** [-kuos], *a.* ácueo, acuoso, aguoso, aguazoso.

aqueousness [-nes], **aquosity** [ekuósiti], *s.* acuosidad.

aquiferous [akuíffœrʊs], *a.* que conduce o surte agua o flúido acuoso.

aquiline [ékuilin], *a.* aguileño.

Arab [éræb], **Arabian** [arébiæn], *s.* y *a.* árabe, arábigo.—**street A.**, pilctte de calle, golfo.—**The Arabian Nights**, las Mil y una Noches.

arabesque [ærebésc], *s.* (b. a.) arabesco.

Arabic [ærebic]. **I.** *s.* árabe, lengua arábiga. **II.** *a.* arábigo.—**A. numeral**, cifra arábiga, número arábigo.

Arabically [arébicali], *adv.* a lo árabe.

Arabism [érebiŝm], *s.* arabismo.

Arabist [érebist], *s.* arabista.

arable [ærebœl], *a.* labrantío, cultivable.

Arachnida [arécnida], *s. pl.* (ent.) arácnidos.

arachnoid [arécnoid], *a.* y *s.* (anat.) aracnoide.

Aragonese [ærægonís], *a.* y *s.* aragonés.

aragonite [ærægonait], *s.* (min.) aragonita.

Aramaic [æraméik], **Aramean** [æramían], *s.* arameo.

araneous [arénus], *a.* semejante a la telaraña.

Araucanian [ærokénian], *a.* y *s.* araucano.

arbalest, arbalist [árbalest, -list], *s.* ballesta.

arbalister [árbalistœr], *s.* ballestero.

arbiter [árbitœr], *s.* arbitrador, árbitro.

arbitrable [árbitrabœl], *a.* arbitrable.

arbitrably [árbitrabli], *adv.* a discreción.

arbitral [árbitræl], *a.* arbitral; arbitrable.

arbitrament [arbítramœnt], *s.* arbitraje; arbitramento; arbitrio.

arbitrarily [árbitrerili], *adv.* arbitrariamente.

arbitrariness [árbitrerines], *s.* arbitrariedad.

arbitrary [árbitreri], *a.* arbitrario, despótico, absoluto; (for.) discrecional.

arbitrate [árbitreit], *va.* y *vn.* arbitrar; decidir como árbitro.

arbitration [arbitréŝʜʊn], *s.* arbitramento, arbitraje, arbitración.—**a. of exchange**, (com.) arbitraje de cambio.

arbitrator [árbitréitœr], *s.* arbitrador, árbitro; tercero; ponente.

arbitratrix [arbitrétrix], **arbitress** [árbitres], *s.* arbitradora.

arbor, arbour [árbœr], *s.* (mec.) árbol, eje; tambor; (bot.) árbol; emparrado, bacelar; glorieta, cenador.—**a. vitæ**, (bot.) tuya, árbol conífero; (anat.) aspecto ramoso de la sección vertical del cerebelo.

arboreal, arboreous [arbóreal, -ʊs], **arborous** [árborʊs], *a.* arbóreo.
arborescence [arborésens], *s.* arborescencia.
arborescent [arborésent], *a.* arborescente.
arboret [árboret], *s.* arbolillo, arbusto; soto, arboleda.
arboretum [arborítʊm], *s.* plantel, almáciga, criadero de árboles.
arboriculture [arboricúlchœr], *s.* arboricultura.
arborist [árborist], *s.* arbolista.
arbuscle [árbʊsœl], *s.* arbustillo.
arbuscule [arbúskiul], *s.* mata, arbusto.
arbute [árbiut], *s.* (bot.) fresal. *V.* ARBUTUS.
arbutean [arbiútean], *a.* perteneciente al fresal.
arbutus [arbiútʊs], *s.* (bot.) madroño.—**trailing a.**, gayuba.
arc [arc]. **I.** *s.* (geom.) arco; (elec.) arco; (astr.) el arco aparente descrito por un astro entre su salida y su puesta.—**a. lamp**, lámpara de arco.— **a. lighter**, dínamo para alumbrado de arco.—**a. lighting**, alumbrado de arco.—**a. process**, (quím.) fijación del nitrógeno del aire combinándolo con el oxígeno por medio del arco eléctrico. —**a. shield**, tabique incombustible de protección que encierra o aísla un arco eléctrico.—**a. stream**, flujo de iones negativos entre el cátodo y el ánodo de un arco eléctrico.—**a. welding**, soldadura eléctrica de arco. **II.** *vn.* (elec) formar arco.
arcade [arkéid], *s.* arcada; pasaje, galería.
Arcadian [arkédian], *a.* y *s.* arcadio, árcade; simple, pastoral.
arcane [arkéin], *a.* arcano, misterioso.
arcanum [arkénʊm], *s.* areano.—*pl.* **arcana**, misterios, arcanos.
arch [arch]. **I.** *va.* arquear, encorvar, enarcar; abovedar. **II.** *vn.* formar bóveda. **III.** *s.* (geom. y arq.) arco; bóveda.—**the a. of heaven**, la bóveda celeste.—**a. of the aorta**, (anat.) la curvatura de la aorta.—**segmental a.**, arco abocinado.—**Gothic a., pointed a.**, arco ojival, arco gótico.—**horseshoe a.**, arco de herradura.— **semicircular a.**, arco de medio punto. **IV.** *a.* travieso, inquieto; picaresco, socarrón, astuto; principal, insigne, de primer orden, grande.
Archaean, Archean [arkían], *a.* (geol.) arqueozoico.
archæology, archæologist. *V.* ARCHEOLOGY, etc.
archaic [arkéic], *a.* arcaico, anticuado.
archaism [árkeism], *s.* arcaísmo.
archangel [arkényel], *s.* arcángel.
archangelic [arkænyélic], *a.* arcangélico.
archbishop [archbíshʊp], *s.* arzobispo, metropolitano.—**archbishopric** [-ric], *s.* arzobispado.
archdeacon [archdíkʊn], *s.* arcediano; archidiácono.
archdeaconry [archdíkʊnri], **archdeaconship** [-ship], arcedianato.
archdiocese [archdáiosis], *s.* arzobispado.
archducal [archdiúcal], *a.* archiducal.
archduchess [archdúches], *s.* archiduquesa.
archduchy [archdúchi], *s.* archiducado.
archduke [archdiúk], *s.* archiduque.
archdukedom [archiúkdom], *s.* archiducado.
arched [archt], *a.* arqueado, abovedado, corvo.
archenemy [archénemi], *s.* el enemigo malo, el demonio.
archeologian [arkeolóyan], **archeologist** [arkeóloyist], *s.* arqueólogo.
archeologic(al [arkeolóyic(al], *a..* arqueológico.
archeology [arkeóloyi], *s.* arqueología.
Archeozoic [árkiośoic], *a.* (geol.) arqueozoico, arcaico.
archer [árchœr], *s.* arquero, ballestero, flechero.
archeress [árchœres], *s.* ballestera, flechadora.
archery [árchœri], *s.* ballestería.
Arches Court [arches cort], *s.* tribunal eclesiástico de Londres.
archetypal [arketáipal], *a.* perteneciente al arquetipo.
archetype [árketaip], *s.* arquetipo, prototipo.
archfiend [árchfínd], *s.* el demonio, el diablo, el enemigo malo.

archidiaconal [arkidiæconal], *a.* perteneciente al arcediano.
Archie [árchi], **Archibald** [-bold], *s.* cañón de defensa contra aeroplanos, cañón antiaéreo.
archiepiscopacy [arkiepíscopasi], **archiepiscopate** [arkiepíscopeit], *s.* arzobispado.
archiepiscopal [arkiepíscopal], *a.* arquiepiscopal o arzobispal.
archil [árchil], *s.* (bot.) orchilla.
archimandrite [arkimǽndrait], *s.* archimandrita.
Archimedean [árquimídiæn], *a.* arquimédico, de Arquimedes.
arching [árching]. **I.** *a.* arqueado. **II.** *s.* arqueo, curvatura.
archipelago [arkipélago], *s.* archipiélago.
architect [árkiteet], *s.* arquitecto; (fig.) artífice.
architectonic [arkitectónic], *a.* arquitectónico.
architectonics [arkitectónics], *s.* arquitectura, arte arquitectónico.
architectural [arkitékchœral], *a.* arquitectural.
architecture [árkitekchœr], *s.* arquitectura.
architrave [árkitrev], *s.* (arq.) arquitrabe
archive [árkaiv], *s.* archivo; documento archivado; estanco.
archivist [árkivist], *s.* archivero, cartulario.
archlike [árchlaik], *a.* en forma de arco.
archly [árchli], *adv.* jocosamente, sutilmente.
archness [árchnes], *s.* travesura, astucia, sutileza de ingenio.
archon [árcon], *s.* aconte.
archpillar [archpílar], *s.* (arq.) columna principal.
archpriest [archpríst], *s.* gran sacerdote; arcipreste.
archvillain [archvílen], *s.* bellaconazo, picarón.
archvillainy [archvíleni], *s.* gran bellaquería.
archway [árchuéi], *s.* pase bajo un arco; pasaje abovedado.
archwise [árchuaís], *a.* en figura de arco.
arcing [árking]. **I.** *s.* (elect.) formación de arco. **II.** *a.* (elec.) que forma arco.
arcograph [árcograf], *s.* arcógrafo.
arctic [árctic], *a.* ártico, septentrional; frígido.
Arcturus [arctúrus], *s.* (astr.) Arturo.
arcuate [árkiuet], *a.* arqueado.
arcuation [arkiuéshʊn], *s.* arqueo, encorvamiento, curvatura.
arcubalist [árkiubalist], *s.* ballesta.
arcubalister [árkiubalíster], *s.* ballestero.
ardency [árdensi], **ardentness** [árdentnes], *s.* ardor, vehemencia, anhelo, calor.
ardent [árdent], *a.* ardiente; vehemente, apasionado, vivo—**a. spirits**, licores espirituosos.
ardently [árdentli], *adv.* apasionadamente, ardientemente, calurosamente.
ardor, ardour [árdor], *s.* ardor, calor; pasión, vehemencia, fervor; acaloramiento.
arduous [áryuus], *a.* arduo, difícil, laborioso; alto, escabroso, enhiesto.
arduously [áryuusli], *adv.* arduamente.
are [ar] (*plural del presente de indicativo del verbo* TO BE).—**we a., you a., they a.**, somos, sois, son, o estamos, estáis, están.
are [éar], *s.* área (medida).
area [érea], *s.* extensión, superficie; patio, corral; (geom.) área, superficie.
areca [aríca], *s.* (bot.) areca y su fruto.
arena [aría], *s.* arena, liza, redondel.
arenaceous [ærenéshʊs], **arenose** [ǽrenous], *a.* arenisco, arenoso, arenáceo.
areola [aríola], *s.* (anat.) aréola.
areolar [aríolar], *a.* areolar.
areometer [areómetœr], *s.* areómetro, pesalicores.
Areopagite [æreópagait], *s.* areopagita.
Areopagus [æreópagʊs], *s.* Areópago.
argal, argali [árgæl, -i], *s.* argalí, carnero salvaje de Siberia; carnero salvaje de los montes Rocallosos.
Argand lamp [árgand læmp], *s.* quinqué.
argent [áryent], *a.* (blas.) argén.
argentation [áryentéshʊn], *s.* plateado, baño de plata.

argentiferous [arȝentífœrʊs], *a.* argentífero.
argentine [árȝentin]. **I.** *a.* argentino. **II.** *s.* metal blanco plateado; precipitado de estaño y cinc; materia plateada de las escamas de los peces.
Argentine, Argentinean [-tíniæn], *s.* y *a.* argentino, de la Argentina.
argentite [-tait], *s.* (min.) argirosa, argentita.
argil [árȝil], *s.* arcilla; aluminita.
argillaceous [arȝiléǝhʊs], **argillous** [arȝílʊs], *a.* arcilloso
argonaut [árgonot], *s.* (ict.) argonauta.
argol [árgol], *s.* tártaro.
argon [árgon], (quím.) argón, argo.
argosy [árgosi], *s.* bajel con cargamento valioso.
argot [árgot], *s.* jerga, jerigonza; germanía; lenguaje vulgar, caló.
argue [árguiu]. **I.** *va.* disputar, discutir, argüir; sostener; convencer. **II.** *vn.* disputar, argüir.
arguer [árguiuœr], *s.* argumentador, arguyente, opinante; discutidor, ergotista.
arguing [árguiuing], *s.* razonamiento, argumento.
argument [árguiumœnt], *s.* argumento, tema, asunto; debate, controversia, disputa; (mat.) argumento; (for.) alegación, alegato.
argumentation [árguiumentéȝhun], *s.* argumentación, raciocinio.
argumentative [arguiuméntativ], *a.* demostrativo: argumentador, argumentista.
Argus [árgʊs], *s.* argos; faisán de China.
argute [arguiút], *a.* agudo, sutil; astuto, perspicaz; penetrante (sonido); (bot.) dentado.
arguteness [arguiútnes], *s.* argucia, agudeza, sutileza, perspicacia.
aria [ária], *s.* (mús.) aria.
Arian [érian], *s.* arriano.—**Arianism** [-iṡm], *s.* arrianismo.
arid [érid], *a.* árido, seco.
aridity [aridíti] *o* **aridness** [éridnes], *s.* aridez.
Aries [ériiṡ], *s.* (astr.) Aries.
arietta [ariéta], *s.* (mús.) arieta.
aright [arráit], *adv.* acertadamente, rectamente, justamente.—**to take a.**, rectificar.
aril [éril], **arillus** [arílʊs], *s.* aril.
arilated [æriléted], *a.* que tiene arilo.
ariolation [arioléṡhun], *s.* adivinación.
arise [aráiṡ], *vn.* (pret. AROSE, *pp.* ARISEN) subir, elevarse; surgir, aparecer; levantarse, ponerse en pie; proceder (de); provenir (de); presentarse, ofrecerse; suscitarse, originarse, sobrevenir; sublevarse, alzarse.
arista [arísta], *s.* (bot.) arista. *V.* AWN.
aristocracy [æristócrasi], *s.* aristocracia.
aristocrat [æristocrat], *s.* aristócrata.
aristocratic(al [-crétic, -al], *a.* aristocrático.
aristocratically [-i], *adv.* aristocráticamente.
aristol [éristoul], *s.* (farm.) aristol.
Aristotelian [éristotílian], **Aristotelic** [-télic], *a.* y *s.* aristotélico.
Aristotelianism [-tílianiṡm], *s.* aristotelismo.
arithmancy [arízmansi], *s.* aritmancia.
arithmetic [arízmetic], *s.* aritmética.
arithmetical [arizmétical], *a.* aritmético.
arithmetician [arizmetíṡhan], *s.* aritmético.
ark [arc], *s.* arca; (mar.) lanchón; (E. U.) bote de fondo plano para transporte interior.—**A. of the Covenant**, arca de la alianza.
arm [arm]. **I.** *s.* brazo (del cuerpo, de una silla, de mar); rama (de planta); rama; canal; arma (instrumento e instituto); (fig.) brazo, mano (de la ley, etc.); (mar.) cabo de una verga; brazo de ancla; (mec.) brazo, palanca; brazo de palanca. —*pl.* armas, servicio militar; ramos del servicio militar; ciencia o profesión de las armas; blasones.—**a. in a.**, de bracete, del brazo.—**a.'s reach**, alcance del brazo.—**at a.'s length**, a una brazada: a distancia prudente; en circunstancias desfavorables.—**fire arms**, armas de fuego.—**in arms**, en hostilidad armada; en fuerte oposición. —**side arms**, armas de cinto, armas de oficiales, espadas.—**to arms!** ¡a las armas!.—**under arms**, sobre las armas. **II.** *va.* armar; fortalecer; proveer de medios o elementos. **III.** *vn.* armarse.

armada [arméda *o* armáda], *s.* armada, flota.
armadillo [armadílo], *s.* (zool.) armadillo.
armament [ármamœnt], *s.* armamento.
armature [ármachuœr], *s.* (elec.) armadura (de un imán); inducido (de una dínamo); (mil.) armadura; armamento, equipo; (hist. nat.) armas naturales, medios de defensa (de los animales y plantas).
armchair [ármchéar], *s.* sillón, butaca, silla de brazos.
Armenian [armínian], *a.* y *s.* armenio.
armful [ármful], *s.* brazada.
armhole [ármjoul], *s.* sobaquera.
armiger [ármiȝœr], *s.* armígero, caballero; escudero.
armillary [ármilœri], *a.* armilar, anular.—**a. sphere**, esfera armilar.
armings [ármingṡ], *s. pl.* (mar.) empavesadas.
armipotent [armípotent], *a.* armipotente.
armisonant [armísonant], *a.* armisonante.
armistice [ármistis], *s.* armisticio.
armless [ármles], *a.* desarmado; manco.
armlet [ármlet], *s.* brazuelo; brazal o brazalete, avambrazo.
armo(u)r [ármœr]. **I.** *s.* armadura, arnés; canillera; coraza, blindaje. **II.** *va.* acorazar, blindar.
armorer [ármœrœr], *s.* armero; mallero.
armorial [armórial], *a.* heráldico.
armoring [ármoring], *s.* acorazamiento, blindaje
armory [ármori], *s.* armería; (E. U.) arsenal; maestranza; cuartel; armadura, armas; blasón, heráldica; escudo de armas.
armour, armoured, etc. = ARMOR. etc.
armpit [ármpit], *s.* sobaco, axila.
armseye [ármsai], *s.* sobaquera.
army [ármi], *s.* ejército; multitud, muchedumbre.—**a. corps**, cuerpo de ejército.
arnatto [arnáto], **arnotto** [arnóto], (bot.) bija, achiote. *V.* ANNATTO.
arnica [árnica], *s.* (bot., farm.) árnica.
aroint [aróint], *vr.* irse, apartarse. Más usado en el imperativo:—**a. thee!** ¡vete, lárgate!
aroma [aróma], *s.* (quím.) aroma; fragancia.
aromatic(al [aromátic(al], *a.* aromático.
aromatics [æromátics], *s. pl.* aromas, especias.
aromatization [-tiséȝhun], *s.* aromatización.
aromatize [arómataiṡ], *va.* aromatizar.
aromatizer [arómataiȝœr], *s.* aromatizador
arose [aróuṡ], *pret.* del verbo TO ARISE.
around [arráund]. **I.** *adv.* alrededor o en derredor, a la redonda; a la vuelta; por todos lados; de un lado para otro. **II.** *prep.* al volver de, alrededor de, cerca de.
arousal [arráuṡal], *s.* despertamiento.
arouse [arráuṡ], *va.* despertar; mover, excitar
arow [arró], *adv.* (poét.) en fila, en línea.
arpeggio [arpéyo], *s.* (mús.) arpegio.
arquebus [árkuebuṡ], *s.* arcabuz.
arquebusier [árkuebusíœr], *s.* arcabucero.
arraign [arréin], *va.* (for.) procesar criminalmente; acusar, denunciar.
arraignment [arréinmœnt], *s.* (for.) proceso, causa criminal; acusación, denuncia.
arrange [arrény]. **I.** *va.* arreglar, acomodar, preparar, aprestar; hacer arreglos para; disponer, convenir, concertar; (mús.) arreglar, adaptar. **II.** *vn.* prevenir, hacer arreglos; concertarse, convenir.
arrangement [arrénymœnt], *s.* colocación; orden; arreglo, distribución; preparativo, medida, providencia, disposición.
arranger [arrényœr], *s.* arreglador, ordenador.
arrant [érrant], *a.* notorio, redomado, consumado, de siete suelas.—**a. fool**, (fam.) tonto de marca.
arrantly [érrantli], *adv.* redomadamente.
arras [érras], *s.* tapicería de Arras.
array [arréi], *s.* orden de batalla, formación; pompa, aparato; adorno, gala, atavío.—**to challenge the a.**, (for.) recusar todo el jurado.

---

array, *va.* poner en orden de batalla; formar las tropas; guarnecer, ataviar, adornar; (for.) colocar los jurados.

arrear [ærrícer], *s.* (ú. más en *pl.*) atrasos, caídos.

arrearage [arrícerey], *s.* atrasos, caídos.

arrest [ærrést], *s.* prisión o arresto; detención; aprehensión; (mec.) parada, interrupción.

arrest *va.* impedir, detener, retener, atajar, reprimir; arrestar, prender; atraer y fijar (la atención).

arrester [ærréstcer], *s.* detenedor.

arrhizous, arrhizal [ærráiôus, -ôal], *a.* sin raíces.

arris [ærris], *s.* esquina, ángulo externo; filo.

arrival [arráival], *s.* arribo, llegada; entrada; logro, consecución; advenimiento; persona que llega.—**a new a.,** un recién venido.

arrive [ærráiv], *vn.* llegar.—**to a. at,** llegar a (un resultado, etc.).—**to a. at, o in,** llegar a (un pueblo, un punto).

arrogance [ærrogans], **arrogancy** [ærrogansi], **arrogantness** [ærrogantnes], *s.* arrogancia.

arrogant [ærrogant], *a.* arrogante.

arrogantly [ærrogantli], *adv.* arrogantemente.

arrogate [ærroguet], *va.* arrogarse, usurpar.

arrogation [ærroguéshun], *s.* arrogación.

arrow [ærro], *s.* flecha, saeta.—**a. grass,** triploquín, planta acuática.

arrowhead [-hed], *s.* punta de flecha.

arrowroot [-rut], *s.* (bot.) arrurruz.

arrowy [ærroui], *a.* en forma de flecha o saeta; rápido como la flecha.

arroyo [arroyo], *s.* arroyo; barranco, torrentera.

arsenal [ársenal], *s.* arsenal; maestranza, atarazana.

arsenate, arseniate [ársenet, -niet], *s.* arseniato.

arsenic [ársenic], *s.* arsénico.

arsenic [arsénic], *a.* (quím.) arsénico.

arsenical [-nical], *a.* arsenical.

arsenid, arsenide [ársenid, -naid], *s.* arseniuro.

arsenious [arsínius], *a.* arsenioso.

arsenite [ársenait], *s.* arsenito.

arsenopyrite [arsénopáirait], *s.* arsenopirita, piritas arsenicales.

arsis [ársis], *s.* sílaba acentuada; inflexión de voz; (mús.) parte no acentuada de un compás.

arson [ársun], *s.* incendio premeditado.

art [2*a. pers. indicat. de.* TO BE], eres, estás.

art [art], *s.* arte; habilidad, maña, destreza; astucia, artificio; oficio, gremio.—**arts and crafts,** artes y oficios.

arterial [artírial], *a.* arterial.

arterialize [artírialaiz], *va.* arterializar.

arterialization [-éishun], *s.* arterialización.

arteriole [artíriol], *s.* arteriola.

arteriosclerosis [-sclerósis], *s.* arteriosclerosis.

arteriotomy [artiriótomi], *s.* (cir.) arteriotomía.

arteritis [árteraitis], *s.* arteritis.

artery [ártceri], *s.* arteria.

Artesian [artíyan], *a.* artesiano.—**A. well,** pozo artesiano.

artful [ártful], *a.* artificial; artero, mañero, ladino, astuto; diestro, ingenioso.

artfully [ártfuli], *adv.* artificiosamente, diestramente; con arte; insidiosa, socarronamente.

artfulness [ártfulnes], *s.* arteria, astucia; habilidad, industria, alicantina.

arthritic(al [arzrític(al], *a.* artrítico; artético.

arthritis [arzráitis *o* zrítis], *s.* artética, artritis.

arthrology [arzróloyi], *s.* artrología.

arthropod [árzropod], *s.* artrópodo.

Arthropoda [arzrópoda], *s. pl.* artrópodos.

arthropodal [arzrópodal], **arthropodous** [arzrópodus], *a.* relativo a los artrópodos.

arthrosis [arzrósis], *s.* articulación.

artichoke [ártichouk], *s.* (bot.) alcachofa, areacil, aguaturma.—**Jerusalem a.,** (bot.) especie de girasol; cotufa, chufa.

article [árticœl]. **I.** *s.* artículo (literario, definido, indefinido, de una ley, de doctrina, de comercio); cosa, objeto; parte.—*pl.* escritura, cédula; constitución; reglamento, ordenanza.—**articles of partnership,** (for.) escritura de so-

ciedad.—**articles of religion,** reglas o constitución (de una iglesia o secta); declaración de fe.—**articles of war,** código militar.—**small articles,** menudencias.—**to be under articles,** estar escriturado.—**to sign articles,** escriturarse.—**to surrender under articles,** capitular. **II.** *va.* formular en artículos; escriturar; contratar; dividir o colocar en artículos; acusar por escrito; comprometer (a un abogado, aprendiz, etc.) por contrato. **III.** *vn.* pactar.

articular [artíkular], *a.* articular.—**articularly** [-li], *adv.* articuladamente.

Articulata [-leitæ], *s. pl.* (zool.) articulados.

articulate [artíkiulet]. **I.** *va.* articular, enunciar; unir, atar. **II.** *vn.* articular, énunciar; estar unido por articulación. **III.** *s.* (zool.) articulado. **IV.** *a.* articulado; claro, distinto.

articulately [artíkiuletli], *adv.* articuladamente.

articulateness [artíkiuletnes], *s.* la calidad de ser articulado.

articulation [artikiuléshun], *s.* (anat.) articulación; coyuntura; (bot.) nudo; (pros.) articulación, pronunciación.

artifice [ártifis], *s.* artificio; ardid, maña, artería.

artificer [artífiscer], *s.* artífice; inventor, autor; artesano hábil, oficial.

artificial [ártifíshal], *a.* artificial, fabricado; imitado, falso; ficticio, fingido; postizo; afectado; artificioso.—**a. person,** persona jurídica.

artificiality [artifíshiáliti], **artificialness** [artifíshalnes], *s.* calidad de artificial o artificioso; apariencia; afectación.

artificially [artifíshali], *adv.* artificialmente.

artillerist [artílcerist], *s.* artillero.

artillery [artílceri], *s.* artillería.—**a. park,** parque de artillería.

artilleryman [-man], *s.* artillero.

artisan [ártiŝan], *s.* artesano, artífice, oficial.

artist [ártist], *s.* artista; artífice; actor.

artistic [artístic], *a.* artístico.

artistically [artisticali], *adv.* artísticamente.

artless [ártles], *a.* natural, sin arte, sencillo; sin dolo; (fam.) chabacano; charanguero, cándido.

artlessly [ártlesli], *adv.* sencillamente, cándidamente; chabacanamente.

artlessness [ártlesnes], *s.* sencillez, candidez, naturalidad.

arum [érum *o* árum], *a.* (bot.) arum, tragontina, sarillo, malanga.

arundinaceous [arúndinéshus], **arundineous** [arundíniuŝ], *a.* perteneciente o semejante a las cañas.

aruspex [arúspex], **aruspice** [-pis], *s.* arúspice.

Aryan [árian], *s.* y *a.* ario.

as [aŝ]. **I.** *adv., conj.* y *pron. rel.* como; a medida que; mientras; cuando; en el momento en que; que (sobre todo después de *such* y *same*); según, como.—**a. . . . again a.,** dos veces más . . . que, vg. *as large again as this room,* dos veces mayor que este cuarto.—**a. against,** por, comparado con.—**a. . . . a.,** tan . . . como, vg., *as large as this one,* tan grande como éste; *as soon as he comes,* tan pronto como él venga.—**a. far a.,** hasta, hasta donde.—**as for,** en cuanto a, por lo que toca a.—**a. good a.,** expresión que se usa para indicar que algo puede darse por hecho o seguro, vg., *that is as good as lost,* eso puede darse por perdido.—**a. is** (com. fam.) como está.—**a. it is,** como está, como están las cosas.—**a. it were,** por decirlo así.—**a much,** tanto; otro tanto; eso en substancia.—**a. much a.,** tanto como; hasta.—**a. much a. to say,** como quien dice.—**a. per,** según, de acuerdo con.—**a. to** =A. FOR.—**a. though,** como si.—**a. well a.,** tan bien como; así como.—**a. yet,** aún, todavía. **II.** *s.* as (moneda).

asafœtida [æsaféida], *s.* asafétida.

asarabacca [æsarabǽca], **asarum** [ǽsarum], *s.* (bot.) ásaro, asarabácara.

asbestic [asbéstic], **asbestine** [æsbéstin], *a.* asbestino; incombustible.

asbestos [æsbéstos], *s.* asbesto, amianto.

ascarid [ǽscarid], *s.* (zool.) ascáride.

Ascaris [ǽscaris], *s.* (zool.) ascáridos.

ascend [asénd], *va.* y *vn.* ascender, subir; adelantar; elevar, encumbrarse; subir de grado.

ascendable [aséndabœl], *a.* accesible, que se puede subir.

ascendant [aséndant], **ascendent** [-ent]. **I.** *s.* altura, elevación; ascendiente, influjo, poder; predominio; padre, antepasado; (astr.) ascensión. **II.** *a.* ascendente; superior, predominante.

ascendancy [-ansi], **ascendency** [-ensi], *s.* ascendiente, influjo, poder.

ascension [asénshun], *s.* ascensión, subida; (igl.) la Ascensión de Jesucristo.

ascensional [asénshunal], *a.* (astr.) ascensional.

ascent [asént], *s.* subida, elevación, ascensión; ascenso, promoción; cuesta, pendiente.

ascertain [ascœrtéin], *va.* averiguar, descubrir, determinar.

ascertainable [-abœl], *a.* averiguable, descubrible.

ascertainer [-œr], *s.* averiguador, indagador.

ascertainment [-mœnt], *s.* averiguación, indagación, determinación.

ascetic [asétic]. **I.** *a.* ascético. **II.** *s.* asceta.

asceticism [asétisiâm], *s.* ascetismo.

ascians [áskiæns], **ascii** [áskiai], *s.* (geo.) ascios.

ascidian [asídiæn], *s.* y *a.* (zool.) ascidia.

ascites [asáitis], *s.* (med.) ascitis.

ascitic(al [asític(al], *a.* ascítico, hidrópico.

ascribable [ascráibabœl], *a.* atribuíble.

ascribe [ascráib], *va.* atribuir; aplicar.

ascription [ascrípshun], *s.* atribución.

ascus [áscus], *s.* (bot.) teca, asco.

asea [así], *adv.* en el mar.

asepsis [asépsis], *s.* asepsia.

aseptic [aséptic], *a.* aséptico.

asepticism [aséptisiâm], *s.* tratamiento aséptico.

asepticize [aséptisaiś], *va.* (med.) aseptizar, hacer aséptico.

asexual [aséxyual], *a.* asexual; sin sexo.

ash [æsh], (sing. de ASHES), *s.* ceniza, cenizas.— **a.-colored,** cenizo, ceniciento.—**a. fire,** fuego lento cubierto con cenizas.—**a. hole, a. pan, a. pit,** cenicero.—**a. tub,** coladero, cubeta de lejía. **A. Wednesday,** miércole de ceniza.

ash, *s.* (bot.) fresno.—**mountain a.,** serbal.

ashamed [ashéimd], *a.* avergonzado, corrido.— **to be a.,** avergonzarse. sonrojarse.

ashen [áshœn], *a.* de fresno; ceniciento; pálido.

ashes [áshes], *s. pl.* ceniza o cenizas.

ashlar, ashler [áshlœr], *s.* (const.) sillar; sillería.

ashlaring, ashlering [áshlaring, áshlœring], *s.* ligazones de los cabrios del techo; sillería.

ashore [áshóar], *adv.* en tierra, a tierra.—**to get a.,** desembarcar.—**to run a.,** encallar, varar.

ashweed [áshuid], (bot.) angélica.

ashy [áshi], *a.* cenizoso, ceniciento.—**a.-pale,** pálido, lívido.

Asian [éshian], **Asiatic** [éshiátic], *a.* asiático.

Asiaticism [ashiátisiâm], *s.* imitación de las costumbres asiáticas.

aside [asáid]. **I.** *adv.* a un lado, al lado; aparte. **II.** *s.* (teat.) aparte.

asinine [ásinin], *a.* asinino, asnal.

ask [ask]. **I.** *va.* preguntar; pedir, solicitar, suplicar; invitar, convidar.—**to a. a question,** hacer una pregunta. **II.** *vn.* preguntar; pedir.—**to a. for,** preguntar por; pedir.—**to a. one down, in, up,** rogar a uno que baje, entre, suba.

askance [askáns], *adv.* al sesgo, de soslayo, oblicuamente, de refilón; con desdén; con recelo.

asker [áskœr], *s.* inquiridor; suplicante.

askew [askiú], *adv.* y *a.* sesgado, oblicuo; de soslayo.

asking [ásking], *s.* súplica, ruego; publicación (de amonestaciones).—**for the a.,** sin más que pedirlo.—**third time of a.,** tercera amonestación.

aslant [aslánt]. **I.** *adv.* y *a.* oblicuamente, inclinado. **II.** *prep.* al través de.

asleep [aslíp], *adv.* dormido, durmiendo.—**to fall a.,** dormirse, quedarse dormido.

aslope [aslóup], *adv.* en declive, en pendiente.

asp [asp], **aspic** [áspic], *s.* áspid.

aspalathus [aspálazus], *s.* (bot.) aspálato.

asparagin [aspárayin], *s.* (quím.) esparraguina.

asparagus [aspáragus], *s.* (bot.) espárrago.

aspect [áspect], *s.* aspecto, semblante; apariencia; fase.

aspen [áspen]. **I.** *s.* (bot.) tiemblo. **II.** *a.* perteneciente al álamo temblón; tembloroso.

asper [áspœr], *s.* aspro (moneda).

asperate [áspœret], *va.* hacer áspera alguna cosa.

aspergill [áspœryil], *s.* (igl.) hisopo.

asperifolious [asperifólius], *a.* (bot.) de hojas ásperas.

asperity [aspériti], *s.* aspereza; rudeza.

aspermatous, aspermous [aspérmatus, -mus], *a.* (bot.) sin semilla.

asperse [aspœrs], *va.* difamar, calumniar, denigrar, infamar.

asperser [aspœrsœr], *s.* infamador.

aspersion [aspœrshun], *s.* defamación, calumnia; mancha, mácula, tacha, deshonra; aspersión, rociadura; (fam.) rociada, reprensión; (igl.) asperges.

aspersive [-siv], *a.* calumnioso, defamatorio.

asphalt [æsfælt], *va.* asfaltar.

asphalt [æsfælt] *o* **asphaltum** [asfæltum], *s.* asfalto; (Cuba) chapapote.

asphalter [æsfæltœr], *s.* asfaltador.

asphaltic [æsfæltic], *a.* asfáltico, bituminoso.

asphodel [æsfodel], *s.* (bot.) asfodelo o gamón.

asphyxia [æsfícsia] (med.), **asphyxiation** [æsfixiéshun], *s.* asfixia, sofocación.

asphyxial [æsfícsial], *a.* asfíctico.

asphyxiate [æsfixieit], *va.* asfixiar, sofocar.

asphyxiating [-éiting], *a.* asfixiante.

aspic [áspic], *s.* (bot.) espliego; (zool.) áspid.

aspirant [aspáirant], *s.* aspirante, pretendiente, candidato.

aspirate [áspireit]. **I.** *va.* aspirar, pronunciar con aspiración; (fisiol.) aspirar. **II.** *a.* aspirado.

aspiration [aspiréshun], *s.* aspiración, anhelo, deseo, ambición; (gram.) aspiración; (fisiol.) aspiración.

aspirator [aspirétœr], *s.* aspirador.

aspiratory [aspáiratori], *a.* aspiratorio.

aspire [aspáicœr], *vn.* aspirar, ambicionar; subir, ascender.

aspirer [aspáircœr], *s.* aspirante.

aspirin [áspirin], *s.* aspirina.

aspiring [aspáiring], *a.* ambicioso; aspirante.

asquint [askuínt], *adv.* al soslayo, de través.

ass [æs], *s.* asno, burro, borrico (sentido recto y fig.).—**young a.,** pollino.

assagai, assegai [ásægai, -egai], *s.* azagaya, saeta sudafricana; (bot.) árbol de azagayas, de que éstas se hacen.

assail [asséil], *va.* asaltar, atacar.

assailable [-œbœl], *a.* que puede ser asaltado.

assailant [-lænt], **assailer** [-lœr], *s.* y *a.* asaltador, agresor.

assailment [-ment], *s.* asalto, agresión.

assart [æsárt]. **I.** *s.* (agr.) roza. **II.** *va.* (agr.) rozar.

assassin [æséesin], *s.* asesino.

assassinate [æséesineit]. **I.** *va.* asesinar. **II.** *vn.* ser asesino, cometer asesinato.

assassination [æsœsinéishun], *s.* asesinato.

assassinator [-éitœr], *s.* asesino.

assault [æsólt]. **I.** *s.* asalto, ataque. **II.** *va.* asaltar, atacar; violar o tratar de violar (a una mujer).

assaulter [-sóltœr], *s.* asaltador, asaltante.

assay [æséi]. **I.** *va.* probar, examinar, investigar; tratar de; verificar, contrastar (moneda, pesas); (metal.) ensayar; (quím.) analizar. **II.** *s.* prueba, determinación, verificación; contraste (de pesas, moneda, etc.); (metal., quím.) ensaye, ensayo; substancia que se ensaya; muestra de ensaye; resultado de un ensaye.—**a. balance,** balanza de ensayes, balanza de precisión.—**a. master,** ensayador, contraste.—**a. pound,** pequeña pesa patrón empleada en ensayes de oro, plata, etc.; es de peso arbitrario—generalmente de unos 5 dg.—**a. ton,** pesa patrón empleada en los ensayes—como 292 dg.

assayer [æséicer], *s.* (met.) ensayador; contraste.
assaying [æséiing], *s.* (met.) ensaye; docimacia.
assemblage [æsémbley], *s.* reunión, unión; grupo; asociación; arreglo (de partes, datos, etc.); (mec.) montaje.
assemble [-sembœl]. **I.** *va.* juntar; allegar; convocar; (mec.) montar, armar. **II.** *vn.* reunirse.
assembler [-blœr], *s.* el que junta o reúne; miembro de una junta o asamblea; (mec.) montador (de máquinas, etc.).
assembling [-bling], *s.* acción de juntarse o de reunir; (mec.) montaje, montadura.
assembly [-bli], *s.* reunión; asamblea; (mec.) grupo, juego, conjunto de piezas; (E. U. y otros países) asamblea, cuerpo legislativo de un estado, departamento, etc.; (mil.) asamblea (llamada).—**a. room,** sala de sesiones, conferencias, juntas, diversiones, etc.
assemblyman [æsémbliman], *s.* individuo de un congreso o asamblea.
assent [æsént]. **I.** *vn.* asentir, convenir. **II.** *s.* asenso, asentimiento; beneplácito.
assentation [æsentéshun], *s.* condescendencia o complacencia servil.
assentient [æsénshœnt]. **I.** *a.* que conviene o asiente. **II.** *s.* consentidor.
assentingly [æséntingli], *adv.* con asenso, mostrando asentimiento.
assentor [æséntœr], *s.* (for. Ingl.) sancionador, confirmante (de un nombramiento, etc.)
assert [æscért], *va.* afirmar, asegurar, aseverar; mantener, defender; hacer valer.—**to a. oneself,** hacerse sentir, hacer valer sus derechos.
assertion [æscérshun], *s.* aserción, aseveración.
assertive [æscértiv], *a.* asertivo.
asserter, assertor [-œr], *s.* afirmador, defensor.
assertory [æscértori], *a.* afirmativo; declaratorio.
assess [æsés], *va.* gravar con impuesto, imponer contribución; fijar o determinar (un impuesto, una indemnización); tasar, avaluar.
assessable [-æbœl], *a.* gravable, sujeto a contribución o impuesto.
assessment [-ment], *s.* imposición o distribución de contribuciones, etc., avalúo; impuesto o contribución.
assessor [æséscœr], *s.* imponedor de contribuciones; (for.) asesor.
asset [æset], *s.* (com.) cada partida del activo; (fig.) posesión, ventaja, elemento de buen éxito.—*pl.* assets, (com.) activo; haber; capital; (for.) haberes disponibles que deja una persona.
asseverate [æsévœreit], *va.* aseverar, afirmar.
asseveration [æsevœréshun], *s.* aseveración.
assibilate [æsíbilet], *va.* pronunciar con sonido sibilante.
assiduity [æsidiúiti], *s.* asiduidad.
assiduous [æsídiuus], *a.* asiduo, constante, aplicado, hacendoso, diligente.
assiduously [æsídiuusli], *adv.* asiduamente.
assiduousness [æsídiuusnes], *s.* diligencia, asiduidad, constancia.
assign [æsáin], **I.** *va.* asignar, fijar, señalar, destinar; (for.) consignar, ceder, traspasar. **II.** *vn.* hacer traspaso o cesión de bienes. **III.** *s.* (for.) cesionario; apoderado.
assignable [æsáinabœl], *a.* asignable, transferible, negociable.
assignat [æsiná o æsignæt], *s.* asignado.
assignation [æsignéshun], *s.* asignación, consignación; cesión, traspaso; cita, señalamiento de hora y lugar.
assignee [æsiní], *s.* cesionario; poderhabiente, apoderado; síndico. *V.* ASSIGN.
assigner [æsáincœr], **assignor** [æsinór], *s.* cesionista, cedente, asignante, transferidor.
assignment [æsáinmœnt], *s.* asignación, señalamiento, cesión; (for.) escritura de cesión de bienes, dejación, traspaso, renuncia, o traslación de dominio.
assimilable [æsímilabœl], *a.* asimilable.
assimilate [æsímileit]. **I.** *va.* asimilar; asemejar, comparar. **II.** *vn.* (fisiol.) asimilarse.

assimilation [-éishun], *s.* asimilación; semejanza.
assimilative [æsímiletiv], *a.* asimilativo.
assist [æsíst]. **I.** *va.* asistir, socorrer; ayudar. **II.** *vn.* ayudar; asistir, concurrir.
assistance [æsístans], *s.* auxilio, socorro, ayuda.
assistant [æsístant]. **I.** *s.* ayudante, auxiliar, asistente, adjutor, portanveces, acólito. **II.** *a.* ayudador, auxiliar; segundo; sub- (vg. *assistant secretary,* subsecretario; *assistant editor,* subredactor).
assize [æsáis], *s.* tasa; sesión de un tribunal. (Usase más en plural.)
associable [æsóshiabœl], *a.* sociable.
associate [æsóshiet]. **I.** *va.* asociar, juntar, unir. **II.** *vn.* asociarse, juntarse, mancomunarse.
associate. I. *a.* asociado; confederado. **II.** *s.* socio o companero, consocio, apercero, coadjutor; miembro, individuo de una sociedad; cómplice; (filos.) imagen asociada.
association [æsoshiéshun], *s.* asociación; unión; sociedad, compañía.—**a. of ideas,** asociación de ideas.
associative [æsóshiativ], *a.* asociativo.
assoil [æsóil], *va.* absolver, perdonar; expiar.
assonance [æsonans], *s.* asonancia.
assonant [æsonant], *a.* y *s.* asonante.
assonate [æsonet], *vn.* asonar, asonantar.
assort [æsórt], *va.* ordenar, clasificar, separar, surtir con variedad.
assorted(-ed), *a.* variado, mezclado.
assortment [æsórtmœnt], *s.* clasificación, distribución; surtido variado, acopio.
assuage [æsuéy], *va.* mitigar, calmar, ablandar, aliviar.
assuagement [-mœnt], *s.* mitigación, alivio.
assuasive [æsuésiv], *a.* mitigativo, calmante.
assume [æsiúm]. **I.** *va.* tomar, asumir, arrogar; appropiar, usurpar; presumir, suponer, dar por sentado. **II.** *vn.* arrogarse, atribuirse, apropiarse.
assumed [æsiúmd], *a.* supuesto, dado por sentado; falso, fingido, pretendido.
assuming [æsiúming], *a.* arrogante, altivo, presuntuoso.
assumpsit [æsúmpsit], *s.* (for.) promesa o pacto verbal.
assumption [æsúmpshun], *s.* suposición; toma, asunción, arrogación; arrogancia; (igl.) asunción; fiesta de la asunción de la Virgen.
assumptive [æsúmptiv], *a.* supuesto; que puede asumirse; arrogante, presuntuoso.
assurance [æshúrans], *s.* seguridad, certeza, confianza, convicción; audacia, arrojo, resolución; descoco, descaro, desvergüenza; (com.) seguro. *V.* INSURANCE.
assure [æshúcer], *va.* asegurar, afirmar; infundir confianza; confirmar; (com.) asegurar contra algún riesgo.
assured [æshúcerd]. **I.** *a.* seguro, cierto; descarado, atrevido, audaz. **II.** *s.* (com.) asegurado (contra algún riesgo).
assuredly [æshúredli], *adv.* ciertamente, indubitablemente, sin duda; con toda seguridad.
assuredness [æshúrednes], *s.* certeza, seguridad; arrogancia.
assurer [æshúrœr], *s.* asegurador; asegurado.
Assyrian [æsírian], *a.* asirio.
astasia [æstéiyia], *s.* astasia, falta de coordinación muscular.
astatic [æstétic], *a.* (fís.) astático.—**a. pair,** par de agujas astáticas.
astatize [æstætaiz], *va.* hacer astático.
aster [æstœr], *s.* (bot.) aster, planta asteroidea; (biol.) aster.—**a. ray** (biol.), estría radial que parte de la esfera atractiva.
Asterias [æstíriæs], *s.* (zool.) astéridos; estrellamares.
asterisk [æstírieited], *a.* (min.) que tiene la propiedad del asterismo.—**a. sapphire,** zafiro de ojo de gato.
asterisk [æstœrisc], *s.* asterisco.

asterism [ǽsteriŝm], s. (astr.) asterismo, constelación; grupo de estrellas; (impr.) grupo triangular de tres asteriscos; (min.) asterismo, reflexión de la luz en forma de estrella.

asterium [æstíriʊm], s. asterio, cuerpo simple que se supone existir en las estrellas.

astern [astœrn], adv. por la popa, a popa.

asteroid [ǽstœroid], s. (astr.) asteroide.

Asteroidea [æsteróideæ], s. (zool.) asteriados, estrellamares.

asthenia [æszenáia o aszínia], s. (med.) astenia, debilidad general.

asthenic [æszénic], a. asténico, flaco, débil.

asthma [ǽsma], s. (med.) asma.—**a. paper,** papel impregnado de salitre.

asthmatic(al [æsmǽtic(al], a. y s. asmático.

**astigmatic, [ǽstigmǽtic], a. astigmático.

astigmatism [ǽstígmatiŝm], s. (ópt. y med.) astigmatismo.

astigmometer [æstigmómetœr], s. astigmómetro.

astir [astœr], adv. activo, en movimiento.

astomatous [astómatʊs], a. (biol.) sin boca ni poros respiratorios.

astonish [æstóniŝh], va. asombrar, pasmar.

astonished [astóniŝht], pp. y a. atónito, pasmado, estupefacto.

astonishing [astóniŝhing], a. sorprendente, asombroso, pasmoso.—**astonishingly** [-li], adv. pasmosamente, asombrosamente.

astonishment [astóniŝhmœnt], s. pasmo, asombro, espanto, sorpresa.

astound [astáund], va. y vn. pasmar, sorprender; aturdir, confundir; aterrar.

astounding [astáunding], a. asombroso, pasmoso, sorprendente.

astraddle [astrǽdœl], adv. a horcajadas.

astragal [ǽstragal], s. (arq. y arti.) astrágalo, collarino; (anat.) astrágalo.—pl. dados, tabas.

astragalus [æstrǽgalʊs], s. (anat.) astrágalo, talón, empeine, taba, chita; (bot.) astrágalo, alquitira.

astral [ǽstræl]. I. a. astral, estelar.—**a. body,** cuerpo astral; fantasma.—**a. lamp,** lámpara astral (que no arroja sombras). II. s. lámpara astral.

astrand [æstrǽnd], a. encallado, varado.

astray [æstréi], adv. desviada o descarriladamente; por el mal camino.

astrict [æstríct], va. (ant.) astringir.

astriction [æstríŝhʊn], s. astricción.

astride [astráid], adv. a horcajadas.

astringe [æstríny], va. astringir; apretar, comprimir; restringir.

astringency [æstrínyensi], s. astricción, astringencia; aspereza de carácter.

astringent [æstrínyent], a. y s. astringente, estíptico; austero; áspero, agrio.

astrography [æstrógrafi], s. astrografía.

astroite [ǽstroait o it], s. (bot.) astroite.

astrolabe [ǽstroleb], s. astrolabio.

astrologer [æstróloyœr], s. astrólogo.

astrologic(al [æstrolóyic(al], a. astrológico, judiciario.—**astrologically** [-li], adv. astrológicamente.

astrology [æstróloyi], s. astrología.

astronomer [æstrónomœr], s. astrónomo.

astronomic(al [æstronómic(al], a. astronómico.—**astronomically** [-li], adv. astronómicamente.

astronomy [æstrónomi], s. astronomía.

astrophysical [æstrofíŝicæl], a. astrofísico.

astrophysics [æstrofíŝics], s. astrofísica, estudio de la constitución física de los astros.

astrophere [ǽstrosfiær], s. (biol.) esfera atractiva del aster.

astrut [æstrút], adv. hinchadamente, pomposamente, con ínfulas.

astute [æstiút], a. astuto, agudo, sagaz.

astuteness [æstiútnes], s. astucia, sagacidad.

asunder [asúndœr], adv. separadamente; en dos, a pedazos.—**to put a.,** separar.

aswim [æsuím], adv. y a. flotante, flotando; a nado, nadando.

asylum [æsáilʊm], s. asilo, refugio; casa de beneficencia.

asymmetric(al [æsimétric(al], a. asimétrico, no simétrico.

asymmetry [æsímetri], s. asimetría.

asymptote [ǽsimtot], s. (mat.) asíntota.

asynchronism [asíncroniŝm], s. asincronismo.

asynchronous [asíncronʊs], a. asincrónico.

asyndeton [asíndeton], s. (ret.) asíndeton.

at [æt], prep. a; con; de; por; de acuerdo con; vg. at the door, a, o en, la puerta; at six dollars, a seis dólares; at your disposal, a su disposición; at nine o'clock, a las nueve; angry at me, enfadado conmigo; surprised at his conduct, sorprendido de su conducta; at one stroke, de un golpe; at Rome, en Roma; at that time, en ese tiempo; at war, en guerra; enter at this gate, entre por esta puerta; I did it at his command, lo hice por órden suya, o según sus órdenes. Con un substantivo de acción, at forma frases adverbiales que se traducen por el gerundio: vg. at play, jugando; at work, trabajando. En leguaje fam., se usa por sí solo después de where y to be para indicar confusión, atolondramiento, o simplemente lugar (como en una narración); vg. I didn't know where I was at, yo estaba perplejo, o confundido; no sabía por dónde andaba; where were we at in the story? ¿por dónde íbamos en el cuento? Antes de nombres propios en el caso posesivo forma expresiones elípticas en que se sobrentiende casa, tienda, etc.; vg. I bought this at Johnson's, compré esto en la tienda de Johnson; we were at Porter's, estábamos en la casa (o restaurante, hotel, tienda, etc.) de Pórter.

atabal [ǽtabæl], s. atabal.

ataghan [ǽtagæn], s. V. YATAGHAN.

atamasco [ætamésco], s. (bot.) lirio atamasco.

ataunt [ætónt], adv. y a. en orden, bien arreglado; (mar.) enteramente aparejado.

atavism [ǽtaviŝm], s. atavismo.

ataxia [atǽxia], s. ataxia.

ataxic [atǽxic], a. atáxico.

ate [éit], pretérito del verbo TO EAT.

atelier [ateliĕ], s. taller, estudio.

athanasia [æzænéiÿiæ], s. atanasia, inmortalidad.

atheism [ézeiŝm], s. ateísmo.

atheist [ézeist], s. ateísta, ateo.

atheistic(al [ezeístic(al], a. ateo, ateístico.

atheistically [-li], adv. ateamente.

atheneum [æzeníʊm], s. ateneo.

Athenian [azínian], a. y s. ateniense.

athermancy [æzœrmænci], s. atermancia, impermeabilidad al calor radiante.—**athermanous** [-mænʊs], a. atérmano, atérmico.

athirst [azœrst], adv. sediento.

athlete [ǽzlit], s. atleta; gimnasta.

athletic [æzlétic], a. atlético; fornido.

athletics [æzlétics], s. agonística, gimnasia; deportes, atletismo.

athwart [azuórt]. I. prep. al o a través de, por el través de; contra.—**a. ship,** (mar.) de babor a estribor. II. adv. contrariamente, a tuertas.

atilt [atílt], adv. en postura inclinada; en ristre.

Atlantean [ætlantían], a. atlántico.

atlantes [ætlǽntiŝ], s. pl. (arq.) atlantes.

Atlantic [ætlǽntic]. I. a. atlántico; (arq.) atlántico. II. s. el mar Atlántico.

atlas [ǽtlas], s. atlas; (arq.) atlante o telamón.

atmometer [ætmómetœr], s. atmómetro.

atmosphere [ǽtmosfiær], s. atmósfera, aire, medio ambiente; alcance, esfera de influencia; (fís.) atmósfera, o atmósfera C.G.S. (centímetrogramo-segundo), unidad de presión, equivalente a una altura barométrica de 750.08 mm. al nivel del mar, 0° C. y latitud de 45°.

atmospheric(al [ætmosféric(al], a. atmosférico.

atmospherics [ætmosférics], s. (rad.) perturbaciones eléctricas atmosféricas (=STATIC).

atoll [atól], s. atol, isla madrepórica.

atom [ǽtom], s. átomo.

atomic(al [ætómic(al], a. atómico; diminuto; atomista.—**a. heat,** calor atómico.—**a. number,** número de cargas eléctricas positivas de un átomo. —**a. weight,** peso atómico.

atomicity [ætomísiti], s. (quím.) atomicidad.

atomism [ǽtomiŝm], s. atomismo.

atomist [átomist], *s.* atomista.
atomistic(al [-místic, -al], *a.* atómico; atomístico, atomista.
atomization [-maišéšhɒn], *s.* pulverización.
atomize [-maiš], *va.* pulverizar, rociar.—**atomizer** [-maišœr], *s.* pulverizador, aromatizador.
atomy [átomi], *s.* átomo; motita; esqueleto; (fam.) enano, pigmeo.
atone [atóun], *va.* y *vn.* expiar, purgar; reparar, compensar, dar reparación; propiciar, aplacar.
atonement [atóunmœnt], *s.* expiación, reparación; compensación, satisfacción; propiciación, sacrificio.
atonic [atónic], *a.* débil, falto de vigor.
atony [átoni], *s.* (med.) atonía.
atop [atóp], *adv.* encima.
atrabilarian [átrabilérian], **atrabilarious** [-ʊs], *a.* atrabiliario, atrabilioso.
atrichia [atríquia], **atrichosis** [átricósis], *s.* pérdida o ausencia de pelo; calvicie.
atrium [étrium o átrium], *s.* atrio.
atrocious [atróšʊs], *a.* atroz.—**atrociously** [atróšʊsli], *adv.* atrozmente.—**atrociousness** [atróšʊsnes], **atrocity** [atrósiti], *s.* atrocidad, maldad horrible.
atrophic [atrófic], **atrophous** [átrofʊs], *a.* atrófico, descaecido.
atrophy [átrofi]. **I.** *s.* (med.) atrofia. **II.** *va.* atrofiar. **III.** *vn.* atrofiarse.
atropia [atrópia], **atropine** [átropin], *s.* atropina.
attach [atéch]. **I.** *va.* pegar, juntar, atar; enganchar; prender, coger; asignar; dar, atribuir (importancia, etc.); ganar, granjearse; acompañar, adjuntar; (for.) embargar, secuestrar, decomisar. **II.** *vr.* pegarse, adherirse.
attachable [-abœl], *a.* pegadizo; secuestrable.
attaché [atašhé], *s.* (dipl.) agregado.
attachment [atéchment], *s.* unión, enlace; adminículo, accesorio; afecto, cariño; adhesión, fidelidad; (for.) secuestro, embargo.
attack [atéc]. **I.** *va.* y *vn.* atacar. **II.** *s.* ataque.
attain [atéin], *va.*, *vn.* lograr, alcanzar, obtener.
attainable [atéinabœl], *a.* asequible, accesible, realizable.—**attainableness** [atéinabœlnes], *s.* calidad de alcanzable o realizable.
attainder [atéindœr], *s.* (for.) proscripción o muerte civil.
attainment [atéinmœnt], *s.* logro, consecución, obtención, adquisición.—*pl.* dotes, prendas.
attaint [atéint]. **I.** *va.* deshonrar, infamar; corromper, viciar; (for.) condenar, proscribir. **II.** *s.* mancha, baldón; (for.) muerte civil.
attar [átar], *s.* aceite escencial. *V.* OTTAR.
attemper [atémpœr], **attemperate** [-eit], *va.* atemperar, diluir, molificar. *V.* TEMPER.
attempt [atémpt]. **I.** *va.* intentar, atentar; aventurar; tentar; probar, ensayar. **II.** *vn.* probar, pretender. **III.** *s.* prueba, ensayo, esfuerzo, tentativa.—**attemptability** [atémptabíliti], *s.* la cualidad de poderse intentar.—**attemptable** [atémptabœl], *a.* que puede intentarse.
attend [aténd]. **I.** *va.* atender, cuidar; servir; acompañar, asistir; concurrir; seguir (como efecto o consecuencia). **II.** *vn.* atender; prestar atención, oír; asistir, concurrir.—**to a. on,** o **upon,** servir a.
attendance [aténdans], *s.* presencia, asistencia; (for.) comparecencia; corte, obsequio; tren, séquito, comitiva, acompañamiento; público, concurrencia, auditorio; servidumbre, asistencia, servicio.—**to dance a.,** (fam.) estar de plantón, o de poste, hacer antesala.
attendant [aténdant]. **I.** *s.* sirviente, servidor; cortesano; seguidor, acompañante; cortejo, galán, obsequiante.—**attendants,** *s.* subalternos, tren, séquito, servidumbre. **II.** *a.* concomitante.
attent [atént], *a.* atento, cuidadoso, solícito.
attention [aténšhɒn], *s.* atención, miramiento, cuidado; (mil.) voz de mando ¡atención!—*pl.* cortejo; galanteo, agasajo, obsequio.
attentive [aténtiv], *a.* atento, solícito, aplicado; galante, obsequioso, cortés.—**attentively** [a-

téntivli], *adv.* atentamente, con atención y cuidado.—**attentiveness** [aténtivnes], *s.* cuidado; cortesía, finura.
attenuant [aténuant], *a.* atenuante.
attenuate [aténiueit]. **I.** *va.* atenuar, adelgazar, disminuir; extenuar. **II.** *a.* atenuado, delgado.
attenuating [ateniuéiting], *a.* extenuativo.
attenuation [ateniuéšhɒn], *s.* atenuación, adelgazamiento, flaqueza; extenuación; dilución.
attest [atést], *va.* atestiguar, atestar, deponer, declarar, certificar; garantizar; autenticar, confirmar; (for.) dar fe.
attest, attestation [atestéšhɒn], *s.* atestación, deposición, testimonio, confirmación, auténtica, certificado.
attestor [atéstœr], *s.* testigo; certificador.
attic [átic], *s.* desván, guardilla, sotabanco, camaranchón; (arq.) ático.
Attic(al [átic(al], *a.* ático, clásico.
Atticism [átisišm], *s.* aticismo.
attire [atáiœr]. **I.** *va.* vestir, ataviar, adornar. **II.** *s.* atavío, adorno, traje; astas de ciervo.
attitude [átitiud], *s.* actitud, ademán, postura; (aer., obst.) posición.—**attitudinal** [atitiúdinal], *a.* referente a la actitud.
attitudinarian [atitiudinérian], **attitudinizer** [atitiúdinaišœr], *s.* el que se coloca en posturas afectadas.—**attitudinize** [atitiúdinaiš], *vn.* pavonearse, tomar posturas afectadas.
attollent [atólent], *a.* elevador (músculo).
attorney [atórni], *s.* (for.) abogado; apoderado.—**a. at law,** procurador público, procurador de oficio en los tribunales.—**a. general,** (Ing.) fiscal de la corona; (E. U.) ministro de justicia, que actúa como consejero y apoderado o abogado de la nación.—**a. in fact** o PRIVATE ATTORNEY.—**district a.,** fiscal de un distrito judicial.—**private a.,** apoderado, agente, representante, encargado por otro de asuntos extrajudiciales.—**public a.** = A. AT LAW.—**by a.,** por poder (P. P.)
attorneyship [-ship], *s.* procuraduría.
attract [atráct], *va.* y *vn.* atraer; cautivar, seducir.—**to a. attention,** llamar la atención.
attractability [-tabíliti], *s.* cualidad de atraíble.
attractable [atráctabœl], *a.* atraíble.
attracter, attractor [atráctœr], *s.* el que atrae.
attraction [atrácšhɒn], *s.* atracción; atractivo, aliciente, interés.
attractive [atráctiv], *a.* atractivo, atrayente, interesante; agradable, simpático.—**attractively** [-li], *adv.* atractivamente.—**attractiveness** [-nes], *s.* atracción, calidad de atractivo; gracia; hechizos.
attributable [atríbiutabœl], *a.* atribuíble.
attribute [atríbiut], *va.* atribuir.
attribute [átribiut], *s.* atributo; característica; honra, reputación.
attribution [-biúšhɒn], *s.* atribución.
attributive [atríbiutiv]. **I.** *a.* atributivo; (b. a.) atribuído. **II.** *s.* (gram.) calificativo.
attrite [atráit], *a.* estregado, frotado; (teol.) pesaroso, atrito.
attrition [atríšhɒn], *s.* rozadura, frotación, refregón, molimiento, desgaste; (teol.) atrición.
attune [atiún], *va.* armonizar, acordar, afinar.
atwain [atuéin], *adv.* en dos.
atwirl [atuérl], *a.* y *adv.* en rotación, girando, dando vueltas.
atwist [atuíst], *adv.* y *a.* torcidamente, al través, sesgado.
auburn [óbœrn], *a.* castaño rojizo.
auction [ócšhɒn]. **I.** *s.* almoneda, subasta, remate; (Amér.) venduta.—**a. by inch of candle,** a vela y pregón.—**a. room,** martillo.—**to put up at a.,** o **to a.,** poner en pública subasta. **II.** *va.* subastar, rematar.
auctioneer [ócšhœnœr], *s.* subastador, pregonero. **II.** *va.* vender a pública subasta.
audacious [odéšhʊs], *a.* audaz, osado; descarado.
audaciously [odéšhusli], *adv.* atrevidamente; descaradamente.
audaciousness [odéšhusnes], **audacity** [odási-til], *s.* audacia, osadía; impudencia, descaro.
audible [ódibœl], *a.* audible.

audibility [odibíliti], **audibleness** [ódibœlnes], *s.* capacidad de ser oído.

audibly [ódiblij], *adv.* audiblemente.

audience [ódiens], *s.* auditorio, concurso, público; audición; audiencia o entrevista.—**a. chamber,** sala o cámara de recepción; (for.) audiencia.

audio-frequency [ódiofrícuensi], *s.* (rad.) audiofrecuencia.

audiometer [odiómetœr], *s.* audiómetro, instrumento para probar la audición.

audion [ódion], *s.* (rad.) audión.

audiphone [ódifoun], *s.* audífono, aparato para transmitir el sonido a los sordos por los dientes.

audit [ódit]. **I.** *s.* intervención y ajuste de cuentas. **II.** *va.* intervenir una cuenta.—**auditing of accounts,** intervención de cuentas.

audition [odíshun], *s.* audición.

auditive [óditiv], *a.* auditivo. *V.* AUDITORY.

auditor [óditœr], *s.* interventor, revisor de cuentas, ordenador de pagos, oyente, oidor, auditor.

auditorium [oditórium], *s.* sala, anfiteatro, teatro; conjunto de asientos o recinto para los oyentes o espectadores.

auditorship [óditorship], *s.* oficio de interventor; intervención.

auditory [óditori]. **I.** *s.* auditorio, público; oyentes; sala, teatro. **II.** *a.* auditivo.

Augean [oyíæn], *a.* referente a Augias; sucísimo; corrompidísimo.—**the A. stables,** los establos de Augias (apl. a lugares muy sucios y a gente o asociaciones corrompidas o desmoralizadas).

auger [ógœr], *s.* barrena; taladro; sonda de taladrar.—**a. bit,** hoja de corte en forma de barrena.—**a. worm,** gusano horadador.

aught [ot]. **I.** *s.* algo; cero; (con negación) nada. **II.** *adv.* absolutamente; en cualquier respecto; en cualquier, o algún, grado.

augite [óyait], *s.* (min.) augita.

augment [ogmént], *va.* y *vn.* aumentar.

augmentation [ogmentéshun], *s.* aumentación, aumento.

augmentative [ogméntativ], *a.* aumentativo.

augur [ógœr], **augurer** [ógœrœr], *s.* augur, agorero, adivino, arúspice.

augur, augurate [ógœr, -eit], *va.* y *vn.* augurar, pronosticar, predecir, agorar, ominar.

augural [óguiural], **augurial** [oguiúrial], *a.* augural.

augury [óguiuri], *s.* augurio, agüero, pronóstico.

august [ogúst], *a.* augusto, majestuoso.

August [ógust], *s.* agosto (mes).

Augustan [ogústan], *a.* augustal, de Augusto.

Augustinian [ogustínian], *a.* agustiniano; agustino (monje, orden).

augustness [ogústnes], *s.* majestuosidad, grandeza, majestad.

auk [ok], *s.* (orn.) nombre de un ave marítima.

auld [óuld], *a.* (Esco.) viejo, antiguo.—**a. lang syne** [óuld lang sáin], antaño, tiempos que fueron.

aulic [ólic], *a.* áulico, palaciego.

aunt [ánt], *s.* tía.

aunty, auntie [ánti], *s. dim.* tía; vieja; (E. U. del Sur) negra vieja.

aura [óra], *s.* magnetismo animal; influencia psíquica; aura, céfiro; (med.) aura epiléptica o histérica.

aural [óral], *a.* auditivo, auricular.

aurantiaceous [oréntieishus], *a.* auranciáceo.

aurate [óret], **aurated** [óreted], *a.* con orejas; dorado, áureo.

aurate, *s.* (quím.) aurato.

aurelia [orília], *s.* crisálida, ninfa.

aureola [oríola], **aureole** [óreol], *s.* aureola, corona.

auric [óric], *a.* de oro, del oro; (quím.) áurico.

auricle [órikœl], *s.* (anat.) aurícula del corazón; pabellón de la oreja.

auricula [oríkiula], *s.* (bot.) oreja de oso; (zool.) apéndice en forma de oreja.

auricular [oríkiular], *a.* auricular; oíble; confidencial, secreto, aicho al oído; tradicional.

auricularly [-li], *adv.* al oído, secretamente.

auriculate, *o* **auriculated** [oríkiuleit, -eited], *a.* orejudo; en forma de oreja.

auriferous [orífœrus], *a.* (poét.) aurífero.

auriform [óriform], *a.* en forma de oreja.

auriga [oráiga], *s.* auriga, (A-, astr.) Auriga.

aurist [órist], *s.* aurista.

aurochs [órocs], *s.* (zool.) uro.

aurora [oróra], *s.* aurora, alba, alborada.—**a. australis,** aurora austral.—**a. borealis,** aurora boreal.

auroral [oróral], *a.* matutino; rosáceo.

aurum [órum], *s.* oro.

auscultate [ósculteit], *va.* y *vn.* auscultar.

auscultation [oscultéshun], *s.* (med.) auscultación; atención.

auspicate [óspiket], *va.* principiar con buenos auspicios.

auspice [óspis], *s.* auspicio, presagio; protección, favor, dirección, auspicio (gen. *pl.*).

auspicial [ospíshal], *a.* perteneciente al auspicio.

auspicious [ospíshus], *a.* feliz, favorable; benigno, propicio.

auspiciously [ospíshusli], *adv.* con buenos auspicios, felizmente.

auspiciousness [ospíshusnes], *s.* prosperidad; buenos auspicios.

austere [ostíœr], *a.* austero, severo, rígido; rudo, adusto; agrio, ácido, acerbo.—**austerely** [ostíœrli], *adv.* austeramente.—**austereness** [ostíœrnes], **austerity** [ostériti], *s.* austeridad, rigorismo, severidad.

Austin Friars [óstin fráiars], *s. pl.* frailes Agustinos.

austral [óstral], *a.* austral.

Australian [ostrélian], *a.* australiano.

Austrian [óstrian], *a.* austríaco.

authentic(al [ozéntic(al], *a.* auténtico, legítimo, fehaciente, original.

authentically [ozéenticali], **authenticly** [ozénticli], *adv.* auténticamente.

authenticalness [ozénticalnes], **authenticity** [ozentísiti], *s.* autenticidad.

authenticate [ozéntikeit], *va.* autenticar, autorizar, refrendar.

authentication [ozéntikéshun], *s.* (for.) autenticación, refrendación.

author [ózœr], *s.* autor; escritor.

authoress [ózores], *s.* autora, escritora.

authoritarian [ozoritériæn], *s.* y *a.* autoritarista, defensor de la autoridad absoluta o excesiva.—**authoritarianism** [-ism], *s.* autoritarismo.

authoritative [ozóritetiv], *a.* autorizado, que autoriza; autoritario; positivo, perentorio, terminante.—**authoritatively** [ozóritetivli], *adv.* autorizadamente.—**authoritativeness** [ozóritetivnes], *s.* calidad de autorizado o autoritario.

authority [ozóriti], *s.* autoridad.—**I have it from the best a.,** lo sé de buena tinta; lo tengo de buena mano.—**printed by a.,** impreso con licencia.

authorization [ózorishéshun], *s.* autorización, sanción, legalización.

authorize [ózorais], *va.* autorizar, facultar, sancionar, acreditar, otorgar, legalizar.

authorship [ózorship], *s.* estado, calidad o profesión de autor; invención; paternidad literaria.

auto [óto]. **I.** *s.* (fam.) automóvil, auto. **II.** *va.* (fam.) pasear o viajar en automóvil.

autobiographic(al [ótobaiográfic(al], *a.* autobiográfico.

autobiography [-baiógrafi], *s.* autobiografía.

autoboat [-bóut], *s.* lancha o bote automóvil.

autobus [-bús], *s.* ómnibus automóvil.

autocar [-cár], *s.* coche automóvil.

autochthonic *o* **autochthonous** [otoczónic, otóczonus], *a.* autóctono.

autoclave [ótocleiv], *s.* autoclave, marmita hermética.

autocoherer [-cohíercœr], *s.* (rad.), autocohesor, autodetector.

autocracy [otócrasi], *s.* autocracia.

autocrasy [otócrasi], *s.* (med.) autocrasia.

autocrat [ótocræt], *s.* autócrata.

autocratic(al [ótocrǽtic(al], *a.* autocrático.

autocycle [-saicœl], *s.* motocicleta.

auto-da-fé [auto dæ féi], *s.* auto de fe.

autogamous [otógæmᴜs], *a.* (bot.) autógamo, autofecundante.

autogamy [-gami], *s.* autofecundación.

autogenesis [ótoyénesis], *s.* autogénesis.

autogenous [otóyenᴜs], *a.* autógeno.—**a. soldering, a. welding,** (elec.) soldadura eléctrica autógena.

autograph [ótograf], *a.* y *s.* autógrafo.

autography [otógrafi], *s.* autografía.

autographic(al [otográ̈fic(al], *a.* autógrafo, autográfico.

autohypnosis [ótojipnósis], **autohypnotism** [-hípnotiᵶm], *s.* autohipnotismo.

autoinfection [ótoinfécᶴhᴜn], *s.* autoinfección.

autointoxication [ótointóxikéiᶴhᴜn], *s.* autointoxicación, autoenvenenamiento del organismo.

automatic(al [otomǽtic(al], *a.* automático.

automatism [ótomatiᵶm], *s.* automatismo; (filos.) automatismo, doctrina según la cual la inteligencia no dirige ninguna función ni acto, siendo sólo fenómeno concomitante; (fisiol.) automatismo de los fenómenos inconscientes, como el parpadeo; mecanismo que los produce.

automaton [otómaton], *s.* autómata.

automobile [ótomobíl]. **I.** *s.* automóvil. **II.** *a.* automóvil, automovilista.

automobiling [-ling], *s.* automovilismo; pasear o ir en automóvil.

automobilism [ótomóbiliᵶm], *s.* automovilismo.

automobilist [-list], *s.* automovilista.

automotive [-mótiv], *a.* automotor, automotriz, automóvil, automovilista (apl. con especialidad a los automóviles; vg. *automotive industry*, industria automovilista).

automotor [-mótor], *s.* automóvil.

autonomic [otonómic], *a.* autonómico.

autonomist [otónomist], *s.* autonomista.

autonomous [otónomᴜs], *a.* autónomo.

autonomy [otónomi], *s.* autonomía.

autopsy [ótopsi], *s.* autopsia, necropsia.

autosuggestion [ótosᴜgréscͪᴜn], *s.* autosugestión.

autotomy [otótomy], *s.* autotomía, división espontánea de un organismo.

autotoxemia [ótotoxímiæ], *s.* autointoxicación.

autotransformer [-trænsfórmœr], *s.* (elec.) autotransformador.

autotruck [-trúc], *s.* autocamión.

autotype [ótotáip], *s.* facsímil, copia exacta.

autumn [ótᴜm], *s.* otoño.

autumnal [otúmnal], *a.* otoñal, autumnal.

auxetophone [oxétofoun], *s.* auxitófono, aparato neumático empleado en fonógrafos para reproducir el sonido.

auxiliar [ogᶴíliar], **auxiliary** [ogᶴíliari]. **I.** *a.* auxiliar; auxiliatorio, subsidiario. **II.** *s.* auxiliador, coadyuvante, sufragáneo.

avail [ævéil]. **I.** *vr.* (*to avail oneself of*), aprovechar, aprovecharse. **II.** *va.* aprovechar, beneficiar. **III.** *vn.* aprovechar, ser útil o conducente. **IV.** *s.* provecho, utilidad; eficacia.—*pl.* beneficios, producto (de una venta).

available [-æbœl], *a.* aprovechable, disponible, asequible.

availableness [-æbœlness], **availability** [-æbíliti], *s.* disponibilidad, calidad de aprovechable; eficacia, valor.

availably [avéilabli], *adv.* eficazmente, provechosamente, útilmente.

avalanche [ávalanᶴh], *s.* lurte, alud; torrente.

avant-guard [avánt-gard], *s.* vanguardia.

avarice [ǽvaris], *s.* avaricia, codicia, sordidez.

avaricious [ævaríᶴhᴜs], *s.* avaro, avariento, miserable.—**avariciously** [-li], *adv.* avaramente, avarientamente.—**avariciousness** [-nes], *s.* avaricia.

avast [avást], *interj.* (mar.) ¡forte! ¡basta!

avaunt [avánt], *interj.* ¡fuera! ¡atrás!

Ave Mary, Ave Maria [évi méri o ave maría], *s.* avemaría.

avena [avína], *s.* (bot.) avena.

avenge [avény], *va.* y *vn.* vengar, vindicar.

avengement [avénymœnt], *s.* venganza.

avenger [avényœr], *s.* vengador.

avens [ǽvens], *s.* (bot.) gariofilea.

aventail, *s.* = VENTAIL.

aventurin(e [avéntiurin], *s.* (min.) venturina.

avenue [ǽveniu], *s.* avenida, calzada; alameda, carrera; vía, entrada, pasadizo.

aver [avœr], *va.* asegurar, afirmar; declarar.

average [ǽvereix]. **I.** *s.* promedio, término medio; cosa o persona ordinaria o de término medio; (com.) avería; compensación por averías; obvención que se da al capitán de un barco por el buen cuidado de mercancías.—**a. bond,** fianza que se da al capitán de un barco por indemnización de averías.—**on an a.,** por término medio. **II.** *a.* medio, de término medio; común, ordinario, corriente. **III.** *va.* calcular el término medio o hallar el promedio de; prorratear. **IV.** *vn.* ser por término medio.

averment [avœrmœnt], *s.* aseveración.

averruncator [ǽverrúnkéitœr], *s.* podadera para escamondar.

averse [avœrs], *a.* renuente, adverso, contrario.

aversely [avœrsli], *adv.* con repugnancia.

averseness [avœrsnes], *s.* repugnancia, renuencia, mala gana.

aversion [-ᶴhᴜn], *s.* aversión, aborrecimiento, inquina; tirria, odio.

avert [avœrt], *va.* desviar, apartar, separar; prevenir, impedir, conjurar.

avian [évian], *a.* perteneciente a las aves.

aviary [évicœri], *s.* pajarera, avería, averío.

aviate [éivieit], *vn.* volar en avión.

aviation [éiviéiᶴhᴜn], *s.* aviación.

aviator [-éitœr], *s.* aviador.

aviculture [éivicúlchœr], *s.* avicultura.

avid [ǽvid], *a.* ávido, ansioso, codicioso.

avidity [avíditi], *s.* avidez, ansia, codicia.

avifauna [éivifónæ], *s.* aves.

avocado, [ávocádo], *s.* (bot.) aguacate.

avocation [ævokéᶴhᴜn], *s.* distracción, diversión, pasatiempo, entretenimiento; (úsase incorrectamente en lugar de **vocation** para denotar una profesión u ocupación seria); (for.) avocamento o avocación.

avocet, avoset [ǽvoset], *s.* (orn.) avoceta.

avoid [avóid]. **I.** *va.* evitar, salvar, eludir, esquivar; (for.) anular. **II.** *vn.* retirarse, zafarse.

avoidable [avóidabœl], *a.* evitable, eludible; revocable.

avoidance [avóidans], *s.* acto y efecto de evitar alguna cosa; (for.) anulación, invalidación.

avoider [avóidœr], *s.* el que evita o evade.

avoidless [avóidles], *s.* inevitable o irremediable.

avoirdupois [ǽvordupóiᶴ], *s.* sistema de pesos vigente en Inglaterra y los E. U., cuya unidad es la libra de 16 onzas; (fam.) peso, gordura.

avouch [aváuch], *va.* afirmar, sostener, alegar, testimoniar, protestar.

avow [aváu], *va.* reconocer, admitir.

avowable [aváuabœl], *a.* que se puede declarar.

avowal [aváual], *s.* confesión, admisión.

avowed [aváud], *a.* reconocido, admitido.

avowedly [-li], *adv.* sin rebozo, reconocida o confesadamente.

avulsion [avúlᶴhᴜn], *s.* separación; (cir.) avulsión.

avuncular [avúnkiular], *a.* de un tío, como un tío; (fam.) como usurero.

await [auéit]. **I.** *va.* aguardar, esperar. **II.** *vn.* esperar, estar aguardando.

awake [auéik], **awaken** [auéikœn]. **I.** va. (pret. AWOKE; pp. AWAKED) despertar (al que está dormido); mover, excitar. **II.** vn. despertar, dejar de dormir.

awake, a. despierto.

awakener [auéiknœr], s. despertador.

awakening [auéikning], s. despertamiento, despertar.

award [auórd], va. y vn. juzgar, otorgar, conferir, conceder; (for.) adjudicar.

award, s. sentencia, laudo, decisión, ajudicación, concesión; premio.

awardable [auórdabœl], a. adjudicable.

awarder [auórdœr], s. juez árbitro.

aware [auéær], a. enterado, sabedor.

awareness [-nes], s. conocimiento; (filos.) mera conciencia de un hecho, sin atención.

awash [auósh], a. y adv. (mar.) a flor de agua.

away [æuéi]. **I.** adv. lejos; a lo lejos; ausente; alejándose, en dirección opuesta, vg. away from the sun, alejándose del sol, en dirección opuesta a la del sol; continuamente, con empeño, vg. he is working away, él está trabajando con ahinco; (fam.) sin empacho, lo que, o cuanto, se quiera (a veces enfático y no se traduce), vg. talk away, diga lo que quiera, eche usted lo que quiera, diga usted. Se usa después de muchos verbos para indicar alejamiento o acción lenta continua, vg. to go away, alejarse, irse; to take away, arrebatar, quitar; to wither away, irse marchitando. Frases de esta clase se dan bajo los verbos respectivos. A veces el verbo se suprime por elipsis, vg. let us (go) away, vámonos; whither (are you going) away? ¿adónde va Vd.? **II.** interj. ¡fuera de aquí! ¡márchese Vd.! ¡vámonos!—**a. with you!** ¡márchese Vd.! ¡lárguese Vd.!

awe [o]. **I.** temor reverente; pavor.—**a.-struck,** despavorido, aterrado, espantado.—**to stand in a. of,** temer; reverenciar sumisamente. **II.** va. infundir terror a, aterrorizar.

aweary [auíri], a. (poét.) cansado, fatigado.

aweather [auéðœr], adv. (mar.) a barlovento.

awesome [ósum], a. terrible, aterrador, pavoroso.

aweigh [auéi], adv. V. ATRIP.

awful [óful], a. tremendo; terrible; majestuosamente abrumador; (fam.) muy malo, enorme.

awfully [óful], adv. terriblemente, horrorosamente; (fam.) muy, excesivamente.

awfulness [ófulnes], s. veneración, respeto o temor reverencial; (fam.) enormidad.

awhile [ajuáil], adv. un rato, algún tiempo.—**not yet a.,** por ahora no, todavía no.

awhirl [ajuœrl], adv. en rotación; en giro, en torbellino.

awkward [ókuard], a. desmañado, desgarbado, torpe, chambón, chabacano; embarazoso, difícil, delicado, peliagudo.

awkwardly [ókuardli], adv. torpemente, desmañadamente; embarazosamente, en una posición difícil, delicada.

awkwardness [ókuardnes], s. torpeza, desmaña.

awl [ol], s. lesna, subilla, punzón.—**pegging a.,** estaquillador de zapatero.—**sailmaker's a.,** aguja de veleros.—**sewing a.,** lesna de coser.—**scratch a.,** punzón fino de marcar.

awn [ón], s. (bot.) arista.

awning [óning], s. toldo, tendal, entalamadura, marquesina; (mar.) toldo, toldilla, cenefa; (hort.) abrigaña.

awoke [auóc], pret. del verbo TO AWAKE.

aworking [auœrking], adv. trabajando.

awry [arái], adv. y a. oblicuo, sesgado, torcido, oblicuamente, de través; fuera de razón, erradamente.

ax, axe [æx], s. hacha.—**to have an a. to grind,** tener algún fin interesado, ir taimadamente tras algo.

axes [æxis], s. pl. de AXIS.

axhammer [æxjæmœr], s. martillo o hacha de dos filos o cabezas.—**axhammered** [-mœrd], a. trabajado o desbastado con el hacha de dos cabezas.

axial [æxiæl], **axil** [æxil], a. axil; (bot.) axilar.—**a.-flow turbine, a. turbine,** turbina paralela.—**a. skeleton,** esqueleto de la cabeza y el tronco, sin las extremidades.

axil, axilla [æxil, æxíla], s. (bot. y anat.) axila.

axillar [æcsilar], **axillary** [-i], a. (hist. nat.) axilar.

axinite [æcsinait], s. (min.) axinita.

axiom [æcsium], s. axioma; postulado.

axiomatic(al [æcsiomætic(al], a. axiomático.

axiometer [acsiómetœr], s. (mar.) axiómetro.

axis [æxis], s. (mat., bot., etc.) eje; (anat.) axis, segunda vértebra cervical; (zool.) venado o ciervo de manchas blancas de la India.—**a. cylinder,** eje de una fibra nerviosa.—**a. of collimation,** (top.) línea de colimación.—**axes of coordinates,** (mat.) ejes de las coordenadas.

axle [æxœl], s. eje (de un vehículo); eje, árbol (de una rueda o máquina).—**a. bar,** eje de hierro de una rueda.—**a. box,** (mec.) caja de eje.—**a. guard,** (f. c.) guía o resbaladera de la caja del eje; (carr.) placa de guarda.—**a. shaft,** (aut.) puente o eje trasero.

axletree [-tri], s. eje (de ruedas de carruaje).

axman [æxmæn], s. hachero; leñador; (top.) ayudante encargado de preparar las estacas, despejar el terreno con el hacha, etc.

axolotl [æxolotœl], s. (Méx.) ajolote, especie de anfibio.

ay [ai], interj. ¡ay!—**ay me!** ¡ay de mí!

ay [ei], **aye** [ei], adv. siempre, por siempre.—**for aye,** por siempre jamás.

aye [ai]. **I.** adv. sí. **II.** s. voto afirmativo.

aye-aye [ái-ái], s. (zool.) aye aye.

azalea [aséla], s. (bot.) azalea.

azarole [æserol], s. (bot.) acerola.

azimuth [æsimuz], s. (astr. y top.) azimut.—**a. compass,** brújula de azimut.

azoic [asóic], a. azoico.

azonic [asónic], a. que no es local.

azote [æsout], s. ázoe.

azoth [æsoz], s. azogue, mercurio.

Aztec [æstec], a. y s. azteca.

azure [æyuær], **azured** [-d]. **I.** a. y s. azulado, claro, azul celeste; (blas.) azur, blao. **II.** va. azular.

azurine [æyurin], a. azulado.

azurite [æyurait], s. azurita, malaquita azul.

azyme [æsim], s. pan ázimo.

azymic, azymous [asímic, æsîmus], a. ázimo, sin levadura.

B

b [bi], s. b; (B, mús.) sí, séptima nota de la escala musical.

baa [ba]. **I.** s. be (balido). **II.** vn. balar.

babbit [bæbit]. **I.** s. metal antifricción (llamado también b. metal). **II.** va. revestir de metal antifricción.

babble [bæbœl], va. y vn. balbucear; charlar; parlar, garlar; murmurar (un arroyo).

babble, s. charla, parla, charlatanería; susurro, murmullo.

babbler [bæblœr], s. charlador, garlador, charlatán, hablador; parlero, bachiller, trapalón.

babbling [bæbling]. **I.** a. murmurante. **II.** s. cháchara, garrulería.

babe [béib], s. criaturita, infante, nen^o, bebé.

Babel, Babeldom [béibel, -dom], s. Babel, confusión, desorden.

babirousa, babirusa [bæbirusæ], s. (zool.) babirusa.

baboon [bæbún], s. (zool.) mandril.

baboosh, babouche [bæbúsh], s. babucha.

baby [béibi]. **I.** s. = BABE.—**b. blue,** azul claro.—**b. farm,** casa en que se crían por paga niños ajenos.—**b. grand piano,** piano de media cola.—**b. jumper,** aro suspendido en que se pone a un niño para impedir que se caiga.—**b. ribbon,** cintilla muy angosta. **II.** a. de niño, semejante a un niño; pequeño. **III.** va. tratar como niño; mimar.

babyish [béibiiŝh], *a.* niñero; pueril, infantil.
babyishness [bébiiŝhnes], *s.* puerilidad, niñada.
babyhood [bébijud], *s.* niñez.
Babylonian [bæbilónian], *a.* babilónico.
baccalaureate [bæcalóriet], *s.* bachillerato.
baccate [bǽkeit], *s.* (bot.) parecido a una baya.
bacchanal [bǽcanal], **bacchanalian** [-éiliaen], **I.** *s.* bacanal. **II.** *a.* borracho, ebrio, báquico.
Bacchanalia [-éiliæ], **Bacchanals** [-alŝ], *s. pl.* bacanales.
bacchant, bacchante [bǽcant, bacǽnte], *s.* bacante, ménade; persona disoluta o borracha.
Bacchic(al [bǽkic(al], *a.* báquico.
bacciferous [bæcsífœrus], *a.* que produce bayas.
baccivorous [bæcsívorus], *a.* que se alimenta de bayas.
bachelor [bǽchelœr], *s.* soltero; bachiller.—**b.'s-button,** (bot.) botón de oro.—**bachelors' apartments, rooms,** etc., apartamientos, cuartos, etc., para solteros.
bachelorship [bǽchelorŝhip], *s.* celibato, soltería; bachillerato.
bacillary [bǽsilœri], *a.* bacilar.
bacillus [basílus], *s.* (*pl.* BACILLI) bacilo, microbio.
back [bæc], *s.* espalda; lomo, espinazo (de un animal); respaldo, espaldar (de un asiento, etc.); reverso, lado de atrás; parte posterior o de atrás; lomo (de una montaña, de un cuchillo, de un libro); (teat.) foro.—**b. to b.,** espalda con espalda.—**at one's b.,** detrás de uno (sea persiguiéndolo, sea apoyándolo).—**behind one's b.,** a espaldas de uno, sin conocimiento de uno (con la implicación de perfidia o cobardía).—**on one's b.,** a cuestas.—**to be,** *o* **lie, on one's b.,** estar en cama; estar postrado, ser impotente.—**to break the b. of,** agobiar.—**to cast behind the b.,** olvidar y perdonar.—**to get,** *o* **put, one's b. up,** (fam.), obstinarse.—**to give,** *o* **make, a b.,** agacharse para que otro salte por encima (en los juegos de muchachos).—**to see the b. of,** deshacerse o librarse de.
back, *a.* trasero, posterior, de atrás; del interior; atrasado; anterior, pasado (apl. al tiempo); apartado, lejano.—**b. door,** puerta de atrás; modo indirecto e indigno.—**b. excentric,** (m. v.) excéntrica de inversión o de cambio de marcha.—**b. electromotive force,** fuerza contraelectromotriz.—**b. filling** (const.), relleno de trasdós.—**b. number,** número atrasado (de un periódico); persona desprestigiada o rezagada.—**b. pressure,** (m. v.) contrapresión.—**b. sight,** (top.) visual inversa, visual de comprobación u orientación dirigida hacia atrás; visual inicial dirigida a un punto de referencia para determinar la altura del ojo, en la nivelación.—**b. stairs,** escalera de atrás; escalera secreta; medios indirectos y solapados.—**b. step,** (mil) marcha atrás, paso a retaguardia.—**b. stream,** contracorriente; remolino.—**b. tooth,** muela.
back, *adv.* atrás, detrás; otra vez, de nuevo; de vuelta, de regreso. Después de un verbo indica en general retroceso, y a veces equivale al prefijo *re*, vg. *to come back,* regresar; *to give back,* devolver; *to beat back,* rechazar.—**b. and forth,** de arriba para abajo, de una parte a otra; de uno a otro.—**b. in 1800,** allá por el año de 1800.—**as far b. as 1800,** ya en 1800, desde 1800.
back. I. *va.* mover, empujar o tirar hacia atrás; hacer retroceder; reforzar; sostener, apoyar; favorecer, apostar a (en carreras, etc.); endosar, certificar al reverso; montar (un caballo).—**to b. up,** sostener, apoyar, defender.—**to b. water,** recular (apl. a las embarcaciones). **II.** *vn.* recular, retroceder.—**to b. down, to b. out,** volverse atrás, abandonar una empresa o resolución.
backache [bǽkéic], *s.* dolor de espalda.
backbite [bǽcbait], *va.* y *vn.* difamar, calumniar solapadamente.—**backbiter** [-báitœr], *s.* calumniador, detractor solapado.—**backbiting** [-báiting], difamación solapada.—**backbitingly** [-li], *adv.* por difamación o calumnia solapada.
backboard [bǽcbord], *s.* respaldo, forro.
backbone [bǽcboun], *s.* espinazo; firmeza, nervio; fundamento; sostén.—**to the b.,** hasta la médula.

backdown [bǽcdaun], *s.* (fam.) cesión; rendición; palinodia.
backed [bact], *a.* apoyado, respaldado.
backer [bǽkœr], *s.* sostenedor, defensor, auxiliador; (com.) refaccionista, aviador; (dep.) sostenedor, apostador.
backgammon [bæcgǽmun], *s.* juego de chaquete.—**b. board,** tablas reales; (Mex.) pretera.
background [bǽcgráund], *s.* posición subordinada o sin influencia; olvido, oscuridad; (b. a.) fondo; último término, lontananza.
backhanded [bǽcjǽnded], *a.* dado con el revés de la mano; inclinado a la izquierda; falto de sinceridad; irónico.
backhouse [bǽcjaus], *s.* trascuarto; el común, la necesaria.
backing [bǽking], *s.* apoyo, sostén, garantía; refacción, avío; retroceso; refuerzo; respaldo, forro, espaldar.
backmost [bǽcmoust], *a. super.* de más atrás.
backpiece [bǽcpis], *s.* (arm.) espaldar.
backsaw [bǽcsó], *s.* serrucho.
backset [bǽcset], *s.* contratiempo, contrariedad, revés, infortunio, recaída; remolino.
backshop [bǽcŝhop], *s.* trastienda.
backside [bǽcsaid], *s.* trasero, nalgas; espalda; trascorral.
backslide [bǽcsláid], *vn.* reincidir, volver a las andadas.
backslider [bǽcsláidœr], *s.* apóstata; reincidente.
backsliding [-ding], *s.* apostasía; reincidencia.
backstairs [bǽcstéœrs], *s. pl.* escalera secreta.
backstay [bǽcstéi], *s.* soporte, refuerzo posterior; tirante; (mar.) brandal, traversa.
backstitch [-stích]. **I.** *s.* pespunte, punto atrás. **II.** *va.* y *vn.* pespuntar.—**backstitching** [-ing], *s.* pespunte, pespuntar.
backsword [bǽcsóœrd], *s.* sable, alfanje.
backward [bǽkuœrd], *a.* vuelto o dirigido hacia atrás; retrógrado, que retrocede; retraído, corto; lerdo, pesado, tardo, atrasado, tardío.—**backward, backwards,** *adv.* de espaldas, atrás; hacia atrás; atrasadamente.—**to go b. and forward,** ir y venir.
backwardly [bǽkuardli], *adv.* con repugnancia, de mala gana; torpemente.
backwardness [bǽkuardnes], *s.* torpeza, pesadez; negligencia; atraso, retraso.
backwater [-uótœr], *s.* contracorriente, remolino; agua de rechazo (de una turbina, etc.); entrada o brazo de mar.
backwoods [-udŝ], *s.* región apartada, el monte.
bacon [béicun], *s.* tocino.—**fitch of b.,** lonja de tocino.—**gammon of b.,** jamón, pernil.—**to save one's b.,** (vulg.) salvar el pellejo.—**to sell one's b.,** (fam.) venderse.
bacteria [bæctíria], *pl.* de BACTERIUM.
bacterial [bæctírial], *a.* bacteriano, bactérico.
bactericidal [-sáidal], *a.* destructor de las bacterias.
bactericide [bæctírisaid], *s.* bactericida.
bacterin [bæcterin], *s.* bacterina, vacuna bacteriana.
bacteriological [bæctíriolóyical], *a.* bacteriológico, microbiológico.
bacteriologist [bæctírióloyist], *n.* bacteriólogo.
bacteriology [bæctirióloyi], *s.* bacteriología, microbiología.
bacteriolysis [bæctiriólosis], *s.* bacteriólosis, descomposición causada por bacterias, sin aire; descomposición de las células.
bacterioscopy [-rióscopi], *s.* bacterioscopia, estudio microscópico de las bacterias.
bacterium [bæctírium], *s.* (*pl.* BACTERIA) bacteria, microbio.
bad [bæd]. **I.** *a.* mal, malo, perverso, depravado; infeliz, desgraciado; dañado, podrido; nocivo, dañoso; indispuesto, enfermo.—**b. blood,** enemistad, encono, mala sangre.—**from b. to worse,** del mal en peor. **II.** *s.* (con me.) lo malo; la perdición; gente mala.
bad, bade, *pret.* del verbo TO BID.

badge [bæʏ], *s.* escarapela, insignia, condecoración, divisa, distintivo, símbolo.

badge, *va.* condecorar, dar una insignia.

badgeless [bǽʏles], *a.* sin divisa.

badger [bǽʏœr]. **I.** *s.* (zool.) tejón, tepezcuinte, **II.** *va.* molestar, cansar, fatigar, fastidiar.

oadinage [bǽdineʏ, badináʏ], *s.* jocosidad, burla, chanza, chirigota; cháchara.

badly [bǽdli], *adv.* mal, malamente.—**b. off,** mal en sus negocios; mal de fortuna; maltrecho.

badness [bǽdnes], *s.* maldad; demasía.

baffle [bǽfl]. **I.** *va.* frustrar, impedir, desconcertar, desbaratar, contrariar. **II.** *vn.* luchar en vano. **III.** *s.* (mec.) cualquier artificio que sirve para desviar, guiar o regular el flujo de un gas o líquido; (m. v.) contrapuerta (del hogar); placa de desviación o de choque (llamada t. **b. plate**); reductor de velocidad o de tiro.—**b. tube,** conducto con placas de desviación para reducir la temperatura de los gases.—**b. wall,** superficie o tabique de choque o desviación.

baffler [bǽflœr], *s.* impedimento, contrariedad; el que desbarata.

bag [bæg]. **I.** *s.* saco, costal, talega; saquito de mano; (zool.) bolsita o vejiguilla de algunos animales; ubre, teta; bolsa (de un marsupial).—**b. net,** nasa.—**to pack up bag and baggage,** liar el hato, liar el petate, tomar el tole. **II.** *va.* ensacar, enzurronar, entalegar, imbursar; coger, capturar, cazar. **III.** *vn.* hacer bolsa o pliegue (la ropa); abotagarse, hincharse.

bagasse [bagǽs], *s.* bagazo, gabazo.

bagatelle [bægatél], *s.* bagatela, leria.

baggage [bǽgueʏ], *s.* (E. U.) equipaje; (mil.) bagaje; (fam.) ramera, prostituta; maula.—**b. car,** o **wagon,** vagón de equipajes.—**b. check,** marbete, contraseña de equipaje.

bagging [bǽguing], *s.* arpillera, malacuenda.

bagnio [bǽño], *s.* lupanar, burdel; casa de baños.

bagpipe [bǽgpáip], *s.* gaita, cornamusa.

bagpiper [bǽgpáiper], *s.* gaitero.

bah [ba], *interj.* ¡bah!

bail [béil]. **I.** *s.* caución, fianza; fiador; asa, cogedero (de cubo, caldero); división entre los compartimentos de un establo; achicador; cubo o vertedor para achicar.—**b. bond,** escritura de fianza. **II.** *va.* caucionar, dar fianza o salir fiador por otro; caucionar en libertad bajo fianza; desaguar, vaciar; achicar.

bailable [béilabœl], *a.* caucionable.

bailee [beilí], *s.* (for.) depositario.

bailer, bailor [béilœr], *s.* (for.) fiador.

bailey [béili], *s.* patio de castillo o fortaleza.— **Old Bailey,** tribunal central de lo criminal en Londres.

bailie, baillie [béili], *s.* alcalde, baile.

bailiff [béilif], *s.* alguacil, corchete; baile, ministril; mayordomo.

bailment [béilmœnt], *s.* (for.) depósito, entrega; libertad bajo fianza.

bailiwick [béiliuik], *s.* alguacilazgo; bailía; mayordomía.

bairn [bǽrn], *s.* niño.

bait [béit]. **I.** *va.* cebar, dar un pienso; poner cebo para atraer animales; azuzar; atormentar, molestar, acosar. **II.** *vn.* hacer parada o alto para tomar un refrigerio; aletear. **III.** *s.* cebo, carnada; pastura, añagaza, señuelo; refrigerio o refresco en una jornada; pienso.—**to take the b.,** tragar el anzuelo, caer en un lazo.

baize [béiš], *s.* bayeta.—**green b.,** tapete verde.—**long-napped b.,** bayeta de pellón, cachera.—**scarlet b.,** bayeta de grana.

bake [béik]. **I.** *va.* cocer en horno; desecar, endurecer, calcinar; hornear.—**baked meat,** guisado. **II.** *s.* cosa cocida en horno.

bakelite [béikelait], *s.* bakelita, producto de alquitrán para barnices.

baker [béikœr], *s.* hornero, panadero, tahonero. —**a b.'s dozen,** trece, docena de fraile.

bakery [békœri], **bakehouse** [békjaus], *s.* horno, panadería, tahona.

baking [béking], *s.* hornada; cocimiento.—**b. pan,** tortera o tartera.—**b. powder,** levadura.

balance [bǽlans]. **I.** *s.* (fís.) balanza; cotejo; equilibrio; balance; péndola, volante de reloj; (astr.) Libra; (com.) balance; saldo, resto, alcance.—**b. of power,** (pol.) equilibrio europeo.— **b. of trade,** balanza del comercio.—**b. sheet,** balance, avanzo.—**b. wheel,** rueda catalina, volante, péndola de reloj.—**to strike a b.,** hacer o pasar balance. **II.** *va.* equilibrar; balancear, contrapesar; dar finiquito, saldar; pesar; considerar, examinar. **III.** *vn.* equilibrarse; contrarrestarse; igualarse, saldarse; vacilar, dudar; balancearse, agitarse, mecerse.

balancer [bǽlansœr], s. pesador; fiel de balanza; equilibrista.

balancing [bǽlansing]. **I.** *s.* equilibrio; balance; balanceo. **II.** *a.* compensador, equilibrador. **b. pole,** balancín.

balcony [bǽlconi], *s.* balcón; antepecho; galería; (teat.) galería, anfiteatro.

bald [bold], *a.* calvo; escueto; pelado; desnudo, pelón, raído; desabrido, grosero.—**b.-faced,** cariblanco.—**b.-headed,** calvo.

baldachin [bóldakin], *s.* (arq.) dosel, baldaquín.

balderdash [bóldœrdæsh], *s.* (fam.) disparate, jerigonza; mezcolanza, calabriada.

baldhead [bóldjed], *s.* persona calva.

baldly [-li], *adv.* chabacanamente, groseramente.

baldness [bóldnes], *s.* calvicie, alopecia, pelona.

baldpate [bóldpait], *s.* (=BALDHEAD.)

baldric [bóldric], *s.* tahalí; (astr.) zodíaco.

bale [béil]. **I.** *s.* fardo; tercio (de tabaco); bala, paca (de algodón); bala (de papel—10 resmas).—**b. fire,** lumbrada, luminaria; pira funeraria. **II.** *va.* embalar, empaquetar; (mar.) achicar.

baleful [béilful], *a.* triste, funesto.

balefully [-i], *adv.* desgraciadamente, tristemente.

baling [béiling], *s.* achique.

balk, baulk [bok]. **I.** *va.* frustrar, desbaratar, impedir, poner obstáculo; amontonar formando lomo. **II.** *vn.* rebelarse (un caballo); resistirse.

balk, *s.* obstáculo, impedimento, contrariedad; fracaso, yerro; lomo entre surcos; (carp.) viga.

balky [bóki], *a.* rebelón; harón.

ball [bol]. **I.** *s.* bola, pelota, globo; bala de cañón; juego (de pelota); manera de arrojar la pelota; yema (del dedo); copa, trago de licor con hielo y agua (llamado también **high b.**); baile; (agr.) cepellón.—**b.-and-socket joint,** articulación esférica.—**b. bearing,** cojinete de bolas.—**b. blue,** añil.—**b. cartridge,** cápsula con bala.—**b. cock,** llave o válvula de flotador.—**b. flower,** (arq.) decoración en forma de bola con flores.—**b. governor,** regulador de bolas o de fuerza centrífuga.—**b. valve,** válvula esférica; válvula de flotador.—**dress b.,** sarao; baile de etiqueta.—**fancy b.,** baile de trajes.—**masquerade b.,** baile de máscaras. **II.** *va.* y *vn.* convertir o convertirse en bolas.

ballad [bǽlad], *s.* balada, copla, trova, cantinela; jácara, romance.—**b. monger,** coplero, coplista, jacarista, trovista.

ballast [bǽlæst]. **I.** *s.* (mar.) lastre; (f. c.) balasto.—**b. lighter,** lanchón de deslastrar.—**b. ports,** portas de lastrar.—**to go in b.,** ir en lastre.—**washed b.,** lastre lavado, o guijarro. **II.** *va.* (mar.) lastrar; (f. c.) balastar; (fig.) asegurar, sostener, reforzar.

ballasting [bǽlasting], *s.* acto de lastrar o balastar; (f. c.) balasto; (mar.) lastre.

ballet [bǽlé], *s.* baile, bailable, danza.

ballista [bǽlísta], *s.* balista; ballesta.

ballistic [bǽlístic], *a.* balístico.

ballistics [bǽlístics], *s.* balística.

ballonet [bǽlonét], *s.* (aer.) globillo compensador, que va dentro de un dirigible para regular el ascenso, etc.

balloon [bǽlún], *s.* globo aerostático; (quím.) redoma.—**b. bed,** amarradero para dirigibles.— **b. tire,** (aut.) neumático de baja presión (llamado a veces en el comercio "neumático de balón" y "neumático fláccido").

balloonist [bælúnist], *s.* aeronauta.

ballot [bǽlot], **I.** *s.* balota; papeleta para votar; voto; votación.—**b. box,** urna electoral. **II.** *vn.* balotar; insacular; votar.

balm [bam], *s.* bálsamo, ungüento; (bot.) balsamila mayor, toronjil.—**b. of Gilead, b. of Mecca,** bálsamo de Canarias.

balmy [bámi], *a.* balsámico; untuoso; fragrante; calmante, reparador.

balneary [bǽlneeri], *a.* y *s.* balneario.

balsam [bólsam], *s.* bálsamo.—**b. apple,** balsamina.

balsamic(al [bolsǽmic(al], *a.* balsámico; untuoso.

balsamine [bólsamin], *s.* (bot.) balsamina.

baluster [bǽlustœr], *s.* (arq.) balaústre.

balustered [-d], *a.* balaustrado, barandado.

balustrade [-treid], *s.* balaustrada, barandilla.

bamboo [bambú], *s.* (bot.) bambú, caña.

bamboozle [bambúsœl], *va.* (fam.) capotear, engañar; burlar, embaucar.

bamboozler [bambúslœr], *s.* (fam.) engañador, embaucador.

ban [bæn], **I.** *s.* bando, edicto, proclama, pregón; excomunión; entredicho; tejido de abacá.—**bans of marriage,** amonestaciones. **II.** *va.* y *vn.* encartar, proscribir.

banal [bǽnal], *a.* trivial, vulgar; feudal.

banality [banǽliti], *s.* trivialidad, lugares comunes; feudo.

banana [banǽna], *s.* (bot.) guineo; banana, banano; (S. A.) cambur.—**b. tree,** banano, bananero, plátano.—**red b.,** guineo morado.

banc [bænc], *s.* (for.) tribunal.—**court in b.,** tribunal en pleno.

band [bænd], **I.** *s.* faja, fleje, venda, tira, lista, cinta, franja, precinta; abrazadera, zuncho; lazo, enlace, unión, conexión, coyunda; cuadrilla, gavilla, partida, bandería; (mús.) banda; (arq.) filete, listón.—**b. brake,** freno de cinta.—**b. pulley,** polea para correa ancha, tambor de transmisión. **II.** *va.* congregar, abanderizar; fajar, vendar, atar, precintar. **III.** *vn.* asociarse, ir en pandilla o en manada.

bandage [bǽndey], **I.** *s.* (cir.) vendaje, venda, faja, longuetas. **II.** *va.* (cir.) vendar.

bandanna [bændǽna], *s.* pañuelo de hierbas.

bandbox [bǽndbox], *s.* caja de cartón.

banderole [bǽnderol], *s.* (mil.) banderola, corneta.

bandit [bǽndit], *s.* bandido, bandolero.

banditry [-ditri], *s.* bandolerismo.

bandlet [bǽndlet], *s.* (arq.) filete, listón.

bandmaster [bǽndmǽstœr], *s.* músico mayor.

bandog [bǽndog], *s.* mastín, perro de presa atado.

bandoleer [bǽndolœr], *s.* (mil.) bandolera.

bandoline [bǽndolin], *s.* bandolina.

bandore [bændóœr], *s.* (mus.) bandurria.

bandy [bǽndi]. **I.** *va.* cambiar, trocar; pelotear; pasar de uno a otro. **II.** *s.* juego de pelota; palo corvo para ese juego. **III.** *a.* arqueado, combado; estevado.—**b.-legged,** estevado, lo contrario de zambo.

bane [béin], *s.* ruina; azote, calamidad; veneno.

baneful [béinful], *a.* pernicioso, dañino, mefítico, ponzoñoso, funesto.

banefulness [béinfulnes], *s.* calidad de pernicioso o ponzoñoso.

banewort [béinuœrt], *s.* (bot.) cualquiera planta venenosa.

bang [bæng], **I.** *va.* arrojar, disparar, golpear con ruido; cascar, sacudir, zurrar; cortar el cabello en cerquillo; desmochar la cola de un caballo. **II.** *vn.* hacer estrépito; saltar. **III.** *s.* puñada, porrazo; detonación; ruido de un golpe; cerquillo de cabello sobre la frente; salto, brinco. **IV.** *adv.* con un golpe violento; con estrépito; de repente. **V.** *interj.* ¡pum!

bangle [bǽngœl], *s.* ajorca.

banian [bǽnian], *s.* (bot.) higuera de Bengala; comerciante de la India oriental; bata, ropón.

banish [bǽnish], *va.* desterrar, deportar, proscribir, confinar; relegar, ahuyentar, exterminar.

banisher [bǽnishœr], *s.* el que destierra.

banishment [bǽnishmœnt], *s.* destierro, deportación, extrañación, expulsión.

banister [bǽnistœr], *s.* baranda, pasamano.

banjo [bǽnyo], *s.* (E. U.) banjo, especie de guitarra de cinco cuerdas, con caja redonda a modo de pandero.—**b.-shaped housing,** (aut.) tubos de trompeta.

bank [bænc], *s.* orilla, ribera, margen (de un río, lago, arroyo, etc.); terreno, loma; bajo, bajío, banco (de arena, etc.); banda (de mesa de billar); banca (dinero del banquero en el juego); banco de remeros en una galera; (mús.) teclado; (aer.) inclinación lateral de un aeroplano en una curva; (com.) banco, casa de banca.—**b. account,** cuenta de banco, o en un banco.—**b. bill,** billete de banco; obligación de banco (expedida o aceptada por un banco).—**b. book,** libreta de depósitos del depositante.—**b. discount** (com. y arit.) descuento corriente o por fuera en el cual se deduce del valor nominal el interés de éste hasta la fecha de vencimiento.—**b. money,** valores de banco.—**b. note,** billete de banco.—**b. of circulation** = B. OF ISSUE.—**b. of deposit,** banco de depósito.—**b. of issue,** banco de emisión.—**b. paper,** papel moneda; obligaciones negociables en los bancos.—**b. rate,** tipo de descuento de un banco, o de los bancos.

bank. **I.** *va.* represar, estancar o resguardar con dique o reparo; amontonar, apilar; depositar en un banco.—**to b. up a fire,** cubrir un fuego (con cenizas). **II.** *vn.* ocuparse en negocios de banca, ser banquero.—**to b. on,** (fam.) apostar a; tener absoluta confianza en. **III.** *va.* y *vn.* (aer.) ladear(se).

bankable [-abœl], *a.* recibidero por un banco.

banker [bǽnkœr], *s.* banquero; cambista.

banking [bǽnking]. **I.** *s.* banca, operaciones de banco. **II.** *a.* bancario.—**b. house,** casa de banca.

bankrupt [bǽncrupt]. **I.** *s.* y *a.* quebrado, fallido, insolvente. **II.** *va.* quebrar, arruinar.

bankruptcy [-si], *s.* (com.) bancarrota, quiebra.

banner [bǽnœr]. **I.** *s.* bandera, insignia, estandarte, pendón, gonfalón. **II.** *a.* digno de llevar la bandera; primero en dignidad. **III.** *va.* proveer de una bandera.

banneret [bǽnœret], *s.* *dim.* bandereta; caballero con bandera.

bannerol [bǽnœrol], *s.* banderola.

banns [bæns], *s.* amonestaciones. *V.* BAN.

banquet [bǽnkuet]. **I.** *s.* banquete, festín. **II.** *va.* y *vn.* banquetear.

banquette [bænkét], *s.* (fort.) banqueta; (E. U. del Sur) acera; andén.

bantam [bǽntam], *s.* gallinilla de Bantam.

banter [bǽntœr], *va.* zumbar o zumbarse, dar matraca, fisgar, chotear, torear.

banter, *s.* zumba, burla, fisga, matraca.

banterer [-œr], *s.* zumbón, burlón, fisgador.

bantling [bǽntling], *s.* chicuelo o chicuela.

banyan, *v.* BANIAN.

banzai [bǽnsai], *interj.* ¡viva!

baobab [béobab], *s.* (bot.) baobab.

baptism [bǽptism], *s.* (igl.) bautismo; bautizo.

baptismal [bæptísmal], *s.* bautismal.—**b. name,** nombre de bautismo o de pila.

Baptist [bǽptist], *s.* bautista.—**Saint John the B.,** San Juan Bautista.

baptistery [bǽptistœri], *s.* (igl.) bautisterio.

baptistic(al [baptístic(al], *s.* bautismal; perteneciente a los bautistas.

baptize [bæptiš], *va.* bautizar, cristianar.

baptizer [bæptišœr], *s.* bautizante.

bar [bar], *s.* barra, varilla; palanca; lista, faja; valla, barrera; bocado (del freno); barra, banco de arena, lodo, etc.; cantina; mostrador de taberna; impedimento; reja; barrote; balaústre; tribunal (de justicia, de la opinión pública); abogacía; cuerpo de abogados licenciados; (for.) foro, estrados; recinto de los acusados; (mús.) raya perpendicular que divide los compases y cada compás del pentagrama; (arq.) listón de marco de ventana; (fís.) = ATMOSPHERE, unidad

de presión.—**b. iron,** hierro forjado en barras.
b. loom, telar de barras.—**b. shot,** (arti.) bala de cadena, bala enramada.—**at b.,** (for.) en pleno tribunal.—**in b. of,** para impedir; como razón suficiente para impedir.—**to be admitted,** o **called, to the b.,** recibirse de abogado.
bar, *va.* atrancar, barrear, trancar, impedir, estorbar, obstruir; prohibir; exceptuar, excluir.—**to b. out,** excluir, cerrarle la puerta a.
barb [barb]. **I.** *s.* púa; lengüeta (de saeta, anzuelo, etc.); caballo berberisco; (bot.) barba, arista.—**b. bolt,** perno dentado. **II.** *va.* armar con lengüetas; hacer incisivo o mordaz.
barbacan, *s. V.* BARBICAN.
barbarian [barbérian], *a* y *s.* bárbaro, barbárico.
barbaric [barbǽric], *a.* de ruda magnificencia.
barbarism [bárbarism], *s.* barbarie; barbarismo.
barbarity [barbǽriti], *s.* barbaridad, ferocidad.
barbarize [bárbaraiŝ], *va.* y *vn.* barbarizar.
barbarous [bárbarus], *a.* bárbaro, inculto; barbárico; troglodita; cruel, inhumano; áspero y bronco.—**barbarously** [-li], *adv.* bárbaramente.
barbate [bárbet], *a.* barbado; (bot.) barbado, aristado.
barbecue [bárbekiu]. **I.** *va.* asar un animal entero; (Méx.) hacer barbacoa. **II.** *s.* animal asado entero; (Méx.) barbacoa.
barbed [barbd], *a.* barbado, armado con lengüetas o púas; bardado. *V.* BARD.—**b. wire,** alambre de púas (para cercas).
barbel [bárbel], *s.* barbilla de ciertos peces; (ict.) barbo, comiza; (vet.) tolano.
barber [bárbœr], *s.* barbero, rapador.—**b. fish** (ict.), barbada.—**b.'s itch,** herpes o tiña tonsorial.
barberry [bárbœri], *s.* (bot.) bérbero, agracejo.
barbet [bárbet], *s.* (orn.) ave tropical; variedad del perro de lanas.
barbette [barbét], *s.* (mil.) barbeta.—**en b.,** en barbeta.
barbican [bárbicæn], *s.* (fort.) barbacana; tronera, aspillera.
barcarole [bárcœroul], *s.* barcarola.
bard [bard]. **I.** *s.* poeta, bardo, vate; barda, arnés, jaez, arreo; (coc.) albardilla; (ict.) mustela de río. **II.** *va.* poner barda a un caballo; enjaezar; (coc.) emborrazar.
bardic, bardish [bárdic, -iŝh], *a.* que pertenece a los bardos o poetas.
bare [béar]. **I.** *a.* desnudo; raso, pelado; raído, gastado, usado; liso, llano; sencillo, simple; desarmado; descubierto; público; mero, puro, solo.—**b. of money,** sin un cuarto, sin blanca.—**to be b. of,** estar desprovisto de.—**to lay b.** desnudar, descubrir. **II.** *va.* desnudar, descubrir, privar, despojar.
bareback [béarbǽc]. **I.** *a.* montado en pelo; sin silla. **II.** *adv.* en pelo, sin silla.—**barebacked** [-bǽct], *a.* desensillado, sin silla.
barebone [béarbôun], *s.* persona muy flaca.
bareboned [-bóund], *a.* muy flaco, descarnado.
barefaced [béarfeist], *a.* descarado, desfachatado, insolente, atrevido.—**barefacedly** [-li], *adv.* descaradamente; con la cara descubierta.—**barefacedness** [-nes], *s.* descaro, desfachatez.
barefoot, barefooted [béarfút, -ed], *a.* descalzo.
bareheaded [-jéded], *a.* destocado, sin sombrero.
barelegged [béarlegd], *a.* en pernetas.
barely [béarli], *adv.* solamente, meramente; escasamente.
barenecked [béarnect], *a.* descotado, con escote.
bareness [béarnes], *s.* desnudez, desabrigo; flaqueza; laceria, miseria.
bareribbed [béarribd], *a.* muy flaco.
bargain [bárguen]. **I.** *s.* convenio, pacto; negocio, trato de compra o venta; ganga, precio muy ventajoso para el comprador; artículo a precio reducido.—**b. day,** día de gangas, día de precios rebajados.—**b. driver,** regateador.—**b. sale,** venta a precios rebajados.—**at a b.,** baratísimo, con gran rebaja.—**to give into the b.,** dar de más o de ñapa; (Méx.) dar de pilón.—**to make a b.,** hacer un convenio o un trato.—**to strike a b.,** cerrar un trato, llegar a un convenio; hallar

una ganga, comprar muy barato. **II.** *va.* y *vn.* negociar, tratar.—**to b. away,** permutar, vender; dar por una bicoca, sacrificar, vender regalado.
bargainee [bárgueni], *s.* (for.) el que pacta para comprar.
bargainer [bárguencœr], *s.* el que hace un pacto de compra o venta.
bargaining [bárguening], *s.* regateo.
bargainor [bárguenor], *s.* (for.) el que pacta para vender.
barge [báry], *s.* (mar.) alijador, lanchón, lancón, barcaza, gabarra.—**b. canal,** canal interior para barcos de carga.—**bargeman** [mæn], barger [œr], *s.* barquero, lanchero.—**bargemaster** [-mǽstœr], *s.* patrón de barca o lanchón.
baric [bǽric], *a.* barométrico; (quím.) bárico.
barilla [baríla], *s.* barrilla (planta o cenizas), aguazur, mazacote, natrón.
barite [bérait], *s.* baritina. *V.* BARYTES.
baritone, *s.* =BARYTONE.
barium [bériʊm], *s.* (quím.) bario.
bark [barc]. **I.** *s.* corteza; ladrido (del perro); latido (de la zorra); barca, barco.—**b. beetle,** escarabajo horadador que ataca el abeto.—**b. mill,** triturador de casca. **II.** *va.* descortezar; raspar; cubrir; curtir o teñir en una infusión de cortezas. **III.** *vn.* ladrar, latir.—**to b. up the wrong tree,** (fam.) ir descaminado, tomar el rábano por las hojas.
barkantine, barkentine [bárkentin], *s.* (mar.) bergantín.
barkeeper [bárkípœr], *s.* tabernero, cantinero.
barker [bárkœr], *s.* ladrador; vociferador, criticón; descortezador.
Barker's mill [-mil], *s.* torniquete hidráulico, molinete de Bárker.
barking [bárking], *s.* ladrido, ladra.
barky [bárki], *a.* cortezudo.
barley [bárli], *s.* cebada.—**b. bin,** cebadera.—**b. sugar,** alfeñique.—**b. water,** hordiate.
barleycorn [-corn], *s.* grano de cebada; tercio de pulgada; ancho de un grano de cebada (como 4 mm.).—**B.,** o **John B.,** personificación del licor, Baco.
barm [barm], *s.* jiste; levadura.
barmaid [bármeid], *s.* cantinera, moza de taberna.
barmecide [bármesaid], *a.* ilusorio.
barmy [bármi], *a.* espumoso; activo.
barn [barn], *s.* granero, pajar, troje; establo; cobertizo para cambios y despacho de coches de tranvía.—**b.-door fowl,** aves de corral.—**b. owl,** autillo, especie de lechuza.
barnacle [bárnacœl], *s.* broma, lapa; (orn.) barnacla; (herr.) acial.—**barnacles,** (fam.) anteojos, antiparras.
barnyard [-yard], *s.* patio de granja.—**b. fowl** = BARN-DOOR FOWL.
barograph, barometrograph [bérograf, bérométrograf], *s.* barógrafo, barometrógrafo.
barometer [barómetœr], *s.* barómetro.
barometrical [barométrical], *a.* barométrico.
baron [bérʊn], *s.* barón.
baronage [bérʊney], baronía, *s.* baronía.
baroness [bérʊnes], *s.* baronesa.
baronet [bérʊnet], *s.* título hereditario de barón en Inglaterra.—**baronetage** [bérʊnetey], **baronetcy, baronetship** [bérʊnetsi, -ship], *s.* dignidad de *baronet*.
baronial [barónial], *a.* perteneciente a barón o baronía.
baroscope [bérʊscop], *s.* baroscopio.
barouche [barúsh], *s.* birlocho.
barracan [béracan], *s.* barragán.
barrack [bérrac], *s.* (gen. *pl.*) (mil.) cuartel; caserna; barraca.
barracoon [bérracún], *s.* barracón.
barrage [bérrey], *s.* (hidrául.) presa de contención; (mil.) cortina de fuego, fuego concentrado de artillería para impedir el avance de tropas de refuerzo.
barrator [bérator], *s.* camorrista; (for.) el culpable de baratería.
barratry [bérratri], *s.* (for.) baratería.

barrel [bǽrel]. **I.** *s.* barril o barrica, candiota; capacidad de un barril (E. U. = 31 galones vino = 196 lbs. harina = 2¾ bushels manzanas); cubeta, rodillo, tambor de cabrestante o molinete; cañón de escopeta; cañón de pluma; cuerpo de bomba.—**b. copper,** cobre nativo en pequeños fragamentos de mineral, que se despacha en barriles.—**b. maker,** barrilero.—**b. organ,** organillo.—**b. process,** (min.) extracción del oro y la plata por tratamiento en cilindros giratorios.—**b. vault,** (arq.) bóveda de cañón. **II.** *va.* envasar, embarrilar.

barreled, barrelled [bǽrreld], *a.* a manera de cañón o cilindro; provisto de cañón o cañones.

barren [bǽren], *a.* estéril, infructuoso, árido.— **barrenly** [bǽrenli], *adv.* infructuosamente, estérilmente.—**barrenness** [bǽrennes], *s.* esterilidad, infecundidad.

barretter [bǽrretœr], *s.* (elec.) detector de oscilaciones eléctricas.

barricade, barricado [bǽriked, -o]. **I.** *s.* barrera, empalizada, barricada. **II.** *va.* obstruir; cerrar con barricadas.

barrier [bǽricœr], *s.* barrera, valla; cerca; (fort.) espaldón; fortaleza; impedimento, obstáculo, estacada, atasco; término, límite.

barring [bárring], *pa.* de TO BAR (*expresión adverbial* salvo, excepto, quitando.

barring-out [bárring-aut], *s.* exclusión; cerrarle las puertas al maestro.

barrister [bǽrrister], *s.* abogado, curial; (Amér.) licenciado.

barroom [bárrúm], *s.* taberna, cantina.

barrow [bǽro], *s.* angarillas; túmulo; escurridor; marrano o puerco.—**b. hog,** verraco.

barshot [bárshót], *s.* (arti.) palanqueta.

bartender [bárténdœr], *s.* tabernero, cantinero.

barter [bártœr]. **I.** *vn.* baratar, traficar, feriar, trujamanear. **II.** *va.* trocar, cambiar, permutar. **III.** *s.* cambio, trueque, permuta.

barterer [bártœrcœr], *s.* traficante, barratador.

baryta [baráita], *s.* (quím.) barita.

barytes [baráitis], *s.* barita.

barytic [barític], *a.* barítico.

barytone [bǽriton], *a.* y *s.* barítono.

basal [bésal], *s.* fundamental; básico.

basalt [basólt], *s.* basalto.

basaltic [basóltic], *a.* basáltico.

bascule [bǽskiul]. *s.* palanca basculante u oscilante.—**b. bridge,** puente levadizo.

base [béis]. **I.** *a.* que sirve de base; de referencia; bajo, ruin; humilde; bajo de ley; (mús.) bajo, grave.—**b. bullion,** plomo en bruto que contiene plata, antimonio, etc.—**b. circle,** (mec.) círculo primitivo (de una rueda dentada).—**b. course,** (arq.) hilada inferior, primera hilada.—**b. court,** patio; tribunal inferior.—**b. line,** (top.) línea de base.—**b. metal,** metal común (no precioso); (fig.) cosa o persona de poco mérito. **II.** *s.* base, fundamento; (quím., mat.) base; (mús.) bajo, grave; (baseball) cada uno de los cuatro puestos que forman cuadro. **III.** *va.* basar, fundar; sostener, sustentar.

baseball [béisból], *s.* baseball; pelota de baseball.

baseboard [béisbórd], *s.* tabla o plancha que sirve de base; (arq.) tabla o listón de resguardo en la base de una pared.

baseborn [béisbórn], *a.* bajo, plebeyo; bastardo.

baseburner, baseburning furnace [béisbœrnœr, -bœrning fœrnæs], *s.* horno de alimentación automática.

baseless [béisles], *a.* desfondado; infundado, sin fundamento.

basely [béisli], *adv.* bajamente, vilmente.

basement [béismœnt], *s.* (arq.) basamento; cuarto bajo, sótano.

baseness [béisnes], *s.* bajeza, vileza.

bashful [bǽshful], *a.* vergonzoso, ruboroso; tímido; esquivo.—**bashfully** [bǽshfuli], *adv.* tímidamente, turbadamente, modestamente.—**bashfulness** [bǽshfulnes], *s.* vergüenza, timidez, cortedad, encogimiento; esquivez.

basic [bésic], *a.* fundamental; (quím.) básico.

basidium [bæsídium], *s.* (bot.) báside, célula esporífera de algunos hongos.

basify [béisifai], *va.* (quím.) basificar.

basil [bǽsil], *s.* (bot.) albahaca, alabega; (carp.) filo achaflanado de escoplo o cepillo; badana.

basilic [basílic], *s.* (anat.) basílica.

basilic, basilical [basílic, al], *a.* (anat.) basílica; real, regio; basilicón.

basilica [basílica], *s.* (arq.) basílica; túmulo endoselado.

basilicon [basílicon], *s.* ungüento basilicón.

basilisk [bǽsilisc], *s.* basilisco.

basin [béisn], *s.* jofaina, bacía, palangana; (P. Rico) ponchera; alcubilla, cámbija, estanque; represa, dársena; arca o depósito de agua; concha de un puerto; taza o tazón de fuente; charca, laguna; cuenca de un río, hoya, valle; cavidad de la pelvis; fuente; platillo de balanza.

basinet [bǽsinet], *s.* bacinete, capacete.

basis [béisis], *s.* base; fundamento, principio fundamental; elemento principal.

bask [basc]. **I.** *va.* asolear, calentar al sol. **II.** *vn.* tomar el sol.

basket [bǽsket], *s.* cesta, canasta; guarnición reticulada o cazoleta de la espada (llamada también **b. hilt**); la espada que la tiene.—**b. ball,** juego de balón.—**b. maker,** cestero.—**b. making** =BASKETRY.—**b. salt,** sal gema filtrada en cestas.

basketful [básketful], *s.* cestada.

basketry [bésketri], *s.* fabricación de cestas.

Basque [bask], *a.* vascongado; vascuence, éuscaro; jubón, ajustador.

bas-relief [bas-relíf], *s.* (b. a.) bajo relieve.

bass [bas]. **I.** *s.* esparto; atocha. *V.* BASSWOOD y BASS; (mús.) bajo profundo; (ict.) lobina. **II.** *a.* (mús.) bajo, grave.—**b.** o **b. viol,** violoncelo.

basset [bǽset], *s.* pinta, juego de naipes; casta de perro de caza, de piernas cortas y orejas largas.—**b. horn,** clarinete de tenor.

bassinet [bǽsinet], *s.* cuna; (mil.) bacinete.

basso [bǽsso], *s.* (mús.) bajo, cantante.—**b.- relievo** [bǽsso], *s.* (b. a.) bajo relieve.

bassoon [bæssún], *s.* (mús.) bajón; fagot, piporro.

basswood [bǽsud], *s.* tilo americano.

bast [bast], *s.* líber; estera, cuerda, etc., hecha de líber.

bastard [bǽstœrd]. **I.** *s.* bastardo, hijo natural. **II.** *a* bastardo; falso, espurio; degenerado; anormal, extraordinario.—**b. ash,** fresno rojo.— **b. cedar,** cedro de la costa del Pacífico de los E. U.—**b. file,** lima bastarda.—**b. ipecac,** (bot.) flor de la sangre.—**b. plantain,** plátano silvestre.

bastardize [bǽstardaiś], *va.* probar que alguno es bastardo; bastardear.

bastardly [bǽstardli], *adv.* como bastardo.

bastardy [bǽstardi], *s.* bastardía.

baste [béist], *va.* (cost.) hilvanar, bastear, embastar; (coc.) pringar, lardar, emborrazar; (fam.) dar de palos.

bastile, bastille [bæstíl], *s.* castillo, fortaleza, prisión; bastilla.

bastinade, bastinado [bǽstineid, -nádo]. **I.** *s.* paliza, bastonada. **II.** *va.* dar una paliza.

basting [bésting], *s.* (cort.) hilván, basta, embaste; (fam.) paliza.

bastion [bǽstiun o bǽstchun], *s.* (fort.) bastión, baluarte.

bat [bæt]. **I.** *s.* garrote, palo con que se juega baseball; albarda; (orn.) murciélago. **II.** *va.* y *vn.* dar, golpear o volear con un *bat;* pestañear; moverse, agitarse.

batch [bætch], *s.* cochura, hornada; número o cantidad de cosas que se reciben, se despachan o se confeccionan de una vez.—**b. mixer,** hormigonera.

bate [béit]. **I.** *s.* contienda, altercación, debate, disputa. **II.** *va.* minorar, disminuir; rebajar el precio; (ten.) poner en remojo; separar y ablandar. **III.** *vn.* minorarse, mermar.

bath [baz], *s.* baño; cuarto de baño; bañadera. **b. brick,** piedra para limpiar cuchillos.—**b. robe,**

bata de baño.—**Order of the B.**, (Ing.) Orden del Baño.—**Knight of the B. (K. B.)**, Caballero de la Orden del Baño.—**to take a b.**, bañarse.

bathe [béið]. **I.** *va.* bañar, lavar. **II.** *vn.* bañarse.

bathhouse [báz-jáus], *s.* casa de baños; casilla o desvestidero en un balneario.

bathing [béiðing]. **I.** *s.* baño. **II.** *a.* de baño.—**b. place,** bañadero, baño, balneario.—**b. suit,** traje de baño.

bathometer [bæzómetœr], *s.* batómetro.

bathos [béizos], *s.* paso de lo sublime a lo ridículo.

bathroom [bázrum], *s.* cuarto de baño.

bathtub [-tub], *s.* bañadera, baño, tina de baño.

bathymeter [bæzímetœr], *s.* batómetro.

bathymetry [-tri], *s.* batometría, determinación de profundidades en el mar.

bating [béiting], *prep.* excepto, exceptuando, deduciendo.

batiste [batíst], *s.* batista; olán.

batlet [bǽtlet], *s.* batidera.

baton [bǽtun]. **I.** *s.* bastón de mando; (mús.) batuta. **II.** *va.* bastonear.

Batrachia [batrékia], *s. pl.* (zool.) batracios.

batrachian [batrékian], *a.* y *s.* batracio.

batsman [bǽtsmæn], *s.* el que volea la pelota con el *bat* en el baseball.

battalion [batǽlliun], *s.* (mil.) batallón.

batten [bǽtœn]. **I.** *s.* lata, tabla de chilla, listón, alfajía, tablilla, tejamanil. **II.** *va.* cebar, engordar; (agr.) abonar la tierra; (carp.) construir con lata, tablillas, o tablas de chilla.—**to b. down the hatches,** (mar.) cerrar las escotillas y asegurarlas con listones de madera. **III.** *vn.* engordar, ponerse gordo; medrar a expensas de otro; saciar un deseo.

batter [bǽtœr]. **I.** *va.* apalear, cascar, golpear, batir, cañonear; romper, desmenuzar; destruir, demoler, derribar, mellar, estropear. **II.** *vn.* golpear. **III.** *s.* batido, pasta culinaria; golpeo, golpeadura; batidor de yeso; (tip.) estropeo de tipos o de una plancha; (ing. y arq.) talud; (dep.) *v.* BATSMAN.

batterer [bǽtœrœr], *s.* apaleador.

battering piece [bǽtœring pis] *o* **gun**, *s.* (arti.) pieza de batir.—**b. train,** batería de sitio.—**b. ram,** ariete.

battery [bǽtœri], *s.* (arti., y mec.) batería; (for.) agresión; (elec.) pila; batería.

batting [bǽting], *s.* agramaje, espadillaje; (cerá.) moldeaje; algodón o lana en hojas; (dep.) voleo.

battle [bǽtœl]. **I.** *s.* batalla, combate; lucha, lidia.—**b. array,** orden de batalla.—**b. ax, b. axe,** hacha de combate.—**b. piece,** (b. a.) cuadro o composición que representa o simboliza una batalla.—**b. royal,** riña promiscua, pelotera.—**to do b.,** batallar, luchar.—**to offer b.,** presentar batalla. **II.** *vn.* batallar, luchar. **III.** *va.* luchar o batirse con.

battled, [bǽtœld], *a.* almenado.

battledore [bǽtœldor], *s.* raqueta.—**b. and shuttlecock,** raquetas y volante.

battlement [bǽtœlmœnt], *s.* muralla almenada, almenaje; pretil con crestería.

battlemented [bǽtœlmented], *a.* almenado.

battleplane [bǽtœlpléin], *s.* avión de combate.

battleship [bǽtœlship], *s.* acorazado mayor o grande de combate.

battology [bætóloyi], *s.* batología.

battue [batiú], *s.* batida, montería de caza mayor; matanza inicua.

bauble, bawble [bóbœl], *s.* chuchería, fruslería, futesa, friolera.

baulk, *vn.* = BALK.

bauxite [bóusait], *s.* (min.) bauxita (hidrato ferroso de aluminio).

Bavarian [bavérian], *a.* y *s.* bávaro.

bavin [bǽvin], *s.* fagina.

bawd [bod], **I.** *s.* alcahuete, alcahueta. **II.** *vn.* alcahuetear.

bawdily [bódili], *adv.* obscenamente.

bawdiness [bódines], *s.* obscenidad; alcahutería; suciedad.

bawdry [bódri], *s.* alcahuetería.

bawdy [bódi], *a.* indecente, obsceno, impúdico.—**b. house,** lupanar, burdel, mancebía.

bawl [bol]. **I.** *vn.* gritar, vocear, chillar, desgañitarse. **II.** *va.* pregonar.

bawler [bólœr], *s.* voceador, vocinglero, alborotador, gritador, chillón.

bay [béi]. **I.** *a.* bayo. **II.** *va.* ladrar a, acorralar. **III.** *vn.* ladrar, aullar. **IV.** *s.* bahía; abra; entrada (de agua en tierra, de un valle en el flanco de una montaña, etc.); ladrido, aullido; caballo bayo; acorralamiento; pajar de almacenar heno; corona de laurel; (bot.) laurel; (arq.) intercolumnio, crujía, entrepaño; vano; recuadro; (hidrául.) agua de una entrada o compartimiento a la cabeza de una esclusa, a la entrada de una turbina, etc.; (ing.) ojo de puente.—**b. rum,** ron con aceite esencial de laurel o de malagueta.—**b. salt,** sal morena o de mar.—**B. State,** estado de Massachusetts (E. U.).—**b. tree,** laurel.—**b. window,** mirador, ventana saliente, balcón cerrado, bow window.—**b. work,** entramado.—**at b.,** acosado, a raya.

bayadere [bayadiær], *s.* bayadera.

bayberry [bébœri], *s.* (bot.) arrayán.—**b. tallow,** cera del arrayán brabántico.

baying [béing], *s.* ladrido; balido.

bayonet [béonet]. **I.** *s.* bayoneta. **II.** *va.* cargar o herir con bayoneta.

bayou [báiu], *s.* canalizo; brazo de río.

baywood [béiud], *s.* caoba tosca de Campeche y Honduras.

bazaar, bazar [bašár], *s.* bazar, feria.

bdellium [délium], *s.* bedelio, joya, perla o ámbar.

be [bi], *vn.* (*ind.* AM, ART, IS; ARE; *pret.* WAS, WAST; WERE; *pp.* BEEN) ser; estar; existir. Con el expletivo *there* equivale al impersonal "haber," pero concuerda en número con el substantivo que le sigue, vg., *there is a man in the room,* hay un hombre en el cuarto; *there are two men,* hay dos hombres. Con algunos adjetivos que indican sensaciones forma frases que se traducen por "tener" seguido del substantivo correspondiente, vg., *to be hungry,* tener hambre. Tales frases se hallarán bajo los adjetivos respectivos. Con algunos verbos neutros es equivalente al auxiliar *to have,* haber: *he was gone,* se había ido; *the time is come,* ha llegado el tiempo. Seguido de infinitivo equivale a deber, tener que: *I am to be there,* debo estar allí. Seguido de *being* y un participio forma frases de construcción pasiva muy comunes aunque censuradas por muchos gramáticos: *the house is being built,* la casa se está construyendo. Seguido de gerundio, forma frases equivalentes a estas últimas, pero más correctas: *the house is building,* la casa se está construyendo.—**to b. coming,** venir, ir: *he is coming tomorrow,* él viene mañana; *I am coming,* ya voy.—**to b. going,** ir: *I am going to the theater,* voy (o pienso ir) al teatro; *where are you going?* ¿adónde va Vd.?.—**to b. off,** irse, marcharse; estar errado o equivocado.—**to b. up to,** (fam.) ser suficiente o competente para; estar al nivel o a la altura de; estar haciendo o urdiendo, andar en (travesuras, intrigas, etc.); depender de; tocar a.

beach [bich]. **I.** *s.* costa, ribera, playa, orilla. **II.** *va.* impeler a la playa. **III.** *vn.* desembarcar en una playa.

beached [bicht], *a.* varado en la playa; playado.

beachy [bichi], *a.* playado.

beacon [bíkun]. **I.** *s.* (mar.) baliza, boya; faro, fanal, almenara, ángaro, alcondora, atalaya; guía. **II.** *va.* señalar con almenara; iluminar, guiar.

beaconage [bíkuney], *s.* derechos de faros.

bead [bid]. **I.** *s.* cuenta, cañutillo, chaquira, abalorio; burbuja; espuma; bolita, gota, glóbulo; saliente, pestaña, listoncillo o tira convexa; mira globular de un arma; (aut.) pestaña o reborde de un neumático; (arq.) moldura convexa; (quím.) botón, glóbulo de bórax, etc. empleado en el análisis al soplete para determinaciones por el color; (min.) glóbulo de metal precioso obtenido por cupelación.—*pl.*, rosario.—**b. tree** (bot.) cinamomo.—**to draw a b. on,** apuntar a con un arma de fuego.—**to say**, o **tell, one's beads**, rezar el rosario. **II.** *va.* adornar con abalorios; redondear los bordes (de un tubo ensanchado, etc.); proveer de molduras convexas, pestañas, etc. (*v.* I.). **III.** *vn.* formar espuma; burbujear.

beading [bíding], *s.* abalorio; preparación para formar espuma en los licores; (tec.) listón; moldura convexa; pestaña, reborde.

beadle [bídœl], *s.* pertiguero o macero, muñidor, bedel, alguacil, ministril.

beadleship [bídœlŝhip], *s.* bedelía.

beady [bídi], *a.* parecido a abalorio; que tiene espuma o jiste.

beagle [bígœl], *s.* sabueso; alguacil; tiburón pequeño.

beak [bíc], *s.* pico; hocico; (fam.) rostro; cabo, promontorio; (mar.) saltillo de proa; espolón.

beaked [bíct], *a.* picudo.

beaker [bíkœr], *s.* vaso o copa de boca ancha; (quím.) vaso picudo para los análisis.

beam [bím]. **I.** *s.* viga; vigueta; rayo (de luz); (mar.) bao; manga de un buque; (tej.) enjulio o vara de empaño; brazo de una báscula o romana; palanca oscilante.—**b. balance**, balanza ordinaria o de brazos.—**b. compass**, compás de regla o de barra.—**b. engine**, máquina de balancín.—**on the b.**, (mar.) por el través.—**to be on her b. ends**, (mar.) estar de costado, estar ladeado (apl. a los barcos). **II.** *vn.* destellar, fulgurar; estar rozagante o rebosando de alegría.

beaming [bíming], *a.* radiante; brillante; alegre, vivo.

beamless [bímles], *a.* sin rayos.

beamy [bími], *a.* radiante; alegre, vivo; (mar.) ancho de manga.

bean [bin], *s.* haba, judía, frijol; grano, semilla, almendra.—**in the b.**, en grano.

bear [béar], *va.* (pret. BORE, *pp.* BORNE, O BORN) sostener, aguantar; llevar, cargar; mostrar, dar muestras; soportar, sufrir, tolerar; sufragar; asumir o tener una obligación, carga o responsabilidad; usar alguna insignia de autoridad o distinción; comportarse (como *vr.*); profesar o tener (amor, odio); tener, guardar (relación, etc.); producir; parir, dar a luz (en este sentido, el *pp.* es **born**); dar (testimonio); ejercer por derecho o autoridad; ser susceptible de, admitir; llevar, tener (una marca, inscripción, etc.); impeler, empujar; deprimir; (com.) hacer bajar el valor, jugar a la baja.—**to b. a hand**, ayudar.—**to b. arms**, servir de soldado.—**to b. away**, llevarse; ganarse.—**to b. company**, acompañar.—**to b. date**, estar fechado.—**to b. down**, reducir a un lugar inferior, rendir, deprimir; derribar, vencer, postrar.—**to b. in**, socavar, aflojar (el carbón de una mina).—**to b. in mind**, tener presente o en cuenta.—**to b. off**, contener, separar; ganar, llevarse (un premio, etc.); (mar.) salvar, apartarse de, para no rozar o chocar.—**to b. out**, sostener, apoyar; confirmar; hacer llevadero.—**to b. the bag**, tener la bolsa, dominar o manejar los fondos.—**to b. up**, sostener.—**to b. witness**, atestiguar.

bear, *vn.* padecer; sufrir; aguantar, soportar; fructificar; dirigirse o encaminarse; tener o llevar cierta dirección, señalar (vg. *the ship bears north*, el barco lleva dirección norte; *this line bears east*, esta línea tiene dirección o rumbo, este).—**to b. away**, (mar.) cambiar la dirección de un barco, sobre todo a sotavento.—**to b. back**, retroceder, retirarse.—**to b. down on**, o **upon**, acosar, atacar despiadadamente, caer sobre.—**to b. off**, (mar.) alejarse.—**to b. up**, cobrar ánimo, resignarse; (mar.) = TO B. AWAY.—**to b. upon**, (mil.) estar dirigido a, dominar.—**to b. with**, tener paciencia con, ser indulgente con.

bear, *s.* (zool.) oso; (com.) bajista.—(**B-**, astr.) Osa.—**b. garden**, patio de osos; (fam.) merienda de negros.—**b.'s-breech**, (bot.) branca ursina, acanto.—**b.'s-ear**, (bot.) oreja de oso.—**b.'s foot**, (bot.) eléboro negro.

bearable [bérabœl], *a.* sufrible, soportable.

bearberry [bérberri], *s.* = BEARWOOD.

beard [bíœrd]. **I.** *s.* barba o barbas; (bot.) raspa, brizna, arista; lengüeta de flecha; barbas de pluma. **II.** *va.* arrancar las barbas, mesar; retar.

bearded [bíœrded], *a.* barbado; barbudo; (bot.) aristado; (astr.) caudato.

beardless [bíœrdles], *a.* imberbe, lampiño; (bot.) derraspado.—**b. wheat**, trigo chamorro.

bearer [béarœr], *s.* portador, dador; faquín; muñidor, zacatecas; árbol frutífero; (tec.) soporte; (print.) calzo.

bearing [béaring]. **I.** *s.* aguante, paciencia, sufrimiento; porte, maneras, presencia, talante; relación, connexión; fuerza, sentido, valor de una expresión; producción, fructificación, cosecha; gestación, preñez; (mec.) punto de apoyo; cojinete; soporte; (arq.) apoyo, sostén; (mar.) orientación, marcación, situación; (top. y mar.) rumbo.—*pl.* orientación, rumbo; línea de flotación (de un barco).—**b. metal**, metal para cojinetes; metal antifricción.—**to bring one to one's bearings**, hacer ver a uno las cosas, abrirle los ojos.—**to lose one's bearings**, confundirse, aturdirse.—**to take a b.**, (top.) determinar un rumbo (de una línea).—**to take bearings**, abalizarse, marcarse; orientarse. **II.** *a.* de apoyo, de contacto; productivo.—**b. rein**, gamarra.—**b. surface**, superficie de apoyo; superficie de contacto o de rozamiento. A veces equivale a la *term.* "-ífero," vg., *gold-bearing*, aurífero.

bearish [béarish], *a.* osuno; rudo, áspero.

bearskin [béarskin], *s.* piel de oso; morrión de granadero.

bearwood [bérud], *s.* (bot.) arbusto cuya corteza es la cáscara sagrada.

beast [bíst], *s.* bestia, bruto, cuadrúpedo; hombre brutal.—**b. of burden**, acémila.—**b. of prey**, animal de rapiña.

beastlike [bístlaic], *a.* bestial, abrutado.

beastliness [bístlines], *s.* bestialidad, brutalidad.

beastly [bístli]. **I.** *a.* bestial, brutal; (fam.) muy malo, detestable. **II.** *adv.* brutalmente; (fam.) sumamente.

beat [bit], *va.* (pret. BEAT; *pp.* BEATEN, BEAT) batir (un metal, huevos, la costa, las alas, etc.); revolver; pegar, aporrear; golpear; vencer; ganarle a; llegar o acabar primero que; correr, recorrer, andar por; indicar, marcar (tiempo, el compás, etc.); (fam.) sobrepasar, dejar atrás (en cuanto a calidad, etc.); confundir, estar más allá de los alcances o capacidad de; (vulg.) engañar; (caz.) dar una batida; (mil.) tocar (tambor u otro instrumento); (agr.) trillar; (ind.) abatanar; espadillar, agranar, majar.—**to b. all hollow**, (fam.) dejar tamañito.—**to b. a parley**=TO SOUND A PARLEY.—**to b. down**, regatear, lograr rebaja regateando.—**to b. it**, (fam.) escaparse, escurrirse, irse.—**to b. off**, rechazar.—**to b. out of**, privar de.—**to b. the band** (fam.), hasta más no poder, con sumo ahinco o empeño.—**to b. the Dutch** (fam.) ser extraordinario o sorprendente.—**to b. the record**, sobrepujar el record, alzar el record.—**to b. time**, marcar el compás.—**to b. up**, sorprender (al enemigo); batir (huevos, etc.).

beat, *vn.* latir, palpitar, pulsar; batir, golpear repetidamente; ganar, vencer; dar un toque (de tambor, etc.); poderse batir o revolver; sonar; (mar.) tentar el vado; (caz.) correr; mover las matas, ramas, etc., para levantar la caza.—**to b. about**, barloventar; andar buscando.—**to b. about the bush**, andarse por las ramas; divagar, andar con rodeos.

beat, **I.** *s.* golpe; pulsación, latido; sonido repetido; toque de tambor; (mil.) ronda.—**b. reception**, (radtlf.) recepción heterodina. **II.** *a.* (fam.) fatigado.

beaten [bítœn]. **I.** *pp.* de TO BEAT. **II.** *a.* trillado, asendereado; batido, vencido.

beater [bítœr], *s.* martillo, maza, pisón, golpeador, batidor, sacudidor, molinillo; apaleador.

beatific(al [biatífic(al], *a.* beatífico.

beatifically [biatíficali], *adv.* beatíficamente.

beatification [biatifikéshun], *s.* beatificación.

beatify [biátifai], *va.* beatificar.

beating [bíting], *s.* paliza, zurra, somanta, tunda; latido, pulsación; golpeo, batidura.

beatitude [biátitiud], *s.* beatitud.—**the Beatitudes**, las bienaventuranzas.

beau [bo], *s.* (*pl.* BEAUX *o* BEAUS) galán, petimetre, pisaverde, currutaco; cortejo.—**b. ideal,** bello idea.—**b. monde,** gente de moda.

beauteous [biútius], *a.* bello, hermoso.

beauteously [-li], *adv.* = BEAUTIFULLY.

beauteousness [-nes], *s.* belleza, encantos.

beautification [-fikéishun], *s.* embellecimiento.

beautifier [biútifáicer], *s.* hermoseador.

beautiful [biútiful], *a.* bello.—**the b.,** lo bello.

beautifully [biútifuli], *adv.* bellamente.

beautifulness [biútifulnes], *s.* belleza.

beautify [biútifai]. **I.** *va.* hermosear, embellecer, acicalar, adornar. **II.** *vn.* hermosearse.

beauty [biúti], *s.* belleza; beldad.—**b. parlor,** salón de belleza para señoras.—**b. sleep,** primer sueño, el de antes de media noche.—**b. spot,** parche o lunar postizo.

beaver [bívcer], *s.* (zool.) castor; piel de castor; sombrero de copa; guante de piel de castor; (arm.) babera, baberol.

beavered [bívcerd], *a.* con babera.

beaverteen [bivcertín], *s.* (tej.) fustán.

becalm [becám], *va.* calmar, serenar, sosegar; (mar.) encalmar.

became [bikéim], *pret.* del verbo TO BECOME.

because [bicós], *conj.* porque.—**b. of,** a causa de.

beccafico [becafíco], *s.* (orn.) papafigo.

bechance [becháns], *va.* y *vn.* acaecer, acontecer.

beck [bec]. **I.** *va.* y *vn.* =BECKON. **II.** *s.* señas, ademán; riachuelo; valle; (tint.) cubeta.—**at one's b. and call,** a disposición de uno, a la mano.

beckon [békun]. **I.** *va.* llamar con señas. **II.** *vn.* hacer señas o ademanes. **III.** *s.* seña o ademán de cabeza.

becloud [bicláud], *va.* obscurecer, anublar.

become [bicúm]. **I.** *va.* convenir a, sentar a; ser propio de. **II.** *vn.* hacerse, convertirse en, ponerse, llegar a ser. Seguido de un adjetivo, se traduce a veces por un solo verbo que indica el cambio correspondiente: vg., *to become angry,* enojarse; *to become old,* envejecer; *to become useless,* inutilizarse.—**to b. of,** ser de, hacerse: *what will become of me?* ¿qué será de mí? *what has become of John?,* ¿qué se ha hecho (o qué hay de) Juan?

becoming [bicúming]. **I.** *a.* correcto, decoroso, propio; decente, conveniente; que sienta bien, que va bien. **II.** *s.* transformación, paso de un estado a otro.

becomingly [bicúmingli], *adv.* decorosamente, correctamente; a propósito.

becomingness [bicúmingnes], *s.* decoro, corrección; propiedad, compostura.

bed [bed]. **I.** *s.* cama, lecho; (geol.) capa, estrato; madre,álveo, cauce; (mec.)asiento,banco,lecho, fondo; armadura, fundación, base; macizo de jardín; tablar de una huerta; (com.) tonga, tongada, camada; (min.) yacimiento, capa.—**b. cover,** cubrecama, colcha.—**b. joint,** (const.) junta horizontal; (geol.) grieta paralela al terreno.—**b. linen,** ropa de cama. **II.** *va.* acostar, poner en cama; dar cama a; sembrar en un macizo; meter; asentar, apoyar; (const.) labrar o preparar la superficie de. **III.** *vn.* acostarse; cohabitar; descansar, apoyarse.

bedabble [bidǽbœl], *va.* rociar, mojar.

bedaub [bedób], *va.* salpicar, ensuciar, embadurnar; vilipendiar.

bedazzle [bidǽsl], *va.* deslumbrar.

bedbug [bédbúg], *s.* (zool.) chinche.

bedchamber [bédchéimbœr], *s.* dormitorio, alcoba; (Méx.) recámara.

bedclothes [bédclózs], *s. pl.* ropa de cama (sábanas, mantas, etc.).

bedding [béding], *s.* colchones y ropa de cama; asiento, fundamento; (geol.) estratificación.

bedeck [bidéc], *va.* adornar, engalanar, acicalar.

bedevil [bidévl], *va.* endemoniar, endiablar; maleficiar; hechizar; enloquecer.

bedew [bidiú], *va.* rociar, regar.

bedfellow [bédfélo], *s.* compañero o compañera de cama.

bedhangings [bédjǽngings], *s.* pabellón, cortinas de cama.

bedhead [bédjed], *s.* cabecera de cama.

bedim [bidím], *va.* obscurecer, ofuscar; desvistar, deslumbrar.

bedizen [bidísn], *va.* adornar, aderezar, acicalar.

bedlam [bédlam], *s.* casa de orates; manicomio; bullicio, Babel; desbarajuste.

bedlamite [bédlamait], *s.* loco, orate.

Bedouin [béduin], *s.* beduíno; vago.

bedpan [bédpæn], *s.* silleta para enfermos, chata.

bedplate [bédpléit], *s.* (mec.) bancaza, cama, platina, plancha de asiento.

bedpost [bédpost], *s.* poste de la cama.

bedquilt [bédkuilt], *s.* cubrecama, colcha.

bedraggle [bidrǽgœl], *va.* ensuciar o manchar arrastrando por el suelo.

bedrid, bedridden [bédrríd, -œn], *a.* postrado en cama.

bedrock [bédrróc], *s.* (min.) lecho de roca.

bedroom [bédrrúm], *s.* alcoba, cuarto de dormir; (Méx.) recámara.

bedside [bédsaid], *s.* lado de cama.

bedsore [bédsoar], *s.* llaga causada por la prolongada permanencia en el lecho.

bedspread [bédspred], *s.* cubrecama, sobrecama.

bedstead [bédsted], *s.* cuja, armadura de la cama.

bedtick [bédtíc], *s.* cotí.

bedtime [bédtaim], *s.* hora de acostarse.

bedward [béduard], *adv.* hacia la cama; hacia la noche.

bee [bi], *s.* abeja; (fam.) reunión, tertulia.—**b. eater,** (orn.) abejarruco.—**b. fiy,** mosca abeja.—**b. glue,** cera aleda, tanque.—**b. line,** línea recta, derechura.—**to have a b. in one's bonnet,** *o* **head,** estar destornillado; estar haciendo castillos en el aire o lleno de esperanzas vanas.

beebread [bíbréd], *s.* polen almacenado por las abejas.

beech [bich], *s.* haya.—**b. mast** = BEECHNUT.—**b. oil,** aceite de fabuco.

beechen [bíchœn], *a.* de haya.

beechnut [bíchnut], *s.* fabuco, hayuco, nuez de haya.

beef [bif], *s.* carne de vaca; res.—**b.-witted,** lerdo, estúpido.

beefeater [bífítœr], *s.* alabardero; criado rollizo; (fam.) un inglés (apodo).

beefsteak [bífsteic], *s.* bistec.

beehive [bíjáiv], *s.* colmena, abeja, abejar.

beekeeper [bíkpœr], *s.* colmenero, abejero.—**b.-keeping** [-kiping], *s.* cría de abejas, apicultura.

been [bin], *pp.* de TO BE.

beer [bíar], *s.* cerveza.—**b. garden,** cervecería (lugar donde se sirve cerveza).—**b. saloon,** taberna, cantina.

beestings [bístings], *s.* calostro.

beeswax [bîs-uax], *s.* cera de abejas.

beet [bít], *s.* (bot.) remolacha, betarraga; (Méx.) betabel.—**b. root,** *o* **beetroot,** remolacha, raíz de la remolacha.

beetle [bítœl]. **I.** *s.* (ent.) escarabajo; pisón, maza, aplanadera; martinete; mallo; batán; estúpido, imbécil.—**b.-browed,** cejudo.—**b.-head,** peso del martinete.—**b.-headed,** lerdo, pesado.—**b. stock,** mango de pisón. **II.** *vn.* hacer barriga, combar; sobresalir; (ind.) abatanar, batanear.

beetling [bítling]. **I.** *a.* saliente, pendiente, colgante. **II.** *s.* (tej.) bataneo.—**b.-machine,** (tej.) batán.

beeves [bívs], *s.* (*pl.* de BEEF) ganado; reses.

befall [bifól], *vn.* (*pret.* BEFELL) *pp.* BEFALLEN) suceder, acontecer, sobrevenir.

befit [bifít], *va.* venir bien, cuadrar, ser propio o digno de.

befitting, *a.* conveniente, propio, digno.

befog [bifóg], *va.* envolver en niebla; confundir, obscurecer.

befool [bifúl], *va.* infatuar, entontecer.

before [bifócer]. **I.** *adv.* delante, al frente; antes, anteriormente, con prioridad **II.** *prep.* delante de, enfrente de; ante, en presencia de; antes de. **III.** *conj.* antes que, primero.

beforehand [bifóœrjænd]. **I.** *adv.* de antemano, a prevención, previamente, con antelación. **II.** *a.* acomodado, con recursos.

befoul [bifául], *va.* ensuciar, emporcar.

befriend [bifrénd], *va.* favorecer, patrocinar, amparar, proteger.

beg [beg]. **I.** *vn.* mendigar, pordiosear, vivir de limosna. **II.** *va.* rogar, pedir, suplicar, implorar.—**to b. the question**, cometer petición de principio.—**to b.** (**leave**) **to,** permitirse.

began [bigǽn], *pret.* del verbo TO BEGIN.

beget [biguét], *va.* (*pret.* BEGOT—ant. BEGAT— *pp.* BEGOTTEN) engendrar; producir, causar.

begetter [biguétœr], *s.* engendrador.

beggar [bégar]. **I.** *s.* mendigo, mendigante, pobre de solemnidad.—**beggardom, beggarhood,** pobrismo o pobrería. **II.** *va.* empobrecer, arruinar; apurar, agotar.—**to b. description**, no haber palabras para describir.

beggarliness [bégarlines], **beggary** [bégari], *s.* mendicidad o mendiguez, pordiosería, pobreza.

beggarly [bégarli]. **I.** *a.* pobre, miserable. **II.** *adv.* pobremente.

begging [béguing]. **I.** *a.* mendicante. **II.** *s.* mendicación, pordioseo.—**to go b.,** andar mendigando.

begilded [biguílded], *a.* dorado.

begin [biguín], *va.* y *vn.* (*pret.* BEGAN O BEGUN; *pp.* BEGUN) empezar; nacer.

beginner [biguínœr], *s.* iniciador, originador; principiante; novicio, novato.

beginning [biguíning], *s.* principio, origen.

begohm [bégóum], *s.* (elec.) begohmio, kilomegohmio.

begone! [bigón], *interj.* ¡fuera! ¡vete!

begonia [bigónia], *s.* (bot.) begonia.

Begoniaceæ [bigoniéisii], *s. pl.* (bot.) begoniáceas.

begored [bigócœrd], *a.* ensangrentado.

begot [bigót], *pret.; ***begotten,** *pp.* de TO BEGET.

begrime [bigráim], *va.* embarrar.

begrudge [bigrúy], *va.* envidiar; regatear, repugnar.

beguile [bigáil], *va.* engañar, seducir; defraudar; entretener, pasar el tiempo, divertir.

beguiler [bigáilœr], *s.* engañador, seductor.

begun, *pp.* y *pret.* de TO BEGIN.

behalf [bijáf], *s.* (precedido de **in, on** o **upon**) por; a favor, en nombre, interés o defensa de.

behave [bijéiv], *va.* y *vn.* proceder, obrar, conducirse, comportarse o portarse (bien o mal). —**b.!** ¡estése Vd. quieto! ¡pórtate bien!

behavior, behaviour [bijéviœr], *s.* proceder, conducta, comportamiento; funcionamiento.

behaviorism, behaviourism [bijéiviœrism], *s.* (psicol.) sistema que sostiene que la psicología debe fundarse exclusivamente en la observación y el análisis de los actos humanos objetivamente observables. (Podría llamarse *objetivismo*).—**behaviorist** [-ist], *s.* partidario del *behaviorism.*— **behavioristic** [-ístic], *a.* relativo al *behaviorism.*

behead [bijéd], *va.* decapitar, descabezar.

beheading [bijéding], *s.* decapitación.

beheld [bijéld], *pret.* y *pp.* de TO BEHOLD.

behest [bijést], *s.* mandato, precepto, requerimiento.

behind [bijáind]. **I.** *adv.* atrás, detrás; en zaga; hacia atrás; por detrás; en pos; con retraso. **II.** *prep.* tras, detrás de; después de.—**b. one's back,** en ausencia o a espaldas de uno.—**b. time,** tarde.—**to be b. the times,** estar atrasado; estar atrasado de noticias.

behindhand [bijáindjænd]. **I.** *adv.* con atraso, con retraso. **II.** *a.* atrasado, retrasado.

behold [bijóld], *va.* (*pret.* y *pp.* BEHELD) mirar, contemplar.—**b.!** *interj.* ¡mirad! ¡he aquí!

beholden [bijóldœn], *a.* obligado por gratitud.

beholder [bijóldœr], *s.* espectador.

beholding [-ing], *s.* contemplación; espectáculo.

behoney [bijóni], *va.* dulcificar.

behoof [bijúf], *s.* provecho, utilidad, ventaja.

behoove, behove [bijúv], *vn. impers.* tocar, corresponder, incumbir, importar.

beild [[bild], *v.* y *s.* = BIELD.

being [bíing]. **I.** *ger.* de TO BE: siendo.—**for the time b.,** por el momento, por ahora; por entonces.—**it b. that,** siendo así que. **II.** *s.* ser, ente, criatura; existencia.

belabor, belabour [bilébœr], *va.* apalear, pegar, cascar; trabajar, elaborar.

belaced [biléist], *a.* muy adornado con encaje, muy galoneado.

belate [biléit], *va.* tardar; trasnochar.

belated [-léited], *a.* demorado, atrasado, tardío.

belay [biléi], *va.* (*pret.* y *pp.* BELAYED O BELAID) amarrar dando vueltas; sitiar, bloquear, cercar, rodear.—**belaying pins,** (mar.) cabillas.

belch [belch]. **I.** *va.* arrojar, echar de sí; vomitar; ventosear. **II.** *vn.* regoldar, eructar; vomitar; salir con fuerza (una llama, etc.).

belch, belching [bélching], *s.* regüeldo, eructo, eructación.

beldam, beldame [béldam, dem], *s.* bruja, vejestorio.

beleaguer [bilíguœr], *va.* sitiar, bloquear.

beleaguerer [-œr], *s.;* **beleaguering,** *a.* sitiador.

belemnite [belémnait], *s.* (min.) belemnita.

belfry [bélfri], *s.* campanario.

Belgian [bélyian], *s.* y *a.* belga.

Belial [bílial], *s.* Belial; Satanás; ángel caído.

belibel [biláibel], *va.* calumniar.

belie [biláí], *va.* desmentir; dar un mentís a; calumniar; disfrazar.

belief [bilíf], *s.* fe, creencia, crédito; confianza; credo, religión; opinión, parecer.

believable [bilívabœl], *a.* creíble.

believe [bilív], *va.* y *vn.* creer; confiar en o fiarse de; opinar.—**to b. in,** creer en; ser partidario de; aprobar; tener fe en o a.

believer [bilívœr], *s.* creyente, fiel.

believingly [bilívingli], *adv.* con fe o creencia, confiadamente.

belike [biláik], *adv.* quizá, acaso, tal vez.

belittle [bilítœl], *va.* deprimir, achicar, dar escasa importancia.

bell [bel], *s.* campana; campanilla; (elec.) timbre; esquila o cencerro; cascabel; campanada.— **b. bird,** (ornit.) campanero.—**b. boy,** muchacho, mozo de hotel encargado de llevar recados, etc.— **b. cow, horse, mule,** julo.—**b. crank,** palanca angular o de brazos en ángulo recto.—**b.-faced,** de cabeza convexa (apl. a martillos).—**b. glass,** campana de cristal.—**b. metal,** bronce de campanas.—**b.-mouthed,** abocinado, acampanado.— **b. pull,** cuerda de campana.—**b. punch,** sacabocados con timbre.—**b. ringer,** campanero.—**b. rope** = B. PULL.—**b. tree,** (mús.) chinascos.—to **bear away the b.,** ganar el premio.—**to bear the b.,** ser el primero, ir en la delantera.—**to deserve the b.,** merecer el premio, los honores, etc. —**to lose the b.,** perder el premio.

bell, *vn.* (bot.) crecer en figura de campana.

belladonna [beladóna], *s.* (bot.) belladama o belladona.

belle [bel], *sf.* beldad, mujer bella.

belles-lettres [bel-letr], *s.* bellas letras.

bellflower [bélfláucœr], *s.* (bot.) ruiponce o reponchigo; campanilla; variedad de manzana.

bellhanger [béljænguer], *s.* campanillero.

bellhanging [-ing], *s.* instalación de campanas.

bellicose [bélicos], *a.* belicoso, bélico, guerrero.

bellied [bélid], *a.* ventrudo, barrigón; panzudo; combado, convexo.

belligerent [belíycœrent]. **I.** *s.* beligerante. **II.** *a.* beligerante, belicoso, guerrero.

bellman [bélman], *s.* pregonero.

bellow [bélo], *vn.* bramar, berrear, mugir, rugir.

bellower [bélocœr], *s.* bramador.

bellowing [-ing], *s.* bufido, bramido rugido.

bellows [bélos], *s.* (*sing.* y *pl.*) fuelle.—**b. maker,** barquinero.

belluppadoer [bélueóœr], *s.* manso.

belly [béli], *s.* (*pl.* BELLIES) vientre; barriga, panza; estómago; seno; entrañas; combadura, barriga de una botella, etc.; frente, parte anterior; base; caja de eje; (min.) ensanche (de una veta).—**b. god,** glotón.—**b.-pinched,** ham-

briento.—**b. worm,** lombriz intestinal. **I.** *vn.*
pandear. **II.** *va.* combar, inflar, hinchar.

bellyache [-eik], *s.* (fam. o vulg.) dolor de barriga.

bellyband [-bænd], *s.* cincho; ventrera, tripera.

bellybound [-baund], *a.* estreñido de vientre.

bellyful [-ful], *s.* panzada, hartazgo.

bellypinch [-pinch], *s.* dolor de estómago causado por hambre.

belong [bilóng], *vn.* pertenecer; tocar, atañer, concernir, incumbir; residir en, ser natural de.—**to b. in,** pertenecer a (una clase, etc.).

belonging [bilónging]. **I.** *a.* perteneciente. **II,** *s.* pertenencia, propiedad.—*pl.* anexos, anexidades; bártulos.

beloved [bilʊ́vt], *pp.* de BELOVE, amado; [bilʊ́ved]. **I.** *a.* caro, dilecto, querido, amado. **II.** *s.* persona amada.

below [biló]. **I.** *adv.* abajo, bajo, debajo, más abajo; en el infierno. **II.** *prep.* bajo, debajo de, después de.

belt [belt]. **I.** *s.* cinto o cinturón, faja, ceñidor, pretina; (mec.) correa de transmisión; (geog.) zona, faja.—**b. line,** *o* **b. railroad,** vía de circunvalación.—**b. saw,** sierra de cinta. **II.** *va.* faiar; cercar, rodear.

belting [bélting], *s.* correaje, correas de transmisión.

beluga [belúga], *s.* (ict.) ballena blanca; esturión blanco.

belvedere [bélvedíœr], *s.* torre, mirador.

bemire [bimáiœr], *va.* enlodar, embarrar, atarquinar, encenagar, emporcar.

bemoan [bimóun], *va.* lamentar, deplorar.

bemoaner [bimóunœr], *s.* lamentador, plañidor.

bemoaning [-ing], *s.* lamento, lamentación.

bench [bench]. **I.** *s.* banco, banca; banco de carpintero; tabla, saliente horizontal; escalón, banqueta; plataforma o serie de bancos para la exhibición de animales; ramo, división (de un cuerpo deliberante, etc.); (for.) tribunal; (top.), =B. MARK.—**b. hardening,** estiramiento del alambre después de recocido.—**b. mark,** (top.) punto de referencia de cota conocida.—**b. plane,** garlopa.—**b. root,** (agr.) raíces trabadas o deformadas.—**b. screw,** tornillo de banco.—**b. show,** exposición de perros u otros animales.—**b. warrant,** auto de prisión.—**the King's,** *o* **Queen's, B.,** tribunal superior de justicia. **II.** *va.* exhibir (animales); proveer de bancos, etc.; poner en un tribunal. **III.** *vn.* ser miembro de un tribunal.

bencher [bénchœr], *s.* decano de los colegios de abogados; frecuentador de tabernas.

bend [bend]. **I.** *va.* (*pret.* y *pp.* BENT) encorvar, doblar, plegar, torcer, combar, empandar, acodillar; dirigir o encaminar; inclinar (la cabeza); dedicar, aplicar; doblegar, sujetar, vencer; humillar, hacer bajar; (mar.) entalingar, amarrar.—**to b. the brow,** fruncir el entrecejo.—**to b. the oars,** hacer fuerza de remos. **II.** *vn.* encorvarse, doblarse, torcerse; doblegarse, someterse. **III.** *s.* comba, encorvadura, curvatura; vuelta, curva; codillo; (mar.) nudo; gaza; (blas.) barra.

bendable [béndabœl], *a.* flexible, plegable.

bender [béndœr], *s.* torcedor; doblador; flexor.

bending [bénding]. **I.** *s.* comba; codillo; inflexión, cimbreo; declive; rodeo, vuelta. **II.** *a.* de flexión.—**b. moment,** (mec.) momento flexor.—**b. strength,** resistencia a la flexión.

Bendix drive [béndix dráive], (aut.) transmisión Béndix.

beneath [biníz], *adv.* y *prep.* bajo, debajo, abajo; en lo más hondo.

benedick [bénedic], **benedict** [-dict], *s.* recién casado.

benedictine [-díctin], *s.* y *a.* benedictino, benito.

benediction [-dicshʊn], *s.* bendición.

benefactor [-féctor], *s.* benefactor, bienhechor; fundador; patrón.—**benefaction** [-fécshʊn], *s.* beneficio, favor, gracia, merced.—**benefactress** [-féctres], *sf.* bienhechora; fundadora, patrona.

benefice [bénefis], *s.* (igl.) beneficio, prebenda.

beneficed [bénefist], *a.* (igl.) beneficiado, prebendado.

beneficence [bénéfisens], *s.* beneficencia; caridad.

beneficent [bénéfisent], *a.* benéfico.

beneficently [-li], *adv.* benéficamente.

beneficial [benefíshal], *a.* beneficioso, provechoso, ventajoso.—**beneficially** [-li], *adv.* provechosamente.

beneficiary [benefíshiari]. **I.** *s.* beneficiario; (igl.) beneficiado; portador de una libranza postal. **II.** *a.* beneficial.

benefit [bénefit]. **I.** *s.* beneficio, utilidad, provecho, ventaja; pro, bien, privilegio; gracia; (teat.) función de beneficio. **II.** *va.* beneficiar, aprovechar. **III.** *vn.* aprovecharse o utilizarse; prevalerse.

benevolence [bénévolens], *s.* benevolencia, gracia, merced.

benevolent [bénévolent], *a.* benévolo, caritativo; gracioso.—**benevolently** [-li], *adv.* benévolamente.

Bengal [bengól], *s.* (tej.) Bengala.—**B. light,** luz de Bengala.—**B. rose** = MONTHLY ROSE.

Bengalee [bengalí], *s.* y *a.* bengalí.

benight [bináit], *va.* cogerle a uno la noche; obscurecer.

benighted [bináited], *a.* anochecido; descarriado, extraviado; ignorante.

benign [bináin], *a.* benigno, afable, humano; (med.) benigno, ligero.

benignant [bínígnant], *a.* benéfico, propicio, saludable.

benignity [bínígniti], *s.* benignidad, bondad, dulzura; salubridad.

benignly [bináinli], *adv.* benignamente.

benison [bénisʊn], *s.* (bot.) benjuí.

benjamin [bényamin], *s.* (bot.) benjuí.

bent [bent]. **I.** *s.* encorvadura, curvatura, comba; inclinación, propensión; grado máximo de tensión; (ing.) palizada o sostén de viaducto. **II.** *a.* encorvado, torcido, combo, gacho; inclinado, determinado, resuelto.—**b. on,** *o* **upon,** resuelto a, empeñado en.

benthos [bénzos], *s.* (biol.) fauna y flora del fondo del mar.

benumb [binʊm], *va.* entorpecer, pasmar, entumecer, envarar, aterir.

benumbedness [binʊ́mednes], **benumbment** [-ment], *s.* entumecimiento, insensibilidad.

benzaldehyde [bensǽldijaid], *s.* aldehido benzoico.

benzene [bénsin], *s.* bencina (C_6H_6).—**b. nucleus, b. ring,** núcleo o anillo bencénico, hexágono o fórmula de Kekulé.

benzil [bénsil], *s.* (quím.) bencilo.—**benzilic** [bensílic], *a.* bencílico.

benzin, benzine [bénsin], *s.* bencina (gen. la del petróleo).

benzoate [bénsoeit], *s.* benzoato.

benzoic [bénsoic], *a.* benzoico.

benzoin [bénsoin], *s.* (quím.) benzoína; (bot.), =SPICEBUSH.

benzol, benzole [bénsoul], *s.* benzol.

benzolin [bénsolin], *s.* benzol.

bequeath [bikuíz], *va.* (for.) dejar, legar (en testamento); transmitir.

bequeather [bikuízœr], *s.* testador.

bequest [bikuést], *s.* (for.) manda, donación o legado.

berate [birréit], *va.* zaherir, reñir, regañar, poner a uno como nuevo.

Berber [bérbœr], *s.* bereber, berberisco.

Berberidaceæ [bœrbœridéisii], *s. pl.* (bot.) berberídeas.

berberine [bœrbœrin], *s.* (quím.) berberina.

Berberis [bœrbœris], *s.* (bot.) berberis.

bereave [birív], *va.* despojar, privar; desolar, acongojar.

bereavement [birívmœnt], *s.* pérdida muy sensible, privación, despojo, desamparo; aflicción, desgracia, luto, duelo.

berg [bœrg], *s.* témpano de hielo.

bergamot [bœrgamot], *s.* (bot.) bergamota (pera); el bergamoto y su fruto; tapiz ordinario; rapé perfumado con bergamota.

beriberi [béribéri], s. beriberi.

berm [bœrm], s. (fort.) lisera, berma.

Berlin [bérlin], s. berlina.—**B. blue,** azul de Prusia.—**B. wool,** estambre.

bernicle [bœrnicœl], s. V. BARNACLE.

berry [bérri]. **I.** s. baya; grano (de café, etc.).— **Avignon b.'s,** granas de Aviñón, pizacantas. **II.** vn. producir bayas; coger fresas, moras, etc.

berth [bœrz]. **I.** s. (mar. y f. c.) litera; camarote; (mar.) anclaje, amarradero; (fam.) empleo, destino.—**to give a wide b. to,** apartarse de. **II.** va. proporcionar o dar litera, anclaje o empleo.

Bertha [bérzæ], s. (fam.) Berta, gran granada Krupp; cañón Krupp de gran calibre.

berthage [bœrzeɣ], s. anclaje.

berthing [bœrþing], s. disposición de los camarotes y literas en un buque o tren; (mar.) anclaje; obra muerta.

beryl [béril], s. (min.) berilo, agua marina.

beryllium [berílium], a. (quím.) glucinio.

beseech [bisích], va. suplicar, rogar, implorar.

beseecher [bisíchœr], s. rogador, suplicante.

beseeching [bisíching]. **I.** s. ruego, súplica. **II.** a. suplicante, de súplica.

beseem [bisím]. **I.** va. cuadrar, parecer bien. **II.** vn. aparecerse, parecer.

beseemly [bisímli], a. decoroso, gracioso, decente.

beset [bisét]. **I.** va. (pret. y pp. BESET) acosar, perseguir; bloquear, obstruir; rodear. **II.** a. adornado, engastado, recamado.

beside [bisáid]. **I.** adv. cerca, al lado, a la mano. **II.** prep. al lado de; en comparación de.—**b. himself,** fuera de sí.

besides [bisáidŝ]. **I.** adv. además, también. **II.** prep. además de.

besiege [bisíɣ], va. (mil.) sitiar; (fig.) asediar; acosar.—**besieger** [-œr], s. sitiador; asediador.

besmear [bismíœr], va. ensuciar, embadurnar.

besmearer [bismíœrœr], va. embadurnador.

besmirch [bismœrch], va. manchar; ensuciar.

besom [bísum], s. escoba.

besot [bisót], va. embeleñar; entontecer; embrutecer; infatuar.

besottedly [bisótedli], adv. estúpidamente; fatuamente.

besottedness [bisótednes], s. entontecimiento, embrutecimiento.

besought [bisót], pret. y pp. de TO BESEECH.

bespangle [bispángœl], va. adornar con lentejuelas.

bespatter [bispætœr], va. salpicar, manchar; disfamar.

bespeak [bispík], va. (pret. BESPOKE; pp. BESPOKE O BESPOKEN) encomendar, encargar, apalabrar; indicar, demostrar; (poét.) hablar a.

bespread [bispréd], va. cubrir.

besprent [bisprént], a. (poét.) rociado, esparcido.

besprinkle [bispríngkœl], va. rociar, regar.

besprinkler [bispríngklœr], s. rociador.

Bessemer [bésemœr], s. acero Béssemer.—**B. iron,** fundición Béssemer, fundición pobre en fósforo.—**B. process,** procedimiento Béssemer.— **B. steel,** acero Béssemer.

bessemerize [bésemœraiŝ], va. someter al procedimiento Béssemer.

best [best], a. y adv. super., mejor. Con el artículo *the* forma la frase substantiva the **b.,** el mejor, los mejores, lo mejor.—**b. b.** (abreviado BB), mejor, mejor de primera, mejor de lo mejor—expresión común en la ind. y el com. para indicar productos, sobre todo hierro, de la más alta calidad, y que a menudo se deja en el original inglés, como nombre que describe determinados productos o materiales. De modo análogo se usan second b., segundo de primera, **third b.,** tercero de primera, **common b.,** mejor ordinario, etc.—**b. bower,** (juego) = JOKER; (mar.) ancla de ayuste.—**b. girl,** (fam.) amiga preferida, mujer querida, novia.—**b. man,** padrino de boda.—**b. of all,** mejor que los demás o lo demás; el que o lo que más.—**b. seller,** favorito, el que más se vende o de más venta (apl. sobre todo a libros).—**as b. one can,** como mejor pueda uno.—**at b.,** at the b., a lo más, aun en las mejores circunstancias.—**for the**

b., con las mejores intenciones; conducente o encaminado al bien o a buenas cosas (everything is for the best, todo sucede para los mejores fines, todo resulta bien a la larga).—**it is b.,** eso es lo mejor; lo mejor es.—**to be at one's b.,** estar en su máximo, obrar con su acostumbrada habilidad o maestría, hacer lo mejor.

bestead [bistéd]. **I.** va. y vn. (pret. BESTEADED; pp. BESTEADED O BESTED) beneficiar, aprovechar, servir. **II.** va. (pp. BESTED O BESTEAD) rodear, cercar, acosar. En esta acepción sólo se usa el participio.

bestial [béstial], a. bestial, brutal.—**bestiality** [bestiáliti], s. brutalidad.—**bestialize** [béstialaiŝ], va. embrutecer.—**bestially** [béstiali], adv. bestialmente.

bestir [bistœr], va. mover; incitar.

bestow [bistó], va. conferir, otorgar, agraciar; regalar; emplear, gastar.

bestowal [bistóal], s. dádiva, presente, gracia.

bestower [bistóœr], s. donador.

bestride [bistráid], va. (pret. BESTRODE O BESTRID; pp. BESTRIDDEN O BESTRODE) montar a horcajadas en; cruzar de un tranco.

bestrew, bestrow [bistrú, bistró], va. (pret. BESTREWED; pp. BESTREWED O BESTREWN) rociar, esparcir, derramar.

bet [bet]. **I.** s. apuesta. **II.** vn. apostar.—**to b. on,** apostar a. **II.** va. apostar, ir (en el juego).— **you b.,** o **you b. your life,** (fam.) ya lo creo, sin la menor duda.

beta [béitæ, bí-], s. beta (letra griega).—**b. rays,** (fís.) rayos beta.

betake [bitéic], vr. (pret. BETOOK; pp. BETAKEN) recurrir, acudir; irse, trasladarse; aplicarse a, darse a, emprender.

betel, beti [bítœl], s. (bot.) betel.—**b. nut,** fruto de la areca.

bethel [bézel], s. capilla para marineros.

bethink [bizínk]. **I.** va. (pret. y pp. BETHOUGHT) recordar. **II.** vn. pensar, reflexionar.

Bethlehem, Bethlehemite, V. BEDLAM, BEDLAMITE.

betide [bitáid]. **I.** va. pronosticar, ser señal de, presagiar. indicar. **II.** vn. suceder, acontecer.

betime [betáim], **betimes** [betáimŝ], adv. con tiempo, en sazón; pronto.

betoken [bitókœn], va. significar; representar; prometer, dar muestras de.

betony [bétoni], s. (bot.) betónica.

betook [bitúk], pret. de TO BETAKE.

betray [bitréi], va. traicionar, vender; revelar, descubrir; violar, seducir; mostrar, dejar ver.

betrayal [bitréal], **betrayment** [bitrémœnt], s. traición, perfidia; seducción, violación; abuso de confianza.

betrayer [bitréœr], s. traidor, descubridor.

betroth [bitróz], va. desposarse, contraer esponsales; dar palabra de casamiento.—**betrothal** [bitrózal], s. esponsales, desposorio.—**betrothed** [bitrózt], pp. y s. prometido, novio.

better [bétœr]. **I.** a. y adv. compar., mejor.— **b. and b.,** de mejor a mejor.—**b. half,** cara mitad (esposo o esposa).—**b. off,** en mejores circunstancias; más acomodado; mejor librado. **II.** s. superioridad, ventaja; persona superior (a uno).— **for the b.,** hacia cosas o condiciones mejores.—**so much the b.,** tanto mejor.—**to be b. than,** ser mejor que; valer más que.—**to change for the b.,** mejorar, mejorarse.—**to get the b. of,** ganarle a, vencer a.—**our betters,** nuestros superiores. **III.** va. mejorar.—**to b. oneself,** mejorar de situación, adelantar. **IV.** vn. mejorar, progresar.

better o **bettor,** s. apostador, ponedor.

betterment [bétœrmœnt], s. mejora, mejoría; mejoramiento, adelantamiento.

betting [béting], s. apuesta; (el) apostar.

betty [béti], s. cominero; (E. U.) matraz.

Betulaceæ [bétiuléisii], s. pl. (bot.) betuláceas.

betulin [bétiulin], s. (quím.) betulina.

between [bituín], **betwixt** [-tuíxt], **I.** adv. en medio, entremedias, entre los dos. **II.** prep. entre.—**b. decks,** (mar.) entrepuentes.—**b. you and me,** entre nos.

bevel [bévœl]. **I.** *s.* bisel, chaflán; derrame, sesgo (de puerta o ventana); falsa escuadra; rueda dentada cónica.—**b. gear, b. gearing,** engranaje cónico.—**b. protactor, b. square,** falsa escuadra.—**b. wheel,** rueda cónica de engranaje. **II.** *a.* chaflanado, biselado. **III.** *va.* chaflanar, biselar; inclinar; (arq.) falsear. **IV.** *vn.* inclinarse.

bevelling [-ing], *s.* chaflán, bisel; (arq.) falseo.

beverage [bévœrey], *s.* brebaje, bebida.

bevy [bévi], *s.* bandada; grupo de mujeres.

bewail [biuéil]. **I.** *va.* lamentar, deplorar. **II.** *vn.* plañir.

bewailing [biuéiling], *s.* lamentación, lloro.

beware [biuéar]. **I.** *va.* (*defect.; sólo se usan el imp. y el imper.*) guardarse de, cuidarse de, estar alerta contra. **II.** *vn.* guardarse, recelarse, precaverse.

bewilder [biuíldœr], *va.* aturdir, aturrullar, azorar, dejar perplejo.—**bewilderment** [-mœnt], *s.* aturdimiento, azoramiento, perplejidad.

bewitch [biuích], *va.* embrujar, aojar; encantar, hechizar, arrobar, fascinar, embelesar.—**bewitcher** [-chœr], *s.* encantador, brujo, hechicero.—**bewitchment** [-mœnt], *s.* encantamiento, hechizo; aojo; embeleso, encanto.—**bewitching** [-ching], *a.* encantador, hechicero.—**bewitchingly** [-chingli], *adv.* de un modo encantador.

bey [béi], *s.* bey, gobernador turco.

beyond [biyónd]. **I.** *adv.* más allá, más lejos. **II.** *a.* de más allá; de ultratumba. **III.** *s.* lo que está más allá; vida futura. **IV.** *prep.* más allá de, tras; fuera de; superior a; no capaz o susceptible de.—**b. compare,** incomparablemente.—**b. doubt,** fuera de duda.—**b. expression,** indeciblemente.—**b. measure,** excesiva o desmesuradamente.

bezant [bišánt], *s.* moneda bizantina; (blas.) bezante, roel.

bezel [bésel]. **I.** *va.* sesgar, abiselar, chaflanar. **II.** *s.* bisel; (joy.) engaste; faceta o bisel; sello de oro grabado.

bezique [bešíc], *s.* juego de naipes.

bezoar [bízoœr], *s.* bezar o bezoar; antídoto.

bezoardic [bešoárdic], *a.* bezoárico.

bi- [bai], *prefijo* que significa dos o doble; (quím.) bi-, di-.

biangular [baiánguiular], *a.* biangular.

biannual [baiániuœl], *a.* semianual, semestral.

bias [báias]. **I.** *s.* sesgo, oblicuidad; parcialidad, preferencia, predisposición, prejuicio.—**to cut on the b.,** cortar al sesgo. **II.** *a.* sesgado. **III.** *va.* (*pret. y pp.* BIASED o BIASSED) influir, predisponer, torcer.

bib [bib]. **I.** *s.* babador, babero, pechero. **II.** *va.* beber a menudo, beborrotear.

bibasic [baibésic], *a.* (quím.) bibásico.

bibb [bib], **bibcock** [bíbcóc], *s.* grifo de boca dirigida hacia abajo.

bibber [bíbœr], *s.* bebedor, chispero.

Bible [báibœl], *s.* Biblia.—**B. Christian** = BRYANITE.—**B.,** *o* **b., paper,** papel indio, especie de papel para libros ligero, delgado, opaco y durable.—**B. text,** (imp.) texto (tipo).

biblical [bíblical], *a.* bíblico.

bibliographer [bibliógrafœr], *s.* bibliógrafo.

bibliographical [bíbliográfical], *a.* bibliográfico.

bibliography [bibliógrafi], *s.* bibliografía.

bibliomania [bíbliománia], *s.* bibliomanía.

bibliomaniac [bíbliomániac], *s.* bibliómano.

bibliophile [bíbliofail], *s.* bibliófilo.

bibliopolist [bibliópolist], *s.* librero.

bibulous [bíbiulus], *a.* bebedor, borrachín; relativo al beber; absorbente.

bicapsular [baicápsiular], *a.* (bot.) bicapsular.

bicarbonate [baicárbonet], *s.* bicarbonato.

bice [báis], *s.* azul de Armenia.

bicentenary [baisénteneri], **bicentennial** [-senténiœl]. **I.** *a.* que ocurre cada 200 años. **II.** *s.* segundo centenario.

bicephalous [baiséfalus], *a.* bicéfalo.

biceps [báiseps], *s.* (anat.) biceps.

bichloride [baiclórid], *s.* (quím.) bicloruro.

bichromate [baicrómet], *s.* (quím.) bicromato.

bicker [bíkœr]. **I.** *vn.* altercar, argumentar trivialmente; correr murmurando (como un arroyo); charlar, gorjear (como los pájaros). **II.** *s.* altercado, quisquilla, discusión ociosa; corrida.—**bickerer** [-œr], *s.* camorrista.—**bickering** [-ing], *s.* disputa ociosa, guerra de palabras.

bickern [bíkœrn], *s.* pico de bigornia.

biconcave [baicónkev], *a.* bicóncavo.

biconvex [baicónvex], *a.* biconvexo.

bicornous [baicórnus], *a.* bicorne.

bicron [báicrun], *s.* (fís.) bicrón, milimicrón, millonésima de milímetro.

bicuspid [baikúspid]. **I.** *a.* bicúspide. **II.** *s.* la muela inmediata al colmillo.

bicycle [báisikœl]. **I.** *s.* bicicleta. **II.** *vn.* andar en bicicleta.

bicycling [báisikling], *s.* biciclismo.

bicyclist, bicycler [báisiklist, -œr], *s.* biciclista.

bid [bid]. **I.** *s.* postura, licitación. **II.** *va.* (*pret.* BADE, BAD o BID; *pp.* BIDDEN o BID) ofrecer, pujar, licitar; pedir, rogar, convidar; mandar, ordenar; proclamar; dar (la bienvenida, el saludo, etc.).—**to b. adieu, farewell, good-bye,** decir adiós a, despedirse de.—**to b. defiance,** desafiar.—**to b. in,** pujar fraudulentamente para hacer subir el precio.—**to b. up,** pujar u ofrecer más. **III.** *vn.* pujar.—**to b. fair,** prometer, dar indicios de o tener probabilidad de.

bidder [bídœr], *s.* postor, licitador, pujador.—**the highest b.,** el mejor postor.

bidding [bíding], *s.* orden, mandato; invitación; licitación, postura.

bide [báid]. **I.** *va.* (*pp.* BIDED, o BODE) esperar, aguardar; sufrir, aguantar. **II.** *vn.* residir.—**to b. by,** sostenerse en, cumplir con.

bidental [baidéntal], *a.* bidentado.

bidet [bidét], *s.* caballito, jaca; bidé.

biding [báiding], *s.* espera; residencia, estancia.

biennial [baiénnial]. **I.** *a.* bienal, dosañal. **II.** *s.* planta bienal; exámenes bienales.

bier [bíœr], *s.* andas funerales, féretro.

bifer [báifœr], *s.* planta que produce flores o frutos dos veces al año.—**biferous** [-us], *a.* que da dos cosechas al año.

bifilar [baifáilœr], *a.* bifilar.

bifurcate(d [baifœrket(ed], *a.* bifurcado.

bifurcation [baifœrkéshun], *s.* bifurcación.

big [big], *a.* grande, abultado, voluminoso; lleno; preñada; hinchado, fatuo.—**b. brother,** hermano mayor o grande, considerado como protector, etc.—**b. bug,** (fam.) persona de influencia o importancia.—**b. end,** (m. v.) cabeza (de la biela).—**b. game,** animales de caza mayor.—**b. gun,** (fam.) = **b.** BUG.—**b. head,** (fam.), envanecimiento.—**b. jaw,** antinomicosis (enfermedad del ganado).—**b.-sounding,** altisonante.—**b. words,** disputa acalorada, palabras mayores; palabras altisonantes.—**to speak, o talk, b.,** (fam.) echaria de savihondo o importante; echar roncas o bravatas. Con participios derivados de substantivos, indica gran tamaño del objeto denotado por el substantivo: *big-mouthed,* boquigrande; *big-bellied,* barrigón; *big-ended,* de extremo grande; *big-footed,* de pies grandes.

bigamist [bígamist], *s.* bígamo.

bigamy [bígami], *s.* bigamia.

bigger [bígœr], *a. compar.* de BIG: mayor, más grande.—**biggest** [biguest], *a. superl.* de BIG: mayor, más grande.

biggin [bíguin], *s.* cafetera; gorra; capillo de niño.

biggish [bíguish], *a.* grande; presuntuoso.

bighorn [bíghórn], *s.* (zool.) carnero de grandes cuernos (E. U.).

bight [báit], *s.* (mar.) caleta, caney.

bigly [bígli], *adv.* pomposa o engreídamente.

bigness [bígnes], *s.* grandor; gran tamaño; importancia.

bigot [bígot], *s.* fanático.

bigoted [bígoted], *a.* fanático, intolerante.

bigotry [bígotri], *s.* fanatismo, intolerancia.

bilabiate [bailébiet], *a.* bilabiado.

bilander [bílandœr], *s.* (mar.) balandra.

bilateral [bailátœral], *a.* bilateral.

bilberry [bílberi], *s.* (bot.) arándano.

bilbo [bílbo], s. (poet.) espada.
bilboes [bílboŝ], s. pl. cepo con grillos.
bile [báil], s. bilis; cólera, ira, mal genio.—**b. duct,** conducto biliar.
bilestone [báilstóun], s. = GALLSTONE.
bilge [bilγ]. I. vn. (mar.) abrirse una vía de agua, hacer agua; combar; hacer barriga. II. s. (mar.) pantoque, sentina; (ton.) barriga de barril.—**b. pump,** bomba de carena.—**b. water,** agua de pantoque.
biliary [bíliari], a. biliario.
bilingual [bailíngual], a. bilingüe.
bilious [bílius], a. bilioso.
biliousness [bíliusnes], s. exceso de bilis.
bilk [bilk]. I. va. engañar, defraudar, pegarla. II. s. trampista, estafador; estafa, trampa.
bill [bil]. I. s. proyecto de ley; ley; certificado; escrito, documento; declaración, formulación; pedimento; lista; cartel, aviso; pico (de ave); uña (de ancla); billete de banco: podón, podadera; pica (arma); alabarda (arma); (com.) cuenta, factura; letra; giro; pagaré; (for.) pedimento, reclamo.—**b. book,** (com.) libro de obligaciones (cuentas por pagar, por cobrar, etc.).—**b. broker,** corredor de cambios.—**b. of credit,** carta de crédito; (E. U.) billete de banco emitido por un estado.—**b. of debt,** pagaré en pago de una deuda.—**b. of entry,** cuenta o lista de artículos recibidos en la aduana.—**b. of exchange,** letra de cambio.—**b. of fare,** lista de platos o comidas.—**b. of health,** patente o certificado de sanidad.—**b. of indictment,** (for.) acusación oficial escrita.—**b. of lading,** conocimiento de embarque.—**b. of material,** (const.) lista de material o de piezas.—**b. of rights,** declaración de derechos; ley fundamental.—**b. of sale,** escritura de venta.—**b. payable,** obligación por pagar. —**b. receivable,** obligación por cobrar. II. va. cargar en cuenta; enviar una cuenta a; anunciar por carteles. III. vn. acariciarse, besarse (a veces **b. and coo**).
billboard [bílbórd], s. cartelera.
billed [bild], a. picudo.
billet [bílet]. I. s. billete, esquela; zoquete de leña; (mil.) boleta; (fund.) lingote; tocho.— **b. doux,** carta amorosa. II. va. (mil.) alojar, aposentar.
billhead [bíljed], modelo o esqueleto de factura.
billiards [bíliardŝ], s. billar.
billingsgate [bílingŝguet], s. lenguaje bajo y soez (como el que usan las pescaderas en el mercado **Billingsgate** de Londres).
billion [bíliun], s. (arit.) billón, millón de millones (en España e Inglaterra); mil millones (en Francia y los E. U.).
billionth [bíliunz], a. y s. billonésimo.
billow [bílo]. I. s. oleada, ola; onda. II. vn. crecer o hincharse como una ola.
billowy [bíloi], a. ondulado, ondeante, undoso.
billposter [bílpóustœr], s. fijador de carteles.
billy [bíli], s. porra, palitroque; cachiporra.— **b. goat,** (fam.) cabra macho, cabrón.
bilobate [bailóbet], a. de dos lóbulos.
Bimana [bímana o baiméina], s. pl. (zool.) bimanos.—**bimanous** [bímænus], a. bimano.
bimetallic [baimetǽlic], a. bimetálico.
bimetalism [baimétaliŝm], s. bimetalismo.
bimonthly [baimónzli], a. y adv. bimestral (mente), cada dos meses.
bin [bin]. I. s. hucha, arcón, arca; depósito; barril, cajón; sección de una bodega. II. va. guardar en hucha o arcón.
binary [báinari], a. binario, doble.—**b. star,** estrella doble.
binate [báinet], vn. (igl.) binar.
binaural [binóral], a. de dos orejas; para ambos oídos.
bind [báind]. I. va. (pret. y pp. BOUND), atar, apretar, amarrar; juntar, unir; ligar; ceñir; envolver; obligar, precisar; (cir.) vendar; (cost.) ribetear; constipar, restreñir; trabar, trincar; encuadernar; escriturar o contratar (a alguno); (for.) compeler.—**to b. over,** obligar a comparecer ante el juez.—**to b. up in,** dedicarse con afán a (una

cosa). II. vn. endurecerse; trabarse; pegarse; ser obligatorio. III. s. lazo, ligadura; (mús.) ligado.
binder [báindœr], s. encuadernador; atadero; (agr.) atador, agavilladora; (carp.) traviesa, ligazón, amarra; (cost.) ribeteador.
bindery [báindœri], s. taller de encuadernación.
binding [báinding]. I. s. ligazón, ligamiento; venda, tira, faja, cinta, ligadura; encuadernación; (cost.) ribete; galón; (mar.) ligazón.— **full b.,** pasta entera.—**half b.,** media pasta. II. a. obligatorio; valedero; constipante, que estriñe.—**b. post, b. screw,** (elec.) tornillo de conexión o de contacto, borne.—**b. streaks,** (mar.) cuerdas o esloras.
bindweed [báinduid], s. (bot.) corregüela, enredadera, altabaquillo.
binnacle [bínæcœl], s. (mar.) bitácora.
binocle [bínocœl], s. (ópt.) binóculo, gemelos.
binocular [binókiular]. I. a. binocular. II. s. anteojo, microscopio, gemelo, lente, etc., para ambos ojos.
binomial [bainóumiœl]. I. a. de dos nombres; (mat.) binomio.—**b. theorem,** binomio de Newton. II. s. (mat.) binomio.
bioblast [báioblæst], s. = BIOPLASM.
biochemistry [-kémistri], s. bioquímica.—**biochemical** [-micœl], a. bioquímico.
biodynamics [báiodainámics], s. biodinámica.
biogenesis [-γénesis], s. (biol.) biogénesis.
biogeny [baióγeni], s. biogenia.
biographer [baióγrafœr], s. biógrafo.
biographical [báioγráfical], a. biográfico.
biography [baióγrafi], s. biografía.
biologic(al [báiolóγic(al], a. biológico.
biology [baióloγi], s. biología.
biologist [baióloγist], s. biólogo.
bionomy [baiónomi], s. bionomía.
bioplasm [báioplaŝm], s. (biol.) bioplasma, protoplasma reproductivo.
biostatics [báiostǽtics], s. (biol.) estudio de la relación entre estructura y función, biostática (en el sentido descrito).
biota [báiouta], s. seres organizados, o flora y fauna (de una región, época, etc.).
biotite [báiotait], s. (min.) biotita.
bipartible [baipártibœl], a. divisible en dos.
bipartite [baipártait], a. bipartido; de dos partes.
biped [báiped], s. bípedo.
bipedal [bípedal], a. bípede, bípedo.
biplane [báiplein], (aer.) biplano.
bipolar [baipóular], a. bipolar.
biquadratic [báikuodrátic]. I. s. (álg.) ecuación del cuarto grado. II. a. del cuarto grado.
birch [bœrch], s. (bot.) abedul; madera de ese árbol; vara de abedul (como férula).
birchen [bœrchen], a. de abedul.
bird [bœrd], s. ave, pájaro; (fam.) tipo, persona rara o singular.—**b. bolt,** saetilla roma de matar pájaros.—**b. cage,** jaula.—**b.-eyed,** de ojos de pájaro; penetrante, observador.—**b. foot.=B.'S FOOT.—b. louse,** piojillo.—**b. mite,** (ent.) ácaro, arador.—**b. of freedom,** (E. U.) águila.—**b. of Minerva,** buho.—**b. of paradise,** ave del paraíso. —**b. of passage,** ave de paso.—**b. of prey,** ave de rapiña.—**b.'s-eye,** moteado; visto de arriba y rápidamente; general, o sin pormenores; (bot.) ojo de pájaro.—**b.'s-eye view,** vista de pájaro.— **b.'s-foot,** (bot.) pie de pájaro.—**b.'s nest,** nido de pájaro.—**b. tick** = B. MITE.—**a b. in the hand is worth two in the bush,** más vale pájaro en mano que buitre volando.—**birds of a feather flock together,** cada cual con los de su oficio; Dios los cría y ellos se juntan.
bird, vn. andar a caza de pájaros.
birdcall [bœrdcol], s. reclamo; añagaza.
birdcatcher [bœrdcǽchœr], **birder** [bœrdœr], s. pajarero.
birding [bœrding], s. caza de pájaros.—**b. piece,** escopeta.
birdlime [bœrdlaim], s. liga, liria, hisca, ajonje, almuérdago.

---

birdling [-ling], **birdlet** [-let], *s.* pajarillo.
birdman [-mæn], *s.* pajarero; ornitólogo.
birdseed [-sid], *s.* alpiste; cualquier grano menudo de alimentar pájaros.
birectangular [bairrectǽnguiulær], *a.* (mat.) birrectángulo.
birr [bœrr]. **I.** *s.* zumbido. **II.** *vn.* zumbar.
birth [bœrz], *s.* nacimiento; principio, origen; parto, alumbramiento; camada, lechigada; linaje, alcurnia.—**b. control,** limitación del número de nacimientos, o de la fecundidad, prevención voluntaria de la preñez; esterilidad voluntaria.—**b. rate,** natalidad, proporción de nacimientos.—**by b.,** de nacimiento.
birthday [bœrzdé], **birthnight** [bœrznáit], *s.* cumpleaños, natal, natalicio.—**b. present,** cuelga.
birthmark [bœrzmárc], *s.* estigma, marca de nacimiento.
birthplace [bœrzpléis], *s.* suelo nativo.
birthright [bœrzrait], *s.* derechos de nacimiento; naturalidad; primogenitura, mayorazgo.
birthwort [bœrzuœrt], *s.* (bot.) guaco, aristoloquia.
bis [bis], *adv.* e *interj.* bis; repítase; ¡otro!
Biscayan [biskéian], *a.* vizcaíno.
biscuit [bískit], *s.* (Ing.) galleta; (E. U.) bizcocho, molleta.
bisect [baiséct], *va.* bisecar, dividir en dos partes iguales.
bisection [baisécshun], *s.* bisección.
bisector [-tœr], *s.* (mat.) bisectriz.
bisexual [baiséxiual], *a.* (bot.) hermafrodita.
bishop [bíshup]. **I.** *s.* obispo; afil; bebida de vino caliente con especias.—**b.'s lawn,** linón, batista. **II.** *va.* hacer obispo.
bishopric [bíshupric], *s.* obispado, episcopado.
bisk [bisc], *s.* sopa o caldo; guisado a modo de pepitoria.
bismuth [bísmuz], *s.* bismuto.
bison [báisun], *s.* (zool.) bisonte.
bisque [bisk], *s.* =BISK; bizcocho, ventaja.
bister, bistre [bístœr], *s.* tinta de China.
bistort [bístort], *s.* (bot.) bistorta.
bistoury [bísturi], *s.* (cir.) bisturí.
bisulphite [baisúlfait], *s.* bisulfito.
bit [bit]. **I.** *s.* taladro; hoja de corte; bocado del freno; paletón de una llave; parte o porción pequeña; trozo, miaja, pizca, triza, jota; bocadito; poquito; moneda pequeña, ardite.—**b. of a cable,** (mar.) bitadura del cable.—**not a b.,** nada, ni miaja, ni pizca.—**to take the b. between the teeth,** rebelarse; desbocarse. **II.** *va.* enfrenar; refrenar; (mar.) abitar. **III.** *pret.* y *pp.* del verbo TO BITE.
bitbrace [-breis], *s.* =BITSTOCK.
bitch [bich], *s.* perra; (vulg.) ramera.
bite [báit]. **I.** *va.* y *vn.* (*pret.* BIT; *pp.* BITTEN o BIT) morder; picar, mordicar (un insecto); picar (el pez); picar, resquemar (la pimienta, etc.); (mec.) agarrar, sujetar; corroer (un ácido); murmurar o satirizar; engañar, clavar, defraudar.—**to b. the dust,** morder el polvo, morir, caer vencido. **II.** *s.* mordedura, tarascada, dentellada; bocado; picada, picadura; resquemo; (mec.) asimiento, cogedura.
biter [báitœr], *s.* mordedor.
bithulitic [biziulític]. **I.** *a.* (ing.) de piedra partida y betún o asfalto. **II.** *s.* pavimento de este material.
biting [báiting], *a.* penetrante; mordaz; picante, cáustico.—**bitingly** [-li], *adv.* mordazmente, con mofa; satíricamente.—**bitingness** [-nes], *s.* resquemo, causticidad, mordacidad.
bitstock [bítstoc], *s.* manubrio de taladro, berbiquí.
bitt [bit]. **I.** *va.* (mar.) abitar. **II.** *s.* V. BITTS.
bitten, *pp.* del verbo TO BITE.
bitter [bítœr]. **I.** *a.* amargo, áspero; agudo, cruel, severo; mordaz, satírico; rudo; enconado, encarnizado; penoso, desagradable.—**b. cold,** frío picante.—**to the b. end,** sin tregua, hasta vencer o morir, sin piedad. **II.** *s.* amargor, amargo, amargura.—*pl.* **bitters,** licor de raíces amargas.
bitterish [bítœrish], *a.* amargoso.

bitterly [bítœrli], *adv.* amargamente; agriamente, severamente.
bittern [bítœrn], *s.* (orn.) alcaraván, bitor, ardea; agua madre de sal; composición amarga para adulterar la cerveza.
bitterness [bítœrnes], *s.* amargor o amargura; odio, rencor o encono; severidad, dureza de genio; mordacidad.
bittersweet [bítœrsuít], *s.* (bot.) dulcamara.
bittervetch [bítœrvech], *s.* (bot.) alcarceña.
bitterwood [bítœrúd], *s.* (bot.) tiquistiquis.
bitterwort [bítœruœrt], *s.* (bot.) genciana.
bitts, *s. pl.* (mar.) bitas, barraganetes.—**pawl b.,** bitas del linguete.—**topsail b.,** abitones.
bitumen [bitiúmen], *s.* betún.
bituminize [bitiúminaiŝ], *va.* embetunar.
bituminous [bitiúminus], *a.* bituminoso.—**b. coal,** carbón bituminoso, hulla grasa.
bivalence, bivalency [baivéilens, lensi], *s.* (quím.) bivalencia.—**bivalent** [-ent], *a.* bivalente.
bivalve [báivælv], **bivalvular** [baivǽlviular], *a.* bivalvo.
bivouac [bívuœc]. **I.** *s.* (mil.) vivac o vivaque. **II.** *vn.* vivaquear.
biweekly [baiuícli], *a.* quincenal, de cada dos semanas; (erróneamente) bisemanal.
bizarre [bišár], *a.* raro, grotesco.
blab [blæb]. **I.** *va.* revelar, divulgar, parlar. **II.** *vn.* chismear.
blab, blabber [blǽbœr], *s.* chismoso, parlador; hablador.
blabbing [blǽbing], *s.* habladuría.
black [blæc]. **I.** *va.* dar o teñir de negro; dar betún y lustre a (los zapatos), dar bola, embolar. **II.** *vn.* ennegrecerse.
black. **I.** *s.* color negro; negro, el etíope; luto; mancha.—**in b. and white,** por escrito. **II.** *a.* negro, obscuro; horrible, atroz; triste; perverso; lizanado.—**b. and blue,** amoratado, lívido.—**b. art,** nigromancia.—**b. beetle,** cucaracha.—**b. bread,** pan de centeno.—**b. cattle,** ganado vacuno.—**b. death,** (hist.) la peste europea del siglo XIV.—**b. eye,** ojo amoratado por un golpe.—**b.-eyed,** ojinegro.—**b.-eyed pea,** garbanzo.—**b.-faced,** carinegro.—**b. friar,** fraile dominicano.—**B. Friday,** viernes santo; viernes aciago o fatal.—**b.-haired,** pelinegro.—**b.-hearted,** perverso, malvado.—**b. lead,** grafito; lápiz.—**b. letter,** letra gótica antigua.—**b. list,** lista de personas sospechosas, enemigas, etc.—**b. Maria,** (fam.) vagón negro de prisión; (mil.) granada humeante.—**b. pepper,** pimienta negra.—**b. pudding,** morcilla.—**b. rust,** (agr.) carbón (honguillo y enfermedad que causa).—**b. sheep,** el hijo malo.—**b. spruce,** abeto falso o negro.—**b. vomit,** vómito negro, fiebre amarilla.
blackball [blǽcbol]. **I.** *s.* bola negra; bola de betún. **II.** *va.* dar bola negra; votar en contra de; dar bola o betún a (los zapatos).
blackberry [blǽcberi], *s.* (bot.) zarza; zarzamora.
blackbird [blǽcbœrd], *s.* (orn.) mirlo o merla.
blackboard [blǽcbord], *s.* pizarra; encerado.
blackcap [blǽccap], *s.* el que lleva gorra negra; (orn.) alondra, silvia; (bot.) frambueso negro y su fruta; enea, espadaña.
blackcock [blǽccóc], *s.* gallo silvestre.
blacken [blǽcœn]. **I.** *va.* dar de negro o teñir de negro; betunar; atezar; ennegrecer u obscurecer; difamar, denigrar. **II.** *vn.* ennegrecerse, obscurecerse.
blackguard [blǽcgard], *s.* (fam.) pillastrón, pelagatos, galopo, tunante, pillo.
blackhead [blǽkjed], *s.* espinilla.
blacking [blǽking], *s.* betún o bola de zapatos.
blackish [blǽkish], *a.* negruzco, bruno.
blackjack [blǽcyæc], *s.* (bot.) pequeño roble (*v.* BLENDE); pabellón pirata; cachiporra; escudilla de metal charolado.
blackleg [blǽcleg], *s.* petardista; fullero, tramposo; obrero no agremiado; (vet.) morriña negra.

blackly [blǽkli], *adv.* atrozmente.
blackmail [blǽkmeil]. **I.** *s.* chantaje, exacción por medio de amenazas. **II.** *va.* arrancar dinero por chantaje, o sea, con amenaza de escándalo o de denuncia.
blackmailer [-méilœr], chantajista.
blackmailing [-méiling], *s.* chantaje.
blackness [blǽcnes], *s.* negrura; obscuridad.
blacksmith [blǽcsmiz], *s.* herrero, chispero, forjador.—**b.'s shop,** herrería.
blacksnake [blǽcsnéik], *s.* culebra negra; látigo, fuete de cuero retorcido.
blackthorn [blǽczorn], *s.* (bot.) endrino.
bladder [blǽdœr], *s.* vejiga; bolsa; ampolla.—**b. senna,** (bot.)espantalobos.
bladderwort [-uœrt], *s.* (bot.) utricularia.
blade [bled], *s.* hoja de espada, etc.; palla de remo; brinza de hierba; joven calavera, tronera; ala o paleta (de la hélice).
bladebone [bléidboun], *s.* (anat.) omoplato.
bladed [bléded], *a.* que tiene hojas.
bladesmith [blédsmiz], *s.* espadero.
blain [bléin], *s.* llaga, ampolla.
blamable [blémabœl], *a.* culpable, vituperable.
blamableness [blémabœlnes], *s.* culpabilidad.
blamably [blémabli], *adv.* culpablemente.
blame [bléim]. **I.** *va.* culpar, echar la culpa a, censurar, tachar. **II.** *s.* vituperación, reproche, reprobación, censura; culpa, falta.
blameful [-ful], *a.* censurable, culpable; censurador.—**blameless** [-les], *a.* inculpable.—**blamelessly** [-lesli], *adv.* inculpablemente.—**blamelessness** [-lesnes], *s.* inculpabilidad.
blameworthy [bléimuœrϑi], *a.* culpable, censurable.—**blameworthiness** [-nes], *s.* culpabilidad, censurabilidad.
blanch [blǽnch]. **I.** *va.* blanquear; hacer palidecer; (coc.) pelar, mondar; escaldar. **II.** *vn.* blanquear, perder el color; palidecer. **III.** *s.* mineral de plomo incrustado en la roca.
blancher [blǽnchœr], *s.* blanqueador.
blanching [blǽnching], *s.* blanquecimiento, blanqueo.—**b. liquor,** agua de blanquear.
blancmange [blamány], *s.* (Fr.) manjar blanco.
bland [blǽnd], *a.* blando, suave, dulce.
blandish [blǽndish], *va.* engatusar, acariciar, halagar o lisonjear.—**blandisher** [-dishœr], *s.* halagador, lisonjeador.—**blandishment** [-mœnt], *s.* halago, requiebro, zalamería.
blandly [blǽndli], *adv.* blandamente, suavemente.
blandness [blǽndnes], *s.* suavidad, blandura.
blank [blǽnk]. **I.** *a.* en blanco, no escrito; vacío, sin adorno; sin interés; confuso, turbado, pálido, descolorido.—**b. analysis,** análisis preliminar hecho con una substancia que no contiene la que se busca en el análisis principal, a fin de determinar errores debidos a los reactivos.—**b. cartridge,** cartucho sin bala.—**b. signature,** firma en blanco.—**b. tire,** llanta sin pestaña.—**b. verse,** verso libre. **II.** *s.* blanco, espacio, laguna, hueco; (arq.) vano; suerte o cédula de la lotería que no gana nada; papel o forma en blanco; pedazo de tejo o metal de forma apropiada para trabajarlo, tejuelo.
blankly [blǽngkli], *adv.* en blanco.
blankness [blǽngknes], *s.* laguna, espacio; turbación, confusión.
blare [bléar]. **I.** *vn.* sonar a modo de trompeta. **II.** *s.* sonido como de trompeta.
blarney [blárni]. **I.** *s.* adulación, lisonja, zalamería. **II.** *va.* y *vn.* lisonjear.
blasé [blaśé], *a.* hastiado, gastado.
blaspheme [blæsfím]. **I.** *va.* blasfemar; vilipendiar. **II.** *vn.* decir blasfemias, renegar.

blasphemer [blæsfímœr], blasfemo, blasfemador.—**blaspheming** [-fíming], *s.* blasfemia, acto de blasfemar.
blasphemous [blǽsfimus], *a.* blasfemo, impío.—**blasphemously** [-li], *adv.* blasfemamente.
blasphemy [blǽsfimi], *s.* blasfemia, reniego.
blast [blast]. **I.** *s.* ráfaga, golpe de aire; resoplido; soplo (de un fuelle, soplete, etc.); carga de un taladro; voladura (de roca, etc.); explosión; sonido o toque repentino (de corneta, etc.); influjo maligno; tizón, añublo; (fund.) carga, hornada.—**b. draft,** tiro forzado o de ventilador.—**b. furnace,** alto horno.—**b. hole,** (min., etc.) taladro (agujero); (hidrául.) agujero de entrada de una bomba.—**b. indicator, b. meter,** indicador de tiro.—**b. pipe,** tubo de escape.—**at full b.,** a todo tiro, a pleno tiro (apl. a hornos, hogares de caldera, etc.).—**in full b.,** en pleno ejercicio. **II.** *va.* volar, reventar; secar, agostar; añublar, atizonar los granos; maldecir, infamar. **III.** *vn.* secarse, marchitarse, perderse.
blasted [blásted], *a.* marchito; maldito.
blastema [blæstíma], *s.* (biol.) blástema.
blasting [blásting], *s.* (min.) voladura; marchitamiento, marchitez.—**b. fuse,** espoleta de barreno.
blastoderm [blǽstodœrm], *s.* blastodermo.
blastogenesis [-yénesis], *s.* (biol.) blastogénesis.
blastula [blǽstiula], *s.* (biol.) blástula.
blatant [blétant], *a.* bramante; voznglero.
blather [blǽϑœr]. **I.** *va.* y *vn.* charlar, charlatanear. **II.** *s.* charla, charlatanería; charlatán.
blatherskite [-scait], *s.* fanfarrón; fanfarronada.
blaw [blo]. **I.** *vn.* jactarse, fanfarronear. **II.** *va.* adular, lisonjear. **III.** *s.* flor.
blaze [bléiś]. **I.** *s.* llama, llamarada, fogarada, hoguera; luz brillante; ardor; estrella o mancha blanca en la frente del caballo o la vaca; señal hecha en los troncos de los árboles, para servir de guía en un bosque.—**in a b.,** en llamas, resplandeciente. **II.** *va.* templar (acero); encender, inflamar; publicar, proclamar; marcar los árboles para que sirvan de guía en un bosque. **III.** *vn.* encenderse en llama; arder con llama; flamear, resplandecer, lucir.
blazer [bléśœr], *s.* chaqueta ligera de franela o seda; brasero, braserillo.
blazing [bléśing], *a.* flameante; en llamas.
blazon [blésn]. **I.** *va.* publicar, proclamar; blasonar; adornar,decorar. **II.** *s.* blasón; divulgación, publicación.
blazoner [blésnœr], *s.* autor de heráldica; heraldo; blasonador.
blazonry [blésunri], *s.* blasón; boato.
bleach [blích]. **I.** *va.* blanquear al sol, emblanquecer; descolorar. **II.** *vn.* ponerse blanco, descolorirse; palidecer.
bleacher [blíchœr], *s.* blanqueador.
bleachery [blíchœri], *s.* blanquería; (E. U.) gradas o tendido de sol.
bleaching [blíching], *s.* blanqueo, blanqueamiento.—**b. powder,** cloruro de cal.
bleak [blík]. **I.** *a.* desierto, desabrigado, yermo; frío, helado. **II.** *s.* (ict.) albur, alburno.
bleakness [blíknes], *s.* intemperie, destemplanza; frío, frialdad.
blear [blíœr]. **I.** *a.* lagañoso; nublado; bañado en lágrimas.—**b.-eyed,** *a.* legañoso; torpe de entendimiento.
blear, *va.* hacer legañoso ; ofuscar; nublar.
blearness [-nes], *s.* lagaña, turbación de la vista.
bleat [blít]. **I.** *s.* balido. **II.** *vn.* balar.
bleating [blíting], *s.* balido. **II.** *vn.* balante.
bleb [bléb], *s.* ampolla, vejiga.
bled [bled], pret. y pp. de TO BLEED.
bleed [blíd]. **I.** *va.* (pret. y pp. BLED), sangrar (a una persona, una planta, etc.); arrancar dinero a; (fam.) purgar un sablazo. **II.** *vn.* sangrar, echar sangre; derramar su sangre; sufrir; exudar (apl. a las plantas).—**to b. at,** echar sangre por.—**to b. to death,** morir de desangramiento o de hemorragia.
bleeder [blídœr], *s.* sangrador.

bleeding [-ing], *s.* sangría; sangradura.—**b. heart,** (bot.) dicentra.
blemish [blémiŝh]. **I.** *va.* afear, manchar, empañar; denigrar, infamar. **II.** *s.* tacha, defecto, desperfecto, lunar; deshonra, baldón.
blemishless [blémiŝhles], *a.* sin tacha.
blench [blench], *vn.* cejar, recular, retroceder.
blend [blend]. **I.** *va.* (*pp.* BLENDED o BLENT) mezclar, combinar; (pint.) casar colores. **II.** *vn.* mezclarse. **III.** *s.* mezcla, mixtura; (pint.) degradación.
blende [blend], *s.* (min.) blenda.
blender [bléndœr], *s.* mezclador.
blennorrhagia [blenorréyia], *s.* blenorragia.
blennorrhœa [blenorría], *s.* (med.) blenorrea.
blent [blent], *pret.* y *pp.* de TO BLEND.
blenny [bléni], *s.* (zool.) blenia.
blepharitis [blefærítis], *s.* blefaritis.
bless [bles], *va.* bendecir; hacer feliz; santificar, consagrar; alabar, exaltar, glorificar.—**b. me!** *interj.* ¡válgame Dios!—**God bless him,** que Dios lo bendiga, bendito sea.
blessed [blésed], *a.* bendito, santo, santísimo; beato, bienaventurado; feliz; escogido.
blessedly [blésedli], *adv.* bienaventuradamente, dichosamente.
blessedness [blésednes], *s.* felicidad, santidad, beatitud, gloria.
blessing [blésing], *s.* bendición; beneficio, bien; gracia, favor divino; santiguada; culto.
blest, *part. adj.* =BLESSED.
blet [blet]. **I.** *vn.* pasarse, echarse a perder, podrirse (la fruta). **II.** *s.* podredumbre incipiente.
blew [blu], *pret.* del verbo TO BLOW.
blight [bláit]. **I.** *s.* tizón; pulgón; (agr.) añublo; alheña, roña; contratiempo, mala suerte, plaga, **II.** *va.* atizonar, agostar, esterilizar, añublar; ajar, marchitar. **III.** *vn.* atizonarse, añublarse, agostarse.
blind [bláind]. **I.** *a.* ciego; ignorante, insensato; confuso, difícil de entender; tapado, sin salida; oculto, secreto; obscuro, tenebroso.—**b. flange,** placa de tapa de un tubo.—**b. gut,** intestino ciego —**b. man's buff,** juego de la gallina ciega.—**b. of one eye,** tuerto.—**b. side,** el lado de menor peligro aparente.—**b. spot,** (anat.) punto ciego. **II.** *va.* cegar, quitar la vista; obcecar, ofuscar; deslumbrar. **III.** *s.* biombo, pantalla, cancel, postigo, venda, velo, cualquiera cosa que estorba la vista o quita la luz; persiana (de ventana); persona ciega; puesto donde se esconde el cazador; evasiva, pretexto, engaño; disfraz, tapujo.—*pl.* (fort.) blindajes, blinda; anteojeras de los arreos.
blinded [bláinded], *a.* enceguecido, cegado.
blindfold [bláindfold]. **I.** *va.* vendar de ojos; hacer la vista gorda; despistar, ofuscar. **II.** *a.* con los ojos vendados; ofuscado; a ciegas, sin saber. **III.** *s.* ardid, engaño, superchería.
blindly [bláindli], *adv.* ciegamente, a ciegas.
blindness [bláindnes], *s.* ceguedad o ceguera.
blindstitch [bláindstich], *va.* (cost.) coser de modo que no se vean las puntadas.
blink [blink]. **I.** *vn.* pestañear, parpadear; disimular; fulgurar. **II.** *va.* guiñar; mirar con los ojos entreabiertos; eludir, hacer la vista gorda; paliar, cohonestar. **III.** *s.* pestañeo, guiñada; destello, reflejo, ardentía.—*pl.* **blinks,** ardid de caza.
blinkard [blínkard], *s.* cegajoso.
blinker [blínkœr]. **I.** *s.* anteojera; pantalla. **II.** *va.* poner anteojeras a; engañar, ofuscar.
bliss [blis], *s.* gloria, bienaventuranza; felicidad, arrobamiento, deleite.
blissful [blísful], *a.* bienaventurado, dichoso.—**blissfully** [-fuli], *adv.* felizmente.—**blissfulness** [-fulnes], *s.* suprema felicidad.
blissless [blísles], *a.* infeliz, desgraciado.
blister [blístœr], *s.* ampolla, vejiga; vejigatorio, cantárida; cámara de aire o de agua que protege de torpedos la quilla de un acorazado. **D. beetle,** cantárida, carraleja.—**b. copper,** cobre metálico de superficie negra amorfa refinado por calcinación.—**b. fly** =B. BEETLE.—**b., o blistering, plaster,** vejigatorio.—**b. steel,**

acero cementado. **II.** *vn.* ampollarse, avejigarse. **III.** *va.* ampollar; aplicar vejigatorio o cantárida.
blithe [bláiz], **blitheful** [bláizful], *a.* alegre, contento, gozoso.—**blithely** [bláizli], *adv.* alegremente.
blitheness [bláiznes], **blithesomeness** [bláizsumnes], *s.* alegría, júbilo, gozo, jovialidad.
blithesome [-sum], *a.* =BLITHE.
blizzard [blíŝard], *s.* ventisca; descarga cerrada; golpe violento; desastre; respuesta desconcertante; chubasco de nieve.
bloat [blóut]. **I.** *va.* hinchar, henchir; ahumar, curar (arenques, etc.). **II.** *vn.* entumecerse, abotagarse. **III.** *a.* hinchado, abotagado; ahumado.—**IV.** *s.* calavera, borrachín.
bloated [blóuted], *a.* hinchado, abotagado.
bloatedness [-nes], *s.* turgencia, hinchazón.
bloater [blóutœr], *s.* arenque ahumado.
blob [blob], *s.* gota, burbuja, pompa, ampolla.
blobber, blobber lip. *V.* BLUBBER, etc.
bloc [bloc], *s.* grupo político, "bloc."—**in b.,** en una pieza, en monobloque (apl. a los cilindros de un motor, etc.)
block [bloc], *s.* bloque, trozo, canto; bloque de cilindros de un motor (llám. t. **cylinder b.** y **motor b.**); manzana de casas, (Amér.) cuadra; horma de sombrero; estampa, dado; cepo (de yunque); polea; rodaja de polea; refuerzo (tira, tabla, etc.), cuña, calzo (de un cañón, etc.); soporte; armazón de soporte para trozas de madera; número o partida de varias cosas de una misma clase (acciones, etc.); tableta o bloc de papel; división, compartimiento; hilera, fila; boliche o bolín, en el juego de bochas; plataforma en que se vendían los esclavos en subasta; banco patibulario, patíbulo; (fam.) testa, cabeza; (f. c.) tramo, sección o block en un sistema de señales; (imp.) montadura de una plancha electrotípica; plancha o estampa grabada para imprimir en tela o en papel.—**b. and tackle,** aparejo de poleas.—**b. letter** (imp.) tipo de madera.—**b. pavement,** pavimento de bloques.—**b. signal,** (f. c.) señal que gobierna el movimiento de trenes en una sección o block.—**b. system** (f. c.) sistema de señales por secciones o blocks.
block, *va.* bloquear, obstruir, cerrar; (alb.) tapar, tapiar, condenar; (tip.) montar una plancha; cerrar una forma; (sombr.) conformar; (carp.) reforzar un ángulo; calzar una rueda; (dep.) parar la pelota.—**b. in,** o **out,** delinear, esbozar.
blockade [blokéid]. **I.** *s.* bloqueo; bloque; obstrucción. **II.** *va.* bloquear.
blockader [blokéidœr], *s.* bloqueador.
blockhead [blócjed], *s.* tonto, estúpido, mentecato.
blockhouse [blócjaus], *s.* (fort.) blocao, fortín.
blockish [blókiŝh], *a.* estúpido, tonto.
blockishly [-li], *adv.* neciamente, tontamente.
blockishness [-ness], *s.* estupidez, tontería.
blond, blonde, [blond], *a.* y *s.* rubio, blondo.
blood [blud]. **I.** *s.* sangre; linaje o parentesco; ira, cólera; jugo o zumo; vida, temperamento, pasión; carnicería, matanza; hombre animoso; sávia de algunos árboles; caballo de pura raza.—**b. cupping,** ventosa sajada.—**b.-curdling,** horrible.—**b. heat,** calor de sangre.—**b. horse,** caballo de pura raza.—**b. money,** precio que se pagaba como indemnización por un asesinato; dinero que se recibe por ayudar a la muerte o ruina de otro.—**b. red,** color de sangre.—**b. relative,** pariente consanguíneo.—**b. relationship,** consanguinidad.—**b.-stained,** manchado de sangre. —**b. vessel,** vaso sanguíneo. **II.** *va.* sangrar; hacer olfatear sangre a un perro de caza.
blooded [blúded], *a.* que tiene sangre o temperamento de tal o cual carácter; de pura casta, de buena raza.
bloodflower [-fláuœr], *s.* (bot.) flor de la sangre.
bloodguilt, bloodguiltiness [blúdgíltines], *s.* culpable de homicidio.
bloodhound [blúdjaund], *s.* sabueso.
bloodily [blúdili], *adv.* cruentamente, encarnizadamente.
bloodiness [blúdines], *s.* ensangrentamiento, derramamiento de sangre; sanguinolencia; calidad de sangriento.

bloodless [blúdles], *a.* exangüe, desangrado, muerto; incruento.

bloodroot [blúdrut], *s.* (bot.) sanguinaria.

bloodshed [blúdshed], *s.* efusión de sangre; matanza.

bloodshedder [blúdshédœr], *s.* homicida, asesino.

bloodshedding [blúdshéding], *s.* derramamiento de sangre.

bloodshot [blúdshot], *a.* ensangrentado, inyectado de sangre.

bloodstain [blúdstein], *s.* mancha de sangre.

bloodstone [blúdstoun], *s.* (min.) hematites, albín; heliotropo.

bloodsucker [blúdsúkœr], *s.* sanguijuela; usurero.

bloodthirstiness [blúdzœrstines], *s.* encarnizamiento, sed de sangre.

bloodthirsty [blúdzœrsti], *a.* sanguinario, cruel, carnicero.

bloody [blúdi], *a.* sangriento; sanguinario; ensangrentado; sanguinolento; mezclado con o acompañado de sangre.—**b. fiux,** flujo de sangre, disentería.—**B. Mary,** (hist.) María la Sanguinaria (María I de Ingl.).—**b.-minded,** cruel, sanguinario.

bloom [blum]. **I.** *s.* (bot.) floración, florecimiento, florescencia; cualquiera flor; pelusilla de algunas frutas y hojas; belleza, lozanía; pasa de calidad superior; (fund.) tocho, lingote.—**b. of youth,** lozanía de la juventud. **II.** *va.* hacer florecer; abigarrar. **III.** *vn.* florecer; ostentar lozanía.—**to b. out,** eflorecerse.

bloomery [blúmœri], *s.* forja; horno de pudelar.

bloomer [blúmœr], *s.* traje de mujer de falda corta y calzones anchos.—*pl.* calzones cortos y holgados.

blooming [blúming], *a.* lozano, fresco; próspero.
—**bloomingly** [-li], *adv.* florida, prósperamente.

bloomy [blúmi], *a.* florido.

blossom [blósum]. **I.** *s.* (bot.) flor, capullo, botón; floración. **II.** *vn.* florecer, echar flor.

blossomy [-i], *a.* lleno de flores, floreciente.

blot [blot]. **I.** *va.* emborronar, manchar de tinta; ensuciar, empañar; denigrar; secar con papel secante; obscurecer.—**to b. out,** rayar lo escrito, tachar; borrar. **II.** *vn.* correrse la tinta, emborronarse. **III.** *s.* borrón; mancha, mancilla; testación, testadura: en ciertos juegos, peón o jugada arriesgada; lado flaco.

blotch [bloch]. **I.** *s.* mancha, borrón, pintarrajo; roncha. **II.** *va.* marcar o cubrir con manchas o ronchas.

blotter [blótœr], *s.* papel secante; (com.) libro borrador.

blotting paper [-ing péipœr], *s.* papel secante.

blouse [bláus], *s.* blusa.

blow [blo], *s.* golpe; ventarrón, vendabal; soplido, resoplido; trompetazo; (bot.) floración, florescencia; (met.) mineral fundido de una hornada; (fund.) escarabajo. Esta voz se traduce a menudo por medio del sufijo -*azo*: *blow with the fist,* puñetazo; *blow with a hat,* sombrerazo.—**b. lamp,** lámpara de soldar.—**b.-off,** expulsión del agua, vapor, etc., por presión; aparato que sirve para esta operación.—**b.-off valve,** válvula de descarga.—**b.-out,** limpia (de una caldera, etc.) por un chorro de vapor; (elec.) bobina de extinción de chispas (llamada t. **b.-out coil**); (aut.) reventazón, pinchazo.—**at a b., at a single b.,** de una vez, repentinamente.—**to come to blows,** venir a las manos, pelear.

blow. **I.** *va.* (*pret.* BLEW; *pp.* BLOWN) soplar, afollar; inflar, henchir (con aire); tocar (un instrumento de viento); soplar (vidrio); limpiar con un cherro de vapor, aire, etc.; quitar soplando o por presión de vapor, etc.; depositar huevos en (apl. a insectos); divulgar; (fam.) gastar con profusión.—**to b. away,** quitar soplando.—**to b. down,** derribar (apl. al viento).—**to b. in,** meter soplando; (metal.) poner a funcionar.—**to b. off,** (m. v.) vaciar o descargar (una caldera); limpiar con un chorro de vapor, aire, etc.—**to b. one's brains out,** levantarse la tapa de los sesos, darse un tiro.—**to b. one's nose,** sonarse las narices.—

to **b. one's own horn,** *o* **trumpet,** alabarse, celebrar uno sus propias acciones.—**to b. out,** hacer salir soplando; apagar soplando; apagar, o suspender el funcionamiento de (un horno); vaciar o expeler por un chorro de vapor, etc.; (elec.) quemar (un fusible).—**to b. up,** inflar (sentido recto y figurado); volar (una roca, un fuerte); (fam.) regañar. **II.** *vn.* soplar; sonar (una corneta, etc.); jadear; hacer viento (*it blows,* hace viento); (fam.) fanfarronear, echar roncas.—**to b. close,** *o* **shut,** cerrarse por el viento (*the door blew shut,* el viento cerró la puerta).—**to b. great guns,** soplar (el viento) violentamente.—**to b. off,** (m. v.) descargarse.—**to b. out,** apagarse por causa del viento; (aut.) estallar, reventar; (elec.) quemarse, fundirse (un fusible).—**to b. over** disiparse, pasar.—**to b. up,** estallar, reventarse.

blower [blóœr], *s.* soplador, aventador, fuelle; tapadera de chimenea.

blowfly [blóflai], *s.* (ent.) moscarda.

blowgun [blógún], *s.* cerbatana, bodoquera.

blowing [blóing]. **I.** *s.* soplo, soplido; sopladura. **II.** *a.* soplador.—**b. weather,** tiempo tempestuoso.—**b. fan,** soplador rotatorio.

blown [blóun], *pp.* de TO BLOW.

blowout [blóáut], *s.* (aut. y elec.) =BLOW-OUT. *V.* BLOW, s.

blowpipe [-paip], *s.* soplete.

blowtorch [-tórch], *s.* lámpara de soldar.

blowup [blóúp], *s.* (azú), pieza destinada a la disolución del azúcar crudo.—**b. pan,** paila de disolución.

blowze [bláuš], *s.* pandorga, mujer gorda y coloradota.

blowzy [bláuši], *a.* coloradote; desaliñado, sucio.

blubber [blúbœr], *s.* esperma o grasa de ballena; (bot.) ortiga marina; gimoteo.—**b.-lip,** bezo, jeta; (Cuba) bemba.—**b.-lipped,** befudo.

blubber, *vn.* llorar hasta hincharse los carrillos; gimotear.

bluchers [blúchœrs], *s.* borceguíes; botines o medias botas.

bludgeon [blúyun], *s.* porra, garrote, clava.

blue [blu]. **I.** *s.* azul.—*pl.* the blues, esplín, morriña. **II.** *a.* azul; triste, melancólico; severo, estricto, puritánico; fiel, leal; genuino; lívido, amoratado; literata, bachillera.—**B. Book** (Ingl.) Libro Azul (de informes oficiales); (E. U.) registro de los empleados del gobierno.—**b. devils,** alucinación; melancolía.—**b. gum,** (bot.) eucalipto: (med. *pl.*) descoloración de las encías.—**b. jay,** (zool.) azulejo.—**b. laws,** leyes puritánicas severas, sobre todo las relativas a la observancia del domingo.—**b. paper,** papel heliográfico.—**b.-pencil,** *va.* marcar o corregir con lápiz azul; (fam.) desaprobar, criticar.—**b. vitriol,** vitriolo azul.

blue, *va.* azular; pavonar.

bluebird [-bœrd], *s.* (orn.) azulejo.

bluebottle [-bótœl], *s.* (ent.) moscarda; (bot.) azulejo, liebrecilla.

bluefish [-fish], *s.* (ict.) pez de la costa norteamericana del Atlántico.

bluejacket [-yéket], *s.* marinero de buque de guerra.

blueprint [-print], *s.* heliografía.

bluestocking [-stóking], *s.* mujer docta; bachillera, literata, marisabidilla.

bluestone [-stoun], *s.* (quím.) sulfato de cobre, vitriolo azul; (min.) arenisca arcillosa azulosa.

bluet [blúet], *s.* (bot.) planta de flores azuladas.

bluff [bluf]. **I.** *a.* francote; escarpado, enhiesto. **II.** *s.* risco, escarpado, morro, farallón; fanfarronada; (E. U.) lance del juego llamado *poker.* **III.** *va.* rechazar o impedir algo, valiéndose de una baladronada. **IV.** *vn.* alardear, baladronar.

bluffness [blúfnes], *s.* asperidad, rudeza.

bluing [blúing], *s.* azul en pasta para lavandera; añil puro, pavonado.

bluish [blúish], *a.* azulado, azulino.

bluishness [blúishnes], *s.* color azulado.

blunder [blúndœr]. **I.** *vn.* desatinar, disparatar; equivocarse, confundir las especies. **II.** *s.* disparate, equivocación, error craso, patochada.

blunderbuss [blúndœrbus], *s.* trabuco, encaro.

---

blunderer [blúndœrœr], **blunderhead** [blúndœrjed], s. desatinado, atronado.
blunderingly [-ingli], adv. desatinadamente.
blunge [blʊnʤ], va. (cerá.) mezclar la pasta.
blunger [blʊ́nʤœr], s. (cerá.) paleta para mezclar la pasta.
blunt [blʊnt]. **I.** a. embotado, romo, obtuso; brusco; descortés, lerdo.—**to grow b.**, entorpecerse; embotarse. **II.** va. embotar, enromar; calmar o mitigar.
bluntly [-li], adv. sin filo; lisa y llanamente, claramente; bruscamente.
bluntness [blʊ́ntnes], s. embotadura; grosería, brusquedad, aspereza.
blur [blœr]. **I.** s. trazo borroso o confuso; borrón, mancha. **II.** va. hacer borroso o indistinto; embotar, entorpecer; empañar, manchar. **III.** vn. ponerse borroso.
blurred [blœrd], a. borroso, confuso.
blurt [blœrt], va. decir o soltar abruptamente.—**to b. out**, hablar sin consideración.
blush [blʊsh]. **I.** vn. ruborizarse, sonrojarse. **II.** va. enrojar, embermejar; sonrojar. **III.** s. rubor, bochorno, sonrojo; color rojo; ojeada, mirada, vistazo.—**blushful** [-ful], a. encarnado.—**blushing** [-ing], s. sonrojo, rubor.—**blushingly** [-li], adv. ruborosamente.—**blushless** [-les], a. desvergonzado, descarado.
bluster [blʊ́stœr]. **I.** s. ruido, tumulto; jactancia, fanfarria. **II.** vn. soplar con furia; fanfarrear, bravear. **III.** va. proferir con ira.
blusterer [blʊ́stœrœr], s. fanfarrón.
blustering [blʊ́stœring]. **I.** s. = BLUSTER. **II.** a. fanfarrón; jactancioso, hinchado; tempestuoso; tumultuoso.
blusterous [blʊstœrʊs], a. tumultuoso, ruidoso, tempestuoso.
bo [bo], interj. bú.
boa [bóa], s. boa (sierpe); boa (cuello de pieles).
boar [bóar], s. verraco.—**wild b.**, jabalí.
board [bord], s. tabla; tablero; tablilla; mesa; comida, comidas, alimentos; pupilaje; tribunal; consejo, junta; cartón; (mar.) bordo; borda.—pl. **boards**, tablazón; (teat.) escenario, las tablas.—**b. and lodging**, mesa y habitación, cuarto y comidas.—**b. foot** (pl. **b. feet**), unidad de medida para madera—como 2 360 cm. cúb.—**b. measure** medida en board feet.—**b. of admiralty**, almirantazgo.—**b. of directors**, junta directiva.—**b. of education**, junta de educación.—**b. of health**, junta de sanidad.—**b. of trade**, junta de comercio.—**b. of trustees**, junta directiva.—**b. rule**, regla graduada para medir board feet.—**b. wages**, alojamiento y comida en pago de servicios; dinero que se da a los criados para mantenerse; sueldo o salario que escasamente alcanza para vivir.—**b. walk**, entablado de tablas, sobre todo a la orilla del mar.—**(bound) in boards**, (enc.) encartonado.—**on b.**, a bordo.—**to go by the b.**, (mar.) caer un mástil roto por el costado del buque; (fig.) arruinarse por completo, frustrarse, fracasar.
board. I. va. (mar.) abordar; acometer, acercarse a; (carp.) entablar, entarimar, enmaderar; dar manutención por dinero, tomar a pupilaje. **II.** vn. estar a pupilaje.
boardable [bórdabœl], a. accesible, abordable.
boarder [bórdœr], s. huésped, pupilo; (mar.) abordador.
boarding [bórding], s. tablazón; entablado; tabique de tablas; pupilaje; (mar.) abordaje.—**b. house**, casa de huéspedes.—**b. pike** (mar.) chuzo de abordar.—**b. pupil**, o **student**, estudiante interno, pensionista.—**b. school**, escuela de internos.
boarish [bórish], a. brutal, cruel.
boast [bóust]. **I.** vn. alardear, jactarse, vanagloriarse. **II.** va. ponderar, exaltar; ostentar; (esc. y cant.) desbastar. **III.** s. jactancia, ostentación, baladronada.
boaster [bóustœr], s. fanfarrón, jaque.
boastful [bóustful], a. jactancioso.
boasting [bóusting], **boastfulness** [bóustfulnes], s. jactancia, ostentación, ronca.

boastingly [bóustingli], adv. jactanciosamente, ostentosamente.
boastless [bóustles], a. simple, sencillo.
boat [bóut]. **I.** s. (mar.) buque, barco; bote, barca, lancha, batel, chalupa.—**b. hook**, bichero, botador.—**b. house**, casilla de botes.—**b. race**, regata a remos.—**b. seaplane**, aerobote, aeroplano de armadura de flotación. **II.** va. poner o llevar a bordo.—**to b. oars**, desarmar los remos. **III.** vn. navegar, remar, ir en bote.
boatable [bóutabœl], a. navegable para botes; que se puede transportar en botes.
boatage [bóuter], s. barcaje, lanchaje; cabida total de los botes de un buque.
boatful [bóutful], s. barcada.
boating [bóuting], s. ir o pasear en bote; manejo de un bote; transporte en bote.
boatload [bóutlóud], s. barcada.
boatman [bóutman], **boatsman** [bóutsman], s. barquero, botero, lanchero.
boatswain [bóutsuein o (mar.) bósʊn], s. contramaestre.—**b.'s mate**, segundo contramaestre.
bob [bob]. **I.** va. y vn. menear(se) o mover(se) con sacudidas; pescar con anzuelo; desmochar, cercenar; cortar corto (apl. esp. al pelo). **II.** va. golpear con algún objeto redondeado o nudoso; dar con el codo o la mano. **III.** s. corcho y cebo para el anzuelo de pescar; perendengue, zarcillo; borla; plomo de plomada; lenteja o disco del péndulo; (maq.) balancín; saludo, cortesía; toque de campanas; (fam.) chelín (en Inglaterra); cola cortada de un caballo; pelo cortado corto.
bobbin [bóbin], s. canilla, broca; carrete, carretel, argadijo, husillo; (elec.) carrete, bobina.
bobbinet (o **bobbin net**) [bóbinet], s. imitación de encaje.
bobsled [bóbsled], **bobsleigh** [-slei], s. rastra corta; trineo de carga de dos rastras.
bobstay [bóbstéi], s. (mar.) barbiquejo.
bobtail [bóbteil]. **I.** va. cortar la cola a. **II.** a. colimocho; incompleto, insuficiente.—**b. car**, coche pequeño de tranvía. **III.** s. animal colimocho; rabo mocho; populacho, canalla.
bobwhite [bóbjuait], s. (orn.) codorniz común (E. U. del Norte); perdiz (E. U. del Sur).
bobwig [bóbuig], s. peluquín.
bocasine [bócasin], s. bocací delgado.
bode [bóud]. **I.** va. presagiar, pronosticar, presentir. **II.** vn. predecir; prometer.
bodice [bódis], s. corpiño, jubón, cuerpo de vestido, almilla.
bodied [bódid], a. corpóreo.
bodiless [bódiles], a. incorpóreo.
bodiliness [bódilines], s. corporalidad, corporeidad.
bodily [bódili]. **I.** a. corpóreo, corporal; real, verdadero. **II.** adv. corporalmente; en conjunto, en peso.
boding [bóuding], s. presagio, pronóstico. **II.** s. ominoso, presagioso.
bodkin [bódkin], s. (cost.) punzón; pasador de jareta; alfiler para el tocado o sombrero; (imp.) punzón o punta.
body [bódi], s. cuerpo; una persona, un individuo; realidad; cuerpo, gremio, corporación; colección, agregado; cuerpo, espesor (del aceite, etc.), consistencia; cuerpo del vino; caja de un carruaje; (aut.) carrocería (sólo se aplica a coches, no a camiones, de los cuales se dice caja); parte principal o central; (mar.) quilla; vista de la quilla; (aer.) armazón de un aeroplano; (impr.) cuerpo (del tipo).—**b. cloth**, manta para caballos.—**b. of a church**, nave de una iglesia.—**b. of heaven**, cielo.—**b. of water**, extensión de agua.—**b. plan**, (mar.) corte transversal de un buque.—**b. politic**, estado o nación; entidad política.—**b. snatcher**, ladrón de cadáveres.—**b. varnish**, laca de apomazar.
body, va. dar cuerpo o forma a; representar; formar un cuerpo, gremio, etc. de.
bodyguard [-gard], s. guardia de corps.
Bœotian [bióshan], a. beocio.

Boer [búœr], *s.* bóer, del Transvaal.
bog [bog], *s.* pantano, fangal.—**b. bean,** (bot.) trifolio fibrino.—**b. oak,** lignito de encina.—**b. ore,** limonita.
bogey, bogy [bógui], *s.* espectro, espantajo.
boggle [bógucœl]. **I.** *va.* hacer una patochada. **II.** *vn.* recular, retroceder; cejar, vacilar.
boggle, *s.* retroceso de un caballo asustado; objeción, dificultad; patochada.
boggy [bógui], *a.* pantanoso, palustre.
bogie [bógui], *s.* carretilla de un taller de aserrar madera; (f. c.) bogie, truck.—**b. engine,** locomotora con bogie giratorio.
bogland [bóglænd], *s.* tierra pantanosa.
bogus [bógʊs], *a.* (fam. E. U.), falso, espurio.
bohea [bojí], *s.* té de calidad inferior.
Bohemian [bojímian], *a.* y *s.* bohemio.
boil [bóil]. **I.** *va.* y *vn.* hervir; cocer, salcochar, herventar.—**to b. away,** consumir un líquido a fuerza de cocerlo.—**to b. down,** reducir por medio de la cocción; reducir(se) a su más simple forma o expresión; reducir(se) a.—**to b. over,** hervir hasta rebosar.—**to b. the clear,** (azú.) melar. **II.** *s.* hervor, ebullición; (med.) divieso, furúnculo; (Cuba) nacido; (Méx.) clacote.
boiler [bóilœr], *s.* marmita, olla, caldero; paila; (m. v.) caldera; (azú.) tacho.—**b. compound,** (m. v.) antiincrustante, desincrustante, preparación para impedir o quitar incrustaciones.—**b. head,** fondo de caldera.—**b. iron, steel,** palastro de hierro, acero, para calderas.—**b. maker,** calderero.—**b. shell,** cuerpo de caldera.
boiling [bóiling], *s.* hervor, ebullición, cocción, cochura.—**b. kettle,** caldero, marmita, hervidor.—**b. point,** punto de ebullición.
boisterous [bóistœrʊs], *a.* turbulento, ruidoso, tumultuoso; borrascoso.—**boisterously** [-li], *adv.* ruidosamente, tumultuosamente.—**boisterousness** [-nes], *s.* turbulencia, tumulto, vocinglería.
bold [bóuld], *a.* arrojado, denodado, valiente; atrevido, osado, temerario; impudente, descarado; (mar.) escarpado, acantilado.—**b.-faced,** descarado.—**b.-faced type,** (imp.) letra negra, negrilla.
boldface [bóuldfeis], *s.* descaro; persona desfachatada; (imp.) =BOLD-FACED TYPE.
boldly [bóuldli], *adv.* libremente; osadamente, audazmente; descaradamente.
boldness [bóuldnes], *s.* arrojo, intrepidez; descaro; atrevimiento, osadía, audacia.
bole [bóul], *s.* tronco de un árbol; arménico. *V.* BOLL (medida).
boll [bóul]. **I.** *s.* (bot.) cápsula (de algodón, etc.). —**b. weevil,** gorgojo; gorgojo del algodón; gusano capsular del algodón (larva del gorgojo).—**b. worm,** gusano del maíz (que ataca también el algodón). **II.** *vn.* formarse en cápsulas; producir cápsulas.
Bolognese [bólofiiš], *a.* boloñés.
bolometer [bolómitœr], *s.* (elec.) bolómetro, detector bolométrico de ondas.—**bolometric** [bolométric], *a.* bolométrico.
Bolshevik [bólšhevic], *s.* y *a.* bolchevique.—**Bolsheviki** [-viki], *s. pl.* bolcheviques.—**Bolshevikism** [-kišm], **Bolshevism** [-višm], *s.* bolchevismo.—**Bolshevist** [-vist], *a.* bolchevista.—**bolshevize** [-vaiš], *va.* hacer bolchevique; "bolchevicar," "bolcheviquificar."—**Bolshevy** [-vi], *s.* mundo bolchevique, bolchevismo.
bolster [bóulstœr]. **I.** *s.* travesero, almohadón; (Filip.) abrazador; soporte, refuerzo; (cir.) cabezal; (mar.) almohada de los palos; borrenes de la silla de montar; (t. c.) solera de carro; (constr.) travesaño; cancelillo; caballete. **II.** *va.* sostener, reforzar, auxiliar, apoyar.
bolstering [bóulstœring], *s.* apoyadero, apoyo.
bolt [bóult]. **I.** *s.* (cerr.) cerrojo, pasador, pestillo, falleba; (carp.) perno, tornillo grande; (art.) lingote, proyectil cilíndrico; dardo, flecha; centella, rayo; suceso repentino; salto rápido; fuga; pieza o rollo (de paño); (mar.) perno, cabilla; tamiz muy fino para harina; (pol., E. U.) disidencia.—*pl.* bolts, grillos, grilletes. **II.** *adv.* recto como una flecha, rígidamente.—**b. upright,** enhiesto, empinado. **III.** *va.* acerrojar; empernar

encabillar; cerner; examinar, escudriñar; (pol. E. U.) disidir de; engullir, tragar sin mascar; soltar; arrojar, echar. **IV.** *vn.* saltar de repente; lanzarse; resistirse; caer como rayo.—**to b. in,** entrar de repente.—**to b. out,** salir de golpe.
bolter [bóultœr], *s.* cedazo, criba; cordel de pescar; (pol. E. U.) disidente.
bolthead [bóultjed], *s.* (quím.) recipiente.
bolting [bóulting], *s.* cernido o cernidura.—**b. cloth,** tela de cedazo.—**b.-house,** cernedero.—**b-hutch, b.-tub,** tina para cerner harina.
boltrope [bóltróup], *s.* (mar.) relinga.
bolus [bólʊs], *s.* bolo, píldora gruesa; pelotilla, bola; medicamento difícil de tomar.
boma [bóma], *s.* estacada circular.—**b. nut,** nuez africana para curtir.
bomb [bom]. **I.** *s.* (art.) bomba, granada; (piro.) petardo.—**b. carrier,** portabombas.—**b. cell,** (aer.) depósito para bombas.—**b. ketch, o vessel,** (mar.) bombarda.—**b. thrower** (arti.) mortero; (aer.) lanzabombas. **II.** *va.* bombardear, sobre todo desde un avión.
bombard [bombárd], *va.* bombardear.
bombardier [bómbardíœr], *s.* bombardero.—**b. beetle,** escarabajo bombardero o escopetero.
bombardment [bombárdmœnt], *s.* bombardeo.
bombast [bómbast], *s.* ampulosidad.
bombast, bombastic [bombást, ic], *a.* ampuloso, altisonante, retumbante.
bombax [bómbæx], *s.* (bot.) ceiba.
bombazine [bómbašín], *s.* alepín.
bombic [bómbic], *a.* del gusano de seda.
bombproof [bómpruf], *a.* a prueba de granadas.
bombshell [bómšhel], *s.* bomba, granada.
bombycid [bómbisid], *s.* y *a.* (ent.) bombícido.
bombyx [-ix], *s.* (ent.) gusano de seda, bómbice.
bona fide [bóna fáidi], *a.* y *adv.* de buena fe, sin engaño, honradamente.—**bona fides** [-fáidiš], *s.* buena fe, honradez, fe guardada.
bonanza [bonǽnša], *s.* (E. U.) mina o veta rica en mineral; (com.) operación lucrativa.
bonbon [bónbón], *s.* confite, dulce.
bond [bond]. **I.** *s.* lazo, vínculo; unión, ligazón; traba, trabadura; cualquier cosa que une o liga; (arq.) aparejo, trabazón; (elec.) conexión eléctrica de dos rieles; (quím.) grado de afinidad; (com.) bono, obligación; título de la deuda; fiador; fianza.—*pl.* **bonds,** cadenas, cautiverio; (const.) maderamen, enmaderado.—**in b.,** en depósito. **II.** *a.,* siervo; esclavizado, cautivo. **III.** *va.* unir; conectar eléctricamente; obligar por fianza; hipotecar; poner mercancías en depósito. **IV.** *vn.* unirse, adherirse.
bondage [bóndey], *s.* cautiverio y esclavitud, servidumbre; obligación.
bonded [bónded], *a.* garantido por obligación escrita; hipotecado; asegurado; depositado bajo fianza para el pago de derechos arancelarios.—**b. goods,** mercancías en depósito.—**b. warehouse,** almacén de depósito.
bondholder [bóndjóuldœr], *s.* tenedor de bonos, obligacionista, rentista.
bondmaid [bóndmeid], *s.* esclava, sierva.
bondman [bóndman], *s.* esclavo, siervo.
bondsman [bóndšman], *s.* fiador, dita.
bondstone [bóndstoun], *s.* (arq.) perpiaño.
bondswoman [bóndšúman], *s.* fiadora, dita.
bone [bóun], *s.* hueso; espina del pez; cuesco de fruta; barba de ballena.—*pl.* espalillos, especie de castañuelas.—**b. black,** negro animal.—**b. dust,** huesos molidos, harina de huesos.—**b. -dry,** enteramente seco; (fam.) que no vende ni gota (de licor); absolutamente temperante.—**b. of contention,** asunto de disputa o desavenencia.—**b. porcelain,** porcelana de fosfato de cal, hecha con polvo de huesos.—**a b. to pick,** una cuestión que averiguar o arreglar.—**to have a b. to pick with some one,** tener que habérselas con alguno.—**to take no bones,** *o* not to make any bones, no andarse con rodeos, no tener empacho—**without more bones,** sin empacho, sin vacilación.
bone, *va.* desosar; emballenar; poner ballenas; (pol.) hurtar.
boneache [bóuneik], *s.* dolor de huesos.

boneblack [-blæc], *s.* =BONE BLACK. *V.* BONE.
boned [bóund], *a.* osudo, huesudo.
bonelace [bóunléis], *s.* encaje hecho a mano.
boneless [bóunles], *s.* mollar, sin huesos.
boneset [bóunset], *s.* (bot.) eupatorio.
bonesetter [bóunsétœr], *s.* componehuesos.
bonfire [bónfaiœr], *s.* hoguera, fogata.
bonhomie [bónomi], *n.* afabilidad.
Boniface [bónifes], *n.* hostelero.
bonification [bonifikéshun], *n.* bonificación.
boning [bóuning], *n.* acción de deshuesar; abono de tierras; nivelación por medio de estacas.
bonito, *s.* (ict.) bonito.
bon mot [bon mó], *s.* agudeza, frase.
bonnet [bónet]. **I.** *s.* gorra, gorro, sombrero de mujer; solideo, bonete; (fort.) bonete; (mec.) sombrerete; (mar.) boneta. **II.** *va.* cubrir; apabullar.
bonnet rouge [boné ruy], *s.* gorro encarnado; ultrarradical.
bonnily [bónili], *adv.* bonitamente.
bonny [bóni], *a.* bonito, lindo, gentil; alegre, festivo.
bonnyclabber [-clǽbœr], *s.* cuajo, leche cuajada.
bonton [bóngtóng], *s.* el gran mundo; buen tono.
bonus [bónus], *s.* adehala; estipendio; (Amér.) ñapa, contra.
bony [bóuni], *a.* osudo, huesudo.
booby [búbi], *s.* y *a.* zote, bobo, pajuncio.
boodle [búdœl], *s.* (fam. E. U.) dinero, blanca; sobomo; (Amér.) chanchullo; hato, partida, cuadrilla. *V.* CABOODLE.
boodler [búdlœr], *s.* (fam. E. U.) el que se deja sobornar.
book [buk]. **I.** *s.* libro; libreta.—**b.-learned,** erudito, leído, de ciencia aprendido en libros.—**b. learning,** saber aprendido en libros, teoría. **B. of Common Prayer,** ritual de la secta episcopal.—**b. of pilotage,** derrotero.—**b. of rates,** arancel de aduana.—**by the b.,** según las reglas; con exactitud. **II.** *va.* asentar en un libro; notar en un registro; inscribir.
bookbinder [búkbáindœr], *s.* encuadernador.
bookbinding [búkbáinding], *s.* encuadernación.
bookcase [búkkés], *s.* armario o estante para libros.
booking [búking], *s.* registro, asiento.—**b. clerk,** (Ingl.) vendedor de billetes de pasaje o teatro.—**b. office,** (Ingl.) expendeduría de billetes.
bookish [búkish], *a.* estudioso; versado en libros; pedante, teórico.
bookishness [búkishnes], *s.* estudiosidad; falta de sentido práctico.
bookkeeper [búkkípœr], *s.* tenedor de libros.
bookkeeping [-kíping], *s.* teneduría de libros, contabilidad.
booklet [búclet], *n.* libretín, folleto, opúsculo.
bookmaker [-méikœr], *s.* el que hace libros; (dep.) apostador de profesión en las carreras de caballos.
bookmaking [-méiking], *s.* ocupación del bookmaker.
bookmark [-marc], *s.* señal o marcador de libro.
bookrack [-ræc], *s.* atril.
bookseller [-sélœr], *s.* librero.
bookstore [-stóar], *s.* librería.
bookworm [-uœrm], *s.* polilla o gusano que roe los libros; bibliófilo, ratón de biblioteca.
boom [bum]. **I.** *s.* (mar.) botalón; botavara; cadena para cerrar un puerto; estampido; (E. U.) torrente crecido y bramador; (fig.) auge, actividad o prosperidad repentina.—**b. iron,** (mar.), zuncho de botalón.—**b. sail,** (mar.) cangreja. **II.** *vn.* hacer estampido; moverse con violencia; ir a velas desplegadas; (fam. E. U.) estar en auge, medrar. **III.** *va.* favorecer, anunciar, fomentar, dar bombo.
boomerang [búmœrang], *s.* bumerang.
boon [bun]. **I.** *s.* dádiva, regalo; gracia, merced; dicha, bendición. **II.** *a.* genial, festivo; liberal, generoso; afortunado, próspero.
boor [bur], *s.* patán, aldeano; rústico holandés.

boorish [búrish], *a.* rústico, agreste; guajiro, jíbaro.—**boorishly** [-li], *adv.* rústicamente, toscamente.—**boorishness** [-nes], *s.* rusticidad, tosquedad, grosería.
boost [bust]. **I.** *va.* (fam. E. U.) empujar, levantar; alzar desde abajo; fomentar, promover; hacer subir. **II.** *s.* alza; ayuda, asistencia.
booster [bústœr], *s.* impulsador, fomentador; (elec.) elevador de potencial.
boot [but]. **I.** *va.* y *vn.* aprovechar, valer, servir, importar; calzarse uno las botas. **II.** *s.* bota; calzado; ganancia, provecho; adehala; ñapa.—**b. hook,** tirabotas.—**b. maker,** zapatero.—**b. tree,** horma de botas.—**to be in another's boots,** estar en el pellejo de otro.—**to b.,** además; de ñapa.—**to put the b. on the wrong leg,** culpar al inocente.
bootblack [bútblæk], *n.* limpiabotas.
booted [búted], *c.* calzado con botas.
booth [buz], *s.* garita, casilla.
boothose [-jóus], *s.* calcetones.
bootjack [-yæc], *s.* sacabotas.
bootleg [bútlég], *va.* y *vn.* (fam. E. U.) contrabandear en licores.—**bootlegger** [-légœr], *s.* contrabandista de licores.—**bootlegging** [-léguing], *s.* contrabando de licores.
bootless [bútles], *a.* descalzo; inútil, sin provecho.
boots [buts], *s.* limpiabotas de hotel.
booty [búti], *s.* botín.—**to play b.,** trampear en el juego.
booze [bus]. **I.** *vn.* embriagarse, emborracharse. **II.** *s.* licor; borrachera, pítima.
boozy [búsi], *a.* (fam.) borracho.
bopeep [bopíp], *s.* escondite.
borable [bórabœl], *a.* que puede ser taladrado.
boracic [borǽsic], *s.* bórico.
boracite [bórasait], *s.* (min.) boracita, borato de magnesio.
borage [bóriy], *s.* (bot.) borraja.
borate [bóret], *s.* borato.
borax [bóræx], *s.* bórax, atíncar.
border [bórdœr]. **I.** *s.* orilla, borde, margen; arriate de un jardín; frontera, límite, confín; orla, guarnición, banda, cenefa, cerco, ribete, franja, farfalá. **II.** *vn.* confinar, lindar; rayar, aproximarse, acercarse.—**to b. on,** *o* **upon,** lindar con, tocar; rayar en. **III.** *va.* (cost.) orlar, repulgar, guarnecer, ribetear; tocar o lindar con.
borderer [bórdœrœr], *s.* limítrofe, comarcano; (cost.) orlador, ribeteador.
bordering [bórdœring]. **I.** *s.* orladura. **II.** *a.* fronterizo, contiguo, lindante.
bore [bóœr]. **I.** *va.* taladrar; barrenar, trepar, horadar, perforar; hacer o abrir a taladro o barrena; (fam.) aburrir, fastidiar. **II.** *vn.* hacer agujeros; adelantarse, avanzar. **III.** *pret.* del verbo TO BEAR. **IV.** *s.* taladro, barreno, agujero que se hace taladrando o barrenando; (artl.) calibre, alma; (mec.) diámetro interior (de un cilindro); luz o diámetro (de un pozo); (fam.) ola grande causada por la marea; (fam.) machaca, pelmazo, persona pesada.
boreal [bóreal], *a.* septentrional, boreal.
boreas [bóreas], *s.* cierzo, bóreas.
borecole [bóœrcol], *s.* (bot.) bróculi; bretón.
boredom [bóœrdum], *s.* fastidio, aburrimiento, tedio; gente pesada en general.
borer [bóœrœr], *s.* barrena; taladro, perforadora; cualquier animal que horada; barrenillo, insecto xilófago (horadador).
boric [bóric], *a.* bórico.
boride [bórid], *s.* (quím.) boruro.
boring [bóœring]. **I.** *s.* trepa, horadación; taladro.—*pl.* **borings,** partículas que se desprenden al taladrar o barrenar. **II.** *a.* de taladrar; xilófago, horadador (insecto).—**b. bar,** barra o árbol postiza barrenas.—**b. block,** bloque de barrenar; portabarrena.—**b. frame,** bastidor de perforadora.—**b. rod,** tientaguja, barra de perforadora.—**b. trestle** =B. FRAME.
born [born], *a.* nacido; destinado.—**to be b.,** nacer.—**to be b. again,** renacer, volver a nacer.
borne [born], *pp.* de TO BEAR.

borneol [bórnioul], *s.* (quím.) borneol, producto del alcanforero de Borneo.
boron [bóron], *s.* (quím.) boro.
borough [bǽɪo], *s.* villa; distrito administrativo de una ciudad.—**municipal b.,** (Ingl.) corporación municipal.—**parliamentary b.,** (Ingl.) pueblo con derecho de representación en el Parlamento.
borrow [bórro], *va.* y *vn.* pedir prestado; apropiarse, hacerse suyo; copiar.—**to b. from,** pedir prestado a; tomar de.
borrow, borrow pit [-pit], *s.* (ing.) zanja de préstamo, zanja de que se saca tierra para terraplenes.
borrower [bórroœr], *s.* prestatario, el que pide o toma prestado.
borrowing [-ing], *s.* acto de pedir o conseguir prestado.
boscage [bóskeiy], *s.* boscaje, espesura.
bosh [boŝ], *s.* (fam.) palabrería, tontería; etalaje de alto horno; embudo del cabilote.
bosk [bosk], *s.* matorral.
bosket [bósket], *s.* bosquecillo, bosquete.
bosky [bóski], *a.* frondoso, nemoroso.
Bosnian [bósnian], *s.* y *a.* bosnio.
bosom [búsʊm]. **I. s.** seno, pecho, corazón; amor, inclinación, cariño; (cost.) pechera. **II. a.** íntimo, querido; secreto.—**b. friend,** amigo íntimo. **III. va.** guardar en el pecho; ocultar.
boss [bos]. **I. s.** clavo o tachón; giba, joroba, corcova, protuberancia; copa (de freno); lomo (de libro); (arq.) pinjante; (fam. E. U.) amo, patrón; jefe, cabecilla; (pol.) cacique, gamonal. **II. va.** trabajar en relieve. (*v.* EMBOSS); (fam. E. U.) regentear, mandar; dominar.
bossage [bósey], *s.* (arq.) almohadilla.
bossed [bost], **bossy** [bósi], *a.* tachonado; turgente, abultado, saliente.
bossism [-iŝm], *s.* caciquismo, gamonalismo.
bossy [bósi], *a.* (fam.) mandón, autoritario.
bot [bot], *s.* larva de estro.
botanic(al [botǽnic(al], *a.* botánico.
botanically [botǽnicali], *adv.* botánicamente.
botanist [bótanist], *s.* botánico.
botanize [bótanaiŝ], *vn.* herborizar.
botany [bótani], *s.* botánica.
botch [boch]. **I. s.** remiendo, chapucería; remendón, chapucero. **II. va.** remendar, chapucear.
botcher [bóchœr], *s.* remendón, chapucero.
botchy [bóchi], *a.* culcusido.
botfly [bótflai], *s.* (ent.) estro.
both [bóuz]. **I. a.** y *pron.* ambos, los dos, dos [*both his sons are here,* sus dos hijos están (ambos) aquí].—**b. of,** los dos, ellos dos, ambos, etc.: *both of them,* ellos dos, los dos, ambos; *both of us,* nosotros dos. **II. conj.** y *adv.* tanto como, así como, a un mismo tiempo: *both he and I,* tanto él como yo; *both cheap and durable,* tanto barato como durable, a un mismo tiempo barato y durable.
bother [bóðœr]. **I. va.** (fam.) incomodar, molestar. **II. s.** molestia, incomodidad, pejiguera.
botheration [bóðœréŝʊn], *s.* molestia, fastidio, vejación.
bothersome [bóðœrsʊm], *a.* molesto, fastidioso.
botryoidal [botrióidal], *a.* arracimado.
bottie [bótœl]. **I.** botella; frasco.—**b. gourd,** (bot.) güira, calabaza vinatera.—**b. green,** verde botella.—**b. imp,** (fís.) diablillo de Descartes. **II. va.** (a veces con **up**) embotellar (un líquido, un ejército, una armada); envasar.
bottleflower [bótœlflǽuœr], *s.* (bot.) centaurea.
bottleful [-ful], *s.* botellada.
bottleholder [bótœljóldœr], *s.* partidario; padrino (en duelo); asistente de un pugilista; portabotellas.
bottler [bótlœr], *s.* embotellador.
bottling [bótling], *s.* envase.
bottom [bótʊm]. **I. s.** fondo; lecho de un río; parte inferior, lo más bajo, pie; trasero; nalgatorio; zanja, cimiento, fundamento; (mar.) casco, nave, barco, buque; base, motivo; poso, sedimento; asiento de una silla.—**to be at the b. of,** ser el causante de.—**to stand on one's own**

b., depender de uno mismo.—**to touch b.,** tocar fondo, quedarse en una parte. **II. a.** hondo, bajo; ínfimo; fundamental; (fam.) último. **III. va** poner fondo o asiento a; cimentar, fundar, apoyar (tec.) acabar, repasar. **IV. vn.** apoyarse.
bottomless [-les], *a.* insondable; visionario.
bottoming [bótʊming], *s.* (f. c.) balasto.
bottomry [bótʊmri], *s.* (com.) préstamo o contrato a la gruesa, o sobre casco y quilla.
boudoir [buduár], *s.* gabinete de señora, tocador.
bouffe [buf], *a.* bufo, cómico.
bough [bau], *s.* rama.—**boughpot** [-pot], *s.* florero.
bought [bot], *pret.* y *pp.* de TO BUY.
boughten [bótœn], *a.* (fam.) comprado (a diferencia de lo casero).
bougie [búyi], *s.* (cir.) candelilla, tienta.
bouillon [búllóng], *s.* caldo, consumado.
boulder [bóldœr], *s.* canto rodado.
boulevard [búlevard], *s.* bulevar.
bounce [búns]. **I. vn.** rebotar; brincar, saltar; lanzarse; echar fieros o bravatas; fanfarronear. **II. va.** hacer saltar o botar; (fam. E. U.) despedir, echar. **III. s.** salto, brinco; bote, rebote, repullo, respingo; golpazo, porrazo; fanfarronada; bola, mentira, filfa; echada, despedida.
bouncer [báunsœr], *s.* guapo, fanfarrón; bola, filfa; embustero; (fam. E. U.) guardián fornido que echa a los alborotadores de un café.
bouncing [báunsing], *a.* fuerte, vigoroso, robusto; exagerado; fanfarrón.
bound [báund]. **I. s.** límite, término, lindero; bote, brinco, corcovo, salto, respingo; resalto, rebote. **II. va.** deslindar, parcelar, confinar, limitar, ceñir; hacer saltar, botar. **III. vn.** saltar, brincar; botar; corvetear.
bound. I. *pret.* y *pp.* del verbo TO BIND. **II. a.** atado, amarrado, sujeto, ligado; confinado; moral o legalmente obligado; encuadernado; destinado; sentenciado; decidido, resuelto; puesto en aprendizaje; estreñido.—**b. for,** (mar.) con destino a.—**b. up,** absorto, engolfado; enfrascado.—**to be b. for,** (fam.) ir a, ir para.
boundary [báundari]. **I. s.** límite, linde, lindero; término, coto; muga, mojón. **II. a.** limítrofe, divisorio.
bounden [báunden], *a.* obligatorio, preciso; indispensable.
boundless [báundles], *a.* ilimitado, infinito.—**boundlessness** [-nes], *s.* inmensidad, infinidad.
bounteous [báunteus], *a.* liberal, generoso.—**bounteously** [-li], *adv.* liberalmente, generosamente.—**bounteousness** [-nes], *s.* munificencia o liberalidad, generosidad.
bountiful [báuntiful], *a.* liberal, dadivoso, generoso.—**bountifully** [-li], *adv.* liberalmente, generosamente.—**bountifulness** [-nes], *s.* generosidad, liberalidad, largueza.
bounty [báunti], *s.* generosidad, liberalidad, munificencia; merced, gracia; concesión, subvención, prima.—**b. money,** enganche.
bouquet [buké], *s.* ramillete de flores; nariz (del vino).
Bourbon [búrbʊn], *s.* Borbón; (fam. E. U.) conservador, recalcitrante.—**B. whisky,** aguardiente de maíz o de centeno.
bourdon [búrdon], *s.* bordón; registro de órgano.
bourgeois [buryuá], *a.* y *s.* burgués; capitalista; ordinario; comerciante, industrial.
bourgeois [bœryóis], *s.* (impr.) tipo de nueve puntos.
bourgeoisie [buryuaŝí], *s.* clase media, burguesía; clase capitalista.
bourgeon [bœryʊn]. **I. vn.** brotar, retoñar. **II. s.** yema, retoño.
bourn [born], *s.* límite, linde; meta; arroyo, riachuelo.
bourse [burs], *s.* (com.) bolsa, lonja; (anat.) bolsa.
bouse, bousy, *V.* BOOZE, BOOZY.
bout [báut], *s.* vez, turno; ataque (de borrachera, de enfermedad); curva o vuelta; encuentro, combate.
Bovidæ [bóuvidi], *s. pl.* (zool.) bóvidos, bovídeos.

bovine [bóvin], *a.* bovino, vacuno; paciente; sufrido; lerdo, bruto.

bow [báu]. **I.** *va.* saludar; hacer reverencia o cortesía; doblar, inclinar; agobiar, oprimir, agravar. **II.** *vn.* inclinarse, arquearse, agacharse; doblarse, torcerse; agobiarse; ceder, someterse. **III.** *s.* saludo; cortesía, venia; (mar.) proa.—b. **chaser**, cañón de caza o de tiro hacia adelante.—b. **oar**, remo o bogador más cercano a la proa.—**on the b.** (mar.) por la serviola.

bow [bo]. **I.** *s.* arco (para disparar flechas); (mús.) arco de violín; lazo (de corbata, de cinta, etc.); arzón de silla. **II.** *a.* arqueado, encorvado.—b. **compass(es)**, bigotera, compás de bomba (compás pequeño de resorte).—b. **hand**, la mano del arco; la mano izquierda (de donde **on the b. hand**, erradamente, por el mal camino).—b.-**legged**, estevado, patituerto.—b. **net**, red de pescar langostas; red para coger pájaros.—b. **pen** = B. COMPASS.—b. **saw**, sierra de arco.—b. **window**, bow window,ventana saliente; mirador. **III.** *va.* arquear, encorvar.

Bowdlerize [báudlœraiŝ], *vt.* recortar, mutilar (un escrito).

bowel [báuel], *s.* intestino, tripa.—*pl.* entrañas.

bower [báuœr], *s.* glorieta, emparrado, cenador, enramada; morada retirada; ancla de proa o de servidumbre (llám. t. **b. anchor**).—b. **bird**, tilonorinco (pájaro australiano).

bower [bóœr], *s.* músico de arco; arquero, hacedor de arcos.

bowery [báuœri]. **I.** *s.* cortijo, granja.—**the B.**, calle de Nueva York frecuentada por el pueblo bajo. **II.** *a.* frondoso, sombreado.

bowie knife [búi naif], *s.* cuchillo de monte.

bowing [báuing], *a.* inclinado.

bowknot [bónot], *s.* nudo corredizo, lazada.

bowl [bóul]. **I.** *s.* escudilla, cuenco; hueco, concavidad; tazón de fuente; palangana; bolo, rulo, bocha; copa, vaso (de vino, etc.).—b. **of a pipe**, hornillo de la pipa.—b. **of a spoon**, paleta de la cuchara.—*pl.* juego de bolos; rodillos de calandria. **II.** *va.* tumbar con una bola; derribar; hacer rodar. **III.** *vn.* jugar a las bochas.

bowlder, *s.* = BOULDER.

bowleg [bóuleg], *s.* pierna corva.

bowler [bólœr], *s.* jugador de bolos.

bowline [bólin], *s.* (mar.) bolina.

bowling [bóuling], *s.* juego de bolos; chirinola.—b.-**alley**, b.-**green**, bolera.

bowman [bóman], *s.* arquero, flechero.

bowse [báus], *vn.* (mar.) halar a un tiempo.

bowshot [bóŝhot], *s.* tiro de flecha.

bowsprit [bósprit], *s.* (mar.) bauprés.

bowstring [bóstring], *s.* cuerda de arco; dogal para ahorcar.

bowwow [báuáu], *s.* ladrido, guau.

bowyer [bóyœr], *s.* arquero.

box [box], *s.* caja; estuche, excusabaraja; cofre, arca; palco de teatro; bofetada; establo; casilla; compartimento, sección, encierro; cavidad, corte, (en un árbol), (mar.) bitácora; (carr.) pescante; (impr.) cajetín; (mec.) buje, caja, manguito; cajera; casilla, compartimiento, (bot.) box o boj.—b. **boat**, sobretodo (apl. esp. al de viaje).—b. **car**, (f. c.) furgón, vagón cubierto.—b. **coupling**, acoplamiento de manguito.—b. **culvert**, (ing.) alcantarilla rectangular o de techo plano.—b. **end**, (m. v.) cabeza integral de biela (de una pieza con ésta).—b. **girder**, viga de cajón o tubular.—b. **office**, (teat.) taquilla.—b. **plaiting**, (cost.) plegado, pliegue de tabla.—**to be in a b.**, hallarse en un aprieto.

box. **I.** *va.* encajonar; [apuñear, abofetear.—**to b. the compass**, (mar.) cuartear. **II.** *vn.* boxear.

boxen [bócsœn], *a.* hecho de boj.

boxer [bócsœr], *s.* boxeador, púgil; embalador; bóxer, miembro de la sociadad patriótica china de los boxers.

boxhaul [bócsjol], *vn.* (mar.) virar en redondo; abroquelar.

boxing [bócsing], *s.* empaque, embalaje; madera para encajonar; boxeo, pugilato; (carp.) marco de puerta o de ventana.

boxthorn [bóxzorn], *s.* (bot.) licio, tamujo.

boxwood [bóxud], *s.* madera de box.

boy [bói], *s.* muchacho, niño; hijo varón; mozo; criado, lacayo.—b. **scout**, niño explorador (perteneciente a la asociación de Niños Exploradores).—**the old b.**, el diablo.

boycott [bóicot]. **I.** *va.* excluir, boicotear. **II.** *s.* exclusión, boicoteo.

boyhood [bóijud], *s.* muchachez, puericia.

boyish [bóiiŝh], *a.* amuchachado; pueril.

boyishly [bóiiŝhli], *adv.* como muchacho.

boyishness [bóiiŝhnes], *s.* muchachada, niñada; talante de muchacho.

brabble [brébœl]. **I.** *vn.* armar camorra. **II.** *s.* camorra, riña, pendencia.

brabbler [bréblœr], *s.* camorrista.

braccate [bréket], *a.* (orn.) paticalzado.

brace [bréis]. **I.** *va.* ligar, asegurar; reforzar; fortalecer, vigorizar; (carp.) ensamblar, empatar; (mar.) bracear; cercar, rodear; (impr.) abrazar con llave o corchete. **II.** *s.* abrazadera, laña, grapón, broche, manija, traba, braza; (carp.) berbiquí; tornapunta; (arq.) riostra, tirante, puntal; (carr.) sopanda; un par (de pistolas, perdices, etc.); (cir.) braguero; (impr.) corchete, llave, { }; (arq.) anclaje, silla, mordaza; can, canecillo—b. **bit**, taladro o barrena de berbiquí.—*pl.* tirantes del pantalón; (mar.) brazas.—**braces of a rudder**, (mar.) hembras del timón.—b. **pendants**, brazalotes.

bracelet [bréslet], *s.* brazalete, ajorca, pulsera, manilla; (arm.) brazal.

bracer [brésœr], *s.* brazal; (med.) medicamento tónico y fortificante; (fam.) bebida fortificante, copa, trago; abrazadera, afianzador, laña; cinto, venda.

brachial [brékial], *a.* braquial.

brachiopod [brékiopod], *s.* (zool.) braquiópodo.

Brachiopoda [-pouda], *s. pl.* braquiópodos.

brachium [brékium], *s.* (pl. BRACHIA) (zool.) brazo superior.

brachycephalic [brékisefélic], **brachycephalous** [-séfœlus], *a.* (anat.) braquicéfalo.

brachypodous [braekípodus], *a.* (zool. y bot.) braquípodo.

bracing [brésing]. **I.** *a.* fortificante, tónico. **II.** *s.* amarra, ligazón, refuerzo, trabazón.

bracken [brékn], *s.* (bot.) helecho; helechal.

bracket [bréket], *s.* ménsula, soporte asegurado en la pared; brazo o sostén de lámpara, mechero de gas, etc. asegurado en la pared; (arq.) modillón, ménsula.—*pl.* paréntesis angulares [ ].

brackish [brékiŝh], *a.* salobre; nauseabundo.

brackishness [brékiŝhnes], *s.* sabor salobre.

bract [bráct], *s.* (bot.) bráctea.

bractlet [bréctlet], *s.* (bot.) bractéola.

brad [bræd], *s.* clavo de ala de mosca; puntilla, hita, espiga, saetín.

bradawl [brédól], *s.* punzón recto afilado para agujeros de clavos, etc.

brag [bræg]. **I.** *s.* jactancia, fanfarronada; farolero, fanfarrón; juego de naipes. **II.** *va. y vn.* jactarse (de), fanfarronear.

braggadocio [brægadóŝhio], *s.* fanfarria, ronca; fanfarrón.

braggardism [brégardiŝm], *s.* jactancia o fanfarronería.

braggart [brégart], *a.* jactancioso, bravucón.

bragger, **bragger** [brégœr], *s.* jaque, matasiete.

bragget [bréguet], *s.* aguamiel.

braggingly [bréguingli], *adv.* jactanciosamente.

Brahman [bráman], *s.* bracmán.

Brahmanical, Braminical [bramánical, -ínical], *a.* bracmánico.

braid [bréid]. **I.** *va.* trenzar; (cost.) acordonar, bordar con cordoncillo o de realce; galonear. **II.** *s.* galón, alamar, trencilla; trenza, crizneja.

brail [bréil], *va.* (mar.) cargar las velas.

brails [bréilŝ], *s. pl.* (mar.) candelizas.

brain [bréin]. **I.** *s.* cerebro.—b. **fever**, fiebre cerebral, meningitis. **II.** *va.* descerebrar, romper la crisma a.

brainless [bréinles], *a.* sin sesos; tonto, insensato.
brainpan [bréinpæn], *s.* cráneo.
brainsick [bréinsic], *a.* chiflado.—**brainsickly** [-li], *adv.* locamente.—**brainsickness** [-nes], *s.* vértigo;^veleidad; chifladura.
brainy [bréini], *a.* (fam.) sesudo, inteligente.
braize [bréiß], *s.* (ict.) pargo.
brake [bréic]. **I.** *s.* (bot.) helecho (*v.* BRACKEN); agramadera; jaral, matorral; (f. c., aut., etc.) freno; (mar.) guimbalete de bomba; amasadera; bocado de canutillo para caballo; (agr.) grada, palanca, espeque.—**b. band**, cinta del freno.—**b. block**, portazapata del freno; zapata. —**b. horsepower**, potencia al freno.—**b. pedal**, (aut.) pedal del freno.—**b. power** = B. HORSE-POWER.—**b. rod**, varilla del freno.—**b. shoe**, zapata del freno. **II.** *va.* (f. c., aut.) frenar, enfrenar; espadar o espadillar el cáñamo; amasar pan; (agr.) desterronar con la grada.
brakeman [-mæn], *s.* (f. c., etc.) guardafrenos.
braky [bréiki], *a.* espinoso, áspero.
bramble [brémbœl], *s.* (bot.) zarza, cambrón; jijallar.
brambled [brémbœld], *a.* breñoso, zarzoso.
brambling [brémbling], *s.* (ornit.) pinzón.
brambly [brémbli], *a.* zarzoso.
bran [brén], *s.* salvado, afrecho.—**b. bread**, acemita.
branch [branch]. **I.** *s.* rama de árbol; sarmiento (de vid, etc.); ramo, dependencia, división o sección; ramal, brazo; tributario; (com.) sucursal; (f. c.) ramal.—*pl.* ramas, ramaje. **II.** *a.* dependiente, tributario, sucursal. **III.** *vn.* ramificarse; echar pitones, astas o ramas.—**to b. off**, bifurcarse, separarse, dividirse.—**to b. out**, divergir, ampliar, extenderse. **IV.** *va.* ramificar, dividir en ramas; bordar.
brancher [bránchœr], *s.* (cetr.) halcón ramero.
branchiæ [bránkie], *s. pl.* (ict.) branquias.
branchial [bránkial], *a.* branquial.
branchiness [bránchines], *s.* frondosidad.
Branchiopoda [bránkiópodæ], *s. pl.* (zool.) branquiópodos.
branchless [bránchles], *a.* sin ramas.
branchlet [bránchlet], *s. dim.* ramita.
branchy [branchi], *a.* ramoso.
brand [brænd]. **I.** *s.* tizón o tea; (poet.) espada, rayo; sello o marca de fábrica; calidad; hierro de marcar reses y la marca; estigma, mancha, baldón.—**b. goose**, (zool.) oca silvestre.—**b. iron, branding iron**, hierro de marcar.—**b.-new**, enteramente nuevo, nuevecito. **II.** *va.* marcar con hierro candente; tiznar (de malo, etc.); infamar, desdorar.
brandish [brándiß]. **I.** *va.* blandir, blandear, cimbrar. **II.** *s.* (esgr.) floreo, molinete.
brandling [brándling], *s.* gusano para cebo.
brandreth [brándrez], *s.* brocal de pozo; andamio, maderamen, armazón.
brandy [brándi], *s.* brandy, coñac.
brandyshop [brándißhóp], *s.* taberna.
branlin [brénlin], *s.* salmón pequeño.
branny [bréni], *a.* parecido al salvado.
brant [brént], *s.* especie de ganso.
brasen, *V.* BRAZEN.
brash [bræßh]. **I.** *a.* (fam.) impetuoso; temerario. **II.** *s.* acedía; erupción; ataque, asalto; montón de escombros.
brasier, *V.* BRAZIER.
brasil, *V.* BRAZIL.
brass [bræs], *s.* latón (aleación amarilla de cobre y cinc, que en algunas partes se llama *bronce*); bronce (aleación de cobre y estaño; hoy se usa poco el término en este sentido, excepto con algún calificativo); plancha conmemorativa de latón.—*pl.* **brasses**, (mec.) bronces, anillos de cojinete; cojinetes.—**b. band**, charanga, murga.—**b.-visaged**, descarado.
brassart [bræssært], *s.* brazal.
brassica [brésicæ], *s.* (bot.) berza.
Brassicaceæ [brésikéisii], *s. pl.* (bot.) crucíferas.
brassière [brésíar], *s.* corpiño, justillo o ajustador bajo y apretado para sostener los pechos.

brassiness [brésiness], *s.* calidad de bronceado; desfachatez, descaro; bajeza.
brassy [brási], **brassish** [-ißh], *a.* de latón; descarado, desvergonzado.
brat [bræt], *s.* rapaz, mocoso.
brattle [brétœl]. **I.** *vn.* repiquetear; (Cuba) chaquetear; poner pies en polvorosa. **II.** *s.* estampido; repiqueteo; redoble.
bravado [bravédo], *s.* bravata, baladronada.
brave [bréiv]. **I.** *a.* bravo, valiente, denodado; excelente. **II.** *va.* desafiar, arrostrar. **III.** *s.* valiente; guerrero (apl. a los indios); jaque, fanfarrón.
bravely [bréivli], *adv.* valerosamente, valientemente; perfectamente.
bravery [bréivœri], *s.* valentía, valor, ánimo; proeza, heroísmo; esplendor, magnificencia.
bravo [bravo]. **I.** *s.* asesino pagado o asalariado. **II.** *interj.* ¡bravo!
brawl [brol]. **I.** *s.* alboroto, disputa, camorra, pendencia; baile, y su música. **II.** *vn.* alborotar, armar camorra; vociferar, vocinglear. **III.** *va.* decir gritando.
brawler [brólœr], *s.* camorrista, pendenciero.
brawling [broling], *s.* alboroto, vocinglería.
brawn [bron], *s.* pulpa, carne mollar; fuerza muscular; carne dura.
brawniness [brónines], *s.* fortaleza, musculatura.
brawny [bróni], *a.* fuerte, musculoso, membrudo.
braxy [bréxi]. **I.** *s.* fiebre carbuncular de las reses; res lanar atacada de este mal. **II.** *a.* atacado de dicha fiebre.
bray [bréi]. **I.** *va.* majar, triturar, moler, pulverizar. **II.** *vn.* rebuznar. **III.** *s.* rebuzno; ruido bronco.
brayer [bréœr], *s.* rebuznador; (impr.) moleta; (cir.) braguero.
braying [bréing], *s.* grito; rebuzno.
braze [bréiß]. **I.** *va.* soldar con soldadura fuerte o de latón; broncear. **II.** *s.* soldadura.
brazen [bréißn]. **I.** *a.* de latón; como de latón; descarado.—**b.-browed, b.-faced,** *a.* descarado.—**b. face**, *s.* cara de vaqueta, sinvergüenza. **II.** *va.* **to b. it out,** *o* **through,** hacer frente a; sostener o llevar a cabo con desfachatez.
brazenness [bréißennes], *s.* descaro, desvergüenza.
brazier [bréyœr], *s.* latonero, calderero; brasero, copa, maridillo, rejuela.
braziery [bréyœri], *s.* latonería.
brazil, brazilwood [brasilud], *s.* palo Brasil.— Brazil nut, nuez del Brasil.
braziletto [brasiléto], *s.* (bot.) brasilete.
Brazilian [brasilian], *a.* y *s.* brasileño.
brazilin [brésilin], *s.* (quím.) brasilina.
breach [brích], *s.* rotura, fractura; rompimiento; infracción, violación; brecha, abertura; disensión, escisión, rompimiento de las relaciones; (mar.) rompiente, oleaje; salto de ballena.—**b. of faith,** *o* **of trust,** abuso de confianza, prevaricación.—**b. of promise,** violación de la palabra de casamiento.—**b. of the peace,** perturbación del orden público.
bread [bred], *s.* pan.—**b. and butter,** pan con mantequilla; (fig.) pan, sustento, diario; (usado como adjetivo, mercenario; menesteroso; relativo a la subsistencia).—**b. corn,** grano de que se hace pan.—**b. line,** fila de menesterosos que piden pan o se distribuye gratis.—**to earn one's b.,** *o* **one's b. and butter,** ganarse el pan o la vida.—**to know on which side one's b. is buttered,** saber dónde aprieta el zapato. **II.** *va.* dar pan a; (coci.) envolver en masa de harina.
breadfruit [brédfrut], *s.* árbol del pan y su fruto.
breadstuff [brédstúf], *s.* cereales, granos, harinas, etc., que sirven para pan; pan, productos de harina.
breadth [bredz], *s.* anchura, ancho; holgura; latitud; liberalidad; (cost.) paño, ancho de una tela.—**b. of beam,** (mar.) manga.
breadthwise [brédzuaiß], *adv.* a lo ancho.
breadwinner [bréduínœr], *s.* el que se gana la vida; productor.

break [brek], *va.* (*pret.* BROKE O BRAKE (poét.); *pp.* BROKEN O BROKE) romper, quebrar; romper, suspender (relaciones, etc.); infringir, violar (la ley, etc.); abrir brecha en; domar, amansar; degradar (a un oficial, etc.); quebrar, arruinar; interrumpir; dividir, reducir a fragmentos o partes, quebrantar; cambiar (un billete, etc.); moderar, amortiguar; exceder, ir más allá de; dar o comunicar suave o cautelosamente (una mala noticia, etc.).—**to b. a house**, entrarse a una casa con intentos criminales.—**to b. a lance with**, batirse con. —**to b. a straw**, reñir.—**to b. asunder**, separar, dividir.—**to b. bread**, comulgar o dar de comulgar.—**to b. bread with**, sentarse a la mesa o a comer con; gozar de la hospitalidad de.—**to b. bulk**, (mar.) descargar la bodega, principiar a descargar.—**to b. camp**, levantar el campo.—**to b. down**, destruir, demoler; desmembrar.—**to b. ground**, abrir o remover la tierra; empezar a cavar; principiar una empresa; (mar.) levar ancla.—**to b. in**, forzar, romper o abrir empujando hacia adentro; domar, amansar; adiestrar. —**to b. in pieces**, despedazar, hacer añicos. —**to b. jail**, escaparse de la cárcel.—**to b. one's neck**, (fam.) desalarse, precipitarse.—**to b. open**, abrir a la fuerza, forzar.—**to b. out**, forzar, quitar; aflojar, abrir; sacar (carga) de la bodega. —**to b. the back**, quebrar la espalda; agobiar, postrar; pasar de lo peor o más difícil.—**to b. the bank**, hacer saltar la banca (en el juego). — **to b. the heart of**, acongojar, matar (fig.) de dolor.—**to b. the ice**, pasar de las primeras dificultades; cobrar confianza; comenzar.—**to b. the record**, exceder o sobrepujar el record.—**to b. up**, dividir en partes, desmenuzar; abrir (una mina, etc.); forzar (una puerta etc.); disolver (un parlamento, etc.); desconcertar, confundir; levantar (casa, el campo, etc.).—**to b. upon the wheel**, enrodar.

break, *vn.* romperse, quebrarse; reventar (una apostema, etc.); quebrar, hacer bancarrota; fracasar, frustrarse; romper (con una persona, etc.); separarse, desprenderse violentamente; salir, brotar; apuntar, rayar (el día); saltar (un pez); estallar; brotar, florecer; desfallecer; ceder, dispersarse; partir antes de tiempo.—**to b. away**, desprenderse; zafarse; escaparse; desaparecer; disiparse.—**to b. down**, desbaratarse; irse abajo; perder la salud, el valor o el ánimo; abatirse, desesperarse.—**to b. forth**, salir, brotar; exclamar.—**to b. from**, desprenderse de.—**to b. in**, entrarse (sobre todo forzando puertas, etc.). —**to b. in upon**, aparecerse a de sopetón, sorprender.—**to b. into**, soltarse en, pasar repentinamente a; forzar.—**to b. loose**, separarse, desprenderse; escaparse o fugarse.—**to b. off**, separarse, desprenderse; desistir.—**to b. out**, brotarse; estallar (una guerra); empezar (una epidemia); echar a hablar; (arq.) sobresalir.—**to b. through**, abrirse paso por o por entre; salvar.—**to b. up**, desmenuzarse, hacerse pedazos o fragmentos; dispersarse: disolverse; levantarse (una sesión).

break, *s.* rotura; abertura, grieta, raja; comienzo, principio; pausa, intervalo, interrupción; vacío; piña, disparate (**to make a b.**), cometer un disparate o piña, obrar con desacierto); gallo, nota falsa (en el canto); (elec.) interruptor; abertura, distancia entre contactos; (com.) baja (en el mercado).—**b. of day**, alba, amanecer.

breakable [brékabœl], *a.* quebradizo, frágil, rompible.

breakage [brékeɣ], *s.* fractura, rotura; destrozo, estropicio; indemnización por cosas quebradas.

breakax [brécæx], *s.* (bot.) quiebrahacha.

breakdown [bréikdaun], *s.* vuelco, caída, derrumbamiento; desbarajuste, trastorno, fracaso; (E. U.) zapateado de negros; debilidad, agotamiento, postración.

breaker [bréikœr], *s.* roturador; infractor; quebrantador, rompedor; (aut.) capa de tela que va entre la rodadura y el esqueleto de un neumático.—*pl.* rompientes, cachones.

breakfast [brékfast]. **I.** *vn.* desayunarse, almorzar. **II.** *s.* desayuno, almuerzo.—**b. food**, gacha.

breaking [bréking], *s.* fractura, quebrantamiento; desgaje; interrupción; (agr.) tierra roturada.

—**b. load**, (ing.) carga de fractura.—**b. up**, cierre, disolución, dispersión.

breakneck [bréknec]. **I.** *s.* despeñadero, precipicio. **II.** *a.* precipitado, rápido.

breakwater [bréikuótœr], *s.* rompeolas, escollera

bream [brím], *s.* (ict.) sargo.

bream, *va.* (mar.) limpiar fondos.

breast [brest]. **I.** *s.* pecho, seno; teta; (arm.) peto; pechuga de ave; pecho, corazón, interior del hombre; (arti.) testera; (arq.) toro; (min.) frente o cara de veta o filón; (carr.) comba del cubo de una rueda.—**b.-deep**, de hondura que da al pecho.—**b. harness**, arnés de pretal.— **b.-high**, de alto que da al pecho.—**b. pump**, mamadera.—**b. wheel**, (hidr.), rueda de costado —**to make a clean b. of**, confesar, reconocer con franqueza. **II.** *va.* arrostrar resueltamente; amamantar, dar el pecho a.

breastband [bréstbænd], *s.* pretal.

breastbone [-boun], *s.* esternón.

breastfast [-fæst], *s.* (mar.) amarra del través.

breasthooks [-jucs], *s.* (mar.) buzardas.

breastpin [-pin], *s.* broche, prendedor.

breastplate [-pléit], *s.* peto; pretal; pectoral.

breastplough, breastplow [-pláu], *s.* arado de pecho.

breastrail [-réil], *s.* antepecho.

breastsummer [-súmœr], *s.* (arq.) cabio superior de puerta o ventana.

breastwork [-uœrk], *s.* (mil., gen. *pl.*) trinchera, defensa, valla; (mar.) propao.

breath [brez], *s.* aliento, respiración, resuello; hálito, soplo; pausa, respiro; sobreseimiento; instante, momento.—**in a b.**, de un resuello.— **out of b.**, sin aliento, sofocado, jadeante.— **under one's b.**, en voz baja.

breathable [brídabœl], *a.* respirable.

breathe [bríð]. **I.** *vn.* respirar, resollar; vivir; descansar, tomar aliento; tomar el fresco; soplar, avahar; aspirar, exhalar. **II.** *va.* inspirar, respirar; exhalar; dar aire o deshogo; sugerir, revelar.—**to b. one's last**, dar el último suspiro, morir, expirar.

breather [bríðœr], *s.* respirador; viviente; inspirador.

breathing [bríðing], *s.* respiración; resuello, vaharada; aire suave; inspiración; aspiración. —**b. hole**, respiradero.—**b. place**, pausa; respiradero, lugar de descanso.—**b. spell**, tregua, descanso, respiro.—**b. time**, huelga, asueto, reposo.

breathless [brézles], *a.* falto de aliento, sin resuello; jadeante; intenso, expectante.

breathlessness [-nes], *s.* desaliento; muerte.

breccia [brétcia], *s.* (min.) brecha.

bred, *pret.* y *pp.* DE TO BREED.

breech [brích]. **I.** *s.* posaderas, nalgas; (arti.) recámara.—**b.-loading** (arti.) de retrocarga. **II.** *va.* poner calzones; zurrar; poner recámara a un arma.

breeches [bríches], *s. pl.* calzones, bragas, pantalones.—**b. buoy**, salvavidas en forma de bragas. —**to wear the b.**, llevar los calzones.

breeching [bríching], *s.* grupera del arnés; zurra; (mar.) bragueros de cañón.

breechloader [-lódœr], *s.* arma de retrocarga.

breed [bríd]. **I.** *va.* criar, engendrar, multiplicar; empollar; parir; ocasionar, producir; educar.—**to b. in-and-in**, procrear sin mezclar razas. **II.** *vn.* multiplicarse; parir; sacar cría. **III.** *s.* casta, raza, progenie; generación; lechigada; ralea.

breeder [brídœr], *s.* criador; padre; paridera.

breeding [bríding]. **I.** *s.* cría; crianza; modales. **II.** *a.* de criar, que cría.—**b. cage**, jaula de criar, criadera.—**b. place**, criadero.

breeze [bríz], *s.* brisa; (fam.) agitación, excitación, embullo; vago rumor, murmuración; cisco de coque; (ent.) tábano.

breezeless [brísles], *a.* sin aire.

breezy [brísi], *a.* ventilado; animado, vivo.— **to be b.** (con *it* por sujeto), hacer brisa.

bregma [brégmæ], *s.* (anat.) bregma.

brethren [brébren], *s. pl.* hermanos (apl. esp. a los miembros de una fraternidad, iglesia, etc.)

Breton [brétön], *a.* y *s.* bretón.

breve [brív], *s.* (mús.) breve; (pros.) marca de sílaba breve.

brevet [brévet]. **I.** *s.* (mil.) graduación honoraria (sin el sueldo correspondiente), grado. **II.** *a.* (mil.) honorario, de grado. **III.** *va.* (mil.) conferir grado honorario a.

breviary [brívieri], *s.* (igl.) breviario.

brevier [brevíœr], *s.* (impr.) breviario, tipo de ocho puntos.

brevipennate [brevipénnet], *s.* y *a.* (zool.) brevipenne, corredor.

brevirostrate, brevirostral [brevirróstret, -tral], *a.* (orn.) corto de pico.

brevity [bréviti], *s.* brevedad; concisión.

brew [bru], **I.** *va.* hacer cerveza, o ponche; fraguar, urdir, tramar. **II.** *vn.* elaborar cerveza; formarse, prepararse: *a storm is brewing*, se prepara, o amenaza, una tormenta. **III.** *s.* mezcla.

brewage [brúœr], *s.* brebaje.

brewer [brúœr], *s.* cervecero.

brewery [-ri], *s.* cervecería, fábrica de cerveza.

brewing [brúing], *s.* elaboración de cerveza; cantidad de cerveza que se hace de una vez; señales de borrasca.

brewis [brúis], *s.* sopa; caldo espeso.

briar [bráiar]. *V.* BRIER.

bribe [bráib]. **I.** *s.* cohecho, soborno. **II.** *va.* cohechar, sobornar.

briber [bráibœr], *s.* cohechador, sobornador.

bribery [bráibœri], *s.* cohecho, soborno.

bric-a-brac, *s.* bric-à-brac.

brick [bric]. **I.** *s.* ladrillo, ladrillos; briqueta, losilla; (fam.) buen chico, persona simpática.— **b. clay,** arcilla de ladrillos.—**b. dust,** polvo de ladrillo; (med.) sedimentos de uratos en la orina. —**b. earth** = B. CLAY.—**to have a b. in one's. hat,** (fam.) estar borracho. **II.** *va.* enladrillar.

brickbat [brícbæt], *s.* tejoleta, tejuela.

brickkiln [bríckil], *s.* horno de cocer ladrillos.

bricklayer [brikléiœr], *s.* enladrillador.

brickmaker [brícméikœr], *s.* ladrillero.

brickmaking [brikméiking], *s.* fabricación de ladrillos.

brickwork [brikuœrc], *s.* enladrillado, obra de ladrillos.

bricky [bríki], *a.* ladrilloso.

brickyard [bríkyard], *s.* ladrillal, adobería.

bridal [bráidal]. **I.** *a.* nupcial.—**b. song,** epitalamio.—**b. trip,** viaje de novios: (apl.) vuelo de la reina para ser fecundada por el zángano. **II.** *s.* boda, fiesta nupcial.

bride [bráid], *s.* novia, desposada.—**bridecake,** torta o pan de la boda.—**bridechamber,** tálamo.

bridegroom [bráidgrum], *s.* novio, desposado.

bridesmaid [bráidsméid], *s.* madrina de boda, pronuba.

bridesman [bráidsmæn], *s.* = GROOMSMAN.

bridewell [bráiduel], *s.* casa de corrección de Londres; calabozo.

bridge [briy]. **I.** *s.* (ing., mar., etc.) puente; caballete de la nariz; puente de violín, etc.; violín del billar; bridge (juego de naipes); (m. v.) altar (del hogar); (fund.) tabique; (f. c.) puente o travesaño elevado de señales.—**B. of Sighs,** Puente de los Suspiros.—**in b.** (elec.) en paralelo. **II.** *va.* (a menudo con *over*), tender un puente sobre; salvar (un obstáculo); llenar (un vacío, etc.); ayudar a salir del paso; (elec.) conectar en paralelo.

bridgehead [bríyjed], *s.* cabeza de puente (defensas a la entrada de un puente).

bridgeward [bríyuard], *s.* custodio de puente; guarda principal de una llave.

bridle [bráidœl]. **I.** *s.* brida o freno del caballo; freno, sujeción; (mar.) frenillo.—**b. hand,** mano izquierda.—**b. path,** camino de herradura.—*pl.* **bridles,** (mar.) poas. **II.** *va.* embridar, enfrenar; reprimir, refrenar. **III.** *vn.* levantar la cabeza, erguirse.

bridler [bráidlœr], *s.* enfrenador; refrenador.

bridoon [brídun], *s.* bridón, filete.

brief [brif], *a.* breve, conciso, corto, sucinto, sumario; fugaz, pasajero, rápido.

brief, *s.* epítome, resumen; (for.) escrito, relación, alegato, memorial, informe; (mús.) breve; (igl.) breve, buleto, apostólico.

briefless [brífles], *a.* sin clientes.

briefly [brífli], *adv.* brevemente, sucintamente; en resumen.

briefness [brífnes], *s.* brevedad, concisión.

brier [bráiœr], *s.* (bot.) escaramujo, agavanzo, rosal silvestre; zarza.

briery [bráiœri], *a.* zarzoso.

brig [brig], *s.* (mar.) bergantín.

brigade [briguéd], *s.* brigada.

brigadier general [brígadiœr yénœral], *s.* (mil.) brigadier.

brigand [brígand], *s.* bandido, bandolero.

brigandage [brígandœr], *s.* salteamiento, latrocinio, bandolerismo.

brigandine [brígandin], *s.* cota de malla.

brigantine, *s.* = BRIG.

bright [bráit], *a.* claro, lustroso, brillante; subido (apl. a colores); preclaro, eximio; vivo, alegre; talentoso, inteligente.—**b.-eyed,** ojialegre.

brighten [bráitœn]. **I.** *va.* pulir o abrillantar; alegrar, consolar; ennoblecer o hacer ilustre; mejorar; avivar. **II.** *vn.* (a veces con **up**) aclarar, despejarse (el cielo); avivarse, animarse.

brightly [bráitli], *adv.* brillantemente.

brightness [bráitnes], *s.* lustre, esplendor, brillantez; resplandor, claridad; agudeza o viveza de ingenio.

Bright's disease [bráits disís], *s.* (med.) albuminuria.

brill [bril], *s.* (ict.) mero. *V.* BRET.

brilliance [bríllans], **brilliancy** [-si], *s.* brillantez, brillo; resplandor; esplendor, lustre.

brilliant [bríllant]. **I.** *a.* brillante, refulgente; talentoso; excelente. **II.** *s.* (joy.) brillante; diamante; (impr.) tipo de 3½ puntos.

brillantine [bríllantin], *s.* brillantina.

brilliantly [bríllantli], *adv.* espléndidamente, brillantemente.

brilliantness [bríllantnes], *s.* brillantez.

brim [brim]. **I.** *s.* borde, orilla; labio de un vaso; ala de sombrero. **II.** *va.* llenar hasta el borde. **III.** *vn.* estar de bote en bote.

brimful [brímful], *a.* lleno hasta el borde.

brimfulness [-nes], *s.* llenura hasta el borde.

brimless [brímles], *a.* sin labio, borde o ala.

brimmer [brímœr], *s.* copa o vaso lleno.

brimming [bríming], *a.* lleno hasta el borde.

brimstone [brímstoun], *s.* azufre.

brinded [brínded], *a.* moteado, mosqueado.

brindle [bríndœl], *s.* variedad de colores como la del tigre.—**brindled,** *a.* mosqueado, abigarrado.

brine [bráin], *s.* salmuera; mar; lágrimas.

brinepit [bráinpit], *s.* ojo de agua salada.

bring [bring], *va.* (pret. y pp. BROUGHT) traer; llevar; conducir; inducir, persuadir; aportar; causar, producir; valer, venderse a (buen precio, etc.).—**to b. about,** efectuar, poner por obra; causar.—**to b. away,** llevarse una cosa de donde estaba.—**to b. back,** traer de vuelta, devolver.—**to b. down,** matar (caza); hacer bajar; deprimir, humillar; continuar, prolongar. —**to b. down the house,** promover grandes aplausos.—**to b. forth,** producir; parir; dar a luz; poner de manifiesto.—**to b. forward,** empujar; (com.) llevar una suma a otra cuenta **(brought forward,** suma y sigue, suma anterior).— **to b. home,** demostrar indisputablemente; hacer sentir o ver claramente.—**to b. in,** presentar (una cuenta, etc.); producir; recoger; entrar, meter; servir (una comida); introducir (una moda, etc.); dar (un fallo); presentar, entablar (juicio, queja, etc.).—**to b. off,** rescatar; disuadir.—**to b. on,** causar; comenzar; inducir.—**to b. out,** presentar; sacar a luz; publicar; sacar; poner de manifiesto; (teatro) poner en escena; revelar, descubrir.—**to b. over,** persuadir, convertir; traer.—**to b. round,** ganar, convertir; curar.— **to b. suit,** entablar o seguir pleito.—**to b. to,** sacar de un desmayo; reanimar; (mar.) ponerse a la capa o en facha.—**to b. to book,** obligar a dar cuenta.—**to b. to light,** descubrir, revelar; hacer ver.—**to b. to pass,** realizar, efectuar.—**to b. to ruin,** perder, arruinar.—**to b. to task,** reprender, regañar, censurar.—**to b. to terms,** hacer ceder o convenir; someter.—**to b. under,** sojuzgar, someter.—**to b. up,** criar, educar; traer a colación o discusión; hacer parada.—**to b. up the rear,** cubrir o ir a la retaguardia.

bringer [bríngœr], s. portador.

brinish [bráiniŝh], a. salado, salobre.

brinishness [-nes], s. sabor de sal.

brink [brink], s. orilla, margen, borde.—**on the b. of,** al borde de; a punto de.

briny [bráini], a. salado, salobre.—**the b. deep,** el mar.

briquet, briquette [brikét], s. briqueta, losilla.

brisk [brisc]. **I.** a. vivo, activo, animado, enérgico; rápido; efervescente; bueno—en el sentido de conveniente, suficiente, etc., v.g., *brisk wind,* buen viento. **II.** va. (con *up*), avivar, animar, acelerar; atizar. **III.** vn. (con *up*), animarse.

brisket [brísket], s. pecho de un animal o un pedazo cortado de él.

briskly [brískli], adv. vivamente, aprisa.

briskness [brísknes], s. viveza, actividad, vivacidad, despejo, gallardía.

bristle [brísœl]. **I.** s. cerda, porcipelo. **II.** va. erizar, poner tieso. **III.** vn. erizarse.—**to b. up,** montar en cólera; hacer ademán de resolución.—**to b. with,** estar erizado o rodeado de (dificultades, etc.)

bristly [brístli], a. cerdoso, hirsuto, erizado.

Bristol board [brístol bord], s. Bristol, cartulina Bristol.—**B. brick,** piedra silícea para limpiar cuchillos.—**B. metal,** latón como de 4 % de cinc.—**B. paper** =B. BOARD.

britannia [britænia] (metal.), s. metal inglés.

Britannic [britænic], a. británico.

British [brítiŝh], a. británico; inglés.

Briton [brítœn], a. y s. britano, inglés.

brittle [brítœl], a. quebradizo, frágil.

brittleness [-nes], s. fragilidad, friabilidad.

broach [bróuch]. **I.** s. (carp.) broca, mecha; espetón, lezna, punzón; terraja de relojero; (joy.) prendedor, broche; (arq.) aguja, chapitel. **II.** va. mencionar por primera vez; introducir; hacer público; espetar, ensartar; espitar un tonel; decentar, encentar.

broad [brod], a. ancho, anchuroso, extenso, vasto; claro; general, comprensivo; liberal, tolerante; descomedido, rudo, tosco, indelicado; lleno, abierto (apl. a letras y sonidos); pronunciado, marcado (apl. a la pronunciación, tono, etc.); pleno (*in broad daylight,* en pleno día, a la luz del sol).—**b.-blown,** enteramente formado.—**b.-breasted,** ancho; de pechos.—**b.-brimmed,** de borde ancho de alas anchas.—**B. Church,** iglesia o doctrina liberal o tolerante.—**b.-faced,** b.-fronted, cariancho.—**b. gage, b. gauge,** s. (f. c.) vía ancha; a. de vía ancha.—**b.-leafed, b.-leaved,** de hojas anchas.—**b.-minded,** tolerante, liberal.—**b. seat,** sello real o nacional.—**b.-shouldered,** espaldudo.—**as b. as long, as b. as it is long,** igual, lo mismo del un modo que del otro.

broadaxe [bródǽcs], s. hacha de carpintero; doladera.

broadbrim [-brím], s. sombrero de ala ancha; sombrero de cuáquero.—**broadbrimmer** [-brímœr], s. (fam.) cuáquero.

broadcast [-cæst]. **I.** a. y vn. (p. y pp. BROADCAST), esparcir, diseminar; propalar; (agr.) sembrar al vuelo; (rad.) perifoniar, radiar, radiodifundir. **II.** s. (agr.) siembra al vuelo. **III.** adv. esparcidamente; por todas partes.

broadcasting [-césting]. **I.** s. (agr.) siembra al vuelo; (rad.) perifonía, radiodifusión. **II.** a. (rad.) emisor, difusor, radiodifusor.

broadcloth [bródcloz], s. paño fino de más de 29 pulgadas de ancho.

broaden [bródœn], va. y vn. ensanchar(se).

broadish [bródiŝh], a. algo ancho.

broadly [bródli], adv. anchamente, ampliamente; de una manera general.

broadness [bródnes], s. ancho o anchura; liberalidad, liberalismo; amplitud.

broadside [bródsáid], s. (mar.) costado de un buque; (arti.) andanada; (impr.) cada lado de un pliego de papel.

broadsword [bródsord], s. espadón, chafarote, montante.

broadwise [bróduaiŝ], adv. a, o por, lo ancho.

brocade [brokéd]. **I.** s. brocado. **II.** va. espolinar; decorar con brocado.

brocaded [brokéded], a. espolinado.

brocage [bróukeY], s. = BROKERAGE.

brocatel [brócatel], s. brocatel.

broccoli [brócoli], s. bróculi, brécol.

brochure [bróŝhuœr], s. folleto; bosquejo.

brock [broc], s. (zool.) tejón.

brocket [bróket], s. gamo de dos años.

brogan [brógæn], s. zapato basto.

brogue [brog], s. abarca; acento de los irlandeses cuando hablan inglés.

broil [bróil]. **I.** s. riña, camorra, pendencia; alboroto, tumulto, sedición; carne asada al fuego; calor intenso. **II.** va. asar carne sobre las ascuas o en parrillas; soasar, tostar, turrar. **III.** vn. asarse, padecer calor.

broiler [bróilœr], s. parilla; pollo a propósito para asar; camorrista.

broiling [-ing], a. extremamente cálido; tórrido.

brokage [bróukeY], s. = BROKERAGE.

broke [bróuk]. **I.** vn. hacer de corredor. **II.** pret. de TO BREAK; (fam. o vulg.), sin blanca, sin un real, (Amér.) pelado, en la lata.

broken [bróukœn], pp. de TO BREAK; quebrado, roto; imperfecto; suelto, separado; interrumpido; domado; mal pronunciado, chapurrado; barrancoso; irregular, áspero, disparejo; quebrado (apl. al terreno); desalentado; debilitado, agotado; arruinado.—**b. ashlar,** mampostería de piedras de distintos tamaños.—**b.-backed,** deslomado; (mar.) quebrantado.—**b. down,** estropeado, agotado; descorazonado, afligido; arruinado.—**b.-hearted,** angustiado, traspasado de dolor.—**b. language,** lenguaje chapurrado, hablado con acento extranjero.—**b. line,** línea quebrada.—**b. sleep,** sueño interrumpido o intranquilo.—**b. voice,** voz cascada.—**b. wind,** (vet.) huélfago.—**b.-winded,** falto de resuello; (vet.) atacado de huélfago.

brokenly [brókœnli], adv. interrumpidamente, a ratos.—**brokenness** [-nes], s. desigualdad.

broker [brókœr], s. (com.) corredor; cambista.

brokerage [brókœreY], s. (com.) corretaje.

broma [bróma], s. harina de cacao; bebida que con ella se hace; (med.) alimento sólido.

bromal [brómal], s. (quím.) bromal.

bromate [brómet]. **I.** va. tratar con bromo. **II.** s. (quím.) bromato.

Bromelia [bromílïæ], s. (bot.) bromelia.—**Bromeliaceæ** [bromiliéisii], pl. (bot.) bromeliáceas.—**bromeliaceous** [-ŝhus], a. (bot.) bromeliáceo.

bromide [brómaid, -mid], s. (quím.) bromuro; (fam. o vulg.) Perogrullo, formalista.—**b. paper,** (fot.) papel de gelatinobromuro.

bromidic [-mídic], a. (fam.) común, trivial, cansado, fastidioso.

bromine [brómin], s. (quím.) bromo.—**b. water,** agua bromurada.

bromoform [brómoform], s. bromoformo.

bronchi [brónkai], s. pl. bronquios.

bronchia [brónkia], s. pl. (anat.) subdivisiones de los bronquios.

bronchial [brónkial], **bronchic** [brónkic], a. bronquial.—**b. tubes,** bronquios.

bronchiole [brónkioul], s. (anat.) bronquíolo.

bronchitis [bronkáitis, kítis], s. bronquitis.

bronchocele [bróncosil], s. (med.) papera.

bronchotomy [broncótomi], s. (cir.) traqueotomía.

bronchus [brónkus], s. (anat.) bronquio.

bronco [bronco], s. potro cerril.

bronze [bronŝ]. **I.** s. bronce; (b. a.) objeto de bronce; color de bronce. **II.** va. broncear; pavonar; tostar por el sol.

---

bronzing [brónŝing], _s._ bronceado.

brooch [broch _o_ bruch], _s._ (joy.) broche, prendedero, alfiler de pecho.

brood [brud]. **I.** _va._ empollar; cobijar; acariciar; tolerar. **II.** _vn._ empollar.—**to b.** over, cavilar ó rumiar. **III.** _s._ cría, nidada, camada; progenie, raza. **IV.** _a._ clueca.

brooder [-œr], _s._ clueca; incubadora; rumión.

broody [brúdi], _a._ clueca.

brook [bruc]. **I.** _s._ arroyo, quebrada. **II.** _va._ sufrir, aguantar, tolerar.

brooklet [brúclet], _s._ arroyuelo.

brooklime [brúclain], _s._ (bot.) becabunga.

brookmint [brúcmint], _s._ (bot.) menta de agua.

brooky [brúki], _a._ lleno de arroyos.

broom [brum], _s._ (bot.) hiniesta, retama; escoba. —**b. brush** = BRUSH BROOM.—**b. corn,** (bot.) millo de escoba, carquexia.—**b. maker,** escobero.

broomstick, broomstaff [brúmstic, -stæf], _s._ palo de escoba.

broomy [brúmi], _a._ retamoso.

broth [broz], _s._ caldo.

brothel [bróþel], _s._ burdel, lupanar.

brother [brúÐœr], _s._ hermano; cofrade, colega.— **brother-in-law,** cuñado.—**B. Jonathan,** el hermano Jonatás (los E. U.).

brotherhood [-jud], _s._ fraternidad; hermandad, confraternidad, cofradía.—**brotherless** [-les], _a._ que no tiene hermanos.—**brotherlike** [-laic], _a._ fraternal.—**brotherly** [-li]. **I.** _a._ fraternal. **II.** _adv._ fraternalmente.

brougham [bróum], _s._ coche cerrado; brougham.

brought [brot], _pret._ y _pp._ del verbo TO BRING.

brow [bráu], _s._ ceja; sienes, frente, rostro; semblante; cresta, cima, cumbre.

browbeat [bráubit], _va._ imponerse a; intimidar; mirar con ceño torvo.

browbeating [bráubíting]. **I.** _s._ ceño; intimidación. **II.** _a._ ceñudo.

browless [bráules], _a._ descarado.

brown [bráun]. **I.** _a._ pardo, castaño, moreno.— **b. bear,** oso pardo.—**b. Betty,** pudín de manzana y pan.—**b. bill,** alabarda.—**b. bread,** pan bazo o moreno.—**b. coal,** lignito.—**b. holland,** holanda cruda.—**b. ochre,** ocre carmelita.—**b. paper** papel de estraza.—**b. race,** raza malaya.—**b. study,** arrobamiento.—**b. sugar,** azúcar terciada. **II.** _s._ color pardo, moreno o castaño. **III.** _va._ poner moreno o tostado; broncear; quemar (el sol).

brownie [bráuni], _s._ duende moreno y benéfico.

brownish [bráuniŝh], _a._ que tira a moreno.

brownness [bráunnes], _s._ color moreno.

brownstone [-stoun], _s._ piedra arenisca de color pardo rojizo.

brownwort [bráunuœrt], _s._ (bot.) escrofularia.

browse [bráuŝ]. **I.** _va._ y _vn._ ramonear, rozar, tascar, herbajar. **II.** _s._ pimpollos, renuevos o ramones que roza el ganado.

browsing [bráuŝing], _s._ ramoneo.

brucite [brúŝait], _s._ (min.) brucita.

bruin [brúin], _s._ oso.

bruise [brúŝ]. **I.** _va._ magullar, golpear, machacar, abollar, majar; pulverizar. **II.** _s._ magulladura, contusión; abolladura.

bruiser [brúŝœr], _s._ púgil; bruñidor de lentes.

bruising [brúŝing], _s._ pugilato; magullamiento; (ten.) majado del cuero; acto de agramar; presión de uvas.

bruit [brut]. **I.** _s._ ruido, rumor, noticia, fama; [brui] (med.) sonido que se oye por la auscultación. **II.** _va._ esparcir, divulgar, publicar.

brumal [brúmal], _a._ brumal.

brume [brum], _s._ bruma, neblina.

brumous [brúmus], _a._ brumoso.

brunette [brunét], _a._ y _s._ moreno, trigueño.

brunt [brunt], _s._ embate más fuerte; lo más reñido.

brush [bruŝh]. **I.** _s._ cepillo, escobilla, bruza; brocha, pincel; (elec.) escobilla; escaramuza, pelea, zacapela, sarracina; batida de caza; haz de leña menuda; matorral, monte, breñal. **II.** _va._ acepillar; limpiar con cepillo; quitar frotando (con un trapo, la mano, etc.); frotar, rozar, restregar;

rasar; pintar con brocha. **III.** _vn._ moverse apresuradamente.—**to b. aside,** echar a un lado.—**to b. away,** restregar duro.—**to b. up,** retocar, refrescar, repasar.

brusher [brúŝhœr], _s._ acepillador.

brushwood [brúŝhud], _s._ matorral, breñal, zarzal; broza, ramojo, ramalla.

brushy [brúŝhi], _a._ cubierto de matojos.

brusk _o_ **brusque** [brusc, brusc]. **I.** _a._ brusco, rudo. **II.** _va._ tratar con rudeza.

Brussels [brúŝelŝ], _s._ Bruselas.—**B. carpet,** alfombra de Bruselas.—**B. lace,** encaje de Bruselas. —**B. sprouts** (bot.) bretones.

brutal [brútal], _a._ brutal, bestial, cruel.

brutality [brutǽliti], _s._ brutalidad; barbaridad.

brutalize [brútalaiŝ], _va._ embrutecer; tratar con crueldad.

brutally [brútali], _adv._ brutalmente.

brute [brut]. **I.** _s._ bruto, bestia. **II.** _a._ brutal; bruto.—**b. force,** fuerza bruta.

brutify [brútifai], _va._ y _vn._, embrutecer, embrutecerse.

brutish [brútiŝh], _a._ brutal, bestial; abrutado; sensual, salaz.—**brutishly** [-li], _adv._ brutalmente.

brutishness [-nes], _s._ brutalidad.—**brutism** [brútiŝm], _s._ bruteza.

bryony [bráioni], _s._ (bot.) brionia.

bubble [búbœl]. **I.** _s._ burbuja, ampolla; borbollón; bagatela; engañifa.—**b. tube,** tubo de nivel de burbuja; el nivel mismo. **II.** _vn._ burbujear, hacer ampollas; bullir, hervir; murmurar el río; brotar, surgir (el agua); trinar los pájaros. **III.** _va._ engañar, estafar.

bubbler [búblœr], _s._ engañador, fullero.

bubbly [búbli], _a._ espumoso.

bubo [búbo], _s._ (med.) incordio, bubón.

bubonic [biubónic], _a._ bubónico.

buccal [búcal], _a._ bucal.

buccaneers [búcaníœrŝ], _s. pl._ filibusteros.

Buccinum [buksínum], _s._ (zool.) buccino.

Bucentaur [biuséntor], _s._ bucentauro.

buchu [búkiu], _s._ (bot.) buchú.

buck [buc]. **I.** _s._ gamo; cabrón; macho de algunos otros animales (ciervo, antílope, liebre, conejo, etc.); (E. U.) indio o negro varón y adulto; petimetre; banquillo de aserrar leña; lejía; salto de carnero del potro cerril; caja de carruaje. **II.** _va._ colar, enjebar; (mil.) castigar atando los codos, muñecas y rodillas; tirar el caballo al jinete por las orejas; romper mineral con martillo. **III.** _vn._ juntarse gamo y gama en tiempo de brama.

buckbasket [búcbásket], _s._ cesto de la colada.

buckbean [búcbin], _s._ (bot.) trébol de pantano.

buckboard [búcbord], _s._ (E. U.) carretón sin muelles.

bucket [búket], _s._ cubo, balde; baldada, contenido de un balde; (hidr.) cangilón; paleta (de turbina u otra rueda); émbolo de (con) válvula de una bomba elevadora; (ing.) cucharón, cubo (de draga, excavadora, etc.).—**b. chain,** (ing.) cadena o transportador de canjilones.—**b. excavator,** excavadora de cucharón.—**b. shop,** (E. U.) oficina o agencia donde se hacen apuestas relativas a los valores de la lonja, en forma de transacciones ficticias (la ley la prohíbe como casa de juego).—**b. wheel,** rueda de cangilones.

bucketful [búketful], _s._ cantidad que puede contener un cubo.

buckeye [búcai], _s._ (bot.) castaña de Indias.

buckle [búcœl]. **I.** _s._ hebilla; arricés; bucle. **II.** _va._ hebillar, abrochar con hebilla; embrozar, hacer bucles. **III.** _vn._ doblarse, encorvarse; prepararse.—**to b. to,** dedicarse con empeño a.— **to b. with,** empeñarse, encontrarse con.

buckler [búclœr], _s._ escudo, broquel, adarga, rodela.

buckmast [búcmast], _s._ fabuco.

buckram [búcram], _s._ bucarán.

bucksaw [búcso], _s._ sierra de bastidor.

buckshorn [búcsjorn], _s._ (bot.) estrellamar.

buckshot [búcshot], _s._ posta, perdigón grande.

buckskin [búcskin]. **I.** _s._ piel de ante; coturno. **II.** _a._ de ante.

buckstall [búcstol], _s._ red tumbadera.

buckthorn [búczorn], *s.* (bot.) ladierno, tamujo, cambrón.

buckwheat [búcjuit], *s.* (bot.) alforfón, trigo sarraceno.—**b. coal,** antracita menuda.

bucolic [biucólic]. **I.** *a.* bucólico, pastoril. **II.** *s.* bucólica.

bud [bud]. **I.** *s.* pimpollo, brote, cogollo, botón o yema de las plantas; capullo de una flor; niña que entra en la sociedad. **II.** *vn.* brotar, germinar, crecer, florecer, abotonar, pimpollecer. **III.** *va.* (agr.) injertar o ingerir de escudete.

Buddha [búda], *s.* Buda.—**Buddhic** [búdic], **Buddhistic** [budístic], *a.* búdico.—**Buddhism** [-ism], *s.* budismo.—**Buddhist** [-ist], *s.* budista.

budding [búding]. **I.** *a.* en capullo. **II.** *s.* brotadura; injerto de escudete; (bot.) gemación.

buddle [búdœl]. **I.** *s.* (min.) lavadero, artesa. **II.** *va.* lavar el mineral.

buddy [búdi], *s.* (fam.) camarada, compañero; soldado; niño, muchachito.

budge [búy]. **I.** *va.* mover. **II.** *vn.* moverse, menearse; hacer lugar. **III.** *a.* guarnecido con piel de cordero; pomposo, imponente, formal. **IV.** *s.* piel de cordero.

budget [búyet], *s.* morral, saco, mochila; colección de noticias; presupuesto.

buff [buf]. **I.** *s.* piel de ante; pulidor rotatorio, rueda pulidora; color de ante; (med.) linfa cuajada.—**in b.,** en cueros. **II.** *a.* de ante; anteado; sólido, firme. **III.** *va.* pulimentar; (ten.) adelgazar el cuero; parar un golpe; amortiguar un choque.

buffalo [búfalo], *s.* (zool.) búfalo; piel de búfalo. —**b. moth,** antreno, polilla de las alfombras.—**b. robe,** piel de búfalo con pelo.

buffer [búfœr], *s.* amortiguador de choques; (f. c.) tope.—**b. block,** (f. c.) tope.—**b. state,** estado o país que sirve de valla entre dos naciones rivales.

buffet [búfet]. **I.** *s.* bofetada; embate; ajetreo. **II.** *va.* abofetear; dar golpes; luchar contra. **III.** *vn.* combatir a puñadas.

buffet [bufé], *s.* aparador, copero; repostería, alacena; caja de órgano.—**b. car,** (f. c.) vagón donde se sirven refrigerios.

buffeter [búfetœr], *s.* púgil, abofeteador.

buffeting [búfeting], *s.* mano de bofetadas.

buffing [búfing], *s.* (ten.) raspado del cuero; separación de dicho respaldo; pulimentación.—**b. block** (f. c.) = BUFFER BLOCK.—**b. spring,** resorte amortiguador.

buffleheaded [búfœljéded], *a.* cabezudo, estúpido, majadero.

buffoon [bufún], *s.* bufón, juglar.—**buffoonery** [-eri], *s.* bufonada, chocarrería.—**buffoonlike** [-laic], *a.* truhanesco, chocarrero, burlesco.

buffy [bufi], *a.* anteado.

bug [bug], *s.* (Ingl.) chinche; sabandija (cucaracha, chinche, etc.).—**b. house,** (vulg.) manicomio.

bugaboo, bugbear [búgabú, búgbear], *s.* espantajo, coco.

buggy [búgi]. **I.** *s.* coche ligero; carro, carretilla; (f. c.) vagón de cola. **II.** *a.* lleno de chinches, gusanos u otros insectos; (vulg.) bobo, destornillado.

bugle [biúgœl], **bugle horn** [-jorn], *s.* corneta, trompeta.—**b. call,** toque o llamada de corneta.

bugle. I. *s.* cañutillo; *pl.* abalorios; (bot.) consuelda menor. **II.** *a.* de abalorio.

bugler [biúglœr], *s.* trompetero, corneta.

bugloss [biúglos], *s.* (bot.) buglosa.

buhl [bul], **buhlwork** [búlcœrk], *s.* taracea.— **b.-saw,** segueta.

buhrstone [bœrstoun], *s.* V. BURRSTONE.

build [bild]. **I.** *va.* y *vn.* (pret. y *pp.* BUILT) edificar, fabricar, construir; formar; cimentar; fundar.—**to b. on,** *o* **upon,** edificar o levantar sobre; contar con, confiar en.—**to b. up,** reconstruir, vigorizar; formar de piezas; (mec.) armar. **II.** *s.* estructura; forma, figura.

builder [bildœr], *s.* arquitecto, maestro de obras, constructor.

building [bilding]. **I.** *s.* casa, fábrica, edificio; obra, construcción, edificación. **II.** *a.* de con-

strucción; para construcciones; de o relativo a casas o edificios.

built [bilt], *pret.* y *pp.* de TO BUILD.—**b. up,** hecho de varias piezas, armado.

bulb [bulb], *s.* (bot.) bulbo o cebolla; (anat.) bulbo; cubeta del barómetro; ampolleta del termómetro.—**b. angle,** (constr.) escuadra con un ala ensanchada.

bulbar [búlbar], *a.* perteneciente a un bulbo.

bulbous [búlbus], *a.* bulboso; que nace de bulbos.

Bulgar [búlgær], *s.* búlgaro.

Bulgarian [bulguérian], *s.* y *a.* búlgaro.

bulge [búly], *s.* pandeo, comba.

bulge. I. *va.* combar, pandear. **II.** *vn.* combarse; (mar.) hacer agua la embarcación.

bulginess [búlvines], *s.* pandeo, combadura; (alb.) desplome.

bulimy [biúlimi], *s.* bulimia, hambre canina.

bulk [bulk], *s.* volumen, tamaño; corpulencia; parte principal, tronco; la mayor parte, el grueso; la mayoría; (mar.) capacidad o carga de un buque; bodega.—**in b.,** al granel.

bulkhead [búlkjed], *s.* (mar.) mamparo, frontón, propao.

bulkiness [búlkines], *s.* volumen o bulto, masa, magnitud.

bulky [búlki], *a.* voluminoso, abultado; corpulento.

bull [bul], *s.* (zool.) toro; (T-, astr.) Tauro; bula pontificia; disparate, despropósito; (com.) alcista.—**b. baiting,** combate de toros y perros. —**b. calf,** ternero.—**b. chain,** cadena para arrastrar trozas con perros.—**b.-faced,** cariancho. —**b. moose,** macho de anta; (fam. pol, E. U., B- M-) progresista (partido fundado por Teodoro Roosevelt).—**b.'s-eye,** [búls-ai], *s.* claraboya, tragaluz; linterna sorda; centro de blanco; tiro que da en el blanco; (astr.) Aldebarán; (mar.) bigota o motón ciego.

bulla [búla], *s.* bula (medalla); (med.) flictena.

bullary [búlari], *s.* (igl.) bulario.

bulldog [búldog], *s.* perro dogo pequeño, bulldog; revólver de calibre grande.

bulldoze [búldoś], *va.* (E. U.) intimidar.

bullet [búlet], *s.* bala (de fusil o pistola); plomada de pescador.—**b. forceps,** sacabalas.— **b.-proof,** a prueba de bala.

bulletin [búletin], *s.* boletín.—**b. board,** tablilla en que se fijan listas, noticias, etc.

bullfight [búlfait], **bullfighting** [-ing], *s.* corrida de toros.—**bullfighter** [-faitœr], *s.* torero, toreador.

bullfinch [-finch], *s.* (ornit.) pinzón real.

bullfrog [-frog], *s.* rana (apl. esp. a la rana mugidora norteamericana).

bullhead [-jed], *s.* (ict.) siluro; gobio; (orn.) chorlito, zote.

bullheaded [-jéded], *a.* cabeza de buey; obstinado, terco.

bullion [búliun], *s.* (com.) metálico; oro o plata en barras.—**b. fringe,** galón o franja de oro.

bullish [búlish], *a.* disparatado; (com.) en alza.

bullock [búlœc], *s.* buey, cebón.

bullpen [-pen], *s.* toril; (fam.) prevención de policía.

bully [búli]. **I.** *s.* espadachín, camorrista, jaque, matón, rufián, matasiete. **II.** *a.* (fam.) magnífico, excelente. **III.** *va.* intimidar, amedrentar. **IV.** *vn.* bravear, gallear, fanfarronear.

bulrush [búlrush], *s.* junco, enea.

bulrushy [búlrushi], *a.* juncoso.

bulwark [búluarc]. **I.** *s.* (fort.) baluarte; (mar.) amurada. **II.** *va.* poner baluartes.

bum [bum]. **I.** *va.* hacer girar y zumbar (una peonza). **II.** *vn.* (fam. E. U.) holgazanear, vivir a expensas de otro. **III.** *s.* (fam. E. U.) holgazán; sablacista; trasero.

bumbailiff [búmbeilif], *s.* corchete, alguacil.

bumblebee [búmbœlbi], *s.* moscón, abejarrón.

bumboat [búmbout], *s.* (mar.) bote vivandero.

bumkin [búmkin], *s.* (mar.) pescante de la amura del trinquete.—**b. shrouds,** vientos de los pescantes de amura.

bummer [búmœr], s. (fam.) holgazán.

bump [bʌmp]. **I.** s. topetazo, porrazo; chichón; giba, corcova; abolladura; barriga, comba; protuberancia. **II.** va. y vn. chocar contra, topetar o topetarse con.

bumper [búmpœr], s. copa o vaso lleno; lo que da golpes; (f. c. y mar.) tope; (aut.) para choques.

bumpkin [búmpkin], s. patán.

bumptious [búmpshʌs], a. (fam.) engreído, envanecido, presuntuoso.—**bumptiousness** [-nes], s. presunción, engreimiento.

bun [bʌn], s. bollo; rabo de conejo; gazapo.

bunch [bʌnch]. **I.** s. manojo, atado; ristra (de cebollas, etc.); mazo, montón; racimo; bulto o tumor; (fam.) manada (de gente). **II.** va. agrupar, juntar, arracimar. **III.** vn. arracimarse, amacollarse.

bunchbacked [búnchbact], a. gibado, corcovado.

bunchiness [búnchines], s. calidad de ser racimoso o nudoso.

bunchy [búnchi], a. racimoso o arracimado, amacollado; giboso.

bunco [búnco]. **I.** va. (E. U.) estafar. **II.** s. estafa.

buncombe, bunkum [búncʌm], s. palabrería.

bundle [búndœl]. **I.** s. atado, lío, mazo, haz, manojo, paquete, envoltorio. **II.** va. liar, atar, enfardelar, empaquetar, envolver.

bundook [búnduc], s. rifle, fusil.

bung [bʌng]. **I.** s. tapón, tarugo, bitoque. **II.** va. atarugar.

bungalow [búngalo], s. en la India, choza con galerías; (E. U.) casa de un piso, gen. de campo.

bunghole [búngjol], s. boca de tonel.

bungle [búngœl]. **I.** va. chapucear, chafallar, estropear. **II.** vn. hacer chapucerías. **III.** s. chapucería.—**bungler** [búnglœr], s. chapucero.—**bunglingly** [búnglingli], adv. chapuceramente, chabacanamente.

bunion [búniʌn], s. hinchazón en el juanete del pie.

bunk [bʌnc]. **I.** s. tarima, litera; (fam.) baladronada, faramalla; hojarasca. **II.** vn. acostarse en tarima; a costarse.

bunker [búnkœr], s. arión; carbonero; (mar.) pañol del carbón.

bunko [búnco], s. = BUNCO.

bunn [bʌn], s. V. BUN.

bunny [búni], s. (fam.) conejito; ardilla.

bunt [bʌnt]. **I.** va. topetar; (baseball) dar un mal voleo a la pelota. **II.** vn. (mar.) hincharse. **III.** s. hinchazón; barriga o seno de una vela o una red; (agr.) añublo, tizón; empellón, topetazo; (baseball), voleo corto o defectuoso.

bunting [búnting], s. lanilla, estameña; banderas; soporte de madera; (orn.) calandria.

buntlines [búntlinš], s. (mar.) brioles.

buoy [boi]. **I.** s. (mar.) boya, baliza.—**b. rope,** orinque. **II.** va. boyar, mantener a flote.—**to b. up,** apoyar o sostener.

buoyage [bóiey], s. sistema de boyas.

buoyancy [bóiansi], s. fluctuación; alegría, animación; (aer.) fuerza ascensional; (fís.) presión hacia arriba.

buoyant [bóiant], a. boyante; alegre, animado, vivaz.

bur, burr [bœr]. **I.** s. carda, cabeza erizada de la cardencha, envoltorio de la castaña, etc.; (tej.) nudillo, moto; (mec.) disco; arandela. **II.** va. (tej.) desmotar; (dent.) raspar con el buril.

burbot [bœrbot], s. (ict.) mustelo.

burden [bœrdœn]. **I.** s. carga, peso, gravamen; cuidados y aflicciones del ánimo; (mar.) porte, capacidad, tonelaje; (poét.) estribillo. **II.** va. cargar, agobiar, gravar.

burdensome [bœrdœnsʌm], a. gravoso, pesado, oneroso, molesto.—**burdensomeness** [-nes], s. molestia, pesadez.

burdock [bœrdoc], s. (bot.) bardana.

bureau [biúro], s. cómoda, tocador; escritorio; oficina, agencia, negociado; ramo, division, departamento.

bureaucracy [biurócrasi] s. burocracia.

bureaucratic [biúrocrétic], a. burocrático.

burette [biurét], s. bureta, probeta.

burg [bœrg], s. villa, aldea.

burganet [bœrganet], s. (arm.) borgoñota.

burgeon [bœryʌn], v. y s. = BOURGEON.

burgess [bœryes], s. burgués, ciudadano libre; (pol.) diputado por un borough.

burgessship [bœryesship], s. oficio y calidad de diputado de borough.

burgh [bœrg], s. = BOROUGH.

burgher [bœrgœr], s. ciudadano, vecino de un burgh.—**burghership** [-ship], s. ciudadanía.

burglar [bœrglar], s. ladrón que escala una casa. —**b. alarm,** alarma contra ladrones.—**b.-proof,** a prueba de ladrones.

burglarious [bœrglárius], a. referente a un escalo.

burglary [bœrglari], s. robo con escalo.

burgomaster [bœrgomástœr], s. burgomaestre.

burgonet [bœrgonet], s. = BURGANET.

Burgundian [bœrgúndian], s. y a. borgoñón.

Burgundy [bœrgʌndi], s. Borgoña.—**B. helmet,** celada borgoñona.—**B. wine,** vino de Borgoña.

burial [bérial], s. entierro.—**b. ground, b. place,** cementerio.

burier [bérioer], s. enterrador, sepulturero.

burin [biúrin], s. (b. a.) buril, cincel.

burl [bœrl]. **I.** va. (tej.) desmotar, despinzar, desborrar. **II.** s. (tej.) borra, nudillo, mota; (carp.) nudo; chapa de madera nudosa.

burlap [bœrlap], **burlaps,** s. arpillera.

burler [bœrlœr], s. desmotador.

burlesque [bœrlesc]. **I.** a. burlesco. **II.** s. (teat.) parodia. **III.** va. [-lésc], chufar, parodiar.

burletta [bœrléta], s. zarzuelita.

burling iron [bœrling áiœrn], s. (tej.) despinzadera.

burly [bœrli], a. corpulento; nudoso.

burn [bœrn]. **I.** va. (pret. y pp. BURNED o BURNT) quemar; incendiar; cocer (ladrillos, etc.), calcinar; (cir.) cauterizar.—**to b. away,** quemar o disipar lentamente por el calor o el fuego.—**to b. daylight,** perder tiempo.—**to b. on,** (tec.) soldar.—**to b. one's boats,** quemar las naves.—**to b. out,** quemar, destruir quemando; hacer salir con fuego.—**to b. the midnight oil,** quemar las cejas.—**to b. to ashes,** reducir a cenizas. **II.** vn. quemarse; arder; consumirse; abrasarse; (elec.) formar arco en las escobillas.—**to b. up,** quemarse o consumirse por completo.—**to b. with,** arder de, abrasarse de (celos, ira, etc.). **III.** s. quemadura; marca de hierro candente.

burnable [bœrnabœl], a. combustible.

burner [bœrnœr], s. quemador, abrasador; quemador de lámpara, mechero (de gas, etc.).

burnet [bœrnet], s. (bot.) pimpinela.

burning [bœrning]. **I.** s. ardor; quemadura; quema, incendio. **II.** a. abrasador, ardiente; vehemente.—**b. glass,** espejo o vidrio ustorio.

burnish [bœrnish]. **I.** va. bruñir, pulir, acicalar, (fot.) satinar. **II.** vn. tomar lustre; medrar. **III.** s. bruñido, satinado.—**burnisher** [-œr], s. bruñidor, pulidor; acicalador; (fot.) satinador.

burnoose, burnous [bœrnús], s. albornoz.

burnt [bœrnt], (pret. y pp. de TO BURN) quemado; abrasado; cocido; calcinado.—**b. offering, o sacrifice,** holocausto.

burr [bœr]. **I.** s. (V. BUR) rebaba del metal; (dent.) buril; (carp.) rondana de perno, virola; canal auricular; piedra de molino; impedimento, fardo; sonido fuerte de la **r**; protuberancia; nudo (de un árbol); raíz de las astas o cuerno de un ciervo. **II.** va. y vn. pronunciar la erre con sonido gutural.

burro [bœrro, búrrou], s. burro.

burrow [bœrro]. **I.** s. madriguera, conejera; (min.) cata. **II.** vn. amadrigar; minar, horadar; (min.) hacer calicatas.

burrstone [búrstoun], s. piedra de molino.

bursa [bœrsa], s. (anat.) bolsa o saco.

bursary [bœrsari], s. tesorería de una orden religiosa.

burse [bœrs], s. (igl.) cubierta para cáliz, etc.

Para la pronunciación de æ, œ, D, š, šh, U, ÿ, Y, z, véase la clave al principio del libro.

burst [bœrst]. **I.** *va.* (*pret.* y *pp.* BURST) romper; reventar.—**to b. open**, forzar, romper (una puerta, etc.) **II.** *vn.* reventarse; estallar; volarse.—**to b. into**, deshacerse en (lágrimas), desatarse en (improperios, amenazas, etc.).—**to b. out**, reventarse, estallar; dasatarse, prorrumpir. **III.** *s.* reventón, estallido, explosión; supremo esfuerzo.

burstwort [bœrstuœrt], *s.* (bot.) herniaria.

burthen [bœrɒen], *s.* = BURDEN.

burton [bœrton], *s.* (mar.) polispastos.

bury [béri], *va.* enterrar, sepultar; soterrar, esconder, ocultar; sumergir, meter.—**to be buried in thought**, estar absorto en la meditación.—**to b. the hatchet**, hacer la paz.

burying [bériing], *s.* entierro; exequias.—**b. ground, b. place**, cementerio.

bus [bʊs], *s.* (fam.) ómnibus; (Cuba) guagua.—**b. bar, busbar**, (elec.) barra colectora (apl. esp. a las barras de cuadros de distribución).

bush [bʊsh]. **I.** *s.* arbusto; manigua; ramo colgado a las puertas de las tabernas; cola de zorra; (mec.) *V.* BUSHING.—**b. bean**, frijol enano. **II.** *vn.* crecer espeso o contiguo. **III.** *va.* poner grano a un cañón, buje a una rueda, tejuelo a un eje, etc.; apoyar, sostener con matas; (agr.) gradar o igualar el terreno arrastrando matas; labrar (piedra) a escuadra con martillo.

bushel [búshel], *s.* medida de áridos (Ingl., 36.35 litros; E. U., 35 litros). **bushelage** [-eʏ], *s.* derecho que se paga por *bushel*.

bushing [búshing], *s.* (mec.) forro de metal; manguito; (aut.) casquillo; boquilla, guía, dado, tejo, tejuelo; (arti.) grano de un cañón.

bushman [búshmæn], *s.* campesino; (**B-**) bosquimano (salvaje nómada sudafricano).

bushwhacker [-juǽkœr], *s.* montonero.

bushy [búshi], *a.* matoso; peludo.

busily [bísili], *adv.* solícitamente, diligentemente; atareadamente.

business [bísnes], *s.* oficio; asunto, cuestión; tarea, trabajo; (com.) negocio o negocios, comercio.—**to be one's b.**, importarle o atañerle a uno.—**to make it one's b.**, proponerse.

businesslike [-laik], *a.* serio, formal, directo.

busk [bʊsk], *s.* ballena de corsé.

buskin [búskin], *s.* borceguí, coturno; (teat.) tragedia.

buskined [búskind], *a.* de alto coturno.

bust [bʊst], *s.* (b. a.) busto; retrato de busto; pecho de mujer.

bust [bʊst] (fam. y vulgar). **I.** *va.* reventar. **II.** *vn.* reventarse; quebrarse; arruinarse, quedar sin un real; salir mal, pifiarse.

bustard [bústard], *s.* (orn.) avutarda.

buster [búster], *s.* (vulg. o fam.) cosa notable, maravilla.

bustle [búsœl]. **I.** *vn.* bullir, menearse, no parar. **II.** *s.* bullicio, animación, bulla, ruido; (cost.) caderillas, tontillo, polizón.

bustler [búslœr], *s.* bullebulle.

busy [bísi]. **I.** *a.* ocupado; activo; bullicioso; entremetido. **II.** *va.* ocupar, emplear. **III.** *vr.* ocuparse.—**busybody** [-bódi], *s.* entremetido, refitolero, chismoso.—**busybrain** [-bréin], *s.* proyectista.

but [bʊt]. **I.** *conj., prep.* y *adv.* pero, mas; excepto, menos; solamente, no más que; sino; que no (*there was nobody* **but** *was tired*, no había nadie que no estuviese cansado); sin que, sin (*he never speaks* **but** *he yells*, nunca habla sin gritar, o sin que grite). Úsase a veces como expletivo enfático: **but** *it rains!* ¡vea que llueve! ¡cómo llueve!—**b. for**, a no ser por.—**cannot b.** no puedo (puede, etc.) menos de, o dejar de (*I could not* **but** *laugh*, no pude dejar de reir; *I cannot but be true*, no puedo dejar de ser cierto).—**none b.**, solamente.

butcher [búchœr]. **I.** *s.* carnicero; hombre sanguinario.—**b. bird**, (orn.) alcaudón.—**b.'s broom**, (bot.) brusco. **II.** *va.* matar reses; dar muerte cruel; hacer una carnicería en.—**butchering** [-ing]. **I.** *s.* carnicería, matanza. **II.** *a.* cruel, inhumano.—**butcherly** [-li], *a.* perteneciente al carnicero.—**butchery** [-ri], *s.* carnicería, matanza; oficio de carnicero; matadero.

butler [bútlœr], *s.* despensero, mayordomo; repostero; sumiller.—**b.'s pantry**, repostería.

butlerage [-eʏ], *s.* departamento del despensero (Ingl.) antiguo derecho sobre vinos.—**butlership** [-ship], *s.* oficio de despensero; sumillería.—**butlery** [-ri], *s.* despensa.

butt [bʊt]. **I.** *s.* cabo, extremo; (carp.) cabeza o tope de tablón; empalme plano; (arm.) culata; mocho de un taco de billar; mango de látigo, etc.; blanco, hito; límite, fin, término; bota, pipa, tonel; topetada, topetazo; mochada; estocada; punta (de cigarro).—**b. cut**, primera troza arriba de la cepa.—**b. end**, cabo, mango, extremo mayor; cabeza (de biela).—**b. hinge**, bisagra.—**b. joint**, junta a tope o de yuxtaposición.—**b. weld**, soldadura a tope. **II.** *va.* topar, topetar; acornear; apoyar; (mec.) juntar a tope. **III.** *vn.* embestir, acornear; sobresalir.—**to b. in**, (fam.) entremeterse.

butte [biut o but], *s.* monte aislado.

butter [bútœr]. **I.** *s.* manteca (de vaca), (Amér.) mantequilla; (quím.) manteca; topador, acorneador, el que da topetazos.—**b. dish**, mantequillera.—**b. knife**, cuchillo mantequillero.—**b. print, o stamp**, troquel o estampa para mantequilla; pedazo de mantequilla moldeada.—**b. spreader**, cuchillo mantequillero (para untar con ella). **II.** *va.* untar con manteca; doblar las puestas en el juego; (fam.) adular.

buttercup [-cʊp], *s.* (bot.) ranúnculo.

butterfly [-flai], *s.* (ent.) mariposa.

butterine(e) [-in], *s.* manteca artificial.

butteris [-is], *s.* (herr.) pujavante.

buttermilk [-milk], *s.* suero de manteca.

buttermold [-mould], *s.*, **butterprint** [-print], *s.* molde para mantequilla.

butternut [-nʊt], *s.* (bot.) nogal blanco americano; nuez del mismo.

butterscotch [-scóch], *s.* dulce de azúcar con mantequilla.

butterwort [-uœrt], *s.* (bot.) sanícula.

buttery [-i]. **I.** *s.* despensa; bodega, botillería. **II.** *a.* mantecoso.

buttock [bútoc], *s.* nalga; anca; (mar.) llenos de popa.

button [bútn]. **I.** *s.* botón; tirador de puerta; (elec.) botón de timbre; botón de florete; (arti.) cascabel; (agr.) botón o capullo.—*pl.* **buttons**, paje, lacayo. **II.** *va.* abotonar. **III.** *vn.* abotonarse.—**buttonhole** [-joul]. **I.** *s.* ojal, presilla. **II.** *va.* (cost.) hacer o abrir ojales; importunar, fastidiar.

buttonhook [-juc], *s.* abotonador de calzado.

buttonwood [-ud], *s.* (bot.) plátano de Occidente.

buttress [bútres]. **I.** *s.* sostén, apoyo, refuerzo; (arq. y geog.) contrafuerte. **II.** *va.* estribar, afianzar, apoyar, sostener.

butyraceous [bʊt-o biutiréshʊs], *o* **butyrous** [bútirʊs o biútirʊs], *a.* mantecoso, butiráceo.

butyric [biutíric], *a.* butírico.

butyrin(e) [biútirin], *s.* butirina.

buxom [búcsʊm], *a.* frescachona, rolliza, mocetona; vivo, alegre, festivo.

buy [bai]. **I.** *va.* (*pret.* y *pp.* BOUGHT) comprar.—**to b. a pig in a poke**, comprar un trato a ciegas.—**to b. at first hand**, comprar de primera mano.—**to b. in**, comprar (en una subasta) por cuenta del dueño.—**to b. off**, librarse con dinero, comprar (a una persona).—**to b. out**, comprar la parte (de un socio).—**to b. up**, acaparar.—**to b. upon tick**, comprar al fiado. **II.** *vn.* hacer compras, comprar.

buyable [báiaboel], *a.* comprable.

buyer [báicer], *s.* comprador, marchante.

buzz [bʊs]. **I.** *s.* zumbido.—**b. saw**, sierra circular. **II.** *vn.* zumbar, cuchichear.

buzzard [búsard], *s.* (orn.) buharro; gallinazo.

buzzer [búsœr], *s.* zumbador, murmurador; (elec.) zumbador.

by [bai]. **I.** *prep.* por (cuando denota el agente, el instrumento, la causa, el modo y el medio por el cual se ejecuta alguna cosa); a, en; para; por, junto a, cerca de, al lado de (cuando denota proximidad); a, de, con, en; según, de acuerdo con.—**b. and b.**, pronto, luego.—**b. and large**, en todo respecto.—**b. day, b. night**, de noche, de día.—**b. one's self**, solo, sin ayuda.— **b. then**, para entonces.—**b. the way**, entre paréntesis; de paso.—**b. this time**, ahora, a la hora de ésta, ya. **II.** *adv.* cerca, al lado de; aparte, a un lado.

by, bye [bái], *s.* asunto secundario; (dep.) meta.— **by the bye**, de paso, entre paréntesis.

by-election [bai-iléckshun], *s.* elecciones especiales, sobre todo para llenar puestos vacantes.

bygone [báigon], *a.* pasado.—**let bygones be bygones**, olvidemos lo pasado.

by-lane [bái-lein], *s.* vereda.

by-law [bái-ló], *s.* estatutos o reglamento.

by-name [bái-neim], *s.* apodo.

by-pass [bái-pæs], *s.* (mec. y elec.) derivación.— **b.-pass valve** (m. v.) válvula auxiliar o de derivación; (hidr.) válvula de sobrecarga o adicional.

bypath [báipaz], *s.* senda, vereda.

byplay [báiplei], *s.* (teat.) escena muda, juego escénico; pasatiempo.

by-product [bái-próduct], *s.* producto accesorio, residuo.

byrlady [bœrléidi], *interj.* ¡por la Virgen!

by-road [bái-roud], *s.* atajo, andurrial.

Byronic [bairónic], *a.* byroniano; romántico, apasionado.

by-room [bái-rum], *s.* retrete.

by-speech [bái-spich], *s.* digresión.

bystander [báisténdœr], *s.* mirón.—*pl.* circunstantes.

by-street [bái-strit], *s.* callejuela.

by-view [bái-viu], *s.* fin particular, propio interés.

byway [báiue], *s.* camino desviado.

byword [báiucœrd], *s.* objeto de burla u oprobio; apodo; mote; máxima, refrán; perogrullada.

Byzant. *V.* BEZANT.

Byzantian, Byzantine [bishénshæn, bishéntin], *a.* bizantino.

C

c [si], *s.* c; (mús., C) do, primera nota de la escala.

cab [cæb], *s.* cab, cabriolé; (Cuba) pesetera; (f. c.) casilla del maquinista.

cabal [cabǽl]. **I.** *s.* cábala, intriga. **II.** *vn.* maquinar, tramar.

cabala [cábala], *s.* cábala de los judíos.

cabalism [cǽbalishm], *s.* cabalismo—**cabalist** [-list], *s.* cabalista.—**cabalistic(al** [-listic(al], *a.* cabalístico.—**cabalistically** [-ticalí], *adv.* cabalísticamente.

caballer [cabǽlœr], *s.* maquinador.

cabaret [cǽbæré], *s.* restaurant teatro, restaurant donde se dan representaciones teatrales.— **c. show**, juego de té o de café.

cabas [cǽba], *s.* bolsa de labor.

cabbage [cǽbey]. **I.** *s.* berza, col, repollo.— **c. beetle, c. bug, c. worm**, etc., nombres de various insectos y orugas que attacan la col. **II.** *va.* sisar (los sastres); hurtar. **III.** *vn.* (agr.) repollar.

cabin [cǽbin]. **I.** *s.* cabaña, choza, bohío; (mar.) cámara, camarote.—**c. boy**, (mar.) paje de escuela; camarero. **II.** *vn.* vivir en cabaña o choza. **III.** *va.* encerrar en cabaña o choza.

cabinet [cǽbinet]. **I.** *s.* (pol.) gabinete, ministerio; colección de objetos artísticos o curiosos; sala donde se exhiben; escaparate, vitrina, estuche; armario; botiquín, (impr.) chibalete.— **c. council**, consejo de ministros o de gabinete.— **c. work**, ebanistería. **II.** *a.* ministerial; (b. a.) digno de figurar en una sala; secreto, reservado. **cabinetmaker** [-méicœr], *s.* ebanista.—**c.'s wood**, madera de ebanistería.—**cabinetmaking** [-ing], *s.* ebanistería.

cable [kéibœl]. **I.** *s.* cable; (mar.) cable, maroma, amarra; telégrafo submarino; (fam.) cablegrama.—**c. bit**, bitadura o media bitadura.—**c. car**, vagón movido por tracción de cable.—**c. grip**, grapa, fiador de cable.—**c. railroad**, ferrocarril de tracción o de cable, ferrocarril funicular.—

c.'s length, cable, medida longitudinal ($\frac{1}{10}$ de milla náutica).—**c. tier**, pozo de cables. **II.** *va.* y *vn.* cablegrafiar.

cablegram [-gram], *s.* (fam.) cablegrama.

cablet [kéiblet], *s.* (mar.) estacha.

cableway [kéibœluéi], *s.* cable aéreo de transporte.

cabman [cǽbman], *s.* calesero, cochero, simón.

caboose [cabús], *s.* (mar.) fogón o cocina; (f. c.) vagón del conductor en un tren de carga; vagón de cola.

cabriolet [cabriolé], *s.* cabriolé.

caburn [cǽbœrn], *s.* (mar.) cajeta.

cacao [cakéo], *s.* (bot.) cacao.

cachalot [cǽchalot], *s.* (ict.) cachalote.

cache [cæsh]. **I.** *va.* depositar en un escondrijo. **II.** *s.* escondite, escondrijo.

cachectic(al [cakéctic(al], *a.* caquéctico.

cachexia [cakéxia], **cachexy** [cakéxi], *s.* (med.) caquexia.

cachinnation [cækinéshun], *s.* carcajada, risotada.

cacique [casíc], *s.* cacique; (orn.) oropéndola.

cackle [cǽkœl]. **I.** *vn.* cacarear, cloquear; reírse; chacharear. **II.** *s.* cacareo; charla, cháchara.

cackler [cǽklœr], *s.* cacareador; chismoso, parlanchín.

cackling [cǽkling], *s.* cloqueo; cháchara.

cacochymia [cæcokímiæ], *s.* (med.) cacoquimia.

cacodemon [cæcodímon], *s.* diablo.

cacography [cacógrafi], *s.* cacografía.

cacomistle [cǽcomiscœl], *s.* (Mex.) cacomixtle.

cacophony [cacófoni], *s.* cacofonía.

cactus [cǽctus], *s.* (bot.) cacto.

cacumen [cakiúmen], *s.* ápice, cumbre.

cad [cæd], *s.* (fem. CADDESS) persona de modales groseros; ayudante o peón; mandadero; conductor de ómnibus.

cadastre, cadaster [cædǽstœr], *s.* catastro.

cadaver [cadéivœr], *s.* cadáver.

cadaverous [cadǽvœrus], *a.* cadavérico.

caddie [cǽdi], *s.* mensajero, recadero; muchacho que en el juego de golf lleva los bastones.

caddis [cǽdis], *s.* (tej.) jerguilla; trencilla de estambre.

caddish [cǽdish], *a.* grosero, mal educado.

caddy [cǽdi], *s.* bote, lata, cajita para té.

cade [kéid]. **I.** *a.* manso, domesticado. **II.** *s.* barril; banasta.

cadence, cadency [kéidens(i], *s.* cadencia.— **cadent** [-ent], *a.* cadencioso.

cadet [cædét], *s.* (mil.) cadete; hermano menor.

cadi [kédi], *s.* cadí.

cadmium [cǽdmium], *s.* (quím.) cadmio

cadre [cádr], *s.* núcleo; armazón; plan; (mil.) cuadro, conjunto de jefes.

caduceus [cadiúseus], *s.* caduceo.

caducous [cadiúcus], *a.* caduco; perecedero; (bot.) caduco.

cæcal [sécal], *a.* cecal.

cæcum [sécum], *s.* intestino ciego

Cæsarean [sisériæn], *a.* cesáreo.—**C. operation, C. section**, (cir.) operación cesárea.

Cæsarism [sísærism], *s.* cesarismo.

cæsura [sisiúra], *s.* (poét.) cesura.

café *s.* café, cantina.

caffein [cǽfein], *s.* cafeína.

cafeteria [cæfétériæ], *s.* restaurant sin criados, donde los parroquianos se sirven a sí mismos.

caftan [cǽftan], *s.* vestimenta turca.

cage [key]. **I.** *s.* jaula, gayola; trena; prisión. **II.** *va.* enjaular.

cageling [kéyling], *s.* pájaro enjaulado.

caic, caique [caic], *s.* (mar.) caique.

cairn [kéarn], *s.* montón de piedras para señal.

caisson [kéison], *s.* arcón; (mil.) furgón; (ing.) cajón sumergible dentro del cual se hacen cimientos bajo el agua; (mar.) camello; compuerta de dique; (arq.) artesón, casetón.

caitiff [kétif], *a.* y *s.* pícaro redomado, belitre.

cajole [cayól], *va.* lisonjear, adular; halagar, engatusar, lagotear.

cajoler [cayólœr], s. adulador, zalamero.

cajolery [cayólœri], s. adulación, lisonja; requiebro, zalamería, carantoña.

cake [kéic]. I. vn. conglutinarse, aterronarse (apl. al carbón), formar costra. II. s. tortita, hojaldre, pastelillo; pastilla o pan de jabón, de cera, etc.; terrón.

cakewalk [-uóc], s. (E. U.) danza de negros, en que se premia con un pastel a la pareja que mejor se contonea.

calaba [cǽlaba], s. (bot.) calaba, calambuco.

calabash (tree) [cǽlabǽshtri], s. (bot.) calabaza; (Cuba) güiro.

caladium [calédiUm], s. (bot.) caladio.

calamar, calamary [cǽlamar, cǽlameri], s. (ict.) calamar. V. squid.

calamine [cǽlamain], s. calamina, cadmia.

calamint [cǽlamint], s. (bot.) calamento.

calamitous [calǽmitUs], a. calamitoso.

calamity [calǽmiti], s. calamidad.

calamus [cǽlamUs], s. (bot.) cálamo aromático.

calash [calǽsh], s. calesa, carretela; capota de carruaje; capota de señora.

calcaneum [cælcáneUm], s. (anat.) calcáneo; calcañar.

calcar [cǽlcar], s. espolón; cárquesa; (met.) horno de reverbero.

calcareous [cælkériUs], a. calcáreo, calizo, calero.

calceate [cǽlsiet], a. calzado.

calcedony, s. =chalcedony.

calcic [cǽlsic], a. cálcico.

calciferous [cælsífœrUs], a. que contiene cal.

calcification [cælsifikéshUn], s. conversión en sustancia pétrea por la deposición de sales de cal; petrificación.—**calcify** [-fai], va. y vn. hacer o hacerse pétreo, depositando cal.

calcimine [cǽlsimain]. I. s. lechada. II. va. dar lechada.

calcinable [cǽlsinabœl], a. calcinable.

calcinate, va. = calcine.

calcination [cælsinéshUn], s. calcinación.

calcinatory [cælsínatori], s. calcinatorio.

calcine [cǽlsin]. I. va. calcinar. II. vn. calcinarse.

calcite [cǽisait], s. (min.) calcita.

calcium [cǽlsiUm], s. (quím.) calcio.—**c. light**, luz de calcio.

calcspar [cǽlcspar], s. calcita.

calculable [cǽlkiulabœl], a. calculable.

calculate [cǽlkiuleit]. I. va. calcular; preparar, disponer, proyectar; (fam.) suponer, creer (I calculate it will rain, creo que lloverá). II. vn. calcular.

calculated [-ted], pp. de to calculate; proyectado, ideado.—**to be c. for**, o **to**, tener la probabilidad de, conducir a.

calculating [-ting], ger. de to calculate; de calcular; que calcula; interesado, artero.—**c. machine**, aritmómetro, máquina de calcular.

calculation [-léishUn], s. cálculo, cómputo.

calculative [-letiv], a. perteneciente al cálculo.

calculator [-léitœr], s. calculador, calculista.

calculi [cǽlkiulai], s. pl. de calculus.

calculous [cǽlkiulUs], **calculose** [-los], a. calculoso.

calculus [cǽlkiulUs], s. (mat. y med.) cálculo.

caldron [cóldrUn], s. caldera o caldero, paila.

Caledonian [cæledónian], a. escocés.

calefacient [cælefǽshient], a. calentador.

calefaction [cælefǽcshUn], s. calefacción.

calefactory [cælefǽctori], s. (igl.) calefactorio.

calendar [cǽlendœr]. I. s. calendario; lista o tabla de pleitos; orden del día.—**c. year**, año civil, año corriente (el que principia el 1° de enero). II. va. poner en el calendario o en una lista; reducir a lista, índice, etc.

calender [cǽlendœr]. I. s. calandria, satinador. II. va. cilindrar, satinar.—**calenderer** [-œr], s. aprensador.

calends [cǽlendẑ], s. pl. calendas.—**at**, o **on, the Greek c.**, en las calendas griegas, nunca.

calendula [caléndiula], s. (bot.) caléndula, maravilla.

calf [caf], s. (pl. calves [cavẑ]), becerro, ternero; cervatillo; piel de becerro; pantorrilla; bobo, mentecato.—**c.'s foot jelly**, gelatina de manos de ternera.

calflike [cáflaic], a. aternerado.

calfskin [cáfskin], s. (ten.) becerrillo, piel de becerro.

caliber, calibre [cǽlibœr], s. (arti.) calibre; peso total del armamento de un buque; calibre, aptitud, capacidad.—**calibrate** [-breit], va. calibrar; graduar; regular; rectificar (graduaciones, dimensiones, etc.).—**calibration** [-bréishUn], s. calibración; rectificación, corrección.

calico [cǽlico], s. (tej.) indiana, zaraza; percal, cotonada; (Mex.) angaripola.—**c. printer**, (tej.) estampador de indiana.—**c. printing**, s. estampado en indiana.

calif [kélif], s. califa.

califate [cǽlifet], s. califato.

Californian [cælifórniæn], s. y a. californiano.

caligraphy, s. = calligraphy.

calipash [cǽlipash], s. substancia verdusca gelatinosa de la tortuga próxima a la concha superior.

calipee [cǽlipi], s. substancia amarillenta de la tortuga próxima a la concha inferior.

caliper [cǽlipœr], s. calibrador.

caliph [kélif], s. = calif.

caliphate, s. = califate.

calisaya [cǽliseya], s. calisaya.

calisthenic, a. = callisthenic.

calix [kélix], s. = calyx.

calk, caulk [cok], va. calafatear; afolar; rellenar, tapar; apretar a martillo; hacer ramplón en la herradura.

calk [cælk], va. y vn. marcar con tiza; calcar.

calk, calkin [cok, cókin], s. ramplón de herradura.

calker [cókœr], s. calafate.—**c.'s boy**, calafatín.

calking [cóking], s. calafateadura, calafateo.

calking, caulking [-ing], a. de calafatear; de afolar.—**c. chisel**, escoplo de calafatear.—**c. hammer**, martillo de afolar.—**c. iron**, escoplo de calafatear; punzón de afolar.

call [col], va. llamar (he called me, me llamó; he called me his friend, me llamó su amigo; they called him John, lo llamaron Juan; this is called cement, esto se llama cemento); citar; llamar, atraer; pronunciar, enunciar, o decir en alta voz; suponer; suponer aproximadamente, dar como valor aproximado; exigir el pago de, (Amér.) cobrar; pasar (lista); recibir, admitir (en la expresión pasiva to be called to the bar, ser admitido como abogado, recibirse de abogado).—**to e. a bluff**, cogerle la palabra a un baladrón.—**to c. away**, llamar (a alguien de alguna parte; la traducción se hace a veces cambiando el giro: I was called away to Boston, me llamaron de Boston; I was called away yesterday, ayer me llamaron y tuve que ausentarme).—**to c. back**, mandar volver; revocar, retirar.—**to c. down**, pedir al cielo; hacer bajar; regañar.—**to c. in**, retirar; llamar (un médico, etc.); exigir la presentación de (bonos, etc.); pedir (a uno) que entre, hacer entrar.—**to c. in doubt**, o **in question**, poner en duda.—**to c. into** (being, existence, etc.) dar el ser, producir, crear; poner en.—**to c. names**, insultar con epítetos ofensivos.—**to c. off**, = to c. away; distraer; suspender; aplazar; desistir de.—**to c. one's own**, disponer de, tener.—**to c. out**, llamar de afuera; poner de manifiesto; desafiar.—**to c. to account**, llamar a cuentas; censurar, impugnar, regañar.—**to c. to memory**, o **to mind**, recordar.—**to c. to order**, llamar al orden; abrir la sesión, dar principio a las deliberaciones.—**to c. up**, llamar de arriba; citar, llamar a comparecencia; poner (un proyecto) en discusión; exigir la continuación o discusión de (un proyecto, etc.); llamar por teléfono.

call, vn. llamar, dar voces; visitar; ir, venir (a ver a alguien), estar (en alguna parte a ver a alguien).—**to c. after**, llamar a.—**to c. again**, volver.—**to c. at**, ir a; parar en.—**to c. for,**

pedir; exigir, necesitar; ir o venir por.—**to c. on,** *o* **upon,** visitar a; pedir a, exhortar, exigir; en la voz pasiva, **to be called on,** *o* **upon,** tener la obligación de.

call, *s.* llamada; llamamiento; citación; convocatoria; reclamo de un ave; vocación; seña, señal, aviso; silbo, señuelo, balitadera; visita; toque, llamada; acción de pasar lista; exigencia; (com.) demanda, pedido; contrato, obligación; mandato de presentación de bonos, etc., para redimirlos.—**c. bell,** timbre de llamada.—**c. bird,** pájaro de reclamo.—**c. loan,** préstamo pagadero a solicitud.—**c. money,** dinero listo para prestar cuando se pida, a la orden.—**c. note,** reclamo (de ave).—**at c.,** *o* **on c.,** a solicitud, al pedir (apl. a obligaciones de pago).—**within c.,** al alcance de la voz.

calla (lily) [cǽla], *s.* (bot.) cala.

caller [cólœr], *s.* llamador; visita, visitante.

calligraph [cǽligraf], *s.* ejemplar o muestra de caligrafía.—**calligraphic** [-gráfic], *a.* caligráfico. —**calligraphy** [cǽligrafi], *s.* caligrafía.

calling [cóling], *s.* profesión, vocación, oficio; acción de llamar, visitar, etc. *V.* CALL.

callipers [cǽlipœrŝ], *s.* compás calibrador.

callisthenic [cæliszénic], *a.* gimnástico.

callisthenics [cæliszénics], *s.* gimnasia.

callosity [cælósiti], **callousness** [cǽlʊsnes], *s.* callosidad, dureza; insensibilidad.

callous [cǽlʊs], *a.* calloso; córneo; endurecido.— **callously** [-li], *adv.* insensiblemente, duramente.

callow [cǽlo], *a.* pelado o desplumado; joven, inexperto.

callus [cǽlʊs], *s.* callo, dureza.

calm [cam]. **I.** *s.* calma, tranquilidad. **II.** *a.* quieto, tranquilo, sereno, bonancible. **III.** *va.* tranquilizar, aquietar; apaciguar, calmar; aplacar, sosegar. **IV.** *vn.* (gen. con **down**), calmarse; abonanzarse.—**calmer** [-œr], *s.* apaciguador, pacificador.—**calmly** [-li], *adv.* sosegadamente.—**calmness** [cámnes], *s.* calma.—**calmy** [-i], *a.* tranquilo, apacible.

calomel [cǽlomel], *s.* calomel.

calorescence [cælorésens], *s.* conversión de rayos caloríficos en rayos luminosos.

caloric [calóric]. **I.** *a.* referente al calor. **II.** *s.* calórico; calor.

calorie [cǽlori], *s.* (fís.) caloría.

calorific [cælorífic], *a.* calorífico.

calorification [cælorífikéŝhʊn], *s.* calorificación.

calorimeter [[cælorímetœr], *s.* calorímetro.

calorimetric [cælorimétric], *a.* calorimétrico.

calorimetry [cælorímetri], *s.* calorimetría.

calorite [cǽlorait], *s.* (marca de fábrica) calorita (aleación de níquel, hierro y cromo).

calorize [cǽloraiŝ], *va.* alear superficialmente con aluminio por tratamiento térmico.

calory [cǽlori], *s.* = CALORIE.

caltha [cǽlza], *s.* (bot.) calta.

caltrop [cǽltrop], *s.* (mil.) abrojo; (bot.) tríbulo, abrojo.

calumet [cǽlyumet], *s.* pipa de los indios de Norte América.

calumniate [calúmnieit], *va.* y *vn.* calumniar.

calumniation [-éiŝhʊn], *s.* calumnia.

calumniator [-éitœr], *s.* calumniador.

calumniatory [calúmniatori], **calumnious** [calúmniʊs], *a.* calumnioso, injurioso, difamatorio.—**calumniously** [-li], *adv.* injuriosamente, calumniosamente.—**calumniousness** [-nes], *s.* calumnia, maledicencia, infamación.

calumny [cǽlʊmni], *s.* calumnia.

Calvary [cǽlvari], *s.* Calvario.

calve [cav], *vn.* parir la vaca.

Calvinism [cǽlviníŝm], *s.* calvinismo.

Calvinist [-ist], *s.* calvinista.—**Calvinize** [-aiŝ], *va.* enseñar la doctrina de Calvino.

calvish [cávíŝh], *a.* aternerado.

calx [calx], *s.* (*pl.* CALXES *o* CALCES) (min.) cenizas o residuos; cal, yeso.

calycle [cǽlikœl], *s.* (bot.) doble cáliz.

calyx [kélix], *s.* (bot.) cáliz; (anat.) pelvis del riñón.

cam [cæm], *s.* (mec.) leva.—**c. gear,** (aut.) engranaje del eje de levas; (mec.) distribución por levas.—**c. shaft,** (aut.) eje de levas.—**c. wheel,** rueda de (con) levas.

camber [cǽmbœr]. **I.** *s.* comba, combadura, alabeo. **II.** *vn.* y *va.* combar(se), arquear(se).

cambist [cǽmbist], *s.* (com.) cambista.

camblet [cǽmlet], *s.* = CAMLET.

Cambrian [cǽmbriæn], *s.* y *a.* (geol.) cámbrico.

cambric [kémbric], *s.* batista, holán cambray.

came [kéim], *pret.* de TO COME.

camel [cǽmœl], *s.* camello; (mar.) camello

camellia [camélia], *s.* (bot.) camelia.

camelopard [camélopard], *s.* camello pardal, jirafa.

cameo [cǽmeo], *s.* camafeo.

camera [cǽmœra], *s.* cámara fotografica; kodak; (anat.) cavidad; (for., Ingl.) cámara particular para los jueces.—**c. lucida,** cámara lúcida.—**c. obscura,** cámara obscura.

cameral [-al], *a.* relativo a una cámara, oficina o tesorería.

cameralistic [-lístic], *a.* perteneciente a la hacienda.

cameraman [-man], *pl.* **-men,** *s.* fotógrafo (apl. esp. al de cinematógrafo y al de cámara portátil).

camion [camión], *s.* camión automóvil militar.

camisado [camisádo], *s.* (mil.) encamisada.

camise [camís], *s.* camisón o bata holgada.

camomile [cǽmomail], *s.* (bot.) camomila, manzanilla.

camouflage [ca-mu-flaŷ]. **I.** *s.* disfraz; (mil.) disfraz de protección (apl. a cañones encubiertos, buques pintados, etc.). **II.** *va.* disfrazar; (mil.) disfrazar; ocultar (un cañón, etc.); encubrir bajo falsas apariencias.

camp [cæmp]. **I.** *s.* (mil.) campo, campamento; vida o servicio militar, vida de cuartel; conjunto de tiendas o cabañas que sirven de alojamiento transitorio; tienda o cabaña donde se vive transitoriamente en el campo; caserío, alojamientos (como cerca de las minas); colonia (como las escolares de verano); campo, terreno (de actividad, de acción); cuerpo, agrupación, clase, partido; multitud (de hechos, razones, etc.); division, sucursal (de una confraternidad). —**c. chair,** silla ligera plegadiza de tijera.—**c. fire,** fogata de campamento; reunión o fiesta militar alrededor de una fogata.—**c. meeting,** reunión religiosa en el campo.—**c. stool,** catrecillo. **II.** *vn.* acampar; (gen. con **out**) vivir transitoriamente en tiendas.

campaign [cæmpéin]. **I.** *s.* (mil.) campaña; (pol., etc.) campaña; propaganda; (ind.) período de trabajo, etc. sin interrupción. **II.** *vn.* hacer campaña o propaganda.—**campaigner** [-œr], *s.* el que hace campaña: propagandista; veterano.

campanero [cæmpǽneiro], *s.* (zool.) campanero.

campaniform [cæmpǽniform], **campanulate** [cæmpǽnyulet], *a.* (bot.) campanudo.

campanile [cæmpaníle], *s.* campanario.

campanology [cæmpanóloyi], *s.* arte de fundir y de tañer las campanas.

campanula [cæmpǽnyula], *s.* (bot.) campánula.

campeachy [cæmpíchi], *s.* = CAMPECHE.

campestral [cæmpéstral], **campestrian** [cæmpéstrian], *a.* campesino, campestre.

camphene, camphine [cæmfín], *s.* aceite de trementina rectificado.

camphor [cæmfœr]. **I.** *s.* alcanfor.—**c. tree,** (bot.) alcanforero. **II.** *va.* alcanforar.

camphorate [-et]. **I.** *a.* alcanforado. **II.** *s.* canforato. **III.** *va.* alcan'orar.

campion [cæmpion], *s.* (bot.) colleja.

campus [cǽmpus], *s.* (E. U.) patio de un colegio o universidad.

camshaft [cǽmŝhæft], *s.* = CAM SHAFT.—**c. gear,** (aut.) engranaje del eje de levas.

camwood [cǽmud], *s.* madera roja de Angola.

can [cæn]. **I.** *s.* lata, bote de lata; portaviandas. **c. hooks,** (mar.) gafas.—**c. opener,** abridor de latas. **II.** *vn. def. usado sólo en el pres. y pret. de indicativo* (*pret.* COULD) poder; saber. **III.** *va.* conservar en latas.—**canned goods** (en Ingl. **tinned goods**) conservas alimenticias.

Canadian [canéidian], *a.* y *s.* canadiense.

canadium [cænéidiʊm], *s.* (quím.) canadio.

canaille [canéil], *s.* canalla, gentuza.

canal [canǽl], *s.* canal; (Filip.) silanga; (arq.) estría, media caña.—**c. rays,** (fís.) iones positivos de un tubo de vacío con un cátodo perforado.

canalage [canǽley], *s.* construcción de canales; sistema de canales; derechos de transporte por un canal.

canaliculate [cænalékiulet], *a.* acanalado, estriado.

canalize [canǽlaiś], *va.* canalizar.

canalization [-éiśhʊn], *s.* canalización.

canard [cænárd], *s.* embuste, filfa; (aer.) aeroplano de mando delantero, de motor propulsor, o de vuelo al revés (con la cola hacia adelante).

canary [canéri], **canary bird,** *s.* (orn.) canario; color de canario; vino de Canarias.—**c. seed,** alpiste, triguero.

cancel [cǽnsel]. **I.** *va.* cancelar, revocar, rescindir; tachar, borrar; invalidar, anular; (mat.) suprimir. **II.** *s.* (impr. y enc.) supresión.

cancelation [cænseléśhʊn], *s.* cancelación, rescisión; (mat.) supresión de factores comunes.

cancellate [cǽnselet], *a.* reticular, celular, poroso.

cancellation [cænseléśhʊn], *s.* retículo.

cancer [cǽnsœr], *s.* cáncer; (astr., **C-**) Cáncer.

cancerate [cǽnsœret], *vn.* cancerarse.

canceration [cænsœréśhʊn], *s.* principio o formación de cáncer.—**cancerous** [-ʊs], *a.* canceroso.—**cancerousness** [-ness], *s.* cancerismo, calidad de canceroso.

cancroid [cǽncroid]. **I.** *s.* (med.) cancro. **II.** *a.* cancroideo.

candelabrum [cændelébrʊm], *s.* (*pl.* CANDELABRA) hachero, blandón; candelabro.

candid [cǽndid], *a.* cándido, sincero.

candidacy [cǽndidasi], **candidature** [-datiuœr], *s.* candidatura.

candidate [-det], *s.* candidato; aspirante.

candidly [cǽndidli], *adv.* cándidamente, ingenuamente.—**candidness** [-nes], *s.* candidez o sinceridad.

candied [cǽndid], *a.* confitado, almibarado, garapiñado.

candle [cǽndœl]. **I.** *s.* vela, bujía; candela; (fís.) bujía, unidad lumínica.—**c. end,** cabo de vela.—**c. foot,** (fís.) bujía-pie, intensidad de la luz de una bujía normal inglesa a 1 pie inglés de distancia.—**c. hour,** bujía-hora.—**c. meter,** bujía-metro, intensidad de la luz de una bujía métrica normal a 1 metro.—**c. power,** intensidad de la luz, o potencia lumínica, expresada en bujías.—**c. snuffer,** despabilador. **II.** *va.* probar (huevos, etc.) por medio de la luz, poniendo entre el ojo y una lámpara, cada uno.

candleberry [-beri], *s.* (bot.) árbol de la cera (llám. t.—**c. myrtle, c. tree**).

candleholder [-jóuldœr], *s.* portavela.

candlelight [-lait], *s.* luz de vela; luz artificial; oración, entrada de la noche.

candlelighter [-láitœr], *s.* encendedor de velas; acólito.

Candlemas [-mas], *s.* Candelaria.

candlepower [-pauer], *s.* = CANDLE POWER.

candlestick [-stic], *s.* candelero.

candlewick [-wic], *s.* pabilo.

cando(u)r [cǽndœr], *s.* candor, sinceridad.

candy [cǽndi]. **I.** *s.* bonbón, dulce.—**c. pull,** (fam.) tertulia en que se hace melcocha. **II.** *va.* almibarar, garapiñar. **III.** *vn.* acaramelarse.

candytuft [cǽndituft], *s.* (bot.) carraspique.

cane [kéin]. **I.** *s.* caña; bengala; bejuco; bastón, báculo; caña de azúcar; pezón; palo; (tej.) urdimbre.—**c. juice,** guarapo.—**c. mill,** ingenio de azúcar.—**c. press,** prensa de exprimir caña.—**c. sugar,** azúcar de caña.—**c. trash,** bagazo. **II.** *va.* apalear; poner asiento o espaldar de mimbre, bejuco, etc.

canebrake [-breik], *s.* cañaveral.

canella [cænélæ], *s.* (bot.) canelo; canela (= c. BARK).

canephorous [cænéforʊs], *s.* canéfora.

canicula [cæníkiulæ], *s.* canícula.—**C.,** Sirio.

canicular [caníkiular], *a.* canicular.

canine [canáin], *a.* canino, perruno.

canister [cǽnistœr], *s.* bote, frasco o lata para té, tabaco, etc.—**c. shot,** bote de metralla.

canker [cǽnkœr]. **I.** *s.* llaga gangrenosa; úlcera en la boca; enfermedad de los árboles frutales. **II.** *vn.* gangrenarse. **III.** *va.* gangrenar, roer, corromper; contaminar.—**cankerous** [-ʊs], *a.* gangrenoso, corrosivo.

cankerworm [cǽnkœrucœrm], *s.* oruga.

cannabic [cǽnabic], *a.* cañameño.

Cannabis [cǽnabis], *s.* (bot.) cáñamo.—**C. indica,** cáñamo de la India; haxix.

Cannaceæ [cænéisii], *s. pl.* (bot.) canabíneas.

cannel [cǽncel], **cannel coal** [coul], *s.* carbón mate, hulla de llama brillante, rica en substancias volátiles.

canner [cǽncœr], *s.* el que pone conservas en latas.

cannery [cǽneri], *s.* fábrica de conservas alimenticias.

cannibal [cǽnibal], *s.* caníbal, antropófago.—**cannibalism** [-iśm], *s.* canibalismo.

cannikin [cǽnikin], *s.* lata o vaso de metal.

cannon [cǽnʊn]. **I.** *s.* oreja de campana; (arti.) cañón; (mec.) manguito, cañón, guardaeje; (billar) carambola.—**c. metal,** bronce de cañón.—**c. shot,** bala de cañón. **II.** *va.* y *vn.* cañonear.

cannonade [cǽnʊned]. **I.** *va.* cañonear. **II.** *s.* cañoneo.

cannoneer [cǽnʊniœr]. **I.** *va.* cañonear. **II.** *s.* cañonero o artillero.

cannot [cǽnnot], *contr.* de CAN y NOT. *V.* CAN.

canny, cannie [cǽnil], *a.* (Esco.) sagaz, prudente, cuerdo; agradable; garboso; digno.

canoe [canú], *s.* canoa.

canoeist [canúist]. **I.** *s.* canoero. **II.** *vn.* llevar o pasear en canoa.

canon [cǽnon], *s.* canon; (igl.) canon o cánones; canónigo; (impr.) canon, tipo grande.

canoness [cǽnones], *s.* canonesa.

canonic(al [canónic(al], *a.* canónico.—**canonically** [-li], *adv.* canónicamente.

canonicals [canónicalś], *s. pl.* hábitos eclesiásticos.

canonicate [canóniket], *s.* canonjía.

canonist [cǽnonist], *s.* canonista.—**canonization** [-aiśéshʊn], *va.* canonizar.—**canonry** [-ri], **canonship** [-śhip], *s.* canonjía, canonicato, prebenda.

canopied [cǽnopid], *a.* endoselado.

canopy [cǽnopi]. **I.** *s.* dosel, pabellón (de cama, etc.); patio; cielo; (elipo.) campana (de una guarnición, etc.). **II.** *va.* endoselar.

canorous [cænórʊs], *a.* canoro.

can't [cant], (fam.) *contr.* de CANNOT.

cant [cænt]. **I.** *s.* canto, esquina, chaflán; desplomo, sesgo, inclinación; tumbo, vaivén; tabla, toza, etc., descanteada; hipocresía, gazmoñería; jerga, jerigonza, germanía, caló; lenguaje afectado o hipócrita. **II.** *va.* poner al sesgo o inclinar; ladear; arrojar, lanzar; voltear, invertir; descantear. **III.** *vn.* hablar con gazmoñería; hablar en jerga.

cantaloup [cǽntalup], *s.* (bot.) melón.

cantalever, *V.* CANTILEVER.

cantankerous [cæntǽkœrʊs], *a.* (fam.) quimerista, pendenciero.

cantata [cæntáta], *s.* (mús.) cantata.

canted [cǽnted], *a.* oblicuo, inclinado; (arq.) chaflanado.

canteen [cæntín], *s.* (mil.) cantina.

canter [cǽntœr]. **I.** *s.* medio galope. **II.** *vn.* andar el caballo a paso largo y sentado.

cantharides [cænzæridis], *s.* cantáridas.

canthus [cǽnzœs], *s.* rabo del ojo.

canticle [cǽntikœl], *s.* cántico.—*pl.* **Canticles,** el Cantar de los Cantares.

cantilever [cæntilévœr], *s.* (ing.) viga voladiza; soporte; modillón.—**c. bridge,** puente de vigas voladizas o de modillones.

cantle, cantlet [cǽntlet], *s.* trozo, pedazo, fragmento, porción; borrén del arzón.

canto [cǽnto], *s.* (mús. y poét.) canto.

canton [cǽnton], *s.* canton.—**C. crèpe,** burato. —**C. flannel,** moletón.

canton, cantonize [cǽntonaiŝ], *va.* acantonar, acuartelar.—**cantonal** [-al], *a.* cantonal.—**cantonalism** [-aliŝm], *s.* cantonalismo.—**cantonment** [-mœnt], *s.* acuartelamiento, acantonamiento.

cantor [cǽntor], *s.* chantre.

Canuck [canúc], *s.* y *a.* (fam.) (E. U.) canadiense; (Can.) canadiense de origen francés.

canvas [cǽnvas], *s.* lona; cañamazo; (pint.) lienzo; (mar.) lona, vela, velamen.

canvasback [-bǽc], *s.* (orn.) variedad de pato marino.

canvass. I. *s.* correría en solicitud de votos, opiniones, pedidos, etc.; examen, inspección; investigación, escrutinio. **II.** *va.* escudriñar, examinar; recorrer un distrito o comarca solicitando votos, pedidos, etc.

canvasser [cǽnvasœr], *s.* solicitador (de votos, pedidos, etc.); (E. U.) agente electoral.

cany [kéni], *a.* lleno de cañas.

canzonet [cǽnŝonet], *s.* cancioncilla, copla.

caoutchouc [cúhuc], *s.* caucho.

canyon, cañon [cǽñon], *s.* garganta, congosto, desfiladero.

cap [cæp]. **I.** *s.* gorro, gorra, casquete, birrete; tapa; bonete, capelo; cima, cumbre; (arq.) capitel; (mec.) casquete, sombrerete, chapaleta; guardapolvo de reloj· (fot.) tapa (de lente); (mar.) tamboretes; (aut.) tapa (de biela).—**c. paper,** papel de estraza. El nombre se aplica además a ciertos tamaños de papel de escribir.—**c. screw,** tornillo grande sin tuerca.—**the c. fits,** viene de perilla.—**to set one's c. for,** proponerse conquistar a uno para novio.—**to put on one's thinking c.,** reflexionar con madurez. **II.** *va.* cubrir con gorra; poner tapa; coronar, poner cima o remate; saludar a uno; dar la última mano, acabar; sobrepujar.—**to c. the climax,** pasar del límite, para colmo (de ridiculez, sinrazón, etc.) **III.** *vn.* descubrirse para saludar en señal de reverencia o cortesía.

capability [kéipabíliti], *s.* capacidad, idoneidad, aptitud, inteligencia.

capable [kéipabœl], *a.* capaz; idóneo, competente; suficiente.—**capableness** [-nes], *s.* capacidad, idoneidad, competencia.

capacious [capéhus], *a.* capaz, espacioso.—**capaciously** [-li], *adv.* capazmente, holgadamente. —**capaciousness** [-nes], *s.* capacidad, cabida.

capacitancy [cæpǽsitænsi], *s.* (elec.) capacitancia.

capacitate [-teit], *va.* habilitar, hacer capaz, autorizar.

capacitive [-tiv], *s.* (elec.) relativo a la capacidad. —**c. coupling** (radtlg.) acoplamiento de (por) condensadores.

capacity [capǽsiti], *s.* capacidad, cabida; inteligencia, aptitud, suficiencia; facultad, poder; calidad, condición, carácter; empleo, destino; (mar.) tonelaje.

cap-a-pie [cæp-a-pi], *adv.* de pies a cabeza, de punta en blanco.

caparison [capǽriscœn]. **I.** *s.* caparazón, paramento, gualdrapa, telliz. **II.** *va.* enjaezar, engualdrapar; (fam.) vestir soberbiamente.

cape [kéip], *s.* (geog.) cabo; capa corta, esclavina, manteleta.

caper [kéipœr]. **I.** *s.* cabriola, zapateta; travesura; (bot.) alcaparra, tápara; corsario holandés del siglo XVII.—**to cut a c.,** cabriolar. **II.** *vn.* cabriolar; chozpar.

caperbush [-buŝh], *s.* (bot.) alcaparro.

caperer [-œr], *s.* saltarín.

caper-spurge [-spœrv], *s.* (bot.) tártago.

capias [képias], *s.* orden de arresto.

capillaceous [cæpiléŝhus], *a.* capilar.

capillarity [cæpilériti], *s.* capilaridad.

capillary [cǽpileri]. **I.** *a.* capilar. **II.** *s.* (anat.) vaso capilar.

capillose [cǽpilos], *a.* cabelludo.

capital [cǽpital]. **I.** *a.* capital; principal; excelente, magnífico; mayúscula.—**c. punishment,** pena de muerte.—**c. ship,** acorazado grande (de más de 10,000 toneladas).—**c. sin,** pecado mortal. —**c. stock** (com.) capital; capital nominal en acciones, o valor nominal total de las acciones (de una compañía). **II.** *s.* capital (ciudad); (arq.) capitel o chapitel; (com.) capital; (fort.) capital.

capitalist [-ist], *s.* capitalista.—**capitalistic** [-ic], *a.* capitalista (sistema, teoría, etc.).

capitalize [-aiŝ], *va.* capitalizar; principiar una palabra con mayúscula.

capitalization [-iŝéŝhun], *s.* capitalización; empleo de letras mayúsculas.

capitally [cǽpitali], *adv.* excelentemente; capitalmente.

capitate [cápiteit], *a.* (bot.) capitado.

capitation [cæpitéŝhun], *s.* capitación.

capitol [cǽpitol], *s.* capitolio.

capitoline [cǽpitolain], *a.* capitolino.

capitula [cæpítiulæ], *s. pl.* de CAPITULUM.

capitular [capítiular], *a.* capitular.

capitularly [capítiularli], *adv.* capitularmente.

capitulary [capítiulari]. **I.** *a.* capitular. **II.** *s.* capitular, ordenanza real (gen. *pl.*).

capitulate [capítiulet], *vn.* (mil.) capitular.

capitulation [capitiuléŝhun], *s.* capitulación.

capitulator [capítiuletor], *s.* capitulante.

capitulum [cæpítiulum], *s.* (bot., anat.) cabezuela.

capon [kéipon], *s.* capón.

capote [capót], *s.* capote; (carr.) capota.

cappadine [cǽpadin], *s.* cadarzo.

capparidaceous [cæparidéŝhus], *a.* (bot.) caparídeo.

Capparis [cǽparis], *s.* (bot.) alcaparro.

capper [cǽpœr], *s.* gorrero; soldador de latas de conserva.

capping [cǽping], *s.* (arq.) coronamiento.

capreolate [cǽpreolet], *a.* (bot.) que tiene zarcillos.

caprice [caprís], **capriciousness** [capríŝhusnes], *s.* capricho, antojo.

capricious [capríŝhus], *a.* caprichoso.

capriciously [-li], *adv.* caprichosamente.

Capricorn [cǽpricorn], *s.* (astr.) Capricornio; (ent.) especie de escarabajo.

caprificate [cǽprifikeit], *va.* (agr.) cabrahigar.

caprification [cæprifikéŝhun], *s.* (agr.) cabrahigadura.

Caprifoliaceæ [cǽprifoliéisii], *s. pl.* (bot.) caprifoliáceas.—**caprifoliaceous** [-ŝhus], *a.* caprifoliáceo.

capriole [cǽpriol], *s.* corveta.

capsicum [cǽpsicum], *s.* (bot.) pimiento, ají.

capsize [cǽpsaiŝ], *va.* y *vn.* volcar(se); (mar.) zozobrar.

capstan [cǽpstan], **capstern** [cǽpstœrn], *s.* cabrestante, argüe; (min.) malacate.—**c. barrel,** cuerpo de cabrestante.—**c. bars,** barras del cabrestante.—**to rig the c.,** guarnir el cabrestante.

capstone [cǽpstoun], *s.* (arq.) coronamiento.

capsular(y [cǽpsiular(i], *a.* capsular.

capsulate(d [cǽpsiulet(ed], *a.* cerrado en forma de cápsula.

capsule [cǽpsiul], *s.* (biol., quím., farm.) cápsula.

captain [cǽpten], *s.* capitán.—**captaincy** [-si], **captainship** [-ŝhip], *s.* capitanía.

caption [cǽpŝhun], *s.* encabezamiento; título; captura, prisión.

captious [cǽpŝhus], *a.* quisquilloso, caviloso; capcioso, falaz.—**captiously** [-li], *adv.* quisquillosamente, falazmente, capciosamente.—**captiousness** [-nes], *s.* cavilosidad.

captivate [cǽptiveit], *va.* cautivar, fascinar.

captivating [-ing], *a.* encantador, seductivo, atractivo.—**captivation** [-véiŝhun], *s.* encanto, fascinación.

captive [cǽptiv], *s.* y *a.* cautivo, prisionero.— **c. balloon,** globo de observación atado a tierra.

captivity [cæptíviti], *s.* cautiverio o cautividad, prisión; obsesión, fascinación.

captor [cǽptœr], *s.* apresador.

capture [cǽpchœr]. **I.** *s.* captura, apresamiento; (mil.) toma; presa, botín. **II.** *va.* apresar, prender; (mil.) tomar.

capuchin [cǽpiuchin], *s.* monje capuchino; capuchón o capotillo con capucha; (orn.) paloma copetuda; (zool.) mono sapajú.

capucin [cǽpiusin], *s.* color anaranjado; (bot.) capuchina.

caput mortuum [cǽput mórtuum], (quím.) cólcotar; residuo.

capybara [cæpibáræ], *s.* (zool.) capibara.

car [car], *s.* coche (automóvil, de f. c., de tranvía); vagón, furgón de f. c.; carreta; barquilla (de un globo); camarín o vehículo (de ascensor).

carabao [carabao], *s.* (zool.) carabao.

carabine, carabineer. *V.* CARBINE, CARBINEER.

carac [cǽrac], *s.* carraca.

caracara [caræcǽræ], *s.* (zool.) caracará.

caracole [cǽracol]. **I.** *s.* caracoleo. **II.** *vn.* caracolear.

carafe [caráf], *s.* garrafa.

caramel [cǽramel], *s.* caramelo; azúcar quemado.

caramelize [cǽramelais], *va.* acaramelar.

carapace [cǽrapes], *s.* carapacho.

carat [cǽrat], *s.* (joy.) quilate.

caravan [cǽravan], *s.* caravana.

caravansary [cæravǽnsari], *s.* posado.

caravel [cǽravel], *s.* carabela.

caraway (seed) [cǽraue sid], *s.* (bot.) alcaravea, carvi.

carbid(e [cárbid, -baid], *s.* (quím.) carburo.

carbine [cárbain], *s.* carabina.—**carbineer** [carbinfœr], *s.* carabinero.

carbohydrate [cárbojáidreit], *s.* (quím.) hidrato de carbono.

carbolic [carbólic], *a.* fénico.

carbolize [cárbolais], *va.* impregnar con fenol.

carbon [cárbon], *s.* copia en papel carbón; (quím.) carbono; (elec.) carbón (de batería, de filamento, de lámpara de arco).—**c. copy,** copia en papel carbón.—**c. dioxide,** anhídrido carbónico.—**c. light,** (elec.) lámpara de arco.—**c. paper,** papel carbón, usado en máquinas de escribir y en fotografía.—**c. steel,** acero ordinario (no de aleación; puede llamarse acero carbono).—**c. tube,** (quím.) vaso de vidrio empleado en la determinación del carbono del acero.

carbonaceous [cárbonéshus], *a.* carbonoso.

carbonate [cárbonet]. **I.** *s.* carbonato. **II.** *va.* carbonatar.

carbonic [carbónic], *a.* carbónico.—**c. acid,** ácido carbónico, (impropia pero muy comúnmente) anhídrido carbónico (ll. t. **c.-acid gas**).

carboniferous [cárbonífœrus], *a.* carbonífero; (geol. **C.-,** *a.* y *s.*) carbonífero.

carbonization [-nɪséshun], *s.* carbonización, carboneo.—**carbonize** [-aíś], *va.* carbonizar.

carborundum [carborúndum], *s.* carborundo (carburo de silicio).

carboy [cárboi], *s.* garrafón, damajuana.

carbuncle [cárbunkœl], *s.* (joy.) carbúnculo o carbunclo; (med.) carbunco, carbunclo.

carbuncular [carbúnkiular], *a.* carbuncal.

carburet [cárbiuret], *s.* carburo.

carburetant [cárbiurétant], *a.* (quím.) carburante.

carbureter, carburetor, carburettor [carbiurétœr], *s.* (m. comb. int.) carburador; carburante (hidrocarburo).

carburize [cárbiuraiś], *va.* combinar o impregnar con carbono.

carcanet [cárcanet], *s.* gargantilla.

carcass, carcase [cárcas], *s.* res muerta; armazón, esqueleto; (mar.) casco o armazón; (arti.) carcasa; (aut.) esqueleto (de neumático).

carcel [cársœl], *s.* (elec.) carcel, patrón Carcel de intensidad lumínica.—**c. lamp,** lámpara Carcel.

carcer [cársœr], *s.* cárcel, prisión.

carcinoma [carsinóma], *s.* cáncer.

carcinomatous [carsinómatus], *a.* canceroso.

card [card]. **I.** *s.* tarjeta, papeleta; aviso, anuncio; naipe, carta; cartón, cartulina; cardencha, carda; almohaza.—**c. index,** índice en tarjetas.—**c. party,** tertulia de baraja (en que se juega baraja).—**c. table,** mesa de baraja.—**to speak by the c.,** hablar con conocimiento de causa. **II.** *va.* cardar, carduzar; almohazar.

cardamine [cárdamin], *s.* (bot.) mastuerzo de prado.

cardamom [cárdamom], *s.* (bot.) cardamomo.

cardboard [cárdbord], *s.* cartón.

cardcase [-keis], *s.* tarjetero.

cardanic [cardǽnic], *a.* cardánico.

Cardan joint [cárdæn yóint], *s.* junta universal, articulación o junta cardánica.—**C. shaft,** cardán (tem.), eje cardánico.

carder [cárdœr], *s.* cardador, carduzador; abejorro.

cardia, *s.* (anat.) cardias.

cardiac [cárdiac], *a.* cardiaco.

cardialgia, cardialgy [cárdiælyria, -i], *s.* (med.) cardialgia.

cardigan [cárdigan], *s.* chupetín de punto.

cardinal [cárdinal]. **I.** *a.* cardinal, fundamental; rojo, purpurado; (gram.) cardinal. **II.** *s.* (igl.) cardenal; púrpura; capa de mujer del siglo XVIII.—**c. bird** (orn.) cardenal.

cardinalate [cárdinalet], **cardinalship** [-ship], *s.* cardenalato.

carding [cárding], *s.* cardadura.—**c. machine,** carda mecánica.

carditis [cardáitis *o* -ditis], *s.* (med.) carditis.

cardmaker [cárdmekœr], *s.* fabricante de naipes o de cardas.

cardoon [cardún], *s.* (bot.) cepacaballo.

care [kéar]. **I.** *s.* cuidado, solicitud, cautela; ansiedad, inquietud, sozobra; cargo, custodia. **II.** *vn.* tener cuidado, ansiedad o interés por algo o alguien; importarle a uno; estimar, apreciar, hacer caso.—**to c. for,** desear, gustar; interesarse en; gustarle a uno (una cosa, una persona).

careen [carín]. **I.** *va.* (mar.) carenar **II.** *vn.* hecharse de costado, dar a la banda.—**careenage** [-ey], *s.* (mar.) carenero; gasto de carena.—**careening** [-ing], *s.* (mar.) carena.—**c. gear,** aparejo de carenar.—**c. wharf,** carenero, despalmador.

career [caríær]. **I.** *s.* carrera, curso, corrida; profesión. **II.** *vn.* correr a carrera tendida.

careful [kéarful], *a.* cuidadoso; cauteloso, prudente.—**carefully** [-li], *adv.* cuidadosamente, esmeradamente.—**carefulness** [-nes], *s.* cuidado, cautela, atención.

careless [kéarles], *a.* descuidado, negligente, indiferente; abandonado; desatento, desaplicado, atolondrado; inconsiderado.

carelessly [-li], *adv.* descuidadamente, negligentemente; sin esmero.

carelessness [-nes], *s.* descuido, abandono, indiferencia; desaseo, desaliño.

caress [carés]. **I.** *va.* acariciar, halagar, mimar. **II.** *s.* caricia, halago, mimo, cariño.

caret [cǽret *o* kéret], *s.* (impr.) signo de intercalación (∧).

caretaker [kéartéikœr], *s.* curador, celador, guardián, vigilante.

careworn [-uórn], *a.* cargado de cuidados; agobiado de inquietud.

carex [kérex *o* cárex], *s.* (bot.) espadaña, estoque.

cargo [cárgo], *s.* (com.) carga, cargamento; consignación.

Carib [cérib], **Caribean** [cæribíæn], *s.* y *a.* caribe.—**C. sea,** mar Caribe o de las Antillas.

caribou [céribu], *s.* (zool.) caribú.

caricature [céricæchuœr]. **I.** *s.* caricatura. **II.** *va.* caricaturar, caricaturizar.—**caricaturist** [-churist], *s.* caricaturista.

caried [kérid], *a.* cariado.

caries [kéris], **cariosity** [keriósity], **cariousness** [kériusnes], *s.* caries.

carinate [cérinet], *a.* aquillado.

carious [kérius], *a.* cariado.

carking [carking], *a.* devorador, acerbo.

carl [carl], *s.* patán, rústico; villano.

carline, carling [cárlin, -ling], *s.* (mar.) carlinga; atravesaños de las latas; galeotas de las escotillas.

carline thistle [cárlin *z*isl], *s.* (bot.) carlina.

carload [cárlod], *s.* galerada; (f. c.) vagonada, furgonada (de 20,000 a 32,000 libras).

carlock [cárloc], *s.* colapez rusa.

Carlovingian [carlovín*y*ian], *a.* carlovingio.

carman [cárman], *s.* carretero, carromatero, carretonero.

Carmelite [cármelait], *s.* Carmelita; tela fina de lana; variedad de pera.

carminative [carmínativ], *a.* carminativo.

carmine [cármin], *s.* carmín, carmesí, albín.

carnage [cárne*y*], *s.* carnicería, matanza.

carnal [cárnal], *a.* carnal; lascivo.

carnalist [cárnalist], *s.* hombre salaz.

carnality [carnáliti], *s.* carnalidad, lujuria, concupiscencia, lascivia.

carnalize [cárnalaiŝ], *va.* excitar la sensualidad.

carnally [cárnali], *adv.* carnalmente.

carnation [carnéŝhun], *s.* (pint.) encarnación, encarnado; (bot.) clavel doble.

carnelian [carnílian], *s.* (min.) cornerina.

carneous [cárneus], *a.* carnoso; encarnado.

carnification [carnifikéŝhun], *s.* carnificación.

carnify [cárnifai], *vn.* criar carne.

carnival [cárnival], *s.* carnaval; holgorio.

Carnivora [carnívora], *s. pl.* (zool.) carnívoros.

carnivorous [carnívorus], *a.* carnívoro, carnicero.

carnose [cárnous], *a.* carnoso, carnudo.

carnosity [carnósiti], *s.* carnosidad.

carnotite [cárnotait], *s.* (min.) carnotita (uno de los minerales de que se extrae el radio).

carob [cérob], *s.* (bot.) algarrobo.—**c. bean**, algarroba, arveja.

caroche [caróŝh], *s.* carroza.

carol [cérol]. **I.** *s.* villancico; canto alegre. **II.** *va.* cantar villancicos. **III.** *vn.* gorjear.

Carolinian [cærolínian], *a. y s.* natural de la Carolina.

carom [cérom]. **I.** *s.* carambola. **II.** *vn.* hacer carambola.

carotid(al [carótid(al], *a.* (anat.) carótida.

carousal [caráuŝal], *s.* festín, holgorio, parranda, francachela.

carouse [caráuŝ]. **I.** *vn.* jaranear, andar de parranda; (fam.) correrla; embriagarse. **II.** *s.* parranda, francachela.

carousel [cérušel], *s.* tiovivo; liza, justa.

carouser [caráuŝœr], *s.* bebedor, jaranero.

carp [carp]. **I.** *s.* (ict.) carpa. **II.** *vn.* censurar, criticar, vituperar.

carpal [cárpal]. **I.** *a.* carpiano. **II.** *s.* hueso carpiano.

carpel [cárpel], *s.* (bot.) carpelo.

carpenter [cárpentœr], *s.* carpintero; (min.) ademador.—**carpentry** [-tri], *s.* carpintería; obra de carpintero.

carper [cárpœr], *s.* criticón; reparón.

carpet [cárpet]. **I.** *s.* alfombra, tapiz; tapete.—**c. beetle**, (zool.) antreno.—**c. knight**, soldado de gabinete o de parada.—**c. maker**, alfombrero.—**c. stretcher**, atesador de alfombras.—**c. sweeper**, abarredera de alfombras. **II.** *va.* alfombrar, entapizar.

carpetbag [-bæg]. **I.** *s.* saco de noche. **II.** *a.* explotador.

carpetbagger [-béguœr], *s.* explotador; aventurero; (hist. E. U.) politicastros del norte que tras la guerra de secesión iban al sur a intrigar y enriquecerse.

carpeting [-ing], *s.* tela para alfombras; alfombrado.

carphology [carfóloyi], *s.* (med.) carfología.

carping [cárping]. **I.** *a.* capcioso, reparón, caviloso. **II.** *s.* censura.

carpingly [cárpingli], *adv.* mordazmente.

carpology [cœrpóloyi], *s.* (bot.) carpología.

carpus [cárpus], *s.* carpo, muñeca.

carrageen [cæraguín], *s.* musgo de Irlanda.

carriage [cérri*y*], *s.* carruaje, coche, carroza; vehículo; (Ingl. f. c.) vagón; (arti.) cureña; (mec.) jinete, carro, carretilla, soporte; (com.) porte, acarreo, transporte; presencia, continente, aire de una persona; (aer.) barquilla; tren de aterrizaje. [a-te-rri-za-je].—**c. and four**, carroza de cuatro caballos.—**c. free**, franco de porte.—**c. horse**, caballo de tiro.—**c. paid**, porte pagado.

carrier [cérriœr], *s.* portador; acarreador, trajinante, faquín; arriero, ordinario, carretero o conductor de carga o mercaderías; mensajero, mandadero; aseguiador; persona o animal que transmite una enfermedad.—**c. pigeon**, paloma mensajera.

carrion [cérriun]. **I.** *s.* carroña; persona despreciable. **II.** *a.* que se alimenta de carroña; mortecino; podrido; asqueroso; vil.—**c. crow**, cuervo negro europeo.—**c. buzzard**, caracará; aura, gallinazo.

carronade [cérroned], *s.* (mil.) carronada.

carrot [cérot], *s.* (bot.) zanahoria.

carroty [céroti], *a.* amarillo rojizo.

carry [cérri], *va.* (*pret.* y *pp.* CARRIED) llevar, transportar, acarrear; ajobar; traer, llevar encima, tener consigo; contener; incluir, comprender; llevar aparejado; implicar; dirigir, impulsar, mover, influir; ganar, tomar, conquistar, conseguir, lograr; mantener; aguantar, sostener; portarse, comportarse; (com.) tener existencia o surtido de.—**to c. about**, llevar de un lado a otro, de acá acullá.—**to c. all**, o **everything, before one**, vencer toda dificultad.—**to c. along**, llevarse consigo.—**to c. arms**, llevar armas; ser militar; cuadrarse.—**c. away**, llevarse; arrebatar (de la vida); seducir, encantar, entusiasmar.—**to c. away the palm**, llevarse la palma, triunfar.—**to c. coals to Newcastle**, llevar hierro a Vizcaya, llevar leña al monte, perder el tiempo.—**to c. forward**, llevar, pasar ("suma y sigue," en las cuentas).—**to c. into effect**, realizar, ejecutar, llevar a cabo.—**to c. off**, llevar, retirar; ganar.—**to c. on**, continuar; ocuparse en practicar, ejercer.—**to c. one's point**, ganar, triunfar; salirse uno con la suya.—**to c. out**, llevar a cabo, realizar; llevarse, retirar, sacar; llevar hasta el fin.—**to c. over**, ganar (a una persona); traspasar; trasladar, pasar a otra cuenta o página.—**to c. the day**, salir adelante, ganar, triunfar.—**to c. the prize**, etc., ganar el premio, etc.—**to c. through**, llevar a cabo; sostener, ayudar hasta el fin.—**to c. up**, llevar arriba; erigir.—**to c. weight**, ser de peso o de influencia.

carry, *vn.* portear (como oficio); alcanzar, llegar, tener alcance.—**to c. on**, continuar, funcionar, permanecer en el puesto o en la tarea; (fam.) travesear.

carry, *s.* transporte de una canoa en hombros; trecho no navegable de un río; alcance (de arma de fuego); celaje.

carryall [-ol], *s.* (E. U.) faetón.

cart [cart]. **I.** *s.* carro, carromato, carreta, carretón; tílburi.—**c. horse**, caballo de tiro.—**c. load**, carretada.—**to put the c. before the horse**, tergiversar, trastrocar. **II.** *va.* carretear, acarrear. **III.** *vn.* usar carretas o carros.

cartage [cártey], *s.* carretaje, acarreamiento, acarreo, conducción, porteo.

carte [cart], *s.* tarjeta; papeleta; lista de platos; (esgr.) cuarta.—**c. blanche**, carta blanca.—**c. de visite**, (fot.) retrato de tarjeta.

cartel [cártel], *s.* cartel (para cambio de prisioneros; de desafío).

carter [cártœr], *s.* carretero, carromatero.

Cartesian [cartíŝian], *s. y a.* cartesiano.—**C. devil, diver**, o **imp**, (fís.) diablillo cartesiano.

cartful [cártful], *s.* carretada.

Carthaginian [cárza*y*inian], *a. y s.* cartaginés.

carthamus [cárzamus], *s.* (bot.) cártamo.

Carthusian [carziuŝian], *s.* cartujo.

cartilage [cártiley], *s.* (anat.) cartílago.

cartilaginous [cartiléyinus], *a.* cartilaginoso.

cartman [cártmæn], *s.* carretero.

cartographer [cartógrafœr], *s.* cartógrafo.—**cartography** [-fi], *s.* cartografía.

carton [cárton], s. caja de cartón fino.
cartoon [cartún]. **I.** s. (pint.) caricatura; boceto. **II.** va. y vn. caricaturizar, hacer caricaturas; bosquejar.—**cartoonist** [-ıst], s. caricaturista.
cartouch [cœrtúsh], s. (arq.) cartela; (mil.) cartucho; cartuchera.
cartridge [cártriɣ], s. (armas) cápsula; cartucho.—**c. belt,** canana.—**c. box,** cartuchera; caja de municiones, portabombas (caja en que se llevan proyectiles a los cañones).—**c. case,** cápsula de proyectil.
cartulary [cártiuleri], s. cartulario.
cartwright [cártrait], s. carretero.
caruncle [cœrunkœl], s. carúncula.
caruncular [carúnkiular], a. parecido a una carúncula.—**carunculate** [-leit], a. que tiene carúnculas.
carve [carv], va. y vn. esculpir; cincelar, tallar; entallar, grabar; trinchar carne.—**carved work,** entallado, obra de talla.
carvel [cárvel], s. (mar.) carabela.—**c.-built,** (mar.) con juntas a tope.—**c. joint,** junta a tope.
carven [cárvn], a. (poét.) esculpido, entallado, grabado.
carver [cárvœr], s. escultor; grabador, entallador; trinchador; trinchante.
carving [cárving], s. escultura, entalladura, arte de trinchar.—**c. knife,** trinchante.—**c. table,** trinchero.
caryatid [cœriǽtid], s. cariátide.
caryophyllaceous [cœriofiléshus], a. (bot.) cariofíleo.
casal [késal], a. (gram.) perteneciente a los casos.
cascabel [cǽscabel], s. (arti.) cascabel.
cascade [cǽskeid]. **I.** s. cascada, catarata. **II.** a. (elec.) en cascada.
cascarilla [cǽscarila], s. cascarilla.
casco [cǽsco], s. casco (bote filipino).
case [kéis]. **I.** s. caso; (for.) causa, acción, pleito; (med.) caso; (gram.) caso; caja, estuche, vaina, funda, cubierta; caja de reloj, guarda-polvo; (com.) caja de mercancías; (mec.) chaqueta, camisa, manguito, forro, cubierta; (carp.) marco, bastidor; (impr.) caja.—**c. in law,** (for.) causa, proceso.—**c. knife,** cuchillo de mesa; cuchillo provisto de vaina.—**c. law,** ley de precedentes, o fundada en decisiones y sentencias.—**c. of pistols** = BRACE OF PISTOLS.—**c. shot,** matralla.—**c. system,** sistema de casos particulares o concretos (en que cada caso se trata por sí solo).—**in any c.,** en todo caso, sea como fuere.—**to make out one's c.,** demostrar lo que uno se proponía. **II.** va. embalar; enfundar; cubrir.
caseharden [-jardán], va. (met.) templar superficialmente.—**casehardening** [-ing], s. temple superficial.
casein [késein], s. caseína.
caseation [keseéshun], s. caseación.
casemate [késmeit], s. (fort.) casamata.
casement [kéismœnt], s. puerta ventana; ventano; cubierta, caja.
caseous [kéisius], a. caseoso.
casern [cašœrn], s. caserna, cuartel.
cash [cæsh]. **I.** s. dinero contante, numerario, efectivo; pago al contado; (com.) caja.—**c. down,** dinero en mano; al contado.—**c. payment,** pago al contado.—**c. register,** caja registradora (de dinero).—**c. store,** tienda de ventas al contado. **II.** adv. al contado. **III.** va. cambiar, cobrar, hacer efectivo (un cheque, etc.)
cashbook [-buc], s. libro de caja.
cashew [cašhú], s. (bot.) anacardo.—**c. nut,** anacardo, marañón.
cashier [cœshícœr]. **I.** s. cajero, contador. **II.** va. destituir; desaforar, degradar.
cashmere [cǽshmiœr], s. -t. (tej.) casimir.
cashoo [cašhú], s. = CATECHU.
casing [késing], s. cubierta, funda, envoltura; marco de ventana o puerta; (aut.) cubierta (de neumático).—pl. **casings,** (E. U.) tripas para embutidos; (Ingl.) boñiga seca para combustible.
casino [casíno], s. casino, círculo; quinta de recreo; casino (juego de naipes).

cask [cask]. **I.** s. pipa, barril, tonel; cuba; casco; tina de tintoreros; casco o capacete. **II.** va. entonelar, envasar.
casket [cásket], s. arquilla, cofrecito, escriño, estuche, joyelero; (E. U.) ataúd.
casque [casc], s. casco, almete, capacete.
cassation [cœsésĥun], s. (for.) casación, anulación, revocación.
cassava [cœsáva], s. casabe.
casserole [cǽseroul], s. cacerola; (quím.) platillo con mango.
cassia [cǽshia], s. (bot.) casia; cañafístula.
cassimere [cǽsimir], s. (tej.) casimir.
cassiterite [cœsítœrait], s. casiterita.
cassock [cǽsoc], s. sotana o balandrán.
cassoon [cœsún], s. (arq.) artesón.
cassowary [cǽsouœri], s. (zool.) casuario.
cassweed [cǽsuid], s. (bot.) bolsa de pastor.
cast [cæst], va. (pret. y pp. CAST) tirar, arrojar, lanzar; soltar, despedir; echar, verter, derramar; tumbar, derribar; echar, bajar (el ancla); tirar (dados), echar (suertes o balotas); mudar (la piel); perder (pelo, dientes, etc.); desechar; volver, dirigir (la mirada o el pensamiento); vaciar, moldear; electrotipar; calcular; imputar, echar la culpa; (teat.) repartir (papeles de un drama); (for.) ganar un pleito; (agr.) aventar; volver a arar; dar (un voto); echar, depositar (una balota, etc.).—**to c. a shoe,** desherrarse, perder una herradura.—**to c. aside,** desechar.—**to c. away,** desechar, abandonar; echar a pique (un buque) (**to be c. away,** naufragar).—**to c. down,** abatir, derribar; descorazonar.—**to c. forth,** exhalar, despedir.—**to c. lots,** echar suertes.—**to c. off,** abandonar, soltar; mudar (la pluma, etc.); descartar.—**to c. out,** echar fuera, arrojar.
cast, vn. idear, pensar; hacerse al molde; calcular; pronosticar, suponer; alabearse; pescar con caña, especialmente con cebo artificial.—**to c. about,** buscar medios, o trazas.
cast [pp. de TO CAST], a. vaciado, fundido.—**c. iron,** hierro colado, fundición.—**c.-iron,** a., de hierro colado; rígido; inflexible.—**c. net,** atarraya.—**c.-off,** a., descartado; echado; s. persona o cosa que no se necesita; (imp.) cálculo de espacio.—**c. steel,** acero colado, acero fundido.
cast, s. echada, lanzamiento, tiro, tirada; distancia, alcance; lo que se tira; pieza fundida; plancha estereotipada; molde, forma; mascarilla; estampa, aspecto, formación; tinte, tono, matiz; tendencia; (teat.) reparto de papeles.—**a c. of the eye,** defecto en la mirada.
castanets [cǽstanets], s. pl. castañuelas.
castaway [cástauéi]. **I.** s. naufrago; réprobo, malhechor; proscrito. **II.** a. desechado, abandonado; perdido.
caste [cast], s. casta; clase social.—**to lose c.,** desprestigiarse.
castellan [cástelan], s. castellán.
castellany [cásteleni], **castelry** [cástelri], s. castellanía.
castellated [cásteleted], a. encastillado.
caster, castor [cástœr], s. tirador, echador; adivino; calculador; fundidor, vaciador, moldeador; rodaja de mueble; ampolleta.—**casters,** vinagreras, convoy de mesa.
castigate [cǽstiguet], va. castigar.
castigation [cǽstiguéiśhun], s. castigo.
castigator [cǽstiguéitœr], s. castigador.
castigatory [cǽstigatori], a. penal.
Castile [cæstíl], s. Castilla.—**C. soap,** jabón de Castilla.
Castilian [cæstíllan], s. y a. castellano.
casting [cásting]. **I.** s. (fund.) vaciado; pieza fundida o vaciada; invención, distribución, arreglo; plan, modelo; (cetr.) curalle. **II.** a. ger. de TO CAST.—**c. line,** tanza.—**c. net,** esparavel.—**c. vote,** voto decisivo o de calidad.
castle [cǽscl]. **I.** s. castillo; torre de ajedrez.—**c. builder,** proyectista imaginario, visionario.—**c. in the air, in Spain, o in the skies,** castillo en el aire. **II.** vn. enrocar (ajedrez).
castled [cǽscld], a. fortificado, encastillado.

castlet [cǽstlet], s. castillejo.

castling [cástling], s. aborto.

castor [cástœr], s. (zool.) castor; pelo o paño de castor; sombrero de castor; castóreo.—**c. oil**, aceite de ricino.—**c.-o. plant**, ricino, higuerilla.

Castor and Pollux [cástœr ænd pólux], s. (mar.) fuego de Sant⟨elmo; ⟨astr.) Astillejos.

castor bean [bin], s. (bot.) ricino, higuerilla; semilla de esta planta.

castoreum [castóreum], s. castóreo.

castrametation [cæstrametéshun], s. (mil.) castrametación.

castrate [cǽstreit], va. castrar.—**castration** [-tréishun], s. capadura, castración.—**castrator** [-tréitœr], s. castrador.

castrel = KESTREL.

casual [cǽsuæl], a. casual, fortuito.—**casually** [-li], adv. casualmente.—**casualness** [-nes], s. contingencia.

casualty [cǽsiualti], s. accidente, desastre; muerte violenta; (mil.) baja; casualidad, contingencia; (for.) caso fortuito.

casuist [cǽsiuist], s. casuista.

casuistical [cæsiuístical], a. casuístico.

casuistry [cǽsiuistri], s. casuística.

casus belli [kéisus bélai], s. casus belli, motivo de guerra.

cat [cæt], s. (zool.) gato; (mar.) gata.—**c.-o'-nine tails**, disciplina o azote con nueve ramales.—**c.'s-eye** (min.) cimófana.—**c. tackle**, (mar.) aparejo de gata.—**to bell the c.**, poner el cascabel al gato.—**to let the c. out of the bag**, revelar un secreto.—**to see which way the c. will jump**, ver qué sesgo toma un asunto.

catabolic [cætæbólic], a. catabólico.—**catabolism** [cætæbolism], s. catabolismo.

catachresis [cætacrísis], s. catacresis.

catachrestic(al [cætacréstic(al], a. forzado, traído por los cabellos.

cataclysm [cátæclism], s. cataclismo; diluvio, inundación.—**cataclysmal, cataclysmic** [-mæl, -mic], a. referente al cataclismo.—**cataclysmist** [-mist], s. = CATASTROPHIST.

catacomb [cátacom], s. catacumba.

catacoustics [cætacústics], s. catacústica.

catadioptric(al [cátadaióptric(al], a. catadióptrico.

catafalque [cǽtafælc], s. catafalco.

Catalan [cátælæn], s. y a. catalán.

catalectic [cætaléctic], a. (ret.) cataléctico.

catalepsy [cætalépsi], s. catalepsia.—**cataleptic** [-éptic], a. cataléptico.

catalog(ue [cátalog], I. s. catálogo, lista, nómina. II. va. catalogar.

catalpa [catálpa], s. (bot.) catalpa.

catalysis [cætálisis], s. (quím.) catálisis.

catalytic [cætælític], a. (quím.) catalizador. II. s. (quím.) catalizador; (med.) restaurativo.—**catalyzer** [-láisœr], s. (quím.) catalizador.

catamaran [cætamarǽn], s. embarcación formada por dos tozas o dos bates unidos.

catamenia [cætamína], s. pl. menstruación.

catamite [cátamait], s. sodomita.

cataphract [cátafræct], s. armadura de escamas de metal.

cataplasm [cátaplæsm], s. cataplasma.

catapult [cátapult], s. catapulta.

cataract [cátaræct], s. catarata, cascada; (med.) catarata.

catarrh [catár], s. (E. U.) catarro crónico; (Ing.) catarro o romadizo fuerte.

catarrhal [-al] **catarrhous** [-us], a. catarral.

catastrophe [cætástrofi], s. catástrofe.—**catastrophic** [cætastrófic], a. de carácter de catástrofe.—**catastrophism** [cætástrofism], s. (geol.) teoría que atribuye a catástrofes repentinas los cambios geológicos.—**catastrophist** [-ist], s. partidario de esa teoría.

catbird [cátbœrd], s. tordo mimo.

catboat [cátbout], s. (mar.) laúd.

catcall [cátcol], s. silba, chifla, rechifla.

catch [cæch]. I. va. (pp. y prep. CAUGHT) coger, agarrar, asir; atrapar; alcanzar; prender,

capturar; sorprender, coger desprevenido; enganchar, engranar, endentar, engarzar; comprender, discernir; ser atacado o contagiarse de.—**to c. cold**, resfriarse.—**to c. fire**, inflamarse, encenderse.—**to c. hold of**, agarrar, asir.—**to c. it**, (fam.) ganarse una zurra, un regaño, etc.—**to c. one's eye**, llamar la atención; ver por casualidad.—**to c. sight of**, ver, alcanzar a ver.—**to c. tne**, o **one's breath**, suspender el resuello.—**to c. up**, alcanzar; acoger con entusiasmo. II. vn. enredarse, engancharse; agarrar; ser contagioso.—**to c. at**, tratar de coger o agarrarse de.—**to c. on**, (fam.) comprender, ver, caer en la cuenta.—**to c. up**, salir del atraso; ponerse al día.—**to c. up with**, alcanzar; marchar con la época, etc.); comprender.

catch, s. acción de coger; lo que se coge (pescados, etc.); presa, botín; captura, prendimiento; enganche; trampa, engañifa; (dep.) acto de parar la pelota al vuelo; (cost.) gancho, corchete; (mec.) leva, tope; botón, fiador, tarabilla, pestillo, cerradera, detenedor, trinquete; alzaprima; pesca, redada; triquiñuela, trampa; impedimento, obstrucción; atractivo; buen partido.

catch, a. **c. basin**, cisterna de desagüe a la cloaca (gen. en las esquinas).—**c. crop** (agr.) siembra intermedia entre dos cosechas o siembras, o entre las hileras de la siembra principal.—**c. drain**, cuneta o tubo de desagüe.

catcher [cáchœr], s. el que o lo que coge; (baseball) catcher, parador de la pelota, situado detrás del batter.

catching [-ing]. I. s. (mec.) engranaje. II. a. contagioso, pegadizo.

catchment [-mœnt], s. desagüe.

catchpenny [-peni]. I. s. baratija. II. a. de pacotilla.

catchpoll [-pol], s. alguacil.

catchup [-up], s. = CATSUP.

catchword [-uœrd], s. reclamo; (teat.) pie.

catechism [cátekism], s. catecismo.

catechist [cátekist], s. catequizante.—**catechistical** [-kísticæl], s. catequístico.—**catechize** [-kaîs], va. catequizar.—**catechizer** [-kaîsœr], s. catequizante.—**catechizing** [-kaîsing], s. s. catequismo.

catechu [cátekiu o chu], s. cato, cachú, cachunde.

catechumen [cætekiúmen], s. catecúmeno.

categoric(al [cætegóric(al], a. categórico.—**categorically** [-li], adv. categóricamente.

category [cátegori], s. categoría, clase.

catenarian [cæténárian], a. catenario; eslabonado.

catenary [cáteneri], s. y a. (geom.) catenaria.

catenate [cátenet], va. encadenar.

catenation [cæténáshun], s. encadenamiento, encadenadura, engarce.

cater [kéitœr], vn. abastecer, proveer.

cater-cousin [-cúsœn], s. pariente lejano; amigo íntimo.

caterer [kéitœrœr], s. proveedor, veedor, abastecedor, despensero.—**cateress** [kéitœres], s. proveedora, abastecedora.

caterpillar [cátœrpilar], s. oruga, gusano.—**c. tractor**, tractor oruga.

caterwaul [cátœruol], vn. maullar.

caterwauling [cátœruoling], s. maullido.

catfish [cátfish], s. (ict.) siluro, barbo.

catgut [cátgœt], s. cuerda de guitarra.

Catharine wheel [cǽzarin juil], s. rueda catalina; (arq.) rosa; rosetón; (piro.) rueda de fuegos artificiales; (arq.) rosa.

catharpin [cátjarpin], s. (mar.) jareta.

catharsis [cazársis], s. (med.) purga.

cathartic [cazártic], I. a. catártico, purgante. II. s. purga.

cathead [cátjed], s. (mar.) serviola.

cathedra [cæzedra], s. cátedra.

cathedral [cazídral], I. s. catedral. II. a. episcopal; dogmático.

catheretic [cæzerétic], a. caterético.

Catherine wheel, s. = CATHARINE WHEEL.

catheter [cǽzetœr], s. (cir.) catéter, algalia, sonda, tienta.

catheterize [cǽzetœraiš], va. introducir el catéter.

cathetometer [cǽzetómitœr], s. catetómetro.

cathode [cǽzod], s. (elec.) cátodo.

catholic [cǽzolic]. **I.** a. católico, universal; liberal. **II.** s. y a. (**C-**) católico romano.

Catholicism [cazólisišm], s. catolicismo.

catholicize [cazólisaiš]. **I.** va. convertir al catolicismo. **II.** vn. hacerse católico.

catholicly [cazóliclí], adv. católicamente.

catholicon [cazólicon], s. catolicón, panacea.

cation [cǽtaion], s. (elec.) catión.

catkin [cǽtkin], s. (bot.) amento.

catlike [cǽtlaic], a. gatesco, gatuno.

catling [cǽtling], s. (cir.) legra.

catmint [cǽtmint], **catnip** [cǽtnip], s. (bot.) calamento, nébeda.

Catonian [ca- o ketónian], a. catoniano.

catoptrical [catóptrical], a. catóptrico.

catoptrics [catóptrics], s. catóptrica.

catsup [cǽtsup], s. salsa de setas o de tomate.

cattail [cǽtteil], s. (bot.) espadaña.

cattish [cǽtiš], a. gatuno, gatesco.

cattle [cǽtœl], s. ganado (gen. se aplica sólo al vacuno).—**c. pump**, bomba automática para ganado.—**c. raising**, ganadería.—**c. ranch**, hacienda de ganado.—**c. rancher**, ganadero.—**c. range**, o **run**, potrero o campo para el ganado.—**c. show**, exposición de ganado.—**c. thief**, abigeo. —**c. tick**, garrapata.—**c. wire**, alambre de púas.

Caucasian [cocǽšhian o cokéšhan], a. caucáseo.

caucus [cócus], s. (pl.) conventículo o junta secreta.

caudad [códad], adv. hacia la cola.

caudal [códal], a. caudal (de la cola).

caudate [códet], a. caudato, raboso.

caudex [códex], s. (bot.) tallo; tronco.

caudicle [códikœl], s. (bot.) caudícula.

caudle [códœl], s. cordial, bebida caliente de vino, huevos, etc.

caught pret. y pp. de TO CATCH.

caul [col], s. (zool.) omento, redaño; membrana; redecilla.

cauldron [cóldrun], s. = CALDRON.

caulescent [colésent], a. (bot.) caulescente.

caulicle [cólikœl], s. (bot.) rejo.

cauliculus [colíkiulus], s. (arq.) caulículo.

cauliferous [colífœrus], a. colífero.

cauliflower [cólifláuœr], s. coliflor.

cauliform [cóliform], a. (bot.) cauliforme.

caulk, caulker, etc. = CALK, CALKER, etc.

causal [cósal], a. causal.

causality [cosǽliti], **causation** [coséšhun], s. causalidad; causa, origen, principio.

causally [cósali], adv. de un modo causal.

causative [cósativ], a. causante.

causatively [cósativli], adv. efectivamente.

cause [coš]. **I.** s. causa; autor; motivo, razón; (for.) causa, litigio, proceso. **II.** va. causar; hacer (to cause to move, hacer mover); mover, inducir, compeler.

causeless [cósles], a. sin causa; infundado, sin razón.—**causelessly** [-li], adv. infundadamente, sin causa.

causer [cósœr], s. causador, causante, autor.

causerie [cosrí], s. conversación; discusión o deliberación de confianza.

causeway [cóšue], **causey** [cóši], s. arrecife; calzada, terraplén; acera.

casidical [cosídical], a. causídico.

caustic(al [cóstic(al], a. y s. cáustico.

causticity [costísiti], **causticness** [cósticnes], s. causticidad, mordacidad.

cauterization [cotœriséšhun], s. cauterización, cauterio.

cauterize [cótœraiš], va. cauterizar.

cauterizing [-ing]. **I.** s. cauterización. **II.** a. cauterizante.

cautery [cótœri], s. cauterio.

caution [cóšhun]. **I.** s. cautela, precaución; amonestación, advertencia, aviso. **II.** va. caucionar, precaver, prevenir, amonestar.—

cautionary [-eri], a. preventivo, admonitorio, avisador.

cautious [cóšhus], a. cauto, prudente.

cautiously [-li], adv. cautamente, prudentemente.—**cautiousness** [-nes], s. cautela, previsión, prudencia, precaución.

cavalcade [cavalkéid], s. cabalgata.

cavalier [cœvalíœr]. **I.** s. caballero; galán, cortejo; jinete; (fort.) caballero. **II.** a. caballeresco; altivo, desdeñoso; alegre, desenvuelto.—**cavalierly** [-li], adv. caballerescamente; caballerosamente.

cavalry [cǽvalri], s. (mil.) caballería.

cave [kev]. **I.** s. cueva, caverna.—**c. in**, hundimiento, atierre.—**c. dweller**, **c. man**, hombre de las cavernas. **II.** vn. (gen. con **in**) hundirse; (fam.) ceder, rendirse. **III.** va. excavar.

caveat [kéviat], s. (for.) intimación a un juez o funcionario para que suspenda un procedimiento; (E. U.) inscripción previa en la oficina de patentes de un invento no perfeccionado todavía.

cavern [cǽvœrn], s. caverna, antro.—**cavernous** [-nus], a. cavernoso.

cavi [kéivi, o cávi], s. (zool.) capincho, (Am.) capiguara o capibara.

caviar [cœviar], s. cavial, caviar.

cavil [cǽvil]. **I.** s. cavilosidad, cavilación. **II.** vn. cavilar, sutilizar.

caviller [cǽvilœr], s. hombre caviloso.—**cavilling** [cǽviling], s. cavilación, cavilosidad.—**cavillingly** [-li], adv. cavilosamente.

cavity [cǽviti], s. cavidad.

cavort [cavórt], vn. (fam. E. U.) corvetear, travesear.

caw [có]. **I.** vn. graznar. **II.** s. graznido.

cay [ke], s. cayo, peñasco o isleta.

cayenne [kéién], s. (bot.) pimentón.—**c. pepper** = RED PEPPER.

cayman [kéiman], s. caimán.

coyote [cáiot], s. = COYOTE.

cazique [cœsík], s. = CACIQUE.

cease [sis]. **I.** vn. cesar, dejar de, parar; fenecer. **II.** va. parar, suspender.

ceaseless [sísles], a. incesante.—**ceaselessly** [-li], adv. perpetuamente, incesantemente.

ceasing [sísing], s. cese, cesación.

cecum, s. = CÆCUM.

cedar [sídar], s. (bot.) cedro; tuya.—**c. bird**, (orn.) pájaro del cedro.—**c. like**, a. semejante al cedro.

cedarn [sídarn], a. cedrino.

cede [sid], va. ceder, traspasar, transferir.

cedilla [sedíla], s. cedilla.

cedrine [sídrin], a. cedrino.

ceil [sil], va. techar con cielo raso.

ceiling [síling], s. techo interior o cielo raso; (mar.) vágara; (aer.) altura máxima que un avión puede alcanzar.

celadon [séladon], s. verdeceledón.

celandine [sélandin], s. (bot.) celidonia, glaucio, golondrinera.

celature [sélatiur], s. arte de grabar o repujar los metales.

celebrant [sélebrant], s. celebrante.—**celebrate** [-breit], va. celebrar, solemnizar; alabar, encomiar.—**celebrated** [-ted], a. célebre, famoso.—**celebration** [-shun], s. celebración.—**celebrator** [-tœr], s. celebrador, celebrante.

celebrity [selébriti], s. celebridad, fama, renombre; persona célebre.

celerity [selériti], s. celeridad, prontitud.

celery [séleri], s. (bot.) apio.

celestial [seléschal]. **I.** a. celeste; celestial, divino.—**c. sphere**, esfera celeste. **II.** s. morador del cielo.

celestially [seléschali], adv. celestialmente.

celestite [sélestait], s. (min.) celestina.

celiac [síliac], a. (med.) celíaco.

celibacy [sélibasi], s. celibato.—**celibate** [-bet], a. y s. célibe.

cell [sel], s. celda, calabozo; (biol.) célula; nicho, cavidad, alvéolo; (api.) celdilla; (elec.) elemento de una pila; (aer.) celda.

cellar [sélar], *s.* sótano, bodega.

cellarage [sélarey], *s.* cueva, sótano, candiotera; almacenaje en una bodega.

cellarer [sélarœr], **cellarist** [sélarist], *s.* cillerero; repostero.

cellaret [sélaret], *s.* frasquera.

cello [chélo], *s.* (mús.) violoncelo.

cellular [séliular], *a.* celular, celuloso.

cellule [séliul], *s.* celulilla; (aer.) celdilla.

celluloid [séliuloid], *s.* celuloide.

cellulose [séliulos]. **I.** *a.* celular, celuloso. **II.** *s.* celulosa.

celsitude [sélsitiud], *s.* celsitud.

Celt [selt], *s.* celta; hacha prehistórica de piedra.

Celtiberian [seltibírian], *a.* y *s.* celtíbero.

Celtic [séltic], *a.* céltico.

Celticism [séltisism], *s.* celticismo.

celtium [sélshium], *s.* (quím.) celtio (uno de los cuerpos simples).

cement [simént]. **I.** *s.* cemento; aglutinante; vínculo; (fund.) cemento.—**c. gun,** manguera de rociar cemento. **II.** *va.* pegar, aglutinar; estrechar, asegurar; (fund.) cementar. **III.** *vn.* pegarse, aglutinarse; unirse.

cementation [sémentéshœn], *s.* ligazón, aglutinación; (fund.) cementación.

cementite [siméntait], *s.* carburo de hierro del acero antes de endurecerse.

cemetery [sémeteri], *s.* cementerio.

cenesthesis [sineszísis], *s.* (psicol.) cenestesia.

Cenobite [sénobait], *s.* cenobita.

Cenobitic(al [senobític(al], *a.* cenobítico.

cenotaph [sénotaf], *s.* cenotafio.

Cenozoic [sinosóic], *s.* y *a.* (geol.) cenozoico; terciario.

cense [sens], *va.* incensar.

censer [sénsœr], *s.* incensario, naveta.

censor [sénsor], *s.* censor; crítico.

censorial [sensórial], *a.* censorio.

censorious [sensórius], *a.* severo, rígido; crítico, hipercrítico.—**censoriously** [-li], *adv.* severamente, críticamente.—**censoriousness** [-nes], *s.* inclinación a censurar.

censorship [sénsorship], *s.* censura.

censual [sénshual], *a.* censual.

censurable [sénshurabœl], *a.* censurable.—**censurableness** [-nes], *s.* calidad de censurable.—**censurably** [-bli], *adv.* censurablemente.

censure [sénshur]. **I.** *s.* censura, reprimenda; reprobación, crítica. **II.** *va.* censurar, reprender; criticar, reprobar.—**censurer** [-œr], *s.* censurador, reprensor, criticador.—**censuring** [-ing], *a.* censurante.

census [sénsœs], *s.* censo, empadronamiento.

cent [sent], *s.* centavo (moneda).

cental [séntal]. **I.** *s.* quintal. **II.** *a.* relativo a un ciento.

centare [sentéar], *s.* centiárea.

centaur [séntor], *s.* centauro.

centaury [séntori], *s.* (bot.) centaura.

centenarian [séntenérian], *s.* y *a.*, centenario, quintañón.

centenary [sénteneri], **centennial** [senténiael], *s.* y *a.* centenario.

center [séntœr]. **I.** *s.* centro; (arq.) cimbra; (top.) eje vertical (de un teodolito, etc.); (mec.) punta (de torno); centro, portapuntas (de torno).—**c. of curvature,** (mat.) centro de curvatura.—**c. of figure,** centro de figura, centro geométrico.—**c. of gravity,** centro de gravedad.—**c. of gyration,** (mec.) centro de giro.—**c. of inertia, c. of mass,** centro de masa, centro de gravedad.—**c. of motion,** centro de rotación, punto fijo.—**c. of population,** centro de población, centro de gravedad de una región cuya superficie se considera proporcional a la población. **II.** *a.* central; relativo al centro.—**c. lathe,** torno de puntas.—**c. line,** eje (de una vía, una caldera, etc.); línea central.—**c. punch,** punzón de marcar; punzón de perforar.—**c. rail,** (f. c.) riel central (para corriente eléctrica, cremallera, etc.). **III.** *va.* centrar; concentrar; determinar el centro de. **IV.** *vn.* concentrarse; estar en el centro.

centerboard [-bórd], *s.* (mar.) orza de deriva.

centering [-ing], *s.* enfocamiento; determinación del centro de un objeto; acción de centrar; (arq.) cimbra de arco.

centerpiece [-pis], *s.* paño (gen. encaje u otra labor) para el centro de la mesa; cualquier cosa que va en el centro; centro de mesa (vaso, florero, etc.).

centessimal [sentésimæl], *a.* centesimal; centésimo.

centibar [séntibar], *s.* centiatmósfera, centésimo de atmósfera.

centigrade [séntigreid], *a.* centígrado.

centigram, centigramme [séntigram], *s.* centigramo.

centiliter, centilitre [-lítœr], *s.* centilitro.

centime [santím], *s.* céntimo.

centimeter, centimetre [séntimítœr], *s.* centímetro.—**c.-gram-second** (C. G. S.), centímetro-gramo-segundo (sistema de unidades).

centipede [séntipid], *s.* cientopiés o ciempiés.

centner [séntnœr], *s.* quintal (45.36 kilos); en docimástica, dracma.

cento [sénto], *s.* centón.

centrad [séntrad], *adv.* (zool.) hacia el centro.

central [séntral], *a.* central, céntrico.—**centralism** [séntralism], *s.* (pol.) centralismo.—**centralist** [-list], *s.* centralista.—**centrality** [sentrálíti], *s.* centralidad.—**centralization** [séntraliséshun], *s.* centralización.—**centralize** [-aís], *va.* centralizar.—**centrally** [-li], *adv.* centralmente.

centre [séntœr] = CENTER.

centric(al [séntric(al], *a.* central, céntrico.—**centrically** [-li], *adv.* centralmente.

centrifugal [sentrífiugæl]. **I.** *a.* centrífugo.—**c. force,** fuerza centrífuga.—**c. pump,** bomba centrífuga.—**c. sugar,** azúcar separada del líquido por acción centrífuga. **II.** *s.* (azú.) centrífuga.

centrifugalize, [-aís], **centrifuge** [séntrifiuy], *va.* someter a acción centrífuga.

centripetal [sentrípetal], *a.* centrípeta.

centrist [séntrist], *s.* (pol.) centrista.

centrobaric [sentrobáric], *a.* (mec.) centrobárico.

centroid [séntroid], *s.* centro de gravedad.—**centroidal** [sentróidæl], *a.* relativo al centro de gravedad.

centrosome [séntrosoum], *s.* (biol.) centrosoma.

centrosphere [séntrosfiær], *s.* (geol.) la parte central o núcleo de la tierra; (biol.) esfera de atracción.

centumvir [sentúmvœr], *s.* centunviro.—**centumvirate** [-viret], *s.* centunvirato.

centuple [séntiupœl], *a.* céntuplo centuplicado.

centuplicate [sentiúpliket], *va.* centuplicar.

centurial [sentiúrial], *a.* secular.

centurion [sentiú- (o tú-) riun], *s.* centurión.

century [sénchuri], *s.* centuria; siglo.

cephalalgia [séfalælyia], *s.* cefalalgia.

cephalic [sefélic], *a.* cefálico.

cephalopod [séfalopod], *s.* cefalópodo.

cephalous [séfalus], *a.* céfalo, que tiene cabeza.

Cepheus [sífius], *s.* (astr.) Cefeo.

ceraceous [seréshus], *a.* ceráceo.

ceramic [serémic], *a.* cerámico.

ceramics [serémics], *s.* cerámica; alfarería.

cerate [síret], *s.* cerato, cerapez.

cerated [síreted], *a.* encerado.

Cerberean [sœrbírean], *a.* parecido al cancerbero o relativo a él.

cere [síœr], *va.* encerar, dar con cera.

cereal [síreal]. **I.** *a.* cereal. **II.** *s.* grano.

cerebellar [sérebélar], *a.* perteneciente al cerebelo.

cerebellum [sérebélum], *s.* cerebelo.

cerebral [sérebral], *a.* cerebral.

cerebration [sérebréishun], *s.* función cerebral.

cerebrin [sérebrin], *s.* (quím.) cerebrina.

cerebrospinal [sérebrospáinæl], *a.* cerebroespinal.—**c. axis,** eje cerebroespinal.

cerebrum [sérebrum], *s.* cerebro, encéfalo.

cerecloth [síœrcloz], *s.* encerado, hule.

Para la pronunciación de æ, œ, D, S, Sh, U, Y, Y, Z, véase la clave al principio del libro.

cerement [síœrmœnt], s. enceramiento; mortaja encerada.

ceremonial [séremónial], a. y s. ceremonial; rito externo o ritual.

ceremonious [-móniŭs], a. ceremonial; ceremonioso.—**ceremoniousness** [-nes], s. ceremonia. —**ceremoniously** [-li], adv. ceremoniosamente.

ceremony [séremoni], s. ceremonia, ceremonial; cumplido, formalidad, etiqueta.

cereous [síriŭs], a. de cera.

Cereus [síreŭs], s. género de cactos.

cerise [serís], s. y a. color de cereza.

cerite [sírait], s. (min.) cerita.

cerium [sírium], s. (quím.) cerio.

cernuous [sœrniŭŭs], a. inclinado.

cero [síroŭ], s. priste, pez sierra.

cerograph [sírograf], s. grabado sobre cera.

cerography [sírografi], s. cerografía.

ceroon [serún], s. V. SEROONS.

ceroplastic [síroplástic] s. ceroplástica.

cerotic [serótic], a. (quím.) cerótico.

certain [sœrten], a. cierto, algún, alguna; seguro, indudable.—**certainly** [-li], adv. ciertamente, sin duda; seguramente, sin falta; con mucho gusto; no hay que dispensar.—**certainty** [-ti], s. certeza, certidumbre.

certificate [sœrtífiket], certification [sœrtifikéshŭn], s. certificado, testimonio; (for.) auténtica, atestado, certificación; acta notarial; (com.) bono, obligación.—c. of baptism, fe de bautismo.—c. of death, partida de defunción. —c. of residence, carta de vecindad.

certificate, va. certificar.

certifier [sœrtifaiœr], s. certificador.

certify [sœrtifai], va. certificar, atestiguar.

certiorari [sœrshiorérai], s. (for.) auto de avocación.

certitude [sœrtitiud], s. certidumbre, certeza.

cerulean [serúlean], a. cerúleo.

cerumen [serúmen], s. cerumen, cerilla.

ceruse [sírus], s. cerusa, albayalde.

cervical [sœrvical], a. cervical.

cervin(e [sœrvin], a. cervino, cervuno.

cervix [sœrvix], s. cerviz, nuca.

Cesarean, a. = CÆSAREAN.

cespitose [séspitos], a. de cesped.

cess [ses]. I. va. amillarar. II. s. amillaramiento.

cessation [seséshŭn], s. cese, cesación, paro, discontinuación.

cession [séshŭn], s. cesión, traspaso.

cessionary [séshŭneri], a. y s. cesionario.

cesspipe [séspaip], s. tubo de desagüe.

cesspool [séspul], s. pozo negro, rezumadero.

cesure, s. = CÆSURA.

cestus [séstŭs], s. cesto de púgil; ceñidor, cinturón.

cetacean [setéshæn], s. (ict.) cetáceo.

cetaceous [setéshŭs], a. cetáceo.

chafe [chéif]. I. va. excoriar, escaldar; calentar frotando; enfadar, irritar. II. vn. desgastarse, raerse; sahornarse; irritarse, acalorarse. III. s. sahorno, excoriación; acaloramiento; rabia.— **chafer** [-œr], s. lo que roza o excoria; estufilla; escarabajo.—**chafery** [-œri], s. fragua o forja.

chaff [chaf]. I. s. barcia, aechaduras; desperdicios, broza; cascabillo; burla, fisga. II. va. y vn. fisgar, dar matraca.

chaffer [cháfœr]. I. vn. regatear, baratear. II. s. regateo.—**chafferer** [-œr], s. regatero.

chaffinch [cháfinch], s. (orn.) pinzón.

chafing [chéfing], s. sahorno, excoriación, desolladura.—c. dish, escalfeta, escalfador, chufeta, anafe.

chagrin [shagrín]. I. s. mortificación, sofocón, disgusto, desazón. II. va. mortificar, enfadar.

chain [chéin]. I. s. cadena (la cadena misma y su longitud tomada por unidad); cadena de Gúnter (66 pies ing., o como 20.117 m.).—c. drive, (aut.) mando o transmisión por cadenas.—c. gang, cuadrilla de presidiarios encadenados entre sí.—c. gear, c. gearing, (mec.) transmisión por rueda y cadena.—c. lightning, relámpagos o relampagueo en zigzag.—c. pump,

noria.—c. riveting, remachado paralelo o de cadena.—c. shot, balas enramadas.—c. stitch, (cost.) punto de cadeneta.—c. store, tienda de un sistema de ellas pertenecientes a una misma empresa y todas de una misma clase, situadas en distintos barrios, pueblos, etc.—c. wheel, rueda dentada para cadena. II. va. encadenar; enlazar, unir.

chainless [-les], a. desencadenado; sin cadenas.

chainman [-mæn], s. cadenero.

chainwork [-uœrk], s. cadeneta.

chair [chéar], s. silla, asiento; silla de manos; sillón de la presidencia; por extensión, presidencia, presidente (de una junta, etc.); (f. c.) cojinete; base, asiento.

chairman [-mæn], s. presidente de una junta; silletero; sillero.—**chairmanship** [-ship], s. presidencia (de una junta directiva).—**chairwoman** [-umæn], s. presidenta.

chaise [shés], s. silla volante, calesín.

chalcedony [cælsédoni], s. (min.) calcedonia.

chalcocite [cælcosait], s. (min.) calcosina o calcocita (mineral de sulfuro de cobre).

chalcograph [-græf], s. calcografía, grabado calcográfico.

chalcography [cælcógrafi], calcografía (arte).

chalcopyrite [cælcopáirait], (min.) calcopirita.

Chaldaic [cældéic], **Chaldean** [-díæn], a. **Chaldee** [-di], a. y s. caldeo.

chaldron [chóldrun], s. chaldrón, medida de carbón, 2,500 a 2,900 libras.

chalet [shalé], s. casita de campo.

chalice [chális], s. (igl.) cáliz.

chalk [choc]. I. creta; tiza, yeso.—c. for cheese, gato por liebra.—c. rock, roca cretácea. II. va. enyesar; marcar o dibujar con tiza; apuntar, llevar cuenta.

chalkstone [-stoun], s. tiza; (med.) concreción gotosa en las coyunturas.

chalky [chóki], a. cretoso, yesoso.

challenge [chæleny]. I. va. desafiar, retar; demandar, exigir; disputar, contradecir; sobrepasar; ofrecer; (for.) recusar; (mil.) dar el quienvive. II. s. desafío; cartel de desafío; demanda, pretensión; (for.) recusación; (mil.) quienvive; concurso, oposición.—**challengeable** [-œbl], a. expuesto a desafío; recusable.—**challenger** [-œr], s. desafiador, retador; demandante.

challis [shæli], s. (tej.) chalí.

chalybeate [calíbiet]. I. a. calibeado, ferruginoso. II. s. agua ferruginosa.

chamade [shamád], s. (mil.) llamada.

chamber [chéimbœr]. I. s. cámara; gabinete, cuarto, alcoba, dormitorio; (for.) cámara, tribunal o sala de justicia; (arti.) cámara.—c. concert, concierto de salón.—c. council, junta secreta.—c., counsel, abogado consultor.—c. fellow, compañero de cuarto.—c. music, música de salón.—c. of commerce, cámara de comercio — c. practice, práctica (de la abogacía) de oficina, profesión de abogado consultor. II. va. hacer la cámara de un cañón; proveer de cámara; ahuecar; ajustar a la cámara. III. vn. (arti.) ajustarse la carga en un cartucho.

chamberlain [-len], s. chambelán; camarlengo. —**chamberlainship** [-ship], s. oficio o dignidad de chambelán.

chambermaid [-meid], sf. camarera; criada de mano; (teat.) graciosa.

chamberpot [-pot], s. orinal (vaso).

chameleon [camíleon], s. camaleón.

chamfer [chémfœr], va. (carp.) acanalar; achaflanar, biselar.

chamfer, chamfret [chémfret], s. (carp.) canal, estría; bisel, chaflán.

chamfrain [chémfren], s. (arm.) testera.

chamois [shémi], s. ante, gamuza; piel de ante.

chamomile [cémomail], s. = CAMOMILE.

champ [chæmp], va. morder, mascar, mordiscar.

champagne [shæmpéin], s. champaña.

champaign [shæmpéin]. I. s. campiña. II. a. abierto o llano.

champak [chæmpak], s. (bot.) ampac.

champion [chǽmpiʊn]. **I.** *a.* y *s.* campeón, paladín, adalid; defensor; (dep.) campeón. **II.** *va.* defender.—**championess** [-es], *s.* campeona; defensora.

chance [chans]. **I.** *s.* azar, acaso, casualidad, ocasión, oportunidad, coyuntura; riesgo; peligro; billete de lotería, rifa, etc.; probabilidad.—**by c.**, por casualidad.—**there is no c.**, no hay esperanza.—**to take chances**, correr el albur, aventurarse. **II.** *a.* casual, accidental.—**c. medley**, (for.) homicidio en defensa propia, en una reyerta. **III.** *adv.* casualmente. **IV.** *vn.* acaecer, suceder, acontecer. **V.** *va.* (fam.) probar, arriesgar.

chancel [chǽnsel], *s.* (igl.) presbiterio.

chancellor [chǽnselœr], *s.* canciller o chanciller; magistrado.—**C. of the Exchequer**, (Ingl.) Ministro de Hacienda.—**chancellorship** [-ship], *s.* cancillería.

chancery [chǽnseri], *s.* chancillería.

chancre [shǽnkœr], *s.* chancro.—**chancrous** [-crʊs], *a.* chancroso.

chancy [chánsi], *a.* (fam.) arriesgado.

chandelier [shændelíœr], *s.* araña de luces.

chandler [chǽndlœr], *s.* cerero o velero; tendero, vendedor.—**c.'s shop**, abacería, (Amér.) pulpería.

chandlery [chǽndlœri], *s.* mercería.

chanfrin [shǽnfrin], *s.* frente o faz del caballo.

change [chéiny]. **I.** *va.* cambiar, alterar, convertir; reemplazar; cambiar (moneda).—**to c. colour**, ruborizarse; demudarse, palidecer.—**to c. hands**, cambiar de dueño.—**to c. one's mind**, mudar de opinión. **II.** *vn.* mudar, cambiar, alterarse; corregirse, transformarse. **III.** *s.* cambio; alteración, mudanza; substitución, reemplazo, permutación, trueque; muda (de ropa); vuelta o sobrante de un pago; menudo o moneda suelta; vaivén, vicisitud; (com.) lonja o bolsa.—**c. of life**, (med.) menopausia.—**c. of the moon**, interlunio, cuarto de luna.—**for a c.**, para variar, por cambiar, por variedad.—**on 'c.**, en la bolsa.

changeability [chéinyabíliti], *s.* mutabilidad.

changeable [chéinyabœl], *a.* variable; inconstante, veleidoso; alterable; cambiante, tornasolado.—**changeableness** [-nes], *s.* mutabilidad; volubilidad; instabilidad.—**changeably** [-bli], *adv.* inconstantemente; variablemente.—**changeful**, [-ful]. *a.* inconstante, variable, veleidoso; variado.—**changeless** [-les], *a.* inmutable.—**changeling** [-ling]. **I.** *a.* variable, inconstante; trocado. **II.** *s.* niño cambiado por otro; bobo, tonto.

changer [chényœr], *s.* cambiador; cambista.

channel [chǽnel]. **I.** *s.* canal; álveo, cauce, madre de un río; (geog.) estrecho; zanja, caño, cacera, saetín; conducto; (carp.) cacera, ranura; (arq.) estría; (tec.) hierro en U (ll. t. **c. iron**).—*pl.* **channels**, (mar.) mesas de guarnición.—**c. of a block**, (mar.) cajera de motón.—**c. wale**, (mar.) cinta de la segunda cubierta. **II.** *va.* acanalar, estriar; surcar; encauzar, conducir.

chant [chant]. **I.** *va.* y *vn.* cantar; discantar. **II.** *s.* canto llano; salmo; sonsonete.

chantage [shantáy], *s.* (for.) *chantage*, explotación con amenazas de difamación.

chanter [chántœr], *s.* cantor, chantre.

chantey [chánte], *s.* saloma.

chantlate [chántlet], *s.* (arq.) alero.

chanticleer [chǽnticlœr], *s.* gallo.

chantress [chántres], *s.* cantora, cantatriz.

chantry [chántri], *s.* capilla; enrejado de una tumba.

chaos [kéos], *s.* el caos.—**chaotic** [keótic], *a.* caótico.

chap [chap]. **I.** *va.* hender, rajar, resquebrajar, agrietar. **II.** *vn.* rajarse, agrietarse, cuartearse. **III.** *s.* grieta, raja, rendija, hendidura; (fam.) mozo, chico; tipo.—*pl.* **chaps** = CHAPARAJOS.

chap [chop], *s.* mandíbula; quijada de un tornillo de banco.

chaparajos [cháparrájos], *s. pl.* chaparreras, zamarros.

chaparral [chæparél], *s.* (E. U.) chaparral.

chape [chéip], *s.* chapa; contera, regatón; charnela de hebilla.

chapel [chǽpel], *s.* capilla; (impr.) personal de una imprenta.—**chapelmaster**, maestro de capilla.

chapeless [chéiples], *a.* sin contera.

chapelet [chǽpelet], *s.* (equit.) doble estribo; (hidr.) draga de cubos; bomba de rosario.

chapelry [chǽpelri], *s.* jurisdicción de una capilla.

chaperon [shǽpœron]. **I.** *s.* acompañadora de señoritas. **II.** *va.* acompañar y escudar a una o más señoritas en lugares públicos.

chapfallen, chopfallen [chópfoln], *a.* boquihundido; (fig.) cariacontecido, alicaído.

chaplain [chǽplen], *s.* capellán; capellán castrense.—**chaplaincy** [-si], **chaplainship** [-ship], *s.* capellanía.

chaplet [chǽplet], *s.* guirnalda, corona de flores; rosario; gargantilla, collar; penacho; (arq.) moldura de cuentas.

chapman [chǽpman], *s.* buhonero.

chappie, chappy [chǽpi], *s.* (fam.) chico; mozalvete, petimetre.

chappy [chǽpi], *a.* agrietado, rajado.

chapter [chǽptœr], *s.* capítulo; (igl.) capítulo, cabildo; sucursal de una confraternidad.—**c. house**, sala capitular.—**to read one a c.**, (fig.) leer a uno la cartilla.—**to the end of the c.**, hasta el fin.

char [char]. **I.** *va.* y *vn.* carbonizar(se). **II.** *s.* carbón de leña, (ict.) umbra.

character [cǽræctœr]. **I.** carácter, índole, genio; fama, reputación; referencia; testimonio de conducta; clave secreta; marca, distintivo, propiedad; persona, sujeto; (teat) parte, papel; carácter de letra, tipo. **II.** *va.* grabar, esculpir; caracterizar.

characteristic(al [-ístic(al], *a.* característico, distintivo, propio.—**characteristic**, *s.* distintivo, peculiaridad; (mat.) característica.—**characteristically** [-ísticali], *adv.* característicamente.—**characterization** [-íséshʊn], *s.* descripción, representación.—**characterize** [-aíś], *va.* caracterizar.—**characterless** [-les], *a.* sin carácter.

charactery [cǽræctœri], *s.* simbolismo.

charade [sharéd], *s.* charada, sobre todo aquella en que la palabra o sus sílabas se indican por acciones dramáticas.

charbon [shárbon], *s.* fiebre esplénica, ántrax.

charcoal [chárcoul], *s.* carbón de leña; carboncillo de dibujar; dibujo al carbón.—**c. burner**, carbonero (que hace carbón).—**c. burning**, quema de madera para hacer carbón.—**c. drawing**, dibujo al carbón.—**c. furnace**, o **oven**, horno de hacer carbón por destilación.—**c. iron**, hierro de carbón de leña (en que éste es el combustible).

chare [chéar], *s.* tarea suelta o de ocasión, trabajo por ratos.

charge [chary]. **I.** *va.* cargar (un horno, un acumulador, etc.); gravar, imponer a; instruir, dar órdenes o instrucciones; exhortar, pedir a, mandar; pedir, llevar (precio); (com.) cargar, poner en cuenta; atacar, embestir; preparar, apuntar (un arma); blasonar.—**to c. on**, echar la culpa a.—**to c. with**, acusar de, imputar a. **II.** *vn.* pedir, llevar (precio); cargarse; cargar (a la bayoneta, etc.); agacharse, tenderse (los perros).

charge, *s.* carga, embestida, ataque; carga, tiro (de cañón); carga (de un horno, un acumulador, etc.); cargo, custodia; persona o cosa de que uno está encargado; obligación; precio; (gen. *pl.*) honorarios; partida o suma cargada en cuenta; impuesto, gravamen; instrucciones (a un jurado, etc.), orden, mandato; cargo, acusación.—**in c.**, encargado; interino.

chargeable [cháryabœl], *a.* que puede cargarse o atribuirse; costoso.

chargé d'affairs [sharyéi dæféar], *s.* encargado de negocios (de una legación).

charger [cháryœr], *s.* caballo; (arti.) medida para una carga de pólvora.

charily [chéarili], *adv.* cautelosamente.

chariness [chéarines], *s.* cautela.

chariot [chǽriot], *s.* carroza.

charioteer [chæriotícœr], s. auriga.

charitable [chéritabœl], a. caritativo.—**charitableness** [-nes], s. caridad.—**charitably** [chéritabli], adv. caritativamente.

charity [chériti], s. caridad; limosna; benevolencia.—**c. box**, cepillo de los pobres.

charivari [shárivári], s. cencerrada.

charlatan [shárlatan], s. charlatán, curandero.

charlatanic [-tænic], a. empírico.—**charlatanry** [-tanri], s. charlatanismo, embaimiento.

charlock [chárloc], s. (Ingl.) mostaza silvestre.

charlotte [shárlot], **charlotte russe** [-rus], s. natilla o compota rodeada de bizcochuelo.

charm [charm]. **I.** s. encanto, embeleso, hechizo; encantamiento, maleficio; talismán, amuleto; (joy.) dije. **II.** va. ensalmar, hechizar; encantar, embelesar, prendar; aojar.

charmer [chármœr], s. encantador, hechicero, fascinador.

charming [chárming]. a. encantador.—**charmingly** [-li], adv. encantadoramente.

charnel [chárnel], a. sepulcral.—**c. house**, carnerario, osario.

charpie [shárpi], s. hilas.

charring [chárring], s. carboneo.

charry [chárri], a. carbonoso.

chart [chart]. **I.** va. poner en una carta hidrográfica. **II.** s. (mar.) carta de navegar o de marear; carta hidrográfica; mapa, cuadro.

chartaceous [cartéshus], a. que tiene la textura de papel.

charter [chártœr]. **I.** s. cédula, título, encartación, carta de privilegio; carta constitucional; (com.) fletamento.—**c. party**, contrata de fletamento. **II.** va. estatuir; (com.) fletar un barco.—**chartered** [-d], a. privilegiado; (mar.) fletado.—**charterer** [-œr], s. fletador.

chartless [-les], a. sin rumbo, desorientado

chartographer, etc. V. CARTOGRAPHER, etc.

chartulary, s. = CARTULARY.

charwoman [chárúman], s. mujer asalariada por hora o día para faenas domésticas.

chary [chéari], a. cuidadoso, cauteloso, circunspecto; económico, frugal.

chase [chéis]. **I.** va. cazar; perseguir; (joy.) engastar, montar; cincelar.—**to c. away, o off,** ahuyentar, espantar; disipar. **II.** s. caza; persecución; montería, partida de caza; cazadero; (impr.) rama; (mec.) ranura, muesca, encaje; (art.) caña de un cañón.

chaser [chéisœr], s. cazador; perseguidor; persona o caballo que se dedica a carreras de obstáculos; (mar.) cazasubmarinos; (aer.) avión ligero de defensa y perseguida.

chasing [-ing], s. cinceladura; seguimiento, caza.

chasm [cæsm], s. vacío, laguna, abismo; quiebra, grieta.

chasse [shas], s. caja, cofre; pluscafé.

chassis [shæsi], s. armazón, bastidor, marco; (art.) riel de cureña; (aut.) chasis; (en fot.) portaplacas.

chasseur [shasœr], s. (mil.) cazador.

chaste [chéist], a. casto; virtuoso, puro; castizo, neto.—**chastely** [-li], adv. castamente; púdicamente; correctamente.

chasten [chéisœn], va. corregir, castigar; purificar.

chastener [chéisnœr], s. castigador, corrector, depurador.—**chasteness** [chéistnes], s. pureza, castidad.—**chastening** [chéisning], s. castigo, corrección; disciplina.

chastisable [chæstáisabœl], a. punible, castigable.

chastise [chæstáis], va. castigar, corregir.—**chastisement** [-ment], s. castigo, corrección.—**chastiser** [-œr], s. castigador.

chastity [chæstiti], s. castidad, pureza.

chasuble [chæsiubœl], s. (igl.) casulla.

chat [chæt]. **I.** vn. charlar, platicar. **II.** s. conversación, plática, charla; (orn.) pájaro.

chateau [sható], s. = CASTLE.

chatelaine [shátelein], s. castellana; (joy.) muelle de dijes.

chattel [chætel], s. bienes muebles, enseres.

chatter [chætœr]. **I.** vn. rechinar los dientes; cotorrear, parlotear, charlar; vibrar. **II.** s; rechinido; garla, charla; garrulería; vibración.—**chatterbox** [-box], s. charlador, tarabilla.—**chatterer** [-œr], s. charlador, gárrulo, hablistán.—**chattering** [-ing]. **I.** s. chirrido; rechinamiento; garrulidad, cotorreo. **II.** a. locuaz, hablanchín.

chatty [chæti], a. hablantín, picotero, gárrulo.

chatwood [chætud], s. ramojo.

chauffer [shófœr], s. (quím.) hornillo.

chauffeur [shofœr], s. cochero de automóvil, chauffeur. (Muchos usan chófer.)

chauvinist [shóvinist], s. patriotero.

chaw [cho]. **I.** va. (vul.) mascar. V. CHEW. **II.** s. (vul.) mascada.

cheap [chíp], a. barato; de pacotilla.

cheapen [chípœn], va. abaratar; regatear.

cheapener [chípnœr], s. regatón.

cheaply [chípli], adv. barato, a bajo precio.

cheapness [chípnes], s. baratura.

cheat [chit]. **I.** va. engañar, defraudar; trampear, enfullar; chasquear. **II.** s. trampa, fraude, engaño; trampista, timador.

cheater [chítœr], s. trampista, fullero; estafador, engañador, defraudador.

cheatery [chítœri], s. fraude, trampa, fullería.

cheating [chíting], s. engaño, fraude, trampa.

check. **I.** va. reprimir, refrenar, detener; verificar y marcar; registrar, facturar (equipajes, etc.); dejar a guardar, dejar (algo por lo cual se recibe contraseña); dar jaque a (ajedrez). **II.** vn. detenerse; rajarse, agrietarse; dar jaque. **III.** s. lo que contiene o detiene; detención; rechazo; obstáculo, impedimento; contratiempo; contraseña, billete de reclamo (de equipajes, etc.); cuadro, jaquel (en tela, etc. de cuadros); jaque (ajedrez); ficha (en el juego); grieta; muesca, entalladura; cuenta (de restaurante); (mec.) tope; (com.) cheque; talón.—**c. book**, libreta de cheques.—**c. chamber**, cámara de la válvula de retención.—**c. nut** = LOCK NUT.—**c. valve**, válvula de retención.

checker, chequer [chékœr]. **I.** va. formar escaques o cuadros; diversificar. **II.** s. el que reprime o refrena; cada pieza del juego de damas; escaque.—pl. juego de damas.—**checkerberry** [-bœri], s. (bot.) gaulteria y su baya.

checkerboard [-bórd], s. tablero de damas.

checkered [chékœrd], a. escaqueado, jaquelado; variado.

checkless [chékles], a. desenfrenado.

checkmate [chécmeit]. **I.** va. dar jaque mate; desconcertar, derrotar. **II.** s. jaque mate.

cheek [chíc], s. carrillo, mejilla; (art.) gualdera de cureña; (mec.) quijada, montante, larguero; banzo, cárcel; (fam.) tupé, descaro, desfachatez; jamba (de puerta o ventana), derrame; cachola (de mástil).—**c. of the pump**, (mar.) picota.—**cheeks of the head**, (mar.) tajamar.—**c. by jowl**, (fam.) cara a cara.

cheekbone [chícboun], s. pómulo.

cheep [chíp]. **I.** vn. piar, chirriar. **II.** s. pío, chirrido.

cheer [chíar]. **I.** s. vivas, vítores, aplausos; alegría, regocijo; banquete, festín. **II.** va. alentar, consolar, alegrar; vitorear, aplaudir. **III.** vn. alegrarse.—**to c. up**, tomar o cobrar ánimo.—**c. up!** ¡ánimo, valor!

cheerer [-œr], s. regocijador, vitoreador.

cheerful [-ful], a. alegre, animado, jovial.—**cheerfully** [-fuli], **cheerily** [-lil], adv. alegremente, con júbilo.—**cheerfulness** [-fulnes], s. alegría, jovialidad.—**cheerless** [-les], a. triste.

cheery [chíari], a. = CHEERFUL.

cheese [chís], s. queso.—**c. curds**, cuajadas.—**c. mite**, ácaro de queso.—**c. parings**, cortezas de queso.—**c. rennet**, cuajaleche.—**c. vat**, quesera.

cheesecake [-keic], s. quesadilla.

cheesecloth [-cloz], s. estopilla de algodón.

cheesemonger [-móngœr], s. quesero.

cheesy [chísi], a. caseoso.

chef [shef], s. jefe; primer cocinero, cocinero en jefe.

chef-d'œuvre [she-dœvr], s. obra maestra.

cheka [chícæ], cheka, policía secreta del gobierno soviético.

chela [kílæ], s. (zool.) quelicero.

Chelonia [kelónia], s. pl. (zool.) quelonios.

chemical [kémical]. **I.** a. químico. **II.** s. producto químico; reactivo.—**chemically** [-li], adv. químicamente.

chemise [shemís], s. camisa de mujer: (fort.) camisa.

chemisette [shemisét], s. camiseta o camisolín de mujer.

chemism [kémism], s. afinidad química; fenómenos químicos.

chemist [kémist], s. químico; farmaceuta.

chemistry [kémistri], s. química.

chenille [sheníl], s. felpilla.

chenopod [kínopod], s. (bot.) quenopodácea.

chenopodium [-pódium], s. (bot.) quenopodio.

cheque [chek], s. (com.) cheque o talón.

cherish [chérish], va. apreciar, estimar, fomentar; alimentar, abrigar, acariciar.

cheroot [sherút], s. (Filip.) trompetilla.

cherry [chérri]. **I.** s. (bot.) cereza; cerezo. **II.** a. hecho de cereza o de cerezo; de color de cereza. **c. red**, rojo cereza.

chert [chœrt], s. (min.) horsteno.

cherty [chœrti], a. que tiene cuarzo.

cherub [chérub], s. (pl. CHERUBIM) querubín.

cherubic(al [cherúbic(al], a. angélical.

cherup [chérup], vn. chirriar, piar.

chervil [chœrvil], s. (bot.) perifolio.

chess [ches], s. ajedrez.—**chessboard**, tablero de ajedrez.—**chessman**, pieza de ajedrez.

chessel [chésel], s. encella.

chest [chest], s. arca, cofre, caja, cajón; pecho, tórax; (mec.) receptáculo para gases o líquidos. —**c. of drawers**, cómoda.—**c. protector**, peto de lana para abrigo.

chestnut [chésnut]. **I.** s. (bot.) castaña; castaño; color de castaña; (E. U. fam.) broma o frase gastada.—**to take**, o **pull, another's c.'s out of the fire**, sacarle a otro el ascua, dejar que otro saque el ascua por mano de uno. **II.** a. castaño; pinar.

chetah [chíta], s. leopardo de Asia.

cheval [shevál], s. caballo, caballete; apoyo, sostén.—**c. de-frise** = CHEVEAU-DE-FRISE.—**c. glass**, espejo de vestir.

chevalier [shevalícer], s. caballero.

chevaux-de-frise [shevó-de-frís], s. (mil.) caballo de frisa.

Cheviot [chéviot], s. (zool.) carnero inglés; (tej.) cheviot.

chevron [shévron], s. (mil.) cheurón.—pl. (blas.) cheurón; (arq.) cabrio.

chevy [chévi]. **I.** va. acosar; cazar. **II.** s. caza; seguimiento; grito de caza.

chew [chu]. **I.** va. mascar, masticar. **II.** vn. mascar tabaco; rumiar, meditar. **III.** s. mascadura.

chewing [chúing], a. de o para mascar.

chewink [cheuínk], s. (orn.) emberiza.

chiaroscuro [kiaroscúro], s. claroscuro.

chibouk [chibúk], s. chibuca.

chic [shic]. **I.** a. gentil, elegante, mono. **II.** s. elegancia, buen tono, gentileza.

chicane [shikén], s. tramoya, trampa.

chicanery [shikénceri], s. trapacería, trampería, embrollo, trampa legal.

chick, chicken [chik, -en], s. polluelo o pollo; (fig.) jovencito; niño.—**c.-hearted**, cobarde, gallina, medroso.—**c. pox**, varicela, viruelas locas.

chickadee [chícadi], s. (orn.) paro americano.

chickpea [chícpi], s. (bot.) garbanzo.

chickweed [chícuid], s. (bot.) pamplina.

chicle [chíccel], s. (bot.) chicle.

chicory [chícori], s. (bot.) achicoria.

chide [chaid]. **I.** va. (pret. CHID: pp. CHID o CHIDDEN) increpar, reprender, regañar; ahuyentar. **II.** vn. regañar, refunfuñar.

chider [chídcer], s. regañón, regañador.

chiding [cháiding], s. regaño, reprimenda.

chidingly [-li], adv. en tono de reprensión.

chief [chif]. **I.** a. principal; primero, primer, en jefe.—**c. clerk**, oficial mayor.—**c. judge, o c. justice**, presidente de sala; (E. U.) presidente de la corte suprema. **II.** s. jefe.—**c. of general staff**, jefe de estado mayor general.—**c. of staff**, jefe de estado mayor.

chiefless [chífles], a. sin jefe.

chiefly [chífli], adv. principalmente, mayormente.

chieftain [chíften], s. jefe, comandante; caudillo, capitán; cabeza.—**chieftaincy** [-si], **chieftainship** [-ship], s. jefatura.

chiffer, chiffre [shífcer], s. (mús.) cifra.

chiffon [shífon], s. gasa, soplillo.

chiffonier [shifonícer], s. mueble de cajonería.

chignon [shífion], s. moño, castaña, poso.

chigoe [chígo], s. nigua.

chilacayote [chilacayóte], s. (bot.) chilacayote.

chilblain [chílblein], s. sabañón.

child [cháild], s. (pl. CHILDREN) niño o niña; hijo o hija.—**c.'s play**, de clavo pasado, muy fácil.—**with c.**, preñada, embarazada.

childbearing [-béœring], s. parto.

childbed [-bed], s. sobreparto.—**c. fever**, fiebre puerperal.

childbirth [-bœrz], s. parto, alumbramiento.

Childermas Day [chíldœrmas dei], **Childermastide** [-taid], s. día de inocentes.

childhood [cháildjud], s. infancia, niñez.

childish [cháildish], a. pueril, aniñado, frívolo, trivial.—**childishly** [-li], adv. puerilmente.—**childishness** [-nes], s. puerilidad, niñada o niñería.

childless [cháildles], a. sin hijos.

childlike [cháildlaic], a. pueril, infantil.

children [chíldren], s. pl. de CHILD.

Chilean [chílean], a. y s. chileno.

chiliad [kíliad], s. mil años.

chiliasm [kíliæsm], s. doctrina milenaria.

chiliast [kíliast], s. milenario.

chill [chil]. **I.** a. frío, desapacible. **II.** s. frío, calofrío o escalofrío; enfriamiento; estremecimiento.—**chills and fever**, (E. U.) = AGUE. **III.** va. enfriar, resfriar, pasmar, helar; desanimar, desalentar; (fund.) vaciar en coquilla; templar superficialmente por enfriamiento rápido. **IV.** vn. escalofriarse.

chilli [chíli], s. chile, ají.

chilliness, chillness [chílnes], s. frialdad.

chilly [chíli]. **I.** a. frío, calofriado; friolento. **II.** adv. fríamente.

chimæra, s. V. CHIMERA.

chimb [cháim], s. jable; gárgol.

chime [cháim]. **I.** s. juego de campanas; campaneo, repique, repiquete; armonía, ritmo; conformidad, analogía; (ton.) jable o gárgol, muesca, ranura de la duela. **II.** va. tocar, tañer las campanas. **III.** vn. repicar, repiquetear (las campanas); sonar con armonía; convenir, concordar.

chimera [kimíra], s. quimera; ilusión.

chimere [shimícer], s. sobrepelliz.

chimerical [kimérical], a. quimérico, imaginario. —**chimerically** [-li], adv. quiméricamente.

chimney [chímni], s. chimenea; bombillo o tubo de lámpara.—**c. corner**, chimenea, hogar.—**c. piece**, delantero de chimenea.—**c. sweep**, limpiador de chimeneas.—**c. top**, caperuza o sombrerete de chimenea.

chimpanzee [chimpánsi], s. chimpancé.

chin [chin], s. barba.—**c. strap**, carrillera, barboquejo.

china [cháina], s. porcelana, loza.—**c. closet**, chinero.—**C. ink**, tinta china.—**c. orange**, naranja china; naranja dulce.—**c. wedding**, vigésimo aniversario.

Chinaman [cháinæmæn], s. chino.

chinaroot [-rut], s. (bot.) china.

chinaware [-uéœr], s. = CHINA.

chinchilla [chinchíla], s. chinchilla y su piel.

chine [chain]. **I.** s. espinazo; lomo; solomo. **II.** va. deslomar.

Chinese [chainís]. **I.** *a.* chino, chinesco.—
C. anise, badián.—**C. white,** blanco de cinc,
óxido de cinc. **II.** *s.* chino, lengua china.

chink [chink], *s.* grieta, hendedura, resquebradura, rajadura; sonido metálico; (fam.) dinero,
blanca. **II.** *vn.* henderse, abrirse; sonar, resonar.

chinkapin [chínkapin], *s.* castaño enano, y su
fruto.

chinky [chínki], *a.* hendido, rajado, resquebrajadizo.

chinned [chind], *a.* barbado.

chinquapin [chincæpin], *s.* = CHINKAPIN.

chinse [chins], *va.* (mar.) calafatear, embromar
costuras.

chints, chintz [chints], *s.* quimón, zaraza.

chip [chip]. **I.** *va.* desmenuzar, picar; astillar,
descantillar. **II.** *vn.* romperse, quebrarse,
desconcharse.—**to c. in,** (fam.) poner la apuesta
(en el juego); contribuir. **III.** brizna, astilla;
pedacito; ficha.—*pl.* chamada, doladura; támaras.
—**c. ax,** o **axe,** azuela.—**a c. of the old block,** de
tal palo tal astilla.

chipper [chípcœr], *a.* (E. U. fam.) vivo, alegre,
jovial; sano, robusto.

chipmunk [chípmunk], *s.* especie de ardilla.

chirk [chœrk]. **I.** *a.* (fam.) alegre, jovial. **II.** *s.*
horsteno. *V.* CHERT.

chirograph [cáirograf], *s.* quirógrafo.

chirographer [cairógrafœr], *s.* escribano, escribiente.—**chirography** [-fi], *s.* quirografía, carácter de letra.

chiromancer [cáiromanser], *s.* quiromántico.

chiromancy [cáiromansi], *s.* quiromancia.

chiropodist [cairópodist], *s.* pedicuro, callista.

chiropractic [cáiropréctic], *s.* "quiropráctica"
(método de tratamiento médico manipulando
la columna vertebral).—**chiropractor** (-præctœr),
"quiropráctico," el que ejerce la "quiropráctica."

chirp [chœrp]. **I.** *vn.* chirriar, gorjear, pipiar.
II. *s.* chirrido; gorjeo; canto.

chirper [chœrpœr], *s.* chirriador, piador.

chirping [chœrping]. **I.** *s.* chirrido, piada. **II.** *a.*
parlero, gárrulo.

chirrup [chírup]. **I.** *va.* y *vn.* gorjear, trinar.
II. *s.* gorjeo, trino.

chisel [chísel]. **I.** *s.* escoplo, cincel, formón. **II.** *va.*
escoplear, cincelar, esculpir.

chit [chit]. **I.** *s.* (despec.) chiquilla, muchacha;
tallo, germen, botón, yema. **II.** *va.* quitar los
brotes o renuevos.

chitchat [chítchæt], *s.* charla, palique.

chitterlings [chítcœrlings], *s. pl.* despojos; asadura, menudos.

chivalric [shívalric], *a.* caballeresco.—**chivalrous**
[-rus], *a.* caballeroso.—**chivalry** [-ri], *s.* caballería;
caballerosidad, hidalguía.

chive [chaiv], *s.* cebollino, cebollana.

chlamys [clémis *o* clámis], *s.* clámide.

chloral [clóral], *s.* cloral.

chlorate [clóret], *s.* (quím.) clorato.

chloric [clóric], *a.* clórico.

chlorid, chloride [clórid, clóraid], *s.* cloruro.

chloridize [clóridais], **chlorinate** [clórineit], *va.*
clorar, tratar con cloro; (metal.) clorurar.

chlorination [-néishu̯ʌ], *s.* cloración; clorura-
ción.—**chlorinator** [-tœr], *s.* clorador, aparato
de clorar.

chlorine [clórin], *s.* (quím.) cloro.

chlorite [clórait], *s.* (min.) clorita.

chloroform [clóroform]. **I.** *s.* cloroformo. **II.** *va.*
cloroformizar.—**chloroformic** [-fórmic], *a.* clo-
rofórmico.—**chloroformization** [-miséishun], *s.*
cloroformización.

chlorometer [clorómitœr], *s.* (quím.) cloró-
metro.—**chlorometry** [-metri], *s.* clorometría.

chlorophyl, chlorophyll [clórofil], *s.* clorofila.

chlorosis [clorósis], *s.* (med.) clorosis.

chlorotic [clorótic], *a.* clorótico, clorótica.

chlorous [clórus], *a.* cloroso.

chock [choc]. **I.** *s.* calzo, cuña, tornapunta;
(mar.) choque. *V.* CHUCK. **II.** *va.* afianzar,
soportar, calzar. **III.** *vn.* cerrar, tapar, llenar
un hueco.

chock-full [chóc-ful], *a.* colmado, atestado, de
bote en bote.

chocolate [chócolet], *s.* chocolate.—**c. cup,**
pocillo, jícara.—**c. pot,** chocolatera.—**c. tree,**
cacao (árbol).

choice [chóis]. **I.** *s.* elección, preferencia; opción;
cosa elegida; lo selecto, lo más escogido. **II.** *a.*
escogido, selecto, exquisito.

choicely [-li], *adv.* escogidamente, primorosamente.—**choiceness** [-nes], *s.* delicadeza; discernimiento.

choir [cuáicœr], *s.* (igl.) coro.

choke [chóuk]. **I.** *va.* y *vn.* ahogar, sofocar; estrangular; agarrotar; suprimir, oprimir.—
to c. up, cerrar, obstruir, tapar; atragantarse,
atorarse. **II.** *s.* estrangulación—**c.-full** = CHOCK-
FULL.—**c. pear,** pera áspera; tapaboca.

choker [chóukœr], *s.* ahogador, agarrotador;
corbatín; tapaboca; (aut.) regulador de aire.

choking coil [chóuking coil], *s.* (elec.) bobina de
reacción o de reactancia.

choky [chóki], *a.* sofocante.

cholagogue [cólagog], *s.* colagogo.

choler [cólœr], *s.* cólera, ira.

cholera [cólera], *s.* (med.) cólera-morbo; cólera
asiático.—**c. infantum,** cólera infantil, enteritis
coleriforme de los niños.

choleraic [cóleraic], *a.* colérico (referente al cólera).

choleric [cólœric], *a.* colérico, irascible.

choleriform [cólœriform], *a.* coleriforme.

cholerine [cólerin], *s.* colerín o colerina.

cholesterine [colésterin], *s.* colesterina.

choose [chuš]. **I.** *va.* escoger, elegir, preferir,
optar por; desear. **II.** *vn.* preferir, querer.

chooser [chúšœr], *s.* escogedor; elector.

choosing [chúšing], *s.* escogimiento, elección.

chop [chop]. **I.** *va.* tajar, cortar, separar; picar
carne; (carp.) desbastar; rajar, hender;
cambiar, trocar; hablar a borbotones.—**to c. off,**
tronchar. **II.** *vn.* dar cuchilladas; interrumpir;
rajarse, cuartearse; virar (el viento).—**to c.
about,** girar, virar.—**to c. at,** zampar. **III.** *s.*
porción, parte; tajada, posta de carne; chuleta o
costilla; raja, hendedura, grieta; quijada, mandíbula; tenazas; cabo, promontorio.—*pl.* **chops,**
quijadas; boca, entrada.—**c. logic,** quisquilla,
casuística; persona quisquillosa o pelillosa.

chophouse [chópjáus], *s.* bodegón; restaurante.

chopine [chopín], *s.* chapín.

chopped [chópd], *pp.* de TO CHOP.—**c. meat,**
carne picada; picadillo.

chopper [chópœr], *s.* cuchilla de carnicero.

chopping [chóping]. **I.** *a.* variable (viento);
picado (mar). **II.** *s.* tajadura, cortadura.—
c. block, tajo de cocina, tajadera, cortafrío.—**c.
board,** tajador.—**c. knife,** cuchillo de picar.—
c. bowl, c. tray, artesilla de picar (carne, etc.)

choppy [chópi], *a.* rajado, hendido; picado,
agitado (mar).

chopstick [chópstic], *s.* palillo chino y japonés
para comer.

choral [córal], *a.* (mús.) coral.

chord [córd]. **I.** *s.* (mús.) cuerda; acorde;
armonía; (geom.) cuerda; (fig.) fibra, cuerda
sensible. **II.** *va.* (mús.) encordar. **III.** *va.* y *vn.*
templar; armonizar.

chore [chóœr], *s.* tarea doméstica.

chorea [coría], *s.* corea, baile de San Vito.

choreograph [córeograf], *s.* coreógrafo.

choreography [córeografi], *s.* coreografía.

choree, choreus [córi, coríus], *s.* coreo, troqueo,
pie de verso (— ◡).

choriambic [coriémbic]. **I.** *s.* coriambo, pie de
verso (— ◡ ◡ —). **II.** *a.* coriámbico.

choroid [córoid]. **I.** *a.* coroideo.—**c. coating,**
coroides. **II.** *s.* coroides.

chorion [córion], *s.* (anat.) corión.

chorist [córist], **chorister** [córistœr], *s.* corista;
clerizón.

chorographer [corógrafœr], *s.* corógrafo.

chorographical [córográfical], *a.* corgráfico.

chorography [corógrafi], *s.* corografía.

chorus [córus], *s.* (mús.) coro.

chose, chosen [chóuŝ, chóuŝn], *pret.* y *pp.* de TO CHOOSE.—**chosen people**, pueblo escogido.

chose [ŝhoŝ], *s.* (for.) cualquier objeto de propiedad personal.

chough [chuf], *s.* (orn.) chova.

chouse [chaus]. **I.** *va.* engañar, estafar. **II.** *s.* engaño, fraude, estafa; bribón, estafador.— **chousing** [-ing], *s.* bellaquería, fraude.

chowchow [cháucháu], *s.* mezcla de encurtidos con mostaza.

chowder [cháuder], *s.* especie de sancocho de almejas o pescado; partida de campo en que se toma *chowder*.

chrestomathy [crestómazi], *s.* crestomatía.

chrism [crism], *s.* (igl.) crisma.

chrismatory [crísmatori], *s.* crismera.

chrisom [crísum], *s.* (igl.) ropaje de bautizar.— **c. child**, niño inocente.

crisscross, *s.* = CRISTCROSS.

Christ [cráist], *s.* Cristo.

christcross [crís̄cros], *s.* cristus (cruz puesta al principio del abecedario).

christen [crísn], *va.* bautizar, cristianar.

Christendom [crísœndum], *s.* cristiandad.

christening [crísœning]. **I.** *s.* bautizo; bautismo. **II.** *a.* baut:smal.

Christian [críschan], *a.* y *s.* cristiano.—**C. name**, nombre de bautismo o de pila.—**C. box**, regalo de Navidad, esp. de dinero.—**C. Science**, ciencia cristiana, eddyismo, secta cristiana fundada por Mary Baker Eddy.—**C. Scientist**, sectario del eddyismo.

Christianism, Christianity [críschaniŝm, crischiǽniti], *s.* cristianismo.

Christianize [críschanaiŝ], *va.* cristianizar.

Christianlike [críschanlaic], *a.* cristiano.

Christianly [críschanli], *adv.* cristianamente.

Christless [cráistles], *a.* anticristiano, herético.

Christmas [crísmas], *s.* natividad de Jesús; pascua de Navidad.—**C. carol**, villancico, cántico de Navidad.—**C. Eve**, víspera de Navidad, nochebuena.—**C. tree**, árbol de Navidad, árbol o rama (gen. de pino) condecorado que se usa en la celebración de las Pascuas.

chroma [cróma], *s.* intensidad de color.

chromate [crómet], *s.* cromato.

chromatic [cromǽtic], *a.* cromático; (mús.) cromático.

chromatics [cromǽtics], *s.* cromática, ciencia del colorido.

chromatography [cromatógrafi], *s.* cromatografía.

chrome [cróum]. **I.** *s.* (quím.) cromo; (tint.) dicromato potásico.—**c. yellow**, amarillo de cromo, cromato de plomo. **II.** *va.* (tint.) tratar con dicromato potásico.—**chromic** [-ic], *a.* crómico.

chromite [cróumait], *s.* (quím.) cromito.

chromium [crómium], *s.* (quím.) cromo.— **c. steel**, acero cromo (aleación de acero y cromo).

chromo, chromolithograph [cromo-lízograf], *s.* cromo, cromolitografía.—**chromolithographer** [-zógrafœr], *s.* cromolitógrafo.—**chromolithography** [-zógrafi], *s.* cromolitografía.

chromosphere [-sfíær], *s.* cromosfera, envoltura de gases que rodea la atmósfera del sol.

chromotype [-taip], *s.* cromotipia; cromolitografía.

chromotypography [-taipógrafi], *s.* cromotipografía.

chromous [crómus], *a.* cromoso.

chronic [crónic], *a.* crónico, inveterado.

chronicity [crónisiti], *s.* estado o calidad de crónico.

chronicle [crónikœl]. **I.** *s.* crónica.—**Chronicles**, Paralipómenos. **II.** *va.* escribir una crónica.

chronicler [cróniclœr], *s.* cronista.

chronogram [crónogræm], *s.* cronograma.

chronograph [crónograf], *s.* cronógrafo.

chronographer [cronógrafœr], *s.* cronologista.

chronography [cronógrafi], *s.* cronografía.

chronologer [cronóloyœr], *s.* cronologista, cronólogo.—**chronologic(al** [cronolóyic(al], *a.* cronológico.—**chronologically** [-l], *adv.* crono-

---

lógicamente.—**chronology** [cronóloyi], *s.* cronología.—**chronologist** [-yist], *s.* = CHRONOLOGER.

chronometer [cronómetœr], *s.* cronómetro.

chronometric(al [crónométric(al], *a.* cronométrico.

chronometry [cronómetri], *s.* cronometría.

chronoscope [crónoscoup], *s.* cronógrafo.

chrysalis [crísalis], *s.* crisálida.

chrysanthemum [crisǽnzemum], *s.* (bot.) crisantemo, santimonia.

chrysoberyl [crisobéril], *s.* (min.) crisoberilo.

chrysolite [crísolait], *s.* (min.) crisólito.

chrysoprase [crísopreŝ], *s.* (min.) crisoprasa.

chub [chub], *s.* (ict.) coto.—**c.-faced**, cariancho.

chubby [chúbi], *a.* regordete, gordiflón, rechoncho.

chuck [chuc]. **I.** *vn.* cloquear; cacarear. **II.** *va.* hacer la mamola; echar, tirar. **III.** *s.* mamola; echada; cloqueo; golpe seco; (mec.) manguito portaherramienta; cuña: calzo; mandril (de un torno).—**c. farthing**, hoyuelo (juego).—**c. full** = CHOCKFULL.—**c. hole**, hoyo en una rodada.

chuckle [chúkœl]. **I.** *vn.* reir entre dientes; cloquear. **II.** *s.* risa ahogada, risita. **III.** *a.* cabezón, cabezudo.

chucklehead [-jéd], *s.* tonto, cabezota.

chuff [chuf], *a.* áspero, gruñón.

chuffy [chúfi], *a.* gordote, gordiflón.

chum [chum]. **I.** *va.* y *vn.* ser camarada. **II.** *s.* camarada, compinche; condiscípulo.

chump [chump], *s.* zoquete, tronco, tarugo; lomo del carnero; (fam.) masturzo.

chunk [chunk], *s.* pedazo, trozo, animalote.

chunky [chúnki], *a.* (E. U.) trabado, rechoncho.

church [chœrch]. **I.** *s.* iglesia (institución y edificio).—**c. book**, registro de la iglesia.—**c. invisible**, congregación de todos los cristianos, muertos y vivos, sin distinción de sectas.—**c. militant**, iglesia militante (de todas las sectas).— **C. of England**, iglesia (secta) anglicana.—**c. school** = SUNDAY SCHOOL.—**c. triumphant**, iglesia triunfante; nombre de dos sectas protestantes (C. Triumphant).—**C. visible**, iglesia militante. —**to go to c.**, asistir al servicio de iglesia (ir a misa, si es éste el servicio). **II.** *va.* llevar (una persona) a la iglesia a ciertos ritos practicados en su beneficio; ejecutar estos ritos.

churchgoer [-gócœr], *s.* persona que asiste regularmente a la iglesia.

churchlike [-laik], *a.* como iglesia, como de iglesia.

churchman [-man], *s.* miembro de alguna iglesia; sacerdote, eclesiástico.

churchwarden [-uórden], *s.* (igl.) capiller, obrero, fabriquero.

churchyard [-yard], *s.* cementerio.

churl [chœrl], *s.* patán, palurdo; avaro.

churlish [chœrliŝh], *a.* rudo, rústico; ruin, avaro.—**churlishly** [-li], *adv.* rudamente.—**churlishness** [-nes]. *s.* rusticidad, tosquedad; rudeza, grosería.

churn [chœrn]. **I.** *s.* mantequera. **II.** *va.* agitar, menear, revolver; batir manteca.— **c. owl**, (orn.) chotacabras.—**churning** [-ing], *s.* batido.—**churnstaff** [-stæf], *s.* batidera.

chute [ŝhút], *s.* saetín; conducto; canal (fem.)

chylaceous [kailéŝhus], *a.* quiloso.

chyle [káil], *s.* quilo.—**chylification** [káilifikéŝhun], *s.* quilificación.—**chylifactive** [-fǽctiv], *a.* quilificativo.—**chylify** [-fai], *vn.* quilificar.— **chylous** [káilus], *a.* quiloso.

chyme [káim], *s.* quimo, cibario.

cibol [síbol], *s.* cebolleta; chalota.

ciborium [sibórium], *s.* dosel de altar; copón.

cicada [sikéda], *s.* cigarra o chicharra.

cicatrice [sícœtris], *s.* cicatriz.—**cicatricial** [-tríŝhœl], *a.* cicatrizal.—**cicatricula** [-tríkiula], *s.* galladura.—**cicatrisant** [-tráiŝant], *s.* cicatrizante. —**cicatrisive** [-tráisiv], *a.* cicatrizativo.—**cicatrix** [-trix], *s.* = CICATRICE.—**cicatrization** [-triŝéŝhun], *s.* cicatrización.—**cicatrize** [-traiŝ], *va.* cicatrizar.

cicely [síseli], *s.* (bot.) perifollo.

cicerone [chicheróne], *s.* cicerone.

Ciceronian [siserónian], *a.* ciceroniano.

---

cicisbeo [chichisbéo], *s.* amante de una mujer casada.

cicuta [sikiúta], *s.* (bot.) cicuta.

cider [sáidœr], *s.* sidra.

ci-devant [si-deván], *a.* anterior, pasado.

cigar [sigár], *s.* cigarro, puro, tabaco.—**c. case,** petaca, cigarrera.—**c. holder, boquilla.—c. maker,** cigarrero, torcedor de tabaco.—**c. store,** *o* **shop,** tabaquería, cigarrería.

cigarette [sígarét], *s. dim.* cigarrillo, pitillo.— **c. case,** pitillera, cigarrillera.

cilia [sília], *s. pl.* de CILIUM.

ciliary [sílieri], *a.* ciliar.

ciliate [síliet], *a.* ciliado, pestañoso.

cilicious [síliśhʊs], *a.* cerdoso.

cilium [sílium], *s.* pelito; pestaña.

cima [śáima], *s.* = CYMA.

Cimbri [símbrai], *s. pl.* cimbros.

Cimbrian [símbrian], **Cimbric** [-ic], *a.* y *s.* cimbro, címbrico.

cimeter [símetœr], *s.* cimitarra.

Cimmerian [simírian], *a.* cimerio.—**C. darkness,** obscuridad espantosa.

cinch [sinchj. **I.** *va.* (fam. E. U.) cinchar; apretar, forzar. **II.** *s.* cincha, cinchú; (fam.) ganga.

cinchona [sinçóna], *s.* (bot.) quina, cinchona.

cinchonine [sínconin], *s.* (quím.) cinconina.

cinchonism [cínconiśm], *s.* cinconismo, quininismo (estado anormal debido al exceso de quinina).

cinchonize [-ñaiś], *va.* poner bajo la influencia de la quinina.

cincture [síncchur], *s.* cinto, ceñidor, cincho; cercado, cerca.

cinder [síndœr], *s.* carbón; cernada.—*pl.* cenizas, pavesas; rescoldo.

Cinderella [síndœrélæ], *s.* la Cenicienta.

cinema [sínemæ], *s.* cine.

cinematograph [-métogræf], *s.* cinematógrafo. —**cinematographer** [-mætógræfœr], *s.* cinematografista.—**cinematographic** [-mætográfic], *a.* cinematográfico.—**cinematographically** [-all], cinematográficamente.

cineraceous [sineráśhʊs], *a.* ceniciento.

cineraria [sineréria], *s.* (bot.) cineraria.

cinerary [sínereri], *a.* cinerario.

cineration [sineréśhʊn], *s.* incineración.

cinereous [sinírius], *a.* ceniciento, cinéreo.

cineritious [sineríśhʊs], *a.* cenizoso.

cinnabar [sínabar], *s.* cinabrio.

cinnamic [sinǽmic], *a.* de canela.

cinnamon [sínamʊn], *s.* canela; canelo (árbol).— **c. stone** = ESSONITE.

cinquecento [chinkuechénto], *s.* siglo XVI del arte y la literatura italianos.

cinquefoil [síncfoil], *s.* (arq.) ventana de cinco puntas; (bot.) cincoenrama.

cipher [sáifœr]. **I.** *s.* (arit.) cero; nulidad; cifra, clave; monograma. **II.** *va.* calcular; cifrar con clave. **III.** *vn.* numerar.

Circassian [sœrcǽśhan], *a.* circasiano.

circensial [sœrsénśhal], **circensian** [-śhan], *a.* circense.

circle [sœrcœl]. **I.** *s.* (geom.) círculo; circunferencia; esfera; anillo; disco; cerco, ruedo; círculo (social), agrupación, clase; circunloquio, rodeo; (lóg.) círculo vicioso; (top., astr.) limbo, placa (de instrumento). **II.** *va.* circundar, rodear. **III.** *vn.* dar vueltas, remolinear.

circled [sœrclœd], *a.* redondo; rodeado.

circlet [sœrclet], *s.* círculo, anillo; collar, brazalete; faja circular.

circuit [sœrkit], *s.* circuito; vuelta, rodeo; gira; radio, ámbito; distrito, contorno; (elec.) circuito.—**c. breaker,** (elec.) disyuntor, interruptor automático.

circuitous [sœrkiúitʊs], *a.* tortuoso.—**circuitously** [-ll], *adv.* tortuosamente.—**circuitousness** [-nes], *s.* tortuosidad, rodeo.

circulable [sœrkiulabœl], *a.* que puede circular.

circular [sœrkiular]. **I.** *a.* circular; redondo.— **c. measure,** (geom.) medida (de un ángulo)

en radianes.—**c. mil,** milipulgada circular, área de un círculo cuyo diámetro es una milipulgada (milésimo de pulgada).—**c. pitch,** paso (de un engranaje).—**c. saw,** sierra circular. **II.** *s.* circular (carta, aviso).

circularity [sœrkiulǽriti], *s.* circularidad.

circularize [sœrkiulæraiś], *vt.* hacer circular; enviar circulares a.

circularly [sœrkiularli], *adv.* circularmente.

circulate [sœrkiuleit]. **I.** *va.* propalar, divulgar; poner en circulación. **II.** *vn.* circular; propagarse.

circulating [-ing], *a.* circulante.—**c. decimal,** fracción decimal periódica.—**c. library,** librería circulante.—**c. medium,** moneda corriente.

circulation [-léiśhʊn], *s.* circulación; propaganda; moneda corriente.

circulatory [sœrkiulatori], *a.* circulatorio.

circumambiency [sœrcʊmǽmbiensi], *s.* medio ambiente.—**circumambient** [-bient], *a.* circumambiente.

circumambulate [-ǽmbiuleit], *vn.* andar al rededor.

circumcise [sœrcʊmsaiś], *va.* circuncidar.— **circumcised** [-sáiśd], *a.* circunciso.—**circumciser** [-sáiśœr], *s.* circuncidante.—**circumcision** [-síyʊn], *s.* circuncisión.

circumference [sœrcʊmfœrens], *s.* circunferencia, periferia; perímetro, contorno.

circumferential [-ferénśhal], *a.* referente a la circunferencia; con rodeo.

circumferentor [-feréntœr], *s.* (top.) brújula de agrimensor.

circumflex [sœrcʊmflex]. **I.** *s.* acento circunflejo; (impr.) capucha. **II.** *a.* (gram.) pronunciado con acento circunflejo; (anat.) circunflejo, encorvado. **III.** *va.* marcar con acento circunflejo.

circumfluence [sœrcʊmfluens], *s.* derrame circular.—**circumfluent** [-ent], **circumfluous** [-ʊs], *a.* circunfluente.

circumfuse [sœrcʊmfiúś], *va.* verter o derramar al derredor.—**circumfusion** [-fiúyʊn], *s.* esparcimiento en derredor.

circumgyrate [-yáiret], *va.* girar.

circumgyration [-yairéśhœn], *s.* giro.

circumjacent [-yésent], *a.* circunvecino.

circumlocution [-lokiuśhʊn], *s.* circunlocución, circunloquio, rodeo.

circumlocutory [-lókiutori], *a.* circunlocutorio, perifrástico.

circumnavigable [-nǽvigabœl], *a.* circumnavegable.

circumnavigate [-nǽvigueit], *va.* circumnavegar. —**circumnavigation** [-éiśhʊn], *s.* circumnavegación.—**circumnavigator** [-éitœr], *s.* el que navega al rededor.

circumpolar [-pólar], *a.* circumpolar.

circumrotation [-rotéśhʊn], *s.* rotación; circunvolución.—**circumrotatory** [-rótatori], *a.* giratorio, rotatorio.

circumscissile [-sísil], *a.* (bot.) dehiscente.

circumscribable [sœrcʊmscráibæbœl], *a.* circunscriptible.

circumscribe [-scráib], *va.* circunscribir, fijar, limitar.—**circumscribed,** circunscrito.

circumscription [-crípśhʊn], *s.* circunscripción; limitación, restricción; periferia.

circumscriptive [-críptiv], *a.* circunscriptivo.

circumspect [-spect], *a.* circunspecto, discreto. —**circumspection** [-péćśhʊn], *s.* circunspección, prudencia, reserva, cautela; recato, decoro.— **circumspectly** [-péctli], *adv.* circunspectamente, con cautela.

circumstance [sœrcʊmstǽns], *s.* circunstancia, incidente, acontecimiento; detalle, menudencia.—*pl.* circunstancias, medios, recursos.— **in easy circumstances,** acomodado.

circumstantial [-tǽnśhal], *a.* circunstanciado, minucioso; indirecto, circunstancial.—**c. evidence,** prueba circunstancial, prueba indiciaria. —**circumstantiality** [-śhiǽliti], *s.* minuciosidad.

circumstantially [-śhali], *adv.* circunstanciadamente, minuciosamente.

Para la pronunciación de æ, œ, ᴅ, ś, śh, ʊ, ȳ, ɤ, z, véase la clave al principio del libro.

circumstantiate [sœrcumstǽnŝhieit], va. relatar circunstanciadamente, detallar.

circumvallate [-vǽlet], va. (fort.) circunvalar.—**circumvallation** [-væléiŝhun], s. circunvalación.

circumvent [-vént], va. entrampar, enredar, embaucar.—**circumvention** [-vénŝhun], s. trampa, enredo, estratagema.—**circumventive** [-véntiv], a. engañoso, delusorio.

circumvest [-vést], va. circundar, rodear, cercar.

circumvolution [-volúŝhun], s. circunvolución; vuelta, rodeo.

circumvolve [-vólv], va. enrollar, envolver.

circus [sœrcus], s. circo; compañía (actores) y animales de circo; arena; hipódromo; plaza circular, redondel.—**c. track**, pista.

cirrhose [sirós], a. cirroso.

cirrhosis [sirósis], s. (med.) cirro.

cirrus [sirrus], s. (bot.) cirro, zarcillo; (meteor.) cirros.—**c. cumulus**, cielo aborregado.

Cisalpine [sisǽlpin], a. cisalpino.

cisatlantic [sísætlǽntic], a. cisatlántico.

cissoid [císoid], s. (mat.) cisoide.

cist [sist], s. arquilla, estuche.

Cistercian [sistœrŝhan], s. cisterciense.

cistern [sístœrn], s. cisterna, aljibe.

cistus [sístus], s. (bot.) cisto, cergazo.

citadel [sítadel], s. ciudadela.

citation [saitéiŝhun], s. cita, mención; citación, comparendo, emplazamiento.

citatory [sáitatori], a. citatorio.

cite [sáit], va. citar, referirse a; (for.) citar.

citer [sáitœr], s. citador.

cithara [sízara], s. lira griega.

cithern [sizœrn], s. cítara.

citizen [sítiŝœn], s. ciudadano; munícipe, vecino.—**citizenship** [-ŝhip], s. ciudadanía.

citrate [sítret], s. (quím.) citrato.

citric [sítric], a. (quím.) cítrico.

citrine [sítrin], a. cetrino.

citron [sítrun], s. (bot.) cidra; cidro.

citronella [sítronelæ], **citronella grass** [græs], s. (bot.) cidronela, toronjil.

citrous [sítrus], a. (bot.) auranciáceo.

city [síti], I. s. ciudad. II. a. municipal, de ciudad; de la ciudad; urbano.—**c. council**, ayuntamiento.—**c. editor**, redactor encargado de las noticias de la ciudad, o locales.—**c. hall**, casa municipal o del ayuntamiento.—**C. of Churches**, Brooklyn (E. U.)—**C. of God**, Ciudad de Dios, Paraíso.—**c. of the dead**, cementerio.—**C. of the Prophet**, Medina (Arabia).

civet [sívet], a. algalia.—**c. cat**, gato de algalia.

civic [sívic], a. cívico.—**civicism** [-siŝm], s. civismo; ciencia del gobierno civil.—**civics**, s. ciencia del gobierno civil.

civil [sívil], a. civil, de lo civil; civil, cortés.—**c. engineer**, ingeniero civil, ingeniero de caminos y construcciones.—**c. engineering**, ingeniería civil, o de caminos y construcciones.—**c. law**, derecho civil.—**c. marriage**, matrimonio civil.—**c. power**, autoridad civil.—**c. service**, servicio civil oficial, ramo civil de la administración pública.—**c. year**, año civil.

civilian [sívilian], s. paisano (no militar); jurisperito, jurisconsulto.

civility [sivíliti], s. civilidad, cortesía.

civilization [síviliséiŝhun], s. civilización.

civilize [sívilaiŝ], va. civilizar.—**civilized**, [-d], a. civilizado.—**civilizer** [-œr], s. civilizador.

civilly [sívili], adv. civilmente; cortésmente.

civism [sívism], s. civismo, patriotismo; ciudadanía.

clabber [clǽbœr], I. vn. cuajarse. II. s. cuajo.

clack [clæc], I. s. ruido, golpeo; charla; (mec.) tarabilla, cítola; triquitraque.—**c. valve**, válvula de charnela, chapaleta. II. vn. restallar; repiquetear, castañetear; charlar, picotear.

clad [clæd], a. vestido, cubierto, aderezado.

claim [cléim], I. va. demandar, pedir en juicio; reclamar; denunciar (una mina); sostener, pretender. II. s. demanda, pedimento; reclamación, petición, ocurso; pretensión, título, derecho; (min.) pertenencia, denuncia.

claimable [-abœl], a. que se puede reclamar.

claimant [-ant], **claimer** [-mœr], s. reclamante; denunciante (de una mina).

clairvoyance [clœrvóians], s. doble vista.

clairvoyant [-ant], a. y s. lúcido; vidente.

clam [clæm], I. s. almeja, tellina. II. vn. pescar almejas.

clamant [clǽmant], a. clamante.

clambake [-beik], s. partida de campo en que se asan almejas.

clamber [clǽmbœr], vn. gatear, trepar, encaramarse.

clamminess [clǽmines], s. viscosidad.

clammy [clǽmi], a. viscoso, pegajoso.

clamo(u)r [clǽmor], I. s. clamor, vocería, clamoreo, algarabía. II. vn. clamar, gritar, vociferar.

clamorous [clǽmœrus], a. clamoroso, ruidoso.—**clamorously** [-li], adv. clamorosamente; ruidosamente.

clamp [clæmp], I. s. montón; pisadas recias; (mec.) abrazadera; grapa, grampa; cárcel; barrilete; prensa de sujeción; tornillo de banco; tornillo de sujeción o de fijación (llám. t. **c. screw**); afianzador; mordaza; (ind.) horno de cocer ladrillos; (min.) montón de mineral. II. va. empalmar; lañar, asegurar, afianzar, sujetar.

clamshell [clǽmshel], s. concha de almeja; (ing.) cucharón de quijadas (ll. t. **c. bucket**).

clan [clæn], s. tribu; clan; fratría; asociación, cuerpo.

clandestine [clændéstin], a. clandestino.—**clandestinely** [-li], adv. clandestinamente.—**clandestineness** [-nes], s. clandestinidad.

clang [clæng], I. s. sonido metálico o retintín. II. vn. sonar, resonar, rechinar. III. vn. hacer sonar.

clango(u)r [clǽngor], s. estruendo, estrépito.—**clangorous** [-us], a. estrepitoso.

clank [clænk], I. s. rechinamiento, ruido estridente. II. vn. rechinar. III. va. hacer rechinar.

clannish [clǽniŝh], a. gregario, unido; exclusivista.

clanship [clǽnŝhip], s. unión bajo un jefe.

clansman [clǽnsman], s. miembro de un clan.

clap [clæp], I. va. batir, golpear; cerrar de golpe; aplicar, pegar; aplaudir. II. vn. aplaudir, dar palmadas; cerrarse ruidosamente; guachapear. III. s. ruido o golpe seco; trueno; palmoteo, aplauso; (vul.) gonorrea.

clapboard [clǽpbœrd], s. tabla de chilla.

clapper [clǽpœr], s. palmoteador; badajo; (mol.) tarabilla, cítola; tableta, tejoleta; aldaba; chapaleta; (mar.) chapaletas de los imbornales.

clapperclaw [-clo], va. (fam.) golpear y arañar.

clapping [clǽping], s. aleteo; palmoteo.

claptrap [-træp], s. artificio para alcanzar popularidad y aplauso; faramalla, música celestial.

clarence [clǽrens], s. carruaje, clarence.

clare-obscure [clǽr-obskiúr], s. claroscuro.

claret [clǽret], s. clarete, vino tinto.

clarification [clærifikéiŝhun], s. clarificación.

clarify [-fai], va. clarificar, defecar, purgar; aclarar; esclarecer.

clarinet [clǽrinet], s. (mús.) clarinete.

clarinettist [clǽrinétist], s. clarinete.

clarion [clǽrion], s. (mús.) clarín.

clarionet [clǽrionet], s. = CLARINET.

clarity [clǽriti], s. claridad; resplandor, luz.

clary [cléri], s. (bot.) salvia silvestre.

clash [clæŝh], I. vn. chocar, entrechocarse, batir; antagonizar, oponerse. II. va. batir, golpear. III. s. choque, fragor, encontrón, colisión; oposición, antagonismo, disputa.

clashingly [clǽŝhingli], adv. en oposición, en conflicto.

clasp [clasp], I. s. broche, chapeta, corchete, presilla, gafete, traba, hebilla, abrazadera; cierre de un libro; (mec.) grapa, cárcel; abrazo.—**c. knife**, navaja, sobre todo la grande de una cuchilla.—**c. nail**, clavo de ala de mosca. II. va. abrochar, encorchetar, enganchar; asegurar; abrazar, embrazar, ceñir.

clasper [cláspœr̃], *s.* el que o lo que abrocha o abraza.

class [clas]. **I.** *s.* clase; condición, categoría; clase en las escuelas. **II.** *va.* clasificar.

classic(al [clásic(al], *a.* clásico.—**c. scholar**, humanista, erudito en las lenguas clásicas (latín y griego).

classic, *s.* autor clásico; obra clásica (apl. esp. a las griegas y latinas).

classically [clǽsicali], *adv.* clásicamente.—**classicism** [clǽsisĭsm], *s.* clasicismo.—**classicist** [clǽsisist], *s.* clásico.

classification [clǽsifikéishʊn], *s.* clasificación.

classify [-fai], *va.* clasificar.

classis [clǽsis], *s.* tribunal eclesiástico.

classmate [clǽsmet], *s.* condiscípulo.

classroom [-rum], *s.* sala de clase, aula.

classy [clǽsi], *a.* (fam.) excelente; elegante.

clastic [clǽstic], *a.* quebradizo; compuesto de fragmentos.

clatter [clǽtœr̃]. **I.** *vn.* repiquetear, guachapear; gritar, charlar. **II.** *s.* repique, martilleo; gresca, alboroto, bulla.

claudication [clodikéishʊn], *s.* cojera.

clause [cloŝ], *s.* cláusula; (gram.) cláusula, período, proposición de relativo.

claustral [clóstral], *a.* claustral.

clavate(d [clévet(ed], *a.* en forma de maza o clava; claveteado.

clavichord [clǽvicord], *s.* (mús.) clave, manicordio.

clavicle [clǽvicœl], *s.* (anat.) clavícula.

clavicular [clavíkiular], *a.* clavicular.

clavier [clǽviœr̃], *s.* (mús.) teclado; [clavíœr̃], instrumento con teclado.

claw [clo]. **I.** *s.* garra; garfa; (mec.) gancho, garfio, uña, diente, garabato; (mar.) uñas de espeque o pie de cabra; (bot.) pecíolo.—**c. bar**, sacaclavos de horquilla; barra con extremo de horquilla.—**c. coupling**, (aut.) acoplamiento de diente.—**c. hammer**, martillo de orejas.—**c.-hammer coat** (fam.) casaca.—**c. hand**, (med.) gafedad. **II.** *va.* arpar, gafar; desgarrar; arañar; rasgar, despedazar. **III.** *vn.* arañar.

clawed [clod], *a.* armado de garras o zarpas.

clay [cléi]. **I.** *s.* arcilla, greda, barro; (fig.) el cuerpo humano; restos mortales.—**c.-cold**, frío helado; sin vida.—**c. marl**, marga.—**c. pit**, gredal. —**c. stone**, piedra arcillosa o formada sobre arcilla. **II.** *va.* engredar; filtrar en barro (apl. al azúcar).

clayey [cléi], **clayish** [cléish], *a.* arcilloso.

claymore [cléimor], *s.* espada escocesa.

cleading [clíding], *s.* (mec.) forro, funda, cubierta, envoltura, camisa.

clean [clín]. **I.** *a.* limpio; puro, inocente; aseado; desembarazado, despejado; neto, distinto, nítido; perfecto; completo; bien hecho; diestro.—**c. acceptance**, (com.) aceptación absoluta o incondicional.—**c. bill**, o **c. bill of health**, patente limpia de sanidad.—**c. bill of lading**, conocimiento de embarque limpio o sin restricciones.—**to make c.**, limpiar.—**to show a c. pair of heels**, tomar las de Villadiego. **II.** *adv.* enteramente.—**c.-bred**, de pura raza.—**c.-cut**, bien definido, claro.—**c.-handed**, con las manos limpias, sin culpa. **III.** *s.* limpia, acción de limpiar.—**c.-out**, limpia.—**c.-up**, limpia; recogida de metal o residuos útiles en molinos, etc.; ganancia. **IV.** *va.* limpiar, asear; purificar; depurar (oro, aire, etc.); mondar; abrir, sacar el menudo a (un pollo, un pescado, etc.).—**to c. out**, vaciar.—**to c. up**, limpiar completamente; acabar, salir de; recoger; desembarazar; (mec.) corregir, rectificar; (min.) recoger; (vulg.) ganar, sacar de ganancia, hacerse a.

cleaner [clínœr̃], *s.* limpiador; sacamanchas; depurador (de aire, etc.).

cleaning [clíning], *s.* aseo, limpia; abaleo, monda.

cleanlily [clénlili], *adv.* aseadamente.

cleanliness [clénlines], *s.* limpieza, aseo, aliño; tersura.

cleanly [clénli]. **I.** *a.* limpio, aseado; puro, delicado. **II.** *adv.* [clínli] primorosamente, aseadamente.

cleanness [clínnes], *s.* limpieza, aseo; pureza.

cleansable [clénsabœl], *a.* purificable; limpiable.

cleanse [clenŝ], *va.* limpiar, purificar; purgar; expurgar, absterger, depurar.

cleanser [-œr̃], *s.* evacuante, purgante; limpiador, purificador.

cleansing [-ing]. **I.** *s.* limpiamiento, detersión, purificación. **II.** *a.* detersorio, mundificativo.

clean-up [clínŭp], *s.* recogida.

clear [clíœr̃]. **I.** *a.* claro; despejado; raso, abierto, franco, libre; limpio, inocente; neto, líquido; desempeñado, sin deudas; puro, sin mezcla; sin desperfectos; cierto, seguro; claro, distinto; completo, total.—**c.-eyed**, penetrante, perspicaz. —**c.-headed**, inteligente, listo.—**c. of**, libre de; salvando, evitando.—**c.-sighted**, previsivo, perspicaz. **II.** *s.* claro, espacio entre objetos; (azú.) meladura; clara. **III.** *adv.* claramente; enteramente (gen. con *away*, *off*, *out*).

clear, *va.* desembarazar, quitar estorbos; limpiar, purificar, aclarar, disipar; justificar; absolver; desenredar, desembrollar (un negocio); satisfacer (una hipoteca); saltar o pasar por encima o un lado de, salvar, franquear; (agr.) tumbar, desmontar, rozar, mondar; (com.) despachar en la aduana; ganar, sacar.—**to c. away**, quitar (estorbos).—**to c. (a ship) for action**, ejecutar el zafarrancho de combate, despejar las cubiertas, alistar (un buque de guerra) para el combate.—**to c. (an equation) of fractions**, quitar los denominadores (de una ecuación).—**to c. out**, echar, sacar; vaciar, desocupar; despachar (un barco) en la aduana.—**to c. the decks** = TO C. FOR ACTION.—**to c. the table**, levantar la mesa.—**to c. up**, sacar estorbos de, desembarazar; dilucidar, explicar; arreglar (una deuda, etc.).

clear, *vn.* aclararse, serenarse; desembarazarse, desenredarse; despacharse en la aduana; liquidar cuentas.—**to c. of fractions**, (álg.) quitar o hacer desaparecer los denominadores.—**to c. off**, o **up**, aclarar, abonanzar; despejarse (el cielo).—**to c. out**, despacharse y salir (un barco); irse, escabullirse, salirse.—**to c. up**, despejarse (el cielo), aclararse.

clearage [clírey], *s.* despejo; desmonte.

clearance [clírans], *s.* despacho de aduana; beneficio líquido; (mec., ing.) juego, espacio libre; (m. v.) espacio muerto (del cilindro); (hidr.) intersticio (de una turbina).

clearer [clírœr̃], *s.* carda fina.

clearing [clíring]. **I.** *s.* aclaramiento, despejo; justificación, vindicación; claro, raso; espacio libre; (com.) liquidación de balances.—**c. of fractions**, (álg.) supresión de denominadores. **II.** *a.* —**c. house**, banco de liquidación (entre bancos).—**c. pan**, (azú.) paila de clarificar, clarificadora.—**c. sale**, venta de liquidación.

clearly [clíœrli], *adv.* claramente; evidentemente; libremente; llanamente; abiertamente.

clearness [clíœrnes], *s.* claridad.

clearstarch [clíœrstárch], *va.* almidonar.

clearstory [clíœrstori], *s.* sobretecho con ventanas laterales.

cleat [clít], *s.* (tec.) listón; abrazadera, manija; mordaza; cepo; (mar.) cornamusa; tojino; galápago.

cleavage [clívey], *s.* hendidura, resquebradura; (min.) crucero.

cleave [clív]. **I.** *va.* (pret. CLEFT, CLOVE o CLAVE; *pp.* CLEFT, CLOVEN o CLEAVED), rajar, hender; abrir en canal; penetrar, abrirse paso. **II.** *vn.* resquebrar, henderse, partirse. **III.** *vn.* (pret. CLEAVED; *pp.* CLEAVED o CLAVE) pegarse, unirse; ajustarse, adherirse.

cleaver [clívœr̃], *s.* hendedor; destralero; hacha, destral; cuchilla de carnicero.

cleavers [clívœr̃ŝ], *s.* (bot.) presera.

clef [clef], *s.* (mús.) clave, llave.

cleft [cleft]. **I.** pret. y *pp.* de TO CLEAVE. **II.** *a.* agrietado, hendido.—**c. grafting**, injerto de hendidura.

cleftgraft [cléftgraft], *va.* injertar por hendidura.

clematis [clématis], *s.* (bot.) clemátide.

clemency [clémensi], *s.* clemencia, piedad.

clement [clément], *a.* clemente, indulgente.—**clemently** [-li], *adv.* clementemente.

clench [clench]. **I.** *va.* agarrar; cerrar el puño o los dientes; asegurar; remachar. **II.** *a.* agarro.—**clencher** [-œr], *s.* agarrador; remachador; (fig.) argumento sin réplica.

clepsydra [clépsidra], *s.* clépsidra.

cleptomania = KLEPTOMANIA.

clergy [clœryi], *s.* clero, clerecía.

clergyman [-man], *s.* clérigo; cura, sacerdote, eclesiástico.

cleric [cléric]. **I.** *s.* clérigo. **II.** *a.* clerical.

clerical [clérical], *a.* clerical, eclesiástico; de dependientes (apl. al trabajo de oficinas).

clericalism [-ism], *s.* clericalismo.

clerk [clœrk; clark en Ingl.], *s.* oficial de secretaría; amanuense, escribiente; dependiente, empleado de oficina; clérigo; escolar, estudiante; (for.) escribano, actuario.

clerkship [clœrcship], *s.* oficio u ocupación de dependiente, clérigo, o escribiente; escribanía; secretaría.

clever [clévœr], *a.* diestro, hábil; avisado, listo, inteligente.—**cleverly** [-li], *adv.* diestramente, hábilmente.—**cleverness** [-nes], *s.* talento; destreza, maña.

clevis [clévis], *s.* abrazadera (del arado, etc.); (mec.) correón.

clew [clu], *s.* ovillo; pista, indicio; (mar.) puño (de vela).—**c. garnet,** palanquín, cargapuños.—**c. lines,** chafaldetes.

cliché [clishé], *s.* (impr.) clisé; (fot.) negativo.

click [clic]. **I.** *s.* golpe seco; (mec.) trinquete, seguro, gatillo, fiador, lingüete. **II.** *va.* y *vn.* sonar con uno o más golpes secos; hacer tictac; piñonear un arma de fuego.

client [cláient], *s.* cliente.

cliental [cláiental], *a.* perteneciente al cliente o a la clientela.

cliented [cláiented], *a.* que tiene clientes.

clientele [cláientl], *s.* clientela.

clientship [cláientship], *s.* clientela, patrocinio.

cliff [clif], *s.* risco, farallón, escarpa, escollera.—**c. dweller,** "cliff dweller," hombre de las rocas, antiguo indio norteamericano que vivía en las rocas.

cliffy [clífi], **clifty** [clífti], *a.* acantilado, escarpado; escabroso.

climacteric [climæctœric], *s.* período climatérico.

climacteric(al [climæctéric(al], *a.* climatérico.

climate [cláimet], *s.* clima.

climatic(al [claimætic(al], *a.* climático.

climatology [claimatóloyi], *s.* climatología.

climax [cláimacs], *s.* clímax; culminación.

climb [cláim]. **I.** *va.* trepar, subir, escalar. **II.** *vn.* trepar, subir, encaramarse. **III.** *s.* trepa; subida, ascenso.—**c. indicator,** (av.) indicador de ascensión.—**climber** [-œr], *s.* trepador, escalador; trepadera; (bot.) enredadera; (zool.) trepador.—**climbing** [-ing]. **I.** *s.* trepa, subida. **II.** *a.* trepador; de subir; de ascensión.—**c. shaft,** tubo de subida (de un dirigible).

clime [cláim], *s.* clima; (poét.) región.

clinch [clinch]. **I.** *va.* remachar, roblar; agarrar; afirmar, fijar, afianzar; establecer, confirmar; (mar.) entalingar. **II.** *vn.* agarrarse. **III.** *s.* remache, robladura; (fig.) argumento sin réplica; (mar.) entalingadura; (E. U.) forcejeo, lucha cuerpo a cuerpo.

clincher [clínchœr], *s.,* clavo remachado; clavo de remachar; junta de clavos remachados; remachador; (fam.) argumento decisivo.—**c. rim,** (aut.) aro con pestaña para neumático de talón.—**c. tire,** (aut.) neumático de talón.—**c. work,** obra con juntas de solapa; (mar.) tinglado.

clinching [clínching], *s.* remachado o robladura; (mar.) solapadura.

cling [cling], *vn.* (pret. y pp. CLUNG) adherirse, pegarse, unirse.

clinging [clínguing], *a.* colgante, pendiente; adhesivo.

clingstone [clíngstoun]. **I.** *a.* peladillo. **II.** *s.* (bot.) pavía (llám. t. **c. peach**).

clinic [clínic], *s.* clínica.—**clinical** [-al], *a.* clínico.

clinician [cliníshan], *s.* médico que practica.

clink [clink]. **I.** *va.* hacer sonar metales. **II.** *vn.* retiñir. **III.** *s.* tañido, retintín.

clinker [clíncœr]. **I.** *s.* lo que retiñe; escoria; pedazo o fragmento de escoria o de lava porosa; ladrillo vítreo; ladrillo holandés.—**c.-built,** (mar.) de tinglad illo. **II.** *vn.* formar escorias; obstruirse con escorias. **III.** *va.* causar la formación de escorias en.

clinkstone [clínkstoun], *s.* perleta, fonolita.

clinometer [clainómetœr], *s.* clinómetro.

clinometric [clainométric], *a.* clinométrico.

clinometry [clainómetri], *s.* clinometría.

clip [clip]. **I.** *va.* esquilar, trasquilar; cortar a raíz; (a veces con **off**) cercenar, recortar; podar, mondar; pellizcar, escatimar, acortar; chapurrear; abrazar, ceñir, agarrar. **II.** *vn.* moverse o deslizarse con rapidez. **III.** *s.* tijeretada, tijeretazo, talla; recorte; trasquila, esquileo; cantonera; grapa, mordaza, pinza, sujetapapeles.

clipper [clípœr], *s.* cercenador, recortador; esquilador, trasquilador; maquinilla para cortar el pelo; cizalla; (mar.) clíper.—*pl.* tijeras podaderas.

clipping [clíping], *s.* recorte; cercenadura, retal; tijereteo.—**c. machine,** maquinilla de repelar.—*pl.* desbroce.

clique [clik]. **I.** *s.* pandilla, camarilla, asociación exclusivista, compadraje. **II.** *va.* y *vn.* apandillar y apandillarse.

clitoris [clítoris], *s.* clítoris.

cloaca [clœicæ], *s.* cloaca; (zool.) cloaca.

cloak [clóuc]. **I.** *s.* capa, manto; palio; excusa, disimulo. **II.** *vn.* encapotar; embozar; ocultar, encubrir, paliar.

cloche [clóush], *s.* (aer.) palanca de mando de campana.

clock [cloc], *s.* reloj (de mesa o pared); cuadrado (de las medias).—**c. maker,** relojero.

clockwise [clókuais], *adv.* en la dirección de las agujas del reloj.

clockwork [clókucœrc]. **I.** *s.* movimiento de reloj. **II.** *a.* de movimiento regular.

clod [clod]. **I.** *s.* terrón; tierra, suelo, césped; masa, trozo; gaznápiro, zoquete.—**clodcrusher,** desterronador.— **II.** *vn.* aterronarse; coagularse. **III.** *va.* tirar terrones.

cloddy [clódi], *a.* terroso.

clodhopper [-jópœr], *s.* destripaterrones.

clodpate [-péit], **clodpoll** [-póul], *s.* mentecato.

clog [clog]. **I.** *va.* cargar, embarazar, empachar; obstruir, entorpecer; apiñar, amontonar. **II.** *vn.* apiñarse, atestarse; agolparse, amontonarse; atorarse; obstruirse; atascarse. **III.** *s.* traba, obstáculo; carga, hipoteca; galocha, chapín, chanclo.—**c. dance,** zapateado.

clogginess [clóguines], *s.* embarazo, impedimento, obstáculo.

cloggy [clógui], *a.* embarazoso.

cloister [clóistœr]. **I.** *s.* claustro; monasterio, convento. **II.** *va.* enclaustrar; proveer de claustros.—**cloisteral** [clóistœral], **cloistral,** *a.* claustral.—**cloistered** [-tœrd], *a.* enclaustrado.—**cloisterer** [-tœrœr], *s.* monje, religioso.—**cloistress** [-tres], *s.* monja.

clonic [clónic], *a.* clónico, convulsivo.

close [clóus]. **I.** *va.* cerrar; tapar; terminar; fenecer.—**to c. out,** vender en liquidación; saldar por ventas (mercancías, géneros, etc.).—**to c. up,** cerrar, cerrar por completo. **II.** *vn.* cerrar; cerrarse; terminar; fenecer; arreglarse (a veces con *on, upon* antes del sustantivo o frase que indica lo convenido).—**to c. in,** acercarse rodeando.—**to c. in on, to c. on, o upon,** rodear, estrechar.—**to c. out,** vender en liquidación.—**to c. with,** cerrar con (el adversario). **III.** *s.* fin; lucha cuerpo a cuerpo; unión, cierre; recinto; solar, parcela.

close [clóus], *a.* cerrado; apretado, ajustado; íntimo o estrecho (amistad, etc.); sofocante; mal ventilado; tupido, compacto, denso; incomunicado; inmediato, contiguo, conexo; unido; estrecho, angosto; breve, compendioso, sucinto; oculto, secreto; avaro, tacaño; retirado, solitario;

atento, nimio, concienzudo; perfecto; notable; marcado; casi igual, casi empatado; reservado, callado; parejo, igual; limitado, restringido.— **c.-bodied**, ajustado; tupido.—**c. call**, (fam.) escape difícil o (fam.) milagroso (**to have a c. call**, escapar en una tabla).—**c. corporation**, compañía o sociedad anónima cuyos dignatarios son por lo general dueños de las acciones.—**c.-coupled circuit**, [elec.] circuito compuesto de dos, uno abierto y otro cerrado.—**c. fertilization** (bot.) autofecundación, fecundación por polen de la misma flor.—**c.-fisted**, tacaño, cicatero.—**c. formation**, (mil.) columna cerrada.—**c.-grained**, tupido.—**c.-hauled** (mar.) de bolina.—**c.-mouthed**, callado, reservado.—**c. order = c. FORMATION.**—**c. quarters**, lugar demasiado pequeño o estrecho.—**c. season**, veda.—**c. shave**, afeitada lisa, a ras o a contrapelo.—**c. stool**, sillico.

close [clóus], adv. cerca, de cerca; estrechamente, apretadamente.—**c. by**, muy cerca.

closed [clóused], a. cerrado.—**c. car** (aut.) coche cerrado.—**c.-coil** (elec.) de arrollamiento cerrado.—**c. sea**, (der. int.) mar enteramente jurisdiccional.—**c. shop**, taller exclusivo, que no admite sino miembros de los gremios obreros.

closely [clóusli], adv. estrechamente, contiguamente; fuertemente, sólidamente; atentamente; cuidadosamente.

closeness [clóusnes], s. encierro; estrechez; densidad; apretamiento; falta de ventilación; solidez, firmeza; reclusión, soledad; reserva; tacañería; conexión, dependencia, unión; exactitud, fidelidad (de copia o traducción).

closet [clóset]. **I.** s. retrete, gabinete; armario, alacena; común, excusado, letrina. **II.** va. encerrar o esconder en un retrete. **III.** vn. encerrarse; conferenciar a puerta cerrada.

close-up [-up], s. fotografía a quema ropa, o de cerca.

closing [-ing]. **I.** s. cierre, acción de cerrar; final, conclusión. **II.** a. de cierre; último, final; de clausura.—**c. price**, último curso (en la bolsa).

closure [clóyur], s. (neol.) procedimiento para poner término a un debate; clausura; encierro; cierre; cercado; fin, conclusión.

clot [clot]. **I.** s. grumo, coágulo, cuajarón. **II.** vn. coagularse, cuajarse, aburujarse, engrumecerse.

cloth [cloz], s. paño, tela, género tejido; mantel; vestido o ropa clerical; el clero.—**c. nipper**, desmotador.—**c. press**, prensa de paños.—**c. prover**, cuentahílos.—**c. yard** yarda de 27 pulgadas.

clothe [clóþ], va. vestir; trajear; revestir; investir.—**to c. with authority**, investir de autoridad.

clothes [clóþs], s. pl. vestido, vestuario, ropa de toda especie; ropa de cama.—**c. brush**, cepillo de ropa.

clothesbars [-bars], s. **clotheshorse** [-jors], s. secarropa de travesaños.

clothesline [-lain], s. tendedera.

clothesman [-mæn], s. ropero, ropavejero.

clothespin [-pin], s. pinzas de tendedera.

clothespress [-pres], s. guardarropa, armario.

clothier [clóþiœr], s. pañero, ropero.

clothing [clóþing], s. vestidos, ropa; pelaje.

clotted, clotty [clóti], a. grumoso, coagulado.

cloture [clótiur], s. V. CLOSURE.

cloud [clául]. **I.** s. nube; nublado, nubarrón; (joy.) mancha, nube; muchedumbre, multitud. —**c.-capt**, o **capped**, altísimo, coronado de nubes. **II.** va. anublar, obscurecer; cegar; abigarrar, motear; empañar, manchar, difamar. **III.** vn. anublarse; obscurecerse.

cloudberry [-beri], s. (bot.) camemoro.

cloudburst [-bœrst], s. turbión, chaparrón.

cloudily [cláudili], adv. obscuramente; con mucha niebla.

cloudiness [-nes], s. nebulosidad, obscuridad.

cloudless [-les], a. sin nubes, despejado.

cloudy [cláudi], a. nublado, nubiloso; vaporoso; obscuro, sombrío; (pint.) nubarrado.

clough [cluf], s. presa, represa; cañada, garganta.

clout [cláut]. **I.** s. rodilla, paño o trapo para limpiar; pañal, remiendo; (mec.) cibica, cibicón.—**c. nails**, clavos de zapato. **II.** va. remendar toscamente; vendar; fregar con trapo.

clove [clóuv], s. clavo de especia; diente de ajo; (E. U.) garganta, cañada.—**c. tree**, (bot.) jirofié.

cloven [clóvœn], pp. y a. partido, hendido.—**c.-foot**, **c.-footed**, **c.-hoofed**, patihendido, bisulco; diabólico.—**to betray**, o **show, the c. foot**, (fam.) enseñar la oreja.

clover [clóvœr], s. (bot.) trébol.—**to be**, o **live, in c.**, vivir en la abundancia.

clovered [clóvœrd], a. lleno de trébol.

clown [cláun], s. patán, paleto; bufón, payaso.

clownery [-œri], s. rusticidad; payasada.

clownish [-ish], a. ridículo, rudo, grosero; tosco, basto.—**clownishly** [-li], adv. toscamente, groseramente.—**clownishness** [-nes], s. rusticidad, grosería, rustiquez.

cloy [clói], va. empalagar; saciar, hartar, tapar, obstruir; clavar un cañón.

cloysome [clóisum], a. empalagoso.

club [clœb]. **I.** s. porra, cachiporra, garrote; basto (en los naipes); club, círculo; maza de gimnasia.—**c. moss**, (bot.) licopodio; pinillo. **II.** vn. contribuir, o concurrir a gastos comunes; unirse o juntarse para un mismo fin. **III.** va. escotar, pagar a prorrata la parte que a cada uno le toca.

clubbed [clœbd], a. ahusado; de extremo ensanchado; (bot.) de raíces atacadas de hongos.

clubbist [clœbist], s. miembro de club o casino.

clubfoot [-fut], s. pateta, pie de piña.—**clubfooted** [-fúted], a. patituerto.

clubhouse [-jaus], s. casino, club.

clubman [-mæn], s. miembro (hombre) de un club.

clubrush [-rush], s. (bot.) espadaña.

clubwoman [-úmæn], s. miembro (mujer) de un club.

cluck [clœc]. **I.** va. y vn. cloquear, enclocar. **II.** s. cloqueo.

clue [clu], s. guía, norte; indicio, pista.

clump [clœmp], s. grupo (de árboles o arbustos); zoquete, tarugo; suela gruesa.

clumsily [clœmsili], adv. zafiamente, groseramente.

clumsiness [clœmsines], s. zafiedad, desmaña.

clumsy [clœmsi], a. desmañado, chapucero, chabacano; incómodo, difícil de manejar.

clung [clœng], pret. y pp. de TO CLING.

cluster [clœstœr]. **I.** s. racimo; grupo.—**c. pine** = SEASIDE PINE. **II.** vn. arracimarse, agruparse. **III.** va. apiñar, amontonar.

clustery [clœstœri], a. arracimado; apiñado; agrupado.

clutch [clœch]. **I.** va. agarrar; empuñar, apretar; embragar. **II.** s. agarro, presa; uña, espolón; grapa, garra, nidada; (aut.) embrague.

clutter [clœtœr]. **I.** s. (fam.) barahúnda, batahola; desorden, confusión. **II.** vn. alborotar; poner en desorden.

clyster [clístœr], s. clistel, enema, lavativa.

coach [cóuch]. **I.** s. coche; carroza; (f. c.) coche de viajeros, esp. el ordinario, o que no es coche salón; preceptor; (dep.) entrenador.—**c. and four**, coche o carroza de cuatro caballos.—**c. box**, pescante.—**c. car** (f. c.) coche ordinario de viajeros.—**c. dog**, perro dalmático. **II.** va. llevar en coche; enseñar, preparar; (dep.) entrenar. **III.** vn. pasear en coche; prepararse con un preceptor; (dep.) entrenarse.

coachee [cóchi], s. cochero, carruajero.

coachful [cóchful], s. coche lleno de gente.

coachman [cóchmæn], s. cochero.

coachmanship [-ship], s. arte de manejar.

coachwhip [-júip], s. manopla (látigo).

coact [coæct]. **I.** va. compeler, forzar, obligar. **II.** vn. cooperar.

coaction [coæcshun], s. coacción.

coactive [coæctiv], a. cooperante.

coadjument [coǽdyumœnt], *s.* mutua y recíproca asistencia.—**coadjutant** [-tænt], *a.* coadyuvante, auxiliar.—**coadjutor** [-tœr], *s.* coadjutor.—**coadjutrix** [-trics], *s.* coadjutora; abadesa.—**coadjuvancy** [-vansi], *s.* coadjutoría.

coadministrator [cóædmínistretœr], *s.* coadministrador.

coagent [coérent], *s.* coagente, cooperador.

coagulability [coæguiulabíliti], *s.* propiedad de coagularse.

coagulable [coǽguiulabœl], *a.* coagulable.

coagulant [-lant], *a.* y *s.* coagulante.—**coagulate** [-let]. I. *va.* coagular, cuajar. II. *vn.* coagularse, cuajarse, espesarse.—**coagulation** [-léshun], *s.* coagulación; cuajamiento; coágulo.—**coagulative** [-lætiv], *a.* coagulativo.—**coagulator** [-léitœr], *s.* coagulatorio.—**coaguline** [-lin], *s.* (quím.) coagulina, coagulasa.—**coagulum** [-lum], *s.* coágulo, cuajarón.

coak [cóuk]. I. *s.* (mar.) dado, macho. II. *va.* unir con dados.

coal [cóul]. I. *s.* hulla, carbón de piedra; brasa.—**c. bin, o box,** area o depósito de carbón, carbonera.—**c. black,** negro como tinta, absolutamente negro.—**c. breaker,** molino de carbón.—**c. field,** yacimiento de carbón.—**c. gas,** gas de hulla.—**c. heaver,** cargador de carbón.—**c. measures,** yacimientos de carbón; (geol.) estratos carboníferos explotables.—**c. oil,** petróleo (esp. kerosina).—**c. pipe,** (min.) veta de carbón delgada e irregular.—**c. rake,** badila, hurgón.—**c. scuttle,** cubo de (para) carbón.—**c. ship,** barco carbonero.—**c. tar,** alquitrán de hulla.—**c. tongs,** tenazas de chimenea. II. *va.* y *vn.* proveer o proveerse de carbón.

coalesce [coalés], *vn.* unirse, juntarse.

coalescence [coalésens], *s.* unión, enlace.

coalfield [cóulfíld], *s.* = COAL FIELD. *V.* COAL.

coalition [coalíshun], *s.* coalición.

coaly [cóuli], *a.* carbonoso, hornaguero.

coaming [cóuming], *s.* brazola, brocal.

coaptation [coæptéshun], *s.* coaptación.

coarctate [coárctet], *a.* comprimido, contraído.

coarctation [coarctéshun], *s.* (med.) contracción, estrechez.

coarse [córs], *a.* basto, ordinario; tosco; vulgar, soez; grueso, burdo.—**c. count,** (tej.) número grueso o bajo (del hilo).—**c. wool,** lana burda.

coarsely [-li], *adv.* toscamente; groseramente.

coarseness [-nes], *s.* calidad de basto o burdo; tosquedad, vulgaridad.

coassume [coæsiúm], *va.* asumir aunadamente.

coast [cóust]. I. *s.* costa; litoral.—**c. guard,** guarda de costas.—**the c. is clear,** ha pasado el peligro; no hay moros en la costa. II. *va.* (mar.) costear. III. *vn.* deslizarse cuesta abajo en un trineíllo raso u otro vehículo movido únicamente por la gravedad: (f. c., aut., etc.) deslizarse, marchar cuesta abajo por gravedad (en aut., con palanca en posición neutra; en camión, con regulador cerrado).

coaster [cóuster], *s.* piloto práctico; barco de cabotaje; habitante de la costa; deslizador.—**c. brake,** freno de bicicleta para marchar cuesta abajo.

coasting [cóusting], *s.* (mar.) cabotaje; acto o diversión de deslizarse cuesta abajo.

coastwise [cóustuaís], *a.* y *adv.* a lo largo de la costa; costanero.

coat [cóut]. I. *s.* levita; saco; casaca, frac; chaqueta; pelo, lana, pelaje; (mec.) cubierta o envoltura, funda, caperuza; túnica del ojo; capa o mano (de pintura, albúmina, etc.).—**c. of arms,** escudo de armas.—**c. of mail,** cota de malla.—**c. room,** guardarropa; cuarto donde se dejan abrigo, sombrero, etc.—**c. shirt,** camisa abierta por el frente.—**c. tail,** faldón.—**to turn one's c.,** volver casaca, cambiar de partido. II. *va.* cubrir, vestir, revestir; bañar, dar una mano o capa de; azogar.

coatee [coutí], *s.* (Ingl.) casaquilla, levitín.

coati [coáti], *s.* (zool.) coatí.

coating [cóuting], *s.* revestimiento, capa, mano de pintura, etc.; (alb.) blanqueo, jalbegue; enlucido; (tej.) bayetón.

co-author [co-ózœr], *s.* coautor.

coax [cóucs], *va.* tentir; instar; engatusar.

coaxer [cóucsœr], *s.* engatusador, marrullero.

coaxial [coǽcsiæl], *a.* coaxil, de un mismo eje.

coaxing [cóucsing], *s.* ruego; engatusamiento.

cob [cob], *s.* bulto, montón; cabeza; tusa de maíz; jaca, caballito; cisne; araña; peso fuerte español; gaviota de Inglaterra; mezcla de arcilla y paja.

cobalt [cóubolt], *s.* cobalto.

cobaltic [coubóltic], *a.* cobáltico.—**cobaltine** [-tin], **cobaltite** [-tait], (min.) cobaltina.—**cobaltous** [-tus], *a.* (quím.) cobaltoso.

cobble [cóbœl], *va.* remendar zapatos; chapucear; empedrar con guijarros.

cobble, cobblestone [-stóun], *s.* guijarro.

cobbler [cóblœr], *s.* zapatero de viejo, remendón; chapucero.

cobelligerent [cobelírœrœnt], *a.* y *s.* cobeligerante.

cobnut [cóbnut], *s.* avellana grande.

cobra [cóubræ], **cobra di capello** [di cæpélo], (zool.) cobra.

cobweb [cóbueb], *s.* telaraña; añagaza.

cobwebbed [cóbuebd], *a.* entelarañado.

coca [coca], *s.* coca.

cocain, cocaine [cócain], *s.* cocaína.

cocainize [cócainaís], *va.* poner bajo la influencia anestésica de la cocaína.

cocciferous [cocsífœrus], *a.* que produce bayas.

cocculus [cókiulus], *s.* (bot.) coca de Levante.

coccus [cócus], *s.* (biol.) coco (bacteria).

coccygeal [cocsíyeal], *a.* perteneciente al coxis o la cola.

coccyx [cócsix], *s.* coxis, cóccix.

cochineal [cóchinil], *s.* cochinilla; grana.

cochlea [cóclea], *s.* caracol del oído.

cochleary [cócleœri], **cochleated** [cócliéited], *a.* caracoleado.

cock [coc]. I. *s.* (orn.) gallo; macho de cualquier ave en palabras compuestas; (Ingl.) caudillo, campeón; veleta, giraldilla; llave, grifo, espita; llave, percusor o martillo de armas de fuego; seguro; vuelta del ala del sombrero; montón de paja, heno, etc.; yola, estilo o gnomon de reloj de sol.—**c. and bull,** exagerado, increíble.—**c.-brained,** temerario.—**c.-eyed,** bizco.—**c. of the walk, o of the loft,** gallito del lugar. II. *va.* montar o amartillar (un arma de fuego); levantar, erguir, enderezar; encandilar el sombrero; hacinar o amontonar heno. III. *vn.* entonarse, engreírse.

cockade [cokéid], *s.* escarapela, cucarda.

cock-a-hoop [cóc-a-júp], *a.* alegre, achispado, engreído.

cockatoo [cocatú], *s.* (orn.) alo, cacatúa.

cockatrice [cócatrais], *s.* basilisco.

cockboat [cócbout], *s.* (mar.) barquilla.

cockchafer [cókchéfœr], *s.* escarabajo.

cockcrow(ing [cócrou(ing], *s.* canto del gallo; la aurora.

cocked hat [cókd jæt], *s.* sombrero de candil o de tres picos.

cocker [cókœr]. I. *va.* acariciar, mimar. II. *s.* sabueso; el que pelea gallos.

cockerel [cókœrel], *s.* gallipollo.

cocket [cóket], *s.* sello de la aduana; guía.

cockfight(ing [cóc-fáit(ing], *s.* riña de gallos.—**cockfighter** [-fáitœr], *s.* gallero.

cockhorse [cócjors], *s.* caballito (juguete).

cockle [cókœl]. I. *s.* coquina; cúpula de horno; barquichuelo; (bot.) vallico, zizaña, joyo. II. *va.* y *vn.* arrugar, hacer arrugas.

cockled [cócœld], *a.* granoso (apl. esp. al papel); arrugado, ondulado.

cockloft [cócloft], *s.* desván, zaquizamí.

cockmaster [cócmæstœr], *s.* gallero.

cockmatch [cócmæch], *s.* riña de gallos.

cockney [cócni], *s.* hijo de Londres de clase baja.

cockpit [cócpit], *s.* gallera; reñidero de gallos; (mar.) entarimado del sollado; (aer.) casilla del piloto y el observador, cámara.

cockroach [cócrouch], *s.* cucaracha.

cockscomb [cócscoum], *s.* (bot.) amaranto, moco de pavo; gorro de bufón; bufón; baladrón.

cockspur [cócspœr], *s.* espolón o navaja de gallo; (bot.) níspero.

cocksure [cócshúœr]. **I.** *a.* absolutamente seguro. **II.** *adv.* con entera seguridad.

cockswain, *V.* COXSWAIN.

cocktail [cócteil], *s.* cocktail, coctel.

cocoa [cóco], *s.* (bot.) coco o cocotero; cacao molido; bebida de cacao.

cocoanut, coconut [cóconut], *s.* coco (fruto).

cocobolo [cocobólo], *s.* (bot.) cocobolo.

cocoon [cocún], *s.* capullo del gusano de seda.

cocoonery [-œri], *s.* criadero de gusanos de seda.

coctile [cóctil], *a.* cocido en horno.

coction [cócshun], *s.* cocción.

cod [cod], *s.* abadejo, bacalao; (bot.) vaina, vainilla; (anat.) escroto.—**c.-liver oil**, aceite de hígado de bacalao.

coddle [códœl], *va.* criar con mimo; sancochar.

code [cóud], *s.* (for.) código, compilación; clave, cifra.—**c. of henour**, código de honor.

codein [codíin], *s.* codeína.

codex [códex], *s.* códice.

codfish [códfîsh], *s.* bacalao.

codger [códyœr], *s.* (despec.) chiflado; tipo.

codicil [códisil], *s.* (for.) codicilo.

codification [códifikéshun], *s.* codificación (de las leyes).—**codify** [-fai], *va.* codificar, compilar (leyes).

codling [códling], *s.* pijota; manzana.

coeducation [coédyukéshun], *s.* educación de ambos sexos en comunidad.

coefficacy [coéficasi], *s.* coeficacia.

coefficiency [coefíshensi], **I.** *s.* coeficiencia.

coefficient [coefíshent]. **I.** *a.* coeficiente. **II.** *s.* (mat.) coeficiente.—**c. of contraction**, (hidr.) coeficiente de contracción.—**c. of discharge**, (hidr.) coeficiente de salida.—**c. of efficiency**, (mec.) rendimiento.—**c. of expansion**, coeficiente de dilatación.—**c. of friction**, (mec.) coeficiente de rozamiento.—**c. of (magnetic) leakage**, coeficiente de dispersión magnética.—**c. of safety**, coeficiente o factor de seguridad.—**c. of sensitiveness**, (elec.) coeficiente de sensibilidad.—**c. of velocity** [hidr.] coeficiente de velocidad.

coefficiently [coefíshentli], *adv.* cooperativamente.

coemption [coémpshun], *s.* coención.

cœnæsthesis, cœnesthesis [síneszesís], (psicol.) *s.* cinestesia.

cœnenchyma [sinénkimæ], *s.* (biol.) cenénquima.

coequal [coíkual], *a.* igual, coigual.

coequality [coikuóliti], *s.* igualdad.

coerce [coœrs], *va.* forzar u obligar; coercer, contener, refrenar; restringir.

coercible [coœrsibœl], *a.* que puede o debe ser refrenado.

coercion [coœrshun], *s.* coerción.

coercive [coœrsiv], *a.* coercitivo; coactivo, obligatorio.

coessential [coesénshal], *a.* coesencial.

coessentiality [-shiæliti], *s.* coesencia.

coessentially [-li], *adv.* coesencialmente.

coetaneous [coeténeœs], *a.* coetáneo.

coeternal [coetœrnal], *a.* coeterno.

coeval [coíval], *s.* y *a.* contemporáneo.

coexecutor [coexékiutœr], *s.* coalbacea.

coexist [coegsíst], *n.* coexistir.—**coexistence** [-tens], *s.* coexistencia.—**coexistent** [-tent], *a.* coexistente.

coextend [coexténd], *va.* coextenderse.—**coextension** [-ténshun], *s.* coextension.—**coextensive** [-ténsiv], *a.* coextensivo.—**coextensively** [-li], *adv.* coextensivamente.

coffee [cófi], *s.* café (grano, bebida y árbol); cafeto.—**c. bean**, grano de café.—**c. berry**, fruto, cereza del cafeto.—**c. cake**, rosca que gen. se come con el café.—**c. grinder, c. mill**, molinillo de café.—**c. grounds**, heces o asientos del café.—**c. tree**, cafeto; cafeto de Kentucky, árbol de los E. U. parecido al cafeto y de cuyo fruto se hace un líquido semejante al café.

coffeehouse [-jaus], *s.* café (establecimiento).

coffeepot [-pot], *s.* cafetera.

coffer [cófœr]. **I.** *s.* arca, cofre; (arq.) artesón hondo. *V.* CAISSON.—*pl.* tesoro, fondos. **II.** *va.* meter en arca; atesorar; artesonar.

cofferdam [cóferdæm], *s.* (hid.) ataguía; (mar.) cófferdam.

coffin [cófin]. **I.** *s.* ataúd, féretro; parte del casco del caballo. **II.** *va.* meter en ataúd; (fig.) encerrar, ocultar.

cog [cog]. **I.** *va.* puntear o poner dientes a una rueda.—**to c. a die**, cargar un dado. **II.** *vn.* trampear, hacer fullerías. **III.** *s.* (mec.) diente de rueda; cama, leva; (carp.) espiga; fraude, o engaño; dado falso; botequín.

cogency [córensi], *s.* fuerza lógica o moral.

cogent [córent], *a.* covincente.

cogged [cogd], *a.* dentado, engranado.

cogitable [córitabœl], *a.* cogitable.

cogitate [córiteit], *vn.* pensar, meditar.—**cogitation** [coritéshun], *s.* reflexión, meditación.—**cogitative** [córitetiv], *a.* cogitativo, reflexivo.

cognac [cóñæc], *s.* coñac.

cognate [cógnet], *a.* y *s.* cognado, consanguíneo; pariente, deudo; afín; semejante, análogo.

cognatic [cognátic], *a.* cognático.

cognation [cognéshun], *s.* cognación; origen común; afinidad, entronque.

cognition [cogníshun], *s.* conocimiento.

cognitive [cógnitiv], *a.* cognoscitivo.

cognizable [cógnisabœl], *a.* conocible; (for.) de la competencia de.—**cognizance** [-sans], *s.* conocimiento, comprensión; divisa, señal; (for.) competencia, jurisdicción.—**cognizant** [-sant], *a.* sabedor, informado.—**cognize** [-nais], *va.* conocer.

cognomen [cognómen], *s.* apellido.—**cognominal** [-mínæl], *a.* tocayo.—**cognominate** [-mineit] *va.* apellidar.—**cognomination** [cognominéshun], *s.* sobrenombre, cognomento.

cognoscible [cognósibœl], *a.* conocible.

cognoscitive [cognósitiv], *a.* cognoscitivo.

cognovit [cognóvit], *s.* (for.) conocencia.

cograil [cógreil], *s.* riel dentado, cremallera.

cogwheel [cógjuil], *s.* rueda dentada.

cohabit [cojébit], *vn.* cohabitar.

cohabitant [-ant], *s.* convecino.

cohabitation [-éishun], *s.* cohabitación, contubernio.

coheir [coéœr], *s.* coheredero.

coheiress [coéœres], *s.* coheredera.

cohere [cojíœr], *vn.* adherirse, pegarse, unirse; enlazarse, adaptarse.

coherence, coherency [cojíœrens, i], *s.* cohesión, coherencia, enlace; conformidad.

coherent [cojírent], *a.* coherente; consecuente.

cohesion [cojíyun], *s.* cohesión.

cohesive [-siv], *a.* coherente, adherente.—**cohesively** [-li], *adv.* coherentemente.—**cohesiveness** [-nes], *s.* calidad o propiedad coherente.

cohort [cójort], *s.* cohorte.

coif [cóif], *s.* cofia, escofieta, toca.

coifed [cóift], *a.* adornado con cofia.

coiffure [cóifiur], *s.* tocado, peinado.

coign [cóin], *s.* esquina; saliente.—**c. of vantage**, posición ventajosa.

coil [cóil]. **I.** *s.* rollo; arrollamiento espiral; vuelta (de tal arrollamiento); serpentín; (mar.) adujada; aduja; (elec.) arrollamiento; bobina. **II.** *va.* enrollar, arrollar; (mar.) adujar. **III.** *vn.* enrollarse; enroscarse.

coin [cóin]. **I.** *s.* moneda acuñada; cuño; casa de moneda; (fam.) blanca, dinero. **II.** *va.* acuñar, inventar, forjar. **III.** *vn.* amonedar, hacer moneda.

coinage [cóiney], *s.* acuñación; braceaje; sistema monetario; invención.

coincide [coinsáid], *vn.* coincidir; convenir.

coincidence [coínsidens], **coincidency** [-i], *s.* coincidencia; casualidad; conformidad.

coincident [-ent], **coincidental** [-éntæl], *a.* coincidente, acorde.

coincidentally [-i], **coincidently** [-i], *adv.* coincidentalmente; al mismo tiempo.

coindicant [coíndicant], *a.* concurrente, confirmante.

coindication [coindikéshun], *s.* indicio que coincide con otro.

coiner [cóinœr], *s.* acuñador; monedero falso; inventor, fabricador.

coinheritance [-injœritæns], *s.* herencia en común.

coinsurance [-inshúræns], *s.* seguro en que el asegurado figura como coasegurador.

coir [cóir, cáir], *s.* bonote.

coition [coíshœn], *s.* coito, concúbito, cópula.

coke [cóuc], **I.** *s.* cok, coque. **II.** *va.* y *vn.* convertir(se) en coque.

colaborer [coléborœr], *s.* colaborador.

colander [cœlendœr], *s.* colador; escurridor.

colatitude [cœlĕtitiud], *s.* colatitud.

colchicum [cólchicum], *s.* (bot.) cólquico.

colcothar [cólcozar], *s.* (quím.) colcótar.

cold [cóuld], *a.* frío; desalentado; desalentado; apartado, lejos (de algo que se busca, como en ciertos juegos infantiles); (quím.) en frío.—**c. abscess**, absceso crónico.—**c.-blooded**, de sangre fría; en sangre fría; impasible, inhumano, cruel; friolento; espurio (de raza).—**c. cream**, crema (cosmético).—**c. cuts**, fiambre.—**c.-drawn**, estirado en frío.—**c. feet**, (hort.) decaimiento debido a exceso de agua; (fama.) miedo, desánimo.—**c.-hearted**, insensible, impasible.—**c. meat**, carne fría, carne fiambre.—**c. press**, preusa de satinar en frío.—**c.-roll**, *va.* laminar en frío.—**c. saw**, sierra de cortar en frío.—**c.-short**, frágil, quebradizo.—**c. shoulder**, frialdad, indiferencia (vg., *to give one the cold shoulder*, tratar a uno con frialdad, despedirlo con cajas desempladas, o con desaire).—**c. storage**, conservación en frigoríficos o instalaciones refrigerantes.—**c.-storage house**, frigorífico, instalación refrigerante.—**c. wave**, ola de frío.—**in c. blood**, a sangre fría.—**to be c.**, tener frío; (con *it* por sujeto) hacer frío.

cold, *s.* frío; resfriado, catarro.—**c. in the head**, romadizo, catarro.—**c. sore**, (med.) fuego en los labios.—**to catch**, o **take, c.**, resfriarse.—**to leave out in the c.**, dejar colgado, dejar a la luna de Valencia.

coldly [-li], *adv.* fríamente; indiferentemente.

coldness [-nes], *s.* frialdad, frigidez; tibieza, indiferencia.

cole [cóul], *s.* (bot.) col, berza, colza.

Coleoptera [coleóptera], *s. pl.* (ent.) coleópteros.

coleopterous [coleóptœrus], *a.* coleóptero.

coleorhiza [coliorráìšæ], *s.* (bot.) coleorriza.

coleseed [óulsid], *s.* semilla de col.

coleslaw [-slo], *s.* ensalada de col.

colessee [colesí], *s.* (for.) mediero.

colessor [colésor], *s.* coarrendatario.

colewort [cóuluœrt], *s.* (bot.) colza, berza.

colic [cólic], *s.* cólico.—*a.* cólico (del colon); relativo al cólico.

colicky [cóliki], *a.* que tiene o produce cólico; parecido al cólico.

coliseum [colisíum], *s.* coliseo.

collaborate [coléboreit], *va.* colaborar.—**collaboration** [-réishun], *s.* colaboración.—**collaborator** [-réitœr], *s.* colaborador.

collapse [coláps], **I.** *s.* aplastamiento; derrumbamiento, desplome; hundimiento; fracaso; (med.) colapso, postración.—**c. ring**, (m. v.) anillo de refuerzo. **II.** *va.* hacer caer o arruinar; aplastar, juntar los lados opuestos de (un tubo, etc.); plegar, reducir a menor volumen doblando o desarmando (un bote portátil, etc.). **III.** *vn.* arruinarse, fracasar; desfallecer, sufrir colapso; aplastarse, plegarse, doblarse.

collapsible [colápsibœl], *a.* que puede aplastarse, desarmarse, etc. *V.* COLLAPSE, *va.*

collar [cólar]. **I.** *s.* cuello (de camisa, levita, etc.); golilla; collar; collera; cabezada; (mec.) aro, anillo, cárcel, zuncho, horcajo, virola, manguito; (mar.) collar, encapilladura; (arq.) anillo, collarín.—**c. band** = NECKBAND.—**c. bone**, clavícula.—**to slip the c.**, escaparse,

desenredarse. **II.** *va.* apercollar; poner cuello, collar, zuncho, etc.

collate [colét], *va.* comparar, cotejar; (igl.) colacionar.

collateral [colétœral]. **I.** *a.* colateral; subordinado, accesorio.—**c. security**, garantía subsidiaria. **II.** *s.* (com.) garantía, resguardo.—**collaterally**, [-li], *adv.* colateralmente, subsidiariamente.

collation [coléshun], *s.* cotejo, comparación; calación, merienda; refacción.

colleague [cólig]. **I.** *s.* colega, compañero. **II.** *vr.* coligarse; conspirar.

collect [colét]. **I.** *va.* recoger; congregar, juntar; coleccionar; copilar; cobrar, recaudar, colectar.—**to c. one's self**, volver en sí; reponerse. **II.** *vn.* congregar, reunirse; acumularse. **III.** *s.* (igl.) colecta.

collectable [-œbœl], *a.* cobrable.

collected [colécted], *a.* reunido, juntado; sosegado, vuelto en sí.

collectedly [coléctedli], *adv.* juntamente; sosegadamente.

collectible [coléctibœl], *a.* cobrable.

collection [coléshun], *s.* colección, conjunto, agregación; cobra, recaudación; cuestación o colecta; compilación.

collective [coléctiv]. **I.** *s.* (gram.) nombre colectivo. **II.** *a.* colectivo.—**c. bargaining**, (e. p.) trato colectivo (entre entidades, cuerpos, etc.).—**c. noun**, substantivo colectivo.

collectively [-li], *adv.* colectivamente.—**collectiveness** [-nes], *s.* colectividad.

collectivism [coléctivišm], *s.* colectivismo, socialismo pacífico o evolucionista.—**collectivist** [-vist], *s.* colectivista, socialista pacífico.

collector [coléctœr], *s.* colector, coleccionador, coleccionista; cobrador, recaudador; compilador.—**c. of a port**, administrador de aduana. **c. of taxes**, recaudador de contribuciones.—**c. of tithes**, diezmero.

collectorate [-et], **collectorship** [-ship], *s.* colecturía.

collegatary [colégateri], *s.* colegatario.

college [cólej]. **I.** *s.* colegio superior; colegio (de cardenale, etc.). **II.** *a.* de colegio; estudiantil.

collegial [colíyial], *a.* colegial.

collegian [colíyian], *s.* **collegiate** [-yiet], *s.* colegial, estudiante.—**collegiate**, *a.* colegial.

collet [cólet], *s.* (mec.) collar; (joy.) engaste.

collide [coláid], *vn.* chocar, topar; contradecir, estar en conflicto.

collie [cóli], *s.* perro de pastor.

collier [cólicer], *s.* obrero de las minas de carbón; barco carbonero; mercader de carbón.

colliery [cóliceri], *s.* mina de carbón; comercio de carbón.

colliflower, = CAULIFLOWER.

colligate [cóliguet], *va.* atar, juntar, amarrar.

colligation [-éishun], *s.* coligación.

collimate [cólimeit], *va.* (opt.) ajustar la visual de (un anteojo); alinear.—**collimation** [-méishun], *s.* colimación.—**collimator** [-méitœr], *s.* (opt.) colimador.

collinear [colíniær], *a.* en línea recta; (mec.) que obran según una misma línea (apl. a fuerzas).

collineation [-éishun], *s.* alineación.

collision [colíyun], *s.* colisión, choque; oposición, antagonismo.

collocate [cóloket], *va.* colocar.

collocation [colokéshun], *s.* colocación.

collodion [colódion], *s.* colodión.

colloid [cóloid]. **I.** *a.* gelatinoso; no cristalizable; amorfo en parte. **II.** *s.* substancia gelatinosa.

colloidal [colóidæl], *a.* (quím.) coloide.—**c. fuel**, combustible coloide (polvo de carbón suspendido en petróleo, alquitrán, etc.)

collop [cólup], *s.* bocado, tajada; pedacito.

colloquial [colócuial], *a.* familar (apl. al lenguaje) —**colloquialism** [-išm], *s.* expresión familiar.—**colloquially** [-li], *adv.* en lenguaje familiar.

colloquy [cólocui], *s.* coloquio, conversación.

collotype [cólotaip], *s.* fotografía de colotipia.—**collotypy** [-taipi], *s.* colotipia.

collude [coliúd], *vn*. obrar de connivencia.
collusion [coliúÿʊn], *s*. colusión.—**collusive** [coliúsiv], *a*. colusorio.—**collusively** [-li], *adv*. colusoriamente.
colly, *s*. *V*. COLLIE.
collyrium [colíriœm], *s*. colirio.
colocynth [cólosinz], *s*. (bot.) coloquíntida.
colon [cólon], *s*. (gram.) dos puntos (:); (anat.) colon.
colonel [cœrnel], *s*. coronel.—**colonelcy** [-si], **colonelship** [-ship], *s*. coronelía.
colonial [colónial], *a*. colonial.
colonist [cólonist], *s*. colono.—**colonize** [-aiš]. I. *va*. colonizar, poblar. II. *vn*. establecerse en colonia.—**colonization** [-éishʊn], *s*. colonización. —**colonizer** [-œr], *s*. colonizador.
colonnade [colonéd], *s*. peristilo, columnata.
colony [cóloni], *s*. colonia.
colophon [cólofon], *s*. (impr.) colofón.
colophony [colófoni], *s*. colofonia.
color, colour [cúlœr]. I. *s*. color, colores, pintura; (pint.) colorido; pretexto; palo (en los naipes).—**colours**, *pl*. bandera, estandarte; enseña.—**c. bearer**, abanderado, portaestandarte. —**c.-blind**, daltoniano.—**c.-blindness**, daltonismo.—**c. filter**, (fot.) filtro cromofotográfico.— **c. guard**, guardia de la bandera.—**c. photography**, cromofotografía, fotografía en colores.—**c. screen**, (fot.) pantalla de color, pantalla de interceptación de colores.—**c. sergeant**, sargento abanderado.— **under c. of**, so color de.—**with flying colors**, a banderas desplegadas. II. *va*. colorar, dar color; paliar, desfigurar. III. colorearse; ruborizarse, encenderse.
colorable [cúlœræbœl], *a*. especioso, plausible.— **colorably** [-bli], *adv*. especiosamente.
coloration [-éishʊn], *s*. coloración; colorido.
colorature [-achur *o* tiur], *s*. (mús.) floreos y cadencias.
colored [cúlœrd], *a*. de color (ni negro ni blanco); negro (apl. a personas); disfrazado, desfigurado; adornado.
colorful [cúlœrful], *a*. lleno de colorido; vívido.
colorific [cúlœrífic], *a*. colorativo.
colorimeter [-ímetœr], *s*. colorímetro.—**colorimetric** [-imétric], *a*. colorimétrico.—**colorimetry** [-ímitri], *s*. colorimetría.
coloring [-ing], *s*. colorante; coloración; estilo o aire particular; (pint.) colorido.
colorist [-ist], *s*. colorista.
colorless [-les], *a*. descolorido, incoloro.
colorman [-mæn], *s*. el que hace y vende colores.
colossal [colósal], *a*. coliseo.
colosseum [colosíum], *s*. coliseo.
colossean [colóssean], **colossean** [colossían], *a*. colosal, descomunal.
colossian [colóshæn], *s*. y *a*. colosense.
colossus [colóscœs], *s*. coloso.
colostrum [colóstrœm], *s*. calostro.
colour *s*. y *v*. = COLOR.
colporteur [cólporteur], *s*. vendedor o repartidor de escritos religiosos.
colpotomy [colpótomi], *s*. colpotomía.
colt [cóult], *s*. potro; mozuelo sin juicio; azote con un nudo.—**c.'s-foot** [cóults-fut], *s*. (bot.) tusílago, fárfara.
colter [cóultœr], *s*. reja del arado.
coltish [cóultish], *a*. juguetón, retozón.
coltishly [-li], *adv*. juguetonamente.
colubrine [cóliubrain], *a*. culebrino; astuto.
columbarium [cólʊmbériʊm], **columbary** [-beri], *s*. palomar; mechinal.
columbiad [colúmbiad], *s*. (mil.) cañón de; ánima lisa.
Columbian [colúmbian], *a*. colombiano; relativo a Cristóbal Colón; colombino.
columbine [cólʊmbin], *a*. columbino.
columbine [cólʊmbain], *s*. (bot.) aguileña o pajarilla.
columbium [colúmbiʊm], *s*. (quím.) columbio.
columella [coliuméla], *s*. eje central, columnilla.
column [cólʊm], *s*. columna; pilar; (mil.) columna.
columnar [colúmnar], *a*. columnario.

columned [cólʊmd], *a*. con columnas.
columniation [colʊmniéshʊn], *s*. columnata.
colure [colúr], *s*. (astr.) coluro.
colza [cólša], *s*. (bot.) colza.
coma [cóma], *s*. (med.) coma; (astr.) cabellera, cola; (bot.) manojito de hebras sedosas.
comate [coméit], *s*. camarada, compañero.
comate [cómeit], *s*. cabelludo.
comatose [cómatos], *a*. comatoso, letárgico.
comb [cóum]. I. *s*. peine; peineta; rasqueta, almohaza; carda, rastrillo, carducha; cresta; (api.) panal; avispero.—**c.-brush**, bruza para limpiar peines.—**c. foundation**, (api.) panal artificial.—**c. maker**, peinero. II. *va*. peinar; cardar, carduzar; rastrillar. III. *vn*. encresparse y romper las olas.
combat [cómbat]. I. *s*. combate, lucha, batalla. II. *va*. y *vn*. combatir.
combatable [combætabœl], *a*. combatible.
combatant [cómbætant], *s*. y *a*. luchador, combatiente.
combative [-tiv], *a*. peleador, belicoso.
combativeness [-nes], *s*. combatividad, acometividad.
comber [cóumœr], *s*. cardador; ola encrestada, cabrilla, rompiente.
combinable [combáinabœl], *a*. combinable.
combination [cómbinéshʊn], *s*. combinación; unión, liga; mezcla; cabala; reunión.
combinative [combáinativ], *a*. combinatorio.
combine [-báin]. I. *s*. combinar; mezclar; reunir, aunar. II. *vn*. combinarse; unirse; maquinar, conspirar. III. *s*. monopolio; camarilla, rosca.
combined [-báind], *a*. juntos, unidos; aunado, unido; compuesto; mixto.
combustibility [combústibíliti], *s*. combustibilidad.—**combustible** [-tibœl], *a*. y *s*. combustible.—**combustion** [-chʊn], *s*. combustión; tumulto, alboroto.
comby [cóumi], *a*. en forma de panal.
come [cʊm], *vn*. (*pret*. CAME) (*pp*. COME) venir; ir; llegar; ser (de), provenir; resultar; entrar (en acción, etc.); estar, halearse; aparecer; salir; acontecer, suceder.—**to c. about**, rodear; acaecer; efectuarse.—**to c. across**, atravesar; encontrarse con; ver; (fam.) pagar, entregar, dar. —**to c. again**, volver.—**to c. after**, seguir, venir detrás o después; (fam.) venir por, en busca de. —**to c. asunder**, deshacerse, desunirse.—**to c. along**, venir; andar, caminar.—**to c. at**, alcanzar; conseguir; llegar a; venirse a; atacar.—**to c. away**, retirarse, irse.—**to c. back**, retroceder, volver; (fam.) rehabilitarse, recobrarse; reflorecer. —**to c. back again**, volver.—**to c. before**, anteponerse.—**to c. between**, interponerse, inmiscuirse.—**to c. by**, pasar junto a; venir por; hacerse a, obtener.—**to c. down**, bajar, descender; desplomarse, demolerse.—**to c. down on**, *o* **upon**, caer sobre.—**to c. downstairs**, bajar (de un piso a otro).—**to c. for**, venir a buscar; venir por.—**to c. forth**, salir; aparecer; adelantarse.—**to c. forward**, avanzar, medrar; adelantarse.—**to c. high** *o* **low**, venderse caro o barato.—**to c. home**, volver a casa; (fig.) tocar la cuerda sensible.—**to c. in**, entrar; llegar; desembocar; consentir, acceder; introducirse; empezar; encajar; parir la vaca; empezar a dar leche.—**to c. in for**, pretender, reclamar; corresponderle a uno; tener parte en, tocarle a uno.—**to c. in**, *o* **into sight**, *o* **view**, aparecer; asomar, empezar a verse.—**to c. into**, entrar a. —**to c. into the world**, venir al mundo, nacer. —**to c. into trouble**, meterse en trabajos; tener algún percance.—**to c. near**, acercarse.—**to c. next**, venir después, ser el que sigue.—**to c. of**, proceder, venir de.—**to c. of age**, llegar a mayor edad.—**to c. off**, zafarse, soltarse, salir; verificarse, tener efecto.—**c. off!** (fam.) ¡déjate de tonterías!.—**to c. on**, avanzar; marchar; medrar. **c. on!** ¡vamos! ¡ven! ¡venga!—**to c. over**, venir, cruzar.—**to c. over to**, pasarse a.—**to c. out**, salir; crecer; brotar; finalizar; trascender; ver la luz; hacerse público; manifestarse, declararse.—**to c. out with**, publicar, revelar;

decir, echar afuera.—**to c. round**, acontecer o efectuarse; convenir, asentir; restablecerse; volver en sí; engatusar.—**to c. short of**, faltar (cambiando un poco el giro), no llegar a; estar lejos de; no tener más o suficiente.—**to c. to**, recobrar los sentidos; ascender a; parar en.—**to c. to a head**, madurar, llegar a condición decisiva o definitiva, definirse; (med.) madurar.—**to c. to anchor**, anclar.—**to c. to an end**, acabarse; morir.—**to c. to an estate**, heredar.—**to c. to blows**, *o* **to close quarters**, venirse a las manos.—**to c. to grief**, fracasar; salir mal parado.—**to c. to hand**, llegar a manos (de uno), recibirse; venir a la mano.—**to c. to life**, nacer.—**to c. to life again**, renacer; revivir; resucitar.—**to c. to mind**, venir a la memoria, ocurrirse.—**to c. to naught**, *to* **nothing**, *o* **to nought**, frustrarse, reducirse a nada; no quedar en nada.—**to c. to one's self**, volver en sí.—**to c. to pass**, suceder.—**to c. together**, venir juntos; juntarse, reunirse.—**to c. to terms**, aceptar condiciones; convenirse; zanjar un negocio.—**to c. to the point**, llegar al punto; venir al caso; venir al grano.—**to c. true**, realizarse, resultar cierto.—**to c. undone**, deshacerse, desatarse.—**to c. up,**, subir; aparecer; brotar; nacer; surgir.—**to c. upon**, encontrarse con, dar con.—**to c. up to**, acercarse a; estar a la altura de; dar alcance; abordar (un buque).—**to c. upstairs**, subir (de un piso o otro).—**to c. up with**, alcanzar a.

comeback [cúmbǽc], *s.* (fam.) rehabilitación, vuelta al puesto u oficio (ú. gen. en dep.); respuesta aguda.

comedian [comídiæn], *s.* cómico, actor.—**comédienne** [comidién], *s.* cómica, actriz.

comedietta, *s.* juguete cómico.

comedo [cómedo], *s.* (med.) espinilla.

comedown [cúmdáun], *s.* (fam.) revés de fortuna.

comedy [cómedi], *s.* comedia.

comelily [cúmlili], *adv.* donosamente.

comeliness [cúmlines], *s.* gracia, donaire.

comely [cúmli]. **I.** *a.* gentil, donoso, bien parecido. **II.** *adv.* gentilmente.

come-off [cúm-of], *s.* salida, pretexto, escapatoria.

comer [cúmœr], *s.* llegado; recién venido.—**all comers**, (dep.) todos los aspirantes, todos los contendientes.

comestible [coméstibœl], *a.* y *s.* comestible.

comet [cómet], *s.* (astr.) cometa.

cometarium [cométériœm], *s.* (astr.) cometario.

cometary [cómeteri], *a.* perteneciente a los cometas.

cometography [cometógrafi], *a.* cometografía.

comfit [cúmfit], *s.* confite.

comfort [cúmfœrt]. **I.** *va.* confortar, fortificar, vivificar; animar, alentar, consolar; alegrar, solazar; (for.) ayudar, apoyar. **II.** *s.* confortación, consuelo, alivio; solaz, satisfacción; bienestar; comodidad, conveniencia, regalo.

comfortable [cúmfœrtabœl]. **I.** *a.* confortativo; cómodo; consolador. **II.** *s.* cobertor, traspuntín.—**comfortableness** [-nes], *s.* comodidad, bienestar; consuelo.—**comfortably** [-bli], *adv.* agradablemente, cómodamente.

comforter [cúmfœrtœr], *s.* confortador, consolador; el Espíritu Santo; cobertor, colcha; bufanda, tapabocas.

comfortless [cúmfœrtles], *a.* desconsolado, sin consuelo, inconsolable.

comfrey [cúmfri], *s.* (bot.) consuelda.

comic(al [cómic(al], *a.* cómico; gracioso.

comically [-li], *adv.* burlescamente, cómicamente.—**comicalness** [-nes], *s.* gracia, chiste.

coming [cúming]. **I.** *s.* venida, llegada; advenimiento.—**c. out**, (fam.) entrada en la sociedad; estreno, *debut*. **II.** *a.* próximo, que viene.

comitial [comíshal], *a.* comicial.

comitiva [cómitiva], *s.* cuadrilla de bandidos.

comity [cómiti], *s.* cortesía, urbanidad, bienquerencia; (der. intern.) cortesía, deferencia.

comma [cóma], *s.* (gram.) coma (,); (mús.) coma.—**c. bacillus**, (biol.) microbio del cólera.

command [cománd]. **I.** *va.* mandar; imponer; atraer; (fort.) dominar. **II.** *vn.* mandar; imponerse. **III.** *s.* mando; mandamiento, o mandato; autoridad, imperio; comandancia, dominación; alcance, perspectiva; facilidad, recursos; disposición, órdenes.—**at one's c.**, a la disposición de uno; de que uno dispone.

commandant [cómandánt], *s.* comandante.

commandeer [cómændiær], *va.* reclutar forzosamente; expropiar, sobre todo para usos militares.

commander [cómændœr], *s.* jefe; teniente de navío; maza para empedrar.—**c. in chief**, generalísimo, general en jefe.

commandery [-dœri], *s.* comandancia; encomienda.

commanding [-ding], *pa.* dominante, imperativo; imponente; convincente, atrayente; quemando.—**c. officer**, comandante en jefe.

commandingly [-dingli], *adv.* imperativamente.

commandment [comándmœnt], *s.* mandato, precepto.—**the Commandments**, los mandamientos.

commando [cómændo], *s.* cuerpo militar; invasión.

commatic [cométic], *a.* breve, sucinto.

commatism [cómatism], *s.* concisión, brevedad.

commemorable [commémorabœl], *a.* memorable.—**commemorate** [-moreit], *va.* conmemorar.—**commemoration** [-moréishʊn], *s.* conmemoración.—**commemorative** [-morativ], *a.* conmemorativo.—**commemoratory** [-moratori], *a.* conmemoratorio.

commence [coméns], *va.* y *vn.* comenzar.

commencement [-ment], *s.* principio, comienzo; (escuelas, etc.) función de fin de año o de distribución de diplomas.

commend [coménd], *va.* encomendar, recomendar, encargar; alabar, ensalzar, loar.

commendable [-abœl], *a.* recomendable, loable; autorizado.

commendably [-abli], *adv.* loablemente.

commendatary [coméndatæri], *s.* comendatario, beneficiado.

commendation [cómendéishʊn], *s.* recomendación, encomio, alabanza.

commendator [-déitœr], *s.* comendatario.

commendatory [cœméndatori], *a.* recomendatorio; de comendatario.

commender [coméndœr], *s.* alabador.

commensal [coménsal], *a.* comensal; (biol.) asociado.

commensalism [coménsalism], *s.* comensalía.

commensurability [coménshurabíliti], **commensurableness** [-bœlnes], *s.* conmensurabilidad.—**commensurable** [-bœl], *a.* conmensurable; proporcionado.

commensurate [-shureit]. **I.** *va.* conmensurar. **II.** *a.* proporcionado.—**commensurately** [-li], *adv.* proporcionadamente.

commensuration [-éishʊn], *s.* conmensuración, proporción.

comment [cóment]. **I.** *va.* comentar; discutir, juzgar, tratar de. **II.** *vn.* comentar.—**to c. on**, comentar, juzgar, expresar opinión acerca de. **III.** *s.* comentario; observación.

commentary [cómentœri], *s.* comentario; interpretación.

commentator [cómentéitœr], **commenter** [cómentœr], *s.* comentador.

commerce [cómœrs]. **I.** *s.* comercio.—**c. destroyer**, buque ligero y rápido para atacar o capturar buques mercantes. **II.** *vn.* [comœrs], comunicarse, intimarse.

commercial [comœrshal], *a.* comercial, mercantil.—**c. law**, derecho mercantil.

commercialism [-ism], *s.* mercantilismo.—**commercialize** [-aiś], *va.* hacer objeto de comercio.—**commercially** [-li], *adv.* comercialmente, mercantilmente.

commerge [comœry], *va.* y *vn.* mezclar, unir o unirse.

commination [cominéshun], *s.* conminación, amenaza.

comminatory [commínatori], *a.* conminatorio.

commingle [comíngœl]. **I.** *va.* mezclar. **II.** *vn.* mezclarse, unirse; barajarse.

comminute [cómíniut], *va.* moler, triturar.—**comminuted fracture,** fractura conminuta.

comminution [-niúshun], *s.* trituración, división; atenuación; (cir.) fractura conminuta.

commiserable [comíseraboel], *a.* lastimoso.

commiserate [comísœret], *va.* apiadarse, compadecerse.—**commiseration** [-éishun], *s.* conmiseración, piedad.

commissar [cómisar], *s.* comisario de gobierno, miembro del gabinete soviético.

commissariat [comisériæt], *s.* (mil.) comisaría; Administración Militar; departamento de gobierno (en Rusia).

commissary [cómisæri], *s.* comisario, delegado; (mil.) comisario de guerra.—**c. general,** jefe superior de Administración Militar.—**commissaryship** [-ship], *s.* comisaría, comisariato.

commission [comíshun]. **I.** *s.* comisión; misión, encargo; cometido; patente, despacho, nombramiento; (com.) comisión; (for.) comisión, perpetración; (E. U.) junta de gobierno municipal.—**c. government,** (E. U.) gobierno municipal dirigido por un administrador o gerente nombrado por una junta municipal o por el alcalde y un concejo.—**c. merchant,** (com.) comisionista.—**out of c.,** (fam.) inservible, inutilizado, arruinado.—**to put into c.,** poner (un buque) en servicio activo.—**to put out of c.,** jubilar, retirar del servicio; (fam.) arruinar; poner fuera de combate (en los dep.), acabar con, despachar. **II.** *va.* comisionar, encargar; nombrar; poner en servicio activo.—**commissioned officer,** (mil.) oficial (apl. al alférez y los oficiales y jefes de mayor grado, que son nombrados por escrito).

commissional [-al], **commissionary** [-æri], *a.* comisionado.

commissioner [comíshunœr], *s.* comisario; comisionado, apoderado, factor; (E. U.) miembro de la junta municipal. (*V.* COMMISSION GOVERNMENT).—**c. of deeds,** (E. U.) notario autorizado por el gobierno federal.

commissure [cómishur], *s.* (anat.) comisura.

commit [comít], *va.* cometer, perpetrar; confiar, depositar, entregar; encarcelar, encerrar; encargar, encomendar; trasladar.—**to c. one's self,** soltar prendas, comprometerse; declararse.—**to c. to memory,** aprender de memoria.—**to c. to writing,** poner por escrito.

commitment [-ment], **committal** [comítal], *s.* perpetración, comisión; traslado a una comisión; (for.) auto de prisión; encierro, encarcelamiento; compromiso, promesa.

committee [comíti], *s.* comisión, diputación, delegación; junta.—**c. of the whole,** comisión de la totalidad de los miembros de una asamblea reunidos en junta con carácter puramente deliberativo.

commode [comód], *s.* cómoda; lavabo cubierto; inodoro.

commodious [comódius], *a.* cómodo, espacioso, holgado.—**commodiously** [-li], *adv.* cómodamente, holgadamente.—**commodiousness** [-nes], *s.* conveniencia, comodidad; holgura.

commodity [comóditi], *s.* comodidad, conveniencia; artículo de comercio o de consumo (apl. gen. a los de primera necesidad), mercancía (sin incluir animales ni bienes raíces).

commodore [cómodor], *s.* (mar.) comodoro; jefe de escuadra.

common [cómun]. **I.** *a.* común, corriente, usual, ordinario; vulgar; público, general; bajo, inferior; adocenado; (gram.) común o apelativo.—**c. carrier,** cargador, porteador, empresa de transporte público (no oficial).—**c. council,** ayuntamiento, concejo.—**c. councilman,** concejal.—**c. crier,** pregonero.—**c. era,** era vulgar o cristiana.—**c. fraction,** (arit.) quebrado.—**c. herd,** gentuza, común de las gentes.—**c. law,** derecho consuetudinario.—**c.-law marriage,** matrimonio consensual.—**c. pleas,** causas ajenas al dominio de la corona; COURT OF COMMON PLEAS.—**c. school,** escuela primaria elemental.—**c. soldier,** soldado raso.—**c. stock,** (com.) acciones ordinarias. **II.** *s.* común, comunal; pastos comunes.—**commonable** [-æbœl], *a.* común, comunal.—**commonage** [-ey], *s.* derecho de pastar en común.—**commonalty** [-alti], *s.* comunal, sociedad, comunidad.

commoner [cómunœr], *s.* plebeyo, pechero; comunero; (Ingl.) miembro de la cámara de los comunes; estudiante de segunda clase en la universidad de Oxford.

commonly [-li], *adv.* comúnmente, usualmente; vulgarmente.

commonness [-nes], *s.* comúnidad; frecuencia; ordinariez, vulgaridad.

commonplace [-pléis]. **I.** *a.* común, vulgar, trivial. **II.** *s.* lugares comunes; apunte, nota.—**c. book,** minuta, libro de memoria.

commons [cómuns], *s. pl.* el vulgo o pueblo bajo; (Ingl.) la cámara baja; mesa redonda; víveres, bucólica.

commonweal [cómunuil], *s.* bien público.

commonwealth [-uelz], *s.* estado; nación; cosa pública; república.—**the C.,** (hist.) la república de Cromwell.

commorant [cómorænt], *s.* y *a.* (for.) vecino.

commotion [comóshun], *s.* conmoción, perturbación, tumulto.

communal [cómyunal], *a.* comunal, público.

commune [cómyun]. **I.** *s.* (pol.) comuna; comunión, intimidad. **II.** *vn.* [comiún], conversar, platicar; comunicarse, ponerse en contacto; comulgar.

communicability [comiúncabíliti], *s.* comunicabilidad.—**communicable** [-cabœl], *a.* comunicable; comunicativo.

communicant [-cant], *s.* comunicante, comulgante.

communicate [-keit]. **I.** *va.* comunicar, hacer partícipe, notificar; transmitir, pegar (una enfermedad); dar la comunión. **II.** *vn.* comunicarse, tener correspondencia; abrir, dar a; comulgar.—**communication** [-kéishun], *s.* comunicación.

communicative [comiúncætiv], *a.* comunicativo; expansivo.—**communicativeness** [-nes], *s.* comunicabilidad.—**communicatory** [-catori], *a.* comunicatorio.

communion [comiúnion], *s.* comunión; contacto, intimidad; confraternidad; (igl.) comunión; congregación.

communiqué [comiúnikéi], *s.* comunicación, oficio.

communism [cómiunism], *s.* comunismo.

communist [-nist], *s.* comunista.—**communistic** [-ic], *a.* perteneciente al comunismo; común.

community [comiúniti], *s.* comunidad, común, público; sociedad, generalidad; corporación, sociedad; comunidad, propiedad o goce común.—**c. chest,** fondo de contribuciones voluntarias para gastos municipales de caridad.

commutability [comiútabíliti], *s.* conmutabilidad.

commutable [-taboel], *a.* conmutable.

commutation [comiutéshun], *s.* mudanza, alteración; conmutación.—**c. ticket,** billete de abono.

commutative [comiútativ], *a.* conmutativo.—**commutatively** [-li], *adv.* conmutativamente.

commutator [cómyutéitœr], *s.* (elec.) colector.—**c. bar,** *o* **segment,** segmento colector.

commute [comiút]. **I.** *vn.* conmutar, cambiar; rescatar; igualarse, ajustarse; abonarse; (elec.) cambiar. **II.** *vn.* conmutar, pagar por medio de conmutación.

commuter [comiútœr], *s.* (f. c.) viajero de conmutación.

compact [cómpæct]. **I.** *s.* pacto, convenio. **II.** *a.* compacto; cerrado, apretado; breve, compendioso; compuesto. **III.** *va.* consolidar, apretar, comprimir; pactar, convenir; compaginar, formar. **IV.** *vn.* coligarse, unirse a o con.

compacted [compécted], *a.* consolidado, apretado, firme.

compactedly [-li], *adv.* = COMPACTLY.

compactedness [-nes], *s.* = COMPACTNESS
compactible [compǽctibœl, *a.* que se puede hacer compacto o reducido.
compactly [-li], *adv.* sólidamente, densamente; reducidamente.
compactness [-nes], *s.* densidad; forma o tamaño reducido.
companion [compǽñun], *s.* compañero; consorte; acompañante; caballero de una orden; (mar.) lumbrera.—**c. ladder,** escala de toldilla.— **c. way,** escalera de la cámara.
companionable [-abœl], *a.* sociable.
companionably [-abli], *adv.* sociablemente.
companionship [-ŝhip], *s.* compañerismo; unión; compañía.
company [cómpani], *s.* compañía, acompañamiento; visitante, huésped; visita (personas); asociación, gremio; compañero, acompañante; (com., mil., tea.) compañía; (mar.) tripulación.
comparable [cómparabœl], *a.* comparable.
comparably [-bli], *adv.* comparablemente.
comparative [compǽrativ], *a.* comparativo, relativo; comparado; (gram.) comparativo.—**c. science,** ciencia de observación (esp. biol.)
comparatively [-li], *adv.* comparativamente, relativamente.
compare [compǽar]. I. *va.* comparar. II. *vn.* poderse comparar; ser comparable; ser igual. —**to c. favorably with,** no perder por comparación con, no ser inferior a.
comparison [compǽrisun], *s.* comparación.— **beyond c.,** sin comparación, incomparablemente; incomparable.
compartment [compártmœnt], *s.* compartimiento, división, departamento; tablero; cajoncito, gaveta; (her.) cuartel.
compass [cœmpas]. I. *va.* conseguir, lograr; idear, maquinar; circuir, cercar; sitiar. II. *s.* círculo, circuito, ámbito; recinto; alcance; extensión; moderación; límites; (mús.) extensión de la voz o de un instrumento; brújula; (gen. *pl.* **compasses**) compás.—**c. card,** rosa de los vientos.—**c. needle,** aguja de brújula; aguja imanada.—**c. saw,** serrucho de calar.—**c. surveying,** levantamiento de planos con la brújula.
compassable [cœmpasabœl], *a.* asequible.
compassion [compǽŝhun], *s.* compasión.
compassionable [-œbœl], *a.* lastimoso, digno de compasión.—**compassionate** [-et]. I. *a.* compasivo. II. *va.* compadecer.—**compassionately** [-li], *adv.* compasivamente.
compatibility [compǽtibíliti], **compatibleness** [compǽtibœlnes], *s.* compatibilidad.
compatible [compǽtibœl], *a.* compatible.
compatibly [-bli], *adv.* compatiblemente.
compatriot [compǽtriot], *a.* y *s.* compatriota.
compeer [compíœr], *s.* igual; compañero.
compel [compél], *va.* compeler, obligar; dominar; arrancar por la fuerza; someter.— **compellable** [-abœl], *a.* que puede ser compelido. —**compellably** [-abli], *adv.* a viva fuerza.
compellation [cómpeléiŝhun], *s.* tratamiento; acción de dirigir la palabra.
compeller [compélœr], *s.* compulsor, apremiador.
compend [cómpend], *s.* compendio
compendious [compéndius], *a.* compendioso, breve.—**compendiously** [-li], *adv.* compendiosamente.—**compendiousness** [-nes], *s.* brevedad.— **compendium** [-dium], *s.* compendio.
compensate [cómpenséit]. I. *va.* compensar, indemnizar; remunerar; (mec.) compensar. II. *vn.* compensar; (con *for*), igualar, equivaler.
compensating [-ing], *a.* (fís., mec., etc.) compensador.
compensation [-séiŝhun]. I. *s.* compensación; remuneración; reparación, desagravio; (psicol.) neutralización. II. *a.* (tec.) compensador, de compensación.
compensative [compénsativ], *a.* = COMPENSATORY.
compensator [cómpenséitœr], *s.* compensador.
compensatory [compénsætori], *a.* compensatorio.

compete [compít], *vn.* competir.
competence, competency [cómpetens, i], *s.* suficiencia, competencia; subsistencia; (for.) competencia.
competent [-ent], *a.* competente, capaz; (for.) competente.
competently [-li], *adv.* competentemente.
competition [-tíŝhun], *s.* (e. p.) competencia, concurrencia; rivalidad; certamen, concurso, oposición.
competitive [compétitiv], *a.* que compite, competidor.—**c. examination,** examen de concurso u oposición.
competitor [compétitor], *s.* competidor, rival.
compilation [compiléŝhun], *s.* compilación, recopilación.
compilatory [cómpáilatori], *a.* perteneciente a una compilación.
compile [compáil], *va.* compilar, recopilar.
compiler [-œr], *s.* compilador; recopilador.
complacence, complacency [compléisens, i], *s.* complacencia, satisfacción.
complacent [-ent], *a.* complaciente; satisfecho. —**complacently** [-li], *adv.* complacientemente; con satisfacción.
complain [compléin], *vn.* quejarse, lamentarse; (for.) querellarse, demandar.
complainant [-ant], *s.* querellante; (for.) demandante.
complainer [-œr], *s.* querellador.
complainingly [-ingli], *adv.* quejosamente.
complaint [compléint], *s.* queja; lamento; querella, agravio; mal, enfermedad; (for.) demanda.
complaisance [compléiŝans], **complaisantness** [-nes], *s.* afabilidad, cortesía, complacencia.—**complaisant** [-ant], *a.* cortés, complaciente.—**complaisantly** [-li], *adv.* cortésmente.
complanate [cómplanet], *a.* aplanado, llano.
complected [complécted], *a.* entretejido, enlazado; complicado.
complement [cómplement]. I. *s.* complemento; accesorio; cantidad o número completo; (gram., geom.) complemento; (biol.) complemento, alexina o citosa. II. *va.* completar.
complemental [-méntæl], *a.* completivo; (geom.) complementario.
complementary [-méntari], *a.* complementario.
complete [complít]. I. *a.* completo. II. *va.* completar, acabar.—**completely** [-li], *adv.* completamente, enteramente.—**completeness** [-nes], *s.* entereza, calidad de completo.
completion [complíŝhun], *s.* terminación, consumación, fin.
completive [complítiv], *a.* completivo.
complex [cómplecs]. I. *a.* complejo; compuesto; (mat.) complejo, imaginario.—**c. fraction,** (arit.) fracción de términos fraccionarios.—**c. sentence** (gram.) oración que contiene una o más proposiciones subordinadas. II. *s.* complexo; (psicol.) grupo de ideas o tendencias reprimidas asociadas con un estado afectivo o emocional.
complexion [complécŝhun], *s.* tez; cutis; naturaleza; estado; carácter, calidad.
complexional [-al], *a.* complexional.
complexionally [-ali], *adv.* por complexión.
complexioned [complécŝhund], *a.* de tal o cual tez.
complexity [-plécsiti], **complexness** [-plécsnes], *s.* complejidad.
complexly [-li], *adv.* complexamente.
complexus [complécsus], *s.* complicación; (anat.) músculo complexo.
compliable [compláiabœl], *a.* = COMPLIANT.
compliance [compláians], *s.* docilidad, sumisión; complacencia; condescendencia, anuencia, consentimiento.—**in c. with,** de acuerdo con, accediendo a.
compliant [-ant], *a.* dócil, obediente, sumiso; condescendiente, complaciente.—**compliantly** [-li], *adv.* rendidamente, complacientemente.
complicate [cómplikeit]. I. *va.* complicar. II. *a.* complicado; (hist. nat.) plegado.

complicated [-keited], *a.* complicado.
complicately [-li], *adv.* complicadamente.
complicateness [-nes], *s.* complicación.
complication [-kéishʋn], *s.* complicación.
complicative [-keitiv], *a.* que produce complicaciones.
complicity [complísiti], *s.* complicidad.
complier [compláiœr], *s.* consentidor, contemporizador.
compliment [cómplimœnt]. **I.** *s.* galantería, requiebro; favor, fineza; cumplimiento; cumplido; obsequio, regalo.—*pl.* recados, memorias; saludo. **II.** *va.* requebrar; galantear; cumplimentar, felicitar; obsequiar. **III.** *vn.* hacer cumplimientos.
complimentary [-méntari], *a* lisonjero, galante; cumplido, cortés, obsequioso; de obsequio, de regalo.—**complimenter** [-mentœr], *s.* adulador; cumplimentero.
complin(e [cómplin], *s.* (igl.) completas.
complot [cómplot]. **I.** *s.* conspiración. **II.** [complót], *va.* conspirar.
Complutensian [compluténshæn], *a.* complutense.
compluvium [complúviʋm], *s.* (arq.) compluvio.
comply [complái], *vn.* obedecer, condescender consentir.—**to c. with,** obrar de acuerdo con, acceder a, satisfacer.
component [compóunent], *a.* y *s.* componente.
comport [compórt], *vn.* y *va.* convenir, concordar; portarse, comportarse.
comportment [-mœnt], *s.* comportamiento.
compose [compóus]. **I.** *va.* componer, formar; redactar, escribir; ajustar, arreglar; apaciguar, sosegar. **II.** *va.* y *vn.* (mús. e impr.) componer.
composed [compóus̄d], *a.* sosegado, tranquilo, sereno.—**composedly** [compóus̄edli], *adv.* tranquilamente, sosegadamente, con calma, serenamente.—**composedness** [-s̄ednes], *s.* compostura, modestia, tranquilidad, serenidad, calma.
composer [compróuâœr], *s.* autor, escritor; conciliador, mediador; (mús.) compositor.
composing [compóusẖing], *ger.* de TO COMPOSE.—**c. frame,** (imp.) chibalete.—**c. rule,** (imp.) regleta, filete.—**c. stand** = c. FRAME.—**c. stick,** (imp.) componedor.
Compositæ [compós̄iti], *s. pl.* (bot.) compuestas
composite [compós̄it]. **I.** *a.* compuesto, formado de partes; (arq.) compuesto; (bot.) compuesta.—**c. carriage,** (f. c.) coche mixto.—**c. number,** (arit.) número no primo.—**c. photograph,** o **c. portrait,** retrato compuesto o de superposición, formado sacando una sobre otra fotografías de diversas cosas o personas. **II.** *s.* cosa compuesta; (bot.) planta compuesta.
composition [compós̄íshʋn], *s.* composición; componenda, arreglo, ajuste; (b. a.) composición.
compositive [compós̄itiv], *a.* compositivo.
compositor [compós̄itœr], *a.* (impr.) cajista, componedor; conciliador.
compost [cómpoust]. **I.** *s.* abono, estiércol. **II.** *va.* abonar la tierra.
composure [compóuŷœr], *s.* compostura, serenidad, calma.
compote [cómpot], *s.* compota, dulce.
compotier [compotié], *s.* dulcera, compotera.
compound [compáund]. **I.** *va.* componer, combinar, mezclar, confeccionar; transigir, componer. **II.** *vn.* avenirse, transigir, arreglarse.
compound [cómpaund]. **I.** *s.* mezcla, mixtura; preparación; (quím.) cuerpo compuesto. **II.** *a.* compuesto; (m. v., elec.) compound (es el término usado en español, italiano, francés, alemán, etc.).—**c. circuit,** (elec.) circuito compuesto de uno cerrado conectado con uno abierto.—**c. dynamo,** dínamo compound.—**c. engine,** (m. v.) máquina compound.—**c. fracture,** (cir.) fractura complicada o abierta (en que el hueso rompe los tejidos).—**c. interest,** interés compuesto.—**c. locomotive,** locomotora compound.—**c. number,** (arit.) número denominado.—**c. steel,** acero de aleación.—**c. winding,** (elec.) arrollamiento compound.

compoundable [compáundabœl], *a.* componible.
compounder [compáundœr], *s.* mezclador; mediador.
compounding [compáunding], *s.* (elec.) composición, compoundaje (el segundo lo prefieren los técnicos).
comprehend [cómprejénd], *va.* comprender, concebir; contener, encerrar.
comprehensible [-s̄ibœl], *a.* comprensible, inteligible.—**comprehensibleness** [-nes], *s.* comprensibilidad.—**comprehensibly** [-bli], *adv.* comprensiblemente.
comprehension [-s̄hʋn], *s.* comprensión.
comprehensive [-s̄iv], *a.* comprensivo, amplio; perspicaz.—**comprehensively** [-li], *adv.* comprensivamente.—**comprehensiveness** [-nes], *s.* extensión, alcance; comprensión, entendimiento.
compress [comprés̄], *va.* comprimir, apretar, estrechar, condensar; abreviar, reducir.
compress [cómpres], *s.* (cir.) compresa.
compressibility [comprés̄ibiliti], **compressibleness** [-s̄ibœlnes], *s.* compresibilidad.
compressible [-s̄ibœl], *a.* compresible.
compression [-s̄hʋn], *s.* compresión.
compressive [-s̄iv], *a.* compresivo.
compressor [-s̄œr], *s.* compresor.
comprisal [compráís̄al], *s.* inclusión, comprensión.
comprise [compráis̄], *va.* comprender, contener, abarcar, abrazar.
compromise [cómpromais̄]. **I.** *s.* arreglo, avenencia, componenda; término medio; compromiso, obligación. **II.** *va.* arreglar, zanjar; comprometer, exponer. **III.** *vn.* transigir.
compromiser [-s̄œr], *s.* compromisario.
comptograph [cómtogræf], *s.* contógrafo.—**comptometer** [comtómitœr], *s.* contómetro. (Estos son nombres de fábrica dados a dos máquinas de calcular.)
comptrol, *v.* y *s.* = CONTROL.
comptroller [comtróulœr], *s.* contralor, interventor; sobrestante.—**comptrollership** [-s̄hip], *s.* contraloría, intervención.
compulsative [compúlsativ], **compulsatory** [-satori], *a.* compulsorio, coactivo.
compulsatively [-li], *adv.* por fuerza.
compulsion [compúls̄hʋn], *a.* compulsión, apremio, coacción.
compulsive [-s̄iv], *a.* compulsivo.—**compulsively** [-li], *adv.* compulsivamente.—**compulsiveness** [-nes], *n.* calidad de compulsivo.
compulsory [compúls̄ori], *a.* obligatorio.—**compulsorily** [-li], *adv.* obligatoriamente.
compunction [compúncs̄hʋn], *s.* compunción, escrúpulo.—**compunctious** [-hʋs], *a.* compungido, contrito.
compurgation [compœrguéshʋn], *s.* compurgación.—**compurgator** [-guétœr], *s.* compurgador
computable [compiútabœl], *a.* calculable.
computation [cómpiutéishʋn], *s.* computación, cálculo.—**compute** [compiút], *va.* computar, calcular.—**computer** [-œr], *s.* calculador, calculista.
comrade [cómræd], *s.* camarada, compañero.
con, *va.* estudiar, leer con atención; (mar.) gobernar (el buque).
concatenate [concát̄eneit]. **I.** *va.* concatenar, encadenar. **II.** *a.* eslabonado.
concatenation [-éishʋn], *s.* concatenación, eslabonamiento, sucesión, serie.
concave [cónkev]. **I.** *a.* cóncavo. **II.** *s.* hueco, hondón.—**concaveness** [-nes], calidad de cóncavo, concavidad.—**concavity** [-cáviti], *s.* concavidad.—**concavo-concave** [conckévo-cónkev], *s.* cóncavo-cóncavo.—**concavo-convex,** cóncavo-convexo.
conceal [consíl], *va.* ocultar, encubrir, callar, tapar, disimular.—**concealable** [-abœl], *a.* ocultable, escondible.—**concealer** [-œr], *s.* ocultador, encubridor.—**concealment** [-mœnt], *s.* secreto, encubrimiento; reticencia; escondrijo, escondite.
concede [consíd]. **I.** *va.* conceder, admitir. **II.** *vn.* asentir, convenir.
conceit [consít]. **I.** *s.* presunción, engreimiento, vanagloria; noción, idea, fantasía; pensamien-

to; capricho, chifladura; concepción, comprensión. **II.** *va.* conceptuar, concebir, imaginar; engreírse; encapricharse.

conceited [consíted], *a.* vanidoso, engreído.— **conceitedly** [-lii], *adv.* engreídamente.—**conceitedness** [-nes], *s.* presunción, vanidad.

conceivable [consívabœl], *a.* concebible.— **conceivableness** [-nes], *s.* conceptibilidad.— **conceivably** [-bli], *adv.* de un modo conceptible.

conceive [consív]. **I.** *va.* concebir, comprender, formar idea; coger (odio, etc.); engendrar, concebir. **II.** *vn.* concebir, imaginar, pensar; concebir, hacerse preñada la hembra.

concenter, *v.* = CONCENTRE.

concentrate [cónsentreit]. **I.** *va.* concentrar, reconcentrar. **II.** *vn.* reunirse; reconcentrarse. **III.** *a.* concentrado. **IV.** *s.* (quím.) substancia o producto concentrado: (met.) resultado de la concentración de minerales o su reducción a menor volumen.

concentrated [-tréited], *a.* (quím.) concentrado.

concentration [-tréishun], *s.* concentración, reconcentración.—**concentrator** [-tœr], *s.* concentrador.

concentre [conséntœr]. **I.** *vn.* reconcentrarse. **II.** *va.* concentrar, enfocar.

concentric(al [conséntric(al], *a.* concéntrico.

concentrically [-lii], *adv.* concéntricamente.

concentricity [cónsentrísiti], *s.* concentricidad.

concentus [conséntus], *s.* concento, armonía, consonancia.

concept [cónsept], *s.* concepto, noción, idea.

conception [consépshun], *s.* concepción, idea, concepto, sentimiento; conocimiento, comprensión; (biol.) concepción, preñez.—**conceptive** [-tiv], *a.* conceptible.

conceptual [consépchuæl], *a.* conceptual, relativo al concepto; de carácter de concepto.— **conceptualism** [-ism], *s.* conceptualismo.— **conceptualist** [-ist], *s.* conceptualista.

concern [consœrn]. **I.** *va.* concernir, importar, interesar, atañer o incumbir; afectar; mover, excitar, preocupar, inquietar, desasosegar. **II.** *s.* asunto, negocio, ocupación; interés, incumbencia; empresa, establecimiento, casa de comercio; importancia, consecuencia; afecto, amor, cariño; inquietud, ansiedad.

concerned [consœrnd], *a.* interesado; comprometido; ansioso, intranquilo.—**as far as I am c.,** en cuanto a mí.—**concernedly** [-nedli], *adv.* ansiosamente, etc.—**concerning** [-ning], *prep.* por lo concerniente a, respecto a.

concernment [-mœnt], *s.* interés; asunto; importancia; ansiedad, cuidado.

concert [consœrt], *va.* concertar, acordar, ajustar.

concert [cónsœrt], *s.* concierto, convenio, acuerdo; (mús.) concierto.

concertina [consœrtína], *s.* (mús.) concertina.

concerto [conchœrto], *s.* (mús.) concerto.

concession [conséshun], *s.* concesión.

concessionary [-eri]. **I.** *s.* concesionario. **II.** *a.* otorgado por concesión.

concessive [consésiv], *a.* concedente.

concessively [-lii], *adv.* concedentemente.

concessory [-sori], *a.* concedente, otorgante.

conch [conc], *s.* caracol marino; concha; fotuto; pabellón de la oreja; (arq.) concha.

concha [cónca], *s.* cavidad del pabellón de la oreja.

Conchifera [conkíferæ], *s. pl.* (zool.) lamelibranquios, conchíferos.

conchiform [cónkiform], *a.* conquiforme.

conchoid [cóncoid], *s.* (geom.) concoide.

conchoidal [concóidal], *a.* concoideo.

conchologist [concóloyist], *s.* conquiliólogo.

conchology [concóloyi], *s.* (zool.) conquiliología.

concierge [consiéry], *s.* conserje, portero.— **conciergerie** [consiéryeri], *s.* portería, conserjería.

conciliate [consíliet], *va.* conciliar, propiciar, grangear, ganar, atraer.

conciliation [consíliéshun], *s.* conciliación.

conciliator [-tœr], *s.* conciliador.

conciliatory [-liætori], *a.* conciliativo.

concise [consáis], *a.* conciso, breve.—**concisely** [-lii], *adv.* concisamente.—**conciseness** [-nes], *s.* concisión, laconismo.

concision [consíyun], *s.* corte, cortadura; concisión; circuncisión.

conclave [cónclev], *s.* conclave.

conclude [conclúd]. **I.** *va.* concluir; inferir; hacer (arreglo, etc.); excluir; decidir; restringir, coartar. **II.** *vn.* finalizar, fenecer; inferir.

conclusion [conclúyun], *s.* conclusión; determinación, decisión.

conclusive [conclúsiv], *a.* concluyente; terminante.—**conclusively** [-lii], *a.* concluyentemente.— **conclusiveness** [-nes], *s.* calidad de concluyente o terminante.

concoct [concóct], *va.* mezclar, confeccionar; trazar, proyectar, urdir.

concoction [concócshun], *s.* mezcla o mixtura; maquinación, trama; trazo.

concoctive [-tiv], *a.* relativo a una mezcla, o un trazo.

concolo(u)r [concólœr], **concolorate** [-et], *a.* de un mismo color.

concomitance, concomitancy [concómitans(i], *s.* concomitancia.—**concomitant** [-tant], *a.* y *s.* concomitante.—**concomitantly** [-lii], *adv.* acompañadamente.

concord [cóncord], *s.* concordia; armonía, buena inteligencia; (mús. y gram.) concordancia.

concordance [concórdans], *s.* concordancias; conformidad, armonía.

concordant [concórdant], *a.* concordante, conforme.—**concordantly** [-lii], *adv.* concordemente, de común acuerdo.

concordat [concórdat], *s.* concordato.

concourse [cóncors], *s.* concurso, concurrencia, gentío; confluencia; campo o lugar de reunión; gran salón (de estación, etc.).

concrescence [concrésens], *s.* concrescencia, crecimiento.

concrete [concrít]. **I.** *va.* concretar; concrecionar, espesar; (alb.) cubrir con hormigón. **II.** *vn.* cuajar, condensarse, coagularse.

concrete [cóncrit]. **I.** *a.* concreto; cuajado; de hormigón. **II.** *s.* masa de azúcar que se forma hirviendo guarapo; concreción; término concreto; (constr.) hormigón.—**c. mixer,** hormigonera.

concretely [concrítli], *adv.* concretamente.

concreteness [-nes], *s.* calidad de concreto.

concretion [concríshun], *s.* concreción; (met.) cálculo.

concretive [concrítiv], *a.* formando concreciones.

concubinage [conkiúbiney], *s.* concubinato.

concubine [cónkiubain], *sf.* concubina.

concupiscence [conkiúpisens], *s.* concupiscencia.

concupiscent [-sent], *a.* libidinoso, lascivo.

concur [concœr], *vn.* concurrir, encontrarse; convenir, conformarse, hallarse de acuerdo; unirse, juntarse, adunarse.

concurrence, concurrency [concœrens, i], *s.* concurrencia; coincidencia, casualidad; acuerdo, cooperación, ayuda; punto de intersección.

concurrent [-ent]. **I.** *a.* concurrente; concomitante, coexistente. **II.** *s.* rival, competidor.—**concurrently** [-lii], *adv.* concurrentemente.

concussion [concúshun], *s.* concusión, sacudida; golpe; (med.) desorden funcional debido a concusión o golpe.—**concussional** [-æl], *a.* (med.) causado por o relativo a concusión.—**concussive** [-cúsiv], *a.* (med.) que causa concusión.

condemn [condém], *va.* condenar; prohibir oficialmente el uso de (edificio, etc. declarado inseguro o peligroso); expropiar.

condemnable [condémnabœl], *a.* culpable, censurable, condenable.

condemnation [cóndemnéshun], *s.* condenación.

condemnatory [condémnatori], *a.* condenatorio.

condemner [condémnœr], *s.* condenador.

condensable [condénsabœl], *a.* condensable.

condensate [cóndenset]. **I.** *a.* condensado, espesado. **II.** *s.* objeto condensado.

condensation [condenséshun], *s.* condensación.

condensative [condénsativ], *a.* condensativo.

condense [condéns]. **I.** *va.* condensar, comprimir; espesar; reducir, abreviar. **II.** *vn.* condensarse, comprimirse, espesarse.

condenser [-œr], *s.* (mec., elec. y ópt.) condensador.

condensing [-ing], *a.* condensante.—**c. engine**, máquina de condensación.

condescend [cóndesénd], *vn.* condescender.

condescendence [-ens], *s.* condescendencia.

condescending [-ing], *a.* condescendiente.

condescendingly [-li], *adv.* condescendientemente.

condescension [-shun], *s.* = CONDESCENDENCE.

condign [condáin], *a.* condigno, merecido.

condignity [condígniti] (teol.), **condignness** [condáinnes], *s.* merecimiento.—**condignly** [condáinli], *adv.* merecidamente, condignamente.

condiment [cóndiment, *s.* condimento.

condition [condíshun]. **I.** *s.* condición; estado, circunstancia; examen de habilitación por presentar (apl. gen. al nuevo examen cuando el alumno ha fracasado en el ordinario). **II.** *va.* estipular, convenir; determinar, modificar; depender, hacer depender (gen. con **on,** vg. *his position is conditioned on his competence,* su puesto depende de su competencia); reprobar (a un estudiante); acondicionar; (com.) probar (telas, etc. para determinar su humedad); (ind.) rehumedecer (telas, etc.) por tratamiento químico.

conditional [condíshunal], *a.* condicional.

conditionality [condíshunéliti], *s.* limitación.

conditionally [condíshunali], *adv.* condicionalmente.

conditioned [condíshund], *a.* condicionado, condicional; acondicionado.

condole [condóul], *vn.* condolerse, dar el pésame.

condolement [-mœnt], **condolence** [condóulens], *s.* pésame.

condonation, condonement [cóndonéshun, condóunment], *s.* condonación, perdón, indulto.

condone [condóun], *va.* condonar.

condor [cóndor], *s.* (orn.) cóndor.

conduce [condiús], *vn.* conducir, tender.

conducive [condiúsiv], *a.* conducente.—**conduciveness** [-nes], *s.,* conducencia, tendencia.

conduct [cóndUct], *s.* conducta; dirección, manejo, gobierno; (mil.) escolta, conducta.

conduct [condUct], *va.* conducir, guiar, dirigir, gestionar, manejar; (vr.) comportarse, proceder; llevar; mandar (un ejército).—*vn.* (fís.) ser conductor; llevar la batuta.

conductible [condUctibœl], *a.* conductible.

conductibility [-tibíliti], *s.* conductibilidad.

conduction [condUcshun], *s.* transmisión, conducción, traída.

conductive [-tiv], *a.* conductivo; (elec.) que obra por conducción.

conductivity [cóndUctíviti], *s.* conductividad; conductibilidad.

conductor [condUctœr], *s.* conductor, guía; director de orquesta;.(É. U., f. c.) recogedor de billetes, cobrador; (arq.) canalón; (cir.) ductor; (elec.) conductor.

conductress [-tres], *s.* conductora, directora.

conduit [cóndit], *s.* conducto; (elec.) tubo, o caja o túnel para conductores.—**c. railway, c. system,** (elec.) ferrocarril de alimentador subterráneo encerrado en un tubo.

condyle [cóndil], *s.* (anat.) cóndilo.

condyloma [condilóma, *s.* (med.) condiloma.

cone [cóun]. **I.** *s.* cono; cucurucho; pan (de azúcar); (bot.) piña.—**c. bearing,** cojinete de cono.—**c. brake,** freno de cono.—**c. clutch,** embrague de cono.—**c. coupling,** acoplamiento de cono.—**c. gear,** engranaje cónico. **II.** *va.* dar forma cónica; ahusar; biselar; arrollar en carrete cónico; (bot.) producir piñas.

coney, *s.* = CONY.

confab, *contr.* de CONFABULATION.

confabulate [confébiuleit], *vn.* confabular; platicar, departir, conferir.—**confabulation** [-éishun], *s.* confabulación, plática, conferencia.

confection [confécshun], *s.* confitura, dulce.—**confectionary** [-eri]. **I.** *a.* confitado. **II.** *s.* confitería; dulces.—**confectioner** [-ncer], *s.* confitero, repostero.—**confectionery** [-eri], *s.* dulces, confites; confitería.—**c. shop,** *o* **store,** confitería, dulcería.

confederacy [confédcerasi], *s.* confederación; cábala.

confederate [confédcoret]. **I.** *va.* y *vn.* confederar(se) **II.** *a.* y *s.* confederado; compinche, socio.

confederation [-éishun], *s.* confederación.

confer [confér]. **I.** *vn.* conferenciar; conferir, tratar, consultar. **II.** *va.* (gen. con **on**) conferir, dar, otorgar (a).—**to c. holy orders,** conferir órdenes sagradas, ordenar.

conference [cónfœrens], *s.* conferencia, entrevista, junta; conversación, plática.

conferrable [confœrabœl], *a.* que puede conferirse.

confess [confés]. **I.** *va.* confesar. **II.** *vn.* confesarse; hacer una confesión.

confessant [confésant], *s.* confesante.

confessed [confést], *a.* confesado, declarado, reconocido.

confessedly [-fésedli], *adv.* reconocidamente, admitidamente, según se admite.

confession [conféshun], *s.* confesión; credo; (igl.) confesión.—**confessional, confessionary** [-al, -eri]. **I.** *s.* confesonario. **II.** *a.* referente a la confesión.

confessor [conféscer], *s.* confesor; penitente; confesante.

confetti [conféti], *s. pl.* confeti, tirillas y bolillas de papel de colores que se arrojan a los concurrentes en los carnavales y otras fiestas.

confidant [cónfidant], *s.* confidente.

confide [confáid]. **I.** *vn.* confiar, fiarse. **II.** *va.* fiar, confiar, depositar.

confidence [cónfidens], *s.* confianza, fe; presunción; confidencia, secreto.

confident [-ent], *a.* cierto, seguro, confiado.

confidential [cónfidénshal], *a.* reservado, confidencial; íntimo.—**confidentially** [-li], *adv.* en confianza, confidencialmente.

confidently [cónfidentli], *adv.* confiadamente.

confider [confáidœr], *s.* el que confía.

confiding [confáiding], *a.* seguro, confiado.

configuration [configuiuréishun], *s.* configuración; (astr.) aspecto.

confinable [confáinabœl], *a.* limitable.

confine [cónfain]. **I.** *s.* confín. **II.** [confáin], *va.* confinar; encerrar, aprisionar; limitar.—**to be confined,** estar de parto. **III.** *vn.* lindar.

confineless [confáinles], *a.* ilimitado.

confinement [-mœnt], *s.* prisión, encierro, destierro, cautiverio; estreñimiento, restricción; parto; sobreparto.

confirm [confœrm], *va.* confirmar, corroborar; verificar, establecer; sancionar, revalidar o ratificar; fortalecer; (igl.) confirmar.—**confirmable** [-bœl], *a.* capaz de ser confirmado o ratificado.

confirmation [cónfœrméshun], *s.* confirmación; ratificación, revalidación; (igl.) confirmación.

confirmative [confœrmativ], *a.* confirmativo.

confirmatively [-li], *adv.* confirmativamente.

confirmatory [-tori], *a.* confirmativo, confirmatorio.

confirmed [confœrmd], *a.* comprobado, corroborado; ratificado; establecido, demostrado; inveterado, consumado.

confirmedness [confœrmednes], *s.* certeza, firmeza.

confiscable [confíscabœl], *a.* confiscable.

confiscate [cónfiskeit], *va.* confiscar.

confiscation [confiskéishun], *s.* confiscación.

confiscator [cónfiskéitœr], *s.* confiscador.

confiscatory [confiscatori], *a.* que confisca.

confiteor [confítiœr], *s.* confíteor.

confiture [cónfichur], *s.* confitura, dulce.

conflagration [conflagréshʊn], s. conflagración, incendio.

conflict [cónflict], s. conflicto, oposición, antagonismo; lucha.

conflict [conflíct], vn. luchar; chocar, pugnar.—**conflicting** [-ing], a. antagónico, encontrado; contradictorio.

confluence [cónfluens], s. confluencia; concurso, concurrencia.

confluent [-ent]. I. a. confluente. II. s. río confluente.

conflux [cónflʊcs], s. confluencia; concurso o concurrencia.

conform [confórm]. I. va. conformar, ajustar, concordar. II. vn. conformarse, allanarse, acatar, someterse.

conformability, conformableness [conformabíliti, confórmabœlnes], s. conformidad.

conformable [-abœl], a. conforme, proporcionado; sumiso.—**conformably** [-bli], adv. conformemente.

conformation [cónforméishʊn], s. conformación, figura, arreglo.

conformator [-tœr], s. conformador (aparato).

conformist [confórmist], s. conformista.

conformity [confórmiti], s. conformidad.

confound [confáund], va. confundir, embrollar; turbar, aturrullar, azorar, desconcertar; mezclar, trabucar.

confounded [confáunded], a. (fam.) maldito.—**confoundedly** [-li], adv. detestablemente, horriblemente.

confrère [confráternity], s. cofradía, confraternidad.

confrère [confréœr]. s. compañero, colega.

confront [confrúnt], va. afrontar, arrostrar, hacer frente a; carear; cotejar, comparar.

confrontation [confrúntéshʊn], **confrontment,** [-mœnt], s. confrontación; careo.

Confucian [confiúshan], a. relativo a o partidario de Confucio.

confuse [confiúś], va. confundir; turbar, azarar; desordenar; mezclar, trabucar; obscurecer.

confused [confiúśd], a. confuso, azarado; turbio, indistinto.

confusedly [confiúśedli], adv. confusamente, atropelladamente.—**confusedness** [-nes], s. = CONFUSION.

confusion [confiúyʊn], s. confusión, desorden; azoramiento, perturbación, vergüenza.—**c.** of tongues, confusión de las lenguas; torre de Babel.

confutable [confiútabœl], a. refutable.

confutant [-tænt], s. refutador.

confutation [cónfutéshʊn], s. confutación, refutación.

confute [confiút], va. confutar, refutar.

confuter [-œr], s. confutador.

congé [conyé], s. despedida.

congeal [conyíl]. I. va. congelar, helar; cuajar, coagular. II. vn. congelarse, helarse, cuajarse.

congealable [conyílabœl], a. congelable.

congealedness [conyílednes], **congealment** [conyílmœnt], s. congelación.

congee [cónyi]. I. vn. despedirse cortésmente; saludar. II. s. despedida.

congelation [conyeléshʊn], s. congelación.

congener [cónyenœr], s. congénere.—**congeneric** [conyenéric], **congenerous** [-yénerʊs], a. congénere.

congenetic [conyenétic], a. de igual origen.

congenial [conyínial], a. congenial, análogo, cognado; simpático.—**congeniality** [conyiniǽliti], **congenialness** [conyíniahnes], s. afabilidad.

congenital [conyénitǽl], a. congénito.

conger, congereel [cóngœr, ill], s. (ict.) congrio.

congeries [conyíriis], s. congerie, cúmulo.

congest [conyést]. I. va. apiñar, aglomerar; (med.) congestionar. II. vn. congestionarse.—**congested** [-ed], a. (med.) congestionado; hiperémico; apretado, apiñado, obstruido.—**congestible** [-ibœl], a. acumulable, amontonable.—**congestion** [-chʊn], s. congestión; apiñamiento.—**congestive** [-iv], a. congestivo.

conglobate [cónglobet]. I. a. conglobado. II. va. y vn. conglobar.

conglobation [conglobéshʊn], s. conglobación.

conglobulate [conglóbiulet], vn. conglobarse.

conglomerate [conglómœret]. I. va. y vn. conglomerar, aglomerar, redondear. II. a. conglomerado; congregado, redondeado. III. s. conglomeración; (geol.) conglomerado.

conglomeration [-éishʊn], s. conglomeración.

conglomeritic [conglomœrític], **conglomeratic,** a. conglomerado.

conglutinate [conglútinet]. I. va. y vn. conglutinar(se); pegar(se). II. a. conglutinado.

conglutination [-éishʊn], s. conglutinación.

conglutinative [-eitiv], a. conglutinativo.

conglutinator [-éitœr], s. conglutinador.

congratulant [congrǽtiulant], a. congratulorio.

congratulate [-eit], va. congratular, felicitar.

congratulation [congrǽtiuléishʊn], s. congratulación; felicitación, enhorabuena, parabién.—**congratulator** [-eitœr], s. congratulador; congraciador.—**congratulatory** [-atori], a. congratulatorio.

congregate [cóngregueit]. I. va. congregar, convocar, reunir. II. vn. juntarse, afluir. III. a. agregado, reunido.

congregation [-śhʊn], s. concurso, auditorio; asamblea, reunión; agregado, colección; (igl.) congregación; conjunto de los fieles o miembros de una iglesia; feligreses.

congregational [-æl], a. perteneciente a una congregación; (C-) congregacionalista.—**Congregationalism** [-ism], s. congregacionalismo.—**Congregationalist** [-ist], s. congregacionalista.

congress [cóngres], s. congreso.

congressional [congréshʊnæl], a. perteneciente o relativo al congreso.—**C.** district, (E. U.) distrito electoral que envía un diputado a la cámara de representantes.

congressman [cóngresmæn], s. miembro de un congreso cualquiera; diputado al congreso. (En los E. U. apl. esp. a los miembros de la cámara de representantes.).—**c.** at large, (E. U.) diputado que representa todo un estado, en vez de un distrito electoral.

congresswoman [-úmæn], s. mujer congresista.

congruence [cóngruens], **congruency** [-ensi], **congruity** [congrúiti], s. congruencia, armonía; (álg.) congruencia; (geom.) coincidencia, superponibilidad, igualdad.—**congruent** [-ent], **congruous** [cóngruʊs], a. congruente, apropiado; (álg.) congruente; (geom.) superponible, igual.—**congruously** [-li], adv. congruentemente, apropiadamente, armónicamente.—**congruousness** [-nes], s. = CONGRUENCE.

conic [cónic]. I. a. cónico.—**c. section,** sección cónica. II. s. cónica, sección cónica.

conical [-æl], a. cónico.—**conically** [-li], adv. a manera de cono.—**conicalness** [-nes], s. conicidad.

conics [cónics], s. teoría de las cónicas.

conidium [conídium], s. (bot.) conidia.

conifer [cónifœr], s. (bot.) conífero.

Coniferæ [conífœri], s. pl. coníferas.

coniferous [conífœrus], a. conífero.

coniform [cóniform], a. coniforme, cónico.

conin(e [cónin], s. (quím.) conicina, cicutina.

conirostral [coniróstral], a. conirrostro.

conium [cónium], s. (bot.) cicuta.

conjecturable [conyékchœrabœl], a. conjeturable, presumible.

conjectural [-ral], a. conjetural.—**conjecturally** [-li], adv. conjeturalmente, presuntamente.

conjecture [-chœr]. I. s. conjetura. II. va. conjeturar.—**conjecturer** [-œr], s. conjeturador.

conjoin [conyóin]. I. va. juntar, unir; asociar; conectar. II. vn. confederarse, unirse, ligarse.

conjoint [conyóint], a. asociado, confederado.—**conjointly** [-li], adv. unidamente, de mancomún.

conjugable [cónyugabœl], a. (gram.) conjugable.

conjugal [cónyugal], a. conyugal.—**conjugally** [-i], adv. conyugalmente.

conjugate [cónyuguet]. I. va. (gram.) conjugar. II. vn. (biol.) unirse en conjugación. III. s.

palabra análoga. **IV.** *a.* apareado; (mat.) conjugado.

conjugation [-éishʊn], *s.* conjunción, unión; (gram.) conjugación; (biol.) unión o fusión.

conjunct [conyʊ́nct], *a.* conjunto, allegado, unido.

conjunction [conyʊ́ncˢhʊn], *s.* conjunción, unión, liga; (gram. y astr.) conjunción.

conjunctiva [cónyʊnctáiva *o* tíva], *s.* (anat.) conjuntiva.—**conjunctival** [-val], *a.* relativo a la conjuntiva.

conjunctive [conyʊ́nctiv], *a.* conjunto; conjuntivo.—**conjunctively** [-li], *adv.* conjuntamente, de mancomún.

conjunctivitis [conyʊnctiváitis *o* vítis], *s.* (med.) conjuntivitis.

conjunctly [conyʊ́nctli], *adv.* juntamente.

conjuncture [conyʊ́nkchuœr], *s.* coyuntura, oportunidad; unión, conexión.

conjuration [cónyuréshʊn], *s.* deprecación, petición, súplica; conjuro; sortilegio.

conjure [cónyuœr]. **I.** *va.* hechizar, encantar; conjurar; exorcizar. **II.** *vn.* hacer juegos de manos.—**to c. away**, exorcizar.—**to c. up**, evocar; suscitar.

conjurer [cónyurœr], *s.* brujo, nigromante.

connate [connéit], *a.* congénito; innato; (bot.) connato.

connation [-shʊn], *s.* calidad de connato; unión congénita.

connatural [connǽchural], *c.* connatural.

connaturality [-réliti], **connaturalness** [-nǽchuralnes], *s.* connaturalidad.—**connaturally** [-nǽchura'¹l], *ʌdv.* connaturalmente.

connect [conéct]. **I.** *va.* juntar, unir; relacionar; coordinar; aparear, reunir; (mec.) conectar, acoplar; (elec.) conectar. **II.** *vn.* unirse, juntarse; relacionarse; enlazarse, encadenarse;

connected [-ed], *a.* unido, conexo; relacionado; encadenado, hilado; asociado; emparentado.— **to be c. with (a firm,** etc.), estar asociado con (una casa, etc.); estar con o empleado por (una casa, etc.).—**connectedly** [-li]. *adv.* coherentemente; con ilación.

connecting [-ing], *a.* que une, conecta, etc.; de unión, conexión, etc.; comunicante, comunicado. —**c. cell** (bot.) heterociste.—**c. link,** (m. v.) sector (de la excéntrica).—**c. rod,** (m. v.) biela.

connection [conécshʊn], *s.* conexión; unión o enlace; encadenamiento, ilación, coherencia; relación; parentesco; asociación, filiación; pariente; coito; (mec.) acoplamiento, junta, unión; (elec.) conexión.—**in c. with,** con respecto a, hablando de, a propósito de.—**in this c.,** con respecto a esto, a propósito.

connective [-tiv]. **I.** *a.* conexivo, conjuntivo. **II.** *s.* (bot.) conectivo; (gram.) palabra conjuntiva (conjunción, preposición, relativo).— **c. tissue,** (anat.) tejido conjuntivo.

connectively [-li], *adv.* conjuntamente, unidamente.

connector [conéctœr], *s.* conector.

conner [cóncr], *s.* inspector; observador; (mar.) oficial de derrota; (ict.) esparo, crenilabro.

connexion, *s.* = CONNECTION.

conning tower [cóning táuœr], *s.* timonera blindada.

conniption [conípshʊn], *s.* (E. U.) pataleta, histerismo.

connivance [connáivans], *s.* connivencia, consentimiento.—**connive** [connáiv], *vn.* tolerar, disimular, hacer la vista gorda.—**conniver** [-œr], *s.* cómplice; consentidor.

connoisseur [conisúœr], *s.* perito, conocedor.

connotate [cónnotet], *va.* connotar.

connotation [-téishʊn], *s.* connotación.

connote [connót], *va.* connotar.

connubial [connúbial], *a.* conyugal, connubial.

connumeration [conniumœréshʊn], *s.* connumeración.

conoid [cónoid], *s.* (geom.) conoide.—**conoidal** [conóidal], **conoidic** [-ic], *a.* conoidal.

---

conquer [cónkœr]. **I.** *va.* conquistar; vencer, superar. **II.** *vn.* triunfar.—**conquerable** [-abœl], *a.* vencible, conquistable, domable.—**conqueress** [-es], *s.* conquistadora.—**conquering** [-ing], *a.* victorioso; conquistador.

conqueror [cónkœror], *s.* conquistador; vencedor.

conquest [cóncuest], *s.* conquista.—**the C.** (hist.) la conquista de Inglaterra por Guillermo el Conquistador.

consanguineous [consængüínius], *a.* consanguíneo.

consanguinity [-niti], *s.* consanguinidad.

conscience [cónshens], *s.* conciencia (moral).— **c. clause,** cláusula de conciencia, cláusula de una ley que exime de observarla a aquellos a quienes su conciencia (sobre todo en materias religiosas) no se lo permita.

conscienced [cónshenst], *a.* concienzudo.

conscienceless [cónshensles], *a.* desalmado, sin conciencia.

conscientious [conshién̄shus], *a.* concienzudo, escrupuloso.—**c. objector,** pacifista por conciencia; refractario por conciencia (apl. esp. al que rehusa servir de soldado por dictarle su conciencia que la guerra es una acción inmoral).—**conscientiously** [-li], *adv.* escrupulosamente.—**conscientiousness** [-nes], *s.* rectitud, equidad; escrupulosidad.

conscionable [cónshʊnabœl], *a.* justo, razonable.

conscionably [-bli], *adv.* en conciencia, razonablemente.

conscious [cónshus], *a.* consciente.

consciously [-li], *adv.* conscientemente, con conocimiento, a sabiendas.—**consciousness** [-nes], *s.* conocimiento, sentido; (psicol.) consciencia (de sí mismo), estado consciente.

conscript [cónscript], *a.* conscripto.—*s.* conscripto, recluta, quinto.

conscript [conscrípt], *va.* reclutar.

conscription [conscrípshʊn], *s.* reclutamiento, quinta, alistamiento.

consecrate [cónsecret]. **I.** *va.* consagrar, santificar; ungir; dedicar, ofrecer; canonizar. **II.** *a.* (poét.) consagrado.—**consecration** [-créishʊn], *s.* consagración; dedicación; canonización.—**consecrator** [-créitœr], *s.* consagrante, consagrador.

consecutive [consékiutiv], *s.* consecutivo; sucesivo.—**consecutively** [-li], *adv.* consecutivamente.

consensual [consénshual], *a.* (for.) consensual; (fisiol.) excitado por medio de acción simpática o refleja.

consensus [consénsus], *s.* conseaso; acuerdo general; (fisiol.) simpatía.—**c. of opinion,** opinión general.

consent [consént]. **I.** *s.* consentimiento, anuencia, permiso, beneplácito. **II.** *vn.* consentir, condescender; avenirse.

consenter [conséntœr], *s.* consentidor.

consentient [consén̄shent], *a.* anuente, consentiente.

consequence [cónsecuens], *s.* consecuencia; importancia.

consequent [cónsecuent]. **I.** *a.* consecuente, consiguiente, lógico.—**c. points, o poles,** (magn.) polos consecuentes o intermedios. **II.** *s.* (lóg.) consiguiente; (mat.) consecuente.

consequential [consecuén̄shal], *a.* fachendista; consiguiente; importante.—**consequentially** [-li], *adv.* con fachenda.—**consequentialness** [-nes], *s.* fachenda, engreimiento.

consequently [cónsecuentli], *adv.* por lo tanto, por consiguiente, en consecuencia.

conservable [consérvabœl], *a.* conservable.

conservancy [consérvansi], *s.* conservación; junta para la conservación y fomento de viveros y pesquerías.

conservant [consérvænt], *a.* conservador, preservador.

conservation [consérvéishʊn], *s.* conservación, preservación.—**c. of energy, of force** (fís.) conservación de la energía, de la fuerza.

conservatism [consérvætiêm], *s.* conservatismo.

conservative [-tiv]. **I.** *s.* conservador. **II.** *a.* preservativo; conservador; moderado.

---

conservator [cónsœrvéitor], *s.* conservador; defensor, protector.
conservatory [consérvatori]. **I.** *a.* conservatorio. **II.** *s.* invernáculo, invernadero; conservatorio, academia.
conservatrix [cónsœrvetrics], *s.* conservadora.
conserve [consérv], *va.* conservar, preservar; hacer conserva.
conserve [cónsœrv], *s.* conserva, dulce; (farm.) confección.
conserver [consérvœr], *s.* conservador; conservero.
consider [consídœr]. **I.** *va.* considerar, pensar, examinar; distinguir, tratar con respeto; creer, opinar; remunerar. **II.** *vn.* pensar, reflexionar, deliberar.
considerable [-abœl], *a.* considerable.—**considerableness** [-nes], *s.* importancia, entidad, valor.—**considerably** [-bli], *adv.* considerablemente, grandemente.
considerate [consídœret], *a.* considerado.
considerately [-li], *adv.* consideradamente.
considerateness [-nes], *s.* consideración; circunspección, moderación.
consideration [consídœréshʊn], *s.* consideración; deliberación; entidad, importancia; retribución, retorno, remuneración.
considering [consídœring], *prep.* en atención a, considerando, visto que.—**consideringly** [-li], *adv.* seriamente, atinadamente.
consign [consáin], *va.* confiar, traspasar; relegar; (com.) consignar.
consignation [cónsignéshʊn], *s.* consignación.
consignatory [consígnatori], *s.* confirmante.
consignee [consainí], *s.* consignatario; depositario.
consigner, *s.* = CONSIGNOR.
consignment [consáinment], *s.* (com.) consignación, partida.
consignor [consinór, consáinœr], *s.* consignador.
consist [consíst], *vn.* consistir; subsistir; armonizar, ser compatible.—**to c. of,** constar de, componerse de.
consistence, consistency [consístens, i], *s.* consistencia; correspondencia, compatibilidad, conveniencia; permanencia, estabilidad.
consistent [consístent], *a.* consecuente, compatible; consistente, denso.
consistently [-li], *adv.* conformemente; consecuentemente; firmemente.
consistorial [cónsistórial], *a.* consistorial.
consistory [consístori], *s.* consistorio; asamblea, junta, congreso.
consociate [consóshiet]. **I.** *vn.* asociar, congregar. **II.** *vn.* asociarse, congregarse. **III.** *a.* asociado.—**consociation** [-éishʊn], *s.* alianza o liga; asociación, sociedad.
consolable [consóulabœl], *a.* consolable.
consolation [cónsoléshʊn], *s.* consolación, consuelo, alivio, confortación.
consolatory [consólatori], *s.* consolativo.—*pl.* discurso o escrito consolatorio.
console [consóul], *va.* consolar; confortar.
console [cónsol], *s.* consola; mesa o tabla sostenida por cartelas (ll. t. **c. table**); (arq.) cartela.
consoler [consólœr], *s.* consolador.
consolidant [consólidant], *s.* consolidativo.
consolidate [consólidet]. **I.** *va.* consolidar; solidar, unir. **II.** *vn.* consolidarse, endurecerse.—**c. annuities,** *v.* CONSOLS.
consolidation [consolidéshʊn], *s.* consolidación, unión, conjunción.
consolidative [consólidetiv], *a.* consolidativo.
consoling [consóuling], *a.* consolador.
consols [cónsolš], *s. pl.* (Ingl.) títulos de la deuda consolidada.
consommé [consomé], *s.* consumado, caldo.
consonance [cónsonans], **consonancy** [-i], *s.* consonancia.
consonant [cónsonant]. **I.** *a.* consonante, cónsono. **II.** *s.* (gram.) consonante.

consonantal [cónsonéntal], *a.* perteneciente a las consonantes.—**consonantly** [-li], *adv.* conformemente, consonantemente.—**consonantness** [-nes], *s.* consonancia, conformidad.
consort [cónsort], *s.* consorte; compañía, compañerismo.
consort [consórt]. **I.** *vn.* asociarse, acompañarse, ir (con). **II.** *va.* casar, juntar, asociar.
consortism [cónsortišm], *s.* (biol.) simbrosis.
consortium [consórtium], *s.* consorcio comercial o financiero (apl. esp. a la asociación de bancos).
conspectus [conspéctʊs], *s.* ojeada, vista general; sumario, digesto.
conspicuity [conspikiúiti], **conspicuousness** [conspíkiuʊsnes], *s.* claridad, visibilidad; evidencia; fama, nombradía.—**conspicuous** [conspíkiuʊs], *a.* conspicuo, visible.—**conspicuously** [-li], *adv.* visiblemente, claramente.
conspiracy [conspírasi], *s.* conspiración.
conspirant [conspáirant], *a.* conspirante.
conspirator [conspíratœr], *s.* conspirador.
conspire [conspáiœr]. **I.** *vn.* conspirar; concurrir, juntarse. **II.** *va.* tramar, urdir; preparar.
conspirer [conspáirœr], *s.* conspirador.
conspiringly [conspáiringli], *adv.* conspirando, criminalmente.
constable [cœnstabœl], *s.* condestable, alguacil, ministril.—**constableship** [-ship], *s.* condestablía.
constabulary [constábiuleri]. **I.** *a* perteneciente a los alguaciles. **II.** *s.* cuadrilla de alguaciles; guardia civil.
constancy [cónstansi], *s.* constancia.
constant [cónstant]. **I.** *a.* constante. **II.** *s. y a.* (mat.) constante.
constantly [-li], *adv.* constantemente.
constellation [cónsteléishʊn], *s.* (astr.) constelación, pléyade.
consternation [constœrnéishʊn], *s.* consternación.
constipate [cónstipeit], *va.* estreñir; cerrar, tupir, obstruir.—**constipation** [-éishʊn], *s.* (med.) estreñimiento de vientre, constipación.
constituency [constítuensi], *s.* (pol.) distrito electoral; grupo de comitentes.
constituent [constítuent]. **I.** *s.* elemento, ingrediente o componente; hacedor o autor; (pol.) elector; (for.) poderdante. **II.** *a.* constitutivo; constituyente (asamblea, etc.); elector.
constitute [cónstitiut], *va.* constituir, formar; nombrar, diputar; hacer, dar poder a; establecer, dar, ejecutar (una ley, etc.).
constitution [constitiúshʊn], *s.* constitución; (for.) ley, estatutos; decreto.
constitutional [-æl]. **I.** *a.* constitucional; complexional.—**c. law,** derecho constitucional o político; constitución, ley orgánica. **II.** *s.* (fam.) caminata, paseo.
constitutionalism [-išm], *s.* (pol.) constitucionalismo.—**constitutionalist** [-ist], *s.* constitucional.—**constitutionality** [-nǽliti], *s.* constitucionalidad, conformidad con la constitución.—**constitutionally** [-tiúshʊnǽli], *adv.* constitucionalmente, legalmente.
constitutive [cónstitiutiv], *a.* constitutivo; legislativo.
constrain [constréin], *va.* constreñir, compeler, obligar, forzar; restringir, impedir, detener; estrechar, comprimir, apretar.
constrainable [-abœl], *a.* constreñible.
constrainedly [constréinedli], *adv.* constreñidamente; por fuerza.
constrainer [constréinœr], *s.* el que obliga.
constraint [constréint], *s.* constreñimiento, coacción, compulsión; coartación, represión.
constrict [constríct], *va.* apretar, estrechar, ligar.
constriction [constríkshʊn], *s.* constricción, contracción, encogimiento.
constrictive [constríctiv], *a.* constrictivo.
constrictor [constríctœr], *s.* constrictor; (zool.) boa constrictor.
constringe [constríny], *va.* constreñir, comprimir, estrechar, ligar.

constringent [con̂strínyent], _a._ constrictivo, constringente.

construct [constrúct], _va._ construir; fabricar; proyectar, idear, inventar, componer.

construct [cónstrúct], _s._ frase gramatical; percepción.

constructer, constructor [-œr], _s._ constructor.

construction [constrúcŝhun̄], _s._ construcción; estructura, obra, fabricación; interpretación, explicación, sentido; (gram.) construcción.

constructional [-æl], _a._ referente a la construcción o a la interpretación.

constructive [constrúctiv], _a._ constructivo; tácito, sobreentendido; afirmativo.

constructively [-li], _adv._ constructivamente; por inducción.—**constructiveness** [-nes], _s._ constructividad; ingeniosidad, aptitud mecánica.

construe [cónstru], _va._ construir, interpretar, explicar.

consubstantial [cónsubstǽnŝhal], _a._ consubstancial, coesencial.—**consubstantiality** [-ŝhiǽliti], _s._ consubstancialidad.

consubstantiate [-ŝhieit], _va._ unir en una misma substancia o naturaleza.

consubstantiation [-ŝhiéiŝhun̄], _s._ consubstanciación.

consuetude [cónsuetiud], _s._ costumbre.

consuetudinary]cónsuetiúdineri], _a._ consuetudinario.

consul [cónsul], _s._ cónsul.—**c. general**, cónsul general.

consular [cónsular], _a._ consular.—**c. agent**, agente consular.—**c. invoice**, factura consular.

consulate [cónsulet], _s._ consulado.—**c. general**, consulado general.

consulship [cónsulŝhip], _s._ consulado (dignidad o puesto).

consult [consúlt], **I.** _va._ consultar; considerar, estudiar, examinar. **II.** _vn._ consultarse, asesorarse. **III.** _s._ (ant.) consulta.

consultant [consúltant], _a._ y _s._ consultante.

consultation [consvltéŝhun̄], _s._ consulta, junta; deliberación.

consultative [consúltætiv], **consultatory** [-tori], _a._ consultivo.—**consulter** [-tœr], _s._ consultor, consultante.—**consulting** [-ting], _a._ consultor.

consumable [consiúmabœl], _a._ consumible.

consume [consiúm]. **I.** _va._ consumir. **II.** _vn._ consumirse.—**consumer** [-œr], _s._ consumidor; disipador, destructor.

consummate [cónsumet]. **I.** _va._ consumar, acabar, completar. **II.** _a._ consumado, cabal, completo.—**consummately** [-li], _adv._ consumadamente.—**consummation** [-suméiŝhun̄], _s._ consumación, acabamiento.

consumption [consúmpŝhun̄], _s._ consunción, extinción; (e. p.) consumo; (med.) consunción, tisis.

consumptive [-tiv]. **I.** _a._ consuntivo; relativo a la tisis; de tisis; de tísicos. **II.** _s._ y _a._ (med.) tísico.—**consumptively** [-li], _adv._ consuntivamente.—**consumptiveness** [-nes], _s._ consunción.

contabescence [contabésens], _s._ (med.) tabes, marasmo, atrofia.

contact [cóntæct], _s._ contacto; relaciones.

contagion [contéyun], _s._ cóntagio; virus; contaminación.

contagious [contéyus], _a._ contagioso.

contagiousness [-nes], _s._ carácter contagioso.

contagium [-yum], _s._ (med.) virus.

contain [contéin]. **I.** _va._ contener, tener cabida para; abarcar, incluir; encerrar; (mat.) ser exactamente divisible. **II.** _vn._ contenerse, refrenarse.—**containable** [-abœl], _a._ contenible.

contaminate [contǽminet], _vn._ contaminar, corromper; contagiar o inficionar; depravar, pervertir.

contamination [-éiŝhun̄], _s._ contaminación.

contemn [contém], _va._ despreciar, menospreciar. —**contemner** [-nœr], _s._ despreciador, menospreciador.

contemplate [cóntempleit]. **I.** _va._ contemplar, estudiar, meditar; proyectar, tener la intención de. **II.** _vn._ meditar, reflexionar.—**contemplation** [-éiŝhun̄], _s._ contemplación, meditación; proyecto; expectación.

contemplative [contémplativ], _a._ contemplativo.

contemplatively [-li], _adv._ con atención y cuidado; contemplativamente.

contemplator [cóntempléitœr], _s._ contemplador.

contemporariness [contémporerines], **contemporaneousness** [-réneusnes], _s._ calidad de contemporáneo.—**contemporaneous** [-réneus], _a._ contemporáneo.—**contemporaneously** [-li], _adv._ contemporáneamente.—**contemporary** [-oreri]. **I.** _a._ y _s._ contemporáneo, coetáneo. **II.** _s._ colega (apl. a periódicos).

contempt [contémpt], _s._ desprecio, menosprecio. —**c. of court**, (for.) contumacia; rebeldía.

contemptibility [-tibíliti], **contemptibleness** [-tibœlnes], _s._ vileza, bajeza.

contemptible [-tibœl], _a._ despreciable.

contemptibly [-blii], _adv._ vilmente.

contemptuous [contémpchuus], _a._ desdeñoso, despreciativo.—**contemptuously** [-li], _adv._ desdeñiosamente, con menosprecio.—**contemptuousness** [-nes], _s._ desdén, desprecio, altanería.

contend [conténd]. **I.** _va._ sostener o afirmai. **II.** _vn._ contender, disputar; competir, lidiar, altercar.—**contending parties**, partes contenciosas o litigantes.

contendent, contender [-ent, -œr], _s._ contendedor, competidor.

content [contént]. **I.** _a._ contento, satisfecho.— **c. o not c.**, (Ingl.) voto en pro o en contra. **II.** _va_ contentar, satisfacer. **III.** _s._ contento, contentamiento, satisfacción.

content [cóntent], _s._ cantidad, proporción; (gen. _pl._) contenido; cabida, capacidad; área; volumen.

contented [conténted], _a._ contento, satisfecho resignado.—**contentedly** [-li], _adv._ tranquilamente, contentamente.—**contentedness** [-nes], _s._ contento, satisfacción.

contention [conténŝhun̄], _s._ contención, contienda, disputa; tema; pretensión; lo que se pretende o sostiene; argumento.

contentious [conténŝhus], _a._ contencioso, litigioso o disputador.—**contentiously** [-li], _adv._ contenciosamente.—**contentiousness** [-nes], _s._ espíritu de contradicción.

contentment [conténtment], _s._ contentamiento, contento, satisfacción.

conterminal [contœrminal], o **conterminous** [-nus], _a._ contérmino, vecino, limítrofe; coextensivo.

contest [contést]. **I.** _va._ contender; disputar; discutir. **II.** _vn._ competir.

contest [cóntest], _s._ contienda, debate; pugna, lid, torneo; concurso, oposición.

contestable [contéstabœl], _a._ contestable.

contestant [-tænt], _s._ contendiente, litigante.

context [cóntext], _s._ contexto, contenido; contextura.

contextual [contéxtiual], _a._ relativo al contexto.

contextural [contéxchural], _a._ perteneciente a la contextura.

contexture [contéxchur], _s._ contextura; entretejido, enlazamiento.

contiguity [cóntiguiúiti], _s._ contigüidad, inmediación; continuidad.

contiguous [contíguiuus], _a._ contiguo.

contiguously [-li], _adv._ contiguamente, junto al lado.—**contiguousness** [-nes], _s._ contigüidad.

continence [cóntinens], o **continency** [-si], _s._ continencia, templanza.

continent [-ent]. **I.** _a._ continente, moderado. **II.** _s._ (geog.) continente.—**the C.**, la Europa continental (en que se excluyen las Islas Británicas).

continental [cóntinéntæl], _a._ continental; de la Europa continental.

contingence, contingency [contínyens, -si], _s._ contingencia, eventualidad.

contingent [-ent]. **I.** *a.* contingente, eventual. **II.** *s.* contingencia, casualidad; contingente, cuota.—**contingently** [-li], *adv.* contingentemente.

continual [contíniual], *a.* continuo, incesante.

continually [-i], *adv.* continuamente.

continuance [-æns], *s.* continuación; persistencia; prolongación; (for.) aplazamiento.

continuation [contíniuéishun], *s.* continuación; prolongación.—**continuator** [-éitœr], **continuer** [contíniuœr], *s.* continuador.

continue [contíniu], *va.* y *vn.* continuar.

continued [contíniud], *a.* continuo, continuado, prolongado.—**c. fraction**, (mat.) fracción continua.—**to be c.**, continuará.

continuedly [-li], *adv.* continuadamente.

continuity [continiúiti], *s.* continuidad; drama o adaptación para cinematógrafo.

continuous [contíniuus], *a.* continuo, sin solución de continuidad (ú, esp. en mat.).—**continuously** [-li], *adv.* continuamente.

continuum [contíniuum], *s.* continuo, cosa continua (en el sentido matemático).

conto [cóntou], *s.* conto (moneda portuguesa y del Brasil).

contort [contórt], *va.* torcer, retorcer.

contortion [-shun], *s.* contorsión.

contortionist [-ist], *s.* contorsionista.

contour [contúr], *s.* contorno; (top.) curva de nivel.

contraband [cóntrabænd]. **I.** *s.* contrabando. **II.** *a.* prohibido, ilegal.—**contrabandism** [-ism], *s.* contrabando, matute.—**contrabandist** [-ist], *s.* contrabandista.

contrabass [cóntrabes], *s.* contrabajo

contraception [cóntrasépshun], *s.* prevención de la preñez, esterilidad voluntaria.

contract [contrǽct]. **I.** *va.* contraer, reducir, apretar; fruncir, arrugar; abreviar, compendiar; contraer (una enfermedad, una deuda, esponsales); opilarse; **comprometerse** por contrato. **II.** *vn.* contraerse, encogerse; opilarse; comprometerse por contrato.

contract [cóntrǽct]. **I.** *s.* contrato; escritura; esponsales; contrata, escritura. **II.** *a.* contraído, abreviado.

contracted [contrǽcted], *a.* contraído; fruncido; estrecho; escaso.—**contractedly** [-li], *adv.* estrechamente, de manera mezquina.—**contractedness** [-nes], *s.* contracción; estrechez; mezquindad.

contractility [contrǽctíliti], *s.* contractilidad.

contractile [contrǽctil], *a.* contráctil.

contracting [contrǽcting], *a.* contrayente; contratante.

contraction [-shun], *s.* contracción; abreviación.

contractor [-tœr], *s.* contratista, asentista.

contractual [contrǽcchuæl], *a.* contractual, relativo a contratos; de o por contrato.

contradance [cóntrædæns], *s.* contradanza.

contradict [cóntradíct], *va.* contradecir, negar; repugnar, oponerse, contrariar.

contradicter [-díctœr], *s.* contradictor.

contradiction [-díshun], *s.* contradicción; renuncio.

contradictorily [-díctorili], *adv.* contradictoriamente.

contradictoriness [-díctorines], *s.* espíritu de contradicción; calidad de contradictorio.

contradictory [-díctori]. **I.** *a.* contradictorio; contrario, opuesto. **II.** *s.* (lóg.) contradictoria.

contradistinct [-distínct], *a.* opuestamente distinto.

contradistinction [-distíncshun], *s.* distinción por calidades opuestas; distinción.—**in c. to**, o **with**, a distinción de, a diferencia de, en contraste con.

contradistinguish [-distíngüish], *va.* distinguir por calidades opuestas.

contrafissure [-físhuœr], *s.* (cir.) contraabertura.

contraflexure [-flécshuœr], *s.* (mec.) inflexión (de una viga).

contraindicant [-índicant], **contraindication** [-índikéshun], *s.* (med.) contraindicante, contraindicación.

contraindicate [-índiket], *va.* contraindicar.

contralto [contrǽlto], *s.* y *a.* (mús.) contralto; de contralto.

contraplex [cóntraplex], *a.* (tlg.) de transmisión simultánea en direcciones opuestas.

contraposition [-poshíshun], *s.* contraposición.

contrapunto [cóntrapúnto], *s.* (mús.) contrapunto.

contrariety [-áieti], *s.* contrariedad; oposición.

contrarily [cóntrarili], *adv.* contrariamente, opuestamente.—**contrariness** [-nes], *s.* contrariedad, oposición; testarudez.—**contrariwise** [-uais], *adv.* al contrario, al revés, inversamente.

contrary [cóntrari]. **I.** *a.* contrario; adverso; contradictorio; divergente. **II.** *s.* contrario; contraria.—**on the c.**, al contrario, por el contrario.—**to the c.**, en contrario.

contrast [cóntrast], *s.* contraste.

contrast [contrást], *va.* y *vn.* contrastar.

contravallation [cóntravæléishun], *s.* (fort.) contravalación.

contravene [cóntravín], *va.* contravenir.

contravener [-œr], *s.* contraventor, infractor.

contravention [-vénshun], *s.* contravención o infracción.

contredance [cóntrœdæns], *s.* contradanza.

contribute [contríbiut], *va.* y *vn.* contribuir, cooperar, concurrir; colaborar.

contribution [cóntribiúshun], *s.* cooperación; contribución; cuota, dádiva; colaboración; artículo, escrito (con que se colabora).

contributive [contríbiutiv], **contributory** [-tori], *a.* cooperante o contribuyente.

contributor [contríbiutœr], *s.* contribuidor, contribuyente; colaborador.

contrite [cóntrait], *a.* contrito.—**contritely** [-li], *adv.* contritamente.—**contriteness**, o **contrition** [-nes, contríshun], *s.* contrición.

contrivance [contráivans], *s.* idea, plan, invención; utensilio, aparato, artefacto; traza, ingenio, artificio; estratagema.

contrive [contráiv]. **I.** *va.* idear, inventar, ingeniar, arbitrar; tramar, urdir. **II.** *vn.* darse maña, buscar un medio, maquinar.

contriver [contráivœr], *s.* autor, inventor, autor.

control [contróul]. **I.** *s.* mando, dirección, dominio; inspección, intervención; restricción, freno; contrarregistro, regulador (mec., aut.) mando, gobierno; aparato de mando o de gobierno; (fís.) factor, causa, agente; (aer.) estación de aterrizaje transitorio, estación de auxilio.—**c. experiment**, experimento de eliminación, en que se omiten ciertos elementos o circunstancias cuya influencia se trata de estudiar. (*V.* BLANK ANALYSIS).—**c. column**, (aer.)=C. STICK.—**c. gear**, (aut.) mecanismo de mando.—**c. lever**, palanca de mando.—**c. stick**, (aer.) palanca de mando o de gobierno. **II.** *va.* dominar, dirigir, gobernar; tener a raya; tener predominancia en; intervenir; reprimir, restringir.—**controlling** [-ing], *a.* que manda, que gobierna; decisivo, determinante; predominante.—**c. interest**, (com.) mayoría, interés predominante.

controllable [-abœl], *a.* gobernable, dominable, manejable.

controller [contrólœr], *s.* interventor, contralor; director, superintendente, inspector; regulador; (fís.) factor, causa, agente; (mar.) retén de cadena; (elec.) combinador (de coche eléctrico).— **C. of the Currency** [E. U.] interventor de los bancos nacionales.

controllership [-ship], *s.* oficio y oficina de **controller.**

controlment [-mœnt], *s.* restricción, sujeción; superintendencia, inspección.

controversial [cóntrovœrshal], *a.* polemístico, contencioso.—**controversialist** [-ist], *s.* polemista.

controversy [cóntrovœrsi], *s.* controversia, disputa, debate, polémica.—**controvert** [-vœrt], *va.* controvertir, disputar.—**controverter** [-œr], *s.* controversista, argumentador, polemista.—**controvertible** [-vœrtibœl], *a.* controvertible, disputable, discutible.

contumacious [contiuméshus], a. contumaz, rebelde, tenaz.—**contumaciously** [-li], adv. contumazmente.—**contumaciousness** [-nes], **contumacy** [cóntiumesi], s. contumacia, terquedad.

contumelious [contiumílius], a. contumelioso, injurioso, ofensivo.—**contumeliously** [-li], adv. contumeliosamente.—**contumeliousness** [-nes], **contumely** [cóntiumeli], s. contumelia, ultraje, injuria.

contuse [contiús], va. contundir.

contusion [contiúyun], s. contusión.

conundrum [conúndrum], s. acertijo, adivinanza.

convalescence, convalescency [cónvalésens, i], s. convalecencia.

convalescent [-ent], a. convaleciente.

convection [convécshun], s. difusión del calor.

convene [convín]. I. va. convocar, citar; emplazar. II. vn. juntarse, reunirse.

convener [convíncer], s. convocador.

convenience, conveniency [convínyens, i], s. conveniencia, comodidad, oportunidad.—**at one's c.**, a beneñácito de uno, cuando le sea cómodo.—**at one's earliest c.**, a la primera oportunidad que uno tenga, tan pronto como le sea posible.

convenient [-ent], a. conveniente, cómodo, útil, oportuno.—**conveniently** [-li], adv cómodamente; convenientemente.

convent [cónvent], s. convento.

conventicle [convénticœl], s. conventículo, conciliábulo.

convention [convénshun], s. convención, asamblea, congreso, junta; convenio.

conventional [-al], a. convencional; estipulado; convenido.

conventionalism [-lism], s. respeto a las costumbres.

conventionality [convénshunæliti], s. regla impuesta por la costumbre.

conventionally [convénshunali], adv. convencionalmente.

conventual [convénchual], a. y s. conventual.

converge [convéry], vn. converger.

convergence, convergency [convérryens, yensi], s. convergencia.

convergent [convéryent], **converging** [-ying], a. convergente.

conversable [convérsabœl], a. conversable; sociable.—**conversableness** [-nes], s. sociabilidad. —**conversably** [-abli], adv. sociablemente, afablemente.

conversant [convérsant], a. (gen. seguido de with) versado, experimentado, experto (en) ocupado (en).

conversation [convœrséshun], s. conversación, plática, conferencia; trato carnal.

conversational [-al], a. perteneciente a la conversación; de conversación.

conversationalist [-alist], s. el que conversa.

converse [convérs], vn. conversar; platicar; departir, tener trato.

converse [cónvœrs]. I. s. conversación, plática; familiaridad, trato; (mat., lóg.) recíproca. II. a. traspuesto, inverso; (mat., lóg.) recíproco.— **conversely** [-li], adv. a la inversa, recíprocamente.

conversible [convérsibœl], a. convertible.

conversion [convérshun], s. conversión, transformación; mudanza; (mil.) conversión; (for.) apropiación ilícita de los bienes de otro para uso propio.

conversive [convérsiv], a. conversivo.

convert [convért]. I. va. convertir; transmutar, transformar, cambiar; (fund.) convertir, reducir; (com.) convertir o cambiar (valores). II. vn. convertirse, mudar.

convert [cónvœrt], s. neófito, converso.

converter, convertor [convértœr], s. (lenguaje común, fund., elec.) convertidor.

convertibility [-tibíliti], s. convertibilidad.

convertible [-ibœl], a. convertible; (aut.) transformable (de cerrado en abierto y recíprocamente).—**convertibly** [-tibli], adv. recíproca o mutuamente.

convex [cónvecs]. I. a. convexo. II. s. convexidad.

convexed [convécst], a. convexo.

convexity [convécsiti], **convexness** [convécsnes], s. convexidad.

convexly [convécsli], adv. convexamente.

convey [convéi], va. transportar, llevar; transmitir; enviar; transferir, traspasar; comunicar; causar, dar (a entender).

conveyable [-abœl], a. conductible.

conveyance [convéians], s. conducción, transporte; conducta; vehículo; entrega, cesión, traspaso, traslación de dominio; escritura de traspaso.

conveyancer [-sœr], s. escribano que hace escrituras de traspaso.—**conveyancing** [-ing], s. oficio de preparar escrituras de traspaso.

conveyer, conveyor [convéicœr], s. conductor, mensajero; portador; cedente; (mec.) transportador.

convict [convíct], va. (for.) condenar; convencer de culpa o delito.

convict [cónvict], s. reo convicto; penado, presidiario.—**c. system**, sistema penal.

convictible [convíctibœl], a. a quien se le puede probar un crimen.

conviction [convícshun], s. convicción, convencimiento; (for.) convicción, prueba y fallo de culpabilidad.

convince [convíns], va. convencer, persuadir.

convincible [-ibœl], a. convencible, que puede convencerse; convincente.

convincing [-ing], a. convincente.

convincingly [-li], adv. convincentemente.

convincingness [-nes], s. calidad de convincente.

convivial [convívial], a. convival.

conviviality [convívilæliti], s. jovialidad, buen humor.

convocation [convokéshun], s. convocación; asamblea.

convoke [convóuk], va. convocar.

convolute, convoluted [cónvolut, o liut, ted]. I. a. convoluto. II. s. enroscadura.

convolution [cónvolúshun], s. repliegue, pliegue; enroscadura; (anat.) circunvolución (cerebral).

convolve [convólv]. I. va. arrollar, enrollar, retorcer. II. va. retorcerse, enroscarse.

convolvulaceous [convólviuléshus], a. (bot.) convolvuláceo.

convolvulus [convólviulus], s. convólvulo.

convoy [convói], va. convoyar.

convoy [cónvoi], s. convoy, conducta; (mar.) conserva.

convulse [convúls], va. dar convulsiones, crispar. —**to be convulsed with laughter**, morirse de risa. II. vr. crisparse.

convulsion [convúlshun], s. convulsión, espasmo; conmoción; (geol.) cataclismo.

convulsionary [convúlshuneri], **convulsive** [convúlsiv], a. convulsivo, espasmódico.

convulsively [convúlsivli], adv. convulsivamente.

cony [cóuni], s. gazapo, conejo.

coo [cu]. I. vn. arrullar; (fam.) pelar la pava. II. s. arrullo.

cooer [cúœr], s. paloma, tórtola; requebrador, cortejo.

cooing [cúing], s. arrullo; requiebro.

cook [cuk], va. y vn. cocinar; aderezar, falsear. —**to c. up**, tramar.

cook, s. cocinero, cocinera.

cookery [cúkœri], s. arte de cocina.

cooky [cúki], s. pequeño bollo dulce.

cool [cul]. I. a. fresco; tibio, indiferente.— **c.-headed**, sereno. II. s. frescura o fresco. III. va. enfriar, refrescar, entibiar, atemperar; calmar. —**to c. one's heels off**, (fam.) hacer antesala, esperar largo tiempo. IV. vn. refrescar, enfriarse, templarse, apaciguarse.

cooler [cúlœr], s. enfriadera, garapiñera; refrigerador; (med.) refrigerante.

coolie [cúli], s. peón chino o indio.
cooling [cúling], a. refrescante, refrigerativo; atemperante.
coolish [cúlish], a. fresco, fresquito.
coolly [cúli], adv. frescamente, serenamente, fríamente.
coolness [cúlnes], s. fresco; frialdad, tibieza; frescura, calma, serenidad.
coom [cum], s. hollín, pringue.
coon [cun], s. V. RACCOON; (E. U. fam.) negro.— **c. song**, canción de negros.—**c.'s age**, mucho tiempo.—**old c.**, viejo marrullero.
coop [cup]. I. s. caponera, gallinero; tonel o cuba. II. va. enjaular; encarcelar.
cooper [cúpœr]. I. va. hacer barriles. II. s. tonelero.
cooperage [-ey], **coopering** [-ing], s. tonelería.
cooperant [coópœrant], a. cooperante.
cooperate [-eit], vn. cooperar.
cooperation [-éishun], s. cooperación.
cooperative [-etiv], a. cooperativo; cooperante, coadyutorio.
cooperator [-éitœr], s. cooperador.
coordinate [coórdinet]. I. va. coordinar. II. s. igual, semejante; (mat.) coordenada. III. a. coordenado; (mat.) relativo a las coordenadas. —**c. axes**, (mat.) ejes de las coordenadas.—**c. geometry**, geometría analítica.
coordinately [-li], adv. coordinadamente.
coordinateness [-nes], **coordination** [-néshun], s. coordinación.
coot [cut], s. (orn.) negreta; (E. U.) especie de pato marino; (fam.) zopenco.
cop [cop], s. cima, cumbre; montón; rimero; rollo ahusado; tubo de enrollar (seda, etc.); (E. U. fam.) polizonte.
copaiba [copéiba], s. copaiba.
copal [cópal], s. copal (resina).
coparcenary [copárseneri], **coparceny** [copárseni], s. (for.) participación en una herencia de bienes raíces.
coparcener [copársenœr], s. (for.) coheredero.
copartner [copártnœr], s. copartícipe; socio.
copartnership [-ship], s. compañía, sociedad, asociación.
cope [cóup]. I. s. arco, bóveda, cúpula; (alb.) albardilla; (igl.) capa pluvia. II. vn. contender; (con with) hacer frente a, superar; rivalizar, competir. III. va. (alb.) poner albardilla o caballete; (igl.) poner la capa pluvial.
copeck [cóupec], s. copec (moneda rusa).
copepod [cóupipod], a. (zool.) copépodo.
Copepoda [coupépodæ], s. pl. (zool.) copépodos.
Copernican [copérnican], a. copernicano.
copestone [cóupstoun], s. (alb.) piedra de albardilla o caballete.
copier [cópiœr], s. copiante, copista; copiador, plagiario.
coping [cóuping], s. (alb.) albardilla.
copious [cópius], a. copioso; prolijo.
copiously [-li], adv. copiosamente.
copiousness [-nes], s. prolijidad, redundancia; profusión, copia.
coplanar [copléinær], a. en un mismo plano.
copped [copt], a. copado, copetudo.
copper [cópœr]. I. s. cobre; calderilla (moneda de cobre); vasija de cobre; lámina de cobre; grabado en cobre; penique norteamericano (en tiempos coloniales); (E. U.) centavo; (E. U., fam.) polizonte.—**c. barilla**, barrilla (cobre granular nativo arenoso).—**c.-bottomed**, de fondo de cobre.—**c.-fastened**, con tornillos, pernos, etc. de cobre.—**c. glance**, (min.) calcocita, sulfuro nativo de cobre.—**c. loss**, (elec.) pérdida en el cobre (en los conductores de cobre).— **c. money**, calderilla.—**c. pyrites**, pirita de cobre, calcopirita. II. a. de cobre; cobrizo (en color). III. va. revestir de cobre.
copperas [cóperas], s. caparrosa.
copperhead [cópœrjed], s. culebra norteamericana muy venenosa; (E. U. pol.) apodo que se daba durante la guerra civil al habitante

de los Estados del norte que simpatizaba con los confederados del sur.
copperish [cópœrish], **coppery** [cóperi], a. cobrizo, cobreño, encobrado.
copperplate [cópœrpleit]. I. s. lámina de cobre para grabar; grabado en cobre (llám. t. **c. engraving**). II. va. grabar en cobre.
coppersmith [cópœrsmiz], s. calderero.
copperworm [cópœrucerm], s. (ento.) broma, teredo; polilla, arador.
coppice [cópis], **coppice woods** [-uds], s. soto, tallar, maleza.
copra, s. (com.) almendra del coco puesta a secar, copra.
copræmia, o **copremia** [coprímiæ], s. (med.) copremia.
coprolite [cóprolait], **coprolith** [-liz], (pal. y pat.) coprolito.
coprophagous [coprófægus], a. coprófago.— **coprophagy** [-yi], s. coprofagia (costumbre o manía de comer excrementos).
coproprietor [copropráietor], s. copropietario.
copse [cops], s. matorral.
Coptic [cóptic]. I. a. cóptico. II. s. copto.
copula [cópiula], s. (gram.) cópula; (anat.) ligamiento.
copulate [cópiulet]. I. va. unir, juntar. II. vn. ayuntarse, copularse.
copulation [cópiuléshun], s. cópula o coito; unión, ayuntamiento.
copulative [cópiuletiv]. I. a. (gram.) copulativo, conjuntivo. II. s. (gram.) conjunción copulativa.
copulatory [cópiuletori], a. copulativo.
copy [cópi]. I. s. copia; ejemplar (de una obra), número (de un periódico); muestra o modelo, plana; (impr.) original, material, manuscrito.— **c. book**, copiador (de cuentas); cuaderno de escritura. II. va. y vn. copiar; imitar.
copygraph [cópigraf], s. hectógrafo.
copyhold [cópijóuld], s. (for.) especie de enfiteusis.
copyholder [cópijóuldœr], s. lector de pruebas (que lee al corrector); (der.) enfiteuta, arrendador, censualista.
copying [cópiing], a. de copiar; para copias.
copyist [cópist], s. = COPIER.
copyright [cópirrait]. I. s. propiedad literaria. II. va. hacer patentar o registrar como propiedad literaria.
coquet [cokét], va. y vn. coquetear, hacer cocos, requebrar, cortejar, galantear.
coquetry [cóketri], s. coqueteo; coquetería.
coquette [cokét], s. coqueta, carantoñera.
coquettish [cokétish], a. coquetón, coquetona.
coracle [córacœl], s. barquilla de cuero.
coracoid [córacoid], s. (anat.) coracoides.
coral [córal]. I. s. coral. II. a. coralino, de coral.
coralline [córalin]. I. a. coralino, de coral. II. s. coralina.
coralloid [córaloid], a. coralino.
corb [corb], s. (min.) barril de extracción.
corban [córban], s. (igl.) ofrenda, exvoto.
corbeil [córbel], s. (mil.) cestón.
corbel [córbel], **corbil** [córbil], s. (arq.) modillón, can, voladizo, repisa.
cord [córd]. I. s. cordel, cuerda, cordón; tendón; torzal; cordoncillo; (tej.) pana; cuerda (medida de leña).—**c. tire**, (aut.) neumático de cordones. II. va. encordelar; encordonar.
cordage [córdey], s. cordaje, cordelería.
cordate [córdet], a. cordiforme.
corded [córded], a. encordelado; acordonado, barrado, hecho de cuerdas.
corder [córdœr], s. encordonador.
cordial [córyal o córdial]. I. s. cordial, licor. II. a. sincero, cordial.
cordiality [cordiéliti], **cordialness** [córdialnes], s. cordialidad, sinceridad.—**cordially** [córdiali], adv. cordialmente.
cordite [córdait], s. cordita (explosivo).
cordon [córdon], s. cordón; cíngulo; (mil.) cordón; (arq.) bocel, cordón.

cordovan [córdovan], **cordwain** [córduein], s. cordobán.

corduroy [córdiuroi], s. (tej.) pana.—**c. road,** camino con piso de troncos.

cordwood [córdud], s. leña apilada o vendida en cuerdas (v. CORD), o de apilar en cuerdas.

core [cóær]. I. s. centro, corazón, alma; parte central; escencia, substancia; fondo (del corazón, fig.); núcleo; (ing.) cilindro de roca sacado con un taladro anular; pared central (de una presa, etc.); interior, núcleo de un terraplén; (fund.) macho o ánima (de molde); (elec.) núcleo (de bobina, etc.); alma (de cable); (vet.) enfermedad de las ovejas causada por gusanos en el hígado.—**c. bit, c. drill,** taladro o barrena tubular.—**c. hole,** abertura para el ánima (de un molde).—**c. iron,** (fund.) parrilla de refuerzo (del ánima).—**c. loss,** (elec.) pérdida en el núcleo.—**c. ratio,** (elec.) relación entre el diámetro del alma (de un cable) y el espesor del aislamiento.—**c. transformer,** (elec.) transformador de núcleo. II. va. quitar el corazón o centro (a menudo con out); despepitar; (fund.) formar con un macho.

cored [cord], a. que tiene gusanos en el hígado (apl. a las ovejas); de núcleo, con núcleo.

coregency [corríyensi], s. corregencia.

coregente [corríyent], s. corregente.

corer [córær], s. despepitador.

corespondent [córespóndent], s. (for.) cómplice del demandado en una demanda de divorcio.

coriaceous [coriéshus], a. coriáceo, correoso.

coriander [coriéndœr], s. (bot.) coriandro, culantro.

Corinthian [corínzian], a. (arq.) corinto; libidinoso.

cork [corc]. I. s. corcho; tapón.—**c. jacket,** salvavidas de corcho.—**c. oak, c. tree,** alcornoque —**c. squeezer,** prensacorchos. II. va. tapar con corcho; pintarse con corcho quemado.

corkage [córkœy], s. acción de tapar con corcho; estipendio que se exige por descorchar una botella (en realidad, recargo de precio por botella).

corkcutter [-cútœr], s. taponero.

corker [córkœr], s. (fam.) argumento irrefutable; cosa o persona extraordinaria, non plus ultra.

corkscrew [córkscru]. I. s. tirabuzon, sacacorchos. II. a. en forma de tirabuzón, en espiral.

corky [córki], a. de corcho, suberoso.

cormorant [córmorant], s. (orn.) corvejón; glotón o avaro.

corn [corn], s. grano, cereal; (E. U.) maíz; mies (no segada); callo (dureza en los pies).— **c. bread,** pan de maíz.—**c. crake,** (orn.) tiptoste. —**c. cutter,** máquina de cortar maíz; pedicuro, callista.—**c. field,** maizal.—**c. flag,** (bot.) estoque, espadilla.—**c. flour,** harina de maíz u otro grano. —**c. flower,** (bot.) aciano, coronilla.—**c. husk,** perfolla del maíz.—**c. land,** tierra de pan llevar.— **c. law,** ley de granos.—**c. meal,** harina de maíz. —**c. mill,** molino harinero.—**c. plaster,** emplasto para los callos.—**c. protector,** anillo adhesivo para los callos.—**c. shuck = c. HUSK.—**c. worm,** gusano del maíz.

corn, va. curar, salar, acecinar; granular.

Cornaceæ [cornéisii], s. (bot.) cornáceas.— **cornaceous** [-shus], a. (bot.) cornáceo.

cornchandler [córnchéndlœr], s. trigaero.

corncob [-cob], s. tusa de maíz.

corncrib [-crib], s. granero para maíz.

cornea [córnea], s. (anat.) córnea.

corned [cornd], a. acecinado.—**c. beef,** cecina.— **c. pork,** puerco salado.

cornel [córnel], s. cornalina.

cornelian [cornílien], s. cornelina.—**c. cherry, c. tree,** cornejo.

corniculate [corníkiulet], a. (bot.) corniculado.

corneous [córneus], a. córneo; calloso.

corner [córnœr]. I. s. esquina; esconce; rincón; recodo, escondrijo; aprieto o apuro; (E. U. com.) acaparamiento, monopolio.—**c. stone,** piedra angular; mocheta; primera piedra. II. va. arrinconar; acochinar; poner en aprieto; copar; (E. U. com.) monopolizar, acaparar.

cornered [córnœrd], a. angulado, esquinado; copado; en aprieto.

cornerwise [córnœruaiš], adv. diagonalmente.

cornet [córnet], s. (mil.) corneta; portaestandarte; (mús.) cornetín; cucurucho; (vet.) corona del casco.—**cornetcy** [-si], s. empleo y grado de portaestandarte.

cornettist [cornétist], s. cornetín (el que lo toca).

cornice [córnis], s. (arq.) cornisa; sobrepuerta.

cornicle [córnicœl], s. cuernecillo.

Cornish [córnish]. I. a. de Cornualles. II. s. dialecto de Cornualles.

cornstalk [córnstoc], s. tallo del maíz.

cornstarch [córnstarch], almidón de maíz, especialmente el purificado para la mesa.

cornucopia [córnucópia], s. cornucopia, cuerno de la abundancia; alcartaz, cucurucho.

cornute(d [cornút(ed], a. cornudo.

corny [córni], a. córneo; calloso.

corolla [coróla], s. (bot.) corola.

corollary [córoleri], s. corolario.

corona [coróna], s. (arq.) corona, alero; (art.) corona, halo; (biol.) coronilla; (elec.) fulguración, descarga luminosa de un conductor de diámetro inadecuado.—**c. loss,** (elec.) pérdida por fulguración, o por descargas luminosas.

coronal [córonal]. I. s. (anat.) coronal; corona, guirnalda. II. a. coronal.

coronary [córoneri], a. coronario.

coronation [córonéshun], s. coronación.

coroner [córonœr], s. pesquisidor del crimen; (Ingl.) administrador del patrimonio real.— **c.'s inquest,** pesquisa dirigida por el pesquisidor.

coronet [córonet], s. corona de un título nobiliario; guirnalda, cintillo; (vet.) corona del casco.

coronium [coróunium], s. (quím.) coronio.

corpora [córporæ], s. pl. (anat.) tubérculos, lóbulos.—**c. quadrigemina,** tubérculos cuadrigéminos.

corporal [córporal]. I. s. (mil.) cabo. II. a. corporal, corpóreo.—**corporality** [-céliti], s. corporalidad, corporeidad.—**corporally** [-ali], adv. corporalmente.

corporate [córporet], a. social; colectivo; incorporado.—**corporately** [-li], adv. corporalmente; en corporación.

corporation [córporéishun], s. corporación; sociedad mercantil (apl. esp. a las muy grandes); cabildo; cuerpo, sociedad, gremio.

corporeal [corpóreal], a. corpóreo, material, tangible.—**corporeally** [-li], adv. materialmente, corporalmente.

corporeity [corporíiti], s. corporeidad, materialidad.

corposant [córpošant], s. (mar.) fuego de Santelmo.

corps [cor], s. cuerpo, corps.—**c. de ballet,** cuerpo de baile.

corpse [corps], s. cadáver.

corpulence, corpulency [córpiulens, i], s. corpulencia.—**corpulent** [-lent], a. corpulento.

corpus [córpus], s. cuerpo; (anat.) lóbulo, tubérculo (for.) bienes tangibles, corporales.— **c. delicti;** cuerpo del delito.

corpuscle [córpuscœl], s. corpúsculo.

corpuscular [corpúskiular], a. corpuscular.

corradiate [corrédiet], va. concentrar los rayos de luz.

corral [corrél]. I. va. (E. U.) acorralar. II. s. corral.

correct [corréct]. I. va. corregir, rectificar; reprender, castigar; reparar, subsanar, remediar. II. a. correcto; exacto, justo; bueno, bien hecho; propio.

correctable, o **correctible** [-æbœl ibœl], a. corregible.

correction [corrécshun], s. corrección, rectificación; castigo, reforma; censura, pena.

correctional [-al]. I. a. penal. II. s. casa de corrección.

corrective [corréctiv]. I. a. correctivo, correccional, reformatorio. II. s. correctivo, castigo.

Para la pronunciación de æ, œ, D, š, šh, U, ȳ, Y, z, véase la clave al principio del libro.

correctly [corréctli], *adv.* correctamente; bien, apropiadamente.—**correctness** [-nes], *s.* corrección; exactitud; validez.

corrector [corréctœr], *s.* corrector, revisor, enmendador.

correlate [córrelet]. **I.** *va.* poner en correlación. **II.** *vn.* tener correlación.—**correlate, correlative** [corrélativ], *a.* y *s.* correlativo.—**correlation** [córreléišhun], *s.* correlación.

correlatively [corrélativli], *adv.* correlativamente.

correlativeness [-nes], *s.* correlación.

correspond [córrespónd], *vn.* y *vr.* corresponder, convenir, adaptarse; mantener correspondencia, escribirse.—**correspondence, correspondency** [-ens, -ensi], *s.* correspondencia; reciprocidad; (com.) correspondencia.—**correspondent** [-ent]. **I.** *a.* correspondiente, conforme, conveniente. **II.** *s.* correspondiente, corresponsal.—**correspondently** [-entli], *adv.* correspondientemente.

corresponding [córresponding], *a.* correspondiente; similar; conforme, congruente.—**c. secretary,** secretario correspondiente.

correspondingly [-li], *adv.* correspondientemente.

corridor [córridor], *s.* galería, pasillo, pasadizo; (fort.) galería; (geo.) paso, vía de salida; tira de tierra de una nación que atraviesa el territorio de otra.

corrigible [córriyibœl], *a.* corregible.

corrival [corráival], *a.* y *s.* émulo.

corroborant [corróborant], *a.* y *s.* corroborante, tónico.

corroborate [-eit], *va.* corroborar, confirmar; confortar, fortalecer.—**corroboration** [-éišhun], *s.* corroboración, confirmación, fe.—**corroborative** [-ætiv], **corroboratory** [-ætori], *a.* corroborativo.—**corroboratively** [-li], *adv.* corroborativamente.

corrode [corróud], *va.* y *vn.* corroer(se).

corrodibility [corrodibíliti], **corrossibility** [-sibíliti], *s.* corrosibilidad.

corrodible, corrosible [corródibœl, sibœl], *a.* corrosible.

corrosion [corróyun], *s.* corrosión.

corrosive [-siv], *a.* y *s.* corrosivo, corroyente, mordicante; mordaz.—**c. sublimate,** sublimado corrosivo, solimán.—**corrosively** [-li], *adv.* corrosivamente.—**corrosiveness** [-nes], *s.* calidad de corrosivo o mordicante.

corrugant [córrugant]. **I.** *a.* que arruga. **II.** *s.* medicamento astringente.

corrugate [córrugueit], *va.* arrugar, acanalar; encarrujar.—**corrugate(d,** *a.* arrugado, ondulado (apl. al hierro en lámina, etc.); acanalado, encarrujado.—**corrugation** [-éišhun], *s.* arruga.

corrupt [corrúpt]. **I.** *a.* corrompido; putrefacto, pútrido; (fig.) desmoralizado. **II.** *va.* malear, adulterar; sobornar, seducir, pervertir; infectar, podrir. **III.** *vn.* corromperse, podrirse.—**corrupter** [-tœr], *s.* corruptor, seductor, pervertidor, sobornador.—**corruptibility** [-tibíliti], *s.* corruptibilidad.—**corruptible** [-tibœl], *a.* corruptible.—**corruptibleness** [-nes], *s.* corruptibilidad.—**corruptibly** [-bli], *adv.* corruptiblemente.—**corruption** [-šhun], *s.* corrupción, descomposición, podredura; inmoralidad; cohecho, soborno; depravación, maldad; perversión; pus, materia.—**corruptive** [corrúptiv], *a.* corruptivo.—**corruptless** [-les], *a.* incorruptible, íntegro, recto.—**corruptly** [corrúptli], *adv.* corruptamente, corrompidamente.—**corruptness** [-nes], *s.* corrupción, putrefacción, infección; vicio.—**corruptress** [-tres], *s.* corruptora, corrompedora.

corsage [córsey], *s.* corpiño, cuerpo.

corsair [córseœr], *s.* corsario, pirata.

corse [cors], *s.* cinta para hábitos.

corselet [córslet], *s.* corselete; peto.

corset [córset], *s.* corsé; cotilla.—**c. cover,** canesú, corpecico, justillo.

ocrsetier [corsetiér], *s.* corsetero.—**corsetière** [-tiéar], *s.* corsetera.

Corsican [córsican], *a.* corso.

cortège [córtey], *s.* comitiva, séquito.

cortex [córtecs], *s.* corteza.

cortical [córtical], *a.* cortical.

corticate(d [córtiket(ed], *a.* cortezudo.

corticose [córticos], *a.* parecido a una **corteza.**

corundum [corúndum], *s.* corindón.

coruscate [córuskeit], *vn.* fulgurar.

coruscation [-éišhun], *s.* coruscación, fulgor.

corvette [corvét], *s.* (mar.) corbeta.

corvetto [corvéto], *s.* (equit.) corveta.

corvine [córvin], *a.* corvino.

corymb [córimb], *s.* (bot.) corimbo.

corypheus [corífrus], *s.* corifeo.

coryza [coráiša], *s.* (med.) coriza.

cosecant [cosícant], *s.* (geom.) cosecante.

cosentient [cosénšhent], *a.* que percibe o siente con otro.

cosey [cóši], *a.* = COZY.

cosher [cóšhœr]. **I.** *va.* (fam.) pedir o dar gollerías; mimar. **II.** *vn.* ser compadre o comadre; chismear.

cosine [cósain], *s.* (geom.) coseno.

cosmetic [cošmétic], *a.* y *s.* cosmético

cosmic(al [cošmic(al], *a.* cósmico, vasto; metódico.

cosmism [cósmism], *s.* teoría de la evolución cosmogónica.

cosmogonal, cosmogonic(al [cošmógonal, cošmogónic(al], *a.* cosmogónico.

cosmogony [cošmógoni], *s.* cosmogonía.

cosmographer [cošmógrafœr], *s.* cosmógrafo.

cosmographical [cošmográfical], *a.* cosmográfico.

cosmographically [-i], *adv.* cosmográficamente.

cosmography [cošmógrafi], *s.* cosmografía.

cosmological [cošmolóyical], *a.* cosmológico.

cosmologist [cošmóloyist], *s.* cosmólogo.

cosmology [cošmóloyi], *s.* cosmología.

cosmopolitan [cošmopólitan], **cosmopolite** [cošmópolait], *a.* y *s.* cosmopolita.

cosmorama [cósmorǽmæ], *s.* cosmorama.

cosmos [cósmos], *s.* cosmos, universo.

Cossack [cósæc], *s.* cosaco.

cosset [cóset]. **I.** *s.* cordero criado sin la madre. **II.** *va.* acariciar, mimar.

cost [cost]. **I.** *s.* costa, coste, costo.—*pl.* costas.—**c., insurance and freight** (c. i. f.), costo, seguro y flete (c. s. f.).—**at all costs,** cueste lo que cueste, a toda costa, a todo trance.—**at c., a** coste y costas.—**to my c.,** a mis expensas. **II.** *vn.* costar.—**c. what it may,** cueste lo que cueste.

costal [cóstal], *a.* (anat.) costal.

costate [cóstet], *a.* con costillas.

costermonger [cóstœrmóngœr], *s.* vendedor ambulante de frutas.

costive [cóstiv], *a.* estreñido, estíptico.

costiveness [cóstivnes], *s.* constipación o estreñimiento de vientre.

costless [cóstles], *a.* de balde.

costliness [cóstlines], *s.* calidad de costoso; suntuosidad.

costly [cóstli]. **I.** *a.* costoso, caro; magnífico o suntuoso. **II.** *adv.* costosamente.

costmary [cóstmeri], *s.* (bot.) atanasia.

costume [cóstium], *s.* traje, vestido; disfraz; indumentaria.

costumer [costiúmœr], *s.* sastre de teatro.

cosy, *a.* = COZY.

cot [cot], *s.* cabaña, choza; catre, camilla; dedal.

cotangent [cotényent], *s.* (geom.) cotangente.

cote [cóut], *s.* corral, aprisco.

contemporaneous, cotemporary, *V.* CON-
TEMPORANEOUS, etc.

coterie [coterí], *s.* agrupación, grupo, círculo.

coterminous, *a.* = CONTERMINOUS.

cothurnus [coźúrnus], *s.* coturno.

cotillon [cotílon], *s.* (danz.) cotillón.

cotquean [cótkuin], *s.* cominero, refitolero, cazolero; maricasera.

cotrustee [cotrustí], *s.* fideicomisario o curador en unión de otro.

cotswold [cótsuold], *s.* majada.

cotta [cota], *s.* (igl.) cota, sobrepelliz.

cottage [cóteᵧ], s. choza, casucha; (E. U.) casa de campo, quinta.—**c. cheese**, requesón.

cottaged [cóteᵧd], a. poblado de chozas.

cottager [cóteᵧœr], **cotter** [cótœr], s. el que vive en *cottage*.

cotter [cótœr], s. (mec.) chabeta, llave, pasador.

cotton [cótᴜn], s. algodón (planta y fibra); tela de algodón; hilo de algodón; lanilla o pelillo vegetal algodonoso.—*pl.* géneros de algodón; ropa de algodón.—**c. bagging**, lienzo de algodón para sacos, y los sacos mismos.—**c. batting**, algodón en hojas.—**c. cake**, torta de harina de semillas de algodón.—**c. flannel**, moletón.—**c. gin**, despepitadora o (Amér.) desmotadora de algodón.—**c. moth**, mariposa del gusano del algodón.—**c. opener**, abridora, máquina para abrir y limpiar el algodón al desembalarlo.—**c. plant**, algodonero. —**c. plantation**, algodonal.—**c. powder**, pólvora que contiene algodón pólvora.—**c. seed** = COTTONSEED.—**c. tree**, viburno; ceiba y otros árboles bombáceous análogos; álamo.—**c. waste**, desperdicios de hilaza de algodón.—**c. wool**, algodón en rama.—**c. worm**, gusano de las hojas (no de la cápsula) del algodón.

cotton. I. *vn.* cubrirse de pelusa o borra; convenir, avenirse. **II.** *va.* envolver o rellenar con algodón; mimar.

cottonlike [-laic], **cottony** [-i], a. algodonoso.

cotonseed [-sid], s. semilla del algodón.—**c. meal**, harina de bourujo de algodón.—**c. oil**, aceite de semillas de algodón.

cottonwood [-úd], s. álamo.

cotyledon [cotilídon], s. cotiledón.

couch [cáuch]. **I.** *va.* acostar; poner en capas o tongadas; depositar; indicar, expresar; encubrir, disimular; enristrar, poner (la lanza) en ristre; (cir.) batir las cataratas o nubes de los ojos. **II.** *vn.* acostarse, recostarse, tenderse, echarse; agacharse; agobiarse, doblarse. **III.** *s.* canapé; yacija; tonga, tongada, capa.—**c. fellow**, compañero de cama.—**c. grass**, (bot.) grama.

couchant [cáuchant], a. (blas.) acostado.

coucher [cáuchœr], s. cartulario.

cougar [cúgar], s. (zool.) cuguar, puma.

cough [cof]. **I.** *s.* tos. **II.** *vn.* toser. **III.** *va.* esputar; arrojar del pecho tosiendo.

coughing [cófing], s. tos, tosidura.

could [cud], *pret. imp.* de CAN.

coulisse [culís], s. ranura de corredera; (tea.) bastidor; entrebastidor.

couloir [cúlúár], s. garganta, barranca; draga de cangilones.

coulomb [culóm], s. (elec.) culombio.

coulter [cóltœr], s. = COLTER.

coumaric [cumáric], a. (quím.) cumárico.— **coumarin** [cúmaerin], (quím.) cumarina.

council [cáunsil], s. concilio; consejo; concejo, junta.—**c. board**, sesión del consejo; mesa del consejo.

councilman [-mæn], s. concejal.

councilor, councillor [-œr], s. concejal; consejero.

counsel [cáunsel]. **I.** *s.* consejo; deliberación; determinación; prudencia, secreto, sigilo; trama, plan, designio; abogado consultor, asesor.— **to keep one's c.**, ser reservado, no decir nada. —**to take c.**, deliberar, aconsejarse. **II.** *va.* aconsejar, dirigir, guiar.

counsel(l)or [cáunselœr], s. consultor, consejero; abogado, causídico; asesor.—**c. at law**, abogado.—**c.'s robe**, garnacha.

counsellorship [-ship], s. empleo o dignidad de consejero.

count [cáunt]. **I.** *va.* contar, numerar; considerar, reputar; imputar, atribuir.—**to c. noses**, [contar cabezas (personas). **II.** *vn.* contar; valer. —**to c. on** o **upon**, contar con, confiar en. **III.** *s.* cuenta, cálculo; partida, cláusula; valor, cuantía; atención, cuidado; conde (título); (for.) demanda, cargo, capítulo; (tej.) número o tamaño (del hilo). —**c. palatine**, conde palatino.

countable [cáuntabœl], a. contadero, contable.

countenance [cáuntenans]. **I.** *s.* semblante, cara, talante, aspecto; patrocinio, protección, apoyo.—**out of c.**, desconcertado, turbado, corrido.

—**to give c.**, apoyar, favorecer, proteger, auxiliar. **II.** *va.* sostener, apoyar, fomentar, aprobar.

counter [cáuntœr]. **I.** *s.* calculista; contador; mostrador; tablero; ficha, tanto; (mar.) bovedilla; lo opuesto, lo contrario; porción del zapato que ciñe el talón; pecho del caballo; (mús.) contrapunto. **II.** *adv.* contra, al contrario. —**c. electromotive force**, fuerza contraelectromotriz.—**to run c.**, oponerse a, violar. **III.** *a.* contrario, opuesto.—**IV.** *va.* combatir; contradecir. **V.** *vn.* contraatacar; oponerse.

counteract [éct], *va.* contrariar, impedir; neutralizar, contrarrestar.

counteraction [-écshᴜn], s. oposición; impedimento.

counteractive [-éctiv]. **I.** *a.* contrario, opuesto. **II.** *s.* opositor.

counterapproach [-ᴣpróuch], s. (fort.) contraaproches o contraataques.

counterattack [-ætéc]. **I.** *s.* contraataque, ataque de reacción. **II.** *va.* y *vn.* contraatacar, hacer un contraataque.

counterattraction [-ætrǽcshᴜn], s. atracción contraria.

counterbalance [-bǽlans]. **I.** *va.* contrapesar, equilibrar; compensar. **II.** *s.* contrapeso, equilibrio, compensación.

counterchange [-chéiny]. **I.** *s.* contracambio. **II.** *va.* trocar, cambiar.

countercharge [-chary], s. recriminación.—*va.* (for.) reconvenir.

countercheck [-chéc]. **I.** *va.* contrastar, contrarrestar. **II.** *s.* oposición, repulsa, rechazo.

counterclockwise [-clókuaiŝ], a. y *adv.* contrario, o en sentido contrario, al de las agujas del reloj; a la izquierda, izquierdo (apl. a arrollamientos, etc.)

countercurrent [-cœrrent], s. contracorriente.— **c. boiler**, caldera de corrientes invertidas.—**c. condensation**, (m. v.) condensación por contracorriente.

counterdraw [-dró], *va.* calcar.

counterevidence [-évidens], s. contraprueba.

counterfeit [-fit]. **I.** *va.* falsear, falsificar, forjar. **II.** *vn.* fingir, disimular. **III.** *s.* impostura, falsificación; copia, imitación; moneda falsa. **IV.** *a.* falsificado, espurio.

counterfeiter [-fitœr]. **I.** *s.* falsario, falsificador, falseador, imitador; monedero falso.

counterfiler [-fáilœr], a. (elec.) contrafilar.

counterfort [-fort], s. contrafuerte, estribo.

counterguard [-gard], s. (fort.) contraguardia.

counterirritant [-íritant], s. (med.) contrairritante.

counterlight [-lait], s. contraluz.

countermand [-mǽnd]. **I.** *va.* contramandar; revocar, invalidar, cancelar. **II.** *s.* contramandato, contraorden.

countermarch [-march]. **I.** *s.* contramarcha. **II.** *vn.* [marcontramārchar, contramarchar].

countermark [-marc]. **I.** *s.* contramarca. **II.** *va.* contramarcar, resellar.

countermine [-main]. **I.** *s.* contramina. **II.** *va.* contraminar; contravenir.

countermotion [-móshᴜn], s. movimiento contrario; proposición contraria.

countermove [-múv], *va.* y *vn.* mover(se) en dirección contraria.

counteropening [-óupning], s. (cir.) contraabertura.

counterpace [-péis], s. contrapaso.

counterpane [-péin], s. colcha de cama, cubrecama; cobertor.

counterpart [-part], s. contraparte; duplicado; copia, imagen.

counterplea [-plí], s. (for.) reconvención.

counterplot [-plót]. **I.** s. contratreta. **II.** *va.* contraminar.

counterpoint [-póint], s. (mús.) contrapunto.

counterpoise [-póiŝ]. **I.** *va.* equilibrar, contrapesar, contrabalancear. **II.** s. contrapeso; compensación, equilibrio; pilón de una romana.

counterpoison [-póiŝʊn], *s.* contraveneno; antídoto.
counterpressure [-préŝhœr], *s.* contrapresión.
counterproject [-próyect], *s.* contraproyecto.
counterproof [-prúf], *s.* contraprueba.
counterproposition [-própoŝiŝhʊn], *s.* contraproposición.
counterrevolution [-révolúŝhʊn], *s.* contrarrevolución.
counterscarp [-scarp], *s.* (fort.) contraescarpa.
counterseal [-síl], *va.* contrasellar.
countersense [-séns], *s.* contrasentido, sentido opuesto.
countershaft [-ŝhæft], *s.* eje intermedio; (aut.) eje secundario del cambio de marcha.
countersign [-sáin]. **I.** *va.* visar, refrendar. **II.** *s.* (mil.) santo y seña, consigna, contraseña.
countersignal [-sígnal], *s.* (mar.) señal que responde a otra.
countersignature [-sígnachur], *s.* refrendata.
countersink [-sínk]. **I.** *va.* abocardar, avellanar. **II.** *s.* avellanador.—**countersinking drill**, abocardo.
counterstroke [-stróuc], *s.* (med.) contragolpe; (m. v.) golpe o carrera de retroceso.
countersunk [-súnc], *pp.* de COUNTERSINK.—**c. rivet**, remache de cabeza embutida.
countertenor [-ténœr], *s.* (mús.) contralto.
countertide [-táid], *s.* (mar.) contramarea.
countertrench [-trénch], *s.* (mil.) contratrinchera.
countervail [-véil]. **I.** *va.* contrapesar, compensar. **II.** *s. V.* COUNTERBALANCE.
counterweight [-uŝit], *s.* contrapeso.
counterwork [-uœrc], *va.* contrarrestar, contrariar; contraminar.
countess [cáuntes], *sf.* condesa.
countinghouse [cáuntingjáus], *s.* despacho, escritorio, oficina.
countless [cáuntles], *a.* innumerables, sin cuento.
countrified [cúntrifaid], *a.* rústico, campesino, agreste.
countrify [cúntrifai], *va.* hacer rústico o campesino.
country [cúntri]. **I.** *s.* país; región, tierra; patria; campo, campiña. **II.** *a.* rústico, rural, campesino; rudo o agreste; campestre, de campo.—**c. dance**, baile campestre, charrada; (Amér.) changüí, guateque.—**c. rock**, (min.) roca madre.—**c. seat**, casa de campo.—**c. squire**, caballero de provincia.
countryman [cúntriman], *s.* (*pl.* COUNTRYMEN) paisano, compatriota; paisano, aldeano, patán; labrador; paleto; (Cuba) montuno, guajiro; (P. Rico) jíbaro; (Méx.) payo.
countrywoman [-úman], *s.* paisana; aldeana; labriega.
county [cáunti], *s.* condado, distrito territorial, jurisdicción.—**c. palatine**, palatinado.
coup [cu], *s.* estratagema, golpe maestro.—**c. de grace**, golpe de gracia.—**c. d'état**, golpe de estado.—**c. de main**, ataque o movimiento repentino e imprevisto.
coupé [cupé], *s.* cupé, berlina.
couple [cúpœl]. **I.** *s.* par, pareja; (mec.) par (de fuerzas, motor).—**married c.**, matrimonio, marido y mujer. **II.** *va.* acoplar, ensamblar, enganchar; unir, juntar, casar. **III.** *vn.* tener cópula o coito.
coupler [cúplœr], *s.* aparato de conexión; acoplamiento; (f. c.) enganche.
couplet [cúplet], *s.* par, pareja; copla; pareado, dístico.
coupling [cúpling], *s.* acoplamiento; junta o unión; (f. c.) enganche.—**c. pin**, (f. c.) pasador del enganche.
coupon [cupón], *s.* cupón, talón.—**c. ticket**, billete talonario.
courage [cúrey], *s.* coraje, valor, denuedo.
courageous [curéyus], *a.* animoso, valiente, valeroso.—**courageously** [-li], *adv.* valerosamente.—**courageousness** [-nes], *s.* valor, intrepidez.
courbaril [cúrbaril], *s.* curbaril.
courier [cúricer], *s.* correo, estafeta, expreso, ordinario.

course [cors]. **I.** *s.* marcha; recorrido; vía; dirección; serie; curso (de estudios); curso, marcha (de los sucesos); camino, proceder, conducta; método, sistema; plato (cada uno de los que forman una comida, vg., *a five-course dinner*, una comida de cinco platos); estadio; carga, encuentro; (mar. y top.) rumbo; (top.) línea (determinada por rumbo y distancia); (arq.) hilada; (min., geol.) dirección de un afloramiento según la horizontal transversal del filón; (min.) galería; (mar.) papahigo.—*pl.* menstruación, regla.—**matter of c.**, cosa común y corriente, cosa de cajón.—**of c.**, por supuesto, naturalmente.—**the last c.**, los postres. **II.** *va.* correr por, o sobre; hacer correr; cazar, dar caza, perseguir. **III.** *vn.* corretear.
courser [córsœr], *s.* corcel; cazador de liebres.
coursing [córsing], *s.* caza de liebres; (min.) ventilación.
court [cort]. **I.** *s.* (for.) tribunal; estrados, sala de justicia; juez; corte; palacio; comitiva, séquito, cortejo; patio, atrio; frontón; cancha; mansión suntuosa; callejuela; plazoleta; cortejo, galanteo.—**c. card**, figura (en la baraja).—**c. day**, día de reunión del tribunal.—**c. lands**, tierras señoriales.—**c. martial**, *s.* consejo de guerra; *va.* seguir, o someter a, consejo de guerra.—**C. of Common Pleas**, tribunal de primera instancia.—**c. of first instance**, tribunal de primera instancia.—**c. officer**, alguacil, ministril.—**c. plaster**, esparadrapo. **II.** *va.* enamorar, galantear; hacer la corte; solicitar, buscar; inducir, incitar.
courteous [cŏrtius], *a.* cortés, atento.
courteously [-li], *adv.* cortésmente.
courteousness [-nes], *s.* cortesía, cortesanía.
courtesan [cŏrtiŝan], *s.* dama cortesana; mujer pública.
courtesy [cŏrtesi]. **I.** *s.* cortesía, finura; gracia, favor, merced; consentimiento, beneplácito; [cŏrtŝi] cortesía, reverencia. **II.** [cŏrtsi], *vn.* hacer una cortesía o reverencia.
courtezan, *s.* = COURTESAN.
courthand [cŏrtjend], *s.* letra gótica.
courthouse [-jaus], *s.* audiencia; palacio de justicia, tribunal.
courtier [cŏrticer], *s.* cortesano o palaciego; cortejo, cortejante.
courtlike [cŏrtlaic], *a.* cortesano.
courtliness [cŏrtlines], *s.* cortesanía, cortesía, urbanidad; elegancia.
courtly [cŏrtli], *a.* cortesano, elegante, galante, cortés.
courtship [cŏrtŝhip], *s.* corte, cortejo; galanteo; noviazgo.
courtyard [cŏrtyard], *s.* patio.
cousin [cŏŝœn], *s.* primo o prima.—**c. german**, primo hermano.—**cousinhood** [-jud], **cousinship** [-ŝhip], *s.* primazgo.
cove [cóuv]. **I.** *s.* abra, ancón, caleta, ensenada; (arq.) bovedilla. **II.** *va.* abovedar, arquear.
covenant [cúvenant]. **I.** *s.* contrato, ajuste, convenio, pacto; escritura de contrato; (bib.) alianza; testamento.—**the New C.**, el Nuevo Testamento. **II.** *va.* prometer, empeñar. **III.** *vn.* convenir, pactar, estipular.
covenantee [-i], *s.* contratante.
covenanter, covenantor [-œr, -or], *s.* contratante; firmante del pacto escocés de la reforma religiosa.
cover [cúvœr]. **I.** *va.* cubrir; tapar, ocultar; cobijar, abrigar, proteger; abarcar, abrazar; describir o investigar (apl. al trabajo de repórters); resarcir, compensar, indemnizar; (recorrer, andar; cubrir (el macho a la hembra); empollar; cubrirse, ponerse el sombrero; paliar, disimular; (com.) cubrir, remesar fondos; (arti.) apuntar a, dominar, cubrir. **II.** *s.* cubierta, tapa, tapadera, cobertera; sobre, sobrecarta; capa, pretexto, velo; abrigo, techado, albergue; cubierto (tenedor, cuchillo y cuchara); funda; forro; tapete, cobertor; (caz.) huidero; guarida.—**c. charge**, precio de admisión (apl. a restaurantes, salas de baile, etc.).—**c. crop**, (agr.) siembra de abono o de protección.—**c. glass**, tapa de vidrio

(de la platina de un microscopio).—**under c.**, bajo techado; oculto, cubierto; bajo sobre o cubierta (apl. a cartas, etc.)

covered [cúvœrd], a. cubierto, tapado; cubierto, con el sombrero puesto; (com.) asegurado, respaldado.— **c. way**, (fort.) camino cubierto, estrada, encubierta.

covering [-ing], s. ropa, abrigo; funda, cobija, envoltura; pelaje, tegumento; cubrimiento.

coverlet, coverlid [-let, -lid], s. colcha, sobrecama, cubrecama, cobertor.

coversed sine [covúrst sáin], s. (mat.) cosenoverso.

covert [cúvœrt]. **I.** s. cubierto o cubierta; refugio, asilo; guarida, huidero; bandada. **II.** a. cubierto, tapado; secreto, escondido; (for.) que está bajo la autoridad o protección del marido (ap. a la mujer casada).—**c. way** = COVERED WAY.

covertly [-li], adv. secretamente, en secreto.

coverture [cúvœrchœr], s. escondrijo, escondite; ocultación; (for.) estado o condición de una mujer casada.

covet [cúvet]. **I.** va. codiciar, apetecer, ambicionar. **II.** vn. aspirar.

covetable [-æbœl], a. codiciable.—**covetous** [-us], a. codicioso, ambicioso, sórdido.—**covetously** [-li], adv. codiciosamente, avariciosamente. —**covetousness** [-nes], s. codicia, avaricia; ambición, avidez, sordidez.

covey [cúvi], s. banda o bandada.

cow [cáu]. **I.** va. acobardar, intimidar. **II.** s. vaca; hembra de otros cuadrúpedos grandes; sombrerete de chimenea.—**c. dung**, boñiga.—**c. house**, boyera; establo para ganado.

coward [cáuard], a. y s. cobarde.—**cowardice** [-is], **cowardliness** [-lines], s. cobardía.—**cowardly** [-li]. **I.** a. cobarde. **II.** adv. cobardemente.

cowboy [cáubói], s. vaquero, gaucho (jinete ganadero).

cowcatcher [-cǽchœr], s. (f. c.) trompa, quitapiedras, barredor (de locomotora).

cower [cáuœr], vn. agacharse, alebrarse.

cowherd [cáujœrd], s. vaquero, pastor de ganado vacuno.

cowhide [-jaid]. **I.** s. cuero; corbacho. **II.** va. azotar, zurriagar.—**cowhiding**, zurribanda.

cowl [cául], s. cogulla, capucha; cubierta; sombrerete de chimenea; (aut.) bóveda del tablero; (aer.) cubierta o caja del motor.

cowled [cáuld], a. encapuchado.

cowlick [cáulic], s. tupé, mechón de pelo.

cowlike [-laic], a. avacado.

cowman [-mæn], s. ganadero, hacendado.

coworker [cóuœrkœr], s. coadjutor, colaborador.

cowpea [cáupi], s. garbanzo.

cowpox [-pocs], s. vacuna.

cowpuncher [-púnchœr], s. (E. U., fam.) = COWBOY.

cowslip [cáuslip], s. (bot.) vellorita.

coxalgia [cocsǽliæ], s. (med.) coxalgia.

coxcomb [cócscoum], s. mequetrefe; farolón, fachendista.—**coxcombical** [-ical], a. fachendoso. —**coxcombry** [-ri], s. fachenda.

coxswain [cócsuein, cósen], s. (mar.) patrón, nostramo.

coy, coyish [coi, cóish], a. recatado, modesto; tímido, esquivo; retrechero.

coy, va. acariciar; engatusar, embaucar.—vn. recatarse.

coyly [-li], adv. con esquivez.—**coyness** [-nes], s. timidez, esquivez; recato, modestia.

coyote, s. (zool.) coyote.

coypu [cóipu], s. (zool.) coipo, coipú.

coz [cus], s. (fam.) primo, prima.

cozen [cúscen], va. engañar.—**cozenage** [-ey], s. engaño, trampa, superchería.—**cozener** [-œr], s. engañador, embaucador.

cozily [cóusili], adv. cómodamente, agradablemente.

cozy, cosey, cosy, cozey [cóusi], a. cómodo, agradable.

crab [cræb]. **I.** a. agrio, áspero. **II.** s. cámbaro, (en Cuba) jaiba; cangrejo; (mec.) molinete,

malacate, torno, cabrestante; (astr.) Cáncer. —**c. apple**, manzana silvestre.—**c. louse**, ladilla.

crabbed [crǽbed], a. avinagrado, áspero, ceñudo, bronco; escabroso, desigual.

crabstone [crǽbstoun], s. ojo de cangrejo.

crack [cræc]. **I.** s. hendedura, grieta, rajadura; crujido, chasquido, estallido; mentecatez, chifladura; mentecato, chiflado; mudanza de la voz.—**c. of doom**, juicio final. **II.** a. (fam.) de calidad superior; de primer orden.—**c. brain**, s. loco, destornillado.—**c.-brained**, a. alelado, chiflado. **III.** va. hender, rajar; hacer chasquear, restallar o crujir; trastornar, enloquecer; decir o contar con gracejo; romper, destruir.—**to c. a bottle**, despachar una botella.—**to c. a joke**, decir un chiste. **IV.** vn. reventar, abrirse, agrietarse; crujir, estallar.

crackajack [crǽkæyæc], **crackerjack** [crǽcœryæc], s. (fam.) gran maravilla, non plus ultra.

cracker [crǽkœr], s. petardo, triquitraque; galletica; (fam.) patraña.

crackle [crǽcœl]. **I.** va. hacer crujir; agrietar. **II.** vn. crujir; agrietarse. **III.** s. crujido, crepitación; superficie finamente estriada o rayada.—**c. ware**, artículos (de porcelana, vidrio, etc.) de superficie estriada o rayada.

crackling [crǽcling]. **I.** s. crepitación; chicharrón. **II.** a. crepitante.

cracknel [crǽcnel], s. coscarana, galletica.—pl. chicharrones.

cradle [créidœl]. **I.** s. cuna; (cir.) tablilla para fracturas; arco de protección para una herida; (agr.) guadaña, agavilladora; (min.) artesa oscilante; (mar.) cuna o basada; (const.) plataforma colgante; (aut.) armazón de retroceso de la cureña; (aut.) artefacto para impedir pinchazos en el neumático; (m. v.) caballete de soporte (de una caldera). **II.** va. cunear. **III.** vn. mecerse. en la cuna; segar con guadaña agavilladora.

craft [craft], s. artificio, astucia, treta; maña, habilidad, pericia; arte u oficio; gremio; (mar.) embarcación, barco.

craftily [cráftili], adv. astuta o mañosamente.

craftiness [cráftines], s. astucia, maña.

craftsman [cráftsman], s. artífice, artesano.

crafty [cráfti], a. astuto, taimado, ladino.

crag [cræg], s. despeñadero, risco.—**cragged** [crǽgued], a. escabroso, peñascoso.—**craggedness** [-ednes], **cragginess** [-ines], s. escabrosidad o fragosidad.

craggy [crǽgui], a. escabroso, escarpado.

cram [cræm]. **I.** va. rellenar, henchir, atestar, embutir; hartar, cebar. **II.** vn. darse un atracón. **III.** s. atracón, atestamiento.

crambo [crǽmbo], s. consonante (en verso); juego de hallar consonantes.

cramming [crǽming], s. repaso.

cramp [cræmp]. **I.** s. calambre; retortijón; entumecimiento; sujeción; estrechez, aprieto; laña; cárcel; grapa.—**c. iron**, laña. **II.** a. contraído; apretado. **III.** va. entumecer; dar calambre; sujetar; lañar; engrapar; apretar.

crampfish [-fish], s. (ict.) torpedo, tremielga.

crampon, crampoon [crǽmpon, crǽmpún], s. raicilla trepadora de la hiedra; púa o espolón para trepar o andar sobre el hielo; tenazas de garfios.

cranberry [crǽnberi], s. (bot.) arándano.

cranch s. = CRAUNCH.

crane [créin]. **I.** s. (orn.) grulla; (mec.) grúa; sifón o cantimplora; cigüeña o aguilón de chimenea; brazo de soporte; (mar.) abanico.— **c. fly**, (ent.) típula. **II.** va. levantar con la grúa; estirar, extender. **III.** vn. estirarse, alargarse.

cranesbill [créinsbil], s. (bot.) geranio.

cranial [créinial], a. craniano.

craniological [creiniolóyical], a. craneológico.

craniology [creinióloyi], s. craneología.

craniometer [creiniómetœr], s. craneómetro.

craniometry [-metri], s. craneometría.

craniotomy [-tomi], s. craneotomía, perforación del cráneo del feto.

cranium [créinium], s. cráneo.

crank [crænk]. **I.** *s.* manubrio; (fam.) maniático; persona caprichosa; (mec.) manivela.—**c. arm**, manivela, brazo de la manivela.—**c. axle**, eje motor acodado; (aut.) cigüeñal.—**c. case**, (aut.) cárter del cigüeñal o del motor.—**c. effort**, par motor de la manivela.—**c. pin**, botón manivela o de la manivela.—**c. radius**, brazo de palanca del botón de la manivela.—**c. shaft**, (aut.) cigüeñal. **II.** *a.* vivo, alegre; inseguro; (mar.) mal lastrado, inestable. **III.** *va.* (aut.) voltear el cigüeñal para hacer arrancar el motor.

crankcase [-keis], *s.* = CRANK CASE. *V.* CRANK.

crankiness [crænkines], *s.* chifladura; desequilibrio; calidad de caprichoso o singular.

crankshaft [-šhæft], *s.* = CRANK SHAFT. *V.* CRANK.—**c. gear**, (aut.) engranaje del cigüeñal.

cranky [crænki], *a.* chiflado, lunático; torcido; destartalado, inseguro; caprichoso, testarudo.

crannied [crænid], *a.* grietoso.

cranny [cræni]. **I.** *s.* grieta, hendedura. **II.** *vn.* grietarse, cuartearse.

crape [crep]. **I.** *s.* crespón. **II.** *va.* encrespar, rizar; poner crespón.

crapefish [-fiśh], *s.* bacalao seco.

crapulence [cræpiulens], *s.* crápula.

crapulent [-lent], **crapulous** [-lus], *a.* crapuloso.

crash [cræsh]. **I.** *vn.* romperse, caerse estrepitosamente; rechinar, crujir; (aer.) aterrizar bruscamente. **II.** *va.* despedazar estrepitosamente; abrirse (paso); (aer.) echar a pique.

crash, crashing [cræsh(ing], *s.* estallido, estampido, estrépito; fracaso; quiebra o bancarrota; (tej.) cutí burdo; (E. U.) lienzo estirado sobre una alfombra para bailar; (aer.) morrón, aterrizaje violento.

crass [cræs], *a.* grueso, gordo; basto, tosco; espeso; craso; torpe.

crassamentum [cræsaméntum], *s.* coágulo de la sangre.

crassness [cræsnes], *s.* crasitud.

crate [créit], *s.* cuévano, canasto, banasta, huacal, (Mex.) cacaxtle.

crater [créitœr], *s.* cráter.

craunch [cránch], *va.* = CRUNCH.

cravat [cravæt], *s.* corbata, corbatín.

crave [créiv]. **I.** *va.* pedir humilde pero vehementemente; anhelar, desear. **II.** *vn.* (con **for**) pedir o desear con vehemencia.

craven [créivœn], *s. y a.* cobarde.

craving [créiving]. **I.** *s.* (con **for**), regosto, sed, deseo vehemente (de). **II.** *a.* insaciable; pedigüeño.

craw [cro], *s.* buche.

crawfish [crófíśh]. **I.** *s.* (zool.) cabrajo o bogavante de río. **II.** *vn.* (fam.) volverse atrás, faltar a lo prometido.

crawl [crol]. **I.** *vn.* arrastrarse; andar a gatas, gatear; humillarse, pedir o someterse abyectamente; marchar paso a paso, a paso de tortuga; (fam.) volverse atrás. **II.** *s.* arrastramiento; bajeza; pozo, corral (de agua).

crawler [crólœr], *s.* reptil; persona rastrera; coche (de alquiler); (bot.) planta rastrera.

crawly [króli], *a.* (fam.) pavoroso; de pavor; que causa hormigueo.

crayfish [créfiśh], *s.* = CRAWFISH.

crayon [créiun], *s.* lápiz, creyón; gis, tiza; dibujo al creyón.

craze [créis]. **I.** *va.* enloquecer; cuartear, grietar. **II.** *vn.* perder la razón; cuartearse, grietarse. **III.** *s.* locura, manía; delirio, furor; antojo, capricho, moda; grieta, cuarteadura (en la cerámica).

crazed [-d], *s.* enloquecido, arrebatado; grietoso.

crazily [créiśili], *adv.* loca o insensatamente.

craziness [créiśines], *s.* locura; desequilibrio mental; inseguridad.

crazy [créiśi], *a.* loco; extravagante; desvencijado, roto, dilapidado; (fam.) exageradamente deseoso o ansioso.—**c. quilt**, (cost.) centón.

creak [crík], *vn.* crujir, rechinar, chirriar.

creaking [críking]. **I.** *s.* crujido, rechinamiento; chirrido. **II.** *a.* crujidero, chirriadero.

creaky [críki], *a.* crujidero, chirriador.

cream [crím]. **I.** *s.* crema, nata; lo mejor, la nata y flor.—**c. cheese**, queso de nata.—**c. of tartar**, crémor tártaro.—**c. puff**, bollo de crema. **II.** *vn.* criar nata. **III.** *va.* desnatar.

creamery [crímœri], *s.* lechería.

creamy [crími], *a.* que parece o contiene nata.

crease [crís]. **I.** *s.* pliegue, repliegue, doblez, arruga, plegadura. **II.** *va.* plegar o doblar; acanalar o estriar; (cost.) repulgar, (enc.) filetear.

creaser [críscœr], *s.* (enc.) fileteador; (cost.) repulgador, marcador.

create [criéit], *va.* criar o crear, producir, causar; engendrar, procrear; crear, establecer; constituir, elegir.

creation [criéiśhun], *s.* creación; producción; obra; fundación; nombramiento, elección.

creationism [-iśm], *s.* doctrina de la creación divina tanto del mundo como de las especies opuesta a la teoría de la evolución.—**creationist** [-ist], *s.* partidario de dicha doctrina.

creative [criéitiv], *a.* creativo, creador.

creativeness [-nes], *s.* facultad creadora, genio inventivo.

creator [criéitor], *s.* creador.—**the C.**, el Criador.

creatress [criétres], *s.* creadora.

creature [críchœr, tiur], *s.* criatura; ser viviente; animal; hechura, paniaguado.

crèche [creśh], *s.* DAY NURSERY; inclusa, casa de expósitos.

credence [crídens], *s.* creencia, asenso, fe; crédito.

credential [cridénśhal]. **I.** *a.* credencial. **II.** *s.* (gen. *pl.*) credenciales.

credibility [cridibíliti], *s.* credibilidad, verosimilitud.

credible [-bœl], *a.* creíble.—**credibleness** [-nes], *s.* credibilidad; veracidad.—**credibly** [-bli], *adv.* creíblemente.

credit [crédit]. **I.** crédito, fe; reputación; encomio; buen nombre; confianza; influencia o autoridad; (com.) crédito; haber; saldo a favor; plazo.—**c. union**, banco cooperativo (gen. de obreros).—**on c.**, al fiado.—**to give c.**, dar crédito; abonar; reconocer el mérito; hacer justicia; reconocer o nombrar como autor (de una obra, cita, etc.); citar o nombrar (una obra de que se copia, etc.). **II.** *va.* creer; atribuir; reconocer; (com.) abonar.—**to c. one with**, atribuir a uno; reconocer a uno (como autor, inventor, etc.); (com.) abonarle a uno.

creditable [crédítabœl], *a.* fidedigno, abonado; apreciable, loable.—**creditability** [-bíliti], *s.* reputación.—**creditably** [crédítabli], *adv.* honorablemente, honrosamente; hábilmente.

credited [crédited], *a.* acreditado, estimado; reputado; creído; (com.) acreditado, abonado en cuenta; pasado al haber.

creditor [créditœr], *s.* acreedor; (com.) haber.

credo [crído], *s.* (igl.) credo.

credulity [crediúliti], **credulousness** [crediulusnes], *s.* credulidad.

credulous [crédiulus], *a.* crédulo.

creed [críd], *s.* credo, creencia, profesión de fe, doctrina.

creek [críc], *s.* abra, cala, caleta, ensenada, estero; riachuelo.

creeky [críki], *a.* lleno de recodos.

creel [críl], *s.* cesta de pescador; jaula de mimbres; (tej.) estízola.

creep [críp]. **I.** *vn.* (*pret. y pp.* CREPT) arrastrarse, serpear; gatear; deslizarse, insinuarse; sentir hormigueo; moverse o acercarse lenta y cautelosa o furtivamente; pedir o someterse abyectamente; humillarse; trepar; correrse (una cosa sobre otra); (elec.) desviarse (una corriente).—**to c. on**, acercarse insensiblemente.—**to c. out**, escurrirse; resbalarse hacia afuera.—**to c. up**, encaramarse, treparse; subir gradualmente. **II.** *s.* arrastramiento.—*pl.* pavor, sobrecogimiento; crispatura.—**c. mouse**, ladino.

creepage [crípey], *s.* = CREEPING.

creeper [crípœr], *s.* el que o lo que se arrastra; reptil; (bot.) enredadera; (orn.) trepador; garfio, garabato; ramplón de zapato.

creephole [crípjóul], *s.* huronera; escapatoria; pretexto.

creeping [críping]. **I.** *a.* que se arrastra; rastrero; lento; pavoroso, crispador; (bot.) rastrera.— **c. palsy, o paralysis,** atrofia muscular progresiva – **c. sickness,** (med.) ergotismo. **II.** *s.* pavor, crispatura, horror; hormigueo; escurrimiento, deslizamiento; arrastramiento; abyección; corredura (de una cosa sobre otra); (elec.) desviación (de una corriente); (fís.) ascenso por atracción capilar; (f. c.) resbalamiento longitudinal (de los rieles); (mec.) resbalamiento (de una correa).

creepingly [-li], *a.* a paso de tortuga; abyectamente.

creepy [crípi], *a.* = CRAWLY.

creese [crís], *s.* (Filip.) cris.

cremate [crímeit], *va.* incinerar.

cremation [-éishun], *s.* cremación, incineración.

crematory [crímatori], *s.* horno de incineración.

cremona [cremóna], *s.* violín de Cremona.

cremor [crímœr], *s.* crémor.

crenate(d [crínet(ed], *a.* (bot.) dentado.

crenelate [crénelet], *va.* almenar.

creole [críol], *s.* y *a.* criollo.

creosol [críosol], *s.* (quím.) creosol.

creosote [críosot], *s.* creosota.

crêpe [créip], *s.* = CRAPE.

crepitate [crépitet], *vn.* crepitar, chisporrotear; chirriar.—**crepitation** [-éishun], *s.* crepitación, chisporroteo, chirrío.

crept, *pret.* y *pp.* de TO CREEP.

crepuscular [cripúsculær], *a.* crepuscular.

crescendo [cresshéndo], *a.* y *s.* (mús.) crescendo.

crescent [crésent]. **I.** *a.* creciente. **II.** *s.* lúnula; media luna; (astr.) cuarto de luna.

cresol [crísol], (quím.) cresol.

cress [cres], *s.* (bot.) lepidio, mastuerzo.

cresset [créset], *s.* fanal o farol, fogaril; hachón, antorcha, antorchero; trébedes.

crest [crest]. **I.** *s.* cresta; copete, penacho; crestón; cimera; (blas.) timbre; cima, cumbre; cresta de una ola. **II.** *va.* coronar. **III.** *vn.* encrestarse; encresparse.

crested [crésted], *a.* crestado, encopetado, penachudo; (blas.) timbrado.—**c. heron,** airón.

crestfallen [créstfólœn], *a.* cabizbajo, abatido.

cretaceous [cretéshus], *a.* cretáceo.

Cretan [crítan], *a.* cretense.

cretin [crítin], *s.* cretino.

cretinism [crítinism], *s.* cretinismo.

cretonne [cretón], *s.* (tej.) cretona.

crevasse [crevás], *s.* hendedura profunda en un alud; (E. U.) brecha en un malecón.

crevice [crévis], *s.* hendedura, grieta.

crew [cru], *s.* (mar.) tripulación o dotación; cuadrilla, banda, hato.

crewel [crúel], *s.* ovillo de estambre.

crib [crib]. **I.** *s.* pesebre; pesebrera; camita de niño; arcón, artesa; granero; (min.) brocal de entibación; (hidr.) cofre, cajón; (constr.) armazón o cajón de sustentación; balsa pequeña; estribo flotante; ratería; plagio; choza, casucha, chiribitil. **II.** *va.* estribar; entibar; enjaular; hurtar; plagiar.

cribbage [críbey], *s.* juego de naipes.

cribble [críbœl]. **I.** *s.* criba, harnero; salvado, afrecho. **II.** *va.* cerner.

cribbled [críbœld], *a.* punteado; agujereado.

cribwork [críbuœrc], *s.* cajón o armazón de apoyo, gen. lleno de piedra.

crick [cric], *s.* torticoli.

cricket [críket], *s.* (ent.) grillo; vilorta; cáncana, banquillo, taburete.

cricketer [críketœr], *s.* vilortero.

crier [cráiœr], *s.* pregonero; baladrero.

crime [cráim], *s.* crimen.

criminal [criminal], *s.* y *a.* criminal.—**c. law,** derecho penal.—**criminality** [-ǽliti], **criminal-**

ness [-alnes], *s.* criminalidad.—**criminally** [-li], *adv.* criminalmente.

criminate [críminet], *va.* acriminar, acusar.

crimination [-éishun], *s.* acriminación, acusación.

criminative [-netiv], *a.* acusatorio.—**criminator** [-atœr], *a.* acriminador, acusador.

criminology [críminóloyi], *s.* criminología.

crimp [crimp]. **I.** *va.* rizar, encrespar; alechugar; doblar hacia dentro (el borde de un tubo, etc.); dar forma doblando; hacer incisiones en. **II.** *a.* quebradizo, desmenuzable; contradictorio; tieso, rígido. **III.** *s.* rizador; el que sirve de señuelo en garitos, etc.

crimper [-œr], *s.* = CRIMPING MACHINE; máquina para cerrar cápsulas doblando los borde hacia adentro.

crimping [-ing], *ger.* de TO CRIMP.—**c. iron,** tenacillas de rizar.—**c. machine,** máquina de combar u ondular.

crimple [crímpœl]. **I.** *va.* y *vn.* encrespar, encoger, arrugar, rizar. **II.** *s.* arruga, pliegue.

crimpy [crímpi], *a.* encrespado.

crimson [crímshun]. **I.** *a.* y *s.* carmesí. **II.** *va.* teñir de carmesí. **III.** *vn.* enrojecerse; sonrojarse.

cringe [criny]. **I.** *vn.* rebajarse, adular. **II.** *s.* adulación, bajeza.

cringer [crínyœr], *s.* adulador servil.

cringing [crínying], *a.* bajo, rastrero.

cringle [críngœl], *s.* (mar.) garrucho.

crinite [cráinait], *a.* crinado, peludo.

crinkle [críncœl]. **I.** *vn.* serpentear. **II.** *va.* arrugar, rizar, acanalar. **III.** *s.* recodo; sinuosidad, ondulación.

crinoid [cráinoid], *s.* crinóideo.

Crinoidea [crinóidiæ], *s. pl.* (zool.) crinóideos.

crinoline [crínolin], *s.* crinolina; ahuecador o miriñaque.

Crioceras [craióceræs], *s.* (pal.) Crioceras (género de cretáceos).

criosphinx [cráiosfincs], *s.* criosfinje, criocéfalo.

cripple [crípœl]. **I.** *s.* y *a.* zopo, cojo o manco, tullido, estropeado, inválido. **II.** *va.* lisiar, mutilar, estropear, encojar; tullir, baldar; descabalar.

crippled [crípœld], *a.* lisiado, estropeado, zopo, mútilo; (mar.) desarbolado, desmantelado.

crisis [cráisis], *s.* crisis.

crisp [crisp]. **I.** *a.* quebradizo, frágil; tostado; crespo, rizado; terso; vigoroso; refrescante. **II.** *va.* encrespar, engrifar, torcer, rizar; undular; hacer quebradizo o frágil.

crispation [crispéshun], *s.* crispatura.

crisping-iron [crisping-áiœrn], **crisping-pin** [-pin], *s.* encrespador.

crispness [críspnes], *s.* rizado, encrespadura; fragilidad.

crispy [críspi], *a.* crespo, rizado; desmenuzable, frágil; fresco, vigorizante.

crisscross [criscrós]. **I.** *a.* cruzado o entrelazado. **II.** *s.* cruz o firma del que no sabe escribir; líneas cruzadas; juego de niños. **III.** *adv.* en cruz.

criterion [craitírion], *s.* criterio.

critic [crític], *s.* crítico, censor; crítica; juicio crítico.

critical [crítical], *a.* crítico; criticón, criticador; exacto, escrupuloso; difícil, peligroso; decisivo; (med.) crítico.

critically [-li], *adv.* críticamente; exactamente, rigurosamente.

criticaster [críticæstœr], *s.* criticastro.

criticism [crítisism], *s.* crítica; juicio crítico; (de un libro, etc.), censura.

criticize, criticise [crítisais̀]. **I.** *vn.* criticar; critiquizar. **II.** *va.* censurar, fiscalizar.—**criticizer** [-œr], *s.* crítico, criticador.

critique [crític], *s.* crítica; revista, juicio crítico.

croak [cróuk]. **I.** *vn.* graznar, crascitar; croar; gruñir. **II.** *s.* graznido; canto de ranas.

croaker [eróukœr], *s.* graznador; gruñidor refunfuñador.

Croat [cróat], **Croatian** [croéishan], *s.* croata.

crocein [crósiin], *s.* (quím.), croceína.

crochet [crŏshé]. **I.** *va.* y *vn.* hacer crochet. **II.** *s.* labor de crochet.—**c. needle**, aguja de gancho para hacer crochet.

crock [croc], *s.* escudilla, cazuela, orza; olla de barro; hollín.

crockery [crókœri], *s.* loza, cacharros.

crocodile [crócodail], *s.* cocodrilo.

crocoite [crócoait], *s.* crocoísa, crocoíta

crocus [crócus], *s.* (bot.) azafrán.

croft [croft], *s.* heredad.

cromlech [crómlec], *s.* monumento megalítico.

crone [cróun], *s.* vieja arrugada.

crony [cróni], *s.* compinche, camarada.

crook [cruk]. **I.** *s.* curvatura, curva; gancho, garfio; cayado; artificio, trampa; (fam.) fullero, petardista. **II.** *va.* encorvar; torcer. **III.** *vn.* encorvarse, corcovarse.

crookback [crúkbæk], *s.* **crookbacked** [-bækd], *a.* jorobado, gibado.

crooked [crúked], *a.* corvo, encorvado, curvo; torcido; oblicuo, ladeado; pícaro, avieso, deshonesto, pervertido.—**c. legs**, patituerto.

crookedly [-lij], *adv.* torcidamente, de través; de mala manera; picaramente.—**crookedness** [-nes], *s.* corvadura, corcova; claudicación, perversidad; vuelta, sinuosidad.

Crookes layer [crúks léicœr], *s.* (fís.) capa de vapor entre un cuerpo en estado esferoidal y la superficie sobre que se forma.—**Crookes tube** [-tiúb], *s.* (fís.) tubo Crookes.—**Crookes vacuum** [-vákiŭm], *s.* (fís.) vacío Crookes, o de tubo Crookes.

crookneck [-nec], *s.* (bot.) calabaza de cuello retorcido.

croon [crun], *va.* y *vn.* canturrear.

crop [crop]. **I.** *s.* cosecha, recolección, agosto; siembra, lo que se siembra; crecimiento de cabellos o barba; cortadura; látigo mocho; buche de ave.—*pl.* mieses; producción. **II.** *va.* segar, cosechar, recoger los frutos; pacer; desorejar, rapar, trasquilar, rabotear, desmochar.—**to c. out**, (min.) aflorar, campear.

cropper [crópœr], *s.* cultivador; planta de cosecha; (orn.) V. POUTER.

croquet [croké, (Ingl.) cróki]. **I.** *s* juego de croquet. **II.** *va.* apartar de una bolada la bola del contrario.

croquette [crokét], *s.* (coc.) croqueta.

crosier, *s.* = CROZIER.

cross [cros]. **I.** *s.* cruz (sentidos recto y figurado); aspa; mercado (donde hay cruz); pieza en cruz; tubo de unión en cruz; cruce; querella, encuentro; cruzamiento (de razas); (top.) escuadra de agrimensor; (elec.) cruzamiento o contacto de dos conductores. **II.** *a.* relativo o perteneciente a la cruz; atravesado; transversal; cruzado; opuesto, contrario, adverso; contradictorio; mal humorado, de mal genio; serio, enojado, enfadado. —**c. arm**, cruceta, brazo en cruz.—**c.-armed**, cruzado de brazos.—**c.-bearer**, cruciferario; (tec.) barra o riostra transversal.—**c.-bedded**, (geol.) de láminas o capas cruzadas.—**c. bill**, (for.) contraquerella.—**c. birth**, (med.) feto atravesado. —**c. bond** (elec.) conexión entre el riel y el alimentador.—**c.-bun**, bollo de viernes santo (marcado con una cruz).—**c.-compound**, (m. v.) compound cruzada, cross-compound.—**c.-country**, a campo traviesa, cross-country.—**c.-examination**, interrogatorio (esp. repregunta).—**c.-examine**, *va.* interrogar (esp. repreguntar).—**c.-eyed**, bizco, bisojo.—**c.-fertilization**, (bot.) fecundación por polinización cruzada (de una planta por otra); (zool.) fecundación de los huevos de un animal por otro.—**c. girder**, viga trasnversal.—**c. grain**, repelo, fibras oblicuas.—**c.-grained**, repeloso, de fibra transversal u oblicua; intratable, terco.—**c.-interrogate**, (for.) *va.* = CROSS-EXAMINE.—**c.-interrogatory** = CROSS-EXAMINATION.—**c.-lots**, a campo traviesa; (fam.) derecho, del modo más corto.—**c.-pollinate**, fecundar por polinización de una planta por otra.—**c.-pollination**, polinización cruzada (de una planta por otra).—**c.-purpose**, propósito o hecho contrario.—**(at c.-purposes**, involuntariamente en pugna, por vías

opuestas).—**c.-question** = CROSS-EXAMINATION.— **c. reference**, referencia de una parte de un libro a otra.—**c. section**, sección transversal.—**c.-sectional**, transversal; de la sección transversal. —**c.-section paper**, papel cuadriculado.—**c.-staff**, (top.) escuadra de agrimensor.—**c. stitch**, punto cruzado, punto de escarpín.—**c. street**, calle traviesa.—**c. wire** (top., astr.) hilo, pelo (del retículo de un anteojo).

crossbar [crósbar], *s.* travesaño.—**c. shot**, (arti.) palanqueta, bala enramada.

crossbeak [-bíc], *s.* = CROSSBILL.

crossbeam [-bím], *s.* viga; viga transversal.

crossbill [-bil], *s.* (orn.) piquituerto.

crossbolt [-bóult], *s.* macho doble de dos direcciones (apl. a cerraduras).

crossbones [-bóuns], *s. pl.* canillas cruzadas (símbolo de la muerte).

crossbow [-bóu], *s.* ballesta (arma).—**crossbowman** [-boumœn], *s.* ballestero (soldado).

crossbred [-bréd], *s.* y *a.* cruzado (de raza), mestizo.

crossbreed [-bríd]. **I.** *s.* planta o animal cruzados; híbrido; mezclado. **II.** *va.* cruzar (animales o plantas).

crosscut [-cŭt], *s.* corte transversal; corte en cruz; atajo; (min.) galería transversal.—**c. chisel**, cincel agudo de ranuras.—**c. file**, lima de picadura cruzada.—**c. saw**, sierra de trozar (al través de la fibra).

crossed [crost], *a.* cruzado; de través; transversal.—**c. belt**, (mec.) correa cruzada.—**c. riveting**, remachado alternado o al tresbolillo.

crosshead [crósjed], *s.* (mec.) cruceta (esp. la de la biela); (imp.) título de columna (de periódico).

crossing [-ing], *s.* cruce, intersección; paso, vado (de un río); acción de cruzar y lugar por donde se cruza; (f. c.) cruzamiento (de dos vías).

crossly [-lij], *adv.* enojadamente, con enfado.— **crossness** [-nes], *s.* enfado; mal humor.

crossover [-óuvœr], *s.* (f. c.) vía de traspaso.

crosspatch [-pæch], *s.* (fam.) gruñón, de mal genio.

crosspiece [-pís], *s.* pieza transversal; cruceta; travesaño; (mar.) cruz de las bitas.

crossroad [-róud], *s.* vereda; junta de dos caminos.

crosstie [-tái], *s.* (f. c.) traviesa, durmiente.

crosstrees [-tríš], *s. pl.* (mar.) crucetas, baos de gavia.

crossway [-uéi], *s.* travesía, encrucijada.

crossways [-uéiš], **crosswise** [-uaiš], *adv.* de través, al través; de parte a parte; en cruz.

crosswort [-uœrt], *s.* (bot.) cruciata.

crotalum [crótalum], *s.* crótalo.

crotch [croch], *s.* bifurcación, cruce, cruz; bragadura, pique.

crotchet [cróchet], *s.* rareza, excentricidad, chifladura; (mús.) semínima; ganchito; (impr.) corchete, [ ]; instrumento de obstetricia.

crotchety [crócheti], *a.* excéntrico, raro, chiflado.

Croton [cróutun], *s.* (bot.) croton.—**c. bug**, cucaracha.—**c. oil**, aceite de crotontiglio o de croton.

crouch [cráuch], *vn.* agacharse, acuclillarse, agabarse; rebajarse.

croup [crup], *s.* rabadilla; anca, grupa; (med.) crup o garrotillo.

croupier [crúpiœr], *s.* gurrupié.

crow [cro]. **I.** *s.* (orn.) cuervo; corneja; cacareo, canto del gallo; barra, palanca de hierro; descalzador.—**c.-quill**, pluma de ave; pluma fina de canutillo para dibujar.—**c.'s foot**, pata de gallo (arrugas); marca en forma de pata de gallo, o de rayas convergentes; (mil.) abrojo; (aer.) bolina.—**as the c. flies**, en línea recta.—**to eat c.**, (fam.) cantar la palinodia. **II.** *vn.* cacarear, cantar el gallo; gallear, alardear, cantar victoria; bravear.

crowbar [cróbar], *s.* barra o palanca de hierro.

crowd [cráud]. **I.** *s.* gentío, multitud; apretura; muchedumbre, tumulto; agolpamiento; caterva, populacho, vulgo; antiguo instrumento parecido al violín. **II.** *va.* amontonar, atestar, apretar, apiñar.—**to c. sail,** (mar.) hacer fuerza de vela. **III.** *vn.* apiñarse, agolparse, remolinarse.

crowded [cráuded], *a.* apiñado, apretado, amontonado; lleno, tupido.

crowder [cráudœr], *s.* amontonador.

crowfoot [crófut], *s.* (bot.) ranúnculo; (mar.) araña; (mil.) abrojo.

crown [cráun]. **I.** *s.* corona; diadema; guirnalda, láurea; premio, galardón; coronilla; copa, cima; complemento, colmo; (Ingl.) moneda de plata (cinco chelines); copa de sombrero; corona del diente; (arq.) corona, coronamiento; (bot.) unión de tallo y raíz.—**c. grafting,** injerto de coronilla.—**c. lands,** (Ingl.) patrimonio de la corona.—**c. law,** (Ingl.) derecho penal.—**c. prince,** príncipe heredero.—**c. glass,** crown glass, vidrio de ornamentación y de instrumentos ópticos. —**c. princess,** consorte del príncipe heredero.— **c. saw,** sierra tubular giratoria. **II.** *va.* coronar; recompensar, premiar; completar.

crowner [-œr], *s.* coronador; remate.

crownland [-lænd], *s.* patrimonio o tierras de la corona.

crownless [-les], *a.* sin corona.

crownlet [-let], *s.* corona pequeña.

crowning [-ing], *s.* remate; coronamiento; coronación.

croze [cróuš]. **I.** *s.* argalle; argallera, jabladera. **II.** *va.* runar.

crozier [cróyœr], *a.* báculo del obispo; (astr.) constelación del sur.

crucial [crúšial], *a.* decisivo, conclusivo; cruzado, atravesado.

cruciate [crúšhiet], *a.* cruciforme.

crucible [crúsibœl], *s.* crisol.

crucifer [crúsifœr], *s.* (igl.) cruciferario.

Cruciferæ [crusífœri], *s. pl.* (bot.) crucíferas.— **cruciferous** [-fœrus], *a.* (bot.) crucífera.

cruciferous [crusífœrus], **crucigerous** [-yœrus], *a.* crucífero; (bot.) crucíferas.

crucifier [crúsifaiœr], *s.* crucificador.

crucifix [-fics], *s.* crucifijo.—**crucifixion** [-fícšhun], *s.* crucifixión.—**cruciform** [-form], *a.* cruciforme.—**crucify** [-fai], *va.* crucificar.

crude [crud]. **I.** *a.* crudo; imperfecto; no sazonado, no refinado; tosco, mal acabado; bruto. —**c. gypsum,** aljez. **II.** *s.* petróleo bruto.

crudely [-li], *adv.* crudamente.—**crudeness** [-nes], **crudity** [-iti], *s.* crudeza, dureza.

cruel [crúel], *a.* cruel.—**cruelly** [-i], *adv.* cruelmente.—**cruelty** [-ti], *s.* crueldad.

cruet [crúet], *s.* ampolleta, vinagrera.—**c. stand,** angarillas, vinagreras.

cruise [cruš]. **I.** *vn.* (mar.) cruzar; (fam.) andar de arriba para abajo, vagar. **II.** *s.* viaje por mar; (mar. mil.) acción de cruzar.

cruiser [crúšœr], *s.* navegante; (mar.) crucero; guardacosta.

cruller [crúlŗr], *s.* buñuelo.

crum, crumb [crum]. **I.** *s.* miga, migajón; pizca, miaja, brote. **II.** *va.* migar, desmigajar; desmenuzar.

crumble [crúmbœl]. **I.** *va.* desmigajar, desmenuzar, destrizar. **II.** *vn.* desmigajarse, desmoronarse.

crummable [crúmbœl], *a.* desmenuzable.

crummy [crúmi], *a.* blando, miguero.

crumpet [crúmpet], *s.* bollo blando.

crumple [crúmpœl]. **I.** *va.* arrugar, apañuscar, ajar. **II.** *vn.* contraerse, encogerse.

crunch [crunch], *vn.* ronchar, tascar, cascar.

cruor [crúor], *s.* crúor (de la san,·re).

crupper [crúpœr], *s.* grupera, baticola, ataharre; grupa.

crural [crúral], *a.* crural.

crus [crus], *s.* caña de la pierna; pedúnculo.

crusade [cruséid], *s.* cruzada.

crusader [cruséidœr], *s.* cruzado.

cruse [crus], *s.* ampolleta, cantarillo, frasco, redomita, botellita.

cruset [crúset], *s.* crisol de orífice.

crush [crušh]. **I.** *va.* romper por compresión; aplastar; quebrantar, triturar; moler, majar; abrumar; vencer; debelar, reprimir; anonadar; empujar. **II.** *vn.* aplastarse; romperse o deformarse por compresión. **III.** *s.* colisión, choque; estrujamiento o deformación por compresión o choque; apiñamiento, aglomeración (de gente).—**c. hat,** sombrero flexible (que puede doblarse), clac.

crusher [-œr], *s.* triturador; trituradora, quebrantadora (máquina); molino; (fam.) polizonte; (fam.) argumento o acontecimiento decisivo o abrumador.

crushing [-ing], *a.* triturador; moledor o de moler; de compresión; abrumador.—**c. strength,** resistencia a la compresión.

crust [crust]. **I.** *s.* costra; corteza; mendrugo de pan; pasta de una torta o pastel; carapacho, concha. **II.** *va.* encostrar, incrustrar. **III.** *vn.* encostrarse.

Crustacea [crustéshea], *s. pl.* (zool.) crustáceos.

crustacean [-šhæn], *a.* y *s.* crustáceo.

crustaceous [-šhus], *a.* crustáceo; conchado.

crustate [crústet], *a.* cubierto con corteza o costra.

crustation [crustéšhun], *s.* incrustación, cobertura.

crustily [crústili], *adv.* enojada o broncamente.

crustiness [-tines], *s.* dureza de la costra; mal genio, aspereza.

crusty [-ti], *s.* costroso; sarroso; rudo, brusco.

crutch [cruch]. **I.** *s.* muleta; muletilla, horquilla.—**crutches** (mar.) horquetas. **II.** *va.* ahorquillar.

crux [crux], *s.* enigma, misterio; problema arduo o peliagudo; lo esencial, el punto de partida.

cry [crái]. **I.** *va.* y *vn.* gritar, vocear; pregonar; exclamar; lamentarse; llorar; aullar, bramar.— **to c. down,** culpar; hacer callar a uno a fuerza de voces; menospreciar; reprimir.—**to c. for,** clamar; pedir llorando; llorar de.—**to c. one's eyes out,** llorar amargamente.—**to c. out,** exclamar. **II.** *s.* (*pl.* CRIES) alarido, grito; lamento, lloro; gritería, clamor, grito; pregón, promulgación; muta, cuadrilla de perros de caza.—**a far c.,** camino largo, gran distancia o diferencia.

crying [cráiing]. **I.** *s.* grito; lloro, lamento; dolores de parto. **II.** *a.* enorme, atroz; urgente.

cryolite [cráiolait], *s.* (min.) criolita.

cryometer [craiómetœr], *s.* criómetro, medidor de bajas temperaturas.

cryoscopy [craióscopi], *s.* (fís.) crioscopia, estudio de las bajas temperaturas y de la congelación por evaporación.

crypt [cript], *s.* gruta, cripta; (anat.) cripta, folículo.

cryptic(al [críptic(al], *a.* escondido, secreto.

cryptically [críplicali], *adv.* ocultamente.

cryptogam [críptogæm], *s.* criptógama.

Cryptogamia [criptogué- (*o* gá) mia], *s. pl.* acotiledóneas.

cryptogamous [criptógamus], *a.* (bot.) criptógamo.

cryptogram [críptogræm], *s.* cifra.

cryptography [criptógrafi], *s.* criptografía.

cryptology [criptóloyi], *s.* criptología.

crystal [cristal], *s.* (quím.) cristal; (min.) cristal de roca; cristal de reloj.—**c. detector, c. tube,** (rad.) detector de cristales; galena.—**c. glass,** cristal.—**c. wedding,** decimoquinto aniversario.

crystal, *o* **crystalline** [cristalin], *a.* cristalino; claro, transparente.

crystallizable [crístalaíšabœl], *a.* cristalizable.

crystallization [-lišéšhun], *s.* cristalización.— **crystallize** [-laíš]. **I.** *va.* cristalizar. **II.** *vn.* cristalizarse.—**crystallography** [-lógrafi], *s.* cristalografía.—**crystalloid** [-loid], *a.* y *s.* cristaloide.

cub [cub], *s.* cachorro; ballenato; zopenco; badulaque.

Cuban [kiúban], *s.* y *a.* cubano.

cubature [kiúbachur], *s.* (geom.) cubicación.

cube [kiúb]. **I.** *s.* (geom. y mat.) cubo.—**c. root,** raíz cúbica. **II.** *va.* cubicar; elevar al cubo.

cubeb [kiúbeb], *s.* cubeba.

eubic [kiúbic]. **I.** *a.* cúbico.—**c. contents,** volumen; capacidad.—**c. equation,** ecuación del tercer grado.—**c. measure,** medida de capacidad. **II.** *s.* = C. EQUATION.

cubical [-æl], *a.* cúbico. *V.* CUBIC.

cubically [-i], *adv.* cúbicamente.

cubicalness [-nes], *s.* calidad de cúbico.

cubicular [kiubíkiular], *a.* perteneciente a la alcoba; privado.

cubiculum [kiubíkiulʊm], *s.* cubículo; cámara de entierro.

cubiform [kiúbiform], **cuboid** [kiúboid], *a.* cúbico.

cubism [kiúbiŝm], *s.* (b. a.) cubismo.—**cubist** [kiúbist], *s.* cubista.

cubit [kiúbit], *s.* codo, antigua medida.

cubital [kiúbital], *a.* cubital; codal.

cuboid [kiúboid], *s.* (anat.) cuboideo.

cuckold [kʊ́cold], *s.* marido cornudo.

cuckoo [cúcu], *s.* (orn.) cuclillo o cuco.

cucullate(d [kiucʊ́let(ed], *a.* en forma de capucha; con capucha.

cucumber [kiúcʊmbœr], *s.* cohombro o pepino.

cucurbit [kiucœ́rbit], *s.* cucúrbita, retorta de alambique; (bot.) calabaza.

cucurbitaceous [kiucœrbitéŝhʊs], *s.* (bot.) cucurbitáceo.

cud [cʊd], *s.* rumia; panza. *V.* QUID.

cudbear [cʊ́dbear], *s.* orchilla.

cuddle [cʊ́dœl]. **I.** *va.* abrazar. **II.** *vn.* estar abrazados.

cuddy [cʊ́di], *s.* (mar.) tumbadillo; fogón.

cudgel [cʊ́yœl]. **I.** *s.* garrote, tolete, porra.—**c. play,** lid deportiva con garrotes.—**to take up the cudgels,** (fig.) entrar en una controversia, entrar en la lucha; (con *for*) salir a la defensa (de). **II.** *va.* apalear, tundir, aporrear.—**to c. one's brains,** devanarse los sesos.

cudgeller [cʊ́yelœr], *s.* apaleador.

cudweed [cʊ́duid], **cudwort** [cʊ́duœrt], *s.* (bot.) algodonera, lanaria, perpetua.

cue [kiu], *s.* cola, rabo; coleta, trenza de cabello. (*v.* QUEUE); (teat.) pie, apunte; indirecta, sugestión; genio, humor; taco de billar.

cuff [cʊf]. **I.** *s.* trompada, bofetón; puño de camisa; bocamanga. **II.** *va.* abofetear. **III.** *vn.* dar de puñadas, luchar, boxear.

cuirass [cuirás], *s.* coraza.

cuirassier [cuirasíœr], *s.* coracero.

cuish [cuíŝh], *s.* (arm.) escarcela, muslera, quijote.

cuisine [cuiŝín], *s.* cocina, arte culinario.

cul-de-sac [pronunciación francesa], *s.* callejón o conducto cerrado o tapado en un extremo.

culex [kiúlex], *s.* (ent.) mosquito.

culinary [kiúlineri], *a.* culinario.

cull [cʊl], *va.* escoger, elegir, entresacar.

cullender, *s.* = COLANDER.

culler [cʊ́lœr], *s.* escogedor.

cullion [cʊ́liʊn], *s.* bulbo; órquide; belitre, tunante.

cullis [cʊ́lis], *s.* canal de tejado.

culm [cʊlm], *s.* (bot.) caña; (E. U.) polvo o desperdicios de carbón; cisco.

culmen, *s.* = SUMMIT.

culmiferous [cʊlmífœrʊs], *a.* culmífero.

culminate [cʊ́lminet], *vn.* culminar; lograr o alcanzar, terminar.

culmination [cʊlminéŝhʊn], *s.* culminación.

culpability [cʊlpabíliti], *s.* culpabilidad.

culpable [cʊ́lpabœl], *a.* culpable.—**culpableness** [-nes], *s.* culpa, culpabilidad.—**culpably** [-li], *adv.* culpablemente.

culprit [cʊ́lprit], *s.* reo, delincuente, criminal.

cult [cʊlt], *s.* culto; homenaje; devoción.

cultivable [cʊ́ltivabœl], *a.* cultivable.

cultivate [-veit], *va.* cultivar, beneficiar, labrar; estudiar, ejercer, practicar; darse a; criar (gusanos de seda, etc.); (agr.) dar las labores a.

cultivation [-véiŝhʊn], *s.* cultivación, cultivo; labranza; labor, mejora, adelantamiento; cultura; (agr.) labores.

cultivator [-véitœr], *s.* cultivador, labrador, agricultor; cultivadora; escarificador, extirpador.

cultural [cʊ́lchural], *a.* cultural, perteneciente a la cultura.

culture [cʊ́lchur]. **I.** *s.* cultura; cultivación; cultivo (de bacterias, etc.); civilización; ilustración. **II.** *va.* educar, enseñar, criar; refinar.

cultured [cʊ́lchœrd], *a.* culto, ilustrado.

culverin [cʊ́lvœrin], *s.* (arti.) culebrina.

culvert [cʊ́lvœrt], *s.* (f. c., caminos) alcantarilla, atarjea.

cumber [cʊ́mbœr], *va.* oprimir, obstruir, embrollar, estorbar; molestar, incomodar.

cumbersome [cʊ́mbœrsʊm], **cumbrous** [cʊ́mbrʊs], *a.* pesado, engorroso, enfadoso, incómodo, fastidioso, molesto.

cumbersomely [-li], **cumbrously** [-li], *adv.* pesadamente, incómodamente.

cumbersomeness [-nes], *s.* incomodidad.

cumbrance [cʊ́mbrans], *s.* carga, impedimento, molestia.

cumin [cʊ́min], *s.* (bot.) comino.

cumulate [kiúmiulet], *va.* y *vn.* acumular(se) amontonar(se).

cumulation [kiumiuléŝhʊn], *s.* acumulación, amontonamiento, hacinamiento.

cumulative [kiúmiuletiv], *a.* cumulativo, acumulativo.

cumulus [kiúmiulʊs], *s.* cúmulo.

cuneal [kiúneal], **cuneate(d** [kiúniet(ed], **cuneiform** [kiúniiform], *a.* cuneiforme.

cunner [cʊ́nœr], *s.* pez lábrido.

cunning [cʊ́ning]. **I.** *a.* astuto, artero, marrullero; socarrón, ladino, solapado; sagaz; (E. U.) gracioso, divertido, mono (apl. gen. a los niños). **II.** *s.* astucia, ardid, disimulo, artificio; bellaquería, malicia, marrullería; sagacidad.

cunningly [-li], *adv.* astutamente; ladinamente.

cup [cʊp]. **I.** *s.* taza, jícara; cubeta; (igl.) cáliz; (fig.) suerte, fortuna; trago; (dep.) copa o jarrón que se da como premio en las regatas, etc.; (med.) ventosa.—**c.-shaped,** acopado.—**in his cups,** ebrio, chispo. **II.** *va.* aplicar ventosas; ahuecar en forma de taza, acopar.

cupbearer [cʊ́pbéarœr], *s.* copero o escanciador.

cupboard [cʊ́bord], *s.* aparador.

cupel [kiúpel], *s.* copela.

cupellation [kiupeléŝhʊn], *s.* (metal.) copelación.

cupful [cʊ́pful], *s.* contenido de una taza.

cupid [kiúpid], *s.* cupido.

cupidity [kiupíditi], *s.* codicia, avaricia.

cupola [kiúpola], *s.* (arq.) cúpula, domo; (fund.) cubilote; (mar.) cúpula.

cupper [cʊ́pœr], *s.* aplicador de ventosas.

cupping [cʊ́ping], *s.* reducción a forma acopada; (med.) sajadura o escarificación para ventosa; aplicación de ventosa; (aut.) formación de concavidades (en un neumático).—**c. glass,** ventosa.

cupreous [kiúpreʊs], *a.* cobrizo, cobreño.

cupric [kiúpric], *a.* (quím.) cúprico.

cupriferous [kiuprífœrʊs], *a.* cuprífero.

cuprite [kiúprait], *s.* (min.) cuprita, mineral de óxido de cobre.

cupromanganese, cupronickel [cúpromǽngæniŝ, -níkœl], etc. cupromanganeso, cuproníquel, etc. (aleación de cobre y manganeso, cobre y níquel, etc.)

cuprous [kiúprʊs], *a.* (quím.) cuproso.

cupule [kiúpiul], *s.* hueco acopado; (bot.) cúpula.

cupuliferous [kiupulífœrʊs], *a.* cupulífero.

cur [cœr], *s.* perro de mala ralea; hombre vil.

curable [kiúrabœl], *a.* curable, sanable.—**curableness** [-nes], *s.* curabilidad.

curaçoa [kiurasóu], *s.* curasao, curazao.

curacy [kiúrasi], *s.* oficio de cura, curate.

curare [curáre], *s.* curare.

curassow [kiuráso], *s.* (orn.) guaco.

curate [kiúret], *s.* teniente de cura; cura.

curateship, *s.* = CURACY.

curative [kiúrativ], *a.* curativo, sanativo.

curator [kiurétœr], *s.* curador; guardián, conservador, celador.

curatrix [kiurétrix], *s.* curadora.

curb [cœrb]. **I.** *s.* barbada; freno con barbada; (fig.) sujeción, restricción; brocal de pozo; encintado, o flanco (de acera); mercado de la lonja de la calle, lugar de la calle donde se hacen transacciones de lonja; (vet.) corvaza. **II.** *va.* refrenar, contener, reprimir, poner freno.

curbing [cœrbing], *s.* hilera de *curbstones*.

curbstone [cœrbstóun], *s.* piedra que forma el reborde o flanco de la acera.

curculio [cœrkiúlio], *s.* escarabajo.

Curcuma [cœrkiuma], *s.* cúrcuma.

curd [cœrd]. **I.** *s.* cuajada; requesón. **II.** *va.* cuajar, coagular, condensar.

curdle [cœrdœl]. **I.** *vn.* cuajarse, coagularse, engrumecerse, arrequesonarse. **II.** *va.* coagular, cuajar, espesar.

curdly [cœrdli], *a.* cuajado, coagulado.

cure [kiúœr]. **I.** *s.* cura, curación; remedio; cura (de la madera, etc.); cura, cuidado (del hormigón, etc.); vulcanización (de un neumático, etc.). **II.** *va.* curar, sanar; curar (la madera, la carne, etc.); vulcanizar. **III.** *vn.* curar, sanar; curarse (la madera, etc.); vulcanizarse, poderse vulcanizar.

cureless [-les], *a.* incurable.

curer [-œr], *s.* sanador; preparador de salazones y conservas.

curfew [cœrfiu], *s.* toque de queda.

curia [kiúria], *s.* (for.) curia.

curio [kiúrio], *s.* objeto curioso y raro.

curiosity [kiuriósiti], *s.* curiosidad; rareza.

curious [kiúriœs], *a.* curioso; primoroso; raro, singular; elegante.—**curiously** [-li], *adv.* curiosamente; singularmente; primorosamente.—**curiousness** [-nes], *s.* curiosidad; delicadeza; extrañeza, primor.

curl [cœrl]. **I.** *s.* bucle, rizo; (Cuba) crespo; tortuosidad, sinuosidad, ondulación; enfermedad de algunos árboles; alabeo (de la madera).—**c. paper,** papelito para rizar. **II.** *va.* rizar, encrespar, ensortijar, alechugar, ondear.—**to c. the lip,** fruncir el labio. **III.** *vn.* rizarse, enroscarse, encarrujarse.

curled [cœrld], *a.* rizado, crespo, ensortijado, escarolado.—**c. up,** abarquillado.

curlew [cœrliu], *s.* (orn.) zarapito, chorlito.

curlicue [cœrlikiu], *s.* retortijón, enroscadura; cabriola, brinco.

curliness [cœrlines], *s.* ensortijamiento.

curling [cœrling], *s.* ensortijamiento; (dep.) juego parecido al chito, que se juega con piedras sobre el hielo.—**c. irons,** o **c. tongs,** encrespador, rizador, tenacillas.—**c. stone,** piedra con agarradera para el juego de *curling*.

curlingly [cœrlingli], *adv.* rizadamente.

curly [cœrli], *a.* rizado, crespo, rizo.—**c.-hair(ed,** de pelo crespo.

curmudgeon [cœrmúyun], *s.* tacaño, cicatero.

currant [cœrant], *a.* (bot.) grosellero; grosella; pasa de Corinto.

currency [cœrensi], *s.* moneda corriente; dinero en circulación; uso corriente; valor corriente.

current [cœrent]. **I.** *a.* corriente, común; admitido, en boga; general, popular; circulante, corriente; presente, del día, de la actualidad.—**c. account,** cuenta corriente (en un banco).—**c. events,** sucesos del día, asuntos de la actualidad.—**c. money,** moneda legal. **II.** *s.* (*a.* antes de *s.*) corriente (de agua, aire, etc.); (elec.) corriente; intensidad de la corriente.—**c. coil,** (elec.) bobina de intensidad.—**c. damper,** (elec.) amortiguador de corriente.—**c. density,** (elec.) densidad de la corriente (intensidad por unidad de área), corriente específica.—**c. meter,** (elec.) contador de intensidad; (hidr.) molinete hidrométrico, medidor de corriente; hidrómetro.—**c. wheel,** (hidr.) rueda de paletas planas movida por la corriente.

currently [cœrentli], *adv.* corrientemente; generalmente; a la moda.—**currentness** [-nes], *s.* circulación; calidad de actual; aceptación general.

curricle [cœricœl], *s.* carrocín, carriola.

curriculum [cœrríkiulum], *s.* plan de estudios

currier [cœriœr], *s.* curtidor, zurrador.

curriery [cœrriœri], *s.* tenería.

currish [cœrish], *a.* perruno; arisco; brutal.

curry [cœri]. **I.** *va.* (ten.) zurrar, adobar; aderezar, curtir; almohazar; (coc.) condimentar con *curry*.—**to c. favor,** pedir o buscar favores adulando o abyectamente. **II.** *s.* (coc.) salsa usada en la India como condimento; plato sazonado con esta salsa.—**c. powder,** polvo de ciertas especias para preparar el *curry*.

currycomb [cœricóum], *s.* almohaza.

curse [cœrs]. **I.** *va.* maldecir, anatematizar. **II.** *vn.* renegar, echar ternos, blasfemar. **III.** *s.* maldición; imprecación, anatema; terno, reniego, blasfemia; calamidad, azote.

cursed [cœrsed], *a.* maldito, abominable, execrable.—**cursedly** [-li], *adv.* miserablemente; abominablemente.—**cursedness** [-nes], *s.* malicia, perversidad; abominación.

curser [cœrsœr], *s.* maldiciente.

curship [cœrship], *s.* vileza, bajeza, ruindad.

cursing [cœrsing], *s.* execración, maldición.

cursive [cœrsiv], *a.* y *s.* cursivo, corriente.—**c. hand,** letra cursiva.

cursorily [cœrsorili], *adv.* precipitadamente, de paso, de carrera.—**cursoriness** [-nes], *s.* precipitación, priesa; descuido.

cursory [cœrsori], *a.* precipitado, de carrera, por encima.

curt [cœrt], *a.* corto, conciso; brusco, rudo.

curtail [cœrtéil], *va.* cortar, abreviar, reducir, cercenar, desmembrar; restringir.

curtailment [cœrtéilmœnt], *s.* reducción, abreviación, rebajamiento.

curtain [cœrten]. **I.** *s.* cortina; (tea.) telón de boca; (fort.) cortina; (aer.) compartimiento.—**c. lecture,** regaño privado.—**c. of fire** = BARRAGE.—**c. raiser** (tea.) pieza o representación preliminar.—**to draw the c.,** correr un velo, ocultar. **II.** *va.* poner cortinas.—**to c. off,** separar por cortinas.

curtation [cœrtéshun], *s.* (astr.) curtación.

curtly [cœrtli], *adv.* brevemente; lacónica y bruscamente.

curtness [-nes], *s.* concisión, brevedad; brusquedad, rudeza.

curtsy [cœrtsi], *s.* reverencia, cortesía.

curule [kiúrul], *a.* curul.

curvate(d [cœrvet(ed], *a.* corvo, encorvado.

curvation [-véshun], *s.* curvidad, encorvadura, curvatura.

curvature [cœrvachur], *s.* curvatura.

curve [cœrv]. **I.** *va.* encorvar, torcer. **II.** *vn.* encorvarse, torcerse; voltear en curva. **III.** *a.* curvo, corvo, torcido, encorvado. **IV.** *s.* curva; comba; combadura.

curvet [cœrvet]. **I.** *s.* corveta, corcovo. **II.** *va.* y *vn.* corcovear, corvetear, cabriolar.

curvilinear [cœrvilínear], *a.* curvilíneo.

cushat [cúshæt], *s.* paloma torcaz.

cushion [cúshun]. **I.** *s.* cojín; almohadilla; banda (de mesa de billar); (mec.) amortiguador; blandura o suavidad elástica.—**c. tire,** (aut.) llanta maciza acanalada. (El nombre se aplica a menudo a toda llanta maciza de gran suavidad, y en el comercio se traduce a veces por "llanta de cojín".). **II.** *va.* cubrir con cojines, poner cojines a; amortiguar, suavizar; someter a acción amortiguadora.

cusp [cusp], *s.* cúspide; (astr.) cuerno de la luna.

cuspid [cúspid], *s.* colmillo.

cuspidal [-al], *a.* puntiagudo.

cuspidate(d [-eit(ed], *a.* cuspidado, apuntillado.

cuspidor [cúspidor], *s.* escupidera.

cuss [cus], *s.* (fam. E. U.) terno, reniego; chaval; tunante.

cussedness [cúsednes], *s.* (fam. E. U.) malicia, tunantería.

custard [cústard], *s.* (coc.) flan, natillas.—**c. apple,** (bot.) guanábana, jachalí.

custodial [cústódial], *a.* del custodio o de la custodia.

custodian [custódian], *s.* custodio.

custody [cústodi], *s.* custodia; guardia; cárcel; prisión; cuidado; seguridad; recaudo.

custom [cústʊm], *s.* costumbre, usanza; parroquia de una tienda; venta, salida, despacho; (for.) consuetud.—*pl.* derechos de aduana.— **c.-free**, libre de derechos.—**c.-made**, hecho a la medida.—**c. tailor**, sastre ordinario (que hace ropa a la medida).—**c. work**, trabajo de cualquier clase hecho según pedido.

customable [cústʊmabœl], *a.* adeudable.

customarily [cústʊmœrili], *adv.* comúnmente, ordinariamente.

customariness [-rines], *s.* frecuencia, hábito, costumbre.

customary [cústʊmœri], *a.* usual, acostumbrado; (for. Ingl.) consuetudinario, a fuero.

customer [cústʊmœr], *s.* parroquiano.

customhouse [cústʊmjaus], *s.* aduana.—**c. broker**, corredor de aduana.—**c. officer**, aduanero. **c. seal**, marchamo.

cut [cʊt], *va.* (*pret.* y *pp.* CUT) cortar; picar; rebanar; lastimar, herir; labrar, tallar; desbastar; segar; recortar; negar el saludo a, extrañar; castrar; alzar o cortar (los naipes); faltar o no asistir a (la escuela, etc.); cortar (un traje); ejecutar, hacer (piruetas, etc.).—**to c. across**, cortar al través.—**to c. a figure**, descollar; ser importante.—**to c. asunder**, separar cortando, cortar.—**to c. away**, cortar, quitar cortando. —**to c. capers**, cabriolar, hacer cabriolas.—**to c. down**, cortar, derribar cortando, tumbar; mermar, rebajar, cercenar.—**to c. in**, (elec.) intercalar, introducir.—**to c. off**, cortar, quitar cortando; cortar, interrumpir, suspender el abastecimiento (de vapor, agua, etc.); segar (fig.), destruir, arrebatar; interceptar; desheredar; terminar.—**to c. one's wisdom teeth**, (fam.) salirle a uno la muela del juicio, llegar a la edad de la prudencia, tener uso de razón.—**to c. open**, abrir cortando, abrir.—**to c. out**, quitar o sacar cortando; dar forma a (traje, bosque) cortando; preparar; labrar (el porvenir, etc.); (fam.) desbancar, suplantar (apl. gen. a asuntos de amores); excluir; separar; quitar; (fam., con *it* por acusativo) no hablar más de eso, callarse, dejarse de eso.—**to c. short**, interrumpir; terminar repentina o prematuramente; abreviar.—**to c. teeth**, salirle a (uno) dientes.—**to c. the knot, o the Gordian knot**, cortar el nudo gordiano, no pararse en pelillos.—**to c. the throat**, degollar.—**to c. to pieces**, destrozar.—**to c. to the quick**, herir en lo vivo.—**to c. under**, salir de (un rival) vendiendo barato.—**to c. up**, trinchar; cortar en pedazos; cortar a raíz; despedazar (fig., un libro, una reputación); (fam.) afligir, acongojar.

cut, *vn.* hacer un corte o incisión; cortar, ser cortante; poderse cortar; cortar (los naipes); salir (los dientes) (fam.) escurrirse, escabullirse.—**to c. across**, atravesar; tomar por el atajo. —**to c. in**, interrumpir, interponer interrumpiendo.—**to c. loose**, escaparse; soltarse; echar de lado toda restricción.—**to c. up**, ser divisible, poderse dividir (entre herederos, etc.); (fam.) travesear, jaranear; hacer piruetas.

cut. **I.** *s.* corte; cortadura, (Amér.) cortada; ofensa, zaherimiento, cosa o palabra hiriente; pedazo, cosa cortada; tajada, rebanada; atajo; moda; forma; reducción, rebaja (de sueldos, gastos, etc.); desaire; (f. c.) desmonte; (impr.) clisé; grabado, figura; (fam.) hacer marros; hacer novillos. **II.** *pp.* de CUT. **III.** *a.* labrado, tallado; capado; reducido, rebajado (apl. a precios).—**c. and dried**, preparado, arreglado o convenido de antemano; de ordenanza.—**c. glass**, cristal tallado.—**c. sugar**, azúcar en terrones.—**c. tobacco**, picadura de tabaco.

cutaneous [kiutéiniʊs], *a.* cutáneo.

cutaway [cútaʊéi], **cutaway coat** [-cóut], *s.* chaqué, levita de faldones sesgados o abiertos, (Colombia) sacolevita.

cute, *a.* (fam. E. U.) cuco, mono, lindo.

cuticle [kiúticœl], *s.* cutícula; película.

cuticular [kiutíkiular], *a.* cuticular.

cutlass [cútlas], *s.* alfanje, machete, chafarote.

cutler [cútlœr], *s.* cuchillero.

cutlery [cútlœri], *s.* cuchillería.—**c. brick**, piedra para limpiar cuchillos.

cutlet [cútlet], *s.* (coc.) chuleta, coteleta.

cut-off [-of], *s.* brazo de río que atraviesa una punta de tierra; laguna que queda cuando un río cambia su cauce; atajo; (m. v.) cierre a la admisión; punto de expansión; punto de cierre a la admisión; grado de admisión.—**c.-o. valve**, válvula de expansión; válvula de cierre a la admisión.

cut-out [-áut], *s.* (elec.) cortacircuito; fusible; bloque de fusibles; (mec., aut.) escape libre; válvula de escape libre.

cutpurse [cútpœrs], *s.* salteador, carterista.

cutter [cútœr], *s.* cortador; herramienta o máquina para cortar; grabador, tallador; (mar.) cúter; escampavía; hierro, hoja (parte cortante de una herramienta); (E. U.) trineíllo.—**c.-bar**, portacuchilla, pórtahierro, (E. U.) pequeño trineo.

cut-throat [cút-zrot], *s.* asesino.

cutting [cúting]. **I.** *a.* cortante; de cortar; incisivo, hiriente, mordaz; penetrante; amargo, penoso. **II.** *s.* cortadura; corte; incisión; viruta, retazo; alce (de naipes); (cir.) talla; (agr.) estaca de plantar.

cuttlefish [cútœlfish], *s.* (ict.) pulpo, jibia, sepia.

cuttle bone [cútœl bóun], *s.* jibión.

cutwater [-uótœr], *s.* (mar.) tajamar; nariz de puente.

cutwork [-uœrc], *s.* (cost.) calado.

cutworm [-uœrm], *s.* larva destructora de las plantas tiernas.

cyanate [sáianet], *s.* (quím.) cianato.

cyanic [saiǽnic], *a.* (quím.) ciánico.

cyanid(e [sáianid, naid], *s.* (quím.) cianuro.

cyaniding [sáianaiding], *s.* (metal.) cianuración.

cyanite [sáianait], *s.* (min.) cianita.

cyanogen [saiǽnoyen], *s.* cianógeno.

cyanosis [saiænósis], *s.* (med.) cianosis.

cyanotype [saiænotaip], *s.* fotografía de cianuro.

cyanuric [sáiæniúric], *a.* cianúrico.

cycad [sáicæd], *s.* (bot.) cicadácea.—**Cycadaceæ** [-éisii], *s.* (bot.) cicadáceas.

cyclamen [síclamen], *s.* (bot.) pan porcino, artanita.

cycle [sáicœl], *s.* ciclo; período; bicicleta.

cyclecar [sáicœllcar], *s.* motocicleta de cuatro ruedas.

cyclic(al [síclic(al], *a.* cíclico.

cycling [sáicling], *s.* (dep.) ciclismo.

cyclist [sáiclist], *s.* ciclista.

cycloid [sáicloid], *s.* (geom.) cicloide.

cycloidal [saiclóidal], *a.* cicloidal.

cyclometer [saiclómetœr], *s.* ciclómetro u odómetro.

cyclometric [sáiclómétric], *a.* ciclométrico.

cyclometry [saiclómetri], *s.* ciclometría.

cyclone [sáiclon], *s.* ciclón, prester, huracán.

cyclopædia [sáiclopídiæ], *s.* enciclopedia.

cyclopedic [saiclopédic], *a.* enciclopédico.

Cyclopean [saiclopían], **Cyclopic** [saiclópic], *a.* gigantesco; ciclópeo.

Cyclops [sáiclops], *s.* Cíclope.

cyclorama [sáiclorama], *s.* ciclorama.

Cyclostomata [sáiclostómætæ], *s. pl.* (zool.) ciclóstomos.

cygnet [signet], *s.* pollo del cisne.

cylinder [sílindœr], *s.* cilindro.—**c. bore**, diámetro interior del cilindro.—**c. foot**, soporte del cilindro.—**c. head**, fondo del cilindro; culata del cilindro (esp. en aut.).—**c. metal**, hierro de cilindros; ferromanganeso.—**c. oil**, aceite de cilindros, aceite lubricante espeso.

cylindric(al [silíndric(al], *a.* cilíndrico.

cylindroid [silíndroid], *s.* (geom.) cilindroide.

cyma [sáima], **cymatium** [siméshium], *s.* (arq.) cimacio, gola.—**c. reversa**, talón.

cymbal [símbal], *s.* címbalo, platillo.

cyme [sáim], *s.* (bot.) corimbo.

cynegetic [sineyétic], *a.* cinegético.

cynic [sínic], *s.* cínico.

---

cynic(al [sínic(al], *a.* cínico.
cynically [sínicali], *adv.* cínicamente.
cynicism [sínisiŝm], *s.* cinismo.
cynosure [sáinoŝhur, sínoŝhur], *s.* miradero, blanco; (astr.) Cinosura, Osa Menor.
Cyperaceæ [sáipœréisii], *s. pl.* (bot.) ciperáceas.
—**cyperaceous** [-ŝhus], *a.* ciperáceo.
cypher, *s.* =CIPHER.
cypress [sáipres], *s.* (bot.) ciprés.
Cyprian [síprian], *a.* y *s.* ciprino, chipriota.
cyst(is [sist(is], *s.* quiste o quisto; zurrón.
cystic [sístic], **cystous** [sístus], *a.* cístico.
cystotomy [sistótomi], *s.* (cir.) cistotomía.
Cytherean [sizirían], *a.* citéreo.
cytisus [sítisus], *s.* (bot.) citiso, borne.
cytoblast [sáitoblæst], *s.* (biol.) citoblasto, núcleo (de una célula).
cytology [saitóloyi], citología, estudio de las células.
cytoplasm [sáitoplæŝm], *s.* (biol.) citoplasma.
czar [ŝar], *s.* zar.—**czarevitch, czarowitz** [ŝárevich, ŝárouits], *s.* zarevitz.—**czarevna** [ŝarévna], **czarina** [ŝarína], *s.* zarina.
Czech [chec], *s.* y *a.* checo.—**Czechoslovakian** [chécoslováekiœn], *s.* y *a.* checoeslovaco.

D

d [di], *s.* d; (mús., **D**) re, segunda nota de la gama.
D, *a.* en D, de forma de D.—**D valve,** válvula de corredera.
dab [dæb]. **I.** *va.* frotar suavemente con algo blando; picar, golpear. **II.** *s.* mamola, sopapo, golpecito; picada, picotazo; untadura; brochazo; (ict.) barbada.—*pl.* poso, sedimento.
dabber [dǽbœr], *s.* (impr.) bala.
dabble [dǽbœl]. **I.** *va.* rociar, salpicar; mojar. **II.** *vn.* chapotear, guachapear; meterse en algún asunto o negocio.
dabbler [dǽblœr], *s.* chapuzador; chapucero; chisgarabís, chiquilicuatro.
dabster [dǽbstœr], *s.* (fam.) perito, diestro.
dace [des], *s.* (ict.) albur, pez de río.
dachshund [dáxjunt], *s.* pachón, perro de patas muy cortas y torcidas.
Dacian [déiŝhæn], *s.* y *a.* dacio.
dacker [dǽkœr], *vn.* hacer trabajo de pieza; regatear; agarrarse; vagar; registrar.
dactyl [dǽctil], *s.* (pros.) dáctilo (— ◡ ◡).
dactylic [dæctílic], *a.* dactílico.
dactylography [dǽctilógrafi], *s.* dactiloscopia (sistema de identificación por las impresiones digitales).
dactylology [-lóloyi], *s.* dactilológica.
dad, daddie, daddy [dǽd, i], *s.* (fam.) papá.—**daddy-long-legs,** arácnido de cuerpo corto y largas patas; típula.
dado [dádo *o* dédo], *s.* (arq.) dado, neto; rodapié, arrimadillo.
dædal, dæmon, *V.* DEDAL, DEMON.
daffodil, daffodilly [dǽfodil, i], *s.* (bot.) narciso.
daft [daft], *a.* bobo; venático, chiflado; demente, tronera.
dag, *s.* daga; pistola antigua; asta.
dagger [dǽgœr], *s.* daga, puñal; (impr.) cruz, obelisco [†]; (mar.) tornapunta de columna de basada.—**to look, o to speak, daggers,** mirar airado.
daggle [dǽgœl]. **I.** *va.* embarrar. **II.** *vn.* embarrarse, enfangarse.
dago [déigo], *s.* (fam. E. U.) italiano.
daguerrean [daguérean], *a.* perteneciente al daguerrotipo.
daguerreotype [-rotaip], *s.* daguerrotipo.
dahlia [dália], *s.* (bot.) dalia; pigmento violado.
Dail Eirean [dal éirn], *s.* Dail Eirean, nombre del parlamento irlandés.
daily [déili]. **I.** *a.* diario, cotidiano. **II.** *s.* diario (periódico). **III.** *s. adv.* diariamente.
dainties [déntiŝ], *s.* chochos, confites, golosinas.

daintily [déintili], *adv.* delicadamente; regaladamente.—**daintiness** [-nes], *s.* pulidez, delicadeza.
dainty [déinti]. **I.** *a.* delicado, exquisito, refinado; regalado, gustoso, sabroso; melindroso; afectado. **II.** *s.* regalo, bocado exquisito, golería, golosina.
dairy [déiri], *s.* lechería; quesera o quesería; vaquería.—**dairyman** [-mæn], *s.* lechero, mantequero.—**dairymaid** [-meid], *s.* lechera, mantequera.
dais [déis], *s.* tablado, grada, estrado; dosel.
daisy [déiŝi], *s.* (bot.) margarita; (fam.) primor.
dale [déil], *s.* vallecico.
dalliance [dǽlians], *s.* tardanza, dilación; regodeo, retozo.
dally [dǽli], *vn.* tardar, entretenerse; perder el tiempo, holgar, retozar.
Dalmatian [dælméŝhian], *a.* y *s.* dálmata.
Dalmatic [dælmétic], *s.* dalmática.
dam [dæm]. **I.** *s.* madre (en ganadería); yegua; (hidr.) presa; (fund.) dama. **II.** *va.* (hidr.) represar, estancar; cerrar, tapar.
damage [dǽmey]. **I.** *s.* daño, perjuicio, deterioro, estropeo, damnificación; pérdida; (com.) avería.—*pl.* daños y perjuicios; indemnización, **II.** *va.* dañar, perjudicar, empecer, damnificar. **III.** *vn.* dañarse, averiarse.
damageable [-abœl], *a.* susceptible de daño o de indemnización.
damaging [-ing], *a.* perjudicante, perjudicial.
daman [dǽmæn], *s.* (zool.) damán (especie de marmota de Asia y África).
Damascene [dǽmasin]. **I.** *va.* V. DAMASKEEN. **II.** *a.* damasceno; damasquino.
damask [dǽmasc]. **I.** *s.* (tej.) damasco. **II.** *a.* adamascado, damasquinado.—**d. rose,** rosa de damasco o encarnada.—**d. steel,** acero damasquino. **III.** *va.* hacer labor de ataujía; (tej.) adamascar; florear, matizar.
damaskeen [dæmaskín], *va.* hacer labor de ataujía.—**damaskeening** [-ing], *s.* ataujía.
damassin [dæmasin], *s.* (tej.) damasina.
dame [dem], *s.* dama, señora; (fam.) tía; maestra de niñas.
damn [dæm]. **I.** *va.* condenar a pena eterna; maldecir; reprobar; vituperar.—**d. it!** (fam. o vulg.) ¡maldito sea! ¡cáspita! **II.** *vn.* echar ternos, renegar. **III.** *vn.* maldición.
damnable [dǽmnabœl], *a.* condenable; detestable, infame.—**damnably** [-bli], *adv.* horriblemente, de un modo abominable.—**damnation** [-néŝhun], *s.* condenación, maldición.—**damnatory** [-natori], *a.* condenatorio.
damned [dæmd], *a.* condenado, réprobo; maldito; detestable.
damnify [dǽmnifai], *va.* dañar, perjudicar, lastimar, injuriar.
damp [dæmp]. **I.** *a.* húmedo, mojado. **II.** *s.* humedad; niebla, exhalación deletérea; desaliento, abatimiento.
damp, dampen [dǽmpœn]. **I.** *va.* humedecer; enfriar, desanimar, desalentar; apagar; amortiguar; quitar el fuego. **II.** *vn.* humedecerse.—**to d. off,** (agr.) podrirse por el pie, por los ataques de honguillos.
dampening [dǽmpening]. **I.** *s.* humectación o humedecimiento. **II.** *a.* humectativo.
damper [dǽmpœr], *s.* apagador; registro, regulador de tiro de chimenea; apagador del piano; sordina; desalentador.
dampness [dǽmpnes], *s.* humedad.
damsel [dǽmŝel], *sf.* damisela.
damson [dǽmŝon], *s.* ciruela damascena.
dance [dans]. **I.** *vn.* bailar, danzar; saltar, brincar. **II.** *va.* hacer bailar o saltar.—**to d. attendance,** hacer plantón. **III.** *s.* danza, baile.
danceable [dánsebœl], *a.* bailable.
dancer [dánsœr], *s.* danzante, bailador; bailarina; bailarín, saltarín.
dancing [dánsing]. **I.** *s.* baile. **II.** *a.* de baile; que baila; danzante.—**d. girls,** (bot.) bayadera.—**d. master,** maestro de baile.—**d. room,** sala de baile.—**d. school,** escuela de baile.

dandelion [dǽndelaion], *s.* (bot.) diente de león, o amargón.

dander [dǽndœr], *s.* caspa.

dandle [dǽndœl], *va.* mecer; hacer saltar sobre las rodillas; mimar, acariciar.

dandler [dǽndlœr], *s.* niñero.

dandruff [dǽndruf], *s.* caspa.

dandy [dǽndi], *a.* y *s.* petimetre, currutaco lechuguino; (fam.) persona o cosa excelente; primor, maravilla.—**d. fever,** dengue.

Dane [déin], *s.* danés, dinamarqués.

danger [dényœr], *s.* peligro, riesgo.—**there is no d.,** (fam.) no hay miedo, no hay cuidado.

dangerous [-us], *a.* peligroso.—**dangerously** [-li], *adv.* peligrosamente, gravemente, seriamente. —**dangerousness** [-nes], *s.* peligro, gravedad.

dangle [dǽngœl]. **I.** *va.* colgar, suspender, columpiar. **II.** *vn.* pender, columpiarse, bambolearse; andar al retortero.

dangler [dǽnglœr], *s.* juan de las damas; perico entre ellas.

Danish [déinish], *a.* danés, dánico.

dank(ish [dǽnk(ish], *a.* húmedo, liento.

dankness, dankishness, *s.* = DAMPNESS.

danseuse [dansœs], *s.* bailarina.

Dantesque [dantésc], *a.* dantesco.

Daphne [dǽfne], *s.* (bot.) rododafne.

dapper [dǽpœr], *a.* apuesto, gallardo, gentil; limpio, aseado; vivaracho.

dapple [dǽpœl], *va.* salpicar, pintar con manchas redondas, motear.

dapple(d [dǽpœl(d], *a.* rodado, habado.—**d.-gray, d.-grey,** rucio moteado.

dare [deœr]. **I.** *vn.* (pret. DURST o DARED: pp. DARED) osar, atreverse, arriesgarse. **II.** *va.* arrostrar, hacer frente a; desafiar, retar. **III.** *s.* reto.

dare-devil [déar-dévœl], *a.* y *s.* atrevido, temerario.

daring [déæring]. **I.** *a.* osado, atrevido, temerario; emprendedor. **II.** *s.* bravura, atrevimiento. —**daringly** [-li], *adv.* atrevidamente, osadamente.

dark [dark]. **I.** *a.* obscuro; negro (sentido recto y fig.); trigueño, moreno; enigmático; secreto; ciego, ignorante; triste; desconsolador; atroz. —**D. Ages,** edad del obscurantismo, edad media. —**d. horse,** caballo que no promete; (pol. E. U.) competidor o candidato desconocido o inesperado, candidato de componenda.—**d. lantern,** linterna sorda.—**d. meat,** (coc.) carne del ave fuera de la pechuga. **II.** *s.* obscuridad; (pint.) sombra muy obscura.

darken [dárkœn]. **I.** *va.* obscurecer, cegar, obcecar, ofuscar; confundir, embrollar; denigrar, manchar; (fig.) contrastar, entristecer. **II.** *vn.* obscurecerse.

darkling [dárkling], *a.* obscurecido; cegato.

darkly [dárkli], *adv.* obscuramente; secreta u ocultamente.

darkness [dárknes], *s.* obscuridad, sombra, tinieblas; opacidad; obcecación u ofuscación; ceguera; ignorancia; secreto.

darksome [dárksum], *a.* (poét.) obscuro, opaco, sombrío.

darky [dárki], *s.* (fam.) negro (de raza).

darling [dárling]. **I.** *a.* querido, amado. **II.** *s.* el predilecto, el querido, el favorito.—**my d.,** vida mía, amor mío.

darn [darn], *va.* zurcir; (fam.) maldecir.

darnel [dárnel], *s.* (bot.) cizaña, cominillo, rabillo, joyo.

darner [dárnœr], *s.* zurcidor o zurcidora.

darning [dárning]. **I.** *a.* de zurcir.—**d. needle,** aguja de zurcir; (ent.) libélula. **II.** *s.* zurcidura, recosido.

dart [dart]. **I.** *s.* dardo, saeta, flecha, venablo, virote; tragacete; movimiento rápido; (cost.) sisa. **II.** *va.* lanzar, tirar; flechar. **III.** *vn.* lanzarse, arrojarse, precipitarse; volar como dardo o saeta.

darter [dártœr], *s.* flechador; (ict.) pez pequeño americano; (orn.) pájaro-culebra.

Darwinian [daruínian], *a.* y *s.* darwiniano.

Darwinism [dáruinism], *s.* darwinismo.

dash [dæsh]. **I.** *va.* arrojar, tirar, lanzar; quebrar, estrellar, romper; magullar; reprimir, desanimar; frustrar; rociar, salpicar; mezclar; sazonar.—**to d. off,** escribir de prisa.—**to d. out,** romper o hacer saltar; tachar; salir precipitadamente.—**to d. to pieces,** hacer añicos. **II.** *vn.* chocar, estrellarse, romperse (olas, etc.); saltar; zabullirse. **III.** *s.* arremetida, arranque, ataque; incursión; colisión, choque, embate; guión, raya o línea; tilde, tildón; fachenda, gran papel, ostentación; mezcla, condimento, sabor; (aut.) tablero de instrumentos.—**at one d.,** de un golpe.—**to cut a d.,** hacer gran papel.

dashboard [dǽshbord], *s.* guardafango o parafango; (aut.) tablero de instrumentos.

dashing [dǽshing]. **I.** *a.* precipitado, arrojado; arrollador. **II.** *s.* embate.

dashpot [dǽshpot], *s.* (mec.) amortiguador.

dastard [dǽstard], *s.* collón, cobarde.

dastardize [-aiš], *va.* acobardar, amedrentar.

dastardly [-li], *a.* cobarde, pusilánime, tímido.

dastardliness [-nes], **dastardy** [dǽstardi], *s.* cobardía, pusilanimidad.

dasyure [dásiuœr], *s.* dasiuro (marsupial arbóreo).

data [déta], *s.* (pl. de DATUM) datos.

dataria [dætéiriæ], *s.* (igl.) dataría.—**datary** [déiteri], *s.* datario.

datary [détari], *s.* datario; dataría.

date [déit]. **I.** *s.* data, fecha; plazo; cita; período, duración; tiempo, época; (bot.) dátil.—**d.,** o] **d. palm,** palmera. **II.** *va.* datar, fechar, poner fecha a. **III.** *va.* contar, computar.

dateless [déitles], *a.* sin fecha.

dater [déitœr], *s.* fechador, estampilla de fechar.

dative [déitiv], *a.* y *s.* (gram.) dativo.

datum [déitum], *s.* dato.—**d. plane,** o **d.,** (tcp.) plano de referencia, plano de cota cero, plano de nivel.

Datura [dætiúra], *s.* (bot.), datura, estramonio.—**daturin(e** [dætiúrin], *s.* (quím.) daturina.

daub [dob]. **I.** *va.* embadurnar; untar, manchar, pintorrear; dar lechada; cubrir, disfrazar. **II.** *s.* unto, embarradura; mezcla o argamasa barata; pintarrajo, mamarrachada.

dauber [dóbœr], *s.* embadurnador, pintor de brocha gorda, pintorreador, mamarrachista; cepillo para dar betún al calzado.

daubing [dóbing], *s.* mortero, estuco; afeite; mamarracho.

dauby [dóbi], *a.* viscoso, pegajoso; pintarrajado.

daughter [dótœr], *s.* hija.—**d.-in-law,** nuera.

daughterly [dótœrli], *a.* como una hija.

daunt [dant, dont], *va.* acobardar, desanimar; espantar, intimidar, atemorizar.

dauntless [dántles], *a.* intrépido, impávido.

dauntlessness [-nes], *s.* intrepidez, valor.

Dauphin [dófin], *s.* delfín.

Dauphiness [dófines], *s.* delfina.

davit [dévit], *s.* (mar.) pescante de bote.

daw [do], *s.* corneja.

dawdle [dódœl], *vn.* perder tiempo.

dawdler [dódlœr], *s.* haragán, gandul!

dawn [don]. **I.** *vn.* amanecer; apuntar, asomar, mostrarse.—**to d. on,** o **upon one,** caer uno en la cuenta, empezar uno a ver o comprender. **II.** *s.* alba, aurora, madrugada; principio, comienzo, albores.

dawning [dóning], *s.* alborada.

day [déi], *s.* día; período, época; jornada, horas de trabajo; lid, lucha, combate; (min.) terreno superyacente (de una mina).—**d. after d.,** día tras día.—**d. after tomorrow,** pasado mañana.—**d. before yesterday,** antier.—**d. by d.,** día por día.—**d. in, d. out,** o **d. in and d. out,** día tras día, sin cesar.—**d. labor,** trabajo a jorna.—**d. laborer,** jornalero, peón.—**d. lily,** (bot.) gamón.—**d. nursery,** lugar donde se cuidan niños durante las horas de trabajo de los padres, casa o sala de cunas.—**d. of doom,** día del juicio.—**days of grace,** días de gracia.—**days of obligation,** fiestas de guarda.—**d. scholar,** alumno externo.—**d. school,** escuela de externos; escuela de semana (no dominical); escuela diurna (en que se en-

seña de día).—d. star, lucero del alba.—by¡ d., de día.—from d. to d., de día en día, de un día para otro.—this d. week, hace ocho días; de hoy en ocho días.—to gain the d., salir vencedor, triunfar.—to this d., hasta el día de hoy.
daybook [déibuc], s. diario (libro).
daybreak [déibreik], s. = DAWN.
daydream [-drim], s. ensueño, ilusión, quimera.
daylight [-lait], s. luz del día, luz natural.—d.-saving time, tiempo (hora) de verano (en que los relojes se ponen con una hora de adelanto).
dayspring [-spring], s. aurora.
daytime [-taim], s. día.—in the d., de día.
daze [déiṣ]. I. va. ofuscar, aturdir, privar. II. s. deslumbramiento, ofuscamiento.
dazzle [dǽṣœl], va. deslumbrar, ofuscar, encandilar.—dazzlement [-mœnt], s. deslumbramiento; traslumbramiento.
deacon [dícʊn], s. diácono.—deaconess [-es], s. diaconisa.—deaconry [-ɥi], deaconship [-ṣhip], s. diaconado, diaconía.
dead [ded], a. muerto; inerte; inanimado; entumecido; inactivo; sin uso; marchito, seco (flores, hojas, etc.); completo; silencioso; certero, seguro, indudable; absoluto; monótono; profundo, hondo (silencio, calma); privado de derechos civiles; apagado (carbón, sonido, etc.); mortal; desechado, descartado, inútil; insensible; estéril; (elec.) inactivo, sin corriente (apl. a alambres desconectados y a accesorios, como ciertas lámparas, puramente ornamentales).—d. beat, (fam.) gorrero, petardista.—d. block, (f. c.) bloque amortiguador.—d. calm, calma profunda; (mar.) calma chicha.—d. center (m. v.) punto muerto.—d. dog, d. earth, (elec.) tierra (conexión con tierra) perfecta.—d. end, éxtremo cerrado.— d. ground, (elec.) D. EARTH.—d. freight, (mar.) falso flete.—d. letter, letra muerta; carta no reclamada.—d.-letter office, oficina de cartas no reclamadas.—d. lift, acto de alzar a pura fuerza de brazo; grande urgencia o emergencia.—d. man's button, botón del manubrio de interrupción automática.—d. man's handle, (elec.) manubrio de interrupción automática (que corta la corriente cuando el conductor lo suelta).—d. load, (ing.) carga fija.—d. march, marcha fúnebre.— d. point, DEAD CENTER.—d. reckoning, (mar.) estima.—d. rising, (mar.) delgado, línea del arrufo.—d. short circuit, (elec.) cortocircuito sin resistencia.—d. stock, (agr.) utensilios, abastecimientos y herramientas.—d. stop, parada repentina o en seco.—d. water, agua tranquila; marea muerta; (mar.) reveses, estela.—d. weight, fardo, carga onerosa; peso propio de un vehículo (sin la carga).—to be d., haber muerto; no existir ya; estar muerto.
dead. I. adv. enteramente; sumamente; (mar.) exactamente.—d.-beat, agotado, muerto (fig.) de cansancio.—d.-hearted, empedernido. II. s. (con the) lo más silencioso, desolador, etc. (vg. the dead of night, el profundo silencio de la noche; the dead of winter, lo más inclemente del invierno).— the d., los muertos.
deadbeat [dédbit], a. (elec.) aperiódico (apl. a galvanómetros, descargas, etc.)
deadborn [dédborn], a. nacido muerto.
deaden [dédœn], va. amortiguar, amortecer; desvirtuar; retardar, parar; apagar, quitar brillo, sonido, etc.; hacer insípido (el vino, la cerveza).
deadeye [dédai], s. (mar.) vigota.
deadhead [-jed], s. gorrero; (mar.) boya en forma de bloque de madera; poste o bloque de amarra; (fund.) mazarota; depósito de mazarota.
deadlights [dédlaits], s. (mar.) postigos o portas de correr.
deadlock [dédloc], s. estancación, desacuerdo insuperable o persistente que interrumpe una negociación, etc.
deadliness [dédlines], s. calidad de mortífero.
deadly [dédli]. I. a. mortal.—d. sin, pecado mortal. II. adv. mortalmente, implacablemente.
deadness [dédnes], s. inercia; pérdida de vida; amortiguamiento, entumecimiento.
deaf [def], a. sordo.—d. mute, sordomudo.

deaf, deafen [défn], va. asordar, ensordecer.
deafness [défnes], s. sordera; ensordecimiento.
deal [dil], s. parte, porción, cantidad indefinida; turno o acción de tallar (en el juego); (E. U.) pacto o convenio secreto; (com.) trato, negociación.—pl. tablones de pino.—a d., a good, o great d., adv. mucho.—a d., a good, o great d. of, a. mucho.
deal. I. va. (pret. y pp. DEALT) distribuir, repartir; dar, asestar (un golpe, etc.). II. vn. traficar, tratar, gestionar, negociar; intervenir, mediar; ser mano (en el juego de baraja).—to d. by, portarse para con, tratar a.—to d. in, negociar o comerciar en.—to d. with, tratar con; tratar a; tratar de; ocuparse en; entenderse con; habérselas con; entender en.
dealer [dílœr], s. comerciante, negociante; expendedor; tallador (en el juego); JOBBER.
dealing [díling], s. proceder, conducta, comportamiento; trato, comunicación; tráfico, comercio, negocio.—pl. negocios; relaciones; transacciones; dires y diretes.
dealt [delt], pret. y pp. de TO DEAL.
dean [dín], s. (igl.) deán; decano.
deanery [dínœri], **deanship** [dínṣhip], s. (igl.) deanato; decanato.
dear [díœr]. I. a. querido, amado; caro, costoso (u. t. como adv.) II. s. persona querida, bien amado.—d. me!¡ ¡Dios mío! ¡válgame Dios!—my d., querido mío; amigo mío.
dearly [-li], adv. tiernamente, cariñosamente; costosamente.—dearness [-nes], s. cariño, amor, afecto; benevolencia; carestía.
dearth [dœrz], s. carestía, escasez, hambre.
deary [díœri], s. (fam.) queridito, corazón.
death [dez], s. muerte; mortalidad; mortandad, estrago; condenación, muerte eterna.—d. certificate, partida de defunción, fe de óbito.—d. gurgle, estertor.—d. rate, mortalidad, proporción de defunciones.—d.'s-head, calavera.—d. toll, doble, toque de difuntos.—d. trap, casa o lugar peligroso o inseguro, amenaza constante.— d. warrant, sentencia de muerte; fin de toda esperanza.—d.-watch, (no deathwatch) velación en un cadáver; guardia de un reo de muerte.—d. wound, herida mortal.—to d., muchísimo, sumamente.
deathbed [dézbed], s. lecho de muerte.
deathful [dézful], a. mortal; mortífero.
deathfulness [-nes], s. calidad de mortal; apariencia de muerte.
deathless [-les], a. inmortal.—deathlike [-laic], a. sepulcral; cadavérico; mortal.—deathly [-li], I. a. como la muerte; letárgico; cadavérico; mortal. II. adv. mortalmente, gravemente.
deathwatch [-uoch], s. (ent.) anobia.
debacle [debǽcœl], s. desbordamiento; alud; desastre, caída, ruina.
debar [debár], va. excluir, privar.
debark [debárk], va. y vn. desembarcar.
debarkation [debarkéṣhʊn], s. desembarque.
debase [debéis], va. rebajar, degradar, prostituir; adulterar o falsificar.—debasement, [-mœnt], s. envilecimiento, degradación; adulteración, falsificación.—debaser [-œr], s. el que degrada o envilece; falsificador.
debatable [debétabœl], a. discutible.
debate [debéit]. I. s. discusión, debate. II. va. disputar, controvertir; considerar. III. vn. deliberar, discutir; pensar, reflexionar.
debater [debétœr], s. polemista.
debauch [debóch], va. corromper, relajar, pervertir; seducir, violar; sobornar, sonsacar.—debauchery [-cœri], s. libertinaje, licencia, vicio; seducción; corrupción.—debauchedly [-chedli], adv. licenciosamente.—debauchee [déboṣhi], s. calaverón, libertino.—debaucher [debóchœr], s. corruptor; seductor.
debenture [debénchur], s. (com.) obligación; bono, vale, acción; abonaré expedido por la aduana para el reintegro de derechos pagados; abonaré u orden de pago del gobierno.
debilitant [debílitant], a. y s. (med.) debilitante.

debilitate [-teit], *va.* debilitar.—**debilitation** [-téishun], *s.* debilitación.—**debility** [-biliti], *s.* debilidad.

debit [débit]. **I.** *s.* (com.) débito, cargo, adeudo; data; saldo deudor; "Debe" de una cuenta. **II.** *va.* adeudar, cargar.

debonair [débonéar], *a.* afable, cortés; benigno.

debonairly [débonéarli], *adv.* cortésmente, complacientemente.

debouch [debúsh], *va.* desembocar, descargar; salir.

debouchure [debushúr], *s.* salida, boca de un desfiladero, etc.

débris [débrí], *s.* enrona, escombros, desecho, resto, ruinas; (geol.) despojos.

debt [det], *s.* deuda, débito; obligación.—**d. book,** mayor (libro).

debtor [détor], *s.* deudor; cargo, "Debe."

début [débiu], *s.* (teat.) estreno.

débutant, *m.* **débutante** *f.* [débiután(t], principiante, el que se estrena.

decade [déked], *s.* decenio, década.

decadence, decadency [dekéidens(i], *s.* decadencia.

decadent [-dent], *a.* decadente.

decagon [décagon], *s.* (geom.) decágono.

decagram (me [décagram], *s.* decagramo.

decahedron [décajídron], *s.* decaedro.

decalage [décalay], *s.* (aer.) decalaje, ángulo entre las alas (de un aeroplano).

decalcomania [decalcoménia], *s.* calcomania.

decaliter, decalitre [décalítœr], *s.* decalitro.

decalogue [décalog], *s.* decálogo.

decameter, -metre [décamítœr], *s.* decámetro.

decamp [decémp], *vn.* decampar; fugarse, tomar las de Villadiego.

decampment [-mœnt], *s.* acción de decampar.

decanal [décanal], *a.* que pertenece al deanato o al decanato.

decant [decént], *va.* decantar, trasegar.

decantation [decántéshœn], *s.* decantación; trasiego.

decanter [decéntœr], *s.* ampolla.

decapitate [decápitcit], *va.* decapitar; descabezar. —**decapitation** [-téishun], *s.* decapitación.

decapod [décapod], *s.* decápodo.

decarbonate [dicárboneit], *va.* eliminar el anhídrido carbónico de.

decarbonize, decarburize [dicárbonais, dicárbiuraiš], *va.* (fund.) descarburar.

decarburization [dicárbiurišéíshun], *s.* descarburación.

decasyllable [decasílabœl], *s.* decasílabo.

decay [dikéi]. **I.** *vn.* decaer, declinar; deteriorarse; pudrirse, dañarse; picarse (dientes); pasarse, marchitarse. **II.** *va.* arruinar, destruir, echar a perder. **III.** *s.* descaecimiento, menoscabo, decadencia, mengua; podredumbre; vejez; pobreza.

decease [disís]. **I.** *s.* muerte. **II.** *vn.* morir.

deceased [disíst], *s.* y *a.* muerto, difunto, finado.

decedent [disídent], *s.* (for.) finado.

deceit [disít], engaño, dolo, fraude o falacia; impostura.

deceitful [-ful], *a.* engañoso, falso; mentiroso, solapado; ilusorio, engañador.

deceitfully [-fuli], *adv.* engañosamente.

deceitfulness [-fulnes], *s.* falsía, duplicidad; apariencia engañosa.

deceivable [disívabœl], *a.* engañadizo, cándido.

deceivableness [-nes], *s.* facilidad de ser engañado.

deceive [disív], *va.* engañar.

deceiver [-œr], *s.* engañador, impostor.

decelerate [disélereit], *va.* y *vn.* retardar(se), disminuir la velocidad.

December [disémbœr], *s.* diciembre; (fig.) vejez.

decemvir [disémvœr], *s.* decenviro.—**decemviral** [-viral], *a.* perteneciente al decenvirato.—**decemvirate** [-viret], *s.* decenvirato.

decency [dísensi], *s.* decencia, recato, decoro; pudor, honestidad.

decennary [desénari], *a.* decenario.

decennial [desénial], *a.* decenal.

decent [dísent], *a.* decente, honesto, decoroso; razonable, módico.

decently [dísentli], *adv.* decentemente.

decentralization [diséntrališéshun], *s.* descentralización.—**decentralize** [-aiš], *va.* descentralizar.

deception [disépshun], *s.* decepción, engaño, impostura.

deceptive [diséptiv], *a.* falaz, engañoso, ilusorio.

deceptively [-li], *adv.* falaz o engañosamente.

declare [desiéar], *s.* deciárea.

decidable [disáidabœl], *a.* que se puede decidir.

decide [disáid], *va.* y *vn.* decidir, determinar, resolver, juzgar, sentenciar.

decided [disáided], *a.* decidido; resuelto; incontestable, indudable; categórico, inequívoco.—**decidedly** [-li], *adv.* decididamente, categóricamente, indudablemente.

deciduous [disídiuus], *a.* caedizo.

decigram (me [désigræm], *s.* decigramo.

deciliter, decilitre [désilítœr], *s.* decilitro.

decimal [désimal], *s.* y *a.* decimal.—**decimally** [-l], *adv.* decimalmente.

decimate [désimeit], *va.* diezmar.—**decimation** [-méishun], *s.* gran mortandad.—**decimator** [-méitœr], *s.* gran destructor.

decimeter, decimetre [désimítœr], *s.* decímetro.

decipher [disáifœr], *va.* descifrar, interpretar; aclarar.—**decipherable** [-abœl], *a.* descifrable.— **decipherer** [-œr], *s.* descifrador.

decision [disíyun], *s.* decisión, resolución; firmeza, entereza; (for.) decisión o resolución judicial (providencia, auto o sentencia).

decisive [disáisiv], *a.* decisivo; conclusivo, terminante, perentorio.—**decisively** [-li], *adv.* decisivamente.—**decisiveness** [-ness], *s.* autoridad decisiva; firmeza, entereza.

decistere [désistíœr], *s.* deciesterio.

deck [dec]. **I.** *va.* vestir, ataviar, engalanar. **II.** *s.* cubierta, albergue; baraja, monte; (mar.) cubierta; (f. c.) techo de un vagón.—**d. bridge,** puente de tablero superior.—**d. compartment,** (aut.) compartimiento de equipajes.—**d. hand,** marinero, estibador.—**d.-transom knees,** curvas de la cubierta.—**between decks,** entre puentes.

deckle [dékœl], *s.* (pap.) cubierta; banda de caucho continua; barba del papel.

declaim [dicléim]. **I.** *va.* recitar. **II.** *vn.* declamar, perorar.

declaimer [-œr], *s.* declamador, perorador.

declamation [diclaméishun], *s.* declamación, peroración, arenga.

declamatory [diclámatori], *a.* declamatorio.

declarable [dicléærabœl], *a.* que se puede declarar.

declaration [déclaréíshun], *s.* declaración; aserción; explicación, exposición; manifiesto.

declarative [dicléærativ], *a.* declarativo, expositivo, testificativo.—**declaratorily** [-torili], *adv.* en forma de declaración.—**declaratory** [-tori], *a.* declaratorio; afirmativo, demostrativo.

declare [dicléœr], *va.* y *vn.* declarar; confesar.

declaredly [dicléœredli], *adv.* declaradamente, abiertamente, explícitamente.

declarer [dicléœrœr], *s.* declarante, deponente.

declension [diclénshun], *s.* (gram.) declinación, desinencia; decadencia, decremento, menoscabo; inclinación, declive.

declinable [dicláinabœl], *a.* declinable.

declination [déclinéshun], *s.* declinación; descenso, declive; inclinación; decadencia; decremento, deterioro; (E. U.) excusa; renuncia; desviación; descarrío; (astr., fís.) declinación.

declinatory [dicláinatori], *s.* declinatorio.

declinatory, *a.* que envuelve excusa o renuncia.

declinature [dicláinachur], *s.* recusación.

decline [dicláin]. **I.** *va.* no aceptar; rehusar, rechazar; (gram.) declinar. **II.** *vn.* rehusar, negarse; no aceptar; declinar, inclinarse hacia abajo, bajar; menguar, decaer, desmejorar; desviarse, apartarse. **III.** *s.* declinación, decadencia, menoscabo, descaecimiento; (fam.) consunción; (med.) enfermedad que va cediendo.

declinometer [declinómitœr], *s.* declinómetro.
declivity [diclíviti], *s.* declive.
declivitous, declivous [diclívitus, déclivus], *a.* inclinado, clivoso.
decoct [dicóct], *va.* hacer un cocimiento de.
decoction [dicócšhun], *s.* cocimiento; decocción; cocción o hervor.
decode [dicóud], *va.* descifrar.
decohere [dicojíar], *va.* (elec.) volver el cohesor a su posición normal.—**decoherer** [-œr], *s.* descohesor, aparato para restablecer el cohesor a su posición normal.
decollate [dicólet], *va.* degollar.—**decollation** [dícoléšhun], *s.* degollación, degüello.
décolleté [décoleté], *a.* (cost.) escotado.
decolor, decolour, decolorate [dicúlœr(et], **decolorize, decolourize** [dicúlœairš], *va.* descolorar, descolorir; blanquear; clarificar (azúcar).
decoloration [-éišhun], *s.* descoloramiento.
decomposable [dicompóusaboel], *a.* corruptible; descomponible.
decompose [dicompóuš]. **I.** *va.* descomponer; pudrir. **II.** *vn.* pudrirse, corromperse.
decomposite [dicompóusit], *a.* compuesto de compuestos.
decomposition [dicómpošíšhun], *s.* descomposición; corrupción; combinación de cosas ya compuestas.
decompound [dicómpáund]. **I.** *va.* componer de cosas ya compuestas. **II.** *a.* (bot.) varias veces compuesto.—**decompoundable** [-aboel], *a.* capaz de componerse de compuestos.
decorate [décoret], *va.* decorar.
decoration [-éišhun], *s.* decoración, ornamentación; adorno, ornamento; condecoración, insignia.—**D. Day,** (E. U.) el 30 de mayo, día señalado para decorar las tumbas de los soldados muertos en campaña.
decorative [décorativ], *a.* decorativo.
decorator [décoréitœr], *s.* decorador, adornista.
decorous [dicórus], *a.* decoroso; correcto.
decorously [-li], *adv.* decorosamente, correctamente.—**decorousness** [-nes], *s.* decoro.
decorticate [dicórtikeit], *va.* descortezar, descascarar; pelar, mondar.—**decortication** [-kéišhun], *s.* descortezamiento, peladura.—**decorticator** [-kéltœr], *s.* descortezador, mondador.
decorum [dicórum], *s.* decoro, honor; corrección.
decoy [dicói]. **I.** *va.* atraer con señuelo o añagaza; entruchar. **II.** *s.* añagaza, señuelo, reclamo; entruchón; lazo, trampa; entruchada.—**d. duck,** o **pigeon,** cimbel.
decrease [dicrís]. **I.** *vn.* decrecer, menguar o disminuir. **II.** *va.* disminuir, reducir. **III.** *s.* deeremento, diminución; descaecimiento, decadencia.
decree [dicrí]. **I.** *va.* y *vn.* decretar, determinar, mandar, ordenar. **II.** *s.* decreto, edicto, mandato; auto, pragmática.
decrement [décrimœnt], *s.* decremento.
decrepit [dicrépit], *a.* decrépito.
decrepitate [dicrépitet], *va.* y *vn.* decrepitar.
decrepitation [dicrepitéšhun], *s.* (quím.) decrepitación.
decrepitness [dicrépitnes], **decrepitude** [-tiud], *s.* decrepitud, senectud.
decrescent [dicrésœnt], *a.* menguante.
decretal [dicrítal]. **I.** *a.* decretal. **II.** *s.* decretal (gen. *pl.*)
decretion [dicríšhun], *s.* minoración, merma.
decretist [dicrítist], *s.* decretista, decretalista.
decretive [dicrítiv], *a.* decretal, decretivo.
decretorily [décritorili], *adv.* definitivamente.
decretory [décritori], *a.* decretorio, definitivo, decisivo, perentorio.
decrial [dicráial], *s.* vituperio.
decrier [dicráiœr], *s.* vituperador.
decry [dicrái], *va.* desacreditar, vituperar, afear, rebajar.
decubitus [dekiúbitus], **decumbence, decumbency** [dicúmbens(i], *s.* decúbito.
decumbent [-bent], *a.* tendido, acostado, echado.

decumbiture [dicúmbichur, tíur], *s.* tiempo que el enfermo guarda cama.
decuple [dékiupœl], *a.* décuplo.
decurion [dikiúriun], *s.* decurión.
decurrent [dicérent], **decursive** [dicœrsiv], *a.* (bot.) decurrente.
decury [dékiuri], *s.* decuria.
decussate [dicúset]. **I.** *vn.* cruzarse o entrelazarse. **II.** *a.* entrecruzado.
decussation [dicuséšhun], *s.* cruzamiento.
dedal, dædal [dídal], *a.* primoroso, intrincado; artístico, ingenioso; taimado, engañoso.
dedalous [dídalus], *a.* intrincado.
dedicate [dédiket]. **I.** *va.* dedicar; aplicar, consagrar, destinar. **II.** *a.* consagrado, dedicado. —**dedication** [-kéišhun], *s.* dedicación, consagración; dedicatoria.—**dedicator** [-tœr], *s.* dedicante. —**dedicatory** [-catori], *a.* dedicatorio.
deduce [didiús], *va.* deducir, colegir; derivar.
deducement [-mœnt], *s.* deducción.
deducible [didiúsiboel], *a.* deducible.
deducive [didiúsiv], *a.* deductivo.
deduct [didúct], *va.* deducir, restar, descontar.
deduction [didúcšhun], *s.* deducción; descuento, rebaja.
deductive [didúctiv], *a.* deductivo.—**deductively** [-li], *adv.* deductivamente.
deed [díd]. **I.** *s.* acto, hecho; realidad; hazaña, proeza; (for.) escritura.—**d. of gift,** instrumento o escritura de donación.—**d. of release,** acta de cesión.—**in d., in very d.,** de veras, en verdad; de hecho. **II.** *va.* (for.) hacer una escritura de cesión o traspaso.
deem [dím], *va.* y *vn.* juzgar, considerar, creer, estimar.
deep [dip]. **I.** *a.* profundo, hondo; sagaz, astuto; subido, intenso (color); excesivo; concienzudo, profundamente aplicado o consagrado; ronco; (mús.) grave, profundo.—**d. in,** absorto en (la meditación, el estudio); cargado o lleno de (deudas); muy metido o envuelto en (política, etc.).—**d. mourning,** luto riguroso.—**d. red** = CRIMSON. —**d.-sea,** *a.* de las profundidades del mar; de aguas profundas de mar.—**d.-sea lead,** o **line,** sondaleza de mar para grandes profundidades. **II.** *adv.* profundamente; (con *into*), hasta tarde (de la noche, etc.).—**d.-laid,** dispuesto con sagacidad o astucia.—**d.-seated,** arraigado profundamente. **III.** *s.* profundidad, profundidades; piélago, mar; abismo.
deepen [dípœn]. **I.** *va.* profundizar, ahondar; obscurecer; entristecer. **II.** *vn.* hacerse más hondo, más profundo o más intenso.
deeply [dípli], *adv.* profundamente, hondamente, sumamente, intensamente; obscuramente; sagazmente.
deepness [dípnes], *s.* profundidad, hondura; intensidad; malicia.
deer [díœr], *s.* venado, ciervo.—**d. lick,** salegar. —**d. shot,** balines, postas.
deerhound [-jáund], *s.* galgo de cazar venados.
deerskin [-skín], *s.* piel o cuero de venado.
deerstalking [-stóking], *s.* caza de venados al acecho.
deface [difés], *va.* mutilar, estropear, afear.
defacement [-mœnt], *s.* deterioro, estropeo, mutilación, afeamiento.
defacer [-œr], *s.* el que deteriora, estropea o afea.
de facto [di o de féscto], de hecho.
defalcate [difélket]. **I.** *va.* descabalar, rebajar, deducir. **II.** *vn.* desfalcar, malversar.
defalcation [defalkéšhun], *s.* desfalco, malversación; deducción, diminución; déficit.
defamation [difaméšhun], *s.* difamación, disfamación, calumnia.
defamatory [difématori], *a.* calumnioso, difamatorio.
defame [diféim], *va.* desacreditar, deshonrar, denigrar; calumniar.
defamer [diféimœr], *s.* infamador, calumniador.
default [difólt]. **I.** *s.* omisión, descuido, negligencia; culpa, delito; defecto, falta; (for.) rebeldía.—**in d. whereof,** en cuyo defecto.

II. *va.* y *vn.* faltar; delinquir; (for.) condenar en rebeldía.

defaulter [difóltœr], *s.* delincuente; defraudador, desfalcador; (for.) rebelde, contumaz.

defeasance [difísans], *s.* anulación, abrogación, revocación, nulidad.

defeasible [difísibœl], *a.* anulable, revocable.

defeat [difít]. **I.** *s.* derrota; anulación; rechazamiento. **II.** *va.* derrotar, vencer; frustrar; desechar; (for.) anular, abrogar.

defecate [défiket]. **I.** *va.* defecar, clarificar, purgar, purificar, depurar. **II.** *vn.* purificarse, clarificarse; exonerar el vientre. **III.** *a.* depurado, clarificado, refinado.

defecation [-kéishun], *s.* defecación, purificación, clarificación; exoneración del vientre.

defecator [défekéitœr], *s.* (azú.) defecadora.

defect [diféct], *s.* defecto; omisión.

defection [difécshun], *s.* defección, apostasía; deserción, abandono.

defective [diféctiv]. **I.** *a.* defectuoso; falto, corto; anormalmente escaso o falto de inteligencia (apl. esp. a niños); (gram.) defectivo. **II.** *s.* persona (esp. niño) anormalmente falta de inteligencia, o de baja mentalidad.—**defectively** [-li], *adv.* defectuosamente, deficientemente.—**defectiveness** [-nes], *s.* imperfección.

defence, defenceless, etc. = DEFENSE, etc.

defend [difénd], *va.* defender; mantener, sostener.—**defendable** [-abœl], *a.* defendible.—**defendant** [-ant]. **I.** *a.* defensivo. **II.** *s.* defensor; (for.) demandado, acusado, reo.—**defender** [-œr], *s.* defensor; protector, patrono.

defense, defence [diféns], *s.* defensa; vindicación o justificación; resistencia, resguardo o reparo; (for.) defensa.—*pl.* (fort.) obras de fortificación.—**defenseless** [-les], *a.* indefenso o inerme.—**defenselessly** [-li], *adv.* indefensamente.—**defenselessness** [-nes], *s.* desvalimiento, desamparo, abandono.—**defensible** [-sibœl], *a.* defendible; sustentable.

defensive [difénsiv]. **I.** *a.* defensivo; vindicativo. **II.** *s.* defensiva.—**defensively** [-li], *adv.* defensivamente.

defensory [difénsori], *a.* defensivo, justificativo.

defer [difœr]. **I.** *va.* diferir, dilatar, aplazar, remitir; deferir, ceder. **II.** *vn.* demorarse; aguardar; asentir, consentir.

deference [défœrens], *s.* deferencia.

deferent [-ent], *a.* **deferential** [-rénshal], *a.* deferente, respetuoso.

deferentially [-i], *adv.* deferentemente.

deferred [difœrd], *a.* y *pp.* de TO DEFER.—**d. payment,** pago por plazos periódicos (mensualidades, etc.).—**d. shares,** o **stock,** acciones postergadas.

deferrer [difœrœr], *s.* tardador.

deferring [difœring], *s.* dilación, aplazamiento.

defiance [difáiœns], *s.* desafío; oposición obstinada.—**to bid d. to,** o **to set at d.,** desafiar; despreciar, echar a un lado.

defibrinate [difáibrinet], *va.* desfibrinar.

deficience, deficiency [difíshens(i], *s.* defecto, imperfección; deficiencia; déficit.

deficient [difíshent], *a.* deficiente; defectuoso.

deficiently [-li], *adv.* deficientemente.

deficit [défisit], *s.* déficit; descubierto.

defier [difáiœr], *s.* desafiador, retador.

defile [difáil]. **I.** *va.* manchar, profanar, viciar; corromper, violar, constuprar. **II.** *vn.* (mil.) desfilar. **III.** *s.* desfiladero.—**defilement** [-mœnt], *s.* contaminación, violación, profanación.—**defiler** [-œr], *s.* corruptor, violador, constuprador.

definable [difáinabœl], *a.* definible.

define [difáin]. **I.** *va.* definir; circunscribir; determinar, fijar. **II.** *vn.* definir; decidir, juzgar.—**definer** [-œr], *s.* definidor.

definite [définit], *a.* definido, preciso.

definitely [-li], *adv.* definidamente, determinadamente, ciertamente.—**definiteness** [-nes], *s.* exactitud, precisión.

definition [definíshun], *s.* definición; decisión o determinación; (ópt.) precisión.

definitive [definitiv]. **I.** *a.* definitivo, perentorio. **II.** *s.* lo que define.—**definitively** [-li], *adv.* definitivamente.—**definitiveness** [-nes], *s.* cualidad de definitivo.

deflagrable [déflagrabœl], *a.* combustible.

deflagrate [déflagret]. **I.** *va.* hacer deflagrar. **II.** *vn.* deflagrar.

deflagration [-gréishun], *s.* deflagración.

deflagrator [-gréitœr], *s.* deflagrador.

deflate [difléit], *va.* desinflar; contraer.—**deflation** [-fléishun], *s.* desinflación; contracción.

deflect [difléct]. **I.** *va.* desviar, apartar. **II.** *vn.* desviarse, apartarse, ladearse.

deflection, deflexion [diflécshun], *s.* desviación; (ing.) flecha, ordenada máxima de una pieza en flexión.—**d. angle,** ángulo de desviación; (f. c.) ángulo tangencial (entre una tangente y una cuerda).—**d. survey,** (top.) levantamiento por medida de ángulos externos (el que cada recta que se traza forma con la prolongación de la anterior).

deflective [difléctiv], *a.* que desvía.

deflex [difléx], *va.* desviar, ladear, deprimir.

deflorate [déflœret], *a.* (bot.) que ha cesado de florecer.

defloration [défloréishun], *s.* desfloración; selección.

deflower, deflour [difláuœr], *va.* desflorar; ajar.—**deflowerer, deflourer** [-œr], *s.* estuprador.

defluxion [diflúcshun], *s.* destilación; reuma.

defoliate [difóliet]. **I.** *a.* deshojado. **II.** *va.* deshojar.

defoliation [difoliéishun], *s.* (bot.) defoliación.

deforce [difórs], *va.* detentar.—**deforcement** [-mœnt], *s.* usurpación, detentación.

deforest [difórest], *va.* desboscar, talar bosques.

deform [defórm], *va.* deformar, desfigurar, degradar.

deformation [défœrméishun], *s.* deformación, alteración, desfiguración; (mec.) deformación.

deformed [defórmd], *a.* deformado, desfigurado; contrahecho, disforme.—**deformedly** [-medli], *adv.* feamente, deformemente.—**deformedness** [-mednes], *s.* deformación.

deformity [-miti], *s.* deformidad; deformación.

defraud [defród], *va.* defraudar, estafar; frustrar.

defrauder [-œr], *s.* defraudador, estafador.

defray [difréi], *va.* costear, sufragar.—**defrayer** [-œr], *s.* el que costea o sufraga.—**defrayment** [-mœnt], *s.* gasto.

deft [deft], *s.* diestro, hábil; mañoso, apto.

deftness [déftnes], *s.* habilidad; maña.

defunct [difúnct], *a.* y *s.* difunto.

defy [defái], *va.* desafiar, retar; arrostrar; despreciar; contravenir.

degeneracy [dyénœrasi], *s.* degeneración; degradación, depravación.—**degenerate** [-et]. **I.** *vn.* degenerar. **II.** *s.* y *a.* degenerado.—**degenerately** [-li], *adv.* degeneradamente; indignamente; vilmente.—**degenerateness** [-nes], *s.* degeneración.

degeneration [-éishun], *s.* degeneración.

deglutinate [diglútinet], *va.* despegar.

deglutition [deglútishun], *s.* deglución.

degradation [dégradéishun], *s.* degradación; deposición; degeneración; diminución; descenso; corrupción; (pint.) degradación.

degrade [digréid]. **I.** *va.* degradar, privar, deponer; minorar, rebajar, reducir; (pint.) degradar, atenuar; (biol.) reducir de clase superior a inferior. **II.** *vn.* degenerar; abellacarse, envilecerse.

degrading [-ing], *a.* degradante.—**degradingly** [-li], *adv.* degradantemente.

degree [digrí], *s.* grado.—**d. of curve,** (f. c., E. U.) ángulo central correspondiente a una cuerda de 100 pies, o a varias cuerdas iguales cuya suma es 100 pies (puede llamarse grado de curvatura, o, mejor, expresar la curva en función del radio).—**by d.'s,** gradualmente, poco a poco.—**to a d.,** sumamente.—**to take a d.,** graduarse.

dehisce [dijís], *vn.* hendirse.

dehiscence [-œns], *s.* hendedura, grieta; (bot.) dehiscencia.

dehiscent [-œnt], *a.* dehiscente.

dehorn [dijórn], *va.* descornar.

dehort [dejórt], *va.* disuadir.
dehortation [dejortéishʊn], *s.* disuasión.
dehortatory [dejórtatori], *a.* disuasivo.
dehumanize [dejiúmanaiŝ], *va.* embrutecer.
dehydrate [dijáidret], *va.* deshidratar.
deicide [díisaid], *s.* deicida; deicidio.
deictic [dáictic], *a.* (lóg.) directo.
deific(al [diiffic(al], *a.* deífico, divino.
deification [-éishʊn], *s.* deificación; apoteosis.
deifier [díifaiœr], *s.* deificador.
deiform [díiform], *a.* deiforme, divino.
deify [díifai], *va.* deificar, endiosar.
deign [déin], *va.* dignarse, condescender.
deigning [déining], *s.* dignación.
Deipara [díipæræ], *s.* deípara (esp. la Virgen).—
deiparous [-pærʊs], *a.* deíparo, que da nacimiento a un dios.
deism [díism], *s.* deísmo—creencia en un Dios criador, sin creencia en la revelación ni los otros dogmas cristianos; teísmo—creencia en Dios como distinto del universo. (Ʊ. gen. en el primer sentido).—**deist** [díist], *s.* deísta; teísta.
deistical [diístical], *a.* deístico.
deity [díiti], *s.* deidad, divinidad.—**D., the D.,** Dios.
deject [diréct], *va.* abatir, afligir; desanimar, desalentar, descorazonar.—**dejected** [-ed], *a.* acongojado, abatido.
dejecta [[diⅡécta], *s. pl.* excrementos.
dejectedly [diréctedli], *adv.* abatidamente, descorazonadamente.
dejection [derécŝhʊn], *s.* melancolía; (med.) deposición, evacuación.
de jure [di rúri], (for.) legalmente, legítimamente; de derecho.
dekagram, dekaliter, etc. = DECAGRAM, etc.
delaine [deléin], *s.* muselina de lana.
delapsed [dilǽpst], *a.* (med.) caído.
delation [diléŝhʊn], *s.* (for.) delación, acusación, denunciación.
delay [dilé]. **I.** *va.* dilatar, diferir, demorar, retardar. **II.** *vn.* tardar, demorarse. **III.** *s.* dilación, tardanza, demora, retraso.
dele [díli]. **I.** *va.* (impr.) suprimir. **II.** *s.* dele, signo (δ).
deleble [délebœl], *a.* que se puede borrar.
delectable [deléctabœl], *a.* deleitable, delicioso.
delectableness [-nes], *s.* calidad de deleitoso.
delectably [-bli], *adv.* deleitosamente.
delectation [delectéiŝhʊn], *s.* deleitación, deleite.
delegate [déleguet]. **I.** *va.* delegar, diputar, comisionar. **II.** *a.* y *s.* delegado; comisario.—'**delegation** [-guéŝhʊn], *s.* delegación, diputación.
delete [delít], *va.* suprimir.
deleterious [deletírius], *a.* deletéreo.
deletion [diⅡŝhʊn], *s.* supresión.
delf [delf], *s.* desaguadero; césped.
delf(t [delf(t], *s.* loza fina.
deliberate [delíbœret]. **I.** *va.* y *vn.* deliberar; vacilar, dudar. **II.** *a.* pensado, reflexionado, premeditado; circunspecto, cauto.—**deliberately** [-li], *adv.* deliberadamente o con premeditación.
deliberateness [-nⅿs], **deliberation** [-éiŝhʊn], *s.* deliberación, reflexión; premeditación; intención.—**deliberative** [-ativ], *a.* deliberativo.
delicacy [délicasi], *s.* delicadeza, finura; suavidad, sensibilidad; ternura; delicadez, fragilidad o friabilidad; nimiedad, escrupulosidad; miramiento o consideración; bocado exquisito; golosina, gollería.
delicate [déliket], *a.* delicado; fino, suave, ligero; pulido, fino (como modales, etc.); tierno; escrupuloso; mirado, considerado; de buen gusto, exquisito.
delicately [-li], *adv.* delicadamente, sutilmente.
delicateness [-nes], *s.* delicadeza, delicadez, molicie.
delicatessen [délicætésen], *s.* manjares delicados, esp. fiambres; tienda donde se venden.
delicious [deliŝhus], *a.* delicioso, sabroso, exquisito.—**deliciously** [-li], *adv.* deliciosamente; sabrosamente.—**deliciousness** [-nes], *s.* calidad de ser delicioso.

delight [deláit]. **I.** *s.* delicia, deleite, encanto. **II.** *va.* deleitar, encantar. **III.** *vn.* deleitarse.
delighted [-ed], *a.* encantado, contentísimo.—**to be d. to** (seguido de infinitivo), tener mucho gusto en; alegrarse muchísimo de.
delightful [-ful], *a.* delicioso, deleitable, encantador.—**delightfully** [-i], *adv.* deliciosamente, deleitosamente.—**delightfulness** [-nes], *s.* delicia, deleite, encanto.—**delightsome** [deláitsʊm], *a.* = DELIGHTFUL.—**delightsomely** [-li], *adv.* = DELIGHTFULLY.
delimit [delímit], *va.* delimitar, fijar límites.—**delimitation** [-éiŝhʊn], *s.* delimitación.
delineament [delíniamœnt], **delineation** [-liniéŝhʊn], *s.* delineación, delineamiento; boceto, diseño, bosquejo, esquicio; descripción.
delineate [deⅡniet], *va.* delinear, trazar, diseñar; describir.
delineator [delíniéitœr], *s.* delineador, diseñador, dibujante, descriptor.
delinquency [delíncuensi], *s.* delincuencia.
delinquent [-cuent]. **I.** *a.* delincuente; descuidado, negligente; culpable; adeudado y no pagado; moroso en el pago. **II.** *s.* delincuente.
deliquesce [delicués], *vn.* liquidarse, derretirse, licuarse.—**deliquescence** [-ens], *s.* (quím.) deliquescencia o licuación.—**deliquescent** [-ent], *a.* delicuescente.
deliquium [delícuiʊm], *s.* deliquio, desfallecimiento.
delirious [delírius], *a.* delirante, desvariado.
delirium [delirⅰʊm], *s.* delirio, desvarío.—**d. tremens,** delirium tremens.
deliver [delivœr]. **I.** *va.* librar, libertar; entregar, rendir; comunicar; recitar, pronunciar, decir; dar, asestar (un golpe, etc.).—**to d. of a baby,** partear.—**to d. over,** entregar; traspasar.—**to d. up,** entregar.—**to be delivered,** alumbrar, parir.—**to be delivered of,** dar nacimiento a. **II.** *vn.* (con *in, into*), alimentar, conducir a (apl. a conductos, tubos, etc.)
deliverance [-ans], *s.* rescate; liberación, salvación; dictamen, profesión; alumbramiento.
deliverer [-œr], *s.* entregador, librador, libertador, salvador; relator.
delivery [delivœri], *s.* liberación, rescate; entrega; lo entregado; capacidad; producción; salida (vg. d. *pipe*, tubo de salida); traspaso, dación; rendición; alumbramiento, parto; modo de obrar, expresarse o cantar; expedición, desembarazo; (for.) entrega, cesión; (com.) remesa; distribución (del correo).
dell [del], *s.* vallejuelo, cañada.
Delphian, Delphic [délfian, délfic], *a.* délfico.
Delsarte [delsárt], o **Delsartean system** [delsártiœn sístem], *s.* método calisténico delsarteano, o de Delsarte.
delta [déltæ], *s.* delta.—**d. connection,** (elec.) conexión en triángulo o en delta.—**d. current,** corriente que pasa por conexión delta.—**d. metal,** metal delta (nombre de fábrica—aleación de cobre, cinc y hierro).
deltoid(al [déltoid(al]. **I.** *a.* deltoide, triangular. **II.** *s.* (anat.) deltoides.
delude [deliúd], *va.* engañar, alucinar.
deluder [deliúdœr], *s.* engañador.
deluge [deliuⅰ]. **I.** *s.* diluvio, inundación; golpe, calamidad. **II.** *va.* diluviar, inundar.
delusion [deliúyʊn], *s.* error, embaimiento; ilusión; decepción, engaño.
delusive [deliúsiv], **delusory** [-sori], *a.* engañoso, ilusivo, ilusorio.
de luxe [de lucs], *a.* de lujo.
delve [delv]. **I.** *va.* y *vn.* cavar; penetrar, ahondar; sondear, inquirir. **II.** *s.* hoyo, zanja; hondonada.
demagnetize [dimǽgnetaiŝ], *va.* desimantar.
demagnetiza(o sa)tion [-tiŝéiŝhʊn], *s.* desimanación, desimantación.
demagogic [demagóyic], *a.* demagógico.
demagogism [démagóguiŝm], **demagogy** [-yi], *s.* demagogia.
demagogue [démagog], *s.* demagogo.

demain [deméin], *s.* heredad; tierra solariega.

demand [dimǽnd]. **I.** *va.* y *vn.* exigir, reclamar o pedir perentoriamente; (for.) demandar, requerir, recuestar; interrogar. **II.** *s.* exigencia; (for., e. p.) demanda.—**on d.**, a la presentación; a solicitud.—**to be in d.**, tener demanda, ser solicitado.—**demandant** [-ant], *s.* (for.) demandante, demandador.—**demander** [-œr], *s.* exactor; demandador; pedigüeño, pedigón.

demarcation, demarkation [demarkésʰhun], *s.* demarcación, deslinde; limitación.

demean [dimín], *va.* y *vr.* portarse, conducirse; rebajarse, degradarse.

demeanor, demeanour [dimínœr], *s.* conducta, comportamiento; porte.

demented [diménted], *a.* demente.

dementia [dimênshia], *s.* demencia, locura.—**d. præcox,** demencia precoz.

demerit [dimérit], *s.* demérito, desmerecimiento.

+demersed [dimœrst], *a.* (bot.) sumergido.

demesne [deméin, demín], *s.* =DEMAIN.

demi, *prefijo*, semi, casi.

demigod [démigod], *s.* semidiós.

demijohn [démiyon], *s.* garrafón, damajuana.

demilitarization [dimílitærisʰéishun],, *s.* desmilitarización.

demilitarize [-aisʰ], *va.* desmilitarizar.

demilune [démiliun], *s.* (astr. y fort.) media luna.

demimondaine [démimóndéin], *s.* mujer de vida airada o libre.—**demimonde** [-mónd], vida airada; mujeres de la vida airada.

demise [demáisʰ]. **I.** *s.* muerte, fallecimiento; sucesión o transmisión de la corona; (for.) +traslación de dominio. **II.** *va.* legar, dejar en testamento; transferir, ceder, arrendar.

demisemiquaver [dʰsmisémicuéivœr], *s.* (mús.) fusa.

demission [demíshun], *s.* dimisión.

demit [demít], *va.* dimitir, renunciar.

demi-tasse [démi-tás], *s.* taza cafetera, jícara.

demiurge [démiœry], *s.* demiurgo.

demobilization [dimóbilisʰéishun], *s.* puesta de un ejército en pie de paz.—**demobilize** [-aisʰ], *va.* (mil.) poner (un ejército) en pie de paz.

democracy [demócrasi], *s.* democracia.

democrat [démocrat], *s.* demócrata.

democratic(al [-crétic(al], *a.* democrático.

democratically-[-i], *adv.* democráticamente.

demography [demógrafi], *s.* demografía.

demographic [démográfic], *a* demográfico.

demolish [demólish], *va.* demoler, arruinar.—**demolisher** [-œr], *s.* destructor, demoledor.—**demolishment** [-mœnt], **demolition** [démolíshun], *s.* demolición, destrucción.

demon [dímun], *s.* demonio.

demonetization [dímónetisʰéishun], *s.* suspensión de la circulación (apl. a la moneda).

demonetize [-taisʰ], *va.* suspender la circulación de (una moneda); quitar el valor normal a.

demoniac(al [dimóniac, dimonáiacal], *a.* demoníaco, endemoniado.—**demoniac,** *s.* energúmeno; demoníaco.

demonism [dímonism], *s.* creencia en demonios; carácter de demonio.

demonolatry [-nólatri], *s.* culto del demonio.

demonology [-nóloyi], *s.* demonología.

demonstrability [dimónstræbíliti], *s.* demostrabilidad.

demonstrable [-bœl], *a.* demostrable.

demonstrableness [-nes], *s.* demostrabilidad.—**demonstrably** [-bli], *adv.* demostrablemente.

demonstrate [démónstreit, démonstreit], *va.* demostrar.

demonstration [démonstréishun], *s.* demostración; muestra; manifestación; exposición, presentación; (mil) demostración de fuerza; manifestación pública.

demonstrative [démónstrativ], *a.* demostrativo.

demonstratively [-li], *adv.* demostrativamente.

demonstrator [démónstréitœr], *s.* el que demuestra; expositor (el que explica); maestro o profesor de una ciencia objetiva, demostrador (apl. esp. al de anatomía).

demoralization [demóralisʰéishun], *s.* desmoralización.

demoralize [-aisʰ], *va.* desmoralizar, corromper; descorazonar; (fam.) desarreglar o desbarajustar.

demotic [demótic], *a.* demótico.

demountable [dimáuntæbœl], *a.* (aut.) desmontable.

demulcent [demulsent], *a.* y *s.* (med.) emoliente, demulcente, dulcificante.

demur [demœr]. **I.** *vn.* objetar, poner dificultades; vacilar, fluctuar; (for.) admitir los hechos aducidos por la parte contraria, pero negando que sean causa suficiente de litigio. **II.** *s.* duda, escrúpulo, vacilación, objeción.

demure [demiœr], *a.* serio, formal; recatado, modesto; gazmoño, pacato.—**demurely** [-li], *adv.* modestamente; con gazmoñería.—**demureness** [-nes], *s.* gravedad, recato; gazmoñería.

demurrage [demœrey], *s.* demora, detención; (com.) estadía.—**demurral** [-al], *s.* demora, detención; vacilación.—**demurrer** [-œr], *s.* (for.) — admisión de los hechos aducidos por la parte contraria, pero negando que sean causa suficiente de litigio.

demy [demái], *s.* papel marquilla.

den [den], *s.* caverna, guarida, escondrijo; rincón, retrete; (fam.) cuchitril.

denary [dénari]. **I.** *a.* decimal. **II.** *s.* decena.

denarius [dinérius], *s.* denario.

denationalize [dinésʰhunalaisʰ], *va.* desnaturalizar; cambiar la nacionalidad.

denationalization [-isʰéishun], *s.* pérdida o cambio de nacionalidad.

denaturalize [dinéchuralaisʰ], *va.* desnaturalizar; desfigurar.

denature [dinéichur], *va.* (quím.) desnaturalizar, alterar (esp. haciendo que no se pueda comer o beber).—**denatured alcohol,** alcohol metilado o desnaturalizado, alcohol impotable.

dendriform [déndriform], **dendritic** [déndrític], *a.* dendrítico.

dendrite [déndrait], *s.* (min.) dendrita.

dendrology [dendróloyi], *s.* dendrografía.

dendrometer [dendrómitœr], *s.* dendrómetro.

dengue, *s.* (med.) dengue.

deniable [dináiabœl], *a.* negable.

denial [dináial], *s.* negación, negativa; denegación.

denier [dináiœr], *s.* negador.

denier [diníœr], *s.* penique de plata.

denigrate [dénigret], *va.* ennegrecer; denigrar.

denitrification [dinítrifikéisʰhun], *s.* desnitrificación, eliminación del nitrógeno.—**denitrify** [-trifai], *va.* desnitrificar.

denization [denisʰéishun], *s.* naturalización, ciudadanía.

denizen [dénisʰen]. **I.** *s.* ciudadano, habitante, residente; (Ingl.) extranjero naturalizado. **II.** *va.* naturalizar.

denominable [denóminabœl], *a.* denominable.

denominate [denóminet]. **I.** *va.* denominar, nombrar. **II.** *a.* denominado.

denomination [-éishun], *s.* denominación, título, designación; secta; religión.—**denominational** [-æl], *a.* sectario.

denominative [-nativ], *a.* denominativo.

denominator [denóminéitœr], *s.* (arit.) denominador.

denotable [denótabœl], *a.* capaz de ser denotado o distinguido.

denotation [denotéishun], *s.* denotación.

denotative [denótativ], *a.* denotativo.

denote [denóut], *va.* denotar.

denouement [denúman], *s.* éxito; desenlace.

denounce [denáuns], *va.* denunciar, delatar; denunciar (una mina); atacar, censurar; amenazar; significar la resolución de terminar (un pacto, tratado); promulgar.

denouncement [-ment], *s.* denuncia; ataque, censura; declaración de la intención de terminar (un tratado, etc.)

denouncer [-œr], *s.* denunciador, delator.

dense [dens], *a.* denso; cerrado, estúpido.
densely [dénsli], *adv.* densamente.
denseness [dénsnes], **density** [dénsiti], *s.* densidad; estupidez.
densimeter [densímitœr], *s.* densímetro.
dent [dent]. **I.** *s.* abolladura; mella; diente, indentación. **II.** *va.* abollar; mellar.
dental [déntal], *a.* y *s.* dental.
dentate(d [déntet(ed], *a.* dentado; (blas.) danchado, dantellado, endentado.
dented [dénted], *a.* abollado; mellado, dentellado.
denticle [dénticœl], *s.* dientecillo; (arq.) dentículo.
denticulate(d [dentíkulet(ed], *a.* (bot.) dentado, dentellado, denticular; (arq.) con dentículos, de dentículos.—**denticulation** [-éishun], *s.* (arq.) formación de dentículos; obra de dentículos, que tiene dentículos;(hist. nat.) denticulación.
dentifrice [déntifris], *a.* dentífrico.
dentil [déntil], *s.* (arq.) dentículo, dentellón.
dentilingual [dentilíngual], *a.* linguodental.
dentin(e [déntin], *s.* dentina.
dentirostral [dentiróstral], *a.* dentirrostro.
dentist [déntist], *s.* dentista.
dentistry [déntistri], *s.* cirugía dental; dentistería.
dentition [dentíshun], *s.* dentición; dentadura.
dentoid [dentóid], *a.* parecido a un diente.
denture [dénchœr], *s.* dientes de un animal; dentadura postiza.
denudate [deniúdet], *a.* desnudo; despojado, deshojado.
denudation [déniudéishun], *s.* denudación.
denude [deniúd], *va.* desnudar, despojar, desvestir; dejar desnudo.
denunciate [denúnshiéit], *vn.* denunciar, amenazar.—**denunciation** [-éishun], *s.* denunciación, acusación.—**denunciator** [-éitœr], *s.* denunciador, denunciante.—**denunciatory** [-siatori], *a.* denunciatorio, conminatorio.
deny [dinái]. **I.** *va.* negar; rehusar o denegar; renunciar, desconocer; negarse a, no dejarse ver de.—**to d. one's self**, hacer abnegación de sí mismo; negarse. **II.** *vn.* negar.
deobstruct [diobstrúct], *va.* desembarazar, desobstruir, abrir.
deobstruent [dióbstruent], *a.* y *s.* (med.) desopilativo.
deodar [diodár], *s.* (bot.) cedro de la India.
deodorant [diódœrant], **deodorizer** [-áiscœr], *s.* desinfectante, sahumador.—**deodorization** [-rišéishun], *s.* desinfección o sahumerio.—**deodorize** [-aiš], *va.* desinfectar, sahumar.
deontology [diontóloyi], *s.* deontología.
deoxidation [diócsidéshun], *s.* desoxidación.
deoxidize [-aiš], **deoxidate** [-eit], *va.* (quím.) desoxigenar, desoxidar.
depart [depárt[, *vn.* irse, partir, salir; apartarse, desviarse, salirse; morir.
department [depártmœnt], *s.* departamento; división, ramo.—**d. store**, bazar (tienda de variedades en grande escala).
departmental [-æl], *a.* departamental; del departamento, ramo, etc.; dividido u organizado en departamentos.
departure [dipárchœr], *s.* partida, salida; desviación; muerte; (mar. y top.) coordenada de longitud, distancia entre los dos meridianos que pasan por el extremo de una recta; (mar.) posición o coordenada (longitud y latitud) de un barco a su salida.
depauperate [depóperet], *va.* empobrecer, depauperar.
depend [depénd], *vn.* pender, colgar.—**to d. on**, o **upon**, depender de; confiar en, contar con, estar seguro de.
dependable [-abœl], *a.* confiable, seguro.
dependance, dependancy, dependant. *V.* DEPENDENCE, DEPENDENCY, etc.
dependence [-dens], *s.* confianza, seguridad; dependencia; posesión, colonia; subordinación; sostén, apoyo; (for.) litispendencia.

dependency [-ensi], *s.* dependencia, pertenencia, sucursal; edificio anexo.—*pl.* anexidades.
dependent [-ent]. **I.** *a.* dependiente, subalterno; subordinado, sujeto; condicional, contingente; necesitado; pendiente, colgante. **II.** *s.* dependiente, subalterno; persona que hay que mantener; mantenido, manutenido; persona falta de lo necesario.
dependently [-ently], *adv.* dependientemente.
depending [-ing], *a.* pendiente; colgante, suspendido; dependiente.—**d. on**, según.
depict [depíct], **depicture** [depícchœr], *va.* pintar; representar; retratar; describir.
depilate [dépilet], *va.* quitar el vello o pelo.
depilation [depiléshun], *s.* depilación.
depilatory [depílatori]. **I.** *a.* atanquía. **II.** *a.* depilatorio.
deplete [deplít], *va.* agotar o disipar; vaciar; (med.) depauperar.—**depletion** [-shun], *a.* vaciamiento; agotamiento.
depletive, depletory [deplítiv, dépletori], *a.* que vacía o agota.
deplorable [deplórabœl], *a.* deplorable, lamentable; lastimoso.—**deplorableness** [-nes], *s.* estado deplorable.—**deplorably** [-bli], *adv.* deplorable o lastimosamente.
deplore [deplóar], *va.* deplorar, lamentar.
deploy [deplói]. **I.** *va.* y *vn.* (mil.) desplegar. **II.** *s.* despliegue.
deplumate [deplúmet], *a.* sin plumas.
deplumation [depluméshun], *s.* muda, desplumadura.
deplume [deplúm], *va.* desplumar.
depolarize [dipólaraiš], *va.* (elec.) despolarizar.
depolarization [-šéshun], *s.* (elec.) despolarización.
depone [depóun], *va.* (for.) deponer.
deponent [-ent], *a.* y *s.* (for.) deponente, declarante; (gram.) verbo deponente.
depopulate [depópiuleit], *va.* despoblar.
depopulation [-léishun], *s.* despoblación; despueblo, asolamiento.—**depopulator** [-léitœr], *s.* despoblador, asolador.
deport [depórt]. **I.** *va.* deportar, desterrar. **II.** *vr.* portarse, conducirse.
deportation [deportéishun], *s.* deportación, destierro.
deportment [depórtmœnt], *s.* proceder; conducta, comportamiento; porte.
deposable [depóusabœl], *a.* capaz o digno de ser depuesto.
depose [dipóuš]. **I.** *va.* deponer, destituir; destronar; degradar; (for.) deponer o declarar. **II.** *vn.* deponer, testificar.
deposit [dipóšit]. **I.** *va.* depositar; (quím.) precipitar, asentar. **II.** *vn.* depositarse. **III.** *s.* depósito, sedimento; (com. y for.) depósito.
depositary [-itœri], *s.* depositario, guardián; almacén, depósito.
deposition [depošíshun], *s.* (for.) deposición o testimonio, declaración; deposición o destitución; depósito, acumulación.
depositor [dipóšitœr], *s.* depositador o depositante.
depository [-tori], *s.* depositaría, depósito, almacén.
depot [dípo], *s.* pósito, depósito, almacén; (f. c. E. U.) estación, paradero.
depravation [[dipravéishun], *s.* depravación, perversión, estragamiento.
deprave [dipréiv], *va.* depravar.—**depraved** [dipréivd], *a.* depravado.—**depravedly** [-vedli], *adv.* depravadamente.—**depravedness** [-vednes], *s.* depravación, estragamiento, corrupción.
depraver [-vœr], *s.* depravador.
depravity [dipræviti], *s.* depravación.
deprecate [déprekeit], *va.* deprecar; lamentar, desaprobar.
deprecation [-kéishun], *s.* deprecación o desaprobación.—**deprecative** [déprecœtiv], **deprecatory** [-œtori], deprecativo; de desaprobación.—**deprecator** [-kéitœr], *s.* deprecador; desaprobador.

---

depreciate [dipríshieit]. **I.** *va.* depreciar, rebajar, abaratar; menospreciar, desapreciar. **II.** *vn.* bajar de precio, abaratarse; depreciarse.

depreciation [-éishun], *s.* depreciación; descrédito, desestimación; baja, reducción de precio.

depreciative, depreciatory [dipríshietiv, ætori], *a.* depreciativo, despectivo.

depreciator [dipríshiéitœr], *s.* deprimidor, despreciador.

depredate [dépredet], *va.* y *vn.* depredar.

depredation [-éishun], *s.* depredación.

depredator [dépredéitœr], *s.* depredador.

depredatory [déprédatori], *a.* de depredación.

depress [diprés], *va.* deprimir, abatir; bajar, inclinar; abaratar, rebajar el precio de; desalentar o desanimar; humillar; (mat.) reducir el grado de.

depressant [-ænt], *s.* y *a.* (med.) deprimente, debilitante.

depressed [diprést], *a.* deprimido; rebajado; desanimado, alicaído.

depression [dipréshun], *s.* depresión; abatimiento.—**d. of the horizon, o of the visible horizon** (mar.) depresión de horizonte.

depressive [-siv], *a.* depresivo; deprimente.

depressor [-sœr]. **I.** *a.* depresor.—**d. nerve,** nervio depresor o de Cyon. **II.** *s.* músculo depresor; (cir.) depresor.

deprivable [depráivabœl], *a.* amovible, revocable.

deprivation [déprivéishun], *s.* privación, carencia; pérdida.

deprive [dipráiv], *va.* privar, despojar; excluir; impedir; destituir.

depth [depz], *s.* profundidad; fondo; espesor, grueso; parte interior o recóndita; lo más profundo o intenso; viveza (del color); gravedad (del sonido); sagacidad, penetración; (mar.) puntal.—**d. bomb, o d. charge,** bomba o granada contra submarinos.—**d. of the hold,** puntal de la bodega.—**beyond, o out of one's d.,** en agua más honda que uno, o que se lo traga; más allá de los alcances de uno.

de profundis [di profúndis], *s.* de profundis.

depurant [dépiurant], **depurative** [-retiv], *a.* depurativo.

depurate [dépiuret]. **I.** *va.* (med.) depurar. **II.** *a.* depurado.

depuration [-éishun], *s.* depuración.

deputation [depiutéishun], *s.* diputación, delegación, comisión.

depute [depiút], *va.* diputar, delegar.

deputize [dépiutaiš], *va.* (E. U.) diputar.

deputy [dépiuti], *s.* diputado; delegado, comisionado, enviado, agente; (for.) lugarteniente.—**d. governor,** teniente gobernador.

deraign [diréin], *va.* probar; vindicar; reclamar.

derail [dirréil], *va.* descarrilar.

derailment [dirréilmœnt], *s.* descarrilamiento.

derange [dirrénY], *va.* desarreglar, desordenar; descomponer; trastornar.—**derangement** [-mœnt], *s.* desarreglo, desorden; descompostura; desbarajuste; locura.

derby [(E. U.) dœrbi, (Ingl.) dárbi], *s.* sombrero hongo; carrera Derby, famosa carrera anual de caballos; (alb.) llana.

derelict [dérelict]. **I.** *a.* negligente, remiso; derrelicto. **II.** *s.* (for.) buque abandonado.

dereliction [dérelicshun], *s.* desamparo, abandono; dejación.

deride [deráid], *va.* ridiculizar.—**derider** [-œr], *s.* burlón, zumbón; ridiculizador, mofador, escarnecedor.—**deriding,** [-ing], *a.* mofador.—**deridingly** [-li], *adv.* irrisoriamente, con mofa.

derision [derívun], *s.* irrisión, mofa, escarnio.

derisive [deráisiv], **derisory** [deráisori], *a.* irrisorio, burlesco.

derisively [deráisivli], *adv.* irrisoriamente.

derivable [deráivabœl], *a.* derivable, deducible.

derivation [dérivéishun], *s.* derivación; deducción; etimología; (biol.) descendencia; (med.) derivación.

derivative [dérivativ], *a.* derivativo.—*s.* derivado; (mat.) derivada.

derive [diráiv]. **I.** *va.* deducir (una conclusión, una fórmula); establecer (una fórmula); (gram.) derivar; (quím.) derivar, obtener (un compuesto de otro); (elec.) derivar.—**to d. from,** deber a; hacer provenir de; sacar (ganancia, etc.) de. **II.** *vn.* provenir, emanar, descender.

derived [diráivd], *a.* derivado; obtenido; resultante; (elec.) derivado.—**d. function,** (mat.) derivada.

derm [dœrm], **derma, dermis** [dœrma, mis], *s.* dermis, cutis.

dermal, dermic [dœrmal, dœrmic], *a.* dérmico, cutáneo.

dermatologist [dœrmatóloyist], *s.* dermatólogo.

dermatology [dœrmatóloyi], *s.* dermatología.

derogate [déroqueit], *vn.* (con **from**) derogar, detractar.—**derogation** [-éishun], *s.* detracción; derogación.—**derogative** [deróqativ], o **derogatory** [-tori], *a.* derogatorio.

derrick [dérric], *s.* grúa; torre o armazón de taladrar (situada en la boca de un pozo artesiano, de petróleo, etc.)

dervish [dœrvish], *s.* derviche, santón.

descant [déscænt]. **I.** *s.* comentario, disertación; (mús.) discante. **II.** [descént], *vn.* discurrir, comentar; (mús.) discantar.

descend [descénd], *va.* y *vn.* descender, bajar; (con **from**) descender, desviarse; (con **to**) rebajarse a, descender a; (con **on** o **upon**) invadir, caer en o sobre; (astr.) declinar, ponerse.

descendant, descendent [-ant, ent], *a.* descendiente; descendente.—**descendible** [-lbœl], *a.* que se puede descender o heredar.

descending [disénding], *a.* descendiente.

descension [desénshun], *s.* descendimiento; descenso; declinación; degradación.

descent [desént], *s.* descenso, bajada; descendimiento; descensión; declive; alcurnia, origen, descendencia, posteridad, sucesión; (for.) herencia; (mil.) invasión, incursión, rebajamiento, humillación, degradación.

describable [descráibæblœ], *a.* descriptible.

describe [descráib], *va.* describir.

describer [descráibœr], *s.* descriptor.

descrier [descráiœr], *s.* descubridor.

description [descripshun], *s.* descripción; trazado; representación; clase, género, naturaleza, calidad.

descriptive [descríptiv], *a.* descriptivo.—**d. anatomy, astronomy, botany, geometry,** etc., anatomía, astronomía, etc., descriptiva.

descry [descrái], *va.* columbrar, avistar, divisar; descubrir.

desecrate [désecreit], *va.* profanar.

desecration [-shun], *s.* profanación.

desert [désœrt]. **I.** *s.* desierto, yermo; páramo. **II.** *a.* desierto, yermo; del desierto.

desert [desœrt]. **I.** *s.* merecimiento o mérito. **II.** *va.* desamparar, dejar solo, abandonar. **III.** *va.* y *vn.* (mil.) desertar.—**deserter** [-œr], *s.* desertor.—**desertion** [-shun], *s.* deserción, defección, abandono.

deserve [desœrv]. **I.** *va.* merecer. **II.** *vn.* tener merecimientos.—**deservedly** [desœrvedli], *adv.* merecidamente, condignamente.

deserver [desœrvœr], *s.* merecedor.

deserving [-ing]. **I.** *a.* meritorio; acreedor, merecedor o digno. **II.** *s.* mérito, merecimiento.—**deservingly** [-li], *adv.* dignamente, merecidamente.

desiccation [desikéishun], *s.* desecación; resecación.

desiccant [désicant], *a.* y *s.* (med.) desecante.

desiccate [désikeit]. **I.** *va.* desecar, enjugar; secar, pasar. **II.** *vn.* resecarse.

desiccative [désikætiv], **desiccatory** [désicatori], *a.* desecativo.

desiccator [désikéitœr], *s.* aparato para desecar; (azú.) evaporadora.

desiderate [desídœret], *va.* desear, querer; faltar, necesitar.

desideratum [desidœrétʊm], s. desiderátum.

design [desáin]. **I.** va. idear, inventar; proyectar, calcular (una máquina, un puente); destinar, dedicar; idear, concebir; diseñar, delinear. **II.** vn. hacer proyectos, diseños, planos, planes. **III.** s. proyecto, cálculo (de máquinas, puentes, etc.); disposición, arreglo, hechura, construcción; plan; propósito, intención; plano; diseño, croquis. —by o through, d., intencionalmente.

designable [desígnabœl], a. demarcable, definible; distinguible.

designate [designeit], va. apuntar, señalar; distinguir; designar, nombrar, destinar.

designation [designéshʊn], s. designación, señalamiento, título, nombramiento.

designative [designætiv], a. designativo, especificante.

designedly [desáinedli], adv. adrede, de propósito, intencionadamente.

designer [desáincœr], s. dibujante; diseñador; proyectista (de máquinas, obras, etc.); delineador, tracista; inventor; maquinador.

designing [desáining], a. insidioso, astuto, artero, intrigante.

designingly [desáiningli], adv. insidiosamente.

desilverize [disílveraiś], va. desplatar, extraer o separar la plata de.

desinence [désinens], s. desinencia.

desirability [desáirabíliti], **desirableness** [desáirabœlnes], s. calidad de deseable; conveniencia.

desirable [desáirabœl], a. deseable, de desearse, conveniente.

desire [desáicœr]. **I.** s. deseo. **II.** va. y vn. desear.

desirous [desáirʊs], a. deseoso.—**desirously** [-li], adv. deseablemente, ansiosamente, con deseo.— **desirousness** [-nes], s. deseo vivo, anhelo.

desist [desíst], vn. desistir.—**desistance** [-æns], s. desistencia, cesación.

desk [desc], s. escritorio, pupitre; carpeta.

desman [désmæn], s. (zool.) desmán.

desmography [desmógrafi], s. desmografía.

desmoid [désmoid], s. (anat. y med.) ligamentoso; fibroso.

desolate [désolet]. **I.** a. desolado; desierto, solitario. **II.** va. desolar o arrasar; despoblar, devastar, arruinar.—**desolately** [-li], adv. desoladoramente.—**desolateness** [-nes], s. desolación.

desolater, desolator [désoléitœr], s. desolador, asolador.—**desolation** [-éishʊn], s. desolación, asolación; aflicción, desconsuelo.

despair [dispéœr]. **I.** s. desesperación. **II.** vn. desesperar, perder toda esperanza.

despairing [-ing], a. desesperante; desesperado; sin esperanza.—**despairingly**, [-li], adv. desesperadamente.

despatch [despéch], va. despachar, expedir; enviar o remitir; aviar, apresurar, concluir; matar, rematar.

despatch, dispatch [des- o dispéch], s. despacho, expedición, prontitud; parte, comunicación; medio rápido de transporte.—**d. boat**, (mar.) aviso.

despatcher [despéchœr], s. despachador; expedidor.

desperado [desperédo o ádo], s. malhechor, bandido temerario.

desperate [désperet], a. desesperado; arrojado, arriesgado o temerario; irremediable, desesperanzado, perdido; furioso, violento, terrible; (for.) incobrable.—**desperately** [-li], adv. desesperadamente; perdidamente.—**desperateness** [-nes], s. temeridad, arrojo, furia, violencia.—**desperation** [-réishʊn], s. desesperación, furor, encarnizamiento.

despicable [déspicabœl], a. despreciable, vil.

despicableness [-nes], s. vileza, ruindad.

despicably [-bli], adv. vilmente, bajamente.

despisable [despáisabœl], a. despreciable.

despise [despáiś], va. despreciar.

despite [despáit]. **I.** s. despecho, malquerencia, aversión, inquina. **II.** prep. a despecho de, a pesar de.

despiteful [-ful], a. malicioso, rencoroso, vengativo, maligno.—**despitefully** [-li], adv. malignamente, maliciosamente.—**despitefulness** [-nes], s. malignidad, rencor, odio, inquina.

despoil [despóil], va. despojar; robar.

despoiler [-œr], s. pillador, saqueador, robador.

despoliation [despoliéishʊn], s. despojo.

despond [despónd], vn. desalentarse, abatirse; perder la esperanza, desesperarse, abandonarse.

despondence, despondency [-ens(i], s. desaliento, descaecimiento.

despondent [-ent], a. desalentado, abatido, desesperanzado.

despondingly, despondingly [-tli, -ingli], adv. desalentadamente.

despot [déspot], s. déspota.—**despotize** [déspotaiś], vn. despotizar.—**despotic(al** [despótic, al], a. despótico.—**despotically** [-li], adv. despóticamente.—**despoticalness** [-nes], s. despotismo.— **despotism** [déspotiśm], s. despotismo.

despumation [despiuméshʊn], s. despumación.

desquamate [déscuameit], vn. exfoliarse.

desquamation [descuaméishʊn], s. descamación, exfoliación.

dessert [diśért], s. postre.—**d. spoon**, cuchara de postre, cuchara de tamaño intermedio entre la de sopa y la cafetera.

destination [destinéishʊn], s. destinación, destino; paradero; meta.

destine [déstin], va. destinar; dedicar, consagrar; predestinar.

destiny [déstini], s. destino, hado, sino.

destitute [déstitiut], a. destituído; desamparado; falto, desprovisto.

destitution [destitiúshʊn], s. destitución, privación; miseria, indigencia, inopia.

destroy [destrói] va. y vn. destruir; matar.

destroyer [destróicœr], s. destruidor, destructor; (mar.) cazatorpedero.

destructibility [destrúctibíliti], s. destructibilidad.—**destructible** [-tibœl], a. destructible.

destruction [distrʊ́cshʊn], s. destrucción; perdición, muerte eterna; (ing.) fractura, rotura (vg. to load a beam to d., cargar una viga hasta la fractura, o hasta romperla).

destructive [-tiv], a. destructor, destructivo.— **d. distillation**, destilación seca.

destructively [-li], adv. destructivamente.— **destructiveness** [-nes], s. espíritu de destrucción; destructividad.

desudation [desiudéishʊn], s. sudor excesivo.

desuetude [désuetiud], s. desuso.

desulphurize [disúlfœraiś], va. desulfurar.

desulphurization [-iśéishʊn], s. desulfuración.

desultorily [désultórili], adv. sin plan ni ilación, inconexamente, inmetódicamente.—**desultoriness** [-rines], s. falta de plan; desconexión.

desultory [désultori], a. inconexo; parentético.

detach [detéch], va. separar, despegar o desprender; destacar.

detachable [ditéchæbœl], a. separable, de quitar y poner, de quitapón.

detached [detécht], a. suelto, distinto, separado.

detachment [detéchmœnt], s. separación, despegadura; destacamento.

detail [ditéil]. **I.** va. detallar, particularizar, circunstanciar. **II.** s. detalle, pormenor, (mil.) destacamento; (b. a.) detalle.

detain [ditéin], va. detener, retardar, contener; retener.—**detainer** [-œr], s. (for.) detentador, retenedor; detención.

detect [detéct], va. descubrir; hallar.

detecter [-œr], s. descubridor.

detection [detécshʊn], s. averiguación, descubrimiento.

detective [detéctiv], a. hábil para descubrir o averiguar.—s. detectivo, detective.

detector [ditéctœr], (m. v.) indicador de nivel; (mar.) detector de torpedos; (elec.) detector.— **d. bar**, (f. c.) barra de fijación o de cierre (en un cambiavías).

detent [detént], s. retén, trinquete; fiador, seguro; escape de un reloj.

detention [deténshŭn], *s.* detención, retención; arresto, encierro.

detentive [det-éntiv], *a.* que retiene o asegura.

deter [detœr], *va.* acobardar; disuadir; desanimar.—**to d. from,** disuadir de, impedir.

deterge [detœrv], *vc.* (med.) absterger.

detergent [detœryent], *a.* y *s.* detergente, detersivo; detersorio; abstergente.

deteriorate [ditírioreit], *va.* y *vn.* deteriorar.—**deteriorating** [-ing], *a.* que deteriora, perjudicial.—**deterioration** [-éishŭn], *s.* deterioro, deterioración.—**deteriorative** [-éitiv], *a.* DETERIORATING.

determent [detœrmœnt], *s.* disuasión.

determinable [detœrminabœl], *a.* determinable; terminable.—**determinably** [-bli], *adv.* determinablemente.

determinant [detœrminant]. **I.** *a.* determinativo. **II.** *s.* causa determinante; (mat.) determinante.

determinate [detœrminet], *a.* determinado, definido; decidido, resuelto; concluyente; (bot.) de inflorescencia limitada.—**determinately** [-li], *adv.* determinadamente.—**determinateness** [-nes], *s.* calidad de determinado.

determination [detœrminéishŭn], *s.* determinación; (for.) decisión, fallo; (lóg.) especificación; (med.) congestión.

determinative [-ativ], *a.* determinativo, determinante.

determine [detœrmin]. **I.** *va.* determinar; (for.) concluir, terminar; restringir. **II.** *vn.* terminar, acabar, concluir; resolverse, decidirse.

determined [-d], *a.* determinado, resuelto.

determinism [ditœrminĭsm], *s.* (fil.) determinismo, negación del libre albedrío.—**determinist** [-ist], *s.* y *a.* (fil.) determinista.

deterrent [detœrœnt]. **I.** *a.* que disuade. **II.** *s.* lo que disuade.

detersion [detœrshŭn], *s.* detersión.

detersive [detœrsiv], *a.* y *s.* detergente, abstergente.

detest [detést], *va.* detestar.—**detestable** [-abœl], *a.* detestable.—**detestableness** [-bœlnes], *s.* calidad de detestable.—**detestably** [-abli], *adv.* detestablemente.—**detestation** [-téishŭn], *s.* detestación, execración.

dethrone [dezróun], *va.* destronar.

dethronement [-mœnt], *s.* destronamiento.

detinue [détiniu], *s.* (for.) auto contra el detentador de alguna cosa.

detonate [détoneit]. **I.** *vn.* estallar, hacer explosión. **II.** *va.* hacer estallar.

detonating [-ing], *a.* detonante.—**d. fuse,** mecha de explosión o detonante.—**d. gas,** gas o mezcla detonante (dos volúmenes de hidrógeno y uno de oxígeno).—**d. powder,** pólvora detonante.—**d. tube,** eudiómetro detonante.

detonation [detonéishŭn], *s.* detonación.

detonator [détonéitœr], *s.* explosivo detonante; señal detonante.

detonator [[détonéitœr], *s.* explosivo detonante o de explosión instantánea; detonador, mezcla o artefacto para producir explosión; (f. c.) señal detonante.

detorsion [detórshŭn], *s.* acto de destorcer.

detour [detúr], *s.* vuelta, rodeo.

detract [detréct]. **I.** *va.* detraer, disminuir o quitar. **II.** *vn.* detraer, detractar, denigrar.—**to d. from,** disminuir, hacer desmerecer, quitar mérito a, afear.

detracter, detractor [detréctœr], *s.* detractor, infamador.

detraction [detrécshŭn], *s.* detracción, maledicencia, difamación.

detractive [-tiv], **detractory** [-tori], *a.* difamatorio, derogatorio.—**detractively** [-tivli], difamatoriamente.

detrain [ditréin]. **I.** *va.* (mil.) sacar (soldados) del tren. **II.** *vn.* salir del tren.

detriment [détrimœnt], *s.* detrimento.

detrimental [detriméntal], *a.* perjudicial.

detrital [detráital], *a.* detrítico.

detrition [detríshŭn], *s.* desgaste.

detritus [detráitus *o* tritus], *s.* (geol.) detritus; escombros, desperdicios.

detrude [detrúd], *va.* empujar o lanzar hacia abajo o hacia afuera.

detruncate [detrŭnkeit], *va.* recortar, podar.

detruncation [-kéishŭn], *s.* recorte, poda.

detrusion [detrúyun], *s.* empuje hacia afuera o hacia abajo.

deuce [diús], *s.* dos (en naipes o dados); pata (en otros juegos); (fam.) demonio, diantre, demontre.

deuced [diúsed], *a.* excesivo.

deuterogamist [diutœrógamist], *s.* deuterógamo, el que contrae segundas nupcias.

deuterogamy [-gami], *s.* deuterogamia, segundas nupcias.

Deuteronomy [diútœrónomi], *s.* Deuteronomio.

devastate [dévasteit], *va.* devastar.

devastation [devastéishŭn], *s.* devastación, desolación, ruina.

develop [dévélop]. **I.** *va.* desenvolver, desarrollar; desplegar; descubrir; fomentar; producir; perfeccionar; explotar (minas, etc.); (fot.) revelar. **II.** *vn.* progresar; avanzar; formarse, crecer, desarrollarse.

developer [-œr], *s.* (fot.) revelador, baño.

development [-mœnt], *s.* desarrollo, evolución; fomento; producción; cambio; acontecimiento nuevo; explotación; (f. c.) desarrollo (vía curva en pendiente); (fot.) revelamiento.

developmental [-mentœl], *a.* relativo al desarrollo; evolucionista.

devest [devést], *va.* y *vn.* (for.) enajenar.

deviate [díviet], *va.* y *vn.* desviar(se).

deviation [diviéishŭn], *s.* desviación; deriva; desvío, extravío, error.

device [deváis], *s.* invento, invención; artefacto, artificio; plan, traza, proyecto; expediente, recurso; ardid; dibujo o patrón (de tela o bordado); lema, divisa, mote, cifra, empresa.

devil [dévil]. **I.** *s.* diablo; demonio; aprendiz de imprenta; manjar muy sazonado con picante; (mec.) terraja para labrar tornillos de madera; máquina de moler o desgarrar; máquina de descargar granos. (Apl. a varias otras máquinas, cuya clase gen. se indica por un modificativo.).—**d.'s advocate,** (igl. y fig.) abogado del diablo.—**d.'s darning needle,** (ent.) caballito del diablo, libélula; (bot.) peine de Venus.—**a poor d.,** un pobre diablo.—**the d.!** (fam.) ¡caramba! ¡diablos! **II.** *va.* condimentar con mucho picante; someter a la acción de una máquina *devil.*

devilfish [-fish], *s.* (zool.) raya grande del golfo de México; pulpo.

devilish [dévilish], *a.* diabólico; perverso; travieso; excesivo.—**devilishly** [-li], *adv.* diabólicamente, endiabladamente.—**devilishness** [-nes], *s.* diablura; perversidad.

devilry [dévilri], **deviltry** [-tri], *s.* diablura, diablería.

devilship [-ship], *s.* calidad o estado de demonio o diablo.

devious [díviœs], *a.* desviado, descarriado, extraviado; tortuoso; errante.—**deviously** [-li], *adv.* tortuosamente.—**deviousness** [-nes], *s.* extravío, descarrío; desviación.

devisable [deváisabœl], *a.* que se puede inventar; (for.) que se puede legar.

devisal [deváisal], *s.* invención; (for.) legado o manda.

devise [deváis]. **I.** *va.* idear, inventar, proyectar; (for.) legar. **II.** *vn.* formar proyectos; maquinar. **III.** *s.* (for.) legado de bienes raíces.

devisee [deviší], *s.* (for.) legatario.

deviser [deváisœr], *s.* inventor, autor.

devisor [deváisor], *s.* testador que lega bienes raíces.

devitalize [diváitalaiš], *va.* quitar vitalidad.

devitrification [devitrifikéishŭn], *s.* desvitrificación.—**devitrify** [-fai], *va.* desvitrificar, quitar al vidrio su transparencia.

devoid [devóid], *a.* libre, exento; desprovisto.

devoir [devuár], *s.* homenaje.

devolution [devolúshʊn], **devolvement** [devólvment], s. entrega, traspaso; (neol.) degeneración.

devolve [devólv]. **I.** va. transmitir, traspasar, entregar. **II.** vn. (seguido de **to, on** o **upon**) recaer, pasar a, tocar, incumbir a.

Devonian [devónian], s. devoniano, devónico.

devote [devóut]. **I.** va. dedicar; consagrar; maldecir. **II.** vr. entregarse, consagrarse.

devoted [devóted], s. devoto, ferviente; adicto, afecto; infeliz, malhadado, condenado.—**devotedly** [-li], adv. devotamente.—**devotedness** [-nes], s. devoción; dedicación; afecto.

devotee [dévotí], s. beato; fanático; aficionado.

devotion [devóshʊn], s. devoción, piedad; celo; afecto; constancia.—pl. preces, rezo.—**devotional** [-œl], a. devoto, piadoso; devocionero.

devour [deváuœr], va. devorar.—**devourer** [-œr], s. devorador, engullidor, tragón; destructor. —**devouring** [-ing], a. devorador.—**devouringly** [-li], adv. devoradoramente.

devout [deváut], a. devoto, pío, piadoso.

devoutly [-li], adv. devotamente, piadosamente.

devoutness [-nes], s. piedad, devoción.

dew [diú]. **I.** s. rocío, relente, sereno.—**d. point,** temperatura a que se forma el rocío. **II.** va. rociar; apaciguar, refrescar.

Dewar vessel [diúœr vésel], s. (quím.) frasco de Dewar, frasco Dewar.

dewberry [diúberi], s. (bot.) zarzamora.

dewdrop [diúdrop], s. gota de rocío.

dewlap [diúlap], s. papada.

dewlapt [diúlapt], a. papudo.

dewworm [-uœrm], s. lombriz de tierra.

dewy [diúi], a. rociado; lleno de rocío.

dexiocardia [décsiocárdiæ], s. (med.) dexiocardia, desviación del corazón hacia la derecha.

dexter [décstœr], a. diestro o derecho; favorable, propicio.

dexterity [decstériti], **dexterousness** [décstœrusnes], s. destreza.

dexterous [décstœrus], a. diestro.—**dexterously** [-li], adv. diestramente.

dextrad [déxtræd], adv. a la derecha.

dextral [décstral], a. derecho, diestro; favorable, propicio.

dextrality [decstráliti], s. situación a la mano derecha.

dextrin(e [déxtrin], s. (quím.) dextrina.

dextrocardia [décstrocárdiæ], s. = DEXIOCARDIA.

dextrose [déxtros], s. (quím.) dextrosa o glucosa.

dey [déi], s. bey o dey.

diabase [dáiabeis], s. (geol.) diabasa.

diabetes [daiabítis], s. (med.) diabetes.

diabetic [daiabétic], a. diabético.

diabolic(al [daiabólic(al], a. diabólico.

diabolically [-i], adv. diabólicamente.

diabolicalness [-nes], s. calidad de diabólico.

diabolo [diæbolo], s. diábolo (juego y juguete).

diacaustic [dáiæcóstic], s. y a. (fís.) diacáustico.

diachylon [daiækilon], **diachylum** [daiækilʊm], s. diaquilón.

diaconal [diæconal], a. diaconal.

diaconate [diæconet], a. diaconato.

diacoustics [dáiacústics], s. diacústica.

diacritic(al [dáiacrític(al], a. diacrítico.

diactinic [dáiactínic], a. diactínico.

diactinism [daiæctinísm], s. diactinismo.

diadelphous [dáiadélfʊs], a. (bot.) diadelfo.

diadem [dáiadem], s. diadema.

diæresis o **dieresis** [daiérisis], s. (gram.) diéresis, crema.

diagnose [dáiægnóuš], va. (med.) diagnosticar.

diagnosis [-nósis], s. (med.) diagnosis.

diagnostic [-nóstic]. **I.** s. (med.) diagnóstico. **II.** a. diagnóstico, diacrítico.

diagnosticate [dáiægnóstikeit] = DIAGNOSE.

diagnostics, s. diagnosis.

diagonal [daiægonal], a. y s. diagonal; (mat.) diagonal.—**d. cloth,** diagonal (tela).

diagonally [daiǽgonali], adv. diagonalmente.

diagram [dáiagræm], s. diagrama.

diagraph [dáiagraf], s. diágrafo.

dial [dáial], s. reloj de sol, cuadrante; muestra, esfera de reloj; brújula.

dialect [dáialect], s. dialecto.

dialectic(s [dáialéctic(s], s. dialéctica, lógica.

dialectic(al [-tic(al], a. dialéctico, lógico.

dialectician [-lectíshan], s. dialéctico, lógico.

dialist [dáialist], s. constructor de relojes solares.

dial(l)ing [-ing], s. gnomónica, levantamiento del plano de una mina.

dialog, s. y vn. = DIALOGUE.

dialogic(al [dáialóyic(al], a. dialogal.

dialogism [daiǽloyism], s. dialogismo.

dialogist [daiǽloyist], s. dialoguista.

dialogically [dáialóyicali], **dialogistically** [-loyísticali], adv. en forma de diálogo.

dialogize [daiǽloyaiš], vn. dialogar, dialogizar.

dialogue [dáialog]. **I.** s. diálogo. **II.** va. y vn. dialogar, dialogizar.

dialysis [daiǽlisis], s. solución de continuidad; (quím.) diálisis; (gram.) diéresis, crema; (ret.) asíndeton; (med.) languidez; herida abierta.

dialytic [daialític], a. dialítico.

diamagnetic [dáiæmægnétic], diamagnético.—**diamagnetism** [-mægnetísm], s. diamagnetismo.

diamantine [daiamǽntin], a. adamantino, diamantino.

diameter [daiǽmetœr], s. diámetro.

diametral [daiǽmetral], **diametrical** [dáiamétrical], a. diametral.—**diametrically** [-i], adv. diametralmente.

diamide [dáiæmid], s. (quím.) diamida.

diamine [-min], s. (quím.) diamina.

diamond [dáiamʊnd]. **I.** s. diamante; cortavidrios; oros (de baraja); (impr.) tipo de letra de 4 o 4½ puntos; (geom.) rombo; demarcación; rombal en el juego de baseball.—**d. anniversary,** aniversario 60.—**d. cutter,** diamantista.—**d. drill,** taladro de punta de diamante.—**d. setter,** joyero.—**d. wedding,** aniversario 75. **II.** a. diamantado; adiamantado; rombal.

diandrous [daiǽndrʊs], a. (bot.) diandro.

diapason [daiapéišʊn], s. (mús.) diapasón.

diaper [dáiapœr]. **I.** s. lienzo adamascado; servilleta; pañal, braga; (b. a.) arabesco, adorno, labor. **II.** va. y vn. labrar, formar arabescos, adamascar.

diaphaneity [daiafanéiti], s. diafanidad.

diaphanous [daiǽfanʊs], a. diáfano o transparente; terso, claro.

diaphoresis [daiaforísis], s. (med.) diaforesis, sudor.—**diaphoretic(al** [daiaforétic(al], a. diaforético, sudorífico.

diaphragm [dáiafræm], s. diafragma.

diaphragmatic [-frægmætic], a. diafragmático.

diaphysis [-fisis], s. diáfasis.

diapophysis [-pófisis], s. (anat.) diapófosis.

diarrhea, diarrhœa [daiarría], s. diarrea.

diarrheal [daiarríal], **diarrheic** [daiaréic], a. diárrico.

diarist [dáiarist], s. diarista.

diarthrosis [dáiarzrósis], s. diartrosis.

diary [dáiari], s. diario, jornal.

diastase [dáiastes], s. diastasia.

diastole [daiǽstoli], s. diástole.

diaspore [dáiaspoœr], s. diásporo.

diastyle [dáiastail], s. (arq.) diástilo.

diatessaron [daiatésaron], s. (mús.) diatesarón.

diathermanous [daiazérmanʊs], a. diatérmano.

diathesis [diǽzesis], s. (med.) diátesis.

diathetic [diazétic], a. diatésico.

diatomic [daiatómic], a. (quím.) diatómico.

diatomically [-ally], adv. diatómicamente.

diatonic [daiatónic], a. (mús.) diatónico.—**d. key,** llave de do natural; tecla blanca.

diatribe [dáitraib], s. diatriba.

dibble [díbœl]. **I.** s. plantador, almocafre. **II.** va. almocafrar, escarbar.

dibstone [díbstoun], s. taba.

dice [dáis]. **I.** s. (pl. de DIE) dados.—**d. box,** cubilete de dados. **II.** vn. jugar a los dados.

dicer [dáisœr], s. jugador de dados.

dichotomize [daicótomaîŝ], *va.* separar, dividir.

dichotomous [daicótomuŝ], *a.* dicotómico.

dichotomy [daicótomi], *s.* dicotomía.

dichroism [dáicroiŝm], *s.* dicroísmo.

dichromate [dicrómet], *s.* dicromato, bicromato.

dichromatism [daicrómatiŝm], *s.* dicromatismo, incapacidad de percibir más de dos colores del espectro.

dichromic [-crómic], *a.* dicromático, de dos colores; que sufre dicromatismo.

dickens [díkenŝ], *s.* (fam.) el diablo.

dicker [díkœr]. **I.** *va.* regatear. **II.** *s.* cambalache, chama; decena; partida.

dick(e)y [díki], *s.* camisola; pechera postiza; delantal; babero; (carr.) zaga.—**d.-bird,** pajarito.

diclinous [dáiclinuŝ], *a.* (bot.) diclino.

dicotyledon [daicótilidon], *s.* dicotiledón.

dicotyledonous [-lídonuŝ], *a.* dicotiledóneo.

dicta [díctæ], *s. pl.* de DICTUM.

dictagraph [díctagræf], **dictograph** [-tográf], *s.* dictógrafo (nombre de fábrica), instrumento telefónico con un amplificador del sonido, que hace innecesaria la bocina.

dictaphone [díctæfoun], *s.* dictáfono, fonógrafo de dictado (es nombre de fábrica).

dictate [díctet]. **I.** *va.* y *vn.* dictar; mandar, imponer(se). **II.** *s.* dictamen; máxima, precepto; dictado.

dictation [dictéiŝhun], *s.* dictado; mando arbitrario.

dictator [dictéitœr], *s.* dictador; el que dicta o prescribe.

dictatorial [dictatórial], *a.* dictatorial, dictatorio.

dictatorially [-i], *adv.* dictatorialmente.

dictatorship [dictéitœrŝhip], *s.* dictadura.

dictatory [díctatori], *a.* dominante.

diction [dícŝhun], *s.* dicción, estilo; locución, lenguaje.

dictionary [dícŝhunæri], *s.* diccionario.

dictum [díctum], *s.* sentencia, aforismo; (for.) fallo.

did, *pret.* de TO DO.

didactic(al [daidǽctic(al], *a.* didáctico.

didactically [-i], *adv.* didácticamente.

didactics [didǽctics], *s.* didáctica.

didapper [dídapœr], *s.* (orn.) somormujo.

diddle [dídœl]. **I.** *va.* (fam.) engañar, entrampar. **II.** *vn.* vacilar, anadear.

didst, *pret. seg. pers.* de TO DO.

didymium [daidímium], *s.* (quím.) didimio.

die [dai]. **I.** *vn.* (*ger.* DYING) morir, morirse; marchitarse, secarse; pasarse, desvirtuarse (un licor, un reactivo).—**to d. away, down,** o **out,** acabarse o desaparecer gradualmente; pasar.—**to d. the death,** sufrir la pena de muerte.—**to be dying to** (fig., fam.) estarse muriendo (de curiosidad, deseo, etc.) por, anhelar. **II.** *va.* cortar o estampar con troquel.

die, *s.* (*pl.* DICE) dado, para jugar; suerte, azar; (*pl.* DIES) cuño, matriz, troquel; molde, estampa; cojinete o caja de terraja; (arq.) cubo.

dielectric [daieléctric], *a.* dieléctrico.

dieresis, *s.* = DIÆRESIS.

dies [díiŝ], *s. día,* días.—**d. non,** (for.) día feriado.

diesinker [dáisínkœr], *s.* grabador en hueco.

diesis [dái- (o dí) esis], *s.* (mús.) diesis.

diestock [dáistoc], *s.* (mec.) terraja.

diet [dáiet]. **I.** *s.* (med.) dieta, régimen alimenticio; dieta (asamblea).—**d. kitchen,** institución de caridad donde se preparan alimentos para los enfermos pobres. **II.** *va.* adietar, poner a dieta. **III.** *vn.* estar a dieta.

dietary [dáieteri]. **I.** *a.* dietético. **II.** *s.* dieta medicinal.

dietetic(al [daietétic(al], *a.* dietético.

dietetics [daietétics], *s.* dietética.

dieting [dáieting], *s.* dieta.

diffarreation [difærêiéiŝhun], *s.* difarreación.

differ [dífœr], *vn.* diferir; disentir.—**to d. from,** diferir de.—**to d. from,** o **to d. with,** no estar de acuerdo con.

difference [dífœrens]. **I.** *s.* diferencia; distinción (de personas, etc.). **II.** *va.* diferenciar, distinguir.

different [dífœrœnt], *a.* diferente.

differential [dífœrénŝhæl]. **I.** *s.* y *a.* (mat.) diferencial; (aut.) diferencial. **II.** *a.* preferente, parcial; (fís., tecn.) diferencial (apl. a gran número de instrumentos y aparatos).—**d. coefficient,** (mat.) primera derivada.—**d. duties,** (e. p.) derechos diferenciales de entrada, en que se tienen en cuenta no sólo la naturaleza de los artículos gravados, sino también su procedencia.—**d. gear,** (turbinas de vapor) compensador; (aut.) piñón del diferencial.—**d. pulley,** polea o aparejo diferencial.—**d. rates,** (f. c.) flete preferente o rebajado (concedido a determinadas ciudades o regiones); flete menor o rebajado (de dos o más vías competidoras).

differentially [-i], *adv.* diferencialmente.

differentiate [dífœrénŝhieit]. **I.** *va.* diferenciar. **II.** *vn.* diferenciarse.

differentiation [-ŝhun], *s.* diferenciación.

differently [dífœrentli], *adv.* diferentemente.

difficult [díficult], *a.* difícil; apurado, penoso.

difficulty [díficulti], *s.* dificultad; obstáculo, tropiezo; objeción, reparo; (E. U.) riña o pelea. —*pl.* aprieto, apuro.

diffidence [dífidens], *s.* falta de confianza en sí mismo; timidez, modestia.—**diffident** [-ent], *a.* desconfiado de sí mismo; tímido o modesto.— **diffidently,** [-li], *adv.* tímidamente; modestamente.

diform [díform], *a.* disforme, deforme.

difformity [dífórmiti], *s.* deformidad.

diffraction [dífrǽcŝhun], *s.* difracción.

diffuse [difiús]. **I.** *va.* difundir; derramar o verter; repartir. **II.** *a.* (difiús], difuso, prolijo.

diffused [difiúŝd], *a.* difundido o extendido; difuso.—**d. light,** luz difusa.—**diffusedly** [-ŝedli], *adv.* difusamente.—**diffusedness** [-nes], *s.* esparcimiento; prolijidad.

diffusely [difiúsli], *adv.* difusamente, copiosamente; prolijamente.—**diffuseness** [-nes], *s.* prolijidad, difusión.

diffuser [difiúŝœr], *s.* difundidor, esparcidor; difusor.

diffusible [difiúŝibœl], *a.* difusible.

diffusion [difiúyun], *s.* difusión; prolijidad.

diffusive [difiúsiv], *a.* difusivo.—**diffusively** [-li], *adv.* difusamente.—**diffusiveness** [-nes], *s.* dispersión; difusión.

dig [dig]. **I.** *va.* (*pret.* y *pp.* DUG o DIGGED) cavar; excavar; ahondar; escarbar; minar; extraer.— **to d. down,** echar abajo socavando.—**to d. up,** desenterrar (sentidos recto y fig.).—**to d. up the hatchet,** o **the tomahawk,** declarar o emprender la guerra. **II.** *vn.* cavar; (fam.) trabajar (esp. estudiar) con desafuero, como un peón, sudar la gota gorda; (mec.) entrar demasiado (apl. a herramientas cortantes).—**to d. in,** (mil., fam.) afosarse, enterrarse, abrirse trincheras.

digastric [daigǽstric], *a.* digástrico.

digest [dáiyest]. **I.** *va.* recopilar, abreviar y clasificar; codificar; sufrir, tolerar; (fisiol., quím. y fig.) digerir. **II.** *vn.* digerir; digerirse.

digester [diréstœr], *s.* digestor.

digestible [diréstibœl], *a.* digerible, digestible.

digestion [diréschun], *s.* digestión; asimilación; (quím.) digestión; solución; absorción.

digestive [diréstiv], *a.* digestivo.

digger [dígœr], *s.* cavador; azadón.

digging [díguing], *s.* acción de cavar.—*pl.* lo que se saca excavando; lavaderos de oro.

dight [dáit], *va.* (poét.) adornar, embellecer.

digit [díyit], *s.* dedo; (astr. y mat.) dígito; tecla del piano.

digital [díyital], *a.* digital.

digitalin [díyitælin], *s.* (quím.) digitalina.

digitalis [díyitélis o tális], *s.* (bot.) dedalera, digital.

digitate(d [díyitet(ed], *a.* digitado.

digitigrade [díyitigred], *a.* digitígrado.

diglot [dáiglot], *a.* bilingüe.

diglyph [dáiglif], *s.* (arq.) diglifo.

dignified [dígnifaid], a. serio, grave; digno, decoroso.

dignify [dígnifai], va. dignificar, honrar.

dignitary [dígniteri], s. dignatario.

dignity [dígniti], s. dignidad; cargo, empleo; destino, puesto, posición.

digress [digrés], vn. divagar.—**digression** [-shṷn], s. digresión o divagación.—**digressional** [-al] o **digressive** [-iv], a. digresivo.—**digressively** [-li], adv. digresivamente.

dihedral [daijídral], a. (geom.) diedro.—**d. angle**, diedro, ángulo diedro.

dike [dáik]. I. s. dique, malecón, represa; (min.) contraveta. II. va. represar; desaguar con zanjas.

dilapidate [dilápideit]. I. va. dilapidar. II. vn. arruinarse.—**dilapidation** [-éishṷn], s. dilapidación, ruina.—**dilapidator** [-éitœr], s. dilapidador.

dilatability [diletabíliti], s. dilatabilidad.

dilatable [dilétabœl], a. dilatable.

dilatant [[dilétant], a. y s. dilatador.

dilatation [dilatéishṷn], **dilation** [diléishṷn], s. dilatación.

dilate [diléit]. I. va. dilatar, amplificar, explayar. II. vn. dilatarse, espaciarse, extenderse.

dilated [-ed], a. dilatado, extendido; hinchado; prolijo, difuso.

dilatedly [-edli], adv. dilatadamente.

dilater [-œr], s. dilatador.—**dilative** [-tiv], a. dilatativo.—**dilator** [-œr], s. (cir.) dilatador.

dilatorily [dílatorili], adv. lentamente, detenidamente.—**dilatoriness** [-nes], a. lentitud, tardanza.—**dilatory** [dílatori], a. dilatorio; tardo, lento.

dilemma [diléma], s. dilema.

dilettante [diletánte], s. aficionado.

diligence [díliyens], s. diligencia, asiduidad; diligencia, coche grande.

diligent [-ent], a. diligente, aplicado, asíduo, activo.—**diligently** [-li], adv. diligentemente, solícitamente.

dill [dil], s. (bot.) eneldo, guijones.

Dill dust cap [dṷst cæp], s. (aut.) tapa Dill de válvula.

dillydally [dílidáli], vn. (fam.) perder el tiempo.

diluent [díliuent], a. y s. diluente.

dilute [dilút o liút]. I. va. desleir, diluir, disolver; aguar. II. vn. desleirse. III. a. deluído; disuelto.

dilution [diliúshṷn], s. desleidura, dilución o dilución.

diluvial, diluvian [dilúvial, -vian], a. diluviano.

diluvium [dilúviṷm], s. (geol.) depósito no estratificado; depósito arrastrado por fuertes corrientes.

dim [dim]. I. a. obscuro, poco claro; confuso, indistinto; lerdo. II. va. obscurecer; ofuscar; reducir la intensidad (de una luz).

dime [dáim], s. diezmo; (E. U.) moneda de diez centavos.

dimension [diménshṷn], s. dimensión.—**dimensional** [-æl], a. dimensional.

dimidiate [dimídieit]. I. va. dimidiar. II. a. partido por la mitad.

dimidiation [dimidiéishṷn], s. acto de partir en dos mitades.

diminish [dimíniśh]. I. va. disminuir; rebajar, degradar. II. vn. disminuir.

diminishing [-ing], a. decreciente.—**d. return.** V. LAW.—**diminishingly** [-li], adv. decrecientemente.

diminuendo [diminuéndo], a. y adv. (mús.) disminuyendo.

diminution [diminiúshṷn], s. diminución.

diminutive [dimíniutiv]. I. a. diminuto; diminutivo; pequeño, mezquino. II. s. (gram.) nombre diminutivo.

diminutively [-li], adv. diminutamente, diminutivamente.—**diminutiveness** [-nes], s. pequeñez.

dimissory [dímisori], a. dimisorio; que despide o traslada.

dimity [dímiti], s. (tej.) cotonía.

dimly [dímli], adv. obscuramente.

dimmer [dímœr], s. lo que obscurece, mitiga o reduce (gen. la luz); (elec.) bobina de reacción reguladora; (aut.) reductor de intensidad (de las luces).

dimness [dímnes], s. ofuscamiento; obscuridad u obscurecimiento; deslustre.

dimorph [dáimorf], s. una de las formas de un dimorfo.

dimorphism [daimórfiśm], s. dimorfismo.

dimorphous [daimórfṷs], s. dimorfo.

dimple [dimpœl]. I. s. hoyuelo. II. va. y vn. formar o formarse hoyuelos.

dimpled [dímpœld], **dimply** [dímpli], a. que tiene hoyuelos.

din [din]. I. s. ruido, estrépito. II. va. ensordecer, asordar; clamorear, aturdir.

dine [dáin]. I. vn. comer (la comida principal). II. va. dar de comer; dar un convite a.

diner [dáinœr], s. coche comedor; persona que va a comer (a un restaurante) o está comiendo.—**d.-out** (fam.) persona que come fuera de casa.

ding [ding]. I. va. golpear, batir; arrojar, lanzar; repicar; instar, urgir. II. vn. sonar (las campanas). III. s. golpe, porrazo.

dingdong [díngdóng], s. dindán, tintín (sonido de las campanas).

ding(e)y, dingee [díngui], s. lancha, bote; (f. c.) vagón del servicio.

dinginess [dínyines], s. obscuridad; deslustre.

dingle [díngœl], s. cañada.

dingy [dínyi], a. empañado, deslustrado, deslucido; manchado, sucio; obscuro.

dining [dáining], ger. de TO DINE.—**d. car**, coche comedor.—**d. room**, comedor.

dinner [dínœr], s. comida (principal).—**d. pail**, portaviandas, o fiambrera.—**d. set**, vajilla.—**d. time**, hora de la comida, hora de comer.

dinosaur [dáinosor], s. (pal.) dinosauro.

dinotherium [-zíriṷm], s. dinoterio.

dint [dint], s. abolladura, mella; fuerza, eficacia.—**by d. of**, a fuerza de.

diocesan [daiósesan o daiosísan], a. y s. diocesano.

diocese [dáiosis], a. diócesis, obispalía.

diecious, diecious [daiíshṷs], a. (bot.) dioico.

dionæa [dáioníæ], s. (bot.) dionea, atrapamoscas.

diopter [daióptœr], s. dioptra.

dioptic(al [daíoptic(al], **dioptric(al** [daióptric(al], a. dióptrico.

dioptrics [daióptrics], s. dióptrica.

diorama [daioráma], s. diorama.

dioramic [daiorámic], a. diorámico.

diorite [dáiorait], s. (min.) diorita.

diorthosis [daiorzósis], s. (cir.) diortosis.

dioxide [daióxid], s. (quím.) bióxido.

Dionysiac [dáionísiæc], **Dyonysian** [-níshæn], a. dionisíaco.

dip [dip]. I. va. meter, sumergir; zabullir; saludar con (la bandera); achicar, vaciar. II. vn. sumergirse, zabullir; hundirse; penetrar; empeñarse o meterse en algún negocio; inclinarse hacia abajo. III. s. inmersión, zambullida; baño corto; vela de sebo chorreada; depresión; baño o líquido en que algo está sumergido; inclinación; caída, declivio; (mec.) cuchara de lubricación; (aer.) bache, agujero.—**d. of the horizon** (mar.) depresión de horizonte.—**d. of the needle**, inclinación de la brújula.

dipetalous [daipétalṷs], a. (bot.) dipétalo.

diphase [dáifeis], a. (elec.) bifásico.

diphther(it)ic [difœr(it)ic], a. diftérico.

diphthong [dífzong], s. (gram.) diptongo.

diplegia [-plíyiæ], s. diplegia, hemiplegia bilateral.

diplex [dáipleks], a. (tlg.) díplex, que transmite simultáneamente dos comunicaciones en una misma dirección. (Algunos aplican el término español a comunicaciones en sentidos opuestos. El término inglés no tiene ese significado.)

diploma [diplóma], s. diploma.

diplomacy [diplómasi], s. diplomacia; tacto, cautela; cuerpo diplomático.

diplomat [díplomat], **diplomatist** [diplómatist], *s.* diplomático.—**diplomatic**(al [-mǽtic(al], *a.* diplomático.—**diplomatically** [-ali], *adv.* diplomáticamente.—**diplomatics** [-mǽtics], *s.* diplomática.

diplopia [daiplóupiæ], *s.* (med.) diplopia.

dipper [dípœr], *s.* cazo, cucharón.—**the D.**, (astr.) la Osa Mayor.

dipping [díping], *a.* que se inclina; inclinado; de inclinación; de sumergir.—**d. circle, d. compass,** brújula de inclinación.—**d. needle,** aguja (magnética) de inclinación.

dipsomania [dípsoméiniæ], *s.* dipsomanía.—**dipsomaniac** [-níæc], *a.* dipsómano.

dipterous [díptœrus], *a.* (ent.) díptero.

diptych [díptic], *s.* (igl.) díptica.

dire [dáiœr], *a.* horrendo u horrible; de mal agüero; deplorable, lamentable.

direct [diréct]. **I.** *a.* directo; derecho; claro, inequívoco; en línea recta (descendencia, sucesión, etc.).—**d. action,** acción directa, métodos sindicalistas extremos (huelgas generales, sabotaje, y aun la fuerza), a diferencia de métodos políticos. —**d. current** [(elec.) corriente continua.—**d. examination,** primer interrogatorio (de un testigo). —**d. object,** (gram.) acusativo.— **d. primary,** (E. U.) comicios que nombran candidatos directamente.—**d. tax,** contribución directa. **II.** *va.* dirigir; gobernar; enviar (una persona a otra, a un lugar, etc.). **III.** *vn.* dirigir. **IV.** *adv.* directamente.—**d.-acting,** (mec.) de acción directa.— **d.-connected, d.-coupled,** (mec.) acoplado directamente, de acoplamiento directo; (elec.) conectado directamente; de conexión directa.

directed [-ed] *a.* que tiene dirección.—**d. quantity,** cantidad dirigida o vectorial.

directer [diréctœr], *s.* = DIRECTOR.

direction [dirécshun], *s.* dirección; orden, instrucción, mandato; designio, mira, fin; tendencia.—*pl.* instrucciones.—**d. finder,** (rad.) radiogoniómetro.

directive [diréctiv], *a.* directivo, directorio.

directly [diréctli], *adv.* directamente; inmediatamente, en seguida, al instante; exactamente, precisamente.

directness [diréctnes], *s.* derechura.

director [diréctœr]. **I.** *s.* director; regente; administrador; guía; vocal de una junta directiva; director de orquesta. **II.** *a.* (mat.) director, directriz.—**directorate** [-ct], *s.* dirección o junta directiva.

directorial [directórial], *a.* directorio, directivo; directorial.

directory [diréctori], *s.* directorio; guía comercial; (igl) analejo.

directress [diréctres], *s.* directora.

directrix [-trics], *s.* (geom. y arti.) directriz.

direful [dáiœrful], *a.* horrible, calamitoso, terrible.—**direfulness** [-fulnes], **direness** [-nes], *s.* horror, espanto.

dirge [dœry], *s.* endecha; canto fúnebre.

dirigible [dírigibœl]. **I.** *a.* dirigible. **II.** *s.* (aer.) dirigible.

dirk [dœrc], *s.* daga, puñal; cutó.

dirt [dœrt]. **I.** *s.* lodo, barro; polvo; partículas extrañas; basura, porquería; mugre; excremento; (fam. E. U.) tierra, marga; vileza, bajeza. **II.** *a.* hecho de tierra.

dirtily [dœrtili], *adv.* puercamente, suciamente, vilmente.—**dirtiness** [-nes], *s.* suciedad; deseaseo; porquería; bajeza, villanía.

dirty [dœrti]. **I.** *a.* sucio; manchado, enlodado; indecente; cochino, bajo. **II.** *va.* emporcar, ensuciar, manchar.

disability [disabíliti], *s.* impotencia; inhabilidad, incapacidad.

disable [diséibœl], *a. va.* imposibilitar; inhabilitar, incapacitar; (mar.) desaparejar, desmantelar; (for.) incapacitar legalmente.

disabled [-bœld], *a.* incapacitado; lisiado.

disablement [diséibœlmœnt], *s.* impedimento; inhabilitación.

disabuse [disabiúš], *va.* desengañar, sacar de un error.

disaccustom [dísæcústum], *va.* desacostumbrar.

disadjust [disadjúst], *va.* trastornar, desarreglar.

disadvantage [disædvántey]. **I.** *s.* desventaja, menoscabo; detrimento, disconveniencia.—**at a d.,** en situación o circunstancias desventajosas. **II.** *va.* perjudicar; estorbar.

disadvantageous [disædvantéiyus], *a.* desventajoso.

disadvantageously [-li], *adv.* desventajosamente.

disaffect [disæféct], *va.* descontentar; indisponer con, malquistar.—**disaffected** [-ted], *a.* desafecto.—**disaffectedly** [-li], *adv.* con desafecto. —**disaffection** [-fécshun], *s.* desafección, desamor, descontento.

disaffirm [disæfœrm], *va.* contradecir, negar, impugnar; (for.) anular; renunciar, rechazar.

disaffirmance [disæfœrmans], **disaffirmation** [disæfœrméishun], *s.* confutación, impugnación.

disafforest [disæfórest], *va.* desacotar.

disagree [disagrí], *vn.* desconvenir; disentir, diferir, desavenirse; contender o altercar.—**to d. with,** no estar de acuerdo con; no sentar bien a, hacer daño a (apl. a comidas, etc.)

disagreeable [disagríabœl], *a.* desagradable; repugnante; descortés, rudo.—**disagreeableness** [-nes], *s.* desagrado; rudeza.—**disagreeably** [-bli], *adv.* desagradablemente.

disagreement [disagrímœnt], *s.* desacuerdo, desavenencia; discordia; disensión; discordancia, discrepancia.

disallow [disæláu], *va. y vn.* denegar, desaprobar; rechazar.—**disallowable** [disæláuabœl], *a.* negable; inadmisible; censurable.—**disallowance** [disæláuans], *s.* denegación, prohibición, vedamiento.

disappear [disæpíœr], *vn.* desaparecer.

disappearance [-ans], *s.* desaparición.

disappoint [disæpóint], *va.* chasquear, frustrar; faltar a una cita con o promesa a; defraudar una esperanza; desilusionar.—**to be disappointed,** llevarse chasco o camelo; verse contrariado; quedar plantado o colgado.—**disappointment** [-mœnt], *s.* desengaño; chasco, camelo.

disapprobation [disæprobéishun], **disapproval** [disæprúval], *s.* desaprobación.

disapprobatory [-batori], *a.* desaprobador, que desaprueba.

disapprove [disæprúv], *va. y vn.* desaprobar.

disapprovingly [-vingli], *adv.* con desaprobación.

disarm [disárm]. **I.** *va.* desarmar. **II.** *vn.* deponer las armas; licenciar tropas, desguarnecer.

disarmament [disármamœnt], *s.* desarme.

disarming [disárming], *s.* desarme, desarmadura.

disarrange [disærrény], *va.* desarreglar, descomponer.—**disarrangement** [-mœnt], *s.* desarreglo, desorden.

disarray [disærré]. **I.** *s.* desarreglo, desorden, confusión; desatavío, paños menores, trapillo. **II.** *va.* desordenar, derrotar; desarreglar; desnudar.

disarticulate [disartíkiuleit]. **I.** *va.* desarticular. **II.** *vn.* desarticularse, descoyuntarse.

disarticulation [-éishun], *s.* desarticulación.

disassociate [disæsóhieit], *va.* disociar.—**disassociation** [-shiéishun], *s.* disociación.

disaster [dissástœr], *s.* desastre.

disastrous [-trus], *a.* desastroso, funesto.—**disastrously** [-li], *adv.* desastrosamente.

disavow [disaváu], *va.* repudiar, desconocer; desaprobar; desautorizar.

disavowal [disaváual], **disavowment** [disaváumœnt], *s.* repudiación.

disband [disbánd]. **I.** *va.* (mil.) licenciar las tropas; despedir, expulsar. **II.** *vn.* dispersarse, desbandarse.

disbandment [-mœnt], *s.* licenciamiento.

disbar [disbár], *va.* (for.) excluir del foro.

disbarment [-mœnt], *s.* (for.) exclusión del foro.

disbelief [disbilíf], *s.* incredulidad, escepticismo.

disbelieve [-lív], *va. y vn.* descreer.—**disbeliever** [-œr], *s.* descreído, incrédulo.

disburden [disbœrden]. **I.** *va.* descargar, aligerar. **II.** *vn.* quitarse un peso de encima.

disbursable [disbǽrsabœl], a. desembolsable, pagable.—**disburse** [disbǽrs], va. desembolsar, pagar, gastar.—**disbursement** [-mœnt], s. desembolso; gasto.—**d. office,** pagaduría.

disburser [-cer], s. pagador.

disc, s. = DISK.

discard [discárd]. **I.** va. descartar; despedir, deponer. **II.** vn. descartarse (en el juego). **III.** s. descarte (en el juego).—**to put, o throw, in the d.,** (fam.) echar a un lado, descartar.

discern [disǽrn], va. y vn. discernir, percibir.

discernible [disǽrnibœl], a. perceptible, discernible.—**discernibleness** [-nes], s. visibilidad, perceptibilidad.—**discernibly** [-bli], adv. perceptiblemente, visiblemente.

discerning [disǽrning], a. discernidor, sagaz, perspicaz.—**discerningly** [-li], adv. juiciosamente, sagazmente.

discernment [disǽrnmœnt], s. discernimiento.

discharge [dischárY]. **I.** va. descargar; disparar; pagar, saldar; desempeñar, ejecutar, cumplir; relevar, exonerar, eximir, dispensar; absolver, dar libertad; desembarazar de alguna dificultad; despedir, remover; lanzar, arrojar; vomitar; vaciar; emitir, dar salida a (tint.) descolorar, desteñir; (mil.) licenciar. **II.** vn. descargarse, soltarse; salir, vaciarse; desaguar; correrse la tinta. **III.** s. (arti.) descarga; disparo; (mar.) descarga; (com.) descargo; finiquito, carta de pago, quitanza; desempeño; separación, remoción, deposición; (mil) licencia; absolución, exoneración; derrame, desagüe; (elec.) descarga; (hidr.) salida; gasto (cantidad que sale por unidad de tiempo); (tint.) antimordente, descolorante.

discharger [-cer], s. descargador, disparador.

discharging arch [-ing arch], s. sobrearco.

disciple [disáipœl]. **I.** s. discípulo. **II.** va. hacer discípulos, convertir.

discipleship [-ship], s. discipulado.

disciplinable [disíplinabœl], a. disciplinable.

disciplinal [disíplinal], **disciplinarian** [-érian], **disciplinary** [-ri], a. disciplinal o disciplinario.—**disciplinant** [-ant], s. & a. disciplinante.—**disciplinarian** [-eriæn], s. ordenancista.

discipline [dísiplin]. **I.** s. disciplina; instrucción, enseñanza; orden, regla, conducta; educación; castigo; curso, materia (de estudio). **II.** va. disciplinar, instruir; castigar; corregir, reformar.

disclaim [discléim], va. repudiar, desconocer, rechazar; (for.) renunciar.—**disclaimer** [-cer], s. negador; (for.) renuncia, abandono.

disclose [disclóus], vn. descubrir, destapar; exponer, revelar, publicar.

disclosure [disclóYœr], s. descubrimiento, revelación, declaración.

discobolus [discóbolus], s. discóbolo, atleta que arroja el disco.

discoid [díscoid], **discoidal** [discóidal], a. discoideo, de forma de disco.

discolo(u)r [discúlœr], va. descolorar, desteñir.—**discolo(u)ration** [-éishun], s. descoloramiento; mancha.—**discolo(u)red** [-d], a. descolorido, descolorado, desteñido.

discomfit [discúmfit], va. derrotar; desconcertar, frustrar.—**discomfiture** [-fichur], s. derrota, desconcierto, desbarato.

discomfort [discúmfœrt]. **I.** s. incomodidad; malestar. **II.** va. incomodar; molestar; apenar, afligir.

discommode [discomóud], va. incomodar, molestar, hacer mala obra.

discompose [discompóus], va. turbar, desconcertar; descomponer, desarreglar.

discomposure [discompóYœr], s. descompostura, agitación, desorden; inquietud, destemple.

disconcert [disconcǽrt], va. desconcertar.

disconformity [dísconfórmiti], s. disconformidad.

disconnect [dísconéct], va. desunir o separar; disociar; (mec.) desacoplar, desconectar; (elec.) desconectar.

disconnected [-ed]. **I.** pp. de DISCONNECT. **II.** a. inconexo, incoherente.

disconnection, disconnexion, [disconécshun], s. desunión, separación; desencajamiento; inconexión; (elec.) desconexión.

disconsolate [discónsolet], a. desconsolado, inconsolable.—**disconsolately** [-li], adv. desconsoladamente.—**disconsolateness** [-nes], s. tristeza, desconsuelo.

discontent [díscontént]. **I.** s. descontento, disgusto, desagrado. **II.** a. descontento; quejoso, disgustado. **III.** va. descontentar, desagradar, disgustar.

discontented [-ed], a. descontentadizo; disgustado, desatisfecho; malcontento.—**discontentedly** [-li], adv. de mala gana, a regañadientes.—**discontentedness** [-nes], **discontentment** [-téntmœnt], s. descontento.—**discontenting** [-ténting], a. descontentador.

discontinuance [díscontíniuans], **discontinuation** [díscontiniuéshun], s. cesación, interrupción, intermisión; suspensión; desabono.—**discontinuance,** (for.) sobreseimiento.

discontinue [díscontíniu], va. y vn. interrumpir, parar, cesar; suspender; desabonarse.

discontinuity [díscontiniúiti], s. descontinuidad.

discontinuous [díscontíniuus], a. descontínuo.

discord [díscord], s. discordia; (mús.) discordancia, disonancia.

discordance, discordancy [discórdans, i], s. discordancia; discensión.—**discordant** [-ant], a. discorde; discordante, disonante.—**discordantly** [-li], adv. discordemente.

discount [discáunt]. **I.** va. (com.) descontar; rebajar, deducir; desestimar; anticipar. **II.** s. descuento; rebaja, menoscuenta.—**at a d.,** al descuento; mal acogido.

discountable [-abœl], a. (com.) descontable.

discountenance [discáuntenans], va. desfavorecer, desaprobar.

discounter [discáuntœr], s. prestamista; corredor de cambio.

discourage [discúreY], va. desalentar, desanimar; desaprobar, oponerse a.—**discouragement** [-mœnt], s. desaliento, desánimo, desmayo.

discourse [discórs]. **I.** s. discurso; plática, conversación; disertación; (lóg.) raciocinación. **II.** vn. discurrir, discursar; disertar; razonar. **III.** va. hablar de; pronunciar, expresar.

discourteous [discǽrteus], a. descortés.—**discourteously** [-li], adv. descortésmente.—**discourteousness** [-nes], **discourtesy** [-tesi], s. descortesía, desatención, grosería.

discous [díscus], a. en forma de disco.

discover [discúvœr]. **I.** va. descubrir. **II.** vn. mostrarse.

discoverable [-abœl], a. que se puede descubrir; distinguible.

discoverer [-cer], s. descubridor.

discovery [discúvœri], s. descubrimiento.

discredit [discrédit]. **I.** s. descrédito, desconfianza; deshonra, oprobio. **II.** va. discreer, dudar; desautorizar, desvirtuar; desacreditar.

discreditable [-abœl], a. vergonzoso, ignominioso.

discreet [discrít], a. discreto, circunspecto.

discreetly [-li], adv. discretamente, cuerdamente.

discreetness [-nes], s. discreción, prudencia.

discrepance, discrepancy [discrépans, -i], s. discrepancia, diferencia.

discrepant [-ant], a. discrepante.

discrete [discrít], a. distinto, desunido, separado; opuesto, contrario; (mat. y med.) discreto.

discretion [discréshun], s. discreción, prudencia, sindéresis; albedrío; juicio.—**at d.,** a discreción; a voluntad.

discretional [-al], **discretionary** [-neri], a. discrecional.—**discretionally** [-li], adv. discrecionalmente, a discreción.

discretively [discrítivli], adv. disyuntivamente, separadamente, de por sí.

discriminable [discríminabœl], a. discernible, distinguible.

discriminant [discríminænt], s. (mat.) discriminante.

Para la pronunciación de æ, œ, D, š, šh, U, y̆, Y, z, véase la clave al principio del libro.

discriminate [discrímineit]. **I.** *va.* discernir, distinguir, diferenciar; entresacar. **II.** *vn.* distinguir; hacer distinciones parciales o injustas.—**to d. against,** hacer distinción en perjuicio de, tratar desfavorablemente o sin equidad. **III.** *a.* definido, distinguible; discernidor, discerniente.

discriminately [-li], *adv.* con discernimiento; con distinciones.

discriminateness [-nes], *s.* discernimiento; distincion; favoritismo.

discriminating [-ing], *a.* discerniente; característico, diferencial; preferente, parcial.

discrimination [discríminéishun], *s.* discernimiento, sindéresis; distinción, diferencia; parcialidad, favoritismo.

discriminative [discríminativ], **discriminatory** [discríminatori], *a.* discerniente, discernidor; parcial, injusto.

discriminatively [-li], *adv.* con discernimiento; con parcialidad.

discrown [discráun], *va.* destronar.

discursive [discœrsiv], *a.* digresivo; discursivo; razonador. razonado.—**discursively** [-li], *adv.* razonadamente, o con ilación.—**discursiveness** [-nes], *s.* calidad de digresivo; ilación.

discus [díscus], *s.* disco. *V.* DISK.

discuss [discús], *va.* discutir; tratar; (fam.) probar; catar.

discussion [discúshun], *s.* discusión; exposición; presentación; estudio, artículo, memoria.

discutient [diskiúshent], *s.* y *a.* (med.) resolvente.

disdain [disdéin]. **I.** *va.* desdeñar, despreciar. **II.** *vn.* desdeñarse. **III.** *s.* desdén, desprecio.—**disdainful** [-ful], *a.* desdeñoso; altivo, altanero. —**disdainfully** [-i], *adv.* desdeñosamente, con desprecio.—**disdainfulness** [-nes], *s.* desprecio altanero.

disease [disís]. **I.** *s.* enfermedad. **II.** *va.* enfermar, hacer daño.—**diseased** [-d], *a.* enfermo; morboso, mórbido.

diselectrify [diseléctrifai], *va.* deselectrizar.

disembark, =DEBARK.

disembarkation, disembarcation [disémbarkúishun], *s.* desembarque o desembarco.

disembarrass [disembéras], *va.* desembarazar; zafar.

disembarrassment [-mœnt], *s.* desembarazo, desencogimiento.

disembody [dísembódi], *va.* librar, separar del cuerpo o de la carne; (mil.) licenciar, dispersar.

disembogue [dísembóg], *va.* y *vn.* desembocar; descargar, desaguar, vaciar.

disembogue(ment [-(mœnt], *s.* desembogue, desagüe, salida al mar.

disembowel [dísembáucel], *va.* desentrañar, sacar las entrañas.

disenchant [dísenchánt], *va.* desencantar, deshechizar; desilusionar.

disenchantment [-ment], *s.* desencanto.

disencumber [dísencúmbœr], *va.* desembarazar, descombrar.—**disencumbrance** [-brans], *s.* desembarazo, descombro.

disendow [disendáu], *va.* retirar la subvención a.

disengage [dísenguéy]. **I.** *va.* desunir; desasir; soltar, desenganchar; librar, eximir. **II.** *vn.* librarse, zafarse, soltarse, desligarse.

disengaged [dísenguéiyd], *a.* desembarazado, libre; suelto; vacante; desocupado; sin empleo.

disengagement [-guéirmœnt], *s.* soltura; desempeño, desembarazo; ocio; desembrague.

disentangle [dísentǽngœl], *va.* desenredar, desenmarañar.—**disentanglement** [-mœnt], *s.* desenredo, desembarazo.

disenthral(l [dísenzról], *va.* libertar, emancipar, manumitir.—**disenthral(l)ment** [-mœnt], *s.* emancipación, manumisión.

disentomb [dísentúm], *va.* desenterrar, exhumar.

disentrance [dísentráns], *va.* deshechizar, desilusionar; hacer volver en sí.

disestablish [dísestǽblish], *va.* separar (la iglesia del Estado).—**disestablishment** [-mœnt], *s.* privación del apoyo de un Estado; separación (de la iglesia y el Estado).

disesteem [dísestím]. **I.** *s.* desestimación. **II.** *va.* desestimar; desaprobar.

disfavo(u)r [disféivœr]. **I.** *va.* desairar; desfavorecer. **II.** *s.* disfavor, malquerencia; desgracia; desaprobación.

disfiguration [disfiguiuréishun], **disfigurement** [-mœnt], *s.* desfiguración, deformidad; daño, deterioro.

disfigure [disfíguiur], *va.* desfigurar, afear.

disforest [disfórest], *va.* desmontar, talar.

disfranchise [disfrénchais], *va.* privar de derechos civiles.—**disfranchisement** [-mœnt], *s.* privación de los derechos civiles.

disgorge [disgóry], *va.* vomitar; arrojar; desembuchar; devolver lo robado.

disgorgement [-mœnt], *s.* vómito; entrega, devolución.

disgrace [disgréis]. **I.** *s.* ignominia, vergüenza; deshonra, estigma.—**in d.**, con ignominia; (fam.) desacreditado, deslucido. **II.** *va.* deshonrar, causar oprobio; despedir con ignominia.

disgraceful [-ful], *a.* vergonzoso.

disgracefully [-i], *adv.* vergonzosamente, ignominiosamente.—**disgracefulness** [-nes], *s.* ignominia, vergüenza.

disgregation [dísgreguéshun], *s.* disgregación.

disgruntle [disgrúntœl], *va.* (fam.) disgustar, enfadar.

disguise [disgáis]. **I.** *va.* disfrazar; desfigurar; embriagar. **II.** *s.* disfraz, máscara; embriaguez.

disgust [disgúst]. **I.** *s.* repugnancia; asco. **II.** *va.* inspirar repugnancia o aversión; fastidiar. —**disgusted** [-ed], *a.* disgustado, fastidiado, chocado o desatisfecho.—**disgusting** [-ing], *a.* repugnante; odioso; asqueroso.—**disgustingly** [-li], *adv.* repugnantemente, asquerosamente.

dish [dish]. **I.** *s.* plato; vasija de bordes bajos; (quím.) cápsula (de evaporar, etc.); concavidad; artesa, gamella (de lavar mineral); caja de medir mineral.—*pl.* vajilla de mesa. **II.** *va.* servir en platos; formar una concavidad en; (fam.) engañar, burlar; (mec.) avellanar.—**to d. out,** servir (manjares); acanalar, ahondar. **III.** *vn.* deprimirse, ahondarse.

dishabille [disabíl], *s.* paños menores, ʼrapillo; desabillé.

dishcloth [díshclóz], **dishclout** [-claut], *s.* albero, paño de secar platos.

dishearten [disjárten], *va.* desanimar, desalentar, descorazonar.

dished [disht], *a.* cóncavo; ahondado.

disherison [disjérisun], *s.* desheredación.

dishevel [dishével], *va.* desgreñar, desmelenar.

dishful [dishful], *s.* contenido de un plato lleno.

dishing [díshing], *a.* cóncavo.

dishonest [disónest], *a.* no honrado, pícaro; fraudulento, falso.—**dishonestly** [-li], *adv.* fraudulentamente, de mala fe.—**dishonesty** [-i], *s.* improbidad, picardía; dolo, fraude.

dishono(u)r [disónœr]. **I.** *s.* deshonor, deshonra. **II.** *va.* deshonrar, infamar; (com.) no aceptar o no pagar (un giro).

dishono(u)rable [-abœl], *a.* deshonroso, indecoroso; deshonrado, infamado.

dishono(u)rably [-bli], *adv.* ignominiosamente, deshonrosamente.

dishpan [díshpæn], *s.* paila de fregar platos.

dishwater [díshuótœr], *s.* agua en que se lavan los platos.

disillusion [dísilúyun], **disillusionize** [-ais], *va.* desilusionar.—**disillusion, disillusionment** [-ment], *s.* desilusión.

disimpassioned [dísimpǽshund], *a.* desapasionado.

disinclination [disinclinéshun], *s.* desafecto o desamor; aversión.

disincline [disincláin], *va.* desinclinar, malquistar, indisponer.

---

disincorporate [dísincórporet], va. desincorporar.—**disincorporation** [-éishun], s. desincorporación.

disinfect [-féct], va. desinfectar.—**disinfectant** [-ant], a. y s. desinfectante.—**disinfection** [-shun], s. desinfección.—**disinfector** [-tœr], s. agente o aparato desinfectante.

disingenuous [dísinyéniuus], a. doble, falso, disimulado.—**disingenuously** [-li], adv. doblemente, falsamente.—**disingenuousness** [-nes], s. doblez, astucia, mala fe.

disinhabited [dísinjǽbited], a. deshabitado.

disinherison [disinjérisun], **disinheritance** [-tans], s. desheredación, exheredación.

disinherit [dísinjérit], va. desheredar.

disintegrate [dísíntegreit]. I. va. desagregar, disgregar. II. vn. desmoronarse, deshacerse.

disintegration [-éishun], s. desagregación, disgregación.

disinter [dísintœr], va. exhumar, desenterrar.

disinterested [dísíntœrested]. a. desinteresado.

disinterestedly [-li], adv. desinteresadamente.

disinterestedness [-nes], s. desinterés.

disinterment [dísíntœrmœnt], s. exhumación, desenterramiento.

disinthrall, va. = DISENTHRALL.

disjoin [disyóin], va. desunir, apartar, separar, despegar.

disjoint [disyóint], va. dislocar, desarticular; desgozar, desunir, desarreglar; trinchar (un ave).—**disjoint(ed** [-ed], a. dislocado, descoyuntado; desarticulado.—**disjointedness** [-tednes], s. descoyuntamiento.

disjunct [disyúnct], a. descoyuntado, dislocado.

disjunction [disyúncshun], s. disyunción, descoyuntamiento, dislocación.

disjunctive [disyúnctiv], a. y s. disyuntivo.

disjunctively [-li], adv. disyuntivamente.

disk [disk], s. disco; (igl.) patena.

dislike [disláik]. I. s. aversión, antipatía, tirria. II. va. tener aversión a, no gustar de.

disliked [disláikt], a. malquisto, malmirado.

dislocate [díslokeit], va. dislocar, descoyuntar.

dislocation [-kéishun], s. dislocación, descoyuntamiento.

dislodge [dislóy]. I. va. desalojar, echar fuera. II. vn. desalojar, mudarse.

disloyal [díslóial], a. desleal.—**disloyally** [-li], adv. deslealmente.—**disloyalty** [-ti], s. deslealtad.

dismal [dísmal], a. triste, funesto, lúgubre.—pl. esplín, morriña.—**dismally** [-li], adv. funesta o tristemente.—**dismalness** [-nes], s. tristeza, melancolía; lobreguez.

dismantle [dismǽntœl], va. desguarnecer, desamueblar; desmantelar; desaparejar.

dismast [dismást], va. (mar.) desarbolar.

dismay [dismé]. I. s. desmayo, congoja; espanto, consternación. II. va. desanimar, espantar, aterrar.

dismember [dismémbœr], va. desmembrar.

dismemberment [-mœnt], s. desmembración.

dismiss [dismís], va. despedir, echar, destituir; descartar, echar a un lado; disolver (una junta, jurado, etc.); licenciar.

dismissal [dismísal], **dismission** [dismíshun], s. destitución, deposición; liberación; acción de desechar, despedir o disolver.

dismissory, dismissive [dismísori, dismísiv], a. que despide, destituye o licencia; dimisorio.

dismount [dismáunt]. I. va. desmontar; desarmar; (arti.) desplantar. II. vn. desmontar o descabalgar, apearse; bajar.

disobedience [disobídiens], s. desobediencia.

disobedient [-ent], a. desobediente.

disobediently [-li], adv. desobedientemente.

disobey [dísobéi], va. y vn. desobedecer.

disoblige [disobláiy], va. desobligar, desplacer, no complacer.—**disobliging** [-ing], a. poco complaciente, poco servicial.—**disobligingly** [-li], adv. desatentamente.

disorder [disórdœr]. I. s. desorden, desarreglo; irregularidad; alboroto o motín; enfermedad;

enajenación mental. II. va. desordenar, desarreglar; inquietar; perturbar.

disorderliness [-lines], s. desorden, confusión; perturbación, turbulencia.

disorderly [-li]. I. a. desordenado, desarreglado; turbulento, alborotador; escandaloso; inmoral; perturbador.—d. house, casa de vicio (esp. burdel). II. adv. desordenadamente; turbulentamente; escandalosamente.

disordinate [disórdinet], a. desordenado, desmedido.

disorganization [disórganiséshun], s. desorganización.

disorganize [disórganais], va. desorganizar.

disorganizer [-œr], s. desorganizador.

disown [disóun], va. repudiar, negar, desconocer; renunciar, renegar de.

disparage [dispérey], va. rebajar, menospreciar, desdorar, desacreditar.

disparagement [-mœnt], s. menosprecio, detracción.

disparaging [dispǽreying], a. menospreciativo, detractivo.—**disparagingly** [-li], adv. desdeñosamente; con desdoro.

disparate [dísparet], a. desigual, discorde; desemejante, diferente.

disparity [dispériti], s. disparidad; (igl.) disparidad de cultos.

dispart [dispárt]. I. va. despartir, apartar, dividir, separar. II. vn. partirse, dividirse, rajarse. III. s. (arti.) punto de mira.

dispassionate [dispǽshuneit], a. desapasionado, imparcial.—**dispassionately** [-li], adv. imparcialmente, sin pasión, desapasionadamente.

dispatch, v. y s. = DESPATCH.

dispauperize [dispópœraiš], va. suprimir el pauperismo en.

dispel [dispél], va. dispersar; disipar.

dispensable [dispénsabœl], a. dispensable.

dispensary [dispénsari], s. dispensario.

dispensation [dispenséishun], s. distribución, reparto; dispensación, dispensa o exención; (teo.) revelación.

dispensatory [dispénsatori]. I. s. farmacopea, dispensaría. II. a. dispensador.

dispense [dispéns], va. distribuir, repartir; administrar (justicia); dispensar, excusar, eximir.—to d. with, hacer caso omiso de, renunciar a, pasar sin.

dispenser [dispénsœr], s. dispensador.

dispeople [dispípœl], va. despoblar.

dispersal [dispœrsal], s. dispersión.

disperse [dispœrs]. I. va. dispersar; disipar; propalar; (opt.) separar (la luz) en sus colores componentes. II. vn. dispersarse; disiparse; desaparecer. III. a. disperso.—d. phase, (quím.) estado coloide (el de una substancia suspendida en un líquido).

dispersedly [-edli], adv. esparcidamente.

disperser [-sœr], s. dispersador.

dispersion [dispœrshun], s. dispersión; esparcimiento; difusión.

dispersive [-iv], a. dispersivo.—d. power, poder dispersivo.

dispersoid [dispœrsoid], (quím.) substancia en suspensión.

dispirit [dispírit], va. desalentar, descorazonar.

dispiritedness [-tednes], s. desaliento, desánimo.

displace [displéis], va. dislocar; remover; desalojar, quitar el puesto a.—**displacement** [-mœnt], s. desalojamiento; remoción; cambio de situación; (mar.) desplazamiento; (quím.) coladura; (geol.) falla, quiebra.—**displacer** [-œr], s. (quím.) colador.

displant [displǽnt], va. arrancar.

display [displéi]. I. va. desplegar, abrir, extender; exhibir, mostrar, lucir, exponer; poner de manifiesto; (impr.) componer con tipo grande o de adorno. II. s. despliegue; exhibición, ostentación, manifestación; pompa o fausto.—d. type, (impr.) tipo de adorno.

displease [displíš], va. y vn. desagradar.—**displeasing** [-ing], a. desagradable.

displeasure [displéyœr], s. desagrado, disfavor.

displume [displúm], *va.* desplumar; degradar; destituir.

disport [dispórt]. **I.** *va.* lucir, gastar, ostentar. **II.** *vn.* y *vr.* entretenerse, retozar, divertirse. **III.** *s.* diversión, pasatiempo.

disposable [dispósabœl], *a.* disponible.

disposal [dispóuȿal], *s.* disposición; colocación, arreglo; distribución, repartimiento; venta; donación; enajenación.

dispose [dispóuȿ], *va.* disponer, arreglar, adaptar; inclinar el ánimo; ordenar, mandar.

disposition [disposíȿhɐn], *s.* disposición; orden, arreglo; genio, natural, índole; inclinación, propensión; tendencia.

dispossess [dispoȿȿés o disposés], *va.* desposeer, desalojar, desaposentar; (for.) desahuciar.

dispossession [-ȿéȿhɐn], *s.* desposeimiento; (for.) desahucio.

dispossessor [-œr], *s.* quien desposee o desahucia.

dispraise [dispréiȿ]. **I.** *va.* menospreciar; criticar, censurar. **II.** *s.* menosprecio; censura o desaprobación.

disproof [disprúf], *s.* confutación, refutación.

disproportion [dispropórȿhɐn]. **I.** *s.* desproporción, desigualdad. **II.** *va.* desproporcionar.

disproportionable [-abœl], **disproportional** [-al], **disproportionate** [-et], *a.* desproporcionado. —**disproportionableness** [-abœlnes], **disproportionality** [-æliti], **disproportionateness** [-etnes], *s.* desproporción, desigualdad.—**disproportionably** [-abli], **disproportionally** [-ali], **disproportionately** [-etli], *adv.* desproporcionadamente.

disprovable [disprúvabœl], *a.* refutable.

disproval [disprúval], *s.* refutación.

disprove [disprúv], *va.* confutar.

disputability [dispiutabíliti], **disputableness** [-abœlnes], *s.* calidad de disputable.

disputable [-abœl], *a.* disputable.—**disputant** [-ant], *a.* y *s.* disputador.—**disputation** [-éiȿhɐn], *s.* disputa.—**disputatious** [-éiȿhɐs], **disputative** [displútativ], *a.* disputador.

dispute [dispiút]. **I.** *va.* refutar, impugnar; disputar, luchar por. **II.** *vn.* disputar, discutir, pleitear. **III.** *s.* disputa, discusión, altercado, reyerta.

disputer [-œr], *s.* disputador; controversista.

disqualification [discuólifikéiȿhɐn], *s.* inhabilitación; impedimento.

disqualified [discuólifaid], *a.* inhabilitado; incompetente.

disqualify [discuólifai], *va.* inhabilitar.

disquiet [discuáiet], *s.* inquietud, intranquilidad, desasosiego.—*va.* inquietar, intranquilizar, desasosegar.

disquietness [-nes], **disquietude** [-iud], *s.* inquietud, desasosiego, intranquilidad.

disquisition [discuiȿíȿhɐn], *s.* disertación, disquisición.

disregard [dísregárd]. **I.** *va.* desatender, no hacer caso de; descuidar; despreciar. **II.** *s.* descuido, omisión; desprecio.—**disregardful** [-ful], *a.* desatento; negligente.—**disregardfully** [-i], *adv.* desatentamente.

disrelish [disrélȿh]. **I.** *s.* repugnancia, aversión, disgusto; desazón, desabrimiento. **II.** *va.* sentir repugnancia o aversión a; desazonar.

disreputability [disrépiutabíliti], *s.* mala reputación.

disreputable [disrépiutabœl], *a.* deshonroso, desdoroso; desacreditado, despreciable.

disreputably [-bli], *adv.* ignominiosamente.

disrepute [dísrepiút], *s.* descrédito, mala fama, mal nombre.

disrespect [dísrespéct], *s.* desatención, desacato, falta de respeto.—**disrespectful** [-ful], *a.* irrespetuoso.—**disrespectfully** [-fuli], *adv.* irrespetuosamente.

disrobe [disróub]. **I.** *va.* desnudar, desvestir; (fig.) despojar. **II.** *vn.* desnudarse.

disroot [disrút], *va.* desarraigar.

disrupt [disrúpt], *va.* romper; reventar, hacer pedazos; desorganizar, desbaratar; (elec.) cortar (un arco).

disruption [disrúpȿhɐn], *s.* desgarre, abrimiento; separación; desorganización o rompimiento; (elec.) interrupción (de un arco), desrupción.

disruptive [disrúptiv], *a.* desgarrador, destrozador, destructor.—**d. discharge**, (elec.) descarga desruptiva, descarga violenta que vence la resistencia del aislamiento.—**d. spark**, (elec.) chispa de descarga.—**d. strength**, (elec.) resistencia dieléctrica, resistencia a la perforación por chispas.—**d. voltage**, (elec.) tensión de perforación de un aislador o aislamiento.

dissatisfaction [disætisfæcȿhɐn], *s.* descontento, disgusto.—**dissatisfactoriness** [-torines], *s.* incapacidad de contentar.—**dissatisfactory** [-tori], *a.* poco o nada satisfactorio.

dissatisfy [disætisfai], *va.* descontentar o desagradar.

dissect [diséct], *va.* anatomizar, disecar; (fig.) criticar, analizar.—**dissecting knife**, escalpelo.

dissection [diséȿhɐn], *s.* disección, anatomía; análisis; objeto disecado.

dissector [diséctœr], *s.* disecador, disector.

disseisin [disíȿin], *s.* (for.) usurpación de tierras o heredades.

disseize [disíȿ], *va.* (for.) usurpar el dominio.

disseizor [disíȿœr], *s.* (for.) usurpador.

dissemble [disémbœl], *va.* y *vn.* disimular, fingir, encubrir.—**dissembler** [-blœr], *s.* hipócrita, fingidor, disimulador.—**dissemblingly** [-li], *adv.* fingidamente, disimuladamente.

disseminate [disémineit], *va.* diseminar.—**dissemination** [-éiȿhɐn], *s.* diseminación.—**disseminator** [-éitœr], *s.* diseminador; propalador.

dissension [disénȿhɐn], *s.* disensión, desunión, discordia; oposición.

dissent [disént]. **I.** *vn.* disentir, diferir, disidir; rehusar adhesión. **II.** *s.* disensión, desavenencia; disidencia.

dissenter [diséntœr], *s.* disidente.

dissentient [disénȿhent]. **I.** *a.* desconforme u opuesto. **II.** *s.* disidente.

dissentious [disénȿhɐs], *a.* contencioso, pendenciero.—**dissentiously** [-li], *adv.* contenciosamente.

dissertation [disœrtéiȿhɐn], *s.* disertación.

dissertator [-téitœr], *s.* disertador.

disserve [disœrv], *va.* deservir.—**disservice** [-is], *s.* deservicio.—**disserviceable** [-visabœl], *a.* perjudicial, dañoso.

dissever [disévœr], *va.* partir, dividir, separar, desmembrar.

disseverance [disévœrans], *s.* división.

dissidence [dísidens], *s.* disidencia.

dissident [dísident], *a.* disidente.

dissilience, dissiliency [disíliens, i], *s.* (bot.) dehiscencia.—**dissilient** [-ient], *a.* dehiscente.

dissimilar [disímilar], *a.* desemejante, diferente.

dissimilarity [disimilériti], **dissimilitude** [disimílitiud], *s.* desemejanza.

dissimulate [disímiuleit], *va.* y *vn.* disimular.

dissimulation [-éiȿhɐn], *s.* disimulo, disimulación.

dissipable [dísipabœl], *a.* disipable.

dissipate [dísipeit], *va.* y *vn.* disipar(se); desvanecer(se).—**dissipated** [-péited], *a.* disipado, relajado.—**dissipation** [-péiȿhɐn], *s.* disipación; libertinaje.

dissociable [disóȿhiabœl], *a.* incongruo; insociable; separable.

dissocial [disóȿhal], *a.* insociable, huraño.

dissociate [disóȿhieit], *va.* disociar, dividir, separar.—**dissociation** [-éiȿhɐn], *s.* disociación, separación, desunión.

dissociative [disóȿhietiv], *a.* disociador.

dissoluble [dísolubœl], *a.* disoluble.

dissolubility [disolubíliti], *s.* disolubilidad.

dissolute [dísolut], *a.* disoluto.—**dissolutely** [-li], *adv.* disolutamente.—**dissoluteness** [-nes], *s.* disipación, relajación.

dissolution [dísolúȿhɐn], *s.* disolución; muerte.

dissolvable, dissolvible [diȿólvabœl, ibœl], *a.* disoluble.

dissolve [diȿólv]. **I.** *va.* disolver, disipar; (for.) derogar, revocar, anular; (fot.) desvanecer gra-

dualmente una fotografía cinematográfica e irla cambiando en otra. **II.** *vn.* disolverse; descomponerse; descaecer, languidecer; desvanecerse.
dissolvent [diŝólvent], *a.* y *s.* disolvente.
dissolving [diŝólving], *ger.* de TO DISSOLVE.— **d. view,** (fot.) fotografía cinematográfica que gradualmente se desvanece y se va cambiando en otra.
dissonance, dissonancy [dísonans, i], *s.* disonancia, desentonación; desconcierto, discordia.
dissonant [dísonant], *a.* disonante, discordante; contrario, discorde, opuesto.
dissuade [disuéid], *va.* disuadir.—**dissuasion** [éiўun], *s.* disuasión.
dissuasive [disuéisiv]. **I.** *a.* disuasivo. **II.** *s.* disuasión, consejo.
dissyllabie [disílæbic], *a.* disílabo.
dissyllable [disílabœl, *s.* (gram.) disílabo.
dissymmetric(al [disimétric, -al], *a.* disimétrico, no simétrico.—**dissymmetry,** [disímetri], *s.* disimetría, falta de simetría.
distaff [dístaf], *s.* rueca.
distain [distéin], *va.* manchar, teñir; deslustrar.
distal [dístal], *a.* (biol.) distante del centro.
distance [dístans]. **I.** *s.* distancia; lejanía, lontananza; trecho; intervalo; respeto, miramiento; esquivez, frialdad, altivez.—**at a d.,** lejos, remoto; lejos o a lo lejos.—**in the d.,** en lontananza, al lo lejos.—**to keep one's d.,** mantenerse a distancia; no familiarizarse. **II.** *va.* alejar; sobrepasar; espaciar; tomar la delantera, pasar, dejar atrás; sobrepasar. **III.** *vn.* adelantarse.
distant [dístant], *a.* distante, lejano, remoto; serio, esquivo, extraño.—**to be d. with one,** tratar a uno con frialdad.
distantly [dístantli], *adv.* a distancia, de lejos; en lontananza.
distaste [distéist], *s.* fastidio, aversión, disgusto.
distasteful [-ful], *a.* desabrido, desagradable.
distastefulness [-fulnes], *s.* aversión, desagrado.
distemper [distémpœr]. **I.** *s.* mal, enfermedad; (fig.) mal humor, destemplanza; desproporción; perturbación política; (pint.) templa; destemple. **II.** *va.* destemplar, desordenar, perturbar; enfermar.
distemperature [distémpœrachur *o* tiur], *s.* destemplanza, desarreglo; indisposición, dolencia; desorden.
distend [disténd], *va.* ensanchar, dilatar, inflar.
distensibility [disténsibíliti], *s.* dilatabilidad.
distensible [disténsibœl], *a.* dilatable.
distension, distention [disténŝhun], *s.* dilatación, inflación.
distich [dístic], *s.* dístico.
distil(l [distíl], *va.* y *vn.* destilar.—**distillable** [-æbœl], *a.* destilable.—**distillate** [dístilet], *s.* líquido o producto de destilación.—**distillation** [-léiŝhun], *s.* destilación.
distillatory [dístilatori]. **I.** *a.* destillatorio. **II.** *s.* alambique.
distiller [distílœr], *s.* destilador, refinador; condensador de alambique.
distillery [distílœri], *s.* destilería.
distinct [distínct], *a.* distinto, claro, preciso, diferente, diverso.
distinction [distíncŝhun], *s.* distinción; discernimiento, juicio; distintivo.
distinctive [distínctiv], *a.* distintivo, característico, privativo.
distinctively [-li], **distinctly** [distínctli], *adv.* distintamente, claramente.
distinctness [distínctnes], *s.* distinción, claridad.
distinguish [distíngüiŝh], *va.* distinguir, diferenciar, discernir; clasificar, marcar; individuar, singularizar.—**distinguishable** [-æbœl], *a.* distinguible, discernible, perceptible.
distinguished [distíngüiŝht], *a.* distinguido, notable, famoso; especial, marcado, señalado.
distort [distórt], *va.* torcer, retorcer; deformar, desfigurar; falsear, pervertir, tergiversar.—**distortion** [distórŝhun], *s.* esguince, contorsión, torcimiento; deformación; perversión, tergiversación.

distract [distráct], *va.* distraer; perturbar, interrumpir; enloquecer, volver loco.—**distracted** [-ed], *a.* aturrullado, aturdido; demente.—**distractedly** [-li], *adv.* locamente.—**distraction** [-ŝhun], *s.* distracción, confusión, perturbación; frenesí, locura; desorden, alboroto.—**distractive** [-iv], *a.* que distrae, perturba o enloquece.
distrain [distréin], *va.* y *vn.* (for.) embargar, secuestrar.
distrainer [distréinœr], *s.* embargador.
distraint [distréint], *s.* (for.) embargo, secuestro.
distraught [distrót], *a.* = DISTRACTED.
distress [distrés]. **I.** *s.* pena, dolor; angustia, zozobra; desgracia, miseria, apuro, escasez; peligro; (for.) embargo, secuestro.—**to put in in d.,** (mar.) entrar de arribada. **II.** *va.* angustiar, afligir; poner en aprieto; (for.) embargar, secuestrar.
distressful [-ful], *a.* = DISTRESSING.
distressfully [-fuli], *adv.* acongojadamente, desdichadamente.
distressing [-ing], *a.* penoso, congojoso, aflictivo.
distributary [distríbiuteri]. **I.** *a.* distributivo. **II.** *s.* brazo de río que no se reune con éste.
distribute [distríbiut]. **I.** *va.* distribuir; clasificar, arreglar, disponer. **II.** *vn.* hacer distribución; (impr.) distribuir.—**distributer** [-œr], *s.* distribuidor, repartidor, dispensador.
distribution [distribiúŝhun], *s.* distribución; arreglo, disposición, clasificación; esparcimiento; (arq.) distribución; (impr.) distribución.
distributive [distríbiutiv], *a.* distributivo.
distributively [-li], *adv.* distributivamente.
district [dístrict], *s.* distrito, comarca o territorio; región, jurisdicción.—**d. attorney,** fiscal de un distrito judicial.
distrust [distrúst]. **I.** *va.* desconfiar, recelar, sospechar. **II.** *s.* desconfianza, recelo, sospecha; descrédito.
distrustful [distrústful], *a.* desconfiado, receloso; sospechoso; difidente o modesto.—**distrustfully** [-li], *adv.* desconfiadamente.—**distrustfulness** [-nes], *s.* desconfianza, sospecha.
disturb [distœrb], *va.* alterar, perturbar; distraer, interrumpir; inquietar, desasosegar; desordenar, revolver.—**disturbance** [-ans], *s.* disturbio, confusión, desorden, alboroto, tumulto; perplejidad, irresolución.—**disturber** [-œr], *s.* perturbador, inquietador, desordenador.
disulfid, disulphid(e [daisúlfid], *s.* bisulfuro.
disunion [disiúñœn], *s.* desunión; discordia, desavenencia.
disunionist [disiúñonist], *s.* (pol.) separatista.
disunite [disiunáit]. **I.** *va.* desunir; dividir; desavenir. **II.** *vn.* desunirse, separarse; desavenirse.
disunity [disiúniti], *s.* desunión, separación.
disusage [disiúŝeiv], *s.* desuso, deshabituación.
disuse [disiús]. **I.** *s.* desuso, deshabituación. **II.** *va.* desusar, desacostumbrar.
disutility [disiútiliti], *s.* (e. p.) incomodidad; inconveniencia, impedimento.
disutilize [disiútilaiŝ], *va.* inutilizar.
disyoke [disyók], *va.* desuncir.
ditch [dich], *s.* zanja, caz; (fort.) foso, cárcava; (hidr.) presa, badén.—*va.* y *vn.* zanjar.
ditcher [díchœr], *s.* cavador de zanjas; máquina de hacer zanjas.
ditheism [dáizeiŝm], *s.* diteísmo, creencia en un dios bueno y uno malo.
dithionic [dáizaiónic], *a.* (quím.) ditiónico, hiposulfúrico.
dithyramb [díziræmb], *s.* ditirambo.
dithyrambic [diziræmbic]. **I.** *s.* ditirambo. **II.** *a.* ditirambico.
dittany [ditani], *s.* (bot.) díctamo.
ditties [ditíŝ], *s.* tela burda para taleguillo de costura de marineros.
ditto [díto], *a.* ídem.
ditty [díti], *s.* (mús.) cantinela.—**d.-bag, d. box,** (mar.) saco, caja de costura.
diuresis [daiurísis], *s.* (med.) diuresis.
diuretic [daiurétic], *a.* y *s.* diurético.

diurnal [daiœrnal]. **I.** *a.* diurno; de día. **II.** *s.* (igl.) diurno.

diurnally [daiœrnali], *adv.* diariamente.

diva [dáivæ, díva], *s.* gran cantatriz.

divagate [dívæguéit], *vn.* vagar perdido; divagar. —**divagation** [-guéishun], *s.* vagancia; divagación.

divan [divǽn], *s.* diván; cámara; café, fumadero; otomana.

divaricate [di- (*o* dai) vǽrikeit]. **I.** *va.* y *vn.* bifurcar o bifurcarse. **II.** *a.* esparrancado.

divarication [-éishun], *s.* bifurcación; cruzamiento.

dive [dáiv]. **I.** *vn.* zabullirse; bucear; sumergirse, enfrascarse, profundizar; (aer.) picar, descender en fuerte declive con la cabeza hacia abajo. **II.** *s.* zabullidura, buceo; enfrascamiento; (fam.) garito, leonera, lupanar; (aer.) picado, descenso rápido de cabeza.

diver [dáivœr], *s.* buzo; (orn.) somorgujo.

diverge [divœry], *vn.* divergir, diferir.

divergence, **divergency** [divœrvens, i], *s.* divergencia.—**divergent** [-ent], *a.* divergente.

divers [dáivœrš], *a.* varios, diversos.

diverse [divœrs], *a.* diverso; multiforme, variado. —**diversely** [-li], *adv.* diversamente, distintamente.

diversification [divœrsifikéishun], *s.* diversificación, variación.—**diversify** [-fai], *va.* diversificar.

diversion [divœrshun], *s.* desviación; diversión, entretenimiento.

diversity [divœrsiti], *s.* diversidad, variedad; diferencia, desemejanza.

divert [divœrt], *va.* desviar, apartar; divertir, recrear.

divertisement [divœrtismœnt], *s.* diversión, holgura; intermedio de baile.

divertissement [divœrtismán], *s.* (tea.) pieza o representación ligera; (mús.) divertimiento, pieza ligera; baturrillo.

divertive [divœrtiv], *a.* diversivo; recreativo, divertido.

divest [divést], *va.* desnudar; despojar; desposeer.

divestiture [divéstichur, *o* tiur], *s.* despojo; (for.) desposeimiento.

dividable [diváidabœl], *a.* divisible.

divide [diváid]. **I.** *va.* dividir; separar; deslindar; graduar. **II.** *vn.* dividirse. **III.** *s.* (geog.) vertiente; cordillera o cresta divisorias de dos cuencas o valles.—**the Great D.**, (E. U.) los montes Rocosos.

divided [-ed], *pp.* de TO DIVIDE.—**d. skirt**, enagua partida en forma de pantalones anchos (úsase para montar, deportes, etc.).

dividedly [-li], *adv.* separadamente; por separado.

dividend [dívidend], *s.* (arit. y com.) dividendo.

divider [diváidœr], *s.* partidor, distribuidor; (arit.) divisor.—*pl.* compás de división de puntas fijas.

divi-divi [dívi-dívi], *s.* (bot.) dividivi.

divination [divinéishun], *s.* divinación, adivinación.

divine [diváin]. **I.** *a.* divino. **II.** *s.* sacerdote, ministro del culto; teólogo. **III.** *va.* adivinar; vaticinar.

divinely [-li], *adv.* divinamente.—**divineness** [-nes], *s.* divinidad.

diviner [diváinœr], *s.* adivino, agorero; adivinador, conjeturador.—**divineress** [-es], *s.* adivina, profetisa.

diving [dáiving], *s.* buceo; (aer.) picado (=DIVE). —**d. bell**, campana de bucear.—**d. dress**, escafandro o vestidura de bucear.

divining [diváining], *ger.* de TO DIVINE.—**d. rod**, vara de adivinar, vara mágica; (min.) vara buscadora, que sirve para determinar la presencia de agua o mineral subterráneos.

divinity [divíniti], *s.* divinidad; deidad, numen; teología; atributo divino.

divinize [divinaiš], *va.* divinizar.—**divinization** [-nišéishun], *s.* divinización.

divisibility [divišibíliti], **divisibleness** [divíšibœlnes], *s.* divisibilidad.

divisible [divíšibœl], *a.* divisible; (for.) dividuo.

division [divíȳun], *s.* división; ramo, departamento; sección; parte, grupo; desunión; votación por paso de los votantes a cuartos distintos; (arit., mil., mar.) división.—**d. of labor**, (e. p.) división del trabajo.—**d. plate**=INDEX PLATE.—**d. wheel**, rueda graduada en la circunferencia.

divisional, o **divisionary** [divíȳunael, -eri], *a.* divisional, divisorio.

divisive [diváisiv], *a.* divisivo.

divisor [diváišœr], *s.* (arit.) divisor.

divorce [divórs]. **I.** *s.* divorcio. **II.** *va.* divorciar; divorciarse de.—**divorceable** [-ibœl], *a.* que se puede divorciar.—**divorcee** [-i], *s.* esposa divorciada.—**divorcement** [-mœnt], *s.* divorcio.—**divorcer** [-œr], *s.* divorciador.

divulge [divúly], *va.* divulgar, revelar, propalar. —**divulger** [-œr], *s.* propalador.

divulsion [divúlshun], *s.* arrancamiento; (cir.) dislaceración, divulsión.

Dixie [díxi], *n. pr.* el sur de los Estados Unidos.

dixit [dícsit], *s.* afirmación dogmática.

dizen [díšœn], *va.* ataviar, adornar.

dizzily [díšili], *adv.* vertiginosamente.

dizziness [díšines], *s.* vértigo, vahido; desvanecimiento.

dizzy [díši]. **I.** *a.* vertiginoso, vaguido, desvanecido. **II.** *va.* causar vértigos o vahidos; aturdir.

do [du], *va.* (*pret.* DID; *pp.* DONE), hacer (justicia, bien, mal, un favor, el honor, daño, etc.); ejecutar; causar (peligro, daño, etc.); cumplir con (un deber, etc.); rendir, tributar (homenaje, etc.); cocinar (*to be done*, estar suficientemente cocinado, asado, etc.); componer, arreglar (la cama, un cuarto); aprender (una lección); hacer, ejecutar (un ejercicio, una suma); terminar; dejar de (*she has done weeping*, ella ha dejado de llorar); traducir; hacer de, desempeñar el papel de; agotar, abrumar; recorrer, andar (una distancia); (fam.) visitar, explorar, ver; (fam.) engañar, estafar; (vulg.) (seguido de una expresión de tiempo) cumplir una condena de (el tiempo mencionado), estar o pasar en la cárcel o el presidio (el tiempo mencionado), vg., *he did a year in the penitentiary*, estuvo un año en la penitenciaría.—**to d. away**, o **away with**, quitar, suprimir.—**to d. one's best**, hacer cuanto pueda.—**to d. one's level best**, o **one's utmost**, hacer cuanto pueda, hacer lo posible.—**to d. over**, volver a hacer, hacer de nuevo; repetir; cubrir, revestir.—**to d. reverence**, rendir homenaje; inclinarse.—**to d. to death**, matar, despachar.—**to d. up**, componer, arreglar, poner en orden; planchar; envolver; llevar a cabo completamente; fatigar, cansar.—**to have nothing (something) to d.**, no tener nada (tener algo) que hacer.

do, *vn.* conducirse; hacerlo (bien o mal); hallarse, estar (bien, mal, etc.: *to be doing*, ir; vg. *the patient is doing well*, el enfermo va bien); moverse, hacer algo, no estar ocioso; obrar, actuar; ser suficiente; servir; (con *to*) que hacer (*what is to do?* ¿qué hay que hacer?).—**to do by**, tratar a, portarse con.—**to d. for**, servir o bastar para; (en la voz pasiva, **to be done for**, estar arruinado o echado a perder; estar muerto o desahuciado).—**to d. with**, tratar, entenderse, habérselas con.—**to d. without**, pasarse sin; prescindir de.—**how do you do?** (saludo) ¿cómo está Vd.? buenos días, etc.—**that will d.**, eso basta; eso sirve; (fam.) deja, déjate de eso; calla, no digas más.—**that will never d.**, **that won't d.**, (fam.) eso no se hace; eso no se hace así; así no se irá a ninguna parte.—**to have done**, terminado; desistir; no seguir adelante.—**to have done with**, haber terminado; no tener más que ver con.—**to have to d. with**, tener que ver con; tener que entenderse o habérselas con; tratar de (*arithmetic has to do with numbers*, la aritmética trata de los números).

do, *aux.* Como auxiliar, *do* se emplea:—1°. Para indicar interrogación o negación: *do you see?* ¿ve usted? *I do not see*, no veo; *she did not come*, ella no vino. 2° Como reproductor del verbo, para evitar su repetición; puede entonces traducirse repitiendo el verbo, o por los adverbios *sí*, *no*: *do you see him?* ¿lo ve usted?—*I do*, *I do* *not*, lo veo, no lo veo (o sí, no). 3º. Antes de un verbo, para dar mayor fuerza a su significado: *he does write well*, el ciertamente escribe bien; *I do tell the truth*, yo sí digo la verdad; *do sing for us*, le ruego que nos cante; *do come tomorrow*, venga mañana sin falta. El traductor puede escoger la palabra o forma enfática que le parezca más apropiada. 4º. Expletivamente, después de adverbios y conjunciones, cuando el sujeto va después del verbo: *nor do I believe*, ni creo yo; *seldom did he complain*, él rara vez se quejaba.

do [dóu], *s.* (mús.) do.

doable [dúœbœl], *a.* factible.

do-all [du-ol], *s.* factótum.

doaty [dóuti], *a.* manchado, descolorido por putrefacción incipiente (apl. a la n.adera).

dobla [dóubla], *s.* dobla (antigua moneda).

doblon [doublón], *s.* doblón.

doby [dóubi], *s.* (fam., E. U.) adobe.

docile [dósil], *a.* dócil, sumiso; fácil de manejar. —**docility** [dosíliti], *s.* docilidad.

docimastic [dosimǽstic], *a.* docimástico.

docimasy, docimacy [dósimasi], *s.* docimasia.

dock [doc]. **I.** *s.* (bot.) bardana, lampazo; muñón de la cola cercenada de un caballo; (mar.) dique, dársena; desembarcadero, muelle; (for.) barra.—**d.-tailed**, o **docked**, curto, rabón, rabicorto. **II.** *va.* cortar, cercenar; descolar, derrabar; (for.) rescindir; (mar.) poner en dique; (*va.* y *vn.*) entrar en muelle.

dockage [dókeɣ], *s.* entrada de un buque en dique; muellaje; reducción, rebaja.

docket [dóket]. **I.** *s.* minuta, sumario, extracto; rótulo, marbete; (for.) lista, turno, orden del día. **II.** *va.* extractar, hacer el sumario o minuta; rotular; dar turno, poner en el orden del día.

dockyard [dócyard], *s.* (mar.) arsenal.

doctor [dóctœr]. **I.** *s.* doctor; médico. **II.** *va.* (fam.) medicinar, recetar; alterar y adulterar; repɛrar, componer. **III.** *vn.* tomar medicinas; practicar la medicina.

doctoral [-al], *a.* doctoral.—**doctorate** [-et], *s.* doctorado.—**doctoress** [-es], *s.* doctora o médica. —**doctorship** [-ʃhip], *s.* doctorado.

doctrinaire [doctrinéar], **doctrinarian** [doctrinérian], *a.* y *s.* doctrinario; visionario, teorista.

doctrinal [dóctrinal], *a.* doctrinal; didáctico o instructivo.

doctrinally [-i], *adv.* magistralmente.

doctrine [dóctrin], *s.* doctrina; teoría.

document [dókiumœnt]. **I.** *s.* documento. **II.** *va.* documentar; probar con documentos.

documental [-méntal], **documentary** [-méntɛri], *a.* documental.

dodder [dódœr], *s.* (bot.) cúscuta.

doddered [dódœrd], *a.* decrépito, quebrantado.

dodecagon [dódécagon], *s.* dodecágono; **dodecagonal** [dódecǽgonœl], *a.* (geom.) dodecágono.—**dodecahedral** [-jídral], *a.* dodecaédrico.—**dodecahedron** [-jídron], *s.* (geom.) dodecaedro.—**dodecasyllable** [-sílabœl], *s.* verso dodecasílabo.

dodge [doɣ]. **I.** *va.* escabullirse, regatear (el cuerpo); evadir; seguir con disimulo. **II.** *vn.* hacer quites; dar un quiebro o esquinazo; trampear, entrampar. **III.** *n.* regate; evasiva; esquinazo.

dodger [dóɣœr], *s.* trampista, sablacista; (E. U.) cartel o anuncio pequeño.

dodo [dódo], *s.* (orn.) dido.

doe [do], *s.* hembra del gamo, de la liebre, del conejo, del canguro y del antílope.—**d. rabbit**, coneja.

doer [dúœr], *s.* hacedor; actor, agente; persona activa.

does [duʃ], 3a. *pers. del pres. de indic. de* TO DO.

doeskin [dóuskin], *s.* ante, piel de gama; tejido fino de lana.

doff [dof], *va.* quitar; quitarse (el sombrero, la ropa, etc.).

dog [dog], *s.* perro; macho de algunos cuadrúpedos, v. gr.: *dog fox*, zorro; (mec.) grapa, cárcel, barrilete; fiador; morillo; llave de arma de fuego); (astr.) Can (Mayor o Menor).—*pl.* tenazas

de tracción.—**d. ape**, (zool.) mandril.—**d. cheap**, muy barato, regalado.—**d. days**, canícula.—**d.-ear** = DOG'S EAR.—**d. fancier**, perrero.—**d.-faced ape**, mandril.—**d. fight**, riña de perros.—**d. grass**, grama y otras clases de yerba.—**d. hook**, gancho, gancho de arrastre.—**d. house**, perrera.—**d. iron**, morillo; llave de destornillar; gafa; grapa.—**d. Latin**, låtinajo.—**d. power**, mecanismo movido por el peso de perros colocados en el flanco de un cilindro giratorio o una cadena sin fin.—**d.-rose**, (bot.) escaramujo, zarza perruna.—**d.'s ear**, esquina doblada de una hoja de un libro. —**d.'s meat**, comida de perros; comida de desperdicios para perros.—**D. Star**, (astr.) Sirio.—**d.'s tongue**, (bot.) cinoglosa.—**d.'s tooth**, (bot.) diente de perro.—**a dead d.**, (fam.) una persona caída (que ha perdido su importancia o influencia). —**a d. in the manger**, el perro del hortelano.—**to go to the dogs** estar arruinado o perdido.—**to throw to the dogs**, tirar o descartar como inútil.—**to put on d.**, (fam.) darse ínfulas.

dog, *va.* seguir los pasos o pisadas de alguno a, espiar, perseguir; (mec.) asegurar o afianzar con grapa, barrilete, etc.

dogbane [dógbein], *s.* (bot.) matacán.

dogberry [-bérri], *s.* cornejo y su fruto.

dogbolt [-bóult], *s.* perno dobladizo para unir piezas en ángulo recto.

dogcart [-cárt], *s.* dogcart, coche de dos ruedas con dos asientos situados espalda con espalda.

doge [doɣ], *s.* dux.

dogfish [dógfish], *s.* (ict.) lija, cazón; tiburón pequeño.

dogged [dógued], *a.* terco, tenaz.—**doggedly** [-li], *adv.* tenazmente.—**doggedness** [-nes], *s.* tenacidad, terquedad, pertinacia.

dogger [dógœr], *s.* (mar.) dogre, urca.

doggerel [dóguerel], *s.* coplas de ciego, aleluyas.

doggery [dógueri], *s.* los perros; farsante, trampista; conducta soez; (vulg.) garito, leonera.

doggish [dóguish], *a.* gruñón, regañón, rudo.

doggy [dógui], *s.* (fam.) perro; perrito.

dogma [dógma], *s.* dogma.

dogmatic(al [dogmǽtic(al], *a.* dogmático.

dogmatically [-i], *adv.* dogmáticamente.—**dogmaticalness** [-nes], *s.* magisterio; calidad de dogmático.—**dogmatics** [dogmǽtics], *s.* (teol.) estudio de los dogmas y doctrinas de una religión. —**dogmatism** [dógmatism], *s.* dogmatismo.—**dogmatist** [-tist], *s.* dogmatizador; dogmatista.—**dogmatize** [-aiʃ], *vn.* dogmatizar.—**dogmatizer** [-aiʃœr], *s.* dogmatizador.

dogskin [dógskin], *s.* piel de perro.

dogsleep [-slip], *s.* sueño fingido; sueño intranquilo o interrumpido.

dogtrot [-trót], *s.* trote suave.

dogvane [-véin], *s.* (mar.) catavientos.

dogwatch [-uóch], *s.* guardia de cuartillo.

dogwood [-ud], *s.* (bot.) cornejo.

doily [dóili], *s.* paño pequeño de adorno o para poner platos.

doing [dúing]. **I.** *ger.* de TO DO.—**nothing d.** (a menudo con **there is, was**, etc.) (fam.) no hay (había, etc.) nada; nada de eso.—**something d.** (fam.) algo pasa (pasaba, etc.).—**to be d.**, estarse haciendo.—**to be up and d.**, moverse, darse prisa, rebullirse. **II.** *s.* acción, hecho.—*pl.* acciones, obras; (fam.) acontecimientos, cosas (que ocurren).—**great d.**, (fam.) grande actividad; grandes (o muchas) cosas; tremolina.

doit [doit], *s.* blanquillo (moneda).

dolce [dólche], *a.* (mús.) dolce, dulce.—**d. far niente** [farniente], *dolce farniente*, dulce ociosidad.

doldrums [dóldrums], *s. pl.* (mar.) zona de calmas ecuatoriales.

dole [dóul]. **I.** *s.* distribución, repartimiento en raciones o pequeñas porciones; dádiva, don, limosna; (poét.) suerte, hado; angustia, congoja; arrullo de tórtola. **II.** *va.* (gen. con *out*) repartir, distribuir, dar (gen. de limosna).

doleful [dóulful], **dolesome** [dóulsum], *a.* triste.—**dolefully** [-i], **dolesomely** [-li], *adv.* tristemente.—**dolefulness** [-nes], **dolesomeness** [-nes], *s.* tristeza.

Para la pronunciación de æ, œ, ᴅ, ʃ, ʃh, ᴜ, ȳ, ɣ, z, véase la clave al principio del libro.

dolerite [dólœrait], *s.* (min.) dolerita.

dolichopcephalic, dolichocephalous [dólicose-féelic, -séfœlus]. (zool.) dolicocéfalo.

doll [dol]. I. *s.* muñeca. II. *va.* (gen. con *up*), (fam.) engalanar.

dollar [dólœr], *s.* dólar.—**d. diplomacy,** diplomacia del dólar o mercantilista, cuyo único móvil son los intereses comerciales; imperialismo del dólar, diplomacia plutocrática, que se aprovecha del poder o la superioridad financieros.—**d. mark,** el signo $.

dolly [dóli], *s.* (fam.) muñequita; (min.) revolvedor de mineral; (mec.) cazoleta de remachar; remachador; rodillo, plataforma de (con) rodillo; (constr.) bloque de protección para la cabeza de un pilote; (f. c.) locomotora de maniobras o de arrastrar mineral.—**d. tub,** tina de lavar mineral.

dolman [dolman], *s.* dolman.

dolmen [dólmen], *s.* dolmen.

dolomite [dólomait], *s.* (min.) dolomía.

dolomitic [dolomític], *a.* dolomítico.

Jolo(u)r [dólœr], *s.* (poét.) dolor, pena.

dolorous [dólorus], *s.* lastimoso; triste.

dolorously [-li], *adv.* dolorosamente.

dolphin [dólfin], *s.* (ict.) delfín, tonina; (mar.) poste de amarra; boya de anclaje; (astr.) Delfín.—**d. striker,** moco del bauprés.

dolt [dóult], *s.* bobalicón, mastuerzo, bodoque.

doltish [dóultiâh], *a.* lerdo, estúpido.

doltishness [-nes], *s.* estupidez.

domain [doméin], *s.* dominio; imperio, soberanía; propiedad, heredad, finca.

domanial [doméinial], *a.* perteneciente al dominio o a la finca.

dome [dóum], *s.* (arq., m. v., fund.) cúpula; (geol.) techo, bóveda (de una caverna, etc.); (aut.) techo; (poét.) edificio majestuoso.—**d. light,** (aut.) lámpara de techo.

domesday, *s.* = DOOMSDAY.

domestic [doméstic]. I. *a.* doméstico, casero; nacional, del país, interior; intestino.—**d. commerce,** comercio interior. II. *s.* doméstico, criado, sirviente.—*pl.* artículos del país.

domestically [-ali], *adv.* domésticamente.

domesticate [doméstikeit], *va.* domesticar; hacer adquirir costumbres domésticas.

domestication [-éishun], *s.* domesticación.

domesticity [dómestísiti], *s.* domesticidad.

domical [dóumical], *a.* en forma de cúpula o que la tiene.

domicile [dómisil]. I. *s.* domicilio, residencia. II. *va.* domiciliar.

domiciliary [dómisílicœri], *a.* domiciliario.

domiciliate [dómisílieit], *va.* avecindarse, establecerse.

domiciliation [-éishun], *s.* fijación de domicilio.

dominant [dóminant]. I. *a.* dominante. II. *s.* (mús.) dominante.

dominate [dómineit], *va.* y *vn.* dominar.

domination [-éishun], *s.* dominación, imperio; tiranía; gobierno, autoridad.—*pl.* (rel.) dominaciones.

dominative [-ativ], *a.* dominativo, dominante; imperioso, altivo.

dominator [-éitœr], *s.* dominador.

domineer [dóminíœr], *va.* y *vn.* dominar, tiranizar.—**domineering** [-ing], *a.* dominante, tiránico, mandón.

domine [dómine], *s.* clérigo.

dominical [domínical], *a.* dominical.

dominican [domínicœn]. I. *a.* dominical.—(D-) dominicano. II. *s.* letra dominical.—(D-) dominicano.

dominie [dómini], *s.* dómine.

dominion [domínion], *s.* dominio; territorio; distrito; (for.) posesión, propiedad, dominio.

dominium [domínium], *s.* (for.) dominio.

domino [dómino], *s.* dominó (disfraz); ficha del juego de dominó.—*pl.* **dominos,** dominó (juego).

don [don], *va.* vestirse, ponerse, calar.

don [don], *s.* caballero, señor; don (título); personaje de alta categoría; (Ingl.) rector de universidad.

donate [dóneit], *va.* donar, contribuir.

donation [donéshun], *s.* donación, dádiva.

Donatism [dónatism], *s.* donatismo.

Donatist [dónatist], *s.* donatista.

donative [dónativ], *s.* donativo.

donator [donéitœr], *s.* donador.

done [dun], *pp.* de TO DO y *a.*: hecho, ejecutado; fecho; convenido; acabado, concluido; bien cocido o asado; fatigado, consumido.

donee [doní], *s.* donatario.

donjon [dúnyun], *s.* = DUNGEON.

donkey [dónki], *s.* asno, burro.—**d. boiler,** (mar.) caldera auxiliar.—**d. engine,** máquina pequeña auxiliar; (m. v.) máquina de alimentación.—**d. pump,** bomba de volante acoplada directamente a la máquina de vapor.

donor [dónœr], *s.* donador, donante.

donship [dónship], *s.* nobleza, caballería.

don't [dóunt], *abrev.* de **do not** y [erróneamente] de **does not.**

doom [dum]. I. *va.* sentenciar a muerte; predestinar a la ruina o destrucción; condenar, imponer, destinar. II. *s.* sentencia, juicio, condena; predestinación; sino, hado, perdición, ruina.

doomsday [dúmsdei], *s.* día del juicio universal.—**D. Book,** (Ingl.) registro del gran catastro hecho por orden del rey Guillermo el Conquistador.

door [dóœr], *s.* puerta.—**d. bell,** timbre o campanilla de llamada.—**d. check,** amortiguador de puerta (para cerrarla suavemente).—**d. knob,** tirador o botón de puerta.—**d. knocker,** aldaba o llamador de puerta.—**out of doors,** afuera, al aire libre.—**to lay at one's d.,** echarle a uno la culpa de.—**to lie at one's d.,** tener uno la culpa de.—**within doors,** adentro (de la casa).—**without doors,** afuera (de la casa).

doorcase [-kéis], *s.* marco de puerta, jambaje.

doorframe [-fréim], *s.* marco de puerta.

doorkeeper [-kípœr], *s.* portero; (igl.) ostiario.

doornail [-néil], *s.* clavo grande de clavar puertas.—**as dead as a d.,** (fam.) absolutamente muerto.

doorpost [-póust], *s.* jamba de puerta.

doorsill [-sil], *s.* umbral.

doorplate [-pléit], *s.* placa de nombre, que se pone a una puerta con el nombre del dueño de la casa.

doorstep [-stép], *s.* escalón de la puerta delantera.

doorstop [-stóp], *s.* tope de puerta.

doorway [-uéi], *s.* entrada, puerta; vano de puerta; portal.

dope [dóup]. I. *s.* pasta o preparación semifluida; grasa lubricante; pasta de opio; material absorbente que se mezcla con los explosivos; (aer.) material para revestir la tela de aeroplanos y dirigibles; (fam.) narcótico, estimulante—**d. fiend,** (fam.) morfinómano, persona que tiene el vicio de los narcóticos o estimulantes. II. *va.* pronosticar; formar el plan de (gen. con *out*); (fam.) estimular o entorpecer con un estimulante o narcótico. III. *vn.* tener el vicio de los narcóticos.

dor, dor-bug [dór, bug], *s.* escarabajo.

Dorian [dórian], **Doric** [dóric], *a.* dórico.

dormancy [dórmansi], *s.* sueño, letargo.

dormant [dórmant], *a.* latente; inactivo.—**d. partner** = SILENT PARTNER.

dormant, dormer [dórmœr], *s.* fiambre; viga maestra.—**dormer window,** buharda.

dormitive [dórmitiv], *s.* dormitivo, soporífero.

dormitory [dórmitori], *s.* dormitorio.

dormouse [dórmáus], *s.* lirón.

dorp [dorp], *s.* aldea, lugarcito.

dorsad [dórsad], *adv.* hacia la espalda.

dorsal [dórsal], *a.* dorsal.

dorsum [dórsum], *s.* (anat.) espalda; lomo.

dory [dóri], *s.* (ict.) gallo, ceo; (mar.) bote pescador de fondo plano y extremos puntudos.

dosage [dóseɪ], *s.* toma de un medicamento en dosis regulares.

dose [dóus]. **I.** s. (med.) dosis; (fig.) píldora, mal trago; ingrediente que se agrega al vino. **II.** va. administrar una dósis; dividir en porciones dosimétricas. **III.** vn. medicarse con frecuencia.

dossal, dossel [dósal], s. (igl.) dosel, colgadura.

dosser [dóscer], s. vago. V. DOSSAL.

dossil [dósil], s. (cir.) lechino; tarugo.

dost [dust], 2da. pers. pres. ind. de TO DO.

dot [dot]. **I.** s. (leng. ord. y mús.) punto. **II.** va. poner punto a (una letra).

dotage [dóteу], s. chochera, chochez; cariño excesivo; extravagancia, delirio.

dotal [dótal], a. dotal.

dotard [dótard], s. viejo chocho, ñoño.

dotation [dotéshun], s. dotación.

dote [dóut], vn. chochear, caducar.—**to d. upon,** amar con exceso.

doter [dóutcer], s. el que ama con exceso.

doth [duz], (ant.) 3a. pers. pres. ind. de TO DO.

doting [dóuting], a. locamente cariñoso o enamorado; bobo, chocho; podrido o pudriéndose de viejo (apl. a las plantas).—**dotingly** [-li], adv. con cariño excesivo, ciegamente.

dotted, a. punteado, de puntos; mosqueado.— **d. line,** línea de puntos.

dotterel [dótcerel], s. (orn.) calandria marina.

doty [dóti], s. =DOATY.

double [dúbœl], a. doble; dos veces; ambiguo; engañoso; (bot.) doble; (mús.) una octava más bajo.—**d. barrel,** escopeta de dos cañones.— **d.-barreled,** de dos cañones.—**d. base, o bass,** (mús.) contrabajo.—**d.-beat valve,** válvula de campana.—**d. boiler,** baño de María.—**d.-break switch,** interruptor doble (para ambos polos del generador).—**d. chin,** papada.—**d. consciousness,** (psicol.) doble personalidad.—**d.-cross,** s. traición hecha a un cómplice; va. traicionar (a un cómplice).—**d.-current dynamo, o generator,** dínamo doble o de dos corrientes (continua y alterna).—**d. dealer,** hombre falso, traidor.—**d. dealing,** falsía, perfidia.—**d. ender,** cosa que tiene extremos iguales; (f. c.) locomotora de dos direcciones (de dos bogíes pilotos); (mar.) barco de dos direcciones (de timón en ambos extremos). —**d. entry,** partida doble (en contabilidad).— **d.-flow turbine,** turbina de dos corrientes contrarias.—**d.-header,** tren con dos locomotoras.— **d-pole switch,** interruptor bipolar.—**d.-quick,** (mil.) paso ligero o rápido.—**d. star** = BINARY STAR.—**d. track,** vía doble.—**d.-track,** de vía doble.

double, adv. doblemente; dos juntos; en par. Empléase sobre todo en adjetivos compuestos, como los que se dan a continuación.—**d.-acting,** (mec.) de doble efecto.—**d.-barreled,** de dos cañones.—**d.-breasted,** de traslapo, de dos hileras de botones.—**d.-edged,** de dos filos.—**d.-ended,** de extremos iguales.—**d.-ended spanner,** o **wrench,** (mec.) llave de dos bocas, llave doble.— **d.-faced,** de dos caras; acabado por ambos lados; doble, falso, hipócrita.—**d.-lock,** va. cerrar con dos machos; asegurar doblemente.—**d.-minded,** vacilante, inconsecuente.—**d.-tongued,** falso, pérfido.

double. I. s. doble, duplo; pliegue, plegadura, doblez, duplicado; contrafigura; copia, retrato (persona muy parecida a otra); (fig.) aparecido, fantasma. **II.** va. doblar, duplicar; redoblar, repetir; pasar por, doblar, remontar.— **to d. up, o over,** doblar, plegar, replegar. **III.** vn. doblarse, duplicarse; volver atrás.—**to d. up,** dormir dos en una misma cama.

doubleness [dúbœlnes], s. doblez, dobladura.

doubler [dúblœr], s. doblador, plegador, plegadera; (elec.) excitador.

doublet [dúblet], s. par, pareja; jubón, ropeta; (joy.) doblete.

doubling [dúbling], s. doblez, pliegue; (cost.) forro.—pl. (mar.) almohadas de las bitas; embón.

doubloon [dublún], s. doblón español.

doubly [dúbli], adv. doblemente; por duplicado; con dolo.

doubt [dáut]. **I.** va. y vn. dudar. **II.** s. duda.

doubtable [-abœl], a. dudable.—**doubter** [-œr], s. el que duda.

doubtful [-ful], a. dudoso.—**doubtfully** [-i], adv. dudosamente.—**doubtfulness** [-nes], s. duda, diffidencia; calidad de dudoso.

doubtingly [dáutingli], adv. dudosamente.

doubtless [dáutles]. **I.** a. cierto; confiado. **II.** adv. indubitablemente, sin duda.—**doubtlessly** [-li], adv. indubitablemente.

douceur [dusćer], s. (fr.) recompensa; gratificación.

douche [dush], s. ducha, regadera.

dough [dóu], s. pasta, masa, amasijo; cochura.

doughboy [dóubói], s. (fam.) soldado norteamericano.

doughnut [dóunut], s. buñuelo.

doughtily [dáutili], adv. con denuedo.

doughtiness [dáutines], s. valentía, denuedo.

doughty [dáuti], a. bravo, valeroso; jactancioso, fanfarrón.

doughy [dóui], a. pastoso.

douma [dúmæ], s. =DUMA.

dourine [dúrín], s. (vet.) durina, sífilis equina.

douse [dáus], va. zabullir; (mar.) recoger; arriar.

dove [duv], s. paloma.—**dovecot, dovecote** [-cot], s. palomar.—**dovelike** [-laic], a. columbino.

dovetail [duvtéil]. **I.** s. (carp.) ensambladura a cola de milano; cola de milano, o de pato.— **d. hinges,** bisagras de cola de pato.—**d. plane,** guillame de ensamblar. **II.** va. machihembrar o ensamblar a cola de milano; ajustar, amoldar. **III.** vn. (a veces con into) unirse a cola de milano; ajustarse; corresponder, estar de acuerdo.

dovetailed [-teild], a. machihembrado; denticulado.

dowable [dáuabœl], a. capaz de ser dotado.

dowager [dáuaрœr], s. viuda con viudedad (apl. esp. a reinas, etc., vg. **d. queen,** reina viuda).

dowdy [dáudi]. **I.** a. zafio, desaliñado, sucio. **II.** s. maritornes.

dowel [dáuel], s. (carp.) tarugo, clavija, espiga; nudillo; torillo.—**d. (bar),** barra de alineación que atraviesa una junta de dilatación.

dower [dáucer]. **I.** s. viudedad; bienes gananciales de una viuda; don, beneficio; prendas personales. **II.** va. señalar viudedad o legar bienes gananciales; (fig.) dotar, adornar, favorecer —**dowerless** [-les], a. sin viudedad.

dowery [dáuri], s. = DOWRY.

down [dáun]. **I.** adv. abajo; hacia abajo; (golf) atrás, atrasado. Después de un verbo indica a menudo diminución, reducción, etc., vg. to boil down, reducir o mermar hirviendo; (fig.) compendiar, reducir a su más simple expresión; to cut down, recortar, rebajar. En leng. familiar se usa (sobre todo con referencia a posición en el mapa) en el sentido de "allá," "por allá," "en," y a veces no se traduce: vg. down West, (allá) en el oeste: I went down to Texas, fuí a Tejas.—**d. and out,** (fam.), fuera de combate (esp. en el boxeo); vencido irremisiblemente; arruinado.—**d. from,** desde. —**d. grade** = DOWNGRADE.—**d. in the mouth,** cariacontecido.—**d. the river, the stream,** etc., río abajo, agua abajo, etc.—**d. to,** hasta.—**d. on one's knees,** de rodillas.—**d. with . . . !** ¡abajo! ¡muera!—**to be d. on, o upon,** tener inquina a. **II.** s. plumón, flojel; bozo, vello; lana fina o pelo suave, pelusa; revés de fortuna, baja, caída; colina, duna; (football) colocación de la pelota en el suelo para una rebatiña.—**d. bed,** edredón, colchón de pluma. **III.** a. pendiente; descendente; abatido, alicaído; de abajo. **IV.** va. (fam.) derribar, echar por tierra; vencer.

downcast [-cast]. **I.** a. inclinado, descendente; deprimido, abatido. **II.** s. (min.) pozo de ventilación.

downcomer [-cúmœr], s. (m. v.) tubo de descenso; (min.) tubería de gases combustibles.

downed [dáund], a. cubierto o henchido con plumón.

downfall [dáunfol], s. caída; ruina.

downgrade [-gréid], a. y adv. pendiente abajo, cuesta abajo.

downhaul [-jol], *s.* (mar.) cargadera.
downhearted [-járted], *a.* abatido, desmayado, descorazonado.
downhill [-jil]. **I.** *a.* pendiente, inclinado, en declive. **II.** *s.* declive, bajada. **III.** *adv.* cuesta abajo, ladera abajo.
downiness [-nes], *s.* vellosidad.
downpour [-pócr], *s.* aguacero, chaparrón.
downright [-rait]. **I.** *a.* vertical; claro, categórico; absoluto, completo. **II.** *adv.* claramente; completamente.
downstairs [-stéærs̈]. **I.** *adv.* abajo, en el piso de abajo. **II.** *s.* piso inferior, primer piso.
downstream [-strím], *adv.* aguas abajo.
downtown [-táun], *a.* y *adv.* de la o en la parte baja de la ciudad.
downtrod(den [-tródœn], *a.* pisoteado; oprimido, esclavizado.
downward, *a.* inclinado, descendente.
downward(s [-uærd, -dŝ], *adv.* hacia abajo.
downy [-i], *a.* velloso, felpudo; blando, suave; dulce, tranquilo.
dowry [dáuri], *s.* dote; dotación.
dowse [dáus], *va.* = DOUSE.
doxology [docsóloyi], *s.* (igl.) Gloria Patri; Gloria in excelsis.
doze [dóuŝ]. **I.** *vn.* dormitar. **II.** *s.* sueño ligero; sopor, adormecimiento.
dozen [dúŝn], *s.* docena.
doziness [dóŝines], *s.* somnolencia, modorra.
dozy [dóŝi], *a.* soñoliento, amodorrado.
drab [dræb]. **I.** *a.* pardusco. **II.** *s.* color entre gris y amarillento; pipa de saladar.
drabble [dræbœl], *va.* arrastrar.
drabbler [dræblœr], *s.* (mar.) vela barredera.
drachm [dræm], *s.* =DRAM.
drachma [dræcma], *s.* dracma; antigua medida griega de peso; en griego moderno, gramo.
Draconian [dracónian], *a.* draconiano.
dracunculus [dracúnkiulvs], *s.* (bot.) dragóntea; (zool.) dracúnculo.
draff [draf], *s.* desperdicios; heces.
draffish [-ish], **draffy** [-i], *a.* inútil, despreciable.
draft, draught [draft], *s.* corriente de aire; tiro (de chimenea, etc.); succión, aspiración; trago, bebida; (mar.) calado; tracción, atracción, tiro, tirón, estirón; (mil.) atelaje; carga, carretada; redada; traza, trazado, delineación; plan, plano; anteproyecto; borrador, minuta, apuntación; esquema; proyecto, propuesta (de ley, reglamento, etc.); (com.) giro, libranza, letra de cambio; libramiento, póliza, orden de pago; (mil.) quinta, conscripción, leva; destacamento.—*pl.* juego de damas.—**d. animal,** animal de tiro.—**d. furnace,** alto horno.—**d. hook,** (arti.) gancho de arrastre de la cureña.—**on d.,** por vaso, sacada del barril (cerveza).
draft, draught, *va.* hacer un borrador, minuta, apuntación de; redactar, escribir; bosquejar, delinear; dibujar; (mil.) reclutar, quintar; '(tej.) hacer pasar entre los lizos del telar.
draftboard, draughtboard [-bord], *s.* tablero de damas.
draftsman, draughtsman [dráftsman], *s.* dibujante.
drag [dræg]. **I.** *va.* arrastrar, tirar; (mar.) rastrear; (E. U. agr.) rastrillar; (fig.) escudriñar. **II.** *vn.* arrastrar por el suelo; garrear; ir tirando, avanzar penosa o lentamente; (fig.) decaer la acción o interés. **III.** *s.* (mar.) rastra; draga; jábega, brancada; (agr.) rastrillo; rastra; (carr.) galga; naria; carruaje alto; (min.) hierro de limpiar pozos; (fig.) rémora, traba; cosa que retarda el movimiento o acción; (aer.) resistencia al avance.—**d. chain,** (f. c.) cadena de acoplamiento.—**d. link,** (mec.) contramanivela; (f. c.) barra de enganche.—**d. sail,** ancla flotante.—**d. wire,** (aer.) tirante de tracción.
dragbar [drægbar], *s.* (f. c.) barra de enganche.
dragbolt [-boult], *s.* (f. c.) pasador de enganche.
draggle [drægœl]. **I.** *va.* ensuciar arrastrando. **II.** *vn.* ensuciarse arrastrando.

draggle-tail [-téil], *s.* mujer desaliñada o puerca.
dragnet [drægnet], *s.* brancada, red barredera; (fig.) pesquisa, sistema o artificio para recoger datos, coger personas sospechosas, etc.
dragoman [drægoman], *s.* dragomán, trujamán.
dragon [drægun], *s.* dragón; hombre o mujer feroz; (bot.) dragontea; (D-, astr.) Dragón.— **d. balloon,** (aer.) globo cometa.—**d. fly,** (ent.) libélula, caballito del diablo, (Colombia) matacaballos.—**d.'s blood,** (bot.) sangre de drago.— **d.'s mouth,** (bot.) dragón, becerra, boca de dragón.—**d. tree,** drago.
dragoon [dragún]. **I.** *s.* (mil.) dragón. **II.** *va.* acosar, intimidar.
drain [dréin]. **I.** *va.* desaguar, avenar; escurrir; sacar (el agua); agotar, secar, desangrar, empobrecer, disipar.—**to d. off,** sacar, vaciar. **II.** *vn.* desaguarse, vaciarse; (a veces con *off*) escurrirse, salir (el agua). **III.** *s.* desagüe; desaguadero; tubería o zanja de desagüe; sumidero; desangre; agotamiento. **IV.** *a.* de desagüe, de drenaje o avenamiento.—**d. cock,** (m. v.) llave de purga. —**d. pipe, d. tile** = DRAINPIPE, DRAINTILE.
drainable [-abœl], *a.* desaguable.
drainage [-ey], *s.* desagüe, avenamiento, drenaje; arroyada, cuenca de un río.
drainpipe [-páip], *s.* tubo o tubería de desagüe.
draintile [-táil], *s.* atanor, tubo de desagüe hecho de barro cocido u hormigón.
drake [dréik], *s.* (orn.) pato.
dram [dræm], *s.* dracma ($\frac{1}{8}$ de onza) (*v.* DRACHMA); trago de aguardiente; porción pequeña.
drama [dréma], *s.* drama.
dramatic(al [dramétic(al], *a.* dramático.
dramatically [-i], *adv.* dramáticamente.
dramatis personæ [drématis persóni], (tea.) personajes dramáticos.
dramatist [drématist], *s.* dramaturgo.—**dramatize** [-aiŝ], *va.* dramatizar.
dramaturge, dramaturgist [-œry, ist], *s.* dramaturgo.
dramaturgy [-tœrryi], *s.* dramática, dramaturgia.
drank [d-ænk], *pret.* del verbo TO DRINK.
drape [dréip], *va.* vestir; colgar, entapizar; formar ropaje o pliegues artísticos en un ropaje o colgadura.—**draper** [-œr], *s.* pañero.—**drapery** [-œri], *s.* ropaje, cortinas, colgaduras, tapicería; pañería; paños.
drastic [dréstic], *a.* extremo, fuerte; (med.) drástico.
draught [dræft], *s.* y *v.* = DRAFT.
draughtsman [dráftsman], *s.* peón del juego de damas. *V.* DRAFTSMAN.
Dravidian [drævídiæn], *s.* y *a.* dravidiano.
draw [dro], *va.* (*pret.* DREW) *pp.* DRAWN) tirar, arrastrar; atraer; estirar; sacar, (clavo, agua, consecuencia); desenvainar; hacer salir; chupar o mamar; aspirar, respirar, inspirar (ap. al aliento); cobrar (un sueldo); sacarse (un premio); procurarse, proporcionarse (medios o recursos); correr o descorrer (cortinas); dibujar; trazar; hacer (descripción, etc.); redactar, escribir o extender; alargar, estirar; (com.) devengar; girar, librar; tender (un arco); hacer un cocimiento; destripar; en el billar, picar bajo; (mar.) calar.—**to d. a prize,** sacarse un premio.—**to d. along,** arrastrar.—**to d. away,** quitar, llevarse; disuadir; distraer.—**to d. asunder,** separar.— **to d. back,** reintegrarse de, recibir devuelto.—**to d. breath,** respirar.—**to d. forth,** hacer salir, sacar.—**to d. in,** atraer; seducir, embaucar.— **to d. it fine,** (fam.) hilar muy delgadito.—**to d. it mild,** sin exagerar.—**to d. lots,** echar suertes. —**to d. off,** sacar, extraer; retirar; trasegar; distraer; disuadir.—**to d. on,** ocasionar.—**to d. out,** sacar; alargar, extender; sondear; sonsacar —**to d. over,** persuadir, sonsacar.—**to d. the curtain,** correr el telón; (fig.) correr el velo (ya para tapar, ya para destapar).—**to d. the line** (a menudo con *at*) hacer la cruz, no pasar o ir más allá (de).—**to d. the long bow,** exagerar. —**to d. to an issue,** acabar, concluir.—**to d. up,** tirar hacia arriba, subir tirando; redactar; extender (un giro); (mil.) formar.

draw, vn. tirar arrastrando; atraer gente, con-'currencia; tirar bien (el fuego, la chimenea); encogerse, arrugarse; adelantarse, moverse; dibujar; echar suertes; sacar la espada; ir al robo (en los naipes); (mar.) calar; (com.) girar. Con ciertos adverbios indica movimiento, vg., *to draw nigh,* o *near,* acercarse; *to draw away,* alejarse.—**to d. against,** (com.) girar contra o sobre (fondos).— **to d. back,** retroceder; cejar.—**to d. near,** o **nigh,** acercarse.—**to d. off,** retirarse.—**to d. on,** acercarse; (com.) girar contra (persona, casa).— **to d. to a head,** madurar, empezar a supurar; aproximarse o llegar a un estado, situación, etc. definitivos, estar al culminar o (fig.) al reventar.

draw, s. tirada, tiro, tracción, arrastre; función muy favorecida, que atrae mucha gente; en el billar, retroceso; en los naipes, robo; en damas y ajedrez, tablas; en dep., votaciones, empate; en juegos de azar, suerte, premio; (tej.) pasada, carrera; parte levadiza o giratoria de ciertos puentes; (E. U.) barranco.—**d. poker,** juego de *poker,* con opción de descartarse e ir al robo.—**d.-well,** pozo de noria.

drawback [dróbǽc], s. rebaja, descuento; reintegro de derechos de aduana; desventaja, inconveniente.

drawbar [-bár], s. (f. c.) barra de tracción.

drawbench [-bénch], s. (mec.) hilera (máquina de estirar); banco de estirar.

drawbridge [-bríy], s. puente levadizo o giratorio.

drawee [-í], s. (com.) girado, librado.

drawer [-œr], s. gaveta, cajón; extractor; (com.) librador, girador.—pl. **drawers,** calzoncillos.

drawgear [-guíær], s. (f. c.) aparato de tracción o de enganche.

drawing [dróing], **I.** s. dibujo; tiro, tirante; sorteo; extracción, saca. **II.** ger. de TO DRAW. —**d. awl,** lezna de ojo.—**d. bench** = DRAWBENCH.—**d. block,** tambor de estirar.—**d. board,** tablero de dibujar; (tej.) DRAWING FRAME.—**d. frame,** (tej.) estirador; carda mecánica.—**d. knife** = DRAWKNIFE.—**d. paper,** papel de dibujo. —**d. pen,** tiralíneas.—**d. press,** prensa de cortar y estampar metal en lámina.—**d. room,** sala (de una casa); recibimiento (sala y acción o función). —**d. table,** mesa de dibujar.

drawknife [drónáif], s. cuchilla desbastadora de dos mangos.

drawl [drol], **I.** va. pronunciar despacio. **II.** vn. arrastrar las palabras. **III.** s. enunciación penosa y lenta.

drawn [dron], pp. de TO DRAW y a. desenvainado; destripado, desentrañado; movido, inducido; tablas, empatado; (mil.) indeciso (el triunfo); abierto (un puente); estirado; fundido, derretido. —**d. butter,** mantequilla derretida.

drawplate [drópléit], s. (mec.) hilera (placa perforada de estirar); (f. c.) plancha de enganche (de la locomotora).

drawtube [-tiúb], s. tubo telescópico de enchufe, esp. el portalentes del microscopio.

dray [dréi], s. carro, carretón, camión pequeño.

drayage [-ey], s. acarreo, carretaje.

drayhorse [-jórs], s. caballo de tiro.

drayman [-mæn], s. carromatero, carretonero.

dread [dred], **I.** s. miedo, terror, pavor. **II.** a. terrible, espantoso; venerable. **III.** va. y vn. temer, tener miedo o temor.

dreadful [drédful], a. terrible, espantoso.

dreadfulness [-nes], s. terribilidad, horridez.

dreadfully [-i], adv. terrible u horrendamente.

dreadless [drédles], a. intrépido, sin temor.

dreadlessness [-nes], s. intrepidez, arrojo.

dreadnaught, dreadnought [drédnot], s. el que nada teme; paño muy doble; capote de capucha; (mar.) dreadnaught, grande acorazado.

dream [drím], **I.** s. sueño, ensueño.—**d. world** = DREAMLAND. **II.** va. y vn. (pret. y pp. DREAMED y DREAMT) soñar.—**to d. of,** soñar con.

dreamer [drímœr], s. soñador.

dreamily, dreamingly [drímili, drímingli], adv. como en sueños.

dreamland [drímland], s. región de los sueños.

dreamless [drímles], a. sin sueños.

dreamlike [-laic], a. como soñado; vaporoso, nebuloso, vago.

dreamt [dremt], pret. y pp. de TO DREAM.

dreamy [drími], a. desvariado; soñador, contemplativo; propio de un sueño.

drear [dríœr], a. = DREARY.—**drearily** [drírili], adv. funestamente, tristemente.—**dreariness** [drírines], s. tristeza; lobreguez.

dreary [dríri], a. triste, melancólico; monótono, pesado.

dredge [drey], **I.** va. dragar; rastrear; (coc.) polvorear. **II.** s. draga; pontón de dragar; rastra; brancada.—**d. box,** (coc.) polvorera.

dredger [-œr], s. el que draga o rastrea; pescador de ostras; draga; pontón de limpia; (coc.) polvorera.

dredging [-ing], pa. y s. dragado.—**d. machine,** draga.—**d. spoon,** cucharón o cubo de draga.—**d. tube,** caño o tubo de una draga de succión.

dreggish [dréguish], **dreggy** [-gui], a. feculento, turbio.

dregs [dregs], s. pl. hez o heces; poso, sedimento; madre (del vino); escoria, barreduras, desperdicio.

dreibund [dráibunt], s. triple alianza.

drench [drench]. **I.** va. empapar, ensopar; (vet.) purgar con violencia. **II.** s. tragantada; mojada; (vet.) bebida purgante; inundación, diluvio; (ten.) solución para remojar.

dress [dres]. **I.** va. (pret. y pp. DRESSED y DREST) vestir; ataviar, adornar, engalanar; curar (las heridas); almohazar; preparar, arreglar; cocinar, guisar; aderezar, aliñar (la ensalada); poner (la mesa); amortajar; peinar, arreglar (el pelo); podar; (ten.) adobar y curtir (pieles); preparar (cáñamo, etc.); (carp.) desbastar (madera); (cant.) labrar (piedra); (albañ.) allanar, aplanar, revocar; (mil.) alinear. **II.** vn. vestirse; componerse, ataviarse; (mil.) formar en línea, alinearse.— **d. left, right!** (mil.) ¡a la izquierda, a la derecha, alinearse!—**to d. up,** (fam.) vestirse de etiqueta, prenderse de veinticinco alfileres. **III.** s. vestido, traje.—**d. circle,** (teat.) galería o grada principal. —**d. coat,** frac, casaca.—**d. goods,** géneros para vestidos.—**d. parade,** (mil.) parada.—**d. rehearsal,** (teat.) ensayo.—**d. suit,** traje de etiqueta.— **d.-suit case,** maleta plana.

dresser [drésœr], s. el que suele acicalarse; ayuda de cámara, moza de cámara; tocador; mesa de cocina; aparador; cocinero; (ten.) zurrador, abobador.

dressing [drésing], s. y pa. adorno, aderezamiento; (tej.) aderezo; (ten.) adobo; (coc.) condimento, aliño, salsa; relleno; (cir.) hilas, vendajes, etc.; (agr.) abono, estercoladura; poda; (fam.) (gen. con *down*) rapapolvo, regaño.—pl. (arq.) molduras, adornos.—**d. gown, jacket,** o **sack,** peinador, bata.—**d. room,** trasalcoba, cuarto de tocador; (teat.) camarín.—**d. table,** mesa de tocador; mesa de limpiar y concentrar (mineral, etc.)

dressmaker [drésméikœr], s. modista.

dressmaking [-méiking], s. arte de modista.

dressy [drési], a. (fam.) acicalado; elegante, vistoso.

drew, pret. de TO DRAW.

dribble [dríbœl], va. y vn. gotear; (dep.) avanzar el football a trechos. V. DRIBEL.

driblet [dríblet], s. trozo, pedacito, pizca; pico (de dinero); gota.

dried [dráid], **I.** part. y pret. de TO DRY. **II.** a. seco; paso.—**d. peaches,** orejones.—**d. plums,** ciruelas pasas.

drier [dráiœr], s. enjugador; secante; desecativo; desecador.

drier, driest, comp. y superl. de DRY.

drift [drift]. **I.** s. todo objeto llevado por una corriente (nubes, restos de un naufragio, etc.); montón formado por el viento, el mar o el deshielo (ventisquero, dunas, alud, témpano, etc.); rumbo, tendencia, objeto, impulso, impulsión; móvil; manada o gentío que va en una dirección. (mec.) mandril de ensanchar (agujeros para remaches, etc.); escariador; (min.) galería horizontal; socavón; rumbo (de una galería; (geol.) terrenos de acarreo, esp. los arrastrados por ventisqueros; en (Ing.) túnel de comunicación (entre otros dos) o de exploración; (aer.) deriva, movimiento o velocidad lateral; (mar.) dirección de la corriente; red flotante (llám t. **d. net**).—**d. angle**, (aer.) ángulo de deriva.—**d. bar**, (aer.) varilla de deriva.—**d. meter**, derivómetro. **II**. *va.*'impeler, llevar; apilar, amontonar; (min.) abrir un socavón o galería. **III**. *vn*. derivar, devalar; apilarse, amontonarse; flotar a la ventura o sin rumbo; ir arrastrado por la corriente; (aer.) derivar, abatir.

driftage [dríftey], *s.* (mar, aer.) deriva; (arti.) desviación.

driftbolt [-bóult], *s.* perno largo; botapernos, clavo o perno para sacar pernos empujándolos.

drifting [-ing[. **I**. *a.* flotante, a flote. **II**. *s.* flotacion, flote; (aer.) deriva, abatimiento.

driftway [-uey], *s.* (min.) galería horizontal (gen. galería de avance o exploración); socavón.

driftwind [-wínd], *s.* ventisca.

driftwood [-ud], *s.* madera flotante o arrojada a la playa por el agua; cosa inestable; basura.

drill [dril]. **I**. *va.* taladrar, barrenar; hacer a barrena; sembrar, plantar en hileras o surcos; derramar gota a góta; (mil.) enseñar el ejercicio. **II**. *vn.* (mil.) hacer el ejercicio; plantar en surcos; gotear. **III**. *s.* taladro, barrena; parahuso; (joy.) árbol; (agr.) sembradora mecánica; hilera de semillas sembradas con esa máquina; (zool.) dril, especie de mono; (mil.) ejercicio; disciplina, pericia; (tej.) dril, tela cruda.—**d. plow**, arado sembrador.—**d. press**, taladradora, perforadora.

drilling [dríling], *s.* perforación, trepa; (mil.) ejercicio; material extraído por un taladro; (tej.) dril.

drillstock [drílstoc], *s.* portabarrena; mangо de taladro.

drink [drink]. **I**. *va.* y *vn.* (*pret.* DRANK, (ant.) DRUNK; *pp.* DRUNK, (ant.) DRUNKEN) beber; chupar, absorber.—**to d. down**, tragar; beber; ahogar (el dolor, etc.) en vino.—**to d. in**, chupar; absorber.—**to d. off, o up**, beber de un trago o a grandes tragos.—**to d. the health of, o to the health of**, beber a la salud de o por; brindar por. **II**. *s.* bebida; trago, copa.

drinkable [drínkaboel]. **I**. *a.* potable. **II**. *s.* bebida.

drinker [drínkœr], *s.* bebedor.

drinking [-ing]. **I**. *s.* acción de beber (ap. esp. a las bebidas alcohólicas). **II**. *a.* de beber, para beber.—**d. cup, glass**, taza, vaso de beber agua.—**d. trough**, abrevadero.

drip [drip]. **I**. *va.* y *vn.* verter o caer gota a gota, gotear, chorrear; escurrir. **II**. *s.* gotera; reguero; humedad condensada; chorrera; goteadero, escurridero. —**d. band, o flap**, faldilla de escurrimiento (de un dirigible).

dripping [dríping], *s.* chorreo, chorreadura, gotera; pringue.—*pl.* miel de descarga.—**d. pan**, grasera, pringuera.

drive [dráiv]. **I**. *va.* y *vn.* (*pret.* DROVE; *pp.* DRIVEN) impeler, impulsar; echar, arrojar; estimular; llevar, conducir, gestionar; compeler, forzar; esclavizar, arrear; meter, clavar; cochear, guiar o manejar (caballos); conducir, gobernar (como un automóvil); ir en coche; abrir un túnel, socavón; (mec.) actuar, mover.—**to d. a good bargain**, hacer un buen negocio.—**to d. at**, aspirar a, tender a, proponerse.—**to d. away**, ahuyentar, desterrar; trabajar asiduamente.—**to d. back**, rechazar.—**to d. in, o into**, meter a macha martillo.—**to d. mad**, volver loco.—**to d. off**, ahuyentar, apartar.—**to d. to the wall**, acosar, poner entre la espada y la pared. **II**. *s.* jornada o paseo en coche; calzada para coches; urgencia, presión, exigencia; manada de reses; montón de leños o trozos de árboles; (com.) saldo, liquidación o quemazón, venta a bajo precio; (mil.) traslado, embate, ataque violento y rápido; (fig.) campaña vigorosa para lograr algún fin; (aut.) conducción, gobierno; mecanismo de dirección o de transmisión; asiento del conductor; (mec.) mecanismo de transmisión; método o sistema de

actuación, de impulsión (*accionamiento*, que erróneamente se usa a menudo) o de hacer funcionar, mecanismo de funcionamiento (llámase también **d. gear, o driving gear**).

drivel [drívœl]. **I**. *vn.* babear; bobear, chochear. **II**. *s.* baba; noñería, cháchara.

drivel(l)er [drívlœr], *s.* fatuo, simple; baboso.

driven [drívn], *pp.* de TO DRIVE.—**d. pulley**, polea impulsada.—**d. well**, pozo perforado o de tubo (perforado con un tubo de penetración).

driver [dráivœr], *s.* el que conduce o gobierna un vehículo; cochero; carretonero; (aut.) conductor; (f. c.) maquinista; rueda motriz (de locomotora); (mec.) rueda (o cualquiera otra pieza) impulsora; polea impulsora; hincador, martinete; (mar.) maricangalla.—**d.'s seat**, pescante (de un coche de tiro); (aut.) asiento del conductor.

driving [dráiving]. **I**. *s.* conducción, manejo de coches u otros vehículos; acción de impulsar, actuar y demás acciones comprendidas en TO DRIVE. **II**. *a.* motor, motriz; impulsor; de actuación, de dirección, de mando, etc. (V. TO DRIVE).—**d. axle**, eje de las motrices.—**d. belt**, correa de transmisión.—**d. flange**, (aut.) platillo de transmisión.—**d. gear** = DRIVE GEAR. V. DRIVE.—**d. pulley**, polea impulsora.—**d. shaft**, árbol o eje de transmisión.—**d. wheel**, rueda motriz.

driveway [dráivuéi], *s.* calzada para coches.

drizzle [drísl]. **I**. *va.* rociar, salpicar. **II**. *vn.* lloviznar, molliznar, garuar.—**drizzling rain**, llovizna. **III**. *s.* llovizna, mollina, cernidillo, chipichipi, garúa.

drizzly [drisli], *a.* lloviznoso.

drogue [dróug], *s.* (aer.) ancla flotante.

droll [drol]. **I**. *a.* festivo, jocoso, chistoso; raro. **II**. *s.* chusco, bufón. **III**. *vn.* bromear, chocarrear.

drollery [drólœri], *s.* chuscada, chocarrería, bufonería.

dromedary [drómederi], *s.* dromedario.

drone [dróun]. **I**. *s.* (ent.) zángano, abejón; zangandungo, haragán; roncón de gaita; zumbido. —**d. fly**, abejorro, moscardón. **II**. *vn.* zanganear, holgazanear; zumbar.

drool [drul], *vn.* babear.

droop [drup]. **I**. *va.* inclinar, bajar. **II**. *vn.* inclinarse, caer; colgar, pender; descaecer, decaer; desanimarse; consumirse, marchitarse.—**drooping lashes**, pestañas caídas. **III**. *s.* inclinación, caimiento.

drop [drop]. **I**. *s.* gota; pizca; (joy.) pendiente, zarcillo; caída, caimiento; pendiente, declive; pastilla; (com.) baja, caída; (mec.) artefacto (plataforma, martillo, etc.) que cae o se abre hacia abajo; (elec.) indicador de disco levadizo (en el tablero de un ascensor, hotel, etc.).—**d. annunciator** (elec.) indicador de disco.—**d. box**, buzón.—**d. by d.**, gota a gota.—**d. curtain**, telón de boca.—**d.-forge**, *va.* forjar a martinete; forjar a troquel.—**d. forging**, forjadura o forjado a martinete.—**d. hammer**, martinete.—**d. of a sail**, (mar.) caída de una vela.—**d. press** = DROP HAMMER.—**d. scene**, telón de foro.—**d. sulphur, tin**, azufre, estaño granulado vaciándolo fundido en agua fría. **II**. *va.* verter o echar a gotas; soltar, dejar caer; abandonar, desprenderse de; renunciar a, desistir de; despedir; echar; polvorear, rociar; escribir (una esquela); parir los animales; (fam.) tumbar, derribar de un tiro.—**to d. a courtesy**, hacer una cortesía.—**to d. a hint**, soltar una indirecta.—**to d. anchor**, anclar.—**to d. a subject**, poner fin a una cuestión, cambiar de asunto. —**to d. the curtain**, correr el telón, echar un velo. **III**. *vn.* gotear, chorrear; bajar, descender; caer; cejar, parar, detenerse.—**to d. in**, entrar al pasar. —**to d. off**, decaer; dispersarse; quedar dormido; morir de repente.—**to d. out**, desaparecer; separarse, retirarse; quedarse atrás.

droplet [dróplet], *s.* gotita.

droplight [dropláit], *s.* (elec.) lámpara movible unida a un cordón de derivación; lámpara colgante; cordón para dichas lámparas.

dropper [drópœr], *s.* cuentagotas.

dropping [dróping], *s.* estilicidio.—**d. bottle,** o **tube,** gotero.—*pl.* (fam.) excrementos de animales domésticos.—**droppingly** [-li], *adv.* a gotas, gota a gota.

dropsical [drópsical], **dropsied** [-sid], *a.* hidrópico.

dropsy [drópsi], *s.* hidropesía.

droshky, drosky [dróski], *s.* carruaje ruso de cuatro ruedas; coche de plaza.

dross [dros], *s.* escoria; horrura, espuma; basura, borra; sedimento, hez.

drossiness [drósines], *s.* calidad de impuro.

drossy [drosi], *a.* que tiene escoria, espuma o heces; impuro.

drought, drouth [dráut, dráuz], *s.* seca, sequía; carestía, escasez; sed.

droughty, drouthy [dráuti, dráuzi], *a.* seco; sediento; árido.

drove [dróuv], *s.* manada, recua, arria, piara, gentío, muchedumbre; cincel de pedrero.

drove, *pret.* de TO DRIVE.

drover [dróuvœr], *s.* ganadero.

drown [dráun]. **I.** *va.* ahogar, anegar; sumergir; inundar. **II.** *vn.* anegarse; ahogarse.

drowse [dráus]. **I.** *va.* adormecer. **II.** *vn.* amodorrarse, adormecerse.

drowsily [dráušili], *adv.* soñolientamente.

drowsiness [dráusines], *s.* somnolencia, modorra.

drowsy [dráuši], *a.* soñoliento, amodorrado; soporífero.

drub [drub]. **I.** *va.* apalear, sacudir, pegar, tundir. **II.** *s.* golpe, puñada.—**drubbing** [-ing], *s.* paliza, zurra, tunda.

drudge [druy]. **I.** *va.* y *vn.* afanarse, fatigarse; insudar. **II.** *s.* ganapán; marmitón, galopín.

drudgery [druyœri], *s.* faena o trabajo penoso, tráfago.

drudgingly [dryingli], *adv.* laboriosamente, penosamente.

drug [drug]. **I.** *s.* droga, medicamento; artículo de poca venta o demanda; narcótico; estimulante.—**d. [habit,** morfinomanía, vicio de los narcóticos.—**d. store,** farmacia, botica. **II.** *va.* mezclar con drogas; narcotizar; poner narcótico en. **III.** *vn.* tomar drogas (esp. narcóticos).

drugget [drúguet], *s.* droguete, buriel.

druggist [-guist], *s.* droguero, droguista, especiero; (E. U.) boticario, farmacéutico.

Druid [drúid], *s. m.*, **Druidess,** *s. f.* druida.

Druidic(al [druídic(al], *a.* druídico.

drum [drum]. **I.** *s.* tambor; (mec.) tambor, cilindro, rodillo; (com.) cuñete o barrilito; (arq.) campana; vaso de capitol, cuerpo de columna; (anat.) tímpano (del oído).—**d. major,** tambor mayor. **II.** *va.* y *vn.* tocar el tambor; tamborilear, repetir, machacar; teclear; (com.) solicitar parroquianos o pedidos.—**to d. out,** (mil.) expeler a tambor batiente.

drumfire [drúmfáiœr], *s.* fuego graneado.

drummer [drúmœr], *s.* tambor, redoblante; (com.) viajante.

drumstick [drúmstic], *s.* bolillo de tambor; (fam.) pierna (de un ave cocinada).

drunk [drunk], *pp.* de TO DRINK. y *a.* borracho, ebrio, beodo.

drunkard [drúnkard], *s.* borrachín.

drunken [drúnken], *a.* ebrio, borracho.

drunkenly [-li], *adv.* ebriamente.—**drunkenness** [-nes], *s.* embriaguez, beodez; crápula.

drupaceous [drupéišhus], *a.* (bot.) drupáceo.

drupe [drup], *s.* (bot.) drupa.

dry [drái]. **I.** *a.* árido, seco, sediento; pobre, estéril, frío; jocoso, satírico; chocarrero; agudo, incisivo; seco (hablando de vinos); (b. a.) duro, crudo; (met.) impuro y basto; (fam. y pol.) prohibicionista, partidario de la temperancia; observante de la temperancia; (quím.) por vía seca.—**d. battery,** batería seca; pila seca.—**d. beef,** cecina.—**d. casting,** fundición en arena seca.—**d. cell,** (elec.) pila seca, elemento seco.—**d. concentration,** (met.) separación por gravedad al aire.—**d. cup,** ventosa seca.—**d. cupping,** aplicación de ventosas secas.—**d. dock,** dique de carena.

—**d. farming,** cultivo seco (sin riego).—**d. fruit,** frutas pasas.—**d. goods,** (E. U.) mercancías generales, esp. telas, ropa y menudencias; (Ingl.) víveres, comestibles.—**d. masonry,** construcción de fábrica a hueso.—**d. mass,** (igl.) misa en seco.—**d. measure,** medida o sistema de medidas para áridos.—**d. nurse,** niñera.—**d. plate,** (fot.) plancha seca.—**d. rot,** enfermedades de las patatas, etc. debidas a honguillos; pudrimiento de la madera debido a causas semejantes.—**d. shod,** a pie enjuto.—**d. weight,** (aer.) peso seco. **II.** *s.* (fam., pol.) prohibicionista, neftalista. **III.** *va.* secar, desecar; pasar (fruta); enjutar, enjugar; desaguar; dar sed; acecinar. **IV.** *vn.* secarse, enjugarse.—**to d. up,** secarse (esp. completa o rápidamente).

dryad [dráiæd], *s.* dríada; lirón.

dryer [dráiœr], *s.* secante; (quím.) desecativo.

dryly [dráili], *adv.* secamente, fríamente.

dryness [dráines], *s.* sequedad, aridez.

drynurse [dráincœrs], *va.* ser niñera de, cuidar de (un niño).

drysalter [dráisóltœr], *s.* traficante en viandas saladas y secas; droguista.

dual [diúal], *a.* binario; (gram.) dual.

dualism [diúališm], *s.* dualismo; dualidad.

dualist [diúalist], *s.* dualista.

duality [diuéliti], *s.* dualidad.

dub [dub]. **I.** *va.* apellidar, dar apodo; armar caballero; alisar; (mar.) aparar.—**to d. out,** (alb.) revocar. **II.** *vn.* redoblar.—**d.-a-d.,** rataplán.

dubbing [dúbing], *pa.* y *s.* (ten.) adobo impermeable; (mar.) aparado.—**d. tool,** azuela.

dubious [diúbius], *a.* dudoso; indeciso.

dubiously [-li], *adv.* dudosamente.—**dubiousness** [-nes], *s.* duda, incertidumbre.

dubitable [diúbitabœl], *a.* dubitable, dudable.

dubitably [-bli], *adv.* dudosamente.

ducal [diúcal], *a.* ducal.

ducat [dúcat], *s.* ducado (moneda).

duchess [dúches], *s.* duquesa.

duchy [dúchi], *s.* ducado.

duck [duc], *s.* (orn.) ánade, pato; acción de agacharse; capuz o chapuz; (tej.) dril, brin; (fam.) pichoña, vida mía.—**to make o to play at ducks and drakes,** hacer saltar una piedra sobre el agua; (fig.) derrochar.—*pl.* (fam.) pantalones de dril. **II.** *va.* zabullir. **III.** *vn.* zabullirse.

ducking [dúking], *s.* chapuz, zambullida.—**d. stool,** silla de chapuzar (antiguo castigo).

duckling [dúcling], *s.* anadeja, patito; monina (voz cariñosa).

duct [duct], *s.* conducto, canal, tubo.

ductile [dúctil], *a.* dúctil, flexible, blando, correoso, dócil, tratable.—**ductility** [ductíliti], *s.* ductilidad; docilidad.

dude [diúd], *s.* petimetre, lechuguino.

dudish [diúdišh], *a.* lechuguino, afectado.

dudgeon [dúyun], *s.* inquina; enojo; puño de daga.

duds [duds], *s. pl.* (fam.) trapos, pingajos, andrajos; ropa vieja.

due [diú]. **I.** *a.* debido, cumplido, vencido; pagadero; apto, propio, conveniente, oportuno; legítimo; esperado, que debe llegar.—**d. bill,** pagaré, abonaré.—**d. to,** ocasionado por, debido a.—**in d. time,** a su debido tiempo. **II.** *adv.* exactamente.—**d. west,** (mar.) poniente derecho. **III.** *s.* deuda u obligación; derechos, tributo, impuesto.—*pl.* cuota.—**to give the devil his d.,** ser justo hasta con el diablo.

duel [diúel]. **I.** *s.* duelo, desafío; certamen. **II.** *vn.* batirse en duelo.—**dueller** [-œr], **duellist** [-ist], *s.* duelista.—**duelling** [-ing], *s.* desafíos, duelos.

duenna [diuéna], *sf.* dueña.

duet [diuét], *s.* (mús.) dúo, dueto; pieza a cuatro manos.

duffel [dúfœl], *s.* (tej.) moletón; equipo, pertrechos.

dug [dug]. **I.** *pret.* y *pp.* del verbo TO DIG. **II.** *s.* teta, ubre.

dugout [dúgaut], *s.* piragua; cueva; (mil.) defensa subterránea cueva, de protección.

duke [diúk], *s.* duque.—**dukedom** [-dum], *s.* ducado.

dulcet [dúlset], *a.* dulce, suave, armonioso.
dulcification [dùlsïkéshʊn], *s.* dulcificación.
dulcify [dúlsïfai], *va.* dulcificar, endulzar.
dulcimer [dúlsimœr], *s.* (mús.) dulcémele.
dulia [duláia *o* diúlia], *s.* (igl.) dulía.
dull [dʊl]. **I.** *a.* embotado, obtuso, sin puntu, sin filo; apagado, sordo; lerdo, negado; insípido, soso, insulso; flojo, perezoso, pesado; lánguido, desvaído; insensible; triste, murrio; lento pero no intenso (dolor); deslustrado, empañado; opaco, obscuro, ofuscado, nebuloso; soñoliento, modorro; (com.) desanimado, paralizado, inactivo, muerto.—**d.-brained,** estúpido, tonto, lerdo.—**d.-browed,** cejijunto.—**d.-eyed,** ojiapagado.—**d. of hearing,** duro de oído, medio sordo.—**d. pain,** dolor sordo.—**d.-sighted,** cegato.—**d.-witted,** lerdo, estúpido. **II.** *va.* embotar, enromar; entontecer; entorpecer, obstruir; contristar; amortiguar, aliviar, moderar, mitigar; ofuscar, deslumbrar; empañar, deslustrar; mermar, enfriar (el entusiasmo, etc.). **III.** *vn.* embotarse; ponerse romo, gastarse la punta o el filo; empañarse; apagarse, mitigarse.
dullard [dúlard]. **I.** *s.* bestia, estólido. **II.** *a.* estúpido.
dullhead [dúljéd], *s.* tonto, zopenco.
dully [dúli], *adv.* lentamente; estúpidamente; sin brillo.
dul(l)ness [dúlnes], *s.* falta de punta o filo; estupidez; somnolencia, pereza, pesadez; prosaísmo; deslustre; (com.) depresión, desanimación.
dulse [dʊls], *s.* alga marina comestible.
duly [diúli], *adv.* debidamente, puntualmente, a su tiempo.
Duma [dúma], *s.* duma, parlamento ruso.
dumb [dʊm], *a.* mudo; callado; oculto, latente.—**d.-bell,** palanqueta de gimnasia.—**d. creature,** bestia, bruto.—**d. motions,** señas.—**d. show,** pantomima, signo, gesto.—**d. waiter,** ascensor o estante giratorio para el servicio del comedor.—**dumbly** [dúmli], *adv.* mudamente.—**dumbness** [-nes], *s.* mudez; silencio; estupidez.
dumdum, dumdum bullet [dúmdʊm búlet], *s.* bala de expansión o dilatación.
dumfound, dumbfound [dúmfáund], *va.* (fam.) confundir, dejar sin habla.
dummy [dúmi]. **I.** *a.* fingido, falseado, imitado.—**d. car,** vagón que lleva su propio motor o locomotora. **II.** *s.* (fam.) testaferro; (teat.) personaje que no habla; ascensor doméstico; objeto simulado; maniquí para vestidos, cabeza para pelucas, etc.; figurón; (imp.) libro en blanco con o sin páginas de muestra que enseña la forma general de un libro; libro u hojas con galeras recortadas, ilustraciones, etc., pegadas por páginas; (f. c.) DUMMY CAR; locomotora de máquina condensadora.
dump [dʊmp]. **I.** *va.* vaciar de golpe; descargar, verter. **II.** *s.* (E. U.) vaciadero; vaciamiento; (min.) terrero.—*pl.* melancolía, morriña.—**d.,** o **dumping car** o **wagon,** carro o vagón de volteo de fondo caedizo.—**to be in the dumps,** tener murria.
dumping [dúmping], *s.* (com.) inundación del mercado con artículos de precios rebajados, esp. para suprimir la competencia.
dumpish [dúmpish], *a.* murrio.—**dumpishness** [-nes], *s.* murria.
dumpling [dúmpling], *s.* pudín de pasta rellena de fruta o carne.
dumpy [dúmpi], *a.* regordete.—**d. level,** (top.) nivel de Troughton (nivel de anteojo corto muy usado en Inglaterra).
dun [dʊn]. **I.** *va.* importunar a un deudor, (Amér.) cobrar; apremiar. **II.** *va.* y *vn.* salar y conservar pescado; obscurecer. **III.** *a.* bruno, pardo, castaño obscuro; sombrío. **IV.** *s.* acreedor importuno; apremio; loma fortificada.
dunce [dʊns], *s.* zote, zopenco, bolo, tonto.
dunderhead, dunderpate [dúndœrjed, -péit], *s.* zamacuco, bodoque, badulaque.
dune [diún], *s.* duna, marisma.
dunfish [dúnfish], *s.* bacalao seco.
dung [dʊng]. **I.** *s.* estiércol.—**d. yard,** estercolero. **II.** *va.* y *vn.* estercolar.

dungeon [dúnɣʊn]. **I.** *s.* calabozo, mazmorra. **II.** *va.* encalabozar.
dungfork [dúngforc], *s.* horca o pala para estiércol.
dunghill [dúngjil]. **I.** *s.* estercolero, muladar, basurero. **II.** *a.* bajo, vil.
dunnage [dúney], *s.* (mar.) abarrote.
dunnite [dúnait], dunita, explosivo Dunn (explosivo compuesto en gran parte de ácido pícrico).
duo [dúo], *s.* (mús.) dúo.
duodecimal [diuodésimal], *a.* duodecimal.
duodecimo [diuodésimo], *s.* libro en dozavo.
duodenum [diuodínum], *s.* duodeno.
duogravure [diúograeviúœr], *s.* fotograbado en un color con dos placas.
duotype [-táip], *s.* fotografía obtenida de dos fotograbados a media tinta.
dupe [diúp]. **I.** *s.* incauto, primo, víctima de engaño o dolo. **II.** *va.* engañar, embaucar.
duple [diúpœl], *a.* doble.
duplex [diúplex], *a.* duplo; doble, dúplice; (tecn.) dúplex.
duplicate [diúplikeit]. **I.** *va.* y *vn.* duplicar, copiar, reproducir; repetir. **II.** *s.* duplicado, copia. **III.** *a.* duplicado, doble, en pares.—**duplication** [-éishʊn], *s.* duplicación; repetición, reduplicación; plegadura, pliegue, doblez.
duplicative [-ketiv], *a.* que duplica o se duplica.
duplicator [-kéitœr], *s.* duplicador, copiador.
duplicity [diuplisiti], *s.* duplicidad, engaño.
durability [diúrabíliti], *s.* estabilidad, permanencia; duración, durabilidad.
durable [diúraboel], *a.* durable, duradero.
durably [diúrabli], *adv.* duraderamente.
dura mater [diúra méitœr], *s.* (anat.) duramáter o duramadre.
duramen [diuréimen], *s.* (bot.) duramen.
durance [diúrans], *s.* cautividad, prisión.
durant [diúrant], *s.* (tej.) sempiterna.
duration [diuréishʊn], *s.* duración.
duress [diúres, durés], *s.* compulsión, coacción; prisión, encierro.
during [diúring], *prep.* durante.
durst, *pret. irr.* de TO DARE.
dusk [dʊsk]. **I.** *a.* (poét.) obscuro. **II.** *s.* crepúsculo vespertino, oraciones; obscuridad.
duskily [dúskili], *adv.* obscuramente.
duskiness [dúskines], *s.* obscuridad.
dusky [dúski], *a.* fusco, obscuro; moreno, pardo.
dust [dʊst]. **I.** *s.* polvo; polvareda; altercado; la tierra, la sepultura; (fig.) abyección, humillación; basura, barreduras; escombros; (fam.) oro en polvo; dinero.—**d.-born,** nacido del polvo.—**d. cap,** (aut.) tapa de válvula.—**d.-devil,** remolino móvil de arena.—**d. guard,** guardapolvo.—**to bite the d.,** morder el polvo.—**to kick up,** o **raise, a d.,** armar un alboroto. **II.** *va.* despolvorear, despolvar, desempolvar, sacudir o quitar el polvo; polvorear, espolvorear.
dustbrush [dústbrúsh], *s.* plumero, cepillo de despolvar.
duster [dústœr], *s.* el que quita el polvo; plumero; guardapolvo; utensilio para espolvorear.
dustguard [dústgard], *s.* guardapolvo.
dustiness [dústines], *s.* calidad de empolvado o polvoroso.
dustman [dústman], *s.* basurero, barrendero.
dustpan [-pæn], *s.* pala de recoger la basura.
dusty [dústi], *a.* empolvado.
Dutch [dʊch], *s.* y *a.* holandés; (E. U., fam. o vulg.) alemán.—**D. bond,** (alb.) aparejo longitudinal o de sogas y tizones alternados.—**D. brass,** tombac (aleación de cobre y cinc).—**D. cheese,** queso de Flandes.—**D. foil, D. metal,** hoja de tombac.—**D. pink,** áncora de Flandes.—**D. treat,** (fam.) convite a escote, convite en que cada cual paga por lo que bebe o come.—**D. wife,** (Fil.) abrazador.
Dutchman [dúchman], *s.* holandés; (fam., en E. U.) alemán.
duteous [diúteʊs], *a.* obediente, obsequioso, respetuoso.

dutiable [diútiabœl], *a.* imponible; sujeto a adeudo.

dutiful [diútiful], *a.* deferente, respetuoso; concienzudo.—**dutifully** [-li], *adv.* obedientemente, respetuosamente; concienzudamente.—**dutifulness** [-nes], *s.* obediencia; respeto; escrupulosidad.

duty [diúti], *s.* deber, obligación; obediencia, sumisión, acatamiento; (mil.) facción, servicio; impuesto, adeudo, derechos de aduana o de puertas; (mec.) trabajo, servicio; (mec.) rendimiento; (ing.) cantidad de agua necesaria para el riego de un área dada (gen. 1 acre); área que una cantidad dada de agua puede regar.—**d. free,** (com.) franco, libre de derechos.

duumvir [diuúnvœr], *s.* duunviro.

duumvirate [diuúmviret], *s.* duunvirato.

dwale [duéil], *s.* (bot.) belladama.

dwarf [duórf]. **I.** *s.* enano. **II.** *a.* diminuto, enano. **III.** *va.* impedir el crecimiento de; empequeñecer, achicar. **IV.** *vn.* empequeñecerse, achicarse.

dwarfish [-fish], *a.* enano, pequeño, diminuto.—**dwarfishly** [-li], *adv.* como un enano.—**dwarfishness** [-nes], *s.* pequeñez de estatura.

dwell [duél], *vn.* habitar, morar, residir, vivir; (con **on** o **upon**) espaciarse (en), tratar (de).

dweller [duélœr], *s.* morador, habitante.

dwelling [duéling]. **I.** *s.* morada; casa. **II.** *a.* de habitación.

dwindle [duíndœl], *vn.* menguar, disminuirse; degenerar; decaer; consumirse.

dyad [dáiæd]. **I.** *a.* (quím.) bivalente. **II.** *s.* (quím.) átomo o cuerpo bivalente.

dye [dái]. **I.** *va.* (*pp.* y *pret.* ger. DYEING) teñir, tinturar. **II.** *s.* tinte; tintura; color, matiz.—**to d. in (the) grain, o in the wool,** teñir (la lana) en rama.—**dyed-in-the-wool,** acérrimo, intransigente.

dyehouse [dáijáus], *s.* tintorería.

dyeing [dáiing]. **I.** *s.* tintorería; tinte, teñidura, tintura. **II.** *a.* colorante.

dyer [dáiœr], *s.* tintorero.—**d.'s broom,** (bot.) ginesta.—**d.'s weed,** (bot.) gualda.

dyestuff [dáistuf], *s.* materia de tinte.

dyewood [-úd], *s.* madera de tinte.

dying [dáiing], *pa.* de TO DIE; moribundo, agonizante; mortal.—**d. eyes,** ojos lánguidos.

dyke [dáik], *s.* = DIKE.

dynactinometer [dainæctinómetœr], *s.* (fot.) dinactinómetro.

dynam [dáinæm], *s.* dinamia.

dynameter [dainémetœr], *s.* (ópt.) dinámetro.

dynamic(al [dainémic(al], *a.* dinámico; eficaz.

dynamics [dainémics], *s.* dinámica; mecánica (estática y dinámica).

dynamism [dáinæmism], *s.* (filos.) dinamismo.—**dynamist** [-ist], *s.* dinamista.

dynamite [-mait]. **I.** *s.* dinamita. **II.** *va.* volar con dinamita.—**dynamiter** [-œr], *s.* dinamitero.

dynamo [dáinamo], *s.* (elec.) dínamo.

dynamo-electric(al [dáinamo-eléctric(al], *a.* dinamoeléctrico.

dynamogenesis [dáinæmoyénesis], *s.* (psic.) dinamogénesis, actividad muscular debida a estimulación de los sentidos.

dynamogeny [-móyeni], *s.* dinamogenia, estado debido a dinamogénesis.

dynamograph [dainémograf], *s.* dinamógrafo, dinamómetro registrador de esfuerzo muscular.

dynamometer [-mómetœr], *s.* dinamómetro.

dynamometric(al [-mométric(al], *a.* dinamométrico.

dynastic(al [dainéstic(al], *a.* dinástico.

dynasty [dáinasti], *s.* dinastía.

dyne [dáin], *s.* (mec.) dina (unidad de fuerza).

dyscrasia, o **dyscrasy** [discréisia, díscrasi], *s.* discrasia.

dysenteric [disentéric], *a.* disentérico.

dysentery [dísenteri], *s.* disentería.

dyspepsia, dyspepsy [dispépsia, -i], *s.* dispepsia.

dyspeptic [dispéptic], *a.* y *s.* dispéptico; mórbido, quejoso; indigesto.

dysphagia [disféyia], *s.* disfagia.

dysphonia, o **dysphony** [disfónia, dísfoni], *s.* disfonía.

dyspnœa [dispnía], *s.* disnea.

dyspnœal, dyspnœic [dispníal, dispníic], *a.* disneico.

dysuria, dysyry [disyúria, dísyuri], *s.* disuria.

E

e [i], *s.* e; (**E**, mús.) mí, tercera nota de la escala.

each [ich]. **I.** *a.* cada, todo. **II.** *pron.* cada uno, todos.—**e. other,** mutuamente, el uno al otro; unos a otros.

eager [ígœr], *a.* ansioso, anhelante; vehemente, impaciente.—**eagerly** [-li], *adv.* ansiosamente, con anhelo.—**eagerness** [-nes], *s.* ansia, avidez, anhelo, ahínco; vehemencia.

eagle [ígœl], *s.* (orn.) águila; (E. U.) águila, moneda de oro ($10).—**e.-eyed,** de ojo avizor.

eaglet [íglet], *s.* aguilucho.

eaglestone [ígœlstóun], *s.* ⟨min.⟩ etites.

eaglewood [-ud], *s.* madera de águila.

ear [íær]. **I.** *s.* oído; oreja; asa, asidero; (bot.) mazorca; espiga.—**e. muff,** orejera.—**e.-piercing,** penetrante (sonido).—**e. trumpet,** trompetilla.—**by e.,** de oído; de oídas.—**by the ears,** en pugna abierta.—**to set by the ears,** enemistar, malquistar.—**up to the ears,** (fam.) en calzas prietas. **II.** *vn.* espigar. **III.** *va.* arar.

earache [íæreic], *s.* dolor de oído.

eardrop [-dróp], *s.* pendiente, arete, zarcillo.

eardrum [-drúm], *s.* tímpano (del oído).

eared [íærd], *a.* espigado; en mazorca.

earing [íring], *s.* (mar.) empuñidura.

earl [œrl], *s.* conde.—**e.-marshal,** rey de armas.

earlap [íærlæp], *s.* punta de la oreja.

earldom [œrldvm], *s.* condado.

earless [íærles], *a.* desorejado.

earlier [-œr], *a.* y *adv.* más temprano; anterior, antiguo.—**earliest** (-est), *a.* y *adv.* más temprano (superl.); más antiguo, más remoto; antiguo, primitivo.

earliness [œrlines], *s.* precocidad, anticipación; presteza, prontitud; calidad de temprano.

earlock [íærloc], *s.* aladar.

early [œrli]. **I.** *a.* primitivo; temprano, tempranero; avanzado, precoz, anticipado; matinal; cercano, próximo.—**e. fruit,** fruto temprano.—**e. riser,** madrugador. **II.** *adv.* temprano, tempranamente; al principio.

earmark [íærmárc], *s.* marca en la oreja; señal inequívoca.

earn [œrn], *va.* ganar; merecer; captarse; devengar.

earnest [œrnest]. **I.** *a.* serio, formal; extremo, fervoroso; activo, celoso, diligente; atento, cuidadoso; grave, importante. **II.** *s.* seriedad, buena fe; arras, prenda, señal.—**e. money,** caparra.—**in (good) e.,** de buena fe, en serio.

earnestly [-li], *adv.* seriamente, de veras; encarecidamente.—**earnestness** [-nes], *s.* seriedad, formalidad, buena fe.

earnings [œrnings], *s. pl.* salario, estipendio, jornal, paga; (com.) ganancias, ingresos.

earpick [íærpic], *s.* mondaoídos, escarbaorejas.

earring [íærring], *s.* = EARDROP.

earshot [-shot], *s.* alcance del oído.

earth [œrz]. **I.** *s.* tierra (globo terráqueo); suelo; madriguera; (elec.) tierra; (quím.) óxido metálico terroso.—**e.-borer,** (min.) barrena.—**e.-eating,** geófago.—**e. system,** (rad.) sistema de toma de tierra. **II.** *va.* enterrar, cubrir con tierra. **III.** *vn.* retirarse debajo de tierra.

earthbank [œrzbænc], *s.* malecón o terraplén.

earthboard [-bórd], *s.* orejera del arado.

earthborn [-bórn], *a.* terrígeno, bajo, innoble.

earthen [œrdœn], *a.* térreo, terreno, terrizo; de barro.

earthenware [-uéar], *s.* loza de barro, cacharros.

earthiness [œrdines], *s.* terrosidad.

earthliness [œrzlines], *s.* terrenidad, mundanalidad.

earthling [ə́rzling], s. habitante de la tierra, ser mortal.

earthly [ə́rzli], a. terreno, terrero; terrenal, mundano.

earthnut [-nút], s. (bot.) castañuela; cacahuete, maní.

earthquake [ə́rzcuéik], s. temblor de tierra, terremoto.

earthwork [ə́rzuə́rk], s. (fort. e ing.) terraplén; movimiento de tierras.

earthworm [ə́rzuœrm], s. lombriz de tierra.

earthy [ə́rði], a. terroso, terrizo; basto, grosero.

earwax [íæruács], s. cerumen, cera de oído.

earwig [-uig], s. (ent.) tijereta; ciempiés.

earwitness [-uítnes], s. testigo auricular.

ease [iš]. I. s. tranquilidad; ocio, reposo; comodidad, alivio, descanso; holgura; facilidad, desembarazo o desenvoltura, naturalidad.—**at e.**, con desahogo, descansadamente.—**with e.**, con facilidad. II. va. aliviar, mitigar, suavizar, aligerar, descargar, desembarazar.—**to e. away,** o **off,** aflojar gradualmente; (mar.) arriar (cable, cadena).—**to e. nature,** o **one's self,** hacer del cuerpo.—**to e. the ship,** (mar.) orzar.

easel [iŝœl], s. caballete de pintor.

easement [íŝmœnt], s. alivio, apoyo, descarga; (for.) servidumbre.

easily [iŝili], adv. fácilmente.

easiness [iŝines], s. facilidad; suavidad; holgura, comodidad; tranquilidad, quietud; despejo, desembarazo.

East [ist]. I. s. Oriente, Levante; este, leste. II. a. oriental, de oriente, levantino; del este. III. adv. hacia el este.

Easter [iśtœr], s. Pascua florida.—**E. day,** día de Pascua.—**E. eve,** sábado santo.—**E. Sunday,** domingo de Resurrección.

Eastertide [íśtœrtáid], s. aleluya, tiempo de Pascua.

easterly [íśtœrli], a. y adv. oriental, del este, al este; hacia el este.—**e. wind,** aire de levante, solano.

eastern [iśtœrn], s. oriental.

eastward [iśtuard]. I. a. de dirección o en dirección oriental. II. adv. hacia el este.

easy [iŝi], a. fácil; cómodo, holgado; acomodado; complaciente, condescendiente; accesible o asequible; suelto, libre; tranquilo; aliviado; simple, natural; suave; manual, mañero; quedito, despacio; (fam.) (com.) flojo; abundante; (fam.) confiado, fácil de engañar.—**e. chair,** butaca, sillón, poltrona.—**e. going,** de movimiento fácil o suave; lento, despacioso; calmado, sereno, filosófico.—**e. labor,** parto feliz.

eat [it]. I. va. (pret. ATE, EAT (et), pp. EATEN, EAT) comer, alimentarse; corroer; consumir.—**to e. away,** corroer, destruir.—**to e. breakfast, dinner, supper,** desayunarse, comer, cenar.—**to e. crow,** (fam.) cantar la palinodia.—**to e. humble pie,** humillarse y dar excusas.—**to e. one's heart,** sufrir uno la amargura en silencio.—**to e. one's words,** retractarse, retirar uno sus palabras. II. vn. comer; ser comible; saber (a); (a menudo con into, through, etc.) corroer, destruir. III. s. (fam., gen. pl.) refrescos, golosinas.

eatable [itœbœl]. I. a. comestible, comedero. II. s. pl. comestibles, víveres, vituallas.

eater [itœr], s. comedor.

eating [iting]. I. s. la acción de comer; cosa de comer; comidas. II. a. de comer; corrosivo; consumidor.—**e.-house,** restaurante; bodegón.

eaves [ivŝ], s. pl. socarrén, alero, tejaroz.

eavesdrop [ivŝdrop], vn. escuchar a las puertas, fisgonear.—**eavesdropper** [-œr], s. el que escucha escondido.

ebb [eb]. I. vn. menguar la marea; decaer, disminuir. II. s. (mar.) menguante, reflujo; decadencia.—**e. of life,** vejez.—**e. tide,** (mar.) marea menguante.

ebon [ébon], a. de ébano, negro.—**ebonist** [-ist], s. ebanista.

ebonite [ébonait], s. ebonita.—**ebonize** [-aiŝ], va. ebonizar.

ebony [éboni], s. (bot.) ébano.

ebullience, ebulliency [ebúlliens, -i], s. ebullición; entusiasmo.

ebullient [-ent], a. hirviente; entusiasta.

ebullition [ébulíŝhun], s. ebullición; (fig.) viva emoción o agitación; entusiasmo.

eburnated [ébœrneted], a. endurecido como hueso.

eburnean [ebœrnian], a. ebúrneo.

eccentric [ecséntric], s. persona excéntrica o rara; (mec.) excéntrica.

eccentric(al [-al], a. (geom. y mec.) excéntrico; extravagante, excéntrico, estrambótico, estrafalario, raro.

eccentrically [-i], adv. excéntricamente.

eccentricity, [écsentrísiti], s. excentricidad.

ecchymosis [ekimósis], s. equimosis, moretón, aporisma.

Ecclesiastes [eclíŝiéstiŝ], s. Eclesiastés.

ecclesiastic(al [eclíŝiéstic(al], a. eclesiástico.—**ecclesiastic,** s. eclesiástico.—**ecclesiastically** [-ali], adv. eclesiásticamente.—**ecclesiasticism** [-siŝm], s. clericalismo.

Ecclesiasticus [-cus], s. (bib.) Eclesiástico.

ecclesiology [eclesióloyi], s. (teol.) ciencia de la Iglesia; (b. a.) arquitectura y decorado de iglesias.

echape [echép], s. caballo de casta cruzada.

echelon [éŝhelon], s. (mil.) escalón.

echinate(d [ékinet(ed], a. erizado.

echinoderm [ekáinodœrm], a. y s. equinodermo.—**echinodermatous** [-dœrmatus], a. equinodermo.

Echinoidea [ékinóidia], s. pl. (zool.) equinoideos.

echinus [ekáinus], s. (arq.) gallón; erizo; equino.

echo [éco]. I. s. eco. II. vn. resonar, reverberar, repetir. III. va. repercutir.

echoic [écoic], a. (filol.) onomatopéyico.—**echoism** [-ism], s. onomatopeya.

éclair [ecléœr], s. bollo de crema.

éclaircissement [ecleœrsísman], s. aclaración, explicación, ilustración.

éclat [eclá], s. esplendor, magnificencia; aclamación, aplauso; renombre, celebridad.

eclectic [ecléctic]. I. s. y a. ecléctico.

eclecticism [-siŝm], s. eclecticismo.

eclipse [eclips]. I. s. eclipse. II. va. eclipsar.

ecliptic [ecliptic]. I. s. (astr.) eclíptica. II. a. eclíptico.

eclogue [éclog], s. égloga.

ecology [ecóloyi], s. (biol.) ecología, mesología, relación entre un organismo y su medio.

economic(al [iconómic, -al], a. económico.

economically [-i], adv. económicamente.

economics [económics], s. economía política.

economist [económist], s. economista.

economize [económiŝ], va. economizar.

economy [económi], s. economía.

écraseur [ecraŝœr], s. (cir.) triturador.

écru [ecrú]. I. a. crudo, sin blanquear. II. s. color de lino sin blanquear; géneros de lino crudo.

ecstasied [écstasid], a. extático.

ecstasy [écstasi], s. éxtasis.—**ecstatic(al** [-tétic-al], a. extático.

ectoblast [éctoblæst], s. (biol.) ectoblasto, ectodermo.

ectoderm [éctodœrm], s. (biol.) ectodermo, ectoblasto.—**ectodermal** [-dœrmæl], **ectodermic** [-ic] a. ectodérmico.

ectogenous [ectóyenus], a. ectógeno, que puede desarrollarse sin el organismo a que se adhiere como parásito (apl. a ciertas bacterias).

ectopia [ectópiæ], s. desplazamiento (de un órgano).

ectoplasm [éctoplæsm], s. ectoplasma, substancia tenue o exhalación que, según algunos, se desprende del cuerpo durante ciertos fenómenos psíquicos, como los mediumísticos; (zool.) ectoplasma, ectosarca; (bot.) ectoplasma, exoplasma, parte periférica del citoplasma.

ectropion, ectropium [ectrópion, -pium], s. (med.) ectropión, inversión de los párpados.

ecumenical [ekiuménical], a. ecuménico.

Para la pronunciación de æ, œ, ɒ, ŝ, ŝh, u, ȳ, y, z, véase la clave al principio del libro.

eczema [écŝema], s. (med.) eczema.
eczematous [ecŝématuŝ], a. eczematoso.
edacious [edéiŝhuŝ], a. voraz.—**edaciousness** [-nes], **edacity** [edǽsiti], s. voracidad, glotonería.
eddy [édi]. **I.** s. remanso; remolino.—**e. current** (elec.) corriente de Foucault, corriente parásita. **II.** vn. remolinar.
edema, œdema [edíma], s. edema.
edematous [edématuŝ], a. edematoso.
Eden [ídœn], s. Edén.
Edentata [identéta], s. (zool.) desdentados.
edentate [edéntet], a. desdentado.
edge [ey]. **I.** s. filo; canto; borde, orilla; ribete. —**e. tool**, herramienta o instrumento de filo.—**on e.**, de canto; impaciente, ansioso.—**to set the teeth on e.**, dar dentera. **II.** va. afilar, aguzar; (a menudo con on) aguijonear, incitar; (cost.) ribetear, guarnecer; bornear; abrirse (paso) marchando de lado. **III.** vn. avanzar de lado, escurrirse.
edged [eyd], a. afilado, cortante.
edgeless [éyles], a. embotado, obtuso; sin filo.
edgewise [éyuaiŝ], adv. de filo o de canto, de lado o sesgo.
edging [éying], s. orla, orilla, ribete; trepado; pestaña; guarnición.
edibility [édibíliti], **edibleness** [édibœlnes], s. cualidad de comestible.
edible [édibœl], a. y s. comestible.
edict [ídict], s. edicto.
edification [edifikéŝhun], s. edificación.
edificatory [édificatori], a. edificativo, edificante.
edifice [édifis], s. edificio.
edifier [édifaiœr], s. edificante.
edify [édifai], va. edificar, fortalecer.
edifying [-ing], a. edificante.—**edifyingly** [-li], adv. edificantemente.
edile [ídail], s. edil.
edit [édit], va. redactar; dirigir (un periódico); corregir.
edition [edíŝhun], s. edición.
editing [éditing], s. redacción; corrección.
editor [éditœr], s. redactor, compilador; director de un periódico.
editorial [éditórial]. **I.** a. editorial. **II.** s. artículo de fondo.
editorship [éditœrŝhip], s. cargo de redactor; dirección de un periódico.
educable [édiucæbœl], a. educable.
educate [édyuket], va. educar, instruir; acostumbrar.
education [édyukéiŝhun], s. educación, enseñanza; instrucción, ilustración; cultura.
educational [-al], a. docente; de enseñanza; educativo.
educationalist [-ist], **educationist** [-kéiŝhunist], s. pedagogo, persona versada en asuntos de educación, educador.
educator [-kéitœr], s. educador, pedagogo.
educe [ediúŝ], va. educir; sacar, extraer.
eduction [edœcŝhun], s. educción.
edulcorate [edúlcoret], va. edulcorar.
edulcoration [edulcoréŝhun], s. edulcoración, dulcificación.—**edulcorative** [edúlcoretiv], a. dulcificante.
eel [íl], s. (ict.) anguila.
eelpot [ílpót], nasa para anguilas.
eelpout [ílpaut], s. = BURBOT.
e'en [ín], adv. contracción de EVEN.
e'er [éœr], adv. contracción de EVER.
eery, eerie [íri], a. imponente; atemorizado.
efface [eféis], va. borrar, raspar, destruir.
effaceable [-abœl], a. deleble.—**effacement** [-mœnt], s. tachón, raspadura.
effect [eféct]. **I.** s. efecto; impresión; eficacia, eficiencia; tenor, significado, substancia; fuerza, vigor, operación; realización, cumplimiento.—pl. efectos, bienes, caudal.—**in e.**, en operación, vigente; en substancia, en realidad (nunca en efecto, en el razonamiento).—**into e.**, en vigencia, en práctica, en operación.—**of no e.**, sin resultado, vano. **II.** va. efectuar.

effective [-iv]. **I.** a. efectivo, eficaz; de buen efecto, que causa buena impresión; real, verdadero; (mec.) útil, efectivo.—**to make e.**, llevar a efecto; hacer cumplir. **II.** s. (com. y e. p.) metálico, numerario; (mil.) soldados disponibles para el servicio; ejército.—**effectively** [-li], adv. eficazmente.—**effectiveness** [-nes], s. eficacia.
effectless [eféctles], a. ineficaz.
effectual [-chual], a. eficaz.—**effectually** [-i], adv. eficazmente; efectivamente, de facto.
effectuate [efékchueit], va. efectuar, ejecutar.
effeminacy [eféminasi], **effeminateness** [-etnes], s. afeminamiento, afeminación.
effeminate [-et]. **I.** a. afeminado. **II.** va. afeminar. **III.** vn. afeminarse.
effeminately [-li], adv. afeminadamente.
effendi [eféndi], s. efendi, título turco semejante a Don.
efferent [éfœrœnt], a. eferente.
effervesce [efervéŝ], vn. hervir, fermentar, estar en efervescencia.—**effervescence** [-ens], s. efervescencia.—**efferverscent** [-ent], a. efervescente.
effete [efít], a. usado, gastado, cascado; estéril, infructuoso.
efficacious [éfikéiŝhuŝ], a. eficaz.—**efficaciously** [-li], adv. eficazmente.—**efficaciousness** [-nes], **efficacy** [éficasi], s. eficacia, eficiencia.
efficiency [efíŝhensi], s. eficacia; eficiencia; habilidad, competencia; economía; (mec.) rendimiento.
efficient [-ŝhent], a. eficiente, eficaz; (mec.) de rendimiento (vg. a very efficient engine, una máquina de gran rendimiento).
efficiently [-li], adv. eficientemente; eficazmente; con buen rendimiento.
effigy [éfiri], s. efigie, retrato, imagen.
efflation [efléŝhun], s. soplo; emanación.
effloresce [efloréŝ], vn. (quím.) eflorescerse.
efflorescence, efflorescency [-sens, i], s. eflorescencia; (med.) roncha; erupción; (bot.) florescencia.—**efflorescent** [-sent], a. (quím.) eflorescente; (bot.) en flor.
effluence [éfluens], s. emanación, efluvio; efusión; efluxión.—**effluent** [-ent]. **I.** a. efluente. **II.** s. líquido que sale.
effluvium [eflúvium], s. efluvio, exhalación, emanación, tufo, vaho.
efflux [éflvcs], s. efusión, emanación; flujo, derrame.—**effluxion** [-ŝhun], s. emanación, efluvio, exhalación, efluxión.
effort [éfort], s. esfuerzo, conato, empeño.
effrontery [efrúnteri], s. desfachatez, impudencia.
effulge [efúly], vn. brillar, resplandecer.
effulgence [-yens], s. esplendor, fulgor, brillantez.
effulgent [-yent], a. resplandeciente, refulgente.
effuse [efiúŝ]. **I.** va. derramar, verter, esparcir. **II.** vn. emanar. **III.** a. (bot.) esparcido.
effusion [efiúyun], s. efusión, derrame; expansión; desahogo.
effusive [-siv], a. expansivo, comunicativo, demostrativo.—**effusively** [-li], adv. demostrativamente, ardientemente.—**effusiveness** [-nes], s. ardor o pasión.
eft [eft], s. lagartija.
egest [iyést], va. excretar, expeler.—**egesta** [-æ], s. pl. excremento, excrescencia.—**egestion**, [-ŝhun], s. defecación.
egg [eg], s. huevo.—**e. coal**, antracita gruesa. —**e. cup**, huevera.—**e. glass**, reloj de arena de 3 minutos para hervir huevos; huevera de vidrio. —**e.-laying**, ovíparo.—**e.-shaped**, oviforme. **II.** va. mezclar o cubrir con huevo; (E. U.) arrojar huevos a una persona; (seguido de on) hurgar, incitar, provocar. **III.** vn. coleccionar huevos de aves.
eggnog [égnog], s. caldo de la reina, yema mejida.
eggplant [-plant], s. (bot.) berenjena.
eggshell [-shel], s. cáscara de huevo, cascarón.—**e. china**, loza muy fina.
egis, ægis [éyis], s. egida, escudo.
eglantine [églantain], s. (bot.) eglantina; agavanzo.
ego [ígo, égo], s. (filos.) (cl) yo.

egoism [égo- o ígoiŝm], *s.* egoísmo.—**egoist** [-ist], *s.* egoísta.—**egoistic** [-istic], *a.* egoísta.—**egotism** [ígotiŝm], *s.* egotismo.—**egotist** [-ist], *s.* egotista.—**egotistic(al** [-tístic(al], *a.* egotista.

egregious [egríγus], *a.* egregio; extraordinario, estupendo.—**egregiously** [-li], *adv.* egregiamente.

egress [ígres], **egression** [egréŝhun], *s.* salida.

egret [égret o ígret], *s.* moño, penacho, plumero; (orn.) airón.

Egyptian [iγípŝhan], *a.* y *s.* egipcio.—**E. pea,** garbanzo.

Egyptologist [iγiptóloγist], *s.* egiptólogo.

Egyptology [-γi], *s.* egiptología.

eh [e], *interj.* ¿qué? ¿eh?

eider, eider duck [áidœr, duc], *s.* (orn.) ganso del norte.—**e. down,** edredón, plumazón, plumón.

eidograph [áidograf], *s.* eidógrafo.

eidolon [aidólon], *s.* representación, imagen; fantasma.

eight [éit], *a.* y *s.* ocho.—**eighteen** [éitín], *a.* y *s.* dieciocho.—**eighteenth** [éitínz], *a.* décimoctavo; dieciochavo; dieciocho (ordinal).

eightfold [éitfould], *a.* ocho veces tanto.

eighth [éitz], *a.* octavo.

eightieth [éitiez], *a.* octogésimo; ochenta (ordinal); ochentavo.

eighty [éiti], *a.* y *s.* ochenta.

either [ídœr o áidœr]. **I.** *a.* y *pron.* uno u otro, cualquiera de los dos; uno y otro, ambos, entrambos. **II.** *conj.* o. **III.** *adv.* (después de *not, nor*) tampoco.

ejaculate [eγækiuleit], *va.* exclamar, proferir.

ejaculation [-ŝhun], *s.* jaculatoria, exclamación.

ejaculatory [-latori], *a.* jaculatorio.

eject [eréct], *va.* arrojar, expeler, echar.

ejection [-ŝhun], *s.* expulsión, evacuación.

ejectment [eγéctmœnt], *s.* (for.) desahucio; expulsión, exclusión.

ejector [eγéctoer], *s.* expulsador; (armas) eyector, botacápsulas; (mec.) bomba de chorro (ll. t. **e. pump**).—**e. condenser,** condensador de chorro.

eke [ik], *va.* obtener o producir con dificultad.—**to e. out,** dar o aumentar poco a poco, escatimar; ganar a duras penas.

elaborate [eláboret]. **I.** *va.* labrar, elaborar. **II.** *a.* elaborado, trabajado, detallado, primoroso; esmerado; estudiado.—**elaborately** [-li], *adv.* primorosamente, con muchos detalles.—**elaborateness** [-nes], *s.* primor, perfección.—**elaboration** [-éiŝhun], *s.* elaboración; obra acabada. **elaborative, elaboratory** [-ativ, -tori], *a.* elaborativo.—**elaborator** [-éitœr], *s.* artífice.

eland [ílænd], *s.* (zool.) anta; grande antílope sudafricano.

elapse [eláps], *vn.* pasar, transcurrir.

elastic(al [elǽsti(œl]. **I.** *a.* elástico.—**e. gum,** caucho.—**e. limit** (tecn.) límite elástico; (com.) límite variable de emisión (de un banco). **II.** *s.* faja o tira de caucho.

elasticity [élas-, o ílæstísiti], *s.* elasticidad.

elate [eléit]. **I.** *a.* exaltado, triunfante, gozoso. **II.** *va.* exaltar, elevar, endiosar; engreír, ensoberbecer.—**elatedly** [-tedli], *adv.* exaltadamente, triunfantemente.

elaterin [elǽterin], *s.* (quím.) elaterina.

elaterium [élætírium], *s.* (bot.) elaterio.

elation [eléiŝhun], *s.* júbilo, elación.

elbow [élbo]. **I.** *s.* codo; recodo, ángulo, codillo; brazo de sillón.—**e. grease,** (fam.) trabajo asiduo.—**e. pipe,** codo, tubo acodado.—**at one's e.,** a la mano, muy cerca. **II.** *va.* codear, dar codazos. **III.** *vn.* formar recodos o ángulos.

elbowed [élbod], *a.* acodado.

elbowroom [élbourrúm], *s.* amplio espacio; espacio suficiente; amplia oportunidad.

elbowchair [-chéær], *s.* silla de brazos, poltrona.

elder [éldœr]. **I.** *a.* mayor, de más edad.—*comp. irr.* de OLD, preferido a OLDER cuando denota la mayor de dos personas. **II.** *s.* anciano; señor; mayor; antepasado; (igl.) jefe de tribu o familia; dignatario; eclesiástico; (bot.) saúco.

elderberry [-berri], *s.* (bot.) baya del saúco.

elderly [-li], *a.* de edad madura.—**eldership** [-ŝhip], *s.* presbiterato.

eldest [éldest], *a. sup.* de OLD: el mayor, primogénito.

Eleatic [éliætic], *s.* y *a.* eleático.

elecampane [elecampéin], *s.* (bot.) énula, campana, olivarda.

elect [eléct]. **I.** *va.* elegir. **II.** *a.* electo; escogido, predestinado. **III.** *s.* escogido, escogidos.

electant [eléctant], *s.* elector.

election [elécŝhun], *s.* elección; (teol.) predestinación.

electioneer [elecŝhuníœr], *vn.* (pol.) solicitar votos; hacer campaña electoral.

elective [eléctiv], *a.* electivo.—**electively** [-li], *adv.* electivamente.

elector [eléctœr], *s.* elector.

electoral [-al], *a.* electoral.—**e. college,** (E. U.) colegio electoral, asamblea de electores que elige al presidente.

electorate [eléctoret], *s.* electorado.

electric(al [eléctric(al], *a.* eléctrico; (fig.) vivo, fogoso; inquieto, activo.—**e. balance,** puente de Wheatstone; electrómetro de balanza.—**e. candle,** bujía eléctrica, bujía de Jablochkoff.—**e. chair,** silla de electrocución, patíbulo eléctrico.—**e. column,** pila voltaica.—**e. engineer,** ingeniero electricista.—**e. engineering,** electrotecnia, ingeniería eléctrica.—**e. fan,** ventilador eléctrico.—**e. fish,** pez eléctrico.—**e. furnace,** horno eléctrico.—**e. generator,** generador eléctrico, dínamo.—**e. lighting,** alumbrado eléctrico.—**e. meter,** contador eléctrico.—**e. motor,** electromotor, motor eléctrico.—**e. plant,** instalación eléctrica.—**e. ray,** (zool.) torpedo, tremielga.—**e. rings,** anillos de Nobili.—**e. seal,** piel de conejo a imitación de foca.—**e. steel,** acero hecho en el horno eléctrico.—**e. tape,** cinta aislada o de aislamiento.—**e. vane,** o **whirl,** molinete eléctrico.—**e. varnish,** barniz aislador.—**e. welding,** soldadura eléctrica.

electrician [eléctríŝhan], *s.* electricista.

electricity [-trísiti], *s.* electricidad.

electricute, electrocute [eléctri- (*o* tro) kiut], *va.* electrocutar.—**electricution, electrocution** [-kiúŝhun], *s.* electrocución.

electrification [eléctrifikéiŝhun], *s.* electrización; electrificación (aplicación de energía eléctrica —a un f. c., etc.).

electrify [-fai], *va.* electrizar; electrificar (un ferrocarril, etc.).

electrine [eléctrin], *a.* ambarino.

electrize [traiŝ], *va.* electrizar.—**electrization** [-triséiŝhun], *s.* electrización.—**electrizer** [-trálŝœr], *s.* (med.) electrizador.

electrobus [eléctrobús], *s.* ómnibus eléctrico.

electrochemical [-kémical], *a.* electroquímico.

electrochemistry [-kémistri], *s.* electroquímica.

electrocute, electrocution. *V.* ELECTRICUTE, ELECTRICUTION.

electrode [eléctrod], *s.* electrodo.

electrodeposit [-depósit]. **I.** *va.* depositar electrolíticamente. **II.** *s.* deposición electrolítica.—**electrodeposition** [-dépoŝíŝhun], *s.* deposición electrolítica, galvanoplastia.

electrodynamic [-dainémic], *a.* electrodinámico.

electrodynamics, *s.* electrodinámica.

electrograph [-grǽph], *s.* electrógrafo, telégrafo registrador; gráfico de funcionamiento de un electromotor; cámara cinematográfica de luz de arco; radiografía.

electrokinetic [-kinétic], *a.* electrodinámico o electrocinético.—**electrokinetics,** *s.* electrocinética, electrodinámica.

electrolier [-líœr], *s.* candelabro o araña de lámparas eléctricas.

electrolysis [eléctrólisis], *s.* electrólisis.

electrolyte [eléctrolait], *s.* electrólito.

electrolytic [-lític], *a.* electrolítico.—**e. detector,** (rad.) detector electrolítico.

electrolyzation [laiŝéŝhun], *s.* electrolización.

electrolyze [-laiŝ], *va.* electrolizar.

electrolyzer [-laiŝœr], *s.* electrolizador; (med.) instrumento para el tratamiento electrolítico de la estrechez uretral.

electromagnet [-mǽgnet], *s.* electroimán.

---

electromagnetic [-mægnétic], *a.* (elec.) electromagnético.

electromagnetism [-mægnetiśm], *s.* electromagnetismo.

electrometallurgy [-métælœrri], *s.* electrometalurgia.

electrometer [electrómetœr], *s.* electrómetro.

electrometric(al [electrométric(al], *a.* electrométrico.

electrometry [electrómetri], *s.* electrometría.

electromotion [eléctromoushun], *s.* circulación de una corriente eléctrica; movimiento producido por energía eléctrica.

electromotive [-mótiv], *a.* electromotor, electromotriz.—**e force,** fuerza electromotriz.

electromotor [-mótœr], *s.* motor eléctrico, electromotor.

electron [eléctron], *s.* (fís. y quím.) electrón.—**electronic** [electrónic], *a.* electrónico.

electron, electrum [-um], *s.* plata alemana; electro; oro argentífero.

electronegative [eléctronégætiv], *a.* electronegativo.

electropathy [electrópazi], *s.* electroterapia.

electrophorus [electróforus], *s.* electróforo.

electroplate [eléctropleit]. **I.** *va.* galvanizar. **II.** *s.* artículo galvanizado.—**electroplating** [-pléiting], *s.* galvanoplastia.

electropositive [-pósitiv], *a.* y *s.* electropositivo.

electropuncturation [-púnkchuréishun], *s.* electropuntura.

electroscope [-scoup], *s.* electroscopio.

electrostatic [-stétic], *a.* electrostático.—**electrostatics,** *s.* electrostática.

electrotechnics [-téknics], *s.* electrotecnia.

electrotelegraphic [-telegráfic], *a.* electrotelegráfico.—**electrotelegraphy** [-telégrafi], *s.* telegrafía eléctrica.

electrotherapeutic(al [-zerapiútic(al], *a.* electroterapéutico.—**electrotherapeutics** [-zerapiútics], **electrotherapy** [-zérapi], *s.* electroterapia.

electrotonus [electrótonus], *s.* cambio producido en un nervio por la corriente eléctrica.

electrotype [-taip]. **I.** *s.* electrotipo; impresión de dicho grabado. **II.** *va.* reproducir por la electrotipia.—**electrotyper** [-œr], *s.* el que hace electrotipos; baño para la electrotipia.—**electrotypic** [-típic], *a.* electrotípico.—**electrotypy** [-taipi], **electrotyping** [-táiping], *s.* electrotipia.

electuary [elékchu- (*o* tiu) eri], *s.* (farm.) confección, electuario.

eleemosynary [élemósinœri]. **I.** *a.* caritativo; de limosna. **II.** *s.* mendigo.

elegance, elegancy [élegans, -i], *s.* elegancia.

elegant [-ant], *a.* elegante.—**elegantly** [-li], *adv.* elegantemente, galanamente.

elegiac(al [elíyiac *o* eleyáiac(al], *a.* elegíaco.

elegize [éleyáiś], *va.* y *vn.* hacer una elegía; lamentar, deplorar.

elegy [éleyi], *s.* elegía, epicedio.

element [élemœnt], *s.* elemento; medio ambiente, esfera de acción; celdilla *o* unidad morfológica; (elec.) elemento, par; (quím.) cuerpo simple. —*pl.* nociones, elementos; intemperie; naturaleza, agentes naturales; los cuatro elementos (tierra, aire, fuego y agua); (igl.) el pan y el vino de la misa.

elemental [eleméntal], **elementary** [-tari], *a.* elemental.

elemi [élemi], *s.* elemí.

elephant [élefant], *s.* elefante.

elephantiasis [elefantáiasis], *s.* (med.) elefancía, elefantíasis.

elephantine [elefántin], *a.* elefantino.

Eleusinian [élusíniæn], *a.* eleusino.

elevate [éleveit], *va.* elevar; alzar; animar, alegrar; inspirar.

elevated [-ed]. **I.** *a.* elevado, alzado, excelso.—**e. railroad,** ferrocarril aéreo *o* elevado. **II.** *s.* = ELEVATED RAILROAD.

elevation [-éishun], *s.* elevación; exaltación, encumbramiento; altura; eminencia; alteza; (dib.) alzado, proyección vertical; (igl.) elevación (de la hostia); ll. t. **E. of the Host).**

elevator [-éitœr], *s.* ascensor; elevador (esp. de granos); almacén o depósito de granos; noria; (aer.) timón de profundidad o elevador.—**e. shaft,** caja o pozo de ascensor.

eleven [ilévn], *a.* y *s.* once.

eleventh [ilévœnz]. **I.** *a.* onceno, undécimo, once (ordinal). **II.** *s.* y *a.* onzavo.

elf [elf], *s.* (*pl.* ELVES) duende, trasgo, diablillo; enano.

elfin [élfin]. **I.** *a.* de duendes. **II.** *s.* diablillo; niño travieso.

elfish [élfish], *a.* aduendado, fantástico; travieso.

elfland [élflænd], *s.* región encantada.

elflock [élflóc], *s.* greña de pelo.

elicit [elísit]. **I.** *va.* sacar, atraer; producir, despertar. **II.** *a.* (filos.) espontáneo, de motu propio.

elide [eláid], *va.* elidir.

eligibility [eliyibíliti], *s.* elegibilidad.

eligible [éliyibœl], *a.* y *s.* elegible, preferible, deseable.—**eligibleness** [-nes], *s.* elegibilidad.

eligibly [-bli], *adv.* de modo elegible.

eliminate [elímineit], *va.* eliminar.

elimination [-éishun], *s.* eliminación.

elision [elíyun], *s.* (gram.) elisión.

elite [elít], *s.* lo selecto, la flor y nata.

elixir [elícscœr], *s.* elíxir; cordial, tónico.

Elizabethan [elísæbízæn], *a.* isabeliano, relativo a la reina Isabel o su tiempo.

elk [elk], *s.* alce o anta; gran bestia.

ell [el], *s.* ana (medida); cualquier cosa en forma de L.

ellipse [elíps], *s.* (geom.) elipse.

ellipsis [elípsis], *s.* (gram.) elipsis.

ellipsoid [elípsoid], *s.* elipsoide.

ellipsoidal [elipsóidal], *a.* elipsoidal.

elliptic(al [elíptic(al], *a.* elíptico.

elliptically [elípticali], *adv.* elípticamente.

elm [elm], *s.* (bot.) olmo.

elmy [élmi], *a.* ulmáceo.

elocution [élokiúshun], *s.* elocución; declamación.

elocutionary [-eri], *a.* declamatorio.

elocutionist [-ist], *s.* declamador.

éloge [élox], **elogy** [éloyi], *s.* apología, panegírico.

elongate [elónguet]. **I.** *va.* alargar; extender. **II.** *vn.* alargarse, prolongarse.

elongation [élongéishun], *s.* alargamiento; (astr.) elongación.

elope [elóup], *vn.* fugarse con un amante; escapar, huir, evadirse.—**elopement** [-mœnt], *s.* fuga.

eloquence [élocuens], *s.* elocuencia.—**eloquent** [-ent], *a.* elocuente.—**eloquently** [-li], *adv.* elocuentemente.

else [els]. **I.** *a.* otro.—**nobody e., no one e.,** ningún otro.—**nothing e.,** nada más. **II.** *adv.* más, además; en vez de.—**or e.,** o bien, o en su lugar, de otro modo, en otro caso; si no.

elsewhere [élsjueœr], *adv.* en cualquiera otra parte, a otra parte, de otra parte.

elucidate [elúsideit], *va.* dilucidar.—**elucidation** [-shun], *s.* elucidación.—**elucidative, elucidatory** [-eitive, -atori], *a.* explicativo.—**elucidator** [-éitœr], *s.* dilucidador, expositor.

elude [eliúd], *va.* eludir, evadir, esquivar.

eludible [-ibœl], *a.* eludible, evitable.

elusion [eliúyun], *s.* evasión, escapatoria; esquinazo; fraude.

elusive [eliúsiv], **elusory** [-sori], *a.* evasivo, esquivo, fugaz.

elution [elúshun], **elutriation** [elutriéshun], *s.* levigación.—**elutriate** [-trieit], *va.* levigar.

elves [elvs], *s. pl.* de ELF: duendes.

elve, elvish, *V.* ELF, ELFISH.

Elysian [elíyæn], *a.* ameno, delicioso.—**E. fields,** campos elíseos.

elytron, elytrum [élitron, -trum], *s.* élitro.

Elzevir [élśevœr], *a.* elzeviriano.

em [em], *s.* nombre de la letra *M;* (impr.) eme, unidad de medida.

'em, *pron.* (fam.) elisión de THEM.

emaciate [eméshiet], *va.* extenuar, adelgazar.

---

emaciate(d, *a.* enflaquecido, flaco; (med.) extenuado.—**emaciation** [emēāhiéiāhun], *s.* extenuación, acabamiento.

emanant [émanant], *a.* emanante.—**emanate** [-eit], *vn.* emanar.—**emanation** [-éiāhun], *s.* emanación.—**emanative** [-nativ], *a.* emanante.

emancipate [emǽnsipeit], *va.* emancipar, libertar.—**emancipation** [emǽnsipéiāhun], *s.* emancipación.—**emancipator** [-eitœr], *s.* emancipador, libertador.

emarginate [emárγineit]. **I.** *va.* quitar el margen, recortar. **II.** *a.* (bot.) recortado.

emasculate [emǽskiuleit]. **I.** *s.* castrar, capar: afeminar, enervar; mutilar. **II.** *a.* afeminado; viciado; castrado.—**emasculation** [-éiāhun], *s.* castradura, castración; afeminación; mutilación.

embalm [embám], *va.* embalsamar; conservar; perfumar.—**embalmer** [-œr], *s.* embalsamador.—**embalmment** [-œnt], *s.* embalsamamiento.

embank [embǽnk], *va.* represar, terraplenar.

embankment [-mœnt], *s.* malecón, riba, presa, dique; terraplén.

embarcation, *s.* = EMBARKATION.

embargo [embárgo]. **I.** *s.* embargo, detención; prohibición. **II.** *va.* embargar, detener.

embark [embárk], *va.* y *vn.* (mar.) embarcar(se).

embarkation [embarkéiāhun], *s.* embarco; embarque.

embarrass [embǽras], *va.* turbar, aturdir, desconcertar; poner en aprieto; estorbar.

embarrassment [-mœnt], *s.* turbación, peturbación, perplejidad; compromiso; embarazo, estorbo; (com.) apuros, dificultades.

embassador = AMBASSADOR.

embassy [émbasi], *s.* embajada.

embattle [embǽtl], *va.* (mil.) formar en batalla; (fort.) almenar.—**embattled** [-tœld], *a.* en orden de batalla; ocupado por combatientes; (fort. y blas.) almenado.—**embattlement** [-tœlmœnt], *s.* almena; almenaje.

embed [embéd], *va.* encajar, encastrar, meter, empotrar.—**embedment** [-mœnt], *s.* empotramiento, encaje.

embellish [embélish], *va.* hermosear, embellecer.

embellishment [-mœnt], *s.* embellecimiento.

embers [émbœrā], *s.* ascua, pavesa, chispa.—*pl.* rescoldo.—**e. days,** (igl.) cuatro témporas.

embezzle [embéāl], *va.* desfalcar.—**embezzlement** [-mœnt], *s.* desfalco, peculado.—**embezzler** [-œr], *s.* desfalcador.

embitter [embítœr], *va.* amargar, agriar.

emblaze [embléiā], *va.* adornar con colores brillantes; hacer resplandecer.

emblazon [embléiāun], *va.* blasonar; esmaltar con colores brillantes; ensalzar, alabar.

emblazoner [-œr], *s.* blasonador, decorador; heraldo.—**emblazonry** [-ri], *s.* blasón.

emblem [émblœm], *s.* emblema.

emblematic(al [-ǽtic(al], *a.* emblemático.

emblematically [-i], *adv.* emblemáticamente.

emblematicize [-mǽtisaiā], *va.* dar carácter emblemático; alegorizar.

emblematize [emblémataiā], *va.* representar, simbolizar.

emblements [émblemœnts], *s. pl.* (for.) cosecha; derecho de un arrendatario a su cosecha.

emblemize [emblemaiā], *va.* representar por medio de un emblema.

embodiment [embódimœnt], *s.* incorporación; personificación.

embody [embódi]. **I.** *va.* dar cuerpo, informar, incorporar; incluir, englobar, formular, sintetizar. **II.** *vn.* unirse, incorporarse.

embolden [embóuldœn], *va.* animar, envalentonar.

embolism [émbolism], *s.* (astr.) embolismo, intercalación; (med.) embolia.

embolismic [-lísmic], *a.* (astr.) embolismal.—**e. year,** año embolismal o de trece lunaciones.

embolus [émbolus], *s.* (med.) émbolo, coágulo u obstrucción que causa embolia.

embonpoint [angbongpuáng], *s.* (fr.) redondez de cuerpo.

emborder [embórdœr], *va.* guarnecer con marco o borde.

embosom [embúāum], *va.* poner en el seno; envolver, encerrar, ocultar; querer, proteger.

emboss [embóā], *va.* abollonar, repujar, relevar, realzar, estampar en relieve.

embossment [-mœnt], *s.* abolladura, realce, relieve, resalte.

embouchure [angbushúœr], *s.* boca, desembocadura; (mús.) embocadura.

embowel [embáuel], *va.* desentrañar, destripar; enterrar, empotrar.—**embowelment** [-mœnt], *s.* acción de destripar.—*pl.* entrañas.

embower [embáuer], *va.* emparrar.

embrace [embréis]. **I.** *va.* abrazar; abarcar, rodear, ceñir, contener, comprender; admitir, recibir, adoptar, aceptar, aprovechar; (for.) cohechar. **II.** *vn.* abrazarse. **III.** *s.* abrazo.—**embrace(ment** [-mœnt], *s.* abrazo.—**embracer** [-œr], *s.* cohechador.—**embracery** [-eri], *s.* (for.) cohecho.—**embracing** [-ing], *s.* abrazamiento; abrazadura; *a.* comprehensivo.

embrasure [embréiϑœr], *s.* (fort.) tronera, aspillera, cañonera; (arq.) alféizar.

embrocate [émbrokeit], *va.* sobar con emolientes; soba o tratamiento con emolientes.—**embrocation** [-kéiāhun], *s.* emoliente; soba o tratamiento con emolientes.

embroglio, *s.* = IMBROGLIO.

embroider [embróidœr], *va.* bordar, recamar.

embroiderer, embroideress [-œr, -es], *s.* bordador, recamador; bordadora.

embroidery [embróidœri], *s.* bordado, bordadura.—**e. frame,** bastidor.—**e. yarn,** hilo de bordar.

embroil [embróil], *va.* embrollar, enredar.

embroilment [-mœnt], *s.* alboroto, confusión; embrollo, intriga.

embrown [embraun], *va.* y *vn.* hacer o volverse moreno u obscuro.

embryo [émbrio]. **I.** *s.* embrión; rudimento, germen. **II.** *a.* embrionario.

embryogeny [embrióyeni], *s.* embriogenia.

embryologist [embrióloyist], *s.* embriólogo.

embryology [embrióloyi], *s.* embriología.

embryonic [embriónic], *a.* embrionario.

emend [eménd], *va.* enmendar, corregir.

emendable [-abœl], *a.* corregible.

emendation [emendéiāhun], *s.* enmienda o corrección.—**emendator** [-éitœr], *s.* corrector, enmendador.

emendatory [eméndatori], *a.* enmendador.

emerald [émœrald]. **I.** *s.* esmeralda; color de esmeralda; (Ingl.) tipo de 6½ puntos. **II.** *a.* de color de esmeralda.—**e. green** = PARIS GREEN.—**E. Isle,** Irlanda.

emerge [emœry], *vn.* emerger, brotar, surgir.

emergence [-yens], *s.* emergencia, salida; aparición.

emergency [-yensi], *s.* emergencia, aprieto o necesidad urgente.—**emergent** [-yent], *a.* emergente, perentorio, repentino, subitáneo.

emeritus [iméritus], *s.* emérito, jubilado, retirado.

emersion [emérāhun], *s.* emersión; (astr.) emersión, reaparición.

emery [émœri], *s.* esmeril.—**e. paper,** papel de lija.—**e. wheel,** rueda de esmeril.

emesis [émesis], *s.* vómito.

emetic [emétic], *s.* y *a.* emético.

emetic(al [emétic(al], *a.* y *s.* emético, vomitivo.

emetin(e [émetin], *s.* (quím.) emetina.

emeu, emew [ímiu], *s.* (orn.) dromeo.

emigrant [émigrant], *a.* y *s.* emigrante.—**emigrate** [-gréit], *vn.* emigrar.—**emigration** [-gréiāhun], *s.* emigración.

emigré [émigréi], *s.* emigrado.

eminence, eminency [éminens, i], *s.* altura, cima, eminencia, encumbramiento, distinción; (igl.) eminencia (título).

eminent [-ent], *a.* eminente; supremo.—**e. domain,** (for.) dominio eminente.

eminently [éminentli], *adv.* eminentemente, en sumo grado.

Emir [emír], *s.* emir o amir.
emissary [émisæri]. **I.** *s.* emisario; canal, desaguadero; orificio de salida; (anat.) conducto excretorio. **II.** *a.* perteneciente al emisario; enviado.
emission [emíšhun], *s.* emisión, salida.
emissive [emísiv], *a.* emisivo.
emissory [émisori]. **I.** *a.* emisivo. **II.** *s.* desaguadero.
emit [emít], *va.* emitir, arrojar, despedir; exhalar; (com.) emitir.
emmenagogue [eménagog], *s.* emenagogo.
emmet [émet], *s.* hormiga, aluda.
emmetropia [émetrópiæ], *s.* emetropía, visión normal.—**emmetropic** [-pic], *a.* emétrope, normal (apl. al ojo.)
emollescence [emolésens], *s.* ablandamiento, reblandecimiento.
emollient [emólyent], *s.* y *a.* emoliente.
emolument [emólyumœnt], *s.* emolumento, gaje; utilidad, provecho.
emotion [emóšhun], *s.* emoción.—**emotional** [-al], *a.* impresionable; sentimental.—**emotionalism** [-alism], *s.* sentimentalismo.—**emotive** [-mótive], *a.* impresionable; emocionante.
empale [empéil], *va.* empalar; cercar.
empalement [-mœnt], *s.* empalamiento; empalizada.
empanel, *va.* = IMPANEL.
empathy [émpæzi], *s.* (psicol.) atribución de una emoción a la causa externa que la estimula.
empennage [an pe nağ], *s.* (aer.) emplumadura, (fam.) cola.
emperor [émpœrœr], *s.* emperador.—**e. moth**, mariposa nocturna grande.
empery [émpœri], *s.* soberanía, dominio; imperio.
emphasis [émfasis], *s.* énfasis, recancanilla.
emphasize [émfasaiš], *va.* recalcar, acentuar; hacer hincapié o insistir en; subrayar.
emphatic(al [emfǽtic(al], *a.* enfático, categórico.
emphatically [-i], *adv.* enfáticamente.
emphraxis [emfráxis], *s.* infarto, opilación.
emphysema [emfisíma], *s.* (med.) enfisema, tumefacción.—**emphysematous** [-sématus], *a.* enfisematoso.
emphyteusis [emfitiúsis], *s.* (for.) enfiteusis.
emphyteutic [emfitiútic], *a.* (for.) enfitéutico.
empire [émpaiær], *s.* imperio.
empiric(al [empíric(al]. **I.** *a.* empírico. **II.** *s.* empírico, medicastro, curandero.
empirically [-i], *adv.* empíricamente.
empiricism [empírisišm], *s.* empirismo.
emplacement [empléismœnt], *s.* emplazamiento.
emplastic [emplǽstic]. **I.** *a.* emplástrico, glutinoso, pegajoso. **II.** *s.* emplasto.
employ [emplói]. **I.** *va.* emplear. **II.** *s.* empleo.
employable [-abœl], *a.* empleable.
employee, employé [émploí], *s.* empleado.
employer [emplóiœr], *s.* el que emplea; (e. p.) patrono, empresario.
employment [emplóimœnt], *s.* empleo, destino; uso, aplicación.
emporium [empórium], *s.* emporio, plaza; bazar.
empower [empáuœr], *va.* autorizar, facultar, comisionar, habilitar, dar poder.
empress [émpres], *s.* emperatriz.
emprise [empráiš], *s.* empresa; aventura; hazaña.
emptier [émpticer], *s.* vaciador.
emptiness [émptines], *s.* vaciedad, vacío, vacuidad; futilidad.
empty [émpti]. **I.** *a.* vacío; desocupado; vaco, vacante; vano, inútil; ignorante; hambriento, frívolo, superficial.—**e.-handed**, manivacío. **II.** *va.* vaciar, evacuar, desocupar, descargar. **III.** *vn.* vaciarse; desaguar, desembocar.
emptyings [émptiingš], *s. pl.* heces de la cerveza usadas como levadura.
empurple [empœrpœl], *va.* purpurar, teñir de púrpura.
empyema [empaíma], *s.* (med.) empiema.

empyreal [empíreal], *a.* empíreo.
empyreal [empiríal], **empyrean** [empirían], *s.* empíreo.
empyreuma [empirúma], *s.* empireuma.
empyreumatic, o empyreumatical [empirumǽtic, al], *a.* empireumático.
emu [imiu], *s.* (orn.) dromeo.
emulate [émiuleit], *va.* emular, competir con, imitar.
emulation [-éišhun], *s.* emulación.
emulative [-lativ], *a.* emulativo.
emulator [-léitœr], *s.* émulo, rival, competidor, emulador.
emulgent [emúlyent], *a.* emulgente.
emulous [émiuluš], *a.* émulo, rival;
emulously [-li], *adv.* con emulación, a competencia.
emulsifier [emúlsifáiœr], *s.* substancia emulsiva.
emulsify [-sifai], *va.* emulsionar, convertir en emulsión, formar emulsión con o de.—**emulsion** [-šhun], *s.* emulsión.—**emulsive** [-siv], *a.* emulsivo.
emunctory [emúnctori]. **I.** *a.* (med.) excretorio. **II.** *s.* emuntorio.
en [en], *s.* nombre de la letra *n*; (impr.) mitad de una eme.
enable [enéibœl], *vn.* habilitar, hacer capaz, permitir.
enact [enǽct], *va.* promulgar, dar (una ley); decretar; (teat.) hacer el papel o desempeñar la parte de.
enactable [enǽctabœl], *a.* que puede ser estatuído, efectuado o representado.
enactment [enǽctmœnt], *s.* ley, estatuto; promulgación (de una ley).
enallage [enǽlaye], *s.* (gram.) enálage.
enambush [enámbuš], *va.* emboscar.
enamel [enǽmel]. **I.** *va.* esmaltar. **II.** *s.* esmalte.
enamel(l)er [-œr], *s.* esmaltador.
enamelling [-ing], *s.* esmaltadura.
enamo(u)red [enǽmœrd], *pp.* (con **of** o **with**) enamorado o prendado (de)
enarthrosis [enarzrósis], *s.* (anat.) enártrosis.
encage [enkéiy], *va.* enjaular.
encamp [encǽmp], *va.* y *vn.* (mil.) acampar.
encamping [encǽmping], *s.* castrametación.
encampment [encǽmpmœnt], *s.* campamento.
encase [enkéis], **encasement** = INCASE, etc.
encave [enkéiv], *va.* encovar.
encaustic [encóstic]. **I.** *a.* (pint.) encáustico. **II.** *s.* encausto, adustión, combustión.—**e. painting**, pintura al encausto.
enceinte [angsǽnt]. **I.** *a.* (fr.) preñada, embarazada, encinta; cesa. **II.** *s.* (fort., arq.) recinto.
encephalic [énsefǽlic], *a.* encefálico.
encephaloid [enséfaloid], *a.* encefaloideo.
encephalon [-falon], *s.* encéfalo, cerebro.
encephalous [-faluš], *a.* con cabeza.
enchain [enchéin], *va.* encadenar.
enchant [enchánt], *va.* encantar, hechizar; deleitar, fascinar, embelesar.—**enchanter** [-œr], *a.* encantador, hechicero.—**enchanting** [-ing], *a.* encantador.—**enchantingly** [-ingli], *adv.* encantadoramente.—**enchantment** [-mœnt], *s.* encantamiento, hechicería; fascinación, encanto, embeleso.—**enchantress** [-res], *s.* maga, bruja; encantadora, seductora.
enchase [enchéis], *va.* engastar, embutir o incrustar.
enchorial [encórial], *a.* peculiar de un país, demótico; endémico; indígena, autóctono.
encircle [ensœrcœl], *va.* cercar, circuir, rodear.
enclitic [enclític], *a.* y *s.* (gram.) enclítico.
encloister [enclóistœr], *va.* enclaustrar.
enclose [enclóuš], *va.* cercar, circunvalar, circuir; rodear, circundar; incluir; encerrar.
enclosure [enclóyœr], *s.* cercamiento; cerca, vallado, tapia; cercado, corral; recinto; (com.) contenido, incluso.
encomiast [encómiæst], *s.* encomiasta, panegirista.
encomiastic(al [-miǽstic(al], *a.* encomiástico.
encomium [encómium], *s.* encomio, elogio.

encompass [encómpas], *va.* cercar, circundar, rodear, encerrar; abarcar.—**to e. the globe**, dar la vuelta al mundo.

encore [angcór]. **I.** *adv.* otra vez, de nuevo. **II.** *interj.* ¡otra! ¡que se repita! **III.** *s.* (teat.) repetición. **IV.** *va.* (teat.) pedir la repetición.

encounter [encáuntœr]. **I.** *s.* encuentro, choque; combate. **II.** *va.* y *vn.* encontrar; dar o tropezar con; batirse.

encourage [encúreɣ], *va.* animar, alentar; estimular, incitar, fomentar; aprobar; dar pábulo.

encouragement [-mœnt], *s.* estímulo, incentivo; fomento; tolerancia.

encouraging [-ing], *a.* alentador, halagüeño, favorable.—**encouragingly** [-lij], *adv.* alentadoramente.

encrinite [éncrinait], *s.* encrinita.

encroach [encróuch], *vn.* (con **on**) pasar los límites de, inmiscuirse en.

encroachingly [-inglij], *adv.* por usurpación o intrusión.—**encroachment** [-mœnt], *s.* usurpación, intrusión, abuso.

encrust, *va.* = INCRUST.

encumber [encúmbœr], *va.* embarazar, sobrecargar, gravar, estorbar.

encumbrance [-brans], *s.* embarazo, impedimento, estorbo; pensión, carga, gravamen.—**free from encumbrances**, libre de gravamen.

encyclical [ensíclical], *s.* y *a.* encíclica.

encyclopædia, encyclopedia [ensáiclopídia], *s.* enciclopedia.

encyclopædic, o encyclopedic(al [ensáiclopídic(al], *a.* enciclopédico.

encyclopedist [-ist], *s.* enciclopedista.

encysted [ensísted], *a.* (cir.) enquistado.

end [end]. **I.** *s.* fin; extremidad; cabo (del mundo); remate; final; fondo.—**e. for e.**, con los extremos invertidos.—**e. on**, de punta: (mar.) de frente.—**e. paper** (imp.) hoja en blanco.—**e. plate**, (m. v.) fondo (de caldera).—**e. play**, (mec.) juego longitudinal.—**e. thrust**, empuje longitudinal.—**e. to e.**, cabeza con cabeza, punta con punta, por los extremos.—**at loose ends**, en desorden, desarreglado.—**in the e.**, al fin.—**no e. of**, sin fin, muchísimo.—**on e.**, de cabeza, de pie, derecho; de punta, erizado (el pelo).—**to make an e. of**, acabar con.—**to make both ends meet**, pasar con lo que se tiene.—**to no e.**, sin efecto, en vano.—**to the e. that**, a fin de que, para que. **II.** *va.* y *vn.* terminar, finalizar, cesar.

end-all [-ol], conclusión definitiva, punto final.

endanger [endényœr], *va.* poner en peligro, arriesgar, comprometer.

endarteritis [endárteráitis], *s.* end(o)arteritis, inflamación de la túnica interior de las arterias.

endear [endíœr], *va.* hacer querer.

endearing [-ing], *s.* cariñoso.—**endearment** [-mœnt], *s.* encariñamiento.

endeavo(u)r [endévœr]. **I.** *s.* esfuerzo, conato, empeño. **II.** *va.* intentar, probar, tratar de. **III.** *vn.* esforzarse, hacer un esfuerzo.

endemic(al [endémic(al], *a.* endémico.

ender [éndœr], *s.* acabador.

endermic [endérmic], *a.* endérmico.

ending [énding], *s.* fin, conclusión; cesación; terminación, supensión; desenlace; (mús.) coda; (gram.) terminación.

endive [éndiv], *s.* (bot.) escarola, endibia.

endless [éndles], *a.* sin fin; infinito; interminable.—**e. cable, chain, screw**, cable, cadena, tornillo sin fin.—**e. tube**, (aut.) cámara de aire continua (de extremos unidos a tope con sobrejunta).

endlessly [-lij], *adv.* infinitamente, sin fin, perpetuamente.—**endlessness** [-nes], *s.* perpetuidad; calidad de interminable.

endlong [éndlong], *adv.* a lo largo, extendido; en línea recta; continuadamente; de pie, a plomo.

endmost [-most], *a.* extremo, último.

endoblast [éndoblæst], *s.* (biol.) endoblasto.—**endoblastic** [-ic], endoblástico.

endocardiac, endocardial [-cárdiac, al], *a.* endocardíaco.—**endocarditis** [-cardáitis], *s.* (med.) endocarditis.—**endocardium** [-cárdium], *s.* (anat.) endocardio.—**endocarp** [-carp], *s.* (bot.) endocarpo.

endocrine [-crain]. **I.** *a.* (anat.) de secreción interna. **II.** *s.* secreción interna (de las glándulas sin conductos).—**endocrinology** [-crinóloɣi], *s.* estudio de las secreciones internas.

endoderm [-dœrm], *s.* endodermo, endoblasto.

endogamy [endógami], *s.* endogamia, matrimonio dentro de la clase, casta, tribu, fratría, clan, etc.

endogen [éndoɣen], *s.* (bot.) planta que se desarrolla por endogénesis.

endogenous [endóɣenus], *a.* (bot.) monocotiledóneo.

endogeny [endóɣeni], *s.* (biol.) endogénesis, reproducción por división interior.

endolymph [éndolinf], *s.* (anat.) endolinfa.

endometritis [-metráitis], *s.* (med.) endometritis, inflamación de la mucosa uterina.

endorse, endorsee, etc. = INDORSE, etc.

endosmose [éndosmos], *s.* endósmosis.

endosmotic [-smótic], *a.* endosmótico.

endosperm [-spœrm], *s.* (bot.) endospermo.

endothermic [-ɵérmic], *a.* endotérmico.

endow [endáu], *va.* dotar; fundar.

endower [endáuœr], *s.* dotador.

endowment [endáumœnt], *s.* dote, dotación, fundación; dotes, prendas, gracias.—**e. insurance policy**, seguro, póliza dotal.

endue [endiú], *va.* dotar, privilegiar; investir; ponerse, vestirse; asumir.

endurable [endiúrabœl], *a.* sufrible, soportable.

endurance [-ans], *s.* paciencia, sufrimiento; resistencia; duración, continuación.

endure [endiúœr]. **I.** *va.* soportar, sufrir, resistir, aguantar; tolerar, sobrellevar. **II.** *vn.* durar, perdurar; sufrir, tener paciencia.

enduring [-ing], *a.* paciente, sufrido; durable, permanente; constante.

endwise [enduáis], *adv.* de punta, de pie, derecho.

enema [énema], *s.* enema, lavativa.

enemy [énemi], *s.* enemigo.

energetic(al [encœrrétic(al], *a.* enérgico.

energetically [-i], *adv.* enérgicamente.

energetics [éncœryétics], *s.* (mec.) ciencia de la energía.

energize [éncœryaiŝ]. **I.** *va.* excitar o dar energía; dar vigor o actividad. **II.** *vn.* obrar con energía.

energumen [encœrguiúmen], *s.* energúmeno, endemoniado.

energy [éncœrri], *s.* energía, vigor; (mec.) energía.

enervate [éncœrveit]. **I.** *va.* enervar, desmadejar; contrarrestar, desvirtuar; cortar los nervios o los tendones. **II.** *a.* debilitado, enervado.

enervation [-éiŝhun], *s.* enervación; debilidad, desmadejamiento.

enfeeble [enfíbœl], *va.* debilitar, enervar.

enfeeblement [-mœnt], *s.* debilidad, desfallecimiento, flojedad.

enfeoff [enfef], *va.* (for.) enfeudar.

enfeoffment [enféfmœnt], *s.* enfeudación.

enfilade [enfiléd]. **I.** *s.* fuego o tiro de enfilada; ringlera, fila, hilera. **II.** *va.* (mil.) enfilar.

enfold, *V.* INFOLD.

enforce [enfórs], *va.* dar fuerza o vigor; hacer cumplir, observar o ejecutar (una ley); hacer valer; violentar, forzar; hacer hincapié en.

enforcement [enfórsmœnt], *s.* ejecución de una ley; observancia forzosa, coacción.

enfranchise [énfrénchaiŝ], *va.* franquear, conceder franquicia o derechos civiles; libertar, manumitir, emancipar; adoptar, dar carta de naturaleza.—**enfranchisement** [-mœnt], *s.* franquicia, ciudadanía; manumisión, emancipación.

engage [enguéiɣ]. **I.** *va.* ajustar, apalabrar, comprometer; escriturar; tomar en alquiler; ocupar, emplear; entretener, distraer; atraer, halagar, ganar; (mil) entrar en lucha o en batalla con, combatir; (mec.) engranar; engranar con; endentar con. **II.** *vn.* empeñarse, obligarse; dar palabra, comprometerse; ocuparse, estar atareado; pelear, venir a las manos.

engaged [enguéiɣd], *a.* ocupado; comprometido, apalabrado; comprometido para casarse.

engagement [enguéiᴙmœnt], s. ajuste, contrato; palabra de casamiento, esponsales; cita, compromiso; obligación; (teat.) escritura, ajuste, contrato; (mil.) acción, batalla o combate.— **e. ring,** anillo de esponsales.

engaging [enguéiᴙing], a. atractivo, insinuante, simpático.

engender [enɾéndœr]. **I.** va. engendrar. **II.** vn. engendrarse, producirse, causarse.

engild [enguíld], va. dorar, abrillantar.

engine [énᴙin], s. máquina; locomotora; motor (esp. los de combustión interna); instrumento, agente.—**e. builder,** fabricante de máquinas.—**e. driver,** (f. c.) maquinista.—**e. house,** casa de máquinas.—**e. lathe,** torno mecánico ordinario.—**e. room,** sala de máquinas; cuarto de la máquina. —**e.-room telegraph,** (mar.) campana o mecanismo de señales (entre el timonel o el puente y el maquinista).—**e. runner,** maquinista.—**e. running,** manejo de máquinas.—**e.-sized,** aprestado a máquina (apl. al papel).

engineer [énᴙiníær]. **I.** s. ingeniero; maquinista. [Ú. gen. en este último sentido, a no ser que las circunstancias o algún modificativo (civil, mechanical, etc.) indiquen otra cosa.]—**E. Corps,** (E. U.) Cuerpo de Ingenieros del ejército o de la armada.—**e.'s chain,** (top.) cadena de 100 pies, con eslabones de 1 pie.—**e.'s level,** nivel ordinario de topografía (a distinción de los de carpinteros, albañiles, etc.).—**e.'s valve,** llave del maquinista (para el freno). **II.** va. gestionar, manejar, dirigir.

engineering [énᴙiníæring]. **I.** s. ingeniería; dirección, manejo. **II.** a. de ingeniería, relativo a la ingeniería.

enginery [énᴙinri], s. artillería; maquinaria, ingenios de guerra.

engird [engœrd], va. ceñir, cercar.

engirdle [engœrdœl], va. circundar, ceñir.

Englify [ínglifai], va. hacer inglés.

English [ínglish], s. y a. inglés; (en el billar) efecto.—**E. bond,** (alb.), aparejo inglés, o de hiladas alternadas de sogas y tizones.—**E. Channel,** Canal de la Mancha.

Englishman [-man], s. inglés (hombre); (mar.) buque inglés.—**Englishwoman** [-úman], s. inglesa.

engorge [engóɾy], va. y vn. atracar, engullir.

engraft [engráft], va. = INGRAFT.

engrail [engréil]. **I.** va. dentar. **II.** vn. tener borde dentellado.

engrain [engréin], va. pintar imitando la trepa de la madera. V. INGRAIN.

engrave [engréiv], va. grabar; cincelar, burilar, esculpir; tallar; (fig.) grabar (en la memoria, etc.).—**engraver** [-œr], s. grabador.—**engraving** [-ing], s. grabado; lámina, estampa.

engross [engrós], va. poner en limpio, copiar o transcribir caligráficamente; absorber, embargar; (ant.) acaparar, monopolizar.—**engrosser** [-œr], s. pendolista, calígrafo; (ant.) monopolista, acaparador.—**engrossment** [-mœnt], s. monopolio; transcripción caligráfica; embebecimiento, embelesamiento, abstracción.

engulf [engúlf], va. engolfar. V. INGULF.

enhance [enjáns], va. mejorar, acrecentar, aumentar el valor de; realzar.

enhancement [-mœnt], s. acrecentamiento, mejoría; realce.

enharmonic [enjarmónic], a. enarmónico.

enigma [enígma], s. enigma.—**enigmatic(al** [énigmǽtic(al], a. enigmático.—**enigmatically** [-l], adv. enigmáticamente.—**enigmatize** [enígmataís], vn. usar de enigmas.

enjoin [enᴙóin], va. mandar, ordenar, prescribir; imponer.—**to e. from,** prohibir.

enjoy [enᴙói], va. gozar de, gozarse en; gustarle a uno; disfrutar de, gozar de; tener, poseer; saborear.—**to e. one's self,** gozar, divertirse.

enjoyable [-abœl], a. deleitable, agradable.

enjoyment [-mœnt], s. goce, disfrute, placer; uso, usufructo.

enkindle [enkíndœl], va. encender.

enlace [enléis], va. enlazar, entrelazar.

enlarge [enláɾy]. **I.** va. agrandar, aumentar, ensanchar; abultar, engrosar; ampliar o ampli-

ficar; desencarcelar. **II.** vn. ensancharse o agrandarse; (gen. con on) explayarse (en), tratar detalladamente; exagerar.

enlargement [-mœnt], s. agrandamiento, ensanchamiento; ensanche, aumento, ampliación; liberación; dilatación, expansión; amplificación; (fot.) ampliación.

enlighten [enláitœn], va. iluminar, instruir, informar.—**enlightened** [-d], a. ilustrado, culto.—**enlightener** [-œr], s. instructor, esclarecedor.—**enlightenment** [-mœnt], s. instrucción, esclarecimiento; civilización, cultura.

enlist [enlíst]. **I.** va. alistar; (mil.) enganchar, reclutar; atraer, conseguir. **II.** vn. (mil.) sentar plaza; poner empeño en algo.—**enlistment** [-mœnt], s. alistamiento, enganche.

enliven [enláivœn], va. vivificar, animar, alentar; avivar, alegrar, regocijar.

enmesh [enmésh], va. coger en la red; entrampar.

enmity [énmiti], s. enemistad.

enmoss [enmós], va. cubrir con musgo.

ennead [éneæd], s. número nueve; novena.

ennoble [ennóbœl], va. ennoblecer.

ennoblement [-mœnt], s. ennoblecimiento o esclarecimiento.

ennui [anuí], s. aburrimiento, tedio, fastidio.

enormity [enórmiti], **enormousness** [-musnes], s. enormidad, demasía; atrocidad.—**enormous** [-mus], a. enorme, descomunal; perverso, atroz.—**enormously** [-li], adv. enormemente.

enough [inúf]. **I.** a. bastante, suficiente. **II.** s. lo suficiente. **III.** interj. ¡basta! ¡no más! **IV.** adv. bastante, suficientemente.—**curiously e., strange e.,** etc., cosa curiosa, extraña, etc. Estas expresiones pueden a veces traducirse cambiando un poco el giro: lo curioso es que, es curioso que, lo cual no deja de ser curioso, etc.

enounce [enáuns], va. declarar; anunciar.

enow [enáu] = ENOUGH.

enquire, enquirer, etc. = INQUIRE, etc.

enrage [enréy], va. enfurecer, encolerizar.

enrapt [enrǽpt], a. arrebatado, extasiado.

enrapture [enrǽpchœr], va. arrebatar, enajenar, arrobar, extasiar.

enrich [enrích], va. enriquecer; fecundar, fertilizar; adornar, embellecer.

enrichment [-mœnt], s. enriquecimiento; abono, beneficio; adorno, embellecimiento.

enring [enríng], va. cercar, rodear.

enrobe [enróub], va. vestir, adornar.

enrol(l) [enróul]. **I.** va. alistar; empadronar, encartar, matricular; envolver, enrollar. **II.** vn. alistarse; maticularse; (mil.) sentar plaza.—**enrol(l)er** [-œr], s. registrador, empadronador.—**enrol(l)ment** [-mœnt], s. alistamiento, empadronamiento; padrón; matriculación.

enroot [enrút], va. arraigar, radicar.

en route [ang rut], adv. en el camino.

ens [ens], s. ente, ser.

ensanguine [ensǽngüin], va. ensangrentar.

ensconce [enscóns], va. acomodar, situar; ocultar; poner en seguro.

ensemble [angsámbœl], s. conjunto; grupo.

ensheathe [enshíþ], va. envainar.

enshrine [enshráin], va. guardar como reliquia.

enshroud [enshráud], va. amortajar; envolver.

ensiform [énsiform], a. (bot.) ensiforme.

ensign [énsain], s. bandera, pabellón, enseña; insignia, divisa; (mil.) alférez; subteniente.—**e. bearer,** abanderado.

ensigncy [énsainsi], s. alferazgo.

ensilage [énsiley]. **I.** s. (agr.) ensilaje. **II.** va. ensilar.

enslave [ensléiv], va. esclavizar, avasallar.

enslavement [-mœnt], s. esclavitud, cautiverio, servidumbre; avasallamiento.

ensnare [ensnéær], va. entrampar; tender un lazo; engañar, embaír.

ensoul [ensóul], va. dar alma a; llevar al alma.

ensphere [ensfíœr], va. colocar en esfera; redondear.

ensue [ensiú]. **I.** vn. seguir, suceder, sobrevenir. **II.** va. (ant.) seguir, perseguir.

ensure [enŝhúœr], *va.* = INSURE.
entablature [entǽblachur], **entablement** [entébœlmœnt], *s.* (arq.) entablamento, cornisamento.
entad [éntæd], *adv.* (anat. y zool.) hacia el centro.
entail [entéil]. **I.** *s.* (for.) vinculación, vínculo, mayorazgo; herencia. **II.** *va.* vincular, asegurar, perpetuar, transmitir, legar; imponer, ocasionar; envolver; (for.) vincular.
ental [éntal], *a.* (anat. y zool.) de lo interior.
entangle [entǽngœl], *va.* enredar, embrollar; intrincar; implicar.—**entanglement** [-mœnt], *s.* enredo, embrollo, complicación.
entelechy [entélequi], *s.* (filos.) entelequia.
entente [éntœr], *s.* pacto; alianza.—**e. cordiale**, pacto o convenio cordial o de amistad.—**E. Powers**, potencias aliadas contra Alemania en la guerra de 1914.—**the E.**, los aliados (en la misma guerra); la triple alianza de Francia, Inglaterra y Rusia.
¡**enter** [éntœr]. **I.** *va.* entrar a, por o en; penetrar; meter, introducir; ingerir, insertar; asentar, anotar, registrar; hacerse miembro de, ingresar en; alistarse en, matricularse, afiliarse; (com.) declarar, aduanar; (for.) incoar; registrar. **II.** *vn.* entrar, introducirse, ingresar; (teat.) entrar en escena.—**to e. into**, entrar en; formar parte de; hacer, celebrar (un contrato, etc.)—**to e. on, o upon**, comenzar, emprender.
enteric [entéric], *a.* entérico.—**e. fever**, fiebre tifoidea.
entering [éntering], *a.* que entra; de entrada.—**e. chisel**, gubia, cincel de media caña.—**e. edge**, (aer.) borde de ataque (el anterior de un plano) —**e. file**, lima plana de punta.—**e. tap**, macho de aterrajado preliminar.—**e. wedge**, (fig.) operación o medida que abre camino o prepara el terreno; primer paso.
enteritis [éntœráitis o rítis], *s.* enteritis.
enterocele [énterosil], *s.* (cir.) enterocele, hernia inguinal o femoral.
enterocolitis [-colítis, láitis], *s.* enterocolitis.
enteromphalos [entœrómfalos], *s.* (cir.) enterónfalo, hernia umbilical.
enteron [éntœron], *s.* canal intestinal.
enterotome [éntœrotom], *s.* (cir.) enterótomo.
enterotomy [entœrótomi], *s.* enterotomía.
enterozoa [entœroŝóa], *s. pl.* entozoarios, parásitos intestinales.
enterprise, enterprize [éntœrpraiŝ], *s.* empresa; actividad, calidad de emprendedor.—**enterpriser** [-œr], *s.* emprendedor; progresista.—**enterprising** [-ing], *a.* emprendedor.
entertain [entœrtéin]. **I.** *va.* hospedar, festejar u obsequiar; entretener o divertir; tomar en consideración; mantener, acariciar, abrigar. **II.** *vn.* dar saraos, tertulias.
entertainable [-abœl], *a.* digno de tomarse en consideración.
entertainer [-œr], *s.* anfitrión; festejador.
entertaining [-ing], *a.* entretenido, chistoso, alegre, divertido, jovial.—**entertainingly** [-li], *adv.* divertidamente, entretenidamente.
entertainment [-mœnt], *s.* recibimiento, hospitalidad; convite, agasajo, festín, festejo; entretenimiento, diversión, pasatiempo; consideración.
enthetic [enzétic], *a.* proveniente de agentes externos; comunicado por inoculación (apl. a enfermedades infecciosas).
enthrall [enzról], *va.* dominar (el ánimo); esclavizar, sojuzgar.
enthrone [enzróun], *va.* entronizar.
enthronement [-mœnt],¹ **enthronization** [enzroniŝéŝhun], *s.* entronización.
enthuse [enziúŝ], *va. y vn.* (fam.) entusiasmar(se).
enthusiasm [enzúsiæŝm], *s.* entusiasmo.
enthusiast [enzúŝiæst], *s.* entusiasta; fanático.
enthusiastic(al [enzusiǽstic(al], *a.* entusiástico; entusiasmado; caluroso.
enthymeme [énzimim], *s.* entimema.
entice [entáis], *va.* tentar, seducir, halagar.

enticement [-mœnt], *s.* tentación, seducción; incitación; atractivo.—**enticer** [entáisœr], *s.* incitador, tentador.—**enticing** [-ing], *a.* seductor. —**enticingly** [-li], *adv.* seductoramente.
entire [entáiœr], *a.* entero; (vet.) entero, cojudo. —**entirely** [-li], *adv.* enteramente.—**entireness** [-nes], *s.* entereza, calidad de entero.—**entirety** [-ti], entereza; cosa entera; todo.
entitle [entáitœl], *va.* titular; intitular; dar derecho; habilitar; autorizar.
entity [éntiti], *s.* entidad; ente, ser.
entoblast [éntoblæst], **entoderm** [-dœrm], *s.* endodermo.
entomb [entúm], *va.* enterrar, sepultar.
entombment [-mœnt], *s.* entierro, sepultura.
entomogenous [éntomóyenus], *a.* parásito de insectos (apl. a ciertos hongos).
entomologic(al [-molóyic(al], *a.* entomológico.
entomologist [-molóyist], *s.* entomólogo.
entomology [-móloyi], *s.* entomología.
entomophagous [-mófagus], *a.* insectívoro.
entomophilous [-mófilus], *a.* entomófila, de polinización por insectos.—**entomophily** [-fili], *s.* entomofilia, polinización por insectos.
entourage [angturáy], *s.* (fr.) compañía, cortejo, séquito; medio ambiente.
entozoa [entoŝóa], *s. pl.* entozoarios.—**entozoan** [-ŝóan], *a.* y *s.* entozoario.—**entozoic** [-ŝóic], *a.* entozoico.
entr'acte [ángtráct], *s.* (fr.) entreacto.
entrain [entréin], *va. y vn.* despachar o ir por tren (apl. a tropas).
entrails [éntreilŝ], *s. pl.* entrañas, vísceras; tripas, intestinos.
entrammel [entrǽmœl] = TRAMMEL.
entrance [éntrans], *s.* entrada; puerta, portal; zaguán; embocadura; ingreso; entrada en la aduana.
entrance [entráns], *va.* extasiar, fascinar, arrebatar.
entrant [éntrant]. **I.** *a.* entrante. **II.** *s.* principiante, novicio.
entrap [entrǽp], *va.* coger con trampa, entrampar.
entreat [entrít], *va.* rogar, suplicar, implorar.
entreating [-ing], *a.* suplicante.—**entreatingly** [-li], *adv.* suplicantemente.
entreaty [entríti], *s.* ruego, súplica.
entrée [angtré], *s.* (fr.) entrada; privilegio de entrar; (coc.) principio o entrada.
entremets [antrœmé], *s. pl.* (coc., teat.) entremés.
entrench [entrénch]. **I.** *va.* atrincherar. **II.** *vn.* atrincherarse; (con *on*) invadir, infringir.
entrenchment [-mœnt], *s.* atrincheramiento, trinchera; parapeto, reparo; infracción, invasión, transgresión.
entrepot [ángtrœpo], *s.* (fr.) factoraje; almacén.
entrepreneur [antrprœnœr], *s.* empresario (esp. de teatro).
entropion [entrópion], *s.* (med.) entropión, inversión de los párpados.
entropy [éntropi], (fís.) entropía.
entrust [entrúst], *va.* (con **with**) entregar, confiar, depositar.
entry [éntri], *s.* entrada; vestíbulo, portal, pórtico, zaguán; ingreso; asiento, anotación o apuntamiento; (min.) bocamina; (mar.) registro, declaración de entrada; (com.) partida.
entwine [entuáin], *va.* enlazar, entrelazar, entretejer.
entwist [entuíst], *va.* torcer; ensortijar.
enucleate [eniúcléeit], *va.* descascarar; desenvolver, abrir; extraer el núcleo de; (en cir.) extirpar, extraer sin cortar;
enucleation [-éiŝhun], *s.* (cir.) extracción de un tumor entero.
enumerate [eniúmœreit], *va.* enumerar.
enumeration [eniúmœréiŝhun], *s.* enumeración; (ret.) recapitulación.
enumerative [eniúmœrativ], *a.* enumerativo.
enunciate [enúnŝhieit], *va. y vn.* enunciar.
enunciation [-éiŝhun], *s.* pronunciación, articulación; enunciación, manifiesto.

enunciative [-ŝhiativ], **enunciatory** [-ŝhiatori], *a.* enunciativo, declarativo.

enure [enyûcer], *vn.* tener efecto. *V.* INURE.

envelop [envélup], **envelope** [ánveloup]. **I.** *va.* envolver; aforrar, cubrir. **II.** *s.* envoltura; funda; cubierta, sobre; (mat.) envolvente (curva); (bot.) túnica, envoltura.

envelopment [envélupmœnt], *s.* envolvimiento; funda, cubierta.

envenom [envénum], *va.* envenenar o emponzoñar.

enviable [énviabœl], *a.* envidiable.

envious [énvius], *a.* envidioso.—**enviously** [-li], *adv.* envidiosamente.—**enviousness** [-nes], *s.* envidia; calidad de envidioso.

environ [enváirun], *va.* rodear, ceñir.

environment [-mœnt], *s.* cercanía; medio ambiente.

environs [enváircœnŝ], *s. pl.* alrededores, cercanías, inmediaciones, afueras.

envisage [envíŝey], *va.* hacer frente a; mirar; contemplar, representarse mentalmente.

envoy [énvoi], *s.* enviado; mensajero; (poét.) tornada.

envy [énvi]. **I.** *va.* y *vn.* envidiar. **II.** *s.* envidia.

enwrap [enrǽp], *va.* envolver.

enwrapment [-mœnt], *s.* cubierta, funda, envoltura.

enwreathe [enríþ], *va.* enguirnaldar.

enzootic [énŝoótic], *a.* enzoótico, endémico (apl. a las enfermedades de los animales).—**enzooty** [enŝóoti], *s.* enzootia, enfermedad enzoótica o de carácter local.

Eocene [íosin], *a.* (geol.) eoceno.

Eolian [eólian], **Eolic** [eólic], *a.* eolio, eólico.— **E. harp,** arpa eolia.

eolipile [eólipail], *s.* (fís.) eolípilo.

eolithic [íolízic], *a.* (geol.) eolítico, relativo al principio de la edad de piedra.

eon, æon [íon], *s.* evo; eón.

eosin [íosin], *s.* (quím.) eosina.

Eozoic [ioŝóic], *s.* y *a.* (geol.) eozoico (apl. a los terrenos subyacentes al paleozoico).

eozoon [ioŝóon], *s.* (pal.) eozoon, masa calcárea que antes se creía ser el fósil más antiguo.

epact [épact], *s.* epacta.

epaulet [épolet], *s.* (mil.) charretera, capona.

ependyma [epéndimæ], *s.* (anat.) epéndimo, membrana que cubre partes del cerebro y la medula.

epenetic [epenétic], *a.* laudatorio, panegírico.

epenthesis [epénzesis], *s.* (gram.) epéntesis.

epergne [epérn], *s.* centro de mesa.

ephemera [efémœra], *s.* (med.) efémera o efímera; (fam.) causón; insecto efímero; cosa efímera.

ephemeral [efémœral]. **I.** *a.* efímero. **II.** *s.* cosa efímera.

ephemeris [efémœris], *s.* (pl. EPHEMERIDES) efemérides, tablas astronómicas.

ephemerist [efémœrist], *s.* astrólogo.

Ephesian [efíŷan], *a.* efesio, de Efeso.

ephialtes [efiǽltiŝ], *s.* pesadilla.

ephod [éfod], *s.* efod; superhumeral.

epiblast [épiblæst], *s.* ectodermo.

epic(al [épic(al]. **I.** *a.* épico. **II.** *s.* poema épico, epopeya.

epicardium [epicárdium], *s.* (anat.) epicardio.

epicarp [épicarp], *s.* (bot.) epicarpo.

epicene [épisin], *a.* (gram.) epiceno.

epicure [épikiur], *s.* epicúreo, sibarita.

epicurean [-rían], *a.* y *s.* epicúreo.

epicurism [-riŝm], *s.* epicureísmo.

epicycle [épisaicœl], *s.* epiciclo.

epicycloid [-sáicloid], *s.* epicicloide.

epidemic(al [-démic(al]. **I.** *a.* epidémico, epidemial. **II.** *s.* epidemia, peste, plaga.

epidermal [-dérmal], *a.* epidérmico.

epidermic(al [dérmic(al], *a.* epidérmico.

epiderm(is, epiderm [-dérmis, -derm], *s.* epidermis, cutícula; piel; (bot.) epidermis.

epididymis [-dídimis], *s.* (anat.) epidídimo.

epidote [-dout], *s.* (min.) epidota.

epigastric [-gǽstric], *a.* epigástrico.

epigastrium [-gǽstrium], *s.* epigastrio.

epigenesis [-yénesis], *s.* (biol.) epigénesis.

epiglottis [-glótis], *s.* epiglotis, lengüeta.

epigram [épigram], *s.* epigrama.—**epigrammatic(al** [-mǽtic(al], *a.* epigramático.—**epigrammatically** [-l], *adv.* epigramáticamente.—**epigrammatist** [-grǽmatist], *s.* epigramatista.

epigraph [-graf], *s.* epígrafe, título; inscripción, epitafio.

epilepsy [-lepsi], *s.* epilepsia.—**epileptic(al** [-tic(al], *a.* y *s.* epiléptico.

epilogistic [epilorístic], *a.* epilogal.

epilogize [epílorais], *va.* y *vn.* epilogar; titular.

epilogue [épilog], *s.* epílogo.

epineurium [épiniúrium], *s.* (anat.) epineuro, envoltura de tejido conjuntivo que rodea un haz de nervios.

Epiphany [epífani], *s.* (igl.) Epifanía, día de los Reyes.

epiphonema [épifoníma], *s.* epifonema.

epiphyte [-fait], *s.* (bot.) epífita, planta no parásita que vive en otra; hongo parásito de un animal.

epiphysis [epífisis], *s.* (anat.) epífisis.—**e. cerebri,** glándula pineal.

episcopacy [epíscopasi], *s.* episcopado.

episcopal [epíscopal], *a.* episcopal; obispal.

Episcopalian [epíscopélian], *a.* y *s.* episcopal, perteneciente a la secta protestante episcopal.— **Episcopalianism** [-ism], *s.* doctrina de la secta protestante episcopal.

episcopally [epíscopali], *adv.* episcopalmente.

episcopate [-pet], *s.* obispado, episcopado.

episode [épisod], *s.* episodio; episodio; procinta.

episod(i)al [-sod(i)al], **episodic(al** [-sódic(al], *a.* episódico.—**episodically** [-l], *adv.* episódicamente.

epispastic [epispǽstic], *a.* y *s.* epispástico; vejigatorio.

episperm [épispœrm], *s.* (bot.) episperma.

epistaxis [epistǽxis], *s.* (med.) epistaxis.

epistemology [épistemólori], *s.* epistemología, teoría del conocimiento.

epistle [epísœl], *s.* epístola, carta.

epistler [epíslœr], *s.* escritor de epístolas o cartas; (igl.) epistolero.

epistolary [epístoleri], **epistolic(al** [epistólic(al], *a.* epistolar(io.

epistrophe [epístrofe], *s.* (ret.) epístrofe, conversión; (mús.) estribillo.

epistyle [épistail], *s.* arquitrabe.

epitaph [épitaf], *s.* epitafio.

epitaphic [epitáfic], *a.* relativo al epitafio.

epitasis [epítæsis], *s.* (teat.) epítasis.

epithalamium [épizalémium], *s.* epitalamio.

epithelial [epizílial], *a.* epitelial.

epithelium [epizílium], *s.* (anat.) epitelio.

epithem [épizem], *s.* (med.) epítema.

epithet [épizet], *s.* epíteto.

epitome [epítome], *s.* epítome, resumen, sumario.—**epitomize** [epítomaiŝ], *va.* epitomar, abreviar.—**epitomizer** [-œr], **epitomist** [-ist], *s.* abreviador, compendiador.

epitrochlea [épitrócliæ], *s.* (anat.) epitróclea, cóndilo interior del húmero.

epitrope [epítropi], *s.* (ret.) epítrope.

epizoa [épisœ], *s. pl.* (zool.) epizoarios.

epizoan [épiŝóan], *a.* y *s.* epizoario.

epizoon [-ŝóon], *s.* epizoario.

epizootic [-ŝoótic], *a.* epizoótico.—**epizooty** [-ti], *s.* epizootia.

epoch [époc], *s.* época, era.—**e.-making,** que forma época, trascendental.

epode [épod], *s.* (poét.) epodo.

eponym [éponim], *s.* héroe, epónimo.

eponymous [epónimus], **eponymic** [eponímic], *a.* epónimo.

epopee [épopi], *s.* epopeya, poema épico.

Epsom salt [épsum solt], *s.* (quím.) sal de la Higuera, epsomita.

equability [ícuabíliti], **equableness** [-bœlnes], *s.* igualdad, uniformidad.—**equable** [-bœl], *a.* igual, uniforme, ecuable.—**equably** [-bli], *adv.* igualmente.

equal [ícuæl]. **I.** *a.* igual; parejo; equitativo; adecuado, suficiente, adaptado.—**to be e. to,** ponerse al nivel de, ser capaz de, sentirse con fuerzas para, servir para, poder hacer frente a, poder desempeñar o ejecutar. **II.** *s.* igual; cantidad igual. **III.** *va.* ser igual a; igualarse a, ponerse al nivel de; ser a propósito para; igualar, emparejar; compensar.—**not to be equalled,** sin igual. **IV.** *vn.* ser igual.

equality [icuóliti], *s.* igualdad; uniformidad; paridad; lisura.

equalization, equalisation [ícualiséíshun], *s.* igualamiento, igualación.—**equalize,** *o* **equalise** [ícualaíś], *va.* y *vn.* igualar; compensar.

equalizer [ícualáíšœr], *s.* igualador, compensador; (elec.) conductor compensador o de compensación; dínamo compensadora.

equalizing [-ing], *a.* igualador; (tec.) compensador, de compensación.

equally [ícuali], *adv.* igualmente; por igual.

equalness [ícualnes], *s.* uniformidad, igualdad.

equanimity [icuanímiti], *s.* ecuanimidad.

equate [ecuéit], *va.* igualar.

equation [ecuéishun], *s.* ecuación.—**e. of payments,** (arit.) regla para reducir a uno solo varios pagos de distintos plazos.—**e. of time,** (astr.) ecuación de tiempo.

equator [icuéitœr], *s.* ecuador.

equatorial [icuatórial], *a.* y *s.* ecuatorial.

equerry [écueri], *s.* caballerizo mayor; caballeriza.

equestrian [ecuéstrian]. **I.** *a.* ecuestre. **II.** *s.* jinete.

equestrianism [-ism], *s.* equitación.

equiangular [icuiénguiular], *a.* equiángulo.

equidistance [-dístans], *s.* equidistancia.

equidistant [-dístant], *a.* equidistante.

equidistantly [-li], *adv.* a una misma distancia.

equiformity [-fórmiti], *s.* uniformidad.

equilateral [-lǽtœral], *a.* y *s.* equilátero.

equilibrant [ecuílibrænt], *s.* (mec.) fuerza igual y contraria a la resultante de un sistema, fuerza equilibrante.

equilibrate [ícuiláibreit], *va.* equilibrar.

equilibration [bróishun], *s.* equilibración; equilibrio.

equilibrator [-bréitœr], *s.* equilibrador; compensador.

equilibrist [ecuílibrist], *s.* equilibrista.

equilibrium [icuilíbrium], *s.* equilibrio, balance.

equine [ícuin *o* ícuain]. **I.** *a.* caballar, hípico, equino. **II.** *s.* caballo; cebra.

equinoctial [icuinócshal]. **I.** *a.* equinoccial.— **e. line,** línea equinoccial, ecuador. **II.** *s.* línea equinoccial; tempestad equinoccial.

equinoctially [-li], *adv.* en dirección equinoccial.

equinox [ícuinocs], *s.* (astr.) equinoccio.

equip [ecuíp], *va.* equipar, pertrechar, aprestar, aparejar, proveer, habilitar, aviar.

equipage [écuipeϒ], *s.* equipaje, equipo; tren; carruaje.

equipment [ecuípmœnt], *s.* equipo, equipaje, habilitación; apresto, armamento; avíos; vestuario; adherentes, arreos; (mec.) equipo, tren, juego, conjunto de aparatos, accesorios, etc.

equipoise [ícuipoiś], *s.* equilibrio; contrapeso.

equipollence, equipollency [-pólens, i], *s.* equipolencia o equivalencia.—**equipollent** [-ent], *a.* equipolente.

equiponderance, equiponderancy [-póndœrans, i], *s.* equiponderancia.

equiponderant [-ant], *a.* equiponderante.

equiponderate [-pónderet], *vn.* equiponderar.

equitable [écuitabœl], *a.* equitativo.—**equitableness** [-nes], *s.* equidad, imparcialidad, justicia. —**equitably** [-bli], *adv.* equitativamente.

equitancy [écuitansi], *s.* equitación.

equitant [écuitant], *a.* (bot.) acaballado.

equitation [ecuitéshun], *s.* equitación.

equity [écuiti], *s.* equidad, justicia; (E. U.) diferencia entre el valor de una propiedad y la cantidad por que está hipotecada.

equivalence, *o* **equivalency** [ecuívalens, i], *s.* equivalencia.—**equivalent** [-ent], *a.* y *s.* equivalente.—**equivalently** [-li], *adv.* equivalentemente.

equivocal [ecuívocal]. **I.** *a.* equívoco, ambiguo. **II.** *s.* equívoco.—**equivocally** [-li], *adv.* equívocamente, ambiguamente.—**equivocalness** [-nes], *s.* ambigüedad.

equivocate [ecuívokeit], *vn.* usar palabras o frases equívocas o ambiguas.—**equivocation** [-éishun], *s.* equívoco, anfibología.—**equivocator** [-tœr], *s.* el que usa de equívocos.

era [íra], *s.* era, época; (geol.) edad, época.

eradiate [eréidiet], *vn.* radiar, irradiar.

eradiation [-éishun], *s.* radiación.

eradicate [erǽdikeit], *va.* desarraigar, erradicar; destruir, extirpar.—**eradication** [-éishun], *s.* desarraigo, extirpación.—**eradicative** [-cativ], *a.* erradicativo.

erasable, [irréisǽbœl], **erasible** [-ibœl], *a.* borrable.

erase [erréis], *va.* borrar, raspar; tachar.

eraser [irréisœr], *s.* raspador; goma de borrar.

erasion [irréiϒun], *s.* (med.) extirpación o eliminación por raspadura.

erasure [irréiϒœr], *s.* raspadura, borradura.

ere [éœr], *prep.* antes de, antes que.

erect [eréct]. **I.** *va.* erigir, levantar; enderezar; montar, instalar; erguir, enhestar o alzar; enaltecer. **II.** *a.* derecho, erguido, enhiesto; vertical; engallado, firme.

erectile [eréctil], *a.* eréctil.

erectility [írectíliti], *s.* erectilidad.

erecting [erécting], *pa.* de TO ERECT; (ópt., top.) de imagen recta (apl. a lentes, anteojos, telescopios, etc.)

erection [erécshun], *s.* erección; montaje, instalación; elevación, erguimiento; estructura.

erective [-tiv], *a.* que tiende a levantar o construir.

erectness [eréctnes], *s.* erección, erguimiento.

erector [eréctœr], *s.* erector.

erelong [éœrlong], *adv.* antes de mucho.

eremite [éremait], *s.* ermitaño.

eremitic(al [-mític(al], *a.* eremítico.

erenow [éœrnau], *adv.* antes de ahora.

erethism [érezism], *s.* (med.) eretismo.

erg [œrg], *s.* erg o ergio, unidad de energía.

ergatocracy [érgætócrasi], *s.* gobierno o dominación de (por) las clases obreras.

ergot [érgot], *s.* (bot.) cornezuelo de centeno.

ergotism [érgotism], *s.* (med.) ergotismo.

Ericaceæ [erikéisii], *s.* (bot.) ericáceas.—**ericaceous** [-kéishus], *s.* (bot.) *a.* ericáceo.

Erin [írin], *s.* Erin (Irlanda).

eristic [erístic], *a.* erístico; pendenciero.

ermine [érmin], *s.* armiño; piel de armiño; (fig.) toga, judicatura; pureza del cargo judicial.

ermined [érmind], *a.* arminado.

erode [eród]. **I.** *va.* corroer, roer; comer. **II.** *vn.* (geol.) desgastarse.—**erodent** [-œnt], *a.* (med.) corrosivo, cáustico.

erosion [eróϒun], *s.* corrosión; desgaste; (geol.) erosión.

erosive [erósiv], *a.* caterético; desgastador o corroedor.

erotic(al [erótic(al], *a.* erótico.—**eroticism** [-ticism], *s.* erotismo.—**erotomania** [-toménia], *s.* erotomanía.

erpetology, *s.* = HERPETOLOGY.

err [œr], *vn.* errar, equivocarse; descarriarse, pecar; errar, no dar en el blanco.

errancy [érransi], *s.* propensión a errar.

errand [érand], *s.* recado, mensaje, mandado, diligencia.—**e. boy,** mandadero.

errant [érrant], *a.* errante, vagabundo, vagaroso; errático.—**errantry** [-tri], *s.* vida errante; caballería andante.

errata [erréita], *s. pl.* de ERRATUM; fe de erratas.

erratic(al [errátic(al], **I.** *a.* errático, excéntrico; errante, vagabundo; (med.) errático. **II.** *s.*

persona excéntrica; canto rodado.—**erratically** [-1], *adv.* de un modo errático; irregularmente.

erratum [erréitum], *s.* (*pl.* ERRATA) errata.

errhine [érrin], *s.* remedio tomado por la nariz.

erring [érring], *a.* errado, errante.

erroneous [erróneus], *a.* errado, erróneo.

erroneously [-li], *adv.* erróneamente.

erroneousness [-nes], *s.* calidad de erróneo.

error [érrœr], *s.* error.—**errors and omissions excepted,** salvo error u omisión.

Erse [œrs], *s.* lenguaje de los montañeses de Escocia.

erst [œrst], **erstwhile** [œrstjuail], *adv.* y *a.* antiguamente, antes; en otro o de otro tiempo.

erubescence, erubescency [erubésens, i], *s.* erubescencia, rubor.

erubescent [-ent], *a.* ruboroso.

eruct(ate) [erúct(et], *va.* eructar, regoldar.

eructation [eructéishun], *s.* eructación, eructo.

erudite [érudait], *a.* y *s.* erudito, letrado.

erudition [-díshun], *s.* erudición.

eruginous [irúyinus], *a.* ruginoso.

erupt [irupt], *vn.* salir con fuerza; hacer erupción.

eruption [irúpshun], *s.* erupción; irrupción.

eruptive [irúptiv], *a.* eruptivo.

eryngo [iríngo], *s.* (bot.) eringe, cabezuela.

erysipelas [érisípelas], *s.* erisipela.

erysipelatous [erisipélatus], *a.* erisipelatoso.

erythema [érisimæ], *s.* (med.) eritema.

erythrin [érizrin], *s.* (quím.) eritrina.

escadrille [éscædríl], *s.* escuadrilla aérea.

escalade [éscaléid]. **I.** *s.* (mil.) escalada. **II.** *va.* (mil.) escalar.

escalator [éscæléitor], *s.* escalera movible sin fin, que funciona como una correa sin fin.

escalop [escólup], *s.* = SCALLOP.

escapade [éscapéid], *s.* escapada, travesura; correría, aventura; fuga; caracoleo del caballo.

escape [eskéip]. **I.** *va.* escaparse de; evadir, evitar, eludir. **II.** *vn.* escapar, escaparse. **III.** *s.* escapada, huída, fuga; escapatoria, evasión, zafada; fuga o escape (de gas o líquido).

escapement [-mœnt], *s.* escape de reloj.

escarp [escárp], *va.* (mil.) escarpar.

escarpment [escárpmœnt], *s.* escarpa.

esc(h)ar [éscar], *s.* escara, costra.

escharotic [escarótic]. **I.** *a.* escarótico. **II.** *s.* cáustico.

eschatology [éscætóloyi], *s.* escatología.

escheat [eschít]. **I.** *s.* (for.) reversión de bienes mostrencos o abintestatos al estado; confiscación de bienes. **II.** *vo.* confiscar, apropiarse el estado de bienes mostrencos o abintestatos. **III.** *vn.* revertir al estado (bienes mostrencos o abintestatos).—**escheatable** [-tabœl], *a.* confiscable; revertible al estado.

eschew [eschú], *va.* huir de, evitar, evadir.

Eschscholtzia [éshshóltsia], *s.* (bot.) amapola.

escort [éscort]. **I.** *s.* escolta, convoy; acompañante. **II.** [escórt], *va.* escoltar, convoyar; acompañar, cortejar.

escritoire [escrituár], *s.* escritorio, escribanía, arquimesa.

escrow [escró], *s.* (for.) plica.

Esculapian [eskuléipian], *a.* medicinal.

esculent [éskulent], *a.* y *s.* comestible; comedero.

escutcheon [escúchun], *s.* escudo de armas; guarnición.—**escutcheoned** [-d], *a.* blasonado.

Eskimo, Eskimau [éskimo], *s.* esquimal.

esophagus [esófagus], *s.* esófago, gola.

esoteric [ésotéric], *a.* esotérico; oculto, reservado; confidencial.

espalier [espáliœr], *a.* espaldera, varaseto.

esparto, esparto grass, *s.* (bot.) esparto.

esparver [espárvœr], *s.* pabellón de cama.

especial [espéshal], *a.* especial.—**especially** [-i], *adv.* especialmente.

Esperanto [éspœránto], *s.* esperanto (lengua universal).

espial [espáial], *s.* espionaje.

espionage [éspioney], *s.* espionaje.

esplanade [ésplanéid], *s.* ribera; (fort.) explanada, glacis.

espousal [espáushal]. **I.** *s.* desposorio, esponsales; adhesión a una causa. **II.** *a.* esponsalicio.

espouse [espáush], *va.* y *vn.* desposar o desposarse, contraer esponsales o matrimonio; defender, abogar por.

esprit [esprí], *s.* espíritu; chiste, agudeza.—**e. de corps,** compañerismo; espíritu de partido o de solidaridad.

espy [espái]. **I.** *va.* divisar, alcanzar a ver, descubrir; espiar. **II.** *vn.* velar, vigilar.

esquire [escuáiœr], *s.* título correspondiente a *don* (se usa pospuesto al apellido); acompañante de una dama; (en Ingl.) labrador o hacendado; escudero.

essay [esséi], *va.* ensayar, probar.

essay [ésci], *s.* ensayo (literario); connato, esfuerzo, ensayo.—**essayist** [éseist], *s.* escritor de ensayos.

essence [ésens], *s.* esencia (de una cosa), substancia; medula; esencia, perfume.

Essene [esín], *s.* y *a.* esenio, eseniano.

essential [esénshal], *a.* esencial, vital, indispensable; constitutivo.—**e. oil,** aceite esencial.

essentiality [esenshiéliti], *s.* cualidad de esencial. —**essentially** [-i], *adv.* esencialmente.

essoin [esóin], *s.* (for.) excusa.

essonite [ésonait], *s.* (min.) grosularia canela.

establish [estéblish], *va.* establecer, fundar; probar, demostrar; restablecer, solidar; ratificar, sancionar.

establishment [-mœnt], *s.* establecimiento (comercial, de educación, etc.); fundación; institución; pensión o renta vitalicia.

estacade [éstækeid], *s.* estacada.

estafet [estafét], *s.* estafeta, correo.

estate [estéit], *s.* bienes, propiedades, patrimonio, herencia; heredad, finca, fundo, hacienda; estado, clase o condición, posición.—**the fourth e.,** la prensa, el periodismo: (Ingl.) galería de los reporteros en la cámara de los comunes.

esteem [estím]. **I.** *va.* estimar, apreciar; reputar, juzgar; tener en o por, creer. **II.** *s.* estimación, aprecio; mérito; juicio, opinión.

ester [éstœr], *s.* (quím.) éster.

esthesia [eszíyiæ], *s.* estesia, sensibilidad; capacidad de sentir.

esthete [észit], *s.* admirador del arte o de la estética.

esthetic [eszétic]. **I.** *a.* estético. **II.** *s.* estética.

esthetically [eszéticali], *adv.* estéticamente.

esthetics [eszétics], *s.* estética.

estimable [éstimabœl], *a.* estimable; calculable.

estimableness [-nes], *s.* estimabilidad.

estimate [éstimeit]. **I.** *va.* apreciar, tasar; calcular (gen. aproximadamente); hacer un presupuesto. **II.** *s.* tasa, cálculo (gen. aproximado); opinión; (com.) presupuesto.

estimation [-éishun], *s.* cálculo; presupuesto; estima, aprecio; opinión; suposición.

estimator [-eitœr], *s.* estimador, calculador.

estivage [estíveir], *s.* (mar.) estiva.

estival [éstival]. **I.** *a.* estival. **II.** *s.* (med.) colerina.

estivation [éstivéishun], *s.* veraneo; veranada; (bot.) prefloración; (zool.) letargo o adormecimiento estival.

estop [estóp], *va.* (for.) impedir una afirmación contraria a otras anteriores.

estoppel [estópel], *s.* (for.) acto o afirmación que no puede negarse posteriormente ante la ley; imposibilidad en que se coloca uno de negar lo que ha afirmado previamente.

estrange [estréiny], *va.* extrañar, apartar.

estrangement [-mœnt], *s.* enajenamiento; extrañamiento, desvío.

estray [estréi], *s.* (for.) animal descarriado o mostrenco.

estuary [éschuœri], *s.* estuario, estero.

étagère [etayér], *s.* estante, juguetero.

et cetera [etcétéræ], etcétera.

etch [ech], *va.* grabar al agua fuerte.

etcher [-œr], *s.* grabador al agua fuerte.

etching [-ing], *s.* grabado al agua fuerte.

etern [-itœrn], **eternal** [etœrnal, *a.* eterno.—**e. flower**, (bot.) perpetua.—**eternally** [-i], *adv.* eternamente.—**eternity** [-iti], *s.* eternidad.— **eternize** [etœrnaiš], *va.* eternizar.

etesian [etíyæn], *a.* etesio, periódico.

ethane [ézein], *s.* (quím.), etano, dimetilo.

ether [ízœr], *s.* éter.—**ethereal** [ezírial], **ethereous** [ezíriuš], *a.* etéreo.

etherealize [ezírialaiš]. **I.** *va.* hacer etéreo, espiritualizar; convertir en éter. **II.** *vn.* hacerse etéreo.

etherealization [-aliśéišhun], *s.* conversión en éter.

etheriform [ízœriform], *a.* etéreo.

etherization [ízœraišéšhun], *s.* eterización.

etherize, etherise [ízœraiš], *va.* (med.) eterizar; (quím.) convertir en éter.

ethic(al [ézic(al], *a.* ético.—**ethically** [-i], *adv.* moralmente.—**ethics** [écics], *s. pl.* ética.

Ethiop [íziop], *s.* etíope.—**Ethiopian** [iziópian]. **I.** *a.* etiópico. **II.** *s.* etíope.—**Ethiopic** [iziópic], *s.* lengua etiópica.

ethmoid [ézmoid], *s.* (anat.) etmoides.

ethnic(al [éznic(al], *a.* étnico; pagano, gentil.

ethnicism [éznicišm], *s.* paganismo, gentilismo.

ethnogeny [eznóyeni], *s.* etnogenia, estudio del origen de las razas.

ethnographer [eznógrafœr], *s.* etnógrafo.

ethnographic(al [eznográfic(al], *a.* etnográfico.

ethnography [eznógrafi], *s.* etnografía.

ethnologic(al [eznolóyic(al], *a.* etnológico.

ethnologist [eznóloyist], *s.* etnólogo.

ethnology [eznóloyi], *s.* etnología.

ethological [ezolóyical], *a.* que trata del carácter.

ethology [ezóloyi], *s.* ciencia que estudia el carácter humano.

ethyl [ézil], *s.* (quím.) etilo.—**e. alcohol**, alcohol etílico.—**e. ether, e. oxide**, éter.

ethylene [ézilin], *s.* (quím.) etileno.

ethylic [ezílic], *a.* etílico.

etiolate [ítiolet], *va.* y *vn.* blanquear(se).

etiolation [-léišhun], *s.* (bot.) palidez, descoloración.

etiology [itióloyi], *s.* (med.) etiología.

etiquette [étiket], *s.* etiqueta.

Etruscan [etrúscan], **Etrurian** [etrúrian], *a.* etrusco.

etui, etwee [etuí], *s.* estuche, caja.

etymological [étimolóyical], *a.* etimológico.

etymologically [-i], *adv.* etimológicamente.

etymologist [étimóloyist], *s.* etimologista.

etymologize [étimóloyaiš], *va.* etimologizar.

etymology [étimóloyi], *s.* etimología.

etymon [étimon], *s.* (gram.) raíz.

eucaine [yúcæin], *s.* eucaína, base de ciertos anestésicos locales.

eucalyptus [yucalíptus], *s.* (bot.) eucalipto.

eucharist [yúcarist], *s.* eucaristía.

eucharistic(al [yucarístic(al], *a.* eucarístico.

euchology [yucóloyi], *s.* eucologio.

euchre [yúkœr]. **I.** *s.* euchre, juego de naipes. **II.** *va.* en dicho juego, dar codillo; (fig.) ganar, vencer.

Euclidean, Euclidian [yuclídiæn], *a.* euclidiano, de Euclides.—**E. construction**, (geom.) construcción euclidiana, sin otros instrumentos que el compás y la regla.—**E. geometry**, geometría euclidiana, en que se admite la validez del postulado de Euclides acerca de las paralelas.—**E. space**, espacio euclidiano, al cual es aplicable la geometría euclidiana.

eudemonics [yudemónics], *s.* tratado de la felicidad.

eudemonism [yudímonišm], *s.* eudemonismo, doctrina según la cual la felicidad es el sumo bien.

eudiometer [yudiómetœr], *s.* (quím.) eudiómetro.

eugenic [iurénic], *a.* eugenésico.—**eugenics**, *s.* eugenesia (apl. esp. a la humana, que trata del perfeccionamiento de la raza).

eugenol [yúrenol], *s.* (quím.) eugenol.

eulogist [yúloyist], *s.* elogiador, panegirista.

eulogistic [-rístic], *a.* laudatorio.—**eulogize** [-yaiš], *va.* elogiar, loar.—**eulogy, eulogium** [yúloyi, yulóyium], *s.* elogio, panegírico, apología.

eunuch [yúnuc], *s.* eunuco.

eupatrid [iupǽtrid; *pl.* EUPATRIDÆ], *s.* (hist.) eupátrida.

eupatorium [yupatórium], *s.* (bot.) eupatorio.

eupepsia [iupépsiæ], *s.* (med.) eupepsia, digestión normal.

euphemism [yúfemišm], *s.* eufemismo.

euphemistic(al [-místic(al], *a.* eufemístico.— **euphemize** [-maiš], *vn.* hacer uso del eufemismo.

euphonic(al [yufónic(al], **euphonious** [yufónius], *a.* eufónico.—**euphoniously** [-li], *adv.* eufónicamente.—**euphony** [yúfoni], *s.* eufonía.

Euphorbiaceæ [yúforbiéicii], *s. pl.* (bot.) euforbiáceas.—**euphorbiaceous** [-šhus], *a.* euforbiáceo.

euphorbium [yufórbium], *s.* (bot.) euforbio.

euphuism [yúfiuišm], *s.* culteranismo, alambicamiento, gongorismo.—**euphuist** [-ist], *s.* gongorista, culterano.—**euphuistic** [-ístic], *a.* culterano, gongórico, alambicado.

Eurasian [yuréiyæn], *a.* y *a.* eurasio, eurasiático: apl. a lo relativo a Eurasia (Europa y Asia) y también al mestizo de europeo y asiático.

eureka [yurícæ], *interj.* ¡eureka! (¡lo he hallado!)

European [yúropiæn], *s.* y *a.* europeo.—**E. concert**, concierto europeo (relativo a la política europea en el Oriente).—**E. plan**, hospedaje sin alimentos, cuarto sin comida.—**Europeanize** [-aiš], *va.* europeizar.

eurythmy [yurízmi], *s.* (b. a.) euritmia.

Eustachian tube [yustéiquiæn tiub], *s.* (anat.) trompa de Eustaquio.

eustyle [yústail], *s.* (arq.) éustilo.

eutectic [yutéctic], *a.* (fís.) eutéctico, de máxima fusibilidad (apl. a aleaciones en que ciertas proporciones de los componentes dan el punto mínimo de fusión).

euthanasia [yúzanéyiæ], *s.* eutanasia, muerte tranquila.

euthenics [yuzénics], *s.* ciencia que trata de mejorar la raza humana mejorando las condiciones de la vida.

Eutychian [yutíkian], *a.* eutiquiano.

euxinite [yúcsinait], *s.* (miner.) euxinita.

evacuant [evǽkiuant], *s.* (med.) evacuante.

evacuate [evǽkiueit]. **I.** *va.* evacuar, desocupar; sacar. **II.** *vn.* vaciarse; evacuar.—**evacuation** [-éišhun], *s.* evacuación.—**evacuative** [-ativ], *a.* purgativo, evacuativo.—**evacuator** [-éitœr], *s.* evacuador.

evade [evéd], *va.* y *vn.* evadir.

evaluate [evǽliueit], *va.* avaluar; (mat.) hallar el valor numérico de.—**evaluation** [-éishun], *s.* avalúo; (mat.) determinación del valor numérico.

evanesce [evanés], *vn.* desaparecer, disiparse; desvanecerse, evaporarse.—**evanescence** [-sens], *s.* disipación.—**evanescent** [-ent], *a.* que se disipa o desvanece; (mat.) que se aproxima a cero; (biol.) instable.

evangel [evǽnyel], *s.* buena nueva, evangelio.

evangelic(al [evanyélic(al], *a.* evangélico.

evangelically [-i], *adv.* evangélicamente.

evangelism [evǽnyelišm], *s.* evangelismo.

evangelist [-list], *s.* evangelista; evangelizador.

evangelistary [-yelístæri], *s.* (igl.) evangeliario.

evangelize [-yelaiš], *va.* evangelizar.—**evangelizer** [-œr], *s.* evangelizador.

evaporable [evǽporabœl], *a.* evaporable.

evaporate [evǽporeit], *va.* y *vn.* evaporar(se).— **evaporation** [-éishun], *s.* evaporación.—**evaporative** [evǽporœtiv], *a.* evaporatorio.—**evaporator** [-réitœr], *s.* evaporador; desecador; (azú.) desecadora, evaporadora.

evasion [ivéiyun], *s.* evasión, evasiva.—**evasive** [ivéisiv], *a.* evasivo.—**evasively** [-li], *adv.* evasivamente.

eve [iv], *s.* vigilia; víspera.—**on the e. of**, la víspera de, en víspera de.

evection [evécshun], *s.* evección, de desviación de la luna por atracción solar.

Para la pronunciación de æ, œ, ᴅ, š, šh, ᴜ, ȳ, ʏ, z, véase la clave al principio del libro.

even. I. *a.* llano, plano, liso; igual; uniforme; apacible, inmutable; par (divisible por dos); recto, justo; constante, firme; redondo (número); situado al mismo nivel, parejo (con).—**of e. date**, de la misma fecha.—**to be e. with**, estar en paz con, estar mano a mano.—**to be e. with one**, cancelar la cuenta con uno; vengarse, pagar en la misma moneda.—**to make e.**, allanar, igualar, compensar. **II.** *adv.* aun, hasta, también; exactamente, precisamente, enteramente; de un modo igual y fácil.—**e. as**, así como.—**e. if**, aun cuando.—**e. so**, así; aun así, suponiendo que así sea.—**e. though** = EVEN IF.—**not e.**, ni siquiera, ni aun. **III.** *va.* (a veces con *up*) igualar, emparejar, allanar, enrasar, nivelar; unir; desquitar, liquidar cuentas. **IV.** *vn.* emparejarse, igualarse, nivelarse.

evening [ívning], *s.* tarde; noche (primeras horas); vísperas.—**e. clothes**, o **dress**, traje de etiqueta.—**e. star**, estrella vespertina.

evenly [-li], *adv.* igualmente; con suavidad; a nivel; imparcialmente.

evenness [-nes], *s.* igualdad, uniformidad; llanura, lisura; imparcialidad.

even-song [ivn-song], *s.* vísperas, oraciones.

event [évént], *s.* acontecimiento, suceso; éxito, consecuencia, resultado.—**at all events, in any e.**, sea lo que fuere, en todo caso, de cualquier modo.—**in the e. of**, en caso de.

eventful [evéntful], *a.* lleno de acontecimientos; memorable.

eventide [ívœntaid], *s.* caída de la tarde.

eventual [evénchual], *a.* consiguiente; eventual, fortuito.—**eventuality** [-chuéliti], *s.* eventualidad.—**eventually** [-i], *adv.* eventualmente, finalmente; con el tiempo.

eventuate [-chuéit], *vn.* acontecer, acaecer, suceder.

ever [évœr], *adv.* siempre; alguna vez, en cualquier tiempo; nunca (vg.: *the best book ever written*, el mejor libro que se haya escrito nunca).—**e. and anon**, de cuando en cuando, de vez en cuando.—**e. since**, desde entonces, después.—**e. so**, muy, -ísimo (*I am ever so happy*, soy muy feliz; *we saw ever so many things*, vimos muchísimas cosas).—**e. as**, como siempre; (con *as*) tanto como, lo más, vg.: *run as fast as ever you can*, corra lo más aprisa que pueda.—**did you e.?** (fam.) ¿habráse visto? ¡qué cosa! ¡qué ocurrencia!.—**for e. and e.**, por siempre jamás.—**hardly e.**, casi nunca.—**nor e.**, ni nunca.—**not e.**, nunca.—**scarcely e.**, casi nunca.

everduring [-diúring], *a.* eterno, sempiterno.

everglade [-gleid], *s.* terreno pantanoso cubierto de altas hierbas.

evergreen [-grin]. **I.** *a.* siempre verde, vivaz. **II.** *s.* (bot.) siemprevira.

everlasting [-lásting]. **I.** *a.* eterno, sempiterno. **II.** *s.* eternidad; ser eterno; (tej.) sempiterna; (bot.) siemprevira.

everlastingly [-lástingli], *adv.* eternamente.

everliving [-líving], *a.* inmortal, eterno, perdurable.

evermore [-móœr], *adv.* eternamente,—**e.**, o **for e.**, para siempre jamás.

everpleasing [-plísing], *a.* que deleita siempre.

eversion [evœrshun], *s.* eversión; vuelta al revés.

evert [evœrt], *va.* trastornar; voltear al revés.

every [éveril, *a.* cada; todo, todos los.—**e. bit**, (fam.) enteramente.—**e. day, month**, etc., todos los días, meses, etc.—**e. now and then**, o **e. once in a while**, de cuando en cuando.—**e. one**, cada uno, cada cual; todos, todo el mundo.—**e. one of them**, todos, todos sin excepción—**e. other**, cada dos, uno sí y otro no (*every other day*, un día sí y otro no).—**e. which way**, (fam.) por todas partes, en toda dirección.—**e. whit**, enteramente.

everybody [-bódi], *s.* todos; todo el mundo; cada uno, cada cual.

everyday [-déi], *a.* de cada día, ordinario, diario, cuotidiano.

everyone [-uónl, *s.* todo el mundo; todos.

everything [-zíng], *s.* todo.

everywhere [-juéœr], *s.* en o por todas partes.

evict [evíct], *va.* desalojar, desaposentar, desahuciar; excluir, expulsar; usurpar.

eviction [evícshun], *s.* (for.) desahucio.

evidence [évidens]. **I.** *s.* evidencia; demostración; (for.) prueba; testimonio, deposición, declaración.—**to be in e.**, dejarse ver, mostrarse.—**to give e.**, dar testimonio, deponer, declarar. **II.** *va.* evidenciar, patentizar, probar.

evident [-ent], *a.* evidente.

evidential [évidénshal], *a.* indicativo; de carácter de prueba, probatorio.

evidently [évidentli], *adv.* evidentemente.

evil. I. *a.* malo; maligno, perverso; aciago.—**e. fame, e. repute**, mala reputación.—**e. speaking**, maledicencia, murmuración.—**the e. eye**, aojo, aojadura.—**the E. One**, el diablo, Satanás. **II.** *s.* mal; maldad, perversidad.—**sufficient unto the day is the e. thereof**, le basta al día su propio afán.—**the social e.**, la prostitución. **III.** *adv.* mal; malignamente.—**e.-eyed**, aojador.—**e.-favored**, repugnante, feo.—**e.-minded**, malicioso mal intencionado.—**e.-starred**, desafortunado, de mala suerte.

evildoer [-dúœr], *s.* persona perversa o maligna.

evilly [ívili], *adv.* malamente; perversamente.

evilness [ívœlnes], *s.* maldad.

evince [evíns], *va.* hacer patente, probar terminantemente; revelar, indicar.—**evincible** [-íbœl], *a.* demostrable.—**evincibly** [-íbli], *adv.* demostrablemente.—**evincive** [-iv], *a.* convincente.

eviscerate [evíseret], *va.* destripar, desentrañar.

evitable [évitabœl], *a.* evitable.

ev'n [ívn], *contracción de* EVEN.

evocation [evokéshun], *s.* evocación o llamamiento; (for.) avocación.

evoke [evóc], *va.* evocar, llamar.

evolute [évoliut], *s.* (geom.) evoluta.

evolution [évoliúshun], *s.* evolución, desarrollo; (mil.) evolución, maniobra; (mat.) extracción de raíces.—**evolutionary** [-eri], *a.* evolucionista, evolucionario.—**evolutionism** [-ism], *s.* evolucionismo, teoría de la evolución.—**evolutionist**, [-ist], *s.* y *a.* evolucionista.

evolve [evólv]. **I.** *va.* desenvolver, desarrollar; (biol.) producir por evolución; despedir (gases). **II.** *vn.* desarrollarse; evolucionar.

evolvent [evólvœnt], *s.* (geom.) evolvente.

evulsion [evúlshun], *s.* (cir.) evulsión, arranque.

ewe [yu], *s.* oveja.

ewer [yúœr], *s.* aguamanil, jarro, múcura.

exacerbate [egsásœrbeit], *va.* exacerbar; agravar.

exacerbation [-béishun], *s.* exacerbación; agravación.

exact [egséect]. **I.** *a.* exacto. **II.** *va.* exigir, imponer.

exacter, exactor [-œr], *s.* exactor, opresor.

exacting [-ing], *a.* exigente.

exaction [egséœcshun], *s.* exacción, extorsión.

exactitude [-itiud], *s.* exactitud.—**exactly** [-li], *adv.* exactamente.—**exactness** [-nes], *s.* exactitud.

exaggerate [egsáœvereit], *va.* y *vn.* exagerar.—**exaggeration** [-éishun], *s.* exageración.—**exaggerative** [-œtiv], *a.* exagerativo.—**exaggeratingly** [-ætivl], *adv.* exagerativamente.—**exaggerator** [-eitœr], *s.* exagerador.

exalt [egsólt]. **I.** *va.* exaltar, elevar, enaltecer, glorificar; alegrar o regocijar; reforzar, sublimar. **II.** *vn.* promover.

exaltation [egsoltéishun], *s.* exaltación, elevación; ensalzamiento, promoción; contento, regocijo.

exalted [egsólted], *a.* exaltado, elevado, eminente.

examinable [egséminabœl], *a.* investigable, averiguable.

examination [-éishun], *s.* examen; inspección, reconocimiento; registro; ensayo, prueba; (for.) interrogatorio.

examine [egsémin], *va.* examinar; inspeccionar; reconocer, registrar; explorar; preguntar, inquirir; ensayar, aquilatar, analizar; (for.) interrogar.—**examiner** [-nœr], *s.* examinador, inspector, escrutador.

example [egsǽmpœl], s. ejemplo.
exanimate [egsǽnimet], a. exánime.
exanimation [-éishʊn], s. muerte; desmayo, síncope.
exanthem(a [ecsénzem, écsænzíma], s. (med.) exantema, erupción, sarpullido.
exanthematous [écsænzématʊs], a. exantemático.
exarch [écsarc], s. exarca.
exarchate [ecsárket], s. exarcado.
exasperate [egsǽspœreit], va. exasperar, irritar; agravar, amargar, agriar.—**exasperation** [-éishʊn], s. exasperación, provocación, enojo; agravación, recargo.
ex cathedra [ecs cæzídræ], adv.ˉy a. exˉcáthedra.
excavate [éxcaveit], va. excavar, cavar; vaciar, ahondar.
excavation [-éishʊn], s. excavación; desmonte; zanja; material extraído por excavación; (agr.) excava.
excavator [-eitœr], s. excavador; (ing.) excavadora (máquina).
exceed [ecsíd]. I. va. exceder; aventajar, sobrepujar. II. vn. excederse, propasarse; preponderar.
exceeding [-ing]. I. a. grande, extraordinario. II. adv. sumamente, muy, -ísimo.
exceedingly [-ingli], adv. sumamente, muy, -ísimo (he is exceedingly rich, él es sumamente rico, o riquísimo).
excel [ecsél], va. y vn. aventajar, ser superior a; sobresalir.
excellence, excellency [écselens, i], s. excelencia. —**His E.**, su Excelencia.
excellent [-ent], a. excelente.—**excellently** [-li], adv. excelentemente.
excelsior [ecsélsior]. I. a. más alto; hacia arriba. II. s. madera en hebras para empaquetar.
excentric [ecséntric], a. = ECCENTRIC.
except [ecsépt]. I. va. exceptuar. II. vn. (for.) excepcionar; recusar. III. prep. excepto, con excepción de, menos. IV. conj. sino, a menos que.—**excepting** [-ing], prep. a excepción de, salvo, exceptuando.—**exception** [-shʊn], s. excepción, salvedad; (for.) excepción, recusación; objeción.—**to take e.**, objetar, oponerse, desaprobar.
exceptionable [-abœl], a. recusable, tachable.
exceptional [-al], a. excepcional.
exceptionally [-i], adv. excepcionalmente.
exceptive [ecséptiv], a. que implica excepción; susceptible, quisquilloso.
exceptor [-tœr], s. el que pone excepciones.
excerpt [ecsérpt]. I. va. extractar. II. s. extracto, excerta.
excerption [ecsérpshʊn], s. acto de extractar; extracto, excerta.
excerptive [-tiv], a., **excerptor** [-tœr], s. extractador.
excess [ecsés], s. exceso; excedente; inmoderación o destemplanza; transgresión; (com.) sobrante, superávit.—**e. profits**, ganancias excesivas, o sea, en exceso de las ordinarias o de término medio.—**to e.**, en exceso, inmoderadamente.
excessive [-iv], a. excesivo, demasiado, inmoderado.—**excessively** [-li], adv. excesivamente, demasiadamente.
exchange [exchénʏ]. I. va. cambiar; canjear, trocar, permutar; hacerse, darse, etc. (vg. to exchange bows, hacerse cortesías).—**to e. cards**, desañarse.—**to e. guns, pistols, o shots**, darse o tirarse pistoletazos.—**to e. signs**, hacerse señas.—**to e. words**, cambiar, decirse algunas palabras. II. s. cambio, trueque, permuta; canje (de periódicos, prisioneros, credenciales); periódico de canje; (com.) bolsa, lonja; cambio (de la moneda); centro; (elec.) estación telefónica.—**e. on checks**, (com.) comisión de cobro de cheques foráneos.
exchangeable [exchénʏabœl], a. cambiable.
exchanger [exchénʏœr], s. cambista.
exchequer [exchékœr], s. real hacienda, erario, tesorería; fondos; (E-), (Ingl.) tribunal de hacienda.—**E. bills**, (Ingl.) abonaré de la Tesorería.

excipient [exípient], s. (farm.) excipiente.
excisable [ecsáisabœl], a. sujeto al derecho de sisa.
excise [ecsáis]. I. s. sisa, impuesto sobre consumos. II. va. cortar; imponer consumos sobre.
exciseman [-man], s. oficial del resguardo.
excision [ecsíyʊn], s. (cir.) excisión; extirpación.
excitability [ecsáitabíliti], s. excitabilidad.
excitable [-tabœl], a. excitable.—**excitant** [-tant], a. y s. excitante.
excitation [ecsitéishʊn], s. excitación; instigación, incitamiento.
excitative, excitatory [ecsáitativ, tori], a. excitativo, provocativo.
excite [ecsáit], va. excitar, acalorar, provocar; animar, estimular; (elec.) excitar.
excited [-ed], a. excitado, agitado, acalorado.—**excitedly** [-li], adv. agitadamente, acaloradamente.
excitement [-mœnt], s. excitación; estimulación; agitación, conmoción; acaloramiento.
exciter [-œr], s. incitador agitador, instigador; (elec.) excitatriz.
exciting [-ing], a. excitante, estimulante; excitador.
excitingly [-ingli], adv. de un modo excitante o provocativo.
exclaim [excléim], va. y vn. exclamar, clamar.
exclamation [éxclaméishʊn], s. exclamación.—**e. mark**, punto de admiración (!).
exclamative, exclamatory [exclémativ, tori], a. exclamativo, exclamatorio.
exclude [exclúd], va. excluir, desechar, rechazar; (biol.) expeler, arrojar.
exclusion [exclúyʊn], s. exclusión; exclusiva, eliminación; recusación; expulsión.
exclusionist [-ist], s. el que quiere excluir a otros.
exclusive [exclúsiv], a. exclusivo; privativo; exceptuado.—**exclusively** [-li], adv. exclusivamente.—**exclusiveness** [-nes], s. exclusiva, repulsa; calidad de exclusivo.—**exclusivism** [-ism], s. exclusivismo.
excogitate [excóyitet], va. excogitar.
excogitation [-téishʊn], s. acción de excogitar.
excommunicable [éxcomiúnicabœl], a. digno de excomunión.—**excommunicate** [-keit]. I. va. excomulgar. II. a. y s. excomulgado.—**excommunication** [-kéishʊn], s. excomunión.—**excommunicator** [-kéitœr], s. excomulgador.
excoriate [excórieit], va. desollar, excoriar; sahornarse.—**excoriation** [-éishʊn], s. desolladura; excoriación.
excortication [-excortikéishʊn], s. descortezadura.
excrement [éxcremœnt], s. excremento.
excremental, excrementary [-méntal, tæri], **excrementitial, excrementitious** [-mentíshal, tíshʊs], a. excrementicio, excrementoso.
excrescence, excrescency [excrésens, i], s. excrecencia, carnosidad, fungosidad.
excrescent [-ent], a. superfluo, que forma excrecencia.
excrete [excrít], va. excretar.—**excrete** [éxcret], s. excremento.—**excretion** [excríshʊn], s. excreción; excremento.—**excretive** [excrítiv], **excretory** [éxcretori], a. excretorio, emuntorio.
excruciate [excrúshieit], va. atormentar.
excruciating [-ing], a. agudísimo (dolor), penosísimo; (fam. E. U.) extremado, afectado.—**excruciatingly** [-ingli], adv. extremadamente, vivísimamente.—**excruciation** [-éishʊn], s. tormento.
exculpable [excúlpabœl], a. disculpable.—**exculpate** [-peit], va. disculpar, justificar, sincerar.—**exculpation** [-péishʊn], s. disculpa.—**exculpatory** [-patori], a. disculpador, justificatorio, sincerador.
excursion [excúrshʊn], s. excursión, romería, viajata; (mil.) correría; expedición, salida; digresión; (fís.) mitad del movimiento de oscilación; (mec.) recorrido, curso.—**e. ticket, train**, billete de ida y vuelta, tren de excursión.
excursionist [excérshʊnist], s. viajero, romero.
excursive [excérsiv], a. errante, vagante; (fig.) digresivo, errático.—**excursively** [-li], adv. de un modo vago, digresivo.—**excursiveness** [-nes], s. calidad de digresivo o errante.

excursus [ecscœrsus]. *s.* apéndice explicativo; digresión.

excusable [exkiúsabœl], *a.* excusable, disculpable.

excusableness [-nes], *s.* disculpabilidad.

excusably [-bli], *adv.* disculpablemente.

excusatory [exkiúsatori], *a.* apologético.

excuse [exkiús]. **I.** *va.* excusar, disculpar, dispensar; sincerar, justificar; eximir, exentar; paliar; despedir. **II.** *s.* excusa, justificación; disculpa; pretexto.

execrable [écsecrabœl], *a.* execrable.

execrably [-bli], *adv.* execrablemente.

execrate [écsecreit], *va.* execrar.—**execration** [-créíshun], *s.* execración.

executant [egsékiutant], *s.* (mús.) ejecutante.

execute [écsekiut]. **I.** *va.* ejecutar, llevar a cabo; cumplir; (mús. y teat.) ejecutar, desempeñar; (for.) legalizar, perfeccionar o finalizar un documento; ejecutar, ajusticiar. **II.** *vn.* obrar; (mús. y teat.) ejecutar, desempeñar.

executed [-ed], *a.* ejecutado; legalizado; fecho.

executer [écsekiutœr], *s.* ejecutor.

execution [écsekiúshun], *s.* ejecución, cumplimiento; (for.) ejecución, mandamiento judicial; legalización de un documento; ejecución (de la pena de muerte); (b. a.) ejecución, desempeño.

executioner [-œr], *s.* verdugo.

executive [egsékiutiv]. **I.** *a.* ejecutivo. **II.** *s.* poder ejecutivo.

executor [egsékiutœr], *s.* albacea, testamentario.

executorship [-ship], *s.* albaceazgo.—**executory** [-tori], *a.* ejecutorio, ejecutivo; administrativo.—**executress** [-tres], **executrix** [egsékiutrics], *s.* albacea (mujer), testamentaria.

exegesis [écseyísis], **exegetics** [-yétics], *s.* exegesis. —**exegete** [écseyit], *s.* exegeta.—**exegetic(al** [-yétic(al], *a.* exegético.—**exegetically** [-i], *adv.* exegéticamente.

exemplar [egsémplar], *s.* ejemplar, modelo o dechado.—**exemplarily** [-lil], *adv.* ejemplarmente. —**exemplariness** [-nes], *s.* calidad de ejemplar.— **exemplary** [-i], *a.* ejemplar.

exemplification [egsémplifikéíshun], *s.* ejemplificación; (for.) copia certificada.—**exemplify** [-fai], *va.* ejemplificar, declarar, manifestar; trasladar, copiar.

exempt [egsémpt]. **I.** *va.* exentar, eximir, franquear. **II.** *a.* exento; libre, franco.

exemptible [egsémptibœl], *a.* exento, privilegiado, libre.

exemption [egsémphun], *s.* exención, franquicia, dispensa, inmunidad.

exequatur [ecsecuéitœr, cuátœr], *s.* exequátur.

exequies [écsecuis], *s. pl.* exequias, funerales.

exercisable [ecsœrsáisabœl], *a.* ejercitativo.

exercise [écsœrsais]. **I.** *s.* ejercicio; ejercicio corporal; gimnasia.—*pl.* exámenes; certamen literario; servicio religioso. **II.** *va.* ejercitar, poner en ejercicio; formar, adiestrar, habituar; atarear; emplear; preocupar, causar ansiedad; ejercer; comunicar. **III.** *vn.* y *vr.* adiestrarse, ejercitarse; hacer ejercicio o gimnasia.

exercitation [egsœrsitéishun], *s.* ejercicio, ejercitación, práctica.

exergue [ecshœrg], *s.* exergo.

exert [egshœrt]. **I.** *va.* esforzar; ejercer. **II.** *vr.* empeñarse, hacer esfuerzo, apurarse.

exertion [egshœrshun], *s.* esfuerzo, conato.—*pl.* diligencias, pasos, medios.

exeunt [écseunt], (lat.) (teat.) vanse.—**e. omnes**, vanse todos.

exfoliate [exfóliet]. **I.** *vn.* (cir.) exfoliarse; escamarse. **II.** *va.* exfoliar, escamar.

exfoliation [-éishun], *s.* exfoliación.

exhalable [exjéilabœl], *a.* exhalable, evaporable.

exhalant [exjéilant], *a.* y *s.* exhalador.

exhalation [exjaléshun], *s.* exhalación, efluvio, vapor, vaho, tufo.

exhale [exjéil]. **I.** *va.* exhalar, emitir, despedir; vahar. **II.** *vn.* disiparse, evaporarse, desvanecerse.

exhaust [egsóst]. **I.** *va.* apurar, extraer, vaciar, agotar; acabar, gastar, consumir o disipar; depauperar o empobrecer; debilitar, enflaquecer, postrar. **II.** *s.* (m. v.) escape, educción; lumbrera de escape o de educción; (fís. y mec.) vacío; succión, aspiración.—**e. chamber**, cámara de escape.—**e. curve**, o **line**, (m. v.) curva de escape.—**e. draft**, tiro de aspiración o por succión. —**e. fan**, ventilador aspirador.—**e. feed heater**, (m. v.) calentador de (con) vapor de escape.—**e. lap**, (m. v.) recubrimiento interior.—**e. lead**, (m. v.) avance al escape; (aut.) avance al encendido.—**e. port**, lumbrera de escape o de educción. —**e. valve**, válvula de escape o de educción.

exhauster [-œr], *s.* agotador; (mec.) aspirador, bomba.—**exhaustible** [-tibœl], *a.* agotable.

exhaustion [egsóschun], *s.* agotamiento; evacuación, vaciamiento.

exhaustive [-iv], *a.* agotador, apurador; cabal, completo.—**exhaustively** [-li], *adv.* cabalmente, completamente, detenidamente.—**exhaustiveness** [-es], *s.* calidad de completo o cabal.—**exhaustless** [-les], *a.* inagotable.

exhibit [egsíbit]. **I.** *va.* exhibir; presentar, manifestar, mostrar; (for.) exhibir; (med.) administrar (un remedio). **II.** *s.* cualquier objeto o instalación de objetos expuestos al público; manifestación; (for.) documento fehaciente presentado como prueba.

exhibiter, **exhibitor** [-œr], *s.* expositor; (for.) el que exhibe.

exhibition [egsibíshun], *s.* exhibición, exposición; manifestación, presentación u ostentación; (med.) administración de un remedio; (Ingl.) beca de merced, prebenda de estudiante.

exhibitioner [-œr], *s.* estudiante pensionado.

exhibitive [egsíbitiv], *a.* representativo.

exhibitor [-bitœr], expositor.

exhibitory [egsíbitori], *a.* que exhibe.

exhilarant [egsílarant], *a.* regocijador; estimulante, vigorizante.

exhilarate [egsílareit], *va.* alegrar, regocijar o alborozar.

exhilarating [-ing], *a.* = EXHILARANT.—**e. gas**, gas hilarante.

exhilaration [egsilaréshun], *s.* regocijo, alborozo.

exhort [egsórt], *va.* y *vn.* exhortar.—**exhortation** [egsortéshun], *s.* exhortación.—**exhortative**, **exhortatory** [egsórtativ, -tori], *a.* exhortatorio.— **exhorter** [egsórtœr], *s.* exhortador.

exhumation [éxjiuméshun], *s.* exhumación.

exhume [exjiúm], *va.* exhumar, desenterrar.

exigence, exigency [écsiyens, i], *s.* exigencia, urgencia.—**exigent** [-ent], *a.* exigente; urgente.— **exigible** [-ibœl], *a.* exigible, exigidero.

exiguous [egsíguiuus], *a.* exiguo, pequeño.

exile [écsail]. **I.** *s.* destierro; desterrado, expatriado. **II.** *va.* desterrar.

exist [egsíst], *vn.* existir.—**existence** [-ens], *s.* existencia; entidad, ente.—**existent** [-ent], *a.* existente.

exit [écsit], *s.* salida; partida, muerte; (teat.) mutis, vase.

ex libris [ecs láibris], ex-libris.

exoderm [écsodœrm], *s.* ectodermo, exodermo.

exodus [écsodus], *s.* salida, emigración, éxodo; (E-) Éxodo, segundo libro del Pentateuco.

ex officio [ecs ofíshio], ex officio, en virtud de autoridad; oficial.

exogamy [ecsógœmi], *s.* exogamia, matrimonio con miembros de tribus extrañas.

exogen [écsoyen], *s.* (bot.) planta exógena.

exogenous [ecsóyenus], *a.* exógeno.

exonerate [egsónœreit], *va.* exonerar, desculpar; aliviar, relevar.—**exoneration** [-éishun], *s.* exoneración; exculpación, descargo.—**exonerative** [-ativ], *a.* exonerativo.

exorable [écsorabœl], *a.* exorable.

exorbitance, exorbitancy [egsórbitans, i], *s.* exorbitancia, exceso.—**exorbitant** [-ant], *a.* exorbitante, excesivo.—**exorbitantly** [-li], *adv.* exorbitantemente.

exorcise [écsorsais], *va.* exorcizar.—**exorciser** [-œr], **exorcist** [-ist], *s.* exorcista, conjurador.— **exorcism** [-ism], *s.* exorcismo, conjuro.

exordial [egsórdial], *a*. preliminar, previo.

exordium [egsórdiᴜm], *s*. exordio, preámbulo; (ret.) isagoge.

exosmose [écsosmous], *s*. (fis.) exósmosis.

exosmotic [ecsosmótic], *a*. exosmótico.

exospore [écsospoær], *s*. exospora, membrana exterior de una espora.

exoteric(al [ecsotœric(al], *a*. exotérico, público.

exothermic [écsozœrmic], *a*. exotérmico.

exotic(al [ecsótic(al]. **I.** *a*. exótico; forastero, extraño. **II.** *s*. (bot.) planta exótica.

expand [ecspǽnd], *a*. y *vn*. extender(se), tender-(se); dilatar(se); ensanchar(se); agrandar(se); abrir(se); (mat.) desarrollar.

expander [-œr], *s*. (mec.) ensanchador.

expanding [-ing], *a*. de expansión, de dilatación; de ensanchar; regulable, ensanchable (apl. a varias herramientas de taladrar, ensanchar, etc., como barrenas, escariadores, etc., que pueden regularse para adaptarlas a agujeros de distintos diámetros).—**e. brake**, freno de cinta.—**e. pulley**, polea de diámetro regulable.—**e. tool**, ensanchador.

expanse [ecspǽns], *s*. extensión, espacio.

expansibility [ecspǽnsibíliti], *s*. expansibilidad; dilatabilidad.

expansible [-sibœl], dilatable.

expansion [ecspǽnshᴜn], *s*. expansión; ensanche; aumento; prolongación; extensión (de terreno, etc.); (fis.) dilatación; (mat.) desarrollo.—**e. bolt**, perno de expansión o de ensanche.—**e. curve**, curva de expansión.—**e. engine**, máquina de expansión.—**e. joint**, junta de dilatación.—**e. plate**, placa de expansión; placa de la válvula de expansión.—**e. valve**, válvula de expansión.

expansive [expǽnsiv], *a*. expansivo.—**expansively** [-li], *adv*. expansivamente.—**expansiveness** [-nes], *s*. expansibilidad, dilatabilidad.

ex parte [ex parte], (for.) de una de las partes.

expatiate [expéishieit]. **I.** *vn*. espaciarse, extenderse. **II.** *va*. extender, alargar, amplificar.

expatiation [-éishᴜn], *s*. digresión, difusión, prolijidad.

expatiatory [-shiatori], *a*. difuso, prolijo.

expatriate [expétrieit], *va*. expatriar.

expatriation [-éishᴜn], *s*. expatriación.

expect [expéct], *va*. esperar, aguardar; contar con; (fam.) suponer.—**expectable** [-abœl], *a*. expectable.—**expectance, expectancy** [-ans, i], *s*. expectativa, esperanza.—**expectant** [-ant]. **I.** *a*. expectante; preñada. **II.** *s*. el que espera.—**expectation** [éxpectéishᴜn], *s*. expectativa, esperanza; probabilidad.—**expectative** [-ativ]. **I.** *a*. que hace esperar. **II.** *s*. expectativa.

expectorant [expéctorant], *a*. y *s*. (med.) expectorante.—**expectorate** [-eit], *va*. y *vn*. expectorar, desgarrar.—**expectoration** [-réishᴜn], *s*. expectoración; esputo, gargajo.—**expectorative** [-ativ], *a*. y *s*. expectorante.

expedience, expediency [expídiens, i], *s*. aptitud, propiedad; conveniencia, utilidad, comodidad; oportunidad.

expedient [-ent]. **I.** *a*. oportuno, conveniente; prudente, propio. **II.** *s*. expediente, medio, recurso.—**expediently** [-li], *adv*. aptamente, convenientemente.

expedite [éxpedait], *va*. acelerar, apresurar, dar prisa; facilitar; despachar, expedir, cursar, dar curso a.

expedition [éxpedíshᴜn], *s*. expedición; jornada de muchas personas; prisa, diligencia, despacho.—**expeditionary** [-ari], *a*. expedicionario.

expeditioner [-œr], *s*. expedicionero.

expeditious [expedíshᴜs], *a*. pronto, activo, expeditivo, sumarísimo.—**expeditiously** [-li], *adv*. expeditamente, prontamente.

expel [expél], *va*. expeler, expulsar; despedir.

expellable [-abœl], *a*. expulsable.—**expellant** [-ant], *a*. expelente.—**expeller** [-œr], *s*. expulsor.

expend [expénd], *va*. expender, gastar.

expenditure [expéndichur], *s*. gasto, desembolso.

expense [expéns], *s*. gasto, coste; desembolso, egreso; detrimento, pérdida.—**at any e.**, a toda costa.—**at one's e.**, a costa de uno.

expenseless [-les], *a*. poco o nada costoso.

expensive [-iv], *a*. costoso; caro.—**expensively** [-li], *adv*. costosamente.—**expensiveness** [-nes], *s*. dispendio; costo; calidad de costoso.

experience [expíriens]. **I.** *s*. experiencia, práctica; lance, paso, aventura, incidente; ejercicio espiritual; conocimiento experimental; conversión.—**e. is the mother of wisdom**, la experiencia es la madre de la sabiduría. **II.** *va*. experimentar; sentir, sufrir.—**to e. religion**, (fam.) convertirse, reformarse.

experienced [expírienst], *a*. experimentado, experto, perito; hábil; amaestrado o aleccionado.

experiencer [expíriensœr], *s*. experimentador.

experiment [expérimœnt]. **I.** *s*. experimento. **II.** *vn*. experimentar, hacer una prueba, un experimento.

experimental [-al], *a*. experimental.

experimentalist [-ist], **experimenter** [-œr], **experimentist** [-ist], *s*. experimentador.

experimentally [-méntali], *adv*. experimentalmente.

experimentation [-mentéishᴜn], *s*. experimento.

expert [expœrt]. **I.** *a*. experimentado, experto, perito. **II.** [éxpœrt], *s*. experto, perito, juez.—**expertly** [-li], *adv*. expertamente, pericialmente.—**expertness** [-nes], *s*. destreza, habilidad, pericia.

expiable [éxpiabœl], *a*. que se puede expiar.

expiate [éxpieit], *va*. expiar.—**expiation** [-éishᴜn], *s*. expiación.—**expiatist**, o **expiator** [éxpietist, éxpiéitœr], *s*. el que expia, quien hace expiación.—**expiatory** [éxpiatori], *a*. expiatorio.

expiration [éxpiréishᴜn], *s*. terminación; (com.) vencimiento, cumplimiento; (fisiol.) espiración; muerte.

expire [expáiær]. **I.** *va*. expirar, expeler (el aire respirado). **II.** *vn*. expirar, terminar; vencerse.

expiry [ecspáiæri], *s*. terminación, expiración, caducidad (apl. esp. a contratos, pólizas, etc. que expiran después de complido su plazo).

explain [expléin], *va*. explicar.—**explainable** [-abœl], *a*. explicable.—**explanation** [éxplanéishᴜn], *s*. explicación.—**explanatory, explanative** [explǽnatori, explǽnativ], *a*. explicativo.

expletive [éxpletiv]. **I.** *a*. expletivo. **II.** *s*. interjección, reniego; partícula expletiva, o ripio.

explicable [éxplicabœl], *a*. explicable.

explicate [éxplikeit], *va*. y *vn*. explicar.—**explication** [-éishᴜn], *s*. explicación.—**explicative** [-ætiv], **explicatory** [éxplicatori], *a*. explicativo.—**explicator** [-éitœr], *s*. expositor, ilustrador.

explicit [explísit], *a*. explícito.—**explicitly** [-li], *adv*. explícitamente.—**explicitness** [-nes], *s*. calidad de explícito, claridad.

explode [explóud]. **I.** *va*. volar, hacer saltar (una mina); refutar, desbaratar, confundir; expeler con violencia y estrépito. **II.** *vn*. volar, estallar; reventar; desplomarse; (med.) declararse súbitamente.

exploder [-œr], *s*. causa cualquiera de explosión.

exploit [explóit]. **I.** *s*. hazaña, proeza. **II.** *va*. explotar, sacar partido o utilidad de; buscar; referir con pormenores.—**exploitable** [-abœl], *a*. explotable.—**exploitation** [éxploitéishᴜn], *s*. explotación.

exploration [éxploréishᴜn], *s*. exploración.

explorator [éxploréitœr], *s*. explorador.

exploratory [éxplóratori], *a*. exploratorio.

explore [explóær], *va*. explorar; averiguar; examinar, sondear; (min.) catar.

explosion [explóyᴜn], *s*. explosión, voladura.

explosive [explósiv], *a*. y *s*. explosivo, fulminante.—**e. ball**, bala explosiva.—**e. cotton**, algodón pólvora.

explosively [-li], *adv*. con explosión.

explosiveness [-nes], *s*. calidad de explosivo.

exponent [expóunent], *s*. representante; expositor; (mat.) exponente.

exponential [éxponénshal], *a*. (mat.) exponencial.

export [expórt]. **I.** *va*. (com.) exportar. **II.** *s*. exportación.—*pl*. artículos de exportación.

exportable [-abœl], *a*. exportable.

exportation [éxportéiŝhʊn], s. (com.) exportación.
exporter [expórtœr], s. exportador.
expose [expóuŝ], va. exponer, poner en peligro, arriesgar; poner de manifiesto, mostrar, descubrir; publicar, divulgar; revelar, desenmascarar; comprometer; abandonar.
exposé [éxpoŝéi], s. revelación comprometedora o escandalosa.
exposed [expóuŝd], a. descubierto, no abrigado.
exposition [éxpoŝíŝhʊn], s. exposición, exhibición; análisis retórico; desenlace de un drama.
expositive [expóŝitiv], a. expositivo.
expositor [expóŝitœr], s. expositor; comentador.
expository [expóŝitori], a. expositivo, explicativo.
ex post facto [ecs poust fǽcto], ex post facto, tras el hecho; retroactivo.
expostulate [expóschuleit], vn. altercar, contender.—**to e. with**, reconvenir a, debatir con.
expostulation [-léiŝhʊn], s. debate, reconvención, disuasión.—**expostulator** [-leitœr], s. el que reconviene.—**expostulatory** [-latori], a. de reconvención.
exposure [ecspóuŷœr], s. exposición; acción de exponer o exponerse (al aire, agua); (estar expuesto a) la intemperie; revelación, desenmascaramiento; (geol.) afloramiento; (fot.) exposición.
expound [expáund], va. exponer, explicar.
expounder [-œr], s. expositor.
express [exprés]. **I.** va. expresar, manifestar; exprimir, prensar; extraer el jugo; enviar, expedir por expreso. **II.** vr. **to e. one's self,** expresarse, producirse, explicarse. **III.** a. expreso; claro; especial; hecho 'le encargo; llevado por expreso; pronto, rápido, veloz; exacto, parecido, pintiparado. **IV.** s. tren expreso; expreso, servicio de porteo o de transportes de mercancías; mensajero.—**e. company**, compañía de porteo, de expreso.—**e. train,** tren expreso.
expressage [exprésey], s. porte por expreso; lo que se envía por expreso; servicio del expreso.
expressible [exprésibœl], a. decible; expresable; exprimible.—**expressibly** [-bli], adv. de modo expresable o exprimible.
expression [expréŝhʊn], s. expresión; gesto; semblante; vocablo, término, palabra; (b. a.) expresión; (farm.) expresión, zumo.
expressive [-siv], a. expresivo.—**expressively** [-li], adv. expresivamente.—**expressiveness** [-nes], s. significación, expresión, energía.
expressly [exprésli], adv. expresamente; explícitamente.
expressman [-man], s. empresario de expresos o servicio de porteo; repartidor de artículos enviados por dicho servicio; trajinante, ordinario.
expressness [-nes], s. exactitud, claridad.
expropriate [exprópriei̧t], va. enajenar, expropiar.
expropriation [-éiŝhʊn], s. enajenamiento, expropiación.
expugn [expiún], va. (mil.) expugnar.
expugnable [expúgnabœl], a. expugnable.
expulsion [expúlŝhʊn], s. expulsión.
expulsive [-siv], a. expulsivo.
expunge [expúnɣ], va. borrar, cancelar; expurgar, destruir.—**expunction** [expúnkŝhʊn], s. canceladura.
expurgate [éxpurgueit], va. expurgar.
expurgation [-guéiŝhʊn], s. expurgación, expurgo.
expurgator [-guéitœr], s. expurgador.
expurgatory [expérgatori], a. expurgatorio.
exquisite [éxcuiŝit]. **I.** a. exquisito; almibarado, remilgado; intenso, excesivo, agudo.—**e. pain,** dolor agudísimo.—**e. pleasure,** vivo placer. **II.** s. elegante, petimetre.
exquisitely [-li], adv. exquisitamente, primorosamente.—**exquisiteness** [-nes], s. primor, delicadeza, excelencia, perfección.
exsanguine [ecsǽngüin], a. exangüe.
exscind [ecsínd], va. cortar; excluir.
exsect [ecséet], va. (cir.) amputar.

exsection [ecsécŝhʊn], s. (cir.) amputación.
exserted [ecscérted], a. (bot.) exserto.
exsiccant [ecsícant], a. y s. desecativo, desecante.
exsiccate [écsikeit], va. desecar, secar.
exsiccation [-kéiŝhʊn], s. desecación.
exsiccative [ecsíccativ], a. desecativo, desecante.
extant [écstant], a. estante, existente; viviente; conspicuo.
extemporal [extémporæl], **extemporaneous** [extémporéineʊs], extemporary [-œri], a. repentino, improvisado.
extemporaneously [-li], adv. repentinamente, de improviso.
extempore [extémpori o re]. **I.** a. sin estudio previo, improvisado. **II.** adv. de improviso, de repente, in promptu.
extemporize [-aiŝ], va. improvisar, repentizar.
extemporizer [-poraiŝœr], s. improvisador, repentista.
extend [exténd]. **I.** va. extender, tender, alargar; ensanchar, amplificar; prolongar; proyectar; ampliar; ofrecer, conceder, dar o comunicar; explayar, dilatar; prorrogar, diferir. **II.** vn. extenderse; prolongarse, estirarse.—**to e. the arm, the hand,** alargar el brazo, tender la mano. —**to e. the time of payment,** dar prórroga, alargar el plazo.
extended [-ed], a. extenso, prolongado, estirado; diferido; (impr.) tipo abierto.—**extendedly** [-li], adv. prolongadamente.—**extendible** [-ibœl], a. extensible.—**extensibility** [-sibíliti], **extensibleness** [-sibœlnes], s. extensibilidad.—**extensible** [-sibœl], a. extensible.
extension [exténŝhʊn], s. extensión; dilatación, expansión; aumento; prolongación; ensanche; adición, anexo; (com.) prórroga, respiro.—**e. bar,** alargadera (de un compás).—**e. bell,** (elect.) timbre intermedio.—**e. ladder,** escalera de alargar y acortar, o de largueros corredizos.—**e. table,** mesa de extensión, mesa con hojas de quitapón.—**e. tripod,** trípode con piernas de corredera, de alargar y acortar.
extensity [exténsiti], s. extensión; (psíc.) elemento de la sensación relativo al espacio; el espacio como parte de la sensación.
extensive [exténsiv], a. extenso, extensivo, extendido; general.—**extensively** [-li], adv. extensivamente, extensamente; generalmente.—**extensiveness** [-nes], s. extensión; generalidad.
extensometer [extensómetœr], s. extensómetro, medidor de deformaciones (empleado en ensayos de materiales).
extensor [exténsœr], s. (anat.) extensor.
extent [extént], s. extensión; alcance; (for.) ejecución; entredicho, embargo; grado.—**to a certain e.,** hasta cierto punto.—**to a great e.,** en sumo grado, grandemente.—**to the full e.,** en toda su extensión, completamente.
extenuate [extényueit], va. minorar, mitigar, atenuar.—**extenuating** [-ing], a. atenuante.—**extenuation** [-éiŝhʊn], s. atenuación, mitigación.
exterior [extírɪœr]. **I.** a. exterior, externo; visible, manifiesto.—**e. angle,** ángulo externo. **II.** s. lo exterior; aspecto, porte, exterioridad.
exteriority [extiríóriti], s. exterioridad.
exteriorly [extiríœrli], adv. exteriormente.
exterminate [extérminéit], va. exterminar.
extermination [-éiŝhʊn], s. exterminio, extirpación.
exterminator [-éitœr], s. exterminador.
exterminatory [-atori], a. exterminador.
extern(e, s. alumno externo; médico o practicante de un hospital que no habita en el edificio; lo externo.
external [extérnal]. **I.** a. externo, exterior; extranjero, exterior; objetivo.—**e. diameter,** diámetro exterior.—**e. trade,** comercio exterior o extranjero. **II.** s. lo exterior o externo; exterioridad.
externality [éxtœrnéliti], s. exterioridad; percepción externa.
externalize, externalise [extérnalaiŝ], va. ex teriorizar; dar cuerpo o forma.
externally [extérnali], adv. exteriormente, externamente, de fuera.

exterritorial [extérritóriæl], a. extraterritorial.—**exterritoriality** [-toriέliti], s. extraterritorialidad.

extersion [extœ́rshʊn], s. borradura, raspadura.

extinct [extínct], a. extinto; extinguido, apagado; abolido, suprimido.—**to become e.**, extinguirse: apagarse; caducar; morir, desaparecer.

extinction [extíncshʊn], s. extinción.

extinguish [extíngüish], va. extinguir; apagar; sofocar; suprimir, destruir; obscurecer.

extinguishable [-abœl], a. extinguible; apagable.

extinguisher [-œr], s. apagador; matacandelas.

extinguishment [-mœnt], s. extinción; apagamiento; abolición, aniquilamiento; terminación; amortización.

extirpable [extœ́rpabœl], a. extirpable.

extirpate [éxtœrpeit], va. extirpar.

extirpation [-péishʊn], s. extirpación; (cir.) excisión, extirpación.—**extirpator** [-péitœr], s. extirpador, arrancador.

extol [extól], va. ensalzar, enaltecer.

extort [extórt], I. va. sacar u obtener por fuerza; arrancar, arrebatar; exigir dinero sin derecho. II. vn. cometer extorsión, exacción o concusión.

extortion [extórshʊn], s. extorsión; exacción, concusión; gabela injusta.

extortionary [-eri], a. que implica extorsión, exacción o concusión.

extortionate [-eit], a. opresivo, injusto, gravoso.

extortioner [-œr], **extortionist** [-ist], s. opresor, concusionario.

extra [extræ]. I. a. extraordinario; adicional, de más; de repuesto.—**e. hand**, empleado supernumerario.—**e. pay, e. work**, paga, trabajo por extraordinarios. II. s. exceso; recargo, sobreprecio; gasto extraordinario; suplemento o alcance de un diario.

extract [extrǽct], va. extraer, sacar (una muela, etc.); escoger (pasajes) y citar; (quím.) extraer; tratar para extraer por disolución; (mat.) extraer (una raíz).

extract [éxtrǽct], s. extracto, excerta, resumen; cita; (quím.) extracto.

extractable, extractible [extrǽcta- (o i) bœl], a. que se puede extraer.

extraction [éxtrǽcshʊn], s. extracción; origen, descendencia; (quím.) extracción.

extractive [-tiv]. I. a. que sirve para extraer o extractar. II. s. lo que puede extraerse o extractarse; (quím.) parte insoluble de un extracto.

extractor [-tœr], s. extractor, extractador; (cir.) fórceps; sacabalas; (arti.) sacatrapos; extractor de cartuchos.

extradite [éxtradait], va. entregar por extradición.

extradition [éxtradíshʊn], s. extradición.

extrados [extrédos], s. (arq.) trasdós.

extrafoliaceous [éxtrafóliéishʊs], a. extrafoliáceo.

extrajudicial [-yudíshal], a. extrajudicial.

extrajudicially [-i], adv. extrajudicialmente.

extramundane [-múnden], a. extramundano.

extramural [-miúral], a. extramuros.

extraneous [extréinius], a. extraño.

extraordinarily [extrórdinerili], adv. extraordinariamente.—**extraordinariness** [-nes], s. singularidad, rareza.—**extraordinary** [-ri]. I. a. extraordinario; especial. II. s. cualquier cosa extraordinaria.

extraprofessional [-proféshʊnal], a. fuera de la profesión, ajeno a la profesión.

extraterritorial [-térritóriæl], **extraterritoriality** [-térritoriǽliti] = EXTERRITORIAL, EXTERRITORIALITY.

extra-uterine [-iúterin], a. extrauterino.

extravagance, extravagancy [extrǽvagans, i], s. lujo desmedido, profusión, derroche; extravagancia; disparate, locura, desbarro.—**extravagant** (-ant), a. extravagante, estrafalario; exorbitante; disparatado; pródigo, manirroto, gastador.—pl. (igl.) extravagantes.—**extravagantly** [-li], adv. extravagantemente; pródigamente, profusamente; estrafalariamente.—**extravagantness** [-nes], s. extravagancia, desarreglo, exceso.

extravaganza [extrǽvagǽnša], s. composición extravagante y fantástica.

extravasate [extrǽvaset]. I. va. y vn. (med.) extravasarse, trasvenarse. II. a. extravasado.

extravasation [-éishʊn], s. extravasación.

extreme [extrím]. I. a. extremo, extremado, último, postrero; riguroso, estricto, severo. II. s. extremo, extremidad, ápice; fin, cabo.—**in the e.**, en o con extremo, en sumo grado.—**to go to extremes**, tomar medidas extremas; exagerar.

extremely_[extrímli], adv. extremamente, sumamente.

extremism [-iśm], s. radicalismo.

extremist [-ist], s. radical.

extremity [extrémiti], s. extremidad; agudeza, rigor; necesidad, apuro.—pl. medidas extremas; (zool.) extremidades.

extricable [éxtricabœl], a. que se puede desenredar.

extricate [-ket], va. desenredar, desembrollar; sacar (de una dificultad).

extrication [-kéishʊn], s. desembarazo, desenredo.

extrinsic(al [extrínsic(al], a. extrínseco.

extrinsically [-i], adv. extrínsecamente.

extrude [extrúd], va. forzar hacia fuera; echar, arrojar; (met.) estirar por presión.—**extruded metal**, metal estirado por presión (forzado por orificios mediante presión hidráulica).

extrusion [extrúyʊn], s. expulsión; (metal.) estiramiento por presión; (geol.) efusión de lava por grietas de rocas.—**e. process**, (metal.) procedimiento de estirar por presión.

exuberance, exuberancy [exiúbœrans, i], s. exuberancia.—**exuberant** [-ant], a. exuberante.—**exuberantly** [-li], adv. abundantemente.

exudation [éxiudéishʊn], s. exudación.

exude [exiúd], vn. exudar, transpirar; rezumarse, revenirse.

exult [egšúlt], vn. regocijarse, alegrarse.

exultant [-ant], a. triunfante, regocijado, alborozado.

exultation, exultance, exultancy [égšʊltéishun, egšúltans, i], s. triunfo; exregocijo, exultación, transporte.

exultingly [egšúltingli], adv. con exultación.

exutory [egšýutori], s. (med.) exutorio.

exuviæ [exyúvii], s. pl. despojos de los animales, (geol.) fósiles.

exuviate [exyúviet], va. mudar, echar, soltar (las plumas, la piel, los cuernos, etc.).

exuviation [exyuviéshʊn], s. la muda (de aves, crustáceos, etc.).

eyas [áias], s. halcón niego.

eye [ai], s. ojo (de la cara, del queso, de aguja, de hacha, de armella, etc.); argolla; vista; aspecto, talante; juicio, discernimiento; concepto, opinión; orificio de observación (de un horno); vigilancia; (cost.) corcheta; (arq.) ojo de cúpula (abertura circular en la parte superior); (bot.) yema o botón.—**e.-minded**, (psic.) en que predominan las imágenes visuales como elementos de la memoria y otros fenómenos mentales.—**e. of a stay**, ojo de un estay.—**e. of the anchor**, (mar.) ojo del ancla.—**e. opener**, todo lo que hace abrir los ojos, literal o figuradamente; cuento maravilloso, noticia increíble o inesperada; (fam.) copa de licor, trago.—**e. shade**, visera, guardavista.—**e.-splice**, (mar.) gaza.—**e. tube**, (opt.) tubo del ocular.—**before one's eyes**, a la vista, en presencia de uno.—**half an e.**, ojeada, vistazo.—**in the twinkling of an e.**, en un abrir y cerrar de ojos.—**the e. of day, of heaven, o of the morning**, el sol.—**to have a cast in the eye**, ser ligeramente bisojo, tener tendencia al estrabismo.—**to have in one's e.**, intentar, proponerse.—**to have one's e. on**, haberle echado el ojo a.—**to keep an e. on**, vigilar.—**with an e. to**, con la intención de, pensando en.

eye, va. mirar de hito en hito, clavar la mirada a; hacer ojos o agujeros a.

eyeball [áiból], s. globo del ojo.

eyebar [-bár], s. barra de ojo (con un ojo en cada extremo).

eyebolt [-bóult], s. perno de ojo; armella roscada; (mar.) cáncamo.

eyebright [-bráit], s. (bot.) eufrasia.

eyebrow [-bráu], s. ceja.

eyecup [-cúp], s. ojera, copilla para los ojos.

eyeflap [-flǽp], s. anteojera.

eyeglance [-gláens], s. ojeada, vistazo.

eyeglass [-glǽs], s. (ópt.) ocular.

eyeglasses [-glǽses], pl. lentes, quevedos.

eyehole [-jóul], s. (cost.) ojete; atisbadero.

eyelash [-lǽsh], s. pestaña.

eyeless [-les], a. ciego; sin ojos.

eyelet [-let], s. resquicio, abertura; (cost.) ojete; (mar.) ollao.

eyeleteer [ailetíær], s. punzón para abrir ojetes.

eyelid [áilid], s. párpado, palpebra.

eyepiece [áipis], s. (ópt.) ocular.

eyesalve [-sav], s. colirio para los ojos.

eyeservant [-sǽrvænt], s. criado que sólo trabaja cuando lo vigilan.

eyeshot [-shót], s. alcance de la mirada.

eyesight [áisait], s. vista; alcance de la vista.

eyesore [áisoær], s. mal de ojos; cosa que ofende la vista.

eyestone [-stóun], s. opérculo empleado para sacar del ojo objetos extraños menudos.

eyestring [-stríng], tendón del ojo.

eyetooth [-túz], s. colmillo.

eyewater [-uótœr], s. colirio, loción para los ojos.

eyewink [-uínk], s. guiñada.

eyewitness [-uítnes], s. testigo ocular.

eyre [éær], s. (anat.) vuelta, circuito.

eyry [éæri], s. nido de ave de rapiña.

F

f [ef], s. f; (F, mús.) fa.

fa [fa] s. (mús.) fa.

faba [féiba o faba], s. (bot.) haba.

fable [féibœl]. I. s. fábula; argumento de un poema o drama. II. va. y vn. fingir, mentir, inventar o contar fábulas.

fabric [fǽbric], s. tejido, tela, género, paño; fábrica, obra, edificio; manufactura; textura.

fabricate [fǽbrikeit], va. fabricar; construir, hacer (apl. esp. a la fabricación en serie o en grande escala de piezas normalizadas inter-cambiables, y a la construcción—de buques, edificios, máquinas, etc.—con dichas piezas); inventar (una mentira).

fabrication [-kéishun], s. fabricación; edificio; obra; mentira, fábula.

fabricator [-kéitœr], s. fabricador; embustero.

fabrikoid [fǽbricoid], fabricoide (nombre de fábrica), imitación de cuero hecha de tela revestida de una disolución de piroxilina.

fabulist [fǽbiulist], s. fabulista.—fabulize, fabulise [-laiŝ], va. decir o narrar como fábula.— fabulous [-lus], a. fabuloso, ficticio.—fabulously [-li], adv. fabulosamente.—fabulousness [-nes], s. fabulosidad.

façade [fasád], s. (arq.) fachada, frontispicio, portada, frente.

face [fes], s. cara; lado; haz, superficie; facie (de un cristal); fachada, frontis; frente (mil., constr.); aspecto, cariz; muestra (de reloj); conocimiento inmediato, vista; descaro, desfachatez; mueca, gesto; (com.) valor neto; (impr.) ojo de la letra; (mec.) cabeza (de un diente de rueda); superficie de trabajo o de contacto (de la válvula de corredera); ancho (de una polea); cotillo (de un martillo); (ing.) paramento (de un muro); fondo, frente, cara de trabajo (de galería, túnel, socavón, etc.).—f. ache, f. ague, neuralgia facial.—f. angle, (geom.) cara (de un ángulo poliedro).— f. card, figura (en la baraja).—f. cloth, sudario. —f. cog, diente lateral (de una rueda).—f. guard, careta, carilla, máscara.—f. joint, junta super-ficial o de paramento.—f. lathe, torno de plato.— f. to f., cara a cara.—f. value, significado literal o al pie de la letra; (com.) valor nominal.—f. wheel,

rueda de dientes laterales.—to fly in the f. of, ir contra viento y marea, nadar contra la corriente.— to one's f., en la cara de uno, en su presencia.— face. I. va. volverse o mirar hacia; hacer frente a, arrostrar; pulir, revestir, cubrir, forrar; (tec.) labrar, acabar, alisar.—to f. it out, hacer frente a todo, no cejar.—to f. out, persistir en o sostener descaradamente.—to f. the music, (fam.) hacer frente a las consecuencias.—to f. with, carear con. II. vn. volver la cara; dar, mirar (a, hacia).—to f. about, voltear la cara; cambiar de frente.

faceplate [féispleit], s. placa de revestimiento o de protección; plato o disco (de torno).

facer [fésœr], s. puñetazo dado en la cara; per-cance o revés.

facet [fǽset]. I. va. (joy.) labrar facetas. II. s. faceta; (arq.) filete de las estrías de una co-lumna; (ento.) faceta del ojo de un insecto.

faceted [fǽseted], pp. y a. labrado en facetas.

facetious [fasíŝhus], a. salado, chistoso, gracioso.

facetiously [-li], adv. chistosamente.

facetiousness [-nes], s. sal, chiste, gracia.

facial [féshial o fásial], a. facial.—f. angle, ángulo facial.

facile [fǽsil], a. fácil; obediente, dócil; vivo, listo; accesible, afable.

facilitate [fasíliteit], va. facilitar.—facilitation [-éishun], s. facilitación.

facility [fasíliti], s. facilidad; destreza; docili-dad; afabilidad.

facing [féising], s. paramento; revestimiento; (cost.) vueltas; cubierta; cara; encaramiento.

fac-simile [fac-símili], a. y s. facsímile.

fact [fæct], s. hecho; realidad.—in f., en reali-dad; de hecho.—in the very f., en el mero hecho.

faction [fǽcshun], s. facción, bando; alboroto, tumulto.—factional [-al], a. faccionario.—fac-tionist [-ist], s. faccioso.—factious [fǽcshus], a. faccioso, sedicioso, revoltoso.—factiously [-li], adv. sediciosamente.—factiousness [-nes], s. espíritu de partido o facción.

factitious [fæctíŝhus], a. facticio; artificial.

factor [fǽctor]. I. s. elemento, factor; agente comisionado; (mat.) factor; coeficiente.—f. of safety, coeficiente de seguridad. II. va. (mat.) descomponer en factores.

factorage [fǽctorey], s. (com.) comisión; fac-toraje.

factorial [fæctóriæl], s. (mat.) factorial, pro-ducto de todos los números enteros desde 1 hasta el número de que se trata (f. n, factorial n).

factoring [fǽctoring], s. (mat.) descomposición en factores, factorización.

factorize [fǽctoraiŝ], va. (mat.) descomponer en factores.—factorization, [-iŝéiŝhun], s. descom-posición en factores, factorización.

factorship [fǽctorŝhip], s. agencia, factoría.

factory [fǽctori], s. fábrica, taller, factoría.

factotum [fæctótum], s. factótum.

facula [fǽkiula], s. (astr.) fácula.

facultative [fǽcultetiv], a. facultativo; (for.) potestativo.

faculty [fǽculti], s. facultad, aptitud; facultad, cuerpo de doctores o maestros de una ciencia; cuerpo de profesores.

fad [fæd], s. novedad, moda; manía, chifladura.

fade [féid]. I. va. marchitar, poner pálido, desco-lorar; debilitar, desmejorar. II. vn. palidecer, descolorarse; decaer, marchitarse.—to f. in (out), hacer aparecer (desaparecer) gradualmente (una imágen cinematográfica).—to f. away, des-vanecerse, desaparecer.

fadeless [-les], a. que no palidece o se descolora.

fady [féidi], a. que decae o se marchita.

fæcal, fæces, fæcula, V. FECAL, FECES, etc.

faerie, faery [féœri], a. (ant.) V. FAIRY.

fag [fæg]. I. va. fatigar, cansar; hacer trotar o trabajar a uno. II. vn. desfallecer de cansancio; trabajar como un galopín. III. s. esclavo, galopín, marmitón, ganapán.—f.-end, cadillos, pestañas; sobra o desperdicio; (mar.) cordón.

fagot [fǽgot]. **I.** *s.* haz, manojo, gavilla de leña; (fort.) fajina; haz de barras de hierro o acero (120 libras de peso); tormento de ser quemado vivo; montón de pescado para curarlo; vieja, bruja. **II.** *va.* liar, hacer líos o haces; recoger, recaudar.

Fahrenheit [fárenjait], *a.* Fahrenheit (grados, temperatura).

faience [fayáns], *s.* loza fina.

fail [féil]. **I.** *va.* abandonar, dejar; frustrar, engañar, chasquear. **II.** *vn.* faltar, fallar, inutilizarse, romperse, ceder; frustrarse, malograrse; consumirse, acabarse, desvanecerse, decaer, menguar; (com.) quebrar, hacer bancarrota; salir mal (en examen, etc.)—**not to f.**, no dejar de. **III.** *s.* falta; defecto; fracaso.—**without f.**, sin falta.

failing [féiling], *s.* falta, desliz; defecto, flaqueza; decadencia, malogro.

failure [féiliuær], *s.* fracaso, fiasco, malogro; falta, culpa, omisión, descuido, desliz; (com.) quiebra, bancarrota.—**f. of issue**, (for.) no dejar prole.

fain [féin]. **I.** *a.* dispuesto, conforme, resignado; contento. **II.** *adv.* gustosamente, de buena gana.

faint [féin]. **I.** *vn.* desmayarse; desfallecer; desalentarse; descaecer, desvanecerse. **II.** *a.* lánguido, abatido, tímido; indistinto, tenue; débil, desfallecido.—**to be f. with**, morirse de, estar muerto de (hambre).—**f.-hearted**, medroso, pusilánime, apocado.—**f.-heartedly**, medrosamente.—**f.-heartedness**, miedo, pusilanimidad.

faint, fainting [féinting], *s.* deliquio, desmayo; desfallecimiento.—**f. fit**, o **spell**, síncope, desmayo; (med.) lipotimia.

faintish [féintiŝh], *a.* desfalleciente.

faintishness [féintiŝhnes], *s.* desfallecimiento.

faintly [féintli], *adv.* desmayadamente, débilmente; tenuemente, indistintamente.

faintness [féintnes], *s.* falta de claridad; languidez, desaliento; timidez.

faints, *s. pl.* productos impuros y débiles del fin de la destilación.

fair [féær]. **I.** *a.* claro, despejado; limpio, terso; inmaculado; bonancible, favorable, próspero; rubio (es el sentido en que se toma gen. cuando se habla del aspecto de una persona); hermoso, perfecto, bello; recto, justo; imparcial; honrado, razonable, franco, cortés, liberal; corriente, regular, mediano, pasable, ordinario; bien formado; distinto; legible.— **f. and square**, honrado a carta cabal.—**f. complexion**, tez blanca (gen. se entiende además pelo rubio).—**f. name**, nombre honrado, sin tacha.—**f. play**, proceder leal, juego limpio.—**f. sex**, bello sexo.—**f. to middling**, bastante bueno.—**f. trade**, comercio internacional fundado en la reciprocidad; comercio legítimo.—**f. weather**, buen tiempo.—**f.-weather friend**, amigo en la prosperidad.—**f. wind**, viento favorable.—**by f. means**, por medios rectos, honrados.—**to be in a f. way to succeed**, estar en buen camino de prosperar.—**to give a f. hearing**, oír, escuchar con imparcialidad.—**to give f. warning**, prevenir, advertir, avisar de antemano.—**to make a f. copy**, poner en limpio. **II.** *adv.* justamente, honradamente; claramente, perfectamente, exactamente; bondadosamente, bien.—**f.-complexioned**, de tez blanca.—**f.-haired**, de cabellos blondos o rubios.—**f.-minded**, imparcial, justo. **III.** *s.* mercado; exposición regional; (poét.) niña hermosa.

fairing [féæring], *s.* ferias, agasajos.

fairly [féærli], *adv.* imparcialmente; bastante, regularmente; justamente; honradamente; totalmente, cabalmente; claramente; favorablemente; primorosamente, bellamente.

fairness [-nes], *s.* hermosura, belleza; honradez, candor; justicia, equidad.

fairway [féæruéi], *s.* (mar.) canalizo.

fairy [féæri]. **I.** *s.* hada, duende, trasgo. **II.** *a.* de duendes, de hadas.—**f. tale**, cuento de hadas.

fairyland [-lǽnd], *s.* tierra de las hadas.

fairylike [-laic], *a.* como hada.

faith [féiz]. **I.** *s.* fe; fidelidad, lealtad.—**f. cure**, curación por fe.—**in f.**, a la verdad.—**in good f.**, de buena fe.—**to break f. with**, faltar a la palabra

dada a.—**upon my f.**, a fe mía. **II.** *interj.* en verdad.

faithful [-ful], *a.* fiel; leal; exacto, puntual; justo, resto; veraz.—**faithfully** [-i], *adv.* fielmente, firmemente; puntualmente.—**faithfulness** [-nes], *s.* fidelidad, honradez; exactitud.—**faithless** [féizles], *a.* infiel, sin fe; pérfido, fementido.—**faithlessness** [-nes], *s.* infidelidad, deslealtad, perfidia.

fake [fek]. **I.** *s.* (mar.) aduja de cable; (fam.) patraña, farsa. **II.** *va.* y *vn.* adujar, enroscar; (fam.) chalanear; fingir, inventar; hurtar.

faker [féikær], *s.* farsante; buhonero.

fakir [fækíær], *s.* faquir; (fam.) buhonero.

falcate(d [fælkeit(ed], *a.* falcado, encorvado.

falcation [-éiŝhun], *s.* encorvadura.

falchion [fólchun], *s.* cimitarra, falce.

falciform [fǽlsiform], *a.* en forma de hoz.

falcon [fócun o fǽlcon], *s.* (orn.) halcón; (arti.) falcón.

falconer [fócunœr], *s.* halconero, cetrero.

falconet [fócnet], *s.* (arti.) falconete.

falconry [fócœnri], *s.* halconería, cetrería.

faldstool [fóldstul], *s.* facistol, atril; faldistorio; silla de tijera.

fall [fol], *vn.* (*pret.* FELL; *pp.* FALLEN) caer, caerse; bajar, menguar, decrecer, disminuir; descaer; renegar, apostatar; ceder, rendirse, entregarse; tocarle o corresponderle a uno; empezar, emprender, echar a.—**to f. aboard**, (mar.) abordar.—**to f. afoul of**, reñir con; (mar.) chocar con.—**to f. asleep**, dormirse.—**to f. a prey to**, ser presa o víctima de.—**to f. away**, enflaquecer; marchitarse; apostatar.—**to f. back**, retroceder, retirarse; retractarse.—**to f. back on**, o **upon**, recurrir a, echar mano de; (mil.) replegarse hacia. —**to f. backward**, caer de espaldas.—**to f. behind**, rezagarse.—**to f. down**, prosternarse, postrarse; caerse.—**to f. due**, (com.) vencerse.— **to f. flat**, caer tendido, caer cuan largo es; no surtir efecto; tener mal éxito.—**to f. from**, abandonar; faltar a; violar.—**to f. in**, caer dentro; desplomarse; ponerse en su lugar, alinearse; expirar, terminar, caducar.—**to f. in line**, formar cola; seguir la corriente; adherirse.—**to f. in love**, enamorarse.—**to f. in with**, encontrarse con; convenir, estar de acuerdo con.—**to f. off**, caer, desprenderse; extrañarse, disgustarse; menguar, disminuir; decaer; (mar.) abatir.—**to f. on**, asaltar, echarse sobre; empezar, emprender; echar mano de, recurrir a; encontrar, descubrir.—**to f. on one's feet**, caer de pie; salir del vado.—**to f. out**, reñir, querellar; suceder.—**to f. over**, desertar; caer.—**to f. short**, faltar; ser deficiente; malograrse; errar (el tiro).—**to f. sick**, enfermar.— **to f. through**, abortar, fracasar.—**to f. to**, principiar a, echar a; tirarse sobre; empezar; cerrarse.—**to f. to one's lot**, o **share**, caber o caer en suerte a uno, tocarle a uno.—**to f. under**, caer debajo; incurrir en, estar sujeto a; ser del número de; estar comprendido en.—**to f. upon**, to F. ON; incumbir a, recaer en.—**to f. within**, estar dentro de, pertenecer a.

fall. **I.** *s.* caída, bajada, descenso; lapso, desliz; salto de agua, cascada, catarata; otoño; decadencia, degradación; caída, desnivel; desembocadura de un río; (com.) baja o disminución de precio; pérdida en los fondos públicos; (mar.) tira de aparejo; (mús.) cadencia; bajada de tono, disminución del sonido. **II.** *a.* otoñal.—**f. wheat**, trigo sembrado en el otoño.—**f. overcoat**, sobretodo de medio tiempo.

fallacious [fæléŝhus], *a.* sofístico, ilógico; engañoso, delusorio.—**fallaciously** [-li], *adv.* falazmente; sofísticamente.—**fallaciousness** [-nes], *s.* falacia; sofisma.

fallacy [fǽlasi], *s.* falacia; sofisma.

fallen [fólun], *pp.* de TO FALL; caído.

fallibility [fælibíliti], *s.* falibilidad.

fallible [fǽlibœl], *a.* falible.

fallibly [fǽlibli], *adv.* faliblemente.

falling [fóling], *pa.* de TO FALL y *s.* caída; baja, diminución; cayente, que cae; (med.) prolapso. —**f.-bodies** (fís.) caída de los cuerpos (parte de la fís.).—**f. off**, caída, decadencia, disminución.—**f. sickness**, o **evil**, epilepsia.—**f. star**, exhalación, estrella fugaz.

fallow [fǽlo]. **I.** *a.* flavo, leonado; (agr.) barbechado; descuidado, abandonado.—**f. deer,** corzo.—**f. finch,** (orn.) triguero. **II.** *s.* barbecho, tierra que descansa.—**to let lie f.,** dejar en barbecho. **III.** *va.* barbechar; desmontar.

fallowing [fǽloing], *s.* barbechera.

fallowness [fǽlones], *s.* (agr.) esterilidad.

false [fols]. **I.** *a.* falso; postizo; de imitación; provisional, temporáneo; de refuerzo; de protección; (biol.) cuasi, seudo; (mús.) desafinado, falso, discordante.—**f. claim,** pretensión infundada.—**f. colors,** bandera falsa.—**f. door,** puerta simulada.—**f. floor,** subpiso.—**f.-heartedness,** perfidia.—**f. imprisonment,** prisión o detención ilegal.—**f. pretenses,** dolo.—**f. window,** ventana simulada. **II.** *adv.* falsamente; pérfidamente.—**f.-faced,** hipócrita, falso.—**f.-hearted,** pérfido.

falsehood [fólsjud], *s.* falsedad.—**falsely** [-li], *adv.* falsamente.—**falseness** [-nes], *s.* perfidia, falsedad.

falsetto [folséto], *s.* (mús.) falsete.

falsidical [folsídicœl], *a.* (psic.) ilusorio, enteramente imaginario.

falsifiable [folsifáiabœl], *a.* falsificable.

falsification [fólsifikéishʊn], *s.* falsificación; confutación.—**falsifier** [-faicœr], **falsificator** [-fikéitœr], *s.* falsificador; falsario.

falsify [fólsifai]. **I.** *va.* falsificar, adulterar; refutar, desmentir. **II.** *vn.* mentir.

falsity [fólsiti], *s.* falsedad, mentira.

falter [fóltœr]. **I.** *va.* balbucear. **II.** *vn.* vacilar; tartamudear. **III.** *s.* vacilación, temblor.

fame [féim]. **I.** *s.* fama. **II.** *va.* afamar; celebrar.

famed [féimd], *a.* afamado, famoso.

familiar [famílîar]. **I.** *a.* familiar, íntimo; muy conocido; confianzudo.—**f. with,** acostumbrado a; versado o ducho en, conocedor de. **II.** *s.* amigo íntimo; demonio familiar; (igl.) familiar.

familiarity [-liériti], *s.* familiaridad, confianza; (con *with*) conocimiento (de).

familiarize [-liaraiŝ], *va.* familiarizar, acostumbrar.

familiarly [-liarli], *adv.* familiarmente, amistosamente, íntimamente.

family [fǽmili]. **I.** *s.* familia; linaje, sangre, raza; (biol.) familia. **II.** *a.* familiar, casero, de la familia.—**f. man,** padre de familia.—**f. tree,** árbol genealógico.—**in the f. way,** (fam.) encinta, embarazada.

famine [fǽmin], *s.* hambre, carestía.

famish [fǽmish], *va.* y *vn.* hambrear; matar o morirse de hambre.

famous [féimʊs], *a.* famoso.—**famously** [-li], *adv.* famosamente; (fam.) admirablemente, a las mil maravillas.

famulus [fámiulʊs], *s.* fámulo.

fan [fæn]. **I.** *s.* abanico; ventalle; (agr.) aventador, bieldo; (mec.) ventilador, volante de molino de viento; aficionado.—**f. blower,** ventilador.—**f. light,** o **window,** (arq.) abanico.—**f. palm,** (bot.) miraguano.—**f.-shaped,** en forma de abanico.—**f. sticks,** varillas de aban'co.—**f. wheel,** ventilador. **II.** *va.* abanicar; ventilar; soplar; (agr.) aventar, aechar.

fanatic [fanǽtic], *a.* fanático.—**fanatic(al** [-(al], *a.* fanático.—**fanatically** [-li], *adv.* fanáticamente.—**fanaticism** [-siŝm], *s.* fanatismo.

fancied [fǽnsid], *a.* imaginario.

fancier [fǽnsiœr], *s.* criador y vendedor de aves y animales; aficionado; visionario.

fanciful [fǽnsiful], *a.* imaginativo, caprichoso; fantástico.—**fancifully** [[-li], *adv.* caprichosamente—**fancifulness** [-nes], *s.* antojo, capricho.

fancy [fǽnsi]. **I.** *s.* fantasía, imaginación, antojo, capricho; imagen, idea; afición, afecto, amor, gusto.—**f.-free,** libre del poder del amor.—**to take a f. to,** aficionarse a; antojarse de; coger cariño a. **II.** *a.* fantástico, imaginario; de fantasía; de ornato; bello, elegante; (com.) de capricho, de gusto.—**f.-dress ball,** baile de trajes, (Méj.) jamaica.—**f. dress,** disfraz, traje de capricho.—**f. goods,** objetos o artículos de fantasía.—**f. woods,** maderas preciosas. **III.** *va.* imaginar, suponer; gustar o encapricharse de, aficionarse a; antojarse, figurarse, fantasear. **IV.** *vn.* tener un antojo o capricho.

fancywork [-uœrk], *s.* labor.

fane [féin], *s.* templo, santuario.

fanfare [fǽnfœr], *s.* son de trompetas; procesión o parada ruidosa; encuadernación vistosa.

fanfaron [fǽnfarón], *s.* fanfarrón.—**fanfaronade** [-éld]. **I.** *s.* fanfarronada. **II.** *vn.* fanfarronear.

fang [fǽng], *s.* colmillo (de un animal); raíz o patas de un diente.—**fanged** [-d], *a.* que tiene colmillos.

fangle [fǽngœl], *s.* novedad trivial.

fangless [-les], *a.* sin colmillos.

fanion [fǽniʊn], *s.* banderola.

fanlight [fǽnlait], *s. V.* FAN WINDOW.

fanlike [fǽnlaik], *a.* en forma de abanico.

fanner [fǽnœr], *s.* ventilador.

fantail [fǽnteil], *s.* variedad de paloma de cola de abanico; (carp.) cola de milano.—**f. burner,** mechero de mariposa.

fantailed [fǽntéild], *a.* de cola en forma de abanico.

fantasia [fantasía o fantǽsia], *s.* (mús.) fantasía.

fantasm [fǽntæŝm], *s.* fantasma.

fantastic(al [fæntǽstic(al]. **I.** *a.* fantástico, grotesco; caprichoso, caprichudo; ilusorio, imaginario. **II.** *s.* persona estrambótica.—**fantastically** [-li], *adv.* fantásticamente.—**fantasticalness** [-nes], *s.* fantasía, capricho.

fantasy [fǽntasi], *s.* fantasía; dibujo fantástico; (mús.) fantasía.

fantom, *s. V.* PHANTOM.

far [far]. **I.** *adv.* lejos; a lo lejos, en lontananza; en alto grado, muy, mucho.—**f. and wide,** por todas partes.—**f. away,** *adv.* muy lejos.—**f.-away,** *a.* lejano, alejado; abstraído, distraído.—**f. be it from me,** lejos de mí, no permita Dios.—**f.-fetched,** forzado, traído por los cabellos.—**f. from,** lejos ni con mucho.—**f. off,** a gran distancia, en lontananza, a lo lejos.—**f.-reaching,** de mucho alcance, trascendente.—**as f. as,** so **f. as,** hasta; hasta donde, en cuanto a, según, que (*as far as I know,* según lo que sé, que yo sepa; *as far as I am concerned,* en cuanto a mí toca).—**by f.,** con mucho.—**in so f. as,** en cuanto a.—**so f., thus f.,** hasta ahora; hasta aquí; hasta ahí. **II.** *a.* lejano, distante, remoto; de grande alcance.—**a f. cry,** una gran distancia (sentidos recto y figurado); gran diferencia (*it is a far cry,* hay gran distancia o diferencia).

farad [fǽræd], *s.* (elec.) faradio.

faradic [farédic], *a.* (elec.) farádico.

faradism [-iŝm], *s.* electricidad por inducción.

faradization [fǽradiŝéishʊn], *s.* (med.) faradización, aplicación de una corriente farádica.

farce [fars]. **I.** *va.* rellenar, embutir; (teat.) meter morcilla. **II.** *s.* entremés, sainete; enredo, tramoya; (coc.) relleno de carne.

farcical [fársical], *a.* entremesado, burlesco, ridículo, bufo.—**farcically** [-i], *adv.* ridículamente.

farcing [fársing], *s.* embutido, relleno.

farcy [fársi], *s.* (vet.) muermo.

fare [féœr]. **I.** *vn.* pasarlo, irle a uno (bien o mal); vivir (bien o mal); ir, viajar. **II.** pasaje (precio); pasajero; comida, comidas.

farewell [-uel]. **I.** *interj.* adiós. **II.** *a.* de despedida. **III.** *s.* despedida, adiós.—**to bid f. to, to take f. of,** despedirse de.

farina [færínæ], *s.* harina de cereales (esp. de maíz); fécula, almidón; (zool.) polvo harinoso.—**farinaceous** [færinéishʊs], *a.* farináceo; harinoso.—**farinose** [-nous], *a.* farináceo; cubierto de polvo harinoso.

farm [farm]. **I.** *s.* granja, labranza, hacienda; (hist.) contribución; terreno agrícola; distrito de contribuciones.—**f. hand,** peón de granja.—**f. produce,** o **products,** productos agrícolas o de campo. **II.** *va.* cultivar, labrar la tierra; arrendar, tomar en arriendo.—**to f. out,** dar en arrendamiento.

farmer [fármœr]. **I.** *s.* labrador; agricultor, hacendado. **II.** *a.* agrícola.

farmhouse [-jáus], *s.* alquería.

farming [-ing]. **I.** *s.* cultivo, labranza; agricultura. **II.** *a.* agrícola; de labranza.

farmstead [-sted], *s.* alquería y sus dependencias.

farmyard [-yard], *s.* corral de una granja.

farness [fárnes], *s.* distancia.

faro [féro o fáro], *s.* faraón o golfo (juego de naipes).

farrago [færrégo], *s.* fárrago, broza.

farrier [færiœr], *s.* herrador; mariscal, albéitar. **—f.'s parer,** pujavante.

farriery [færiœri], *s.* albeitería.

farrow [féro]. **I.** *s.* lechón; lechigada de puercos. **II.** *a.* horra; machorra. **III.** *va.* parir (apl. a la puerca).

farseeing [fársiing], *a.* que ve a gran distancia; previsor, precavido.

farsighted [-sáited], *a.* présbite; presciente, perspicaz.

farther [fárpœr]. **I.** *adv.* más lejos, a mayor distancia; más adelante; además de, demás de, ulteriormente.**—f. on,** adelante. **II.** *a.* más lejano; ulterior, más alejado.

farthermost [fárpœrmoust], **farthest** [fárpest], **I.** *adv.* más lejos (*super.*). **II.** *a.* más lejano (*super.*).

farthing [fárping], *s.* cuarto de penique; ardite, blanca.

farthingale [-gueil], *s.* verdugado, guardainfante.

fasces [fésis], *s. pl.* fasces.

fascia [féshia], *s.* (anat.) aponeurosis; (arq.) faja, imposta; (astr.) faja alrededor de un planeta.

fascial [féshial], *a.* (anat.) fascial.

fasciate(d [féshiet(ed], *a.* fajado, vendado.

fasciation [fæshiéshun], *s.* vendaje.

fascicle [fésicœl], *s.* racimo, manojo; hacecillo; entrega de una publicación.

fascicular [fæsíkiular], *a.* fascicular.

fascinate [fésineit], *va.* fascinar.**—fascination** [-éishun], *s.* fascinación.

fascine [fasín], *s.* (fort.) fajina; haz.

Fascism [fésism], *s.* fascismo.**—Fascist** [-ist], *s.* y *a.* fascista.

fashion [féshun]. **I.** *s.* moda, estilo; elegancia, buen tono; forma, figura, hechura; modo, manera; gente de buen tono, alta sociedad.— **f. plate,** figurín, ilustración (grabado) de modas.— **after a f.,** hasta cierto punto, en cierto modo; así así.**—in f.,** de moda.**—out of f.,** fuera de moda, de moda vieja, pasado. **II.** *va.* formar; adaptar; idear, inventar.

fashionable [-abœl]. **I.** *a.* ajustado a la moda; de moda; elegante, de buen tono. **II.** *s.* lechuguino, currutaco.**—fashionableness** [-nes], *s.* gentileza, elegancia, buen tono.**—fashionably** [-bli], *adv.* a la moda.

fast [fast]. **I.** *vn.* ayunar. **II.** *s.* ayuno; lazo, amarra, cable.**—to break one's f.,** romper el ayuno. **III.** *a.* firme, seguro, fuerte; fijo, inmoble, estable; apretado; invariable; constante, fiel; indeleble, duradero; profundo (sueño); veloz, rápido; adelantado (reloj); gastador, pródigo; disoluto.**—f. color,** color fijo o indeleble.**—f. friend,** amigo seguro.**—f. knot,** nudo apretado, firme. **IV.** *adv.* fuertemente, firmemente; estrechamente, apretadamente; duraderamente; para siempre; profundamente; no lejos; cerca de; aprisa, rápidamente.

fasten [fáscen]. **I.** *va.* afirmar, asegurar, fijar; pegar; echar el cerrojo, aldaba, etc., a; atar, amarrar; (mar.) trincar, abadernar; trabar, unir; abrochar.**—to f. a door,** cerrar una puerta.**—to f. in,** clavar, hincar.**—to f. one's eyes on,** fijar los ojos en.**—to f. on, o upon,** fijar en; imputar a. **II.** *vn.* fijarse, establecerse; agarrarse, asirse, pegarse.

fastener [fásnœr], *s.* el que afirma o asegura; asegurador, pasador, cerrojo, falleba, tarabilla; fiador; afianzador.

fastening [fásning], *s.* (mar.) encapilladura; unión, ligazón, atadura, cierre.

faster [fástœr], *s.* ayunador.

fastidious [fæstídius], *a.* descontentadizo; melindroso, dengoso.**—fastidiously** [-li], *adv.* melindrosamente.**—fastidiousness** [-nes], *s.* melindrería.

fastigiate [fæstiriéit], *a.* ahusado, de lados o flancos convergentes; (bot.) fastigiado.

fasting [fásting], *s.* ayuno

fastness [fástnes], *s.* firmeza, fijeza, solidez; fuerza; fortaleza, plaza fuerte; guájaras, fragosidad; celeridad, velocidad, rapidez; disipación, libertinaje.

fat [fæt]. **I.** *a.* gordo; graso, mantecoso; resinoso; tosco, lerdo, grosero; opulento, rico; ganancioso, provechoso, lucrativo; pura (cal); (impr.) ancho, abierto, claro. **II.** *s.* gordo, gordura; grasa; manteca, sebo; lo más rico o provechoso de alguna cosa. **III.** *va.* y *vn.* engordar.

fatal [féital], *a.* fatal, mortal; inevitable.

fatalism [-ism], *s.* fatalismo.**—fatalist** [-ist], *s.* fatalista.

fatality [fatéliti], *s.* fatalidad, predestinación; desgracia, infortunio; muerte.

fatally [féitali], *adv.* fatalmente; mortalmente.

fatalness [-nes], *s.* fatalidad.

fate [féit], *s.* hado, destino, suerte, fortuna.— **fated** [-ed], *a.* predestinado; fatal, aciago.

fateful [-ful], *a.* fatal, funesto.

father [fápœr]. **I.** *s.* padre.**—f.-in-law,** suegro. **II.** *va.* prohijar, reconocer o adoptar como hijo; tratar como hijo.**—to f. on, o upon,** achacar, imputar, atribuir a.

fatherhood [fápœrjud], *s.* paternidad.

fatherland [fápœrland], *s.* patria; madre patria.

fatherless [-les], *a.* huérfano de padre; desautorizado.

fatherlike [-laik], *a.* como padre, con afecto paternal.

fatherliness [-lines], *s.* ternura o amor paternal.

fatherly [fápœrli]. **I.** *a.* paternal, paterno. **II.** *adv.* paternalmente.

fathom [fépum]. **I.** *s.* (mar.) braza; toesa; alcance. **II.** *va.* sondar, sondear; profundizar, examinar a fondo, tantear; penetrar en, desentrañar, escudriñar.

fathomable [-abœl], *a.* sondable, sondeable, penetrable.

fathomless [-les], *a.* insondable; impenetrable.

fatidical [fatídical], *a.* fatídico.

fatigue [fætíg]. **I.** *s.* fatiga; (mec.) pérdida de resistencia por esfuerzos continuos; (mil.) faena, fajina (il. t. f. duty). **II.** *va.* fatigar.

fatling [fétling]. **I.** *s.* ceboncillo. **II.** *a.* gordo, grueso, engordado.

fatly [fétli], *adv.* corpulentamente.

fatness [fétnes], *s.* gordura, gordo, grasa; fertilidad, fecundidad.

fatten [fétœn]. **I.** *va.* engordar, cebar; (agr.) abonar, fecundar, engrasar. **II.** *vn.* echar carnes, engrosarse; medrar, prosperar.

fattiness [fétines], *s.* gordura.

fattish [fétish], *a.* gordiflón, regordete; grasoso.

fatty [féti], *a.* craso; (fam.) gordiflón; (quím.) graso; (med.) grasoso.**—f. degeneration,** degeneración grasosa.

fatuity [fatiúiti], *s.* fatuidad.

fatuous [fétiuus], *a.* fatuo, insensato.

fauces [fósis], *s. pl.* fauces, gaznate, garganta.

faucet [fóset], *s.* espita, canilla, llave, grifo.

faugh [fo], *interj.* ¡puf! ¡bah!

fault [folt]. **I.** *s.* falta, culpa; defecto, tacha, lunar; pérdida del rastro por los perros de caza; (geol.) falla; (elec.) fuga de corriente.— **at f.,** equivocado; culpable, responsable; extraviado; perplejo.**—in f.,** culpable, responsable.— **to a f.,** excesivamente, con exceso.**—to find f. with,** culpar; hallar defecto en. **II.** *va.* (geol.) producir falla en.

faultfinder [fóltfáindœr], *s.* censurador, criticón; reparón.

faultily [fóltili], *adv.* defectuosamente, erradamente.**—faultiness** [-nes], *s.* culpa; vicio, defecto.**—faultless** [fóltles], *a.* sin tacha, perfecto.—**faultlessly** [-li], *adv.* inculpablemente; perfectamente.**—faultlessness** [-nes], *s.* perfección; inculpabilidad.

faulty [fólti], *a.* defectuoso, imperfecto.

faun [fon], *s.* fauno.

fauna [fóna], *s.* (zool.) fauna.

fauteuil [fotǽi], s. sillón, poltrona; silla presidencial (de una academia, etc.); condición de académico (en Francia); (aer.) asientos; cabina.

favonian [favónian], a. favorable, próspero.

favo(u)r [féivœr]. **I.** va. hacer un favor; favorecer, preferir; mirar con favor, apoyar; contribuir a, conducir a; usar con cuidado o precaución; (b. a.) suavizar; (fam.) asemejarse, parecerse a. **II.** s. favor; fineza, cortesía; preferencia, favoritismo; protección, auspicio, apoyo; mitigación, lenidad o condescendencia; permiso o licencia; acomodación, facilitación; obsequio, agasajo; (com.) carta, grata, atenta.—**to be in f. with**, disfrutar del favor o tener el apoyo de.

favo(u)rable [-abœl], a. favorable.

favo(u)rableness [-nes], s. agrado, benignidad; calidad de favorable.—**favo(u)rably** [-bli], adv. favorablemente, benignamente.

favo(u)red [féivord], a. favorecido; encarado.

favo(u)rite [féivorit], a. y s. favorito.

favo(u)ritism [-išm], s. favoritismo.

fawn [fon]. **I.** s. cervato, cervatillo; color del cervato. **II.** vn. parir la cierva; acariciar, halagar; popar, adular.

fawner [fónœr], s. adulador, adulón.

fawning [fóning], s. adulación, servilismo.

fawningly [-li], adv. servilmente.

fay [féi]. **I.** s. empalme, unión; hada, duende. **II.** va. y vn. unir, empalmar, juntar.

fealty [fíalti], s. homenaje, fidelidad, lealtad.

fear [fíœr]. **I.** s. temor.—**for f.**, por temor o miedo de.—**to be in f.**, temer. **II.** va. y vn. temer.

fearful [-ful], a. medroso, miedoso; tímido, encogido; horrendo, espantoso, terrible.—**fearfully** [-i], adv. temerosamente; terriblemente; (fam.) sumamente.—**fearfulness** [-nes], s. temor, miedo.

fearless [fíœrles], a. intrépido; sin temor.

fearlessly [-li], adv. intrépidamente, sin miedo.

fearlessness [-nes], s. intrepidez, arrojo.

fearnought [fíœrnót], s. acorazado; persona que nada teme.

fearsome [fíœrsʊm], a. temible, espantoso; tímido, miedoso, asustado.

feasance [fíšæns], s. (for.) cumplimiento.

feasibility [fíšibíliti], s. posibilidad.

feasible [fíšibœl], a. factible.—**feasibleness** [-nes], s. factibilidad.—**feasibly** [-bli], adv. de modo factible.

feast [físt]. **I.** s. fiesta; función; banquete; (fam.) comilona. **II.** va. festejar, banquetear, agasajar; regalar, recrear, deleitar. **III.** vn. comer opíparamente; gozarse, deleitarse.

feaster [fístœr], s. goloso; festejador.

feat [fít], s. hecho, acción; hazaña, proeza, valentía; juego de manos.—pl. suertes.

feather [féðœr]. **I.** s. pluma; plumaje; género, clase; (mec.) cuña, rayo; nervio, refuerzo de eje; (carp.) lengüeta, barbilla.—**f. bed**, colchón de plumas, plumón.—**f. duster**, plumero.—**f. joint**, (carp.) encaje de barbilla y farda.—**f. key**, cuña de corredera.—**a f. in one's cap**, un timbre para uno, un triunfo de uno.—**in high f.**, vivo, alegre.—**to cut a f.**, (mar.) cortar el agua, navegar con rapidez; estar hecho un brazo de mar.—**to show the white f.**, volver las espaldas, huir. **II.** va. emplumar, cubrir o adornar con plumas o algo parecido; volver la pala del remo al sacarla del agua, poniéndola casi horizontal; (carp.) machihembrar. **III.** vn. cubrirse de plumas; saltar o cristalizarse un líquido en forma de plumas.—**to f. one's nest**, hacer su agosto.

featherbone [féðœrbóun], s. imitación de ballena para corsés, etc.

featherbrain [-brein], s. imbécil, tonto.

featheredged [-eyd], a. en bisel, achaflanado.

feathered [-d], a. plumado; alado, penígero; emplumado.—**f. tribe**, los pájaros.

feathering [-ing], pa.—**f. float** o **paddle**, (hidr.) álabe o paleta movible.—**f. wheel** (o screw), rueda (o hélice) de paletas movibles.

featherless [-les], a. desplumado; implume.

featherweight [-uéit], s. y a. ligero de peso; de escasa importancia; (dep.) peso pluma.

feathery [-i], a. plúmeo, plumoso.

feature [fíchœr]. **I.** s. rasgo, facción o carácter distintivo; lo más notable o conspicuo; (teat.) pieza o película principal.—pl. facciones, fisionomía, semblante, rostro. **II.** va. (fam.) asemejarse, parecerse a; hacer conspicuo, dar importancia a.

featured [-d], a. formado, cincelado; encarado; anunciado de modo conspicuo.

featureless [-les], a. sin rasgos o facciones características.

febricity [febrísiti], s. febricidad.

febrifacient [febriféišhent], a. **febrific** [febrífic], a. que produce fiebre.

febrifugal [febrífiugal], a. febrífugo.

febrifuge [febrifiuy], s. (med.) febrífugo.

febrile [fíbril o fébril], a. (med.) febril.

February [fébruæri], s. febrero.

fecal [fícal], a. fecal.

feces [físeš], s. pl. excrementos; inmundicias.

fecula [fékiula], s. almidón, fécula.

feculence, feculency [fékiulens, i], s. feculencia; posos, heces.—**feculent** [-ent], a. feculento; inmundo.

fecund [fécʊnd], a. fecundo, fértil.—**fecundate** [-eit], va. fecundar, fecundizar.—**fecundation** [-éišhʊn], s. fecundación.—**fecundity** [fecʊnditi], s. fecundidad.

fed [fed], pret. y pp. de TO FEED.

federal [fédœral], a. federal.—**federalism** [-išm], s. federalismo.—**federalist** [-ist], s. federalista.—**federalize, federalise** [-aiš]. **I.** va. confederar, formar una federación de. **II.** va. confederarse.

federate [fé deret]. **I.** a. confederado, aliado. **II.** va. = FEDERALIZE.—**federation** [-éishʊn] s., confederación, liga, federación.—**federative** [-ativ], a. federativo.

fee [fí]. **I.** s. honorarios; derechos; retribución, gratificación, propina; cuota de ingreso en un club, etc.; feudo; (for.) bienes, hacienda de patrimonio.—**f. farm**, dominio útil.—**f. simple**, dominio absoluto.—**f. tail**, herencia restringida al heredero o a él y especificados herederos suyos. **II.** va. pagar, retribuir; dar propina; alquilar; cohechar, sobornar.

feeable [fíœbœl], a. recompensable.

feeble [fíbœl], a. débil; enfermizo; flojo, endeble; tenue, delicado.—**f.-minded**, imbécil; irresoluto, vacilante.—**f.-mindedness**, idiotez; irresolución.

feebleness [-nes], s. debilidad.—**feebly** [fíbli], adv. débilmente.

feed [fíd]. **I.** va. alimentar; mantener; (mec.) alimentar. **II.** vn. comer, alimentarse.—**to f. on**, o **upon**, alimentarse de. **III.** s. forraje, pienso; alimentación.—**f. bag**, morral.—**f. door**, (fund.) puerta de carga o de alimentación.—**f. head** (no feedhead), carga hidrostática de alimentación.—**f. pipe, pump, roll, valve**, etc., tubo, bomba, rodillo, válvula, etc. de alimentación.—**f. rack**, pesebre, comedero.—**f. slide valve**, válvula de alimentación automática.—**f. water**, (m. v.) agua de alimentación.—**f.-water heater**, (m. v.) recalentador de agua de alimentación.—**f. wire**, (elec.) alimentador.

feeder [fídœr], s. comedor (el que come); gorrista, paniaguado, parásito; afluente de un río; (f. c.) ramal tributario o alimentador; (elec.) alimentador; subalimentador o alimentador derivado; (mec.) alimentador.—**f. pillar**, (elec.) caja de alimentadores en forma de pilar.

feedhead [fídjed], s. (m. v.) depósito de alimentación; (fund.) = SPRUE.

feeding [fíding]. **I.** s. forraje, pasto; alimente. **II.** a. de alimentación.—**f. bottle**, mamadera, biberón.

feedstuff [fídstʊf], s. alimentos para ganado, forraje (en su sentido general).

feel [fíl]. **I.** va. sentir; tocar, tentar; tomar (el pulso); examinar. **II.** vn. sentirse; ser . . . ; al tacto, estar, producir la sensación de (v. gr. this feels rough, esto está áspero, o es áspero al tacto; the room feels warm, el cuarto está caliente).—**to f. cold, hot, warm**, tener frío, mucho calor; (con it por sujeto) hacer frío, etc.—**to f. for**, condolerse de; buscar tentando.—**to f. hungry,**

thirsty, tener hambre, sed.—**to f. of**, tocar, palpar. **III.** *s.* tacto, tocamiento; sensación, percepción.

feeler [fílœr], *s.* el que toca o palpa; probatura, cebo; (ent.) antena, tentáculo; (mec.) lámina calibradora.

feeling [fíling]. **I.** *s.* tacto, tocamiento; sensación; sentimiento, emoción; ternura, compasión; calor, pasión. **II.** *a.* sensible, tierno; conmovedor.

feelingly [-li], *adv.* vivamente, con mucha expresión; conmovidamente; tiernamente.

feet [fít], *s. pl.* de FOOT.

feetless [fítles], *a.* sin pies.

feign [féin]. **I.** *va.* fingir, pretender; inventar, idear o imaginar. **II.** *vn.* fingir, disimular.

feignedly [-edli], *adv.* fingidamente.

feignedness [-nes], *s.* fingimiento.

feigner [-œr], *s.* fingidor.—**feigning** [-ing], *s.* fingimiento.—**feigningly** [-li], *adv.* fingidamente.

feint [féint]. **I.** *s.* ficción, disimulación, treta, artificio; (esgr.) finta. **II.** *vn.* hacer finta.

fel(d)spar [féldspar], **feldspath** [-pæz], *s.* (min.) feldespato.—**feldspathic** [-pæzic], *a.* feldespático.

felicitate [felísiteit], *va.* felicitar.

felicitation [-éishʊn], *s.* felicitación.

felicitous [-us], *s.* feliz, dichoso; bienaventurado; oportuno.—**felicitously** [-li], *adv.* felizmente; con oportunidad.—**felicity** [-ti], *s.* felicidad; ocurrencia oportuna.

Felidæ [fílidi], *s. pl.* (zool.) felinos.

feline [fílain], *s.* gatuno, gatesco; felino.

fell [fel]. **I.** *s.* (cost.) sobrecostura; remate del tejido; pelo, vello; pellejo; cuero, piel; páramo, erial; mineral fino. **II.** *a.* cruel, fiero, feroz. **III.** *pret.* de TO FALL. **IV.** *va.* derribar, tumbar, cortar; acogotar (las reses); (cost.) sobrecoser.—**to f. trees**, desmontar.

fellah [féla], *s.* en Oriente, patán, labriego.

feller [félœr], *s.* máquina taladora; pieza accesoria de una máquina de coser para hacer sobrecosturas.

fellmonger [félmongœr], *s.* mercader de pieles.

felloe [félo], *s.* pina (de rueda).

fellow [félo]. **I.** *a.* asociado; compañero de o en (cambiando un poco el giro; vg.: *fellow sufferer*, compañero en el sufrimiento); parejo, correspondiente.—**f. boarder**, compañero de pupilaje.—**f. citizen**, conciudadano.—**f. feeling**, simpatía, compasión, interés común.—**f. laborer**, colaborador.—**f. man, being, o creature**, prójimo.—**f. member**, compañero, colega.—**f. partner**, consocio.—**f. scholar, f. student**, condiscípulo.—**f. traveller, o passenger**, compañero de viaje.—Este adjetivo entra en la composición de otros vocablos y denota igualdad o compañerismo. **II.** *s.* compañero, camarada; igual; pareja; socio o individuo de un colegio, sociedad, etc.; (fam.) hombre, sujeto, tipo.—**a good f.**, (fam.) buen tipo, buen chico; desprendido. **III.** *va.* aparear.

fellowship [-ship]. **I.** *s.* confraternidad, compañerismo; coparticipación; asociación, mancomunidad; compañía, cuerpo, sociedad; colegiatura, plaza pensionada; beca; (arit.) regla de compañía. **II.** *va. y vn.* admitir, aceptar o unirse con otros en sociedad.

felly [féli], *s.* = FELLOE.

felly, *adv.* cruelmente, ferozmente.

felo-de-se [fílo-de-sí], *s.* (for.) suicida.

felon [félʊn]. **I.** *s.* reo, criminal, felón; panadizo, panarizo. **II.** *a.* malvado, criminal; traidor.

felonious [felónius], *a.* criminal; perverso.—**feloniously** [-li], *adv.* criminalmente; malvadamente.

felony [féloni], *s.* crimen, delito.

felspar [félspar], *s.* (min.) feldespato.

felt [felt]. **I.** *s.* fieltro. **II.** *pp. y pret.* de TO FEEL. **III.** *va.* hacer fieltro; cubrir con fieltro.

felting [félting], *s.* materiales para hacer fieltro; fieltro; (carp.) aserrar al hilo.

felucca [felúca], *s.* (mar.) faluca.

female [fímeil], *s. y a.* (zool. y bot.) hembra.—**f. screw**, hembra de tornillo, tuerca.—El término se aplica a veces a la mujer, sobre todo como *a.*

vg. *a female* (gen. despec.) una mujer; *a female writer*, una escritora. Se usa muy a menudo para distinguir el sexo de los animales: *a female donkey*, una burra; *a female dog*, una perra; *a female fish*, *un pez hembra*.

feme [féim], *s.* (for.) mujer.—**f. covert**, mujer casada.—**f. sole**, soltera; mujer que vive sola.

feminality [féminǽliti], **femineity** [féminíiti], *s.* feminicidad; calidad de femenino.

feminine [féminin], *a.* femenino; mujeril; mujeriego; afeminado.

feminism [féminism], *s.* caracteres femeninos; (pol.) feminismo; (med.) caracteres femeninos en el macho.—**feminist** [-ist], *s. y a.* (pol.) feminista.

femininity [féminíniti], *s.* calidad o estado de femenino; el bello sexo.

femoral [fémoral], *a.* (anat.) femoral.

femur [fímœr], *s.* (anat.) fémur.

fen [fen], *s.* marial, pantano, fangal; enfermedad mohosa del lúpulo.—**f. cress**, (bot.) berro pantanoso.—**f. cricket**, grillotalpa.—**f. duck**, ánade silvestre.

fenberry [fénberri], *s.* zarzamora.

fence [fens]. **I.** *s.* cerca, valla; defensa, reparo; esgrima; (fam.) comprador de efectos robados; (mec.) guarda, guía, resguardo.—**f. mouth**, tiempo de veda.—**to be on the f.**, estar indeciso. **II.** *va.* (a menudo con *in*), cercar, vallar; defender, guardar, custodiar. **III.** *vn.* esgrimir, pelear; defenderse.

fencer [fénsœr], *s.* esgrimidor, floretista; caballo ágil para saltar cercas.

fencible [fénsibœl]. **I.** *a.* defendible. **II.** *s.* (mil.) soldado destinado a la defensa del país.

fencing [fénsing], *s. y pa.* esgrima; habilidad en el debate; materiales para cercas; valladar.—**f. bout**, asalto de armas.—**f. master**, maestro de esgrima.—**f. school**, escuela de esgrima.

fend [fend]. **I.** *va.* (con **off**) parar, apartar, rechazar; defender, guardar, preservar. **II.** *vn.* esgrimir; defenderse.

fender [féndœr], *s.* guardafuegos de chimenea francesa; (mar.) defensas, andullo, pallete; (aut.) guardafango.—**f. bar, o f. rail**, batayola. —**f. beam**, espolón.—**f. board**, guardafango.—**f. pile**, pilote de protección.

fenestella [fénestǽlæ], *s.* ventanilla.

fenestra [fénestræ], *s.* (anat.) ventana (del oído, etc.); orificio a modo de ventana; (ent.) mancha transparente de un órgano fenestrado. —**f. ovalis**, ventana oval.—**f. rotunda**, ventana redonda.—**fenestral** [-træl], *a.* relativo a la estructura fenestrada; a modo de ventana.—**fenestrate** [-tret], *a.* fenestrado.

fenestration [fénestréishʊn], *a.* (arq.) ventanaje.

Fenian [fíniæn], *s. y a.* feniano.—**Fenianism** [-ism], *s.* fenianismo.

fennel [fénel], *s.* (bot.) hinojo.—**f. flower**, neguilla, ajenuz.

fenny [féni], *a.* palustre, pantanoso.

fenugreek [fénugric], *s.* (bot.) fenogreco, alholva.

feod, feodal, feodary, etc. *V.* FEUD, etc.

feoff [fef]. **I.** *va.* (for.) enfeudar. **II.** *s.* feudo.

feoffee [feff], *s.* feudatario.

feoffer, feoffor [féfœr], *s.* el que enfeuda.

feoffment [féfmœnt], *s.* (for.) feudo.

feral [fíral], *a.* feral; salvaje; silvestre.

feria [fíriæ], *s.* (igl.) feria.—*pl.* **feriæ**, (hist.) días de fiestas.

ferial [fírial], *a.* (igl.) ferial.

ferine [fírain]. **I.** *a.* ferino, no domesticado; maligno. **II.** *s.* fiera.

ferineness [fírainnes], **ferity** [fériti], *s.* fiereza, ferocidad.

ferment [fœrmént]. **I.** *va.* hacer fermentar. **II.** *vn.* fermentar; rehervirse, revenirse; agitarse.

ferment [fœrmœnt], *s.* fermento; fermentación, agitación.

fermentability [fœrméntabílity], *s.* fermentabilidad.—**fermentable** [-tabœl], *a.* fermentable.

fermentation [fœrmentéishʊn], *s.* (quím.) fermentación; (fig.) efervescencia, agitación.

fermentative [fœrméntativ], *a.* fermentativo, fermentante.—**fermentativeness** [-nes], *s.* calidad de fermentativo.—**fermentible** [-tibœl], *a.* fermentable.

fern [fœrn], *s.* (bot.) helecho, polipodio.

fernery [-eri], *s.* lugar donde se crían helechos.

ferny [fœrni], *a.* abundante en helechos.

ferocious [feróshus], *a.* feroz.—**ferociously** [-li], *adv.* ferozmente.—**ferociousness** [-nes], **ferocity**, [-siti], *s.* ferocidad.

ferreous, ferrean [férreus, férrean], *a.* férreo, ferrizo.

ferret [férret]. **I.** *s.* (zool.) hurón; (vid.) ferrete; listón, bocadillo, hiladillo, ribete; filadiz. **II.** *va.* (con **out**) indagar, averiguar; cazar con hurones.

ferriage, ferryage [férriey], *s.* barcaje, lanchaje, peaje.

ferric [férric], *a.* (quím.) férrico.

ferricyanic [férrisaiénic], *s.* ferricianhídrico.

ferricyanid(e [-sáianid *o* naid], *s.* ferricianuro.

ferriferous [ferrífœrus], *a.* ferrífero.

ferrocalcite [férrocǽlsait], *s.* ferrocalcita.

ferrochrome [férrocróum], **ferrochromium** [-ium], *s.* ferrocromo, aleación de hierro y cromo.

ferroconcrete [-cóncrit], *s.* hormigón armado.

ferrocyanate [-sáianet], **ferroprussiate** [-prúshiet], *s.* ferroprusiato.—**f. paper** = BLUE-PAPER.

ferrocyanic [-saiénic], *a.* ferrocianhídrico.

ferromagnetic [-mægnétic], *a.* magnético, paramagnético.

ferromanganese [-mǽngænis], **ferrosilicon** [-sílicon], etc. ferromanganeso, ferrosilicio, etc., aleaciones de hierro y manganeso, silicio, etc.

ferrotype [férrotaip], *s.* ferrotipo.

ferrous [férrus], *a.* (quím.) ferroso.

ferruginous [ferrúyinus], *a.* ferruginoso; mohoso, aherrumbrado.

ferrule [férrul], *s.* regatón, virola, casquillo; zuncho; marco de pizarra.

ferry [férri]. **I.** *va.* y *vn.* transportar de una a otra orilla; barquear; cruzar un río en embarcación. **II.** *s.* medio de transporte a través de un río; paso, pasaje; embarcadero, balsadera.—**f. cable**, andarivel.

ferryboat [-bout], *s.* barco o bote de paso (a través de un río).—**ferryman** [-mæn], *s.* balsero, barquero; encargado de un paso (de río) o de un muelle de paso.

fertile [fœrtil], *a.* fértil, fecundo, feraz.

fertilely [-li], *adv.* fértilmente, abundantemente.

fertileness [-nes], **fertility** [fœrtíliti], *s.* fertilidad.

fertilization [-iséishun], *s.* (biol.) fecundación; (agr.) abono.—**fertilize** [-ais], *va.* fertilizar, fecundar; abonar.—**fertilizer** [-aisœr], *s.* (agr.) abono; fructificador.

ferula [férula], *s.* (bot.) férula, cañaheja; cetro.

ferule [férul]. **I.** *s.* férula, palmeta. **II.** *va.* dar palmetazos.

fervency [fœrvensi], *s.* ardor; celo, devoción.

fervent [-vent], *a.* ferviente; fogoso, vehemente; hirviente, ardiente.—**fervently** [-li], *adv.* fervorosamente.—**ferventness** [-nes], *s.* ardor, fervor.

fervid [fœrvid], *a.* férvido, ardiente, fogoso.

fervidity, fervidness, *s.* = FERVENCY.

fervo(u)r [fœrvœr], *s.* fervor, devoción; ardor, vehemencia.

fescue [féskiu], *s.* puntero.—**f. grass**, (bot.) cañuela.

festal [féstal], *a.* festivo; de fiesta, de fiestas.

fester [féstœr]. **I.** *vn.* enconarse, ulcerarse. **II.** *va.* enconar, emponzoñar. **III.** *s.* llaga, úlcera.

festival [féstival]. **I.** *a.* festivo. **II.** *s.* fiesta.

festive [féstiv], *a.* festivo, alegre.

festivity [festíviti], *s.* regocijo, alegría, júbilo, alborozo; fiesta, festividad.

festoon [festún]. **I.** *s.* festón, guirnalda. **II.** *va.* festonear.—**festooned**, *o* **festoony**, afestonado.

fetal, fœtal [fítal], *a.* fetal.

fetch [fech]. **I.** *va.* ir a buscar, ir por; traer; coger; alcanzar, lograr, conseguir; producir, venderse por; derivar, sacar, deducir; llegar a; (fam.) traer a un arreglo, convencer.—**to f. a com-**

pass, hacer un rodeo.—**to f. a pump**, cebar una bomba.—**to f. down**, bajar, abatir, humillar.—**to f. in**, *o* **within**, entrar o meter dentro.—**to f. one's breath**, tomar aliento.—**to f. out**, sacar a luz, hacer resaltar.—**to f. up**, educar, criar; parar, detener; recuperar; alcanzar. **II.** *vn.* moverse, menearse; (mar.) arribar, llegar.—**to f. away**, (mar.) soltarse, dar tumbos. **III.** *s.* acto de ir a buscar o de traer; tirada, alcance; estratagema, treta.

fetcher [féchœr], *s.* el que va por algo.

fête [féit]. **I.** *va.* festejar. **II.** *s.* fiesta.—**f. day**, fiesta onomástica.

fetial [físhial], *a.* fecial.

fetich [fítish], *s.* = FETISH.

feticide [fétisaid], *s.* (for.) feticidio; (med.) producción intencional del aborto.

fetid [fétid], *a.* fétido.

fetidity [fetíditi], **fetidness** [fétidnes], *s.* fetidez.

fetish [fítish *o* fétish], *s.* fetiche.—**fetishism** [-ism], fetichismo.—**fetishist** [-ist], *s.* fetichista.

fetlock [fétloc], *s.* cerneja; menudillo.

fetor [fítœr], *s.* hedor, fetor.

fetter [fétœr]. **I.** *va.* engrillar, encadenar. **II.** *s.* grillete, arropea, calceta: prisión.—**f. bone**, cuartilla.—*pl.* grillos, brete, cadenas: prisiones.

fetterless [fétœrles], *a.* desenfrenado.

fetterlock [-loc], *s.* manea, maniota.

fettle [fétœl], *va.* alisar, quitar rebabas a; (fund.) poner brasca a.

fettling [fétling], *s.* (fund.) brasca.

fetus, fœtus [fítus], *s.* feto.

feud [fiúd], *s.* contienda, enemistad entre familias, tribus, clases, etc.; (for.) feudo.

feudal [fiúdal], *a.* feudal.—**feudalism** [-ism], *s.* feudalismo.—**feudality** [fiudǽliti], *s.* feudalidad.—**feudalize** [fiúdalais], *va.* enfeudar.

feudary [fiúdari]. **I.** *a.* feudal. **II.** *s.* vasallo; feudatario.—**feuda(ta)ry**, **feudatory** [fiúdari, tæri, tori], *a.* y *s.* vassallaje, feudo, feudatario.

feudist [fiúdist], *s.* feudista.

feuilleton [fœlleton], *s.* folletín.

fever [fívœr]. **I.** *s.* fiebre; ventolera, pasión.—**f. blister**, **f. sore**, fuegos en los labios. **II.** *va.* causar fiebre.

feverfew [-fiu], *s.* (bot.) matricaria.

feverish [-ish], *a.* febricitante, calenturiento.

feverishly [-li], *adv.* febrilmente.

feverishness [-nes], *s.* estado febril, calentura.

few [fiú], *a.* y *pron.* pocos.—**a f.**, unos cuantos, unos pocos.—**in a f.**, en una palabra.—**not a f.**, no pocos.

fewer [fiúœr], *a. comp.* de FEW: menos.—**fewest** [-est], *a. super.* de FEW: menos.

fewness [fiúnes], *s.* escasez, poquedad, cortedad, corto número.

fez [fes], *s.* fez, gorro turco.

fiacre [fiácr], *s.* coche de plaza.

fiancé [fiansé], *s.* novio.—**fiancée**, *s.* novia.

fiasco [fiásco], *s.* fiasco, fracaso; frasco, botella.

fiat [fáiat], *s.* fiat, orden, mandato.

fib [fib]. **I.** *s.* embuste, filfa, bola. **II.** *vn.* decir mentirillas, embustear.

fibber [fíbœr], *s.* mentiroso, trapacero.

fiber [fáibœr], *s.* fibra.—**f. silk**, seda artificial hecha de celulosa.—**f. stress**, (mec.) esfuerzo en la fibra más remota (del eje neutro).

fibril [fíbril], *s.* fibrila, pelillo.

fibrilose [-ous], *a.* fibriloso.

fibrin(e [fáibrin], *s.* fibrina.

fibroid [fáibroid], *a.* fibroso.

fibroid, fibroma [faibróma], *s.* (med.) fibroma, tumor fibroso.

Fibrospongiæ [fáibrospónyii], *s. pl.* (zool.) fibrospóngidos.

fibrous [fáibrus], **fibrose** [fáibros], *a.* fibroso.

fibrovascular [fáibrovǽskiular], *a.* fibrovascular.

fibula [fíbiula], *s.* (anat.) peroné; imperdible.

fibular [fíbiular], *a.* peroneo.

fichu [físhú], *s.* pañoleta, fichú.

fickle [fícœl], *a.* voluble, inconstante, veleidoso.—**fickleness** [-nes], *s.* inconstancia, veleidad.—**fickly** [fícli], *adv.* inconstantemente.

fictile [fíctil], *a.* plástico; figulino.

fiction [fícshun], *s.* ficción, invención; literatura novelesca; novela, mentira, embuste, fábula; (for.) ficción de derecho.

fictitious [fictíshus], *a.* ficticio, contrahecho; fingido; fabuloso.—**fictitiously** [-li], *adv.* ficticiamente.—**fictitiousness** [-nes], *s.* calidad de ficticio.

fictive [fíctiv], *a.* fingido, ficticio, imaginario.

ficus [fáicus], *s.* (bot.) higuera.

fid [fid], *s.* barra de sostén; tarugo, cuña.

fiddle [fídæl]. **I.** *s.* violín; utensilio mecánico.— **f. block,** motón de poleas diferenciales.—**f. bow,** arco de violín. **II.** *vn.* tocar el violín; enredar, jugar.

fiddlededee [fídœldedi]. **I.** *interj.* ¡qué simpleza! **II.** *s.* disparate.

fiddle-faddle [fídœlfádœl]. **I.** *s.* (fam.) bagatelas, frioleras; desatino, dislate. **II.** *a.* quisquilloso. **III.** *va.* disparatar.

fiddler [fídlœr], *s.* violinista.

fiddlestick [fídœlstic], *s.* arco de violín; bagatela. —**fiddlesticks!** *interj.* ¡disparate!

fiddlestring [-string], *s.* cuerda de violín.

fidelity [fidéliti], *s.* fidelidad; veracidad.

fidget [fíret]. **I.** *va.* (fam.) molestar, inquietar. **II.** *vn.* ajetrearse, afanarse, cazcalear. **III.** *s.* (gen. *pl.*) afán, agitación.—**fidgety** [-i], *a.* (fam.) inquieto, agitado.

fiducial [fidiúshal], *a.* fiduciario, de confianza; (mat.) fiducial.—**fiducially** [-i], *adv.* confiadamente; confidentemente.

fiduciary [fidiúshiœri]. **I.** *a.* fiduciario; confiado, resuelto. **II.** *s.* (for.) fideicomisario.

fie! [fái], *interj.* ¡uf! ¡abrenuntio!

fief [fif], *s.* (for.) feudo.

field [fild]. **I.** *s.* campo, campiña: (agr.) campo, sembrado, terreno cultivado; (mil.) campo de batalla; batalla, campaña; (ópt.) campo de un anteojo; (elec.) inductor· (magn.) campo magnético; (dep.) campo del baseball fuera del cuadro; cancha, campo de juego; colectividad de competidores en carreras, etc.; todos los caballos que entran en una carrera aparte del favorito.—**f. artillery,** artillería de campaña.—**f. basil,** (bot.) clinopodio, albahaca silvestre.—**f. bean,** judía ordinaria blanca.—**f. bed,** catre de tijera.—**f. day** día de ejercicios atléticos o militares.—**f. glass,** anteojo de larga vista.—**f. gun,** cañón de campaña.— **f. lark,** cugujada.—**f. magnet,** (elec.) inductor; (min.) imán para buscar hierr·.—**f. marshall,** mariscal.—**f. officer,** coronel, teniente coronel o comandante.—**f. of force,** campo de acción de una fuerza.—**fields of ice,** bancos de hielo.—**f. piece,** (arti.) pieza de campaña.—**f. sports,** diversiones de la caza y la carrera.—**f. of view,** campo visual.— **f. winding,** (elec.) arrollamiento del inductor.— **f. work,** (top.) trabajo de campo o en el terreno.— **to keep the f.,** mantenerse firme.—**to take the f.,** entrar en o salir a campaña. **II.** *va.* (dep.) parar y devolver la pelota; poner al aire libre. **III.** *vn.* (dep.) actuar como *fielder;* apostar al *field.*

fielded [fílded], *a.* acampado.

fielder [fíldœr], *s.* (dep.) jugador situado en el *field* para interceptar la pelota; perro de caza.

fieldfare [fíldféœr], *s.* (orn.) zorzal.

fieldworks [-uœrks], *s.* (fort.) obras de campo.

fiend [fínd], *s.* espíritu malo, el demonio; furia, arpía; (fam.) monomaníaco, esp. morfinómano. —**fiendish** [-ish], **fiendlike** [-laic], *a.* diabólico, perverso, malvado.—**fiendishness** [-nes], *s.* maldad, perversidad.

fierce [fícers], *a.* fiero, feroz; bravío; violento, furioso; vehemente, impetuoso.—**fiercely** [-li], *adv.* furiosamente, ferozmente.—**fierceness** [-nes], *s.* fiereza, ferocidad.

fieri facias [fáieri féshias], *s.* auto ejecutorio.

fierily [fáiœrili], *adv.* calurosamente, ardientemente.

fieriness [-nes], *s.* ardor, fogosidad, vehemencia.

fiery [fáiœri], *a.* ígneo; ardiente; encendido; vehemente, fogoso; feroz, furibundo.

fife [fáif]. **I.** *s.* (mús. mil.) pífano. **II.** *va.* y *vn.* tocar el pífano.

fifer [fáifœr], *s.* (tocador de) pífano.

fifteen [fiftín], *a.* y *s.* quince.

fifteenth [fíftínz], *a.* y *s.* décimoquinto; quince (ordinal); quinzavo.

fifth [fifz], *s.* y *a.* quinto; cinco (del mes).—**f. wheel,** rodete.

fiftieth [fíftiez], *s.* y *a.* quincuagésimo; cincuenta; cincuentavo.

fifty [fífti], *a.* y *s.* cincuenta.—**f. f.,** (fam.) por igual, mitad y mitad.

fig [fig], *s.* (bot.) higuera; higo; (fam.) ardite, comino, bledo.—**figpecker,** (orn.) becafigo.

fight [fáit]. **I.** *va.* (*pret.* y *pp.* FOUGHT) pelear, combatir, reñir, luchar con. **II.** *vn.* batallar; luchar; pelear; hacer la guerra.—**to f. against odds,** luchar con desventaja.—**to f. shy,** evadir una contienda. **III.** *s.* batalla, lucha, combate; pelea, riña.

fighter [fáitœr], *s.* guerrero; peleador; batallador; lidiador, luchador, combatiente; duelista, espadachín.

fighting [-ing]. **I.** *a.* aguerrido, combatiente; agresivo; luchador; pugnante. **II.** *s.* combate, querella, riña, el pelear.

figment [fígmœnt], *s.* ficción, invención.

figuline [fíguiulin], *s.* objeto figulino.

figural [fíguiural], *a.* que tiene figuras.

figurante [fíguiurant], *s.* (teat.) figurante; figuranta.

figurate [-et], *a.* figurado; (mús.) floreado, embellecido.

figuration [-éishun], *s.* figuración; figura.

figurative [fí.guiurativ], *a.* figurado, metafórico; florido.—**figuratively** [-li], *adv.* figuradamente.— **figurativeness** [-nes], *s.* calidad de figurativo.

figure [fíguiœr]. **I.** *s.* figura; tipo; maniquí; distinción, papel, viso; (arit.) cifra, guarismo; (com.) precio, valor; (gram.) figura gramatical: (astrol.) horóscopo.—*pl.* números, cifras. **II.** *va.* y *vn.* figurar, delinear, formar; adornar con figuras: figurarse, imaginarse; representar, simbolizar; calcular; (mús.) florear.—**to f. out,** hallar por cálculo, resolver.—**to f. up,** computar, calcular, sumar. **III.** *vn.* figurar; calcular, hacer cuentas.

figured [fíguiœrd], *pp.* y *a.* adornado, floreado, labrado.—**f. velvet,** terciopelo estampado.—**f. silk,** seda floreada.

figurehead [fíguiœrjed], *s.* caudillo nominal, figurón; (mar.) mascarón de proa.

figurine [fíguirin], *s.* figurilla o imagen adornada con dorados o pintura.

figwort [fíguœrt], *s.* (bot.) escrofularia.

Fijian, Feejeean [fíyian]. **I.** *a.* de Fiji. **II.** *s.* habitante o lengua aborigine de las islas Fiji.

filaceous [filéshus], *a.* hebroso, fibroso.

filament [fílamœnt], *s.* filamento.

filamentous, filamentose [filamēntus, ous], *a.* filamentoso.

filar [fáilar], *a.* perteneciente al hilo; filiforme; que contiene hilos.—**f. microscope,** microscopio de ocular reticulado.

filature [fílachur o tiur], *s.* hilandería; fábrica de hilados.

filbert [fílbœrt], *s.* avellana.—**f. tree,** avellano.

filch [filch], *vn.* ratear, hurtar.—**filcher** [-œr], *s.* ratero, garduño, ladroncillo.—**filchingly** [-ingli], *adv.* rateramente.

file [fáil]. **I.** *s.* lima; escofina; archivo; ensartapapeles; guardapapeles; legajo o colección ordenada de periódicos o documentos; fila, hilera; catálogo, lista.—**f. card,** limpialimas.—**f. cutter,** picador de limas.—**f.-hard,** a prueba de lima. **II.** *va.* limar; archivar; ensartar, enhilar; acumular; presentar, registrar, asentar, anotar. **III.** *vn.* (mil.) marchar en filas.—**to f. off,** (mil.) desfilar.

file-fish [fáil-fish], *s.* (ict.) liga.

filer [fáilœr], *s.* limador.

filial [fílial], *a.* filial.

filially [fíliali], *adv.* filialmente.

filiation [filiéishun], *s.* filiación; adopción, prohijamiento; dependencia.

filibuster [fílibústœr]. **I.** *va.* obstruir (la aprobación de una ley). **II.** *vn.* ser filibustero;

(E. U.) obstruir la aprobación de leyes, etc., en un cuerpo legislativo. **III.** *s.* filibustero, pirata; obstruccionista.—**fillbusterism** [-ĭšm], *s.* filibusterismo; obstruccionismo.

filicide [fílisaid], *s.* filicida, que mata a su hijo.

filiform [fíliform], *a.* filiforme.

filigrane [fíligren], **filigree** [fíligri], *s.* filigrana.

filigreed [fíligrid], *a.* afiligranado.

filing [fáiling]. **I.** *s.* limado, acción de limar; acción de archivar; (gen. *pl.*) limadura. **II.** *a.* de limar; de archivar.—**f. card**, tarjeta para archivo.

Filipino [filipíno], *s.* y *a.* filipino.

fill [fil]. **I.** *va.* llenar; rellenar; henchir; satisfacer, contentar; ocupar (un puesto); empastar (un diente); hinchar; macizar; terraplenar.—**to f. in**, terraplenar; rellenar; insertar.—**to f. out**, llenar, completar; llevar a cabo.—**to f. the bill**, (fam.) llenar los requisitos.—**to f. up**, colmar; llenar un blanco; tapar.—**to f. up the time**, emplear el tiempo. **II.** *vn.* (a menudo con *up*), llenarse; echar de beber, llenar el vaso; saciarse, hartarse. **III.** *s.* terraplén; hartura, hartazgo; abundancia.

filler [fílœr], *s.* lo que sirve para llenar o rellenar; henchidor, embudador, envasador; embudo.—*pl.* tripa (tabaco).—**f. rods**, varillas para soldadura.

fillet [fílet]. **I.** *s.* prendedero; venda, tira, faja, cinta; lista, listón; gusanillo de rosca; filete, solomillo; (arq.) filete, tenia, listel; (enc.) nervio. **II.** *va.* vendar, fajar, atar o ceñir con venda, faja o cinta; (arq.) filetear.

filling [fíling]. **I.** *s.* henchimiento; relleno; envase; tripa (tabaco); (dent.) orificación o empastadura. **II.** *a.* de llenar o rellenar; que llena.—**f. sleeve**, (aer.) manguera de inflar.

fillip [fílip]. **I.** *va.* dar un capirotazo; tirar o impeler con un capirotazo; incitar, estimular. **II.** *s.* capirotazo; estímulo, aguijón.

fillister [fílistœr], *s.* (carp.) guillame.

filly [fíli], *s.* potranca; (despec.) muchacha retozona.

film. I. *s.* película, membrana, telilla; nube en el ojo; (foto.) película.—**f. play**, drama cinematográfico, película dramática. **II.** *va.* cubrir con película; fotografiar para el cine. **III.** *vn.* cubrirse de una película.

filminess [fílmines], *s.* apariencia como de película.

filmize [fílmaiš], *va.* (fam.) fotografiar para el cine.

filmy [fílmi], *a.* membranoso, pelicular.

filose [fáilos], *a.* filiforme.

filter [fíltœr]. **I.** *va.* filtrar, colar; depurar. **II.** *vn.* infiltrarse. **III.** *s.* filtro, destiladera, colador, filtrador.—**f. paper**, papel de filtrar.

filth [filz], *s.* suciedad, inmundicia, porquería, mugre.—**filthily** [-lili], *adv.* asquerosamente.—**filthiness** [-nes], *s.* inmundicia, suciedad.

filthy [fílzi], *a.* sucio, puerco, asqueroso.

filtrate [fíltreit]. **I.** *va.* filtrar. **II.** *s.* líquido filtrado.

filtration [-éišŭn], *s.* filtración.

fimbriate [fímbrieit], *va.* franjear; ribetear.

fimbriate(d, fimbricate(d [-(ed, -keit(ed], *a.* franjeado; recortado, laciniado.

fin, *s.* aleta; barba de ballena; (mec.) apendice en forma de aleta; peces.—**f.-footed**, palmeado.

finable [fáinabœl], *a.* multable.

final [fáinal]. **I.** *a.* final, terminal; terminante, conclusivo, decisivo; mortal.—**f. cause**, (filos.) causa final. **II.** *s.* final; el final o último (juego, examen, etc.).

finale [finále], *s.* (teat.) final; (mús.) coda.

finality [finǽliti], *s.* finalidad; decisión, determinación.

finally [fáinali], *adv.* finalmente, en fin.

financial [finǽnšhal], *a.* rentístico; monetario.

financially [-i], *adv.* rentísticamente; en lo relativo a fondos.

finance [fainǽns, finǽns]. **I.** *s.* ciencia o teoría de las operaciones y transacciones monetarias (hacienda, banca, etc.); (gen. *pl.*) asuntos monetarios o financieros; hacienda; fondos, recursos. **II.** *va.* manejar (fondos); dirigir u ocuparse en operaciones financieras o monetarias para; conseguir o suministrar fondos para. **III.** *vn.* ocuparse en operaciones financieras.

financier [finænsíær]. **I.** *s.* financiero. **II.** *va.* y *vn.* = FINANCE.

finback [fínbæk], *s.* (ict.) yubarta.

finch, *s.* (orn.) pinzón, fringilino, picogordo.

find [fáind]. **I.** *va.* (*pret.* y *pp.* FOUND) encontrar, hallar; ver, descubrir; recobrar el uso de; averiguar, adquirir, saber; (for.) fallar, decidir; procurar, proveer; alimentar, mantener.—**to f. fault with**, culpar; censurar; desaprobar.—**to f. one's self**, encontrarse (apl. a la salud); descubrir uno sus aptitudes.—**to f. out**, resolver; descubrir; atrapar, sorprender; adivinar; averiguar. **II.** *vn.* (for.) pronunciar sentencia o fallo. **III** *s.* hallazgo.

finder [fáinder], *s.* el que encuentra; descubridor; (ópt.) anteojo buscador (de un telescopio); portaobjetos cuadriculado (de microscopio); (fot.) aparato reductor (de una cámara) por el cual se obtiene una reproducción en miniatura de la imagen de la placa principal.

fin-de-siécle [fæn de siékl], *a.* del fin del siglo XIX; moderno, al día.

finding [fáinding], *s.* descubrimiento; hallazgo; (for.) fallo, sentencia, decisión, laudo; gasto, mantenimiento.—*pl.* herramientas y avíos de zapateros y talabarteros.

fine [fáin]. **I.** *a.* fino; menudo; refinado, puro; excelente, admirable; bello, hermoso; selecto, escogido o primoroso; guapo, bien parecido o gallardo; claro, transparente; agradable.—**f. arts**, bellas artes.—**f. cut**, picadura fina de tabaco, tabaco fino.—**f. gentleman** (desp.) lechuguino.—**f. lady**, (desp.) mujer de ínfulas.—**f. writing**, estilo afectado o rebuscado. **II.** *s.* multa.—**in f.**, en resumen. **III.** *va.* afinar, refinar; multar. **IV.** *vn.* (con **down**) purificarse; adelgazarse; derretirse. **V.** *adv.* finamente; (fam.) muy bien (apl. a la salud); (billar) apenas tocando.—**f.-corded wool**, estambre.—**f.-looking**, guapo, buen mozo, bien parecido.—**f.-tongued**, zalamero.

finedraw [fáindró], *va.* (*pret.* FINEDREW) *pp.* FINEDRAWN), (cost.) zurcir; (metal.) estirar en hilos finísimos; (fig.) hilar muy delgado en, sutilizar en.

finely [-li], *adv.* finamente; hermosamente, primorosamente; sutilmente.

fineness [-nes], *s.* fineza, delicadeza; primor, excelencia; agudeza, sutileza; pureza, perfección; ley del metal; finura, menudez (de arena, cemento, etc.).

finer [fáiner]. **I.** *a. comp.* de FINE: más fino, mejor, más hermoso. **II.** *s.* refinador de metales.

finery [fáinœri], *s.* gala, adorno, atavío, aderezo; primor, elegancia.

finespun [fáinspun], *a.* sutil; alambicado.

finesse [finés]. **I.** *vn.* valerse de subterfugios y artificios. **II.** *s.* artificio; treta; astucia, sutileza; tino, tacto, diplomacia.

finger [fíngœr]. **I.** *s.* dedo; (mec.) dedo, brazo, apéndice, saliente, etc.—pieza o parte que por su forma u oficio se asemeja a un dedo.—**f. bowl, f. glass**, enjuague, enjuagatorio.—**f. board**, mástil de violín o guitarra; teclado.—**f. mark**, impresión digital, marca que el dedo deja.—**f. nail**, uña.—**f. post**, poste indicador.—**f. reading**, lectura de letras en relieve por el tacto.—**f. stall**, dedil.—**to have a f. in the pie**, meter la cuchara; tener participación en un asunto.—**to have at one's fingers' ends, o tips**, tener en la punta de los dedos. **II.** *va.* tocar, manosear; sisar, hurtar; (mús.) pulsar, tañer, teclear; hacer algo con los dedos. **III.** *vn.* tener destreza en los dedos.

fingerbreadth [-brédz], *s.* anchura de un dedo.

fingering [-ing], *s.* manoseo; digitación.

fingerprint [-prínt], *s.* impresión digital.

finial [fíniæl], *s.* (arq.) pináculo; remate.

finic(al [fínic(al], **finicky** [fíniki], *a.* melindroso, remilgado, demasiado escrupuloso.—**finicality** [-cæliti], *s.* remilgo, melindre.—**finically** [-call], *adv.* melindrosamente.

---

finish [fínish]. **I.** *va.* acabar, terminar; pulir, perfeccionar, retocar, dar la última mano; (fam.) mataro hacer impotente; vencer. **II.** *vn.* acabar, fenecer, finalizar, cesar; morir. **III.** *s.* fin, término; pulimento, última mano; acabado, capa superficial, revestimiento.

finisher [-œr], *s.* consumador; afinador, pulidor.

finishing [-ing]. **I.** *s.* acabamiento, consumación; colmo, perfección; última mano, toque, pincelada.—*pl.* accesorios de madera de un edificio. **II.** *a.* último; de remate, de acabado; de acabar.—**f. blow,** golpe mortal; golpe de gracia.—**f. coat,** última capa, capa de acabado; (pint.) última mano.—**f. school,** escuela de educación social para mujeres.

finite [fáinait], *a.* finito.—**f. verb,** inflexión verbal que denota tiempo (a distinción del infinitivo y los participios).—**finitely** [-li], *adv.* finitamente.—**finiteness** [-nes], *s.* calidad de finito, lo finito.

finless [fínles], *a.* sin aletas, desaletado.

finlike [fínlaic], *a.* de forma de aleta.

Finn [fin], *s.* finlandés, finlandesa.

finned [find], *a.* aleteado.

Finnic [fínic], *a.* y *s.* finés.

Finnish [fínnish], *a.* y *s.* finlandés.

finny [fínni], *a.* armado de aletas; abundante en peces.

fiord [fiord], *s.* fiordo, ría orillada de altas rocas.

fir [fœr], *s.* (bot.) abeto; pino.—**f. tree,** abeto.

fire [fáiœr], *s.* fuego; lumbre; incendio, quema; chispa; ardor, pasión, viveza; desgracia, infortunio; rabia.—**f. alarm,** alarma o llamada de incendios.—**f. board,** mampara de chimenea.—**f. box,** caja de fuegos (de una locomotora).—**f. brick,** ladrillo refractario.—**f. bug,** (fam.) incendiario.—**f. bridge,** (m. v.) altar.—**f. clay,** arcilla refractaria.—**f. damp,** fuego grisú, mofeta.—**f. department,** servicio de bomberos.—**f. door,** puerta de horno u hornillo; boca de hornalla.—**f. eater,** titiritero que finge tragarse brasas; jaque, matamoros, fierabrás; (E. U.) partidario acérrimo de los estados del sur antes de la guerra civil.—**f. engine,** bomba de incendios.—**f. escape,** aparato o escalera de salvamento.—**f. extinguisher,** extintor, matafuego.—**f. insurance,** seguro contra incendios.—**f. opal,** ópalo de fuego.—**f. pan,** brasero, chofeta.—**f. plug,** boca de agua (para incendios).—**f. room,** cuarto de calderas.—**f. screen,** pantalla, mampara.—**f. ship,** brulote.—**f. shovel,** pala de cocina.—**f. surface,** superficie de calefacción.—**f. trap,** edificio sin medios adecuados de escape en caso de incendio.—**f. water,** aguardiente.—**to be on f.,** estar ardiendo.—**to miss f.,** hacer fogonazo, hacer higa.—**to set f. to, to set on f.,** pegar fuego a, incendiar.

fire. I. *va.* incendiar; quemar; encender; disparar; cauterizar. **II.** *vn.* encenderse; inflamarse; disparar, hacer fuego; excitarse, enojarse.

firearm [fáiœrarm], *s.* arma de fuego.

fireback [-béc], *s.* pared posterior de un horno u hogar.

fireball [-ból], *s.* granada de mano.

firebrand [-bránd], *s.* tea, tizón; incendiario.

firecracker [-crécœr], *s.* triquitraque, carretilla, trabuca.

firedog [-dóg], *s.* morillo de hogar.

firefly [-flái], *s.* (ent.) luciérnaga, cocuyo.

firing [-ing]. **I.** *s.* acción de encender, disparar, etc. (*v.* FIRE, *va.*); cuidado del fuego de una caldera, etc. **II.** *a.* de disparar, encender, etc.—**f. iron,** cauterizador.—**f. line,** (mil.) línea principal de batalla.—**f. pin,** aguja de percusión.—**f. squad,** (mil.) pelotón de fusilamiento.

fireless [-les], *a.* sin fuego; apagado.—**f. cooker,** cocina o cocinilla sin fuego, en que el calor se obtiene de receptáculos aisladores.

firelock [-léc], *s.* fusil de piedra o de chispa.

fireman [-mæn], *s.* bombero; fogonero.

fireplace [-pléis], *s.* hogar, chimenea francesa.

fireproof [-prúf]. **I.** *a.* incombustible, calorífugo. **II.** *va.* hacer incombustible.—**fireproofing** [-ing], *s.* acción de hacer incombustible; materiales refractarios.

firewood [-úd], *s.* leña.

fireworks [-uéres], *s.* fuegos artificiales.

firkin [fœrkin], *s.* cuñete, barrilito.

firm [fœrm]. **I.** *a.* firme; fijo, estable; tenaz, inflexible. **II.** *s.* (com.) casa (de comercio); razón social (ll. t. **f. name**).

firmament [fœrmamœnt], *s.* firmamento.

firmamental [-tal], *a.* del firmamento.

firman [fœrman], *s.* firmán.

firmer chisel [fœrmœr chísœl], *s.* formón ancho y corto.

firmly [fœrmli], *adv.* firmemente.

firmness [-nes], *s.* firmeza.

first [fœrst]. **I.** *a.* primero.—**f. or last,** tarde o temprano, un día u otro.—**f. rate,** excelente, de primera clase; (fam.) muy bien.—**at f.,** al principio.—**at f. blush, at f. glance,** a primera vista, sin madura consideración.—**at f. hand,** de primera mano, directamente.—**from the f.,** desde el principio. **II.** *s.* el primero; el principio. **III.** *adv.* primero; en primer lugar; al principio; antes.—**f. begotten, f.-born,** primogénito.—**f.-boiler,** clarificadora (de azúcar).—**f.-class,** de primera clase o calidad.—**f.-cousin,** primo hermano, prima hermana.—**f. fruits,** primicia.—**f.-hand,** (com.) de primera mano.

firstling [-ling], *a.* y *s.* primogénito; primerizo.

firstly [fœrstli], *adv.* primeramente, en primer lugar.

firth [fœrth], *s.* = FRITH.

firwood [fœrud], *s.* madera de abeto.

fisc [fisc], *s.* fisco, erario, hacienda pública.

fiscal [físcal]. **I.** *s.* fiscal; ministro o secretario de hacienda. **II.** *a.* fiscal, perteneciente al fisco; rentístico.—**f. year,** año económico.

fish [fish]. **I.** *s.* pez; pescado; (mar.) gimelga, gemelo, gaburón; (mec.) refuerzo; (f. c.) plancha de empalme, eclisa.—**f. car,** vivero; (f. c.) furgón para llevar pescado.—**f. culture,** piscicultura.—**f. day,** día de pescado.—**f. glue,** cola de pescado, colapez.—**f. joint,** (f. c.) junta de eclisa.—**f. market,** pescadería.—**f. meal,** comida de pescado.—**f. of an anchor,** (mar.) pescante de un ancla.—**f. scale,** escama.—**f. spear,** = FISH-GIG.—**f. story,** cuento increíble, andaluzada.—**f. wire,** (elec.) alambre para tirar conductores por tubos.—**to have another, o other, f. to fry,** tener otras cosas en que pensar. **II.** *va.* pescar; buscar, coger; sacar (a menudo con *out*); intentar, alcanzar, obtener; reforzar, engimelgar; empalmar (rieles, etc.); (elec.) tirar (un conductor) por un tubo. **III.** *vn.* pescar.

fishbone [físhbóun], *s.* espina de pescado.

fisher [físhœr], *s.* pescador; marta de América.

fisherman [-man], *s.* pescador; barca pescadora.

fishery [físhœri], *s.* pesca, pesquería.

fishgig [-yíg], *s.* (mar.) fisga, arpón.

fishhook [-júc], *s.* anzuelo.

fishing [físhing]. **I.** *s.* pesca, pesquera, pesquería. **II.** *a.* de pescar.—**f. bait,** cebo, carnada.—**f. barge, gánguil.—f.-boat,** barca pescadora.—**f. fly,** mosca artificial para carnada.—**f. grounds,** pesquera.—**f. line,** cordel o sedal de pescar.—**f. reel,** carretel.—**f. rod,** caña de pescar.—**f. smack,** balandro o queche.—**f. tackle,** avíos de pescar, aparejo de pescar.—**f. wire** = FISH WIRE.

fishiness [físhines], *s.* forma, olor o sabor de pescado.

fishlike [-laic], *a.* semejante a los peces; a modo de pez.

fishmonger [-móngœr], *s.* pescadero.

fishplate [-pléit], *s.* (f. c.) eclisa, placa de unión.

fishpond [-pónd], *s.* nansa, vivero.

fishskin [-skín], *s.* piel de pescado, piel de lija.

fishwife [-uáif], **fishwoman** [-umæn], *s.* pescadora; marimacho.

fishy [físhi], *a.* pisciforme; que huele o sabe a pescado; habitado por pescados; abundante en pescado; (fam.) inverosímil, inventado.

fissate [físet], *a.* hendido, grietado.

fissile [físil], *a.* fisil, hendible, rajadizo.

fissipedal [fisípedal], *a.* fisípedo, bisulco.

fission [físhun], *s.* agrietamiento, fisura; fisiparidad, reproducción por división.

fissiparism [físípærîŝm], **fissiparity** [físipǽriti], *s.* fisiparidad, reproducción por división.—**fissiparous** [fisípærus], *a.* fisíparo.

fissure [físhuœr]. **I.** *s.* grieta, hendedura, rajadura, fisura. **II.** *va.* hender. **III.** *vn.* agrietarse, cuartearse.

fist. I. *s.* puño; (impr.) llamada, manecilla, ☞ **II.** *va.* apuñear, dar puñetazos a.

fistic [místic], *a.* relativo al puño; pugilístico.

fisticuff [místicuf], *s.* puñada; puñetazo.

fistula [míschula *o* tula], *s.* (cir.) fístula.

fistular [místular], *a.* fistular.

fistulate [míschulet], *a.* tubular.

fistulous [místulus], *a.* fistuloso.

fit. I. *s.* (med.) acceso, paroxismo; ataque (de una enfermedad, esp. de carácter histérico o epiléptico); pasión o capricho; arranque, arrebato; corte, talle o entalladura de un traje; ajuste, encaje; conveniencia, conformidad, adaptación; preparación; punto de saponificación.—**by fits (and starts)**, a tontas y a locas, espasmódicamente.—**to give one fits**, poner a uno como nuevo. **II.** *a.* apto, idóneo, a propósito, adecuado, conveniente, aprestado; hábil, capaz; compatible, apropiado, digno; decente; listo, preparado; (fam.) como si, casi, cuasi.—**to see f.**, juzgar conveniente. **III.** *va.* ajustar, encajar, acomodar, conformar; igualar, adaptar, adecuar; surtir, proveer, equipar, aprestar; disponer, preparar; (cost.) entallar un vestido; calzar, vestir.—**to f. out**, equipar; armar; tripular.—**to f. up**, ajustar, acomodar, componer; adornar, ataviar; amueblar. **IV.** *vn.* convenir, venir bien, corresponder; compadecerse o compaginarse con; ajustarse, entallarse, venir, sentar o caer bien o mal.—**to f. into**, encajar en; concordar con.

fitch [fich], **fitchet** [míchet], **fitchew** [míchu], *s.* (zool.) veso.

fitful [mítful], *a.* espasmódico; caprichoso; incierto, vacilante.—**fitfully** [-i], *adv.* por intervalos; caprichosamente.

fitly [mítli], *adv.* aptamente, adecuadamente, propiamente, acertadamente.

fitness [mítnes], *s.* aptitud, idoneidad; conveniencia, correspondencia; oportunidad; adaptabilidad.

fitter [mítœr], *s.* ajustador; montador; proveedor; (cost.) entallador, cortador.

fitting [míting]. **I.** *a.* propio, digno, adecuado, conveniente. **II.** *s.* ajuste, encaje; (cost.) entalladura, corte.—*pl.* guarniciones, accesorios; adjuntos o añadiduras; herrajes o avíos; herramientas.

fittingly [-li], *adv.* propiamente, aptamente.

five [fáiv], *s.* y *a.* cinco.—**f.-finger, f.-leaf** (bot.) cincoenrama.—**f.-spot**, cinco (en los naipes); (fam.) billete de cinco dólares o libras (llám. t. **fiver**).

fivefold [fáivfold], *a.* quíntuplo.

fives [fáivŝ], *s.* un juego de pelota; (vet.) adivas.

fix. I. *va.* fijar; asegurar, asentar; señalar (una fecha); arreglar, poner en orden; reparar, componer; (quím. y foto.) fijar; (E. U.) sobornar, cohechar; (fam.) castigar a uno, ajustarle las cuentas.—**to f. up**, componer, arreglar; equipar. **II.** *vn.* fijar el domicilio, establecerse; congelarse, cristalizarse, solidificarse.—**to f. on, o upon**, decidir, escoger, elegir. **III.** *s.* (fam.) apuro, aprieto; (fund.) brasea.

fixable [mícsabœl], *a.* fijable.

fixation [ficsáŝhun], *s.* fijación; fijeza, firmeza, estabilidad; (quím.) fijación.

fixative [mícsativ]. **I.** *a.* que fija. **II.** *s.* (tint.) mordente.

fixed [fixt], *pp.* y *a.* fijo; determinado; (com.) a plazo fijo; perentorio.

fixedly [mícsedli], *adv.* fijamente; firmemente; ciertamente.—**fixedness** [-nes], **fixity** [mícsiti], *s.* fijeza, firmeza; coherencia; fijación.

fixing [mícsing], *s.* acción de TO FIX en cualquier sentido; fijación.—*pl.* jaeces, enseres, útiles, accesorios.

fixture [mícxchœr], *s.* cosa fija o enclavada en un sitio; sostén, brazo (de lámpara eléctrica o

gas); adorno, trasto o mueble fijo en el suelo, la pared o el techo; empleado inamovible.—*pl.* habilitación de una tienda; instalación; guarniciones de alumbrado eléctrico y de gas (brazos, sostenes, accesorios, etc.).—**to be a f.**, (fam.) estar constantemente (en alguna parte).

fizgig [mísguig], *s.* arpón, dardo; buscapiés o carretilla; moza callejera.

fizz [fiŝ]. **I.** *vn.* sisear. **II.** *s.* siseo; efervescencia; (fam.) champaña.

fizzle [mísœl]. **I.** *vn.* sisear; hacer fiasco, quedar mal. **II.** *s.* fiasco; champaña o bebida efervecente; (fam.) apuro, aprieto.

flabbergast [flǽbœrgæst], *va.* (fam.) dejar de una pieza, pasmar.

flabby [flǽbi], *a.* flojo, lacio, fofo.

flabellate [flabélet], **flabelliform** [-liform], *a.* flabeliforme.

flaccid [flǽcsid], *a.* flojo, endeble, débil, flaco, laso; (med.) fláccido.—**flaccidity** [flæcsíditi], *s.* flojedad, flaqueza, debilidad.

flag [flæg]. **I.** *va.* hacer señales con banderola; izar bandera; cazar con banderín; asolar o adoquinar con lanchas o losas; hacer (a un tren) señal de parada. **II.** *vn.* flaquear, amilanarse; decaer, debilitarse; colgar, pender; vacilar. **III.** *s.* bandera; estandarte, pabellón; banderola; lajalosa; cola de venado; (*pl.*) (ornit.) plumas largas de las piernas; plumas secundarias del ala; (bot.) gladiolo, espadaña; ácoro; (geol.) FLAGSTONE, roca o piedra laminada; (mar.) FLAGSHIP.—**F. Day**, (E. U.) día de la bandera (14 de junio, aniversario de la adopción de la bandera norteamericana por los patriotas en 1777).—**f. officer**, (mar.) jefe de una escuadra (generalmente un almirante, vicealmirante o contraalmirante).—**f. of truce**, (mil.) parlamentario, bandera de parlamento.

flagellant [flǽelant]. **I.** *a.* flagelante. **II.** *s. pl.* (igl.) flagelantes.—**flagellate** [-leit], *vn.* flagelar.—**flagellation** [-léiŝhun], *s.* flagelación.

flagelliform [flavéliform], *a.* en forma de látigo o de sarmiento.

flagellum [flavélum], *s.* flagelo, azote; (bot.) renuevo, sarmiento.

flageolet [flǽyolet], *s.* caramillo, chirimía, dulzaina.

flagging [flǽguing]. **I.** *s.* enlosado; lajas para adoquinar. **II.** *a.* lánguido, flojo.

flaggy [flǽgui], *a.* parecido a la laja; que contiene espadañas o ácoros; flojo.

flagitious [flayíŝhus], *a.* malvado; atroz.

flagitiousness [-nes], *s.* maldad, atrocidad.

flagon [flǽgun], *s.* frasco, pomo.

flagpole [flǽgpóul], *s.* asta de bandera; (top.) banderola, jalón.

flagrancy [fléigrænsi], *s.* notoriedad, escándalo impudencia.—**flagrant** [-ant], *a.* notorio, escandaloso, público; flagrante.

flagrante delicto [flægrénti dilícto], *adv.* en flagrante, en fraganti.

flagrantly [flégrantli], *adv.* notoriamente.

flagship [flǽgship], *s.* (mar.) capitana, buque en que va el jefe de una escuadra.

flagstaff [flǽgstæf], *s.* asta de bandera.

flagstone [flǽgstóun], *s.* losa grande de embaldosar; (geol.) laja, lancha.

flail [fléil]. **I.** *s.* (agr.) mayal; (mil.) mangual. **II.** *va.* desgranar con mayal. **III.** *vn.* batir, sacudir.

flake [fleik]. **I.** *s.* pedacito, escama, casquito; hojuela, laminilla; clavel rayado.—**f. of fire**, centella, chispa.—**f. of ice**, carámbano.—**f. white**, albayalde. **II.** *va.* y *vn.* formar hojuelas o escamas; descascararse o desconcharse.

flaky [fléiki], *a.* lleno de cascajo o casquitos; escamoso; formando trepa.

flam [flæm]. **I.** *s.* mentira, embuste. **II.** *va.* mentir, engañar.

flambeau [flǽmbo], *s.* antorcha, hachón, candelabro; caldero para hervir azúcar.

flamboyant [-bóiant], *a.* rimbombante; flamígero, flamante; de bordes ondulados.

flame [fléim]. **I.** *s.* llama; (fam.) persona amada.
—**f.-colored**, de color de llama. **II.** *va.* quemar, chamuscar; encender. **III.** *vn.* arder, flamear, llamear, encenderse; brillar, fulgurar; inflamarse.
flameless [fléimles], *a.* sin llama.
flamen [fléimen], *s.* flamen.
flaming [fléiming], *a.* flamante, llameante; excitante; apasionado; llamativo, faustoso.
flamingo [flamíngo], *s.* (orn.) flamenco.
flamy [fléimi], *a.* inflamado, llameante.
flange [flænʒ]. **I.** *s.* (mec.) pestaña, reborde; tapa; herramienta para formar pestañas.— **f. coupling**, acoplamiento con anillos de rebordes.—**f. joint**, junta de pestañas remachadas o empernadas.—**f. nut**, tuerca de reborde o de basa.—**f. pipe**, tubo con pestaña.—**f. rail**, riel en T.—**f. wheel**, rueda de pestaña. **II.** *va.* hacer pestaña o reborde a. **III.** *vn.* ensancharse en forma de pestaña.
flanged [-d], *a.* de reborde, que tiene reborde o rebordes.
flank [flænk]. **I.** *s.* ijar, ijada; flanco, costado; (mil., fort.) flanco. **II.** *a.* lateral, de lado, de costado o por el flanco. **III.** *va.* orillar, estar a cada lado de; (mil.) flanquear. **IV.** *vn.* (con **on**) lindar con.—**flanker** [-œr], *s.* (fort.) flanco; flanqueador.
flannel [flǽnel], *s.* franela.
flanning, *s.* (alb.) derrame, vuelta, alféizar.
flap [flæp]. **I.** *s.* (sast.) cartera, golpe o portezuela; falda, faldilla, faldeta, faldón; ala de sombrero; hoja plegadiza de mesa; oreja de zapato; mosqueador; revés, cachete; (aut.) faja de protección (de la cámara de aire), guardacámara.—**f.-eared**, de orejas grandes y gachas.— **f.-mouthed**, morrudo, bezudo, hocicudo.— **f.-valve**, chapaleta. **II.** *va.* batir, sacudir, golpear, pegar; agitar, columpiar; mosquear; gualdrapear.—**to f. the wings**, aletear. **III.** *vn.* batir, dar gualdrapazos o socolladas; colgar.
flapdragon [flǽpdrægon], *s.* juego en que se arrebatan pasas, etc., de entre las llamas, y se comen.
flapjack [-yǽc], torta de sartén.
flapper [flǽpœr], *s.* batidor; el que o lo que bate, golpea o sacude; recordatorio; patito, anadino, polluelo; (fam.) chica; chica despreocupada.
flapping [flǽping], *s.* batimiento, aleteo, aletazo; (mar.) gualdrapazo, socollada.
flare [fléœr]. **I.** *va.* encender; chamuscar; (fig.) ostentar, enseñar, lucir. **II.** *vn.* lucir, brillar o destellar; deslumbrar; ostentar vestidos o adornos de colores chillones; acampanarse; ensancharse hacia la boca; sobresalir.—**to f. up**, encenderse; encolerizarse. **III.** *s.* llama, llamarada, fulgor, brillo, destello; brillantez, relumbrón; inclinación; derramo, ensanchamiento, reviro.— **f.-up**, llamarada; arrebato de cólera.
flaring [fléring], *a.* rutilante, resplandeciente, fulgurante; chillón; acampanado, abocinado; que proyecta o sobresale.—*s.* = FLARE.
flash [flæʃ]. **I.** *s.* relámpago; llamarada, destello, resplandor; viso; fucilazo; fogonazo; estanque, esclusa, represa; golpe de agua.—**f. light**, relámpago fotogénico.—**f.-light photography**, fotografía instantánea de relámpago.—**f. of lightning**, relámpago.—**f. of the eye**, ojeada, vistazo.—**f. of wit**, agudeza, rasgo de ingenio. **II.** *a.* ladronesco; charro, chillón; (fam.) experto, listo.—**f. burner**, mechero de gas con encendedor eléctrico.—**f. light**, luz titilante o intermitente (de un faro); luz giratoria de intensidad variable (para faros); linterna eléctrica de bolsillo o portátil (llám. t. **f. lamp**); (fot.) luz instantánea.—**f. point**, punto o temperatura de inflamación.—**f. test**, prueba del punto de inflamación; (por extensión) punto de inflamación.—**f. wheel**, rueda de canjilones para elevar agua. **III.** *va.* encender; quemar (pólvora); enviar o despedir con celeridad; sacar a relucir; hacer brillar; (elec.) tratar (un filamento de carbón) por la corriente eléctrica en una mezcla de hidrocarburos. **IV.** *vn.* relampaguear; brillar, destellar; pasar o cruzar como un relámpago.— **to f. in the pan**, dar higa (un fusil).

flashboard [flǽshbord], *s.* tabla de contención puesta sobre una presa, etc., para ahondar el agua.
flasher [flǽshœr], *s.* (elec.) destellador (especie de interruptor empleado en las lámparas de anuncios eléctricos).
flashily [flǽshili], *adv.* con ostentación, con colores chillones.
flashing [flǽshing], *s.* y *pa.* centelleo (*v.* FLASH); soplado del vidrio; (elec.) operación de reforzar los filamentos de lámparas incandescentes; (hid.) golpe de agua; vierteaguas, despidiente de agua, tabla o plancha de escurrimiento o de desviación (de agua).—**f. light, point** = FLASH LIGHT, POINT.
flashy [flǽshi], *a.* de oropel, de relumbrón.
flask [flask], *s.* frasco, redoma, botella, pomo; (fund.) caja de moldear.
flat [flæt]. **I.** *s.* llanura; banco, bajío, escollo; cosa plana, v. gr.: palma de la mano, plano de una hoja cortante, barca chata, pala de remo, carro de plataforma, alma de botón; apartamento, piso; (mús.) bemol, (fam.) mentecato; (agr.) semillero de cajón. **II.** *a.* plano; raso, chato, aplastado; tendido, extendido; arrasado; categórico; fijo; neto; insulso, insípido; (mús.) desafinado (bajo); menor o disminuído.—**f.-bottomed**, de fondo plano.—**f. car**, vagón de plataforma.— **f.-footed**, de pies achatados; (fam.) inflexible, resuelto, determinado.—**f. nose**, nariz chata.— **f.-nosed**, chato.—**f. roof**, azotea.—**f. tire**, o **tyre**, (aut.) neumático desinflado. **III.** *va.* (mus.) bajar de tono; allanar, aplastar, achatar. **IV.** *vn.* (mús.) desafinar por lo bajo; aplastarse; atontarse.
flatboat [flǽtbout], *s.* barco o bote de fondo plano.
flatiron [-áiœrn], *s.* plancha (de planchar).
flatlong [flǽtlong], *adv.* de plano.
flatly [-li], *adv.* horizontalmente, llanamente; de plano; absolutamente; sin animación ni interés.—**flatness** [-nes], *s.* llanura, lisura, chatedad; desabrimiento, insipidez, insulsez.
flatten [flǽtœn]. **I.** *va.* allanar, aplastar, achatar, aplanar; tender; abatir; desabrir, desazonar; deprimir; (aer.) enderezar (un avión), poner horizontal. **II.** *vn.* aplanarse, igualarse; perder el sabor; evaporarse; (aer.) tomar la posición horizontal.
flatter [flǽtœr]. **I.** *comp.* de FLAT: más llano, insípido, etc. **II.** *s.* allanador; hilera de estirar alambre.
flatter . **I.** *va.* adular, lisonjear; hacerse una ilusión; favorecer. **II.** *vn.* adular, lisonjear.— **flatterer** [-œr], *s.* adulador; lisonjero, zalamero.— **flattering** [-ing], *a.* lisonjero, halagüeño.—**flatteringly** [-ingli], *adv.* lisonjeramente, halagüeñamente.—**flattery** [-ri], *s.* adulación, lisonja, halago.
flattish [flǽtish], *a.* achatado.
flatulence, flatulency [flǽtiulens, i], *s.* flatulencia; hinchazón, presunción.
flatulent [-ent], **flatuous** [flǽchius], *a.* flatulento; hinchado, vano.
flatus [fléitus], *s.* flato, ventosidad; hinchazón; ráfaga, soplo.
flatwise [flǽtuais], *adv.* de llano.
flaunt [flant]. **I.** *va.* y *vn.* ostentar, lucir; desplegar, ondear. **II.** *s.* ostentación, alarde.
flautist [flótist], *s.* flautista.
flavescent [flavéscent], *a.* amarillento.
flavo(u)r [fléivœr], **I.** *s.* sabor, gusto, gustillo; (coc.) sazón, sainete. **II.** *va.* saborear, sazonar, condimentar; (fig.) dar cualidad distintiva a una cosa.—**flavo(u)ring** [-ing], *a.* sainete, condimento.—**flavo(u)rless** [-les], *a.* sin sabor, insípido, soso.—**flavo(u)rous** [-us], *a.* sabroso.
flaw [flo]. **I.** *s.* defecto, imperfección; grieta, pelo, paño, paja; falla, mancha; (mar.) ráfaga, racha. **II.** *va.* afear, estropear; agrietar.
flawless [flóles], *a.* entero, sin tacha.
flawy [flói], *a.* agrietado; lleno de faltas o tachas; propenso a rachas.
flax [flæcs], *s.* (bot.) lino.—**f. brake**, agramadera.—**f. comb**, rastrillo.—**f. dresser**, rastrillador.—**f. dressing**, rastrillo del lino.—**to brake f.**, agramar lino.—**to dress f.**, rastrillar lino.

flaxen [flǽcsen], **flaxy** [flǽcsi], a. de lino.—**f.-haired**, blondo.

flaxseed [flǽcsid], s. (bot.) linaza.

flay [fléi], va. desollar; despellejar.

flayer [fléiœr], s. desollador.

flea [flí], s. pulga.—**a f. in one's ear**, amonestación.

fleabane [flíben], s. (bot.) coniza, pulguera.

fleabite [flíbait], s. picadura de pulga.

fleabitten [-bítœn], a. picado de pulgas; salpicado.

fleam [flím], s. (vet.) fleme, lanceta.

fleawort [flíuœrt], s. (bot.) pulicaria.

fleck(er [flék(œr]. **I.** va. abigarrar, varetear. **II.** s. punto o lista de color, mancha, lunar; copo, vedija; lonja (de tocino).

fleckless [flécles], a. sin mancha.

flection [flécshun], s. flexión; corvadura; ojeada o mirada; (gram.) flexión.

fled, pret. y pp. de TO FLEE.

fledged [fleyt], a. plumado, plumoso; con bozo; alado; maduro, sazonado.

fledg(e)ling [fléyling], s. y a. volantón; joven, novel.

flee [flí]. **I.** va. (pret. y pp. FLED) huir de. **II.** vn. huir; fugarse; desaparecer.

fleece [flís]. **I.** s. vellón, lana.—**f. wool**, vellón. **II.** va. esquilar, tonsurar; cubrir con lana o nieve; escamotear.

fleecy [flísi], a. lanudo.—**f. clouds**, nubes aborregadas.

fleer [flíœr]. **I.** va. mofar, burlar. **II.** vn. mofarse; burlarse. **III.** s. burla, mueca; risa falsa.

fleet [flít]. **I.** s. (mar.) armada; flota. **II.** a. veloz, rápido.—**f.-footed**, alípede; ligero.—**f.-winged**, alígero. **III.** va. y vn. volar, desvanecerse; pasar; (mar.) despasar, cambiar.

fleeting [flíting], a. fugaz, efímero.

fleetingly [-li], **fleetly** [flítli], adv. velozmente, fugazmente.

fleetness [flítnes], s. ligereza, rapidez.

Fleming [fléming], s. flamenco.

Flemish [flémiSh], a. y s. flamenco.—**F. bond** = DUTCH BOND.

flesh [fleSh]. **I.** s. carne; género humano; pulpa (de las frutas).—**f. and blood**, carne y hueso; sangre, parentela, progenie.—**f. brush**, cepillo para frotar la piel.—**f. color**, color de carne, encarnado.—**f. diet**, dieta de carne.—**f. fly**, moscarda.—**f. meat**, (coc.) carne.—**f. wound**, herida superficial. **II.** va. hartar; incitar; meter en la carne (la espada, etc.); avezar, habituar; cebar; (ten.) descarnar, pelambrar.

fleshiness [fléShines], s. gordura, corpulencia.

fleshings [fléShingś], s. pl. (teat.) calzas de punto de color de carne; (ten.) descarnaduras, piltrafas.

fleshless [fléShles], a. descarnado.

fleshliness [fléShlines], s. carnalidad.

fleshly [fléShli], a. carnal; corpóreo.

fleshmonger [fléShmóngœr], s. carnicero; alcahuete.

fleshpot [-pót], s. marmita, olla.

fleshy [fléShi], a. gordo; corporal; carnal; carnoso, pulposo; suculento.

fletcher [fléchœr], s. flechero.

fleur-de-lis [flœr-de-lí], s. sing. y pl. flor de lis.

flew [fliú], pret. de TO FLY.

flewed [fliúd], a. boquihendido.

flews [fliúś], s. pl. belfos.

flex [fleks]. **I.** va. doblar, encorvar. **II.** vn. doblarse, encorvarse. **III.** s. doblez, encorvadura.

flexibility [flécsibíliti], **flexibleness** [flécsiboelnes], s. flexibilidad; docilidad.

flexi(b)le [flécsi(bœ)l], a. flexible; dócil; adaptable, doblegable; cimbreño, plástico.

flexion [flécshun], s. = FLECTION.

flexor [flécsor], s. (anat.) músculo flexor.

flexuose [fléxyuos], **flexuous** [fléxyuus], a. tortuoso; vario, inconstante; (bot.) flexuoso.

flexure [fléxyuœr], s. flexión; corvadura.

flick. I. va. dar ligeramente con un látigo, etc. **II.** s. pasagonzalo.

flicker [flíkœr]. **I.** vn. flamear; fluctuar, vacilar, aletear, revolotear. **II.** s. llama vacilante; picamaderos (pájaro).

flier [fláiœr], s. volador; ave voladora; fugitivo; (mec.) volante; (impr.) sacapliegos; escalón, peldaño; (fam.) cosa veloz, v. gr.: buque rápido, caballo de carrera, tren expreso, etc.; (fam.) aventura, tentativa; operación de bolsa.

flight [fláit], s. vuelo, volada; espacio recorrido por un proyectil, pájaro, etc.; bandada de pájaros; ímpetu, arranque; tramo de escalera; huída, fuga; (for.) evasión, escape; (aer.) escuadrilla aérea, compuesta gen. de cuatro aviones.—**f. feather**, remera.—**f. path**, (aer.) trayectoria del centro de gravedad de un avión, línea de vuelo.

flightiness [fláitines], s. veleidad, capricho.

flighty [fláiti], a. volátil; voltario; travieso.

flimflam [flímflam]. **I.** s. (fam.) soflama. **II.** va. soflamar.

flimsily [flímsili], adv. sin consistencia, endeblemente.—**flimsiness** [-nes], s. endeblez, falta de solidez o consistencia.

flimsy [flímsi], a. débil, endeble; baladí, frívolo.

flinch. I. vn. vacilar; acobardarse; echar el cuerpo atrás.—**to f. back**, retroceder; desistir; desdecirse. **II.** s. vacilación, titubeo.

flinder [flíndœr], s. astilla, fragmento, tira.

fling. I. va. (pret. y pp. FLUNG) arrojar, tirar, despedir; derribar, echar al suelo; sobrepujar, vencer.—**to f. about**, desparramar, esparcir.—**to f. away**, arrojar, desechar.—**to f. in one's face**, echar en cara; lanzar al rostro.—**to f. off**, engañar en la caza.—**to f. open**, abrir de repente.—**to f. out**, arrojar con fuerza; hablar violentamente, echar chispas.—**to f. up**, abandonar, dejar. **II.** vn. lanzar un arma arrojadiza; escarnecer, mofarse, murmurar; alborotarse, cocear, brincar. saltar, lanzarse. **III.** s. tiro; echada, echamiento; indirecta, sarcasmo, pulla; brinco, salto; coz; honda; libertad de acción; bravata, atrevimiento; baile escocés muy vivo.

flint, s. pedernal; piedra de chispa; cualquiera cosa sumamente dura.—**f. glass**, cristal.—**f.-heart(ed**, empedernido.—**f. stone**, pedernal.

flintiness [flíntines], s. excesiva dureza.

flintlock [-lóc], s. llave o fusil de chispa.

flinty [flínti], a. aperdernalado o pedernalino; empedernido, inexorable.

flip. I. va. lanzar, soltar; chasquear; dar un golpe rápido; quitar de golpe. **II.** s. pasagonzalo, capirotazo; bebida de vino o cerveza con ron y azúcar.

flippancy [flípansi], s. petulancia, locuacidad, impertinencia.—**flippant** [-ant], a. petulante, locuaz, impertinente.—**flippantly** [-li], adv. locuazmente, impertinentemente.

flipper [flípœr], s. aleta o pata de tortuga o de foca.

flirt [flœrt]. **I.** vn. coquetear; corretear, travesear; burlarse, mofarse. **II.** va. tirar, sacudir o menear con ligereza; hacer burla de. **III.** s. coqueta; coquetón; golpe o meneo rápido; mofa, gesto.

flirtation [flœrtéiShun], **flirting** [flœrting], s. coquetería, coqueteo.—**flirtatious** [-téiShus], a. coqueta; coquetón.

flit, vn. volar, revolotear; deslizarse, pasar rápidamente.

flitch [flich], s. hoja de tocino; mojama; (carp.) costero.—**f. beam**, viga armada.

flitter [flítœr], s. revoloteador; harapo, andrajo; lentejuela, adorno de oropel.

flitting [flíting]. **I.** s. fuga, vuelo rápido. **II.** a. fugaz.

flivver [flívœr], s. (fam.) automóvil barato.

flix, s. borra, tamo, pelusa.

float [flóut]. **I.** va. poner, mantener o llevar a flote; (com.) emitir, poner en circulación; (alb.) enlucir con llana o talocha; regar; (dep.) cazar en bote. **II.** vn. flotar, sobrenadar; boyar; fluctuar; cernerse; nadar.—**to f. up**, soldar por dentro. **III.** s. flotador; cualquier cosa que flota; balsa,

boya, armadía, maderada; (mar.) jangada; salvavidas; cercho de una caña de pescar; palo (de
remo); (alb.) regla o tabla aplanadora; bote de
cazar patos; carromato; carroza para espectáculos
públicos. **IV.** *a.* de flotador (apl. a varios artificios
mecánicos, como válvulas, indicadores de nivel,
etc.).—**f.-cut file,** lima de picadura sencilla.—**f.
seaplane,** hidroavión de flotadores.

floatable [flótabœl], *a.* flotable.

floatage, *s.* = FLOTAGE.

floatboard [flóutbórd], *s.* álabe, paleta de rueda.

floater [flótœr], *s.* flotador.

floating [flóting]. **I.** *s.* flote, flotación; (alb.)
revestimiento. **II.** *a.* flotante, boyante; a
flote, suelto, no anclado; fluctuante, movible,
variable; (com.) flotante, en circulación.—**f.
battery,** (elec.) pila compensadora.—**f. debt,**
deuda flotante.—**f. island,** especie de flan en que
flotan las claras de huevos batidas.—**f. kidney,**
riñón flotante.—**f. population,** población flotante,
de tránsito.—**f. rib,** (anat.) costilla flotante.—**f.
tapers,** mariposas.

floccose [flócos], *a.* (bot.) velludo.

flocculence [flókiulens], *s.* vellosidad.

flocculent [-ent], *a.* velludo, lanudo; (orn.) parecido al flojel.

flock. I. *s.* manada, rebaño; grey; bandada;
congregación; multitud; borra, tamo, flojel,
pelusilla; copo o vedija de lana.—**f. bed,** colchón
de borra.—**f. paper,** papel aterciopelado. **II.** *vn.*
congregarse, juntarse, reunirse, atroparse.

floe [flo], *s.* masa de hielo flotante.

flog, *va.* azotar, vapular, tundir.

flogging [flóguing], *s.* flagelación; azotes.

flood. I. *s.* diluvio; avenida, creciente;
inundación; (min.) aguada; chorro, menstruo
excesivo.—**f. light,** lámpara proyectante de rayos
concentrados, para iluminar objetos especiales.—
f. lighting, sistema de alumbrado uniforme sin
sombras.—**f. tide,** pleamar. **II.** inundar; anegar.

floodgate [-guéit], *s.* compuerta de esclusa, paradera.

flooding [-ing], *s.* inundación; (med.) hemorragia
uterina.

floodmark [-márc], *s.* nivel de la marea alta.

flook [fluc], *s.* (mar.)=FLUKE.

floor [flóœr]. **I.** *s.* suelo, piso; piso de una casa
(primero, segundo); (agr.) era; (mar.) fondo,
plan; en una asamblea, lugar destinado a los
diputados, y, por extensión, el uso de la palabra
(*to have the floor,* tener la palabra). **II.** *va.* solar,
tillar, entarimar; echar al suelo; (fig.) abrumar;
vencer, derrotar; poner en el suelo.

floorcloth [-clóz], *s.* hule para cubrir el suelo.

flooring [-ing], *s.* suelo, piso; material para
pisos.

floorwalker [-uókœr], *s.* superintendente de una
división de un bazar.

flop. I. *va.* batir, sacudir. **II.** *vn.* aletear; caer
flojamente; colgar; caerse, venirse abajo; (fam.)
pasarse de un partido a otro.

flora, *s.* flora.

floral [flóral], *a.* floral.

Florentine [flórentin], *s.* florentino.

florescence [florésens], *s.* (bot.) florescencia.

florescent [florésent], *a.* floreciente.

floret [flóret], *s.* (bot.) flósculo.

floriculture [flóricúlchœr], *s.* floricultura.

floriculturist [-ist], *s.* floricultor.

florid [flórid], *a.* florido; encarnado, rojo; vivo;
(b. a.) florido.

floridity [floríditi], **floridness** [flóridnes], *s.* floridez.

floridly [flóridli], *adv.* floridamente.

floriferous [florífœrus], *a.* florífero.

florin [flórin], *s.* florín (moneda).

florist [flórist], *s.* florero, florera.

floscule [flóskiul], *s.* (bot.) flósculo.

floss, *s.* seda floja; atanquía, cadarzo; penacho
del maíz; (fund.) escorias que sobrenadan.—
f. silk, seda floja.

flossy [flósi], *a.* len.

flotage [flótey], *s.* objetos que flotan; pecio; flotación.

flotation [flotéishun], *s.* flotación; teoría de los
cuerpos flotantes.

flotilla [flotíla], *s.* flotilla.

flotsam [flótsam], *s.* pecios; objetos flotantes.

flounce [fláuns]. **I.** *va.* (cost.) guarnecer con
volantes o vuelos. **II.** *vn.* pernear; brincar de
impaciencia. **III.** *s.* (cost.) volante, fleco, farfalá, cairel.

flounder [fláundœr]. **I.** *s.* (ict.) lenguado, rodaballo; tumbo, tropiezo. **II.** *vn.* forcejar; tropezar y caer.

flour [fláuœr]. **I.** *s.* harina; polvo; salitre fino.—
f. bolt, tamiz, cedazo.—*l.* **of powder,** pólvora de
mostacilla. **II.** *va.* pulverizar; rociar con harina.
III. *vn.* dividirse en granos, pulverizarse.

flourish [flœrish]. **I.** *va.* florear, blandir, menear;
embellecer. **II.** *vn.* florecer; medrar, prosperar;
rasguear; jactarse; blandear; (mús.) florear.
III. *s.* rasgo, plumada; rúbrica; floreo, adorno;
(esgr.) molinete; (mús.) floreo, preludio.

flourishing [-ing], *a.* floreciente; próspero.

flourishingly [-li], *adv.* floridamente; prósperamente.

floury [fláuœri], *a.* harinoso.

flout [fláut]. **I.** *va.* y *vn.* burlarse, mofarse, befar.
II. *s.* mofa, befa, burla, escarnio.

flow [flóu]. **I.** *vn.* fluir, manar; correr; dimanar;
seguirse; ondear, flotear; salir; crecer (la
marea); desembocar, desaguar.—**to f. away,**
deslizarse, pasar.—**to f. with,** abundar en, o manar.
II. *s.* corriente, torrente; flujo; salida; flujo de la
marea; (hidr.) gasto, cantidad que sale o pasa por
unidad de tiempo.

flower [fláuœr]. **I.** *s.* (bot.) flor; planta en flor;
flor y nata; figura retórica; adorno, belleza.—
pl. (quím.) flor; regla, menstruación.—**f. bed,**
cuadro, macizo, era de jardín.—**f. bud,** capullo,
botón de flor.—**f. de luce,** flor de lis, iris.—**f.
garden,** jardín.—**f. girl,** florera, ramilletera.—
f. leaf, pétalo.—**f. of an hour,** hibisco.—**f. piece,**
ramillete; (pint.) florero.—**f. stalk,** pedúnculo,
pezón.—**f. stand,** jardinera (mueble).—**f. vase,**
florero.—**flowers of zinc,** cinc sublimado. **II.** *va.*
florear. **III.** *vn.* florecer.

flowered [fláuœrd], *a.* floreado, espolinado.—**f.
silk,** seda agrisetada.

floweret [fláuœret], *s.* florecilla, florecita.

flowcriness [-ines], *s.* abundancia de flores;
floreo de palabras.

flowering [-ing]. **I.** *a.* (bot.) fanerógamo. **II.** *s.*
floración, florescencia.

flowerless [fláuœrles], *a.* sin flores.

flowerpot [-pót], *s.* tiesto, maceta de flores.

flowery [fláuœri], *a.* florido; ornado.

flowing [flóing]. **I.** corriente, fluente, ondeante,
fluctuoso; suelto; colgante; fluido. **II.** *s.* derrame, salida; corriente, flujo; fluidez.—**flowingly**
[-li], *adv.* copiosamente.—**flowingness** [-nes], *s.* dicción fluida.

flown [flóun], *pp.* de TO FLY; vidriado.

fluctuant [flúkchuænt], *a.* fluctuante, fluctuoso.

fluctuate [-eit], *vn.* fluctuar; oscilar, ondear.

fluctuation [-éishun], *s.* fluctuación.

flue [flu], *s.* cañón de chimenea; tubo de caldera;
pelusa, borra, tamo.—**f. boiler,** caldera de tubos
de humos o de conductos interiores.

fluency [flúensi], *s.* fluidez; afluencia, facundia,
labia.

fluent [-ent]. **I.** *a.* facundo, afluente; suelto,
fácil; fluido, fluente. **II.** *s.* (mat.) fluente,
función.—**fluently** [-li], *adv.* con facundia o labia.

fluff [flvf]. **I.** *s.* pelusa, lanilla, pelillo, vello, borra, mota, tamo, plumón. **II.** *va.* mullir borra,
plumón, etc.—**fluffiness** [flúfines], *s.* calidad de
mullido o sedoso.—**fluffy** [flúfi], *a.* cubierto de
plumón o vello; blando, mullido.—**f. hair,** cabello
sedoso.

fluid [flúid], *s.* y *a.* flúido.—**f. dram,** o **drachm,**
la octava parte de una *fluid ounce.*—**f. ounce,**
medida de capacidad para líquidos (29.6 mililitros
o centímetros cúbicos).

fluidity [fluíditi], **fluidness** [flúidnes], *s.* fluidez.

fluke [fluc], *s.* uña del ancla; uña del arpón; aleta de la cola de la ballena; (fam.) chiripa (en el billar); lombriz del ganado lanar; (ict.) platija.

flume [flum], *s.* saetín, caz, canal; cañada; canal de descargar (carbón, etc.).

flummery [flúmœri], *s.* manjar blanco; pelitrique.

flung [flung], *pret.* y *pp.* de TO FLING.

flunk(e)y [flúnki], *s.* lacayo; adulón, lavacaras.

flunkyism [flúnkiìsm], *s.* servilismo.

fluor [flúor], *s.* **f. spar**, (min.) espato flúor.

fluorescence [fluorésens], *s.* fluorescencia.

fluorescent [fluorésent], *a.* fluorescente.

fluoric [fluóric], *a.* (quím.) fluórico.

fluorid(e [flúorid, -aid], *s.* (quím.) fluoruro.

fluorin(e [flúorin], *s.* (quím.) flúor.

fluorite [flúorait], *s.* (min.) fluorita.

fluoroscope [fluóroscoup], *s.* fluoroscopio.

flurry [flœri]. **I.** *s.* agitación, conmoción; ráfaga, racha. **II.** *va.* confundir, aturdir.

flush [flush]. **I.** *va.* abochornar, sonrojar; engreír, alentar; igualar, nivelar o emparejar; inundar; limpiar con un chorro de agua. **II.** *vn.* salirse, derramarse, llenarse de agua; echar a volar; sonrojarse, ponerse colorado. **III.** *a.* igual, parejo, ras, niveladas; copioso, abundante; rico, adinerado; robusto, lleno de vida.—**f. bolt**, perno de cabeza embutida.—**f. box**, (elec.) caja de inspección e introducción de conductores subterráneos, de tapa pareja con el pavimento.—**f. joint**, junta machihembrada ras en ras.—**f. rivet**, remache de cabeza embutida.—**f. switch**, (elec.) interruptor embutido de tapa al ras con la pared. —**f. tank**, depósito de agua para limpia (de inodoros, etc.).—**f. with**, a flor de, ras en ras o parejo con. **IV.** *s.* rubor, sonrojo, color (en las mejillas); animación, agitación, emoción; vuelo súbito de un pájaro o una bandada; floración; flujo rápido o copioso; copia, abundancia; flux (de naipes).

fluster [flústœr]. **I.** *va.* embriagar; confundir, aturdir. **II.** *s.* confusión, aturdimiento; borrachera.

flustered [flústœrd], *a.* calamocano.

flute [flut]. **I.** *s.* (mús.) flauta; (arq.) estría; rizado, pliegue. **II.** *va.* estriar, acanalar, encañutar; (cost.) alechugar, rizar, plegar, (Méx.) encarrujar. **III.** *vn.* tocar la flauta.

fluted [flúted], *a.* acanalado, ondulado.

fluting [-ing], *s.* (arq.) estría, estriadura, acanaladura; (cost.) rizado, alechugado.—**f. iron**, hierro de rizar.—**f. plane**, cepillo bocel.

flutist [-ist], *s.* flautista.

flutter [flútœr]. **I.** *va.* agitar, menear, sacudir; aturdir. **II.** *vn.* agitarse, menearse, alterarse; aletear, revolotear. **III.** *s.* alboroto, confusión; agitación; vibración; ondulación.

fluvial [flúvial], **fluviatile** [flúviatil], **fluviatic** [fluviætic], *a.* fluvial.

fluviograph [flúviogræf], *s.* fluviógrafo, fluviómetro.

flux [flvcs]. **I.** *s.* flujo; derretimiento, fusión; (med.) fluxión, flujo; (quím. y met.) fundente. **II.** *va.* fundir, derretir; mezclar con un fundente; (med.) purgar.

fluxion [flúcshun], *s.* flujo; fusión; (med.) fluxión, congestión; (mat.) fluxión, derivada; (mat.) diferencial.—**fluxional** [-al], *a.* variable, inconstante.

fly [flái]. **I.** *va.* (*pret.* FLEW [flu]; *pp.* FLOWN [flóun]) hacer volar; elevar (una cometa, etc.); enarbolar; evitar, evadir, huir de; (impr.) sacar pliegos; (aer.) dirigir (un avión); cruzar o atravesar en avión. **II.** *vn.* volar; lanzarse, precipitarse; correr, pasar rápidamente; saltar, reventar, estallar; huir, escaparse; desaparecer, desvanecerse.—**to f. about**, (mar.) cambiar el viento con frecuencia.—**to f. around**, ir de un lado a otro.—**to f. at**, arrojarse o lanzarse sobre.—**to f. away**, irse volando; escaparse.—**to f. down**, bajar volando.—**to f. from**, huir de.—**to f. in the face of**, ir contra, hacer frente a.—**to f. into a passion**, montar en cólera; irse del seguro.—**to f. off**, desprenderse súbitamente; separarse, suble-

varse.—**to f. off at a tangent**, tomar repentinamente una resolución extraña, o salir con alguna extravagancia.—**to f. off the handle**, (fam.) perder la chaveta, irse del seguro.—**to f. on**, lanzarse sobre, arremeter a.—**to f. open**, abrirse repentinamente.—**to f. out**, disparararse, salir a espetaperros; TO FLY OFF THE HANDLE.—**to f. to arms**, correr a las armas.—**to f. to pieces**, romperse en añicos.

fly, *s.* mosca; (dep.) mosca artificial (cebo para pescar); cabriolé, calesín, volanta; fruslería, bagatela; uno de varios objetos de movimiento rápido, v. gr.: 1) (impr.) sacapliegos; 2) brazo de romana; 3) rueda volante; 4) escape de reloj; 5) brazo de veleta; 6) vuelo de una bandera; 7) lanzadera, etc.; (sast.) bragueta; vuelo de un proyectil, pelota, etc.; tapa del teclado de un piano; (teat.) bambalina.—**f.-bitten**, manchado por las moscas.—**f. blister**, cantárida (parche).—**to f.-fish**, *v.* pescar con moscas artificiales.—**f.-fishing**, pesca con moscas artificiales.—**f. net**, mosquitero.—**f. paper**, papel para coger o matar moscas.—**on the f.**, al vuelo.

flyaway [fláieuéi], *a.* instable, inquieto; inconstante.

flyblow [-blou]. **I.** *s.* cresa, huevo de mosca. **II.** *va.* corromper la carne llenándola de cresas.

flyboat [-bout], *s.* (mar.) flibote.

flycatcher [-cæchœr], *s.* (orn.) doral, muscaria, papamoscas.

flyflap [-flæp], **flytrap** [-træp], *s.* mosqueador, espantamoscas, mosquero.

flying [fláing]. **I.** *a.* volante; volador; de volar; volátil; rápido, veloz; flotante, undulante; desplegado.—**f. boat**, hidroavión.—**f. buttress**, (arq.) botarel, arbotante.—**f. fish**, pez volador.— **f. jib**, petifoque, cuarto foque.—**f. report**, noticia volandera.—**f. squadron**, escuadra ligera.—**to shoot f.**, tirar al vuelo. **II.** *s.* vuelo.

flyleaf [fláilif], *s.* (impr.) guarda de un libro.

flyspeck [fláispec], *s.* mancha de mosca.

flywheel [fláijuíl], *s.* (mec.) volante.

foal [fóul]. **I.** *s.* potro; potrillo; buche. **II.** *va.* y *vn.* parir (una yegua o burra).

foam [fóum]. **I.** *s.* espuma. **II.** *va.* hacer espuma. **III.** *vn.* espumar, echar espuma o espumarajos.

foamy [fómi], *a.* espumajoso, espumoso.

fob [fob]. **I.** *s.* faltriquera del reloj.—**f. chain**, leopoldina. **II.** *va.* engañar, defraudar, pegársela a uno.

focal [fócal], *a.* focal; céntrico.—**f. distance**, o **length**, distancia focal.

focus [fócus]. **I.** *s.* foco; distancia focal.—**f. screen**, pantalla o visera para poner en foco. **II.** *va.* enfocar, afocar; concentrar.

fodder [fódœr]. **I.** *s.* forraje. **II.** *va.* dar forraje a.

foe [fóu], **foeman** [-man], *s.* enemigo.

foelike [fólaic], *a.* hostil.

foetus [fítus], *s.* feto.

fog. **I.** *s.* niebla, neblina, confusión, perplejidad; (foto.) velo.—**f. bell, signal, whistle**, campana, señal, sirena de nieblas o de alarma. **II.** *va.* obscurecer; (foto.) velar. **III.** *vn.* ponerse brumoso; (foto.) velarse.

fog, fogge, foggage [fóguey], *s.* segunda cosecha de hierba de una estación.

foggily [fóguili], *adv.* brumosamente.

fogginess [fóguines], *s.* calidad de nublado o brumoso.

foggy [fógui], *a.* brumoso; obscuro; calamocano; (bot.) mohoso; (foto.) velado.

foghorn [fógjórn], *s.* sirena.

fogy [fógui], *s.* vejestorio.

fogyism [fóguiìsm], *s.* cosas de viejos.

foh [fo], *interj.* ¡quita allá!

foible [fóibœl], *s.* lado flaco, flaqueza; parte media de la hoja de una espada.

foil [fóil]. **I.** *va.* frustrar; embotar; adormecer, amortiguar. **II.** *s.* hoja delgada de metal; oropel; chapa; pan u hoja de oro o plata; azogado de un espejo; (arq.) hoja, lóbulo; (esgr.) florete; (caza) huella, pista, rastro.

foiling [fóiling], *s.* freza, rastro.

foist [fóist], *va.* meter clandestinamente; (gen. con *on*) imponer (a); meterle (a), engañar con.

fold [fóuld]. **I.** *s.* doblez, pliegue, repliegue, arruga, recogido; abrazo; envoltorio; redil, corral, aprisco; hato, rebaño; (fig.) congregación de fieles. Usado como sufijo denota veces (*twofold*, dos veces, doble). **II.** *va.* doblar, plegar; abrazar, enlazar; cerrar, incluir, envolver, encerrar; arredilar; meter en redil.—**to f. the arms**, cruzar los brazos. **III.** *vn.* doblarse, plegarse, cerrarse.

folder [fóuldœr], *s.* plegador, doblador; plegadera; hoja, circular, etc., plegadizas.

folderol [fólderol]. **I.** *a.* absurdo o desatinado. **II.** *s.* pamema, pampirolada.

folding [fóulding]. **I.** *a.* plegadizo, plegable, replegable; doblador, plegador.—**f. bed**, cama plegadiza, catricofre.—**f. camera**, cámara plegadiza.—**f. chair**, silla plegadiza; catrecillo.—**f. door**, puerta de dos hojas o plegadiza; puerta corrediza.—**f. knife**, navaja; cuchillo de caza.—**f. machine**, máquina de plegar, plegadora mecánica.—**f. screen**, biombo.—**f. seat**, asiento levadizo. **II.** *s.* plegado, plegadura; pliegue, repliegue.

foldnet [fóuldnét], *s.* arañuelo, red para coger pájaros.

foliaceous [foliéîshus], *a.* foliáceo; laminado.

foliage [fóliey], *s.* follaje, frondosidad, fronda.

foliate [fólieit]. **I.** *va.* (metal.) batir hoja; azogar un espejo. **II.** *a.* frondoso; batido, laminado.

foliated [-ed], *a.* (metal.) batido, laminado; (arq.) lobulado; azogado; chapeado; (bot.) foliado.

feliation [foliéîshun], **foliature** [fóliachur], *s.* (metal.) batimiento; exfoliación; azogamiento; (bot.) foliación.

folio. I. *s.* infolio; folio, página; (for.) unidad para medir la extensión de un documento (Ingl. 90 palabras; E. U. 100 palabras); cartera para grabados, etc. **II.** *a.* de a folio. **III.** *va.* foliar.

foliose [fólious], *a.* frondoso.

folk [fóuc], *s.* gente; nación, raza, pueblo.—*pl.* (fam. E. U.) parientes, parentela.—**f. song**, cantar de gesta; copla, jácara, romance.—**f. speech**, lenguaje vulgar.

folklore [fóuclóœr], *s.* folklore, tradiciones y leyendas populares; estudio de ellas.

folkloric [-lóric], *a.* folklórico. (*V.* FOLKLORE.)

folklorist [-lórist], *s.* folklorista. (*V.* FOLKLORE.)

follicle [fólicœl], *s.* (anat.) folículo; (bot.) folículo, hollejo; (ento.) capullo.

follicular [folíkiular], *a.* folicular.

follow [fólo]. **I.** *va.* seguir, ir detrás de; venir después de; perseguir; ejecutar, poner por obra; observar, poner atención; resultar de, seguirse (*it follows*, síguese).—**to f. one's nose**, ir o seguir derecho.—**to f. out**, poner por obra, llevar hasta el fin.—**to f. suit**, jugar el mismo palo (en los naipes); seguir el ejemplo o la corriente; hacer lo mismo.—**to f. up**, perseguir con ahinco; llevar hasta el fin; continuar; reforzar. **II.** *vn.* seguir, ir detrás; seguirse.—**to f. in one's tracks**, seguir a uno, seguir en las pisadas de uno.—**to f. on**, continuar; seguir en la misma dirección (que otro).—**as follows**, como sigue(n).

follower [fólocœr], *s.* seguidor; acompañante, secuaz; ayudante; criado; (mec.) pieza impulsada; polea impulsada; bloque de protección de un pilote que se hinca.—*pl.* comitiva, séquito.

following [fóloing]. **I.** *a.* siguiente; próximo; subsiguiente; consiguiente. **II.** *s.* séquito, comitiva, cortejo; oficio, carrera, profesión.

folly [fóli], *s.* tontería, locura, desatino.

foment [fomént], *va.* fomentar, provocar, instigar; (med.) fomentar, dar baños calientes.

fomentation [fóméntéîshun], *s.* (med.) fomentación, fomento; provocación, instigación.

fond, *a.* aficionado, enamorado; tierno, cariñoso; querido, acariciado.—**to be f. of**, ser amigo de o aficionado a; estar encariñado con.

fondle [fóndœl], *va.* mimar, acariciar.

fondling [fóndling], *s.* acariciar, mimar; acariciador; niño mimado.

fondly [-li], *adv.* tiernamente, afectuosamente, cariñosamente.

fondness [-nes], *s.* afecto, cariño; afición, apego, inclinación.

fonetic, fonograf=*V.* PHONETIC, etc.

font, *s.* pila de bautismo; fuente; (impr.) fundición, torta.

fontanel [fontanél], *s.* (anat.) fontanela.

food [fud], *s.* alimento, comida; pasto de los animales; pábulo, materia.—**f. for thought**, materia en que pensar, cosa que da que pensar.

fool [fúl]. **I.** *s.* tonto, necio; bufón, truhán, payaso. **II.** *va.* chasquear; embromar; engañar, embaucar.—**to f. away**, malbaratar. **III.** *vn.* tontear, divertirse, chancear.

foolhardiness [fúljárdines], *s.* temeridad.

foolhardy [fúljárdi], *a.* temerario.

fooling [fúling], *s.* broma, chacota; engaño.—**no f., without f.**, (fam.) sin broma, hablando en serio.

foolproof [-prúf], *a.* que los curiosos o chambones no pueden dañar o desarreglar; seguro.

foolish [fúlish], *a.* tonto; disparatado; bobo.—**foolishly** [-li], *adv.* tontamente.—**foolishness** [-nes], *s.* simpleza, tontería.

foolscap [fúlscæp], *s.* papel grande de escribir (35 × 43 centímetros), papel de oficio.

foot [fut], *s.* pie (de animal, mesa, etc.); pata; base; pie, medida lineal; (mil.) infantería; (pros.) pie.—**f. bath**, pediluvio.—**f. candle**, intensidad de la luz de una bujía normal a distancia de un pie.—**f. guard**, guardacascos, especie de bota para los caballos; cualquier cosa que protege los pies.—**F. Guards**, (Ing.) infantería de la guardia real.—**f. post**, cartero pedestre; el correo que lleva.—**f. pound** = FOOTPOUND.—**f.-pound-second**, pie-libra-segundo (apl. al sistema de unidades en que las fundamentales son el pie, la libra y el segundo).—**f. rule**, pie, regla de 1 pie dividida en pulgadas y fracciones (corresponde, en cuanto al uso, al doble decímetro).—**f. second**, pie por segundo.—**f. soldier**, soldado de infantería.—**f. stove**, estufilla para los pies.—**f. tub**, baño de pies.—**f. warmer**, calientapiés.—**by f.**, a pie.—**on f.**, de pie; levantado, activo; progresando.—**to put one's best f. foremost**, (fam.) poner sus cinco sentidos; poner todas sus fuerzas; andar con actividad, con la mayor diligencia posible.—**to put one's f. down**, (fam.) tomar una resolución decidida.—**to put one's f. in it**, hacer una plancha.—**to set on f.**, iniciar, emprender, poner alguna cosa en movimiento, darle el primer impulso.—**to trample, o tread, under f.**, pisotear.—**under f.**, debajo de los pies; el suelo; con el pie sobre el pescuezo.

foot. I. *va.* recorrer, andar; hollar, pisotear; sumar y poner la suma al pie; poner pies a alguna cosa; (fam., E. U., gen. con *up*), pagar (una cuenta); costear, sufragar. **II.** *vn.* andar, caminar, patear; (fam.) sumar guarismos.

footage [fútey], *s.* (min.) paga por pie (u otra unidad lineal) de trabajo; (cine) longitud en pies.

football [fútbol], *s.* football, futbol, balompié (la segunda palabra parece preferible).

footboard [-bórd], *s.* pie (barandilla del pie) de cama; trasera (de coche); tabla del pescante para los pies del cochero; pedal.

footboy [-bóy], *s.* lacayo.

footbreadth [-brédz], *s.* ancho de un pie.

footbridge [-bríy], *s.* puente para gente de a pie.

footcloth [-clóz], *s.* alfombrilla; gualdrapa.

footed [-ed], *a.* que tiene pies o patas; sumado.

footfall [-fól], *s.* paso, pisada (con respecto al ruido).

footgear [-guíœr], *s.* calzado.

foothill [-jil], *s.* colina al pie de una montaña.

foothold [-jóuld], *s.* espacio en que cabe el pie; pie firme; posición establecida; chanclo de goma sin tacón.

footing [-ing], *s.* pie, base, fundamento; zarpa; piso, paso; baile, danza; estado, condición; estribo, zócalo saliente; (arit.) suma de una columna.—**on a war f.**, bajo pie de guerra.—**to be on equal f.**, estar en iguales condiciones.

footless [-les], *a.* sin pies; sin fundamento; (fam.) estúpido, chambón.
footlights [-láits], *s.* (tea.) candilejas; las tablas.
footling [-ling], *a.* y *adv.* (obst.) con los pies hacia afuera.
footman [-mæn], *s.* lacayo.
footmark [-márc], *s.* huella.
footnote [-nóut], *s.* nota al pie de una página.
footpace [-péis], *s.* descanso de escaleras; paso lento.
footpad [-pad], *s.* salteador de caminos.
footpath [-paz], *s.* senda para gente de a pie.
footpound [-páund], *s.* librapié, unidad de trabajo—el ejecutado por una fuerza de 1 libra en una distancia de 1 pie (0.14 kgm.)
footprint [-prínt], *s.* huella, pisada, rastro
foots [futs], *s. pl.* sedimentos, heces, poso.
footsore [-sóær], *a.* que tiene los pies doloridos o lastimados, despeado.
footstalk [-stóc], *s.* (bot.) pedúnculo, pezón.
footstep [-stép], *s.* huella, pisada, paso.
foostool [-stúl], *s.* escabel, escañuelo.
footwalk [-uóc], *s.* acera.
footwear [-uéær], *s.* calzado.
footworn [-uórn], *a.* cansado de caminar; asendereado, trillado.
fop, *s.* petimetre; mentecato.
fopling [fópling], *s.* lechuguino.
foppery [fópœri], *s.* afectactión en el vestir; perifollos.
foppish [fópish], *a.* vanidoso, afectado.: alechuguinado.—**foppishly** [-li], *adv.* afectadamente; con perifollos.—**foppishness** [-nes], *s.* = FOPPERY.
for. **I.** *prep.* por (cuando significa a causa de, en consideración a, con respecto o relación a, en cuanto a, en busca de, en nombre o representación de, en lugar o sustitución de, a cambio de); para (cuando denota destinación, aplicación, dedicación, fin, intento, provecho, beneficio); v. gr.: *I speak for him*, hablo por él: *this is for him*, esto es para él; no obstante, a pesar de: durante, por espacio de; de (*to cry for joy*, llorar de gozo). **II.** *conj.* porque, pues; (mat.) en efecto.
forage [fórey]. **I.** *va.* y *vn.* forrajear, apasturar. **II.** *s.* forraje.
forager [fórœyœr], *s.* forrajeador.
foramen [forémen o rámen], *s.* foramen, apertura, agujero.
foraminifer [fóræmínífœr], *s.* (zool.) foraminífero.—**Foraminifera** [forǽminíferæ], *s. pl.* foraminíferos.—**foraminiferal** (-al), **foraminiferous** [-us], *a.* foraminífero.
forasmuch as [forasmúch as̆], *conj.* puesto que, por cuanto.
foray [fóre]. **I.** *s.* correría, irrupción; saqueo, pillaje. **II.** *va.* saquear, pillar, despojar.
forbade [forbǽd], *pret.* de FORBID.
forbear [forbéær], *va.* y *vn.* (*pret.* FORBORE [forbóœr]; *pp.* FORBORNE [forbórn]) abstenerse, contenerse, dejar de, reprimirse.
forbearance [-ans], *s.* indulgencia o lenidad; abstención; (for.) morosidad.—**forbearing** [-ing], *a.* paciente, indulgente.
forbid [forbíd], *va.* (*pret.* FORBADE; *pp.* FORBIDDEN) prohibir; impedir, estorbar.
forbidding [-ing], *a.* prohibitivo; repulsivo, aborrecible, repugnante.
forbore [forbóœr], *pret.* de FORBEAR.
force [fors]. **I.** *s.* fuerza; vigor; energía, animación; virtud, poder, eficacia; móvil, motivo, coacción, violencia; valor, validez; peso, importancia; (mil.) fuerzas, tropa.—**f. majeure**, fuerza mayor.—**f. pump**, bomba impelente.—**In f.**, vigente, en vigor. **II.** *va.* forzar; violentar; violar; (coc.) rellenar, embutir, mechar; (agr.) forzar, hacer madurar temprano.—**to f. along**, hacer avanzar o adelantar.—**to f. away**, obligar a alejarse.—**to f. back**, rechazar, hacer retroceder. —**to f. down**, obligar a bajar.—**to f. from**, obligar a salir, echar de.—**to f. in**, o **through**, clavar, meter o entrar por fuerza.—**to f. out**, arrancar, sacar u obtener por fuerza.—**to f. up**, hacer subir por fuerza.

forceful [fórsful], *a.* enérgico; lúcido; potente; violento.
forceless [-les], *a.* endeble, débil.
forcemeat [fórsmit], *s.* (coc.) relleno, embutido, salpicón.
forceps [fórseps], *s.* (cir.) forceps, pinzas.
forcer [fórsœr], *s.* forzador; émbolo.
forcible [fórsibœl], *a.* fuerte, potente; eficaz; violento; enérgico; de peso.—**forcibleness** [-nes], fuerza; violencia.—**forcibly** [-bli], *adv.* fuertemente; enérgicamente; lúcidamente; forzosamente; violentamente.
forcing [fórsing]. **I.** *pa.* y *a.* impelente; madurador; clarificador de vino. **II.** *s.* forzamiento. —**f. bed**, almajara.—**f. house**, invernadero.
ford. **I.** *s.* vado. **II.** *va.* vadear, esguazar.
fordable [fórdabœl], *a.* vadeable, esguazable.
fore [fóœr]. **I.** *a.* anterior, delantero; (mar.) proel, de proa.—**f. hatching**, escotilla de proa.— **f.-topgallant**, juanete de proa.—**f.-topsail**, velacho. **II.** *adv.* anteriormente, delante, antes; (mar.) de proa.—**f. and aft**, de popa a proa.
forearm [fóœrarm], *s.* antebrazo.
forearm [fóœrárm], *va.* armar de antemano.
forebode [fóœrbód], *vn.* y *va.* pronosticar, presagiar; presentir, antever.—**foreboding** [-ing], *s.* presentimiento, presagio; corazonada.
forecast [fóœrcást], *va.* y *vn.* proyectar, trazar; prever, predecir, pronosticar.
forecast [fóœrcast], *s.* pronóstico; previsión; proyecto, traza, plan.
forecastle [fóœrcascœl o (mar.) fócscœl], *s.* (mar.) castillo de proa.
forecited [fóœrsáited], *a.* precitado.
foreclose [fóœrclóus̆], *va.* impedir, excluir; (for.) entablar, sustanciar y decidir un juicio hipotecario.—**foreclosure** [-clóuy̆œr], *s.* (for.) juicio hipotecario.
foredoom [-dúm], *va.* predestinar.
forefather [-fáœr], *s.* ascendiente, antepasado.
forefinger [-fíngœr], *s.* dedo índice.
forefoot [-fút], *s.* mano o pata delantera; (mar.) gorja, tajamar.
forefront [-frúnt], *s.* frente, puesto delantero, primera fila.
forego [fóœrgó], *va.* (*pret.* FOREWENT: *pp.* FORGONE) privarse de, renunciar a; ceder, abandonar.
foregoing [-góing], *a.* precedente, anterior.
foregone [-gón], *a.* predeterminado, decidido de antemano; inevitable, seguro.
foreground [-graund], *s.* (pint.) primer plano, frente.
forehanded [-jǽnded], *a.* temprano; (E. U.) acomodado, adinerado.
forehead [fóred], *s.* la frente; descaro.
foreign [fóren], *a.* extranjero; exterior; extraño, advenedizo; ajeno, remoto.—**f.-built**, **f.-born**, etc., construido, nacido, etc., en el extranjero.—**f. commerce**, comercio exterior.—**F. Office**, (Ingl.) ministerio de negocios extranjeros.—**f. trade,** = FOREIGN COMMERCE.
foreigner [-œr], *s.* extranjero, forastero.
foreignness [-nes], *s.* calidad de extraño o extranjero.
forejudgment [fóœry̆úymœnt], *s.* prejuicio.
foreknow [-nó], *va.* prever, tener presciencia de.
foreknowable [-nóœbœl], *a.* que se puede prever.
foreknowledge [-nóley], *s.* presciencia.
foreland [fóœrlænd], *s.* cabo, promontorio.
foreleg [-lég], *s.* pierna o pata delantera.
forelock [-lóc], *s.* melena, guedeja; chaveta.
foreman [-mæn], *s.* capataz; mayoral, sobrestante; (impr.) regente; (for.) presidente del jurado.
foremast [-mast], *s.* (mar.) palo de trinquete.
forementioned [-ménshund], *a.* susodicho, precitado, antedicho.
foremost [fóœrmost], *a.* delantero; primero.
forename [fóœrnéim], *s.* primer nombre, nombre de pila.
forenamed [-néimd], *a.* susodicho.

forenoon [fôœrnun], *s.* la mañana.

forensic [forénsic], *a.* forense; causídico.

foreordain [fóœordéin], *va.* preordinar, pre-destinar.—**foreordination** [-dinéíshun],| *s.* pre-determinación; predestinación.

forerun [fóœrrún], *va.* (*pret.* FORERAN: *pp.* FORERUN) preceder; **adelantarse**; anunciar.

forerunner [-rúnœr], *s.* precursor; presagio, pronóstico; nuncio; (mil.) explorador.

foresaid [fóœrsed], *a.* antedicho, susodicho.

foresail [-séil *o* (mar.) fóscœl], *s.* trinquete.

foresee [fóœrsí], *va.* (*pret.* FORESAW: *pp.* FORE-SEEN) prever, barruntar.

foreseer [fóœrsíœr], *s.* previsor.

foreshadow [fóœrshǽdo], *va.* indicar, anunciar.

foreshorten [fóœrshórtœn], *va.* (pint.) escorzar.

foreshortening [-ing], *s.* (pint.) escorzo.

foresight [fóœrsait], *s.* previsión, prevención, perspicacia; presciencia; (top.) visual hacia adelante; visual de cota del ojo, para deter-minar la altura del ojo en la nivelación.

foreskin [fóœrskin], *s.* (anat.) prepucio.

foreskirt [fóœrskœrt], *s.* (cost.) delantero.

forest [fórest]. **I.** *s.* monte, bosque, selva, floresta.—**f. ranger**, guardabosques. **II.** *va.* arbolar.

forestal [fórestal], *a.* forestal.

forestall [fóœrstól], *va.* antuviar, anticipar; im-pedir, prevenir; (com.) acopiar, monopolizar, acaparar.—**forestaller** [-œr], *s.* monopolista; aco-piador.—**forestalling** [-ing], *s.* monopolio, acopio, estanco.

forestation [fórestéíshun], *s.* silvicultura prác-tica; plantación o extensión de montes.

forestay [fóœrstéi], *s.* estay del trinquete.

forestaysail [-séil], *s.* trinquete.

forester [fórestœr], *s.* silvicultor; ingeniero fores-tal o de montes; guardamonte.—**forestry** [-tri], *s.* silvicultura; ingeniería forestal o de montes.

foretackle [fóœrtǽccœl], *s.* aparejo del trinquete.

foretaste [fóœrtést]. **I.** *va.* gustar o conocer de antemano. **II.** *s.* goce anticipado.

foretell [-tél], *va.* y *vn.* predecir, pronosticar, profetizar, presagiar.—**foreteller** [-œr], *s.* profeta.—**foretelling** [-ing], *s.* profecía, pronóstico.

forethought [-zót], *s.* presciencia, providencia; prevención; premeditación.

foretoken [-tóukœn], *va.* y *s.* = FORESHADOW.

foretop [-top], *s.* copete, tupé; (mar.) cofa de trinquete.

forever [forévœr], **forevermore** [-moœr], *adv.* por siempre, por siempre jamás.—**forever and a day**, *o* **forever and ever**, eternamente, por siem-pre jamás.

forewarn [fóœruórn], *va.* prevenir, advertir, avisar.—**forewarning** [-ing], *s.* advertencia, aviso.

forewoman [fóœruman], *s.* primera oficiala de un taller de mujeres.

foreword [fóœruœrd], *s.* advertencia, preámbulo, prefacio.

foreyard [-yard], *s.* (mar.) verga del trinquete.

forfeit [fórfit]. **I.** *s.* pérdida legal de cosa o derecho por incumplimiento de obligaciones. **II.** *a.* perdido por incumplimiento. **III.** *va.* perder el derecho a, por incumplimiento o viola-ción.—**forfeitable** [-æbœl], *a.* alienable, invali-dable, revocable; perdible.—**forfeiture** [-chur], *s.* pérdida legal por incumplimiento o violación de obligaciones; lo que se pierde por tales causas.

forgave [forgéiv], *pret.* de TO FORGIVE.

forge [fory]. **I.** *s.* fragua; forja, hornaza; herre-ría.—**f. mill**, fragua.—**f. roll**, cilindro de laminar —**f. train**, fragua de laminar. **II.** *va.* forjar, fraguar; contrahacer, falsificar, falsear; inventar; tramar.—**to f. off, on,** *o* **over**, empujar, empeler. **III.** *vn.* avanzar despacio; tropezarse (las bestias).

forger [fóryœr], *s.* forjador, fraguador; falsificador.

forgery [fóryœri], *s.* falsificación.

forget [forguét], *va.* y *vn.* (*pret.* FORGOT: *pp.* FORGOTTEN) olvidar.—**to f. one's self,** excederse, desmedirse; ser distraído; olvidarse de sí mismo por los demás, ser abnegado.

forgetful [-ful], *a.* olvidadizo.—**forgetfulness** [-fulnes], *s.* olvido; calidad de olvidadizo.

forget-me-not [forguét-mi-not], *s.* (bot.) mio-sota, nomeolvides.

forging [fórying], *s.* tropezadura de algunas caballerías; forjadura, pieza forjada.

forgivable [forguívabœl], *a.* perdonable.

forgive [forguív], *va.* (*pret.* FORGAVE; *pp.* FOR-GIVEN) perdonar.

forgiven [forguíven], *pp.* de TO FORGIVE.

forgiveness [forguívnes], *s.* perdón; remisión; clemencia, misericordia.

forgot, forgotten, *pret.* y *pp.* de FORGET.

fork [fork]. **I.** *s.* tenedor; (agr.) horca, horcón, horqueta, horquilla; horcadura; bifurcación; confluencia de un río. **II.** *va.* hacinar o cargar con horca; ahorquillar. **III.** *vn.* ahorquillarse, bifur-carse.

forked [forkt *o* fórked], *a.* ahorquillado, bifurcado.

forkhead [fórkjed], *s.* lengüeta de saeta o flecha.

forlorn [forlórn], *a.* abandonado, olvidado, de-samparado.—**f. hope,** (mil.) destacamento encar-gado de un servicio peligroso; empresa deses-perada.

form [form]. **I.** *s.* forma; figura; hechura; hoja, modelo que ha de llenarse, (Amér.) esqueleto; condición; estado; práctica, ritual, formali-dad, ceremonia; estilo; horma, matriz, patrón; porte, conducta, modales; aparición, sombra; banco, asiento largo; (gram.) forma, inflexión; (impr.) forma; (constr.) molde; (fort.) cestón.—**f. letter,** (com.) carta general, que no requiere más cambio que el del nombre y dirección.—**in due f.,** en debida forma.—**for f.'s sake,** por pura fórmula.—**of f.,** de pura forma o de apariencia. **II.** *va.* formar, construir, labrar, modelar; idear, concebir; ordenar, componer, arreglar; hacer, constituir. **III.** *vn.* formarse.

formal [fórmal], *a.* formal, relativo a la forma; aparente; de pura forma; ceremonioso, eti-quetero; esencial, constitutivo.

formaldehyde [fórmáldijaid], *s.* (quím.) for-maldehído, aldehído fórmico.

formaline [fórmælin], *s.* (quím.) formalina, disolución de aldehído fórmico.

formalism [fórmalism], *s.* formalismo.

formalist [fórmalist], *s.* formalista.

formality [formǽliti], *s.* formalidad, ceremonia, etiqueta.

formally [fórmali], *adv.* formalmente, con toda solemnidad; realmente.

format [formát, fórmá], *s.* forma de un libro, inclusos detalles tipográficos, tamaño, etc., (Amér.) formato (palabra tachada de "galicis-mo," si bien el español no tiene ninguna que ex-prese su significado).

formate [fórmet], *s.* (quím.) formiato.

formation [forméíshun], *s.* formación; de-sarrollo; disposición, arreglo; (geol.) formación.

formative [fórmativ], *a.* formativo.

former [fórmœr]. **I.** *a.* primero; (con *the*) aquél, aquélla, aquéllos, etc.; pasado, anterior, antiguo. **II.** *s.* formador, plasmador; molde, matriz.

formerly [-li], *adv.* antiguamente, en tiempos pasados.

formic [fórmic], *a.* hormigoso; fórmico.

formicant [fórmicant], *a.* (med.) formicante.

formicary [-keri], *s.* hormiguero.

formication [fórmikéíshun], *s.* hormigueo.

formidable [fórmidabœl], *a.* formidable.

formidably [-bli], *adv.* formidablemente.

formless [fórmles], *a.* informe, sin forma.

formula [fórmiula], *s.* fórmula.

formulæ [-li], *pl.* de FORMULA.

formulary [fórmiuleri]. **I.** *a.* formal; sujeto a fórmula. **II.** *s.* formulario.

formulate [-leit], *va.* formular.—**formulation** [-éíshun], *s.* formulación.

formulize [-laiŝ], *va.* y *vn.* formalizar; formular.

formyl [fórmil], *s.* (quím.) formilo.

fornicate [fórnikeit], *vn.* fornicar.—**fornicate(d** [-ed], *a.* abovedado.—**fornication** [-kéíshun], *s.* fornicación; (arq.) bóveda.—**fornicator** [-kéitœr], *s.* fornicador.—**fornicatress** [-kéitres], *s.* con-cubina; manceba.

forsake [forséik], *va.* (*pret.* FORSOOK: *pp.* FORSAKEN) dejar, abandonar, desamparar, desertar; separarse de; renegar de; desechar, rechazar.

forsooth [forsúz], *adv.* ciertamente, en verdad.

forswear [forsuéær]. **I.** *va.* (*pret.* FORSWORE: *pp.* FORSWORN) abjurar; desjurar.—**to f.** one's self, perjurarse. **II.** *vn.* perjurar.

forsworn, *pp.* de FORSWEAR.

fort [fort], *s.* fuerte, castillo, fortaleza.

fortalice [fórtalis], *s.* fortín.

forte [fort], *s.* fuerte (afición o mérito).

forte [fórte], *a.* y *s.* (mús.) forte.

forth [forz], *adv.* delante; adelante; fuera, afuera; a la vista, públicamente; hasta lo último.—**and so f.,** y así de lo demás; etcétera.

forthcoming [forzcúming], *a.* futuro, próximo, que viene.

forthwith [forzuíz], *adv.* inmediatamente.

fortieth [fórtiez], *s.* y *a.* cuadragésimo; cuarentavo; cuarenta (ordinal).

fortifiable [fórtifáiabœl], *a.* fortificable.

fortification [-fikéishvn], *s.* fortificación; fortalecimiento.

fortifier [-faicer], *s.* fortificador; fortalecedor.

fortify [fórtifai]. **I.** *va.* fortificar; fortalecer; reforzar; corroborar. **II.** *vn.* construir defensas.

fortissimo [fortísimo], *a.* y *adv.* (mús.) fortísimo.

fortitude [fórtitiud], *s.* fortaleza; fuerza.

fortlet [fórtlet], *s.* fortín.

fortnight [fórtnait], *s.* quincena, dos semanas.—**fortnightly** [-li]. **I.** *a.* quincenal. **II.** *adv.* quincenalmente.

fortress [fórtres], *s.* fuerte; plaza fuerte.

fortuitous [fortiúitvs], *a.* fortuito.—**fortuitously** [-li], *adv.* fortuitamente.—**fortuitousness** [-nes], *s.* calidad de fortuito.

fortuity [fortiúiti], *s.* caso fortuito; accidente.

fortunate [fórchunet], *a.* afortunado.

fortunately [-li], *adv.* afortunadamente.

fortune [fórchun *o* tiun], *s.* fortuna.—**f. book,** libro de la buena ventura.—**f. hunter,** el que anda en busca de esposa rica.—**f. teller,** sortílego, adivino.—**f. telling,** buenaventura, sortiaria, sortilegio.

fortuneless [-les], *a.* sin fortuna, sin bienes.

forty [fórti], *a.* y *s.* cuarenta.

forum [fórvm], *s.* plaza; foro; tribunal.

forward [fóruard]. **I.** *adv.* adelante, en adelante; hacia adelante, más allá. **II.** *a.* delantero; (mar.) proel; precoz; adelantado; anterior; pronto, activo; desenvuelto, descocado; apresurado, vivo, listo; audaz, emprendedor; inexorable. **III.** *va.* reenviar; transmitir, remitir; apresurar, activar; fomentar.—**forwarder, o forwarding merchant,** comisionista expedidor.

forwardly [-li], descocada o descaradamente.—**forwardness** [-nes], *s.* adelantamiento, progreso; prontitud, apresuramiento; precocidad; descaro, descoco.

forwards [fóruardŝ], *adv.* = FORWARD.

foss, fosse [fos], *s.* (fort.) foso.

fossa, *s.* (anat.) fosa.

fossil [fósil], *a.* y *s.* fósil.—**fossiliferous** [-ífervs], *a.* fosilífero.—**fossilist** [-list], *s.* paleontólogo.—**fossilization** [-iśéishvn], *s.* fosilización.—**fossilize** [-ais]. **I.** *va.* fosilizar; petrificar; hacer anticuado. **II.** *vn.* fosilizarse, petrificarse.—**fossilology** [-óloyi], *s.* paleontología.

fossorial [fosórial], *a.* cavador.—**f. wasp,** avispa cavadora.

foster [fóstœr]. **I.** *va.* criar, nutrir; dar alas, alentar, fomentar. **II.** *a.* Como adjetivo, se aplica comúnmente a nombres que por sí solos denotan parentesco, para expresar condición analoga debida a crianza o, general pero no necesariamente, adopción.—**f. brother, child, sister,** hermano, hijo, hermana de leche, adoptivos, o criados como hijos, etc.—**f. mother, father,** madre, padre adoptivos, o que han criado a los *foster children* correspondientes.—**f. earth,** (agr.) suelo o tierra de almáciga.—**f. home,** casa de crianza, donde se crían niños ajenos.—**f. nurse,** nodriza.

fosterage [fósterey], *s.* crianza de niños.

fosterling, *s.* = FOSTER CHILD.

Foucault current [fucó cœrrent], corriente de Foucault, corriente parásita.

fought [fot], *pret.* y *pp.* de FIGHT.

foul [fául]. **I.** *a.* sucio, puerco, impuro, inmundo; fétido, pestilente; viciado (aire); detestable, vil; injusto, sin derecho; enredado, atascado, obstruído; contrario, desagradable; obsceno; (impr.) lleno de errores y correcciones.—**f. ball,** (juego de baseball) pelota que cae fuera de las *foul lines,* que son las dos líneas que forman el ángulo del *home base.*—**f. bill of health,** (mar.) patente sucia.—**f. breath,** aliento fétido.—**f. dealing,** dolo, mala fe.—**f. language,** palabras injuriosas; lenguaje obsceno.—**f.-mouthed,** mal hablado.—**f. play** = F. DEALING.—**f. weather,** mal tiempo.—**to fall f. of,** enredarse con; atacar; (mar.) abordar, chocar con. **II.** *s.* acción de ensuciar, de ludir o enredarse una cosa en otra; violación de las reglas establecidas; en baseball, caída de la pelota fuera del cuadro. **III.** *va.* ensuciar, emporcar; (mar.) abordar, chocar, trabarse; (dep.) violar las reglas establecidas. **IV.** *vn.* ensuciarse; (mar.) chocar; (dep.) en baseball, caer la pelota fuera del cuadro.

foulard [fulárd], *s.* fular, seda fina.

foully [fáuli], *adv.* suciamente.—**foulness** [-nes], *s.* asquerosidad, porquería.

found [fáund], *pret.* y *pp.* de FIND.

found [fáund], *va.* cimentar; edificar; instituir, fundar, establecer; asentar, fijar; (fund.) fundir, derretir.

foundation [fáundéishvn], *s.* fundación, establecimiento; fundamento, base, apoyo, entibo, polo; dotación; (mec.) asiento, lecho, pie; (ing.) firme; cimiento, embasamiento, fundamento; (cost.) forro, refuerzo.—**f. school,** escuela dotada.

founder [fáundœr]. **I.** *s.* fundador; fundidor; (vet.) despeadura. **II.** *va.* (mar.) hacer zozobrar; despear los pies del caballo. **III.** *vn.* (mar.) irse a pique; fracasar; desplomarse.

foundry [fáundri], *s.* fundición (fábrica).—**f. iron,** fundición bruta de moldeo, o para piezas fundidas.

foundling [fáundling], *s.* niño expósito.—**f. hospital,** inclusa, casa de expósitos.

foundress [fáundres],₊*s.* fundadora.

fount [fáunt], **fountain** [fáunten], *s.* fuente; manantial; fontana.—**f. pen,** pluma estilográfica, pluma fuente.—**f. syringe,** (med.) jeringa o inyector de gravedad.

fountainhead [-jed], *s.* fuentes, cabeceras (de un río); fuente; origen.

four [fóœr], *a.* y *s.* cuatro.—**f.-cornered,** cuadrangular.—**f.-footed,** cuadrúpedo.—**f.-handed,** cuadrúmano; para o de cuatro jugadores; (mús.) de o a cuatro manos.—**f.-hundred,** (fam.) la alta sociedad, la nata social.—**f.-in-hand,** carruaje tirado por cuatro caballos; corbata larga de nudo corredizo.—**f.-o'clock,** (bot.) dondiego de noche, arrebolera.—**f. of a kind,** quínola.—**f.-way,** de cuatro direcciones.—**f.-wheel, f.-wheeler,** carruaje de cuatro ruedas.—**f.-wheeled,** de cuatro ruedas.—**all fours,** las cuatro patas.

fourfold [-fould], *a.* cuádruplo.—**fourpence** [fórpens], *s.* (Ingl.) cuatro peniques.—**fourscore** [-scoœr], *a.* cuatro veintenas de; octogenario.—**foursquare** [-scuéær], *a.* = F.-CORNERED.

fourteen [fóœrtin], *a.* y *s.* catorce.

fourteenth [fóœrtinz]. **I.** *a.* catorceno; décimocuarto, catorce (ordinal). **II.** *s.* y *a.* catorzavo.

fourth [forz], *s.* y *a.* cuarto, cuarta parte; cuatro [del mes].—**f. state,** la prensa.—**the F.,** (E. U.) el 4 de julio.

fourthly [fórzil], *adv.* en cuarto lugar.

fowl [fául]. **I.** *s.* gallo, gallina; pollo; aves en general.—*pl.* volatería, aves de corral. **II.** *vn.* cazar (aves), ir de caza (de aves).

fowler [-œr], *s.* cazador (de aves).

fowling [-ing], *s.* volatería; caza (de aves).—**f. net,** red de cazar pájaros.—**f. piece,** escopeta; (pint.) bodegón de volatería.

---

*P*ara la pronunciación de æ, œ, ᴅ, ŝ, ŝh, ᴜ, ȳ, ʏ, z, véase la clave al principio del libro.

fox [focs]. **I.** *s.* zorra, raposa; zorro, bellaco, taimado.—**f. brush**, rabo de zorra.—**f. chase**, caza de zorras.—**f. terrier**, fox térrier (perro). —**f. trot**, trote corto; apl. t. a cierto baile. **II.** *vn.* cazar zorras; disimular; agriarse, acedarse; ponerse rojizo, descolorarse. **III.** *va.* acedar; (fam.) atisbar.

foxed [foxt], *pp.* y *a.* descolorido.

foxfire [fócsfáicer], *s.* luz fosforescente de la madera podrida.

foxglove [-glúv], *s.* (bot.) dedalera, digital.

foxhound [-jáund], *s.* perro jateo, zorrero o raposero.

foxiness [fócsines], *s.* astucia; acedía, agrura; descolorimiento.

foxish [fócsish], **foxlike** [fócslaic], *a.* astuto, taimado, bellaco.

foxtail [fóxteil], *s.* (bot.) carricera.

foxwood [fóxud], *s.* madera podrida.

foxy [fócsi], *a.* raposuno, zorruno; taimado, astuto; rojizo; agriado, tomado; descolorido, manchado.

foyer [fuayé], *s.* (teat.) salón de descanso; (fund.) cubilote.

fracas [frécas], *s.* zacapela, riña.

fraction [frécshun], *s.* fracción.

fractional [-æl], *a.* fraccionario; fracionado.— **f. distillation**, destilación fraccionada.

fractionate [-eit], *va.* (quím.) separar por destilación fraccionada.

fractious [frécshus], *a.* reacio; rebelón.

fracture [frékchœr]. **I.** *s.* rotura, fractura; (cir.) fractura. **II.** *va.* fracturar, quebrar.

fragile [fréyil], *a.* frágil.—**fragility** [frayíliti], **fragileness** [fráyilnes], *s.* fragilidad.

fragment [frégmœnt], *s.* fragmento; trozo.

fragmentary [-eri], *a.* fragmentario.

fragrance, fragrancy [frégrans, i], *s.* fragancia, perfume, aroma.—**fragrant** [-ant], *a.* fragante, oloroso, aromático.—**fragrantly** [-li], *adv.* con fragancia.

frail [fréil]. **I.** *a.* frágil, quebradizo, deleznable; débil, delicado, endeble. **II.** *s.* canasta, junco. —**frailness** [-nes], **frailty** [-ti], *s.* fragilidad o friabilidad; flaqueza, debilidad.

frame [fréim]. **I.** *va.* fabricar, formar, construir; armar; componer, ajustar; arreglar, dirigir; forjar, idear; enmarcar.—**to f. up**, (fam.) arreglar de antemano clandestinamente, sobre todo en perjuicio de alguien.—**framed structure**, construcción reticulada o de celosía. **II.** *s.* marco; armazón; estructura; figura; arreglo, construcción; armadura, esqueleto, entramado, bastidor; banco de tornero; molde para barras de jabón; (tej.) telar; (impr.) chibalete; (cost.) bastidor para bordar; (mar.) cuadernas, ligazones, costillaje; (fig.) talante, disposición.—**f. house**, casa hecha de madera.—**f. of mind**, estado de ánimo.—**f. saw**, sierra montada o de bastidor.

framer [-œr], *s.* constructor, armador; fabricante de marcos.

framework [-œrk], *s.* armadura, armazón, esqueleto, entramado.

framing [-ing], *s.* armadura, armazón.

frame-up [-up], *s.* (fam.) conspiración o trama.

franc [frænc], *s.* franco, moneda francesa.

franchise [frénchais o frénchish]. **I.** *s.* derecho político; franquicia, privilegio; exención; encartación; asilo, santuario. **II.** *va.* exentar.

franchisement [frénchishment], *s.* liberación.

Franciscan [transíscan], *s.* y *a.* franciscano.

francolin [fréncolin], *s.* (zool.) francolín.

frangible [frényibœl], *a.* frágil; perecedero.

frangipani [frényipáni], *s.* franchipán.

frank [frænk]. **I.** *a.* franco, sincero; francote, campechano; franco, exento, libre. **II.** *s.* franquicia de correos; carta franca. **III.** *s.* y *a.* franco, galo. **IV.** *va.* enviar (carta) exenta de franqueo.

Frankenstein [frénkenstain], *s.* persona cuyas obras le causan su propia ruina.

frankincense [frénkinsens], *s.* incienso.

Frankish [frénkish], *a.* franco (de los francos).

franklin [frénclin], *s.* (Ingl.) = FREEHOLDER.

frankly [fréncli], *adv.* francamente.

frankness [fréncnes], *a.* franqueza.

frantic [fréntic], *a.* frenético.

frantically [-ali], *adv.* frenéticamente.

frap, *va.* (mar.) atortorar.

frappé [frapéi]. **I.** *a.* refrescado con hielo. **II.** *s.* bebida (vino, licor) con hielo, *frappé.*

fraternal [fratœrnal], *a.* fraternal.

fraternally [-i], *adv.* fraternalmente.

fraternity [fratœrniti], *s.* fraternidad; confraternidad.

fraternize [frétœrnais], *vn.* fraternizar.

fratricidal [frétrisáidal], *a.* fratricida.

fratricide [-said], *s.* fratricidio; fratricida.

fraud [frod], *s.* fraude; farsante; engañador, timador.—**fraudful** [-full], *a.* pérfido, engañador; fraudulento.—**fraudfully** [-li], *adv.* engañosamente.—**fraudless** [-les], *a.* sin fraude.—**fraudulence, fraudulency** [fródyulens, i], *s.* fraude, engaño.—**fraudulent** [-ent], *a.* fraudulento.—**fraudulently** [-li], *adv.* fraudulentamente.

fraught [frot], *a.* cargado, lleno, atestado.

fraxinella [frécsinéla], *s.* (bot.) fresnillo.

fray [fré]. **I.** *s.* riña, refriega; raedura, desgaste. **II.** *va.* ludir, raer, tazar; alarmar. **III.** *vn.* deshilacharse.

frazzle [frésl]. **I.** *va.* y *vn.* (fam.) deshilachar(se). **II.** *s.* cosa deshilachada; hilachas, añicos.

freak [frik]. **I.** *s.* capricho, antojo; rareza, monstruosidad, curiosidad, extravagancia.—**f. of nature**, aborto de la naturaleza. **II.** *va.* varetear; abigarrar, gayar.

freakish [-ish], *a.* caprichoso, antojadizo; raro, extravagante.—**freakishly** [-li], *adv.* caprichosamente.—**freaki(sh)ness** [-nes], *s.* ealidad de caprichoso, monstruoso o ridículo.

freckle [frécœl]. **I.** *s.* peca.—**f.-faced**, pecoso. **II.** *va.* motear. **III.** *vn.* ponerse pecoso.

freckled [frécœld], **freckly** [frécli], *a.* pecoso; moteado.

freckledness [frécœldnes], *s.* estado de pecoso.

free [frí]. **I.** *a.* libre; despejado, franco; desocupado, vacante; licencioso, atrevido; liberal, generoso; exento, privilegiado; inmune; permitido; voluntario, discrecional; gratuito, de balde; gallardo, vivo, activo; zafo, flojo, suelto, desatado; escotero.—**f. agency**, libre albedrío. —**f. and easy**, despreocupado, sin restricción.—**f. born**, (for.) ingenuo.—**f. goods**, mercancías exentas de derechos.—**f.-hand drawing**, dibujo a pulso.—**f.-handed**, libre de manos; exento de trabas; liberal, dadivoso.—**f.-hearted**, franco, abierto.—**f. lance**, lanza, soldado libre; hombre despreocupado e independiente.—**f. labor**, trabajo libre.—**f. list**, (com.) lista de artículos exentos de derechos; lista de personas exentas de pago.—**f. liver**, comilón.—**f. of charge**, gratis, de balde.— **f. on board** (**f. o. b.**), (com.) libre de gastos a bordo (l. a b.).—**f. port**, puerto franco.—**f. pass**, pase, permiso.—**f. school**, escuela gratuita.—**f.-spoken**, sin reserva, franco.—**f.-tongued**, lenguaraz, deslenguado.—**f. trade**, (com.) libre cambio.—**f. trader**, librecambista.—**f. will**, libre albedrío. **II.** *va.* libertar; librar, rescatar; manumitir; desvedar; exentar, eximir; desembarazar, zafar.

freeboard [fríbord], *s.* (mar.) obra muerta.

freebooter [fríbútœr], *s.* saqueador; filibustero, forbante.

freebooting [fríbúting], *s.* saqueo, pillaje.

freedman [frídman], *s.* liberto.

freedom [frídum], *s.* libertad; exención, inmunidad; licencia, franqueza o familiaridad atrevida; facilidad, soltura.—**f. of a city**, concesión de inmunidades y privilegios especiales en una ciudad. —**f. of speech**, libertad de palabra.—**f. of the press**, libertad de imprenta.—**f. of the will**, libre albedrío.—**f. of worship**, libertad de cultos.

freehold [fríjold], *s.* (for.) feudo franco, dominio absoluto.—**freeholder** [-œr], *s.* dueño, propietario absoluto de una finca.

freely [fríli], *adv.* libremente; sin reserva; espontáneamente; desembarazadamente.

freeman [fríman], *s.* hombre libre; ciudadano; (ant.) hacendado.

Freemason [fríméisn], *s.* francmasón.

Freemasonry [fríméisœnri], *s.* masonería, francmasonería.

freeness [frínes], *s.* libertad; franqueza, sinceridad; liberalidad.

freer [fríer]. **I.** *s.* libertador. **II.** *a. comp.* de FREE: más libre.

Freesoiler [frísóilœr], *s.* (pol., E. U.) abolicionista.

freestone [frístóun]. **I.** *s.* piedra franca. **II.** *a.* y *s.* abridero (durazno).

freethinker [-zíncœr], *s.* librepensador.

freethinking [-zínking], *s.* librepensamiento.

freewoman [-umæn], *s.* mujer libre, no esclava.

freeze [fríś]. **I.** *va.* (*pret.* FROZE, *pp.* FROZEN, FROZE) congelar, helar; no hacer caso a, tratar con desprecio.—**to f. out**, excluir o hacer salir tratando con frialdad o desprecio. **II.** *vn.* helarse; helar, escarchar.

freezer [fríśœr], *s.* refrigerador, congelador; sorbetera.

freezing [fríśing], *a.* congelante, frigorífico; glacial.—**f. point**, punto de congelación.

freight [fréit]. **I.** *va.* fletar; cargar. **II.** *s.* carga, cargazón; flete.—**f. car**, vagón o carro de carga.— **f. free**, libre de flete.—**f. home**, o **return f.**, flete de vuelta.—**f. out and in**, flete de ida y vuelta. —**f. outwards**, flete de ida.—**f. train**, tren de mercancías o de carga.—**by f.**, como carga.

freightage [fréitey], *s.* carga, cargamento; flete; transporte.—**freighter** [fréitœr], *s.* fletador; cargador; busque de carga.

French [french], *a.* y *s.* francés; idioma francés.— **F. beans**, judías en lata tratadas químicamente.— **F. bread**, pan francés.—**F. fried potatoes**, patatas fritas en trozos.—**F. horn**, bocina, trompa.—**F. leave**, despedida a la francesa, a la chita, callando. —**F.-like**, afrancesado, a la francesa.—**F. roof**, mansarda.—**F. woman**, francesa (mujer).—**the F.**, los franceses.

Frenchify [frénchifai], *va.* afrancesar.

Frenchman [frénchman], *s.* francés.

Frenchwoman [-umæn], *s.* francesa.

frenetic [frenétic], **frenzied** [frénśid], *a.* frenético.

frenzy [frénśi], *s.* frenesí.

frequency [frícuensi], *s.* frecuencia; (elec.) frecuencia, número de períodos o ciclos por segundo.—**f. meter**, (elec.) frecuencímetro, medidor de frecuencia.

frequent [frícuent], *a.* frecuente.

frequent [frecuént], *va.* frecuentar.

frequentation [frícuentéishun], *s.* frecuentación.

frequentative [frecuéntativ], *a.* frecuentativo.

frequenter [frecuéntœr], *s.* frecuentador.

frequently [frícuentli], *adv.* frecuentemente.

fresco. I. *s.* (b. a.) pintura al fresco. **II.** *va.* pintar al fresco.

fresh [freśh]. **I.** *a.* fresco, nuevo; reciente; recién llegado; refrigerante; puro (aire, agua); lozano (flor, planta, etc.); sano, robusto; inexperto, novicio; (fam.) descocado, descarado; oficioso, entremetido.—**f. from**, acabado de llegar, sacar, etc. de.—**f. hand**, novicio.—**f. water**, agua dulce. **II.** *s.* avenida, riada, inundación; manantial; mezcla de agua dulce y salada en los ríos.

freshen [fréśhœn]. **I.** *va.* refrescar, refrigerar. **II.** *vn.* refrescarse, avivarse.

freshet [fréśhet], *s.* avenida, crecida, creciente.

freshly [-li], *adv.* frescamente; recientemente.

freshman [-man], *s.* estudiante de primer año.

freshness [-nes], *s.* frescura, frescor; lozanía; verdor; descaro.

fret. I. *va.* gastar estregando, rabosear; raer, corroer; enojar, irritar; recamar, bordar en realce; adornar con calados. **II.** *vn.* gastarse, incomodarse, impacientarse, inquietarse; lamentarse.—**fretted**, calado. **III.** *s.* roce, rozamiento; raspadura, raedura; desgaste; irritación, enojo; hervor; empeine, herpes; (b. a.) relieve, realce, cinceladura; greca; calado; traste de guitarra.— **f. saw**, sierra de calados, segueta.

fretful [frétful], *a.* displicente, irritable, mohíno; incómodo, molesto.—**fretfully** [-li], *adv.* con mal

humor; de mala gana.—**fretfulness** [-nes], *s.* mal humor.

fretwork [frétuœrk], *s.* (b. a.) greca, adorno; calado.

Freudian [fróidiæn], *a.* (filos.) freudiano, de Freud.—**Freudianism** [-iśm], *s.* freudianismo, teoría de Freud.

friability [fráiabíliti], *s.* friabilidad.

friable [fráiabœl], *a.* friable, desmenuzable.

friar [fráiar], *s.* fraile.—**friary** [-ri]. **I.** *s.* convento de frailes. **II.** *a.* frailero, frailesco.

fribble [fríbœl]. **I.** *vn.* bobear. **II.** *a.* vano, frívolo. **III.** *s.* persona frívola; fruslería.

fricassee [fricasí]. **I.** *s.* (coc.) fricasé. **II.** *va.* hacer fricasé.

fricative [frícativ], *a.* (gram.) fricativo.

friction [fríćshun], *s.* fricción; frotación, frotamiento; rozamiento (el término que debe usarse cuando se trata de resistencia al movimiento). Se usa mucho adjetivamente en mecánica, y casi siempre se traduce "de fricción," vg.: **f. clutch, cone, gearing**, embrague, cono, engranaje de fricción.—**f. band**, cinta de fricción (de un freno).—**f. block**, zapata (de un freno).—**f. factor**, coeficiente de rozamiento.—**f. matches**, fósforos de fricción.

frictional [-æl], *a.* de o producido por rozamiento o frotamiento.—**f. resistance**, resistencia de rozamiento.

Friday [fráide], *s.* viernes.

fried [fráid], *a.* frito; freído (*pp.* de TO FRY).

friend [frend], *s.* amigo, amiga; cuáquero.

friendless [-les], *a.* desamparado, desvalido, sin amigos.

friendliness [fréndlines], *s.* amistad.

friendly [-li]. **I.** *a.* amigable, amistoso; servicial, favorable, benévolo, propicio. **II.** *adv.* amigablemente, amistosamente.

friendship [-śhip], *s.* amistad.

frieze [fríś], *s.* (tej.) frisa; (arq.) friso, arrocabe.

frigate [fríguet], *s.* (mar.) fragata.

fright [fráit], *s.* susto, espanto, terror; espantajo.

frighten [fráitœn], *va.* espantar, asustar, amedrentar, aterrorizar, amilanar.—**to f. away**, ahuyentar, espantar.

frightful [fráitful], *a.* espantoso, horroroso, terrible, tremebundo; feísimo.—**frightfully** [-li], *adv.* espantosamente, terriblemente.—**frightfulness** [-nes], *s.* horror, espanto; terror.

frigid [fríyid], *a.* frío, frígido, gélido.

frigidity [fríyíditi], *s.* frialdad, frigidez, frío; impotencia.

frigidly [fríyidli], *adv.* fríamente.

frigorific [frigoríific], *a.* frigorífico.

frill [fril]. **I.** *s.* (cost.) lechuga, escarola; faralá, chorrera; tiritón de las aves.—*pl.* (E. U. fam.) ringorrangos, arrequives. **II.** *va.* (cost.) alechugar, escarolar. **III.** *vn.* escarolarse.

fringe [friny]. **I.** *s.* (cost.) fleco; orla. **II.** *va.* guarnecer con fleco; orlar.—**fringeless** [-les], *a.* sin fleco.—**fringy** [-i], *a.* floqueado.

fripper(er [frípœr(œr], *s.* chamarilero, ropavejero, baratillero; prendero.

frippery [frípœri]. **I.** *s.* prendería; trapería; baratillo; ropa vieja; fruslería. **II.** *a.* despreciable, frívolo.

frisk. I. *vn.* saltar, brincar, cabriolar; retozar, travesear. **II.** *s.* retozo; brinco, salto.

frisker [-œr], *s.* retozón, juguetón.—**frisket** [-et]. *s.* (impr.) frasqueta.—**friskiness** [-s], *s.* calidad de retozón.—**frisky** [-i], *a.* retozón, vivaracho.

frit [frit]. **I.** *s.* (vid.) frita. **II.** *va.* derretir.

fritter [frítœr]. **I.** *s.* fritura, frisuelo, fruta de sartén; quesadilla; fragmento, trozo, triza. **II.** *va.* desmenuzar; desperdiciar.—**to f. away**, desperdiciar o malgastar a poquitos.

frivolity [frivóliti], *s.* frivolidad, trivialidad.

frivolous [frívolus], *a.* frívolo, trivial, vano, baladí—**frivolously** [-li], *adv.* frívolamente, trivialmente.—**frivolousness** [-nes], *s.* trivialidad.

frizz, frizzle [friś, fríśœl]. **I.** *va.* frisar; rizar, encrespar. **II.** *s.* rizo, bucle.

frizzler [fríślœr], *s.* rizador, frisador.

fro, *adv.* atrás, hacia atrás.—**to and f.**, de una parte a otra, de arriba para abajo.

frock, *s.* (cost.) túnico, vestido de mujer o de niño; blusa.—**f. coat**, levita.

frog [frog], *s.* (zool.) rana; (f. c.) crucero, corazón, (Cuba) rana; (elec.) rana, desvío.—**f. eye**, parches blancos hongosos del tabaco.

froggy [frógui], *a.* lleno de ranas.

frolic. I. *s.* juego, retozo, travesura. **II.** *a.* alegre, juguetón, travieso. **III.** *vn.* juguetear, retozar, triscar, jaranear.—**frolicsome** [-sum], *a.* juguetón, travieso, retozón.

from, *prep.* de; desde; de parte de; a fuerza de;. por, a causa de; según; con.—**f. behind**, desde atrás, por detrás.—**f. memory**, de memoria.—**f. nature**, del natural.—**f. off**, desde lejos, fuera de. —**f. on high**, desde lo alto.—**f. out**, de, desde, del fondo de.

frond, *s.* (bot.) fronda; hoja.

frondage [fróndey], *s.* frondosidad, follaje.

frondose [fróndos], *a.* (bot.) frondoso.

frondescence [frondésens], *a.* (bot.) foliación; frondosidad.

frondiferous [frondífœrus], *a.* (bot.) frondoso, frondífero.

front [frunt]. **I.** *s.* frente, faz, cara; audacia, descaro; (arq.) frontispicio, fachada; (igl.) frontal; (teat.) sala, auditorio; (cost.) pechera, delantera, camisolín; (carr.) testera; (zap.) caña de una bota. **II.** *a.* anterior, delantero, frontero; frontal.—**f. room**, cuarto que da a la calle.—**f. view**, vista de frente. **III.** *va.* hacer frente a, mirar, dar o caer a; poner frente o fachada a; arrostrar. **IV.** *vn.* estar al frente de.

frontage [fróentey], *s.* extensión lineal de frente.

frontal [fróntal]. **I.** *a.* frontero, anterior; frental o frontal. **II.** *s.* (anat.) hueso frontal; frentero; (igl.) frontal; (arq.) frontón.

frontier [fróntíœr]. **I.** *s.* frontera; confines de la parte civilizada o explorada de un país, fronteras de las tierras vírgenes. **II.** *a.* fronterizo; de exploración o colonización; de explorador o colonizador (con referencia a regiones incultas o inexploradas).—**frontierman** [-mæn], *s.* colonizador; explorador.

frontispiece [fróntispis], *s.* (impr.) portada (de un libro); (arq.) frontis, frontispicio.

frontless [frœntles], *a.* sin frente.

frontlet [fróntlet], *s.* venda para la frente.

frost [frost]. **I.** *s.* escarcha, rosad; helada, hielo. —**f. nail**, tacón de herradura. **II.** *va.* escarchar; congelar; dañar (el frío); deslustrar. **III.** *vn.* helar, congelarse.

frostbitten [fróstbiten], *a.* helado.

frosted [frósted], *pa.* y *a.* escarchado; deslustrado; mate; garapiñado.

frostiness [-ines], *s.* escarcha.

frosting, *s.* en pastelería, capa de clara de huevo batida con azúcar; imitación de escarcha en los metales.

frostwork [-uœrk], *s.* garapiña; ramajes de la escarcha.

frosty [frósti], *a.* que tiene o parece escarcha; frío, indiferente; cano, canoso.

froth [froz]. **I.** *s.* espuma; bambolla, frivolidad. **II.** *vn.* espumar, hacer espuma; echar espuma. —**to f. at the mouth**, echar espuma por la boca.

frothily [frózili], *adv.* con espuma; frívolamente. —**frothiness** [-nes], *s.* espumosidad; frivolidad.— **frothy** [frózi], *a.* espumoso; frívolo, vano.

frouzy [fráusi], *a.* = FROWSY.

frow [fráu], *s.* (fam.) dama holandesa o alemana; mujer casada.

froward [fróuard], *a.* indócil, díscolo; insolente.— **frowardly** [-li], *adv.* díscolamente; protervamente. —**frowardness** [-nes], *s.* indocilidad; insolencia.

frown [fráun]. **I.** *va.* mirar con ceño. **II.** *vn.* fruncir el entrecejo, enfurruñarse. **III.** *va.* echar en cara; desaprobar, enojo.—**frowns of fortune**, reveses de fortuna.

frowning [fráuning], *a.* fosco, torvo, ceñudo.

frowningly [-li], *adv.* con ceño, de mal ojo.

frowzy [fráusi], *a.* desaliñado, desaseado, sucio; mal peinado.

froze [fróus], *pret.* de FREEZE.

frozen [fróusn], *pp.* de FREEZE.

fructescence [fructésens], *s.* fructificación.

fructiferous [frúctífœrus], *a.* fructífero.

fructification [frúctifikéishun], *s.* (bot.) fructificacion; fruto.—**fructify** [frúctifai]. **I.** *va.* fertilizar, fecundar. **II.** *vn.* fructificar.

fructose [frúctous], *s.* (quím.) fructosa, levulosa extraída de frutas o miel.

frugal [frúgal], *a.* frugal.—**frugality** [frugéliti], *s.* frugalidad.—**frugally** [frúgali], *adv.* frugalmente.

frugiferous [fruyífœrus], *a.* fructífero.

frugivorous [fruyívorus], *s.* frugívoro.

fruit [frut]. **I.** *s.* fruto; fruta; frutas.—**f. basket**, cesta para frutas.—**f.-bearing**, frutal.— **f. dryer**, secador de frutas.—**f.-eating**, frugívoro. —**f. jar**, vaso o tarro para frutas.—**f. parer**, perero.—**f. piece**, (pint.) frutaje.—**f. press**, aparato para prensar frutas.—**f. sugar** = FRUCTOSE.—**f. tree**, árbol frutal. **II.** *vn.* producir frutas; dar fruto.

fruitage [frútey], *s.* fruta; fruto.

fruiter [frútœr], *s.* (mar.) buque frutero.

fruiterer [frútœrœr], *s.* frutero.

fruitery [frútœri], *s.* fruta; frutería.

fruitful [frútful], *a.* feraz, fértil; productivo; prolífico o fecundo; fructuoso, provechoso.—

fruitfully [-i], *adv.* fructuosamente; fértilmente, prolíficamente.—**fruitfulness** [-nes], *s.* fertilidad; fecundidad.

fruition [fruíshun], *s.* fruición; goce, gusto, complacencia.

fruitless [frútles], *a.* estéril, infructuoso, vano.

fruitlessly [-li], *adv.* infructuosamente.

fruitlessness [-nes], *s.* esterilidad; infructuosidad.

fruity [frúti], *a.* de olor o sabor de fruta.

frumentaceous [frúmenteáishus], *a.* frumenticio.

frumenty [frúmenti], *s.* manjar hecho de trigo cocido con leche.

frump [frump], *s.* vieja regañona.

frush [frush], *s.* (vet.) arestín.

frustrate [frústreit]. **I.** *va.* frustrar; anular. **II.** *a.* frustrado, burlado; nulo.—**frustration** [-tréishun], *s.* contratiempo, chasco; privación.— **frustrative** [frústrativ], *a.* frustratorio.

frustum [frústum], *s.* (geom.) cono o pirámide truncados, tronco de cono o de pirámide.

frutescence [frutésens], *s.* (bot.) calidad de fruticoso o leñoso.

frutescent [-ent], *a.* (bot.) fruticoso.

fruticose [frúticos], *a.* fruticoso.

fry [frái]. **I.** *s.* (*pl.* FRIES) (coc.) fritada; (fam.) brete, sofocón.—*sing.* y *pl.* pececillos recién nacidos; enjambre, muchedumbre.—*pl.* criadillas. **II.** *va.* freír. **III.** *vn.* freírse; achicharrarse. —**frying pan**, sartén.

fuchsia [fiúshia], *s.* (bot.) fucsia.

fuchsin(e [fúcsin], *s.* (quím.) fucsina.

fucoid [fiúcoid]. **I.** *a.* fucáceo. **II.** *s.* (bot.) alga parecida al fuco.

fucus [fiúcus], *s.* afeite, aderezo; artimaña; (bot.) fuco, ova.

fuddle [fúdœl]. **I.** *va.* emborrachar; confundir. **II.** *vn.* emborracharse.

fudge [fuy]. **I.** *s.* embuste, cuento; dulce de chocolate. **II.** *interj.* ¡quita allá!

Fuegian [fiuíyæn], *s.* y *a.* fueguino, de la Tierra del Fuego.

fuel [fiúel], *s.* combustible; pábulo, aliciente.— **f. oil**, aceite combustible, aceite de quemar.

fugacious [fiuguéishus], *a.* fugaz.—**fugaciously** [-li], *adv.* fugazmente.—**fugaciousness** [-nes], **fugacity** [fiugásiti], *s.* fugacidad; calidad de fugitivo.

fugh [fu], *interj.* ¡fo!

fugitive [fiúyitiv]. **I.** *a.* fugitivo, prófugo; fugaz, pasajero, perecedero. **II.** *s.* fugitivo, tránsfuga. —**fugitiveness** [-nes], *s.* fugacidad; calidad de fugitivo.

fugleman [fiúgœlman], *s.* (mil.) jefe de fila.

fugue [fiúg], *s.* (mús.) fuga.

fulcrum [fúlcrum], *s.* (mec.) fulcro, punto de apoyo; (bot.) apéndice.

fulfil(l) [fulfíl], *va.* colmar, llenar; cumplir; realizar.

fulfil(l)ment [-mœnt], *s.* cumplimiento, desempeño, ejecución, realización, colmo.

fulgency [fúlɣensi], *s.* fulgor, esplendor.

fulgent [fúlɣent], *a.* fulgente.

fuliginous [fiulíɣinus], *a.* fuliginoso.—**fuliginously** [-li], *adv.* de un modo fuliginoso.

full [ful]. **I.** *va.* dar amplitud; hacer espeso o grueso; (tej.) batanar o abatanar. **II.** *vn.* llenarse, espesarse; llegar la luna a su plenilunio. **III.** *a.* lleno; completo; pleno; cumplido; amplio; harto, ahíto; copioso, abundante; plenario; borracho; maduro, perfecto; fuerte; suficiente.— **f. back,** en el juego de football, puesto trasero.— **f. bloom,** pleno tiro.—**f.-bloom,** abierta (una flor); maduro, cabal; desarrollado.—**f. brother, sister,** hermano (-na) de padre y madre.—**f. cock,** montado, amartillado.—**f. dress,** uniforme de gala; traje de etiqueta.—**f. house,** concurrencia plena, todos los puestos ocupados.—**f.-length,** de tamaño natural, de cuerpo entero.—**f. load,** (mec.) plena carga; (aer.) peso total.—**f. moon,** plenilunio, luna llena.—**f. of play,** muy juguetón o retozón.—**f. powers,** facultades amplias, plenos poderes.—**f. sea,** mar bravío.—**f. speed,** plena, o toda, velocidad.—**f. stock,** (com.) acciones de valor nominal de 100 dólares.—**f. stop,** punto final.— **f.-tide** = HIGH TIDE.—**f. weight,** peso cabal.— **in f. swing,** en plena operación. **IV.** *s.* lleno, complemento; colmo; saciedad; total, totalidad; plenilunio.—**in f.** completamente, detalladamente; completo; total; por completo. **V.** *adv.* enteramente, del todo, de lleno; totalmente, en pleno; derechamente.—**f.-blooded,** pletórico; de pura raza.—**f.-faced,** carrilleno, carigordo; (impr.) letra negra.-—**f.-fledged,** completo, acabado.—**f.-grown,** maduro, crecido, completamente desarrollado.—**f. manned,** con la dotación completa.— **f. well,** muy bien, perfectamente.

fullage [fúleɣ], *s.* lo que se paga por abatanar el paño.

fullam [fúlœm], *s.* dado falso; fraude.

fuller [fúlœr], *s.* batanero.—**f.'s earth,** (tej.) tierra de batán, galactita.—**f.'s thistle,** cardo de bataneros.

fullery [fúlœri], *s.* batán.

fulling mill [fúlingmíl], *s.* batán.

fully [fúli], *adv.* enteramente, completamente.

fulminant [fúlminant], *a.* fulminante.

fulminate [fúlminet]. **I.** *va.* y *vn.* volar, hacer explosión, estallar; tronar, detonar; fulminar. **II.** *s.* (quím.) fulminato.

fulminating [fúlmineting], *a.* fulminante.—**f. cap,** cápsula fulminante.—**f. compound, f. powder,** pólvora fulminante.—**f. mercury,** fulminato de mercurio.

fulmination [fúlminéśhun], *s.* fulminación, detonación.

fulminatory [fúlminatori], *a.* fulminante, fulminoso, fulmíneo.

fulmine [fúlmin]. **I.** *va.* fulminar. **II.** *vn.* tronar.

ful(l)ness [fúlnes], *s.* plenitud, copia, llenura, abundancia; hartura, saciedad; complemento.

fulminic [fulmínic], *a.* (quím.) fulmínico.

fulsome [fúlsum], *a.* bajo, repugnante, indecente.—**fulsomely** [-li], *adv.* asquerosamente, indecentemente.—**fulsomeness** [-nes], *s.* asquerosidad.

fulvous [fúlvus], **fulvid** [fúlvid], *a.* leonado, amarillo rojizo.

Fumaria [fiumériæ], *s.* (bot.) género de las fumarieas.

fumaric [fiuméric], *a.* (quím.) fumárico.

fumarole [fiúmœroul]. *s.* fumarola, grieta que arroja vapores volcánicos.

fumble [fúmbœl], *va.* y *vn.* chapucear, manosear; parar una pelota desmañadamente.—**to f. along,** andar a tientas.

fumbler [-blœr], *s.* chapucero.—**fumblingly** [-blingli], *adv.* chapuceramente.

fume [fiúm]. **I.** *s.* vapor, gas, humo; emanación; cólera, acaloramiento.—*pl.* (quím.) vapores. **II.** *va.* ahumar; sahumar; fumigar; avahar;

exhalar. **III.** *vn.* humear; exhalar vapores; encolerizarse, enojarse.

fumigate [fiúmigueit], *va.* fumigar, ahumar; perfumar.—**fumigation** [-éiśhun], *s.* sahumerio, sahumo; (med.) fumigación.—**fumigator** [-éitœr], *s.* fumigador.—**fumigatory** [-atori], *s.* fumigatorio.

fuming [fiúming]. **I.** *s.* sahumerio; enojo. **II.** *a.* humeante.

fumitory [fiúmitori], *s.* (bot.) fumaria, palomina.

fumy [fiúmi], *a.* humoso, fumoso.

fun [fun], *s.* broma, chacota, chanza, chiste, chuscada, burla; diversión, holgorio.—**for f.,** o **in f.,** en broma.—**to be f.,** (fam.) ser divertido.—**to have f.,** (fam.) divertirse, pasar un buen rato.

funambulatory [fiunémbiulatori], *a.* propio de volatines.—**funambulist** [-ist], *s.* funámbulo, volatín.

function [fúncśhun]. **I.** *s.* (leng. ord., mat., fisiol., etc.) función. **II.** *vn.* funcionar.—**functional** [-œl], *a.* funcional.—**functionary** [-eri], *s.* funcionario.

fund [fund]. **I.** fondo (dinero); caja (de caridad, etc.); acopio; reserva.—*pl.* fondos, dinero. **II.** *va.* consolidar (una deuda).

fundable [fúndabœl], *a.* consolidable.

fundament [fúndamœnt], *s.* fundamento, principio, cimiento; (fam.) nalgas, trasero.

fundamental [fúndaméntal]. **I.** *a.* fundamental. —**f. colours,** colores elementales. **II.** *s.* fundamentalista.

Fundamentalism [-ism], *s.* ortodoxia, fundamentalismo, adhesión a la interpretación literal de la Biblia (entre los protestantes).—**Fundamentalist** [-ist], *s.* ortodoxo, fundamentalista, literalista.

fundamentally [-li], *adv.* fundamentalmente.

funded [fúnded], *a.* consolidado; acumulado e invertido.—**f. debt,** deuda consolidada.

fundholder [fúndjóuldœr], *s.* rentista.

fundus [fúndus], *s.* fondo.

funeral [fiúncœral]. **I.** *a.* funeral, funerario, fúnebre.—**f. procession,** cortejo fúnebre. **II.** *s.* funeral, funerales, exequias; entierro; duelo.

funereal [fiuníreal], *a.* fúnebre; funéreo.

fungi [fúnyai], *pl.* de FUNGUS.

fungicide [fúnyisaid], *s.* funguicida, substancia para destruir hongos.—**fungiform** [fúnyiform], *a.* fungiforme, de forma de hongo.

fungoid [fúngoid], *a.* fungoso.

fungosity [fungósiti], *s.* fungosidad.

fungous [fúngus], *a.* fungoso; hongoso.

fungus [fúngus], *s.* (bot.) hongo; honguillo; moho; (med.) hongo, fungosidad.

funicle [fiúnicœl], *s.* cuerdecilla, funículo.

funicular [fiuníkiular], *a.* funicular.—**f. railroad,** o **railway,** (f. c.) ferrocarril funicular, esp. el de gravedad.

funiculus [-kiulus], *s.* (bot.) funículo; (anat.) cordón umbilical.

funnel [fúnel], *s.* embudo; túnel, cañón, humero; (mar.) chimenea de un vapor; (fund.) boca de carga.—**f.-shaped,** de forma de embudo.

funny [fúni], *a.* cómico, divertido, gracioso, chistoso; (fam.) extraño, curioso.—**f. bone,** (fam.) cóndilo interno del húmero junto al cual pasa el nervio ulnar en el codo.—**f. business,** (fam.) treta; picardía, fraude.

fur [fœr]. **I.** *s.* piel (para abrigo o adornos); borra, sarro, rova. **II.** *va.* cubrir, forrar o adornar con pieles; depositar sarro; (alb.) separar de la pared con tiras los listones de enlucir; (mar.) forrar un buque; quitar incrustaciones a las calderas. **III.** *vn.* formarse incrustaciones.

furbelow [fœrbelo]. **I.** *s.* (cost.) farfalá, volante, (Cuba) vuelo. **II.** *va.* adornar con volantes.

furbish [fœrbiśh], *va.* acicalar, pulir, limpiar.

furcate [fœrket], *a.* ahorquillado.

furcation [fœrkéiśhun], *s.* bifurcación.

furfur [fœrfœr], *s.* (med.) fúrfura.

furfuraceous [fœrfœréśhus], *a.* parecido al salvado o la caspa.

furious [fiúrius], *a.* furioso.—**furiously** [-li], *adv.* furiosamente.

furl [fœrl], *va.* plegar, recoger; (mar.) aferrar, empanicar.—**f. lines,** aferravelas.

furlong [fœrlong], *s.* estadio (⅛ milla).

furlough [fœrlo]. **I.** *s.* (mil.) licencia. **II.** *va.* licenciar.

furnace [fœrnes], *s.* horno; fornalla; hogar (de caldera).—**f. bridge,** (m. v.) altar.—**f. charger,** cebadura.

furnaceman [-mæn], *s.* hornero (encargado de un horno).

furnish [fœrnish], *va.* surtir, suplir, suministrar, proporcionar; aparejar, equipar; amoblar.

furnished [-d], *a.* amueblado.

furnisher [-œr], *s.* amueblador, decorador; proveedor.

furnishing [-ing], *s.* habilitación, equipo, suministro.—*pl.* equipos, accesorios, útiles, fornituras, avíos, adminículos.—**f. goods,** (com.) artículos para caballero.

furniture [fœrnichur *o* tiur], *s.* mobiliario; muebles; equipo; adornos, accesorios; avíos; (impr.) fornitura; (mar.) aparejo.

furor (e [fiúror, fiuróre], *s.* furor, furia, rabia; frenesí; entusiasmo.

furred [fœrd], *a.* forrado o cubierto de piel; cubierto con sarro.

furrier [fœriœr], *s.* peletero, manguitero.

furriery [fœriœri], *s.* peletería.

furring [fœring], *s.* forro o guarnición de pieles; incrustaciones de una caldera, y operación de limpiarla; sarro; (alb.) tiras o tablas que van bajo los listones de enlucido.

furrow [fœro]. **I.** *s.* (agr.) surco; zanja; (fig.) arruga; (carp.) encaje, gárgol, muesca; (arq.) estría, mediacaña. **II.** *va.* surcar; estriar; arar. —**furrowing** [-ing], *s.* corrosión electrolítica; acción de arar o de surcar.

furry [fœri], *a.* adornado con pieles; sarroso.

further [fœrdœr]. **I.** *a.* (*compar.* de FAR) más; más distante; más amplio; adicional. **II.** *adv.* más lejos, más allá; nuevamente, con nuevos informes o detalles; además; aun; además de eso. **III.** *va.* adelantar, promover, fomentar, apoyar.

furtherance [-ans], *s.* adelantamiento, promoción, ayuda, apoyo, fomento.

furtherer [-œr], *s.* promotor, patrón, protector.

furthermore [-mœr], *adv.* además; otrosí.

furthermost [-moust], *a. superl.* más lejano, más remoto.

furthest [fœrδest], *a.* y *adv. superl.* más lejos, más remoto; extremo.

furtive [fœrtiv], *a.* furtivo.—**furtively** [-li], *adv.* furtivamente.

furuncle [fiúruncœl], *s.* furúnculo, divieso, nacido.

furuncular [fiurúnkiular], *a.* furunculoso.

fury [fiúri], *s.* furia; frenesí, entusiasmo.

furze [fœrs], *s.* (bot.) tojo, hiniesta, argoma, aliaga.

furzy [fœrsi], *a.* retamero.

fuscous [fúscus], *a.* fusco.

fuse [fiús]. **I.** *va.* fundir, derretir.—*vn.* fundirse, derretirse. **II.** *s.* espoleta, pebete, cebo, mecha, pajuela; (f. c.) llama de señales.—(elec.) fusible.—**f. block,** o **board,** (elec.) tabla o bloque de fusibles.—**f. link,** (elec.) fusible.—**f. plug,** tapón fusible.—**f. wire,** alambre para fusibles.

fusee [fiusí], *s.* fósforo de yesca o cartón; (arti.) espoleta, pipa; caracol o husillo de reloj.

fuselage [fiúsilex], *s.* (aer.) fuselaje.

fusel oil [fiúsel oil], *s.* (quím.) líquido que contiene principalmente alcohol amílico.

fusibility [fiusibíliti], *s.* fusibilidad.

fusible [fiúsibœl], *a.* fusible, fundible.

fusiform [fiúsiform], *a.* fusiforme.

fusil [fiúsil], *s.* fusil de chispa.

fusileer, fusilier [fiusilíœr], *s.* (mil.) fusilero.

fusillade [fiusiléd], *s.* (arti.) descarga cerrada.

fusing [fiúsing], *a.* fundente.—**f. point,** punto de fusión.

fusion [fiúῨun], *s.* fusión; unión.

fusionist [-ist], *s.* (pol.) unionista, fusionista.

fuss [fus]. **I.** *s.* bulla, bullicio, alboroto; alharaca. **II.** *va.* encocorar. **III.** *vn.* ajetrearse, agitarse, inquietarse.

fussy [fúsi], *a.* inquieto, remilgado, exigente.

fust [fust], *s.* fuste de la columna.

fustian [fúschan]. **I.** *s.* (tej.) fustán, pana; cultedad, culteranismo. **II.** *a.* hecho de fustán; culterano, altisonante, retumbante.

fustic [fústic], *s.* fustoc, fustete.

fustigate [fústiguet], *va.* fustigar.

fustigation [-guéishun], *s.* castigo o pena de azotes, palos o latigazos.

fustiness [-nes], *s.* enmohecimiento; rancidez.

fusty [fústi], *a.* mohoso, rancio; husmeador, fisgón, entrometido.

futile [fiútil], *a.* vano, inútil.

futility [fiutíliti], *s.* inutilidad, ineficacia.

futtock [fútoc], *s.* (mar.) genol, estamenara, singlón, barraganete; arraigada.—**f. shrouds,** pernadas de las arraigadas.

future [fiúchœr]. **I.** *a.* futuro. **II.** *s.* lo futuro, porvenir; (com.) artículo de entrega futura.

Futurism [fiúchœrism], *s.* (b. a.) futurismo.—**Futurist** [-ist], *s.* (b. a.) futurista; (teol.) el que cree que muchas de las profecías de la Biblia se cumplirán en lo futuro.

futurity [fiutiúriti], *s.* lo futuro, porvenir.

fuze [fiús] = FUSE.

fuz(z [fus]. **I.** *vn.* soltar pelusa o borra. **II.** *s.* pelusa, borra, tamo.

fuzzball [fúsbol], *s.* (bot.) bejín.

fuzziness [fúsines], *s.* vellosidad.

fuzzy [fúsi], *a.* velloso, cubierto de pelusa.

fy [fái], *interj.* ¡qué vergüenza!

fyke [fík], *s.* nasa para pescar.

G

g [yi], *s.* g; (mús. G) sol.—**G clef,** clave de sol.—**G string,** primera cuerda del contrabajo, tercera del violoncelo, viola y guitarra, y cuarta del violín; pampanilla.

gab [gæb], *s.* va. y *vn.* parlotear, charlar. **II.** *s.* (fam.) locuacidad, charla; gancho.

gabardine [gæbardín], **gaberdine** [gæbœrdín], *s.* gabacha, gabardina.

gabble [gæbœl]. **I.** *va.* y *vn.* charlar, cotorrear. **II.** *s.* algarabía; cotorreo, charla; graznido.

gabbler [gæblœr], *s.* charlador, picotero.

gabion [guébion], *s.* (fort.) gavión, cestón.

gable [guéibœl], *s.* (arq.) gablete, tímpano triangular de edificio o pared; pared lateral.—**g. end,** pared lateral de gablete o de remate triangular.—**g. roof,** tejado de caballete o de dos aguas.—**g. wall,** pared de caballete o de remate triangular.

gablet [guéiblet], *s.* (arq.) frontón, tímpano.

gad [gæd]. **I.** *vn.* andorrear, callejear. **II.** *s.* (min.) cuña, punzón, aguja, taladro; aguijón, chuzo. **III.** *interj.* (fam. o vulg.) ¡por Dios!

gadabout [gǽdabaut]. **I.** *a.* callejero, cantonero. **II.** *s.* placero; pindonga.

gadder [gǽdœr], *s.* callejero, andorrero.

gadding [gǽding], *s.* vagancia, briba.

gadfly [gǽdflái], *s.* tábano.

gadolinium [gædolínium], *s.* (quím.) gadolinio.

Gael [guéil], *s.*, **Gaelic** [-ic], *s.* y *a.* gaélico.

gaff [gæf], *s.* arpón o garfio; (mar.) botavara.—**g. boom,** verga de cangreja.—**g. sail,** escandalosa.

gaffer [gǽfœr], *s.* viejo, vejete.

gaffle [gǽfœl], *s.* (œp.) espolón de acero, navaja de gallo.

gag [gæg]. **I.** *va.* amordazar; hacer callar; provocar bascas o náuseas; (teat.) meter morcilla. **II.** *vn.* nausear, arquear. **III.** *s.* mordaza; (vet.) acial; asco; lo que produce bascas; (teat.) morcilla.

gage [guéi]. **I.** *s.* prenda, caución; (ant.) guante, gaje, reto; variedad de ciruela. **II.** *va.* (ant.) empeñar, dar en prenda; apostar.

gage, gauge [guéiɣ]. **I.** *s.* regla de medir; medida, norma, escantillón; calibrador; indicador; (mar.) calado; (m. v.) manómetro; (f. c.) ancho de la vía, entrevía, (Amér.) trocha.—**g. cock,** (m. v.) grifo o llave de nivel.—**g. glass,** (m. v.) tubo indicador de nivel.—**g. rod,** calibre cilíndrico de diámetros.—**g. pressure,** (m. v.) presión manométrica. **II.** *va.* aforar, medir; graduar, calibrar, escantillar; estimar, apreciar, avaluar; (mar.) arquear.

gager, gauger [guéiɣœr], *s.* aforador, arqueador, graduador.

gagger [gǽgœr], *s.* el que amordaza.

gaiety [guéieti], *s.* jovialidad, alegría, alborozo; broma, algazara; viveza, ufanía.

gaily [guéili], *adv.* alegremente, jovialmente.

gain [guéin]. **I.** *s.* ganancia, beneficio, provecho; usura; logro; (carp.) gárgol, ranura. **II.** *va.* ganar, reportar, lograr; granjear; vencer, conquistar; conciliar; propiciar; (carp.) hacer gárgoles.—**to g. ground,** ganar terreno.—**to g. the wind,** (mar.) ganar el barlovento. **III.** *vn.* (con **in**) ganar, aumentar, crecer; (con **on** o **upon**) avanzar, adelantarse (a), aproximarse, acercarse.

gainable [guéinabœl], *a.* ganable, asequible.

gainful [guéinful], *a.* lucrativo, ventajoso.—**gainfully** [-i], *adv.* ventajosamente.—**gainfulness** [-nes], *s.* provecho, ganancia.

gainless [guéinles], *a.* desventajoso; infructuoso.

gainlessness [-nes], *s.* inutilidad.

gainsay [guéinséi], *va.* (*pret.* y *pp.* GAINSAID) contradecir, negar.—**gainsayer** [-œr], *s.* contradictor.—**gainsaying** [-ing], *s.* contradicción.

gairish, gairishly, etc.=GARISH, etc.

gait [guéit], *s.* marcha, paso, andadura; porte, continente; viaje, camino.

gaiter [guéitœr], *s.* borceguí, polaina, botín, botina.

gala [guéila], *s.* gala, fiesta.

galactic [galǽctic], *a.* galáctico.

galactometer, s. = LACTOMETER.

Galatian [galéishæn], *s.* y *a.* gálata.

Galaxy [gǽlæcsi], *s.* (astr.) Galaxia, Vía Láctea; grupo notable, constelación (fig.)

galbanum [gǽlbanum], *s.* gálbano.

gale [guéil], *s.* viento fuerte, ventarrón; (fig.) algazara.

galea [guélea], *s.* yelmo, gálea, casco.

galena [galína], *s.* (min.) galena; triaca, antídoto, contraveneno.

galenic(al [galénic(al], *a.* galénico.

Galenism [guélenišm], *s.* galenismo.

Galenist [guélenist], *s.* galenista.

Galilean [gǽlilían], *s.* y *a.* galileo.

galiot [gǽliot], *s.* (mar.) galeota.

galipot [gǽlipot], *s.* galipodio.

gall [gol]. **I.** *s.* hiel, bilis; amargura, aspereza; odio, rencor; (fam.) descaro, (vet.) rozadura o matadura.—**g., g. apple,** (bot.) agalla.—**g. bladder,** vesícula biliar, vejiga de la bilis. **II.** *va.* y *vn.* ludir, raspar; irritar, hostigar.

gallant [gǽlænt]. **I.** *a.* galante, cortés; galanteador, cortejador. **II.** *s.* galán; cortejo; chichisbeo. **III.** *va.* galantear, cortejar, requebrar.

gallant [gǽlant], *a.* valeroso, valiente.

gallantly [-li], *adv.* valerosamente; galantemente.

gallantry [gǽlantri], *s.* valentía, gallardía, valor; galantería, galanteo.

gallate [gǽlet], *s.* (quím.) galato; agallato.

galleon [gǽleon], *s.* (mar.) galeón.

gallery [gǽlœri], *s.* galería; tribuna; balcón corrido; pasadizo; crujía, corredor (apl. esp. al exterior); (b. a.) colección, galería; (teat.) paraíso, cazuela, gallinero; público que ocupa el paraíso o las tribunas; (fort.) galería; (min.) socavón, galería; (mar.) galería, crujía.

galley [gǽli], *s.* (mar.) galera; fogón, cocina; (Ingl.) falúa; (impr.) galera.—**g. proof,** (impr.) galerada.—**g. slave,** galeote.—**g. tiles,** azulejos.

gallfly [gólfläi], *s.* insecto que produce las agallas.

Gallic(an [gǽlic(an], *a.* galicano, galo; (quím.) agállico.

Gallicism [gǽlisišm], *s.* galicismo.

Gallicize [gǽlisaiš], *va.* afrancesar.

galligaskins [gǽligǽskiñš], *s. pl.* botarga, calzacalzón.

gallinaceous [gǽlinéishus], *a.* gallináceo.

galliot, s.=GALIOT.

gallipot [gǽlipot], *s.* orza, bote, pote.

gallium [gǽlium], *s.* (quím.) galio.

gallivant [gǽlivænt], *vn.* (fam.) callejear, pindonguear.

gallnut [gólnut], *s.* = GALL APPLE.

gallon [gǽlun], *s.* galón (Ingl. 4,543 litros; E. U. 3,785 litros); medida inglesa para áridos (⅛ bushel).

galloon [gǽlún], *s.* (tej.) galón, trencilla.

gallop [gǽlup]. **I.** *s.* galope. **II.** *vn.* galopar; ir aprisa.

gallopade [-péid], *s.* caracoleo; (danz.) galop.

Galloway [gǽlouei], *s.* jaca escocesa.

gallows [gǽloš], *s.* horca; armazón, montante.—**g. bird,** malhechor digno de la horca o que ha sido ahorcado; carne para la horca.

gallstone [gólstóun], *s.* cálculo biliario.

gally [góli], *a.* amargo.

galore [galór], *a.* y *adv.* muchísimos; en abundancia.

galosh, galoche [galósh], *s.* galocha, choclo, chanclo, zueco, zapatón; botín, polaina.

Galtonian [goltóniæn], *a.* galtoniano.

galvanic [gælvénic], *a.* galvánico.

galvanism [gǽlvanišm], *s.* galvanismo.

galvanization [-éishun], *s.* galvanización.

galvanize [gǽlvanaiš], *va.* galvanizar.—**galvanized iron,** hierro galvanizado.—**galvanized plate,** palastro galvanizado.

galvanometer [gǽlvanómetœr], *s.* galvanómetro.

galvanometric [-nométric], *a.* galvanométrico.

galvanometry [-nómetri], *s.* galvanometría.

galvanoplasty [-noplésti], *s.* galvanoplastia.

galvanoscope [-noscoup], *s.* galvanoscopio.

gambade, gambado [gæmbéid, gæmbéido], *s.* polaina.—*pl.* guardaestribos de cuero.

gambier [gǽmbiær], *s.* (bot.) gambir de la India, cato (arbusto) amarillo.

gambit [gǽmbit], *s.* gambito.

gamble [gǽmbœl]. **I.** *va.* aventurar o perder una coca en el juego. **II.** *vn.* jugar por dinero. **III.** *s.* (fam.) jugada.

gambler [gǽmblœr], *s.* jugador, tahur.

gambling [gǽmbling]. **I.** *s.* juego (por dinero). **II.** *a.* de juego; jugador.—**g. den,** (fam.), **g. hell** (fam.), **g. house,** garito, casa de juego.

gamboge [gæmbóɣ], *s.* guta, resina o gutagamba.

gambol [gǽmbol]. **I.** *vn.* brincar, saltar, chozpar, caracolear; jugetear, travesear. **II.** *s.* cabriola, brinco, zapateta, travesura.

gambrel [gǽmbrel], *s.* corvejón, tarso, jarrete; garabato, gancho.—**g. roof,** (arq.) techo a la holandesa.

game [guéim]. **I.** *s.* juego; partida de juego; chanza, burla, mofa; caza (animales, antes o después de cazados).—**g. bag,** zurrón, morral.—**the g. is up,** se ha levantado la caza; (fam.) el proyecto se ha frustrado. **II.** *va.* y *vn.* jugar; jugar fuerte. **III.** *a.* relativo a la caza o al juego; dispuesto a pelear; valeroso.—**g. bird,** ave de caza; gallo de pelea.—**g. fish,** pez difícil de pescar y que es por eso el favorito de los pescadores deportivos.—**g. fowl,** raza de gallos de pelea.

gamecock [guéimcóc], *s.* gallo de pelea.

gamekeeper [-kípœr], *s.* guardamontes, guardabosques.

gamesome [-sum], *a.* juguetón, retozón.

gamesomeness [-sumnes], *s.* festividad, alegría, jugueteo.

gamester [guéimstœr], *s.* tahur; garitero.

gamin [gǽmin], *s.* pilluelo, golfo.

gaming [guéiming], **gambling** [gǽmbling], *s.* juego.—**g. house,** garito, casa de juego.—**g. table,** mesa de juego.

gammer [gǽmœr], *s.* vieja; tía, abuelita.

gammon [gǽmon]. **I.** *s.* jamón; lance del juego de chaquete; (fam.) añagaza, trola, chasco.

II. *va.* engañar, chasquear; ganar doble partida de chaquete; curar jamón; (mar.) trincar.—**gammoning**, trinca.—**gammoning hole**, groera de trinca.

gamogenesis [gǽmoɣénesis], *s.* generación o reproducción sexual.

gamopetalous [-pétalʊs], *a.* (bot.) gamopétalo.

gamosepalous [-sépalʊs], *a.* (bot.) gamosépalo.

gamut [gǽmʊt], *s.* (mús.) gama, escala.

gamy [guéimi], *a.* (coc.) maido, salvajino; (fam.) peleón, bravo, indómito.

ganch [gænch], *va.* empalar.

gander [gǽndœr], *s.* (orn.) ánsar, ganso.

gang [gæng], *s.* cuadrilla, pandilla; revezo; juego, grupo; (min.) ganga.—**g. plough, o plow**, arado de reja múltiple.—**g. saw**, sierra múltiple.

gangboard [gǽngbord], *s.* (mar.) plancha, andamio.

ganglion [gǽngliʊn], *s.* (anat.) ganglio.

ganglionic [gængliónic], *a.* ganglionar.

gangplank [gǽnplænc], *s.* pasamano, plancha.

gangrene [gǽngrin], **I.** *va.* gangrenar. **II.** *vn.* gangrenarse. **III.** *s.* gangrena.

gangrenous [gǽngrenʊs], *a.* gangrenoso.

gangster [gǽngstœr], *s.* miembro de una cuadrilla de rufianes.

gangue [gæng], *s.* (min.) ganga.

gangway [gǽngüéi], *s.* (mar.) pasamano, portalón, tilla.

gannet [gǽnet], *s.* (orn.) bubia.

ganoid [gǽnoid], *a.* (ict.) ganoideo.

ga(u)ntlet [gántlet], *s.* (mil.) baquetas.

gantry [gǽntri], *s.* = GAUNTRY.

gaol, gaoler [ʝéil, -œr] = JAIL, JAILER.

gap [gæp], **I.** *s.* portillo, abertura, raja, resquicio, brecha; vacío, claro, laguna; quebrada; barranca, hondonada; (aer.) entreplano, distancia mínima entre los planos de un biplano. **II.** *va.* hacer una muesca o brecha en.

gape [gap]. **I.** *vn.* bostezar; boquear; estar con la boca abierta; abrirse o estar abierta una cosa.—**to g. at**, embobarse, papar moscas. **II.** *s.* bostezo; boqueada; brecha, abertura, hendedura.

gaper [gápœr], *s.* bostezador; bobalicón, papamoscas.

gar [gar], *s.* (ict.) sollo o belona.

garage [(gǽráɣ], *s.* garaje, cochera para automóviles.

garb, *s.* vestido, vestidura, vestiduras, traje; forma literaria; apariencia, exterior, aspecto.

garbage [gárbey], *s.* basura, desperdicios.

garbel [gárbel], *s.* (mar.) aparadura.

garble [gárbœl]. **I.** *va.* pervertir, mutilar; garbillar; entrescar, escoger. **II.** *s. pl.* (com.) desecho de especias y drogas.

garbler [gárblœr], *s.* garbillador; pervertidor.

garboard (plank) [gárbord], *s.* (mar.) aparadura.

garden [gárdœn]. **I.** *s.* huerta, huerto; jardín.—**g. balsam**, balsamina de jardín.—**g. bed, o plot**, plantío; era, cuadro.—**g. mould**, tierra vegetal.—**g. stuff**, hortalizas, legumbres. **II.** *va. y vn.* cultivar jardines o huertos.

gardener [gárdnœr], *s.* jardinero; hortelano.

gardenia [gardínia], *s.* (bot.) gardenia.

gardening [gárdning], *s.* jardinería; horticultura.

garfish [gárfîsh], *s.* (ict.) belona.

gargarism [gárgarišm], *s.* gargarismo.

gargarize [gárgaraiš], *va.* gargarizar.

garget [gárguet], *s.* (vet.) enfermedad del ganado, que consiste sobre todo en hinchazón de la garganta; inflamación de la ubre.

gargle [gárgœl]. **I.** *va. y vn.* gargarizar. **II.** *s.* gárgara, gargarismo; enjuague, colutorio.

gargoyle [gárgoil], *s.* (arq.) gárgola.

garish [guérîsh], *a.* deslumbrante; charro.

garishly [-li], *adv.* deslumbradora o llamativamente.—**garishness** [-nes], *s.* relumbrón, oropel.

garland [gárland]. **I.** *s.* guirnalda, corona; lauro; crestomatía; (arq.) festón; (mar.) roñada. **II.** *va.* enguirnaldar.

garlic [gárlic], *s.* (bot.) £jo.

garlicky [gárliki], *a.* que huele o sabe a ajo.

garment [gármœnt], *s.* prenda de vestir; vestido, vestidura.

garner [gárnœr]. **I.** *va.* entrojar, almacenar el grano. **II.** *s.* granero, hórreo, acopio.

garnet [gárnet], *s.* granate; color rojo; (mar.) aparejo de carga.

garnish [gárnîsh]. **I.** *va.* (coc.) aderezar; guarnecer, ornar, ataviar; (for.) prevenir, notificar; aprestar. **II.** *s.* (coc.) aderezo; guarnición, adorno.—**garnisher** [-œr], *s.* aderezador; guarnecedor.—**garnishment** [-mœnt], *s.* ornamento, adorno; (for.) entredicho.

garniture [gárnichur], *s.* guarnición, adorno, gayadura.

garpike [gárpaik], *s.* (ict.) belona; nombre de varios otros peces de agua dulce.

garret [gǽret], *s.* guardilla, buharda.

garrison [gǽrisʊn]. **I.** *s.* (mil.) guarnición. **II.** *va.* guarnecer; guarnicionar.

garrote [gœrrót]. **I.** *va.* agarrotar; estrangular para robar. **II.** *vn.* hacer fullerías. **III.** *s.* garrote.

garrulity [gœrrúliti], *s.* garrulidad.

garrulous [gǽrulʊs], *a.* gárrulo, lenguaz.

garter [gártœr]. **I.** *s.* liga, cenojil, ataderas, jarretera.—**g. fish**, (ict.) lepidopo.—**G. King-at-arms**, rey de armas.—**g. snake**, nombre de una culebrilla no venenosa.—**the G.**, orden de la Jarretera, y su insignia. **II.** *va.* atar con liga o cenojil; investir con la orden de la Jarretera.

gas [gæs], *s.* gas; (fam., esp. en aut.) gasolina.—**g. bracket**, brazo de mechero de gas.—**g. burner**, mechero de gas.—**g. carbon**, carbón de las retortas (en las fábricas de gas).—**g. engine**, motor de gas.—**g. fitter**, gasista, instalador de cañerías de gas y accesorios.—**g. fittings**, tubos y accesorios de distribución interior de gas.—**g. fixtures**, mecheros y accesorios de gas.—**g. holder**, gasómetro.—**g. jet**, mechero de gas o su llama.—**g. lighter**, encendedor de gas.—**g. main**, cañería maestra o alimentadora de gas.—**g. mask**, (mil. careta de protección contra el gas.—**g. meter**, contador de gas.—**g. oil**, aceite para gas de alumbrado, obtenido del petróleo.—**g. pipe**, tubo o tubería de gas.—**g. producer**, gasógeno.—**g. range**, fogón o cocina de gas.—**g. tank**, gasómetro.—**g.-tight**, hermético.—**g. works**, fábrica de gas.

gas. I. *va.* (tej.) exponer a una llama de gas o a calor fuerte para aflojar las fibras; chamuscar; (quím.) saturar de gas; (mil) asfixiar, envenenar o atacar con gas. **II.** *vn.* desprender gas.

gasconade [gǽsconéid]. **I.** *s.* gasconada, fanfarronada. **II.** *vn.* jactarse, fanfarronear.

gaseous [gǽseʊs], *a.* gaseoso.

gash [gæsh]. **I.** *va.* dar una cuchillada, hacer un chirlo. **II.** *s.* cuchillada; incisión grande.

gasification [gǽsifikéishun], *s.* gasificación.

gasify [gǽsifai], *va.* gasificar.

gasiform [gǽsiform], *a.* gasiforme.

gasket [gǽsket], *s.* (mec.) relleno, empaquetadura.—*pl.* (mar.) tomadores, cajetas.

gaskins [gǽskinš], *s. pl.* empaquetadura de cáñamo o estopa.

gaslight [gǽslait], *s.* luz de gas; mechero de gas.

gasogen(e [gǽsoɣen, -yin], *s.* = GAZOGENE.

gasoline [gǽsolin], *s.* gasolina.

gasometer [gæsómetœr], *s.* gasómetro.

gasometry [gæsómetri], *s.* gasometría.

gasp. I. *va. y vn.* emitir sonidos entrecortados; boquear. **II.** *s.* boqueada.

gast(e)ropod [gǽstœropod], *n. y s.* gasterópcdo.

gastralgia [gæstrályia], *s.* gastralgia.

gastric [gǽstric], *a.* gástrico.

gastritis [gæstráitis o tritis], *s.* gastritis.

gastronomer, gastronomist [gæstrónomœr, -mist], *s.* gastrónomo.—**gastronomic(al** [gæstronómic(al], *a.* gastronómico.—**gastronomy** [gæstrónomi], *s.* gastronomía.

gastrotomy [gæstrótomi], *s.* (cir.) gastrotomía.

gastrula [gǽstrula], *s.* (zool.) gástrula.

gate [guéit], *s.* puerta; entrada; portal; pórtico; (f. c.) barrera; rastrillo, poterna; compuertas de esclusa; vía, camino; garganta, paso; (fund.)

vaciadero de un molde, conducto de colada.—**g. valve**, válvula de tipo de compuerta.

gatekeeper [guéitkípœr], **gateward** [-uord], s. portero; (f. c.) guardabarrera.

gateway [guéituéi], s. entrada, paso (con portillo).

gather [gǽɒœr]. **I.** va. reunir, coger, recoger, ganar; acopiar, acumular; recolectar; juntar, congregar; (cost.) fruncir; colegir, inferir.—**to g. breath**, tomar aliento.—**to g. dust**, cubrirse de polvo.—**to g. flesh**, criar carnes.—**to g. grapes**, vendimiar.—**to g. strength**, recuperarse, tomar fuerzas. **II.** vn. unirse, reunirse, juntarse, congregarse; amontonarse, acumularse; aumentarse; concentrarse, condensarse, contraerse; formarse pus. **III.** s. (cost.) frunce, pliegue, plegado.

gatherable [gǽɒœrabœl], a. deducible; que puede juntarse o cosecharse.

gatherer [gǽɒœrœr], s. colector, segador, vendimiador; (cost.) fruncidor.

gathering [gǽɒœring], s. asamblea; reunión; amontonamiento, hacinamiento, acumulación; fruncimiento, contracción; cuesta, demanda, colecta; absceso; (cost.) fruncido.

Gatling gun [gǽtling gɒn], s. (arti.) ametralladora Gatling.

gauche [góšh], a. zurdo, torpe.

gaucherie [goshœrí], s. torpeza.

gaud [god], s. objeto charro.

gaudily [gódili], adv. ostentosamente, fastosamente, charramente.

gaudiness [-nes], s. oropel, fausto, pompa; charrada.

gaudy [gódi], **gaudish** [gódišh], a. brillante, lucido; llamativo, charro, chillón.

gauge [geiy], **gauger** = GAGE, etc.

gauging [guéiying], s. aforo, aforamiento; medición; (mar.) arqueaje.

Gaul [gol], s. Galia antigua, Francia; galo.

Gaulish [gólishh], a. galicano, galo.

gaultheria [golzíriæ], s. (bot.) gauteria, gualteria; aceite de gauteria.

gaunt [gant], a. flaco, delgado, desvaído.

gauntlet [gántlet], s. manopla; guantelete. V. GANTLET.

gauntry [góntri], s. caballete para barril, poíno; (f. c.) puente transversal de señales.—**g. crane**, puente grúa, grúa de puente.

gauze [goš], s. gasa, cendal.

gauziness [góšines], s. diafanidad.

gauzy [góši], a. diáfano como gasa.

gavage [gaváỹ], s. alimentación forzada.

gave [guéiv], pret. de TO GIVE.

gavel [gǽvel], s. mazo; mallo, mallete; haz, gavilla, mostela.

gavelock [gǽveloc], s. barra o palanca de hierro.

gavial [guévial], s. gavial, cocodrilo del Ganges.

gavot [gǽvot o gavót], s. gavota.

gawk [gok]. **I.** s. páparo, bobo, payo. **II.** vn. cometer torpezas.

gawky [góki]. **I.** s. zote, papanatas. **II.** a. bobo, tonto, rudo, torpe, desgarbado.

gay [guéi], a. alegre, festivo, gayo, ledo, ufano, llamativo; ligero de cascos, calavera.

gayety, gayly = GAIETY, GAILY.

gayness [guéines], s. V. GAIETY.

gaze [guéiš]. **I.** vn. mirar con fijeza, clavar la mirada. **II.** s. contemplación, mirada fija o penetrante.

gazogene [gǽšoyin], s. (met.), gasógeno, horno para la producción de gases combustibles.

gazehound [guéisjáund], s. perro que sigue la presa con la vista.

gazelle [gašél], s. gacela.

gazer [guéišœr], s. mirón.

gazette [gašét]. **I.** s. gaceta; nombramiento o anuncio oficial. **II.** va. publicar o anunciar en la Gaceta; nombrar oficialmente.

gazetteer [gǽšetíær], s. gacetero; nomenclador o diccionario geográfico.

gear [guíær]. **I.** s. (mec.) engranaje, encaje; mecanismo de transmisión, de distribución o de gobierno; juego; rueda dentada; (mar.) aparejo, maniobra; en general, equipo, vestidos, adornos o atavíos, herramientas, aperos, utensilios caseros, arneses o aparejos de tiro.—pl. (mar.) drizas.—**g. box, g. case**, caja de engranajes; (aut.) caja de velocidades.—**g. cutter**, fresa para dientes de ruedas.—**g.-cutting machine**, máquina de fresar o cortar dientes.—**g. ratio**, relación de multiplicación.—**g.-shift lever**, (aut.) palanca de cambio de marcha.—**ꭓ. wheel**, rueda dentada.—**in g.**, en juego, engranado, encajado.—**out of g.**, fuera de juego, desencajado, desengranado.—**to put in g.**, relacionar, conexionar; engranar.—**to throw into g.**, poner en juego; engranar.—**to throw out of g.**, desengranar; desencajar; desmontar. **II.** va. aparejar, enjaezar; equipar, preparar; montar, armar; (mec.) engranar, encajar, endentar, embrazar. **III.** vn. venir o estar en juego; engranar; estar engranado.

gearing [gíæring], s. (mec.) mecanismo; de engranaje; engranaje; (mar.) drizas y aparejos.

geat [yit], s. (fund.) boca del molde.

gee [ɣí]. **I.** va. arrear hacia la derecha. **II.** vn. torcer hacia la derecha. **III.** interj. ¡Ave María! ¡caramba!

geese [guís], s. pl. de GOOSE.

Gehenna [guejéna], s. gehena, infierno.

gel [ɣel], s. (biol., quím.) substancia gelatinosa.

gelatin(e [ɣélatin], s. gelatina, jaletina.

gelatinate, gelatinize [ɣelǽtinet, naišh], va. y vn. convertir o convertirse en substancia gelatinosa.

gelatinous [ɣelǽtinus], a. gelatinoso.

geld [gueld], va. (vet.) castrar, capar; (api.) castrar las colmenas.—**gelder** [guéldœr], s. castrador, capador.—**gelding** [-ing], s. animal capado.

gelid [ɣélid], a. gélido.—**gelidity** [ɣelíditi], **gelidness** [ɣélidnes], s. frío extremo.

gem [ɣem]. **I.** s. gema; joya, alhaja; preciosidad. **II.** va. adornar con piedras preciosas.

gemel [ɣémel], a. y s. gemelo, mellizo.—**g. ring**, sortija de alianza.

gemellus [ɣemélus], s. músculo gemelo.

geminate [ɣémineit], a. (bot.) geminado.

gemination [-éishun], s. geminación.

Gemini [ɣéminai], s. (astr.) Géminis.

gemma [ɣéma], a. (bot.) botón, yema.

gemmate [ɣémet], a. que tiene yemas o botones. **—gemmation** [ɣeméishhun], s. (zool. bot.) gemación.

gemmule [ɣémiul], s. (bot.) botoncillo.

gemot [guemót], s. (ant.) asamblea.

gendarme [yendárm, ỹandárm], s. gendarme, polizonte armado.—**gendarmerie** [-eri, erj], s. gendarmería.

gender [ɣéndœr]. **I.** s. (gram.) género; (fam.) sexo. **II.** va. engendrar; producir, causar.

genealogical [ɣénealóyical], a. genealógico.—**g. tree**, árbol genealógico.

genealogist [ɣénealóyist], s. genealogista.

genealogy [ɣéneáloyi], s. genealogía.

genera [ɣéneræ], pl. de GENUS.

generable [ɣénerabœl], a. generable.

general [ɣéneræl]. **I.** a. general.—**g. officer**, (mil.) jefe de grado superior al de coronel. **II.** s. (mil.) general; generala (toque).—**in g.**, en general, por regla general.

generalissimo [ɣéneralísimo], s. generalísimo.

generality [ɣénœréliti], s. generalidad.

generalization [ɣénœrališéishun], s. generalización.

generalize [ɣénœralaišh], va. generalizar.—**generally** [ɣénœrali], adv. generalmente.

generalship [ɣénœralshhip], s. generalato; táctica; habilidad en el manejo.

generant [ɣénœrant]. **I.** a. generativo. **II.** s. generante.

generate [ɣénœret], va. engendrar; producir, causar; (mec.) producir; (mat.) engendrar.

generation [ɣénœréshhun], s. generación; procreación, reproducción; (mat. y fís.) generación, producción.

generative [ɣénœrativ], a. generativo, prolífico, fecundo.

generator [yénœréitœr], *s.* padre, procreador, engendrador; (elec.) generador, dinamo; (mec.) generador; (mat.) generatriz.

generatrix [-trix], *s.* (mat.) generatriz; (elec.) dinamo; madre.

generic(al [yenéric(al], *a.* genérico.

generically [yenéricali], *adv.* genéricamente.

generosity [yénœrósiti], *s.* generosidad.

generous [yénœrus], *a.* generoso; noble, magnánimo; amplio, holgado; estimulante.—**generously** [-li], *adv.* liberalmente, generosamente.—**generousness** [-nes], *s.* generosidad.

genesis [yénesis], *s.* génesis, origen, formación; (G-) Génesis, primer libro del Pentateuco.

genet [yénet], *s.* haca, jaca.

genet [yenét], *s.* gineta, y su piel.

genetic [yenétic], *a.* genesíaco; genésico.

genetics [yenétics], *s.* ciencia del desarrollo natural de los seres organizados; estudio experimental de la formación de especies nuevas.

Genevan [yenívan], *a. y s.* ginebrino, ginebrés; calvinista.

genial [yíñal *o* yínial], *a.* genial, cordial, afable; nupcial.—**geniality** [yiniéliti], *s.* afabilidad.—**genially** [yíniali], *adv.* cordialmente.

geniculate(d [yeníkiuleit(ed], *a.* articulado, doblado.—**geniculation** [-éiśhun], *s.* genuflexión; (bot.) articulación, nudosidad.

genii [yíniai], *s. pl.* de GENIUS.

Genista [yenísta], *s.* (bot.) retama.

genital [rénital]. I. *a.* genital. II. *s. pl.* órganos genitales, partes pudendas.

genitive [yénitiv], *a. y s.* (gram.) genitivo.

genius [yínius], *s.* genio (fuerza intelectual extraordinaria); genio (sujeto dotado de esa fuerza; (en esta acepción el plural es GENIUSES); prototipo; genio, numen; (b. a.) angel, cupidillo.

Genoese [yénóís], *a. y s.* genovés.

genteel [yentíl], *a.* urbano, cortés, gentil; gallardo, airoso; elegante.—**genteelly** [-li], *adv.* cortésmente, gentilmente.—**genteelness** [-nes], *s.* gentileza, gracia, garbo.

gentian [yénśhian], *s.* (bot.) genciana.

Gentile [yéntail], *a. y s.* gentil; (gram.) gentilicio.

gentilism [yéntiliśm], *s.* gentilismo, gentilidad.

gentilitious [yéntiliśhus], *a.* gentilicio.

gentility [yentíliti], *s.* nobleza, gentileza, donosura, gracia, garbo, donaire.

gentle [yéntœl], *a.* suave, apacible; dócil, manso; dulce, benévolo, benigno; bien nacido.— **g. craft**, zapatería; pesca.—**g. passion**, amor.— **g. sex**, bello sexo.

gentlefolk [-fóuc], *s.* gente bien nacida.

gentleman [yéntœlman], *s.* caballero, hombre decente.—**g. in waiting**, gentilhombre de servicio.—**gentlemanlike** [-laic], *a.* acaballerado, caballeroso.

gentlemanliness [-lines], *s.* caballerosidad, hidalguía.

gentlemanly [-li], *a.* caballeroso, civil, urbano; hidalgo.

gentlemen [-men], *s. pl.* de GENTLEMAN; señores; (en cartas) muy señores míos (nuestros).—**g.'s agreement**, pacto de caballeros, sin valor oficial pero que obliga moralmente.

gentleness [yéntœlnes], *s.* dulzura; docilidad, mansedumbre; urbanidad, delicadeza, nobleza.

gentlewoman [yéntœluman], *s.* señora, dama; dama de honor.

gently [yéntli], *adv.* dulcemente, suavemente; silenciosamente; mansamente; poco a poco, despacio, con tiento.

Gentoo [yentú], *s.* indio oriental.

gentry [yéntri], *s.* clase media.

genuflection [yéniuflecśhun], *s.* genuflexión.

genuine [yéñuin], *a.* genuino, verdadero; sincero; (zool.) típico.—**genuinely** [-li], *adv.* genuinamente, sinceramente.—**genuineness** [-nes], *s.* puerza, autenticidad, legitimidad.

genus [yínus], *s.* (biol.) género.

geocentric [yíoséntric], *a.* geocéntrico.

geochemical [-kémicœl], *a.* geoquímico, relativo a agentes geológicos y químicos.

geochemistry [-kémistry], *s.* geoquímica, geología química.

geode [yíod], *s.* (geol.) géoda.

geodesist [yíodesist], *s.* geodesta.

geodesy [yeódesi], *s.* geodesia.

geodetic(al [yíodétic(al], *a.* geodésico.

geogenic [yíoyénic], *a.* geogénico, geogónico.

geogeny [yióyeni], *s.* geogenia.

geognosy [yiógnosi], *s.* geognosia.

geographer [yiógrafœr], *s.* geógrafo.

geographic(al [yíográfic(al], *a.* geográfico.—**g. mile** = NAUTICAL MILE.

geographically [-i], *adv.* geográficamente.

geography [yiógrafi], *s.* geografía.

geoid [yíoid], *s.* geoide, la tierra considerada como sólido geométrico.

geologic(al [yíolóyic(al], *a.* geológico.

geologist [yióloyist], *s.* geólogo.

geologize [yióloyaiś], *vn.* estudiar la geología.

geology [yióloyi], *s.* geología.

geomancy [yíomænsi], *s.* geomancia.

geometer [yiómetœr], *s.* geómetra.

geometric(al [yíométric(al], *a.* geométrico.

geometrically [-i], *adv.* geométricamente.

geometrician [yíometríśhan], *s.* geómetra.

Geometridæ [yiómétridi], *s. pl.* (ent.) geometrinos.

geometry [yiómetri], *s.* geometría.

geomorphy [yíomorfi], *s.* geomorfia.

geonomic [yíonómic], *a.* geonómico.

geonomy [yíonomi], *s.* geonomía.

geophagous [yiófagus], *a.* geófago.

geophysics [yíofísics], *s.* geofísica, estudio de los caracteres y cambios físicos de la tierra—incluye la geografía física y la geodinámica.

geoponic(al [yíopónic(al], *a.* geopónico.

geoponics [-s], *s.* geoponía, agricultura.

georama [yíoréma, yeoráma], *s.* georama, globo geográfico.

george [yory], *s.* placa de la orden de la Jarretera; (sast.) cuello; antigua peluca; (mar.) garganta de polea.

Georgian [yóryian], *a. y s.* georgiano.

georgic(al [yóryic(al], *a.* geórgico.

geoscopy [yióscopi], *s.* geoscopia.

geosyncline [yíosínclain], *s.* (geol.) geosinclinal, pliegue cóncavo.

geotectonic [yíotectónic], *a.* (geol.) geotectónico.

geothermic [yíozérmic], *a.* geotérmico.

geotropism [yiótropiśm], *s.* (bot.) geotropismo, tendencia hacia el centro de la tierra.

Geraniaceæ [yeréiniéisii], *s. pl.* (bot.) geraniáceas.—**geraniaceous** [-śhus], *a.* geraniáceo.

geranium [yerénium], *s.* (bot.) geranio.

gerfalcon [yérfokun], *s.* (orn.) gerifalte.

germ [yœrm], *s.* germen; (biol.) embrión; (bot.) yema, botón, simiente, embrión, ovario; principio, origen, rudimento; (med.) microbio.

german [yœrman], *a.* de unos mismos padres o abuelos.

German, *s. y a.* alemán; germánico, tudesco.— **G. measles**, rubéola.—**G. silver**, plata alemana, metal blanco.—**G. text**, (imp.) tipo alemán.—**G. tinder**, yesca.—**the g.**, el cotillón.

germander [yœrmándœr], *s.* (bot.) pinillo, maro.

germane [yœrméin], *a.* pariente; afín; pertinente, relacionado, aplicable.

Germanic [yœrmǽnic], *a.* germánico, alemanisco.

Germanism [yœrmaniśm], *s.* germanismo.

germanium [yœrméinium], *s.* (quím.) germanio.

germicidal [yœrmisáidal], *a.* germicida.

germicide [yœrmisaid], *s.* bactericida.

germiculture [yœrmicúlchœr], *s.* (biol.) cultivo de bacterias.

germinal [yœrminal], **germinative** [-etiv], *a.* germinal, germinativo.—**germinate** [-eit], *vn.* germinar.—**germination** [-éiśhun], *s.* germinación.

germplasm [yœrmplæsm], *s.* parte del protoplasma que se transmite de generación a generación y es la causa de la herencia.

gerund [yérund], *s.* (gram.) gerundio.

gerundive [rerʊndiv], *s.* (gram.) gerundio adjetivado.

gest [rest], *s.* (ant.) gesta, romance.

gestation [restéishʊn], *s.* gestación, preñez, embarazo.

gestatory [réstatori], *a.* gestatorio.

gesticulate [restíkiuleit], *vn.* gesticular, accionar. —**gesticulation** [-éishʊn], *s.* gesticulación.—**gesticulator** [-éitœr], *s.* gestero.—**gesticulatory** [restíkiulatori], *a.* gesticular.

gesture [réschur]. **I.** *s.* gesto, acción, ademán, signo. **II.** *vn.* accionar; gesticular o hacer gestos.

get [guet], *va.* (*pret.* GOT: *pp.* GOT o GOTTEN) conseguir, obtener, adquirir; ganar; llevar (premio, ventaja, etc.); reportar, recibir; aprender de memoria; engendrar, procrear; mandar, disponer, hacer que; persuadir, inducir, incitar; procurar, lograr; traer; poner(se); entender.—**to g. a footing,** establecerse.—**to g. back,** recobrar.—**to g. by heart,** aprender de memoria. —**to g. down,** descolgar, bajar; tragar.—**to g. it,** (fam.) recibir castigo o un regaño.—**to g. off,** enviar; disponer de; librar, sacar (de un aprieto, etc.).—**to g. one's hand in,** aprender por experiencia o con la práctica.—**to g. on the brain,** tener (algo) metido en la cabeza.—**to g. out,** publicar, editar, sacar.—**to g. the better,** o **the best, of,** llevar ventaja a; engañar a; ganar a.— **to g. the sack,** (fam.) recibir calabazas.—**to g. the start of,** coger la delantera a.—**to g. the worse,** o **the worst,** llevar la peor parte, quedar mal parado; perder.—**to g. up,** arreglar, preparar; idear, inventar; vestir, engalanar.—**to g. wind of,** recibir aviso de, tener noticia de, descubrir.—**to have got,** (fam.) tener, poseer.—**g. you gone!** ¡váyase Vd! ¡larga de aquí!

get, *vn.* ganar dinero; llegar; ponerse o volverse; (seguido de participio) hacerse (seguido de infinitivo), ser; hallarse, estar; introducirse, meterse.—**to g. abroad,** divulgarse, hacerse público; levantarse y moverse (un convaleciente).—**to g. abroad,** divulgarse.—**to g. ahead,** adelantarse, ganar la delantera.—**to g. ahead of,** adelantarse a; ganar a.—**to g. along,** adelantar; hallarse; ir pasando.—**to g. among,** hacerse uno de.—**to g. at,** ir a; llegar a; atacar; averiguar, descubrir.— **to g. away,** irse; partir; huir, escaparse.—**to g. away with,** llevarse; vencer, ganarle a.—**to g. back,** volver, regresar.—**to g. behind,** penetrar; enterarse de los secretos de; quedarse atrás.—**to g. better,** mejorar.—**to g. clear,** salir bien, quedar absuelto; vindicarse; zafarse, librarse.—**to g. down,** bajar, descender.—**to g. even with,** hacérselas pagar a; vengarse de.—**to g. forward,** adelantar, medrar.—**to g. home,** llegar a casa o a la meta.—**to g. in,** (lograr) entrar; llegar.—**to g. in the habit of,** acostumbrarse a, contraer el hábito de.—**to g. into,** entrar, penetrar; montarse en (cólera, etc.); meterse en.—**to g. in with,** relacionarse con.—**to g. left,** (fam.) quedarse colgado o a la luna de Valencia.—**to g. loose, o free,** zafarse; quedar libre.—**to g. married,** casarse.—**to g. near,** acercarse.—**to g. off,** salir de un asunto; escapar, huir; irse; salir; apearse.—**to g. on,** adelantar, medrar; ponerse encima de; subir; montar; entrar en un coche; armonizar.—**to g. on one's legs,** levantarse; mejorar de fortuna. —**to g. on one's nerves,** (fam.) irritar, cansar o fastidiar a uno.—**to g. on with,** llevarse con uno. —**to g. out,** salir, salirse.—**to g. out of,** evadir; evitar; escaparse de.—**to g. out of order,** descomponerse, desajustarse.—**to g. out of the way,** apartarse o hacerse a un lado.—**to g. over,** pasar por encima; vencer (obstáculos); recuperarse de; olvidar.—**to g. ready,** aparejarse.—**to g. rid of,** zafarse o librarse de.—**to g. round,** evadir, evitar; refutar.—**to g. square** = TO GET EVEN.—**to g. there,** (fam.) llegar al fin que se desea, salirse con la suya.—**to g. through,** pasar, penetrar; terminar.—**to g. through with,** acabar con.—**to g. together,** juntarse, reunirse.—**to g. up,** levantarse; subir, ascender.—**to g. under way,** partir, salir; zapar, hacerse a la vela.—**to have got to,** o **to've got to,** (fam.) haber de, tener que.

get, *s.* engendro; engendramiento; raza; cría.

gettable [guétæbœl], *a.* obtenible, asequible.

getter [-œr], *s.* persona que consigue o logra.

get-up [-ʊp], *s.* arreglo, disposición; atavío; traje.

gewgaw [guiúgo]. **I.** *s.* miriñaque, adorno cursi. **II.** *a.* cursi, chillón.

geyser [gáiscœr], *s.* géiser, fuente termal intermitente.

ghastliness [gástlines], *s.* palidez cadavérica.

ghastly [gástli]. **I.** *a.* livido; horrible. **II.** *adv.* horriblemente; lívidamente.

ghee [gui], *s.* aceite de manteca clarificada.

gherkin [gœrkin], *s.* pepinillo, cohombrillo.

Ghetto [géto], *s.* ghetto, barrio de los judíos.

Ghibelline [guíbelin], *s.* gibelino.

ghost [góust], *s.* aparecido, espectro, sombra, fantasma; ánima en pena; alma, espíritu; imagen, traza leve; (foto. y ópt.) imagen falsa o secundaria; mancha.—**not a g. of a doubt,** ni sombra de duda.—**to give up the g.,** dar, o exhalar, el espíritu, morir, morirse.

ghostliness [góustlines], *s.* espiritualidad.

ghostly [góustli], *a.* espiritual; de duendes o aparecidos.

ghoul [gul], *s.* vampiro.

ghurry [gœri], *s.* (Anglo-ind.) clepsidra; reloj; hora india.

giant [ráiant]. **I.** *a.* gigantesco. **II.** *s.* gigante. —**g.-powder,** dinamita.

giantess [ráiantes], *s.* giganta.

giaour [rǽuar], *s.* infiel (en el sentido musulmán).

gib [rib]. **I.** *s.* chaveta, cuña, contraclavija; aguilón, brazo de grúa.—**cotter** (**o key**) **and g.,** clavija y contraclavija. **II.** *va.* acuñar, asegurar con chaveta. **III.** *vn.* rebelarse el caballo.

gib [guib], *s.* gato castrado.

gibber [guíbœr], *vn.* farfullar.

gibberish [guíbœrish]. **I.** *s.* jerigonza, jerga. **II.** *va.* falto de sentido.

gibbet [ríbet]. **I.** *s.* horca. **II.** *va.* ahorcar.

gibbon [guíbon], *s.* (zool.) gibón.

gibbosity [guibósiti], *s.* giba, corcova.

gibbous [guíbʊs], *a.* convexo; giboso, jorobado.

gibbousness [-nes], *s.* convexidad; corvadura.

gibe [ráib]. **I.** *va.* escarnecer, ridiculizar, mofarse de. **II.** *vn.* burlarse. **III.** *s.* escarnio, mofa.

gibingly [ráibingli], *adv.* con burla.

giblet [ríblet], *s.* menudillo de ave.—*pl.* andrajos, guiñapos; menudillo.

giddily [guídili], *adv.* vertiginosamente; atolondradamente.

giddiness [guídines], *s.* vértigo, vahído, desvanecimiento; aturdimiento, atolondramiento, veleidad; devaneo, desvarío.

giddy [guídi], *a.* vertiginoso; voltario, voluble, inconstante; aturdido, atolondrado.—**g. girl,** muchacha casquivana.—**g.-brained, headed o pated,** ligero de cascos, frívolo.—**g.-head,** o **pate,** persona frívola, con los cascos a la jineta.

gift [guift]. **I.** donación; dádiva, regalo, obsequio; don, dote, prenda.—**g. of tongues,** don de las lenguas. **II.** *va.* dotar; agraciar.

gifted [guífted], *a.* talentoso; agraciado.

gig [guig]. *s.* birlocho, calesín, quitrín; máquina para tundir paño; (mar.) bote, lancha, falúa; parón; trompo, peonza, perinola; chacota; calaverada.

gigantean [raigantían], *a.*; **gigantic** [raigǽntic], *a.* gigantesco; giganteo.

giggle [guígœl]. **I.** *vn.* reírse tratando de suprimir u ocultar la risa; reírse sin motivo; reírse por nada. **II.** *s.* risa falsa, risita. **III.** *vn.* reírse.

giggler [guíglœr], *s.* persona de risa falsa o de risita.

gild [guild], *s.* = GUILD.

gild [guild], *va.* (*pret.* y *pp.* GILDED o GILT) dorar; iluminar; dar brillo o lustre.

gilder [guíldœr], *s.* dorador; charolista.

gilding [guílding], *s.* doradura; dorado; latón de dorar (con como 95% de cobre) (ll. t. **g. metal**).

gilia [rília], *s.* (bot.) gilia.

gill [ʏil], s. medida de líquidos (¼ litro); moza, pelandusca; (bot.) hiedra terrestre.

gill [guil], s. (ict.) agalla, branquia; (fam.) papada; barranco; rambla; estría de chapa ondulada; carretón de dos ruedas sin cama.

gillyflower, gilliflower [ʏiliflaúœr], s. (bot.) alelí.

gilt [guilt]. **I.** pret. y pp. de GILD. **II.** a. dorado, aureo.—**g. edges,** o **leaves,** cortes dorados. **III.** s. dorado; oro en hojuelas; oropel; falso brillo.

gilthead [guíltjed], s. (ict.) dorada; salema.

gimbals [ʏímbalš], s. pl. (mar.) balancines de la brújula.

gimcrack [ʏímcrac]. **I.** a. cursi, de baratillo. **II.** s. chuchería, cosa cursi.

gimlet [guímlet], s. barrena pequeña.

gimp [guimp], s. (tej.) bocadillo, alamar.—**g. nail,** tachuela para tapicería.

gin [ʏin], s. almarra, alijadora, despepitadora o (Amér.) desmotadora de algodón; cabria, malacate, molinete, husillo; bomba movida por un molino de viento; martinete; trampa, armadijo; ginebra (licor de enebro).—**g. fizz,** bebida de ginebra y gaseosa.—**g. mill,** o **shop,** (fam., E. U.) taberna.—**g. palace,** taberna lujosa. **II.** va. coger con trampa: despepitar (el algodón).

ginger [ʏínʏœr], s. (bot.) jengibre.—**g. beer,** o **pop,** cerveza de jengibre.

gingerbread [-bred], s. pan de jengibre.—**g. work,** adorno cursi.

gingerly [ʏínʏœrli]. **I.** a. cauteloso, escrupuloso. **II.** adv. cuidadosamente.

gingerness [ʏínʏœrnes], s. escrupulosidad.

gingernut [ʏínʏœrnút], s. = GINGERSNAP.

gingersnap [-snæp], s. galletita de jengibre.

gingham [guíngam], s. carranclán, guinga.

gingili [ʏínʏili], s. (bot.) sésamo.

gingival [ʏíu̯ʏival], a. gingival, perteneciente a las encías.

ginseng [ʏínseng], s. (bot.) ginseng, ginsen.

gip [ʏip], va. destripar los pescados.

gipsy [ʏípsi]. **I.** s. gitano; jerga, germanía; muchacha desparpajada.—**g. winch,** grúa de soporte lateral. **II.** a. gitanesco; pícaron.

gipsydom [-dom], **gipsyhood** [-jud], s. gitanismo, gitanería.

gipsyism [ʏípsiism], s. gitanismo.

giraffe [ʏiræf], s. (zool.) jirafa; (**C-,** astr.) constelación Cameloparalis.

girandole [ʏírandol], s. araña, candelabro; (piro.) girándula; (joy.) pendiente.

girasol [ʏírasol], s. especie de ópalo.

gird [ʏœrd]. **I.** va. (pret. y pp. GIRDED o GIRT) ceñir; cercar, rodear. **II.** vn. mofarse, burlarse. **III.** s. escarnio, mofa, burla.

girder [ʏœ́rdœr], s. (constr.) viga.—**g. rail,** riel de doble T para tranvías.

girdle [ʏœ́rdœl]. **I.** s. cinto, cinturón, ceñidor, cíngulo, pretina, faja, cincho; circunferencia, cerco, círculo, zona; zodíaco. **II.** va. ceñir, cercar, rodear, circundar.

girl [ʏœrl], s. muchacha, niña; (fam.) sirvienta, criada.—**g. scout,** niña exploradora, miembro de la asociación de las Niñas Exploradoras.

girlhood [ʏœ́rljud], s. cualidad o estado de muchacha; vida o edad de muchacha.

girlish [ʏœ́rliš], a. de carácter de muchacha; característico de las muchachas; como de muchacha.

girlishly [-li], adv. como una muchacha.

Girondist [ʏírondist], s. y a. girondino.

girt [ʏœrt], pret. de TO GIRD, pp. y a. (mar.) amarrado; (ento.) braceado.

girth [ʏœrz]. **I.** s. cincha; faja, cinto; periferia. **II.** va. cinchar, ceñir.

girtline [ʏœ́rtlain], s. (mar.) andarinel.

gist [ʏist], s. substancia, quid, busilis.

give [ʏiv], va. (pret. GAVE; pp. GIVEN) dar; otorgar; sacrificar; pagar; producir o causar; dedicar, consagrar.—**to g. a good account of one's self,** salir bien, hacerlo bien.—**to g. a lift to one,** ayudar a uno a levantarse o a levantar algo.—**to g. a piece of one's mind to,** decir las verdades del barquero, decir cuántas son cinco.—**to g.**

away, dar, regalar; deshacerse de; vender regalado (casi de balde); contar, divulgar (un secreto); descubrir, traicionar.—**to g. back,** restituir, devolver.—**to g. birth to,** dar a luz, parir; producir.—**to g. chase,** perseguir.—**to g. ear to,** prestar oídos a; escuchar.—**to g. fire,** mandar hacer fuego; disparar.—**to g. forth,** publicar, divulgar.—**to g. it to one,** (fam.) dar de palos a uno, echarle un sermón o (Amér.) una raspa; poner a uno como nuevo; regañar a uno.—**to g. mouth to,** proferir, expresar.—**to g. notice,** advertir, hacer saber, informar.—**to g. off,** arrojar, echar, despedir, emitir.—**to g. one the cold shoulder,** recibir a uno fríamente.—**to g. one's self up,** entregarse, rendirse; abandonarse, desesperarse.—**to g. out,** publicar, divulgar; proclamar; declarar, decir; repartir, distribuir.—**to g. over,** entregar; abandonar; desistir de; desahuciar.—**to g. place,** ceder su puesto; ir seguido (de); dejar el puesto (a).—**to g. rein,** dar licencia, dar salida.—**to g. rise to,** causar, ocasionar.—**to g. room,** hacer lugar; retirarse, apartarse.—**to g. the lie,** desmentir.—**to g. the rod,** azotar, castigar.—**to g. the sack** (fam.) dar calabazas.—**to g. the slip,** dar esquinazo; echar.—**to g. up,** renunciar a; entregar; abandonar; dar por perdido; desahuciar.—**to g. vent to,** dar salida a; desatarse en.—**to g. warning,** prevenir, advertir.—**to g. way,** ceder; cejar; retroceder; ceder su puesto; aflojarse; hundirse; bajar en, caer en (seguido de un número) (apl. a precios). **II.** vn. dar libremente, ser dadivoso; dar de sí, aflojarse; ablandarse; ceder; cejar, recular; desteñirse; aguarse; deteriorar.—**to g. back,** retirarse; cejar.—**to g. in,** ceder; acceder; asentir.—**to g. out,** faltar; consumirse, acabarse, agotarse; apagarse; perder las fuerzas; pararse (una máquina, un órgano).—**to g. over,** cesar, suspender; ceder.—**to g. up,** desistir; darse por vencido; perder la esperanza.

give, s. acción de ceder físicamente (como una cuerda); elasticidad.

give-and-take [-ænd téic]. **I.** s. concesiones mutuas, componenda; réplicas y contrarréplicas. **II.** a. de componenda, de concesiones mutuas; de réplicas y contrarréplicas compensadas, de dares y tomares.

give-away [-euéi], s. revelación indiscreta; dejar ver (algo que se trata de ocultar), o (fam., fig.) mostrar el juego; ganapierde (en el juego de damas).

given [ʏivn], a. y pp. de TO GIVE; dado; citado, especificado; (mat.) conocido.—**g. name,** nombre bautismal.—**g. that,** suponiendo que, sabiendo que.

giver [ʏívœr], s. donador, dador, donante.

gizzard [ʏuísard], s. molleja (de ave); primer estómago (de un insecto).

glabrous [glébrus], a. liso, calvo, llano; sin pelo ni pelusa.

glacé [glaséi], a. liso y lustroso; glaseado.

glacial [gléšhial], a. glacial.—**g. acetic acid,** ácido acético puro.

glaciate [gléšhiet]. **I.** va. (geol.) cubrir con hielo glacial; producir sobre una superficie un efecto pareido al hielo. **II.** vn. helarse.

glaciation [gléšhiéšhun], s. helamiento, congelación.

glacier [glésiœr] o gléišhiœr], s. helero, glaciar.

glacis [gléšis], s. (fort.) glacis o explanada.

glad [glæd], a. alegre, contento, gozoso; agradable; agradecido.—**to be g.,** alegrarse, tener gusto (I am glad to see you, me alegro de ver a Vd.; I shall be glad to go, tendré gusto en ir).

gladden [glédœn], va. alegrar, regocijar.

glade [gléid], s. claro, raso; ciénaga.

gladiator [glédiéitœr], s. gladiador.

gladiatorial [glédiatórial], **gladiatory** [-tori], a. gladiatorio.

gladiole [glédiol], **gladiolus** [glædiólus], s. (bot.) gladio.

gladiolus [gladáiolus], s. (bot.) espadaña, gladiolo; (anat.) esternón.

gladly [glédli], adv. alegremente; de buena gana, gustosamente.

gladness [glédnes], s. alegría, placer, gozo.

gladsome [gládsᴜm], *a.* alegre, contento.—**gladsomely** [-li], *adv.* alegremente.—**gladsomeness** [-nes], *s.* alegría, regocijo.

glair [gléær]. **I.** *s.* (enc.) clara de huevo; cualquier substancia viscosa. **II.** *va.* untar con clara de huevo.

glairy [gléæri], *a.* viscoso, pegajoso.

glaive [gléiv], *s.* alabarda.

glamo(u)r [glámœr]. **I.** *s.* encanto, hechizo; encantamiento, embeleso; brujería. **II.** *va.* y *vn.* hechizar, encantar.

glance [glans]. **I.** *s.* mirada, ojeada, vistazo; vislumbre; fulgor; desviación (por choque); (min.) mineral lustroso.—**g. coal,** antracita.—**at the first g.,** al primer aspecto, a primera vista. **II.** *va.* mirar de o al soslayo, o de reñlón. **III.** *vn.* dar un vistazo o una ojeada; tocar o herir oblicuamente; brillar, centellear.—**to g. at,** referirse a, aludir a.—**to g. off,** desviarse (al chocar).—**to g. over,** echar un vistazo a; hojear (un libro).

gland [glænd], *s.* (anat. y bot.) glándula; bellota; (mec.) cuello, collarín, gola; casquillo del prensaestopas.

glanderous [glǽndœrus], *a.* muermoso.

glanders [glǽndœrs], *s.* (vet.) muermo.

glandiferous [glændíferᴜs], *a.* glandífero.

glandiform [glǽndiform], *a.* abellotado.

glandular [glǽndiular], **glandulous** [glǽndiulus], *a.* glanduloso, glandular, adenoso.

glandule [glǽndiul], *s.* glandulilla.

glandulosity [-lósti], *s.* calidad de glanduloso.

glans [glæns], *s.* (*pl.* GLANDES) bellota; (anat.) bálano; clítoris.

glare [gléær]. **I.** *vn.* relumbrar, brillar; tener colores chillones; (con *at*) mirar fija y penetrentemente (fig.) echando fuego por los ojos. **II.** *s.* resplandor; mirada feroz y penetrante; superficie lisa y vidriosa. **III.** *a.* liso, lustroso y resbaladizo.

glaring [gléæring], *a.* deslumbrador; evidente, notorio; de mirada penetrante.—**glaringly** [-li], *adv.* notoriamente, evidentemente; fijamente, penetrantemente.

glass [glæs]. **I.** *s.* vidrio; vaso; copa; vidrio o cristal de ventana; espejo; lente, catalejo; ampolleta; anteojo; reloj de arena; contenido de un vaso o copa (*a glass of water*, un vaso de agua; *a glass of brandy*, una copa de brandy).—*pl.* **glasses,** anteojos, gafas; quevedos, lentes.—**g. blower,** soplador de vidrio, vidriero.—**g. blowing,** fabricación de objetos de vidrio.—**g. furnace,** carquesa. —**g. metal,** materiales fundidos de que se hace el vidrio. **II.** *a.* de vidrio.—**g. bead,** abalorio, cuenta de vidrio.—**g. case,** escaparate.—**g. window,** vidriera. **III.** *va.* glasear, satinar; cubrir con, encerrar en vidrio; reflejar.

glassful [glásful], *s.* vaso (contenido de un vaso).

glasshouse [-jáus], *s.* vidriería; fábrica de vidrio o cristal; invernadero; galería fotográfica.

glassiness [-ines], *s.* calidad de vidrioso.

glasslike [-laic], *s.* transparente como vidrio; vidrioso.

glassmaker [-méicœr], **glassman** [-mæn], *s.* vidriero.

glassware [-uéær], *s.* cristalería, vajilla de cristal.

glasswork [-ucrk], *s.* fabricación de vidrio; artículos de vidrio.—**glassworks** [-ucrks], *s.* fábrica de vidrio o cristales.

glasswort [-ucrt], *s.* (bot.) sosa, barrilla, almarjo, matojo, sapina.

glassy [-i], *a.* vítreo, cristalino, vidrioso.

Glauber's salts [gláubœrs, *o* glóbœrs, solts], *s. pl.* sal de Gláuber.

glaucoma [glocóma], *s.* (med.) glaucoma.

glaucous [glócus], *a.* glauco, verde claro; (bot.) cubierto de una pelusilla blanca azulosa.

glaze [gléís]. **I.** *va.* poner vidrios a una ventana; vidriar; barnizar; satinar, glasear; apomazar. —**glazed,** vidriado; satinado; glaseado. **II.** *s.* superficie lisa y lustrosa; barniz, lustre.

glazier [gléíyœr], *s.* vidriero.

glazing [gléísing], *s.* vidriado, mogate; barnizado; satinado; superficie lustrosa; barniz, lustre; vidriería, cristalería.

gleam [glím]. **I.** *s.* destello, fulgor, viso, centelleo. **II.** *vn.* centellear, fulgurar.

gleamy [glími], *a.* centelleante, fulgurante.

glean [glín]. **I.** *va.* espigar, respigar; recoger, juntar; rebuscar. **II.** *s.* moraga; rebusca, rebusco.—**gleaner** [-œr], *s.* espigadera; respigador, rebuscador, recogedor.—**gleaning** [-ing], *s.* moraga, arrebañadura, rebusco.

glebe [glíb], *s.* gleba, césped, terrón; (Ingl.) tierras beneficiales; (min.) mineral terroso.

glede [glíd], *s.* (orn.) molano.

glee [glí], *s.* alegría, gozo, júbilo; (mús.) canción alegre para voces solas.

gleeful [glíful], **gleesome** [-sᴜm], *a.* alegre, gozoso, contento.

gleek [glic], *s.* mirada seductora.

gleet [glít], *s.* (med.) gonorrea crónica, gota militar; blenorrea.

gleety [glíti], *a.* blenorrágico.

glen, hocino, hoyada, vallecico.

glenoid [glénoid], *a.* que tiene una pequeña cavidad; (anat.) glenoideo.

gliadin(e [gláiadin *o* glíadin], *s.* (quím.) gluten.

glib, *a* voluble, suelto de lengua.—**glibly** [glíbli], *adv.* volublemente.—**glibness** [-nes], *s.* volubilidad, facundia.

glide [gláid]. **I.** *vn.* resbalar, deslizarse, escurrirse; (aer.) planear. **II.** *s.* deslizamiento, escurrimiento; (aer.) planeo.

glider [-œr], *s.* el o lo que se desliza; (aer.) deslizador, aeroplano de gravedad (sin motor), planeador (éste es el nombre usado en España).

gliding [-ing]. **I.** *s.* deslizamiento; (aer.) planeo. **II.** *a.* deslizador, que se desliza; (aer.) de planear, de planeo.—**g. angle,** (aer.) ángulo de deslizamiento, ángulo de planeo.—**g. boat,** (nav.) hidrodeslizador, barco deslizador, que se desliza por la superficie del agua.—**g. machine,** (aer.) = GLIDER.

glimmer [glímœr]. **I.** *vn.* rielar, centellear, brillar con luz vacilante. **II.** *s.* luz trémula; vislumbre, visión momentánea.—**glimmering** [-ing]. **I.** *pa.* vatilante, luciente. **II.** *s.* vislumbre, viso.

glimpse [glimps]. **I.** *s.* ojeada, vistazo; vislumbre, resplandor fugaz; reflejo. **II.** *va.* ver con una ojeada. **III.** *vn.* ojear, dar un vistazo; lucir a intervalos.

glint, **I.** *va.* reflejar. **II.** *vn.* lucir, brillar, destellar; saltar de rechazo.

glioma [glaiómæ], *s.* (med.) glioma, especie de tumor de ciertas partes del sistema nervioso.

glisten [glísn], *vn.* brillar, resplandecer, rielar.

glister [glístœr]. **I.** *vn.* brillar, lucir. **II.** *n.* brillo, destello.

glitter [glítœr]. **I.** *vn.* resplandecer, centellear, rutilar, brillar. **II.** *s.* brillo, resplandor; oropel. —**glittering** [-ing], *a.* reluciente, resplandeciente, corruscante.—**glitteringly** [-li], *adv.* lustrosamente, con lustre o brillo.

gloam [glóum], *va.* y *vn.* obscurecer u obscurecerse, anochecer.—**gloaming** [-ing], *s.* crepúsculo vespertino, el anochecer, la oración.

gloat [glóut], *vn.* (con *on, over*) deleitarse, gozarse (en).

globate(d [glóbet(ed], *a.* esférico, globular.

globe [glóub], *s.* esfera, globo; pecera globular; globo de una lámpara.—**g. sight,** (arm.) mira esférica.—**g. valve,** válvula esférica.

globefish [glóubñsh], *s.* (ict.) orbe.

Globigerina [glóbiyeráinæ], *s.* (zool.) globigerina.

globin [glóubin], *s.* (quím.) globina.

globose [glóbos], *a.* globoso, redondo.

globosity [globósiti], *s.* esfericidad, redondez.

globular [glóbiular], *a.* globular, esférico.

globule [glóbiul], *s.* glóbulo, globulillo.

globulin [glóbiulin], *s.* (quím.) globulina.

globulose, globulous [glóbiulus], *a.* globuloso.

glomerate [glómœret]. **I.** *va.* aglomerar, ovillar, formar una bola. **II.** *a.* aglomerado, conglomerado.

glomeration [glómœréshᴜn], *s.* conglobación.

glomerule [-mœrul], *s.* (anat., bot.) glomérulo.

glonoin [glónoin], *s.* nitroglicerina o glonoína.

gloom [glum]. **I.** *s.* obscuridad, lobreguez, tenebrosidad, tinieblas; melancolía, tristeza. **II.** *vn.* encapotarse, obscurecerse; entristecerse. **III** *va.* encapotar, obscurecer.

gloomily [glúmili], *adv.* obscuramente; tétricamente, lúgubremente, tenebrosamente.

gloominess [-nes], *s.* obscuridad, tenebrosidad, lobreguez; melancolía, tristeza; adustez.

gloomy [glúmi], *a.* tenebroso, sombrío, lóbrego; nublado; triste, melancólico.

gloria [glóuriæ], *s.* tela de lana y seda usada para reemplazar la seda pura; (igl.) gloria; (b. a.) aureola.

glorification [glórifikéishun], *s.* glorificación, apoteosis; (fam.) celebración.

glorify [glórifai], *va.* glorificar.

gloriole [glóriol], *s.* aureola.

glorious [glóriŭs], *a.* glorioso; (fam.) excelente, magnífico.—**gloriously** [-li], *adv.* gloriosamente.—**gloriousness** [-nes], *s.* gloria, calidad de glorioso.

glory [glóri]. **I.** *s.* gloria.—**to be in one's g.**, estar uno en sus glorias. **II.** *vn.* gloriarse, jactarse; deleitarse.

gloss. I. *s.* lustre, brillo; pulimento; barniz; apariencia falaz, oropel; glosa, comentario; disculpa, paliativo. **II.** *va.* pulir, pulimentar, satinar, glasear; disculpar, paliar. **III.** *va.* y *vn.* glosar, comentar, postillar, escoliar.

glosa, *s.* (anat.) lengua.

glossarial [glosérial], *a.* referente a una glosa.

glossarist [glósarist], *s.* glosador.

glossary [glósari], *s.* glosario, nomenclador.

glossiness [glósines], *s.* pulimento, lustre.

glossitis [glosáitis], *s.* glositis, inflamación de la lengua.

glossographer [glosógrafœr], *s.* glosador, comentador.

glossography [-fi], *s.* arte de glosar o de hacer glosarios; (anat.) descripción de la lengua.

glossology [glosóloyi], *s.* clasificación de las lenguas; filología comparativa.

glossy [glósi], *a.* lustroso, glaseado, satinado; especioso, plausible.

glottis [glótis], *s.* (anat.) glotis.

glove [gluv]. **I.** *s.* guante.—**g. fight**, boxeo con guantes.—**g. hook, o buttoner,** abotonador de guantes.—**g. money** (Ingl.) gratificación a los criados; gajes.—**g. stretcher,** abridor de guantes.—**to be hand and g.,** ser inseparables, ser uña y carne.—**to handle without gloves,** tratar sin con templaciones. **II.** *va.* enguantar.

glover [glúvœr], *s.* guantero.

glow [glóu]. **I.** *vn.* dar luz o calor sin llama; brillar o lucir suavemente; fosforescer; ponerse incandescente; enardecerse, agitarse. **II.** *s.* brillo sin llama; incandescencia; calor intenso; vehemencia.

glower [-œr]. **I.** *vn.* mirar con fijeza. **II.** *s.* lo que brilla; mirada fija; (elec.) varilla o filamento de incandescencia.

glowing [-ing], *a.* resplandeciente, incandescente; ardiente.—**glowingly** [-li], *adv.* de un modo resplandeciente o vehemente.

glowlamp [-læmp], *s.* lámpara incandescente.

glowworm [-uœrm], *s.* luciérnaga, cocuyo.

gloxinia [gloxíniæ], *s.* (bot.) gloxinia.

gloze [glóus], *vn.* paliar, colorear, excusarse.

glozing [glóusing], *s.* paliativo; adulación.

glucase [glúkeis], *s.* (quím.) glucasa, fermento de la sangre y otros fluidos.

glucin [glúsin], **glucina** [glusáina], *s.* (quím.) glucina.

glucinum [glusáinŭm], *s.* (quím.) glucinio.

glucose [glúcos], *s.* glucosa.

glucosid(e [-cosid, -said], *s.* glucósido.

glucosuria [-cosiúriæ], *s.* (med.) glucosuria.

glue [glu]. **I.** *s.* cola, ajicola; gluten. **II.** *va.* encolar; pegar con cola.

gluey [glúi], **gluish** [glúish], *a.* pegajoso, glutinoso.—**glueyness** [-nes], *s.* glutinosidad.

glum [glŭm], *a.* malhumorado, displicente.

glumaceous [gluméishŭs], *a.* (bot.) glumáceo.

glume [glum], *s.* (bot.) gluma.

glumpy [glúmpi], *a.* (fam.) malhumorado, de mal humor.

glut [glŭt]. **I.** *va.* hartar, saciar; saturar; colmar; atascar, atarugar.—**to g. the market,** (com.) inundar el mercado. **II.** *vn.* devorar, engullir; **III.** *s.* hartura, hartazgo; plétora; cuña de madera; (alb.) ripio de ladrillo.

gluteal [glutíal], *a.* glúteo, nalgar.

gluten [glútœn], *s.* (quím.) gluten.

gluteus [glútiŭs], *s.* músculo glúteo.

glutinosity [glútinósiti], **glutinousness** [glútinŭsnes], *s.* glutinosidad, viscosidad.

glutinous [glútinŭs], *a.* glutinoso.

glutted [gluted], *a.* harto, ahito.

glutton [glútŭn], *s.* glotón.

gluttonous [glútŭnŭs], *a.* glotón; goloso.

gluttonously [-li], *adv.* vorazmente, glotonamente.

gluttony [glútŭni], *s.* glotonería, gula.

glyceric [glíseric], *a.* de glicerina.

glycerid(e [glicerid], *s.* (quím.) glicérido.

glycerin(e [-in], *s.* glicerina.

glycerite [-ait], *s.* (med.) medicamento que contiene glicerina.

glycerol [-oul], *s.* glicerina o glicerol.

glyceryl [-il], *s.* (quím.) glicerilo.

glycogen [gláicoyen], *s.* y *a.* glicógeno.

glycol [gláicoul], *s.* (quím.) glicol.

glycolate [gláicolet], *s.* (quím.) glicolato.

glycolic [glaicólic], *a.* (quím.) glicólico.

glycosuria [gláicosiúriæ], *s.* = GLUCOSORIA.

glyph [glif], *s.* (arq.) glifo; estría.

glyptic [glíptic], *a.* glíptica.

glyptodont [glíptodont], *s.* gliptodonte.

glyptography [gliptógrafi], *s.* gliptografía.

gnarl [narl]. **I.** *vn.* refunfuñar, gruñir. **II.** *s.* nudo (en el árbol o la madera).

gnarled [narld], **gnarly** [nárli], *a.* nudoso, retorcido.

gnash [næsh], *va.* rechinar o crujir los dientes.

gnashing [næshing], *s.* rechinamiento o crujido de los dientes.

gnat [næt], *s.* jején.

gnaw [no], *va.* roer; morder, mordicar; carcomer; corroer.—**gnawer** [nóœr], *s.* roedor.

gneiss [náis], *s.* (geol.) gneis.—**gneissic** [-ic], *a.* (geol.) gneísico.

gnetaceous [netéishŭs], *a.* gnetáceo.

gnome [nóum], *s.* máxima, aforismo; gnomo, trasgo, enano; (orn.) especie de colibrí.

gnomic(al [nómic(al], *a.* sentencioso, gnómico.

gnomon [nómon], *s.* gnomon; saeta.

gnomonic(al [nomónic(al], *a.* gnomónico.

gnomonics [nomónics], *s.* gnomónica.

Gnostic [nóstic], *s.* gnóstico.

Gnosticism [nóstisism], *s.* gnosticismo.

gnu [nu], *s.* (zool.) bucéfalo.

go [góu], *va.* (*pret.* WENT; *pp.* GONE) interesar; contribuir con, tener participación en; responder por; en el juego, ir, apostar, envidar.—**to g. bail,** salir fiador.—**to g. better,** apostar más.—**to g. halves,** ir a medias.—**to g. it,** (fam.) embestir, ir adelante; sufrir, soportar.—**to g. it alone,** obrar solo, sin ayuda.—**to g. one better,** aventajar, ir más allá.—**to g. one's way,** proseguir uno su camino.—**to g. shares,** entrar o ir a la parte.—**to g. smacks,** ir a medias.—**to g. the limit,** (fam.) ir hasta lo último o hasta el non plus ultra.—**to g. the rounds,** ir de ronda.—**to g. the way of all flesh, o of all the earth,** devolver el polvo al polvo, morir.

go, *vn.* ir, irse; andar; marchar; (mec.) funcionar, andar; acudir, recurrir; sentar, venir, ir, o caer bien; contribuir, concurrir, tender; morirse, estarse muriendo; venderse, tener venta; valer, ser válido, aceptarse.—**to g. about,** hacer, emprender; maniobrar; dar rodeos; atender a; (mar.) virar de bordo.—**to g. about one's business,** meterse uno en lo que le importa.—**to g. abroad,** ir a otro país; divulgarse.—**to g. after,** seguir a, ir tras de; ir por; caerle a, atacar.—**to g.**

against, oponerse a, chocar con, ir en contra de.—**to g. ahead**, adelantar, seguir, proseguir.—**to g. along**, seguir, proseguir; irse, marcharse (gen. *imp.*).—**to g. along with**, acompañar a.—**to g. around**, alcanzar para todos; TO GO ROUND.—**to g. aside**, retirarse, separarse; extraviarse, caer en la tentación.—**to g. astray**, extraviarse; cometer un desliz.—**to g. at**, atacar, acometer; emprender; empezar, atacar (un problema, etc.); ejecutar, hacer.—**to g. away**, desaparecer; irse, marcharse.—**to g. back**, retirarse, retroceder; regresar; ceder, desistir, volverse atrás.—**to g. back of**, mirar más allá de; poner en tela de juicio.—**to g. back on one**, (fam.) faltar a lo pactado, traicionar.—**to g. back to**, remontarse hasta, datar de.—**to g. backward**, retroceder.—**to g. behind**, ir atrás o atrás de; investigar las causas de o lo que está más allá de.—**to g. between**, interponerse entre; mediar entre.—**to g. by**, pasarse por alto; pasar por el lado de; pasar cerca, pasar (por aquí, por mi casa, etc.); ajustarse o atenerse a; regirse por.—**to g. down**, bajar; descender; ponerse (el sol); hundirse; caer, caerse; (com.) quebrar, fracasar; (fam.) poderse tragar o creer; pasar por cierto.—**to g. down on one's knees**, arrodillarse; implorar, rogar.—**to g. downstairs**, bajar (de un piso a otro).—**to g. far**, ir lejos; servir de mucho; alcanzar para mucho.—**to g. far towards**, ayudar o contribuir mucho a.—**to g. for**, favorecer; (fam.) embestir, atacar, acometer (real o figuradamente).—**to g. for a walk**, ir a pasear, dar un paseo.—**to g. forth**, salir; publicarse.—**to g. forward**, adelantar, adelantarse.—**to g. hard with one**, irle mal a uno; costarle a uno caro; ser para uno de graves consecuencias.—**to g. in**, entrar; encajar.—**to g. in and out**, entrar y salir; vivir; pasarlo.—**to g. in for**, (fam.) apoyar, favorecer, consagrarse a; buscar, solicitar.—**to g. into**, participar en; investigar, discutir o ventilar; caber en; entrar en.—**to g. into liquidation**, (com.) liquidarse, suspender negocios.—**to g. mad**, enloquecerse, perder el juicio.—**to g. near**, acercarse.—**to g. off**, abandonar; dispararse, hacer explosión; morirse; irse, largarse, despedirse; tener efecto, salir o quedar (bien o mal).—**to g. on**, continuar, proseguir; ir adelante; progresar; entrar (un guante, etc.).—**to g. on the road**, viajar como agente o en el ejercicio de una profesión (esp. la del teatro).—**to g. on the stage**, hacerse actor.—**to g. out**, salir; apagarse, extinguirse.—**to g. out of fashion**, pasar de moda.—**to g. out of the way**, apartarse; descarriarse; molestarse.—**to g. over**, examinar, estudiar, repasar; recorrer; aplazar; pasarse (al otro lado, partido, etc); pasar por encima de.—**to g. round**, andar al rededor de; dar vueltas.—**to g. through**, realizarse, llevarse a cabo; registrar, examinar detenidamente; pasar, sufrir; atravesar; penetrar; pasar por; derrochar, malbaratar.—**to g. to bed**, acostarse, ir a acostarse.—**to g. together**, andar o ir juntos; armonizar entre sí, avenirse.—**to g. to law**, recurrir a los tribunales.—**to g. to pieces**, desvencijarse, desbarajustarse (apl. esp. a la salud); confundirse, afligirse, echarse a morir.—**to g. to pot**, arruinarse.—**to g. to rack and ruin**, arruinarse.—**to g. to sleep**, dormirse.—**to g. to smash**, arruinarse, frustrarse, quebrar.—**to g. to the bottom**, irse a pique; profundizar.—**to g. to the country** = TO APPEAL TO THE COUNTRY.—**to g. to the wall**, quedarse atrás, darse por vencido; fracasar.—**to g. to the wreck**, arruinarse, perderse.—**to g. under**, quebrar, quedar arruinado, vencido o destruido; hundirse.—**to g. up**, subir; (fam.) quebrar, arruinarse.—**to g. upon an assumption**, proceder u obrar según una suposición.—**to g. upstairs**, subir (de un piso a otro).—**to g. up the spout**, (fam.) fracasar; evaporarse (fig.).—**to g. West**, (fam.) irse al otro mundo, morir.—**to g. with**, acompañar; seguir.—**to g. without**, pasarse de o sin.—**to g. without saying**, sobreentenderse.—**to g. wrong**, salir mal, fracasar; perderse, irse a la mala vida; ir por mal camino.

go, *s*. (fam.) moda, usanza; energía, empuje; giro, marcha, curso; predicamento; pacto, convenio; buen éxito; oportunidad, turno.—**it is all the go.**, es la gran moda, hace furor.—**is it a g.?** ¿está resuelto? ¿estamos convenidos?—**it is no g.**, es inútil, esto no marcha.—**on the g.**, en actividad, moviéndose.

goad [góud]. **I.** *s*. aguijón; focino para elefantes.—**g. spur**, acicate.—**g. stick**, garrocha, rejo. **II.** *va*. aguijonear, agarrochar; estimular, incitar.

go-ahead [gó-ajed]. *a*. (fam.) emprendedor, activo, enérgico.

goal [goul], *s*. meta, fin, objeto.

go-as-you-please [-æs-yu-plíś], *a*. y *adv*. (fam.) al paso que uno quiera; libre, sin restricción.

goat [góut], *s*. cabra; víctima que carga con la culpa ajena.—**g. buck**, cabrón, macho cabrío.—**g. milker**, (orn.) chotacabras.—**g.'s hair**, pelote.—**g.'s rue**, (bot.) gálega.—**g.'s horn**, (bot.) tragacanto, alquitira.

goatbeard [góutbíard], *s*. (bot.) barba cabruna.

goatee [goutí], *s*. pera, perilla.

goatherd [góutjœrd], *s*. cabrero.

goatish [góutiśh], *a*. cabrerizo; cabruno, chotuno; lascivo.

goatskin [-skin], *s*. piel de cabra.

goatsucker [-súccœr], *s*. = GOAT MILKER.

gob [gob], *s*. pedazo; (min.) escombro; (fam.) marinero de guerra.

gobbet [góbet], *s*. canto de piedra; bocado.

gobble [góbœl]. **I.** *va*. engullir, tragar. **II.** *vn*. hacer ruido en la garganta como los pavos. **III.** *s*. voz del pavo.

gobbler [góblœr], *s*. glotón, tragón, tragador; (fam.) pavo.

go-between [-bituín], *s*. mediador; alcahuete.

goblet [góblet], *s*. copa grande de mesa, vaso de pie (gen. para beber agua).

goblin [góblin], *s*. trasgo, duende.

goby [góubi], *s*. (ict.) gobio.

go-by [go-bai], *s*. desaire; esquinazo.

gocart [gócart], *s*. carretilla, andaderas.

god, God [god], *s*. dios, Dios.—**G.-fearing**, temeroso de Dios.—**G. forbid**, no lo quiera Dios.—**G.-forsaken**, dejado de la mano de Dios, desamparado.—**G.'s Day**, domingo; fiesta del Corpus.—**G.'s house**, iglesia, templo.—**G. willing**, Dios mediante, si Dios quiere.—**for G.'s sake**, por Dios, por el amor de Dios.

godchild [gódcháild], *s*. ahijado, ahijada.

goddaughter [góddótœr], *f*. ahijada.

goddess [gódes], *s*. diosa.

goddesslike [-laic], *a*. de diosa; como de diosa.

godfather [gódfáœœr], *s*. padrino.

Godhead [gódjed], *s*. Deidad, Divinidad.

godless [gódles], *a*. infiel, impío.—**godlessness**, [-nes], impiedad; ateísmo.

godlike [gódlaic], *a*. deiforme, de dios, como dios.

godlily [gódlili], *adv*. piadosamente.

godliness [gódlines], *s*. piedad, santidad.

godly [gódl], *a*. piadoso, religioso.

godmother [gódmúdœœr], *s*. madrina.

godown [godáun], *s*. almacén chino o indio.

godsend [gódsend], *s*. divina merced; (fam.) fortuna, buena suerte.

godship [gódśhip], *s*. divinidad.

godson [gódsún], *s*. ahijado.

Godspeed [gódspíd]. *s*. bienandanza.—**G.!** o **G. speed!** ¡buena suerte! ¡buen viaje!

Godward [góduard], *adv*. hacia Dios.

godwit [gódwit], *s*. (orn.) francolín.

goer [góœr], *s*. andador, paseante.

goffer [gófœr]. **I.** *va*. rizar, encrespar; estampar cuero. **II.** *s*. rizado.

goggle [gógœl]. **I.** *va*. y *vn*. torcer o abrir extremadamente los ojos. **II.** *s*. torcimiento de los ojos, mirada afectada.—*pl*. **goggles**, anteojos de camino; anteojeras.—**g.-eyed**, de ojos saltones.—**g.-eyes**, ojos saltones.

going [góing]. **I.** *a*. y *ger*. de TO GO; activo, que funciona.—**a g. concern**, una empresa que funciona o marcha.—**to be g.**, ir, irse (*I am going to London tomorrow*, voy a Londres mañana; *where are you going?*, ¿adónde va Vd.?; *are you going so soon?* ¿se va Vd. tan pronto?). **II.** *s*. paso, andar, andadura; marcha, ida, partida; estado del camino.—*pl*. **goings**, idas y venidas.—**goings on**, ocurrencias, sucesos.

goiter, goitre [góitœr], *s*. papera.—**goitered** [góitœrd], **goitrous** [-trus], *a*. que tiene papera.

gola [góla], *s.* (arq.) gola, cimacio.

gold [góuld], *s.* oro; color de oro.—**g.-bearing**, aurífero.—**g. brick**, añagaza, embuste.—**g. dust**, oro en polvo; (bot.) aliso.—**g. fever**, fiebre de oro.—**g.-filled**, revestido de oro.—**g. foil**, oro batido o en hojas.—**g. lace**, galón o encaje de oro; entorchado.—**g. leaf**, pan de oro.—**g. plate**, vajilla de oro.—**g.-plated**, dorado.—**g. size**, cera de dorar.—**g. standard**, (com., e. p.) patrón de oro.—**g. thread**, gusanillo de oro.

goldbeater [-bítœr], *s.* batihoja, batidor de oro.

golden [góldœn], *a.* áureo, de oro; brillante; excelente, precioso; feliz; rubio, amarillento.—**g. calf**, becerro de oro; riquezas, oro (fig.).—**g. fleece**, vellocino de oro.—**g. number**, (astr.) número áureo.—**g. rule**, regla áurea.—**g. thistle**, (bot.) cardillo.—**g. wedding**, bodas de oro.

goldfinch [-finch], *s.* (orn.) cardelina; pintacilgo.

goldfish [góldfish], *s.* (ict.) carpa pequeña de color rojo dorado.

goldsmith [góldsmiz], *s.* orífice, orfebre.

goldstone [góldstoun], *s.* venturina.

golf, *s.* golf, juego escocés.—**g. club**, palo para jugar al golf; grupo de personas que lo juegan.

Golgotha [gólgoza], *s.* Calvario.

gondola [góndolæ], *s.* góndola; (aer.) barquilla o (si es muy grande) cabina.—**g. car**, vagón largo de plataforma.

gondolier [gondolíœr], *s.* gondolero.

gone [gon], *pp.* de TO GO; ido; perdido, arruinado; pasado; apagado. Ú. a veces con *to be* en vez de *to have* para formar tiempos compuestos, vg., *he was gone*, él se había ido.—**g. on**, (fam.) locamente enamorado de.

gonfalon [gónfalon], *s.* gonfalón, pendón.

gonfalonier [gónfaloníœr], *s.* confalonier.

gong, *s.* batintín, gongo.

goniometer [gónió mitœr], *s.* goniómetro.

goniometric(al [goniométric(al], *a.* goniométrico.

goniometry [goniómitri], *s.* goniometría.

gonococco, *s.* gonococo.

gonophore [gónofœr], *s.* (bot.) gonóforo, prolongación del eje de la flor.

gonorrhœa [gónorría], *s.* gonorrea.

gonorrhœal [gónorríal], *a.* gonorreico.

good [gud]. **I.** *a.* bueno; apto, conveniente, ventajoso, útil; genuino, legítimo; de buena índole, dócil u obediente; hábil, capaz o competente; amplio, grande o considerable; digno.—*pl. V.* GOODS.—**g. afternoon**, buenas tardes.—**g. and collectable**, (com.) valedero y cobrable.—**g. day**, buenos días.—**g. enough**, suficientemente bueno; pasadero, suficiente.—**g. even, g. evening**, buenas noches (saludo).—**g. for nothing**, inútil, sin valor; haragán, pelafustán.—**G. Friday**, viernes santo.—**g.-humored**, jocoso, vivo, jovial.—**g.-humoredly**, jocosamente, alegremente.—**g.-looking**, guapo, buen mozo, bien parecido.—**g. morning, g. morrow**, buenos días (por la mañana).—**g. nature**, bondad, buen corazón.—**g.-natured**, bonachón, afable, paciente.—**g.-naturedly**, tolerantemente, afablemente.—**g. night**, buenas noches (despedida).—**g. offices**, buenos oficios.—**g. pay**, buena paga; buen pagador.—**G. Shepherd**, Buen Pastor (Jesucristo).—**g. speed**, buena suerte.—**g.-tempered**, de buen genio o carácter.—**g. time**, rato, día, etc., agradable o divertido; diversión, holgorio.—**g. will**, buena voluntad; benevolencia; (com.) popularidad, reputación, buen nombre, bienquerencia.—**a g. way**, un buen trecho, larga distancia.—**as g. as** (seguido de participio), casi (*this is as good as done*, esto está casi terminado, o puede darse por terminado).—**in g. part**, en buena parte.—(**to be**) **in g. repute**, (tener) buena reputación.—**in g. time**, a tiempo; a propósito con oportunidad. **II.** *s.* bien; provecho, ventaja.—**for g.**, permanentemente, para siempre.—**for g., for g. and all**, terminantemente, una vez por todas.—**much g. may it do you**, que le aproveche.—(**to be**) **to the g.**, (tener) ganado de sobra, en favor o el haber (de uno). **III.** *adv.* bien, rectamente. **IV.** *interj.* ¡bueno! ¡magnífico! ¡muy bien!

good-by, good-bye [-bái], *s.* e *interj.* adiós.

good-for [-fœr], *s.* (com.) pagaré.

goodish [gúdish], *a.* algo bueno, regular; amplio, holgado.

goodliness [gúdlines], *s.* belleza, hermosura, gracia, elegancia.

goodly [gúdli], *a.* hermoso, guapo, bien parecido; excelente; atractivo, agradable o vistoso; abultado; considerable; algo numeroso.—**a g. prospect**, hermosa perspectiva; buenas esperanzas.

goodman [gúdmæn], *s.* señor; amo de casa.

goodness [gúdnes]. **I.** *s.* bondad, benevolencia; favor, fineza. **II.** *interj.* ¡Ave María!

goods [gudš], *s. pl.* géneros, mercancías, efectos.—**g. shed**, almacén, cobertizo.—**g. train**, (Ingl.) tren de mercancías o de carga.—**g. truck, wagon, o van**, (f. c.) furgón.

goodsman [gúdsmæn], *s.* agarrochador, boyero.

goody [gúdi], *a.* y *s.* bonachón, pazguato, Juan Lanas, mojigato.—**g.-g.**, santurrón, beato.

goosander [gusǽndœr], *s.* (orn.) mergánsar, patín.

goose [gus], *s.* (*pl.* GEESE [guís]) ganso; plancha de sastre; bobo, necio; juego de la oca.—**g. barnacle**, percebe, escaramujo.—**g. flesh**, carne de gallina (aplicado a la piel humana).—**g. quill**, pluma de ave, pluma de ganso.—**g. skin = GOOSE FLESH.**—**g. step**, ejercicio en que uno descansa alternativamente sobre un pie y levanta el otro, como marcando el paso; (mil.) paso en que se mantienen las piernas tesas.

gooseberry [gúš- o gúsberi], *s.* (bot.) uva espina o crespa; variedad de grosella.

goosecap [gúscæp], *s.* bobo, tonto, pazguato.

goosefoot [-fút], *s.* (bot.) chual.

gooseherd [-jœrd], *s.* ansarero.

gooseneck [-néc], *s.* (mar.) gancho de botalones; arbotante, cuello de cisne; pescante de bote; (tecn.) barra, tubo, etc., curvos; conexión en S o de doble codo con articulación universal.

goosewings [-uíngs], *s.* (mar.) calzones.

goosy [gúsi], *a.* tonto, estúpido; atacado de carne de gallina (apl. a personas).

gopher [gófœr], *s.* (zool.) variedad de topo, de ardilla, de tortuga y de culebra.

gopher wood, *s.* (bot.) árbol de madera amarilla.

Gordian knot [górdiœn not], *s.* nudo, gordiano.

gore [gócr]. **I.** *s.* sangre, cuajarón; crúor; (cost.) cuchillo, nesga, sesga, fonas; pedazo de terreno triangular; (mar.) tabla triangular, cuchillo. **II.** *va.* herir con arma blanca o con los cuernos; acornear; poner nesga o cuchillo.

gorge [gory]. **I.** *s.* gorja, gola, garganta, gaznate; abra, desfiladero, barranco, cañada; cuello de un vestido; trago, bocado; apretujón. **II.** *va.* engullir, tragar, atiborrar; hartar, saciar. **III.** *vn.* hartarse, saciarse.

gorgeous [górɣus], *a.* vistoso, magnífico, suntuoso.—**gorgeously** [-li], *adv.* magníficamente, suntuosamente—**gorgeousness** [-nes], *s.* esplendor, magnificencia, suntuosidad.

gorget [góryet], *s.* (arm.) gola, gorguera, gorjal; (cost.) gorguera; (orn.) collar de ciertas aves; (mil.) golilla; (cir.) cuchilla para fístulas.

Gorgon [górgon], *s.* gorgona, esperpento.

Gorgonean [gorgóniæn], *a.* gorgóneo.

gorgonzola [górgonšóulæ], *s.* queso de Gorgonzola.

gorilla [goríla], *s.* (zool.) gorila.

gormand [górmand], **gourmand** [gúrmand], *s.* glotón, goloso.—**gormandize** [-aiš], *vn.* glotonear.—**gormandizer** [-aišœr], *s.* glotonazo, tragamallas.

gorse [gors], *s.* (bot.) argomón, aulaga.

gory [góri], *a.* ensangrentado; sangriento.

goshawk [góšjoc], *s.* (orn.) azor.

gosling [gósling], *s.* (orn.) ansarino, gansarón.—**g. green**, color verdoso amarillento.

gospel [góspel]. **I.** *s.* evangelio; cosa cierta e indudable.—**g. truth**, verdad palmaria. **II.** *va.* evangelizar.

gospeller [góspelœr], *s.* evangelista; evangelistero; misionero.

gossamer [gósamœr], *s.* hilo finísimo; telaraña;

(tej.) gloria, gasa sutilísima; tela delgada impermeable.

gossamer(y [gósamœr(i], *a.* sutil, delgado.

gossip [gósip]. **I.** *s.* chismografía, chismería, murmuración, hablilla; chismoso, murmurador; padrino, madrina. **II.** *vn.* charlar; murmurar, chismear.

got, *pret.* y *pp.* del verbo TO GET.

Goth [góz], *s.* godo.—**Gothic** [gózic]. **I.** *a.* gótico. **II.** *s.* lengua goda.—**Gothicism** [gózisiŝm], *s.* idioma godo; estilo gótico; barbarie.

gotten, *pp.* de TO GET.

gouge [gáuy]. **I.** *s.* (carp.) gubia, mediacaña; ranura, canal o estría. **II.** *va.* escoplear con una gubia; arrancar, sacar, vaciar; sacar ventaja, engañar.

goulash [guláŝh], *s.* guiso húngaro, compuesto de ternera, patatas y harina con fuertes condimentos.

gourd [gócerd *o* gurd], *s.* (bot.) calabaza, calabacera; güiro, calabacino.

gourmand, gourmandize = GORMAND, etc.

gourmet [gurmé], *s.* (fr.) gastrónomo.

gout [gáut], *s.* (med.) gota, artritis.—**g. of,** o **in, the feet,** podagra.

gout [gu], *s.* gusto; inclinación.

goutiness [gáutines], *s.* afección gotosa.

goutwort [gáutuœrt], *s.* (bot.) angélica.

gouty [gáuti], *a.* gotoso.

govern [gúvœrn], *va.* y *vn.* gobernar; guiar, regir, dirigir, mandar; manejar; domar, embridar, enfrenar; (gram.) regir.

governable [-abœl], *a.* dócil; manejable.

governance [-ans], *s.* gobierno, ejercicio del poder, autoridad.

governess [-es]. **I.** *s.* aya, institutriz. **II.** *va.* y *vn.* instruir o enseñar como institutriz.

government [-mœnt], *s.* gobierno; dominio, autoridad; dirección, manejo; conducta, porte; (gram.) régimen.—**for your g.,** (com.) para su gobierno.

governmental [-mœntal], *a.* gubernamental, gubernativo.

governor [-œr], *s.* governador; administrador; tutor, ayo; (mec.) regulador.

governorship [-ŝhip], *s.* dignidad de gobernador; período que dura la gobernación; territorio sujeto a un gobernador.

gown [gáun]. **I.** *s.* traje de mujer; túnica; toga, vestidura talar. **II.** *va.* y *vn.* poner o ponerse toga o vestido de mujer.

gowned [gáund], *a.* vestido.

gownman [gáunman], **gownsman** [gáunŝman], *s.* togado; paisano, civil.

grab [grœb]. **I.** *va.* asir, agarrar; arrebatar; posesionarse. **II.** *s.* (fam.) agarro, toma, asimiento; presa; arrebatiña; copo; (fam.) robo, sisa; (mec.) gancho, garfio.—**g. tool,** arrancasondas.

grabble [grœbœl], *vn.* ir a tientas; postrarse.

grace [gréis]. **I.** *s.* gracia, garbo, donaire; favor, merced, indulgencia; concesión o privilegio; gana, disposición, talante; (teol.) gracia; (Ingl.) título de honor que se daba al soberano y se da a los duques y arzobispos, y equivale a Alteza; jaculatoria que se dice antes o después de comer.—**days of g.,** (com.) días de gracia.—**to say g.,** dar gracias o bendecir la mesa.—*pl.* **good graces,** favor, amistad, bienquerencia.—**the Graces,** las tres Gracias. **II.** *va.* adornar; agraciar, favorecer.

graceful [gréisful], *a.* gracioso, agraciado, donairoso; fácil, natural; decoroso.—**gracefully** [-li], *adv.* graciosamente, donosamente, airosamente.—**gracefulness** [-nes], *s.* gracia, donosura, garbo, donaire.

graceless [gréisles], *a.* réprobo, malvado; dejado de la mano de Dios.—**gracelessly** [-li], *adv.* depravadamente.—**gracelessness** [-nes], *s.* depravación.

gracile [grésil], *a.* grácil.

gracious [gréiŝhus], *a.* benigno, bondadoso; afable, cortés; gracioso, grato, agradable.—**g. me!** o **good(ness g!** ¡válgame Dios!

graciously [-li], *adv.* benignamente, cortésmente, gratamente.—**graciousness** [-nes], *s.* gracia, afabilidad, bondad, benignidad.

grackle [grǽcœl], *s.* (orn.) especie de grajo.

gradate [gréidet], *va.* graduar, (pint.) degradar.

gradation [gradéŝhun], *s.* graduación; paso gradual; grado; serie; (mús.) gradación; escalonamiento; (pint.) degradación (de tamaño, de color o de luz).

gradatory [grǽdatori]. **I.** *a.* graduado o gradual; dispuesto para andar. **II.** *s.* (arq.) gradas.

grade [gréid]. **I.** *s.* grado, graduación; clase, calidad; animal de raza mixta; pendiente; rasante; superficie del firme, del terreno, etc.—**g. crossing,** (f. c.) paso a nivel.—**g. of repose,** pendiente máxima de equilibrio, más allá de la cual un vehículo rueda por la sola acción de la gravedad.—**at g.,** a nivel. **II.** *va.* clasificar u ordenar según tamaño, calidad, etc., graduar; (ing.) nivelar, explanar.—**to g. up,** cruzar castas de animales.

grader [gréidœr], *s.* (ing.) nivelador; grada; (agr.) separadora de granos.

gradient [gréidient]. **I.** *a.* ambulante, moviente; pendiente. **II.** *s.* (ing.) pendiente, inclinación; (meteor.) grado del aumento o diminución (de temperatura, presión, etc.); diagrama que lo representa.—**g. post,** (f. c.) poste indicador del declive.

gradienter [gréidiéntœr], *s.* (top.) nivel de círculo vertical para establecer pendientes; tornillo tangencial micrométrico del tránsito (teodolito norteamericano) empleado para determinar ángulos de inclinación por sus tangentes y para calcular distancias horizontales.

gradin(e [gréidin], *s.* grada, escalón; gradino de escultor.

grading [gréiding], *s.* (ing.) nivelación.

gradual [grédyual]. **I.** *a.* gradual; graduado. **II.** *s.* (igl.) gradual.—**gradually** [-i], *adv.* gradualmente.—**gradualness** [-nes], *s.* calidad de gradual.

graduate [grédyueit]. **I.** *va.* graduar (conferir un grado); graduar (dividir y señalar por grados); modificar, aumentar o disminuir gradualmente. **II.** *vn.* graduarse, recibirse; cambiar gradualmente. **III.** *a.* graduado, recibido (de doctor, etc.). **IV.** *s.* el que se ha recibido en alguna facultad; (quím.) graduador, probeta; vasija o frasco graduados.

graduation [-éiŝhun], *s.* graduación.

graduator [-éitœr], *s.* graduador.

graffito [grǽfito], *s.* inscripción tosca hallada en antiguos sepulcros y ruinas; (arq.) obra esgrafiada.

graft [grǽft]. **I.** *s.* injerto; parte donde el injerto se aplica al patrón; mezcla; (cir.) transferencia de tejidos de un animal a otro; el tejido así transferido; (fam.) dinero mal habido, esp. aprovechándose de puestos públicos; concusión; peculado; latrocinio; soborno político. **II.** *va.* injertar; ingerir; mezclar; (cir.) transferir tejidos de un animal a otro.—**to g. by approach,** injertar por aproximación. **III.** *vn.* injertar; transferir; (fam.) traficar con los puestos públicos, recibiendo sobornos; cometer concusión o peculado.

grafter [grǽftœr], *s.* injertador; (fam.) el que trafica con los puestos públicos; concusionario.

grafting [grǽfting], *s.* enjertación, ingeridura, injerto.—**g. knife,** abridor.—**g. twig,** estaca.

Graham bread [gréam bred], *s.* acemita.

grail [gréil], *s.* cáliz.—**the Holy G.,** el grial.

grain [gréin]. **I.** *s.* grano (en todas sus acepciones); grano, peso equivalente a 0.06 gramos; finura (de una muela o piedra de esmerilar); fibra, veta, o trepa de la madera, el mármol, etc.; granilla del paño; flor del cuero; genio, disposición, índole; (tint.) grana, cochinilla, color rojo.—**g. cleaner,** aventador.—**g. elevator,** elevador de granos; depósito de granos con elevador.—**g. fork,** bieldo, -a, horca.—**g. moth,** polilla de granos.—**grains of paradise,** granos del Paraíso, amomo.—**g. screen,** (fot.) pantalla reticular.—**g. weevil,** gorgojo de los granos.—**across the g.,** transversalmente a la fibra (de la madera).—**against the g.,** contra la dirección de la fibra, a contrapelo.—**in g.,** de color vivo; arraigado; innato.—**with a g. of salt,** recortándole o quitándole algo de los adornos de la exageración (*cum grano salis,* en latín). **II.** *va.* granular; granear; granelar; vetear, imitar la trepa de la madera, etc.

grained [gréined], a. granular; áspero; teñido en rama.

grainer [gréinœr], ·s. brocha o instrumento de granear; evaporadora de sal; solución de remojar.

grainy [gréini], a. graneado; granoso.

grama grass [gráma græs], s. (bot.) grama.

gram(me [græm], s. gramo.

gram [græm], s. garbanzo de la India.

gramercy [gramœrsi], intsrj. (ant.) ¡muchas mercedes! ¡gracias!

graminaceous [graminéshus], **gramineous** [gramíneus], a. gramíneo.

Gramineæ [graminii], s. pl. gramíneas.

graminivorous [gréminívorus], a. graminívoro.

grammar [græmar], s. gramática; elementos de una ciencia.—g. school, (Ingl.) escuela de humanidades; (E. U.) escuela pública de enseñanza elemental.

grammarian [græmérian], s. gramático.

grammatic(al [græmætic(al], a. gramatical.

grammatically [-i], s. gramaticalmente.

grammaticalness [-nes], s. corrección gramatical.

gramophone [græmofoun], s. gramófono.

grampus [græmpus], s. (ict.) orco, orca.

Gram's solution, Gram's stain [gram solúshun, stéin], s. (bact.) solución Gram.

granary [grænari], s. granero.

grand [grænd], a. grande, grandioso; magnífico, majestuoso; ilustre, augusto.—g. climacteric, año 63 de la vida.—g. juror, miembro de un grand jury.—g. jury, gran jurado de acusación.—g. larceny, robo.—g. master, gran maestre.—G. Mogul, gran mogol.—g. plano, piano de cola.—g. stand, andanada, tribuna o asientos principales para espectadores.

grandee [grandí], s. noble, grande.

grandam(e [grændæm], s. abuela; anciana.

grandaunt [-ant], s. tía (hermana del abuelo o de la abuela).

grandchild [-cháild], s. nieto.

granddaughter [-dótœr], s. nieta.

grandeur [grényur], s. grandeza, magnificencia, fausto.

grandfather [grændfáðœr], s. abuelo.

grandiloquence [grændílocuens], s. grandilocuencia.—grandiloquent [-ent], grandiloquous [-us], a. grandílocuo.

grandiose [grændios], a. grandioso; hinchado, bombástico.

grandly [grændli], adv. grandiosamente.

grandma [-mæ], s. (fam.) abuelita.

grandmother [-mópœr], s. abuela.

grandnephew [grændnéfiu], s. sobrino (nieto de un hermano o de una hermana).

grandness [-nes], s. grandiosidad.

grandniece [-nís], s. sobrina (nieta de un hermano o de una hermana).

grandpa [-pa], s. (fam.) abuelito.

grandparent [-pérent], s. abuelo (apl. a ambos sexos).

grandsire [-sáiar], s. abuelo, antepasado.

grandson [-sún], s. nieto.

granduncle [-úncœl], s. tío (hermano del abuelo o de la abuela).

grange [grenγ], s. granja, cortijo, a¹quería, hacienda; (E. U.) logia de la sociedad Patrons of Husbandry, para el fomento de la agricultura.

granger [grénγœr], s. (E. U.) miembro de una GRANGE; labriego, patán.

graniferous [granífœrus], a. granoso.

granite [grænit], s. (min.) granito.—g. ware, utensilios de hierro con esmalte de color de granito; obra de alfarería semejante al granito.

granitic(al [granític(al], a. granítico.

granivorous [granívorus], a. granívoro.

granny [gréni], s. (fam.) abuelita; comadre.

grant [grant], I. va. conceder; otorgar, dispensar; ceder, transferir, transmitir el título de una propiedad, etc.; asentir, convenir en, dar de barato.—to take for granted, presuponer, dar por supuesto. II. s. concesión, dádiva, donación;

permiso, privilegio, subvención, asenso, asentimiento; (for.) carta forera o de gracia; documento que confiere un privilegio o concesión.

grantable [grántabœl], a. que se puede otorgar o conceder; dable, permisible.

grantee [grantí], s. cesionario, concesionario, adjudicatario.

grantor [grántœr], s. cesionista, otorgante.

granular [gréniular], **granulary** [-leri], a. granoso, granular, granuloso.

granulate [gréniuleit]. I. va. granular; granear; granar (pólvora); (fund.) granallar. II. vn. granularse; (surg.) encarnar.—granulated [-ed], pp. y a. graneado, granulado; en grano; moteado. —g. steel, acero hecho con hierro granulado.

granulation [-éishun], s. granulación; granazón; superficie granulada; (med.) encarnación; formación de tubérculos.

granule [gréniul], s. gránulo, granito.

granulize [gréniulaiš], va. granular; convertir en píldoras.

granulous [gréniulus], a. granuloso.

grape [gréip], s. uva; vid.—g. hyacinth, (bot.) almizcleña.—g. stone, granuja, simiente de uva. —g. sugar, glucosa, dextrosa.

grapefruit [-frut], s. (bot.) toronja.

grapeless [-les], a. sin uva.

grapery [-eri], s. invernadero o criadero de uvas.

grapeshot [-shót], s. (art.) metralla.

grapevine [-váin], s. vid, parra.

graph [græf]. I. s. gráfica, representación gráfica. II. va. construir la gráfica de, representar gráficamente.

graphic(al [gréfic(al], a. gráfico.—g. accent, acento ortográfico.—g. statics, grafostática.

graphically [gréficali], adv. gráficamente.

graphite [gréfait], s. (min.) grafito; lápiz.

graphitic [gréfitic], a. grafítico.

grapholite [gréfolait], s. pizarra.

graphalloy [gréfalói], s. aleación de grafito impregnado de metal.

graphometer [grafómeter], s. grafómetro.

graphophone [gráfofon], s. grafófono.

grapline [gréplin], **grapnel** [grépnel], s. (mar.) anclote, rezón; arpeo, cloque, rastra, rebañadera, garabato.

grapple [grépœl]. I. va. agarrar, agarrafar, asir; amarrar. II. vn. agarrarse, engarrafarse; (mar.) atracarse, aferrarse, abordarse. III. s. lucha, riña, pelea; arpeo, garabato, gafa, cloque, rastra.

grappling [grépling], s. (mar.) rezón; aferramiento.—g. iron, cloque, arpeo.

graptolite [gréptolait], s. piedra con marcas naturales semejantes a dibujos; (pal.) graptolito, orden de hidrozoos (medusas) fósiles.

grapy [gréipi], a. lleno o hecho de uvas.

grasp [grasp]. I. va. empuñar, asir; apoderarse de, usurpar, tomar; ver, entender. II. vn. agarrarse fuertemente. III. s. asimiento, agarro; usurpación; puño, puñado; garras; comprensión.

grasper [gráspœr], s. agarrador.

grasping [grásping], a. codicioso.

grass [gras]. I. s. hierba, herbaje; pasto; césped.—g. cloth, batista de cantón.—g.-green, verde como la hierba.—g.-grown, cubierto de hierba.—g. mower, dallador.—g. widow, mujer separada de su marido.—to let the g. grow under one's feet, perder el tiempo, haraganear. II. va. cubrir de hierba; blanquear lino; apacentar.

grasshopper [grásjopœr], s. (ent.) saltamontes, saltón; palanca de cada tecla del pianoforte.

grassiness [grasines], s. abundancia de hierba.

grassless [grásles], a. sin hierba.

grassplat [grésplæt], **grassplot** [græsplót], s. prado, terreno cubierto de césped.

grassy [grási], a. herboroso; herbáceo.

grate [gréit]. I. s. reja; verja, enrejado; (m. v.) parrilla de hogar.—g. bar, barra de parrilla. II. va. rallar; raspar; frotar, hacer rechinar; enrejar; emparrillar. III. vn. rozar, ludir; raer; rechinar, chirriar; (gen. con on o upon) molestar, irritar.

grateful [gréitful], *a.* agradecido; grato, gustoso. —**gratefully** [-li], *adv.* agradecidamente; gratamente.—**gratefulness** [-nes], *s.* gratitud; agrado.

grater [gréitœr], *s.* rallo, rallador, raspador.

graticulate [grætíkiulet], *va.* cuadricular.

graticule [grǽtikiul], *s.* ocular cuadriculado.

gratification [grǽtifikéshun], *s.* satisfacción, complacencia; gratificación, recompensa.

gratify [grǽtifai], *va.* satisfacer, complacer, dar gusto; gratificar, recompensar.

grating [gréiting.] **I.** *va.* rechinante, chirriante, discordante, mal sonante; irritante, ofensivo, áspero. **II.** *s.* reja, verja, enrejado; emparrillado; escurridero; chirrido, rechinamiento; (ópt.) reticula de microscopio, etc.—*pl.* (mar.) ajedrez, enjaretado.

gratis [gréitis], *adv.* y *a.* gratis.

gratitude [grǽtitiud], *s.* gratitud.

gratuitous [gratúitus], *a.* gratuito; injustificado.

gratuitously [-li], *adv.* gratuitamente.

gratuity [gratúiti], *s.* gratificación; propina.

gratulate [grǽtyuleit], *va.* gratular.—**gratulation** [-éishun], *s.* gratulación.—**gratulatory** [-lætori], *a.* gratulatorio.

gravamen [gravéimen], *s.* gravamen; agravio.

grave [gréiv], (*pret.* GRAVED: *pp.* GRAVED O GRAVEN) grabar; esculpir, cincelar; (mar.) despalmar.

grave [gréiv]. **I.** *s.* sepultura, sepulcro, tumba; (gram.) acento grave. **II.** *a.* grave, serio; solemne; (mús.) grave, bajo, profundo; (gram.) grave.

graveclothes [-clóuds], *s.* mortaja.

gravedigger [-dígœr], *s.* sepulturero.

gravel [grǽvel]. **I.** *s.* cascajo, grava; (med.) litiasis, mal de piedra, cálculos.—**g. pit**, cascajar.— **g. walk**, paseo enarenado. **II.** *va.* arenar, enarenar; confundir, embarazar.

gravelly [grǽveli], *a.* cascajoso, guijoso.

gravely [gréivli], *adv.* seriamente, gravemente.

graven [gréivn], *pp. irr.* de TO GRAVE.

graveness [gréivnes], *s.* gravedad, seriedad.

graver [gréivœr], *s.* (b. a.) buril, chaple; punzón; gradino; cincel; grabador, cincelador.

graves [gréivs], *s. pl.* residuo o sedimento del sebo derretido.

gravestone [gréivstóun], *s.* lápida sepulcral.

graveyard [gréivyard], *s.* cementerio.

gravid [grǽvid], *a.* preñada.—**gravidity** [grævíditi], *s.* preñez.

gravimeter [gravímetœr], *s.* gravímetro.

gravimetric [grǽvimétric], *a.* gravimétrico, relativo a la determinación por medio del peso.

gravimetry [grævímetri], *s.* gravimetría, determinación de pesos o densidades.

gravitate [grǽviteit], *vn.* gravitar; tender.

gravitation [-éishun], *s.* gravitación.

gravitational [-ael], de gravitación, referente a la gravitación.

gravity [grǽviti], *s.* gravedad, pesantez; seriedad; majestad; importancia.

gravy [gréivi], *s.* salsa, jugo.

gray, [gréi]. **I.** *va.* y *vn.* poner(se) gris o cano; encanecer. **II.** *a.* gris; tordo, rucio; cano, encanecido.—**g.-bearded**, barbicano.—**g.-eyed**, ojizarco. —**g.-haired**, canoso, encanecido; envejecido.—**g. horse**, caballo tordo.—**g. matter**, (anat.) substancia gris. **III.** *s.* color gris; animal gris.

graybeard [-bíard], *s.* barbicano; hombre entrado en años.

grayhound, *s.* = GREYHOUND.

grayish [gréish], *a.* pardusco, gríseo, agrisado; entrecano; tordillo.

graylag [gréilæg], *s.* ganso gris silvestre.

grayling [gréiling], *s.* (ict.) tímalo.

graze [gréis]. **I.** *vn.* pacer, pastar; tascar; rozar, rasar. **II.** *va.* pastorear, apacentar; dar pienso o forraje; pasar rozando, raspar, rasar. **III.** *s.* roce, raspadura; pasto, apacentamiento.

grazier [gréiyœr], *s.* ganadero.

grease [grís]. **I.** *s.* grasa; (vet.) aguajas.—**g. box**, o **cup**, (máq.) caja de grasa. **II.** *va.* engrasar, untar; lubricar; sobornar con dinero.

greaser [grísœr], *s.* engrasador; lubricador; lubricante; (E. U. despec.) apodo que se da a los hispanoamericanos.

greasily [grísili], *adv.* crasamente.

greasiness [grísines], *s.* calidad de grasiento.

greasy [grísi], *a.* grasiento.

great [gréit], *a.* grande; magno; admirable, excelente; lleno, preñado. Indica la tercera, cuarta o quinta generación, vg.: *great-grandson*, biznieto: *great-granddaughter*, biznieta: *great-grandfather*, bisabuelo: *great-grandmother*, bisabuela; *great-grandchildren*, biznietos: *great-great-grandfather*, rebisabuelo o tatarabuelo: *great-great-grandmother*, rebisabuela o tatarabuela.—**G. Bear**, (astr.) Osa Mayor.—**g.-bellied**, barrigudo; preñada.—**g. cattle**, ganado mayor.—**g. circle**, (geom. y astr.) círculo máximo.—**G. Dane**, mastín danés. —**g. grandsire**, bisabuelo.—**g. gross**, doce gruesas.—**g. gun**, cañón de artillería.—**g.-hearted**, animado, de alma grande.—**G. Lakes**, los Grandes Lagos—Superior, Michigan, Huron, Erie y Ontario.—**g. mogul**, gran mogol.—**g. nettle**, ortiga mayor.—**g. primer**, texto (tipo de 18 puntos).—**g. pyramid**, pirámide de Cheops o Gran Pirámide.— **g. seal**, gran sello.—**G. War**, gran guerra (la de 1914).—**G. White Way**, Broadway, calle principal de Nueva York.—**a g. deal**, mucho, gran cantidad.—**a g. many**, muchos.—**a g. way off**, muy lejos.—**a g. while**, largo rato.—**the g.**, los grandes.

greatcoat [gréitcóut], *s.* levitón, casacón; gabán.

greaten [grétœn]. **I.** *va.* agrandar, engrandecer. **II.** *vn.* crecer, aumentarse.

greater [gréitœr], *a. comp.* de GREAT: mayor, más grande.—**G. Britain**, el imperio colonial de la Gran Bretaña.

greatest [gréitest], *a. sup.* de GREAT: más grande; máximo; sumo.—**g. common divisor**, máximo común divisor.

greatly [gréitli], *adv.* muy, mucho; grandemente, magnánimamente; en gran parte.

greatness [gréitnes], *s.* grandeza; grandiosidad; magnitud, extensión; fausto.

greaves [grivs], *s. pl.* (arm.) grebas, canilleras, espinilleras; (coc.) chicharrones.

grebe [grib], *s.* (orn.) colimbo.

Grecian [gríshan], *s.* y *a.* griego; helenista.

Grecianize [gríshanaiš], **Grecize** [grísaiš], *va.* y *vn.* grecizar, greguizar.

Grecism [grísišm], *s.* grecismo, helenismo.

Greco-Latin [gríco-lǽtin], *a.* grecolatino.—**G.-Roman**, grecorromano.

greed [gríd], **greediness** [grídines], *s.* voracidad, gula; codicia; anhelo.

greedily [grídili], *adv.* vorazmente; vehementemente.

greedy [grídi], *a.* voraz, guloso; anhelante; codicioso.

Greek [grík]. **I.** *s.* griego; helenista; (fam.) jerga, gringo. **II.** *a.* griego.—**G. calends**, calendas griegas.—**G. fire**, fuego friego.

green [grín]. **I.** *a.* verde (de color y de sazón); inexperto o novato; crudo; nuevo o fresco, reciente, acabado de hacer; pálido, descolorido; floreciente, lozano.—**g. cloth**, tapete verde, mesa de juego; (Ingl.) mayordomía de palacio.— **g.-colored**, verde, verdoso; pálido, enfermizo.— **g. corn**, maíz tierno; (Méx.) elote; (Ingl.) trigo nuevo.—**g.-eyed**, ojiverde.—**g.-eyed monster**, celotipia.—**g. gage**, ciruela verdal.—**g. goods**, (E. U.) billetes de banco falsificados.—**g. hand**, novicio, tirón.—**g. laver**, alga marina comestible. —**g. lead ore**, piromorfita, fosfato de plomo.— **g. sand** (no *greensand*), (fund.) arena de moldear, rica en sílice y mezclada con carbón pulverizado.— **g. stoke.** = LAVER.—**g. vitriol**, caparrosa, vitriolo verde.—**g. ware**, loza cruda. **II.** *s.* color verde; verdor, verdura; prado o pradera; césped. —*pl.* (coc.) verduras, hortalizas. **III.** *va.* pintar o teñir de verde. **IV.** *vn.* verdear.

greenback [grínbéc], *s.* (E. U.) papel moneda, billete del gobierno o de un banco nacional.— **G. party**, (E. U.) partido político que sostenía que la moneda debía limitarse a billetes emitidos por el gobierno.

greenfinch [-fínch], *s.* (orn.) verdecillo, verderón.

greengage [-gueiy], *s.* ciruela verdal.

greengrocer [-gróscœr], *s.* verdulero.

greenheart [-járt], *s.* (bot.) bebeerú, especie de laurel de Guayana.

greenhorn [grinjórn], *s.* (fam.) tirón, novicio, aprendiz; paleto, palurdo.

greenhouse [-jáus], *s.* invernáculo.

greening [-ing], *s.* acto de verdear; variedad de manzana verdosa.

greenish [-ish], *a.* verdoso, verdusco.

greenly [-li], *adv.* nuevamente, recientemente; sin madurez.

greenness [-nes], *s.* verdura, verdor; vigor, frescura; falta de experiencia; novedad.

greenroom [-rúm], *s.* (teat.) sala de espera de los actores.

greensand [-sǽnd], *s.* (geol.) arenisca verde.

greensick [-síc], *a.* clorótico.—**greensickness** [-nes], *s,* clorosis.

greenstall [-stól], *s.* puesto o tabla para vender frutas y verduras.

greenstone [-stóun], *s.* amoladera de instrumentos quirúrgicos; roca verde eruptiva (diorita, dolerita, etc.); jade, piedra nefrítica.

greensward [-suord], *s.* césped.

greenwood [-ud], *s.* selva frondosa.

greet [grít]. **I.** *va.* saludar, dar la bienvenida. **II.** *vn.* encontrarse y saludarse.

greeting [gríting], *s.* salutación, saludo; ¡salud!

gregarious [greguérius], *a.* gregario.—**gregariously** [-li], *adv.* gregariamente.—**gregariousness** [-nes], *s.* calidad de gregario.

Gregorian [gregórian], *a.* gregoriano.

greisen [gráisn], *s.* (geol.) gres.

gremial [grímiæl], *s.* (igl.) gremial.

grenade [grenéid], *s.* granada, bomba.

grenadier [grenadícœr], *s.* granadero.

grenadine [grenadín], *s.* (tej.) granadina.

grew [gru], *pret.* de TO GROW.

grey [grei], *a.* gris, *V.* GRAY.

greyhound [-jáund], *s.* galgo; lebrel; **vapor de** alta mar muy veloz.

grice [gráis], *s.* gorrino, lechón; osezno.

grid [grid], *s.* red; parrilla; reja, rejilla; (elec.) rejilla (de una pila); (rad.) parrilla, malla, ánodo auxiliar reticulado de la lámpara termiónica; (f. c.) GRIDIRON.—**g. accumulator**, (elect.) acumulador de rejilla.—**g. circuit, g. current**, etc., (rad.) circuito, corriente, etc., de la parrilla.—**g. leak** (rad.) resistencia de protección del circuito de la parrilla.—**g. potentiometer**, (rad.) potenciómetro regulador del voltaje de la parrilla.—**g. resistance**, (elec.) reóstato o resistencia de rejillas.

griddle [grídœl], *s.* (coc.) tortera; tapadera de fogón.

griddlecake [-kéic], *s.* tortita de harina que se asa en la tortera o sobre una plancha caliente.

gridiron [grídáicœrn], *s.* parrillas; red (de vigas, tubos, etc.); (mar.) andamiada, basada de esqueleto; (f. c.) red de rieles; (teat.) telar; (dep.) campo demarcado para el juego de football.

grief [gríf], *s.* pesar, aflicción, dolor.

griefless [grífles], *a.* exento de pena.

grievance [grívans], *s.* injusticia, perjuicio; motivo de queja.

grieve [grív]. **I.** *va.* afligir, lastimar; apesadumbrar. **II.** *vn.* apesadumbrarse, dolerse, penar.

grievingly [grívingli], *adv.* apesaradamente.

grievous [grívus], *a.* penoso, doloroso, lastimoso; oneroso; fiero, atroz, cruel.—**grievously** [-li], *adv* penosamente, lastimosamente, afligidamente.—**grievousness** [-nes], *s.* calidad de penoso, cruel, etc. *V.* GRIEVOUS.

griffin [grífin], **griffon** [grífon], *s.* grifo; buitre; guardián, vigilante.

grig, *s.* (ent.) grillo; (ict.) anguila pequeña.

grill [gril]. **I.** *va.* asar en parrillas; atormentar, molestar. **II.** *s.* parrilla; manjar asado en parrillas. *V.* GRILLROOM.

grillade [griléd], *s.* manjar asado en parrillas o carbonada.

grillage [gríley], *s.* emparrillado; enrejado.

grille [gril], *s.* verja, reja.

grillroom [grílrúm], *s.* restaurante de servicio rápido.

grim, *a.* torvo, ceñudo; feo, horrendo; inflexible; formidable.—**g.-faced**, o **g.-visaged**, malcarado.

grimace [griméis], *s.* mueca, gesto.

grimalkin [grimǽlkin o grimólkin], *s.* gatazo, gata vieja.

grime [gráim]. **I.** *s.* tizne, mugre, porquería. **II.** *va.* ensuciar, tiznar.

grimly [grímli]. **I.** *a.* espantoso, horrible; ceñudo. **II.** *adv.* horriblemente, ásperamente.

grimness [grímnes], *s.* grima, horror, espanto.

grimy [gráimi], *a.* tiznado, sucio, manchado.

grin. I. *vn.* hacer muecas mostrando los dientes; sonreír sarcásticamente. **II.** *s.* mueca; sonrisa burlona.

grind [gráind]. **I.** *va.* (*pret.* y *pp.* GROUND) moler, quebrantar, triturar; pulverizar; amolar, afilar; vaciar; frotar, rallar, estregar, refregar; pulir, bruñir; mascar; dar vueltas a un manubrio; gravar, acosar, molestar, agobiar, oprimir; (fam.) estudiar con ahinco; dar matraca. **II.** *vn.* hacer molienda; rozar, frotar, ludir; pulirse o deslustrarse con el roce.

grinder [gráindœr], *s.* molinero, molendero; moledor; muela, piedra de molino o de amolar; molino, molinillo; amolador; muela, diente molar.

grinding [gráinding]. **I.** *s.* pulverización, moledura, molienda; amoladura; bruñido, pulimento. **II.** *pa.* de GRIND; moliente.—**g. lathe**, torno de pulir.—**g. mill**, trapiche.—**g. plate**, disco para pulir vidrio.—**g. roll**, maza de trapiche.—**g. stand**, torno esmerilador.—**g. wheel**, muela; rueda de amolar o de esmerilar.

grindstone [gráindstóun], *s.* amoladera, muela; esmeriladora.

gringo [gríngo], *s.* (fam.) *gringo*, yanqui.

grip. I. *s.* apretón de mano; empuñamiento, agarro; modo de darse la mano; saco de mano; asidero, puño, mango; garras (fig.); (f. c.) mordaza de arrastre del cable de tracción; capacidad de agarrar y frenar, o de comprender; (med.) GRIPPE. **II.** *va.* agarrar, empuñar, asir, cerrar. **III.** *vn.* agarrarse con fuerza.

gripe [gráip]. **I.** *va.* agarrar, empuñar; pellizcar; (mec.) morder; dar cólico; afligir, acongojar. **II.** *vn.* agarrar fuertemente; padecer cólico; sacar dinero por exacción. **III.** *s.* agarro, asimiento; sujeción; (fig.) esclavitud; garra; (mec.) uña, grapa, abrazadera, freno de malacate; puño, mango, manija, agarradera; opresión; aprieto, apuro; (mar.) pie del tajamar.—*pl.* dolor, cólico, retortijón; (mar.) obenques o bozas de lancha; trincas.

grip(pe [grip], *s.* (med.) gripe.

gripman [grípmæn], *s.* (f. c.) encargado de la mordaza de arrastre.

gripper [grípœr], *s.* (impr.) uña; (elec.) soporte del carbón de una lámpara de arco.

grippy [grípi], *a.* semejante a o con caracteres de gripe; tenaz, testarudo; avaro.

gripsack [grípsæc], *s.* (fam.) saco de noche, maletica.

grisette [grisét], *s.* griseta (tela.); griseta, obrera o modistilla alegre.

grisly [grísli], *a.* espantoso, terrible.

grison [gráison], *s.* (zool.) grisón, pequeño mamífero carnívoro.

grist, *s.* molienda; provisión, abasto, suministro.

gristle [grísœl], *s.* cartílago, ternilla.

gristly [grísli], *a.* cartilaginoso.

gristmill [grístmil], *s.* molino harinero.

grit, *s.* arena, cascajo; (geol.) arenisca silícea; firmeza; entereza; valor, ánimo; moyuelo.—*pl.* sémola, farro.

grittiness [grítines], *s.* contextura arenosa; fortitud entereza.

gritty [gríti], *a.* arenoso, arenisco; valeroso, esforzado.

grizzle [grísœl], *s.* color gris; mezclilla.

grizzled [grísœld], *a.* tordillo.

---

grizzly [grísli]. **I.** a. gríseo, pardusco.—**g. bear,** oso pardo. **II.** s. (min.) criba grande.

groan [gróun]. **I.** vn. gemir; lanzar quejidos. **II.** s. gemido, quejido.

groat [gróut], s. (Ingl.) moneda (cuatro peniques); bicoca, ardite.—pl. sémola, avena mondada.

grocer [grósœr], s. especiero, abacero.—**g.'s shop,** abacería, especiería.

grocery [grósœri], **grocery store** [stóœr], s. (E. U.) abacería.—pl. **groceries,** especierías, comestibles, víveres; (Amér.) abarrotes.

groceteria [grósetíriæ], s. especiería donde los parroquianos toman ellos mismos lo que quieren, y pagan al salir.

grog, s. brebaje o bebida alcohólica, grog.

groggy [grógui], a. medio borracho, calamocano; (dep.) vacilante; turulato.

grogram [grógram], s. (tej.) cordellate.

grogshop [grógshop], **groggery** [grógueri], s. taberna.

groin. I. s. ingle, empiene; (arq.) arista de encuentro, esquina viva; espolón. **II.** va. (arq.) formar aristas.

groined [groind], a. de arista (apl. a arcos, etc.).

grommet [grómet], s. anillo para cordones de talegas, velas, zapatos, etc.

groom [grum]. **I.** s. mozo de mulas o de cuadra; establero; palafrenero; lacayo; novio.—**g. in waiting,** camarero de semana.—**g. of the bed chamber,** ayuda de cámara del rey.—**g. of the chamber,** caballerizo de cámara. **II.** va. cuidar, almohazar los caballos; (fam.) peinar y vestir.

groomsman [grúmsmæn], s. padrino de boda.

groove [gruv]. **I.** s. muesca, encaje, rebajo, encastre, gárgol, acanaladura, ranura, estría; surco; (arm.) rayadura; rutina.—**g. and tongue,** s. (carp.) ranura y lengüeta, unión machihembrada; va. machihembrar.—**g. grafting,** injerto de canutillo. **II.** va. acanalar; (ton.) ruñar.

grooved [grúvd], a. acanalado.

grope [gróup], va. y vn. tentar, andar a tientas; buscar tentando.

gros, grosgrain [gró(gréin], s. (tej.) gro.

grosbeak [grósbik], s. (orn.) cardenal.

gross [grós]. **I.** a. craso; grueso; espeso, denso; indecoroso, obsceno; tosco, grosero, descortés; lerdo, estúpido; (com.) bruto.—**g. amount,** importe total.—**g. ton**=LONG TON.—**g. weight,** peso bruto. **II.** s. (pl. GROSS) gruesa (doce docenas); grueso, la mayor parte; la totalidad, el conjunto.—**by the g.,** por mayor; por gruesas.—**in g., in the g.,** en grueso, por junto, en conjunto.

grossly [grósli], adv. en bruto; crasamente, toscamente, groseramente.

grossness [grósnes], s. grosería, incivilidad, ordinariez; densidad; grosura.

grossularite [grósiularait], s. (min.) grosularia.

grot, s. (poét.) gruta.

grotesque [grotésc]. **I.** a. grotesco; (b. a.) grutesco. **II.** s. (b. a.) grutesco.

grotesquely [-li], adv. grotescamente.

grotesqueness [-nes], s. calidad de grotesco.

grotto [gróto], s. gruta, antro, covacha.

grouch [gráuch]. **I.** s. (fam.) gruñón, descontento.—**to have a g.,** estar de mal humor. **II.** vn. gruñir, refunfuñar, estar de mal humor.—**groucher** [-œr], s. (fam.) gruñón, persona de mal humor.—**grouchy** [-i], a. (fam.) mal humorado.

ground [gráund]. **I.** s. tierra, terreno, suelo; territorio; base, fundamento; razón, motivo, causa; (pint.) fondo o campo; baño, capa; (elec.) tierra; (mil.) campo de batalla; (pl.) poso, sedimento, heces; jardín, parque, terrenos; cancha (de juego).—**on, o upon, the g.,** en tierra, en el suelo.—**to be on one's own g.,** estar uno en su elemento—**to break g.,** desmontar; roturar; empezar un trabajo.—**to come, o fall, to the g.,** caer al suelo; fracasar.—**to gain g.,** ganar terreno; hacer progresos.—**to give, o to lose, g.,** perder terreno, retroceder, atrasar.—**to stand, o to hold, one's g.,** mantenerse firme.—**to take the g.,** encallar. **II.** a. situado en el suelo o al nivel del suelo; fundamental.—**g. floor,** piso bajo.—**g. hog,** marmota.—**g.-hog day,** (E. U.) día de la mar-

mota (2 de feb.) en que, según la tradición, este animal descubre si el invierno será corto o largo.—**g. ivy,** (bot.) hiedra terrestre.—**g. pine,** (bot.) pinillo.—**g. plate,** (elec.) placa de (conexión con) tierra; (f. c.) plancha de asiento; (arq.) carrera inferior.—**g. plot,** solar, lote; (arq.) plano.—**g. rent,** censo.—**g. speed,** (aer.) velocidad horizontal de un avión con respecto a la tierra.—**g. tackle,** (mar.) amarrazones.—**g. water,** agua subterránea; agua de pozo.—**g. wire,** (elec.) alambre de tierra; (aer.) cable del palo, que se une al de toma de tierra. **III.** va. fundar, apoyar, establecer; enseñar los elementos de alguna ciencia; poner en tierra; (elec.) conectar con tierra. **IV.** vn. (mar.) encallar, embarrancar, varar.

ground, pp. de TO GRIND.—**g. glass,** vidrio deslustrado.

groundage [-deY], s. (mar.) derecho de puerto o de anclaje.

grounding [-ing], s. (mar.) encalladura.

groundless [-les], a. infundado.—**groundlessly** [-li], adv. infundadamente, sin razón.—**groundlessness** [-nes], s. falta de razón o fundamento.

groundling [-ling], s. animal terrestre; (ict.) loche, loja; villano.

groundnut [-nút], s. (bot.) cacahuete, maní.

groundsel [-sel], s. (bot.) zuzón, hierba cana.

groundsill [-sil], s. (arq.) carrera inferior; solera, umbral.

groundwork [-uœrk], s. plan, plano, pie, base, fundamento, cimiento; principio, razón fundamental.

group [grup]. **I.** s. grupo. **II.** va. agrupar.

grouse [gráus], s. (orn.) guaco; chachalaca.

grout [gráut]. **I.** s. (alb.) lechada; enlucido; sémola, farro.—pl. heces, sedimento. **II.** va. rellenar con lechada.

grouty [gráuti], a. turbio, fangoso, sucio; regañón, arisco, intratable.

grove [gróuv], s. arboleda, alameda, enramada, soto, bosquecillo, boscaje.

grovel [gróvel], vn. serpear, arrastrarse; envilecerse, rebajarse.—**grovel(l)er** [-œr], s. hombre servil y rastrero.—**grovel(l)ing** [-ing], a. servil, rastrero.—**grovelingly** [-ingli], adv. servilmente, rastreramente.

grow [gróu]. **I.** va. (pret. GREW; pp. GROWN) cultivar; criar; producir. **II.** vn. crecer; darse (frutas, plantas, etc.); (seguido de adjetivo o adv.) volverse, ponerse (vg.: to grow old, ponerse viejo, envejecer; to grow angry, ponerse colérico, encolerizarse; to grow late, hacerse tarde; to grow better, ponerse mejor, mejorar; to grow less, disminuir; to grow loose, aflojarse); proceder, provenir, resultar; (con ro) fijarse, arraigarse (en).—**to g. on, o upon,** desarrollarse en, ir dominando a; ganar o aventajar a; hacerse cada vez más querido, admirable, etc., a.—**to g. out of,** resultar o provenir de, ser causado por, originarse en; brotar de; salir o pasar de con la edad (he will grow out of this whim, este capricho se pasará con la edad, o cuando crezca).—**to g. sad,** entristecerse.—**to g. up,** crecer, desarrollarse, salir de la niñez; desarrollarse y establecerse (una costumbre, etc.)

grower [gróuœr], s. cultivador, agricultor.

growing [gróuing], **I.** s. cultivo; cría; crecimiento, desarrollo. **II.** a. creciente; que crece, que aumenta.—**g. pains,** dolores debidos a desarrollo prematuro.

growl [grául]. **I.** vn. gruñir; rezongar, refunfuñar. **II.** va. decir gruñendo. **III.** s. gruñido; refunfuño.

growler [gráulœr], s. perro gruñidor; regañón, refunfuñador; (E. U., fam.) jarro para cerveza.

grown [gróun], a. y pp. crecido, espigado, desarrollado; cubierto o lleno de hierbas, maleza, etc.; prevalente, dominante, adulto.—**g. up,** crecido, adulto.

growth [gróuz], s. crecimiento, desarrollo; aumento; producto, producción; acrecencia.

grub [grub]. **I.** va. y vn. rozar; desyerbar, desmalezar; quitar insectos nocivos; (fam.) alimentar(se), manducar; cavar; emplearse en oficios bajos. **II.** s. gorgojo; larva; (vulg.) ali-

mento, manducatoria; persona desaliñada; (E. U.)
raíz arrancada.—**g. ax**, legón,¸picaza.—**grubbing
hoe**, escarda.

grubber [grúbœr], *s.* desyerbador; arrancador de
raíces.

grubby [grúbi], *a.* gusarapiento.

grudge [grʊy]. **I.** *va.* envidiar, codiciar; escatimar, dar de mala gana. **II.** *s.* rencor, inquina,
tema, tirria; renuencia, mal grado.

grudging [grʊ́ying], *s.* envidia, mala voluntad;
refunfuño; repugnancia, aversión.—**grudgingly**
[-li], *adv.* de mala gana.

gruel [grúel]. **I.** *s.* atole, avenate. **II.** *va.* incapacitar, agotar; estropear, desbaratar.

gruesome, [grúsum], *a.* horrible, horripilante.

gruff [grʊf], *a.* ceñudo, áspero.—**gruffly** [grúfli],
adv. ásperamente.—**gruffness** [-nes], *s.* aspereza,
ceño, mal humor.

grugru [gru grʊ], *s.* grugrú, especie de palmera
americana.

grum [grum], *a.* áspero, severo; gutural.

grumble [grúmbœl]. **I.** *vn.* refunfuñar, gruñir,
rezongar, quejarse. **II.** *s.* regaño, quejumbre,
refunfuñadura.

grumbler [grúmblœr], *s.* refunfuñador, gruñidor,
rezongador, malcontento.

grumbling [grúmbling], *s.* queja, descontento,
refunfuñadura.—**grumblingly** [-li], *adv.* refun-
fuñando.

grume [grum], *s.* grumo, cuajarón.

grumous [grúmus], *a.* grumoso; (bot.) amacollado.

grumpy [grúmpi], *a.* gruñón, quejoso, áspero.

grunt [grunt], *vn.* gruñir; arruar; refunfuñar.

grunt(ing [grúnt(ing], *s.* gruñido; (ict.) nombre
de un pez americano.

grunter [grúntœr], *s.* gruñidor; cerdo.

gruntingly [grúntingli], *adv.* regañando, refun-
fuñando.

gruntling [grúntling], *s.* lechón, cochinillo.

guacharo [guácharo], *s.* (ornit.) guácharo.

guaco, *s.* (bot.) guaco.

guaiac(um [guáiac(um], *s.* (bot.) guayaco o
guayacán; resina de este árbol.

guaiacol [guáiæcol], *s.* guayacol.

guanaco [guanáco], *s.* (zool.) guanaco.

guanin(e [guánin], guanina.

guano [guáno]. **I.** *s.* guano. **II.** *va.* abonar con
guano.

guarantee [gærantí]. **I.** *va.* garantir, garantizar;
salir fiador de; dar fianza o caución. **II.** *s.*
(for.) persona de quien otra sale fiadora; úsase
también, aunque incorrectamente, unas veces en
el sentido de GUARANTY y otras en el sentido de
'GUARANTOR.

guarantor [gærantor], *s.* garante, fiador.

guaranty [gæranti]. **I.** *s.* (for.) garantía, caución, fianza. **II.** *va.* garantizar.

guard [gard]. **I.** *va.* y *vn.* guardar, custodiar;
vigilar; atalayar; estar prevenido; guardarse.
—**to g. against**, guardarse de. **II.** *s.* guarda;
guardia; guardián, custodio; resguardo, protección,
custodia, defensa; vigilancia; atalaya, centinela,
vigilante; precaución, cautela; estado de defensa;
guarnición de un vestido o de una espada; (f. c.)
conductor de tren.—**g. mounting**, relevo de
guardia o de centinela.—**on g.**, alerta; (esgr.) en
guardia.—**to be off one's g.**, estar desprevenido.
—**to be on one's g.**, estar alerta. **III.** *a.* de guardia, de protección.—**g. rail**, (f. c.) contracarril;
(mar.) barandilla.—**g. ship**, navío de guardia, de
ronda o de estación.

guardedly [gárdedli], *adv.* cautelosamente.

guardedness [-nes], *s.* cautela, precaución.

guardhouse [gárdjaus], *s.* cuartel de la guardia;
prisión militar.

guardian [gárdian]. **I.** *s.* guardián, guarda, custodio; (for.) tutor o curador. **II.** *a.* que guarda,
tutelar.—**g. angel**, ángel de la guarda, ángel custodio.

guardianship [-ship], *s.* tutela, patronato; (for.)
tutoría, curaduría; protección, amparo, guarda,
custodia.

guardroom, [gárdrrum], *s.* cuarto de guardia;
calabozo.

guardsman [gárdsmæn], *s.* soldado de guardia;
centinela.

guava [guáva], *s.* (bot.) guayabo; guayaba.

guayule [guayúle], *s.* (bot.) guayule.

gubernatorial [guiúbœrnatórial], *a.* gubernativo;
del gobernador.

gudgeon [gúdyun], *s.* (ict.) gobio; bobo, mentecato; chiripa, ganga; (mec.) muñón, cuello
de eje; (mar.) hembra (del timón).—**g. socket,**
cojinete.

Guelf, Guelph [güelf], *s.* güelfo.

guerdon [gœrdun], *s.* galardón, premio.

guerrilla [guerríla]. **I.** *s.* (mil.) guerrillero. **II.** *a.*
de guerrillas, de guerrilleros.

guess [gues]. **I.** *va.* y *vn.* conjeturar, suponer, barruntar; adivinar, acertar; (fam.) pensar, creer.
II. *s.* conjetura, suposición, adivinación.

guesser [guéšœr], *s.* conjeturador; adivinador.

guesswork [guésuœrk], *s.* conjetura, ojo de buen
cubero.

guest [guest], *s.* huésped, convidado; forastero;
visita; pensionista o inquilino; animal parásito
o intruso.—**g. chamber, g. room**, cuarto de reserva, cuarto para convidados.

guestrope [guéstróup], *s.* (mar.) guía de falsa
amarra.

guffaw [gufó], *s.* carcajada, risotada.

guidance [gáidans], *s.* guía, gobierno, dirección,
conducta.

guide [gáid]. **I.** *va.* guiar; arreglar, gobernar.
II. *s.* guía, mentor; corredera; (impr.) mordante.—**g. lines**, pauta, falsilla.—**g. rope**, cuerda
lateral de guía; (aer.) cuerda de arrastre colgada
de la barquilla para mantener un dirigible a una
misma altura.

guideboard [gáidbo.d], *s.* = GUIDEPOST.

guidebook [-búc], *s.* guía del viajero.

guideless [-les], *a.* sin guía, sin gobierno.

guidon [gáidon], *s.* (mil.) guión; portaguión.

guidepost [gáidpóst], *s.* hito, poste indicador.

guild [guild], *s.* gremio, cuerpo, comunidad, hermandad, corporación.

guilder [guíldœr], *s.* florín holandés.

guildhall [guíldjol], *s.* casa consistorial, casa de
ayuntamiento.

guile [gáil], *s.* dolo o engaño; estratagema.—
guileful [gáilful], *a.* aleve, engañoso.—**guilefully**
[-i], *adv.* insidiosamente, engañosamente.—**guileless**
[-les], *a.* sencillo, cándido.—**guilelessness** [-lesnes],
s. franqueza, sinceridad.

guillotine [guílotin]. **I.** *s.* guillotina. **II.** *va.*
guillotinar.

guilt [guilt], *s.* delito, culpa, delincuencia; pecado.

guiltily [guíltili], *adv.* criminalmente, culpablemente.

guiltiness [guíltines], *s.* maldad; culpabilidad.

guiltless [guíltles], *a.* inocente, libre de culpa;
puro, sin tacha; virgen; ignorante, nesciente.
—**guiltlessly** [-li], *adv.* inocentemente.—**guiltlessness** [-nes], *s.* inocencia, inculpabilidad.

guilty [guílti], *a.* reo, delincuente, convicto; culpable.—**g. of death**, reo de muerte.

guimpe [guimp], *s.* (cost.) canesú.

guinea [guíni], *s.* guinea (unidad monetaria
inglesa, 21 chelines).—**g. fowl, g. hen**, gallina de
Guinea, pintada.—**g. pepper**, (bot.) pimiento de
Guinea.—**g. pig**, conejillo de Indias, cobayo, curí.
g. worm, filaria.

guise [gáis], *s.* modo, manera; apariencia; máscara, capa, pretexto.—**under the g. of**, socolor,
bajo capa de.—**in this g.**, de este modo.

guiser [gáisœr], *s.* disfrazado.

guitar [guitár], *s.* guitarra.

gula [guiúla], *s.* parte superior de la garganta.—
gular (-r), *a.* relativo o perteneciente a la garganta.

gulch [gulch], *s.* quebrada, cañada.

gulden [gúlden], *s.* gulden (moneda); florín
(austrico, alemán, etc.).

gules [guiuls], *s.* (her.) gules.

gulf [gʌlf], *s.* golfo; seno; sima, abismo, vorágine·
—**G. stream,** corriente del Golfo de Méjico.—**the
G.,** (E. U.) el golfo de México.
gulfweed [gʌ́lfuid], sargazo, alga marina.
gull [gʌl]. **I.** *va.* engañar, timar, estafar. **II.** *s.*
(orn.) gaviota; bobo, bodoque, primo; engaño,
petardo.—**g.-catcher,** engañador, petardista.
gullery [gʌ́lœri], *s.* engaño, petardo.
gullet [gʌ́let], *s.* fauces, gaznate, gola; (anat.)
esófago; zanja, trinchera profunda.
gullibility [gʌ́libíliti], *s.* credulidad.
gullible [gʌ́libœl], *a.* bobo, crédulo.
gully [gʌ́li]. **I.** *va.* formar canal. **II.** *s.* cárcava;
barranca, hondonada; zanja honda.
gullyhole [gʌ́lijóul], *s.* sumidero, albañal.
gulp [gʌlp]. **I.** *va.* engullir, tragar.—**to g. up,**
vomitar, vaciar. **II.** *s.* trago.
gum [gʌm]. **I.** *s.* goma; encía.—**g.-arabic,**
guacia, goma arábiga.—**g. dragon,** tragacanto.—
g. elastic, goma elástica, caucho.—**g. lac,** goma
laca.—**g. resin,** gomorresina.—**g. tree,** árbol que
da goma.—**g. water,** aguagoma. **II.** *va.* engomar;
pegar con goma.
gumbo [gʌ́mbo], *s.* (bot.) quimbombó; dialecto
criollo de Luisiana.
gumboil [gʌ́mboil], *s.* flemón, párulis.
gumdrop [gʌ́mdrop], *s.* pastilla de goma.
gummiferous [gʌmífœrʊs], *a.* gomífero.
gumminess [gʌ́mines], *s.* gomosidad.
gummy [gʌ́mi], **gummous** [gʌ́mʊs], *a.* gomoso;
engomado.
gump [gʌmp], *s.* (fam.) páparo, payo.
gumption [gʌ́mpshʊn], *s.* (fam.) perspicacia,
sindéresis; (pint.) arte de preparar colores.
gun [gʌn], *s.* arma de fuego; cañón; fusil; escopeta de caza; (E. U., fam.) pistola o revólver;
disparo de arma de fuego; cañonazo.—**g. barrel,**
cañón de fusil o de escopeta.—**g. carriage,** cureña.
—**g. deck,** (mar.) cubierta principal, batería.—**g.
metal,** bronce de cañón.—**g. port,** porta, cañonera.—**g. room,** (mar.) Santa Bárbara, polvorín.
gunboat [gʌ́nbout], *s.* (mar.) cañonero.
guncotton [gʌncótʊn], *s.* algodón pólvora.
gunflint [gʌ́nflint], *s.* piedra de chispa, pedernal.
gunlock [gʌ́nloc], *s.* llave de fusil.
gunman [gʌ́nmæn], *s.* bandido de calle o de ciudad, apache.
gunnage [gʌ́nœy], *s.* número y peso de los cañones
de un buque.
gunnel, *s.* (mar.) = GUNWALE.
gunner [gʌ́nœr], *s.* (mar.) condestable; artillero;
escopetero.
gunnery [gʌ́nœri], *s.* artillería.
gunning [gʌ́ning], *s.* (dep.) caza.
gunpowder [gʌ́npáudœr], *s.* pólvora.
gunpower [gʌ́npáuœr], *s.* (mar.) potencia de
artillería (de un acorazado), peso total de los
proyectiles que las piezas mayores pueden disparar simultáneamente.
gunreach [gʌ́nrích], *s.* alcance.
gunshot [gʌ́nshót], *s.* tiro de fusil, alcance; escopetazo.
gunsling [-sling], *s.* aparejo de artillería; charpa,
portafusil.
gunsmith [gʌ́nsmiz], *s.* armero.
gunstock [gʌ́nstoc], *s.* caja de fusil o de escopeta.
Gunter's chain [gʌ́ntœrs chéin], *s.* (top.)
cadena de Gunter (2,0117 Dm.)
gunwale [gʌ́nueil o gʌ́nel], *s.* regala, borda.
gurgitation [gœryitéshʊn], *s.* vorágine, remolino.
gurgle [gœ́rgœl]. **I.** *vn.* gorgotear. **II.** *s.* gorgoteo, murmullo.
gurglet [gœ́rglet], *s.* alcarraza.
gurnard [gœ́rnard], **gurnet** [gœ́rnet], *s.* (ict.)
trilla, alcotana.
gush [gʌsh]. **I.** *va.* derramar, verter. **II.** *vn.*
brotar, fluir, manar, chorrear; ser extremoso.
III. *s.* chorro, borbotón; efusión, extremo.
gusher [gʌ́shœr], *s.* pozo de chorro de petróleo.
gushing [gʌ́shing], *a.* extremoso.
gusset [gʌ́set], *s.* (cost.) escudete, contrete, fonas;
codo de hierro, hierro angular de refuerzo.

gust [gʌst], *s.* ráfaga, racha, ventolera; (mar.)
fugada, sobreviento; acceso, arrebato; gusto,
sentido del paladar; deleite, inclinación, afición.
gustation [gʌstéshʊn], *s.* gustadura.
gustatory, gustative [gʌ́statori, tiv], *a.* del sentido del gusto.
gusto [gʌ́sto], *s.* gusto, placer.
gusty [gʌ́sti], *a.* borrascoso, chubascoso.
gut [gʌt]. **I.** *s.* intestino, tripa; cuerda de tripa;
(mar.) estrecho. **II.** *va.* desventrar, destripar;
desentrañar.
gutta [gʌ́ta], *s.* (farm. y arq.), gota.
gutta-percha [gʌ́ta-pœrchá], *s.* gutapercha.
guttated [gʌ́teited], *a.* goteado.
gutter [gʌ́tœr]. **I.** *s.* canal, gotera; badén,
cuneta; arroyo de la calle; arbollón, albañal,
zanja, acequia; cámara; estría, canal de ebanistería. **II.** *va.* acanalar, estriar; poner canalones;
construir albañales, etc. **III.** *vn.* acanalarse.
guttural [gʌ́tʊral], *a.* gutural.—**gutturality**
[-æliti], **gutturalness** [-nes], *s.* calidad de gutural.
—**gutturally** [-i], *adv.* guturalmente.
guy [gái]. **I.** *s.* tirante, viento, guía; (mar.) retenida, patarraez; tipo, sujeto; adefesio, ente
ridículo, mamarracho. **II.** *va.* (mar.) sujetar
con vientos o retenidas; (fam., E. U.) hacer burla o
mofa.
guzzle [gʌ́sœl]. **I.** *va.* y *vn.* beber mucho; tragar,
engullir. **II.** *vn.* emborracharse.
guzzler [gʌ́slœr], *s.* bebedor, borrachín.
gybe [yaib] = JIBE.
gymnasium [yimnéisium], *s.* gimnasio; escuela
secundaria superior.
gymnast [yímnæst], *s.* gimnasta.
gymnastic(al [yimnǽstic(al], *a.* gimnástico.
gymnastics [yimnǽstics], *s. pl.* gimnasia.
gymnobase [yímnobeis], *s.* (bot.) gimnobase.—
gymnobasic [-bǽsic], *a.* gimnobásico.
gymnosophist [yimnósofist], *s.* gimnosofista.
gymnosperm [yímnospœrm], *s.* (bot.) planta
gimnosperma.
gymnospermous [yímnospœrmʊs], *a.* (bot.)
gimnospermo
gynarchy [yínarki], **gynæcocracy** [yiniócrasi],
gynecocracy [-necócrasi], *s.* ginecocracia.
gynecium [yinésium], *s.* gineceo.
gynecologist [yinecóloyist], *s.* ginecólogo.
gynecology [yinecóloyi], *s.* ginecología.
gyniatrics [yáiniǽtrics], *s.* ginecología aplicada.
gypseous [yípseus], **gypsine** [yípsin], *a.* yesoso.
gypsum [yípsum], *s.* yeso.—**g. pit,** yesal.
gypsy [yípsi], *s.* = GIPSY.
gyral [yáiral], *a.* giratorio; (anat.) referente a la⁵
circunvoluciones del cerebro.
gyrate [yáiret], *vn.* girar, rodar.
gyration [yairéshʊn], *s.* giro, vuelta.
gyre [yáicœr], *s.* giro, girada, vuelta.
gyrfalcon [yœr], *s.* = GERFALCON.
gyrocompass [yáirocómpæs], *s.* (mar.) compás
giroscópico o brújula giroscópica.
gyro level [lévœl], *s.* (aer.) nivel giroscópico.
gyromancy [yáiromænsi], *s.* giromancia.
gyroscope [yáiroscoup], *s.* giroscopio.
gyrostat [yáirostæt], *s.* giróstato.
gyrostatic [-stétic], *a.* girostático, giroscópico.—
g. compass = GYROCOMPASS.—**gyrostatics,** *s.*
girostática.
gyve [yáiv], *va.* encadenar; apiolar.
gyves [yáivs], *s. pl.* grillos.

H

h [éich]. **I.** *s.* h. **II.** (H) *a.* en H, en forma de H
(apl. a vigas, postes, inducidos, etc.)
ha [ja], *interj.* ¡ah! ¡ja, ja!
haak, *s.* (ict.) = HAKE.
habeas corpus [jéibias córpus], *s.* (for.) habeas
corpus.
haberdasher [jǽbœrdǽshœr], *s.* camisero, mercero, tendero.—**haberdashery** [-i], *s.* camisería,
mercería.

habergeon [jǽbœryʊn], *s*. cota de malla.
habiliment [jabílimœnt], *s*. prenda de vestir.— *pl*. vestuario, ropa.
habilitate [jabíliteit]. **I.** *va*. (E. U.) pertrechar, habilitar, aviar. **II.** *vn*. hacerse idóneo.
habilitation [-éishʊn], *s*. habilitación; aptitud.
habit [jǽbit]. **I.** *s*. hábito, costumbre; estado o condición habitual; carácter, manera de vivir (gen. *pl*.); vicio; vestido, hábito; (equit.) traje de amazona.—**h.-forming**, enviciador; que forma o crea hábito. **II.** *va*. ataviar; vestir.
habitable [jǽbitabœl], *a*. habitable.
habitableness [-nes], *s*. habitabilidad.
habitant [jǽbitant], *s*. habitante, morador.
habitat [jǽbitat], *s*. región donde crece y vive un animal o planta; habitación, morada.
habitation [-éishʊn], *s*. habitación, domicilio, morada.
habitual [jabítiual], *a*. habitual, acostumbrado.
habitually [-i], *adv*. habitualmente.
habituate [jabítiuet], *va*. y *vn*. habituar(se).
habitude [jǽbitiud], *s*. hábito, costumbre; trato, relaciones.
habitué [jabitué], *s*. concurrente, parroquiano.
hachure [jǽshur]. **I.** *s*. (dib.) líneas de sombra; líneas de declive (en dibujo topográfico). **II.** *va*. sombrear con líneas.
hack [jæc]. **I.** *s*. caballo de alquiler, rocín, cuartago; alquilón; (E. U.) simón o coche de alquiler; peón, trabajador; hacha, azuela, cuchilla; muesca, corte, tajo, cuchillada; puntapié en la canilla; (fam.) tos seca.—**h. saw**, sierra para cortar metal. **II.** *va*. tajar, cortar, picar; acuchillar, machetear; picar piedra; hacer muescas, mellar; alquilar (coche o caballo). **III.** *vn*. cortar; toser con tos seca; alquilarse, venderse.
hackamore [jǽcæmore], *s*. cabezada de cuero crudo.
hackle [jǽcœl]. **I.** *va*. rastrillar; romper en pedazos. **II.** *s*. rastrillo ; fibra no hilada; mosca para pescar.
hackman [jǽcmæn], *s*. simón, cochero de alquiler.
hackmatack [jǽcmatác], *s*. (bot.) alerce.
hackney [jǽcni]. **I.** *s*. caballo de alquiler, rocín, cuartago; alquilón. **II.** *a*. alquilado; común. —**h. coach**, coche de alquiler, simón.—**h. coachman**, cochero de alquiler.—**h. writer**, escritor mercenario. **III.** *va*. repetir, gastar, vulgarizar; llevar en coche de alquiler.—**hackneyed**, trillado, manoseado, gastado.
hacqueton [jǽketon], *s*. jubón antiguo.
had [jǽd], *pret*. de TO HAVE.
haddock [jǽdoc], *s*. róbalo, cecial.
hade [jéid], *s*. (min.) buzamiento.
Hades [jéidis], *s*. el otro mundo; los infiernos.
hæma- [jíma, jéma], **hæmo-** [jímo, jémo]. (En composición estas partículas se reemplazan generalmente por HEMA-, HEMO-).
hæmal [jímæl], *s*. = HEMAL.
hæmetite [jémetait], *s*. hematites.
hæmatosis, **hæmorrhage**, etc. = HEMATOSIS, HEMORRHAGE, etc.
haft [jaft], *s*. mango, asa, puño, guarnición.
hag [jæg]. **I.** *s*. bruja, hechicera. **II.** *va*. aterrar, acosar, atormentar.
haggard [jǽgard]. **I.** *a*. trasnochado, macilento, ojeroso; zabareño, montaraz, intratable. **II.** *s*. halcón; fiera, sujeto indómito.
haggardly [jǽgardli], *adv*. ansiosamente.
haggish [jǽguish], *a*. feo como bruja.
haggle [jǽgœl]. **I.** *va*. tajar, destrozar, machetear. **II.** *vn*. regatear; cavilar.
haggler [jǽglœr], *s*. tajador; regatero.
hagiarchy [jǽyiarki], **hagiocracy** [-ócræsi], *s*. gobierno de (por) sacerdotes.
hagiographa [jeyiógrafa], *s*. *pl*. hagiógrafos.— **hagiographal** [-al], *a*. hagiógrafo.—**hagiographer** [-œr], *s*. hagiógrafo.—**hagiography** [-i], *s*. hagiografía.—**hagiolatry** [lætri], *s*. culto de los santos.
hah [ja], *interj*. = HA.
ha-ha [ja-ja], *s*. foso con escarpa.
haik [jáik], *s*. jaique árabe.

hail [jéil]. **I.** *s*. granizo; saludo; grito, llamada· —**h. fellow**, compañero, camarada.—**H. Mary**, Ave María.—**within h.**, al habla. **II.** *interj*. ¡salve! ¡salud! **III.** *va*. saludar; aclamar; llamar.— **to h. a ship**, (mar.) ponerse al habla con un buque. **IV.** *vn*. granizar; vocear.—**to h. from**, venir o proceder de.
hailshot [jéilshot], *s*. perdigones, munición menuda.
hailstone [jéilstóun], *s*. piedra de granizo.
hailstorm [-stórm], *s*. granizada, pedrisquero.
haily [jéili], *a*. lleno de granizo.
hair [jéœr], *s*. pelo; vello; cabello; cerda; hebra, fibra, pelillo, filamento; pelusa.—**h. dye**, tinte para el pelo.—**h. net**, albanega.—**h. pencil**, pincel.—**h. shirt**, cilicio.—**h. switch**, añadido — **h. trigger**, pelo (de una pistola).—**against the h.**, a contrapelo.—**to a h.**, exactamente, perfectamente.
hairbrained [-bréind], *a*. (por error) = HARE-BRAINED.
hairbreadth [-bredʒ], *s*. ancho de un pelo; casi nada.—**to have a h. escape**, escapar por un pelo.
hairbrush [-brŏsh], *s*. cepillo para la cabeza.
haircloth [-clóʒ], *s*. tela de crin.
hairdresser [-drésœr], *s*. peluquero, peinador o peinadora.
hairdressing [-drésing], *s*. peinado.
haired [-d], *a*. peludo, cabelludo.
hairiness [-ines], *s*. pelaje.
hairlace [-léis], *s*. cinta o venda para atar el pelo.
hairless [-les], *a*. pelado, pelón, calvo; sin pelo.
hairpin [-pín], *s*. horquilla, gancho.
hairsieve [-sív], *s*. tamiz de cerda.
hairsplitting [-splíting]. **I.** *a*. quisquilloso. **II.** quisquilla; hilar muy delgado.
hairspring [-spríng], *s*. pelo o muelle (de reloj).
hairy [jéœri], *a*. peludo, velludo, velloso, cabelludo, peloso.
Haitian [jéitian o jáitian], *a*. = HAYTIAN.
hake [jéic], *s*. (ict.) merluza, pescada; (com.) pescada, cecial.
halation [jaléshʊn], *s*. (fot.) halo o aureola.
halberd [jǽlbœrd], *s*. alabarda.
halberdier [jælbœrdíœr], *s*. alabardero.
halcyon [jǽlsion]. **I.** *a*. quieto, apacible, tranquilo.—**h. days**, días tranquilos; veranillo de San Martín. **II.** *s*. (orn.) alcedón, alción.
hale [jéil]. **I.** *a*. sano, robusto, fuerte. **II.** *va*. tirar de, arrastrar, halar.
half [jaf]. **I.** *s*. (*pl*. HALVES, javś) medio; mitad. **h. and h.**, mitad y mitad, mezcla de dos cervezas. **II.** *a*. y *adv*. medio; casi; (en composición) semi.— **h. binding**, (enc.) media pasta, a la holandesa.— **h. blood**, mestizo; (for.) medio hermano, media hermana.—**h.-bred**, *a*. mestizo; incivil, inculto.— **h-breed**, *s*. mestizo.—**h. brother**, hermanastro.— **h.-caste**, mestizo.—**h-cock**, (arm.) montar en seguro.—**h.-cocked**, medio amartillado, montado en seguro.—**h.-hearted**, frío, indiferente; mezquino.—**h.-heartedly**, friamente, sin entusiasmo. —**h. hose**, calcetines.—**h.-mast**, *s*. media asta (apl. a la bandera); *va*. poner a media asta.—**h. measure**, media o medias, paños tibios.—**h. moon**, semilunio.—**h. mourning**, medio luto.— (mús.) mínima.—**h.-past one, two, etc.**, la una, las dos, etc., y media.—**h. pay**, media paga.—**h. round**, semicircular.—**h.-round file**, lima de media caña.—**h.-seas over**, achispado, medio borracho.—**h. sister**, hermanastra.—**h. sole**, media suela.—**h.-sole**, *va*. echar o poner media suela a.— **h.-timer**, obrero que trabaja sólo la mitad del tiempo ordinario.—**h. tone**, fotografiado a media tinta; (mús.) semítono.—**h.-tone plate**, clisé fotografiado a media tinta.—**h.-witted**, bobo, imbécil.—**h. year**, semestre.—**h.-yearly**, semestral; semestralmente.
halfpenny [jáfpéni, (Ing.) jépeni, *s*. medio penique.
halfway [jáfuei], *a*. y *adv*. equidistante, a medio camino, hasta la mitad.—**to go h.**, **to meet one h.**, hacer concesiones en cambio de otras, estar dispuesto a hacer un compromiso.
halibut [jólibut], *s*. (ict.) hipogloso (pez grande, sin espinas, de carne muy estimada).

halitus [jǽlitus], *s.* hálito.

hall [jóil], *s.* vestíbulo, zaguán; pasadizo, corredor; salón, edificio (apl. a los destinados a reuniones, funciones, estudios, etc.); colegio; casa señorial.—**h. mark**, marca del contraste.

halleluiah, hallelujah [jǽlelúya], *s.* aleluya.

halliard [jǽlyard], *s.*=HALYARD.

hallo, halloa [jaló], *interj.* con que se llama o saluda: ¡hola! ¡oiga! ¡eh!

halloo [jaló *o* jalú]. **I.** *s.* grita, vocería. **II.** *interj.* ¡sus! ¡busca! voz de los cazadores. **III.** *va.* y *vn.* gritar, vocear, azuzar o llamar a gritos.

hallooing [jalúing], *s.* grita, vocería.

hallow [jǽlo], *va.* consagrar, santificar; reverenciar.

Hallowmass [jǽlomas], *a.* fiesta de Todos los Santos.

Hallowe'en [jǽloin], *s.* víspera de Todos los Santos.

hallucinate [jælúsineit], *va.* alucinar.

hallucination [néisshun], *s.* alucinación.

hallway [jóluéi], *s.* pasadizo; zaguán.

halm [jom], *s.* paja larga. *V.* HAUM.

halo [jélo], *s.* halo, nimbo, aureola.

halogen [jǽloyen], *s.* (quím.) halógeno.

halography [jælógrafi], *s.* halografía.

haloid [jéloid]. **I.** *a.* haloideo. **II.** *s.* sal haloidea.

halophilous [jælófilus], *a.* halófilo.

halt [jolt]. **I.** *vn.* cojear, renguear; vacilar; tartamudear; estar imperfecto; parar, hacer alto. **II.** *va.* parar, detener. **III.** *s.* cojera; detención; parada, alto. **IV.** *a.* cojo; lisiado.

halter [jóltœr]. **I.** *s.* cabestro, ronzal, jáquima; cuerda de ahorcar, dogal. **II.** *va.* cabestrar; echar el ronzal; poner el dogal.

haltingly [jóltingli], *adv.* a cox cox; vacilantemente.

halve [jav], *va.* dividir en dos partes iguales; ser o formar la mitad de; machihembrar.

halves [javs], *pl.* de HALF.—**to g. h.,** ir a medias.

halyard [jǽlyard], *s.* (mar.) driza.

ham [jæm], *s.* jamón; (anat.) corva.—*pl.* (fam.) nalgas.

hamadryad [jǽmadraiæd], *s.* hamadríada.

hame [jem], *s.* horcate.

Hamite [jǽmait], *s.* camita, descendiente de Cam; caucasiano antiguo del nordeste de África.

Hamitic [jæmític], *a.* camítico.

hamlet [jǽmlet], *s.* aldea, villorrio, caserío.

hammer [jǽmœr]. **I.** *s.* martillo; llave, rastrillo o percutor de arma de fuego; macillo del piano; martinete; pilón o maza de martinete.—**h.** and **tongs,** (fam.) con violencia, bruscamente; en discordia, como perros y gatos.—**h.-hard,** endurecido o forjado en frío a martillo.—**h.-harden,** *va.* martillar en frío.—**h.-refined,** afinado a martillo. **II.** *va.* martillar; batir, golpear, cutir, machacar; clavar; forjar; lucubrar.—**to h. one's brains,** devanarse los sesos. **III.** *vn.* martillar, dar golpes; repiquetear; trabajar asiduamente.

hammercloth [-clóz], *s.* paño del pescante de un coche.

hammerer [jǽmœrœr], *s.* martillador.

hammerhead [-jéd], *s.* (ict.) cornudilla, pez martillo.

hammering [jǽmœring], *s.* martilleo; ruido de martillazos; repuleo.

hammock [jǽmoc], *s.* hamaca.

hamper [jǽmpœr]. **I.** *s.* canasta, cesto grande; (mar.) aparejo; traba, impedimento. **II.** *va.* embarazar, estorbar; encestar, encanastar.

hamstring [jǽmstring]. **I.** *s.* tendón de la corva. **II.** *va.* desjarretar.

hanaper [jǽnapœr], *s.* canasto para documentos u objetos de valor.

hand [jænd]. **I.** *s.* mano; maña, destreza; ejecución, mano de obra; lado (derecho o izquierdo); operario, obrero; peón, jornalero, brazo, bracero; aguja, manecilla (de reloj, etc.); carácter de letra; firma, rúbrica; palmo menor; dominación, poder, posesión; mano, en el juego; acción, trabajo, agencia.—**h.and glove,** uña y carne.—**h. in h.,** parejas; junto; de concierto, de acuerdo.—**h.**

over head, inconsideradamente.—**hands down,** sin dificultad, con los ojos cerrados (fig.).—**hands off,** no tocar; no meterse, abstenerse (cambiando un poco el giro).—**hands up!** ¡alce(n) las manos! (para seguridad de que quien recibe la orden no saca arma).—**all hands below!** ¡todo el mundo abajo! —**all hands on deck!** ¡todo el mundo arriba!— **at h.** o **near at h.,** a la mano, cerca.—**by h.,** a mano; con biberón.—**by the h.,** de la mano.—**from h. to h.,** de mano a mano.—**from h. to mouth,** de manos a boca.—**given under my h. and seal,** firmado y sellado de mi mano.—**in h.,** de contado, dinero en mano; entre manos.—**in one's h.,** en mano o manos de uno.—**off one's hands,** desechado; despachado.—**on all hands,** por todas partes.— **on h.,** disponible; (com.) en existencia; pendiente, por hacer; por venir; presente, a la mano.—**on one's hands,** entre manos; a cargo de uno.—**on the one h.,** por una parte.—**on the other h.,** por otra parte; en cambio; al contrario.—**out of h.,** luego, inmediatamente; terminado; desbocado (fig.), incontenible.—**to get the upper h.,** llevar la ventaja; tomar cuerpo, agravarse.—**to h.,** a la mano; listo.—**to have a h. in,** tener mano o parte en.— **to have one's hands full,** estar ocupadísimo, tener muchísimo que hacer.—**to set the h. to,** meter mano en, emprender; firmar.—**under my h.,** firmado de mi puño y letra. **II.** *va.* dar, entregar, poner en manos (de alguien), pasar; conducir, guiar por la mano.—**to h. down,** transmitir; bajar, entregar o pasar de arriba abajo.—**to h. in,** o **into,** dar la mano para entrar.—**to h. over,** entregar.—**to h. round,** o **around,** hacer pasar, pasar de uno a otro. **III.** *a.* de mano; hecho a mano; para la mano.—**h. basket,** cestilla, cesta.—**h. bell,** campanilla.—**h. glass,** espejo de mano; lente para leer; (agr.) vaso de protección.—**h. grenade,** granada de mano.— **h. language,** lenguaje de los mudos.—**h. lead** = LEAD LINE.—**h. mill,** molinillo.—**h. organ,** organillo.—**h. sails,** (mar.) velas manuales.—**h. screw,** gato de mano, cornaquí.—**h. vise,** entenalla.

handball [jǽndbol], *s.* pelota; juego de pelota; bola hueca para rociar, etc.

handbarrow [-bárro], *s.* angarillas, parihuela.

handbill [-bíl], *s.* hoja suelta.

handbook [-búk], *s.* manual; guía.

handbreadth [-bréz], *s.* palmo menor.

handcart [-cárt], *s.* carretilla de mano.

handcuff [-cuf]. **I.** *s.* manilla, esposas. **II.** *va.* maniatar.

handed [-ed], *a.* que tiene manos; de mano.

handful [-ful], *s.* puñado, manojo, manípulo.

handicap [jǽndicæp]. **I.** *va.* (dep.) igualar a los competidores imponiendo ciertos impedimentos a los que llevan ventajas o dando a los otros ventajas especiales; de aquí, poner trabas u obstáculos, estorbar. **II.** *s.* (dep.) iguala que se hace imponiendo restricciones a los competidores que tienen ventaja; carrera con caballos de peso igualado; obstáculo, impedimento o desventaja.— **handicapped** [-d], *a.* impedido.

handicraft [jǽndicraft], *s.* mano de obra; oficio, arte mecánica.—**handicraftsman** [-sman], *s.* artesano, artífice.

handily [jǽndili], *adv.* diestramente.

handiness [-nes], *s.* habilidad, destreza.

handiwork [-uœrc], *s.* artefacto, maniobra.

handkerchief [jǽnkœrchif], *s.* pañuelo.

handle [jǽndœl]. **I.** *va.* tocar, manosear; manipular, manejar; hacer tratable; tratar; dirigir; comerciar en; poner mango a. **II.** *vn.* usar las manos o trabajar con ellas; ser manejado. **III.** *s.* mango, puño, asa, manigueta, manubrio, tirador; (fam.) título.

handless [jǽndles], *a.* manco.

handling [jǽndling], *s.* manejo; manoseo, tocamiento; maniobra; manipulación; toque.

handmade [jǽndméid], *s.* hecho a mano.

handmaid [-méid], **handmaiden** [-méidœn], *s.* criada de mano, asistenta.

handrail [-réil], *s.* pasamano.

handsaw [-só], *s.* serrucho.

handsel, hansel [jǽndsel, jǽnsel]. **I.** *s.* estrena, prenda y señal. **II.** *va.* estrenar.

handsome [jǽnsum], *a.* hermoso; excelente; amplio, liberal, generoso; elegante, fino.

handsomely [-li], *adv.* hermosamente; generosamente.—**handsomeness** [-nes], *s.* hermosura; generosidad.

handspike [jǽndspáic], *s.* palanca.

handspring [jǽndspríng], *s.* voltereta sobre las manos.

handwork [-uǽrc], *s.* obra hecha a mano.

handwriting [-ráiting], *s.* carácter de letra, quirografía; escritura.

handy [jǽndi], *a.* manual, manuable; fácil de manejar; próximo, a la mano; diestro, hábil.

handywork [-uǽrc], *s.* = HANDIWORK.

hang [jæng]. **I.** *va.* (*pret.* y *pp.* HUNG o HANGED) colgar, suspender; fijar (en la pared, etc.); empapelar (pared); poner colgaduras en; endoselar; ahorcar (en este último sentido el participio pasado es HANGED solamente).—**to h. fire**, fallar el tiro, hacer higa; estar una cosa en suspenso; vacilar.—**to h. out**, enarbolar.—**to h. the helm**, calar el timón.—**to h. the rudder**, (mar.) montar el timón.—**to h. up**, levantar, suspender en el aire; colgar; arrinconar, dejar pendiente, suspender; empeñar.—**to h. with tapestry**, entapizar. **II.** *vn.* colgar, pender, caer; fluctuar, vacilar; ser ahorcado; ser inminente, amenazar; pegarse, agregarse a uno, ir al retortero; colgarse o abrazarse al cuello de uno; vigilar, aguardar; depender, estar pendiente de; vacilar, estar en duda; (E. U.) no avenirse, no convenir.—**to h. around**, rondar, haraganear.—**to h. back**, plantarse, resistirse; vacilar.—**to h. down**, colgar, estar pendiente.—**to h. loose**, colgar flojamente. —**to h. in the balance**, estar pendiente de un hilo.—**to h. off**, no decidirse, hacerse el remolón. —**to h. on**, colgarse de, apoyarse en; quedarse, permanecer; insistir; persistir.—**to h. on the sleeve of**, estar sujeto a la voluntad de.—**to h. out**, estar enarbolado o colgado; sobresalir; ser inflexible, no ceder; (fam.) pasar la noche, dormir, alojarse.—**to h. over**, colgar arriba de; destacarse sobre.—**to h. together**, permanecer unidos; tener cohesión. **III.** *s.* caída; modo como cuelga una cosa; (fam.) maña, destreza; quid, busilis; (mar.) curva.

hangar [hángár], *s.* cobertizo; (aer.) hangar.

hangbird [jǽngbǽrd], *s.* pájaro que fabrica nido colgante.

hangdog [jǽngdog], *a.* y *s.* camastrón.

hanger [jǽngœr], *s.* soporte colgante; colgadero; barra, plancha, hierro, etc., de suspensión; artefacto de suspensión; (impr.) espito; alfanje.

hanger-on [jǽngœr-on], *s.* dependiente; mogollón, gorrista; familiar; paseante en corte.

hanging [jǽnging]. **I.** *s.* ahorcadura, muerte en la horca.—*pl.* colgaduras, tapices, cortinajes, etc. **II.** *a.* colgante, suspendido; patibulario.—**h. compass**, brújula de cámara.—**h. sleeves**, mangas perdidas.

hangman [jǽngman], *s.* verdugo.

hangnail [jǽngnéil], *s.* padrastro, respigón.

hangnest [jǽngnést], *s.* nido colgante.

hank [jǽnk]. **I.** *s.* madeja; adujada, rollo de cuerda. **II.** *vn.* hacer madejas; adujar.

hanker [jǽnkœr], *vn.* (gen. con *for* o *after*), ansiar, apetecer.

hankering [jǽnkœring], *s.* anhelo, deseo.

hansard [jǽnsard], *s.* actas del parlamento inglés; anseático.

hanse [jæns], *s.* ansa; unión mercantil.

Hanseatic [jǽnsiǽtic], *a.* anseático.

hansom (**cab** [jǽnsʊm], *s.* cabriolé con el pescante en la zaga.

hap [jæp]. **I.** *s.* lance, acaso; azar, suerte, casualidad. **II.** *vn.* acontecer.

haphazard [jǽpjǽsǽrd]. **I.** *s.* suerte, casualidad. **II.** *a.* casual, fortuito. **III.** *adv.* al acaso, casualmente.

hapless [jǽples], *a.* desventurado, miserable.

haply [jǽpli], *adv.* quizá; casualmente.

happen [jǽpœn], *vn.* acontecer, suceder, pasar, sobrevenir; parar en; hallarse por casualidad en.—**to h. in**, entrar o llegar casualmente.—**to h. on**, encontrar o tropezar con.—**no matter what**, o **whatever**, **happens**, suceda lo que suceda.

happening [jǽpœning], *s.* suceso.

happily [jǽpili], *adv.* afortunadamente.

happiness [jǽpines], *s.* felicidad.

happy [jǽpi], *a.* feliz.—**to be h. to**, alegrarse de, celebrar, tener gusto en; tener la fortuna de.—**h. hunting grounds**, la tierra feliz de la caza, paraíso de los indios norteamericanos.

happy-go-lucky [-go-lʊ́ki]. **I.** *a.* y *s.* descuidado, confiado en la buena ventura. **II.** *adv.* a la buena ventura; de cualquier modo.

haptophore [jǽptofœœr], *s.* (biol.) haptóforo.

haptophile [-fail], *a.* (bact.) haptóforo.

hara-kiri [járakíri], *s.* harakiri, suicidio japonés que consiste en abrirse las entrañas.

harangue [jarǽng]. **I.** *s.* arenga, perorata. **II.** *va.* arengar a. **III.** *vn.* pronunciar un discurso.

harass [jǽras], *va.* acosar, fatigar, atormentar, vejar; (mil.) hostigar, hostilizar, perseguir.— **harassment** [-mœnt], *s.* hostigamiento; persecución, vejamen.

harbinger [járbinyœr], **I.** *s.* precursor; presagio. **II.** *va.* presagiar, anunciar.

harbo(u)r [járbœr]. **I.** *s.* puerto; seguro; asilo, abrigo, albergue.—**h. dues**, derechos de puerto.— **h. master**, capitán de puerto. **II.** *va.* abrigar, amparar; acoger, hospedar; guardar, conservar; profesar, acariciar. **III.** *vn.* ampararse, refugiarse.

harbo(u)rage [járbœrey], *s.* puerto; refugio, amparo, asilo.

harbo(u)rer [járbœrœr], *s.* amparador, albergador, acogedor; encubridor.

harbo(u)rless [járbœrles], *s.* desamparado.

hard [jard]. **I.** *a.* duro; inflexible, tieso; difícil, arduo; empedernido; fuerte, recio, riguroso, severo; injusto, opresivo; ofensivo; áspero, tosco; vigoroso, sufrido; mezquino, miserable; cruda (agua); penoso; fuerte, fermentado; (fam.) malvado, perverso.—**h. and fast**, de calicanto, o a macha martillo.—**h. cash**, (com.) numerario, efectivo.—**h. coal**, antracita.—**h. drink**, bebida fuertemente alcohólica; licor.—**h. drinking**, mucho beber.—**h.-heartedness**, insensibilidad, empedernimiento.—**h. labor**, trabajo forzado.— **h. lines**, **h. luck**, mala suerte.—**h. money** = H. CASH.—**h. of hearing**, duro de oído.—**h. knot**, nudo apretado.—**h. rubber**, ebonita, vulcanita.— **h. sauce**, salsa espesa de azúcar y mantequilla.— **h. soap**, jabón duro.—**h. solder**, soldadura fuerte o dura, o de alto punto de fusión.—**h. steel**, acero rico en carbono.—**h.-tack**, pan de marinero.—**h. to deal with**, intratable.—**h. words**, palabras injuriosas.—**h. work**, trabajo difícil; trabajo fuerte.—**to be h. up**, hallarse en apuros, estar a la cuarta pregunta. **II.** *s.* piso o camino duro. **III.** *adv.* diligentemente, con ahínco, con inquietud, con impaciencia, vejación o pesar; difícilmente; reciamente, con fuerza, con dureza; (mar.) todo, enteramente.—**h. a-port**, a babor todo.—**h. a-weather**, todo a barlovento.—**h. by**, inmediato, muy cerca.—**h.-earned**, ganado con dificultad.— **h.-favored**, o **featured**, de aspecto áspero, cariagrio.—**h.-fisted**, de manos callosas; avaro, agarrado.—**h.-handed**, de manos encallecidas o ásperas; cruel; despótico.—**h.-headed**, terco; perspicaz.—**h.-hearted**, empedernido.—**h.-heartedly**, empedernidamente.—**h. pressed**, **h. pushed**, escaso o falto de recursos, apurado.—**h.-set**, resuelto; inflexible, obstinado.—**h.-working**, asiduo, que trabaja con tesón.—**to drink h.**, beber con exceso.—**to rain h.**, llover a cántaros.—**to work h.**, aporrearse, trabajar con ahínco.

harden [járdœn]. **I.** *va.* endurecer; solidar; curtir, encallecer; robustecer; templar; hacer insensible o indiferente. **II.** *vn.* endurecerse, empedernirse.

hardihood [járdijud], *s.* atrevimiento, temeridad.

hardiness [járdines], *s.* ánimo, valor, intrepidez; robustez, vigor.

hardly [járdli], *adv.* difícilmente, apenas, escasamente; no del todo; duramente, severamente.

hardness [járdnes], *s.* dureza; firmeza, solidez; escasez, penuria; crueldad, rigor; desabrimiento; obduración; crudeza (del agua); (b. a.) dureza, tosquedad.

---

hardpan [járdpæn], s. (min.) capa roqueña debajo de terreno blando; base sólida; fondo.

hardship [járdship], s. penalidad, trabajo; opresión, gravamen, injusticia.

hardware [járduéær], s. quincalla, ferretería, quincallería.

hardwareman [-mæn], s. quincallero, ferretero.

hardwood [járdud], s. madera dura.

hardy [járdi], a. fuerte, robusto, endurecido; bravo, intrépido; (bot.) resistente.

hare [jéær], s. liebre; (astr.) constelación Lepus. —**h. and hounds,** juego en que se imita la caza de liebres.—**h.'s-ear,** (bot.) perfoliada.—**h.-hearted,** alebrado, medroso.

harebell [-bel], s. (bot.) campanilla.

harebrained [-bréind], a. cabeza de chorlito, ligero de cascos, tolondro.

harefoot [-fút], s. pie de liebre; corredor ágil.

harefooted [-fúted], a. ligero, ágil.

harehound [-jáund], s. lebrel, galgo lebrero.

harelip [-lip], s. labio leporino.—**harelipped** [-lipt], a. labihendido, de labio leporino.

harem [jéæem], s. harén, serrallo.

haremint [jéærmint], s. (bot.) yaro, manto de Santa María.

haricot [jéæricot], s. guisado con habichuelas y otras legumbres; frijol, habichuela.

hark [jark], **harken, hearken** [járkœn], va. y vn. oír con atención, escuchar, atender.—**to h. back,** volver al asunto.

harl [jarl], s. hebras de lino; filamento.

harlequin [járlekuin o kin]. **I.** s. arlequín, bufón. **II.** va. y vn. bufonear, chasquear.—**harlequinade** -éid], s. arlequinada, pantomima.

harlot [járlot]. **I.** s. ramera. **II.** a. meretricio.

harlotry [járlotri], s. prostitución.

harm [jarm]. **I.** s. daño, perjuicio, mal. **II.** va. dañar, perjudicar; ofender, herir.

harmful [jármful], a. dañoso, dañino, nocivo, perjudicial.—**harmfully** [-li], adv. dañosamente, perniciosamente.—**harmfulness** [-nes], s. calidad de nocivo.

harmless [jármles], a. innocuo; inocente; ileso, libre de daño; sano y salvo.—**harmlessly** [-li], adv. inocentemente; sin daño.—**harmlessness** [jármlesnes], s. inocencia; innocuidad.

harmonic, s. armónico, tono secundario.

harmonica [jarmónica], s. (mús.) armónica.

harmonic(al [jarmónic(al], a. armónico.

harmonically [-i], adv. armónicamente.

harmonicon [jarmónicon], s. (mús.) armónica, organillo.

harmonious [jarmóniu̶s], a. armónico; armonioso; simétrico, proporcionado.—**harmoniously** [-li], adv. armoniosamente, armónicamente.—**harmoniousness** [-nes], s. armonía.

harmonist [jármonist], s. armonista.

harmonium [jarmóniu̶m], s. (mús.) armonio.

harmonize, harmonise [jármonaı̶s]. **I.** va. armonizar, concertar, poner de acuerdo. **II.** vn. armonizarse, congeniar; armonizar, convenir, corresponder.—**harmonizer** [-œr], s. conciliador; (mús.) armonista.

harmony [jármoni], s. armonía.

harness [járnes]. **I.** s. guarniciones de caballerías; (arm.) arnés; (mec.) aparejo; equipo; (fig.) servicio activo.—**h. maker,** guarnicionero, talabartero.—**h. room,** guardarnés. **II.** va. poner las guarniciones a (una caballería); enjaezar; armar con arnés.

harp [jarp]. **I.** s. (mús.) arpa; (astr.) Lira. **II.** vn. tocar o tañer el arpa.—**to h. on,** o **upon,** repetir, machacar, porfiar.—**to h. on,** o **upon, one string,** o **the same string,** estar siempre con la misma cantinela.

harper [járpœr], s. arpista.

harping [járping], s. tañido del arpa; repetición enfadosa.—pl. (mar.) cucharros; jarretas.

harpist [járpist], s. = HARPER.

harpoon [jarpún]. **I.** s. arpón. **II.** va. arponear. —**h. gun,** cañón para disparar el arpón.—**harpooner** [-œr], s. arponero.

harpsichord [járpsicord], s. clavicordio.

harpy [járpi], s. arpía; (orn.) arpella.

harquebuss [járcuebu̶s], s. arcabuz.

harquebussier [-fær], s. arcabucero.

harridan [jéridan], s. vieja regañona.

harrier [jéricœr], s. lebrel pequeño; pillador, asolador; molestador; ave de rapina.

harrow [jéro]. **I.** s. (agr.) grada, rastro, trilla; escarificador. **II.** va. (agr.) gradar; perturbar, atormentar.—**harrowing** [-ing], a. horripilante.

harry [jéri], va. pillar, asolar, saquear; acosar, molestar.

harsh [jarsh], a. áspero, agrio, bronco, duro, riguroso, desagradable; tosco.—**harshly** [-li], adv. ásperamente, severamente, duramente, agriamente. —**harshness** [-nes], s. aspereza, rudeza, acerbidad; bronquedad; rigor, severidad.

hart [jart], s. ciervo de cinco años.

hartshorn [jártsjorn], s. amoníaco; cuerno de ciervo; (bot.) variedad de llantén.

harum-scarum [jéærum-skéærum], a. atolondrado; al tuntún, a troche y moche.

haruspex, haruspice [jarúspex, pis], s. arúspice.

harvest [járvest]. **I.** s. cosecha; siega, agosto; fruto, producto, recolección.—**h. bug,** (ento.) nita, arador.—**h. fly,** cigarra, chicharra.—**h. home,** (ingl.) fiesta o coro de segadores.—**h. moon,** luna de la cosecha.—**h. mouse,** ratón del campo.—**h. time,** mies. **II.** va. recoger la cosecha, segar, esquilmar; cosechar; (fig.) recoger el fruto.

harvester [-œr], s. agostero, cosechero; segadora, máquina de segar.

harvestman [-mæn], s. (ento.) típula.

has [jæs], 3a. pers. pres. ind. de TO HAVE.

hash [jæsh]. **I.** s. picar, desmenuzar, hacer picadillo. **II.** s. picadillo.

hasheesh, hashish, [jéshish], s. haxis.

haslet [jéslet], s. asadura de puerco.

hasp [jasp]. **I.** s. aldaba de candado; broche. **II.** va. abrochar; cerrar con aldaba.

hassock [jésoc], s. banqueta, escabel; cojín; ruedo de estera.

hastate [jéstet], a. (bot.) alabardado.

haste [jéist], s. prisa.—**in h.,** de prisa.

haste, hasten [jéiscœn]. **I.** va. acelerar, apresurar, activar; precipitar. **II.** vn. darse prisa, apresurarse.

hastily [jéistili], adv. apresuradamente, precipitadamente, a la carrera.

hastiness [-nes], s. prisa, prontitud; impaciencia.

hasty [jéisti], a. pronto; apresurado; precipitado, arrojado; temprano.—**h. pudding,** (coc.) papilla, gachas.

hat [jæt], s. sombrero; capelo, dignidad de cardenal.—**h. money,** (mar.) capa y sombrero.—**hats off!** ¡descubrámonos! ¡descubrirse!—**to pass the h.,** o **to pass the h. around,** pasar el cepillo, hacer una colecta.

hatable [jéitæbœl], a. odioso.

hatband [jétbænd], s. cintillo del sombrero, cinta.

hatbox [-bóx], **hatcase** [-kéis], s. sombrerera.

hatch [jæch]. **I.** va. criar pollos, empollar, incubar o encobar; fraguar, tramar, maquinar; sombrear con líneas. **II.** vn. empollarse, salir del cascarón; madurarse. **III.** s. cría, nidada; salida del cascarón; portezuela; trampa; (mar.) escotilla, cuartel; (hidr.) paradera, compuerta.— **h. bar,** (mar.) barra de escotilla.

hatchel [jéchel]. **I.** s. restrillo. **II.** va. rastrillar; contrariar, impacientar.

hatchery [jéchei̶ı], s. incubadero, criadero (esp. de peces).

hatchet [jéchet], s. destral, machado, hacha pequeña.—**h. face,** cara delgada.—**h.-faced,** de facciones enjutas.

hatching [jéching], s. cloquera, incubación; (b. mar.) sombra hecha con líneas.

hatchway [jéchuei], s. (mar.) escotilla.

hate [jéit]. **I.** va. odiar, aborrecer. **II.** s. odio, aborrecimiento.

hateful [jéitful], a. aborrecible, odioso; maligno, rencoroso, malévolo.—**hatefully** [-li], adv. odiosamente.—**hatefulness** [-nes], s. odiosidad.

hater [jéitœr], s. aborrecedor; enemigo.

hath [jæz], 3a. *pers. pres. ind.* de TO HAVE.

hatpin [jǽtpin], *s.* pasador o aguja de sombrero; rascamoño.

hatred [jéitred], *s.* odio.

hatted [jǽted], *a.* que lleva sombrero.

hatter [jǽtœr], *s.* sombrerero.—**h.'s jack**, carda.

hauberk [jóberk], *s.* (arm.) plaquín, camisote.

haughtily [jótili], *adv.* arrogantemente.

haughtiness [-nes], *s.* arrogancia; ínfulas, humos.

haughty [jóti], *a.* arrogante; vano, entonado.

haul [joll]. **I.** *va.* tirar de, arrastrar; transportar; (mar.) halar, ronzar, aballestar, cazar.—**h. aft the sheets**, cazar las escotas.—**to h. down the colours**, arriar la bandera.—**to h. over the coals**, culpar; regañar, echar una raspa a.—**to h. the wind**, abarloar, ceñir el viento. **II.** *s.* tirón o estirón, hala; arrastre, transporte; redada.

haulage [jóleɤ], *s.* arrastre, acarreo, transporte; carretaje; coste o gastos de acarreo; (f. c.) movimiento de tierras; precio que se paga por el uso de una vía férrea (gen. por los trenes de otra).

hauling [jóling], *s.* estirón, hala; acarreo, transporte, arrastre.—**h. line**, guía.

haulm, haum [jom], *s.* paja, rastrojo.

haunch [janch], *s.* anca, grupa, culata; pernil; (arq.) riñón de una bóveda.

haunt [jant o jont]. **I.** *va.* frecuentar; rondar; perseguir una idea a uno; causar obsesión; aparecerse en, andar por (apl. a los muertos que se suponen espantar como fantasmas). **II.** *s.* guarido; lugar que uno frecuenta; hábito, costumbre.

haunted [jónted], *a.* visitado por aparecidos; donde se aparecen fantasmas o los muertos espantan.

haustellum [jostélum], *s.* trompa de las mariposas, moscas, etc.

hautboy [jóboi], *s.* (mús.) oboe; (bot.) variedad de fresa.

hauteur [jótœr], *s.* arrogancia; altivez.

have [jæv]. **I.** *aux.* (*pret.* y *pp.* HAD) haber. El pretérito **had** se usa a veces en vez de *if* (*I, you, etc.*), *had*, si (yo, Vd., etc.) hubiera (*had I been there*, si hubiera estado allí; *had it rained*, si hubiera llovido).—**had as soon, had as lief**, expresa buena voluntad, pero sin preferencia: *I had as lief go*, iré de buena gana, no tengo inconveniente en ir.—**had better**, (le, me, etc.) sería mejor o convendría (*you had better wait*, le sería mejor aguardar, mejor es que aguarde; *we had better ask*, mejor es que preguntemos).—**had rather**, más bien, (yo, etc.) preferiría (*I had rather go*, yo preferiría ir; *I had rather be free than famous*, yo preferiría ser libre a ser famoso, más quisiera ser libre que famoso). **II.** *va.* tener; recibir (carta, noticia, tec.); tolerar, permitir; decir, asegurar; (fam.) vencer, ganar; engañar; saber, poseer (un idioma). Seguido de infinitivo indica, ya deseo, ya mandato (*I would have you come*, deseo que Vd. venga; *I will have my servant take the letter*, haré que mi criado lleve la carta). Antes de participio, equivale a "hacer" seguido de infinitivo (*I had the letter copied*, hice copiar la carta), o al tiempo del verbo correspondiente con dativo (*he had a leg broken*, le quebraron una pierna).—**to h. a care**, tener cuidado. —**to h. a mind to**, querer, tener ganas de.—**to h. an eye to**, vigilar, observar.—**to h. at**, dar (golpes, etc.) a, atacar.—**to h. at heart**, desear con vehemencia.—**to h. in hand**, estar ocupado en, tener entre manos.—**to h. it**, ganar; recibir golpes, castigo, etc.—**to h. it hard** (se emplea algún otro giro; vg. *he had it hard*, le dieron recio, le pegaron bien).—**to h. it out**, terminar el negocio, ponerle punto final, poner fin al asunto (por discusión, riña, etc.); decir verdades, cantar claro.—**to h. on**, tener puesto (traje, etc.).—**to h. one's eye on**, vigilar, no perder de vista; haberle echado el ojo a.—**to h. one's self to blame**, tener la culpa.—**to h. one's way**, hacer uno lo que quiera; salirse con la suya.— **to h. recourse**, recurrir.—**to h. to**, tener que, deber.—**as fate, o fortune, would h. it**, quiso la suerte que, según quiso la suerte.—**will h.**, deseo, desea, etc. (*I will have it so*, así lo quiero; *what will you have?* ¿qué desea Vd.?

havelock [jǽvloc], *s.* (mil.) cogotera.

haven [jéivn], *s.* puerto, fondeadero, abra; abrigo, asilo.

haversack [jǽvœrsæc], *s.* (mil.) mochila, barjuleta.

having [jǽving], *s.* bienes, hacienda, haber.

havoc [jǽvoc]. **I.** *s.* estrago, estragos.—**to cry h.**, dar la orden de degüello y saqueo.—**to play h.**, hacer estragos. **II.** *va.* y *vn.* asolar, talar, hacer estragos.

haw [jo]. **I.** *s.* (bot.) acerola; baya o simiente del espino blanco; balbucencia. **II.** *va.* y *vn.* volver o hacer volver a la izquierda.—**to h. and gee**, ir de un lado a otro. **III.** *vn.* tartamudear.

Hawaiian [jauáyan], *a.* de Hawaii.

hawk [jok]. **I.** *s.* (orn.) halcón; gavilán.—**h.-eyed**, lince, de ojo avizor.—**h.-nosed**, aguileño, de nariz aguileña.—**h. owl**, (orn.) úlula, autillo. **II.** *vn.* cazar con halcón; pregonar mercancías; gargajear, arrancar flema.

hawker [jókœr], *s.* buhonero; pregonero; falconero.

hawkweed [jokuíd], *s.* (bot.) pelosilla.

hawse [još], *s.* (mar.) proa del buque; distancia, largo o cumplido de un cable.—**h. hole**, escobén.— **h. pipes**, bocinas o canales de los escobenes.—**h. plugs**, tacos de los escobenes.

hawser [jóšœr], *s.* (mar.) cable, estacha.

hawthorn [józorn], *s.* (bot.) espino, blanca espina, acerolo, oxiacanto.

hay [jéi], *s.* paja de heno u otras hierbas para forraje, bálago; (esgr.) estocada.—**h. cold, h. fever**, catarro anual de la nariz y los ojos.— **h.-spreader, h.-tedder**, esparcidora de heno.— **to make h. while the sun shines**, golpear el hierro cuando está en ascua, aprovechar la oportunidad, hacer su agosto.

haycock [jéicoc], *s.* almiar, niara.

hayfield [-fild], *s.* henar.

hayfork [-fórc], *s.* horca, bieldo.

hayloft [-lóft], *s.* henal o henil.

hayrake [-réic], *s.* rastrillo para heno.

hayrick [-ríc], *s.* = HAYSTOCK.

hayseed [-síd], *s.* simiente de heno o de hierbas; patán, rústico.

haystack [-stǽc], *s.* niara, almiar; hacina de heno.

Haytian [jéitian o jáitian], *a.* haitiano.

hazard [jǽšard]. **I.** *s.* azar, albur; peligro, riesgo; juego de azar a los dados; tronera del billar. **II.** *va.* arriesgar, aventurar, exponer. **III.** *vn.* arriesgarse, aventurarse.

hazardous [jǽšardus], *a.* arriesgado, peligroso.— **hazardously** [-li], *adv.* peligrosamente, arriesgadamente.—**hazardousness** [-nes], *s.* riesgo, peligro; lo arriesgado.

haze [jéiš]. **I.** *s.* niebla, bruma; ofuscamiento mental. **II.** *vn.* abrumarse la atmósfera. **III.** *va.* dar culebra (en los colegios); (mar.) fatigar con trabajos pesados.

hazel [jéišl]. **I.** *s.* (bot.) avellano.—**h. grouse**, (orn.) ortega. **II.** *a.* castaño.

hazelnut [-nut], *s.* avellana.

haziness [jéišines], *s.* fosca, calígine.

hazing [jéišing], *s.* culebra, culebrazo, novatada (en los colegios).

hazy [jéiši], *a.* anieblado, brumoso; confuso, vago.

he [ji], *pron. pers.* él. Se emplea también para denotar el macho, vg.: *he-goat*, macho cabrío; *he-bear*, oso (macho).—**he-man**, (fam.) todo un hombre, hombre cabal.—**h. who, h. that**, el que, quien.

head [jed], *s.* cabeza; cima; parte superior o principal; título, encabezamiento; división, sección (de un escrito, etc.); cabecera (de cama, de río); fondo, tapa (de cilindro); (aut., etc.) culata (de cilindro); jefe, caudillo; director; res, cabeza de ganado (en este sentido el *pl.* es como el *sing.*); avance, progreso; crisis; astas de ciervo o venado; punta (de flecha, etc.); (mar.) proa; fuente, nacimiento; (hidr.) carga hidrostática o de presión, diferencia de nivel.—**h. fast**, cabo de retenida de proa.—**h. of an arrow**, punta de un dardo.—**h. of a sail**, gratil.—**h. of cabbage**, etc. repollo de col, etc.—**h. of hair**, cabellos.—**h. on,**

de frente, cabeza con cabeza.—**h. or tail, o heads or tails,** cara o cruz, cara o sello.—**h. over heels,** precipitadamente, temerariamente.—**from h. to foot,** o **to heels,** de pies a cabeza.—**neither h. nor tail,** ni pies ni cabeza.—**off one's h.,** (fam.) destornillado, loco.—**on this h.,** sobre este punto, asunto o particular.—**out of one's h.,** con el conocimiento perdido, delirante.—**over h. and ears,** hasta las orejas.—**over one's h.,** por encima de uno, sin hacer caso de uno; fuera del alcance de uno.—**to bring to a h.,** (med.) madurar; ultimar, traer a un estado o situación decisivos.—**to come to a h.,** llegar a un estado definitivo, culminar; (med.) madurar.

head, *a.* principal; de o para la cabeza; de frente; (mar.) de proa; (hidr.) relativo a la carga hidrostática.—**h. cook,** primer cocinero.— **h. money,** capitación.—**h. post,** pilar o poste de cabecera.—**h. sea,** (mar.) mar o marejada de proa. —**h. timber,** gambota de proa.—**h. tone, h. volce,** voz de cabeza.

head. **I.** *va.* encabezar; mandar, dirigir; interceptar; deterner (gen. con *off*); descabezar, degollar; poner cabeza, puño, cabo; poner título; podar; (con *in*), recortar o mochar (árboles). **II.** *vn.* dirigirse; supurar; repollar, acogollarse; nacer en, salir o provenir de.

headache [jédéík], *s.* dolor de cabeza, cefalalgia.

headband [-bǽnd], *s.* cabezada de libro; venda para cabeza.

headblock [-blóc], *s.* bloque de levante bajo el extremo de un madero, etc.; (f. c.) traviesa de apoyo de las agujas de un cambiavía.

headboard [-bórd], *s.* cabecera de cama.

headcheese [-chís], *s.* queso de cerdo.

headdress [-drés], *s.* cofia, tocado, redecilla o escofieta.

headed [-ed], *a.* que tiene cabeza; titulado.—**h. for,** en dirección a, con rumbo a.

header [-œr], *s.* (ton.) el que pone fondos a las cubas; caída de cabeza o zambullida; golpe en la cabeza; descabezador de las mieses; cabecilla; (arq.) tizón, piedra o ladrillo a tizón; (m. v.) colector, cámara de circulación.

headfirst [-fœrst], **headforemost** [-fóœrmost], *adv.* de cabeza.

headgear [-guíær], *s.* tocado o cofia de mujer; jaez, cabezada; (mar.) aparejo de las velas de proa.

headiness [-ines], *s.* terquedad, obstinación; encabezamiento del vino.

heading [-ing], *s.* título, encabezamiento; membrete; (ton.) témpano, tapa; (min.) galería, socavón; frente; (arq.) paramento o frente de un tizón.—**h. bond,** (arq.) aparejo de tizones.—**h. joint,** (carp.) junta de dos maderos con las fibras en ángulo recto.

headland [-land], *s.* promontorio, punta.

headledge [-ley], *s.* (mar.) contrabrazola.

headless [-les], *a.* descabezado, degollado; acéfalo.

headlight [-láit], *s.* linterna delantera; (mar.) farol de tope.

headline [-láin], *s.* título; epígrafe.

headlong [-long]. **I.** *a.* temerario, arrojado; precipitado; precipitoso. **II.** *adv.* de cabeza; precipitadamente, de sopetón; sin pensarlo; de hoz y de coz.

headmost [-moust], *a.* delantero, de la cabeza.

headpiece [-pís], *s.* morrión, bacinete, casco, yelmo; (impr.) viñeta; (fam.) cholla, mollera.

headquarters [-cuórtœrs], *s.* (mil.) cuartel general; oficina principal; centro de dirección o de operaciones.

headrace [-réis], *s.* acequia, saetín.

headrail [-réil], *s.* (mar.) percha.

headrest [-rést], *s.* apoyo para la cabeza.

headrope [-róup], *s.* relinga de gratil.

headsail [-séil], *s.* (mar.) vela delantera.

headshake [-shéic], *s.* cabezada.

headsman [-sman], *s.* verdugo, degollador.

headspring [-spring], *s.* fuente, origen.

headstall [-stól], *s.* cabezada del freno, testera; (Méx.) bozal.

headstock [-stóc], *s.* portaherramienta (de un torno, de cepilladora); (tej.) bastidor de la carretilla de la despepitadora de algodón.

headstone [-stóun], *s.* lápida mortuoria.

headstrong [-strong], *a.* terco, testarudo, obstinado.—**headstrongness** [-nes], *s.* terquedad, obstinación, testarudez.

headtire [-táiœr], *s.* escofieta.

headwaters [-uótœrs], *s.* cabeceras.

headway [-uéi], *s.* marcha de un buque; avance, ímpetu; progreso; (f. c.) intervalo o distancia entre dos trenes.

headwork [-uœrc], *s.* trabajo mental; obra intelectual; (arq.) cabeza de adorno en una clave.

heady [jédi], *a.* temerario, arrojado; fuerte, encabezado (vino); violento, impetuoso.

heal [jíl]. **I.** *va.* curar; remediar; reconciliar, componer. **II.** *vn.* sanar; recobrar la salud.— **to h. up,** cicatrizarse.

healable [jílabœl], *a.* curable, sanable.

heald [jíld], *s.* (tej.) lizo.

healer [jílœr], *s.* sanador; curador.

healing [jíling]. **I.** *s.* sanativo, curativo. **II.** *s.* cura, curación.

health [jelz], *s.* salud; sanidad.—**h. guard, h. officer,** oficial de sanidad o de cuarentena.—**h. lift,** máquina de alzar pesos como ejercicio.—**h. giving,** salubre, saludable.—**h. resort,** lugar de curas, colonia de enfermos.—**your h.!** ¡a su salud!

healthful [jélzful], *a.* sano, saludable.

healthfully [-i], *adv.* saludablemente.

healthfulness [-nes], *s.* salubridad, calidad de saludable.

healthily [jézili], *adv.* saludablemente.

healthiness [jélzines], *s.* sanidad, estado sano, goce de buena salud.

healthless [jélzles], *s.* enfermizo, sin salud.

healthy [jélz], *a.* sano; fuerte, de buena salud; saludable.

heap [jíp]. **I.** *s.* montón; multitud, gentío.— **in heaps,** a montones. **II.** *va.* amontonar, apilar, acumular; colmar, llenar completamente.

heaping [-ing], *a.* llenado con exceso o hasta que se desborde.

hear [jíœr]. **I.** *va.* (pret. y pp. HEARD) oír; oír decir; saber, tener noticia de; dar audiencia; otorgar, conceder.—**to h. it said,** oír decir. **II.** *vn.* oír.—**to h. from,** saber de (directamente, como por carta).—**to h. of,** saber de (de oídas); tener noticia de.

heard [jœrd], *pret.* y *pp.* de TO HEAR.

hearer [jíœrœr], *s.* oyente.

hearing [jíœring], *s.* oído; audiencia; (for.) examen de testigos; acción de oír; alcance del oído.—**within h.,** al alcance del oído.

hearken [járkœn], *vn.* = HARKEN.

hearsay [jíœrséi], *s.* rumor, voz común, fama.— **by h.,** de oídas.

hearse [jœrs]. **I.** *s.* carro fúnebre; ataúd, féretro. **II.** *va.* colocar en un ataúd.

hearsecloth [jœrscloz], *s.* palio, paño mortuorio.

hearselike [-laic], *a.* lúgubre, fúnebre.

heart [jart], *s.* corazón; ánimo; figura de corazón en los naipes, que equivale a la copa de los naipes españoles. (En lo que sigue se usa *c.* en vez de *corazón*).—**h. alive!** ¡Ave María! ¡caramba! —**h. and soul,** en cuerpo y alma.—**h. block,** retardación rítmica de los latidos del c.—**h. consuming, h. corroding,** que consume o corroe el c.—**h. disease,** enfermedad del c.—**h. rending,** agudo, desgarrador, que parte el c.—**h. shaped,** corazonado, en forma de c.—**h. to h.,** sincero, franco.—**h. trouble,** enfermedad del c.—**h. whole,** desamorado; valiente, intrépido; sincero. —**h. wounded,** herido en el alma.—**h. worn,** agobiado.—**after one's own h.,** de todo el gusto de uno, que armoniza en todo con las ideas de uno. —**at h.,** en el fondo, esencialmente; en verdad.— **by h.,** de memoria.—**from one's h.,** de todo c., con sinceridad.—**out of h.,** descorazonado; en mal estado.—**to have the h. in the mouth,** estar muerto de miedo.—**with all one's h.,** con todo el c., de todo c.

heart. *va.* = HEARTEN.

heartache [jártéik], *s.* angustia, congoja, pesar.

heartbeat [-bít], *s.* latido del corazón; profunda emoción.

heartbreak [-bréic], *s.* angustia, pesar, dolor.

heartbreaking [-bréiking], *a.* congojoso, doloroso.

heartbroken [-bróukn], *a.* acongojado, transido de dolor, muerto (fig.) de pesar.—**heartbroken·y** (-ll), *adv.* con el corazón partido, dolorosísimamente.

heartburn [-bœrn], *s.* acedía.—**heartburning** [-ing]. **I.** *s.* acedía; rencilla, animosidad. **II.** *a.* intenso, profundo, sentido.

hearted [-ed], *a.* que tiene corazón.

hearten [-œn], *va.* animar, alentar; (agr.) abonar.

heartfelt [-félt], *a.* cordial, sincero; sentido.

heartgrief [-gríf], *s.* congoja, angustia.

hearth [jarz], *s.* hogar, fogón, chimenea; hogar doméstico.—**h. money,** fogaje, tributo antiguo.

heartily [jártili], *adv.* sinceramente, cordialmente.

heartiness [-nes], *s.* cordialidad, sinceridad.

heartless [tles], *a.* sin corazón; empedernido, cruel; tímido, pusilánime.—**heartlessly** [-li], *adv.* cruelmente, sin piedad; pusilánimemente, tímidamente.—**heartlessness** [-nes], *s.* falta de corazón; falta de ánimo; empedernimiento.

heartsease [jártsiŝ], *s.* (bot.) trinitaria, pensamiento.

heartsick [-síc], *a.* dolorido; desconsolado.

heartsore [-sóœr], *a.* afligido, acongojado.

heartstricken [-stríken], *a.* afligido, angustiado.

heartstrings [-stríngs], *a.* fibras del corazón.

heartstruck [-strúc], *a.* fijo en el corazón; afligido.

heartwood [-úd], *s.* madera de corazón.

hearty [járti], *a.* cordial, sentido, sincero; sano, robusto, vigoroso; voraz; gustoso, grato.

heat [jít]. **I.** *s.* calor; acaloramiento, ardor, vehemencia; celo de los animales; (fund.) carga de un horno, hornada; colada; (dcp.) carrera o corrida de uno o varios caballos.—**h. engine,** máquina térmica.—**h. lightning,** fucilazos, relámpagos sin trueno.—**h. stroke,** insolación.—**h. unit,** unidad térmica.—**in h.,** en celo, salida (perra, gata, etc.). **II.** *va.* calentar, caldear; acalorar; excitar. **III.** *vn.* fermentar, hervir; calentarse; acalorarse.

heater [jítœr], *s.* calentador; calorífero; aparato de calefacción.

heath [jiz], *s.* (bot.) brezo; brezal, matorral.—**h. cock,** (orn.) gallo silvestre.

heathen [jíðœn], *s.* gentil, pagano.—**heathen·ish** [-iŝh], *a.* gentílico, pagano.—**heathenism** [-iŝm], *s.* gentilismo, paganismo.—**heathenize** [-aiŝ], *va.* hacer pagano.

heather [jéðœr], *s.* (bot.) brezo, bermejuela.

heathery [jéðœri], **heathy** [jíŝi], *a.* cubierto de brezos, matoso.

heating [jíting]. **I.** *s.* calefacción; calda. **II.** *a.* caluroso; calefaciente; de calefacción (superficie, área, etc.).—**h. power,** potencia calorífica.

heatless [jítles], *a.* frío, sin calor.

heave [jív]. **I.** *va.* (pret. y *pp.* HEAVED) alzar, levantar, elevar; (mar.) izar; virar; lanzar, echar fuera, arrojar; exhalar, prorrumpir.—**to h. overboard,** echar al agua.—**to h. the lead,** escandallar.—**to h. a sigh,** exhalar un suspiro. **II.** *vi.* levantarse y bajarse alternativamente, v. gr., el pecho, el mar; suspirar hondo; palpitar; jadear trabajar penosamente; tener náuseas; (mar.) virar.—**to h. to,** ponerse al pairo o en facha. **III.** *s.* elevación; alzadura, levantamiento; henchidura de una ola; náusea, arcada; (geol.) falla.—**h. offering,** sacrificio de los judíos.

heaven [jevn], *s.* cielo; firmamento.—**h.-born,** celeste, divino, angelical.—**h.-kissing,** que llega hasta el cielo.

heavenliness [jévnlines], *s.* calidad de celestial.

heavenly [-li]. **I.** *a.* celeste; celestial. **II.** *adv.* celestialmente.

heavenward [-uard], *adv.* hacia el cielo.

heaver [jívœr], *s.* (mar.) alzaprima; cargador.

heaves [jivs], *s. pl.* (vet.) huérfago.

heavily [jévili], *adv.* pesadamente, lentamente; tristemente; excesivamente, sumamente.

heaviness [jévines], *s.* pesantez, peso; tardanza, torpeza; languidez, modorra; abatimiento o tristeza; opresión, carga.

heaving [jíving], *s.* palpitación; oleada.—**h. line,** estacha, calabrote.

heavy [jévi]. **I.** *a.* pesado; grueso; fuerte; duro, riguroso; opresivo; molesto; denso, espeso; oneroso, gravoso; cargado, recargado; difícil; pesaroso, triste; considerable, importante; tardo, lento, estúpido; indigesto.—**h. rain,** o **shower,** lluvia fuerte, turbión, aguacero. **II.** *adv.* HEAVILY. —**h.-armed,** armado de armas o armadura pesadas.—**h.-hearted,** triste, abatido.—**h.-laden,** recargado; agobiado, oprimido.

heavyweight [-wéit], *s.* boxeador de primer peso o de peso mayor.

hebdomad [jébdomœd], *s.* hebdómada.

hebdomadal [jebdómadal], **hebdomadary** [jebdómadœri], *a.* hebdomadario, semanal.

hebetation [jebetéiŝhun], **hebetude** [jébetiud], *s.* estupidez, entorpecimiento.

Hebraic [jebréic], *a.* hebreo, hebraico.

Hebraism [j.braiŝm], *s.* hebraísmo.

Hebraist [jibraist], *s.* hebraísta.

Hebraise [jíbraaiŝ]. **I.** *va.* hebraizar, hacer hebreo. **II.** *vn.* volverse hebreo.

Hebrew [jíbru], *s.* y *a.* hebreo.

Hecate [jécœti], *s.* (mit.) Hécate.

hecatomb [jécatom], *s.* hecatombe.

heck [jec], *s.* enrejado, verja.

heckle [jéccœl], *va.* interrumpir con preguntas irrisorias y sátiras.

hectare [jéctœær], *s.* hectárea.

hectic(al [jéctic(al], *a.* hético; agitado, turbulento.—**hectic,** *s.* tisis; fiebre hética; tísico.

hecto [jécto], *prefijo* que significa ciento.—**hectogram, hectogramme** [-grœm], *s.* hectogramo.—**hectoliter, hectolitre** [-lítœr], *s.* hectólitro.—**hectometer, hectometre** [-mítœr], *s.* hectómetro.—**hectograph,** hectógrafo.

hector [jéctœr]. **I.** *s.* matasiete, matón, fanfarrón. **II.** *vn.* baladronear, bravear. **III.** *va.* amenazar, intimidar con bravatas.

heddle [jédœl], *s.* malla, lizos de un telar.

hedge [jeɟ]. **I.** *s.* seto, vallado de zarzas.—**h. creeper,** vagamundo.—**h. hyssop,** (bot.) graciola.—**h. mustard,** (bot.) jaramago, aliaria.—**h.-note,** escrito mal pergeñado.—**h. parson, h. priest,** clérigo ambulante inculto.—**h. sparrow,** (orn.) curruca.—**h. school,** escuela al aire libre. **II.** *va.* cercar con seto, vallar; defender, circundar; rodear. **III.** *vn.* ponerse al abrigo; cubrirse; compensar o igualar una apuesta o jugada de bolsa con otra en sentido contrario.

hedgeborn [jéyborn], *a.* de baja ralea.

hedgehog [-jog], **hedgepig** [-pig], *s.* (zool.) erizo.

hedger [jeɟœr], *s.* el que hace setos; el que compensa o iguala sus apuestas.

hedgerow [jéyro], *s.* seto vivo.

hedging bill [jéying bil], *s.* podadera de setos.

hedonics [jedónics], *s.* ciencia del placer; parte de la ética que estudia el placer en su aspecto moral.

hedonism [jédoniŝm], *s.* hedonismo.—**hedonist** [-st], *s.* hedonista.

hedonol [jédonol], *s.* (quím., farm.) hedonal, polvo ligeramente hipnótico.

heed [jid]. **I.** *va.* atender, escuchar; observar, tener en cuenta. **II.** *vn.* prestar atención, hacer caso. **III.** *s.* cuidado, atención.

heedful [jídful], *a.* atento, cuidadoso.—**heedfully** [-li], *adv.* atentamente, cuidadosamente.—**heedfulness** [-nes], *s.* cautela, atención, cuidado.

heedless [jídles], *a.* desatento, descuidado; atolondrado, incauto.—**heedlessly** [-li], *adv.* incautamente, descuidadamente.—**heedlessness** [-nes], *s.* descuido, negligencia, imprudencia.

heel [jil]. **I.** *s.* (mat.) talón o calcañal; (zap.) tacón; talón de una media; pie, parte inferior; (mar.) coz o pie de palo; (agr.) estaca, pie; (t. c.) talón (de una aguja).—**h. blank, o lift,** (zap.) tapa.—**heels over head,** patas arriba; precipitadamente a tontas.—**down at the heels,** desvalido, en aprietos; desaliñado.—**to be at the**

heels of, perseguir estrechamente; seguir servilmente. **II.** *a.* poner talón a (zapatos o medias); asir, agarrar por los talones; poner espolones al gallo; (fam.) proveer de dinero.—**to h. in,** plantar estacas o pies; cubrir provisionalmen con tierra las raíces. **III.** *vn.* (mar.) tumbarse o escorar.

heeler [jílœr], *s.* gallo que clava los espolones; (fam.) paniaguado de un cacique político; (zap.) taconero; andarín.

heelpiece [jílpís], *s.* talón.

heft [jcft]. **I.** *s.* mango, asa, cabo; (fam.) peso, pesadez; (fam.) la mayor parte. **II.** *va.* (fam.) sompesar. **III.** *vn.* (fam.) pesar.

Hegelian [jegué- (*o* jeguí) lian], *a.* hegeliano.

Hegelianism [-ĭsm], *s.* hegelianismo.

hegemony [jíye- (*o* jégue) moni], *s.* hegemonía.

hegira [jéyira *o* jeyáira], *s.* hégira.

heifer [jéfœr], *s.* vaquilla, novilla.—**h. calf,** ternera.

heigh-ho [jái-jo], *interj.* ¡ay! ¡oh!

height [jáit], *s.* altura; colmo.—**h. gage, o h. gauge,** calibre de alturas.—**the h. of folly,** el colmo de la locura.

heighten, highten [jáitœn], *va.* realzar, levantar, elevar; mejorar; adelantar, ascender; sublimar, exaltar; avivar.

heinous [jéinᴜs], *a.* atroz, nefando, horrible.—**heinously** [-oi], *adv.* atrozmente, horriblemente.—**heinousness** [-nes], *s.* atrocidad, perversidad.

heir [éœr], *s.* heredero.—**h. apparent,** heredero forzoso.—**h. at law,** heredero legal.—**h. presumptive,** presunto heredero.

heirdom [éœrdᴜm], **heirship** [-ship], *s.* herencia, derecho de heredar.—**heiress** [-es], *s.* heredera.—**heirless** [-les], *a.* sin heredero.—**heirloom** [-lum], *s.* bienes muebles heredados; herencia; atavismo.

heliac(al [jcláiac(al], *a.* (astr.) helíaco.

helical [jélical], *a* espiral, helicoidal

Helianthemum [jeliǽnzemᴜm], *s.* (bot.) heliantemo.

helicoid [jélicoid]. **I.** *a.* helicoidal. **II.** *s.* (geom.) helicoide.

Helicon [jélicon], *s.* Helicón, Parnaso.

heliocentric(al [jílioséntric, al], *a.* heliocéntrico.

heliochrome [jíliocroum], *s.* heliocromía, fotografía con colores naturales.

heliochromy [jilióchromi], *s.* fotocromía.

heliograph [jíliográf]. **I.** *s.* heliógrafo; helióstato. **II.** *va.* hacer señales con el heliógrafo o el helióstato.

heliographic [jíliográfic], *a.* heliográfico.

heliography [jiliógrafi], *s.* transmisión de señales por medio del heliógrafo; descripción de la superficie del sol.

heliogravure [jíliogræviúœr], *s.* heliograbado.

heliolatry [jiliólatri], *s.* culto del sol.

heliometer [jiliómetœr], *s.* heliómetro.

helioscope [jílioscoup], *s.* helioscopio.

heliostat [jíliostæt], *s.* helióstato.

heliotrope [jíliotroup], *s.* (bot.) heliotropo; olor o color de esta flor; (fís.) heliógrafo; (min.) heliotropo, ágata verdosa.

heliotype [jíliotaip]. **I.** *s.* heliotipo, heliograbado. **II.** *va.* reproducir por medio del heliotipo. **III.** *vn.* imprimir un heliotipo.

heliotypy [jíliotaipi], *s.* procedimiento del heliograbado o heliotipo.

helium [jílium], *s.* (quím.) helio.

helix [jílix], *s.* hélice; (anat.) hélix, reborde del pabellón de la oreja; caracol de tierra.

hell [jel], *s.* infierno; garito; desván; (impr.) caja de letras inscribles.—**h.-cat,** bruja.—**h.-doomed,** réprobo.—**h.-fire,** fuego o tormento del infierno.—**h.-gate,** puerta del infierno.

hellborn [jélbórn], *a.* infernal.

hellbox [-bóx], *s.* (imp., fam.) caja de tipo roto o inservible.

hellbroth [-broz], *s.* caldo alterado, caldo mágico maligno.

hellebore [jéleᴮor], *s.* (bot.) eléboro, veratro, verdegambre.

Hellenic [jelénic], *a.* heleno.

Hellenism [jéleniŝm], helenismo.—**Hellenist** [-ist], *s.* helenista.—**Hellenistic** [-istic], *a.* helenístico.—**Hellenistically** [-ísticali], *adv.* a la manera de los griegos.—**Hellenize** [-aiŝ], *vn.* grecizar.

hellgrammite [jélgramait], *s.* (ento.) larva que se emplea como carnada en la pesca.

hellhound [jéljáund], *s.* Cancerbero; perseguidor cruel.

hellish [jéliŝh], *a.* infernal.—**hellishly** [-li], *adv.* infernal o diabólicamente.—**hellishness** [-nes], *s.* malicia infernal, diablura.

hello [jéló], *interj.* = HALLO.

hellward [jéluard], *adv.* hacia el infierno.

helm [jelm], *s.* (mar.) timón, gobernalle; (ant.) yelmo, capacete.

helmet [jélmet], *s.* yelmo, celada, casco.—**h. flower,** (bot.) acónito, matalobos.

helmeted [jélmeted], *a.* que lleva yelmo.

helminth [jélminz], *s.* lombriz, helminto.

helminthic [jelmínzic], *a.* helminto; vermífugo.

helminthology [jélminzóloyi], *s.* helmintología.

helmless [jélmes], *a.* sin timón.

helmsman [jélmŝman], *s.* timonero, timonel.

helot [jélot], *s.* ilota.—**helotism** [-iŝm], *s.* ilotismo.—**helotry** [jélotri], *s.* la clase ilota; servidumbre, esclavitud.

help [jelp]. **I.** *va.* ayudar, asistir; servir o servirse (comida); aliviar; remediar, reparar; evitar; dejar de hacer.—**to h. down,** ayudar a alguno a bajar.—**to h. forward,** adelantar, activar, promover.—**to h. on,** ayudar.—**to h. one's self to,** servirse (carne, sopa, etc.)—**to h. one to,** servir a uno (carne, sopa, etc.); proporcionar.—**to h. out,** ayudar; ayudar a salir; sacar de algún peligro o mal pasao.—**to h. over,** ayudar a salir de (una dificultad, etc.).—**to h. up,** ayudar (a una persona) a levantarse.—**cannot h.** (seguido de gerundio), no puedo (puede, pueden, etc.) dejar de, menos de (seguido de infinitivo) (*I cannot help believing it,* no puedo menos de creerlo; *he could not help doing it,* él no pudo dejar de, o menos de, hacerlo).—**so h. me God,** así Dios me salve. **II.** *vn.* ayudar; contribuir; servir (en la mesa).—**to h. out,** ayudar. **III.** *s.* ayuda; remedio; criados, sirvientes; empleados, dependientes; trabajadores.—**by the h. of,** con ayuda de.—**there is no h. for it,** eso no tiene remedio.

helper [jélpœr], *s.* auxiliador, ayudador; asistente, ayudante.

helpful [jélpful], *a.* útil, servicial; provechoso; saludable.—**helpfulness** [-lnes], *s.* calidad de provechoso, servicial, etc.; utilidad.

helpless [jélples], *a.* desvalido; imposibilitado, impotente; inútil; irremediable.—**helplessly** [-li], *adv.* irremediablemente o desamparadamente.

helplessness [-nes], *s.* desamparo; impotencia.

helpmate [jélpmeit], *s.* compañero; asistente, ayudante.

helter-skelter [jéltœr-skéltœr], *adv.* a trochemoche, sin orden ni concierto.

helve [jelv]. **I.** *s.* ástil de hacha o de destral; mango. **II.** *vn.* poner mango o cabo a.

Helvetian [jelvéŝhan], **Helvetic** [jelvétic], *a.* helvético, helvecio.

hem [jem]. **I.** *s.* (cost.) dobladillo, bastilla, repulgo. **II.** *interj.* ¡ejem! **III.** *va.* (cost.) dobladillar, bastillar, repulgar; (gen. con *in*), rodear, encerrar. **IV.** *vn.* tartamudear; fingir tos, toser de fingido.

hemal [jímal], *a.* perteneciente a la sangre; relativo al lado del cuerpo que contiene el corazón.

hematemesis [jémætémesis], *s.* hematemesis, vómito de sangre.

hematic [jemétic], *a.* hemático, de la sangre, que afecta la sangre.

hematin [jématin], *s.* (quím.) hematina.

hematite [jématait], *s.* (min.) hematites.

hematoblast [jémætoblæst], *s.* hematoblasto.

hematocele [jémætosíl], *s.* hematocele, tumor sanguíneo.

hematogenesis [-yénesis], *s.* hematogénesis, formación de sangre.

hematoid [-toid], *a.* hematoideo, de sangre o semejante a la sangre.

hematology [-tóloyi], s. hematología.

hematoma [-tómæ], s. hematoma, tumor sanguíneo.

hematose [jématous], a. lleno o recargado de sangre; sanguíneo.

hematosis [jématósis], s. hematosis.

hematoxylin [-tóxilin], s. hematoxilina, principio colorante del palo de Campeche.

hematuria [-turiæ], s. (med.) hematuria, orina con sangre.

hemi [jémi], a. prefijo que equivale a medio o semi.

hemialgia [-ǽlyiæ], s. hemialgia, dolor en un solo lado, esp. de la cabeza (llám. entonces t. **hemicrania**).

hemic [jémic], a. hémico, de la sangre, relativo a la sangre.

hemicrania, hemicrany [-créinia, creni], s. hemicránea.

hemicycle [-sálcœl], s. hemiciclo.

hemihedral [-jídral], (min.) hemiédrico.—**hemihedron** [-jídron], s. hemiedro.

hemiplegia, hemiplegy [-plíyia, -plíyi], s. hemiplejía.—**hemiplegic** [-yic], a. hemipléjico.

hemipterous [jemípterʊs], a. (ento.) hemíptero.

hemisphere [jémisfiær], s. hemisferio.

hemispheric(al [-sféric(al], a. hemisférico.

hemistich [jémistic], s. hemistiquio.

hemitropism [-tropism], **hemitropy** [jemítropi], (min.) hemitropía.

hemlock [jémloc], s. (bot.) pinabete o abeto, pícea; (bot.) cicuta.—**h. spruce**, (bot.) abeto del Canadá.

hemoglobin [jémoglóbin], s. hemoglobina.

hemorrhage [jémorey], s. hemorragia.

hemorrhoids [jémoroidš], s. pl. hemorroides, almorranas.

hemorrhoidal [-róidal], a. hemorroidal.

hemostatic [jémostátic], a. hemostático.

hemp [jemp], s. (bot.) cáñamo.—**h. beater**, espadador o espadillador.—**h. breaker**, agramador.—**h. close**, o **h. field**, cañamar.—**h. comb**, rastrillo.—**h. dresser**, batidor.

hempen [jémpœn], a. cañameño.

hempseed [jémpsid], s. cañamón.—(fam.) villano, malhechor.

hemstitch [jémstich]. I. va. (cost.) hacer una vainica en. II. s. (cost.) vainica.

hempy [jémpi], a. cañameño.

hen [jen], s. gallina; hembra de cualquier ave. Se usa adjetivalmente en el sentido de hembra.—(hen canary, canario hembra).—**h. dung**, gallinaza.

henbane [jénbein], s. (bot.) beleño.

hence [jens], adv. de aquí; de aquí a (two months hence, de aquí a dos meses); desde aquí; fuera de aquí; por tanto, por esto, en consecuencia; de esto.

henceforth [jénsforz], adv. de aquí en adelante, en adelante, en lo futuro.

henceforward [-fóruard], adv. de aquí en adelante; en lo venidero.

henchman [jénchman], s. hechura, paniaguado, secuaz servil.

hencoop [jéncúp], s. gallinero.

hendecasyllable [jéndecasílabœl], s. endecasílabo.

henhouse [jénjáus], s. = HENCOOP.

henna [jéna], s. (bot.) alheña.

hennery [jéneri], s. gallinero.

henotheism [jénoziišm], s. henoteísmo, creencia en el poder alternativo de varios dioses, o en el poder de dioses regionales.

henpeck [jénpéc], va. dominar e importunar la mujer al marido.—**henpecked** [jénpect], a. gurrumino.—**h. husband**, marido cuya mujer lleva los calzones, gurrumino.

henroost [jénrúst], s. = HENCOOP.

henry [jénri], s. (elec.) henrio.

hep [jep], s. fruto del agavanzo.—**h. bramble**, o **brier**, escaramujo, agavanzo.

hepatic(al [jepǽtic(al], a. hepático.

hepatica [jepǽtica], s. (bot.) hepática.

hepatite [jépatait], s. (min.) hepatita.

hepatitis [jépætáitis], s. hepatitis, inflamación del hígado.

hepatization [-tiśéíšhʊn], s. hepatización.

heptachord [jéptacord], s. heptacordo.

heptad [jéptad], s. setena.

heptagon [jéptagon], s. heptágono.

heptane [jéptein], s. (quím.) heptano.

heptarchy [jéptarki], s. heptarquía.

Heptateuch [jéptatiuc], s. Heptateuco.

her [jœr], pron. (caso objetivo o acusativo de SHE) la, le, ella, a ella: I saw her, la ví: I told her, le dije: this is for her, esto es para ella; (caso posesivo o genitivo de SHE, y adjetivo posesivo) su, de ella: her book, her house, su libro, su casa (de ella).

herald [jérald], s. heraldo, rey de armas; precursor; publicador.

heraldic [jeráldic], a. heráldico, genealógico.

heraldry [jéraldri], s. heráldica, blasón.

heraldship [jéraldship], s. oficio de heraldo.

herb [jœrb], s. hierba, yerba.

herbaceous [jœrbéšhʊs], a. herbáceo.

herbage [jœrbey o œrbey], s. hierba, nerbaje; pasto.

herbal [jœrbal], a. herbario.—**herbalism** [-išm], s. conocimiento de las hierbas.—**herbalist** [-ist], s. botánico herbario.

herbarium [jœrbérium], s. herbario seco.

herbarize [jœrbaraiš], vn. herborizar.

herbary [jœrbari], s. jardín de hierbas.

herbescent [jœrbésent], a. herbáceo.

herbiferous [jœrbíferʊs], a. herbífero.

Herbivora [jerbívoræ], s. pl. herbívoros.

herbivore [jérbivor], s. herbívoro.

herbivorous [jœrbívorʊs], a. herbívoro.

herbless [jœrbles], s. sin hierbas, yermo.

herborization [jœrborišéíšhʊn], s. herborización.

herborize [jœrboraiš], vn. herborizar.

herborizer [jœrboraišœr], herborizador.

herbose [jœrbos], **herbous** [jœrbʊs] o **herby** [jœrbi], a. herboso, herbáceo.

herbwoman [jœrbúman], s. herbolaria; verdulera.

herculean [jœrkiúlian], a. herculéo.

herd [jœrd]. I. s. hato, grey, rebaño; piara; multitud, chusma; manadero, vaquerizo. II. vn. ir en manadas o hatos; asociarse. III. va. reunir el ganado en hatos o rebaños.

herdsman [jérdšman], s. pastor, vaquerizo, manadero.

here [jíær], adv. aquí; acá; por aquí; ahora, en este momento, en este punto.—**h. I am, he is**, etc., aquí estoy, está, etc., o heme aquí, helo aquí, etc.—**h. is to you, him**, etc., a la salud de Vd., él, etc.—**that is neither h. nor there**, eso no viene al caso.

hereabouts [jíærabáuts], adv. por aquí, en estas cercanías, por aquí cerca.

hereafter [jíæráftœr]. I. adv. en adelante, en lo futuro. II. s. estado futuro.

hereat [jíæréet], adv. a esto, en esto, por eso.

hereby [jíærbái], adv. por éstas, por la presente, por este medio.

hereditable [jíærédabœl], a. que puede ser heredado.—**hereditament** [-tamœnt], s. (for.) todo lo que puede heredarse.—**hereditarily** [-teríli], adv. por herencia, hereditariamente.—**hereditary** [jéréditery], a. hereditario.

heredity [jéréditi], s. (biol.) herencia.

herefrom [jíærfróm], adv. de aquí, desde aquí; a causa de esto.

herein [jíærín], **hereinto** [jíæríntu], adv. aquí dentro; incluso.

hereinafter [jíærinǽftœr], adv. después, más abajo, más adelante.

hereof [jíæróv], adv. de ésto, de eso, acerca de esto, de aquí.

hereon [jíærón], adv. sobre esto, sobre este punto.

heresiarch [jéresiarc o jerísiarc], s. heresiarca.

heresy [jéresi], s. herejía.
heretic [jéretic], s. hereje.—**heretic(al** [jerétic-(al], a. herético.—**heretically** [-li], adv. herética-mente.
hereto [jíærtú], adv. a esto, a este fin.
heretofore [jíærtufór]. **I.** adv. en otro tiempo, antes, en tiempos pasados; hasta aquí, hasta ahora. **II.** s. el tiempo pasado, antaño.
hereunder [jíærúndœr], adv. bajo esto, en virtud de esto.
hereunto [jíæruntú], adv. a esto, a eso.
hereupon [jíærupón], adv. a esto; sobre esto.
herewith [jíæruiz], adv. con esto, junto con esto, adjunto.
heritable [jéritabœl], a. que se puede heredar.
heritage [jéritey], s. herencia.
hermaphrodite [jœrmǽfrodait]. **I.** a. (zool. y bot.) hermafrodita. **II.** s. hermafrodito o her-mafrodita, andrógino; (mar.) bergantín, goleta.
hermaphroditic(al [-dític(al], a. hermafrodita.
hermaphroditism, hermaphrodism [-dai-tiŝm], s. hermafroditismo.
hermeneutic(al [jœrmeniútic(al], a. hermenéu-tico.
hermeneutics [-tics], s. hermenéutica.
hermes [jœrmiŝ], s. herma.
hermetic(al [jœrmétic(al], a. hermético.—**the h. art,** alquimia.
hermetically [-li], adv. herméticamente.
hermit [jœrmit], s. ermitaño.—**h. crab,** (zool.) ermitaño, crustáceo que se aloja en conchas de moluscos.
hermitage [jœrmitey], s. ermita.
hermites [jœrmites], s. ermitaña.
hermitical [jœrmítical], a. eremítico.
hern, s. = HERON.
hernia [jœrnia], s. hernia.
hernial [jœrnial], a. herniario.
hernshaw [jœrnŝho], s. (orn.) garza.
hero [jíro], s. héroe; protagonista.—**h. worship,** culto extremado de los héroes.
Herodian [jeródian], s. herodiano.
heroic(al [jeróic(al], a. heroico, épico; grande, sublime; valeroso, magnánimo.—**heroically** [-li], adv. heroicamente.—**heroicalness** [-nes], s. heroi-cidad.
heroics [jeróics], s. pl. rimbombancia, ampulo-sidad.
heroin [jéroin], s. (quím.) heroína, uno de los derivados acetílicos de la morfina.
heroine [jéroin], s. heroína.
heroism [jéroiŝm], s. heroísmo.
heron [jéron], s. (orn.) ardeida; garzota —**h.'s-bill,** (bot.) pico de garza.
herony [jéronii], s. lugar en que se crían las garzas o garzotas.
herpes [jœrpiŝ], s. (med.) herpes.
herpetic [jœrpétic], a. herpético.
herpetism [jœrpetism], s. herpetismo.
herpetology [jœrpetóloyi], s. (zool.) herpetología, estudio de los reptiles.
herring [jéring], s. arenque.
hers [jœrŝ], pron. pos. f. suyo, suya, de ella; el suyo, la suya, los suyos, las suyas (de ella).
herse [jœrs], s. (fort.) rastrillo; caballo de frisia; enrejado.
herself [jœrsélf], pron. ella misma, ella, sí, sí misma. V. HIMSELF.
hesitancy [jés- o jésitansi], s. irresolución, vacila-ción.—**hesitant** [-ant], a. vacilante, indeciso.—**hesitate** [-eit], vn. vacilar, titubear; balbucear, tartamudear.—**hesitation** [-éiŝun], s. irresolu-ción, titubeo, vacilación; balbucencia.
Hesper [jéspœr], s. Héspero, estrella vespertina.
Hesperian [jespírian]. **I.** a. hespérido; occiden-tal. **II.** s. habitante de un país occidental.
Hessian [jésiæn], s. y a. hessiano, de Hesse; (fam.) mercenario, venal; (s.) arpillera.—**H. crucible,** crisol de arcilla refractaria.—**H. fly,** nombre de una mosca muy nociva al trigo.
hetæra [jitíræ], **hetaira** [-táiræ], s. hetera, es-pecie de cortesana griega.

heterochromous [jéterocróumus], a. (bot.) heteócromo.
heteroclite [-clait], s. y a. heteróclito, irregular.
heterodox [-dox], a. heterodoxo.
heterodoxy [-docsi], s. heterodoxia.
heterodyne [-dain], a. (rad.) heterodina.
heterogamous [jétœrógamus], a. (bot.) heteró-gamo.—**heterogamy** [-mi], s. heterogamia.
heterogeneity [jétœroyeníiti], **heterogeneous-ness** [jétœroyíniusnes], s. heterogeneidad.
heterogeneous [jétœroyíniuŝ], a. heterogéneo.
heterogenesis [-yénesis], s. generación espon-tánea; heterogenia, producción de una especie por otra.
heteromorphic, heteromorphous [-mórfic, -us], a. heteromorfo.
heteronym [-nim], s. palabra que tiene la misma ortografía¡que otra, pero sonido y sentido dife-rentes, v. gr.: lead [lid], guiar, y lead [led], plomo.
heteroplasty [-plásti], s. heteroplastia.
Heteroptera [jéterópteræ], s. pl. (zool.) heteróp-teros.
heteroscians [jéteróŝhans], a. y s. pl. heteroscios.
heterosexual [jéterosécŝhuæl], a. heterosexual—**heterosexuality** [-éliti], s. heterosexualidad.
heterostatic [-stætic], a. (elec.) heterostático.
hetman [jétmæn], s. atamán.
heuristic [jiurístic], a. heurístico, que ayuda al descubrimiento o interpretación de hechos y verdades.
hew [jiú]. **I.** va. (pret. HEWED: pp. HEWN y HEWED) tajar, cortar, picar; hachear, des-bastar; trabajar una cosa.—**to h. a stone,** picar o labrar (una piedra).—**to h. in pieces,** destrozar, destroncar.—**to h. out,** hachear, cortar; modelar en bruto; abrir paso. **II.** vn. golpear.—**to h. right and left,** acuchillar a diestra y siniestra.
hewer [jiúœr], s. cantero; picapedrero; desbas-tador.
hexachord [jéxacord], s. (mús.) hexacordo.
hexagon [jéxagon], s. hexágono, exágono.
hexagonal [jexǽgonal], a. hexagonal, exagonal.
hexahedron [jexajídron], s. hexaedro.
hexameter [jexémetœr], s. hexámetro.
hexametric(al [jexamétric(al], a. hexámetro.
hexangular [jexéngular], a. hexángulo.
hexapod [jéxapod], a. y s. (ento.) hexápodo.
hexastyle [jéxastail], s. (arq.) hexástilo.
Hexateuc [jéxætiuc], s. Hexateuco, los seis prime-ros libros del Antiguo Testamento.
hexavalent [jéxævéilent], a. (quím.) hexavalente.
hey [je], interj. ¡he! ¡eh!
heyday [jéde]. **I.** s. colmo, apogeo de vitalidad y vigor. **II.** interj. ¡hola!
hiatus [jaiétus], s. laguna, vacío, solución de con-tinuidad; hiato, cacofonía.
hibernal [jaibœrnal], a. invernizo, invernal.
hibernate [jáibœrneit], vn. invernar; estar re-tirado e inactivo, vegetar.
hibernation [jáibœrnéiŝhun], s. invernada.
Hibernian [jaibœrnian], s. irlandés, hibernés.
Hibernianism, Hibernicism [jaibœrnianiŝm, nisiŝm], s. idiotismo irlandés.
hibiscus [jaibíscus, hibíscus], s. hibisco.
hiccough, hiccup, hickup [jícup]. **I.** s. hipo. **II.** vn. hipar, tener hipo.
hickey [jíki], s. encorvador tubular en T.
hickory [jícori], s. (bot.) nogal americano.—**h. nut,** nuez del nogal americano.
hid [jid], pret. y pp. de TO HIDE.
hidden [jidœn], a. y pp. de TO HIDE; oculto, recóndito, escondido, secreto, latente.
hiddenly [-li], adv. escondidamente.
hide [jáid], s. cuero, piel, pellejo.—pl. corambre.
hide. I. va. (pret. HID: pp. HIDDEN o HID) es-conder, ocultar, encubrir; dar latigazos o fue-tazos, cruzar con un vergajo. **II.** vn. escon-derse, ocultarse.
hide and seek [-ænd sic], s. juego del escondite.
hidebound [jáidbaund], a. obstinado, fanático, de ánimo estrecho; (med.) que tiene la piel endurecida.

hideous [jídiυs], *a.* horrible, espantoso.—**hideously** [-li], *adv.* horriblemente.—**hideousness** [-nes], *s.* horribilidad; fealdad, deformidad.

hiding [jáidiŋ], *s.* ocultación, encubrimiento; retiro, retrete: (fam.) zurra, paliza.—**h. place,** escondite.

hie [jái]. **I.** *vn.* darse prisa, apresurarse. **II.** *va.* activar, apresurar; correr, pasar con rapidez.— **h. thee,** date prisa.—**h. thee home,** apresúrate a volver a casa.

hierarch [jáiœrarc], *s.* jerarca, pontífice.—**hierarchal** [-al], **hierarchical** [-kical], *a.* jeráquico.— **hierarchism** [-iŝm], *s.* jerarquía.—**hierarchy** [-i], *s.* jerarquía.

hieratic(al [jáiœrǽtic(al], *a.* hierático, sacerdotal; consagrado.—**h. writing,** escritura hierática.

hieroglyph(ic [jáiœroglíf(íc], *s.* jeroglífico.

hieroglyphic(al [-al], *a.* jeroglífico.

hieroglyphically [-i], *adv.* simbólicamente.

hierologic [jaiœrolóyic], *a.* hierológico.

hierology [jaicróloyi], *o.* hierología.

hieromancy [jáiœromǽnsi], *s.* hieroscopia.

hierophant [jáiœrofant], *s.* hierofante.

hifalutin, *a.* y *s.* = HIGHFALUTIN.

higgle [jigœl], *vn.* regatear, altercar.

higgledy-piggledy [jígœldi-pígœldi], *adv.* (fam.) confusamente.

higgler [jíglœr], *s.* zarracatín.

high [jai], *a.* alto; de alto (con *to be,* que entonces es tener: *this is two inches high,* esto tiene dos pulgadas de alto); encumbrado o eminente, superior; sumo (sacerdote); supremo (tribunal, etc.); elevado, digno; picante, muy sazonado; rico (en carbono, cemento, etc.); vivo, intenso; arrogante, estirado; fuerte, violento (viento); fuerte, oliscada (la carne); poderoso; (fam.) achispado.— **h. altar,** altar mayor.—**h. and dry,** en seco.—**h. and mighty,** (fam.) arrogante, hinchado.—**h. Church,** iglesia ortodoxa o ritualista (en la secta episcopal).—**h. day,** día de fiesta.—**h. explosive,** explosivo instantáneo de gran potencia.—**h. gear,** (aut.) posición de toma directa.—**h. hat,** sombrero de copa.—**h. jinks,** (fam.) francachela; hilaridad.— **h. living,** abuso de los placeres de la mesa, epicurismo.—**H. Mass,** misa cantada o mayor.— **h. noon,** pleno mediodía.—**h. pressure,** alta presión.—**h.-pressure,** de alta presión.—**h.priest,** sumo sacerdote.—**h. relief,** alto relieve.—**h. road,** camino real; vía pública; carretera.—**h. school,** escuela secundaria.—**h. sea,** mar gruesa.—**h. seas,** alta mar.—**h.-speed steel,** acero rápido o de corte rápido.—**h. spirits,** alegría, buen humor (**in h. spirits,** alegre).—**h. steel,** acero rico en carbono.—**h. tide,** pleamar.—**h. treason,** alta traición, delito de lesa majestad.—**h. water,** marea alta; agua alta.—**h. words,** palabras ofensivas o ásperas.—**in h. terms,** en términos lisonjeros.—**the Most H.,** el Altísimo.—**to be h. time,** ser ya hora o tiempo de, no deberse hacer esperar más (algo que debe hacerse).

high, *adv.* altamente; muy, sumamente; a grande altura; arrogantemente; a precio elevado; lujosamente.—**h. and low** (fam.) por doquiera.—**h.-colored,** subido de color.—**h.-flown,** de alto vuelo; presuntuoso, altivo, orgulloso; hinchado.—**h.-grown,** muy crecido o muy alto.— **h.-handed,** despótico, arbitrario.—**h.-heaped,** colmado.—**h.-hearted,** animoso, denodado.—**h.-keyed,** impresionable, sensitivo; (mús.) agudo. —**h.-minded,** magnánimo.—**h.-pitched** = H.-KEYED.—**h.-priced,** caro.—**h.-seasoned,** picante. —**h.-sounding,** altisonante o retumbante.—**h.-spirited,** gallardo, bizarro.—**h.-stepped,** picador (caballo).—**h.-strung** = H.-KEYED.—**h.-toned,** honorable, caballeroso; (mús.) agudo; (fam.) aristocrático, de buen tono.—**h.-wrought,** primorosamente labrado; muy agitado.—**on h.,** en las alturas, en el cielo.

highball [jáibol], *s.* licor con hielo y agua.

highborn [-bórn], *a.* noble, de alta alcurnia, linajudo.

highbrow [-bráu], *s.* erudito engreído y arrogante; petulante.—**highbrowed** (-d) *a.* hinchado, arrogante.

higher [-œr], *a. comp.* de HIGH: más alto; superior (álgebra, matemáticas, etc).—**h. classes,**

clases altas.—**h. criticism,** crítica textual (fundada en el texto) de la Biblia.—**h.-up,** (fam.) *a.* superior, de mayor jerarquía; *s.* funcionario de mayor jerarquía.

highest [-est], *a. superl.* de HIGH: más alto; sumo, supremo; mayor; máximo.—**h. common divisor,** o **factor,** máximo común divisor.

highfalutin [jáifaliútin], *a.* (fam.) hinchado, pomposo, retumbante.

highflier [-fláiœr], *s.* pájaro de alto vuelo; extremista; despilfarrador.

highland [jáiland], *s.* región montañosa.—*pl.* tierras altas; montañas.—**highlander** [-œr], *s.* montañés; serrano; montañés de Escocia.

highlandish [-iŝh], *a.* montañés.

highly [jáili], *adv.* altamente; levantadamente, elevadamente; sumamente; arrogantemente, ambiciosamente; encarecidamente.

highness [jáines], *s.* altura, elevación; celsitud; Alteza (título).

hight [jait], *va.* y *vn.* llamar(se).

hight, highten = HEIGHT, HEIGHTEN.

highty-tighty = HOITY-TOITY.

highway [jáiuéi], *s.* camino real; vía pública; carretera, calzada.—**h. robber** = HIGHWAYMAN.

highwayman [-mæn], *s.* bandido, salteador de caminos.

hilarious [jailériυs], *a.* alegre, bullicioso.

hilarity [jailériti], *s.* hilaridad, júbilo.

hill [jil]. **I.** *s.* collado, colina, cerro, otero, altozano.—**h. of beans,** montoncillo de judías (sembradas). **II.** *va.* aporcar. **III.** *vn.* amontonarse.

hilling [jíliŋ], *s.* amontonamiento.

hilliness [jílines], *s.* montuosidad.

hillman [jílman], *s.* arribeño.

hillock [jíloc], *s.* altillo, loma, montecillo, otero.

hillside [jílsaid], *s.* ladera.

hilltop [jíltop], *s.* cima, cumbre de una colina.

hilly [jíli], *a.* montañoso, montuoso.

hilt [jilt], *s.* (arm.) puño, empuñadura.

hilted [jílted], *a.* que tiene puño o guarnición.

hilum [jáilum o jílυm], *s.* (bot.) ombligo de una semila; núcleo de un grano de almidón; ojo de un fréjol.

him [jim], *pron. pers. m.* (caso oblicuo de HE), él, a él, le, lo.

himself [jimsélf], *pron. pers.* (reflexivo en los casos oblicuos) él, él mismo, se, sí, sí mismo.— **by h.,** solo, por sí, por su cuenta.—**for h.,** por su cuenta, por cuenta propia.—**he h.,** él mismo; en persona.—**he said to h..** se di°o a sí mismo.

hind [jáind]. **I.** *a,* trasero, zaguero, posterior.— **h.-bow,** taja de la silla de montar.—**h.-foremost,** lo de atrás delante.—**h. wheel,** juego trasero del coche. **II.** *s.* cierva.

hinder [jíndœr], **I.** *va.* impedir, estorbar, obstruir. **II.** *vn.* poner obstáculos, poner trabas; oponerse.

hinder [jáindœr], *a.* posterior, trasero.

hinderer [jíndœrœr], *s.* obstructor, estorbador.

hindermost [jáindœrmoust], **hindmost** [jáindmoust], *a.* postrero, último.

hindhand [jáindhænd], *s.* cuarto trasero de un caballo.

Hindi [jíndi], *s.* indi, el idioma moderno del Indostán.

Hindoo, Hindu [jíndu], *s.* y *a.* indostánico.

hindrance [jíndrans], *s.* impedimento, obstáculo, estorbo.

Hinduism [jínduiŝm], *s.* indoísmo.

Hindustani [jíndustǽni], *s.* indostani, lengua principal de la India.

hinge [jiny]. **I.** *s.* gozne; bisagra; punto capital o principal.—**h. joint,** (anat.) gínglimo angular; (mec.) articulación de bisagra. **II.** *va.* engoznar; enquiciar. **III.** *vn.* girar sobre un gozne; (con *on*) depender (de).

hinny [jíni]. **I.** *vn.* relinchar. **II.** *s.* macho, mulo.

hint [jint]. **I.** *va.* insinuar, indicar, intimar, sugerir. **II.** *vn.* echar una pulla o indirecta. —**to h. at,** aludir a. **III.** *s.* indirecta, sugestión, pulla, insinuación.

hinterland [jíntœrlænd], s. región interior (de un país, etc.).

hip [jip]. **I.** s. (anat.) cadera; (bot.) fruto del escaramujo; (arq.) caballete.—**h. bath**, baño de asiento, semicupio.—**h. bone**, cía, hueso de la cadera.—**h. roof**, (arq.) techo a cuatro vertientes. **II.** va. descaderar; echar sobre la cadera; (arq.) construir un techo con cubierta a cuatro aguas.

hippish [jípiȟh], a. (fam.) melancólico, abatido.

hippocampus [jípocǽmpʊs], s. hipocampo.

hippocentaur [jíposéntor], s. hipocentauro.

hippocras [jípocras], s. hipocrás.

Hippocratic [jípocrǽtic], a. hipocrático.

hippodrome [jípodrom], s. hipódromo, circo.

hippogriff [jípogrif], s. hipogrifo.

hippophagy [jipófayi], s. hipofagia, costumbre de comer carne de caballo.

hippopotamus [jipopótamʊs], s. hipopótamo.

hipshot [jípȟhot], a. renco.

hircine [jœrsin], a. cabrío, cabruno, hircino.

hire [jáiœr]. **I.** va. alquilar, dar o tomar en arriendo; arrendar; ajornalar, asalariar.—**to h. out**, alquilar, alquilarse. **II.** s. alquiler, arriendo; salario, jornal; soborno.

hireling [jáirling]. **I.** s. alquilón; persona asalariada. **II.** a. mercenario, venal.

hirer [jáirœr], s. alquilador, arrendador.

hirsute [jœrsiút], a. hirsuto, peludo.

hirsuteness [jœrsiútnes], s. vellosidad.

hirundine [jirúndine], a. de golondrina, semejante a la golondrina.

Hirundinidæ [jírundínidæ], s. pl. (zool.) hirundíneos.

his [jis], posesivo. su, sus (de él); suyo, suyas, el suyo, la suya, los suyos, las suyas (de él).

hispid [jíspid], a. híspido, cerdoso.

hiss [jis]. **I.** va. y vn. silbar; sisear. **II.** s. silbido, siseo.

hissing [jísing], s. silbido, chifla; siseo.

hissingly [jísingli], adv. a silbidos.

hist [jist], interj. ¡chito! ¡chito!

histologic(al [jistolóric(al], a. histológico.

histologist [jistóloyist], s. histólogo.

histology [jistóloyi], s. histología.

historian [jistórian], s. historiador.

historic(al [jistóric(al], a. histórico.—**h. present**, (gram.) el presente usado metafóricamente en vez del pretérito, etc.—**h. tense**, (gram.) HISTORIC PRESENT.

historically [-i], adv. históricamente.

historiographer [jístoriógrafœr], s. historiógrafo.

historiography [-grafi], s. historiografía.

history [jístori], s. historia.—**h. piece**, (pint.) cuadro o tapiz histórico.—**to have a h.**, ser persona de historia (de malos antecedentes).

Hispanic [jispénic], a hispánico.—**hispanicism** [-ciȟm], s. hispanismo, españolismo.

histogenesis [jístoyénesis], **histogeny** [jistóyeni], s. histogenia, formación de los tejidos vivos.

histolysis [jistólisis], s. (biol.) histólisis, disgregación de los tejidos; (entom.) disolución de los órganos larvales en la crisálida.

histrionic(al [jistriónic(al], a. histriónico.—**histrionically** [-i], adv. cómicamente, teatralmente.—**histrionism** [jistrionȟm], s. histrionismo.

hit [jit]. **I.** va. (pret. y pp. HIT) dar, pegar, golpear; atinar, acertar; encontrar, dar con o en.—**to h. off**, improvisar; describir o expresar bien o lucidamente.—**to h. the mark**, dar en el blanco.—**to h. the nail on the head**, dar en el hito o en el clavo.—**to h. the trail**, (fam.) convertirse, hacer votos tras un sermón o exhortación. **II.** vn. rozar, chocar; acaecer o acontecer felizmente, salir bien; encontrar por casualidad; acertar.—**h. or miss**, (fam.) congenial, llevarse bien con otro. **III** s. tolondro.—**to h. against**, dar contra alguna cosa, chocar.—**to h. on**, o **upon**, dar con, hallar; acordarse de. **III.** s. golpe, choque, coscorrón; rasgo de ingenio.—**a lucky h.**, golpe de fortuna, ocurrencia feliz.—**to make a h.**, (fam.) dar golpe.

hitch [jich]. **I.** va. atar, ligar; enganchar; (mar.) amarrar; mover a tirones. **II.** vn. moverse a saltos; rozarse los pies (los caballos); enredarse; (fam.) congeniar, llevarse bien con otro. **III** s.

alto, parada; tropiezo, dificultad; tirón; (mar.) vuelta de cabo.

hither [jíðœr]. **I.** adv. acá, hacia acá.—**h. and thither**, acá y allá. **II.** a. citerior.—**on the h. side of**, aquende, de este lado de.

hithermost [-moust], a. más cercano o próximo.

hitherto [jíðœrtu], adv. hasta ahora, hasta aquí.

Hittite [jítait], s. heteo, hitita.

hive [jáiv]. **I.** s. colmena; enjambre de abejas; emporio.—pl. (med.) urticaria, ronchas. **II.** va. (api.) enjambrar, encorchar. **III.** vn. vivir juntos como en colmena.

ho, hoa! [jo], interj.! ¡eh! ¡basta!

hoar [jóœr], a. blanco, cano; nevado.

hoard [jóœrd]. **I.** va. y vn. atesorar, acumular y guardar. **II.** s. provisión; montón; acumulamiento, repuesto; tesoro escondido.

hoarder [jórdœr], s. atesorador.

hoarding [jórding], s. atesoramiento; cerca provisional; tablilla de avisos.

hoarfrost [jóœrfrost], s. escarcha en agujas.

hoarhound, horehound [jóœrjáund], s. (bot.) marrubio.

hoariness [jóœrines], s. blancura; canicie.

hoarse [jórs], a. ronco, rauco.—**hoarsely** [-li], adv. roncamente.—**hoarseness** [-nes], s. ronquera, carraspera.

hoary [jóœri], a. blanco, blanquecino; cano, canoso; carchado.

hoax [jocs]. **I.** s. engaño, burla, bola, petardo, mentira. **II.** va. engañar, burlar.

hob [job], s. repisa interior del hogar; cubo de rueda; mandril para hacer roscas de tornillo; punzón de embutir; juego del chito; tángano. —**to play h. with**, trastornar.

hobble [jóbœl]. **I.** va. poner trabas, maniotar. **II.** vn. cojear. **III.** s. cojera; traba, maniota; dificultad, atolladero.

hobbledehoy [jóbœdejói], s. adolescente.

hobby [jóbi], s. (fam.) tema, manía, chifladura; caballico (juguete); jaca; (orn.) sacre.

hobbyhorse [jóbijórs], s. tema, manía; caballico (juguete); velocípedo.

hobgoblin [jóbgóblin], s. duende, trasgo.

hobnail [jóbneil]. **I.** s. clavo de herradura. **II.** va. clavar con dichos clavos.

hobnob [jóbnób], vn. beber juntos; tener intimidad, rozarse.

hock [joc]. **I.** s. vino del Rin; tarso; corva. **II.** va. desjarretar.

hockey [jóki], s. juego de pelota con palo encorvado.

hocus [jócʊs], va. engañar, chasquear; atontar con drogas.—**h. pocus**, treta, birlibirloque.

hod [jod], s. (alb.) cuezo.

hodcarrier [jódcǽrriœr], s. manobre, peón de albañil.

hodgepodge [jóypóy], s. almodrote, bodrio; baturillo.

hodman [jódman], s. peón de albañil, manobre.

hoe [jo]. **I.** s. azada, azadón. **II.** va. azadonar, sachar.—**hoeing**, sachadura.

hog [jog]. **I.** s. puerco, cerdo, marrano; (fam.) persona sucia, tragona o egoísta; (mar.) escobón.—**h. fennel**, (bot.) servato, ervato.—**h.'s bristle**, cerda.—**to go the whole h.**, (fam.) llegar hasta el último límite. **II.** va. (mar.) afretar, limpiar fondos; partir una embarcación por el medio; rapar el pelo. **III.** vn. arquearse, combarse.

hoggish [jóguiȟh], a. porcuno, porcino; egoísta; guloso, comilón.—**hoggishly** [-li], adv. puercamente, cochinamente; vorazmente.—**hoggishness** [-nes], s. porquería, cochinada; glotonería; egoísmo.

hogherd [jógjœrd], s. porquero, porquerizo.

hogpen [jógpén], **hogsty** [-stai], s. pocilga.

hogshead [jógȟȟed], s. pipa, bocoy, tonel.

hoiden [jóiden]. **I.** a. atrevida, desenvuelta.—s. muchacha traviesa, tunantuela. **II.** vn. retozar de un modo indecoroso.

hoist [jóist]. **I.** va. alzar, elevar; izar, enarbolar. **II.** s. cabria, pescante, grúa, malacate, montacarga, elevador, ascensor; levantamiento, ascensión, enarboladura; medida vertical de una vela o una bandera.

hoity-toity [jóiti-tóiti]. **I.** *a.* fachendero, engreído. **II.** *interj.* ¡ola! ¡tate!

hold [jóuld]. **I.** *va.* (*pret.* y *pp.* HELD: *pp.* (ant.) HOLDEN) tener; asir, coger, agarrar; retener, reservar; detener, contener; sostener, apoyar; tener de reserva; restringir, estrechar, limitar; hacer, tener cabida o capacidad para; mantener; sostener, opinar; juzgar, reputar, entender; poseer, ocupar, disfrutar, gozar; celebrar (sesión, reunión); continuar, seguir; conservar; guardar, observar; obligar; hacer (responsable, etc.)—**to h. a bet**, o **a wager**, apostar.—**to h. back**, retener; contener.—**to h. down**, oprimir, tener sujeto.—**to h. forth**, expresar, publicar; mostrar.—**to [h. hands**, cogerse de la mano; estar mano en mano.—**to h. in**, sujetar, refrenar.—**to h. in play**, tener ocupado.—**to h. off**, apartar, alejar.—**to h. one's hand**, detenerse; abstenerse.—**to h. one's own**, defenderse bien; no salir perdiendo; resistir, aguantar (una enfermedad, etc.).—**to h. one's peace**, o **one's tongue**, callar, no decir nada.—**to h. out**, ofrecer, proponer; extender.—**to h. over**, tener suspendido o en suspenso; diferir, aplazar; (mús.) prolongar (una nota).—**to h. sway**, gobernar, mandar.—**to h. up**, levantar, alzar; apoyar, sostener; asaltar para robar, saltear.—**to h. up one's hands**, alzar las manos en señal de sumisión; rendirse, darse por vencido.—**to h. water**, ser estanco (un cubo, etc.); (fig.) ser lógico o válido (un argumento); (mar.) ciar. **II.** *vn.* valer, ser válido, estar en vigor; mantenerse firme, sostenerse, aguantar; seguir, proseguir; estar en posesión; refrenarse, abstenerse; aplicarse, ser aplicable.—**to h. back**, detenerse, contenerse; abstenerse.—**to h. fast**, agarrarse bien.—**to h. fast to**, afirmarse en; agarrarse bien de.—**to h. forth**, arengar, exponer (uno) sus ideas.—**to h. good**, subsistir; aplicarse.—**to h. in**, contenerse, refrenarse.—**to h. off**, mantenerse a distancia.—**to h. on**, seguir, proseguir, persistir; detenerse; aguardar.—**to h. on to**, asirse de.—**to h. out**, mantenerse firme, no cejar; durar; resistir, aguantar.—**to h. over**, continuar desempeñando un cargo después del término legal.—**to h. to**, pegarse, adherirse a.—**to h. together**, mantenerse o estar juntos o reunidos.—**to h. up**, cesar, parar.—**to h. with**, convenir con. **III.** *s.* presa, asimiento, agarro; asa, mango; influencia, dominio; freno; refugio, amparo; fortificación; posesión, custodia; celda (en una prisión); (mar.) bodega; (mús.) calderón.

hold! hold on! *interj.* ¡tente! ¡para! ¡quieto! (mar.) ¡top!

holdback [jóuldbæc], *s.* restricción, freno; (carr.) cejadero.

holder [jóuldœr], *s.* tenedor, posesor; mantenedor; agarradero, asidero, mango, asa; porta—(vg. *lamp holder*, portalámpara; *tool holder*, portaherramienta); sostén; (for.) tenedor; propietario; arrendatario; inquilino; (mar.) marinero de la bodega.—**h. of a bill**, tenedor o portador de una letra.—**h. of a share**, accionista.

holdfast [jóuldfast], *s.* (mec.) barrilete, grapón, grapa, laña; prensa, mordaza; sostén.

holding [jóulding], *s.* tenencia, pertenencia, posesión; arrendamiento, inquilinato.—*pl.* valores habidos.

holdup [jóuldúp], *s.* salteamiento, asalto de ladrones.

hole [jóul]. **I.** *s.* agujero, orificio; cavidad, hueco, hoyo; seno; perforación; pozo, charco (de un río, arroyo, etc.); cueva; (fam.) atolladero, aprieto.—**a h. to crawl out of**, escapatoria, excusa, refugio. **II.** *va.* agujerear, taladrar, perforar, horadar; meter una bolade billar en la tronera. **III.** *vn.* encuevarse; hacer un agujero u hoyo.

holiday [jólidéi]. **I.** *s.* día festivo, fiesta, festividad; día feriado; aniversario.—**holidays**, vacaciones, asueto. **II.** *a.* alegre, festivo.

holily [jóulili], *adv.* piadosamente, santamente.

holiness [jóulines], *s.* santidad, beatitud.—**His H.**, Su Santidad.

holing [jóuling], *s.* perforación; taladro para alojar un clavo, perno, cabilla, etc.

holland [jóland], *s.* (tej.) holanda.—*pl.* ginebra.

hollo, holl(o)a [jólo]. **I.** *interj.* ¡eh! ¡hola! **II.** *s.* grito, grita.

hollow [jólo], *a.* hueco, vacío; hundido; falso, insincero.—**h.-hearted**, solapado.—**h. newel**, ojo de escalera.—**h. ware**, ollas, pucheros, marmitas. **II.** *s.* cavidad; depresión, concavidad; canal, ranura; hueco; hoyo; valle; cañada. **III.** *va.* excavar; ahondar; ahuecar; acopar.

hollowness [jólones], *s.* cavidad, hueco, vacío; doblez, falsía.

hollowroot [jólorut], *s.* (bot.) moscatelina, palomilla.

holly [jóli], *s.* (bot.) acebo; agrifolio.

hollyhock [jólijóc], *s.* (bot.) malva hortense.

holm [jolm], *s.* isleta de río; rambla; (bot.) acebo.—**h. oak**, encina.

holmia [jólimæ], *s.* holmia, óxido de holmio.

holmium [jólmium], *s.* (quím.) holmio.

holocaust [jólocost], *s.* holocausto.

holograph [jólogræf], *s.* hológrafo.

holographic [-gráfic], *a.* hológrafo.

holohedron [-jidron], *s.* holoedro.—**holohedral** [-jídræl], *a.* holoédrico.

holophrasis [jolófræsis], *s.* holofrasia, polisintetismo.—**holophrastic** [jólofræstic], *a.* holofrástico, polisintético.

holothurian [jóloziuriæn], *s.* (bot.) holoturia, cohombro de mar.

Holotricha [jolótricæ], *s. pl.* (zool.) holótricos, holotríquidos.

holster [jólstœr], *s.* pistolera.—**h. cap**, tapafundas.

holy [jóuli], *a.* santo, pío; puro, inmaculado; sacro, sagrado; consagrado, santificado; bendito.—**H. Communion**, sagrada comunión.—**h. cross**, santa cruz.—**h. cup**, cáliz.—**h. day**, fiesta de guardar, disanto.—**H. Father**, santo padre (el papa).—**H. Ghost**, Espíritu Santo.—**H. Grail**, grial.—**h. lamb**, agnusdéi.—**H. Land**, Tierra Santa.—**H. Office**, Santo Oficio.—**h. of holies**, santo de los santos, sanctasanctórum.—**h. oil**, crisma, óleo santo.—**H. One**, Dios; Jesucristo.—**h. order**, o **orders**, orden sacerdotal.—**h. rood**, crucifijo; santa cruz.—**H. See**, santa sede.—**H. Spirit** = HOLY GHOST.—**h. tide**, festividad.—**h. water**, agua bendita.—**h.-water sprinkler**, hisopo.—**h. week**, semana santa.—**h. writ**, la Sagrada Escritura.

holystone [jóulistóun]. **I.** *s.* (mar.) piedra de cubierta. **II.** *va.* (mar.) dar piedra y arena.

homage [jómeʏ]. **I.** *s.* homenaje. **II.** *va.* reverenciar, honrar, acatar.

homager [jómeʏœr], *s.* el que rinde homenaje.

home [jóum]. **I.** *s.* hogar, casa; morada; patria, suelo patrio; domicilio, residencia; asilo, hospedería, albergue, refugio; (dep.) meta; límite o término.—**at h.**, en casa; en el país de uno; con toda comodidad; en su elemento; dispuesto a recibir visitas; recepción.—**to hit**, o **strike, h.**, dar en el blanco; herir en lo vivo, llegar al alma. **II.** *a.* doméstico, de casa, casero; nativo, natal, indígena; regional; nacional, del país; certero, eficaz, que da en el blanco, que llega a la meta.—**h. base**, (dep.) puesto del *batsman* en baseball.—**h.-born**, doméstico; nacido en casa.—**h.-bound**, en dirección a casa, hacia el hogar; imposibilitado de salir de casa.—**h.-bred**, nativo, natural; doméstico; casero, de casa; sencillo, inculto.—**H. Department, H. Office**, (Ingl.) Ministerio de lo Interior.—**h. office**, oficina matriz.—**h. rule**, (pol.) autonomía.—**h. ruler**, autonomista.—**h. run**, (dep.) en baseball, carrera del *batsman* alrededor del cuadro; carrera de regreso al punto de partida.—**H. Secretary**, (Ingl.) Secretario de lo Interior.—**h. stretch**, (dep.) último trecho de una carrera. **III.** *adv.* a casa; en casa; al país o en la tierra de uno; en el punto o lugar en que debe estar una cosa.

homeless [jóumles], *a.* destituído; sin casa ni hogar; mostrenco.

homelike [-laik], *a.* como de casa, semejante al hogar doméstico; sosegado y cómodo.

homeliness [-lines], *s.* simpleza, sencillez; fealdad, mal aspecto.

homely [jóumli]. **I.** *a.* casero, doméstico; sencillo, liso, llano; feo; rústico, inculto, vulgar. **II.** *adv.* llanamente, simplemente; como de casa; groseramente.

homemade [jóumméid], *a.* hecho en casa; fabricado en el país.

homeopathic, homœopathic [jómeopǽzic]. **I.** *a.* homeopático. — **homeopathically** [-ali], *adv.* homeopáticamente.—**homeopath**(**ist**, **homœopath**(**ist** [-pæz, -ópazist], *s.* homeópata.—**homeopathy, homœopathy** [jómeópazi], *s.* homeopatía.

Homeric [joméric], *a.* homérico.

homesick [jóumsíc], *a.* nostálgico.

homesickness [-ness], *s.* nostalgia, añoranza.

homespun [jóumspʊn]. **I.** *a.* casero, hecho en casa; basto, tocho. **II.** *s.* tela tejida en casa.

homestead [jóumsted], *s.* casa de habitación y sus terrenos; heredad; hogar.

homeward [jóumuard], *adv.* hacia casa, hacia su país; de vuelta.—**h. bound,** de regreso.

homicidal [jómisáidal], *a.* homicida.

homicide [jómisaid], *s.* homicidio; homicida.

homiletic(**al** [jomilétic(al], *a.* referente a la oratoria sagrada.

homiletics [jomilétics], *s.* oratoria sagrada.

homilist [jómilist], *s.* predicador de homilías.

homily [jómili], *s.* homilía; sermón.

homing [jóuming], *a.* mensajera (paloma).

hominy [jómini], *s.* maíz molido.

homochromous [jómocrómʊs], *a.* (bot.) de un mismo color.

homogen [jómoyen], *s.* estructura o parte homogénea.

homogeneous [jómoyínius], *a.* homogéneo.— **homogeneously** [-li], *adv.* homogéneamente.— **homogeneousness** [-nes], *s.* homogeneidad.

homogenous [jomóyenus], *a.* de un mismo origen; (geol.) de una misma estructura.

homograph [jómogræf], *s.* vocablo homógrafo.

homographic [jomogrǽfic], *a.* homógrafo.

homologation [jomóloguéshʊn], *s.* (for.) homologación.

homologous [jomólogus], *a.* homólogo.

homolog(**ue** [jómolog], *s.* cosa homóloga.

homonym [jómonim], *s.* vocablo homónimo.

homonymous [jomónimus], *a.* homónimo; equívoco, ambiguo.

homonymy [jomónimi], *s.* homonimia; equivocación, ambigüedad.

homophone [jómofoun], *s.* palabra o letra homófona.

homophonous [jomófonus], *a.* homófono.

homophony [jomófoni], *s.* identidad de sonido de dos palabras de distinta significación.

homopterous [jomópterus], *a.* homóptero.

homosexual [jomosécshiuel], *a.* homosexual, por el propio sexo, por individuos del mismo sexo (pasión).—**homosexuality** [-æliti], homosexualidad, inversión sexual.

homotonous [jomótonus], *a.* que tiene el mismo tono; parecido, uniforme.

homunculus [jomúnkiulus], *s.* homúnculo.

hone [jóun]. **I.** *s.* piedra de afilar. **II.** *va.* afilar, asentar.

honest [ónest], *a.* honrado, probo, recto; sincero; equitativo; honesta (mujer).

honestly [-li], *adv.* honradamente; de veras; francamente; honestamente.

honesty [ónesti], *s.* honradez, probidad; franqueza; honestidad.

honey [jʊ́ni], *s.* miel de abejas. Empléase a veces como voz de cariño, en el sentido de *vida mía, mi querido,* etc.—**h. ant,** hormiga melífera.— **h. bag,** órgano melífero de la abeja.—**h. cell,** alvéolo.— **h. creeper,** (orn.) pipí.— **h. flower,** ceriflor.—**h. harvest,** recolección de la miel.— **h.-mouthed,** adulador, melifluo.—**h.-pot,** colmena de abejas silvestres. — **h. stalk,** trébol. —**h.-tongue,** lengua melosa. **II.** *va.* enmelar, cubrir con miel. **III.** *vn.* hablar con cariño.

honeybee [-bí], *s.* abeja neutra u obrera.

honeycomb [-cóum], *s.* bresca, panal de miel; (fund.) escarabajos, rebolludura, magaña.

honeycombed [-cóumd], *a.* apanalado, alveolar; (mar.) abromado; horadado por gusanos.

honeydew [-diú], tabaco moteado; secreción dulce de algunos insectos y plantas.

honeyed [jʊ́nid], *a.* dulce, meloso, melifluo.—

honeyedness [-nes], *s.* dulzura, halago.

honeyless [jóniles], *a.* sin miel.

honeymoon [-mún], *s.* luna de miel.

honeysuckle [-súcœl], *s.* (bot.) madreselva.

honeysweet [-suít], *a.* melar.

honeywort [-uórt], *s.* ceriflor.

hono(**u**)**r** [ónoer]. **I.** *s.* honor, honra.—*pl.* en algunos juegos de naipe, tantos adicionales, semejantes a los que se acusan en el tute.— **h. bright,** (fam.) de veras, a fe de caballero.—**on,** o upon, **my h.,** por mi fe, por mi palabra de honor. —**your H.,** usía, vuestra señoría (apl. a jueces, alcaldes, etc.). **II.** *va.* honrar; (com.) honrar, aceptar, pagar.

hono(**u**)**rable** [ónœrabœl], *a.* honorable; pundonoroso; honrado; honorífico, honroso.— **H.,** honorable (tratamiento).

hono(**u**)**rableness** [-nes], *s.* honradez; honorabilidad.

hono(**u**)**rably** [-bli], *adv.* honorablemente; honrosamente.

honorarium [jónorériʊm], *s.* honorarios.

honorary [ónœræri]. **I.** *a.* honorario, honorífico; honroso. **II.** *s.* honorarios.

hooch [juch], *s.* bebida fuertemente alcohólica; licor de contrabando.

hood [jud]. **I.** *s.* capucha, capirote, caperuza; muceta; (mar.) caperuza de palo; carroza de la escalera; fuelle de carruaje; (aut.) cubierta del motor; campana del hogar; sombrerete (de chimenea, etc.), cubierta, tapa. **II.** *va.* cubrir con caperuza, capucha o capirote; tapar, ocultar.

hoodlum [júdlʊm], *s.* (fam.) pillo, tunante, rufián.

hoodman-blind [júdman-blaind], *s.* juego de la gallina ciega.

hoodoo [júdu]. **I.** *va.* (fam.) aojar.—**hoodooed,** aojado. **II.** *s.* mal de ojo; aojador.

hoodwink [júduinc], *va.* vendar los ojos; encubrir, tapar; engañar, deslumbrar.

hoof [juf]. **I.** *s.* casco, pezuña; animal ungulado; (geom.) cono o cilindro truncado.—**on the h.,** en pie (ganado), vivo. **II.** *vn.* andar o ir a pie.

hoofbound [júfbáund], *a.* corto de cascos.

hoofed [juft], *a.* ungulado.

hook [juk]. **I.** *s.* gancho, garabato, garfio; anzuelo; aprón, grapón; garra; corchete, prendedero; atractivo, aliciente; (mús.) rabo de una corchea.—**h. nose,** nariz aguileña.—**h.-nosed,** de nariz aguileña.—**hooks and eyes,** (cost.) corchetes y corchetas, broches.—**by h. or by crook,** a tuertas o a derechas.—**off the hooks,** agitado, distraído. —**on one's own h.,** (fam.) por cuenta propia, sin depender de otro. **II.** *va.* enganchar, engafar, garfear, atraer, engatusar; encornar, dar una cornada; (fam.) birlar, hurtar.

hookbill [júcbíl], *s.* pico encorvado.

hooked [jukt], *a.* enganchado; encorvado, ganchudo.

hookedness [júkednes], *s.* encorvadura.

hook-up [-úp], *s.* (rad.) circuito.

hookworm [-uérm], *s.* anquilóstomo, lombriz intestinal.—**h. disease,** anquilostomiasis.

hooky [júki], *a.* ganchudo.

hoop [jup]. **I.** *s.* aro; fleje, zuncho; (mec.) collar, collarín; anilla, argolla, vilorta; virola; (joy.) sortija, ajorca; miriñaque; grito.—**h. la!** ¡arriba! ¡upa!—**h. poles,** cujes.—**h. skirt,** miriñaque. **II.** *va.* poner aro a ; zunchar; cercar, ceñir. **III.** *vn.* gritar; ojear.

hooper [júpœr], *s.* tonelero.

hooping cough, *s.* = WHOOPING COUGH.

hoopoe, hoopoo, [júpo, júpu], *s.* (orn.) abubilla.

hoot [jut]. **I.** *vn.* gritar, ulular, huchear; dar grita. **II.** *va.* ojear la caza. **III.** *s.* grito, grita, ruido, clamor; sofión.—**h. owl,** buho que ulula.

hooting [júting], *s.* grito, grita.

hoove, hooven [juv, juvn], *s.* (vet.) enfermedad del ganado (distensión del abdomen por gases).

hop [jop]. **I.** *va.* saltar, brincar; recoger lúpulo; mezclar el lúpulo en la cerveza. **II.** *vn.* cojear; (a menudo con *off*) alzarse o partir (en aeroplano) **III.** *s.* salto, brinco; baile, sarao; (bot.) lúpulo; (aer.) trayecto de vuelo; vuelo.—**hops**, (com.) lúpulo.

hopbine [jópbain], *s.* vástago de lúpulo.

hope [jóup]. **I.** *s.* esperanza.—**h. box, o chest,** colección o acumulación de prendas de vestir, etc. que una joven hace en la esperanza de usarlas cuando se case.—**in hopes,** en o con la esperanza. **II.** *va.* y *vn.* esperar, tener esperanza.—**to h. against h.,** esperar lo imposible.

hopeful [jóupful], *a.* lleno de esperanzas; que da esperanza o promete; (fam.) esperanzado.—**hopefully** [-li], *adv.* con esperanza.—**hopefulness** [-nes], *s.* esperanza; aspecto prometedor.

hopeless [jóuples], *a.* desahuciado; desesperanzado; incurable.—**hopelessly** [-li], *adv.* sin esperanza.—**hopelessness** [-nes], *s.* falta de esperanza o de remedio.

hopingly [jóupingli], *adv.* con esperanza.

hoplite [jóplait], *s.* hoplita.

hopper [jópœr], *s.* persona que salta a la pata coja (mol.) tolva; (agr.) sementero.

hopple [jópœl]. **I.** *va.* trabar o manear un caballo. **II.** *s.* traba, manea, maniota.

hopscotch [jópscoch], *s.* coxcojilla, infernáculo o reina mora.

horal [jóral], **horary** [-ari], *a.* horario; por horas.

Horatian [joréshan], *a.* horaciano.

horde [jord]. **I.** *s.* horda, aduar. **II.** *vn.* formar hordas.

hordeolum [jordíolum], *s.* orzuelo.

horehound [joœrjáund], *s.* = HOARHOUND.

horizon [joráisŏn], *s.* horizonte.

horizontal [jórisŏntal], *a.* horizontal.

horizontality [-tæliti], *s.* horizontalidad.

horizontally [jórisŏntali], *adv.* horizontalmente.

horn [jorn]. **I.** *s.* cuerno, asta; cuerna, cacho; (zool.) tentáculo; palpo o antena; (música) trompa; corneta de monte, cuerno de caza; (fonóg., aut., etc.) bocina; callosidad o dureza en la piel; cuerno de la luna; vaso u objeto de cuerno; (aer.) palanca de gobierno.—**h. fly,** mosca que se posa en enjambres sobre los cuernos del ganado vacuno.—**h. of plenty,** cuerno de la abundancia. **II.** *va.* poner cuernos; proveer de cuernos; dar una cornada; dar una concertada.

hornbeam [jórnbim], *s.* (bot.) carpe.

hornbill [-bil], *s.* (orn.) cálao.

hornblende [-blénd], *s.* (min.) hornablenda.

hornblower [-blóœr], *s.* trompetero, bocinero.

hornbook [-bŭc], *s.* cartilla.

horned [jornd], *a.* cornudo, cornígero; encornado; enastado: de cuerno.—**h. cattle,** ganado vacuno.—**h. owl,** (orn.) especie de bulho de los E. U.—**h. toad,** especie de iguana.

hornet [jórnet], *s.* crabrón.—**h. fly,** avispón.

hornfish [jórnfish], *s.* (ict.) aguja.

horning [jórning], *s.* media luna.

hornish [jórnish], *a.* duro; córneo.

hornpipe [jórnpaip], *s.* (Ingl.) baile predilecto de los marineros, que ejecuta una sola persona; (mús.) gaita o chirimía.

hornsilver [jórnsilvœr], *s.* (min.) plata córnea.

hornwork [jórnuœrk], *s.* (fort.) hornabeque u obra a cuerno.

horny [jórni], *a.* hecho de cuerno; córneo; calloso.

horography [jorógrafi], *s.* gnomónica.

horologe [jóroloy], *s.* reloj.—**horologic(al** [lóyic(al], *a.* referente a la gnomónica.—**horology** [joróloyi], *s.* horología.

horometry [jorómetri], *s.* horometría.

horoscope [jóroscŭup], *s.* horóscopo.

horrent [jórent], *a.* erguido; horrendo.

horrible [jórribœl], *a.* horrible.—**horribleness** [-nes], *s.* horribilidad.—**horribly** [-bli], *adv.* horriblemente.

horrid [jórrid], *a.* horrible o hórrido; ofensivo; dañoso.—**horridly** [-li], *adv.* horriblemente.—**horridness** [-nes], *s.* horridez, horror.

horrific [jórrific], *a.* horrífico.

horrify [jórrifai], *va.* horrorizar, horripilar.

horrifying [jórrifaiing], *a.* horripilante.

horrisonous [jorrísonus], *a.* horrísono.

horror [jórrœr], *s.* horror.—**the horrors,** (fam.) melancolía, morriña; espasmo de horror.

horripilation [jorrípiléishun], *s.* (med.) horripilación.

horse [jors]. **I.** *s.* caballo; (mil.) caballería, caballos; caballete de secar ropa, borriquete, banco, bastidor, burro, borrico; tendedor, mesa de papel, etc.; (ten.) garatura o tabla de descarnar; (mar.) marchapié, guardamancebo, guindaste; manía, tema, chifladura, muletilla.—**h. aloes,** acíbar caballuno.—**h. ant,** hormiga roja.—**h. armour,** barda.—**h. artillery,** artillería montada o volante.—**h. bean,** haba panosa o caballuna.—**h. block,** apeadero; montador, montadero.—**h. boat,** tafurca.—**h. bot,** lombriz de caballo.—**h. boy,** mozo de cuadra.—**h. breaker,** picador o domador de caballos.—**h. brush,** bruza.—**h. car,** tranvía de fuerza de sangre; carro de transportar caballos.—**h.-chestnut,** (bot.) castaño de Indias; castaña que produce.—**h. cloth,** manta de caballo.—**h. dealer,** chalán.—**h. doctor,** albéitar; veterinario.—**h. drench,** toma de medicina para caballo.—**h. dung,** cagajón, estiércol de caballo.—**h.-faced,** de cara acaballada.—**h. guards,** guardias montadas; (Ingl.) cuartel general del ejército.—**h. keeper,** establero, mozo de cuadra.—**h. litter,** litera montada o tirada por caballos.—**h. mackerel,** (ict.) chicharro.—**h. mill,** molino de sangre.—**h. milliner,** fabricante de adornos para caballos.—**h. of a sail,** (mar.) nervio de vela.—**h. pistol,** pistola de arzón.—**h. power** = HORSEPOWER; fuerza de sangre.—**h. race,** carrera de caballos.—**h. racing,** carreras de caballos.—**h. sense,** sentido común práctico.—**h. thief,** cuatrero.—**h. trappings,** arneses.—**to get on, o mount, the high h.,** asumir una actitud arrogante.—**to h!** (mil.) ¡a caballo! **II.** *va.* montar a caballo; poner o llevar a caballo; (mil.) remontar, proveer de caballos: cubrir el caballo a la yegua; (mar.) forzar el trabajo. **III.** *vn.* cabalgar, andar a caballo; estar (la yegua) salida.

horseback [jórsbæc], *s.* lomo de caballo o asiento del jinete.—**to ride h.,** montar a caballo.

horsefair [-féær], *s.* feria de caballos.

horseflesh [-flésh], *s.* carne de caballo; conjunto de caballos; variedad de caoba de las Bahamas.

horsefly [-flái], *s.* tábano; rezno.

horsehair [-jéær], *s.* pelo de caballo (esp. de la crin y la cola); tela de crin.

horsejockey [-yóki], *s.* (dep.) postillón.

horselaugh [-láf], **horselaughter** [-láftœr], *s.* risotada.

horseleech [-lích], *s.* sanguijuela; albéitar, veterinario; posma.

horseload [-lóud], *s.* carga de caballo.

horseman [-man], *s.* jinete, caballero; (mil.) soldado de caballería.—**horsemanship** [-ship], *s.* manejo, equitación.

horsemint [-mínt], *s.* (bot.) mastranzo.

horseplay [-pléi], *s.* payasada.

horsepond [-pónd], *s.* estanque donde beben los caballos.

horsepower [-páucœr], *s.* caballo de vapor o de fuerza.

horseradish [-rædish], *s.* (bot.) rábano picante o rústico.

horseshoe [-shu], *s.* herradura; lo que tiene forma de herradura; (zool.) límulo, cangrejo.

horsetail [-téil], *s.* cola de caballo; (bot.) belcho.

horsewhip [-juíp]. **I.** *s.* látigo, (Am.) fuete. **II.** *va.* azotar, zurriagar, cruzar con látigo, dar fuetazos a.

horsewoman [-úman], *s.* amazona.

horsey [jórsi] = HORSY.

horsiness [jórsines], *s.* afición a los caballos.

horsing [jórsing], *s.* asiento del amolador de cuchillos; azoles.

horsy [jórsi], *a.* caballar, caballuno, chalán.

hortation [jortéshun], *s.* exhortación.

hortative [jórtativ], **hortatory** [-tori], *a.* exhortatorio.

hortensial [jorténshal], *a.* hortense, hortelano.

horticultural [jórticúlchural], *a.* hortícola.
horticulture [-chur], *s.* horticultura.
horticulturist [-ist], *s.* horticultor.
hortus siccus [jórtus sícus], *s.* herbario.
hosanna [josǽna], *s.* hosana.
hose [jóuś], *s.* calceta; medias o calzas; manguera.—**h. reel,** carretel de manguera.
hoseman [jóusmæn], *s.* manguero.
hosier [jóyœr], *s.* mediero, calcetero.
hosiery [jóyœri], *s.* calcetería.—**h. yarn,** hilo de punto o de calcetería.
hospice [jóspis], *s.* hospicio, hospedería.
hospitable [jóspitabœl], *a.* hospitalario.—**hospitableness** [-nes], *s.* hospitalidad.—**hospitably** [-tabli], *adv.* hospitalariamente.
hospital [jóspital], *s.* hospital.—**h. ship,** buque hospital.—**h. wagon,** carro de ambulancia.—**h. ward,** sala o crujía de hospital.
hospitality [jóspitǽliti], *s.* hospitalidad.
hospital(l)er [jóspitalœr], *s.* hospitalario; hospiciano; hospitalero.
hospitium [jospíshum *o* pítium], *s.* hospicio.
host [jóust], *s.* hospedero, mesonero, posadero; huésped, anfitrión; hueste; multitud; (igl.) hostia.
hostage [jóstey], *s.* rehén, prenda, gaje.
hostel [jóstel], *s.* posada, hostería; hotel; casa de huéspedes para estudiantes.
hostelry, hostlery [-ri], *s.* fonda, mesón, hotel.
hostess [jóstes], *s.* posadera, mesonera, patrona, huéspeda, ama.
hostile [jóstil], *a.* hostil, enemigo.
hostilely [jóstil-li], *adv.* hostilmente.
hostility [jóstíliti], *s.* hostilidad.
hostilize [jóstilaíś], *va.* hostilizar.
hostler [jóslœr], *s.* establero, palafrenero.
hot [jat], *a.* cálido, caliente; caluroso; ardiente, fogoso; picante, acre; violento, furioso; (fam.) intolerable; en caliente; (fam.) cercano (de algo que se busca).—**h. and heavy,** (fam.) furioso.—**h. blast,** tiro de aire caliente.—**h.-blooded,** apasionado, de sangre ardiente.—**h. chisel,** cincel para metal caliente.—**h.-head,** persona fogosa o exaltada.—**h.-headed,** fogoso, exaltado.—**h.-livered,** irascible, botafuego.—**h. mustard,** mostaza muy picante.—**h.-press,** *s.* prensa de satinar papel en caliente; prensa térmica para la extracción del aceite; *va.* satinar (papel) en caliente.—**h. pursuit,** perseguimiento enérgico; (der. int.) perseguimiento extraterritorial de violadores del territorio nacional.—**h. riveting,** remachado en caliente.—**h.-roll,** laminar en caliente.—**h.-rolled,** laminado en caliente.—**h. saw,** sierra de cortar metal en caliente.—**h.-water bottle,** calientapiés de caucho para agua caliente.—**h.-wire,** térmico (apl. a varios instrumentos eléctricos).—**to be burning h.,** estar que quema; hacer mucho calor.—**to be in h. water,** (fam.) estar en ascuas o en calzas prietas.
hotbed [jótbed], *s.* almajara; (fig.) foco, plantel.
hotchpotch [jóchpóch], *s.* mezcolanza; sancocho.
hotel [jotél], *s.* hotel; palacio.
hothouse [jótjaus], *s.* invernadero, invernáculo.
hotly [jótli], *adv.* calurosamente; vehementemente; lascivamente.
hotness [jótnes], *s.* calidad de caliente; calor.
hotspur [jótspœr], *s.* y *a.* temerario, impulsivo, atolondrado.
Hottentot [jótentot], *s.* y *a.* hotentote.
hough [joj], = HOCK.
hound [jáund]. **I.** *s.* sabueso, podenco; collón, hombre vil; (mar.) cacholas.—**h.'s-tongue,** (bot.) cinoglosa, viniebla.—**h.-tree,** (bot.) cornejo. **II.** *va.* cazar con perros; soltar los perros; seguir la pista; perseguir; azuzar.
hour [áuœr], *s.* hora.—*pl.* horas (rezos).—**h. angle** (astr.) ángulo horario.—**h. circle,** (astr.) círculo horario.—**h. hand,** horario (del reloj).
hourglass [-glæs], *s.* ampolleta o reloj de arena.
houri [júri *o* jáuri], *s.* hurí.
hourly [áuœrli]. **I.** *adv.* a cada hora; por horas, frecuentemente. **II.** *a.* por horas, frecuente.

house [jáus]. **I.** *s.* casa; hogar, residencia, domicilio; casilla del tablero de ajedrez; (com.) casa de comercio, razón social, establecimiento mercantil; cámara de un cuerpo legislativo; (teat.) sala, público; (mec.) caja, cubierta.—**h. duty,** (Ingl.) impuesto sobre las casas.—**h. fly,** mosca ordinaria.—**h. of cards,** castillo de naipes.—**H. of Commons,** Cámara de los Comunes.—**H. of Lords,** o **of Peers,** Cámara de los Lores o de los Pares.—**h. of prayer** = H. OF WORSHIP.—**H. of Representatives,** Cámara de Representantes.—**h. of worship,** iglesia, templo.—**h. party,** convite de varios días; los convidados.—**h. physician,** médico residente o de asiento (en un hospital, casa, etc.).—**h. rent,** alquiler de casa.—**h. tax** = H. DUTY. **II.** *va.* albergar, alojar; (agr.) entrojar; poner a cubierto; almacenar; (mar.) afianzar o cubrir cuando hay borrasca; (carp.) encajar. **III.** *vn.* residir, tener alojamiento.
housebreaker [-bréicœr], *s.* ladrón que escala una casa.—**housebreaking** [-bréiking], *s.* escalo.
household [jáusjold], *s.* casa, familia.—**h. bread,** pan casero o bazo.—**h. furniture,** ajuar o menaje de casa.
householder [-jóldœr], *s.* amo de casa.
housekeep [-kíp], *vn.*, manejar casa, tener hogar propio; cocinar.
housekeeper [-kípœr], *s.* ama de gobierno o ama de llaves; casera; mujer de casa.
housekeeping [-kíping]. **I.** *s.* manejo de casa (se subentiende que comprende la cocina). **II.** *a.* casero, de casa; provisto de facilidades para cocinar.
houseleek [-lic], *s.* (bot.) siempreviva o hierba puntera.
houseless [-les], *a.* sin casa ni hogar.
housemaid [-méid], *s.* criada.
houseroom [-rúm], *s.* cabida de una casa.
housetop [-tóp], *s.* tejado; lugar público.
housewarming [-uórming], *s.* tertulia con que se celebra el estreno de una casa.
housewife [-uáif], *s.* ama de casa; madre de familia; ama de gobierno o de llaves; agujetero; estuche o neceser de costura.
housewifely [-suáifli]. **I.** *adv.* con economía doméstica. **II.** *a.* económica y cuidadosa.
housewifery [-uáifri], *s.* gobierno de una casa; economía doméstica.
housework [-uœrc], *s.* tareas domésticas.
housing [jáusing], *s.* alojamiento; abrigo, albergue; almacenaje; (mec.) muesca, rebajo, encaje; chumacera; caja; (aut.) caja, cárter; (arq.) nicho; (mar.) piola.—*pl.* mantilla, gualdrapa.
hove [jóuv]. **I.** *pret.* de TO HEAVE. **II.** *s.* enfermedad del ganado. *V.* HOOVE.
hovel [jóvel]. **I.** *s.* cobertizo; choza, cabaña, bohío. **II.** *va.* abrigar en cabaña.
hover [júvœr *o* jóvœr]. **I.** *va.* cubrir con las alas. **II.** *vn.* revolotear; rondar; estar suspenso; dudar.—**hovering** [-ing], *s.* revoloteo.
how [jáu]. **I.** *adv.* y *relat.* como; cuán, cuánto; a cómo; como (que).—**h. do you do?** ¿cómo le va a Vd.? ¿cómo está Vd.? para servir a Vd.?—¿a qué distancia? ¿hasta dónde?—**h. early?** ¿cuándo, a más tardar?—**h. late?** ¿a qué hora? ¿hasta qué hora? ¿cuándo?—**h. long?** ¿cuánto tiempo?—**h. many?** ¿cuántos?—**h. much?** ¿cuánto?—**h. now?** ¿y bien? ¿pues qué? ¿qué significa eso?—**h. so** = HOWSOEVER.—**h. so?,** cómo así?—**h. soon?** ¿cuándo?—**h. that,** como, que. **II.** *s.* cómo.
howbeit [jáubíit], *adv.* sea como fuere, así como así; no obstante, aunque.
howdah [jáuda], *s.* castillo que se pone sobre un elefante o camello.
howel [jáuel], *s.* (ton.) doladera.
however [jáuévœr]. **I.** *adv.* como quiera que, de cualquier modo; por muy.—**h. much,** por mucho que. **II.** *conj.* no obstante, sin embargo.
howitzer [jáuitsœr], *s.* (arti.) obús.
howl [jául]. **I.** *vn.* aullar, dar alaridos; ulular; rugir, bramar. **II.** *va.* gritar; (con *down* o *out*) condenar o echar a gritos. **III.** *s.* aullido, ululato; alarido; gemido; rugido; bramido.

howler [jáulœr], *s.* aullador; gemidor; gritador; mono chillón, araguato.

howlet [jáulet], *s.* lechuza.

howling [jáuling], *s.* aullido; grito; lamento.

howsoever [jáusoˆvœr], *adv.* como quiera; aunque; sin embargo.

hoy [joi]. **I.** *s.* (mar.) cáraba. **II.** *interj.* (mar.) ¡hola!

hoyden [jóiden], *s.* = HOIDEN.

hub [jʊb], *s.* (carr.) cubo de la rueda; por extensión, centro, eje; chito; calzo; manguito de doble bocina para juntas o empalmes; punzón para hacer troqueles.—**h.-and-spigot joint**, junta de enchufe de campana.—**the H.** (E. U., fam.) la ciudad de Boston.

hubbub [jʌbʊb], *s.* grita, alboroto, bulla.

huckaback [jʌcabæc], *s.* (tej.) alemanisco.

huckleberry [jʌcœlberi], *s.* (bot.) variedad de gayuba.

hucklebone [jʌcœlboun], *s.* (anat.) cía.

huckster [jʌcstœr]. **I.** *s.* vendedor ambulante al pormenor, esp. de productos agrícolas; sujeto ruin. **II.** *va.* y *vn.* regatonear, andar menudeando.

hucksterage [jʌcstœrey], *s.* regatonería.

huckst(e)ress [jʌcstœres], *s.* regatona.

huddle [jʌdl]. **I.** *va.* amontonar, desordenadamente; atrabancar. **II.** *vn.* acurrucarse; amontonarse, agruparse. **III.** *s.* tropel, confusión, baraúnda.

huddler [jʌdlœr], *s.* chapucero.

hue [jiú], *s.* matiz, tinte; grita, clamor.—**h. and cry**, alarma, somatén.

huff [jʌf]. **I.** *s.* enfado, enojo. **II.** *va.* hinchar, inflar; bravear; maltratar, injuriar; soplar una dama en el juego. **III.** *vn.* hincharse; engreírse; bufar; enfadarse.

huffish [jʌfɪʃ], *a.* irascible; petulante.

huffishly [-li], *adv.* con petulancia; insolentemente; con enfado.—**huffishness** [-nes], *s.* petulancia, arrogancia, impertinencia.

huffy [jʌfi], *a.* arrogante; irascible, malhumorado; hinchado.

hug [jʌg]. **I.** *va.* abrazar; abrazarse a; navegar muy cerca de (la costa).—**to h. one's self**, congratularse.—**to h. the wind**, (mar.) ceñir el viento.—**II.** *s.* abrazo.

huge [jiúy], *a.* inmenso, enorme.—**hugely** [-ii], *adv.* enormemente, inmensamente.—**hugeness** [-nes], *s.* enormidad, inmensidad.

hugger-mugger [jʌgœr-mʌgœr]. **I.** *s.* reserva, secreto; confusión, desorden. **II.** *a.* secreto, reservado; dejado, descuidado.

Huguenot [jiúguenot], *s.* hugonote.

hulk [jʌlc]. **I.** *s.* casco (de barco); carraca, barco viejo; armatoste, gordiflón. **II.** *va.* (min.). sacar (roca) antes de una voladura. **III.** *vn.* (gen. con *up*) convertirse en armatoste.

hulking [jʌlking], **hulky** [jʌlki], *a.* tosco, grueso, pesado.

hull [jʌl]. **I.** *s.* cáscara, corteza; vaina de legumbre; casco (de un buque). **II.** *va.* pelar, descortezar, descascarar; dar un proyectil en el casco de un buque.

hullabaloo [jʌlabalú], *s.* alboroto, batahola.

hullo [jʌló], *v.*, *s.* e *interj.* = HALLOO.

hully [jʌli], *a.* cascarudo.

hum [jʌm]. **I.** *va.* canturrear, tararear. **II.** *vn.* zumbar; susurrar; hervir (fig.). **III.** *s.* zumbido, susurro; voz inarticulada (¡hum!); engaño, filfa, burla, chasco. **IV.** *interj.* ¡ya! ¡hum!

human [jiúman]. **I.** *a.* humano.—**h. race**, género humano. **II.** *s.* mortal, ser humano.

humane [jiuméin], *a.* humanitario.

humanely [-li], *adv.* humanitariamente.

humanism [jiúmanism], *s.* letras humanas; humanidad.

humanist [jiúmanist], *s.* humanista.

humanitarian [jiumænitérian]. **I.** *a.* humanitario. **II.** *s.* filántropo; el que cree que Jesucristo no fué más que un hombre; el que cree en la perfectibilidad de la naturaleza humana; el que basa la religión únicamente en la filantropía.

humanitarianism [-ism], *s.* humanitarismo.

humanity [jiuméniti], *s.* humanidad; filantropía, benevolencia.—*pl.* **humanities**, humanidades.

humanize [jiúmanaiß] *va.* y *vn.* humanizar(se).

humankind [jiúmankáind], *s.* humanidad, género humano.

humanly [jiúmanli], *adv.* humanamente.

humble [jʌmbœl]. **I.** *a.* humilde.—**humble pie** [pái], *s.* empanada de entrañas de venado.—**to eat h. p.**, humillarse, pedir misericordia. **II.** *va.* humillar.

humblebee [-bí], *s.* = BUMBLEBEE.

humbleness [jʌmbœlnes], *s.* humildad.

humbles [jʌmbœlß], *s. pl.* entrañas de venado.

humbling [jʌmbling], *s.* humillación, abatimiento, rendimiento.

humbly [jʌmbli], *adv.* humildemente.

humbug [jʌmbʌg]. **I.** *s.* farsa, patraña, fraude; farsante, embaucador. **II.** *va.* y *vn.* embaucar.

humdrum [jʌmdrʊm]. **I.** *a.* monótono, pesado, cansado. **II.** *s.* fastidio, aburrimiento; lata; charla o cantilena fastidiosa; posma, zorrocloco, persona cargante.

humeral [jiúmœral], *a.* humeral.

humerus [jiúmœrus], *s.* (anat.) húmero.

humic [jiúmic], *a.* húmico, relativo al mantillo; (quím.) húmico.

humid [jiúmid], *a.* húmedo.—**h. process, way,** etc., (quím.) vía húmeda.

humidification [jiumídifikéißhun], *s.* humedecimiento.

humidify [jiumídifai], *va.* humedecer.

humidity [jiumíditi], *s.* humedad.

humiliate [jiumílieit], *va.* humillar.

humiliation [-éißhun], *s.* humillación.

humility [jiumíliti], *s.* humildad.

humming [jʌming]. **I.** *s.* zumbido, susurro. **II.** *a.* zumbador.—**h. ale**, cerveza fuerte y espumosa.—**h. bird**, (orn.) colibrí, pájaro mosca, tominejo.

hummock [jʌmoc], *s.* montecillo, morón, colina, mogote.

humo(u)r [jiúmœr]. **I.** *s.* humor, carácter, índole; humorada, fantasía, capricho; sal, agudeza, chiste, jocosidad; (med.) humor; buen humor; aguadija; (fam.) erupción cutánea. **II.** *va.* complacer, dar gusto, acceder; consentir en; mimar; adaptarse, acomodarse a; desempeñar bien.

humoral [jiúmoral], *a.* (med.) humoral.

humorism [-ism], *s.* (med.) humorismo; ingenio, gracejo; gracia, chiste.

humorist [jiúmorist], *s.* humorista; chocarrero.

humorous [jiúmorus], *a.* jocoso, chistoso; voluntarioso, caprichoso.—**humorously** [-li], *adv.* jocosamente; caprichosamente.—**humorousness** [-nes], *s.* jocosidad, gracejo, donaire; humorada.

humorsome [-sʊm], *a.* caprichoso.

humous [jiúmus], *a.* que contiene humus o mantillo.

hump [jʌmp]. **I.** *s.* giba, joroba, corcova. **II.** *vn.* encorvarse, doblar la espalda.—**humped** [-d], *a.* jorobado, corcovado.

humpback [jʌmpbæc], *s.* giba, joroba; **jorobado.** —**humpbacked** [-d], *a.* jorobado, giboso.

humpy [jʌmpi], *a.* giboso.

humus [jiúmus], *s.* humus, mantillo.

Hun [jʊn], *s.* huno.

hunch [jʌnch]. **I.** *vt.* empujar, dar empellones; doblar la espalda. **II.** *vn.* abalanzarse. **III.** *s.* giba, corcova; empujón, empellón, codazo.

hunchback(ed, = HUMPBACK(ED.

hundred [jʌndred]. **I.** *a.* (precedido de *a* o *one*) ciento, cien.—**h.-legs**, ciempiés. **II.** *s.* ciento; (arit.) centena; centenar.—**by hundreds**, a o por centenares.—**by the h.**, por ciento; por centenares.

hundredfold [-fóuld], *a.* céntuplo.

hundredth [jʌndredz], *a.* centésimo, ciento (ordinal).

hundredweight [-uéit], *s.* (E.U.)100 libras (como 45.4 kg.); (Ingl.) 100 ó 112 libras (como 45.4 ó 50.8 kg.).

hung [jʌng], *pret.* y *pp.* de TO HANG.—**h. beef**, tasajo.—**h. jury**, (fam.) jurado en desacuerdo.

Hungarian [jʊnguérian], *a*. húngaro.

hunger [jʌ́ngœr]. **I**. *s*. hambre.—**h. strike**, recurso al suicidio por hambre (apl. a ciertos encarcelados). **II**. *va*. hambrear. **III**. *vn*. tener hambre.

hungrily [jʌ́ngrili], *adv*. hambrientamente.

hungry [jʌ́gri], *a*. hambriento; ganoso, deseoso; estéril, pobre.—**to be, o to feel, h.**, tener hambre.

hunk [jʌnk], *s*. (fam.) buen pedazo; rebanada gruesa.

Hunker [jʌ́ncœr], *s*. (hist. E. U.) conservador.

hunks [jʌncs], *s*. avaro.

hunky [jʌ́nki], *a*. (fam.) muy bien hecho; en buen estado.

Hunnish [jʌ́niś], *a*. huno.

hunt [jʌnt]. **I**. *va*. cazar; seguir, perseguir; recorrer buscando, registrar.—**to h. up**, buscar.—**to h. up and down**, buscar por todos lados. **II**. *vn*. cazar; hacer un registro minucioso; buscar.—**to h. after**, buscar, anhelar.—**to h. counter**, ir contra la pista. **III**. *s*. caza, cacería, montería; perseguimiento, acosamiento; asociación de cazadores.

hunter [jʌ́ntœr], *s*. montero, cazador; podenco; caballo de caza.—**h.'s cap**, montera, gorra de caza.

hunting [jʌ́nting], *s*. montería, caza, cacería.—**h. box**, pabellón de caza.—**h. case**, tapa de saboneta.—**h.-case watch**, saboneta.—**h. ground**, cazadero.—**h. horn**, corneta de montería, trompa de caza.—**h. horse**, caballo de caza.—**h. jacket**, cazadora.—**h. lodge**= H. BOX.—**h. match**, o **party**, batida, partida ⊃ caza.—**h. season**, tiempo de caza.

huntress [jʌ́ntres], *s*. cazadora.

huntsman [jʌ́ntsman], *s*. montero, cazador.

hurdle [jœ́rdœl]. **I**. *s*. zarzo, valla, cañizo; encañado, encujado; adral; (dep.) valla portátil en carreras de caballos; (mil) fagina, gabión, cestón; persona que toma parte en una carrera de obstáculos.—*pl*. carrera de obstáculos (ll. t. **h. race**). **II**. *va*. hacer o colocar cañizos; defender con faginas. **III**. *vn*. saltar vallas.

hurdy-gurdy [jœ́rdi-gœ́rdi], *s*. (mús.) gaita, zanfonia; rueda de choque, rueda Pelton.

hurl [jœrl]. **I**. *va*. tirar, lanzar, arrojar; pegar (un grito). **II**. *vn*. lanzarse, arrojarse. **III**. *s*. tiro, lanzamiento.

hurling [jœ́rling], *s*. antiguo juego parecido al football; en Irlanda, el juego llamado *hockey*.

hurlyburly [jœ́rlibœ́rli], *s*. batahola, baraúnda, alboroto.

hurra(h [jʊrrá]. **I**. *interj*. ¡viva! ¡hurra! **II**. *va*. y *vn*. aclamar, vitorear.

hurricane [jœ́rrikein], *s*. huracán.

hurried [jœ́rrid], *a*. y *pp*. de TO HURRY; precipitado, apresurado, hecho de prisa.—**hurriedly** [-li], *adv*. apresuradamente, precipitadamente.

hurry [jœ́rri]. **I**. *va*. y *vn*. apresurar(se); dar(se) prisa; afanar(se); obrar o hacer obrar a la carrera o con precipitación.—**to h. after**, correr detrás o en pos de.—**to h. away**, salir precipitadamente.—**to h. back**, volver de prisa; apresurarse a volver.—**to h. in**, hacer entrar de prisa; entrar con precipitación en.—**to h. into**, arrastrar, impeler hacia.—**to h. off**, huir, salir o hacer marchar de prisa.—**to h. on**, apresurar, precipitar; impulsar, empujar; apresurarse.—**to h. over**, pasar o hacer pasar rápidamente; despachar, expedir.—**to h. up**, apresurarse, darse prisa. **III**. *s*. prisa, premura, precipitación.

hurry-skurry (o **scurry**) [jœ́rri-scœ́rri], *adv*. confusamente, en tropel.

hurt [jœrt]. **I**. *va*. (pret. y *pp*. HURT) dañar, hacer mal o daño, lastimar, lisiar, estropear, herir; injuriar, ofender; perjudicar, damnificar.—**to h. one's feelings**, apenar a uno; herirle a uno el amor propio, venderlo. **II**. *vn*. doler. **III**. *s*. lesión, herida, contusión, lastimadura; mal, daño, perjuicio, detrimento. **IV**. *a*. lastimado, herido, lisiado; perjudicado.

hurtful [jœ́rtful], *a*. perjudicial, pernicioso, nocivo, dañino.—**hurtfully** [-i], *adv*. dañosamente, perniciosamente; injuriosamente.—**hurtfulness** [-nes], *s*. calidad dañosa, perjudicial; naturaleza dañina, peligrosa, perniciosa.

hurtle [jœ́rtœl]. **I**. *vn*. lanzarse, arrojarse con violencia. **II**. *va*. menear, blandir; lanzar o arrojar.

hurtleberry, *s*. V. HUCKLEBERRY y WHORTLEBERRY.

hurtless [jœ́rtles], *a*. inocente; ileso, intacto.

husband [jʊ́sband]. **I**. *s*. marido, esposo. **II**. *va*. ahorrar; manejar con economía; procurar marido a; ser o pasar por marido de.

husbandman [-man], *s*. agricultor, granjero.

husbandry [-dri], *s*. labranza, agricultura; producción agrícola; frugalidad, parsimonia; economía doméstica.

hush [jʊś]. **I**. *va*. apaciguar, aquietar; hacer callar.—**to h. up**, tapar, ocultar, mantener secreto. **II**. *vn*. estar quieto, callar, enmudecer, estar callado. **III**. *s*. silencio, quietud.—**h. money**, dinero con que se compra el silencio de alguien.—**h. boat**, **h. ship** = MYSTERY BOAT, etc. **IV**. *interj*. ¡chito! ¡silencio!

husk [jʊsk]. **I**. *s*. cáscara, vaina, pellejo, hollejo; bagazo; desperdicio. **II**. *va*. descascarar, desvainar, pelar, mondar, despellejar, deshollejar.

husked [jʊskt], *a*. que tiene cáscara, vaina o pellejo.—**husker** [-œr], *s*. descascarador, desgranador; abridor de ostras.

huskily [jʊ́skili], *adv*. roncamente; secamente.

huskiness [jʊ́skines], *s*. ronquera; calidad de cascarudo o cortezudo.

husking [jʊ́sking], *s*. acto de descascarar y desgranar maíz.—**h. bee**, reunión de vecinos para desgranar maíz.

husky [jʊ́ski], *a*. cascarudo, cortezudo; sin valor; ronco, rauco; (fam.) fuerte, fornido.

hussar [jʊśár], *s*. (mil.) húsar.

Hussite [jʊ́sait], *s*. husita, discípulo de Huss.

hussy [jʊ́si], *s*. buena pieza, tunanta, pícara; estuche o bolsa de costura.

husting [jʊ́sting], *s*. asamblea, junta.—*pl*. (Ingl.) tribuna pública para discursos electorales; consejo o tribunal de autoridades municipales.

hustle [jʊ́sl]. **I**. *va*. mezclar, confundir; empujar, atropellar, sacudir. **II**. *vn*. andar a empellones; (fam. E. U.) pernear, patear, moverse con actividad.

hustler [jʊ́slœr], *s*. (fam. E. U.) trafagón, buscavidas, persona enérgica.

hut [jʊt]. **I**. *s*. choza, cabaña, barraca; huta, bohío.—**h. urn**, urna cineraria. **II**. *va*. y *vn*. alojar o vivir en una choza.

hutch [jʊch]. **I**. *s*. arca, cofre; artesa; cesto; hucha; ratonera; conejera; amasadera; (min.) cuba. **II**. *va*. guardar en cofre.

huzza [jʊśá], *vn*., *s*. y *interj*. = HURRAH.

hyacinth [jáiasinz], *s*. (bot. y min.) jacinto.

hyacinthine [jaiasínzin], *s*. jacintino.

hyæna, *s*. = HYENA.

hyalin(e [jáiœlin], *s*. (quím.) hialino.

hyaline [-lin], *a*. vítreo, vidrioso, transparente.

hyaloid [-loid], *a*. hialoideo, hialino.

hybridism [jáibridiśm], **hybridity** [jaibríditi], *s*. hibridismo.

hybridize [jáibridaiś], *va*. y *vn*. producir o generar híbridos; ser capaz de cruzamiento.

hybridizing [-ing], *s*. hibridación.

hybrid(ous [jáibrid *o* jíbrid(ʊs], *a*. híbrido.

hydatid [jáidœtid], *s*. (med. y zool.) hidátide.

hydra [jáidra], *s*. hidra.

hydracid [jaidrǽsid], *a*. (quím.) hidrácido.

hydragog [jáidrægog], *s*. hidragogo.

hydrangea [jaidrǽnyea], *s*. (bot.) hortensia.

hydrant [jáidrant], *s*. boca de riego; boca de agua para incendios.

hydrargyric [jáidraryíric], *a*. hidrargírico.

hydrargyrum [-ʊm], *s*. hidrargiro, mercurio.

hydra(ta)tion [jáidr(at)éśhʊn], *s*. (quím.) hidratación.

hydrate [jáidret]. **I**. *s*. (quím.) hidrato. **II**. *va*. hidratar.

hydraulic(al [jaidrólic(al], *a*. hidráulico.—**h. cement**, cemento hidráulico.—**h. elevator**, ascensor hidráulico; draga hidráulica.—**h. forging**, forjadura hidráulica, forjadura en caliente por presión hidráulica.—**h. gage,** o **gauge,** manómetro hidráulico.—**h. gradient,** línea de alturas piezométricas.—**h. jack,** gato hidráulico.—**h. main,** receptáculo con agua para depurar el gas de alumbrado.—**h. mean depth,** o **mean radius=** H. RADIUS.—**h. mining,** minería hidráulica.—**h. power,** energía hidráulica, fuerza hidráulica.—**h. press,** prensa hidráulica.—**h. radius,** radio hidráulico, radio hidráulico medio, profundidad media (área dividida por el perímetro mojado).— **h. ram,** ariete hidráulico.—**h. valve,** válvula de máquina hidráulica; tapa acopada con los bordes sumergidos en agua.

hydraulic. **I.** *va.* y *vn.* excavar o demoler por chorros hidráulicos. **II.** *vn.* explotar minas por el método hidráulico.

hydraulician [jáidrolíshæn], *s.* hidráulico.

hydraulicking [jaidróliking], *s.* (min.) minería hidráulica; explotación hidráulica.

hydraulics [jaidrólics], *s. pl.* hidráulica.

hydrazin(e [jáidræšin], *s.* (quím.) hidracina.

hydric [jáidric], *a.* (quím.) hídrico.

hydrid(e [jáidrid, -draid], *s.* hidruro.

hydriodic [jáidriódic], *a.* (quím.) yodhídrico.

hydroaeroplane, hydroairplane [jáidroéiceropléin, -éærpléin], hidroaeroplano, hidroavión.

hydrobromic [jáidrobrómic], *a.* bromhídrico.

hydrocarbon [jáidrocárbœn], *s.* (quím.) hidrocarburo.

hydrocele [jáidrosil], *s.* (cir.) hidrocele.

hydrocephalus [jáidroséfalus], *s.* (med.) hidrocefalia.

hydrochlorate [-clóret], *s.* clorhidrato.

hydrochloric [-clóric], *a.* clorhídrico.

hydrocyanic [-saiænic], *a.* cianhídrico o prúsico.

hydrodynamic(al [-dainæmic(al], *a.* hidrodinámico.

hydrodynamics [-dainæmics], *s.* hidrodinámica.

hydroelectric [-eléctric], *a.* hidroeléctrico.

hydrofluoric [-fluóric], *a.* (quím.) fluorhídrico.

hydrogen [jáidroyen], *s.* (quím.) hidrógeno.

hydrogenate, hydrogenize [jáidroyenet, -naiš], *va.* (quím.) hidrogenar.

hydrogenous [jaidróyenus], *a.* hidrogenado.

hydrographer [jaidrógrafœr], *s.* hidrógrafo.

hydrographic(al [jáidrográfic(al], *a.* hidrográfico.

hydrography [jaidrógrafi], *s.* hidrografía.

hydrokinetic [jáidrokinétic], *a.* hidrocinético o hidrodinámico.—**hydrokinetics** [-s], *s.* hidrocinética o hidrodinámica.

hydrologic(al [jáidrolóyic(al], *a.* hidrológico.

hydrology [jaidróloyi], *s.* hidrología.

hydrolysis [jaidrólosis], *s.* hidrólisis.—**hydrolitic** [jáidrolític], *a.* hidrolítico.

hydromancy [jáidromænsi], *s.* hidromancía.

hydromechanics [jáidromecænics], *s.* hidromecánica.

hydromedusa [-mediúsæ], *s.* (zool.) hidromedusa.

hydromel [jáidromel], *s.* hidromel, aguamiel.

hydrometallurgy [-métalœrri], *s.* hidrometalurgia.

hydrometeor [-mítior], *s.* hidrometeoro.

hydrometer [jaidrómetœr], *s.* areómetro; (hidr.) medidor de velocidad de una corriente, velocímetro.

hydrometric [jáidrométric], *a.* hidrométrico.— **h. pendulum,** péndulo hidrométrico.

hydrometry [jaidrómetri], *s.* areometría, teoría y uso del areómetro.

hydropathic [jáidropæzic], *a.* hidropático.

hydropathy [jaidrópazi], *s.* hidropatía.

hydrophobia [jáidrofóbia], **hydrophoby** [-fóbi], *s.* hidrofobia.

hydrophone [-foun], *s.* (mar., hidr.) hidrófono; (med.) estetoscopio de columna de agua.

hydroplane [-pléin], *s.* hidroplano, hidroavión.

hydroquinone [-cuinoun], *s.* hidroquinona.

hydroscope [-scoup], *s.* instrumento para observar el fondo del mar.

hydrostat [-stæt], *s.* (m. v.) indicador eléctrico de nivel.

hydrostatic(al [jáidrostǽtic(al], *a.* hidrostático. —**h. balance, joint. press, pressure,** balanza, conexión, prensa, presión hidrostática.—**hydrostatically** [-i], *adv.* hidrostáticamente.

hydrostatics [jáidrostǽtics], *s.* hidrostática.

hydrosulphide [jáidrosúlfaid], *s.* hidrosulfuro.

hydrosulphuric [-fiúric], *a.* sulfhídrico.

hydrotherapeutic [-zœrapiútic], *a.* hidroterápico.

hydrotherapeutics, hydrotherapy [-zœrapi], *s.* hidroterapia, hidropatía.

hydrothermal [-zœrmal], *a.* hidrotermal.

hydrothorax [-zóracs], *s.* (med.) hidrotórax.

hydrovane [-véin], *s.* timón horizontal para el movimiento vertical de un submarino.

hydrous [jáidrus], *a.* acuoso, aguado; hidratado.

hydroxid(e [jaidróxid, -aid], *s.* hidróxido.

hydroxyl [jaidróxil], *s.* oxhidrilo.

hyena [jaina], *s.* hiena.

hyetal [jáietal], *a.* pluvial; lluvioso.

hygiene [jáiyiin], **hygienics** [-ics], *s.* higiene.

hygienic [jaiyiénic], *a.* higiénico.

hygienically [-ali], *adv.* higiénicamente.

hygienist [jáiyienist], *s.* higienista.

hygrometer [jaigrómetœr], *s.* higrómetro.

hygrometric(al [jáigrométric(al], *a.* higrométrico.

hygrometry [jaigrómetri], *s.* higrometría.

hygroscope [jáigroscoup], *s.* higroscopio.

hygroscopic(al [-cópic(al], *a.* higroscópico.

hyli(ci)sm [jáili(si)šm], *s.* materialismo.

hylotheism [jáiloziism], *s.* panteísmo.

hylozoism [jáilošóišm], *s.* hilozoísmo, doctrina según la cual la vida y la materia son inseparables.

hymen [jáimen], *s.* himeneo; (anat.) himen.

hymeneal, hymenean [jaimenial, -an]. **I.** *s.* epitalamio. **II.** *a.* nupcial.

Hymenoptera [jaimenóptœra], *s. pl.* (ent.) himenópteros.—**hymenopteran** [-æn], **[hymenopterous** [-us], *a.* himenóptero.

hymn [jim]. **I.** *s.* himno. **II.** *va.* alabar con himnos. **III.** *vn.* cantar himnos.

hymnal [jímnal], *s.* himnario.—**hymnic** [-ic], *a.* perteneciente a los himnos.—**hymnology** [jimnóloyi], *s.* estudio, tratado o colección de himnos.

hyoid [jáioid]. **I.** *s.* (anat.) hioides. **II.** *a.* hioideo.—**h. arch,** arco hioideo.

hyoscine [jáiosin], *s.* (quím.) hioscina.

hyoscyamine [-saiæmin], *s.* (quím.) hiosciamina.

hypallage [jípæley], *s.* (ret.) hipalaje.

hyperacidity [jáipœræsiditi], *s.* hiperacidez, exceso de ácido en el estómago.

hyperæmia, hyperemia [jáipœrímia], *s.* (med.) hiperemia.

hyperæsthesia, hyperesthesia [-eszíšiæ], *s.* hiperestesia.

hyperbaton [jaipœrbaton], *s.* (ret.) hipérbaton.

hyperbola [jaipœrbola], *s.* (geom.) hipérbola.

hyperbole [jaipœrboli], *s.* (ret.) hipérbole.

hyperbolic(al [jaipœrbólic(al], *a.* hiperbólico.

hyperbolically [jaipœrbólicali], *adv.* hiperbólicamente.

hyperbolist [jaipœrbolist], *s.* exagerador.

hyperborean [jáipœrbórian], *a.* y *s.* hiperbóreo.

hypercompound [-cómpaund], *a.* (elec.) hipercompound.—**hypercompounding** [-ding], *s.* hipercompoundaje.

hypercritic [jáipœrcrític], *s.*, **hypercritical** [-al], *a.* hipercrítico.

hyperdulia [jáipœrdiúlaiæ], **hyperduly** [jáipœrdiúli], *s.* hiperdulía.

hyperemia = HYPERÆMIA.

Hypericaceæ [jáipœrikései o cásee], *s. pl.* (bot.) hipericíneas.

hypericum [jaipéricum], *s.* (bot.) hipérico.

hypermeter [jaipœrmetœr], *s.* hipermetría.

hypermetrope [jáipœrmétroup], *s.* y *a.* hipermétrope o présbita.—**hypermetropia** [-metróupiæ], *s.* hipermetropía, presbicia.

hypertrophic [jáipœrtrófic], *a.* hipertrófico.
hypertrophy [jaipœrtrofi]. **I.** *s.* (med.) hipertrofia; (fig.) aumento excesivo. **II.** *va.* y *vn.* hipertrofiar(se).
hyphæmia, hyphemia [jaifímiæ], *s.* hifemia, anemia; extravasación de la sangre, esp. en el ojo.
hyphen [jáifen], *s.* guión (-).
hyphenate [jáifeneit], *va.* separar con guión.
hyphenated [-ed], *a.* (E. U.) de doble nacionalidad (apl. a extranjeros nacionalizados, esp. a los que prefieren su país natal al adoptivo).
hyphenation [-éishʊn], *s.* separación de sílabas con guiones.
hypnosis [jipnósis], *s.* hipnosis.
hypnotic [jipnótic], *a.* hipnótico.
hypnotism [jípnotism], *s.* hipnotismo.
hypnotize [jípnotaiś], *va.* hipnotizar.
hypnotizer [-œr], *s.* hipnotizador.
hypo [jáipou], *s.* (fot.) hiposulfito.
hypoblast [-blæst], *s.* hipoblasto, endodermo.
hypocaust [-cost], *s.* hipocausto.
hypochlorous [-clóʊrus], *a.* hipocloroso.—**hypochlorite** [-clóʊraitl, *s.* hipoclorito.
hypochondria [jipo- o jáipocóndria], **hypochondriasis** [jipocondríasis], *s.* hipocondría.
hypochondriac [-cóndriac], *s.* hipocondríaco.
hypochondriac(al [-condriáiacal], *a.* hipocondríaco, hipocóndrico.
hypocondrium [-cóndriʊm], *s.* (anat.) hipocondrio.
hypocrisy [jipócrisi], *s.* hipocresía.
hypocrite [jipócrit], *s.* hipócrita.—**hypocritical** [-crítical], *a.* hipócrita.—**hypocritically** [-i], *adv.* hipócritamente.
hypocycloid [jáiposáicloid], *s.* (geom.) hipocicloide.
hypoderm [-dœrm], *s.* (ento.) hipodermis.
hypodermic [-dérmic], *a.* hipodérmico.—**h. injection, syringe** (o simplemente **hypodermic,** *s.*) inyección, jeringa hipodérmicas.
hypogastric [-gǽstric], *a.* hipogástrico.
hypogastrium [-gǽstriʊm], *s.* hipogastro.
hypogeal [-yízl], *a.* subterráneo; (geol.) hipogénico, de formación subterránea, plutónico.
hypogene [-yin], *a.* (geol.) hipogénico, plutónico.
hypogeous [-yíʊs], *a.* subterráneo; (bot.) de crecimiento subterráneo.
hypogeum [jipoyíʊm], *s.* hipogeo.
hypoglossal [jáipoglóssæl], **I.** *a.* hipogloso. **II.** *s.* nervio hipogloso.
hypogynous [jaipóyinʊs], *a.* (bot.) hipógino.
hyponitrous [jáiponáitrʊs], *a.* hiponitroso.
hypophosphite [-fósfait], *s.* hipofosfito.
hypophyge [jipófiyi], *s.* (arq.) nacela.
hypophysis [jaipófisis], *s.* (anat.) hipófisis, glándula pituitaria (llám. t. **h. cerebri**); (bot.) hipófisis, célula proveniente del suspensor contiguo.
hypostasis [jaipóstasis], *s.* base, fundamento; (teol.) hipóstasis; (med.) sedimento de la orina.
hypostatic(al [jaipostǽtic(al], *a.* hipostático; constitutivo; personal.
hypostatically [-i], *adv.* hipostáticamente.
hypostatize [jaipóstætaiś], *va.* objetivar, atribuir existencia real a.
hyposulphate [jáiposúlfeit], *s.* hiposulfato.
hyposulphite [-fait], *s.* hiposulfito.
hypotenuse [jaipótenius], *s.* (geom.) hipotenusa.
hypothec [jaipózec], *s.* (for.) hipoteca.
hypothecate [jaipózekeit], *va.* hipotecar, empeñar, pignorar.
hypothecation [jaipózekéishʊn], *s.* pignoración.
hypothecator [jaipózekeitœr], *s.* el que pignora o da en hipoteca.
hypothenuse [jaipózenius] = HYPOTENUSE.
hypothesis [jaipózesis], *s.* hipótesis.
hypothetic(al [jáipozétic(al], *a.* hipotético.
hypothetically [-i], *adv.* hipotéticamente.
hypsometer [jipsómetœr], *s.* hipsómetro.
hypsometric(al [jípsométric(al], *a.* hipsométrico.

hypsometry [jipsómetri], *s.* hipsometría.
hyrse [jœrs], *s.* (bot.) mijo.
hyson [jáisʊn], *s.* (com.) cha o te verde.
hyssop [jísʊp], *s.* (bot.) hisopo.
hysterectomy [jísteréctomi], *s.* histerectomía, extirpación del útero.
hysteresis [jistérisis], *s.* (elec.) histéresis.—**h. cycle,** ciclo o lazo de histéresis.—**h. loss,** pérdida por histéresis.—**h. loop** = H. CYCLE.
hysteria [jistíria], *s.* (med.) histeria, histerismo.
hysteric(al [jistéric(al], *a.* histérico.
hysterics [jistérics], *s.* = HYSTERIA.
hysteritis [jisteráitis], *s.* histeritis, metritis.
hysterotomy [-rótomi], *s.* histerotomía; operación cesárea; incisión uterina.

I

i [ái], *s.* i.
I, *pron. pers.* (siempre con mayúscula) yo.
I, *s.* el yo (en metafísica).
I, *a.* en I; de doble T.—**I bar,** barra de doble T.—**I beam, I girder,** viga de doble T.—**I iron** = I BAR.—**I rail,** riel de doble T.
iambic [aiémbic]. **I.** *a.* (poét.) yámbico. **II.** *s.* (pros.) yambo; verso yámbico.
iambus [aiémbus], *s.* (pros.) yambo
Iberian [aibírian], *a.* ibérico.
ibex [áibecs], *s.* íbice, cabra montés.
ibis [áibis], *s.* (orn.) ibis.
Icarian [ai- o ikérian], *a.* icario; arriesgado.
ice [áis]. **I.** *s.* hielo; sorbete, granizado, garapiña.—**I. boat,** bote con patines que anda sobre el hielo; barco rompehielos.—**I. box,** nevera, refrigerador.—**I. breaker,** espolón rompehielos.—**I. chest** = I. BOX.—**I. cream,** helado.—**I.-cream parlor,** heladería, tienda donde se sirve y se vende helado.—**I. drift, I. field, I. float, I. floe,** témpano de hielo flotante.—**I. house,** nevera o nevería.—**I. pick,** punzón para romper hielo.—**I. plant,** (bot.) escarchada.—**I. water,** agua de nieve, agua enfriada con hielo. **II.** *va.* helar; enfriar con hielo; garapiñar; cubrir con alfeñique.
iceberg [áisbœrg], *s. iceberg,* témpano grande de hielo flotante.
icebound [áisbáund], *a.* rodeado de hielo; pegado en el hielo o detenido por él.
iced [áisd], *a.* escarchado, congelado; enfriado con hielo; cubierto con alfeñique.
Icelander [áislǽndœr], *s.* islandés.
Icelandic [aislǽndic], *a.* islandés.
Iceland moss [áisland mos], *s.* (bot.) liquen o musgo de Islandia.—**I. spar** [spar], *s.* espato de Islandia.
iceman [áismæn], *s.* nevero, vendedor de hielo.
ichneumon [icniúmon], *s.* (zool.) icneumón, mangosta (cuadrúpedo); icneumón (mosca) (ll. t. **i. fly**).
ichnographical [ícnográfical], *a.* icnográfico.
ichnography [icnógrafi], *s.* icnografía.
ichor [áicor], *s.* (med.) icor.
ichorous [áicorus], *a.* icoroso.
ichthyocolla [ícziocóla], *s.* colapez o cola de pescado.
ichthyoid [íczioid], *a.* ictioideo.
ichthyol [íicziol], **ichthyol oil** *s.* ictiol.
ichthyologic(al [ícziolóyic(al], *a.* ictiológico.
ichthyologist [íczioloyist], *s.* ictiólogo.
ichthyology [-loyi], *s.* ictiología.
ichthyophagous [-fagus], *a.* ictiófago.—**ichthyophagy** [-yi], *s.* ictiofagia.
ichthyornis [ícziórnis], *s.* (pal.) ictiornis, odontotormes, pájaro con dientes en el pico.
Ichthyosauria [-sóriæ], *s. pl.* ictiosaurios.—**ichthyosaurus** [-ʊs], *s.* ictiosauro.
icthyosis [icziósis], *s.* ictiosis.
icicle [áisicœl], *s.* cerrión; carámbano.
icily [áisili], *adv.* fríamente, frígidamente.
iciness [áisines], *s.* frigidez.
icing [áising], *s.* capa de azúcar batida con clara de huevo (en tortas).
icon [áicon], *s.* imagen, representación; ilustración, grabado; icón, icono (imagen rusa.)

iconoclast [aicónoclæst], s. iconoclasta.
iconoclastic [aiconoclǽstic], a. iconoclasta.
iconography [áiconógrafi], s. iconografía.
iconolater [áiconólatœr], s. iconólatra.
iconology [áiconóloyi], s. iconología.
icosahedron [áicosajídron], s. icosaedro.
icteric(al [ictéric(al], a. y s. ictérico.
ictus [íctus], s. (med.) pulsación; latido; (pros.) acento tónico.
Icy [áisi], a. helado, frío, álgido.
I'd [áid], contr. de **I would**, o **I had.**
idea [aidía], s. idea.—**ideal** [aidíal], s. y a. ideal; prototipo.—**idealism** [aidíalĭsm], s. idealismo.—**idealist** [-ist], s. idealista.—**idealistic** [-lístic], a. idealista.
ideality [áidiǽliti], **idealness** [aidíalnes], s. idealidad.
idealization [aidíalĭséishun], s. idealización.
idealize, idealise [aidíalaiŝ], va. y vn. idealizar.
ideally [aidíali], adv. idealmente.
identical [aidéntical], a. idéntico.—**i. with**, idéntico a.—**identically** [-li], adv. idénticamente.—**identicalness** [-nes], s. identidad.
identification [aidéntifikéishun], s. identificación.
identifier [-faiær], s. identificador.
identify [-fai], va. identificar.
identity [aidéntiti], s. identidad.
ideograph [áidi- (o íde) ograef], s. ideograma.
ideographic [aidíográfic], a. ideográfico.
ideography [aidíografi], s. ideografía.
ideologist [aidíóloyist], s. ideólogo; idealista.
ideology [aidíóloyi], s. ideología.
ideomotor [áidiomótœr], s. ideomotor.
ides [áidŝ], s. pl. idus.
idiocy [ídiosi], s. idiotez, necedad.
idiom [ídium], s. modismo, idiotismo; habla, lenguaje, jerga; genio, índole de una lengua.
idiomatic(al [idiomǽtic(al], a. idiomático.
idiopathic(al [idiopǽzic(al], a. idiopático.
idiopathy [idiópazi], s. idiopatía.
idiosyncrasy [idiosíncrasi], s. idiosincrasia.
idiosyncratic [ídiosincrétic], a. idiosincrásico.
idiot [ídiot], s. idiota.
idiotic [idiótic], a. idiota.
idiotism [ídiotĭsm], s. idiotismo; idiotez.
idiopathy [idiópæzi], s. idiopatía.
idle [áidœl]. **I.** a. ocioso, desocupado; perezoso, haragán; inútil, vano.—**i. current**, (elec.) corriente devatiada o anérgica.—**i. fellow**, haragán.—**i.-headed**, desrazonable.—**i.-pated**, majadero.—**i. pulley**, polea de guía; polea de tensión.—**i. wheel**, rueda intermedia o de transmisión. **II.** vn. holgazanear o haraganear; holgar, estar ocioso; (aut.) funcionar (el motor) con el coche parado. **III.** va. (gen. con away) gastar ociosamente.
idleness [áidœlnes], s. ociosidad, ocio; pereza, holgazanería, haraganería, frivolidad; inutilidad.
idler [áidlœr], s. holgazán, azotacalles; (mec.) = IDLE PULLEY, IDLE WHEEL. V. IDLE.
idly [áidli], adv. ociosamene; desidiosamente; inútilmente, vanamente.
idol [áidol], s. ídolo.
idolater [aidólatœr], s. idólatra.—**idolatress** [-tres], s. mujer idólatra.—**idolatrous** [-trus], a. idólatra.—**idolatrously** [-li], adv. idolatradamente.
idolatry [-tri], s. idolatría.
idolize [áidolaiŝ], va. idolatrar.
idyl [áidil], s. idilio.
idyllic [aidílic], a. idílico; pastoral.
if [if]. **I.** conj. si.Ú. elípticamente en vez de if it is, if they are, etc.; vg. this, if true, is strange, esto, si es cierto, es extraño; if sold (= if it is sold), it must be sold well, si se vende, debe venderse bien.—**i. that**, si. **II.** s. hipótesis, suposición.
igad [igéd], interj. = EGAD.
igneous [ígneus], a. ígneo, vulcanio.
ignis fatuus [ígnis fǽtiuus], s. fuego fatuo.
ignitable, ignitible [ignáitibœl], a. inflamable.
ignite [ignáit]. **I.** va. encender, pegar fuego; (quím.) incinerar. **II.** vn. encenderse, inflamarse.

ignition [igníshun], s. ignición, inflamación; (m. comb. int.) encendido.
ignivomous [ignívomus], a. (poét.) ignívomo.
ignobility [ignobíliti], s. villanía, bajeza.
ignoble [ignóubœl], a. innoble, indigno; bajo, humilde.
ignobleness [-nes], s. bajeza.
ignobly [-bli], adv. innoblemente.
ignominious [ignomínius], a. ignominioso.
ignominiously [-li], adv. ignominiosamente.
ignominy [ignomini], s. ignominia.
ignoramus [ignorémus o ramus], s. ignorante.
ignorance [ignorans], s. ignorancia; desconocimiento; rusticidad, falta de cultura.—**ignorant** [-ant], a. ignorante, indocto; inculto o rústico.—**ignorantly** [-tli], adv. ignorantemente, neciamente, legamente.
ignore [ignóœr], va. desconocer, pasar por alto, no hacer caso de; ignorar; (for.) sobreseer; dar un fallo de "no ha lugar."
iguana [iguána], s. (zool.) iguana.
iguanadon [-don], s. iguanadonte.
ileac [íleæc], a. ilíaco.
ileum [íleum], s. (anat.) íleon (intestino).
ileus [íleus], s. (med.) íleo, cólico miserere.
ilex [áilecs], s. (bot.) acebo; coscoja.
iliac [íliæc], a. (med.) ilíaco.
Iliad [íliæd], s. Ilíada.
ilium [ílium], s. (anat.) íleon (hueso).
ilk [ilc], a. cada; ordinario; mismo (ú. a menudo pero erróneamente en el sentido de raza, clase).—**of that i.**, del mismo nombre.
ill [il]. **I.** a. enfermo; malo; mal; nocivo, dañino.—**i. blood**, animosidad, inquina.—**i. breeding**, malos modales.—**i. fame**, mala fama; reputación de inmoral (ap. esp. a la prostitución).—**i. nature**, mala disposición; malevolencia.—**i. temper**, mal genio.—**i. turn**, partida serrana, mala jugada.—**i. will**, mala voluntad, malquerencia.—**In i. part**, en mala parte. **II.** s. adversidad, calamidad; mal; malquerencia. **III.** adv. mal, malamente.—**i.-advised**, malaconsejado; mal pensado; desacertado.—**i.-affected**, descontento; malintencionado.—**i. at ease**, intranquilo, ansioso.—**i.-bred**, malcriado, descortés.—**i.-contrived**, mal pensado, mal dispuesto.—**i.-disposed** = I.-AFFECTED.—**i.-fated**, malhadado, malaventurado.—**i.-favored**, feo, repulsivo.—**i.-founded**, mal fundado, infundado.—**i.-gotten**, mal habido.—**i.-grounded** = I.-FOUNDED.—**i.-humored**, malhumorado.—**i.-minded**, maligno, mal intencionado.—**i.-natured**, avieso.—**i.-pleased**, malcontento.—**i.-shaped**, malhecho.—**i.-sorted**, mal juntado; mal pareado, incompatible.—**i.-sounding**, malsonante.—**i.-spoken of**, de mala reputación.—**i.-starred**, malaventurado, desdichado.—**i.-tempered**, áspero, de mal genio.—**i.-willed**, malévolo; de mal genio; reunente, maldispuesto.
I'll [áil], contr. de I SHALL o I WILL.
illation [iléshun], s. ilación, consecuencia, inferencia.
illative [ílativ]. **I.** a. ilativo. **II.** s. conjunción ilativa.
illatively [ílativli], adv. por ilación o inferencia.
illegal [ilígal], a. ilegal, ilegítimo.
illegality [ilegǽliti], **illegalness** [ilígalnes], s. ilegalidad; desaguisado.
illegally [ilígali], adv. ilegalmente.
illegibility [iléyibíliti], s. ilegibilidad.—**illegible** [-bœl], a. ilegible.—**illegibly** [-bli], adv. ilegiblemente.
illegitimacy [ileyítimasi], s. ilegitimidad.
illegitimate [ileyítimet], a. ilegítimo; espurio, falso; desautorizado. **II.** va. ilegitimar.—**illegitimately** [-li], adv. ilegítimamente.—**illegitimation** [-méishun], s. ilegitimidad.
illiberal [ilíbœral], a. iliberal, mezquino; estrecho de miras.—**illiberality** [-rǽliti], s. tacañería, ruindad; poquedad, apocamiento.—**illiberally** [-ali], adv. mezquinamente.
illicit [ilísit], a. ilícito; ilegal.—**illicitly** [-li], adv. ilícitamente.—**illicitness** [-nes], s. calidad de ilícito; ilegalidad.
illimitable [ilímitabœl], a. ilimitado; indefinido.

illimitably [-bli], *adv.* ilimitadamente.
illiquid [ílícuid], *a.* (for.) incierto, sin fundamento legal.
illision [ilíyʊn], *s.* choque, colisión.
illiteracy [ilítœrasi], **illiterateness** [ilítœretnes], *s.* analfabetismo; ignorancia.—**illiterate** [-tœret], *a.* analfabeto; ignorante.
illness [ílnes], *s.* mal, enfermedad.
illogical [ilóyical], *a.* ilógico.—**illogically** [-i], *adv.* ilógicamente.—**illogicality** [ilóyicæliti], **illogicalness** [-lóyicalnes], *s.* falta de lógica.
illtreat [íltrít], *va.* maltratar; acocear.
illtreated [-ed], *a.* maltrecho.
illume [iliúm], *va.* (poét.) iluminar; dorar.
illuminant [iliúminant. **I.** *a.* iluminador, iluminante. **II.** *s.* substancia iluminativa.
illuminate [-neit]. **I.** *va.* iluminar, alumbrar; aclarar, esclarecer; (b. a.) iluminar. **II.** *vn.* hacer luminarias.
illuminati [iliúminétai *o* náti], *s. pl.* secta de los iluminados.
illumination [-éishʊn], *s.* iluminación, alumbrado; luminarias; brillo, esplendor; inspiración; (b. a.) iluminación en colores.
luminative [-ativ], *a.* iluminativo.
illuminator [-eitœr], *s.* iluminador, reflector (lámpara, lente, etc.); (b. a.) iluminador.
illumine [iliúmin], *va.* iluminar.
illusion [iliúyʊn], *s.* ilusión.—**illusive** [iliúsiv], *a.* ilusivo, ilusorio.—**illusively** [-li], *adv.* ilusoriamente.—**illusiveness** [-nes], *s.* ilusión, calidad de ilusorio; embaimiento.—**illusory** [iliúsori], *a.* ilusorio; engañoso.
illustrate [ilʊstreit], *va.* ejemplificar; ilustrar, esclarecer con ejemplos; representar con grabados; ilustrar con grabados, etc.
illustration [ilʊstréíshʊn], *s.* ejemplo; (b. a.) ilustración, lámina.
illustrative [ilʊstrativ], *a.* ilustrativo.
illustratively [-li], *adv.* ilustrativamente.
illustrator [ilʊstreitœr], *s.* ilustrador.
illustrious [ilʊstriʊs], *a.* ilustre.—**illustriously** [-li], *adv.* ilustremente.—**illustriousness** [-nes], *s.* excelencia, grandeza.
I'm [áim], *contr.* de I AM, soy, estoy.
image [iméy]. **I.** *s.* imagen.—**i. worship,** culto de las imágenes. **II.** *va.* imaginar; formar imagen o idea clara de; representarse en la mente; pintar (fig.) vívidamente; parecerse a.
imagery [iméyri], *s.* imaginación, fantasía; conjunto de imágenes; exterioridad, apariencia; (b. a.) imaginería.
imaginable [imæyinabœl], *a.* imaginable.
imaginal [imæyinæl], *a.* relativo al insecto en su forma final o adulta. *V.* IMAGO.
imaginary [-neri]. **I.** *a.* (leng. ord. y mat.) imaginario. **II.** *s.* (mat.) imaginaria, cantidad imaginaria.
imagination [-néishʊn], *s.* imaginación; imaginativa, inventiva.
imaginative [-netiv], *a.* imaginativo; imaginario.
imagine [imæyin], *va.* imaginar; concebir; idear, inventar; figurarse, imaginarse. **II.** *vn.* imaginar, fantasear.
imagist [ímagist], *s.* poeta que escribe en verso absolutamente libre y con abundancia de imágenes o figuras.
imago [iméigo], *s.* imagen; (zool.) imago, forma adulta o final de un insecto.
imam [imám], *s.* imán (sacerdote, califa, etc. mahometanos).
imbecile [ímbesil], *a.* y *s.* imbécil.
imbecility [imbesíliti], *s.* imbecilidad.
imbed [imbéd], *va.* = EMBED.
imbibe [imbáib]. **I.** *va.* embeber, absorber; empaparse, saturarse de; esponjarse; (fig.) empaparse de alguna idea. **II.** *vn.* (fam.) beber (vino); empinar el codo.
imbibition [imbíbíshʊn], *s.* imbibición.
imbricate(d [ímbrikeit(ed], *a.* imbricado, encaballado, sobrepuesto.—**imbrication** [-éishʊn], *s.* imbricación, superposición.

imbroglio [imbróllo], embrollo, enredo.
imbrown [imbráun], *va.* = EMBROWN.
imbrue [imbrú], *va.* mojar, calar, empapar.
imbrute [imbrút], *va.* y *vn.* embrutecer(se).
imbue [imbiú], *va.* calar, empapar, infiltrar; tinturar, teñir; imbuir, infundir.
imitability [imitabíliti], *s.* calidad de imitable.
imitable [-bœl], *a.* imitable.
imitate [-teit], *va.* imitar.—**imitation** [-téishʊn]. **I.** *s.* imitación. **II.** *a.* de imitación, imitado; falso (joya, etc.).—**imitative** [-tativ], *a.* imitativo; imitatorio.—**imitator** [imitéitœr], *s.* imitador.
immaculacy [imækiulesi], **immaculateness** [-letnes], *s.* pureza, inocencia.
immaculate [-let], *a.* inmaculado.—**I. Conception,** Inmaculada Concepción.
immaculately [-li], *adv.* inmaculadamente.
immanacle [immænacœl], *va.* aprisionar con esposas; reprimir.
immanence, immanency [ímanens, i], *s.* calidad de inmanente; inherencia.
immanent [ímanent], *a.* inmanente.
immaterial [imatírial], *a.* inmaterial, incorpóreo; sin importancia, que no importa.—**to be i,** no importar, no tener importancia, ser indiferente.
immaterialism [-ism], *s.* espiritualismo; idealismo.—**immaterialist** [-ist], *s.* espiritualista; idealista.
immateriality [imatíríáliti], *s.* inmaterialidad, incorporeidad.
immaterialized [imatírialaisd], *a.* incorpóreo, espiritual.
immaterially [-i], *adv.* espiritualmente.
immaterialness [-nes], *s.* inmaterialidad.
immature [imatiúœr], *a.* inmaturo, verde; prematuro; imperfecto.—**immaturely** [-li], *adv.* prematuramente; sin madurez.—**immatureness** [-nes], **immaturity** [imatiúriti], *s.* calidad de inmaturo, falta de sazón.
immeasurability [iméyurabíliti], *s.* inconmensurabilidad.—**immeasurable** [-abœl], *a.* inmedible, desmesurado.—**immeasurably** [-bli], *adv.* inmensamente, desmesuradamente.
immediacy [imídiasi], *s.* inmediación, proximidad, contigüidad.
immediate [imídiet], *a.* inmediato, cercano; perentorio, próximo, instantáneo, urgente; directo; intuitivo.—**i. truths,** verdades intuitivas.—**immediately** [-li], *adv.* inmediatamente; directamente, intuitivamente.—**immediateness** [-nes], *s.* inmediación.
immedicable [imédicabœl], *a.* incurable, irremediable.
immemorial [imemórial], *a.* inmemorial.
immemorially [-i], *adv.* inmemoriablemente.
immense [iméns], *a.* inmenso.—**immensely** [-li], *adv.* inmensamente.—**immenseness** [-nes], **immensity** [-siti], *s.* inmensidad.
immensurability [imenshurabíliti], *s.* inconmensurabilidad.
immensurable [iménshurabœl], *a.* inmensurable.
immerge [iméry]. **I.** *va.* sumergir, zambullir. **II.** *vn.* ocultarse, perderse de vista.
immerse [imœrs], *va.* sumergir; anegar, sumir; bautizar por la inmersión.
immersion [imœrshʊn], *s.* inmersión, sumersión; bautismo por inmersión.
immesh [imésh], *va.* entrampar, enredar.
immethodical [imezódical], *a.* inmetódico.
immethodically [-i], *adv.* inmetódicamente.
immigrant [ímigrant], *s.* y *a.* inmigrante.
immigrate [ímigret], *vn.* inmigrar.
immigration [imigréíshʊn], *s.* inmigración.
imminence [íminens], *s.* inminencia.
imminent [íminent], *a.* inminente.
immiscibility [immisibíliti], *s.* (quím.) inmiscibilidad.
immiscible [immísibœl], *a.* inmiscible.
immission [-íshʊn], *s.* introducción, inyección.
immitigable [irnítigabœl], *a.* inmitigable.
immix [imícs], *va.* mezclar, juntar.
immobile [imóbil], *a.* inmóvil, inmovible.
immobility [imobíliti], *s.* inmovilidad.

immobilize [imóbilaiŝ], va. inmovilizar; paralizar.

immoderate imódœret], a. inmoderado, excesivo; desarreglado.—**immoderately** [-li], adv. inmoderadamente. — **immoderateness** [-nes], o **immoderation** [-éiŝhυn], s. inmoderación, exceso, desarreglo.

immodest [immódest], a. impúdico, indecoroso, indecente; impudente, atrevido.—**immodestly** [-li], adv. inmodestamente.—**immodesty** [-i], s. inmodestia, impudicia, falta de pudor.

immolate [ímolet], va. inmolar.—**immolation** [-éiŝhυn], s. inmolación.—**immolator** [-éitœr], s. inmolador.

immoral [imóral], a. inmoral; corrompido, vicioso.

immorality [imoráliti], s. inmoralidad.

immortal [imórtal], a. y s. inmortal.—**immortality** [imortǽliti], s. inmortalidad.—**immortalization** [-ŝéiŝhυn], s. perpetuación.—**immortalize** [imórtalaiŝ], va. inmortalizar.—**immortally** [imórtali], adv. inmortalmente.

immortelle [imortél], s. (bot.) siempreviva, perpetua.

immotile [imótil], a. (bot.) inmoto, fijo.

immovability [imúvabíliti], **immovableness** [imúvabœlnes], s. inmovilidad; inamovilidad; inmutabilidad; inalterabilidad; insensibilidad.

immovable [imúvabœl], a. inmóvil, inmovible, inamovible; inmutable, firme, inalterable; impasible, apático; (for.) inmueble.—pl. bienes raíces.—**immovably** [-bli], adv. inmutablemente, inalterablemente.

immune [imiún]. a. y s. inmune.

immunity [iniúniti], s. inmunidad.

immunize [imiúnaiŝ], va. inmunizar.

immunization [-niŝéiŝhυn], s. inmunización.—**immunology** [imiunóloϳi], s. ciencia que trata de la inmunidad.

immure [imiúœr], va. emparedar.

immutability [imiutabíliti], s. inmutabilidad, firmeza, constancia.—**immutable** [imiútabœl], a. inmutable.—**immutably** [-bli], adv. inmutablemente.

imp [imp], s. diablillo, trasgo; picaruelo, tunantuelo.

impact [impǽct], va. empaquetar.

impact [ímpæct], s. choque.

impaction [impǽcŝhυn], s. (med.) infarto; presión.

impair [impéœr], va. .mpeorar, dañar, perjudicar, menoscabar, deteriorar.—**impairment** [-mœnt], s. empeoramiento, deterioro, menoscabo.

impale, va. = EMPALE.

impalpability [impǽlpabíliti], s. impalpabilidad.

impalpable [-bœl], a. impalpable, intangible.

impanate [impǽnet], a. (teol.) existente en el pan de la eucaristía.

impanel [impǽnel], va. (for.) formar la lista de los jurados; elegir (jurado).

imparity [impǽriti], s. desigualdad, desproporción; disparidad.

impart [impárt], va. impartir, comunicar, dar; conceder; compartir.

impartial [impárŝhal], a. imparcial.

impartiality [impárŝhiǽliti], s. imparcialidad.

impartially [impárŝhali], adv. imparcialmente.

impartible [impártibœl], a. impartible, indivisible; comunicable; concedible.

impartment [-pártmœnt], s. participación; comunicación.

impassability [impǽsabíliti], **impassableness** [-bœlnes], s. calidad de intransitable o de insuperable.—**impassable** [-bœl], a. intransitable, impracticable; insuperable.

impasse [ǽnpás], s. atolladero, dificultad insuperable, desavenencia irreconciliable.

impassibility [impǽsibíliti], **impassibleness** [-bœlness], s. impasibilidad.

impassible [-ibœl], a. impasible.

impassion [impǽŝhυn], va. (poét.) conmover.

impassionable [-æbœl], a. conmovible.

impassionate [-eit], va. apasionar; conmover o afectar.

impassioned [impǽŝhυnd], a. apasionado, vehemente, extremoso.

impassive [impǽsiv], a. impasible.

impassiveness [-nes], s. impasibilidad.

impastation [impastéŝhυn], s. (cerá.) pasta, empaste.

impaste [impéist], va. hacer pasta; (pint.) empastar.

impatience [impéiŝhens], s. impaciencia.

impatient [-ŝhent], a. impaciente.

impatiently [-li], adv. impacientemente.

impeach [impích], va. acusar (a un funcionario ante un tribunal); poner en tela de juicio.—**impeachable** [-abœl], a. delatable, censurable.—**impeacher** [-œr], s. acusador, denunciador, delator.—**impeachment** [-mœnt], s. acusación; imputación, delación, residencia.

impearl [impérl], va. aljofarar.

impeccability [impecabíliti], s. impecabilidad.

impeccable [impécabœl], a. impecable.

impecuniosity [impekiúniósiti], s. inopia.

impecunious [impekiúnius], a. pobre.

impedance [impídœns], s. (elec.) impedancia.—**I. coil,** bobina de reacción.

impede [impíd], va. impedir, estorbar.

impediment [impédimœnt], s. impedimento; obstrucción, traba, cortapisa.

impedimenta [impédiménta], s. pl. (mil.) impedimenta.

impeditive [impéditiv], a. impeditivo.

impel [impél], va. impeler, impulsar.—**impellent** [-ent]. I. a. impelente; impulsor. II. s. empuje, motor, móvil.—**impeller** [-œr], s. impulsor, motor.

impend [impénd], vn. pender; amenazar, amagar, por inminente.—**Impendence, Impendency** [-dens, i], s. inminencia, amago, amenaza.—**impendent** [-ent], **Impending** [-ing], a. inminente, amenazante.

impenetrability [impénetrabíliti], s. impenetrabilidad.—**Impenetrable** [-bœl], a. impenetrable.—**impenetrableness** [-nes], s. impenetrabilidad.—**impenetrably** [-bli], adv. impenetrablemente.

impenitence, impenitency [impénitens, i], s. impenitencia.—**impenitent** [-tent], a. y s. impenitente.—**impenitently** [-li], adv. sin contrición.

imperative [impérativ]. I. a. imperativo, imperioso. II. s. mandato perentorio; (gram.) imperativo.

imperatively [-li], adv. imperativamente.

imperator [imperéitœr], s. (hist. rom.) emperador, imperátor.

imperceptibility [impœrséptibíliti], **imperceptibleness** [-bœlnes], s. imperceptibilidad.

imperceptible [impœrséptibœl], a. imperceptible.—**imperceptibly** [-bli], adv. imperceptiblemente.—**imperceptive** [-tiv], a. incapaz de percibir.

imperfect [impœrfect]. I. a. imperfecto, defectuoso. II. s. (gram.) imperfecto.

imperfection [impœrfécŝhυn], s. imperfección, desperfecto, defecto.

imperfectly [impœrfectli], adv. imperfectamente.

imperfectness [-nes], s. imperfección.

imperforate(d [impœrforet(ed], a. imperforado.

imperforation [impœrforéŝhυn], s. imperforación, cerramiento, obstrucción.

imperial [impírial]. I. a. imperial. II. s. pera, perilla; (arq.) cúpula morisca; cosa superior en su clase.—**Imperialism** [-iŝm], s. imperialismo.—**Imperialist** [-ist], s. (pol.) imperial, imperialista.—**Imperially** [-i], adv. imperialmente.

imperil [impéril], va. poner en peligro, arriesgar.

imperious [impíríus], a. imperioso.—**imperiously** [-li], adv. imperiosamente.—**Imperiousness** [-nes], s. autoridad, mando; arrogancia.

imperishable [impériŝhabœl], a. imperecedero.

imperium impíriuɔm], s. (hist. rom.) imperio, mando absoluto; (for.) potestad, poder.

impermanence [impǽrmanens], s. instabilidad.

impermanent [-nent], a. que no es permanente.

impermeability [impǽrmiabíliti], s. impermeabilidad.—**impermeable** [-bœl], a. impermeable.

impersonal [impǽrsʊnal], a. impersonal.

impersonally [-i], adv. impersonalmente.

impersonate [impǽrsʊneit], va. personificar; (teat.) representar; imitar, remedar.

impersonation [-éishʊn] s. personificación; (teat.) representación, papel; imitación, remedo.

impersonator [-éitœr], s. personificador; (teat.) el que hace papel; imitador, remedador.

impertinence, impertinency [impǽrtinens, i], s. impertinencia; insolencia.—**impertinent** [-nent], a. impertinente; oficioso; insolente, atrevido.—**impertinently** [-li], adv. impertinentemente; insolentemente.

imperturbability [impœrtœbabiliti], s. imperturbabilidad, serenidad.—**imperturbable** [-bœl], a. imperturbable.—**imperturbably** [-bli], adv. imperturbablemente.—**imperturbation** [impœrtœrbéshʊn], s. calma, serenidad.—**imperturbed** [impœrtœrbd], a. sereno, sosegado.

impervious [impǽrviʊs], a. impermeable.

imperviously [-sli], adv. impenetrablemente.

imperviousness [-nes], s. impermeabilidad.

impetrative [ímpetretiv], a. impetrante.

impetuosity [impetiuósiti], s. ímpetu, impetuosidad.

impetuous [impétiuʊs], a. impetuoso, arrebatado.—**impetuously** [-li], adv. impetuosamente.—**impetuousness** [-nes], s. impetuosidad.

impetus [ímpetʊs], s. ímpetu, impulso.

imphee [ímfi], s. caña africana de azúcar.

impiety [impáieti], s. impiedad.

impinge [impíny], vn. tropezar, chocar.

impious [ímpiʊs], a. impío.—**impiously** [-li], adv. impíamente.—**impiousness** [-nes], s. impiedad.

impish [ímpish], a. travieso, endiablado.

implacability [implecabíliti], **implacableness** [impléecabœlnes], s. implacabilidad.

implacable [impléicabœl], a. implacable; inexorable.—**implacably** [-bli], adv. implacablemente.

implacental, implacentate [implaséntal, tet]. I. a. (biol.) que no tiene placenta. II. s. mamífero que no tiene placenta.

implant [implǽnt], va. plantar, acodar, ingerir; inculcar.

implantation [implǽntéshʊn], s. injertación, plantación; inculcación.

implead [implíd], va. (for.) demandar, poner pleito.—**impleader** [-œr], s. (for.) demandante, parte actora.

implement [ímplemœnt], s. herramienta, utensilio.—pl. utensilios, útiles, aperos, enseres.

implicate [ímpliket], va. implicar, envolver; enredar, embrollar.—**implication** [-éishʊn], s. deducción, inferencia; implicación; complicidad.

implicative [ímplicativ], a. deductivo, que se infiere.—**implicatively** [-li], adv. por deducción o inferencia.

implicit [implísit], a. implícito, sobrentendido; absoluto, sin reserva.—**i. faith**, fe ciega.

implicitly [-li], adv. implícitamente, tácitamente; sin reserva.—**implicitness** [-nes], s. calidad de implícito.

implied [impláid], a. implícito, sobrentendido.—**to be i.**, sobrentenderse.

impliedly [-li], adv. implícitamente.

imploration [imploréshʊn], s. imploración.

implore [implóœr], va. implorar.

imploringly [-ingli], adv. suplicantemente, con súplicas.

impluvium [implúviʊm], s. impluvio, estanque en el atrio de las casas romanas.

imply [implái], va. querer decir; significar, denotar; envolver; enredar; adscribir, atribuir.

impolicy [impólisi], s. impolítica.

impolite [impoláit], a. descortés, incivil.

impoliteness [-nes], s. descortesía, desatención; falta de urbanidad.

impolitic [impólitic], a. imprudente, indiscreto; impolítico.

imponderability [impóndœrabíliti], s. imponderabilidad.—**imponderable** [-bœl], a. imponderable, impesable.

imporosity [imporósiti], s. falta de porosidad.

imporous [impórʊs], a. no poroso.

import [impórt]. I. va. (com.) importar; denotar, significar; importar, interesar. II. vn. convenir, importar, tener importancia.

import [ímport], s. sentido, significación; importancia, valor.—pl. (com.) artículos importados.—**i. duty**, derechos de entrada o de importación.

importable [impórtabœl], a. importable.

importance [impórtans], s. importancia; consecuencia; vanidad, presunción, fachenda.—**important** [-tant], a. importante; presuntuoso, fachendero.—**importantly** [-li], adv. importantemente; engreídamente.

importation [importéshʊn], s. (com.) importación, entrada; artículo importado.

importer [impórtœr], s. importador.

importunate [impórchu- (o tiu) net], a. importuno, pesado, insistente.—**importunately** [-li], adv. importunamente.—**importunateness** [-nes], s. importunidad.

importune [impórtiun], va. y vn. importunar, instar, porfiar, machacar.

importuner [-œr], s. importunador.

importunity [importiúniti], s. importunidad, porfía.

imposable [impóʊsabœl], a. imponible.

impose [impóʊs], va. imponer; hacer pasar como bueno; (igl.) imponer las manos el obispo; (impr.) imponer.—**to i. on, o upon**, engañar, embaucar.

imposer [impóʊsœr], s. imponedor.

imposing [impóʊsing], a. imponente; tremendo.—**i. stone, o table**, (impr.) piedra, o mesa, de imponer.

imposition [impoʃíshʊn], s. imposición; impuesto, carga, tributo, gabela; abuso; impostura, engaño; (impr.) imposición.—**i. of hands**, (igl.) imposición de manos.

impossibility [impósibíliti], s. imposibilidad.

impossible [-ibœl], a. imposible; (for.) impracticable.—**impossibly** [-bli], adv. imposiblemente.

impost [ímpost], s. impuesto, tributo, gabela; (arq.) imposta.

impostor [impóstœr], s. impostor.

imposture [impóschœr], s. impostura.

impotence, impotency [ímpotens, i], s. impotencia; agenesia.—**impotent** [ímpotent], a. impotente.—**impotently** [-li], adv. impotentemente.

impound [impáund], va. encerrar, acorralar; recoger (agua) en un depósito; aprisionar; (for.) depositar.

impoverish [impóvœrish], va. empobrecer; menguar, deteriorar.—**impoverishment** [-mœnt], s. empobrecimiento.

impracticability [imprǽcticabíliti], **impracticableness** [-bœlnes], s. impracticabilidad.—**impracticable** [-bœl], a. impracticable; intratable, irrazonable, terco.

imprecate [ímprekeit], va. imprecar, maldecir.

imprecation [imprekéshʊn], s. imprecación.

imprecatory [imprecatori], a. imprecatorio.

impregnable [imprégnabœl], a. inexpugnable; impregnable.—**impregnably** [-bli], adv. inexpugnablemente.

impregnate [imprégnet]. I. va. empreñar, fecundizar; impregnar; imbuir. II. a. impregnado; preñada.

impregnation [impregnéshʊn], s. fecundidad, impregnación; fertilización; infusión.

impresario, s. (teat.) empresario.

imprescriptible [imprescríptibœl], a. imprescriptible.

impress [imprés], va. imprimir, grabar, estampar; marcar; fijar; imprimir, impresionar; inculcar, influir; (mil.) reclutar, enganchar; expropiar.

impress [ímpres], s. impresión, señal, huella; empresa, divisa, lema; (mil.) leva, enganche; expropiación.

impressibility [imprésibíliti], *s.* facilidad de impresionarse.

impressible [-bœl], *a.* impresionable; que se puede estampar.

impression [impréshʊn], *s.* impresión, estampa, sigilación; marca, señal; sello, estampado; impresión producida en el ánimo; idea o recuerdo vago; (impr.) impresión, edición.

impressionable [-abœl], *a.* impresionable, susceptible.

impressional [-nal], *a.* referente a la impresión.

impression(al)ist [impréshʊn(al)ist], *s.* (b. a.) impresionista.—**impressionism** [-íşm], *s.* (b. a.) impresionismo.—**impressionistic** [-ístic, *a.* (b. a.) impresionista.

impressive [imprésiv], *a.* que causa impresión; solemne, grandioso, imponente.—**impressively** [-li], *adv.* de modo poderoso o eficaz; imponentemente.—**impressiveness** [-nes], *s.* calidad de causar impresión; grandiosidad.

impressment [imprésmœnt], *s.* expropiación; (mil.) leva, enganche; requisición, requisa.

imprest [imprést]. **I.** *va.* (Ingl.) hacer (el Erario) un anticipo. **II.** *s.* anticipo que hace el Erario

imprevision [imprevíyʊn], *s.* imprevisión.

imprimatur [ímpriméitœr], *s.* imprimátur.

imprimis [impráimiş], *adv.* en primer lugar.

imprint [imprínt], *va.* imprimir, estampar; fijar, grabar en el ánimo, etc.

imprint [imprint], *s.* impresión, marca, señal, huella; (impr.) pie de imprenta.

imprison [impríşʊn], *va.* encarcelar, poner preso, aprisionar.—**imprisonment** [-mœnt], *s.* prisión, encarcelación.

imprisonment [-mœnt], *s.* prisión, encarcelación.

improbability [impróbabíliti], *s.* improbabilidad. —**improbable** [-babœl], *a.* improbable.—**improbably** [-bli], *adv.* improbablemente.

improbity [impróbiti], *s.* improbidad.

impromptu [imprómptiu *o* tu]. **I.** *a.* impremeditado, improvisado. **II.** *adv.* de repente, en el acto. **III.** *s.* repente, ímpetu; improvisación.

improper [imprópœr], *a.* impropio.—**i. fraction,** quebrado impropio.—**improperly** [-li], *adv.* impropiamente.

impropriate [impróprieit]. **I.** *va.* apropiarse; expropiar o secularizar bienes eclesiásticos. **II.** *a.* secularizado.—**impropriation** [-éishʊn], *s.* secularización de bienes eclesiásticos.

impropriety [impropráieti], *s.* impropiedad, incongruencia, indecoro.

improvability [imprúvabíliti], **improvableness** [imprúvabœlnes], *s.* mejoramiento, calidad de mejorable.—**improvable** [-bœl], *a.* mejorable; laborable, cultivable.—**improvably** [-bli], *adv.* mejorablemente.

improve [imprúv]. **I.** *va.* mejorar; enmendar; utilizar; aprovechar; hacer más útil o valioso. **II.** *vn.* mejorarse; mejorar; adelantar, progresar.—**to i. on,** o **upon,** mejorar, hacer mejor.

improvement [-mœnt], *s.* mejora; mejoramiento; adelanto, progreso; alivio, mejoría; adición o cambio valioso.—**i. on,** progreso sobre o con respecto a.

improver [imprúvœr], *s.* adelantador, mejorador, beneficiador; aprendiza de costurera.

improvidence [impróvidens], *s.* improvidencia, descuido, imprevisión, desprevención.—**improvident** [-dent], *a.* impróvido.—**improvidently** [-li], *adv.* impróvidamente.

improvisation [impróviséishʊn], *s.* improvisación.—**improvise** [improváiş], *va.* improvisar.—**improviser** [-œr], *s.* improvisador.

imprudence [imprúdens], *s.* imprudencia.—**imprudent** [-dent], *a.* imprudente.—**imprudently** [-li], *adv.* imprudentemente.

impudence [ímpiudens], *s.* impudencia, desfachatez, atrevimiento; impudicia.—**impudent** [-dent], *a.* impudente, descarado; impúdico.—**impudently** [-li], *adv.* descaradamente, impudentemente; impúdicamente.

impudicity [ímpiudísiti], *s.* impudicicia.

impugn [impiún], *va.* impugnar.—**impugnable** [impʊ́gnabœl], *a.* impugnable.—**impugnation**

[impʊgnéishʊn], *s.* impugnación.—**impugner** [impiúnœr], *s.* impugnador.—**impugnment** [impiúnmœnt], *s.* impugnación.

impulse [impʊls], *s.* impulso, ímpetu; estímulo, instigación, motivo; arranque, corazonada.

impulsion [impʊ́lshʊn], *s.* impulsión, impulso.

impulsive [-siv], *a.* y *s.* impulsivo.—**impulsively** [-li], *adv.* impulsivamente.

impunity [impiúniti], *s.* impunidad.

impure [impiúœr], *a.* impuro; sórdido; impúdico, deshonesto; manchado por el pecado; incorrecto (lenguaje).—**impurely** [-li], *adv.* impuramente. —**impureness** [-nes], **impurity** [-riti], *s.* impureza; adulteración; torpeza, deshonestidad.

imputable [impiútabœl], *a.* imputable.

imputability [-bíliti], **imputableness** [-nes], *s.* imputabilidad.

imputation [impiutéishʊn], *s.* imputación, acusación; reconvención, censura.

imputative [impiútativ], *a.* imputador.

impute [impiút], *va.* imputar, achacar.

imputer [impiútœr], *s.* imputador.

in. I. *prep.* en, de, por, con, durante, mientras, dentro de, de aquí a (según que denote situación, división, estado, modo, disposición, duración, causa, objeto, fin, etc.), v. gr.: *he is in Paris,* está en París; *the best hotel in Paris,* el mejor hotel de París; *in the morning,* por la mañana; *in writing,* por escrito; *in fun, in jest,* en broma, por broma; *in deference,* por deferencia; *in ink,* con tinta; *in anger,* con ira; *in his sleep,* durante el sueño, cuando está dormido; *he will come in a week,* vendrá de aquí a una semana.—**i. as much as,** o **inasmuch as,** en cuanto, hasta donde; tanto como; por cuanto, porque, a causa de que.—**i. that,** en que; por cuanto. **II.** *adv.* dentro, adentro; en casa, en su oficina, etc.; hacia adentro; en el poder; en su turno.—**i. - and - i.,** de una misma casta.—**i. here, there,** etc. aquí dentro, allí dentro, etc.—**i.- and-out,** que sale y entra alternativamente; a veces bueno y a veces malo; (mec.) de vaivén; (alb.) de sogas y tizones alternados verticalmente.—**to be i.,** haber entrado o llegado; estar en casa, la oficina, etc.—**to be i. for,** estar expuesto a, echarse a cuestas, estar metido en (trabajos, etc.).—**to be i. with,** gozar del favor de. **III.** *s.* rincón, recodo; miembro (de un partido) a quien se le ha dado empleo público; persona que está adentro; jugador del lado que lleva el *bat.*— **ins and outs,** interioridades, pormenores minuciosos. **IV.** *a.* de adentro; interior, interno; que está en el poder; que está en su turno.

inability [inabíliti], *s.* inhabilidad, incapacidad, ineptitud; impotencia.

inaccessibility [inæcsésibíliti], *s.* inaccesibilidad. —**inaccessible** [-bœl], *a.* inaccesible.—**inaccessibly** [-bli], *adv.* inaccesiblemente.

inaccuracy [inækiurasi], *s.* inexactitud, incorrección, error.—**inaccurate** [-kiuret], *a.* inexacto, erróneo.—**inaccurately** [-li], *adv.* incorrectamente; inexactamente.

inaction [inæcshʊn], *s.* inacción.

inactive [inæctiv], *a.* inactivo, inerte.—**inactively** [-li], *adv.* inactivamente.—**inactivity** [inæctíviti], *s.* inactividad, ociosidad.

inadequacy [inædecuæsi], *s.* insuficiencia; falta de adecuación.—**inadequate** [inædecuet], *a.* inadecuado.—**inadequately** [-li], *adv.* inadecuadamente.—**inadequateness** [-nes], *s.* imperfección, falta de adecuación.

inadmissible [inædmísibœl], *s.* inadmisible.

inadvertence, inadvertency [inædvœrtens, i], *s.* inadvertencia.—**inadvertent** [-tent], *a.* inadvertido, accidental; negligente, descuidado.—**inadvertently** [-li], *adv.* inadvertidamente.

inaffable [inæfabœl], *a.* poco afable.

inalienable [inélienabœl], *a.* inalienable.

inalienably [-bli], *adv.* inalienablemente.

inalterability [inólteorabíliti], *s.* inalterabilidad.

inalterable [inólterabœl], *a.* inalterable.

inamorata [inæmorátæ], *s.* mujer amada; mujer enamorada.

inane [inéin]. **I.** *a.* sandio, mentecato; inane, vacío, insubstancial. **II.** *s.* vacío; espacio infinito.

inanimate(d [ínǽnimeit(ed], *a.* inanimado; exánime.

inanimateness [-meitnes], **inanimation** [-méishŭn], *s.* falta de animación, de vida.

inanition [inaníshŭn], *s.* inanición; vaciedad.

inanity [inǽniti], *s.* inanición; insubstancialidad, sandez, mentecatada.

inappeasable [inæpísaboel], *a.* implacable.

inappetence, inappetency [inǽpetens, i], *s.* inapetencia.

inapplicability [inǽplicabíliti], *s.* falta de aplicabilidad.

inapplicable [inǽplicaboel], *a.* inaplicable.

inapposite [inǽposit], *a.* inoportuno; inaplicable; discordante.

inappreciable [inæpríshiaboel], *a.* inapreciable, inestimable.

inapprehensible [inæprejénsiboel], *a.* ininteligible, incomprensible.

inapproachable [inæpróchaboel], *a.* inaccesible, inasequible.

inappropirate [inæprópriet], *a.* inadecuado, impropio, inapropiado.—**inappropriately** [-li], *adv.* impropiamente, fuera del caso.—**inappropriateness** [-nes], *s.* impropiedad, incorrección.

inaptitude [inǽptitiud], *s.* ineptitud.

inarable [inǽraboel], *a.* incultivable.

inarch [inárch], *va.* injertar por aproximación.

inarticulate [inartíkiulet], *a.* inarticulado.—**inarticulately** [-li], *adv.* de modo inarticulado.—**inarticulateness** [-nes], *s.* calidad de inarticulado.

inartificial [inártifíshal], *a.* natural, simple, sencillo, sin artificio.

inasmuch as [inasmŭch ǽs], = IN AS MUCH AS. V. IN, *prep.*

inattention [inaténshŭn], *s.* desatención, distracción, inadvertencia.—**inattentive** [inaténtiv], *a.* desatento.—**inattentively** [-li], *adv.* descuidadamente, sin atención.

inaudibility [inódibíliti], **inaudibleness** [boelnes], *s.* calidad de inaudible.

inaudible [inódiboel], *a.* inaudible.

inaugural [inóguiural], *a.* inaugural.

inaugurate [inóguiuret], *va.* inaugurar; investir, instalar.—**inauguration** [-éishŭn], *s.* inauguración, instalación, estreno.

inauspicious [inospíshus], *a.* impropicio, desfavorable, infeliz.—**inauspiciously** [-li], *adv.* desgraciadamente, bajo malos auspicios.

inauspiciousness [-nes], *s.* malos auspicios.

inbeing [inbíing], *s.* inherencia, inseparabilidad.

inboard [ínbórd], *a.* y *adv.* (mar.) interior, dentro del casco; (mec.) hacia dentro.

inborn [ínborn], *a.* innato, ingénito.

inbound [inbáund], *a.* de entrada; de venida, que viene.

inbreathe [inbríd], *va.* inspirar.

inbred [ínbred], *a.* ínsito, innato.

inbreed [inbríd], *vn.* criar sin mezclar razas.

Inca [inca], *s.* inca; orejón.

incage [inkéy], *va.* enjaular, encerrar.

incalculable [incǽlkiulaboel], *a.* incalculable.

incandesce [íncændés], *va.* y *vn.* incandescer(se), poner(se) incandescente.

incandescence, incandescency [incændésens, i], *s.* incandescencia.

incandescent [-sent], *a.* incandescente, candente. **i. lamp,** lámpara incandescente.

incantation [íncantéishŭn], *s.* encantamiento.

incantator [-téitcer], *s.* encantador.

incantatory [incántatori], *a.* mágico.

incapability [inkéipabíliti] o **incapableness** [-boelnes], *s.* incapacidad.

incapable [inkéipaboel], *a.* incapaz.

incapacitate [incapǽsiteit], *va.* incapacitar.

incapacitation [-téishŭn], *s.* inhabilitación.

incapacity [incapǽsiti], *s.* incapacidad.

incapsulate [incǽpsiuleit], *va.* enchufar.

incarcerate [incársœreit], *va.* encarcelar.

incarceration [-éishŭn], *s.* encarcelación, encarcelamiento, prisión; (cir.) estrangulación (de una hernia).

incardinate [incárdineit], *va.* instalar, nombrar; ascender a cardenal.

incarnadine [incárnadin]. **I.** *va.* encarnar, dar color de carne. **II.** *s.* encarnadino, color de carne.

incarnate [incárnet]. **I.** *va.* encarnar, tomar carne. **II.** *a.* encarnado.

incarnation [incarnéishŭn], *s.* encarnación; (cir.) encarnamiento.

incarnative [incárnativ], *s.* encarnativo.

incase [inkéis], *va.* encajar, embutir, meter; empotrar; encerrar, encajonar.

incasement [-ment], *s.* acción de encajar, meter o encerrar; empotramiento, introducción; cubierta, caja.

incautious [incóshus], *a.* incauto.—**incautiously** [-li], *adv.* incautamente.—**incautiousness** [-nes], *s.* falta de cautela, descuido.

incavation [incavéishŭn], *s.* ahuecamiento; depresión; hueco.

incendiarism [inséndiarism], *s.* incendio malicioso; vicio de incendiar.

incendiary [inséndiæri], *a.* y *s.* incendiario.

incense [ínsens], *s.* incienso.—**i. bearing,** turífero.

incense [inséns], *va.* exasperar, irritar, encolerizar; [ínsens] (igl.) incensar.

incensement [-mœnt], *s.* ira, furia, desagrado.

incensive [insénsiv], *a.* provocativo.

incensory [insénsori], *s.* incensario.

incentive [inséntiv]. **I.** *s.* incentivo, estímulo, aliciente. **II.** *a.* incitativo.

incept [insœpt]. **I.** *va.* recibir. **II.** *vn.* (Ing.) hacerse candidato para el bachillerato de artes.

inception [insœpshŭn], *s.* principio, comienzo.

inceptive [-tiv], *a.* incipiente, incoativo.

inceptor [inséptœr], *s.* (Ingl.) examinando para recibir el grado de maestro en artes.

incertitude [insórtitiud], *s.* incertidumbre.

incessant [insésant], *a.* incesante.

incessantly [-li], *dv.* incesantemente.

incest [ínsest], *s.* incesto.

incestuous [inséstus- (o tius)os], *a.* incestuoso.

incestuously [-li], *adv.* incestuosamente.

inch [inch]. **I.** *s.* pulgada (2.54 centímetros); pizca.—**i. by i.,** palmo a palmo, pulgada por pulgada.—**i. of water** = WATER INCH.—**i.-pound,** (mec.) pulgada-libra, unidad de momento y de energía cuando las de fuerza y longitud son la libra y la pulgada respectivamente.—**by inches,** paso a paso, con gran lentitud, (fam.) a poquitos.—**every i.,** cabal, en todo respecto (cambiando un poco el giro).—**within an i. of,** a dos dedos de, al (seguido de infinitivo). **II.** *a.* de una pulgada.—**i. board,** tablón de a pulgada. **III.** *va.* marcar por pulgadas.

inched [incht], *a.* dividido en pulgadas.

inchmeal [ínchmíl], *adv.* poco a poco.

inchoate [íncoet], *a.* principiado, incoado.

inchoately [-li], *adv.* en el primer grado.

inchoation [incóéshŭn], *s.* principio.

inchoative [incóativ], *a.* incipiente, incoativo.

inchworm [ínchucœrm], *s.* = MEASURING WORM.

incidence [ínsidens], *s.* incidencia; gabela, gravamen.—**i. wires,** (aer.) = STAGGER WIRES.

incident [-ent]. **I.** *a.* incidente; probable, acontecedor; casual, fortuito; concomitante. **II.** *s.* incidente; casualidad; acontecimiento, episodio, lance.

incidental [insidéntal], *a.* incidental, incidente, contingente; concomitante.—**i. to,** que acompaña, inherente a.—**incidentals,** circunstancias imprevistas; imprevistos (gastos).

incidentally [insidéntal], *adv.* incidentemente, incidentalmente.

incinerate [insínœret], *va.* incinerar.

incineration [-éishŭn], *s.* incineración.

incinerator [-éitœr], *s.* incinerador.

incipience, incipiency [insípiens, i], *s.* principio.

incipient [-ent], *a.* incipiente.—**incipiently** [-li], *adv.* en los comienzos.

incise [insáis], *va.* tallar, grabar; cortar.

incised [-d], *a.* (h. n.) irregularmente denticular o serrado.

incision [insíȳʋn], *s.* incisión; muesca; denti-culación.

incisive [insáisiv], *a.* incisivo.

incisor [insáisœr]. **I.** *a.* incisivo. **II.** *s.* diente incisivo.

incisory [insáisori], *a.* incisorio.

incitant [ínsitant]. **I.** *a.* provocativo, incitante, incitativo. **II.** *s.* estímulo, incentivo.

incitation [insitéshʋn], *s.* incitación, instigación.

incite [insáit], *va.* incitar, instigar.—**incitement** [-mœnt], *s.* incitación, instigación; estímulo, incentivo, aliciente.—**inciter** [-œr], *s.* incitador, instigador.—**inciting** [-ing], *a.* estimulante o incitante.—**incitingly** [-ingli], *adv.* incitantemente.

incivility [insivíliti], *s.* incivilidad, descortesía.

inclemency [inclémensi], *s.* inclemencia, intemperie; revés, desgracia; crueldad, severidad.

inclement [-ent], *a.* inclemente, duro; riguroso, borrascoso; adverso, contrario.

inclinable [incláinabœl], *a.* favorable, inclinado a.

inclination [inclinéishʋn], *s.* inclinación (de dos líneas, de un terreno); pendiente, declive; inclinación, propensión; reverencia, venia; (fís.) inclinación (de la brújula); (farm.) decantación.

inclinatory [incláinatori], *a.* inclinado.

incline [incláin]. **I.** *va.* inclinar, ladear; doblar, doblegar. **II.** *vn.* inclinarse, ladearse, bajar, hacer pendiente; hacer reverencia o acatamiento; propender, tender a, tirar a (un color); sentir inclinación o predilección. **III.** *s.* declivio; declive, pendiente.

inclined [incláind], *a.* inclinado, oblicuo; propenso, proclive.—**i. plane**, plano inclinado.

inclose, inclosure = ENCLOSE, ENCLOSURE.

include [incliúd], *va.* incluir, encerrar; comprender, abrazar, contener.

included [-ed], *a.* inclusive, incluso; (geom.) comprendido (ángulo).

inclusion [incliúȳʋn], *s.* inclusión; contenido; (min.) partícula extraña, intrusión.

inclusive [incliúsiv], *a.* inclusivo.

inclusively [-li], *adv.* inclusivamente, inclusive.

incognito [incógnito], *adv., a.* y *s.* incógnito; de incógnito.

incoherence, incoherency [incojírens, i], *s.* incoherencia, inconexión.—**incoherent** [-ent], *a.* incoherente, inconexo.—**incoherently** [-li], *adv.* incoherente o inconexamente, sin conexión.

incombustibility [incombŏstibíliti], **incombustibleness** [-bœlnes], *s.* incombustibilidad.

incombustible [-bœl], *a.* incombustible.

income [íncʋm], *s.* renta, entrada, ingreso, rédito, censo; alimento asimilado.—**i. tax**, impuesto sobre rentas.

incomer [íncʋmœr], *s.* recién llegado.

incoming [íncʋming]. **I.** *a.* entrante, que está por llegar. **II.** *s.* llegada, arribo, entrada.

incommensurability [incomênshurabíliti], *s.* inconmensurabilidad.—**incommensurable** [-ménshurabœl], *a.* inconmensurable.

incommensurate [-ménshuret], *a.* desproporcionado.—**incommensurately** [-li], *adv.* desproporcionadamente.

incommode [incomóud], *va.* incomodar, desacomodar, molestar.

incommodious [-diʋs], *a.* incómodo, inconveniente, molesto.—**incommodiously** [-li], *adv.* incómodamente.—**incommodiousness** [-nes], **incommodity** [incomóditi], *s.* incomodidad, inconveniencia, molestia.

incommunicability [íncomiúnicabíliti], **incommunicableness** [incomiúnicabœlnes], *s.* incomunicabilidad.—**incommunicable** [-miúnicabœl], *a.* incomunicable; indecible.—**incommunicably** [-bli], *adv.* sin comunicación.

incommunicado [-miúnicado], *s.* y *a.* incomunicado.

incommunicative [incomiúnicativ], *a.* insociable, reservado.—**incommunicativeness** [-nes], *s.* carácter intratable, reserva.

incommutability [incomiútabíliti], *s.* inconmutabilidad.—**incommutable** [-miútabœl], *a.* inconmutable.—**incommutably** [-bli], *adv.* inconmutablemente.

incomparable [incómparabœl], *a.* incomparable, sin igual.—**incomparableness** [-nes], *s.* excelencia incomparable.—**incomparably** [-bli], *adv.* incomparablemente.

incompassionate [incompǽshʋnet], *a.* incompasivo, desapiadado.—**incompassionately** [-li], *adv.* desapiadadamente.

incompatibility [incompǽtibíliti], *s.* incompatibilidad.—**incompatible** [-pǽtibœl],|*a.*|incompatible.—**incompatibly** [-bli], *adv.* incompatiblemente.

incompetence, incompetency [incómpetens, i], *s.* incompetencia.—**incompetent** [-tent], *a.* incompetente; (for.) inadmisible.—**incompetently** [-li], *adv.* incompetentemente.

incomplete [íncomplít], *a.* incompleto.—**incompletely** [-li], *adv.* incompletamente.—**incompleteness**, [-nes], *s.* estado incompleto, calidad de incompleto.

incomplex [íncomplex], *s. a.* incomplejo.

incompliance [incompláians], *s.* falta de condescendencia; inflexibilidad; terquedad.

incomprehensibility [íncomprejénsibíliti], **incomprehensibleness** [-bœlnes], *s.* incomprensibilidad.—**incomprehensible** [-bœl], *a.* incomprensible.—**incomprehensibly** [-bli], *adv.* incomprensiblemente.—**incomprehension** [-jénshʋn], *s.* falta de comprensión.

incomprehensive [-jénsiv], *a.* limitado, de poco alcance.—**incomprehensiveness** [-nes], *s.* limitación, poco alcance.

incompressibility [incomprésibíliti], *s.* incompresibilidad.—**incompressible** [-sibœl], *a.* incompresible.

inconcealable [inconsílabœl], *a.* que no se puede ocultar.

inconceivable [inconsívabœl], *a.* inconcebible.—**inconceivability** [-bíliti], **inconceivableness** [-bœlnes], *s.* inconcebibilidad.—**inconceivably** [vabli], *adv.* inconcebiblemente.

inconclusive [inconclúsiv], *a.* inconcluyente, que no convence; inconcluso; indeciso.—**inconclusively** [-li], *adv.* de un modo que no convence; indecisamente; inconcluyentemente.—**inconclusiveness** [-nes], *s.* calidad de indeciso, inconcluso o inconcluyente.

incongruence, o incongruity [incóngruens, incongrúiti], *s.* inconexión, discordancia, anomalía.—**incongruent** [incóngruent], **incongruous** [-gruʋs], *a.* discordante, mal adaptado; inconsecuente; incoherente; (alg.) incongruente; (geom.) insuperponible.—**incongruently, incongruously**, [-li], *adv.* discordantemente, inconexamente, contradictoriamente, inapropiadamente.—**incongruousness** [-nes], calidad de discordante, inapropiado, anómalo, etc.

inconsequence [incónsecuens], *s.* inconsecuencia.—**inconsequent** [-cuent], *a.* inconsecuente, ilógico.—**inconsequential** [-cuénshal], *a.* inconsecuente, inconexo; de poca importancia.

inconsiderable [inconsídœrabœl], *a.* insignificante, despreciable.—**inconsiderableness** [-nes], *s.* insignificancia.

inconsiderate [inconsídœret], *a.* irreflexivo; desconsiderado.—**inconsiderately** [-li], *adv.* inconsideradamente; irreflexivamente.—**inconsiderateness** [-éishʋn], *s.* falta de consideración.

inconsistence, inconsistency [inconsístens, i], *s.* incompatibilidad, contradicción, inconsecuencia.—**inconsistent** [-tent], *a.* incompatible, contradictorio, inconsecuente.—**inconsistently** [-li], *adv.* inconsecuentemente, contradictoriamente.

inconsolable [inconsóulabœl], *a.* inconsolable.

inconstancy [incónstansi], *s.* inconstancia.—**inconstant** [-tant], *a.* inconstante.—**inconstantly** [-li], *adv.* inconstantemente, volublemente.

inconsumable [incnsiúmabœl], *a.* inconsumible.

incontestable [incontéstabœl], *a.* incontestable.

incontestably [bli], *adv.* incontestablemente.

incontinence, incontinency [incóntinens, i], *s.* incontinencia; lascivia; (med.) incontinencia.

incontinent [-ent], *a.* incontinente, desenfrenado; incesante; (med.) incontinente; (fam.) inmediato.—**incontinently** [-li], *adv.* incontinentemente; inmediatamente, incontinenti.

incontrollable [incontróulabœl], *a.* ingobernable.—**incontrollably** [-bli], *adv.* ingobernablemente, sin restricción.

incontrovertible [incóntrovœrtibœl], *a.* incontrovertible.—**incontrovertibly** [-bli], *adv.* indisputablemente.

inconvenience, inconveniency [ínconvíniens, i]. **I.** *s.* inconveniencia, inconveniente; incomodidad, molestia. **II.** *va.* incomodar, estorbar, molestar.—**inconvenient** [-ent], *a.* incómodo, molesto, inconveniente, inoportuno.

inconveniently [-li], *adv.* incómoda o molestamente.

inconvertible inconvœrtibœl], *a.* inconvertible.

inconvincible [inconvínsibœl], *a.* inconvencible, incontrastable.

incorporate [incórporeit]. **I.** *va.* dar cuerpo o forma material; incorporar; formar corporación, gremio, etc. **II.** *vn.* incorporarse, unirse, asociarse. **III.** *a.* incorporado; conmisto; incorporal, inmaterial; no constituído en corporación o asociación.

incorporation [-éishun], *s.* incorporación; organización, asociación.

incorporeal [incorpóreal], *a.* incorporal, incorpóreo.—**incorporeally** [-i], *adv.* incorporalmente.

incorporeity [incórporïiti], *s.* incorporeidad.

incorrect [incorréct], *a.* incorrecto; falso, inexacto, erróneo; inmoral.—**incorrectly** [-li], *adv* incorrectamente; inexactamente.—**incorrectness** [-nes], *s.* inexactitud; incorrección; impropiedad.

incorrigible [incórriyibœl], *a.* incorregible.—**incorrigibility** [incórriyibíliti], **incorrigibleness** [incórriyibœlnes], *s.* incorregibilidad.—**incorrigibly** [incórriyibli], *adv.* incorregiblemente.

incorrupt [incorrúpt], *a.* incorrupto; íntegro, probo.—**incorruptibility** [-tibíliti], *s.* incorruptibilidad.—**incorruptible** [-tibœl], *a.* incorruptible, probo.—**incorruption** [-shun], *s.* incorrupción.—**incorruptive** [-tiv], *a.* incorrupto.—**incorruptness** [-nes], *s.* incorrupción.

incrassate [incrǽset]. **I.** *va.* espesar, encrasar. **II.** *vn.* espesarse, engrosarse. **III.** *a.* encrasado.

incrassation [-éishu a], *s.* encrasación.

incrassative [incrǽsativ], *a.* incrasante.

increasable [incrísabœl], *a.* aumentable.

increase [incrís], *va.* y *vn.* aumentar(se); multiplicar(se).

increase [íncris], *s.* aumento, incremento; ascenso, crecida (de las aguas); creciente (de la luna); ganancia, interés; multiplicación; progenie; productos agrícolas; (tecn.) adaptador, tubo cónico de unión.

increaser [incrísœr], *s.* lo que sirve para aumentar; (tecn.) refuerzo; adaptador, tubo cónico de unión.

increasing [-ing], *a.* creciente.—**increasingly** [-li], *adv.* crecientemente.

increate [incriet], *a.* increado.

incredibility [incrédibíliti], **incredibleness** [incrédibœlnes], *s.* incredibilidad.—**incredible** [-bœl], *a.* increíble.—**incredibly** [-bli], *adv.* increíblemente.

incredulity [incrediúliti], **incredulousness** [incrédiulusnes], *s.* incredulidad.

incredulous [incrédiulus], *a.* incrédulo.

increment [incremœnt], *s.* incremento; (ret.) gradación, clímax.

incriminate [incrímineit], *va.* criminar, acriminar o incriminar.

incrimination [incriminéishun], *s.* criminación, acriminación o incriminación.

incrust [incrúst(et)], *va.* encostrar; incrustar.—**incrustation** [incrústéishun], *s.* incrustación.

incubate [ínkiubeit], *va.* y *vn.* empollar, incubar; pensar, madurar.—**incubation** [ínkiubéishun], *s.* incubación, empolladura; (med.) incubación.—**incubator** [ínkiubeitœr], *s.* empollador; incubadora.

incubus [ínkiubus], *s.* íncubo; carga, obligación; (med.) pesadilla, íncubo.

inculcate [incúlkeit], *va.* inculcar.—**inculcation** [íncvlkéishun], *s.* inculcación.—**inculcator** [incúlkeitœr], *s.* inculcador.

inculpable [incúlpabœl], *a.* inculpable.—**inculpableness** [-bœlnes], *s.* inculpabilidad.—**In-**

culpably [-bli], *adv.* inculpablemente.—**inculpate** [-pet], *va.* inculpar.—**inculpation** [ínculpéishun], *s.* inculpación.—**inculpatory** [incúlpatori], *a.* que inculpa.

incumbency [incúmbensi], *s.* posesión o goce de un empleo; duración del mismo.

incumbent [-ent]. **I.** *a.* obligatorio; colocado sobre, apoyado en, sostenido por. **II.** *s.* (igl.) beneficiado; empleado con posesión de su cargo.

incumber, incumberance, = ENCUMBER, ENCUMBRANCE.

incunabula [ínkiunǽbiulæ], *s. pl.* orígenes, cuna; incunables.

incur [incœr], *va.* incurrir; atraerse.—**to i. a debt,** contraer una deuda.

incurability [inkiúrabíliti], **incurableness** [inkiúrabœlnes], *s.* incurabilidad.—**incurable** [inkiúr.bœl]. **I.** *a.* incurable, insanable, irremediable. **II.** *s.* incurable.—**incurably** [-bli], *adv.* incurablemente.

incuriosity [inkiúriósiti], *s.* incuria.—**incurious** [inkiúrius], *a.* indiferente; incurioso, descuidado.—**incuriously** [-li], *adv.* sin curiosidad; descuidadamente.—**incuriousness** [-nes], *s.* falta de curiosidad o interés.

incursion [incœrshun], *s.* incursión.

incurvate [incœrvet], **incurve** [incœrv]. **I.** *va.* encorvar, doblar, torcer. **II.** *a.* encorvado, torcido.—**incurvation** [incœrvéshun], *s.* encorvadura, curvatura; genuflexión; (med.) uñero.—**incurvity** [incœrviti], *s.* corvadura.

incuse [inkiús]. **I.** *a.* incuso. **II.** *s.* medalla incusa, figura incusa. **III.** *va.* estampar golpeando.

indebted [indéted], *s.* adeudado, endeudado, obligado, reconocido.—**indebtedness** [-nes], *s.* adeudo; deuda, pasivo; obligación.—**indebtment** [-mœnt], *s.* adeudo.

indecency [indísensi], *s.* indecencia.—**indecent** [-sent], *a.* indecente, indecoroso.—**indecently** [-li], *adv.* indecentemente, indecorosamente.

indecision [indesíyun], *s.* indecisión, irresolución.—**indecisive** [indesáisiv], *a.* indeciso, irresoluto.—**indecisiveness** [-nes], *s.* indecisión, irresolución.

indeclinable [indecláinabœl], *a.* indeclinable.—**indeclinably** [-bli], *adv.* sin declinación.

indecorous [indecórus], *a.* indecoroso.—**indecorously** [-li], *adv.* indecorosamente.—**indecorousness** [-nes], **indecorum** [indecórum], *s.* indecoro, indecencia.

indeed [indíd], *adv.* verdaderamente, realmente, de veras, a la verdad, sí, claro está.—**i.?** ¿de veras? ¿es posible?

indefatigability, indefatigableness [indefǽtigabíliti, -bœlnes], *s.* calidad de infatigable o incansable.—**indefatigable** [-bœl], *a.* incansable.—**indefatigably** [-bli], *adv.* incansablemente.

indefeasibility [indefísibíliti], *s.* irrevocabilidad.—**indefeasible** [indefísibœl], *a.* (for.) inabrogable, irrevocable.

indefectibility [indeféctibíliti], *s.* indefectibilidad.—**indefectible** [-bœl], *a.* indefectible.—**indefectibly** [-bli], *adv.* indefectiblemente.

indefensible [indefénsibœl], *a.* indefendible, insostenible.

indefensive [indefénsiv], *a.* indefenso.

indefinable [indefáinabœl], *a.* indefinible.

indefinite [indéfinit], *a.* indefinido, vago.—**indefinitely** [-li], *adv.* indefinidamente.—**indefiniteness** [-nes], *s.* calidad de indefinido.

indehiscence [indejísens], *s.* (bot.) indehiscencia.—**indehiscent** [-sent], *a.* (bot.) indehiscente.

indeliberate(d [indelíbœret(ed)], *a.* indeliberado, impremeditado.

indelibility [indelíbíliti], *s.* calidad de indeleble.—**indelible** [-bœl], *a.* indeleble.—**indelibly** [-bli], *adv.* indeleblemente.

indelicacy [idélicasi], *s.* indelicadeza, indecoro.—**indelicate** [-ket], *a.* indecoroso, falto de delicadeza.

indemnification [indémnifikéishun], *s.* indemnización.—**indemnify** [-fai], *va.* indemnizar.—**indemnity** [indémniti], *s.* indemnización, resarcimiento; indemnidad.—**i. bond,** contrafianza.

indemonstrable [indemónstrabœl], *a.* indemostrable.

indent [indént]. **I.** *va.* dentar, endentar, mellar; (impr.) sangrar. **II.** *vn.* mellarse. **III.** *s.* mella, diente, muesca.

indentation [índentéiŝhun], *s.* mella, muesca, corte, piquete.

indented [indénted], *a.* dentado, enmuescado, serrado; (bot.) dentellado.

indention [indénŝhun], *s.* abolladura; mella; (impr.) sangría.

indenture [indénchœr]. **I.** *s.* (for.) escritura, instrumento,‚contrato, carta; partida, documento. **II.** *va.* escriturar, obligar por contrato.

independence, independency [índepéndens, i], *s.* independencia; posición holgada; bienandanza.—**I. Day,** (E. U.) fiesta de la independencia (4 de julio).

independent [-ent], *a.* independiente; libre; acomodado, capaz de mantenerse; altivo, altanero.—**independently** [-li], *adv.* independientemente; altivamente.

indescribable [indescráibabœl], *a.* indescriptible.—**indescribably** [-bli], *adv.* indescriptiblemente.

indestructibility [indestrŭctibíliti], *s.* indestructibilidad.—**indestructible** [-bœl], *a.* indestructible.

indeterminable [indetœrminabœl], *a.* indeterminable.—**indeterminate** [-et], *a.* indeterminado.—**indeterminately** [-li], *adv.* indeterminadamente.—**indeterminateness** [-nes], **Indetermination** [-éiŝhun], *s.* indeterminación, duda.—**Indetermined** [-mind], *a.* indeterminado.

indeterminism [indetérminiŝm], *s.* indeterminismo.—**indeterminist** [-ist], *s.* indeterminista.

index [index]. **I.** *s.* índice (indicio, tabla de materias, lista, indicador, manecilla, aguja); dedo índice; (mat. y fís.) índice.—**I. card,** tarjeta para índices o archivos.—**I. correction,** corrección para eliminar el error instrumental.—**I. error,** error instrumental, error del cero (en el teodolito, etc.); error del índice (en el sextante).—**I. Expurgatorious,** índice expurgatorio.—**I. finger,** dedo índice. —**I. gage,** o **gauge,** compás de graduación.—**I. hand,** indicador, aguja.—**I. number,** (com., e. p.) índice de precio, relación entre el precio de un artículo en un tiempo dado y un precio fijo tomado por unidad o patrón.—**I. plate,** círculo graduador. **II.** *va.* poner índice a; poner en un índice; indicar.

indexical [indéxical], *a.* en forma de índice; indicativo.

india [índia], *s.* India.—**I. ink,** tinta china.—**I. paper,** papel de China.—**I. proof,** prueba en papel de China.—**I. rubber,** caucho, goma elástica.

Indiaman [índiamæn], *s.* buque que hace el comercio con la India.

Indian [índian]. **I.** *a.* indio; indo, índico; indiano.—**I. berries,** cocas de Levante.—**I. clubs,** mazas de gimnasia.—**I. corn,** máiz.—**I. cress,** (bot.) capuchina.—**I. fig.** tuna, higo chumbo.—**I. meal,** narina de maíz.—**I. millet,** (bot.) alcandía.—**I. pink,** (bot.) clavelón de Indias.—**I. red,** almagre.—**I. summer,** (E. U.) veranillo de San Martín. **II.** *s.* indio; indo.

Indic [índic], *a.* índico; indio.

indicate [índikeit], *va.* indicar.—**indication** [-kéiŝhun], *s.* indicación.

indicative [indícativ], *a.* indicativo.—**i. mode** (o **mood**), modo indicativo.

indicatively [-li], *adv.* indicativamente.

indicator [indikéitœr], *s.* indicador; índice, aguja; (m. v.) indicador; (quím.) indicador.— **i. bosses,** (m. v.) tetón de indicador.—**I. card,** o **diagram,** (m. v.) diagrama o gráfica del indicador. —**i. telegraph,** telégrafo de agujas.

indicatory [índicatori], *a.* demostrativo, indicatorio.

indices [índisis], *s. pl.* de INDEX.

indicia [indíŝhiæ], *s. pl.* indicios, señales.

indicial [indíŝhæl], *a.* indicativo, que indica; (anat.) índice, del índice.

indict [indáit], *va.* acusar ante el juez; (for.) procesar, encausar.—**indictable** [-tabœl], *a.* (for.)

---

procesable, denunciable.—**indictee** [-ti], *s.* acusado, procesado.—**indicter** [-tœr]. *s.* (for.) denunciante, fiscal, acusador.

indiction [indícŝhun], *s.* indicción.

indictment [indáitmœnt], *s.* (for.) sumaria; denuncia, acusación; proceso.

indifference [indífœrens], *s.* indiferencia; apatía, tibieza; imparcialidad, neutralidad.

indifferent [-ent], *a.* indiferente; apático; neutral, imparcial; pasadero, mediano.

iadifferentism [-iŝm], *s.* indiferencia habitual; (teol.) indiferentismo teológico, doctrina de que las diferencias de fe no son de importancia; (fil.) doctrina de que existir en el pensamiento y existir en la realidad son una misma cosa.

indifferently [-li], *adv.* indiferentemente; imparcialmente; pasaderamente, medianamente.

indigence, indigency [índivens, i], *s.* indigencia, penuria, inopia.

indigenous [indívinus], *a.* indígena, nativo, natural; innato.

indigent [índivent], *a.* indigente, pobre, necesitado; falto.

indigested [indivésted], *a.* no digerido; confuso, desordenado.

indigestible [indivéstibœl], *a.* indigesto.

indigestion [-chun], *s.* indigestión.

indignant [indígnant], *a.* indignado.—**indignantly** [[-li], *adv.* con indignación.

indignation [índignéiŝhun], *s.* indignación.

indignity [indígniti], *s.* indignidad, ultraje o afrenta; oprobio.

indigo [índigo], *s.* añil, índigo.—**i. blue,** azul de añil.—**I. plant,** o **tree,** (bot.) índigo, jiguilete.

indirect [índirect], *a.* indirecto.—**indirection** [-ŝhun], *s.* **indirectness** [indiréctnes], *s.* oblicuidad, rodeo, tortuosidad; conducta torcida; efugio; indirectas.—**indirectly** [-li], *adv.* indirectamente.

indiscernible [indiŝérnibœl], *a.* indiscernible, imperceptible.

indiscreet [indiscrít], *a.* indiscreto.

indiscreetly [-li], *adv.* indiscretamente.

indiscrete [indiscrít], *a.* que no está separado o desunido.

indiscretion [indiscréŝhun], *s.* indiscreción.

indiscriminate [indiscríminet], *a.* que no hace distinciones; promiscuo.—**indiscriminately** [-li], *adv.* indistintamente, promiscuamente.—**indiscriminating** = UNDISCRIMINATING.—**indiscrimination** [-éiŝhun], *s.* falta de distinción.—**indiscriminative** [-œtive], *a.* que no distingue.

indispensability, indispensableness [indispénsabíliti, -bœlnes], *s.* calidad de indispensable, necesidad.—**indispensable** [-bœl], *a.* indispensable; preciso.—**indispensably** [-bli], *adv.* indispensablemente.

indispose [indispóuŝ], *va.* indisponer.

indisposition [indíspoŝíŝhun], *s.* indisposición, destemplanza; falta de inclinación

indisputable [indíspiutabœl], *a.* disputable, incontestable.—**indisputableness** [-nes], *s.* indisputabilidad.—**indisputably** [-bli], *adv.* indisputablemente.

indissolubility [indísolubíliti], **indissolubleness** [-bœlnes], *s.* indisolubilidad.—**indissoluble** [-bœl], *a.* indisoluble, insoluble; obligatorio, forzoso.—**indissolubly** [-bli], *adv.* indisolublemente.

indistinct [índistinct], *a.* indistinto, confuso; obscuro, vago.—**indistinction** [-tincŝhun], *s.* obscuridad, falta de claridad.—**indistinctly** [-li], *adv.* indistintamente, confusamente, vagamente.—**indistinctness** [-nes], *s.* falta de claridad, obscuridad.

indistinguishable [indistíngüiŝhabœl], *a.* indistinguible.

indite [indáit]. **I.** *va.* redactar, escribir. **II.** *vn.* poner por escrito.—**inditement** [-mœnt], *s.* redacción.—**inditer** [indáitœr], *s.* redactor, escritor.

indium [índium], *s.* (quím.) indio.

individual [indivídyual]. **I.** *a.* solo, único, individual, particular, singular, individuo; para o de uno; personal; separado; para uno solo. **II.** *s.* individuo, particular, persona.

---

individualism [índivídyualîŝm], s. individualismo.—**individualist** [-ist], s. individualista—**individualistic** [-ístic], a. individualista.

individuality [índivídyuéliti], s. individualidad, personalidad; individuación, particularidad; originalidad.

individualize [indivídyualaiŝ], va. individualizar, particularizar.

individually [indivídyuali], adv. individualmente, particularmente, personalmente.

individuate [indivídyueit]. I. va. individuar; individualizar.—**individuation** [-éiŝhvn]. II. s. individuación; producción de individuos.

indivisibility [índivíŝibíliti], s. indivisibilidad.—**indivisible** [-bœl], a. indivisible.—**indivisibly** [-bli], adv. indivisiblemente, indivisamente.

Indo-Chinese [índo-chainís]. I. a. indochino. II. s. mongol de Indochina.

indocile [indósil], a. indócil, cerril.

indocility [indosíliti], s. indocilidad.

indoctrinate [indóctrinet], va. doctrinar, enseñar, disciplinar.—**indoctrination** [-éiŝhvn], s. instruc ción, enseñanza.

Indo-European [indo-iúropían], **Indo-Germanic** [-γœrmánic], a. indoeuropeo, indogermánico.

indolence [índolens], s. indolencia, desidia; (med.) ausencia de dolor.—**indolent** [-ent], a. indolente, desidioso; (med.) sin dolor, insensible.—**indolently** [-li], adv. indolentemente.

indomitable [indómitabœl], a. indomable.

indoor [índor], a. interno, interior, de casa; de puertas adentro.

indoors [indóœrs], adv. dentro; en casa.

indorsable [indórsabœl], a. endosable, endorsable; confirmable.

indorse [indórs], va. (com.) endosar; respaldar; garantizar, abonar; apoyar, sancionar.

indorsee [índorsí], s. (com.) endosado, portador.

indorsement [indórsmœnt], s. (com.) endoso; respaldo, rótulo; aval, garantía; sanción.

indorser, indorsor [indórsœr], s. (com.) endosante.

indow, indowment, = ENDOW, etc.

indraft, indraught [índraft], s. absorción, succión, aspiración.

indrawn [índron], a. sorbido, inspirado; con voz ahogada; abstraído.

indubitable [indiútabœl], a. indubitable.—**indubitableness** [-nes], s. certeza.—**indubitably** [-bli], adv. indubitablemente.

induce [indiús], va. inducir, mover, incitar; causar, producir; (lóg. y elec.) inducir.

inducement [-mœnt], s. móvil, aliciente; persuasión.

inducible [-íbœl], a. inducible; que se puede causar o producir.

induct [indúct], va. instalar; iniciar.

inductance [-æns], s. (elec.) inductancia; bobina de inductancia o de reacción.

induction [-ŝhvn], s. introducción, preámbulo; instalación (en un puesto, dignidad, etc.); (elec. y lóg.) inducción.—**i. balance**, balanza de inducción.—**i. coll**, bobina de inducción.—**i. pipe, port, valve**, tubo, lumbrera, válvula de admisión.

inductive [-tiv], a. inductivo, ilativo; introductor; (elec.) inductivo, inductor, inductriz.—**inductively** [-li], adv. inductivamente.

inductivity [indvctíviti], s. (elec.) inductividad.

inductophone [indúctofoun], s. (elec.) inductófono, aparato para telefonear desde un tren en marcha a una estación.

inductor [indúctor], s. (igl.) instalador; (elec.) inductor.

indue [indiú], va. vestir; investir; dotar.

indulge [indúly]. I. va. dar rienda suelta a; acceder a la voluntad o a los caprichos de (apl. esp. a la indulgencia excesiva de los padres); dar (a un niño) cuanto pide; gratificar, dejarse dominar por (el vicio, etc.); (igl.) conceder indulgencia a; (com.) dar plazo o prorrogar el plazo a. II. vn. (con in) entregarse a; gustar de.

indulgence [-rens], **indulgency** [-rensi], indul, gencia, lenidad; gratificación; exceso; com, placencia, favor; (com.) prórroga, extensiór de plazo; (igl.) indulgencia.—**indulgent** [-rent], a. indulgente.

indulgential [indvlrénŝhal], a. (igl.) indulgente, **indulgently** [indúlrentli], adv. indulgentemente.

indult [indúlt], s. (igl.) dispensa.

indurate [índiuret]. I. va. endurecer. II. vn. endurecerse, empedernirse. III. a. duro, endurecido.

induration [índiuréŝhvn], s. endurecimiento; dureza de corazón; (med.) dureza.

industrial [indústrial]. I. a. industrial. II. s. industrial; (com.) acción u obligación de una sociedad industrial anónima.—**industrialism** [-iŝm] s. industrialismo.—**industrialize** [-aiŝ], va. industrializar.—**industrially** [-i], adv. industrialmente.

industrious [-trivs], a. industrioso, diligente.

industriously [-li], adv. industriosamente.

industry [índvstri], s. industria; laboriosidad.

indwell [induél], va. y vn. residir, morar.—**indweller** [-œr], s. morador.—**indwelling** [-ing], a. morador, residente.

inebriant [iníbriant]. I. a. embriagador. II. s. lo que embriaga.

inebriate [iníbrieit]. I. va. embriagar; infatuar; cegar. II. a. ebrio, borracho. III. s. borracho, beodo.

inebriation [iníbriéiŝhvn], **inebriety** [ínibráiiti], s. embriaguez.

inedited [inédited], a. inédito.

ineffable [inéfabœl], a. inefable.—**ineffableness** [-nes], s. inefabilidad.—**ineffably** [-bli], adv. inefablemente.

ineffaceable [ineféisabœl], a. indeleble.

ineffaceably [-bli], adv. indeleblemente.

ineffective [ineféctiv], a. ineficaz.

ineffectual [inefékchual], a. ineficaz.

ineffectually [-i], adv. ineficazmente.

ineffectualness [-nes], s. ineficacia.

inefficacious [inéfikéiŝhvs], a. ineficaz.

inefficaciously [-li], adv. ineficazmente.

inefficaciousness [-nes], s. ineficacia.

inefficacy [inéficasi], **inefficiency** [ínefíŝhensi], s. ineficacia.

inefficient [inefíŝhœnt], a. ineficaz.

inelastic [inelástic], a. inelástico.

inelasticity [-læstísiti], s. falta de elasticidad.

inelegance, inelegancy [inélegans, i], s. falta de elegancia.—**inelegant** [-ant], a. inelegante, falto de elegancia.—**inelegantly** [-li], adv. sin elegancia.

ineligibility [ineliyibíliti], s. ineligibilidad.

ineligible [inéliyibœl], a. ineligible.

ineloquent [inélocuent], a. infacundo

inept [inépt], a. inepto; absurdo.—**ineptitude** [-itiud], **ineptness** [-nes], s. ineptitud.—**ineptly** [-li], adv. ineptamente.

inequality [inecuóliti], s. desigualdad; aspereza, escabrosidad; injusticia.

inequitable [inécuitabœl], a. injusto.

inerrable [inérrabœl], **inerrant** [inérrant], a. inerrable, infalible.—**inerrancy** [-si], s. infalibilidad.

inert [inért], a. inerte, inactivo.

inertia [inérŝhia], s. inercia.

inertly [inértli], adv. pesadamente, flojamente, indolentemente.—**inertness** [-nes], s. flojedad; falta de actividad.

inestimable [inéstimabœl], a. inestimable, inapreciable.—**inestimably** [-bli], adv. de modo inestimable.

inevitable [inévitabœl], a. inevitable.—**inevitability** [-bíliti], **inevitableness** [-bœlnes], s. calidad de inevitable.—**inevitably** [-bli], adv. inevitablemente.

inexact [inegŝáect], a. inexacto.—**inexactly** [-li], adv. inexactamente.

inexcusable [inexkiúŝabœl], a. inexcusable, imperdonable.—**inexcusableness** [-nes], s. calidad de inexcusable.—**inexcusably** [-bli], adv. inexcusablemente.

inexhaustible [inegŝóstibœl], o **inexhaustive** [-tiv], a. inagotable.—**inexhaustibleness** [-bœl-nes], s. calidad de inagotable.

inexistence [inegsístens], s. inexistencia.

inexistent [inegsístent], a. inexistente.

inexorable [inécsorabœl], a. inexorable.

inexorability [-bíliti], **inexorableness** [-bœlnes], s. inexorabilidad.—**inexorably** [-bli], adv. inexorablemente.

inexpedience, inexpediency [inexpídiens, i], s. inoportunidad o inconveniencia.—**inexpedient** [-ent], a. inoportuno, inconveniente.

inexpensive [inexpénsiv], a. barato.

inexperience [inexpíriens], s. inexperiencia, impericia.—**inexperienced** [-t], **inexpert** [inexpœrt], a. inexperto, novel.

inexpiable [inexpiabœl], a. inexpiable.

inexpiably [-bli], adv. de un modo inexpiable.

inexplicable [inéxplicabœl], a. inexplicable.—**inexplicability, inexplicableness** [inéxplicabíliti, -bœlnes], s. calidad de inexplicable.—**inexplicably** [-bli], adv. inexplicablemente.

inexplorable [inexplórabœl], a. inexplorable.

inexpressible [inexpréslbœl]. I. a. indecible. II. s. pl. (fam.) los pantalones.—**inexpressibly** [-bli], adv. indeciblemente.

inexpressive [inexprésiv], a. falto de expresión; (poét.) indecible.

inexpugnable [inexpúgnabœl], a. inexpugnable.

inextensible [inexténsibœl], a. inextensible.

inextinguishable [inextíngüíshabœl], a. inextinguible.

inextricable [inéxtricabœl], a. inextricable, intrincado.—**inextricableness** [-nes], s. calidad de inextricable.—**inextricably** [-bli], adv. inextricablemente.

infallibility [infælibíliti], **infallibleness** [-bœlnes], s. infalibilidad.—**infallible** [-bœl], a. infalible.—**infallibly** [-bli], adv. infaliblemente.

infamous [ínfamus], a. infame; infamante, infamatorio.—**infamously** [ínfamusli], adv. infamemente.—**infamousness** [-nes], **infamy** [ínfami], s. infamia.

infancy [ínfansi], s. infancia; (for.) minoridad.

infant [ínfænt]. I. s. infante, niñito, criatura, nene; (for.) menor. II. a. infantil; menor de edad; de niños; naciente.

infanta [infánta], s. infanta.—**infante** [infánte], s. infante.

infanticidal [infǽntisaidœl], a. relativo al infanticidio; de infanticidio.—**infanticide** [-said], s. infanticidio.

infantile [ínfantil], a. infantil.—**i. paralysis,** parálisis infantil o poliomielitis anterior aguda.—**i. scurvy,** escorbuto infantil o mal de Barlow.

infantry [ínfantri], s. (mil.) infantería.

infarct [infárct], s. (med.) infarto.

infarction [infárcshun], s. (med.) infartación.

infatuate [infǽtiueit], va. infatuar, cegar, atontar.—**infatuate(d** [-eit(ed], a. infatuado, locamente enamorado.—**infatuation** [-éishun], s. infatuación, apasionamiento.

infeasibility [infísibíliti], **infeasibleness** [infísibœlnes], s. impracticabilidad, infactibilidad.

infeasible [infísibœl], a. impracticable.

infect [inféct], va. infectar, inficionar, contagiar; (for.) exponer a pena o a proceso.

infection [-shun], s. infección, contagio; corrupción de costumbres; miasma; (for.) tacha de ilegalidad.

infectious [-shus], a. contagioso; (med.) infeccioso; (for.) antilegal, que viola la ley.—**infectiously** [-li], adv. infecciosamente.—**infectiousness** [-nes], s. carácter de infeccioso.—**infective** [-iv], a. infeccioso.

infecundity [infecúnditi], s. infecundidad, esterilidad.

infelicitous [infelísitus], a. desatinado, mal pensado.—**infelicity** [-ti], s. infelicidad, infortunio; falta de tino.

infer [infœr]. I. va. inferir, colegir; indicar, probar. II. vn. inferir.—**inferable** [-abœl], a. deducible.—**inference** [ínferens], s. inferencia, deducción.—**inferential** [inferénshal], a. ilativo.—**inferentially** [-li], adv. por inferencia.

inferior [inffricœr], s. y a. inferior.—**inferiority** [-órity], s. inferioridad.

infernal [infœrnæl], a. infernal.—**i. machine,** máquina infernal.—**infernally** [-i], adv. infernalmente.

inferrible [inférribœl], a. deducible, colegible.

infertile [infœrtil], a. estéril.

infertility [ínfertíliti], s. esterilidad.

infest [infést], va. infestar, plagar.

infestive [inféstiv], a. triste, melancólico.

infeudation [ínfiudéishun], s. enfeudación.

infidel [ínfidel]. I. s. infiel; librepensador (en el sentido de descreído). II. a. infiel; librepensador; de infieles, de los infieles.

infidelity [ínfidéliti], s. infidelidad, descreimiento; infidelidad conyugal.

infield [ínfíld], s. = DIAMOND en baseball.

infiltrate [infíltret]. I. va. infiltrar, calar. II. vn. infiltrarse, penetrar.

infiltration [infíltréshun], s. infiltración.

infinite [ínfinit]. I. a. infinito; (mús.) sin final. II. s. infinito.—**infinitely** [-li], adv. infinitamente.—**infiniteness** [-nes], s. infinidad.

infinitesimal [ínfinitésimal]. I. a. (mat.) infinitesimal. II. s. cantidad infinitésima.

infinitive [infínitiv], s. y a. infinitivo.

infinitude [infínitiud], s. infinidad.

infinity [infíniti], s. infinidad; infinito.

infirm [infœrm], a. enfermizo, achacoso; instable, poco firme; (for.) anulable.—**infirmary** [-mari], s. enfermería, casa de salud.—**infirmity** [-miti], s. enfermedad, dolencia, achaque; flaqueza, fragilidad.—**infirmly** [-li], adv. débilmente.

infix [infícs], va. clavar, encajar; inculcar.

inflame [infléim]. I. vn. inflamar, encender; enardecer, acalorar, azuzar; provocar, irritar. II. vn. arder, encenderse; (med.) inflamarse, hincharse.—**inflamer** [-œr], s. inflamador.

inflammability, inflammableness [inflæmabíliti, -bœlnes], s. inflamabilidad.

inflammable [-bœl], a. inflamable.

inflammation [inflaméshun], s. inflamación.

inflammatory [inflǽmatori], a. inflamatorio, inflamante; (med.) inflamatorio.

inflate [infléit], va. inflar, hinchar.—**inflated** [-ted], a. hinchado, inflado; afectado, pomposo.—**inflation** [-shun], s. inflación, hinchazón; emisión excesiva de papel moneda; plétora.—**inflationist** [-shunist], s. partidario de la emisión de papel moneda.

inflect [infléct], va. torcer, doblar; modular, acentuar; (gram.) declinar.

inflection [-shun], s. inflexión, dobladura; acento, modulación de la voz; (gram.) inflexión.—**inflectional** [-œl], a. (gram.) que tiene inflexiones.—**inflective** [-iv], a. capaz de doblar o torcer; (gram.) = INFLECTIONAL.

inflexibility [inflécsibíliti], **inflexibleness** [-bœlnes], s. inflexibilidad.—**inflexible** [-bœl], a. inflexible.—**inflexibly** [-bli], adv. inflexiblemente.

inflexion, s. = INFLECTION.

inflict [inflíct], va. (gen. con on) infligir, imponer, descargar.—**infliction** [-shun], s. imposición, aplicación; pena, castigo.—**inflictive** [-tiv], a. que se impone o inflige.

inflorescence [infflorésens], s. (bot.) inflorescencia; florescencia.

inflow [ínflo], s. flujo, afluencia; entrada.

influence [ínfluens]. I. s. influencia, valimiento, influjo. II. va. influir; inducir, persuadir; ejercer presión (fig.) sobre.—**influential** [-énshal], a. influyente.—**influentially** [-i], adv. influyentemente.

influenza [ínfluénsa], s. influenza.

influx [ínflux], s. flujo; afluencia; instilación, intromisión; desembocadura, entrada.

infold [infóuld], va. envolver; incluir; abrazar.

inform [infórm]. I. va. informar, avisar, comunicar, enterar; instruir, enseñar; informar o dar forma a, modelar; animar. II. vn. (con on o against) denunciar; delatar (a).

informal [infórmal], a. informal, irregular; sin ceremonia, de confianza.

informality [infórmǽliti], s. informalidad, irregularidad; acto sencillo, sin ceremonia.

informally [infórmali], adv. informalmente; sin ceremonia.

informant [infórmant], s. informante.

information [ínforméiåhʊn], s. informe, información; saber, conocimientos; (for.) acusación, delación.

informative [infórmativ], a. informativo.

informer [infórmœr], s. delator, denunciador; soplón; informante, informador.

infraction [infrǽcåhʊn], s. infracción, violación; (med.) fractura.—**Infractor** [-tœr], s. infractor.

inframaxilary [ínfræmǽcsilary]. **I.** a. submaxilar. **II.** s. maxilar inferior.

infrangible [infrǽnyibœl], a. infrangible, inquebrantable.—**infrangibleness** [-bœlnes], s. calidad de infrangible.

infraorbital [infraórbital], a. situado debajo de la órbita del ojo.

infra-red [ínfræ-red], a. (fís.) infrarrojo o ultrarrojo.

infrequence, infrequency [infrícuens, i], s. rareza, raridad.—**infrequent** [-cuent], a. raro, infrecuente.

infringe [infríny]. **I.** va. infringir, violar. **II.** vn. (con **on** o **upon**) violar.—**infringement** [-mœnt], s. infracción, violación.—**infringer** [infrínyœr], s. violador, infractor.

infundibular, infundibuliform [infʊndíbiular, -liform], a. infundibuliforme.

infuriate [infiúreit], va. enfurecer, irritar.

infuriated [-ed], a. enfurecido, furioso.

infuse [infiuś], va. vaciar; (farm.) macerar; (con *into*) inculcar, infundir; (con *with*) inspirar, dar, comunicar.

infusible [infiúśibœl], a. infusible.

infusibility [infiúśibíliti], **infusibleness** [infiúśibœlnes], s. infusibilidad.

infusion [infiúyʊn], s. infusión; instilación; (farm.) maceración.

Infusoria [ínfiusória], s. infusorios.—**infusorial** [-al], a. infusorio.—**I. earth,** tierra de infusorios.—**infusorian** [-n], s. y a. infusorio.

ingate [inguct], s. (fund.) bebedero; (min.) boca de una galería.

ingathering [ingǽɒcœring], s. cosecha.

ingeminate [inyéminet]. **I.** va. reiterar. **II.** a. repetido.—**ingemination** [-éiåhʊn], s. repetición.

ingenerate [inyéneret], a. innato, ingénito; increado.

ingenious [inyíniʊs], a. ingenioso.—**ingeniously** [-li], adv. ingeniosamente.

ingeniousness [nes], s. ingeniosidad, ingenio.

ingenuity [ínyeniúiti], s. ingeniosidad, inventiva.

ingenuous [inyéniuʊs], a. ingenuo, sincero.—**ingenuously** [-li], adv. ingenuamente.

ingenuousness [-nes], s. ingenuidad.

ingest [inyést], va. introducir en el estómago.

ingesta [inyésta], s. pl. alimento tomado; (fig.) cosas ingeridas.

ingestion [inyéschʊn], s. introducción de una cosa en el estómago.

inglorious [inglóriʊs], a. afrentoso, ignominioso; obscuro.—**ingloriously** [-li], adv. ignominiosamente; obscuramente.—**ingloriousness** [-nes], s. ignominia; obscuridad.

ingoing [ingóing]. **I.** a. entrante, que entra, que llega. **II.** s. entrada, ingreso.

ingot [íngot], s. lingote; tejo de oro, galápago de cobre; barra de metal.

ingraft [ingráft], va. (agr.) injertar.

ingraftment [-mœnt], s. injerto.

ingrain [íngrein]. **I.** a. teñido en rama; inculcado. **II.** s. alfombra ordinaria.

ingrain [ingréin], va. teñir en rama; teñir con grana o cochinilla; fijar o impregnar.

ingrate [íngreit], a. y s. ingrato.

ingratiate [ingréiåhiéit], va. recomendar; hacer aceptable.—**to i. one's self with,** hacerse a la buena voluntad de, conquistarse el favor de.

ingratitude [ingrǽtitud], s. ingratitud.

ingredient [ingrídient], s. ingrediente.

ingress [íngres], s. ingreso, entrada; acceso.

ingrowing [íngròing], a. que crece hacia dentro.—**i. nail,** uñero.

inguinal [inguinal], a. inguinal.

ingulf [ingúlf], va. sumir, engolfar.

ingurgitation [ingœryitéåhʊn], s. voracidad, glotonería, ingurgitación.

inhabit [injǽbit]. **I.** va. habitar; ocupar. **II.** vn. (ant.) habitar, vivir, residir.—**inhabitable** [-abœl], a. habitable.—**inhabitance** [-tans], s. habitación, morada, residencia.

inhabitant [injǽbitant], s. habitante.

inhabitation [injǽbitéåhʊn], s. habitación, acción de habitar; domicilio, morada.

inhalation [injaléiåhʊn], s. inspiración; (med.) inhalación.

inhale [injéil], va. inspirar, inhalar, aspirar.

inhaler [injéilœr], s. inhalador.

inharmonic(al [injarmónic(al], a. inarmónico.

inharmonious [injarmóniʊs], a. discordante, inarmónico.—**inharmoniously** [-li], adv. inarmónicamente, discordantemente.—**inharmoniousness** [-nes], s. desarmonía.

inhere [injíœr], vn. ser inherente.—**inherence, inherency** [-ens, i], s. inherencia.—**inherent** [-œnt], a. inherente, inmanente; innato, esencial.—**inherently** [-li], adv. inherentemente.

inherit [injérit]. **I.** va. heredar. **II.** vn. suceder como heredero.—**inheritable** [-abœl], a. heredable.—**inheritably** [-abli], adv. por herencia.—**inheritance** [-ans], s. herencia; patrimonio.—**inheritor** [-œr], s. heredero.—**inheritress, -trix** [-tres, -trix], s. heredera.

inhesion [injíyʊn], s. inherencia.

inhibit [injíbit], va. inhibir, prohibir; (igl.) prohibir a un sacerdote que ejerza sus funciones espirituales.

inhibition [injibíåhʊn], s. inhibición, prohibición, impedimento.

inhibitory, inhibitive [injíbitori, tiv], a. inhibitorio.

inhive [injáiv], va. (api.) enjambrar.

inhospitable [injóspitabœl], a. inhospitalario.—**inhospitableness** [-nes], **inhospitality** [injóspitǽliti], s. inhospitalidad.—**inhospitably** [-bli], adv. inhospitalariamente.

inhuman [injiúman], a. inhumano, desalmado.—**inhumanity** [injiumǽniti], s. inhumanidad, crueldad.—**inhumanly** [injiúmanli], adv. inhumanamente.

inhume [injiúm], va. inhumar; (quím.) exponer a un calor constante enterrando el recipiente en tierra o estiércol caliente.

inhumation [injiuméiåhʊn], s. inhumación.

inimical [inímical], a. enemigo, hostil.—**inimically** [-al], adv. enemigamente, hostilmente.

inimitability [inímitabíliti], s. imposibilidad de ser imitado.—**inimitable** [-bœl], a. inimitable.—**inimitableness** [-nes], s. calidad de inimitable.—**inimitably** [-bli], adv. inimitablemente.

iniquitous [inícuitʊs], a. inicuo.—**iniquitously** [-li], adv. inicuamente.—**iniquity** [inícuiti], s. iniquidad.

initial [iníshal]. **I.** a. inicial, incipiente. **II.** s. letra inicial.

initiate [iníshieit]. **I.** va. iniciar. **II.** a. adepto, iniciado.

initiation [iníshiéiåhʊn], s. iniciación.

initiative [iníshietiv]. **I.** a. iniciativo. **II.** s. iniciativa; originalidad; (der. y pol.) iniciativa, derecho (de una asamblea, etc.) de introducir propuestas, etc.; (con *the*) iniciativa popular directa, derecho del pueblo de proponer directamente medidas legislativas, como en Suiza.

initiator [iníshiéitœr], s. iniciador.

initiatory [iníshiatori], a. iniciativo.

inject [inyéct], va. inyectar, jeringar; introducir.

injection [-åhʊn], s. inyección; (med.) enema, inyección, lavativa; (mec.) inyección.

injector [inyéctœr], s. (mec.) inyector.

injudicious [inyudíshʊs], a. indiscreto, poco juicioso, imprudente.—**injudiciously** [-li], adv. indiscretamente, tontamente.—**injudiciousness** [-nes], s. indiscreción, imprudencia.

Injunction [inɣʊncŝhʊn], s. mandato, mandamiento; requerimiento; prohibición (for.) entredicho.

Injure [ínɣœr], va. injuriar, agraviar; dañar, damnificar, menoscabar; averiar; lastimar, lisiar.

Injurer [ínɣurœr], s. perjudicador.

Injurious [ínɣúrious], a. dañoso, perjudicial, dañino.—**Injuriously** [-li], adv. dañosamente, perjudicialmente.—**Injuriousness** [-nes], s. calidad de perjudicial.

Injury [ínɣuri], s. daño, avería; perjuicio, mal, detrimento, menoscabo, damnificación.

Injustice [inɣústis], s. injusticia.

Ink [inc], **I.** s. tinta; (ict.) tinta de calamar.—**i.**, o **inking, ball**, bala de entintar.—**I. fountain**, (impr.) tintero de prensa.—**i.**, o **inking, roller**, (impr.) rulo, rodillo. **II.** va. (a veces con in) entintar, dar tinta.

Inkhorn [ínkjorn]. **I.** s. tintero de bolsillo. **II.** a. pedantesco, pomposo.

Inkle [ínkœl], s. cinta ancha de hilo.

Inkling [ínkling], s. insinuación; sospecha; vislumbre, indicio.

Inkmaker [ínkméikœr], s. fabricante de tinta.

Inknot [innót], va. atar o añudar.

Inkstand [ínkstænd], s. tintero.

Inkwell [-uel], s. tintero; frasco de tintero.

Inky [ínki], a. parecido a la tinta; manchado de tinta.

Inlace [inlés], va. = ENLACE.

Inlaid [inléid], pret. y pp. de INLAY.—**i. work**, embutido, taracea, incrustación, ataujía.

Inland [ínland]. **I.** a. interior; del país, nacional, regional.—**I. commerce, duty, navigation**, etc., comercio, impuesto, navegación, etc. interior. **II.** s. el interior de un país. **III.** adv. tierra adentro.

Inlander [ínlandœr], s. el que habita tierra adentro; (Amér.) tierradentreño.

Inlay [inléi], va. (pret. y pp. INLAID) embutir; ataracear, taracear, hacer ataujía o mosaico; incrustar.

Inlay [ínlei], s. ataracea, embutido.

Inlayer [inléicœr], s. incrustador, obrero que hace taracea.

Inlaying [inléing], s. arte de ataracear, embutir o incrustar.

Inlet [ínlet], s. entrada; abra, caleta, ensenada, estero, estuario; boca de entrada.

Inlook [ínluc], s. = INTROSPECTION.

Inly [ínli], adv. interiormente.

Inmate [ínmeit], s. ocupante, residente (enfermo, si se trata de hospital; preso, si de cárcel, etc.); inquilino, huésped.

Inmesh [inméŝh], va. = ENMESH.

Inmost [ínmoust], a. íntimo, recóndito, profundo.

Inn [in], s. posada, fonda, mesón, hospedería.—**I. of court**, (Ingl.) colegio de abogados.

Innate [innéit], a. innato, ingénito, connatural.—**Innately** [-li], adv. por modo ingénito.—**Innateness** [-nes], s. calidad de innato.

Innavigable [innǽvigabœl], a. innavegable

Inner [ínœr], a. interior.

Innermost [ínœrmoust], a. = INMOST.

Innervate [ínnœrvet], va. proveer de nervios; causar inervación.—**Innervation** [-éiŝhʊn], s. (fisiol.) inervación.—**Innerve** [innœrv], va. vigorizar.

Inning [íning], s. en baseball y otros juegos, turno del batman; por extensión, turno en el mando o gobierno.

Innkeeper [ínkípœr], s. posadero, mesonero, hospedero, hostelero.

Innocence, innocency [ínosens, i], s. inocencia.

Innocent [ínosent], s. y a. inocente.

Innocently [-li], adv. inocentemente.

Innocuous [innókiuus], a. innocuo, inofensivo.—**Innocuously** [-li], adv. innocuamente, sin daño.—**Innocuousness** [-nes], s. calidad de inocuo.

Innominate [innóminet], a. (anat.) innominado; anónimo.

Innovate [ínoveit], va. innovar.—**Innovation** [-éiŝhʊn], s. innovación.—**Innovator** [-éitœr], s. innovador.

Innoxious [innókŝhius], a. innocuo.

Innuendo [iniuéndo], s. indirecta, insinuación.

Innumerability [inniúmœrabíliti], s. innumerabilidad.—**Innumerable** [-bœl], a. innumerable. —**Innumerableness** [-nes], s. innumerabilidad.— **Innumerably** [-bli], adv. innumerablemente.— **Innumerous** [-us], a. innumerable.

Inoculate [inókiuleit], va. y vn. (med.) inocular; (agr.) injertar en escudo; fertilizar (el suelo) con bacterias; (fig.) imbuir, infundir; infectar, inficionar.

Inoculation [-éiŝhʊn], s. (med.) inoculación; contaminación, infección; (agr.) injertación en escudo; fertilización con bacterias.

Inoculator [inókiuléitœr], s. inoculador.

Inodorous [inódœrus], a. inodoro.

Inoffensive [inofénsiv], a. inofensivo.—**Inoffensively** [-li], adv. inofensivamente.—**Inoffensiveness** [-nes], s. calidad de inofensivo.

Inofficious [inofíŝhus], a. (for.) inoficioso.

Inoperative [inópœretiv], a. ineficaz.

Inopportune [inóportiún], a. inoportuno, a mal tiempo.—**Inopportunely** [-li], adv. inoportunamente.—**Inopportuneness** [-nes], s. inoportunidad.

Inordinacy [inórdinasi], s. desarreglo, desorden; exceso.—**Inordinate** [inórdinet], a. inordenado, desarreglado; excesivo.—**Inordinately** [-li], adv.. inordenadamente; desmedidamente.—**Inordinateness** [-nes], s. desorden; exceso, demasía.

Inorganic(al [ínorgǽnic(al], a. inorgánico.

Inosculate [inóskiulet]. **I.** va. unir por anastomosis. **II.** vn. anastomarse.

Inosculation [inoskiuléŝhʊn], s. anastomosis.

Inoxidize [inócsidaiŝ], va. hacer inoxidable.

Inphase [ínféiŝ], a. (elec.) de la misma fase.

Input [ínput], s. dinero contribuído o gastado; (mec.) energía recibida por una máquina; (fisiol.) cantidad de sangre recibida por el cuerpo.

Inquest [íncuest], s. (for.) indagación, averiguación, examen, (información o pesquisa judicial con ayuda de un jurado; jurado que hace dicha pesquisa; juicio de indemnización.

Inquietude [incuáietiud], s. inquietud, desasosiego, descontento.

Inquirable [incuáiœrabœl], a. investigable.

Inquire [incuáier], va. y vn. inquirir, preguntar; averiguar.—**to I. about, after o for**, preguntar por.—**to i. into**, investigar, examinar.

Inquirer [incuáircœr], s. inquiridor, investigador, averiguador; persona que pregunta.

Inquiry [incuáiri], s. pregunta; consulta; indagación, averiguación; investigación, estudio.— **i. into**, investigación de, estudio de.

Inquisition [incuiŝíŝhʊn], s. inquisición; Santo Oficio; escudriñamiento, investigación.

Inquisitional [-al], a. inquisitorial.

Inquisitive [incuiŝítiv], a. inquisitivo, preguntón; investigador.—**Inquisitively** [-li], adv. inquisitivamente.—**Inquisitiveness** [-nes], s. curiosidad, manía de preguntar.

Inquisitor [incuiŝítœr], s. inquisidor; juez investigador; inquiridor.

Inquisitorial [incuiŝítórial], a. inquisitorial.

In re [in ri], concerniente o relativo a.

Inroad [ínroud], s. incursión, irrupción.

Inrush [ínruŝh], s. empuje, invasión.

Insalivate [insǽliveit], va. insalivar.

Insalivation [insǽliveiŝhʊn], s. insalivación.

Insalubrious [insalúbrius], a. insalubre, malsano.

Insalubrity [insalúbriti], s. insalubridad.

Insane [inséin], a. loco; de locos o para locos.— **i. asylum**, casa de locos, manicomio.

Insanity [insǽniti], s. locura.

Insatiable [inséŝhiabœl], a. insaciable, que no se sacia.—**Insatiableness** [-nes], s. insaciabilidad.— **Insatiably** [-bli], adv. insaciablemente.

Insatiate [-ŝhiet], a. insaciable.—**Insatiately** [-li], adv. insaciablemente.

Inscribable [inscráibabœl], a. inscribible.

Inscribe [inscráib], va. inscribir; grabar; dedicar; apuntar.

Inscription [inscrípŝhʊn], s. inscripción; rótulo, letrero; registro; dedicatoria.

inscriptive [inscríptiv], *a.* inscrito, inscripto.
inscrutability [-crútabíliti], *s.* inescrutabilidad.
inscrutable [-bœl], *a.* inescrutable.—**inscrutably** [-bli], *adv.* inescrutablemente.
insect [ínsect], *s.* insecto.—**i. powder**, polvos insecticidas.
Insecta [inséctæ], *s. pl.* insectos.
insectarium [ínsectéiriʊm], *s.* lugar donde se crían insectos.
insectean [inséctean], **insectile** [inséctil], *a.* insectil.
insecticide [inséctisaid], *s.* insecticida.
insection [insékshʊn], *s.* incisión.
Insectivora [ínsectívoræ], *s. pl.* insectívoros.
insectivorous [ínsectívorʊs], *a.* insectívoro.
insecure [insekiúœr], *a.* inseguro.
insecurely [-li], *adv.* inseguramente.
insecurity [insekiúriti], *s.* inseguridad, incertidumbre; peligro, riesgo.
insensate [insénset], *a.* insensato.
insensibility [insénsibíliti], *s.* insensibilidad.
insensible [-bœl], *a.* insensible; imperceptible; impasible.—**Insensibleness** [-nes], *s.* insensibilidad.—**insensibly** [-bli], *adv.* insensiblemente.
insentient [insénshent], *a.* insensible.
inseparability [inséparabíliti], **inseparableness** [-bœlness], *s.* inseparabilidad.—**inseparable** [-bœl], *a.* inseparable.—**inseparably** [-bli], *adv.* inseparablemente.
insert [insert], *s.* cosa insertada, intercalada, etc. (*V.* INSERT, *va.*); (enc.) hoja o lámina, etc. intercalada en un libro; (en el correo) circular o anuncio metido en un periódico o libro que se envía por correo; (cine) letrero explicativo proyectado sobre la pantalla.
insert [insért], *va.* insertar, ingerir; introducir, meter, encajar; intercalar.
insertion [insérshʊn], *s.* inserción, metimiento, introducción; (cost.) entredós; (bot.) inserción.
inserviceable [insérvisabœl], *a.* inservible.
inset [ínset], *s.* intercalación; flujo o marea montante; (enc.) INSERT.
inshore [ínshor]. **I.** *a.* cercano a la orilla. **II.** *adv.* hacia la orilla o cerca de ella.
inshrine, *va.* = ENSHRINE.
inside [ínsaid]. **I.** *a.* interior, interno.—**to have the l. track**, (dep.) seguir la pista interior en una carrera; tener ventaja sobre un competidor. **II.** *s.* el interior, la parte de dentro; contenido; forro; guarnición interior (de válvula, etc.).—*pl.* entrañas; interioridades. **III.** *adv.* dentro, adentro, en el interior.—**l. out**, de dentro afuera; al revés.
insidious [insídiʊs], *a.* insidioso, solapado.—**insidiously** [-li'], *adv.* insidiosamente.—**Insidiousness** [-nes], *s.* calidad de insidioso.
insight [ínsait], *s.* discernimiento, perspicacia; penetración; comprensión; conocimiento, idea; percepción de la naturaleza interior de una cosa.
insignia [insígnia], *s. pl.* insignias.
insignificance, insignificancy [insigníficans, i], *s.* insignificancia.—**insignificant** [-cant], *a.* insignificante.—**Insignificantly** [-li], *adv.* insignificantemente.
insincere [insinsíœr], *a.* falto de sinceridad.—**insincerely** [-li], *adv.* sin sinceridad.—**insincerity** [-séroti], *s.* falta de sinceridad. camandulería.
insinuate [insíniueit]. **I.** *va.* insinuar, indicar, sugerir.—**i. one's self**, insinuarse, introducirse, intimar. **II.** *vn.* echar pullas o indirectas.
insinuating [-ing], *a.* insinuativo.
insinuation [insiñuéishʊn], *s.* insinuación; sugestión, indirecta, pulla.
insinuative [insíñuetiv], *a.* insinuante, insinuativo.
insinuator [insíñuéitœr], *s.* insinuante, insinuador.
insipid [insípid], *a.* insípido.—**insipidity** [insipidíti], **Insipidness** [insípidnes], *s.* insipidez, insulsez, sosería.—**Insipidly** [-li], *adv.* insulsamente, insípidamente, sosamente.
insist [insíst], *vn.* insistir; persistir, porfiar.—**insistence, insistency** [-ens, i], *s.* insistencia, porfía.—**insistent** [-ent], *a.* insistente, persistente; porfiado.

in situ [in sáitu], (geol.) *in situ*, en el lugar de origen.
insnare [insnéær], *va.* = ENSNARE.
insobriety [insobráiti], *s.* falta de sobriedad; embriaguez, borrachera.
insofar as, in so far as [in so far æs], en cuanto a, en cuanto, en lo que, hasta donde.
insolate [ínsolet], *va.* insolar.
insolation [insoléshʊn], *s.* acto de secar al sol, blanqueo; (med.) insolación.
insole [ínsoul], *s.* (zap.) plantilla.
insolence [ínsolens], *s.* insolencia.—**insolent** [-lent], *a.* insolente.—**Insolently** [-li], *adv.* insolentemente.
insolubility [insóliubíliti], **insolubleness** [-bœlnes], *s.* insolubilidad.—**Insoluble** [-bœl], *a.* insoluble.
insolvable [insólvabœl], *a.* inexplicable; insoluble; que no se puede saldar.
insolvency [insólvensi], *s.* insolvencia.
insolvent [insólvent], *a.* insolvente.
insomnia [insómnia], *s.* insomnio, desvelo.
insomnious [-ʊs], *a.* insomne, desvelado.
insomnolence [-nolens], *s.* falta de sueño.
insomuch [insomúch], *conj.* (seguido de *as* o *that*) de manera que, de suerte que, de tal modo que, hasta el punto que.
inspect [inspéct], *va.* reconocer, registrar; inspeccionar.—**Inspection** [inspécshʊn], *s.* inspección; reconocimiento, registro.—**by i.**, a la simple vista.—**Inspector** [inspéctœr], *s.* inspector.—**Inspectorate** [inspéctoret], **Inspectorship** [-ship], *s.* distrito, cargo o empleo de un inspector.
insphere [insfir], *va.* = ENSPHERE.
inspiration [inspiréishʊn], *s.* inspiración (en todas sus acepciones).
inspirational [-æl], *a.* inspirativo; inspirado.
inspiratory [inspáiratori], *a.* inspirador, inspirativo.
inspire [inspáiœr]. **I.** *va.* inspirar; insinuar, sugerir; autorizar (por funcionarios públicos). **II.** *vn.* inspirar.—**Inspirer** [-œr], *s.* inspirador; insinuador.—**Inspiring** [-ing], *a.* inspirador; inspirativo, fortificante.
inspirit [inspírit], *va.* alentar, animar.
inspissate [inspíseit]. **I.** *va.* espesar, condensar, incrasar. **II.** *a.* espeso.—**Inspissation** [-séishʊn], *s.* condensación, acto de espesar.
instability [instabíliti], *s.* instabilidad.
instable [instábœl], *a.* instable.
install [instól], *va.* instalar; colocar.
installation [instoléishʊn], *s.* instalación; montaje.
instal(l)ment [instólmœnt], *s.* instalación; entrega; plazo.—**I. plan**, pago por plazos (por mensualidades, si los pagos son mensuales).
instance [ínstans]. **I.** *s.* ejemplo; caso; instancia, ruego, solicitación; (for.) instancia, expediente; ocasión, lugar.—**for i.**, por ejemplo.—**in the first i.**, desde el principio. **II.** *va.* ejemplificar; citar, mencionar.
instancy [ínstansi], *s.* insistencia.
instant [ínstant]. **I.** *a.* inminente, inmediato, perentorio; corriente, presente, actual. **II.** *s.* instante.
instantaneous [-téiniʊs], *a.* instantáneo.
instantaneously [-li], *adv.* instantáneamente.—**instantaneousness** [-nes], *s.* calidad de instantáneo.
instanter [instæntœr], **instantly** [instantli], *adv.* al instante.
instate [instéd], *va.* instalar, colocar.
instead [instéd], *adv.* en lugar, en vez; en lugar de eso, ello, él, etc.
instep [ínstep], *s.* empeine del pie; parte anterior de la pata trasera.
instigate [ínstiguet], *va.* instigar.—**instigation** [-éishʊn], *s.* instigación.—**Instigator** [-éitœr], *s.* instigador.
instil(l [instíl], *va.* instilar; inspirar, inculcar, infundir.
instillation [instiléishʊn], **instil(l)ment** [instílmœnt], *s.* instilación; insinuación.

---

instinct [instínct], *a.* (con *with*) animado, impulsado, movido por.

instinct [instinct], *s.* instinto.

instinctive [instínctiv], *a.* instintivo.—**instinctively** [-li], *adv.* instintivamente.

institor [institœr], *s.* (for.) institor, factor.

institute [institiut]. **I.** *va.* instituir, fundar; iniciar; nombrar; (igl.) conferir un beneficio. **II.** *s.* instituto, establecimiento; regla, principio, máxima.—*pl.* instituta; instituciones.—**Institutes of Justinian,** Instituta de Justiniano.—**Institutes of medicine,** instituciones de medicina.

institution [institiúshun], *s.* institución; establecimiento; instituto; comienzo, acto incoativo; (for.) nombramiento de heredero; (igl.) institución canónica.—**institutional** [-nal], o **institutionary** [-eri], *a.* institucional; elemental, rudimentario.—**institutive** [-tiv], *a.* instituente o instituyente; establecido, instituido.—**institutor** [-tœr], *s.* instituidor, institutor, fundador.—**institutress** [-tres], *s.* fundadora.

instruct [instrúct], *va.* instruir, enseñar, amaestrar; dar instrucciones, dar órdenes, mandar.

instructer, *s.* = INSTRUCTOR.

instruction [instrúcshun], *s.* instrucción, educación, enseñanza; conocimiento, saber.—*pl.* instrucciones; órdenes.

instructive [-tiv], *a.* instructivo.—**instructively** [-li], *adv.* instructivamente.—**instructiveness** [-nes], *s.* calidad de instructivo.

instructor [-tœr], *s.* instructor, maestro.

instructress [-tres], *s.* instructora, institutriz.

instrument [instrumœnt]. **I.** *s.* instrumento; (for.) instrumento, documento. **II.** *va.* (mús.) instrumentar.

instrumental [-méntæl], *a.* instrumental; influyente, servicial, cooperador; conducente; sujeto.—**instrumentalism** [-méntalism], *s.* (filos.) sistema que hace de la utilidad el criterio de la verdad.—**instrumentalist** [-méntalist], **instrumentist** [instruméntist], *s.* (mús.) instrumentista.—**instrumentality** [-mentæliti], *s.* agencia, mediación.—**instrumentally** [-méntali], *adv.* instrumentalmente.—**instrumentation** [-mentéishun], *s.* (mús.) instrumentación; ejecución instrumental; agencia.

insubordinate [insubórdinet], *a.* insubordinado.

insubordination [-néishun], *s.* insubordinación.

insufferable [insúfœrabœl], *a.* insufrible.—**insufferably** [-bli], *adv.* insufriblemente.

insufficience, insufficiency [insufíshens, i], *s.* insuficiencia.—**insufficient** [-físhœnt], *a.* insuficiente; incapaz, inepto.—**insufficiently** [-li], *adv.* insuficientemente.

insufflate [insúflet], *va.* insuflar.—**insufflation** [insufléishun], *s.* soplo, insuflación.—**insufflator** [-fleitœr], *s.* insuflador.

insular [ínsular], *a.* insular, isleño; estrecho de miras.—**i. sclerosis,** esclerosis cerebroespinal.

insularity [-lériti], *s.* calidad de insular o isleño; estrechez de miras.

insulate [ínsuleit], *va.* aislar.—**insulating** [-ing], *a.* aislador, aislante.—**insulation** [-éishun], *s.* aislamiento.—**insulator** [-eitœr], *s.* aislador.

insulin [ínsulin], *s.* insulina, producto pancreático antidiabético.

insult [ínsult], *s.* insulto.

insult [insúlt], *va.* insultar.—**insulter** [-œr], *s.* insultador.—**insulting** [-ing], *a.* insultante.—**insultingly** [-li], *adv.* insultantemente.

insuperability, insuperableness [insiúpœrabílity, -bœlnes], *s.* calidad de insuperable.—**insuperable** [-pœrabœl], *a.* insuperable.—**insuperably** [-bli], *adv.* invenciblemente.

insupportable [insupórtabœl], *a.* insoportable, inaguantable o insufrible.—**insupportableness** [-nes], *s.* calidad de insoportable o inaguantable.—**insupportably** [-bli], *adv.* insoportablemente.

insuppressible [insuprésibœl], *a.* que no se puede ocultar o suprimir.

insurable [inshúrabœl], *a.* asegurable.

insurance [inshurans], *s.* garantía, seguridad; (com.) seguro, aseguramiento; sistema de seguros; prima o premio del seguro; cantidad total de seguro.—**i. agent,** agente de seguros.—**i. bonds,** bonos u otras propiedades en que las compañías de seguros pueden legalmente invertir sus fondos.—**i. broker,** corredor de seguros.—**i. company,** compañía de seguros.—**i. policy,** póliza de seguro.

insurant [inshúrænt], *s.* asegurado.

insure [inshúær]. **I.** *va.* (com.) asegurar; garantizar, afianzar; dar o tener seguridad de; lograr. **II.** *vn.* asegurarse.

insurer [inshúrœr], *s.* asegurador.

insurgent [insœrvent], *a.* y *s.* insurgente.

insurmountable [insœrmáuntabœl], *a.* insuperable.—**insurmountably** [-bli], *adv.* insuperablemente.

insurrection [insœrrécshun], *s.* insurrección.—**insurrectional, insurrectionary** [-al, -eri], *a.* revolucionario, rebelde.—**insurrectionist** [-ist], *s.* insurrecto.

insusceptible [insuséptibœl], *a.* no susceptible, insensible.

inswept [ínsuépt], *a.* (aut.) estrechado hacia adelante.

intact [intáct], *a.* intacto.—**intactness** [-nes], *s.* integridad.

intaglio [intéllo o intállo], *s.* obra de talla; (joy.) entalle.

intake [inteik], *s.* producto de una finca; (tej.) punto con que se empieza a estrechar; admisión; orificio de entrada, o de toma; rigola.

intangibility o **intangibleness** [intænyibíliti, -bœlnes], *s.* calidad de intangible.

intangible [-bœl], *a.* intangible.

integer [íntevœr], *s.* número entero.

integral [íntegræl]. **I.** *a.* íntegro; integrante, inherente; (mat.) entero (número, función, etc.); integral (cálculo); (mec.) de una pieza. **II.** *s.* (mat.) integral.

integralism [-gralism], **integrality** [-græliti], *s.* integridad.

integrally [-grali], *adv.* integralmente.

integrand [-grænd], *s.* (mat.) función o diferencial por integrar.

integrant [-grænt], *a.* integrante, constitutivo.

integrate [-greit]. **I.** *va.* integrar, formar un todo; (mat.) integrar. **II.** *vn.* integrarse, completarse.—**integrating** [-gréiting], *a.* integrante; de integración.—**integration** [-gréishun], *s.* integración.—**integrator** [-gréitœr], *s.* integrador (instrumento).

integrity [intégriti], *s.* integridad.

integument [intéguiumœnt], *s.* integumento, túnica.—**integumental, integumentary** [-æl, -eri], *a.* integumentario.

intellect [íntelect], *s.* intelecto, inteligencia; gente de talento.

intellection [-lékshun], *s.* intelección.

intellective [-léctiv], *a.* intelectivo.

intellectual [íntelékchual], *s.* y *a.* intelectual.—**intellectuality** [-lékchuæliti], *s.* intelectualidad.—**intellectually** [-lékchuali], *adv.* intelectualmente.

intelligence [intélivens], *s.* inteligencia; penetración; informe; noticia, aviso; correspondencia mutua, armonía, acuerdo; un ser inteligente.—**i. bureau** o **department,** oficina de información.—**i. office,** agencia de sirvientes.

intelligencer [-vensœr], *s.* noticiero, mensajero; espía.

intelligent [-vent], *a.* inteligente; bien fundado, con conocimiento.—**intelligently** [-li], *adv.* inteligentemente; con conocimiento del asunto.

intelligentsia [-véntsiæ], *s. pl.* las clases cultas o ilustradas.

intelligibility [intéliyibíliti], **intelligibleness** [-bœlnes], *s.* comprensibilidad, claridad.

intelligible [-bœl] *a.* inteligible.—**intelligibly** [-bli], *adv.* inteligiblemente.

intemperance [intémpœrans], *s.* intemperancia; exceso en la bebida.—**intemperate** [-et], *a.* destemplado; inmoderado, desmandado; intemperante; excesivo, desmedido.—**intemperately** [-li], *adv.* destempladamente; inmoderadamente.—**intemperateness** [-nes], *s.* inmoderación, intemperancia; exceso, demasía.

intend [inténd], *va.* intentar, tener intención de; proponerse; destinar; aplicar, determinar; querer decir; tener por objeto.

intendancy [inténdansi], *s.* intendencia.

intendant [inténdant], *s.* intendente.

intended [inténded]. **I.** *s.* (fam.) desposado, prometido, futuro. **II.** *a.* deseado, pensado, que se tiene en mira.—**intendedly** [-li], *adv.* adrede, intencionalmente.

intendment [inténdmœnt], *s.* (for.) intento o espíritu de una ley.

intense [inténs], *a.* intenso, fuerte, vivo, violento; extremado, sumo; esforzado; (fot.) duro (negativo).—**intensely** [-li], *adv.* intensamente.—**intenseness** [-nes], *s.* calidad de intenso, intensidad.

intensifier [inténsifaiœr], *s.* (fot.) baño para reforzar un negativo.

intensify [-fai]. **I.** *va.* intensar, hacer más intenso; (fot.) reforzar. **II.** *vn.* volverse intenso.

intension [inténshun], *s.* intensión; tensión; intensidad; (lóg.) contenido, comprensión.

intensity [inténsiti], *s.* intensidad; (fot.) fuerza de un negativo.

intensive [inténsiv], *a.* intensivo; entero, completo; (lóg.) relativo al contenido; (gram.) enfático.—**intensively** [-li], *adv.* intensivamente.

intent [intént]. **I.** *a.* atento; asiduo, dedicado; (con *on*) decidido, resuelto a. **II.** *s.* intento, designio, intención, propósito.—**to all intents and purposes,** en realidad, en el fondo.

intention [inténshun], *s.* intención; (for.) propósito deliberado; (cir.) curso o procedimiento natural.—**by first, second i.,** (cir.) por primera, segunda intención.

intentional [-al], *a.* intencional.—**intentionally** [-l], *adv.* intencionalmente.

intently [inténtli], *adv.* asiduamente; atentamente; resueltamente.—**intentness** [-nes], *s.* aplicación asidua, atención.

inter [intœr], *va.* enterrar, sepultar.

interact [intœréct]. **I.** *va.* obrar entre sí, o recíprocamente. **II.** *s.* (teat.) entreacto; intermedio.

interaction [-œcshun], *s.* acción recíproca.

interallied [-æláid], *a.* de los aliados.

interborough [-bœrou], municipal, interseccional, que una las secciones o distritos (*boroughs*) de una gran ciudad (apl. esp. a los ferrocarriles de Nueva York).

interbreed [-bríd], *va.* y *vn.* = HYBRIDIZE.

intercalary [intœrcaleri], *a.* intercalar.—**intercalate** [-leit], *va.* intercalar.—**intercalation** [-léishun], *s.* intercalación.

intercede [intœrsíd], *vn.* interceder.

interceder [-sídœr], *s.* intercesor.

intercellular [-séliular], *a.* intercelular.

intercept [-sépt]. **I.** *va.* interceptar; atajar, detener. **II.** *s.* (mat.) ordenada en el origen.—**interception** [-sépshun], *s.* intercepción; atajo.

intercession [-séshun], *s.* intercesión.—**intercessor** [-sésœr], *s.* intercesor.—**intercessory** [-sésori], *s.* intercesorio.

interchain [-chéin], *va.* encadenar, entrelazar.

interchange [-chéin]. **I.** *va.* alternar; cambiar, trocar; permutar. **II.** *vn.* alternarse, trocarse. **III.** *s.* intercambio; comercio, tráfico.—**interchangeability** [-abíliti], **interchangeableness** [-abœlnes], *s.* calidad de intercambiable.—**interchangeable** [-abœl], *a.* intercambiable; permutable; mutuo, recíproco.—**interchangeably** [-abli] *adv.* recíprocamente; intercambiablemente.

interclude [-clúd], *va.* obstruir, tapar.

interclusion [-clúyun], *s.* interceptación, obstrucción.

intercolumnar [-colúmnar], *a.* intercolumnar.

intercolumniation [-colúmniéishun], *s.* (arq.) intercolumnio.

intercommon [-cómun], **intercommune** [-comiún]. **I.** *va.* (Ingl.) deportar o denunciar a uno por sostener comunicación con malhechores o insurrectos. **II.** *vn.* tener prados en común.

intercommunicate [-comiúnikeit], *vn.* comunicarse con otro.—**intercommunication** [-éishun], *s.* comunicación mutua.

intercostal [-cóstal], *a.* intercostal.

intercourse [-cors], *s.* comercio, tráfico; intercambio; comunicación, correspondencia, trato, roce.

intercrop [-crop]. **I.** *va.* hacer una siembra entre los surcos de otra; hacer siembra accesoria intermedia de cosecha rápida entre la cosecha de la siembra principal y el tiempo de sembrar para otra análoga. **II.** *s.* siembra de entre surcos; siembra accesoria intermedia de cosecha rápida.

intercross [-crós], *va.* entrecruzar; cruzar castas, hibridar.

intercrossing [-crósing], *s.* cruzamiento.

intercurrent [-cœrrent], *a.* intercurrente.

intercutaneous [-kiuténius], *a.* intercutáneo.

interdependence [-depéndens], *s.* dependencia mutua.—**interdependent** [-ent], *a.* dependiente uno de otro.

interdict [-díct], *va.* interdecir; prohibir, vedar; poner entredicho.

interdict [-dict], **interdiction** [-dicshun], *s.* veto, prohibición; interdicto, entredicho.

interdictive [-díctiv], **interdictory** [-díctori], *a.* que interdice o veda.

interdigital [-díyital], *a.* interdigital.

interest [intœrest]. **I.** *va.* interesar. **II.** *s.* interés; provecho; simpatía; (com.) interés, rédito; participación en una empresa; influencia, empeño, influjo.

interesting [interesting], *s.* interesante, atractivo.—**in an i. condition,** en estado interesante, encinta.

interfere [intœrfíœr], *vn.* ingerirse, inmiscuirse, interponerse, meterse; intervenir; (con **with**) embarazar, impedir, estorbar; (vet.) tropezar, rozarse un pie con el otro los caballos.

interference [-fírens], *s.* ingerencia, interposición; intervención; obstáculo, impedimento; (ópt.) interferencia.

interferential [-ferénshæl], *a.* interferente.

interferometer [-ferómetœr], *s.* instrumento para medir distancias, desplazamientos, etc., por medio de la interferencia; instrumento para el análisis espectral de gases incadescentes.

interfering [fíring], *s.* (vet.) alcance, tropezón, rozadura.

interfuse [-fiúś]. **I.** *va.* hacer fluir juntamente, mezclar. **II.** *vn.* fluir uno en otro; mezclarse. —**interfusion** [fiúyun], *va.* mezcla, combina ción.

interim [intœrim], *a.* intermedio, ínterin.—**i. certificate,** certificado provisional.—**in the i.,** en el ínterin.

interior [intíriœr]. **I.** *a.* interior, interno. **II.** *s.* interior, parte de adentro.

interiorly [-li], *adv.* interiormente.

interjacent [intœrréishent], *a.* interyacente, interpuesto.

interject [-réct]. **I.** *va.* interponer, insertar. **II.** *vn.* interponerse, intervenir.

interjection [-récshun], *s.* (gram.) interjección; exclamación; intervención, interposición.

interjoin [-yóin], *va.* unir mutuamente.

interlace [-léis], *va.* entrelazar, entremezclar.

interlard [-lárd], *va.* (coc.) mechar; interpolar, insertar.

interleave [-lív], *va.* interfoliar, interpaginar, intercalar hojas en.

interline [-láin], *va.* interlinear.—**interlinear** [-líniar], **interlineary** [-líniari], *a.* interlineal.—**interlineation** [-liniéishun], *s.* interlineación.—**interlining** [-láining], *s.* interlineación; (cost.) entretela.

interlink [-línc], *va.* eslabonar.

interlock [-lóc], *va.* y *vn.* trabar, engranar, engarzar; unirse, entrelazarse; cerrar.—**interlocking** [-lóking], *a.* que engranan, que se traban; de traba; de fijación mutua; de cierre.—**i. directorates,** juntas directivas entrelazadas de empresas comerciales, en que varios miembros lo son de juntas de empresas diferentes, las cuales pueden en realidad ser dominadas por unas mismas personas.

interlocution [-lokiúshʊn], s. interlocucion, plática.

interlocutor [-lókiutœr], s. interlocutor.

interlocutory [-lókiutori], a. dialogístico; interlocutorio.

interlope [-lóup], vn. entrementerse sin derecho; traficar sin licencia.—**interloper** [-œr], s. entremetido, intruso; (com.) intérlope.

interlude [-liud], s. intermedio, entremés; (mús.) interludio.

interlunar(y [-lúnar(i], a. perteneciente al interlunio.

intermarriage [-mǽrriy], s. matrimonio de personas de distintas razas, o entre parientes.

intermarry [-mǽrri], vn. casarse personas emparentadas o de distintas razas.

intermaxilary [-mǽxileri]. **I.** a. intermaxilar. **II.** s. hueso intermaxilar (ll. t. **i. bone**).

intermeddle [-médœl], vn. ingerirse, inmiscuirse, meterse.—**Intermeddler** [-médlœr], s. entremetido

intermedial, intermediate [-mídial, diet] a. intermedio.—**Intermediary** [-mídiæri], a. y s. intermediario.—**intermediate** [-mídiet], vn. intervenir.—**Intermediately** [intœrmídietli], adv. por intervención.—**Intermediation** [-mídiéíshʊn], s. intervención, mediación. ◢

interment [intœrmœnt], s. entierro.

intermezzo [íntœrmédso], s. (mús.) intermedio, intermezzo.

interminable [intœrminabœl], a. interminable. —**interminably** [-bli], adv. interminablemente.—**Interminate** [intœrminet], a. interminable.

intermingle [íntœrmíngœl]. **I.** va. entremezclar, entreverar. **II.** vn. mezclarse.

intermission [-míshʊn], s. intermisión, interrupción, tregua; intermitencia; (tea.) intermedio, entreacto.

intermissive [-mísiv], a. intermitente.

intermit [-mít]. **I.** va. intermitir, interpolar. **II.** vn. interrumpirse, cesar.—**Intermittent** [-mítœnt], a. intermitente.—**Intermittingly** [-mítingli], adv. con intermisión, a intervalos.

intermix [-mícs]. **I.** va. entremezclar, entreverar, entretejer, interpolar. **II.** vn. entremezclarse, compenetrarse. — **intermixture** [-mícschœr], s. entremezcladura; mezcla.

intern [intœrn]. **I.** va. encerrar, poner a buen recaudo. **II.** a. interno. **III.** s. practicante de hospital.

internal [intœrnal], a. interno, interior; doméstico, intestino; íntimo.—**i.-combustion engine**, motor de combustión (interna).—**i. diameter**, diámetro interior.—**i. gear**, (mec.) engranaje de dientes interiores.—**i. revenue**, rentas interiores, rentas provenientes de impuestos sobre artículos y operaciones interiores.—**i. valve gear**, (mec.) distribución interior.—**i. work**, (mec.) trabajo interno.

internally [-i], adv. internamente; interiormente; adentro.

international [intærnǽshʊnæl]. **I.** a. internacional.—**i. law**, derecho de gentes, derecho internacional. **II.** s. (**I-**), Internacional (asociación); miembro de la Internacional.

internationalist [-ist], s. internacionalista.

internationalize [-ais], va. hacer internacional.

internecine [íntœrnísin], a. intestino; sanguinario.

internod(i)al [íntœrnód(i)al], a. colocado entre dos nudos.

internode, internodium [íntœrnód(ium], s. (bot.) internodio, cañuto.

inter nos [íntœr nos], entre nos.

internuncio [-núnshio], s. internuncio.

interosseous [-osius], a. interóseo.

interpellant [-pélænt], a. y s. interpelante.—**Interpellate** [-pélet], va. interpelar.

interpellation [-peléíshʊn], s. interpelación.

interpenetrate [-pénetreit], va. y vn. compenetrar(se).

interphone [interfóun], s. teléfono de servicio interior.

interplane [-pléin], a. situado entre dos planos.

interplead [-plíd], vn. (for.) litigar entre sí varios demandantes, para determinar el mayor derecho a la demanda.—**interpleader** [-plídœr], s. (for.)-procedimiento para determinar cuál de varios de mandantes tiene derecho a la demanda.

interpolate [intœrpoleit], va. interpolar.—**interpolation** [intœrpoléíshʊn], s. interpolación.—**interpolator** [intœrpoléitœr], s. interpolador.

interposal [intœrpóusal], s. interposición, mediación, intervención.—**interpose** [-póus]. **I.** va. interponer. **II.** vn. interponerse, intermediar, intervenir; interrumpir.—**interposer** [-póusœr], s. mediador.—**interposition** [-posíshʊn], s. interposición.

interpret [intœrpret], va. interpretar, descifrar, traducir; representar, ilustrar.

interpretable [-abœl], a. interpretable.

interpretation [íntœrpretéíshʊn], s. interpretación, traducción, explicación, exposición.

interpretative [intœrpretativ], a. interpretativo. —**interpretatively** [-li], adv. interpretativamente.

interpreter [intœrpretœr], s. intérprete.

interregnum [interrégnum], s. interregno.

interrogate [intérrogeit]. **I.** va. interrogar, preguntar, examinar. **II.** vn. hacer preguntas.

interrogation [interroguéíshʊn], s. interrogación, pregunta, pesquisa.—**i. point**, (impr.) interrogación, punto interrogante (?).

interrogative [interrógativ]. **I.** a. interrogativo. **II.** s. palabra interrogativa. — **interrogatively** [-li], adv. interrogativamente.

interrogator [intérrogueitœr], s. interrogante.

interrogatory [interrógatori]. **I.** s. interrogatorio, examen. **II.** a. interrogativo.

interrupt [intœrrúpt], va. interrumpir.—**interruptedly** [-tedli], adv. interrumpidamente, descontinuamente.—**interrupter** [-tœr], s. interruptor; (elec.) interruptor.—**interruption** [-shʊn], s. interrupción.

interscapular [-scǽpiular], a. interescapular.

intersect [-séct]. **I.** va. cortar. **II.** vn. cortarse, intersecarse.

intersection [-sécshʊn], s. intersección.

interspace [-spéis]. **I.** va. dejar espacio entre; llenar el espacio entre; espaciar. **II.** s. espacio intermedio.

intersperse [-spœrs], va. esparcir, entremezclar; diseminar.—**interspersion** [-spœrshʊn], s. esparcimiento de una cosa entre otras.

interspinal, o interspinous [-spáinal, -nʊs], a. interespinal.

interstate [intœrstéit], a. entre estados, de entre estados (de un mismo país).

interstellar [-stélar], a. interestelar.

interstice [intœrstis o intœrstis], s. intersticio.

interstitial [intœrstíshal], a. que tiene intersticios.

intertexture [intœrtéxchœr], s. contexto, entretejedura, entretejimiento.

intertropical [intœrtrópical], a. intertropical.

intertwine, intertwist [íntœrtuáin, tuíst], va. entretejer, entrelazar; (mar.) acolchar.

interval [íntœrval], s. intervalo.

intervene [íntœrvín], vn. intervenir, mediar; atravesarse, interponerse; ocurrir, sobrevenir. —**intervening** [-ing], a. intermedio, intercurrente.

intervention [íntœrvénshʊn], s. intervención, mediación; interposición.

interventionist [-vénshʊnist], s. partidario de la intervención; (med.) el que sostiene que una enfermedad debe atacarse en vez de dejarla seguir su curso natural; intervencionista, partidario del paternalismo o de la intervención del estado en disputas económicas.

intervertebral [-vœrtebral], a. intervertebral.

interview [íntœrviu]. **I.** s. entrevista, conferencia, abocamiento. **II.** va. entrevistar, tener entrevista con.

interviewer [-viúœr], s. reportero que se avista con personas para indagar opiniones, obtener información, etc.

intervolve [-vólv], va. envolver una cosa dentro de otra.

interweave [-uív], *va.* y *vn.* (*pret.* INTERWOVE o INTERWEAVED; *pp.* -WOVEN o WEAVED) entretejer, entrelazar.—**interweaving** [-ing], *s.* entretejimiento, entrelazamiento.—**interwoven**, *pp.* de INTERWEAVE; *a.* entrelazado, entretejido, vinculado.

interwreathe [-ríᴅ], *va.* tejer en forma de guirnalda.

intestable [intéstabœl], *a.* legalmente incapacitado para hacer testamento.

intestacy [intéstasi], *s.* falta de testamento.

intestate [intéstet], *a.* intestado, abintestato.

intestinal [intéstinal], *a.* intestinal; interior, intestino.

intestine [intéstin]. **I.** *a.* interior, intestino, doméstico; interno. **II.** *s.* intestino.

inthrall, inthralment, etc. = ENTHRALL, etc.

intimacy [íntimasi], *s.* intimidad.

intimate [íntimet]. **I.** *a.* íntimo. **II.** *s.* amigo íntimo, confidente. **III.** *va.* insinuar, indicar, intimar.—**intimately** [-li], *adv.* íntimamente.

intimation [intiméshun], *s.* insinuación, intimación, indirecta, pulla; indicio.

intimidate [intímideit], *va.* intimidar o amenazar.—**intimidation** [-éishun], *s.* intimidación.

intitle [intáitœl], *va.* = ENTITLE.

into [íntu], *prep.* en, dentro, adentro, hacia el interior (según que denote ingreso, penetración, inserción, inclusión, transformación o multiplicación).—**i. the bargain, por** añadidura.

intolerability [intólœrabíliti], **intolerableness** [-bœlnes], *s.* intolerabilidad.—**intolerable** [-bœl], *a.* intolerable, insufrible, inaguantable.—**intolerably** [-bli], *adv.* intolerablemente.—**intolerance**, **intolerancy** [-ans, i], *s.* intolerancia.—**intolerant** [-ant], *a.* y *s.* intolerante.—**intolerantly** [-li], *adv.* con intolerancia.

intomb [intúm], *va.* enterrar, sepultar.

intonate [íntoneit], *vn.* entonar, solfear, cantar.—**intonation** [-éishun], *s.* entonación.

intone [intóun], *va.* y *vn.* entonar; cantar o recitar en un solo tono; (igl.) salmear, salmodiar.

intortion [intórshun], *s.* intorsión.

intoxicant [intóxicant], *s.* bebida alcohólica.

intoxicate [intócsikeit]. **I.** *va.* embriagar; (med.) envenenar, intoxicar. **II.** *a.* ebrio.—**intoxication** [-éishun], *s.* embriaguez; (med.) intoxicación, envenenamiento.

intra-atomic [íntræ-ætómic], *a.* intraatómico, del interior del átomo.

intractability [intréctabíliti], **intractableness** [-bœlnes], *s.* hurañería.—**intractable** [-bœl], *a.* intratable.—**intractably** [-bli], *adv.* hurañamente.

intra.los [intrédos o intrádos], *s.* (arq.) intradós.

intramolecular [intramolékiular], *a.* intramolecular

intramural [íntramiúral], *a.* situado intramuros.

intranquillity [intræncuíliti], *s.* intranquilidad.

intransigent [intrénsiyent], *a.* **intransigentist** [-ist], *s.* intransigente.

intransitive [intrénsitiv], *a.* intransitivo.

intransitively [-li], *adv.* intransitivamente.

intransmutability [intrænsmiútabíliti], *s.* intransmutabilidad.

intransmutable [-miútabœl], *a.* intransmutable.

intrench, intrenchment = ENTRENCH, etc.

intrepid [intrépid], *a.* intrépido.

intrepidity [intrepíditi], *s.* intrepidez.

intrepidly [intrépidli], *adv.* intrépidamente.

intricacy [íntricasi], **intricateness** [-ketnes], *s.* intrincación, intrincamiento, embrollo, enredo.

intricate [íntriket], *a.* intrincado, enredado.

intricately [-li], *adv.* intrincadamente.

intrigue [intríg]. **I.** *s.* intriga, manejo, trama; arte, amaño; intriga amorosa, galanteo, lío; enredo de una comedia. **II.** *vn.* intrigar; tramar; tener intrigas amorosas. **III.** *va.* ganarse mañosamente, seducir.

intriguer [intrígœr], *s.* intrigante.

intriguing [intríguing], *a.* intrigante; seductor.—**intriguingly** [-li], *adv.* por medio de intrigas.

intrinsic(al [intrínsic(al], *a.* intrínseco.

intrinsically [-li], *adv.* intrínsecamente.

intrinsicalness [-nes], *s.* calidad de intrínseco.

introduce [introdiús], *va.* introducir, meter; presentar (una persona a otra); dar entrada; hacer adoptar, poner en uso.—**to i. a bill**, presentar un proyecto de ley.

introducer [-diúsœr], *s.* introductor.

introduction [introdúcshun], *s.* introducción; presentación.

introductive [-tiv], *a.* introductivo.

introductor [-tœr], *s.* introductor.

introductory [-tori], *a.* de introducción, introductivo; preliminar.

introit [intróit], *s.* (igl.) introito.

intromission [intromíshun], *s.* introducción; admisión, iniciación.

intromit [-mít]. **I.** *va.* introducir, insertar; enviar adjunto; dar entrada, admitir. **II.** *vn.* entremeterse, ingerirse.

introspect [-spéct]. **I.** *va.* mirar lo interior de alguna cosa. **II.** *vn.* hacer examen de introversión.—**introspection** [-shun], *s.* introversión.

introversion [-vœrshun], *s.* introversión.

introvert [-vœrt], *va.* volver hacia dentro.

intrude [intrúd]. **I.** *vn.* intrusarse, entremeterse, inmiscuirse. **II.** *va.* meter, forzar.

intruded [-ed], *a.* (geol.) intrusivo.

intruder [intrúdœr], *s.* intruso, entremetido.

intrusion [intrúyun], *s.* intrusión, entremetimiento, impertinencia; (geol.) intrusión.

intrusional [-al], **intrusive** [-siv], *a.* intruso; (geol.) de intrusión, intrusivo.—**intrusively** [-li], *adv.* intrusamente.—**intrusiveness** [-nes], *s.* tendencia a i..rusarse.

intrust [intrúst], *va.* = ENTRUST.

intubate [íntiubeit], *va.* intubar.—**intubation** [-béishun], *s.* intubación.

intuition [intiuíshun], *s.* intuición.

intuitional [-al], *a.* intuitivo; de o por intuición.—**i. ethics**, doctrina de que los sentimientos e ideas morales son intuitivos.

intuitionalism [-alism], **intuitionism** [-ism], *s.* doctrina de que ciertas verdades fundamentales se adquieren por intuición; doctrina de que las ideas y sentimientos morales son intuitivos.

intuitive [intiúitiv], *a.* intuitivo.

intuitively [-li], *adv.* intuitivamente.

intumesce [intiumés], *vn.* hincharse.—**intumescence, intumescency** [-ens, i], *s.* intumescencia, hinchazón.—**intumescent** [-ent], *a.* intumescente, hinchado.

intussusception [íntususépshun], *s.* intususcepción.

intwine [intuáin], *va.* = ENTWINE.

inula [íniula], *s.* (bot.) énula, campana, ínula.

inulin [íniulin], *s.* (quím.) inulina.

inunction [inuncshun], *s.* untura, frotación.

inundate [inúndeit], *va.* inundar.

inundation [inundéishun], *s.* inundación.

inurbane [incœrbéin], *a.* inurbano, descortés, incivil.—**inurbaneness, inurbanity** [-nes, -bǽniti], *s.* inurbanidad.

inure [iniúœr]. **I.** *va.* avezar, acostumbrar, habituar. **II.** *vn.* tener efecto; quedar para, pasar (a).—**inured** [-d], *a.* avezado, hecho (a), endurecido.—**inurement** [-mœnt], *s.* práctica, hábito, costumbre.

inurn [incœrn], *va.* poner en una urna cineraria.

inutility [iniutíliti], *s.* inutilidad.

invade [invéid], *va.* invadir.—**invader** [-œr], *s.* invasor.

invaginate [invǽyineit]. **I.** *va.* envainar, enchufar; (cir.) invaginar. **II.** *a.* envainado, enchufado.—**invagination** [-éishun], *s.* enchufamiento; intususcepción, invaginación.

invalid [invǽlid], *a.* inválido, nulo.

invalid [ínvalid], *a.* inválido, persona baldada, impedida o lisiada.—**i. chair**, sillón para inválidos.

invalid [ínvalid], *va.* matricular en el registro de inválidos; lisiar, incapacitar.

invalidate [invǽlideit], *va.* invalidar, anular.

invalidation [-éishun], *s.* invalidación, irritación.

invalidism [ínvalidism], *s.* baldadura crónica.

invalidity [invalíditi], **invalidness** [invǽlidnes], *s.* (for.) nulidad; falta de salud; inhabilitación, incapacidad.

invaluable [inváeliuabœl], *a.* inestimable, inapreciable.—**Invaluably** [-bli], *adv.* inestimablemente.

invariability [invériabíliti], **invariableness** [invériabœlnes], *s.* invariabilidad.—**invariable** [-bœl], *a.* invariable.—**Invariably** [-bli], *adv.* invariablemente.

invariant [invériænt]. **I.** *a.* invariable, constante; (mat.) relativo a las invariantes. **II.** *s.* (mat.) invariante.

invasion [invéiyun], *s.* invasión.

invasive [invéisiv], *a.* hostil; agresivo, invasor.

invective [invéctiv]. **I.** *s.* invectiva. **II.** *a.* ultrajante, injurioso.—**Invectively** [-li], *adv.* injuriosamente.

inveigh [invéi], *vn.* prorrumpir en invectivas.

inveigher [invéiœr], *s.* el que lanza una filípica.

inveigle [inví- (o invéi) gœl], *va.* seducir, engañar, engatusar.—**Inveiglement** [-gœlmœnt] *s.* engañifa, embalmiento.—**Inveigler** [-glœr], *s.* seductor.

inveil [invéil], *va.* cubrir con un velo.

invent [invént], *va.* inventar.

inventible [-tibœl], *a.* que puede ser inventado.

invention [-shun], *s.* invención, invento; inventiva, ingenio; mentira, falsedad, embuste.—**I. of the Cross,** Invención de la Santa Cruz.

inventive [-tiv], *a.* inventivo.

inventor [-œr], *s.* inventor.

inventorial [inventórial], *a.* perteneciente al inventario.—**inventorially** [-i], *adv.* con inventario.

inventory [inventori]. **I.** *s.* inventario. **II.** *va.* inventariar.

inverse [invœrs], *a.* inverso, invertido.—**i. ratio,** razón inversa.—**Inversely** [-li], *adv.* inversamente.

inversion [invœrshun], *s.* inversión, transmutación, trastrocamiento.

invert [invœrt]. **I.** *va.* invertir; volver al revés; trastrocar; transponer. **II.** *a.* invertido.

invertebral, invertebrate [invœrtebral, breit], *a. y s.* invertebrado.

Invertebrata [-bréitæ], *s. pl.* invertebrados.

invertedly [-tedli], *adv.* invertidamente.

invest [invést], *va.* (com.) invertir, interesar, emplear o imponer dinero; (con **with** o **in**) vestir, cubrir, adornar, poner; investir, conferir, dar; sitiar, cercar.

investigable [invéstigabœl], *a.* averiguable, investigable, escudriñable.

investigate [invéstigueit], *a.* investigar, indagar, averiguar; estudiar o analizar.—**Investigation** [-guéishun], *s.* investigación, pesquisa, indagación; estudio, análisis.—**investigative** [-gativ], *a.* investigador.—**Investigator** [-guéitœr], *s.* investigador; indagador, averiguador.

investiture [invéstichur], *s.* investidura, instalación.

investment [invéstmœnt], *s.* (com.) inversión; (mil.) sitio, cerco; investidura, instalación; cubierta; envoltura.

investor [invéstœr], *s.* (com.) persona que invierte dinero; interesado.

inveteracy [invétœrasi], **inveterateness** [-etnes], *s.* hábito o costumbre inveterada.—**Inveterate** [-et], *a.* inveterado.—**inveterately** [-li], *adv.* inveteradamente.

invidious [invídius], *a.* denigrante, difamatorio; odioso.—**Invidiously** [-li], *adv.* denigrantemente; odiosamente.—**Invidiousness** [-nes], *s.* calidad de difamatorio.

invigorate [invígoreit], *va.* vigorizar, fortificar.—**Invigorating** [-eiting], *a.* vigorizante, fortaleciente.—**Invigoration** [-éishun], *s.* acto y efecto de vigorizar.

invincibility [invínsibíliti], **invincibleness** [-bœlnes], *s.* calidad de invencible.—**Invincible** [-bœl], *a.* invencible.—**Invincibly** [-bli], *adv.* invenciblemente.

inviolability [inváiolabíliti], **inviolableness** [-bœlnes], *s.* inviolabilidad.—**Inviolable** [-bœl], *a.* inviolable, inquebrantable.—**inviolably** [-bli], *adv.* inviolablemente.—**Inviolate(d** [-let(ed], *a.* inviolado, incorrupto, íntegro.

invisibility [invísibíliti], **invisibleness** [-bœlnes], *s.* invisibilidad.—**Invisible** [-bœl], *a.* invisible.—**Invisibly** [-bli], *adv.* invisiblemente.

invitation [invitéishun], *s.* invitación.

invitatory [inváitatori]. **I.** *a.* invitador. **II.** *s.* (igl.) invitatorio.

invite [inváit], *va.* convidar, invitar; atraer; provocar, incitar, tentar; instar.

inviter [inváitœr], *s.* convidador, invitador.

inviting [inváiting], *a.* atractivo, seductivo; incitante.—**invitingly** [-li], *adv.* de un modo atractivo.—**Invitingness** [-nes], *s.* calidad de atractivo.

invocation [invokéishun], *s.* invocación; (for.) suplicatorio, exhorto, mandamiento.

invoice [invois]. **I.** *s.* (com.) factura.—**i. book,** libro de facturas.—**i. price,** precio de factura. **II.** *va.* facturar.

invoke [invóuc], *va.* invocar; (for.) expedir suplicatorio, exhorto o mandamiento.

involucel [invóliusel], *s.* (bot.) involucro secundario.

involucral [involúcral], *a.* involucral.—**involucrate** [-cret], **involucred** [-kœrd], *a.* involucrado.

involucre [-kœr], **involucrum** [-crum], *s.* (bot.) involucro; (anat.) involutura.

involuntarily [invólunterili], *adv.* involuntariamente.—**Involuntariness** [-nes], *s.* involuntariedad.—**involuntary** [-teri], *a.* involuntario.

involute [ínvoliut]. **I.** *a.* intrincado; vuelto hacia dentro; enrollado en espiral. **II.** *s.* (geom.) evolvente, involuta.

involution [ínvolúshun], *s.* envolvimiento; complicación, enredo; (mat.) elevación a potencias; teoría de las potencias.

involve [invólv], *va.* envolver, enrollar; implicar, comprometer; torcer, enredar, enmarañar, complicar; involucrar; (mat.) elevar a una potencia, hallar una potencia de.

involved [invólvd], *a.* complicado, difuso (apl. esp. al estilo).

involvedness [-vednes], **involvement** [invólvment], *s.* envolvimiento; complicación, intrincación.

invulnerability [invúlnœrabíliti], **invulnerableness** [-bœlnes], *s.* invulnerabilidad.—**Invulnerable** [-bœl], *a.* invulnerable.

invulnerably [-bli], *adv.* invulnerablemente.

inwall [inuól], *va.* rodear o proteger con muros.—**Inwall** [ínwall], *s.* pared interior; revestimiento interior (de un horno, etc.)

inward(s [ínuard(ŝ], *adv.* hacia dentro, hacia lo interior; adentro.

inward. I. *a.* interior, interno; secreto, oculto. **II.** *s.* el interior; entraña.—**Inwardly** [-li], *adv.* interiormente, internamente.—**Inwardness** [-nes], *s.* calidad, naturaleza o estado interior; lo interior; esencia; fondo.

inweave [inuív], *va.* entretejer, enlazar.

inwrap [inráp], *va.* envolver (= ENWRAP).

inwreathe, *va.* = ENWREATHE.

inwrought [inrót], *a.* labrado, embutido, incrustado.

iodate [áiodet], *s.* yodato.

iodic [aiódic], *a.* yódico.

iodid(e [áiodid *o* daid], *s.* yoduro.

iodin(e [áiodin o daiŋ], *s.* (quím.) yodo.

iodinate [áiodineit], *va.* tratar o combinar con yodo.

iodism [áiodiŝm], *s.* (med.) yodismo.

iodize [áiodaiŝ], *va.* yodurar.

iodoform [aiódoform], *s.* yodoformo.

ion [áion], *s.* (quím.) ion.

ionic [aiónic], *a.* de o relativo a iones.

Ionic [aiónic], *a.* jónico.

ionium [aiónium], *s.* ionio, uno de los cuerpos simples.

ionize [áionaiŝ], *va.* ionizar, disociar.—**ionization** [áionišéishun], *s.* ionización, disociación.

iota [aióta], *s.* jota, ápice, tilde, punto.

I O U [áioíú] (abreviatura fonética de *I owe you,* yo le debo), *s.* vale, abonaré.

ipecac [ipecæc], **ipecacuanha** [ípecækiuéna], *s.* (bot.) ipecacuana.

Ipomœa [ipomía], *s.* (bot.) convolvuláceas.

ipse dixit [ipse díxit], afirmación dogmática.

ipso facto [ípso fáecto], *ipso facto,* por el mismo hecho, por eso mismo.

---

irascibility [irǽsibíliti], **irascibleness** [-bœlnes], s. iracundia.—**irascible** [-bœl], a. irascible.
irate [airét], a. encolerizado, airado.
ire [áiær], s. ira, cólera.—**ireful** [-ful], a. iracundo, colérico.—**irefully** [-il], adv. airadamente.
irenic(al [airénic(al], a. pacífico, conciliador.
iridaceous [airidéíshus], **irideous** [airídeus], a. (bot.) irídeo.
iridectomy [iridéctomi], s. (cir.) iridectomía, escisión parcial del iris.
iridesce [iridés], vn. irisar.
iridescence [iridésens], s. cambiante, tornasol.—**iridescent** [-ent], a. iridiscente, tornasolado.
iridium [irídium], s. (quím.) iridio.
iris [áiris], s. (anat. y ópt.) iris; arco iris; (bot.) efémero, flor de lis.—**I. root** = ORRIS-ROOT.
Irish [áirish], a. y s. irlandés.—**I. moss**, musgo de Irlanda.—**the I.**, los irlandeses.
Irishism [-ism], s. locución irlandesa; rasgo irlandés.
Irishman [-mæn], s. irlandés.
Irishwoman [-úmæn], s. irlandesa.
iritis [airáitis o irítis], s. (med.) iritis.
irk [œrc], v. impers. fastidiar, aburrir, cansar.
irksome [-sum], a. tedioso, fastidioso, cansado.—**irksomely** [-li], adv. cansadamente, fastidiosamente.—**irksomeness** [-nes], s. calidad de tedioso.
iron [áiœrn]. **I.** s. hierro (metal); hierro, hoja (parte cortante de una herramienta); hierro (pieza de construcción—escuadra, viga, etc.— de hierro o acero); plancha (de planchar); herramienta; utensilio; arma de hierro.—**I. in the fire**, negocio, empresa, asunto a que atender.—**in irons**, aherrajado, en prisiones. **II.** a. férreo, de hierro; relativo al hierro.—**I. age**, edad de hierro.—**I. alum**, alumbre de pluma, alumbre ferropotásico.—**I. black**, polvo de antimonio.—**I. -bound**, unido o sujeto con hierro; escabroso; aherrojado; inflexible, rígido.—**I. chest**, arca de hierro.—**I. foundry**, fundición de hierro.—**I. horse**, (fig.) locomotora.—**I. law of wages**, la supuesta ley de que el salario tiende al mínimo necesario para la subsistencia.—**I. loss**, (elec.) pérdida en el hierro.—**I. Mask**, (hist.) el hombre de la máscara de hierro.—**I. mill**, ferrería.—**I. sand**, arena ferruginosa; limaduras de hierro.—**I. scrap**, hierro forjado viejo; hierro colado de desecho. **III.** va. planchar; aherrojar, poner grilletes a.—**to I. out**, planchar, emparejar, alisar; allanar.
ironclad [-clæd]. **I.** a. (mar. y elec.) acorazado; riguroso; leonino. **II.** s. acorazado; horno para calcinar mineral de mercurio.
ironed [áiœrnd], a. planchado, aplanchado; aherrojado; armado.
ironer [áiœrnœr], s. planchadora.
ironic(al [airónic(al], a. irónico.
ironically [-i], adv. irónicamente.
ironing [áiœrning]. **I.** s. planchado, acción de planchar; ropa por planchar. **II.** a. de planchar.—**I. board**, palo de planchar.
ironmaster [áiœrnmǽster], s. fabricante de hierro (apl. esp. a los grandes industriales).
ironmonger [-múngœr], s. mercador o traficante en hierro; quincallero, ferretero.—**I.'s shop**, ferretería.
ironmongery [-i], s. ferretería, cerrajería.
ironside [-said], s. hombre fuerte o terrible; héroe, acorazado.—**Ironsides**, Oliverio Cromwell; caballería de Cromwell.
ironsmith [-smiz], s. herrero.
ironstone [-stóun], s. mineral de hierro (gen. siderita o hematites).
ironware [-uéær], s. artículos de ferretería.
ironwood [-ud], s. palo hacha.
ironwork [-uœrk], s. herraje, obra de hierro.
ironworks [-uœrks], s. fundición de hierro, ferrería.
ironwort [-uœrt], s. (bot.) sideritis.
irony [áironi]. **I.** s. ironía. **II.** [áiœrni], a. ferruginento.
Iroquois [irocuói], s. iroqués.
irradiance, irradiancy [irrédians, i], s. irradiación; lustre, esplendor.

irradiate [irréidiet]. **I.** va. irradiar, iluminar; inspirar; esparcir. **II.** vn. lucir, brillar. **III.** a. (poét.) resplandeciente.—**irradiation** [-éishun], s. irradiación; brillo, esplendor; iluminación.
irradiative [-diœtiv], a. radiante, refulgente.
irradicate [irrédiket], va. arraigar.
irrational [irréshunal], a. irracional; absurdo, ilógico; (álg.) irracional.—**irrationality** [-nǽliti], s. irracionalidad.—**irrationally** [-nali], adv. irracionalmente.
irreclaimable [irrecléimabœl], a. incorregible; irredimible; inutilizable.—**irreclaimably** [-bli], adv. incorregiblemente; irremediablemente.
irreconcilable [irrécunsáilabœl]. **I.** a. irreconciliable, inconciliable; intransigente. **II.** s. (pol.) intransigente.—**irreconcilableness** [-lnes], s. imposibilidad de reconciliarse.—**irreconcilably** [-bli], adv. irreconciliablemente; irremediablemente.
irrecoverable [irrecúvœrabœl], a. irreparable o irrecuperable; incobrable.—**irrecoverableness** [-nes], s. calidad de irrecuperable.—**irrecoverably** [-bli], adv. irremediablemente, irreparablemente.
irrecuperable [irrekiúpœrabœl], a. irrecuperable; irremediable.
irredeemable [irredímabœl], a. irredimible; irremisible.—**irredeemably** [-bli], adv. de un modo irredimible; irremisiblemente.
irredenta [irredéntæ]. **I.** a. irredimido. **II.** s. región irredimida.
irreducible [irrediúsibœl], a. irreducible; (mat.) irreductible.
irreflective [irrefléctiv], a. irreflexivo.
irrefragability [irréfragabíliti], s. irrefragabilidad.—**irrefragable** [-bœl], a. irrefragable.—**irrefragably** [-bli], adv. irrefragablemente.
irrefrangible [irrefrǽnyibœl], a. (ópt.) irrefrangible.—**irrefrangibility** [-bíliti], s. irrefrangibilidad.
irrefutable [irrefiútabœl], a. irrefutable.
irrefutably [-bli], adv. irrefutablemente.
irregular [irréguiular], a. irregular; anormal.—**irregularity** [-lǽriti], s. irregularidad; demasía, exceso.—**irregularly** [-li], adv. irregularmente.
irrelative [irrélativ], a. inconexo, sin relación, regla, ni orden.
irrelatively [-li], adv. inconexamente.
irrelevancy [irrélevansi], s. inaplicabilidad; impertinencia, inconexión; calidad de ajeno (a un asunto).—**irrelevant** [-vant], a. que está fuera de lugar, ajeno, inaplicable, que no viene al caso.—**irrelevantly** [-li], adv. inconexamente, impertinentemente, saliéndose del asunto.
irrelievable [irrelívabœl], a. irremediable, irreparable.
irreligion [irrelíyun], s. irreligión.—**irreligious** [-yus], a. irreligioso.—**irreligiously** [-li], adv. irreligiosamente.
irremediable [irremídiabœl], a. irremediable.—**irremediableness** [-nes], s. calidad de irremediable.—**irremediably** [-bli], adv. irremediablemente.
irremissible [irremísibœl], a. irremisible, imperdonable.—**irremissibleness** [-nes], s. calidad de irremisible.—**irremissibly** [-bli], adv. irremisiblemente.
irremovable [irremúvabœl], a. inamovible; inmutable.
irreparability [irréparabíliti], s. calidad de irreparable.—**irreparable** [irréparabœl], a. irreparable.—**irreparably** [-bli], adv. irreparablemente.
irrepealable [irrepílabœl], a. inabrogable, irrevocable.
irrepleviable [irrepléviabœl], a. (for.) irredimible.
irreprehensible [irréprejénsibœl], a. irreprensible.—**irreprehensibly** [-bli], adv. irreprensiblemente.
irrepressible [irreprésibœl], a. indomable, incorregible.
irreproachable [irrepróuchabœl], a. intachable.—**irreproachably** [-bli], adv. intachablemente.
irresistibility [irrésistibíliti], **irresistibleness** [-bœlnes], s. irresistibilidad.—**irresistible** [-tibœl], a. irresistible.—**irresistibly** [-bli], adv. irresistiblemente.

irresoluble [irrésólubœl], *a.* irresoluble.—**irresolubleness** [-nes], *s.* calidad de irresoluble.
irresolute [irrésólut *o* liut], *a.* irresoluto, vacilante, indeciso.—**irresolutely** [-li], *adv.* irresolutamente. —**irresoluteness** [-nes], *s.* irresolución, vacilación, indecisión.—**irresolution** [irrésólu- *o* llúshun], *s.* irresolución, indecisión.
irresolvable [irresólvabœl], *a.* que no puede descomponerse.
irrespective of, irrespectively of [irrespéctivli ov), con independencia de, sin consideración a, prescindiendo de.
irrespirable [irrespáirabœl, *o* irréspirabœl], *a.* irrespirable.
irresponsibility [irrespónsibíliti], *s.* irresponsabilidad.—**irresponsible** [-bœl], *a.* irresponsable. —**irresponsibly** [-bli], *adv.* irresponsablemente.
irretraceable [irretréisabœl], *a.* que no se puede desandar.
irretrievable [irretrívabœl], *a.* irrecuperable, irreparable; incobrable.—**irretrievably** [-bli], *adv.* irreparablemente.
irreverence [irrévœrœns], *s.* irreverencia.
irreverent [-œnt], *a.* irreverente.—**irreverently** [-li], *adv.* irreverentemente.
irreversible [irrevœrsibœl], *a.* irreversible; irrevocable.
irreversibility [-bíliti], **irreversibleness** [-bœlnes], *s.* irreversibilidad; irrevocabilidad.—**irreversibly** [-bli], *adv.* irreversiblemente; irrevocablemente.
irrevocability [irrévocabíliti], **irrevocableness** [irrévocabœlnes], *s.* irrevocabilidad.
irrevocable [irrévocabœl], *a.* irrevocable.
irrevocably [-bli], *adv.* irrevocablemente.
irrigable [írigabœl], *a.* regadizo, regadío.
irrigate [írigueit], *va.* regar; bañar, mojar, humedecer; (med.) irrigar.—**irrigation** [-guéishun], *s.* riego, regadura; (med.) irrigación.—**irrigator** [-guéitœr], *s.* carro de riego; (med.) irrigador.
irrision [irríyun], *s.* irrisión, mofa.
irritability [irritabíliti], *s.* irritabilidad.
irritable [-bœl], *a.* irritable.—**irritableness** [-nes], *s.* irritabilidad.
irritant [iritant], *a.* y *s.* irritante.
irritate [íriteit], *va.* irritar.—**irritation** [írritéishun], *s.* irritación.—**irritative** [íritativ], *a.* irritador, irritante.
irruption [irrúpshun], *s.* irrupción.
irruptive [irrúptiv], *a.* invasor.
is [is], 3d. pers. sing. pres. ind. de TO BE.
isagogical [isagóyical], *a.* isagógico.
isagogics [áisægóyics], *s.* estudio crítico literario de la Biblia; introducción a la exégesis.
isagon [ísagon], *s.* (geom.) iságono.
ischiatic [iskiǽtic], *a.* isquiático.
ischium [ískium], *s.* (anat.) isquion.
iserine [áisœrin], *s.* (min.) iserina.
Ishmaelite [íshmaelait], *s.* ismaelita.
isinglass [áisinglas], *s.* colapez (llám. t. **l. glue**); (min.) mica.
Islam [íslam], **Islamism** [íslamism], *s.* islam, islamismo.
Islamic [islǽmic], *a.* islámico.
island [áiland], *s.* isla, ínsula.—**islander** [-œr], *s.* isleño.
isle [áil], *s.* isla, ínsula.—**islet** [-et], *s.* isleta, cayo.
ism [ism], *s.* (despec.) doctrina, *ismo*.
isobaric [áisobáric], *a.* isobárico.
isocheim [-caim], *a.* isoquímeno.
isochromatic [-crómǽtic], *a.* isocromático.
isochronal *o* **isochronous** [aisócronal, nus], *a.* isócrono.
isochronism [aisócronism], *s.* isocronismo.
isoclinal [áisoclánal], *a.* de igual inclinación.—**i line**, línea que une los puntos de igual inclinación de la brújula.
isocline [-clain], *s.* (geol.) isoclinal, pliegue isoclinal.
isodynamic [-dainǽmic], *a.* isodinámico.
isogonal [aisógonal], *a.* isógono.
isogonic [áisogónic], *a.* isogónico.—**i. line**, línea isogónica.

isolate [ísoleit *o* áisoleit], *va.* aislar, separar, apartar.—**isolated** [-ed], *a.* aislado; solitario, retirado; incomunicado.—**isolation** [-éishun], *s.* aislamiento. —**isolator** [-eitœr], *s.* aislador.
isomeric [áisoméric], *a.* (quím.) isomérico.
isomerism [aisómœrism], *s.* (quím.) isomería.
isometric(al [áisométric(al], *a.* isométrico.
isometropia [áisometrópiæ], *s.* isometropia, igualdad en la refracción de los dos ojos.
isomorphism [-mórfism], *s.* (min.) isomorfismo, isomorfia.—**isomorphous** [-fus], *a.* isomorfo.
isopathy [aisópazi], *s.* isopatía, doctrina de que toda enfermedad contagiosa produce ella misma el virus que la cura.
Isopoda [aisópodæ], *s. pl.* isópodos.—**isopod** [áisopod], *s. y a.* isópodo.
isosceles [aisósœlis], *a.* isósceles.
isosporous [áisospórus], *a.* (bot.) isospóreo.—**isospory** [áisóspori], *s.* calidad de isospóreo.
isotherm [íso- (*o* áiso) zœrm], *s.* línea isoterma.—**isothermal** [-al], *a.* isotermo.
isotropic [áisotrópic], *a.* isotrópico.
Israelite [ísraelait], *s.* israelita.
Israelitish, Israelitic [-ish, lític], *a.* israelita, israelítico.
issuable [íshuabœl], *a.* emisible.
issue [íshu]. **I.** *s.* (impr.) edición, tirada, impresión; prole, progenie, sucesión; emisión de valores; rentas, réditos, producto, beneficios; salida, egreso; flujo (de sangre, etc.); fuente, principio, nacimiento; evento, consecuencia, resultado, éxito; decisión; tema de discusión, problema; (med.) exutorio; (for.) punto en disputa.—**l. of blood**, pérdida de sangre.—**at l.**, *o* **in l.**, en disputa. **II.** *va.* echar, brotar, arrojar; dar; dictar, expedir, despachar; (com.) librar, emitir, poner en circulación; dar a luz, publicar. **III.** *vn.* salir, brotar, fluir, proceder, provenir; nacer; resultar; acabarse, terminarse, resolverse; litigar.
issueless [íshules], *a.* sin sucesión.
isthmian [ístmian], *a.* ístmico; istmeño.
isthmus [íst- *o* ísmus], *s.* istmo.
istle [istl], *s.* = IXTLE.
it, *pron. neutro* (*pl.* THEY). Se aplica a cosas inanimadas, a niños de teta y a los animales cuyo sexo no puede determinarse; por consiguiente corresponde en español a *él, ella, eso, ello, lo, la, le,* según los géneros y casos de las cosas a que se refiere; v. gr.: *have you the book?*—I have it, ¿tiene Vd. el libro?—Lo tengo. No se traduce cuando es sujeto gramatical de una oración que no tiene sujeto lógico (como las de verbos impersonales) o cuyo sujeto lógico (y gramatical en español) es un infinitivo o una frase: *it rains*, llueve; *it is late*, es tarde; *it is easy to promise*, es fácil prometer; *it is evident that he was there*, es evidente que él estaba allí. Tampoco se traduce cuando se refiere a la hora (*what time is it?* ¿qué hora es? *it is six o'clock*, son las seis); ni en las expresiones *who is it?* ¿quién es? *it is I*, soy yo; *it is they*, son ellos; *it was he who spoke*, fué él quien habló, y otras análogas.—**Is l.?** ¿de veras?—**Is l. not (so)**? ¿no es verdad? ¿verdad? ¿no es así?—**not to be in l. with**, (fam.) no poderse comparar con, ser muy inferior a.
Italian [itǽlian], *a.* y *s.* italiano.—**I. oak**, roble de bellotas.—**I. paste**, pasta de macarrones.—**Italianism** [-ism], *s.* italianismo.—**Italianize** [itǽlianaiz], *va.* italianizar.
Italiot, Italiote [itǽliot], *s.* italiota, antiguo habitante griego de Italia.
italic [itǽlic], *a.* itálico; (impr.) bastardilla.
italicize [itǽlisais], *va.* poner en letra bastardilla; subrayar, dar énfasis.
itch [itch]. **I.** *s.* sarna; comezón, picazón; prurito.—**i. insect, l. mite**, (ent.) ácaro, arador. **II.** *vn.* picar; sentir picazón o comezón; antojarse, tener prurito por algo; desear vehementemente.
itching [ítching], *s.* escozor, picazón, comezón; prurito, deseo vehemente.
itchy [íchi], *a.* sarnoso; picante, hormigoso.
item [áitem]. **I.** *adv.* ítem; otro sí, aun más. **II.** *s.* partida; artículo; párrafo; detalle.
itemize [áitemais], *va.* detallar, especificar.
iterable [ítœrabœl], *a.* iterable.

---

iterant [ítœrant], *a.* iterativo.
iterate [ítœreit], *va.* repetir, reiterar; inculcar.
iteration [-éiŝhʊn], *s.* iteración, repetición.
iterative [ítœrativ], *a.* iterativo; (gram.) frecuentativo.
itinerant [aitínœrant], *a.* itinerante, viandante; ambulante, errante.
itinerary [-æri]. **I.** *s.* itinerario, ruta; relación de un viaje; guía de viajeros. **II.** *a.* itinerario, hecho en viaje.
itinerate [-éit], *vn.* seguir una ruta o itinerario.
its, *pron.* posesivo neutro (genitivo de *it*) su (de él, de ella, de ello), v. gr.: *a house with its furniture*, una casa con sus muebles.
it 's, abreviatura de *it is*.
itself [itsélf], *pron.* (se aplica solamente a las cosas) él mismo, la misma, lo mismo; v. gr.: *it moves of itself*, eso se mueve por sí mismo; *she is virtue itself*, es la virtud misma.
I 've [áiv], contracción familiar de *I have*, yo he, yo tengo.
ivied [áivid], *a.* cubierto de hiedra.
ivory [áivori]. **I.** *s.* marfil.—*pl.* cosas hechas de marfil; bolas de billar; (fam.) los dientes. **II.** *a.* ebúrneo, de marfil.—**i. nut**, marfil vegetal, tagua.—**i. palm**, (bot.) tagua.
ivy [áivi], *s.* (bot.) hiedra o yedra; cazuz.
ixtle [íxtle], **ixtli** [-tli], *s.* istle, ixtle; fibra de Tampico o de istle.—**i. grass**, istle (la planta).
izzard [íŝard], *s.* (ant.) la letra *z*.—**from A to i.**, de cabo a rabo, de pe a pa.

J

j [yéi], *s.* **j**.
jab [yæb]. **I.** *va.* (fam.) pinchar. **II.** *s.* hurgonazo, pinchazo.
jabber [yǽbœr]. **I.** *vn.* charlar; farfullar; (fam.) disparatar. **II.** *s.* jerga, jerigonza, guirigay.
jabberer [yǽbœrœr], *s.* farfullador, parlanchín.
jabiru [yǽbiru], *s.* (zool.) jabirú.
jaborandi [yǽborándi], *s.* (bot.) jaborandi, pilocarpo.
jacamar [yǽcæmar], *s.* (orn.) jacamar, ave americana.
jacana [yǽcænæ], *s.* (orn.) jácana, ave zancuda americana.
jacaranda [yǽcaránda], *s.* (bot.) jacaranda.
jacent [yéisent], *pa.* yacente.
jacinth [yéisinz], *s.* (bot.) = HYACINTH; (min.) = ZIRCON.
jack [yæc], *s.* mozo; hombre; marinero; macho del burro y otros animales; (mec.) gato, cric; barrilete, cárcel, prensa, burro, borriquete; sacabotas; martinete o macillo del piano; torno de asador; cota de malla; (dep.) boliche; sota (de la baraja); (mar.) bandera de proa; (tlf.) jack; (fam.) blanca, dinero; linterna manual de proyección (para cazar, etc.).—**j. afloat**, (fam.) marinero.—**j. boots**, botas grandes y fuertes.—**j. by the hedge**, (bot.) erísimo.—**j.-in-the-box**, muñeco en una caja de resorte; (mar.) cric.—**j. of all trades** aprendiz de todo y oficial de nada, sábelo todo.—**j.-o'lantern**, fuego fatuo.—**j. plane**, (carp.) cepillo desbastador.—**j. rabbit**, liebre americana.—**j. shaft**, eje intermedio.—**j.-tar**, (fam.) marinero.—**j. towel**, toalla de un rodillo giratorio.
jackal [yǽcol], *s.* chacal.
jackanapes [yǽcaneips], *s.* mequetrefe.
jackass [yǽcas], *s.* garañón, asno, borrico; (fig.) asno, tonto, necio.
jackdaw [yǽcdo], *s.* (orn.) grajo, chova.
jacket [yǽket]. **I.** *s.* chaqueta, jubón, jaqueta; envoltura, cubierta; (mec.) chaqueta, camisa. **II.** *va.* enchaquetar.
jackknife [yǽcnáif], *s.* navaja sevillana.
jackpudding [yǽcpúding], *s.* arlequín, titiritero, payaso.
jackscrew [yǽcscru], *s.* (mar.) gato, cric, lirón.
jackstaff [yǽcstaf], *s.* (mar.) asta de bandera.
jackstone [yǽcstóun], *s.* taba, pito.
jackstraw [yǽcstro], *s.* efigie de paja; espantapájaros.—*pl.* juego con pajitas.

Jacobin [yǽcobin], *s.* (igl.) dominico; (pol.) jacobino; demagogo; pichón capuchino.
Jacobinic(al [-bínic(al], *s.* jacobínico.
Jacobinism [yǽcobiniŝm], *s.* jacobinismo.
Jacobite [yǽcobait], *a.* y *s.* jacobita.
Jacob's-ladder [yéicobŝ-lǽdœr], *s.* (bot.) polemonio; (mar.) escala de jarcias.—**J.'s staff**, bordón de peregrino; bastón con estoque; báculo de Jacob; ballestilla; (top.) estaca con un regatón que se usa en vez de trípode.
jaconet [yǽconet], *s.* (tej.) chaconá, chaconada.
jac(ti)tation [yæc(ti)téŝhʊn], *s.* agitación, desasosiego; fanfarronería, jactancia.
jaculate [yǽkiuleit], *va.* lanzar, arrojar.
jaculatory [-latori], *a.* disparado; jaculatorio.
jade [yéid]. **I.** *s.* rocín, jamelgo; mujercilla; picarona, mala pécora; (min.) jade. **II.** *va.* cansar, acosar. **III.** *vn.* jadear, desalentarse.
jadish [yéidiŝh], *a.* viciosa (yegua); impúdica (mujer).
jag [yæg]. **I.** *va.* dentar, mellar. **II.** *s.* diente, punta; perno de lengüeta; melladura, mella, muesca; carga para un caballo; (fam.) pítima, turca, chispa.
jagged [yægd], **jaggy** [yǽgui], *a.* mellado, dentado.—**jaggedness** [yǽguednes], *s.* melladura.—**jaggy** [yǽgui], *a.* dentado, dentellado, serrado.
jaguar [yaguár], *s.* (zool.) jaguar.
jail [yéil], *s.* cárcel.—**j. fever**, tifo.
jailbird [-bœrd], *s.* el que ha estado en presidio; presidiario, malhechor.
jailer [yéilœr], *s.* carcelero.
jalap [yǽlap], *s.* jalapa.
jalapin [yǽlæpin], *s.* (quím.) jalapina.
jalousie [yaluŝi], *s.* celosía.
jam [yæm]. **I.** *s.* compota, conserva; apretura, apiñadura, agolpamiento.—**j. nut** = LOCK NUT. **II.** *va.* apiñar; acuñar, apretar, estrechar, apachurrar, estrujar; (rad.) causar interferencia o perturbaciones en las ondas transmitiendo ondas extrañas del mismo largo. **III.** *vn.* atorarse, agolparse.
Jamaican [yaméicæn], *a.* jamaicano.
Jamaica wood [úd], *s.* brasilete.
jamb [yæm], *s.* jamba, quicial.
jambe [yæmb], *s.* (arm.) canillera, greba.
jamboree [yǽmborí], *s.* lance del juego de *euchre;* (fam.) francachela.
jangle [yǽngœl]. **I.** *vn.* reñir, altercar. **II.** *va.* hacer sonar. **III.** *s.* sonido discordante; disputa, querella, altercado.
jangling [yǽngling], *s.* sonido discordante; riña, pendencia; charla.
janitor [yǽnitœr], *s.* portero; conserje.
janizary [yǽniŝæri], *s.* jenízaro.
jannock [yǽnoc], *s.* pan de avena.
Jansenism [yǽnseniŝm], *s.* jansenismo.
Jansenist [-ist], *s.* jansenista.
January [yǽniuæri], *s.* enero.
Japan [yæpǽn]. **I.** *s.* charol; obra japonesa charolada. **II.** *va.* charolar; barnizar. **III.** *a.* (J-) japonés, japónico.—**J. earth**, tierra japónica, cateчú.
Japanese [yæpanís o níŝ], *a.* y *s.* japonés.—**J. persimmon**, níspero del Japón.
Japhetic [yafétic], *a.* jafético.
japonica [yapónica], *s.* (bot.) camelia japonesa.
jar [yar]. **I.** *va.* sacudir, agitar, hacer vibrar o trepidar. **II.** *vn.* chirriar, hacer ruido desagradable; vibrar, trepidar; ludir, chocar; discordar.—**to j. on**, irritar, fastidiar. **III.** *s.* jarro o jarra; tinaja, cántaro, tarro, botija; vibración, trepidación; sacudida; choque; pendencia, riña; chirrido, ruido desagradable.—**on a j.**, **on the j.**, entreabierto.
jardinière [yárdiniéær], *s.* jardinera, florero.
jargon [yárgon], *s.* jerga, jerigonza; caló.
jashawk [yæsjóc], *s.* halconcillo.
jasmine [yǽsmin], *s.* (bot.) jazmín.
jasper [yǽspœr(ait], *s.* (min.) jaspe.
jaundice [yándis]. **I.** *s.* (med.) ictericia; celotipia, predisposición. **II.** *va.* causar ictericia; predisponer, torcer.

jaundiced [yándist], *pp.* y *a.* ictérico, cetrino, aciguatado, aliacanado.

jaunt [yant]. **I.** *vn.* corretar, ir y venir. **II.** *s.* excursión, caminata, paseata.

jauntiness [yántines], *s.* viveza, gentileza, garbo, ligereza.

jaunty [yánti], *a.* vistoso, airoso, garboso.

Javanese [yévanís], *a.* y *s.* javanés.

javelin [yévlin], *s.* jabalina, venablo.

jaw [yo]. **I.** *s.* quijada, mandíbula; (mec.) boca, quijada, telera; mordaza; (fig.) abismo; garras; (fam.) charla, palabrería; vituperio. **II.** *a.* de quijadas; de las quijadas; de mordaza.— **j. clutch,** embrague de mordaza.—**j. crusher,** triturador de quijadas.—**j. teeth,** las muelas. **III.** *va.* y *vn.* (vulg.) regañar, refunfuñar; charlar.

jawbone [yóbóun], *s.* quijada, mandíbula (apl. esp. a la inferior).

jawbreaker [-bréiccer], *s.* (fam.) terminacho impronunciable.

jay [yéi], *s.* rústico, chambón; simplón; (orn.) grajo; chova.

jaycrossing [-crósing], *s.* (fam.) acción de cruzar la calle descuidada y estúpidamente, esp. en lugares peligrosos⁴ (apl. a grandes ciudades, donde hay gran tráfico).

jaywalker [-uóccer], *s.* (fam.) persona que cruza la calle en puntos peligrosos. *V.* JAYCROSSING.

jazz [yæŝ], *s. jazz,* música sincopada discordante; estilo rimbombante y excéntrico.

jealous [yélus], *a.* celoso; envidioso.

jealously [-li], *adv.* celosamente.

jealousy [yélusi], **jealousness** [yélusnes], *s.* celos, encelamiento.

jean [yéin], *s.* (tej.) coquillo, cotí.

jeer [yícer]. **I.** *va.* y *vn.* befar, mofar, burlarse. **II.** *s.* befa, mofa,⁹burla.—*pl.* **jeers,** o **jears,** (mar.) guindaste con sus drizas.

Jehovah [yejóva], *s.* Jehová.

jehu [yíjiu], *s.* cochero, auriga.

jejune [yeyún], *va.* falto; seco, estéril, árido; insípido.

jejuneness, jejunity [yeyúnnes, niti], *s.* carestía, esterilidad; aridez, sequedad; pobreza; tibieza.

jejunum [yeyúnum], (anat.) yeyuno.

jellied [yélid], *a.* gelatinoso.

jellify [yélifai], *va.* y *vn.* hacer(se) gelatinoso.

jelly [yéli]. **I.** *s.* jalea. **II.** *va.* y *vn.* convertir(se) en jalea.

jellyfish [-fíŝh], *s.* (zool.) medusa, aguamar.

jennet [yénet], *s.* jaca española.

jenny [yéni], *s.* torno, máquina para hilar; hembra; burra, jumenta; (orn.) = WREN; (mᵒc.) grúa locomóvil.

jeopard [yépard], **jeopardize** [-aíŝ], *va.* arriesgar, exponer, comprometer.—**jeopardy** [-i], *s.* riesgo, peligro.

jerboa [yérboa o yerbóa], *s.* (zool.) gerbo.

jeremiad [yéremáiad], *s.* jeremiada.

jerk [yœrk]. **I.** *s.* tirón, sacudida, sacudimiento, vibración; salto, brinco, respingo; (mar.) socollada, gualdrapazo; (equit.) sobarbada. **II.** *va.* arrojar, dar un tirón, mover a tirones; sacudir, traquetear; atasajar carne.—**jerked beef,** tasajo. **III.** *vn.* moverse a tirones.

jerkin [yérkin], *s.* justillo; chaquetón.

jerky [yœrki], *a.* espasmódico.

jerry [yérri], *a.* de inferior calidad; mal hecho, hecho a la diabla.—**j.-build,** *va.* y *vn.* edificar a la diabla, mal o con malos materiales.—**j.-builder,** constructor de casas baratas de inferior calidad.

jerrymander, *s.* = GERRYMANDER.

Jersey [yœrŝi], *s.* estambre fino; camiseta, jubón o elástica de lana o de seda; toro o vaca de la isla de Jersey (Ingl.).

Jerusalem artichoke [yerúsalem ártichouk], *s.* (bot.) cotufa.

jess [yes], *s.* pihuela.

jessamine [yésamin], *s.* (bot.) jazmín.

jesse [yési], *s.* candelabro.

jest [yest]. **I.** *vn.* bromear, jaranear, chancearse. **II.** *s.* chanza, broma.

jester [yéstœr], *s.* bufón; burlón, fisgón.

jestingly [yéstingli], *adv.* de burlas, por broma.

Jesuit [yéŝiuit], *s.* jesuíta; intrigante.—**J.'s bark,** quina.—**Jesuitic(al** [-ític(al], *a.* jesuítico; ajesuitado.—**Jesuitically** [-i], *adv.* jesuíticamente. —**Jesuitism** [-iŝm], *s.* jesuitismo.

jet [yet]. **I.** *s.* azabache; chorro; surtidor; caño de salida.—**j.-black,** negro como el azabache. **II.** *va.* echar, arrojar, lanzar. **III.** *vn.* salir en chorro.—**to j. out,** sobresalir.

jetsam [yétsam], **jetson** [-sum], *s.* (mar.) echazón; (for.) pecio.

jettee, *s.* = JETTY.

jettison [yétisun]. **I.** *va.* (mar.) echar mercancías al mar. **II.** *s.* (mar.) echazón; (for.) pecio.

jetty [yéti]. **I.** *a.* de azabache; negro. **II.** *s.* malecón, rompeolas, dique, muelle, espolón; (arq.) salidizo, vuelo.

Jew [yu], *s.* judío.

jewel [yúel]. **I.** *s.* joya, alhaja; gema, piedra preciosa; piedra (de reloj de bolsillo).—**j. box, case** o **casket,** joyero, joyelero, escriño. **II.** *va.* adornar con piedras preciosas.

jewel(l)er [yúelœr], *s.* joyero, platero.—**jewelers' putty** = PUTTY POWDER.—**jeweler's shop,** joyería, platería.

jewel(le)ry [yúelri], *s.* aderezo; joyas, pedrería; prendería, joyería.

Jewess [yúes], *s.* judía.

jewfish [yúfiŝh], *s.* (ict.) guasa.

Jewish [yúiŝh], *a.* judío; ajudiado.

Jewishly [yúishli],*adv.* como judío, a la judía.

Jewry [yúri], *s.* Judea; Judería.

jews'-harp [yúŝ-járp], *s.* birimbao.

Jezebel [yéŝebel], *s.* mujer viciosa y cruel.

jib [yib], *s.* (mar.) foque.—**j. boom,** botalón de bauprés, tormentín.—**j. of a crane,** aguilón, pescante o pico de una grúa.

jibe [yáib], *va.* (mar.) mudar un botavante.

jiffy [yífi], *s.* (fam.) instante, periquete.

jig [yig]. **I.** *s.* (mús. y danz.) jiga; chasco, bromazo, petardo; (min.) criba; anzuelo cargado de plomo; (mec.) conductor o guía para fabricar piezas idénticas.—**j. saw,** sierra de vaivén. **II.** *va.* (mús.) cantar o tocar una jiga; sacudir de abajo hacia arriba; separar minerales con criba; (mec.) formar o adaptar por medio de guías; dar un bromazo. **III.** *vn.* bailar una jiga; pescar con anzuelo emplomado.

jigger [yígœr], *s.* bailador de jiga; cualquier utensilio que tiene movimiento de vaivén, v. gr. criba para minerales; rueda de alfarero; indicador eléctrico de precios; (mar.) aparejuelo, palanquín de socaire; (rad.) jigger, transformador Marconi; (ent.) nigua, pulga, garrapata u otra sabandija; (fam.) cosilla; aparato, artefacto, herramienta.

jill [yil], *s.* moza; querida; hurón hembra; taza, jícara. *V.* GILL.

jilt [yilt]. **I.** *s.* la mujer que da calabazas a su pretendiente. **II.** *va.* despedir o dar calabazas; (fam.) plantar, dejar colgado. **III.** *vn.* coquetear.

jim-crow [yímcróu], *s.* encorvador de rieles.

jimmy [yími], *s.* pie de cabra de los salteadores en poblado.—**j. bar** = CROWBAR.

jingle [yíngœl]. **I.** *va.* y *vn.* retiñir, sonar o resonar; rimar. **II.** *s.* retintín, sonido metálico; cascabel; rima pueril, aleluya.—**jiaglet,** escrupulillo de cascabel.

jingo [yíngo], *s.* jingoísta, partidario de una política exterior agresiva.—**by j.!** ¡caramba! ¡por Dios!

jingoism [-iŝm], *s.* jingoísmo, política agresiva; odio de lo extranjero.

jinny [yíni], *s.* (min.) máquina fija de arrastre; JINNY ROAD.—**j. road,** (min.) plano inclinado para arrastre por gravedad.

jinx [yinx], *s.* = HOODOO.

jippo [yípo], *s.* jubón, jaqueta, cotilla.

jitney [yítni], *s.* moneda de cinco centavos; bicoca; ómnibus.

job [yob]. **I.** *s.* tarea; destajo; remiendo; agiotaje; socaliña, engañifa; (fam.) empleo, ocupación, trabajo; tarea, empresa; suceso; circunstancia.—**j. lot,** mercancías varias vendidas en montón.—**j. printing,** impresión de remiendos **II.** *va.* y *vn.* comprar al por mayor y revender al por menor; alquilar(se) al destajo; hacer destajo; especular con los fondos públicos.

jobber [yóbœr], *s.* agiotador, agiotista; intrigante, destajero, destajista; remendero, remendón; (com.) negociante o traficante medianero, corredor.

jobbery [yóbœri], *s.* engañifa; agiotaje.

jobbing [yóbing], *s.* negocio de comprar por mayor y revender por menor; agio; cambalache.— **j. house,** (com.) casa medianera entre los fabricantes o importadores y los detallistas.

jockey [yóki]. **I.** *s.* (dep.) jockey; chalán; engañabobos, petardista. **II.** *va.* trampear, engañar; ponerse delante de otro caballo en una carrera.

jocose [yocóus], *a.* jocoso.—**jocosely** [-li], *adv.* jocosamente.—**jocoseness** [-es], **jocosity** [yocóusiti], *s.* jocosidad, alegría, chanza.

jocular [yókiular], *a.* jocoso, chancero; burlesco. —**jocularity** [-lǽriti], *s.* jocosidad.—**jocularly** [larli], *adv.* jocosamente.

jocund [yócund], *a.* alegre, festivo, jovial.— **jocundity** [yócúnditi], *s.* alegría, jovialidad.— **jocundly** [yócúndli], *adv.* alegremente.

jog [yog]. **I.** *va.* empujar; dar un golpecito para llamar la atención; excitar suavemente, estimular. **II.** *vn.* **to j. on,** o **along,** moverse o ir despacio o a un trote corto. **III.** *s.* empujoncito, golpecito; estímulo; zangoloteo; trote lento; (mec.) muesca cuadrada.

joggle [yógœl], *va.* y *vn.* empujar o moverse con sacudidas suaves.

John [yon], *s.* Juan. ɩ́. para denotar un tipo nacional o genérico.—**j.-apple,** (bot.) especie de manzana tardía.—**J. Bull,** John Bull (Inglaterra; el pueblo inglés); armazón de taladro.—**J. Chinaman,** cualquier chino; los chinos en general.—**J. Doe,** N. N., Fulano de Tal.—**j. dory,** (ict.) dorado. —**J. Trot,** rústico, patán.

johnycake [yónikéic], *s.* (E. U.) torta o pan de maíz.

join [yóin]. **I.** *va.* juntar, unir, ensamblar, empalmar; añadir; unir, casar; asociar; agregarse, incorporarse o unirse a, ingresar en, abrazar (un partido, etc.); empeñarse juntos, aunarse; chocar, embestir.—**to j. battle,** librar batalla.—**to j. company,** incorporarse.—**to j. issue,** ponerse de punta; disputar; contradecirse mutuamente.—**to j. issues,** zurcir voluntades. **II.** *vn.* unirse, juntarse, estar junto a.

joinder [yóindœr], *s.* (for.) junta, unión, asociación.

joiner [yóinœr], *s.* ebanista, ensamblador, carpintero de obra prima.

joinery [yóinœri], *s.* ensambladura; ebanistería.

joining [yóining], *s.* unión, juntura.—**J. press,** (carp.) cepo.

joint [yóint]. **I.** *s.* juntura, junta, unión, empalme, ensambladura; conexión, enganche; coyuntura, articulación; nudillo; gozne, bisagra; charnela; (alb.) degolladura; cuarto de un animal; encuentro de un ave; (bot.) nudo.—**out of j.,** desunido; descoyuntado, desbarajustado. **II.** *a.* unido, agrupado, colectivo; copartícipe; asociado; mixto.—**j. author,** coautor.—**j. bolt,** perno para juntas en T.—**j. commission,** comisión mixta.— **j. consent,** común acuerdo.—**j. file,** lima de acanalar bisagras.—**j. heir,** coheredero.—**j. meeting** = **j. session.**—**j. pipe,** manguito, golilla.—**j. property,** propiedad indivisa.—**j. responsibility,** responsabilidad solidaria.—**j. session,** sesión plena. —**j. stock,** capital social, fondos en común.—**j. stock company,** compañía por acciones.—**j. tenancy,** tenencia en mancomún, con derecho absoluto del sobreviviente.—**j. tenant,** inquilino mancomunado. **III.** *va.* juntar, unir, agregar; formar nudos, articulaciones o coyunturas; descuartizar. **IV.** *vn.* unirse por medio de articulaciones.

jointed [yóinted], *a.* nudoso; articulado.

jointer [yóintœr], *s.* (carp.) juntera.

jointly [yóintli], *adv.* juntamente, colectivamente mancomunadamente, in sólidum.—**j. and severally,** todos y cada uno de por sí,in sólidum.

jointure [yóinchur o yóintiur], *s.* (for.) bienes parafernales.

joist [yóist], *s.* (arq.) viga, vigueta.

joke [yóuc]. **I.** *s.* chanza; chiste; chuscada.— **in j.,** en chanza, de broma. **II.** *vn.* chancear, chancearse.

joker [yóukœr], *s.* burlón, bromista, chancero; en el juego de *euchre,* naipe adicional que es el triunfo más alto.

jokingly [yóukingli], *adv.* de burlas, en chanza.

jolliness, jollity [yólines, ti], *s.* jovialidad, broma, alegría, regocijo.

jolly [yóli]. *a.* alegre, festivo, jovial; jaranero; divertido.—**j.-boat,**(mar.) botequín, serení. **II.** *va.* (fam.) candonguear.

jolt [yolt]. **I.** *va.* y *vn.* traquetear, sacudir, dar sacudidas. **II.** *s.* sacudida, traqueteo, salto.

jongleur [yonglœr], *s.* trovador; bufón.

jonquil [yóncuil], *s.* (bot.) junquillo.

joss [yos], *s.* ídolo o dios chino.—**j. house,** templo para ídolos chinos.—**j. stick,** pajuela perfumada que los chinos queman ante sus ídolos.

jostle [yósœl]. **I.** *va.* y *vn.* rempujar, empellar; codear. **II.** *s.* empellón, empujón.

jot [yot]. **I.** *s.* pizca, ápice, tilde. **II.** *va.* (con **down**) apuntar, tomar notas.

joule [yául], *s.* (elec.) julio.

jounce [yæuns]. **I.** *va.* y *vn.* (fam.) sacudir, traquetear. **II.** *s.* sacudimiento, traqueteo.

journal [yœrnal], *s.* diario, periódico diario; revista (publicación); acta; diario (apuntes personales); (com.) diario (libro); (mec.) gorrón, manguleta.—**j. bearing, j. box,** cojinete, chumacera.

journalism [yœrnalism], *s.* periodismo.—**journalist** [-ist], *s.* periodista.—**journalistic** [-listic], *a.* periodístico.

journalize [-aiš]. **I.** *va.* (com.) pasar al jornal. **II.** *vn.* apuntar en un diario.

journey [yœrni]. **I.** *s.* jornada; viaje por tierra; tránsito, pasaje. **II.** *vn.* viajar; recorrer un trayecto.—**journeyer** [-œr], *s.* viajero.

journeyman [-mæn], *s.* jornalero.—**j. tailor,** oficial de sastre.—**journeywork** [-uœrc], *s.* jornal.

joust [yust]. **I.** *s.* justa, torneo. **II.** *vn.* justar

jovial [yóval], *a.* jovial.—**joviality, jovialness** [yoviǽliti, yóvialnes], *s.* jovialidad.—**jovially** [yóviali], *adv.* jovialmente.

jowl [yoi o yául], *s.* carrillo, quijada; cabeza de pescado aderezada.

jowler [yólœr o yáulœr], *s.* especie de perro.

joy [yói], *s.* alegría, júbilo, regocijo; felicidad.— **j. ride,** paseo subrepticio en automóvil, en que se violan las ordenanzas, esp. las que restringen la velocidad.—**j. stick** (aer.) palanca de gobierno.

joyful [yóiful], *a.* alegre, gozoso; festivo.—**joyfully** [-i], *adv.* gozosamente.—**joyfulness** [-nes], *s.* gozo, júbilo.

joyless [yóiles], *a.* triste, sin gozo.—**joylessly** [-li], *adv.* tristemente.—**joylessness** [-nes], *s.* tristeza, abatimiento.

joyous [yóius], *s.* alegre, gozoso.—**joyously** [-li], *adv.* gozosamente.—**joyousness** [-nes], *s.* gozo, dicha, júbilo.

jubilant [yúbilant], *a.* alborozado, regocijado, alegre.—**jubilate** [-eit], *vn.* alegrarse, regocijarse.— **jubilation** [-léišhun], *s.* júbilo, regocijo.

jubilee [yúbili], *s.* jubileo.

Judaic(al [yudéic(al], *a.* judaico.

Judaically [-i], *adv.* a manera de judío.

Judaism [yúdæišm], *s.* judaísmo.—**Judaize** [-aiš] *vn.* judaizar.—**Judaizer** [-aišœr], *s.* judaizante.

judge [yuy], *s.* juez; magistrado de un tribunal de justicia; magistrado de la corte suprema; perito.—**J. Advocate,** auditor de guerra.—**to be no j. of,** no ser juez en, no entender de, no conocer. **II.** *va.* juzgar; sentenciar, fallar. **III.** *vn.* juzgar.—**judging by,** o **from,** a juzgar por.

judg(e)ment [yúymœnt], *s.* juicio, criterio, discernimiento; sentir, opinión; fallo; sentencia ejecutoria; juicio final.—**j. day,** día del juicio.—**j.**

of God, juicio de Dios.—**J. seat**, tribunal.—**to the best of one's j.**, según el leal saber y entender de uno.

judgeship [-ship], *s.* judicatura, magistratura.

judicable [yúdicabœl], *a.* que puede ser juzgado. —**judicative** [-tiv], *a.* judicativo.—**judicatory** [-tori]. **I.** *s.* tribunal de justicia; judicatura. **II.** *a.* judicial; jurídico.—**judicature** [-chur], *s.* judicatura, magistratura; juzgado.

Judicial [yudíshal], *a.* judicial.—**J. separation**, separación legal o judicial (de marido y mujer)— exime a los cónyuges de sus deberes como tales, pero no disuelve el matrimonio.

judicially [-i], *adv.* judicialmente.

judiciary [yudíshiæri]. **I.** *a.* judiciario; judicial. **II.** *s.* administración de justicia; magistratura; poder judicial.

judicious [-shus], *a.* juicioso, cuerdo, sensato.— **judiciously** [-li], *adv.* juiciosamente, cuerdamente. —**judiciousness** [-nes], *s.* cordura, sensatez.

jug [yug]. **I.** *va.* introducir o cocer en una botija o cacharro; (vulg.) encarcelar. **II.** *vn.* reclamarse (algunos pájaros); juntarse las perdices. **III.** *s.* botijuela, botijo; jarro, cacharro, cántaro, porrón; reclamo del ruiseñor.

juggle [yúgœl]. **I.** *vn.* hacer juegos de manos; engañar, hacer trampas. **II.** *s.* juego de manos; impostura, engaño.

juggler [yúglœr], *s.* prestidigitador; escamoteador; impostor.

jugglery [yúgleri], *s.* prestidigitación; engaño, trampa.

Jugoslav [yúgoslav], *s*, **Jugoslavian, Jugoslavic** [-ian, -ic], *a.* yugoeslavo.

jugular [yúgiular]. **I.** *a.* yugular. **II.** *s.* vena yugular.

juice [yus], *s.* zumo; jugo, substancia; (fam.) electricidad.—**j. of the sugar-cane**, zumo de caña, guarapo.

juiceless [yúsles], *a.* seco, sin jugo.

juiciness [yúsines], *s.* jugosidad, suculencia.

juicy [yúsi], *a.* jugoso, zumoso.

jujube [yúyub], *s.* azufaifa, yuyuba, jínjol, guinja. —**j. tree**, (bot.) guinjo, azufaifo.

jujutsu [yuyútsu], *s.* método japonés de combatir brazo a brazo sin armas.

julep [yúlep], *s.* (farm.) julepe.

Julian [yúliæn], *a.* juliano.

julienne [yulién], *s.* sopa Juliana.

July [yulái], *s.* julio.

jumble [yúmbœl]. **I.** *va.* mezclar, arrebujar, emburujar; confundir. **II.** *vn.* mezclarse, revolverse, confundirse. **III.** *s.* mezcla, revoltillo, embrollo, mezcolanza; bollito delgado y dulce.

jumbo [yúmbo]. **I.** *s.* (fam.) coloso, cosa o animal enorme. **II.** *a.* colosal, gigantesco.

jump [yump]. **I.** *va.* saltar por encima de o al otro lado de; hacer saltar; saltarse, omitir; en el juego de damas, comer un peón.—**to j. one's ball**, fugarse uno estando bajo fianza. **II.** *vn.* saltar; brincar; convenir, concordar.—**j. at**, apresurarse a aprovechar.—**to j. on**, arremeter a; (fam.) poner como nuevo.—**to j. over**, saltar por encima de.— **to j. to a conclusion**, sacar precipitadamente una conclusión. **III.** *s.* salto, brinco; (min.) falla de una vena.—**j. joint**, junta a tope; junta en ras.—**j. spark**, (elec.) chispa en el entrehierro o en cualquier otro espacio de separación.—**j. weld**, soldadura a martillo en caliente.—**on the j.**, de un salto, al vuelo.

jumper [yúmpœr], *s.* saltador, brincador; (E. U.) blusa de obrero; zamarra de pieles; narria, rastra; usurpador de una mina denunciada por otro; (mec.) barreta de mina, taladro de mano; (elec.) alambre de cierre.

jumping jack [yúmping yæc], *s.* títere.

junction [yúncshun], *s.* junta, unión; trabadura, acopladura; (f. c.) confluencia de dos o más vías.—**j. box**, (elec.) caja de conexiones; caja de derivación.

juncture [yúnchur], *s.* junta, juntura; coyuntura, articulación; ocasión, oportunidad; trance.

June [yun], *s.* junio.

jungle [yœngœl], *s.* maraña, matorral, zarzal.— **j. fever**, fiebre palúdica de la India.

jungly [yúngli], *a.* enmarañado, lleno de matorrales.

junior [yúniœr]. **I.** *s.* estudiante de penúltimo (gen. de tercer año); joven. **II.** *a.* más joven; hijo (gen. en la forma abreviada *jr.* o *Jr.*, v. gr. *Alexander Dumas, Jr.*, Alejandro Dumas, hijo); de penúltimo año (estudiante); menor; más nuevo o reciente; menos antiguo; posterior; segundo, subordinado.—**j. high school**, escuela secundaria inferior (escuela intermedia entre la elemental y la secundaria).—**j. partner**, socio menos antiguo, socio menor.—**J. Red Cross**, Cruz Roja Juvenil, o de la Juventud.

juniorate [yúnioret], *s.* jovenado.

juniority [yunióriti], *s.* condición de *junior*.

juniper [yúnipœr], *s.* (bot.) enebro; junípero.— **j. berries**, nebrina.

junk [yunc], *s.* (mar.) junco, champán; trozada, chicote; hierro viejo; cecina; (fam.) basura, hojarasca.

junker [yúnker], *s.* joven noble alemán; aristócrata reaccionario alemán.

junket [yúnket]. **I.** *va.* y *vn.* tener o dar un convite; festejar, obsequiar; andar de parranda. **II.** *s.* manjar de leche, cuajo y azúcar.

junket(ing [yúnket(ing], *s.* festín, francachela, tiberio.

junta [yúnta], *s.* junta.

junto [yúnto], *s.* cábala, cabildeo.

jupon [yupón], *s.* jubón.

jurant [yúrænt], *a.* juramentado.

Jurassic [yurésic], *a.* jurásico.

juratory [yúratori], *a.* juratorio.

jurel [jurél], *s.* (ict.) jurel.

juridic(al [yurídic(al], *a.* jurídico, judicial.

juridically [-i], *adv.* jurídicamente.

jurisconsult [yúriscónsult], *s.* jurisconsulto.

jurisdiction [-dícshun], *s.* jurisdicción; potestad, poderío; fuero.—**jurisdictional** [-al], *a.* jurisdiccional.

jurisprudence [-prúdens], *s.* jurisprudencia.— **jurisprudent** [-prúdent], *a.* y *s.* jurisperito, jurisconsulto.

jurist [yúrist], *s.* jurista, jurisconsulto.

juristic [yurístic], *a.* jurídico.—**j. person**, persona jurídica, entidad jurídica.

juror [yúrœr], *s.* (for.) jurado (individuo).

jury [yúri], *s.* (for.) jurado (cuerpo e institución). —**j. box**, tribuna del jurado.

juryman [-mæn], *s.* jurado (persona).

jurymast [yúrimast], *s.* (mar.) bandola.

just [yust]. **I.** *a.* justo; legal; legítimo, bien fundado; fiel, exacto. **II.** *adv.* justamente, exactamente; casi; sólo, no más que; apenas; simplemente; hace un momento —**j. as**, al momento que, al tiempo que; cuando; no bien; lo mismo que, semejante a.—**j. as you please**, como Vd. guste.—**j. beyond**, un poco más allá.—**j. by**, aquí cerca.—**j. now**, ahora mismo, en este mismo instante, poco hace.—**to have but j. time**, tener el tiempo preciso.—**to have j.** (seguido de participio), acabar de (seguido de infinitivo: *I have just arrived*, acabo de llegar).

just, joust [yust]. **I.** *s.* justa, torneo. **II.** *vn.* justar, lidiar.

justice [yústis], *s.* justicia; razón, derecho; (for.) juez; magistrado.—**j. of the peace**, juez de paz, alcalde.

justiceship [yústisship], *s.* justiciazgo, judicatura.

justiciable [yustíshiæbœl], *a.* justiciable.

justiciary [yustíshiæri]. **I.** *a.* judicial. **II.** *s.* juez, magistrado.

justifiable [yústifáiabœl], *a.* justificable.—**justifiableness** [-nes], *s.* calidad de justificable.—**justifiably** [-bli], *adv.* justificadamente.—**justification** [-ñkéishun], *s.* justificación; descargo, defensa.

justificative [yústifiketiv], **justificatory** [-catori], *a.* justificativo, defensivo.

justifier [yústifaicœr], *s.* justificador, ajustador; justificante; calibrador.

justify [yústifai], *va.* justificar, probar en justicia; sincerar, vindicar; absolver; (teol.) absolver, perdonar; (impr.) justificar, ajustar.

justle, *s.* y *v.* = JOSTLE.

justly [yústli], *adv.* justamente, rectamente; debidamente, dignamente; exactamente, precisamente.—**justness** [-nes], *s.* justicia; exactitud; propiedad; regularidad; primor.

jut [yʊt]. **I.** *vn.* sobresalir; combarse. **II.** *s.* salidizo, vuelo, retallo, resalto.—**j. window**, ventana saliente, mirador.

jute [yʊt], *s.* yute, cáñamo de las Indias.

juvenescence [yúvenésens], *s.* renovación de la juventud.—**juvenescent**]-sent], *a.* rejuveneciente, que se remoza.

juvenile [yúvenil], *a.* juvenil, joven.—**j. court**, tribunal juvenil o del niño.—*s.* mocito, joven, galancete.

juvenility [yúveníliti], *s.* mccedad, juventud.

juxtapose [yúxtapóus], *va.* yuxtaponer.

juxtaposition [-poŝíŝhʊn], *s.* yuxtaposición, contigüidad.

K

k [kéi], *s.* k.

Kabyle [kabáil], *s.* cabila.

Kafir, Kaffir [kǽfœr], *s.* cafre; infiel (entre los mahometanos).

kaiak [ká- o kéyæk], *s.* canoa de los esquimales.

kail, kale [kéil], *s.* (bot.) bretón.

Kaiser [káiŝœr], *s.* káiser.

kakapo [cácapó], *s.* papagayo nocturno australiano (puede llamarse cacapó).

kaki [cáki], *s.* caqui, kaki, níspero del Japón.

kaleidoscope [kaláidoscoup], *s.* calidoscopio.

kaleidoscopic [-cópic], *a.* calidoscópico; variado, pintoresco.

kalendar, = CALENDAR.

kali [káli], *s.* (bot.) barrilla.

kalif, kalifate, = CALIF, CALIFATE.

kalium [kéiliʊm], *s.* potasio.

kalmia [kǽlmia], *s.* (bot.) kalmia.

Kalmuck [kǽlmʊc], *s.* calmuco.

kalsomine, *v.* y *s.* = CALCIMINE.

kamerad [cámerad]. **I.** *s.* camarada (usado exclusivamente por los soldados alemanes en señal de rendición). **II.** *vn.* (fam.) rendirse, dar el *camarada*.

Kanaka [kanáka], *s.* natural de las islas de Hawái.

kangaroo [cǽngarú], *s.* (zool.) canguro.

Kantian [kǽntian], *s.* kantiano.

Kantianism [kǽntianiŝm], *s.* kantismo.

kaolin [kéolin], *s.* caolín.

kapellmeister [kapélmaistœr], *s.* maestro de capilla; director de un coro.

kapok [cápoc], *s.* kapoc, especie de lana de ceiba.

karat, *s.* = CARAT.

karma [cármæ], *s.* karma, efecto persistente que todo acto individual deja en su autor; ley de retribución.

karn, *s.* montón de piedras. *V.* CAIRN.

karyokinesis [cáriokinísis], *s.* (biol.) mitosis, multiplicación de las células por división indirecta.

katydid [kétidid], *s.* insecto ortóptero.

kauri [káuri], **kawrie** [kóri], *s.* pino de la Nueva Zelandia, y su resina.

kayak [ka- o keyæc], *s.* = KAIAK.

kazoo [kaŝú], *s.* chicharra (instrumento).

keck [kec]. **I.** *vn.* arquear. **II.** *s.* tallo hueco.

keckle [kécœl], *va.* (mar.) aforrar un cable.

keckson, kecksy, *s.* = KEX.

keddah [kédæ], *s.* trampa de elefantes.

kedge [keу], *s.* (mar.) anclote.

keel [kíl]. **I.** *s.* (mar.) quilla. **II.** *va.* poner la quilla; surcar el mar; dar carena.

keelage [kíleу], *s.* (mar.) derechos de quilla.

keelhaul [kíljol], *va.* (mar.) pasar por debajo de la quilla (castigo).

keelson [kílsʊn], *s.* (mar.) sobrequilla.

keen [kín], *a.* afilado; aguzado; agudo, penetrante, sutil, vivo; astuto, ladino; perspicaz; ansioso, vehemente; acre, mordaz, incisivo.

keenly [kínli], *adv.* agudamente, profundamente; sutilmente.

keenness [kínnes], *s.* agudeza; sutileza, perspicacia, penetración; ansia, anhelo.

keep [kip], *va.* (*pret.* y *pp.* KEPT) guardar (una cosa, un secreto, un mandamiento, la cuaresma, cama, un rebaño); tener (criados, secretario, un perro); dirigir, manejar (hotel, tienda, etc.); alojar, dar hospedaje a por paga, tener (*he keeps boarders*, tiene huéspedes, da hospedaje, o tiene casa de huéspedes); llevar (cuentas, libros); cumplir (la palabra, una promesa); mantener; detener, demorar; contener; mantenerse en.—**to k. an eye on**, vigilar.—**to k. away**, tener o retener alejado; no dejar venir, entrar, etc.—**to k. back**, detener; ocultar; impedir; preservar, guardar o reservar; restringir.—**to k. bad hours**, acostarse tarde.—**to k. cash**, ser cajero.—**to k. company**, acompañar; tener amores o casamiento arreglado.—**to k. company with**, pasar el tiempo en compañía de; tener amores con.—**to k. down**, sujetar; reprimir.—**to k. good hours**, acostarse temprano.—**to k. house**, tener hogar propio; manejar casa.—**to k. in**, mantener dentro; no dejar salir.—**to k. late hours**, acostarse tarde.—**to k. off**, detener; tener a distancia; cerrar el paso a.—**to k. on**, mantener; continuar.—**to k. one at bay**, entretener a uno.—**to k. one's counsel**, callar, no decir nada.—**to k. one's countenance**, no alterarse, permanecer inmutable.—**to k. one's distance**, mantenerse dentro de propios límites, no tomarse libertades.—**to k. one's eyes open**, mantenerse alerta, no dormirse (fig.).—**to k. one's ground**, mantenerse en su puesto, defenderse bien.—**to k. one's hands off**, no tocar, no meterse en.—**to k. one's head**, no perder la cabeza, mantener su sangre fría.—**to k. one's temper**, obrar con calma.—**to k. one's word**, cumplir su palabra, tener palabra.—**to k. open house**, mantener la puerta abierta (fig.), ofrecer hospitalidad o hacer invitaciones de continuo.—**to k. out**, no dejar entrar; excluir.—**to k. out of sight**, no dejar ver; quitar de delante.—**to k. pace with**, marchar con, ir al mismo paso que.—**to k. tally**, llevar la cuenta.—**to k. the ball rolling**, mantener el fuego ardiendo (fig.), mantener la animación, conversación, etc.—**to k. the bowels open**, mantener libre el vientre.—**to k. the land aboard**, (mar.) mantenerse inmediato a la costa.—**to k. the peace**, mantener la paz o el orden público.—**to k. the pot boiling**, ganarse la vida; mantener la actividad.—**to k. the wind**, navegar de bolina.—**to k. the wolf from the door**, guardarse del hambre o la pobreza.—**to k. time**, marcar la hora, andar (el reloj); llevar el compás.—**to k. track of**, seguir la pista a, no perder de vista.—**to k. under**, sujetar, oprimir.—**to k. up**, mantener, conservar.—**to k. up one's spirits**, mantener su valor, no desalentarse.

keep [kip] *vn.* mantenerse, sostenerse; durar sin dañarse; acostumbrarse, soler; continuar; preservar; permanecer, quedarse.—**to k. along**, continuar, seguir, proseguir.—**to k. aloof**, permanecer apartado, no meterse, no tomar parte.—**to k. at it**, (fam.) perseverar, persistir.—**to k. at home**, quedarse en casa.—**to k. away**, mantenerse apartado, no acercarse.—**to k. from**, abstenerse de; no meterse en.—**to k. in**, permanecer dentro; estarse en casa.—**to k. off**, no entrar a; no tocar; no andar sobre o por; mantenerse fuera o lejos de.—**to k. on**, seguir, proseguir.—**to k. out of**, no meterse en, evitar.—**to k. out of sight**, mantenerse oculto, no mostrarse.—**to k. out of the way**, estarse o hacerse a un lado; esconderse, sacar el cuerpo.—**to k. to**, adherirse estrictamente a; seguir por.—**to k. up**, mantenerse firme; persistir; no cejar; estar de jarana.

keep, *s.* manutención, subsistencia; receptáculo, depósito; torreón, alcázar; castillo; custodia; cuidado.—**for keeps**, para guardar, para quedarse con ello; permanentemente.

keeper [kípœr], *s.* guarda, guardián, custodio, defensor; tenedor; carcelero; guardabosque.—**k. of the great seal**, guardasellos del rey.—**k. of the records**, archivero.

keepership [-ŝhip], *s.* guardería, alcaidía.

keeping [kíping], *s.* cargo, custodia, mantenimiento; cuidado, preservación, defensa; guarda.—**in k. with**, en armonía con, de conformidad con.

Para la pronunciación de æ, œ, D, ŝ, ŝh, ʊ, ȳ, Y, z, véase la clave al principio del libro.

keepsake [kípseic], *s.* regalo, recuerdo.

keeve [kiv], *s.* cuba o tina en que fermenta la cerveza.

keg, *s.* cuñete, barrilito.

keir [kíær], *s.* cuba, tanque de blanquear.

kell [kel], *s.* redaño. *V.* CAUL.

kelp [kelp], *s.* algas marinas y sus cenizas, de las que se obtiene el yodo; sosa.

Kelt, Keltic [kelt, ic], = CELT, etc.

kelter [kéltœr], *s.* = KILTER.

Kelvin scale [kélvin skéil], escala absoluta (de temperaturas).

ken [ken]. **I.** *va.* saber, conocer; divisar. **II.** *s.* alcance de la vista.

kenotron [kénotron], *s.* (elec.) transformador de tubo de vacío.

kennel [kénel]. **I.** *s.* perrera; jauría; canal, desagüe; zorrera; cuchitril. **II.** *va.* y *vn.* tener o estar en perrera.

kentledge [kéntleɣ], *s.* (mar.) enjunque.

kept, *pret.* y *pp.* de verbo TO KEEP.—**k. mistress,** o **woman,** manceba, querida.

keramic [kœrǽmic], *a.* = CERAMIC.

keratitis [kératáitis *o* trtis], *s.* (med.) queratitis.

kerbstone, = CURBSTONE.

kerchief [kérchif], *s.* pañuelo.

kerf [kœrf], *s.* corte que hace la sierra en la madera; cortadura que hace una máquina de tundir.

kerite [kérait], *s.* aislador compuesto de alquitrán, aceite y azufre.

kermes [kœrmiŝ], *s.* quermes, grana.—**k. oak,** coscoja.—**k. berry,** grana.

kermess [kœrmes], *s.* bazar, fiesta, romería.

kern [kœrm]. **I.** *s.* última gavilla de la cosecha, y fiesta con que se celebra; (impr.) hombro, cran de una letra; patán; soldado irlandés. **II.** *vn.* (agr.) granar.

kernel [kœrnel]. **I.** *s.* almendra, pepita, meollo o semilla carnosa de cualquier fruto drupáceo; grano de maíz; (fig.) meollo, medula. **II.** *vn.* formarse almendra.

kernel(l)ed [kœrneld], *a.* que tiene almendra o pepita.

kernelly [kœrneli], *a.* almendrado.

kernelwort [-uœrt], *s.* (bot.) escrofularia, ruda canina.

kerosene [kérosin], *s.* kerosina, keroseno, petróleo de arder.

kersey [kœrŝi], *s.* (tej.) buriel.

kerseymere, kerseynette [-míœr, -net], *s.* casimir.

kestrel [késtrel], *s.* (orn.) cernícalo.

ketch [kech], *s.* (mar.) queche.

ketchup [kéchup], *s.* = CATCHUP.

ketone [kíton], *s.* (quím.) ketona.

kettle [kétœl], *s.* caldera, marmita.

kettledrum [-drum], *s.* (mús.) timbal, atabal, tímpano; tertulia de confianza por la tarde.

kettledrummer [-drúmœr], *s.* timbalero, atabalero.

kettlepins [-pinŝ], *s.* juego de bolos.

kevel [kével], *s.* (mar.) manigueta; (zool.) gacela.

kex [kex], *s.* cicuta; tallo hueco.

key [kí]. **I.** *s.* llave; clave, buscapié; (mec.) llave, destornillador; chaveta; cuña; (arq.) clave, dovela; (enc.) clavija; (arti.) sotrozo; (elec.) llave, conmutador; tecla (del piano, de máquina de escribir o de las de componer y distribuir tipos); pistón o llave de los instrumentos de viento; (mús.) clave, llave, tono; (mar.) cayo, isleta; muelle.— **k. action,** teclado y mecanismo de un órgano o piano.—**k. bolt,** perno de chaveta.—**k. bugle,** corneta de llaves.—**k. rack,** taquilla.—**k. ring,** llavero.—**k. seat,** cajera de cuña.—**k. tone** = KEYNOTE.—**in k.,** templado, de acuerdo, en armonía. **II.** *va.* enchavetar, calzar, acuñar; poner llaves; afinar, templar con llave.

keyboard [kíbord], *s.* teclado.

keyed [kid], *a.* que tiene llaves o teclas; estirado; templado, afinado.—**k. up,** excitado, agitado.

keyhole [kíjóul], *s.* ojo de la cerradura.—**k. saw,** sierra de punto o de calador.

keynote [-nóut], *s.* (mús.) nota tónica; principio fundamental, piedra angular.

keystone [-stóun], *s.* (arq.) clave, llave de arco.

keyway [-uéi], *s.* = KEY SEAT.

khaki [cáki], *s.* kaki, caqui (tela y color).

khan [kan], *s.* kan o khan; posada o mesón en Turquía.

khedive [kedív], *s.* jedive (virrey).

kibe [káib], *s.* grieta en la piel; sabañón ulcerado.

kibed [káibd], **kiby** [-bi], *a.* lleno de sabañones.

kick [kic]. **I.** *va.* acocear, dar patadas a.—**to k. out,** echar a puntapiés o a patadas.—**to k. the bucket,** (fam.) irse al otro mundo, morirse.—**to k. up a dust,** o **a row,** (fam.) armar un bochinche, ponerse por las nubes.—**to k. up one's heels,** (fam.) morirse. **II.** *vn.* cocear, patear; (fam.) respingar: oponerse; quejarse.—**to k. against the pricks,** cocear contra el aguijón. **III.** *s.* patada, coz; puntapié; (fam.) respingo; oposición; queja.

kicker [kíkœr], *s.* coceador, pateador; (fam.) reparón, quejumbroso.

kicking [kíking]. **I.** *s.* acoceamiento, pateadura; pataleo; respingo, queja. **II.** *a.* **k. coil** = CHOKING COIL.—**k. piece,** resguardo.

kickshaw [kíkŝho], *s.* fruslería, bagatela; pisto.

kid. **I.** *s.* cabrito, chivo, chivato; cabritilla; carne de cabrito; (fam.) niño; muchachito; chico, chica; (mar.) gamella.—*pl.* guantes o zapatos de cabritilla. **II.** *va.* y *vn.* engañar por broma.

kidder [kídœr], *s.* monopolista de granos; chancero, bromista.

kidling [kídling], *s.* choto.

kidnap [kídnæp], *va.* plagiar; secuestrar.—**kidnapper** [-œr], *s.* ladrón de niños u otras personas, secuestrador.—**kidnapping** [-ing], *s.* plagio; secuestro.

kidney [kídni], *s.* riñón; (ant.) afectos, índole, temperamento.—**k. bean,** judía, frijol ordinario.— **k. stone,** piedra nefrítica.—**k. vetch,** vulneraria.

kidneyshaped [-ŝhéipd], *a.* reniforme.

kidneywort [-uœrt], *s.* (bot.) ombligo.

kier [kíær], *s.* = KEIR.

kilampere [kílæmpíær], *s.* kiloamperio.

kilderkin [kíldœrkin], *s.* (Ingl.) medio barril (18 galones).

kilerg [kílœrg], *s.* (fís.) kiloergio.

kill [kil]. **I.** *va.* matar; destruir; amortiguar; neutralizar; descartar; anular, cancelar, suprimir. **II.** *s.* acción de matar; animal muerto (matado); arroyo, riachuelo.

killdee(r [kíldi(r), *s.* (orn.) frailecillo norteamericano.

killer [kílœr], *s.* matador.

killing [kíling]. **I.** *a.* matador; destructivo; irresistible; (fam.) ridículo, risible. **II.** *s.* acto de matar, occisión, matanza.

kiln [kil], *s.* horno, estufa; horno de cochura.

kilndry [kíldrái], *va.* secar al horno.

kilo [kílo], kilo.—**kilocalorie** [-cǽlori], kilocaloría. —**kilogram(me** [-græm], *s.* kilogramo.—**kilogrammeter** [-græmítœr], kilográmetro.—**kilojoule** [-yú], kilojulio.—**kiloliter** [-lítœr], kilolitro. —**kilometer** [-mítœr], kilómetro—**kilometric** [-metric], kilométrico.—**kilovolt** [-vóult], kilovoltio.—**kilowatt** [-uót], kilovatio.—**kilowatt-hour** [-áuœr], kilovatio-hora.

kilt, *s.* tonelete; enagüillas, falda corta.

kilter, [kíltœr], *s.* buena condición, buen estado.

kimono [kimóno], *s.* bata de quimón.

kin. **I.** *s.* parentesco, vínculo; parientes, parentela, familia, linaje. **II.** *s.* pariente, allegado.

kind [káind]. **I.** *a.* bueno, benévolo, bondadoso; manso; afectuoso.—**k.-hearted,** bondadoso, de buen corazón.—**k.-heartedness,** benevolencia, bondad de corazón.—**k. regards,** cordial saludo, saludes; sentimientos de consideración. **II.** *s.* género, clase, calidad.—**k. of,** (fam.) algo, un poco; en cierto modo.—**in k.,**' del mismo modo, en la misma moneda (fig.); (e. p.) en especie (no en dinero).

kindergarten [kíndœrgártœn], *s.* kindergarten, escuela de párvulos.

kindle [kíndœl]. **I.** *va.* encender; inflamar, enardecer. **II.** *vn.* prender, arder: inflamarse, avivarse.

kindler [-dlœr], *s.* encendedor (persona o cosa).

kindliness [káindlines], *s.* benevolencia; buena índole.

kindling wood [kíndling ud], leña.

kindly [káindli]. **I.** *adv.* bondadosamente; (cir.) por primera intención. **II.** *a.* bondadoso, benévolo; favorable, propicio; (mⁱn.) que promete; (hist.) lícito: legítimo.

kindness [káindnes], *s.* bondad, benevolencia, favor, gracia.

kindred [kíndred]. **I.** *s.* parentesco; parentela, casta, tribu. **II.** *a.* emparentado, deudo, connotado; hermano, parejo; conexo, congénere.

kinemacolor [kínemæcólœr], *s.* cinematografía en colores.

kinematics [kínemæetics], *s.* cinemática.

kinematograph [-mætograf], *s.* cinematógrafo.

kinesiatrics [kinísiæetrics], **kinesitherapy** [-zérapl], *s.* cinesis o cinesia, tratamiento de las enfermedades por movimientos musculares.

kinesthesia [kineszísiæ], **kinesthesis** [-zísis], *s.* sentido muscular, percepción de los movimientos musculares propios.

kinetic [kinétic], cinético, dinámico.—**k. energy,** energía cinética.—**kinetics,** *s.* cinética, dinámica.

kinetograph [kinétogræf], *s.* cinematógrafo; cinetógrafo (cinematógrafo parlante).

kinetophone [kinétofoun], **kinetophonograph** [-fónograf], *s.* cinematógrafo parlante (en combinación con un fonógrafo).

kinetoscope [-scoup], *s.* kinetoscopio.

king, *s.* rey; en los naipes y el ajedrez, rey; en el juego de damas, dama.—**k. crab,** (zool.) límulo.— **k. pin,** KINGBOLT; pivote; en el juego de bolos, el de adelante; (fam.) persona de suma importancia. —**k. post,** montante, pendolón.—**k.-post bridge, o truss,** puente o armadura triangular de pendolón.—**k.'s evil,** escrófula.—**k.'s household,** casa real.—**k.'s yellow,** oropimento.—**the k.'s speech,** discurso de la Corona.

kingbird [kíngbœrd], *s.* (orn.) tirano, musícapa.

kingbolt [-bóult], *s.* (carr.) pivote que une la caja al eje delantero; (constr.) tirante; (min.) perno de suspensión.

kingcraft [-craft], *s.* arte de reinar.

kingcup [-cup], *s.* (bot.) botón de oro.

kingdom [kíngdum], *s.* reino.

kingfisher [kíngfíshœr], *s.* (orn.) guardarrío, martín pescador.

kinghood [kíngjud], *s.* dignidad real.

kinglet [kínglet], *s.* reyezuelo; (orn.) abadejo, régulo.

kinglike [kínglaic], **kingly** [kíngli], *a.* real, regio; majestuoso.

kingly, *adv.* regiamente, majestuosamente.

kingship [kíngship], *s.* majestad, dignidad real; monarquía; reino.

kink. I. *s.* retorcimiento, ensortijamiento; (mar.) coca; (fam.) capricho, chifladura. **II.** *va.* y *vn.* formar cocas, ensortijarse, encarrujarse.

kinky [kínki], *a.* ensortijado, encarrujado, grifo; (fam.) chiflado.

kino [kíno], *s.* quino.

kinsfolk [kínsfouc], *s.* parentela, parientes.

kinship [kínship], *s.* parentesco.

kinsman [kínsman], *s.* pariente, deudo.

kinswoman [kínsuman], *s.* parienta.

kiosk [kiósk], *s.* kiosco o quiosco.

kip, *s.* (ten.) piel de res pequeña.—**k.-leather** = KIPSKIN.

kipe [káip], *s.* nasa, butrón o buitrón.

kipper [kípœr]. **I.** *s.* salmón o arenque ahumado. **II.** *va.* curar (pescado) al humo.

kipskin [kípskin], *s.* becerro.

kirk [kœrk], *s.* iglesia.

kirtle [kœrtœl], *s.* manto; chupa larga.

kismet [kísmet], *s.* hado, destino.

kiss [kis]. **I.** *va.* besar; en el billar, tocarse suavemente dos bolas.—**to k. the dust,** morder el polvo.—**to k. the rod,** someterse a un castigo. **II.** *s.* beso; en el billar, pelo; merengue; dulce.— **k.-curl,** aladar.

kisser [kísœr], *s.* bescuador, besador.

kit, *s.* colodra, tineta; cubo; equipo, avíos, juego o caja de herramientas; violín de tres cuerdas; tiple (guitarrita); gatito; (fot.) marquito interior del chasis o portaplanchas.—**k.-cat,** (pint.) lienzo o retrato de medio cuerpo; (agr.) rodillo para tierras de labranza.

kitchen [kíchen], *s.* cocina; fogón portátil.—**k. boy,** pinche, galopillo.—**k. furniture,** utensilios de cocina.—**k. garden,** huerta.—**k. knave** = K. BOY.—**k. maid,** fregona, fregatriz.—**k. range,** fogón a la inglesa, fogón movible de hierro.—**k. stuff,** material o hierbas de cocina, legumbres; grasa, pringue.—**k. wench** = K. MAID.

kitchener [kíchenœr], *s.* estufa de cocinar; cocinero.

kitchenette [-et], *s.* cocina reducida o pequeña.

kite [káit], *s.* cometa; (com.) papel negociable u obligación de valor dudoso; (orn.) milano; (mar.) sobrejuanete, foque volante.—**k. balloon, k. sausage,** globo cautivo.

kiteflier [-fláiœr], *s.* (fam.) el que negocia pagarés sin valor.

kiteflying [-fláiing], *s.* acción de remontar una cometa; (fam.) negociación de pagarés sin valor.

kith [kiz], *s.* conocidos, amistades.—**k. and kin,** parientes y amigos.

kitten [kítœn], **kitling** [kítling]. **I.** *s.* gatito. **II.** *vn.* parir la gata.

kittiwake [kítiéuic], *s.* (orn.) risa, especie de gavión o gaviota.

kitty [kíti], *s.* gatito, minino.

kiva [kíva], *s.* cuarto o cámara de ceremonias de ciertos indios norteamericanos, con la entrada por arriba.

kiwi [kíui], *s.* kiwí, aptérix, pájaro áptero australiano.

kleptomania, *s.* = CLEPTOMANIA.

knack [næc], *s.* tino, don, destreza, acierto, arte; treta; chuchería.

knaggy [nǽgui], *a.* nudoso; áspero.

knapping [nǽping], *s.* quebrantamiento o corte de piedras.—**k. hammer,** martillo de picapedrero.

knapsack [nǽpsæc], *s.* (mil.) mochila; barjuleta, alforja, fardel.

knapweed [nǽpuid], *s.* (bot.) cabezuela.

knarled [narld], *a.* nudoso. *v.* GNARLED.

knave [néiv], *s.* bribón, pícaro, bellaco; sota de los naipes.—**knavery** [-ceri], **knavishness** [-íshnes], *s.* picardía, bellaquería, bribonada.—**knavish** [-íshl, *a.* bribón, pillo; travieso.—**knavishly** [-li], *adv.* bellacamente.

knead [níd], *va.* amasar, sobar, heñir.

kneader [nídœr], *s.* panadero, amasador.

kneading [-ing], *s.* amasadura; soba.—**k. trough** [trof], amasadera, artesa.

knee [ní], *s.* rodilla; (mec.) codo, codillo, ángulo, escuadra.—**k. breeches,** calzón corto.—**k. crooking,** obsequioso.—**k.-deep,** metido hasta las rodillas.—**k.-high,** hasta la rodilla.—**k. jerk,** patada o sacudida causada por golpe en el tendón de la rótula.—**k. joint,** articulación de la rodilla; junta de codillo.—**k. jointed,** encorvado o angular. —**k. of the head,** curva capuchina.—**k. timber,** madera para curvas.—**k. tribute,** genuflexión; (mar.) curva.

kneecap [nícǽp], *s.* rodillera; (anat.) rótula.

kneed [níd], *a.* articulado, acodillado.

kneeholly [níjoli], *s.* (bot.) brusco.

kneel [níl], *vn.* (a veces con *down*) arrodillarse.

kneeler [nílœr], *s.* el que se arrodilla.

kneepan [nípæn], *s.* (anat.) rótula.

knell [nel]. **I.** *s.* doble, toque de difuntos; mal agüero. **II.** *va.* y *vn.* doblar, tocar a muerto.

knew [niú], *pret.* de TO KNOW.

Knickerbocker [níkœrbókœr], *s.* descendiente de una de las primeras familias holandesas que se establecieron en Nueva York.—*pl.* calzón corto, braga.

knickknack [nícnæc], *s.* (fam.) chuchería. bujería, juguete.

knife [náif], *s.* cuchillo; navaja.—**k.-edge**, arista, filo; cuchillito, soporte de cuchillo.— **k. sharpener**, chaira, amolador.—**k. switch**, (elec.) interruptor de cuchillo. **II.** *va.* (fam.) acuchillar; (E. U.) frustrar o arruinar por intrigas.

knight [náit], *s.* caballero; campeón; caballo del ajedrez.—**k.-errant**, caballero andante.—**k.-errantry**, caballería andante.—**k. of St. Crispin**, zapatero.—**K. of the Order of the Garter**, caballero de la orden de la Jarretera.—**k. of the shears**, sastre. **II.** *va.* armar caballero; encomendar; (en Ingl.) hacer caballero, conferir el título de *Sir*.

knighthead [náitjed], *s.* (mar.) tragante exterior del bauprés.—**k. of the windlass**, cepos o bitas del molinete.—**knightheads of the gears**, guindastes.

knighthood [-jud], *s.* caballería; encomienda.

knightliness [-lines], *s.* calidad de caballeresco.

knightly [-li]. **I.** *a.* caballeresco. **II.** *adv.* caballerosamente, caballerescamente.

knit [nit], *va.* y *vn.* (pret. y *pp.* KNIT O KNITTED) hacer malla, hacer media o calceta, hacer punto de aguja; atar, enlazar, entretejer; contraer; unirse, trabarse.—**k. stockings**, medias de punto. —**to k. the eyebrows**, fruncir las cejas.

knitter [nítœr], *s.* calcetero, mediero.

knitting [níting], *s.* unión o junta; acción de hacer calceta; trabajo de punto.—**k. machine**, máquina de hacer punto de media.—**k. needle**, aguja de medias.—**k. work**, trabajo de punto.

knives [-lines], *pl.* de KNIFE.

knob [nob], *s.* prominencia, bulto, protuberancia; nudo en la madera; borlita o borlilla, perilla; botón; gorrón; (arq.) abollón; (mar.) tojino.

knobbed [nobd], **knobby** [nóbi], *a.* lleno de bultos o nudos; montañoso.

knock [nok]. **I.** *va.* y *vn.* chocar, topar; tocar, llamar a una puerta; pegar, cutir; golpear, dar o pegar golpes, aporrear.—**to k. about**, vagar, rodar.—**to k. down**, derribar; (com.) abatir, desarmar.—**to k. down to the highest bidder**, rematar al mejor postor.—**to k. in**, martillar o amartillar; hacer entrar a golpes.—**to k. off**, hacer saltar una cosa a fuerza de golpes; cesar, descontinuar, suspender; (fam.) hacer o ejecutar prontamente; rebajar, descontar.—**to k. on the head**, dar en la cabeza; frustrar.—**to k. out**, hacer salir a golpes; acogotar; dejar o poner fuera de combate (en el boxeo).—**to k. together**, construir toscamente o de prisa.—**to k. the bottom out of**, desfondar; echar a perder, frustrar.—**to k. under**, someterse, rendirse. **II.** *s.* choque, golpe, porrazo, topetazo; aldabonazo, llamada, toque.

knockdown [nócdáun]. **I.** *a.* mínimo (apl. al precio mínimo a que se venderá una cosa en subasta); desarmable; abrumador. **II.** *s.* golpe que derriba o abruma; cosa desarmada.

knocker [nókœr], *s.* golpeador; llamador, aldaba, aldabón.

knocking [nóking], *s.* aldabazo, aldabonazo, llamada a la puerta.

knock-kneed [nóc-nid], *a.* patituerto, zambo.

knock-out [-áut]. **I.** *a.* que pone fuera de combate; abrumador.—**k. drops**, (fam.) gotas narcóticas. **II.** *s.* golpe que pone fuera de combate; destapadero (lugar de una plancha donde puede botarse el metal a martillo para formar un agujero).

knoll [nol]. **I.** *va.* y *vn.* doblar, tocar las campanas a muerto. **II.** *s.* loma, otero; cumbre o cima de una loma; doble de las campanas.

knop, *s.* (ant.) = KNOB; (arq.) florón.

knosp [nosp], *s.* (bot.) capullo; (arq.) florón.

knot [not]. **I.** *s.* nudo; lazo, vínculo; nudo de la madera o de plantas; enredo de un drama; dificultad; grupo, corrillo; quid, busilis; moño o castaña; (mar.) milla náutica, nudo; (orn.) canuto, tríngido.—**k. hole**, agujero que deja en la madera un nudo desprendido.—**k. wood**, madera. nudosa.—**knots of the log line**, nudos de la corredera. **II.** *va.* anudar; atar con nudos; enredar, juntar; fruncir (las cejas); hacer nudos en; intrincar; unir. **III.** *vn.* echar nudos las plantas; formar nudos; enredarse.

knotgrass [nótgras], *s.* (bot.) centinodia; grama.

knotless [nótles], *a.* sin nudos.

knotted [nóted], *a.* nudoso, anudado.

knottiness [nótines], *s.* abundancia de nudos; desigualdad; dificultad.

knotty [nóti], *a.* nudoso; duro, áspero; intrincado, difícil.

knout [náut], *s.* azote, instrumento de suplicio usado antes en Rusia.

know [no]. **I.** *va.* conocer; saber; distinguir, discernir.—**to k. best**, ser el mejor juez de. **II.** *vn.* saber.—**to k. best**, ser el mejor juez, saber lo que más conviene.—**to k. of**, saber de, tener noticia o conocimiento de; conocer de oídas.

knowable [nóabœl], *a.* conocible.

knower [nóœr], *s.* sabio, conocedor.

knowing [nóing], *a.* instruído, hábil, entendido; diestro; inteligente; sabihondo; como de quien sabe (gen. desp.). **II.** *s.* conocimiento.

knowingly [-li], *adv.* hábilmente; a sabiendas, con conocimiento de causa.

knowledge [nóley], *s.* conocimiento; erudición; inteligencia, destreza, pericia.—**to my k.**, que yo sepa.—**to the best of my k.**, según mi leal saber y entender.

known [nóun], *pp.* de TO KNOW.

Know-Nothing [-nózing], *s.* ignorante; (**K.-N.**), (hist. E. U.) miembro de un partido secreto (llamado **Know-Nothingism**) opuesto a la naturalización de extranjeros.

knuckle [núcœl]. **I.** *s.* coyuntura, articulación de los dedos; jarrete de ternero; (mec.) charnela; (mar.) codillo de una curva. **II.** *vn.* someterse, rendirse; abandonar la partida.

knuckled [núcœld], *a.* nudoso.

knur(l [nœr(l], *s.* nudo, protuberancia.

knurled [nœrld], *a.* nudoso.

kob [cob], *s.* antílope africano.

kobold [kóbold], *s.* gnomo.

kodak [kódæk], **I.** *s.* (fot.) kodak. **II.** *va.*. (fot.) sacar una instantánea de.

kohl rabi [cóul ræbi], *s.* (bot.) colirrábano.

komitaji [cómitáyi], *s.* guerrillero balcánico.

kopeck [kópek], *s.* = COPECK.

Koran [korán o córan], *s.* Corán.

kotow [kotáu], *s.* reverencia o saludo de los chinos.

koumiss, *s.* = KUMISS.

kraal [kral], *s.* población de hotentotes; corral, redil.

kremlin [krémlin], *s.* kremlín, fortaleza de una ciudad rusa.

kreasote [kríasot], *s.* = CREOSOTE.

krypton [crípton], *s.* cripto.

Ku-Klux Klan [kiú clux clæn], *s.* (E. U.) sociedad secreta organizada en los estados del Sur después de la guerra civil para hostigar, amedrentar y alejar a los negros y a sus defensores, y revivida más tarde para hostilizar a los negros, judíos, católicos y extranjeros. Ll. t. **Ku-Klux** o **Kuklux**.

kultur [cultúær], *s.* cultura, civilización.

kumiss, koomiss [kúmis, *s.* kumis, leche fermentada de burra.

Kurd [cœrd], *s.* y *a*, **Kurdish** [-diśh], *a.* kurdo.

kyanize, kyanise [káianaiś], *va.* dar a la madera un baño de sublimado corrosivo.

kymograph [cáimograf], *s.* instrumento para medir los movimientos de rotación de un aeroplano.

Kyrie [kírii], *s.* (igl.) kirie.—**K. eleison**, kirie-leisón.

kyriologic(al [kiriolóvic(al], *a.* kiriológico; simbólico.

L

l (el), *s.* l.

L [el]. **I.** *s.* ferrocarril elevado o aéreo; tubo en L o de ángulo recto. **II.** *a.* de o relativo a ferrocarril aéreo; en L, en forma de L.—**L.-head**, (m. comb. int.) culata en L, culata con válvulas de un mismo lado.—**L-square**, escuadra de carpintero.

la [la], *s.* (mús.) la.

labarum [læbarum], *s.* lábaro; norma.

labefaction [læbefǽcắhʊn], s. decadencia, decaimiento; enflaquecimiento; declinación.

label [lébœl]. **I.** s. marbete, rótulo. **II.** va. rotular o marcar; poner marbete o rótulo a; designar, clasificar.

labellum [labélʊm], s. (bot.) labelo; (ent.) parte de la trompa de un insecto díptero.

labial [léibial]. **I.** a. labial; que tiene bordes. **II.** s. letra labial.

labiate(d [lébiet(ed], a. y s. (bot.) labiado.

labiodental [lebiodéntal]. **I.** a. labiodental. **II.** s. articulación labiodental.

labionasal [lebionéssal]. **I.** a. labionasal. **II.** s. sonido labionasal.

labium [lébiʊm], s. (pl. LABIA) labio.

laboratory [léboratori], s. laboratorio; (mil.) taller de maestranza.

labo(u)r [léibœr]. **I.** s. trabajo; las clases obreras; tarea, faena; obra; quehacer, tráfago; aprieto, apuro; dolores de parto; (mar.) balanceo y cabeceo de un buque.—**L. Party**, (Ingl.) laborismo, partido obrero.—**l.-saving**, que ahorra trabajo. **II.** vn. trabajar; forcejar; estar de parto; (mar.) balancearse, cabecear, trabajar el buque contra mar y viento. **III.** va. elaborar, labrar, fabricar, pulir, perfeccionar; hacer trabajar, activar.

labo(u)red [léibœrd], a. hecho con dificultad; forzado, antinatural.

labo(u)rer [léibœrœr], s. peón, jornalero, bracero; trabajador.

labo(u)ring [léibœring], **I.** s. trabajo, esfuerzo. **II.** a. trabajador; de trabajo.—**l. beast**, bestia de carga.

laborious [labóriʊs], a. laborioso, trabajoso, difícil, arduo; diligente, industrioso.—**laboriously** [-li], adv. laboriosamente.—**laboriousness** [-nes], s. laboriosidad, diligencia; dificultad.

Labo(u)rite [léibœrait], s. (Ingl.) laborista, miembro o defensor del partido del trabajo o laborista (Labour Party).

labo(u)rsome [léibœrsʊm], a. trabajoso, penoso, ímprobo, arduo.

labradorite [lébradorait], s. (min.) labradorita.

labrum [lébrʊm], s. (ent.) labro.

laburnum [labérnʊm], s. (bot.) laburno.

labyrinth [lébirinʒ], s. laberinto, dédalo; (anat.) laberinto.

labyrinthic [-ínʒic], **labyrinthian** [-ínʒiæn], a. laberíntico, intrincado.

lac [læc], s. laca.

lace [léis]. **I.** s. encaje; cuerda; cordón, cinta; cordón del corsé o del zapato.—**l. bobbin**, pasillo o majaderillo.—**l. frame**, telar para hacer encajes.—**l. pillow**, almohadilla para encajes.—**l.-winged**, provisto de alas como de gasa o encaje. **II.** va. atar, ajustar, abrochar (corsé, zapatos, vestidos, etc.) con lazos o cordones; acordonar, enlazar; galonear, guarnecer con encajes, galones o cordones; entrelazar; rayar con líneas muy finas; (fam.) azotar.—**laced ruffles**, vueltas de encaje.

Lacedæmonian [læsedemóniæn], s. y a. lacedemonio.

laceman [léismæn], s. pasamanero.

lacerable [lésœrabœl], a. que se puede lacerar.

lacerate [lésœreit], va. lacerar, despedazar; lastimar.—**laceration** [-éishʊn], s. laceración, desgarradura.

lacertian [lasœrshan]. **I.** a. lacertídeo. **II.** s. lagarto.

lacewing [léisuing], s. (ent.) crisopo.

lacewoman [léisúmæn], s. vendedora de encajes, randas, etc.; pasamanera.

lachrymal, lachrymary, etc., = LACRIMAL, etc.

lacing [léising], s. acto de atar con cordones, en particular el uso de corsés; cordón, cordoncillo; pieza de espaldar, curva de barco; (fam.) zurra, tunda.

lacinia [lasínia], s. (bot.) lacinia.

laciniate(d [lasíniet(ed], a. laciniado.

lack [læc]. **I.** va. y vn. carecer, necesitar, faltar. **II.** s. falta, carencia, escasez, necesidad.

lackadaisical [lækadéishical], a. sentimental, lánguido.

lackaday [lékadéi], interj. ¡mal día! ¡día aciago! ¡mal haya!

lackbrain [lécbrein], s. simple, pelele.

lacker [lékœr], s. = LACQUER.

lackey [léki]. **I.** s. lacayo. **II.** va. y vn. servir como lacayo; ser criado.

lacking [léking], a. falto, defectuoso.—**to be l.**, faltar.

lacklove [léclʊv], s. desamorado.

lackluster [léclustœr], a. deslustrado.

laconic(al [lacónic(al], a. lacónico.—**laconically** [-i], adv. lacónicamente.—**laconism** [léconism], s. laconismo.

lacquer [lékœr]. **I.** va. barnizar; dar laca. **II.** s. laca.—**l.**, o **l. work**, objetos de laca.

lacquering [lékœring], s. barnizado de laca.

lacrimal [lécrimal]. **I.** a. lacrimal, lagrimal. **II.** s. (anat.) lagrimal.—**lacrimary** [-meri], a. lacrimal.—**lacrimation** [-méishʊn], s. llanto, lloro.—**lacrimatory** [-matori], a. lacrimatorio.—**lacrymose** [-mos], a. lacrimoso.

lacrosse [lacrós], s. cierto juego de pelota común en el Canadá.

lactary [léctari]. **I.** a. lácteo, lactario. **II.** s. lechería.

lactate [léctet]. **I.** s. (quím.) lactato. **II.** va. convertir en leche. **II.** vn. lactar, amamantar.

lactation [lactéishʊn], s. lactancia, crianza; lactación.

lacteal [lécteal], a. lácteo, quilífero.

lacteous [lécteʊs], a. lácteo, lactario.

lactescence [lactésens], s. lactescencia.

lactescent [lactésent], a. lácteo, lactario.

lactic [léctic], a. láctico.

lactiferous [lactífœrʊs], a. lactífero, lechal.

lactifuge [léctifiur], s. lactífugo.

lactometer [lactómetœr], s. lactómetro.

lactone [léctoun], s. (quím.) lactona.

lactoscope [léctoscoup], s. lactoscopio.

lactose [-tous], s. lactosa, azúcar de leche.

lactucarium [læctiukériʊm], s. (farm.) lactucario.

lactumen [læctiúmen], s. (med.) lactumen.

lacuna [lakiúna], s. laguna, espacio; hoyo o hueco.

lacunar, lacunal [lakiúnar, -nal], **lacunose** [lækiunos], a. que tiene lagunas, claros u hoyos.

lacunar, s. lagunar, lacunario, artesonado.

lacustral, lacustrine [lacústral, trin], a. lacustre.

lad [léd], s. mozo, mozalbete.

ladanum [lédanʊm], a. ládano.

ladder [lédœr], s. escalera, escala.—**l. ropes**, brandales.

lade [léid]. **I.** s. canal de desagüe; embocadero, desembocadero. **II.** va. (pp. LADED O LADEN) cargar; achicar; echar en. **III.** vn. (mar.) hacer agua.

laden [léidn], a. cargado; abrumado, oprimido.

ladies' man [léidis mæn], s. hombre de salón, hombre galante.

lading [léiding], s. acción de cargar; carga, cargamento; achicamiento.

ladle [léidœl], s. cucharón, cuchara grande; cazo; (fund.) cazo o cuchara de colada; (hidr.) álabe, paleta; (arti.) cuchara. **II.** va. achicar; sacar o servir con cucharón.—**ladleful** [-ful], s. cucharada.

lady [léidi], s. señora, dama; (Ingl.) voz de tratamiento que se da a la esposa o hija de algún título del reino.—**l.** q. adjetivadamente para indicar sexo: a lady doctor, una doctora; a lady friend, una amiga.—**l. fern**, helecho hembra.—**l. finger**, L.'s FINGER; especie de torta o bizcocho largo y angosto.—**l. in attendance**, camarera mayor.—**l. in waiting**, azafata de una reina o princesa.—**l.-killer**, Don Juan, Tenorio; galanteador, coquetón.—**l. love** = LADYLOVE.—**l. of the house**, ama o señora de la casa.—**l.'s-bower**, (bot.) la especie británica de la clemátide.—**l.'s-finger**, (bot.) vulneraria; guisante silvestre; aplícase también a variedades de manzanas, uvas, etc.—**l.'s maid**, doncella.—**l.'s-mantle**, (bot.) estrellada.—**l.'s-slipper**, (bot.) zueco, planta orquídea.—

l.'s-smock, (bot.) cardamina.—l. superior, supe‐
riora.—l.'s thumb, (bot.) persicaria.

ladybird [léidibœrd], ladybug [-búg], ladycow
[-cáu], ladyfly [flái], s. (ento.) coquito de San
Antón, mariquita.

ladylike [-láic], a. delicado, tierno, elegante; afe‐
minado, amujerado.

ladylove [-lúv], s. amada, mujer querida.

ladyship [-ship], sf. (Ingl.) señoría, tratamiento
que se da a las esposas e hijas de títulos de
reino.

lag [læg]. I. a. rezagado, postrero, último. II. s.
(mec.) retardación de movimiento; listón de
revestimiento o de forro de caldera.—l. screw,
tornillo para madera con cabeza poligona. III. vn.
retrasarse; remolonear, roncear, rezagarse; que‐
darse atrás.

lager [lágœr], s. especie de cerveza.

laggard [lǽgard], lagger [lǽgœr], a. y s. tardo,
perezoso, holgazán.

lagging [lǽguing], s. movimiento retardado;
listones de madera con que se forman reves‐
timientos, forros, cubiertas, etc.

lagoon [lagún], s. laguna, lagunajo, charca.

laic(al [léic(al], a. laico, lego, secular, seglar.—
laic, s. lego, seglar.

laid [léid], pret. y pp. de TO LAY.

lain [léin], pp. del verbo TO LIE.

lair [léœr], s. cubil; cueva de fieras.

laird [léœrd], s. lord; hacendado.

laitance [léitáns], s. exudación o excreción gelati‐
nosa del cemento y el hormigón.

laity [léiti], s. los legos.

lake [léik], s. lago; (pint.) laca.—l. dweller,
hombre lacustre.—l. dwelling, habitación la‐
custre.

lakelet [léklet], s. laguna, laguito.

lama [láma], s. lama (sacerdote).

la(ma)ism [lá(ma)ism], s. lamaísmo.

Lamarckian [lœmárkiœn], a. de Lamarck.

lamb [læm], s. cordero, borrego.—l. fry, turma,
criadilla.—l.'s-lettuce, (bot.) macha, valerianilla.

lambative [lǽmbativ]. I. a. que se lame. II. s.
(fam.) lamedor.

lambent [lǽmbent], a. ligero, undulante; ra‐
diante.

lambkin [lǽmkin], s. corderito.

lamblike [-láic], a. manso; inocente; sumiso.

lambrequin [lǽmbœrkin], s. guardamalleta, so‐
brepuerta.

lambskin [lǽmskin], s. corderina.

lame [léim]. I. a. cojo, renco; lisiado, estropea‐
do, derrengado; imperfecto.—l. account, relación
imperfecta.—l. duck, persona incapacitada; deu‐
dor insolvente.—l. excuse, disculpa frívola.—l.
expression, expresión manca.—l. verses, versos
cojos o defectuosos.—to go l., cojear, andar co‐
jeando. II. va. lisiar, estropear; encojar, derrengar.

lamella [laméla], s. laminilla; hojuela.

lamellar [lǽmelar], a. laminar.

lamellate(d [-leit(ed], a. laminado; hojaldrado.

lamellibranch [lǽmélibrænk], s. y a. (zool.)
lamelibranquio.—Lamellibranchia [-kiœ], La‐
mellibranchiata [-kiétœ], s. pl. lamelibranquios.

lamellicorn [-corn], s. y a. lamelicornio.

lamelliform [-form], a. lameliforme.

lamely [léimli], adv. con cojera; defectuosa‐
mente; débilmente.

lameness [léimnes], s. cojera, derrengadura;
falta, defecto, imperfección.

lament [lament]. I. va. y vn. lamentar(se);
plañir, dolerse. II. s. lamento, queja.

lamentable [lǽmentabœl], a. lamentable, deplo‐
rable.—lamentably [-bli], adv. lamentablemente.—
lamentation [-éishun], s. lamentación, lamento.

lamented [lǽménted], a. lamentado.—lamenter
[-tœr], s. lamentador.—lamenting [-ting], s. la‐
mentación.

lamina [lǽmina], s. lámina, hoja.—laminable
[-nabœl], a. laminable.—laminar [-nar], a. lami‐
nar.—laminate(d [-net(ed], a. laminado.

laminitis [-náitis], s. (vet.) despeadura.

Lammas [lǽmas], s. (igl.) festividad del día
primero de agosto.

lammergeier [lǽmœrgayœr], s. (orn.) quebran‐
tahuesos.

lamp [læmp], s. lámpara; farol; linterna.—l.
burner, mechero, piquera.—l. chimney, tubo de
lámpara.—l. globe, globo.—l. holder, porta‐
lámparas.—l. post, pie de farol de la calle.—l.
shade, pantalla de lámpara.

lampass [lǽmpas], s. (vet.) inflamación en la
parte superior de la boca de los caballos.

lampblack [lǽmpblæc], s. negro de humo.

lampers [lǽmpœrs], s. = LAMPASS.

lamplight [lǽmplait], s. luz de una lámpara; luz
artificial.—lamplighter [-œr], s. farolero, lampa‐
rero; encendedor, cerillero.

lampoon [læmpún]. I. s. pasquín, libelo. II. va.
satirizar, pasquinar.—lampooner [-œr], s. escritor
de pasquines.

lamprey [lǽmpri], s. (ict.) lamprea.

lanary [lénari], s. almacén para lana.

lanate(d [léinet(ed], a. lanoso; (bot.) lanudo.

lance [lans]. I. s. lanza; pica, asta; lanceta;
lancetazo, lanzada; lanza, lancero.—l. bucket,
cuja. II. va. lancear, dar una lanzada; penetrar,
cortar; (cir.) abrir con lanceta.

lanceolate [lǽnseolet], a. lanceolado.

lancer [lánsœr], s. alanceador; (mil.) lancero.—
pl. = LANCIERS.

lancet [lánset], s. (cir.) lanceta; (arq.) arco
puntiagudo; (ent.) trompetilla.

lancewood [lánsud], s. palo de lanza; (bot.) yaya.

lanch [lanch], va. lanzar. V. LAUNCH.

lanciers [lánsiœrs], s. pl. (danz.) lanceros.

lancinate [lǽnsineit], va. lancinar.—lancination
[-éishun], s. dolor lancinante.

land [lænd]. I. s. tierra; terreno; suelo, terruño;
l. agent, corredor de fincas rurales.—l. forces,
fuerzas terrestres.—l. jobbing, especulación en
la compra y venta de bienes raíces.—l. measure,
medidas agrarias.—l. office, oficina del catastro.—
l. of promise, tierra prometida o de promisión.—
l. plane, (aer.) avión terrestre, o de tierra.—l.
poor, poseedor de muchas tierras improductivas.
—l. surveying, topografía; agrimensura.—l. sur‐
veyor, agrimensor.—l. tax, contribución terri‐
torial.—l. waiter, guardapuerto, guardacostas.—
l. wind, terral. II. va. y vn. desembarcar.

landau [lǽndou], s. (carr.) landó.

landed [lǽnded], a. hacendado.

landfall [lǽndfol], s. herencia de tierras; des‐
prendimiento de tierras; (mar.) recalada; (aer.)
aterrizaje.

landgrave [lǽndgréiv], s. langrave.

landgraviate [-iet], s. langraviato.

landholder [lǽndjóuldœr], s. hacendado, terra‐
teniente.

landing [lǽnding]. I. s. descanso (de escalera);
desembarque; desembarcadero o apeadero;
(aer.) aterrizadero, aterrizaje. II. a. de desem‐
barque; de aterrizaje.—l. gear, (aer.) subestruc‐
tura (de un aeroplano), armazón de sustentación
en tierra, tren de aterrizaje.—l. net, red para alzar
un pescado cogido con el anzuelo.—l. wire, (aer.)
cable de toma de tierra.

landlady [lǽndléidi], s. ama, casera, mesonera,
posadera, patrona; arrendadora, propietaria.

landless [lǽndles], a. sin bienes o sin tierras; sin
fortuna, pobre.

landlocked [lǽndloct], a. cercado de tierra.

landloper [lǽndloupœr], s. venturero, vaga‐
mundo. V. LANDLUBBER.

landlord [lǽndlord], s. propietario o dueño de
tierras o casas; arrendador; amo, huésped,
posadero o casero, patrón; patrón.—landlordism [-ism], s.
autoridad del propietario; hacendados en general.

landlubber [lǽndlúbœr], s. (despec.) marinero
bisoño.

land(s)man [lǽnd(s)man], s. el que vive en tierra.

landmark [lǽndmark], s. mojón, marca, coto;
punto o acontecimiento culminante; progreso
o rasgo sobresaliente.—pl. (mar.) marcas.

landowner [lǽndóunœr], s. hacendado, terra‐
teniente, propietario.

landplane [-pléin], s. (aer.) aeroplano de tierra
o terrestre (a distinción del hidroaeroplano).

landscape [lǽndskeip], s. paisaje, campiña, vista; (pint.) paisaje.

landslide, landslip [lǽndslaid, slip], s. derrumbamiento, derrumbe.

Landsturm [lántshtúrm], s. (mil.) leva, enganche general; últimas reservas.

landward [lǽnduard], adv. hacia tierra.

Landwehr [lántvéær], s. milicia disciplinada licenciada, que sirve de reserva en tiempo de guerra.

lane [léin], s. senda, vereda; calle, callejuela.

langsyne [lángsáin]. **I.** adv. mucho ha, tiempo ha. **II.** s. tiempo, tiempos (en la expresión escocesa auld langsyne, o auld lang syne, los felices tiempos de antaño).

language [lǽngüey], s. lenguaje; idioma.

languaged [lǽngüeyd], a. poligloto.

Languedocian [lǽngüedóšhan], a. lemosín.

languet [lǽnguet], s. lengüeta, orejeta.

languid [lǽngüid], a. lánguido.—**languidly** [-li], adv. lánguidamente.—**languidness** [-nes], s. languidez.

languish [lǽngüišh], va. y vn. languidecer, extenuarse, consumirse; agostarse, ponerse mustio; aflojar, encalmarse; mirar con ternura.

languishing [-ing]. **I.** s. languidez, flaqueza. **II.** a. lánguido, afligido.—**languishingly** [-li], adv. lánguidamente.—**languishment** [-mœnt], s. languidez; consumimiento, angustia.

languor [lǽngœr], s. desfallecimiento, languidez, postración.

languorous [-us], a. lánguido, débil.

laniard [lǽñard], s. V. LANYARD.

laniary [léniæri]. **I.** a. propio para rasgar. **II.** s. colmillo, diente canino.

laniferous [laníferus], **lanigerous** [-yœrus], a. lanudo, lanoso, lanífero, lanuginoso.

lank [lænc], a. flaco, seco, descarnado; delgado.— **l. hair**, cabellos largos y lacios.—**lankly** [lǽncli], adv. flacamente.—**lankness** [lǽncnes], s. flacura; delgadez.—**lanky** [lǽnki], a. (fam.) larguirucho, langaruto, delgaducho.

lanner [lǽnœr], s. (orn.) alcotán, borní.

lanolin [lǽnolin], s. (farm.) lanolina.

lansquenet [lǽnskenet], s. sacanete; cascarela; (ant.) lancero de a pie.

lantana [læntéinæ], s. (bot.) lantana.

lantern [lǽntœrn], s. linterna, farol; (mar.) faro, fanal; (arq.) linterna.—**l. maker**, linternero.—**l. jack**, fuego fatuo.—**l. jaws**, quijadas de farol (apodo).—**l. jawed**, carienjuto.—**l. pinion**, o **wheel**, (mec.) piñón de linterna.—**l. slide**, diapositiva.

lanthanum [lǽnzanum], s. (quím.) lantano.

lanuginous [læniúyinus], a. lanuginoso.

lanyard [lǽñard], s. (mar.) acollador; cuerda, cabo; (arti.) cuerda y gancho de disparo.—**lanyards of the buoy**, rebenques de cabeza de la boya.—**lanyards of the stoppers**, mojeles de las hozas.

Laodicean [leódisían], a. laodicense; tibio, indiferente.

lap [læp]. **I.** s. falda; regazo; traslapo (dep.) vuelta completa de la pista o redondel; (mec.) rueda de amolar, pulir o labrar joyas o metales; lamedura; susurro del agua; (m. v.) recubrimiento (de la válvula de corredera).—**l. dog**, perrillo faldero.—**l.-eared**, de orejas gachas o pendientes.— **l. hemmer**, rebatidor.—**l. joint**, junta de solapa, de traslapo o de recubrimiento.—**l. seam**, (cost.) costura rebatida.—**l. table** = LAPBOARD. **II.** va. traslapar; recubrir; envolver, cubrir, rodear; juntar a traslapo; pulir, labrar; lamer; tocar, besar (apl. al agua). **III.** vn. traslaparse; susurrar.

laparotomy [læparótomi], s. (cir.) laparotomía.

lapboard [lǽpbórd], s. tabla faldera de sastre.

lapel [lapél], s. (sast.) solapa.

lapful [lǽpful], s. lo que puede caber en el regazo o enfaldo.

lapidary [lǽpideri]. **I.** s. lapidario. **II.** a. lapidario; inscrito sobre piedra; lapídeo.

lapidate [lǽpideit], va. labrar las piedras finas y preciosas.—**lapidation** [-déišhun], s. lapidación,

apedreamiento.—**lapidescence** [-désens], s. lapidificación.—**lapidescent** [-désent], a. que petrifica. —**lapidific** [-dific], a. lapidífico.—**lapidification** [-dínkéišhun], s. (quím.) lapidificación.—**lapidist** [-dist], s. lapidario.

lapis [lépis], s. procedimiento para estampar indianas con añil.—**l. infernalis**, piedra infernal, nitrato de plata.—**l. lazuli**, lapislázuli, lazulita.

Laplander [lǽplandœr], s. lapón.

lapling [lǽpling], s. (despec.) hombre ocioso o salaz.

Lap(p [læp], s. lapón.

lappet [lǽpet], s. caídas de toca o escofieta; moco de pavo.

lapsable [lǽpsabœl], a. (for.) prescriptible; susceptible de caer.

lapse [læps]. **I.** s. caída, lapso; intervalo de tiempo, curso, transcurso; desliz, traspié, equivocación, falta; (for.) prescripción; translación de derecho o dominio.—**in the l. of time**, con el transcurso del tiempo, andando el tiempo. **II.** vn. pasar, transcurrir; decaer, deslizarse; caer en algún defecto, desliz o error; (for.) prescribir, caducar.

lapsed [læpst], a. caído; deslizado; cumplido, caducado; omitido; prescrito.

lapstone [lǽpstóun], piedra de batir el cuero.

lapwing [lǽpuing], s. (orn.) frailecico.

lapwork [lǽpuœrk], s. obra entrelazada o entretejida.

lar, 2 s. (pl. LARES) lar, dios doméstico.—**l. watch**, guardia de babor.

larboard [lárbord], s. (mar.) babor.—**l. watch**, guardia de babor.

larcener, larcenist [lársnœr, -ist], s. ladrón, ratero.

larceny [lárseni], s. (for.) ratería, hurto.

larch, s. (bot.) alerce, lárice.

lard [lard]. **I.** s. manteca de puerco.—**l. oil**, aceite de manteca de cerdo. **II.** va. (coc.) mechar; lardar o lardear; entreverar, guarnecer.

lardaceous [lardéšhus], a. lardoso, grasiento; (med.) craso, gordo.

larder [lárdœr], s. despensa, reposte.

larderer [lárdœrœr], s. despensero.

lardy [lárdi], a. graso, lardoso, mantecoso.

large [larv]. **I.** a. grande; liberal, espléndido; pródigo; lleno, fuerte (pulso); largo (viento).— **l.-handed**, de manos grandes; codicioso; liberal, dadivoso.—**l.-hearted**, magnánimo, desprendido o generoso.—**l.-minded**, de ideas liberales.— **l.-size(d)**, grande, de tamaño grande.—**at l.**, en libertad, suelto; extensamente; sin limitación, libre; al acaso; (E. U.) que representa un todo (estado, región, etc.), a distinción del que representa una de las divisiones (distrito electoral, etc.) **II.** adv. (mar.) con viento a la cuadra; (fam.) con jactancia.

largely [lárylil], adv. grandemente; liberalmente; ampliamente; mayormente; en gran manera, considerablemente; muy.

largeness [lárynes], s. grandor, calidad de grande; liberalidad; grandeza de ánimo.

largess [láryes], s. don, dádiva, regalo; largueza.

larghetto [larguéto], a. y s. (mús.) lento.

largo [lárgo], a. y s. (mús.) largo, lento.

lariat [lériæt], s. reata; lazo, mangana.

lark [larc], s. (orn.) alondra, calandria; (fam.) calaverada, francachela, parranda, holgorio.—**l. mirror**, espejuelo.—**to be, o to go, on a l.**, andar de parranda; echar una cana al aire.

larkspur [lárkspœr], s. (bot.) espuela de caballero, consólida real.

larrup [lǽrup], va. (fam.) zurrar, tundir.

larva [lárva], s. larva.—**larval** [-l], a. larval.

larvate(d [lárvet(ed], a. (med.) larvado.

laryngeal [larínyial], a. laríngeo.

laryngitis [lærinyái- (o yí) tis], s. (med.) laringitis.

laryngology [læringóloyi], s. laringología.

laryngoscope [laríngoscop], s. laringoscopio.

laryngoscopy [læringóscopi], s. laringoscopia.

laryngotomy [-gótomi], s. (cir.) laringotomía.

larynx [lérincs], s. (anat.) laringe.

lascar [læscár], s. láscar.

---

lascivious [lᴂsívius], *a.* lascivo.—**lasciviously** [-li], *adv.* lascivamente.—**lasciviousness** [-nes], *s.* lascivia.

lash [læsh]. **I.** *s.* látigo; azote, latigazo; chasquido; sarcasmo, invectiva; embate de las olas; pestaña. **II.** *va.* dar latigazos; azotar; romper contra (como las olas); satirizar, censurar, reprochar; (mar.) amarrar, ligar, trincar. **III.** *vn.* chasquear el látigo.—**to l. out**, desenfrenarse, desordenarse.

lashing [lᴂshing], *s.* ligadura, atadura; (mar.) amarra, amarradura; castigo de azotes.—**l. rings**, (mar.) argollas de amura.—**l. rope**, braga.

lasket [lᴂsket], *s.* (mar.) badaza de boneta.

lass [læs], *s.* doncella, moza, muchacha.

lassie [lᴂsi], *f.* muchachita, mozuela.

lassitude [lᴂsitiud], *s.* lasitud.

lasso [lᴂso]. **I.** *va.* lazar, manganear. **II.** *s.* lazo, mangana, guaso.

lassoer [lásœr], *s.* lazador.

last [læst]. **I.** *a.* último; pasado (*last week*, la semana pasada; *March last*, el marzo pasado). **l. but not least**, último en orden pero no en importancia.—**l. but one**, penúltimo.—**l. but two**, antepenúltimo.—**l. day**, día del juicio.—**l. evening**, anoche, ayer por la noche.—**l. honors**, honores fúnebres.—**L. Judgment**, juicio final.—**l. night**, anoche.—**L. Supper**, última cena (de Jesucristo).—**at l.**, por fin, al fin, al cabo.—**to the l.**, hasta el fin, hasta lo último. **II.** *adv.* la última vez, finalmente, al fin. **III.** *s.* fin, término; durabilidad; (lo, el) último; (zap.) horma. **IV.** *vn.* durar, perdurar.

lastage [lástey], *s.* (mar.) espacio para la estiva; cargamento; lastre.

laster [lástœr], *s.* (zap.) ahormador.

lasting [lásting]. **I.** *a.* duradero, durable, constante, perdurable. **II.** *s.* (tej.) sempiternas.—**lastingly** [-li], *adv.* para siempre.—**lastingness** [-nes], *s.* duración, calidad de durable.

lastly [lástli], *adv.* en conclusión, por fin, finalmente, por último.

lastmaker [lástméikœr], *s.* hormero.

latch [læch]. **I.** *s.* aldaba, aldabilla, cerrojo, picaporte. **II.** *va.* cerrar con aldaba; colar con lejía.

latchet [lᴂcnet], *s.* agujeta o cordón de zapato.

latchkey [lᴂchkí], *s.* llavín.

latchstring [lᴂchstríng], *s.* cordón de aldaba.—**the l. is out**, venga Vd. cuando guste; será Vd. siempre bienvenido.

late [léit]. **I.** *a.* tardío; postrero, lejano; tardo, lento; último, postrero; difunto; reciente, moderno.—**l. arrival**, recién llegado.—**l. in years**, de edad provecta. **II.** *adv.* tarde; poco ha, últimamente; antes.—**l. in the year**, al fin del año.—**of l.**, recientemente, últimamente.—**to be l.**, llegar tarde; estar atrasado; ser tarde.

lateen [latín], *a.*—**l. sail**, (mar.) vela latina o de burro.

lately [léitli], *adv.* poco ha, no ha mucho; recientemente, últimamente.

latency [léitensi], *s.* estado latente.

lateness [léitnes], *s.* calidad de tardo o de reciente.

latent [léitent], *a.* latente.

later [léitœr], *adv.* y *a.* (*comp.* de LATE) más tarde; luego, después; posterior, subsecuente. **l. on**, más tarde, después.

lateral [lᴂtœral], *a.* lateral.—**laterally** [-i], *adv.* lateralmente.

Lateran [lᴂteran], *a.* lateranense.

laterite [lᴂtœrait], *s.* arcilla roja ferruginosa.

latescent [latésent], *a.* que se va obscureciendo u ocultando.

latest [léitest], *a.* y *adv.* (*superl.* de LATE) último; novísimo.

latex [léitex], *s.* (bot.) látex, jugo lechoso y viscoso.

lath [laz]. **I.** *s.* (alb.) lata, listón. **II.** *va.* (alb.) listonar, hacer un enlatado a o en.

lathe [léiƌ], *s.* (mec.) torno; (tej.) marco de telar.—**l. bed**, banco del torno.—**l. dog**, trinquete de mandril.—**l. drill**, torno de taladrar.

lather [lᴂƌœr]. **I.** *va.* enjabonar para afeitar; (fam.) azotar. **II.** *s.* jabonadura, espuma de jabón. **III.** *vn.* espumar, hacer espuma.

lathing [lᴂzing], *s.* (alb.) enlatado, enlistonado.

lathy [lᴂzi], *a.* largo y delgado como un listón.

Latin [lᴂtin]. **I.** *a.* latino. **II.** *s.* latín.—**Latinism** [-ism], *s.* latinismo.—**Latinist** [-ist], *s.* latinista.—**Latinity** [latíniti], *s.* latinidad.—**Latinize** [lᴂtinais]. **I.** *va.* latinizar. **II.** *vn.* emplear latinismos.

latish [léitish], *a.* (fam.) algo tarde, tardecito.

latirostrous [lᴂtiróstrus], *a.* (orn.) latirrostro.

latitude [lᴂtitiud], *s.* latitud, anchura; difusión; amplitud; laxitud; libertad; (geog.) latitud.

latitudinal [-tiúdinal], *a.* latitudinal.

latitudinarian [-tiudinérian], *a.* y *s.* latitudinario.—**latitudinarianism** [-ism], *s.* latitudinarismo.

latria [latráia], *s.* culto de latría.

latrine [lᴂtrín], *s.* letrina.

latten [lᴂten], *s.* latón en láminas; metal en lámina.—*pl.* láminas metálicas muy delgadas.

latter [lᴂtœr], *a.* posterior, más reciente, moderno.—**l.-day**, de nuestros días.—**L.-Day Saints**, mormones.—**the l.**, éste, esto.

latterly [-li], *adv.* recientemente; poco ha.

lattice [lᴂtis]. **I.** *va.* enrejar, poner celosías; entrelazar, entretejer. **II.** *s.* celosía, enrejado de listoncillos.—**l. bar**, listón de celosía, listón de sujeción (apl. esp. a los que, trabados, unen dos piezas paralelas de una construcción).—**l. bridge**, puente de celosía.—**l. girder, l. truss**, viga de celosía.—**l. web**, alma de celosía.

Latvian [lᴂtvian], *s.* y *a.* latvio, de Latvia.

laud [lod]. **I.** *s.* (igl.) laudes. **II.** *va.* alabar, loar, elogiar.

laudability [lódabíliti], **laudableness** [-bœlnes], *s.* calidad de laudable.—**laudable** [-bœl], *a.* laudable, loable.—**laudably** [-bli], *adv.* laudablemente.

laudanum [lódanum], *s.* láudano.

laudative, laudatory [lodativ tori]. **I.** *a.* laudatorio. **II.** *s.* panegírico.

laugh [laf]. **I.** *vn.* reír, refrse.—**l. and lay down**, un juego de naipes.—**to l. at**, reírse de, mofarse, ridiculizar.—**to l. at one to his face**, reírsele a uno en las barbas.—**to l. in one's sleeve**, reírse interiormente.—**to l. out**, reírse a carcajadas. **II.** *va.* causar o hacer (salir, callar, dormir, cesar) a risa o a carcajadas; ahogar en o con risa.—**to l. away**, ahogar en risa; echar a risa o a risotadas.—**to l. down**, hacer callar a risotadas; matar o acabar con (una reforma, etc.) ridiculizando.—**to l. to scorn**, ridiculizar, poner en ridículo. **III.** *s.* risa; risotada.

laughable [láfabœl], *a.* risible; divertido.

laugher [láfœr], *s.* reidor.

laughing [láfing]. **I.** *s.* risa, reír. **II.** *a.* risueño, reidor.—**l. eyes**, ojos alegres, reidores.—**l. gas**, gas hilarante.—**l. jackass**, martín pescador insectívoro australiano.

laughingly [-li], *adv.* riendo, con risa.

laughingstock [-stóc], *s.* hazmerreír.

laughter [láftœr], *s.* risa.

launch [lanch]. **I.** *va.* botar o echar al agua; dar principio a, acometer; lanzar, arrojar. **II.** *vn.* arrojarse, salir, lanzarse. **III.** *s.* (mar.) botadura de un buque; lanzamiento; (mar.) lancha, chalupa.

launder [lándœr], *va.* lavar la ropa.

launderer [lándœrœr], *s.* lavandero.

laundress [lándres], *s.* lavandera.

laundry [lándri], *s.* lavadero; lavandería, establecimiento de lavar ropa; tren de lavado; (fam.) ropa lavada. **II.** *va.* lavar y planchar (la ropa).

laureate [lórieit], *a.* laureado.

laureateship [lorieitship], *s.* dignidad de poeta laureado.

laureation [-éishun], *s.* acto de recibir algún grado académico.

laurel [lórel], *s.* (bot.) laurel; lauro, lauréola; honor, distinción.

laurelled [lóreld], *a.* laureado.

Laurentian [lorénshæn], *s.* y *a.* (geol.) laurentino.

laurestine [lórestin], **laurestinus** [lórestáinus], s. (bot.) durillo.

lauric [lóric], a. láurico.

lava [láva], s. lava.

lavation [lavéshun], s. lavadura, lavatorio, lavado.

lavatory [lǽvatori], s. lavatorio; loción.

lave [léiv], va. y vn. lavar(se), bañar(se)].—**to l. water**, sacar agua.

lavender [lǽvendœr], s. (bot.) espliego, alhucerna, lavándula; color de alhucema.—**l. cotton**, santolina.—**l. water**, agua de lavanda.

laver [léivœr], s. aguamanil, jofaina, palangana; ova, alga comestible.

lavish [lǽvish]. I. a. pródigo, gastador; profuso. II. va. disipar, malbaratar, prodigar.—**lavisher** [-œr], s. pródigo, gastador.—**lavishly** [-li], adv. pródigamente.—**lavishment, lavishness** [-mœnt, nes], s. prodigalidad, profusión.

lavolta [lavólta], s. antigua danza.

law [lo], s. ley; código de leyes; jurisprudencia, derecho, leyes (en general); tora o libro de la ley judía; (bib.) ley (de Moisés, del Antiguo Testamento).—**l.-abiding**, observante de la ley.— **l. day**, día en que están abiertos los tribunales.— **l. of definite proportions**, ley de las proporciones definidas.—**l. of diminishing return**, (e. p.) ley de que, pasado cierto límite, los productos de la tierra dejan de aumentar proporcionalmente al aumento de capital y trabajo que se le consagre.— **l. of multiple proportions**, ley de las proporciones múltiples.—**l. of nations**, derecho internacional; derecho de gentes.—**l. of nature**, ley natural.—**l. school**, escuela de derecho.—**laws of motion**, leyes del movimiento.—**laws of war**, derecho de guerra.

lawbreaker [lóbréikœr], s. transgresor, violador de la ley.

lawful [lóful], a. legal, lícito, legítimo, conforme a la ley; permitido, válido.—**l. goods**, géneros permitidos o lícitos.—**l. prize**, presa legítima.

lawfully [lófuli], adv. legalmente, legítimamente, lícitamente.

lawfulness [lófulnes], s. legalidad, legitimidad.

lawgiver [lóguívœr], s. legislador.

lawless [lóles], a. ilegal; licencioso; foragido; desaforado.—**lawlessly** [-li], adv. ilegalmente; licenciosamente.—**lawlessness** [-nes], s. desorden, licencia; desobediencia.

lawmaker [lóméikœr], s. legislador.

lawmaking [-méiking]. I. s. legislación. II. a. legislativo.

lawn [lon]. I. s. prado, césped; linón, estopilla. —**l. hose**, manguera de regar.—**l. mower**, cortadora de césped.—**l. tennis**, tenis (juego). II. a. de linón.

lawny [lóni], a. que tiene campos de césped; hecho o vestido de linón.

lawsuit [lósiút], s. pleito, litigio, juicio.

lawyer [lóyœr], s. abogado, jurisconsulto.

lax [læcs], a. suelto, flojo, fláccido; laxo, relajado; vago, indeterminado; corriente de vientre.

laxation [læcséishun], s. laxación.

laxative [lǽxativ]. I. a. laxativo, laxante. II. s. laxante, purgante.

laxativeness [-nes], s. propiedad laxante.

laxity [lǽcsiti], **laxness** [lǽxnes], s. laxidad, laxitud; flaccidez, aflojamiento, flojedad; relajamiento; relajación, descuido, indiferencia.

laxly [lǽxli], adv. flojamente, sueltamente.

lay [léi], pret. de TO LIE.

lay [léi], va. (pret. y pp. LAID) poner, colocar; tender (tuberías, cables, etc.), instalar; derribar; poner (un huevo, la mesa, etc.); matar, asentar (el polvo); enterrar; calmar, aquietar, sosegar, apaciguar; propagar (las plantas); imponer (cargas, tributos, etc.); (impr.) poner; calzar; proyectar, trazar, discurrir; imputar, atribuir; apostar; exhibir, presentar, exponer, hacer manifiesto.—**to l. a bill on the table**, dar carpetazo a un proyecto de ley.—**to l. against**, acusar de achacar a.—**to l. apart**, reservar, poner aparte.—**to l. aside**, desechar, echar o poner a un lado; arrinconar, abandonar; ahorrar.—**to l. a**

wager, apostar.—**to l. away**, dejar, echar a un lado; guardar.—**to l. bare**, exponer, revelar, desnudar, poner al descubierto.—**to l. by**, poner a un lado, descartar; reservar, ahorrar.—**to l. claim to**, reclamar; pretender.—**to l. down**, abatir; abandonar; entregar, rendir, dimitir; sentar, formular; dictar, dar (la ley, etc.); proyectar; tragar; guardar, reservar; apostar.—**to l. eyes on**, ver.—**to l. hands on**, sentar la mano a, pegar a; tocar; coger, atrapar; (igl.) dar imposición de manos a, bendecir u ordenar por imposición de manos.—**to l. hold of**, asir, agarrar, coger; prender.—**to l. in**, proveerse de, comprar; bosquejar.—**to l. level**, igualar, allanar; arrasar.—**to l. off**, quitarse de encima; trazar, delinear; medir; despedir, suspender.—**to l. on**, descargar (golpes) sobre, pegar a; dar (pintura, etc.); distribuir (agua, gas); imponer a.—**to l. one's self out**, esforzarse.—**to l. open**, descubrir, revelar, demostrar.—**to l. out**, gastar, emplear, desembolsar; exhibir, mostrar; trazar; proyectar; disponer; arreglar; amortajar.—**to l. over**, cubrir, sobreponer; aplazar.—**to l. siege to**, sitiar; importunar.—**to l. stress on**, insistir o hacer hincapié en.—**to l. the blame on**, echar la culpa a.—**to l. to heart**, tomar a pechos.—**to l. up**, guardar, atesorar, reservar; obligar a guardar cama; encerrar; guardar, poner a un lado; desarmar.—**to l. wait**, formar emboscada; acechar.—**to l. waste**, asolar.

lay, vn. poner, aovar (las gallinas, etc.); apostar; (mar.) situarse, colocarse; (incorrecta pero muy frecuentemente TO LIE), acostarse, hallarse o estar acostado, etc.—**to l. about**, dar palos de ciego.—**to l. aft**, ir a popa.—**to l. by** = TO L. TO.— **to l. for**, (fam.) acechar.—**to l. off**, parar (en el trabajo).—**to l. on**, virar hacia.—**to l. out**, procurar, esforzarse.—**to l. over**, demorarse, detenerse; sobrepasar.—**to l. to**, (mar.) estar parado o flotando en la dirección del viento.

lay. I. a. laico, lego, secular, seglar; profano, incompetente.—**l. brother**, lego, converso, monigote.—**l. clerk**, capiscol, sochantre.—**l. days**, (mar.) estadía.—**l. figure**, maniquí.—**l. race**, (tej.) curso de la lanzadera.—**l. sister**, lega, freila. II. s. caída, sesgo, dirección; contorno; oficio, ocupación, negocio; cantidad determinada de hilo; (tej.) marco de telar; participación en una ganancia; trama (de un cable); canción, balada, lay.

layer [léœr]. I. s. capa; (ten.) tina de remojar; (agr.) serpa, acodo; gallina ponedora. II. va. (agr.) acodar.

layering [léiering], s. (agr.) acodadura.

layette [leyét], s. canastillo.

laying [léing]. I. s. colocación; postura (del huevo); (alb.) primera capa de un enlucido. II. a. situado; (mar.) anclado.—**l. hook**, manubrio del cordelero.—**l. on of hands**, imposición de manos.—**l. press**, (enc.) prensa de cepillo.—**l. top**, galápo.—**l. walk**, cordelería.

layman [léiman], s. lego, seglar.

layout [léiaut], s. (fam.) equipo; mesa puesta para un banquete; plan, disposición, arreglo.

laystall [léistol], s. establo.

lazar [léisar], s. leproso, lazarino.

lazaret [lǽsaret], **lazaretto** [-réto], **lazarhouse** [-jáus], s. lazareto.

lazily [léisili], adv. perezosamente.

laziness [léisines], s. pereza.

lazuli, s. V. LAPIS LAZULI.

lazy [léisi], a. perezoso.

lea [li], s. prado, pradera; llanura.

leach [lich]. I. va. lixiviar; colar la ropa. II. s. cenizas de lejía; lixiviación; colada.—**l., l. tub**, colador de ropa.

leachy [lichi], a. permeable, poroso.

lead [led]. I. s. núcleo o grafito del lápiz; (min.) plomo; (impr.) interlínea, regleta; (mar.) sondaleza, escandallo.—**l. pencil**, lápiz.—**l. pencil**, lápiz. II. va. (pret. y pp. LEADED) emplomar, forrar o guarnecer con plomo; (impr.) interlinear, regletear, espaciar verticalmente.

lead [lid]. I. s. primacía, primer lugar; dirección; mando; delantera; en el juego, mano; salida (palo que juega el que es mano). II. va. (pret. y pp. LED) llevar de la mano, de cabestro, etc.;

guiar, dirigir; mandar; ir a la cabeza de, (mús.) llevar la batuta; enseñar, amaestrar, adestrar; encauzar; derivar; llevar (buena, mala vida); atraer, inducir, mover; gastar o emplear el tiempo en alguna cosa.—**to l. along,** conducir, acompañar.— **to l. a new life,** enmendarse.—**to l. astray,** descarriar, seducir.—**to l. by the nose,** manejar a su gusto, llevar del cabestro, tener agarrado por las narices.—**to l. in,** o **into,** introducir en; llevar o conducir a.—**to l. off,** o **out,** desviar; principiar. —**to l. out of the way,** descarriar.—**to l. the way,** mostrar el camino, llevar la delantera, ir adelante. **III.** *vn.* mandar en jefe; guiar, enseñar el camino; sobresalir, ser el primero; ir adelante; conducir; dominar; ser mano en el juego de naipes.—**to l. off,** ir adelante; principiar.—**to l. on,** ir adelante, guiar, enseñar el camino.—**to l. up to,** conducir a.

leaded [léded], *pp.* y *a.* (impr.) interlineado; emplomado, plomado.

leaden [lédœn], *a.* plomizo, plomoso; aplomado; pesado.—**l.-footed,** lento, tardo.—**l.-hearted,** insensible, empedernido.—**l.-heeled, l.-stepping** =L.-FOOTED.—**l.-pated, l.-skulled,** lerdo, estúpido.

leader [lídœr], *s.* guía, conductor; guión; jefe, caudillo, cabecilla; (alb.) condutal, canalera; canalón; caballo delantero; (cine) tílvlo o letrero; (mús.) director de orquesta; primer violín; (impr.) puntos suspensivos; artículo de fondo; (mec.) rueda motriz; (min.) nervadura, vena, filón; (pesca) sedal corto de trifa unido al extremo del principal.

leadership [lídœrship], *s.* dirección.

lead-in [lid-in]. **I.** *a.* (elec.) de toma, de entrada. **II.** *s.* conductor de entrada; (rad.) parte vertical de una antena.

leading [líding]. **I.** *a.* principal, primero; capital; dominante, sobresaliente.—**l. edge,** (aer.) borde de ataque.—**l.-in,** (elec.) de entrada.—**l. man,** jefe, cabecilla.—**l. question,** pregunta que sugiere o insinúa la respuesta.—**l. strings,** andadores.—**l. wheels,** ruedas delanteras de una locomotora. **II.** *s.* guía, conducción; dirección de orquesta.

leading [léding], *s.* emplomadura; (impr.) interlineación.

leadsman [lédsman], *s.* (mar.) sondeador.

leadwort [lédœrt], *s.* (bot.) vclesa.

leady [lédi], *a.* aplomado, plomizo.

leaf [lif]. **I.** *s.* (*pl.* LEAVES [livs]) (bot.) hoja; hoja (de un libro, de una mesa, de puerta, etc.); hoja o plancha de metal.—**l. brass,** oropel.—**l. bud,** yema, botón de planta.—**l. lard,** manteca en rama. —**l. of gold, silver,** hoja o pan de oro, plata.—**l. tobacco,** tabaco en rama. **II.** *vn.* echar hojas; hacerse frondoso.

leafage [lifey], *s.* follaje, frondaje.

leafblade [lifbléid], *s.* lámina (parte ensanchada de la hoja).

leafed [lift], **leafy** [lifi], *a.* frondoso.

leafiness [lifines], *s.* follaje, frondaje.

leafless [lifles], *a.* afilo; deshojado.

leaflet [liflet], *s.* hojilla, hojuela.

leafstalk [lifstók], *s.* pecíolo, pezón.

league [lig]. **I.** *s.* liga, confederación; sociedad o asociación; pandilla.—**L. of Nations,** Sociedad de las Naciones. **II.** *va.* y *vn.* aliar(se); confederar(se) asociar(se).

leagued [lígd], *a.* confederado o aliado; conjurado.

leaguer [lígœr], *s.* miembro de una liga.

leak [lik]. **I.** *s.* gotera en un techo; fuga o escape de gas, vapor, etc.; salida, fuga (lugar por donde de algo se escapa); (mar.) vía de agua. **II.** *vn.* gotear; hacer agua; salirse, dejar escapar (el agua, vapor, etc.); tener fugas o salidas.—**to l. out,** saberse, traslucirse.

leakage [likey], *s.* escape, fuga, salida; (magn.) dispersión; (elec.) fuga, escape; (com.) avería, pérdida, merma, derrame.

leaky [liki], *a.* llovedizo; resquebrajado; que se sale o deja fugar el contenido; permeable; (mar.) que hace agua; (fam.) locuaz, indiscreto.

lean [lin]. **I.** *vn.* apoyarse, recostarse, inclinarse; ladearse, encorvarse.—**to l. on,** o **upon,** apoyarse en; buscar o tener apoyo en.—**to l. over,** incli-

narse. **II.** *va.* apoyar, reclinar; inclinar; encorvar. **III.** *a.* flaco; magro; pobre, improductivo; necesitado; pobre en cemento (apl. al hormigón y al mortero).—**l.-witted,** tonto, necio. **IV.** *s.* carne mollar, carne pulpa, carne magra; inclinación, propensión.

leaning [líning]. **I.** *a.* inclinado. **II.** *s.* (a veces en plural) inclinación, propensión, tendencia; preferencia.

leanly [línli], *adv.* pobremente; sin gordura.

leanness [línnes], *s.* flacura; magrez; pobreza.

lean-to [lin-tu], *s.* (arq.) colgadizo; tejado de una sola agua, o lo que lo tiene.

leap [líp]. **I.** *vn.* saltar, brincar; corvetear; brotar, salir con ímpetu; batir el corazón. **II.** *va.* saltar, cubrir el macho a la hembra. **III.** *s.* salto, brinco.—**l. day,** día intercalar.—**l. year,** año bisiesto.

leaper [lípœr], *s.* saltador, brincador.

leapfrog [lípfróg], *s.* a la una la mula (juego de muchachos).

learn [lœrn], *va.* y *vn.* (*pret.* y *pp.* LEARNED o LEARNT) aprender; enterarse de, tener noticia de, saber; instruirse.

learnable [lœrnabœl], *a.* que puede aprenderse.

learned [lœrned], *a.* docto, erudito, ilustrado; —**the l.,** los doctos.

learnedly [-li], *adv.* doctamente, eruditamente.

learner [-œr], *s.* aprendiz; alumno, estudiante.

learning [lœrning], *s.* saber, ciencia, erudición; aprendizaje.

leasable [lísabœl], *a.* arrendable.

lease [lis]. **I.** *s.* (for.) arriendo, escritura de arrendamiento, censo; locación, inquilinato; (tej.) paso, cruce. **II.** *va.* arrendar, dar en arriendo.

leasehold [lísjóuld], *n.* censo, inquilinato.

leash [lísh]. **I.** *s.* pihuela, traílla, correa; tres, par y medio; (tej.) lizo. **II.** *va.* atraillar.

least [líst]. **I.** *a.* (*sup.* de LITTLE) mínimo; el menor, el mínimo, el más pequeño.—**l. common multiple,** mínimo común múltiplo, menor múltiplo común.—**l. reading,** apreciación (de un nonio, etc.).—**l. squares,** mínimos cuadrados.—**at l.,** o **at the l.,** al menos, a lo menos, por lo menos.—**not in the l.,** de ninguna manera, bajo ningún concepto.—**the l.,** lo menos. **II.** *adv.* menos (*sup.*).

leather [lépœr]. **I.** *s.* cuero, cordobán. **II.** *a.* de cuero.—**l. beater,** batidor.—**l. belt,** correa.—**l. belting,** correaje.—**l. cutter,** vendedor de cuero por menor.—**l. dresser,** curtidor, noquero.—**l. shield,** adarga. **II.** *va.* forrar o guarnecer con cuero; hacer cuero; dar una tunda.

leatherette [lépœret], *s.* cuero artificial.

leatherhead [lépœrjéd], *s.* (orn.) frailecico; tonto, bodoque.

leathern [lépœrn], *a.* de cuero.

leatheroid [lépœroid], *s.* imitación de cuero, de fibra vegetal.

leathery [lépœri], *a.* coriáceo, correoso.

leave [lív]. **I.** *s.* licencia, permiso; despedida.— **l. of absence,** licencia.—**l.-taking,** despedida.—. **by your l.,** con permiso de Vd. **II.** *va.* (*pret.* y *pp.* LEFT) dejar; abandonar; salir o partir de; separarse de.—**to l. alone,** dejar quieto; no meterse con, no menealo.—**to l. behind,** dejar atrás; dejar en pos de sí.—**to l. in the lurch,** abandonar en un apuro.—**to l. no stone unturned,** no dejar piedra por mover.—**to l. off,** suspender; dejar (un vicio, una costumbre).—**to l. out,** omitir, excluir. —**to l. out in the cold,** dejar colgado, olvidarse de.—**to l. undone,** no hacer, dejar de hacer; dejar sin terminar. **II.** *vn.* irse; salir; partir: (gen. con *off*) cesar, desistir; (*pret.* y *pp.* LEAVED) echar hojas.

leaved [lívd], *a.* hojoso; de hojas.

leaven [lévœn]. **I.** *s.* levadura, fermento. **II.** *va.* fermentar, leudar; corromper, pervertir, viciar.—**l. bread,** pan de levadura.

leavening [lévning], *s.* fermento.

leavenous [lévnus], *a.* que contiene fermento.

leaves [lívs], *s. pl.* de LEAF.

leaving [líving], *s.* partida, marcha.—*pl.* sobras, desechos, desperdicios; residuo, sobra.

lecher [léchœr], *s.* libertino.

lecherous [léchœrʊs], _a._ lujurioso, lascivo.— **lecherously** [-li], _adv._ lujuriosamente.

lecherousness_[-nes], **lechery** [échœri], _s._ lujuria, salacidad.

lecithin [lésizin], _s._ (quím.) lecitina.

lectern [léctœrn], _s._ atril, facistol.

lection [lécšhʊn], _s._ (igl.) lección; letra de un texto.

lectionary [lécšhʊnœri], _s._ (igl.) leccionario.

lector [léctœr], _s._ (igl.) lector.

lectorate [léctoret], _s._ (igl.) lectorado.

lecture [lékchœr]. **I.** _s._ disertación, conferencia; instrucción, clase; (fam.) sermoneo, regaño **II.** _vn._ disertar, discursar; dar una conferencia; hablar ex cáthedra. **III.** _va._ (fam.) regañar, sermonear.

lecturer [lékchurœr], _s._ conferenciante; catedrático.

lectureship [lékchurŝhip], _s._ lectoría; cátedra.

led, _pp._ y _pret._ de TO LEAD.

ledge [leɥ], _s._ anaquel; borde, capa, tonga, tongada; retallo; arrecife; (mar.) latas de los baos.

ledger [léɥœr]. **I.** _s._ (com.) libro mayor; solera de emparrillado; traviesa de andamio.

lee [líɥ]. **I.** _s._ (mar.) sotavento; socaire. **II.** _a._ (mar.) sotaventado.—**l. shore,** (mar.) costa de sotavento.—**l. side,** banda de sotavento.—**l. tide,** marea de donde viene el viento.

leeboards [líbórds], _s._ (mar.) orzaderas.

leech [lích]. **I.** _s._ sanguijuela; gorrón; ventosa; (mar.) gratil; médico.—**l. lines,** apagapenoles.— **l. rope,** relinga de las caídas. **II.** _va._ V. LEACH.

leek [líc], _s._ (bot.) puerro, ajete.

leer [lícœr]. **I.** _s._ mirada de soslayo; (vid.) templador. **II.** _va._ atraer. **III.** _vn._ mirar de soslayo.

leeringly [líringli], _adv._ mirando de soslayo.

lees [líš], _s._ _pl._ heces, sedimento, poso.

leeward [líuard], _s._ (mar.) entre marineros, lúard], _a._ (mar.) sotavento.—**l. ship,** buque roncero.—**l. tide,** marea en la dirección del viento.—**to l.,** a sotavento.

leeway [líuéi], _s._ (mar.) deriva, abatimiento; decadencia, desviación; plazo, tiempo; libertad.

left [left]. **I.** _pret._ y _pp._ de TO LEAVE.—**l. off,** puesto a un lado o desechado. **II.** _a._ izquierdo. —**l. bower,** triunfo que sigue al primero (_right bower_) en el _euchre._—**l. drive,** (aut.) conducción a la izquierda.—**l.-hand,** izquierdo (lado, etc.); con la mano izquierda; torcido hacia la izquierda (un cable, etc.); de movimiento hacia la izquierda.— **l.-handed,** zurdo; torpe, desmañado; torcido, malicioso; de movimiento, funcionamiento, etc., hacia la izquierda.—**l-handedness,** zurdería.— **l.-handed screw,** tornillo zurdo, tornillo a la izquierda. **III.** _s._ mano izquierda, lado izquierdo. —**at, on, o to the l.,** a la izquierda.

leg, _s._ pierna; pata (de las aves y otros animales); pie o pata (de un mueble); pierna de pantalón; pierna de compás, teodolito, etc.); caña de media o de bota; (mar.) bordada; (geom.) cateto; trayecto, jornada; (elec.) circuito derivado; alambre exterior de un circuito trifilar; (m. v.) placa de agua.—**on,** o **upon, its legs,** en pie, firmemente establecido.—**on one's last legs,** acabándose; agonizante; sin recursos.

legacy [légasi], _s._ legado, manda; herencia.—**l. duty,** derechos de herencia.

legal [lígæl], _a._ legal.—**l. cap,** papel grande para documentos legales.—**l. tender,** moneda de curso forzoso.

legality [llegǽliti], _s._ legalidad, legitimidad.

legalization [légaliŝéishʊn], _s._ legalización; refrendación, refrendc.

legalize [lígalaiŝ], _va._ legalizar, autorizar, legitimar; refrendar; interpretar a la letra.

legally [lígali], _adv._ legalmente.

legate [légueit], _s._ legado, enviado.

legatee [légatí], _s._ legatario.

legateship [léguetŝhip], _s._ legacía.

legatine [légatin _o_ tain], _a._ hecho por un legado o que pertenece a él.

legation [leguéishʊn], _s._ legación; misión.

legato [legáto], _adv._ (mús.) ligado.

legator [lleguéitœr _o_ legatór], _s._ testador.

legend [léɥend], _s._ leyenda; letrero, inscripción, titulillo.—**legendary** [-deri], _a._ legendario.

leger [léɥœr]. **I.** _a._ ligero, delicado.—**l. lines,** (mús.) rayas adicionales al pentagrama.— **l. space,** espacio comprendido por esas rayas adicionales. **II.** _s._ _V._ LEDGER.

legerdemain [léɥœrdeméin], _s._ juego de manos, prestidigitación.

legged [légued], _a._ de piernas o pies. ú. gen. en composición; _vg._ _long-legged,_ de piernas largas; _three-legged,_ de tres pies o patas; _two-legged,_ bípedo; de dos pies o patas.

legging [léguing], _s._ polaina, sobrecalza, guardapierna.

Leghorn [léɥjorn], _s._ sombrero de paja de Italia; casta de gallinas.

legibility [lléɥibíliti], **legibleness** [-bœlnes], _s._ legibilidad.—**legible** [-bœl], _a._ legible.—**legibly** [-bli], _adv._ legiblemente.

legion [líɥun], _s._ legión.—**legionary** [-œri], _a._ y _s._ legionario.

legislate [léɥisleit], _va._ y _vn._ legislar.—**legislative** [-léŝhun], _s._ legislación.—**legislative** [-lativ], _a._ legislativo.—**legislator** [-léitœr], _s._ legislador.— **legistorial** [-latórial], _a._ de legislación o legislatura.—**legislatorship** [-léitœrŝhip], _s._ oficio o dignidad de legislador.—**legislature** [-lechœr], _s._ legislatura, asamblea.

legist [líɥist], _s._ legista, jurisconsulto.

legitimacy [leɥítimasi], _s._ legitimidad.

legitimate [-timet]. **I.** _a._ legítimo.—**II.** _va._ legitimar.—**legitimately** [-li], _adv._ legítimamente.— **legitimateness** [-nes], _s._ legitimidad.—**legitimation** [-timéiŝhʊn], _s._ legitimación.—**legitime** [léɥitim], _s._ (for.) legítima.—**legitimist** [leɥítimist], _s._ (pol.) legitimista.—**legitimize** [-timaiŝ], _va._ _V._ = LEGITIMATE.

legume [léguium _o_ leguiúm], **legumen** [leguiúmen], _s._ (bot.) legumbre, vaina.

leguminous [leguiúminʊs], _a._ (bot.) leguminoso.

leisure [líɥœr], _s._ ocio, ociosidad, holganza; comodidad.—**l. hours,** horas libres o desocupadas. —**at l.,** despacio, con sosiego, en un rato de ocio.— **to be at l.,** estar desocupado.

leisurely [-li]. **I.** _a._ pausado, deliberado. **II.** _adv._ despacio; desocupadamente.

lemma [léma], _s._ (lóg. y mat.) lema.

lemna [lemna], _s._ (bot.) lenticula.

lemnaceous [lemnéisʊs], _a._ (bot.) lemnáceo.

lemon [lémʊn]. **I.** _s._ (bot.) limón.—**l.-colored,** cetrino.—**l. squeezer,** exprimidor de limón.—**l. tree,** limonero. **II.** _a._ de limón; hecho o sazonado con limón; cetrino.

lemonade [lémʊneid], _s._ limonada.

lemur [límœr], _s._ (zool.) lémur.

Lemures [lémiuris], _s._ _pl._ (mit.) lemures.

Lemuridæ [lemiúridi], _s._ _pl._ (zool.) lemúridos.

lend, _va._ prestar.—**to l. a hand** (to), dar una mano, ayudar.—**to l. aid,** dar ayuda, prestar auxilio.—**to l. an ear,** prestar atención, dar oídos.

lender [léndœr], _s._ prestador, prestamista; logrero, mutuante.

lending [lénding], _s._ empréstito; préstamo.

lene [líni _o_ léne]. **I.** _a._ (gram.) suave, no aspirado. **II.** _s._ consonante no aspirada.

length [lenɥz], _s._ longitud, largo; espacio, duración de tiempo; alcance (de un tiro, etc.); (dep.) echada.—**at l.,** al fin, finalmente; extensamente.— **at full l.,** a lo largo, de todo el largo.

lengthen [lénɥzen]. **I.** _va._ alargar, estirar; prolongar, dilatar. **II.** _vn._ alargarse, prolongarse.

lengthening [lénɥzening]. **I.** _s._ alargamiento; prolongación. **II.** _a._ de alargar.—**l. bar,** alargadera.

lengthwise [lénɥzuaiŝ], _adv._ longitudinalmente; a lo largo.

lengthy [lénɥzi], _a._ largo; demasiado largo, larguísimo.

leniency [líniensi], _s._ suavidad, lenidad.

lenient [línient], _a._ y _s._ indulgente, lenitivo.

Leninism [léninism], _s._ leninismo, sistema de Lenín.—**Leninite** [-nait], _s._ leninista.

lenitive [lénitiv], *s.* y *a.* lenitivo.
lenity [léniti], *s.* lenidad, blandura.
lens [lenŝ], *s.* (ópt.) lente; (anat.) cristalino.
lent. **I.** *pret.* y *pp.* de TO LEND; prestado. **II. (L-')**, *s.* cuaresma.—**L. dinner,** comida de viernes.
lentando [lentándo], *adv.* (mús.) con lentitud creciente.
lenten [lénten], *a.* cuaresmal; escaso.
lenticel [léntisel], *s.* (bot.) lentejuela.
lenticular [lentíkiular], **lentiform** [léntiform], *a.* lenticular.
lentiginous [lentírinus], *a.* (bot. y zool.) pecoso; casposo.
lentil [léntil], *s.* (bot.) lenteja.
lentiscus [lentíscus], **lentisk** [léntisc], *s.* (bot.) lentisco.
lento [lénto], *a.* y *adv.* (mús.) lento, lentamente.
Leo [lío], *s.* (astr.) León.
leonine [líonin *o* nain], *a.* leonino.
leopard [lépard], *s.* (zool.) leopardo o pardal.—**l.'s-bane,** (bot.) dorónico.
lepadid(e [lépadid], *s.* lápade, percebe.
leper [lépœr], *s.* leproso, lazarino.
leperous [lépœrus], *a.* = LEPROUS.
lepidolite [lépidolait], *s.* lepidolita.
Lepidoptera [lépidóptera, *s.* (ent.) lepidópteros, diurnos.—**lepidopterous** [-terus], *a.* lepidóptero.
leporine [léporin *o* rain], *a.* lebruno, leporino.
leprosarium [léprosérium], *s.* lazareto, hospital de leprosos.
leprose [léprous], *a.* (bot.) casposo, escamoso.
leprosity [leprósiti], *s.* calidad de casposo o escamoso.
leprosy [léprosi], *s.* lepra, elefancía.
leprous [léprus], *a.* leproso, lazarino.
leprousness [-nes], *s.* leprosidad.
Lepus [lípus], *s.* (astr.) Liebre.
lese majesty [liŝ-mǽyesti], *s.* lesa majestad.
lesion [líȝun], *s.* lesión.
less [les]. **I.** *a.* (*comp.* de LITTLE) menor, menos, inferior. **II.** *adv.* menos, en grado más pequeño; en grado más bajo.—**l. and l.,** de menos en menos, cada vez menos.
lessee [lesí], *s.* arrendatario, rentero, inquilino.
lessen [léscœn]. **I.** *va.* minorar, disminuir, mermar; menoscabar; rebajar, degradar. **II.** *vn.* mermar, disminuirse; degradarse, rebajarse.
lesser [léscœr], *a.* (comp. de LITTLE) menor, más pequeño.—**l. prophets,** profetas menores.
lesson [lesn], *s.* lección; (igl.) lección.
lessor [lésor], *s.* arrendante, arrendador, censualista, que da una cosa en arrendamiento.
lest [lest], *conj.* para que no, por miedo de o de miedo que, no sea que.
let. **I.** *va.* (*pret.* y *pp.* LET) dejar, conceder, permitir; arrendar, alquilar, dar en arrendamiento. Como auxiliar, se usa para formar el subjuntivo e imperativo de algunos verbos anteponiéndolo al infinitivo: *let him go,* que se vaya; *let us fly,* huyamos; *let the children play,* que jueguen los niños; *let x be the price,* sea *x* el precio. Las circunstancias indican cuándo es auxiliar y cuándo no. Así, *let us see* puede significar "veamos" o "déjeme ver," según el caso. El infinitivo se usa a menudo elípticamente por sí solo en el sentido de "dejar," "permitir," "se arrienda," "de alquiler," etc.—**to l. alone,** dejar en paz, no molestar; no tocar; no meterse con o en; sin hablar de; sin mencionar; mucho menos (*he cannot buy a horse, let alone an automobile,* no puede comprar un caballo, mucho menos un automóvil).—**to l. be,** no molestar; no meterse con.—**to l. bygones be bygones,** olvidar lo pasado.—**to l. down,** dejar caer; bajar.—**to l. fall a word,** soltar inadvertidamente una palabra.—**to l. fly,** (fam.) disparar.—**to l. go,** soltar.—**to l. in,** dejar entrar, admitir, recibir; introducir; hacer entrar.—**to l. into,** dejar o hacer entrar en; dejar conocer; iniciar o admitir en.—**to l. know,** hacer saber, avisar.—**to l. loose,** soltar, aflojar; desatar, desencadenar.—**to l. off,** disparar, descargar; dejar salir o ir, dejar libre.—**to l. out,** dejar salir; poner en libertad, soltar; hacer salir; divulgar; arrendar, alquilar; largar (un rizo, etc.), aflojar.—**to l. the cat out of the**

bag, revelar un secreto. **II.** *vn.* alquilarse o arrendarse.—**to l. go,** soltar.—**to l. pass,** dejar pasar.—**to l. up,** (fam.) cesar; disminuir, moderarse.
let, *s.* estorbo, obstáculo.—**without l. or hindrance,** sin estorbo ni obstáculo.
lethal [líȝal], *a.* letal.
lethargic(al [leȝárric(al], *a.* letárgico.—**lethargically** [-i], *adv.* letárgicamente.—**lethargize, lethargise** [léȝarraiŝ], *adv.* aletargar.—**lethargy** [léȝarri], *s.* (med.) letargo.
Lethean [liȝían], *a.* léteo.
lethiferous [leȝífœrus], *a.* somnífero.
letter [létœr]. **I.** *s.* letra; carta, comunicación.—*pl.* letras, literatura.—**l. book,** (com.) copiador de cartas.—**l. box,** buzón; apartado; taquilla.—**l. carrier,** cartero.—**l. case,** cartera, carpeta.—**l. drop,** buzón.—**l. file,** cartera, guardacartas, archivo.—**l. man** = L. CARRIER.—**l. of advice,** (com.) carta de aviso.—**l. of attorney,** poder, procuración.—**l. of credit,** carta de crédito.—**l. of license,** moratoria, espera.—**l. of marque,** carta de marca, patente de corso.—**l. paper,** papel de cartas.—**l.-perfect,** que sabe su papel, discurso. etc. de memoria.—**l. press,** prensa de copiar cartas —**l. rogatory,** (for.) suplicatoria.—**l. scale,** balanza para pesar cartas.—**l. stamp,** cancelador de sellos de correo; sello para fechar cartas en el correo.—**l. writer,** memorialista.—**letters of safe conduct,** guía, salvoconducto.—**letters patent,** título o patente de privilegio. **II.** *va.* estampar con letras; rotular; poner letras, título o letreros a.
lettered [létœrd], *a.* letrado, instruído, erudito, literato, docto.
letterer [létœrœr], *s.* el que pone letras y letreros (en un dibujo, etc.)
lettergram [-græm], *s.* telegrama largo, a manera de carta, que se envía con rebaja de precio pero sin garantía de entrega inmediata (puede llamarse carta telegráfica).
letterhead [-jéd], *s.* membrete; hoja o pliego de papel con membrete.
lettering [létœring], *s.* letrero, inscripción, rótulo; estampilla; puesta de letras a un dibujo.
letterpress [-préss], *s.* impresión, impreso; texto (a distinción de grabados o figuras).—**l. printing,** impresión directa con tipo (a distinción de la hecha con planchas).
Lettish [létish], *s.* y *a.* letón.
lettre de caché (letr dœ cáshé], *s.* carta real cerrada.
lettuce [létis], *s.* (bot.) lechuga.
let-up [let up], *s.* diminución, calma; cesación, interrupción; descanso.
leucin(e [liúsin], *s.* (quím.) leucina.
leucite [liúsait], *s.* (min.) leucita.
leucocyte [liúcosait], *s.* leucocito.
leucoma [liucóma], *s.* (med.) albugo.
leucorrhea [liúcorría], *s.* leucorrea.
Levant [levánt]. **I.** *s.* levante, oriente. **II.** *a.* oriental.—**L. trade,** comercio de levante.
Levanter [-œr], *s.* viento del levante.
levantine [levéntin], *a.* levantino.—**levantines,** *s.* (tej.) levantín.
levator [levéitœr], *s.* músculo elevador; (cir.) levantador.
levee [lévi], *s.* corte, besamanos, recepción; [leví], dique, malecón.
level [lévœl]. **I.** *a.* plano, llano, igual, parejo; igual, uniforme; derecho, recto; honrado, probo; (fam.) juicioso, discreto; a nivel; horizontal.—**l. crossing,** (f. c.) paso a nivel.—**l.-headed,** juicioso, discreto. **II.** *s.* nivel (instrumento, altura); llanura; puntería; línea visual; (min.) galería horizontal, piso.—**on the l.,** abiertamente, sin dolo. **III.** *adv.* a nivel, ras; en derechura; con puntería; igualmente; lisa y llanamente. **IV.** *va.* igualar, allanar; nivelar; arrasar, derribar; apuntar, dirigir, asestar; proporcionar, adaptar, ajustar; igualar, emparejar; (alb.) enrasar. **V.** *vn.* apuntar (un arma); (top.) nivelar, hacer nivelaciones.
level(l)er [-œr], *s.* allanador, igualador, aplanador; nivelador; aplanadera.

level(l)ing [-ing]. **I.** *s.* nivelación; (alb.) enrasado. **II.** *a.* de nivelar; de enrasar.—**l. rod,** mira de nivelar.

levelness [-nes], *s.* igualdad; horizontalidad.

lever [lévœr, lívœr], *s.* palanca; brazo; manecilla; escape de reloj.—**l. arm,** brazo de palanca.— **l. watch,** reloj de escape.

leverage [-eiɣ], *s.* brazo de palanca; acción de una palanca; sistema de palancas; influencia, poder, ventaja.

levert [lévœret], *s.* lebrato.

leviable [léviabœl], *a.* exigible.

leviathan [leváiaᵹan], *s.* leviatán.

levigate [lévigueit], *va.* levigar; pulverizar.

levigation [-óiŝhᴜn], *s.* levigación; pulverización.

levitate [léviteit], *va.* aligerar; alzar o hacer subir contra la acción de la gravedad y sin medios físicos (apl. a los fenómenos espiritistas).— **levitation** [-téiŝhᴜn], *s.* aligeramiento; suspensión o levantamiento de cuerpos pesados sin medios físicos.

Levite [lívait], *s.* levita; tacaño; (ant.) diácono.

Levitic(al [levític(al], *a.* levítico.

levity [léviti], *s.* levedad, ligereza; veleidad.

levulose [léviulʊs], *s.* (quím.) levulosa.

levy [lévi]. **I.** *va.* reclutar, enganchar; exigir tributos; (for.) embargar, ejecutar. **II.** *s.* recluta, enganche; exacción de tributos; (for.) embargo, ejecución.

lewd [lud o liúd], *a.* lujurioso, lascivo.—**lewdly** [-li], *adv.* lascivamente; impúdicamente.—**lewdness,** [-nes], *s.* lascivia, lujuria; prostitución.

lewis [liúis(on], *s.* clavija para alzar piedras; castañuela de cantera.

lexical [léxical], *a.* lexicográfico.

lexicographer [-cógrafœr], *s.* lexicógrafo.—**lexicographic** [-cográfic], *a.* lexicográfico.—**lexicography** [-cógrafi], *s.* lexicografía.—**lexicological** [-colóyical], *a.* lexicológico.—**lexicologist** [-cóloyist], *s.* lexicólogo.—**lexicology** [-cóloyi], *s.* lexicología.

lexicon [léxicon], *s.* léxico.

lex talionis [lex tæliónis], ley del talión.

Leyden jar [láiden ɣar], *s.* (fís.) botella de Leiden.

liability [láibíliti], *s.* riesgo, exposición; obligación, responsabilidad.—*pl.* **liabilities,** (com.) pasivo.

liable [láiabœl], *a.* sujeto, expuesto; obligado, responsable, deudor; propenso.

liaison [lieŝón], *s.* concubinaje; unión, coordinación; (gram.) unión de una consonante final a la vocal siguiente.

liana, liane [liéna, lián], *s.* (bot.) jagüey.

liar [láiar], *s,* embustero, mentiroso, falsario.

lias [láias], *s.* (geol.) lías.

libation [laibéŝhᴜn], *s.* libación.

libel [láibel]. **I.** *s.* libelo; difamación. **II.** *va.* y *vn.* difamar, calumniar.—**libel(l)ant** [-ant], *s.* (for.) actor o demandante ante el tribunal del Almirantazgo.—**libel(l)er** [-œr], *s.* libelista, difamador.—**libel(l)ing** [-ing], *s.* difamación.—**libel(l)ous** [-ᴜs], *a.* infamatorio, difamatorio.

libellula [laibéliula], *s.* (ento.) libélula.

liber [láibœr o líbœr], *s.* libro, registro; (bot.) líber.

liberal [líbœral], *a.* liberal, generoso; abundante; (pol.) liberal; (trad.) liberal (traducción, etc.); noble, bien nacido.—**l. arts,** artes liberales.

liberalism [-aliŝm], *s.* liberalismo.

liberality [-éliti], *s.* liberalidad.

liberalize [-alaiŝ], *va.* liberalizar.

liberally [-ali], *adv.* liberalmente; generosamente.

liberate [-eit], *va.* libertar, librar; manumitir; descargar.

liberation [-óiŝhᴜn], *s.* liberación, redención.

liberator [-éitœr], *s.* libertador.

libertarian [-tériæn]. **I.** *s.* el que cree en el libre albedrío. **II.** *a.* relativo a la doctrina que defiende el libre albedrío.

libertinage [-tiney], **libertinism** [-tiniŝm], *s.* libertinaje.

libertine [-tin]. **I.** *a.* y *s.* libertino, disoluto. **II.** *s.* (for.) libertino, hijo de liberto.

liberty [líbœrti], *s.* libertad; exención, prerrogativa, inmunidad; osada familiaridad; liberación de presos o cautivos; licencia, permiso.— **L. Bell,** campana de la libertad (la que se repicó cuando los E. U. declararon su independencia).

libidinous [libídinᴜs], *a.* libidinoso, lujurioso.— **libidinously** [-li], *adv.* libidinosamente. —**libidinousness** [-nes], *s.* lascivia, lujuria.

Libra [láibra], *s.* (astr.) Libra.

librarian [laibrérian], *s.* bibliotecario.—**librarianship** [-ŝhip], *s.* empleo de bibliotecario.

library [láibrari], *s.* biblioteca.

librate [láibret], *va.* balancear, equilibrar.

libration [-éiŝhᴜn], *s.* libración, balance; (astr.) libración.

libratory [láibratori], *a.* de libración, oscilatorio; que balancea.

librettist [librétist], *s.* libretista.

libretto, *s.* (teat.) libro, libreto.

lice [láis], *s. pl.* de LOUSE; piojos.

licebane [láisben], *s.* (bot.) albarraz, hierba piojera.

licensable [láisensabœl], *a.* permisible.

license [láisens]. **I.** *s.* licencia, permiso; despacho, cédula, título; licencia, libertinaje. **II.** *va.* licenciar, dar licencia o permiso; autorizar, facultar; dar cédula, despacho o privilegio.

licensee [láisensí], *s.* persona que obtiene licencia o permiso.

licenser [láisensœr], *s.* el que da la licencia.

licentiate [laisénŝhiet], *s.* el que usa de licencia; licenciado.

licentious [-ŝhᴜs], *a.* licencioso, desenfrenado, disoluto.—**licentiously** [-li], *adv.* licenciosamente.—**licentiousness** [-nes], *s.* disipación, libertinaje.

lichen [láiken], *s.* (bot.) liquen; (med.) salpullido causado por el calor.

licit [lísit], *a.* lícito.—**licitly** [-li], *adv.* lícitamente.—**licitness** [-nes], *s.* calidad de lícito.

lick [lic]. **I.** *va.* lamer; (mec.) absorber, chupar; (fam.) cascar, dar una tunda o felpa; sobrepujar, vencer.—**to l. the dust,** morder el polvo. **II.** *vn.* flamear. **III.** *s.* lamedura, lengüetada; salagar, lamedero; (fam.) mojicón, bofetón.

licker [líkœr], *s.* lamedor; (mec.) lubricador automático.

lickerish [líkœriŝh], *a.* regalado, delicado, sabroso; salaz, libidinoso.—**lickerishly** [-li], *adv.* deliciosamente, regaladamente.—**lickerishness** [-nes], *s.* delicadeza de paladar, regalo.

licking [líking], *s.* (fam.) tunda, felpa.

lickspittle [lícspítœl], *s.* quitapelillos, parásito, hombre servil.

licorice [lícoris], *s.* (bot.) regaliz, orozuz, alcazuz.

lictor [líctœr], *s.* lictor.

lid, *s.* tapa, tapadera; párpado; (bot.) opérculo; guardapolvo de reloj.

lie [lái]. **I.** *s.* mentira, embuste; desmentida, mentís; postura, posición; yacimiento, caída; cubil; (f. c.) desviadero.—**to give the l. to,** dar un mentís a, desmentir. **II.** *vn.* (*pret.* y *pp.* LIED: *pa.* LYING) mentir.

lie, *vn.* (*pret.* LAY: *pp.* LAIN) echarse, tenderse; descansar recostado; apoyarse; acostarse, estar acostado o en cama; yacer, ubicar, estar situado; pernoctar; consistir, depender; estar en, tocar o corresponder a; estar pendiente.—**to l. about,** estar esparcido.—**to l. along,** dar a la banda.—**to l. at,** importunar, molestar; estar expuesto.—**to l. at the heart,** ser objeto de afecto, ansiedad o deseo.—**to l. at the point of death,** estar expirando.—**to l. by,** estar cerca o a la mano; parar, descansar.—**to l. down,** echarse, acostarse; alocarse.—**to l. in,** estar de parto.—**to l. in one,** estar en uno, estar de manos de uno.—**to l. in state,** estar en capilla o cámara ardiente.—**to l. in wait,** espiar, acechar.—**to l. low,** estar postrado; permanecer oculto o en la oscuridad.—**to l. off,** descansar; contenerse al principio (de una carrera, etc.).—**to l. on,** o **upon,** ser obligatorio a, pesar sobre; depender de.—**to l. on one's head,** tener uno la culpa de.—**to l. on the oars,** cesar de remar: descansar del trabajo.—**to l. over**, aplazarse; (com.) caducar.—**to l. to**, estar a la capa.—**to l. under**, estar bajo el peso de.—**to l. up**, descansar. —**to l. with**, vivir o dormir con; tocar o corresponder a; tener coito con.

lief [lif], *adv*. de buena gana, de buen grado.

liege [liʏ]. **I**. *a*. ligio; feudatario. **II**. *s*. vasallo súbdito; señor feudal.—**liegeman** [líʏman], *s*. vasallo.

lien [líen, lin], *s*. (for.) embargo preventivo para el cobro de una deuda; obligación, gravamen.

lienteric [laientéric], *s*. lientérico.

lientery [láienteri], *s*. (med.) lienteria.

lieu [liú], *s*.—**in l. of**, en lugar de, en vez de.

lieutenancy, lieutenantship [liuténænci, -ship], tenientazgo (first l.); alferazgo (second l.)

lieutenant [-nænt], *s*. teniente (**first l.**); alférez (**second l.**); lugarteniente.—**l. colonel**, teniente coronel.—**l. general**, teniente general.—**l. governor**, (E. U.) vicegobernador, dignatario que reemplaza al gobernador cuando éste no puede funcionar; (Ingl.) lugarteniente del gobernador general de una colonia; gobernador de provincia.

life [láif]. **I**. *s*. vida.—**for l.**, de por vida, por toda la vida.—**from l.**, del natural. **II**. *a*. de la vida; relativo a la vida; de toda la vida, vitalicio. —**l. annuity**, renta vitalicia.—**l. assurance** = L. INSURANCE.—**l. belt**, cinto de salvamento.—**l. box** = L. SLIDE.—**l. buoy**, boya o guíndola salvavidas.—**l.-giving**, vivificante.—**l. guard**, guardia de corps; empleado de una estación de salvamento; (f. c.) guardarrueda.—**l. insurance**, seguro sobre la vida.—**l. line**, cuerda salvavida; andarivel horizontal de verga.—**l. policy**, póliza vitalicia o de seguro ordinario sobre la vida, pagadera sólo al fallecimiento del asegurado.—**l. preserver**, salvavidas.—**l.-saving apparatus**, aparato salvavidas.—**l.-saving gun**, o **mortar**, cañón u obús para lanzar proyectiles de salvamento.—**l.-saving station**, estación de salvamento en la costa.—**l. sentence**, sentencia de prisión vitalicia.—**l. slide**, celdilla de vidrio para el estudio microscópico de animálculos.

lifeblood [-blúd], *s*. sangre vital; alma, nervio.

lifeboat [-bóut],ᵃ *s*. lancha salvavidas.

lifeless [-les], *a*. sin vida; inanimado.—**lifelessly** [-li], *adv*. sin vigor.

lifelike [-laic], *a*. que parece vivo, natural.

lifelong [-long], *a*. de toda la vida.

lifestring [-string], *s*. fibra que se suponía esencial a la vida.

lifetime [-táim], *s*. curso de la vida; toda la vida.

lift. **I**. *va*. alzar, levantar; quitar la presión; (fam.) hurtar; quitar, llevarse. **II**. *vn*. hacer fuerza para levantar algo; disiparse (la niebla).—**to l. the feet**, acudir presuroso al socorro de alguno.—**to l. the hat**, quitarse el sombrero para saludar.—**to l. the horn**, tratar con insolencia, con desdén; establecer en autoridad.—**to l. up**, alzar (la partícula a veces da énfasis, pero generalmente no es más que cuestión de uso).—**to l. up the hand**, prestar juramento levantando la mano.—**to l. up the heel against**, tratar con insolencia y desprecio. **II**. *vn*. hacer fuerza para levantar; disiparse (la niebla). **III**. *s*. esfuerzo para levantar; acción de alzar; lo que sirve para alzar (aparejo, gancho, etc.); elevación, altura a que algo se alza; ayuda; carrera (de un martinete, etc.); (aut.) maniqueta de ventana; (Ingl.) ascensor; (min.) diferencia de nivel; (min.) juego de bombas; (aer.) fuerza ascensional, componente vertical de la presión aerodinámica.—**l. bridge**, puente levadizo.—**l. lock**, esclusa.—**l. pump**, bomba aspirante.—**l. valve**, válvula de movimiento vertical.—**l. wire**, (aer.) cable o cinta de sustentación.—**at one l.**, de un golpe.

lifter [líftœr], *s*. alzador, cualquier cosa que sirve para alzar; elevador; leva; ratero; (m. v.) brazo de la válvula de una máquina de blancín.

lifting [lífting]. **I**. *s*. acción de alzar. **II**. *a*. de alzar o elevar.—**l. bridge**, puente levadizo.—**l. injector**, (m. v.) inyector aspirante.—**l. jack**, gato, cric.—**l. pump**, bomba aspirante.—**l. rod**, (m. v.) vástago vertical que en una máquina de balancín mueve el brazo de la válvula.

ligament [lígamœnt], *s*. ligamento.

ligamental, ligamentous [ligaméntal, us], *a*. ligamentoso.

ligan [láigan], *s*. (for.) pecio.

ligate [láiguet], *va*. (cir.) atar con ligadura.

ligation [liguéishun], *s*. ligación.

ligature [lígachur *o* tiur], *s*. (cir., mec. y mús.) ligadura; ligación; (impr.) letras ligadas, como fi, fl, etc.

light [láit]. **I**. *s*. luz; luminar, notabilidad (dicho de los grandes hombres); claraboya, tragaluz; vidrio de ventana; fuego (de un cigarro, etc.); fósforo, cerilla; aspecto; situación, posición; punto de vista; día, alba; (pint.) luz.—*pl*. *V*. LIGHTS.— **l. dues**, derechos de faro.—**l. keeper**, torrero.—**l. port**, (mar.) portilla.—**l. vessel** = LIGHTSHIP.—**l. year**, unidad sideral de distancia, espacio que la luz recorre en un año.—**in the l. of**, a la luz de, según.—**in this l.**, desde este punto de vista. **II**. *a*. ligero, leve; sutil; (mar.) boyante; llevadero; suelto, fácil; fútil, frívolo, superficial; ágil, desembarazado; inconstante, mudable; alegre, vivo; liviano, incontinente; claro (apl. esp. al color); de tez blanca; blondo, rubio.—**l. complexion**, tez blonda.—**l.-complexioned**, de tez blonda.—**l.-headedness**, delirio; atolondramiento, aturdimiento.—**l. heavyweight**, (dep.) boxeador de peso medio (que no pasa de 175 libras). —**l. horse**, caballería ligera.—**l. literature**, literatura amena, literatura ordinaria.—**l. soil**, terreno arijo. **III**. *va*. encender; alumbrar, iluminar. **IV**. *vn*. encenderse, prender (el fuego o la luz); lucir; descender, posarse; (con *on* o *upon*), encontrarse con, hallar por casualidad; apearse. **V**. *adv*. ligeramente; fácilmente.—**l.-fingered**, largo de uñas, ligero de dedos.—**l. foot** (el, **l. heeled**, ligero de pies.—**l.-headed**, ligero de cascos, casquivano: delirante; atolondrado, aturdido.—**l.-hearted**, alegre, festivo.—**l.-legged**, ligero de piernas, activo.—**l.-minded**, voluble; atolondrado.—**l.-witted**, chalado, cascabelero.

lightbrain [láitbréin], *s*. casquivano.

lighten [láiten]. **I**. *va*. iluminar, alumbrar; aclarar; aligerar, quitar peso; aliviar; alegrar, regocijar. **II**. *vn*. ponerse ligero, disminuir de peso; relampaguear.

lightening [láitening], *s*. alba, alborada, aligeramiento.

lighter [láitœr]. **I**. *a*. *comp*. de LIGHT: más ligero; más claro. **II**. *s*. (mar.) barcaza, chalana; alumbrador, encendedor; mecha. **III**. *va*. y *vn*. transportar o llevar en chalana.

lighterage [láitœrey], *s*. (mar.) gastos de chalana.

lighterman [láitœrman], *s*. (mar.) lanchonero, gabarrero.

lighthouse [láitjaus], *s*. (mar.) faro.

lighting [láiting], *s*. alumbrado; iluminación.

lightless [láitles], *a*. obscuro, sin luz.

lightly [láitli], *adv*. ligeramente, levemente; fácilmente; prontamente, ágilmente; alegremente, de buena gana; sin seriedad, con liviandad; irrespetuosamente, con desprecio.

lightness [láitnes], *s*. levedad, ligereza; agilidad; velocidad; inconstancia, frivolidad; liviandad.

lightning [láitning], *s*. relámpago; relampagueo; rayo.—**l. arrester, conductor, rod**, (elec.) pararrayos.—**l. proof**, a prueba de rayos.

lightroom [láitrúm], *s*. pañol de los faroles; lampión de pañol de pólvora; linterna de un faro.

lights [láits], *s*. *pl*. pulmones, bofes.

lightship [láitship], *s*. buque fanal.

lightsome [láitsum], *a*. alegre, festivo; (poét.) luminoso.—**lightsomeness** [-nes], *s*. claridad: alegría, jovialidad.

lightweight [láitueit], **I**.*a*. de poco peso; (dep.) de peso ligero (apl. a boxeadores); (fam.) de poca monta. **II**. *s*. boxeador de peso ligero.

lightwood [-úd], *s*. (E. U.) pino resinoso. Apl. t. a otras maderas que contienen substancias volátiles inflamables.

lignaloes [lignéloš], *s*. (bot.) lináloe.

ligneous [lígneus], *a*. leñoso.

ligniferous [lignífœrus], *a*. leñífero.

lignify [lígnifai], *va.* y *vn.* convertir(se) en madera.

lignin [lígnin], *s.* (quím.) lignina.

lignite [lígnait], *s.* lignito.

lignum-vitæ [lígnum-váiti], *s.* (bot.) guayaco, guayacán, palo santo.

ligroin [lígroin], *s.* ligroína, una de las fracciones del petróleo.

ligula [líguiulæ], *s.* (bot.) lígula.

ligulate [líguiulet], *a.* (bot.) ligulado.

ligule [líguiul], *s.* (bot.) lígula.

ligure [líguiur], *s.* ligurio.

like [láik]. **I.** *a.* semejante, parecido; igual; lo mismo que, equivalente; creíble, probable; prometedor; ganoso, deseoso.—**l. figures,** (geo.) figuras semejantes.—**l. for l.,** en la misma moneda. —**l. master, l. man,** tal para cual.—**in l. manner,** análogamente, del mismo modo.—**not to have one's l.,** no tener (uno) igual.—**to be as l.as two peas,** parecerse como dos gotas de agua. **II.** *s.* semejante, igual; gusto, simpatía (gen. en la frase **likes and dislikes,** simpatías y antipatías, gustos y aversiones). **III.** *adv.* y *prep.* como, semejante a; del mismo modo que, a semejanza de; probablemente; (fam., pospuesto), como con, como de, al parecer (cambiando un poco el giro, v. gr.: *he spoke wisely like,* él habló como con sabiduría; *she answered unwillingly like,* ella contestó como de mala gana).—**l. as,** como, así como.—**l. mad,** como loco, furiosamente, vehementemente.

like [láic]. **I.** *va.* gustar de (*he likes the pleasures of the table,* él gusta de los placeres de la mesa); (fam.) amar. Gen. se traduce por *gustar,* pero con construcción distinta: el nombre o pronombre que en inglés es sujeto, en español es dativo, y el que en inglés es acusativo es en español sujeto: *I like this,* me gusta esto; *do you like music?* ¿le gusta a Vd. la música? En oraciones subjuntivas o condicionales, puede traducirse análogamente, o por "querer": *I should like to see him,* me gustaría (o quisiera) verlo; *what would you like to eat?* ¿qué quisiera Vd. (o le gustaría a Vd.) comer?—**to l. best, better,** gustar (a uno) más (*I like Japan better than China,* me gusta más el Japón que la China; *I like this best,* me gusta más (sup.) esto, esto es lo que más me gusta). **II.** *vn.* (común en autores antiguos) gustar, agradar (*this likes me not,* esto no me gusta).—**as you l.,** como Vd. quiera, como Vd. guste.

likelihood, likeliness [láih-lijud, nes], *s.* probabilidad.

likely [láikli]. **I.** *a.* probable; prometedor; apto, idóneo, a propósito. **II.** *adv.* probablemente.— **l. enough,** no sería extraño.

liken [láikœn], *va.* asemejar, comparar.

likeness [láiknes], *s.* semejanza, parecido; conformidad, igualdad; apariencia, aire; retrato.

likewise [láikuaiŝ], *adv.* también, asimismo, además, igualmente.

liking [láiking], *s.* afición; gusto; simpatía; preferencia.

lilac [lílac]. **I.** *s.* (bot.) lila. **II.** *a.* de color de lila, aberenjenado.

Lilliaceæ [líliéisii], *s. pl.* liliáceas.—**liliaceous** [-éishus], *a.* (bot.) liliáceo.

lilied [lílid], *a.* adornado con lirios.

Lilliputian [líllipiúŝhan], *a.* y *s.* liliputiense, enano.

lilt [lilt]. **I.** *va.* y *vn.* cantar alegremente. **II.** *s.* jácara.

lily [líli], *s.* lirio, azucena; flor de lis.— **l.-livered,** cobarde, ruin.—**l. of the valley,** lirio de los valles, muguete.

lilywort [líliucœrt], *s.* (bot.) liliácea.

Lima [láima o líma], *n. pr.* Lima (Perú).—**L. bean,** haba, faséolo.—**L. wood,** brasilete.

limaceous [liméshus], *a.* limáceo.

Limax [láimax], *s.* babosa, babaza.

limb [lim], *s.* miembro (del cuerpo), especialmente la pierna; rama (de árbol); miembro, individuo; (top., astr.) limbo; (fam.) joven travieso.

limbed [limd], *a.* membrudo; ramoso.

limber [límbœr]. **I.** *a.* flojo, flexible, blando. **II.** *s.* (arti.) avantrén de cureña, armón; (mar.) groera del canal del agua.—**l. boards,** (mar.) panas imbornaleras de las varengas.—**l. holes,** imbornales de las varengas.—**l. rope,** cabo imbornalero de las varengas. **III.** *va.* poner flexible o blando; (con **up**) poner o colocar el armón; poner el avantrén a una cureña.

limberness [límbœrnes], *s.* flexibilidad, flojedad.

limbless [límles], *a.* desmembrado.

limbo [límbo], *s.* limbo; prisión.

lime [láim]. **I.** *s.* cal; liga; (bot.) limón mejicano, limoncito, limoncillo (limón pequeño muy ácido— *Cítrus acida*).—**l. burner,** calero.—**l. nitrogen,** cianamida cálcica.—**l. pit,** calera, cantera de cal; pelambrera.—**l. tree,** (bot.) tilia, tilo (= LINDEN).—**l. twig,** vareta. **II.** *va.* encalar; untar o coger con liga; (alb.) unir con argamasa, mortero o mezcla; (agri.) abonar con cal; (ten.) pelambrar.

limehound [-jáund], *s.* sabueso.

limekiln [-kil], *s.* calera (horno de quemar caliza para extraer la cal).

limelight [-láit], *s.* luz de calcio; posición conspicua, vista del público.

limen [láimen], *s.* (psic.) umbral de la conciencia, punto en que un estimulante empieza a producir su efecto en la conciencia.

limerick [límeric], *s.* lira o quintilla jocosa.

limestone [láimstóun], *s.* piedra caliza.

limewater [láimuótœr], *s.* agua de cal.

liminal [líminæl], *a.* relativo al umbral.

limit [límit]. **I.** *s.* límite; lindero, aledaño, meta, limitación. **II.** *va.* limitar, fijar; restringir.

limitable [-æbœl], *a.* restringible.

limitary [-æri], *a.* limitáneo, fronterizo, limítrofe.

limitation [-éishun], *s.* limitación, coartación, restricción.

limited [límited], *a.* limitado, poco, escaso; restricto; finito.—**l. company (Ltd.), l.-liability company,** compañía de responsabilidad limitada al valor de las acciones de cada socio.—**l. divorce,** divorcio restringido.—**l. express,** (f. c.) tren compuesto sólo de coches de primera clase.—**l. partnership,** sociedad en comandita.—**l. train** = L. EXPRESS.

limitedly [-li], *adv.* limitadamente.

limitless [límitles], *a.* ilimitado.

limn [lim], *va.* pintar, iluminar; dibujar; retratar.

limonene [límonin], *s.* (quím.) limoneno.

limonite [láimonait], *s.* (min.) limonita.

limous [láimus], *a.* cenagoso, fangoso.

limousine [límuŝin], *s.* (aut.) limosina.

limp. **I.** *s.* cojera. **II.** *a.* débil, flojo; flexible; blando, débil de carácter. **III.** *vn.* cojear, renquear; (med.) cojear.—**limper** [-œr], *s.* cojo.

limpet [límpet], *s.* lepada o lepas.

limpid [límpid], *a.* límpio, cristalino, límpido.

limpidity [limpíditi], **limpidness** [límpidnes], *s.* limpidez, claridad.

limpingly [límpingli], *adv.* con cojera.

limy [láimi], *a.* calizo; viscoso, pegajoso.

Linaceæ [lainéisii], *s. pl.* (bot.) lináceas.

linaceous [-ŝhus], *a.* (bot.) lináceo.

linchpin [línchpin], *s.* sotrozo, pezonera.

linden (tree) [línden, tri], *s.* (bot.) tilo; patagua.

line [láin], *s.* (leng. ord., geom., f. c., mar., mili., elec.) línea; (geom.) línea recta (usada sola, la palabra tiene casi siempre esta acepción); (ing.) tubería; raya; veta; renglón; cuerda, cabo; sedal (de pescar); frontera, límite; línea, sucesión; (imp., etc.) línea, renglón; (com.) renglón, ramo, clase; surtido; (geog.) línea (equinoccial), ecuador; curso, camino; método, plan; línea de conducta o de acción; rumbo; hilera, fila; versos (una línea); especialidad, conocimientos.— *pl.* contornos, apariencia; versos; (tea.) texto de un drama; parte de un actor; curso, plan, método; (fam.) certificado de matrimonio.—**l. drawing,** dibujo de líneas, dibujo instrumental.—**l. drop,** (elec.) caída de potencial en la línea debida a pérdidas.—**l. engraving,** grabado al buril; plancha para grabado al buril.—**l. fishing,** pesca con sedal y anzuelo.—**l. geometry,** geometría de Plücker.—**l. keeper,** (f. c.) guardavía.—**l. of apsides,** (ast.) línea de los ápsides.—**l. of centers,** (geom.) línea de los centros.—**l. of collimation,** (top.) línea de

colimación o de fe.—**l. of departure,** (arti.) dirección de salida de un proyectil.—**l. of flotation,** (mar.) línea de flotación.—**l. of force,** (fís., mag.) línea de fuerza.—**l. of levels,** (top.) línea acotana, línea de nivelación.—**l. of nodes,** (astr.) línea de los nodos.—**l. of sight,** visual.—**l. shaft,** árbol de transmisión.—**in one's l.,** en la especialidad o dentro de los conocimientos de uno.—**out of one's l.,** ajeno a la especialidad o tarea de uno; (asunto) de que uno no entiende.

line. I. va. rayar, trazar líneas en; alinear; enseñar; leer en alta voz línea por línea; forrar, revestir. **II.** vn. alinearse; estar alineado; (gen. con *up*) estar en fila, formar fila; formarse, ponerse en formación.

lineage [líney], s. linaje, prosapia.

lineal [línial], a. lineal; descendiente, hereditario.

lineament [líniamœnt], s. lineamento, facción del rostro.

linear [líniar], a. lineal; longitudinal; (zool. y bot.) linear.—**l. equation,** ecuación del primer grado.—**l. measure,** medida de longitud.

lineate(d [líniéit(ed], a. señalado con líneas.

lineation [líniéshʊn], s. delineación.

lined [láind], a. rayado; forrado.—**l. paper,** papel rayado.

lineman [láinmæn], s. (f. c., tlg., tlf.) recorredor y reparador de la línea; (top.) cadenero.

linen [línen], s. lienzo, lino; género de lino; ropa blanca.—**l. cambric,** olán, batista, cambray.—**l. damask,** damasco de hilo, alemanisco.—**l. draper,** lencero.—**l. goods,** géneros de lino, lencería.—**l. trade,** lencería.—**l. hosiery,** medias de hilo.—**l. prover,** cuentahilos.—**l. weaver,** tejedor de lienzos.

liner [láinœr], s. vapor o avión de una línea establecida; delineador; rayador; forrador; forro; forro tubular de quitapón; placa de cuña: en baseball, pelota voleada horizontalmente.

linesman [láinsmæn], s. (f. c., tlg., tlf.) = LINE MAN.—**l.'s detector,** galvanoscopio probador.

line-up, lineup [-ʊp], s. formación, agrupación; fila; división definida en grupos o partidos.

ling, s. (bot.) brezo; (ict.) curadillo.

linger [língœr]. **I.** vn. demorarse, dilatarse, ir despacio. **II.** va. (con **out** o **away**) prolongar, dilatar, demorar.—**lingerer** [-œr], s. el que se demora.

lingerie [lǽnʏœrí], s. ropa blanca.

lingering [língœring]. **I.** a. lento, prolongado, moroso. **II.** s. tardanza, dilación.—**lingeringly** [-li], adv. lentamente, con dilación.

lingo [língo], s. (fam.) jerga, algarabía.

lingot [língot], s. molde de lingote.

linguadental [línguadéntal], a. linguodental.

lingual [língual]. **I.** a. lingual. **II.** s. letra lingual.

linguist [língüist], s. lingüista, poligloto.

linguistic [língüístic], a. lingüístico.

linguistics, s. lingüística.

liniment [línimœnt], s. linimento, untura.

lining [láining], s. forro; (mar.) embono, encofrado.

link [linc]. **I.** eslabón; enlace, enganche; (top.) 0.01 de cadena de Gúnter (201.2 mm.); (mec.) articulación, gozne; vástago de unión o transmisión; cada una de las partes de un sistema articulado; (m. v.) sector de la excéntrica; (fam.) salchichón.—pl. cancha de golf.—**l. block,** (m. v.) taco del sector de la excéntrica.—**l. fuse,** (elec.) fusible descubierto.—**l. motion,** (m. v.) distribución, sistema o mecanismo de distribución. **II.** va. y vn. enlazar(se), eslabonar(se), encadenar(se); unir(se).

linkage [línkey], s. eslabonamiento, encadenamiento; unión; (mec.) sistema articulado; (elec.) flujo magnético por espira de un arrollamiento.

linkboy [líncbói], **linkman** [-man], s. paje de hacha.

linnet [línet], s. (orn.) jilguero.

linoleum [línólium], s. linóleo.

linotype [línotaip], s. (impr.) linotipo (línea de tipos fundida en una sola pieza]; linotipia, máquina de componer y fundir linotipos.

linseed [línsid], s. linaza.—**l. meal,** harina de linaza.—**l. oil,** aceite de linaza.

linsey-woolsey [línsi-úlsi], a. y s. de hilo y lana mezclados; basto.

lin(t)stock [línstoc], s. botafuego.

lint, s. hilaza; plumón; (cir.) hilas; red.

lintel [líntel], s. (arq.) dintel.

linty [línti], a. hilachoso.

lion [láiʊn], s. león; persona muy festejada; (astr.) León.—**at,** = ANT LION.—**l.-heart,** persona valerosa y noble.—**L.-Heart,** Corazón de León (Ricardo I de Inglaterra).—**l.-hearted,** valeroso y noble.—**l.'s share,** la parte del león, lo mejor.

lioness [-nes], s. leona.

lionize [-aiȥ], va. poner en las nubes.

lionlike [-laic], a. de león, leonino.

lip, s. labio; por extensión, boca, habla; labio de una herida; borde; pico de jarro.—**l. glue,** cola de boca.—**l. devotion,** devoción de boca.—**l. good,** farisaico.—**l. labour,** = L. WISDOM.—**l. reading,** interpretación del movimiento de los labios.—**l. salve,** ungüento para los labios.—**l. stick,** barrita para pintarse los labios.—**l. wisdom,** jarabe de pico, palabras vanas.

lipoma [lipómæ], s. (med.) lipoma.

lipomatosis [-tósis], s. degeneración crasa.

lipothymy [lipózimi], s. lipotimia, síncope.

lipped [lipt], a. que tiene labios.

liquable [lícuabœl], a. licuable, liquidable.

liquate [láikueit]. **I.** va. liquidar(se), derretir(se), fundir(se). **II.** va. extraer por fusión.—**liquation** [laicuéshʊn], **liquefaction** [licuefæcshʊn], s. licuación, licuefacción.—**liquefiable** [lícuefaiabœl], a. liquidable.—**liquefy** [lícuefai], va. y vn. liquidar(se).

liquescence, liquescency [licuésens, si], s. (fís.) licuescencia.

liquescent [-sent], a. (fís.) licuescente.

liqueur [licœr], s. cordial, pluscafé.

liquid [lícuid], s. y a. líquido.—**l. assets,** valores realizables.—**l. fire,** petróleo ardiendo.—**l. measure,** medida para líquidos.—**l. securities** = L. ASSETS.

liquidambar [lícuidámbar], s. liquidámbar.—**l. tree,** (bot.) ocozol, estoraque.

liquidate [lícuideit], va. liquidar, saldar cuentas.—**liquidation** [-éishʊn], s. (com.) liquidación.—**liquidator** [lícuidéitœr], s. (for.) = RECEIVER.

liquidity [licuíditi], **liquidness** [lícuidnes], s. liquidez, fluidez.

liquor [lícœr], s. licor, aguardiente; solución, baño, licor.—**l. case,** cantina, frasquera; [láicuor o lícuor] (farm.) solución (simple o química).

liquorice, s. = LICORICE.

lira [líra], s. lira (moneda).

lisp. I. va. y vn. balbucir o balbucear, cecear. **II.** s. ceceo; balbucencia.

lisper [líspœr], s. el que cecea.

lisping, a. ceceoso; balbuciente.—**lispingly** [-li], adv. con ceceo.

lissom(e [lísʊm], a. = LITHSOME.

list. I. s. lista; (tej.) orilla, borde del paño; lista, tira, cenefa; (arq.) filete, listel, orla, listón, barandal; (carp.) tabloncillo; (poét.) borde, límite; (mar.) falsa banda, bandeo.—pl. liza, palestra.—**l. price,** precio de tarifa o corriente. **II.** va. registrar, poner en lista, matricular, inscribir; catalogar; (com.) cotizar, facturar; (mil.) alistar; cercar (liza) para torneos; guarnecer con listones o cenefas; (poét.) escuchar; (mar.) dar carena al buque. **III.** vn. inclinarse a la banda, escorar.

listed [listed], a. listado, listeado; (com.) cotizado.

listel [lístel], s. (arq.) listel, filete.

listen [lisn], vn. (con *to*) escuchar.—**to l. in,** (tlg., tlf.) escuchar a hurtadillas, intercalar o arreglar un instrumento receptor para enterarse subrepticiamente de comunicaciones enviadas a otras personas; escuchar.

listener [lísnœr], s. escuchador, oyente.

listening [lísning], a. de escuchar, de escucha.—**l. cam, l. key, l. plug,** clavija de intercalación o de escucha, por medio de la cual el telefonista

conecta su receptor con el circuito de un suscritor.
—**l. post,** escucha.
lister [lístœr], *s.* (agr.) arado sembrador.
listerine [lístœrin], *s.* (farm.) listerina.
Listerism [-iŝm], *s.* listerismo (procedimiento antiséptico).
listing [lísting], *s.* orilla de paño, tira, cenefa.
listless [lístles], *a.* desatento; indiferente, descuidado.—**listlessly** [-li], *adv.* indiferentemente.—**listlessness** [-nes], *s.* descuido, indiferencia.
lit [lit], *pret.* y *pp.* de TO LIGHT.
litany [lítani], *s.* letania.
liter [lítœr], *s.* litro.
literacy [líteræsi], *s.* capacidad de leer y escribir.
literal [lítœral], *a.* literal; positivista.—**literalism** [-iŝm], *s.* exactitud literal; (b. a.) naturalismo.—**literalist** [-ist], *s.* escrupulosamente exacto; positivista.—**literally** [-li], *s, adv.* literalmente.—**literalness** [-nes], *s.* exactitud literal; materialidad, positivismo.
literary [lítœreri], *a.* literario.—**l. property,** propiedad literaria.
literate [lítœret], *a.* y *s.* literato; que sabe leer y escribir.
literati [lítœrétai], *s.pl.* literatos, doctos, eruditos.
literatim [lítœrétim *o* átim], *adv.* letra por letra, a la letra; literalmente.
literature [lítœræchur], *s.* literatura; obras literarias; trabajo literario; (com.) escritos de publicidad (circulares, catálogos, etc.).
litharge [lízary], *s.* litargirio.
lithate [lízet], *s.* urato.
lithe [láiᴅ], *a.* flexible, delgado, blando.
lithemia [liᵭímiæ], *s.* exceso de uratos y ácido úrico en la sangre.
litheness [láiᴅnes], *s.* flexibilidad, flojedad; blandura.
lithesome [-sᴜm], *a.* (poét.) flexible.
lithia [lízia], *s.* (quím.) litina.
lithiasis [lizái- (*o* zí-) asis], *s.* (med.) litiasis, mal de piedra.
lithic [lízic], *a.* lítico.
lithium [líziᴜm], *s.* (quím.) litio.
lithocolla [lízocóla], *s.* litocola.
lithograph [lízograf]. **I.** *va., vn.* litografiar. **II.** *s.* litografía (impresión).
lithographer [lizógrafœr], *s.* litógrafo.
lithographic [lízográfic], *a.* litográfico.—**l. stone,** piedra litográfica.
lithography [lizógrafi], *s.* litografía (arte.)
lithoid(al [lízoid, lizóidal], *a.* litoideo.
litholapaxy [lizolapéxi], *s.* (cir.) litotricia.
litholatry [lizólætri], *s.* culto de las piedras.
lithologic(al [lízolóyic(al], *a.* litológico.
lithologist [lizóloyist], *s.* litólogo.
lithology [lizóloyi], *s.* (geol.) litología; (med.) tratado sobre los cálculos.
lithontriptic [lizontríptic], *a.* y *s.* litotrípico, litagogo.
lithophone [lízofoun], *s.* litoscopio.
lithophyte [lízofait], *s.* litófito.
lithotomist [lizótomist], *s.* (cir.) litotomista.
lithotomy [lizótomi], *s.* (cir.) litotomía, talla.
lithotrity [lizótriti *o* lízotraiti], *s.* (cir.) litotricia.
lithotrite [lízotrait], *s.* litotrictor.
litigant [lítigant], *s.* y *a.* litigante.—**litigate** [-gueit], *va.* y *vn.* litigar, pleitear.—**litigation** [-guéiŝhᴜn], *s.* litigio, pleito.—**litigator** [-guéitœr], *s.* pleiteador.
litigious [litíyᴜs], *a.* litigioso.—**litigiously** [-li], *adv.* de un modo litigioso.—**litigiousness** [-nes], *s.* inclinación a pleitear.
litmus [lítmᴜs], *s.* tornasol en pasta.—**l. paper,** papel de tornasol.
litotes [lítotiŝ], *s.* (ret.) lítotes.
litre [lítœr], *s.* litro.
litter [lítœr]. **I.** *s.* litera; camilla, parihuela; cama de paja para las caballerías; parto; cría, camada; (fig.) objetos en desorden. **II.** *va.* parir; esparcir, poner en desorden; extender. **III.** *vn.* parir.

litterateur [lítœratœr], *s.* literato.
little [lítœl]. **I.** *a.* poco; pequeño; insignificante; apocado; despreciable, ruin, mezquino. Se traduce a menudo por una desinencia diminutiva: *a little girl,* una muchachita; *a little watch,* un relojito.—**L. Bear,** (atr.) Osa Menor.—**l. brain,** cerebelo.—**L. Corporal,** Cabito (Napoleón).—**l. finger,** dedo meñique.—**l. hours,** (igl.) horas menores.—**l. office,** (igl.) oficio parvo.—**l. one,** niñito, muchachito.—**a l.** (seguido de sustantivo), un poco de. **II.** *adv.* poco. **III.** *s.* poco.—**l. by l.,** o **by l. and l.,** poco a poco.
littleness [-nes], *s.* pequeñez, poquedad; ruindad, mezquindad, bajeza.
littoral [lítoral], *s.* y *a.* litoral.
liturgic(al [litœryic(al], *a.* litúrgico.
liturgy [lítœryi], *s.* (igl.) liturgia.
live [liv]. **I.** *va.* pasar, llevar (tal o cual vida); habituarse a, hacerse a. **II.** *vn.* vivir; mantenerse, subsistir; (mar.) salvarse.—**to l. down,** sobrevivir a; refutar una calumnia, borrar una falta.—**to l. from hand to mouth,** vivir al día.—**to l. on,** vivir de.—**to l. up to,** vivir en conformidad con, vivir dentro de.—**to l. up to one's promise,** cumplir lo prometido.
live [láiv], *a.* vivo, viviente; de la vida, vital; encendido, en ascua; activo, listo; de interés actual; hirviendo de (fig.), repleto de; (imp.) útil, disponible; (artl.) cargado; (elec.) cargado (de electricidad), activo.—**l. axle,** eje motor.—**l. bait,** carnada viva (apl. esp. a pececillos que sirven de cebo en el anzuelo).—**l. box,** portaobjetos para el examen de animales microscópicos; cajón perforado para mantener vivos los pescados.—**l. coal,** brasa de carbón.—**l. load,** carga móvil, carga variable.—**l. oak,** encina perenne (siempre verde) norteamericana.—**l. spindle,** nuso o tambor (de torno).—**l. steam,** vapor vivo o de la caldera (no de escape).—**l. stock,** ganado.—**l. wire,** (elec.) alambre cargado o activo; (fam.) trafagón, persona de grande actividad.
livelihood [lívlijud], *s.* vida, subsistencia.
liveliness [láivlines], *s.* vida, animación; agilidad, actividad.
livelong [lívlong], *a.* todo, entero.—**all the l. day,** todo el santo día.
lively [láivli]. **I.** *a.* vivo, vivaz, vivaracho; gallardo, airoso; rápido; animado, bullicioso. **II.** *adv.* enérgicamente; vivamente; aprisa.
liver [lívœr], *s.* vividor; hígado; higadilla.—**l. colour,** color carmelita.—**l. complaint,** mal de hígado.
livered [lívœrd], *a.* de hígado.
liveried [lívœrid], *a.* que lleva librea.
liverwort [lívœruœrt], *s.* (bot.) hepática.
livery [lívœri], *s.* librea; uniforme; cochería de alquiler; (for.) entrega, acto de dar posesión de tierras; (ant.) ración.—**l. carriage,** o **l. coach,** carruaje de alquiler.—**l. horse,** caballo de alquiler.—**l. stable,** pensión de caballos; cochería de alquiler.
liveryman [mæn], *s.* dueño de cochería de alquiler; criado de librea; (Ingl.) individuo de algún gremio.
liverymen [-men], *s. pl.* de LIVERYMAN.
lives [láivŝ], *s. pl.* vidas.
livid [lívid], *a.* lívido.
lividity [lividiti], **lividness** [lívidnes], *s.* lividez.
living [líving]. **I.** *s.* vida; subsistencia, mantenimiento; vida, potencia vital; beneficio eclesiástico.—**the l.,** los vivientes, los vivos. **II.** *a.* vivo, viviente.—**l. language,** lengua viva.—**l. rock,** roca viva.—**l. room,** sala de confianza, cuarto general de habitación y recibo.—**l. wage,** salario natural, salario de subsistencia plena (inclusas las necesidades higiénicas, morales e intelectuales del obrero y su familia).
lixivial [liksívial], **lixiviate** [lixívieit], *a.* lixiviado.—**lixiviate,** *va.* lixiviar; hacer lejía.—**lixiviation** [-éiŝhᴜn], *s.* lixiviación.
lixivium [liksíviᴜm], *s.* lejía.
lizard [líŝard], *s.* (zool.) lagarto, lagartija.
llama [lâma], *s.* (zool.) llama.
lo, *interj.* he aquí, ved aquí, mirad.
loach [lóuch], *s.* (ict.) locha, lobo.

---

load [lóud]. **I.** *s.* carga; (pint.) adición de color blanco, para obtener opacidad; (fam., gen. *pl.*) montón, montones, gran cantidad o número, muchísimo; (fam.) borrachera.—**l. line,** línea de flotación; (mec.) línea o diagrama de cargas. **II.** *va.* y *vn.* cargar; recargar; agregar al premio de un seguro para cubrir ciertos gastos; (pint.) agregar color blanco para producir opacidad.

loader [lóudœr], *s.* cargador, embarcador.

loading [-ing]. **I.** *a.* de cargar; que carga.—**l. coil,** (rad.) bobina de inducción para cambiar la longitud de la onda. **II.** *s.* acción de cargar; recargo aumentado al premio de una póliza para cubrir ciertos gastos; (rad.) cambio de la longitud de la onda de un instrumento.

loadstar [lóudstar], *s.* = LODESTAR.

loadstone [lóudstoun], *s.* piedra imán.

loaf [lóuf]. **I.** *s.* hogaza de pan.—**l. of sugar,** pan de azúcar.—**l. sugar,** azúcar de pilón.—**loaves and fishes,** gajes, ganancias; (pol.) turrón. **II.** *va.* (con **away**) haraganear, holgazanear.

loafer [lóufœr], *s* haragán, holgazán; cantonero, arrimón, corrillero.

loam [lóum]. **I.** *s.* barro, marga; arcilla plástica; (fund.) tierra de moldeo. **II.** *va.* untar con marga; cubrir con arcilla o barro.—**loamy** [-i], *a.* margoso, gredoso.

loan [lóun]. **I.** *s.* préstamo; prestación, presti-monio; (com.) empréstito; (for.) mutuo, como-[dato.—**l. office,** casa de empeños. **II.** *va.* pres-[tar.

loath [lóuz], *a.* poco dispuesto.

loathe [lóub]. **I.** *va.* detestar, abominar. **II.** *vn.* tener hastío, sentir fastidio, disgusto o aborreci-miento.—**loather** [-œr], *s.* el que siente disgusto o aborrecimiento.—**loathful** [-ful], *a.* lleno de tedio o aversión.—**loathing,** [-ing], *s.* aversión, asco, repugnancia.—**loathingly** [-ingli], *adv.* de mala gana, con repugnancia.—**loathsome** [-sum], *a.* aborrecible, repugnante, asqueroso.—**loathsome-ly** [-li], *adv.* asquerosamente.—**loathsomeness** [-nes], *s.* calidad de repugnante o asqueroso.

loaves [lóuvs], *pl.* de LOAF.

lob. I. *s.* lombriz para cebo; masa, mezcla blan-da y espesa; en tenis, voleo alto y tendido de la pelota; en el *cricket,* voleo bajo. **II.** *va.* hacer un *lob* con la pelota.

lobar [lóubar], *a.* lobular.

lobate(d [lóubet(ed], *a.* lobulado.

lobby [lóbi]. **I.** *s.* paso, pasillo, corredor; salón de entrada (de un hotel); antecámara, vestí-bulo; (E. U., pol.) camarilla de cabilderos. **II.** *va.* y *vn.* (E., U. pol.) cabildear.

lobbying [lóbiing], *s.* (E. U., pol.) cabildeo.

lobbyist [lóbiist], *s.* (E. U., pol.) cabildero.

lobe [lóub], *s.* lóbulo, lobo.

lobed [lóubd], *a.* lobado, lobulado.

lobelia [loblfia], *s.* (bot.) lobelia.

lobster [lóbstœr], (ict.) langosta americana; can-grejo de mar.

lobulate [lóbiulet], *a.* lobulado.

lobule [lóbiul], *s. dim.* lobulillo.

local [lóucœl]. **I.** *a.* local; regional.—**l. attrac-tion,** (top.) atracción anormal, perturbación (de la brújula) debida a la presencia de hierro en la vecindad; (fís., etc.) atracción de la plomada (por montañas, etc.).—**l. battery,** (tlg.) batería local, batería del receptor.—**l. government,** auto-nomía en asuntos puramente locales.—**l. horizon,** horizonte sensible.—**l. option,** (E. U.) derecho u obligación de una división territorial (distrito, ciu-dad, etc.) de establecer por sí y para sí ciertas ordenanzas (esp. las relativas a la venta de licores). —**l. time,** hora local, tiempo local.—**l. train,** tren seccional, que circula sólo en un tramo de un fe-rrocarril.—**l. value,** (arit.) valor relativo (de una cifra). **II.** *s.* (E. U.) tren seccional; (Ingl.) tren suburbano; (fam.) noticia de interés local.

localism [lóucalism], *s.* costumbre o locución local; provincialismo.

locality [locœliti], *s.* situación; localidad, lugar, plaza.

localization [lócalisêshun], *s.* localización.

localize [lócalais], *va.* localizar.

locally [lóucali], *adv.* localmente.

locate [lókeit], *va.* poner, colocar, situar; (f. c.) trazar la vía de.—**located** [-ed], *a.* sito, situado.

location [lokéshun], *s.* ubicación, colocación; sitio, localidad; situación, posición; (f. c.) trazado de la vía.

loch [loj], *s.* lago; ensenada.

lochia [lókia], *s. pl.* loquios.

lock [loc]. **I.** *s.* cerradura, cerraja; llave (de las armas de fuego); esclusa; abrazo estrecho y apretado; cerca, vallado; calabozo; bucle, guedeja; borla; trabas, maniotas.—*pl.* cabellos.—**l. nut,** tuerca de seguridad.—**l. stitch,** punto de cadeneta.—**l., stock and barrel,** el todo; por completo.—**under l. and key,** bajo llave. **II.** *va.* cerrar con llave, acerrojar, candar; poner cerra-dura; hacer pasar por una esclusa; juntar, atar, entrelazar, trabar; (impr.) acuñar, cerrar la forma; abrazar; fijar, trincar; cerrar.—**to l. in,** encerrar, poner bajo llave; abrazar.—**to l. one out,** cerrar la puerta a uno; dejar en la calle.—**to l. up,** en-cerrar; encarcelar. **III.** *vn.* cerrarse con llave; unirse, enlazarse; trabarse; sujetarse.

lockage [lóker], *s.* materiales u obra de una esclusa; diferencia de nivel en un canal de esclusas; derechos o portazgo de esclusa.

locker [lókœr], *s.* cajón, gaveta; alacena, ropero, armario; cerrador.—*pl.* cajonada.

locket [lóket], *s.* guardapelo, relicario.

locking [lóking], *a.* fijador, de fijación; de cierre; de traba.—**l. plate,** platillo fijador.—**l. wire,** (aer.) alambre fijador.

lockjaw [lócyo], *s.* (med.) trismo, tétano.

locknut [lócnŏt], *s.* = LOCK NUT. *V.* LOCK.

lockout [lócaut], *s.* cierre (de fábrica); paro (en las huelgas).

lockram [lócram], *s.* lienzo basto.

locksmith [lócsmiz], *s.* cerrajero.

lockup [lócup], *s.* calabozo; cárcel; encarcela-miento.

locomobile [lócomóubil], *a.* locomóvil.

locomotion [-móshun], *s.* locomoción.

locomotive [-mótiv]. **I.** *a.* locomotor, locomóvil. **II.** *s.* locomotora.—**l. boiler,** caldera de locomo-tora o de tipo locomotora.—**l. engine,** (máquina) locomotora.

locomotor [-mótœr], *a.* locomotor, locomotriz.— **l. ataxia,** ataxia locomotriz.

locust [lócust], *s.* (ento.) langosta, saltamontes; (E. U.) cigarra.—**l., o l. tree,** (bot.) curbaril; robinia; algarrobo.

locution [lokiúshun], *s.* locución, frase.

locutory [lókiutori], *s.* (igl.) locutorio.

lode [lóud], *s.* (min.) filón, veta, vena; (hidr.) reguera, acequia.

lodestar [lóudstar], *s.* estrella de guía; estrella polar.

lodestone [lóudstóun], *s.* piedra imán.

lodge [loy]. **I.** *va.* alojar, hospedar, albergar; colocar; plantar, introducir, fijar; dar a guar-dar, poner a recaudo.—**to l. a complaint,** dar una queja. **II.** *vn.* vivir, morar, parar, hospedarse; tenderse, echarse. **III.** *s.* casa de guarda; pabellón; casita accesoria; logia.

lodgment [lóymœnt], *s.* colocación; alojamiento; amontonamiento, acumulación; (mil.) atrin-cheramiento.

lodger [lóyœr], *s.* huésped, inquilino.

lodging [lóying], *s.* posada, hospedería; vivienda; albergue; hospedaje; (mil.) alojamiento; rada, residencia.—**l. house,** casa de huéspedes o de pupilos.—**l. knees,** (mar.) curvas valonas.

loft [loft], *s.* piso, sobrado, desván; almacén.

loftily [lóftili], *adv.* elevadamente, levantada-mente; hinchadamente.

loftiness [-nes], *s.* altura, elevación; excelsitud; altanería, orgullo; majestad.

lofty [lófti], *a.* altísimo, elevado, encumbrado; eminente, excelso; altivo, orgulloso.

log [log]. **I.** *s.* leño, palo; tronco, troza; (mar.) corredera; barquilla de la corredera.—**l. board,** (mar.) tableta de bitácora.—**l. book,** cuaderno de bitácora; diario de navegación.—**l. cabin, l. hut,** cabaña rústica, caney.—**l. line,** (mar.) corredera.

—**l. reel,** carretel, devanadera. **II.** *vn.* cortar aserrar y transportar trozas; extraer madera.

logarithm [lógarizm], *s.* logaritmo.

logarithmic(al [lógarízmic(al], *a.* logarítmico.

loggerhead [lógœrjed], *s.* zote, necio; tortuga marina. —**at loggerheads,** en desacuerdo, en disputa; de uñas. —**to fall, get o go to logger-heads,** venir a las manos.

logging [lóguing], *s.* corte y transporte de trozas.

logia [lóguiæ], *s. pl.* de LOGION: máximas y palabras atribuídas a Jesucristo pero que no se hallan en los libros canónicos.

logic [lóyic], *s.* lógica.—**logical** [lóyical], *a.* lógico; natural. —**logically** [-l], *adv.* lógicamente.

logician [loyíshæn], *s.* lógico.

logistic [loyístic], *a.* logístico (logaritmo).

logistics [loyístics], *s. pl.* (mil.) arte de transportes y abastecimientos.

logman [lógman], *s.* leñero.

logogram [lógogræm], *s.* abreviatura o signo que indica una palabra, como **lb.,** £, $; logogrifo, enigma en verso.

logograph [lógograf], *s.* palabra escrita.

logogriph [lógogrif], *s.* logogrifo.

logomachy [logómaki], *s.* logomaquia; juego de formar anagramas.

Logos [logos], *s.* (teol.) Verbo; (fil.) el principio racional del universo.

logroll [lógrrol], *vn.* hacer rodar tozas.

logrolling, tarea de rodar tozas; (E. U.) junta o cabildeo de politicastros.

logwood [lógúd], *s.* palo de Campeche o de tinte.

loin [lóin], *s.* ijada, ijar.—*pl.* lomos.

loiter [lóitœr]. **I.** *vn.* holgazanear, haraganear, vagar. **II.** *va.* malgastar (tiempo).—**loiterer** [-œr], *s.* vagabundo, haragán u holgazán.—**loitering** [-ing]. **I.** *a.* vago, haragán. **II.** *s.* vagancia.

loll [lol]. **I.** *vn.* apoyarse, recostarse, tenderse; colgar, estar colgando. **II.** *va.* sacar la lengua.

lollypop [lólipop], *s.* variedad de melcocha o arropía.

loment [lómœnt], *s.* (bot.) lomento.

Londoner [lœnduncœr], *s.* londinense.

lone [lóun], *a.* solitario, solo; soltero.—**loneliness** [-lines], *s.* soledad; tristeza del aislamiento.—**lonely** [-li], *a.* solitario; solo; amante de la soledad; triste.—**loneness** [-nes], *s.* soledad; tristeza.

lonesome [-sum], *a.* solitario, desierto; triste.—**lonesomely** [-li], *adv.* solitariamente; tristemente.—**lonesomeness** [-nes], *s.* soledad; tristeza.

long [long]. **I.** *a.* largo; de largo (a veces con *to be,* que entonces es tener: *this tape is 2 inches long,* esta cinta tiene 2 pulgadas de largo); tardío, dilatorio; excesivo, de más; remoto, distante; (com.) recargado, esperando alza de precios (apl. esp. al tenedor de valores de bolsa).—**l. clothes,** ropón de niño, pañales.—**l.-cut tobacco,** tabaco en hebras.—**l. division,** (arit.) división en que se escriben los productos parciales, división no abreviada.—**l.-distance** (tlf.) de larga distancia (apl. gen. a comunicaciones más allá de los límites dentro de los cuales se paga el abono ordinario).—**l. dozen,** docena del fraile—trece.—**l. measure,** medida de longitud.—**L. Parliament,** (hist.) Parlamento Largo.—**l. primer,** (impr.) entredós, letra de 10 puntos.—**l. staple,** fibra o hebra larga.—**l. sufferance,** fortitud.—**l. suffering,** paciencia en el sufrimiento.—**l. ton,** tonelada de 2240 libras.—**how l.,** de qué largo. **II.** *adv.* a gran distancia; mucho, mucho tiempo.—**l. ago,** mucho tiempo ha. —**l.-drawn,** (ort.) lento, pesado, prolongado.—**l.-eared,** orejudo.—**l.-headed,** astuto, listo, sagaz. —**l.-legged,** zanquilargo.—**l.-lived,** longevo, de larga vida.—**l.-shanked** = L.-LEGGED.—**l.-sighted,** présbite; sagaz, previsor, precavido.—**l. since** = L. AGO.—**l.-stapled,** de hebra larga.—**l.-suffering,** paciente, sufrido.—**l.-tongued,** lenguaraz, chismoso.—**l.-winded,** largo, pesado, prolijo.—**all,** o **the whole, day, year,** etc., **l.,** todo el santo día, año, etc.—**as l.** as, mientras. —**how l.,** cuánto tiempo.—**how l. is it since?** ¿cuánto (tiempo) hace que? ¿cuánto tiempo hace?—**not l. before,** poco tiempo antes.—**so l. as,**mientras que, en tanto que. **III.** *s.* longitud, largo; (mús.) longa; (pros.) sílaba larga.—*pl.* (com.) los que guardan acciones en

espera de alza.—**the l. and the short,** el meollo. **IV.** *vn.* (con *for*) anhelar, suspirar (por).

longboat [lóngbóut], *s.* lancha, chalupa, falúa.

longe [lony], *s.* estocada; pista.

longer [lóngœr]. **I.** *a. comp.* de LONG; más largo. **II.** *adv.* comparativo de LONG; más tiempo.—**ho** **much l.,** cuánto tiempo más.—**no l.,** ya no.

longeron [lónjerón], *s.* (aer.) larguero.

longest [lónguest], *a. y adv. super.* de LONG.—**at the l.,** a más tardar, cuando más.

longeval, longevous [lonyíval, vus], *a.* longevo.

longevity [lonyéviti], *s.* longevidad.

longhand [lóngjænd], *s.* escritura corrida, sin abreviaciones.

longicorn [lónyicorn], *a. y s.* (ent.) longicornic.

longimanous [lonyímanus], *a.* longimano.

longimetry [lonyímetri], *s.* longimetría.

longing [lónguing], *s.* deseo vehemente, anhelo, ansia.

longingly [-li], *adv.* vehementemente; anhelantemente.

longish [lónguish], *a.* algo largo, largucho.

longitude [lónyitiud], *s.* (geog.) longitud.

longitudinal [-tiúdinal], *a.* longitudinal.

longitudinally [-i], *adv.* longitudinalmente, a lo largo.

longly [lóngli], *adv.* por mucho tiempo; prolijamente; extensamente.

longshoreman [lóngshócerman], *s.* estivador, trabajador de muelle.

longspun [-spún], *a.* = LONG-DRAWN OUT. *V.* LONG.

longways [-uéis], *adv.* (fam.) = LENGTHWISE.

loof [luf], *s.* (mar.) lof.

look [luc]. **I.** *va.* mirar, pasar la vista a; examinar, estudiar; causar (vergüenza, silencio, etc.) en, con la mirada; expresar, indicar con la mirada o el ademán.—**to l. a gift horse in the mouth,** mirarle el diente a caballo regalado.—**to l. daggers,** echar chispas; (con *at*) mirar con amenaza, o echando chispas.—**to l. in the face,** mirar cara a cara; mirar sin vergüenza.—**to l. over,** examinar.—**to l. up,** buscar, averiguar. **II.** *vn.* mirar; parecer; poner cuidado; tener cuidado; lucir (bien o mal); tener o estar de buen o mal semblante.—**to l. about,** mirar alrededor; observar.—**to l. about one,** estar alerta, tener vigilancia.—**to l. after,** cuidar; tener cuidado de; prestar atención; buscar, inquirir, investigar.—**to l. alike,** parecerse.—**to l. at,** mirar; considerar; atender.—**to l. back,** reflexionar; mirar atrás.—**to l. down upon,** despreciar.—**to l. for,** esperar; buscar.—**to l. forward,** prever; mirar al o pensar en el porvenir.—**to l. forward to,** esperar.—**to l. into,** examinar, estudiar, averiguar.—**to l. like,** parecerse a; dar o haber señales de (mejor es cambiar el giro: *it looks like rain,* parece que va a llover).—**to l. on,** considerar, estimar, juzgar; mirar, ver; ser espectador; dar o caer a.—**to l. out,** tener cuidado.—**to l. out for,** buscar; esperar; tener cuidado con.—**to l. out of,** asomarse a.—**to l. sharp,** tener ojo avizor.—**to l. through,** examinar, inspeccionar, hacer un registro de.—**to l. to,** cuidar de, velar por; atender a; hacer responsable; esperar de.—**to l. up to,** respetar, estimar.—**to l. upon,** considerar; estimar, dar o caer a. **III.** *s.* mirada, ojeada, vistazo; (gen. *pl.*) aspecto, semblante, cara aire, ademán.

looker, looker-on, [lúkœr, on], *s.* mirón; espectador.

looking [lúking], **I.** *s.* apariencia. **II.** *a.* de mirar, paramirar,—**l. glass,** espejo.

lookout [lúkaut], *s.* vigía, vigilancia; observación; mirador, garita, atalaya; guardia.—**to be on the l.,** estar a la mira.

loom [lum]. **I.** *s.* telar; (mar.) guión del remo; (elec.) tubo flexible; presencia, aparición.—**l. shuttle,** lanzadera mecánica. **II.** *vn.* asomar, aparecer; descollar; lucir, relucir.

looming [lúming], *s.* (ópt.) espejismo.

loon [lun], *s.* bobo, tonto; (orn.) somorgujo.

loop [lup]. **I.** *s.* gaza, lazo, bucle; ojal, presilla, alamar; curva, vuelta; (cost.) onda; (fort.) aspillera; (mec.) abrazadera, anilla; espira o vuelta vertical de un ferrocarril centrífugo; (f. c.)

vuelta (de un desarrollo).—**l. aerial, o antenna,** (rád.) antena de cuadro —**l.-the-l.,** ferrocarril centrífugo con espiras verticales. **II.** *va.* asegurar con presilla; hacer gazas en; formar festones o curvas en.—**to l. in,** (elec.) intercalar (en un circuito); formar gaza o vuelta en un alimentador e intercalar en ella la estación intermedia, en vez de emplear un conductor separado de derivación.—**to l. the l.,** dar una vuelta en una espira vertical de un ferrocarril centrífugo; (aer.) hacer el rizo, dar una vuelta vertical; (fam.) salir bien en una empresa ardua. **III.** *vn.* andar haciendo curvas; formar gaza.

looper [lúpœr], *s.* engazador.

loophole [lúpjóul], *s.* abertura, mirador; (fort.) aspillera, tronera; escapatoria, excusa.

loopholed [-dị, *a.* que tiene troneras o aspilleras.

loose [lus]. **I.** *va.* desatar, desprender; desliar; aflojar; soltar, libertar, librar; desenredar; desocupar.—**to l. one's hold,** soltar. **II.** *a.* suelto; desatado, desenredado; flojo, holgado; vago, indefinido; suelto de vientre; libre, relajado, disoluto; suelto, en libertad; descuidado, negligente, remiso.—**l.-bodied,** suelto, ancho, holgado (vestido).—**l. in the bowels,** suelto de vientre. —**l. morals,** moral relajada. **III.** *s.* libertad; soltura.—**to give l.,** to, dar rienda suelta a.

loosely [lúsli], *adv.* flojamente; sin cohesión; vaga o indefinidamente.

loosen [lúsen]. **I.** *va.* aflojar, soltar, desunir, desatar, desligar; solver; relajar; ablandar; librar, libertar; soltar el vientre.—**to l. the sails,** (mar.) largar o descargar las velas. **II.** *vn.* desunirse, aflojarse, desatarse, desasirse, separarse.

looseness [lúsnes], *s.* aflojamiento, flojedad, holgura; relajación, licencia; soltura; flujo de vientre; vaguedad.

loosening [lúsning]. **I.** *a.* laxante. **II.** *s.* aflojadura, desatadura.

loot [lut]. **I.** *va.* saquear, pillar; llevarse como botín. **II.** *s.* botín; pillaje.

lop. **I.** *va.* desmochar, chapodar; maestrear; cortar y doblar hacia abajo. **II.** *vn.* colgar. **III.** *s.* rama podada; oreja gacha.

lope [lóup]. **I.** *va.* y *vn.* galopar; saltar. **II.** *s.* galope tendido.

lophobranch [lófobrænc], *a.* (zool.) lofobranquio. —**Lophobranchii** [-brænkiai], lofobranquios.

lopping [lóping], *s.* poda, desmoche.

lopsided [lópsaided], *a.* más pesado de un lado que de otro; desequilibrado; maniático.

loquacious [locuéśhʋs], *a.* locuaz, lenguaz.

loquaciousness [-nes], **loquacity** [locuǽsiti], *s.* locuacidad, habladuría.

lord. **I.** *s.* señor; amo, dueño, patrón; castellano; marido; lord.—**L. Chamberlain,** camarero mayor.—**L. Chief Justice,** presidente del tribunal supremo de Inglaterra.—**L. Deputy,** virrey. —**L. High Chancellor,** ministro de justicia, o gran canciller.—**L. High Steward,** mayordomo mayor. —**L. Lieutenant,** virrey y gobernador de Irlanda. —**L. Mayor,** alcalde o corregidor de Londres.— **L.'s day,** domingo, día del Señor.—**L.'s Prayer,** padre nuestro.—**L.'s Supper,** la última cena; Sacramento de la Eucaristía.—**L.'s table,** altar de la sagrada comunión; comunión, Eucaristía.— **Our L.,** Nuestro Señor.—**the L.,** el Señor. **II.** *va.* investir con la dignidad de lord; dar el título de lord; gobernar, mandar.—**to l. it over,** dominar, mandar despótica o altaneramente, imponerse a. **III.** *vn.* mandar imperiosamente.—**to l. over** = TO L. IT OVER.

lordliness [lórdlines], *s.* dignidad, señorío; altivez, orgullo.

lord(l)ing [lórd(l)ing], *s.* (despec.) hidalguillo, señorito, pequeño lord.

lordly [lórdli]. **I.** *a.* perteneciente a un lord; señoril; orgulloso, imperioso. **II.** *adv.* señorilmente, imperiosamente.

lordship [lórdśhip], *s.* señorío, dominio, poder; señoría, excelencia.—**your l.,** usía; vuecencia.

lore [lóœr], *s.* erudición, saber, ciencia.

lorgnette [lornét], *s.* impertinentes; gemelos de teatro con mango.

lorica [lorǽica *o* lorǐca], *s.* (ant.) loriga; (zool.) cubierta protectora; brasca o luten para los crisoles.

loricate [lóriket]. **I.** *va.* enchapar, planchear; esmaltar. **II.** *a.* planchado, enchapado.

lorication [-éishʋn], *s.* enchapado; esmalte.

loris, *s.* (zool.) especie de lemur.

lorn, *a.* sin parientes ni amigos.

lorry [lórri], *s.* autocamión; carro de plataforma de cuatro ruedas.

lory [lóri], *s.* (orn.) especie de loro.

los(e)able [lúsabœl], *a.* fácil de perder.

lose [lúś]. **I.** *va.* (*pret.* y *pp.* LOST) perder; malograr; entregar a la ignominia o a la ruina; quitar, hacer perder.—**to l. ground,** perder terreno.—**to l. heart,** desanimarse.—**to l. one's heart,** enamorarse.—**to l. one's mind,** enloquecerse.—**to l. one's temper,** perder los estribos, encolerizarse.—**to l. one's way,** perderse, andar perdido.—**to l. sight of,** perder de vista. **II.** *vr.* perderse, extraviarse. **III.** *vn.* perder, tener una pérdida.

loser [lúśœr], *s.* perdedor, el que pierde algo o no logra lo que desea.

loss [los], *s.* pérdida.—**at a l.,** perdiendo, con pérdida; perplejo, en duda, sin saber que hacer.

lost [lost], *a.* y *pret.* y *pp.* de TO LOSE: perdido.— **l. cause,** (hist. E. U.) la causa de los esclavistas.— **l. motion,** (mec.) juego inútil, juego muerto, pérdida debida a conexiones flojas o inadecuadas.—**l. or not l.,** (com.) cláusula especial del seguro que cubre todos los riesgos.—**l. to,** insensible a; perdido para.

lot. **I.** *s.* lote; suerte, hado, sino; cuota, partija, parte, porción; solar de terreno; (fam., a veces *pt.*) gran cantidad; mucho; muchos. **II.** *va.* asignar, repartir.

lotah [lóta], *s.* escudilla de cobre.

lote [lóut], *s.* = LOTUS.

loth [louz], *a.* = LOATH.

lothario [lozé- (*o* zá) rio], *s.* libertino.

lotion [lóśhʋn], *s.* loción, ablución.

lotos *o* **lotus** [lótʋs], *s.* (bot.) loto, ninfea.— **l.-eater,** lotófago; lujurioso.—**l. tree,** loto, almez.

lottery [lótœri], *s.* lotería, rifa.

lotto [lóto], *s.* lotería, juego casero.

loud [láud]. **I.** *a.* ruidoso, fuerte, recio; alta (la voz); turbulento, estrepitoso; (fam.) urgente; (fam.) charro, chillón, vulgar.—**l. laugh,** risotada. **II.** *adv.* ruidosamente, en alta voz, con ruido.

loudly [-li], *adv.* ruidosamente, recio; en alta voz.

loudness [-nes], *s.* ruido, sonoridad; (fam.) vulgaridad, mal gusto.

loud-speaker [-spícœr], *s.* (radtlf.) altavoz, altoparlante.

lough [loj], *s.* lago, laguna.

louis [lúi], *s.* luis de oro.

lounge [láunŷ]. **I.** *vn.* haraganear, holgazanear, callejear; tenderse, repantigarse; ponerse uno a sus anchas. **II.** *s.* haraganería, holgazanería; siesta; lugar donde se sesta; canapé, yacija.—

lounger [-œr], *s.* holgazán, azotacalles.

lounging room [-ing rum], antesala.

louse [láus], *s.* piojo, cáncano.

lousewort [láusuœrt], *s.* (bot.) albarraz; estafisagria; hierba piojera.

lousily [láusili], *adv.* con piojería.

lousiness [láusines], *s.* piojería.

lousy [láusi], *a.* piojoso, piojento; pedicular; astroso, miserable.

lout [láut]. **I.** *s.* patán, rústico, zafio. **II.** *vn.* demorarse, perder el tiempo.—**loutish** [-iśh], *a.* rústico, tosco.—**loutishly** [-li], *adv.* groseramente.

louver [lúvœr], *s.* (arq.) lumbrera, lucerna.—**l. boards,** tejadillos.

lov(e)ability [lʋvabíliti], **lov(e)ableness** [-bœlnes], *s.* atractivo, bondad, simpatía.—**lov(e)able** [-bœl], *a.* amable; digno de ser amado.

lovage [lívey], *s.* (bot.) ligústico.

love [lʋv]. **I.** *va.* amar, querer; (fam.) gustar mucho de, tener grande afición a. **II.** *vn.* amar. **III.** *s.* amor; grande afición; (en tenis y otros juegos) falla, nada.—**l. affair,** intriga amorosa.— **l. bird,** (orn.) periquito.—**l. feast,** ágape.—**l.**

knot, lazo de amor.—**l.-maker,** galanteador, enamorado.—**l.-making,** amorío, galanteo, amores. —**l. potion,** filtro de amor.—**in l. with,** enamorado de.

lovelace [lúvléis], *s.* seductor, libertino.

loveless [lúvles], *a.* desamorado; hurón.

loveliness [lúvlines], *s.* amabilidad, agrado, encanto; belleza.

lovelock [lúvloc], *s.* (ant.) rizo largo con lazo.

lovelorn [-lorn], *a.* abandonado de su amante; suspirando de amor.

lovely [-li]. **I.** *a.* amable, cariñoso; hermoso, bello; agradable, atractivo; ameno, deleitoso. **II.** *adv.* amablemente.

lover [lúvœr], *s.* amante; galán; amigo, aficionado.

lovesick [-sic], *a.* herido de amor.

loving [lóving], *a.* amante, afectuoso, amoroso, cariñoso; aficionado; benigno, apacible.— **l. cup,** copa con varias asas, que pasa de mano en mano entre amigos; copa de premio (gen. ll. *copa* simplemente.)—**l.-kindness,** favor desinteresado.

lovingly [-li], *adv.* afectuosamente, amorosamente.

lovingness [-nes], *s.* cariño, afecto.

low [lóu]. **I.** *a.* bajo, de poca altura o profundidad; bajo (tono, voz); módico, barato; abatido, desanimado; gravemente enfermo; bajo, vil, ruin; pobre, humilde; muerto; inferior; débil, debilitado.—**l. area,** área o región de baja presión barométrica.—**l. brass,** similor.—**L. Church,** iglesia o secta no ritualista.—**L. Churchman,** sectario opuesto al ritualismo.—**l. comedy,** sainete.—**l. count,** (tej.) número grueso o bajo (del hilo).—**L. Countries,** Países Bajos.—**l. day,** día de trabajo.—**l. expressions,** expresiones vulgares. —**l. fever,** calentura lenta.—**L. Latin,** bajo latín. —**l. latitude,** latitud cercana al ecuador.—**l. mass,** misa rezada.—**l. pressure,** baja presión.— **l.-pressure cylinder,** cilindro de baja presión.— **l. relief,** bajo relieve.—**l. spirits,** abatimiento.— **l. steel,** acero pobre en carbono.—**l. water,** marea baja; nivel mínimo (de un río, lago, etc.).—**l.-water line,** o **mark,** línea de nivel mínimo.—**in l. spirits,** abatido. **II.** *adv.* bajo, cerca del suelo; en la parte inferior; barato, a precio bajo; bajamente, vilmente; sumisamente; en voz baja; en tono profundo.—**l.-minded,** ruin.—**l.-necked,** escotado.—**l.-spirited,** abatido, acobardado. **III.** *vn.* mugir, berrear. **IV.** *s.* mugido, berrido; en los naipes, triunfo más bajo.

lowbell [lóbél]. **I.** *s.* cencerro; campanilla para coger pájaros por la noche. **II.** *va.* cazar pájaros con campanilla y luz.

lowborn [-born], *a.* de humilde cuna.

lower [lóœr]. **I.** *va.* agachar, humillar, abatir; bajar, poner más bajo; rebajar, minorar, disminuir.—**to l. the flag,** abatir la bandera.—**to l. the sails,** (mar.) arriar las velas. **II.** *vn.* bajar, menguar, disminuirse. **III.** *a. comp.* de LOW; más bajo; inferior.—**l. case,** (impr.) caja baja, letras minúsculas.—**l. futtock riders,** (mar.) genoles de sobreplanes.—**l. house,** cámara de representantes o diputados.—**l. world,** averno.

lower [láuœr], *vn.* mirar sañudo, fruncir el ceño; encapotarse o encubrirse el cielo.

lowering [láuœring], *a.* encapotado, nebuloso; amenazador.—**loweringly** [-li], *adv.* nubladamente, con ceño.

lowermast [lóœrmæst], *s.* (mar.) palo principal.

lowermost [lóœrmoust], *a.* el más bajo.

lowing [lóing], *s.* mugido, bramido.

lowland [lóulænd], *s.* tierra baja.—**the Lowlands,** las tierras bajas de Escocia.

lowlander [-lænder], *s.* abajeño.

lowlily [lóulili], *adv.* bajamente; vilmente; humildemente.

lowliness [lóulines], *s.* humildad; bajeza, vileza, ruindad.

lowly [lóuli]. **I.** *a.* humilde; vil, bajo. **II.** *adv.* humildemente; vilmente.

lowness [lóunes], *s.* bajeza o vileza; humildad; sumisión; abatimiento, póstración; baratura; gravedad o profundidad del tono; suavidad o debilidad del sonido.

loxodrome [lóxodroum], *s.* loxodromía.

loxodromic [-drómic], *a.* loxodrómico.—**l. line,** línea loxodrómica.

loyal [lóial], *a.* leal, fiel.—**loyalist** [-ist], *s.* (pol.) realista.—**loyally** [-li], *adv.* lealmente.—**loyalty** [-ti], *s.* lealtad, fidelidad.

lozenge [lóśenγ], *s.* (geom.) rombo; (farm.) pastilla; (blas.) losanje, lisonja.

lozenged [lóśenγd], *a.* rombal.

lozengy [lóśenγi], *a.* (blas.) lisonjado.

lubber [lúbœr], *s.* gordiflón; bobalicón; marinero de agua dulce.—**l.'s hole,** (mar.) boca de lobo.

lubberly [-li]. **I.** *a.* poltrón. **II.** *adv.* toscamente, zafiamente.

lubricant [lú- (o liú) bricant], *s.* y *a.* lubricante.

lubricate [lúbrikeit], *va.* lubricar.—**lubricating** [-kéiting], *a.* de lubricar, lubricante.—**lubrication** [-kéiśhun], *s.* lubricación.—**lubricator** [-kéitor], *s.* lubricador.

lubricity [lubrísiti], *s.* lubricidad, lisura; veleidad, inconstancia; lujuria, lascivia.

lubricous [lúbrikus], *a.* lúbrico; deslizadero; incierto; inconstante.

luce [liús o lus], *s.* (ict.) lucio.

lucern [lusœrn], *s.* alfalfa.—**l. field,** alfalfal.

lucernal [lusœrnæl], *a.* referente a lámparas.—**l. microscope,** microscopio proyector de lámpara.

lucid [liúsid], *a.* diáfano; brillante; lúcido.

lucidity [liucídity], **lucidness** [liúcidnes], *s.* lucidez, brillantez.

Lucifer [lúsifœr], *s.* lucero del alba; Lucifer, Luzbel.—**l.,** o **l. match,** fósforo de fricción .

Luciferian [-fírian], *a.* luciferino, diabólico, endiablado.

luck [luc], *s.* azar, acaso; suerte.—**for l.,** para que traiga suerte.—**to be in l.,** estar de buena suerte.

luckily [lúkili], *adv.* por fortuna, afortunadamente.

luckiness [lúkines], *s.* buena suerte.

luckless [lúkles], *a.* desafortunado, desgraciado.

lucky [lúki], *a.* afortunado; propicio, favorable.

lucrative [lú- (o liú) crativ], *a.* lucrativo.

lucratively [-li], *adv.* lucrativamente.

lucre [lúkœr], *s.* lucro; ganancia; usura.

lucubrate [liúkiubreit], *va.* lucubrar.

lucubration [-śhun], *s.* lucubración.

luculent [liúkiulent], *a.* luciente, claro; evidente, indubitable.

ludicrous [lú- (o liú) dicrus], *a.* ridículo, cómico, risible.—**ludicrously** [-li], *adv.* ridículamente, cómicamente.—**ludicrousness** [-nes], *s.* ridiculez.

lues [liúis], *s.* sífilis.

luetic [liuétic], *a.* sifilítico.

luetin [liúetin], *s.* emulsión del parásito sifilítico.

luff [luf]. **I.** *s.* (mar.) gratil; orzada, cachete de proa.—**l. tackle,** (mar.) aparejo de bolinear. **II.** *va.* (mar.) ceñir el viento, orzar, bolinear.—**to l. alee,** o **round,** orzar a la banda.—**to l. up,** tomar por avante.

lug [lug]. **I.** *s.* (fam.) tirón, estirón; cosa tirada; cosa lenta y pesada; oreja; anillo, argolla; saliente; lóbulo de la oreja; argadera, asa; jamba de chimenea; correa de las varas de un carruaje; pértiga. **II.** *va.* tirar de (algo); (mar.) halar.—**to l. away,** o **off,** llevarse arrastrando.— **to l. in** o **into,** arrastrar hacia dentro; (fam.) introducir.

luggage [lúguedź], *s.* equipaje; trastos, petate.

lugger [lúgœr], *s.* (mar.) lugre.

lugsail [lúgséil], *s.* (mar.) vela de tercio.

lugubrious [lugiúbrius], *a.* lúgubre, lóbrego.

lugworm [lúgüœrm], *s.* lombriz de cebo.

lukewarm [lúcuorm], *a.* tibio, templado; indiferente, frío.—**lukewarmly** [-li], *adv.* tibiamente; indiferentemente.—**lukewarmness,** [-nes], *s.* tibieza; frialdad.

lull [lul]. **I.** *va.* arrullar, adormecer; calmar, moderar. **II.** *s.* momento de calma o de silencio.

lullaby [lúlabai], *s.* arrullo.

luller [lúlœr], *s.* niñero.

lum [lúm], *s.* chimenea.

lumbago [lumbégo], *s.* lumbago.
lumbar [lúmbar], *a.* lumbar.
lumbricales [lúmbrikéilis], *s. pl.* músculos lumbricales.
lumber [lúmbœr]. **I.** *s.* madera aserrada; armatoste; balumba; (fam.) trastos o muebles viejos.—**l. room,** camaranchón, cuarto de trastos. **II.** *va.* amontonar trastos viejos. **III.** *vn.* andar pesadamente; avanzar con ruido sordo.
lumbering [-ing], *s.* explotación de bosques maderables.
lumberman [-man], *s.* hachero; negociante en madera, maderero.
lumberyard [-yard], *s.* maderería, depósito de maderas.
lumen [liúmen], *s.* (fís.) lumen, unidad de radiación de la luz.
luminary [liúmineri], *s.* astro, luminar; lumbrera.
luminescence [liúminésens], *s.* luminescencia, emisión de luz sin incandescencia.—**luminescent** [-ent], *a.* luminescente, luminoso sin incandescencia.
luminiferous [liúminífœrus], *a.* luminoso.
luminosity [liúminósiti], *s.* luminosidad.
luminous [liúm:nus], *a.* luminoso; lúcido.
luminously [-li] *adv.* luminosamente.
luminousness [-nes], *s.* luminosidad.
lump [lump]. **I.** *s.* masa, bulto, burujón; protuberancia, hinchazón; pitón; bollo; terrón; (fund.) lupia.—**l. of sugar,** terrón de azúcar.—**l. sugar,** azúcar de terrón o en terrones.—**by the l.,** (com.) a bulto, en globo, a ojo, por grueso o por junto. **II.** *va.* amontonar, aborujar; comprar a bulto, en globo. **III.** *vn.* trabajar como estivador; aborujarse, apelotonarse, aterronarse.
lumping [lúmping], *a.* grande, pesado.
lumpish [lúmpish], *a.* pesado, macizo; tosco; torpe, estúpido.—**lumpishly** [-li], *adv.* lerdamente, estúpidamente.—**lumpishness** [-nes], *s.* pesadez; estupidez; majadería.
lumpy [lúmpi], *a.* aterronado.
lunacy [lúnasi], *s.* locura.
lunar [lúnar], *a.* lunar; lunario; lunado; lunático; (quím. y med.) relativo a la plata.—**l. caustic,** lunar cáustico, nitrato de plata.—**l. year,** año lunar (354¼ días).
lunarian [lunérian]. **I.** *a.* lunar. **II.** *s.* supuesto habitante de la Luna.
lunary [lúnari]. **I.** *a.* lunar. **II.** *s.* (bot.) hierba de la plata, lunaria anual.
lunate(d [lúnet(ed], *a.* lunado.
lunatic [lúnatic], *s.* y *a.* loco.—**l. asylum,** casa de locos, manicomio.
lunation [lunéshun], *s.* lunación.
lunch [lunch], **luncheon** [lúnchun]. **I.** almuerzo (comida del mediodía, gen. ligera); merienda, colación.—**l. basket,** fiambrera.—**l. room,** merendero. **II.** *vn.* almorzar; merendar.
lune [lun], *s.* (geom.) lúnula.
lunette [lunét], *s.* cualquier cosa de figura lunada; (forti.) luneta; (arq.) luneto.
lung [lung], *s.* pulmón.—**l. trouble,** (fam.) tisis.
lunge [luny]. **I.** *s.* (esgr.) estocada; (fam.) embestida, arremetida. **II.** *vn.* (esgr.) irse a fondo, dar una estocada; abalanzarse, embestir.
lungwort [lúngœrt], *s.* (bot.) pulmonaria.
luniform [lúniform], *a.* lunado.
lunisolar [lunisólar], *a.* lunisolar.
lunular, lunulate [lúniular, let], *a.* lunado.
lunule [lúniul], *s.* (geom.) lúnula; blanco de las uñas.
Lupercalia [liúpœrkéiliæ], *s. pl.* Lupercales.
lupine [lúpin]. **I.** *s.* (bot.) altramuz, lupino. **II.** *a.* lupino, de lobo; voraz; (zool.) perteneciente a la familia que comprende los perros y los lobos.
lupuline [lúpiulin], *s.* lupulino.
lupus [lúpus], *s.* (astr.) el Lobo; (med.) lupus.
lurch [lœrch]. **I.** *s.* sacudida, vaivén; balance brusco; (mar.) bandazo, guiñada; en algunos juegos, partida doble. **II.** *vn.* (mar.) cabecear, dar bandazos; ganar una partida doble.—**lurcher** [lœrchœr], *s.* acechador; perro de caza.—**lurching** [-ing], *s.* celada.

lure [liur]. **I.** *s.* añagaza; reclamo; armadijo; cebo; engaño; tentación. **II.** *va.* atraer, inducir, tentar.
lurid [lúrid], *a.* cárdeno; fantástico, espeluznante.
lurk [lœrk], *vn.* espiar, acechar; esconderse.—**lurking place,** escondite, guarida; rincón; emboscada.
lurker [lœrkœr], *s.* acechador, espía.
lurry [lœri], *s.* (min.) carretón.
luscious [lúshus], *a.* sabroso, delicioso; empalagoso, meloso.—**lusciously** [-li], *adv.* melosamente.—**lusciousness** [-nes], *s.* dulzura que empalaga, melosidad; calidad de sabroso.
lush [lush]. **I.** *a.* suculento, jugoso; fresco y lozano; fácil de arar. **II.** *va.* y *vn.* beber licor o cerveza. **III.** *s.* licor, cerveza; borracho.
lust [lust]. **I.** *s.* anhelo vehemente, codicia; lujuria, concupiscencia. **II.** *vn.* codiciar, anhelar; lujuriar.
luster [lústœr]. **I.** *s.* lustre, brillo; viso, aguas; lucimiento, esplendor; araña de cristal; lustro. **II.** *va.* lustrar.
lusterless [-les], *a.* sin brillo, deslustrado.
lustful [lústful], *a.* lujurioso, sensual.—**lustfully** [-i], *adv.* lujuriosamente.—**lustfulness** [-nes], *s.* lascivia, lujuria.
lustily [lústili], *adv.* fuertemente, vigorosamente.
lustiness [lústines], *s.* lozanía, vigor, robustez.
lustral [lústral], *a.* lustral, lústrico.
lustrate [lústret], *va.* lustrar.
lustration [lustréshun], *s.* lustración.
lustre [lústœr], *s.* = LUSTER.
lustrical [lústrical], *a.* (igl.) lustral.
lustring [lústring], *s.* (tej.) lustrina.
lustrous [lústrus], *a.* lustroso, brillante.
lustrum [lústrum], *s.* lustro, quinquenio; lustración, purificación.
lusty [lústi], *a.* lozano, fuerte, robusto, vigoroso.
lutation [lutéshun], *s.* lutación.
lute [liút]. **I.** *s.* (mús.) laúd; (quím.) lodo para junturas; arandela de goma para cerrar tarros herméticamente; raspador de ladrillales. **II.** *va.* enlodar, tapar o embarrar con lodo o cemento; enrasar un ladrillal.
lutecium [liutíshium], *s.* (quím.) luvecio.
lutein [lútein], *s.* (quím.) luteína.
lutestring [lútstring], *s.* cuerda de laúd; (ent.) mariposa nocturna.
Lutheran [lúœran], *s.* y *a.* luterano.
Lutheranism [lúœranishm], *s.* luteranismo.
luthern [lúœrn], *s.* (arq.) lumbrera.
lutist [liútist], *s.* tañedor de laúd.
lutose [liútous], *a.* lodoso, cenagoso.
luxate [lúxeit], *va.* dislocar, descoyuntar.
luxation [-éishun], *s.* luxación, dislocación.
lux [lucs], *s.* lux, unidad de intensidad luminosa, igual a una bujía-metro.
luxe [pron. francesa], *s.* lujo (esp. en la expresión de luxe, de lujo).
luxuriance, luxuriancy [lugyúrians o luxiúrians, i], *s.* exuberancia, lozanía; frondosidad; demasía.
luxuriant [-ænt], *a.* exuberante, lozano, superabundante; superfluo; frondoso; lujuriante.
luxuriantly [-li], *adv.* abundantemente; lozanamente.
luxuriate [-eit], *vn.* ostentar lozanía; crecer o brotar con exuberancia; vivir con lujo; (fig.) gloriarse, complacerse.
luxurious [-us], *a.* lujoso; lujurioso; sibarítico; exuberante; frondoso.—**luxuriously** [-li], *adv.* con lozanía o exuberancia; frondosamente; lujosamente.—**luxuriousness** [-nes], *s.* lujo.
luxury [lúcshuri], *s.* lujo; gastos superfluos; manjar delicioso; cosa que deleita los sentidos.
lyceum [laisíum], *s.* liceo, ateneo; escuela secundaria; escuela de enseñanza por conferencias.
Lycopodiaceæ [láicopodiéisii], *s. pl.* (bot.) licopodiáceas.—**lycopodium** [-dium], *s.* (bot. y farm.) licopodio.
Lydian [lídian], *a.* y *s.* lidio, de la Lidia.
lye [lái], *s.* lejía, (ingl., f. c.) desviadero.

lying [láing]. **I.** *pa.* de TO LIE, y *a.* falso, mentiroso; echado, tendido; sito, situado.—**l.-to**, (mar.) al pairo o en facha.—**l.-in**, parto.—**l.-in hospital**, casa de maternidad.—**l.-in woman**, mujer parida. **II.** *s.* mentira, embuste.

lyingly [-li], *adv.* mentirosamente, falsamente.

lymph [limf], *s.* linfa, aguosidad; virus para inocular.—**l. duct**, vaso linfático.

lymphadenoma [limfǽdenóumæ], *s.* linfadenoma.

lymphangitis [línfænɣáitis], *s.* linfangitis.

lymphatic [limfǽtic]. **I.** *a.* linfático; flemático. **II.** *s.* vaso linfático.

lymphatism [límfætiŝm], *s.* linfatismo.

lymphoid [límfoid], *a.* linfoideo.

lynch [linch], *va.* linchar.—**l. law**, (E. U.) ley de Lynch, suplicio impuesto por particulares sin procedimiento ni forma legal.

lynching [linching], *s.* linchamiento.

lynx [lincs], *s.* lince.—**l.-eyed**, de ojos linces.

lyonnaise [láionéis], *a.* a la lionesa (apl. a papas fritas con cebollas).

lyrate [láiret], *a.* de forma de lira.

lyre [láiær], *s.* (mús.) lira; (astr.) Lira.—**l. bird**, (orn.) pájaro lira.

lyric(al [líric(al], *a.* lírico.—**lyric**, *s.* poema lírico; letra de una canción.—**lyricism** [lírisiŝm], *s.* lirismo.—**lyrist** [láirist], *s.* tocador de lira; poeta lírico.

lysimachia [láisiméikia], *s.* (bot.) lisimaquia.

lysis [láisis], *s.* (med.) lisis.

lysol [láisol], *s.* lisol (nombre de fábrica), desinfectante extraído del alquitrán.

lyssa [lísa], *s.* rabia canina.

lythraceous [lizréiŝʊs], *a.* (bot.) litrarico.

M

m [em], *s.* m.

ma, *contr.* de MA(M)MA, mamá.

ma'am [mam *o* mæm], *s. contr.* de MADAM, señora.

Mac, *prefijo* que significa "hijo de" en nombres patronímicos escoceses o irlandeses (suele abreviarse así: **Mc**, **Mᶜ**, o **M'**).

macadam [mæcǽdam]. **I.** *s.* macádam. **II.** *a.* de macádam, macadamizado.—**macadamize** [-aiŝ], *va.* macadamizar.

macaque [macǽc], *s.* (zool.) macaco.

macaroni [mǽcaróni], *s.* macarrones; mezcla estrambótica; pisaverde.

macaronic [-ónic]. **I.** *s.* macarronea; mezcla estrambótica. **II.** *a.* macarrónico.

macaroon [mǽcarún], *s.* almendrado, macarrón de almendras.

macassar [macǽsar], *s.* aceite macasar.

macaw [macó], *s.* (orn.) guacamayo, macagua.

maccaboy [mǽcaboi], *s.* rapé macuba.

mace [méis], *s.* maza (insignia); (arm.) maza, clava, porra; forma de taco de billar; macis o macías.—**macer**, o **mace bearer**, macero, ballestero.

macerate [mǽscæreit], *va.* macerar.

maceration [-éiŝʊn], *s.* maceración.

Machiavel(l)ian [mǽkiavélian]. **I.** *s.* maquiavelista. **II.** *a.* maquiavélico.—**Machiavelism** [-iŝm], *s.* maquiavelismo.

machicolation [mǽchicoléŝʊn], *s.* (fort.) matacán o ladronera.

machinate [mǽkineit], *va.* y *vn.* maquinar.—**machination** [-éiŝʊn], *s.* maquinación, intriga.—**machinator** [-eitœr], *s.* maquinador.

machine [maŝhín]. **I.** *s.* máquina; (Ingl.) vehículo, coche, calesa; (E. U., pol.) camarilla.—**m. gun**, ametralladora.—**m. made**, hecho a máquina.—**m. shop**, taller de maquinaria.—**m. tool**, máquina herramienta. **II.** *va.* fresar, trabajar a máquina.

machinery [maŝhínœri], *s.* maquinaria.

machinist [maŝhínist], *s.* maquinista, mecánico.

mackerel [mǽcœrel], *s.* (ict.) escombro, caballa.—**m. sky**, cielo aborregado.

Mackinaw [mǽkino], *s.* (E. U.) bote de fondo plano y extremos agudos; manta gruesa de tela burda.—**M. coat**, saco corto de frente traslapado.

mackintosh [mǽkintoŝh], *s.* impermeable.

mackle [mǽcœl]. **I.** *va.* (impr.) repintar, macular, remosquear. **II.** *s.* maculatura.

macle [mǽcl], *s.* (min.) cristal gemelo; andalucita teselada; mancha oscura.

macrobian [mæcróbian], *s.* macrobiano.

macrobiosis [mǽcrobaiósis], *s.* longevidad.

macrobiotics [-tics], macrobiótica.

macrocephalous [-séfalʊs], *a.* macrocéfalo.

macrocosm [-coŝm], *s.* macrocosmo.

macropodian [-pódiæn], *s.* y *a.* macrópodo.

macroscopic [-scópic], *a.* macroscópico.

macula [mǽkiula], *s.* mácula, mancha, lunar.

maculate [mǽkiuleit]. **I.** *va.* macular, manchar. **II.** *a.* manchado, maculado.—**maculation** [-éiŝhʊn], *s.* mancilla, mácula, lunar.

mad [mæd]. **I.** *a.* loco; enojado, encolerizado; hidrófobo; bulliciosamente alegre.—**m. apple**, berenjena.—**m. as a March hare**, loco de atar.—**m. doctor** (fam.) alienista.—**m.-headed** = MADBRAIN. **II.** *va.* = MADDEN.

madam [mǽdam], **madame** [madám], *s.* madama, señora.

madapollam [mǽdapólam], *s.* (tej.) madapolán.

madbrain, **madcap** [mǽdbrein, cæp], *a.* y *s.* fogoso; temerario; calavera.

madden [mǽden], *va.* y *vn.* enloquecer(se).

madder [mǽdœr], *s.* (bot.) rubia.—**m. bloom**, o **color**, granza.

made [méid], *pret.* y *pp.* de TO MAKE.—**m. mast**, (mar.), palo compuesto.—**m.-up**, artificial; pintado (el rostro); acabado; (con *of*) compuesto (de).

Madeira wine [madéira uáin], *s.* vino de Madera.

madhouse [mǽdjáus], *s.* manicomio.

madly [mǽdli], *adv.* locamente; furiosamente.

madman [mǽdman], *s.* loco.

madness [mǽdnes], *s.* locura.

madonna [madóna], *s.* señora, madama; imagen de la Virgen, madona.

madrepore [mǽdrepoœr], *s.* (zool.) madrépora.

madrier [mǽdricœr], *s.* tablón, albitana.

madrigal [mǽdrigal], *s.* madrigal; (mús.) canción pastoral.

Madrilenian [mǽdrilénian], *a.* y *s.* madrileño.

madroño [madroña], *s.* (bot.) madroño.

madwort [mǽducœrt], *s.* (bot.) marrubio, aliso.

maelstrom [mélstrʊm], *s.* remolino.

mænad [mínæd], *s.* bacante.

maestoso [maestóso], *u.* (mús.) maestoso.

magazine [mǽgaŝin], *s.* almacén; (arti.) cámara para cartuchos en un rifle de repetición; polvorín, pañol de pólvora o Santabárbara; (impr.) revista.

magaziner, magazinist [mǽgaŝíncœr, ist], *s.* el que escribe para las revistas.

magdalen [mǽgdalen], *s.* ramera arrepentida.

Magellanic [mǽyelǽnic], *a.* magallánico.

magenta [maɣénta], *s.* color magenta.

maggot [mǽgot], *s.* (ent.) cresa; capricho, antojo.—**maggoty** [-i], *a.* gusaniento.

Magi [méirai], *s. pl.* magos, sabios.

Magian [méiyiæn], *a.* y *a.* mago.

magic [mǽyic]. **I.** *s.* magia; prestidigitación. **II.** *a.* mágico; encantador.—**m. lantern**, linterna mágica.

magical [mǽyical], *a.* mágico; encantado.

magically [-i], *adv.* mágicamente, por arte de encantamiento.

magician [mayíŝhan], *s.* mago, mágico, nigromante; prestidigitador.

magilp [maguílp], *s.* (pint.) aceite secante.

magisterial [mǽyistírial], *a.* magistral, magisterial; absoluto.—**magisterially** [-i], *adv.* magistralmente.—**magisterialness** [-nes], *s.* magisterio; autoridad magistral.

magistery [mǽyisteri], *s.* decreto magisterial; obra maestra; piedra filosofal; panacea; (quím.) magisterio, precipitado.

magistracy [mǽyistrasi], *s.* magistratura.

magistral [mǽyistral], *a.* y *s.* magistral, magisterial; (farm.) magistral, preparado según prescripción; (metal.) magistral, piritas de cobre pulverizadas.

magistrate [mǽyistreit], s. magistrado; justicia, juez de paz.

magma [mǽgmæ], s. magma, bagazo; (geol.) magma, materia fundida de que se forman las rocas ígneas; base vidriosa de una roca ígnea.

Magna Charta [mǽgna cárta], s. Carta Magna.

magnanimity [mægnanímiti], s. magnanimidad. —**magnanimous** [mægnǽnimʊs], a. magnánimo. —**magnanimously** [-li], adv. magnánimamente.

magnate [mǽgneit], s. magnate.

magnesia [mægníÿiæ], a. magnesia.

magnesian [-æn], **magnesic** [mægnésic], a. magnésico, magnesiano.

magnesite [mǽgnesait], s. (min.) magnesita, espuma de mar.

magnesium [mægníÿiʊm], s. magnesio.

magnet [mǽgnet], s. imán; piedra imán.

magnetic(al [mægnétic, -al], a. magnético.—**m. battery,** imán hojeado o compuesto.—**m. bearing,** rumbo magnético.—**m. creeping,** histérisis viscosa.—**m. explorer,** bobina de prueba.—**m. field,** campo magnético.—**m. flux,** flujo magnético. —**m. lag,** retardo de imanación.—**m. leakage,** dispersión magnética.—**m. pyrites,** pirita magnética.

magnetically [-i], adv. de un modo atractivo.

magnetism [mǽgnetišm], s. magnetismo.

magnetite [-ait], s. (min.) magnetita.

magnetizable [-taišabœl], a. magnetizable.

magnetization [-tišéišʊn], s. magnetización, imanación.

magnetize [-taiš], I. va.(fís.) magnetizar, imanar. II. vn. imanarse.

magnetizer [-táišœr], s. magnetizador; imanador.

magneto [mægníto, mǽgneto], s. máquina magnetoeléctrica; (aut., etc.) magneto.

magneto-dynamo [mǽgneto-dáinamo], s. magneto, dínamo de imanes permanentes.

magneto-electric [-eléctric], a. magnetoeléctrico.

magneto-electricity [-electríciti], s. magnetoelectricidad.

magneto-generator [-yéneréitor], s. = MAGNETO-DYNAMO.

magnetometer [mǽgnetómetœr], s. magnetómetro.

magnetomotive [mǽgnetomótiv], a. magnetomotriz (fuerza).

magneton [mǽgneton], s. magnetón, elemento magnético semejante al electrón en electricidad.

magnetoscope [mægnétoscoup], s. (fís.) magnetoscopio.

magnifiable [mǽgnifaiabœl], u. capaz de ser aumentado o enaltecido.

Magnificat [magnífficæt], s. (igl.) Magníficat.

magnification [mǽgnifikéšhʊn], s. (opt.) amplificación; aumento; enaltecimiento; alabanza, glorificación; exageración.

magnificence [mægnífisens], s. magnificencia.— **magnificent** [-ent], a. magnífico.—**magnificently** [-li], adv. magníficamente, espléndidamente.

magnifier [mǽgnifaiœr], s. (ópt.) amplificador; vidrio de aumento; exagerador; panegirista.

magnify [mǽgnifai], va. aumentar, amplificar; magnificar, alabar; exagerar. —**m. glass,** vidrio de aumento, lente.

magnifying [-inŋ], a. amplificador, de aumento.

magniloquent [magnílocuent], s. grandílocuo.

magnitude [mǽgnitiud], s. magnitud.

magnolia [mægnólia], s. (bot.) magnolia.

Magnoliaceæ [-liésiai], s. pl. magnoliáceas.

magnum [mǽgnʊm], s. botella de dos litros.

magpie [mǽgpai], s. (orn.) urraca, picaza; pega.

Magyar [mǽyár], s. magiar.

Maharaja [majaráya], s. maharajá, príncipe de la India; gran predicador (India).

mahatma [majátma], s. mahatma, título que se da en la India a los más elevados seguidores del budismo esotérico y la teosofía.

mahlstick [málstic], s. (pint.) tiento.

mahogany [majógani], s. caoba.

Mahometan, Mahomedan [majómetæn, -dæn]. etc. = MOHAMMEDAN, etc.

maid [méid], s. doncella, soltera; virgen; criada, sirvienta; (ict.) lija. —**m. of honor,** dama o doncella de honor.

maiden [méiden]. I. a. virgíneo, virginal; soltera; prístino, primero, nuevo, inicial; intacto.— **m. name,** apellido de soltera.— **m. speech,** primer discurso de un orador. II. s. virgen, doncella, joven soltera; zagala.

maidenhair [-jeær], s. (bot.) brenea, culantrillo.

maidenhead, maidenhood [-jed, -jud], s. doncellez, virginidad.

maidenliness [-lines], s. modestia, pudor.

maidenly, maidenlike [-li, laic]. I. a. virginal, pudoroso. II. adv. modestamente.

maidhood [méidjud], s. virginidad.

maidservant [-sœrvænt], s. criada.

mail [méil]. I. s. correo; correspondencia; mala, valija; (arm.) cota de malla.—**m. bag,** mala, valija; portacartas.—**m. carrier,** cartero.—**m. catcher,** (f. c.) garra para la correspondencia.— **m. chute,** buzón tubular.—**m. pouch,** = M. BAG. —**m. sack,** saco de lona para impresos.—**m. steamer,** vapor correo.—**m. train,** tren correo. II. va. armar con cota de malla; echar al correo.

mailable [méilabœl], a. que se puede enviar por el correo.

mailed [méild], pp. de TO MAIL, y a. cubierto con cota de malla.

maim [méim]. I. va. mutilar, estropear, lisiar. II. s. mutilación, manquera.

maimed [méimd], pp. y a. mútilo, manco, zopo, mocho, contrecho.

maimedness [méimednes], s. mutilación, mancamiento, estropeamiento.

main [méin]. I. a. principal, de mayor importancia.—**m. braces,** brazos mayores.—**m. floor,** primer piso.—**m. hatchway,** (mar.) escotilla mayor.—**m. tackle,** aparejo real.—**m.-topgallant,** mastelero de juanete mayor.—**m.-topmast,** mastelero, mayor.—**m. topsail,** vela de gavia.— **m. wale,** cinta principal o mayor.—**m. wall,** pared maestra.—**m. yard,** verga mayor.—**by m. force,** por la fuerza. II. s. océano; alta mar; continente; cañería maestra (de gas o agua); fuerza, violencia; partida o pareja de gallos; jugada de dados.— **upon the m.,** al fin.

mainland [-land], s. continente, tierra firme.

mainly [-li], adv. principalmente, (ant.) poderosamente.

mainmast [-mast], s. (mar.) palo mayor.

mainsail [-seill], s. (mar.) vela mayor.

mainsheet [-šhit], s. escota mayor.

mainstay [-stéi], s. estay mayor.

maintain [meintéin], va. tener, guardar, mantener; sostener, afirmar.

maintainable [-abœl], a. defendible, sostenible.

maintainer [-œr], s. mantenedor; defensor; partidario, patrón.

maintenance [méintenans], s. mantenimiento, apoyo, protección; manutención; sostén, sostenimiento; conservación (de una vía, máquina, camino, etc.)

maintop [méintóp], s. cofa mayor o de gavia.— **m. braces,** brazos de gavia.

maize [méiš], s. (bot.) maíz.

majestic [mayéstic], a. majestuoso.

majestically [-ali], adv. majestuosamente.

majesty [mǽyesti], s. majestad; majestuosidad.

majolica [mayó- (o mayó) lica], s. mayólica.

major [méyœr]. I. a. mayor, más grande (en número, en cantidad, en extensión, en dignidad o importancia); principal; (mús.) mayor, normal. II. s. (mil.) [comandante; (for.) mayor de edad.—**m. general,** (mil.) mariscal de campo.— **m. mode, o scale,** (mús.) modo mayor.

majordomo [méiycœrdómo], s. mayordomo.

majority [mayóriti], s. mayoría, el mayor número; (for.) mayoría, mayor edad.

make [méik], va. (pret. y pp. MADE) hacer; producir; ganar; ser (buen material, empleado útil, mal maestro, etc.); formar, ser, ser igual a (en arit.); causar, ocasionar; poner (triste, alegre); componer, trabajar; decir, pronunciar; constituir, disponer, aderezar; granjear, proporcionar; recoger, allegar; ganar; lograr; alcanzar, llegar a; atravesar, pasar por, cruzar; (mar.) descubrir, avistar; hacer (la cama, el tocado, etc.), arreglar; inferir, deducir; adiestrar, enseñar; dar, prestar (excusas, juramento); andar, recorrer (leguas, distancia, etc.); dar (vueltas, revoluciones); cometer (error, equivocación). Seguido de acusativo modificado por un adjetivo indica acción que causa la calidad o estado que el adjetivo denota, y se traduce por "poner" o "hacer" seguido del adjetivo, o por un solo verbo (*to make sad*, poner triste, entristecer; *to make round*, redondear, dar forma redonda; *to make public*, hacer público, publicar).—**to m. a clean breast of**, confesar, admitir francamente un error.—**to m. a figure**, hacer papel, hacer figura.—**to m. a fool of**, engañar, embaucar; poner en ridículo.—**to m. again**, rehacer, hacer de nuevo.—**to m. a great deal of** = TO M. MUCH OF.—**to m. a hit**, (fam.) causar buena impresión.—**to m. a litter**, ensuciar, desordenar. —**to m. amends**, indemnizar, resarcir, reparar, compensar.—**to m. a mistake**, equivocarse.—**to m. a move**, hacer una jugada; dar un paso, obrar. —**to m. and break**, (elec.) abrir y cerrar un circuito.—**to m. a pass**, tirar una estocada.—**to m. a point**, lograr (uno) su objeto; esmerarse en.— **to m. a point of**, dar importancia a; proponerse. —**to m. a practice of**, acostumbrar, tener por costumbre.—**to m. a record**, establecer un record; tomar nota, apuntar.—**to m. a (bad, good) show**, hacerlo (mal, bien), salir (mal, bien).—**to m. a show of**, ostentar, hacer gala de; poner en ridículo.—**to m. a stop**, detenerse; hacer una pausa. —**to m. both ends meet**, pagar uno sus gastos, vivir con lo que gana o tiene.—**to m. clear**, poner claro; aclarar.—**to m. fast**, amarrar, afianzar, asegurar.—**to m. friends**, granjearse amigos; amistarse.—**to m. fun of**, burlarse de.—**to m. good**, mantener, defender; hacer bueno, probar; mejorar, cumplir; garantizar, responder de; resarcir, indemnizar; lograr, llevar a cabo.—**to m. haste**, darse prisa.—**to m. head**, avanzar, progresar.—**to m. head against**, hacer frente a, resistir a.—**to m. headway**, adelantar.—**to m. hot**, calentar.—**to m. into**, convertir en.—**to m. it a practice**, o **rule**, tener por regla.—**to m. it hard for one**, causarle a uno trabajo.—**to m. it hot for one**, causarle a uno molestia o embarazo.—**to m. known**, hacer saber.—**to m. level**, nivelar, allanar; (alb.) enrasar.—**to m. light of**, burlarse de; no dar importancia a.—**to m. little (o nothing) of**, hacer poco o ningún caso de, despreciar.—**to m. love**, enamorar.—**to m. money**, ganar dinero.—**to m. more sail**, largar las velas.—**to m. much of**, dar grande importancia a; estimar, apreciar; festejar.— **to m. neither head nor tail of**, no comprender, no ver pies ni cabeza a.—**to m. no bones of**, no tener escrúpulo, no pararse en pelillos acerca de.— **to m. no difference**, o **no matter**, ser indiferente, no importar.—**to m. nothing of**, no reparar en; no dar importancia a; no ganar en; no comprender.—**to m. of**, sacar de, inferir, deducir, entender, aprovecharse de.—**to m. one of**, ser uno de.—**to m. one's escape**, escaparse, zafarse.—**to m. one's mark**, firmar con una cruz; señalarse, distinguirse.—**to m. one's mouth water**, hacerle a uno la boca agua.—**to m. one's self known**, darse a conocer.—**to m. one's self miserable**, entristecerse, afligirse.—**to m. one's self scarce**, largarse, marcharse.—**to m. one's way**, avanzar; progresar; dirigirse; abrirse paso; salir bien.—**to m. out**, comprender, descifrar, descubrir; probar, justificar; suplir, abastecer, completar; componer, redactar; escribir, hacer (recibo, etc.); llenar, formular.—**to m. out of**, hacer o formar de.—**to m. over**, rehacer, hacer de nuevo; ceder, traspasar; confiar.—**to m. progress**, progresar, hacer progresos.—**to m. ready**, preparar, alistar; (impr.) imponer.—**to m. room**, abrir paso, hacer lugar.—**to m. room for**, dar paso a; dejar campo, lugar o puesto para; dar lugar, puesto a.—**to m. sail**, dar a la vela.—**to m. sense**, tener sentido (una frase); (con *of*) comprender.—**to m. shift**, sacar partido.—**to m. short work of**, disponer de prontamente, sin rodeos.—**to m. sick**, enfermar;

(fam.) fastidiar; inspirar desprecio; causar repugnancia.—**to m. slight of**, tener en poco, menospreciar.—**to m. speed**, darse prisa.—**to m. sport of**, burlarse de.—**to m. sure**, cerciorarse.— **to m. the best of**, sacar el mayor provecho de; hacer frente a, minorar en lo posible los efectos de. —**to m. the land**, descubrir la tierra, acercar la nave a la costa, tomar tierra.—**to m. the most of**, aprovecharlo todo; sacar el mejor partido de.—**to m. things hum**, (fam.) desplegar actividad.—**to m. tired**, cansar; fastidiar.—**to m. up**, reunir, formar; componer (un tren, etc.); completar; sumar; compensar, resarcir, indemnizar; saldar, ajustar; conciliar, apaciguar; inventar (cuentos, etc.); (impr.) compaginar; enumerar, contar.—**to m. up one's mind**, resolverse, determinar.—**to m. use of**, servirse de, hacer uso de.—**to m. water**, hacer aguas, orinar; (mar.) hacer agua.—**to m. way**, abrir paso.

make, vn. (con *at*, *for*, o *toward*) dirigirse o encaminarse a, abalanzarse a; (con *for* o *to*) contribuir a, servir para, tender o propender a; crecer (la marea); formarse (el hielo).—**to m. after**, tratar de coger, seguir.—**to m. against**, estar en oposición a; ser contrario o nocivo a.—**to m. as if**, o **as though**, fingir; hacer como si.—**to m. away**, largarse, huirse.—**to m. away with**, derrochar; llevarse, hurtar; suprimir, matar.—**to m. believe**, fingir, pretender.—**to m. free with**, no gastar cumplidos con; servirse de sin pedir. —**to m. good**, salir bien, cumplir.—**to m. merry**, divertirse; regodearse.—**to m. off** = TO M. AWAY. —**to m. off with**, llevarse, quitar de delante; quitar.—**to m. out**, salir (bien o mal), tener (buen, mal) éxito.—**to m. sure**, asegurarse, cerciorarse. —**to m. up**, hacer las paces; componerse con afeites.—**to m. up for**, compensar, equiparar. —**to m. up to**, acercarse a; obsequiar a; galantear.

make, s. hechura, forma, figura; estructura; fábrica, producción, manufactura; producto; marca, nombre (de fábrica).—**m. -and-break** (elec.), cortacircuitos.

make-believe [méik-belív]. **I.** a. fingido, falso, de mentirillas. **II.** s. artificio, artimaña; pretexto.

maker [méikœr], s. artífice; constructor, fabricante; autor.—**M.**, Hacedor.

makeshift [méikshíft]. **I.** a. temporero, provisional. **II.** s. expediente, tapaagujeros.

make-up [méik-ʊp], s. conjunto; carácter, modo de ser; (impr.) imposición; (teat.) caracterización, modo de pintarse y arreglarse.

makeweight [méikuéit], s. complemento de peso o contrapeso en una balanza; suplente; adulterante.

making [méiking], s. composición, estructura; hechura; preparación; formación; germen, elementos.—**m. iron**, hierro de calafate.

Malaccan, a. = MALAKKAN.

Malaceæ [maléisii], s. pl. (bot.) pomáceas.— **malaceous** [-shʊs], a. pomácea.

malachite [málakait], s. malaquita.

malacology [málacóloyi], s. malacología.

malacopterygian [-cóptyrían], a. (zool.) malacopterigio.

maladdress [málædrés], s. descortesía, falta de tacto.

maladjustment [málædyʊstmœnt], s. ajuste defectuoso; desconformidad, discordancia.

maladministration [málædministréshun], s. mal manejo.

maladroit [málædróit], a. torpe, desmañado, falto de tino o de tacto.

malady [máladi], s. mal, enfermedad.

Malaga [málaga], s. vino o uva de Málaga.

malaise [malés], s. indisposición, malestar.

Malakkan [málækœn], s. y a., malayo, de Malaca.

malanders [málandœrs], s. (vet.) ajuagas, esparavanes.

malapert [málapœrt], a. desvergonzado, descomedido, descarado.

malapropos [málapropó], a. impropio, fuera de propósito.

malar [méilar], a. malar.—**m. bone**, hueso malar, pómulo.

malaria [maléria], *s.* (med.) paludismo; fiebre palúdica.—**malarial, malarious** [-al,-us], *a.* palúdico.

malate [mélet], *s.* (quím.) malato.

Malay(an [malé(an], *a.* malayo.

malcontent [mǽlcontént], *a.* malcontento.

male [méil]. **I.** *a.* masculino; varón; macho; varonil; compuesto de varones; (bot.) estaminado.—**m. issue,** hijos varones, sucesión masculina.—**m. screw,** tornillo. **II.** *s.* varón, hombre; animal macho.

malediction [mældícshun], *s.* maldición.

malefactor [mǽlefǽctœr], *s.* malhechor.

malefic(ent [maléfic, fisent], *a.* maléfico.

malevolence [malévolens], *s.* malevolencia.—**malevolent** [-ent], *a.* malévolo; malhadado.—**malevolently** [-li], *adv.* malignamente.

malfeasance [mǽlfísans], *s.* fechoría, desaguisado.

malformation [mǽlforméishun], *s.* formación defectuosa.—**malformed** [mælfórmd], *a.* mal formado, contrahecho.

malic [mélic], *a.* málico.

malice [mǽlis], *s.* malicia, mala intención, malignidad.

malicious [malíshus], *a.* malicioso, maligno, maléfico.—**maliciously** [-li], *adv.* maliciosamente.—**maliciousness** [-nes], *s.* mala intención, malicia.

malign [maláin]. **I.** *a.* maligno; pernicioso, perjudicial. **II.** *va.* difamar; calumniar.

malignancy [malígnansi], *s.* malignidad, malicia, malevolencia.

malignant [malígnant]. **I.** *a.* maligno, malévolo; perverso; nocivo; virulento.—**m. fever,** fiebre perniciosa.—**m. tumor,** tumor maligno. **II.** *s.* hombre malintencionado.

malignantly [-li], *adv.* malignamente.

maligner [maláincœr], *s.* detractor, difamador.

malignity [malígniti], *s.* malignidad.

malignly [maláinli], *adv.* malignamente.

malinger [malíngcœr], *vn.* fingirse enfermo.

malingerer [malíngcœrœr], *s.* maula.

malison [mélisun], *s.* (poét.) maldición.

malkin [mólkin], *s.* aljofifa; escobillón, deshollinador de horno; fregona, mujer soez, criada sucia; espantajo, gato.

mall [mol]. **I.** *s.* mazo, mallo; [mal *o* mel] alameda, paseo; tribunal. **II.** *va.* = MAUL.

mallard [mǽlard], *s.* (orn.) pato.

malleability, o malleableness [mǽleabíliti, -bœlnes], *s.* maleabilidad.

malleable [mǽliæbœl], *a.* maleable.—**m. cast iron,** fundición maleable, fundición dulce de moldeo.—**m. iron,** (E. U.) M. CAST IRON; (Ingl.) hierro forjado.

malleate [mǽlieit], *va.* martillar.

malleation [mǽliéshun], *s.* maleación.

mallein [mǽlein], *s.* (vet.) maleína.

malleolar [mǽlíolar], *a.* maleolar.

malleolus [malíolus], *s.* (anat.) maléolo.

mallet [mǽlet], *s.* mazo, maceta.

malleus [mǽleus], *s.* (anat.) martillo.

mallow(s [mǽlo(s], *s.* (bot.) malva.

malmsey [mámsi], *s.* malvasía.

malnutrition [mǽlnutríshun], *s.* desnutrición, nutrición defectuosa; alimentación deficiente.

malodorous [mælódorus], *a.* hediondo; desagradable.

malpighia [mælpíguiæ], (bot.) paralejo.—**Malpighiaceæ** [mælpíguiéisii], *s. pl.* (bot.) malpigiaceas.—**malpighiaceous** [-eishus], *a.* malpigiáceo.

Malpighian [mælpíguiæn], *a.* malpighiano, de Malpighi.—**M. bodies, o corpuscles,** corpúsculos malpighianos (del bazo); glomérulo malpighiano (del riñón).—**M. pyramids,** pirámides malpighianos (del riñón).

malposition [mǽlposíshun], *s.* posición anormal, defectuosa.

malpractise, malpractice [-prǽctis], *s.* (med. y cir.) tratamiento erróneo, perjudicial o ilegal; inmoralidad.

malt [molt]. **I.** *s.* malta; cerveza.—**m. dust,** polvo de malta.—**m. kiln,** horno para secar la

malta.—**m. liquor,** cerveza.—**m. mill,** molino para la malta. **II.** *va.* hacer germinar la cebada; preparar la malta.

Maltese [moltís], *a.* y *s.* maltés; gato maltés.—**m. cross,** cruz de Malta o de Jerusalén.

maltha [mǽlza], *s.* brea mineral.

Malthusian [mælziúÿæn] *s.* y *a.* maltusiano.—**Malthusianism** [-ism], *s.* maltusianismo.

maltman [móltman], **maltster** [móltstœr], *s.* preparador de malta.

maltose [móltous], *s.* (quím.) maltosa.

maltreat [mæltrít], *va.* maltratar.

Malvaceæ [mælvéisii], *s. pl.* malvaceas.—**malvaceous** [-shus], *a.* malváceo.

malversation [mǽlvœrséshun], *s.* malversación.

mam(m)a [mamá *o* máma], *s.* mamá.

Mameluke, Mamaluke [mǽmeliuc], *s.* mameluco.

mamey [maméi], **mamey apple,** *s.* mamey.

mamma [mǽma], *s.* mama, teta.

mammal [mǽmal], *s.* mamífero.

Mammalia [mamélia], *s. pl.* mamíferos.

mammalian [mamélian], *a.* mamífero.

mammalogy [mamǽloyi], *s.* mamalogía.

mammary [mǽmari], *a.* mamario.

mammee tree [mæmí tri], *s.* (bot.) mamey.

mammet [mǽmet], *s.* = MAUMET.

mammiferous [mæmífœrus], *a.* mamífero.

mammiform [mǽmiform], *a.* atetado.

mammilla [mæmíla], *s.* mamella, mamila.

mammillary [mǽmilæri], *a.* mamilar.

mammillate(d [mǽmilet(ed], *a.* mamellado.

Mammon [mǽmun], *s.* espíritu de la codicia, becerro de oro; dios de las riquezas.

mammonist [mǽmunist], *s.* avaro, codicioso.

mammoth [mǽmuz]. **I.** *a.* enorme, gigantesco. **II.** *s.* mamut.

mammy [mǽmi], *s.* (fam.) madre, mamá; (E. U. del Sur) negra, ama de leche; (Ingl.) abuela.

man [mæn], *s.* hombre; varón; persona, sujeto; criado, servidor; peón (de ajedrez); dama (del juego de damas); soldado (vg.: *officers and men,* oficiales y soldados).—**m. and wife,** marido y mujer.—**m. at arms,** soldado (esp. el caballero armado).—**m. eater,** antropófago; animal que ataca al hombre (apl. esp. a tiburones, tigres y leones).—**m. Friday,** criado que sirve para todo.—**m.-hater,** misántropo; mujer que aborrece al sexo masculino.—**m.-killer,** homicida, asesino.—**m. midwife,** partero, comadrón.—**M. of Destiny,** Hombre del Destino (Napoleón).—**m. of straw,** testaferro.—**m. of the world,** hombre de mundo.—**m.-of-war,** buque de guerra.—**m.'s estate,** edad viril.—**m. slayer,** homicida.—**to a m.,** todos a una, como un solo hombre, unánimemente.

man, *va.* (mar.) tripular, dotar; armar; (mil.) guarnecer, poner guarnición a.—**to m. the capstan,** (mar.) armar o guarnir el cabrestante.—**to m. the pumps,** (mar.) armar las bombas.—**to m. the yards,** disponer la gente sobre las vergas.

manacle [mǽnacœl]. **I.** *s.* manilla.—*pl.* esposas. **II.** *va.* maniatar, poner esposas o manillas a.

manage [mǽnœy]. **I.** *va.* y *vn.* manipular, hacer andar o funcionar; manejar, dirigir, administrar; gestionar, procurar, amansar, domar. **II.** *vn.* ingeniarse, arreglarse, componérselas; llevar la batuta.

manageable [mǽneyabœl], *a.* manejable; dócil, tratable.—**manageableness** [-nes], *s.* calidad de manejable; docilidad; flexibilidad, mansedumbre.

management [mǽneymœent], *s.* manejo, gobierno, dirección, administración; (com.) gerencia; gestión, negociación; proceder, conducta, régimen; uso, empleo; prudencia, destreza; dirección, cuerpo de directores.

manager [mǽnayœr], *s.* administrador, director; empresario; superintendente; regente; (com.) gerente; proyectista diestro; intrigante.

managerial [mǽneyírial], *a.* directivo, administrativo.

manatee [mǽnatí], *s.* (zool.) manatí.

manchineel [mænchiníl], *s.* (bot.) manzanillo.

mancipation [mænsipéshun], *s.* (for.) mancipación; emancipación de la patria potestad.

---

manciple [mǽnsipœl], s. mayordomo de un colegio.

mandamus [mændéimʊs], s. (for.) mandamiento, carta orden, despacho.

mandarin [mǽndarín], s. mandarín; lengua mandarina; (tint.) amarillo de mandarín; naranja mandarina.

mandatary [mǽndatæri], s. mandatario; agente.

mandate [mǽndet]. **I.** s. mandato; encargo, comisión; legacía o mandato de la Sociedad de las Naciones. **II.** va. asignar por mandato.

mandator [mændétœr], s. mandante.

mandatory [mǽndatori]. **I.** a. (for.) preceptivo, obligatorio. **II.** s. mandatario.

mandible [mǽndibœl], s. mandíbula, quijada.

mandibular [mændíbiular], a. mandibular.

mandibulate [mændíbiulet], a. mandibulado.

mandolin(e [mǽndolin], s. (mús.) bandolín.

mandragora [mændrǽgora], **mandrake** [mǽndrek], s. (bot.) mandrágora.

mandrel [mǽndrel], s. mandril de torno; taladro, parahuso.

mandrill [mǽndril], s. (zool.) mandril.

mane [méin], s. crin; melena.

maned [méind], a. crinado, crinito.

manège [manéy], s. equitación, manejo; picadero.

manequin [mǽnekin], s. = MANIKIN.

manes [méiniś], s. manes.

maneuver, manœuvre [manúvœr]. **I.** s. (mar.) maniobra; (mar. y mil.) evolución; manejo, artificio. **II.** va. y vn. maniobrar; ejecutar maniobras o evoluciones; intrigar, tramar.

manful [mǽnful], a. viril.—**manfully** [-i], adv. varonilmente.—**manfulness** [-nes], s. virilidad.

manganate [mǽngænet], s. manganato.

manganese [mǽngæniś], s. manganeso.—**m. bronze**, bronce mangánico; (tint.) color pardo debido a sales de manganeso (llám. t. **m. brown**).— **m. steel**, acero mangánico, acero manganeso.—**m. spar**, rodonita, espato mangánico.

manganic [mængǽnic], a. mangánico.

manganite [mǽngænait], s. (min.) manganita; (quím.) manganito.

manganous [mǽngænʊs], a. manganoso.

mange [menƴ], s. roña, sarna, caracha.

manger [ménƴœr], s. pesebre; (mar.) caja de agua.

manginess [ménƴines], s. sarnazo, roña.

mangle [mǽngœl]. **I.** va. mutilar, destrozar, estropear, lacerar; echar a perder, chafallar; satinar, alisar, pasar las telas por la calandria. **II.** s. (mec.) calandria; máquina de aplanchar.

mangler [mǽnglœr], s. destrozador, despedazador; lustrador.—**mangling** [-gling], s. despedazamiento; acto de lustrar telas.

mango [mǽngo], s. (bot.) mango.

mangonel [mǽngonel], s. catapulta.

mangosteen [mǽngostin], s. (bot.) mangostán.

mangrove [mǽngrouv], s. (bot.) mangle.

mangy [ménƴi], a. sarnoso.

manhandle [mænƴǽndœl], va. mover o manipular a brazo, sin fuerza mecánica; maltratar, tratar ruda o violentamente.

manhole [mǽnjoul], s. agujero de hombre.

manhood [mǽnjud], s. naturaleza humana; virilidad; (for.) masculinidad.

mania [mǽinia], s. manía.

maniac [méiniac], s. loco maniático.

maniac(al [manáiac(al], a. maniático.

Manichean [mǽnikiæn], **Manichee** [-nikí], s. maniqueo.

Manicheism [-kíiśm], s. maniqueísmo.

manichord [mǽnicord], s. manicordio.

manicure [mǽnikiuœr]. **I.** s. manicuro. **II.** va. cuidar y arreglar (manos y uñas). **III.** vn. ejercer el oficio de manicuro.—**manicurist** [-ist], s. manicuro.

manifest [mǽnifest]. **I.** a. manifiesto, claro. **II.** s. (com.) manifiesto. **III.** va. hacer patente; presentar el manifiesto de; poner o declarar en el manifiesto. **IV.** vn. dar un manifiesto; manifestarse (un espíritu).

manifestable [-féstabœl], a. manifestable, demostrable.

manifestation [-festéśhʊn], s. manifestación.

manifestly [-festly], adv. manifiestamente.

manifestness [-festnes], s. evidencia clara o patente; perspicuidad.

manifesto [-fésto], s. manifiesto, proclama.

manifold [mǽnifould]. **I.** a. múltiple, multíplice, vario, numeroso; diverso. **II.** va. sacar varias copias al mismo tiempo. **III.** s. copia o duplicado; agregado; (aut.) múltiple, tubo múltiple.— **manifolder** [-œr], s. copiador múltiple.

manifoldness [mǽnifoldnes], s. multiplicidad.

Manihot [mǽnijot], **Manioc** [mǽnioc], s. (bot.) casabe.

manikin [mǽnikin], s. maniquí, muñeco.

manila [manila], s. trompetilla, cigarro filipino; (bot.) abacá.—**m. hemp**, abacá, cáñamo de Manila.—**m. paper**, papel de Manila.

manil(le [manil], **manilio** [manillo], s. manilla, ajorca; en algunos juegos de naipes, mala o malilla.

maniple [mǽnipœl], s. manípulo.

manipular [manípiular], a. manuable; perteneciente al manípulo.

manipulate [manípiulet]. **I.** va. manipular; manejar. **II.** vn. trabajar con las manos.—**manipulation** [-léiśhʊn], s. manipulación; manipuleo.— **manipulative, manipulatory** [-lativ, tori], a. manipulante.—**manipulator** [-létœr], s. manipulador.

manitou [mǽnitu], s. espíritu; fetiche.

mankind [mǽnkáind], s. la humanidad.

manlike [mǽnlaik], a. varonil; hombruno.

manliness [mǽnlines], s. virilidad, hombría.

manly [mǽnli], a. varonil, viril.

manna [mǽna], s. maná.—**m. sugar**, manita.

manner [mǽncer], s. manera, modo; modo de ser; suerte, género, especie; traza, aire, además, porte.—pl. modales; costumbres.—**manners bit**, porción de un manjar que por el buen parecer se deja en el plato.—**after (o in) this m.**, así, de este modo—**by all m. of means**, de todos modos; de cualquier modo.—**by no m. of means**, de ningún modo.—**in a m.**, en cierto modo, hasta cierto punto.—**to the m. born**, avezado (a ello) desde la cuna; de noble cuna, bien nacido.

mannerism [-iśm], s. amaneramiento; (teat.) latiguillo.—**mannerist** [-ist], s. artista amanerado.

mannerliness [-lines], s. urbanidad.

mannerly [-li]. **I.** a. cortés, urbano, atento, bien educado. **II.** adv. urbanamente.

mannite [mǽnait], s. (quím.) manita.

mannish [mǽniśh], a. ahombrado, hombruno, machuno.—**m. woman**, marimacho.

manœuvre, s. y v. = MANEUVER.

manometer [manómetœr], s. manómetro.

manometric(al [mænométric(al], a. manométrico.

manor [mǽncer], s. feudo; (E. U.) hacienda, finca solariega.—**m. house, m. seat**, casa solariega.

manorial [manórial], a. señorial, solariego.

mansard (roof [mænsard (ruf)], s. (arq.) techo Mansard.—**m. truss**, armadura Mansard.

manse [mæns], s. rectoría; (ant.) manso, masada.

mansion [mǽnśhʊn], s. mansión, morada, residencia.—**m. house**, quinta, hotel; palacio del Lord Mayor o alcalde de Londres.

manslaughter [mǽnslótœr], s. homicidio sin premeditación pero criminal.

manteau [mǽnto o mantó], s. manto.

mantel(piece [mǽntœl(pis], s. manto de chimenea francesa.

mantelet [mǽntelet], s. capotillo, manteleta; (mil.) mantelete, galápago.

manteletta [mænteléta], s. (igl.) mantelete.

mantelshelf [-śhelf], s. = MANTLEBOARD.

mantilla [mæntíla], s. mantilla, mantón.

mantis [mǽntis], s. (ent.) cortón.

mantissa [mæntísa], s. (mat.) mantisa.

mantle [mǽntœl]. **I.** s. manto, manteo, capa; (zool.) manto, palio, capa; caperusa de gasa incandescente. **II.** *va.* y *vn.* cubrir, tapar; extender las alas, extenderse, desparramarse.

mantleboard [-bórd], *s.* repisa, mesilla o tablero de chimenea.

mantling [mǽntling], *s.* mantelete, lambrequín.

mantua [mǽntua], *s.* manto.—**mantuamaker** [-méicœr], *s.* modista.

manual [mǽniuœl]. **I.** *a.* manual; manuable.— **m. alphabet,** alfabeto dactilológico (letras indicadas con los dedos).—**m. training,** enseñanza de trabajo manual (a menudo incluye las tareas domésticas); enseñanza de artes y oficios.—**m. work,** trabajo manual. **II.** *s.* manual; (mús.) teclado de órgano; (mil.) ejercicio de armas.

manubrium [mæniúbrium], *s.* (anat.) apófisis; (zool.) manubrio (de las medusas).

manufactory [mǽniufǽctori], *s.* fábrica, taller; manufactura.

manufacture [-fǽkchœr]. **I.** *s.* fabricación; manufactura. **II.** *va.* hacer, manufacturar, fabricar. **III.** *vn.* manufacturar, ser fabricante.

manufactured, *a.* manufacturado, fabricado.

manufacturer [-œr], *s.* fabricante.

manufacturing [-ing]. **I.** *a.* manufacturero, fabril. **II.** *s.* fabricación.

manumission [-míshun], *s.* manumisión.

manumit [-mít], *va.* manumitir.

manumotor [mǽnumóutœr], *s.* cochecito para inválidos.

manure [maniúœr]. **I.** *va.* (agr.) abonar, estercolar. **II.** *s.* abono, estércol.

manus [mǽnus], *s.* mano (de un animal).

manuscript [mǽniuscript]. **I.** *a.* manuscrito. **II.** *s.* manuscrito; (impr.) original.

Manx [mænx], *a.* y *s.* de la isla de Man; lenguaje, y pueblo de dicha isla.

many [méni], *a.* muchos, muchas. A menudo va seguido de nombre en singular con el artículo indeterminado; pero denota más de uno y se traduce en plural; v. gr.: *many a man,* muchos hombres. Forma con adjetivos en *-ed* derivados de sustantivos expresiones adjetivas, que se traducen por *de muchos* seguido del sustantivo correspondiente, o alguna otra expresión equivalente: *many-sided,* de muchos lados o aspectos; variado; *many-legged,* de muchos pies; *many-colored,* de muchos colores, policromo.—**a great m.,** muchos, muchísimos.—**as m.,** igual número, otros tantos; más *(twice as many,* dos veces más).—**as m. as,** tantos como; cuantos; más que; hasta.—**one, two,** etc., **too m.,** uno, dos, etc. de más o de sobra.—**the m.,** la mayoría, la mayor parte de la gente.—**very m.,** muy muchos, muchísimos.

manyplies [méniplaiś], *s.* ventrículo.

map [mæp]. **I.** *s.* mapa, carta geográfica, plano topográfico. **II.** *va.* delinear mapas; (a veces con *out*), hacer planes, formar (un plan).

maple [méipœl], *s.* (bot.) arce, meple.—**m. sugar,** azúcar de arce.—**m. wax,** dulce de jarabe de arce.

maqui [mǽki], *s.* (bot.) maqui.

mar. I. *va.* echar a perder, estropear, dañar, desfigurar; frustrar, aguar; malear, viciar, corromper. **II.** *s.* mancha, borrón daño, desperfecto.

marabou [mǽrabu], **marabout** [mǽrabut], *s.* (orn.) marabú; pluma de marabú.—**Marabout,** *s.* maribito.

maraschino, marasquino [mǽrræskíno], *s.* marrasquino.

marasmus [marǽsmus], *s.* (med.) marasmo, demacración.

maraud [maród], *va.* merodear.—**marauder** [-œr], *s.* merodeador.—**marauding** [-ing], *s.* merodeo, pillaje.

maravedi [mǽravédi], *s.* maravedí.

marble [márbœl]. **I.** *s.* mármol; bola (de mármol, vidrio, etc., con que juegan los niños); (impr.) piedra de imponer.—*pl.* juego de bolas. —**m. cutter,** marmolista.—**m. works,** marmolería (taller). **II.** *a.* marmóreo, de mármol.—**m.-hearted,** duro, empedernido. **III.** *va.* jaspear.— **marbled leaves,** (enc.) cortes jaspeados.—**marbled paper,** papel jaspeado.

marbleize [márblaiś], *va.* jaspear.

marbling [márbling], *s.* marmoración, jaspeadura.

marbler [márblœr], *s.* marmolista; jaspeador.

marbly [márbli], *a.* marmóreo, marmoleño.

marc, *s.* orujo, hollejo.

marcasite [márcasait], *s.* (min.) marcasita.

marcel [marsél], *va.* rizar el pelo a la Marcel— **M. wave,** rizo Marcel.

marcescent [marsésent], *a.* (bot.) marcescente.

march. I. *va.* poner en marcha, hacer marchar. **II.** *vn.* marchar, caminar; lindar; estar contiguo o vecino.—**to m. in,** entrar.—**to m. off,** irse, marcharse.—**to m. on,** marchar, caminar; seguir adelante.—**to m. out,** salir o hacer salir.— **to m. up,** avanzar, adelantar. **III.** *s.* marcha; (geogr.) marca; **(M-)** marzo.

marcher [márchœr], *s.* jefe de fuerzas que defendían una frontera.

marching [márching]. **I.** *s.* marcha. **II.** *pa.* marchando, de o en marcha.—**m. order,** orden de marcha.

marchioness [márshunes], *s.* marquesa.

marchpane [márchpen], *s.* mazapán.

marcid [mársid], *a.* marchito, macilento.

Marcionite [márshunait], **Marcionist** [-ist], *s.* y *a.* marcionista.

marconigram [marcónigræm], *s.* marconigrama, radiotelegrama.

Mardi gras [márdi gra], *s.* martes de carnaval.

mare [mǽœr], *s.* yegua.—**m.'s nest,** agua de cerrajas.—**m.'s tall,** (bot.) cola de caballo.

mare clausum [méri clósum], *s.* marcerrado.

marekanite [mǽrecanait], *s.* (min.) marecanita.

mareograph [mǽreograf], *s.* mareógrafo.

margarate [márgaret], *s.* margarato.

margaric [margéric], *a.* margárico.

margarin(e [márgarin], *s.* imitación de mantequilla; (quím.) margarina.

margarite [márgarai], *s.* (min.) margarita.

margay [márguei], *s.* (zool.) margay, mamífero fétido americano.

marge [mary], *s.* (poét.) = MARGIN.

margent [márγent]. **I.** *a.* marginal. **II.** apostilla, acotación.

margin [márγin]. **I.** *s.* margen, borde, orilla; reserva (para futuras contingencias); ganancia bruta; sobrante, excedente; (en el seguro) LOADING. **II.** *va.* marginar, margenar, apostillar, poner borde o margen. **III.** *vn.* depositar fondos como margen para ciertas jugadas de bolso.

marginal [márγinal], *a.* marginal.—**m. note,** apostilla, acotación.—**marginally** [-i], *adv.* al margen.—**marginate(d** [-eit/ed], *a.* marginado.

margrave [márgrev], *s.* margrave.

marguerite [márguerit], *s.* (bot.) margarita.

Marian [mérian], *a.* mariano; (Ingl.) adicto o referente a la reina Mary.

marigold [mérigould], *s.* (bot.) caléndula.

marinade [mérineid], *s.* escabeche.—**marinate** [mérineit], *va.* escabechar o marinar pescado.

marine [mærín]. **I.** *a.* marino, de mar.—**m. belt,** (der. int.) aguas jurisdiccionales.—**m. boiler,** caldera marina.—**m. corps,** cuerpo de soldados de marina.—**m. engine,** máquina marina.—**m. league,** legua marina (5.56 km.).—**m. stores,**= NAVAL STORES. **II.** *s.* marino, soldado de marina; marina (mercante); (pint.) marina.

mariner [mérinœr], *s.* marinero, marino.

Mariolatry [meriólatri], *s.* (igl.) hiperdulía.

marionette [marionét], *s.* títere.

marital [mérital], *a.* marital, matrimonial.

maritime [méritim], *a.* marítimo.—**m. insurance,** seguro marítimo.—**m. law,** código marítimo. —**m. perils,** riesgos marítimos.

marjoram [márγoram], *s.* (bot.) mejorana.

mark [marc]. **I.** *s.* marca; seña o señal; nota, importancia *(a man of mark,* un hombre de nota); calificación (de escuela, etc.); límite; fin, propósito; blanco (a que se tira); marco (moneda); signatura, sigilación; señal o signo que sirve de firma (de quien no sabe escribir); depresión en el colmillo de una bestia, que indica edad. **II.** *va.* marcar, señalar; notar, acotar; advertir, observar; caracterizar.—**to m. down,** anotar, poner por escrito; marcar a un precio más bajo.—**to m. out,** mostrar, señalar; elegir o escoger; cancelar, borrar. **III.** *vn.* advertir, notar, reparar.

marked [markt], *a.* marcado, notable.

markedly [márkedli], *adv.* marcadamente.

marker [-œr], *s.* marcador; marca, ficha; coime.

market [márket]. **I.** *s.* mercado; plaza; tienda (esp. carnicería o especiería).—**m. bell,** (Ingl.) campana de mercado.—**m. day,** día de mercado.—**m. garden,** huerta.—**m. man,** placero.—**m. place,** mercado; plaza de mercado.—**m. price,** precio corriente.—**m. rate,** tipo del mercado.—**m. stand,** banca de plaza; puesto en el mercado o la plaza. **II.** *va.* llevar al o vender en el mercado; vender; dar salida a; hallar mercado para. **III.** *vn.* comprar o vender en un mercado; hacer compras en un mercado o una tienda (apl. esp. a la compra de provisiones caseras).

marketable [márketabœl], *a.* vendible, comerciable; corriente, de venta; venal.

marketing [márketing], **I.** *s.* despensa; gasto de plaza; compra o venta en el mercado.

marking [márking]. **I.** *s.* acción de marcar; marca; detalles y distribución de coloridos. **II.** *a.* de marcar; que marca.—**m. ink,** tinta de marcar.—**m. iron,** hierro de marcar, cercador.—**m. machine,** máquina de acordonar monedas.—**m. nut,** agalla de caoba.

marksman [márcsmæn], *s.* tirador.

marksmanship [-ŝhip], *s.* puntería.

marl. I. *s.* marga, greda. **II.** *va.* (agr.) margar, abonar con marga; (mar.) trincafiar, empalomar.—**marlpit** [-pit], *s.* gredal, margal.

marlaceous [marléŝhus], *a.* margoso.

marline [márlin], *s.* (mar.) merlín.

marlinspike [márlinspáic], **marling-spike** (márling-], *s.* pasador.

marly [márli], *a.* margoso, gredoso.

marmalade [mármaleid], *s.* mermelada.

marmatite [mármatait], *s.* (min.) marmatita.

marmoration [marmoréŝhun], *s.* marmoración, estuco.

marmoreal, o **marmorean** [marmóreal, an], *a.* marmóreo.

marmoset [mármoŝet], *s.* (zool.) tití.

marmot [mármot], *s.* (zool.) marmota.

maroon [marún]. **I.** *va.* abandonar a uno en una costa desierta. **II.** *a.* castaño. **III.** *s.* color castaño; (bot.) castaña.—**m.,** o **marooner,** negro cimarrón; persona abandonada en una isla.

marplot [márplot], *s.* aguafiestas.

marque [mark], *s.* corso.

marquee [markí], *s.* marquesina; gran tienda de campaña; toldo de ventana.

marquetry [márketri], *s.* marquetería, taracea o ataracea, embutido.

marquis [márcuis], *s.* marqués.—**marquisate** [-et], *s.* marquesado.—**marquise** [-cuis], *s.* marquesa.

marriage [mérriy], *s.* matrimonio; casamiento; (fig.) enlace, íntima unión.—**m. articles,** contrato matrimonial o contratos esponsalicios.—**m. bell,** campana de bodas.—**m. licence,** licencia para casarse.—**m. portion,** dote.—**m. song,** epitalamio.

marriageable [mérriyabœl], *a.* casadero, núbil.

married [mérrid], *a.* casado; matrimonial, conyugal, connubial.—**m. couple,** cónyuges, marido y mujer, matrimonio.—**m. state,** estado conyugal, vida conyugal.

marron [marún], *s.* (piro.) petardo; color castaño; (bot.) castaña.

marrow [mæro], *s.* tuétano, medula, meollo.—**marrowbone** [-bóun], *s.* caña o hueso con tuétano.—**marrowfat** [-fæt],*s.* (bot.) guisante.—**marrowish** [-iŝh], *a.* meduloso.—**marrowless** [-les], *a.* falto de medula o tuétano.—**marrowy** [mæroi], *a.* lleno de tuétano, meduloso; medular.

marry [mæri]. **I.** *va.* casar, unir en matrimonio; casarse con; unir, juntar; (mar.) ayustar (cabos). **II.** *vn.* casarse. **III.** *interj.* ¡canastos! ¡cáspita! ¡por mi fe! ¡justo!

Mars [marŝ], *s.* (mito. y astr.) Marte.

Marseillais(e [márselléiŝ]. **I.** *a.* marsellés. **II.** *s.* la Marsellesa.

marsh [marsh], *s.* marjal, pantano.—**m. gas,** gas de los pantanos, metano.—**m. mallow,** (bot.) malvavisco, altea; pastilla de altea.—**m. marigold,** (bot.) hierba centella.

marshal [márŝhal]. **I.** *s.* mariscal; bastonero o maestro de ceremonias; (mil.) mariscal; (E. U.) ministril; alguacil; jefe de policía en alguasn ciudades. **II.** *va.* ordenar, poner en orden; dirigir, mandar; adiestrar, disciplinar. **III.** *vn.* juntarse, reunirse.

marshaller [-œr], *s.* arreglador, ordenador.

Marshalsea [márŝhalsi], *s.* cárcel de Londres.

marshalship [-ŝhip], *s.* mariscalía, mariscalato.

marshy [márŝhi], *a.* pantanoso, cenagoso.

marsupial [marsiúpiœl], *a.* y *s.* marsupial.

marsupium [-pium], *s.* bolsa de los didelfos.

Marsupialia [marsiúpiéilie], **Marsupiata** [-piéitæ], *s. pl.* marsupiales, didelfos.

mart, *s.* mercado; comercio; día de [San Martín.

martel [mártel], *s.* (blas.) martillo.

marteline [mártelin], *s.* martellina.

marten [márten], *s.* (zool.) marta, fuina, garduña; piel de marta.

martial [márŝhæl], *a.* marcial.—**m. law,** gobierno militar; estado de guerra (*to be under martial law,* estar en estado de guerra).

martialism [-iŝm], *s.* marcialidad.

martialist [-ist], *s.* guerreador, guerrero.

Martian [márŝhian], *a.* de Marte, marciano.

martin(et [mártin(et], **martlet** [mártlet], *s.* (orn.) avión, arrejaco, vencejo.

martinet [mártinét], *s.* (mil.) ordenancista; [mártinet] (mar.) apagapenoles.

martingale [mártingueil], *s.* gamarra; (mar.) moco del bauprés.

Martinmas [mártinmas], *s.* día de S. Martín (11 de noviembre).

martyr [mártœr]. **I.** *s.* mártir. **II.** *va.* martirizar; atormentar.—**martyrdom** [-dum], *s.* martirio.—**martyrize** [-aiŝ], *va.* martirizar.—**martyrological** [-olóyical], *a.* perteneciente al martirologio.—**martyrologist** [-óloyist], *s.* escritor de martirologios.—**martyrology** [-óloyi], *s.* martirologio.

marvel [márvel]. **I.** *s.* maravilla, prodigio.—**m. of Peru,** (bot.) maravilla del Perú. **II.** *vn.* maravillarse, admirarse, pasmarse.—**to m. at,** admirarse de.

marvelous [márvelus], *a.* maravilloso.—**marvelously** [-li], *adv.* maravillosamente.—**marvelousness** [-nes], *s.* calidad de maravilloso; maravilla.

mascalonge [mæscalony], *s.* (ict.) sollo.

mascot [mæscot], *s.* (fam.) mascota, el que o lo que trae buena suerte.

masculine [mæskiulin], *a.* masculino; varonil; macho, machuno.—**m. woman,** marimacho, mujer varonil.

masculinely [mæskiulinli], *adv.* varonilmente.

masculinity [mæskiulíniti], *s.* masculinidad.

mash [mæŝh]. **I.** *s.* amasijo, masa; malta; (fam.) conquista amorosa.—**m. tub,** cuba de bracear la cerveza. **II.** *va.* amasar, magullar, majar; (fam.) hacer cocos, cocar, hacer una conquista amorosa.—**mashed potatoes,** patatas majadas.

mashlin, mashlim, = MASLIN.

mashy [mæŝhi], *a.* magullado.

mask. I. *s.* máscara, careta; mascarilla de una persona muerta; mascarada (*v.* MASQUERADE); máscara (persona disfrazada); (fort.) parapeto provisional.—**m. ball,** o **masked ball,** baile de máscaras. **II.** *va.* enmascarar, disfrazar; encubrir, disimular.—**to m. a ship,** (mar.) disfrazar la bandera. **III.** *vn.* andar enmascarado o disfrazado.

masker [máskœr], *s.* máscara, mascarón.

maskinonge [mæskinony], *s.* (ict.) sollo.

maslin [mæŝlin], *s.* comuña, tranquillón.

mason [méisn], *s.* albañil; francmasón; abeja albañila.—**m. bird,** (orn.) trepatroncos o herrerillo.—**m. wasp,** avispa que construye celdas de barro.

masonic [masónic], *a.* masónico; albañil...

masonry [méisonri], *s.* albañilería; mampostería (de piedra o de ladrillo); materiales de albañilería; francmasonería.

Masorah [mésora *o* masóra], *s.* Masora.

Masoretic(al [mæsorétic(al], *a.* masorético.

Masorite [mésorait], *s.* masoreta.

masque [masc], *s.* = MASK.

masquerade [méskœreid]. **I.** *s.* mascarada, comparsa; máscara, disfraz.—**m. ball** = MASK BALL. **II.** *vn.* enmascararse, disfrazarse.

masquerader [-œr], *s.* máscara, mascarón.

mass. I. *s.* montón, mole; revoltijo, baturrillo; bulto, volumen; (mec.) masa; (igl., mús.) misa.—**m. book,** libro de misa; misal.—**m. formation,** (mil.) columna cerrada.—**m. for the dead,** misa de réquiem o de ánima.—**m. meeting,** gran mitin, mitin popular.—**m. production,** producción en serie.—**in m., in the m.,** en masa, en conjunto.—**the masses,** el pueblo, el vulgo. **II.** *va.* juntar, reunir en masa, amasar. **III.** *vn.* formarse, juntarse en masas.

massacre [mésakœr]. **I.** *s.* carnicería, matanza, destrozo. **II.** *va.* matar atrozmente, hacer una carnicería, destrozar.

massacrer [mésacrœr], *s.* matador, asesino.

massage [mésey *o* masáy]. **I.** *s.* masaje, soba. **II.** *va.* sobar.

masseter [mæsítœr], *s.* (anat.) masetero.

massicot [mésicot], *s.* masicote, almártaga.

massi(ve)**nes** [mási(v)nes], *s.* peso, bulto, mole; solidez.

massive [másiv], **massy** [mási], *a.* macizo, pesado, sólido.

mast. I. *s.* (mar.) palo, mastelero, mástil, árbol; bellota, fabuco.—*pl.* (mar.) arboladura. —**m.-coat,** capa de palo.—**m.-hole,** fogonadura.— **m. hoop,** arrucho.—**m. sprung,** palo rendido.— **m. trunk,** cajera. **II.** *va.* (mar.) árbolar un palo; cebar con bellotas, fabucos, etc.

mastabe [méstæbæ], *s.* mastaba, especie de capilla mortuoria de los antiguos egipcios.

masted [másted], *a.* arbolado.

master [mástœr]. **I.** *s.* amo, señor; maestro, preceptor; ingenio; director, gobernador, jefe; señorito; (mar.) capitán, maestre, patrón, arráez; perito, experto; oficial, maestro (de un oficio).—**m. builder,** maestro de obras; contratista de construcciones; sobrestante de albañilería.—**m. mason,** masón de grado tres; maestro u oficial de albañilería.—**m. mechanic,** maestro mecánico.— **m. of,** profundo conocedor de; perito o docto en.— **m. of arts,** maestro en artes.—**m. of the horse,** caballerizo mayor.—**m. of the ordnance,** director general de artillería.—**m. of the robes,** jefe de la guardarropa.—**m. of the rolls,** (Ingl.) archivero mayor o gran archivero.—**m. warden of the mint,** director de la casa de moneda.—**m. workman,** maestro, sobrestante.—**the M.,** el Maestro (Jesucristo). **II.** *a.* magistral, superior, principal.—**m. hand,** mano maestra, maestría.— **m. key,** llave maestra.—**m. stroke,** golpe maestro. **III.** *va.* vencer, domar; dominar, conocer a fondo; ser maestro o perito en. **IV.** *vn.* ser superior en alguna cosa.

masterdom [-dvm], *s.* dominio, mando.

masterful [-ful], *a.* imperioso, dominante, arbitrario; perito, experto; sobresaliente, excelente.

masterless [-les], *a.* indómito, rebelde; mostrenco.

masterliness [-lines], *s.* maestría, destreza.

masterly [-li]. **I.** *a.* magistral; maestro; imperioso. **II.** *adv.* magistralmente.

masterpiece [-pis], *s.* obra maestra.

mastership [-ship], *s.* magisterio; maestría; superioridad, preeminencia; obra maestra.

masterwork [-uœrk], *s.* = MASTERPIECE.

masterwort [-uœrt], *s.* (bot.) imperatoria, astrancia.

mastery [mástœri], *s.* dominio, poder, gobierno; maestría, destreza, habilidad; superioridad, ventaja, victoria; conocimiento.

masthead [mástjed], *s.* (mar.) tope, espiga; vigía, gaviero.

mastic [méstic], *s.* (bot.) alfóncigo, lentisco; almáciga; cemento, bituminoso.

masticate [méstikeit], *va.* masticar.—**mastication** [-éishvn], *s.* masticación.—**masticator** [-éitœr], *s.* masticador.—**masticatory** [méstikatori], *s.* masticatorio.

mastiff [mástif], *s.* mastín, perro alano.

mastitis [mæstáitis], *s.* mastitis.

mastless [mástles], *a.* que no produce bellotas, fabucos o castañas; (mar.) desarbolado.

mastodon [méstodon], *s.* mastodonte.

mastoid [méstoid], *a.* mastoides.—**m. process,** apófisis mastoides.

mastoiditis [-áitis], *s.* mastoiditis.

masturbate [méstœrbeit], *vr.* masturbarse.

masturbation [-éishvn], *s.* masturbación, onanismo.

mat [mæt]. **I.** *s.* estera, esterilla, felpudo; rejilla, emparrillado; (mar.) palleta, pallete; borde de cartón alrededor de un grabado, etc.; mate del metal; herramienta para dar mate. **II.** *va.* enredar, desgreñar (pelo, lana, etc.); esterar; producir (en los metales) una superficie mate. **III.** *vn.* enredarse, formarse greñas.

matador [mætadócœr], *s.* diestro, primer espada; en juegos de naipes, matador.

match [mæch]. **I.** *s.* compañero, pareja; igual, semejante; competidor, contrincante; (dep.) partido; partida, juego, contienda, lucha, certamen; noviazgo, casamiento, alianza, boda; fósforo, cerilla, mecha, pajuela; (arti.) mecha, cuerdamecha, cuerdacalada.—**m. board,** tabla de machihembrar, con ranura en un borde y lengüeta en el otro.—**m. box,** fosforera.—**m. cord, m. line,** mecha.—**m. mark,** marca de apareamiento o de armar, que indica el orden o posición en que deben ponerse las piezas de un artefacto desarmado.—**m. safe** = M. BOX.—**m. staff,** botafuego. **II.** *va.* hermanar, aparear, casar; igualar a, equiparar; ser igual a; competir con.—**to m. horses,** emparejar caballos. **III.** *vn.* casarse; hermanarse, casar.

matchable [méchabœl], *a.* que puede emparejarse con otro.

matchless [méchles], *a.* incomparable, sin igual, sin rival.—**matchlessly** [-li]. *adv.* incomparablemente.—**matchlessness** [-nes], *s.* calidad de incomparable.

matchlock [méchloc], *s.* llave de los mosquetes antiguos; mosquete.

matchmaker [máchméikœr], *s.* casamentero; fabricante de fósforos.—**matchmaking** [-ing], *s.* andar arreglando bodas o haciendo casamientos; fabricación de fósforos.

mate [méit]. **I.** *s.* consorte, cónyuge; compañero, compañera; macho o hembra entre los animales; mate (ajedrez); (mar.) piloto. **II.** *va.* casar, desposar; igualar; aparear; competir; en ajedrez, dar jaque mate.

maté, *s.* mate, te del Paraguay.

mateless [méitles], *a.* solo, sin compañera, falto de consorte, desparejado.

materia medica [mætíriæ médicæ], *s.* (med.) materia médica.

material [matírial]. **I.** *a.* material; importante, substancial, esencial; serio, grave. **II.** *s.* material o ingrediente; materia o asunto; ropa, género.

materialism [-ism], *s.* materialismo.

materialist [-ist], *s.* materialista.—**materialistic** [-istic], *a.* materialista.

materiality [mætiriéliti], *s.* materialidad; importancia.

materialization [matírialiséishvn], *s.* encarnación de un espíritu.

materialize [matírialaiš]. **I.** *va.* materializar; dar cuerpo, exteriorizar; hacer común o vulgar. **II.** *vn.* (fam.) hacerse visible o corpóreo; cuajar, encarnar; tomar forma; (fam.) aparecer.

materially [matíriali], *adv.* materialmente, físicamente; esencialmente, importantemente; notablemente.

materialness [-nes], *s.* materialidad; importancia, indispensabilidad.

maternal [matœrnal], *a.* maternal, materno.

maternally [matǽrnali], *adv.* maternalmente.

maternity [matǽrniti], *s.* maternidad; casa de maternidad.—**m. hospital,** casa de maternidad.

matgrass [mǽtgræs], *s.* = MATWEED.

mathematic(al [mǽzeimǽtic(al], *a.* matemático.

mathematically [-i], *adv.* matemáticamente.

mathematician [mǽzematíśhan], *s.* matemático.

mathematics [mǽzemǽtics], *s. pl.* matemáticas.

matico [matíco], *s.* (bot.) matico.

matin [mǽtin]. **I.** *a.* matutino. **II.** *s.* mañana. —*pl.* (igl.) maitines.

matinal [mǽtinal], *a.* matinal.

matinée [mǽtiné], *s.* (teat.) [matiné, función de tarde; chambra, peinador.

mating [méiting], *s.* apareamiento; casamiento.

matrass [mǽtras], *s.* (quím.) matraz.

matriarch [méitriarc], *s.* matriarca, mujer que gobierna su familia y su tribu o clan.—**matriarchate** [-keit], **matriarchy** [-ki], *s.* matriarcado, sistema en que la mujer da su nombre a sus hijos y la descendencia se determina por la línea materna; gobierno de las mujeres.

matrices [mǽtrisiŝ], *s. pl.* de MATRIX.

matricidal [-sáidal], *a.* referente al matricidio.

matricide [-said], *s.* matricidio; matricida.

matricula [matríkiula], *s.* matrícula.

matriculate [-eit]. **I.** *va.* y *vn.* matricular(se). **II.** *s.* y *a.* matriculado.—**matriculation** [-éiśhun], *s.* matriculación.

matrimonial [mǽtrimónial], *a.* matrimonial; marital.—**matrimonially** [-i], *adv.* matrimonialmente.

matrimony [-moni], *s.* matrimonio, casamiento.

matrix [métrix o mǽtrix], *s.* (anat.) matriz, útero; (biol.) substancia intercelular; (impr. y fund.) matriz, molde; quijo.

matron [méitron], *s.* matrona; mujerona; ama de llaves; directora de instituto.

matronal [métronal o mǽtronal], *a.* matronal.

matronly [-li]. **I.** *a.* como de matrona; de alguna edad. **II.** *adv.* como una matrona; maternalmente.

matronymic [métronímic]. **I.** *a.* perteneciente al nombre de la madre o derivado de él. **II.** *s.* nombre así derivado.

matt [mæt], *a.* y *s.* mate.

matte [mæt], *s.* (fund.) mata.

matter [mǽtœr]. **I.** *s.* materia; substancia; materia, asunto, cuestion; material; cosa, negocio; importancia, entidad; (med.) materia, pus; (impr.) tipo compuesto.—**m. of course,** cosa natural o de cajón.—**m. of fact,** hecho, realidad. —**a m.-of-fact man,** hombre positivista.—**as a m. of fact,** como cuestión de hecho; en realidad.—**for the m. of that,** en cuanto a eso.—(**it is**) **no m.,** no importa.—**small m.,** cosa de poca entidad. —**what is the m.?** ¿qué pasa? ¿qué ocurre?— **what is the m. with this (it, him,** etc.)? ¿qué inconveniente tiene, qué defecto le encuentra a, por qué no, qué le parece (esto, él, etc.)?—**what is the m. with you (him, her,** etc.)? ¿qué (achaque) tiene Vd. (él, ella, etc.)? ¿qué le pasa a usted (él, ella, etc.)? **II.** *vn.* importar; convenir, hacer al caso; supurar, formarse materia o pus.

matterless [mǽtœrles], *a.* fútil.

matting [mǽting], *s.* estera; esterado; borde de cartón para un grabado, acuarela, etc.; (mar.) empalletado.

mattock [mǽtoc], *s.* zapapico.

mattress [mǽtres], *s.* colchón; (hidr.) defensa de ramas, varas y troncos trabados.

maturant [mǽtiurant], **maturative** [mǽtiurativ]. **I.** *s.* madurativo. **II.** *a.* madurante.

maturate [mǽtiuret]. **I.** *va.* (cir.) madurar. **II.** *vn.* supurar, formar pus.—**maturation** [-éiśhun], *s.* maduración; (med.) supuración.

mature [matiúœr]. **I.** *a.* maduro, sazonado; juicioso; acabado, completo o perfecto; (com.) vencido, pagadero. **II.** *va.* madurar, sazonar. **III.** *vn.* madurar o madurarse; (com.) vencer, cumplirse un plazo.—**maturely** [-li], *adv.* maduramente, sesudamente.—**matureness** [-nes], *s.* madurez.

maturity [matiúriti], *s.* madurez; maduración; edad madura; perfección; (com.) vencimiento.

matutinal [matiútinal o mǽtiutáinal], *a.* matutino, matinal; matutinal.

matweed [mǽtuid], *s.* (bot.) esparto, albardín.

matzoth [mǽtsouz], *s.* galleta de pan sin levadura.

maudlin [módlin]. **I.** *a.* peneque, calamocano. **II.** *s.* (bot.) agerato, balsamina menor.

maul [mol]. **I.** *va.* apalear, aporrear; maltratar. **II.** *s.* mazo, machota, porra, mandarria.

maulstick [mólstic], *s.* = MAHLSTICK.

maunder [móndœr], *vn* gruñir, refunfuñar.

maunderer [móndœrœr], *s.* regañón.

Maundy [móndi], *s.* (igl.) mandato, lavatorio de pies.—**M. Thursday,** jueves santo.

Mauritanian [móriténian], *a.* y *s.* mauritano.

mausolean [mósolían], *a.* sepulcral.

mausoleum [-um], *s.* mausoleo.

mauve [mov], *s.* color de malva.

mauveine [móvin], *s.* malveína, violeta de anilina.

mavis [mévis], *s.* (orn.) malvís, zorzal.

maw [mo], *s.* buche de las aves; cuajar; vejiga de aire en los peces.

mawkish [mókiŝh], *a.* asqueroso, nauseabundo.

mawkishness [mókiśhnes], *s.* asquerosidad.

mawky [móki], *a.* gusaniento.

mawseed [mósíd], *s.* semillas secas de amapola, para pájaros.

mawworm [-uœrm], *s.* lombriz intestinal.

maxilla [mæxíla], *s.* hueso maxilar.

maxillary [mǽxíleri], *s.* y *a.* maxilar.—**m. bone,** maxilar.—**m. sinus,** antro de Highmore, o seno maxilar.

maxim [mǽxim], *s.* máxima; axioma.

maximite [mǽximait], *s.* maximita, explosivo Maxim.

maximize [-aiŝ], *va.* llevar hasta el máximo; exagerar; interpretar liberalmente.

maximum [mǽximum], *s.* y *a.* máximo.

maxwell [mǽxuel], *s.* máxwel, unidad de flujo magnético.

may [méi], *vr. irr.* y *def.* (*imperf.* MIGHT) poder, tener facultad o permiso, ser posible, lícito o permitido; poderse (v. gr.: *I may go,* puede que yo vaya: *you may go,* puede Vd. marcharse: *may I come in?* ¿puedo entrar?: *it may be,* puede ser: *if I may say so,* si me es lícito decirlo). Usado elípticamente, suceder, ser (v. gr.: *be the result what it may,* sea cual fuere el resultado: suceda lo que suceda). A veces denota deseo vivo, y se traduce por ojalá, Dios quiera, o se omite y el verbo se pone en subjuntivo, v. gr.: *may it be so,* ojalá que así sea: *may you live long and happy years,* viva Vd. largos y felices años.

May [méi]. **I.** *s.* mes de mayo; (fig.) primavera de la vida; (bot.) acerolo.—**M. apple,** (bot.) mandrágora.—**M. day,** primero de mayo.—**M. drink** = M. WINE.—**M. fly,** (ent.) mosca de mayo; mosca de un día.—**M. lady** = M. QUEEN.—**M. lily,** (bot.) lirio de los valles.—**M. queen,** maya, joven que preside la fiesta de mayo. **II.** *vn.* úsase solo en la frase **to be, o go, a-maying,** coger flores la mañana del día primero de mayo.

Maya [máya], *a.* y *s.* maya, de los mayas.

maybe [méibi], **mayhap** [méijæp], *adv.* acaso, quizá, tal vez.

Mayflower [méifláuœr], *s.* (bot.) maya; (E. U., bot.) gayuba.

mayhem [méijem], *s.* (for.) mutilación criminal de una parte del cuerpo.

maying [méiing], *s.* festividad del primero de mayo.

mayonnaise [méionéŝ], *s.* (coc.) salsa mayonesa.

mayor [méiœr], *s.* alcalde.

mayoralty [méioralti], *s.* alcaldía.

maypole [méipóul], *s.* mayo, poste o vara alta con adornos que se clava en el centro del lugar donde se celebran las fiestas del primero de mayo.

mayweed [méiwid], *s.* (bot.) manzanilla loca.

mazard [mǽŝard], *s.* (bot.) guinda.—**m. tree,** guindo.

mazarine [mǽ§arín], *s.* color azul subido.

mazdaism [mǽsdæism], **mazdeism** [deiâm], *s.* mazdeísmo.

mazda lamp [mǽsdæ læmp], *s.* lámpara de tungsteno.

maze [méis]. **I.** *s.* laberinto; perplejidad, confusión.—**to be in a m.**, estar perplejo. **II.** *va.* extraviar; asombrar, confundir. **III.** *vn.* vacilar.

mazer [mésœr], *s.* escudilla de madera.

mazurka [masúrka], *s.* mazurca.

mazy [mési], *a.* perplejo; embrollado.

me [mi], *pron. pers.* (caso oblicuo de **I**) me, mí: *do me the favour*, hágame Vd. el favor: *for me*, para mí: *with me*, conmigo.

mead [mid], *s.* aguamiel, hidromel, aloja, meloja.

meadow [médo], *s.* **mead** (poét.), pradera, pradería, vega, prado.—**m. lark**, (orn.) alondra de los prados.—**m. saffron**, (bot.) villorita, quitameriendas.

meadowsweet [-suit], **meadowwort** [-uœrt], *s.* (bot.) ulmaria, barba de cabra.

meadowy [médoi], *a.* de pradera; como prado; lleno de prados.

meager, meagre [mígœr], *a.* magro, flaco, enjuto; escaso, pobre; cuaresmal, de vigilia.—**meagerly, meagrely** [-li], *adv.* pobremente, estérilmente.—**meagerness, meagreness** [-nes], *s.* flaqueza, flacura; escasez.

meal [mil], *s.* comida; (en general) sustento; harina. —**m. time**, hora de comer.

mealiness [mílines], *s.* calidad de harinoso; melosidad.

mealman [mílmæn], *s.* harinero.

mealy [míli], *a.* harinoso; de pintas blancas.—**m. mouthed**, pacato, tímido; meloso, falso.

mean [min]. **I.** *a.* humilde; mediano; inferior, pobre; bajo, vil; (fam.) malo, desconsiderado, indigno; desazonado, de mal humor; obscuro, despreciable; tacaño, mezquino, sórdido; insignificante; medio, intermedio; (mat.) medio.—**m.-born**, de humilde cuna; de baja estofa.—**m. pressure**, presión media.—**m. proportional**, medio proporcional.—**m.-spirited**, bajo, ruin.—**m. sun**, sol medio.—**m. time**, tiempo medio.—**m. velocity**, velocidad media.—**m. wall**, pared medianera. **II.** *s.* medio (punto medio); medio (de una proporción); mediocridad, medianía.—*pl.* medio, recurso, modo, forma, instrumento, arbitrio, expediente; (com.) medios, caudal, fondos, recursos, riquezas.—**by all means**, sin duda, sin falta; por todos los medios posibles.—**by fair means**, por medios lícitos; a las buenas.—**by foul means**, por malos medios, por la fuerza.—**by no means**, by no manner of means, de ningún modo.—**by some means**, de alguna manera.—**by this means**, por este medio. **III.** *va.* (pret. y *pp.* MEANT) significar, querer decir, dar a entender; pensar, proponerse, pretender.—**what do you m.?** ¿qué quiere Vd. decir? ¿qué se propone Vd.? **IV.** *vn.* (con adverbio) tener intención o propósito, v. gr.: *he means well*, tiene buenas intenciones; *a well-meaning man*, un hombre de buena fe, bien intencionado.

meander [miǽndœr]. **I.** *s.* meandro, laberinto, camino tortuoso.—**m. line**, (top.) línea quebrada auxiliar. **II.** *vn.* serpear, serpentear.

meandrian [miǽndrian], *a.* serpentino, tortuoso.

meaning [míning]. **I.** *a.* significativo. **II.** *s.* intención, voluntad, designio; sentido, significado.—**meaningless** [-les], *a.* insensato; sin sentido, vacío.—**meaningly** [-li], *adv.* significativamente; con intención.

meanly [mínli], *adv.* bajamente, vilmente; con desprecio; probremente, miserablemente; medianamente, mediocremente.

meanness [mínnes], *s.* bajeza; vileza: humildad; tacañería, miseria, mezquindad.

meant [ment], *pret.* y *pp.* de TO MEAN.

meantime [míntaim], **meanwhile** [mínjuail]. **I.** *adv.* mientras tanto, entretanto. **II.** *s.* ínterin.—**in the m.**, mientras tanto, en el ínterin, hasta entonces.

measled [mísld], *a.* atacado del sarampión; roñoso (cerdo); (vulg.) despreciable.—**measledness** [-nes], *s.* estado de los cerdos roñosos.

measles [mísœls], *s. pl.* sarampión; roña de los cerdos; (bot.) cáncer de los árboles.

measly [misli], *a.* = MEASLED,

measurable [méѱurabœl], *a.* medible, mensurable; moderado.—**measurableness** [-nes], *s.* mensurabilidad.—**measurably** [-bli], *adv.* mediblemente; con moderación.

measure [méѱœr]. **I.** *s.* medida; unidad de medida; compás, metro, cadencia; modo, grado; moderación; proyecto de ley; (mús.) compás.—*pl.* (geol.) capas, yacimientos.—**beyond m.**, con exceso.—**in a great m.**, en gran manera; en gran parte.—**in some m.**, hasta cierto punto, en cierto modo.—**out of m.** = BEYOND M.—**to take measures**, tomar las medidas necesarias.—**to take one's m.**, o **the m. of**, tomar la medida a uno. **II.** *va.* medir, mensurar, señalar, distribuir; estimar, juzgar; valuar; comparar, oponer;—**to m. one's length**, medir el suelo, caer tendido.—**to m. out**, asignar o dar según medida: medir (algo a alguien).—**to m. swords**, medir espadas. **III.** *vn.* medir, tener tal o cual dimensión.—**to m. up to**, elevarse a la altura de, ser igual a.

measured [-d], *pp.* y *a.* medido, moderado; uniforme; lento, rítmico; limitado, restringido.

measureless [-les], *a.* inmensurable, ilimitado.

measurement [-mœnt], *s.* medición; dimensión; medida; (mar.) cubicación, arqueo.—**m. bill,** (mar.) certificación del porte de los buques.

measurer [-œr], *s.* medidor.

measuring [-ing]. **I.** *s.* medición, medida. **II.** *a.* de medir.—**m. tape**, cinta de medir.—**m. worm**, (ent.) oruga geómetra.

meat [mit], *s.* carne, vianda; substancia, jugo; comida.—**m. ball**, albóndiga.—**m. fly**, mosca de carne.—**m. hook**, escarpia.—**m. market**, carnicería.—**m. spit**, espiche.

meatus [miétus], *s.* (anat.) meato.

meaty [míti], *a.* carnoso; jugoso, substancioso.

mechanic [mecǽnic]. **I.** *a.* mecánico, maquinal. **II.** *s.* mecánico, artesano, obrero, menestral.

mechanical [mecǽnical], *a.* mecánico; maquinal. —**m. equivalent of heat**, equivalente mecánico del calor.

mechanically [-i], *adv.* mecánicamente; maquinalmente.—**mechanicalness** [-nes], *s.* calidad de mecánico.

mechanician [mecaníshan], *s.* mecánico, perito en la ciencia de la mecánica; maquinista.

mechanics [mecǽnics], *s.* mecánica.

mechanism [mecǽnism], *s.* mecanismo.

mechanist [mécænist], *s.* mecanicista, el que sostiene que todos los fenómenos universales son puramente físicos o mecánicos.—**mechanistic** [-nistic], *a.* mecanicista.

mechanize [mécænais], *va.* construir mecánicamente; convertir en máquina.

Mechlin [méclin], *a.* encaje o puntas de Malinas.

mechoacan [mechóacan], *s.* (bot.) mechoacán.

meconate [méconet], *s.* (quím.) meconato.

meconic [mecónic], *a.* (quím.) mecónico.

meconium [mecónium], *s.* meconio, alhorre.

medal [médal], *s.* medalla.

medallic [medǽlic], *a.* numismático.

medallion [medǽliun], *s.* medallón.

medal(l)ist [médalist], *s.* numismático, colector de medallas; grabador de medallas; el que ha sido agraciado con una medalla.

meddle [médœl], *vn.* (gen. con *with*) meterse, entremeterse, ingerirse.

meddler [médlœr], *s.* entremetido.

meddlesome [médœlsum], *a.* entremetido, oficioso.—**meddlesomeness** [-nes], *s.* entremetimiento, oficiosidad.

meddling [médling], *s.* entremetimiento, interposición impertinente y oficiosa.

Mede [mid], *s.* y *a.* medo.

media [mídia]. **I.** *s.* (anat.) túnica media de un vaso. **II.** *pl.* de MEDIUM.

mediæval [mediíval], *a.* = MEDIEVAL.

medial [mídial], *a.* medio, del centro.

median [mídian]. **I.** *a.* del medio; (geom.) mediana. **II.** *s.* (geom.) mediana.

Median, *s.* y *a.* medo.

---

mediastinum [midiæstáinʊm], *s.* (anat.) mediastino.

mediate [mídɪet]. **I.** *va.* y *vn.* mediar, intervenir, intermediar, interponerse. **II.** *a.* mediato, medio; **i**nterpuesto.

mediately [mídietli], *adv.* mediatamente.

mediation [mídiéishʊn], *s.* mediación, intercesión; interposición, intervención; tercería.

mediator [-éitœr], *s.* mediador, intercesor, medianero, avenidor, tercero.

mediatorial [mídiatórial], *a.* medianero.

mediatorship [mídiéitœrship], *s.* oficio de mediador.

mediatress, mediatrix [mídiétres, trix], *s.* medianera, abogada.

medic [médɪc], *s.* (bot.) alfalfa, mielga.

medicable [médɪcabœl], *a.* medicable.

medical [médɪcal], *a.* médico.—**m. school**, escuela de medicina.—**medically** [-i], *adv.* en calidad de médico, facultativamente.

medicament [-mœnt], *s.* medicamento.

medicamental [-méntal], *a.* medicamentoso, curativo.

medicaster [médɪcæstœr], *s.* medicastro.

medicate [médɪkeit], *va.* medicinar; hacer medicinal (alguna cosa).—**medication** [-éishʊn], *s.* medicación.

medicative [médɪketiv], *a.* medicinal.

medicinal [medísinal], *a.* medicinal.

medicinally [-i], *adv.* según la medicina.

medicine [médisin], *s.* medicina, medicamento, remedio; medicina (arte o ciencia); (E. U.) entre los indios, ensalmo.—**m. chest**, botiquín.—**m. lodge**, casilla o tienda del exorcista.—**m. man**, exorcista, hechizador.

medicolegal [medicolígal], *a.* medicolegal.

medieval [mídíval], *a.* medioeval.

mediocre [mídiokœr], *a.* mediocre; vulgar, trivial, baladí.

mediocrity [midiócriti], *s.* mediocridad.

meditate [méditeit]. **I.** *va.* meditar, idear, tramar. **II.** *vn.* meditar.

meditation [-éishʊn], *s.* meditación.

meditative [méditativ], *a.* meditativo.—**meditatively** [-li], *adv.* meditativamente.

mediterranean, mediterraneous [mediterréni-an, niʊs], *a.* mediterráneo.

medium [mídiʊm]. **I.** *s.* (*pl.* MEDIUMS o MEDIA) medio; expediente; instrumento, intermediario; médium; (fís.) medio ambiente; circunstancias rodeantes; (pint.) aceite.—**at a m.**, uno con otro, por término medio. **II.** *a.* mediano, intermedio; mediocre; (coc.) no muy cocido.— **m. fine**, entrefino.—**m.-sized**, de tamaño mediano. —**m. steel**, acero de construcciones (de entre 0,15 y 0,30 de carbono).

mediumistic [-ístic], *a.* de o relativo a médiums.

medlar [médlar], *s.* (bot.) níspero.

medley [médli]. **I.** *s.* miscelánea, mezcla, mescolanza, baturrillo; (mús.) miscelánea, *potpourri*. **II.** *a.* mezclado, confuso.

medulla [medúla], *s.* (anat.) médula.—**m spinalis** o **oblongata**, médula espinal.

medullary [médʊlæri], *a.* medular.

medusa [medúsa], *s.* (ict.) medusa.

meed [míd], *s.* premio, galardón.

meek [mík], *a.* manso, humilde, dócil.—**meekly** [-li], *adv.* mansamente, humildemente.—**meekness** [-nes], *s.* mansedumbre, humildad, docilidad.

meerschaum [mícœrshom o mérshaum], *s.* espuma de mar; pipa de espuma de mar.

meet [mít]. **I.** *va.* (*pret.* y *pp.* MET) encontrarse con; encontrar, chochar con; convenir a, satisfacer, llenar; pagar, saldar, honrar (un pagaré, etc.); sufragar, correr con, hacer frente a; refutar, destruir con argumentos; combatir, batirse o pelea.· con; conocer o tratar personalmente (*I am glad to meet you*, me alegro de conocer a Vd.)—**to m. a charge**, refutar, responder a una acusación. —**to m. expenses**, hacer frente a los gastos.—**to m. half way**, partir el camino con; partir la diferencia con; hacer algunas concesiones a. **II.** *vn.*

reunirse, juntarse; verse; encontrarse; luchar, combatir, batirse; entenderse, convenirse; confluir.—**to m. with**, juntarse con; encontrar; tener, sufrir (un accidente, una desgracia, etc.).—**to m. with one's match**, dar uno con la horma de su zapato.—**till we m. again**, hasta más vernos. **III.** *a.* apto, idóneo, apropiado, conveniente. **IV.** *s.* reunión de cazadores para una cacería, y lugar donde se reúnen.

meeting [míting], *s.* mitin; reunión, sesión; entrevista, conferencia; (igl.) capítulo; confluencia de dos ríos; encuentro, duelo o desafío.—**m. of creditors**, concurso de acreedores.

meetinghouse [-jáus], *s.* capilla o templo protestante.

meetly [mítli], *adv.* convenientemente.

meetness [mítnes¹], *s.* aptitud, propiedad, conveniencia.

mega- [mégæ], sufijo que se usa con los nombres de varias unidades mecánicas y eléctricas para indicar un millón; vg. *megadyne* (-dain), megadina (un millón de dinas); *megafarad*, (-færæd), megafaradio.

megacephalic [-sefélic], **megacephalous** [-séfælʊs], *a.* = MEGALOCEPHALOUS.

megalith [mégaliz], *s.* megalito.

megalithic [megalízic], *a.* megalítico.

megalocephalous [-loséfælʊs], *a.* megalocéfalo.

megalomania [-méiniæ], *s.* megalomanía.

megalomaniac [-niæc], *s.* y *a.* megalómano.

megalosaur [-sor], *s.* megalosauro.

megaphone [-foun], *s.* megáfono, bocina, portavoz.

megapode [-poud], *s.* megalópodo.

megascope [-scoup], *s.* megascopio; cámara fotográfica ampliadora.

megatherium [-zíriʊm], *s.* megaterio.

megohm [mégóum], *s.* megohmio, un millón de ohmios.

megrim [mígrim], *s.* hemicránea.

meikle, *y* *s.* = MICKLE.

melancholia [mélancólia], *s.* lipemanía.—**melancholic** [-cólic], *a.* y *s.* melancólico, lipemaníaco. —**melancholically** [-cólicali], *adv.* de una manera melancólica.—**melancholy** [mélancoli]. **I.** *s.* lipemanía; melancolía, tristeza. **II.** *a.* melancólico.

melange [mélany *o* melány], *s.* mezcla.

melanism [mélæriism], *s.* melanodermia.

melanite [mélanait], *s.* (min.) melanita, granate.

melanosis [-nósis], *s.* (med.) melanosis, cáncer negro.

melanuria [-niúriæ], *s.* melanuria o melanuresis, formación de pigmentos negros en la orina.

mêlée [melé], *s.* rebujiña, pelotera.

meliaceous [mílieíshʊs], *a.* (bot.) meliáceo.

melic [mélic], *a.* mélico, lírico.

melilot [mélilot], *s.* (bot.) meliloto.

meliorate [mílioreit]. **I.** *va.* mejorar; adelantar; bonificar. **II.** *vn.* mejorarse.—**melioration** [-éishʊn], *s.* mejoramiento, mejora, adelanto.

melissa [melísa], *s.* (bot.) melisa.

melliferous [melífœrʊs], *a.* melífero.

mellifluence [-fluens], *s.* melifluidad.—**mellifluent** [-ent], **mellifluous** [-ʊs], *a.* melifluo; dulce.

mellow [mélo]. **I.** *a.* maduro, sazonado; meloso; tierno, blando, suave; pastoso, mantecoso; melodioso; blando, friable; mórbido; calamocano. **II.** *va.* sazonar, madurar, ablandar, suavizar. **III.** *vn.* madurar, madurarse.

mellowly [-li], *adv.* suavemente, dulcemente.

mellowness [-nes], *s.* madurez, sazón; melosidad, suavidad; pastosidad, morbidez.

mellowy [-i] = MELLOW.

melocoton, melacotoon [melocotún], *s.* (bot.) membrillo o membrillero.

melodic [melódic], *a.* melódico.

melodious [melódiʊs], *a.* melodioso.—**melodiously** [-li], *adv.* melodiosamente.—**melodiousness** [-nes], *s.* melodía.

melodist [mélodist], *s.* melodista, compositor o cantor de melodías.

melodize [mélodaiȝ]. **I.** *va.* hacer melodioso. **II.** *vn.* hacer melodía.

melodrama [mélodráma], **melodrame** [-dram], *s.* melodrama.—**melodramatic** [-dramǽtic], *a.* melodramático.—**melodramatically** [-dramǽtically], *adv.* melodramáticamente.—**melodramatist** [-drǽmatist], *s.* autor de melodramas.

melody [mélodi], *s.* melodía; canción o aire melódico.

melon [mélun], *s.* (bot.) melón.—**m. beetle,** (ent.) diabrótico.

melrose [mélrouŝ], *s.* miel de rosas.

melt. I. *va.* derretir, fundir; disolver; ablandar, aplacar; consumir, gastar. **II.** *vn.* fundirse, derretirse;. deshelar; ablandarse; amilanarse; confundirse, mezclarse; (**a** veces con *away*) disiparse, desvanecerse.—**to m. into tears,** deshacerse en lágrimas. **III.** *s.* substancia derretida; fusión, derretimiento; (metal.) hornada; colada.

melter [méltœr], *s.* fundidor; crisol.

melting [mélting]. **I.** *a.* fundente. **II.** *s.* derretimiento, fusión.—**m. pan,** cazo.—**m. point,** punto de fusión.—**m. pot,** crisol.

melton [méltun], *s.* (tej.) paño melton.

member [mémbœr], *s.* miembro (del cuerpo, de una igualdad); parte de un todo; miembro, individuo, socio; pieza (de un puente, etc.)

membered [mémbœrd], *a.* membrudo, fortachón, fornido; (blas.) membrado.

membership [-ŝhip], *s.* calidad de miembro o socio; número de socios o miembros; personal.

membranaceous, *o* **membranous** [mémbranéŝhus,-braenus], *a.* membranoso.—**membranous croup,** difteria.

membrane [mémbren], *s.* membrana; panículo; trozo de pergamino.

membraniferous [mémbræníferus], *a.* que produce membranas.

memento [meménto], *s.* recuerdo, memento; memoria.

memoir [mémuar], *s.* memoria, informe,—*pl.* memorias.

memorabilia [mémorabília], *s. pl.* cosas dignas de recordación.

memorable [mémorabœl], *a.* memorable.

memorably [-bli], *adv.* memorablemente.

memorandum [mémorǽndum], *s.* memorándum.—**m. book,** memorándum, cartera de apuntes.—**m. clause,** cláusula de exenciones (en una póliza), que exime de ciertas obligaciones al asegurador.

memorial [mémórial]. **I.** *a.* conmemorativo.— **M. Day**= DECORATION DAY. **II.** *s.* monumento conmemorativo; memorial, instancia, petición, (Méx.) ocurso; (for.) nota, apuntamiento.

memorialist [-ist], *s.* solicitante, suplicante.

memorialize [-aiŝ], *va.* presentar una petición o memorial a; conmemorar.

memoritor [mémóritœr], *adv.* de memoria.

memorize [mémorais], *va.* aprender de memoria; memorar, recordar.

memory [mémori], *s.* memoria, recuerdo.

men, *s. pl.* de MAN.

menace [ménes]. **I.** *va.* y *vn.* amenazar. **II.** *s.* amenaza.

ménage [menáy], *s.* familia; manejo de casa, economía doméstica.

menagerie [menǽyœri], *s.* colección de animales; casa de fieras.

mend. I. *va.* remendar; componer; mejorar; enmendar, reformar, remediar. **II.** *vn.* enmendarse, reformarse; mejorar; restablecerse. **III.** *s.* mejoría; reforma; remiendo.—**on the m.,** mejorando (se).

mendable [méndabœl], *a.* reparable, componible; reformable.

mendacious [mendéiŝhus], *s.* mendaz.—**mendaciously** [-li], *adv.* mendazmente.—**mendaciousness** [-nes], **mendacity** [mendǽsiti], *s.* mendacidad.

mender [méndœr], *s.* componedor, reformador; reparador; remendón.

mendicancy [méndicansi], **mendicity** [mendísiti], *s.* mendicidad.

mendicant [méndicant], *a.* y *s.* mendicante.

mendole [méndoul], *s.* (ict.) boga.

menhaden [menjéidœn], *s.* (ict.) especie de sábalo.

menhir [ménjir], *s.* menhir.

menial [mínial], *a.* y *s.* doméstico, sirviente, servil, bajo; criado, lacayo.

meningeal [meninyeal], *a.* meníngeo.

meninges [meníniŝ], *s. pl.* de MENINX; (anat.) meninges.

meningitis [méninyáitis], *s.* (med.) meningitis.

meninx [míninx], *s.* (anat.) meninge.

meniscus [meniscus], *s.* lúnula, media luna; (ópt.) menisco.

Menispermaceæ [ménispœrméisii], *s. pl.* (bot.) menispermáceas.—**menispermaceous** [-ŝhus], *a.* menispermáceo.

menology [menóloyi], *s.* menologio.

menopause [ménopoŝ], *s.* (med.) menopausia.

menorrhagia [menorréyia], *s.* menorragia.

menses [ménsiŝ], *s. pl.* menstruo, reglas.

menstrual [ménstrual], *a.* menstrual.

menstruate [ménstrueit], *vn.* menstruar.

menstruation [-éiŝhun], *s.* menstruación.

menstruous [ménstruus], *a.* menstruo, menstruoso; (bot.) mensual.

menstruum [ménstrum], *s.* (quím.) menstruo, disolvente.

mensurability [ménŝhurabíliti], *s.* mensurabilidad.

mensurable [ménŝhurabœl], *a.* mensurable.

mensural [ménŝhural], *a.* mensural.

mensuration [ménŝhuréiŝhun], *s.* medición; medida; cálculo de magnitudes geométricas; (arit.) aplicaciones geométricas.

mental [méntæl], *a.* mental.—**m. blindness,** afección cerebral que impide la interpretación de las imágenes visuales.—**m. deafness,** afección cerebral que impide la interpretación o identificación de las impresiones auditivas.—**m. healer,** curador mental, o por fe.—**m. healing,** arte de curar mediante procedimientos mentales.—**m. reservation,** reserva mental.

mentality [mentǽliti], *s.* mentalidad.

mentally [méntali], *adv.* mentalmente.

mentha [ménza], *s.* (bot.) menta, hierbabuena.

menthol [ménzol], *s.* mentol.

mention [ménŝhun]. **I.** *s.* mención, recuerdo, alusión. **II.** *va.* mencionar, mentar, aludir.— **don't m. it,** (fam.) no hay de qué.

mentionable [ménŝhunabœl], *a.* mencionable.

mentor [méntœr], *s.* mentor, guía.

menu [méniu], *s.* lista de platos; comida.

meow [méu], *s.* y *vn.* = MEW.

mephitic(al [mefític(al], *a.* mefítico.

mephitis [mefáitis *o* fítis], *s.* mefitis, vapor fétido; (min.) mofeta.

mercantile [mœrcantil], *a.* mercantil.

mercantilism [-iŝm], *s.* mercantilismo.

mercenariness [mœrsenerines], *s.* venalidad.

mercenary [mœrseneri]. **I.** *a.* mercenario; venal, interesado. **II.** *s.* mercenario.

mercer [mœrsœr], *s.* sedero, mercero.

mercerize [-aiŝ], *va.* mercerizar.

mercership [-ŝhip], *s.* sedería, mediería, mercería.

merchandise [mœrchandaiŝ]. **I.** *s.* mercadería, mercancía, efectos, géneros. **II.** *vn.* traficar, comerciar, negociar.

merchant [mœrchænt]. **I.** *s.* comerciante. **II.** *a.* mercante, mercantil.—**m. iron,** hierro o acero en barras de ciertos tamaños.—**m. marine, m. service,** marina mercante.—**m. tailor,** sastre comerciante (que vende géneros).

merchantable [-abœl], *a.* comerciable; vendible; de recibo, corriente.

merchantlike [-laic], *a.* propio de comerciantes.

merchantman [-man], *s.* buque mercante.

merciful [mœrsiful], *a.* misericordioso, compasivo.—**mercifully** [-l], *adv.* misericordiosamente. —**mercifulness** [-nes], *s.* misericordia, compasión.

merciless [mœrsiles], *a.* desapiadado.

mercilessly [-li], *adv.* sin piedad.—**mercilessness** [-nes], *s.* falta de compasión, endurecimiento.

mercurial [mœrkiúrial]. **I.** *a.* mercurial; vivo, activo, jovial; volátil. **II.** *s.* preparación mercurial.—**mercurialism** [-iŝm], *s.* mercurialismo, estado causado por abuso del mercurio; salivación.—**mercurialize** [-aiŝ]. **I.** *va.* (med.) someter a un tratamiento mercurial; salivar; (foto.) desarrollar con mercurio. **II.** *vn.* ser voltario.

mercuric [mœrkiúric], *a.* mercúrico.

mercurize [mœrkiuraiŝ], *va.* tratar o combinar con mercurio.

mercurous [mœrkiurʊs], *a.* mercurioso.

mercury [mœrkiuri], *s.* mercurio, azogue, hidrargirio; (astr.) Mercurio; (bot.) mercurial.—**m.'s wand**, caduceo.

mercy [mœrsi], *s.* misericordia, clemencia, compasión; merced, gracia, perdón; arbitrio, discreción, poder.—**m. me!** ¡Ave María!—**m. seat**, propiciatorio.—**at the m. of**, a la merced de.—**for m.!** o **for m.'s sake!** ¡por piedad!

mere [mîœr]. **I.** *a.* mero, puro; sólo, no más que (lo mencionado). **II.** *s.* laguna; (Esco.) el mar; (Ingl.) lindero, límite.—**merely** [-li], *adv.* solamente, meramente; simplemente; puramente.

meretricious [meretríŝhʊs], *a.* meretricio; chillón.—**meretriciously** [-li], *adv.* meretriciamente.—**meretriciousness** [-nes], *s.* mal gusto; calidad de meretricio.

merganser [mœrgǽnsœr], *s.* (orn.) mergo, mergánsar, gallipato, somorgujo.

merge [mœry]. **I.** *va.* unir, fundir, combinar. **II.** *vn.* fundirse, absorberse, mezclarse.

merger [mœryœr], *s.* combinación, unión, consolidación.

meridian [merídiæn]. **I.** *s.* meridiano; mediodía. **II.** *a.* meridiano.—**m. instrument**, meridiana, anteojo meridiano.—**m. line**, meridiana.—**m. sailing**, navegación según la meridiana, siguiendo la meridiana.

meridional [merídional], *a.* meridiano; meridional.

meridionally [-i], *adv.* en o según el meridiano.

meringue [merǽng], *s.* merengue.

merino [mœríno]. **I.** *a.* merino; hecho de merino. **II.** *s.* carnero merino; paño merino.

merit [mérit]. **I.** *s.* mérito; premio. **II.** *va.* merecer, ser digno de.

meritorious [-tóriʊs], *a.* meritorio.

meritoriously [-li], *adv.* merecidamente.

meritoriousness [-nes], *s.* merecimiento, mérito.

merle [mœrl], *s.* (orn.) merla, mirlo.

merlin [mœrlin], *s.* (orn.) esmerejón, merlín.

merlon [mœrlʊn], *s.* (fort.) merlón.

merluce [mœrliusʼ], *s.* (ict.) merluza.

mermaid [mœrmeid], *s.* sirena, pejemuller.

merman [mœrman], *s.* tritón.

merops [mírops], *s.* abejarruco.

Merovingian [mérovínyian], *a.* merovingio.

merrily [mérrili], *adv.* alegremente, con júbilo.

merriment [-mœnt], *s.* alegría, júbilo; fiesta, diversión.

merry [mérri], *a.* alegre, festivo, divertido; feliz; gozoso, regocijado; risueño, placentero, agradable.—**m.-andrew**, bufón, truhán, chocarrero.—**m.-go-round**, tío vivo, caballitos.—**m. Christmas**, felices Pascuas.

merrymake [mérrimeik]. **I.** *s.* gaudeamus, francachela, holgorio. **II.** *vn.* divertirse, ir de parranda.—**merrymaker** [-œr], *s.* fiestero, parrandista.

merrythought [-zot], *s.* hueso de la pechuga de las aves.

mescal [mɛscál], *a.* mescal.—**m. maguey**, mescal (planta).

meseems [misîms], *v. impers.* me parece, tengo para mí.

mesencephalon [mésenséfælon], *s.* mesencéfalo, cerebro medio.

mesenchyma [mesénkimæ], *s.* mesénquima.—**mesenchymatous** [mésenkimætʊs], *a.* mesenquimatoso.

mesenteric [mésentéric], *a.* mesentérico.

mesentery [-teri], *s.* (anat.) mesenterio, entresijo.

mesh [meŝh]. **I.** *s.* malla de una red; obra de malla; trampa, lazo; (mec.) engrane; engra-

nado.—*pl.* red, randa. **II.** *va.* enredar, coger con red. **III.** *vn.* enredarse; endentarse.

meshy [méŝhi], *a.* reticular, de malla.

mesial [mésial o míŝial], *a.* mediano, del medio.—**m. plane**, plano mediano del cuerpo.

mesmeric [mesméric], *a.* mesmeriano.—**mesmerism** [mésmœriŝm], *s.* mesmerismo.—**mesmerist** [-ist], **mesmerizer** [-aiŝœr], *s.* magnetizador.—**mesmerize**, **mesmerise** [-aiŝ], *va.* magnetizar, hipnotizar.

mesne [min], *a.* intermedio.—**m. profits**, beneficios de una tierra durante ocupación ilícita.

mesoblast [mésoblæst], *s.* (biol.) mesoblasto.

mesocarp [-carp], *s.* mesocarpio.

mesoderm [-dœrm], *s.* mesodermo.—**mesodermal** [-dœrmæl], **mesodermic** [-dœrmic], *a.* mesodérmico.

mesogastrium [-gǽstriʊm], *s.* mesogastrio.—**mesogastric** [-tric], *a.* mesogástrico.

meson [méson], *s.* = MESIAL PLANE.

mesoplast [mésoplæst], *s.* núcleo celular.

mesothoracic [-zorǽsic], *a.* mesotorácico.—**mesothorax** [-zóræx], *s.* mesotórax.

Mesozoic [mésoŝóic], *a.* (geol.) mesozoico; secundario.

mesquite [meskit], *s.* (bot.) mezquite.

mess. **I.** *s.* plato (cantidad de vianda); ración, porción; rancho, comistrajo o matalotaje; (fam.) lío, confusión, revoltijo.—**m. kit**, utensilios de cocina y vajilla en que se llevan. **II.** *va.* dar de comer; dar rancho; desarreglar, desordenar; ensuciar. **III.** *vn.* comer en rancho o hacer rancho; arrancharse; hacer un revoltijo.

message [mésey], *s.* mensaje; recado, parte, aviso.

messenger [mésenyœr], *s.* mensajero, mandadero; heraldo, nuncio; (mar.) aparejo para levar el ancla.

Messiah [mesáia], *s.* Mesías.

messieurs [méŝicœrŝ], *s. pl.* de MISTER, señores; se escribe **Messrs.**, en abreviatura.

messmate [mésmet], *s.* comensal.

messuage [mésueˠ], *s.* casa de vivienda y anexas.

mestizo, mestino [mestíŝo, -tíno], *s.* mestizo; cambujo.

met, *pret.* y *pp.* de TO MEET.

metabolism [metǽboliŝm], *s.* (biol.) metabolismo; (ent.) metamorfosis.

metacarpal [métacárpal]. **I.** *a.* del metacarpo. **II.** *s.* cada hueso del metacarpo.

metacarpus [-cárpʊs], *s.* (anat.) metacarpo.

metacentre [-séntœr], *s.* metacentro.

metachronism [metǽcroniŝm], *s.* metacronismo.

metagenesis [métæyénesis], *s.* metagénesis.

metageometry [-yiómetri], *s.* geometría no euclidiana.

metal [métal], *s.* metal; liga, aleación; material (piedra partida, escorias, etc.) para caminos; balasto; vidrio en fusión; cualidad esencial; (mar.) peso de los proyectiles que un acorazado puede disparar a un tiempo.—**m. industry**, metalistería.

metalepsis [métalépsis], *s.* (ret.) metalepsis.

metalled [métald], *a.* (f. c.) terraplenado, afirmado.

metallic [metǽlic], *a.* metálico; libre, puro.

metalliferous [métalífœrʊs], *a.* metalífero.

metallist [métalist], *s.* metalario.

metallization [-iŝéŝhun], *s.* metalización.

metallize [-aiŝ], *va.* metalizar.

metallography [-ógrafi], *s.* metalografía.

metalloid [-oid], *a.* y *s.* (quím.) metaloide.

metallotherapy [-óŝrapi], *s.* metaloterapia.

metallurgic(al [-œrvic(al], *a.*, **metallurgist** [-œrist], *s.* metalúrgico.—**metallurgy** [-œryi], *s.* metalurgia.

metalman [métalman], *s.* metalario.

metamer [métæmœr], *s.* (quím.) cuerpo metámero; (bot.) parte de una planta.—**metamere** [-miær], *s.* (zool.) metámero.—**metameric** [-méric], *a.* (quím. y zool.) metámero.—**metamerism** [-meriŝm], *s.* (quím.) metamería; (zool.) estructura metámera.

metameric [métaméric], *a.* (quím.) metamérico.

metamorphic [-tamórfic], *a.* metamórfico.—
metamorphism [-ñăm], *s.* (geol.) metamorfismo;
metamorfosis.—**metamorphize, metamorphose**
[-fais, foă], *va.* metamorfosear.—**metamorphosis**
[-fosis], *s.* metamorfosis.
metaphor [-for], *s.* (ret.) metáfora.—**meta-**
phoric(al [-fóric(al], *a.* metafórico.—**metaphoric-**
ally [-i], *adv.* metafóricamente.—**metaphorist**
[metæforist], *s.* metaforista.
metaphrase [métafreiă], *s.* metáfrasis, traducción
literal.—**metaphrast** [-frast], *s.* traductor literal.
metaphrastic [-fræstic], *a.* literal.
metaphysic(al [métafísic(al], *a.* metafísico.
metaphysically [-i], *adv.* metafísicamente.
metaphysician [-fiăĭshan], *s.* metafísico.
metaphysics [-fíăics], *s.* metafísica.
metaplasm [métaplaăm], *s.* (gram.) metaplasmo;
(biol.) metaplasma.
metastasis [metéăstæsis], *s.* metamorfosis; (med.)
metástasis; (teol.) regeneración bautismal;
(biol.) metabolismo.
metatarsal [métatársal], *a.* metatársico.
metatarsus [-társus], *s.* (anat.) metatarso.
metathesis [metéăzesis], *s.* (ret.) metátesis;
(quím.) substitución.
metathorax [métazóræx], *s.* metatórax.
Metazoa [-ăóæ], *s. pl.* metazoarios.
mete [mít] *va.* repartir, prorratear; servir de
norma.
metempsychosis [métempsicósis], *s.* metempsicosis.
meteor [mítior], *s.* metéoro; exhalación, estrella
fugaz.
meteoric [mítióric], **meteoritic** [mítiorític], *a.*
meteórico; atmosférico, meteorológico.—**m. iron,**
o **stone,** aerolito.—**m. showers,** lluvia de estrellas
fugaces.
meteorism [mítiorism], *s.* (med.) meteorismo.
meteorite [mítiorait], **meteorolite** [mitiórolait],
meteoroid [mítioroid], *s.* aerolito, meteorito, bólido.
meteorological [mítiorolóyical], *a.* meteorológico.—**meteorologist** [-ólóyist], *s.* meteorologista.
—**meteorology** [-ólóyi], *s.* meteorología.
meteorous [mítiorus], *a.* meteórico.
meter [mítœr], *s.* (pros.) metro (medida del
verso); metro (medida de longitud); medidor,
mensurador; contador (de gas, agua, etc.)
methane [mézen], *s.* (quím.) metano.
metheglin [mezéglin], *s.* aguamiel, hidromel.
methinks [mezíncs], *v. impers.* me parece, creo,
pienso.
method [mézud], *s.* método; (mús.) ejecución,
técnica.
methodic(al [mezódic(al], *a.* metódico.
methodically [-i], *adv.* metódicamente.
methodism [mézodiăm], *s.* método.—**(M-)** metodismo.—**Methodist** [-ist], *s.* metodista.
methodistic(al [mézodístic(al], *a.* metodístico.
methodize [mézodaiă], *va.* metodizar.
methodology [mézodólóyi], *s.* metodología.
methought, *pret.* de METHINKS.
methyl [mézil], *s.* (quím.) metilo.—**m. alcohol,**
alcohol metílico.—**m. orange,** anaranjado de metilo.
methylate [mézileit]. **I.** *s.* metilato. **II.** *va.*
mezclar con metilo o alcohol metílico.—**methyl-**
ated spirit, mezcla de alcohol etílico y alcohol
metílico.
methylene [mézilin], *s.* (quím.) metileno.
methylic [mezílic], *a.* metílico.
meticulous [metíkiulus], *a.* escrupuloso en demasía.
metonymical [métonímical], *a.* metonímico.—
metonymically [-i], *adv.* metonímicamente.—
metonymy [metóniml], *s.* metonimia.
metope [métopi], *s.* (arq.) metopa, plato; frente,
faz.
metoposcopy [mítopóscopi], *s.* metoposcopia.
metre [mítœr], *s.* = METER.
metric(al [métric(al], *a.* métrico.
metrically [métricali], *adv.* métricamente.
metrician [metríăhan], o **metrist** [mítrist], *s.*
versificador, metrista.

metritis [metráitis o trítis], *s.* (med.) metritis.
metrograph [métrograf], *s.* (f. c.) metrógrafo.
metrological [métrolóyical], *a.* metrológioo.
metrology [metróloyi], *s.* metrología.
metronome [métronoum], *s.* (mús.) metrónomo.
metropolis [metrópolis], *s.* metrópoli; urbe.
metropolitan [métropólitan]. **I.** *a.* metropolitano. **II.** *s.* (igl.) metropolitano; ciudadano
de una metrópoli.
metrorrhagia [mítrorréyia], *s.* (med.) metrorragia.
mettle [métœl], *s.* temple, brío, valor; vivacidad,
fuego.
mettled [métœld], **mettlesome** [métœlsum], *a.*
brioso, vivo, fogoso.—**mettlesomely** [-li], *adv.*
briosamente, vivamente.—**mettlesomeness** [-nes],
s. brío, fuego, vivacidad.
mew [miú]. **I.** *s.* maullido, maúllo; (orn.) gaviota; jaula; cercado o corral.—*pl.* establo, caballeriza. **II.** *va.* enjaular, encerrar. **III.** *vn.*
maullar, miar.
mewing [miúing], *s.* maullido, maúdo.
mewl [miúl]. **I.** *vn.* llorar como un niño. **II.** *s.*
lloro de niño.
Mexican [méxican], *a.* y *s.* mejicano.
mezereon [mesírion], *s.* (bot.) lauréola.
mezzanine [mésanin], *s.* (arq.) entresuelo.
mezzo-rilievo [médăo-rillévo], *s.* medio relieve
mezzotint(o [médăotint(o], *s.* media tinta.
mi, *s.* (mús.) mi.
miasm(a [miéăm(a], *s.* miasma.
miasmal [-al], **miasmatic** [-ætic], *a.* miasmático,
infecto, palúdico.
mica [máica], *s.* (min.) mica.—**m. schist,** mica-
quisto.
micaceous [maikéăhus], *a.* micáceo.
mice [máis], *s. pl.* de MOUSE.
Michaelmas [míkælmas], *s.* sanmiguelada.
microbe [máicroub], *s.* microbio.
microbial [micróbial], **microbic** [micróbic], *a.*
micróbico, microbiano.
microbicide [micróbisaid], *s.* microbicida.
microbiological [máicrobiolóyical], *a.* microbiológico.—**microbiologist** [-baiólóyist], *s.* microbiólogo.—**microbiology** [-baiólóyi], *s.* microbiología.
microcephalic [-sefélic], **microcephalous** [-sé-
falus], *a.* microcéfalo.
microcóccal [-cócal], *a.* micrococal.
micrococcus [-cócus], *s.* micrococo.
microcosm [-coăm], *s.* microcosmos.
microcosmic(al [-mic(al], *a.* microcósmico.
microcoulomb [-culóm], *s.* microculombio.
microcyte [-sait], *s.* (patol.) microcito.
microfarad [-fárad], *s.* microfaradio.
microgram [-græm], *s.* micrógramo.
micrograph [-græf], *s.* micrógrafo, pantógrafo.
micrographer, micrographist [maicrógrafœr,
fist], *s.* micrógrafo.
micrographophone [máicrográfofoun], *s.* micro-
gráfófono.
micrography [maicrógrafi], *s.* micrografía.
microhm [máicroum], *s.* microhmio.
micrometer [maicrómetœr], *s.* micrómetro.—**m.**
caliper, gauge, o **gage,** compás micrométrico.
—**m. screw,** tornillo micrométrico.
micrometric(al [máicrométric(al], *a.* micrométrico.
micrometry [maicrómetri], *s.* micrometría.
micromillimiter [máicromilímetœr], *s.* micra,
micromilímetro.
micromotion [-móuăhun], *s.* movimiento de
objetos diminutos amplificado en el microscopio.
micron [máicron], *s.* micra, micrón (millonésima
de metro).
microorganism [máicroórgæniăm], *s.* microrganismo.
microphone [-foun], *s.* micrófono.
microphotograph [-fótogræf], *s.* microfotografía.
microphyte [-fait], *s.* (bot.) micrófito.
micropyle [-pail], *s.* (bot. y zool.) micrópilo.

micropyrometer [-pairómetœr], micropiróme tro, instrumento óptico para determinar la temperatura y otras propiedades relacionadas con la luz y el calor.

microscope [máicroscoup], s. microscopio.

microscopic(al [-cópic(al], a. microscópico.

microscopist [maicróscopist], s. microscopista.

microscopy [maicróscopi], s. microscopia, micros cópica.

microseism [máicrosaiŝm], s. microsismo.— **microseismometer, microseismograph** [-saismómetœr, -sáismogræf], s. microsismógrafo.

microtelephone [-télefoun], s. microteléfono.

microtome [máicrotom], s. micrótomo.

microvolt [-voult], s. microvoltio.

microwatt [-wot], s. microvatio.

microzyme [-ŝaim], s. microcima, microzima.

miction [mícŝhun], **micturition** [mictiuríŝhun], s. micturición, micción.

micturate [míctiuret], vn. orinar.

mid. I. a. medio. Úsase en composición.— **m.-age,** edad madura.—(**in**) **m. air,** (en) el aire. —**m.-course,** media carrera o medio camino.— **m.-hour,** medio día.—**m.-Lent,** media cuaresma. —**m.-sea,** alta mar. II. prep. (poet.) entre, en medio de.

midday [míddéi]. I. s. mediodía (tiempo, hora). II. a. del mediodía.

middle [mídœl]. I. a. medio, intermedio.—pl. (agric.) lomos, caballones.—**m.-aged,** de edad madura.—**M. Ages,** Edad Media.—**M. America,** Méjico y la América Central.—**m.-class,** de la clase media.—**m. class,** clase media.—**m. ear,** (anat.) tímpano; oído medio.—**m. earth,** (poet.) tierra, el mundo.—**m. finger,** dedo del corazón.— **m. jib,** (mar.) segundo foque.—**M. Kingdom,** imperio chino.—**m.-shot wheel** = BREAST WHEEL. —**m.-sized,** de mediana estatura o tamaño.—**m. wall,** tabique. II. s. medio, centro, mitad, cora zón; promedio; cintura.—**m. of,** mediados de.

middleman [-man], s. (com.) agente de negocios; revendedor.

middlemost [-moust], a. del medio; en el medio o más cercano al medio.

middleweight [-uéit], a. de peso medio o me diano.

middling [mídling]. I. a. mediano, regular, pasadero. II. s. pl. acemite.—**middlingly** [-li], adv. medianamente, regularmente, pasaderamente.

middy [mídi], s. dim. (fam.) guardiamarina.

midge [miy], s. mosca de agua; enano.

midget [míyet], s. enanillo; chiquillo vivaracho.

midheaven [mídjévn], s. el medio del cielo; el meridiano superior.

midland [mídland]. I. a. mediterráneo, tierra adentro, interior. II. s. corazón de un país.

midnight [mídnáit]. I. s. media noche. II. a. nocturno; oculto, secreto.

midrib [mídrrib], s. (bot.) vena central.

midriff [mídrif], s. (anat.) diafragma.

midship [mídŝhip]. I. a. en medio del buque. II. s. pl. bao o cuaderna maestra.—**m. beam,** bao maestro.

midshipman [-mæn], s. (mar.) guardiamarina.

midst. I. s. medio, centro; (fig.) rigor, fragor.— **in our, their, your m.,** en medio de nosotros, ellos, vosotros.—**in the m. of,** en medio de, entre; en lo más (reñido, agitado, etc.) de. II. adv. en medio. III. prep. entre.

midstream [mídstrím], s. el medio de una co rriente.

midsummer [mídsúmœr], s. solsticio estival; la mitad del verano; pleno verano.—**M. Day,** día de San Juan (24 de junio).

midway [míduéi]. I. s. medio camino, mitad del camino. II. a. situado a mitad del camino; entre. III. adv. en medio del camino; a medio camino.—**m. between,** equidistante de.

midweek [míduíc]. I. s. medio o mediados de la semana.—**M.** (entre los cuáqueros) mitad de se mana (miércoles). II. a. de la mitad de la semana.

midwife [míduáif]. I. s. (pl. MIDWIVES) partera. II. va. y vn. partear.—**midwifery** [-ri], s. obstetri cia, partería.

midwinter [míduíntœr], s. solsticio hiemal; mitad del invierno; pleno invierno.

mien [mín], s. semblante, aire, talante, facha.

miff. I. s. (fam.) sofocón, bochorno. II. va. desa gradar, enojar; amoscar.

might [máit], imperf. ind. y subj. de MAY: podía, podría.

might [máit], s. poder, fuerza.—**with m. and main,** con todas sus fuerzas, a más no poder.

mightily [máitili], adv. poderosamente.

mightiness [máitines], s. poder, poderío; poten cia, fuerza; grandeza.

mighty [máiti]. I. a. potente, poderoso; fuerte, vigoroso; enorme; eficaz, importante. II. adv. (fam.) extremamente, sumamente.

mignonette [miñonét], s. (bot.) reseda.

migraine [migréin], s. (fr.) = MEGRIM.

migrate [máigreit], vn. emigrar.—**migrating** [-ing], a. migratorio, peregrino; de paso.

migration [-gréiŝhun], s. migración.

migratory [máigratori], a. = MIGRATING.

mihrab [miráb], s. mihrab, hornacina.

Mikado [mikádo], s. micado.

mil, s. (elec.) milipulgada, milésima de pulgada.

milady [miléidi], s. miladi, dama noble inglesa.

milch [milch[, a. lactífera, lechera, que da leche. —**m. cow,** vaca de leche.

mild [máild], a. suave, moderado, apacible, man so; leve, ligero.—**m. humus,** buen mantillo pa ra la vegetación.—**m. steel,** acero dúctil, acero pobre en carbono (menos de 0,15 por ciento).

mildew [míldiu]. I. s. añublo, moho, tizón, roya. II. va. y vn. enmohecer, alheñar; enmohecerse, añublarse, atizonarse.

mildly [máildli], adv. suavemente, blandamente, con indulgencia.—**mildness** [-nes], s. suavidad, lenidad; apacibilidad; mansedumbre, indulgencia.

mile [máil], s. milla (5,280 pies ingleses = 1,609 metros).—**m. post,** o stone, piedra miliaria, poste miliar, mojón.

mileage [máiliy], s. longitud en millas; derecho de peaje por milla; (aut.) kilometraje, recorrido (apl. esp. a la duración de llantas medida por la distancia total que recorren).—**m. ticket,** billete kilométrico.

Milesian [miliŝhan], a. milesio; irlandés o hi bernés.

milfoil [mílfoil], s. (bot.) milenrama.

miliaria [míliériæ], s. erupción miliar.

miliary [míliæri], a. (med.) miliar.

militancy [mílitansi], s. guerra; actitud belicosa o de combate.

militant [-tant], a. militante, combatiente; beli coso, guerrero.

militarily [-tærili], adv. militarmente.

militarism [mílitariŝm], s. militarismo.

militarist [-ist], s., **militaristic** [-istic], a. mili tarista.

military [mílitæri]. I. a. militar; de tropa; de guerra.—**m. law,** código militar.—**m. stores,** municiones de guerra. II. s. ejército, milicia, militares.

militate [mílitet], vn. combatir, pelear; (con **against** o **with**) militar contra, oponerse a.

militia [milíŝha], s. milicia, guardia nacional.— **militiaman,** miliciano.

milk. I. s. leche.—**m. abscess,** absceso del pecho.—**m.-and-water,** (fam.) vacilante, débil de carácter.—**m. bag,** ubre.—**m. can,** lecherón, ca mella.—**m. fever,** fiebre láctea.—**m. food,** lacticinio.—**m. leg,** ede ma doloroso puerperal.—**m.-livered,** timorato, miedoso.—**m. of almonds,** almendrada.—**m. pail,** colodra, ordeñadero.—**m. pan,** lechera.—**m. sugar,** lactina, lactosa.—**m. tester,** lactómetro.— **m. thistle,** (bot.) titímalo, cardo lechero o silibo. —**m. tooth,** diente incisivo.—**m. vetch,** astrá galo, regaliz silvestre.—**m. -warm,** tibio.—**m. white,** blanco como la leche. II. va. ordeñar; (fam.) agotar; extraer de. III. vn. dar leche.

milker [mílkœr], s. ordeñador; vaca de leche.

milkiness [mílkines], s. lactescencia.

milkmaid [mílkméid], s. lechera; mantequera.

milkman [mílkmæn], s. lechero.

milksop [mílksop], s. marica, mantecón.
milkweed [mílkuid], s. (bot.) vencetósigo.
milkwort [mílkuœrt], s. (bot.) polígala.
milky [milki], a. lácteo, lactífero; lechoso, lactícíneo, lechar o lechal; blando, tierno, suave, tímido.—**M. Way**, Vía Lactea.
mill [mil]. **I.** s. molino; taller, fábrica; (mec.) prensa; hilandería o tejeduría; fábrica de hilados o de tejidos; (fam.) pugilato; una milésima parte; (E. U.) milésimo de dólar.—**m. clack**, tarabilla, cítola.—**m. construction**, construcción anticombustible, que en sí misma minora el peligro de incendio, sin ser de materiales incombustibles. (Es expresión que debe explicarse al traducirla.)—**m. course**, canal de molino, saetín, caz.—**m. dust**, harija.—**m. hand**, obrero.—**m. hopper**, tolva de molino.—**m. horse**, caballo de tahoma.—**m. pond**, alberca, alcubilla.—**m. race**, saetín.—**m. run** = M. RACE; (min.) ensayo de molino.—**m. wheel**, ruejo, rueda de molino.— **to go through the m.**, saber una cosa por experiencia. **II.** va. moler, desmenuzar; acordonar (moneda), estriar; fresar.
millboard [míldbord], s. cartón de encuadernar.
milldam [míldæm], s. esclusa, represa; dique.
millenarian [mílenérian], **millenary** [mílenæri], a. y s. milenario.
millennial [mílénial], a., **millennium** [míléniüm], s. milenario.
milleped [míleped], s. (ent.) ciempiés.
millepore [mílepoœr], s. milépora.
miller [mílœr], s. molinero, molendero, tahonero; (ent.) mariposa con manchas blancas. —**m.'s-thumb**, (ict.) gobio.
millet [mílet], s. (bot.) mijo.
milliampere [míliampíœr], s. (elec.) miliamperio.
milliamperimeter [-amperímetœr], s. (elec.) miliamperímetro.
milliard [míliard], s. mil millones.
milliary [míliæri]. **I.** a. miliario. **II.** s. piedra miliar.
milliare [míliéær], s. miliárea.
millier [míliéi], s. tonelada métrica.
millifarad [mílifærad], s. milifaradio.
milligram(me [míligram], s. miligramo.
millilitre, millilitre [-litœr], s. mililitro.
millimeter, millimetre [-mitœr], s. milímetro.
millimicron [-máicron], s. milimicrón, milimicra.
milliner [mílinœr], s. modista.
millinery [mílineri], s. cintas, flores, etc., para sombreros de señora; ocupación o tienda de modista.
milling [míling]. **I.** s. molienda; acordonamiento, acuñación; cordoncillo de la moneda. **II.** a. de moler, de fresar, etc. V. MILL, va.—**m. cutter**, fresa.—**m. machine**, fresadora.—**m. saw**, sierra circular de cortar metales.
million [mílün], a. y s. millón.
millionaire [mílünéær], s. y a. millonario.
millioned [mílünd], a. amillonado.
millionth [mílünθ], s. y a. millonésimo.
millstone [mílstoun], s. muela, piedra molar o de molino.—**m. hammer, o pick**, martellina.
millwork [mílüœrc], s. maquinaria de molino.
millwright [mílrait], s. constructor de molinos.
milord [milórd], s. milord.
milreis [mílris o réis], s. milréis.
milt. **I.** s. (anat.) bazo; lechecillas de los peces. **II.** va. impregnar las huevas de los peces.
milter [míltœr], s. pez macho.—**m. and spawner**, pez macho y hembra.
Miltonian [miltóniæn], **Miltonic** [-tónic], a. miltónico, miltoniano.
miltwaste [míltueist], s. (bot.) doradilla.
mime [máim], s. mimo; truhán, bufón, farsante; pantomima, farsa.
mimeograph [mímeograf], s. mimeógrafo.
mimesis [mimésis], s. (ret.) mimesis.
mimetic(al [mimétic(al], a. imitativo, mímico.
mimic [mímic]. **I.** va. remedar, imitar. **II.** s. mimo, pantomimo, remedador. **III.** a. mímico,

imitativo, burlesco.—**mimically** [-cali], adv. burlescamente, mímicamente.—**mimicry** [-cri], s. bufonería; monería, remedo; (biol.) mimetismo.
mimosa [mi- (o mai) mósa], s. (bot.) mimosa o sensitiva.
mimosis [mimósis], s. (med.) semejanza.
mimulus [mímiulvs], s. (bot.) mímulo.
minaret [mínaret], s. (arq.) minarete.
minatory [mínatori], a. amenazador.
mince [mins]. **I.** va. desmenuzar, destrizar, capolar; picar (carne), hacer picadillo; medir (las palabras); paliar, atenuar. **II.** vn. ser afectado o melindroso. **III.** s. afectación.—**m. meat** = MINCEMEAT.—**m. pie**, pastel relleno de picadillo de carne, fruta y especias.
mincemeat [mínsmít], s. carne picada con frutas, etc., para hacer pasteles.—**to make m. of**, destruir, aniquilar.
mincingly [mínsingli], adv. a pedacitos; con afectación.
mind [máind]. **I.** s. mente, entendimiento, pensamiento, inteligencia; espíritu, ánimo; gusto, propensión, inclinación, afición, afecto; voluntad, gana; intención, resolución; opinión, juicio, parecer, dictamen.—**m. blindness** = MENTAL BLINDNESS.—**m. cure**, sistema de curar que supone que toda enfermedad se debe a causas psicológicas.—**m. deafness** = MENTAL DEAFNESS.— **m. reader**, adivinador del pensamiento ajeno.— **m. reading**, adivinación del pensamiento ajeno.— **of one m.**, unánimes.—**out of m.**, olvidado.—**to give someone a piece of one's m.**, decir a alguien cuántas son cinco, ponerlo como nuevo.— **to have a m. to**, tener gana de, querer; proponerse.—**with one m.**, unánimemente. **II.** va. notar, observar; atender a; cuidar; cuidarse de; recordar; tener inconveniente en; oponerse a; hacer caso a o de; obedecer; proponerse.—**to m. one's business**, meterse uno en lo que le importa.—**to m. one's p's and q's**, poner los puntos sobre las íes, tener gran cuidado en lo que se hace o dice. **III.** vn. atender, obedecer, hacer caso; tener cuidado.—**never m.**, no importa.
minded [máinded], a. inclinado, dispuesto, propenso.
mindful [máindful], a. atento, cuidadoso.
mindfully [-i], adv. atentamente, cuidadosamente.—**mindfulness** [-nes], s. calidad de cuidadoso o atento.
mindless [máindles], a. sin mentalidad; descuidado, negligente; necio, insensato.
mine [máin], pron., pos. mío, el mío (ambos géneros y números), lo mío; (ant.) mi: this book is mine, este libro es mío; your book and mine, su libro y el mío.—**of m.**, mío.—**It is m.** (seguido de infinitivo), a mí me toca o me cae en suerte; yo puedo a mi arbitrio.
mine [máin]. **I.** s. (min., fort., art.) mina; (mar.) mina submarina.—**m. layer**, barco plantaminas.— **m. sweeper**, dragaminas.—**m. thrower**, obús. **II.** va. minar; contraminar; zapar; destruir; extraer (mineral), explotar (una mina). **III.** vn. hacer una mina; explotar minas; dedicarse a la minería; hacer trabajos de zapa; dañar secretamente.
miner [máinœr], s. (min.) minero, barretero; (arti.) minador, zapador.—**m.'s inch** = WATER INCH.—**m.'s pick**, pica de hoja de salvia.
mineral [míneræl], s. y a. mineral.—**m. cotton**, = M. WOOL.—**m. oil**, petróleo.—**m. jelly**, vaselina.—**m. pitch**, asfalto.—**m. right**, derecho al subsuelo.—**m. wax**, ozocerita.—**m. wool**, lana de escoria.
mineralization [-aiśéiśhun], s. mineralización.
mineralize [-aiś], va. mineralizar.
mineralizer [-œr], s. (quím.) mineralizador.
mineralogic(al [-óyic(al], a. mineralógico.— **mineralogist** [mincœrǽloyist], s. mineralogista.
mineralogize [-yaiś], va. recoger y estudiar minerales.
mineralogy [-loyi], s. mineralogía.
mingle [míngœl], va. mezclar; confundir.—vn. mezclarse, juntarse.—**m. mangle**, mixtura, miscelánea, almodrote.
mingledly [míngœldli], adv. confusamente.
miniate [míniet], a. rojo.

miniature [míniachur o tiur]. **I.** a. en miniatura. **II.** s. (b. a.) miniatura.—**m. painter,** miniaturista.

minify [mínifai], va. empequeñecer, achicar; despreciar.

minikin [mínikin], s. cosa menuda o chiquirritica; alfilerito.

minim [mínim], s. (farm.) medida flúida (0.95 grano de agua; casi una gota); (mús.) mínima; enano, pigmeo.

minimal [mínimal], a. mínimo.

minimize [mínimaiś], va. reducir al mínimo; achicar; menospreciar, tener en menos.

minimum [mínimum], s. y a. mínimo, mínimum.

mining [máining]. **I.** s. mineria, laboreo o explotación de minas. **II.** a. minero, de mina.— **m. camp,** colonia de mineros.—**m. engineer,** ingeniero de minas.—**m. engineering,** ingeniería de minas.—**m. ship** = MINE LAYER.

minion [míniun], s. privado, valido o paniaguado; esbirro; (impr.) tipo miñona (tipo de 7 puntos).

minister [mínistœr]. **I.** s. ministro (en todas sus acepciones). **II.** va. y vn. dar, ministrar, administrar, suministrar; surtir o proveer de. **III.** vn. atender, asistir, auxiliar; (igl.) oficiar, decir misa; tender, contribuir.

ministerial [ministírial], a. ministerial; sacerdotal, parroquial.—**m. benches,** bancos del gobierno (en el Congreso).

ministerially [-i], adv. ministerialmente.

ministerialism [-ism], s. ministerialismo.

ministrant [mínistrant]. **I.** a. ministrante. **II.** s. (igl.) oficiante.

ministration [-éiŝhun], s. servicio, agencia, comisión; (igl.) ministerio, oficio eclesiástico.

ministry [mínistri], s. ministerio, oficio, servicio; (pol.) ministerio, gabinete; (igl.) ministerio, clero; ayuda, intervención.

minium [mínium], s. (quím.) minio.

miniver [mínivœr], s. (zool.) gris.

mink, s. (zool.) visón, su piel.

minnie [míni], s. (fam.) obús; bomba, granada.

minnie [míni], **minnow** [míno], s. (ict.) pez pequeño de agua dulce que se usa como cebo.

minor [máinœr]. **I.** a. menor; secundario, inferior; (mús.) menor.—**m. key,** tono menor.—**m. mode,** modo menor.—**M. Prophets,** profetas menores. **II.** s. menor (de edad); (lóg.) menor; (mús.) tono menor.

minorite [máincœrait], s. menor, franciscano.

minority [minóriti], s. minoridad o menor edad; minoría, los menos.

Minotaur [mínotor], s. minotauro.

minster [mínstœr], s. monasterio; basílica, catedral.

minstrel [mínstrel], s. trovador, cantor; (E. U.) cantor cómico que se tizna la cara e imita a los negros; (poét.) bardo.—**minstrelsy** [-si], s. arte u ocupación del minstrel; gaya ciencia; canturía; compañía de minstrels.

mint. **I.** s. casa de moneda; mina, potosí; (bot.) menta, hierbabuena; matapulgas.—**m. julep,** aguardiente de hierbabuena.—**m. master,** director de la casa de moneda. **II.** va. acuñar; inventar; forjar, fraguar.

mintage [míntey], s. monedería; braceaje; derechos de cuño.

minter [míntœr], s. acuñador; inventor.

minuend [mínuend], s. (arit.) minuendo.

minuet [mínuet], s. (danz.) minué.

minus [máinus]. **I.** a. menos (−); negativo; falto de, sin; sin valor positivo. **II.** s. cantidad negativa; signo menos.

minute [mainiút], a. menudo, pequeño, diminuto; nimio, minucioso.

minute [mínit]. **I.** s. minuto; (arq.) módulo; minuta, nota, apuntamiento;—pl. minutas, actas; memoria auténtica.—**m. book,** minutario, o libro de minutas.—**m. glass,** ampolleta de un minuto.—**m. guns,** cañonazos disparados de minuto en minuto.—**m. hand,** minutero.—**m. of arc,**

minuto de la circunferencia, arco de 1 minuto.— **m. watch,** reloj de minutero.—**m. wheel,** rueda de los minutos. **II.** va. minutar, anotar, apuntar.

minutely [mainiútli], adv. minuciosamente.— [mínitli], por minutos, a intervalos de un minuto.

minuteman [mínitmæn], s. miliciano pronto para prestar servicio en el acto.

minuteness [mainiútnes], s. minuciosidad; suma pequeñez.

minutia [miniúŝhia], s. minucia, detalle menudo o minucioso.

minutiae [-ŝhii], s. (pl. de MINUTIA) menudencias, trivialidades.

minx [mincs], s. moza descarada.

miny [máini], a. subterráneo.

Miocene [máiosin], a. (geol.) mioceno.

miracle [míracœl], s. milagro; (teat.) auto dramático.—**m. monger,** milagrero.—**m. play,** auto, drama en que se representan episodios bíblicos o de personajes religiosos.—**m. worker,** taumaturgo.

miraculous [mirækiulus], a. milagroso.

miraculously [-li], adv. milagrosamente.

miraculousness [-nes], s. calidad de milagroso.

mirage [miráý], s. espejismo.

mire [máiœr]. **I.** s. cieno, lodo, fango; lodazal, cenagal. **II.** va. encenegar, enlodar. **III.** vn. atascarse en el fango.

miriness [máirines], s. calidad de fangoso.

mirk, mirky [mœrki], s. = MURKY.

mirror [mírœr]. **I.** s. espejo; ejemplar, modelo. **II.** va. reflejar, espejear, retratar.

mirth [mœrz], s. alegría, regocijo o júbilo.— **mirthful** [mœrzful], a. alegre; gozoso.—**mirthfully** [-li], adv. alegremente, jovialmente.—**mirthless** [mœrzles], a. triste, abatido.

miry [máiri], a. cenagoso, lodoso, fangoso.

misacceptation [mísæcseptéŝhun], s. mala inteligencia.

misadventure [mísædvénchur], s. desgracia, desventura, revés.

misalliance [mísæláians], s. matrimonio morganático, o con persona de clase inferior.

misanthrope [mísanzroup], **misanthropist** [misǽnzropist], s. misántropo.—**misanthropic(al** [misanzrópic(al], a. misantrópico.—**misanthropy** [misǽnzropi], s. misantropía.

misapplication [mísæplikéŝhun], s. mala aplicación, mal uso.

misapply [mísæpli], va. hacer mal uso de.

misapprehend [mísæprijend], va. entender mal.

misapprehension [-ŝhun], s. error, concepto erróneo, falsa interpretación.

misappropriate [mísæprópriet], va. malversar.

misbecome [mísbicúm], va. no ser propio de, ser indigno de, no convenir a.

misbegot(ten [misbigót(œn], a. bastardo.

misbehave [misbijéiv], vn. y vr. portarse mal.

misbehaved [-d], a. que se porta mal; reacio, travieso.

misbehavio(u)r [-biœr], s. desmán, mal comportamiento.

misbelief [misbelíf], s. error; sospecha, incredulidad.—**misbelieve** [-lív], vn. estar en error.— **misbeliever** [-œr], s. incrédulo.

miscalculate [miscǽlkiuleit], va. calcular mal.

miscalculation [-éiŝhun], s. error, mal cálculo; cuenta errada.

miscall [miscól], va. nombrar impropiamente; ultrajar, difamar.

miscarriage [miscǽrriy], s. aborto, malparto; fracaso, malogro; extravío, desmán.

miscarry [miscǽri], vn. frustarse, malograrse, salir mal; abortar, malparir; extraviarse.

miscegenation [miseyenéiŝhun], s. mezcla de las razas negra y blanca.

miscellanea [miseléinia], s. pl. miscelánea.

miscellaneous [-us], a. misceláneo, mezclado; diverso.

miscellany [miseléni], s. silva, miscelánea.

mischance [mischáns], s. desgracia, infortunio.

mischarge [mischárý], va. cargar indebidamente en cuenta.

mischief [míschif], s. mal, daño; injuria, agravio; travesura, diablura; persona traviesa.—**m.-maker,** dañino; chismoso, enredador.—**m.-making,** dañino, perjudicial.

mischievous [míschivus], a. dañino, dañoso; malicioso o malévolo; chismoso o enredador; travieso.—**mischievously** [-li], adv. perversamente; con o por travesura; perjudicialmente.— **mischievousness** [-nes], s. malicia, perversidad; picardía, travesura.

miscibility [mísibíliti], s. miscibilidad.

miscible [mísibœl], a. miscible.

misclaim [miscléim], s. pretensión mal fundada.

misconceive [mísconsív], va. y vn. formar concepto erróneo, juzgar mal.

misconception [míconsépshun], s. concepto erróneo, equivocación, engaño; mala inteligencia; mala interpretación.

misconduct [miscónduct], s. mala conducta o mal manejo, mal porte.

misconduct [miscondúct], va. y vr. manejar mal; portarse mal.

misconstruction [místconstrúcshun], s. mala interpretación, error.

misconstrue [miscónstru], va. interpretar erróneamente, entender mal.

miscount [miscáunt]. I. va. contar mal. II. vn. descontarse, equivocarse en la cuenta.

miscreant [míscriant], s. malandrín.

miscue [miskiú], s. (billar) pifia.

misdate [misdéit], va. fechar falsamente, o poner fecha equivocada.

misdeed [misdíd], s. fechoría, delito.

misdemean [mísdemín], vn. portarse mal.

misdemeanant [-ænt], reo de delito menor.

misdemeanor [-œr], s. mala conducta; (for.) fechoría, delito de menor cuantía.

misdirect [mísdiréct], va. dirigir erradamente.— **misdirection** [-shun], s. mala dirección; informe falso.

misdo [misdú], va. y vn. errar, hacer mal o disparatadamente; faltar o delinquir.—**misdoer** [-œr], s. malhechor, criminal.—**misdoing** [-ing], s. falta, mala acción; yerro.

mise en scène [miś an sen], s. (teat.) aparato escénico; puesta en escena.

misemploy [misemplói], va. abusar; emplear mal.—**misemployment** [-mœnt], s. abuso.

miser [máiśœr], s. avaro, avariento.—**m.,** o **mizer,** aparato tubular para abrir pozos.

miserable [mísœrabœl], a. miserable, desdichado, infeliz; pobre, menguado; sin valor; despreciable; lastimoso, lastimero..—**miserably** [-bli], adv. miserablemente.

miserere [mísœríri], s. (igl.) miserere.

misericorde [mísœricórd], s. puñal o cachetero envenenado.

miserly [máiśœrli], a. avariento, tacaño, mezquino.

misery [mísœri], s. miseria, desgracia; dolor continuo; lance de ciertos juegos de naipes.

misfaith [misféiz], s. falta de fe.

misfeasance [misfíśans], s. (for.) acto legal hecho de una manera ilegal; infidencia.

misfire [misfáiœr]. I. vn. no dar fuego; no reventar. II. s. hecho de no reventar o dar fuego.

misfit [misfít]. I. va. ajustar o entallar mal, no sentar bien, no encajar. II. s. lo que no sienta, ajusta, entalla o encaja bien.

misfortune [misfórchun o tiun], s. desgracia, infortunio, revés.

misgive [misgív]. I. va. llenar de dudas o recelos; hacer temer o dudar. II. vn. ser receloso o tímido; faltar valor.—**misgiving** [-ing], s. recelo, duda, presentimiento; desconfianza, temor.

misgotten [misgótœn], a. mal habido.

misgovern [misgúvœrn], va. desgobernar, gobernar o administrar mal.—**misgovernment** [-mœnt], s. desgobierno, mala administración.

misguidance [misgáidans], s. dirección errada; extravío, error.—**misguide** [misgáid], va. descarriar, extraviar; maltratar.

mishap [misjǽp], s. desgracia, accidente, contratiempo.

misimprove [mísimprúv], va. desaprovechar o desperdiciar.

misinform [mísinfórm], va. y vn. mal enterar, o informar; dar informes erróneos.—**misinformation** [mísinforméishun], s. información errónea.

misinterpret [mísintérpret], va. interpretar mal, entender mal.—**misinterpretation** [-éishun], s. mala o falsa interpretación.

misjudge [misyúy], va. y vn. errar, juzgar mal.

misjudgment [-mœnt], s. juicio errado o injusto.

mislay [misléi], va. colocar mal, extraviar, traspapelar, perder.

misle [mísl], vn. = MIZZLE.

mislead [mislíd], va. extraviar, descaminar, despistar; conducir a conclusiones erróneas; alucinar, engañar, seducir, pervertir.

misleading [-ing], a. engañoso; de falsas apariencias.

mistletoe [míscœlto], s. = MISTLETOE.

mismanage [mismǽney], va. manejar o administrar mal.—**mismanagement** [-mœnt], s. mal manejo, mala administración.—**mismanager** [-œr], s. mal administrador.

mismarriage [mismǽriy], s. mal matrimonio, matrimonio desacertado; (gram.) concordancia ilógica.

mismatch [-mǽch], va. desigualar; deshermanar, desajustar.

misname [misnéim], va. trasnombrar, equivocar el nombre.

misnomer [misnómœr], s. nombre inapropiado; (for.) nombre erróneo.

misogamist [misógamist], s. misógamo.

misogamy [misógami], s. misogamia.

misogynist [misóyinist], s. misógino.

misogyny [misóyini], s. misoginia.

misperception [míspœrsépshun], s. percepción errónea.

misplace [mispléis], va. colocar mal o fuera de su sitio; extraviar, traspapelar.

misprint [misprínt]. I. va. imprimir con erratas. II. s. (impr.) errata, error de imprenta.

misprision [mispríyun], s. (for.) ocultación de un crimen o delito.

mispronounce [mispronáuns], va. y vn. pronunciar mal.

misproportion [míspropórshun], va. desproporcionar.

misquotation [míscuotéshun], s. cita falsa o equivocada.

misquote [miscuót], va. citar falsa, equivocada o erróneamente.

misreport [misripórt]. I. va. dar una noticia falsa. II. s. informe falso o erróneo.

misrepresent [misrépresént], va. desfigurar, pervertir, tergiversar, disfrazar, falsificar.

misrepresentation [-éishun], s. falsedad, noticia o relación falsa, tergiversación.

misrule [misrúl]. I. va. y vn. gobernar mal; desgobernar. II. s. mal gobierno; desgobierno; confusión, desorden.

miss [mis], s. (pl. MISSES) señorita (título que se da a una soltera: Miss Brown, la señorita Brown; the Misses Brown, las señoritas Brown); muchacha, jovencita (el significado que gen. tiene en el com.)

miss. I. va. errar (el tiro, el golpe, etc.); no acertar con, no ver, no comprender; equivocar; perder (el tren, la función, un goce); echar de menos; pasar sin, abstenerse de, carecer de; pasar por alto, dejar de hacer.—**to m. fire,** fallar el tiro.—**to m. one's mark,** errar el blanco.—**to m. out,** pasar por alto, omitir.—**to m. stays,** (mar.) faltar la virada, no virar.—**to m. the point,** no ver el punto, no comprender el verdadero sentido. II. vn. frustrarse, salir mal, malograrse; errar, faltar; fallar. III. s. malogro, fracaso, marra; pérdida, extravío; falta.

missal [mísal], s. (igl.) misal.

---

missend [missénd], va. (pret. y pp. MISSENT) enviar o dirigir mal.

misshape [misshéip], va. deformar, desfigurar, afear.

missile [mísil]. I. a. arrojadizo. II. s. proyectil; arma arrojadiza.

missing [mísing], a. extraviado, perdido; ausente.—**to be m.**, faltar, estar extraviado, perdido o ausente.

mission [míshun], s. misión.—**m. school**, escuela de caridad donde se da instrucción general y religiosa; escuela preparatoria para misioneros; escuela dirigida por misioneros.

missionary [-œri]. I. s. misionario; (igl.) misionero. II. a. misionero.

missis, missus [mísis], s. (modo usual de pronunciar la palabra **Mistress**, cuya abreviatura es **Mrs.**) señora; (fam.) esposa.

missive [mísiv]. I. a. misivo, enviadizo. II. s. carta, misiva, comunicación escrita.

misspeak [mispíc], vn. y vr. (pret. MISSPOKE; pp. MISSPOKEN) equivocarse al hablar, hablar e- quivocadamente.

misspell [mispél], va. deletrear mal.

misspelling [-ing], s. deletreo erróneo.

misspend [mispénd], va. malgastar, malbaratar.

misstate [mistéit], va. relatar o exponer falsamente.—**misstatement** [-mœnt], s. relación equivocada o falsa, error, falencia, aserción errónea.

misstep [mistép]. I. vn. dar un paso en falso, tropezar. II. s. paso falso, desliz; tropiezo.

missy [mísi], s. (fam.) señorita, niña.

mist [mist]. I. s. niebla, neblina; vapor, vaho. II. va. anieblar, anublar, empañar, obscurecer. III. vn. lloviznar.

mistakable [mistéikabœl], a. que puede ser equivocado.

mistake [mistéik]. I. va. (pret. MISTOOK: pp. MISTAKEN) equivocar, comprender mal; trabucar, tomar una cosa por otra. II. vn. errar, equivocarse, engañarse. III. s. equivocación, error; errata.—**and no m.**, (fam.) sin duda alguna, con toda seguridad.—**to make a m.**, equivocarse.

mistaken [mistéikœn], pp. de TO MISTAKE; erroneo, incorrecto; equivocado; errado, desacertado.

mistakenly [-li], **mistakingly** [-kingli], adv. equivocadamente.

misteach [mistích], va. (pret. y pp. MISTAUGHT) enseñar o instruir mal.

mister [mistœr], s. señor (término de cortesía, cuya abreviatura es **Mr.**).

misterm [mistœrm], va. dar un nombre equivocado o impropio.

mistful [místful], a. caliginoso.

mistimed [mistáimd], pp. y a. inoportuno, extemporáneo, intempestivo.

mistiness [místines], s. caligine.

mistletoe [míscœlto o míscœlto], s. (bot.) muérdago; liga, visco.

mistook [mistúk], pret. y pp. de TO MISTAKE.

mistral [místral], s. viento maestral.

mistranslate [místransléit], va. traducir erróneamente.

mistranslation [-léishun], s. traducción errónea.

mistress [místres], s. señora; concubina, querida; maestra; cortejo, mujer cortejada; (con of) conocedora (de) a fondo, perita (en). Título que se da a las casadas y equivale en español a Señora (se escribe **Mrs.** y en este sercido se pronuncia mísis).—**M. of the Robes**, camarera mayor de una reina o princesa.

mistrial [mistráial], s. (for.) nulidad de juicio por causa de error o por desacuerdo del jurado.

mistrust [mistrúst]. I. s. desconfianza. II. va. desconfiar de, dudar de.—**mistrustful** [-ful], a. desconfiado.—**mistrustfully** [-li], adv. desconfiadamente.—**mistrustfulness** [-nes], s. desconfianza, recelo.—**mistrustingly** [-ingli], adv. con desconfianza.

misty [místi], a. brumoso, caliginoso.

misunderstand [misúndœrstǽnd], va. entender mal; tomar en sentido erróneo.

misunderstanding [-ing], s. concepto falso, equivocación, error, mala inteligencia; desavenencia, disensión.

misusage [misiúsey], **misuse** [misiúś], s. abuso; maltrato, estropeo.

misuse, va. maltratar, tratar mal; estropear; abusar de.—**misused**, maltrecho.

mite [máit], s. pizca, triza, mota; blanca, ardite; óbolo; (ent.) ácaro, gorgojo, arador.

miter, mitre [máitœr]. I. s. (igl.) mitra; dignidad de obispo; (mec.) inglete; caballete, caperuza o sombrerete de chimenea; (cost.) escudete, contrete.—**m. block, m. box**, caja de ingletes.—**m. joint**, junta a inglete. II. va. conferir una mitra a; adornar con mitra o algo parecido; (mec.) juntar con inglete.

mithridate [mízridet], s. mitridato.

mitigable [mítigabœl], a. capaz de ser mitigado.

mitigant [mítigant], a. mitigante, calmante.

mitigate [-gueit], va. mitigar, calmar.—**mitigation** [guéishun], s. mitigación.—**mitigative, mitigatory** [-guetiv, gatori], a. y s. mitigativo, lenitivo, calmante.—**mitigator** [-guétœr], s. mitigador.

mitosis [mitóusis], s. mitosis, carioquinesis.

mitral [máitral], a. mitral.

mitre [máitœr], va. y s. = MITER.

mitred [máitœrd], a. mitrado.

mitt, mitten [mít(œn], s. mitón, confortante; guante con dedo para el pulgar, pero sin separaciones para los otros cuatros dedos; (fam.) calabazas, repulsa de un amante.—**to get (to give) the m.**, recibir (dar) calabazas.

mittimus [mítimuś], s. (for.) auto o decreto de prisión.

mix. I. va. mezclar; embarullar, emburujar; aderezar (ensalada); amasar; hacer, confeccionar (hormigón, etc.); incorporar, asociar, unir, confundir. II. vn. mezclarse.

mixable [mícsabœl], a. que puede mezclarse.

mixed [mixt], a. mezclado; mixto; (gen. con up) confundido; atolondrado.—**m. marriage**, matrimonio entre los de distintas razas o religiones (apl. esp. al entre un católico y un protestante).—**m. metal**, aleación.—**m. number**, número mixto.—**m. pickles**, encurtido mezclado (de varias legumbres).

mixer [míxœr], s. mezclador; (const.) mezcladora; hormigonera; (fam.) persona sociable y adaptable.

mixt (pp. irr. de TO MIX) = MIXED, confuso; misceláneo.

mixtilineal, mixtilinear [míxtilínial, -ar], a. (geom.) mixtilíneo.

mixture [míxchœr], s. mezcla; mixtura; mescolanza, mixtifori.

mizen, mizzen [mísœn], s. (mar.) mesana.—**m. shrouds**, jarcia de mesana.—**mizzenmast** [-mæst], s. palo de mesana.

mizzle [mísœl]. I. vn. lloviznar; confundir, aturdir. II. vn. sucumbir; (fam.) achisparse; fugarse. III. s. m., o **mizzling**, llovizna, chipi-chipi.

mnemonic(al [nemónic(al], a. mnemotécnico.

mnemonics [nemónics], s. mnemónica.

moa [móa], s. diuornis, gran pájaro de Nueva Zelandia ya extinguido.

Moabite [móabait], s. y a. moabita.

moan [móun]. I. s. quejido, gemido. II. va. lamentar, llorar, deplorar. III. vn. gemir, quejarse; lamentarse.

moanful [-ful], a. lamentable, triste; quejumbroso.—**moanfully** [-l], adv. quejumbrosamente, con gemidos o quejidos.

moat [móut]. I. s. (fort.) foso. II. va. rodear con fosos.

mob. I. s. chusma, populacho; multitud; cofia, toca o gorra de mujer. II. va. atropellar, hacer asonada a.

mobbish [móbish], a. tumultuoso.

mobile [móbil], a. movedizo, movible, móvil; inconstante, variable.

mobile [móbili], *s.* (filos.) cosa movible.

mobility [mobíliti], *s.* movilidad; volubilidad, instabilidad.

mobilization [móbiliséshun], *s.* movilización.

mobilize [móbilais], *va.* (mil.) movilizar.

mobocracy [mobócræsi], *s.* gobierno de (por) la muchedumbre; la muchedumbre gobernante.— **mobocrat** [móbocræt], *s.* partidario del gobierno de la muchedumbre; demagogo.

moccasin [mócasin], *s.* mocasín, abarca de piel de gamo; mocasín, serpiente venenosa.

mocha [móca], *s.* café de Moca.

mock [moc]. **I.** *va.* mofar, escarnecer; remedar, imitar, copiar; engañar, burlar. **II.** *vn.* (con **at**) burlarse de, hacer mofa de. **III.** *s.* mofa, escarnio, burla; mímica. **IV.** *a.* ficticio, falso, imitado; cómico, burlesco; irónico.—**m. orange**, (bot.) jeringuilla.—**m. privet**, (bot.) alaterno.— **m. turtle soup**, sopa hecha con cabeza de ternera a imitación de tortuga.—**m. willow** = M. PRIVET.

mocker [mókœr], *s.* mofador, escarnecedor.

mockery [mókœri], *s.* mofa, burla; remedo.

mocking bird [móking bœrd], *s.* (orn.) sinsonte; arrendajo.—**m. thrush**, mirlo burlón.

mockingly [mókingli], *adv.* burlonamente, con mofa.

modal [módal], *a.* modal.

modality [modælitil], *s.* carácter modal, diferencia accidental.

mode [móud], *s.* modo, manera; moda, uso; graduación, grado; (gram., filos., mús.) modo.

model [módel]. **I.** *s.* modelo, ejemplar o patrón; muestra; horma; dechado; plantilla, figurín; mujer que sirve de figurín en tiendas de ropa; (b. a.) modelo vivo. **II.** *a.* modelo, ejemplar.—**m. school**, escuela experimental o de práctica, anexa a una normal y que sirve tanto de modelo como de escuela de prueba en que los alumnos de la normal enseñan bajo la dirección de sus maestros. **III.** *va.* modelar; moldear; (b. a.) modelar; (fund.) hacer un molde de.

model(l)ing [-ing]. **I.** *s.* (b. a.) modelado. **II.** *a.* modelador.—**m. board**, terraja.

modeller [-œret], *s.* modelador, trazador.

moderate [módœret]. **I.** *a.* moderado, quieto, tranquilo; regular, ordinario; razonable, sobrio; bonancible, suave; módico (en precio). **II.** *va.* moderar, reprimir; templar, modificar; calmar. **III.** *vn.* moderarse, calmarse, apaciguarse; presidir.

moderately [-li], *adv.* moderadamente; razonablemente; módicamente; medianamente.

moderateness [-nes], *s.* moderación; modicidad.

moderation [-éishun], *s.* moderación; frugalidad, economía; presidencia, acto de presidir. —*pl.* (Ingl.) exámenes universitarios.

moderator [-éitœr], *s.* moderador, concordador, árbitro; presidente de una congregación protestante; (Ingl.) examinador en las universidades.—**m. lamp**, lámpara de regulador.

moderatrix [-trics], *s.* moderadora; presidenta.

modern [módœrn]. **I.** *a.* moderno.—**m. geometry**, geometría proyectiva.—**m. improvements**, mejoras modernas.—**m. languages**, lenguas vivas. **II.** *s.* modernista.

modernism [-ism], *s.* modernismo; (M-), modernismo, en el sentido católico (sistema condenado por Pío X en 1907); (M-), modernismo, en el sentido protestante (sistema que niega la necesidad de los dogmas teológicos y la inspiración total de la Biblia).—**modernist, M-** (-ist), modernista, partidario del modernismo.

modernize [-ais], *va.* modernizar; resucitar.

modernness [-nes], *s.* calidad de moderno.

modest [módest], *a.* modesto.—**modestly** [-li], *adv.* modestamente.

modesty [módesti], *s.* modestia.—**m. piece**, bobillo (encaje).

modicum [módicum], *s.* pitanza, bocado, porción pequeña; poco.

modifiable [módifáiæbœl], *a.* modificable.

modification [-fikéishun], *s.* modificación.

modificative [-ficativ], *a.* modificativo.

modifier [faicœr], *s.* modificador; (gram.) modificante, palabra modificativa.

modify [-fai], *va.* modificar.—**modifying** [-ing], *a.* modificante, modificativo.

modill(i)on [modíliun], *s.* (arq.) modillón, can, cartela.

modish [móudish], *a.* hecho a la moda; conforme a la moda.

modiste [móudist], *s.* modista.

modular [módiular], *a.* modular.

modulate [módiuleit]. **I.** *va.* modular, entonar. **II.** *va.* y *vn.* (mús.) modular, cambiar de tono.— **modulation** [-éishun], *s.* (mús.) modulación; (arq.) módulo.—**modulator** [-eitœr], *s.* modulador, gorjeador.

module [módiul], *s.* (arq.) módulo.

moduli [módiulai], *s. pl.* de MODULUS.

modulus [módiulus], *s.* (mat.) módulo.

modus [módus], *s.* modo, manera.—**m. operandi**, modo de funcionar.—**m. vivendi**, convenio interino entre dos naciones, modus vivendi.

mofette [mofét], *s.* mofeta.

mogul [mogúl], *s.* mogol; naipe de la mejor calidad; locomotora de gran tamaño.

mohair [mójæær], *s.* pelo de camello; tela de pelo de camello.

Mohammedan [mojæmedan], *s.* y *a.* mahometano.

Mohammedanism [-ism], *s.* mahometismo.

Mohammedanize [-ais], *va.* mahometizar.

Mohican, Mohegan [mojícan, gan], *s.* mohicano, miembro de cierta tribu india.

moidore [móidor], *s.* moidoro (moneda portuguesa).

moiety [móieti], *s.* mitad.

moil [móil]. **I.** *va.* enlodar, ensuciar; cansar, fatigar. **II.** *vn.* fatigarse; inquietarse. **III.** *s.* mancha, suciedad.

moire, moiré [muár, muaré], *s.* (tej.) muer, moaré, muaré.

moist [móist], *a.* húmedo; jugoso, suculento.

moisten [móisœn], *va.* humedecer.

moistener [móisnœr], *s.* humedecedor, remojador.

moistness [móistnes], **moisture** [móischœr], *s.* humedad; jugosidad.

molar, molary [mólar, i], *a.* relativo a la masa; molar.—**m. tooth**, muela, diente molar.

molasses [móleses], *s.* melaza, miel.—**m. candy**, melcocha.

mold, molder, molding, etc. = MOULD, etc.

Moldavian [moldéivian], *s.* y *a.* moldavo.

mole [móul], *s.* lunar; mancha; muelle, dique, malecón, espolón; (zool.) topo; (med.) mola.— **m. cricket**, grillotalpa o topogrillo.—**m.-eyed**, cegato.—**m. furs**=MOLESKIN.—**m. rat**, ratón topo.

molecast [móulcæst], *s.* = MOLEHILL.

molecular [molékiular], *a.* molecular.

molecule [mólekiul], *s.* molécula.

molehill [móuljill], *s.* topinera.

moleskin [móulskin], *s.* piel de topo.

molest [molést], *va.* molestar, vejar; faltar al respeto a (una mujer); meterse con, dañar.

molestation [mólestéshun], *s.* molestia, incomodidad, importunidad; vejación.

mollah [móla], *s.* título mahometano.

mollient [mólient], *a.* molitivo.

mollifiable [mólifaiæbœl], *a.* molificable.

mollification [-fikéishun], *s.* molificación; mitigación.

mollifier [-faicœr], *s.* ablandador, emoliente; mitigador, pacificador.

mollify [-fai], *va.* molificar, ablandar; apaciguar; aliviar; suavizar, mitigar.

mollusc [mólusk], *s.* molusco.

Mollusca [molúsca], *s. pl.* (zool.) moluscos.

molluscan [molúscan], *a.* y *s.* molusco.

Molluscoida [molúscóidæ], *s. pl.* moluscoideos.— **molluscoid** [molúscoid], *s.* y *a.* moluscoideo.

mollusk [mólusc], *s.* molusco.

molly-coddle [móli(códœl], *s.* (fam.) marica.

Moloch [móloc], s. Moloc, deidad de los fenicios; influencia perniciosa.

molossus [molósus], s. (pros.) moloso.

molt, molting, s. = MOULT, MOULTING.

molten [móultœn], a. y pp. irr. de TO MELT.

moly [móuli], s. (bot.) planta fabulosa; ajo silvestre.

molybdate [molíbdeit], s. molibdato.

molybdenous [molíbdenus], a. molibdoso.

molybdenum [molíbdenum], s. (quím.) molibdeno.

molybdic [molíbdic], a. molíbdico.

moment [móumœnt], s. momento; importancia, entidad; (mec.) momento.—**m. of a couple,** momento de un par.—**m. of flexure,** momento de flexión.—**m. of inertia,** momento de inercia.—**m. of momentum,** momento de la cantidad de movimiento.—**m. of resistance,** momento de resistencia, momento del par de las ֽfuerzas elásticas.

momentarily [mómœnterili], adv. momentáneamente.—**momentariness** [-erines], s. momentaneidad.—**momentary** [-teri], a. momentáneo.—**momently** [-li], adv. por momentos.

momentous [moméntus], a. importante, grave, trascendental.—**momentously** [-li], adv. con importancia, gravemente.—**momentousness** [-nes], s. importancia, gravedad.

momentum [moméntum], s. impulso; (mec.) cantidad de movimiento.

monachal [mónacal], a. monacal, monástico.

monachism [mónacism], s. monaquismo.

monacid [monæsid], s. (quím.) monácido.

monad [mónæd], **I.** a. mónada (en todas sus acepciones). **II.** a. que se refiere a o consta de una mónada; (quím.) que tiene poder de combinación equivalente a uno.

Monadelphia [mónædélfiæ], s. pl. (bot.) monadelfas.—**monadelphous** [-fus], a. monadelfo.

monadism [mónadism], **monadology** [monadóloyi], s. monadología.

monarch [mónarc], s. monarca.—**monarchal** [monárcal], **monarchical** [monárkic(al], a. monárquico.—**monarchism** [mónark֭ism], s. monarquismo.—**monarchist** [-ist], s. monarquista.

monarchy [mónarki], s. monarquía.

monastery [mónasteri], s. monasterio.

monastic(al [monástic(al], a. monástico.

monastically [-i], adv. monásticamente.

monatomic [mónætómic], a. monoatómico.

monazite [mónæsait], s. monacita.

Monday [múnde], s. lunes.

monetary [mónetæri], a. monetario, pecuniario. **m. unit,** unidad monetaria.

monetization [mónetiśéiśhun], s. amonedación, monetización.

monetize [-aiś], va. monetizar; acuñar, amonedar.

money [múne], **I.** s. dinero; moneda; sistema monetario.—pl. pagos o recibos al contado.—**m. bill,** ley de hacienda.—**m. box,** alcancía.—**m. broker,** corredor de cambios.—**m. changer, dealer, o jobber,** cambista.—**m. lender,** prestamista, usurero.—**m. making,** lucro, ganancia, prosperidad; ganancioso, lucrativo, provechoso.—**m. market,** mercado monetario.—**m. of account,** moneda imaginaria.—**m. order,** libranza postal.—**m. scales,** pesillo para pesar el oro y la plata.—**m.'s worth,** valor cabal del dinero que se page por algo. **II.** va. acuñar, hacer (moneda); convertir en moneda.

moneybag [-bǽg], s. talega, bolsa, bolsón· —pl. (fam.) ricacho.

moneyed [múnid], a. adinerado.—**m. man,** capitalista.

moneyer [múniœr], s. monedero.

moneyless [múniles], a. falto de dinero, pobre.

monger [múngœr], s. tratante, traficante.

Mongol(ian [móngol, mongólian], a. y s. mogol; idioma mogólico.

mongoos(e [móngus], s. (zool.) mangosta.

mongrel [múngrel], a. y s. mestizo, mixto, a-travesado.

'mongst [mongst], prep. forma apocopada de AMONGST.

monism [mónism], s. (fil.) monismo; (biol.) unidad de origen.—**monist** [-ist], s., **monistic** [monistic], a. monista.

monition [moníśhun], s. amonestación, consejo; aviso.

monitor [mónitœr], s. amonestador o monitor; (mar.) monitor.

monitory [mónitori].֭ **I.** a. instructivo, monitorio. **II.** s. amonestación.

monk [munk], s. monje.

monkery [múnkœri], s. vida monástica, frailía.

monkey [múnki]. **I.** s. (zool.) mono; (mec.) grapa, trinquete, fiador del martinete; crisol para fundir el vidrio.—**m. flower,** (bot.) mímulo.—**m. jacket,** capote o capotón de piloto.—**m. tricks, monerías.—m. wrench,** llave inglesa. **II.** va. y vn. (fam.) remedar, imitar; hacer payasadas. —**to m. with,** meterse con; bregar con.

monkhood [múnkjud], s. monacato, monjía.

monkish [múnkiśh], a. monástico, frailesco.

monkshood [múnksjud], s. (bot.) napelo.

monoceros [monóscœros], s. monocerote, unicornio; (**M-**) Unicornio (constelación).

monochlamydeous [mónoclæmídius], a. (bot.) monoclamídeo.

monoclinal [-cláinæl], s. y a. (geol.) monoclinal.

monochord [-cord], s. monocordio.

monochroic [-croic], **monochromatic** [-crométic], a. monocromático.

monochrome [-croum], s. monocromo.

monocle [mónocœl], s. monóculo.

monoclinic [mónoclínic], a. (min.) monoclínico.

monocotyledonous [-cotilédonus], a. (bot.) monocotiledón(eo.

monocular [monókiuiar], **monoculous** [monókiulus], a. monóculo; de o para un ojo.

monocyclic [mónosáiclic], a. (elec.) monocíclico.

monodactylous [-dáctilus], a. monodáctilo.

Monodelphia [-délfiæ], s. pl. (zool.) monodelfos.—**monodelphian, monodelphous** [-fæn, -fus], s. y a. monodelfo.

monody [mónodi], s. monodia; elegía; (mús.) obligado, solo.

monogamist [monógamist], s. monógamo.

monogamous [monógamus], a. monógamo; (bot.) monógamo.

monogamy [monógami], s. monogamia.

monogenesis [mónoϋénesis], s. unidad de origen; doctrina de la descendencia de todos los seres vivos de una sola celdilla; reproducción asexual.

monogenism [monóϋenism], s. ꞏmonogenismo, doctrina de la unidad de origen de toda la raza humana.

monogram [mónogræm], s. monograma, cifra.

monograph [-græf], s. monografía.

monographic [-gráfic], a. monográfico.

monography [monógrafi], s. dibujo claroscuro, sin colores.

monohydrate [mónojáidreit], s. monohidrato.—**monohydrated** [-ed], a. monohidratado.

monolater [monólætœr], s. el que adora sólo a uno de muchos dioses.—**monolatry** [-tri], s. adoración de sólo uno de varios dioses.

monolith [mónoliϋ], s. monolito.—**monolithic** [-líϋic], a. monolítico.

monologian [mónolóϋian], **monologist** [monóloyist], s. monologista.

monologue [mónolog], s. monólogo, soliloquio.

monomachy [mónómaki], s. monomaquia.

monomania [mónoméinia], s. monomanía.

monomaniac [-méiniac]. **I.** a. monomaníaco. **II.** s. monómano.

monometallism [-métalism], s. monometalismo, teoría económica que defiende el uso de un solo metal como base monetaria.

monomial [monómial], s. y a. (álg.) monomio.

monopetalous [mónopétalus], a. (bot.) monopétalo.

monophobia [-fóubiæ], s. (pat.) terror de la soledad.

monophyletic [-filétic], a. monofilético, referente a un antepasado común y único.

---

monophyllic [-fíiic], *a.* (bot.) monófilo.
Monophysite [monófisait], *s.* **Monophysitic** [-sític], *a.* monofisita.
monoplane [mónopléin], *s.* monoplano.
monoplegia [-plíyiæ], *s.* monoplegia, parálisis de un lado.
monopolism [monópolism], *s.* monopolismo.
monopolist, monopolizer [-ist, -aîœr], *s.* monopolista.—**monopolistic** [-tic], *a.* monopolista.—**monopolize** [-aiš], *va.* monopolizar.
monopoly [monópoli], *s.* monopolio.
monopteron [monópteron], *s.* (arq.) monóptero.
monops [mónops], *s.* tuerto.
monosepalous [mónosépalʊs], *a.* (bot.) monosépalo.
monospermous [-spœrmʊs], *a.* (bot.) monospermo.
monosyllabic(al [-silæbic(al], **monosyllable** [-sílabœl], *a.* monosílabo.
monotheism [mónoziišm], *s.* monoteísmo.
monotheist [mónoziist], *s.*, **monotheistic** [-ic], *a.* monoteísta.
monotone [mónotoun], *s.* monotonía.
monotonic(al [-tónic(al], **monotonous** [monótonʊs], *a.* monótono; machacón, unisonante.
monotony [monótoni], *s.* monotonía; unisonancia.
Monotremata [mónotrémætæ], *s. pl.* (zool.) monotremas.
monotriglyph [mónotráiglif], *s.* (arq.) monotriglifo.
monotype [mónotaip], *s.* monotipia, máquina de componer que funde letras sueltas.
monovalent [monóvælœnt], *a.* (quím.) monovalente.
monoxid(e, monoxid [monóxid], *s.* monóxido.
mousoon [monsún], *s.* monzón.
monster [mónstœr]. **I.** *s.* monstruo. **II.** *a.* enorme, prodigioso, extraordinario.—**m. meeting**, junta magna.
monstrance [mónstrans], *a.* (igl.) custodia, viril.
monstrosity [monstrósiti], *s.* monstruo; monstruosidad.
monstrous [mónstrʊs]. **I.** *a.* monstruoso. **II.** *adv.* (fam.) excesivamente.—**monstrously** [-li], *adv.* monstruosamente.—**monstrousness** [-nes], *s.* monstruosidad.
Montanist [móntænist], *s.* montanista.
month [mʊnz], *s.* mes.—**m. of Sundays,** (fam.) largo tiempo.
monthly [mʊnzli]. **I.** *a.* mensual.—**m. rose,** rosa de todo el año, rosa de China. **II.** *s.* publicación mensual.—*pl.* las reglas, menstruo. **III.** *adv.* mensualmente.
monticle [mónticœl], *s.* montecillo.
monument [móniumœnt], *s.* monumento; memoria, recuerdo; mojón, marca de límites, hito.—**monumental** [-méntal], *a.* monumental; sepulcral; conmemorativo; grandioso, descomunal.—**monumentally** [-i], *adv.* a modo de monumento; (fam.) muy, en alto grado, descomunalmente.
mood [mud], *s.* disposición de ánimo, genio, humor; (lóg.) modo silogístico; (gram.) modo.—**in a bad (good) m.,** de mal (buen) humor.
moodily [múdili], *adv.* caprichosamente; pensativamente.—**moodiness** [-nes], *s.* capricho, extravagancia; mal humor; tristeza, cavilación, melancolía.
moody [múdi], *a.* fantástico, caprichoso; irritable, de mal humor; caviloso; triste, taciturno.
moon [mun], *s.* (astr.) luna: satélite; mes lunar.—**m. blasted,** echado a perder por la influencia de la luna.—**m. daisy,** (bot.) margarita mayor.—**m. dial,** reloj lunar.—**m.-eyed,** ojizaino; bizco, bisojo.—**m. fern,** (bot.) botriquio.
moonbeam [múnbîm], *s.* rayo lunar.
moonblind [-bláind], *s.* cegato, corto de vista.
mooncalf [-cáf], *s.* monstruo; bobo, tonto.
mooned [mund], *a.* lunado.
moonless [múnles], *a.* sin luna.
moonlight [múnlait]. **I.** *s.* luz de la luna. **II.** *a.* iluminado por la luna.

moonlit [múnlit], *a.* iluminado por la luna.
moonseed [múnsíd], *s.* (bot.) cualquier planta menispermácea.
moonshine [múnšháin]. *s.* claridad de la luna; desatino, disparate; música celestial; (E. U.) licor destilado ilegalmente. —**moonshiner** [-œr], *s.* (E. U.) fabricante matutero de aguardiente.
moonstruck [múnstruc], *a.* lunático, loco.
moonwort [múnuœrt], *s.* (bot.) lunaria; botriquio.
moony [múni]. **I.** *a.* lunático; claro como la luna. **II.** *s.* bobo, simplón.
moor [múœr]. **I.** *s.* (Ingl.) páramo, ciénaga; frezal, marjal; (**M-**) moro, sarraceno.—**m. buzzard,** (orn.) circo.—**m. cock, fowl,** o **game,** (orn.) macho de la cerceta.—**m. hen,** (orn.) cerceta, zarceta. **II.** *va.* (mar.) amarrar, aferrar, atar con cables, afirmar con anclas. **III.** *vn.* anclar; estar anclado.
mooring[-ing]. **I.** *s.* (mar.) amarra, noray; cable o calabrote de amarrar. **II.** *a.* de amarre, de amarrar.—**m. buoy,** boya de anclaje.—**m. guy,** amarre de retenida (de un globo).—**m. mast,** (aer.) torre o pilar de amarre para globos.—**m. rings,** (mar.) argollas de amarrar.
moorish [múriš], *a.* pantanoso, cenagoso; árido; (**M-**), moro, morisco.
moorland [-land], *s.* marjal; brezal; erial.
moory [múri], *a.* pantanoso.
moose [mus], *s.* (zool.) anta, alce.
moot [mut]. **I.** *va.* discutir. **II.** *s.* junta; discusión; lugar de reunión. **III.** *a.* discutible; discutido.—**m. court,** tribunal ad hoc, donde se ventilan pleitos supuestos para la enseñanza del derecho.
mop. **I.** *s.* aljofifa, estropajo; (mar.) lampazo; greña, mechón; mueca; muchacha mimada.—**II.** *va.* aljofifar, fregar. —**to m. up,** *vn.* (mil.) acabar con el resto del enemigo.
mopboard [mópbórd], *s.* rodapié.
mope [móup]. **I.** *a.* atontar, abatir. **II.** *vn.* dormitar, entontecerse. **III.** *s.* hombre abatido, atontado o estúpido.—**m.-eyed,** cegato.
mopish [-íšh], *a.* atontado, abatido; adormecido. —**mopishness** [-nes], *s.* abatimiento; adormecimiento.
mopstick [mópstic], *s.* mango de aljofifa.
moquette [mokét], *s.* moqueta.
moraine [moréin], *s.* (geol.) morena.
morainic [moréinic], *a.* (geol.) referente a una morena o formado por ella.
moral [móral]. **I.** *a.* moral, ético; virtuoso; honrado, recto.—**m. faculty,** conciencia.—**m. suasion,** persuasión, influencia moral. **II.** *s.* moralidad, moraleja.—*pl.* costumbres, conducta; ética, moral social.
morale [morál], *s.* moral, estado de ánimo, espíritu.
moralism [móralism], *s.* creencia en una moral sin carácter religioso.—**moralist** [-ist], *s.* moralista, ético; partidario del *moralism.*
morality [moréliti], *s.* ética, moral; moralidad; moraleja; antiguo drama alegórico.
moralization [mórališéishun], *s.* moralización.—**moralize, moralise** [-aiš], *va.* y *vn.* moralizar.—**moralizer** [-œr], *s.* moralizador.
morally [mórali], *adv.* moralmente.
morass [morás], *s.* cenagal, ciénaga, marisma.
morat [móræt], *s.* bebida hecha con miel con jugo de moras.
moratorium [mórætóuriʊm], *s.* moratoria.
moratory [-ri], *a.* moratorio.
Moravian [morévian], *a.* y *s.* moravo.
morbid [mórbid], *a.* mórbido, morboso.
morbidness [-nes], **morbidity** [morbíditi], *s.* morbidez.
morbific(al [morbífic(al], **morbose** [morbóus], *a.* morbífico, morboso, enfermizo.
morceau [morsó], *s.* (fr.) trozo, fragmento, pieza.
mordacious [mordéishʊs], *a.* mordaz.
mordacity [mordásiti], *s.* mordacidad.
mordant [mórdant]. **I.** *s.* mordiente, mordente; (b. a.) agua fuerte. **II.** *a.* mordiente, ácido, corrosivo; acre, mordaz.

mordent [mórdent], s. (mús.) mordente.

more [móær], a. y adv. más.—**m. and m.**, de más en más, cada vez más.—**m. or less**, poco más o menos.—**no m.**, no más; ya no; se acabó.—**so much the m.**, tanto más, cuanto más.—**the m.**, tanto más.—**the m. . . ., the better**, cuanto más . . ., tanto mejor (*the more you give, the better*, cuanto (o mientras) más dé Vd., tanto mejor).— **the m. . . ., the less**, cuanto más . . ., tanto menos.—**the m. . . ., the m.**, cuanto más . . ., tanto más.—**to be no m.**, haber muerto; no existir ya.

moreen [morín], s. filipichín; tabí.

morel [mórel], **moril** [móril]. **I.** s. (bot.) colmenilla, cagarria. **II.** a. moreno, oscuro.

morelle [morél], s. (bot.) hierba mora, solano.

moreover [moróvœr], adv. además.

mores [móris], s. pl. costumbres (apl. esp. a las que envuelven sanción moral); leyes consuetudinarias.

Moresque [morésc]. **I.** a. morisco. **II.** s. (b. a.) arabesco.

morganatic [mórganætic], a. morganático.

morgue [mórg], s. depósito de cadáveres no identificados.

moribund [móribʊnd], a. moribundo.

morion [mórivn], s. morrión, casco.

Morisco [morísco]. **I.** a. morisco. **II.** s. morisco; arábigo; danza morisca; (arq.) arabesco.

Mormon [mórmon], s. mormón.

Mormonism [-iŝm], s. mormonismo.

morning [mórning] (poét. **morn**). **I.** s. mañana (primera parte del día). **II.** a. matutino, matinal, de mañana.—**m. dress**, traje de mañana. —**m. glory**, (bot.) dondiego de día, dompedro, maravilla.—**m. gown**, bata.—**m. star**, (astr.) lucero del alba; (arm.) mangual.

Moro [móuro], s. y a. moro o mahometano filipino.

Moroccan [morócæn], s. y a. marroquí.

morocco [moróco], s. marroquí, tafilete.

moron [móuron], s. hombre de ánimo infantil.

morose [moróus], a. áspero, malhumorado.—**morosely** [-li], adv. broncamente, ásperamente.—**moroseness** [-nes], s. mal humor, acrimonia.

Morpheus [mórfius], s. (mitol.) Morfeo.

morphia [mórfia], **morphin(e** [-fin], s. morfina.

morphinism [mórfiniŝm], s. (med.) morfinismo.

morphology [morfóloyi], s. morfología.

morphological [mórfolóyical], a. morfológico.

morphosis [morfósis], s. (biol.) morfosis.

morrice, morris o **morris-dance** [móris-dans], s. danza morisca; mojiganga; (danz.) especie de bolero.

morrow [móro], s. mañana (día que sigue al de hoy)—**on the m.**, en el día de mañana.

morse [mors], s. = WALRUS.

morsel [mórsel], s. bocado, manjar.

mort, s. muerte; toque de la trompa de caza al morir la res.

mortal [mórtal]. **I.** a. mortal; (fam.) extremo, violento; prolijo, fastidioso.—**m. sin**, pecado mortal. **II.** s. mortal, ser humano.

mortality [mortǽliti], s. mortalidad; muerte; mortandad; humanidad.

mortally [mórtali], adv. mortalmente; (fam.) extremadamente, sumamente.

mortar [mórtar], s. mortero, almirez; (arti.) mortero, obús (llám. t. **m. piece**); (alb.) mortero, mezcla.—**m. board**, (alb.) esparavel (tabla con asa por debajo); gorro estudiantil cuadrado.

mortgage [mórguey]. **I.** s. hipoteca, gravamen. —**m. deed**, título de propiedad depositado en calidad de hipoteca. **II.** va. hipotecar.

mortgageable [mórguæybœl], a. hipotecable.

mortgagee [mórgueyí], s. acreedor hipotecario.

mortgager [mórguevœr], s. deudor hipotecario.

mortiferous [mortífœrus], a. mortífero.

mortification [mórtifikéŝhun], s. mortificación, bochorno; (med.) descomposición, gangrena; maceración.

mortify [mórtifai]. **I.** va. mortificar, humillar, abochornar; macerar o castigar (la carne);

subyugar, domar (las pasiones); (med.) mortificar. **II.** vn. mortificarse, gangrenarse, corromperse.

mortise [mórtis]. **I.** s. (carp.) mortaja, cotana, muesca, entalladura, gárgol; (mar.) alefriz.— **m. hole**, escopleadura.—**m. lock**, cerradura embutida. **II.** va. escoplear, hacer muescas; engargolar, ensamblar, enmechar.

mortmain [mórtmein], s. (for.) manos muertas; amortización.

mortuary [mórchuæri], a. mortuorio, funerario; depósito de cadáveres; osario.

mosaic [moŝéic], a. y s. mosaico, embutido.— M., mosaico, referente a Moisés.

mosey [móusi], vn. (fam.) irse pronto o aprisa; darse prisa.

Moslem [móslem], s. y a. musulmán.

mosque [mosc], s. mezquita.

mosquito [moskíto], s. mosquito, (Méx.) mosco, (P. R., Colomb.) zancudo.—**m. bar**, mosquitero. —**m. fleet**, escuadra de barcos relativamente menores.—**m. net** = M. BAR.—**m. netting**, gasa o redecilla para mosquiteros.

moss [mos]. **I.** s. (bot.) musgo, musco, moho; tremedal, ciénaga.—**m. agate**, ágata musgosa.— **m.-covered**, **m.-grown**, musgoso.—**m. rose**, rosa musgosa. **II.** va. cubrir de musgo.

mossiness [mósines], s. abundancia de musgo.

mosstrooper [móstrúpœr], s. bandido, bandolero.

mossy [mósi], a. musgoso.

most [móust]. **I.** a. (superl. de MUCH, MANY) más (superl.); casi; lo más, los más, el mayor número (de); casi todo(s); la mayor parte de. —**for the m. part**, principalmente, generalmente; en su mayor parte. **II.** adv. más (superl.) sumamente, -ísimo (*most cruel*, muy cruel, cruelísimo).— M. Reverend, reverendísimo, ilustrísimo. **III.** s. lo principal, la mayor parte, el mayor número, lo más, el mayor valor.—**at (the) m.**, a lo más.

mostly [móustli], adv. en su mayor parte, casi todo(s), principalmente.

mote [móut], s. mota, átomo; punto; mecha; junta, asamblea.

mote [móut], v. (ant.) **so m. it be**, así sea, amén.

motet [motét], s. (mús.) motete.

moth [moz], s. (ent.) alevilla; polilla.—**m.-eaten**, apolillado.

mother [mʊ́dœr]. **I.** s. madre; madre, tía, mujer vieja; madre del vino, zurrapa.—**m. hubbard**, bata, ropón de mujer.—**m.-in-law**, suegra. —**m.-of-pearl**, nácar, madreperla.—**m. of thyme**, (bot.) serpol. **II.** a. madre; natural, nativo, natal, materno; vernáculo, nacional; metropolitano.—**m. church**, iglesia metropolitana.—**m. country**, madre patria; metrópoli.—**m. liquid**, m. liquor, (quím.) aguas madres.—M. Superior, superiora (de monjas, etc.).—**m. tongue**, lengua madre o vernácula.—**m. water** = M. LIQUOR.—**m. wit**, chispa, ingenio. **III.** va. servir de madre a. **IV.** vn. criar madre, como el vino.

motherhood [-jud], s. maternidad.

motherless [-les], a. huérfano de madre.

motherliness [-lines], s. maternidad, cariño o cuidado maternal.

motherly [-li]. **I.** a. maternal, materno. **II.** adv. maternalmente.

motherwort [-uœrt], s. (bot.) agripalma.

mothy [mózi], a. lleno de polilla.

motif [motíf], s. motivo, asunto, tema.

motil(e [motíl], a. movible.

motility [motíliti], s. movilidad.

motion [móshun]. **I.** s. movimiento; meneo, aire, ademán; signo, señal, seña; proposición o moción que se hace en una asamblea; (for.) pedimento.—**m. bar**, guía de la crucetа.—**m. picture**, cine; fotografía cinematográfica.—**m. work**, (reloj.) cuadratura (ruedas del movimiento de las manecillas). **II.** vn. hacer señas.

motionless [-les], a. inmóvil; yerto; estupefacto.

motive [móutiv]. **I.** a. motor, motriz.—**m. power**, fuerza motriz. **II.** s. motivo, razón; pie, tema, idea, asunto; (mús.) tema, motivo.

motivity [motíviti], s. potencia motriz.

motley [mótli]. **I.** *a.* abigarrado; mezclado, variado, diverso; vestido de colorines. **II.** *s.* traje abigarrado de payaso; payaso vestido de colorines; mezcla de colores.

motor [móutœr]. **I.** *s.* motor, el que o lo que mueve; (mec.) motor; (aut.) automóvil. **II.** *a.* motor, motriz; de motor, movido por motor (máquina).—**m. boat,** autobote, bote de gasolina. —**m. bus,** autoómnibus.—**m. car,** automóvil.— **m. cycle,** motocicleta.—**m.-driven,** movido por electromotor.—**m. generator,** (elec.) motogenerador.—**m. nerve,** nervio motor.—**m. oil,** aceite lubricante de motores (gen. de gasolina).—**m. truck,** autocamión. **III.** *vn.* pasear, viajar o ir en automóvil.

motordrome [-dróum], *s.* autódromo, pista para carreras de automóviles.

motorman [-mœn], *s.* motorista.

mottle [mótœl]. **I.** *va.* motear, abigarrar, jaspear. **II.** *s.* mancha, veta.

motto [móto], *s.* mote, lema, divisa.

moufflon [múflon], *s.* (zool.) musmón.

mo(u)ld [móuld]. **I.** *s.* tierra vegetal, suelo, mantillo; molde, matriz; modelo, patrón; (arq. y carp.) moldura; materia de que está hecha una cosa; moho, verdín; mancha de orín.—**m. shot,** balines o bolines. **II.** *va.* moldear, vaciar, amasar, formar; cubrir con mantillo; (mar.) galibar. **III.** *vn.* emmohecerse, florecerse.

mo(u)ldable [móuldabœl], *a.* capaz de ser moldeado o amoldado.

mo(u)ldboard [móuldbórd], *s.* vertedero del arado.

mo(u)lder [móuldœr], *s.* moldeador, vaciador; amoldador, plasmador.

mo(u)lder. I. *vn.* convertirse en polvo, desmoronarse, consumirse. **II.** *va.* convertir en polvo, consumir, desgastar.

mo(u)ldering [-ing], *s.* desmoronamiento.

mo(u)ldiness [móuldines], *s.* moho.

mo(u)lding [móulding]. **I.** *s.* (arq. y carp.) moldura, bocel, ataire, lengüeta; vaciado, vaciamiento. **II.** *a.* plasmante.—**m. plane,** bocelete, bocelón.

mo(u)ldy [móuldi], *a.* mohoso.

moulin [mulén], *s.* pozo casi vertical que forma el agua en un ventisquero.

mouline(t [mulín, múlinet], *s.* (esgr.) molinete; tamborilete, rodillo.

mo(u)lt [móult], *vn.* mudar la pluma, desplumar. —**mo(u)lting** [-ing], *s.* muda (de pluma).

mound [máund]. **I.** montón de tierra; montículo, morón; baluarte, defensa, terraplén; túmulo. —**m. builders,** constructores de túmulos (apl. a los aborígenes de los E. U. que dejaron muchos túmulos sepulcrales y terraplenes de defensa. Muchos escritores prefieren la expresión inglesa *mound builders*.) **II.** *va.* atrincherar, fortalecer.

mount [máunt]. **I.** *s.* monte, montaña; baluarte, terraplén; montadura; caballería; montura; apeadero; (mil.) monta, toque de clarín. **II.** *va.* cabalgar, montar; armar, montar (una máquina, etc.); subir, alzar, elevar; enaltecer; subir a, trepar por; proveer de caballos; poner a caballo; (joy.) montar o engastar; (teat.) exornar, poner en escena; preparar una cosa para usarla o exhibirla; (mec.) montar, aparejar; (arti.) montar, armar; (mar.) montar, llevar (cañones).—**to m. a cannon,** (arti.) montar un cañón.—**to m. guard,** (mil.) montar la guardia. **III.** *vn.* subir, ascender, elevarse; montar a caballo; subir, montar, ascender (una cuenta, etc.).

mountable [máuntabœl], *a.* que se puede montar o subir.

mountain [móuntœn]. **I.** *s.* monte, montaña. **II.** *a.* montés, montañés; de montaña.—**m. artillery,** artillería de montaña.—**m. ash,** (bot.) mostajo, serbal de cazadores.—**m. chain,** sierra, cadena de montañas.—**m. dew,** aguardiente de contrabando.—**m. lion,** puma.—**m. side,** falda o vertiente de una montaña.

mountebank [máuntebænc], *s.* saltimbanco o juglar.

mounting [máunting], *s.* subida, ascensión; engaste, montadura; armadura; marco; montaje. —**m. block,** cabalgadero, montador o montadero.

mourn [morn]. **I.** *va.* lamentar, llorar, sentir. **II.** *vn.* lamentarse, dolerse; plañir; vestir o llevar luto.—**to m. for,** llevar luto por; lamentar, llorar.

mourner [mórnœr], *s.* doliente; persona que lleva el duelo en un funeral; lloraduelos, plañidera.

mournful [mórnful], *a.* triste, plañidero; apesadumbrado; funesto, deplorable; fúnebre, luctuoso.—**mournfully** [-li], *adv.* tristemente.— **mournfulness** [-nes], *s.* pesar, tristeza, melancolía, aflicción, desconsuelo, duelo, sentimiento.

mourning [mórning]. **I.** *s.* luto; duelo; dolor, aflicción.—**in m.,** de luto. **II.** *a.* de luto, de duelo; fúnebre, luctuoso.—**m. band,** brazal de luto.— **m. bride, m. widow,** (bot.) escabiosa.—**m. dove,** tórtola gemidora de los E. U.

mouse [máus]. **I.** *s.* ratón; (mar.) barrilete.—**m. = colored,** pardusco, de color de rata.—**m.-ear,** (bot.) miosotis.—**m.-ear chickweed,** vellosillo o pelosilla. **II.** *va.* y *vn.* cazar o coger ratones; cazar a hurtadillas, acechar; desgarrar, hacer trizas; (mar.) amarrar, hacer barriletes.—**to m. a hook,** amarrar un gancho.

mouser [máusœr], *s.* gato o perro ratonero.

mousehole [máusjóul], *s.* agujero.

mousing [-ing]. **I.** *a.* ratonero, taimado. **II.** *s.* caza de ratones; (mar.) acto de amarrar un gancho.—**m. hook,** gancho amarrado.

mousetail [-téil], *s.* (bot.) miosuro, cola de ratón.

mousetrap [-træp], *s.* ratonera, trampa de ratones.

mousquetaire [muskétær], *s.* (mil.) mosquetero; guante de mosquetero.

mousseline [muselín], *s.* (tej.) muselina; vidrio de muselina.

moustache, = mustache.

mouth [máuz]. **I.** *s.* boca; embocadura o desembocadura de un río; labio, lengua, voz; mueca. **II.** *va.* pronunciar, proferir, vocear; mascar, comer; agarrar con la boca o en la boca; reprochar. **III.** *vn.* vociferar, hablar a gritos.

mouthed [máuzd], *a.* que tiene boca.

mouthful [máuzful], *s.* bocado; buchada; miaja, migaja, pizca.

mouthless [máuzles], *a.* desbocado, sin boca.

mouthpiece [máuzpis], *s.* boquilla, estrangul, bocal; el que lleva la voz o habla por otros, intérprete.

mov(e)able [múvabœl]. **I.** *a.* móvil, movible; movedizo, locomovible. **II.** *s. pl.* muebles, menaje, mobiliario, efectos.

movability [múvabíliti], **movableness** [múvabœlnes], *s.* movilidad.

movably [múvabli], *adv.* de un modo movible.

move [muv]. **I.** *s.* movimiento; paso; en varios juegos, suerte, jugada, turno.—**on the m.,** en movimiento; de viaje.—**to get a m. on,** (fam.) rebullirse, darse prisa. **II.** *va.* mover; remover; trasladar, mudar; poner en otro sitio; menear, sacudir; proponer, hacer una moción en una asamblea; conmover, enternecer; hacer mover el vientre.—**to m. to,** causar (cólera, compasión, lágrimas, etc.). a. (A veces se traduce mejor por *hacer o poner,* cambiando el giro; *to move to anger,* poner colérico, hacer enojar; *to move to tears,* hacer llorar). **III.** *vn.* moverse; mudarse (de casa); mudar de lugar o de postura; ir, andar, caminar, ponerse en marcha; obrar, entrar en acción; avanzar, progresar; exonerarse (el vientre); jugar, hacer una jugada.—**to m. away,** alejarse; irse; mudar de casa.—**to m. forward,** adelantarse, avanzar.—**to m. in,** entrar; entrar a habitar una casa.—**to m. off,** quitarse o apartarse de.—**to m. round,** dar vueltas, rodar.

movement [[múvmœnt], *s.* movimiento; (mil.) maniobra, evolución; paso, acto, acción, incidente; (mec.) movimiento; mecanismo; (mús.) movimiento, compás o tiempo; cámara, evacuación, deposición; (com.) circulación; actividad.

mover [múvœr], *s.* motor, movedor, móvil; autor de una moción.

movies [múviš], s. pl. (fam.) cine.

moving [múving]. **I.** s. movimiento; cambio de domicilio. **II.** a. patético, conmovedor; que mueve o traslada.—**m. picture,** fotografía cinematográfica (en pl., cine).—**m. platform,** plataforma movible de correa sin fin.—**m. side-walk,** acera de correa sin fin.—**m. staircase,** o **stairway** = ESCALATOR.—**m. van,** conductora.

movingly [múvingli], adv. patéticamente, conmovedoramente.

movy [múvi], s. (fam.) función de cine; película.

mow [mo]. **I.** va. (pp. MOWED y MOWN [moun]) segar, guadañar. **II.** vn. hacer muecas; burlarse de. **III.** s. mueca.

mow [máu]. **I.** s. granero, troj, henil. **II.** va. entrojar.

mowburn [máubœrn], vn. calentarse o fermentar el grano o heno.

mower [móœr], s. segador, dallador, guadañero; guadañadora, segadora mecánica.

mowing [móing], s. siega; gesto, mueca.—**m. machine,** guadañadora o segadora mecánica.

mown [móun], pp. irr. de MOW.

moxa [móxa], s. (bot. y cir.) moxa.

Mozarab [mošáræb], s. mozárabe.

mozetta [motséta], s. (igl.) muceta.

mucedinous [miusédinus], s. mohoso.

much [mʊch]. **I.** a. mucho.—**m. ado about nothing,** nada entre dos platos; más es el ruido que las nueces. **II.** adv. mucho; casi; (antes de pp.) muy.—**m. of a muchness,** (fam.) poco más o menos lo mismo, casi igual.—**m. the same,** casi lo mismo; poco más o menos lo mismo.—**to be m. of a** (seguido de sustantivo), ser muy, ser todo un (he is much of a gentleman, es todo un caballero; she is much of a woman, ella es muy mujer).—**this m. more,** esto más, tanto así más. **III.** s. mucho.

muchness [múchnes], s. (fam.) cantidad, demasía.

mucilage [miúsilej], s. mucílago.

mucilaginous [-léyinus], a. mucilaginoso.

mucilaginousness [-nes], s. calidad de mucilaginoso.

mucin [miúsin], s. moco, mucosidad.

muciferous, muciparous [miusífœrus, párus], a. mucilaginoso, mucoso.

muck [mʊc]. **I.** s. abono, estiércol, fiemo; porquería, basura; (despec.) dinero.—**m. bar,** hierro de primera laminación.—**m. fork,** horquilla para estiércol.—**m. hill,** o **pit,** estercolero.—**m. rake,** rastrillo para estiércol.—**m. rolls,** primeros rodillos de laminar. **II.** va. estercolar, abonar.

muckiness [múkines], s. suciedad, inmundicia.

muckrake [mʊ́crréic], vn. (pol.) andar escarbando para sacar trapos sucios al sol; sacar trapos sucios al sol o a relucir. —**muckraker** [-œr], s. (pol.) escarbador de vidas ajenas, averiguador y expositor de ruindades.

mucky [mʊki], a. puerco, sucio, asqueroso.

mucoid [miúcoid], a. mucoso.

mucopurulent [miúcopiúrulœnt], a. mucopurulento.

mucor [miúcor], s. moco, mucosidad; moho; (bot.) variedad de hongo.

mucous [miúcus], a. mucoso.—**m. membrane,** membrana mucosa.—**m. râle,** estertor.

mucousness [miúcunes], s. mucosidad, viscosidad, moco.

mucro [miúcro], s. punta.

mucronate(d [miúcronet(ed], a. puntiagudo, mucronato.

mucus [miúcus], s. moco, mucosidad.

mud [mʊd]. **I.** s. fango, cieno, lodo, barro.—**m. baffle,** colector de lodo.—**m. bath,** baño de cieno.—**m. dauber,** (ent.) pelopeo, matador de arañas.—**m. gun,** cernedor de lodo o arcilla.—**m. lighter,** gánguil, lancha de draga.—**m. scow,** pontón, gánguil.--**m. sucker,** (orn.) somormujo. —**m. volcano,** cono volcánico que arroja cieno, (Méx.) hornito.—**m. wall,** tapia, bardal.—**m. walled,** tapiado. **II.** va. enlodar, embarrar; enturbiar, ensuciar.

muddily [múdili], adv. turbiamente.

muddiness [-nes], s. turbieza, suciedad; turbulencia.

muddle [múdœl]. **I.** va. enturbiar; embriagar; atontar; confundir, revolver. **II.** vn. estar atontado; estar peneque. **III.** s. chabacanería; (fam.) embrollo, confusión.—**m.-headed,** estúpido, atontado.

muddy [múdi]. **I.** a. barroso, lodoso, fangoso; sucio, turbio; tonto, estúpido, confuso. **II.** va. enturbiar, ensuciar; entontecer, turbar.

mudsill [múdsil], s. madero colocado en el suelo como cimiento; (E. U.) persona de baja condición social.

mudwort [múdwœrt], s. (bot.) limosela.

muezzin [miuéšin], s. muecín, almuédano.

muff [mʊf]. **I.** s. manguito; estufilla; chabacanería, torpeza; en baseball, falta o falla; torpe, zurdo. **II.** va. hacer algo poco diestramente; en baseball, dejar escapar la pelota.

muffin [mʊ́fin], s. mollete, panecillo, mojicón; platito de barro.

muffle [mʊ́fœl]. **I.** s. (quím.) mufla; horno de esmaltar, horno de arcilla, horno de copela; hocico, morro; funda; guante de púgil.—**m. furnace,** mufla. **II.** va. embozar, arrebozar, encapotar; envolver, encubrir, apagar un sonido. —**to m. a drum,** enfundar o destemplar un tambor.

muffled [mʊ́fœld], a. pagado, sordo.—**m. drum,** tambor destemplado, tambor fúnebre.—**m. noise,** ruido sordo.—**m. oars,** remos silenciosos (cubiertos de trapos para ensordecer su ruido).

muffler [mʊ́fœr], s. bufanda, tapaboca.

mufti [mʊ́fti], s. mufti.

mug [mʊg], s. cubilete, pichel; (vulg.) cara, boca; mueca.

muggy [múgui], **muggish** [múguišh], a. húmedo, caluroso y sofocante (el tiempo); húmedo y mohoso (el heno).

mugginess [múguines], s. calor húmedo.

mugwort [múguœrt], s. (bot.) artemisa.

mugwump [múguʊmp], s. (pol. E. U.) secuaz de un partido que se reserva el derecho de votar con entera independencia.

mulatto [miuláto], s. mulato.

mulberry [múlberi], s. (bot.) mora.—**m. tree,** morera o moral.

mulch [mʊlch]. **I.** va. cubrir (las plantas, etc.) con paja y estiércol. **II.** s. estiércol y paja con que se protegen las plantas.

mulct [mʊlct]. **I.** s. multa. **II.** va. multar.

mule [miúl], s. mulo, mula; (bot.) planta híbrida; (tej.) = M. JENNY.—**m. boy, m. driver,** = MULE-TEER.—**m. chair,** jamuga.—**m. jenny,** hiladora mecánica intermitente (en varias partes llám. selfactina).—**m.-spun yarn, m. yarn,** hilo de hiladora intermitente o de selfactina.

muleteer [miuletœr], s. muletero, arriero.

muliebrity [miuliébriti], s. calidad o estado de mujer.

mulier [miúliœr], s. (for.) mujer casada, esposa.

mulish [miúlišh], a. obstinado o terco como una mula; híbrido, mula.

mull [mʊl]. **I.** s. (Ingl.) confusión, enredo, desorden; muselina clara; (Esco.) cabo, promontorio. **II.** va. calentar vino con especias; moler, triturar; confundir, aturrullar. **III.** vn. afanarse mucho sin resultado.

mulle(i)n [múlen], s. (bot.) verbasco, candelaria.

muller [mʊ́lœr], s. moleta; pulverizador.

mullet [mʊ́let], s. (ict.) múgil, mújol; cabezudo.

mulligatawny [mʊ́ligatóni], s. sopa de arroz y carne sazonada con curry.

mullion [mʊ́liun], s. (arq.) columna que divide el vano de una ventana; montante. **II.** va. dividir (una ventana) mediante una columna.

mulse [mʊls], s. clarea, vino mulso.

multicapsular [mʊlticápsular], a. (bot.) de muchas cápsulas o celdillas.

multidentate [-déntet], a. multidentado.

multifarious [-fériʊs], a. vario, multiplicado.—**multifariously** [-li], adv. diversamente.—**multifariousness** [-nes], s. diversidad; variedad, desemejanza.

multifid(ous [-fid, mʊltífidʊs], *a.* dividido en muchas partes, lóbulos o porciones.

multiflorous [-flórʊs], *a.* multifloro.

multiform [-form], *a.* multiforme.

multigraph [-grǽf]. **I.** *s.* multígrafo (nombre de fábrica), aparato rotatorio que arregla tipo y lo imprime. **II.** *va.* multigrafiar, imprimir con multígrafo.

multiloquent [mʊltílocuent], *a.* parlero, hablador, locuaz.

multimillionaire [mʊltimíllœnéær], *s.* multimillonario.

multinominal [mʊltinóminal], *a.* que tiene muchos nombres; (mat.) multinomio.

multipara [mʊltípara], *f.* (med.) mujer polípara.

multiparous [mʊltíparʊs], *a.* multípara.

multipartite [mʊltipártait], *a.* que consta de muchas partes.

multiped [-ped]. **I.** *a.* multípedo. **II.** *s.* ciempiés, escolopendra.

multiphase [-feis̆], *a.* (elec.) polifásico.

multiplane [-plein], (aer.) poliplano.

multiple [mʊltipœl]. **I.** *s.* múltiplo.—**in m.,** (elec.) en paralelo, en derivación. **II.** *a.* múltiple.—**m. circuit, connection, o series,** (elec.) circuito, o conexión, compuesto o en serie múltipe.—**m.-contact coherer,** (rad.) cohesor de contactos múltiples.—**m. trnasformer,** transformador en paralelo; transformador de varios primarios o secundarios.—**m.-way switch,** (elec.) interruptor de varias direcciones.—**m.-unit system,** (elec.) sistema multifilar; (f. c. eléc.) sistema de tracción de unidades múltiples, sistema de varios carros motores gobernados por un combinador común.—**m.-wire system,** (elec.) sistema multifilar.

multiplex [mʊltiplex], *a.* mʊltíplice; (tlg.) múltiplex.

multipliable [mʊltipláiabœl], **multiplicable** [mʊltiplicabœl], *a.* multiplicable.

multipliableness [-nes], *s.* calidad de multiplicable.

multiplicand [mʊltiplicǽnd], *s.* multiplicando.

multiplicate [mʊltiplikeit], *a.* multiplicado; (bot.) replegado.

multiplication [-éis̆hʊn], *s.* multiplicación.—**m. table,** tabla de multiplicar.

multiplicative [-etiv], *a.* multiplicador, multiplicativo.

multiplicity [-plísiti], *s.* multiplicidad, sinnúmero.

multiplier [-plaiœr], *s.* multiplicador; (elec.) multiplicador; máquina de multiplicar.

multiply [mʊltiplai], *va.* y *vn.* multiplicar(se).

multiplying [-ing], *a.* multiplicador; de multiplicación; reproductor.—**m. gear,** engranaje multiplicador.—**m. glass,** espejo de varias facetas que multiplica el número de las imágenes.—**m. lens,** (fot.) lente multiplicadora.

multipolar [mʊltipólar], *a.* multipolar.

multipresence [mʊltiprésens], *s.* ubicuidad.

multitubular [-tiúbiulær], *a.* multitubular.—**m. boiler,** caldera de tubos de humos.

multitude [mʊltitiud], *s.* multitud.

multitudinous [mʊltitiúdinʊs], *a.* numeroso.

multiturn coil [mʊltitœrn cóil], (rad.) bobina receptora de arrollamiento múltiple empleada en lugar de antena.

multivalent [mʊltivéilœnt], *a.* (quím.) polivalente.

multivalve [-vælv]. **I.** *a.* polivalvo. **II.** *s.* polivalva.

multocular [mʊltókiular], *a.* que tiene muchos ojos.

multure [mʊlchur], *s.* maquila; molienda.

mum [mʊm]. **I.** *interj.* ¡chito! ¡chitón! ¡silencio! **II.** *s.* cerveza fuerte y dulce. **III.** *a.* callado, silencioso. **IV.** *va.* y *vn.* enmascarar(se); disfrazar(se); guardar silencio.

mumble [mʊmbœl], *va.* y *vn.* gruñir, murmurar, refunfuñar; mascar, mascujar.

mumbler [mʊmblœr], *s.* farfulla, gruñidor.

mumbo jumbo, [mʊmbo yʊmbo], *s.* espantajo; fetiche.

mummer [mʊmœr], *s.* máscara.

mummery [mʊmœri], **mumming** [mʊming], *s.* momería, mojiganga, disfraz.

mummification [-ifikés̆hʊn], *s.* momificación.

mummify [mʊmifai], *va.* momificar.

mummy [mʊmi], *s.* momia; cera de injertos.

mump [mʊmp], *va.* mordiscar, morder o mascar; farfullar; mendigar; estafar.

mumper [mʊmpœr], *s.* mendigo.

mumpish [mʊmpis̆h], *a.* arisco, intratable, malhumorado.

mumps [mʊmps], *s.* (med.) paperas, parótidas.

munch [mʊnch], *va.* mascullar, mascar.

mundane [mʊndein], *a.* mundano.

mungo [mʊngo], *s.* garbanzo.

mungoose, *s.* = MONGOOSE.

municipal [miunísipal], *a.* municipal.—**m. government,** gobierno municipal; municipalidad.

municipality [-pǽliti], *s.* municipio; municipalidad.

municipalize [-pælais̆], *va.* transferir a la municipalidad; convertir en propiedad municipal.

munificence [miunífisens], *s.* munificencia.—**munificent** [-sent], *a.* munífico, generoso, liberal.—**munificently** [-li], *adv.* munificamente.

muniment [miúnimœnt], *s.* fortaleza; apoyo, defensa; cualquier documento u objeto valioso y cuidadosamente guardado.

munition [miunís̆hʊn], *s.* (mil.) municiones, pertrechos; equipo.—**m. bread,** pan de munición.—**m. ship,** navío almacén.

munjeet [mʊnyít], *s.* (tint.) rubia.

mural [miúral], *a.* mural; adosado a una pared; escarpado, vertical.—**m. circle,** (astr.) círculo mural.—**m. crown,** corona mural.—**m. tablet,** tablilla fijada en una pared.

murc [mœrc], *s.* orujo, hollejo.

murder [mœrdœr]. **I.** *s.* asesinato.—**m. in the first degree,** homicidio premeditado.—**m. in the second degree,** homicidio impremeditado. **II.** *va.* asesinar.

murderer [-œr], *s.* asesino.—**murderess** [-es], *s.* asesina.—**murderous** [-ʊs], *a.* asesino; sanguinario, cruel; desastroso, fatal.—**murderously** [-li], *adv.* sanguinariamente; desastrosamente; asesinamente.—**murderousness** [-nes], *s.* instinto o intento homicida.

murex [miúrex], *s.* (zool.) múrice.

murexide [muréxid], *s.* murexida.

muriate [miúriet], *s.* (quím.) muriato.

muriatic [miuriǽtic], *a.* muriático.

muricate(d [miúriket(ed], *a.* espinoso.

muricid [miúrisid], *s.* (zool.) múrice.

Muricidæ [miurísidi], *s. pl.* (zool.) murícidos.

Muridæ [miúridi], *s. pl.* (zool.) múridos.

murine [miúrin], *s.* y *a.* (zool.) múrido.

murk(y [mœrk(i], *a.* obscuro, lóbrego.

murmur [mœrmœr]. **I.** *s.* murmullo, susurro; murmuración, queja. **II.** *vn.* murmurar, susurrar; refunfuñar; (con *at* o *against*) gruñir, quejarse de.—**murmurer** [-œr], *s.* gruñidor, murmurador.—**murmuring** [-ing]. **I.** *s.* murmullo; murmuración, queja. **II.** *a.* murmurante, susurrante.—**murmuringly** [-li], *adv.* con murmurio; quejumbrosamente.

muræna [miurí- o réna], *s.* (ict.) morena.

murrain [mœrein], *s.* (vet.) morriña.

murrine [mœrin], *a.* múrrino.

murr(e [mœr], *s.* (orn.) uria. *V.* AUK.

murrey [múre], *a.* morado, castaño.

musa [miús̆a], *s.* (bot.) plátano.

Musaceæ [miuséisii o miusásee], *s. pl.* (bot.) musáceas.—**musaceous** [-séis̆hʊs], *a.* musáceo.

muscadine [mʊscadin], *s.* variedad de vid.

muscardine [mʊscardin], *s.* parásito que ataca a los gusanos de seda.

muscat(el [mʊscat(el], *s.* (bot.) moscatel.

Muscidæ [mʊsidi], *s. pl.* (zool.) múscidos.—**muscid** [-sid], *a.* múscido.

muscle [mʊsœl], *s.* (anat.) músculo; fuerza muscular; (zool.) MUSSEL.

Para la pronunciación de æ, œ, ᴅ, s̆, s̆h, ʊ, ȳ, ʏ, z, véase la clave al principio del libro.

muscoid [múscoid]. **I.** *a.* musgoso. **II.** *s.* planta musgosa.

muscosity [muscósiti], *s.* abundancia de musgo.

muscovado [muscovéido *o* vádo], *s.* azúcar mascabado.

Muscovite [múscovait], *s.* y *a.* moscovita.

muscovy [múscovi], *s.* ánade americano.

muscular [múskiular], *a.* muscular; musculoso, vigoroso, fornido.

muscularity [múskiuléeriti], *s.* calidad de muscular *o* musculoso.

musculation [múskiuléishun], **musculature** [-læchúær]. *s.* musculatura.

Muse [miúś]. **I.** *s.* musa; **(m-)** meditación. **II. (m-)** *vn.* meditar.—**to m.** on, over, *o* upon, meditar en.

museful [miúśful], *a.* cogitabundo, pensativo.

muset [miúśet], *s.* senda de conejos.

museum [miuśíum], *s.* museo; gabinete.

mush [muśh], *s.* (E. U.) gachas, puches; mineral de hierro de primera calidad.

mushroom [múśhrum]. **I.** *s.* (bot.) seta, hongo. **II.** *a.* hecho con hongos o setas; efímero, advenedizo.

mushy [múśhi], *a.* mollar, pulposo.

music [miúśic], *s.* música; composición musical; solfa; (ent.) estridor.—**m. book**, libro de música. —**m. box**, o **musical box**, caja de música.—**m. cabinet**, musiquero.—**m. hall**, salón de conciertos.—**m. of the spheres**, armonía de las esferas celestes.—**m. paper**, papel de pauta.—**m. rack**, atril.—**m. stand**, atril; tablado para una orquesta.—**m. stool**, taburete o banqueta de piano.

musical [miúśical], *a.* musical, músico; melodioso, canoro.—**m. director**, director de música.

musicale [miuśicál], *s.* velada musical, concierto casero.

musically [miúśicali], *adv.* musicalmente, sonoramente.

musicalness [miúśicalnes], *s.* armonía, melodía.

musician [miuśíśhan], *s.* músico.

musing [miúśing]. **I.** *a.* contemplativo, pensativo. **II.** *s.* cogitación, meditación.

musk [musk]. **I.** *s.* almizcle; olor o perfume de almizcle; (zool.) almizclero.—**m. apple**, camuesa o manzana almizcleña.—**m. cat** = civet.—**m. cherry**, cereza almizcleña.—**m. deer**, almizclero. —**m. grape**, moscatel.—**m. melon**, melón.—**m. ox**, carnero almizcleño.— **m. pear**, mosqueruela. —**m. rose**, rosa almizcleña.—**m. seed**, grano de ambarilla.—**m. thistle**, (bot.) cardo nutante. **II.** *va.* almizclar, perfumar con almizcle.

muskalonge, *s.* = maskinonge.

musked [musct], *a.* almizclado.

musket [músket], *s.* mosquete, fusil; (orn.) gavilán macho.—**m. shot**, fusilazo.

musketeer [músketíær], *s.* mosquetero.

musketoon [músketún], *s.* (arti.) tercerola.

musketry [músketri], *s.* fusilería.

muskiness [múskines], *s.* olor de almizcle.

muskmelon [múscmélon], *s.* (bot.) melón.

muskrat [múskrrat], *s.* rata almizclera.

musky [múski], *a.* almizclero, almizclado.

Muslim, *s.* = moslem.

muslin [múślin]. **I.** *s.* (tej.) muselina; percal, camiquí; tarlatana; (enc.) percalina. **II.** *a.* de muselina; de percal.

musquash [múscueśh], *s.* (zool.) almizclera.

musqueteer, *s.* = musketeer.

musquito [muskíto], *s.* mosquito.

muss [mus]. **I.** *s.* (fam.) desorden, confusión; arrebatiña, riña. **II.** *va.* (fam.) desordenar, desarreglar, arrugar; ensuciar.

mussel [múscel], *s.* mejillón, mítulo.

Mussulman [músulmæn], *s.* musulmán.

must [must], *v. def.* cuyas formas equivalen a las de deber, tener que, haber de, deber de (*I must write*, debo escribir, tengo que escribir; *it must be late*, debe de ser tarde). A veces se subentiende el infinitivo que le sigue [*you must*, Vd. debe (hacerlo, escribir, hablar, etc.); *I must (go) to the city*, debo partir para la ciudad).—**m. needs**, debe

(debo, etc.) necesariamente o sin falta.—**it m. not be**, eso no puede ser, eso no debe permitirse.

must [must]. **I.** *s.* mosto, zumo de la uva; pulpa de patatas preparada para la fermentación; moho. **II.** *va.* enmohecer. **III.** *vn.* enmohecerse.

mustache [mustáśh], **mustachio** [mustáchio], *s.* bigote, mostacho; especie de mono; soldado.

mustang [mústæng], *s.* potro mesteño.

mustard [mústærd], *s.* mostaza.—**m. gas**, iperita, líquido para granadas de gas; gas mostaza, gas de iperita.—**m. paper**, **m. plaster**, sinapismo. —**m. pot**, mostacera.

musteline, *o* **musteloid** [mústelain, -teloid], *s.* mustelino.

muster [mústœr]. **I.** *va.* (mil.) juntar para pasar revista, pasar lista, etc.—**to m. in**, *o* **into**, **service**, (mil.) alistar.—**to m. out (of service)** dar de baja.—**to m. up**, tomar (valor, fuerza, resignación, etc.). **II.** *vn.* (mil.) juntarse; pasar lista. **III.** *s.* (mil.) revista, muestra; rol, lista, reseña; alarde, muestra.—**m. book**, rol, lista.— **m. master**, comisario de revistas.—**m. roll**, matrícula de revista; (mil.) muestra; (mar.) rol de la tripulación.

mustily [mústili], *adv.* con moho.

mustiness [mústines], *s.* husmo; moho.

musty [músti], *a.* mohoso; añejo; rancio; pasado; mustio, triste.

mutability [miútabíliti], *s.* mutabilidad.

mutable [-bœl], *a.* mudable.—**mutableness** [-nes], *s.* mutabilidad.—**mutably** [-bli], *adv.* mudablemente.

mutate [miúteit], *va.* y *vn.* transformar(se); (biol.) variar bruscamente.

mutation [-éiśhun], *s.* mudanza, alteración; mutación, variación; (biol.) variación brusca.

mute [miút]. **I.** *a.* mudo; (gram.) mudo. **II.** *s.* mudo; (gram.) letra muda; (mús.) sordina.

mutely [miútli], *adv.* mudamente.

mutilate [miútileit], *va.* mutilar.—**mutilation** [-éiśhun], *s.* mutilación.—**mutilator** [-éitœr], *s.* mutilador.

mutineer [miútiníœr], *s.* amotinador, amotinado, sedicioso.

mutinous [-us], *a.* amotinado, sedicioso, turbulento, faccioso.—**mutinously** [-li], *adv.* amotinadamente, sediciosamente.—**mutinousness** [-nes], *s.* carácter sedicioso.

mutiny [miútini]. **I.** *vn.* amotinarse, rebelarse. **II.** *s.* motín, insubordinación.

mutism [miútiśm], *s.* mudez.

mutoscope [miútoscoup], *s.* mutoscopio, rueda cinematográfica.

mutt [mut], *s.* (fam.) tonto, mentecato; perro atravesado o mestizo.

mutter [mútœr]. **I.** *va.* y *vn.* refunfuñar, gruñir; hablar o decir entre dientes. **II.** *s.* refunfuñadura, gruñido.—**mutterer** [-œr], *s.* rezongador, gruñón.

mutton [mútun], *s.* carne de carnero.—**m. broth**, caldo de carnero.—**m. chop**, costilla de carnero, chuleta.—**m. fish**, (ict.) barbero, antia.— **m. fist**, manaza, mano grande y colorada.

mutual [miúchual, tiual], *a.* mutuo.—**m. insurance**, seguro mutuo.

mutuality [miúchuéliti], *s.* mutualidad.

mutually [miúchuali], *adv.* mutuamente.

mutualness [-nes], *s.* mutualidad.

mutuary [miúchu- *o* miútiuæri], *s.* (for.) mutuatario.

mutule [miútiul], *s.* (arq.) modillón.

mutuum [miúchuum *o* tuum], *s.* (for.) mútuo.

muzzle [múśœl]. **I.** *s.* morro, hocico, jeta; bozal, mordaza, frenillo, esportilla; boca de arma de fuego.—**m. bag**, **cap**, *o* **cover**, tapaboca o sombrerete de cañón.—**m. energy**, energía inicial. —**m.-loader**, arma de antecarga.—**m.-loading**, de antecarga.—**m. ring**, anillo de la boca de un cañón.—**m. velocity**, velocidad inicial o de salida. **II.** *va.* embozar, abozalar, poner bozal; amordazar, imponer silencio. **III.** *vn.* acercar el hocico para husmear o ventear.

muzzy [múśi], *a.* (fam.) borracho, peneque.

my [mái], *a. posses.* mi, mis.—**oh, my!** (fam.)
¡Ave María! ¡cáspita!

myasthenia [máiæzíniæ], *s.* miastenia, astenia
muscular, debilidad muscular.

mycelium [misílium], *s.* (bot.) micelión.

mycology [micóloyi], *s.* (bot.) micetología, mi-
cología.

mydriasis [midráiasis], *s.* (med.) midríasis.

myelitis [maieli- o láitis], *s.* (med.) mielitis.

mynheer [minjíær], *s.* señor, título de cortesía en
Holanda; holandés.

myocarditis [máiocardáitis], *s.* miocarditis.

myocardium [mái-, o míocárdium], *s.* (anat.)
miocardio.

myograph [máiogræf], *s.* miógrafo.

myography [maiógrafi], **myology** [malóloyi], *s.*
(anat.) miografía o miología.

myopathy [-pazi], *s.* enfermedad de los músculos.

myope, myops [máiop, s], *s.* miope.

myopia [maiópia], **myopy** [máiopi], *s.* miopía.

myopic [maiópic], *a.* miope, corto de vista.

myoscope [máioscoup], *s.* = MYOGRAPH.

myosin [máiosin], *s.* (quím.) miosina.

myosis [mái- o miósis], *s.* (med.) miosis.

myosotis [maiosótis], *s.* (bot.) miosotis o mio-
sótide; nomeolvides.

myriad [míriad], *s.* diez mil; millares, un gran
número.

myriagram [míriagræm], *s.* miriagramo.

myrialiter [-lítœr], *s.* mirialitro.

myriameter [-mítœr], *s.* miriámetro.

myriapod [-pod], *s.* miriápodo o miriópodo.

myrmidon [mœrmidon], *s.* esbirro, rufián.

myrobalan [miróbalan], *s.* (bot.) mirobalanos.

myrrh [mœr], *s.* mirra, goma resinosa.

myrrhic [mœric], *a.* mirrado, mirrino.

myrrhin [mœrin], *s.* mirrina.

Myrtaceæ [mœrtéisei o tásei], *s. pl.* (bot.) mir-
táceas.—**myrtaceous** [-šhus], *a.* mirtáceo.

myrtiform [mœrtiform], *a.* mirtino.

myrtle [mœrtœl], *s.* (bot.) mirto, arrayán.—**m.
berry,** murtón, baya del mirto.—**m. wax,** cera del
arrayán.

Myrtus [mœrtus], *s.* (bot.) murtilla.

myself [maiself], *pron.* yo mismo; me, a mí, mí
mismo (*I said to myself,* me dije a mí mismo:
I myself did it, yo mismo lo hice).

mystagogue [místægog], *s.* mistagogo.

mysterious [místírius], *a.* misterioso.—**mysteriously** [-li], *adv.* misteriosamente.—**mysterious-
ness** [-nes], *s.* misterio, calidad de misterioso.

mystery [místœri], *s.* misterio; (teat.) auto sacramental.

mystic(al [místic(al], *a.* místico.—**mystically**
[-l], *adv.* místicamente.—**mysticalness** [-nes], *s.*
calidad de místico.

mysticism [místisiŝm], *s.* misticismo.

mystification [-fikéišhun], *s.* ofuscación, confusión, perplejidad; superchería.—**mystify** [-fai], *va.*
confundir, desconcertar, ofuscar.

myth [miz], *s.* mito, fábula.

mythical [mízical], *a.* mítico; fabuloso.

mythologic(al [mízolóyic(al], *a.* mitológico.

mythologically [-i], *adv.* mitológicamente.

mythologist [mizóloyist], *s.* mitólogo, mitoló-
gista.—**mythologize** [-yaiŝ], I. *va.* convertir en
mito; interpretar mitológicamente. II. *vn.* explicar las fábulas mitológicas.

mythology [-yi], *s.* mitología.

mythopeic [máizopíic], *a.* creador de mitos; de la
edad de los mitos.

myxomycetes [mícsomaisítiŝ], *s. pl.* (bot.) mixo-
micetos.

N

n [en], *s. n.*

nab [næb], *va.* (fam.) prender, atrapar.

nabob [néibob], *s.* nabab; ricacho.

nacelle [naséll], *s.* (aer.) barquilla; casilla.

nacre [néikœr], *s.* nácar, madreperla.

nacreous [néicrius], *a.* nacarado; nacarino.

nadir [néidœr], *s.* (astr.) nadir.

nævose [ní- o névos], *a.* manchado, pecoso.

nævus [ní- o névus], *s.* lunar.

nag [næg]. I. *s.* haca, jaco. II. *va.* y *vn.* (a veces
con *at*) regañar, machacar, encocorar, sermonear.

Naiad [néyad], *s.* (mitol.) náyade.

naif [naíf], *a.* cándido, sencillo; (joy.) lustroso
en bruto; naife.

nail [néil]. I. *s.* uña; pezuña, garra; clavo; tachón, punta; roblón; medida de 2¼ pulgadas.
—**n. cleaner,** limpiauñas.—**n. extractor,** menestrete, arrancaclavos, desclavador.—**n. file,**
lima para las uñas.—**n. plate,** metal en plancha
para clavos.—**n. puller** =N. EXTRACTOR.—**n.
scratch,** uñada, arañazo.—**on the n.,** luego, al
instante, en el acto. II. *va.* clavar, enclavar,
guarnecer o adornar con clavos.—**to n. a lie,**
demostrar que una cosa es mentira.—**to n. down,**
o **nail up,** sujetar con clavos; condenar (una ventana, etc.), clavándola.

nailbrush [-bruŝh], *s.* cepillo para las uñas.

nailer [néilœr], *s.* fabricante de clavos.

nailery [néilœri], *s.* fábrica de clavos.

nainsook [nénsuk], *s.* (tej.) nansú.

naissant [nésant], *a.* (blas.) naciente.

naive [naív], *a.* ingenuo, cándido.—**naively** [-li]
adv. cándidamente, candorosamente.

naiveté [naivté], *s.* candidez, ingenuidad.

naked [néiked], *a.* desnudo; descamisado, indigente; descubierto, sin defensa.—**n. eye,** simple
vista.—**n. sword,** espada desnuda, desenvainada.
—**the n. truth,** la verdad pura o desnuda.

nakedly [-li], *adv.* desnudamente; claramente.—
nakedness [-nes], *s.* desnudez; partes pudendas.

nam(e)able [néimabœl], *a.* que puede recibir
nombre, nombrable.

namby-pamby [næmbi-pémbi]. I. *a.* melindroso, afectado. II. *s.* pamplina, melindre.

name [nem]. I. *s.* nombre; título; nombradía,
fama; reputación, crédito; autoridad, poder,
representación.—**n. day,** día del santo, días de
uno, fiesta onomástica.—**n. plate,** plancha con el
nombre de uno.—**n. saint,** santo de uno.—**n. son,**
tocayo.—**by the n. of,** llamado, nombrado.—**in
n.,** de nombre.—**in the n. of,** en nombre de.—
of the n. of =BY THE N. OF. II. *va.* nombrar,
apellidar, llamar, poner nombre; mentar, mencionar; proferir; especificar, elegir, señalar, designar, fijar.

nameless [néimles], *a.* innominado, anónimo; desconocido.

namely [néimli], *adv.* señaladamente, especialmente; saber.

namesake [néimseik], *s.* tocayo; homónimo.

nanism [néiniŝm], *s.* enanismo, calidad de enano.

nankeen, nankin [nænkín], *s.* (tej.) mahón, nan-
quín.

naos [néios], *s.* (arq.) nave.

nap [næp]. I. *s.* siesta; vello de las plantas,
lanilla, pelusa. II. *va.* (tej.) perchar, carmenar, sacar pelo. III. *vn.* dormitar, echar
una siesta; estar desprevenido, dormirse (fig.).

nape [néip], *s.* nuca, cogote; testuz.

Naperian [neipíriæn], *a.* neperiano.

napery [népœri], *s.* ropa blanca, artículo de
lienzo; mantelería.

naphtha [næfza], *s.* nafta.

naphthalene [næfzalin], *s.* (quím.) naftalina.

naphthol [næfzol], *s.* (quím.) naftol.

Napier [néipiœr], *nombre propio,* Néper.—**N.
analogies,** (mat.) analogías de Néper.—**N.'s
bones,** varillas de Néper (un artefacto de cálculo).
—**Napierian,** *a.* =NAPERIAN.

napiform [néipiform], *a.* de forma de nabo.

napkin [næpkin], *s.* servilleta; toalleta.—**n.
ring,** servilletero.

napless [næples], *a.* raído.

napoleon [napólion], *s.* napoleón (moneda);
juego de naipes; pastelito de hojaldre y crema.

napped [næpt], **nappy** [næpi], *a.* peludo, velloso.

napper [népœr], *s.* (tej.) perchador.

nappiness [nǽpines], s. vellosidad.
nappoo [næpú]. **I.** a. muerto; ido; suficiente. **II.** vn. (fam.) morirse.
nappy [nǽpi], a. soñoliento; encabezado, fuerte (vino).
narcein(e [nársein], s. (quím.) narceína.
narcisism [nársisism], **narcism** [nársism], s. narcisismo, admiración o enamoramiento de sí mismo.
narcissus [narsísus], s. (bot.) narciso.
narcosis [narcósis], s. (med.) narcotismo.
narcotic [narcótic], s. y a. narcótico.
narcotin(e [nárcotin], s. narcotina.—**narcotism** [-ism], s. narcotismo.—**narcotize** [-ais], va. narcotizar.—**narcotization** [-iseishun], s. narcotismo; narcotización.
nard [nard], s. (bot.) nardo.
nardin(e [nárdin], s. nardino.
narghile [nárguile], s. narguile.
nares [néris], s. pl. de NARIS [néris, náris], s. orificio o ventana de la nariz.
narrate [nærréit]. **I.** va. y vn. narrar.—**narration** [-éishun], s. narración.—**narrative** [nærrætiv]. **I.** a. narrativo. **II.** s. narración.—**narratively** [-li], adv. narrativamente.—**narrator** [nærréitœr], s. narrador.—**narratory** [nærrætori], a. narrativo.
narrow [nǽro]. **I.** a. angosto, estrecho; escaso, limitado; apretado, encogido; tacaño, mezquino; de ideas poco liberales; próximo, cercano, aproximado; atento, escrupuloso.—**n. circumstances**, escasez pecuniaria, cortos posibles.—**n. escape**, escapada en una tabla.—**n. gauge**, (f. c.) vía angosta.—**n.-gauge railway**, ferrocarril de vía angosta.—**n.-minded**, apocado, mezquino; intolerante, fanático.—**n. sea**, estrecho de mar.—**n.-spirited**, o **n.-souled** =N.-MINDED. **II.** s. pl. bocal, pasaje angosto; desfiladero. **III.** va. estrechar, angostar, contraer, encoger, disminuir; limitar. **IV.** vn. estrecharse, encogerse, reducirse; reducir el número de puntos al hacer calceta; (equit.) andar con las patas muy juntas. —**to n. down to**, reducirse a.
narrowly [nǽroli], adv. estrechamente, angostamente, reducidamente; por poco, escasamente; mezquinamente.
narrowness [nǽrones], s. angostura, estrechura, apretura; estrechez, pobreza; mojigatería.
narwhal [nárjual], s. (ict.) narval.
nasal [nésal o násal]. **I.** a. nasal. **II.** s. letra nasal; hueso de la nariz; (arm.) barra que protege la nariz.
nasality [nasáliti], s. sonido nasal; nasalidad.
nasalize [nésalais], va. ganguear, pronunciar con sonido nasal.
nasally [nésali], adv. nasalmente, con gangueo.
nasard [nésard], s. (mús.) nasardo.
nascent [nésent], a. naciente; creciente.
nastily [nástili], adv. puercamente, asquerosamente.
nastiness [nástines], s. suciedad, porquería.
nasturtium [næstœrshium], s. (bot.) nasturcia, berro; capuchina.
nasty [násti], a. sucio, asqueroso; obsceno, indecente; impuro, sórdido; (fam.) desagradable; ofensivo; avieso; intratable; detestable.
natal [néital], a. nativo; natal.
natality [natáliti], a. natalidad.
natant [néitant], a. (bot.) nadante, flotante.
natation [netéshun], s. natación.
natatorial [netatórial], **natatory** [nétatori], a. natatorio.
natatorium [-tórium], s. escuela o piscina de natación.
nates [néitis], s. pl. nalgas, nalgatorio.
nation [néshun], s. nación.
national [néshunal], a. nacional.—**N. Guard**, milicia nacional.—**n. debt**, deuda pública.
nationalism [néshunalism], s. nacionalismo, forma reciente del socialismo; amor a la independencia nacional, patriotismo; idiotismo, costumbre, rasgo nacional peculiar o característico.—**nationalist** [-ist], s. nacionalista.

nationality [næshunáliti], s. nacionalidad; nación; ciudadanía, patriotismo.
nationalization [næshunaliséishun], s. conversión en nación, creación en nación; nacionalización, puesta bajo la dirección o en poder de la nación.
nationalize [-ais], va. convertir en nación; poner bajo la dirección o en poder de la nación.
nationally [néshunali], adv. nacionalmente.
native [néitiv]. **I.** a. nativo, natural, oriundo u originario; vernáculo; nacional, del país, patrio; (min.) nativo.—**n. country**, patria, país natal.—**n. place**, suelo o tierra natal.—**n. silver**, plata nativa o virgen.—**n. soil**, país natal. **II.** s. natural, indígena; producto nacional.
natively [-li], adv. naturalmente, originalmente, originariamente.
nativeness [néitivnes], s. calidad de nativo.
nativity [natíviti], s. nacimiento, natividad, natalicio; horóscopo.—**N.**, Navidad.
natrium [néitrium], s. sodio.
natron [nétron], s. (quím.) natrón.
nattily [nétili], adv. garbosamente.—**nattiness** [-nes], s. (fam.) garbo, gentileza.
natty [nati], a. (fam.) elegante, garboso.
natural [néchural]. **I.** a. natural, nativo; sencillo, inafectado; genuino, verdadero; normal, ordinario; bastardo, natural; (mús.) natural.—**n. draft**, o **draught**, tiro natural.—**n. gas, gas** natural.—**n. history**, historia natural.—**n. key** = DIATONIC KEY.—**n. law**, ley natural; derecho natural.—**n. magic**, magia blanca.—**n. philosophy**, física.—**n. pruning**, (agr.) desprendimiento natural de ramas, ya por estar podridas, ya como adaptación de la planta al medio.—**n. science**, ciencias naturales.—**n. selection**, selección natural.—**n. slope**, (ing.) pendiente natural.—**n. theology**, teología natural. **II.** s. idiota, simplón; (mús.) becuadro; tecla blanca; nota natural.
naturalism [néchuralism], s. naturalismo.
naturalist [néchuralist], s. naturalista.
naturalization [néchuraliséshun], s. naturalización; aclimatación.
naturalize [néchuralais], va. naturalizar; habituar; aclimatar.
naturally [néchurali], adv. naturalmente.
naturalness [-nes], s. naturalidad.
nature [néchœr], s. naturaleza; natural, índole, genio, carácter; especie, género, clase; naturalidad, espontaneidad.—**from n.**, (b. a.) del natural.
naught [not]. **I.** s. nada; cero, la cifra 0. **II.** a. nulo, de ningún valor.
naughtily [nótili], adv. pícaramente; malvadamente, perversamente.
naughtiness [nótines], s. maldad, perversidad; travesura.
naughty [nóti], a. perverso; desobediente, díscolo, pícaro.—**n. boy**, picaruelo.—**n. trick**, picardiguela, pillada.
naumachy [nómæki], s. naumaquia.
nausea [nóshia], s. náusea.
nauseant [nóshiant]. **I.** a. nauseabundo. **II.** s. substancia nauseabunda.
nauseate [nóshieit]. **I.** va. dar asco o disgusto. **II.** vn. nausear, asquear.
nauseative [nóshiativ], **nauseous** [nóshus], a. nauseabundo, asqueroso.—**nauseously** [-li], adv. asquerosamente.—**nauseousness** [-nes], s. náusea, asquerosidad.
nautch [noch], s. baile de la India.—**n. girl**, bailarina india.
nautic(al [nótic(al], a. náutico o marino.—**n. mile**, milla marina.
nautilus [nótilus], s. nautilo, caracol de mar; argonauta; fisalia.
naval [néival], a. naval; de marina.—**n. auxiliary**, barco auxiliar.—**n. law**, código naval.—**n. officer**, oficial de marina; (E. U.) capitán de puerto.—**n. stores**, artículos navales; productos resinosos.—**n. tactics**, táctica naval, evoluciones marítimas.
nave [nev], s. (arq.) nave; (car.) cubo de rueda, maza.—**n. box**, buje.—**n. line**, (mar.) perigallo de racamento.

navel [névœl], *s.* ombligo; centro, medio, parte interior.—**n. gall,** (vet.) matadura.—**n. lll,** (vet.) inflamación del ombligo.—**n. orange,** variedad de naranja sin semillas.—**n. string,** cordón umbilical. —**n. shaped,** umbilicado.
nave(l)led [névœld], *a.* umbilicado.
navelwort [névœlucœrt], *s.* (bot.) oreja de monje.
navew [néviu], *s.* (Ingl.) nabiza, colinabo.
navicular [navíkiular]. **I.** *a.* navicular. **II.** *s.* (anat.) fosa navicular; hueso navicular.
navigability [nævigabíliti], **navigableness** [návigabœlnes], *s.* calidad de navegable.
navigable [návigabœl], *a.* navegable.
navigate [návigueit], *va.* y *vn.* navegar.
navigation [-guéiṡhun], *s.* navegación; (poét.) marina, naves.
navigator [-guéitœr], *s.* navegador, navegante; piloto; tratado de náutica.
navvy [névi], *s.* (Ingl.) peón, bracero; máquina excavadora.
navy [néivi], *s.* armada, marina de guerra.—**n. bean,** frijol blanco ordinario.—**n. blue,** azul oscuro.—**N. Department,** (E. U.) Ministerio de Marina.—**N. Office,** (Ingl.) Almirantazgo.—**n. yard,** arsenal.
nawab [nauób], *s.* nababo.
nay [néi]. **I.** *adv.* no; de ningún modo; más aún, y aun. **II.** *s.* voto negativo; negación.
Nazarene [nésarín], *a.* y *s.* nazareno.
Nazarite [násarait], *s.* nazareno (sectario hebreo).
naze [neṡ], *s.* cabo, promontorio.
Neanderthaloid [neándertáloid], *a.* neandertaliano, del tipo del hombre de Neanderthal.
neap [níp], *s.* marea muerta (ll. t. **n. tide).**
Neapolitan [niapólitan], *a.* y *s.* napolitano.
near [níœr]. **I.** *prep.* cerca de, por, hacia. **II.** *adv.* cerca; próximamente.—**n. at hand,** a (la) mano, cerca.—**n. by,** *o* **n.-by,** cerca, cercano. **III.** *a.* cercano, próximo, inmediato; inminente; allegado; íntimo, estrecho; cicatero, tacaño; exacto; literal; imitado (*near silk,* seda imitada, imitación de seda); a punto de, por poco (cambiando el giro: *we were in a near accident,* por poco tenemos un accidente).—**n. beer,** (E. U.) cerveza no embriagante, de muy pequeña proporción de alcohol (puede llamarse cerveza aguada).—**n. relation,** *o* **relative,** pariente cercano. **IV.** *va.* y *vn.* acercar(se).
nearly [níœrli], *adv.* cerca, cerca de; estrechamente; mezquinamente; casi; íntimamente, de cerca; próximamente, aproximadamente.
nearness [níœrnes], *s.* proximidad, cercanía; inminencia; parentesco cercano; amistad estrecha; mezquindad.
nearsighted [-sáited], *a.* miope.
nearsightedness [-nes], *s.* miopía.
neat [nít]. **I.** *a.* limpio, aseado, pulcro; bonito, pulido, lindo; neto, mondo, lirondo; puro, casto, natural; puro, sin mezcla; nítido, claro; gallardo; esmerado; perteneciente al ganado vacuno.—**n. cattle,** ganado vacuno.—**n.-handed,** diestro; con manos limpias. **II.** *s.* ganado vacuno; vaca o buey. —**n.'s-foot oil,** aceite de pata de vaca.—**n.'s leather,** cuero de buey.—**n.'s tongue,** lengua de vaca.
'neath [niṡ], forma apocopada de BENEATH.
neatherd [nítjœrd], *s.* vaquero.
neatly [nítli], *adv.* pulidamente, nítidamente; primorosamente; limpiamente, aseadamente; elegantemente; diestramente, mañosamente.
neatness [nítnes], *s.* aseo, pulcritud; pulidez, elegancia, delicadeza.
neb, *s.* pico, boca; punta, cabo.
nebula [nébiula], *s.* (astr.) nebulosa; nube en los ojos.
nebular [nébiular], *a.* nebuloso; nebular.—**n. hypothesis,** hipótesis nebular, hipótesis de Laplace.
nebulizer [nébiulaiṡœr], *s.* rociador.
nebulosity [nébiulósiti], *s.* nebulosidad.
nebulous [nébiulus], *a.* nebuloso.
necessaries [néseseríṡ], *s. pl.* lo necesario.
necessarily [-li], *adv.* necesariamente.

necessary [néseseri]. **I.** *a.* necesario. **II.** *s.* lo necesario; requisito esencial; necesaria, letrina.
necessitarian [nesésiteriæn], *s.* y *a.* (filos.) determinista.—**necessitarianism** [-iṡm], *s.* determinismo.
necessitate [nesésitet], *va.* necesitar.
necessitous [nesésitus], *a.* necesitado.
necessity [nesésiti], *s.* necesidad.
neck [nek], *s.* cuello, garganta, pescuezo; cuello, gollete (de una botella); clavijero (de guitarra o violín); degüello; (arq.) collarino; (cost.) degolladura; (geog.) istmo, cabo, península.—**n. and crop,** todo junto y a un tiempo; al momento.—**n. and heels,** (fam.) de pies a cabeza, del todo.—**n. and n.,** (dep.) parejos, con igual rapidez en una carrera.—**n. handkerchief** = NECKERCHIEF.—**n. of land,** lengua de tierra.—**n. or nothing,** a toda costa.—**n. yoke,** yugo de colleras; (carr.) volea.—**on the n. of,** *o* **over the n. of,** luego, inmediatamente después.
neckband [nécbænd], *s.* (cost.) cabezón o tirilla de camisa.
neckcloth [néccloz], *s.* corbata, corbatín.
neckerchief [nékœrchif], *s.* corbata, corbatín; bobillo.
necklace [nécleis], *s.* collar, gargantilla.
necktie [néctai], *s.* corbata.
necrologic(al [nécrolóyic(al], *a.* necrológico.
necrologist [necróloyist], *s.* registrador de defunciones.
necrology [necróloyi], *s.* necrología.
necromancer [nécromǽnsœr], *s.* nigromante, (fam.) brujo.—**necromancy** [-si], *s.* nigromancia; brujería.—**necromantic** [-tic], *a.* nigromántico.
necropolis [necrópolis], *s.* necrópolis.
necrosis [necrósis], *s.* necrosis, gangrena.
nectar [néctar], *s.* néctar.—**nectarean** [nectérian], **nectareous** [-us], **nectarial** [-al], *a.* nectáreo.
nectarine [néctarin]. **I.** *a.* nectáreo, nectarino. **II.** *s.* (bot.) variedad de pérsico.
nectary [néctari], *s.* (bot.) nectario; (ent.) tubo para miel.
née [ne], *a.* (fr.) nacida; se usa para designar el apellido paterno de una mujer casada: *Mrs. Kate Brown, née Smith,* Señora Kate Smith de Brown.
need [nid]. **I.** *s.* necesidad; pobreza, miseria.— **if n. be,** si hubiere necesidad, si fuere necesario.— **to be in need,** tener necesidad; estar necesitado. **II.** *va.* necesitar, haber menester. Antes de infinitivo se emplea como una especie de auxiliar invariable, sobre todo en expresiones negativas, en el sentido de no haber que, no ser necesario, no deber: *he need not go,* no es necesario que él vaya; *it need not be done,* no hay que hacerlo, no es necesario que se haga. **III.** *vn.* ser necesario; estar en la necesidad, carecer de lo necesario.
needer [nídœr], *s.* necesitado.
needful [nídful], *a.* necesario.—**needfully** [-li], *adv.* necesariamente.—**needfulness** [-nes], *s.* calidad de necesario.
needily [nídili], *adv.* pobremente.
neediness [nídines], *s.* necesidad, pobreza.
needle [nídœl], *s.* aguja de coser; (mar.) aguja de marear, brújula; (arq.) aguja, chapitel; obelisco; roca o piedra acicular.—**n. bar,** portaaguja de una máquina de coser.—**n. file,** lima de aguja.—**n. gun,** fusil de aguja.—**n. holder,** portaagujas, palillo, acerico.—**n. lace,** encaje de, o a, mano. —**n. of a balance,** lengüeta, fiel de la balanza.— **n. of a dial,** aguja o estilo de un reloj de sol.—**n. point,** N. LACE; punta de aguja del compás y otros instrumentos; (arq.) aguja, chapitel.—**n.-shaped,** acicular.—**n.-threader,** ensartador de agujas.—**n. valve,** válvula de aguja o ahusada.
needlecase [-kéis], *s.* alfiletero.
needlefish [-fíṡh], *s.* (ict.) aguja.
needieful [nídœlful], *s.* hebra de hilo.
needler [nídlœr], *s.* agujero.
needless [nídles], *a.* inútil, innecesario.—**n. to say,** inútil es decir(lo).
needlessly [-li], *adv.* innecesariamente.
needlessness [-nes], *s.* superfluidad, inutilidad.

needlewoman [nídœlúman], *s.* costurera.

needlework [-uǽrc], *s.* costura; labor, bordado de aguja.

needs [nídŝ], *adv.* necesariamente.

needy [nídi], *a.* necesitado, menesteroso.

ne'er [néær], *adv. contr.* de NEVER.

nefarious [niférius], *a.* nefando, nefario.

nefariously [-li], *adv.* nefariamente.

nefariousness [-nes], *s.* calidad de nefario.

negation [neguéŝhun], *s.* negación.

negative [négativ]. **I.** *a.* negativo; (elec.) negativo. **II.** *s.* negativa; denegación; veto, derecho de rehusar; (foto.) negativo; (elec.) electricidad negativa. **III.** *va.* denegar, desaprobar, negar; oponerse a, votar en contra de; poner su veto a; contradecir.

negatively [négativli], *adv.* negativamente.

neglect [negléct]. **I.** *s.* descuido, negligencia; inobservancia; abandono, desdén, indiferencia; desuso. **II.** *va.* descuidar, desatender; olvidar; dejar de; abandonar; desdeñar; arrinconar; (mat.) despreciar.

neglectable [negléctabœl], *a.* =NEGLIGIBLE.

neglecter [negléctœr], *s.* descuidado, negligente; despreciador.

neglectful [negléctful], *a.* negligente, descuidado. —**neglectfully** [-li], *adv.* negligentemente, descuidadamente.—**neglectfulness** [-nes], *s.* negligencia, descuido, incuria, abandono.

negligee [négliŷéi]. **I.** *a.* suelto, libre, inceremonioso, de confianza (apl. a prendas de vestir). **II.** *s.* traje libre o inceremonioso; bata de casa.

negligence [négliŷens], *s.* negligencia.

negligent [négliŷœnt], *a.* negligente.

negligently [-li], *adv.* negligentemente.

negligible [négliŷibœl], *a.* despreciable, insignificante.

negotiable [negóŝhiabœl], *a.* negociable.

negotiate [negóŝhieit]. **I.** *va.* (com.) negociar, cambiar; gestionar, agenciar; (fam.) ejecutar, vencer, disponer de, salvar, superar. **II.** *vn.* negociar.—**negotiating** [-ing], *a.* negociante, contratante.—**negotiation** [-éiŝhun], *s.* negociación.—**negotiator** [-éitœr], *s.* negociador, gestor.

negress [nígres], *s.* negra.

negrillo, negrito, *s.* negrito malayo de raza enana.

negro [nígro]. **I.** *s.* negro. **II.** *a.* negro, de raza negra; de negro; de los negros.

negroid [nígroid], *a.* parecido o referente a los negros.

negus [nígus], *s.* carraspada, sangría.

neigh [néi]. **I.** *vn.* relinchar. **II.** *s.* relincho.

neighbo(u)r [néibœr]. **I.** *s.* vecino; prójimo. **II.** *va.* estar vecino o cercano a; ser vecino de.

neighbo(u)rhood [-jud], *s.* vecindad; vecindario; cercanía, inmediación.

neighbo(u)ring [-ring], *a.* vecino, rayano o cercano.

neighborliness [-lines], *s.* cortesía de vecindad; buena vecindad.

neighborly [-li]. **I.** *a.* urbano, atento. **II.** *adv.* civilmente.

neither [níDœr]. **I.** *a.* ningún, ninguno de los dos. **II.** *conj.* ni; correlativo ordinario de NOR (v. gr.: *neither he nor she*, ni él ni ella); tampoco, ni siquiera (*neither will I do it*, yo tampoco lo haré). **III.** *pron.* ninguno, ni uno ni otro, ni el uno ni el otro.

Nemæan [nimían], *a.* nemeo.

nematode [némætod], *s.* (zool.) nemátodo, nematode.

Nemathelminthes [némæzelmínzis], *s. pl.* nematelmintos.

Nematoda [némætódæ], *s. pl.* nematodos, nematodos, nematodes.—**nematode** [-toud], *s.* y *a.* nemátodo, de carácter o relativo a los nemátodos.

Nemesis [némesis], *s.* Némesis; justicia.

neo- [nío], *prefijo*, neo-, nuevo, reciente. Ú. en composición; v. gr.: *neo-Catholic*, neocatólico; *neo-Malthusianism*, neomaltusianismo.

neodymium [níodímium], (quím.) neodimio.

neolithic [níolízic], *a.* neolítico.

neologic(al [níolóyic(al], *a.* neológico.

neologism [nióloyiŝm], *s.* neologismo.

neologist [nióloyist], *s.* neólogo.

neology [nióloyi], *s.* neología.

neomenia [níomínia], *s.* neomenia.

neon [níon], *s.* (quím.) neón.

neophyte [níofait], *s.* neófito; novicio.

neoplasm [níoplæŝm], *s.* neoplasma.

Neoplatonism [níoplétoniŝm], *s.* neoplatonicismo.—**Neoplatonic**[-plætónic], *a.* neoplatónico.

neosalvarsan [níosælvarsæn], *s.* neosalvarsán (es nombre de fábrica dado a un derivado del salvarsán).

neoteric [níotéric], *a.* neotérico, moderno.

Neozoic [níoŝóic], *a.* (geol.) neozoico.

nepenthe(s [nepénzi(ŝ], *s.* filtro o pócima que se suponía calmar las penas; (bot.) nepenta.

nephew [néfiu o néviu], *s.* sobrino.

nephology [néfóloyi], *s.* tratado de las nubes.

nephoscope [néfoscoup], *s.* instrumento que indica la dirección, elevación, etc., de las nubes.

nephralgia [nefrǽlyiæ], *s.* nefralgia, neuralgia renal.

nephrectomy [nefréctomi], *s.* nefrectomía, excisión del riñón.

nephrite [néfrait], *s.* (min.) piedra nefrítica o jade.

nephritic [nefrític]. **I.** *a.* nefrítico. **II.** *s.* remedio nefrítico.

nephritis [nefráitis o frítis], *s.* nefritis.

nephroptosis [néfroptósis], *s.* riñón flotante o móvil, nefróptosis.

nephrotomy [nefrótomi], *s.* (cir.) nefrotomía.

nepotism [népotiŝm], *s.* nepotismo, sobrinazgo.

Neptune [néptiun], *s.* Neptuno; (fig.) océano; (astr.) Neptuno.

Neptunian [neptiúnian], *a.* neptúneo; (geol.) neptúnico.—**N. theory,** neptunismo.

Nereid [níreid], *s.* nereida.

nerita [niráita o ríta], *s.* nerita.

nerval [nœrval], *a.* nérveo.

nervate [nœrvet], *a.* (bot.) nervioso, nervado.

nervation [nœrvéŝhun], **nervature** [nœrvatiur], *s.* (bot.) nervadura.

nerve [nœrv]. **I.** *s.* (anat. y bot.) nervio; vigor, fibra; desfachatez, descaro.—*pl.* excitabilidad nerviosa. **II.** *va.* vigorizar, dar fuerza; animar, alentar.

nerved [nœrvd], *a.* nervudo, nervoso.

nerveless [nœrvles], *a.* enervado.

nerviduct [nœrviduct], *s.* conducto óseo para dar paso a un nervio.

nervine [nœrvin], *s.* remedio nervino.

nervous [nœrvus], *a.* nervioso; nervoso; nervudo; excitado; vigoroso.—**n. prostration,** neurastenia.—**n. system,** sistema nervioso.

nervously [-li], *adv.* nerviosamente; nervosamente.

nervousness [-nes], *s.* nerviosidad; nervosidad, vigor, fuerza; estado nervioso, irritable.

nervule [nœrviul], *s.* nervezuelo.

nervure [nœrviur], *s.* (arq. y bot.) nervadura; (ent.) vena, nervadura.

nervy [nœrvi], *a.* vigoroso; valeroso; (fam.) descarado.

nescience [néŝhiœns], *s.* nesciencia, necedad.

ness, *s.* promontorio, cabo.

nest. I. *s.* nido; nidada; manida, madriguera; guarida; juego de objetos que encajan unos dentro de otros; (mec.) engranaje; (geol. y min.) bolsa.—**n. egg,** nidal.—**n. of drawers** o **boxes,** juego de gavetas o cajones.—**n.-spring,** muelles en espiral metidos unos en otros. **II.** *va.* y *vn.* nidificar, anidar, hacer un nido; buscar nidos; alojar, anidarse, establecerse; colocar una serie de objetos unos dentro de otro.

nestle [néscœl]. **I.** *va.* abrigar, poner en un nido; acariciar, mimar. **II.** *vn.* anidarse, enjaularse; estar abrigado, como en un nido; apiñarse.

nestling [nésling], *s.* pollo, pichón, volantón.

Nestorian [nestórian], *a.* y *s.* nestoriano.—**Nestorianism** [-ĭsm], *s.* nestorianismo.

net. I. *s.* red; malla; (tej.) tul. **II.** *va.* enredar, prender o coger con red; (com.) obtener, producir una ganancia líquida. **III.** *vn.* redar, echar la red; hacer redes.

net(t, *a.* neto; limpio, puro; reticular, de punto de malla; cogido con red.—**n. embroidery,** bordado reticular.—**n. mackerel,** escombro cogido con red.—**n. produce,** producto neto.—**n. profit,** ganancia o beneficio líquido.—**n. weight,** peso neto.

netbraider [nétbréidœr], *s.* redero, mallero.

nether [néDœr], *a.* inferior, más bajo.—**n. lip,** labio inferior.—**n. world,** el otro mundo, la otra vida; infierno.

nethermost [néDœrmoust], *a.* lo inferior o más bajo en situación.

netmaker [nétméicœr], *s.* =NETBRAIDER.

netted [néted], *a.* cubierto o protegido por una red; reticular; enredado, cogido con red.

netting [néting], *s.* red, randa, obra de malla; operación de hacer redes o redecillas; (mar.) jareta, alambrado, ajedrez.—**n. needle,** aguja de tejer redes o mallas.

nettle [nétœl]. **I.** *s.* (bot.) ortiga.—**n. fever, n. rash,** urticaria.—**n. tree,** (bot.) almez, almezo. **II.** *va.* picar como ortiga; irritar, provocar, espinar.

nettling [nétling], *s.* provocación, irritación.

network [nétuœrc], *s.* red, randa, malla; plexo.

neume [niúm], *s.* (mús.) neuma.

neural [niúræl], *a.* neural.—**n. arch,** arco neural. —**n. axis,** eje cerebroespinal.—**n. canal,** canal neural, canal medular.—**n. spine,** espina neural.

neuralgia [niurélyia], *s.* neuralgia.

neuralgic [niurélyic], *a.* neurálgico.

neurasthenia [niúræszináia *o* zínia], *s.* (med.) neurastenia.

neurasthenic [niuræszínic], *a.* neurasténico.

neuration [niuréshŭn], *s.* = NERVATION.

neuraxis [niuréxis], *s.* neuroeje, neuraxis, eje cerebroespinal.

neuraxon [niuréxon], *s.* (anat.) neuraxon, axon.

neurectomy [niuréctomi], *s.* neurectomía.

neurilemma [niúrilémæ], *s.* (anat.) neurilema.

neuritis [niuráitis *o* rítis], *s.* (med.) neuritis.

neuroblast [niúroblæst], *s.* (biol.) neuroblasto.

neurography [niurógrafi], *s.* neurografía.

neurology [niuróloyi], *s.* neurología.

neuroma [niuróma], *s.* (med.) neuroma.

neuron [niúron], *s.* sistema cerebroespinal; neurona, célula con sus prolongaciones, etc.

neuropath [niúropaz], *s.* neurópata.

neuropathology [niúropæzóloyi], *s.* neuropatología.

neuropathy [niurópazi], *s.* neuropatía.

Neuroptera [niuróptera], *s. pl.* (ento.) neurópteros.

neuropterous, neuropteral [-us, -al], *a.* neuróptero.

neurosis [niurósis], *s.* (med.) neurosis.

neurotic [niurótic], *a.* (med.) neurótico.

neurotome [niúrotoum], *s.* (cir.) neurótomo.

neurotomy [niurótomi], *s.* (cir.) neurotomía.

neuter [niútœr], *a.* (gram.) neutro; (bot. y zool.) sin sexo.

neutral [niútral]. **I.** *a.* neutral, neutro; indiferente, inactivo; mediano; (pint.) neutro, pardusco o azulado; (biol.) neutro, sin sexo; (quím.) neutro; (mec.) neutro (eje, plano, etc.). **II.** *s.* neutral.

neutralism [niútralism], *s.* espíritu y observancia de la neutralidad.

neutrality [niutréliti], *s.* neutralidad, calidad de neutral; (quím.) calidad de neutro.

neutralization, o neutralisation [niútræliséshŭn], *s.* neutralización.

neutralize [niútralaiš], *va.* neutralizar.

neutrally [niútrali], *adv.* neutralmente.

neutrodyne [niútrodain], *a.* (rad.) neutrodino.

never [névœr], *adv.* nunca, jamás; no, de ningún modo.—**n. again,** nunca más, otra vez no.—**n. a whit,** ni pizca.—**n. fear,** no hay cuidado, no hay

miedo.—**n. mind,** no importa.—**n. so,** por muy'¹ por mucho o por más que. Con *never* y un ge. rundio se forman compuestos que indican que la acción o condición denotadas por el verbo no se verifican o no se realizarán nunca, v. gr. *never-ceasing, never-ending,* que nunca termina, continuo, perpetuo, eterno; *never-erring,* que nunca falla, infalible; *never-fading,* que nunca se marchita, inmarcesible; *never-failing,* infalible; *never-tiring,* incansable.

nevermore [névœrmócœr], *adv.* jamás, nunca más.

nevertheless [névœrdelés], *adv.* no obstante, con todo, sin embargo, a pesar de eso.

new [niú]. **I.** *a.* nuevo; moderno; novicio; no habituado; fresco, recién hecho, recién cogido, etc.—**n. departure,** nuevo sistema, nuevo método; nuevo derrotero; cambio, reforma.—**n.-delivered,** recién parida.—**n.-fashioned,** de última moda.— **n.-fledged,** volantón, recién emplumado, novel.— **n.-formed,** reformado; formado de nuevo.—**n. -grown,** recién crecido; recién salido.—**n.-laid,** fresco (huevo); recién puesto, colocado o tendido. —**n. learning,** nueva ciencia, renacimiento del saber; doctrinas de la reforma protestante; crítica bíblica moderna.—**n. moon,** luna nueva.—**N. Style,** (cronología) estilo nuevo, estilo del calendario gregoriano.—**N. Year,** año nuevo.—**N. Year's (Day),** día de año nuevo.—**N. Year's gift,** aguinaldo. **II.** *adv.* nuevamente, de nuevo; (seguido de participio) recién.

newborn [niúbórn], *a.* recién nacido.

newcomer [niúcŭmœr], *s.* recién llegado.

newel [niúel], *s.* (arq.) nabo o bolo (de escalera); (carp.) poste con que termina la baranda de una escalera.

newfangled [niúfǽngœld], *a.* novel, recién inventado, de última moda.

Newfoundland [niúfŭndlænd], *n. pr.* Terranova; perro de Terranova.—**N. fish,** bacalao, abadejo.

newish [niúish], *a.* bastante nuevo.

newly [niúli], *adv.* nuevamente, recientemente, recién.—**n. arrived,** recién llegado.

newness [niúnes], *s.* novedad; innovación; falta de práctica.

news [niúš], *s.* noticia; noticias (siempre en singular: *the news is this,* las noticias son éstas); cosa nueva, noticia fresca; papel para periódicos.—**n. agent, o dealer, o vender,** vendedor de periódicos.—**n. stand,** puesto o mostrador de periódicos.—**n. writer,** gacetillero, noticiero.—**no n. is good n.,** la falta de noticias es buena noticia.

newsboy [niúšboi], *s.* chiquillo vendedor de periódicos.

newsmonger [-mŭngœr], *s.* gacetista, portanuevas, pilonero.

newspaper [niúšpĭpœr], *s.* periódico; papel de periódico.—**n. man,** (fam.) periodista; reportero.

newsprint [-print], *s.* papel para periódicos.

newsroom [niúšrum], *s.* gabinete de lectura de periódicos; tienda de periódicos.

newsy [niúši], *a.* noticioso.

newt [niút], *s.* lagartija acuática.

Newtonian [niutónian], *a.* neutoniano.

New-Yorker [niu-yórcœr], *s.* neoyorquino.

next. I. *a.* siguiente; entrante; próximo, contiguo, adyacente; subsiguiente, futuro, venidero.— **n. day,** el día siguiente, al día siguiente.—**n. door,** la puerta (o casa) siguiente.—**n. door to,** a la puerta (o casa) siguiente de; muy cerca de.—**n. month,** el mes entrante.—**n. of kin,** parientes más cercanos.—**n. time,** la próxima vez, otra vez.— **n. week,** la semana entrante.—**the n. day before,** la víspera.—**the n. life,** la otra vida.—**to be n.,** seguir en turno, tocarle a uno. **II.** *adv.* luego, después, ahora, inmediatamente después.—**n. best,** lo mejor después de eso, o a falta de eso.—**n. to,** junto a, al lado de; después de; casi.—**what n.?** ¿y ahora (o luego) qué? **III.** *prep.* junto a, al lado de.

nexus [néxus], *s.* nexo, lazo, vínculo.

nib. I. *s.* asa de la guadaña; pico, punta, extremo; punto o tajo de una pluma; pico de un ave; grano de cacao o de café. **II.** *va.* hacer punta a, aguzar; cortar la pluma.

---

nibble [níbœl]. **I.** *va.* mordicar o mordiscar, roer, pacer, tascar; rozar. **II.** *vn.* picar, morder (como el pez); (con **at**) satirizar, criticar. **III.** *s.* roedura, ramoneo; mordisco, bocadito.

niblick [níblic], *s.* (dep.) uno de los palos del juego de golf.

nice [náis], *a.* fino, sutil; delicado; diligente, solícito; circunspecto, cauto; exacto, concienzudo; pulcro, pulido, refinado; tierno, frágil; agradable, lindo, bonito; simpático, gentil, amable. —**n.** distinction, sutileza.—**n. point**, punto delicado.

nicely [náisli], *adv.* con finura; delicadamente; primorosamente; sutilmente; (fam.) muy bien.

Nicene [náisin], *a.* niceno.

niceness [náisnes], *s.* finura, gentileza, amabilidad; delicadeza.

nicety [náisiti], *s.* finura, delicadeza, amabilidad; exactitud, esmero; refinamiento, atildadura; sutileza, nimiedad.—**to a n.**, con la mayor precisión, en buen punto.

niche [nich], *s.* nicho, capilleta.

nick. I. *s.* muesca, mella, corte, escote, tarja; (impr.) cran del tipo; muesca en la cabeza de un tornillo; punto crítico, momento oportuno; jugada favorable.—(**Old**) **N.,** el diablo.—**in the n. of time**, en el momento perentorio, a punto, a tiempo. **II.** *va.* mellar, cortar o hacer muescas, descantillar, tarjar; acertar, dar en el clavo; llegar a tiempo. **III.** *vn.* corresponder, igualarse, ser parejo; hacer una buena jugada.

nickel [níkel], *s.* (quím.) níquel; (E. U., fam.) moneda de níquel (5 centavos).—**n. bronze,** aleación de 3 partes de cobre y una de níquel, de que se hacen las monedas de 5 cvos. de los E. U.— **n.-plate**, *va.* niquelar.—**n.-plated,** niquelado.— **n. silver,** metal blanco, plata alemana.—**n. steel,** acero niquel.

nichrome [nícroum], *s.* aleación de níquel y cromo (es nombre de fábrica); puede llamarse nicromo o cromoníquel).

nicknack [nícnæc], *s.* friolera, chuchería.

nickname [nícneim]. **I.** *s.* apodo. **II.** *va.* motejar, apodar.

nicotian [nicóshian], *a.* nicociano.

nicotin(e [nícotin], *s.* nicotina.

nictitate [níctitet], *vn.* pestañear, parpadear.— **nictitating membrane,** membrana nictitante.

nictitation [nictitéshun], *s.* pestañeo.

nidificant [nídificant], *a.* nidificante.

nidification [nídifikéshun], *s.* nidificación.

nidify [nídifai], *vn.* nidificar, anidar.

nidus [náidus *o* nídus], *s.* nido; centro o foco de infección; (anat.) núcleo nervioso.

niece [nís], *s.* sobrina.

niello [niélo]. **I.** *s.* niel. **II.** *va.* nielar.

nig, *va.* cortar el borde (de una moneda); labrar (piedra) a pico.

nigella [nivéla], *s.* (bot.) neguilla.

niggard [nígard], *a.* y *s.* tacaño, mezquino.

niggardish [nígardish], *a.* cicatero.

niggard(li)ness [nígard(li)nes], *s.* tacañería o mezquindad.

niggardly [nígardli]. **I.** *a.* mezquino, miserable. **II.** *adv.* tacañamente, mezquinamente, con mezquindad o cicatería.

nigger [nígœr], *s.* (despec.) negro, negra; uno de varios inventos mecánicos; (ento.) oruga negra.—**n. engine,** máquina rudamente construida.—**n. in the wood pile,** (fam.) gato encerrado. —**n. heaven,** (fam.) paraíso, gallinero (en el teatro).

niggerism [nígœrism], *s.* locución o idiotismo propio de los negros.

niggle [nígœl]. **I.** *va.* burlarse de. **II.** *vn.* ocuparse en menudencias. **III.** *s.* letra menuda o metida.

niggling [nígling], *s.* (b. a.) minuciosidad.

nigh [nái]. **I.** *prep.* cerca, no lejos de, cabe, junto a. **II.** *adv.* cerca, inmediato; casi, cuasi. —*a.* cercano, próximo, vecino; (fam.) de la izquierda (hablando de caballos); allegado, íntimo.

night [náit]. **I.** *s.* noche.—**at n., n., by de** noche, por la noche. **II.** *a.* nocturno; de noche; que funciona, se hace u ocurre de noche, o sirve para la noche.—**n. bell,** campanilla para llamar por la noche.—**n. bird,** pájaro nocturno; (fam.) trasnochador.—**n. brawler,** alborotador nocturno.—**n. chair,** sillico.—**n. clothes,** camisa o traje de dormir.—**n. dog,** perro que caza de noche.—**n. glass,** catalejo nocturno.—**n. heron,** (orn.) gargota.—**n. key,** llavín, llave de noche.— **n. lamp,** mariposa, lamparilla o luz de noche.—**n. latch,** cerradura de resorte.—**n. letter** = LETTER-GRAM.—**n. light** = N. LAMP.—**n. lock** = N. LATCH. —**n. piece,** (b. a.) cuadro o escena nocturna.—**n. rest,** reposo de la noche.—**n. robe**=NIGHTGOWN.— **n. school,** escuela nocturna.—**n. soil,** contenido de las letrinas.—**n. stool** = N. CHAIR.—**n. watch,** sereno, guardia o ronda de noche.

nightcap [náitcæp], *s.* gorro de dormir; (fam.) trago que se toma antes de acostarse.

nightdress [-dres], *s.* camisón, camisa de dormir.

nightfall [-fol], *s.* anochecida.

nightgown [-gáun], *s.* = NIGHTDRESS.

nighthawk [-jóc], *s.* (orn.) chotacabras; pájaro insectívoro crepuscular de los E. U.; (fam.) trasnochador, nocherniego.

nightjar [-yar], *s.* chotacabras.

nightingale [náitingueil], *s.* (orn.) ruiseñor.

nightlong [náitlong], *a.* y *adv.* de toda la noche, durante toda la noche.

nightly [náitli]. **I.** *adv.* por las noches, todas las noches. **II.** *a.* nocturno, de noche.

nightmare [-méœr], *s.* pesadilla.

nightshade [-shéid], *s.* (bot.) dulcamara, solano.

nightshirt [-shœrt], *s.* camisa de dormir.

nighttime [-táim], *s.* noche.

nightwalker [-uócœr], *s.* noctívago, sonámbulo; vago o mujer pública que callejea de noche; lombriz nocturna de tierra, usada para cebo de pescar.

nightward [-uord], *a.* cercano o próximo a la noche.

nigrescence [nigrésens], *s.* ennegrecimiento.

nigrification [nigrifikéshun], *s.* ennegrecimiento.

nigrescent [nigréscent], *a.* negruzco.

nigrify [nígrifai], *va.* ennegrecer.

nihil [náijil], *s.* nada.

nihilism [náijilism], *s.* nihilismo.—**nihilist** [-ist], *s.*, **nihilistic** [-tic], *a.* nihilista.

nikalgin [nicœlyin], *s.* anestésico local de ácido clorhídrico, quinina y urea.

nil, nill [nil], *s.* nada; hojuela que salta del bronce al forjarlo.

nilg(h)au [nílgau], *s.* (zool.) especie de antílope.

nimble [nimbœl], *a.* vivo, listo, ágil, veloz, expedito.—**n.-fingered,** ligero de dedos.—**n.-footed,** ligero de pies, alípedo.—**n.-pinioned,** de vuelo rápido.—**n.-witted,** vivo, despierto, inteligente.

nimbleness [nímbœlnes], *s.* ligereza, agilidad, celeridad; expedición, destreza.

nimbly [nímbli], *adv.* ligeramente, ágilmente.

nimbus [nímbus], *s.* nimbo; aureola.

nincompoop [níncœmpup], *s.* (fam.) badulaque, simplón, tonto, pelele.

nine [náin], *a.* y *s.* nueve.—**the N.,** las nueve musas.

ninefold [náinfold], *a.* y *adv.* nueve veces.

ninepence [náinpens], *s.* nueve peniques; real fuerte o media peseta.

ninepins [náinpins], *s.* juego de bolos.

ninescore [náinscœr], *a.* y *s.* nueve veces veinte.

nineteen [náintin], *a.* y *s.* diecinueve.

nineteenth [náintínz], *a.* décimonono; diecinueveavo; diecinueve (del mes).

ninetieth [náintiez], *a.* nonagésimo; noventa; noventavo.

ninety [náinti], *a.* y *s.* noventa.

ninny [níni], *s.* simple, mentecato, pelele, badulaque, papanatas, bobo.

ninth [náinz], *a.* nono, noveno; nueve (del mes).

ninthly [náinzli], *adv.* noveno o en nono lugar.

niobium [naió- *o* nióbium], *s.* (quím.) niobio.

nip. I. *va.* pellizcar; asir, sujetar, agarrar; mordicar, cortar, recortar, desmochar; helar, escarchar, marchitar; tocar de cerca, interesar.—**to n. in the bud,** o **blossom,** cortar en flor.—**to n. off,** desmochar, despuntar. **II.** *s.* pellizco; pedacito; trago, traguito; uñada, dentellada; helada, escarcha; cogida; daño repentino de las plantas o sembrados.—**n. and tuck,** (fam. E. U.) empate.

Nipa [náipa o nipa], *s.* (bot.) nipa.

nipper [nípœr], *s.* agarrador; pinza; boca de algunos crustáceos; pala, diente delantero del caballo.—*pl.* pinzas, tenazas, tenacillas; (mar.) mojeles, badernas.

nipping [níping]. **I.** *s.* araño, rasguño, mordedura. **II.** *a.* mordaz, picante.—**n. tool,** sacabocados.

nippingly [nípingli], *adv.* mordazmente.

nipple [nípœl], *s.* pezón; tetilla; chimenea de arma de percusión; pezón artificial.—**n. shield,** pezonera.

nipplewort [-uœrt], *s.* (bot.) lapsana.

nisus [náisʊs], *s.* esfuerzo; contracción de los músculos en la evacuación del vientre o de la vejiga; apetito procreativo primaveral de las aves.

nit. I. *s.* liendre; punto pequeño. **II.** *adv.* (fam.) no, ni por pienso.

niter, nitre [náitœr], *s.* nitro, salitre.—**n. bed,** nitral.

nitid [nítid], *a.* (bot.) lustroso.

niton [náiton], *s.* nitón, emanación del radio.

nitrate [náitret], *s.* (quím.) nitrato.

nitric [náitric], *a.* nítrico.

nitrid [náitrid], *s.* (quím.) nitruro.

nitrification [náitrifikéiṡhʊn], *s.* nitrificación.— **nitrify** [-fai], *va.* nitrificar, nitrogenar.—**nitrifier** [-fáiœr], *s.* substancia nitrogenada que sirve para nitrificar.

nitrile [náitril], *s.* (quím.) nitrolo.

nitrite [náitrait], *s.* (quím.) nitrito.

nitrobacteria [náitrobœctíriæ], *s. pl.* de NITRO-BACTERIUM: nitrobacterias (gen. se aplica a las nítricas).

nitrobenzine [-bénṡin], *s.* nitrobencina.

nitrocellulose [-séliulos], *s.* (quím.) nitrocelulosa.

nitrocotton [-cótn], *s.* algodón pólvora.

nitrogelatin [-ɣélœtin], nitrogelatina.

nitrogen [náitroyen], *s.* nitrógeno, ázoe.—**n.-fixing,** nitrogenante, que fija o combina el nitrógeno atmosférico (apl. a bacterias).

nitrogenize [náitroyenaiṡ], *va.* nitrogenar.

nitrogenous [naitróyenʊs], *a.* nitrogenado.

nitroglycerin [náitroglíscœrin], *s.* nitroglicerina.

nitrometer [naitrómetœr], *s.* nitrómetro.

nitroprussid, nitroprussiate [náitroprúsid, -siet], *s.* (quím.) nitroprusiato.

nitrosyl [náitrosil], *s.* (quím.) nitrosilo.

nitrous, nitry [náitrʊs, tri], *a.* nitroso, salitroso. —**n. acid,** ácido nitroso.—**n. bacteria,** bacterias nitrosas.

nitty [níti], *a.* lendroso.

nival [náival], *a.* nevoso.

niveous [nívius], *a.* níveo.

nix(ie [nix(i], *s.* genio de las aguas en la mitología alemana; (E. U. fam.) nitos, nada.

no [no]. **I.** *adv.* no.—**n. more,** no más.—**n. more of that,** o **of this,** basta, bastante; no hablemos más de eso.—**say n. more,** no diga más. **II.** *a.* ninguno, ningún, ninguna. Gen. equivale a NOT y se traduce por no: *I have no time,* no tengo tiempo; *there is no bread,* no hay pan. A menudo se usa en expresiones elípticas en que es preciso suplir el verbo *ser, permitir, haber,* etc.: *no admittance,* no hay admisión, no se permite la entrada; *no public entrance,* ésta no es entrada pública; *no smoking,* no se permite fumar. Después de algunas preposiciones equivale a sin: *to no purpose,* sin objeto; *with no money,* sin dinero.—**n. account,** sin valor, despreciable.—**n. fooling,** (fam.) sin broma, de veras.—**n. man's land,** el campo que separa dos ejércitos enemigos.—**n. matter,** no importa; de ninguna importancia.—**n. matter how much,** por mucho que.—**n. . . , n. . .,** sin . . ., no hay [*no payment, no delivery,*]

sin pago no hay (o habrá) entrega].—**n. one,** nadie, ninguno.—**n. use** (con *to be*), inútil. **III.** *s.* (*pl.* NOES) no, voto negativo.

Noachian [noéikiæn], *a.* relativo a Noé.

nob, *s.* (fam.) la cabeza; protuberancia, bulto; (fam.) noble, persona de viso.

nobby [nóbi], *a.* (fam.) llamativo; ostentoso, vistoso; jarifo.

nobiliary [nobíliæri], *a.* nobiliario.

nobility [nobíliti], *s.* nobleza.

noble [nóubœl], *s.* y *a.* noble; (Ingl.) moneda antigua.—**n. extraction,** de noble alcurnia, sangre azul.—**n. metals,** metales nobles (oro, piata y platino).—**n. opal** = PRECIOUS OPAL.

nobleman [-mæn], *s.* noble, hidalgo.

nobleness [-nes], *s.* nobleza.

noblesse [noblés], *s.* nobleza.

noblewoman [nóubœlúman], *s.* mujer noble, hidalga.

nobly [nóubli], *adv.* noblemente.—**n. born,** noble de nacimiento.

nobody [nóbodi], *s.* nadie, ninguno; persona despreciable.—**n. else,** nadie más, ningún otro.

noctambulist [noctámbulist], *s.* somnámbulo.

noctiflorous [nóctiflórʊs], *a.* (bot.) que florece de noche.

noctiluca [noctilúca], *s.* noctíluco.

nocturn [nóctœrn], *s.* (igl.) maitines.

nocturnal [noctœrnal]. **I.** *a.* nocturno. **II.** *s.* (mar.) nocturlabio.

nocturne [nóctœrn], *s.* (pint.) escena nocturna; (mús.) nocturno.

nod. I. *va.* hacer una seña afirmativa o llamativa con la cabeza; inclinar la cima o parte superior (de una rama, etc.). **II.** *vn.* cabecear, doblar o inclinar la cabeza; descabezar el sueño, dormitar. **III.** *s.* cabeceo; cabezada; signo o seña con la cabeza; reverencia, inclinación de cabeza.

nodal [nódal], *a.* nodal.

nodated [nodéited], *a.* nudoso.

nodding [nóding]. **I.** *a.* (bot.) inclinado, colgante. **II.** *s.* cabeceo; saludo con la cabeza.

noddle [nódœl], *s.* (despec.) mollera, cabeza.

noddy [nódi], *s.* pelele, papanatas; carruaje ligero de dos ruedas; pájaro bobo.

node [nóud], *s.* bulto, protuberancia, chichón; nudo; (cir.) nodo, nudo, tumor, dureza, nódulo; (astr.) nodo; (bot.) nudo; (geom.) nodo; (teat.) enredo, nudo, trama.

nodose [nódos], *a.* nudoso.

nodosity [nodósiti], *s.* nudosidad.

nodular [nódiular], **noduled** [nódiuld], *a.* que tiene nódulos o nudillos.

nodule [nódiul], *s.* nudillo; nódulo.

noetic [noétic], *a.* mental, intuitivo.

nog, *s.* bloque de madera; (mar.) cabilla, clavija.

noggin [nóguin], *s.* cubo; jarro.

nogging [nóguing], *s.* tabique; escora.

noise [nóiṡ]. **I.** *s.* ruido; sonido. **II.** *va.* esparcir, divulgar, turbar con gritos o con estruendo.

noiseful [nóiṡful], *a.* ruidoso.

noiseless [nóiṡles], *a.* silencioso, sin ruido.

noiselessly [-li], *adv.* sin ruido.—**noisily** [nóiṡili], *adv.* ruidosamente.

noisiness [nóiṡines], *s.* estrépito, ruido.

noisome [nóiṡʊm], *a.* apestoso, fétido.—**noisomely** [-li], *adv.* apestosamente.—**noisomeness** [-nes], *s.* mal olor, fetidez, hedor, peste.

noisy [nóiṡi], *a.* ruidoso, turbulento, estrepitoso.

nolens volens [nólenṡ vólenṡ], *adv.* velisnolis, de grado o por fuerza, quieras o no.

noli-me-tangere [nólai-mi-tǽnyere], *s.* (bot.) balsamina; (med.) nolimetángere.

nolition [nolíṡhʊn], *s.* (teol.) nolición.

nolle prosequi [nóle prósecuai, o -sécui], (for.) abandono de acción.

nomad(ic [nómad, nomédic]. **I.** *a.* nómada. **II.** (nomad), *s.* nómada.

nomarch [nómarc], *s.* nomarca.

nom de plume [nom de plum], *s.* seudónimo, nombre falso.

nome [nóum], *s.* provincia, nomo.

nomenclator [nómenclétœr], s. nomenclador, nomenclator.

nomenclature [-cléchœr], s. nomenclatura.

nominal [nóminal], a. nominal.—**nominalism** [-îŝm], s. nominalismo.—**nominalist** [-ist], s. nominalista.—**nominally** [-i], adv. nominalmente.

nominate [nómineit], va. nombrar como candidato, designar; señalar.

nomination [-éishun], s. nombramiento; propuesta.

nominative [nóminativ], s. (gram.) nominativo.

nominator [-éitœr], s. nominador, nombrador.

nominee [nominí], s. nómino, nombrado.

nominor [nóminor], s. nominador.

nomology [nomóloyi], s. nomología, ciencia o formulación de las leyes de una ciencia.

non- [non], partícula negativa que corresponde gen. a in-, no o a falta de en español.—n. assumpsit, (for.) alegación de que una persona no ha hecho una promesa.—the n.-ego, (el) no yo, el mundo externo.—n.-Euclidean (o -dian), no euclidiano.

nonacceptance [nónacséptæns], s. rechazo o falta de aceptación; recusación.

nonactinic [-æctínic], a. no actínico.

nonage [nóney], s. minoridad.

nonagenarian [nónayenérian], a. y s. nonagenario, noventón.

nonagesimal [nónayésimal], a. nonagésimo.

nonappearance [-æpíæræns], s. (for.) contumacia, rebeldía.

nonarrival [-ærráivæl], s. falta de llegada o de arribo.

nonattendance [-æténdæns], s. falta de asistencia, ausencia.

nonce [nons], s. tiempo presente; actualidad.—n. word, palabra ad hoc.—for the n., por esta vez, por ahora, por el momento.

nonchalance [nonŝhaláns o nónŝhalæns], s. indiferencia.—**nonchalant** [-lant], a. indiferente, impasible.

noncommissioned [nóncomíŝhund], a. n. officer, sargento o cabo; oficial nombrado por el jefe de un cuerpo.

noncomittal [-comítæl], a. reservado, evasivo, que no se compromete expresando su opinión.

noncompliance [-compláiæns], s. (gen. con with) falta de cumplimiento, falta de obediencia.

noncombatant [-cómbætænt], s. y a. no combatiente.

non compos (mentis) [non cómpos (méntis)], a. insano, falto de juicio.

nonconcurrence [-concœrrens], s. falta de unión, combinación o cooperación; desacuerdo.

nonconducting [-condúcting], a., **nonconductor** [-condûctœr], s. (fís., elec.) no conductor, mal conductor.

nonconformist [-confórmist], s. disidente (de la iglesia anglicana).

nonconformity [-confórmiti], s. desconformidad, disidencia (de la iglesia anglicana).

nonconsent [-consént], s. falta de consentimiento.

noncontagious [-contéiyus], a. no contagioso.

noncontent [-contént], s. oponente; voto contrario.

nondelivery [-delíveri], s. falta de entrega.

nondescript [-descrípt]. I. a. no descrito; indescribible, raro, estrambótico. II. s. objeto curioso, raro y desconocido.

none [nœn]. I. pron. nadie, ninguno; nada; nada de; no . . . nada, no . . . ninguno (I have none, yo no tengo ninguno, yo no tengo nada).—n. of one's business, cosa que a uno no le importa o atañe.—n. of that, nada de eso. II. adv. no, de ninguna manera, absolutamente no.—n. the less, no menos.—to be n. the better (worse) (a menudo con for, con, a causa de, por) no hallarse mejor (peor), no salir o quedar mejor (peor) librado, no ganar (perder).

nonelectric [nóneléctric], a. aneléctrico.

nonentity [nonéntiti], s. la nada; persona o cosa de ningún valor, cero a la izquierda, nulidad.

nones [nóunŝ], s. pl. nonas; (igl.) nona.

nonessential [nónesénŝhæl], s. y a. no esencial.

nonesuch [núnsúch], a. y s. sin igual, sin par.

nonexistence [nónegŝístœns], s. no existencia.— **nonexistent** [-tœnt], no existente, inexistente.

nonius [nónius], s. = VERNIER.

nonjuror [nónjúrœr], s. (Ingl.) clérigo que no juró fidelidad al trono en 1688.

nonlegal [-lígæl], a. ilegal.

nonmetal [-métæl], s. metaloide.

nonmoral [-móræl], a. no ético, fuera del dominio de la moral.

nonpareil [nónparél]. I. a. sin par, incomparable, sin rival. II. s. persona o cosa de incomparable mérito; (orn.) variedades de pinzón y de loro; (impr.) nomparell, tipo de seis puntos.

nonpartisan [-pártiŝæn], a. (pol.) independiente, no afiliado con ningún partido.

nonpayment [-péimœnt], s. falta de pago.

nonperformance, [-perfórmæns], s. falta de ejecución.

nonplus [nónplus]. I. s. perplejidad, estupefacción. II. va. confundir, aplastar, dejar sin palabra.—**nonplus(s)ed**, confundido, turulato, estupefacto.

nonresidence [-résidens], s. ausencia, residencia en otra parte.

nonresident [-résidént], s. ausente, no residente.

nonresistance [-resístæns], s. obediencia pasiva, falta de resistencia.

nonsectarian [-sectériæn], a. no sectario.

nonsense [nónsens], s. disparate, desatino; tontería, absurdo, necedad; (fam.) música celestial; bagatelas, fruslerías, jerigonza.

nonsensical [nonsénsical], a. disparatado, absurdo, desatinado.—**nonsensically** [-l], adv. disparatadamente, tontamente.—**nonsensicalness** [-nes], s. absurdidad; insensatez.

non sequitur [-sécuitœr], (lóg.) non séquitur, falsa conclusión, conclusión que no se deduce de las premisas.

nonsuit [-siut]. I. s. (for.) abandono de acción; sobreseimiento; caducidad de la instancia. II. va. (for.) absolver de la instancia; sobreseer.

nontechnical [-técnicæl], a. no técnico.

nonunion [-iúniun], a. no perteneciente a los gremios obreros; de fuera de los gremios.

noodle [núdœl], s. tallarín; (fam.) tonto, simplón, mentecato.

nook [nuc], s. rincón, escondrijo.

noon [nun], s. mediodía, meridiano; culminación, apogeo.

noonday [núndei]. I. s. mediodía (mitad del día). II. a. de mediodía.

nooning [núning], s. siesta.

noontide [núntaid]. I. a. del mediodía. II. s. mediodía; apogeo, culminación.

noose [nus o nuŝ]. I. s. lazo corredizo, gaza; dogal.—n. snare, trampa. II. va. [nus], lazar, coger con lazo corredizo, o con trampa.

nopal [nóupal], s. (bot.) nopal; higuera chumba.

nor [nor], conj. ni.

noria [nóriæ], s. noria.

Nordic [nórdic], s. y a. nórdico, del noroeste de Europa (apl. esp. a pueblos y razas, más bien que a las lenguas).

norm [norm], s. norma, pauta, modelo; (biol.) tipo.

normal [nórmæl]. I. a. normal, regular, corriente; típico, ejemplar; (geom., quím.) normal. —n. acid, ácido normal (de las fracciones $\frac{1}{16}$, $\frac{2}{16}$, etc., decinormal, veintinormal, etc., o de un décimo, un veintavo, etc., de la concentración normal).—n. school, escuela normal. II. s. estado normal; (geom.) normal.

normalcy [-si], **normality** [normǽliti], s. normalidad.

normalize [nórmalaiŝ], va. normalizar.

normally [nórmali], adv. normalmente.

Norman [nórmæn], a. y s. normando.

Norse [nors], a. y s. escandinavo.

Norseman [nórsman], s. hombre del norte, normando, antiguo escandinavo.

north [norz]. **I.** *s.* norte; (poét.) cierzo.—**n. by east**, norte, cuarta nordeste.—**n. by west**, norte, cuarta noroeste. **II.** *a.* septentrional, del norte.— **n. pole**, polo norte.—**n. star**, estrella polar, la Polar.—**n. wind**, nordada, cierzo. **III.** *adv.* al norte, hacia el norte.

northeast [nórzíst], *s.* y *a.* nordeste.—**northeaster** [-œr], *s.* tempestad nordestal.—**northeasterly** [-œrli], **northeastern** [-œrn], *a.* nordestal.

norther [nórƋœr], *s.* cierzo, nortada.

northerly [-li], **northern** [nórƋœrn], *a.* septentrional, boreal; del norte o hacia el norte.— **n. lights**, aurora boreal.

northern(er [nórƋœrnœr], *s.* habitante del norte. —**N.**, (E. U.) natural de los estados del norte.

northernmost [-moust], *a.* *superl.* más septentrional.

northing [nórƋing], *s.* (mar.) derrota hacia el norte; diferencia de latitud norte.

Northman [nórzman], *s.* = Norseman.

northward(s [nórzuard(ŝ], *adv.* hacia el norte.

northwest [nórzuést], *s.* y *a.* noroeste.—**n. by north**, noroeste, cuarta norte.—**n. by west**, noroeste, cuarta oeste.—**northwesterly** [-œrli], *a.* hacia el noroeste o del noroeste.—**northwestern** [-œrn], *a.* del noroeste.

Norwegian [noruíyian], *s.* y *a.* noruego.

nose [nóuŝ]. **I.** *s.* nariz; hocico de los animales; olfato; sagacidad; algo parecido a una nariz, v.gr.: proa de un buque; tobera o cañuto de fuelle; pico o boca (de cafetera, jarro, etc.); (aer.) extremo anterior o cabeza de un avión.—**n. bag**, morral, cebadera.—**n. dive**, (aer.) descenso de cabeza o con gran inclinación.—**n. piece**, sobarba, muserola; portaobjetivo (de microscopio); extremo o boquerel de manguera. **II.** *va.* y *vn.* oler, olfatear, husmear, rastrear; restregar la nariz contra; ganguear; encararse; oponerse, hacer frente; (con **out**) descubrir, averiguar.—**to n. about**, husmear, curiosear.

noseband [nóuŝbænd], *s.* muserola, sobarba.

nosebleed [nóuŝblid], *s.* epistaxis, hemorragia nasal; (bot.) milenrama.

nosegay [nóuŝguei], *s.* ramillete; pomo de flores.

noseless [nóuŝles], *s.* desnarigado; sin nariz.

nosography [nosógrafi], *s.* nosografía.

nosological [nosolóyical], *a.* nosológico.

nosologist [nosóloyist], *s.* nosólogo.

nosology [nosóloyi], *s.* nosología.

nostalgia [nostǽlyia], *s.* nostalgia.

nostoc [nóstoc], *s.* liquen.

nostologic [nostolóyic], *a.* senil.—**nostology** [nostóloyi], *s.* ciencia de la senilidad.

nostril [nóstril], *s.* ventana de la nariz.

nostrum [nóstrum], *s.* remedio o medicina secreta o de patente; cúralotodo.

not [not], *adv.* no; ni, ni siquiera (*not a word*, ni una palabra).—**n. at all**, de ningún modo.—**n. but, n. that**, no es decir que no (*not but that I shall go*, no es decir que no vaya).—**n. guilty**, no culpable; absuelto.—**n. one**, ni uno (solo).—**n. proved, n. proven**, (for.) no convicto, absuelto.— **n. so much as**, ni siquiera.—**n. to**, sin, por no (*not to say bad*, por no decir malo; *not to mention more than two*, sin mencionar más que dos).—**I think n.**, no lo creo; creo que no.

notability [notabíliti], *s.* notabilidad.

notableness [nóutabœlnes], *s.* notabilidad.

notable [nóutabœl]. **I.** *a.* notable; hacendoso, cuidadoso, arreglado, económico. **II.** *s.* notabilidad (persona).

notably [nótabli], *adv.* notablemente.

notarial [notérial], *a.* notarial.

notary (**public** [nótari (públic], *s.* notario.

notation [notéiŝhun], *s.* notación; anotación; sentido; significación; numeración escrita.

notch [noch]. **I.** *s.* muesca, corte, incisión, entalladura, ranura, mortaja, hendidura; mella; (mar.) tojino. **II.** *va.* hacer muescas; dentar, mellar; ranurar.

note [nóut]. **I.** *s.* nota; marca, señal; anotación; apunte, memoria; comunicación, nota diplomática; esquela, cartita; conocimiento, noticia, aviso; distinción, nota, importancia; (mús.) nota;

tecla; tono; voz, acento; (com.) vale, pagaré, abonaré.—*pl.* notas, solfa, pieza de música.—**n. of hand** = PROMISSORY NOTE.—**n. paper**, papel para esquelas. **II.** *va.* marcar, distinguir; reparar, observar, advertir; (a veces con *down*), apuntar, registrar.—**to n. an exception**, (for.) anotar en los autos la excepción que pone una de las partes. —**to n. a protest**, protestar una letra o pagaré.

notebook [nóutbúc], *s.* libreta, memorándum, libro de apuntes; (top.) libreta.

noted [nóuted], *a.* afamado, célebre.

notedly [nóutedli], *adv.* notablemente.

noteless [nóutles], *a.* obscuro, desconocido.

noteworthy [nóutuœrƋi], *a.* notable, digno de atención.

nothing [núzing]. **I.** *s.* nada, ninguna cosa; la nada; nadería, friolera; nitos; cero.—**n. doing**, V. DOING.—**n. like**, ni con mucho, ni aproximadamente.—**n. much**, no mucho, poca cosa.—**n. worth**, sin valor, despreciable.—**for n.**, gratis, de balde; inútilmente, sin provecho.—**that is n. to me**, eso nada me importa. **II.** *adv.* de ningún modo, en nada.—**n. daunted**, sin temor alguno, sin inmutarse.

nothingness [núzingnes], *s.* nada; la nada; nonada; insignificancia.

notice [nóutis]. **I.** *s.* nota, observación; atención; aviso, noticia, informe, notificación; mención; artículo, suelto; ojo, llamada; consideración, cortesía.—**at the shortest n.**, al momento, tan pronto como sea posible.—**on short n.**, con poco plazo o tiempo, con poco tiempo de aviso. **II.** *va.* notar, advertir, reparar; hacerse cargo de, atender a, cuidar de; mentar, hacer mención de; (fam.) tratar con atención.

noticeable [nótisabœl], *a.* digno de atención, notable; perceptible.

noticeably [nótisabli], *adv.* notablemente; perceptiblemente.

notification [nótifikéiŝhun], *s.* notificación.

notify [nótifai], *va.* notificar; dar a conocer.

notion [nóŝhun], *s.* noción; idea; parecer, opinión; entendimiento, sentido; (fam.) preocupación; capricho; (fam.) (gen. *pl*) baratija, fruslería.

notional [-al], *a.* imaginario, ideal; fantástico; caprichoso, chiflado, maniático.

notionally [-i], *adv.* idealmente.

notoriety [nótoráieti], *s.* notoriedad, publicidad (esp. de carácter escandaloso).

notorious [notórius], *a.* notorio, público, conspicuo; de mala reputación.

notoriously [-i], *adv.* notoriamente.

notoriousness [-nes], *s.* notoriedad, publicidad; mala reputación.

notornis [notórnis], *s.* (zool.) notornis.

notus [nótus], *s.* noto, austro.

notwheat [nótjuit], *s.* (bot.) trigo chamorro.

notwithstanding [nótuizstǽnding]. **I.** *adv.* no obstante. **II.** *prep.* a pesar de, a despecho de. **III.** *conj.* aun cuando, aunque, bien que; por más que.—**n. that**, aunque.

nought [not], *s.* = NAUGHT.

noumenon [númenon], *s.* (filos.) nóumeno.— **noumenal** [-æl], *s.* noumenal, relativo al nóumeno, de carácter de nóumeno.

noun [náun], *s.* (gram.) nombre, substantivo.

nourish [nœriŝh], *va.* nutrir, alimentar; abrigar, alentar; fomentar; criar, educar. **II.** *vn.* nutrir, dar alimento.

nourishable [-abœl], *a.* que se puede nutrir o fomentar.

nourisher [-œr], *s.* nutridor, alimentador.

nourishing [-ing], *a.* nutritivo, alimenticio.

nourishment [-mœnt], *s.* alimento; nutrición, alimentación; pasto, pábulo, fomento.

nova [nóuvœ], *s.* estrella transitoria.

Novatian [novéiŝhæn], *s.* y *a.* novaciano.

novel [nóvœl]. **I.** *a.* novel, nuevo, original; reciente, moderno. **II.** *s.* novela; (for.) novela.

novelette [nóvelét], *s.* novela corta.

novelist [nóvelist], *s.* novelista.

novelistic [nóvelístic], *a.* novelesco.

novelize [nóvelaiŝ], *va.* novelar.
novelty [nóvelti], *s.* novedad; innovación.
November [novémbœr], *s.* noviembre.
novena [novína], *s.* (igl.) novena.
novenary [nóvenæri], *a.* novenario.
novennial [novénial], *a.* que ocurre cada noveno año o que dura nueve años.
novice [nóvis], *s.* novicio; (igl.) novicio.
novitiate [novíŝhiet], *s.* (igl.) noviciado; novicio.
novocaine [nóvokéin], *s.* novocaína (nombre de fábrica de un anestésico local).
now [náu]. **I.** *adv.* y *conj.* ahora; ahora que; ya, ora; después de esto; ahora bien, esto supuesto; ¡vamos!—**n. and again, n. and then,** de vez en cuando, de cuando en cuando.—**n. . . ., n. . . .,** ya . . . ya, ora . . . ora, alternativamente (*now rich, now poor,* ya rico, ya pobre).—**n. then,** y bien, bien, pues bien. **III.** *s.* actualidad, momento presente.
nowadays [náuedéiŝ], *adv.* hoy día.
noway(s [nóue(ŝ], *adv.* de ningún modo.
nowhere [nójueær], *adv.* en ninguna parte.—**n. else,** en ninguna otra parte.
nowhither [nójuiþœr], *adv.* hacia ninguna parte.
nowise [nóuaiŝ], *adv.* de ningún modo, de ninguna manera, de modo alguno.
noxious [nócshʊs], *a.* nocivo, malsano, mefítico.—**noxiously** [-li], *adv.* perniciosamente.—**noxiousness** [-nes], *s.* calidad de nocivo.
noz(z)le [nóŝœl], *s.* boquerel, boquilla (de manguera); boquilla, gollete, pitón, cuello, alargadera, canuto, tobera; (Ingl.) hocico.
nubbin [núbin], *s.* (fam. E. U.) mazorca imperfecta de maíz.
Nubian [núbian], *s.* y *a.* nubio.
nubile [niúbil], *a.* núbil; doncella casadera.
nucha [núca], *s.* nuca.
nuciferous [niusífœrʊs], *a.* que produce nueces.
nucleal [niúcliæl], **nuclear** [-ar], *a.* nuclear.
nucleate [niúcliet], *va.* y *vn.* formar un núcleo.
nuclein [niúclein], *s.* (quím.) nucleína.
nucleolus [niucliólʊs], *s.* nucléolo.
nucleus [niúcliʊs], *s.* núcleo.
nudation [niudéŝhʊn], *s.* acto de desnudar.
nude [niúd], *a.* desnudo, nudo; escueto.—**the n.,** (b. a.) desnudo, figura humana desnuda.
nudge [nʊy]. **I.** *va.* tocar con el codo. **II.** *s.* toque ligero dado con el codo.
nudity [niúditi], *s.* desnudez, desabrigo.
nugatoriness [niúgatorines], *s.* nulidad.
nugatory [niúgatori], *a.* ineficaz; nugatorio.
nugget [núguet], *s.* (min.) pepita, palacra.
nuggety [núgueti], *a.* en forma de pepitas.
nuisance [niúsans], *s.* incomodidad, molestia, estorbo; engorro, fastidio, lata; indecencia, porquería; (for.) perjuicio, daño, molestia o incomodidad que se causa al prójimo sin derecho para ello.
null [nʊl]. **I.** *vn.* tornear algo en forma de cuentas de rosario; ensortijarse, formar cocas. **II.** *a.* nulo, inválido, írrito, sin fuerza legal.— **n. and void,** nulo, írrito. **III.** *s.* cosa sin validez ni eficacia; nonada, cero; obra de rosario.
nullification [nʊlifikéŝhʊn], *s.* anulación, invalidación; (E. U. pol.) renuncia de un estado a obedecer las leyes federales.
nullify [nʊlifai], *va.* anular, invalidar.
nullity [nʊliti], *s.* nulidad; (for.) acto o documento nulo y sin valor.
numb [nʊm]. **I.** *a.* aterido, entumecido, baldado. **II.** *va.* entumecer, baldar.
number [númbœr]. **I.** *va.* numerar, contar; computar; incluir, contar, ascender a.—**numbering machine,** máquina numeradora. **II.** *s.* número; cifra, guarismo; (gram.) número; (impr.) número o ejemplar (de periódico); (poét., mús.) ritmo, cadencia.—*pl.* aritmética, ciencia de los números.—**Numbers,** Números, libro del Antiguo Testamento.—**n. one,** (fam.) uno mismo, sí mismo.—**a n. of,** varios.
numberer [númbœrœr], *s.* numerador, contador.
numberless [númbœrles], *a.* innumerable, un sinnúmero de.

numbfish [númfiŝh], *s.* (ict.) torpedo.
numbness [númnes], *s.* entumecimiento, aterimiento, envaramiento, adormecimiento.
numerable [niúmœrabœl], *a.* numerable, enumerable.
numeral [niúmœral], *a.* numeral; numerario.—*s.* número, cifra, guarismo; (gram.) nombre o adjetivo numeral.
numerary [niúmœræri], *a.* numerario.
numerate [niúmœreit], *va.* numerar, enumerar, contar.
numeration [-éiŝhʊn], *s.* numeración hablada; enumeración.
numerator [-eitœr], *s.* contador; numerador.
numeric(al [niuméric(al], *a.* numérico.
numerically [-i], *adv.* numéricamente.
numerosity [niumœrósiti], *s.* numerosidad.
numerous [niúmœrʊs], *a.* numeroso; muchos.—**numerously** [-li], *adv.* numerosamente, en gran número.—**numerousness** [-nes], *s.* numerosidad.
Numidian [niumídiæn], *s.* y *a.* númida.
numismatic(ai [niúmismátic(al], *a.* numismático.—**numismatics** [-tics], **numismatology** [niumismatóloyi], **numismatography** [niumismatógrafi], *s.* numismática.—**numismatist** [niumismatist], *s.* numismático.
nummular [númiular], *a.* monetario; (med.) numuláceo.
numskull [númscʊl], *s.* zote, bodoque.
nun [nʊn], *s.* monja; (orn.) una de varias clases de aves—paro, harla, pichón, copetudo, etc.— **n. buoy,** boya de barrilete.—**n.'s velling,** (tej.) velo de monja.
nunciature [núnŝhietiur], *s.* nunciatura.
nuncio [núnŝhio], *s.* nuncio.
nuncupative, nuncupatory [nʊnkiúpativ, tori], *a.* nuncupativo, verbal.
nunnery [núnœri], *s.* convento de monjas.
nunnish [núniŝh], *a.* monjil.
nuptial [núpŝhal], *a.* nupcial.—**n. plumage,** plumaje de un ave durante la cría.—**n. song,** epitalamio.
nuptials [núpŝhalŝ], *s. pl.* nupcias, boda.
nurl [nœrl], *va.* acordonar una moneda.—**nurling tool,** portamoleta.
nurse [nœrs]. **I.** *s.* ama de cría, nodriza; niñera; enfermera, enfermero; protector, padrino; fomentador; especie de tiburón.—**n. balloon,** globo nodriza, globo alimentador.—**n. bee,** abeja de menos de dieciséis días.—**n. child,** niño de teta.—**n. pond,** vivero. **II.** *va.* criar, lactar, amamantar; alimentar, mantener; abrigar, acariciar; cuidar o asistir enfermos; fomentar, dar alas. **III.** *vn.* cuidar de un enfermo; dar de mamar a un niño, criar; mamar, amamantarse; lactar.
nursemaid [-méid], *s.* niñera; criandera, ama.
nurser [nœrsœr], *s.* promotor.
nursery [nœrsœri], *s.* crianza; cuarto o aposento destinado a los niños; (agr.) plantel, plantío, plantario, almáciga, criadero, semillero; vivero, viveral; (fig.) plantel, semillero, seminario.—**n. garden,** vivero, criadero.—**n. tales,** cuentos de niños.
nurserymaid [-méid], *s.* = NURSEMAID.
nursing [nœrsing], *s.* crianza, lactancia.—**n. bottle,** biberón, tetero.
nursling [nœrsling], *s.* niño de teta.
nurture [nœrchœr]. **I.** *s.* nutrimento; alimentación, nutrición; educación, crianza; fomento. **II.** *va.* nutrir, alimentar; criar; educar, enseñar; promover.
nut [nʊt], *s.* (bot.) nuez; fruto parecido a la nuez; (mec.) tuerca, matriz, hembra de tornillo; talón del arco de violín.—**n. oil,** aceite de nueces.—**n. of an anchor,** (mar.) oreja de ancla.—**n. pick,** escoznete.—**n. pine,** pino que da piñones.—**n. wrench,** desvolvedor. **II.** *vn.* coger nueces.
nutant [niútant], *a.* (bot.) inclinado.
nutation [niutéŝhʊn], *s.* (astr.) nutación; inclinación de cabeza.
nutbrown [nútbráun], *a.* avellanado.
nutcracker [nútcrækœr], *s.* cascanueces.
nutgall [nútgol], *s.* (bot.) agalla.

nuthatch [nútjæch], s. (orn.) picamadero.

nuthook [nútjúc], s. horquilla para coger nueces.

nutmeg [nútmeg], s. (bot.) nuez moscada.—**n. grater, tree,** mirística.

nutpecker [nútpécœr], s. = NUTHATCH.

nutria [niútria], s. (zool.) nutria.

nutrient [niútrient]. **I.** a. nutricio, nutritivo. **II.** s. alimento nutritivo.—**nutriment** [-mœnt], s. nutrimento, alimento.—**nutrimental** [-méntal], a. nutrimental.

nutrition [niutríshʊn], s. nutrición, alimentación.

nutritious [niutríshʊs], **nutritive** [niútritiv], a. nutritivo, alimenticio.

nutshell [nútshel], s. cáscara de nuez o avellana. —**In a n.,** en pocas palabras, en su más simple expresión.

nuttiness [nútines], s. sabor de nuez.

nutty [núti], a. abundante en nueces; que sabe a nueces; (fam.) elegante; (con on o upon) entusiasta, loco (por); chiflado.

nux vomica [núx vómica], s. nuez vómica.

nyanza [niǽnša], s. lago, pantano.

nyctalopy [nictǽlopi], s. nictalopia.

nyctalops [níctalops], s. nictálope.

nymph [nimf], s. ninfa; (poét.) mujer joven, zagala; (ent.) ninfa, paloꭑilla, crisálida.

nympha [nímfa], s. (anat.) ninfa de la vulva; (zool.) ninfa, crisálida.

nymphæa [nimfía], s. (bot.) ninfea, neúfar.

Nymphæaceæ [nimfiései o nimfiásee], s. pl. (bot.) ninfeáceas.

nymphal [nímfal], **nymphean** [nimfían], a. perteneciente a las ninfas.

nymphomania, nymphomany [nímfoméinia, -méini], s (med.) ninfomanía, furor uterino.

O

o [óu], s. o.

O! interj. ¡O! ¡oh! ojalá.

oaf [of], s. idiota, zoquete, bobalicón.

oak [óuc], s. (bot.) roble.—**o. apple,** u **o. gall,** bugalla, agalla del roble.—**o. grove,** robledo, robledal.—**o. leather,** cuero curtido con cáscara de roble; hongo duro y correoso que nace en los robles.—**o.-tanned,** curtido con corteza de roble.— **o. tree,** (bot.) roble.

oaken [óukœn], a. roblizo, de hojas o madera de roble.

oakling [óucling], s. roble tierno.

oakum [óukʊm], s. estopa.

oaky [óuki], a. duro, fuerte.

oar [óœr]. **I.** s. remo; remero; ꭇevolvedor. **II.** va. y vn. bogar, remar.

oarage [óœreꭇ], s. conjunto de remos.

oared [óœrd], a. provisto de remos; (zool.) que tiene pies parecidos a remos.

oarlock [óœrloc], s. horquilla, escalamera.

oarsman [óœrsman], s. remero, remador.

oarsmanship [-ship], s. arte de remar; destreza en remar.

oary [óœri], a. formado como remo.

oasis [óásis u oésis], s. oasis.

oast [óust], s. horno para lúpulo.

oat(s [óut(s], s. (bot.) avena; (poét.) avena; poema pastoril.—**oats-peas-beans,** juego de niños que bailan y cantan en corro.—**off one's oats,** indispuesto, desganado.

oatcake [óutkéic], s. torta de harina de avena.

oaten [óutœn], a. aveníceo de avena.

oatfield [óutfíld], s. avenal.

oath [óuz], s. juramento; reniego, mala palabra.— **o.-breaking,** violación de juramento, perjurio.— **on,** u **upon, o.,** bajo juramento.

oatmeal [óutmil], s. harina de avena; gachas de avena.

obbligato [obligáto], s. (mús.) obligado

obduracy [óbdiurasi], s. obduración, obcecación, obstinación.

obdurate [óbdiuret], a. obstinado.—**obdurately** [-li], adv. tercamente, obstinadamente.

obdurateness [-nes] = OBDURACY.

obedience [obídiœns], s. obediencia.—**obedient** [-œnt], a. obediente.—**obediently** [-li], adv. obedientemente.

obeisance [obísans, obésans], s. cortesía, reverencia, homenaje.

obelisk [óbelisk], s. obelisco; (impr.) cruz, obelisco, obelo (†).

obelus [óbelʊs], s. obelo, obelisco, cruz o señal (como —, ÷ o †) puesto al margen.

obese [obís], a. obeso, gordo.—**obeseness** [-nes], **obesity** [obésiti], s. obesidad, gordura, crasitud.

obey [obéi], va. obedecer; estar sujeto a, estar bajo el dominio de.

obfuscate [obfúsket], va. ofuscar, cegar.

obfuscation [-kéishʊn], s. ofuscación, ceguedad.

obi [óbi], s. sortilegio practicado por los negros de las Antillas.

obit [óbit], s. óbito, defunción; exequias, funerales.

obituary [obíchuæri]. **I.** a. obituario, mortuorio. **II.** s. necrología; (igl.) obituario.

object [óbyect], s. objeto, cosa, materia, sujeto; objeto, propósito; blanco, punto; (gram.) complemento.—**o. glass, o. lens,** (ópt.) objetivo. —**o. lesson,** lección práctica u objetiva.—**o. teaching,** enseñanza o método objetivo.

object [obyéct]. **I.** va. objetar, oponer, aducir, poner reparos; imputar, hacer cargos. **II.** vn. oponerse, poner objeción.

objectify [-ifai], **objectivize** [-ivaiŝ], va. (filos.) objetivar.—**objectification** [-iꭍkéishʊn], s. (filos.) objetivación.

objection [obyécshʊn], s. objeción, reparo; réplica; tacha, defecto; inconveniente.

objectionable [-abœl], a. inconveniente; defectuoso; reprensible, censurable.

objective [obyéctiv]. **I.** a. objetivo.—**o. case,** caso complementario.—**o. point,** punto objetivo, meta. **II. s.** (ópt.) objetivo; (gram.) acusativo, caso acusativo; punto objetivo, destinación, objeto, propósito.

objectively [obyéctivli], adv. objetivamente.

objectivism [obyéctiviŝm], s. (filos.) objetivismo.

objectivity [obyéctíviti], s. (filos.) objetividad.

objectless [óbyectles], a. sin objeto.

objector [obyéctœr], s. impugnador, objetante.

objurgate [obyœrgueit], va. reprender, regañar, reconvenir.

objurgation [óbyœrguéshʊn], s. reprensión, reconvención, reprimenda.

objurgatory [obyœrgatori], a. reprobatorio.

oblate [obléit]. **I.** a. achatado por los polos; (igl.) consagrado al culto. **II.** s. beato, misero; (igl.) hostia, oblata.

oblation [obléshʊn], s. (igl.) oblación, ofrenda, sacrificio; eucaristía.

obligate [óbliguet], va. obligar, comprometer, empeñar; precisar, constreñir.

obligation [-guéishʊn], s. obligación, promesa formal; agradecimiento.—**of o.,** obligatorio, de obligación, de precepto.—**to be under o. to one,** deber favores a uno.—**to put, o place, under o.,** hacer favores a; imponer obligación (legal o moral) a.

obligatoriness [óbligatorines], s. calidad de obligatorio.

obligatory [-tori], a. obligatorio.

oblige [obláiꭇ], va. obligar, compeler, constreñir; complacer, agradar, servir, hacer un favor. Ú. a menudo, esp. en la voz pasiva, para expresar agradecimiento, dar las gracias o pedir un favor; v. gr.: I am obliged (o much obliged) to you, muchas gracias, le agradezco mucho; I am very much (o greatly) obliged to you, le agradezco muchísimo, muchísimas gracias; you will greatly oblige me, me hará Vd. un gran favor, le agradeceré muchísimo.

obligee [óbliyí], s. (for.) obligado.

obliger [obláiꭇœr], s. el que obliga.

obliging [-ying], a. servicial, servidor, obsequioso, condescendiente.—**obligingly** [-li], adv. cortésmente, bondadosamente.—**obligingness** [-nes], s. cortesía, condescendencia, bondad.

obligor [obligór], s. (for.) deudor, obligado.

oblique [oblíc *u* obláic]. **I.** *a.* oblicuo, sesgado, diagonal, inclinado; indirecto, evasivo; solapado, doloso, siniestro; colateral (pariente); (gram.) oblicuo.—**o. angle,** ángulo oblicuo.— **o.-angled,** oblicuángulo. **II.** *vn.* oblicuar, torcerse. **III.** *s.* oblicua, línea oblicua.—**obliquely** [-li], *adv.* oblicuamente, al sesgo, de reflón; indirectamente, por rodeos.—**obliqueness** [-nes], [**obliquity** [oblícuiti], *s.* oblicuidad, sesgo, desviación; aberración, extravío.

obliterate [oblítœreit], *va.* borrar; destruir; arrasar; (med.) obliterar.—**obliteration** [-éišhun] *s.* cancelación, testación o testadura, extinción, destrucción; (med.) obliteración.

oblivion [oblívion], *s.* olvido.

oblivious [-vius], *a.* olvidadizo, desmemoriado; abstraído, absorto; que causa olvido.

oblong [óblong]. **I.** *a.* oblongo. **II.** *s.* cuadrilongo.

obloquy [óblocui], *s.* deshonra, baldón; difamación.

obnoxious [obnócšhus], *a.* ofensivo, odioso, detestable; sujeto, expuesto.—**obnoxiously** [-li], *adv.* odiosamente.—**obnoxiousness** [-nes], *s.* odiosidad.

oboe [óboe], *s.* (mús.) oboe.—**oboist** [óboist], *s.* oboe (el que lo toca).

obol, obolus [óbol(us], *s.* óbolo.

obovate [obóvet], *a.* (bot.) trasovado.

obscene [obsín], *a.* obsceno, indecente; (poét.) asqueroso.—**obscenely** [-li], *adv.* obscenamente.— **obsceneness** [-nes], **obscenity** [obsénlti], *s.* obscenidad, indecencia, torpeza.

obscurant(ist [obskiúrant(ist], *s.* obscurantista. —**obscurantism** [-tišm], *s.* obscurantismo.

obscuration [óbskiuréišhun], *s.* obscurecimiento.

obscure [obskiúœr]. **I.** obscuro. **II.** *va.* obscurecer; ocultar, disfrazar, evadir, confundir (*to obscure the issue,* confundir o disfrazar el punto en debate).—**obscurely** [-li], *adv.* obscuramente.

obscureness [-nes], *u* **obscurity** [-kiúriti], *s.* obscuridad.

obsecration [obsecréšhun], *s.* (igl.) cada ruego de la letanía.

obsequial [obsícuial], *a.* funeral, fúnebre.

obsequies [óbsecuiš], *s. pl.* exequias, funeral, ritos fúnebres.

obsequious [obsícuius], *a.* zalamero, servicial; servil, rendido.—**obsequiously** [-li], *adv.* servicialmente; servilmente.—**obsequiousness** [-nes], *s.* servilismo.

observable [obsćérvabœl], *a.* observable; perceptible; visible, conspicuo; ordinario, usual. —**observableness** [-nes], *s.* calidad de observable o notable.—**observably** [-bli], *adv.* notablemente, conspicuamente.

observance [-vans], *s.* observancia; rito o ceremonia; costumbre, uso.

observant [-vant], *a.* observador, vigilante; observante, obediente.

observation [óbsœrvéišhun], *s.* observación; escrutinio, examen.—**o. car,** (E. U., f. c.) coche trasero con mirador.

observatory [obsćérvatori], *s.* observatorio; atalaya; mirador, miradero.

observe [obsćérv], *va.* observar; velar, vigilar; guardar (una fiesta); cumplir (un precepto).

observer [-œr], *s.* observador.

observing [-ing], *a.* observador, atento, cuidadoso; observante.—**observingly** [-li], *adv.* cuidadosamente, atentamente.

obsession [obséšhun], *s.* obsesión; (mil.) sitio (de una plaza).

obsidian [obsídian], *s.* (min.) obsidiana.

obsidional [obsídional], *a.* (mil.) obsidional.

obsolesce [obsolés], *vn.* caer en desuso.—**obsolescence** [-sens], *s.* estado o acto de caer en desuso. —**obsolescent** [-sœnt], *a.* que va haciéndose, anticuado.

obsolete [óbsolit]. **I.** *a.* anticuado; (biol.) atrofiado, imperfecto. **II.** *s.* voz anticuada.

obsoleteness [-nes], *s.* desuso; (biol.) desarrollo imperfecto.

obstacle [óbstacœl], *s.* obstáculo.

obstetric(al [obstétric(al], *a.* obstétrico.

obstetrician [óbstetríšhan], *s.* especialista en obstetricia; partero, comadrón.

obstetrics [obstétrics], *s.* obstetricia.

obstinacy [óbstinasi], *s.* obstinación. porfía.

obstinate [óbstinet], *a.* obstinado, terco.

obstinately [-li], *adv.* obstinada o tercamente.

obstreperous [obstrépœrus], *a.* estrepitoso, ruidoso, turbulento, alharaquero.—**obstreperously** [-li], *adv.* estrepitosamente, turbulentamente. —**obstreperousness** [-nes], *s.* estrépito, bulla, baraúnda alharaca.

obstruct [obstrúct], *va.* obstruir; atorar; dificultar, estorbar; atajar, detener.

obstructer, obstructor [obstrúctœr], *s.* el que estorba, impide o retarda.

obstruction [obstrúcšhun], *s.* obstrucción, estorbo, obstáculo, entorpecimiento.—**obstructionism** [-išm], *s.* (pol.) obstruccionismo.—**obstructionist** [-ist], *s.* (pol.) obstruccionista.

obstructive [obstrúctiv]. **I.** *a.* obstructivo. **II.** *s.* impedimento.—**obstructiveness** [-nes], *s.* calidad de obstructivo.

obstruent [óbstruœnt], *a.* (med.) opilativo.

obtain [obtéin]. **I.** *va.* obtener, adquirir, alcanzar, lograr. **II.** *vn.* prevalecer, privar, ser ley, moda o uso; existir, presentarse; aplicarse.

obtainable [obtéinabœl], *a.* asequible.

obtainer [obtéinœr], *s.* el que obtiene.

obtainment [obtéinmœnt], *s.* obtención, consecución, logro.

obtrude [obtrúd]. **I.** *va.* imponer, meter o introducir a la fuerza. **II.** *vn. y vr.*—**to o. one's self,** entrometerse, intrusarse.

obtruder [obtrúdœr], *s.* entremetido, intruso.

obtruncate [obtrúnkéit], *va.* desmochar.

obtruncation [-kéišhun], *s.* desmoche, desmochadura.

obtrusion [obtrúýun], *s.* intrusión, entremetimiento.

obtrusive [obtrúsiv], *a.* intruso, entremetido; importuno; pretencioso.

obtund [obtúnd], *va.* embotar, amortiguar.

obturate [óbtiureit], *va.* obturar, tapar.

obturation [obtiuréišhun], *s.* obturación.

obturator [óbtiureitœr], *s.* obturador.

obtuse [obtiús], *a.* obtuso; romo, sin punta, embotado; lerdo, torpe; sordo, apagado (ruido).—**o.-angle, o.-angled,** obtusángulo.

obtusely [-li], *adv.* obtusamente; lerdamente.

obtuseness [-nes], *s.* embotadura, embotamiento; torpeza.

obverse [óbvœrs]. **I.** *s.* anverso, frente. **II.** *a.* del anverso.

obversion [obvćéršhun], *s.* vuelta que se da a un objeto para ponerlo de frente.

obvert [obvćért], *va.* volver un objeto de frente a.

obviate [óbviet], *va.* obviar, evitar, salvar.

obvious [óbvius], *a.* obvio, evidente.—**obviously** [-li], *adv.* obvia o evidentemente.—**obviousness** [-nes], *s.* claridad, evidencia.

oca [óca], *s.* (bot.) oca; caví.

occasion [okéiýun]. **I.** *s.* ocasión o; caso; acontecimiento; oportunidad, coyuntura; sazón, tiempo oportuno; motivo, causa, razón; necesidad, falta.—**as o. requires,** en caso necesario, cuando llegue la ocasión.—**by o. of,** a causa de. —**on, o upon, o.,** en su oportunidad o a su debido tiempo; cuando se ofrece, ocasionalmente. **II.** *va.* ocasionar, causar, acarrear.

occasionable [-abœl], *a.* que puede ser causado u ocasionado.

occasional [-al], *a.* ocasional, casual, fortuito; accidental; poco frecuente, que ocurre de cuando en cuando.—**occasionally** [-i], *adv.* a veces, de vez en cuando.

occasioner [-œr], *s.* ocasionador, causante, causador; causa, motivo.

occident [ócsidœnt], *s.* occidente, ocaso.—**O.,** Europa y América.

occidental [ocsidéntal], *s. y a.* occidental.

occipital [ocsípital], *a.* occipital.—**o. bone,** hueso occipital.

occiput [ócsiput], s. occipucio.

occlude [oclúd], va. cerrar, tapar; (quím.) absorber; (med.) ocluir.

occlusion [oclúyun], s. (med.) oclusión; (quím.) absorción de gases.

occult [ocúlt], a. oculto; visible sólo para los que tienen visión espiritual, según la teosofía.

occultation [ócultéíshun], s. (astr.) ocultación; desaparición.

occultism [ocúltism], s. investigación de lo sobrenatural; astrología; teosofía moderna.

occultist [ocúltist], s. teósofo.

occultness [ocúltnes], s. calidad de oculto.

occupancy [ókiupansi], s. ocupación, toma de posesión; tenencia.

occupant [ókiupant], s. ocupante; inquilino.

occupation [ókiupéíshiun], s. ocupación, toma de posesión; tenencia, inquilinato; ocupación, trabajo; oficio, empleo, profesión.

occupational [-æl], a. relativo a ocupaciones u oficio.—**o. disease**, enfermedad causada por el oficio u ocupación.

occupied [ókiupaid], a. ocupado.

occupier [-paiær], s. = OCCUPANT.

occupy [ókiupai], va. ocupar, emplear (tiempo); estar instalado en, vivir en; apoderarse de; dar empleo, ocupación o trabajo a.—**to be occupied with**, ocuparse en.

occur [ocœr], vn. ocurrir, encontrarse; suceder; aparecer; ocurrirse, venir a la imaginación o a la memoria.

occurrence [ocœrœns], s. ocurrencia; suceso, caso, acaecimiento.

ocean [óshæn], s. océano.

oceanic [osheænic], a. oceánico; (zool.) pelágico.

oceanographer [óshanógræfœr], s. oceanógrafo.—**oceanographic** [-nogræfic], a. oceanográfico.—**oceanography** [-nógræfi], s. oceanografía.

ocellate(d [osélet(ed], a. ojoso; manchado, rodado.

ocellus [osélus], s. (zool.) ocelo.

ocelot [óselot], s. (zool.) ocelote.

ochlocracy [oclócrasi], s. oclocracia.

ochra [ócra], s. V. OKRA y GUMBO.

ocher, ochre [ókœr], s. ocre, sil.

ocherous, ochreous [ókœrus], **ochery** [ókœri], a. ocroso.

o'clock [oclóc], loc. contr. de OF THE CLOCK (según el reloj).—**what o. is it?** ¿qué hora es?—**it is eight o.**, son las ocho.

octagon [óctægon], s. octágono.

octagonal [óctægonal], a. octágono, octagonal.

octahedral [óctajídral], a. octaédrico.

octahedron [óctajídron], s. octaedro.

octant [óctant], a. y s. (astr., geom.) octante.

octateuch [óctatiuc], s. octateuco.

octave [óctev]. I. s. (mús. y poét.) octava; (igl.) octava de una fiesta.—**o. coupler**, doblemano de órgano. II. a. octavo, ochavo.

octavo [octévo]. I. a. (impr.) en octavo. II. s. libro, folleto, etc., en 8vo.

octennial [octénial], a. que dura ocho años.

octet [octét], s. (mús.) octeto.

octillion [octíllun], s. octillón; (E. U. y Fr.) unidad con 27 ceros; (Ingl.) unidad con 48 ceros.

October [octóbœr], s. octubre.

octodecimo [óctodésimo], a. (impr.) en décimoctavo; (escríbese por lo común 18mo y se llama **eighteenmo** [éitínmo]).

octoedrical [octoídrical], a. octoédrico.

octogenarian [óctoyenérian], **octogenary** [octóyenæri], a. y s. octogenario, ochentón.

octopetalous [óctopétalus], a. octopétalo.

octopus [óctopus u octópus], s. pulpo, pólipo, jibia octópoda; (fig.) organización monopolizadora o absorbente.

octoroon [óctorún], s. mulato muy claro.

octostyle [óctostail], s. (arq.) octóstilo.

octosyllabic [óctosilábic], a. octosílabo.

octroi [octruá], s. fielato; derechos de puerta o de consumos.

octuple [óctiupœl], a. óctuplo.

ocular [ókiular]. I. a. ocular, visual. II. s. (ópt.) ocular.

ocularly [ókiularli], adv. ocularmente; visiblemente.

oculist [ókiulist], s. oculista, oftalmólogo.

od [óud], s. fuerza misteriosa a que se atribuían los fenómenos del mesmerismo, llamada también **od(y)lic force** y **astral fluid**.

odalisk [ódalisk], s. odalisca.

odd [od]. I. a. impar; non, sobrante; y tantos, y pico (forty odd, cuarenta y tantos, cuarenta y pico); suelto (an odd volume, un tomo suelto; an odd job, una tarea suelta); casual, accidental; extraordinario, singular, raro; excéntrico, extraño; ridículo, estrambótico. II. s. V. ODDS.

oddity [óditi], s. singularidad, rareza; despropósito; ente singular.

oddly [ódli], adv. desigualmente; extrañamente, singularmente; estrambóticamente.

oddness [ódnes], s. disparidad, desigualdad; singularidad, extravagancia, rareza.

odds [ods], s. pl. (y a veces singular) desigualdad, diferencia, disparidad; partido desigual, apuesta desigual; ventaja, superioridad, exceso; riña, pendencia, disputa.—**o. and ends**, retazos, trozos, fragmentos sobrantes.—**to be at o.**, estar de punta o encontrado(s).

ode [óud], s. (poét.) oda.

odeon [odíon], s. odeón.

odic [óudic], a. (poét.) ódico.

odious [ódius], a. odioso, abominable.—**odiously** [-li], adv. odiosamente, abominablemente.—**odiousness** [-nes], s. odiosidad; odio.

odium [óudium], s. odiosidad; odio; mala voluntad, malquerencia.—**o. medicum**, odio mutuo de médicos rivales.—**o. theologicum**, odio teológico.

odometer [odómetœr], s. hodómetro.

odometrical [odométrical], a. hodométrico.

odontalgia [odontælyia], s. odontalgia, dolor de muelas.

odontalgic [odontælyic], a. odontálgico.

odontograph [odóntograf], s. (mec.) instrumento para trazar dientes de engranaje.

odontoid [odóntoid], a. odontoideo.

odontology [odontóloyi], s. odontología.

Odontornithes [odontórnizis], s. pl. (pal.) odontornites, pájaros con dientes.

odontoscope [odóntoscoup], s. (dent.) odontoscopio.

odo(u)r [óudœr], s. olor; aroma, perfume, fragancia; estimación; reputación.

odoriferous [óudœrífœrus], a. odorífero.

odo(u)rless [óudœrles], a. inodoro.

odorous [óudœrus], s. oloroso, fragante.

odorousness [-nes], s. fragancia, aroma.

odyl [óudil], s. V. OD.

Odyssey [ódisi], s. Odisea.

œ [e o i], diptongo con que antes se escribían algunas voces de origen latino o griego que hoy se escriben con e, tales como **œconomics, œcumenical**, y que se hallarán en la **E**.

œnological [enolóical], a. enológico.

œnology [enóloyi], s. enología.

œnometer [enómetœr], s. enómetro.

o'er [ócr], contr. poética de OVER.

œstrum [és- u óistrum], s. brama, celo; estro.

œstrus [éstrus], s. (ent.) tábano.

of [ov], prep. de. Éste es el significado general de of; pero hay algunas expresiones, sobre todo con verbos, e idiotismos en que equivale a otra preposición o no se traduce (to think of, pensar en; to rob a man of his money, robar el dinero a un hombre; to taste of, saber a; of course, naturalmente; of late, últimamente). Tales formas se dan en los artículos sobre los verbos, sustantivos, etc. correspondientes. Cuando un gerundio sigue a un posesivo, el sustantivo que en español es el acusativo del verbo correspondiente va gen. precedido de of: la expresión resultante se traduce mediante el infinitivo o el subjuntivo del verbo español: his writing of that letter, el que él haya (hubiese) escrito esa carta; our ordering of those articles, el pedir (o haber pedido) nosotros esos artículos, o el que nosotros pidamos (hayamos pedido) esos artículos.—**o. an evening,** algunas noches.—**o. myself, himself,** etc., por mí mismo, por sí mismo, etc., solo.—**o. the,** del, de la, de los, de las.—**it is five minutes of three,** faltan cinco minutos para las tres.—**it is very kind of you to do that,** es Vd. muy bondadoso en hacer eso.

off (of]. **I.** *adv.* lejos, a distancia, fuera; enteramente, del todo; quitado, no puesto (*the lid is off,* la tapa está quitada; *my shoes are off,* estoy sin zapatos, me he quitado los zapatos); abandonado, frustrado (*the trip is off,* el viaje se ha abandonado, hemos desistido del viaje, etc.); de menos, de rebaja (*two per cent off,* rebaja o descuento de dos por ciento); a (con respecto a distancia: *two miles off,* a dos millas). Se une a muchos verbos para modificar su sentido, denotando ausencia, diminución, privación o distancia.—**o. and on,** de vez en cuando, algunas veces; a intervalos.—**how far o. is it?** cuánto hay de aquí allá? **II.** *prep.* lejos de; fuera de; de; desde; frente a, a corta distancia de, cerca de (*off the coast,* cerca de la costa; *off New York,* frente a Nueva York).—**o. color,** desteñido; (joy.) de mal color; (fam.) verde, obsceno.—**o. the track,** (fam.) despistado, por los cerros de Úbeda.—**from o.,** de. **III.** *a.* derecho o de la derecha (hablando de una pareja de animales, o bien de las patas de los mismos, v. gr.: el buey de la derecha; *off fore foot,* pata derecha delantera); de fiesta, de asueto (v. gr.: *an off day,* un día libre: *the off season,* la estación muerta); (fam.) equivocado, incorrecto (v. gr.: *in his calculations,* errado en sus cálculos).—**o. side,** lado derecho. **IV.** *interj.* ¡fuera! ¡vete! ¡vamos!—**o. with his head!** ¡que le corten la cabeza!—**o. with you!** ¡márchate! ¡fuera de aquí!

offal [ófal], *s.* asadura, despojos de reses muertas; desecho, desperdicio.

offcast [ófcæst]. **I.** *a.* desechado, descartado. **II.** *s.* cosa descartada.

offence, offenceless=OFFENSE, OFFENSELESS.

offend [ofénd]. **I.** *va.* y *vn.* ofender. **II.** *vn.* pecar, delinquir; desagradar, disgustar.

offender [oféndœr], *s.* delincuente, transgresor; ofensor, agraviador.

offense [oféns], *s.* ofensa; culpa, falta; cualquier delito o desaguisado.—**no o.,** sin ofender a Vd.

offenseless [-les], *a.* inofensivo.

offensive [-iv]. **I.** *a.* ofensivo, desagradable; perjudicial; agresivo.—**o. odor,** olor desagradable.—**o. warfare,** guerra ofensiva. **II.** *s.* ofensiva, ataque.

offensively [-li], *adv.* ofensivamente.

offensiveness [-nes], *s.* calidad de ofensivo o desagradable.

offer [ófœr]. **I.** *va.* ofrecer, prometer; proponer; sacrificar, inmolar. **II.** *vn.* ofrecerse, ocurrir; (con **at**) intentar, tratar de. **III.** *s.* oferta, ofrecimiento, promesa; envite; declaración de amor; esfuerzo, intento; (com.) oferta; proposición o propuesta.

offerable [ófœraboel], *a.* ofrecible.

offerer [ófœrœr], *s.* ofrecedor; oferente.

offering [ófœring], *s.* ofrecimiento, oferta; sacrificio; ofrenda, oblación, tributo.

offertory [-tori], *s.* (igl.) ofertorio; ofrecimiento, ofrenda.

offhand [ófjænd], *a.* y *adv.* improvisado, de repente; sin preparación; a pulso; sin cumplidos ni ceremonia.

office [ófis], *s.* oficio; ministerio, empleo o cargo (sea público o privado); colocación, destino; oficina, despacho, bufete; agencia, negociado, departamento; (igl.) oficios, función solemne, rezo.—*pl.* servicio, favor; buenos oficios; (Ingl.) cocina y cuartos del servicio.—**o. boy,** chico de oficina, muchacho mandadero.—**o. building,** edificio de oficinas.—**o. copy,** copia certificada.—**o. hours,** horas de oficina; (med.) horas de consulta o de clínica.—**o. hunter,** o seeker, pretendiente, buscaempleos.—**o. work,** trabajo de oficina; (ing.) trabajo de gabinete.—**to be in o.,** tener un empleo; estar en el poder.

officeholder [-jóuldœr], *s.* empleado público.

officer [ófiscœr]. **I.** *s.* oficial; funcionario; dignatario; empleado o dependiente de alguna categoría; agente de policía; (mil.) oficial o jefe (desde alférez arriba). **II.** *va.* mandar (como oficial o jefe); proveer de oficiales y jefes.—**officered** [-d], *a.* provisto de oficiales y jefes.

official [ofíshal]. **I.** *a.* oficial; de oficio; autorizado; (farm.) oficinal.—**o. letters,** pliegos de oficio. **II.** *s.* oficial público; funcionario; (Ingl.) provisor o juez eclesiástico; juez de la curia.

officialdom [-dum], *s.* círculos oficiales; funcionarios públicos.

officialism [-ism], *s.* estado, condición, costumbres oficiales; burocracia; formalismo.

officially [-li], *adv.* oficialmente.

officialty [ofíshalti], *s.* (igl.) cargo de oficial o ministro de la curia.

officiate [ofíshieit], *vn.* oficiar; funcionar, ejercer o desempeñar un cargo.

officinal [ofisinal o ofisáinal], *a.* (farm.) oficinal; (bot.) empleado en las artes o como medicamento.

officious [ofíshus], *a.* oficioso, entremetido, intruso; solícito.—**officiously** [-li], *adv.* oficiosamente.—**officiousness** [-nes], *s.* oficiosidad.

offing [ófing], *s.* mar afuera.

offish [ófish], *a.* intratable, arisco.

offlet [óflet], *s.* (hidr.) tubo de desagüe de un canal.

offprint [ófprint], *s.* (impr.) reproducción de un artículo, párrafo, etc.

offscouring [ófscáuring], **offscum** [ófscum], *s.* hez, desecho, basura, lavaduras.

offset [ófset], *s.* balance, compensación, equivalencia, equivalente; (geog.) estribo, estribación; (top.) ordenada; (E. U.) terraplén; cañería en S; (arq. e impr.) = SET-OFF.

offset [ofsét]. **I.** *va.* equiparar, compensar, contrapesar; neutralizar; medir la tierra por el procedimiento de ordenadas; terraplenar. **II.** *va.* (impr.) repetir.

offshoot [ófshut], *s.* renuevo, vástago; ramal.

offshore [ófshœœr], *adv.* de la costa; a corta distancia de la costa.

offspring [ófspring], *s.* hijos, prole, progenie o descendencia.

oft [oft]. **I.** *a.* (poét.) frecuente. **II.** *adv.* a menudo, con frecuencia.

often [ófœn], **oftentimes** [-táims], **ofttimes** [óftaims], *adv.* frecuentemente, a menudo.—**as o.** as, siempre que, tantas veces (o tan a menudo) como.—**how o.,** cada cuánto, cuántas veces.—**not o.,** rara vez.

ogee [oyí], *s.* (arq.) gola, cimacio.

ogive [óyiv u óyaiv], *s.* (arq.) arista de arco carpanel; ojiva, arco apuntado.

ogival [oyáival], *a.* aristado; ojival.

ogle [ógœl]. **I.** *va.* y *vn.* ojear, echar el ojo, comerse con los ojos a. **II.** *s.* mirada al soslayo, ojeada.

ogler [óglœr], *s.* el que echa el ojo.

ogling [ógling], *s.* ojeada, mirada al soslayo.

ogre [ógœr], *s.* ogro, monstruo.

ogress [ógres], *s.* ogro hembra.

oh! [o], *interj.* ¡oh!

ohm [om], *s.* (elec.) ohmio.—**ohmic** [-ic], *a.* (elec.) óhmico.—**ohmmeter** [-mítœr], *s.* ohmímetro.

oho [ojó], *interj.* ¡ajá!

oidium [óidium], *s.* (bot.) oídio.

oil [óil]. **I.** *s.* aceite; petróleo; óleo.—**o. bag,** glándula oleífera.—**o. beetle,** (ent.) carraleja.—**o. bottle**=o. CAN.—**o. box,** (f. c.) caja de aceite o sebo.—**o. cake,** torta de berujo.—**o. can,** alcuza.—**o. car,** vagón tanque para petróleo.—**o. colors,** pinturas al óleo.—**o. cup,** (mec.) aceitera, copa de engrase.—**o. engine,** motor de petróleo.—**o. gas,** gas de petróleo.—**o. meal,** berujo molido, harina de berujo.—**o. mill,** molino de aceite, trujal, almazara.—**o. miller,** almazarero.—**o. motor**= O. ENGINE.—**o. painting,** pintura al óleo, cuadro al óleo; arte de pintar al óleo.—**o. paints**=O. COLORS.—**o. pan,** recogedor de aceite.—**o. pipe,** tubo de engrase.—**o. press**=O. MILL.—**o. safe,** almijara, depósito de aceite.—**o. shop,** aceitería.—**o. stove,** estufa o cocina de petróleo.—**o. tank,** tanque, depósito de aceite (gen. de petróleo).—**o. trough,** canal de aceite.—**o. well,** pozo de petróleo. **II.** *va.* aceitar, engrasar, lubricar; (fig.) hacer liso, suave y agradable; ungir, olear; untar (la mano), sobornar.

oilbird [-bǽrd], *s.* (orn.) guácharo.

oilcloth [-clóz], *s.* encerado, hule.

oiler [óilœr], *s.* aceitero, engrasador; aceitera, aceitador; alcuza; capa de hule; buque aceitero.

oilet [óilet], *s.* (arq.) tronera.

oiliness [óilines], *s.* oleaginosidad, untuosidad.

oilskin [óilskín], *s.* encerado, impermeable.

oilstone [óilstóun]. **I.** *s.* piedra afiladera o de amolar; asperón. **II.** *va.* afilar con asperón.

oily [óili], *a.* aceitoso, oleoso, oleaginoso; grasiento, craso; zalamero, hipócrita.—**o. calm,** tranquilo como una balsa de aceite.—**o. grain,** (bot.) ajonjolí.

ointment [óintmœnt], *s.* ungüento.

okapi [ocápi], *s.* rumiante del Congo semejante a la jirafa.

okra [ókra], *s.* (bot.) quimbombó.

old [óuld], *a.* viejo; antiguo; añejo.—**o. age,** vejez.—**o. bachelor,** solterón.—**o. boy,** (fam.) chico, mi viejo (expresión de amistad).—**O. Boy,** (fam.) el diablo.—**o.-fashioned,** chapado a la antigua; anticuado, fuera de moda.—**O. Glory,** (E. U.) la bandera de los E. U.—**O. Guard,** (E.U.) bando conservador del partido republicano.—**o. Harry,** (fam.) el diablo.—**o. lady,** anciana.—**o. looking,** de aspecto viejo, que parece viejo.—**o. maid,** solterona; la mona (juego de naipes).— **o.-maidish,** que parece u obra como solterona; melindroso, caprichoso.—**o. man,** viejo.—**O. Nick,** (fam.) el diablo.—**o. song,** bagatela.—**o. style,** estilo antiguo (de computar el tiempo); (impr.) tipo de forma antigua.—**O. Testament,** Antiguo Testamento.—**o.-timer,** antiguo residente o concurrente.—**o. timber,** madera usada o de demolición. **o. wheat,** trigo añejo.—**o. wine,** vino añejo.—**o. woman,** vieja.—**O. World,** Viejo Mundo.—**o.-world,** del Viejo Mundo.— **how o. is he, are you,** etc.? ¿cuántos años tiene él, Vd., etc.?—**of o.,** antiguo; antiguamente.—**to be . . . o.,** tener . . . de edad (*he is six years old,* él tiene seis años).—**to be o. enough,** tener bastante edad; no ser niño.

olden [óuldœn]. **I.** *a.* (poét.) viejo, antiguo.—**o. time,** tiempos pasados o antiguos. **II.** *vn.* envejecer, hacerse viejo.

oldish [óuldish], *a.* avejentado.

oldness [óuldnes], *s.* vejez; envejecimiento.

oleaceous [oleéshus], *a.* (bot.) oleáceo.

oleaginous [oleáyinus], *a.* oleoso, oleaginoso.

oleaginousness [-nes], *s.* oleosidad.

oleander [oleǽndœr], *s.* (bot.) adelfa, baladre.

oleaster [oleǽstœr], *s.* (bot.) oleastro, acebuche.

oleate [óliet], *s.* (quím.) oleato.

oleic [ólíic o óleic], *a.* (quím.) oleico.

olein [ólein], *s.* (quím.) oleína.

oleograph [óleogræf], *s.* oleografía.

oleomargarin(e [óleomárgarin], *s.* oleomargarina.

oleoresin [-résin], *s.* oleorresina.

oleose [óleos], **oleous** [óleus], *a.* oleoso.

olfactory [olfǽctori]. **I.** *a.* olfatorio. **II.** *s.* olfato.

olibanum [olíbanum], *s.* incienso, olíbano.

oligarch [óligark], *s.* oligarca.

oligarchic(al [oligárkic(al], *a.* oligárquico.

oligarchy [óligarki], *s.* oligarquía.

oligist(e [óliyist], *s.* (min.) oligisto.

Oligocene [óligosin], *s.* y *a.* (geol.) oligoceno.

oligoclase [-cleis], *s.* (min.) oligoclasa.

olio [ólio], *s.* mezcla, miscelánea; olla podrida, olla.

olivaceous [olivéshus], *a.* oliváceo.

olivary [óliveri], *a.* oliviforme.—**o. body,** (anat.) oliva o cuerpo olivar.

olive [óliv]. **I.** *s.* (bot.) olivo; aceituna, oliva.— **o.-bearing,** olivífero.—**o.-colour(ed,** aceitunado. —**o. dealer,** aceitunero.—**o. grove,** olivar.—**o. oil,** aceite de oliva.—**o. presser,** lagarero.—**o. tree,** (bot.) olivo, aceituno.—**o. yard,** olivar. **II.** *a.* aceitunado.

---

olivin(e [ólivin], *s.* (min.) olivino.

olla [óla], *s.* marmita, puchero, olla.—**o. podrida,** olla podrida; mistifori, mescolanza.

Olympiad [olimpiæd], *s.* olimpíada.

Olympian, Olympic [-pian, -pic], *a.* olímpico.

Olympus [-pus], *s.* olimpo.

Om, *s.* nombre solemne del Ser Supremo entre los bracmanes.

omasum [omé-, omásum], *s.* (anat.) libro, tercer estómago de los rumiantes.

omber, ombre [ómbœr], *s.* tresillo o juego del hombre.

omega [omíga *u* ómega], *s.* omega; fin.

omelet [ómelet], *s.* tortilla de huevos.

omen [ómen], *s.* agüero, pronóstico, presagio.

omened [ómend], *a.* fatídico.

omental [oméntal], *a.* omental.

omentum [oméntum], *s.* omento, redaño.

ominous [óminus], *a.* ominoso, siniestro, nefasto; presagioso, pronosticador.—**ominously** [-li], *adv.* ominosamente; fatalmente.—**ominousness** [-nes], *s.* calidad de ominoso.

omissible [omísibœl], *a.* que se puede omitir o excluir.

omission [omíshun], *s.* omisión; supresión, exclusión; olvido, descuido.

omissive [omísiv], *a.* que omite o excluye; remiso.

omit [omít], *va.* omitir; prescindir de; suprimir, excluir; pasar por alto, olvidar.

omnibus [ómnibus]. **I.** *s.* (carr.) ómnibus; palco grande al nivel del escenario; (fam.) ayudante de mozo de comedor. **II.** *a.* que comprende varios asuntos.

omnifarious [omniférius], *a.* omnímodo.

omniferous [omnífœrus], *a.* que puede producir todas las cosas.

omnific [omnífic], *a.* que todo lo crea.

omniform [ómniform], *a.* omnímodo.

omniformity [ómnifórmiti], *s.* calidad de omnímodo.

omniparous [omníparus], *a.* omníparo.

omnipotence, omnipotency [omnípotens, i], *s.* omnipotencia.

omnipotent [-tœnt], *a.* y *s.* omnipotente.

omnipresence [ómniprésœns], *s.* ubicuidad, omnipresencia.

omnipresent [-œnt], *a.* omnipresente.

omniscience, omnisciency [omníshœns, i], *s.* omnisciencia.

omniscient [-œnt], *a.* omnisciente.

omnium [ómnium], *s.* (Ingl.) agregado de los diversos títulos de la deuda; estante para bric-a-brac.—**o. gatherum,** (fam.) miscelánea, mare mágnum.

omnivorous [omnívorus], *a.* omnívoro; glotón; codicioso; (zool.) omnívoro.

omoplate [ómopleit], *s.* (anat.) omoplato.

omphacin(e [ómfasin], *a.* onfacino.

omphalic [omfélic], *a.* umbilical.

omphalism [ómfalism], *s.* centralización; centralismo.

on [on]. **I.** *prep.* sobre, encima de; en (*on the floor,* en el suelo; *on the train,* en el tren; *on the island,* en la isla; *on the wall,* en la pared; *on the committee,* en la comisión; *he is on his second year,* está en su segundo año; *on that occasion,* en esa ocasión; *on arriving,* en llegando); a, al (*on my arrival,* a mi llegada; *to bet on a horse,* apostar a un caballo; *on seeing,* al ver; *on seeing him,* al verlo; *on the right,* a la derecha); bajo, so, con (*on my responsibility,* bajo mi responsabilidad; *on pain of death,* bajo (so) pena de muerte; *on his word,* por su palabra; *on my part,* por mi parte; *on all sides,* por todos lados; *on condition,* con la condición; *on long terms,* con plazos largos); contra (*an attack on liberty,* un ataque contra la libertad; *draw attack on me,* gire contra mí). Gen. no se traduce cuando le sigue una expresión de tiempo: *on Monday,* lunes; *on that day,* ese día.—**o. an average,** por término medio.—**o. a sudden,** de golpe, de repente.—**o. credit,** al fiado.—**o. duty,** en servicio. —**o. fire,** ardiendo.—**o. foot,** a pie.—**o. guard,** en guardia; de guardia; alerta.—**o. high,** en alto; en

---

lo alto.—**o. horseback**, a caballo.—**o. purpose**, a propósito, adrede.—**o. record**, registrado; que consta; de que se tiene noticia.—**o. second thought**, después de reflexionar, reflexionando.—**o. the contrary**, por el contrario.—**o. the gad**, callejeando, correteando.—**o. the move**, moviéndose, andando.—**o. the run**, corriendo; afanándose.—**o. time**, a la hora debida; puntualmente; (com.) a plazo, al fiado.—**o. to**, a, hacia.—**o. trust**, al fiado. **II.** *adv.* o *a.* puesto (*the lid is on*, la tapa está puesta; *with his hat on*, con el sombrero puesto); principiado, ocurriendo, verificándose (*the game is on*, el juego ha principiado, o se está jugando). Se usa con muchos verbos para indicar continuación o acción continua (*speak on*, continué hablando), o posición o colocación sobre algo que se sobrentiende (*the frying pan is on* [*the fire*], la zartén está sobre el fuego, o ya puesta). Se emplea pleonásticamente con ciertos comparativos, como "más" en español (*later on*, más tarde; *farther on*, más adelante). Indica la parte que va adelante en ciertos movimientos (*head on*, de cabeza).—**o. and off**, a intervalos, de vez en cuando.—**o. and o.**, continuamente, sin cesar.—**and so o.**, y así sucesivamente; etcétera. **III.** *interj.* ¡adelante!

onager [ónayœr], *s.* (zool. y mil) onagro.

onagra [onégra *o* nágra], *s.* (bot.) onagra.

once [uʌns]. **I.** *adv.* una vez; en otro tiempo, otras veces.—**o. and again**, varias veces.—**o. for all**, una vez por todas, por última vez, definitivamente.—**o. in a while**, de cuando en cuando.—**o. more**, otra vez.—**o. upon a time**, en otro tiempo; en tiempo de Maricastaña; érase que se era.—**at o.**, a un mismo tiempo; de una vez, simultáneamente; enseguida, inmediatamente.—**for o.**, una vez siquiera; últimamente; al fin.—**this o.**, esta vez, siquiera esta vez. **II.** *a.* de otro tiempo, pasado, que fué.

oncome [óncʌm], *s.* (med.) ataque repentino; hinchazón.

one [uʌn]. **I.** *a.* un, uno; solo, único; un tal; igual.—**o. day**, un día, cierto día; algún día, un día de éstos.—**o.-eyed**, tuerto.—**o.-handed**, manco.—**o.-horse**, de (o tirado por) un caballo;. de poca importancia.—**o. hundred**, cien, ciento.—**o.-sided**, parcial, injusto, leonino; de un solo lado; desigual.—**o.-story**, de un solo piso.—**o. thousand**, mil.—**it is all o. to me**, lo mismo me da; me es lo mismo.—**of o. height**, de un mismo alto.—**with o. accord**, de común acuerdo, unánimemente. **II.** *s.* y *pron.* uno; la una (hora). Ú. como reproductivo en casos en que un español se usa el artículo o el adjetivo sustantivado: *this one*, éste; *the white one*, el blanco; *the one that came*, el que vino; *the little one*, el chiquillo; *a better one*, uno mejor. Ú. indefinidamente en el sentido de "cosa," "chiste," "sujeto," "tipo," etc.: *this is a good one*, éste es un buen chiste (noticia, jugada, etc., según el caso); *he is a bad one*, es mal sujeto.—**o. and all**, todos, todos sin excepción.—**o. and the same**, idéntico.—**o. another**=EACH OTHER.—**o. by o.**, uno a uno, uno por uno.—**o. or two**, unos pocos.—**o.'s**, de uno, su.—**o. to o.**, de punto por punto o parte por parte.—**all o.**, lo mismo.—**at o.**, a una; de común acuerdo.—**for o.**, por lo menos, uno de los que (*I for one don't believe it*, yo por lo menos no lo creo, yo soy uno de los que no lo creen).

oneness [uʌnnes], *s.* unidad.

onerous [ónœrʌs], *a.* oneroso, gravoso; gravable, sujeto a gravamen.

one's self [uʌnŝ self], **oneself** [uʌnself], *pron.* se, sí, sí mismo, uno mismo, a uno mismo.

ongoing [óngóing]. **I.** *a.* que marcha o va hacia adelante. **II.** *s.* movimiento hacia adelante.—*pl.* acontecimientos; negocios, asuntos.

onion [úniʌn], *s.* (bot.) cebolla.—**o. bed**, cebollar.

onlooker [ónlúkœr], *s.* espectador.

only [ónli]. **I.** *a.* único, solo; singular, raro.—**o. begotten**, unigénito.—**o. child**, hijo único. **II.** *adv.* sólo, solamente, únicamente. **III.** *conj.* sólo que, pero.

onomastic [onoméstic], *a.* onomástico.

onomatechny [onoméchni], *s.* onomancia.

onomatopœia [ónométópíya], *s.* (ret.) onomatopeya.—**onomatopœic, onomatopoetic** [-píic, -poétic], *a.* onomatopéyico.

onrush [ónruŝh], **onset** [-set], *s.* embestida, arremetida, carga, ataque; acceso; arranque.

onslaught [ónslot], *s.* ataque furioso, embestida, arremetida, asalto.

ontogeny [ontóyeni], *s.* ontogenia.

ontologic(al [ontolóyic(al], *a.* ontológico. .

ontologist [ontóloyist], *s.* ontólogo.

ontology [ontóloyi], *s.* ontología.

onus [óunʌs], *s.* carga, responsabilidad.—**o. probandi**, obligación de probar.

onward [ónuard], *a.* avanzado; progresivo.

onward(s, *adv.* adelante, hacia adelante; progresivamente; en adelante.

onyx [ónix], *s.* (min.) ónice, ónix; (med.) absceso en la córnea del ojo.

oolite [óolait], *s.* (min.) oolita.

oolitic [oolític], *a.* oolítico.

oologic(al [oolóyic(al], *a.* oológico.

oology [oolóyi], *s.* (orn.) oología.

oolong [úlong], *s.* variedad de te negro.

oophorectomy [óoforéctomi], *s.* ovariotomía.

oophoritis [-ráitis], *s.* ovaritis.

oosperm [-spœrm], *s.* huevo fecundado.

oosphere [óosfíœr], *s.* (bot.) oosfera, célula reproductiva antes de su fecundación.

ooze [uŝ]. **I.** *va.* sudar. **II.** *vn.* manar, fluir; escurrirse; exudar, rezumarse, trazumarse. **III.** *s.* fango, limo, lama; chorro suave.

oozy [úŝi], *a.* cenagoso, lamoso, legamoso.

opacity [opésiti], *s.* opacidad.

opal [ópal], *s.* (min.) ópalo.—**opalesce** [ópalés], *vn.* irisar.—**opalescence** [-sens], *s.* calidad de opalino.—**opalescent** [-ent], **opaline** [ópalin], *a.* opalino, iridiscente.

opaque [opéic], *a.* opaco; (bot. y ent.) sin brillo, obscuro, mate.

opaqueness [opéiknes], *s.* opacidad.

ope [óup], *va.* (poét.) abrir.

open [óupœn]. **I.** *va.* abrir; descubrir; desenvolver, destapar, desempaquetar; desplegar; establecer; cortar, rajar; romper; exponer, manifestar, descubrir, revelar; explicar; ensanchar, aumentar.—**to o. the ball**, abrir el baile o romper a bailar; dar comienzo.—**to o. the mouth**, hablar.—**to o. up**, explorar, descubrir, hacer accesible. **II.** *vn.* (a veces *con out*) abrirse, desplegarse, destaparse; descubrirse; dividirse, entreabrirse; aparecer, asomarse; desarrollarse, desenvolverse; empezar, comenzar, estrenarse.—**to o. on, o upon**, dar o mirar a. **III.** *a.* abierto, libre, franco; público; descubierto; extendido, desplegado; expuesto a un ataque; desnudo, visible; receptivo, dispuesto a, susceptible de; listo, aparejado; manifiesto, claro; sincero, franco; directo; suave; templado; (gram.) abierta (vocal); (com.) abierto, pendiente.—**o. air**, aire libre.—**o. coil**, (elec.) bobina abierta.—**o. car**, (aut.) coche abierto o descubierto.—**o. credit**, (com.) letra abierta.—**o. door**, (der. int.) puerta abierta, igualdad de derechos.—**o.-eyed**, alerta, vigilante, avizor.—**o. face**, muestra (de reloj) sin tapa.—**o.-faced**, sin tapa; de cara franca.—**o.-handed**, generoso, dadivoso o liberal.—**o.-hearted**, ingenuo, sincero, abierto.—**o.-heartedness**, liberalidad, generosidad; franqueza.—**o.-hearth** (**steel, process,** etc.), (acero, procedimiento, etc.) Siemens-Martin.—**o. letter**, carta abierta.—**o. look**, mirada franca.—**o. market**, mercado público, mercado.—**o. marks**, señales evidentes.—**o.-minded**, razonable, liberal, imparcial.—**o.-mouthed**, con la boca abierta; clamoroso.—**o. notes**, notas blancas (breves, semibreves y mínimas).—**o. pit**, (min.) tajo abierto.—**o. plumbing**, tuberías descubiertas.—**o. port**, puerto abierto al comercio extranjero.—**o. question**, cuestión discutible.—**o. sea**, alta mar.—**o. seam**, junta abierta (sin soldar).—**o. secret**, secreto conocido de todos, secreto de Anchuelos.—**o. sesame**, conjuro mágico para abrir puertas secretas; (fig.) palabra mágica, vara mágica.—**o. shame**, vergüenza pública.—**o. shop**, taller franco, en que se admiten obreros de los gremios y de fuera de los gremios.—**o. winter**, invierno templado, sin heladas.—**in o. court**, en pleno tribunal.—**in the o. air**, al raso, a la intemperie.—**in the o. field**, a campo raso.—**with o. arms**, con los

---

Para la pronunciación de æ, œ, D, ŝ, ŝh, U, ŷ, Y, z, véase la clave al principio del libro.

brazos abiertos. **IV.** *s.* claro, raso, lugar abierto.—**in the open,** a campo raso; al descubierto, abiertamente.

opener [óupnœr], *s.* abridor; (tej.) desmotadora.

opening [óupning]. **I.** *s.* abertura, brecha; orificio; vano (de puerta o ventana); luz; abrimiento; claro, raso, campo abierto; abra, bahía; (min.) socavón, galería; principio, inauguración, apertura; oportunidad, coyuntura. **II.** *a.* aperitivo.—**o. price,** primer curso (en la Bolsa).

openly [óupœnli], *adv.* abiertamente; públicamente.—**openness** [-nes], *s.* franqueza, sinceridad, publicidad.

openwork [-uœrk], *s.* (cost.) deshilado, calado.

opera [ópœra], *s.* (mús.) ópera.—**o. book,** libreto de una ópera.—**o. bouffe,** ópera bufa.—**o. cloak,** abrigo de señora para la salida del teatro.—**o. comique,** ópera cómica, zarzuela.—**o. glasses,** gemelos de teatro.—**o. hat,** clac.—**o. house,** ópera (edificio), teatro de la ópera.—**o. singer,** operista, cantante de ópera.

operameter [opœrémetœr], *s.* operámetro.

operand [óperænd], *s.* (mat.) cantidad sometida a una operación.

operate [ópœreit]. **I.** *va.* hacer funcionar, mover, actuar; gobernar, dirigir, manejar; llevar a cabo, efectuar. **II.** *vn.* (con **in, on** o **upon**) obrar, operar; producir efecto; funcionar; exonerar el vientre, hacer del cuerpo; (cir.) operar; (com.) especular, jugar a la bolsa.

operatic(al [ópœrǽtic(al], *a.* de ópera.

operating [ópœréiting], *a.* de operación; de funcionamiento; de explotación; de manejo, de servicio.—**o. expenses,** gastos de funcionamiento, de explotación o corrientes.—**o. room,** (cir.) sala de operaciones; (fot.) cuarto obscuro. —**o. table,** (cir.) mesa de operaciones.

operation [opœréshʊn], *s.* operación; funcionamiento; manejo, manipulación; acción, efecto; (cir.) operación.

operative [ópœrativ]. **I.** *a.* operativo, eficaz, activo. **II.** *s.* operario, obrero, artesano.

operator [ópœréitœr], *s.* operario; maquinista; telegrafista; telefonista; escribiente con máquina; (cir.) operador; (com.) agente, corredor de bolsa; (E. U.) explotador o empresario de minas de carbón.

opercular [opœrkiular]. **I.** *a.* que tapa. **II.** *s.* opérculo.

operculum [opœrkiulʊm], *s.* (biol.) opérculo.

operetta [ópœréta], *s.* opereta, zarzuela.

ophicleide [óficlaid], *s.* (mús.) figle.

Ophidia [ofídia], *s. pl.* (zool.) ofidios.—**ophidian** [-diæn], *a.* y *s.* ofidio.

ophioglossum [ófioglósʊm], *s.* (bot.) ofiglosa o lengua de serpiente.

ophiolatry [ófiólatri], *s.* ofiolatría, culto de las serpientes.

ophiology [-loʏi], *s.* ofiología, ciencia que trata de las serpientes.

ophite [ófait], *s.* (min.) ofita.—**ophitic** [-fític], *a.* ofítico.

Ophiuroidea [ófiuróideæ], *s. pl.* (zool.) ofiurídeos.

ophthalmia [ofzǽlmia], **ophthalmy** [ofzǽlmi], *s.* (med.) oftalmía.—**ophthalmic** [ofzǽlmic], *a.* oftálmico.—**ophthalmography** [ofzælmógrafi], *s.* oftalmografía.—**ophthalmologic(al** [-molóvic(al], *a.* oftalmológico.—**ophthalmology** [-móloʏi], *s.* oftalmología.—**ophthalmometer** [-mmetœr], *s.* (ópt.) oftalmómetro.—**ophthalmoplegia** [-plíʏiæ], *s.* oftalmoplegia.—**ophthalmoscope** [ofzǽlmoscop], *s.* (ópt.) oftalmoscopio.—**ophthalmoscopy** [ofzælmóscopi], *s.* oftalmoscopía.

opiate [ópiet]. **I.** *s.* opiato, narcótico. **II.** *a.* opiado, narcótico, soporífico. **III.** *va.* (med.) administrar opio; (farm.) componer con opio.

opinable [opáinabœl], *a.* opinable.

opinion [opíniʊn], *s.* opinión.—**to be of o.,** ser de opinión, opinar.

opinionated [opíniʊneted], *a.* porfiado, obstinado, terco.

opinionately [opíniʊnetli], *adv.* porfiadamente, obstinadamente.

opinioned [opíniʊnd], *a.* presumido, obstinado.

opinionist [opíniʊnist], *s.* obstinado.

opisometer [opisómitœr], *s.* opisómetro.

opium [ópiʊm], *s.* opio.—**o. eater,** el que toma opio por vicio.—**o. joint,** fumadero de opio.—**o. pipe,** pipa para fumar opio.

opobalsam [opobólsam], *s.* opobálsamo.

opodeldoc [opodéldoc], *s.* (farm.) opodeldoc.

opopanax [opópanacs], *s.* opopónaco (goma de la pánace).

opossum [opósʊm], *s.* (zool.) zarigüeya.

oppilation [opiléshʊn], *s.* opilación.

opponency [opónœnsi], *s.* oposición a un grado, cátedra, etc.

opponent [opónœnt]. **I.** *s.* antagonista, contrincante, contrario; opositor; competidor. **II.** *a.* opuesto, contrario; (anat.) oponente.

opportune [óportiun], *a.* oportuno, a propósito. —**opportunely** [-li], *adv.* oportunamente.—**opportuneness** [-nes], *s.* oportunidad.

opportunism [óportiunišm], *s.* (pol.) oportunismo.—**opportunist** [-ist], *s.* oportunista.

opportunity [óportiuníti], *s.* oportunidad.

opposable [opóusabœl], *a.* oponible.

oppose [opóuš]. **I.** *va.* oponer, resistir, combatir; oponerse a, hacer frente a, luchar contra; impugnar, contrariar, contrarrestar. **II.** *vn.* oponerse, resistirse; argüir; obstar; estar frente a frente.

opposed [opóusd], *a.* opuesto, contrario.

opposeless [opóušles], *a.* irresistible.

opposer [opóušœr], *s.* adversario, antagonista, rival.

opposite [opósit]. **I.** *a.* opuesto; fronterizo, frontero; al otro lado; del otro lado de; al frente de.—**o. leaves,** hojas opuestas.—**the o. sex,** el otro sexo, el sexo opuesto. **II.** *s.* antagonista, adversario; contrario.—**the o.,** lo opuesto, lo contrario.

oppositely [-li], *adv.* enfrente, opuestamente.

oppositeness [-nes], *s.* contrariedad.

opposition [óposíshʊn], *s.* oposición; contraste; contrariedad; aversión, repugnancia; óbice, impedimento; (astr.) oposición.—**oppositional** [-al], *a.* de oposición; de la oposición.—**oppositionist** [-ist], *s.* (pol.) oposicionista, antiministerial.

oppress [oprés], *va.* oprimir; apretar, aprensar, comprimir.

oppression [opréshʊn], *s.* opresión; miseria, calamidad; presura, opresión de ánimo; fatiga, agobio, ahogo; pesadez.

oppressive [oprésiv], *a.* opresivo, tiránico; gravoso; abrumador; sofocante.—**oppressively** [-li], *adv.* opresivamente.—**oppressiveness** [-nes], *s.* opresión.

oppressor [oprésœr], *s.* opresor.

opprobrious [opróbriʊs], *a.* oprobioso o deshonroso.—**opprobriously** [-li], *adv.* oprobiosamente. —**opprobriousness** [-nes], *s.* oprobio.

opprobrium [opróbriʊm], *s.* oprobio.

oppugn [opiún], *va.* oppugnar, combatir.

oppugnancy [opúgnansi], *s.* oppugnación.

oppugner [opiúnœr], *s.* oppugnador.

optative [óptativ], *a.* y *s.* optativo.

optic(al [óptic(al]. **I.** *a.* óptico.—**optic angle,** ángulo óptico.—**optic nerve,** nervio óptico.—**optical square,** escuadra de reflexión.—**optical telegraphy,** telegrafía óptica, sistema de señales ópticas.—**optical thalamus** (*pl.* **thalami**), tálamo óptico. **II.** *s.* ojo.

optician [optíshan], *s.* óptico.

opticist [óptišist], *s.* perito en óptica.

optics [óptics], *s.* óptica.

optimism [óptimišm], *s.* optimismo.—**optimist** [-ist], *s.,* **optimist(ic** [-ist(ic], *a.* optimista.

option [ópshʊn], *s.* opción, elección, facultad de escoger; alternativa; (com.) opción, plazo para determinar.

optional [-al], *a.* facultativo, discrecional.—**optionally** [-li], *adv.* discrecionalmente, a voluntad.

optometer [optómetœr], *s.* (ópt.) opsiómetro.

optometrist [-trist], *s.* optómetra, optometrista. —**optometry** [-tri], *s.* optometría.

optophone [óptofoun], *s.* optófono, instrumento por cuyo medio los ciegos reconocen la luz por el oído.

opulence, opulency [ópiulens, i], *s.* opulencia, abundancia; lozanía; copia.—**opulent** [-lœnt], *a.* opulento.—**opulently** [-li], *adv.* opulentamente.

opuntia [opúnŝhia], *s.* (bot.) tuna, nopal, chumbera.

opus [ópus], *s.* (*pl.* opera) obra o composición literaria o música.

opuscle [opúscœl], *s.* opúsculo.

or [or]. **I.** *conj.* o, u. **II.** *s.* (blas.) oro (color amarillo).

orach [óræc], *s.* (bot.) orzaga, bledo.

oracle [óracœl], *s.* oráculo.

oracular [orékiular], *a.* fatídico; positivo, magistral, dogmático; obscuro, ambiguo.

oraculously [orékiulusli], *adv.* a modo de oráculo.

oral [óral], *a.* oral; verbal, hablado; bucal; (for.) nuncupativo.

orally [órali], *adv.* verbalmente, de palabra.

orange [órenʏ]. **I.** *s.* (bot.) naranja; color de naranja.—**o. blossom**, azahar.—**o. color**, color de naranja.—**o.-colored**, anaranjado.—**o. dog**, (E. U.) oruga nociva a las naranjas.—**o. musk**, pera anaranjada.—**o. peel**, cáscara de naranja.—**o. scale**, insecto cóccido que se cría en el naranjo.—**o. tree**, naranjo, naranjero.—**o. wife**, o **woman**, naranjera, vendedora de naranjas. **II.** *a.* perteneciente a las naranjas; anaranjado.

orangeade [órenʏéid], *s.* naranjada.

Orangeman [-mæn], *s.* orangista, protestante seguidor de Guillermo de Orange; orangista, miembro de la sociedad secreta irlandesa de los orangistas, fomentadora del protestantismo.

orangery [órenʏri], *s.* naranjal.

orang-(o)utan(g [oráeng-utáeng], *s.* (zool.) orangután.

orarium [orérium], *s.* orario, banda que los romanos se ataban al cuello; estola ancha.

oration [oréŝhun], *s.* oración, discurso.

orator [óratœr], *s.* orador; (for., Ingl.) suplicante.

oratorian [oratórian], *s.* (igl.) sacerdote que pertenece a un oratorio.

oratorical [oratórical], *a.* oratorio.

oratorically [oratóricali], *adv.* oratoriamente.

oratorio [oratório], *s.* (mús.) oratorio; capilla.

oratory [óratori], *s.* oratoria, elocuencia; oratorio, capilla; (igl.) oratorio, congregación.

orb. **I.** *s.* orbe, esfera, globo; astro; círculo, rueda. **II.** *va.* cercar, rodear, englobar; formar círculo.

orbed [orbd], *a.* redondo, circular; esférico; redondeado; lleno; de ojos, que tiene ojos (ú. en composición).—**o. moon**, luna llena.

orbicular [orbíkiular], *a.* orbicular, esférico.

orbicularly [orbíkiularli], *adv.* orbicularmente.

orbicularness [orbíkiularnes], *s.* esfericidad.

orbit [órbit], *s.* (astr. y anat.) órbita.

orbital [órbital], *a.* orbital.

orca, *s.* (ict.) orca, orco.

orcanet [órcanet], *s.* (bot.) orcaneta.

orcein [órsein], *s.* (quím.) orceína.

orchard [órchard], *s.* huerto.—**orcharding** [-ing], *s.* cultivo de huertos.—**orchardist** [-ist], *s.* cultivador de huertos.

orch(e)otomy [ork(e)ótomi], *s.* (cir.) orcotomía.

orchestra [órkestra], *s.* (mús.) orquesta; (teat.) platea.—**o. chair**, o **seat**, butaca de platea.

orchestral [-tral], *a.* instrumental, de orquesta.—**orchestrate** [-treit], *va.* (mús.) instrumentar.—**orchestration** [-tréiŝhun], *s.* (mús.) instrumentación.

orchid [órkid], *s.* (bot.) orquídea.

orchidaceous [orkidéŝhus], *a.* orquídeo.

orchil [órkil], *s.* (bot.) urchilla.

orchis [órkis], *s.* (bot.) órquide; orquídea; abejera.

orchitis [orcáitis o kítis], *s.* (med.) orquitis.

orcin(e [órsin], *s.* (quím.) orcina.

ordain [ordéin], *va.* ordenar, mandar; decretar, constituir, estatuir; (igl.) ordenar.

ordainer [ordéinœr], *s.* ordenador.

ordeal [órdial], *s.* ordalía; juicio de Dios; prueba.

order [órdœr]. **I.** *s.* orden; clase; (com.) pedido.—*pl.* orden sacerdotal; sacramento; (mil.) descanso (de armas).—**o. book**, libro de pedidos.—**o. of knighthood**, orden de caballería.—**o. of the day**, orden del día.—**O. of the Garter**, orden de la Jarretera.—**O. of the Golden Fleece**, orden del Toisón de Oro.—**in good o.**, en buen estado.—**in o. to, in o. that**, para, a fin de, para que.—**on the o. of**, de la clase de.—**till further orders**, hasta nueva orden.—**to give an o.**, hacer un pedido.—**to o.**, a la medida; a propósito, especialmente; cuando o como se pida. **II.** *va.* ordenar, mandar; ordenar, arreglar; mandar hacer; pedir (mercancías, una coche, una copa de vino, el almuerzo); (igl.) ordenar.—**o. arms!** (mil.) ¡descansen! (voz de mando); armas en descanso.—**to o. away**, despedir a uno, decirle que se vaya.—**to o. in**, mandar entrar; mandar traer.—**to o. out**, mandar salir; mandar llevar; echar.

orderer [órdœrœr], *s.* ordenador.

orderless [órdœrles], *a.* desordenado.

orderliness [órdœrlines], *s.* orden, método.

orderly [órdœrli]. **I.** *a.* ordenado, metódico; bien arreglado; quieto o tranquilo.—**o. book**, (mil.) libro de ordenanzas.—**o. officer**, oficial del día. **II.** *s.* (mil.) ordenanza; practicante de medicina, asistente en un hospital. **III.** *adv.* ordenadamente, metódicamente, en orden.

ordinal [órdinal]. **I.** *a.* ordinal.—**o. numeral**, numeral ordinal. **II.** *s.* numeral ordinal; (igl.) ritual.

ordinance [-nans], *s.* ordenanza, ley, reglamento, estatuto; (igl.) rito, ceremonia del culto; (arq.) sistema de arreglo, disposición.

ordinarily [-nerili], *adv.* ordinariamente.

ordinary [órdinæri]. **I.** *a.* ordinario, común, corriente; ordenado, metódico, normal; tosco, plebeyo, vulgar; mediano, adocenado.—**o. shares**, acciones ordinarias. **II.** *s.* la masa, el vulgo; juez ordinario; (igl.) orden de la misa; (ant.) fonda a precio fijo; mesa redonda.—**in o.**, actual servicio, con ejercicio.

ordinate [órdinet]. **I.** *a.* ordenado, metódico. **II.** *s.* (geom.) ordenada.

ordination [órdinéŝhun], *s.* (igl.) ordenación; arreglo, buen orden.

ordnance [órdnans], *s.* artillería, cañones.—**o. stores**, o **supplies**, pertrechos de guerra.

ordonnance [órdonans], *s.* (pint.) composición de lugar; ordenación, ordenanza, estatuto.

ordure [órʏur], *s.* excremento, inmundicia.

ore [óer], *s.* mineral, mena.—**o. crusher**, o **stamp**, bocarte, triturador.

oread [óreæd], *s.* orea, oréade, ninfa.

organ [órgan], *s.* (mús.) órgano; organillo (biol.) órgano; hablando de periódicos, órgano.—**o. blower**, entonador.—**o. builder**, organero.—**o. grinder**, tocador de organillo.—**o. pipe**, cañón de órgano.—**o. stop**, registro de órgano.

organdy [órgandi], *s.* (tej.) organdí.

organic(al [orgénic(al], *a.* orgánico; organizado; sistematizado; constitutivo o fundamental; (quím.) orgánico.—**o. chemistry**, química orgánica.—**o. disease**, afección orgánica.—**o. laws**, leyes orgánicas, fundamentales.—**o. remains**, restos orgánicos, materias orgánicas.

organically [orgénicali], *adv.* orgánicamente.

organism [órganiŝm], *s.* organismo; estructura orgánica; (biol.) órgano.

organist [órganist], *s.* (mús.) organista.

organization [órganiŝéŝhun], *s.* organización; organismo; sociedad, compañía; corporación; cuerpo, entidad.

organize [órganais]. **I.** *va.* organizar, disponer, arreglar, constituir; abanderizar; (biol.) organizar. **II.** *vn.* organizarse, constituirse.

organogenesis [órgænoʏénesis], *s.* organogenia.

organographic(al [órganográfic(al], *a.* organográfico.—**organography** [-nógrafi], *s.* organografía.—**organology** [-nóloʏi], *s.* organología.

organon, organum [-non, num], *s.* (filos.) sistema, método (apl. esp. a la lógica de Aristóteles y a la inductiva de Bacon); medio (de conocer).

organzin(e [órgansin], s. torzal; tela de torzal.

orgasm [órgæsm], s. excitación, incontinencia; (med.) orgasmo.

orgeat [órvæt], s. horchata.

orgiastic [órvɪǽstic], a. orgiástico.

orgy [órvi], s. orgía.—pl. orgies, orgías (esp. las bacanales de los antiguos).

orichalc(um [óricǽlcʊm], s. latón, oricalco.

oriel [óriel], s. (arq.) mirador.

orient [órient]. I. a. naciente; oriental; brillante, resplandeciente. II. s. oriente. III. va. orientar.

oriental [orióntal], a. y s. oriental.—orientalism [-ɪsm], s. orientalismo.—orientalist [-ɪst], s. orientalista.—orientalize [-aiś], va. orientalizar.

orientate [órientóit]. I. va. orientar. II. vn. caer o mirar hacia el este.

orientation [orientéshʊn], s. orientación.

orifice [órifis], s. orificio.

oriflamme [óriflæm], s. oriflama.

origan [órigan], origanum [oríganʊm], s. (bot.) orégano, mejorana.

Origenism [óriyenism], s. origenismo.

Origenist [óriyenist], s. origenista.

origin [óriyin], s. origen.

original [oríyinal]. I. a. original; primitivo, primero; radical; ocurrente.—o. sin, pecado original. II. s. original; prototipo; raíz; ejemplar; persona rara u original.

originality [oriyenǽliti], s. originalidad.

originally [oríyinali], adv. originalmente; en el principio.

originate [oríyineit]. I. va. originar, crear, inventar; producir, ocasionar. II. vn. originarse, nacer, dimanar, emanar.

origination [-néshʊn], s. origen, principio; modo de propagar o de producir.

orillon [orílon], s. (fort.) orejón.

oriole [óriol], s. (orn.) oriol, oropéndola.

Orion [oráiʊn], s. (astr.) Orión.

orison [órisœn o son], s. oración, plegaria.

orle [orl], s. (arq.) orla, filete, listón; (blas.) orla.

orlop [órlop], s. (mar.) sollado, plataforma, entrepuente.—o. beam, (mar.) bao del sollado.

ormolu [órmolu], s. similor; bronce dorado; oro molido para dorar.

ornament [órnamœnt]. I. s. ornamento, adorno, ornato; persona o cosa que honra o enaltece; condecoración, insignia. II. va. ornamentar, adornar.

ornamental [órnaméntal], a. ornamental, decorativo.—o. painter, adornista, decorador.

ornamentally [-i], adv. ornadamente.

ornamentation [órnamentéishʊn], s. ornamentación.

ornamented [-mented], ornate [órnet], a. ornado, ornamentado, adornado.

ornateness [órnetnes], s. ornato, adorno.

ornithologic(al [órnizolóyic(al], a. ornitológico.—ornithologist [-zóloyist], s. ornitólogo.—ornithology [-zóloyi], s. ornitología.

ornithomancy [orníʒomansi], s. ornitomancia.

ornithopod [órnizopód], s. y a. ornitópodo.

ornithorhynchus [órnitoríncus], s. ornitorrinco.

orogenesis [óroyénesis], orogeny [oróyeni], s. (geol.) orogenia.

orogenic [óroyénic], a. orogénico.

orographic [órográfic], a. orográfico.

orography [orógrafi], s. orografía.

oroide [óroaid], s. oroide, similor.

orology [oróloyi], s. (geol.) orología.

orometer [orómetœr], s. barómetro de alturas.

oropharynx [orofǽrinx], s. (anat.) faringe.

orotund [órotʊnd]. I. a. rotundo, sonoro. II. s. voz rotunda.

orphan [órfan]. I. a. y s. huérfano.—o. asylum, orfanato, asilo de huérfanos. II. va. dejar huérfano a.—orphaned, a. huérfano.

orphanage [órfaney], s. orfandad; orfanato.

orphanhood [órfanjud], s. orfandad.

Orphean [orfían u órfian], Orphic [órfic], a. órfico.

---

orpiment [órpimœnt], s. oropimente.

orpin(e [órpin], s. (bot.) telefio, fabacrasa; pigmento de varios matices.

orrery [órrœri], s. planetario.

orris [órris], s. (bot.) lirio de Florencia; bocadillo y galón.—o. root, raíz de lirio o iris florentina.

ort [ort], s. (gen. en pl., orts) sobras, desperdicios.

orthocephalous [órzoséfælʊs], a. ortocéfalo.—orthocephaly [-séfæli], s. ortocefalia.

orthochromatic [-cromǽtic], a. (foto.) ortocromático.

orthoclase [-cleis], s. (min.) ortoclasa, ortosa.

orthodox [órzodocs], a. ortodoxo; correcto, admitido, convencional.

orthodoxness [órzodoxnes], s. calidad o condición de ortodoxo.

orthodoxy [órzodocsi], s. ortodoxia.

orthodromics [órzodrómics], orthodromy [órzodromi], s. (mar.) ortodromía.

orthoepic(al [orzoépic(al], a. prosódico, ortológico.

orthoepist [órzoepist], s. ortólogo.

orthoepy [órzoepi], s. ortología, prosodia.

orthogamy [orzógæmi], s. (bot.) autogamia, autofecundación.

orthogon [órzogon], s. ortogonio.

orthogonal [orzógonal], a. ortogonal.

orthographer [orzógrafer], s. ortógrafo.—orthographic(al [órzográfic(al], a. ortográfico.—orthographically [-i], adv. ortográficamente.—orthographist [orzógrafist], s. ortógrafo.—orthography [orzógrafi], s. ortografía.

orthometry [orzómetri], s. ortometría.

orthopedia, orthopædia [orzopídia], orthopedy [órzopídi], s. (cir.) ortopedia.

orthopedic, orthopædic [orzopídic], a. ortopédico.

orthophony [orzófoni], s. ortofonía, arte de pronunciar y articular bien.

orthophosphoric [órzofosfóric], a. ortofosfórico, fosfórico.

orthopnœa [orzopnía], s. (med.) ortopnea.

orthopter [orzóptœr], s. (aer.) ortóptero, avión de alas oscilantes verticalmente.

Orthoptera [orzóptera], s. pl. (ent.) ortópteros.—orthopterous [-ʊs], a. ortóptero.

orthorhombic [orzorrómbic], a. ortorrómbico.

orthoscopic [-scópic], a. de vista normal; para corregir defectos de la vista.

ortive [órtiv], a. (astr.) ortivo.

ortol [órtoul], s. ortol (un revelador fotográfico).

ortolan [órtolan], s. (orn.) hortelano; verderol; emberiza.

oryx [órix], s. (zool.) órix.

Osage orange [ósey óreny], s. (bot.) árbol americano de las urticáceas, que se emplea para formar setos.

oscillancy [ósilansi], s. vibración u oscilación.

oscillate [ósileit]. I. va. balancear, hacer oscilar. II. vn. oscilar, fluctuar.

oscillating [-ing], a. oscilante.—o. engine, máquina de cilindros oscilantes.—o. valve, válvula oscilante.

oscillation [-léishʊn], s. oscilación.

oscillator [-léitœr], s. oscilador.

oscillatory [ósilatori], a. oscilatorio, oscilante.

osculate [óskiuleit], va. y vn. besar; (geom.) tocar por osculación.

osculation [-léishʊn], s. beso, ósculo; (geom.) osculación.

osculatory [óskiulatori], a. osculatorio.

osier [óʒœr]. I. s. (bot.) mimbrera, sauce, sarga; mimbre. II. a. de mimbre, mimbreño.

osiery [óʒœri], s. mimbreral.

os innominatum [os inómiéitʊm], s. hueso innominado, hueso ilíaco.—o. pubis, [-piubis], pubis, parte anterior del hueso ilíaco.—o. sacrum, [-sécrʊm], sacro (hueso).

osmazome [ósmaʒoum], s. osmazomo.

osmic [ósmic], a. ósmico.

osmium [ósmiʊm], s. (quím.) osmio.

---

osmose [osmos], **osmosis** [osmósis], *s.* ósmosis.
osmotic [osmótic], *a.* osmótico.
osprey [óspre], *s.* (orn.) águila osífraga, quebrantahuesos, atahorma.
ossarium [osárium], *s.* osario.
ossein [ósiin], *s.* oseína.
osseous [óseus], *a.* huesoso, óseo, ososo.
ossicle [ósicœl], *s.* huesecillo.
ossiferous [osífœrus], *a.* osífero.
ossific [osífic], *a.* osífico.
ossification [ósifikéshun], *s.* osificación.
ossified [ósifaid], *a.* osificado.
ossifrage [ósifrey], *s.* (orn.) osífraga, quebrantahuesos.
ossify [ósifai], *va.* y *vn.* osificar(se).
ossivorous [osívœrus], *a.* osívoro.
ossuary [ósiueri], *s.* osario, osar.
ostarthritis [ostarzráitis *o* zrítis], *s.* (med.) reumatismo crónico.
osteitis [osteáitis *o* teítis], *s.* (med.) osteítis.
ostensible [osténsibœl], *a.* aparente; pretendido.
ostensibly [-bli], *adv.* ostensiblemente; aparentemente.
ostensive [osténsiv], *a.* ostensivo.
ostentation [ostentéishun], *s.* ostentación, boato; jactancia.—**ostentatious** [-téishus], *a.* ostentoso, jactancioso, faustoso.—**ostentatiously** [-li], *adv.* pomposamente.—**ostentatiousness** (-nes], *s.* pomposidad; jactancia.
osteoblast [óstioblæst], *s.* osteoblasto, célula característica de los huesos.
osteocolla [-cóla], *s.* osteocola.
osteogenesis [-yénesis], **osteogeny** [óstióyeni], *s.* osteogenia, formación de los huesos.
osteography [-ógræfi], *s.* osteografía.
osteologist [ósteóloyist], *s.* osteólogo.
osteology [óste óloyi], *s.* osteología.
osteoma [óstiómæ], *s.* osteoma.
osteomalacia [-mælái shiæ], *s.* osteomalacia.
osteomyclitis [-máieláitis], *s.* osteomielitis.
osteopath [óstiopæz], *s.* osteópata.—**osteopathic** [-pǽzic], *a.* osteopático.—**osteopathy** [ósteópæzi], *s.* osteopatía.
osteotomy [-ótomi], *s.* osteotomía.
ostiary [óstieri], *s.* (igl.) ostiario.
ostler [óslœr], *s.* V. HOSTLER.
ostosis [ostósis], *s.* osificación.
ostracean [ostréishan], **I.** *a.* ostráceo, conchudo. **II.** *s.* ostra.
ostraceous [ostréshus], *a.* ostráceo, ostrero.
ostracism [óstrasiâm], *s.* ostracismo.
ostracize [óstrasaiŝ], *va.* desterrar.
ostrich [óstrich], *s.* (orn.) avestruz.
Ostrogoth [óstrogoz], *s.* ostrogodo.
otacoustic [otacústic], **I.** *a.* otacústico. **II.** *s.* trompetilla.
otalgia [otǽlyia], *s.* (med.) otalgia.
other [úDœr], **I.** *a.* y *pron.* otro, otra, otros, otras.—**the o. day**, el otro día, hace poco. **II.** *adv.* (con *than*) otra cosa que (*I can not do other than praise him*, no puedo hacer otra cosa que alabarlo, no puedo abstenerme de alabarlo).
otherwise [úDœruaiŝ]. **I.** *adv.* de otra manera, de otro modo; también. **II.** *a.* otro, diferente.
otic [ótic], *a.* ótico, auricular.
otiose [óshios], *a.* ocioso; holgazán.
otitis [otáitis *u* otítis], *s.* (med.) otitis.
otolith [ótoliz], *s.* otolito.
otologist [otóloyist], *s.* otólogo, aurista.
otology [otóloyi], *s.* (med.) otología.
otorrhea, otorrhæa [ótorría], *s.* otorrea
otoscope [ótoscoup], *s.* otoscopio.
otoscopy [otóscopi], *s.* otoscopia.
ottar [ótar], **otto** [óto], *s.* aceite esencial.—**o. of roses**, aceite esencial de rosas.
otter [ótœr], *s.* (zool.) nutria; nutria de mar; (ent.) oruga de una mariposa nocturna.—**o.-colored**, alutrado.—**o. hunting**, caza de nutrias. **o. pike** (ict.) dragón marino.—**o. skin**, piel de nutria.
Ottoman [ótoman]. **I.** *a.* y *s.* otomano, turco. **II.** *s.* otomana.

oubliette [úbliet], *s.* calabozo de prisión perpetua con entrada por arriba.
ouch [áuch]. **I.** *s.* (joy.) montura, engaste; adorno de oro. **II.** *interj.* ¡huy! ¡ay, ay!
ought [ot]. **I.** *s.* algo, alguna cosa; nada—**for o. I know**, por lo que yo puedo comprender.
ought [ot]. **I.** *aux. def.* que se traduce por formas (gen. el presente de ind., el condicional y el pret. de subj.) de deber: *you ought not to go*, Vd. no debe (debiera, debería) ir. En la ética se usa como expresión de obligación moral, y a veces queda mejor traducido por "ser el deber," "tener obligación," cambiando un poco el giro. **II.** *s.* (filos.) deber, obligación.
ouija [úiyæ], **ouija board** [bord], tabla de escritura espiritista.
ounce [áuns], *s.* onza (= 28.35 gramos); onza de oro española ($16); (zool.) onza; jaguar; (farm.) V. LIQUID OUNCE.
our, ours [áur, s], *a.* y *pron. poss.* nuestro, nuestra, nuestros, nuestras. Cuando no va seguido del substantivo, se emplea ours, v. gr.: *your house is larger than ours*, la casa de Vd. es mayor que la nuestra; *this is ours*, esto es nuestro; *those cows are ours*, aquellas vacas son nuestras.
ourang [uræng], *s.* = ORANG-OUTANG.
ourself [aursélf], *pron.* yo mismo, yo misma (en estilo oficial o regio).
ourselves [aursélvŝ], *pron. recíproco o enfático.* nosotros mismos, nosotras mismas. V. MYSELF.
ousel [úŝl] = OUZEL.
oust [áust], *va.* desposeer, desalojar, desaposentar, echar fuera, despedir.
ouster [áustœr], *s.* (for.) desahucio, desposeimiento, despojo.
out [áut]. **I.** *adv.* fuera, afuera; hacia fuera. Se emplea después de muchos verbos para indicar movimiento, dirección, etc., hacia fuera o situación fuera o afuera (*to look out*, mirar hacia fuera; *to be out*, estar afuera), o para cambiar parcial o totalmente el significado de ellos (*to look out*, tener cuidado; *to be out*, estar reñidos). Las frases en que sirve para este último objeto se dan con los verbos respectivos.—**o. and o.**, cabal, completo, sin reserva.—**o. at interest**, a interés.—**o. at the elbows**, agujereado, roto por los codos; andrajoso.—**o. at the heels**, con zapatos rotos.—**o. of**, fuera de; más allá de; sin; por (*out of charity*, por caridad: *out of respect for you*, por respeto a Vd.); seguido de un adjetivo, niega el estado o propiedad que éste denota (*out of vertical*, no vertical, desviado de la vertical; *out of true*, no alineado o arreglado, desalineado, desarreglado).—**o. of breath**, sin aliento, jadeante.—**o. of character**, impropio, inconveniente.—**o. of danger**, fuera de peligro.—**o. of doors** = OUT-DOORS.—**o. of fashion**, fuera de moda, pasado.—**o. of favor**, desvalido, desgraciado; desacreditado, menospreciado.—**o. of hand**, luego, al punto.—**o. of his wits**, fuera de sí, insensato.—**o. of hope**, desesperanzado, sin esperanza.—**o. of humor**, de mal humor, enojado.—**o. of joint**, trastornado, desbarajustado.—**o. of measure**, desmesurado.—**o. of one's way**, apartado del camino de uno (gen. es mejor cambiar el giro: *that store is out of my way*, yo no paso por esa tienda); a un lado (poner, hacerse, etc., según el verbo).—**o. of order**, desordenado, descompuesto, desarreglado; fuera de orden.—**o. of patience**, sin paciencia, con la paciencia agotada (a veces es mejor cambiar el giro: *I am out of patience*, se me ha agotado la paciencia).—**o. of place**, fuera de lugar, impropio, desacomodado.—**o. of print**, agotada (una edición).—**o. of sight**, fuera del alcance de la vista, invisible; (fam.) el non plus ultra, de calidad superior, excelente.—**o. of sorts**, indispuesto; descontento; (impr.) falta de un tipo o de una letra.—**o. of spite**, por despique.—**o. of the way**, donde no estorbe; suprimido; hecho, despachado (a veces se cambia el giro: *I am glad that work is out of the way*, me alegro haber salido de ese trabajo).—**o.-of-the way**, *a.* lejano, apartado; inaccesible; extraordinario.—**o. of the woods**, libre de dudas, dificultades.—**o. of time**, fuera de compás.—**o. of touch with**, apartado de, o alejado de; sin relaciones con; en desacuerdo con.—

o. of trim, de mal humor; en mal estado; (mar.) mal estivado.—**o. of tune**, desentonado; destemplado.—**o. to o.**, de extremo a extremo, total.—**a way o.**, salida; escapatoria.—**the time is o.**, el tiempo (la hora) ha pasado; el plazo ha expirado.—**to be o.**, estar fuera o ausente; no estar en casa (o en el despacho, edificio, etc.); no estar de moda o en boga; quedar cesante: quedarse cortado; perder, haber perdido, salir perdiendo; estar apagado o extinguido; haberse agotado o acabado; haberse publicado, haber salido (un libro, un periódico); estar reñidos; (con *with*) estar reñido (con).—**to be o. of**, no tener más, habérsele acabado a uno (*we are out of coffee*, se nos ha acabado el café, no tenemos más café). **II.** *interj.* ¡fuera!—**o. with it!** ¡fuera con ello! hable Vd. sin rodeos.—**o. upon thee!** ¡vergüenza! **III.** *s.* exterior, parte de afuera; esquina, lugar exterior; exterioridad; cesante; dimisionario; (impr.) olvido, omisión; en baseball, el efecto de echar a un jugador del lugar que ocupaba.—*pl.* (pol.) la oposición. **IV.** *va.* expulsar, desposeer, desalojar, echar fuera. **V.** *a.* exterior, de afuera.

outact [autáct], *va.* propasarse, excederse en.

outbalance [autbǽlans], *va.* sobrexceder, sobrepujar.

outbid [autbíd], *va.* mejorar, pujar.

outbidder [autbídœr], *s.* pujador, ponedor, requintador.

outboard [autbórd]. **I.** *a.* (mar.) fuera del buque. **II.** *adv.* fuera del centro.

outbound [áutbáund], *a.* de travesía; que sale, de salida.

outbrag [áutbrǽg], *va.* exceder o sobrepujar en fanfarronadas.

outbrave [autbréiv], *va.* sobrepujar en valentía o audacia; arrostrar los peligros.

outbreak [áutbréic]. **I.** *s.* erupción; ataque violento; pasión; tumulto, disturbio; principio (de una guerra, epidemia, etc.). **II.** *vn.* brotar; estallar; principiar.

outbuilding [autbílding], *s.* dependencia accesoria.

outburst [áutbœrst], *s.* explosión, erupción; arranque.

outcast [áutcast]. **I.** *a.* desechado, inútil; expulso, proscripto; perdido. **II.** *s.* paria.

outclass [autclás], *va.* exceder, ser superior a.

outcome [áutcum], *s.* éxito, resultado.

outcrop [autcróp], *vn.* (min.) asomar; aflorar.

outcrop [áutcrop], *s.* (min.) afloramiento.

outcry [áutcrai], *s.* clamor, clamoreo; grita; alboroto, gritería, vocería.

outdare [autdéær], *va.* atreverse más que.

outdate [áutdeit], *va.* anticuar.

outdistance [autdístans], *va.* pasar delante de, dejar atrás. *

outdo [autdú], *va.* exceder, sobrepujar, descollar, eclipsar, vencer.—**to o. one's self**, excederse a sí mismo.

outdoor [áutdor], *a.* externo, fuera de la casa, al aire libre.—**o. exercise**, ejercicio al aire libre.—**o. relief**, socorro a domicilio.—**o. sports**, juegos al aire libre, en campo abierto.

outdoors [autdóœrs]. **I.** *s.* el campo raso, el mundo de puertas afuera. **II.** *adv.* fuera de casa, al aire libre, al raso, a la intemperie.

outdrink [autdrínc], *va.* beber más que.

outer [áutœr], *a.* exterior, externo.

outerly [áutœrli], *adv.* hacia fuera; exteriormente.

outermost [áutœrmoust], *a.* extremo; lo más exterior.

outfall [autfól], *s.* salida; boca.

outface [autféis], *va.* humillar; retar.

outfield [áutfild], *s.* campo abierto; campo contiguo; (dep.) campo y jugadores situados fuera del cuadro o de la demarcación.

outfit [áutfit]. **I.** *s.* equipo, apresto; traje; habilitación, desembolso; pertrechos, avíos, menesteres. **II.** *va.* equipar, aviar, habilitar.

outfitter [autfítœr], *s.* armador; abastecedor, proveedor, habilitador.

outflank [autflǽnc], *va.* (mil.) flanquear; llevar la ventaja.

outflash [autflǽsh], *va.* brillar más que, eclipsar.

outflow [áutflo], *s.* efusión, derrame, flujo; salida.

outgeneral [autyénœral], *va.* exceder en táctica militar o en habilidad.

outgo [autgó]. **I.** *va.* exceder, aventajar, pasar, vencer. **II.** *vn.* adelantarse, tomar la delantera. **III.** *s.* [áutgo], gasto, expendio, costas.

outgoer [autgóœr], *s.* el que o lo que sale, parte o se va.

outgoing [áutgoing]. **I.** *s.* ida, salida, partida. **II.** *a.* saliente, cesante; que sale, de salida.

outgrow [autgró], *va.* crecer más que, pasar de la edad de, ser ya viejo para; botar o curarse de con la edad (*the boy has outgrown his clothes*, el muchacho ha crecido tanto que la ropa le está corta; *he will outgrow this ailment*, este achaque le pasará con la edad, o con el tiempo).

outgrowth [áutgroz], *s.* excrecencia, nacencia; resultado, consecuencia.

outguard [áutgard], *s.* (mil.) guardia avanzada.

outhouse [áutjaus], *s.* dependencia, accesoria.

outing [áuting], *s.* salida; paseo, caminata, jira, excursión, esparcimiento.

outlandish [autlǽndish], *a.* extranjero, remoto; extraño, ridículo.

outland [áutlænd], *s.* tierra vecina no cultivada u ocupada.

outlander [áutlǽndœr], *s.* extranjero.

outlast [autlást], *va.* durar más que; sobrevivir a.

outlaw [áutlo]. **I.** *s.* foragido, facineroso; proscrito. **II.** *a.* proscrito; fuera de la ley; rebelde, faccioso. **III.** *va.* proscribir; declarar fuera de la ley.

outlawry [áutlóri], *s.* proscripción; encartamiento.

outlay [áutléi]. **I.** *s.* desembolso, gasto. **II.** *va.* gastar; desplegar.

outlet [áutlet], *s.* salida; orificio de salida; desagüe; desagundero; (min.) agojía.

outlie [autlái]. **I.** *va.* mentir más que. **II.** *vn.* dormir al raso, acampar en tiendas.

outline [áutlain]. **I.** *s.* contorno, perfil; croquis, esbozo, bosquejo, plan general. **II.** *va.* bosquejar, delinear, esquiciar, reseñar.

outlive [autlív], *va.* sobrevivir a; durar más que.

outlook [áutluc], *s.* vista, perspectiva, aspecto; probabilidades; atalaya, vigía, garita; centinela, guardia.

outlying [áutlaing], *a.* distante; extrínseco; exterior, extranjero.

outmarch [autmárch], *va.* dejar atrás a.

outmeasure [autméyœr], *va.* exceder en medida.

outmost [áutmoust], *a.* = OUTERMOST.

outnumber [autnúmbœr], *va.* exceder en número, ser más que.

outport [áutport], *s.* puerto exterior; puerto pequeño.

outpost [áutpoust], *s.* (mil.) avanzada.

outpour [autpóœr]. **I.** *va.* y *vn.* chorrear, verter. **II.** *s.* chorreo, chorro.

outpouring [áutporing], *s.* chorro; efusión, emanación.

output [áutput], *s.* producción total; (mec., elec.) potencia neta o útil; (fisiol.) lo que se expele por los pulmones, los riñones o la piel.

outrage [áutrey]. **I.** *va.* ultrajar, injuriar; maltratar, violentar; violar, desflorar. **II.** *s.* ultraje, afrenta; desafuero, atropello; atrocidad; violación, rapto.

outrageous [autréyus], *a.* afrentoso, injurioso; atroz; desaforado.—**outrageously** [-li], *adv.* ultrajantemente; atrozmente.—**outrageousness** [-nes], *s.* calidad de ultrajante.

outrance [utráns], *s.* el último extremo.

outreach [autrrích], *va.* alcanzar, pasar, tomar la delantera.

outreason [autrrísun], *va.* discurrir mejor que.

outride [autrráid]. **I.** *va.* ganar la delantera a caballo. **II.** *vn.* ir a caballo junto al estribo de un carruaje.

outrider [áutrráidœr], *s.* batidor.

outrigger [autrrígœr], *s.* saliente, vuelo; horqueta, escora, tangón, cuerno; (Filip.) batanga.

(mar.) pescante de banda para carenar; puntal de tope.—*pl.* (mar.) bordones, botantes.

outright [autrráit]. **I.** *a.* sincero, franco. **II.** *adv.* completamente, abiertamente; sin reserva; sin tardanza, al momento, luego.

outrival [autrráival], *va.* sobrepujar en excelencia, ganar, vencer.

outrun [autrrún], *va.* correr más que; pasar, ganar, exceder.

outsail [autséil], *va.* (mar.) ser más velero que, navegar mejor que.

outscouring [áutscáuring], *s.* enjuagadura.

outsell [autsél], *va.* vender más caro o más aprisa que.

outset [áutset], *s.* principio; salida; estreno, inauguración.

outshine [autšháin]. **I.** *va.* exceder en brillantez, dejar deslucido, eclipsar. **II.** *vn.* brillar, lucir, resplandecer.

outshoot [autšhút]. **I.** *va.* tirar más lejos que. **II.** *vn.* sobresalir. **III.** *s.* saliente, vuelo.

outside [áutsaid]. **I.** *a.* exterior, externo; extremo; ajeno, neutral.—**o. shutter,** contraventana. **II.** *s.* exterior, parte de fuera, superfice; apariencia; extremo.—*pl.* resmas costeras.— **at the o.,** a lo sumo, a más tirar. **III.** *adv.* afuera, fuera. **IV.** *prep.* fuera de, más allá de.

outsider [autsáidœr], *s.* forastero, extraño; entremetido, intruso.

outskirt [áutskœrt], *s.* borde, linde, orilla.—*pl.* cercanías, inmediaciones, arrabales.

outspeak [autspíc]. **I.** *va.* hablar alto, hablar claro; hablar mejor o más tiempo que. **II.** *vn.* osar hablar.

outspoken [autspóucœn], *a.* franco; francote.

outspread [autspréd], *va.* extender, difundir.

outstand [autstǽnd], *vn.* combar; sobresalir; quedar pendiente.

outstanding [autstǽnding], *a.* salidizo, saliente; sobresaliente, principal, prominente; pendiente, no pagado.—**o. bills,** obligaciones pendientes.

outstretch [autstréch], *va.* extender, alargar.

outstrip [autstríp], *va.* pasar, rezagar, dejar atrás; aventajar, ganar.

outturn [áuttœrn], *s.* producción; artículos producidos y entregados; resultado (en la venta y entrega de mercancías).

outvalue [autvǽllu], *va.* valer más que.

outvie [autvái], *va.* sobrepujar a.

outvote [autvóut], *va.* ganar a, en el número de votos.

outwalk [autuóc], *va.* andar más que, dejar atrás.

outwall [áutuol], *s.* pared exterior; antemural; exterior, parte externa.

outward [áutuard]. **I.** *a.* exterior, externo, visible; aparente, superficial; extranjero, extraño; extrínseco; (teol.) carnal, corpóreo.— **o. cargo,** o **freight,** cargamento o flete de ida. **II.** *adv.* fuera, afuera, exteriormente; superficialmente; (mar.) de ida; para el extranjero.—**o. bound,** con rumbo a un puerto extranjero; de ida, de salida; que sale.

outwardly [áutuardli], *adv.* exteriormente; aparentemente.

outward(s [áutuard(š], *adv.* = OUTWARD.

outwatch [autuóch], *va.* vigilar o velar más que.

outwear [autuéœr], *va.* durar más que; gastar, consumir.

outweigh [autuéi], *va.* preponderar; pesar más que; sobrepujar.

outwit [autuít], *va.* ser más listo que.

outwork [autuœrk], *va.* trabajar más que.

outwork [áutuœrk], *s.* (fort.) obra exterior o accesoria.

outworn [autuórn], *a.* ajado, gastado, usado.

ouzel [úšœl], *s.* (orn.) mirlo, mirla o merla.

oval [óval]. **I.** *s.* óvalo. **II.** *a.* oval, ovalado.

ovally [óvali], *adv.* en figura de óvalo.

ovarian [ovérian], *a.* ovárico.

ovariotomist [overiótomist], *s.* ovariotomista.

ovariotomy [overiótomi], *s.* (cir.) ovariotomía.

ovaritis [ovaráitis o rítis], *s.* (med.) ovaritis.

ovary [óvari], **ovarium** [ové- *u* ovárium], *s.* ovario; (orn.) overa o huevera; (bot.) ovario.

ovate(d [óvet(ed], *a.* ovado.

ovation [ovéišhun], *s.* ovación.

oven [úvœn], *s.* horno; hornillo.—**o. fork,** hurgón. —**o. rake,** badila, hurgón.

ovenpeel [-píl], *s.* pala de horno

over [óvœr]. **I.** *prep.* sobre, encima, por encima de; allende, al otro lado de; a pesar de; más de; mientras, durante· por, en.—**o. all,** total, de extremo a extremo.—**o. night,** durante la noche, hasta el otro día (cambiando el giro: *to stay over night,* pasar la noche).—**o. one's head,** sin contar con o hacer caso de uno.—**o. one's signature,** bajo su firma.—**o. the top,** (fam., mil.) al ataque, en el ataque, (ir, salir) a la carga (saliendo de las trincheras o defensas). **II.** *adv.* al otro lado; al lado, parte o partido contrario; enfrente; de arriba abajo; al revés; encima; más, de más; otra vez, de nuevo; demasiado, excesivamente; acabado, terminado; a la vuelta, al dorso. Ú. mucho como prefijo equivalente a re-, super-, trans-, ultra-, o para denotar superioridad o exceso, y a menudo puede traducirse por "demasiado" (*overscrup ·lous,* demasiado escrupuloso; *overkind,* demasiado bondadoso).—**o. again,** otra vez, segunda vez, de nuevo.—**o. against,** enfrente.—**o. and above,** además de, en exceso de.—**o. and o.,** repetidas veces, una y otra vez.—**o. the leaf,** a la vuelta.— **o. the left,** (fam.) exactamente lo opuesto.—**o. there,** (fam.) en el frente, en la línea de batalla.— **all the world o.,** o **the world o.,** en o por todo el mundo.—**to be all o.,** haber pasado, haberse acabado.—**to be o.,** haber pasado; haberse acabado; terminar(se).

overabound [óvœrabáund], *vn.* superabundar.

overact [-ǽct], *va.* exagerar.

overalls [-olš], *s. pl.* zahones o zafones.

overanxious [-ǽncšhus], *a.* demasiado ansioso.— **overanxiously** [-li], *adv.* con excesiva ansiedad.

overarch [-árch], *va.* abovedar.

overawe [-ó], *va.* intimidar.

overbalance [-bǽlans]. **I.** *va. y vn.* preponderar; llevar ventaja. **II.** *s.* preponderancia.

overbear [-béœr]. **I.** *va.* (*pret.* OVERBORE: *pp.* OVERBORNE) sojuzgar, reprimir; subyugar, oprimir, agobiar. **II.** *vn.* llevar demasiado fruto.

overbearing [óvœrbéœring], *a.* ultrajoso, despótico; imperioso, altivo. dominante.

overbid [-bid]. **I.** *va.* ofrecer más que, pujar. **II.** *vn.* ofrecer demasiado.

overbidding [-bíding], *s.* puja.

overbig [-bíg], *a.* demasiado grande.

overblow [-blóu]. **I.** *va.* (*pret.* OVERBLEW; *pp.* OVERBLOWN) dispersar; llevarse (el viento); cubrir de flores. **II.** *vn.* dispersarse; pasar; soplar con violencia (el viento).

overboard [-bord], *adv.* (mar.) al mar, al agua.— **man o.!** ¡hombre al agua!

overboil [-bóil], *va.* hervir o cocer demasiado.

overbold [-bóuld], *a.* temerario; descarado.

overborne [-bórn], *a. y pp. de* OVERBEAR.

overburden [-bœrdœn], *vn.* sobrecargar; oprimir.

overcapitalization [-cǽpitælišéišhun], *s.* exageración del capital, capitalización inflada.—

overcapitalize [-aiš], *va.* exagerar el valor de, como capital; capitalizar en más de lo justo.

overcareful [-kéœrful], *a.* demasiado cuidadoso.

overcast [-cást]. **I.** *va.* anublar, obscurecer; entristecer; (costura) sobrehilar; (cir.) cicatrizar; (enc.) hacer un doblez a (una hoja) para coserla. **II.** *vn.* anublarse. **III.** *a.* nublado, sombrío.

overcautious [-cóšhus], *a.* demasiado prudente o precavido.

overcharge [-chary]. **I.** *va.* recargar el precio; cobrar más de lo justo; (arti.) sobrecargar; oprimir; exagerar; hacer cargos exagerados. **II.** *s.* cargo excesivo; extorsión; cargo adicional; recargo de precio.

overcheck [-chéc], *s.* falsarrienda.

overcloud [-cláud], *va.* cubrir de nubes, anublar, entristecer.

overcoat [-cout], *s.* sobretodo, gabán, abrigo, paletó.—**overcoating** [-ing], *s.* paño para gabanes.

overcold [-cóuld], *a.* friolero, friolento.

overcome [-cúm]. **I.** *va.* vencer, rendir, sujetar, domar; sojuzgar, subyugar; superar, vencer; salvar (obstáculos). **II.** *vn.* sobreponerse; hacerse superior. **III.** *a.* agobiado; confundido.

overcompound (**ed** [-cómpaund, -ed], *a.* (elec.) hipercompuesto, hipercompound. —**overcompounding** [-ing], *s.* (elec.) hipercomposición, hipercompoundaje.

overconfidence [-cónfidens], *s.* presunción; demasiada confianza.—**overconfident** [-ent], *a.* demasiado confiado.

overcrowd [-cráud], *va.* apiñar, atestar.—**overcrowded**, atestado, repleto.

overdo [-dú]. **I.** *vn.* (*pret.* OVERDID; *pp.* OVERDONE) hacer más de lo necesario; excederse, extralimitarse. **II.** *va.* agobiar, abrumar de trabajo; exagerar; (coc.) recocer, esturar, requemar; (poét.) eclipsar, sobrepujar.—**overdone**, (coc.) recocido, recocho, demasiado asado.

overdose [-dóus]. **I.** *va.* dar una dosis excesiva. **II.** *s.* dosis excesiva.

overdraft [-draft], *s.* (com.) giro o libranza en exceso de los fondos o el crédito disponibles.

overdraw [-dró], *va.* (*pret.* OVERDREW; *pp.* OVERDRAWN) (com.) exceder, en un giro, del crédito disponible; estirar demasiado; exagerar.

overdress [-drés], *va.* y *vn.* adornar o vestirse con exceso.

overdrink [-drínc], *vn.* beber con exceso, emborracharse.

overdrive [-dráiv], *va.* (*pret.* OVERDROVE; *pp.* OVERDRIVEN). arrear y fatigar los animales; (mec.) hacer funcionar a más de la capacidad normal.

overdue [-diú], *a.* (com.) vencido y no pagado; retrasado.

overeat [-ít], *vn.* tupirse, hartarse.

overestimate [-éstimet]. **I.** *va.* presuponer, avaluar o estimar en valor excesivo; exagerar; tener en más de lo justo. **II.** *s.* estimación, avalúo o presupuesto excesivos.

overexcitement [-ecsáitmœnt], *s.* sobrexcitación.

overexposure [-expóÿœr], *s.* (foto.) demasiada exposición.

overfatigue [-fatíg]. **I.** *va.* fatigar demasiado; rendir, estropear. **II.** *s.* estropeo.

overfeed [-fíd], *va.* alimentar con exceso.

overflow [-fló]. **I.** *vn.* salir de madre; rebosar, rebasar, desbordarse, derramarse. **II.** *va.* sobrellenar, inundar.

overflow [óvœrflo], *s.* inundación, avenida, diluvio; desbordamiento, derrame; exceso, superabundancia; aliviadero.—**o. pipe**, aliviadero de superficie.

overflowing [-flóing], *s.* superabundancia; inundación, anegación, desbordamiento.—**to o.**, hasta derramarse; en exceso; en suma abundancia.

overflowingly [-li], *adv.* superabundantemente.

overfreight [-fréit], *va.* sobrecargar.

overgrow [-gró]. **I.** *va.* (*pret.* OVERGREW: *pp.* OVERGROWN) cubrir con plantas o hierba; crecer más que. **II.** *vn.* crecer o desarrollarse con exceso. Se usa más como *pp.* (**overgrown**): *garden overgrown with weeds*, jardín cubierto de herbaje.—**overgrown child**, niño grandullón o talludo.

overgrowth [óvœrgróuz], *s.* vegetación exuberante, manigua; crecimiento, exuberancia.

overhand [óvœrjænd], *a.* (dep.) voleada (la pelota) por lo alto: (cost.) sobrehilado.

overhang [-jæng]. **I.** *va.* sobresalir horizontalmente por encima de; colgar, suspender; mirar a, dar a, caer a; ser inminente, amenazar; poner demasiadas colgaduras en. **II.** *vn.* colgar o estar pendiente. **III.** *s.* (arq.) alero; vuelo; (aer.) diferencia entre los largos de dos superficies de sustentación de un mismo lado del centro.

overhasty [-jéisti], *a.* demasiado apresurado; precipitado.

overhaul [-jól], *va.* repasar, registrar, recorrer, trastejar; componer, remendar; desarmar y componer; (mar.) alcanzar, o ir ganando un barco en la persecución de otro.—**to o. accounts**, revisar las cuentas.

overhead [-jéd]. **I.** *adv.* arriba, en lo alto; más arriba o hasta más arriba de la cabeza. **II.** *a.* de arriba; mediano, de término medio; aéreo (trole, etc.).—**o. charges**, **o expenses**, gastos generales fijos (alquiler, alumbrado, calefacción, seguro, impuestos, etc.)

overhear [-jíar], *va.* (*pret.* y *pp.* OVERHEARD) alcanzar a oír; oír por casualidad.

overheat [-jít]. **I.** *va.* acalorar, achicharrar; recalentar. **II.** *s.* recalentamiento, calor excesivo.

overhours [óvœráuærs], *s. pl.* horas extraordinarias, fuera de reglamento.

overissue [-ísiu]. **I.** *va.* (com.) emitir con exceso. **II.** *s.* emisión excesiva.

overjoy [-rói]. **I.** *va.* arrebatar o enajenar de alegría. **II.** *s.* arrebato de alegría, éxtasis, enajenamiento.

overjoyed [-róid], *a.* lleno de alegría.

overkind [-káind], *a.* demasiado bondadoso.

overland [óvœrlænd], *a.* y *adv.* por tierra.—**o. route**, ruta por la vía terrestre.

overlap [-læp]. **I.** *va.* sobreponer, solapar, traslapar. **II.** *vn.* sobreponerse, traslaparse. **III.** *s.* solapadura, traslapo, mampuesto.

overlay [-léi]. **I.** *va.* cubrir; dar una capa; dorar, platear; anublar, obscurecer; echar un puente sobre; (impr.) calzar.—**to o. with quicksilver**, azogar. **II.** *s.* capa; (impr.) alza, calzo.

overlaying [-léing], *s.* (impr.) colocación de alzas o calzos; capa, dorado, plateado.

overleap [-líp], *va.* saltar por encima de.

overlie [-lái], *va.* descansar o estar sobre; sofocar echándose encima (v. gr., a un niño).

overlive [-lív]. **I.** *va.* sobrevivir. **II.** *vn.* vivir demasiado activamente.

overload [-lóud]. **I.** *va.* sobrecargar, recargar. **II.** *s.* sobrecarga; sobornal.

overlook [-lúk]. **I.** *va.* mirar desde lo alto; tener vista a, dar o caer a; dominar (con la vista); examinar; vigilar, cuidar de; pasar por alto, disimular, tolerar, perdonar; hacer la vista gorda; descuidar, no hacer caso de: no notar. **II.** *s.* mirada desde lo alto; altura, punto de vista elevado; (bot.) planta trepadora leguminosa.

overlooker [-lúkœr], *s.* sobrestante, celador, inspector, veedor.

overlying [-láiing], *pa.* de TO OVERLIE y *a.* puesto o situado encima de; superyacente.

overman [-mæn], *s.* sobrestante; juez, árbitro; superhombre.

overmaster [-mástœr], *va.* señorear, dominar.

overmatch [-mæch]. **I.** *va.* vencer, superar. **II.** *s.* el que puede más que otro; lucha de fuerzas desiguales.

overmeasure [-méÿœr]. **I.** *s.* colmo. **II.** *va.* dar demasiada importancia a.

overmuch [-múch], *a.* y *adv.* demasiado, más de lo suficiente; en demasía, con exceso.

overmultiplication [-múltiplikéishon], *s.* multiplicación excesiva.

overnice [-náis], *a.* remilgado, escrupuloso.—**overniceness** [-nes], *s.* melindre, escrupulosidad.

overnight [-náit], *adv.* durante la noche; de noche, toda la noche.

overpass [-pás], *va.* atravesar, salvar; mirar con indiferencia, menospreciar; pasar por alto; omitir; sobrepujar, exceder; repasar, considerar.

overpay [-péi], *va.* pagar con exceso.

overpayment [-mœnt], *s.* pago excesivo.

overplus [óvœrplus], *s.* sobrante, superábit.

overpopulation [-pópiuléishun], *s.* exceso de población.

overpower [-páuœr], *va.* subyugar, vencer; supeditar, oprimir, abrumar; colmar.

overpress [-prés], *va.* oprimir, abrumar, aplastar; importunar.

overprize [-práiŝ], va. valuar o apreciar en más de lo justo.

overproduction [-prodúcŝhun], s. exceso de producción.

overproof [-pruf], a. de concentración alcohólica de más de 50 por ciento.

overrate [-rét], va. encarecer; exagerar el valor de.

overreach [-rích]. I. va. ser más listo o astuto que; extender, alargar o estirar demasiado; tirar alto; ir o pasar más allá de lo necesario; alcanzar, extenderse sobre.—**to o. onself,** aventurarse más allá de sus fuerzas; pretender demasiado; salir mal por exceso de astucia o de acción; pasarse de listo. II. vn. (vet.) rozarse la pata trasera con la delantera; (mar.) dar una bordada o virada más allá de lo necesario. III. s. (vet.) rozadura.

override [-ráid], va. pasar por encima, supeditar, vencer; poner a un lado, dar de mano a, rechazar arbitrariamente; anular, contrarrestar; reven-[tar, fatigar un caballo.—**to o. one's commission,** extralimitarse, excederse.

overripe [-ráip], a. demasiado maduro, papandujo.

overrule [-rúl], va. predominar, dominar; ganar, vencer; gobernar, dirigir, regir; (for.) denegar, no admitir un alegato.

overrun [-rún]. I. va. invadir, infestar; excederse; desbordarse, (impr.) retocar, recorrer. II. vn. rebosar; estar muy abundante.

overscrupulous [-scrúpiulus], a. demasiado escrupuloso.

oversea(s [-sí, -síŝ]. I. adv. allende los mares, ultramar. II. a. de ultramar.

oversee [-sí], va. (pret. OVERSAW: pp. OVERSEEN) inspeccionar, superintender, vigilar; descuidar, pasar por alto.

overseer [-síœr], s. sobrestante; veedor, inspector; mayoral.

overset [-sét]. I. va. volcar, voltear, derribar; trastornar, arruinar. II. vn. volcarse, caerse.

overshade [-ŝhéd]. I. va. obscurecer, sombrear. II. vn. dar sombra.

overshadow [-ŝhædo], va. sombrear; eclipsar, obscurecer.

overshoe [-ŝhu], s. chanclo; zapato de goma.

overshoot [-ŝhút]. I. va. (pp. y pret. OVERSHOT) tirar por encima del blanco; ir más allá de, exceder; pasar rápidamente por encima.—**to o. one's self,** pasarse de listo. II. vn. pasar de raya.

overshot wheel [-ŝhot juíl], s. rueda de canjilones alimentada por arriba.

oversight [-sait], s. inadvertencia, descuido; vigilancia, cuidado.

oversize [-sáiŝ]. I. a. de mayor tamaño que el ordinario; extragrande. II. s. tamaño mayor que el regular; tamaño mayor.

overskirt [óvœrskœrt], s. sobrefalda, faldellín.

oversleep [-slíp], vn. y vr. dormir demasiado; no despertar.

oversleeves [-slívs], s. mangotes, contramangas.

overspread [-spréd], va. desparramar, esparcir, regar, tender.

overstate [-stéit], vn. exagerar.

overstay [-stéi]. I. vn. demorarse (en alguna parte); permanecer demasiado tiempo. II. va. (com.) retener (valores de bolsa) demasiado tiempo, con pérdida consiguiente.

overstep [-stép], va. y vn. traspasar, transgredir, excederse, extralimitarse, propasarse.

overstock [-stóc]. I. va. abarrotar. II. s. surtido excesivo.

overstrain [-stréin]. I. va. apretar o estirar demasiado. II. vn. esforzarse demasiado. III. s. tensión o tirantez excesiva.

overstretch [-strétch], va. estirar demasiado.

overstrew, overstrow [-strú, stró], va. esparcir, desparramar.

overstrung [-strúng], a. demasiado tirante; muy sensible; hablando de pianos, que tiene dos juegos de cuerdas cruzadas oblicuamente.

oversubscribe [-subscráib], va. solicitar (bonos, etc.) en exceso de la emisión; contribuir más de

lo pedido. Ú. gen. en la voz pasiva, y en la traducción se cambia el giro: *the loan has been oversubscribed*, la demanda de bonos del empréstito ha sido mayor que la oferta, las subscripciones al empréstito han excedido los bonos, ha habido subscripciones de sobra al empréstito, etc.

overt [óvœrt], a. abierto, público, patente, evidente.—**o. act,** ofensa o transgresión premeditada; acto hostil.

overtake [-ték], va. alcanzar; atajar; coger o pillar en el hecho.

overtax [-tǽcs], va. oprimir con tributos.

overthrow [-zró]. I. va. echar abajo, demoler, derribar; derrocar, destronar; vencer. II. s. derribo, vuelco, derrocamiento; caída; (dep.) voleo demasiado alto.

overtime [óvœrtáim]. I. s. horas extraordinarias de trabajo. II. adv. fuera del tiempo estipulado. III. a. en exceso de las horas regulares de trabajo.

overtire [-táiœr], va. fatigar demasiado.

overtly [óvœrtli], adv. abiertamente, manifiestamente.

overtone [óvœrtoun], s. (mús.) armónico.

overtop [-tóp], va. dominar, descollar sobre, sobresalir entre; sobrepujar.

overture [óvœrchuœr], s. insinuación, proposición, propuesta; (mús.) obertura.

overturn [-tœrn], va. volcar; echar abajo; trastornar.

overvalue [-vǽliu], va. encarecer, ponderar; atribuir valor excesivo a.

overwatch [-uóch], va. y vn. cansar a fuerza de vigilias; vigilar, celar.

overweening [-uíning], a. presuntuoso, arrogante.—**overweeningly** [-li], adv. arrogantemente.

overweigh [-uéi], va. pesar más que, preponderar; prevalecer contra.

overweight [-uéit], s. preponderancia, sobrepeso; superioridad.

overwhelm [-juélm], va. abrumar; anonadar; hundir.—**overwhelming** [-ing], a. abrumador, opresivo; agobiante; irresistible, dominante, arrollador.—**overwhelmingly** [-ingli], adv. abrumadoramente; irresistiblemente.

overwork [-uœrk]. I. va. hacer trabajar con exceso, esclavizar; elaborar la superficie de. II. vn. trabajar demasiado. III. s. trabajo excesivo; trabajo hecho fuera de las horas reglamentarias.

overworn [-uón], a. gastado por el trabajo; abrumado de fatiga.

overwrought [-rót], a. sobrexcitado; muy elaborado o labrado; recargado de adornos.

oviduct [óviduct], s. (anat.) oviducto.

oviferous [ovífœrus], **ovigerous** [ovíyœrus], a. ovífero.

oviform [óviform], a. oviforme.

ovine [óvin], a. ovino, lanar, ovejuno.

oviparous [ovíparus], a. ovíparo.

oviposit [ovipósit], vn. (ent.) poner huevos.

oviposition, ovipositing [óvipóŝihun, ovipóŝiting], s. (ent.) postura.

ovipositor [ovipósitor], s. órgano que sirve a los insectos para depositar sus huevos.

ovoid (al [óvoid, ovóidal], a. ovoide, aovado.

ovolo [óvolo], s. (arq.) equina, cuarto bocel.

ovoviviparous [óvovivipǽrus], a. ovovivíparo.

ovule [óviul], s. óvulo.

ovum [óvum], s. (pl. OVA) (biol.) huevo; (arq.) cuarto bocel, equina.

owe [óu]. I. va. (pa. OWING: pp. OWED; antiguamente OWN u OUGHT) deber, adeudar; (con **to**) ser deudor a o de; estar obligado a.—**owing to,** debido a, por causa de.—**to be owing,** ser debido, imputable o atribuíble. II. vn. estar endeudado, deber.

owl [ául]. I. s. (orn.) lechuza, buho, mochuelo. II. vn. (Ingl.) matutear.

owlet [-et], s. bijuelo del buho.—**o. moth,** (ent.) mariposa nocturna.

owlish [-iŝh], **owl-like** [-laic], a. semejante al buho.

owllight [-lait], *s*. crepúsculo.

own [óun]. **I.** *a*. propio, particular; peculiar, individual; mismo, verdadero, real: *he wrote it with his own hand*, lo escribió de su propio puño: *this is my own*, esto es mío propio; esto es lo mío; *Nero killed his own mother*, Nerón mató a su misma madre.—**o. cousin,** primo hermano, prima hermana.—**my** (**our,** etc.) **o.** (con respecto a la familia) los míos (nuestros, etc.).—**my o. self,** yo mismo.—**of one's o. motion,** espontáneamente, de motu propio. **II.** *va*. poseer, ser dueño de, tener; reconocer, confesar. **III.** *vn*. (con *to*) admitir, confesar, reconocer; poseer, tener, ser dueño.

owner [óuncer], *s*. dueño, poseedor; amo, propietario.

ownerless [-les], *a*. mostrenco.

ownership [-ship], *s*. propiedad.

ox, *s*. (*pl.* OXEN) buey.—**o. bot** = OXFLY.—**o. driver,** boyero.—**o.-eyed,** de ojos grandes.—**o. stall,** boyera, boyeriza.

oxacid [oxǽsid], *s*. (quím.) oxácido.

oxalate [óxalet], *s*. (quím.) oxalato.

oxalic [oxǽlic], *a*. oxálico.

Oxalidaceæ [oxælidéisii], *s*. *pl*. (bot.) oxalídeas.

Oxalis [oxǽlis], *s*. (bot.) acedera.

oxazin(**e** [óxæsin], *s*. oxazina.

oxbow [óxbou], *s*. collera de yugo.

oxcart [óxcart], *s*. carro tirado por bueyes.

oxen, *s. pl*. de OX.

oxeye [óxai], *s*. (mar. y bot.) ojo de buey; (orn.) pajarito.—**o. daisy,** (bot.) manzanilla loca.

oxfly [óxflái], *s*. (ent.) estro.

oxgoad [óxgóud], *s*. aguijada, aguijón.

oxherd [óxjćerd], *s*. = O. DRIVER.

oxhouse [óxjáus], *s*. = O. STALL.

oxidable [óxidabœl], *a*. oxidable.

oxidant [óxidant], *s*. oxidante.

oxidase [óxideis], *s*. (quím.) oxidasa.

oxidate [óxidet], *va*. = OXIDIZE.

oxidation [óxidéishun], *s*. oxidación.

oxide [óxid], *s*. (quím.) óxido.

oxidize [óxidaiš], *va*. oxidar u oxigenar.—**oxidized silver,** plata oxidada.

oxlip [óxlip], *s*. (bot.) prímula.

Oxonian [oxónian]. **I.** *a*. (Ingl.) perteneciente a Oxford o a su universidad. **II.** *s*. habitante de Oxford o estudiante de su universidad.

oxtongue [óxtúng], *s*. (bot.) buglosa.

oxyacetylene [óxiæsétilin], *a*. oxiacetilénico.

oxyacid [óxiǽsid], *s*. oxácido.

oxychlorid(**e** [óxiclórid *o* raid], *s*. (quím.) oxicloruro.

oxygen [óxiyen], *s*. (quím.) oxígeno.

oxygenate [óxiyenet], *va*. oxigenar.

oxygenation [oxiyenéshun], *s*. oxigenación, oxidación.

oxygenic, oxygenous [óxiyénic, oxíyenus], *a*. oxigenoid.

oxygenizable [óxiyenáisǎbœl], *a*. oxígenable.—**oxygenize** [-aiš], *va*. = OXYGENATE.

oxyhæmoglobin [óxijímoglóbin], *s*. (quím.) oxihemoglobina.

oxyhydrogen [óxijáidroyen], *s*. (quím.) gas oxhídrico.—**o. blowpipe,** soplete oxhídrico.

oxymel [óximel], *s*. ojimiel, onfacomeli.

oxysalt [óxisolt], *s*. (quím.) oxisal.

oxysulfid(**e** [-súlfid, aid], *s*. (quím.) oxisulfuro.

oxytocic [-tósic], *s*. y *a*. oxitócico, ocitócico.

oxytone [óxitoun]. **I.** *a*. (pros.) agudo. **II.** *s*. palabra aguda.

oyer [óyœr], *s*. (for.) audición, vista; audiencia.—**o. and terminer,** (Ingl.) tribunal que se reúne dos veces al año en cada condado; (E. U.) tribunal de más alta jurisdicción criminal.

oyes, oyez [óyes], *interj*. (for.) ¡oíd, oíd! voz de los ujieres.

oyster [óistœr], *s*. ostra.—**o. bed,** ostral, criadero de ostras.—**o. culture,** ostricultura.—**o. farm** = O. BED.—**o. farming** = O. CULTURE.—**o. fishery,** pesquería de ostras.—**o. grass,** ulva verde.—**o.-green,** alga marina.—**o. house** [-jáus], *s*. ostrería.—**o. plant,** (bot.) salsifí.—**o. shell,** desbulla.—**o. tongs,** gafas para pescar ostras.

oysterman [-mæn], *s*. ostrero.

ozæna [osínæ], *s*. (med.) ocena.

ozocerite [óšoscérait], *s*. ozocerita.

ozonation [óšounéishun], *s*. ozonización.

ozone [óšoun], *s*. ozono.—**o. paper,** papel para ozono, papel revestido de almidón y yoduro potásico (ll. a menudo *ozonómetro*).

ozonic [osónic], *a*. ozonizado; relativo al ozono.—**o. ether,** disolución de bióxido de hidrógeno en éter.

ozonize [óšonaiš], *va*. ozonizar.—**ozonizer** [-œr], *s*. ozonizador—**ozonometer** [-nómetœr], *s*. medidor de ozono.—**ozonous** [-nus], *a*. = OSONIC.

P

p [pi], *s*. p.

pa [pa], *s*. (fam.) papá.

pabular [pǽbiular], *a*. alimentoso, nutritivo.

pabulum [pǽbiulum], *s*. pábulo.

paca [páca *o* péca], *s*. (zool.) paca.

pace [péis]. **I.** *s*. paso; marcha, modo de andar; (equit.) paso, portante, andadura; paso (medida de longitud); (arq.) estrado, tablado. **II.** *va*. recorrer o medir a pasos; marcar el paso; dirigir. **III.** *vn*. pasear, andar, marchar; (equit.) amblar.

pacer [péisœr], *s*. caballo de paso de andadura; el que mide a pasos o marca el paso.

pacha [pashó], *s*. = PASHA.

Pachydermata [pækidćrmata], *s*. *pl*. (zool.) paquidermos.

pachyderm(**atous,** *o* **pachyderm**(**ous** [pækidćrm(atus, mus], *a*. paquidermo.

pacific [pasífic], *a*. pacífico.

pacificate [pasífikeit], *va*. pacificar.—**pacification** [-éishun], *s*. pacificación.—**pacificator** [-kéitœr], **pacifier** [pǽsifaiœr], *s*. pacificador, apaciguador.—**pacificatory** [pasíficatori], *a*. pacificador.

pacifism [pǽsifiŝm], *s*. pacifismo.—**pacifist** [-ist], *s*. y *a*. pacifista.—**pacifistic** [-ic], *a*. pacifista.

pacify [pǽsifai], *va*. pacificar, apaciguar.

pacing [péising], *s*. paso, andadura.

pack [pæc]. **I.** *s*. lío, fardo; paquete; baraja de naipes; muta, perrada; hato o manada (de animales); cuadrilla, manga (de pícaros); gran de extensión de témpanos flotantes.—**p. animal,** acémila, animal de carga.—**p. cloth,** arpillera.—**p. load,** carga de una acémila.—**p. needle,** aguja de enjalmar, aguja de arria; almarada.—**p. train,** recua, reata. **II.** *va*. empacar, empaquetar; enfardar, enfardelar; embalar, envasar; encajonar, embaular; llenar, atestar, apretar, colmar; (mec.) empaquetar una junta; despachar, enviar; cargar (una acémila); llevar sobre la espalda o lomo: envolver a un enfermo en sábanas mojadas, con mantas secas al exterior. **III.** *vn*. empaquetar; hacer el baúl, arreglar el equipaje; formar una masa compacta, consolidarse; tomar soleta.—**to p. away,** largarse.—**to p. off,** enviar, despedir, despachar; poner de patitas en la calle.

package [pǽkey], *s*. fardo, bulto, lío; atado; paquete; cabo; (mar.) abarrote; embalaje, envase.

packer [pǽkœr], *s*. embalador, empaquetador, envasador, arpillador.

packet [pǽket]. **I.** *s*. paquete, fardo pequeño; paquete de cartas; mala, valija, correo.—**p. boat, p. ship, p. vessel,** paquebote. **II.** *va*. empaquetar, enfardelar.

packing [pǽking]. **I.** *s*. embalaje; envase; enfardeladura; (mec.) empaquetadura, guarnición, (alb.) relleno, enripiado. **II.** *a*. de embalar; de enfardelar; de envolver.—**p. box, p. case,** caja de embalar; envase.—**p. gland,** prensaestopas.—**p. house,** frigorífico.—**p. leather,** cuero para empaquetadura.—**p. liquid,** líquido de obturación.—**p. paper,** papel de envolver.—**p. press,** prensa de embalar.—**p. strip,** (mec.) cuña, tira de refuerzo.

packman [pǽcman], *s*. buhonero.

packsaddle [pǽcsǽdœl], *s*. albarda, basto,(Amér.) enjalma.

packthread [pǽczred], *s.* bramante, hilo de acarreto.

pact [pæct], *s.* pacto, convenio, tratado.

pad [pæd]. **I.** *s.* cojincillo, almohadilla; colchoncillo; postizo; caderillas; (esgr.) peto, plastrón; hoja grande de planta acuática; rastro, huella. **II.** *va.* forrar, rellenar, emborrar; aumentar (un escrito) con material superfluo; formar blocs de papel. **III.** *vn.* llevar postizos.

padding [pǽding], *s.* relleno, almohadilla; algodón guata, (Amér.) huata; (tej.) imprimación; ripio (en un escrito).

paddle [pǽdœl]. **I.** *va.* y *vn.* impeler, bogar o remar con canalete; manosear, tentar, dar palmaditas; chapotear, guachapear. **II.** *s.* canalete, zagual.—**p. board, p. float,** álabe, arcaduz.—**p. staff,** béstola o arrejada.—**p. wheel,** rueda de paletas.—**p.-wheel steamer,** vapor de ruedas.

paddler [pǽdlœr], *s.* remero.

paddock [pǽdoc], *s.* dehesa.

paddy [pǽdi], *s.* (orn.) ánade americano; arroz en cáscara, palay.—**p. drill,** taladro para pozos con perforadores de expansión.—**p. field,** arrozal.

padlock [pǽdloc]. **I.** *s.* candado. **II.** *va.* echar el candado, cerrar con candado.

paduasoy [pǽdiuasoi], *s.* seda de Padua.

pæan [pían], *s.* peán.

pæony [píoni], *s.* = PEONY.

pagan [péigan], *s.* y *a.* pagano.—**paganish** [-iâh], *a.* pagano.—**paganism** [-iŝm], *s.* paganismo.—**paganize** [-aiŝ], *va.* y *vn.* hacer o hacerse pagano.

page [péiy]. **I.** *s.* página; paje, escudero, criado. **II.** *va.* foliar, paginar; buscar llamando (en los hoteles).

pageant [péyant], *s.* procesión cívica, manifestación imponente, pompa; (teat.) espectáculo, aparato escénico.

pageantry [-tri], *s.* fasto, fausto, pompa.

pagehood [péyjud], *s.* oficio de paje.

paginate [péyineit], *va.* paginar, foliar.

pagination [-éishun], *s.* paginación, foliación.

paging [péying], *s.* paginación.—**p. machine,** máquina de foliar.

pagoda [pagóda], *s.* pagoda.

Pahlavi [pálavi], *s.* pelvi, antigua lengua persa.

paid [péid], *pret.* y *pp.* de TO PAY.—**p.-up share,** acción liberada.

paidology [paidóloyi], *s.* estudio científico de los niños.

pail [péil], *s.* cubo, balde.

pailful [-ful], *s.* lo que cabe en un balde.

pain [péin]. **I.** *va.* doler (usado intransitivamente: *my stomach pains me,* me duele el estómago); causar dolor (*this pains me,* esto me causa dolor, o me duele); apenar, afligir. **II.** *vn.* doler. **III.** *s.* dolor; pena (castigo).—*pl.* V. PAINS.—**in p.,** con dolor.—**on p. of,** so pena de.—**to be in p.,** tener dolor, estar con dolor.

pained [péind], *a.* apenado, afligido.

painful [péinful], *a.* penoso, embarazoso; dolorido, afligido; doloroso, aflictivo; arduo, penoso, laborioso.—**to be p.,** doler.—**painfully** [-li], *adv.* dolorosamente; penosamente.—**painfulness** [-nes], *s.* calidad de penoso o doloroso.

painless [péinles], *a.* sin dolor, indoloro.

painlessness [-nes], *s.* ausencia de dolor.

pains [péinŝ], *s.* trabajo, incomodidad, fatiga; esmero, cuidado; ansiedad, inquietud, solicitud; dolores de parto.—**to be at the p. of,** tomarse el trabajo de.—**to have one's labor for one's p.,** trabajar de balde o en vano, no sacar nada.

painstaker [péinŝtéikœr], *s.* trabajador, afanador.

painstaking [péinŝtéiking], *a.* cuidadoso, industrioso; afanoso, esmerado, concienzudo.

paint [péint]. **I.** *va.* pintar, colorar; untar, dar una capa o baño; retratar o copiar con colores; dedicarse a la pintura; afeitarse, pintarse el rostro, arrebolarse; describir.—**to p. the town red,** (fam.) andar de picos pardos, ir de parranda, correrla.—**to p. with,** pintar con; dar una capa de; revestir de. **II.** *vn.* pintar, ser pintor; pintarse (el rostro). **III.** *s.* pintura; color; colorete, afeite, arrebol.—**p. box,** caja de colores o pinturas.—**p. tube,** tubo de color.

paintbrush [péintbrúsh], *s.* brocha, pincel.

painted [péinted], *a.* pintado; de color.—**p. glass,** vidrio de color.

painter [péintœr], *s.* pintor; (mar.) amarra del bote o de la lancha.

painting [péinting], *s.* pintura (arte y oficio); coloración; cuadro o pintura.

paintress [péintres], *s.* pintora.

pair [péær]. **I.** *s.* par; pareja; (pol.) en un cuerpo legislativo, dos miembros de opiniones contrarias, apareados para abstenerse de votar.—**p. of scales,** peso de cruz.—**p. of stairs,** tramo de escalera.—**a p. of scissors, of spectacles,** un par de tijeras, de anteojos. **II.** *va.* parear, aparear; casar. **III.** *vn.* aparearse, hermanarse, igualarse.—**to p. off,** aparearse dos diputados de opiniones contrarias antes de la votación; retirarse de una reunión en parejas.—**to p. with,** hacer pareja con.

pajamas [payámaŝ], *s. pl.* pijama, traje de dormir; pijama, traje oriental.

pal [pæl], *s.* (fam.) compañero.

palace [pǽles], *s.* palacio.—**p. car,** coche salón.

paladin [pǽladin], *s.* paladín.

palæography, palæontology, *s.* = PALEOGRAPHY, PALEONTOLOGY.

palanquin [pǽlankin], *s.* palanquín.

palatability [pǽlatabíliti], *s.* buen sabor.

palatable [pǽlatabœl], *a.* sabroso, apetitoso; agradable, aceptable.

palatal [pǽlatal], *a.* y *s.* paladial.

palate [pǽlet], *s.* paladar; sentido del gusto; paladeo.

palatial [paléíshal], *a.* palaciego, palatino; magnífico, suntuoso.

palatinate [palǽtinet], *s.* palatinado.

palatine [pǽlatin], *a.* palatino; paladial.

palaver [palávœr]. **I.** *s.* palabrería; zalamería; embustes; conferencia, discusión. **II.** *va.* y *vn.* adular; engatusar; charlar.

pale [péil]. **I.** *a.* pálido; descolorido; claro; apagado, albarazado.—**p.-eyed,** de ojos sin brillo.—**p.-faced,** caripálido.—**p. green,** verde claro.—**p.-hearted,** pusilánime.—**p. wine,** vino clarete. **II.** *s.* estaca; palizada, estacada; valla, límite; espacio cerrado, literal o figuradamente; esfera, seno, gremio, sociedad; (blas.) palo.—**p. of the church,** gremio de la iglesia. **III.** *va.* empalizar, cercar, rodear; poner pálido, hacer palidecer; descolorar, o descolorir. **IV.** *vn.* palidecer; perder el color.

palea [pélea], *s.* (bot.) glumilla, arista.

paleface [péilfeis], *s.* caripálido (nombre que dan los indios a los blancos).

palely [péili], *adv.* pálidamente.

paleness [péilnes], *s.* palidez, descoloramiento.

paleobotany [péiliobótæni], *s.* paleofitología, paleobotánica.

Paleogene [-rin], *s.* (geol.) paleoceno, el terciario más antiguo.

paleograph [-græf], *s.* paleógrafo.

paleographic(al [-grǽfic(al, *a.* paleográfico.

paleography [paleógrafi], *s.* paleografía.

paleolith [péilioliz], *s.* (geol.) objeto pétreo de la edad de piedra.—**paleolithic** [-ic], *a.* paleolítico.

paleologist [peilióloyist], *s.* paleólogo.

paleology [-yi], *s.* paleología.

paleontographic(al [péiliontogrǽfic(al], *a.* paleontográfico.—**paleontography** [-tógrafi], *s.* paleontografía.

paleontologic(al [-ontolóyic(al], *a.* paleontológico.—**paleontologist** [-tóloyist], *s.* paleontólogo.—**paleontology** [-tóloyi], *s.* paleontología.

Paleozoic [péilioŝóic], *a.* paleozoico.

paleozoology [-ŝoóloyi], *s.* paleozoología.

palestra, *s.* palestra, gimnasio.

palette [pǽlet], *s.* (pint.) paleta.—**p. knife,** espátula.

palfrey [pólfri], *s.* palafrén.

palfreyed [pólfrid], *a.* montada en palafrén.
Pali [páli], *s.* pali (lengua).
palimpsest [pǽlimpsest], *s.* palimpsesto.
palindrome [pǽlindroum], *s.* palindromia.
paling [péiling], *s.* palenque, estacada, valla, palizada.
palingenesis [pælinyénesis], **palingenesia** [pælinyénsia], *s.* palingenesia.
palinode [pǽlinoud], *s.* palinodia.
palisade, palisado [paliséid, o], *s.* palizada, estacada, frisa.—*pl.* farallón, risco.
palisander [pǽlisǽndœr], *s.* palisandro.
palish [péliʃh], *a.* paliducho.
pall [pol]. **I.** *s.* paño mortuorio; (fig.) lo que ocasiona aflicción o tristeza; (igl.) hijuela, palia; palio. **II.** *va.* evaporar, desvirtuar, quitar el sabor; desalentar; saciar; hartar, empalagar. **III.** *vn.* hacerse insípido, perder el sabor.
palladium [pælédiʊm], *s.* paladio; garantía, salvaguardia; (quím.) paladio.
pallbearer [pólbéærœr], *s.* persona que va al lado del féretro.
pallet [pǽlet], *s.* jergón, camilla; (mec.) paleta de reloj, fiador de rueda, retén, linguete; eslabón de una cadena sin fin; (mar.) caja de lastre; torno de alfarero; (alb.) paleta; (pint.) paleta; (enc.) herramienta para dorar o inscribir los lomos de los libros; válvula de cañón de órgano.
palliate [pǽlieit], *va.* excusar, paliar; mitigar.
palliation [-éiʃhʊn], *s.* paliación, mitigación.
palliative [pǽliativ], *a.* y *s.* paliativo.
pallid [pǽlid], *a.* pálido, descolorido.
pallidity [pælíditi], **pallidness** [pǽlidnes], *s.* palidez.
pallium [pǽliʊm], *s.* palio; manto.
pall-mall [pel-mel], *s.* palamallo; galería o zona donde se juega.—**Pall Mall** [pæl mæl], *s.* nombre de una calle de Londres y del ministerio de guerra que estaba en ella.
pallor [pǽlœr], *s.* palidez.
palm [pam]. **I.** *s.* (bot.) palma, palmera; victoria; palma de la mano: ancho de la mano (medida); (mar.) rempujo.—**p. bird,** (orn.) tejedor.—**p. cabbage,** palmito.—**p. oil,** aceite de palma, aceite del Senegal.—**P. Sunday,** domingo de ramos.—**p. tree,** palmera, palma.—**p. wine,** vino de palmera. **II.** *va.* escamotar; (con **off, on** o **upon**) engañar, defraudar con; manejar, manosear, manipular; cubrir con palmas.
palmaceous [palméiʃhʊs], *a.* palmáceo.
palma Christi [pǽlma crísti], *s.* (bot.) palma-cristi, ricino.
palmar [pǽlmar], *a.* palmar.
palmary [pǽlmari], *a.* principal; digno del premio.
palmate(d [pǽlmeit(ed], *a.* palmeado, palmado.
palmer [pámœr], *s.* palmero, peregrino, romero; fullero, tahur; palmeta.—**p. worm,** oruga velluda; gorgojo.
palmetto [pælméto], *s.* (bot.) palmito, margallón; sombrero de palmito.—**P. State,** Carolina del Sur.
palmiferous [pælmífœrus], *s.* palmífero.
palmiped [pǽlmiped], *a.* palmípedo.
palmister [pǽlmistœr], *s.* quiromántico.
palmistry [pǽlmistri], *s.* quiromancia.
palmitic [pǽlmític], *a.* (quím.) palmítico.
palmitin [pǽlmitin], (quím.) palmitina.
palmy [pámi], *a.* próspero, floreciente; triunfal; palmar.
palp(us [pǽlp(ʊs], *s.* (ent.) palpo.
palpability [pǽlpabíliti], *s.* palpabilidad, evidencia.
palpable [pǽlpabœl], *a.* palpable, evidente.—**palpably** [-bli], *adv.* palpablemente, claramente.
palpation [pælpéiʃhʊn], *s.* palpamiento.
palpebra [pǽlpebra], *s.* pálpebra, párpado.
palpebral [pǽlpebral], *a.* palpebral.
palpitate [pǽlpiteit], *vn.* palpitar, latir.—**palpitating** [-teiting], *a.* palpitante.—**palpitation** [-téiʃhʊn], *s.* palpitación.
palpus [pǽlpʊs], *s.* (zool.) palpo.
palsied [pólsid], *a.* perlático, paralítico.
palsy [pólsi]. **I.** *s.* parálisis, perlesía; ineficacia, apatía. **II.** *va.* paralizar.

palter [póltœr], *vn.* petardear, divertirse con alguno.
palterer [póltœrœr], *s.* petardista.
paltriness [póltrines], *s.* vileza, mezquindad.
paltry [póltri], *a.* vil, miserable, mezquino.
paludamentum [paliúdaméntʊm], *s.* paludamento.
paludine [pǽliudin], *a.* palúdico, de los pantanos.—**paludism** [-iʃm], *s.* paludismo.—**paludous** [-ʊs], *a.* palúdico; de los pantanos, que vive en los pantanos.
paly [péli], *a.* (poét.) pálido, marchito; (blas.) palado.
pampas [pǽmpaʃ], *s. pl.* pampas.—**p. grass,** (bot.) cortadera argentina.
pampean [pampíæn], *a.* y *s.* pampero.
pamper [pǽmpœr], *va.* atracar, engordar; tratar con mimo y regalo.
pamperer [-œr], *s.* mimador.
pampero [pampérou], *s.* pampero (viento, habitante).
pamphlet [pǽmflet], *s.* folleto.
pamphleteer [pǽmfletíœr], *s.* folletista.
pan [pæn]. **I.** *s.* cacerola, cazuela, cuenco; perol; caldero; paila; (min.) gamella; cazoleta de un arma de fuego; (carp.) quicio; cráneo, sesera.—**p. pudding,** pudín cocido en el horno.—**P.'s pipes,** flauta del dios Pan. **II.** *va.* (min.) separar el oro en una gamella; (fam.) alcanzar, sacar, lograr; cocer y servir en una cazuela. **III.** *vn.* (con **out**) dar oro la tierra o arena; (fam.) dar buen resultado o provecho.
panacea [pænasía], *s.* panacea, sanalotodo, catolicón; (bot.) pánace.
panache [panáʃh], *s.* penacho.
panada [panéda], *s.* panetela, panado.
Panama hat [pánamá jæt], *s.* jipijapa, sombrero de jipijapa.—**Panamaian** [pánamáiæn], **Panaman** [-mæn], **Panamanian** [-mániæn], **Panamano** [-mano], *s.* y *a.* panameño.
Pan-American [pǽnæméricæn], *a.* panamericano.—**Pan-Americanism** [-iʃm], *s.* panamericanismo.
Pan-Anglican [-ǽnglicæn], *a.* pananglicano, relativo al conjunto de las divisiones de la iglesia anglicana.
pancake [pǽnkéic], *s.* torta delgada de masa cocida rápidamente en la zarten, la callana o una plancha metálica; (Am.) panquec; (aer.) aterrizaje brusco casi vertical.
pancratic(al [pæncrǽtic(al], *a.* atlético, gimnástico; (ópt.) ajustable.
pancratium [pæncréiʃhʊm], *s.* pancracio.
pancreas [pǽncreas], *s.* (anat.) páncreas.
pancreatic [pæncreǽtic], *a.* pancreático.—**p. juice,** jugo pancreático.
pancreatin [pæncriætin], *s.* pancreatina.
pandanus [pændéinʊs], *s.* (bot.) planta pandanea.
Pandean [pændían], *a.* del dios Pan.—**P. pipes,** = PAN'S PIPES.
pandect [pǽndect], *s.* tratado, recopilación, digesto.—*pl.* pandectas.
pandemonium [-demónium], *s.* pandemónium.
pandemic [pændémic], *a.* muy epidémico.
pander [pǽndœr]. **I.** *s.* alcahuete. **II.** *va.* alcahuetear.
panderage [pǽndœrey], **panderism** [pǽndœriʃm], *s.* alcahuetería, lenocinio.
panderess [pǽndœres], *s.* alcahueta.
pandiculated [pændíkiuleted], *a.* estirado, extendido, abierto.
pandore [pændóœr], *s.* (mús.) bandola.
pandy [pǽndi]. **I.** *s.* palmetazo. **II.** *va.* dar palmetazos.
pane [péin], *s.* hoja de vidrio o cristal de ventana o vidriera; cuadro, cuadrado, tablero; cara, lado, faz, faceta.
paned [péind], *a.* hecho a cuadros.
panegyric(al [pénewíric(al], **panegyric(al** [-ýric(al], *a.* panegírico.—**panegyrist** [pǽnewírist], *s.* panegirista.—**panegyrize** [-yiraiʃ], *va.* panegirizar.

panel [pǽnel]. **I.** *s.* panel; entrepano, cuarterón, artesón, tablero, tabica; (elec.) panel; (pint.) tabla; (cost.) paño (en un vestido); cara de una piedra labrada; (for.) lista oficial de personas que pueden servir como jurados.—**p. board**, tablero de cortacircuitos.—**p. game**, modo de robar mediante postigos o puertas secretas en casas de mal vivir.—**p. house**, burdel donde se practica el robo antedicho. **II.** *va.* formar tableros, cuarterones o artesones.

paneless [péinles], *a.* sin cristales (ventana o vidriera).

panel(l)ing [pǽneling], *s.* artesonado.

panful [pǽnful], *s.* contenido de una cazuela o cacerola.

pang [pæng], *s.* angustia, dolor, tormento.—**pangs of childbirth**, dolores de parto.—**pangs of death**, ansias de la muerte, agonía.

pangenesis [pænyénesis], *s.* pangénesis.—**pangenetic** [-renétic], *a.* pangenésico.

Pan-German [pænyǽrmæn], *a.* pangermanista.—**Pan-Germanism** [-ĭsm], *s.* pangermanismo.

pangolin [pǽngolin], *s.* (zool.) pangolín.

panhandle [pænjǽndœl]. **I.** *vn.* mendigar en las calles. **II.** *s.* (P-) entrada angosta de un territorio en otro.—**P. State**, (E. U.) Virginia Occidental.

Pan-Hellenism [pænjélenĭsm], *s.* panhelenismo.

panic [pǽnic]. **I.** *a.* pánico. **II.** *s.* miedo o terror pánico; consternación; pánico o crisis comercial.—**p. grass**, (bot.) mijo, daza.—**p. stricken**, **p. struck**, sobrecogido de terror.

panicle [pǽnicœl], *s.* (bot.) panoja, panocha.

paniculate(d [paníkiulet(ed], *a.* (bot.) apanojado.

Panicum [pǽnicum], *s.* (bot.) panizo.

panniculus [pæníkiulus], **pannicle** [pǽnicœl], *s.* (biol.) panículo.

pan(n)ier [pǽnœr], *s.* cuévano, serón, canastón; armazón ligera; (ing.) cestón, gabión.

pannikin [pǽnikin], *s.* cazo, cacillo.

panoply [pǽnopli], *s.* panoplia.

panorama [pænoráma], *s.* panorama.

panoramic [pænorámic], *a.* panorámico.

Panslavic [pænslǽvic], *a.* paneslavista.—**Panslavism** [-ĭsm], *s.* paneslavismo.

panspermatism [pænspœrmatĭsm], *s.* (biol.) panspermia.

pansy [pǽnsi], *s.* (bot.) pensamiento.

pant. I. *va.* y *vn.* jadear, anhelar; palpitar.—**to p. for** o **after**, suspirar por, desear con ansia. **II.** *s.* jadeo; palpitación.—*pl.* (fam.) pantalones.

pantagraph [pǽntægræf] = PANTOGRAPH.

pantalets [pǽntaléts], *s. pl.* pantalones largos de mujer.

pantaloon [pǽntælún], *s.* arlequín, bufón.—*pl.* pantalones.

pantelegraph [pæntélegraf], *s.* (elec.) pantelégrafo, instrumento telegráfico que transmite autógrafos, etc.

pantheology [pænzeóloyi], *s.* panteología.

pantheism [pǽnzeĭsm], *s.* panteísmo.—**pantheist** [-ĭst], *s.*, **pantheistic** [-ĭstic], *a.* panteísta.

Pantheon [pǽnzion], *s.* Panteón.

panther [pǽnzœr], *s.* (zool.) pantera.

pantherine [pǽnzœrin], *a.* panterino.

pantile [pǽntail], *s.* teja, canalón.

panting [pǽnting], *a.* jadeante.—**pantingly** [-li], *adv.* sin resuello, con afán.

pantler [pǽntlœr], *s.* panetero.

pantograph [pǽntograf], *s.* pantógrafo.

pantographic [-grǽfic], *a.* pantográfico.

pantometer [pæntómetœr], *s.* pantómetro.

pantomime [pǽntomaim], *s.* mímica; (teat.) pantomima.—**pantomimic** [-mímic], *a.* pantomímico.—**pantomimist** [-máimist], *s.* pantomimo.

pantry [pǽntri], *s.* despensa, reposte.

pap [pæp], *s.* pezón, teta; mogote; papilla, gachas, puches; carne (de la fruta).

papa [papá o pápa], *s.* papá.

papacy [péipasi], *s.* papado.

papain [pápain], *s.* (quím.) papaína.

papal [péipal], *a.* papal, pontifical.—**papalism** [-ĭsm], *s.* papismo.—**papalist** [-ĭst], *s.* papista.

papaveraceous [papaveréšhus], **papaverous** [papǽvœrus], *a.* amapolado, papaveráceo.

papaw [papó], *s.* (bot.) lechosa, papaya; (E. U., bot.) asimina.

paper [péipœr]. **I.** *s.* papel; memoria, artículo, disertación, ensayo; diario, periódico, (com.) valor, vale, letra o pagaré negociable; envoltorio; paquete, papel o papelito que contiene algo; (teat.) billete de favor, pase.—*pl.* papeles (valores, documentos, apuntes, etc.); credenciales; autos; carta de naturaleza.—**p. hanger**, empapelador.—**p. of needles**, cartón o paño de agujas.—**p. of tacks**, cajetilla de tachuelas.—**on p.**, escrito; por escrito; en lo escrito, en teoría. **II.** *a.* de papel; del o relativo al papel; para papel; para papeles; ecrito.—**p. blockade**, (der. int.) bloqueo en el papel.—**p. book**, libro en blanco.—**p. box**, caja de cartón.—**p. case**, papelera.—**p. clip**, sujetapapeles.—**p. currency**, papel moneda.—**p. cutter**, cortapapel; (enc.) máquina de cortar papel.—**p. file**, papelera, guardapapeles.—**p. folder**, plegadera.—**p. hanging**, oficio de empapelador; arte de empapelar.—**p. hangings**, papel de empapelar.—**p. kite**, cometa de papel, papalote.—**p. knife**, cortapapel.—**p. (making) machine**, máquina para hacer papel continuo.—**p. mill**, fábrica de papel.—**p. money**, papel moneda.—**p. muslin**, lustrina.—**p. nautilus**, (zool.) argonauta.—**p. pulp**, pulpa para papel.—**p. stainer**, fabricante de papeles pintados.—**p. wasp**, avispa.—**p. wedding**, primer aniversario de la boda.—**p. weight**, pisapapel, prensapapeles.—**p. wheel**, rueda de papel prensado. **III.** *va.* empapelar; cubrir con papel; pulir con papel de lija.

papery [péipœri], *a.* parecido al papel.

papescent [papésent], *a.* pulposo, carnoso.

papess [péipes], *s.* papisa.

papeterie [papetrí], *s.* cajita de papel y sobres.

papier-maché [papié-mašhé], *s.* cartón piedra.

papilio [papílio], *s.* mariposa.

Papilionidæ [papiliónidi], *s. pl.* (ent.) mariposas.

papilionaceous [papilionéshus], *a.* amariposado; (bot.) papilionáceo.

papilla [papíla], *s.* pezón; papila.

papillary [pæpílæri], **papillous** [papílus], *a.* papilar, mamilar.

papillitis [pæpiláitis], *s.* papilitis, neuritis óptica.

papilloma [pæpilómæ], *s.* papiloma.

papist [péipist], *s.* papista.

papistic(al [pæpístic(al], *a.* papista.

pap(p)oose [pæpús], *s.* niño de los indios norteamericanos.

pappose [pæpos], **pappous** [pæpus], *a.* velloso, velludo.

pappus [pǽpus], *s.* (bot.) vilano, papo.

pappy [pépi], *a.* mollar, jugoso.

paprika [páprika], *s.* pimentón.

papula [pǽpiula], **papule** [pǽpiul], *a.* pápula.

papular [pǽpiular], **papulous** [pǽpiulus], *a.* lleno de pápulas.

papyraceous [pæpiréšhus], *a.* papiráceo; hecho de papiro.

papyrus [papáirus], *s.* (bot.) papiro; papel de papiro; documento escrito en papiro.

par [par], *s.* equivalencia, paridad, nivel; (com.) par.—**p. value**, valor a la par.—**above p.**, a premio, con prima.—**at p.**, a la par.—**below p.**, a descuento.—**to be on a p. with**, ser igual a, estar al par de, correr parejas con.

parable [pǽrabœl], *s.* parábola.

parabola [pærǽbola], *s.* (geom.) parábola.

parabolic(al [pæræbólic, -æl], *a.* parabólico.—**p. geometry**, geometría euclidiana.—**p. space**, espacio euclidiano.

parabolically [-li], *adv.* parabólicamente.

paraboloid [pærǽboloid], *s.* paraboloide.

paracentric(al [pæraséntric(al], *a.* paracéntrico.

parachronism [pærǽcronĭsm], *s.* paracronismo.

parachute [pǽrašhut], *s.* paracaídas; (min.) cuba de seguridad.

Paraclete [pǽraclit], *s.* Paráclito o Paracleto.

parade [paréid]. **I.** *s.* (mil.) parada, revista de tropas; procesión; cabalgata; (Ingl.) paseo público; ostentación, pompa, fachenda; (esg.)

parada, quite.—**p. ground**, plaza de armas. **II.** *va.* y *vn.* (mil.) formar en parada; pasar revista; pasear, cabalgar; fachendear, alardear, ostentar.

paradigm [pǽradim], *s.* paradigma.

paradigmatic [-digmǽtic], *a.* ejemplar.

paradise [pǽradais], *s.* paraíso; (teat.) paraíso.— **p. bird**, ave del paraíso.

paradisiacal, paradisaic [pæradisáiacal, séic], *a.* paradisíaco.

paradox [pǽradox], *s.* paradoja.—**paradoxical** [-dóxical], *a.* paradójico.—**paradoxically** [-i], *adv.* paradójicamente.

paraffin(e [pǽræfin], *s.* parafina.

parage [párey], *s.* igualdad de sangre, de dignidad o terreno (entre coherederos).

paragenesis [pǽrayénesis], *s.* (min.) paragénesis.

paragoge [pæragóye], *s.* (ret.) paragoge.

paragogic [pæragóyic], *a.* paragógico.

paragon [pǽragon], *s.* modelo, ejemplar, dechado; (impr.) parangona (tipo grande de 20 puntos).

paragraph [pǽragraf]. **I.** *va.* dividir en párrafos. **II.** *s.* párrafo, aparte; suelto, gacetilla; (impr.) párrafo, calderón, el signo ¶.

paragrapher [pǽragrafœr], *s.* gacetillero.

paragraphic(al [pǽragrǽfic(al], *a.* escrito en párrafos sueltos; gacetillesco.

paragraphically [-i], *adv.* por párrafos.

Paraguayan [pæraguáian], *a.* y *s.* paraguayo, paraguayano.

paraldehyde [parǽldejaid], *s.* paraldehido.

parale(i)psis [paraláipsis], *s.* (ret.) paralipse.

parallactic(al [pǽralǽctic(áll], *a.* paraláctico.

parallax [pǽralæcs], *s.* (astr.) paralaje.

parallel [pǽralel]. **I.** *a.* paralelo; igual; análogo, semejante.—**p. bars**, paralelas (gimnasio).—**p. motion**, mecanismo de movimiento paralelo; paralelogramo de Watt.—**p. postulate**, postulado de las paralelas, o de Euclides.—**p. ruler**, rcgla para trazar rectas paralelas.—**p. sailing**, navegación paralela.—**p. series**, (elec.) = MULTIPLE SERIES. *V.* MULTIPLE. **II.** *s.* línea paralela; paralelo, cotejo; conformidad, semejanza; análogo; (geog.) paralelo (de latitud); igual, contraparte; (fort.) paralela; (impr.) signo de esta forma ‖.—**p. of latitude**, paralelo de latitud.—**in p.**, (elec.) en paralelo, en derivación. **III.** *va.* ser paralelo o igual a, correr parejas con; poner en dirección paralela; parangonar, cotejar, poner en paralelo.

parallelepiped, *s.* = PARALLELOPIPED.

parallelism [pǽralelism], *s.* paralelismo.

parallelly [pǽraleli], *adv.* paralelamente.

parallelogram [pǽralélogræm], *s.* (geom.) paralelogramo.

parallelopiped [pǽralélopáiped], *s.* (geom.) paralelepípedo.

paralogism, paralogy [parǽlorism, ri], *s.* (lógica) paralogismo.

paralogize, [parǽloyaiŝ], *vn.* paralogizar.

paralysis [pærǽlisis], *s.* (med.) parálisis; paralización estancamiento.

paralytic[pærǽlitic], *s.* paralítico, perlático.

paralytic(al [-al], *a* paralítico, perlático.

paralyzation [pæraliséiŝhun], *s.* parálisis; paralización.

paralyze, paralyse [pǽralaiŝ], *va.* paralizar.

paramagnetic [-mægnétic], *a.* paramagnético.

parameter [pǽrémetœr], *s.* (mat.) parámetro.

paramo [páramo], *s.* paramo.

paramorphism [pæramórfiŝm], *s.* (min.) paramorfismo, paramorfosis.

paramount [pǽramaunt], *a.* superior, supremo, principalísimo.

paramour [pǽramur], *s.* amante; manceba.

paranoia [pæranóia], *s.* paranoia, esp. la persecutoria, o locura de persecución.—**paranoiac** [-æc], **paranoic** [-noic]. **I.** *a.* relativo a la paranoia. **II.** *s.* el que sufre de paranoia.

Para nut [pará nut], *s.* = BRAZIL NUT.

paranymph [pǽraninf], *s.* paraninfo.

parapet [pǽrapet], *s.* (arq.) baranda, antepecho, pretil, mampuesto; (fort.) parapeto, baluarte.

paraphernalia [pǽrafœrnélia], *s.* *pl.* atavíos, arreos; adornos, galas, insignias; (for.) bienes parafernales.

paraphrase [pǽrafreŝ]. **I.** *s.* paráfrasis. **II.** *va.* parafrasear.—**paraphraser** [-freŝœr], *s.* parafraste. —**paraphrasis** [parǽfrasis], *s.* paráfrasis.—**paraphrastic(al** [pǽrafrǽstic(al], *a.* parafrástico.— **paraphrastically** [-i], *adv.* parafrásticamente.

paraplegia [pǽraplíyia], *s.* paraplegía.

paraquet, *s.* = PARRAKEET.

parasceve [pǽrasiv], *s.* parasceve de los judíos; viernes santo.

paraselene [-selín], *s.* paraselene.

parasite [pǽrasait], *s.* parásito; pájaro que pone sus huevos en el nido de otro.—**p. resistance**, (aer.) resistencia pasiva.

parasitic(al [pærasític(al], *a.* parásito; gorrístico; (med.) parasítico.—**p. current**, (elec.) corriente de Foucault o parásita.

parasitically [-i], *adv.* a modo de parásito; a ufo.

parasitism [pǽrasaitiŝm], *s.* parasitismo.

parasol [pǽrasol], *s.* sombrilla, parasol.

paravane [-vein], *s.* artificio para destruir minas submarinas.

parboil [párboil], *va.* sancochar; producir vejiguillas en la piel por el calor.

parbuckle [párbŭcœl]. **I.** *s.* tiravira. **II.** *va.* levantar o bajar por medio de una tiravira.

parcel [pársel]. **I.** *s.* paquete; lío, fardo, bulto; atado; porción, cantidad; hatajo, cuadrilla, partida.—*pl.* (for.) demarcación de linderos.—**p. of ground**, lote de terreno, solar.—**p. post**, servicio de paquetes postales. **II.** *va.* (con **out** o **into**) partir, dividir, distribuir; liar, empaquetar.—**to p. the seams**, (mar.) aforrar las costuras.—**parcelling**, (mar.) capa.

parcenary [párseneri], *s.* herencia indivisa.

parcener [pársenœr], *s.* coheredero.

parch. **1.** *va.* resecar, agostar; tostar, quemar, abrasar. **II.** *vn.* tostarse, quemarse, abrasarse. —**to be parched with thirst**, estarse abrasando de sed.

parching [-ing], *a.* abrasador, ardiente.

parchment [párchmœnt], *s.* pergamino.

parcimony [pársimoni], *s.* parsimonia.

pard, *s.* leopardo; (vulg. E. U.) asociado, compinche.

pardon [párdun]. **I.** *va.* perdonar, absolver; indultar; disculpar, dispensar.—**p. me**, perdone Vd., Vd. dispense.—**to p. a criminal**, conceder gracia a un criminal. **II.** *s.* perdón, gracia, absolución, indulto.—**I beg your p.**, Vd. dispense, perdone Vd. (fórmula de cortesía).

pardonable [párdunabœl], *a.* perdonable; venial. —**pardonableness** [-nes], *s.* disculpabilidad.— **pardonably** [-bli], *adv.* disculpablemente.

pardoner [párdunœr], *s.* perdonador.

pardoning [-ing], *a.* indulgente, perdonante.

pare [péœr], *va.* cortar, recortar; mondar (fruta); pelar (patatas, etc.); rallar, raspar; descantillar, desbastar.—**to p. a horse's hoof**, despalmar el casco de un caballo.—**to p. the nails**, cortar las uñas.

paregoric [pæregóric]. **I.** *a.* paregórico, calmante. **II.** *s.* elixir paregórico.

parenchyma [parénkima], *s.* parénquima.

parenchymous [parénkimus], **parenchymatous** [parenkimatus], *a.* parenquimatoso.

parenetic(al [parenétic(al], *a.* parenético, persuasivo.

parent [pérœnt]. **I.** *s.* padre o madre; autor, causa, origen.—*pl.* padres. **II.** *a.* madre, matriz, materno, principal.—**p. house**, casa principal. —**p. speech**, lengua matriz.

parentage [párentey], *s.* parentela; nacimiento, origen.

parental [paréntal], *a.* paternal.

parentheses [parénzesis], *s.* *pl.* de PARENTHESIS.

parenthesis [parénzesis], *s.* paréntesis.

parenthetic(al [parenzétic(al], *a.* entre paréntesis.—**parenthetically** [-i], *adv.* entre paréntesis.

parenthood [pérentjud], *s.* calidad de padre o madre.

parentless [pérentles], _a._ huérfano.
parer [péærœr], _s._ mondador, pelador.
paresis [péresis], _s._ (med.) paresia.
parétic, [parétic], _s._ y _a._ (med.) parestésico.
par excellence [par éxeláns], por excelencia, sin rival.
parget [páryet]. **I.** _va._ (alb.) enyesar, enlucir. **II.** _s._ yeso; mortero, argamasa; enlucido.
pargeting [páryeting], _s._ (alb.) enlucido; estuco; argamasa.
parhelion [parjílion], _s._ (astr.) parhelia.
Pariah [péria _o_ pária], _s._ paria.
parietal [paráietal]. **I.** _a._ paredaño; parietal; interno; (bot.) parietal. **II.** _s._ (anat.) parietal.
parietary [paráieteri], _s._ (bot.) parietaria.
paring [péæring], _s._ raspadura, peladura, pellejo, cáscara, recorte, desperdicio, desecho.—**p. knife**, cuchilleja, trinchete; descarnador; pujavante.
Paris [péris], _a._ de París.—**P. green**, cardenillo arsenioso, aceto-arsenito de cobre.—**P. white**, blanco de París.
parish [pérish]. **I.** _s._ parroquia, feligresía, curato; (E. U.) en Luisiana, jurisdicción o partido. **II.** _a._ parroquial.—**p. clerk**, sacristán de parroquia.—**p. school**, escuela parroquial.
parishioner [paríshunœr], _s._ parroquiano, feligrés.
Parisian [paríšian], _a._ y _s._ parisiense.
parity [péeriti], _s._ paridad, semejanza.
park. I. _s._ parque; (mil.) parque de artillería. **II.** _va._ cercar o cerrar un coto; arrimar y dejar (un coche) al borde de la acera o a un paradero; depositar, guardar, dar a guardar por poco tiempo (algo que estorba).
parkleaves [párclivš], _s._ (bot.) androsemo, castellar.
parkway [-uéi], _s._ bulevar; carretera para automóviles.
parlance [párlans], _s._ lenguaje, idioma; conversación.
parley [párli]. **I.** _vn._ parlamentar; discutir; conferenciar. **II.** _s._ conferencia, plática.
Parliament [párlimœnt], _s._ (Ingl.) parlamento; cuerpo legislativo.—**P. heel**, (mar.) péndol.
parliamentarian [-térian], _s._ parlamentario.
parliamentarily [parliméntarili], _adv._ parlamentariamente.
parliamentarism [-tarišm], _s._ parlamentarismo.
parliamentary [-tari], _a._ parlamentario.—**p. law**, práctica parlamentaria.
parlo(u)r [párlor], _s._ sala de recibo; (Ingl.) sala de confianza; parlatorio, locutorio.—**p. car**, coche salón.
parlous [párlus],ᵃ _a._ (fam.) peligroso, temible; sorprendente.—**parlously** [-li], _adv._ (fam.) sumamente.
Parmesan [párme̅san], _a._ parmesano.
Parnassus [parnéésus], _s._ Parnaso.
Parnassian [-siæn]. **I.** _a._ del Parnaso; poético. —**P. school**, escuela parnasiana. **II.** _s._ poeta; parnasiano.
parochial [paróikial], _a._ parroquial.
parochially [paróikiali], _adv._ por parroquias.
parodical [paródical], _a._ paródico.
parody [pérodi]. **I.** _s._ parodia. **II.** _va._ parodiar.
parol [pæról], _a._ (for.) verbal, oral; escrito pero no sellado.—**p. contract**, contrato no perfeccionado. —**p. evidence**, prueba verbal.—**by p.**, de palabra.
parole [paról]. **I.** _s._ palabra, promesa de honor de un prisionero; santo y seña; (for.) alegación o alegato. **II.** _va._ (mil.) poner en libertad bajo palabra.
paronomasia [péronoméíyiæ], _s._ (ret.) paronomasia.
paronomastic [-méstic], _a._ paronímico.
paronychia [pæroníkia], _s._ (cir.) panadizo.
paronym [péronim], _s._ voz parónima.—**parony-mous, paronymic** [pærónimus, pærónimic], _a._ parónimo.—**paronymy** [pærónimi], _s._ paronimia.
paroquet [péroket], _s._ (orn.) periquito.
parotid [parótid]. **I.** _a._ próximo a la oreja. **II.** _s._ (anat.) parótida.—**parotitis** [pærotáitis], **parotiditis** [pærótidáitis], _s._ parotiditis.
paroxysm [péroxišm], _s._ paroxismo.

paroxysmal [-mal], _a._ paroxismal; (geol.) producido por una conmoción.
parquet [parkét], _s._ (teat.) platea.—**p. floor, piso** de mosaico de madera.
parquetry [párketri], _s._ mosaico de madera.
parr, _s._ (ict.) esguín, murgón.
parrakeet [pérakit], _s._ (orn.) perico, periquito.
parrel [pérrel], _s._ manto de chimenea; (mar.) racamento.—**p. rope**, troceo.—**p. truck**, (mar.) troza.
parrhesia [paríyia _o_ sia], _s._ parresia.
parricidal [périsáidal], _a._ parricida.
parricide [périsaid], _s._ parricida; parricidio.
parrot [pérrot]. **I.** _s._ (orn.) papagayo, loro, cotorra.—**p. fish o wrasse**, (ict.) escaro. **II.** _va_ y _vn._ repetir o hablar como loro; decir ociosidades.
parry [párri]. **I.** _va._ y _vn._ (esgr.) parar, rechazar, reparar, quitar. **II.** _s._ parada, quite, reparo.
parrying [pérriing], _s._ parada, quite.
parse [pars], _va._ (gram.) analizar.
parsec [pársec], _s._ unidad astronómica igual a 206.265 veces la distancia del sol a la tierra.
Parsee, Parsi [pársi], _s._ parsi.
Parseeism, Parsism [pársiišm], _s._ parsismo, religión de Zoroastro.
parsimonious [pársimónius], _a._ parco, frugal; mezquino.—**parsimoniously** [-li], _adv._ parcamente; mezquinamente.—**parsimoniousness** [-nes]. **parsimony** [pársimoni], _s._ parquedad; mezquindad.
parsing [pársing], _s._ (gram.) análisis.
parsley [pársli], _s._ (bot.) perejil.
parsnip [pársnip], _s._ (bot.) chirivía, berraza, pastinaca.
parson [pársun], _s._ clérigo; párroco, cura.
parsonage [pársuney], _s._ rectoría.
part. I. _s._ parte; miembro; pieza; región, lugar; (teat.) papel; interés, cuidado; obligación, deber; (mús.) parte; entrega de una publicación; raya del cabello.—_pl._ partes, prendas personales, dotes.—**p. and parcel**, uña y carne, carne y hueso.—**p. of speech**, parte de la oración.—**p. owner**, condueño.—**for one's p.**, por lo que a uno toca, en cuanto a uno.—**in good (bad) p.**, sin ofenderse (ofendido).—**in p.**, en parte, parcialmente.—**to do one's p.**, cumplir uno con su obligación; hacer cuanto pueda. **II.** _va._ partir; repartir; separar, dividir; romper, desprender; salir o irse de; apartar.—**to p. company**, separarse.—**to p. the hair**, partir el pelo, hacerse la raya. **III.** _vn._ partirse; separarse; desprenderse, saltar, zafarse; despedirse; partir, irse; morir.— **to p. from**, despedirse de, decir adiós a.—**to p. with**, deshacerse de; enajenar.
partage [pártey], _s._ repartimiento.
partake [parték]. **I.** _va._ (_pret._ PARTOOK: _pp._ PARTAKEN) participar de, tener parte en. **II.** _vn._ (con _of_ o _with_) participar; tomar parte.
partaker [pártekœr], _s._ partícipe, participante.
parterre [partéær], _s._ cuadro de jardín, macizo de flores; (teat.) parte de la platea detrás de las lunetas.
parthenogenesis, parthenogeny [párzenoyénesis, -nóyeni], _s._ partenogénesis.—**parthenogenetic** [yenétic], _a._ partenogenésico.
partial [parshæl], _a._ parcial, prevenido; parcial, no del todo o completo; más aficionado (a), mejor dispuesto (hacia, para, con).—**p. differential**, (mat.) diferencial parcial.—**p. eclipse**, eclipse parcial.—**p. fractions**, (mat.) fracciones parciales, fracciones en que puede descomponerse una fracción algebraica.—**p. payments**, pagos parciales.
partiality [pàrshiéeliti], _s._ parcialidad; predilección, preferencia.
partially [párshali], _adv._ parcialmente, en parte; con parcialidad.
participant [partísipant], _a._ y _s._, **participator** [-pitœr], _s._ participante, partícipe, copartícipe.— **participate** [-peit], _va._ y _vn._ participar.—**participation** [-péishun], _s._ participación; distribución, repartimiento.
participial [partisípial], _a._ participial.
participially [-li], _adv._ participialmente.
participle [pártisipœl], _s._ (gram.) participio.— **past p.**, participio pasado.—**present p.**, gerundio.

particle [párticcel], s. partícula; pizca; (gram.) partícula; (mec.) punto material.

particular [partíkiular]. **I.** a. particular, peculiar; en particular; individual, privado, privativo; singular, notable; distinguido, predilecto; preciso, exacto; delicado, escrupuloso; minucioso, detallado: exigente, quisquilloso. **II.** s. particularidad, detalle, pormenor; circunstancia; caso individual.—**in p.**, particularmente, en particular.

particularity [-lǽriti], s. particularidad.

particularize [-aiŝ], va. particularizar.

particularly [-li], adv. particularmente.

parting [párting]. **I.** s. separación, división; marcha o partida; despedida; rompimiento, rotura; bifurcación.—**to be at the p. of the roads, o of the ways**, haber llegado el tiempo de decidir definitivamente, o de que coja cada cual por su camino. **II.** a. divisorio; de separación; de partida; de despedida; último, al partir.

partisan, a. y s. = PARTIZAN.

partition [partíŝhun]. **I.** s. partición, repartimiento; división, separación; linde, demarcación; (alb.) tabique; (carp.) mampara, camón de vidrios; (for.) partición, partija, repartición; (mús.) partitura.—p. **wall**, tabique; medianería, cerramiento. **II.** va. partir, dividir o separar; repartir, distribuir.

partitive [pártitiv]. **I.** a. partitivo; (gram.) partitivo; distributivo. **II.** s. palabra o caso partitivo.

partizan [pártiŝan]. **I.** a. partidario; parcial; (mil.) de guerrilla.—p. **vote**, votación de partido. **II.** s. partidario, secuaz; (arm.) partesana; bastón de mando.

partizanship, partisanship [pártiŝanŝhip], s. adhesión ciega a un partido, (Am.) partidarismo.

partly [pártli], adv. en parte, en cierto modo.

partner [pártnœr], s. socio; compañero; pareja (de baile); consorte, cónyuge; interesado, partícipe; aparcero, parcionero.

partnership [pártnœrŝhip], s. (com.) compañía; sociedad, interés social; consorcio; aparcería; (arit.) regla de compañía.—p. **in commendam, paen commandite**, sociedad comanditaria, o en comandita.

partook, pret. de TO PARTAKE.

partridge [pártriy], s. (orn.) perdiz.

parturient [partiúrient], a. parturiente.

parturifacient [pártiuriféiŝhœnt], s. y a. ocitócico, que acelera el parto.

parturition [partiuríŝhun], s. parto.

party [parti]. **I.** s. partido (político, etc.); partida (de campo, teatro, etc.); tertulia; cuadrilla, cuerpo; parte, partícipe; (mil.) partida, destacamento; (for.) parte, parte interesada; (fam.) persona, sujeto.—p. **in interest**, (for.) parte interesada; interesado.—p. **of the first (second) part**, (for.) primera (segunda) parte. Estas expresiones se usan en contratos, escrituras, etc., para distinguir las partes contratantes; pero al traducirlas debe cambiarse el giro, para que la frase se adapte a las formas castellanas; v. gr.: a contract between N. N., party of the first part, and X. Y., party of the second part, puede traducirse: "contrato entre N. N., por una parte, y X. Y., por otra parte"; o "contrato entre N. N., otorgante, y X. Y., concesionario," etc., según las circunstancias. Cuando en el cuerpo del documento se diga, the said party of the first part, etc., puede decirse: "el dicho N. N.", "dicho otorgante," "el mencionado otorgante," etc., **II.** a. de partido; partido, dividido.—p.-colored, de varios colores.—p. **jury**, (Ing.) jurado mixto (de ingleses y extranjeros).—p. **line, p. wire**, (elec.) línea de teléfonos agrupados en un mismo circuito.—p. **wall**, pared medianera.

parvenu [párveniu], s. y a. advenedizo.

parvis [párvis], s. (arq.) atrio.

pas [pa], s. paso; baile; precedencia.

paschal [péscal,] a. pascual.—p. **taper**, cirio pascual.

pasha [paŝhá o péŝho], s. bajá.

pasquinade [péscuinéd], pasquil, pasquín [péscuil, cuin], s. pasquín, pasquinada.

pass. I. va. (pp. PASSED O PAST) pasar; pasar de; pasar por; aprobar (un proyecto, a un alumno); dar, promulgar (una ley); pasar por alto; evacuar, orinar (sangre, etc.); ser aprobado en (un examen, una materia); transferir, trasladar; aventajar, exceder; hacer pasar; tolerar; admitir, dar entrada.—**to p. a dividend**, no pagar dividendo. —**to p. along**, pasar de uno a otro.—**to p. away**, gastar (el tiempo).—**to p. by**, dispensar, perdonar; omitir; pasar por alto.—**to p. each other, o one another**, cruzarse.—**to p. judgement** = TO P. SENTENCE.—**to p. muster**, pasar revista; valer algo; ser aceptado.—**to p. off**, dar o circular como legítimo lo que no lo es.—**to p. (something) on**, pasar (algo) de unos a otros; transmitir; pasar (algo) a otras personas.—**to p. one's word for another**, empeñar su palabra por otro.—**to p. over**, pasar por alto, excusar.—**to p. sentence**, pronunciar sentencia.—**to p. the buck**, (fam.) echarle la carga o el muerto a otro.—**to p. the time of day**, saludar, dar los buenos días.—**to p. through**, pasar o hacer pasar por.

pass, vn. pasar; transmitirse; ser aprobado (un proyecto, un alumno); ser admitido, aceptarse; (esgr.) dar una estocada, hacer un pase; (naipes) pasar, abstenerse de hacer una jugada.—**to p. along**, pasar de largo.—**to p. away**, fallecer; desaparecer.—**to p. beyond**, pasar de; ir más allá de. —**to p. by**, pasar por el lado o cerca de.—**to p. current**, ser corriente; aceptarse como bueno.— **to p. for**, pasar por, ser tenido o reputado por.— **to p. into**, pasar a; convertirse en.—**to p. off**, pasar, desaparecer (una enfermedad, tempestad, etc.); disiparse.—**to p. on**, seguir, continuar.—**to p. on, o upon**, formar juicio sobre, examinar y decidir sobre.—**to p. through**, pasar por; atravesar.—**to p. out**, salir.—**to p. over**, atravesar, cruzar.

pass, s. paso; pase (billete, permiso; de manos, de esgrima); billete de favor o de cumplimiento; situación, estado (de los negocios, de las cosas); aprobación (en un examen).—p. **book**, libro de cuenta y razón; libreta de banco.—p. **check**, billete de admisión; billete de ida y vuelta. —p.-key, llave maestra.

passable [pásabœl], a. transitable; pasadero, regular.—**passably** [-bli], adv. pasaderamente.

passage [péser], s. pasaje; paso, pasada, tránsito; viaje, navegación, travesía; pasadizo, pasillo; callejón; pasaje (de un libro, etc.); trámite y aprobación de un proyecto de ley; acontecimiento, episodio; encuentro personal, lance; migración de las aves; cámara, deposición.—p. **boat**, escorchapín.

passage-way [-uéi], s. pasadizo.

passé, passée [paséi], a. pasado, pasada; marchito, marchita (fig.).

passementerie [pasméntri], s. pasamanería.

passenger [pásenyœr], s. pasajero, transeúnte; viajero, viandante.

passe partout [pas partú], s. marco ligero de vidrio y cartón.

passer(-by) [pásœr(-bai)], s. transeúnte, viandante.

passerine [páserin], a. paserino.

passibility [pásibiliti], o **passibleness** [pásibœlnes], s. pasibilidad.

passible [pásibœl], a. pasible.

Passifloraceæ [pésiflorésii], s. pl. (bot.) pasifloráceas.

passim [pásim], adv. pássim, en varias partes.

passimeter [pasimétœr], s. cuentapasos.

passing [pásing]. **I.** a. que pasa; pasajero, transitorio, momentáneo.—p. **bell**, toque de difuntos. **II.** adv. eminentemente, sumamente. **III.** s. paso, pasada; tránsito; muerto; aprobación.—**in p., de paso.

passion [péŝhun], s. pasión; (fam.) cólera; (P-) Pasión (de Cristo).—p. **flower** pasionaria.—P. **play**, drama de la Pasión, drama religioso en que se representa la Pasión.—p. **vine** = P. FLOWER.—P. **Week**, semana de Pasión.

passionate [péŝhunet], a. apasionado; ardiente, impetuoso; colérico, arrebatado.—**passionately** [-li], adv. apasionadamente; ardientemente; coléricamente.—**passionateness** [-nes], s. vehemencia, impetuosidad.

passionless [pǽshʊnles], a. frío, sin pasiones.
passive [pǽsiv]. **I.** a. pasivo; inerte. **II.** s. (gram.) voz pasiva.—**passively** [-li], adv. pasivamente.—**passiveness** [-nes], **passivity** [pǽsiviti), s. pasividad.
Passover [pásovœr], s. pascua de los hebreos.
passport [pásport], s. pasaporte.
password [pásucœrd], s. palabra de pase; santo y seña, contraseña.
past. I. a. pasado, último; concluído; terminado; ex, que fué (presidente, director, etc.).—**p. master of**, experto o sobresaliente en. **II.** s. lo pasado; antecedentes, historia; (gram.) pretérito; pasado. **III.** prep. más de, después de (tiempo); más allá de, fuera de (lugar); fuera de, sin.—**p. a doubt**, fuera de duda.—**p. bearing**, insoportable; infecundo.—**p. cure**, incurable.—**p. dispute**, incontestable, fuera de duda.—**p. question**, fuera de duda, indudable.—**p. recovery**, desahuciado, sin remedio.—**p. remedy**, irremediable.
paste [péist]. **I.** s. pasta; engrudo; (joy.) imitación de piedras preciosas. **II.** va. engrudar, empastar, pegar.
pasteboard [péistbœrd]. **I.** s. cartón. **II.** a. de cartón; acartonado.
pastel [pǽstel], s. (b. a.) pastel; clarioncillo; (bot.) hierba pastel.
pastern [pǽstœrn], s. cuartilla del caballo; trabadera.—**p. bone**, (vet.) falange.—**p. joint**, articulación de las falanges.
Pasteurization [pæstœrizéishʊn], s. pasteurización.—**Pasteurize** [-aiź], va. pasteurizar.—**Pasteurizer** [-aiśœr], s. pasteurizador (persona o aparato).
pastil(le [pǽstil], s. pastilla, tableta; (b. a.) pastel.
pastime [pástaim], s. pasatiempo.
pastor [pástœr], s. pastor espiritual, cura, clérigo; (orn.) estornino copetudo.
pastoral [pástoral]. **I.** a. pastoril, pastoricio; (igl.) pastoral. **II.** s. (poét.) pastoral, bucólica; idilio, pastorela; (igl.) carta pastoral.
pastorate [pástœret], **pastorship** [pástœrship], s. curato; cura de almas.
pastry [péstri], s. pastelería, pasteles, pastas.—**p. cook**, pastelero, repostero.
pasturable [páschurabœl], a. pacedero.
pasturage [páschurey], s. pastos, pastura; pasturaje; apacentamiento, adehesamiento.
pasture [páschur]. **I.** s. apacentador, dehesa; pastura, pasto; apacentamiento, pacedura.—**p. ground**, dehesa, pradera, acampo. **II.** va. pastar, apacentar, pastorear. **III.** vn. pastar, pacer.
pasty [pésti]. **I.** a. pastoso. **II.** s. pastel de carne.
pat [pæt]. **I.** a. exacto, oportuno, propio, bueno, cómodo. **II.** s. caricia, mamola; ruido de pasos; pastilla. **III.** adv. justamente, convenientemente, a propósito. **IV.** va. acariciar, pasar la mano, hacer la mamola.
patache [patǽsh], s. (mar.) patache.
patch [pæch]. **I.** va. remendar, apedazar, apañar; chapuzar, chafallar; ponerse lunares postizos. **II.** vn. echar remiendos, hacer labor de retazos. **III.** s. remiendo; parche, apaño; material para remiendos; pieza embutida en taracea; lunar postizo; placa (en las mucosas); sembrado.—**p. of land**, o **ground**, pedazo de terreno.
patcher [pǽchœr], s. chafallón; remendón.
patchouli [pachúli], s. pachulí.
patchwork [pǽchuœrk], s. obra o labor de retacitos; remiendo; chapucería.
pate [péit], s. (fam.) cabeza.
pâté [paté], s. pastelillo, empanada.
patella [patéla], s. (anat.) rótula; (zool.) parte semejante a una copa; cazoleta.
paten [pǽten], s. (igl.) patena.
patent [pǽtœnt]. **I.** a. patente, manifiesto; público; patentado; de patente; de patentes.—**p. law**, ley de patentes.—**p. leather**, charol.—**p. medicine**, remedio de patente.—**P. Office**, oficina de patentes. **II.** s. patente, privilegio de invención.—**p. applied for**, se ha solicitado patente. **III.** va. patentar.
patentable [-abœl], a. patentable.
patentee [-i], s. el que obtiene una patente.
patentor [-or], s. el que otorga una patente.

patera [pétera], s. patera.
paternal [patœrnal], a. paternal, paterno.
paternally [patœrnali], adv. paternalmente.
paternity [patœrniti], s. paternidad; linaje, alcurnia por parte de padre.
paternoster [péitœrnóstœr], s. padrenuestro.— **p. pump**, bomba de cadena sin fin.
path [paz], s. senda, sendero; vereda; camino, vía; línea; trayectoria.
pathetic(al [pazétic(al], a. patético o conmovedor.—**pathetically** [-i], adv. patéticamente.— **patheticalness** [-nes], s. calidad de patético.
pathless [pázles], a. intransitable.
pathogenic [pazoyénic], a. patógeno.
pathologic(al [pazolóyic(al], a. patológico.
pathologist [pazóloyist], s. patólogo.
pathology [pazóloyi], s. patología.
pathos [péizos o pázos], s. rasgo conmovedor, sentimiento.
pathway [pázuei], s. senda, vereda.
patience [péishens], s. paciencia; (bot.) romaza.
patient [péshent]. **I.** a. paciente, pacienzudo; asiduo, perseverante; sufrido. **II.** s. paciente, sujeto pasivo; (med.) paciente, enfermo, doliente.
patiently [péshentli], adv. pacientemente.
patina [pǽtina], s. pátina.
patly [pǽtli], adv. a propósito, convenientemente.
patness [-nes], s. oportunidad, conveniencia.
patois [patuá], s. jerga, dialecto, patois.
patriarch [péitriarc], s. patriarca.
patriarchal [petriárcal], a. patriarcal.
patriarchate, patriarchship, patriarchy [péitriarket, ship, ki], s. patriarcado.
patrician [patríshan], a. y s. patricio.
patriciate [-shicit], s. patriciado.
patricide [pétrisaid], s. parricida; parricidio.
patrilineal [péitrilínial], a. de o por la línea paterna.
patrimonial [pætrimónial], a. patrimonial.
patrimony [pǽtrimoni], s. patrimonio.
patriot [péitriot], s. patriota.
patrioteer [-tíœr]. **I.** s. patriotero. **II.** vn. alardear de patriotismo, darse a la patriotería.
patriotic [petriótic], a. patriótico.—**patriotically** [-œli], adv. patrióticamente.
patriotism [péitriotiśm], s. patriotismo, civismo.
patristic(al [patrístic(al], a. patrístico.
patristics [patrístics], s. patrística.
patrol [patróul]. **I.** s. patrulla; ronda. **II.** va. y vn. patrullar, rondar; hacer la ronda.
patrolman [patróulman], s. rondador; vigilante de policía.
patrology [patróloyi], s. patrología.
patron [péitrʊn], s. patrón, patrono, patrocinador, protector; santo patrón; parroquiano; (igl.) patrono.
patronage [pétruney], s. patrocinio, amparo, auspicio; clientela; (igl.) patronato, patronazgo.
patronal [pétrunal], a. patronal.
patroness [pétrunes], sf. patrona, protectora; patrocinadora, madrina.
patronize [pétrunaiź], va. patrocinar, proteger; apoyar, fomentar; condescender con arrogancia; tratar con arrogante condescendencia; (fam.) ser concurrente a, o parroquiano de.
patronizer [-œr], s. patrocinador.
patronizing [-ing], a. fatua o desdeñosamente condescendiente; estirado.—**patronizingly** [-li], adv. con arrogante condescendencia, con aire de superioridad.
patronless [pétrʊnles], a. desamparado.
patronymic [pætronímic], s. y a. patronímico.
patten [pǽten], s. zueco, chanclo; (arq.) cimiento, fundamento.
patter [pǽtœr]. **I.** vn. hacer ruido acompasado. —**to p. with the feet**, patalear, patear. **II.** s. sucesión de golpecitos o palmaditas; pataleo; parlería, charla.
pattern [pǽtœrn]. **I.** s. modelo, pauta; ejemplar; muestra; patrón, dechado; molde, plantilla, escantillón. **II.** va. copiar, imitar; servir de ejemplo.

patty [pǽti], *s*. pastelillo, empanada.

pattypan [pǽtipæn], *s*. tartera.

patulous [pǽtiulʊs], *a*. abierto, extendido.

paucity [pósiti], *s*. poquedad, escasez, corto número; exiguidad, insuficiencia.

pauldron [póldrʊn], *s*. hombrera.

Pauline [pólin], *a*. referente a San Pablo.

Paulist [pólist], *s*. paulista.

paulownia [polónia], *s*. (bot.) paulonia.

paunch [ponch *o* panch], *s*. panza, barriga, vientre; panza de los rumiantes; borde de una campana; (mar.) pallete, gimelga.

pauper [pópœr], *s*. pobre, indigente.—**pauperism** [-ísm], *s*. pauperismo.—**pauperization** [-ísếíŝhʊn], *s*. empobrecimiento.—**pauperize, pauperise** [-aiŝ], *va*. depauperar, empobrecer.

pause [poŝ]. **I**. *s*. pausa; hiato, cesura; irresolución, vacilación; (mús.) espera, fermata. **II**. *vn*. cesar, parar, detenerse; tardar, vacilar.

pausingly [póŝingli], *adv*. por pausas; después de un intervalo.

pavan [pǽvan], *s*. (danz.) pavana.

pave [péiv], *va*. pavimentar, empedrar, enladrillar, embaldosar.—**to p. the way**, preparar el terreno, abrir el camino.

pavement [péivmœnt], *s*. pavimento, empedrado, adoquinado, piso.

paver [péivœr], **pavier** [péiviœr], *s*. empedrador, solador.

pavilion [pavíllun], *s*. pabellón, tienda de campaña; quiosco, cenador de jardín; dosel; pabellón, bandera; pabellón de la oreja; (arq.) pabellón, ala.

paving [péiving]. **I**. *s*. pavimento; pavimentación; material de pavimentar. **II**. *a*. de pavimentar, para pavimentos.—**p. hammer**, aciche.—**p. tile**, baldosa.

pavonine [pǽvonin], *a*. relativo al pavo real; iridescente.

paw [po]. **I**. *s*. garra, zarpa. **II**. *va*. y *vn*. patear, piafar; manosear.

pawl [pol], *s*. linguete, trinquete; fiador de rueda; paleta de reloj; diente de encaje, retén, seguro.

pawn [pon]. **I**. *va*. empeñar, dar en prenda. **II**. *s*. prenda, empeño; peón de ajedrez.—**p. ticket**, papeleta de empeño.—**in p.**, en prenda.

pawnbroker [pónbróukœr], *s*. prestamista sobre prendas, prendero, usurero; comodatario.

pawnee [poní], *s*. prestador, prestamista sobre prendas.—**P.**, tribu de indios norteamericanos.

pawner [pónœr], *s*. prendador.

pawnshop [pónŝhóp], *s*. casa de empeños.

pax [pæx], *s*. (igl.) paz (patena y el acto de besarla en la misa).

pay [péi]. **I**. *va*. (*pret*. y *pp*. PAID) pagar; producir ganancia o provecho a; (mar.) embrear. **to p. a call, o a visit**, hacer una visita.—**to p. a compliment**, hacer un cumplido, echar una flor. —**to p. attention**, prestar atención; fijarse; galantear, cortejar.—**to p. back**, devolver, restituir; pagar en la misma moneda, vengarse de.—**to p. by instalments**, pagar a plazos.—**to p. cash**, pagar al contado.—**to p. court**, hacer la corte.— **to p. down**, pagar al contado.—**to p. expenses**, cubrir los gastos.—**to p. in full**, pagar por completo, pagar totalmente.—**to p. off** = TO P. OUT; pagar; pagar a y despedir; redimir (una hipoteca, etc.).—**to p. on account**, pagar a buena cuenta. —**to p. one's addresses to**, cortejar, pretender en matrimonio.—**to p. one's duties**, rendir homenaje.—**to p. one's respects**, presentar u ofrecer sus respetos.—**to p. one's score**, pagar sus deudas, su escote.—**to p. out**, ir aflojado o dando (una cuerda), largar; arriar.—**to p. reverence to**, rendir homenaje a; inclinarse ante.—**to p. the fiddler, o the piper**, pagar el pato, pagar los vidrios rotos. **II**. *vn*. pagar; compensar, ser provechoso; valer la pena.—**to p. by instalments**, pagar a plazos.—**to p. dear, o dearly**, costarle a uno caro.—**to p. in full**, pagar totalmente o del todo.—**to p. off**, pagar; pagar por completo; pagar y despedir el personal (de un taller, buque, etc.). **III**. *s*. paga, sueldo, salario; recompensa, galardón.—**p. bill**, vale, boletín, póliza.—**p. clerk**,

pagador.—**p. day**, día de pagos.—**p. dirt** (**rock**, etc.) (min.) tierra (roca, etc.) que da oro con ganancia.—**p. list, p. roll**, nómina.

payable [péabœl], *a*. pagadero, reembolsable.

payee [peí], *s*. tenedor, persona a quien se paga o debe pagarse una letra, cheque, etc.

payer [péœr], *s*. pagador.

paymaster [péimastœr], *s*. pagador, contador; (mil.) habilitado.

payment [péimœnt], *s*. pago, paga;.—**p. in full**, pago total; saldo, finiquito.—**on the p. of**, mediante el pago de.

paymistress [péimístres], *s*. pagadora.

pea [pí], (*pl*. PEAS *o* PEASE) (bot.) guisante, chícharo, pésol; (orn.) pavo real.—**p. green**, verde claro.—**p. gun o shooter**, bodoquera, cerbatana. —**p. pod, p. shell**, vaina de guisante.—**p. weevil** (ent.) gorgojo.

peace [pis]. **I**. *s*. paz.—**p. at any price**, la paz a toda costa.—**p. be with you**, la paz sea con vosotros.—**p. establishment, o footing**, (mil.) pie de paz.—**p. offering**, sacrificio propiciatorio.—**p. officer**, guardia civil o municipal. **II**. *interj*. ¡paz! ¡silencio!

peaceable [písabœl], *a*. tranquilo, pacífico, apacible.—**peaceableness** [-nes], *s*. tranquilidad. —**peaceably** [-bli], *adv*. pacíficamente, tranquilamente.

peacebreaker [písbréicœr], *s*. perturbador de la paz.

peaceful [písful], *a*. tranquilo; pacífico.—**peacefully** [-i], *adv*. tranquilamente; pacíficamente.— **peacefulness** [-nes], *s*. quietud, calma.

peacemaker [písméikœr], *s*. pacificador; reconciliador.

peach [pich]. **I**. *s*. durazno, melocotón; color de durazno; (fam.) persona o cosa admirable.—**p. tree**, melocotonero, durazno, duraznero. **II**. *vn*. hacerse delator de un cómplice.

peachy [píchi], *a*. semejante al durazno; (fam.) muy agradable.

peacock, peafowl [pícoc, faul], *s*. (orn.) pavón o pavo real.—**p. fish**, (ict.) budión.

peahen [píjén], *s*. pava real.

pea-jacket [pí-yæket], *s*. chaquetón.

peak [pic]. **I**. *s*. cima, cumbre, pico, picacho; cúspide; máximo (ú. t. como *a*.); (mar.) penol, pico, espiga de vela; uña del ancla.—**p. halliards**, (mar.) drizas de la pena. **II**. *vn*. tener apariencia de enfermo. **III**. *va*. (mar.) amantillar el pico, levantar una verga contra el mástil.

peaked [píked], *a*. puntiagudo; (arq.) con caballete; (fam.) enfermizo.

peakish [píkiŝh], **peaky** [píki], *a*. picoteado, picudo; (fam.) flacucho.

peal [píl]. **I**. *s*. repique de campanas; estruendo, estrépito.—**p. of laughter**, carcajada, risotada.— **p.-ringing**, repiqueteo. **II**. *va*. y *vn*. repicar, retronar.

peanut [pínut], *s*. (bot.) cacahué, cacahuete, (Cuba) maní.—**p. butter**, pasta de cacahuetes tostados.—**p. candy**, guirlache de cacahuetes.

pear [péær], *s*. (bot.) pera.—**p. blight**, tizón.— **p.-shaped**, piriforme.—**p. tree**, peral.

pearl [pœrl], *s*. perla, aljófar; nube o catarata en el ojo; (impr.) perla, tipo de 5 puntos.—**p. barley**, cebada perlada.—**p.-eyed**, que tiene una nube en el ojo.—**p. oyster**, ostra que produce perlas.—**p. powder**, blanco de perla.—**p. seed**, aljófar, rostillo.—**p. white** = P. POWDER.

pearlash [pœrlǽŝh], *s*. potasa purificada.

pearled [pœrld], *a*. perlado, aljofarado.

pearlstone [pœrlstoun], *s*. perlita, fonolita.

pearly [pœrli], *a*. perlino; aljofarado.

pearmain [pœrmein], *s*. (bot.) pero.

peart [pírt], *a*. (fam.) jovial, alegre.

peasant [pésant]. **I**. *s*. labriego, labrador. **II**. *a*. campesino, rústico.

peasantry [pésantri], *s*. paisanaje, gente del campo, lugareños.

peascod [píscod], *s*. vaina de los guisantes.

pease [pis], *s*. *pl*. de PEA: guisantes.

peat [pít], *s*. turba.—**p. bog o bed**, turbal, turbera.—**p. charcoal**, carbón de turba.—**p. moss**, musgo de pantano; turbera.

peaty [píti], a. turboso.
pebble(stone [pébœl(stoun]. I. s. guija, china, matacán; cuero abollonado; pólvora gruesa; lente de cristal de roca. II. va. y vn. granular, abollonar cuero; presentar apariencia áspera.
pebbly [pébli], a. guijoso.
pecan [pecǽn], s. (bot.) pacana, pecana.—**p. nut,** pacana.
peccability [pecabíliti], s. fragilidad.
peccable [pécabœl], a. pecable.
peccadillo [pecadílo], s. pecadillo.—**peccadilloes,** peccata minuta.
peccancy [pécansi], s. vicio, defecto.
peccant [pécant], a. pecador, pecante; corrompido, ofensivo; vicioso.
peccary [pécari], s. (zool.) pecarí.
peck [pec]. I. s. medida de áridos (¼ de bushel); (fam.) montón, gran cantidad; picotazo, picotada. II. va. picotear; picar. III. vn. picotear; recoger (alimento) con el pico.—**to p. at,** regañar de continuo.
pecker [pékœr], s. picoteador; pico, zapapico; (orn.) picoverde.
pecten [pécten], s. peine, o algo parecido; (orn.) membrana del ojo; festón de una concha.
pectin, pectine [péctin], s. pectina.
pectinate(d [péctinet(ed], a. pectiniforme.
pectoral [péctorœl]. I. a. pectoral.—**p. cross,** (igl.) pectoral.—**p. fin,** (ict.) aleta pectoral. II. s. adorno para el pecho; (anat.) órgano, músculo pectoral; (med.) pectoral.
pectose [péctous], s. (quím.) pectosa.
peculate [pékiuleit], vn. desfalcar; ratear, hurtar, robar.—**peculation** [-éishun], s. peculado, malversación.—**peculator** [-eitœr], s. peculador, malversador.
peculiar [pekiúliar]. I.'a. peculiar, privativo, especial; raro, extraordinario. II. s. propiedad particular; (igl.) parroquia independiente.
peculiarity [pekiuliǽriti], s. peculiaridad, singularidad; individualidad.
peculiarly [pekiúliarli], adv. peculiarmente, particularmente.
peculium [pekiúlium], s. peculio.
pecuniarily [pekiúniǽrili], adv. pecuniariamente.
pecuniary [-niǽri], a. pecuniario, monetario.
pecunious [-nius], a. rico, adinerado.
pedagogic(al [pedagóyic(al], a. pedagógico.
pedagogics [pedagóyics], s. pedagogía.
pedagogism [pédagoyism], s. pedantismo.
pedagogy [pédagoyi], s. pedagogía; pedantismo.
pedal [pédal]. I. a. del pie o del pedal.—**p. pipe,** cañón del órgano correspondiente a los pedales. II. s. pedal; (mús.) bajo de órgano.
pedant [pédant], s. pedante.—**pedantic(al** [pedǽntic(al], a. pedantesco.—**pedantically** [-li], adv. pedantescamente.—**pedantism** [pédantism], **pedantry** [pédantri], s. pedantería, pedantismo.
Pedata [pedéitæ], s. pl. (zool.) pedatos.
pedate [pédet], a. (zool.) parecido a un pie; (bot.) palmeado.
peddle [pédœl]. I. va. vender como buhonero; vender menudencias (esp. legumbres y frutas) de casa en casa. II. vn. ser buhonero.
peddler [pédlœr], s. buhonero.
pederast [péderast], s. pederasta.
pederasty [pédœrasti], s. pederastia.
pedesis [pedísis], s. agitación de partículas microscópicas en un líquido.
pedestal [pédestal], s. pedestal; peana; soporte; caballete.—**p. chair,** silla giratoria.
pedestrial, pedestrious [pedéstrial, trius], a. pedestre.
pedestrian [pedéstrian]. I. s. caminante, andante. II. a. pedestre; vulgar.
pediatrics [pidiǽtrics], s. (med.) pediatría.
pedicel [pédisel], s. pedúnculo, pedículo, cabillo.
pedicellate [pédiselet], a. pedunculado.
pedicle [pédiccœl], s. (bot.) pedúnculo; (med.) pedículo.

pedicular, o **pediculous** [pedíkiular, lus], a. (med.) pedicular.
pedigree [pédigri], s. genealogía, linaje, árbol genealógico.
pediluvium [pedilúvium], s. pediluvio, baño de pies.
pediment [pédimœnt], s. (arq.) frontón, tímpano.
pedipalp [pédipalp], s. y a. (zool.) pedipalpo.—**Pedipalpida** [-pálpidæ], s. pl. pedipalpos.
pedler [pédlœr], s. buhonero.
pedlery [pédlœri], s. buhonería.
pedling [pédling], a. frívolo, baladí.
pedobaptism [pídobǽptism], s. bautismo de los niños.
pedology [pedóloyi], s. pediatría; estudio de la niñez.
pedometer [pidómitœr], s. hodómetro.
pedotrophy [pidótrofi], s. pedotrofía, arte de criar niños.
pedrail [pédreil], s. mecanismo de rieles de un tractor.
peduncle [pedúncœl], s. (anat. y bot.) pedúnculo.—**peduncular** [-kiular], a. peduncular.—**pedunculat(ed** [-kiuleit(ed], a. (bot.) pedunculado.
peek [píc], vn. (fam.) atisbar.
peekaboo [pícæbú]. I. s. escondite, juego de niños. II. a. (fam.) transparente.
peel [píl]. I. va. descortezar, pelar, deshollejar. II. vn. desconcharse, descascararse, pelarse. III. s. corteza, cáscara; pellejo, hollejo; telilla de cebolla; pala de horno; (mar.) pala del remo; (impr.) espito, colgador.
peeler [pílœr], s. pelador, mondador, descortezador.
peeling [píling], s. peladura, mondadura, desconchadura, hollejo.
peen [pín], s. boca (del martillo).—**p. hammer,** martillo de dos bocas.
peep [píp]. I. vn. atisbar, mirar a hurtadillas; asomar, mostrarse; piar, pipiar. II. s. atisbo, atisbadura; mirada, ojeada; atisbadero; mira; asomo; pío, piada de pájaros.—**p. sight** (arti.) mira regulable de corredera.—**at the p. of day,** al despuntar el día.
peeper [pípœr], s. atisbador; (fam.) ojo; pollito que pía.
peephole [pípjóul], s. mirilla, atisbadero.
peer [píœr]. I. vn. atisbar, fisgar, husmear; (poét.) asomar, salir, aparecer. II. s. par, igual; (Ingl.) par (título).
peerage [píœrey], s. (Ingl.) dignidad de par; la grandeza, la nobleza.
peeress [píœres], s. (Ingl.) mujer que tiene título de nobleza.
peerless [píœrles], a. sin par, incomparable.—**peerlessly** [-li], adv. incomparablemente.—**peerlessness** [-nes], s. calidad de incomparable.
peevish [pívish], a. malhumorado, displicente, rencilloso, enojadizo.—**peevishly** [-li], adv. con displicencia y malhumor.—**peevishness** [-nes], s. displicencia, mal humor.
peg. I. s. clavija, espiga, taco; colgadero; pernete, saetín; (mar.) cabilla; (fig.) pretexto o excusa; (fam.) grado en la posición social.—**p. ladder,** espárrago, escala de cotorra.—**p. top,** peonza. II. va. estaquillar, clavar, enclavijar, encabillar; (a veces con out) estacar.—**pegging awl,** estaquillador.
Pegasus [pégasus], s. Pegaso.
pegmatite [pégmatait], s. (min.) pegmatita.
Pehlevi [pélevi], =PAHLAVI.
pejoration [piyoréshun], s. corruptela, corrupción.
pejorative [piyórativ], a. corruptivo.
pekan [pékan], s. (E. U. zool.) especie de mustela.
pekoe [píco], **pekoe tea** [tí], s. té negro de primera calidad.
Pelagianism [peléyianism], s. pelagianismo.
pelagic [peléyic], **pelagian** [peléyian], a. pelágico, oceánico.—**Pelagian,** pelagiano.
pelargonium [pelargónium], s. (bot.) pelargonio.
Pelasgi [pelǽsyai]. s. pl. pelasgos.—**Pelasgian** [-yian], s. y a., **Pelasgic** [-yic], a. pelasgo.

pelerine [pélœrin], s. esclavina.
pelf, s. dinero, riquezas mal adquiridas.
pelican [pélican], s. (orn.) pelícano, alcatraz; (quím.) alambique; (dent.) sacadientes antiguo.
pelisse [pelís], s. pelliza.
pell [pel], s. pellejo, cuero; rollo de pergamino.
pellagra [pélagra o pelégra], s. (med.) pelagra.
pellet [pélet], s. pella, píldora, pelotilla; bola, bolita; bodoque; perdigón.
pellicle [pélicœl], s. película, cutícula, panículo, túnica, hollejo; lapa, telilla, brinza.
pellicular [pelíkiular], a. pelicular.
pellitory [pélitori], s. (bot.) cañarroya.—**p. of Spain**, pelitre.
pellmell [pélmél], adv. confusamente, atropelladamente, a trochemoche.
pellucid [peliúsid], a. diáfano.—**pellucidity** [peliusíditi], **pellucidness** [peliúsidnes], s. diafanidad.
pelt. **I**. s. cuero, zalea; pelada; golpe, trastazo. —pl. corambre. **II**. va. apedrear, llover (piedras o algo análogo) sobre. **III**. vn. arrojar alguna cosa; caer con fuerza.
pelta [pélta], s. pelta.
peltate(d [péltet(ed], a. peltado; (bot.) peciolado por el centro.
peltry [péltri], s. peletería, pieles, pellejos, corambre.
pelvic [pélvic], a. pélvico.
pelvimeter [pelvímetœr], s. pelvímetro.
pelvis [pélvis], s. (anat.) pelvis.
pemmican [pémican], s. especie de tasajo indio.
pemphigus [pemfígus], **pemphix** [pémfix], s. (med.) pénfigo.
pen. **I**. s. pluma (para escribir); escritura, caligrafía; corral, pocilga, zahurda.—**p. name**, seudónimo. **II**. va. escribir (con pluma); pergeñar, componer; encerrar, acorralar.
penal [pínal], a. penal; sujeto a pena o castigo.— **p. servitude**, presidio, trabajos forzados.
penality [penæliti], s. penalidad; criminalidad.
penalize [pénalaiś], va. imponer pena a.
penalty [pénalti], s. pena (castigo); multa, pena pecuniaria.
penance [pénans], s. penitencia.—**to do p.**, hacer penitencia o acto de contrición.
Penates [penétis o nátes], s. pl. penates.
pencase [pénkéis], s. estuche de plumas.
pence [pens], s. pl. de PENNY.
penchant [panshán o pénchan], s. inclinación, afición, tendencia.
pencil [pénsil]. **I**. s. lápiz; pincel fino; haz (de luz, de rayos).—**p. case**, lapicero.—**p. of rays**, (fís., geom.) haz de rayos.—**p. sharpener**, cortalápiz. **II**. va. dibujar o escribir con lápiz; lapizar.
pend, vn. estar pendiente de arreglo.
pendant [péndant], s. cualquier cosa que cuelga o está pendiente de otra, v. gr.: (joy.) medallón, pinjante, pendiente, arete, zarcillo; apéndice; péndulo; (arq.) adorno que cuelga de un techo; (b. a.) uno de dos objetos que forman juego; (mar.) amante; gallardete.
pendency [péndensi], s. dilación, calidad de pendiente o de colgante.
pendent [péndent], a. pendiente; colgante, suspendido; salidizo; (bot.) pendiente.
pending [pénding]. **I**. a. pendiente; colgante. **II**. prep. durante, mientras.
pendragon [pendrǽgon], s. jefe supremo, dictador.
pendular [péndiular], a. péndulo.—**pendulosity** [-lósiti], **pendulousness** [-lusnes], s. suspensión.— **pendulous** [-lus], a. colgante.—**pendulum** [-lum], s. péndulo; péndola.
penetrability [pénetrabíliti], **penetrableness** [-bœlnes], s. penetrabilidad.—**penetrable** [-bœl], a. penetrable.
penetralia [pénetréiliæ], s. pl. penetral.
penetrancy [pénetransi], s. calidad de penetrante.—**penetrant** [-trant], a. penetrante.
penetrate [pénetreit]. **I**. va. penetrar; taladrar, horadar; atravesar, calar; profundizar; conmover. **II**. vn. introducirse, penetrar.—**penetrat-**

ing [pénetreiting], a. penetrante.—**penetration** [-tréishun], s. penetración.—**penetrative** [-trativ], a. penetrante.—**penetrativeness** [-nes], s. aptitud de penetrar.
penful [pénful], s. plumada.
penguin [péngüin], s. (orn.) alca o pájaro bobo; (aer.) aeroplano de enseñanza, que no vuela; mujer del cuerpo de aviación de Inglaterra.
penholder [pénjóldœr], s. portapluma, mango de pluma.
penicillate [penisílet o pénisilet], a. (biol.) guarnecido de hebras finas.
peninsula [penínsiula], s. península.
peninsular [penínsiular], a. peninsular.—**P. War**, guerras napoleónicas de España y Portugal.
penis [pínis], s. pene, miembro viril.
penitence [pénitens], s. penitencia; contrición.
penitent [pénitent]. **I**. a. penitente; contrito. **II**. s. penitente; arrepentida.
penitential [-ténshal]. **I**. a. penitencial; de arrepentimiento; penal. **II**. s. libro de penitencias.
penitentiary [-ténshari]. **I**. a. penitenciario, de penitencia; de castigo, penal. **II**. s. penitenciaría, presidio; (igl.) penitenciario.
penitently [-tentli], adv. con arrepentimiento, con penitencia.—**penitentness** [-tentnes], s. estado del penitente.
penknife [pén-náif], s. cortaplumas, cuchilla, navaja.
penman [pénman], s. pendolista o calígrafo; maestro de escritura.
penmanship [pénmanship], s. escritura, caligrafía; carácter de letra.
penna [péna], s. (orn.) pena.
pennant [pénant], s. gallardete, banderola, insignia; (mar.) amante, maroma corta.
pennate(d [pénet(ed], a. alado; (bot.) de figura de pluma.
penner [pénœr], s. autor, escritor; estuche de plumas de escribir.
penniless [péniles], a. sin dinero; sin un real; en la miseria.
pennon [pénun], s. pendón, banderola.
penny [péni], s. (pl. PENNIES, cuando denota número, y PENCE, cuando denota valor monetario) (Ingl.) penique; (E. U.) centavo; dinero en general.—**p.-a-liner**, gacetillero.—**p. loaf**, rollo, bollo.—**p.-wise**, dícese del que por ahorrar poco se expone a perder mucho.—**p.-wise and pound-foolish**, que escatima en los gastos pequeños y derrocha sumas cuantiosas.
pennyroyal [péniróial], s. (bot.) poleo.
pennyweight [péni-uéit], s. (joy.) escrúpulo, (peso = 24 granos).
pennyworth [péni-uérz], s. valor de un penique; cantidad pequeña.
penological [penolórical], a. penológico.
penology [penóloyi], s. penología.
penrack [pénrǽc], s. espetera, portaplumas.
pensile [pénsil], a. pensil, colgante.
pensileness [-nes], s. calidad de colgante.
pension [pénshun]. **I**. s. pensión; cesantía; (mil.) retiro; beca; juro. **II**. va. pensionar.— **pensionary** [-eri]. **I**. a. pensionado. **II**. s. pensionado, pensionista.—**pensioner** [-œr], s. pensionista, pensionado; beca; jurista, (mil. y mar.) inválido.
pensive [pénsiv], a. pensativo.—**pensively** [-li], adv. pensativamente.—**pensiveness** [-nes], s. melancolía, tristeza; meditación profunda.
penstock [pénstoc], s. compuerta de esclusa; paradera (del caz); portapluma.
pent, a. y pp. de TO PEN.—**p.-up**, acorralado, enjaulado, encerrado: detenido, reprimido.
pentachord [péntacord], s. pentacordio.
pentacle [péntacœl], s. (geom.) estrella de cinco puntas, ✡.
pentad [péntæd], s. número cinco; grupo de cinco cosas; lustro; (quím.) átomo, radical o elemento que tiene fuerza de combinación de cinco.

Para la pronunciación de æ, œ, ᴅ, ŝ, ŝh, ᴜ, ȳ, ʏ, ᴢ, véase la clave al principio del libro.

pentadactyl [péntadǽctil], **pentadactylous** [-lʊs], *s.* y *a.* (zool.) pentadáctilo, de cinco dedos.— **Pentadactyla** [-læ], *s. pl.* pentadáctilos

pentagon [péntagon], *s.* pentágono.

pentagonal, pentagonous [pentǽgonal, nʊs], *a.* pentagonal.

pentagram [péntagræm], *s.* = PENTACLE.

pentagraph [-graf], *s.* pantógrafo.

pentahedron [-jídron], *s.* pentaedro.

pentahedral, pentahedrous [-jídral, -drʊs], *a.* pentaédrico.

pentamerous [pentǽmerʊs], *a.* (biol.) pentámero.

pentameter [pentámetœr], *s.* pentámetro.

pentane [péntein], *s.* (quím.) pentano.

pentarchy [péntarqui], *s.* pentarquía.

Pentateuch [péntatiuc], *s.* Pentateuco.

Pentecost [péntecost], *s.* Pentecostés.

pentecostal [péntecóstal], *a.* pascual.

penthouse [péntjaus], *s.* tejaroz, tejadillo, colgadizo, cobertizo.

pentice [péntis], *s.* techo inclinado; colgadizo, tejadillo, sotechado.

pentile [péntail], *s.* = PANTILE.

pentosan [péntosæn], *s.* (quím.) pentosana.

pentose [péntous], *s.* (quím.) pentosa, pentaglucosa.

penult [penúlt], *s.* penúltima sílaba.

penultimate [penúltimet], *a.* penúltimo.

penumbra [penúmbra], *s.* (astr. y pint.) penumbra.

penurious [peniúriʊs], *a.* tacaño, miserable; escaso; indigente.—**penuriously** [-lii], *adv.* escasamente; miserablemente.—**penuriousness** [-nes], *s.* tacañería, ruindad, miseria; escasez, carestía.

penury [péniuri], *s.* penuria, miseria.

penwiper [pénuáipœr], *s.* limpiaplumas.

peon [píon], *s.* criado; peón.

peonage [píoney], *s.* sistema de emplear deudores como peones para que paguen con su trabajo lo que deben.

peony [píoni], *s.* (bot.) peonia.

people [pípœl]. **I.** *s.* pueblo; gente, personas. En este último sentido es plural: *people say,* dice la gente, se dice; *many people,* mucha gente; *there were many people asking for their friends,* había muchas personas preguntando por sus amigos. **II.** *va.* poblar.

pep [pep], *s.* (fam.) fuste, espíritu, fuerzas, vigor.

pepastic [pepǽstic], *a.* (med.) madurativo.

peplum [péplʊm], *s.* peplo.

pepper [pépœr]. **I.** *s.* pimienta; pimentero; ají, chile.—**p. box, bottle, caster** o **pot,** pimentero.—**p. mill,** pimentero de molinillo. **II.** *va.* sazonar con pimienta o ají; acribillar; sazonar (una conversación o escrito) con dichos picantes.

peppercorn [-corn], *s.* grano de pimienta; bagatela, chuchería.

peppergrass [-gras], o **pepperwort** [-uœrt], *s.* (bot.) lepidio.

peppering [-ing]. **I.** *a.* caliente, fogoso, colérico. **II.** *s.* perdigonada.

peppermint [-mint], *s.* (bot.) menta, yerbabuena.—**p. drop,** pastilla de menta.

peppery [pépœri], *a.* picante; mordaz; de mal humor o genio.

pepsine [pépsin], *s.* pepsina.

peptic [péptic], *a.* péptico.

peptone [pépton], *s.* peptona.

peptonic [peptónic], *a.* peptónico.

peptonize [péptonaiš], *va.* peptonizar.

per [pœr], *prep.* por.—**p. annum,** al año.—**p. capita,** por cabeza, por persona.—**p. cent., p. centum,** por ciento.—**p. contra,** por el contrario; por otra parte.—**p. diem,** por día.—**p. se,** por sí mismo, en sí mismo.

peradventure [perædvénchur]. **I.** *adv.* quizá, acaso, por ventura. **II.** *s.* posibilidad; duda.

perambulate [pœrǽmbiuleit], *va.* y *vn.* recorrer, transitar, visitar; andar.— **perambulation** [-éišhʊn], *s.* visita de inspección.— **perambulator** [-eitœr], *s.* cochecillo de niño; podómetro.

percale [pœrcál o pœrkél], *s.* (tej.) percal.

percaline [pœrcalin], *s.* percalina.

perceivable [pœrsívabœl], *a.* perceptible.

perceivably [-blii], *adv.* perceptiblemente.

perceive [pœrsív], *va.* percibir.

percentage [pœrséntech], *s.* (com.) tanto por ciento percentaje, (am.) porcentaje.

percept [pœrcept], *s.* (psic.) representación mental de lo percibido; el objeto percibido según lo da la percepción.

perceptibility [pœrséptibíliti], *s.* perceptibilidad.

perceptible [-tibœl], *a.* perceptible.

perceptibly [bli], *adv.* perceptiblemente.

perception [-šhʊn], *s.* percepción; (for.) percibo.

perceptive [-tiv], *a.* perceptivo.

perceptivity [pœrseptíviti], *s.* perceptividad.

perch [pœrch]. **I.** *s.* (ict.) perca; pértica (medida); alcándara, percha. **II.** *vn.* posarse, pararse, empingorotarse, encaramarse; ponerse (las aves) en percha. **III.** *va.* emperchar, empingorotar.

perchance [pœrcháns], *adv.* acaso, tal vez, quizá, por ventura.

Percheron [pœršheron], *a.* y *s.* percherón.

perchglue [pœrchglu], *s.* cola fina de perca.

perchlorate [pœrclóreit], *s.* perclorato.

perchloric [pœrclóric], *a.* (quím.) perclórico.

perchloride [pœrclórid o raid], *s.* (quím.) percloruro.

percipient [pœrsípient], *a.* y *s.* percipiente.

perclose [pœrclouš], *s.* (arq.) barandilla o enverjado.

percolate [pœrcoleit], *va.* y *vn.* colar, filtrar, pasar, rezumarse, infiltrar.

percolation [-éišhʊn], *s.* coladura, filtración, infiltración.

percolator [-eitœr], *s.* filtro, colador; cafetera filtradora.

percuss [pœreús], *va.* herir, golpear, percutir.

percussion [pœrcúšhʊn], *s.* percusión, choque; (med.) percusión.—**p. bullet,** bala explosiva. **p. cap,** fulminante, pistón.—**p. fuse,** pebete o fulminante de percusión o de choque.

percussive [pœrcúsiv], **percutient** [pœrkiúšhent], *a.* percuciente.

percussor [pœrcúscer], *s.* percusor

perdition [pœrdíšhʊn], *s.* perdición.

perdu, perdue [pœrdiú], *a.* perdido de vista, escondido.

perdurable [pœrdiu- o perdiúrabœl], *a.* perdurable.—

perdurably [-bli], *adv.* perdurablemente.

peregrinate [péregrineit], *vn.* peregrinar.— **peregrination** [-éišhʊn], *s.* peregrinación.

peregrine [péregrin], *a.* peregrino, migratorio; extranjero.

peremptorily [péremptorili], *adv.* perentoriamente; absolutamente.

peremptoriness [-nes], *s.* perentoriedad.

peremptory [-tori], *a.* perentorio; absoluto, terminante, definitivo; dogmático, magistral. **p. orders,** órdenes perentorias.—**p. sale,** venta forzosa.

perennial [pœrénial]. **I.** *a.* perenne, perennal; continuo, incesante, permanente, perpetuo; (biol.) que crece continuamente; (bot.) perenne, vivaz. **II.** *s.* (bot.) planta vivaz.

perfect [pœrfect]. **I.** *a.* perfecto; completo, entero; (bot.) completo; (gram.) perfecto; (fam.) muy grande, excesivo. **II.** *s.* (gram.) tiempo perfecto.

perfect [pœrféct o pœrfect], *va.* perfeccionar, mejorar.

perfecter [-œr], *s.* perfeccionador.

perfectibility [pœrféctibíliti], *s.* perfectibilidad. —**perfectible** [-tibœl], *a.* perfectible.—**perfection** [-šhʊn], *s.* perfección.—**perfective** [-tiv], *a.* perfectivo.—**perfectively** [-lii], *adv.* con perfección.—**perfectly** [pœrfectlii], *adv.* perfectamente.

perfervid [pœrférvid], *a.* muy férvido.

perfidious [pœrfídiʊs], *a.* pérfido.—**perfidiously** [-lii], *adv.* pérfidamente.—**perfidiousness** [-nes], *s.* perfidia.

perfidy [pœrfidi], *s.* perfidia.

perfoliate(d [pœrfólieit(ed], a. (bot.) perfoliado.
perforate [pœrforeit], va. perforar.—**perforating**
[-ing], a. perforador, de perforar.—**perforation**
[-éiŝhun], s. perforación.—**perforator** [-eitœr], s.
perforador.
perforce [pœrfórs], adv. por fuerza.
perform [pœrfórm]. **I.** va. ejecutar, hacer, poner
por obra; desempeñar, llenar, cumplir; practicar, ejercer. **II.** vn. (teat.) representar, desempeñar un papel; tocar un instrumento músico;
funcionar.
performance [-ans], s. ejecución; desempeño,
cumplimiento; funcionamiento, acción; capacidad; obra, acción, hecho, hazaña; (teat.)
función, representación.
performer [-œr], s. ejecutante; actor; músico;
acróbata.
perfume [pœrfium, pœrfiúm]. **I.** s. perfume, fragancia, aroma. **II.** va. [pœrfiúm] perfumar, sa-
numar, aromatizar.—**perfuming pan,** perfumador, cazoleja.
perfumer [pœrfiúmœr], s. perfumador; perfumero, perfumista.
perfumery [-fiúmeri], s. perfumería; perfumes.
perfunctorily [pœrfúnctorili], adv. perfunctoriamente, por llenar las apariencias.—**perfunc-
toriness** [-nes], s. descuido, superficialidad.—**perfunctory** [-tori], a. perfuntorio, superficial.
pergola [pœrgolæ], s. cenador; emparrado;
balcón largo, galería exterior.
perhaps [pœrjæps], adv. tal vez, quizá, acaso, por
ventura.
peri [píri o péri], s. perí, hada.
perianth(ium [périænz(ium], s. (bot.) periantio;
perigonio.
pericardial, pericardiac [-cárdial, æc], **pericar-
dian** [-cárdian], a. pericardino.—**pericarditis**
[-cardáitis o dítis], s. (med.) pericarditis.—**pericardium** [-cárdium], s. (anat.) pericardio.
pericarp(ium [-cárp(ium], s. (bot.) pericarpio,
folículo.—**pericarpial, pericarpie** [-cárpial, pic],
a. pericarpial.
perichondrium [-cóndrium], s. pericondrio.
pericranium [-crénium], s. (anat.) pericráneo.
pericycle [-sákœl], s. (bot.) periciclo.
periderm [-dœrm], s. (bot.) corteza exterior.
peridot [-dot], s. (min.) peridoto, crisolito.
peridotite [-dotait], s. (min.) peridotita, mezcla
de olivina y otros minerales ferromagnésicos,
con poco o ningún feldespato.
peridrome [-drom], s. (arq.) peridromo.
periœci [-ísai], s. pl. (geog.) periecos.
perigee [-yi], s. perigeo.
perigeum [-ríum], s. perigeo.
perigon [-gon], s. (geom.) perígono, ángulo de 360°.
perigonium [-gónium], s. (bot.) perigonio.
perihelion, o **perihelium** [-jílion, -um], s. perihelio.
perikon [-con], s. (radtlg.) detector perikon
(nombre de fábrica patentado), compuesto de
calcopirita en contacto con óxido rojo de cinc.
peril [péril]. **I.** s. peligro, riesgo. **II.** va. poner en
peligro; arriesgar. **III.** vn. peligrar; estar en
peligro, riesgo.
perilous [périlus], a. peligroso, arriesgado.
perilously [-li], adv. peligrosamente.
perilousness [-nes], s. calidad de peligroso;
peligro.
perimeter [perímetœr], s. perímetro.
perineal [períníal], a. perineal.
perinephrium [périnéfrium], s. perinefrio, tejido
adiposo que rodea los pulmones.
perineum [níum], s. (anat.) perineo.
period [píriod], s. período; término, fin, conclusión; (gram.) período, cláusula; (impr.) punto
(.); (med.) período; (mús.) período.—**the p.,** el
día de hoy, la actualidad.—pl. las reglas, menstruo.
periodic [peraiódic], a. (quím.) peryódico.
periodic(al [piriódic(al]. **I.** a. periódico. **II.** s.
publicación periódica.
periodically [-i], adv. periódicamente.
periodicalness [-nes], s. periodicidad.
periodicity [píriodísiti], s. periodicidad.
periodide [peráiodaid], s. peryoduro.

periœci [períísai], s. pl. (geog.) periecos.
periosteotome [périósteotom], s. (cir.) legra.
periosteotomy [-ósteótomi], s. (cir.) legración.
periosteum [-óstium], s. (anat.) periostio.
periostitis [-ostáitis o títis], s. (mea.) periostitis.
peripatetic [-patétic], a. y s. peripatético.—**P.
philosophy,** o **Peripateticism,** peripato.
peripheral, peripheric(al [perífœral, fœric(al],
a. relativo a la periferia.
periphery [perífœri], s. superficie exterior; periferia, circunferencia.
periphrase [périfrœiŝ], va. perifrasear.
periphrasis, periphrase [perífrasis, freiŝ], s.
perífrasis, circunlocución.
periphrastic(al [perifrǽstic(al], a. perifrástico.
periphrastically [-i], adv. con perífrasis.
peripteral [-patéral], a. y a. (arq.) períptero.
periptery [-teri], s. (aer.) región del aire alrededor
de un avión agitada por remolinos.
Periscii [perìŝhiai], s. pl. (geog.) periscios.
periscope [périscoup], s. (ópt.) periscopio.
periscopic [periscópic], a. periscópico.
perish [périŝh], vn. perecer; marchitarse, pasarse.
perishable [périŝhabœl], a. perecedero; putrescible, expuesto a podrirse.
perishableness [-nes], s. fragilidad, calidad de
perecedero o putrescible.
perisperm [périspœrm], s. (bot.) perispermo.
perissodactyl [perisòdǽctil], s. (zool.) perisodál-
tico.—**Perissodactyla** [-æ], **Perissodactyli** [-ai]
s. pl. perisodáctilos.
peristalsis [-tǽlsis], s movimiento peristáltico.—
peristaltic [-tic], a. peristáltico.
peristome [péristom], s. (bot.) perístomo.
peristyle [péristail], s. (arq.) peristilo.
perisystole [perísistole], s. (med.) perisístole.
peritoneal [péritonĩæl], a. peritoneal.—**peritoneum** [-níum], s. (anat.) peritóneo.—**peritonitis**
[-náitis o nítis], s. (med.) peritonitis.
perityphlitis [-tifláitis], s. (med.) peritiflitis.
periwig [périuig], s. peluca.
periwinkle [périuincœl], s. litorina, margarita,
caracol de mar; (bot.) pervencha.
perjure [pœrryur], va. y vr. perjurar.—**perjurer**
[-rœr], s. perjuro.—**perjury** [-i], s. perjurio.
perk [pœrc]. **I.** va. adornar, vestir; erguir;
levantar la oreja o la cabeza. **II.** vn. erguirse,
contonearse.
perk(y [pœrk(i], a. gallardo.
permanence [pœrmanens], **permanency** [-si], s.
permanencia, estabilidad, durabilidad.
permanent [-nent], a. permanente, duradero;
fijo.—**p. visor,** (aut.) visera fija.—**p. wave,** ondulación permanente (del pelo).
permanently [-li], adv. permanentemente.
permanganate [pœrmǽnganet], s. (quím.) permanganato.
permanganic [pœrmǽngénic], a. permangánico.
permeability [pœrmiabíliti], s. permeabilidad.
permeable [pœrmiabœl], a. (fís.) permeable.
permeance [pœrmiæns], s. (elec.) permeancia.
permeate [pœrmieit], va. penetrar, pasar a través
de; estar difundido en, afectar, calar.
permeation [-éiŝhun], s. penetración al través de
los poros.
permeative [-ativ], a. penetrativo, permeativo.
Permian [pœrmiæn], s. y a. (geol.) permiano.
permissibile [pœrmísibœl], a. permissibile.
permission [pœrmíŝhun], s. permiso, licencia.
permissive [pœrmísiv], a. permisivo.—**permissively** [-li], adv. permisivamente.
permissory [pœrmísori], a. por o con permiso;
autorizado.
permit [pœrmít]. **I.** va. permitir. **II.** s. [pœr-
mit] permiso, pase; (com.) cédula de aduana.
permittance [pœrmítans], s. (elec.) inductividad.
permittivity [pœrmitíviti], s. (elec.) inductividad específica.
permutable [pœrmiútabœl], a. permutable.
permutation [pœrmiutéiŝhun], s. permuta, trueque; (mat.) permutación.

permutator [-teitœr], s. (elec.) convertidor de núcleo magnético.

permute [pœrmiút], va. permutar, trocar.

pern [pœrn], s. (orn.) buaro.

pernicious [pœrníŝhus], s. pernicioso.—**perniciously** [-li], adv. perniciosamente.—**perniciousness** [-nes], s. perniciosidad.

pernickety [pœrníketi], a. (fam.) quisquilloso, demasiado escrupuloso; difícil, delicado.

peroration [peroréŝhun], s. peroración.

peroxid(e [pœróxid o xaid], s. peróxido.

perpend [pœrpénd], va. (ant.) reflexionar, pensar, considerar.

perpend, perpend stone [pœrpend, stoun], o **perpender** [pœrpéndœr], s. (alb.) perpiaño.

perpendicular [pœrpendíkiular. **I.** a. perpendicular; vertical.—**p. pronoun**, (fam.) pronombre de primera persona (a causa de la forma de la letra I que lo representa); don yo. s. perpendicular.— **perpendicularity** [-lǽriti], s. perpendicularidad.— **perpendicularly** [-li], adv. perpendicularmente.

perpetrate [pœrpetreit], va. perpetrar, cometer. —**perpetration** [-tréiŝhun], s. perpetración, comisión.—**perpetrator** [-treitœr], s. perpetrador.

perpetual [pœrpéchual], a. perpetuo.—**p. calendar**, calendario perpetuo.—**p. motion**, movimiento perpetuo o continuo.

perpetually [-i], adv. perpetuamente.

perpetuate [pœrpéchueit], va. perpetuar.

perpetuation [-éiŝhun], s. perpetuación.

perpetuity [pœrpetiúiti], s. perpetuidad.

perplex [pœrpléx]. **I.** va. confundir, aturdir; embrollar, enredar, enmarañar. **II.** a. intrincado, enredado.

perplexed [-plécst], a. perplejo.—**perplexedly** [-pléxedli], adv. perplejamente.—**perplexedness** [-ednes], **perplexity** [-iti], s. perplejidad.

perquisite [pœrcuiŝit], s. gajes, propina, adehala.

perron [péron], s. (arq.) grada, escalinata.

perroquet [pérokét], s. (orn.) cotorra.

perry [perri], s. sidra de peras.

persecute [pœrsekiut], va. perseguir; vejar; importunar.

persecution [pœrsekiúŝhun], s. persecución; vejación.

persecutive [pœrsekiutiv], a. perseguidor.

persecutor [pœrsekiutœr], s. perseguidor.

perseverance [pœrseviœrǽns], s. perseverancia; (teol.) perseverancia final (II.t. **p. of the saints**, esp. entre los calvinistas, y **final p.**, entre éstos y los católicos).

persevere [-víœr], vn. perseverar; persistir.— **persevering** [-víœring], pa. perseverante; persistente.—**perseveringly** [-li], adv. perseverantemente, persistentemente.

Persian [pœrŝhæn]. **I.** s. persa; lengua persa; (tej.) persiana. **II.** a. persa, persiano, pérsico.—**P. blinds**, celosías, persianas.—**P. Gulf**, golfo Pérsico.—**P. wheel**, noria.

Persic [pérsic]. **I.** a. pérsico, persa. **II.** s. idioma persa.

persienne [pérsien], s. persiana, tela oriental adornada.

persimmon [pœrsímun], s. níspola (fruto del níspero); (bot.) níspero.

Persism [pœrsîsm], s. religión de los antiguos magos de Persia.

persist [pœrsíst], vn. insistir, porfiar, empeñarse; persistir, perseverar.

persistence, persistency [-ens, i], s. insistencia, porfía; persistencia, perseverancia.

persistent, persisting, persistive [-ent, -ing, -iv], a. persistente, perseverante; permanente.

person [pœrsun], s. persona; (desp.) quídam, tipo; (biol.) individuo.—**in p.**, en persona.—**in the p. of**, en lugar o representación de.

persona [pœrsóna], s. persón; (biol.) individuo, organismo particular.—**p. ficta**, persona jurídica. —**p. grata**, persona grata.—**p. non grata**, persona no grata o no acepta.

personable [pœrsunabœl], a. guapo, bien parecido; (for.) que tiene personalidad.

personage [pœrsuney], s. personaje.

personal [pœrsunæl], a. personal; personalmente ofensivo o hiriente a la persona con quien se habla o discute; en persona (acción, comparecencia, etc.).—**p. effects**, bienes o efectos personales o de uso personal.— **p. equation**, ecuación personal.—**p. property**, bienes muebles.

personality [-ǽliti], s. personalidad, individualidad; alusión personal; personaje.

personalize [-alaiŝ], va. personalizar; (ret.) personificar.

personally [-ali], adv. personalmente.

personalty [-alti], s. (for.) bienes muebles.

personate [-eit]. **I.** va. hacerse pasar por; usurpar el nombre de; (teat.) desempeñar o hacer el papel de. **II.** vn. (teat.) representar. **III.** a. (bot.) personada.

personation [-éiŝhun], s. personificación; (for.) usurpación del nombre de otro.

personator [-eitœr], s. el que se hace pasar por otro.

personification [pœrsónifikéiŝhun], s. personificación; (ret.) prosopopeya.

personify [pœrsónifai], va. personificar.

personnel [pœrsunél], s. personal; empleados; tripulación.

perspective [pœrspéctiv]. **I.** s. perspectiva. **II.** a. (pint.) en perspectiva.— **perspectively** [-li], adv. con arreglo a la perspectiva.

perspicacious [pœrspikéiŝhus], a. perspicaz.

perspicaciousness [-nes], **perspicacity** [-cǽsiti], s. perspicacia.

perspicuity [pœrspikiúiti], s. perspicuidad, claridad, lucidez.

perspicuous [pœrspíkiuus], a. perspicuo, claro, lúcido.—**perspicuously** [-li], adv. perspicuamente, claramente.—**perspicuousness** [-nes], s. perspicuidad, claridad de estilo.

perspiration [pœrspiréiŝhun], s. sudor, transpiración, perspiración.

perspirative, perspiratory [pœrspáirativ, tori], a. sudorífico.

perspire [pœrspáiœr], va. y vn. sudar; exhalar, excretar por la piel.

persuadable [pœrsuéidabœl], a. persuasible.

persuade [pœrsuéid], va. persuadir, inducir, mover.—**persuader** [-dœr], s. persuasor, inducidor. —**persuasibility** [-ésibíliti], s. calidad de persuasible.—**persuasible** [-ésibœl], a. persuasible.— **persuasibleness** [-ibœlnes], s. facilidad en persuadir.

persuasion [pœrsuéiÿun], s. persuasión, inducción; creencia, opinión; credo, secta, denominación; persuasiva.

persuasive [-siv]. **I.** a. persuasivo. **II.** s. persuasiva.—**persuasively** [-sivli], adv. persuasivamente.—**persuasiveness** [-sivnes], s. persuasiva.

persulphate [pœrsúlfet], s. (quím.) persulfato.

persulphuric [pœrsulfiúric], a. persulfúrico.

pert [pœrt], a. atrevido, descarado.

pertain [pœrtéin], vn. pertenecer, tocar, concernir, incumbir.

pertinacious [pœrtinéiŝhus], a. pertinaz.—**pertinaciously** [-li], adv. pertinazmente.—**pertinaciousness** [-nes], **pertinacity** [-nǽsiti], s. pertinacia.

pertinence, pertinency [-ens, i], s. pertinencia.

pertinent [-ent], a. pertinente, a propósito, atinado.—**pertinently** [-li], adv. pertinentemente, oportunamente, atinadamente.

pertly [pœrtli], adv. descaradamente.

pertness [pœrtnes], s. descaro, desfachatez.

perturb [pœrtœrb], va. perturbar.

perturbable [pœrtœrbabœl], a. perturbable.

perturbation [pœrtœrbéiŝhun], s. perturbación; (astr.) perturbación, desviación.

perturbator [pœrtœrbéitœr], s. perturbador, **perturber** [pœrtœrbœr, s. perturbador.

pertuse [pertiús], a. horadado, agujereado; (bot.) fistuloso.

pertussis [pœrtúsis], s. (med.) tos ferina.

peruke [perrúk], s. peluca, peluquín.

perusal [perúŝal], s. lectura cuidadosa.

peruse [perús], va. leer con cuidado; examinar, escudriñar.

Peruvian [perúvian], s. y a. peruano.—**P. bark**, quina.

pervade [pœrvéid], va. penetrar, ocupar, llenar.

pervasion [pœrvéiȳun], s. esparcimiento.

pervasive [pœrvéisiv], a. penetrante.

perverse [pœrvœrs], a. perverso; contrario, refractario, contumaz; molesto, petulante.

perversely [-li], adv. perversamente.

perverseness [-nes], **perversity** [-i], s. perversidad; terquedad, contumacia.

perversion [-şhun], s. perversión, corrupción.

perversive [-siv], a. perversivo.

pervert [pœrvœrt]. **I.** va. pervertir, corromper; tergiversar, falsear. **II.** s. [pœrvœrt], renegado, apóstata.

perverter [pœrvœrtœr], s. pervertidor.

pervertible [pœrvœrtibœl], a. pervertible.

pervious [pœrvius], a. penetrable; permeable.—**p. to light**, diáfano.

perviousness [-nes], permeabilidad.

pesade [peséid], s. (equit.) acto de encabritarse el caballo.

pesky [péski], a. (fam. E. U.) molesto, incómodo, cargante.

pessary [pésæri], s. supositorio vaginal; (cir.) pesario.

pessary [pésari], s. (cir.) pesario.

pessimism [pésimişm], s. pesimismo.

pessimist [-ist], s., **pessimistic** [-ístic], a. pesimista.

pest, s. peste, pestilencia, plaga; insectos nocivos.

pester [péstœr], va. molestar, vejar, cansar, incomodar, importunar; (fam.) amolar, cargar.

pesthouse [péstjaus], s. lazareto.

pestiferous [pestífœrus], a. pestífero.

pestilence [péstilens], s. pestilencia.—**pestilent** [-ent], **pestilential** [-lénşhæl], a. pestiente, pestifero; pernicioso, maligno; dañino, perjudicial.—**pestilently** [-lentli], adv. pestiferamente.

pestle [péscel]. **I.** s. mano de almirez; pistadero; martinete; triturador. **II.** va. majar, pistar, triturar, moler.

pet. **I.** va. mimar, acariciar. **II.** a. acariciado, mimado; favorito; domesticado.—**p. name**, diminutivo o epíteto cariñoso. **III.** s. cualquier animal domesticado y mimado; favorito; niño mimado; enojo, enfado, berrinche.

petal [pétal], s. (bot.) pétalo.

petaled, **petalous** [pétald, pétalus], a. (bot.) provisto de pétalos.

petaliferous [pétalífœrus], a. que tiene pétalos.

petalism [pétalişm], s. (hist.) petalismo.

petaloid [pétaloid], a. petaloideo.

petard [petárd], s. petardo.

petardeer [pétardiœr], s. petardero.

petcock [pétcoc], s. llave de escape; (m. v.) llave de purga, llave de desagüe.

petechiæ [petékii], s. pl. (med.) petequias.

petechial [petékial], a. petequial.

peter [pítœr], vn. (con **out**) (min.) disminuir, desaparecer una veta o filón.

Peter's pence, Peter pence [pítœr(s) pens], s. dinero de San Pedro.

petiolar [pétiolar], **petiolate** [pétiolet], a. (bot.) peciolado.

petiole [pétiol], s. (bot.) peciolo.

petit [petít], a. (for.) pequeño; menor.—**p. jury** = PETTY JURY.

petite [petít], a. pequeña, chiquita.

petition [petíşhun]. **I.** s. memorial, instancia, recurso, representación; (Méx.) ocurso; pedimiento, petición, demanda; súplica, ruego. **II.** va. suplicar, rogar; pedir, dirigir un memorial a.

petitionary [-æri], a. demandante, suplicante, petitorio.

petitioner [-œr], s. peticionario, memorialista, representante.

petitory [pétitori], a. petitorio.

petrel [pé- o pítrel], s. (orn.) petrel.

petrescence [petrésens], s. petrificación.

petrescent [-ent], a. que se petrifica.

Petri dish [pétri dişh], platillo de Petri para cultivos microbiológicos.

petrifaction [pétrifæcşhun], s. petrificación; fósil.

petrifactive [pétrifæctiv], **petrific** [petrífic], a. petrífico, petrificante.

petrification [pétrifikéishun], s. petrificación; fósil.—**petrify** [-fai], va. y vn. petrificar(se).

petroglyph [pétroglif], s. petroglifo, escultura o inscripción en roca.

petrography [petrógrafi], s. petrografía.

petrol [pétrol], s. (aut.) gasolina.

petrolatum [pétroléitum], s. (farm.) ungüento de petróleo, obtenido como residuo de la destilación del petróleo y purificado.

petroleum [petrólium], s. petróleo.—**p. ether**, nafta.

petroleur [petrolœr], s. petrolero (incendiario).

petrology [petróloyi], s. petrología, petrografía.

petronel [pétronel], s. V. PISTOL.

petrous [pé- o pítrus], a. petroso, pétreo.

petticoat [péticóut]. **I.** s. enaguas, fustán, basquiña; faldas, guardapiés; (elec.) campana (de aislador); aislador de campanas (ll. t. **p. insulator**); (locom.) tubo compensador de tiro (ll. t. **p. pipe**). **II.** a. de mujer, de mujeres; (elec.) de campana(s).

pettifog [pétifog]. **I.** va. (fam.) mangonear. **II.** vn. ser picapleitos.

pettifogger [pétifógœr], s. leguleyo, picapleitos; (vulg.) tinterillo.—**pettifoggery** [-fógœri], s. triquiñuela de abogado.

pettiness [pétines], s. pequeñez, mezquindad.

pettish [pétişh], a. enojadizo, quisquilloso; áspero, regañón.—**pettishly** [-li], adv. caprichosamente, ásperamente.—**pettishness** [-nes], s. enojo; aspereza; capricho.

pettitoes [pétitoş], s. manos o pies de lechoncillo.

petto [péto], s. pecho.—**in p.**, en lo interior del pecho, secreto.

petty [péti], a. insignificante, mezquino, despreciable; subordinado, inferior.—**p. cash**, (com.) gastos menores de caja.—**p. jury**, jurado de juicio, compuesto de doce individuos, encargado de declarar y determinar el hecho.—**p. king**, reyezuelo.—**p. larceny**, hurto.—**p. prince**, principillo, principote.—**p. treason**, traición menor.—**p. wares**, géneros menudos.

petulance, petulancy [pétiulans, i], s. mal genio, impaciencia.—**petulant** [-ant], a. quisquilloso, enojadizo.—**petulantly** [-li], adv. impacientemente, con aspereza.

petunia [petiúniæ], s. (bot.) petunia.

pew [piú], s. banco de iglesia.—**p. opener**, (igl.) ujier, acomodador.—**p. rent**, alquiler anual de un banco de iglesia.—pl. **pews**, la congregación.

pewee [pí-uí], s. (E. U.) (orn.) especie de tirano. V. PHŒBE.

pewholder [piújouldœr], s. arrendatario de un banco de iglesia.

pe(e)wit [píuit], s. (orn.) PEWEE; avefría, frailecillo; laro, pájaro reidor.

pewter [piútœr], s. peltre.

pewterer [piútœrœr], s. estañador.

phænogam, phænogamic, phænogamous, V. PHANEROGAM, etc.

phaeton [féietun], s. (carr.) faetón.

phagocyte [fágosait], s. (biol.) fagocito.

phalange [falány], s. (pol.) falange ideada por Fourier.

phalangea [falényia], a. falangiano.

phallanger [falényœr], s. falangista (marsupial australiano).

phalanges [falényiş], s. pl. de PHALANX.

Phalangida [félanyáida], s. pl. (ent.) familia de los falangios.

phalansterian [félanstíriæn], s. y a. falansteriano.

phalanstery [félansteri], s. falansterio.

phalanx [félænx o félænx], s. falange.

phallic [félic], a. fálico, relativo al falo o al falismo.

phallism [-lişm], s. falismo, culto del falo o principio generador de la naturaleza.

Para la pronunciación de æ, œ, ᴅ, ş, ş͟h, ᴜ, ȳ, ʏ, з, véase la clave al principio del libro.

phallus [fǽlʊs], s. (anat., relig., bot.) falo.

Phanerogamia [fǽnœroguémia], s. pl. (bot.) cotiledóneas.

phanerogamous, phanerogamic [-œrógamus, -ogǽmic], a. fanerógamo.

phantasm [fǽntæsm], **phantasma** [fæntǽśma], s. fantasma.

phantasmagoria [fæntæsmagória], s. fantasmagoría.

phantasmagori(c)al [fæntæsmagóri(c)al], a. fantasmagórico; ilusorio.

phantasy [fǽntasi], s. = FANTASY.

phantom [fǽntʊm], s. fantasma, espectro, sombra, visión.

Pharaonic [faraónic], a. faraónico.

pharisaic(al [fǽriséic(al], a. farisaico.—**pharisaically** [-i], adv. farisaicamente.—**pharisaism** [-séiśm], s. farisaísmo.

Pharisee [fǽrisi], s. fariseo.

pharmaceutic(al [fármasiútic(al], a. farmacéutico.—**pharmaceutics** [-tics], s. farmacia (ciencia).—**pharmaceutist** [-tist], **pharmacist** [fármasist], s. farmacéutico, boticario.

pharmacological [fármacolóyical], a. farmacológico.—**pharmacologist** [-cóloyist], s. farmacólogo.—**pharmacology** [-cóloyi], s. farmacología.

pharmacopœia [-copíya], s. farmacopea.

pharmacopolist [-cópolist], s. boticario.

pharmacy [fármasi], s. farmacia; botica.

pharos [féros], s. faro.

pharyngeal [fǽrinyial o farínyial], a. faríngeo.

pharyngitis [-yáitis], s. (med.) faringitis.

pharyngoscope [faríngoscoup], s. faringoscopio.

pharyngotomy [færingótomi], s. faringotomía.

pharynx [fǽrinx], s. (anat.) faringe.

phase [féiś], s. fase, aspecto; (astr.) fase; (elec.) fase.—**p. angle**, ángulo de retraso, ángulo de diferencia de fases.—**p. displacement**, desplazamiento de fase.—**p. lag**, o **lagging**, retraso de fase.—**p. lead**, o **leading**, avance de fase.—**to be in p.**, (elec.) tener una misma fase, estar en (concordancia de) fase.—**to be out of p.**, no tener una misma fase, discordar en fase.

phasis [féisiś o fáses], s. (astr.) fase.

pheasant [féśant], s. (orn.) faisán.

pheasantry [féśantri], s. criadero de faisanes.

phenacetin [fenǽsetin], s. fenacetina.

phenakistoscope [fénǽkistoscoup], s. fenaquistoscopio.

phenazone [-śoun], s. antipirina.

phenic [fínic], a. fénico.

Phenician [finíshan], a. y s. fenicio.

Phenix [fínix], s. fénix; prodigio; (astr.) Fénix, constelación austral.—**P. column**, columna redonda compuesta de hierros curvos en U unidos por sus pestañas.

phenogam, etc. V. PHÆNOGAM, etc.

phenol [fínol], s. (quím.) fenol, ácido fénico.

phenology [fenóloyi], s. fenología, ciencia de los efectos del clima en el desarrollo de los seres organizados.

phenomena [fenómenæ], s. pl. de PHENOMENON. Ú. erróneamente en vez del sing.—**phenomenal** [-næl], a. fenomenal.—**phenomenalism** [-nælism], s. (filos.) fenomenalismo.—**phenomenalist** [-ist], s., **phenomenalistic** [-istic], a. fenomenalista.—**phenomenon** [-non], s. fenómeno.

phenyl [fénil], s. (quím.) fenilo.

phenylacetic [-æsític], a. fenilacético.

phenylene [fénilin], s. (quím.) fenileno.—**p. blue**, azul de fenileno.—**p. brown**, pardo de fenileno.

phial [fáial], s. redoma, frasco. V. VIAL.

Philadelphian [filadélfian], a. filadelfo, de Filadelfia.

philander [filǽndœr]. **I.** vn. hacer cocos, galantear. **II.** s. amante, pretendiente.

philanthropic(al [filanzrópic(al], a. filantrópico.

philanthropist [filǽnzropist], s. filántropo.—**philanthropy** [filǽnzropi], s. filantropía.

philately [filǽteli], s. filatelia.—**philatelic(al** [filætélic, -æl], a. filatélico.

philharmonic [filjarmónic], a. filarmónico.

philippic [filípic], s. filípica; invectiva.

Philippine [fílipin], a. filipino.

Philistine [filístin], s. y a. filisteo; positivista, mercenario.

philologist [filóloyist], s. filólogo.

philologic(al [filolóyic(al], a. filológico.

philology [filóloyi], s. filología.

philomath [fílomæz], s. amante del saber.

philomel, philomel(a [fílomel, mila], s. (poét.) filomela, ruiseñor.

philopena [filopína], s. juego en que una persona paga una prenda a otra bajo ciertas condiciones; almendra doble que motiva este juego; regalo o prenda que paga el que pierde.

philosophaster [filósofæstœr], s. filosofastro.

philosopher [filósofœr], s. filósofo.—**p.'s stone**, piedra filosofal.

philosophic(al [filosófic(al], a. filosófico.

philosophically [-i], adv. filosóficamente.

philosophism [filósofiśm], s. filosofismo.—**philosophist** [-fist], s. filosofastro.—**philosophize** [-faiś], vn. filosofar.—**philosophizer** [-faiśœr], s. filosofador.

philosophy [filósofi], s. filosofía.

philter [fíltœr]. **I.** s. filtro, hechizo. **II.** va. hechizar con filtro.

phimosis [fimóusis], s. (med.) fimosis.

phiz [fiś], s. (vulg.) facha, cara.

phlebitis [flibáitis], s. flebitis.

phlebosclerosis [flébosclerósis], s. flebosclerosis, endurecimeinto de las membranas venosas interiores.

phlebotomist [flebótomist], s. flebótomo, flebotomiano, sangrador.

phlebotomize [flebótomaiś], va. sangrar.

phlebotomy [flebótomi], s. flebotomía.

phlegm [flem], s. flema, gargajo; lentitud, cachaza, apatía.

phlegmasia [flegméýia], s. flegmasia, flogosis.

phlegmatic(al [flegmétic(al], a. flemático; cachazudo.

phlegmon [flégmon], s. (med.) flemón.

phlegmonous [flégmonʊs], a. flemonoso.

phlogistic [floyístic], a. flogístico; (med.) inflamatorio.

phlogiston [floyíston], s. (quím.) flogisto.

phlox [flox], s. (bot.) flox.

phlyctena [flictína o téna], s. (med.) flictena.

phobia [fóbiæ], s. temor o aversión mórbidos.

phoca [fóca], s. (ict.) foca.

phœbe bird [fíbi bœrd], s. (orn.) febe.

Phœbus [fíbus], s. Febo.—**Phebean** [fíbiæn], a. febeo.

Phœnician, a. y s.=PHENICIAN.

Phœnix [fínics], s. = PHENIX.

phonation [fonéśhʊn], s. fonación.

phone [fóun], contr. de TELEPHONE; (fam.) teléfono. **II.** va. y vn. telefonear.

phoneidoscope [fonéidoscoup], s. foneidoscopio.

phonetic(al [fonétic(al], a. fonético.

phonetics, phonics [fonétics, fónics], s. fonología, fonética.

phonic [fónic], a. fónico.

phonogram [fónogræm], s. tipo que simboliza un sonido; fonograma; reproducción fonográfica.

phonograph [fónograf]. **I.** s. fonógrafo. **II.** va. reproducir por medio del fonógrafo.

phonographer [fonógrafœr], **phonographist** [fonógrafist], s. taquígrafo fonético; persona versada en el uso del fonógrafo.

phonographic(al [fonogrǽfic(al], a. fonográfico.

phonography [fonógrafi], s. fonografía.

phonolite [fónolait], s. (geol.) fonolita, perlita.

phonologer [fónóloyœr], **phonologist** [fonóloyist], s. fonólogo.

phonologic(al [fonolóyic(al], a. fonológico.

phonology [fonóloyi], s. fonología.

phonometer [fonómetœr], s. fonómetro.

phonometric [fonométric], a. fonométrico.

phonotype [fónotaip], s. (impr.) fonotipo; tipo empleado en la fonotipia.

phonotypic [fónotípic], a. fonotípico.

phonotypy [fónotaipi], *s.* (impr.) fonotipia, impresión con tipos que representan sonidos.

phony [fóuni], *a.* (fam.) falso, falsificado.

phosphate [fósfeit], *s.* fosfato.—**f. rock**, roca fosfatada o rica en fosfato (gen. de calcio).

phosphated [-ed], **phosphatic** [-fǽtic], *a.* fosfático; fosfatado.

phosphene [fósfin], *s.* fosfeno, sensación de luz causada por presión en el ojo.

phosphid(e [fósfaid], *s.* (quím.) fosfuro.

phosphine [fósfin], *s.* (quím.) fosfina.

phosphite [fósfait], *s.* (quím.) fosfito.

Phosphor [fósfœr], *s.* Fósforo, lucero del alba, estrella matutina.—**p. bronze**, bronce fosforado.

phosphorate [fósforet], *va.* combinar con fósforo.—**phosphorated oil**, aceite fosforado.

phosphoresce [fósforés], *vn.* fosforescer.—**phosphorescence** [-ens], *s.* fosforescencia, ardentía.—**phosphorescent** [-ent], *a.* fosforescente.

phosphoric [fosfóric], *a.* fosfórico; fosforescente.

phosphorite [fósforait], *s.* (min.) fosforita.

phosphoroscope [fósforoscoup], *s.* fosforoscopio.

phosphorous [fósforus], *a.* fosforoso.

phosphorus [fósforus], *s.* (quím.) fósforo.

phosphuret [fósfiuret], *s.* fosfuro.

phot [fot], *s.* unidad de luz, igual a 1 lumen por centímetro cuadrado.

photic [fótic], *a.* relativo a la luz y a la producción de la luz.

photo [fóto], *s.* (fam.) estampa fotográfica o retrato.

photochemical [fótokémical], *a.* fotoquímico.

photochemistry [-kémistri], *s.* fotoquímica.

photodrama [-drǽmœ], *s.* drama cinematográfico.—**photodramatist** [-tist], *s.* escritor de dramas cinematográficos.

photoelectron [-eléctron] fotoelectrón, electrón emitido por un metal iluminado.

photoengraving [-engréiving], *s.* fotograbado.

photogen [fótoyen], *s.* organismo fotógeno; fotógeno (nombre de fábrica de un aceite de lámpara extraído de pizarras bituminosas).

photogene [-yin], *s.* imagen persistente en la retina.

photogenic [fótoyénic], *a.* fotogénico.

photograph [fótograf]. **I.** *va.* fotografiar, retratar por la fotografía. **II.** *s.* fotografía (estampa).

photographer [fótografœr], *s.* fotógrafo.

photographical [fótográfic(al], *a.* fotográfico.—**photographically** [-i], *adv.* fotográficamente.

photography [fotógrafi], *s.* fotografía (arte).

photogravure [fótograviúœr], *s.* fotograbado.

photolithograph [-lízograf]. **I.** *va.* fotolitografiar. **II.** *s.* fotolitografía.—**photolithographic** [-lízográfic], *a.* fotolitográfico.—**photolithography** [-lizógrafi], *s.* fotolitografía.

photolysis [fotólisis], *s.* descomposición química por la luz.

photometer [fotómetœr], *s.* fotómetro.

photometric [fótométric], *a.* fotométrico.

photometry [fotómetri], *s.* fotometría.

photophobia [fótofóbia], *s.* (med.) fotofobia.

photophone [-foun], *s.* fotófono.

photoplay [-pléi], *s.* = PHOTODRAMA.—**photoplayer** [-œr], *s.* actor de dramas cinematográficos, actor de cinematógrafo.—**photoplaywright** [-rait], *s.* = PHOTODRAMATIST.

photoprint [-print], *s.* impresión fototipográfica.

photoprocess [-próses], *s.* cualquier procedimiento fototipográfico.

photorelief [-rrelif], *s.* impresión fotográfica de relieve.

photosphere [-sfiœr], *s.* fotosfera.

photostat [fótostæt], *s.* fotóstato (nombre de fábrica de una cámara de fotografía directa para reproducir documentos, grabados, etc., sin necesidad de negativo); reproducción fotostática.

photosynthesis [-sínzesis], *s.* (bot.) fotosíntesis.

phototelegraphy [-telégrafi], *s.* telefotografía.

phototelephone [-télefoun], *s.* = PHOTOPHONE.—**phototelephony** [-léfoni], *s.* fototelefonía, transmisión del sonido por medio de la luz.

phototherapeutics [-zérapiútics], *s.* fototerapia.

phototype [-taip], *s.* clisé fototipográfico.

phototypography [-taipógrafi], *s.* fototipografía.

phrase [freis]. **I.** frase (en gram. se aplica esp. a la que no tiene verbo y a la compuesta de preposición y término); estilo, modo de hablar o de escribir; (mús.) frase musical. **II.** *va.* expresar, formular; (mús.) frasear, dividir en frases.

phraseology [freisióloyi], *s.* fraseología; dicción, construcción, estilo.

phratry [frǽtri], *s.* fratría.

phrenetic [frenétic], *a.* frenético; atacado de fiebre cerebral.

phrenitis [frenáitis o nítis], *s.* (med.) fiebre cerebral; frenesí.

phrenologic(al [frenolóyic(al], *a.* frenológico.

phrenologist [frenóloyist], *s.* frenólogo.

phrenology [frenóloyi], *s.* frenología.

Phrygian [fríyian], *a.* y *s.* frigio.

phthalein [zǽlein], *s.* (quím.) ftaleína.

phthalic [zǽlic], *s.* (quím.) ftálico.

phthisic(al [tísic(al], *a.* tísico; asmático.

phthisis [záisis o zísis], *s.* tisis.

phycology [faicóloyi], *s.* ciencia de las plantas marítimas.

phylacter(y [filǽctœr(i], *s.* filacteria.

phyllis [fílis], *s.* zagala, pastora.

phyllium [fílium], *s.* insecto parecido a una hoja.

phyllome [fílom], *s.* (bot.) hoja.

phyllotaxis [fílotǽxis], *s.* (bot.) filotaxia.

phylloxera [filoxíra], *s.* filoxera.

phylode [fíloud], **phylodium** [fíloudium], *s.* (bot.) filodio.

phylogeny [filóyeni], *s.* (biol.) filogenia.

Phylopoda [filópodæ], *s. pl.* filópodos.—**phylopod** [fílopod]. **I.** *a.* filópodo, de patas anchas semejantes a hojas; filópodo, del orden de los filópodos. **II.** *s.* filópodo, del orden de los filópodos.

physic [físic]. **I.** *va.* medicinar, purgar. **II.** *s.* medicinas, medicamentos, remedios; purgante o purga.

physical [físical], *a.* físico.—**p. herbs**, hierbas medicinales.—**p. point**, punto material.—**p. science**, ciencias físicas.—**p. training**, educación física.

physically [-i], *adv.* físicamente.

physician [fisíshan], *s.* médico.

physicist [físisist], *s.* físico.

physicky [físiki], *a.* purgante.

physics [físics], *s.* física.

physiocracy [físiócræsi], *s.* fisiocracia.—**physiocrat** [físiocræt], *s.* fisiócrata.

physiognomist [fisiógnomist], *s.* fisonomista, fisónomo.—**physiognomic(al** [fisiognómic(al], *a.* fisonómico.

physiognomy [fisiógnomi], *s.* fisonomía.

physiographic(al [físiográfic(al], *a.* fisiográfico.

physiography [fisiógrafi], *s.* fisiografía.

physiologic(al [fisiolóyic(al], *a.* fisiológico.

physiologically [-i], *adv.* fisiológicamente.

physiologist [fisióloyist], *s.* fisiologista, fisiólogo.

physiology [fisióloyi], *s.* fisiología.

physique [fisíc], *s.* físico, figura, presencia.

phytivorous [faitívorus], *a.* herbívoro.

phytogenic [fáitoyénic], *a.* fitógeno, de origen vegetal.

phytography [faitógrafi], *s.* fitografía.

Phytolaccaceæ [fáitolækéisii], *s. pl.* (bot.) fitolacáceas.

phytonomy [faitónomi], *s.* fitonomía.

phytophagous [faitófagus], *a.* fitófago.

phytoid [fáitoid], *a.* fitoide.

phytotoxin [fáitotóxin], *s.* toxina obtenida de substancias vegetales.

pi, pie [pai]. **I.** *va.* (impr.) empastelar. **II.** *s.* (impr.) pastel.

piacular [paiǽkiular], *a.* expiatorio; culpable, criminal.

pia mater [páia méitœr], *s.* piamáter.

pianism [piénism], *s.* arreglo para piano; ejecución en el piano.

pianissimo [pianísimo], *adv.* y *a.* (mús.) muy suavemente, pianísimo.

pianist [piénist], *s.* pianista.

piano [piáno], *a.* y *adv.* (mús.) dulcemente, piano.

piano(forte [piéno(fórte], *s.* (mús.) pianoforte, piano; (com.) ¡con cuidado!—**p. action,** mecanismo de piano.—**p. stool,** taburete o banqueta de piano.

pianola [pianólæ], *s.* pianola, piano mecánico.

plaster, piastre [piéstœr], *s.* piastra; peso.

piazza [piésa], *s.* pórtico, galería.

pibroch [páibroj], *s.* (Esco.) música marcial tocada con la gaita; (poét.) gaita o zampoña.

pica [páica], *s.* (impr.) lectura, cícero (tipo de 12 puntos); (med.) pica, malacia.

picador [picadóær], *s.* picador; polemista listo o perspicaz.

picaresque [pícæræsk], *a.* picaresco.

picaroon [picarún], *s.* picarón; ladrón; pirata.

picayune [pícayún], *s.* (E. U.) medio real; cualquiera moneda o cosa de poco valor.

piccalilli [picalíli], *s.* legumbres en escabeche.

piccaninny [picaníni], *s.* negrito o mulatico.

piccolo [pícolo], *s.* (mús.) flautín, requinto.

piceous [píshus], *a.* píceo; inflamable; (zool.) de color de brea.

pick. I. *va.* picar, aguijerear, romper con pico, picotear; hurtar, ratear; abrir (una cerradura) con ganzúa; escoger; coger, recoger; mondar o limpiar; descañonar (un ave).—**to p. a bone,** roer un hueso.—**to p. a bone with,** reñir o habérselas con.—**to p. a hole in one's coat,** denigrar a uno.—**to p. a quarrel,** buscar camorra, armar pendencia.—**to p. off,** arrancar; ir escogiendo y matando uno a uno (en la guerra).—**to p. one' nose,** hurgarse las narices.—**to p. one's teeth,** mondarse o limpiarse los dientes.—**to p. out,** escoger; tocar (una pieza) o cantar de oídas. —**to p. pockets,** ser carterista o ratero de faltriquera.—**to p. up,** alzar, recoger; aprender de oídas o con la práctica; coger; lograr obtener con trabajo; recobrar (las carnes, ánimo); entablar conversación con, sin presentación previa, metérsele a.—**to have a bone to p. with one,** tener que ajustar cuentas (fig.) o habérselas con uno. **II.** *vn.* picar, comer bocaditos; hurtar; escoger esmeradamente.—**to p. at,** tirar de; criticar, regañar, sermonear.—**to p. up,** restablecerse, recobrar la salud; cobrar carnes;(mec.) desarrollar velocidad. **III.** *s.* pico (herramienta); ganzúa; escogida, derecho de elección; lo más escogido; cantidad de mieses que se recoge con las manos; golpe que empuja la lanzadera del telar; hilo de un tejido; mancha en un pliego impreso.—**p. and p.,** alternación de hilos de diferentes colores.—**p. of hops,** cosecha de lúpulo u hombrecillo.

pickaback, pickapack [pícapæc], *adv.* (fam.) sobre los hombros.

pickax, pickaxe [pícæx], *s.* zapapico.

picked [píked]. **I.** *a.* espinoso, con púas; puntiagudo. **II.** *pp.* y *a.* [pikt], escogido.

picker [pícœr], *s.* escogedor; escardador; (tej.) desmotadora, abridora; recibidor.—**p. of quarrels,** camorrista, pendenciero.

pickerel [pícœrel], *s.* (ict.) lucio; sollo.—**p. weed,** (bot.) hierba acuática perenne.

picket [píket]. **I.** *s.* estaca puntiaguda, piquete; (mil.) piquete; (pol., e. p., etc.), piquete de vigilancia y propaganda, grupo de un bando, partido, etc. estacionado cerca de un establecimiento industrial, lugar de reunión de un cuerpo legislativo, residencia de un funcionario, etc. con el objeto de promover, de acción, de palabra o con la mera presencia, los intereses o propósitos de dicho bando, etc. **II.** *va.* y *vn.* cercar con estacas o piquetes; (mil.) colocar de guardia; poner piquetes (cerca de); desempeñar las funciones de un piquete o miembro de él; (pol., e. p., etc.) estacionar o poner piquetes de vigilancia y propaganda (en, cerca de, a, etc.).

picking [píking], *s.* acción y efecto de *to pick* en todas sus acepciones; v. gr.: recolección, cosecha; arrancamiento; picadura, roedura; limpia, monda; elección, escogida; hurto, robo.— *pl.* desperdicios, residuos; hurtos, raterías.

pickle [píkœl]. **I.** *s.* salmuera, escabeche, adobo; encurtido, pepinillo; (fam.) lío, enredo, brete, apuro. **II.** *va.* escabechar, adobar, conservar, encurtir.—**pickled cucumbers,** pepinillos encurtidos.—**pickled fish,** pescado en escabeche.— **pickled herrings,** arenques salados.—**pickled oysters,** ostras encurtidas.—**pickled salmon,** salmón escabechado.

picklock [píclóc], *s.* ganzúa, llave falsa; ladrón nocturno; lana escogida.

pickpocket [pícpóket], **pickpurse** [pícpœrs], *s.* cortabolsas, carterista, ratero de faltriquera.

pickthank [píczænc], *s.* zalamero.

Pickwickian [picuíkiæn], *a.* oculto, esotérico, no literal.

picnic [pícnic]. **I.** *s.* partida de campo, jira, romería; (fam. E. U.) tortas y pan pintado. **H.** *vn.* ir de romería.

picoline [pícolin], *s.* (quím.) picolina.

picotee [picotí], *s.* clavel moteado.

picrate [pícret], (quím.) picrato.

picric [pícric], *a.* muy amargo; (quím.) pícrico.

pictograph [píctogræf], *s.* pictografía, representación pictográfica.—**pictographic** [-gráfic], *a.* pictográfico.—**pictography** [pictógræfi], *s.* pictografía, arte pictográfico.

pictorial [pictórial], *a.* pictórico, gráfico.

picturable [píkchurabœl], *a.* que puede dibujarse o pintarse.

picture [píkchœr]. **I.** *s.* pintura, cuadro; retrato, fotografía; ilustración, lámina, grabado; descripción.—**p.-book,** libro con láminas.—**p. frame,** marco.—**p. gallery,** pinacoteca, galería de pinturas.—**p.-like,** semejante a una pintura. **II.** *va.* pintar, dibujar; describir; imaginar.—**to p. to one's self,** imaginarse, representarse, concebir.

picturedrome [-droum], *s.* teatro de cine.

picturesque [-ésk], *a.* pintoresco.

picturesqueness [-nes], *s.* carácter pintoresco.

picturize [-aiš], *va.* adaptar al cine.

piddle [pídœl], *vn.* picar o pellizcar la comida; emplearse en bagatelas; (fam.) orinar.

piddler [pídlœr], *s.* el que come sin ganas.

pidgin English [pívin ínglish], *s.* inglés chapurrado usado en China.

pie [pái], *s.* pastel; empanada; (orn.) marica, urraca; (impr.) *V.* PI.—**to have a finger in the p.,** meter cuchara, tener parte.

piebald [páibould], *a.* pío; pintado, de varios colores; mezclado.

piece [pis]. **I.** *s.* pieza, pedazo, trozo, retazo, fragmento; sección, parte, división; pieza (de paño, etc.); (arti.) pieza (cañón, fusil, escopeta); cualquier moneda; composición, obra, escrito; cualquier artefacto; (pint.) cuadro; (teat.) pieza. —**p. goods,** géneros que se venden por piezas. —**p. of advice,** consejo.—**p. of folly,** acto de locura.—**p. of furniture,** mueble.—**p. of ground,** solar, parcela.—**p. of news,** noticia, informe.—**p. of wit,** chiste, agudeza.—**p. price,** precio por artículo o por obra hecha.—**p. wage,** paga por pieza o por obra.—**of a p. (with),** de la misma clase (que), del mismo tenor (que).—**to come to pieces,** desarmarse, desbaratarse. **II.** *va.* apedazar, remendar; pegar, juntar, unir.—**to p. on,** juntar, pegar o poner a.—**to p. out,** completar a pedacitos; completar.—**to p. up,** apedazar, remendar; unir, juntar. **III.** *vn.* juntarse, unirse.

piecemeal [písmil]. **I.** *adv.* en pedazos. **II.** *a.* dividido. **III.** *s.* fragmento, pedazo.—**by p.,** a pedacitos.

piecework [písuœrc], *s.* obra pagada por pieza.

pied [páid], *a.* de varios colores, pintado.

pieplant [páiplænt], *s.* (bot.) ruipóntico, rapóntico.

pier [pícœr], *s.* (arq.) pila, machón; entrepaño de pared; muelle, embarcadero; escollera, espolón. —**p. glass,** espejo alto de pared, que por lo común va en un entrepaño.—**p. table,** consola.

pierage [pícœrey], *s.* muellaje, derechos de muelle.

pierce [pícœrs]. **I.** *va.* aguijerear, taladrar, pinchar; acribillar; atravesar, traspasar; abrir paso o camino.—**pierced with holes,** acribillado. —**pierced with sorrow,** traspasado de dolor. **II.** *vn.* penetrar, internarse, entrar a la fuerza.

piercing [píœrsing]. **I.** *pa.* penetrante, agudo, cortante. **II.** *s.* penetración.—**piercingly** [-li], *adv.* agudamente.

Pierian [paiírian], *a.* pierio.

piert [pícert], *a.* = PEART.

pietism [páietism], *s.* mojigatería; (**P-**), pietismo.—**pietist** [-ist], *s.* beato, misero; (**P-**), pietista.

piety [páieti], *s.* piedad; santidad.

piezometer [páiesómitœr], *s.* piezómetro; tubo indicador de presión.

pig [pig]. **I.** lechón, cochinillo; cerdo, puerco, marrano; (fund.) lingote; molde de lingotes; metal bruto en lingotes (apl. esp. al hierro y al plomo).—**p.-headed,** terco, cabezudo.—**p. iron,** lead, hierro, plomo, en lingotes o para lingotes.— **a p. in a poke,** cosa que se quiere vender sin mostrarla. **II.** *vn.* parir la puerca; conducirse o vivir como cochinos.

pigeon [píyun], *s.* paloma; (fam.) primo, bobalicón.—**p. breast,** deformidad causada por la raquitis.—**p.-breasted,** deformado de pecho por la raquitis.—**p. fancy,** afición a la cría de palomas.— **p.-hearted,** tímido; cobarde.—**p. house,** palomar.—**p.-livered,** = P.-HEARTED.—**p. loft** = P. HOUSE.—**p.'s blood,** (joy.) rubí de color claro.— **p.-toed,** de pies de paloma.

pigeonfoot [-fut], *s.* (bot.) pie de milano.

pigeonhole [-jóul], *s.* casilla.—*pl.* juego de boliche.

pigeonry [-ri], *s.* palomar.

piggery [pígœri], *s.* zahurda, chiquero.

piggin [píguin], *s.* cubeta, balde; cazo; botiho, cacharro.

piggish [pígish], *a.* cochino; voraz; puerco, sucio.—**piggishness** [-nes], *s.* voracidad; porquería, suciedad.

pigment [pígmœnt], *s.* pigmento, color, pintura; bebida de vino con especias y miel.—**pigmentary** [-eri], *a.* pigmentario.—**pigmentation** [-éishun], *s.* pigmentación; (med.) deposición excesiva.

pigmy [pígmi], *s.* pigmeo.

pignoration [pignoréshun], *s.* pignoración.

pignut [pígnut], *s.* (bot. E. U.) variedad de nogal de América y su nuez.

pigpen [pígpén], *s.* zahurda, pocilga.

pigsty [pígstai], *s.* pocilga, gorrinera.

pigtail [pígtéil], *s.* coleta, trenza; andullo de tabaco.

pike [páic], *s.* (ict.) lucio; sollo; pica, chuzo guincho, garrocha; camino de barrera.

piked [páict *o* píked], *a.* puntiagudo.

pikeman [páicman], *s.* piquero, chucero.

pikestaff [páicstaf], *s.* báculo herrado.

pila [páila *o* píla], *s.* (arq.) estribo.

pilar [páilar], *a.* peludo, velloso.

pilaster [piléestœr], *s.* (arq.) pilastra.

pilchard, pilcher [pílchard, pílchœr], *s.* (ict.) sardina.

pile [páil]. **I.** *s.* pila, montón, rimero, hacina; pira, hoguera; pilote; edificio grande y macizo; pelo, pelaje; fibra, pelillo, pelusa; (arti.) montón de balas; (elec.) pila.—*pl.* piles, hemorroides, almorranas.—**p. drawer,** aparato para arrancar pilotes.—**p. driver, p. engine,** martinete para clavar pilotes.—**p. hoop,** virola, loriga o zuncho de pilote.—**p. shoe,** azuche.—**he has made his p.,** (fam.) tiene un riñón cubierto. **II.** *va.* hincar pilotes en; poner pelusa (a una tela); (a veces con *up*), amontonar, apilar; acumular. **III.** *vn.* (a veces con *up*) amontonarse; acumularse.

pileous [páilius], *a.* píleo.

pilework [páiluœrk], *s.* pilotaje.

pilfer [pílfœr], *va.* y *vn.* ratear, hurtar.—**pilferer** [-œr], *s.* ratero, birlador.—**pilfering** [-ing], *s.* ratería, sisa.

pilgrim [pílgrim]. **I.** *s.* peregrino, romero. **II.** *vn.* peregrinar.

pilgrimage [pílgrimey], *s.* peregrinación.

piliferous, piligerous [pilífœrus, yœrus], *a.* peludo, velloso.

piling [páiling], *s.* pilotaje.

pill [pil], *s.* píldora; desazón, sinsabor, mal trago; posma.

pillage [píley]. **I.** *s.* pillaje, saqueo, merodeo. **II.** *va.* pillar, saquear.

pillager [píláyœr], *s.* pillador, saqueador, merodeador.

pillar [pílar], *s.* columna, pilar; (biol.) columela, columna; (fig.) soporte, sostén.—**Pillars of Hercules,** Columnas de Hércules.—**from p. to post,** de Ceca en Meca, de Herodes a Pilatos.

pillared [pílard], *a.* sostenido por columnas.

pillion [píliun], *s.* grupera.

pilloried [pílorid], *a.* empicotado.

pillory [pílori] **I.** *s.* picota, cepo. **II.** *va.* empicotar.

pillow [pílo]. **I.** *s.* almohada, cabezal; almohadón, cojín; (mec.) cojín, cojinete, gorrón, dado. —**p. block,** soporte; cojinete.—**p. of the bowsprit,** (mar.) tragante.—**p. sham,** cubierta de adorno para almohada.—**p. slip** = PILLOWCASE.— **II.** *va.* poner sobre una almohada, cojinete, etc.

pillowcase [-kéis], *s.* funda de almohada.

pilocarpin(e [páilocárpin], *s.* (quím.) pilocarpina.

pilose [páilos], *a.* piloso, velloso.

pilosity [pilósiti], *s.* vellosidad.

pilot [páilot]. **I.** *va.* timonear; gobernar, dirigir, guiar; (aer.) conducir, manejar. **II.** *s.* timonel; piloto, práctico; consejero, guía; (aer.) conductor, aviador; (f. c.) trompa o quitapiedras (de la locomotora).—**p. balloon,** globo piloto, pequeño globo indicador de la dirección y velocidad del viento —**p. bird,** (orn.) pájaro piloto.—**p. biscuit** = P. BREAD.—**p. boat,** bote del práctico.—**p. bread,** galleta.—**p. burner,** mechero encendedor, mechero pequeño que se mantiene encendido y sirve para encender otra mayor.—**p. engine,** locomotora piloto o de descubierta, que va delante de un tren y lo guía.—**p. fish,** (ict.) piloto, pez de mar.—**p. flag,** bandera en demanda de práctico.—**p. flame** = P. BURNER.—**p. house,** timonera.—**p. lamp,** (elec.) lámpara piloto.—**p. valve,** (hidr.) válvula de mano auxiliar para hacer funcionar otra.—**p. wire,** (elec.) alambre piloto.

pilotage [páilotey], *s.* pilotaje, practicaje.

pilotry [páilotri], *s.* náutica.

pil(e)ous [páil(i)us], *a.* piloso, peludo.

pimiento [pimiénto], *s.* pimiento.

pimp [pimp]. **I.** *s.* alcahuete, rufián, echacuervos; chulo. **II.** *vn.* alcahuetear, echacorvear.

pimpernel [pímpœrnel], *s.* (bot.) pamplina.

pimpinel [pímpinel], *s.* (bot.) pimpinela.

pimping [pímping], *a.* (fam.) pequeño, fútil, mezquino, miserable.

pimple [pímpœl], *s.* grano, barro, pupa, barrillos.

pimply [pímpli], *a.* barroso, granujiento.

pin. **I.** *s.* alfiler; prendedor, broche; clavija, pasador, espiga, bolo.—**p. clover,** (bot.) alfilerilla. —**p.-connected,** con juntas de pasador; de ensamble articulado.—**p. connection,** junta de pasador o articulada.—**p. maker,** alfilerero. —**p. money,** dinero para alfileres.—**p. oak,** (bot.) pincarrasco.—**p. point,** punta de alfiler; minuciosidad, nimiedad.—**I don't care a p.,** no se me da un bledo, no me importa un pito. **II.** *va.* prender con alfileres; fijar, clavar, sujetar; (fam.) birlar, sisar.—**to p. down,** acosar; restringir.—**to p. in,** (alb.) llenar con ripio; encerrar, enjaular.—**to p. one's faith to, u on,** confiar absolutamente en.—**to p. up,** arremangar, recoger y asegurar con alfileres.

Pinaceæ [pinéisii], *s. pl.* (bot.) pináceas.—**pinaceous** [-shus], *a.* pináceo.

pinafore [pínafor], *s.* delantal de niño.

pinang [pináng], *s.* (Filip., bot.) areca.

pinaster [pi- (*o* pai) néestœr], *s.* (bot.) pinastro, aznacho.

pincase [pínkéis], *s.* alfiletero.

pincers [pínsœrs], *s. sing.* y *pl* pinzas, tenacillas; tenazas; (zool.) pinza.

pinch. **I.** *va.* pellizcar; repizcar; apretar con pinzas o tenazas; oprimir, perseguir, estrechar; contraer, adelgazar; escatimar, limitar mucho los gastos; (E. U. fam.) prender, arrestar; hurtar, birlar.—**to p. one's self,** privarse de lo necesario. —**to p. out,** exprimir, hacer salir por presión. **II.** *vn.* pellizcar, apretar (*my shoes pinch,* me aprietan los zapatos). **III.** *s.* pellizco, pizco; pulgarada; aprieto, apuro; dolor, tormento.—**p. bar,** palanca o barra con espolón.—**p. fit,** junta de bridas.—**p. of snuff,** toma o polvo de rapé.—**to be in a p.,** hallarse en un aprieto, en un apuro.—**upon a p.,** en caso necesario.

pinchbeck [pínchbec], s. similor.

pinchcock [pínchcoc], abrazadera regulable de compresión.

pinchers [pínchœrs], s. pl. = PINCERS.

pinchfist [pínchfist], s. avaro.

pinching tongs [pínching tongâ], s. (vid.) tenazuelas.

pincushion [píncúshun], s. acerico.

Pindaric [pindéric], a. pindárico.

pindust [píndust], s. limadura de alfileres.

pine [páin]. I. s. (bot.) pino.—**p. cone,** piña.—**p. grove,** pinar, pineda.—**p. marten,** (zool.) marta cibelina.—**p. needle,** pinocha.—**p. nut,** piña; piñón.—**p. tree,** pino.—**P.-tree State,** (E. U.) estado de Maine. II. vn. y vr. (con for) anhelar.

pineal [píaial o páinial], a. de figura de piña.—**p. gland,** glándula pineal.

pineapple [páinæpœl], s. (bot.) piña, anana.

pinene [píainin], s. (quím.) pineno, el elemento principal de la trementina, etc.

pinfeather [pínfépœr], s. pluma rudimentaria.—**pinfeathered** [-d], a. implume.

ping [ping], s. silbido de una bala.

ping-pong [-pong], s. ping-pong, juego de salón semejante al tenis.

pinhead [pínjéd], s. cabeza de alfiler; objeto muy pequeño.

pinhole [pínjoul], s. agujero que hace el alfiler; (fot.) punto transparente en un negativo.

pining [páining], s. languidez.

pinion [píniun]. I. s. ala de ave; alón; piñón (pluma y último huesecillo del ala); (mec.) piñón.—pl. esposas, grillos. II. va. atar las alas; maniatar, poner esposas.

pinioned [píniund], a. alado; maniatado.

pink. I. s. (bot.) clavel; cualquier flor parecida al clavel; color de rosa; (cost.) picadura; dechado, modelo; casaquín encarnado de caza. II. a. rosado.—**p.-sterned,** (naut.) de popa puntuda. III. va. (cost.) picar, calar, ojetear.

pinker [pínkœr], s. el que pica las telas de seda.

pinkeye [pínkai], s. (vet.) catarro epidémico de los caballos, acompañado de oftalmía; (med.) oftalmía purulenta contagiosa.

pinking [pínking], s. (cost.) picadura, picado.—**p. iron,** hierro de picar festones.

pinkish [pínkish], a. que tira a rosado.

pinky [pínki], a. rosado.—**p. eyes,** ojuelos chispeantes.

pinna [pína], s. (bot.) hojuela de hoja pinada; (anat.) oreja, pabellón del oído; (zool.) ala, aleta.

pinnace [pínes], s. (mar.) pinaza.

pinnacle [pínacœl], s. (arq.) pináculo, ápice, remate, fastigio; cima, cumbre.

pinnate(d [pínet(ed], a. (bot.) pinado.

pinnatifid [pinætífid], a. (bot.) pinatífido.

pinner [pínœr], s. el que asegura con alfileres, pernos, clavijas, etc.; delantal; toquilla.

pinnigrade [pínigred], a. (zool.) que se mueve por medio de aletas.

pinniped [píniped], s. y a. pinípedo.—**Pinnipedia** [-pídiæ], s. pl. pinípedos.

pinnule [pínul], s. (zool.) aleta pequeña; (bot.) pínula, hojuela.

pinocle [pínocœl], s., pinocle, juego de naipes.

pint [páint], s. pinta (½ galón).

pintail [pínteil], s. (orn.) ánade de cola larga.

pinto [pínto]. I. a. pintado, de varios colores. II. s. animal pintado.

pintle [píntœl], s. clavija, perno pinzote; macho de timón.

pinwheel [pínjuíl], s. rueda de engranaje con clavijas en vez de dientes; rueda giratoria de fuegos artificiales.

pinworm [pínuœrm], s. gusano.

piny [páini], a. pinoso.

pioneer [páionicœr]. I. s. explorador; iniciador, primer promotor; (mil.) gastador, zapador, palero. II. va. y vn. explorar; abrir un camino; guiar; introducir, promover.

pious [páius], a. pío, piadoso.

piously [-li], adv. piadosamente.

pip. I. s. moquillo, pepita (de las aves); pepita o semilla de una manzana, naranja, etc.; punto de un naipe, dado o dominó. II. va. romper (un polluelo) el cascarón. III. vn. piar.

pipe [páip]. I. s. tubo, caño; tubería; cañería; pipa de fumar; cañón (como de órgano, etc.); (mús.) caramillo, churumbela; pito o silbato del contramaestre; silbo, silbido; pipa, casco, tonel.—pl. gaita.—**p. clay,** blanquizal.—**p. fitter,** montador de tuberías.—**p. fitting,** instalación de tuberías; acoplamientos y accesorios de tuberías.—**p. layer,** tendedor o instalador de cañerías.—**p. laying,** instalación de cañerías.—**p. line,** tubería, cañería; oleoducto.—**p. of peace** = CALUMET.—**p. organ,** órgano de cañones.—**pipes of Pan** = PAN'S PIPES.—**p. stock,** terraja.—**p. tree,** (bot.) lila. II. va. tocar (flauta, caramillo o dulzaina); cantar con voz aguda; llamar con un pito o silbato; conducir por medio de cañerías o tubos; instalar cañerías en; (cost.) hacer un vivo. III. vn. tocar el caramillo o la gaita; pitar; gritar; (fund.) endurecerse en forma de tubo.

pipefish [páipfish], s. un pez de mar.

piper [páipœr], s. flautista, gaitero.

piperin(e [pípœrin], s. (quím.) piperina.

pipestem [páipstém], s. boquilla de pipa de fumar.

pipette [pipét], s. pipeta, probeta.

piping [páiping]. I. a. hirviente; que silba; pastoril.—**p. hot,** hirviendo. II. s. sonido de caramillo; gemido; cañería, tubería; (cost.) vivo, cordoncillo.

pipit [pípit], s. (orn.) especie de alondra.

pipkin [pípkin], s. pucherito, ollita.

pippin [pípin], s. (bot.) camuesa.

piquancy [pícansi], s. picante, acrimonia.

piquant [pícant], a. picante; áspero, mordaz.

piquantly [pícantli], adv. picantemente, agriamente; mordazmente.

pique [pic]. I. s. pique, resentimiento, rencilla. II. va. picar, ofender, irritar. III. vr. preciarse, jactarse; picarse, ofenderse.

piqué [piké], s. (tej.) piqué.

piquet [pikét], s. séptimo, juego de los cientos; (mil.) piquete, guardia avanzada.

piracy [páirasi], s. piratería; plagio.

pirate [páiret]. I. s. pirata; plagiario. II. va. y vn. piratear; plagiar; pillar, robar.

piratical [pairética1], a. pirático, raquero.

pirn [pœrn], s. narigón; (tej.) correte; ovillo de hilo arrollado en la canilla.

pirogue [piróg], s. piragua, canoa.

pirouette [piruét], s. pirueta, girada.

piscary [píscari], s. privilegio de pesca en aguas ajenas.

piscatorial [píscætóriæl], **piscatory** [-tori], a. piscatorio.

pisces [písis], s. pl. los peces; (astr. P-) Piscis.

pisciculture [pisicúlchœr], s. piscicultura.

pisciculturist [pisicúlchurist], s. piscicultor.

piscina [písina], a. piscina, pecina.

piscivorous [písívœrus], a. piscívoro.

pish [pish], interj. ¡bah! ¡quita allá!

pisiform [písiform], a. pisiforme.—**p. bone,** hueso pisiforme.

pismire [pís- o písmaiœr], s. hormiga.

piss. I. vn. (vulg.) orinar. II. s. orina.

pissasphalt [písasfalt], s. pissásfalto.

pistachio [pistésho o pistáchio], s. (bot.) alfóncigo o pistacho.—**p. tree,** alfóncigo, cornicabra.

pistil [pístil], s. (bot.) pistilo.

pistillary [-æri], a. perteneciente al pistilo.

pistillate [pístilet], a. pistilado.

pistol [pístul]. I. s. pistola; revólver.—**p. case,** pistolera, funda de pistolas.—**p. shot,** pistoletazo, tiro de pistola. II. va. tirar con pistola.

pistole [pistól], s. doblón de oro.

pistolet [pistolét], s. pistolete, cachorro.

Para la pronunciación de æ, œ, ᴅ ᴣ. ŝh, ᴜ, ȳ, ᴎ, ᴢ, véase la clave al principio del libro.

píston [pístʊn], *s.* émbolo; (mús.) llave o pistón.—**p. boss,** cubo del émbolo.—**p. pin,** (aut., etc.) eje del émbolo.—**p. ring,** anillo de empaquetadura del émbolo.—**p. rod,** vástago del émbolo.—**p. slide valve,** distribuidor cilíndrico de émbolo.—**p. stroke,** golpe de émbolo; carrera del émbolo.—**p. travel,** carrera del émbolo.—**p. valve** = P. SLIDE VALVE.

pit. I. *s.* hoyo; hoya, cárcava; foso; cacaraña; hueso de ciertas frutas; (teat.) platea.—**p. coal,** hulla.—**p. head,** pozo de mina.—**p. of the stomach,** boca del estómago.—**p. saw,** sierra cabrilla, sierra abrazadera.—**to be at the p.'s brink,** estar al borde del precipicio. **II.** *va.* marear con hoyos; cacarañar; poner en un hoyo; incitar a pelear.

pita [pítæ], *s.* pita, (planta y fibra).—**p. fiber, p. hemp,** pita (fibra). (*Pita* se aplica a veces a la cabuya y otras fibras análogas.)

pitapat [pítæpæt], *adv.* tictac.

pitch [pich]. **I.** *s.* grado de inclinación, pendiente, declive; paso (de tornillo, de rueda dentada, de arrollamiento); (mús.) tono; término, extremo, punto; en ciertos juegos, lanzamiento, echada, tiro; pez, betún, brea, alquitrán; resina.—**p. chain,** cadena articulada que mueve una rueda dentada, cadena de engranaje.—**p. circle,** círculo o circunferencia primitivos (de una rueda dentada).—**p. dark,** obscuro como boca de lobo.—**p. line** = P. CIRCLE.—**p. of an arch,** relación entre la flecha y la luz o la semiluz de un arco (gen. se toma en este último sentido).—**p. of a roof,** inclinación o pendiente de un tejado.—**p. of rivets,** espaciado de remaches, distancia de centro a centro de los remaches.—**p. pine,** pino tea.—**p. pipe,** diapasón de voz.—**p. tree,** (bot.) abeto píceo. **II.** *va.* tirar, arrojar; echar, botar: en el juego de baseball, arrojar la pelota al *batsman;* clavar, plantar o fijar en tierra; armar, asentar (tienda, etc.); colocar, formar, arreglar; embrear, betunar; (mús.) graduar el tono, dar el diapasón. —**to p. tents,** (mil.) armar las tiendas, acamparse. **III.** *vn.* arrojar por bajo mano; caerse hacia abajo; caer de cabeza; instalarse, fijarse, establecerse; arfar, cabecear (el buque).—**to p. in,** (fam.) poner manos a la obra, emprender (algo) con ahínco.—**to p. into,** (fam.) arremeter a; desatarse contra, sermonear, zurrar.

pitchblende [píchblend], *s.* pechblenda, variedad de uraninita, que es un mineral de óxido de uranio.

pitched battle [picht bǽtœl], *s.* batalla campal.

pitcher [píchœr], *s.* jarro, cántaro; arrojador, botador; en baseball, el que tira la pelota al *batsman;* (bot.) ascidia.—**p. plant,** planta provista de ascidias.

pitchfork [píchfork], *s.* (agr.) horca, horquilla, aventador; (mús.) diapasón.

pitchiness [píchines], *s.* obscuridad; negrura, color de pez.

pitching [píching]. **I.** *a.* inclinado, en declive. **II.** *s.* arfada, cuneo, cabezada.—**p. pence,** (Ingl.) contribución por vender en mercado.

pitchstone [píchstoun], *s.* vidrio volcánico.

pitchy [píchi], *a.* embreado, píceo; negro, obscuro, triste.

piteous [pítiʊs], *a.* lastimero, lastimoso; compasivo, tierno.—**piteously** [-li], *adv.* lastimosamente.—**piteousness** [-nes], *s.* compasión, ternura.

pitfall [pítfol], *s.* trampa, hoya cubierta; peligro latente.

pith [piz]. **I.** *s.* meollo, corazón, medula; medula espinal; fuerza, vigor; jugo; substancia. **II.** *va.* quitar el meollo a (una planta); destruir los centros nerviosos de; atronar, descabellar, matar (ganado) cortando la medula espinal.

pithecanthrope pithecanthropus [pizicǽnzroup, pʊs], pitecantropo. — **Pithecanthropus erectus,** pitecantropo de Dubois (llám. gen. pitecantropo).

pithily [pízili], *adv.* enérgicamente, fuertemente.

pithiness [pízines], *s.* energía, eficacia.

pithless [pízles], *a.* falto de meollo; endeble.

pithy [pízi], *a.* enérgico, eficaz; meduloso; expresivo, sentencioso.

pitiable [pítiabœl], **pitiful** [pítiful], *a.* lastimoso, enternecedor; despreciable.

pitifully [-i], *adv.* lastimosamente.

pitifulness [-nes], *s.* calidad de lastimoso.

pitiless [pítiles], *a.* desapiadado, empedernido.—**pitilessly** [-li], *adv.* desapiadadamente, sin compasión.—**pitilessness** [-nes], *s.* empedernimiento.

pitman [pítman], *s.* (*pl.* PITMEN) aserrador de foso; (min.) pocero; (mec.) (*pl.* PITMANS) biela.—**p. arm,** biela; (aut.) biela o brazo de dirección.

pittance [pítans], *s.* pitanza, ración, porción.

pitted [píted], *a.* picado, cacarañado.

pituita [pitúaita o tuíta], *s.* pituita.

pituitary [pítuiteri], *a.* pituitario.—**p. body, p. gland,** glándula pituitaria.

pituitous [-tus], *a.* pituitoso.—**p. fever,** fiebre tifoidea.

pity [píti]. **I.** *s.* piedad, misericordia, lástima.—**for p.'s sake, from p.,** por piedad.—**to have, o take, p. on,** tener piedad de, compadecer. **II.** *va.* compadecer. **III.** *vn.* apiadarse, tener piedad, enternecerse.

pityriasis [pitiráiæsis], *s.* pitiriasis.

pivot [pívʊt]. **I.** *s.* pivote; espiga, espigón, gorrón; centro de rotación; punto o hecho fundamental, corazón (fig.), punto de partida. **p. chair,** silla giratoria.—**p. collar** = P. HOLE.—**p. gun,** cañón giratorio, colisa.—**p. hole,** buje o cuenca de pivote o de eje.—**p. (man),** (mil.) guía, centro de giro de una hilera. **II.** *va.* colocar por medio de un pivote; proveer de pivote. **III.** *vn.* girar sobre un pivote.—**to p. on,** girar sobre dépender de, estribar en.

pivotal [-æl], *a.* cardinal, fundamental, céntrico.

pix, *s.* (igl.) píxide, portapaz.

pixy [píxi], *s.* (Ingl.) hada, duende.

placability [placabíliti], **placableness** [pléca-bœlnes], *s.* placabilidad; dulzura, clemencia.

placable [plécabœl], *a.* placable, aplacable.

placard [plécard]. **I.** *s.* cartel, letrero, anuncio; proclama, edicto. **II.** *va.* (plácard) publicar por medio de carteles; fijar (cartel o aviso).

placate [plékeit], *va.* aplacar, apaciguar.

placation [plekéishʊn], *s.* aplacamiento.

place [pléis]. **I.** *s.* lugar, sitio, paraje, local, puesto; (mil.) plaza, fortaleza, puesto militar; calle corta; callejón; situación; posición; grado, rango; empleo, puesto; dignidad; acomodo; espacio, cabida, asiento.—**p. of arms,** (artí.) plaza de formación del camino cubierto.—**in p.,** en su lugar; apropiado; in situ; en la obra (que se construye).—**in p. of,** en lugar o vez de.—**in the first p.,** en primer lugar.—**in the next p.,** luego, después.—**out of p.,** fuera de lugar o de propósito; indebido, intempestivo. **II.** *va.* colocar, poner, situar; dar colocación o empleo a; recordar pormenores o circunstancias acerca de; prestar a interés, invertir o poner (dinero) en un negocio; (com.) disponer de, vender, dar salida a.

placeman [plésman], *s.* empleado público, oficinista.

placenta [plasénta], *s.* (anat. y bot.) placenta.

placental [plaséntal], *a.* referente a la placenta; provisto de placenta.

placer [plésœr], *s.* placer, lavadero de oro.—**p. mine,** placer de oro.—**p. mining,** minería de placer o de lavado.

placer [pléisœr], *s.* colocador.

placet [pléset o pláset], *s.* permiso.

placid [plésid], *a.* plácido, apacible.

placidity [plasíditi], **placidness** [plǽsidnes], *s.* placidez, apacibilidad, serenidad.

placidly [plǽsidli], *adv.* plácidamente, apaciblemente.

placket [pléket], *s.* abertura en la parte superior de una saya o enagua.

placoid [plécoid], *a.* placoideo.

plagal [pléigal], *a.* (mús.) plagal.

plagiarism [pléiyiarism], *s.* plagio.—**plagiary, plagiarist** [-i, ist], *s.* plagiario.—**plagiarize, -ise,** [-aís], *va.* y *vn.* plagiar.

plague [pléig]. **I.** *s.* plaga, peste, pestilencia; miseria, calamidad. **II.** *va.* vejar, importunar; infestar, plagar.

plaguily [pléiguili], *adv.* (fam.) molestamente.

plaguy [pléigui], *a.* (fam.) enfadoso, molesto.

plaice [pleis], *s.* (ict.) platija.

plaid [pléid]. **I.** *s.* manta escocesa listada a cuadros; (plæd *o* pléid) tartán o género listado a cuadros; muestra o diseño en forma de cuadros. **II.** *a.* [plæd *o* pléid] a cuadros, cuadrícula.

plain [pléin]. **I.** *a.* llano, simple, sencillo; desnudo, sin adornos; franco; natural, ingenuo; ordinario o común; puro, sin mezcla; manifiesto, claro; humilde, de humilde cuna.—**p.** arm, (aut.) biela o brazo de dirección.—**p. as a pikestaff**, obvio, evidente.—**p. chant**, canto llano.—**p. clothes**, traje ordinario (a distinción de uniforme). —**p. dealer**, hombre sincero.—**p. dealing**, sinceridad, buena fe.—**p.-hearted**, bueno, sin doblez.— **p.-heartedness**, sinceridad.—**p. people**, gente sencilla, gente humilde; el común de las gentes.— **p. sailing**, camino fácil, cosa fácil; coser y cantar. —**p. song** = P. CHANT.—**p. speaking**, franqueza. —**p.-spoken**, claro, franco.—**p. truth**, pura, verdad.—**p. work**, costura sencilla, sin adorno.— **in p. English**, en romance, sin rodeos. **II.** *s.* llano, llanura. **III.** *va. y vn.* lamentar(se).

plaining [-ing], *s.* (poét.) queja, lamento.

plainly [-li], *adv.* llanamente; sencillamente; evidentemente; claramente, francamente.

plainness [-nes], *s.* simplicidad, llaneza, sencillez; franqueza; claridad.

plainsman [pléinsmæn], *s.* llanero.

plaint [pléint], *s.* quejido, queja, lamento.

plaintful [-ful], *a.* quejoso; dolorido.

plaintiff [pléintif], *s.* (for.) demandante, actor.

plaintive [pléintiv], *a.* dolorido, quejumbroso.

plaintively [-li], *adv.* quejumbrosamente.—**plaintiveness** [-nes], *s.* calidad de quejumbroso.

plait [pléit]. **I.** *s.* (cost.) pliegue, doblez, alforza, plegado; trenza.—**p. cordage**, cajetas.—**p. laces**, cordones, torzales. **II.** *va.* (cost.) plegar, alechugar, rizar, encañonar, encarrujar; tejer, trenzar.

plaiter [pléitœr], *s.* plegador.

plaiting [pléiting], *s.* plegadura, plegado.—**p. machine**, plegador.

plan [plæn]. **I.** *s.* plan; plano, dibujo; planta, proyección horizontal; (perspectiva) plano óptico, tabla. **II.** *va.* idear, proyectar, planear; hacer planes para; pensar, resolver. **III.** *vn.* hacer planes.

planchet [plénchet], *s.* tejuelo, disco metálico.

planchette [planshét], *s.* brújula de agrimensor; tabla de escritura mesmérica.

plane [pléin]. **I.** *s.* (geom., aer.) plano; (carp.) cepillo; (bot.) plátano falso; (f. c., etc.) plano inclinado; (aer., fam.) aeroplano; (mec.) SURFACE PLATE.—**p. of projection**, plano de proyección.—**p. of sight**, plano visual, plano vertical de la línea visual. **II.** *a.* plano, llano; relativo al plano; (geom.) plano.—**p. angle**, ángulo plano.— **p. geometry**, geometría plana.—**p. sailing**, navegación sobre la carta de marear.—**p. surveying**, (top.) planimetría, topografía ordinaria, en que no se tiene en cuenta la curvatura de la tierra.—**p. table**, (top.) plancheta; (min.) plano inclinado.— **p. tree**, plátano falso.—**p. trigonometry**, trigonometría rectilínea o plana. **III.** *va.* acepillar; desbastar; allanar, alisar. **IV.** *vn.* alisar, acepillar; funcionar (una cepilladora, etc.); (aer.) planear.

planer [pléinœr], *s.* acepillador, cepillo mecánico; (impr.) tamborilete, aplanador.

planet [plénet], *s.* (astr.) planeta.—**p. gear**, engranaje planetario.—**p. stricken, p.-struck**, asombrado, atónito. **p. wheel**, rueda planetaria.

planetarium [plénetérium], *s.* planetario.

planetary [plénetæri], *a.* planetario.—**p. gear**, engranaje planetario.

planetoid [plénetoid], *s.* asteroide.

planifolious [plænifólius], *a.* (bot.) planifolio u hojiplano.

planimeter [plænímetœr], *s.* planímetro.

planimetry [planímetri], *s.* medida de las áreas planas.

planing [pléning], *s.* acepilladura, alisadura.—**p. bench**, banco de carpintero.—**p. machine**, cepillo mecánico, cepilladora.

planipetalous [plænipétalus], *a.* planipétalo.

planish [plénish], *va.* alisar, pulir, aplanar; pulir perfectamente con rodillos.

planisher [plénishœr], *s.* alisador, aplanador, bruñidor.

planisphere [plénisfiœr], *s.* planisferio.

plank [plænc]. **I.** *s.* tablón, tabla gruesa; tablaje, tablazón (gen. en *pl.*); (pol.) cada uno de los principios que forman el programa de un partido.—**p. road**, camino de tablas. **II.** *va.* entablar, enmaderar; (min.) encofrar.

planking [plénking], *s.* tablaje, entabladura, forro.

plankton [pléncton], *s.* vegetación flotante marítima.

planner [plénœr], *s.* trazador, tracista, proyectista.

plano-concave [pléino-cónkeiv], *a.* planocóncavo.—**plano-conical** [-cónicæl], *a.* planocónico. —**plano-convex** [-cónvex], *a.* planoconvexo.

plant [plænt *o* plant]. **I.** *s.* (bot.) planta, mata; (mec.) instalación de maquinaria, etc.—**p. bed**, plantel de tabaco.—**p. louse**, (ent.) brugo, pulgón. **II.** *va.* plantar, sembrar; colocar, instalar; fijar, sentar, asegurar; fundar, establecer; engendrar.

plantain [plénten], *s.* (bot.) plátano; llantén, plantaina.

plantar [pléntar], *a.* plantar.

plantation [plæntéshun], *s.* hacienda, ingenio; plantación, siembra, plantío; ostral, ostrera, criadero de ostras.—*pl.* colonia.—**p. hoes**, azadones.

planter [pléntœr], *s.* plantador, cultivador, hacendado; colono.

plantigrade [pléntigred]. **I.** *a.* (zool.) plantígrado. **II.** *s.* animal plantígrado.

plantlet, plantule [pléntlet, pléntiul], *s.* (bot.) plantita.

plaque [plac], *s.* (b. a.) placa, plato decorativo; broche, medalla; (zool.) disco.

plash [plæsh]. **I.** *s.* chapaleteo; celaje; fucilazo; charco, aguazal, lagunajo; rama cortada y entretejida con otras. **II.** *va. y vn.* chapalear, chapotear; enramar, entretejer (ramas); (pint.) manchar.

plashy [pléshi], *a.* pantanoso; manchado.

plasm [plæsm], *s.* molde, matriz; plasma.

plasma [plésma *o* plésma], *s.* (biol.) plasma; (min.) prasma o plasma.

plasmic [plésmic], *a.* plasmático.

plasmodium [plæsmódium], *s.* (biol.) plasmodio.

plasmosome [plésmosoum], *s.* (biol.) plasmosoma.

plasome [pléisoum], *s.* (biol.) plasoma, bióforo.

plaster [plástœr]. **I.** *s.* yeso; argamasa, mortero, mezcla; enlucido; (farm.) parche, emplasto.— **p. of Paris**, yeso mate. **II.** *va.* (alb.) enyesar, enlucir, revocar; embarrar; poner emplastos.

plasterer [-œr], *s.* revocador, yesero.

plastering [-ing], *s.* (alb.) enlucido, revoque, enyesado; emplastadura.

plasterwork [-uœrc], *s.* enyesado, enlucido.

plastic [pléstic *o* plástic], *a.* plástico; formativo.—**p. art**, plástica.—**p. surgery**, cirugía plástica.

plasticity [plæstísiti], *s.* plasticidad.

plastid [plæstid], *s.* (biol.) plastidio, elemento protoplasmático; célula.

plastron [pléstron], *s.* peto, pechera, plastrón; (zool.) concha inferior de las tortugas.

plat [plæt]. **I.** *s.* (mar.) baderna; solar, parcela; mapa o plano; trenza, cintilla. **II.** *va.* entretejer, trenzar; trazar el plano de; trasladar al papel.

Platanaceæ [plætanésii *o* násee], *s. pl.* (bot.) platáneas.

platane [pléten], *s.* = PLANE-TREE.

platband [plétbænd], *s.* arriate de un jardín; (arq.) faja de la cornisa.

plate [pleit]. **I.** *s.* plancha, chapa, lámina, placa; plato (de comer); vajilla en general; platina (de una máquina neumática); (dep.) palio, copa de oro o plata dada como premio en regata o carrera; (impr.) estereotipo, clisé; electrotipo; ilustración, grabado; (dent.) dentadura postiza; (elec.) elemento de una pila; plancha de blindaje; (foto.) placa; (top.) placa, limbo (de un instrumento).—**p. armor**, blindaje.—**p. cultivation, p. culture**, cultivo de las bacterias en gelatina sobre láminas de vidrio.—**p. frame**, (foto.) portaplaca, bastidor.—**p. girder**, viga de alma llena.—**p. glass**, vidrio cilindrado.—**p. holder** = P. FRAME.—**p. mark**, marca de contraste.—**p. metal**, metal en planchas.—**p. paper**, papel de primera calidad para grabados.—**p. powder**, polvos para pulir vajilla.—**p. press**, prensa para grabados.—**p. printing**, impresión de grabados con planchas.—**p. rack**, escurridero para platos; (foto.) bastidor para sostener las placas mientras se secan.—**p. rail**, riel plano; moldura plana o anaquel para platos ornamentales, etc.—**p. room**, repostería.—**p. shears**, cizalla.—**p. tracery**, labor calada en una piedra.—**p. warmer**, calientaplatos.—**p. wheel**, rueda de disco lleno. **II.** *va.* planchear; platear, dorar, niquelar (por la galvanoplastia); batir hoja; unir con planchas de metal.

plateau [plató], *s.* mesa, meseta, rasa.

plated [pléited], *a.* plateado, niquelado, etc., según el metal (vg: *silver plated*, plateado; *gold plated*, dorado; etc.).—**p. ware**, plaqué.

plateful [pléitful], *s.* un plato lleno.

platen [pléten], *s.* (impr. y mec.) platina.

plater [pléitœr], *s.* plateador (en gen., el que platea, dora, etc.); artífice que trabaja en metales en lámina; platero (que trabaja en plata, oro, joyas, etc.)

platform [plǽtform], *s.* plataforma, tablado, andamio; cadalso; terraplén; tribuna; (f. c.) andén; plataforma de un tranvía; (E. U. pol.) programa, declaración formal de principios.—**p. car**, vagón de plataforma.—**p. scale**, báscula.

platinate [plǽtineit], *s.* platinato.

plating [pléiting], *s.* arte o acción de revestir con una capa metálica (dorado, plateado, etc.); capa o recubrimiento metálico; blindaje.

platinic [plǽtínic], *a.* platínico.—**platiniferous** (plǽtiníferus), *a.* platinífero.—**platiniridium** [-irídium], *s.* platinoiridio, aleación cuyos principales componentes son iridio y platino.—**platinite** [-ait], acero níquel muy rico en este metal (como 46%).—**platinize** [-aiš], *va.* platinar.—**platinoid** [-oid]. **I.** *a.* semejante al platino. **II.** *s.* platinoide, aleación de plata alemana y tungsteno.—**platinotype** [-otaip], *s.* platinotipia.—**platinous** [-us], *a.* platinoso.

platinum [plǽtinum], *s.* platino.—**p. black**, polvo negro de platino.

platitude [plǽtitiud], *s.* perogrullada, trivialidad.

platitudinize [-tiúdinaiš], *vn.* decir perogrulladas o vejeces. —**platitudinous** [-tiúdinus], *a.* insípido, trivial, traqueado.

Platonic [platónic], *a.* platónico.—**P. year**, año platónico.

Platonism [plétonišm], *s.* platonismo.

platoon [platún], *s.* (mil.) pelotón.

platter [plǽtœr], *s.* fuente, platel.

platting [plǽting], *s.* cintillo de paja; dibujo.

plaudit [plódit], *s.* aplauso, aclamación.

Platyrrhina [plǽtirrínæ], *s. pl.* (zool.) platirrinos. —**platyrrhine, platyrrhinian** [-rrin, rríniæn], *s.* y *a.* platirrino.

plausibility [plošibíliti], **plausibleness** [plósibœlnes], *s.* plausibilidad.

plausible [plóšibœl], *a.* plausible.

plausibly [plóšibli], *adv.* plausiblemente.

plausive [plósiv], *a.* laudatorio.

play [ple]. **I.** *va.* jugar (algún juego); mover (la pieza de algún juego); hacerle o jugarle a uno (una mala partida, etc.); (teat.) dar, representar, poner en escena; desempeñar un papel; (mús.) ejecutar, tocar (pieza o instrumento); manejar, menear, manipular; valerse o hacer uso de; arrojar, echar, lanzar.—**to p. a part**, representar un papel.—**to p. a set, o game**, jugar un partido o una partida.—**to p. one a trick**, engañar a uno,

hacerle una mala jugada, pegarle un petardo.—**to p. second fiddle**, estar subordinado, hacer un papel secundario.—**to p. the fool**, hacerse el tonto.—**to p. the game**, jugar limpio.—**to p. the knave**, engañar.—**to p. the mischief**, causar daño.—**to p. the monkey**, hacer monadas.—**to p. (the) truant**, hacer novillos.—**to p. tricks**, hacer suertes; hacer travesuras. **II.** *vn.* jugar, juguetear; burlarse, chancearse, bromear; (mús.) tocar; (mec.) jugar, moverse, funcionar; portarse, conducirse; flotar, ondular, ondear; (teat.) representar. —**to p. at cards**, jugar a los naipes.—**to p. fair**, jugar limpio.—**to p. false**, engañar.—**to p. fast and loose**, embaucar, no ser digno de confianza.— **to p. into the hands of one**, hacer a uno el caldo gordo.—**to p. off**, hacer alarde; pretender, ostentar.—**to p. on**, tocar (un instrumento).—**to p. to the gallery, o to the galleries**, obrar sin más motivo que el aplauso o la aprobación públicos.— **to p. upon one**, burlarse de uno.—**to p. upon words**, hacer equívoco de vocablos. **III.** *s.* juego; jugada; (teat.) drama; función, representación; (mec.) juego, espacio libre; funcionamiento, operación; rienda suelta, libertad de acción, vuelo; movimiento ligero y rápido; reflejo de colores o de luces; (teat.) ejecución, desempeño.—**p. actor**, actor, cómico.—**p. upon words**, equívoco, retruécano.—**in p.**, en chanza, de burlas.

playbill [pléibil], *s.* (teat.) cartel; programa.

playbook [-búc], *s.* libreto.

playday [-déi], *s.* día de huelga o de asueto.

played out [pléid áut], *a.* agotado; acabado, concluído.

player [pléicœr], *s.* jugador; actor, cómico; (mús.) músico, instrumentista; pianola, piano mecánico (ll. t. **p. piano y piano p.**).

playfellow [-félo], *s.* compañero de juego.

playful [-ful], *a.* juguetón, retozón.

playgame [-guéim], *s.* juego de niños.

playgoer [-gócer], *s.* persona que frecuenta los teatros.

playground [-gráund], *s.* patio de recreo.

playhouse [-jáus], *s.* teatro, coliseo.

playing card [pléiing card], *s.* naipe, carta.

playlet [pléilet], *s.* drama corto.

playmate [-méit], *s.* = PLAYFELLOW.

plaything [-zing], *s.* juguete, niñería.

playwright [-rráit], *s.* dramaturgo, autor dramático.

plaza [pláša], *s.* plaza.

plea [plí], *s.* argumento; ruego, súplica; (for.) alegato, defensa; respuesta o declaración (del acusado); acción, litigio, proceso; disculpa, pretexto.—**p. in abatement**, instancia de nulidad.—**p. of the crown**, (Ingl.) causa criminal.

pleach [plích], *va.* entretejer ramas.

plead [plid]. **I.** *va.* defender (un pleito, una causa); aducir como razón, motivo o excusa. **II.** *vn.* suplicar; abogar; declarar o responder el acusado si es culpable o no.—**to p. guilty**, confesarse delincuente.—**to p. not guilty**, declararse inocente.

pleadable [plídabœl], *a.* que se puede alegar en un pleito, o en derecho.

pleader [plídœr], *s.* abogado, defensor.

pleading [plíding], *s.* (for.) alegación, defensa; informe; abogacía.—*pl.* alegatos.

pleasant [plésant], *a.* grato, agradable; simpático, tratable.—**pleasantly** [-li], *adv.* agradablemente.— **pleasantness** [-nes], *s.* agradabilidad.

pleasantry [plésantri], *s.* chuscada, broma, humorada, agudeza, chanza.

please [plíš]. **I.** *va.* gustar, agradar; complacer, dar gusto, satisfacer, placer.—**to be pleased to**, tener gusto en, o el gusto de; alegrarse de.—**to be pleased with**, estar satisfecho de o con; gustarle a uno (cambiando el giro: *I am much pleased with this car*, me gusta mucho este coche).—**to p. one's self**, hacer uno su gusto sin miramientos por los demás. **II.** *vn.*) agradar, satisfacer; querer, gustar. En el imperativo y con *if* se emplea por cortesía en el sentido de "hacer el favor," "tener la bondad," "servirse," etc.: *please speak slowly*, sírvase, o hágame el favor de, hablar despacio; *if you please*, o simplemente *please*, si Vd. me hace el favor, si

Vd. tiene la bondad).—**as one pleases**, como uno quiera o guste.

pleasing [plíşing], _a._ complaciente; agradable, placentero.—**pleasingly** [-li], _adv._ agradablemente, donosamente.

pleasurable [pléÿurabœl], _a._ agradable.

pleasurableness [-nes], calidad de agradable. —**pleasurably** [-bli], _adv._ placenteramente.

pleasure [pléÿœr], _s._ placer; voluntad, arbitrio. **p. ground**, parque, jardín de recreo.—**at one's (own) p.**, como uno quiera, como le plazca.—**at p.**, a voluntad.—**what is your p.?** ¿qué desea Vd.? ¿en qué puedo complacerle?—**with great p.**, **with p.**, con mucho gusto, con placer.

pleat [plít], _va._ (fam.) plegar, arrugar.—**pleating** [ing], (cost.) plegado.

plebe [plíb], _s._ (E. U. fam.) plebeyo, estudiante de primer año.

plebeian [plebíyan], _a._ y _s._ plebeyo.

plebiscite [plébisit], _s._ plebiscito.—**plebiscitary** [plebísiteri], _a._ plebiscitario.

plebs [plebŝ], _s._ plebe, populacho.

plectrum [pléctrṷm], _s._ plectro, púa.

pledge [plex]. **I.** _s._ prenda, señal; empeño, fianza; rehén; promesa, voto; brindis. **II.** _va._ empeñar, dar en prenda, dar fianza; brindar por; prometer, dar (la palabra).

pledgee [pleÿí], _s._ (for.) depositario.

pledger [pléÿœr], _s._ prendador.

pledget [pléÿet], _s._ taruguito; (cir.) tapón.

Pleiades [plíyadiŝ], _s._ (astr.) Pléyades.

Pleistocene [pláistosin], _s._ (geol.) pleistoceno.

plenarily [plínarili], _adv._ plenariamente.

plenary [plínari], _a._ plenario.

plenipotential [plénipoténŝhal], _a._ autorizado con poder pleno.

plenipotentiary [-ŝhieri], _s._ y _a._ plenipotenciario.

plenitude [plénitiud], _s._ plenitud, abundancia.

plenteous [pléntius], _a._ = PLENTIFUL.—**plenteously** [-li], _adv._ abundantemente.—**plenteousness** [-nes], _s._ abundancia.

plentiful [pléntiful], _a._ copioso, abundante; fértil, feraz.—**plentifuliy** [-i], _adv._ abundantemente, copiosamente.—**plentifulness** [-nes], _s._ abundancia, copia; fertilidad.

plenty [plénti]. **I.** _s._ copia, abundancia, profusión. **II.** _a._ (fam.) copioso, abundante.

plenum [plínum], _s._ pleno, plenitud, plétora.

pleochroism [plíocroiŝm], **pleochromatism** [plíocrómatiŝm], _s._ pleocroísmo, propiedad de variar de color según la dirección de la luz.

pleonasm [plíonæŝm], _s._ pleonasmo.—**pleonastic(al** [plionæstic(al], _a._ pleonástico.—**pleonastically** [-i], _adv._ pleonásticamente.

pleroma [plíróma], _s._ plenitud.

plesiosaur [plísiosor], _s._ (pal.) plesiosauro.— **Plesiosauria** [-sóriæ], **Plesiosauri** [-sórai], _s._ _pl._ orden de los plesiosaurianos.—**Plesiosaurus** [-ṷs], _s._ género de los plesiosauros.

plethora [plézora], _s._ plétora, exceso, hartura.

plethoric [plézoric], _a._ pletórico, repleto.

plethysmograph [pleziŝmogræf], _s._ pletismógrafo.

pleura [plúra], _s._ (anat.) pleura.—**pleural** [plúral], _a._ pleurítico; lateral.—**pleurisy** [plú-(o pliú) risi], _s._ (med.) pleuritis, pleuresía.—**pleuritic(al** [plurític(al], _a._ pleurítico.

pleurodynia [plurodínia], _s._ (med.) pleurodinia.

pleuron [plúron], _s._ (zool.) costado.

pleuropneumonia [plúroniumónia], _s._ (med.) pleuroneumonía.

pleurotomy [plurótomi], _s._ pleurotomía, incisión en la pleura.

plexiform [pléxiform], _a._ reticular, complicado.

pleximeter [plexímeter], _s._ pleximetro.

plexus [plécsṷs], _s._ trabazón, entreiazamiento, red; (anat.) plexo.

pliability [pláiabíliti], _s._ flexibilidad, docilidad.

pliable [pláiabœl], _a._ flexible; trefe; doblegable; dócil, manejable.—**pliableness** [-nes], **pliancy** [-pláiansi], _s._ flexibilidad, docilidad.

pliant [pláiant], _a._ flexible, doblegable, cimbreño; dócil, manejable.

plica [pláica], _s._ pliegue; (med.) plica.

plicate(d [pláiket(ed], _a._ (bot.) plegado.

plication [plikéiŝhṷn], _s._ plegadura, pliegue.

pliers [pláicerŝ], _s._ _pl._ alicates, tenacillas.

plight [pláit]. **I.** _va._ empeñar o dar (palabra); prometer en matrimonio, contraer esponsales. **II.** _s._ promesa, compromiso solemne; esponsales, promesa de matrimonio; situación, condición; apuro, aprieto.

plinth [plinz], _s._ (arq.) plinto, orlo.

Pliocene [pláiosin], _a._ (geol.) plioceno.

plod, _vn._ afanarse, trabajar con ahinco.

plodder [plódœr], _s._ trafagón.

plodding [plóding], _s._ tráfago.

plot. I. _s._ solar, parcela, porción de terreno; plano de un terreno; conspiración, complot; entruchada; plan, trama (de drama o novela). **II.** _va._ tramar, urdir, fraguar; hacer el piano o dibujo de; transportar al papel. **III.** _vn._ conspirar, maquinar.

plotter [plótœr], _s._ conspirador, conjurado; tramador, maquinador.

plotting [plóting]. **I.** _s._ dibujo de planos; representación gráfica. **II.** _a._ que conspira; para pianos o diagramas.—**p. paper**, papel cuadriculado.

plough [pláu], **ploughboy**, etc. = PLOW, PLOW-BOY, etc.

plover [plúvœr], _s._ (orn.) avefría.

plow [pláu]. **I.** _s._ arado.—**p. alms**, contribución a la iglesia por cada arado.—**p. beam**, pértigo del arado.—**p. colter**, o **coulter**, cuchilla del arado. —**p. cutter**= P. PRESS.—**p. handle**, esteva.— **p. knife**, (enc.) lengüeta.—**P. Monday**, primer lunes después de la Epifanía.—**p. pin**, telera.—**p. plane**, guillame, acanalador.—**p. press**, (enc.) ingenio.—**p. sole**, capa compacta de tierra formada por el arado en el fondo del surco.—**p. staff**, arrejada.

plowboy [pláuboi], _s._ yuguero, yuntero.

plower [pláucer], _s._ arador, surcador.

plowing [pláuing], _s._ aradura, labranza.

plowland [pláulænd], _s._ tierra labrantía o de pan llevar.

plowman [pláuman], _s._ arador, labrador; yuguero; patán, campesino.

plowpan [pláupæn], _s._ = PLOW SOLE. V. PLOW.

plowshare, **plowsock** [pláuŝheær, soc], _s._ reja de arado.

plowtail [pláutéil], _s._ mancera, mangorrillo.

plowwright [pláurrait], _s._ fabricante de arados.

pluck [plṷc]. **I.** _va._ coger, arrancar; desplumar; (fam.) dar calabazas en los exámenes. **II.** _vn._ (con at) tirar de, dar un tirón.—**to p. a bird's feathers**, desplumar.—**to p. up**, arrancar; cobrar, recobrar. **III.** _s._ valor, ánimo, resolución; tirón, estirón; asadura (hígado, corazón y bofes); reprobado (en los exámenes).

plucky [plṷki], _a._ animoso, denodado, resuelto.

plug [plṷg]. **I.** _s._ tapón, tarugo, taco; (arm.) obturador; (dent.) empastadura; espita; caña; porción de tabaco torcido; (fam.) rocín, penco; sombrero de copa; chistera.—**p. board**, (elec.) conmutador de clavijas.—**p. key**, (elec.) clavija de conexión.—**p. tobacco**, tabaco curado o torcido. **II.** _va._ atarugar, tapar; (dent.) orificar, empastar; (elec.) insertar una clavija de conexión.—**to p. melons**, calar melones, etc.

plugger [plṷgœr], _s._ orificador.

plum [plṷm], _s._ (bot.) ciruela; ciruelo; pasas para guisar; (fig.) golosina, gollería; lo mejor; la nata; (fam. Ingl.) la cantidad de £100,000; riquezas, fortuna.—**p. cake**, bizcocho con pasas. —**p. curculio**, (ent.) curculio, gorgojo.—**p. pie**, pastel de ciruelas o de pasas.—**p. pudding**, pudín inglés.—**p. tree**, ciruelo, cirolero.

plumage [plúmeÿ], _s._ plumaje; adorno.

plumagery [plúmeyri], _s._ plumajería.

plumb [plṷm]. **I.** _a._ perpendículo, a plomo; recto.—**off p.**, **out of p.**, no vertical, desviado de la vertical. **II.** _s._ plomada.—**p. bob**, plomo, plomada (pesa de ella).—**p. line**, tranquil.—**p. rule**, regla plomada. **III.** _adv._ a plomo, verticalmente. **IV.** _va._ sondar, sondear; (alb.) aplomar; instalar cañerías.

Plumbaginaceæ [plʊmbǽyinásii], *s. pl.* (bot.) plumbagíneas.

plumbago [plʊmbéigo], *s.* grafito, plombagina; (bot.) plumbagínea.

plumbean, *o* **plumbeous** [plúmbian, biʊs], *a.* plúmbeo, plomizo, plúmbico.

plumber [plʊ́mœr], *s.* plomero, emplomador; cañero, instalador de cañerías.

plumbic [plʊ́mbic], *a.* plúmbico.

plumbiferous [plʊmbíferʊs], *a.* plumbífero, que contiene plomo.

plumbing [plʊ́ming], *s.* arte u oficio del plomero; plomería, instalación de cañerías; sistema de cañerías interiores.

plumbum [plʊ́mbʊm], *s.* (farm.) plomo.

plumcot [plʊ́mcot], *s.* injerto de ciruelo y albaricoque.

plume [plum *o* pliúm]. **I.** *s.* pluma; plumaje, penacho, plumero.—**p. alum,** alumbre de pluma.—**p. maker,** plumista, plumario.—**p. of feathers,** plumero, penacho. **II.** *va.* adornar con plumas; desplumar; pelar; desbalijar. **III.** *vr.* jactarse o preciarse.

plumed [plumd], *a.* plúmeo, penachudo, empenachado.

plumeless [plúmles], *a.* implume.

plumicorn [plúmicorn], *s.* copete, penacho.

plumigerous [plumíyœrʊs], *a.* plumífero.

plumiped [plúmiped], *s.* ave calzada; (orn.) calzado.

plumist [plúmist], *s.* plumista, plumario.

plummet [plʊ́met], *s.* plomo, plomada, nivel; sonda, sondaleza.

plumose, plumous [plúmos, mʊs], *a.* plúmeo.

plump [plʊmp]. **I.** *a.* rollizo, regordete; brusco, claro, francote. **p.-faced,** carilleno. **II.** *adv.* de golpe; a plomo. **III.** *s.* grupo apretado; bandada de aves; espesura de árboles. **IV.** *va.* soltar, dejar caer, arrojar; engordar, hinchar. **V.** *vn.* caer a plomo; hincharse, engordar, llenarse.

plumpness [plʊ́mpnes], *s.* gordura, corpulencia.

plumpy [plʊ́mpi], *a.* gordo, lleno, rollizo.

plumula [plúmiula], *s.* (orn.) plúmula.

plumule [plúmiul], *s.* (orn. y bot.) plúmula.

plumy [plúmi], *a.* plumado, plumoso.

plunder [plʊ́ndœr]. **I.** *va.* despojar, saquear; expoliar. **II.** *s.* pillaje, saqueo, robo, botín.

plunderer [plʊ́ndœrœr], *s.* saqueador; ladrón.

plunge [plʊny]. **I.** *va.* zambullir, sumergir, chapuzar; ahocicar; meter, hundir; arrojar, precipitar. **II.** *vn.* sumergirse, zambullirse; precipitarse, arrojarse; saltar, lanzarse. **III.** *s.* sumersión, zambullida; chapuz; salto, arrojo, embestida.—**p. bath,** baño de inmersión; tanque para bañarse.

plungeon [plʊ́ndyʊn], *s.* (orn.) somorgujo.

plunger [plʊ́nyœr], *s.* buzo; (hidr.) émbolo buzo; (fam.) jugador o bolsista desenfrenado.—**p. pump,** bomba de émbolo buzo.

plunk [plʊnk]. **I.** *va.* (fam.) golpear o arrojar fuerte o repentinamente. **II.** *vn.* sonar como un golpe seco. **III.** *s.* (fam.) golpe fuerte; ruido seco y repentino; dólar.

pluperfect [plupœ́rfect], *a. y s.* (gram.) pluscuamperfecto.

plural [plúral], *a. y s.* plural.

pluralism [plúrališm], *s.* pluralidad; ocupación de más de un puesto o destino a un mismo tiempo; (filos.) pluralismo, doctrina que sostiene que existe más de una substancia última (opuesto al monismo).—**pluralist** [-ist], el que ocupa más de un puesto a un mismo tiempo; (filos.) pluralista, partidario del pluralismo.

plurality [pluráliti], *s.* pluralidad; mayoría (de votos).

pluralize [plúralaiš], *va.* pluralizar.

plurally [plúrali], *adv.* en plural.

plus [plʊs]. **I.** *a.* más; sobre cero; positivo.—**p. sign,** signo más. **II.** *s.* signo más; cantidad positiva.

plush [plʊšh]. **I.** *s.* (tej.) tripe, felpa. **II.** *a.* afelpado.

plushy [plúšhi], *a.* felpudo, afelpado.

plutarchy [plútarki], **plutocracy** [plutócrasi], *s.* plutocracia.

plutocrat [plútocræt], *s.* plutócrata.

plutocratic [plútocrǽtic], *a.* plutocrático.

Plutonian [plutónian]. **I.** *a.*plutónico. **II.** *s.* plutonista.

Plutonic [plutónic], *a.* plutónico.—**P. theory,** plutonismo.

Plutonist [plútonist], *s.* plutonista.

pluvial [plúvial]. **I.** *a.* pluvial. **II.** *s.* (igl.) capa pluvial.

pluviogram [plúviogræm], *s.* pluviograma, diagrama trazado por el pluviógrafo.

pluviograph [-græf], *s.* pluviógrafo, pluviómetro registrador.

pluviometer [pluviómetœr], *s.* pluviómetro.

pluviometric(al [plúviométric(al], *a.* pluviométrico.

pluvious [plúviʊs], *a.* pluvioso.

ply [plái]. **I.** *va.* trabajar en con ahinco; ejercer, practicar; emplear, ocupar; manejar (la aguja, el remo); importunar, acosar; propinar; atacar. **II.** *vn.* ir y venir, hacer viajes; estar constantemente ocupado o funcionando; solicitar o aguardar compradores; ir de prisa; (mar.) barloventear. **III.** *s.* pliegue, doblez; propensión, inclinación; capa (de tela, etc.).

pneuma [niúma], *s.* respiración, aliento; espíritu.

pneumatic(al [niumǽtic(al], *a.* neumático.—**p. tire,** neumático, llanta neumática.

pneumatics [niumǽtics], *s.* neumática.

pneumatology [niumatóloyi], *s.* neumatología, tratado sobre las cosas espirituales.

pneumatometer [niúmætómetœr], *s.* neumatómetro.

pneumatosis [-tósis], *s.* neumatosis.

pneumobacillus [niúmobǽsilʊs], *s.* neumobacilo, bacilo de Friedländer.

pneumococcus [-cócʊs], *s.* neumococo.

pneumogastric [-gǽstric]. **I.** *a.* neumogástrico. **II.** *s.* nervio neumogástrico.

pneumograph [-graf], *s.* (med.) neumatógrafo.

pneumonia [niumónia], *s.* (med.) neumonía, pulmonía.

pneumonic [niumónic], *a.* neumónico, pulmonar; pulmoníaco.

pneumothorax [niúmozóræx], *s.* acumulación de aire o gases en la cavidad pleural.

poa [póa], *s.* (bot.) poa, género de gramíneas.

Poaceæ [poéisii], *s. pl.* gramíneas.—**poaceous** [poéišhʊs], *a.* gramíneo.

poach [póuch]. **I.** *va.* (coc.) escalfar (huevos); robar caza de algún vedado; invadir; meterse en un fangal. **II.** *vn.* cazar o pescar en vedado; encenagarse un terreno.

poacher [póuchœr], *s.* el que roba caza o pesca en vedado.—**poaching** [-ing], *s.* hurto de caza en vedado.

pochard [póuchard], *s.* (orn.) pato de mar.

pock [poc], *s.* pústula, postilla.

pocket [póket]. **I.** *s.* bolsillo, faltriquera; cavidad, receptáculo; (min.) depósito de pepitas de oro; nasa para pescados.—**p. edition,** edición de bolsillo.—**p. flap,** (sast.), golpe, cartera.—**p. handkerchief,** pañuelo de bolsillo.—**p. money,** alfileres, dinero para gastos particulares.—**p. picking,** ratería de carterista, robo de faltriquera.—**p. pistol,** pistolete, cachorro.—**in p.,** con ganancia.—**out of p.,** con pérdida. **II.** *va.* embolsar, embolsillar; tomar, apropiarse; tragarse (una injuria).

pocketbook [-búc], *s.* portamonedas; cartera.

pocketful [-ful], *s.* bolsillado, lo que cabe en un bolsillo.

pocketknife [-náif], *s.* cortaplumas, cuchilla.

pockiness [pókines], *s.* cacaraña.

pockmark [pócmarc], *s.* cacaraña.

pockmarked, [-d], *a.* picado de viruelas.

pocky [póki], *a.* cacarañoso; sifilítico.

pod. **I.** *s.* (bot.) vaina (de legumbre), cápsula de una planta; manada; ranura o canal longitudinal.—**p. auger,** broca de media caña. **II.** *vn.* llenarse, hincharse; criar vainas.

podagra [pódǽgra], s. (med.) podagra, gota.
podagric(al [pódǽgric(al], a. gotoso.
podesta [podéstæ], s. podesta, primer magistrado.
podium [pódiʊm], s. (arq.) podio; (anat. y zool.) pie; (bot.) sostén, peciolo.
podometer [podómetœr], s. podómetro.
podophyllin [pódofīllin], s. (quím.) podofilina.
Podophyllum [pódofīlʊm], s. (bot.) género de los podofilos.
poem [póem], s. poema; poesía, composición poética.
poesy [póesi], s. poesía; arte poética.
poet [póet], s. poeta.—**p. laureate**, poeta laureado.
poetaster [póetǽstœr], s. poetastro.
poetess [póetes], s. poetisa.
poetic(al [poétic(al], a. poético.—**p. vein**, vena, numen poético.
poetically [poéticali], adv. poéticamente.
poetics [poétics], s. arte poética.
poetize [póetaiš], vn. poetizar.
poetry [póetri], s. poética; poesía.
pogrom [pogróm], s. (Rusia) pogrom, asonada de asesinato y despojo de los judíos instigada por el gobierno.
poh [po], interj. ¡puf! ¡bah! ¡quiá!
poignancy [póinansi], s. acerbidad.—**poignant** [-ant], a. acerbo, punzante, mordaz.—**poignantly** [-li], adv. acremente, mordazmente.
point. **I.** s. punto (en casi todas sus acepciones); punta; herramienta puntiaguda (como un buril, punzón); (Ingl. f. c.) aguja (en plural, cambiavía); agujeta; punta (de tierra), promontorio; peculiaridad, rasgo característico; grado (de una escala); sazón, ocasión, momento crítico; agudeza, sal, chiste ingenioso; instante, momento; (mar.) rumbo; en ciertos juegos, punto, tanto; (com.) entero, en la fluctuación de los valores; (gram.) cualquier signo de puntuación; (impr.) punto tipográfico (unidad de medida); rabo, cola de un animal.—**p. (lace)**, encaje hecho con aguja.—**p. at issue**, punto en cuestión.—**p. of honor**, cuestión de honor.—**p. of inflexion**, (geom.) punto de inflexión.—**p. of law**, cuestión de derecho.—**p. of order**, cuestión de procedimiento, recurso al reglamento.—**p. of view**, punto de vista.—**p. system**, (impr.) sistema de medida por puntos.—**at all points**, por todos lados, enteramente.—**at the p. of death**, en artículo de muerte.—**at the p. of the sword**, a hierro y sangre, por la fuerza.—**in p.**, al caso, a propósito; en cuestión, de que se trata.—**in p. of**, en cuanto a, tocante a.—**in p. of law**, como cuestión de derecho, desde el punto de vista del derecho.—**on the p. of**, a punto de.—**to give points**, dar tantos (en el juego); dar información útil.—**to the p.** = IN P. **II.** va. aguzar, sacar punta; (con **at**, o a **toward**) apuntar, señalar; indicar; encarar, dirigir, asestar; (gram.) puntuar; (alb.) unir con mortero, rellenar (juntas), llenar, fijar. **III.** vn. (con **out**) apuntar, señalar; parar, mostrar la caza.
pointblank [póintblanc]. **I.** a. horizontal; directo, claro, categórico. **II.** adv. a quema ropa; directamente, en línea recta; categóricamente, sin ambajes. **III.** s. tiro a quema ropa, tiro asestado.
pointed [póinted], a. puntiagudo, aguzado; picante, satírico; directo, acentuado; (arq.) ojival, apuntado.—**pointedly** [-li], adv. sutilmente; mordazmente; categóricamente.—**pointedness** [-nes], s. agudeza, aspereza, acrimonia.
pointer [póintœr], s. indicador, índice; manecilla (de reloj), apuntador, puntero; punta, buril; (f. c.) palanca de aguja o cambiavía; perro de muestra, ventor, pachón, braco.—pl. (astr.) las dos estrellas de la Osa Mayor que indican la polar.
pointing [póinting], s. afiladura, aguzadura; señalamiento, indicación; puntuación; (alb.) mamposteado, relleno de juntas; puntería; maduración de un absceso; (mar.) rabo de rata.
pointless [póintles], a. obtuso, sin punta; insubstancial.
pointsman [póintsman], s. (Ingl. f. c.) guardaagujas.

poise [póiš]. **I.** s. equilibrio, contrapeso; balanza; reposo; porte, talante. **II.** vn. equilibrar; contrapesar, equiparar; sompesar; pesar; considerar; abrumar. **II.** vn. posarse, estar suspendido; dudar.
poison [póišʊn]. **I.** s. veneno.—**p. ash**, **p. dogwood**, **p. elder**, **p. ivy**, **p. oak**, **p. plant**, **p. sumac**, etc., variedades de árboles y plantas que causan erupción cutánea.—**p. nut**, nuez vómica.—**p.-pen letter**, paulina, carta anónima ofensiva. **II.** va. envenenar.
poisoner [-œr], s. envenenador.—**poisoning** [-ing], s. envenenamiento.—**poisonous** [-ʊs], a. venenoso.—**poisonousness** [-ʊsnes], s. venenosidad, toxicidad.
poitrel [póitrel], s. (arm.) antepecho.
poke [póuk]. **I.** s. empuje, empujón; hurgonada; hurgonazo; trangallo; hombre tardón; barjuleta, bolsa; saquito; (ict.) vejiga de aire.—**p. bonnet**, papalina de mujer de ala abovedada. **II.** va. picar, aguijonear; atizar, hurgar; asomar, sacar.—**to p. fun at**, burlarse, mofarse de.—**to p. the fire**, hurgar la lumbre; atizar el fuego. **III.** vn. rezagarse; andar a tientas.
poker [póukœr], s. atizador o atizadero, espetón; (fam.) duende; póker, juego de naipes.—**p. picture**, diseño hecho sobre madera con un hierro candente.
pokerish [[póukœriš], a. alarmante.
pokeweed [póukuíd], s. (bot.) hierba carmín, fitolaca.
poking [póuking], a. que sobresale; (fam.) despreciable, servil.
pok(e)y [póuki], a. (fam.) flojo, pesado, lento; (Ingl.) astroso; encogido, apretado.
polacca [poléca], **polacre** [-lácœr], s. (mar.) polacra.
Polander [póulændœr], s. polaco.
polar [póulœr], a. polar.—**p. bear**, oso blanco.—**p. coordinates**, coordenadas polares.—**p. curve**, curva dada en coordenadas polares.—**p. lights**, aurora (boreal o austral).
polarimeter [póularimetœr], s. polarímetro.
Polaris [poléris], s. la (estrella) polar.
polariscope [poláriscoup], s. polariscopio.
polarity [polériti], s. polaridad.
polarization [pólariséšhʊn], s. polarización.
polarize, **polarise** [pólaraiš], va. polarizar.
pole [póul]. **I.** s. (geog. y elec.) polo; pértiga, vara larga, palo largo, asta, paral, estaca; percha (medida); (top.) jalón; (**P-**), polaco.—**p. bean**, frijol de enrame, frijol trepador.—**p. of a coach**, lanza de coche, —**p. prop**, tentemozo. **II.** va. empujar con un palo; llevar, sostener con palos; armar con palos; (metal.) revolver o agitar con varas. **III.** vn. impeler un barco con pértiga.
poleax(e [póulæx], s. hachuela de mano.
polecat [póulcæt], s. (zool.) veso, mofeta.
polemic(al [polémic(al], a. polémico.
polemic, s. polémica; polemista.
polemics, s. polémica, dialéctica.
polemoscope [polémoscoup], s. polemoscopio.
polestar [póulstár], s. estrella polar.
police [políš]. **I.** s. policía. **II.** va. apostar polizontes; poner o mantener servicio de policía en.
policeman [-man], s. polizonte, policía, agente de policía.
policewoman [-úmæn], s. polizonta, policía (mujer).
policlinic [póliclínic], s. dispensario anexo a un hospital; policlínica.
policy [pólisi], s. prudencia, sagacidad; curso o plan de acción; política; regla, sistema; costumbre; póliza de seguro; especie de lotería.—**p. holder**, asegurado, tenedor de una póliza.
polish [póliš]. **I.** va. pulir, pulimentar; lustrar, dar lustre, embolar; educar; civilizar. **II.** vn. recibir lustre o pulimento. **III.** s. pulimento, lustre; cultura, urbanidad; barniz; betún o bola para zapatos; embolada, acción de embolar (zapatos).
Polish [póuliš], a. y s. polaco, polonés.
polished [pólišht], pp. y a. pulido, bruñido, refinado, culto.

polishedness [pólíśhtnes], *s.* bruñidura, tersura; cortesanía, urbanidad.

polisher [pólíśhœr], *s.* pulidor, pulidero.

polishing [pólíśhing], *a.* pulidor, de pulir.—**p. bed,** bruñidor o pulidor mecánico; mesa de pulir. **p. disk,** (dent.) disco pulidor.—**p. iron,** plancha o hierro de abrillantar.

polite [poláit], *a.* cortés, urbano, bien educado.— **politely** [-li], *adv.* cortésmente.—**politeness** [-nes], *s.* urbanidad, buena crianza.—**for p.' sake,** por cortesía; por política.

politic [pólitic], *a.* político; sagaz, astuto, hábil, ladino; apropiado, atinado.

political [pólítical], *a.* político.—**p. economy,** economía política.

politically [pólíticali], *adv.* políticamente.

politician [pólitíśhan], *s.* politicastro, politiquero; político.

politics [pólitics], *s. pl.* política.

polity [póliti], *s.* constitución política, forma de gobierno; política.

polka [pólka], *s.* (danz. y mús.) polca.

poll [pol]. **I.** *s.* cabeza; persona; nómina, padrón, empadronamiento; matrícula; lista electoral; votación; cotillo de destral o martillo; lugar donde se vota, urnas electorales.—**p. evil,** úlcera en la nuca (de un caballo).—**p. tax,** capitación. **II.** *va.* empadronar, matricular, registrar; dar o recibir (votos); someter a la votación de; determinar los votos de; escrutar; descabezar; podar, desmochar; descornar. **III.** *vn.* votar en las elecciones.

pollack, [pólac], *s.* (ict.) abadejo.

pollard [pólard]. **I.** *s.* árbol desmochado o descopado; res descornada; (ict.) coto; salvado. **II.** *va.* desmochar, podar.

pollen [pólen], *s.* (bot.) polen.—**p. mass,** polinia.

pollex [pólex], *s.* pólice, pulgar.

pollinate [pólineit], *va.* (bot.) polinizar, fecundar con polen; fecundar.—**pollination** [-néiśhon], *s.* polinación, polinización; fecundación.

polling [póling], *s.* votación; escrutinio.—**p. booth, p. place,** lugar de votación, urna (en el sentido general, que comprende la urna y el lugar en que se halla).

pollinium [pólíniɴm], *s.* (bot.) polinea, masa coherente de granos de polen.

polliwig, polliwog [póliuig, uog], *s.* (fam.) renacuajo.

pollock [póloc], *s.* =POLLACK.

pollute [polút *o* poliút], *va.* manchar, ensuciar; contaminar o corromper; violar, deshonrar; profanar, mancillar.

pollutedness [polútednes], **pollution** [polúśhɴn], *s.* polución, corrupción, contaminación; violación.

polluter [polútœr], *s.* corruptor, contaminador; violador; profanador.

Pollux [pólʊx], *s.* (astr.) Pólux.

Polly [póli], *s. dim.* de MARY: (fam.) Mariquita; cotorra, lorito.

polo [pólo], *s.* (dep.) polo (juego.)

polonaise [polonéś], *s.* (sast.) polonesa; (mús.) polaca.

polonium [pólóniʊm], *s.* (quím.) polonio.

poltroon [poltrún], *s.* poltrón, cobarde, pusilánime; mandria, haragán.

poltroonery [poltrúneri], *s.* cobardía.

poly [póli], *s.* (bot.) zamarrilla.

polyandry [póliéndri], *s.* poliandria.

polyandrous [póliéndrʊs], *a.* poliándrico; (bot.) poliandro.

polyanthus [-énzʊs], *s.* (bot.) primavera.

polyarchy [-arki], *s.* poliarquía.

polyatomic [-atómic], *a.* poliatómico.

polybasic [-béisic], *a.* (quím.) polibásico.

polycarpous [-cárpʊs], *a.* (bot.) policarpio.

polychroism [-croiśm], *s.* policroísmo.

polychromatic [-crométic], *a.* policromático.

polychrome [-cróum], *s.* obra policroma.— **polychromic** [-crómic], *a.* policromo.

polyclinic [-clínic], *s.* hospital; escuela de clínica.

polygala [polígælæ], *s.* (bot.) polígala.—**Polygalaceæ** [póligæléisii], *s. pl.* poligáleas.

polygamist [poligamist], *s.*, **polygamous** [-mʊs], *a.* polígamo.

polygamy [polígami], *s.* poligamia.

polygenesis [póliyénesis], *s.* (biol.) poligénesis, doctrina de la pluralidad de orígenes.

polygenetic [-yenétic], *a.* relativo a la poligénesis; de orígenes diversos.

polyglot [-ɡlot], *a.* poligloto.

polygon [-gon], *s.* polígono.

polygonal [polígonal], *a.* poligonal, polígono.

Polygonum [poligonʊm], *s.* género de las poligonáceas.

polygraph [póligræf], *s.* polígrafo.

polygraphic(al [-græfic(al], *a.* poligráfico.

polygraphy [polígrafi], *s.* poligrafía.

polygynous [políyinʊs], *a.* (bot.) poliginia.

polygyny [políyini], *s.* poligamia por parte del hombre, posesión de varias esposas.

polyhedral, polyhedrous, polyhedrical [pólijídral, drʊs, drical], *a.* poliédrico, poliedro.— **polyhedral angle,** ángulo poliedro.

polyhedron [pólijídron], *s.* poliedro·

polymeric [-méric], *a.* (quím.) polímero.—**polymerid** [-merid], *s.* cuerpo polímero.—**polymerism** [polimeríśm], *s.* polimerismo.

polymorph [pólimorf], *s.* (quím.) ser u organismo polimorfo.

polymorphism [-mórfíśm], *s.* (quím.) polimorfismo.

polymorphous, polymorphic [-mórfʊs, fic], *a.* polimorfo.

Polynesian [póliníýæn], *s.* y *a.* polinesio, polinesiano.

polynomial [pólinómial]. **I.** *a.* de varios términos. **II.** *s.* (mat.) polinomio; vocablo científico compuesto de más de dos palabras.

polynuclear [-niúcliœr], *a.* polinuclear.

polyp [pólip], *s.* pólipo, zoófito.

polypary [póliperi], *s.* polipero.

polypetalous [-pétalʊs], *a.* polipétalo.

polyphase [-féiś], *a.* (elec.) polifásico.

polyphonism [polifoníśm], *s.* variedad de sonidos.

polypody [pólipodi], *s.* (bot.) polipodio.

polypous [pólipʊs], *a.* poliposo.

polypus [pólipʊs], *s.* (med.) pólipo.

polyscope [póliscoup], *a.* poliscopio.

polysepalous [-sépalʊs], *a.* polisépalo.

polyspermous [-spérmʊs], *a.* (bot.) polispermo, polispermático.

polysyllabic(al [-silæbic(al], *a.* polisílabo.

polysyllable [-sílabœl], *s.* polisílabo.

polysyndeton [-síndeton], *s.* (ret.) polisíndeton.

polytechnic [-técnic]. **I.** *a.* politécnico. **II.** *s.* escuela politécnica; exhibición industrial.

polytheism [-ziíśm], *s.* politeísmo.—**polytheist** [-zíist], *s.* politeísta.—**polytheistic(al** [-zíistic(all, *a.* politeísta.

polyuria [póliiúriæ], *s.* poliuria, secreción excesiva de orina.—**polyuric** [-ric], *a.* poliúrico.

polyzoan [-śóan]. **I.** *a.* compuesto de zoófitos. **II.** *s.* individuo de un cuerpo compuesto de zoófitos.

pomace [púmes], *s.* bagazo de manzanas exprimidas.

pomaceous [poméíśhʊs], *a.* (bot.) pomáceo.

pomade [poméid], *s.* pomada.

pomato [pomato], *s.* injerto de papa y tomate.

pomatum [poméitʊm], *s.* pomada; manteca.

pome [póum], *s.* pomo, fruta de pipa.

pomegranate [pómgrænet], *s.* (bot.) granada.— **p. tree,** granado.

pomelo [pómelo], *s.* (bot.) toronja.

pomiferous [pomíferʊs], *a.* pomífero.

pommel [púmel]. **I.** *s.* pomo (de un arzón, de una espada o de un cañón); culata; (arq.) perilla, bolilla. **II.** *va.* cascar, aporrear.

pomological [pomolóyical], *a.* pomológico.

pomologist [pomóloyist], *s.* pomólogo.

pomology [pomóloyi], *s.* pomología.

pomp, s. pompa, fausto.
pompadour [pómpadur], s. copete. ,
pompano [pompáno], s. (ict.) pámpano, salpa.
Pompeian [pompían o pompéian], a. pompeyano.
pompelmous [pómpelmŭs], s. (bot.) toronja.
pompom [pómpóm], s. cañón automático.
pomposity [pompósitij], **pompousness** [pómpŭsnes], s. fausto, pompa, ostentación; afectación.
pompous [pómpŭs], a. pomposo, ostentoso.
pompously [-li], adv. pomposamente.
pond [pond], s. charca, laguna, laguillo.—**p. lily** = WATER LILY.
ponder [póndœr]. I. va. pesar, estudiar, examinar. II. vn. (con on o over) considerar, reflexionar (acerca de).
ponderable [póndœrabœl], a. ponderable.
ponderosity [póndœrósitij], s. ponderosidad; pesadez, aridez.
ponderous [póndœrŭs], a. ponderoso, pesado; voluminoso; tedioso, cansado.—**ponderousness** [-nes], s. pesadez; aridez, sequedad, pesadez (de estilo).—**ponderously** [-li], adv. pesadamente.
poniard [póniard]. I. s. puñal. II. va. apuñalar.
pontage [póntey], s. pontazgo, pontaje.
pontee [pontí], s. = PONTIL.
Pontic [póntic], a. póntico.
pontifex [póntifex], s. pontífice, sumo sacerdote (apl. esp. al de los antiguos romanos).
pontiff [póntif], s. pontífice.
pontific(al [pontífic(al], a. pontifical; pontificio, papal.—**p. mass**, misa pontifical.
pontifical, s. pontifical.—pl. pontificales.
pontifically [pontíficali], adv. pontificalmente.
pontificate [pontífiket], s. pontificado.
pontil [póntil], **ponty** [pónti], s. (vid.) pontil, puntel.
ponto(o)n [pontún], s. (mil.) pontón; (mar.) chata, barcaza.—**p. bridge**, puente de barca o pontones.
pony [pouni]. I. s. haca, caballito; (fam.) clave o traducción empleada a hurtadillas en un examen; copa o vaso pequeños. II. va. (fam.) traducir con clave o ayuda en un examen. III. vn. (con up) pagar. IV. a. pequeño.—**p. engine**, locomotora de maniobras.—**p. truck**, bogie Bissel, truck o bogie articulado.—**p. truss**, puente bajo sin refuerzos transversales superiores.
poodle [púdœl], s. perro de lanas.
pooh [pu], interj. ¡bah! ¡fu!
pooh-pooh [pú-pú], va. y vn. desdeñar; hacer mofa.—**p.-p. theory**, la teoría de que el lenguaje tuvo su origen en interjecciones.
pool [pul]. I. va. formar una polla; pagar a escote; mancomunar intereses.—**to p. issues**, conciliar diferencias. II. vn. formar un charco. III. s. charco, lagunajo; alberca, balsa; hoya, rebalsa; en ciertos juegos, polla; en el billar, piña, truco; fusión de intereses o de empresas; combinación para especular en fondos o valores públicos.—**p. room**, sala de apuestas, donde se apuesta a carreras, etc. verificadas en otro lugar; sala de trucos.
poop [pup]. I. s. (mar.) popa o toldilla.—**p. ladder**, escala de popa.—**p. royal**, (mar.) chopeta, imperial. II. va. empopar.
poor [púœr]. I. a. pobre; falto, escaso; en mal estado; de poco valor, de poco mérito; malo; de mala calidad; indispuesto, malo, enfermizo.—**p. box**, cepillo de pobres.—**p. devil**, pobre diablo.—**p. laws**, leyes de pobres o acerca de los pobres.—**p. rate**, contribución a la iglesia para limosnas; tasa o contribución para socorrer a los pobres.—**p.-spirited**, abatido, cobarde.—**p.-spiritedness**, poquedad, cobardía, pusilanimidad.—**p. thing**, pobrecito, pobrecilla.—**a p. horse**, un penco.—**a p. night**, una mala noche.—**a p. opinion of one**, mala opinión de uno. II. s. **the p.**, los pobres.
poorfarm [-fárm], **poorhouse** [-jaus], s. hospicio, casa de caridad o de beneficencia.
poorly [-li]. I. adv. pobremente; malamente.—**p. off**, escaso de dinero. II. a. (fam.) indispuesto, enfermizo.
poorness [-nes], s. pobreza, carestía; deficiencia.

pop. I. s. chasquido, ruido seco, detonación; pistoletazo, taponazo; bebida gaseosa; (fam.) concierto popular.—**p. corn**, palomitas de maíz. II. va. soltar, espetar, disparar; chasquear, hacer saltar un tapón.—**to p. the question**, (fam.) hacer una declaración de amor; pedir en matrimonio. III. vn. entrar o salir de sopetón; saltar un tapón; dar un chasquido, detonar.—**to p. off**, (fam.) morir.
pope [póup], s. papa.—**p.'s head**, (Ingl.) escobillón para limpiar bóvedas.—**p.'s nose**, obispillo o rabadilla de ave.
popedom [póupdŭm], s. papado, papazgo.
popery [póupœri], s. (despec.) papismo.
popgun [pópgŭn], s. cerbatana, tirabala.
popinjay [pópinye], s. pisaverde; galancete; (orn.) loro, papagayo; picamaderos.
popish [póupiśh], a. papal, papista.
poplar [póplar], s. (bot.) álamo.
poplin [póplin], s. (tej.) papelina.
popliteal [poplítial, poplíteal], a. poplíteo.
poppet [pópet], s. válvula de movimiento vertical (llám. t. **p. valve**); (mar.) columna de basada.
poppy [pópi], s. (bot.) adormidera, amapola.
poppycock [pópicóc], s. (fam.) farsa, música celestial, farándula.
populace [pópiules], s. pueblo; (despec.) populacho, chusma.
popular [pópiular], a. popular, democrático, comunero; populachero; preferido, en voga, favorecido.—**p. applause**, aura popular.
popularity [-kériti], s. popularidad, prestigio, aceptación o buena acogida general.
popularize [lараiś], va. popularizar, dar a conocer.
popularly [-larli], adv. popularmente.
populate [-let]. I. va. poblar. II. vn. multiplicarse, propagarse.
population [-léiśhŭn], s. población.
Populism [pópulŭm], s. (pol. E. U.) populismo, partido semisocialista.—**Populist** [-ist], s., **Populistic** [-ic], a. populista.
populous [-lŭs], a. populoso.—**populously** [-li], adv. con mucha gente.—**populousness** [-nes], s. abundancia de población.
porcate [pórket], a. surcado.
porcelain [pórselein], s. porcelana, loza fina.—**p. shell**, concha de Venus (marisco).
porcelane(ous [pórselein, léinius], a. de porcelana.
porch, s. pórtico, vestíbulo, atrio, porche, entrada, soportal; corredor, galería (del frente o los lados de una casa).
porcine [pórsin], a. porcuno, porcino.
porcupine [pórkiupain], s. puerco espín.
pore [póœr]. I. s. poro. II. vn. (con on, upon u over) escudriñar, estudiar escrupulosamente.
porgy [pórgui], s. (ict.) pargo.
poriness [póœrines], s. porosidad.
pork [porc], s. carne de puerco; (pol., fam.) favores políticos otorgados por funcionarios públicos, honores mamados, canonjías.—**p. barrel**, (pol., E. U., fam.) partidas de favoritismo provincial, destinadas a determinadas localidades prescindiendo del bien general.
porker [pórkœr], s. puerco.
pornograph [pórnogræf], s. pornografía.
pornographic [-gréfic], a. pornográfico.
pornographer [pórnógrafœr], s. pornógrafo.
pornography [pórnografi], s. pornografía.
porosity [porósiti], **porousness** [pórŭsnes], s. porosidad.
porous [pórŭs], a. poroso, esponjoso.
porphyritic(al [porfirític(al], a. porfídico.
porphyry [pórfiri], s. pórfido.
porpoise, porpus [pórpŭs], s. puerco marino, marsopa.
porridge [pórri], s. gachas, puches, potaje.
porringer [pórrinœer], s. escudilla.
port. I. s. puerto, porta, portañola, tronera; portal, puerta; (m. v.) lumbrera; (mar.) babor; porte, talante; vino de Oporto; porte, capacidad de un buque.—**p. bar**, obstrucción (natural o artificial) a la entrada de un puerto.

—**p. of call**, escala, puerto de arribada.—**p. of delivery**, puerto de destino.—**p. of entry**, puerto (marítimo o seco). **II.** *va.* y *vn.* llevar, cargar; (mar.) poner, o andar, a babor; (mil.) llevar un fusil terciado.

portable [pórtbœl], *a.* manual, portátil.—**p. engine**, máquina locomóvil.—**p. railroad**, ferrocarril portátil.

portableness [pórtbœlnes], *s.* propiedad de ser manual o portátil.

portage [pórteɣ], *s.* porte, portaje, portazgo; transporte, acarreo; carga.

portal [pórtal], *s.* (arq.) portal, portada; vestíbulo.

portcrayon [pórtcréion], *s.* portalápiz de pintor.

portcullis [portcúlis], *s.* (fort.) rastrillo.

Porte (The), *s.* la Puerta otomana.

portemonnaie [pórtmonnéi], *s.* portamonedas.

portend [porténd], *va.* pronosticar, presagiar.

portent [portént o pórtent], *s.* presagio, augurio, portento.

portentous [porténtus], *a.* ominoso, de mal agüero; prodigioso, portentoso.

porter [pórtœr], *s.* portador, porteador, mozo de servicio (en trenes, hoteles, etc.); portero; cerveza oscura.—**p.'s lodge**, portería.

porterage [pórtœreɣ], *s.* oficio de faquín; porte, portaje.

porterhouse [pórtœrjáus], *s.* cervecería; restaurante.—**p. steak**, (E.U.) biftek de solomillo y filete.

portfire [-fáiœr], *s.* lanzafuego, botafuego.

portfolio [portfólio], *s.* cartera, carpeta; (fig.) ministerio.

portico [pórtico], *s.* pórtico, porche, soportal, atrio.

porticoed [pórticod], *a.* provisto de pórtico, o de pórticos.

portière [portiéœr], *s.* cortina de puerta.

portion [pórshun]. **I.** *s.* porción, parte; cuota, dote. **II.** *va.* dividir, repartir; dotar.

portionless [pórshunles], *a.* indotado.

portliness [pórtlines], *s.* porte majestuoso.

portly [pórtli], *a.* rollizo, grueso; majestuoso, serio, grave.

portmanteau [portmǽnto], *s.* portamanteo, maleta ligera.

Porto Rican [pórtorrícan], *a.* y *s.* portorriqueño.

portrait [pórtret], *s.* retrato.—**p. painter**, retratista.

portraitist [-ist], *s.* retratista.

portraiture [pórtretiur o chur], *s.* retrato, pintura, bosquejo.

portray [portré], *va.* retratar, pintar.

portrayal [portréal], *s.* representación gráfica; descripción.

Portuguese [pórchuguís], *a.* y *s.* portugués.

portulaca [portiuléca o lǽka], *s.* (bot.) verdolaga.

pose [póus]. **I.** *va.* (b. a.) colocar en cierta actitud o postura; proponer, afirmar. **II.** *vn.* colocarse en cierta postura; fachendear; confundir con preguntas difíciles.—**to p. as**, pretender ser, darlas de. **III.** *s.* postura, posición, actitud.

poser [póusœr], *s.* pregunta o problema difícil; (Ingl) examinador; persona afectada o vanagloriosa.

posit [póusit], *va.* (lóg.) afirmar, proponer; disponer, colocar.

position [posíshun], *s.* posición; puesto, empleo.

positive [pósitiv]. **I.** *a.* positivo; absoluto, inherente; explícito, categórico; imperativo; escrito, convenido; (filos.) positivista; empírico, experimental; seguro, cierto, convencido; obstinado, terco, porfiado; (mat., elec., foto. gram.) positivo; (mec.) de acción directa, de transmisión rígida; de vaivén; de alimentación continua bajo presión (apl. a la lubricación); (aut.) de curvas concéntricas de giro, de Ackerman (apl. al sistema o eje por cuyo medio las ruedas interior y exterior describen arcos concéntricos en las curvas).—**p. law**, derecho positivo. **II.** *s.* realidad, certeza; (foto.) prueba positiva; (gram.) grado positivo de comparación; (elec.) plancha, polo, etc., positivos.

positively [-li], *adv.* positivamente, absolutamente; categóricamente; sin duda.

positiveness [-nes], o **positivity** [pósitíviti], *s.* seguridad, certeza; porfía.

positivism [-išm], *s.* positivismo; certeza, certidumbre.

positivist [-ist], *s.* positivista.

posse [póse], *s.* posibilidad; (fam.) pelotón; fuerza civil que el *sheriff* tiene autoridad de juntar para evitar desórdenes, tumultos, etc. (ll. t. **p. comitatus**).

possess [posés o posés], *va.* poseer; (como *vr.*), apoderarse, hacerse dueño; señorear, dominar; poner (a uno) en posesión.

possessed [posést], *pp.* poseso, poseído.—**one p.**, energúmeno.

possession [poséshun], *s.* posesión, dominio.—*pl.* patrimonio, propiedades, bienes.

possessive [posésiv], *s.* y *a.* posesivo.

possessor [posésœr], *s.* poseedor, posesor.

possessory [posésori], *a.* posesorio.

posset [póset], *s.* bebida de leche cuajada y mezclada con especias.

possibility [pósibíliti], *s.* posibilidad.

possible [-bœl], *a.* posible.

possibly [-bli], *adv.* posiblemente, quizá.

possum [pósum], *s.* (fam.) = OPOSSUM.

post [póust]. **I.** *s.* poste, pilar, paral; (mil.) puesto, plaza, guarnición, avanzada; empleo, destino, cargo; correo, posta, estafeta, ordinario, propio.—**p. bag**, mala, balija.—**p. card** = POSTAL CARD.—**p. chaise**, **p. coach**, silla de posta, coche de posta.—**p. horse**, caballo de posta. —**p. note**, billete de banco redimible en fecha dada pagaré circulante emitido por un banco.—**p. office**, casa de correos, administración de correos, estafeta.—**p.-office box**, apartado de correos.— **p. road**, camino de posta o correo. **II.** *adv.* con rapidez; por la posta; de prisa. **III.** *va.* anunciar, pegar o fijar (carteles); estigmatizar, infamar; apostar, situar; echar al correo o a la estafeta; pasar los asientos de un libro al libro mayor; (fam.) informar, tener al corriente. **IV.** *vn.* viajar en posta; (equit.) montar a la inglesa.

postage [póstey], *s.* porte de correos, franqueo; viaje en posta.—**p. stamp**, sello de correo, estampilla.

postal [póstal], *a.* postal.—**p. (card)**, tarjeta postal.—**p. convention**, convenio postal.—**p. note**, (E. U.) vale postal por menos de $5.—**p. order**, orden postal de pago.—**p. tube**, canuto para enviar papeles por correo.

postcard [-card], *s.* = POST CARD.

postdate [-déit]. **I.** *va.* posfechar. **II.** *s.* [póustdeit] posfecha.

postdiluvial, postdiluvian [-dilúvial, vian], *s.* y *a.* postdiluviano.

poster [póustœr], *s.* cartel, cartelón, papelón; fijador de carteles; correo; propio; caballo de posta.

posterior [postíricœr], *a.* posterior.—*pl.* nalgas.

posteriority [postirióriti], *s.* posterioridad.

posterity [postériti], *s.* posteridad.

postern [póstœrn], *s.* puerta trasera; (fort.) postigo, poterna.

postfix [póustfix]. **I.** *va.* añadir un sufijo. **II.** *s.* sufijo.

postgraduate [postgrédiueit]. **I.** *a.* de o para graduados (apl. a estudios superiores hechos después de recibir un grado). **II.** *s.* estudiante graduado que hace estudios superiores complementarios.

posthaste [postjéist]. **I.** *a.* urgente, apresurado. **II.** *s.* diligencia, presteza. **III.** *adv.* a toda prisa, a raja tabla.

posthouse [póustjáus], *s.* casa de postas.

posthumous [póstiumus o chumus], *a.* póstumo.

postil [póstil], *s.* postilla, apostilla.

postillate [póstilet], *va.* postilar.

postil(l)ion [postiliun], *s.* postillón.

postimpressionism [póstimpréshunišm], *s.* (b. a.) postimpresionismo.—**postimpressionist** [-ist], *s.* postimpresionista.

postliminium [postliminíum], **postliminy** [postlímini], s. (for.) postliminio.

postlude [póstlud o liud], s. (mús.) postludio.

postman [póustman], s. cartero.

postmark [póstmárk], s. sello o estampa de la oficina de correos.

postmaster [póstmǽstœr], s. administrador de correos.—**p. general**, director general de correos.

postmeridian [postmerídian], a. postmeridiano, de la tarde.

post mortem [post mórtem], adv. (Lat.) después de la muerte.—**p. m., examination**, necropsia, autopsia.

postnatal [postnéitæl], a. postnatal, de después del nacimiento.

postnuptial [-núpŝhal], a. posterior al matrimonio.

postoperative [-óperætiv], a. postoperatorio, de después de la operación.

postorbital [-órbitæl], a. postorbital (apl. esp. a la apófisis postorbital).

postpaid [-péid], a. porte pagado, franco de porte.

postpone [-póun], va. diferir, aplazar; postergar; posponer.—**postponement** [-mœnt], s. aplazamiento; postergación.

postprandial [-prándial], a. de sobremesa.—**p.** (speech), bríndis.

postscript [-script], s. posdata; alcance.

postulant [póschulant, o. tiulant], s. postulante; (igl.) novicio, postulador.

postulate [póstiuleit]. I. va. postular. II. s. postulado.—**postulation** [-léiŝhun], s. suposición, enunciado de una proposición que se da por sentada; (igl.) postulacion.

posture [póschur]. I. s. postura, actitud; situación, estado, disposición. II. va. y vn. poner(se) en alguna postura.

postwar [póstuór], a. de después de la guerra.

posy [póusi], s. ramillete de flores; mote o cifra en verso.

pot. I. s. marmita, olla; pote; piñata, cacharro, caldereta; orinal, tibor; cantidad contenida en una olla; en el juego, apuesta, puesta.—**p.-bellied, p.-belly**, panzudo, barrigón.—**p. cheese**, requesón.—**p. companion**, compañero de taberna.—**p. lead**, graftto.—**p. metal**, aleación de cobre y plomo; vidrio que se colora cuando está fundido.—**p. roast**, (coc.) carne asada en marmita.—**p.-valiant**, valeroso a fuerza de aguardiente. II. va. (coc.) estofar, cocer en olla; plantar en tiestos; conservar en potes. III. vn. tirar o disparar; beber, achisparse.

potable [pótæbœl]. I. a. potable. II. s. bebida.

potableness [-nes], s. potabilidad.

potash [pótæŝh], s. potasa (hidróxido de potasio, o potasa caústica); carbonato de potasio.

potassic [potǽsic], a. potásico.

potassium [potǽsium], s. (quím.) potasio.

potation [potéiŝhun], s. potación; bebida; trago.

potato [potéito], s. patata, papa.—**p. beetle, p. bug**, (ent.) dorífero.—**p. blight**, enfermedad de las patatas.—**p. oat**, avena geórgica.—**p. rot** = P. BLIGHT.—**a small p.**, (fam.) cosa o persona de poca monta, nonada, nulidad.

potboiler [pótbóiler], s. (fam.) obra artística o literaria hecha de prisa para ganarse la vida.

poteen [potín], s. whisky irlandés de contrabando.

potency [pótensi], s. potencia, fuerza; poder, influjo, autoridad.

potent [pótent], a. potente, poderoso.

potentate [pótentet], s. potentado.

potential [poténŝhal]. I. a. potencial, posible; virtual; (fís.) potencial; (gram.) potencial; eficaz, poderoso.—**p. energy**, energía potencial. II. s. (gram.) modo potencial; (fís.) potencial; (elec.) potencial, tensión.

potentiality [poténŝhaliti], s. potencialidad, capacidad.

potentially [poténŝhali], adv. potencialmente, virtualmente.

potentilla [pótentíllæ], s. (bot.) cincoenrama.

potentiometer [poténŝhiómetœr], s. (elec.) potenciómetro.

potently [pótentli], adv. potentemente, poderosamente.

potentness [pótentnes], s. potencia, poder.

pothanger [pótjéngœr], s. gramallera, llares.

pother [pódœr]. I. s. baraúnda, alboroto. II. va. y vn. atormentar, aturdir; alborotar.

potherb [pótœrb], s. hortaliza.

pothook [pótjúc], s. llares, gramallera; garabato.

pothouse [pótjáus]. I. s. taberna. II. a. de taberna.

potion [póŝhun], s. poción, brebaje, pócima.

potlid [pótlíd], s. cobertera o tapadera de olla.

potluck [pótlúc], s. comida ordinaria, sin preparación ni cumplidos.

potpie [pótpái], s. pastel de carne.

potpourri [pópurí], s. baturrillo.

potsherd [pótŝhœrd], s. tiesto, casco.

pottage [pótœy], s. potaje, menestra, acemita.

potter [pótœr], s. alfarero, ollero, alcarracero.—**p.'s clay**, barro de alfareros.—**p.'s field**, cementerio de los pobres, hoyanca—**p.'s ware**, alfarería, cacharros.—**p.'s wheel**, rueda de alfarero.

pottery [pótœri], s. alfarería; alfar, ollería; cacharros.

pottle [pótœl], s. pote, jarro, vaso; azumbre (medida), cesto para frutas.—**p.-bellied**, panzudo.

pouch [páuch]. I. s. saquito, bolsa; (bot.) silícula. II. va. embolsar; tragar, engullir. III. vn. hacer pucheritos, (Amér.) jerimiquear.

poudrette [pudrét], s. abono compuesto.

poulard [pulárd], s. polla capona.

poulterer [póltœrœr], s. pollero, gallinero.

poultice [póltis], s. cataplasma, emplasto. II. va. bizmar.

poultry [póltri], s. aves de corral.—**p. yard**, corral, gallinero.

pounce [páuns]. I. s. zarpada; zarpa, garra; grasa, grasilla.—**p. bag**, cisquero o muñequilla de estarcir.—**p.**, o **pouncet, box**, cajita agujereada para polvos de sandáraca, o para perfumes. II. va. y vn. agujerear; dar una pasada; agarrar; polvorear con grasilla; alisar (un sombrero) frotándolo.

pound [páund]. I. s. libra (peso de 16 onzas); libra esterlina; corral de concejo; depósito.—**p. breach**, soltura ilegal del ganado encerrado en el corral de concejo.—**p.-foolish**, gastador, derrochador.—**p. net**, nasa de pescar.—**p. sterling**, libra esterlina.—**p. weight**, peso de una libra. II. va. golpear, batir; machacar, majar, moler; encerrar; poner a buen recaudo.

poundage [páundey], s. derecho de tanto por libra de peso; costo de rescatar el ganado acorralado.

poundal [páundæl], s. unidad de fuerza que, obrando durante un segundo sobre una masa de 1 libra, le da la velocidad de 1 pie por segundo.

poundcake [páundkéic], s. bizcocho en que entra una libra de cada ingrediente.

pounder [páundœr], s. triturador; golpeador; majador, machacadera, pala de lavar la ropa. Usase en composición para denotar el número de libras: thirty-six pounder, cañón de a treinta y seis; six-pounder, pescado, bala, etc., de seis libras.

poundkeeper, poundmaster [-kípœr, -mǽstœr], s. guardián de un corral de concejo.

pour [pócr]. I. va. derramar; verter, vaciar; echar, emitir, arrojar; gastar pródigamente.—**to p. down**, vaciar con ron.—**to p. out of**, vaciar de. II. vn. fluir, correr, caer; llover a cántaros, diluviar; salir a borbotones.

pourer [pócrœr], s. trasegador, vaciador.

pourparler [pur par lé], s. coloquio, conferencia (esp. diplomática) inceremoniosa.

pout [páut]. I. s. pucherito; berrinche; (ict.) faneca. II. vn. hacer pucheritos; poner mal gesto, enfurruñarse; hinchar el pecho (apl. a las aves).

pouter [páutœr], s. hombre ceñudo; paloma buchona (ll. t. **p. pigeon**, o **pouting pigeon**).

poverty [póvœrti], s. pobreza.

powder [páudœr], s. pólvora; polvo; polvos de tocador; polvera.—**p. box**, polvorera.—**p. chamber**, (art.) cámara de la pólvora en una mina o un `arma' de fuego.—**p. magazine**, polvorín, santabárbara.—**p. room**, pañol de pólvora, santabárbara. **II.** *vn.* pulverizar; empolvar; polvorear, espolvorear. **III.** *vn.* pulverizarse: ponerse polvos.

powderflask [páudœrflæsc], **powderhorn** [-jórn], *s.* frasco para pólvora.

powdermill [-míl], *s.* fábrica de pólvora.

powdery [páudœri], *a.* polvoriento; empolvado; lleno de polvo; deleznable, quebradizo.

power [páucœr], *s.* potencia, virtud; fuerza, poder, poderío; autoridad; ascendiente, influjo; potencia (nación); fuerza mecánica (a distinción de fuerza de sangre); (mat.) potencia; (mec.) potencia; fuerza motriz; energía; (ópt.) potencia (de una lente).—**p. factor**, factor de potencia.—**p. house**, instalación o estación de energía o de fuerza motriz.—**p. of attorney**, (for.) poder, procuración.—**p. of the keys**, (igl.) llaves de la Iglesia.—**p. plant** = P. HOUSE; (aut.) motor y sus accesorios.—**p. transmission**, transmisión de energía.

powerful [-ful], *a.* poderoso, fuerte.—**powerfully** [-li], *adv.* poderosamente.—**powerfulness** [-nes], *s.* poder, potencia; fuerza.

powerless [-les], *a.* impotente.

powwow [páu-uáu]. **I.** *vn.* (entre los indios) conjurar las enfermedades con exorcismos; celebrar una junta; (fam. E. U.) deliberar con algarabía. **II.** *s.* curandero indio; exorcismo; baile, festín, holgorio; concilio.

pox, *s.* cualquiera enfermedad que causa erupciones pustulosas (sífilis, viruelas, etc.).

pozzolana [pótsolána], **pozzuolana** [pótsuolána], *s.* puzolana.

practicable [præcticabœl], *a.* practicable, factible, viable; accesible, transitable.

practicability [-bíliti], **practicableness** [-bœlnes], *s.* practicabilidad, factibilidad.—**practicably** [-bli], *adv.* posiblemente, prácticablemente.

practical [præctical], *a.* práctico; de hecho, real; positivo, prosaico (a distinción de ideal, espiritual, teórico, etc.).—**p. joke**, burla, chanza, chasco.

practicality [præcticæliti], *s.* calidad de práctico; cosa práctica; espíritu práctico.

practically [-li], *adv.* prácticamente; en la práctica; por la práctica; virtualmente, en realidad; casi, poco menos que (a veces se cambia el giro: *he is practically dead*, está casi muerto, puede darse por muerto; *this is practically a refusal*, esto es realmente una negativa. Éste es el uso más general del adverbio, y debe cuidarse de no traducirlo por *prácticamente*.)

practicalness [-nes], *s.* calidad de práctico.

practice, practise [præctis]. **I.** *s.* práctica, uso, costumbre; ejercicio; experiencia; sistema, regla, método; clientela. **II.** *va.* y *vn.* practicar, ejercitar(se); ejercer (una profesión); hacer ejercicios (en el piano, etc.); negociar secretamente.—**to p. at a target**, tirar al blanco.

practiser [præctisœr], *s.* practicante; el que ejerce una profesión; hombre artero.

practitioner [præctíshunœr], *s.* el que ejerce una profesión.

prænomen [prinómen], *s.* = PRENOMEN.

prætexta [pritéxtæ], *s.* pretexta.

pragmatic [prægmætic], *a.* práctico; pragmático, filosófico.—**p.**, o **p. sanction**, pragmática.—**pragmatical** [-al], *a.* entremetido, oficioso; activo, atareado; común o corriente.—**pragmatically** [-i], *adv.* impertinentemente; magistralmente.

pragmatism [prægmætism], *s.* (filos.) pragmatismo, doctrina que sostiene que el criterio de la verdad son los resultados prácticos.—**pragmatist** [-ist], *s.* pragmatista, partidario del pragmatismo.

prairie [præri], *s.* llanura, pradera.—**p. chicken**, (orn.) chocha.—**p. dog**, (zool.) aranata.

praise [preis]. **I.** *s.* alabanza, elogio, loor, encomio; fama, renombre. **II.** *va.* encomiar, alabar, ensalzar.

praiser [préisœr], *s.* loador, ensalzador.

praiseworthily [préisuœrpili], *adv.* laudablemente.—**praiseworthiness** [-nes], *s.* calidad de loable.—**praiseworthy** [-ɒi], *a.* digno de alabanza, laudable.

prance [prans], *vn.* cabriolar; trenzar.

prancer [pránsœr], *s.* caballo pisador.

prandial [prǽndial], *a.* perteneciente a una comida.

prank [prænk]. **I.** *va.* hermosear, adornar. **II.** *vn.* ataviarse con exceso. **III.** *s.* travesura, picardihuela, jugarreta.

prankish [prǽnkish], *a.* travieso, retozón.

praseodymium [préisiodímium], *s.* (quím.) praseodimio.

prate [preit]. **I.** *va.* charlar. **II.** *s.* charla.

prater [préitœr], *s.* hablador, charlatán.

pratique [pratíc], *s.* (mar.) libre plática.

prattle [prǽtœl]. **I.** *va.* balbucear. **II.** *vn.* charlar, parlotear. **III.** *s.* parlería, charla.

prattler [prǽtlœr], *s.* charlador, parlanchín.

prawn [pron], *s.* camarón.

praxis [præcsis], *s.* práctica, ejercicio; crestomatía. **II.** *vn.* rezar, orar. Se emplea como forma de cortesía en el sentido de "sírvase," "si me hace el favor," "sírvase decirme," "decidme," etc.: (*I) pray, where is the station?* ¿me hace el favor de decirme dónde es la estación? *how can we do this, pray?* sírvase decirme cómo podemos hacer esto.

prayer [préœr], *s.* oración, rezo; súplica, ruego.—**p. book**, devocionario.—**p. desk**, reclinatorio.—**p. meeting**, reunión para ejercicios espirituales.

prayerful [-ful], *a.* piadoso, devoto.—**prayerfulness** [-nes], *s.* devoción; inclinación a rezar.—**prayerless** [-les], *a.* sin rezo; que no reza.

preach [prich], *va.* y *vn.* predicar.—**preacher** [-œr], *s.* predicador.—**preaching** [-ing], *s.* predicación.—**preachment** [príchmœnt], *s.* prédica, plática o sermón; arenga.

preacquaint [príæcuéint], *va.* comunicar o advertir de antemano.—**preacquaintance** [-ans], *s.* conocimiento previo.

preadamite [priǽdamait], **preadamitic** [-mític], *a.* y *s.* preadamita.

preamble [priǽmbœl], *s.* preámbulo.

prearrange [priarrény], *va.* arreglar de antemano.

prebend [prébend], *s.* (igl.) prebenda; prebendado.—**prebendal** [-al], *a.* perteneciente a la prebenda.—**prebendary** [-æri], *s.* prebendado.

Pre-Cambrian [pri-cǽmbriæn], *s.* y *a.* (geol.) precambriano, precámbrico.

precarious [prekérius], *a.* precario; peligroso, arriesgado.—**precariously** [-li], *adv.* precariamente.—**precariousness** [-nes], *s.* calidad de precario.

precast [pricǽst], *a.* prevaciado, llevado hecho a la obra (ap. a construcciones y artefactos de hormigón, etc. hechos por sí mismos fuera de la obra y luego llevados a ella).

precaution [pricóshun], *s.* precaución.

precautionary [-æri], *a.* de precaución.

precede [prisíd]. **I.** *va.* anteceder, preceder; sobresalir; anteponer. **II.** *vn.* ir delante; tener la primacía; preceder.

precedence [prisídens], **precedency** [prisídensi], *s.* prioridad, anterioridad, antelación; precedencia, superioridad.

precedent [présedent]. **I.** *s.* precedente; (for.) decisión judicial que forma jurisprudencia. **II.** *a.* [président], precedente.

preceding [prisíding], *a.* precedente, anterior.

precentor [preséntœr], *s.* chantre, capiscol.

precept [prísept], *s.* precepto.

preceptive [preséptiv], *a.* preceptivo.

preceptor [preséptœr], *s.* preceptor.

preceptress [preséptres], *s.* preceptora.

precession [preséshun], *s.* precedencia; (astr.) precesión.

precinct [prísinct], *s.* recinto; distrito, barriada.

precious [préshus]. **I.** *a.* precioso, preciado; de gran valor; caro, querido, amado.—**p. opal** = NOBLE OPAL.—**p. stones**, piedras preciosas. **II.** *adv.* (fam.) muy.

preciously [-li], *adv.* preciosamente.

preciousness [-nes], *s.* preciosidad.

precipice [présipis], *s.* precipicio.

precipitable [presípitabœl], *a.* que puede precipitarse.

precipitance, precipitancy [-tans, -si], *s.* precipitación.

precipitant [-tant]. **I.** *a.* precipitado, arrojado, arrebatado. **II.** *s.* (quím.) precipitante.

precipitantly [-li], *adv.* precipitadamente.

precipitate [-tet]. **I.** *va.* precipitar, arrojar; acelerar, apresurar; (quím.) precipitar. **II.** *vn.* precipitarse, despeñarse, arrojarse; (quím.) precipitarse. **III.** *a.* precipitado, atropellado. **IV.** *s.* (quím.) precipitado.

precipitately [-li], *adv.* precipitadamente.

precipitation [presipitéishun], *s.* precipitación; derrumbamiento; rocío; cantidad de agua de lluvia.

precipitin [presípitin], *s.* (bact.) precipitina, substancia de la sangre que precipita las bacterias.

precipitous [presípitus], *a.* precipitoso, escarpado; arrojado.

precise [prisáis], *a.* preciso, exacto; justo, ni más ni menos; estricto, quisquilloso, escrupuloso; propio, mismísimo, idéntico.

precisely [-li], *adv.* precisamente, exactamente; justamente, cabalmente; formalmente.

preciseness [-nes], *s.* precisión, exactitud; escrupulosidad.

precisian [presíyæn], *s.* rigorista; formulista.

precision [presíyun], *s.* precisión, exactitud; escrupulosidad.

preclude [preclúd], *va.* evitar, impedir; excluir.

precocious [precóshus], *a.* precoz.—**precociousness** [-nes], **precocity** [precósiti], *s.* precocidad.

precognition [pricogníshun], *s.* precognición.

preconceit [priconsít], *s.* = PRECONCEPTION.

preconceive [priconsív], *va.* concebir, opinar o imaginar de antemano.

preconception [-sépshun], *s.* prejuicio, concepto anticipado.

preconcert [priconsсert]. **I.** *va.* concertar de antemano. **II.** *s.* [pricónscert] acuerdo previo.

preconization [príconiséshun], *s.* preconización.

preconsign [priconsáin], *va.* consignar anteriormente.

precontract [pricontréct]. **I.** *va.* contratar con anterioridad. **II.** *s.* [pricóntræct] contrato anticipado.

precordial [pricórdial], *a.* precordial.

precursive, precursory [pricсersiv, sori], *a.* precursor.

precursor [pricсersœr], *s.* precursor.

predaceous [pridéshus], **predatory** [prédatori], *a.* de rapiña, de presa, rapaz, voraz.

predeceased [pridesíst], *a.* muerto antes que otro.

predecessor [prideséscœr], *s.* predecesor.

predestinarian [predéstinérian], *a.* y *s.* partidario de o relativo a la doctrina de la predestinación.—**predestinarianism** [-ism], *s.* fatalismo, doctrina de la predestinación.—**predestinate** [-eit]. **I.** *va.* predestinar. **II.** *a.* y *s.* predestinado.—**predestination** [-éshun], *s.* predestinación.—**predestinator** [-eitcœr], *s.* predestinante.—**predestine** [-tin], *va.* predestinar.

predeterminate [pridetcérminet], *a.* predeterminado.—**predetermination** [-éishun], *s.* predeterminación.—**predetermine** [-min], *va.* predeterminar, prefijar.

predial [prídial], *a.* predial.

predicable [prédicæbœl]. **I.** *a.* predicable. **II.** *s.* (lóg.) predicable, categorema.

predicament [predícamœnt], *s.* predicamento; clase, categoría.

predicate [prédiket]. **I.** *va.* afirmar un predicado. **II.** *vn.* afirmarse. **III.** *s.* (gram. y lóg.) predicado, atributo.

predication [-kéishun], *s.* afirmación, aserción; proclama.

predict [predíct], *va.* predecir, pronosticar.

prediction [predícshun], *s.* predicción, pronóstico.

predictive [predíctiv], *a.* que predice.

predigest [prídaiyést], *va.* digerir artificialmente, peptonizar.

predigestion [prídiyéschun], *s.* digestión artificial o peptonización del alimento.

predilection [pridilécshun], *s.* predilección.

predispose [pridispóus], *va.* predisponer.

predisposition [pridíspoшíshun], *s.* predisposición, propensión.

predominance, predominancy [predóminans, i], *s.* predominio; ascendiente, influencia.

predominant [-ant], *a.* predominante.

predominate [predómineit], *va.* predominar, prevalecer.

preëminence [priéminens], *s.* preeminencia, supremacía.—**preëminent** [-ent], *a.* preeminente, supremo; extraordinario, superlativo.—**preëminently** [-li], *adv.* preeminentemente; sumamente, extraordinariamente.

preëmpt [priémpt]. **I.** *va.* (E. U.) asegurar el derecho de prioridad en la compra de terrenos públicos. **II.** *vn.* apropiarse terreno por derecho de prioridad.—**preëmptible** [-bœl], *a.* sujeto al derecho de prioridad.—**preëmption** [-shun], *s.* derecho de prioridad.—**preëmptor** [-cœr], *s.* el que adquiere derecho de prioridad.

preen [prín], *va.* limpiar y componer sus plumas las aves.

preëngage [prienguéy], *va.* apalabrar.

preëstablish [priestæblish], *va.* preestablecer.

preëxist [priegsíst], *vn.* preexistir.—**preëxistence** [-ens], *s.* preexistencia.—**preëxistent** [-ent], *a.* preexistente.

preface [préfes]. **I.** *s.* prefacio, prólogo. **II.** *va.* poner un prólogo a un libro; hacer un exordio a, decir por vía de introducción a, empezar. **III.** *vn.* empezar.

prefatory [préfatori], *a.* preliminar; por vía de introducción.

prefect [prífect], *s.* prefecto.

prefecture [préfectiur], *s.* prefectura.

prefer [prefсer], *va.* (con **to** o **above**) preterir; elevar, exaltar, adelantar, ascender; presentar ofrecer; dar preferencia, v. gr. a un acreedor.—**preferred shares, o stock,** (com.) acciones privilegiadas.

preferable [préfœræbœl], *a.* preferible.—**preferableness** [-nes], *s.* preferibilidad.—**preferably** [-bli], *adv.* preferiblemente; preferentemente.

preference [préfœrens], *s.* preferencia; prelación; ventaja.—**p. shares,** o **stock,** acciones privilegiadas.

preferential [préferénshæl], *a.* preferente; privilegiado; parcial.—**p. ballot,** (E. U.) papeleta de *preferential voting.*—**p. voting,** votación en que el elector indica en su papeleta el candidato a quien realmente da su voto, y el que prefiere en caso de que aquél no obtenga la mayoría (puede llamarse votación de primera y segunda preferencia, o votación con subpreferencia).

preferment [prefсermœnt], *s.* promoción, elevación, ascenso, adelantamiento.

prefiguration [prefiguiuréshun], **prefigurement** [prefigiuirmœnt], *s.* prefiguración.

prefigurative [prefigiurativ], *a.* que prefigura.

prefigure [prefigiur], *va.* prefigurar.

prefix [prefix]. **I.** *va.* prefijar, anteponer. **II.** *s.* [prífics], (gram.) prefijo, afijo.

prefloration [prifloréishun], *s.* (bot.) prefloración.

preformation [príforméishun], *s.* (biol.) formación previa.

pregnancy [prégnansi], *s.* preñez; fertilidad, fecundidad.

pregnant [prégnant], *a.* preñada; fértil, copioso, fecundo.—**p. with,** repleto, lleno de.

pregnantly [-li], *adv.* abundantemente, plenamente.

prehensible [prejénsibœl], *a.* capaz de ser aprehendido o asido.

prehensile [prejénsil], *a.* prehensil.

prehension [prejénshun], *s.* prehensión.

prehistoric(al [prijistóric(al], *a.* prehistórico.

preignition [príignishun], *s.* (m. comb. int.) encendido anticipado.

prejudge [priyúy], *va.* prejuzgar.

prejudg(e)ment [priyúymœnt], *s.* prejuicio.

prejudication [priyúdikéshun], *s.* prejuicio.

prejudice [préyudis]. **I.** s. prevención, prejuicio, preocupación; parcialidad; perjuicio, detrimento.—**in,** o **to, the p. of,** con perjuicio de. **II.** va. preocupar, prevenir, predisponer; perjudicar.
prejudicial [prevudíshal], a. perjudicial.
prejudicially [-i], adv. perjudicialmente.
prelacy [prélasi], s. prelacía; episcopado.
prelate [prélet], s. prelado.—**prelateship** [-ship], s. prelacía, prelatura.
prelatic(al [prelétic(al], a. de prelado.
prelature(ship [prélatiur(ship], s. prelatura, prelacía.
prelection [prelécshun], s. lección, conferencia.
prelector [preléctœr] s. conferencista.
preliminarily [preliminærili], adv. preliminarmente.
preliminary [-næri]. **I.** a. preliminar; proemial, introductorio. **II.** s. preliminar.—pl. preliminares; (E. U.) exámenes preliminares.
prelude [príliud o préliud]. **I.** s. preludio, prelusión; presagio; (mús.) preludio. **II.** va. y vn. preludiar.
preludial [prelúdial], **prelusive** [prelúsiv], a. previo, introductorio, proemial.
premature [prímatiúær], a. prematuro.
prematurely [-li], adv. prematuramente.—**prematureness** [-nes], **prematurity** [-tiúriti], s. madurez o sazón antes de tiempo.
premaxilla [prímæxílæ], s. hueso intermaxilar.
premeditate [preméditeit], va. y vn. premeditar.
premeditate(d)ly [-(ed)li], adv. premeditadamente.
premeditation [-éishun], s. premeditación.
premier [prímiœr]. **I.** s. primer ministro. **II.** a. primero, principal.
premillennial [primilénial], a. anterior al milenario.—**premillenialism** [-ism], s. doctrina de que el milenario empezará con la segunda venida de Cristo.
premise [premáis], va. sentar o establecer como premisa.
premise [prémis], s. (lóg.) premisa.—pl. (for.) asertos, aserciones anteriores; parte de una escritura o título de dominio en que se expresan la fecha, los nombres de los individuos, la descripción de la propiedad, precio, etc.; predio rústico o urbano, casa, tierra, posesiones.—**in the premises** tocante al asunto de que se trata.
premium [prímium], s. premio; galardón; (com.) prima, premio, interés.—**p. note,** pagaré otorgado en lugar del pago de primas de seguro.—**at a p.,** a premio; en gran demanda, muy solicitado.
premolar [prímólær], **premolar tooth** [tuz], s. colmillo (del hombre y otros mamíferos).
premonition [primoníshun], s. prevención, advertencia; presentimiento.
premonitory [premónitori], a. que advierte o anuncia.
Premonstratensian [prímónstræténshæn], s. y a. premonstratense.
premunition [primuníshun], s. estado de defensa.
prenatal [prinéitæl], a. antenatal, de antes del nacimiento.
prenomen [prenómen], s. prenombre.
prenotion [prenóshun], s. prenoción.
prentice [préntis], s. (fam.) aprendiz.
preoccupant [priókiupant], s. el que ocupa antes que otro.
preoccupation [priókiupéshun], **preoccupancy** [-pansi], s. preocupación; ocupación previa.
preoccupied [priókiupaid], a. preocupado, absorto; ocupado anteriormente; puesto ya en uso.
preoccupy [priókiupai], va. preocupar; ocupar antes que otro.
preordain [priordéin], va. (teol.) preordinar o predestinar.
preordination [príordinéishun], s. (teol.) preordinación, predestinación.
preparation [preparéishun], s. preparación; preparado; preparativo.
preparative [prepárativ]. **I.** a. preparativo, preparatorio. **II.** s. preparativo, apresto.

preparatively [-li], adv. anticipadamente.
preparatorily [-torili], adv. preparatoriamente.
preparatory [-tori], a. preparatorio.—**p. school,** escuela de preparación para estudios universitarios.
prepare [prepéær], va. y vn. preparar(se).
preparedly [prepéærdli], adv. preventivamente.
preparedness [prepéærednes], s. preparación, prevención; preparación militar en tiempo de paz (ú. gen. en este sentido).
preparer [prepéærœr], s. preparador.
prepay [pripéi], va. (pret. y pp. PREPAID) pagar adelantado; franquear una carta.
prepayment [-mœnt], s. pago adelantado; franqueo.
prepense [prepéns], a. premeditado.—**with malice p.,** (for.) maliciosa y premeditadamente.
preponderance, preponderancy [pripóndœrans,-i], **preponderation** [-éishun], s. preponderancia, prepotencia.—**preponderant** [-ant], a. preponderante, predominante.—**preponderate** [-eit], va. y vn. preponderar, pesar más; predominar, prevalecer.
preposition [preposíshun], s. (gram.) preposición.—**prepositional** [-al], a. prepositivo.
prepositive [prepósitiv]. **I.** a. (gram.) antepuesto, prefijo. **II.** s. partícula prepositiva.
prepositor [prepósitœr], s. (Ingl.) decurión.
prepossess [pripošés], va. predisponer, causar buena impresión; preocupar, tomar posesión antes que otro.—**prepossessing** [-ing], a. simpático, atractivo.
prepossession [pripošéshun], s. impresión favorable; simpatía, predisposición favorable; preocupación, ocupación o posesión previa.
preposterous [prepóstœrus], a. prepóstero, absurdo; (fam.) ridículo, tonto.—**preposterously** [-li], adv. absurdamente, prepósteramente.
prepotency [prepótensi], s. prepotencia, predominio.
prepuce [prípius], s. (anat.) prepucio.
Pre-Raphaelite [prirǽfœelait], s. y a. prerrafaelista.—**Pre-Raphaelitism** [-tism], s. prerrafaelismo.
prerequisite [prirrécuisit]. **I.** a. previamente necesario. **II.** s. requisito previo.
prerogative [prerrógativ]. **I.** s. prerrogativa, privilegio, distinción. **II.** a. privilegiado.
presage [présey, presérmœnt]. **I.** s. presagio. **II.** va. [preséiy] presagiar.
presbyope [présbiop], s. présbite.—**presbyopia,** **presbyopy** [-ópia, pi], s. presbicia.—**presbyopic** [-ópic], a. présbite.
presbyter [prés- o présbitœr], s. presbítero, sacerdote.
presbyterial [-tírial], a. presbiteral.
Presbyterian [-tírian], a. y s. presbiteriano.—**Presbyterianism** [-ism], s. presbiterianismo.
presbytery [-biteri], s. presbiterio; presbiterianismo; tribunal eclesiástico de los presbiterianos; (arq.) ábside, presbiterio.
prescience [príshiens], s. presciencia.
prescient [príshient], a. presciente.
prescind [presínd], va. y vn. separar, abstraer.
prescribe [prescráib]. **I.** va. prescribir; (med.) recetar. **II.** vn. dar leyes o reglas; (med.) recetar, prescribir un remedio o tratamiento; (for.) prescribir.
prescriptible [prescríptibœl], a. prescriptible; (for.) adquirible por prescripción.
prescription [prescríphun], s. disposición, precepto, regla; (med.) receta; (for.) prescripción.
prescriptive [prescríptiv], a. sancionado, autorizado por la costumbre; (for.) adquirido por prescripción.
presence [présens], s. presencia; aparición, aparecido; asistencia, corte; sala de corte o de reunión; soberano (rey, etc.).—**p. of mind,** presencia de ánimo, serenidad.
present [présænt]. **I.** a. presente; actual, corriente (mes, semana, etc.).—**p. participle,** participio presente, gerundio.—**p. value, p. worth,** valor actual (de un pagaré, etc.). **II.** s. presente, la actualidad; (gram.) tiempo presente; regalo, dádiva, obsequio.—pl. (for.) las escrituras presen-

tes.—**at p.**, al presente, ahora, por ahora.—**for the p.**, por ahora.—**know all men by these presents,** conste por las presentes.—**to all to whom these presents shall come, greeting,** a cuantos las presentes vieren, salud. **III.** *va.* [preśént], presentar, introducir, dar a conocer; dar, regalar; manifestar, mostrar, exponer; apuntar, asestar (arma); (for.) denunciar, acusar.—**to p. a person with a thing,** regalar una cosa a alguien.—**to p. arms,** (mil.) presentar las armas.—**to p. one's self,** presentarse, personarse.

presentable [preśéntabœl], *a.* presentable.

presentability [preśéntabíliti], *s.* calidad de presentable.

presentation [préśentéśhʊn], *s.* presentación; ntroducción; entrega ceremoniosa de un obsequio; exhibición, representación; (med.) presentación del feto; (psic.) presentación.—**p. copy,** ejemplar de regalo con dedicatoria.—**on p.,** (com.) a presentación.

presentationism [-iśm], *s.* (psic. y filos.) presentacionismo.

presentative [preśéntativ], *a.* (filos.) concerniente a la presentación mental.

presentee [preśénti], *s.* (igl.) presentado.

presenter [preśéntœr], *s.* obsequiador.

presential [preśénśhal], *a.* presencial.

presentiment [-timœnt], *s.* presentimiento.

presently [préśentli], *adv.* luego, ya, dentro de poco, pronto.

presentment [preśéntmœnt], *s.* presentación, introducción; representación, retrato; semejanza; conducta; (for.) denuncia, acusación.

preservable [preśœrvabœl], *a.* preservable, conservable.

preservation [preśœrvéśhʊn], *s.* preservación, conservación, resguardo.

preservative [preśœrvativ]. **I.** *a.* preservativo, conservativo, defensivo; profiláctico. **II.** *s.* preservativo; defensa, salvaguardia.

preservatory [preśœrvatori], *a.* preservativo.

preserve [preśœrv]. **I.** *va.* preservar, guardar; resguardar, proteger; reservar, retener; conservar, mantener; (coc.) curar, confitar, almibarar.—**preserved meats,** viandas conservadas. **II.** *vn.* hacer conservas de frutas. **III.** *s.* conserva, dulce, compota, confitura; vedado, coto.—**p. jar,** bote para conservas.

preserver [preśœrvœr], *s.* preservador, conservador; confitero.

preside [priśáid], *vn.* (con **over**) presidir; gobernar, dirigir.

presidency [préśidensi], *s.* presidencia.

president [préśident], *s.* presidente.

president(i)al [preśidénśhal, tal], *a.* presidencial. —**p. year,** (E. U.) año de elecciones presidenciales.

presidentship [préśidentśhip], *s.* presidencia.

presidial [preśídial], *a.* (mil.) guarnicionado.

press [pres]. **I.** *va.* prensar; apretar, comprimir; planchar (la ropa); abrumar, afligir, oprimir; compeler, obligar; apresurar, apremiar, instar; acosar, perseguir; hostigar, fatigar; recalcar, ajustar; (mil.) hacer levas, enganchar soldados; abrazar, dar un apretón; satinar.—**to p. into service,** enganchar (soldados); poner a trabajar.—**to p. the point,** apurar el punto, insistir en el asunto. **II.** *vn.* pesar, ejercer presión; avanzar, adelantarse; embestir, arremeter; urgir, apremiar; agolparse, apiñarse; ser importuno; influir en el ánimo.—**to p. forward, to p. on,** avanzar; embestir. **III.** *s.* turba, muchedumbre; apiñamiento; empujón, apretón; prisa, presión, urgencia, cúmulo de negocios; (mec.) prensa (máquina); imprenta, estampa; prensa (periódica); escaparate, armario; (mil.) leva, enganche.—**p. money,** (mil.) prima de enganche.—**p. proof,** (impr.) prueba de prensa.— **p. roll,** (pap.) cilindro.

presser [préśœr], *s.* prensador, satinador, lustrador; planchador; pisacostura de una máquina de coser.

pressing [préśing]. **I.** *a.* urgente, apremiante, importante; importuno.—**p. boards,** cartones de satinar; (enc.) tablillas.—**p. iron,** plancha. **II.** *s.* prensado, prensadura, recalcadura.

pressman [préśman], *s.* prensador; tirador; (impr.) prensista; (mil.) reclutador.

pressroom [préśrrúm], *s.* taller de imprenta; sala o cuarto de las prensas.

pressure [préśhœr], *s.* presión; prensadura; urgencia, premura, prisa; ímpetu, impulso, apretón; carga, opresión; (elec.) tensión, potencial.— **p. circuit,** circuito derivado de un contador (que va al contador).—**p. coil,** bobina de tensión, bobina en derivación.—**p. cooker,** estufa o cocina de presión, en que se encierra herméticamente lo que se cocina.—**p. forging,** forjado por presión.— **p. gage,** o **gauge,** manómetro.—**p. nozzle,** (aer.) aparato para medir la presión del aire debida a la velocidad del avión.—**p. wire,** alambre de derivación del voltímetro (que va al voltímetro).

presswork [préśuœrk], *s.* (impr.) impresión, tiro, tirada; encolado de chapas.

prester [préstœr], *s.* preste.

prestidigitation [préstidiyitéíśhʊn], *s.* prestidigitación, juegos de manos.—**prestidigitator** [-téítœr], *s.* prestidigitador.

prestige [préstiy], *s.* prestigio.

prestimony préstimoni], *s.* prestimonio.

presto [présto]. **I.** *adv.* (mús.) presto; rápidamente. **II.** *interj.* ¡pronto!

presumable [preśiúmabœl], *a.* presumible.

presumably [-bli], *adv.* presumiblemente.

presume [preśiúm]. **I.** *va.* presumir, suponer; atreverse a. **II.** *vn.* (con **on** o **upon**) jactarse, presumir, preciarse de.

presumer [preśiúmœr], *s.* presumido; hombre arrogante o presuntuoso.

presumption [preśúmpśhʊn], *s.* presunción, conjetura; suposición, presunción, engreimiento.

presumptive [-tiv], *a.* presunto, presuntivo.

presumptively [-li], *adv.* presuntivamente.

presumptuous [-tiuʊs], *a.* presuntuoso, presumido; insolente; atrevido, temerario.—**presumptuously** [-li], *adv.* presuntuosamente.—**presumptuousness** [-nes], *s.* presunción, presuntuosidad, temeridad.

presuppose [prísʊpóuś], *va.* presuponer.

presupposition [prisʊpoʊśíśhʊn], *s.* presuposición, conjetura.

pretence [preténs], *s.* = PRETENSE.

pretend [preténd], *va.* aparentar, fingir; hacerse el, o que; pretender, intentar; alegar o afirmar falsamente.—**pretender** [-œr], *s.* pretendiente, pretensor; hipócrita.—**pretendingly** [-ingli], *adv.* presuntuosamente.

pretense [preténs], *s.* pretexto, excusa; máscara, capa, velo; pretensión, afectación, simulación; intención, proyecto.—**under false pretenses,** con falsas apariencias, con dolo.—**under p. of,** so pretexto de.

pretension [-śhʊn], *s.* pretensión, demanda; pretexto; simulación, afectación; afirmación gratuita.

pretentious [-śhʊs], *a.* presuntuoso, presumido de pretensiones.

preterit(e [prétœrit], *a.* y *s.* (gram.) pretérito.

preterition [pretœríśhʊn], *s.* preterición, pretermisión; (ret.) preterición.

pretermit [prítœrmít], *va.* pretermitir, omitir, pasar por alto.

preternatural [prítœrnǽchural], *a.* preternatural.—**preternaturally** [-li], *adv.* preternaturalmente.—**preternaturalness** [-nes], *s.* calidad de preternatural.

pretext [prítext o pretéxt], *s.* pretexto.

pretor [prítor], *s.* pretor.

pretorial, pretorian [pretória, an], *a.* pretoriano, pretorial.

prettily [prítili], *adv.* lindamente, bonitamente; agradablemente.

prettiness [prítines], *s.* lindeza.

pretty [príti]. **I.** *a.* lindo, bonito; bastante, pasadero, regular; (desp.) bello, grande, bueno (*a pretty mess you made of the business,* buen (o bello) lo hizo Vd. del negocio).—**a p. penny,** una buena suma, una buena talegada. **II.** *adv.* algo, algún tanto; un poco, bastante (*pretty good,* bas-

tante bueno; *pretty ttreá*, un poco, o algo, cansado).
—**p. much**, casi.—**p. well**, medianamente, así
así, tal cual.
prevail [prevéil], *vn.* reinar, prevalecer, preponderar; (con **over** o **against**) vencer a, triunfar de; sobresalir, predominar.—**to p. on, upon** o **with**, persuadir, inducir, convencer.
prevailing [-ing], *a.* predominante, reinante.
prevalence, prevalency [prévalens, i], *s.* predominio, preponderancia.
prevalent [-ent], *a.* prevaleciente, predominante, reinante.
prevaricate [prevǽrikeit], *vn.* engañar con embuste; (for.) prevaricar.—**prevarication** [-kéishun], *s.* embuste, mentira; dolo; (for.) prevaricato.—**prevaricator** [-kéitœr], *s.* prevaricador.
prevent [privént]. I. *va.* prevenir, precaver, evitar, impedir; (con **from**) impedir (a uno), estorbar, atajar. II. *vn.* empecer, obviar.—**preventable** [-æbœl], **preventible** [-ibœl], *a.* evitable.—**preventability** [-æbiliti], **preventibility** [-ibiliti], *s.* evitabilidad.—**preventer** [-œr], *s.* estorbador; (mar.) soga, berlinga, cadena o perno auxiliar.
prevention [privénshun], *s.* prevención, acción de evitar o impedir; obstáculo, estorbo.
preventive [privéntiv]. I. *a.* impeditivo; preservativo o profiláctico; (for.) preventivo.—**p. service**, resguardo militar. II. *s.* preservativo, profiláctico.
previous [prívius], *a.* previo.—**p. question**, proposición de que se hace uso en las asambleas para poner fin a un debate.—**p. to**, antes de.
previousness [-nes], *s.* prioridad, anterioridad.
prevision [privíyun], *s.* previsión.
prewar [priuór], *a.* de antes de, o anterior a, la guerra.
prey [préi]. [I. *s.* presa; botín, pillaje; rapiña, robo; víctima. II. *vn.* (con **on** o **upon**) devorar (la presa); rapiñar, pillar, robar; consumir, oprimir, agobiar.
price [práis]. I. *s.* precio.—**p. current**, lista o boletín de precios corrientes.—**p. list**, lista de precios, tarifa.—**at any p.**, a toda costa, cueste lo que cueste.—**to set a p. on one's head**, poner a precio la cabeza de uno, poner talla a uno (apl. a criminales). II. *va.* estimar, apreciar, tener en precio (dicho esp. de valor inmaterial); valuar, poner precio a; (fam.) preguntar el precio de.—**priced catalog(ue**, catálogo con precios.
priceless [práisles], *a.* inapreciable; sin precio.
prick [pric]. I. *va.* punzar, picar, pinchar; aguijonear, espolear; (a veces con *up*) erguir, aguzar, levantar (las orejas); marcar, indicar o calcar con agujerillos (en una lista, un mapa, etc.); causar una punzada (dolor punzante); seguir la pista a; mochar, cortar (la cola); (mar.) trazar o puntear sobre la carta de marear.—**to p. off**, (agr.) trasplantar en el viadero.—**to p. on**, o **forward**, aguijonear, aguzar, incitar.—**to p. out**, (agr.) = TO P. OFF.—**to p. up**, enderezar, erguir (las orejas); (alb.) dar la primera capa de enlucido a.—**to p. up one's ears**, aguzar las orejas o los oídos, poner la oreja, escuchar con ahinco. II. *vn.* causar o sentir una punzada o dolor punzante; erguirse o estar erguido; picarse (el vino); correr (a caballo). III. *s.* aguijón; acicate; puntura, picadura, punzada, agujerillo; espina, remordimiento; pista, rastro; punto, momento; blanco a que tiran los ballesteros.—**p.-eared**, amusgado; despierto, vivo.
pricker [príkœr], *s.* punzón, aguijón, lesna; jinete.
pricket [príket], *s.* candelero con punta en que se inserta una bujía; gamo de un año.
prickle [prícœl], *s.* pincho, púa, espina.
prickliness [príclines], *s.* calidad de espinoso; abundancia de abrojos.
prickly [prícli], *a.* lleno de púas o puntas, espinoso.—**p. heat**, erupción y picazón causada por el calor.—**p. pear**, (bot.) nopal, tunal; higo chumbo.—**p. thistle**, acanto.
prickpunch [prícpŭnch], *s.* punzón de acero.
pricktimber, prickwood [príctímbœr, prícud], *s.* (bot.) bonetero.
pride [práid]. I. *s.* orgullo; engreimiento; soberbia; dignidad, respeto de sí mismo; vigor;

causa de satisfacción; majestuosidad, pompa, aparato. II. *vr.* y *vn.* (gen. con **in** o **on**), enorgullecerse (de); jactarse (de).
prideful [práidful], *a.* orgulloso, arrogante.
priedieu [prídiœ], *s.* (igl.) reclinatorio.
prier [práicœr], *s.* escudriñador, atisbador, acechador, husmeador.
priest [príst], *s.* sacerdote; presbítero, cura.—**p.-ridden** = PRIESTRIDDEN.
priestcraft [prístcraft], *s.* superchería, intriga eclesiástica.
priestess [prístes], *s.* sacerdotisa.
priesthood [prístjud], *s.* clero, sacerdocio.
priestliness [prístlines], *s.* comportamiento de un sacerdote.
priestly [prístli], *a.* sacerdotal.
priestridden [prístrrídœn], *a.* dominado por sacerdotes o clérigos.
prig, *s.* pedante.
priggish [príguish], *a.* presumido, afectado.
priggishness, priggism [príguishnes, príguish], *s.* pedantería.
prill [pril], *s.* = BRILL.
prim. I. *a.* etiquetero, relamido, estirado. II. *va.* y *vr.* ponerse de veinticinco alfileres.
primacy [práimasi], *s.* primacía; supremacía; precedencia.
primadonna [prímadóna], *s.* primadonna, primera cantatriz.
prima facie [práima féishie], prima facie, de prima facie.—**p.-f. evidence**, prueba suficiente para justificar la presunción de un hecho.
primage [práimeʏ], *s.* (mar.) capa.
primal [práimal], *a.* prístino; principal.
primarily [práimarili], *adv.* en primer lugar; originalmente; principalmente.
primariness [práimarines], *s.* primacía, prioridad, supremacía.
primary [práimari]. I. *a.* primario, primero; primitivo, prístino; radical, principal, fundamental; elemental, rudimental; (geol.) primario; (elec.) primario.—**p. coil**, bobina primaria, o del circuito primario.—**p. color**, (fís.) color elemental, color espectral.—**p. feathers**, plumas primarias, (astr.) movimiento primario, movimiento aparente de la esfera celeste.—**p. planet**, planeta primario.—**p. point**, (com.) centro de distribución de granos.—**p. school**, escuela primaria, (cir.) cura por primera intención. II. *s.* (lo) primero; mitin de electores para elegir candidatos, delegados, etc.; comicios preliminares; (elec.) circuito primario; (astr.) planeta primario; (zool.) pluma primaria de un ave; ala de un insecto.
primate [práimet], *s.* (igl.) primado.—*pl.* P. [praiméitis], (zool.) cuadrumanos, primates.
primateship [práimetship], *s.* (igl.) primacía.
prime [práim]. I. *s.* flor (de la vida, de la juventud); albor, principio; alba, aurora, amanecer; flor, nata, lo mejor, lo más escogido; (igl.) hora prima; (arit.) número primo; (impr.) virgulilla, signo ('). II. *a.* primero, principal; primoroso, de primera clase o calidad, selecto; original, prístino; (mat.) primo (número); (impr.) marcado con el signo (').—**p. conductor**, colector (de una máquina eléctrica).—**p. cost**, costo de fábrica, costo de producción.—**p. meridian**, primer meridiano, meridiano principal.—**p. minister**, primer ministro.—**p. mover**, fuente natural de energía o fuerza motriz (agua, viento, etc.); máquina generadora de energía (turbina, máquina de vapor, etc.); alma, palanca (de una empresa).—**p. vertical** (astr.), vertical primario. III. *va.* preparar, alistar; informar, prevenir, dar instrucciones; cebar (un arma de fuego, una bomba, etc.); (alb. y pint.) dar la primera capa; (impr.) poner el signo ('). IV. *vn.* (arti. y mec.) estar cebado; estar listo o preparado; (m. v.) arrastrar agua con el vapor; entrar una marea antes de tiempo.
primely [práimli], *adv.* en alto grado, muy bien, excelentemente.
primeness [-nes], *s.* primacía; primor, excelencia.
primer [prímœr], *s.* cartilla, libro primero de lectura.

primer [práimœr]. **I.** *a.* primero, original; primario. **II.** *s.* (arti.) pistón, fulminante; cebador.

primeval [praimíval], *a.* primitivo, prístino.

primigenial [práimiyínial], *a.* primogénito; primigenio, primitivo.

priming [práiming], *s.* preparación; (arti. y mec.) cebo; (m. v.) arrastre de agua con el vapor; (pint.) primera capa.—**p. hole**, oído.—**p. horn**, cebador.—**p. tube**, estopín.

primipara [praimípara], *s.* primeriza, primípara.

primitive [prímitiv], *a.* primitivo; primordial.

primitively [-li], *adv.* primitivamente.

primitiveness [-nes], *s.* calidad de primitivo.

primitivity [-tíviti], *s.* = PRIMITIVENESS.

primly [prímli], *adv.* de veinticinco alfileres.

primness [prímnes], *s.* escrupulosidad, remilgo, dengue.

primogenial, *a.* = PRIMIGENIAL.

primogenitor [práimoyénitœr], *s.* progenitor.

primogeniture [-chur *o* tiur]. *s.* primogenitura.

primordial [praimórdial]. **I.** *a.* primordial, primitivo. **II.** *s.* principio elemental.

primrose [prímrouŝ]. **I.** *s.* (bot.) bellorita, primavera; color amarillo verdoso claro. **II.** *a.* amarillo verdoso claro; florido, gayo.

Primulaceæ [prímiuléisii *o* primulásii], *s. pl.* (bot.) primuláceas.

prince [prins], *s.* príncipe.—**P. of Darkness**, Satanás.—**P. of Peace**, Jesucristo; Príncipe de la Paz (Manuel de Godoy).—**p. of the blood royal**, (ingl.) infante, príncipe de sangre real.—**P. of Wales**, Príncipe de Gales.

princedom [prínsdum], *s.* principado.

princeliness [prínslines], *s.* munificencia, nobleza, magnificencia.

princely [prínsli]. **I.** *a.* semejante a un príncipe, propio o digno de un príncipe, magnífico, regio. **II.** *adv.* como un príncipe.

princess [prínses], *s.* princesa.—**p. royal**, hija mayor de un soberano.

principal [prínsipal]. **I.** *a.* principal; máximo; (arq.) maestro. **II.** *s.* principal, jefe; director (de escuela); (for.) causante, comitente, constituyente; (com.) capital (puesto a interés); (arq.) jamba de fuerza.

principality [-péliti], *s.* principado, soberanía.

principally [-pali], *adv.* principalmente, mayormente, máxime.

principalness [prínsipalnes], *s.* principalidad.

principle, *va.* imbuir, infundir principios o máximas a.—**principled** [-d], *a* de principios, escrupuloso, probo.

principle [prínsipœl], *s.* principio, origen; fundamento, motivo, razón; principio (regla, ley, teorema); (quím.) principio activo.

prink, *vn.* y *va.* ataviar(se), adornar(se); acicalar(se); contonearse, fachendear.

print. **I.** *va.* estampar, imprimir; tirar, hacer una tirada; (foto.) imprimir; (fig.) imprimir o grabar en la memoria, etc.—**printed by**, impreso por; imprenta de.—**print(ed) goods**, (tej.) estampados. **II.** *vn.* ser impresor; (foto.) cambiar de color. **III.** *s.* impresión, estampa; tipo o letra de molde (v. gr. *small print*, tipo menudo); impreso, folleto, volante, periódico, alcance, etc.; papel de imprenta; impresión, marca, señal o huella; lámina, grabado; (tej.) estampado, indiana; molde; muestra, dibujo; (foto.) impresión, positivo impreso.—*pl.* **prints**, (tej.) estampados, cotonada, zarazas.—**p. shop**, estampería.—**p. works**, (tej.) fábrica de estampados.—**in p.**, impreso; publicado; en letra de molde.—**out of p.**, (edición) agotada.

printer [príntœr], *s.* impresor.—**p.'s devil**, aprendiz de impresor.—**p.'s mark**, pie de imprenta.—**p.'s shooting stick**, (impr.) acuñador.

printing [prínting]. **I.** *s.* imprenta, tipografía; impresión; estampa, impreso. **II.** *a.* de imprenta, de imprimir.—**p. frame**, (foto.) marco de imprimir.—**p. machine** = P. PRESS.—**p. office**, imprenta.—**p. press**, prensa, máquina para imprimir o para estampar telas.—**p. types**, caracteres de imprenta, tipo.

prior [práiœr]. **I.** *a.* anterior, precedente, previo.—**p. to**, antes de. **II.** *s.* prior.

priorate [práioret], *s.* priorato.

prioress [práiores], *s.* priora.

priority [praióriti], *s.* prioridad, antelación, prelación.

priorship [práiœrŝhip], *s.* priorazgo. priorato.

priory [práiœri], *s.* priorato.

prism [priŝm], *s.* (geom.) prisma.

prismatic(al [priŝmǽtic(al], *a.* prismático.

prismatically [-i], *adv.* en forma de prisma.

prismoid [priŝmoid], *s.* sólido de forma parecida a la del prisma.

prison [priŝon]. **I.** *s.* prisión, cárcel.—**p. bars**, **p. base** = PRISONER'S BASE.—**p. cell**, celda.—**p. fever** = JAIL FEVER.—**p. house**, cárcel, prisión.—**p. ship**, pontón. **II.** *va.* encarcelar.

prisoner [príŝnœr], *s.* preso, prisionero.—**p.'s base**, rescate, juego de muchachos.

pristine [prístin], *a.* prístino.

pritchel [príchel], *s.* (vet.) contrapunzón.

prithee [prídi], *v. contr.* de **I pray thee**, te ruego.

prittle-prattle [prítœl-prǽtœl], *s.* charla.

privacy [práivasi], *s.* retiro, soledad, aislamiento; reserva, secreto; retrete; condición de estar solo y poder obrar privadamente.

private [práivet]. **I.** *a.* privado; particular (a distinción de público); personal; confidencial; secreto, oculto; solo, retirado; reservado, excusado; callado, reticente.—**p. affair**, o **business**, asunto privado.—**p. family**, familia que no tiene por negocio tomar pupilos.—**p. hearing**, audiencia secreta, a puertas cerradas.—**p. house**, casa particular.—**p. letter**, carta reservada.—**p. lodging**, habitación en una casa particular.—**p. mass**, misa rezada.—**p. office**, gabinete, despacho particular.—**p. school**, escuela particular.—**p. secretary**, secretario particular.—**p. staircase**, escalera secreta o excusada.—**p. theatricals**, comedias caseras o de aficionados; teatro casero; función de aficionados.—**at one's p. expense**, a costa propia.—**in p.**, particularmente; en secreto, en particular.—**to be p.**, estar solo(s); estar ocupado en asuntos privados. **II.** *s.* soldado raso.—*pt.* **partes pudendas.**—**in p.**, privadamente, en reserva.

privateer [práivatíœr]. **I.** *s.* corsario. **II.** *vn.* armar en corso.—**privateering** [-ing], *s.* corso.—**privateersman** [-sman], *s.* corsario.

privately [práivetli], *adv.* privadamente, secretamente, reservadamente.

privateness [-nes], *s.* calidad de privado.

privation [praivéŝhun], *s.* privación; carencia.

privative [práivativ]. **I.** *a.* privativo; (gram.) privativo. **II.** *s.* negación; (gram.) prefijo o adjetivo privativo.—**privatively** [-li], *adv.* privativamente.—**privativeness** [-nes], *s.* calidad de privativo.

privet [prívet], *s.* (bot.) alheña, ligustro.

privilege [prívilej]. **I.** *s.* privilegio; gracia, prerrogativa; inmunidad, exención, dispensa; indulto. **II.** *va.* privilegiar, exceptuar, eximir.

privileged [prívelert], *a.* privilegiado, inmune, exento, libre.—**p. altar**, (igl.) altar privilegiado.—**p. debt**, (for.) deuda preferente.—**p. shares**, **p. stock**, acciones privilegiadas.—**p. witness**, testigo a quien las partes interesadas pueden impedir que declare.

privity [príviti], *s.* informe reservado, confidencia, secreto.

privy [prívi]. **I.** *a.* confidente, cómplice; instruido, informado, enterado; privado, secreto; excusado; particular, propio, personal.—**p. council**, consejo privado.—**p. seal**, sello privado (o pequeño). **II.** *s.* copartícipe; cómplice; retrete, letrina, lugar excusado; (mar.) jardín.

prize [práiŝ]. **I.** *s.* premio, galardón; presa, botín; buque apresado; adquisición, ganancia, ventaja, buena suerte.—**p. court**, tribunal de presas.—**p. crew**, tripulación que lleva un buque apresado a su destino.—**p. fight**, boxeo entre profesionales.—**p. fighter**, boxeador.—**p. master**, capitán o cabo de presa.—**p. money**, parte de una presa.—**p. office**, negociado de las presas de guerra.—**p. ring**, liza de boxear; el boxeo como profesión. **II.** *va.* apreciar, estimar, valuar, tasar.

prizer [práiŝœr], *s.* apreciador; valorador.

pro [pro]. **I.** *adv.* en favor; por. **II.** *s.* voto afirmativo.—**p. and con,** en favor y en contra.—**p. forma,** (com.) simulado.—**p. rata** (pro réita), a prorrata.—**pros and cons,** (el) pro y el contra.—**p. tem(pore,** (pro tem, témpore), interino, interinamente.—**neither p. nor con,** ni en pro ni en contra.

probabilism [próbabilism], *s.* probabilismo.
probabilist [próbabilist], *s.* probabilista.
probability [próbabíliti], *s.* probabilidad.—**in all p.,** según toda probabilidad.—**probable** [-bœl], *a.* probable.—**probably** [-bli], *adv.* probablemente.
probang [próbæng], *s.* sonda esofágica.
probate [próbeit]. **I.** *a.* (for.) testamentario.—**p. court,** tribunal testamentarías. **II.** *s.* (for.) prueba plena y legal de la autenticidad de un testamento; competencia de un juez o tribunal en juicio testamentario. **III.** *va.* validar o legalizar (un testamento tras la muerte del testador).
probation [probéishun], *s.* prueba, ensayo, tentativa; probación, noviciado; (en los tribunales juveniles) libertad vigilada.—**p. officer,** vigilante, agente de vigilancia(en algunas partes se llama *delegado de libertad vigilada.*)—**probational** [-al], **probationary** [-æri], *a.* probatorio.—**probationer** [-œr], *s.* novicio; aprendiz, meritorio.
probationership [-œrship], *s.* noviciado.
probative [próbativ], *a.* probatorio.
probator [probéitœr], *s.* examinador, aprobador.
probatory [próbatori], *a.* probatorio.
probe [próub]. **I.** *s.* (cir.) sonda, tienta, cánula, exploratorio; prueba, ensayo.—**p. scissors,** tijeras de cirujano. **II.** *va.* (cir.) tentar, explorar; escudriñar, indagar.
probity [próbiti], *s.* probidad.
problem [próblem], *s.* problema.
problematic(al [-mætic(al], *a.* problemático.
problematically [-i], *adv.* problemáticamente.
Proboscidea [próbosídiæ], *s. pl.* (zool.) proboscidios.—**proboscidean** [-diæn], *s.* y *a.* proboscídio.
proboscis [probósis], *s.* proboscis, proboscide, trompa (del elefante, etc.); (ent.) trompetilla; (fam.) nariz.
procaine [prokéin], *s.* = NOVOCAINE.
procardium [procárdium], *s.* boca del estómago.
procedure [prosíyur *o* prosídiur], *s.* proceder, procedimiento, conducta; (for.) procedimientos judiciales, tramitación, vía judicial.
proceed [prosíd], *vn.* seguir, proseguir; marchar, adelantar, avanzar; proceder, obrar; empezar, instituir; tramitar; provenir, dimanar, proceder.—**to p. to blows,** llegar a las manos, acudir a los golpes.—**to p. to business,** ir a lo que importa; poner manos a la obra; entrar en materia.
proceeding [-ing], *s.* procedimiento, conducta, proceder; transacción; (for.) providencia, trámite, procedimiento; proceso.—*pl.* actas; expediente, autos, actuaciones.
proceeds [prósids], *s. pl.* producto, réditos.
procephalic [prosefælic], *a.* procefálico; de la parte anterior de la cabeza.
process [próses]. **I.** *s.* procedimiento, método, sistema; proceso (conjunto o serie de fenómenos naturales); progreso, continuación, adelantamiento; curso, serie, sucesión; (for.) causa, proceso, expediente, autos; providencia; (anat. y zool.) protuberancia, excrescencia; (bot.) apéndice.—**p. butter,** mantequilla de inferior calidad que se derrite con leche o crema para "renovarla."—**p. of time,** curso del tiempo.—**p. plate,** placa de fotografía lenta, empleada esp. para dispositivos.—**in p. of time,** con el tiempo.—**in the p.,** haciéndose, en vía de (fabricación, preparación, etc.).—**in the p. of,** en vía de. **II.** *va.* cocinar o esterilizar bajo presión; fotografiar; someter a algún procedimiento especial, tratar.
procession [proséshun], *s.* procesión; cabalgata; desfile de tropa.
processional [proséshunal]. **I.** *a.* procesional. **II.** *s.* procesionario (libro).
processionary [proséshunæri], *a.* procesional.
proclaim [prokléim], *va.* proclamar; promulgar; publicar, pregonar, vocear.
proclaimer [prokléimœr], *s.* proclamador.

proclamation [próclaméishun], *s.* proclamación, publicación; proclama, decreto, edicto, bando.
proclitic [proclític], *a.* (gram.) proclítico.
proclivous [procláivus], *a.* inclinado hacia adelante.
proclivity [proclíviti], *s.* propensión, proclividad.
procœlia [prosília], *s.* (anat.) procelio; (**P-**), *pl.* suborden de cocodrilos.
proconsul [procónsul], *s.* procónsul.—**proconsular** [-siular], *a.* proconsular.—**proconsulate, proconsulship** [-siulet, -sulship], *s.* proconsulado.
procrastinate [procrǽstineit], *va.* y *vn.* diferir, dilatar, trasmañanar, ser moroso.—**procrastination** [-éishun], *s.* dilacion, demora.—**procrastinator** [-éitœr], *s.* hombre moroso.
procreant [prócriant], *a.* procreante.
procreate [prócrieit],*va.* procrear.—**procreation** [-éishun], *s.* procreación.—**procreative** [-éitiv], *a.* procreador.—**procreativeness** [-nes], *s.* facultad o potencia procreadora.—**procreator** [-éitœr], *s.* procreador.
Procrustean [procrústian], *a.* de Procusto.
proctor [próctœr], *s.* procurador; apoderado, agente; censor de una universidad.
proctorage [próctorey], *s.* procuración.
proctorial [proctórial], *a.* referente al procurador o al censor académico.
proctorship [próctœrship], *s.* procura, procuración; procuraduría.
procumbent [procúmbent], *a.* postrado, inclinado; (bot.) rastrero.
procurable [prokiúrabœl], *a.* asequible; proporcionable.
procuracy [prókiurasi], *s.* procuración; gestión, manejo de negocios.
procuration [prokiuréshun], *s.* alcahuetería; (for.) procura, procuración, poder.—**p. fee,** comisión sobre un préstamo.
procurator [prókiuréitœr], *s.* procurador, apoderado.
procuratorial [-ratórial], *a.* hecho por procurador.
procure [prokiúœr]. **I.** *va.* lograr, obtener, conseguir; causar, ocasionar. **II.** *va.* y *vn.* solicitar mozas para un lupanar, alcahuetear.
procurement [-mœnt], *s.* obtención, logro, consecución; solicitud, gestión.
procurer [prokiúrœr], *s.* alcahuete.
procuress [prokiúres], *sf.* alcahueta.
Procyon [prósion], *s.* (astr.) Prócion.
prod. [prod]. **I.** *va.* punzar, picar, aguijonear. **II.** *s.* pincho, aguijada; picadura, pinchazo.
prodigal [pródigal]. **I.** *a.* pródigo. **II.** *a.* y *s.* manirroto, derrochador.
prodigality [-gǽliti], *s.* prodigalidad.
prodigally [pródigali], *adv.* pródigamente.
prodigious [prodíyus], *a.* prodigioso.
prodigiously [-li], *adv.* prodigiosamente.
prodigiousness [-nes], *s.* calidad de prodigioso.
prodigy [pródiyi], *s.* prodigio.
prodrome, prodromus [pródrom(us], *s.* (med.) pródromo; prolegómeno.
produce [prodiús]. **I.** *va.* producir; mostrar, presentar; introducir, presentar al público; (geom.) prolongar. **II.** *vn.* producir. **III.** *s.* (pródius) producto; productos agrícolas, provisiones.—**p. exchange,** lonja de víveres.
producer [prodiúscœr], *s.* productor; gasógeno, generador de gas pobre.—**p. gas,** gas pobre.—**producers' goods,** (e. p.) elementos de producción (materias primas, maquinaria, etc.)
producible [prodiúsibœl], *a.* producible.
producibleness [-nes], *s.* producibilidad.
product [próduct], *s.* producto; artículo.
productile [prodúctil], *a.* dúctil.
production [prodúcshun], *s.* producción; producto; composición, obra del ingenio; (teat.) producción escénica, representación teatral.
productive [-tiv], *a.* productivo.—**productiveness** [-nes], **productivity** [próductiviti], *s.* productividad.
proem [próem], *s.* proemio; exordio.
proemial [proémial], *a.* proemial.
profanation [prófanéishun], *s.* profanación.

profane [proféin]. **I.** *a.* profano, secular; profano, irreverente; indecente; de reniegos. **II.** *va.* profanar.

profanely [-li], *adv.* profanamente.

profaner [proféincer], *s.* profanador.

profaneness [proféinnes], **profanity** [proféeniti], *s.* profanidad, blasfemia; reniego; irreverencia, desacato.

profess [profés]. **I.** *va.* profesar, creer en; declarar, manifestar; pretender; enseñar (como profesor); ejercer (una profesión); (igl.) profesar. **II.** *vn.* hacer profesión, declarar abierta o públicamente.

professed, profest [profést], *a.* profeso, declarado, decidido.

professedly [-sedli], *adv.* declaradamente; pretendidamente.

profession [proféshun], *s.* profesión, carrera, ocupación; profesión o protestación de la fe; declaración, manifestación; (igl.) profesión; (teat.) arte dramático; los cómicos en general.

professional [proféshunal]. **I.** *a.* profesional, facultativo; de profesión (v. gr.: *professional gambler*, jugador de profesión). **II.** *s.* (dep.) deportista de profesión; (teat.) actor o actriz; perito en algún arte o profesión.

professionally [-i], *adv.* profesionalmente, en calidad de o como profesional.

professor [proféscer], *s.* profesor, catedrático; perito.

professorial [profesórial], *a.* de profesor; profesional, pedagógico.

professorship [proféscership], *s.* profesorado, cátedra.

proffer [prófcer]. **I.** *va.* proponer, ofrecer, brindar. **II.** *s.* oferta, propuesta, ofrecimiento.

proficience, proficiency [profíshens, i], *s.* adelanto, adelantamiento; pericia, habilidad.

proficient [-shcent], *s.* y *a.* experto, perito; proficiente, adelantado.

profile [prófil *o* prófail]. **I.** *s.* contorno; recorte; , perfil.—**p. paper,** papel cuadriculado. **II.** *va.* perfilar.

profit [prófit]. **I.** *s.* provecho, beneficio; lucro, ganancia, utilidad.—**p. and loss,** ganancias y pérdidas. **II.** *va.* aprovechar a, servir. **III.** *vn.* sacar utilidad o provecho, ganar; adelantar, mejorarse.—**to p. by,** sacar partido o provecho de.

profitable [prófitabœl], *a.* provechoso, útil; productivo, lucrativo.—**profitableness** [-nes], *s.* calidad de provechoso.—**profitably** [-blii], *adv.* provechosamente; lucrativamente.

profiteer [-tícer]. **I.** *vn.* usurear, logrear, explotar, (ap¹. esp. a la usura que se aprovecha de una necesidad o calamidad nacional). **II.** *s.* usurero, logrero, explotador, buitre (fig.), vampiro (fig.) (Véase la explicación anterior).—**profiteering,** [-ing], *s.* usura, logrería, explotación. (La misma explicación.)

profitless [prófitles], *a.* infructuoso.

profitlessly [-li], *adv.* infructuosamente.

profligacy [prófligasi], *s.* libertinaje, desenfreno, disolución, crápula.

profligate [-guet], *a.* y *s.* libertino, relajado, perdido.—**profligately** [-li], *adv.* disolutamente, licenciosamente.

profound [profáund]. **I.** *a.* profundo. **II.** *s.* sima, abismo; profundo, mar, océano.

profoundly [-li], *adv.* profundamente.

profoundness [-nes], *s.* profundidad.

profundity [profúnditi], *s.* profundidad; hondura.

profuse [profiús], *a.* profuso; pródigo.—**profusely** [-li], *adv.* profusamente; pródigamente.

profusion [profiúyun], *s.* profusión, prodigalidad.

progenitor [proyénitœr], *s.* progenitor.

progeny [próyeni], *s.* progenie, prole.

prognathism [prógnaziśm], *s.* pragnatismo.

prognathous [prógnazus], *a.* prognato.

prognosis [prognósis], *s.* (med.) pronóstico; vaticinio, predicción; presciencia.

prognostic [prognóstic]. **I.** *s.* pronóstico, presagio; (med.) síntoma determinante. **II.** *a.* pronosticador.

prognosticable [-cabœl], *a.* pronosticable.

prognosticate [-keit], *va.* pronosticar; presagiar; augurar.—**prognostication** [-kéishun], *s.* pronosticación; presagio, pronóstico.—**prognosticator** [-kéitœr], *s.* pronosticador, vaticinador.

program(me [prógræm], *s.* programa, cartel; plan, prospecto.—**p. music,** música descriptiva.

progress [prógres]. **I.** *s.* progreso; progresos, aprovechamiento, adelantamiento; desarrollo, mejoramiento; marcha, curso, carrera.—**to make p.,** hacer progresos, progresar. **II.** *va.* [progrés] adelantar, llevar adelante. **III.** *vn.* progresar; avanzar, marchar; adelantar, hacer progresos.

progression [prógréshun], *s.* progresión, adelantamiento, curso; (mat.) progresión.

progressional [-al], *a.* progresivo.

progressionist [-ist], *s.* evolucionista; (biol.) transformista.

progressive [progrésiv], *a.* progresivo; progresista (t. *s.*).—**progressively** [-li], *adv.* progresivamente.—**progressiveness** [-nes], *s.* calidad de progresivo o progresista.

prohibit [projíbit], *va.* prohibir; impedir.

prohibition [prójibíshun], *s.* prohibición; auto prohibitorio, entredicho o interdicto; veto; (E. U.) neftalismo obligatorio, prohibicionismo, prohibición legal de la manufactura y venta de bebidas alcohólicas.—**P. party,** (E. U.) partido prohibicionista, que aboga por la prohibición de bebidas alcohólicas.

prohibitionist [-ist], *s.* (E. U. pol.) prohibicionista, neftalista, afiliado al prohibicionismo.

prohibitive, prohibitory [projíbitiv, tori], *a.* prohibitivo, prohibitorio.

project [proyéct]. **I.** *va.* proyectar; idear; echar, arrojar, despedir. **II.** *vn.* resaltar, sobresalir, salir. **III.** *s.* (próyect), proyecto, plan; empresa.

projectile [proyéctil]. **I.** *s.* proyectil. **II.** *a.* proyectante; arrojadizo.

projecting [-ing], *a.* proyectante (línea); saledizo, voladizo, saliente.—**p. lantern,** (opt.) aparato de proyección, proyector.

projection [-shun], *s.* lanzamiento, echamiento; resalte; vuelo, saliente, plan, proyecto; (geom.) proyección.

projector [-tœr], *s.* proyectista; proyector, aparato de proyección.

projecture [-chur], *s.* (arq.) proyectura, saledizo, vuelo.

prolabium [prolibium], *s.* prolabio.

prolapse [prolæps], *vn.* caer hacia adelante o afuera.

prolapsus [prolæpsus], *s.* (med.) prolapso.

prolate [próleit], *a.* alargado hacia los polos, achatado en el ecuador.

proleg [próleg], *s.* (ent.) pie falso.

prolegomena [prólegómenæ], *s. pl.* (*sing.* **prolegomenon**) prolegómenos.

prolepsis [prolépsis], *s.* (ret.) prolepsis.

proleptic(al [-tic(al], *a.* previo.

proleptically [-li], *adv.* previamente.

proles [prólis], *s.* prole, hijos; descendencia.

proletarian [próletérian], *a.* y *s.* proletario; obrero.

proletariat [-riæt], *s.* proletariado; clase obrera.

prolicide [prólisaid], *s.* infanticidio.

proliferate [prolífœret]. **I.** *va.* (biol.) producir, dar. **II.** *vn.* reproducirse.

proliferous [prolíforus], **prolific(al** [prolífic(al], *a.* prolífico, fecundo.

prolifically [-i], *adv.* prolíficamente.

prolification [prólifikéshun], *s.* generación; (bot.) proliferación.

prolificness [prolíficnes], *s.* fecundidad.

prolix [prólix *o* prolíx], *a.* prolijo.—**prolixity** [prolíxiti], **prolixness** [prolíxnes], *s.* prolijidad.— **prolixly** [prolíxli], *adv.* prolijamente.

prolocutor [prolókiutœr *o* prólokiútœr], *s.* intercesor, portavoz; presidente de una asamblea.

prolog(ue [prólog], *s.* prólogo, introito, proemio.
prolong [prolóng], *va.* prolongar.
prolongation [prolonguéishon], *s.* prolongación.
prolonge [prolóny], *s.* (mil.) prolonga.
prolusion [proliúy̆un], *s.* prolusión, prelusión, preludio; ensayo preliminar.
promenade [prómenád]. **I.** *vn.* pasearse. **II.** *s.* paseo (lugar y acto).—**p. concert,** concierto durante el cual la gente pasea o baila.—**p. deck,** (mar.) cubierta superior.—**p. roof,** azotea de baile y diversión.
promenader [prómenidœr], *s.* paseante.
Promethean [promízian], *a.* de Prometeo.
prominence, prominency [próminens, i], *s.* eminencia, altura; prominencia, protuberancia, saledizo, resalto.
prominent [próminent], *a.* prominente, saliente, conspicuo; eminente, sobresaliente, distinguido.—**p. eyes,** ojos saltones.—**p. figures,** figuras de relieve.
promiscuity [prómiskiúiti], *s.* promiscuidad (apl. esp. a las relaciones sexuales).
promiscuous [promískius], *a.* promiscuo.—**p. intercourse,** relaciones sexuales promiscuas, libre amor.—**promiscuously** [-li], *adv.* promiscuamente; sin distinción.—**promiscuousness** [-nes], *s.* promiscuidad, confusión.
promise [prómis]. **I.** *s.* promesa; promisión; cosa prometida; espectativa, esperanza. **II.** *va.* y *vn.* prometer; dar o hacer concebir esperanzas.—**Promised Land,** Tierra Prometida.
promisee [promisí], *s.* (for.) persona que ha recibido una promesa.
promiser [prómiscœr], **promisor** [prómisor], *s.* prometedor.
promising [prómising], *a.* premetiente, prometedor, que promete.
promissorily [prómisorili], *adv.* promisoriamente.
promissory [prómisori], *a.* promisorio.—**p. note,** pagaré, vale.
promontory [prómontori], *s.* promontorio.
promorphology [promorfóloyi], *s.* morfología geométrica.
promote [promóut], *va.* promover, fomentar; provocar, suscitar; alentar, estimular; mejorar, adelantar, ascender; (com.) agenciar, gestionar; capitalizar y organizar (una empresa).
promoter [promóutœr], *s.* promotor, promovedor, gestor, agente que se dedica a capitalizar y organizar empresas industriales.
promotion [promóshun], *s.* promoción, ascenso, adelantamiento.
promotive [promótiv], *a.* promovedor.
prompt. I. *a.* pronto, listo, expedito; puntual.—**p.-book,** (teat.) libro del apuntador o consueta.—**p. cash,** pago al contado, inmediato.—**p. note,** (com.) nota de aviso, especie de memorándum o factura que se da a quien compra al fiado. **II.** *va.* impulsar, mover, incitar; indicar, sugerir, insinuar; soplar, decir en voz baja (en una clase); (teat.) apuntar.
prompter [prómptœr], *s.* incitador, instigador; (teat.) apuntador, traspunte, consueta.
promptitude, promptness [-titiud, nes], *s.* prontitud, presteza, puntualidad. **promptly** [-li], *adv.* prontamente, prestamente; puntualmente.
promulgate [promúlgueit], *va.* promulgar.
promulgation [promulguéishun], *s.* promulgación, proclama..
promulgator [-guéitœr], **promulger** [promúlyœr], *s.* promulgador.
pronaos [pronéios], *s.* (arq.) pronaos.
pronation [pronéishun], *s.* pronación.
prone [próun], *a.* postrado; inclinado, pendiente; prono, dispuesto, propenso.
proneness [-nes], *s.* postración; inclinación; propensión, tendencia.
pronephros [pronéfros], (anat.) pronefros.
prong, *s.* púa, diente, punta (de tenedor, horquilla, etc.); pitón de asta; punta de colmillo.
prongbuck, pronghorn [próngbúc, jórn], *s.* antílope americano.
pronged [prongd], *a.* dentado, provisto de púas.

pronominal [pronóminal], *a.* pronominal.
pronoun [prónaun], *s.* (gram.) pronombre.
pronounce [pronáuns]. **I.** *va.* pronunciar; declarar; (for.) pronunciar, dar (sentencia). **II.** *vn.* pronunciar; hablar magistralmente.
pronounceable [-abœl], *a.* pronunciable.
pronounced [-t], *a.* pronunciado, marcado, fuerte, subido.—**pronouncement** [-mœnt], *s.* proclama, manifiesto, declaración.—**pronouncing** [-ing], *a.* de pronunciación, con la pronunciación.
pronucleus [proniúclius], *s.* pronúcleo.
pronunciamento [pronúnshiæmento], *s.* proclama, manifiesto, declaración.
pronunciation [pronúnsi- (*o* shi) éishun], *s.* pronunciación.
proof [pruf]. **I.** *s.* prueba, evidencia; demostración; ensayo, experimento; impenetrabilidad; (impr.) prueba; graduación normal de licores alcohólicos; (foto. y b. a.) prueba; (mat.) prueba, comprobación.—**p.-read,** leer y corregir prueba de.—**p. reader,** corrector de pruebas.—**p. reading,** corrección de pruebas.—**p. sheet,** pliego de prueba, prueba. **II.** *a.* empleado en probar, cotejar o corregir; de comprobación; impenetrable, hecho a prueba de; de prueba.—**p. sheet,** prueba (de imprenta).—**p. spirit,** licor de prueba (que contiene 50% de alcohol).—**to be p. against,** ser o estar a prueba de.
proofing [prúfing], *s.* substancia o preparación impermeabilizadora o antipermeable.
proofless [prúfles], *a.* falto de prueba, no probado; sin fundamento.
prop. I. *va.* sostener, apuntalar; entibar, escorar, acodalar, ahorquillar; (fig.) mantener, sustentar. **II.** *s.* apoyo, puntal, paral, apeo, asnilla, madrina, sustentáculo; (min.) entibo, adema; (agr.) rodrigón, tentemozo; machón, contrafuerte; apoyo, amparo, báculo; sostén.
propædeutic(al [própidiútic, al], *a.* propedéutico.—**propædeutics,** [-tics], *s.* propedéutica.
propagable [própagæbœl], *a.* propagable.
propaganda [própagænda], *s.* propaganda.
propagandist [-dist], *s.* propagandista.
propagate [-gueit]. **I.** *va.* propagar, multiplicar; diseminar; propalar; impeler, empujar. **II.** *vn.* propagarse; cundir.
propagation [-guéishun], *s.* propagación; diseminación, difusión.
propagative, propagatory [própaguetiv, tori], *a.* propagativo.
propagator [-guéitœr], *s.* propagador.
propane [própein], *s.* (quím.) propano.
propel [propél], *va.* impeler, empujar.
propellent [-œnt], *a.* motor, propulsor, impelente.
propeller [-œr], *s.* impulsor, propulsor; hélice (de un buque, de un avión).—**p. shaft,** (aut.) eje de propulsión, eje cardán.
propelling [-ing], *a.* de impulsión, de propulsión.—**p. power,** fuerza propulsora.
propense [propéns], *a.* propenso.
propension, propensity [propénshun, siti], *s.* propensión, tendencia.
proper [própœr], *a.* propio, conveniente, apropiado, adecuado; decoroso, formal, correcto; justo, exacto.—**p. fraction,** quebrado propio.—**p. noun,** nombre propio.—**properly** [-li], *adv.* propiamente, apropiadamente; correctamente; oportunamente; decorosamente.
properness [-nes], *s.* propiedad.
propertied [-tid], *a.* propietario.
property [própœrti], *s.* propiedad; hacienda, bienes; posesión, dominio, pertenencia; (teat.) aderezo, cualquier objeto necesario para la representación de una obra.—**p. owner,** propietario (esp. de bienes raíces).
prophecy [prófesi], *s.* profecía.
prophesy [prófesai], *va.* y *vn.* profetizar.
prophet [prófet], *s.* profeta.
prophetess [prófetes], *s.* profetisa.
prophetic(al [profétic(al], *a.* profético.
prophetically [-i], *adv.* proféticamente.
propheticalness [-nes], *s.* calidad de profético.

prophylactic [profiláectic], *a.* profiláctico.
prophylaxis [profiláecsis], *s.* (med.) profilaxis.
prophyll [prófil], *s.* (bact.) bractéola.
propinquity [propíncuiti], *s.* propincuidad, cercanía; parentesco.
propitiable [propíshiabœl], *a.* que se puede propiciar, favorable.
propitiate [propíshieit], *vn.* propiciar.—**propitiation** [-éishūn], *s.* propiciación.—**propitiator** [-etœr], *s.* propiciador.—**propitiatory** [-atori]. **I.** *a.* propiciatorio. **II.** *s.* propiciación; propiciatorio.
propitious [propíshūs], *a.* propicio.—**propitiously** [-li], *adv.* propiciamente.—**propitiousness** [-nes], *s.* calidad de propicio.
propolis [própolis], *s.* (api.) propóleos, tanca, cera aleda.
proponent [propónent], *s.* proponente.
proportion [propórshūn]. **I.** *s.* proporción.— **out of p.**, desproporcionado. **II.** *va.* proporcionar, armonizar; aporcionar.
proportionable [-abœl], *a.* proporcionable, proporcionado.—**proportionableness** [-nes], *s.* calidad de proporcionado.—**proportionably** [-bli], *adv.* proporcionablemente, proporcionadamente.
proportional [-al]. **I.** *a.* proporcional.—**p. dividers**, compás de proporción. **II.** *s* número o cantidad proporcional.
proportionality [-éliti], *s.* proporcionalidad.
proportionally [-ali], *adv.* proporcionalmente.
proportionate [propórshūnet]. **I.** *a.* proporcionado, armónico. **II.** *va.* proporcionar, ajustar.
proportioned [propórshūnd], *a.* proporcionado; formado (un hombre, una mujer, etc.).
proposal [propóšal], *s.* propuesta.
propose [propóuš]. **I.** *va.* proponer; proponerse, tener intención de. **II.** *vn.* proponer (esp. matrimonio).
proposer [propóušœr], *s.* proponente, proponedor.
proposition [própošíshūn], *s.* proposición, propuesta; (lóg. y mat.) proposición; (ret.) exposición, propósito; (mús.) tema. En lenguaje familiar se emplea a veces con alguna vaguedad en el sentido de "cosa," "asunto," "problema," "sujeto," etc.: *the war was a serious proposition*, la guerra fué cosa seria; *the working of those mines was a complicated proposition*, la explotación de esas minas era un problema complicado; *that man seems to be a very tough proposition*, ese hombre parece ser tipo muy difícil.
propositional [-al], *a.* de carácter de proposición; relativo a la proposición.
propound [propáund], *va.* proponer; presentar.
propounder [-œr], *s.* proponente, proponedor.
propretor [proprítœr], *s.* propretor.
proprietary [propráietæri]. **I.** *a.* propietario; privilegiado, patentado (apl. esp. a remedios de patente). **II.** *s.* propietario, dueño; hacendados, propietarios; propiedad.
proprietor [-tœr], *s.* propietario, dueño, amo.
proprietress [-tres], *s.* propietaria, dueña.
propriety [propráieti], *s.* propiedad, corrección; decoro, decencia.—*pl.* **proprieties**, reglas, canones (del arte, sociales, etc.).
propt, *pp. irr.* de **to prop**.
propulsion [propúlshūn], *s.* propulsión; impulso, impulsión.
propulsive, propulsory [-siv, sori], *a.* propulsor, impelente.
propyl [própuil], *s.* (quím.) propilo.
propylæum [própilium], *s.* propíleo.
propylene [própilin], *s.* (quím.) propileno.
prorate [prorréit], *va.* prorratear.
prorogation [proroguéishūn], *s.* prórroga; (Ingl. pol.) suspensión de las sesiones del Parlamento.
prorogue [prorróg], *va.* diferir, aplazar; (ant.) prorrogar; (Ingl. pol.) suspender las sesiones (del Parlamento).
prosaic [prošéic], *a.* prosaico.
prosaically [prošéicali], *adv.* prosaicamente.
prosaism [próšaišm], *s.* prosaísmo.
proscenium [prosínium], *s.* proscenio.

proscribe [proscráib], *va.* proscribir; condenar, reprobar.
proscriber [proscráibœr], *s.* proscriptor.
proscription [proscrípshūn], *s.* proscripción; encartamiento.
proscriptive [proscríptiv], *a.* proscriptivo.
prose [próuš]. **I.** *s.* prosa; discurso pesado. **II.** *a.* de prosa, en prosa; insulso, pesado. **III.** *va.* y *vn.* escribir en prosa, o en estilo pesado.
prosect [proséct], *va.* preparar disecciones anatómicas.
prosecute [prósekiut]. **I.** *va.* continuar, llevar adelante; (for.) acusar, encausar, enjuiciar, procesar. **II.** *vn.* querellarse ante el juez; seguir un pleito; fiscalizar.
prosecution [prosekiúshūn], *s.* prosecución, seguimiento; (for.) parte actora, fiscal.
prosecutor [prósekiútœr], *s.* (for.) actor, acusador; acusador oficial, fiscal.
prosecutrix [-trix], *s.* acusadora, demandante.
proselyte [próselait]. **I.** *s.* prosélito. **II.** *va.* hacer prosélitos.
proselytism [próselitišm], *s.* proselitismo.
proselytize [próselitaiš], *va.* y *vn.* convertir, hacer prosélitos.
prosencephalon [prósenséfælon], *s.* prosencéfalo, parte anterior del cerebro (los hemisferios).
prosenchyma [prosénkimæ], *s.* (bot.) prosénquima.
proser [próšœr], *s.* prosista.
prosily [próšili], *adv.* prosaicamente.
prosiness [próšines], *s.* calidad de prosaico; insulsez, aridez.
proslavery [prosléivœri]. **I.** *a.* esclavista. **II.** *s.* defensa de la esclavitud.
prosodist [prósodist], *s.* versado en prosodia.
prosodic [prosódic], *a.* prosódico.
prosody [prósodi], *s.* prosodia.
prosopopœia [prósopopíya], *s.* (ret.) prosopopeya, personificación.
prospect [próspect]. **I.** *va.* y *vn.* (min.) explorar, catear, buscar; dar buenas esperanzas, prometer. **II.** *s.* perspectiva, vista; probabilidad, señal; expectativa, esperanza; situación, orientación; indicación o señal de veta o criadero; cata, producto de un mineral catado, muestra; (com.) comprador o parroquiano probable o de expectativa.
prospector, prospecter [próspeetœr], *s.* (min.) explorador, buscador.
prospective [prospéctiv]. **I.** *a.* anticipado, venidero, en expectativa; previsor, prevenido; presunto, de expectativa. **II.** *s.* perspectiva, vista; (com.) comprador o parroquiano presunto o de expectativa.
prospectus [prospéctus], *s.* prospecto.
prosper [próspœr]. **I.** *va.* hacer medrar. **II.** *vn.* prosperar, medrar, florecer.
prosperity [prospériti], *s.* prosperidad.
prosperous [próspœrus], *a.* próspero, floreciente; favorable o propicio.—**prosperously** [-li], *adv.* prósperamente.—**prosperousness** [-nes], *s.* prosperidad.
prostate [próstet], *s.* (anat.) próstata.
prostatic [prostétic], *a.* prostático.
prosthesis [prósžesis], *s.* prótesis.
prostitute [próstitiut]. **I.** *va.* prostituir **I . s.** prostituta. **III.** *a.* prostituído, mercenario, degradado.
prostitution [próstitiúshūn], *s.* prostitución.
prostrate [próstret]. **I.** *a.* postrado, humillado, prosternado; (biol.) tendido. **II.** *va.* tender, postrar; demoler, derribar; arruinar; (med.) postrar, debilitar. **III.** *vn.* postrarse, prosternarse.
prostration [prostréshūn], *s.* postración, abatimiento, depresión; (med.) postración o adinamia.
prostyle [próstail], *s.* (arq.) próstilo.
prosy [prósi], *a.* prosaico; insulso, árido.
protagonist [protǽgonist], *s.* protagonista.
protasis [prótasis], *s.* (gram.) prótasis.
protean [prótian], *a.* variable.

protect [protéct], *va.* proteger.

protected cruiser, crucero protegido, que tiene cubierta acorazada y torres blindadas, pero poco o ningún blindaje en los costados.—**protected state,** (der. int.) protectorado (territorio).

protection [protécŝhun], *s.* protección, amparo; resguardo, defensa; salvoconducto, pasaporte, carta de seguridad; (e. p.) protección; proteccionismo.

protectionism [-iŝm], *s.* (e. p.) proteccionismo.

protectionist [-ist], *s.* proteccionista.

protective [protéctiv]. **I.** *a.* protector; (e. p.) proteccionista. **II.** *s.* protección; lo que protege; (cir.) cubierta aséptica para una herida.

protector [protéctœr], *s.* protector.

protectorate [protéctœret], *s.* protectorado.

protectress [protéctres], *s.* protectora.

protégé [proteÿé], *s.* (fr.) protegido, paniaguado.

proteid [próteid], **protein** [prótein], *s.* (quím.) proteína.

Proterozoic [prótœrœŝóic], *s.* y *a.* (geol.) postarqueozóico.

protest [protést]. **I.** *va.* protestar, declarar; (com.) protestar (una letra).—**to p. for non-acceptance,** protestar por falta de aceptación.—**to p. for non-payment,** protestar por falta de pago. **II.** *vn.* protestar. **III.** *s.* [prótest] protestación, protesta; (com.) protesto.

Protestant [prótestant], *a.* y *s.* protestante.

Protestantism [-iŝm], *s.* protestantismo.

protestation [prótestéiŝhun], *s.* protestación; protesta, declaración.

protestor [protéstœr], *s.* el que protesta.

prothallium [prozélium], *s.* (bot.) protalo.

prothesis [prózesis], *s.* (gram.) prótesis.

prothonotary [prozónotœri], *s.* protonotario.—**p. warbler,** (E. U. orn.) pájaro cantor.

prothonotaryship [-ŝhip], *s.* protonotariato.

prothorax [prozóræx], *s.* (ent.) protórax.

Protococcales [prótocockéliŝ], *s. pl.* (bot.) protococales.—**Protococcus** [-cócus], *s.* protococo.

protocol [prótocol]. **I.** *s.* protocolo. **II.** *va.* protocolar.

protolithic [prótolízic], *a.* del primer período de la edad de piedra.

protomartyr [prótomártœr], *s.* protomártir.

protometal [-métal], *s.* metal refinado a altísimas temperaturas, cuyo espectro se aprovecha en el análisis espectral. Para especificar, se pone el nombre del metal: *protocalcium, protovanadium.*

proton [próton], *s.* (fís.) protón, parte del átomo (complemento del electrón).

protoplasm [prótoplaŝm], *s.* (biol.) protoplasma.

protoplasmic, protoplasmal, protoplasmatic [-ic, -al, -ætic], *a.* protoplasmático.

protopope [prótopoup], *s.* protopapa, especie de archidiácono en la iglesia griega.

prototype [prótotaip], *s.* prototipo.

prototyp(ic)al ¡prótotaip(ic)al], *a.* prototípico.

protoxid [prótóxid], *s.* protóxido.

Protozoa [prótoŝóa], *s. pl.* protozoarios, protozoos.

protract [protréct], *va.* alargar, prolongar, demorar; trazar (un plano) por medio del transportador.

protracted [-ed], *a.* largo, prolongado, demorado, lento.

protractile [-til], *a.* que se puede alargar hacia delante.

protraction [protrécŝhun], *s.* prolongación, demora, continuación.

protractive [protréctiv], *a.* dilatorio.

protractor [protréctor], *s.* prolongador; transportador (instrumento); (anat.) músculo extensor; (sast.) molde o regla.

protrude [protrúd]. **I.** *va.* empujar, sacar fuera. **II.** *vn.* salir fuera o sobresalir.—**protrusi(b)le** [-si(bœ)l], *a.* que puede sacarse o alargarse.—**protrusion** [-ÿun], *s.* acción de sacar o empujar hacia afuera; parte que sobresale.—**protrusive** [-siv], *a.* que sobresale o tiende a sobresalir; que empuja hacia adelante.

protuberance, protuberancy [protiúbœrans, i], *s.* protuberancia.—**protuberant** [-ant], *a.* protuberante, resaliente.—**protuberate** [-eit], *vn.* sobresalir, resaltar.

proud [práud], *a.* orgulloso; soberbio, arrogante; brioso, pujante.—**proudly** [-li], *adv.* soberbiamente; orgullosamente.

provable [prúvabœl], *a.* demostrable.

prove [pruv]. **I.** *va.* (pret. PROVED: *pp.* PROVED o PROVEN) probar, demostrar; comprobar; poner a prueba, examinar, experimentar; (for.) abrir y hacer público (un testamento); (impr.) sacar prueba de. **II.** *vn.* resultar, venir a parar, salir (bien o mal); demostrar que es (capaz, etc.)

proven [prúvœn], *pp.* de TO PROVE; (for.) probado, demostrado.—**not p.,** veredicto de no probado.

provender [próvendœr], *s.* forraje.

provenience [províniœns], *s.* (b. a.) procedencia.

proverb [próvœrb], *s.* proverbio; adagio, refrán.—**proverbial** [provœrbial], *a.* proverbial.—**proverbialist** [-ist], *s.* proverbista.—**proverbially** [-li], *adv.* proverbialmente.

provide [prováid]. **I.** *va.* proveer, proporcionar, suplir, abastecer, suministrar; estipular. **II.** *vn.* (con for) proveer lo necesario, sufragar gastos, abastecer de víveres; precaverse, tener cuidado, encargarse de; tomar precauciones, prepararse; estipular, disponer; dar disposiciones con respecto a; providenciar, dar providencias para.—**to p. against,** precaver, prevenir algún riesgo.—**provided that,** con tal que, a condición que.

providence [próvidens], *s.* providencia; previsión; prudencia; frugalidad, economía; (P-) la Providencia.

provident [-ent], *a.* próvido, providente; económico.

providential [-dénŝhal], *a.* providencial.

providentially [-i], *adv.* providencialmente.

providently [próvidentli], *adv.* próvidamente, prudentemente.

provider [prováidœr], *s.* proveedor, suministrador, abastecedor.

province [próvins], *s.* provincia; obligación, incumbencia, competencia.—**that is not my p.,** eso no me toca, no es de mi incumbencia.

provincial [provínŝhal]. **I.** *a.* provincial; rudo, campesino, grosero. **II.** *s.* provinciano; (igl.) provincial.—**provincialism** [-iŝm], *s.* provincialismo.—**provincialist** [-ist], *s.* provinciano.—**provinciality** [-ŝhiéliti], *s.* carácter provinciano.

provincially [-ŝhiali], *adv.* a modo provinciano.

provine [prováin], *va.* (agr.) amugronar.

provision [províÿun], *s.* provisión, aprovisionamiento, abastecimiento; (for.) medida, disposición, estipulación.—*pl.* provisiones, comestibles, víveres.—**till farther p. be made,** hasta más proveer.

provisional [-al], *a.* provisional, interino.—**provisionally** [-i], *adv.* provisionalmente, interinamente.

proviso [prováiŝo], *s.* caución, estipulación, condición, requisito.

provisor [prováiŝœr], *s.* proveedor.

provisorily [-ili], *adv.* condicionalmente.

provisory [-i], *a.* provisorio; condicional.

provocation [provokéŝhun], *s.* provocación; excitación, estímulo.

provocative [provócativ]. **I.** *a.* provocativo. **II.** *s.* estimulante.—**provocativeness** [-nes], *s.* calidad de provocativo.

provoke [provóuk]. **I.** *va.* provocar, irritar, encolerizar; excitar, incitar; causar, promover. **II.** *vn.* causar enojo, excitar cólera.—**provoker** [-œr], *s.* provocador.—**provoking** [-ing], *a.* provocativo, provocante, irritante.—**provokingly** [-li], *adv.* provocativamente.

provost [próvust], *s.* preboste; (Ingl.) director de colegio.—**p. marshal,** (mil.) capitán preboste.

provostship [-ŝhip], *s.* prebostazgo.

prow [práu], *s.* (mar.) proa; tajamar.

prowess [práues], *s.* proeza, hazaña.

prowl [prául], *va.* y *vn.* rondar (para robar).—**prowler** [práulœr], *s.* vago, rondador.

proximal [próximal], a. (biol.) próximo.
proximate [próximet], a. próximo, inmediato.
proximately [-li], adv. próximamente, inmediatamente.
proximity [proxímiti], s. proximidad.
proximo [próximo], adv. del o en el mes próximo (se abrevia **prox.**).
proxy [próxi], s. apoderado, delegado, poderhabiente; procuración, poder.—**by p.**, por poder, mediante apoderado o substituto.
prude [prud], s. mojigata, remilgada, gazmoña.
prudence [prúdens], s. prudencia.
prudent [-ent], a. prudente.
prudential [prudénŝhal], a. prudencial.
prudentially [-i], adv. prudencialmente.
prudently [prúdentli], adv. prudentemente.
prudery [prúdœri], s. melindrería, remilgo, gazmoñería.
prudish [prúdiŝh], a. gazmoño, remilgado, denguero.
prune [prun]. **I.** va. y vn. (agri.) podar, cortar, escamondar; expurgar. **II.** s. ciruela pasa; (bot.) ciruela.
prunella, prunello [prunéla, o], s. (tej.) sempiterna, rompecoches.
pruner [prúnœr], s. podador.
pruniferous [prunífœrus], a. que produce ciruelas.
pruning [prúning], s. poda, monda, remonda, escamonda.—**p. hook** o **knife**, podón, márcola, bodollo.—**p. shears**, podaderas.
prurience, pruriency [prúriens, i], s. comezón, prurito; sensualidad.—**prurient** [-ent], a. salaz. lascivo; anheloso.
prurigo [pruráigo], s. comezón, prurigo.
Prussian [prúŝhan o prúŝhan], a. y s. prusiano.— **P. blue,** azul de Prusia.
Prussianism [-iŝm], s. prusianismo, militarismo opresivo y ambicioso.
prussiate [prúsiet], s. (quím.) prusiato.
prussic [prúsic o prúsic], a. (quím.) prúsico.
pry [prái]. **I.** va. y vn. espiar, acechar, atisbar, observar, registrar o escudriñar; (mec.) alzaprimar.—**to p. into,** fisgar, fiscalizar, curiosear, entremeterse.—**to p. out a secret,** arrancar un secreto. **II.** s. inspección, reconocimiento o registro escrupuloso; persona curiosa o entremetida; (mec.) palanca, barra, alzaprima.
prytaneum [prítæníum], s. pritáneo.
prytanis [prítanis], s. prítano, miembro del senado entre los antiguos atenienses.
psalm [sam], s. salmo; himno.
psalmist [sámist o sælmist], s. salmista.
psalmody [sálmodi o sámodi], s. salmodia.
psalter [sóltœr], s. salterio, salmodia.
psalterium [soltírium], s. tercer estómago de los rumiantes.
psaltery [sóltœri], s. (mús.) salterio.
pseudo [siúdo], a. seudo, falso, pretendido. Se emplea en muchas palabras compuestas cuyo significado es obvio; v. gr.: *pseudo-apostle,* seudo apóstol, falso apóstol; *pseudo-emperor,* pretendido emperador; *pseudo-science,* falsa ciencia.
pseudomorph [-morf], s. (min.) seudomorfo; forma irregular o falsa.—**pseudomorphous** [-fus], a. seudomorfo.—**pseudomorphism** [-fiŝm], s. seudomorfismo.
pseudonym [-nim], s. seudónimo; (biol.) nombre vernáculo.
pseudonymous [siudónimus], a. seudónimo.
pseudopod [siúdopod], s., **pseudopodal** [siudópodæl], a. (biol.) seudópodo.
pseudoscope [siúdoscòup], s. seudoscopio.
pshaw [ŝho], interj. ¡bah! ¡fuera! ¡quita!
Psittaci [sítasai, psítasi], s. pl. (orn.) sitácidos.
psoas [sóœs], s. (anat.) psoas.—**p. magnus,** o **p. major,** gran psoas.—**p. minor,** o **p. parvus,** pequeño psoas.
psora [sóra], s. (med.) sora, sarna.
psoriasis [soráiasis], s. (med.) soriasis.
psyche [sáiki], s. psique, mente.
psychiatrist [sáikiætrist], s. psiquiatrista, psicópata.—**psychiatry** [-tri], s. psiquiatría.

psychic(al [sáikic(al], psíquico.
psycoanalysis [sáicoœnælisis], s. psicoanalisis o psicanalisis.—**psychoanalyst** [-œnælist], s. psicoanalista; alienista.
psychogenesis [-yénesis], s. psicogénesis o psicogenia.—**psychogenetic** [-yenétic], a. psicogenésico.
psychologic(al [sáicolóyic(al], a. psicológico.— **psychologist** [saicóloyist], s. psicólogo.—**psychologize** [-yaiŝ], vn. psicologizar.—**psychology** [saicóloyi], s. psicología.
psychometer [-cómitœr], s. psicómetro.—**psychometry** [-cómetri], s. psicometría.
psychopathology [sáicopæzóloyi], s. psicopatología, patología de la mente.
psychopathy [saicópæzi], s. psicopatía.
psychophysics [sáicofísics], s. psicofísica.
psychosis [saicósis], s. psicosis.
psychotherapeutics [sáicoœzéræpiútics], **psychotherapy** [-zéræpi], psicoterapia.
psychrometer [saicrómitœr], s. psicrómetro.
ptarmigan [tármigan], s. (orn.) chocha.
pteropod [téropod], s. y a. (zool.) pterópodo.— **Pteropoda** [terópodæ], s. pl. pterópodos.
ptisan [tíŝan], s. tisana.
Ptolemaic [tóleméic], a. tolemaico.
ptomain(e [tómain], s. ptomaína.
ptyalin [táiælin], s. (quím.) ptialina.
ptyalism [táialiŝm], s. tialismo, salivación, babeo.
puberty [piúbœrti], s. pubertad, pubescencia; (bot.) período de florescencia.
pubes [piúbis, púbes], s. (anat.) pubis.
pubescence [piubésens], s. (bot.) pelusa, vello; pubescenia, pubertad.—**pubescent** [-ent], a. (bot.) pubescente, velloso; púber.
pubic [piúbic], a. pubiano, púbico.
public [públic]. **I.** a. público.—**p. health,** higiene pública.—**p. house,** posada, hostería, fonda; (Ingl.) cantina.—**p. lands,** tierras incultas nacionales, tierras baldías.—**p. loan,** empréstito. —**p. officer,** funcionario público.—**p. prosecutor,** fiscal.—**p. purposes,** utilidades públicas, usos públicos.—**p.-spirited,** patriótico, de espíritu público.—**p. utility,** obra o empresa de servicio público.—**p. weal,** bien público. **II.** s. público.
publican [públican], s. publicano; (Ingl.) mesonero, posadero, tabernero.
publication [públikéiŝhun], s. publicación.
publicist [públisist], s. publicista.
publicity [publísiti], s. publicidad, notoriedad.
publicly [públicli], adv. públicamente.
publish [públiŝh], va. publicar; editar.
publisher [-œr], s. editor; publicador.
publishing [-ing], a. editorial, de publicaciones. —**p. house,** casa editorial.
puccoon [pucún], s. (bot.) orcaneta.
puck [puc], s. coco, fantasma, duende.
puckball [pucból], s. (bot.) bejín.
pucker [púcœr]. **I.** va. (cost.) fruncir, plegar, recoger, arrugar. **II.** s. (cost.) fruncido, pliegue, arruga; (fam.) agitación, embrollo.
pudding [púding], s. (coc.) pudín o budín.—**p. dish** o **pan,** tartera.
puddle [púdœl]. **I.** s. charco, poza; cimiento hidráulico. **II.** va. (fund.) pudelar; (hidr.) cimentar el fondo de un canal; enlodar, enfangar.
puddler [púdlœr], s. (fund.) pudelador; orno de pudelar.
puddling [púdling], s. (fund.) pudelación, pudelado; cimiento hidráulico; (hidr.) cimentación.—**p. furnace,** horno de pudelar.
puddly [púdli], a. lodoso, cenagoso.
pudency [piúdensi], s. recato, pudor.
pudenda [piudéndæ], s. pl. órganos genitales.— **pudendum** [-um], s. vulva.
pudgy [púyi], a. (fam.) regordete, gordiflón.
pudicity [piudísiti], s. pudicicia, pudor.
pueblo [pueblo], s. pueblo, aldea; casa comunal o aldea de indios.—**P. Indians,** tribus indígenas agrícolas semicivilizadas de México y el sur de los E. U.
puerile [piúœril], a. pueril, infantil.
puerility [piuœríliti], s. puerilidad.

---

puerperal [piucérpœral], *a.* (med.) puerperal.—**p. fever**, fiebre puerperal.

puff [pʊf]. **I.** *s.* resoplido, soplo, bocanada, bombo o elogio exagerado; mota de empolvarse; (cost.) bollo.—**p. adder**, víbora venenosa.—**p. paste**, hojaldre.—**p. of wind**, ráfaga, soplo; ventolera. **II.** *va.* hinchar, inflar, engreír, envanecer; ensalzar, dar bombo; (cost.) abollonar. **III.** *vn.* inflarse, hincharse; engreírse; bufar, dar bufidos; echar bocanadas; resoplar, fumar, resollar, jadear.—**to p. away**, disipar a soplos.—**to p. up**, hincharse, hincharse, ahuecarse; engreírse. **IV.** *interj.* ¡puf! ¡bah!

puffball [pʊfbol], *s.* (bot.) bejín.

puffer [pʊfœr], *s.* soplador; ponderador.

puffin [pʊfin], *s.* (orn.) alca.

puffiness [pʊfines], *s.* hinchazón; (med.) hinchazón, intumescencia.

puffily [pʊfili], *adv.* hinchadamente; jadeando.

puffy [pʊfi], *a.* hinchado, inflado, entumecido.—**p. style**, estilo campanudo.

pug [pʊg]. **I.** *s.* (alb.) torta.—**p. (dog)**, dogo.—**p. mill**, artesa de ladrillería; amasadera.—**p. nose**, nariz respingada.—**p.-nosed**, braco, nacho. **II.** *va.* (hidr.) cimentar; (alb.) embarrar, rellenar con torta o argamasa.

pugh [piú o pu], *interj.* ¡uf! ¡fo!

pugilism [piúyilišm], *s.* pugilato.—**pugilist** [-ist], *s.* pugilista.—**pugilistic** [-istic], *a.* de pugilato.

pugnacious [pʊgnéišus], *a.* pugnaz, belicoso.

pugnacity [pʊgnǽsiti], *s.* pugnacidad.

puisne [piúni], *a.* (for.) juez pedáneo.

puissance [piúisans], *s.* pujanza, poder.

puissant [piúisant], *a.* pujante, fuerte.

puke [piúc]. **I.** *s.* vomitivo. **II.** *va.* y *vn.* vomitar.

pulchritude [pʊ́lcritiud], *s.* pulcritud.

pule [piúl], *vn.* piar, pipiar; gemir, llorar

pulex [piúlex], *s.* (ent.) pulga.

pulic [piúlic], *s.* (bot.) pulguera.

puling [piúling], *s.* piada.

pull [pul]. **I.** *va.* tirar de, tirar hacia sí, halar, arrastrar; estirar; arrancar, sacar; pelar, desplumar; rasgar o desgarrar; bogar o remar; (impr.) sacar (una prueba) con la prensa de mano; (fam.) sorprender y copar un garito.—**to p. a long face**, poner la cara larga.—**to p. asunder**, o **away**, arrancar, separar o quitar con violencia.—**to p. back**, tirar hacia atrás; hacer recular o cejar.—**to p. down**, derribar, demoler; degradar, deponer; humillar, abatir.—**to p. in**, tirar hacia adentro; cerrar.—**to p. in pieces**, hacer trizas, desgarrar, despedazar.—**to p. off**, o **out**, arrancar; deshacer o desbaratar.—**to p. one's leg**, (E. U. fam.) dar un sablazo, pedir o hacer gastar dinero.—**to p. one's self together**, recobrar la calma; arreglarse, componerse.—**to p. the wool over one's eyes**, engañar a uno como un chino.—**to p. through**, sacar de dificultades o de un aprieto.—**to p. up**, extirpar, desarraigar.—**to p. up stakes**, (fam.) prepararse para partir, alzar tiendas (fig.).—**II.** *vn.* tirar con esfuerzo; tirar de una cuerda; dar un tirón.—**to p. ahead**, (mar.) halar avante.—**to p. apart**, romperse por tracción.—**to p. through**, salir de un trance o aprieto.—**to p. up**, detener un caballo; hacer alto. **III.** *s.* tirón, estirón; tirador (de puerta, etc.); (fam.) influjo, influencia; (impr.) impresión hecha con la prensa de mano; (dep.) ejercicio de remos, boga.—**p. box**, (elec.) caja de acceso a los conductores y tubos que los llevan.—**p. switch**, interruptor de tiro o de cadena. **IV.** *interj.* ¡hala!

pullback [púlbæc], *s.* rémora, estorbo.

puller [púlœr], *s.* el o lo que tira o arranca.

pullet [púlet], *s.* polla.

pulley [púli], *s.* polea; (mar.) garrucha, motón, cuadernal; (anat.) trocla, tróclea.—**p. block**, aparejo (de poleas).

pullman [púlman], *s.* (E. U., f. c.) coche salón.

pullulate [púliulet], *vn.* pulular.

pulmonary [púlmonæri], *a.* pulmonar.

Pulmonata [púlmoneitæ], *s. pl.* (zool.) pulmonados.—**pulmonate** [-neit], *s.* y *a.* pulmonado.

pulmonic [pulmónic]. **I.** *s.* pectoral; el que tiene una afección pulmonar. **II.** *a.* pulmonar.

pulmotor [púlmóutœr], *s.* pulmotor (nombre de fábrica), aparato de respiración artificial.

pulp [pulp], *s.* pulpa; (bot.) arilo; (pap.) pulpa, pasta.

pulpiness [púlpines], **pulpousness** [púlpusnes], *s.* calidad de pulposo.

pulpit [púlpit], *s.* púlpito; clero; tribuna.

pulpous [púlpus], **pulpy** [púlpi], *a.* pulposo, carnoso, mollar.

pulpwood [púlpud], *s.* madera de pulpa (para papel).

pulsate [púlset], *vn.* pulsar, latir, batir.

pulsatile [púlsatil], *a.* pulsátil, pulsativo; laniente; (mús.) de percusión.

pulsating [púlseiting], *a.* pulsativo (ú. esp. en elec.).

pulsation [pulséišun], *s.* pulsación, latido.

pulsative [púlsativ], *a.* pulsativo.

pulsator [pulséitœr], *s.* pulsímetro.

pulsatory [púlsatori], *a.* pulsante, latiente.

pulse [púls]. **I.** *s.* pulso; pulsación, vibración; legumbres colectivamente (garbanzos, habas, lentejas, etc.). **II.** *vn.* pulsar, latir, batir.

pulseless [púlsles], *a.* sin pulso.

pulsimeter [pulsímetœr], *s.* (med.) pulsímetro, esfigmómetro.

pulsion [púlšun], *s.* impulso.

pulsometer [pulsómetœr], (med.) esfigmómetro; (hidr.) pulsómetro.

pultaceous [pultéšhus], *a.* pultáceo.

pulverization [pulvœrišéišhun], *s.* pulverización, trituración.—**pulverize** [-aiš], *va.* pulverizar.—**pulverizer** [-áiscer], *s.* pulverizador.

pulverulence [pulvérulens], *s.* abundancia de polvo, polvareda.—**pulverulent** [-lœnt], *a.* polvoriento, pulverulento.

puma [piúma], *s.* (zool.) puma.

pumice [púmis o piúmis], *va.* apomazar.—**p. stone**, piedra pómez.

pumiceous [piumíšhus], *a.* que contiene piedra pómez.

pummel, *v.* y *s.* = POMMEL.

pump [pump]. **I.** *s.* (mec.) bomba; (zap.) escarpín.—**p. barrel** = P. CYLINDER.—**p. brake**, manubrio de bomba; (art.) freno o amortiguador hidráulico.—**p. cylinder**, cuerpo de bomba.—**p. dale**, dala.—**p. handle** = P. BRAKE.—**p. plunger**, émbolo de bomba (apl. esp. al buzo).—**p. rod**, **p. spear**, vástago del émbolo de una bomba.—**p. water**, agua de pozo. **II.** *va.* y *vn.* dar a la bomba, bombear; sondear, tantear, sonsacar.

pumper [púmpœr], *s.* bombero; sonsacador.

pumpernickel [púmpœrnícœl], *s.* pan moreno.

pumping [púmping], *a.* de bombear.—**p. engine**, bomba de vapor.—**p. jack**, aparato de poleas de transmisión para actuar una bomba en un pozo profundo.

pumpkin [púmpkin (fam. púnkin)], *s.* (bot.) calabaza confitera.

pun [pʊn]. **I.** *s.* equívoco, retruécano, juego de vocablos. **II.** *vn.* jugar del vocablo.

punch [pʊnch]. **I.** *va.* punzar, punzonar, horadar con punzón; sacar o cortar con punzón; empujar, hurgar; (fam.) dar puñetazos de hurgón. **II.** *s.* punzón, sacabocados; ponche (bebida); (fam.) puñada o puñetazo de hurgón; energía, actividad; vivacidad.—**P. and Judy**, títeres.—**p. bowl**, bol, ponchera.—**p. pliers**, sacabocados.—**p. press**, punzonadora.—**p. sinker**, tallador, abridor o grabador en hueco.

puncheon [púnchœn], *s.* pipa (medida de líquidos); punzón; contrapunzón, estampador; (carp.) pie derecho.

puncher [púnchœr], *s.* punzón; (E. U.) vaquero, boyero.

punchinello [púnchinélo], *s.* pulchinela; títere.

punctilio [pʊnctílio], *s.* puntillo.

punctilious [pʊnctílius], *a.* puntilloso, pundonoroso; etiquetero.—**punctiliousness** [-nes], *s.* puntillo, pundonor.

puncto [púncto], *s.* (esgr.) toque.

punctual [púnctiual], *a.* puntual.—**punctuality** [pʊnctiuǽliti], *s.* puntualidad.—**punctually** [púnctiuali], *adv.* puntualmente.

punctuate [púnkchueit], *va.* y *vn.* puntuar.

punctuation [-éishʊn], _s._ (gram.) puntuación.
puncture [pʌ́nkchʊr]. **I.** _va._, punzar; pinchar, agujerear, picar.—**punctured wound,** herida penetrante, picadura. **II.** _s._ pinchadura, pinchazo; punzada, picadura; (cir.) punción; (zool.) hoyo.
pundit [pʌ́ndit], _s._ bracmán sabio.
pungency [pʌ́nyensi], _s._ picante, punta, sabor; acerbidad, acrimonia; mordacidad.
pungent [pʌ́nyent], _a._ picante; pungente, mordicante; acre, mordaz, acerbo; (zool.) punzante; (bot.) puntiagudo.
Punic [piúnic], _a._ púnico.
puniness [piúnines], _s._ encanijamiento.
punish [pʌ́niŝh], _va._ castigar.—**punishable** [-abœl], _a._ punibible.—**punishability** [-abíliti], **punishableness** [-abœlnes], _s._ punibilidad.— **punisher** [-œr], _s._ castigador.—**punishment** [-mœnt], _s._ castigo; (fam.) vapuleo, julepe.
punitive, punitory [piúnitiv, tori], _a._ penal, punitivo.
punk [pʊnc]. **I.** _s._ yesca, hupe, pebete; (fam.) tonterías, hojarasca. **II.** _a._ (fam.) muy malo, sin valor ni mérito.
punka [pʌ́nka], _s._ abanico colgante.
punster [pʌ́nstœr], _s._ equivoquista.
punt [pʊnt]. **I.** _va._ impeler una batea apoyando una vara en el fondo del río; (dep.) dar un puntapié al balón en el aire; lanzar. **II.** _vn._ cazar, pescar o ir en batea; despedir el balón con un puntapié; apuntar, en juegos de azar. **III.** _s._ batea, barquichuelo de fondo plano; (mar.) plancha de agua; (dep.) puntapié dado al balón en el aire.
punter [pʌ́ntœr], _s._ el que impele una batea; el que despide un balón a puntapiés; pelete (en juegos de azar).
puny [piúni], _a._ encanijado; pequeño, diminuto; mezquino.
pup [pʊp]. **I.** _vn._ parir la perra. **II.** _s._ cachorro.
pupa [piúpa], _s._ (ent.) ninfa, crisálida.
pupil [piúpil], _s._ pupila; discípulo, alumno.
pupilage [piúpiley], _s._ pupilaje.
pupil(l)ary, pupilar [piúpilæri], _a._ pupilar.—**p. margin,** borde de la pupila.
Pupipara [piupípara], _s. pl._ (ent.) pupíparos.
puppet [pʌ́pet], _s._ títere, muñeco, monigote, maniquí; paniaguado.—**p. (valve)** = POPPET VALVE. —**p. show,** función de títeres.
puppetman [-mæn], _s._ titiritero.
puppy [pʌ́pi], _s._ cachorro, perrillo; (despec.) trasto, monicaco, trompeta.
puppyish [pʌ́piiŝh], _a._ parecido a un cachorro; fatuo.
puppyism [pʌ́piiŝm], _s._ fatuidad.
purblind [pœ́rblaind], _a._ cegato.—**purblindness** [-nes], _s._ ofuscamiento de la vista.
purchaseable [pœ́rchasabœl], _a._ comprable.
purchase [pœ́rches]. **I.** _va._ comprar; lograr, ganar, obtener, adquirir; (mec. y mar.) mover o sujetar con aparejo. **II.** _s._ compra; adquisición; (mec.) aparejo, aparejo, maniobra.—**not to be worth a day's p.,** (fam.) estar en las últimas.
purchaser [pœ́rchescœr], _s._ comprador; adquiridor, adquirente.
pure [piúcœr], _a._ puro (en todas sus acepciones).— **p. mathematics,** matemáticas puras.
purée [piuré], _s._ (coc.) puré.
purely [piúœrli], _adv._ puramente; meramente, simplemente.
pureness [piúœrnes], _s._ pureza.
purfle [pœ́rfœl]. **I.** _s._ orla. **II.** _va._ orlar.
purgation [pœrguéiŝhʊn], _s._ purgación, purgamiento, purificación; (for.) purgación.
purgative [pœ́rgativ]. **I.** _a._ purgador, purgativo, purgante. **II.** _s._ purga, purgante.
purgatorial [pœrgatórial], _a._ del purgatorio; purgativo, expiatorio.
purgatory [pœ́rgatori], _s._ purgatorio.
purge [pœ́ry]. **I.** _va._ purgar, purificar, limpiar, clarificar, acrisolar; justificar; (med.) purgar. **II.** _vn._ purificarse. **III.** _s._ purga, purgante, catártico; purgamiento.

purger [pœ́rɣœr], _s._ purificador, purgador; purga, purgante.
purging [pœ́rɣing]. **I.** _a._ purgativo. **II.** _s._ purgación; purificación, expiación; diarrea.
purifiable [piúrifáiabœl], _a._ depurable.—**purification** [-fikéŝhun], _s._ purificación, depuración; expiación; defecación.—**purificative, purificatory** [-ficativ, tori], _a._ purificatorio, purificante.— **purificator** [-fikéitœr], _s._ (igl.) purificador.— **purifier** [-faicœr], _s._ purificador.—**puriform** [-form], _a._ puriforme.
purify [piúrifai]. **I.** _va._ purificar; purgar, limpiar, refinar, clarificar; expiar; expurgar, depurar; refinar. **II.** _vn._ purificarse.—**purifying** [-ing]. **I.** _s._ purificación. **II.** _a._ purificador; depurador.
purine [piúrin], _s._ (quím.) purina.
purism [piúriŝm], _s._ purismo.
purist [-ist], _s._ purista.
Puritan [piúritan], _s._ puritano.—**puritanic(al** [-tænic(al], _a._ puritano; riguroso, severo, rígido.— **Puritanism** [-taniŝm], _s._ puritanismo.
purity [piúriti], _s._ pureza.
purl [pœrl]. **I.** _va._ arremolinar, envolver; (cost.) orlar, adornar con fleco. **II.** _vn._ murmurar o susurrar los arroyos; ondular; arremolinarse. **III.** _s._ murmullo, susurro; ondulación; (cost.) fleco de oro o plata, orla; pliegue de vestido; encaje del siglo XVI; cerveza aromatizada.
purlieus [pœ́rlius], _s. pl._ cercanías, alrededores.
purlin(e [pœrlin], _s._ (arq.) ejión, jabalcón.
purling [pœ́rling]. **I.** _s._ murmullo, susurro. **II.** _a._ murmurante.
purlman [pœ́rlmæn], _s._ vendedor de cerveza.
purloin [pœrlóin], _va._ hurtar, robar.
purloiner [pœrlóincœr], _s._ ladrón, ratero.
purparty [pœ́rparti], _s._ (for.) parte, división.
purple [pœ́rpœl]. **I.** _a._ purpúreo, morado; imperial, regio; (poét.) purpurino; sangriento. **II.** _s._ púrpura, múrice; trábea.—_pl._ pintas; tabardillo pintado. **III.** _va._ purpurar, teñir de púrpura.
purplish [pœ́rpliŝh], _a._ purpurino.
purport [pœ́rport]. **I.** _s._ significado, tenor, substancia. **II.** _va. y vn._ [pœrpórt] significar, querer decir, implicar.
purpose [pœ́rpus]. **I.** _s._ propósito, fin, objeto; intención; resultado, utilidad; voluntad, resolución, determinación; uso, caso; tenor, significación; proposición, cuestión.—**for what p.?** ¿con qué fin? ¿para qué?—**of p.,** on p., expresamente, de propósito, de intento.—**to no p.,** inútilmente.—**to the p.,** a lo de propósito; al caso; al grano; de perilla.—**to very little p.,** casi para nada, con poco provecho. **II.** _va. y vn._ proponer, proponerse, proyectar.
purposeless [-les], _a._ sin propósito ni fin determinado; vago.
purposely [-li], _adv._ adrede, de intento, de propósito, expresamente.
purposive [-iv], _a._ dirigido o adaptado a un fin; intencional.—**purposively** [-li], _adv._ con propósito, para un fin; intencionalmente.
purpura [pœ́rpiuræ], _s._ = PURPLES; escorbuto.
purpurin [-rin], _s._ (ten.) purpurina.
purr [pœr]. **I.** _s._ murmullo o ronroneo del gato. **II.** _vn._ ronronear o murmurar (el gato). **III.** _va._ decir murmurando.
purse [pœrs]. **I.** _s._ bolsa, bolso o bolsillo; porta-monedas; talega, bolsa de dinero; colecta, derrama; (zool.) buche.—**p. net,** manga de pescar. —**p. proud,** envanecido por la opulencia.—**p. seine** = P. NET.—**p. strings,** cerradero, cordones de la bolsa. **II.** _va._ embolsar, embolsillar; fruncir.
purseful [pœ́rsful]. **I.** _a._ rico. **II.** _s._ la cantidad que contiene una bolsa.
purser [pœ́rsœr], _s._ (mar.) contador, sobrecargo.
pursiness [pœ́rsines], _s._ dificultad en la respiración; gordura.
purslain, purslane [pœ́rslein], _s._ verdolaga.
pursuable [pœrsiúabœl], _a._ proseguible.
pursuance [-ans], _s._ prosecución, seguimiento, cumplimiento.
pursuant [-ant]. **I.** _a._ consiguiente, conforme. **II.** _adv._ (con **to**) de acuerdo con, en cumplimiento de, según.

pursue [pœrsiú]. **I.** *va.* y *vn.* perseguir, dar caza; seguir, continuar; seguir (una carrera), dedicarse a, ejercer. **II.** *vn.* seguir; (for.) demandar, poner pleito, procesar.

pursuer [pœrsiúœr], *s.* perseguidor.

pursuit [pœrsiút], *s.* perseguimiento, caza; práctica, ejercicio; prosecución; busca; ocupación; pretensión; conato, empeño.—*pl.* ocupaciones, estudios, investigaciones, actividades.—**p. of happiness**, busca de la felicidad o del bienestar.

pursuivant [pœrsuivant], *s.* persevante.

pursy [pœrsi], *a.* asmático; obeso.

purulence, purulency [piúruleus, i], *s.* purulencia.—**purulent** [-lent], *a.* purulento.

purvey [pœrvéi], *va.* y *vn.* proveer, surtir, suministrar, abastecer.—**purveyance** [pœrvéians], *s.* abastecimiento: abasto, suministro.—**purveyor** [-œr], *s.* proveedor, abastecedor.

purview [pœrviu], *s.* extensión, esfera, alcance; substancia de un estatuto; límite o alcance de una disposición legal.

pus [pus], *s.* (med.) pus.

push [push]. **I.** *va.* empujar, rempujar; promover, activar; apremiar, obligar, estrechar; importunar, molestar.—**to p. away**, alejar, rechazar; apartar con la mano.—**to p. back**, rechazar, echar atrás.—**to p. down**, abatir, derribar.—**to p. in**, hacer entrar, introducir empujando.—**to p. off**, apartar con la mano.—**to p. on**, incitar, aguijonear; apresurar.—**to p. one's self forward**, abrirse camino; entremeterse.—**to p. out**, empujar hacia fuera; echar, expulsar; desatracar. **II.** *vn.* empujar; dar empellones; apresurarse, darse prisa; acometer.—**to p. forward**, adelantarse dando empujones; avanzar, adelantar.—**to p. further**, seguir adelante.—**to p. in**, entremeterse.—**to p. off**, (mar.) desatracar.—**to p. on**, seguir adelante, avanzar. **III.** *s.* impulso; empuje; rempujón, empellón; embestida, arremetida; apuro, aprieto; energía, iniciativa.—**p. button**, pulsador, botón de presión o de llamada.

pushcart [púshcart], *s.* carretilla de mano.

pusher [púshœr], *s.* empujador; (f. c.) locomotora de empuje o trasera (ll. t. **p. locomotive**).—**p. engine**, (aer.) motor propulsor.—**p. grade**, pendiente que requiere locomotora de empuje.

pushing [púshing], *a.* activo, diligente, emprendedor; agresivo.

pushpin [púshpin], *s.* juego de pajitas; pasador de la caja del reloj.

pusillanimity [piúsilanímiti], *s.* pusilanimidad. **pusillanimous** [-lǽnimus], *a.* pusilánime.

puss, *s.* miz, minino, morro, micho, gata; chiquitín; chica; liebre.—**p. in the corner**, juego de las cuatro esquinas.—**p. moth**, (ent.) oruga.

pussy [púsi], **pussycat** [-cæt], *s.* pussy; (bot.) amento de sauce americano llamado *pussy willow*.

pussyfoot [-fut]. **I.** *vn.* (fam.) andarse con tiento, no declararse. **II.** *a.* (fam.) prohibicionista.—**pussyfooter** [-œr], *s.* (fam.) prohibicionista.

pustular [pústiular], *a.* pustuloso.—**pustulate** [pústiulet]. **I.** *vn.* formarse pústulas. **II.** *a.* pustuloso.

pustule [pústiul], *s.* pústula, pupa.

pustulous [-us], *a.* puposo, pustuloso.

put, *va.* (*ger.* PUTTING: *pret.* y *pp.* PUT) poner; colocar, exponer, proponer, presentar para ser discutido; hacer, dirigir (una pregunta); expresar, declarar, interpretar; arrojar, lanzar; suponer.—**to p. an end to**, poner fin a, terminar.—**to p. a question**, hacer una pregunta o una interpelación.—**to p. a stop to**, poner coto o fin a; acabar con; impedir.—**to p. asunder**, separar, apartar.—**to p. away**, apartar, quitar; poner aparte; echar fuera, despedir; repudiar, rechazar. —**to p. back**, atrasar, retardar; devolver, reponer; rehusar, denegar.—**to p. behind**, poner atrás; relegar a puesto o posición inferior; arrinconar.—**to p. by**, guardar; arrinconar; desviar, apartar.—**to p. down**, sofocar, reprimir; deprimir, abatir; humillar, degradar; depositar; registrar, anotar, apuntar; rebajar, disminuir; hacer callar. **to p. forth**, extender, alargar; publicar, dar a luz; producir, echar; presentar, proponer; ejercer; emplear.—**to p. forward**, adelantar.—**to p. in**,

poner en, echar en o a, meter; poner, insertar, ingerir, introducir, intercalar; presentar; hacer (reclamo, etc.); colocar (en un empleo, etc.); interponer (palabra, observación; (top., dib.) trazar (una curva, etc.).—**to p. in an appearance**, aparecer, ir, llegar; (for.) comparecer.—**to p. in irons**, aherrojar.—**to p. in mind**, recordar.—**to p. in order**, arreglar, ordenar.—**to p. in, o into, practice**, poner en práctica, aplicar.—**to p. in print**, imprimir.—**to p. into**, meter dentro de, guardar en; expresar en.—**to p. into one's head**, meterle a uno en la cabeza.—**to p. in writing**, poner por escrito.—**to p. off**, diferir, dilatar, aplazar; desechar, apartar; evadir, entretener; salir de (con promesas); quitarse, desprenderse de. —**to p. on**, poner sobre; ponerse (ropa, etc.); ganar (carnes); vestir, armarse de; achacar, atribuir a; echar, poner, dar, aplicar (vapor, el freno, etc.); instigar a; engañar con; imponer, poner a.—**to p. on airs**, darse ínfulas.— **to p. on one's thinking cap**, aguzar el seso, parar mientes.—**to p. on shore**, poner en tierra, desembarcar.—**to p. one on**, o to, one's mettle, picar a uno el amor propio.—**to p. one's best foot, o leg, foremost, o forward**, (fam.) hacer uno lo sumo posible, poner sus cinco sentidos.—**to p. one's foot down**, plantarse, obrar resueltamente y sin cejar.—**to p. one's nose out of joint**, suplantar a uno.—**to p. out**, brotar, echar (retoños); despedir, despachar, echar; apagar o matar (la luz, el fuego); publicar, dar a luz; cegar; borrar, tachar; cortar, confundir, desconcertar; dislocar, sacar de quicio; poner (dinero a interés), dar (a logro); extender, sacar, mostrar, enojar, irritar.— **to p. out of all hope**, quitar la esperanza, desahuciar.—**to p. out of doors**, poner en la calle. —**to p. out of one's head**, sacarse de la cabeza, dejarse de.—**to p. out of the way**, quitar, poner (algo) donde no estorbe; suprimir (matar).—**to p. over**, dar a uno el cargo de; diferir, dilatar, conducir al otro lado; llevar a cabo, hacer pasar o triunfar.—**to p. the hand to**, poner manos a, meter las manos en, emprender; meter la mano en, apropiarse.—**to p. to**, agregar, añadir; usar, ejercitar; dejar, abandonar; exponer o someter a; consignar a; echar, juntar (machos con hembras).—**to p. to bed**, acostar, poner en cama. —**to p. to death**, matar; ajusticiar, ejecutar.—**to p. to flight**, poner en fuga.—**to p. together**, acumular, juntar; reunir; armar (una máquina); coordinar, arreglar.—**to p. to it**, causar dificultad a, poner en calzas prietas, poner a parir.—**to p. to rights**, poner en orden; componer; reconciliar.— **to p. to shame**, avergonzar.—**to p. to silence**, hacer callar.—**to p. to sleep**, adormecer, hacer dormir; poner fuera de combate (ú. esp. en el boxeo).—**to p. to the sword**, pasar a cuchillo.— **to p. to the test, to trial, o on trial**, poner a prueba.—**to p. to the vote**, someter a votación; proceder a votar acerca de.—**to p. to use**, usar, utilizar; sacar partido de.—**to p. two and two together**, atar cabos.—**to p. up**, poner en su lugar, guardar, conservar; acondicionar; preparar (vg. conservas, remedios, etc.); construir, erigir; (mec.) montar (una máquina); proponer, presentar (como candidato); ofrecer, elevar; envainar (la espada); oponer, ofrecer (resistencia); (teat.) poner en escena; (fam.) poner dinero en una apuesta; tramar, urdir.—**to p. up for sale**, poner en venta.—**to p. upon**, poner en, colocar encima de; atribuir o imputar a, acusar.—**to p. upon oath**, hacer prestar juramento.—**to p. up to**, incitar, instigar a; presentar o someter a; dejar a, enseñar, dar instrucciones a.

put, *vn.* (mar.) dirigirse, seguir rumbo.—**to p. about**, (mar.) cambiar de rumbo; molestar, aturdir.—**to p. back**, retroceder; regresar.—**to p. forth**, partir, (mar.) zarpar.—**to p. in**, arribar, entrar; tocar en (un puerto); ponerse en salvo, esconderse; pernoctar.—**to p. in for**, pretender, solicitar; hacer oposición a algún destino.—**to p. into port**, (mar.) arribar, entrar de arribada.— **to p. off**, partir, salir.—**to p. on**, apresurarse; avanzar.—**to p. out**, salir, partir.—**to p. to sea**, salir a la mar; hacerse a la vela; salir, partir.—**to p. up**, parar; hospedarse; detenerse (encombate), envainar la espada; poner (la apuesta).—**to p. up with**, aguantar, tolerar, sufrir; conformarse con.

---

put, s. acción de *to put* en cualquiera de sus acepciones; golpe, tiro, lanzamiento; *put,* juego de naipes; (E.U., com.) opción o privilegio que una persona adquiere pagando una prima a otra de venderle, dentro de un plazo determinado, un artículo por un precio estipulado; el mismo privilegio de compra se llama *call.*

putamen [piutéimœn], s. (bot.) hueso, cuesco.

putative [piútativ], a. putativo.

puteal [piútial], s. brocal de pozo.

putlog [pútlog], s. (arq.) almojaya.

putrefaction [piútrefǽcshun], s. putrefacción.

putrefactive [-tiv], a. putrefactivo.

putrefactiveness [-nes], s. calidad de putrefactivo.

putrefiable [-fáiabœl], a. que puede pudrirse.

putrefy [-fai], va. y vn. pudrir(se).

putrescence [piutrésens], s. pudrición, putrefacción.—**putrescent** [-ent], a. podrido, pútrido.—**putrescible** [-ibœl], a. expuesto a pudrirse.

putrid [piútrid], a. podrido, pútrido.

putridity [piutríditi], **putridness** [piútridnes], s. podredumbre, putridez.

putter [pútœr]. I. s. ponedor, uno de los palos del golf.—**p. on,** incitador, instigador. II. vn. V. POTTER.

putting [púting], s. acción de poner, etc. V. PUT.

putty [púti]. I. s. masilla de aceite; cemento (apl. esp. al de cal).—**p. coat,** revestimiento de cemento de cal dado a un enlucido.—**p. knife,** espátula (para masilla).—**p. powder,** cenizas de estaño.—**p. work,** relieves de material plástico (que luego se endurece). II. va. rellenar con masilla; revocar con cemento (gen. de cal).

put-up [put up], a. (fam.) tramado, urdido.—**p.-up job,** trama, confabulación.

puzzle [púsl]. I. s. acertijo, rompecabezas; enigma, misterio; problema arduo. II. va. confundir, poner perplejo, devanar los sesos.—**to p. out,** resolver, descifrar, desenredar. III. vn. estar perplejo.—**to p. over,** tratar de resolver, hincarle el diente a.

pycnometer [picnómetœr], s. picnómetro, frasco para pesos específicos.

pycnostyle [pícnostail], s. (arq.) picnóstila, intercolumnio estrecho (de 1½ diámetros).

pyelitis [páieláitis], s. pielitis.

pyemia [paiímia], s. piohemia, infección de la sangre por materias purulentas.

pygmean [pigmían], s. pigmeo.

pygmy [pígmi] a. y s. pigmeo, enano.

pyjamas, s. pl. = PAJAMAS.

pylon [páilon], s. (arq. egipcia), pilón, portada con torres piramidales: (aer.) torre o poste de señal: soporte de la hélice de un dirigible; torre de lanzamiento.

pyloric [pilóric], a. pilórico.—**p. valve,** esfínter pilórico.

pylorus [pilórus], s. (anat.) píloro.

pyogenesis [páioyénesis], **pyogenia** [-yínia], s. piogenia, formación de pus.—**pyogenetic** [-yenétic], **pyogenic** [-yénic], a. piógeno, que produce pus: relativo a la piogenia.

pyorrhea [páiorriæ], s. piorrea (apl. esp. a la alveolar).

pyralis [píralis], s. (ent.) piral, pirausta.

pyramid [píramid], s. pirámide; (anat.) pirámide (de Malpighi, etc.).—**pyramidal** [pirǽmidal], **pyramidical** [piramídical], a. piramidal.

pyramidally [-il], adv. piramidalmente.

pyre [páiœr], s. pira, hoguera.

pyrargyrite [pirárýriait], s. (min.) plata roja.

Pyrenean [pirenían], a. pirenaico.

pyretic [pairétic]. I. a. pirético, febril. II. a. y s. febrífugo.

pyretology [pairetóloyi], s. (med.) piretología.

pyrexia [pairécsia], s. (med.) pirexia, fiebre esencial.

pyridic [pairidic], a. (quím.) piridico.—**pyridin(e** [píridin], (quím.) piridina.

pyriform [píriform], a. piriforme.

pyrite [páirait], pl. **pyrites** [pirátiš], s. (min.) pirita, piritas. El sing. se aplica esp. a la de hierro, o marcasita.

pyritic, pyritous [pairític, píritus], a. piritoso.

pyro [páiro], s. (fam.) contr. de *pyrogallol,* ácido pirogálico.

pyroacetic [-asétic], a. piroacético.—**p. acid, o spirit,** ácido o espíritu piroacético.

pyroacid [-ǽsid], s. ácido pirogenado.

pyrogallic [-gǽlic], a. pirogálico.—**p. acid, o pyrogallol,** ácido pirogálico.

pyrogenous [pairóyenus], a. pirógeno, ígneo; febril.

pyrograph [páirogrǽf], s. pirografía, pirograbado (cosa pirograbada).—**pyrography** [pairógrafi], **pyrogravure** [páirogrǽviúœr], pirografía, pirograbado (arte).

pyrolign(e)ous [páirolign(i)us], a. piroleñoso.

pyrolusite [páirolúsait], s. pirolúsita.

pyrolysis [pairólisis], s. descomposición química por el calor.

pyromagnetic [páiromægnétic], a. piromagnético.

pyromancy [páiromænsi], s. piromancía.

pyrometer [pai- (o pi) rómetœr], s. pirómetro.

pyromorphous [páiromórfus], a. piromorfo.

pyrophorus [pairóforus], s. piróforo.

pyrophosphate [páirofósfet], s. (quím.) pirofosfato.

pyroscope [páiroscoup], s. piroscopio.

pyrosis [pairósis], s. (med.) pirosis.

pyrotechnic(al [páirotécnic(al], a. pirotécnico.—**pyrotechnist, pyrotechni(ci)an** [-técnist, -tecníshan], s. pirotécnico.—**pyrotechny, pyrotechnics** [-técni, cs], s. pirotecnia.

pyroxene [páiroxin], s. (min.) piroxeno.

pyroxylin [pi- (o pai) róxilin], s. piroxilina, algodón pólvora.

pyrrhic [pírric]. I. s. y a. pírrico (danza griega). II. (P-), a. pírrico, de Pirro.—**P. victory,** triunfo pírrico, victoria demasiado costosa.

Pyrrhonean [pironían], **Pyrrhonist** [píronist], a. y s. pirrónico, pirroniano.

Pyrrhonism [píronišm], s. pirronismo.

Pythagorean [pizǽgorían], a. pitagórico.

Pythian [pízian], a. pitio.

python [páizon], s. serpiente boa; pitón; adivino, agorero; ventrílocuo.

pythoness [pízones], s. pitonisa.

pyuria [paiiúriæ], s. piuria, pus en la orina.

pyx [pics], s. (igl.) copón, píxide.

Q

q [kíu], s. q.

qua [cuá, cuéi], adv. como, en su calidad de.

quack [cuæc]. I. va. y vn. graznar, parpar; charlatanear; echárselas de médico; curar empíricamente o con sortilegios. II. s. y s. graznido del pato. III. s. y a. charlatán; curandero, matasanos: medicucho, medicastro.

quackery [cuæcœri], s. charlatanismo.

quadra [cuódra], s. (arq.) bastidor, marco; plinto.

quadragesima [cuódrayésima], s. cuadragésima, cuaresma.

quadragesimal [-l], a. cuadragesimal.

quadrangle [cuódrængœl], s. cuadrángulo; (arq.) patio.

quadrangular [cuodrænguiular], a. cuadrangular.

quadrant [cuódrant], s. (geom.) cuadrante; (mec.) sector oscilante; (astr.) y mar.) cuadrante de altura.—**q. electrometer,** electrómetro de cuadrante.

quadrantal [cuódrǽntal], a. (mat.) cuadrantal.

quadrat [cuódræt], a. (impr.) cuadrado, cuadratín.

quadrate [cuódret]. I. s. cuadrado. II. s. (anat.) hueso o músculo cuadrado; (astr.) cuadrado; (mús.) becuadro.

quadratic [cuodrǽtic]. I. a. de segundo grado. II. s. ecuación de segundo grado.

quadrature [cuódratiur o chur], s. (mat., elec. y astr.) cuadratura; (mec.) escuadreo.

quadrennial [cuodrénial], a. cuadrienal.

quadriga [cuodráiga], s. cuadriga.

quadrilateral [cuódrilétœral], a. y s. (geom. y mil.) cuadrilátero.

quadrille [cuadríl], s. (danz. y mús.) contradanza, rigodón; cuatrillo, cascarela (juego de naipes); cuadrícula.

quadrillion [cuodríliun], s. cuadrillón (E. U. y Fr., unidad seguida de 15 ceros; Ingl. y Esp., unidad seguida de 24 ceros).

quadripartite [cuódrípártait], a. cuadripartido.

quadrisyllable [cuodrisílabœl], s. cuadrisílabo.

quadrivalent [cuódrivéilent], a. (quím.) tetravalente.

quadrivium [cuodrívium], s. cuadrivio.

quadroon [cuodrún], s. cuarterón.

Quadrumana [cuodrúmana], s. pl. cuadrumanos.

quadrumane [cuódruméin], s. y a. cuadrumano.

quadrumanous [cuodrúmænus], a. cuadrumano.

quadruped [cuódruped], s. cuadrúpedo.

quadrupedal [cuodrúpedal], a. cuadrupedal.

quadruplane [cuódrupléin], s. (aer.) tetraplano, avión de cuatro planos.

quadruple [cuódrupœl]. I. a. cuádruple. II. s. cuádruplo, cuatrotanto. III. va. y vn. cuadruplicar.

quadruplet [cuódruplet], s. serie de cuatro cosas; bicicleta de cuatro asientos.

quadruplex [cuódruplex]. I. a. (elec.) cuadrúplex. II. s. instrumento telegráfico cuadrúplex.

quadruplicate [cuódrúpliket], va. cuadruplicar.

quadruplication [cuódruplikéíshun], s. cuadruplicación.

quadruply [cuódruplii], adv. al cuádruplo.

quaff [cuaf]. I. va. y vn. beber. II. s. trago.

quagga [cuéga], s. (zool.) cuaga.

quaggy [cuégui], a. pantanoso; blando.

quagmire [cuégmaiær], s. tremedal, trembladal.

quahaug, quahog [cuójog], s. almeja.

quail [cuéil]. I. s. (orn.) codorniz.—**q. pipe**, reclamo de codornices. II. vn. acobardarse, descorazonarse; cejar.

quaint [cuéint], a. de prístina belleza o amenidad; de curioso primor, de exquisito arcaísmo.—**quaintly** [-lii], adv. de modo amenamente arcaico, con la curiosa exquisitez de tiempos que fueron.—**quaintness** [-nes], s. amenidad o belleza arcaica.

quake [cuéc]. I. vn. temblar. II. s. temblor; estremecimiento.

Quaker [cuéikœr], s. y a. cuáquero.—**Quakeress** [-es], s. cuáquera.—**Quakerism** [-ísm], s. cuaquerismo.

qualifiable [cuólifáiabœl], a. calificable.

qualification [-fikéishun], s. calificación, requisito; calidad, cualidad, capacidad, idoneidad; atenuación, mitigación.

qualificator [-kéitœr], s. (igl.) calificador.

qualified [-faid], a. calificado, habilitado, idóneo, apto, competente; modificado; (for.) limitado, restringido.

qualifier [-faicœr], s. (gram.) calificativo.

qualify [-fai]. I. va. habilitar, hacer idóneo; calificar; modificar, limitar, restringir; templar, suavizar; diluir (un licor). II. vn. prepararse, habilitarse; llenar los requisitos; (E. U.) prestar juramento antes de entrar en funciones.—**qualified voter**, elector habilitado.

qualifying [-faing], a. preparativo; calificativo.

qualitative [-tativ], a. cualitativo.—**q. analysis**, análisis cualitativo.

quality [cuóliti], s. calidad, cualidad; clase; propiedad, poder o virtud; categoría, alta posición social.

qualm [cuám], s. basca; escrúpulo de conciencia.—**qualmish** [-ish], a. bascoso; escrupuloso.—**qualmishness** [-nes], s. náusea.

quandary [cuóndari], s. incertidumbre, duda, perplejidad.

quantitative [cuóntitativ], a. cuantitativo.—**q. analysis**, análisis cuantitativo.

quantity [cuóntiti], s. cantidad; gran cantidad, gran número; (mús. y pros.) cantidad.—(elec.)

intensidad (de una corriente); (mús. y pros.) cantidad.—pl. **quantities**, (fam.) gran cantidad, gran número.—**q. lever**, (aut.) palanca de regulación de la admisión, palanca de reglaje.—**q. surveying**, medida y cálculo de materiales en las construcciones.—**q. theory** (e. p.) teoría de que las variaciones en la cantidad de la moneda circulante son causa y no efecto de las variaciones en los precios.—**in q.**, (elec.) en paralelo.

quantum [cuóntum], s. tanto; cantidad; (fís.) unidad elemental de energía.

quarantine [cuóræntin]. I. cuarentena; estación de cuarentena; aislamiento (de dolientes de enfermedad contagiosa); prohibición de transportar animales o plantas enfermos que transmiten enfermedades. II. va. poner en cuarentena; aislar.

quarrel [cuórrel]. I. s. reyerta, pendencia, querella, camorra, disputa; diamante de vidrieros; flecha o instrumento cortante de cuatro aristas; vidrio, loseta o adoquín romboidal. II. vn. pelear, altercar, desamistarse, romper.

quarreller [-œr], s., **quarrelsome** [-sum], a. pendenciero.—**quarrelsomeness** [-nes], s. pugnacidad; petulancia.

quarrier [cuórricœr], s. cantero, picapedrero.

quarry [cuórri]. I. s. cantera, pedrera; caza, presa; cuadrado, cuadro, rombo (de vidrio, teja, etc.). II. va. explotar (canteras).—**quarryman** [-mæn], s. cantero, picapedrero.

quart [cuórt], s. cuarto de galón (come un litro); (mús.) cuarta; [cart] (esgr.) cuarta; en el juego de los cientos, cuarta.

quartan [cuórtan]. I. a. cuartanal. II. s. (med.) cuartana.

quartation [cuortéíshun], s. (metal.) incuartación.

quarter [cuórtœr]. I. s. cuarto, cuarta parte; arroba (cuarto de quintal); trimestre; cuarto de hora; cuarto de tonelada; (E. U.) moneda de 25 centavos (un cuarto de dólar); cuarto de luna; (mús.) semínima; (mar.) cuarta; origen, procedencia; región, comarca, distrito (v. gr.: from all quarters, de todas partes); barrio, barriada, vecindad; (carp.) cuarterón, entrepaño; (mar.) cuadra de popa; cuartel, merced o clemencia.—pl. domicilio, vivienda, morada; (mil.) cuartel; alojamiento.—**q. cask**, cuarterola.—**q. day**, día en que principia una estación del año; día en que se paga un trimestre.—**q.-deck**, (mar.) alcázar.—**q.-deck ladder**, escala del alcázar.—**q. ladder**, escala de la toldilla.—**q. netting**, (mar.) redes de combate.—**q.-phase**, (elec.) bifásico.—**q. pieces**, (mar.) montantes.—**q. plates**, (foto.) placa de 3¼ por 4¼ pulgadas.—**q. point**, (mar.) cuarto viento o rumbo de la brújula.—**q.-sawed**, aserrado en cuartones.—**q. section**, (E. U.) cuarto de una milla cuadrada (160 acres).—**q. sessions**, tribunal inferior que se reúne cada trimestre.—**q. wind**, viento al anca o a la cuadra. II. a. cuarto. III. va. cuartear; descuartizar, hacer cuartos; dividir en cuarteles; (mil.) acuartelar, acantonar; alojar, hospedar; (blas.) cuartelar.

quarterage [cuórtœrœy], s. sueldo o salario trimestral; cuartel, alojamientos.

quartered [cuórtœrd], a. hecho de madera aserrada a lo largo en cuartos, para mostrar la veta.—**q. oak**, roble aserrado de dicho modo.

quarterly [cuórtœrli]. I. a. trimestral. II. s. publicación trimestral. III. adv. trimestralmente; en cuartos, por cuartos.

quartermaster [-mástœr], s. (mil.) comisario ordenador; (mar.) cabo de brigadas.—**q.-general**, intendente de ejército.

quartern [cuórtœrn], s. (Ingl.) cuarta.—**q. loaf**, pan de cuatro libras.

quartet(te [cuortét], s. cuatro cosas de una misma clase; (mús., poét.) cuarteto.

quartile [cuórtil], s. (astr.) cuadrado.

quarto [cuórto]. I. a. (impr. y enc.) en cuarto. II. s. libro en cuarto.

quartz [cuorts], s. cuarzo.—**quartziferous** [-íferus], a. cuarcífero.—**quartzite** [-ait], s. cuarcita.—**quartzose, quartzous, quartzy** [-ous, -us, -i], a. cuarzoso.

---

quash [cuósh], *va.* sofocar, reprimir; (for.) anular, invalidar, derogar.

quasi contract [cuésai cóntract], *s.* cuasicontrato.

quassia (wood) [cuáshia *o* cuóshia, ud], *s.* (bot.) palo de casia amarga.

quassin [cuásin], *s.* cuasina, elemento amargo de la casia.

quaternary [cuatœrnari]. **I.** *a.* cuaternario; cuarto en orden; cuadrángulo. **II.** *s.* (geol.) período cuaternario.

quaternion [cuatœrniʊn], *s.* cuaternidad; fila o serie de cuatro; (mat.) cuaternio.

quatrain [cuótrein], *s.* (poét.) cuarteto.

quatrocento [cuátrochénto], *s.* (b. a.*)* período cuatrocentista, Renacimiento (esp. italiano) del siglo XV.

quaver [cuéivœr]. **I.** *vn.* gargantear, gorjear, trinar, temblar, vibrar. **II.** *s.* gorjeo, trino; trémolo, vibración; (mús.) corchea.

quavering [cuéivœring]. **I.** *s.* gorgorito, trinado, trino, gorjeo. **II.** *a.* trémulo.

quay [ki], *s.* muelle; desembarcadero.

quayage [kíey], *s.* = WHARFAGE.

queachy, queechy [cuíchi], *a.* movedizo.

quean [cuín], *sf.* mujercilla; moza, mozuela.

queasiness [cuísines], *s.* propensión a la náusea.

queasy [cuísi], *a.* propenso a la náusea, bascoso; nauseabundo; delicado.

quebracho [kebrácho], *s.* quebracho.

queen [cuín], *s.* reina; en los naipes, figura 'de reina que equivale al caballo; la dama en el juego de damas y la reina en el ajedrez.— **q. (bee)**, abeja reina, enjambrera.— **q. consort**, esposa del rey.— **q. dowager**, reina viuda.— **q. mother**, reina madre.— **q. of the meadow**, (bot.) espírea, ulmaria.— **q. olive**, aceituna de la reina.— **q.-post** (constr.) pendolón.— **q.-post truss**, viga (de puente) o armadura (de techo) de dos pendolones.— **q. regent**, reina regente.— **q. regnant**, reina reinante.— **q.'s English**, inglés castizo o puro.— **Q.'s speech**, discurso de la Corona.— **q.'s ware**, vajilla de color de crema.

queenliness [cuínlines], *s.* majestad de una reina.

queenly [cuínli], *a.* como de reina; como reina; regio; propio de una reina.

queenship [cuínship], *s.* dignidad, dominio o poder de una reina.

queer [cuícœr]. **I.** *a.* extraño, excéntrico, estrafalario, estrambótico; sospechoso, misterioso; (fam.) falso. **II.** *s.* (fam.) moneda falsa. **III.** *va.* (fam.) comprometer, poner a uno en mal lugar.

queerly [-li], *adv.* extrañamente, estrafalariamente; sospechosamente.

queerness [-nes], *s.* rareza, extrañeza.

quell [cuel], *va.* reprimir, sofocar; calmar, mitigar (un dolor).

queller [cuélœr], *s.* opresor, domador, sojuzgador.

quench [cuench], *va.* apagar, matar (luz, fuego); calmar, apagar (la sed); ahogar, sofocar; sosegar; extinguir; templar (hierro).

quenchable [cuénchabœl], *a.* extinguible.

quencher [cuénchœr], *s.* apagador.

quenchless [cuénchles], *a.* inextinguible.

quercin [cuœrsin], *s.* (quím.) cuercina, amargo de roble.— **quercine** [cuœrsin], *a.* cuercino, relativo al roble o a la encina.

quercitrin [cuœrsitrin], *s.* (quím.) cuercitrina.

quercitron [cuœrsítrʊn], *s.* roble negro americano y su cáscara.

Quercus [cuœrcʊs], *s.* (bot.) cuerco, género que comprende los robles y las encinas.

querist [cuírist], *s.* inquiridor, preguntador.

querl, quirl [cuœrl]. **I.** *va.* (E. U.) torcer, enroscar. **II.** *s.* sinuosidad, enroscadura.

quern [cuœrn], *s.* molino de mano.

querulous [cuérulʊs], *a.* querelloso, quejicoso, chinchoso.— **querulously** [-li], *adv.* querellosamente, quejosamente.— **querulousnes** [-nes], *s.* disposición a querellarse.

query [cuíri]. **I.** *s.* pregunta; duda; signo interrogante (?). **II.** *va.* marcar con signo de inte-

rrogación; preguntar, indagar, pesquisar. **III.** *vn.* expresar una duda; preguntar.

quest [cuést]. **I.** *s.* pesquisa, averiguación; busca. **II.** *vn.* averiguar; buscar.

question [cuéschʊn]. **I.** *s.* pregunta; cuestión, asunto; problema; debate, controversia; proposición que ha de discutirse en una asamblea; objeción, discusión.— **q.-begging**, de carácter de círculo vicioso.— **q. mark**, signo de interrogación.— **a fair q.**, una pregunta legítima, justa o cuerda.— **out of q.**, sin duda, de veras.— **that is the q.**, he ahí el problema, o la cuestión; ahí está el quid.— **there is no q. about it**, eso es indiscutible, está fuera de duda.— **to be out of the q.**, ser ajeno al asunto; ser indiscutible; no haber que pensar en.— **what is the q.?** ¿de qué se trata? **II.** *va.* preguntar, examinar, interrogar; dudar, poner en tela de juicio; desconfiar de; oponerse a, objetar; recusar. **III.** *vn.* inquirir, preguntar, escudriñar; dudar.

questionable [-abœl], *a.* discutible, dudoso, sospechoso; dispuesto a ser interrogado (la acepción en *Hamlet*).

questionary [cuéschʊneri]. **I.** *s.* cuestionario. **II.** *a.* interrogativo.

questioner [-œr], *s.* preguntador, interrogador; preguntón.

questionless [-les], *a.* que no pregunta.

questionnaire [kes chʊn er], *s.* cuestionario.

questor [cuéstœr], *s.* cuestor.

quetzal [cuétsal], *s.* (orn.) quetzal.

queue [kiú], *s.* coleta; fila, cola, hilera de personas; apendice, trenza, (de pelo).

quibble [cuíbœl]. **I.** *vn.* sutilizar, buscar escapatorias; hacer uso de argucias o sofismas. **II.** *s.* subterfugio, argucia, sutileza.— *pl.* sofistería, retóricas.

quibbler [cuíblœr], *s.* sofista, equivoquista.

quick [cuíc]. **I.** *a.* rápido, presto, veloz, listo, ágil; ardiente; penetrante, fino; irritable, petulante; disponible, efectivo; vivo.— **q.-fire**, **q.-firing** (art.) de tiro rápido.— **q. grass** = COUCH GRASS.— **q. hedge**, seto vivo.— **q. march**, (mús.) paso doble.— **q. match**, estopín.— **q. sighted-ness**, agudeza de vista, penetración.— **q. time**, (mil.) paso redoblado.— **q. with child**, embarazada, encinta.— **to be q. and the dead**, los vivos y los muertos.— **to be q. about**, o **at**, hacer de prisa, despachar pronto. **II.** *s.* carne viva; lo más hondo o profundo (del alma, de la sensibilidad); lo más delicado.— **to cut (hurt, offend**, etc.) **to the q.**, herir en el alma o profundamente. **III.** *adv.* con presteza, prontamente, velozmente.— **q.-sighted**, de vista aguda, penetrante.— **q.-tempered**, de mal genio, irascible.— **q.-witted**, agudo, perspicaz.

quicken [cuíken]. **I.** *va.* vivificar, dar vida, resucitar; acelerar, urgir, avivar; excitar, aguzar, animar. **II.** *vn.* avivarse, vivificarse, revivir; moverse más aprisa; ser más sensitivo.

quickener [-œr], *s.* vivificador, avivador.

quickening [-ing], *s.* vivificación, avivamiento; (for.) primera señal de vida que da el feto.

quicklime [cuíclaim], *s.* cal viva.

quickly [cuícli], *adv.* prontamente, pronto, aprisa.

quickness [cuícnes], *s.* presteza, vivacidad, prontitud, celeridad; sagacidad, viveza, penetración.

quicksand [cuícsænd], *s.* arena movediza.

quickset [cuícset]. **I.** *s.* espino o abrojo con que se hace un seto.— **q. hedge**, seto vivo. **II.** *va.* cercar con seto vivo.

quicksilver [cuícsílvœr]. **I.** *s.* azogue, mercurio. **II.** *va.* azogar.

quickstep [cuícstép], *s.* (mús.) paso doble, pasacalle; (mil.) paso redoblado.

quid [cuíd], *s.* mascada de tabaco; paja medio mascada que cae de la boca de un caballo; rumiadura; substancia.— **q. pro quo**, quid pro quo.

quiddity [cuíditi], *s.* esencia de una cosa; quid, busilis, sutileza.

quidnunc [cuídnʊnc], *s.* curioso, insaciable, cuentista, refitolero.

quiesce [cuaiés], *vn.* aquietarse, callarse; hacerse muda una letra.— **quiescence, quiescency** [-ens, i], *s.* quietud, reposo.—**quiescent** [-ent], *a.* quieto, inactivo; tranquilo; mudo, que no se pronuncia; (ing.) estático, fijo.

quiet [cuáiet]. **I.** *a.* quieto; sereno, tranquilo, calmado; callado, silencioso; sencillo, modesto, sin ceremonia; ameno, apacible.—**q. market,** mercado calmado o en calma.—**to be, o to keep, q.,** callarse; no hacer ruido. **II.** *s.* quietud; silencio; tranquilidad, calma. **III.** *va.* aquietar, apaciguar; tranquilizar, calmar. **IV.** *vn.* (a veces con *down*) apaciguarse, calmarse.

quieting [-ing], *a.* calmante.—**quietism** [-iŝm], *s.* quietismo.—**quietist** [-iŝt], *v.* y *a.* quietista.—

quietly [-li], *adv.* tranquilamente; calladamente; sin ruido; sin alharaca.—**quietness, quietude** [-nes, iud], *s.* quietud, sosiego, tranquilidad, paz.

quietus [cuaíťus], *s.* carta de pago, finiquito; descanso; muerte; golpe decisivo.

quill [cuíl]. **I.** *s.* pluma de ave; cañón de pluma; cañón o pluma para escribir; escritor; púa del puerco espín; canilla, broca, devanador, canutillo; estria, pliegue cilíndrico de un rizado.— **q. men,** gente de pluma.—**q. pen,** pluma de ave. —**the q.,** la pluma, la profesión literaria. **II.** *va.* desplumar; encanillar; (cost.) rizar, hacer un encañurado.

quilling [cuíling], *s.* (cost.) rizado, encarrujado.

quilt [cuílt]. **I.** *s.* colcha, cobertor acolchado. **II.** *va.* colchar o acolchar, acojinar, estofar.

quilter [cuílťœr], *s.* acolchador; colchero.

quilting [cuílting], *s.* (mar.) cajera; colchadura; material para colchas; hechura de colchas; (tej.) cotín, piqué.—**q. bee,** reunión de amigas para hacer colchas.—**q. cotton,** algodón en hojas para acolchar.

quina [cuáina], *s.* quina.

quinary [cuáinari], *a.* y *s.* quinario.

quince [cuíns], *s.* (bot.) membrillo.—**q. tree,** membrillero.

quincuncial [cuincúnŝhal], *a.* figura de tresbolillo.

quincunx [cuíncuncs], *s.* tresbolillo.

quinia [cuínia], *s.* quinina.

quinidin(e [cuínidin], *s.* quinidina o cincolina.

quinine [cuínin, cuáinain, kinín], *s.* quinina.

quinol [cuínol], *s.* hidroquinona.

quinoline [cuínolin], *s.* (quím.) quinolina.

quinone [cuínoun], *s.* quinona.

quinquagenarian [cuíncuayenérian], *a.* y *s.* quincuagenario.

Quinquagesima [-yésima], *s.* quincuagésima.

quinnat [cuínæt], *s.* (E. U., ict.) variedad de salmón del Pacífico.

quinquefoliate(d [cuíncuefólieit(ed], *a.* quinquefoliado; quinquedigitado.

quinquennial [-cuénial]. **I.** *a.* quinquenal. **II.** *s.* quinto aniversario.

quinquennium [-cuéniŭm], *s.* quinquenio.

quinquina [cuincuáina], *s.* quinaquina.

quinsy [cuínŝi], *s.* (med.) angina.

quint [cuínt], *s.* registro de órgano; conjunto de cinco; cuerda quinta del violín; (mús.) quinta; en algunos juegos de naipes, quinta; (esgr.) quinta.

quintain [cuíntein], *s.* juego de lanza a caballo.

quintal [cuíntal], *s.* quintal.

quintan [cuíntæn]. **I.** *a.* de cada cinco días. **II.** *s.* fiebre intermitente que ocurre cada cinco días.

quintessence [cuintésens], *s.* quinta esencia.

quintessential [cuintesénŝhal], *a.* depuradísimo.

quintet(te [cuintét], *s.* (mús.) quinteto.

quintillion [cuintíllun], *s.* quintillón (E. U. y Fr., sexta potencia de mil; Ingl. y Esp., quinta potencia de un millón.)

quintuple [cuíntiupœl], *a.* quíntuplo.

quip [cuíp], *s.* pulla, chufleta.

quip(p)u [kí- (o cuí) pu], *s.* quipos.

quire [cuáiœr]. **I.** *s.* mano de papel (24 o 25 hojas); (enc.) cuadernos que forman un libro; libro. **II.** *va.* formar manos de papel.

quirk [cuœrk]. **I.** *s.* desviación, vuelta corta, recodo; arranque, capricho; evasiva, argucia

rodeo; (arq.) copada, caveto, avivador. **II.** *va.* acanalar, estriar.—**quirking plane,** cepillo de cavetos, avivador.

quirt [cuœrt], *s.* látigo; (Méx.) cuarta.

quit [cuít]. **I.** *va.* (pret. y pp. QUIT O QUITTED) dejar, parar, cesar o desistir de; dejarse de, soltar, dejar ir, abandonar; renunciar; evacuar, desocupar; irse, salir o marcharse de.—**to q. cost,** pagar los gastos, reembolsar.—**to q. scores,** ajustar cuentas.—**to q. work,** parar (en el trabajo). **II.** *vn.* desistir; parar; cejar; irse; abandonar (una empresa, una causa, a sus amigos, etc.), zafarse.

quit, *a.* libre, descargado, absuelto.—**to be quits,** estar en paz, empatar.

quitch, quitch grass [cuích gras], *s.* grama.

quitclaim [cuítcleim]. **I.** *va.* renunciar o ceder. **II.** *s.* (for.) renuncia; (com.) finiquito.

quite [cuáit], *adv.* completamente, enteramente, absolutamente; (fam.) bastante, más bien.— **q. the,** enteramente lo; justamente el (la).

quitrent [cuítrrent], *s.* (ant.) censo para librarse del servicio feudal.

quits [cuits], *interj.* en paz.

quittance [cuítans], *s.* finiquito, descargo, recibo; liberación; recompensa, remuneración.

quitter [cuítœr], *s.* escorias; (fam.) el que se da por vencido o vuelve el rabo; desertor (de una causa, etc.).

quittor [cuítœr], *s.* inflamación de las patas de los caballos.

quiver [cuívœr]. **I.** *s.* carcaj, aljaba; temblor, tiritón. **II.** *vn.* temblar, estremecerse; palpitar.

quivered [cuívœrd], *a.* armado con aljaba; metido en aljaba.

quivering [cuívœring]. **I.** *s.* tremor, temblor. **II.** *a.* tremulante, temblador.

quixotic [cuixótic], *a.* quijotesco.—**quixotically** [-ali], *adv.* quijotescamente.—**quixotism, quixotry** [cuixótism, tri], *s.* quijotismo, quijotería.

quiz [cuíŝ]. **I.** *s.* chanza, broma, guasa; acertijo, enigma; zumbón, chancero, guasón; (fam.) pregunta hecha a un discípulo o a una clase; apunte tomado de una conferencia. **II.** *va.* chulear, chancearse, tomar a guasa; mirar de hito en hito; (fam.) examinar a un discípulo o clase.— **quizzing glass,** monóculo.

quizzical [cuíŝical], *a.* burlón, zumbón, bromista; raro, extraño, estrambótico.

quod [cuód], *s.* cuadrángulo; (fam.) cárcel.

quodlibet [cuódlibet], *s.* (mús.) fantasía, miscelánea; sutileza.

quoin [cuóin o cóin]. **I.** *s.* (arq.) adaraja, diente; mocheta, piedra angular; esquina, ángulo; clave de arco; (mec. e impr.) cuña. **II.** *va.* acuñar.

quoit [cuóit]. **I.** *s.* tejo, herrón.—*pl.* juego de tejos. **II.** *vn.* jugar al tejo.

quondam [cuóndæm], *a.* antiguo, de otro tiempo, que fué.

quorum [cuórum], *s.* quórum.

quota [cuóta], *s.* cuota.—**q. of troops,** contingente de tropas.

quotable [cuótabœl], *a.* citable; cotizable.

quotation [cuotéŝhŭn], *s.* citación; cita; texto citado; (com.) cotización.—**q. marks,** (impr.) comillas, el signo " ".

quote [cuóut]. **I.** *va.* y *vn.* citar; repetir un texto; (com.) cotizar. **II.** *s.* cita; (fam.) comillas.

quoter [cuótœr], *s.* citador; cotizador.

quoth [cuóz], *pret.* del verbo desusado TO QUETH. —**q. I,** dije yo.—**q. he,** él dijo.

quotha [cuóza], *interj.* ¡de veras! ¡vaya!

quotidian [cuotídian]. **I.** *a.* cotidiano, diario. **II.** *s.* calentura cotidiana.

quotient [cuóŝhent], *s.* (mat.) cociente.

R

r [ar], *s.* r.—**the three r's,** (fam.) lectura, escritura y aritmética (*reading, 'riting, 'rithmetic*).

rabbet [ræbet]. **I.** *va.* (carp.) ensamblar a rebajo, encajar; hacer un rebajo. **II.** *s.* (carp.) rebajo, espera; encaje, ensambladura; batiente; (mar.) alefriz.—**r. plane,** guillame.

rabbi [rǽbai], **rabbin** [rǽbin], *s.* rabí, rabino.

rabbinic(al [ræbínic(al], *a.* rabínico.

rabbinism [rǽbinism], *s.* rabinismo.—**rabbinist** [-ist], *s.* rabinista.

rabbit [rǽbit], *s.* (zool.) conejo.—**r.-ear faucet**, grifo de aletas o de cierre automático.—**r. hole, r. nest**, conejera, madriguera.—**r. warren**, conejera, conejar.

rabble [rǽbœl], *s.* canalla, chusma, populacho; (fund.) barra o agitador de pudelar.

rabid [rǽbid], *a.* (med.) rabioso; fanático, violento, feroz.

rabies [réibiis], *s.* rabia, hidrofobia.

raca [réicæ], *a.* (bib.) raca, vil, despreciable.

raccoon [ræccún], *s.* (zool.) coatí.—**r. skin**, mapache.

race [rés]. **I.** *s.* raza; estirpe; casta; subespecie, variedad; calidad; nariz, sabor (del vino); carrera, corrida, regata, cualquier certamen de velocidad; curso, decurso de la vida; corriente de agua; canal estrecho, caz, saetín; (tej.) paso, carrera de la lanzadera; pista de caballo de noria. —**r. course**, hipódromo; estadio; pista.—**r. cup**, premio de carrera; (hidr.) = RACEWAY.—**r. horse**, caballo de carrera.—**r. suicide**, suicidio de la raza, reducción voluntaria de la población impidiendo la preñez o los partos; neomalthusianismo exagerado.—**r. track**, pista. **II.** *va.* hacer correr de prisa; competir con, en una carrera, echar carrera con. **III.** correr de prisa; (mec.) desbocarse.

raceme [rasím], *s.* (bot.) racimo.

racemiferous [ræsemíferus], *a.* racimífero.

racemose, racemous [rǽsemos, ～mus], *a.* racimoso.

racer [réisœr], *s.* corredor; caballo de carrera.

raceway [réisuéi], *s.* caz, saetín; guía; (elec.) conducto o canal para conductores eléctricos.

rachialgia [rakiǽlyia], *s.* (med.) raquialgia.

rachis [rékis], *s.* (bot.) raquis, raspa; cañón de pluma; espinazo.

rachitic [rakític], *a.* (med.) raquítico; raquidiano raquídeo.

rachitis [rakáitis], *s.* (med.) raquitis.

racial [réishæl], *a.* de raza.

racily [résili], *adv.* de una manera picante.

raciness [résines], *s.* picante; nariz del vino.

rack [ræc]. **I.** *s.* bastidor, rambla; aparato para estirar; potro de tormento; dolor, pena, angustia; (mec.) cremallera o barra dentada; espetera, astillero, percha, cuelgacapas; (coc.) morillos de asador; pesebre, comedero; (carr.) escaleta; nube tenue; trote cochinero.—**r. and pinion**, engranaje de cremallera y piñón.—**r. and ruin**, (fam.) ruina completa, acabóse.—**r. bar**, cremallera.—**r. block**, telera.—**r. rail**, riel de cremallera.—**r. railway**, ferrocarril de cremallera. —**racks of a cart**, adrales, laderas de carro.—**to be on the r.**, estar en el potro (fig.), estar en angustias. **II.** *va.* atormentar; despedazar, rasgar; extorsionar; agobiar, oprimir, vejar; hacer un enrejado para; (mar.) amarrar; trasegar, trasvasar. **III.** *vn.* andar a trote cochinero.

racket [rǽket]. **I.** *s.* baraúnda, ruido, confusión; (fam.) francachela, parranda, raqueta; zapato para andar sobre fango o nieve.—*pl.* juego parecido al tenis. **II.** *vn.* meter bulla.

rackety [rǽketi], *a.* (fam.) ruidoso.

racking [rǽking], *s.* tortura; trasiego.

rackrent [rǽcrrént], *s.* arriendo o arrendamiento exorbitante.

rackwork [rǽcucœrc], *s.* mecanismo de engranaje de cremallera.

racy [réisi], *a.* que tiene aroma (el vino); picante, chispeante (estilo o lenguaje); de raza.

radial [réidiæl], *a.* radial; radiado.

radian [réidiæn], *s.* (geom.) radián, arco igual al radio (como 57° 18′).

radiance, radiancy [réidians, i], *s.* brillo, resplandor, esplendor.

radiant [réidiant]. **I.** *a.* radiante; resplandeciente, brillante; (bot.) radiado. **II.** *s.* (geom.) línea radial; foco irradiador; objeto radiante.

radiantly [-li], *adv.* con brillo, con esplendor; con alegría.

Radiata [réidiéita], *s. pl.* (zool.) radiados.

radiate [réidieit]. **I.** *va.* emitir, irradiar. **II.** *vn.* radiar, brillar.

radiate(d [rédieit(ed], *a.* radiado.

radiation [-éishʊn], *s.* radiación, irradiación.

radiator [-eitœr], *s.* calorífero, aparato de calefacción; (aut., etc.) radiador.

radical [rǽdical]. **I.** *a.* radical; (gram.) radical; (bot.) radical, raigal, radicoso; (quím., mat. y pol.) radical.—**r. sign**, signo radical (√). **II.** *s.* (pol.) radical; (gram.) radical, raíz de una palabra; (quím.) radical; (mat.) radical.

radicalism [-ism], *s.* radicalismo.

radicality [rædicǽliti], **radicalness** [rǽdicalnes], *s.* naturaleza radical, fundamental.

radically [rǽdicali], *adv.* radicalmente.

radicant [rǽdicant], *a.* que echa raíces.

radicate [rǽdikeit]. **I.** *va.* y *vn.* arraigar(se). **II.** *a.* arraigado.

radication [-kéishʊn], *s.* radicación, arraigue.

radicle, radicule [rǽdicœl, kiul], *s.* (bot.) radícula, raiceja.

radii [réidiai], *s. pl.* de RADIUS: radios.

radio [réidio], *s.* radiocomunicación (apl. esp. a la radiotelefonía).—**r.-frequency**, frecuencia de las ondas de radiocomunicación.

radioactive [-éctiv], *a.* radiactivo.—**radioactivity** [-æctiviti], *s.* radiactividad.

radioamplifier [réidioémplifaiær], *s.* radioamplificador.

radiobroadcast [-bródcæst], *va.* y *vn.* perifonear, difundir por radiotransmisión.—**radiobroadcaster** [-cœr], *s.* perífono, aparato de radiodifusión.—**radiobroadcasting**, [-ing.]. **l.** *s.* perifonía, radiodifusión. **II.** *a.* perifónico, de radiodifusión, difusor.

radiocompass [-cómpæs], *s.* (rad.) radiogoniómetro, detector de dirección.

radioconductor [-condúctœr], *s.* (rad.) radioconductor.

radiodetector [-ditéctœr], *s.* (rad.) radiodetector, detector de ondas eléctricas.

radiogoniometer [-goniómetœr], *s.* (rad.) radiogoniómetro, detector de dirección.

radiogram [-græm], *s.* (rad.) radiograma; (fot.) radiografía.

radiograph [-græf]. **I.** *s.* radiografía, fotografía por medio de la radiactividad; radiografía, fotografía con rayos X. **II.** *va.* radiofotografiar; fotografiar con rayos X. **III.** *va.* radiografiar, sacar una radiografía; radiografiar, sacar una radiografía.

radiography [réidiógrafi], *s.* radiografía, fotografía con substancias radiactivas; radiografía, fotografía con rayos X.

Radiolaria [réidiolériæ], *s. pl.* (zool.) radiolarios. —**radiolarian**, *s.* y *a.* radiolario.

radiometer [réidiómetœr], *s.* radiómetro.

radiometry [-tri], *s.* radiometría.

radiophare [-féær], *s.* radiofaro o estación baliza.

radiophone [-réidiofóun], *s.* radioteléfono.

radioscopy [reidióscopi], *s.* radioscopia.

radiotelegraph [réidiotélegræf], *s.* radiotelégrafo, telégrafo sin hilos.—**radiotelegraphy** [-telégrafi], *s.* radiotelegrafía, telegrafía sin hilos.

radiotelephone [-télefoun], *s.* radioteléfono.— **radiotelephony** [-tel⁴foni], *s.* radiotelefonía.

radiotherapeutics [-zéræpiútics], **radiotherapy** [-zéræpi], *s.* radioterapia, empleo terapéutico de los rayos X; raditerapia, empleo terapéutico de la radioactividad.

radiotron [-tron], *s.* (rdtf.) radiotrón (nombre de fábrica), especie de detector y amplificador.

radish [rǽdish], *s.* (bot.) rábano, rabanillo.

radium [réidium], *s.* (quím.) radio.

radius [réidius], *s.* (geom. y anat.) radio.—**r. of curvature**, radio de curvatura.—**r. of gyration**, radio de giro.—**r. of the eccentric**, radio o excentricidad de la excéntrica.—**r. vector**, radio vector.

radix [réidix], *s.* raíz; base (de un sistema de numeración).

raffle [ráefœl]. **I.** *vn.* rifar, sortear. **II.** *s.* rifa, sorteo, lotería.

raft. I. *s.* balsa, almadía; maderada, jangada, zatara.—**r. port,** (mar.) porta. **II.** *va.* convertir en balsa; transportar en balsa; pasar en balsa.

rafter [ráftœr], *s.* (arq.) cabrio.

raftsman [ráftsman], *s.* almadiero.

rag [rӕg], *s.* trapo, andrajo, harapo; (despec.) bandera, vela, periódico, capa; borde o canto mellado; risco; piedra granulosa.—**r. baby,** muñeca de trapo.—**r. bolt,** (mar.) perno harponado.—**r. buffer,** pulidor de alambre.—**r. money,** papel moneda.

ragamuffin [rӕgamúfin], *s.* galopín, pelafustán, pelagatos.

rage [rey]. **I.** *s.* rabia, ira, furor, vehemencia, encarnizamiento; ardor, anhelo o entusiasmo; (fam.) boga, moda. **II.** *vn.* rabiar, bramar, enfurecerse.

ragged [rӕgued], *a.* roto, rasgado, andrajoso, harapiento; mellado, desigual, escabroso o áspero.—**raggedly** [-ly], *adv.* andrajosamente; escabrosamente.—**raggedness** [-nes], *s.* aspereza, escabrosidad; estado andrajoso.

raglan [rӕglӕn], *s.* (sast.) raglán.

ragman [rӕgman], **ragpicker** [rӕgpíkœr], *s.* trapero.

ragout [ragú], *s.* (coc.) guisado.

ragstone [rӕgstoun], *s.* piedra de amolar.

ragtag [rӕgtӕg], *s.* chusma, morralla.

ragtime [rӕgtaim], *s.* (mús.) tiempo sincopado; (fam.) música popular.

ragwort [rӕgucœrt], *s.* (bot.) zuzón.

raid [réid]. **I.** *va.* invadir; (fam.) entrar o apoderarse por fuerza legal. **II.** *vn.* hacer una irrupción. **III.** *s.* (mil.) correría, irrupción, incursión; (fam.) invasión repentina, sorpresa.

rail [réil]. **I.** *s.* baranda, barandilla; (f. c.) riel, carril; ferrocarril (medio de transporte); (mar.) batayola, cairel, galón, brazal; (orn.) ave zancuda.—**r. chair,** (f. c.) cojinete de riel.—**r. guard,** contracarril; limpiavía, artificio unido a los lados de la locomotora para quitar estorbos de los carriles.—**r. train,** tren de laminadores de rieles. **II.** *va.* (a veces con *in* o *off*) poner barandilla, barrera o verja a: transportar por ferrocarril. **III.** *vn.* (con *at* o *against*) escarnecer; mofarse de.

railer [réilœr], *s.* murmurador.

railhead [réiljéd], *s.* término de la vía (los rieles) de un ferrocarril no terminado; (mil.) estación ferroviaria de víveres y municiones.

railing [réiling], *s.* baranda, barandilla, pasamano; cerca, verja, reja, enrejado; (f. c.) carriles, rieles; material para rieles.

raillery [réilœri], *s.* chocarrería, fisga.

railroad [réilróud], *va.* (E. U.) apresurar, hacer algo rápidamente; hacer, llevar, hacer aprobar, etc., con precipitación; transportar por ferrocarril.

railroad, railway [réiluéi]. **I.** *s.* ferrocarril. **II.** *a.* ferroviario, de ferrocarril, para ferrocarriles. —**r. car,** o **carriage,** vagón ferroviario; coche ferroviario.—**r. crossing,** paso a nivel.—**railway spine,** (med.) desorden de la medula espinal debido a concusión.

raiment [réimœnt], *s.* ropa, traje; prendas de vestir.

rain [réin]. **I.** *vn.* llover.—**r. or shine,** que llueva o no; con buen o mal tiempo. **II.** *va.* derramar copiosamente.—**to r. pitchforks,** llover chuzos, llover a cántaros. **III.** *s.* lluvia.—**r.-and-wind storm,** turbonada.—**r. ga(u)ge,** pluviómetro.—**r. spout,** chaparrón, turbión.—**r. water,** agua lluvia, agua llovediza.

rainbow [réinbo], *s.* arco iris.—**r.-hued,** irisado, iridiscente.

raincoat [-cóut], *s.* impermeable (sobretodo).

raindrop [-dróp], *s.* gota de agua.

rainfall [réinfol], *s.* aguacero; cantidad de lluvia que cae durante tiempo determinado (gen. un año).

raininess [réinines], *s.* estado lluvioso.

rainstorm [-stórm], *s.* aguacero, temporal, chubasco; tempestad de agua.

rainy [réini], *a.* lluvioso.

raise [réiś]. **I.** *va.* levantar, alzar, poner en pie; elevar, erguir; erigir; aumentar, subir; promover, ascender, encumbrar; animar, incitar; crear; causar, ocasionar; criar, cultivar; hacer concebir, inspirar, dar lugar a; hacer surgir, hacer brotar; vivificar, revivir; llamar, evocar; reclutar, alistar; allegar, reunir, recoger o juntar (dinero); poner fin a, abandonar; formar en relieve; ofrecer, presentar, suscitar; levantar (en la caza); fermentar (pan.).—**to r. a check,** raspar y aumentar la cantidad de un cheque, etc.—**to r. a dust, a great deal of dust,** (fam.) hacer grande alharaca.—**to r. an objection,** poner una objeción.—**to r. an outcry,** causar gritería, gritar.—**to r. a point,** presentar una cuestión, hacer una observación.—**to r. a row,** armar bochinche o camorra.—**to r. a storm,** levantar cisco, promover desórdenes.—**to r. a racket, a row, a rumpus, Cain, the devil, the dickens, the mischief, the Old Boy,** etc. (fam.) armar un alboroto; causar gran conmoción, trastorno o desbarajuste; armar un lío.—**to r. money on,** empeñar, obtener dinero prestado por.—**to r. steam,** levantar vapor, poner la caldera bajo presión.—**to r. the country,** sublevar, alborotar, revolucionar el país.—**to r. the dead,** despertar a los muertos.—**to r. the dust,** (fam.) hacerse a fondos.—**to r. the nap of the cloth,** perchar los paños, sacarles el pelo.—**to r. to a power,** (mat.) elevar a una potencia. **II.** *s.* levantamiento, alzamiento; (fam.) aumento, subida; ascenso.

raised [réisd], *a.* abollonado, en relieve; de resalto, de realce, que sobresale; (coc.) fermentado (pan).

raiser [réiśœr], *s.* productor, cultivador; educador; fundador.

raisin [réiśœn], *s.* pasa, uva seca.

raising [réiśing], *s.* acción de levantar, erigir, etc. (*V.* RAISE.)

raison d'être [re śon detr], razón de ser.

raj [ray], *s.* (India) soberanía, señorío.

raja(h [ráya], *s.* rajá, príncipe o caudillo de una tribu india.

rake [réik]. **I.** *s.* (agr.) rastro, mielga, rastrillo; inclinación, desviación de la vertical; (aer.) inclinación del extremo de un plano de sustentación al plano de simetría, lanzamiento o caída; calavera, libertino, perdido.—**r. dredge,** draga barredera. **II.** *va.* (agr.) rastrillar; barrer, raspar, rascar, raer; atizar, hurgar; escudriñar; cubrir con tierra; (mil.) enfilar, barrer.—**to r. out,** ahondar raspando. **III.** *vn.* pasar el rastro o la mielga; rascar, ahorrar; pasar con rapidez o violencia; llevar una vida disoluta; (mar.) inclinarse.

rakehell [réikjel], *s.* libertino, perdido.

rake-off [réik-of], *s.* (fam.) ganancia, tajada.

raker [réikœr], *s.* raedera, raspadera; rastrilladora mecánica.

rakish [réikiśh], *a.* libertino, disoluto; (mar.) de mástiles muy inclinados.—**rakishness** [-nes], *s.* disolución, libertinaje; (mar.) caída, inclinación de los palos.

rale [ral], *s.* (med.) estertor.

rally [réli]. **I.** *va.* (mil.) reunir y reanimar, rehacer; ridiculizar; dar matraca o zumba. **II.** *vn.* (mil.) reunirse, rehacerse; reanimarse; recobrar las fuerzas, revivir; chancearse, zumbarse. **III.** *s.* unión o reunión (de tropas dispersas o de gente); recuperación.

ram [rӕm]. **I.** *s.* morueco, carnero padre; (mec.) martinete, pisón; ariete hidráulico; (mar.) espolón; buque con espolón; (mil.) ariete; (astr.) Aries. **II.** *va.* pisonear, apisonar, golpear con un pisón, espolón o ariete; meter por la fuerza, apretar; atacar (un arma de fuego); atestar, henchir; atracar.

Ramadan [rӕmadӕn], *s.* Ramadán.

ramble [rӕmbœl]. **I.** *vn.* vagar, callejear; divagar, ir por las ramas; dar vueltas, serpentear. **II.** *s.* paseo.

rambler [rӕmblœr], *s.* vagabundo, callejero; paseador; divagador.

rambooze [rӕmbuś], *s.* clarea (bebida).

ramekin [rӕmekin], *s.* (coc.) quesadilla; tazuela para quesadillas.

ramie [ræmi], s. (bot.) ramio; ramina.
ramification [ræmifikéishɒn], s. ramificación, ramal.—**ramify** [-fai], va. y vn. ramificar(se).
rammer [ræmœr], s. baqueta de fusil; atacador; pisón de empedrador; (mar.) espolón.
rammish [ræmish], a. que huele a chotuno; libidinoso, salaz.
ramose [ramós], **ramous** [réimɒs], a. ramoso.
ramp [ræmp]. I. s. rampa, declive. II. vn. saltar, brincar; (bot.) trepar.
rampage [ræmpey], s. (fam.) alboroto.
rampancy [rǽmpansi], s. exuberancia, superabundancia, extravagancia.
rampant [rǽmpant], a. exuberante; excesivo; desenfrenado; general y sin coto; ufano, lozano; (blas.) rampante.
rampart [rǽmpart], s. (fort.) terraplén; muro, muralla; baluarte.
rampion [rǽmpiɒn], s. (bot.) rapónchigo.
ramrod [rǽmród], s. baqueta, atacador.
ramshackle [rǽmshæccœl], a. desvencijado, destartalado, ruinoso.
ramulose, ramulous [rǽmiulos, lʊs], a. (biol.) ramoso.
ramus [rémɒs], s. ramal, ramificación.
ran [ræn], pret. de TO RUN.
Rana [réina o rána], s. (zool.) ránido; (R-) príncipe de la India.
ranch [rænch]. I. s. hacienda de ganado; granja. II. vn. tener hacienda de ganado, ser hacendado. —**rancher** [-œr], **ranchman** [-mæn], s. hacendado, ganadero; boyero.
rancid [rǽnsid], a. rancio, acedo; rancioso.
rancidness, rancidity [rǽnsidnes, rænsíditi], s. rancidez.
ranco(u)r [rǽncœr], s. rencor, enemiga, encono, inquina.
rancorous [rǽncœrɒs], a. rencoroso.
rancorously [-li], adv. rencorosamente.
rand [rænd], s. calzo del zapato.
random [rǽndɒm]. I. s. azar, casualidad; desatino, desacierto.—**at r.**, a la ventura, al azar. II. a. fortuito, impensado, casual; sin orden ni concierto. —**r. shot**, tiro sin puntería.
rang, pret. de TO RING.
range [réinɣ]. I. va. recorrer; batir (el monte); (mar.) costear; poner en posición; poner en fila; (a veces con in) alinear; arreglar, clasificar. II. vn. vagar; extenderse; estar en línea; ponerse al lado, adherirse; tener igual grado, estar a la misma altura; variar, fluctuar; (arti.) tener alcance (un proyectil).—**to r. by**, (mar.) pasar, dejar atrás. III. s. distancia que recorre alguna cosa; trascurso, duración; esfera de actividad; vasta extensión de terrenos de pasto; alcance (de un arma o proyectil); fila, hilera, línea; clase, orden; línea de un tiro de artillería; sitio para tirar al blanco.—pl. (mar.) cornamusas.—**r. finder**, (art.) telémetro.—**r. of mountains**, cadena de montañas, cordillera.—**r. pole**, (top.) jalón.—**r. stove**, cocina portátil.—**r. work**, (alb.) mampostería concertada con hiladas de una misma altura.
ranger [réinɣœr], s. batidor; guardamayor de bosque; recorredor, vigilante; perro ventor.
rank [rænk]. I. a. lozano, exuberante, fértil; espeso, cerrado; rancio; fétido; acabado, rematado; (mec.) profundo, hondo. II. s. línea, hilera; grado, graduación; posición (social, etc.); calidad, distinción; (mil.) las filas.—**the ranks, the r. and file**, la tropa; las masas; el cuerpo, los miembros ordinarios (de una asociación, etc., a distinción de los dignatarios). III. va. clasificar, ordenar; colocar por grados; poner en fila; (mil.) tener un grado superior a. IV. vn. tener tal o cual grado o clasificación; ocupar (primer, segundo, etc.) lugar; (con with) estar al nivel (de); (con high, low), ocupar (alta, baja) posición.
rankish [rǽnkisk], a. algo rancio.
rankle [-cœl], vn. enconarse, inflamarse; causar encono, resentimiento o enojo.
rankly [-cli], adv. groseramente; pomposamente; ranciamente.—**rankness** [-nes], s. fertilidad; rancidez, fetidez.

ransack [rǽnsæc], va. escudriñar, explorar, registrar.—**to r. one's brains**, devanarse los sesos, **ransom** [rǽnsɒm]. I. s. rescate, redención. II. va. rescatar, redimir.—**ransomeless** [-les], a. irrescatable, irredimible.
rant [rænt]. I. vn. gritar, desvariar, delirar, desparpajar. II. s. lenguaje campanudo, retumbante.—**ranter** [-œr], s. vociferador, energúmeno.
ranunculaceous [ranɒnkiuléshɒs], a. (bot.) ranunculáceo.—**ranunculus** [-lʊs], s. (bot.) ranúnculo, botón de oro.
rap [ræp]. I. va. y vn. (pret. y pp. RAPPED) golpear, tocar, dar un golpe seco; proferir vivamente, criticar, zaherir, echar púas—**to r. at the door**, tocar o llamar a la puerta. II. va. (pret. y pp. RAPT, RAPPED) arrebatar; transportar con éxtasis (ú. principalmente el participio pasado). III. s. golpe seco, taque; medio penique falso; fruslería, ardite (v. gr.: I don't care a rap, no me importa un bledo); madeja, cadejo de 120 yardas de hilo.—**r. on the nose**, papirote, pasagonzalo.—**r. on the knuckles**, golpecito sobre los artejos.
rapacious [rapéishɒs], a. rapaz.—**rapaciously** [-li], adv. con rapacidad.—**rapaciousness** [-nes], **rapacity** [rapǽsiti], s. rapacidad.
rape [réip]. I. s. violación, estupro; rapto, robo; (bot.) nabo silvestre, colza; filtro para hacer vinagre; granuja.—pl. escobajo. II. va. violar, desflorar.
rapeseed [-sid], s. nabina o simiente de colza o nabo silvestre.—**r. oil**, aceite de colza.
Raphaelesque [ræfæelésc], a. rafaelesco.—**Raphaelism** [-ism], s. rafaelismo, estilo o escuela de Rafael.—**Raphaelite** [-ait], s. rafaelista.
raphe [réfi o ráfe], s. rafe, torillo.
rapid [rǽpid]. I. a. rápido.—**r.-firing gun**, cañón de tiro rápido. II. s. pl. rabión, recial, rápidos. pidez.
rapidity [rapíditi], **rapidness** [rǽpidnes], s. rapidez.
rapidly [rǽpidli], adv. rápidamente.
rapier [réipiœr], s. espadín; estoque.
rapine [rǽpin], s. rapiña, robo.
rappee [ræppí], s. rapé.
rapper [rǽpœr], s. golpeador; medio espiritista; llamador, aldabón.
rapport [ræppórt, rapór], s. armonía, concordancia, simpatía.
rapprochement [ra prosh man], s. restablecimiento de las relaciones o la armonía (entre dos naciones); reconciliación; armonía, buenas relaciones (internacionales).
rapscallion [ræpscǽliɒn], s. vagabundo, canalla.
rapt [ræptɟ], a. transportado, arrebatado o extasiado.
raptorial—**raptorial**. I. a. de presa, rapaz. II. ave rapaz.
Raptores [ræptóris], s. pl. aves rapaces.
rapture [rǽpchur], s. rapto, enajenamiento, arrobamiento, embeleso.
rapturous [-ʊs], a. arrobado, arrebatado, embelesado.—**rapturously** [-li], adv. con éxtasis, con transportes.
rare [réœr], a. raro; precioso; (coc.) poco asado, a medio asar; raro, ralo (de la atmósfera); esparcido.
rarebit [réœrbit], s. V. WELSH RABBIT.
raree-show [réœri-sho], s. tutilimundi, mundinovi.
rarefaction [ræreféeshɒn], s. rarefacción.
rarefiable [-fáiabœl], a. capaz de rarefacción.
rarefy [-fai]. I. va. rarificar; refinar, purificar. II. vn. rarificarse.
rarely [réœrli], adv. raramente, rara vez, por rareza.
rareness [-nes], s. rareza, singularidad.—**rareripe** [réœrraip]. I. a. precoz, temprano. II. s. fruta precoz.
rarity [rǽriti], s. raridad, rareza; curiosidad, preciosidad; tenuidad.
rascal [rǽscal], s. pícaro, bribón, bellaco.
rascality [rascǽliti], s. bellaquería.
rascallion [rascǽliɒn], s. villano, canalla, bergante.
rascally [rǽscali], a. vil, bajo, ruin.

rase [réiš], *va.* arrasar, demoler, destruir.

rash [ræsh]. **I.** *a.* temerario, imprudente, arrebatado, precipitado. **II.** *s.* sarpullido, erupción.

rasher [ræshœr], *s.* lonja, magra.

rashly [ræshli], *adv.* temerariamente, imprudentemente.

rashness [-nes], *s.* temeridad, imprudencia, precipitación.

Rasores [rasóriš], *s. pl.* (orn.) gallináceas.

rasorial [-al], *a.* gallinácea.

rasp. I. *s.* escofina, raspa, raspador, limatón, rallo, escarpelo; sonido estridente. **II.** *va.* raspar, escofinar, rallar.

raspatorium, raspatory [ræspatorium, ri], *s.* (cir.) legra.

raspberry [ræsberi], *s.* (bot.) frambuesa, sangüesa.—**r. bush,** frambueso.

rasper [ráspœr], *s.* raspador, rallo.

rasping [rásping]. **I.** *a.* raedor, raspante; ronco, áspero; irritante. **II.** *s.* raspadura, raedura.

rat [ræt]. **I.** *s.* (zool.) rata; (despec.) esquirol, el que toma el lugar de un huelguista; (Ingl.) desertor, renegado; (E. U.) postizo para el pelo.—**r. catcher,** cazador de ratas.—**r. dung,** cagurruta de ratas.—**r. poison,** veneno para matar ratas.—**r.-tail file,** lima de cola de rata. —**r. trap,** ratonera. **II.** *va.* y *vn.* (fam.) reemplazar obreros agremiados por otros no agremiados; trabajar por jornal menor que el que fija un gremio; tomar el lugar de un huelguista; cazar ratas; (Ingl. pol. fam.) volver casaca.

ratable [réitabœl], *a.* sujeto a contribución; imponible; valuable, que puede tasarse.

ratably [réitabli], *adv.* a prorrata.

ratafia [rætafía], *s.* ratafia.

ratan [ratǽn], *s.* = RATTAN.

ratan(h)y [rætani], *s.* (bot.) ratania.

ratch [ræch], *s.* cremallera; rueda dentada con trinquete.

ratchet [ráchet], *s.* (mec.) trinquete.—**r. brace,** chicharra, berbiquí de trinquete.—**r. drill,** taladro de trinquete.—**r. wheel,** rueda de trinquete.—**r. wrench,** llave de trinquete.

rate [réit]. **I.** *s.* tarifa, precio o valor fijo; valuación; tasa; tipo (de interés, etc.); velocidad; proporción, tanto (por ciento, por unidad, etc.); contribución, impuesto; cuota; clase o clasificación de un buque mercante; error o variación diaria de un reloj; modo, manera; (Ingl.) contribución local. Se emplea a menudo, sobre todo en plural, para denotar sumas de dinero pagadas, exigidas, etc., regularmente, y puede traducirse por "precios," "salarios," "tarifa," "honorarios," "sueldos," etc., según el caso.—**r. of climb,** (aer.) velocidad de ascenso.—**r. of exchange,** cambio (valor relativo de las unidades monetarias), tipo del cambio.—**r. of grade,** (f. c.) pendiente relativa, pendiente (subentendiéndose que se expresa en tanto por ciento, por kilómetro, etc.).—**r. of population,** aumento proporcional de la población (expresado en tantos por 1000, por 100,000, etc.).—**at any r.,** de todos modos, sea como fuere. —**at that r.,** a esa proporción; de ese modo; a ese paso.—**at the r. of,** a razón de. **II.** *va.* tasar, valuar; clasificar; imponer contribuciones, derecho, gravamen, etc.; determinar el error de (un reloj); considerar, justipreciar; calcular, estimar; fijar precio, tarifa, etc.; dar o determinar la capacidad normal de (una máquina). **III.** *vn.* ser considerado (como), tenido (por); estar clasificado (como). **IV.** *va.* y *vn.* regañar, reñir, sermonear.

rateable [réitabœl], *a.* = RATABLE.

rateen, *s.* = RATTEN.

ratel [réitel], *s.* (zool.) ratel.

rather [ræðœr], más bien, un poco, algo (*she is rather pretty,* ella es más bien bonita; *I am rather tired,* estoy un poco cansado); más bien, mejor dicho (*I am tired, or, rather, exhausted,* estoy cansado, o mejor dicho, agotado); por el contrario; (Iron.) muy, mucho.—**r. than,** más bien que, antes que.—**had r.** *V.* HAVE.—**the r., the r. as, the r. that,** tanto más cuanto que.—**would r.,** preferiría, más bien quisiera.—**(I) would r. not,** preferiría no, prefiero no, creo que es mejor no (hacerlo, llevarlo, decirlo, ir. etc.).

rathskeller [rátskélœr], *s.* restaurante o cantina de sótano.

ratification [rétifikéshun], *s.* ratificación.—**ratifier** [-faiœr], *s.* ratificador.—**ratify** [-fai], *va.* ratificar.

rating [réiting], *s.* justiprecio; apreciación; clasificación; marinero de guerra; (mec.) capacidad o potencia normal o de régimen, según la da el fabricante o el proyectista.

ratio [réshio], *s.* razón, relación, proporción; (mat.) razón.

ratiocinate [rœðiósineit]. **I.** *vn.* raciocinar. **II.** *a.* razonado.

ratiocination [réshiosinéshun], *s.* raciocinio.

ration [réshun o ráshun], *s.* (mil.) ración.

rational [réshunal]. **I.** *a.* racional; (mat.) racional. **II.** *s.* ser racional.

rationale [ræshonéli], *s.* exposición razonada.

rationalism [réshunalîsm], *s.* racionalismo.

rationalist [réshunalist], *s.* racionalista.

rationalistic(al [-ic(al], *a.* racionalista.

rationality [ræshunéliti], *s.* racionalidad.

rationalization [réshunælišéishun], *s.* conversión o transformación en ente racional; (mat.) supresión de radicales.—**rationalize** [-aiš], *va.* hacer racional; concebir racionalmente; (mat.) hacer racional, quitar los radicales a.

rationally [réshunali], *adv.* racionalmente.

ratite [rétait], *s.* y *a.* (zool.) corredora (ave).

Ratitæ [rætáiti], *s. pl.* (zool.) corredoras.

ratlin(e [rétlin], **ratling** [rétling], *s.* (mar.) rebenque, flechaste, frenillo.

ratoon [ratún], *s.* retoño; soca de caña de azúcar; hoja del corazón del tabaco.

ratsbane [rétsbein], *s.* arsénico.

rat(t)an [rættæn], *s.* (bot.) roten o rota; junquillo; bastón o varilla de roten.

ratteen [ratín], *s.* (tej.) ratina.

ratten [rétœn], *va.* molestar o vejar a obreros que no quieren agremiarse o que reemplazan a huelguistas.

rattle [rǽtœl]. **I.** *va.* hacer sonar como una matraca; batir o sacudir con ruido; atolondrar, aturrullar; decir a la carrera. **II.** *vn.* matraquear, rechinar, guachaporar; charlatanear, parlotear; moverse o funcionar con matraqueo.—**to r. away,** parlotear; rodar a d stancia, haciendo ruido. **III.** *s.* cascabel; sonajero (juguete); matraca, carraca; parla, charla.—**r.-brained, r.-headed, r.-pated,** ligero de cascos, casquivano.—**r. snake,** crótalo, culebra de cascabel.

rattlebox [-box], *s.* cascabel (juguete).

rattled [rétœld], *a.* aturdido, azarado, confundido.

rattlehead [rétœljéd], **rattlepate** [-péit], **rattleskull** [scúl], *s.* parlanchín.

rattler [rétlœr], *s.* parlanchín, tarabilla; crótalo; (fam.) golpe que aturde.

rattietrap [-træp], *s.* objeto destartalado.

rattlesnake [-snéik], *s.* culebra de cascabel, crótalo.—**r. root,** (bot.) lechera.

rattling [rétling], *a.* (fam.) vivo, sorprendente, alegre.—**r. box,** cascabel.

raucity [rósiti], *s.* ronquera, ronquedad

raucous [rócus], *a.* ronco, rauco, bronco.

ravage [révœl]. **I.** *va.* saquear, pillar; asolar, talar, destruir. **II.** *s.* ruina, estrago, destrucción; saqueo.

ravager [réveɥœr], *s.* saqueador; asolador.

rave [réiv]. **I.** *vn.* delirar, desvariar; devanear, disparatar; bramar, enfurecerse; salirse de sus casillas.—**to r. after,** querer a toda costa, despepitarse por. **II.** *s.* adral de un carro.

ravehook [réivjúc], *s.* (mar.) descalcador.

ravel [révœl]. **I.** *va.* deshilar, deshebrar, deshacer: (con out) desenredar, desenmarañar; enredar (acepción original). **II.** *vn.* (con out) deshilarse, destorcerse; deshacerse; (ant.) enredarse.

ravelin [révlin], *s.* (fort.) rebellín.

ravel(l)ing [révœling], *s.* hilacha, deshiladura.

raven [réivn]. **I.** *s.* (orn.) cuervo. **II.** *a.* negro y lustroso.

raven, ravin [rævn]. **I.** *va.* y *vn.* apresar, prender por fuerza; devorar. **II.** *s.* presa, botín.

ravening [rǽvning]. **I.** *s.* rapiña; voracidad. **II.** *a.* rapaz; (blas.) cebado.

ravenous [rǽvnus], *a.* voraz, famélico; rapaz.— **ravenously** [-li], *adv.* vorazmente.—**ravenousness** [-nes], *s.* voracidad; rapacidad.

ravine [ravín], *s.* barranca, cañada, hondonada.

raving [réiving]. **I.** *s.* desvarío, delirio. **II.** *a.* delirante, desvariado.—**ravingly** [-li], *adv.* desvariadamente, locamente.

ravish [rǽvish], *va.* arrebatar, atraer, encantar; violar, estuprar.—**ravisher** [-œr], *s.* estuprador; arrebatador.—**ravishing** [-ing], *a.* arrebatador, embriagador.—**ravishingly** [-li], *adv.* arrobadoramente.—**ravishment** [-mœnt], *s.* rapto, transporte, arrobamiento; estupro; violación (de una mujer).

raw [ro], *a.* crudo; pelado, despellejado; en carne viva; descarnado; desapacible, frío y húmedo; (com.) en bruto; fresco, nuevo; novato, bisoño; vulgar, tosco, brutal.—**r.** cotton, algodón en rama. —**r.** flesh, carne viva.—**r.** hand, novato, novicio. —**r.** hemp, cáñamo sin peinar.—**r.** material, materia prima.—**r.** silk, seda en rama devanada.— **r.** spirits, licores puros o sin mezcla.—**r.** sugar, azúcar bruto o mascabado.—**r.** tallow, sebo puro o en rama.—**r.** weather, tiempo crudo.

rawboned [róbóund], *a.* huesudo.

rawhead [rójed], *s.* espectro, fantasma, espantajo. —**r.** and bloody bones, coco.

rawhide [rójáid]. **I.** *a.* de cuero crudo. **II.** *s.* cuero crudo; látigo hecho de este cuero.

rawish [róish], *a.* algo crudo, más bien crudo.

rawly [róli], *adv.* crudamente.

rawness [rónes], *s.* crudeza.

ray [réi]. **I.** *s.* rayo (de luz, calor, etc.); (geom.) rayo; línea recta, hilera, raya; (bot.) lígula; (ict.) raya.—**r.** filter, pantalla fotocrómica.—**r.** grass, (bot.) vallico. **II.** *va.* y *vn.* emitir rayos.

raze [réis], *va.* arrasar, demoler, derruir.

razee [raší]. **I.** *va.* rebajar un buque de guerra; reducir, cercenar. **II.** *s.* buque rebajado.

razor [réisœr], *s.* navaja de afeitar; colmillo del jabalí.—**r.** blade, cuchilla de navaja de afeitar de seguridad.—**r.** case, navajero.—**r.** clam, **r.** fish, navaja (marisco).—**r.** grinder, vaciador de navajas de afeitar.—**r.** shell = R. CLAM.—**r.** strap, **r.** strop, asentador de navajas de afeitar.

razorbill [-bil], *s.* (orn.) alca.

razzle-dazzle [rǽsœl-dǽsœl]. **I.** *va.* (E. U. fam.) embriagar; deslumbrar; aturdir. **II.** *s.* borrachera; aturdimiento; especie de tiovivo.

re [réi], *s.* (mús.) re; (for.) [ri] causa, litigio, acción; (com.) acerca de, concerniente a.

reabsorb [riæbsórb], *va.* resorber.

reabsorption [riæbsórpshun], *s.* resorción.

reaccess [riǽcses], *s.* (med.) recidiva.

reach [rích]. **I.** *va.* alargar, llegar a o hasta; alcanzar; penetrar.—**to r.** out one's hand, tender la mano.—**to r.** the heart, llegar al o tocar el corazón. **II.** *vn.* extenderse, llegar, alcanzar, penetrar; esforzarse; coger; (mar.) ceñir el viento, navegar de bolina.—**to r.** after, procurar obtener o coger, hacer esfuerzos para alcanzar o coger.—**to r.** into, penetrar en. **III.** *s.* alcance; extensión, distancia; poder, facultad; capacidad; (carr.) barra que une el juego posterior con la parte delantera; (mar.) bordada.—**beyond one's r.**, out of one's r.**, fuera del alcance de uno.—**within one's r.**, al alcance de uno; dentro del poder de uno.

react [riǽct], *vn.* reaccionar.

reactance [riǽctæns], *s.* (elec.) reactancia.—**r. coil**, bobina de reacción o de reactancia.

reaction [riǽcshun], *s.* reacción.—**reactionary** [-nœri]. **I.** *a.* reaccionario. **II.** *s.* (pol.) retrógrado. —**reactionist** [-nist], *s.* (pol.) reaccionario, retrógrado.

reactive [riǽctiv], *a.* reactivo.

reactivity [riæctíviti], *s.* tendencia reactiva.

reactor [riǽctœr], *s.* (elec.) = REACTANCE COIL.

read [ríd]. **I.** *va.* (pret. y pp. READ [red]) leer; descifrar; enseñar, aconsejar, avisar; (mús.) leer; (seguido de infinitivo) poner a . . . leyendo (*I read him to sleep*, lo puse a dormir, o lo dormí, leyéndole).—**to r.** law, estudiar derecho.—**to r.** off hand, leer de corrido.—**to r.**

out, expulsar (a un miembro de una asociación).— **to r.** over, leerlo todo, recorrer (un escrito).—**to r.** proofs, (impr.) corregir pruebas.—**to. r.** through, leer de cabo a rabo. **II.** *vn.* leer; (con of o about) saber, enterarse de (leyendo); leer, decir, rezar (*the text reads thus*, el texto reza, o dice, así); (mús.) saber leer e interpretar las notas; conferenciar en público; indicar; sonar (bien, mal) al leerlo; ser lectura (amena, difícil, etc.).—**to r.** about, leer acerca de; aprender leyendo.—**to r.** between the lines, leer entre líneas.—**to r.** on, proseguir o continuar leyendo.—**to r.** to, indicar hasta, tener apreciación de (apl. a instrumentos de medida).

readable [rídabœl], *a.* leíble, legible; ameno, interesante.

readability [ridabíliti], *o* **readableness** [rídabœlnes], *s.* calidad de legible; amenidad de estilo.

reader [rídœr], *s.* lector, leyente; declamador; libro de lectura (de texto); (impr.) corrector de pruebas; (igl.) lector.

readership [rídœrship], *s.* lectoría.

readily [rédili], *adv.* fácilmente; prontamente, luego; con placer, de buena gana.

readiness [rédines], *s.* disposición, buena voluntad; prontitud; facilidad; aptitud, desembarazo.—**r.** of wit, viveza o vivacidad de ingenio. —**in r.**, listo, preparado.

reading [ríding]. **I.** *s.* lectura; material de lectura; significado (de algo escrito); conferencia, disertación; lectura de un proyecto de ley; estudio; lectura, indicación de un instrumento graduado; interpretación; leyenda, variante, glosa; solución de un enigma o acertijo; (teat.) desempeño o interpretación de un papel. **II.** *a.* de lectura.—**r.** desk, facistol, atril.—**r.** matter, sección de lectura (de un periódico).—**r.** room, sala de lectura.

readjust [riædjúst], *va.* ajustar de nuevo; readaptar; (impr.) recorrer.—**readjustment** [-ment], *s.* readaptación; (impr.) recorrido.

readmission [riædmíshun], *s.* readmisión.

readmit [riædmít], *va.* admitir de nuevo.

ready [rédi], *a.* listo, pronto, preparado, dispuesto; inclinado, propenso; ágil, diligente; ligero; fácil; manuable, a la mano, al alcance; útil, disponible; (com.) contante, efectivo.— **r.-made**, ya hecho; confeccionado.—**r.** money, dinero contante; dinero al contado.—**r.** payment, paga inmediata.—**r.** wit, genio agudo.—**r.-witted**, de ingenio vivo, pronto.

reaffirm [riæfœrm], *va.* reiterar.—**reaffirmance** [-æns], *s.* reiteración.

reagent [riéyent], *s.* (quím.) reactivo.

real [ríæl]. **I.** *a.* real, verdadero; inmueble; referente a bienes raíces; (mat.) real.—**r.** property, o **r.** estate, bienes raíces. **II.** *s.* real (moneda); (con *the*), (la) realidad, (lo) real. **III.** *adv.* (fam. e incorrecto) muy, bastante.

realgar [riélgar], *s.* rejalgar.

realism [ríálism], *s.* (filos. y b. a.) realismo.

realist [ríalist], *s.* (filos. y b. a.) realista.

realistic [ríalístic], *a.* natural, vivo; (filos. y b. a.) realista.

reality [riǽliti], *s.* realidad.—**in r.**, en realidad.

realizable [ríaláisabœl], *a.* realizable, factible.

realization [ríaliséshun], *s.* realización, verificación; concepción, comprensión.

realize [ríalais], *va.* darse cuenta, hacerse cargo de; comprender; realizar, verificar, efectuar; dar vida; cumplir, llevar a cabo; ganar, reportar; (com.) realizar, convertir en dinero.

really [ríali], *adv.* realmente, verdaderamente.

realm [relm], *s.* reino o región, dominio; (zool.) extensión de una fauna.

realtor [ríaltœr], *s.* (E. U.) corredor de bienes raíces que es miembro de la asociación de las Juntas de Bienes Raíces.

realty [ríalty], *s.* (for.) bienes raíces.

ream [rím]. **I.** *s.* resma. **II.** *va.* escariar.

reamer [rímœr], *s.* escariador.

reanimate [riǽnimet], *va.* reanimar.

reannex [riænécs], *va.* volver a unir.

reap [ríp]. **I.** va. segar; cosechar; obtener o sacar provecho de. **II.** vn. cosechar, hacer el agosto, hacer la cosecha; recibir (uno) la recompensa, o el fruto de su trabajo.

reaper [rípœr], s. segador; segadora mecánica.

reaping [ríping], s. siega, cosecha.—r. hook, hoz, segadera.—r. machine, segadora.—r. time, siega.

reappear [riæppíær], vn. reaparecer.

reappearance [riæppírans], s. reaparición.

reappoint [riæpóint], va. nombrar, designar o fijar de nuevo.

reapportion [riœpórⱥhⱴn], va. proporcionar o repartir de nuevo.

reappraise [riapréis], va. retasar.

reappraisement [-mœnt], s. retasa, revaluación.

rear [ríær]. **I.** a. de atrás, trasero, posterior; último, de más atrás.—r. admiral, contralmirante. —r. axle, (aut.) eje trasero, puente.—r.-axle shaft, (aut.) semieje trasero.—r. guard, retaguardia.—r. rank, última fila.—r. view, vista posterior.—r. wall, pared trasera o posterior. **II.** s. fondo; espalda, parte de atrás o posterior; cola. **III.** va. levantar, alzar, exaltar; erigir, construir; criar, educar. **IV.** vn. encabritarse (el caballo).

rearmost [ríærmoust], a. último, de más atrás.

rearrange [riarrény], va. volver a arreglar, cambiar el arreglo o el orden de.

rearward [ríæruard]. **I.** a. postrero, último. **II.** adv. hacia atrás. **III.** s. cola, último lugar.

reascend [riasénd], va. y vn. subir de nuevo.

reason [rísn]. **I.** s. razón; causa; moderación; sensatez; justicia; (lóg.) premisa.—r. for existence, r. of being, razón de ser.—by r. of, a causa de, en virtud de.—in (all) r., con justicia, con razón.—out of r., out of all r., fuera de razón, desrazonable. **II.** va. (a menudo con out) demostrar o concluir por el razonamiento. **III.** vn. razonar.

reasonable [rísnabœl], a. razonable, justo; módico; regular, mediano.—reasonableness [-nes], s. racionalidad; moderación; justicia.—reasonably [-bli], adv. razonablemente; bastante.

reasoner [rísnœr], s. razonador.

reasoning [rísning], s. razonamiento, raciocinio.

reasonless [rísnles], a. sin razón; desrazonable.

reassemble [riæsémbœl], va. juntar de nuevo.

reassert [riæsœrt], va. afirmar de nuevo.

reassign [riæsáin], va. asignar, destinar o repartir de nuevo.

reassume [riæsiúm], va. reasumir.

reassumption [riæsⱴmpⱥhⱴn], s. reasunción.

reassurance [riæⱥhúrans], s. confianza establecida; afirmación repetida, certeza restablecida; (com.) segundo seguro.

reassure [riæⱥhúær], va. tranquilizar; (com.) volver a asegurar.

reattachment [riætǽchmœnt], s. (for.) reembargo.

rebaptize [ríbæptáiⱥ], va. rebautizar.

rebate [ribéit], va. y vn. rebajar, descontar, hacer rebaja; embotar.—rebate(ment [-(mœnt], s. rebaja, descuento; diminución, reducción; (f. c.) detasa.

rebec [ríbec], s. (mús.) rabel.

rebel [rébⱥl]. **I.** a. y s. rebelde. **II.** vn. [rebél] rebelarse, sublevarse.

rebellion [rebéliⱴn], s. rebelión, sublevación.

rebellious [rebéliⱴs], a. rebelde; refractario.—rebelliously [-li], adv. con rebeldía.—rebelliousness [-nes], s. rebeldía, insubordinación.

reblossom [riblósⱴm], vn. florecer de nuevo.

rebore [ríbœr], va. (mec.) rectificar (un cilindro).

rebound [rebáund]. **I.** vn. repercutir; rebotar, resurtir, saltar. **II.** s. rebote, resurtida, rechazo.

rebounding [ribáunding], s. rebotadura.

rebuff [ribⱴf]. **I.** s. desaire, repulsa, denegación; contrariedad. **II.** va. rechazar, desairar.

rebuild [ribíld], va. (pret. y pp. REBUILT) reedificar.

rebuke [rebiúk]. **I.** va. increpar, reprochar, censurar, regañar. **II.** s. repulsa, reproche, reprimenda; revés, bofetada.

rebus [ríbⱴs], s. jeroglífico, logogrifo, acertijo; quisicosa.

rebut [rebⱴt]. **I.** va. (for.) refutar, contradecir. **II.** vn. replicar.

rebuttal [rebⱴtal], s. refutación.

rebutter [rebⱴtœr], s. (for.) contrarréplica; el que la hace.

recalcitrant [recǽlsitrant], a. recalcitrante.

recalcitrate [recǽlsitret], vn. recalcitrar.

recalescence [ricælésens], s. recalescencia.

recall [ricól]. **I.** va. revocar, anular; llamar, hacer volver; recordar; deponer, destituir de un cargo o empleo.—to r. an ambassador, retirar a un embajador. **II.** s. recordación; revocación; toque o aviso de llamada; (pol. E. U.) derecho de deponer funcionarios o anular sus decisiones por votación popular.

recant [ricǽnt], va. y vn. retractar(se).

recantation [ricæntéiⱥhⱴn], s. retractación.

recanter [ricǽntœr], s. retrayente.

recapacitate [ricapǽsitet], va. recapacitar.

recapitulate [ricǽpitiuleit], va. recapitular.

recapitulation [-léiⱥhⱴn], s. recapitulación.

recapitulatory [-latori], a. que recapitula.

recapture [ricǽpchur]. **I.** va. volver a tomar; represar. **II.** s. represa.

recast [ricást], va. (pret. y pp. RECAST) (fund.) volver a fundir; refundir, volver a escribir; volver a hacer; calcular de nuevo.

recede [risíd], vn. cejar, retroceder; retirarse, alejarse; desistir, volverse atrás; desdecirse; inclinarse, desviarse.

receipt [risít]. **I.** s. recibo, cobranza; descargo, carta de pago; receta, fórmula.—pl. ingresos, entradas.—r. and outgo, entrada y salida.—r. book, registro de recetas; (com.) libro de recibos.—r. in full (of all demads), recibo por saldo de cuenta, quitanza, finiquito.—on r. of, al recibo de. **II.** va. y vn. firmar o extender recibo; poner el recibí.

receipted a. que lleva el recibí.

receivable [risívabœl], a. recibidero; admisible.

receive [risív], va. recibir; admitir; hospedar, agasajar; contener; en tenis, volear la pelota. —received payment, recibí.—to r. the sacrament, comulgar.

receiver [risívœr], s. recibidor, receptor; recipiente, campana (de máquina neumática, etc.); (elec.) receptor; (for.) depositario, síndico; receptador.

receivership [risívœrⱥhip], s. receptoría; sindicatura.

receiving [risíving], a. que recibe; de recibir.—r. teller, (com.) cobrador.

recency [rísensi], recentness [rísentnes], s. novedad; fecha, origen reciente.

recension [risénⱥhⱴn], s. revisión crítica; texto revisado.

recent [rísent], a. reciente.—recently [-li], adv. recientemente.

receptacle [reséptacœl], s. receptáculo.

receptacular [reseptǽkiular], a. perteneciente a un receptáculo.

receptibility [riséptibíliti], s. capacidad para recibir.

receptible [-tibœl], a. capaz de ser recibido.

reception [resépⱥhⱴn], s. recepción, recibimiento, recibo; acogimiento, acogida; audiencia; recibimiento social, besamanos.

receptive [reséptiv], a. receptivo.

receptivity [riceptíviti], s. receptividad; sensibilidad.

recess [resés o ríses], s. nicho; depresión, entrada; tregua, suspensión; vacación, recreación; retiro, lugar apartado, lugar o cosa recónditos.

recession [reséⱥhⱴn], s. receso, retirada, desistimiento.

recessional [reséⱥhunal], s. himno que se canta después del servicio divino.

recherché [reⱥherⱥhé], a. deseado, buscado; excelente.

recidivist [residivist], s. criminal reincidente.

recipe [résipe], *s.* récipe, receta de médico; fórmula.

recipient [resípient], *a.* y *s.* recibidor; recipiente.

reciprocal [resíprocæl]. **I.** *a.* recíproco, mutuo; alterno, alternativo; permutable.—**r. pronoun,** pronombre reflexivo. **II.** *s.* (mat.) inverso (de un número—fracción cuyo numerador es 1 y cuyo denominador es el número).—**reciprocalness** [-nes], *s.* reciprocidad.—**reciprocally** [-li], *adv.* recíprocamente, mutuamente.

reciprocate [resíprokeit]. **I.** *va.* producir un movimiento de vaivén; permutar; corresponder. **II.** *vn.* alternar; ser recíproco; tener movimiento alternativo; estar a la recíproca.

reciprocating [-ing], *a.* de vaivén, alternativo; de movimiento alternativo.—**r. engine,** máquina de movimiento alternativo, máquina de émbolo.— **r. parts,** piezas de movimiento alternativo.

reciprocation [-kéishun], *s.* reciprocación, reciprocidad; correspondencia (de amor, bondad, etc.); alternación.

reciprocity [résiprósiti], *s.* reciprocidad.

recision [risíyun], *s.* resección.

recital [risáital], *s.* relación, narración; recitación; (mús.) sesión musical por un solista.

recitation [résitéishun], *s.* recitación, declamación; clase; acción de decir la lección en la clase.

recitative [résitatív], *a.* y *s.* (mús.) recitativo, recitado.

recite [risáit], *va.* y *vn.* narrar, relatar, contar; recitar; declamar; citar; dar o decir la lección.

reciter [risáitœr], *s.* recitador, declamador.

reckless [récles], *a.* descuidado; temerario; atolondrado; derrochador.—**recklessly** [-li], *adv.* temerariamente; descuidadamente.—**recklessness** [-nes], *s.* temeridad; indiferencia.

reckon [récun], *va.* y *vn.* contar, enumerar; calcular; estimar, considerar; suponer, creer; (con **on** o **upon**) contar con, fiar en.—**to r. without one's host,** hacer la cuenta sin la huéspeda.

reckoner [récunœr], *s.* contador, calculador.

reckoning [récuning], *s.* cuenta; tanteo, cómputo, cálculo; cuenta de gastos en una posada; ajuste de cuentas.—**(dead) r.,** (mar.) rumbo estimado, estima.—**r. book,** libro de cuenta y razón. —**every one must pay his r.,** cada palo que aguante su vela.—**to be out in one's r.,** equivocarse en el cálculo.

reclaim [ricléim], *va.* reclamar (derechos, terrenos, etc.); vindicar; amansar, domesticar, domeñar; reducir; mejorar y utilizar (tierras), hacer labrantío o aprovechable; utilizar (material usado).

reclaimable [ricléimabœl], *a.* reclamable, mejorable, utilizable.

reclamation [reclaméshun], *s.* reclamación; restauración; mejoramiento.

reclinate [réclinet], *a.* reclinado.—**reclined** [ricláind], *a.* reclinado, recostado.

reclination [reclinéshun], *s.* reclinación.

recline [ricláin]. **I.** *va.* reclinar, recostar. **II.** *vn.* recostarse.

recluse [reclús]. **I.** *a.* recluso, solitario. **II.** *s.* solitario, eremita.

recluseness [reclúsnes], **reclusion** [reclúyun], *s.* reclusión, retiro, aislamiento.

reclusive [reclúsiv], *a.* recluso.

recognition [récogníshun], *s.* reconocimiento; agradecimiento.

recognizable [-náisabœl], *a.* que puede ser reconocido.

recognizance [recógnisans], *s.* (for.) reconocimiento; obligación contraída.

recognize [récógnais]. **I.** *va.* reconocer; (filos.) [ricógnais] volver a conocer, a percibir. **II.** *vn.* (for.) subscribir una obligación auténtica.

recognizee [recógnisí], *s.* (for.) aquel a cuyo favor se da algún vale.

recognizor [récognáisœr], *s.* (for.) el que da un vale a favor de otro.

recoil [ricóil]. **I.** *s.* rechazo, reculada; coz, retroceso, rebufo; repugnancia, temor.—**r. spring,**

resorte para disminuir el rebufo. **II.** *vn.* recular; retirarse; cejar, retroceder; rebufar (un arma de fuego).

recoin [ricóin], *va.* resellar.

recoinage [ricóiney], *s.* resello.

recollect [récoléct], *va.* y *vn.* recordar; [ricolléct] recoger, reunir; juntarse de nuevo.

recolle(c)t [récolect], *s.* (igl.) recoleto.

recollection [récolécshun], *s.* recuerdo.

recommence [ricoméns], *va.* empezar de nuevo. —**recommencement** [-mœnt], *s.* acción de comenzar de nuevo.

recommend [récoménd]. **I.** *va.* recomendar. **II.** *s.* (vulg.) carta de recomendación.—**recommendable** [-abœl], *a.* recomendable.—**recommendation** [-mendéishun], *s.* recomendación; (fam.) carta de recomendación.—**recommendatory** [-méndatori], *a.* recomendatorio.

recommit [ricomít], *va.* trasladar de nuevo (un proyecto, etc.) a una comisión informadora; prender de nuevo (a alguno que estaba bajo fianza); enviar otra vez a la cárcel.—**recommitment, recommittal** [-mœnt], -al], *s.* nuevo traslado a una comisión; nuevo arresto; nuevo encarcelamiento.

recompense [récompens]. **I.** *va.* recompensar; indemnizar; resarcir. **II.** *s.* recompensa, compensación, remuneración.

recompose [rícompóus], *va.* tranquilizar de nuevo; recomponer, rehacer.—**recomposition** [rícómposhun], *s.* recomposición.

reconcentrado [recónsentrádo], *s.* reconcentrado, persona obligada en la guerra a vivir dentro de ciertos límites.

reconcilable [récousáilabœl], *a.* reconciliable; conciliable, compatible.—**reconcilableness** [-nes], *s.* calidad de reconciliable o compatible.—**reconcilably** [-bli], *adv.* compatiblemente.

reconcile [réconsail], *va.* y *vr.* reconciliar, componer, conciliar, compadecerse, avenirse; ajustar, componer; resignarse; (igl.) reconciliar.—**reconcilement** [-mœnt], *s.* reconciliación.—**reconciler** [-œr], *s.* reconciliador; conciliador, pacificador.

reconciliation [-siliéishun], *s.* reconciliación; conciliación, ajuste; concordancia, conformidad.

reconciliatory [-síliatori], *a.* reconciliador.

recondite [récondait], *a.* recóndito.

recondition [ricóndishun], *va.* (mec.) reacondicionar, rectificar, corregir.

reconduct [ricondúct], *va.* volver a conducir.

reconnaissance, reconnoissance [recónæsans, -isans], *s.* (mil.) reconocimiento; (f. c.) reconocimiento, exploración.

reconnoitre [récónóitœr]. **I.** *va.* reconocer, explorar, inspeccionar. **II.** *vn.* practicar un reconocimiento.

reconquer [ricónkœr], *va.* reconquistar.

reconquest [rícóncuest], *s.* reconquista.

reconsider [ríconsídœr], *va.* repensar; volver a discutir.—**reconsideration** [-éishun], *s.* nueva discusión o consideración.

reconstitute [ricónstitiut], *va.* reconstituir, reorganizar.—**reconstitution** [-tiúshun], *s.* reconstitución, reorganización.

reconstruct [riconstrúct], *va.* reedificar, reconstruir; reconstituir—**reconstructed ruby,** rubí artificial.—**reconstruction** [-shun], *s.* reconstrucción; reconstitución.

reconvene [riconvín], *va.* convocar, juntar o reunir de nuevo.

reconvey [riconvéi], *va.* traspasar de nuevo; reponer, restituir.

record [ricórd]. **I.** *va.* registrar; inscribir, depositar; apuntar; marcar, indicar; hacer un fonograma (impresión fonográfica) de; (ant.) referir, relatar. **II.** *s.* [récord] registro; constancia; datos; partida, inscripción; acta; documento; relación, crónica, historia; hoja de servicios, antecedentes de una persona; fonograma, cilindro o disco fonográficos; (for.) memorial, informe, expediente; atestación, testimonio; memoria, recuerdo, recordación; (dep.) record.—*pl.* records, archivo; protocolo; fastos; memorias; datos.— **r. breaker,** el que o lo que sobrepasa o sube el

record.—r.-breaking, que pasa del record, que sube el record.—**of r.,** (for.) que consta (en el expediente, la escritura, etc.).—**on r.,** registrado; de que hay o queda constancia; que la historia registra.

recorder [recórdœr], s. registrador, archivero; (for.) juez municipal superior que entiende en causas criminales; (mec.) indicador, contador; aparato inscriptor, trazador o grabador (de un fonógrafo, etc.).—**r. of deeds,** registrador de la propiedad.

recordership [recórdœrship], s. cargo de registrador o archivero.

recording [-ing], a. anotador, registrador; (fís., etc.) registrador (apl. a instrumentos).—**r. secretary,** secretario de actas, secretario escribiente.

recount [ricáunt]. I. va. referir, relatar; recitar; detallar; [rícáunt] recontar, hacer un recuento. II. s. [rícaunt] recuento.

recoup [recúp]. I. va. retener para indemnizarse; reintegrarse, desquitarse de; reparar, indemnizar, resarcir. II. s. desquite, reintegro, resarcimiento.—**recoupment** [-ment], s. desquite; resarcimiento, reembolso.

recourse [recórs], s. recurso, remedio, auxilio, refugio; (for.) recurso.—**to have r. to,** recurrir a.—**without r.,** (com.) sin responsabilidad (de parte del endosante)—expresión que indica que quien endosa una letra, etc., a otro no se hace responsable de su pago.

recover [recúvœr]. I. va. recobrar, recuperar; desempeñar; rescatar; reintegrarse o resarcirse; (for.) obtener fallo judicial contra alguien. II. vn. recobrar la salud; reponerse; (for.) ganar un pleito.

recover [ricúvœr], va. volver a cubrir o tapar.

recoverable [recúvœrabœl], a. recuperable, recobrable.

recovery [recúvœri], s. recobro, recuperación; cobranza; rescate; restablecimiento; (for.) fallo o decisión favorable.

recreancy [récreansi], s. deslealtad; pusilanimidad.—**recreant** [-ant], a. y s. falso, desleal; cobarde.

recreate [ricrièit], va. recrear, divertir.

recreate [rícrièit], va. crear o criar de nuevo.

recreation [recrièishun], s. recreación, recreo; diversión; esparcimiento.

recreation [ricrièishun], s. nueva creación.

recreative [récriativ], a. recreativo.

recrement [récremœnt], s. (med.) recremento; (ant.) hez, escoria.

recremental [recreméntal], a. recrementicio, feculento.

recriminate [recrímineit], va. y vn. recriminar.

recrimination [-éishun], s. recriminación.

recriminative, recriminatory [-ativ, -tori], a., **recriminator** [-eitœr], s. (for.) recriminador.

recross [ricrós], va. volver a pasar o cruzar.

recrudesce [ricrudés], vn. recrudecer, recrudecerse.—**recrudescence** [-sens], s. recrudecimiento, recrudescencia.—**recrudescent** [-ent], a. recrudescente.

recruit [recrút]. I. va. y vn. (mil.) alistar, reclutar; restablecer, reparar; abastecer. II. s. (mil.) recluta; novicio; renuevo, suministro.

recruiting [recrúting], s. recluta, reclutamiento.

rectal [réctal], a. (anat.) del recto.

rectangle [réctængœl], s. rectángulo.—**rectangular** [rectǽnguiular], a. rectangular.—**rectangularity** [-guiulǽriti], **rectangularness** [-guiularnes], s. calidad de rectangular.

rectifiable [réctífáiabœl], a. rectificable.

rectification [-fikéshun], s. rectificación, corrección; (quím.) rectificación, refinación; (geom.) rectificación.

rectifier [-faiœr], s. rectificador; refinador.

rectify [-fai], va. (pret. y pp. RECTIFIED) rectificar, corregir; (quím.) rectificar, refinar; (mat.) rectificar.

rectilineal, rectilinear [-líneal, ar], a. rectilíneo.

rectitude [réctitiud], s. rectitud; corrección.

rector [réctor], s. (igl.) rector, cura párroco; prior, superior; rector de universidad.—**rectoral** [-all], **rectorial** [rectórial], a. rectoral.—**rectorate,** rec-

torship [réctoret, ship], s. rectorado, rectoría.—**rectory** [réctori], s. rectoría.

rectrix [réctrix], s. (orn.) pluma timonera.

rectum [réctum], s. (anat.) recto.

recumbency, recumbence [recúmbensi, ens], s. reclinación.

recumbent [-ent], a. recostado, reclinado.

recuperate [rekiúpœreit]. I. va. recuperar, recobrar. II. vn. recobrar la salud, reponerse.—**recuperation** [-éishun], s. recuperación; recobro, rehacimiento.—**recuperative, recuperatory** [-ativ, -atoril, a. recuperativo.

recur [ricœr], vn. repetirse, volver a ocurrir.

recurrence, recurrency [-ens, -i], s. repetición, reaparición; recurso.—**recurrent** [-ent], a. periódico; (anat.) recurrente.

recurve, recurvate [recœrv, -et], va. y vn. encorvar, torcer o torcerse en sentido opuesto al ordinario; encorvarse hacia abajo.

recurved, recurvous [recœrvd, -vus], a. (bot.) encorvado anormalmente; (zool.) encorvado hacia arriba (el pico).

recusancy [rékiusansi], s. recusación.

recusant [rékiusant], s. y a. recusante.

recusation [-éishun], s. (for.) recusación.

red. I. a. encarnado, colorado, rojo; (pol. y e. p.) rojo (apl. esp. a los comunistas rusos y sus partidarios).—**r. ant,** hormiga colorada.—**r.-bellied,** pechirrojo.—**r. brass,** latón cobrizo, latón rojo.—**r. cedar,** cedro colorado; junípero; tuya de la costa del Pacífico.—**r. chalk,** creta roja; creyón rojo.—**r. clover,** trébol morado.—**r. copper,** cuprita, óxido rojo de cobre.—**r. coral,** coral rojo.—**R. Cross,** Cruz Roja; Cruz de San Jorge.—**r. deer,** ciervo común.—**r. flag,** bandera roja (apl. hoy gen. a la bandera socialista y de revolución social).—**r. gum,** añublo, tizón; erupción que sale en la cara a los recién nacidos.—**r.-haired,** pelirrojo.—**r.-handed,** con las manos ensangrentadas; in fraganti.—**r.-hard,** duro en caliente, o cuando está caliente.—**r. heat,** calor rojo.—**r. herring,** arenque seco y ahumado; artimaña para apartar la atención del asunto de que se trata (ú. esp. en la expresión **to draw a r. herring across the track,** distraer la atención, despistar).—**r.-hot,** candente, enrojecido al fuego; muy caliente; acérrimo, extremo.—**r. iron,** hematites.—**r. lead,** minio.—**r.-lead pencil,** lápiz rojo.—**r.-letter,** marcado con letras rojas.—**r.-letter day,** día de fiesta, día de dos cruces; día feliz o de regocijo, día de piedra blanca.—**r. liquor,** acetato de alúmina.—**r. man,** indio norteamericano.—**r. mordant** = R. LIQUOR.—**r. mullet,** salmonete.—**r. ocher,** ocre rojo o quemado, almagre, almazarrón.—**r. pepper,** pimentón; pimiento, ají, chile.—**r. poppy,** abado, albohol.—**R. Sea,** Mar Rojo.—**r.-short,** frágil o quebradizo en caliente.—**r. silver,** plata roja, pirargirita; proustita.—**r. spider,** ácaro rojo, cresa roja.—**r. spruce,** picea roja.—**r. tape,** balduque; expedienteo, rutina oficinesca, formalismo.—**r. wine,** vino tinto. II. s. color rojo; (pol. y e. p.) rojo, revolucionario. III. va. enrojar, pintar de rojo.

redact [redéct], va. redactar.—**redaction** [-shun], s. redacción.—**redactor** [-tœr], s. redactor.

redan [redǽn], s. (fort.) estrella.

redbird [rédbœrd], s. (orn.) cardenal.

redbreast [rédbrést], s. (orn.) pitirrojo.

redbud [rédbʌd], s. (bot.) ciclamor.

redbug [rédbʌg], s. (ent.) nigua.

redcap [rédcæp], s. (orn.) cardelina.

redcoat [rédcóut], s. (Ingl. fam.) soldado.

Redcross Knight [rédcrós náit], s. caballero templario.

redden [rédœn]. I. va. reojear, teñir de rojo. II. vn. ponerse colorado; ruborizarse.

reddish [rédish], a. rojizo.

reddishness [-nes], s. bermejura.

reddle [rédœl], s. almazarrón, almagre.

redeem [redím], va. redimir; desempeñar; amortizar; rescatar; cumplir; resarcir; compensar.

redeemable [redímabœl], a. redimible, rescatable, amortizable.—**redeemableness** [-nes], s. calidad de redimible.

redeemer [redímœr], s. redentor o rescatador; (**R-**) Redentor.

redeeming [redíming], a. redentor; rescatador; atenuante.—**r. feature**, circunstancia atenuante; rasgo compensador o paliatorio.

redemption [redémpšhʊn], s. redención; rescate; desempeño, amortización de una deuda.

redemptional [-šhʊnal], a. redentor; que redime o se relaciona con la redención, rescate o amortización.

redemptioner [redémpšhʊncœr], s. emigrante que paga su pasaje a América con su servicio personal.

redemptive, redemptory [-tiv, -tori], a.=RE-DEMPTIONAL.

redhibition [redjibíšhʊn], s. (for.) redhibición.

redhibitory [redjíbitori], a. redhibitorio.

redintegrate [redíntegreit]. I. va. reintegrar, restablecer. II. a. reintegrado, restablecido; renovado.—**redintegration** [-éishʊn], s. reintegración, reintegro; restauración, restablecimiento.

redirect [ridiréct], a. (for.) dícese del segundo interrogatorio de un testigo por su abogado, después de las repreguntas del contrario.

redly [rédli], adv. rojizamente.

redness [rédnes], s. rojez, rojura, bermejura.

redolence, redolency [rédolens, -i], s. fragancia. —**redolent** [-ent], a. fragante.

redouble [redúbœl]. I. va. redoblar, aumentar; repetir. II. vn. redoblarse.

redou(b)t [redáut], (fort.) reducto.

redoubtable [-abœl], a. formidable, temible.

redound [redáund], vn. redundar, resultar, contribuir.

redowa [rédoa], s. (danz. y mús.) redova.

redraft [ridráft], s. nuevo dibujo; copia o borrador; (com.) resaca.

redraw [ridró]. I. va. hacer un segundo dibujo o borrador. II. vn. (com.) resacar.

redress [redrés]. I. va. enderezar; reparar, resarcir; remediar; hacer justicia. II. s. reparación, satisfacción, desagravio; remedio; compensación.

re-dress [ri-drés], va. y vn. vestir o vestirse de nuevo.

redresser [redréscœr], s. reparador, remediador.

redsear [redsíœr], vn. quebrarse el hierro candente cuando se martilla.

redshirt [rédšhœrt], s. revolucionario (apl. esp. a los anarquistas y comunistas).

redskin [rédskin], s. piel roja, indio norteamericano.

redstreak [rédstric], s. manzana rosa.

redtop [rédtop], s. (bot.) alfalfa.

reduce [rediús], va. reducir; minorar, rebajar, mermar; sujetar, someter; sojuzgar; (mil.) degradar; (mat., quím., cir. y b. a.) reducir.

reducer [rediúscœr], s. reductor; tubo de reducción; empate cónico de reducción.

reducible [rediúsibœl], a. reducible.—**reducibleness** [-nes], s. calidad de reducible.

reducing [rediúcing], a. reductor; de reducción (llama, agente, escala, etc.)

reduction [redúcshʊn], s. reducción; rebaja, diminución; sujeción, toma, conquista; (mat., quím., cir. y b. a.) reducción.—**r. works**, fundición, horno de reducción.

reductive [redúctiv], a. reductivo.

redundance, redundancy [redúndans, -i], s. redundancia; pleonasmo.—**redundant** [-ant], a. redundante; pleonástico.—**redundantly** [-li], adv. redundantemente, superfluamente.

reduplicate [redúpliket]. I. va. reduplicar, repetir, multiplicar. II. a. reduplicado.—**reduplication** [-kéishʊn], s. reduplicación, repetición.

redwing [réduing], s. (orn.) malvís.

redwood [rédud], s. (bot.) pino gigantesco de California.

reëcho [riéco], vn. responder, repercutir.

reed [rid], s. (bot.) caña, cañuela, junquillo, aguinaldo; (mús.) lengüeta; caramillo, dulzaina, churumbela, chirimía; por extensión, cual-

quier instrumento de boquilla; (fig.) poesía bucólica; (min.) tubo para cebrar un barreno; (arq.) baqueta, junquillo; (tej.) peine (cárcel); (poét.) flecha, saeta; barda; abomaso.—**r. mace**, (bot.) anea, espadaña.—**r. organ**, armonio.

redbird [rídbœrd], s. (orn.) pajarito americano que se cría en los arrozales.

reedwork [ríduœrk], s. lengüetería del órgano.

reedy [rídi], a. cañado, cañoso; de tono delgado y agudo.

reef [rif]. I. s. arrecife, escollo, bajío; (Australia) filón, vena metálica; (mar.) rizo.—**r. band**, faja de rizos.—**r. cringle**, anillo de vela.—**r. knot**, nudo de rizos.—**r. line**, cabo de tomar rizos.—**r. tackles**, (mar.) aparejuelos o palanquines de rizos. II. va. (mar.) tomar rizos, arrizar.

reefer [rífœr], s. (mar.) rizador; (sast.) chaquetón.

reefy [rifi], a. lleno de escollos.

reek. I. va. ahumar. II. vn. (con **with**) humear, vahear, vahar.

reeky [ríki], a. ahumado, ennegrecido.

reel [ril]. I. s. carrete, tambor; devanadera; película de cine (gen. de 30 m.); broca.—**r. click**, trinquete para regularizar el movimiento de la cuerda de pescar.—**r. of a log**, (mar.) carretel. II. va. aspar, devanar. III. vn. hacer eses, tambalear.

re-elect [ri-eléct], va. reelegir.

re-election [ri-elécshʊn], s. reelección.

re-embark [ri-embárk], va. y vn. reembarcar.

re-embarkation [-barkéishʊn], s. reembarco.

re-enact [ri-enéct], va. revalidar (una ley).

re-enactment [-mœnt], s. revalidación (de una ley).

re-enforce [ri-enfórs]. I. va. reforzar, fortalecer. II. s. refuerzo. V. REINFORCE.

re-enforcement [ri-enfórsmœnt], s. refuerzo. V. REINFORCEMENT.

re-engage [ri-enguéj], va. reescriturar, contratar de nuevo.—**re-engagement** [-mœnt], s. nuevo ataque; renovación de una contrata o escritura.

re-enter [ri-éntœr], va. reingresar; registrar o entrar de nuevo; repasar con el buril.

re-entering [-ing], a. = RE-ENTRANT.

re-entrance, re-entry [ri-éntrans, -tri], s. segunda entrada; asiento repetido.—**re-entrant** [-œnt], a. entrante (ángulo, etc.).

re-establish [riestéblish], va. restablecer, instaurar.—**re-establisher** [-œr], s. restablecedor, restaurador.—**re-establishment** [-mœnt], s. restablecimiento, restauración.

reeve [riv], va. (mar.) laborear, guarnir.

re-examine [ri-egsémin], va. reexaminar.

re-examination [-éishʊn], s. reexaminación, repaso, revista.

re-export [ri-expórt], va. reexportar.

re-exportation [-portéshʊn], s. reexportación.

refection [refécshʊn], s. refacción, colación.

refectory [reféctori], s. refectorio.

refer [refér]. I. va. referir, remitir, dirigir; trasladar, someter; asignar. II. vn. referirse, aludir; recurrir, acudir; indicar por medio de marcas.

referable [réfœrabœl], **referrible** [reféribœl], a. referible, asignable.

referee [réfœri], s. árbitro; (for.) secuestro, ponente.

reference [réfœrens]. I. s. referencia, recomendación; remisión; alusión, mención, nota, marca o señal de referencia; persona a quien se puede acudir para referencia; fiador; (for.) arbitramento.—**r. mark**, (impr.) llamada (* † ‡ ‖ § ¶). —**in**, o **with, r. to**, respecto de, en cuanto a. II. a. de referencia; de consulta (libro, etc.).—**r. frame**, (mat.) sistema de coordenadas o de ejes de coordenadas.

referendum [réfœréndʊm], s. (dipl.) referéndum; (pol.) plebiscito.

referential [refœrénšhal], a. referente.

referrible, a. = REFERABLE.

refill [rifíl], va. rellenar, rehenchir, reenvasar.

refine [refáin]. I. va. refinar, purificar, clarificar; acrisolar; pulir, perfeccionar. II. vn. sutilizar; purificarse, refinarse, pulirse.

refined [-d], _a._ refino, refinado; fino, cortés.

refinement [-mœnt], _s._ refinamiento, cortesía, cultura; refinación, refinadura; afinamiento, finura, filigrana; sutileza, afectación.

refiner [refáinœr], _s._ refinador.

refinery [refáinœri], _s._ refinería.

refining [rifáining], _s._ refinación, refinadura.

refit [refít], _va._ reparar, componer; (mar.) embonar.

reflect [refléct]. **I.** _va._ reflejar; reflexionar; indicar, manifestar (gen. en la voz pasiva **to be reflected**, manifestarse, verse, hacerse sentir); traer consigo, dar. **II.** _vn._ reflexionar; reflejar.—**to r. on, o upon,** desprestigiar; herir; hacer desmerecer, desdecir de.

reflected [-ed], _a._ reflejado, reflejo; (anat.) replegado.

reflection [-shʊn], _s._ (fís., psic.) reflexión; reflejo; reproche, tacha, baldón; (anat.) repliegue; acción refleja.—**on o upon r.,** después de pensarlo.

reflective [-iv], _a._ reflexivo; meditativo, meditabundo; reflector; reflejo.

reflectively [-li], _adv._ reflexivamente.

reflector [-œr], _s._ (ópt.) reflector; telescopio de reflexión.

reflex [ríflex]. **I.** _a._ reflejo.—**r. action,** acción refleja. **II.** _s._ acción refleja; reflejo, reverberación. **III.** _va._ [refléx] replegar.

reflexive [-iv], _a._ (gram.) reflexivo; (fís.) reflector, de reflexión.

reflexively [-li], _adv._ reflexivamente.

reflorescence [riflorésens], _s._ acto de reflorecer.

reflourish [riflœrish], _vn._ reflorecer.

reflow [ryfló], _vn._ refluir.

refluence, refluency [réfluens, -i], _s._ reflujo.

refluent [réfluent], _a._ refluente.

reflux [ríflux], _s._ reflujo, menguante.

reform [rifórm]. **I.** _va._ formar de nuevo, rehacer; reformar, corregir. **II.** _vn._ reformarse, enmendarse. **III.** _s._ reforma.

reformation [réforméishʊn], _s._ reforma; **(R-)** (hist.) Reforma; [rɪforméshʊn] nueva formación.

reformative [refórmativ], _a._ reformador.

reformatory [refórmatori]. **I.** _a._ reformatorio. **II.** _s._ casa de corrección.

reformer [refórmœr], _s._ reformador, reformista.

reformist [refórmist], _s._ religioso reformado.

refract [refráct], _va._ refractar.—**refraction** [-shʊn], _s._ refracción.—**refractive** [-tiv], _a._ refringente, refractor.—**r. power,** poder de refracción.

refractometer [rifræctómetœr], (fís.) _s._ refractómetro.

refractor [refráctœr], _s._ telescopio de refracción.

refractorily [-ili], _adv._ tercamente, obstinadamente.—**refractoriness** [-ines], _s._ contumacia, terquedad, porfía.—**refractory** [refráctori], _a._ refractario, díscolo; (equit.) repropio; (quím.) refractario.

refragable [réfragabœl], _a._ impugnable.

refrain [rifréin]. **I.** _va._ refrenar, contener, reprimir. **II.** _vn._ refrenarse, abstenerse de, contenerse. **III.** _s._ (poét.) estribillo.

refrangibility [rifrænyibíliti], **refrangibleness** [-bœlnes], _s._ refrangibilidad.—**refrangible** [-bœl], _a._ refrangible.

refresh [rifrésh]. **I.** _va._ refrescar, renovar, vivificar; templar el calor, enfriar; aliviar. **II.** _vr._ refrescarse, recobrar nuevas fuerzas.—**refresher** [-œr], _s._ refresco; algo que ayuda a recordar.—**refreshing** [-ing], _a._ refrescante; alentador, placentero.—**refreshment** [-mœnt], _s._ refresco.

refrigerant [refríyœrant], _a._ y _s._ refrigerante.

refrigerate [-eit], _va._ refrigerar, enfriar.

refrigerating [-eiting], _a._ refrigerante.—**r. chamber,** refrigerador.—**r. machine,** máquina de hacer hielo.—**r. vault** = R. CHAMBER.

refrigeration [-éishʊn], _s._ refrigeración, enfriamiento.

refrigerative [-ativ], _s._ y _a._ refrigerante.

refrigerator [-éitœr], _s._ refrigerador, nevera; (quím.) refrigerante.—**r. car,** (f. c.) carro de refrigeración; furgón nevera.

refrigeratory [-atori]. **I.** _s._ (quím.) refrigerante. **II.** _a._ refrigerativo, refrigerante.

refuge [réfiur], _s._ refugio, amparo, asilo, albergue; guarida; subterfugio, escapatoria.

refugee [réfiuyí], _s._ refugiado; asilado.

refulgence, refulgency [refúlyens, -i], refulgencia, esplendor.—**refulgent** [-yent], _a._ refulgente, resplandeciente.

refund [refúnd], _va._ restituir, reintegrar, reembolsar, amortizar; consolidar una deuda.

refundable [refúndabœl], _a._ restituíble.

refurbish [rifœrbish], _va._ restaurar; retocar.

refusable [refiúsabœl], _a._ recusable.

refusal [refiúsal], _s._ negativa, denegación; desaire; opción, exclusiva.

refuse [refiús]. **I.** _va._ y _vn._ rehusar; rechazar; desechar; negarse a; resistirse a; saltar por sobre. **II.** _va._ [rifiús] (fund.) refundir. **III.** _s._ [réfius], desecho, basura, desperdicio; sobra, residuo. **IV.** _a._ desechado, de desecho.

refutable [refiútabœl], _a._ impugnable.

refutation [réfiutéishʊn], **refutal** [refiútal], _s._ refutación.

refutatory [refiútatori], _a._ refutatorio.

refute [refiút], _va._ refutar, rebatir.

regain [riguéin], _va._ recobrar, recuperar.

regal [rígal]. **I.** _a._ real, regio. **II.** _s._ (mús.) organillo portátil.

regale [reguéil], _va._ regalar, agasajar, festejar; recrear, deleitar.—**regalement** [-mœnt], _s._ regalamiento, regalo, festejo.

regalia [reguélia], _s. pl._ insignias reales; insignias, distintivos.

regality [regéliti], _s._ realeza, soberanía.

regally [rígali], _adv._ regiamente.

regard [regárd]. **I.** _va._ observar, mirar; considerar, reputar, juzgar; respetar, venerar; tocar, concernir; referirse a, relacionarse con.—**as regards,** tocante a, en cuanto a. **II.** _s._ miramiento, consideración, acatamiento; referencia, relación; mirada; respeto.—_pl._ memorias, expresiones, afectos, recuerdos.—**r. being had to,** atendido a, en vista de.—**in r. to** = WITH REGARD TO.—**with r.,** con sentimientos de consideración.—**with (best, kind) regards**—fórmula que a veces se pone al fin de una carta y que puede traducirse por "con amistoso saludo," "con sentimientos de consideración," "me es grato subscribirme," etc., según el grado de confianza, o no traducirse.—**without any r. to,** sin miramientos por, sin hacer caso de.—**with r. to,** con respecto a.

regardful [-ful], _a._ atento; cuidadoso, mirado.—**regardfully** [-i], _adv._ atentamente.

regarding [-ing], _prep._ relativo a, respecto de.

regardless [-les], _a._ descuidado, indiferente.—**r. of,** sin cuidado de, sin hacer caso de, prescindiendo de.

regardlessness [-nes], _s._ descuido, negligencia; indiferencia.

regatta [regéta], _s._ regata.

regency [ríyensi], _s._ regencia.

regeneracy [reyénœrasi], _s._ regeneración.

regenerate [reyénœreit]. **I.** _va._ regenerar; reproducir; reengendrar. **II.** _s._ regenerado; reengendrado.

regenerateness [-nes], **regeneration** [-éishʊn], _s._ regeneración; renacimiento.

regenerative [-ativ], _a._ regenerador, regenerativo.—**r. furnace,** horno de Siemens.

regenerator [-œr], _s._ regenerador; aparato regenerador del horno de Siemens.

regent [ríyent]. **I.** _a._ regente, reinante. **II.** _s._ regente; gobernador, gobernante; regente de una universidad.

regentship [ríyentship], _s._ regencia.

regicidal [revisáidal], _a._ regicida.

regicide [révisaio], _s._ regicidio; regicida.

régime [reyím], _s._ régimen; administración; sistema social.

regimen [réyimen], _s._ (med.) régimen; gobierno metódico, sujeción, freno; (gram.) régimen.

regiment [réyimœnt], _s._ (mil.) regimiento.

regimental [-al], _a._ perteneciente a un regimiento.—_pl._ uniforme militar.

region [ríyun], _s._ región.—**regional** [-al], _a._ regional.—**regionalism** [-alism], _s._ regionalismo.

---

register [réyistœr]. **I.** s. registro, inscripción; matrícula; lista, archivo, protocolo; libro de parroquia; registrador; indicador, contador; registro (de hornillo, de chimenea, etc.); reja regulable de calefacción; (impr. y enc.) registro; (mús.) registro (de la voz y del órgano); (mar.) matrícula; (com.) certificado de nacionalidad; cédula, albalá, registro de aduana.—**r. book,** registro. **II.** va. registrar, inscribir, matricular, protocolar, encartar; (mar.) matricular, abanderar; indicar, marcar (según escala o graduación); manifestar, indicar.—**to r. a letter,** certificar una carta. **III.** vn. inscribirse; matricularse; (impr.) estar en registro.

registered [réyistœrd], a. registrado, inscrito, matriculado.—**r. bond,** (com.) título nominativo. —**r. letter,** carta certificada.

registrar (y [-trar, -i], s. registrador, archivero.

registration [réyistréishun], s. asiento, registro; inscripción, empadronamiento, encabezamiento.

registry [réyistri], s. asiento, inscripción; matrícula; protocolo, registro; archivo.

reglet [réglet], s. (arq.) filete; (impr.) corondel, regleta.

regnant [régnant], a. reinante.

regress [rígres]. **I.** s. regreso; (astr.) movimiento retrógrado, retrogradación. **II.** vn. [regrés] regresar; (astr.) retrogradar.—**regression** [regréshun], s. regresión.—**regressive** [-iv], a. regresivo.

regret [regrét]. **I.** s. pena, pesar; compunción, remordimiento.—pl. excusa cortés que se envía para rehusar una invitación. **II.** va. sentir, deplorar, lamentar. **regretful** [-ful], a. pesaroso.— **regretfully** [-fuli], adv. sentidamente.

regrettable [-abœl], a. lamentable, sensible.

regrettably [-bli], adv. sensiblemente.

regular [régiular]. **I.** a. regular, normal, corriente; arreglado, ordenado, metódico; uniforme; (geom.) regular; (mil.) regular, de línea; (fam.) completo, cabal, a toda vela; **II.** s. (mil.) soldado de línea; obrero permanente; (igl.) regular.

regularity [-lériti], s. regularidad.

regularization [-lariséishun], s. regularización.— **regularize** [-larais], va. regularizar.

regularly [-li], adv. regularmente o con regularidad.

regulate [-leit], va. regular, regularizar, arreglar, ordenar.

regulation [-léishun]. **I.** s. regulación; reglamento, orden, regla; reglamentación.—pl. reglamento. **II.** a. corriente, ordinario, de ordenanza.

regulative [-lativ], a. regulativo, regulador.

regulator [-léitor]. **I.** s. (tecn.) regulador (de una máquina, turbina, etc.); registro (de reloj); cronómetro regulador. **II.** a. de regulación, regulador.—**r. valve,** (loc.) válvula del regulador.

regulus [régiulus], s. (quím.) régulo; (astr.) Régulo.

regurgitate [rigœryiteit], va. y vn. regurgitar.

regurgitation [-téishun], s. regurgitación.

rehabilitate [rijabíliteit], va. rehabilitar.

rehabilitation [-téishun], s. rehabilitación.

rehash [rijǽsh]. **I.** va. (despect.) recomponer, refundir. **II.** s. refundición; fárrago.

rehearsal [rijœrsal], s. (teat.) ensayo; recitación; relación.

rehearse [rijœrs], va. y vn. (teat.) ensayar; repasar; repetir, recitar, referir.

reheat [rijít], va. recalentar; calentar de nuevo.— **reheater** [-œr], s. recalentador.

Reich [ráij], s. la República Alemana (aunque literalmente la palabra significa imperio).— **Reichsrat(h)** [ráijsrát], s. parlamento austriaco en tiempos del imperio.—**Reichstag** [-tág], s. (en Alemania) cámara baja del parlamento.—**Reichswehr** [-véœr], s. (en Alemania) ejército voluntario de defensa nacional, guardia nacional de voluntarios.

reign [réin]. **I.** vn. reinar. **II.** s. reino, reinado.— **reigning** [-ing], a. reinante.

reimburse [riimbœrs], va. reembolsar, reintegrar, indemnizar.—**reimbursement** [-mœnt], s. reembolso, reintegración, indemnización.

reimpression [riimpréshun], s. (impr.) reimpresión.

rein [réin]. **I.** s. rienda. **II.** va. gobernar; llevar las riendas de; refrenar, contener. **III.** vn. obedecer a las riendas.

reincarnation [riincarnéshun], s. reencarnación.

reincorporate [riincórporeit], va. reincorporar.— **reincorporation** [-éishun], s. reincorporación.

reindeer [réindíœr], s. (zool.) reno, rangífero o rengífero.

reindorse [riindórs], va. (com.) contraendosar.

reinforce [réinfórs], va. = REENFORCE; (ing.) armar, reforzar (hormigón).—**reinforced concrete,** hormigón armado.—**reinforcing bars,** armadura, barras de armadura o de refuerzo (del hormigón armado).—**reinforcement** [-mœnt], s. = REENFORCEMENT; (ing.) armadura (del hormigón armado).

reins [réins], s. riñones, región renal; entrañas; afectos, las pasiones; (arq.) riñón (de una bóveda).

reinsert [riinsœrt], va. insertar o ingerir de nuevo.

reinstall [riinstól], va. reinstalar; rehabilitar, reponer, restablecer.—**reinstallment** [-mœnt], s. reinstalación, rehabilitación, restablecimiento.

reinstate [riinstéit], va. reinstalar, rehabilitar, restablecer; en los seguros contra incendios, reparar o reponer lo dañado.

reinsurance [riinshúrans], s. (com.) reseguro; contraaseguro.

reinsure [riinshúœr], va. reasegurar.

reissue [riíshu]. **I.** va. volver a publicar o emitir. **II.** vn. volver a salir. **III.** s. reimpresión, nueva edición o emisión.

reiterate [ritœreit], va. reiterar.—**reiteratedly** [-tedli], adv. reiteradamente o reiteradas [-éishun], s. reiteración, repetición.

reject [reyéct], va. rechazar, recusar, rehusar, rehuir, repeler; expeler, arrojar; negar, denegar; desechar, despreciar; arrinconar, descartar.

rejectable [-abœl], a. recusable, inadmisible.

rejecter, rejector [-œr], s. el que rechaza, recusa o desecha.

rejection [-shun], s. rechazamiento, desecho, exclusión, repudiación.

rejective [reyéctiv], a. que rechaza, rehusa o excluye.

rejoice [reyóis]. **I.** va. regocijar, alegrar. **II.** vn. regocijarse, gozarse.

rejoicing [-ing], s. alegría, fiesta, regocijo; júbilo, festividad. **II.** a. gozoso, regocijado.

rejoin [reyóin]. **I.** va. reunirse con, volver a la compañía de. **II.** vn. replicar; (for.) triplicar.

rejoinder [reyóindœr], s. respuesta, réplica; (for.) tríplica, contrarréplica.

rejoint [reyóint], va. (alb.) llenar las degolladuras con mortero.

rejuvenate [reyúveneit], va. rejuvenecer.

rejuvenation [-éishun], **rejuvenescence** [-sens], **rejuvenescency** [-i], s. rejuvenecimiento.

rekindle [rikíndœl], va. volver a encender, reavivar, despertar.

relapse [relǽps]. **I.** vn. recaer; rincidir; renegar. **II.** s. recaída; reincidencia; (med.) recidiva.

relate [reléit]. **I.** va. relatar, contar, narrar; relacionar; emparentar. **II.** vn. relacionarse con; ser concerniente a, referirse.

related [reléited], a. relacionado, conexo; afine, emparentado, allegado.

relater [reléitœr], s. relator, narrador.

relation [-shun], s. relación; referencia, alusión; relato, narración; parentesco; pariente.— pl. parentela.—**in r. to,** con relación a, respecto a.

relational [-al], a. que guarda o expresa relación.

relationship [-ship], s. relación; parentesco.

relative [rélativ]. **I.** a. (leng. ord. y gram.) relativo.—**r. wind,** (aer.) viento relativo. **II.** s. pariente, deudo; (gram.) relativo, pronombre relativo.—**relatively** [-li], adv. relativamente.

relativism [rélativiśm], s. (fil. y fís.) relativísmo, teoría de la relatividad en general, y de la relatividad del conocimiento en particular.—**relativist** [-ist], s. relativista.

relativity [-tíviti], s. relatividad.—**r. of knowledge**, relatividad del conocimiento.

relax [reláx]. **I.** va. relajar, aflojar; mitigar; remitir; desatar; aliviar el estreñimiento; causar languidez. **II.** vn. aflojar, ceder; esparcirse, descansar; mitigarse.

relaxation [rí- o rélæxéśhun], s. aflojamiento, flojedad; descanso, reposo; solaz, recreo, distracción; mitigación, lenidad; relajamiento de nervios, músculos, etc.

relay [reléi]. **I.** s. relevo, remuda; (m. v.) máquina auxiliar reguladora (llám. t. **r. cylinder**); (elec.) relevador. **II.** va. enviar por posta; [ríléi], volver a colocar.

release [relís]. **I.** va. soltar; poner en libertad; relevar, exonerar; renunciar a o abandonar; aliviar; poner en circulación, dar al público; [rí-], realquilar. **II.** s. liberación; exoneración; quita; cesión (de un derecho); obra o pieza (de cine, fonógrafo, etc.) lista para darla al público; (m. v.) escape; (mec.) disparador, escape, trinquete.

releasee [relisí], s. (for.) persona a cuyo favor se otorga una escritura de cesión o finiquito.

releasor [relísœr], s. (for.) el que otorga un finiquito o acta de cesión.

relegate [rélegueit], va. relegar; desterrar.

relegation [-éiśhun], s. relegación.

relent [relént], vn. aplacarse, desenojarse; ceder, ablandarse.—**relentless** [-les], a. implacable, inexorable.—**relentlessly** [-nes], s. cualidad de implacable.—**relentlessly** [-li], adv. implacablemente, sin piedad.

relevancy, relevance [rélevansi, -vans], s. pertinencia.—**relevant** [-ant], a. pertinente, a propósito, apropiado.

reliability [reláiæbíliti], **reliableness** [-bœlnes], s. confiabilidad; calidad de seguro o digno de confianza.—**reliable** [-bœl], a. seguro, digno de confianza, confiable.—**reliance** [-ans], s. confianza, seguridad.—**reliant** [-ant], a. confiado.

relic [rélic], s. reliquia, vestigio.

relict [rélict], s. viudo.

relief [relíf], s. alivio, consuelo; relevación, aligeramiento; socorro, limosna; solaz, descanso; (nil.) relevo; (for.) desagravio, satisfacción, compensación, reparación; (b. a.) relieve, realce, resalte o resalto.

relievable [relívabœl], a. consolable; aliviable.

relieve [relív], va. relevar, remediar, socorrer, aliviar; descargar, exonerar; mitigar, suavizar; vivificar; realzar, poner en relieve, hacer resaltar; acopar; (mil.) relevar; (for.) reparar, desagraviar, hacer justicia.—**to r. nature** = TO EASE NATURE.

relieving arch [relíving arch], s. (arq.) sobrearco, arco de descarga.—**r. tackle** [tǽcœl], (mar.) pluma de chata de carga; aparejos de la caña del timón.

relievo [relívo], s. V. RILIEVO.

religion [relíyun], s. religión.

religionary [relíyuneri], a. religioso.

religionist [relíyunist], s. religionario.

religionism [relíyuniśm], s. (despect.) falsa religiosidad, fariseísmo.

religiosity [reliyiósiti], s. religiosidad.

religious [relíyus]. **I.** a. religioso. **II.** s. (igl.) religioso.—**religiously** [-li], adv. religiosamente.—**religiousness** [-nes], s. religiosidad.

relinquish [relíncuiśh], va. abandonar, dejar; ceder; renunciar.—**relinquishment** [-mœnt], s. abandono, dejación, renuncia.

reliquary [rélicuæri], s. relicario; (for.) el que paga a plazos.

relish [réliśh]. **I.** s. gusto, apetencia, sabor grato, dejo; sazón, condimento; entremés; fruición, goce; (carp.) hombro de espiga. **II.** va. saborear, paladear; gustar de; hacer algo con fruición; sazonar, condimentar. **III.** vn. saber bien, ser sabroso; gustar, agradar.

relishable [-abœl], a. gustoso, sabroso.

reload [rilóud], va. recargar; cargar de nuevo.

relucent [relúsent], a. reluciente.

reluctance, reluctancy [relúctans, -i], s. repugnancia, renuencia, desgana, disgusto.—**with r., de mala gana.**—**reluctant** [-tant], a. renuente, maldispuesto, repugnante.—**reluctantly** [-li], adv. de mala gana, a contrapelo.

relume [reliúm], va. volver a encender.

rely [relái], vn. (con **on** o **upon**) confiar o fiar en, contar con, fiarse de.

remain [reméin], vn. quedar, restar o faltar; estarse, permanecer; persistir, continuar.—**to r. silent**, callar; guardar silencio; no chistar.—**to r. undone**, quedar sin hacer.

remainder [reméindœr]. **I.** s. resto; (arit.) residuo; alcance. **II.** a. restante.

remains [reméins], s. pl. restos, cadáver; sobras, reliquias; obras póstumas; esqueletos humanos; ruinas.

remake [riméik], va. rehacer.

reman [rímæn], va. poner un nuevo contingente en; alentar.

remand [remánd], va. enviar o mandar al punto de procedencia, devolver; (for.) reencarcelar; enviar a otro tribunal.

remand(ment [-(mœnt], s. (for.) reencarcelamiento; mandato judicial para el traslado a otro tribunal.

remark [remárk]. **I.** s. observación, advertencia, nota. **II.** va. y vn. hacer una observación, observar, advertir, notar, reparar.

remarkable [-abœl], a. notable, interesante, extraordinario.—**remarkably** [-bli], adv. notablemente.

remarker [-œr], s. observador; anotador.

remarriage [rimǽriy], s. segundas nupcias.

remarry [rimǽri], va. y vn. volver a casar o casarse; contraer segundas nupcias.

remediable [remídiabœl], a. remediable.

remedial [remídial], a. reparador; terapéutico.

remedy [rémedi]. **I.** s. remedio; cura.—**to be past r.**, no tener cura o remedio. **II.** va. curar, remediar.

remember [rimémbœr]. **I.** va. recordar; tener presente; memorar, hacer presente, dar memorias. (remember me to her, déle Vd. expresiones mías). **II.** vn. acordarse.

remembrance [-brans], s. memoria, retentiva; recordación; recuerdo; conmemoración.—**remembrancer** [-brancer], s. recordador, recordatorio; (Ingl.) oficial de Hacienda.

remind [rimáind], va. recordar.—**reminder** [-œr], s. recordativo, señal, recordatorio; advertencia.—**remindful** [-ful] a. recordativo, rememorativo; atento, cuidadoso.

reminisce [reminís], vn. (fam.) hablar de o contar cosas pasadas, contar (uno) sus recuerdos.

reminiscence, reminiscency [réminisens, -i], s. reminiscencia.—pl. memorias.—**reminiscent** [-sent], a. recordativo, rememorativo.

remise [remáiś]. **I.** va. restituir; ceder. **II.** s. restitución, cesión.

remiss [remís], a. remiso, descuidado; flojo.

remissibility [remísibíliti], s. calidad de remisible.—**remissible** [-ibœl], a. remisible.

remission [remíśhun], s. remisión, perdón; relevación, diminución; descanso, asueto; (com.) remesa; (med.) remisión.

remissly [remísli], adv. remisamente.

remissness [-nes], s. flojedad, negligencia.

remissory [remísori], a. remisorio.

remit [remít]. **I.** va. (com.) remesar, remitir, enviar; remitir, perdonar, condonar; exonerar, eximir; relajar, aflojar; referir, someter, trasladar. **II.** vn. enviar; hacer remesas; disminuir; debilitarse, bajar, templarse.

remitment [-mœnt], s. remisión, gracia, exoneración; remesa.—**remittal** [-al], s. cesión, renuncia, abandono; remesa.—**remittance** [-ans], s. (com.) remesa, giro, letra de cambio.—**remittent** [-œnt]. **I.** a. remitente. **II.** s. fiebre o calentura remitente.—**remitter** [-œr], s. remitente; (for.) restitución.

remnant [rémnant], s. remanente, resto, residuo; retal, retazo.

remodel [rimódel], *va.* modelar de nuevo; rehacer, reconstruir.

remonetize [rimúnetaiš], *va.* remonetizar.

remonstrance [remónstrans], *s.* protesta; memorial, representación; represión, amonestación, reconvención; (igl.) *V.* MONSTRANCE.

remonstrant [remónstrant]. **I.** *a.* en son de protesta o de reconvención. **II.** *s.* peticionario, exponente.

remonstrate [remónstret], *vn.* protestar, objetar; (con *with*) reconvenir.

remora [rémora], *s.* (ict.) rémora.

remorse [remórs], *s.* remordimiento.—**remorseful** [-ful], *a.* lleno de remordimientos; arrepentido. —**remorseless** [-les], *a.* cruel, sin conciencia.—**remorselessly** [-li], *adv.* sin remordimiento, sin piedad.—**remorselessness** [-nes], *s.* falta de piedad o remordimiento.

remote [remóut], *a.* remoto, apartado; extraño, ajeno.—**remotely** [-li], *adv.* remotamente.

remoteness [-nes], *s.* calidad de remoto.

remount [rimáunt]. **I.** *va.* y *vn.* remontar; volver a subir; (mil.) remontar, remontarse. **II.** *s.* (mil.) remonta.

removability [remúvabíliti], *s.* removibilidad, amovilidad.—**removable** [-bœl], *a.* removible; separable, de quitapón; transportable; amovible.

removal [remúval], *s.* acción de quitar, llevarse o levantar; remoción; removimiento; deposición; eliminación, extirpación; alejamiento, apartamiento; traslación, mudanza, cambio de domicilio; remudamiento; supresión.

remove [remúv]. **I.** *va.* remover; quitar; suprimir; alejar; mudar, cambiar, trasladar; alzar o levantar la casa; destituir, deponer; derogar; apartar, desarrimar; sacar, extirpar, arrancar; desembarazarse de; poner fin a. **II.** *vr.* mudarse, trasladarse, alejarse; cambiar de sitio, cambiar de domicilio. **III.** *s.* cambio de lugar, mudada; corta distancia, grado, paso, intervalo; grado de parentesco; plato o entrada que se quita en una comida.

remover [remúvœr], *s.* quitador.

remunerable [remiúnœrabœl], *a.* remunerable.

remunerate [-eit], *va.* remunerar.—**remuneration** [-éišhun], *s.* remuneración.—**remunerative** [-ativ], *a.* remuneratorio; lucrativo, remunerador. —**remunerator** [-éitœr], *s.* remunerador.

renaissance [rénesáns], *s.* renacimiento.

renal [rínal], *a.* renal.

renard [rénard], *s.* = REYNARD.

renascence, renascency [renésens, -i], *s.* renacimiento.

renascent [renésent], *a.* renaciente.

rencounter [rencáuntœr]. **I.** *s.* encuentro, combate, refriega, pendencia, riña casual. **II.** *va.* y *vn.* embestirse, acometerse.

rend. **I.** *va.* rasgar, desgarrar; rajar, hender; lacerar, hacer pedazos; separar, desunir; arrancar. **II.** *s.* (mar.) costura de los tablones.

render [réndœr]. **I.** *va.* volver; poner; hacer; dar; suministrar, prestar, rendir; (mús.) interpretar, ejecutar; traducir; devolver, restituir; derretir y clarificar; extraer por fusión; (alb.) dar la primera capa de enlucido a.—**to r. assistance**, prestar auxilio, auxiliar.—**to r. into**, traducir o verter al. —**to r. justice**, hacer justicia. **II.** *s.* pago (esp. en forma de servicio); (alb.) capa de enlucido aplicada sin listonado.

rendezvous [rándevú]. **I.** *va.* y *vn.* acudir, juntarse, reunirse. **II.** *s.* cita; reunión; lugar de la cita.

rendition [rendíšhun], *s.* versión o traducción; (mús.) interpretación, ejecución; rendición, entrega; (com.) rendimiento, producción.

renegade [rénegued], **renegado** [reneguédo], *s.* renegado, apóstata; desertor.

renew [reniú], *va.* y *vn.* renovar, reengendrar; rehacer; reanudar; renovarse; (com.) extender, prorrogar.

renewable [reniúabœl], *a.* renovable.

renewal [reniúal], *s.* renovación, renuevo; reanudación; (com.) prórroga.

reniform [réniform], *a.* reniforme.

renitency [renáitensi], *s.* renitencia.

renitent [renáitent], *a.* renitente.

rennet [rénet], *s.* cuajo; (anat.) cuajar; (bot.) cuajaleche, cardo lechero.

rennin [rénin], *s.* quimosina, fermento del cuajar.

renominate [rinómineit], *va.* nombrar de nuevo.

renomination [-éišhun], *s.* (pol.) segundo nombramiento.

renounce [renáuns], *va.* renunciar; rechazar, repudiar, renegar, abnegar, abandonar, abjurar; abdicar; en los naipes, renunciar.

renouncement [-mœnt], *s.* renuncia.

renovate [rénoveit], *va.* renovar, rehacer; limpiar; purificar.—**renovation** [-éišhun], *s.* renovación, rehacimiento, compostura; renuevo; limpiadura.—**renovator** [-éitœr], *s.* renovador.

renown [renáun], *s.* renombre, fama.

renowned [renáund], *a.* renombrado, famoso.

rent [rent]. **I.** *s.* renta; arrendamiento; alquiler, arriendo; rédito; rasgón, rasgadura, desgarro; raja, grieta, cuarteadura; cisma.—**r. day**, día de pagar el arrendamiento. **II.** *va.* alquilar, arrendar, dar o tomar en arrendamiento.

renfable [réntabœl], *a.* arrendable.

rental [réntal], *s.* renta, arrendamiento, alquiler.

renter [réntœr], *s.* rentero, arrendante, inquilino.

renunciation [renúnšhiéšhun], *s.* renuncia, renunciación.

reopen [riópœn], *va.* volver a abrir.

reorganization [riórganišéšhun], *s.* reorganización.—**reorganize** [riórganaiš], *va.* reorganizar.

rep, *s.* (tej.) rep, género acordonado.

repack [ripǽc], *va.* reempacar; reembalar.

repaint [ripéint], *va.* repintar.

repair [ripéœr]. **I.** *va.* restaurar, reparar, componer; remendar; (zap.) remontar; remediar, subsanar, enmendar; resarcir o indemnizar; restablecer; (mar.) carenar. **II.** *vn.* (con **to**) ir a, dirigirse a. **III.** *s.* reparo, reparación, restauración; compostura, remiendo, recorrida, embonada; (zap.) remonta.—**r. shop**, taller de reparaciones.—**out of r.**, descompuesto, en mal estado.

repairer [ripéœr], *s.* reparador, componedor, restaurador.

repairing [ripéring], *s.* reparación, compostura, restauración; (zap.) remonta.

reparable [réparabœl], **repairable** [repéœrabœl], *a.* reparable.

reparation [reparéšhun], *s.* reparación, satisfacción, resarcimiento; (ant.) restauración.

reparative [repǽrativ], *a.* y *s.* reparativo, restaurativo.

repartee [repartí], *s.* respuesta o réplica aguda, vuelta, agudeza, discreteo.

repartition [ripartíšhun], *s.* repartimiento, repartición.

repass [repás], *va.* repasar, volver a pasar.

repassage [repásey], *s.* repaso.

repast [repást], *s.* comida, alimento.

repatriate [ripéitriet], *va.* repatriar.

repay [ripéi]. **I.** *va.* pagar, recompensar; reintegrar; convenir o aprovechar a; pagar en la misma moneda. **II.** *vn.* hacer un pago.

repayment [-mœnt], *s.* reintegro, pago, retorno.

repeal [repíl]. **I.** *va.* derogar, revocar. **II.** *s.* revocación, derogación.—**repealable** [abœl], *a.* revocable.—**repealer** [-œr], *s.* revocador.—**repealing** [-ing], *a.* derogatorio.

repeat [repít]. **I.** *va.* repetir; repasar, ensayar. **II.** *s.* (mús.) repetición.

repeatedly [repítedli], *adv.* repetidamente, repetidas veces.

repeater [repítœr], *s.* repetidor; reloj de repetición; arma de repetición; (elec.) repetidor; (E. U. pol.) elector que vota varias veces en una misma elección.

repeating [repíting], *a.* repetidor; de repetición. —**r. circle**, (top., ast., etc.) círculo repetidor.—**r. coil**, (elec.) bobina acopladora de inducción.—**r. decimal**, (arit.) fracción decimal periódica.— **r. firearm**, arma de repetición.—**r. instrument**, instrumento repetidor.—**r. watch**, reloj de repetición.

repel [repél]. **I.** va. repeler, rechazar; resistir; alejar, ahuyentar; (med.) repercutir los humores. **II.** vn. ser repelente o repulsivo.

repellent [repélent]. **I.** a. repelente; repercusivo; ahuyentador; impermeable. **II.** s. tela impermeable; (med.) remedio repercusivo.

repent [repént]. **I.** va. y vn. arrepentirse (de). **II.** a. [rípcent] (zool. y bot.) rastrero.—**repentance** [-ans], s. arrepentimiento.—**repentant** [-ant], a. arrepentido, contrito.—**repentant, repenter** [-œr], s. penitente, arrepentido.—**repentingly** [-ingli], adv. arrepentidamente, con arrepentimiento.

repeople [rɪpipœl], va. repoblar.

repercussion [rɪpœrcúshun], s. repercusión, reverberación, rechazo.

repercussive [rípœrcúsiv], a. repercusivo.

repertoire [repœrtuár], s. repertorio.

repertory [répœrtori], s. depósito, colección; repertorio; prontuario, inventario, lista, índice.

repetend [répetend], s. período (de una fracción decimal periódica).

repetition [repetíshun], s. repetición; repaso; redición.

repetitious [repetíshus], a. (E. U.) redundante.

repine [repáin], vn. apurarse, quejarse.—**repiner** [-œr], s. el que se queja.—**repining** [-ing], s. pesar; queja, descontento.

replace [rɪpléis], va. reemplazar; volver a poner; devolver, reembolsar o restituir.—**replaceable** [-abœl], a. reemplazable; renovable.—**replacement** [-mœnt], s. reemplazo, substitución; restitución, reposición.

replait [replét], va. replegar.

replant [riplént], va. replantar.

replenish [riplénish], va. rellenar, rehenchir; llenar.—**replenishment** [-mœnt], s. acción y efecto de llenar o proveer.

replete [replít], a. lleno, repleto.

repletion [replíshun], **repleteness** [replítnes], s. repleción, plenitud.

repleviable [replévíabœl], a. (for.) reivindicable.

replevin [replévin], s. (for.) reivindicación; auto de desembargo.

replevin, o replevy [replévi], va. (for.) desembargar; reivindicar.

replica [réplica], s. (b. a.) duplicado; copia, reproducción; (mús.) repetición.

replicant [réplicant], s. replicador, replicante.

replicate [répliket], a. replegado.

replication [replikéshun], s. réplica, replicato, respuesta; repetición; repliegue; (for.) réplica.

reply [riplái]. **I.** s. respuesta, contestación. **II.** va. contestar, responder, reponer.

report [ripórt]. **I.** va. informar acerca de; referir, contar; redactar un informe o dictamen; propalar, divulgar; quejarse de, acusar, delatar, denunciar.—**to r. progress,** dar cuenta de la marcha de un asunto.—**it is reported,** corre la voz, se dice. **II.** vn. presentar informe o dictamen; servir como reporter o noticiero; comparecer, personarse. **III.** s. relato, parte, noticia, reporte, información; informe, dictamen, memoria; voz, rumor; reportaje (de periódico); fama, reputación; (for.) relación de pleitos o causas; estampido, estallido, trueno, estruendo.—**r. of a gun, musket, pistol,** cañonazo, escopetazo, pistoletazo.—**by r.,** según se dice.

reporter [repórtœr], s. reporter, reportero; (for.) relator.—**reporters' gallery,** tribuna de los periodistas.

reportorial [reportórial], a. reporteril.

repose [repóus]. **I.** va. descansar, reclinar; poner (confianza o esperanza). **II.** vn. reposar, descansar; tener confianza en. **III.** vr. tenderse, reclinarse, recostarse. **IV.** s. reposo, descanso; tranquilidad, calma.

reposite [repósit], va. depositar.

reposition [ríposhshun], s. reposición, restablecimiento.

repositor [repósitœr], s. reponedor, repositor.

repository [repósitori], s. repositorio, depósito; almacén, tienda.

repossess [riposés], va. recobrar, recuperar.

repossession [riposéshun], s. recuperación.

repoussé [repusé], a. repujado.

reprehend [reprijénd], va. reprender.

reprehensible [-sibœl], a. reprensible.—**reprehensibleness** [-nes] s. calidad de reprensible.—**reprehension** [-shun], s. reprensión, regaño; paulina, fraterna, repasata.—**reprehensive, reprehensory** [-siv, -sori], a. reprensor.

represent [repreśént], va. representar; manifestar, exponer; [rí-] presentar de nuevo.

representable [répreśéntabœl], a. representable.

representation [-téishun], s. representación (en todas sus acepciones); [rí-] nueva presentación.

representative [répreśéntativ]. **I.** a. representativo, típico, representante. **II.** s. representante, gestor, apoderado, delegado; símbolo, tipo, ejemplar; (R-) diputado, representante (miembro de la Cámara de Representantes).

repress [représ] va. reprimir, dominar; sojuzgar, sujetar; sofocar; [riprés] volver a prensar.

repression [représhun], s. represión.

repressive [represiv], a. represivo.

reprieve [repriv]. **I.** va. (for.) suspender la ejecución de una sentencia; aliviar, librar temporalmente de peligro, pena o dolor. **II.** s. suspensión temporal de una sentencia o de un dolor.

reprimand [réprimánd]. **I.** va. reprender, regañar, reñir, reconvenir. **II.** s. [réprimand] reprimenda, regaño.

reprint [reprínt]. **I.** va. reimprimir. **II.** s. reimpresión; tirada aparte (de un artículo).

reprisal [repráisal], s. represalia.

reprise [repráis], s. represa; (mús.) estribillo.

reproach [repróuch]. **I.** va. reprochar, increpar, echar en cara; vituperar, censurar. **II.** s. reproche, increpación; contumelia, vituperio.—**reproachable** [-abœl], a. censurable, reprensible.—**reproachableness** [-nes], s. reprensibilidad.

reproachful [-ful], a. increpante, reprensor, vituperioso; ceñudo.—**reproachfully** [-i], adv. vituperiosamente, contumeliosamente.—**reproachfulness** [-res], s. calidad de vituperioso.

reprobate [réprobet]. **I.** a. y s. réprobo, malvado. **II.** va. reprobar, condenar; desaprobar.—**reprobation** [-béishun], s. reprobación, desaprobación, condenación.—**reprobative** [-betiv], a. reprobador.—**reprobatory** [-ori], a. reprobador, reprobatorio.

reproduce [riprodiús], va. reproducir; copiar.—**reproducer** [-œr], s. aparato reproductor (fonográfico, etc.).—**reproducible** [-ibœl], a. reproductible.

reproduction [riprodúcshun], s. reproducción; reminiscencia; (b. a.) copia, traslado, trasunto.—**reproductive, reproductory** [-tiv, -tori], a. reproductivo, reproductor.

reproof [reprúf], s. reprobación, reproche, repensión.—**reprovable** [reprúvabœl], a. censurable, reprensible.

reprove [reprúv], va. reprobar, culpar, censurar; acusar, condenar.—**reprover** [-œr], s. reprensor, reprobador, censor.

reptant [réptant], a. rastrero.

reptile [réptil], s. y a. reptil.—**Reptilia** [reptíliæ], s. pl. reptiles.—**reptilian** [reptílien]. **I.** s. reptil. **II.** a. de reptil, de los reptiles.—**r. age,** (geol.) edad de los reptiles o mesozóica.

republic [republic], s. república.—**republican** [-æn], a. y s. republicano; (orn.) republicano, que anida en manadas.—**republicanism** [-iśm], s. republicanismo.

republication [ripúblikéshun], s. nueva publicación; reimpresión; (for.) renovación de un testamento.

republish [ripúblish], va. publicar de nuevo; reimprimir; renovar.

repudiable [repiúdiabœl], a. repudiable.

repudiate [repiúdieit], va. repudiar.

repudiation [-éishun], s. repudiación.

repugnance, repugnancy [repúgnans, -i], s. repugnancia, mala gana, aversión.—**repugnant** [-nant], a. repugnante; antipático; opuesto, renitente; contrario, incompatible.—**repugnantly** [-li], adv. con repugnancia, de mala gana.

repulse [repúls]. **I.** *s.* repulsa, repulsión; denegación. **II.** *va.* repulsar, desechar, rechazar, repeler.

repulsion [repúlŝhʊn], *s.* (fís.) repulsión; rechazamiento; repugnancia, renitencia.—**repulsive** [-siv], *a.* repulsivo, repugnante, repelente.—**repulsiveness** [-nes], *s.* carácter repugnante o repulsivo.

reputable [répiutabœl], *a.* honroso, honrado, estimable, intachable; lícito.—**reputably** [-bli], *adv.* honrosamente, honradamente.

reputation [répiutéiŝhʊn], *s.* reputación.

repute [repiút]. **I.** *va.* reputar, estimar, juzgar, tener por. **II.** *s.* fama, crédito, reputación, estimación; opinión común.

reputed [repiúted], *a.* considerado, tenido por, supuesto.—**reputedly** [-li], *adv.* según la opinión común; según se cree.

request [recuést]. **I.** *s.* súplica, ruego; petición, pedimento, instancia, solicitud; (com.) demanda.—**at the r. of, o by r.,** a petición, a solicitud de.—**in r.,** en boga, en demanda, pedido, buscado. **II.** *va.* rogar, pedir, suplicar, solicitar.

requiem (mass) [rícuiem (mas)], *s.* (igl. y mús.) misa de réquiem.

requirable [recuáirabœl], *a.* que se puede requerir o solicitar.

require [recuáiœr], *va.* requerir, demandar, pedir, exigir, necesitar.

requirement [-mœnt], *s.* demanda, requerimiento, exigencia; requisito, necesidad; estipulación.—**requirer** [recuáirœr], *s.* requeridor.

requisite [récuiŝit]. **I.** *a.* necesario, forzoso, indispensable. **II.** *s.* requisito.—**requisitely** [-li], *adv.* necesariamente, calidad de indispensable.—**requisiteness** [-nes], *s.* necesidad, calidad de indispensable.

requisition [recuiŝíŝhʊn], *s.* pedimento, petición, demanda, requisición; necesidad, requisito, menester; (com.) demanda, solicitud; (for.) requisitoria.—**in r.,** en demanda, pedido, buscado.

requisitory [recuíŝitori], *a.* requisitorio.

requital [recuáital], *s.* retorno, paga, satisfacción; compensación; desquite; pena del talión.

requite [recuáit], *va.* pagar, recompensar, retornar, devolver; compensar; pagar en la misma moneda.

requiter [-œr], *s.* el que recompensa o devuelve; lo que compensa.

reredos [rícœrdos], *s.* (igl.) retablo; (arq.) trashogar.

rescind [resínd], *va.* rescindir, anular, abrogar.

rescission [resíyʊn], *s.* rescisión, anulación, abrogación.

rescissory [resísori], *a.* (for.) rescisorio.

rescript [ríscript], *s.* rescripto, edicto.

rescue [réskiu]. **I.** *va.* rescatar, redimir; salvar, librar, libertar. **II.** *s.* rescate, salvación, libramiento, recobro; socorro.

rescuer [réskiuœr], *s.* salvador, rescatador, libertador.

research [resœrch]. **I.** *s.* investigación; averiguación, indagación. **II.** *va.* y *vn.* investigar.

resection [resécŝhʊn], *s.* (cir.) resección.

Reseda [resídæ], *s.* (bot.) reseda, género de las resedas.—**Resedaceæ** [résedéiŝi], *s. pl.* (bot.) resedáceas.—**resedaceous** [-ŝhʊs], *a.* resedáceo.

resemblance [reŝémblans], *s.* parecido, semejanza.—**resemble** [-bœl], *va.* asemejarse a, parecerse a.

resent [reŝént], *va.* resentirse de, ofenderse por.—**resentful** [-ful], *a.* resentido, agraviado.—**resentment** [-mœnt], *s.* resentimiento.

reservation [réŝœrvéiŝhʊn], *s.* reservación; reserva, salvedad; doble sentido; (E. U.) territorio reservado para los indios.

reserve [reŝœrv]. **I.** *va.* reservar, guardar, retener, conservar; exceptuar, excluir. **II.** *s.* reserva, reservación; cautela, sigilo, reticencia; (mil.) reserva, retén.—**r. bank,** banco de reserva.—**without r.,** sin reserva, sin excepcion, enteramente.

reserved [reŝœrvd], *a.* reservado; circunspecto, discreto, mesurado; callado; retenido, guardado.—**reservedly** [-vedli], *adv.* reservadamente; con

cautela.—**reservedness** [-vednes], *s.* reserva, cautela, sigilo.

reservist [reŝœrvist], *s.* soldado de reserva.

reservoir [réŝœrvuar], *s.* depósito; receptáculo; (com.) surtido de reserva; (hidr.) depósito de abastecimiento; charca, cámbija, aljibe; presada; depósito (de gas, agua, etc.); cubeta.

reset [risét]. **I.** *va.* reengastar, montar de nuevo. **II.** *s.* nuevo engaste o montadura.

reship [riŝhíp], *va.* y *vn.* reembarcar.—**reshipment** [-mœnt], *s.* reembarco, reembarque.

reside [reŝáid], *vn.* residir, morar, vivir.

residence [réŝidens], *s.* residencia, morada, domicilio; casa; estada, permanencia, mansión; presencia.

residency [réŝidensi], *s.* V. RESIDENCE; en la India inglesa, habitación oficial del representante del gobernador general.

resident [-dent]. **I.** *a.* residente; morador, habitador; permanente; inherente. **II.** *s.* habitante, vecino; (dipl.) ministro residente.

residential [-dénŝhœl], *a.* perteneciente o relativo a la residencia; de habitación, de habitaciones, de casas de habitación.

residentiary [·dénŝhiœri]. **I.** *a.* residencial. **II.** *s.* residente, habitante, vecino.

residual, residuary [reŝídiual, o -iuæri] *a.* restante.—**residual magnetism** [·(elec.) magnetismo remanente.—**residuary legatee,** heredero universal.

residue [réŝidiu], *s.* residuo, resto, sobrante, remanente, superávit.

residuum [riŝíyuʊm], *s.* residuo, resta; desperdicio.

resign [reŝáin]. **I.** *va.* dimitir, renunciar, ceder, dejar, abandonar. **II.** *vr.* resignarse, rendirse, someterse. **III.** *va.* [riŝáin] firmar otra vez.

resignation [réŝignéiŝhʊn], *s.* dimisión, renuncia, dejación; resignación, conformidad.

resigned [reŝáind], *a.* resignado, conforme.—**resignedly** [reŝáindli], *adv.* resignadamente.

resignee [reŝiní o reŝainí], *s.* resignatario.

resigner [reŝáinœr], *s.* resignante.

resilience [reŝíliens], **resiliency** [-i], *s.* elasticidad, resorte, rebote; trabajo de elasticidad.—**resilient** [-ent], *a.* elástico.

resin [réŝin], *s.* resina, colofonia.

resinaceous [reŝináŝhʊs], *a.* resinoso.

resiniferous [reŝiníferʊs], *a.* resinífero.

resinoid [réŝinoid]. **I.** *a.* parecido a la resina. **II.** *s.* substancia que parece resina.

resinous [réŝinʊs], *a.* resinoso.—**resinousness** [-nes], *s.* calidad de resinoso.

resist [reŝíst], *va.* y *vn.* resistir, rechazar, repeler; oponerse; impedir, detener, contrariar, negarse a; aguantar, soportar.

resistance [reŝístæns], *s.* (leng. ord. y tecn.) resistencia.—**r. box,** (elect.) caja de resistencias.—**r. coil,** bobina o carrete de resistencia.—**r. frame,** reóstato de cuadro, cuadro de resistencia.—**r. of materials,** resistencia de materiales.

resistant, resistent [-tænt, -tœnt], *a.* resistente.

resistibility [-tibíliti], *s.* resistibilidad.

resistible [-tibœl], *a.* resistible.

resistivity [-réŝistíviti], *s.* (elec.) resistividad, resistencia específica.

resistless [reŝístles], *a.* irresistible; indefenso.—**resistlessness** [-nes], *s.* calidad de irresistible.

resistor [reŝístœr], *s.* (elec.) resistencia.

resole [risóull], *va.* (zap.) remontar, sobresolar.—**resoling** [-ing], *s.* remonta.

resoluble [réŝolubœl], *a.* soluble; resoluble.

resolute [réŝoliut], *a.* resuelto, determinado; firme, denodado.—**resolutely** [-li], *adv.* resueltamente.—**resoluteness** [-nes], *s.* resolución, determinación, denuedo.

resolution [réŝoliúŝhʊn], *s.* resolución, determinación, denuedo; propósito; resolución, acuerdo (de una junta o asamblea); (mat.) resolución (de un problema); disolución de un todo; análisis (químico, mecánico o mental); descomposición; (med.) resolución (de un tumor, etc.); (mec.) descomposición (de fuerzas, velocidades, etc.)

resolvable [reśólvabœl], *a.* resoluble.
resolve [reśólv]. **I.** *va.*, *vr.* y *vn.* resolver o resolverse; acordar, tomar un acuerdo; descomponer (un cuerpo, una fuerza, etc.); disipar, desvanecer; (med.) resolver (tumores, etc.); (con *into*) transformarse en o reducirse a. **II.** *s.* resolución, determinación, propósito, acuerdo.
resolved [reśólvd], *pp.* acordado, decidido; resuélvese.—**it is r.**, resuélvese, queda acordado.
resolvedly [reśólvedli], *adv.* resueltamente.
resolvent [reśólvent], *a.* resolvente.
resonance [réśonans], *s.* resonancia.—**resonant** [-ant], *a.* resonante, retumbante; sonoro.
resonator [-éitœr], *s.* resonador.
resorption [resórpśhʊn], *s.* reabsorción, resorción.
resorptive [resórptiv], *a.* reabsorbedor.
resort [reśórt]. **I.** *vn.* acudir, recurrir, frecuentar, concurrir; pasar a. **II.** *s.* concurso, concurrencia; punto de reunión; manida; recurso, medio, refugio; lugar frecuentado (gen. el objeto se indica por un substantivo modificativo: *summer resort*, lugar de veraneo; *health resort*, lugar de curación, colonia de enfermos).
resound [reśáund]. **I.** *va.* repetir, repercutir el sonido; cantar, celebrar. **II.** *vn.* resonar, retumbar; formar eco; tener resonancia; tener fama, ser celebrado; [riśáund] *va.* volver a sonar, sonar repetidas veces.
resource [resórs], *s.* recurso, arbitrio, medio, expediente.—*pl.* recursos, posibles, medios pecuniarios; riquezas (inclusas las naturales).
resourceful [-ful], *a.* listo, ingenioso.
resourceless [-les], *a.* desprovisto de recursos o de medios.
respect [respéct]. **I.** *va.* respetar; acatar, observar, guardar; respectar, tocar, corresponder, concernir, referir.—**as respects**, en cuanto a, en lo tocante a. **II.** *s.* respecto; respeto.—*pl.* memorias, recuerdos, respetos, expresiones.—**r. of persons,** acepción de personas.—**in r. that,** puesto que.—**in r. to,** tocante a.—**in this r.,** a este respecto.—**to have r. to,** referirse a.—**without r. to,** sin consideración de, sin distinción de, prescindiendo de.
respectability [-abíliti], **respectableness** [-abœlnes], *s.* respetabilidad, crédito.
respectable [-abœl], *a.* respetable, acreditado, autorizado; pasable, bastante bueno; considerable; mediano.—**respectably** [-abli], *adv.* respetablemente; medianamente.
respecter [-œr], *s.* respetador.—**r. of persons,** aceptor o aceptador de personas.
respectful [-ful], *a.* respetuoso.
respectfully [-fuli], *adv.* respetuosamente.
respectfulness [-fulnes], *s.* conducta respetuosa.
respecting [-ing], *prep.* con respecto a, en cuanto a, por lo que toca a.
respective [-iv], *a.* respectivo; particular, individual.
respectively [-ivli], *adv.* respectivamente.
respirable [réspirabœl], *a.* respirable.
respiration [-éiśhʊn], *s.* respiración, respiro.
respirator [réspiréitœr], *s.* respirador.
respiratory [réspiratori], *a.* respiratorio.
respire [respáiœr], *va.* y *vn.* resollar, respirar; espirar, exhalar.
respite [réspit]. **I.** *s.* tregua, espera, pausa; plaza, prórroga, respiro. **II.** *va.* dar treguas, suspender o diferir, aplazar, prorrogar.
resplendence, resplendency [respléndens, -i], *s.* resplandor, esplendor.—**resplendent** [-ent], *a.* resplandeciente.—**resplendently** [-li], *adv.* esplendorosamente.
respond [respónd], *vn.* responder; reaccionar; corresponder; obedecer; venir bien, ajustarse.
respondent [-ent]. **I.** *a.* respondiente, respondedor, correspondiente. **II.** *s.* (for.) demandado.
response [respóns], *s.* respuesta, contestación.
responsibility [respónsibíliti], *s.* responsabilidad; deber; fideicomiso o depósito; solvencia.
responsible [-bœl], *a.* responsable; garante, fiable, solvente; autorizado; de responsabilidad.—**r. for,** responsable de; causa de; autor de; origen de.
responsibleness [-bœlnes], *s.* responsabilidad.

responsibly [-bli], *adv.* con responsabilidad.
responsive [respónsiv], *a.* respondiente, respondedor; sensible; obediente; interesado; correspondiente, conforme.—**responsiveness** [-nes], *s.* correspondencia, simpatía, conformidad; sensibilidad; obediencia.
responsory [respónsori], *a.* que responde, respondiente.
rest. **I.** *s.* descanso, reposo; paz, quietud, tranquilidad; sueño, paz (de los muertos); sustentáculo, apoyo, base, soporte, arrimo, estribo; portaútil (de torno, etc.); cuja, ristre; resto, residuo, sobra; excedente, sobrante, superávit; saldo semanal (del Banco de Inglaterra); posada, dos cansadero; parada, detención; (mús.) pausa; (poét.) cesura; (con *the*) los demás, los otros; lo demás; el resto.—**a r.,** descanso.—**at r.,** en reposo; en paz (apl. a los muertos); decidido, arreglado, terminado.—**without r.,** sin descanso, sin tregua. **II.** *vn.* descansar, reposar; yacer, reposar en el seno de la muerte; cesar, parar; estar en paz, vivir tranquilo; posarse o asentarse; descansar (sobre), apoyarse (en), cargar (sobre); confiar o fiar (en), contar (con); depender (de); quedar, permanecer; (for.) haber presentado una de las partes todas sus pruebas. **III.** *va.* y *vn.* descansar, proporcionar descanso, dejar descansar, poner, apoyar o asentar; (for.) terminar la presentación de pruebas.
restaurant [réstorant], *s.* restaurante.
restful [réstful], *a.* reposado, quieto, tranquilo.
restfully [-i], *adv.* tranquilamente.
resting place [résting pléis], *s.* descansadero; (fig.) la tumba; meseta de escalera.
restitution [réstitiúśhʊn], *s.* restitución, restablecimiento; devolución, torna, reintegración; reparación, indemnización; recuperación, recobro; (fís.) elasticidad.
restitutive [réstitiutiv], *a.* restitutorio, devolutivo.
restive [réstiv], *a.* (equit.) repropio; ingobernable; impaciente, inquieto.
restiveness [-nes], *s.* impaciencia, inquietud.
restless [réstles], *a.* inquieto, desasosegado, intranquilo; bullicioso, revoltoso, levantisco; insomne, desvelado.—**restlessness** [-nes], *s.* inquietud, impaciencia, desasosiego; insomnio, desvelo.
restock [rístóc]. **I.** *va.* volver a surtir, a llenar o a abastecer; (agr.) renovar, restablecer (un bosque, etc.). **II.** *s.* renovación, restablecimiento (de un bosque, etc.)
restorable [restórabœl], *a.* restituíble.
restoration [réstoréiśhʊn], *s.* restauración, renovación; instauración, rehabilitación, restablecimiento; (teol.) redención final.
restorative [restórativ], *a.* y *s.* restaurativo.
restore [restóœr], *va.* restaurar, rehacer, reconstruir o reedificar; restablecer, instaurar; restituir, devolver, reponer; [rístóœr], depositar o almacenar de nuevo.
restorer [restóroœr], *s.* restaurador; restituidor.
restrain [restréin], *va.* refrenar, reprimir, contener; limitar, coartar, restringir; (for.) prohibir o vedar a.—**restrainable** [-abœl], *a.* restringible.—**restrainedly** [-nedli], *adv.* con restricción.—**restrainer** [-œr], *s.* (foto.) restingente.
restraint [restréint], *s.* sujeción, limitación, restricción, freno; coerción, prohibición.
restrict [restríct], *va.* restringir, limitar, coartar.—**restriction** [restricśhʊn], *s.* restricción, limitación, coartación.—**restrictive** [-tiv], *a.* restrictivo.—**restrictively** [-li], *adv.* restrictivamente.
result [reśúlt]. **I.** *vn.* resultar; (con **in**) venir a parar, acabar o terminar en, conducir a; causar. **II.** *s.* resultado, resulta; conclusión, deducción.
resultant [reśúltant]. **I.** *a.* resultante. **II.** *s.* consecuencia, resultado; (mec.) resultante.
resulting [reśúlting], *a.* resultante; emergente; (for.) **r. use,** usufructo reversible.
resumable [reśiúmabœl], *a.* que se puede reasumir.
resume [reśiúm]. **I.** *va.* reasumir; reanudar; recobrar, reocupar, recuperar; (ant.) resumir. **II.** *vn.* tomar el hilo.

résumé [résiumé], s. resumen, sumario, recapitulación.

resumption [resǘmpšhʊn], s. reasunción, recobro.—**resumptive** [-tiv], a. que vuelve a tomar o a asumir.

resupinate [resiúpineit], **resupine** [resiupáin], a. supino, boca arriba.

resupination [risiupinéšhʊn], s. posición supina.

resurge [risǽry], vn. resurgir, volver a alzarse o a subir.—**resurgence** [-ens], s. reaparición; resurrección.—**resurgent** [-ent], a. resurgente, que surge de nuevo; resurrecto.

resurrect [résʊrréct], va. (fam.) resucitar, desenterrar.

resurrection [-rrécšhʊn], s. resurrección; renovación, restablecimiento.

resurrectionist [-ist], s. (fam.) el que desentierra y vende cadáveres.

resurvey [rísœrvéi], I. va. reexaminar; (top.) levantar un nuevo plano de; volver a medir. II. s. [risǽrvei] nuevo examen, nuevo estudio; (top.) nuevo levantamiento, nueva medición.

resuscitate [risǘsiteit], va. y vn. resucitar, revivir.—**resuscitation** [-téišhʊn], s. resurrección, renacimiento, renovación.—**resuscitative** [-tativ], a. resucitador, que revive.

ret, va. enriar (cáñamo o lino).

retail [ritéil]. I. va. vender al menudeo, o por menor. II. s. [ríteil] menudeo, venta por menor.

retailer [ritéilœr], s. comerciante al por menor, lonjista, tendero, revendedor, mangón.

retain [ritéin]. I. va. retener, guardar, conservar; contratar, ajornalar; ajustar (a un abogado). II. vn. estar ajustado o contratado.

retainable [-abœl], a. que se puede retener.

retainer [ritéinœr], s. adherente, partidario; paniaguado; dependiente, criado, asistente; retenedor; anticipo que se da a un abogado al ajustar sus servicios; (mec.) fiador; mecanismo de cierre; aldaba.

retaining [ritáining], a. que retiene o contiene; de retención, de contención.—**r. fee**, pago anticipado con que se ajusta a una persona.—**r. wall**, muro de sostenimiento o de contención.

retainment [-mœnt], s. retención; ajuste, empleo (de abogado).

retake [ritéic], va. volver a tomar.

retaliate [retǽlieit], va. talionar, desquitarse, vengarse; usar de represalias.

retaliation [-éišhʊn], s. desquite, despique; represalia; desagravio, satisfacción; pago, retorno.

retaliative [retéliativ], a. vengativo.

retaliatory [-tori], a. que usa de represalias.

retard [retárd]. I. va. retardar, atrasar, retrasar. II. s. retraso, atraso, dilación, demora.

retardation [rítardéishʊn], s. retardación, retardo, atraso, retraso.

retardative, o **retardatory** [retárdativ, -tori], a. retardador.

retarder [retárdœr], s. retardador.

retch [rech], vn. arquear.—**retching**, arcada.

rete [ríti], s. (anat.) redecilla.

retention [reténshʊn], s. retención, conservación; retentiva, memoria.—**retentive** [-tiv], a. retentivo.—**retentiveness** [-nes], s. retentiva.

reticence, reticency [rétisens, -i], s. reticencia, reserva; (ret.) reticencia.

reticent [rétisent], a. reticente.

reticle [réticœl], s. (ópt.) retículo.

reticular [retíkiular], a. reticular.—**reticulate** [-leit], va. y vn. formar a modo de red.—**reticulate(d** [-leit, -ed], a. reticular.—**reticulation** [-éišhʊn], s. disposición en forma de red.

reticule [rétikiul], s. ridículo, bolsa.

reticulum [retíkiulʊm], s. retículo (tejido); redecilla, bonete de los rumiantes.

retiform [ré- o rítiform], a. reticular.

retina [rétina], s. retina.

retinitis [rétináitis], s. retinitis, inflamación de la retina.

retinue [rétiniu], s. tren, comitiva, séquito, acompañamiento.

retiral [retáiral], s. (com.) recogida.

retire [retáiœr]. I. vn. retirarse, irse a acostar; retirarse de la vida activa o de un empleo; jubilarse; recogerse, apartarse, separarse. II. va. (com.) recoger, retirar de la circulación; jubilar.

retired [retáiœrd], a. retirado; apartado, aislado; retraído; (com.) recogido; retirado, jubilado.—**r. life**, vida retirada o solitaria.—**r. officer**, oficial retirado.—**to put on the r. list**, dar el retiro, jubilar.

retiredly [retáiœrdli], adv. retiradamente; privadamente.—**retiredness** [-nes], s. retiro, recogimiento, soledad.

retirement [retáiœrmœnt], s. retiro; retraimiento; lugar retirado; jubilación.

retiring [retáiring], a. retraído, austero, recatado; modesto, discreto; referente a la jubilación.

retorsion [retórshʊn], s. talión, represalia.

retort [retórt]. I. va. redargüir; devolver (un insulto); replicar, retorcer. II. s. redargüición; réplica mordaz; (quím.) retorta.

retorter [retórtœr], s. el que replica o redarguye.

retortion [retórshʊn], s. retorcedura, retorcimiento; retorsión; represalia.

retouch [ritʊ́ch]. I. va. retocar, modificar, limar, pulir; (foto.) retocar.—**retouching frame**, bastidor de retocar. II. s. retoque, última mano.

retoucher [ritʊ́chœr], s. (foto.) retocador.

retrace [ritréis], va. seguir (las huellas) retrocediendo; buscar el origen de; repasar un trazado; relatar, narrar.—**to r. one's steps**, volver sobre sus pasos.

retract [retrǽct]. I. va. retractar, retirar; retractarse de; retraer, encoger, esconder. II. vn. retractarse, desdecirse, cantar la palinodia; encogerse.—**retractable, retractible** [-ta(ti)bœl], a. retractable; retráctil.—**retractile** [-til], a. retráctil.—**retraction** [-šhʊn], s. retractation [-téišhʊn], s. retracción; contracción; retractación.—**retractive** [retrǽctiv], a. que tiende a retractar.—**retractor** [retrǽctœr], s. el que o lo que retracta; (cir.) retractor; (anat.) músculo contractor.

retreat [ritrít]. I. s. retiro; soledad, retraimiento; refugio, asilo; (mil.) retirada; retreta; (igl.) retiro. II. vn. retirarse; retroceder; cejar; (esgr.) dar un paso atrás; apartarse, inclinarse o prolongarse hacia atrás.

retrench [retrénch]. I. va. cercenar, cortar, disminuir, abreviar; mondar o podar; (mil.) atrincherar. II. vn. reducirse, economizar o ahorrar.

retrenchment [-mœnt], s. cercenadura, cercenamiento; economía; rebaja, diminución; (mil.) atrincheramiento, trinchera.

retribution [rétribiúšhʊn], s. retribución, pago; justo castigo, pena incurrida.

retributive, retributory [retríbiutiv, -tori], a. retribuyente.

retrievable [retrívabœl], a. recuperable; reparable.

retrievability [-bíliti], **retrievableness** [-bœlnes], s. posibilidad de recuperación.

retrieval [retríval], s. cobranza, recobro, recuperación; reintegración.

retrieve [retrív]. I. va. recuperar, recobrar; restaurar, reparar, remediar; cobrar (la caza). II. vn. cobrar la caza.

retriever [retrívœr], s. perro cobrador; perdiguero, sabueso.

retroact [rítrœct], vn. tener fuerza retroactiva.—**retroaction** [-œcshʊn], s. (for.) retroactividad.—**retroactive** [-œctiv], a. retroactivo.

retrocede [rí- o rítrosid]. I. va. (for.) hacer retrocesión. II. vn. retroceder, recular.

retrocession [rítroséshʊn], s. (for.) retrocesión; retrocession.

retroflex [rétroflex], a. doblado hacia atrás.

retroflexion [-flócshʊn], s. repliegue, inflexión hacia atrás.

retrogradation [rétrogradéishʊn], s. retrogradación.

retrograde [rétrogred]. I. a. retrógrado. II. vn. retrogradar, retroceder, desandar; ciar.

retrogression [rí- o rétrogréshʊn], *s.* retrogradación, retroceso, regresión.

retrogressive [rétrogrésiv], *a.* retrógrado.

retrospect [rétrospect], *s.* mirada retrospectiva.

retrospection [rétrospécshʊn], *s.* memoria; consideración de cosas pasadas.

retrospective [rétrospéctiv], *a.* retrospectivo.

retroussé [retrusé], *a.* respingado.

retroversion [rítrovǽrshʊn], *s.* inclinación hacia atrás.

retrovert [-vǽrt], *va.* desviar hacia atrás.

retry [ritrái], *va.* (for.) rever.

retting [réting], *s.* enriamiento. **II.** *a.* de enriar; relativo al enriamiento; enriador.

return [ritǽrn]. **I.** *va.* volver, devolver; corresponder a, pagar, retornar, dar en cambio, recompensar; dar (gracias, fallo, respuesta, etc.); rendir (informe); redituar, producir; (pol.) elegir, enviar (al congreso, etc.).—**to r. a kindness,** corresponder a un favor. **II.** *vn.* volver, regresar; reaparecer, presentarse de nuevo; represorntar, reponer, replicar; (for.) revertir.—**to r. home,** regresar a casa. **III.** *va.* y *vn.* [ritǽrn] volver de nuevo, dar otra vuelta o doblez. **IV.** *s.* vuelta, regreso; torna, correspondencia (a un favor), pago, recompensa; respuesta; redargüición; restitución, devolución, restablecimiento, reinstalación, instauración; reaparición; ganancia, utilidad, provecho, rédito; cambio, trueque, intercambio; estado, relación, informe o parte oficial; lista, nómina, padrón o censo; curva, vuelta; desviadero; (for.) diligencia; (arq.) ala; vuelta de moldura, marco, etc.; (pol.) elección.—*pl.* tablas, estadísticas; resultado, cifras (de elecciones).—**r. conductor,** (elec.) conductor de retorno.—**r. game,** (match, etc.), juego (lucha, etc.) de desquite.—**r. request,** (E. U.) membrete en que se suplica la devolución de una carta al remitente, caso de no hallarse el destinatario.—**r. shock,** (elec.) choque de retroceso.—**r. stroke,** (mec.) golpe o carrera de retroceso.—**r. ticket,** billete de ida y vuelta.—**r. mail, by r. of post,** a vuelta de correo.—**happy returns,** felices cumpleaños más.—**in r.,** en cambio.

returnable [retǽrnabœl], *a.* restituíble, reintegrable, devolutivo; reversible; (for.) devolutorio, restitutorio.

retuse [rétius], *a.* achatado.

reunion [riyúniʊn], *s.* reunión; reconciliación; tertulia; junta.

reunite [riyunáit]. **I.** *va.* reunir, juntar; volver a unir; reconciliar. **II.** *vn.* reunirse, reconciliarse.

revamp [riváemp]. **I.** *va.* (zap.) poner capellada nueva a; remendar. **II.** *s.* cosa remendada.

revanche [rœvánsh], *s.* venganza, represalias.

reveal [revíl], *va.* revelar; manifestar, descubrir, publicar, divulgar.

revealer [revílœr], *s.* revelador.

reveille [revélle o revélli], *s.* (mil.) diana; alborada.

revel [révl]. **I.** *vn.* jaranear, ir de parranda; gozarse. **II.** *s.* algazara, jarana, parranda.

revelation [-éishʊn], *s.* revelación; (**R-.**) Apocalipsis.

revel(l)er [révelœr], *s.* calavera, borrasquero.

revelry [révelri], *s.* jarana, gresca, francachela, orgía, borrachera.

revenge [revénʒ]. **I.** *va.* y *vn.* vengar, vindicar, vengarse de. **II.** *s.* venganza.—**revengeful** [-ful], *a.* vengativo.—**revengefully** [-i], *adv.* vengativamente.—**revengefulness** [-nes], *s.* calidad de vengativo, carácter vengativo.

revenue [réveniu], *s.* rentas públicas, ingresos del Erario; (com.) renta; rédito; entrada, ingreso, provento; recompensa, beneficio.—**r. cutter,** guardacostas.—**r. officer,** aduanero, empleado de aduana.

reverberant [revǽrbœrant], *a.* repercusivo; retumbante, resonante.—**reverberate** [revǽrbœreit], *va.* y *vn.* retumbar, repercutir, reverberar, reflejar.—**reverberation** [-éishʊn], *s.* eco, repercusión; reverberación, reflexión.—**reverberator** [-éitœr], *s.* reverberador, reverbero.

reverberatory [revǽrbœratori]. **I.** *a* de reverbero, que reverbera o refleja.—*s.* **r.** (furnace), horno de reverbero.

revere [revíœr], *va.* reverenciar, venerar.

reverence [réverens]. **I.** *s.* reverencia, veneración; reverencia (inclinación del cuerpo); (igl.) Reverencia (tratamiento). **II.** *va.* reverenciar, venerar.

reverend [révœrend], *a.* reverendo, venerable; (igl.) Reverendo (tratamiento).

reverent [révœrent], *a.* reverente.—**reverently** [-li], *adv.* reverentemente.

reverential [révœrénshal], *a.* reverencial, respetuoso. —**reverentially** [-li], *adv.* con reverencia, respetuosamente.

reverie [révœri], *s.* ensueño; embelesamiento, arrobamiento; (mús.) fantasía.

reversal [rivǽrsal], *s.* reversión; inversión; (for.) revocación; (ópt.) cambio de una línea obscura en una brillante y viceversa.

reverse [rivǽrs]. **I.** *va.* trastrocar, invertir; trastornar; revocar, anular; (mec.) invertir, dar contravapor. **II.** *vn.* invertirse; volver (a un estado anterior). **III.** *a.* inverso, invertido; opuesto, contrario; (mec.) de inversión, marcha atrás contramarcha.—**r. curve,** (f. c.) curva en S.—**r. gear,** (mec.) mecanismo de marcha atrás.—**r. lever,** palanca de contramarcha.—**r. operation,** (mat.) operación inversa.—**r. running,** marcha hacia atrás.—**r. turn,** (aer.) maniobra de cambio de dirección. **IV.** *s.* lo contrario, lo opuesto; respaldo, dorso, reverso; reversión, inversión; contratiempo, revés, descalabro.

reversed [rivǽrsed], *a.* = REVERSE; invertido, inverso.—**r. ogee,** (arq.) gola reversa.

reversely [-li], *adv.* al revés.

reverseless [-les], *a.* que no se puede trastrocar o invertir, irreversible.

reversible [-ibœl]. **I.** *a.* volvible, versátil; (mec.) reversible; de vaivén; de dos caras; (for.) revocable. **II.** *s.* (tej.) género de dos caras.

reversing [rivǽrsing], *a.* y *ger.* of TO REVERSE; de inversión, de cambio de marcha, etc. **V.** REVERSE, *va.* y *a.*

reversion [-shʊn], *s.* reversión; atavismo; (for.) reversión; futura, derecho de sucesión.

reversionary [-œri], *a.* (for.) reversible.

reversioner [-œr], *s.* el que tiene derecho de reversión.

revert [revǽrt], *vn.* retroceder, volver, resurtir, recudir; (biol.) saltar atrás; (for.) revertir.

revertible [revǽrtibœl], *a.* reversible.

revery, *s.* = REVERIE.

revest [rivést], *va.* revestir; restablecer.

revet [revét], *va.* (alb.) revestir.

revetment [revétmœnt], *s.* (alb.) revestimiento.

review [riviú]. **I.** *va.* rever, remirar; revisar; censurar, escribir una crítica o una síntesis de (un libro, etc.); criticar, analizar; (mil.) revistar, pasar revista a. **II.** *vn.* escribir una revista. **III.** *s.* exámen, análisis; revista, censura, juicio crítico; revista (publicación periódica); (mil.) revista, parada; (for.) revisión.

reviewer [riviúœr], *s.* crítico, revistero; revisor; examinador, inspector.

revile [riváil], *va.* denigrar, vilipendiar.—**revilement** [-mœnt], *s.* denuesto, vilipendio.—**reviler** [-œr], *s.* vilipendiador, denostador.—**revilingly** [-ingli], *adv.* denigrantemente, injuriosamente.

revisal [riváisal], *s.* revista, revisión.

revise [riváis]. **I.** *va.* revisar, rever, releer, repasar; corregir, enmendar.—**revised,** revisado, corregido.—**Revised Version,** traducción corregida de la Biblia (hecha en los años 1870 a 1884). **II.** *s.* revista, revisión; (impr.) segunda prueba.

reviser, revisor [riváisœr], *s.* revisor; (impr.) corrector de pruebas.

revision [reviýun], *s.* revisión; (impr.) corrección de pruebas.

revisit [revísit], *va.* volver a visitar.

revisory [reváisori], *s.* revisor.

revival [riváival], *s.* renacimiento, restauración, restablecimiento; (teat.) representación de obras antiguas; despertamiento religioso.—**revivalist** [-ist], *s.* predicador protestante que recorre un país para despertar la fe.

revive [reváiv]. **I.** *va.* hacer revivir, revivificar; restablecer, restaurar; despertar, avivar; hacer recordar, despertar la memoria. **II.** *vn.* revivir; restablecerse, reanimarse; volver en sí, recobrar los sentidos; renacer.

reviver [reváivœr], *s.* vivificador.

revivification [rivívifikéiŝhʊn], *s.* vivificación, revivificación.

revivify [rivívifai]. **I.** *va.* revivificar, hacer revivir. **II.** *vn.* restablecerse, revivir.

revocable [révocabœl], *a.* revocable.—**revocableness** [-nes], *s.* calidad de revocable.

revocation [-kéiŝhʊn], *s.* revocación; derogación.

revoke [revóukj. **I.** *va.* revocar, derogar, anular. **II.** *vn.* en los juegos de naipes, hacer un renuncio.

revolt [revólt]. **I.** *vn.* rebelarse, sublevarse, amotinarse; sentir repugnancia o repulsión. **II.** *va.* rebelar, sublevar; causar asco o repugnancia; chocar, indignar. **III.** *s.* sublevación, rebelión.—**revolter** [-œr], *s.* rebelde, sublevado.

revolting [revólting], *a.* odioso; repugnante, asqueroso.

revolute [révolut (*o* -liut)], *a.* (bot.) enrollado hacia atrás.

revolution [révoliúŝhʊn], *s.* revolución; (mec.) revolución, vuelta.—**revolutionary** [-œri], *a.* y *s.* revolucionario.—**revolutionist** [-ist], *s.* revolucionario.—**revolutionize** [-aiŝ], *va.* revolucionar.

revolvable [révólvabœl], *a.* giratorio.

revolve [revólv]. **I.** *vn.* girar, dar vueltas; moverse en ciclos, suceder periódicamente; ser considerado bajo todos los aspectos. **II.** *va.* voltear, hacer girar o rodar; revolver (en la cabeza), pensar, meditar acerca de.

revolver [revólvœr], *s.* (arm.) revólver.

revolving [revólving], *a.* giratorio.—**r. chair**, silla giratoria.—**r. light**, luz giratoria.

revue [reviú], *s.* (tea.) sainete de sucesos actuales o recientes.

revulsion [revúlŝhʊn], *s.* cambio repentino, reacción; removimiento, apartamiento, retroceso; reculada; (med.) revulsión, reacción.

revulsive [-siv], *a.* (med.) revulsivo, revulsorio.

reward [riuórd]. **I.** *va.* premiar, galardonar, recompensar. **II.** *s.* premio, recompensa, galardón; merecido; pago, remuneración, gratificación.—**rewardable** [-abœl], *a.* remunerable, digno de premio.—**rewarder** [-œr], *s.* premiador, remunerador.

reweigh [riuiéi], *va.* (com.) repesar.

reynard [réinard], *s.* (zool.) zorro.

Rhamnaceæ [ræmnéisii], *s. pl.* (bot.) rámneas.—**rhamnaceous** [-ŝhʊs], *a.* rámneo.

rhapontic [rapóntic], *s.* (bot.) rapóntico.

rhapsodist [répsodist], *s.* autor de rapsodias; rapsoda.—**rhapsodize** [-daiŝ], *va.* y *vn.* cantar o recitar rapsodias.—**rhapsody** [-di], *s.* rapsodia.

rhea [ría], *s.* (orn.) avestruz de la América del Sur.

Rhenish [réniŝh]. **I.** *a.* renano. **II.** *s.* vino del Rin.

rheometer [reómetœr], *s.* reómetro.

rheophore [ríofor], *s.* (elec.) reóforo.

rheostat [ríostæt], *s.* (elec.) reóstato.

rheostatic [-ic], *a.* reostático.

rhetoric [rétoric], *s.* retórica.—**rhetorical** [retórical], *a.* retórico.—**rhetorically** [-i], *adv.* retóricamente.—**rhetorician** [rétoriŝhan], *s.* retórico.

rheum(a [rum(a], *s.* (med.) reuma, corrimiento, fluxión.

rheumatic [ruméetic], *a.* reumático.

rheumatism [rúmatiŝm], *s.* (med.) reumatismo.

rheumatoid [-toid], *a.* reumatismoso; reumático.

rheumides [rúmaids], *s.* (med.) reumátide.

rhinitis [raináitis *o* rinítis], *s.* (med.) coriza, romadizo, catarro nasal.

rhinoceri(c)al [rainoséri(c)al], **rhinocerotic** [rainoserótic], *a.* rinoceróntico.

rhinoceros [rainóseros], *s.* (zool.) rinoceronte.

rhinology [rainóloɣi], *s.* ciencia de la nariz y sus enfermedades.

rhinoplastic [ráinolpǽstic], *a.* (cir.) rinoplástico, —**rhinoplasty** [-ti], *s.* (med.) rinoplastia.

rhinoscope [-scoup], *s.* rinoscopio.

rhizocarpic [ráiŝocárpic], **rhizocarpous** [-pʊs], *a.* (bot.) rizocárpeo.

rhizome, rhizoma [ráiŝom, raiŝóma], *s.* (bot.) rizoma.

rhizopod [ráiŝopod], *s.* animal rizópodo.

Rhodes grass [róudŝ græs], *s.* pasto Rhodes o yerba Rhodes.

rhodic [ródic], *a.* (quím.) ródico.—**rhodium** [ródiʊm], *s.* (quím.) rodio.

rhododendron [rododéndron], *s.* (bot.) rododendro.

rhodonite [ródonait], *s.* (min.) espato mangánico.

rhomb(us [rómb(ʊs], *s.* (geom.) rombo; (blas.) losange.

rhombic [rómbic], *a.* rombal.

rhombohedron [rómbojídron], *s.* (geom.) romboedro.

rhomboid [rómboid], *s.* (geom.) romboide.

rhomboidal [rombóidal], *a.* romboidal.

rhumb [rʊmb], *s.* (mar.) rumbo.

rhubarb [rúbarb], *s.* (farm.) ruibarbo; (bot.) ruipóntico o rapóntico.

rhyme, rhymer, etc. = RIME. RIMER, etc.

rhythm [riŝm], *s.* ritmo, cadencia; armonía; (med.) periodicidad.—**rhythmic(al** [-mic(al], *a.* rítmico.—**rhythmically** [-i], *adv.* ritmicamente.

rialto [riálto], *s.* mercado, lonja; (E. U.) centro teatral en Nueva York.

rib. I. *s.* costilla; (arq.) faja, listón, nervio, nervadura; cabrio, viga de tejado; arco; resalte, saliente; (mar.) cuaderna; varilla (de paraguas); tirante, varenga de hierro; (mec.) pestaña, reborde; (cost.) vivo; (bot.) costilla, nervadura de las hojas; (fam.) costilla, la mujer propia.—**r. grass,** (bot.) = RIBWORT.—**ribs of a ship,** (mar.) costillaje. **II.** *va.* marcar con rayas, listones o filetes; afianzar con rebordes o pestañas; (cost.) hacer un vivo.

ribald [ríbalq]. **I.** *a.* obsceno, lascivo, ribaldo. **II.** *s.* persona impúdica.

ribaldry [ríbaldri], *s.* ribaldería, cinismo.

riband [ríband], *s.* (ant.) = RIBBON.

ribbon [ríbʊn]. **I.** *s.* cinta, listón, coionia; tira, banda, faja; galón.—*pl.* (fam.) riendas; perifollos.—**r. grass,** (bot.) alpiste. **II.** *va.* encintar. **III.** *a.* hecho de cinta; de forma de cinta.

ribwort [ríbuœrt], *s.* (bot.) llantén.

rice [ráis], *s.* (bot.) arroz.—**r. paper,** papel de paja de arroz; papel de China.

ricebird [-bœrd], *s.* (orn.) = REEDBIRD.

ricefield [-fild], *s.* arrozal.

rich [rich], *a.* rico; vivo (color, etc.); muy sazonado, muy dulce, muy fuerte, etc.; fértil; (fam.) muy divertido; risible, ridículo.

riches [rícheŝ], *s. pl.* riqueza, riquezas.

richly [ríchli], *adv.* ricamente; copiosamente.

richness [ríchnes], *s.* riqueza; suntuosidad; fertilidad; abundancia; suculencia, crasitud.

ricinic [risínic], **ricinoleic** [risínoliic], *a.* (quím.) ricinólico.

rick [ric]. **I.** *s.* niara, fascal, hacina. **II.** *va.* hacer niaras o hacinas de.

rickets [ríkets], *s.* (med.) raquitis, raquitismo.

rickety [ríketi], *a.* desvencijado, destartalado; (med.) raquítico.

ricochet [ricoŝhé]. **I.** *va.* hacer fuego de rebote. **II.** *vn.* rebotar. **III.** *s.* (art.) fuego de rebote.

rictus [ríctus], *s.* ensanche de la boca (en las aves, etc.); esquinas de la boca.

rid, *va.* (*pp.* y *pret.* RID) desembarazar, librar, quitar de encima, zafar.—**to r. one's self of, to get r. of,** salir, desembarazarse, zafarse, deshacerse de.—**to be r. of,** estar libre o exento de.

riddance [rídans], *s.* libramiento o preservación de un mal, expulsión o alejamiento; zafada.

ridden [rídœn], *pp.* de TO RIDE.

riddle [rídœl]. **I.** *s.* acertijo, enigma, adivinanza; busilis, quisicosa; misterio; criba o garbillo. **II.** *va.* resolver, adivinar; cribar, garbillar; acribillar. **III.** *vn.* hablar enigmáticamente.

riddler [rídlœr], *s.* garbillador.

ride [ráid]. **I.** *va.* (*pret.* RODE: *pp.* RIDDEN) cabalgar, correr, dirigir o manejar (un caballo, etc.); ir montado en o sobre; hender o surcar (las olas).—**to r. down**, pasar por encima de, pisotear, derribar y hollar (como en un ataque de caballería).—**to r. out**, hacer frente a, resistir bien (el viento).—**to r. shank's mare**, ir a pie. —**to r. the goat**, (fam.) ser iniciado (en sociedad secreta). **II.** *vn.* montar a caballo, cabalgar; pasear a caballo o en carruaje; ir en coche; flotar; (mar.) estar fondeado; (mec.) rodar, tener juego, funcionar.—**to r. down**, echar el caballo encima; pisotear; tratar con arrogancia.—**to r. easy**, mantenerse bien al ancla, marchar suavemente.— **to r. horseback**, montar a caballo.—**to r. over**, pasar por encima de; mandar con arrogancia.— **to r. roughshod** (a menudo con *over*) obrar con indiferencia del prójimo, pisoteando los derechos ajenos. **III.** *s.* paseo a caballo o en coche; viaje a caballo o en vehículo; camino de herradura.

rider [ráidœr], *s.* caballero, cabalgador, jinete; persona que va en coche, bicicleta, etc.; picador, amansador; cosa que va montada sobre otra; hojuela pegada a un documento; aditamento, añadidura o adición a un proyecto de ley; (mar.) sobreplán, cochinata.

ridge [riy]. **I.** *va.* (agr.) alomar; formar lomos o camellones; acanalar, arrugar, encabalgar. **II.** *vn.* tener lomos o camellones. **III.** *s.* cerro, colina, cordillera, serranía; escollo, arrecife; arruga, costurón; (agr.) caballón, lomo, camellón; (arq.) caballete del tejado.—**ridges of a horse's mouth**, arrugas en el paladar de un caballo.—**r. tile**, teja acanalada.

ridgebeam [ríybím], **ridgepiece** [-pís], **ridgeplate** [-pléit], **ridgepole** [-póul], *s.* (arq.) parhilera.

ridgerope [-róup], *s.* (mar.) cuerda de toldo.

ridgy [ríyi], *a.* acanalado.

ridicule [rídikiul]. **I.** *s.* ridículo. **II.** *va.* ridiculizar, poner en ridículo.

ridiculous [ridíkiulus], *a.* ridículo.—**ridiculously** [-li], *adv.* ridículamente.—**ridiculousness** [-nes], *s.* calidad de ridículo, ridiculez.

riding [ráiding], *s.* paseo a caballo o en coche; cabalgata; camino de herradura; equitación; manejo; movimiento, marcha (de un vehículo). —**r. cloak, r. coat**, redingote.—**r. habit**, traje de amazona.—**r. hood**, capirote, capotín, capuchón. —**r. horse**, caballo de silla.—**r. party**, partida de cabalgata.—**r. rod** = R. WHIP.—**r. school**, picadero, escuela de equitación.—**r. whip**, látigo de montar.

rifacimento [rifáchiménto], *s.* rehacimiento; adaptación.

rife [ráif], *a.* abundante, numeroso; corriente, reinante; (con **with**) lleno de.—**rifely** [-li], *adv.* abundantemente.—**rifeness** [-nes], *s.* abundancia.

riffle [rífœl], *s.* (min.) ranura en el fondo de una gamella.

riffler [ríflœr], *s.* escofina encorvada.

riffraff [rífrœf], *s.* gentuza, canalla; desecho, desperdicio, ripio.

rifle [ráifœl]. **I.** *va.* robar, pillar; (arti.) arrebatar; rayar (un arma); hacer girar un proyectil. **II.** *s.* (arm.) rifle; espiral de rifle; piedra de afilar guadañas.—**r. pits**, pozos para rifleros.—**r. shot**, fusilazo; tiro de fusil.

rifleman [ráifœlman], *s.* riflero.

rifler [ráifœr], *s.* saqueador, salteador.

rift. **I.** *s.* hendedura, rendija, grieta, reventón; cuarteadura; desemboque, vado; ola que lame la playa. **II.** *va.* hender, dividir. **III.** *vn.* reventar; partirse.

rig. **I.** *va.* (con **out**) ataviar, guarnir, adornar; (con **out** o **up**) aparejar, equipar; (mar.) enjarciar. **II.** *s.* (mar.) aparejo; (fam.) traje; tren de carruaje o caballos: apresto, equipo; aparato de pesca; burla, mala partida.

rigadoon [rigadún], *s.* (danz.) rigodón.

rigger [rígœr], *s.* (mar.) aparejador.

rigging [ríguing], *s.* (mar.) aparejo, cordaje, jarcia, enjarciadura; (mec.) aparejo (de poleas); equipo de arrastre (de trozas).

right [ráit]. **I.** *a.* recto, justo, equitativo; propio, conveniente; debido; correcto; fundado; ver-

dadero, cierto, real, genuino, legal, legítimo; derecho, directo, en línea recta; ordenado, ajustado; derecho (lado, mano); sano; cuerdo; derecho (contrario de revés en las telas); que conviene, que se busca, que se quiere (a veces no se traduce, o se cambia el giro: *this is the right man*, éste es el hombre [que se busca]; éste es el hombre que se necesita; éste es el hombre adecuado, etc.).—**r. and left**, a diestra y siniestra.—**r. angle** ángulo recto.—**r. ascension**, (astr.) ascensión recta.—**r. bower**, el mayor triunfo en el juego de *euchre*.—**r.-hand**, de la mano derecha.—**r.-hand drive**, (aut.) conducción a la derecha.—**r.-hand man**, (fam.) hombre de confianza, brazo derecho (fig.), gran palanca.—**r. line**, línea recta.—**r. or wrong**, a tuertas o a derechas; con razón o sin ella; bueno o malo.—**r. side**, lado derecho; lado de afuera, cara. —**r. triangle**, triángulo rectángulo.—**it is r.**, está bien; es justo.—**to be r.**, tener razón.—**II.** *interj.* ¡bien! ¡bueno! **III.** *adv.* rectamente, justamente; exactamente, perfectamente, precisamente; bien; correctamente; debidamente; derechamente, en derechura; muy; inmediatamente, al instante, ahora mismo; mismo (vg. *right here*, aquí mismo).—**r. about**, vuelta a retaguardia; despedida.—**r. along**, sin interrupción, sin cesar; derecho, sin torcer.—**r. angled**, rectangular, rectángulo.—**r.-angled triangle**, triángulo rectángulo.—**r. away**, luego, ya, inmediatamente.—**r. down**, sin rodeos; sin demora.—**r.-handed**, derecho (que usa la mano derecha); diestro, mañoso, hábil; de movimiento a la derecha, o de izquierda a derecha.— **r.-handed screw**, tornillo de rosca a la derecha. —**R. Honorable**, honorabilísimo, muy honorable. —**r.-minded**, recto, honrado.—**r. now, r. off**, al punto, inmediatamente.—**r. reverend**, reverendísimo. **IV.** *s.* derecho; justicia; rectitud; propiedad, dominio, título; poder, autoridad; privilegio, prerrogativa; la diestra, la derecha (lo opuesto a la izquierda).—**r. of search, r. of visit**, (mar.) derecho de visita.—**r. of way**, (for.) servidumbre de paso; derecho a la vía; (f. c.) servidumbre de vía. —**of r.**, de derecho, según derecho.—**on the r.**, a la derecha.—**to be in the r.**, tener razón.—**to have a r.**, tener derecho; (fam.) tener obligación. —**to rights**, derechamente, derecho, sin tocar.— **to the r.**, a la derecha. **V.** *va.* hacer justicia; enderezar, ajustar, corregir; (mar.) adrizar.—**to r. a wrong**, enderezar un entuerto, corregir un abuso.

righteous [ráichús], *a.* justo, recto, virtuoso.— **righteously** [-li], *adv.* virtuosamente, rectamente. —**righteousness** [-nes], *s.* rectitud, virtud.

righter [ráitœr], *s.* enderezador de tuertos o agravios.

rightful [-ful], *a.* legítimo; recto.—**rightfully** [-li], *adv.* legítimamente, rectamente, justamente.— **rightfulness** [-nes], *s.* virtud, justicia, rectitud.

rightly [ráitli], *adv.* rectamente, justamente; bien, como se debe; exactamente, directamente.

rightness [-nes], *s.* rectitud, justicia; derechura; propiedad.

rigid [ríyid], *a.* rígido.—**rigidity** [riyíditi], **rigidness** [ríyidnes], *s.* rigidez.—**rigidly** [ríyidli], *adv.* rígidamente.

rigmarole [rigmaról], *s.* jerigonza, galimatías.

rigo(u)r [rígœr], *s.* rigor, inflexibilidad; inclemencia; severidad, austeridad; tesón, terquedad; rigor, exactitud; [ráigœr o rígœr] (med.) escalofrío.—**r. mortis**, rigor de la muerte, rigidez cadavérica.

rigorism [rígœrism], *s.* rigorismo.

rigorist [-ist], *s.* rigorista.

rigorous [-us], *a.* rigoroso; estricto, severo.— **rigorously** [-li], *adv.* rigorosamente, severamente. —**rigorousness** [rígœrusnes], *s.* severidad, rigor.

rile [ráil], *va.* (fam.) sulfurar, encolerizar.

rill [ril] *s.* riachuelo, arroyuelo.

rillet [rílet], *s.* arroyuelo, reguero.

rim, *s.* canto, borde, margen, orilla; llanta, aro; cerco, reborde, pestaña; ceja.—**r. nut**, (aut.) tuerca de válvula de neumático.—**r. of the belly**, peritoneo.

rime, rhyme [ráim]. **I.** *s.* rima, consonancia, consonante; verso; poesía; escarcha; grieta, hendedura, resquicio; peldaño de escala.—

without r. or reason, sin ton ni son. **II.** *va.* poner en verso; influir en, o mover, con versos; emplear como consonante; rimar. **III.** *vn.* rimar, consonar; corresponder, armonizarse.

rimer [ráimœr], **rimester** [ráimstœr], *s.* rimador, versificador; (carp.) avellanador.

rimose [ráimos *o* raimóus], **rimous** [ráimʊs], *a.* hendido, rajado, cuarteado.

rimple [rímpœl], *va.* arrugar. *V.* RUMPLE.

rimy [ráimi], *a.* escarchado.

rind [ráind]. **I.** *s.* corteza, pellejo, cuero, hollejo. **II.** *va.* descortezar, mondar, pelar, deshollejar.

rinderpest [ríndœrpest], *s.* morriña.

ring. I. *s.* anillo, argolla, anilla; (joy.) sortija, anillo; circo, arena, liza; corro o corrillo de gente; camarilla; ojera; campaneo, tañido o repique de campanas; juego de campanas; campanilleo, toque de campanilla; sonido metálico; rumor, clamor, estruendo; (mar.) arganeo, virola con chaveta.—**r. finger,** dedo anular.—**r. frame,** hiladera continua de anillo.—**r. gage,** o **gauge,** calibre anular; (joy.) calibre para anillos.— **r.-shaped,** anular.—**r. spindle,** huso de hiladera continua de anillo.—**r. spinner** = R. FRAME. **II.** *va.* (*pp.* y *pret.* RINGED) rodear, circundar; poner un anillo a, anillar, ensortijar; adornar con anillos. (hort.) quitar una tira circular de corteza. **III.** *vn.* moverse en círculo o en espiral; formar círculo. **IV.** *va.* (*pret.* RANG, a veces RUNG; *pp.* RUNG) tocar, tañer, repicar (campanas); tocar (timbre o campanilla); anunciar, proclamar, celebrar (con repique de campanas); repetir, reiterar; llamar, convocar, por medio de una campana.—**to r. the bells in a peal,** tocar las campanas a vuelo. **V.** *vn.* sonar, tañer; retumbar, resonar; zumbar los oídos.

ringbolt [ríngbóult], *s.* cáncamo; armella.

ringbone [-bóun], *s.* (vet.) sobrehueso de caballo.

ringdove [-dv́v], *s.* paloma torcaz, zurita o zorita.

ringed [ríngd], *a.* que lleva anillo de matrimonio; comprometido (a casarse); (zool.) anillado.

ringent [rínvœnt], *a.* (bot.) bostezante.

ringer [ríngœr], *s.* campanero.

ringing [rínguing]. **I.** *a.* resonante, retumbante. **II.** *s.* campaneo, repique, retintín.

ringleader [rínglídœr], *s.* cabecilla, abanderizador, promotor.

ringlet [rínglet], *s.* anillejo, círculo; sortija, bucle, rizo; (Cuba) crespo.

ringtail [ríngteil], *s.* (orn.) especie de milano.

ringworm [ríngœrm], *s.* (med.) empeine, culebrilla, serpigo.

rink [rink], *s.* patinadero; sala de patinar; bolera.

rinse [rins], *va.* lavar, limpiar, deslavar, enjuagar, aclarar.

rinser [rínsœr], *s.* lavandero.

rinsing [rínsing], *s.* enjuagadura, escurridura, deslavadura.

riot [ráiʊt]. **I.** *s.* tumulto, sedición; pelotera; motín, asonada, desorden, exceso; borrachera. **II.** *vn.* armar motines.

rioter [ráivetœr], *s.* alborotador; amotinado (fam.) bullanguero, jaranero, libertino.

riotous [ráiʊtʊs], *a.* sedicioso, faccioso; desenfrenado; desarreglado; bullicioso.—**riotously** [-li], *adv.* disolutamente; bulliciosamente.—**riotousness** [-nes], *s.* disolución; desenfreno, desorden.

rip. I. *va.* (con **up, open** o **off**) rasgar, romper; descoser, soltar; (con **out** o **away**) cortar, arrancar, destripar, destrozar; (con **up**) sondear o estudiar a fondo, descubrir; (carp.) aserrar, hilar, linear.—**to r. off a plank,** (mar.) descoser un tablón.—**to r. out an oath,** jurar con violencia, jurar a la ligera, blasfemar. **II.** *vn.* rasgarse, henderse, romperse. **III.** *s.* laceración, rasgadura, rasgón.

riparian [raipérian], *a.* ribereño.—**riparious** [-ʊs], *a.* (bot. y zool.) ribereño.

ripe [ráip], *a.* maduro, sazonado; hecho, acabado; pronto, preparado, a propósito; rosado, colorado.

ripen [ráipœn], *va.* y *vn.* madurar, sazonar.

ripely [ráipli], *adv.* maduramente; a propósito, en sazón.

ripeness [ráipnes], *s.* madurez, sazón.

ripper [rípœr], *s.* rasgador.

ripping [ríping], *s.* rasgadura; deshiladura, descosedura.—**r. iron,** (mar.) descalcador.—**r. line,** (aer.) cabo de desgarre, con que se maneja la faja de desgarre.—**r. panel,** (aer.) faja de desgarre (es un parche que puede rasgarse prontamente).

ripple. I. *va.* rizar, ondear; desgargolar el cáñamo. **II.** *vn.* agitarse, rizarse la superficie del agua; murmurar. **III.** *s.* escarceo, onda, rizo (del agua); murmullo; carda o peine para desgargolar.

riprap [ríprœp]. **I.** *s.* piedras sueltas; cimiento de piedras sueltas. **II.** *va.* poner piedras sueltas sobre; reforzar con piedras sueltas.

ripsaw [-só], *s.* sierra para corte longitudinal de madera.

rise [ráis]. **I.** *vn.* (*pret.* ROSE: *pp.* RISEN) ascender, subir, elevarse, remontarse; levantarse, ponerse en pie; levantarse (de la cama); suspender una sesión; salir (el sol); nacer, salir o brotar (las plantas o los manantiales); levantarse, sublevarse; surgir, aparecer, presentarse; sobrevenir, armarse, suscitarse (una disputa, etc.); medrar, mejorar de posición; hincharse, aumentar de volumen; encarecerse, subir (el precio); resucitar.—**to r. to one's feet,** ponerse en pie, levantarse. **II.** *s.* ascensión, elevación; levantamiento; crecimiento o desarrollo; cuesta, subida; nacimiento (de un manantial); altura, eminencia; inclinación, pendiente: salida (de un astro); encarecimiento, subida, alza (de precios); crecida, creciente (de un río, etc.); fuente, principio, origen, manantial, causa: adelantamiento, medro; ascenso; elevación de la voz; (arq.) flecha de un arco; (carp.) altura de una contrahuella.—**r. of a hill,** pendiente de una colina.—**r. of ground,** elevación del terreno.—**r. of mercury, of temperature,** subida del mercurio o de la temperatura.

risen, *pp.* de TO RISE.

riser [ráisœr], *s.* el que se levanta; (carp.) contrahuella; solivador; cosa que sirve para elevar; (arq.) tubería vertical; (elec.) conductor de un piso a otro u otros; tubo ascendente. (fund.) = FEEDHEAD; respiradero.

risibility [rísibiliti], *s.* risibilidad.

risible [rísibœl], *a.* risible.

rising [ráising]. **I.** *a.* naciente; creciente; ascendiente; que se levanta; saliente; próspero. **II.** *s.* ascenso, subida; resurrección; renacimiento; levantada; levantamiento, insurrección; (astr.) orto, salida; acto de levantarse (una sesión, una persona); levadura, fermento; prominencia o protuberancia; lobanillo, lupia.

risk. I. *s.* riesgo, peligro; en el juego, albur. **II.** *va.* arriesgar, aventurar, exponer.

risky [ríski], *a.* peligroso, arriesgado; imprudente, temerario.

risorial [raisórial], *a.* reidor; risible.

rite [ráit], *s.* rito, ceremonia.

ritornelle [rítornél], *s.* (mús.) retornelo.

ritual [rítiual], *a.* y *s.* ritual, ceremonial.

ritualism [-ism], *s.* ritualismo; ritualidad.— **ritualist** [-ist], *a.* y *s.* ritualista.—**ritualistic** [-istic], *a.* ritualista.—**ritually** [-li], *adv.* según el ritual, conforme a los ritos, de rúbrica.

rival [ráival]. **I.** *s.* rival. **II.** *a.* émulo, competidor, opuesto. **III.** *va.* emular; competir con, rivalizar con. **IV.** *va.* rivalizar.—**rivalry** [-ri], *s.* rivalidad.

rive [ráiv]. **I.** *va.* (*pret.* RIVED: *pp.* RIVED o RIVEN) rajar, hender. **II.** *vn.* henderse.

river [rívœr]. **I.** *s.* río.—**r. basin,** hoya o cuenca de río.—**r. bed,** lecho, álveo, madre de un río.—**r. dragon,** cocodrilo.—**r. horse,** hipopótamo.— **down (the) r.,** río abajo.—**up (the) r.,** río arriba.

riverside [rívœrsaid], *s.* orilla o margen de un río; ribera.

rivet [rívet]. **I.** *s.* remache, roblón.—**r. knob,** embutidera. **II.** *va.* remachar; (fig.) asegurar, afianzar.

rivet(t)ing [ríveting], *s.* remachado, remache.

rivulet [ríviulet], *s.* riachuelo, arroyo.

roach [róuch], *s.* (ict.) escarcho; (ent.) cucaracha.

---

road [róud], *s.* camino, vía; carretera (el significado general en los países civilizados).—*pl.* rada; fondeadero.—**r. agent**, (fam.) salteador.— **r. house**, fonda de paseantes.—**r. metal**, material (grava, escorias, etc.) para caminos.—**r. roller**, rodillo (para caminos).—**r. runner**, (orn.) cuchillo de tierra.—**to be on the r.**, viajar de pueblo en pueblo en el ejercicio de una profesión (apl. esp. a los agentes viajeros y a las compañías cómicas).

roadbed [-béd], *s.* firme (de camino o carretera); (f. c.) balasto, asiento de los durmientes.

roadstead [róudsted], *s.* rada, fondeadero.

roadster [róudstœr], *s.* caballo o bicicleta de aguante; (aut.) roadster.

roadway [róduéi], *s.* carretera, calzada (apl. esp. a la parte central o de tráfico).

roam [róum], *va.* y *vn.* vagar, andar errante.

roamer [róumœr], *s.* vago, vagabundo.

roan [róun]. **I.** *a.* roano o ruano, rosillo, sabino. **II.** *s.* caballo ruano; color ruano; badana de color ruano.

roar [róœr]. **I.** *vn.* rugir, bramar. **II.** *s.* rugido, bramido; estruendo.

roarer [róœrœr], *s.* bramador.

roaring [róring]. **I.** *a.* rugiente, bramador; ruidoso; (fam.) magnífico, superlativo, inmenso. **II.** *s.* (vet.) ronquido.

roast [róust]. **I.** *va.* (coc.) asar; tostar; calcinar; (fam.) hablar mal de; ridiculizar.—**to r. coffee**, tostar café. **II.** *a.* asado; tostado.—**r. beef**, carne de vaca asada, rosbif.—**r. meat**, asado; carne asada o buena para asar.

roaster [róustœr], *s.* cocinero que asa; asador, tostador; pollo o lechón propio para asar.

roasting [róusting]. **I.** *a.* acción de asar; tostadura; (metal.) torrefacción; calcinación, cocción; (fam.) desolladura, despellejada (fig.) **II.** *a.* de asar; de calcinar; de cocción.

rob [rob], *va.* y *vn.* robar.—**to r. one of**, robar a uno (*John robbed me of my money*, Juan me robó mi dinero).

robalo [róbalo], *s.* (ict.) róbalo.

robber [róbœr], *s.* ladrón; salteador.

robbery [róbœri], *s.* robo.

robe [róub]. **I.** *s.* manto; túnico o túnica; ropón; ropaje, toga, traje talar; corte de vestido; manta de coche.—**r. of state**, traje de ceremonia. —**the (long) r.**, la curia. **II.** *va.* vestir de gala o de ceremonia; vestir, ataviar. **III.** *vn.* vestirse, ponerse traje; cubrirse.

robin [róbin], *s.* (orn.) pechicolorado, petirrojo.

roborant [róborant], *a.* roborante, roborativo.

robust [robúst], *a.* robusto, vigoroso, fuerte.

robustness [robústnes], *s.* robustez.

roc [roc, ruc], *s.* rocho, ruc.

rochet [róchet], *s.* (igl.) roquete.

rock [roc]. **I.** *s.* roca, peña, peñasco; arrecife, escollo, laja.—**r. alum (roche alum)**, alumbre de roca, jebe.—**r. bass**, (ict.) papagayo.—**r. bound**, rodeado de peñascos.—**r.-bottom**, *s.* el fondo, lo más profundo; *a.* mínimo, bajísimo.—**r. sugar**, azúcar cande.—**r. crusher**, triturador, bocarte.— **r. crystal**, cristal de roca, cuarzo.—**r. dove**, paloma de las rocas.—**r. drill**, perforadora de rocas.— **r. oil**, petróleo.—**r. quartz**, cristal de roca.—**r. salt**, sal de piedra, o gema.—**r. water**, agua viva de roca. **II.** *va.* mecer, cunear, balancear; arrullar; calmar, sosegar. **III.** *vn.* mecerse, bambolear, oscilar.

rocker [rókœr], *s.* cualquier cosa que mece o se mece; cuna; columpio; cunera; mecedora (silla); soportes del asiento de una mecedora; (mec.) balancín; eje oscilante en sus cojinetes.—**r. arm**, brazo o palanca oscilante.—**r. cam**, leva oscilante.

rocket [róket], *s.* cohete, volador; (bot.) oruga, jaramago, hespéride.

rockiness [rókines], *s.* abundancia de rocas; naturaleza roqueña.

rocking [róking]. **I.** *a.* mecedor; oscilante.— **r. chair**, mecedora, (Cuba) columpio.—**r. horse**, caballo mecedor, caballico.—**r. shaft** = ROCK-SHAFT.—**r. valve**, válvula oscilante. **II.** *s.* balance, balanceo.

rockrose [rócrróus], *s.* (bot.) estepa, cisto, cergazo.

rockshaft [-shæft], *s.* eje que oscila en sus cojinetes.

rockwork [rócuœrc], *s.* gruta artificial.

rocky [róki], *a.* peñascoso, roqueño, roquero, pedregoso, pétreo, duro, endurecido.—**R. Mountains**, Montes Rocallosos, Montañas Roqueñas.

rococo [rocóco], *a.* y *s.* churrigueresco.

rod, *s.* vara, varilla; cetro; bastón de mando; vara de alcalde o de alguacil; disciplinas; varilla de virtudes; caña de pescar; varilla o barra de cortina; vara de medir; pértica (medida); jalón; (mec.) vástago, barra, varilla; azote; disciplina, castigo; alcurnia, linaje; raza, tribu.

rode [róud], *pret.* de TO RIDE.

rodent [ródœnt], *a.* y *s.* (zool.) roedor.

rodman [ródmæn], *s.* (top.) jalonero.

rodomontade [ródomontéid]. **I.** *s.* bravata, baladronada, fanfarronada. **II.** *vn.* baladronear, fanfarronear, bravear.

roe [róu], *s.* (zool.) corzo; hueva, freza, ovas de pescado.

roebuck [róbúc], **roe deer** [ró díœr], *s.* (zool.) corzo.

Roentgen rays [rœntgœn réis], *s. pl.* rayos X o de Roentgen.

rogation [roguéishun], *s.* (igl.) rogativa; ruego, súplica.

rogatory [rógatori], *a.* rogatorio.

rogue [róug], *s.* bribón, pícaro, pillo, bellaco, villano; (fam.) tunantuelo, perillán; (for., Ingl.) pordiosero, vago, vagabundo; elefante feroz y peligroso.—**r.'s gallery**, galería de malhechores, retratos de malhechores que colecciona la policía para su identificación.

roguery [róguœri], *s.* picardía o bellaquería; travesura, retozo.

roguish [róguish], *a.* picaresco, belitre, tuno; travieso, juguetón.—**r. eyes**, ojos picarescos.— **roguishly** [-li], *adv.* picaramente, picarescamente. —**roguishness** [-nes], *s.* picardía, bellaquería.

roily [róil], *va.* enturbiar; vejar, irritar.

roily [róili], *a.* turbio; agitado.

roister [róistœr]. **I.** *vn.* bravear, fanfarronear. **II.** *s.* fanfarrón, baladrón.

rôle [róul], *s.* (teat.) papel, parte.

roll [ról]. **I.** *va.* hacer rodar; volver, girar, voltear; arrollar o enrollar, abarquillar; (fund.) laminar; alisar, allanar, emparejar con rodillo; envolver, fajar; redoblar (el tambor); vibrar la lengua (para pronunciar la **rr**) o la voz (para hacer un trino); mover (los ojos) hacia arriba, ponerlos en blanco.—**to r. up**, enrollar, arrollar; (fam.) acumular; revolver, revolverse. **II.** *vn.* rodar; agitarse (las olas); ondular, fluctuar, flotar; retumbar, retemblar; bambolearse, balancearse; arrollarse, abarquillarse, encarrujarse; dar un redoble de tambores.—**to r. about**, rodar, divagar, andar de acá para allá.—**to r. down**, bajar rodando.—**to r. in money**, nadar en la abundancia. **III.** *s.* rollo; lista, nómina, matrícula, registro; bollo, panecillo; rodillo, cilindro de emparejar, allanar o laminar; laminador; maza de trapiche; redoble (de tambores); retumbo del trueno; balanceo, bamboleo; oleaje; (cir.) mecha; (arq.) voluta.—*pl.* archivos.—**r. call**, acto de pasar lista. —**r. sulphur**, azufre en barretas.—**r.-top desk**, escritorio o pupitre de tapa rodadera.

rolled [róuld], *a.* enrollado, arrollado; alisado, allanado, emparejado; (fund.) laminado.—**r. oats**, avena aplastada que se usa como alimento.

roller [rólœr], *s.* rodillo, tambor, cilindro; arrollador, allanador, aplanadera; alisador; (impr.) ruló, rodillo; ola larga; (cir.) venda, faja; (mar.) polines, rolletes, roldada.—**r. bearing**, cojinete de rodillos.—**r. skate**, patín de ruedas.— **r. towel**, toalla continua o sin fin.

rollick [rólic], *vn.* travesear, retozar.

rollicking [rólicing]. *a.* jovial; juguetón, travieso, retozón.

rolling [róuling]. **I.** *a.* rodador, rodante; rodadero; quebrado, undulado (terreno).—**r. mill**, (metal.) taller de laminar; laminador.—**r. pin**, rodillo de pastelero, rollo, zurullo; hataca.—**r. stock**, (f. c.) material rodante.—**r. stone**, (geol.)

Para la pronunciación de æ, œ, ᴅ, ş, sh, u, ȳ, ʏ, z, véase la clave al principio del libro.

ralga, canto rodado.—r. tackle, (mar.) aparejo de rolín. II. s. rodadura; revuelco; balanceo, cuneo; enrollamiento; fajamiento; (aer.) escora lateral.

roly-poly [róuli-póuli]. I. a. rechoncho, gordiflón. II. s. pudín en forma de rollo; (fam.) persona gordiflona.

Romaic [roméic], a. romaico.

Roman [róumæn]. I. a. romano; romanesco; católico romano.—R. architecture, arquitectura románica.—R. candle, candela romana.—R. law, derecho romano.—R. letter, (impr.) letra romana.—R. nose, nariz aguileña.—R. numeral, número romano.—R. type, (impr.) tipo romano. —R. vitriol, vitriolo azul, sulfato de cobre.

Romance, Romanic [roméns, roménic], a. romance; neolatino.

romance [roméns]. I. s. romance; novela, ficción, cuento, fábula; (mús.) romanza; aventura, drama, episodio extraño y conmovedor. II. vn. mentir; fingir fábulas.—**romancer** [-œr], **romancist** [-ist], s. romancero, novelista; embustero; visionario.

Romanesque [rómanésc], a. romanesco; (arq.) románico.

Romanism [rómanišm], s. catolicismo romano.

Romanist [-ist], s. y a. católico romano.

Romanize [-aiš], va. y vn. convertir al catolicismo.

romantic(al [roméntic(al], a. romántico, novelesco, romancesco; sentimental; fantástico. —**romantic(al)ly** [-li], adv. de un modo romántico.

romanticism [rométisišm], s. romanticismo.

romanticist [-ist], s. escritor romántico.

Romish [róumišh], a. romano.

Rom(m)any [rómani], a. y s. gitano.

romp. I. s. muchacha retozona, saltabardales; retozo. II. vn. retozar, juguetear, travesear.

rompers [rómpœrš], s. pl. traje de juego para niñitos.

rompish [rómpišh], a. retozón.

rondeau, rondel [róndo, del], s. (poét.) rondel.

rondo [róndo], s. (mús.) rondó.

Röntgen rays = ROENTGEN RAYS.

rood [rud], s. cruz, crucifijo; cuarto de acre; pértica inglesa (entre 6 y 8 yardas).

roof [ruf]. I. s. tejado, techado, azotea; cubierta; (poét.) bóveda, cielo; imperial de una diligencia; casa, hogar, habitación.—r. of the mouth, paladar.—r. garden, azotea de baile y diversión.— r. paper, papel cubretechos, papel para tejados.— r. tile, teja.—r. truss, armadura de techo. II. va. techar; abrigar, alojar.

roofage [rúfey], s. materiales para techo.

roofer [rúfœr], s. constructor de tejados.

roofing [rúfing]. I. s. (arq.) techado, cubierta; material para techos; albergue. II. a. para techos o tejados, de techar.

rooftree [-trí], s. cumbrera.

rook [ruc], s. (orn.) corneja, corvato; roque, torre (del ajedrez).

rookery [rúkœri], s. manada de cornejas; lugar donde procrean las aves marinas o las focas; casa destartalada y ruinosa; vecindario escuálido.

rooky [rúki], a. habitado por cornejas.

room [rum]. I. vn. (fam.) tener una habitación o aposento, alojarse. II. s. lugar; paraje, sitio, espacio, puesto; cuarto, aposento, sala, habitación, cámara, pieza; causa, motivo, razón; tiempo, ocasión, oportunidad.—there is no r. for doubt, no cabe duda.

roomful [rúmful], s. cuarto lleno.

roominess [rúmines], s. espaciosidad, holgura, amplitud.

roommate [-méit], s. compañero de cuarto.

roomy [rúmi], a. espacioso, capaz, amplio, holgado.

roorback [rúrbæc], s. (pol. E. U.) filfa, tramoya.

roost [rust]. I. s. percha de gallinero; lugar de descanso; sueño, descanso, reposo (de las aves domésticas); (E. U.) perchada. II. vn. dormir o descansar (las aves) en una percha.

rooster [rústœr], s. gallo.

root [rut]. I. s. raíz (en todas sus acepciones); (mús.) base.—r. gall, hinchazón de las raíces. II. vn. y va. arraigar, echar o criar raíces, arraigarse; hozar, hocicar.—to r. up, o out, arrancar de raíz, desarraigar; extirpar; desterrar.

rootbeer [rútbíœr], s., rootbeer, bebida no alcohólica hecha de varias raíces.

rooted [rúted], a. radical; arraigado.—**rootedly** [-li], adv. radicalmente; fijamente.

rootlet [rútlet], s. dim. raicilla, radícula.

rootstock [rútstóc], s. rizoma.

rooty [rúti], a. lleno de raíces; radicoso.

rope [róup]. I. s. cuerda, cordel, cabo, driza, sirga, toa, reata, cobra; sarta, ristra, trenza; hilera, fila.—r. ladder, escala de cuerdas.—r. of onions, ristra de cebollas.—r.'s end, chicote de cabo.—ropes of a ship, (mar.) jarcia, cordaje.— r. railway = CABLEWAY.—r. yard, cordelería.— r. yarn, filástica.—to be at the end of one's r., estar sin recursos; estar uno en las últimas. II. va. atar, amarrar con una cuerda; rodear con soga; (E. U.) coger con lazo; (fam.) engatusar, embaucar. —to r. in, (fam. E. U.) atraer, embaucar, engañar. —roper-in, gancho, donillero. III. vn. hacer hebras o madeja.

ropebands [-bænds], s. envergues.

ropedancer [-dénsœr], s. volatín, bailarín de cuerda.

ropemaker [-méicœr], s. cordelero, soguero.

ropery [-œri], s. cordelería.

ropewalk [-uoc], s. cordelería.—**ropewalker** [-œr], s. volatinero, maromero.

ropeway [-ueí], s. = CABLEWAY.

ropework [-uœrc], s. trabajo hecho de cuerdas.

ropiness [róupines], s. viscosidad; tenacidad.

ropish [róupišh], **ropy** [róupi], a. viscoso, pegajoso, glutinoso.

roquet [roké]. I. va. en el juego de croquet, dar la bola del que juega contra otra. II. s. choque de dichas bolas.

rorqual [rórcual], s. (ict.) yubarta.

Rosaceæ [roséicii], s. pl. (bot.) rosáceas.— **rosaceous** [roséíshus], a. (bot.) rosáceo.

rosary [rósari], s. (igl.) rosario; guirnalda o corona de rosas; macizo o jardín de rosales; (fig.) crestomatía.

rose [róuš], pret. de TO RISE.

rose [róuš], s. (bot.) rosal; rosa; color de rosa; (arq.) rosetón; remate perforado de una regadera.—r. apple, pomarrosa.—r. beetle, r. bug, r. chafer, nombres de insectos que atacan al rosal. —r.-colored, color de rosa; róseo, halagüeño.— r. geranium, geranio de rosa.—r. of Jericho, rosa de Jericó.—r. spray = ROSEHEAD.—r. window, (arq.) rosetón (ventana).—under the r., bajo cuerda, secretamente.

roseaniline [-énilin], s. (quím.) rosanilina.

roseate [rósiet], a. rosado; róseo.

rosebay [-bé], s. adelfa, baladre.

rosebud [-búd], s. pimpollo, botón o capullo de rosa; niña adolescente.

rosebush [-bušh], s. (bot.) rosal.

rosegall [-gol], s. (bot.) zarzarrosa.

rosehead [-jéd], s. boquilla de regadera; (m. v.) colador.

rosemary [-meri], s. (bot.) romero.

roseola [rošíola], s. (med.) roseola.

roset [róšet], s. rosicler.

rosette [rošét], s. rosa, roseta; escarapela, moña; (arq.) rosetón, florón.

rosewater [-róušuótœr], s. agua de rosas.

rosewood [róušud], s. palo de rosa.

Rosicrucian [rósicrúšhan], s. rosacruz.

rosied [rósid], a. rosado, róseo.

rosin [rósin]. I. s. abietinote, resina. V. RESIN. II. va. dar con resina.

rosiny [rósini], a. resinoso.

Rosmarinus [róusmarínus o rínus], s. (bot.) rosmarino, romero.

rossoli [rósoli], s. rosoli (licor).

roster [róstœr], s. (mil.) lista; orden del día; registro, nómina, matrícula.

rostra [róstræ], *s. pl.* de ROSTRUM.

rostral [róstral], *a.* rostral.

rostrate [róstret], *a.* rostrado.

rostrum [róstrum], *s.* tribuna; (zool.) rostro, pico, hocico; (mar.) rostro, espolón; cañón de alambique.

rosy [rósi], *a.* róseo, rosado, de color de rosa; sonrojado; (fig.) agradable, lisonjero; optimista.—**r.-hued,** rosado.

rot [rot]. **I.** *vn.* pudrirse; padecer de morriña las ovejas; estar estancado; ir a menos. **II.** *va.* pudrir; enriar. **III.** *s.* putrefacción, podre, podredumbre; (vet.) morriña; (bot.) enfermedad de las plantas causada por los hongos; (fam.) tontada, sandez.

rota [róta], *s.* rol, nómina, lista; orden del día, rutina; (**R-**) [igl.] Rota.

rotary [rótari], *a.* giratorio, rotativo, rotatorio.—**r. engine,** máquina rotativa.—**r. press,** (impr.) prensa rotativa.—**r.pump,** bomba rotatoria.—**r. squeezer,** (fund.) forja giratoria.—**r. valve,** distribuidor giratorio.

rotate [róteit]. **I.** *vn.* girar, dar vueltas; alternar, alternarse. **II.** *va.* hacer girar, dar vuelta o vueltas a; alternar; (agr.) alternar, sembrar o cultivar en rotación. **III.** *a.* (bot.) de venas radiales (apl. a las hojas).

rotation [rotéishun], *s.* rotación, giro; turno; cambio, alternación; (agr.) rotación.—**r. of crops,** rotación de cultivos.—**by r., in r.,** por turnos, alternadamente.—**in r.,** (agr.) en rotación.

rotative, rotatory [rótativ, -tori], *a.* rotatorio, giratorio.

rotator [rotéitœr], *s.* lo que hace rodar o girar.

rote [róut], *s.* lo que se aprende de memoria.—**by r.,** de memoria; mecánicamente, como coro.

Rotifera [rotíferæ], *s. pl.* (zool.) rotíferos.—**rotifer** [rótifœr], *s.,* **rotiferal, rotiferous** [rotíferæl, -us], *a.* rotífero.

rotiform [rótiform], *a.* de forma de rueda o estrella; radiado.

rotisserie [rotíserí], *s.* restaurante cuya especialidad son los asados; tienda donde se venden o se preparan asados.

rotogravure [rótogrævíúær], rotograbado.

rotor [róutœr], *s.* pieza giratoria; (hidr.) rotor, rueda móvil (de turbina); (elec.) rotor; pequeño motor para hacer girar discos, etc.

rotten [rótœn], *a.* podrido, carroño, putrefacto; (fam.) malísimo, pésimo; dañado, en mal estado, descompuesto o podrido.—**rottenness** [-nes], *s.* podredumbre, putrefacción.

rottenstone [rótœnstóun], *s.* trípol o trípoli.

rotund [rotúnd], *a.* rotundo, redondo; orbicular.—**rotunda** [-da], *s.* rotonda o rotunda.

rotundity [-iti], *s.* rotundidad, redondez.

rouble [rúbœl], *s.* = RUBLE.

roué [rué], *s.* libertino.

rouge [ruy]. **I.** *s.* colorete, afeite, brasil; (joy.) colcótar. **II.** *a.* colorado, encarnado. **III.** *va.* y *vr.* arrebolar(se), pintar(se), dar(se) colorete.

rough [rúf]. **I.** *a.* áspero; tosco; fragoso, escabroso; erizado; peludo, encrespado; duro, bronco, desapacible; bruto, tosco, cerril; rudo, inculto; grosero, brusco; tempestuoso, borrascoso; chapucero, mal acabado; aproximativo, general; preliminar, preparativo.—**r.-and-ready,** tosco o rudo pero eficaz, pronto pero tosco.—**r.-and-tumble,** desordenado, sin restricción ni regla; a topa tolondro; fuerte, resistente.—**r. coat,** primera capa (de enlucido, etc.).—**r. copy,** borrador, minuta.—**r. diamond,** diamante en bruto; persona ruda pero de buen fondo.—**r. draft,** boceto, bosquejo; borrador.—**r.-draft (to),** hacer un boceto o borrador.—**r. grinding,** desbaste.—**r.-house,** pelotera; algazara.—**r. sea,** mar bravo o alborotado.—**r. sketch** = R. DRAFT.—**r. wind,** viento borrascoso.—**r. wine,** vino áspero.—**as,** o **at, a r. guess,** a ojo de buen cubero. **II.** *s.* estado tosco; matón, belitre, rufián.—**in the r.,** en bruto, sin pulimento. **III.** *va.* poner áspero, tosco, escabroso; labrar toscamente; (fam.) molestar, irritar.—**to r. it,** pasar trabajos, vivir sin comodidades.

roughcast [rúfcæst]. **I.** *va.* bosquejar; picar, hacer áspero; dar una primera capa de mezcla gruesa. **II.** *s.* (alb.) mezcla o mortero gruesos; modelo tosco; obra sin acabar.

roughdry [-drái], *va.* secar (ropa) sin planchar.

roughen [rúfœn], *va.* y *vn.* poner o ponerse áspero o tosco; picar, rascar.—**to r. a horse,** domar un caballo.

roughhew [-jiú], *va.* desbastar.

roughly [-li], *adv.* ásperamente, rudamente; aproximadamente, de un modo general.

roughness [-nes], *s.* aspereza, rudeza, tosquedad, escabrosidad; severidad, dureza; ordinariez, bronquedad; chapucería; tempestad, tormenta.

roughrider [-ráidœr], *s.* picador o domador de caballos; *roughrider,* soldado voluntario norteamericano de caballería durante la guerra entre España y los E. U.—*pl.* **roughriders,** caballería voluntaria norteamericana durante la misma guerra (puede llamarse *Escuadrón de Picadores*).

roughsetter [-sétœr], *s.* (alb.) mampostero.

roughshod [-shod], *a.* herrado con púas o clavos que impiden resbalar en el hielo.

rouleau [ruló], *s.* cartucho de dinero; rollo, cucurucho, alcartaz.

roulette [rulét], *s.* ruleta; roleta de grabador.

Roumanian [rumíiniæn], *s.* y *a.* rumano.

round [ráund]. **I.** *a.* redondo; rotundo, lleno; sonoro; cabal; grande, cuantioso; liberal, amplio; franco, sincero, llano, ingenuo; vivo, veloz; justo, honrado.—**r. assertion,** afirmación clara y categórica.—**r.-head screw,** tornillo de cabeza redonda (de gota de sebo).—**r.house=** ROUNDHOUSE.—**r. iron,** hierro rendondo o en barras redondas (cabilla, varilla o balaústre, según el diámetro).—**r. number,** número redondo.—**r. robin,** memorial firmado en rueda (con las firmas en rueda).—**r. shot,** bala rasa. **r. sum,** cifra o suma redonda.—**r. table,** mesa redonda (sin ceremonia).—**R. Table,** (hist.) Tabla redonda; el rey Arturo y los caballeros de la Tabla redonda.—**r. timber,** madera en troncos.—**r. trip,** viaje redondo o de ida y vuelta.—**r.-trip ticket,** billete de ida y vuelta. **II.** *s.* círculo, orbe, esfera; círculo de personas o cosas; redondez; vuelta, rodeo, giro, rotación, revolución; peldaño (de escala); listón o travesaño (de silla); rodaja de carne; (arq.) mediacaña; (mil.) ronda; andanada, salva, disparo, tiro, descarga; cartucho con bala; ruta, camino, circuito; rutina, serie; (dep.) tanda, suerte, turno; (mús.) rondó; danza. **III.** *adv.* alrededor, en derredor, por todos lados; a la redonda.—**r. about,** por el lado opuesto; por todos lados, a la redonda.—**r.-faced,** carirredondo.—**r.-headed,** repolludo.—**r.-headed bolt,** perno de cabeza de hongo.—**r.-shouldered,** cargado de espaldas.—**all-r.,** completo, que sirve para todo; cabal, experto en todos los detalles de su profesión u oficio.—**all the year r.,** todo el año, el año entero. **IV.** *prep.* alrededor de; a la vuelta de. **V.** *va.* (a veces con *off*) redondear, arredondar; moverse alrededor, cercar, ceñir, dar vuelta a; acabar, perfeccionar; (mar.) (con **in** o **down**) halar.—**to r. up,** recoger, juntar. **VI.** *vn.* redondearse; desarrollarse, perfeccionarse; dar vueltas; rondar.—**to r. on,** volverse contra, cerrar, atacar.—**to r. out,** llenarse, redondearse.—**to r. to,** (mar.) orzar.—**to r. up,** colmar; echar una peluca; (mar.) halar.

roundabout [-abaut]. **I.** *a.* indirecto, vago; desviado. **II.** *s.* chaqueta; tiovivo; danza.

roundel, o **roundelay** [-del, -delei], *s.* (mús.) melodía; rondó; baile en círculo.

rounder [-œr], *s.* libertino, calavera.

roundhand [-jænd], *s.* letra redonda; parrandista.

Roundhead [-jed], *s.* (Ingl.) (despec.) "cabeza redonda," apodo que se daba a los puritanos.

roundhouse [-jaus], *s.* (mar.) toldilla, tumbadillo; (f. c.) rotunda, casa de máquinas.

rounding [-ing], *s.* curvatura; (mar.) forro de cable.

roundish [-ish], *a.* casi redondo, medio redondo.

roundly [-li], *adv.* redondamente; claramente, francamente; aproximadamente.

roundness [-nes], *s.* redondez.

round-up [ráund-úp]. **I.** va. recoger el ganado para reconocerlo, marcarlo, etc., (Am.) rodear (ganado). **II.** s. rodeo de ganado.

roundsman [ráundsman], s. (E. U.) rondador de policía.

roup [rup], s. crup de las aves domésticas.

rouse [ráuŝ]. **I.** va. despertar, animar, excitar, provocar; levantar (la caza); (mar.) halar o arronzar. **II.** vn. despertar o despertarse, despabilarse, animarse, moverse.

rouser [ráuŝer], s. despertador, excitador; (fam.) bola, mentira, embuste.

rousing [ráuŝing], a. vehemente, entusiasmador, entusiasta, ruidoso; activo, animado (el comercio); descarado.

roust [ráust]. **I.** va. (fam.) despertar, sacudir. **II.** vn. moverse con energía.

roustabout [ráustabáut], s. peón, gañán.

rout [ráut]. **I.** s. rota, derrota, huída, destrozo; jabordo, garulla, chusma; alboroto, tumulto, asonada. **II.** va. derrotar, desbaratar, destrozar; arrancar hozando.—**to r. out,** sacar a luz; forzar, echar, hacer salir.

route [rut], s. ruta, vía, camino; marcha, curso, itinerario; trazado, línea.

routinary, routine [rutínari, rutín], a. rutinario.

routine [rutín], s. rutina; costumbre, hábito.

rove [róuv]. **I.** va. (tej.) torcer el hilo antes de encanillarlo; ensartar, enhebrar. **II.** vn. corretear, vagar.—**to r. about the seas,** piratear. **III.** s. correría, paseo; hilado; arandela de remache.

rover [róuvœr], s. errante, andorrero, vagabundo; persona inconstante; pirata; flecha de arquero.

roving [róving]. **I.** s. primera torsión. **II.** a. errante vagabundo.

row [róu]. **I.** s. hilera, fila; paseo en lancha o bote; remadura. **II.** vn. (mar.) remar, bogar. **III.** va. conducir remando.

row [ráu]. **I.** vn. pelearse, armar camorra o bochinche. **II.** s. camorra, bochinche, trifulca.

rowan [róan], s. (bot.) fresno.

rowboat [róubout], s. (mar.) bote de remos.

rowdy [ráudi], s. y a. quimerista, alborotador, zaragatero, rufián.—**rowdyism** [-iŝm], s. rufianismo, bellaquería, tunantería.

rowel [ráucl]. **I.** s, rodaja de espuela; (vet.) sedal. **II.** va. poner sedal.

rowen [ráuen], s. segunda cosecha.

rower [róœr], s. remero, bogador.

rowlock [róulóc], s. escalamera, encaje de remo.

royal [róial]. **I.** a. real, regio, magnífico, magnánimo, excelente, superior.—**r. navy,** real armada. **II.** s. tamaño de papel (19x24 pulgs. para escribir y de 20x25 para imprenta); (mar.) sobrejuanete; punta superior del asta del ciervo.

royalism [-iŝm], s. realismo.—**royalist** [-ist], s. realista.

royally [-i], adv. regiamente.

royalty [-ti], s. realeza, soberanía, majestad real; regalía; participación, tanto por ciento de los ingresos; prerrogativas reales.

rub [rvb]. **I.** va. estregar, refregar, frotar; tocar; ludir; raspar, raer; incomodar, fastidiar.—**to r. away,** quitar frotando.—**to r. down,** limpiar (un caballo, perro, etc.); rebajar o alisar frotando.—**to r. in,** hacer penetrar por los poros frotando; (fam.) machacar.—**to r. off,** quitar; limpiar frotando.—**to r. out,** borrar.—**to r. the wrong way,** frotar a contrapelo; irritar, incomodar.—**to r. up,** aguijonear, excitar; retocar, repasar, pulir. **II.** vn. pasar raspando, rozar; ser desagradable o molesto; ir a contrapelo.—**to r. along, u on,** (fam.) vivir con apuros. **III.** s. frotación, ludimiento, roce, estregamiento; tropiezo, obstáculo o dificultad; sarcasmo, denuesto.

rubadub [rvbadúb], s. tantán.

rubber [rvbœr]. **I.** a. de caucho o goma elástica.—**r. dam,** (dent.) reparo de goma.—**r. band,** faja de goma, o de caucho.—**r. belt,** correa (de trasmisión) de caucho (más propiamente, de tela y caucho).—**r. belting,** correaje de caucho (más propiamente, de tela y caucho).—**r. cement,** cemento o pasta de caucho y azufre.—**r. cloth,** tela engomada. **II.** caucho, goma elástica; fregador, frotador; goma de borrar; estropajo, aljofifa, estregadera; escofina; jugada final que decide un empate; partida de juego.—pl. zapatos de goma.

rubberize [-aiŝ], va. engomar, cubrir o impregnar de caucho.

rubbery [-i], a. semejante al caucho; de consistencia de caucho.

rubbing [rvbing], s. fricción, frotación soba; roce; estregamiento.

rubbish [rvbiŝ], s. basura, desperdicios.

rubble [rvbœl], s. mampuesto, piedra de cantera, piedra bruta o sin labrar ; mampostería común, o de piedra de cantera (sin labrar); ripios, fragmentos de piedra y ladrillo para relleno; mezcla de fragmentos sueltos.—**r.** **masonry,** mampostería concertada (de piedras a medio labrar) ; mampostería de piedra bruta o de cantera (sin labrar).

rubblework [-uœrc], s. = RUBBLE MASONRY. V. RUBBLE.

rubefacient [rúbiféiŝhent], a. y s. (med.) rubefaciente.

rubella [rubélæ], s. rubéola.

rubescence [rubésens], s. rubicundez.

rubescent [rubésent], a. **rubicund** [rúbicvnd], a. rubicundo, sonrosado.

Rubiaceæ [rúbiéisii], s. pl. (bot.) rubiáceas.—**rubiaceous** [-ŝhus], a. rubiáceo.

rubicund [rúbicvnd], a. rubicundo.

rubicundity [-cvnditi], s. rubicundez.

rubidium [rubídivm], s. (quím.) rubidio.

rubied [rúbid], a. adornado con rubíes; color de rubí.

rubiginous [rubíyinus], a. añublado.

rubigo [rubáigo o bígo], s. añublo, tizón.

ruble [rubœl], s. rublo, moneda rusa.

rubric [rúbric]. **I.** a. rubro, rojo, rojizo. **II.** s. rúbrica; título, encabezamiento; división, sección; (igl.) rúbrica.—**rubricate** [-al], a. de rúbrica.—**rubricate** [-eit]. **I.** a. iluminado, escrito o impreso de color rojo. **II.** va. marcar o iluminar con encarnado.

ruby [rúbi]. **I.** s. rubí; carmín, color encarnado vivo; (Ingl. impr.) V. AGATE. **II.** a. rúbeo, rojo. **III.** va. rubificar, enrojecer; arreglar.

ruche [ruŝh], s. (cost.) golilla, lechuguilla.

ruck [rvc]. **I.** va. arrugar, ajar; (gen. con up) enfadar, incomodar. **II.** s. arruga; enojo, enfado.—**to have one's r. up,** estar enojado.

rudder [rúdœr], s. timón, gobernalle.—**r. chain,** varones del timón.—**r. pendants,** varones del timón.—**r. pintles,** machos del timón.

rudderhole [-jóul], s. limera del timón.

rudderpost [-póust], s. (mar.) codaste; (aer.) eje del timón.

rudderstock [-stóc], s. cabeza del timón.

ruddiness [rúdines], s. rojez, rubicundez.

ruddy [rvdi], a. rojo, rojizo; rubicundo.

rude [rud], a. rudo, brusco, descortés; tosco, basto, chabacano, grosero; inculto; fuerte, vigoroso.—**rudely** [-li], adv. rudamente, groseramente, toscamente, descortésmente.—**rudeness** [-nes], s. grosería; patanería, descortesía; rudeza, dureza, aspereza; rusticidad, tosquedad, crudeza, incultura.

rudiment [rúdimœnt], s. rudimento; embrión, germen.—**rudimental** [-méntal], a. = RUDIMENTARY.—**rudimentarily** [-méntarili], adv. rudimentariamente.—**rudimentary** [rudiméntari], a. rudimentario; principiante, embrionario.

rue [ru]. **I.** va. y vn. lamentar(se); arrepentirse (de). **II.** s. arrepentimiento, pesar; acción de volverse atrás (en un negocio, etc.); (bot.) ruda; trago amargo.—**rueful** [rúful], a. lamentable, lastimoso; triste, apesarado; terrible.—**ruefully** [-li], adv. tristemente.—**ruefulness** [-nes], s. tristeza, pena, pesar.

ruff [ruf], s. (cost.) lechuguilla, gorguera, golilla, escarola; collarín de plumas o de pelo de algunos animales; gallineta de collar; (ict.) pavo marino.

ruffed [rvfd], a. de collar, que tiene collar o collarín.—**r. grouse,** guaco norteamericano, especie de perdiz grande con collarín y moño.

ruffian [rúfian], *a.* y *s.* rufián, bergante, belitre.— **ruffianism** [-ism], *s.* bellaquería.—**ruffianly**, **ruffianlike** [-li, -laik], *a.* forajido, arrufianado.

ruffle [rufœl]. **I.** *va.* (cost.) fruncir un volante, rizar; ajar, arrugar, descomponer, desordenar; desazonar, enfadar, irritar; vejar; redoblar (el tambor). **II.** *vn.* rizarse, arrugarse; desarreglarse; tremolar; enojarse, incomodarse. **III.** *s.* (cost.) volante fruncido; desazón, enojo, enfado; escarceo del agua; redoble de tambor.

rufous [rúfus], *a.* rufo, bermejo, leonado.

rug [rug], *s.* alfombrilla, ruedo, tapete; felpudo; manta de viaje; perro de lanas.

rugate [rúguet], *a.* = RUGOSE.

rugged [rúgued], *a.* áspero, escarpado, escabroso; tosco, basto; inculto; desapacible; bronco; descomedido, desvergonzado; arrugado, ceñudo, regañón; desgreñado; (fam. E. U.) robusto, vigoroso; tempestuoso o borrascoso.—**ruggedly** [-li], *adv.* rudamente; ásperamente.—**ruggedness** [-nes], *s.* rudeza; aspereza, escabrosidad; robustez.

rugose, rugous [rúgos, rúgus], *a.* rugoso, arrugado, rizado.

rugosity [rugósiti], *s.* rugosidad.

ruin [rúin]. **I.** *s.* ruina, caída; bancarrota; tala, devastación, degradación, perdición. **II.** *va.* arruinar, echar a perder; desbaratar; estropear; seducir, perder (a una mujer). **III.** *vn.* caer en ruinas, arruinarse; decaer.

ruination [ruinéishun], *s.* arruinamiento, ruina, perdición.

ruinous [rúinus], *a.* ruinoso, desmantelado; desastroso, fatal, funesto.—**ruinously** [-li], *adv.* perniciosa o ruinosamente.—**ruinousness** [-nes], *s.* arruinamiento; calidad de desastroso.

rulable [rúlabœl], *a.* gobernable, dirigible, manejable; permisible.

rule [rul]. **I.** *s.* regla; gobierno, mando, poder, dominio, autoridad; estatuto, precepto, canon; (arq.) ságoma, escantillón; regla graduada; regla de trazar líneas; (for.) auto, fallo de un tribunal; (impr.) pleca, raya, filete; raya, línea trazada.—**r. of false position**, (arit.) regla de falsa posición.—**r. of the road**, reglamento del tráfico (apl esp. al de los automóviles).—**r. of three**, regla de tres.—**rules and regulations**, reglamento.—**r. of thumb**, regla empírica; método empírico.—**as a r.**, por regla general, por lo general.—**to be the r.**, ser la regla; ser de reglamento. **II.** *va.* gobernar, mandar, regir; reprimir, contener; (for.) decidir, determinar, disponer; dirigir, guiar; arreglar, ordenar; rayar (papel), reglar.—**to r. out**, excluir; descartar; no admitir, desechar.—**to r. the roast**, (fam.) mandar, dominar, tener vara alta. **III.** *vn.* gobernar, mandar; establecer una regla, formular una decisión; prevalecer, estar en boga, privar; (com.) mantenerse a un tipo.—**to r. over**, mandar, gobernar, dominar.

ruled surface [ruld sœrfæs], *s.* (geom.) superficie reglada.

ruler [rúlœr], *s.* gobernante; regla (para trazar líneas).

ruling [rúling], *s.* (for.) decisión, fallo, disposición; rayadura; rayado.—**r. grade**, (f. c.) pendiente determinante.—**r. machine**, máquina de rayar.—**r. pen**, tiralíneas.—**r. price**, (com.) precio predominante.

rum [rum]. **I.** *s.* ron; (fam.) aguardiente. **II.** *a.* (fam. Ingl.) extraño, singular; excelente.

rumble [rúmbœl]. **I.** *va.* y *vn.* retumbar, rugir; avanzar con estruendo; alborotar. **II.** *s.* rumor, ruido sordo y prolongado; estruendo; pescante situado detrás de un coche.

rumbler [rúmblœr], *s.* lo que hace un ruido sordo y continuo.—**rumbling** (-biing), *s.* ruido sordo y continuo, retumbo.

rumen [rúmen], *s.* omaso, panza.

ruminant [rúminant], *a.* y *s.* rumiante; meditativo.

Ruminantia [rúminénshiæ], *s. pl.* rumiantes.

ruminate [-eit], *va.* y *vn.* rumiar; considerar, reflexionar.—**rumination** [-éishun], *s.* rumia, rumiadura; meditación.—**ruminative** [-ativ], *a.* reflexivo.

rummage [rúmey]. **I.** *va.* y *vn.* revolver, explorar, escudriñar; agitar (un líquido); (con out o up) hallar, desenterrar. **II.** *vn.* revolverlo todo en busca de algo. **III.** *s.* revuelta, trastorno, desorden.—**r. sale**, venta de cosas usadas con el fin de allegar fondos para obras caritativas; venta de rezagos o de artículos no reclamados.

rummager [rúmeyœr], *s.* saqueador; explorador.

rumo(u)r [rúmœr]. **I.** *s.* rumor, runrún. **II.** *va.* divulgar, propalar.—**it is rumoured**, se dice.

rump [rump], *s.* rabadilla u obispillo de ave; anca; (despec.) trasero, nalga; solomo de vaca.

rumple [rúmpœl]. **I.** *va.* arrugar, ajar, chafar. **II.** *s.* arruga, doblez, ajamiento, estrujadura.

rumpus [rúmpus], *s.* batahola.

run [run]. **I.** *va.* (pret. RAN; *pp.* RUN) correr, hacer correr (*to run a horse*, correr un caballo); meter, clavar, introducir; empujar, impeler, echar; cazar, perseguir; tirar, trazar (una línea, en el papel o el terreno); pasar (la vista); atravesar, cruzar; derramar, verter, manar; correr (un peligro); fundir, moldear; (cost.) bastear; manejar, dirigir (una máquina, institución, empresa).— **to r. a blockade**, violar un bloqueo, burlar un bloqueo.—**to r. a level line**, (top.) hacer una nivelación, trazar una línea de cotas.—**to r. a line**, trazar una línea.—**to r. a line of levels**, (top.) hacer una nivelación, trazar una línea de cotas.—**to r. a race**, luchar a la carrera, a correr.—**to r. a risk**, correr riesgo o peligro.—**to r. down**, dar caza; (mar.) echar a pique; vilipendiar, difamar, hablar mal de; quebrantar, postrar; gastar (la salud, etc.).—**to r. in**, recorrer; encerrar; (impr.) = TO RUN ON.—**to r. into the ground** meter en la tierra; extender hasta más abajo del suelo; (fam.) llevar al exceso.—**to r. off**, desviar; desecar, vaciar; repetir, decir de coro; imprimir. —**to r. on**, (impr.) poner de seguido, sin párrafo.— **to r. one's**, o **the chances**, correr los riesgos.— **to r. the danger**, correr el peligro.— **to r. the gantlet**, pasar por baquetas.—**to r. the hazard** = TO R. THE DANGER.—**to r. through**, atravesar, pasar de parte a parte; traspasar; hojear, leer por encima; gastar, derrochar, malbaratar.—**to r. up**, (cost.) remendar, repasar; incurrir, hacer subir (una cuenta); sumar, hacer una suma; montar o edificar de prisa; izar. **II.** *vn.* correr; pasar, deslizarse, volar; marchar, andar, funcionar, moverse (un buque, un reloj, una máquina); derretirse, fluir, gotear o chorrear; derramarse; competir, lidiar (vg.: *to run a race*, apostar a correr); (med.) supurar; (teat.) representarse consecutivamente; extenderse, ir; correr, transcurrir; inclinarse, tener predilección; continuar, durar; rezar, decir (*the deed runs thus*, la escritura reza así); ser, salir (mineral, carbón, tamaños, etc.); tener curso, circular; salirse, dejar fugar el agua, etc.; ir, andar, hallarse (en manadas, etc.).—**to r. about**, andar de lugar en lugar; andar de una parte a otra; corretear.—**to r. across**, atravesar corriendo; hallar; dar o tropezar con.—**to r. after**, ir tras de, seguir; perseguir; buscar andar buscando.— **to r. against**, chocar, topar, dar contra; oponerse; ser contrario a.—**to r. aground**, encallar.—**to r. ahead**, correr delante; llevar ventaja.—**to r. along**, correr a lo largo de; ir, correr.—**to r. amuck**, perder la chaveta, atacar a diestra y siniestra.—**to r. away**, huir; escaparse, zafarse; desbocarse.—**to r. away with**, arrebatar; fugarse con.—**to r. back**, retroceder, volver atrás.—**to r. behind**, correr detrás; quedarse atrás, atrasarse; no hacer frente a sus gastos.—**to r. counter**, oponerse a; ir en contra de.—**to r. down**, acabarse la cuerda (de un reloj); dejar de funcionar por falta de vapor, agua, etc.; agotarse, debilitarse.—**to r. foul of**, (mar.) chocar, abordar.—**to r. in**, entrar; entrar al pasar; ir un momento. —**to r. in the blood**, o **in the family**, venir de familia, estar en la sangre.—**to r. into**, meterse de cabeza en; topar, chocar con.—**to r. mad**, enloquecerse; ser atacado de hidrofobia.—**to r. off**, (com.) estar pagado (pagaré, etc.); agotarse; salirse de.—**to r. off the rails**, o **off the track**, descarrilarse.—**to r. off**, huirse con.— **to r. on** = TO R. UPON; continuar.—**to r. out**, salir; salirse; esparcirse; escurrirse; derramarse; gastarse, acabarse.—**to r. out of**, no tener más, habérsele acabado a uno.—**to r. over**, repasar, revisar de prisa; rebosar, derramarse; pasar al otro lado; atropellar, pasar por encima de.—**to r. short,** hallarse falto o escaso, habérsele acabado a uno.—**to r. riot,** desenfrenarse, desmandarse, desaforarse; correr a rienda suelta.—**to r. to,** acudir a; correr a o hacia; tener inclinación o propender a.—**to r. to seed,** granar; agotarse.— **to r. true to type,** seguir o conservar el tipo, ser del tipo legítimo (apl. a plantas y animales); no desdecir de sus antecedentes o afiliados; obrar como era de esperarse o como de usanza.—**to r. up,** crecer, aumentar.—**to r. up and down,** correr de una parte a otra; subir y bajar corriendo.—**to r. up into,** o **to,** subir o llegar hasta.—**to r. upon,** versar sobre, referirse a; correr por encima de.— **to r. wild,** volver al estado primitivo; desenfrenarse.—**to r. with,** estar saturado o empapado de; manar, abundar en.—**as they r.,** (com.) al barrer, sin escoger. **III.** *a.* extraído; vaciado; derretido. —**r.** metal, metal derretido. **IV.** *s.* corrida, carrera; curso, marcha; batida de caza; (mil.) marcha forzada; vuelta, viajecito, excursión, jornada; recorrido; distancia; (mar.) singladura; (mec.) marcha, movimiento, funcionamiento; serie, continuación; duración, vida; hilo (del discurso); (teat.) serie de representaciones consecutivas de una pieza; lo que sale o se saca cada vez (hornada, vaciada, etc.); libre uso, discreción o libertad en el uso de algo; mando, dirección; asedio de un banco por los imponedores; terreno de pasto; migración; ribazón; clase, tipo; aspecto, carácter; producto al natural o como sale (de la mina, etc.); (min.) dirección; caída (de la caja de un elevador); galería inclinada, paso; distancia; (mús.) escala; (mar.) racel.—**r. of mine,** producto (mineral, carbón, etc.) tal como sale de la mina.—**in the long r.,** a la larga.—**the (common) run,** el común de las gentes; lo común, lo corriente.

runabout [rŭnabáut], *s.* vagabundo; (carr.) birlocho.

runagate [rŭnaguet], *s.* (ant.) renegado, apóstata; vagamundo.

runaway [rŭnauéi], *a.* y *s.* tránsfuga, fugitivo, desertor; fuga; rapto, secuestro; desbocamiento; caballo desbocado.—**r. marriage,** o **r. match,** casamiento que sigue a un secuestro.

runcinate [rŭnsinet], *a.* (bot.) dentado hacia atrás.

rundlet [rŭndlet], *s.* barrilejo.

rune [run], *s.* runa; misterio.

rung [rŭng]. **I.** *pret.* y *pp.* de TO RING. **II.** *s.* peldaño de escala, travesaño de silla; listón, barrote; (mar.) varengas, planes.

rungheads [rŭnĝjedŝ], *s.* (mar.) escoas o puntas de escoas.

Runic [rŭnic]. **I.** *a.* rúnico, runo. **II.** *s.* (impr.) tipo rúnico.

runlet, runnel [rŭnlet, -nel], *s.* arroyuelo.

runner [[rŭnœr], *s.* corredor; peatón, andarín; pieza o parte giratoria o corrediza; correo, mensajero; correvedidile; tránsfuga, fugitivo; maquinista; agente, factor; alguacil, corchete; corredera, volandera, muela; guía; anillo movible; pasador corredizo; hoja (de un patín); canal (para metal fundido); (bot.) serpa, jerpa; (hidr.) rueda móvil (de turbina); (aer.) patín o zapata de aterrizaje.—**r. of a crowfoot,** (mar.) perigallo de araña.—**r. of a tackle,** (mar.) amante de aparejo.

running [rŭning]. **I.** *s.* carrera, corrida, curso; matute, contrabando; celo de ciertos animales; (med.) corrimiento; laboreo. **II.** *a.* corredor; corriente; correntío, manantío; supurante; rápido, por encima; repetido.—**r. block,** polea movible.—**r. board,** estribo (de coche, locomotora). —**r. expenses,** gastos corrientes.—**r. fight,** combate en retirada.—**r. gate,** bebedero de orificio alimentador (de un molde).—**r. gear,** ejes y ruedas de un vehículo; mecanismo (a distinción de la armazón).—**r. hand,** letra corrida.—**r. knot,** nudo corredizo.—**r. lights,** luces de situación o de costado.—**r. title,** (impr.) título de página, titulillo.—**r. water,** agua corriente, agua viva.

runround [rŭnráund], *s.* panadizo.

runt [rŭnt], *s.* redrojo; enano; paloma.

runway [rŭnue], *s.* lecho, madre, cauce; senda; vía (gen. de rieles).

rupee [rupí], *s.* rupía (moneda).

Rupert's drops [rŭpœrts drops], *s. pl.* lágrimas de Batavia.

rupture [rŭpchœr]. **I.** *s.* rompimiento, rotura; reventazón; ruptura, desavenencia; (med.) potra, hernia, quebradura. **II.** *va.* romper, fracturar, quebrar; reventar. **III.** *vn.* abrirse, romperse, rajarse, reventar.

rupturewort [rŭpchœruœrt], *s.* (bot.) milengrana, herniaria.

rural [rŭral], *a.* rural, campesino, campestre.— **r.** free delivery, distribución gratuita del correo en regiones rurales.

rurally [rŭrali], *adv.* ruralmente.

ruse [ruŝ], *s.* ardid, astucia, artimaña.

rush [rŭsh], *s.* ímpetu, embestida, acometida; prisa, precipitación; torrente, tropel, agolpamiento, asedio; tierra rica en oro; lucha, rebatiña; (bot.) junco, junquillo, enea; friolera, bagatela.—**r.-bottomed,** con asiento de enea.—**r. candle,** vela de junco y sebo.—**r. mat,** estera de junco.—**r. rope,** aderra.—**it is not worth a r.,** no vale un bledo o un ardite. **II.** *vn.* lanzarse, abalanzarse, precipitarse; embestir, acometer; agolparse. —**to r. forward,** lanzarse.—**to r. in,** entrar precipitadamente, entrar a espetaperro.—**to r. in upon,** sorprender.—**to r. out,** salir a espetaperro. —**to r. through,** lanzarse por entre o a través de. **III.** *va.* empujar o arrojar con violencia; activar, despachar con prontitud, acelerar, precipitar; en football, llevar el balón a través del campo enemigo.—**to r. through,** ejecutar de prisa.

rusher [rŭshœr], *s.* embestidor; en football, el que cruza el campo enemigo con el balón.

rushy [rŭshi], *a.* juncoso, juncino.

rusk [rŭsc], *s.* galleta, sequillo, rosca.

russet [rŭset]. **I.** *a.* bermejo; burdo, tosco, grosero.—**r.** leather, cuero bermejo.—**r. shoes,** zapatos de cuero bermejo. **II.** *s.* color bermejo; paño burdo; cuero bermejo; (bot.) variedad de manzana.

russety [rŭseti], *s.* bermejizo.

Russia [rŭsha o rŭsha], *s.* Rusia; piel de Rusia; vaqueta de Moscovia.—**R. leather,** piel de Rusia.

Russian [rŭshan o rŭshan], *a.* y *s.* ruso.

rust [rŭst]. **I.** *s.* orín, herrumbre, rova, moho; (bot.) añublo, tizón; hongo que produce esa enfermedad. **II.** *vn.* enmohecerse, aherrumbrarse; entorpecerse, embotarse. **III.** *va.* enmohecer, aherrumbrar; embotar o entorpecer.

rustic [rŭstic]. **I.** *a.* rústico, rural; aldeano, campesino; sencillo; inculto, morral, palurdo. —**r. work,** cosas (muebles, adornos, etc.) hechas de madera al natural; mampostería acanalada o de juntas rebajada. **II.** *s.* rústico, campesino.

rustically [rŭsticali], *adv.* rústicamente.

rusticate [rŭstiket]. **I.** *vn.* rusticar, veranear. **II.** *va.* enviar al campo; expulsar de un colegio; (arq.) biselar las juntas.

rustication [rŭstikéishun], *s.* rusticación.

rusticity [rŭstísiti], *s.* rusticidad, rustiquez.

rustily [rŭstili], *adv.* con herrumbre, enmohecimiento o falta de uso.

rustiness [rŭstines], *s.* enmohecimiento, herrumbre; torpeza; falta de uso.

rustle [rŭsœl]. **I.** *va.* y *vn.* susurrar, crujir (la seda); (fam. E. U.) = HUSTLE. **II.** *s.* susurro, crujido.

rustler [rŭslœr], *s.* (fam. E. U.) hombre activo o emprendedor.

rusty [rŭsti], *a.* mohoso, herrumbroso; rojizo o amarillento; entorpecido, torpe por falta de práctica; ronco, rudo, bronco.—**r. bacon,** tocino rancio.

rut [rŭt]. **I.** *va.* hacer rodadas o surcos. **II.** *vn.* bramar los venados, etc., estar en celo. **III.** *s.* rodada, surco, releje; rutina, costumbre, hábito arraigado; sendero trillado; brama, toriondez, celo (de los animales); mugido, bramido; ruido, batahola, alboroto.—**rutting time,** tiempo de brama, estación del celo.

rutabaga [rutabéga], *s.* (bot.) naba.

rutaceous [rutéishus], *a.* (bot.) rutáceo.

ruth [ruẑ], *s.* (ant.) compasión.

Ruthene [ruźín], *s.*, **Ruthenian** [-niæn], *s.* y *a.* ruteno.

ruthenium [ruźíníum], *s.* (quím.) rutenio.

ruthless [rúźles], *a.* cruel, despiadado, empedernido.—**ruthlessly** [-li], *adv.* cruelmente, sin piedad.—**ruthlessness** [-nes], *s.* crueldad, empedernimiento.

rutile [rútil], *s.* (min.) rutilio.

ruttish [rútišh], *a.* toriondo; salido.

rutty [rúti], *a.* lleno de rodadas.

rye [rái], *s.* (bot.) centeno; whisky de centeno (llám. t. **r. whisky**).—**r. grass**, (bot.) ballico.—**r. straw**, paja centenaza.

ryot [ráiot], *s.* en la India, labrador, labriego.

S

s [es], *s.* **s.**—**'s**, de, el de (signo del posesivo: *this book is John's*, este libro es de Juan, o el de Juan).—**'s**, contr. de **is**, **es**.

S. I. *a.* en S, de forma de S.—**S. bend**, codo, junta acodada.—**S. brake**, freno de dos zapatas y palanca acodada. **II.** *s.* curva en S; junta en S o acodada; barra, tubo, etc., en S.

Sabæan, Sabean [sæbíæn] = SABIAN.

Sabaoth [sébeoz o sabáoz], *s. pl.* ejércitos.

Sabbatarian [sæbatérian], *a.* y *s.* sabatario (apl. hoy a los que guardan santamente el domingo).

Sabbath [sæbaz], *s.* día de descanso en cada semana (sábado entre los judíos, domingo entre los cristianos).

Sabbatic(al [sæbǽtic(al], *a.* sabático, sabatino.

saber [séibœr]. **I.** *s.* sable. **II.** *va.* acuchillar, herir a sablazos.

Sabian [séibian], *a.* y *s.* sabeo.

Sabianism [séibianišm], *s.* sabeísmo.

sabine [sébin], *s.* (bot.) sabina.—(S-), *s.* y *a.* sabino.

sable [séibœll. **I.** *s.* (zool.) cebellina, marta; su piel. **II.** *a.* (blas.) sable, negro.

sabot [sabó], *s.* zueco, almadreña; (arti.) salero de granada.

sabotage [-taȳ], *s.* sabotaje.

sabre [séibœr], *s.* = SABER.

sabulite [sǽbiulait], *s.* sabulita (un explosivo de gran potencia).

sabulous [sǽbiulus], *a.* sabuloso, arenoso.

sac [sæc], *s.* (biol.) saco, bolsa, cavidad o receptáculo.

saccate [sǽket], *a.* en forma de bolsa o saco.

saccharate [sǽcærǝit], *s.* (quím.) sacarato.

saccharic [sǽcǽric], *a.* (quím.) sacárico.

sacchariferous [sǽcæfíerus], *a.* sacarífero.

saccharification [sǽcærifikéišhun], *s.* sacarificación.

saccharify [-ifai], *va.* sacarificar.

saccharimeter, saccharometer [-rí- (o -ró-) metœr], *s.* sacarímetro, sacarómetro.

saccharin [-in], *s.* sacarina.—**saccharine, saccharous** [-in, -us], *a.* sacarino, azucarado.—**saccharoid** [-oid], *a.* sacaroídeo.—**saccharose** [-ous], *s.* sacarosa.

sacerdotal [sǽscœrdótal], *a.* sacerdotal.

sacerdotalism [-dótališm], *s.* carácter y métodos sacerdotales; clericalismo.

sachem [séichem], *s.* cacique hereditario norteamericano.

sachet [sašhé], *s.* sachet, perfumador.

sack [sæc]. **I.** *s.* saco, costal, talega; (mil.) saco, saqueo; botín; (sast.) saco, americana; vino blanco generoso.—**s. race**, carrera de personas metidas en sacos. **II.** *va.* ensacar, meter en un saco; saquear.—**to s. up**, ensacar.

sackbut [sǽcbut], *s.* (mús.) sacabuche.

sackcloth [sǽccloz], *s.* arpillera; cilicio.

sacker [sǽkœr], *s.* saqueador.

sackful [sǽcful], *s.* costal o saco lleno.

sacque [sæc], *s.* (cost.) saco, chaqueta.

sacrament [sǽcramœnt], *s.* sacramento; eucaristía.—**sacramental** [-méntal], *a.* sacramental.—**sacramentally** [-méntali], *adv.* sacramentalmente.

—**sacramentarian** [-mentérian]. **I.** *a.* sacramental. **II.** *s.* sacramentario.—**sacramentary** [-méntari]. **I.** *a.* sacramental. **II.** *s.* (igl.) sacramentario (libro).

sacrarium [sæcrériǔm], *s.* (igl.) sagrario; (arq.) capillita.

sacred [séicred], *a.* sagrado, sacro; santo.—**sacredly** [-li], *adv.* sagradamente, santamente.—**sacredness** [-nes], *s.* santidad, carácter de sagrado.

sacrifice [sǽcrifais]. **I.** *va.* y *vn.* sacrificar. **II.** (-ais), *s.* sacrificio.—**at a s.**, haciendo un sacrificio; perdiendo, con pérdida.

sacrificer [-faisœr], *s.* sacrificador.—**sacrificial** [-físhal], *a.* sacrificador; de sacrificio, del sacrificio.

sacrilege [sǽcriley], *s.* sacrilegio.—**sacrilegious** [-líȳus], *a.* sacrílego.—**sacrilegiously** [-li], *adv.* sacrílegamente.

sacrist [séicrist], *s.* (igl.) sacristán, sacristan [sæcristan], *s.* (igl.) sacristán.

sacristy [sǽcristi], *s.* (igl.) sacristía.

sacrosanct [sǽcrosænct], *a.* sacrosanto.

sacrum [séicrǔm], *s.* (anat.) sacro.

sad [sæd], *a.* triste.

sadden [sǽdn], *va.* y *vn.* entristecer(se), contristar(se).

saddle [sǽdœll. **I.** silla de montar; enjalma; asiento, silla (de bicicleta); parte trasera de una res; (mec.) asiento, silla, soporte; cojinete, caballete de asiento (de una caldera); silla de los cilindros (de una locomotora); parte posterior del espinazo (de un ave); depresión, garganta, paso (de una montaña).—**s.-backed**, deprimido en la parte superior; (caballo) de espalda baja y cuello largo; de espalda arqueada.—**s. cover**, acitura, telliz.—**s. gall**, matadura.—**s. horse**, caballo de silla.—**s. joint**, junta de resalte, hecha doblando en sus extremos las dos planchas hacia arriba, poniendo a tope las partes dobladas, y doblando la parte superior de la una para cubrir la otra.—**s. maker** = SADDLER.—**s. of mutton**, lomo de carnero.—**s. roof**, tejado de caballete o de dos aguas.—**s. tank**, depósito curvo de agua montado sobre la caldera de una locomotora.—**s.-tank locomotive**, locomotora con tanque sobre la caldera. **II.** *va.* ensillar, enalbardar; cargar, poner a cuestas.—**to s. with**, hacer cargar con; echar a cuestas a.

saddlebag [-bæg], *s.* alforja.

saddlebow [-bów], *s.* arzón.

saddlecloth [-clóz], *s.* sudadero, mantilla de silla.

saddler [sǽdlœr], *s.* sillero, talabartero.

saddlerock [sǽdœlróc], *s.* variedad de ostra grande.

saddlery [sǽdlœri], *s.* talabartería.

saddletree [sǽdœltrí], *s.* fuste de silla; arzón, tejuelo, borrén.

Sadducean [sédiusǽen], *a.*, **Sadducee** [-si], *s.* saduceo.—**Sadduceeism** [-sišm], *s.* saduceísmo.

sadiron [sǽdaicrn], *s.* plancha para la ropa.

sadly [sǽdli], *adv.* tristemente.

sadness [sǽdnes], *s.* tristeza.

saengerfest, sängerfest [séngœrfest], *s.* certamen coral.

safe [séif]. **I.** *a.* seguro; salvo, ileso; sin peligro, innocuo; intacto; leal, digno de confianza; cierto.—**s. and sound**, sano y salvo.—**s.-conduct**, salvoconducto.—**s.-keeping**, guarda, depósito, custodia.—**s. load**, (ing.) carga de trabajo. **II.** *s.* caja de caudales, caja fuerte de hierro; alacena, despensa.

safeguard [-gard]. **I.** *s.* salvaguardia; resguardo; carta de seguridad; defensor, escolta; defensa, abrigo. **II.** *va.* guardar, proteger.

safely [-li], *adv.* seguramente, sin peligro; a salvo, felizmente, sin novedad.

safeness [-nes], *s.* estado o condición de seguridad; ausencia o falta de peligro.

safety [-ti]. **I.** *s.* seguridad; protección; incolumidad; innocuidad; ausencia de todo mal, daño o perjuicio; salud (pública). **II.** *a.* de seguridad.—**s. arch**, arco de descarga.—**s. belt**, salvavidas.—**s. factor**, coeficiente de seguridad.—**s. fuse**, mecha de seguridad, mecha de quema lenta; (elec.) fusible.—**s. isle**, o **island**, plataforma de seguridad (en el centro de una calle).—s. lamp, lámpara de seguridad.—s. match, fósforo de seguridad (llám. en algunas partes fósforo sueco).—s. pin, imperdible.—s. razor, navaja de afeitar de seguridad.—s. valve, (mec.) válvula de seguridad.

safflower [sǽflauœr], s. (bot.) alazor, cártamo.

saffron [sǽfrun]. I. s. (bot.) azafrán. II. a. azafranado.

sag [sæg]. I. va. combar, empandar. II. vn. combarse; estirarse y combarse en el centro; ceder, doblegarse; hundirse; desplomarse, desviarse de la vertical; rezagarse; vagar; (mar.) irse a la ronza. III. s. comba; flecha (de un cable, etc. combado).

saga [séga o sága], s. saga (leyenda).

sagacious [saguéišhus], a. sagaz, perspicaz; ladino, vivo.—sagaciously [-slí], adv. sagazmente, ladinamente.—sagaciousness [-nes], sagacity [sagǽsiti], s. sagacidad, perspicacia; astucia.

sagamore [ságamor], s. cacique inferior.

sagapenum [sægapínum], s. sagapeno.

sage [séiy]. I. s. (bot.) salvia; sabio, filósofo. II. a. sabio; grave; sagaz; cuerdo.—sagely [-li], adv. sabiamente; cuerdamente.—sageness [-nes], s. sabiduría.

sagebrush [-brúšh], s. artemisia.

saggar, sagger [sǽgœr], s. receptáculo refractario de cocción.

sagittal [sǽyital], a. sagital.

Sagittaria [-téria], s. (bot.) sagitaria, saetilla.

Sagittarius, Sagittary [-térius, -teri], s. (astr.) Sagitario.

sago [séigo], s. (bot.) sagú.

saguaro [saguéro], s. (bot.) pitahaya

sahib [sáib], s. señor (tratamiento persa e indio).

said [sed], pp. de SAY; (for.) dicho, antedicho.

sail [séil], s. (mar.) vela; buque, nave (en esta acepción el plural es como el singular); excursión o paseo en barco.—s. loft, tinglado de velas. —s. needle, (mar.) aguja capotera.—s. twine, (mar.) hilo de vela. II. vn. darse a la vela; zarpar; salir (un buque); navegar; dar un paseo o viajar por mar, río o lago; ir embarcado; flotar, mecerse en el aire; deslizarse.—to s. against wind and tide, ir contra viento y marea.—to s. along the coast, costear.—to s. back, tomar puerto.—to s. before the wind, navegar viento en popa.—to s. close with the wind, ceñir el viento, bolinear.—to s. with flowing sheets, navegar a escota larga. III. va. gobernar (una embarcación); navegar por, surcar.

sailable [-abœl], a. navegable.

sailboat [-bóut], s. bote de vela.

sailcloth [-cloz], s. lona.

sailer [-œr], s. buque de vela.—good s., velero.

sailing [-ing]. I. s. salida, partida (de un buque); navegación, náutica. II. a. de vela; de o relativo a la navegación.—s. directions, avisos o noticias marítimas.—s. orders, orden de salida, últimas instrucciones que se dan al capitán de un buque.—s. ship, o vessel, buque de vela.

sailmaker [-méicœr], s. fabricante de velas.

sailor [séilœr], s. marinero; marino.

sailyard [séilyard], s. verga.

sainfoin [sénfoin], s. (bot.) mielga, pipirigallo.

saint [séint]. I. s. santo; ángel. II. a. santo; como título (que generalmente se abrevia así: St.) San, Santo, Santa.—St. Andrew's cross, cruz de San Andrés.—St. Anthony's fire, erisipela.—St. Bernard, perro de San Bernardo.—St. George's Cross, cruz griega de la bandera inglesa. —St. John's bread, (bot.) algarrobo.—St. John's wort, hierba de San Juan, hipérico, corazoncillo.—St. Valentine's Day, día de San Valentín (14 de febrero).—St. Vitus's dance, (med.) corea, baile de San Vito. III. va. (igl.) canonizar. IV. vn. obrar como un santo.

sainted [-ed], a. santo; bendito, canonizado; sagrado.—sainthood [-jud], s. = SAINTSHIP.—saintlike [-laik], a. de santo, como de santo.—saintliness [-lines], s. santidad.—saintly [-li], adv. santamente.—saintship [-ship], s. santidad, carácter de santo.

Saint-Simonian [-saimóniæn], s. y a. sansimoniano.—Saint-Simonianism, [-išm], Saint-Simonism [-sáimonišm], s. sansimonismo.

saith [seth], (ant.) 3d. pers. pres. indic. del verbo TO SAY: dice.

sake [séic], s. causa, motivo, fin, objeto, razón; amor, respeto, consideración. Ú. casi siempre en el caso posesivo precedido de jor, y a veces no se traduce o se cambia el giro: for your sake, por Vd., por su bien, por consideración a Vd.; for brevity's sake, o for the sake of brevity, por brevedad, para mayor brevedad; for policy's sake, por política; for the sake of peace, por amor a la paz, por la paz, para conservar la paz; for the sake of fostering education, a fin de fomentar la educación.—for conscience's., por conciencia, para cumplir con la conciencia.—for God's s., por Dios, por el amor de Dios.—for mercy's s., por piedad, por misericordia.

saker [sékœr], s. (orn.) sacre.

sal [sæl], s. (quím. y farm.) sal.—s. ammoniac, sal amoníaco.—s. soda, sosa, carbonato de sodio. —s. volatile, carbonato amónico.

salaam, salam [salám]. I. va. y vn. hacer zalemas. II. s. zalema.

salability [séilabíliti], salableness [-bœlnes], s. facilidad de ser vendido.

salable [séilabœl], a. vendible.

salacious [saléišhus], a. salaz.—salaciously [-li], adv. salaz o lujuriosamente.—salaciousness [-nes].

salacity [salǽsiti], s. salacidad, lascivia.

salad [sǽlad], ensalada.—s. bowl, s. dish, ensaladera.—s. dressing, aderezo, aliño.—s. oil, aceite de comer.

sale [séil], s. venta; almoneda, venta a pública subasta; demanda, voga, mercado.—s. by auction, almoneda, subasta.—s. on return, (for.) retroventa.—for s., u on s., de venta.

saleable, saleableness = SALABLE, -NESS.

saleratus [sélœrétus], s. (coc.) bicarbonato de sosa o potasa.

Salesian [saléišhæn], s. y a. salesiano.

saleslady [séiIsléidi] = SALESWOMAN.

salesman [-mæn], s. vendedor; dependiente de tienda.

salesmanship [-mænšhip], s. arte de vender.

saleswoman [-uman], s. vendedora; dependiente de tienda.

Salian [séiliæn], s. y a., Salic [sǽlic], a. sálico. —Salic law, ley sálica.

salicaceous [selikéseus], a. (bot.) salicíneo.

salicetum [sélisítum], s. salceda.

salicin(e [sélisin], s. salicina.

salicylate [sélisilet], s. salicilato.

salicylic [-sílic], a. salicílico.

salience, saliency [séiliens, -si], s. calidad de sobresaliente; lo que sobresale; saliente.

salient [-ent]. I. s. saliente, resalto; esquina, ángulo. II. a. saliente, saledizo; que sobresale; prominente, notorio.

saliferous [salifœrus], a. (geol.) salífero.

salifiable [salifiabœl], a. (quím.) salificable.

salify [sélifai], va. (quím.) salificar.

salimeter [sélímetœr], s. pesasales.

salina [sælaína], s. salina (establecimiento); salina marítima, charco artificial de agua de mar para obtener sal.

saline [séilain], a. salino.—salineness [-nes], s. calidad de salino.

salinometer [sélinómetœr], s. pesasales.

salipyrin(e [-pairin], s. salipirina.

saliva [saláiva], s. saliva.—salival [-val], salivary [sǽliværi], a. salival; salivoso.—salivant [sǽlivant], s. (med.) sialogogo.—salivate [sǽliveit], va. (med.) salivar.—salivation [sælivéišhun], s. salivación, desalivación.

sallow [sélo]. I. a. cetrino, pálido, lívido. II. s. (bot.) sarga, sauce.—sallowness [-nes], s. palidez, amarillez.

sally [sǽli]. **I.** *s.* (mil.) salida, surtida; paseo, excursión; ímpetu o arranque; humorada, salida de pie de banco; (arq.) saledizo, saliente, vuelo.—**s. of wit,** agudeza, ocurrencia chistosa. **II.** *vn.* (a veces con *forth*) salir, hacer una salida; tener un arranque; avanzar con denuedo.

sallyport [sǽliport], *s.* (fort.) surtida.

salmagundi [sælmagúndi], *s.* salpicón; mescolanza.

salmon [sǽlmʊn], *s.* (ict.) salmón; color de salmón.—**s. trout,** trucha salmonada.

salmonet [sǽmonet], *s.* salmón joven o aún pequeño.

salol, *s.* (quím.) salol.

Salomonic [sǽlomónic], *a.* salomónico.

salon [salón], *s.* salón, sala; exposición anual de cuadros.

saloon [salún], *s.* salón, gran sala; cámara de un vapor; (E. U.) cantina; (Ingl.) (f. c.) coche salón.—**s. keeper,** tabernero.

salse [sals], *s.* volcán de cieno.

salsify [sǽlsifai], *s.* (bot.) salsifí.

salt [solt]. **I.** *s.* sal; (quím.) sal; sabor, gusto; sal ática, agudeza, ingenio chispeante; (fam.) marinero.—*pl.* sales medicinales; en especial, sal de la Higuera, sulfato de magnesia.—**not worth one's s.,** no valer uno el pan que come. **II.** *a.* salado; salobre; curado o conservado con sal.—**s. box,** salero de cocina.—**s.-bush,** (bot.) hierba de paste.—**s. junk,** (mar.) tasajo de rancho —**s. lick,** salegar, lamedero.—**s. maker,** salinero. —**s. marsh,** saladar o marisma.—**s. meat,** carne salada, cecina.—**s. mine,** mina de sal; salina.— **s. pan,** caldera de saladar.—**s. pit,** saladar, lagunajo; salina.—**s. pork,** tocino salado.—**s. rheum,** (med.) dermatosis reumática.—**s. spring,** fuente de agua salada —**s. tub,** saladero.—**s. water,** agua de mar, agua salada.—**s. well,** pozo de agua salada.—**s. works,** salina. **III.** *va.* salar, salpresar, arencar, curar con sal; (fig.) sazonar; purificar; (fam.) poner mineral secretamente en una mina para darle valor.

saltant [sǽltant], *a.* saltante.

saltation [sæltéishʊn], *s.* saltación, salto; palpitación.

saltatorial [sǽltatórial], **saltatory** [-tori], *a.* saltón.

saltcellar [sóltséllær], *s.* salero de mesa.

salted [sólted], *a.* salado; inmunizado por enfermedad previa; (fam.) perito, experimentado.

salter [sóltœr], *s.* salador; salinero.

saltern [sóltœrn], *s.* salina (fábrica).

saltier [sǽltir], *s.* (blas.) sotuer.

saltigrade [sǽltigred], *a.* saltígrado.

salting [sólting], *s.* saladura.—**s. tub,** saladero.

saltish [sóltish], *a.* salobre, un poco salado.

saltless [sóltles], *a.* sin sal; soso, insulso, insípido.

saltness [sóltnes], *s.* sabor de sal.

saltpan [sóltpæn], *s.* paila o recéptaculo para evaporar agua salada; charco artificial de agua salada.—*pl.* salina (establecimiento).

saltpeter, saltpetre [sóltpítœr], *s.* nitro, salitre. —**s. house** o **works,** nitrería; salitrería.—**s. maker,** salitrero.

saltwort [sóltwœrt], *s.* (bot.) barrilla, sosa.

salty [sólti], *a* salado; salobre.

salubrious [salúbrius], *a.* salubre.—**salubriously** [-li], *adv.* salutíferamente.—**salubrity, salubriousness** [salúbriti, briʊsnes], *s.* salubridad.

salutariness [sǽliutérines], *s.* salubridad.

salutary [-teri], *a.* saludable; salubre, sano, salutífero.

salutation [-téishʊn], *s.* salutación, saludo; bienvenida, enhorabuena, parabién.

salutatory [salútatori]. **I.** *a.* saludador. **II.** *s.* discurso de bienvenida.

salute [saliút]. **I.** *va.* y *vn.* saludar; (mil.) saludar, cuadrarse. **II.** *s.* salutación; saludo; (mil.) saludo, salva.

salvability [sǽlvabíliti], **salvableness** [-bœlnes], *s.* posibilidad de ser redimido o de salvarse.

salvable [-bœl], *a.* que puede salvarse.

Salvadorean, Salvadorian [sǽlvædóriæn], *s.* y *a.* salvadoreño.

salvage [sǽlveу], *s.* salvamento.—**s. money,** derecho de salvamento.

salvarsan [sælvársæn], *s.* salvarsán.

salvation [sælvéshʊn], *s.* salvación.—**S. Army,** Ejército de Salvación (organización religiosa).

Salvationist [-ist], *s.* miembro del Ejército de Salvación.

salve [sav]. **I.** *s.* emplasto, ungüento; socorro, remedio.—**S. Regina,** salve (oración). **II.** *va.* curar (una herida) con ungüentos o emplastos; salvar; socorrer; remediar.

salver [sǽlvœr], *s.* salvilla, bandeja.

Salvia [sǽlvia], *s.* (bot.) salvia.

salvo [sǽlvo], *s.* salvedad, reservación, excepción; salva de artillería.

samara [saméra *o* sǽmara], *s.* (bot.) sámara.

Samaritan [saméritan], *a.* y *s.* samaritano; persona benévola y caritativa.

samarium [sæmérium], *s.* (quím.) samario.

Sambo [sǽmbo], *s.* negro o mulato.

sambuca [sæmbiúcæ], *s.* sambuca (instrumento musico).

same [sem], *a.* mismo; igual.—**all the s.,** a pesar de eso, a pesar de todo.—**if it is the s. to you,** si le es a Vd. lo mismo, o igual; si Vd. no tiene inconveniente.—**it is all the s. to me,** para mí es todo uno; lo mismo me da.—**much the s.,** casi lo mismo.—**much the s. as,** casi como.—**the s.,** lo mismo, el mismo, los mismos; otro tanto; todo uno.—**the s. as,** lo mismo que; el mismo, los mismos que.

sameness [sémnes], *s.* igualdad; parecido exacto; uniformidad monótona, monotonía.

samlet [sǽmlet], *s.* = SALMONET.

Sammy [sǽmi], *s.* (fаɪn.) soldado norteamericano.

Samnite [sǽmnait], *s.* y *a.*, **Samnitic** [sæmnítie], *a.* samnita.

samovar [sámovar], *s.* samovar, urna rusa para agua caliente.

samp [sæmp], *s.* (E. U.) maíz descortezado sin moler; potaje de *samp.*

samphire [sǽmfaiær], *s.* (bot.) hinojo marino.

sample [sǽmpœl]. **I.** *s.* muestra, prueba, espécimen; patrón. **II.** *va.* sacar una muestra; probar, catar.

sampler [sǽmplœr], *s.* probador, catador; catacaldos; dechado, labor de las niñas.

sampleroom [sǽmpœlrúm], *s.* cuarto de muestras; cantina, taberna.

sanative [sénativ], *a.* curativo, sanativo.

sanatorium [sénatórium], *s.* sanatorio.

sanatory [sénatori], *a.* sanador, sanitario.

sanbenito [sénbenito], *s.* sambenito (capotillo de penitente).

sanctification [sénctifikéishʊn], *s.* santificación; consagración.—**sanctifier** [-faicer], *s.* santificador. —**sanctify** [-fai], *va.* santificar.

sanctimonious [sénctimónius], *a.* beato, santurrón, santucho.—**sanctimoniously** [-li], *adv.* con mojigatería, santurronamente, taimadamente.— **sanctimoniousness** [-nes], **sanctimony** [-moni], *s.* santurronería, beatería.

sanction [séncshʊn]. **I.** *s.* sanción; ratificación, confirmación; justificación. **II.** *va.* sancionar, autorizar, ratificar.

sanctity [sénctiti], *s.* santidad.

sanctuary [sénctiueri], *s.* santuario; asilo, refugio sagrado.

sanctum [sénctum], *s.* paraje sagrado; (fam.) retrete.—**s. sanctorum,** sanctasanctórum.

Sanctus [sénctus], *s.* (igl.) sanctus.—**S. bell,** campanilla que anuncia la elevación de la hostia.

sand [sænd]. **I.** *s.* arena; (E. U. fam.) fuerza de carácter; valor; dinero contante, caudales.— *pl.* granos de arena; arenales; momentos de tiempo o de vida.—**s. bank,** banco o bajo de arena, placer, encalladero.—**s. bar,** barra, banco de arena.—**s. bath,** (quím.) baño de arena.— **s.-blast,** soplador o aventador de arena para grabar el vidrio, mármol, etc.; chorro de arena; tempestad de arena.—**s. box,** salvadera, areni-

llero; (f. c.) arenero.—**s.-box tree**, (bot.) hura.—
s. dune, algaida.—**s. fly**, (ent.) jijene.—**s. pit**,
mina de arena, hoyo de donde se saca arena.—**s.**
wasp, avispa de arena. **II.** *va.* arenar, enarenar.
sandal [sǽndal], *a.* sandalia, abarca.
sandalwood [sǽndalud], *s.* (bot.) sándalo.
sandarac(h [sǽndaræc], *s.* sandárica.—**s. tree**,
(bot.) tuya.
sandbag [sǽndbæg]. **I.** *s.* saco de arena. **II.** *va.*
atacar o golpear con sacos de arena.
sanded [sǽnded], *a.* arenoso, arenisco.
sanders [sǽndœrs], *s.* (bot.) sándalo.
sandglass [sǽndglæs], *s.* reloj de arena.
sandiness [sǽndines], *s.* naturaleza arenosa;
rubio bermejizo.
sandiver [sǽndivœr], *s.* anatrón.
sandpaper [sǽndpéipœr]. **I.** *s.* papel de lija.
II. *va.* lijar.
sandpiper [sǽndpáipœr], *s.* (orn.) gallineta.
sandstone [sǽndstoun], *s.* piedra arenisca.
sandwich [sǽnduich]. **I.** *va.* colocar entre dos
capas; intercalar, insertar. **II.** *s.* (coc.) emparedado; combinación de cosas diferentes alternadas.—**s. man**, hombre que va por las calles
con cartelones colgados por delante y por detrás.
sandy [sǽndi], *a.* arenoso, arenisco; rufo.
sane [séin], *a.* cuerdo; sano.
saneness [séinnes], *s.* cordura.
sang [sæng], *pret.* de TO SING.
sangaree [sængarí], *s.* sangría (bebida).
sang-froid [san fruá], *s.* sangre fría.
Sangreal [sangrél], *s.* grial.
sanguiferous [sænguífœrus], *a.* sanguífero.
sanguification [sænguïfikéiʃhun], *s.* sanguificación.—**sanguify** [sǽnguïfai], *vn.* sanguificar.
sanguinariness [sǽnguïnerines], *s.* calidad de
sanguinario.—**sanguinary** [-neri], *a.* sanguinario.
sanguine [sǽngüin], *a.* confiado, lleno de esperanza; sanguíneo, sanguinoso; pletórico.—
sanguinely [-li], *adv.* ardientemente; confiadamente.—**sanguineness** [-nes], *s.* plenitud de esperanza, confianza o entusiasmo; plétora.
sanguineous [sangüíneus], *a.* sanguíneo; sanguinolento.
sanguivorous [sangüívorus], *a.* que se alimenta
de sangre.
Sanhedrin, Sanhedrim [sǽnjedrin, -m], *s.* sanedrín, sinedrio; cualquier asamblea.
sanicle [sǽnicœl], *s.* (bot.) sanícula.
sanies [séniiš], *s.* (med.) sanies, icor.
sanious [sénius], *a.* sanioso, icoroso.
sanitarian [sǽnitérian], *a.* y *s.* sanitario.
sanitarium [-térium], *s.* sanatorio.
sanitary [-teri], *a.* sanitario.
sanitation [-téiʃhun], *s.* saneamiento; aplicación práctica de la ciencia sanitaria.
sanity [sǽniti], *s.* cordura, juicio sano, sentido
común; sanidad.
Sanskrit, Sanscrit [sǽnskrit], *s.* y *a.* sánscrito.
Santalaceæ [sǽntæléisii], *s. pl.* (bot.) santalá-
ceas.—**santalaceous** [-ʃhus], *a.* santaláceo.
santon [sǽnton], *s.* santón.
santonica [sæntónica], *s.* (bot.) santónico.
santoniu(e [sæntonin], *s.* santonina.
sap [sæp]. **I.** *s.* savia; (fort.) zapa. **II.** *va.*
zapar, minar. **III.** *vn.* hacer trabajos de zapa;
obrar por bajo mano.
sapajou [sǽpayu], *s.* (zool.) sapajú, zamba.
sapanwood [sapénud], *s.* sapán.
sapful [sǽpful], *a.* lleno de savia.
saphenous [safínus], *a.* (anat.) superficial, manifiesto.
sapid [sǽpid], *a.* sápido, sabroso.
sapidity, o sapidness [sapíditi, sǽpidnes], *s.*
sabor, gusto, sainete.
sapience [séipiens], **sapiency** [-si], *s.* sabiduría.
sapient [séipient], *a.* sabio.
Sapindaceæ [sæpindéisii], *s. pl.* (bot) sapindá-
ceas.—**sapindaceous** [-ʃhus], *a.* sapindáceo.
sapless [sǽples], *a.* seco, sin jugo.
sapling [sǽpling], *s.* renuevo, vástago, serpollo;
mozuelo, mozalbete.

sapodilla [sæpodíla], *s.* (bot.) chicozapote, zapotillo.
saponaceous [sǽponéiʃhus], *a.* jabonoso, saponáceo.
saponifiable [sapónifáiabœl], *a.* saponificable.
saponification [-fikéiʃhun], *s.* saponificación.
saponify [-fai], *va.* saponificar.
saponifier [-faiœr], *s.* saponificador.
saponin [sǽponin], *s.* (quím.) saponina.
saporific [sǽporífic], *a.* saporífero.
sapota [sapóta], *s.* (bot.) zapote.
Sapotaceæ [sǽpotéisii], *s. pl.* (bot.) sapotáceas.—
sapotaceous [-ʃhus], *a.* sapotáceo.
sapper [sǽpœr], *s.* (mil.) zapador, gastador.
Sapphic [sǽfic]. **I.** *a.* sáfico. **II.** *s.* verso sáfico.
sapphire [sǽfaiœr], *s.* zafiro; color de zafiro,
cerúleo.
sapphirin(e [sǽfirin]. **I.** *a.* zafirino. **II.** *s.*
(min.) zafirina.
sappiness [sǽpines], *s.* abundancia de savia,
jugosidad; sentimentalismo.
sappy [sǽpi], *a.* lleno de savia; jugoso; inmaturo;
ridículamente sentimental.
saprogenic [sǽproyénic], **saprogenous** [sæpró-
yenus], *a.* que produce putrefacción; que vive en la
putrefacción.
saprophyte [sǽprofait], *s.* (biol.) saprofito.
saprophytic [-fític], *a.* saprofítico.
sapwood [sǽpud], *s.* albura, alburno; (carp.)
sámago.
saraband [sǽraband], *s.* zarabanda.
Saracen [sǽrasen], *a.* sarraceno.
Saracenic [sǽrasénic], *a.* sarracénico.
sarbacand [sǽrbacænd], *s.* cerbatana.
sarcasm [sárcæšm], *s.* sarcasmo.—**sarcastic(al**
[sarcǽstic(al], *a.* sarcástico, mordaz.—**sarcastically** [-i], *adv.* sarcásticamente.
sarcenet [sársnet], *s.* = SARSENET.
sarcocarp [sárcocarp], *s.* (bot.) sarcocarpio.
sarcocele [sárcosil], *s.* (med.) sarcocele.
sarcocolla [sárcocóla], *s.* sarcocola.
sarcode [sárcoud], *s.* sarcoda, protoplasma animal.
sarcologic(al [sarcolóyic(al], *a.* sarcológico.
sarcology [sarcóloyi], *s.* sarcología.
sarcoma [sarcóma], *s.* (med.) sarcoma.
sarcomatous [sarcómatus], *a.* sarcomatoso.
sarcophagous [sarcófagus], *a.* carnívoro.
sarcophagus [sarcófagus], *s.* sarcófago, lucillo;
variedad de piedra caliza.
sarcotic [sarcótic], *a.* y *s.* (cir.) sarcótico.
sard [sard], *s.* (joy.) sardio.
sardel [sárdel], **sardine** [sardín], *s.* (ict.) sardina;
(joy.) sardio.
Sardinian [sardínian], *a.* sardo.
sardonic, sardonian [sardónic, -nian], *a.* sardónico, burlón.
sardonyx [sárdonics], *s.* (joy.) sardónice.
sargasso [sargǽso], *s.* sargazo (alga).
sark [sark], *s.* (Ingl.) camisa; mortaja.
Sarmatian [sarméiʃhæn], *s.* y *a.* sármata.
sarment [sármœnt], **sarmentum** [sarméntum],
s. (bot.) sarmiento.
sarmentose [sarméntouš], *a.* sarmentoso.
Sarracenia [sárræsiniæ], *s.* (bot.) género de las
sarracenias.—**Sarraceniaceæ** [-niéisii], *s. pl.* sa-
rraceniáceas.
sarsa [sársa], **sarsaparilla** [-paríla], *s.* (bot.)
zarzaparrilla.
sars(e)net [sársnet], *s.* (tej.) tafetán de Florencia.
sartorial [sartórial], *a.* sartorio; de o relativo a
sastres.
sartorius [-rius], *s.* músculo sartorio.
sash [sæʃh], *s.* (mil.) faja, banda, trena; cíngulo,
cinturón, ceñidor, cinto; (carp.) bastidor o
marco de ventana.
sassafras [sǽsafras], *s.* (bot.) sasafrás.
Sassanid(e [sǽsænid], **s. Sassanian** [sæséiniæn],
a. sasánida.
sat, *pret.* y *pp.* del verbo TO SIT.
Satan [séitan], *s.* Satanás.—**satanic(al** [satǽnic-
(al], *a.* satánico.—**satanically** [-i], *adv.* satánicamente.

satchel [sǽchel], *s.* maleta, maletín.

sate [séit], *va.* hartar, saciar; hastiar.

sateen [sætín], *s.* (tej.) satén, rasete.

satellite [sǽtelait], *s.* satélite.

satiable [séshiabœl], *a.* saciable.

satiate [séishieit]. **I.** *va.* y *vn.* saciar(se); nartar(se); ahitar(se). **II.** *a.* saciado; harto, ahito.—**satiation** [-éishun], *o* **satiety** [satáleti], *s.* saciedad; hartura.

satin [sǽtin], *s.* (tej.) raso.—**satinet** [-et], *s.* (tej.) satinete; rasete.—**satinflower** [-flúœr], *s.* (bot.) lunaria.—**satinwood** [-ud], *s.* palo del águila; doradillo; palo áloe.—**satiny** [-i], *a.* (tej.) arrasado.

satire [sǽtaiœr], *s.* sátira.—**satirical** [satíric(al], *a.* satírico.—**satirically** [-i], *adv.* satíricamente.—**satirist** [sǽtirist], *s.* escritor satírico.—**satirize** [sǽtiraiz], *va.* satirizar.

satisfaction [sǽtisfǽcshun], *s.* satisfacción; recompensa o reparación; desquite; desagravio; finiquito, pago (de una deuda o cuenta).

satisfactorily [-torili], *adv.* satisfactoriamente.—**satisfactoriness** [-torines], *s.* calidad de satisfactorio.—**satisfactory** [-tori], *a.* satisfactorio; expiatorio; suficiente.

satisfy [-fai]. **I.** *va.* satisfacer, contentar; convencer; recompensar, resarcir, pagar. **II.** *vn.* satisfacer, causar satisfacción.

satisfied [-faid], *a.* satisfecho, contento; pagado.

satrap [séitrap, sǽtrap], *s.* sátrapa.

satrapy [séitrapi], *s.* satrapía.

saturable [sǽtiurabœl], *a.* saturable.

saturate [sǽtiuret]. **I.** *va.* saturar; empapar. **II.** *a.* saturado; intenso (color).

saturated [-ed], *a.* saturado; (ópt.), puro, sin mezcla de blanco (apl. a colores).

saturation [sǽtiuréishun], *s.* saturación.

Saturday [sǽtœrde], *s.* sábado.

saturant [sǽtiurant]. **I.** *a.* saturador. **II.** *s.* substancia que neutraliza a otra.

Saturn [sǽtœrn], *s.* (astr.) Saturno.

Saturnalia [-éiliæ], *s.* saturnales.—**Saturnalian** [-éiliæn], *a.* saturnal, licencioso.

Saturnian [satœrnian], *a.* saturnal; feliz, dichoso.

saturnine [sǽtœrnin], *a.* saturnino; melancólico, triste, silencioso; (ant. quím.) plomizo.— **s. poisoning**, envenenamiento por el plomo, saturnismo.

satyr [sǽtœr *o* sétœr], *s.* sátiro.

satyriasis [sǽtœráiasis *o* -ríasis], *s.* satiriasis.

satyric [satíric], *a.* referente a los sátiros.

sauce [sos]. **I.** *s.* (coc.) salsa, aderezo, aliño; compota; verduras; (fam.) lenguaje descomedido. **II.** *va.* condimentar, sazonar; (fam.) ser respondón con, desvergonzarse con o contra, decir insolencias a.

sauceboat [sósbóut], *s.* salsera.

saucebox [-box], *s.* muchacho descarado y atrevido.

saucedish [-dish], *s.* salcera; platillo dulcero.

saucepan [-pæn], *s.* cacerola.

sauceplate [sóspléit], *s.* platillo dulcero.

saucer [sóscœr], *s.* platillo dulcero; salsereta.

saucily [sósili], *adv.* descaradamente, insolentemente.

sauciness [-nes], *s.* insolencia, desmandamiento.

saucisse [sosís], *s.* (arti.) salchicha.

saucy [sósi], *a.* respondón, descarado, insolente.

sauerkraut [sáuœrkráut], *s.* (coc.) col ácida o fermentada.

saunter [sántœr *o* sóntœr], *vn.* vagar; andar despacio y sin objeto; haraganear.

sauntering [-ing], *s.* vagancia; paseo lento.

Sauria [sória], *s. pl.* (zool.) saurios.

saurian [sórian], *s.* y *a.* saurio.

sauropod [sóropod], *s.* y *a.* (pal.) saurópodo.— **Sauropoda** [sorópodæ], *s. pl.* saurópodos.

sausage [sósech], *s.* salchicha, embutido.—**s. balloon** = KITE BALLOON.—**s. stuffer**, jeringa choricera.

savage [sǽvey]. **I.** *a.* salvaje; silvestre; bárbaro, inculto; brutal, feroz; enfurecido. **II.** *s.*

salvaje.—**savagedom** [-dom] = SAVAGERY.—**savagely** [-li], *adv.* bárbaramente, salvajemente, fieramente.—**savageness**, **savagery** [-nes, -ri], *s.* salvajismo; ferocidad, crueldad; los salvajes.

savanna(h [savǽna], *s.* sabana, pradera.

savant [savǽent], *s.* sabio.

save [séiv]. **I.** *va.* salvar, librar; guardar, conservar, reservar; ahorrar, economizar; evitar; aprovecharse de; proteger, eximir; dispensar (*save the word*); séame permitido el vocablo).— **God, o Heaven, s. the mark**, expresión de desprecio o impaciencia; puede traducirse: ¡que mal haya! ¡maldita la cosa! ¡vaya! etc. según el caso. **II.** *prep.* salvo, excepto. **III.** *conj.* sino, a menos que, a no ser que.

sav(e)able [-abœl], *a.* conservable; que se puede salvar o ahorrar.

save-all [-ol], *s.* baloncita, apuracabos; (mar.) vela rastrera.

saver [-œr], *s.* libertador; auxiliador; economizador, ahorrador.

savin [sǽvin], *s.* (bot.) sabina, junípero; cedro rojo.

saving [séiving]. **I.** *a.* ahorrativo, frugal, económico; salvador; calificativo.—**s. clause**, cláusula que contiene una salvedad o reserva. **II.** *s.* economía, ahorro; salvedad.—*pl.* ahorros.—**savings bank**, caja de ahorros. **III.** *prep.* con excepción de, fuera de, excepto, salvo.—**s. your reverence**, con perdón de Vd.

savingly [-li], *adv.* económicamente, parcamente.

savingness [-nes], *s.* ahorro, economía; frugalidad, parquedad.

savio(u)r [séiviœr], *s.* salvador; (S-) Salvador (Jesucristo).

savo(u)r [séivœr]. **I.** *s.* sabor, sainete, dejo, gusto, gustillo; olor, perfume. **II.** *va.* saborear, sazonar, dar sabor y gusto a. **III.** *vn.* (con **of**) saber a, oler a.

savo(u)rily [-ili], *adv.* con gusto, sabrosamente, apetitosamente.

savoriness [-ines], *s.* buen sabor; fragancia.

savo(u)ry [-i]. **I.** *a.* sabroso, apetitoso, delicado; fragante. **II.** *s.* (bot.) ajedrea.

savoy [savói], *s.* (bot.) variedad de col o berza con hojas arrugadas.

Savoyard [savóiard], *a.* y *s.* saboyano.

saw [so]. **I.** *s.* (carp.) sierra; dicho, refrán, proverbio, sentencia.—**s. cut**, corte de sierra; muesca hecha con la sierra.—**s. swage, set, o wrest**, triscador. **II.** *va.* (*pp.* SAWED y SAWN) serrar, aserrar. **III.** *vn.* ser serrado (*this wood saws easily*, esta madera es fácil de aserrar); usar una sierra.

saw, *pret.* del verbo TO SEE.

sawbuck [sóbuc], *s.* cabrilla de aserrar.

sawdust [sódust], *s.* serrín, aserrín.

sawer [sócœr], *s.* aserrador.

sawfish [sófish], *s.* (ict.) pristo, pez sierra.

sawhorse [sójórs], *s.* caballete o cabrilla de aserrar.

sawmill [sómíl], *s.* aserradero.

sawn [son], *pp. irr.* de TO SAW: aserrado.

sawpit [sópit], *s.* aserradero.

sawwort [sóucœrt], *s.* (bot.) serrátula.

sawyer [sóycœr], *s.* aserrador; chiquichaque.

sax [sæcs], *s.* martillo de pizarrero.

saxatile [sǽcsatil], **saxicolous** [sæxícolus], *a.* saxátil.

saxhorn [sǽxjorn], *s.* (mús.) bombardino, bombardón.

saxicoline [sæxícolain], **saxicolous** [-lus], *a.* saxátil, que se cría en las rocas.

Saxifragaceæ [sáxifraguéisii], *s. pl.* (bot.) saxifragáceas.—**saxifragaceous** [-shus], *a.* saxifragáceo.—**saxifrage** [-frey], saxífrago.

Saxon [sǽxun]. **I.** *a.* sajón. **II.** *s.* sajón; lengua sajona; anglosajón; lengua inglesa castiza.

saxophone [sǽxofoun], *s.* (mús.) saxofón.

say [séi]. **I.** *va.* (*pret.* y *pp.* SAID) decir; hablar; recitar.—**to s. a lesson**, recitar una lección.—**to s. in one's sleeve**, decir para su capote o para su sayo.—**to s. one's prayers**, rezar, decir uno sus oraciones.—**to s. over again**, volver a decir, repetir.—**to s. the least**, por lo menos, si no algo peor.—**It is said, they s.,** se dice, dicen. **II.** *vn.* decir.—**s.! I s.!** ¡hola! ¡oiga! ¡digo!—**to s. on,** continuar hablando.—**to s. right,** decir bien, tener razón.—**to s. to,** decir a; opinar de.—**that is to s.,** es decir, esto es. **III.** *s.* uso de la palabra; decisión; expresión de opinión; discurso, afirmación; (fam.) turno de hablar.

saying [séing], *s.* dicho, lo que se dice; aserto, relato; adagio, dicho, refrán.—**as the s. is,** como dijo el otro, como dice el refrán.

'sblood, [sblod], *interj.* ¡por Dios!

scab [scæb], *s.* (cir.) costra, escara; (vet.) roña, escabro; hombre ruin o roñoso; (despec.) esquirol, obrero no agremiado que reemplaza a los agremiados en una huelga.

scabbard [scæbard], *s.* vaina de espada, cuchillera, funda.

scabbed [scæbd], **scabby** [scæbi], *a.* costroso, postilloso; tiñoso, roñoso; vil, ruin.

scabbiness [scæbines], *s.* calidad de costroso, roñoso o tiñoso.

scabies [skéibiis *o* scáibies], *s.* sarna.

scabious [skéibius]. **I.** *a.* sarnoso. **II.** *s.* (bot.) escabiosa.

scabrous [-brus], *a.* escabroso, desigual, áspero.

scabrousness [-nes], *s.* escabrosidad, aspereza.

scabwort [scæbucert], *s.* (bot.) énula campana.

scad [scæd], *s.* (ict.) escombro; alosa.

scaffold [scæfold]. **I.** *s.* andamio, tablado; cadalso, patíbulo. **II.** *va.* construir tablados o andamios para; tender cadáveres sobre andamio.

scaffolding [-ing], *s.* castillaje, andamiada; paral, armazón, bastidor de apoyo, arrimadero.

scaglia [scálla], *s.* piedra caliza italiana.

scagliola [scagliola], *s.* escayola, enlucido de imitación de piedra (mármol, granito, etc.).

scalar [skéilær]. **I.** *a.* (mat.) numérico, no vectorial. **II.** *s.* cantidad puramente numérica o no vectorial.

scal(l)awag [scælauæg], *s.* (fam. E. U.) tuno, bribón; res raquítica.

scald [scold]. **I.** *va.* escaldar, quemar; (coc.) escalfar; limpiar con agua muy caliente. **II.** *s.* quemadura, escaldadura; escalda, bardo escandinavo; (fam.) tiña. **III.** *a.* tiñoso.—**s. head,** (med.) acores, usagre.

scale [skél]. **I.** *s.* escala; platillo de balanza; (gen. en *pl.*) balanza, báscula; (**S-,** astr.) Libra; escama (de peces, reptiles); costra, costrita; (bot.) escama, hoja rudimentaria; incrustación (en las calderas); chispa; escama, laminita, plancha, hojuela; escala, escalera portátil; escalón; escalada; (mat.) escala o pitipié; escala (de un mapa); escala, regla graduada; graduación, división; (mús.) escala, gama.—**s. insect,** (ent.) insecto cóccido, pulgón.—**on a large s.,** en grande escala, en grande.—**on a small s.,** en pequeña escala, en pequeño.—**to s.,** (dib.) según escala. **II.** *va.* escamar o desescamar; descortezar; pelar, descascarar, raspar; cubrir con escamas; incrustar; escalar; (a veces con *off*) medir según escala; dibujar según escala; (con **down**) reducir o rebajar según escala; pesar, romanar; tener (tanto) peso; graduar, igualar. **III.** *vn.* (a veces con *off*) descostrarse; desconcharse, pelarse, descascararse; formarse incrustaciones o escamas; formar escalera; dar facilidad de subir; subir.

scalebeam [-bím], *s.* ástil o brazo de balanza.

scaled [-d], *a.* escamudo, escamoso; costroso.

scalene [scælín]. **I.** *a.* (geom.) escaleno; (anat.) escaleno (músculo). **II.** *s.* triángulo escaleno.—**scalenus** [-línus], *s.* músculo escaleno.

scalepan [skéilpæn], *s.* platillo de balanza.

scaler [skéilcer], *s.* escalador; rascador.

scaliness [-lines], *s.* escamosidad.

scaling [-ling]. **I.** *s.* escamadura; (mil.) escalamiento. **II.** *a.* de escalar.—**s. ladders,** escalas de sitio.

scall [scol], *s.* (med.) tiña.—**scalled** [-d], *a.* tiñoso; costroso.

scallion [scæliun], *s.* (bot.) chalote, ascalonia.

scallop [scólup]. **I.** *s.* (ict.) venera, pechina; venera o concha (distintivo de los romeros); (cost.) festón, recorte, onda; platito en forma

de concha para ostras. **II.** *va.* festonear, ondear; (coc.) asar ostras empanadas.

scalp [scælp]. **I.** *s.* pericráneo; cuero cabelludo (que los indios arrancan como trofeo). **II.** *va.* quitar el pericráneo con la cabellera (como hacen los indios); despelusar (los granos); (fam.) comprar y revender (billetes de f. c.) a precios reducidos.

scalpel [scælpel], *s.* escalpelo.

scalper [scælpœr], *s.* (E. U.) revendedor de billetes (de f. c.) a precios reducidos; máquina de despelusar.

scalping [scælping], *s.* acción de despelusar; acción de desprender la piel del cráneo con cabellera.—**s. iron,** (cir.) raspador.—**s. knife,** cuchillo que usan los indios para desprender la piel del cráneo.

scaly [skéli], *a.* escamoso, conchado; herrumbroso; incrustado (caldera); (fam.) vil, ruin, deshonrado.

scammony [scæmoni], *s.* (bot.) escamonea.

scamp [scæmp]. **I.** *s.* bribón, pícaro. **II.** *va.* hacer (algo) o ejecutar (trabajo) descuidada o malamente, con intención de perjudicar al patrón.

scamper [-œr]. **I.** *vn.* escaparse, escabullirse, huir. **II.** *s.* fuga, huída precipitada.

scamping [-ing], *s.* mala ejecución del trabajo para perjudicar al patrón; producción de un obrero superior a la convenida con sus compañeros, para beneficiarse traicionándolos; sonsacamiento.

scan [scæn], *va.* escudriñar, examinar, registrar; (poét.) escandir.

scandal [scændal], *s.* escándalo; difamación, maledicencia; reproche, censura; oprobio, ignominia.—**s. bearer** = SCANDALMONGER.

scandalize [-aiz], *va.* escandalizar; difamar; acusar falsamente.

scandalmonger [-móngœr], *s.* murmurador, propagador de escándalos.

scandalous [-us], *a.* escandaloso; vergonzoso; calumnioso o difamatorio.—**scandalously** [-lil], *adv.* ignominiosamente; escandalosamente. **scandalousness** [-nes], *s.* carácter escandaloso.

scandent [scændent], *a.* trepador.

scandic [scændic], *a.* (quím.) escándico.

Scandinavian [-dinéivien], *s.* y *a.* escandinavo.

scandium [-dium], *s.* (quím.) escandio.

scansion [scænshun], *s.* (poét.) escansión.

scansorial, scansorious [scænsórial, -rius], *a.* trepador.

scant [scænt]. **I.** *va.* escatimar. **II.** *vn.* (mar.) virar, caer o disminuir el viento. **III.** *a.* escaso, limitado; insuficiente.—**a s.,** poco menos que.

scantily [-lil], *adv.* escasamente, parcamente, a duras penas.—**scantiness** [-ines], *s.* escasez, in suficiencia, exigüidad.

scantling [scæntling], *s.* cuartón, madero, barrote; colección de cuartones; escantillón.— *pl.* (mar.) grúas de tablas.

scanty [scænti], *a.* escaso, escatimado, corto, insuficiente; económico.

scape [skéip], *s.* (bot.) escapo, bohordo; (ent.) cuerno, antena; (orn.) cañón de una pluma; (arq.) fuste de una columna.

scapegoat [-gout], *s.* víctima propiciatoria; persona que paga por las culpas de otras.

scapegrace [-gres], *s.* persona incorregible; pícaro, travieso, bribón.

scapement, *s.* = ESCAPEMENT.

scaphander [scæfændœr], *s.* escafandra.

scaphoid [scæfoid]. **I.** *a.* navicular; escafoideo. **II.** *s.* (anat.) navicular o escafoides.

scapula [scæpiula], *s.* escápula, omoplato.

scapular [-lar]. **I.** *a.* escapular. **II.** *s.* (igl.) escapulario; (cir.) vendaje para el omoplato.

scar. **I.** *s.* cicatriz; chirlo, costurón; (Ingl.) peñasco, farallón. **II.** *va.* marcar con una cicatriz.

Para la pronunciación de æ, œ, d, ş, sh, ʊ, ȳ, γ, z, véase la clave al principio del libro.

scarab(ee [scǽrab, -i], *s.* escarabajo; (arqueol.) escarabajo sagrado de los egipcios, escarabeo.— **Scarabædiæ** [-bidii], *s. pl.* escarabeidos.—**scarabæid** [-bíid], *s.* y *a.* escarabídeo.—**scarabæus** [-bíʊs], *s.* = SCARAB.

scaramouch [scǽramáuch], *s.* botarga, bufón.

scarce [skéɐrs], *a.* raro, escaso.—**scarce(ly** [-li], *adv.* escasamente, apenas, con dificultad; no bien, luego que.—**scarceness, scarcity** [-nes, -siti], *s.* carestía, escasez; rareza; esterilidad.

scarcement [scársment], *s.* vuelo, peldaño.

scare [skéɐr]. **I.** *va.* asustar, espantar; amedrentar, intimidar.—**to s. away,** espantar, ahuyentar. **II.** *s.* susto, sobresalto, alarma.

scarecrow [skéɐrcróu], *s.* espantajo; esperpento, adefesio.

scarf. I. *s.* banda, trena; faja; corbata, chalina; junta de solapa con bordes biselados o enmuescados; junta a diente de sierra (llám. t. **s. joint**). **II.** *va.* (carp.) ensamblar, empotrar, encabezar, charpar; adornar con una banda.

scarfing [scárfing], *s.* acopladura, ensambladura, encabezadura, empalme.

scarfpin [scárfpin], *s.* alfiler de corbata.

scarfskin [scárfskin], *s.* cutícula, epidermis.

scarification [scǽrifikéiʃhʊn], *s.* (cir.) escarificación, saja.—**scarificator** [-kéitœr], *s.* (cir.) escarificador.—**scarifier** [-faiœr], *s.* sajador, escarificador; (agr.) escarificador.—**scarify** [-fai], *va.* (cir.) escarificar, sajar; (agr.) revolver la superficie del terreno; (fig.) criticar severamente.

scarious, scariose [skériʊs, -os], *a.* (bot.) escarioso; seco, delgado.

scarlatina [scarlatína], *s.* escarlatina.

scarlet [scárlet]. **I.** *s.* escarlata, grana. **II.** *a.* de color escarlata.—**s. fever,** (med.) escarlatina, escarlata.—**s. oak,** (bot.) coscoja.

scarp [scarp]. **I.** *va.* hacer escarpa, cortar en declive. **II.** *s.* (fort.) escarpa; declive, pendiente.

scarry [scári], *a.* que tiene cicatrices.

scary [skéɐri], *a.* (fam.) medroso, asustadizo.

scat [scæt], *interj.* ¡zape!

scath [skæz], **scathe** [skeɒ]. **I.** *va.* desbaratar, dañar seriamente. **II.** *s.* daño, perjuicio.

scatheless [skéibles], *a.* sano y salvo.

scatter [scǽtœr]. **I.** *va.* esparcir, regar, desparramar, desperdigar; disipar; dispersar.—**s.-brained,** atolondrado. **II.** *vn.* dispersarse, esparcirse; disiparse.

scatterbrain [-bréin], *s.* (fam.) cabeza de chorlito.

scattered [-d], *a.* disperso, regado, esparcido, desparramado; apartado; irregular.

scatteringly [-ingli], *adv.* esparcidamente.

scaup [scop], *s.* (orn.) pato marino.

scavenge [scǽveny]. **I.** *va.* recoger la basura. **II.** dar salida a los gases (de los cilindros de un motor).

scavenger [scǽvenyœr], *s.* basurero; animal que se alimenta de carroña (aura tiñosa, zopilote, etc.).—**s. beetle,** escarabajo clavicornio.

scenario [senário], *s.* (teat.) argumento, libreto; película, drama o argumento para cinematógrafo.—**s. writer,** escritor de películas.

scend [send]. **I.** *vn.* (mar.) arfar, cabecear. **II.** *s.* arfada.

scene [sín], *s.* escena, vista, paisaje; (teat.) escena; escenario; decoración; teatro, lugar de un acontecimiento; arrebato, escándalo.— **s. painter,** pintor escenógrafo.

sceneful [sínful], *a.* abundante en escenas o en imágenes.

scenery [sínœri], *a.* vista, paisaje; (teat.) decoraciones.

sceneshifter [sínʃhíftœr], *s.* tramoyista.

scenic [sínic], *a.* escénico; artístico; pintoresco.

scenographer [senógrafœr], *s.* escenógrafo.

scenographical [senográfical], *a.* escenográfico. —**scenographically** [-i], *adv.* escenográficamente.

scenography [senógrafi], *s.* escenografía.

scent [sent]. **I.** *s.* olfato; olor, perfume; mal olor; rastro, pista. **II.** *va.* y *vn.* oler, olfatear, husmear, ventear; perfumar; sospechar.

scentless [séntles], *a.* sin olfato; inodoro, sin olor.

sceptic, scepticism = SKEPTIC, SKEPTICISM.

scepter, sceptre [séptœr], *s.* cetro.

sceptred [séptœrd], *a.* que lleva o tiene cetro; real, regio, imperial.

schedule [skédiul]. **I.** *va.* incluir en una lista, catálogo, plan, programa o inventario; inventariar, catalogar. **II.** *s.* cédula; horario (de f. c., etc.); plan, programa; lista, catálogo, cuadro, descripción; (f. c.) cuadro de servicio de trenes.

schema [skíma], *s.* sumario, sinopsis, cuadro; diagrama; esquema.

schematic [skemǽtic], *a.* esquemático.

scheme [skím]. **I.** *s.* plan, proyecto, designio; planta, esquema, modelo; diseño, bosquejo, traza, diagrama; sistema, arreglo, disposición; ardid, treta, artificio. **II.** *va.* y *vn.* proyectar, idear; urdir, tramar.

schemer [skímœr], *s.* proyectista; maquinador, intrigante.

schism [sism], *s.* cisma.—**schismatic** [sismǽtic], *s.* cismático.—**schismatic(al** [-al], *a.* cismático.— **schismatically** [-i], *adv.* cismáticamente, como cismático.—**schismatize** [sismataiz], *vn.* dirigir, causar o fomentar un cisma.

schist [ʃhist], *s.* (geol.) esquisto.

schistic, schistose, schistous [-ic, -ous, -ʊs], *a.* esquistoso.

schnaps [ʃhnæps], *s.* ginebra de Holanda.

scholar [scólar], *s.* escolar, alumno, estudiante; erudito, hombre de letras, docto, letrado; (Ingl.) beca.

scholarly [-li]. **I.** *a.* erudito; ilustrado, docto. **II.** *adv.* eruditamente, doctamente.

scholarship [-ʃhip], *s.* saber, erudición; beca, plaza pensionada.

scholastic [scolǽstic], *a.* escolástico, escolar; (filos.) escolástico; pedantesco.—**scholastically** [-all], *adv.* escolásticamente.—**scholasticism** [scolǽstisism], *s.* escolasticismo.

scholia [scóliæ], *s. pl.* de SCHOLIUM.

scholiast [scóliast], *s.* escoliador.

scholium [scólium], *s.* escolio.

school [scul]. **I.** *s.* escuela; la escuela (*in school,* en la escuela); sala de exámenes; (fam.) cardumen, banco de peces (= SHOAL, que es el término correcto). **II.** *a.* de escuela; para escuela. —**s. board,** junta de educación.—**s. teacher,** maestro o maestra de escuela.—**s. teaching,** enseñanza de escuela; profesión de maestro de escuela. **III.** *va.* instruir, enseñar, aleccionar, amaestrar; reprender, disciplinar. **IV.** *vn.* ir o andar en manadas, como algunos peces; moverse en masa.

schoolbook [scúlbúc], *s.* texto de escuela.

schoolboy [-bói], *s.* muchacho de escuela.

schooled [sculd], *a.* enseñado, amaestrado, aleccionado.

schoolfellow [-félou], *s.* condiscípulo.

schoolgirl [-gœrl], *s.* niña de escuela.

schoolhouse [-jáus], *s.* escuela (edificio).

schooling [-ing], *s.* instrucción elemental; educación, enseñanza; experiencia; precio de la escuela.

schoolman [-mæn], *s.* (filos.) escolástico.

schoolmaster [-mástœr], *s.* maestro de escuela.

schoolmate [-meit], *s.* condiscípulo.

schoolmistress [-místres], *s.* maestra de escuela.

schooner [scúnœr], *s.* (mar.) goleta; (E. U.) galera con toldo que usan los emigrantes; (fam.) vaso alto y grande para cerveza.

schorl [ʃhorl], *s.* (min.) chorlo; turmalina.

sciagraph [sáiagraf], *s.* (arq.) sección vertical.

sciagraphic(al [sáiagréfic(al], *a.* esciagráfico.

sciagraphy [saiágrafi], *s.* esciagrafía.

sciatica [saiética], *s.* (med.) ciática.

sciatic(al [saiétic(al], *a.* ciático, isquiático.—**s. nerve,** nervio ciático.

science [sáiens], *s.* ciencia.

scientific(al [saientific(al], *a.* científico.

scientifically [-i], *adv.* científicamente.

scientist [sáientist], *s.* sabio, hombre de ciencia o científico.

---

seimeter, scimitar, *V.* SIMITAR.
scintilla [sintíla], *s.* centella, chispa.
scintillant [síntilant], *a.* centelleante; titilante.
—**scintillate** [-eit], *vn.* chispear, centellear; titilar.
—**scintillation** [-éishun], *s.* chispazo, centelleo; titilación.
sciolist [sáiolist], *s.* erudito a la violeta, semi-sabio.
scion [sáion], *s.* (agr.) púa, acodo, plantón, esqueje; vástago, renuevo, verdugo; hijo, hija o descendiente.
scioptic [saióptic], *a.* escióptico.
scirrhosity [skirósiti], *s.* calidad de escirroso.
scirrhous [sírus *o* skírus], *a.* (med.) cirroso o escirroso, endurecido; canceroso.
scirrhus [skírus], *s.* (med.) cirro o escirro.
scissel [sísel], *s.* desperdicios o recortes de metal.
scission [síshun, síyun], *s.* corte, división, separación.
scissor [sísœr], *va. y vn.* cortar o cortarse con tijeras.—**scissors** [sísœrs], *s. pl.* tijeras.
scissure [síshœr], *s.* cisura, hendedura; escisión, cisma.
Sclav, Sclavic, *a.* y *s.* = SLAV, SLAVIC.
scleroma [scleróumæ], *s.* escleroma.
sclerosis [-sis], *s.* esclerosis.
sclerotic [-ótic]. **I.** *a.* escleroso, indurado. **II.** *s.* esclerótica.—**sclerotica** [-icæ], *s.* esclerótica.—**sclerotitis** [sclerotáitis], *s.* esclerotitis, inflamación de la esclerótica.—**sclerotomy** [sclerótomi], *s.* esclerotomía.
scobs, *s.* aserraduras, rasuras, limaduras; escoria; álcali.
scoff. I. *vn.* (con **at**) mofarse o burlarse de. **II.** *s.* mofa, escarnio, burla, befa; hazmerreír.
scoffer [scófœr], *s.* mofador, burlón.
scoffingly [scófingli], *adv.* con mofa y escarnio.
scold [scould]. **I.** *va. y vn.* regañar, reñir, reprender, increpar; rezongar, refunfuñar. **II.** *s.* persona regañona.
scolding [-ing], *s.* regaño, reprensión.
scoliosis [scóliósis], *s.* escoliosis, encorvadura lateral de la columna vertebral.
scollop [scólup], *s.* y *v.* = SCALLOP.
Scolopendra [scolopéndra], *s.* (ent.) género de las escolopendras o ciempiés.
scomber [scómbœr], *s.* (ict.) escombro, caballa.
Scombridæ [-bridi], *s. pl.* (zool.) escómbridos.
sconce [scons]. **I.** *s.* cobertizo, salidizo; (fort.) baluarte, fortín; yelmo; (fam.) cabeza; seso, juicio, sentido; anaquel fijo; multa; cornucopia o candelabro de pared; farolillo, linterna sorda. **II.** *va.* fortificar con baluarte; multar.
scoop [scup]. **I.** *s.* pala de mano; cuchara o cucharón de draga; excavación, ahuecamiento; achique; paletada, cucharada; cavidad, hueco; (mar.) vertedor, achicador; (fam.) ganancia; noticia que publica un periódico antes que los demás.—**air s.,** cuchara de aire (de un dirigible).—**s. net,** red barredera. **II.** *va.* sacar con pala o cuchara; achicar, vaciar; ahuecar, cavar, excavar.
scooper [scúpœr], *s.* achicador, vaciador; cavador.
scoot [scut], *vn.* (fam. E. U.) tomar las de Villadiego; pasar, volar.
scooter [-œr], *s.* tablilla horizontal con dos ruedas en tándem y una palanca vertical larga, que usan los niños para diversión, poniendo un pie sobre ella y empujándola con el otro; especie de arado empleado para hacer surcos.
scope [scóup], *s.* alcance, extensión; campo, espacio o esfera de acción o aplicación; propósito, plan, objeto, fin; (mar.) bitadura.
scorbutic(al [scorbiútic(al], *a.* escorbútico.
scorbutically [-i], *adv.* con escorbuto o con propensión a él.
scorbutus [-biútus], *s.* escorbuto.
scorch. I. *va.* chamuscar, socarrar, aburar, rescaldar, tostar; agostar, abrasar (el sol). **II.** *vn.* quemarse, secarse; agostarse, abrasarse (ap. a las plantas); ir (en coche o en bicicleta) con gran velocidad.

scorcher [scórchœr], *s.* (fam.) día muy caluroso; reproche o censura cáustica; jinete o biciclista que va a toda velocidad.
scorching [scórching], *a.* ardiente, abrasador.
scordium [scórdium], *s.* (bot.) escordio.
score [scóœr]. **I.** *s.* muesca, canalita, entalladura; señal, línea, raya; cuenta, tantos (en el juego); deuda; inquina; controversia; cuenta y razón; motivo, consideración; talla (en el juego); (mús.) partitura; veintena.—**on that s.,** a ese respecto, en cuanto a eso.—**on the s. of,** con motivo de.—**on,** o **upon, what s.,** con qué motivo, por qué razón. **II.** *va.* rayar, marcar con líneas, rayas o muescas; escoplear; azotar; censurar severamente; borrar, tachar, testar; apuntar, sentar, poner en cuenta; ganar tantos en un juego; (mús.) instrumentar.—**to s. a point,** (dep.) ganar un tanto; obtener un triunfo. **III.** *vn.* marcar; llevar una cuenta; marcar los tantos en un juego; llevar ventaja en un juego; hacer muescas, rayas o señales.
scorer [scórœr], *s.* marcador; coime.
scoria [scória], *s.* escoria, horrura, cagafierro.—*pl.* scoriæ, escorias volcánicas.
scoriaceous [scoriéshus], *a.* escoriáceo.
scorification [scórifikéishun], *s.* escorificación.
scoriform [-form], *a.* escoriforme.
scorify [-fai], *va.* escorificar.
scorn [scorn]. **I.** *va. y vn.* despreciar, desdeñar; escarnecer. **II.** *s.* desdén, desprecio, escarnio.—**scorner** [scórnœr], *s.* despreciador, escarnecedor.—**scornful** [-ful], *a.* desdeñoso, despreciativo.—**scornfully** [-fuli], *adv.* desdeñosamente; despreciablemente.—**scornfulness** [-fulnes], *s.* desprecio, desdén.
Scorpio [scórpio], *s.* (astr.) Escorpión.
scorpiold [scórpiod], *a.* escorpiónido, semejante al escorpión.
scorpion [scórpiun], *s.* (ent.) escorpión, alacrán; látigo o azote.—(**S-**), (astr.) Escorpión.—**s. fly,** panorpo, escorpión mosca.—**s. grass,** (bot.) miosotis o nomeolvides.
Scorpionida [scórpiónidæ], *s. pl.* (zool.) escorpiónideos.
scorpionwort [-uœrt], *s.* alacranera, alcine.
scot, *s.* (ant.) escote, tasa, contribución; multa; (**S-**) escocés.—**s.-free,** libre de gravámenes; sano y salvo.
scotch [scoch]. **I.** *va.* escoplear, hacer muescas o cortes; herir ligeramente; picar piedra; calzar, poner calza o galga; (fam.) frustrar. **II.** *s.* cortadura, corte, incisión; rasguño; trazo para jugar al hopscotch; calzo o calza, cuña, galga.
Scotch, Scottish, [scótish]. **I.** *a.* escocés.—**S. fir, S. pine,** pino albar.—**S. marriage,** matrimonio por mero acuerdo, sin ceremonia alguna.—**S. reel,** (danz. y mús.) especie de contradanza, muy animada.—**S. snap,** (mús.) ritmo peculiar de los cantos de Escocia. **II.** *s.* el pueblo escocés; la lengua escocesa.
Scotchman, Scotsman [scóchman, scótsman], *s.* escocés.
scoter [scótœr], *s.* (orn.) foja, falaris.
scotfree [scótfri], *a.* = SCOT-FREE. *V.* SCOT.
scotia [scóshia], *s.* (arq.) escocia, nacela.
Scotism [scótism], *s.* escotismo.
Scotist [scótist], *s.* escotista.
scotograph [scótograf], *s.* = SKIAGRAPH.
scotoma [scotóma], *s.* (med.) escotoma.
scotomy [scótomi], *s.* (med.) escotomía.
Scotticism [scótisism], *s.* idiotismo o provincialismo escocés.
scoundrel [scáundrel], *s.* pícaro, bribón.
scoundrelism [-ism], *s.* vida de bribón; bribones colectivamente.
scoundrelly [scáundreli], *adv.* pícaramente.
scour [scáuœr]. **I.** *va. y vn.* fregar, estregar, limpiar; blanquear; purgar; formar cauce; recorrer, batir (el monte); ahuyentar, expeler; pulir, alisar; quitar estregando; lavar con un chorro o una corriente; limpiar (el trigo). **II.** *s.* recorrida; barranco, zanja; limpiador (esp. de lana).—*pl.* diarrea del ganado.

scourer [scáurœr], s. limpiador, desengrasador, sacamanchas; purgante eficaz; azotacalles.

scourge [scœry]. **I.** s. azote.—**the S. of God**, el azote de Dios (Atila). **II.** va. azotar, flagelar; mortificar; acosar.

scouring [scáuring], s. fregado, fregadura, estregadura; desengrase; purga.

scout [scáut]. **I.** s. (mil.) explorador, batidor; niño de la asociación de Niños Exploradores. —**s. commissioner**, director de un cuerpo de niños exploradores.—**s. master**, especie de capitán de varias cuadrillas de niños exploradores. **II.** va. y vn. (mil.) explorar; reconocer.—**to s. at**, burlarse de, escarnecer. **III.** va. rechazar con desdén.

scouting [-ing], a. de reconocimiento, de exploración.

scow [scáu], s. (E. U.) chalana, lanchón.

scowl [scául]. **I.** vn. mirar con ceño, poner mal gesto, enfurruñarse; tener mal cariz. **II.** va. rechazar, repeler. **III.** s. ceño, sobrecejo; mal cariz.

scrabble [scrǽbœl]. **I.** va. escarabajear, garabatear; arrebañar. **II.** vn. emborronar papel, hacer garabatos; (fam.) V. SCRAMBLE. **III.** s. escarabajeo, pataleo.

scrag [scrǽg], s. cualquier cosa flaca y basta o áspera; el cuello; retal.—**scragged, scraggly** [scrǽgued, -gli], a. áspero, escabroso; flaco, descarnado.—**scraggedness, scragginess** [-guednes, -guines], s. flaqueza, extenuación; aspereza, escabrosidad.—**scraggy** [scrǽgui], a. áspero; flaco o descarnado.

scramble [scrǽmbœl]. **I.** va. arrebatar, arrebañar; recoger de prisa o confusamente; (coc.) hacer un revoltillo de (huevos).—**scrambled eggs**, revoltillo, huevos revueltos. **II.** vn. trepar, subir gateando; (bot.) trepar; andar a la rebatina, bregar. **III.** s. trepa; contienda, arrebatiña.— **scrambler** [-blœr], s. trepador; el que anda a la rebatiña.

scrap [scrǽp]. **I.** s. migaja, mendrugo; pedacillo, fragmento; material viejo o de deshecho (apl. esp. al hierro viejo); (fam.) riña, camorra.—pl. cuero tostado (de tocino, etc.); basura, ripios, desperdicios; sobras.—**s. iron**, hierro viejo. **II.** va. echar a la basura; descartar. **III.** vn. (fam.) reñir, armar camorra.

scrapbook [scrǽpbúc], s. álbum de recortes.

scrape [scréip]. **I.** va. y vn. raer, raspar, rascar; arrebañar, recoger; amontonar poco a poco; rascar o tocar mal (un instrumento); restregar los pies; hacer las labores (al algodonero).—**to s. acquaintance**, trabar amistad; lograr amistarse. —**to s. down**, hacer callar (a un actor) con ruido de pies.—**to s. from, off, o out**, quitar raspano.— **to s. together**, juntar a poquitos. **II.** s. raspadura, raedura, rasguño, arañazo; ruido de raspar; restregadura de pies contra el suelo; enredo, lío, berenjenal, aprieto.

scraper [-œr], s. rascador, raspador; estregadera, raedera; arañador, escarbador; rascatripas, mal violinista; (mar.) rasquetas; (ten.) garatura, descarnador.

scraping [-ing], s. raedura, raimiento, raspadura; escarbo.—pl. ahorros; raspaduras.

scrapple [scrǽpœl], s. pasta frita de harina con pedazos de tocino.

scratch [scrǽch]. **I.** va. y vn. rascar, raspar, raer; arañar; rasguñar; rayar (el vidrio); escribir mal, garrapatear; escarbar; cancelar, borrar.— **to s. out one's eyes**, sacar a uno los ojos con las uñas. **II.** s. rasguño, arañazo; rascadura; marca o raya; tachón, borradura, tildón; (dep.) línea de partida en una carrera; peluquín; (E. U.) en el billar, bambarria, chiripa.—pl. (vet.) galápago, espundia.—**s. coat**, capa de base de un enlucido, que es la primera capa, rayada para que la segunda se adhiera mejor.

scratcher [-œr], s. arañador, escarbador.

scratchwork [-ucerc], s. = s. COAT (v. SCRATCH); (b. a.) esgrafiado.

scrawl [scrol]. **I.** va. garrapatear, garabatear. **II.** s. garabatos, garrapatos.

scrawler [scrólœr], s. garabateador.

scrawniness [-nes], s. flacura.

scrawny [scróni], a. flaco y huesoso.

screak [scríc]. **I.** vn. chirriar, rechinar; chillar. **II.** s. chirrido, rechinamiento.

scream [scrím]. **I.** va. y vn. chillar; gritar. **II.** s. grito, alarido, chillido; (fam.) cosa o persona divertidísima, que hace reventar de risa.

screamer [scrímœr], s. chillón; (orn.) palamedea, especie de pájaro cornudo gritador; (fam.) cosa o persona divertidísima.

screaming [scríming]. **I.** s. gritería, grito, gritos; acción de gritar. **II.** a. gritador, que grita; (fam.) divertidísimo.

screech [scrích]. **I.** vn. chillar. **II.** s. chillido, estridor.—**s. owl**, lechuza.

screechy [scríchi], a. chillante, chillón, agudo.

screed [scríd], s. invectiva, arenga; (alb.) maestra, referencia; jirón, tira larga, retazo.

screen [scrín]. **I.** s. biombo, mampara; pantalla; antipara, persiana; tabique, reja; albitana, cerca; reparo, abrigo, defensa; pantalla de chimenea; criba, cedazo, tamiz; pantalla de cinematógrafo.—**s. plate**, (foto.) placa de filtros de colores.—**the s.**, el cine, el teatro de cinematógrafo. **II.** va. cribar, cerner; ocultar, encubrir; escudar, proteger; (teat.) hacer una película de, poner en el cine.

screenings [scríningß], s. pl. residuo, desperdicios de criba.

screw [scru]. **I.** s. tornillo; rosca; hélice (de buque o avión); (fam.) cicatero, tacaño. **II.** a. de tornillo, de rosca, roscado; para tornillos.— **s. bolt**, perno roscado.—**s. conveyor**, transportador de tornillo sin fin.—**s. driver**, destornillador.— **s. eye**, armella roscada.—**s. gear**, rueda dentada; engranaje de rueda dentada y tornillo sin fin.—**s. jack**, gato, cric.—**s. machine**, máquina de hacer tornillos; torno de roscar.—**s. nail**, tornillo para madera.—**s. pile**, pilote con pie metálico de hélice. —**s. plate**, terraja.—**s. propeller**, hélice (de buque o avión).—**s. steamer**, buque de hélice.— **s. stair**, escalera de caracol.—**s. stock**, terraja; material para tornillos.—**s. tap**, macho de terraja. —**s. thread**, filete de tornillo.—**s. wheel**, rueda dentada.—**s. wrench**, llave de atornillar; llave inglesa. **III.** va. atornillar; fijar con tornillos; torcer, retorcer; forzar, apretar, comprimir, oprimir, estrechar; apremiar; hacer visajes, gestos o contorsiones con.—**to s. down**, atornillar, fijar con tornillo; (fam.) apretar los tornillos.—**to s. in**, hacer entrar una cosa en otra dándole vueltas como a un tornillo; insinuar.—**to s. up**, excitar, aguijonear; torcer. **IV.** vn. retorcerse o dar vueltas una cosa en forma de rosca o espiral; ejercer extorsión u opresión.

scribble [scríbœl]. **I.** va. escribir de prisa; borrajear, garrapatear. **II.** s. escrito mal pergeñado; garabato.

scribbler [scríblœr], s. mal escritor.

scribe [scráib]. **I.** s. escriba; calígrafo; amanuense, escribiente; notario publico. **II.** va. marcar, rayar, puntear; (carp.) juntar, ensamblar, ajustar.

scrimmage [scrímey], s. arrebatiña.

scrimp [scrimp]. **I.** va. y vn. escatimar. **II.** a. escaso, reducido, corto. **III.** s. avaro.

scrip [scrip], s. cédula; (com.) póliza, acción o certificado con carácter de vale o abonaré; esquela, apunte; bolsa, zurrón, taleguilla.— **s. holder**, tenedor de vales o certificados provisionales.

script [script], s. letra cursiva; (impr.) plumilla inglesa; (for.) escritura.

scriptural [scrípchural], a. bíblico.

scripturally [-i], adv. conforme a la Biblia.— **Scripture** [scrípchur], s. Escritura (la Biblia).

scrivener [scrívnœr], s. plumista; escribano, tagarote.

scrofula [scrófiula], s. escrófula.—**scrofulism** [-lißm], s. escrofulismo.—**scrofulous** [-luß], a. escrofuloso.

scroll [scrol]. **I.** s. rollo de papel o pergamino; rasgo, rúbrica; hélice; (arq.) cinta (hidr.) caja (de turbina) con conducto de caracol. **II.** a. en espiral; de caracol; en hélice; de o para volutas. **III.** *va.* adornar con volutas; dar forma de voluta o caracol.—**s. saw,** sierra de cinta para contornear.

scrollwork [-uœrc], *s.* obra con volutas, adornos de voluta.

Scrophularia [scrófiulériæ], *s.* (bot.) (género de las) escrofularias.—**Scrophularlaceæ** [-riéisii], *s. pl.* escrofulariáceas.—**scrophulariaceous** [-šhus] *a.* escrofulariáceo.

scrotal [scrótal], *a.* escrotal.

scrotum [scrótum], *s.* (anat.) escroto.

scrub [scrub]. **I.** *va.* fregar, estregar; restregar; limpiar, depurar, lavar (un gas, etc.); limpiar fregando. **II.** *a.* achaparrado, desmirriado; inferior, mezquino; (dep.) de aficionados (carrera, etc.); estropajo; escoba vieja; mequetrefe; monte bajo.

scrubber [scrúbœr], *s.* restregador; limpiasuelos; bruza; (quím. y metal.) limpiador, depurador.

scrubbing [-ing]. **I.** *s.* fregadura, fregado, estregadura; estropajeo (esp. del suelo). **II.** *a.* de estregar, de estropajear.—**s. brush,** bruza para el suelo, estregadera, cepillo limpiasuelos.

scrubby [scrúbi], **scrubbed** [scrúbd], *a.* estropajoso; despreciable; achaparrado.

scruff [scrúf], *s.* nuca; (fund.)=DROSS.

scrumptious [scrúmšhus], *a.* (fam.) elegante; excelente, magnífico.

scrunch [scrunch]. **I.** *va.* y *vn.* (fam.) =CRUNCH; apretar. **II.** *s.* chasquido.

scruple [scrúpœl]. **I.** *s.* escrúpulo; (farm.) escrúpulo (peso de 20 granos); cantidad ínfima. **II.** *vn.* escrupulizar, tener escrúpulos.

scrupulous [scrúpiulus], *a.* escrupuloso, concienzudo.—**scrupulously** [-li], *adv.* escrupulosamente. —**scrupulousness** [-nes], **scrupulosity** [scrupiulósiti], *s.* escrupulosidad.

scrutineer [scrútiníœr], *s.* escrutiñador.

scrutinize [scrútinaiš], *va.* escudriñar, escrutar.

scrutinous [scrútinus], *a.* curioso.

scrutiny [-ni], *s.* escrutinio, escudriñamiento.

scud [scud]. **I.** *vn.* correr, volar o deslizarse rápidamente.—**to s. before the wind,** correr viento en popa. **II.** *s.* carrera rápida; celaje.

scuff [scúf], *va.* y *vn.* (fam.) ponerse áspera una superficie; arrastrar los pies.

scuffle [scúfœl]. **I.** *s.* rebatiña, forcejeo. **II.** *vn.* andar a la rebatiña, forcejear.

sculk, sculker. *V.* SKULK, SKULKER.

scull [scul]. **I.** *s.* remo de espadilla; botequín. **II.** *va* y *vn.* bogar con espadilla.

scullboat [scúlbot], *s.* barquillo, botecito, botequín; (mar.) serení.

sculler [scúlœr], *s.* bote de espadilla; remero de bote.

scullery [scúlœri], *s.* espetera, sollastria o fregadero.

scullion [scúliun], *s.* marmitón, pinche, galopín de cocina; sollastre.—**s. wench,** fregona.

sculper [scúlpœr], *s.* buril, cincel.

sculpin [scúlpin], *s.* (ict.) coto espinoso.

sculptor [scúlptœr], *s.* escultor.—**sculptress** [-tres], *s.* escultora.—**sculptural** [-chural], *a.* escultural.—**sculpture** [-chur]. **I.** *s.* escultura. **II.** *va.* esculpir, entallar, cincelar.—**sculpturesque** [-churésc], *a.* escultural, majestuoso.

scum [scum]. **I.** *s.* espuma, nata, hez, escoria; (fig.) desecho.—**s. of metals,** escoria de metales. **II.** *va.* espumar.

scumble [scúmbœl]. **I.** *va.* (pint.) dar glacis. **II.** *s.* glacis, unión de colores.

scummy [scúmi], *a.* espumoso, natoso.

scup [scup], *s.* (ict.) pez comestible.

scupper(-hole [scúpœr(-jóul], *s.* (mar.) imbornal o embornal.—**s. nails,** estoperoles.

scurf [scœrf], *s.* caspa; costra.—**scurfiness** [-fines], *s.* estado casposo o costroso.—**scurfy** [scœrfi], *a.* casposo, costroso.

scurrility [scœríliti], *s.* grosería, insolencia, procacidad, desvergüenza.—**scurrilous** [scœrilus], *a.* grosero, indecente, procaz; difamatorio.—**scurrilously** [-li], *adv.* injuriosa o groseramente. —**scurrilousness** [-nes], *s.* calidad de procaz o de insolente.

scurry [scœrri]. **I.** *va.* poner en fuga, barrer. **II.** *vn.* echar a correr, escaparse, escabullirse. **III.** *s.* fuga precipitada; ventolera, remolino.

scurvied [scœrvid], *a.* escorbútico.

scurvily [scœrvili], *adv.* vilmente; groseramente; ignominiosamente.—**scurviness** [-nes], *s.* torpeza; vileza.

scurvy [scœrvi]. **I.** *s.* (med.) escorbuto. **II.** *a.* vil, ruin, despreciable.—**s. grass,** (bot.) coclearia.

scutate [skiútet], *a.* (zool.) escutiforme; (bot.) escuteliforme.

scutch [scuch]. **I.** *va.* agramar, espadar, tascar. espadillar. **II.** *s.* estopa.—**s. (blade),** agramadera.

scutcheon [scúchun], *s.* escudo de armas; escudete; planchuela.

scutcher [scúchœr], *s.* agramadera; batidera; aventador.

scutellate(d [skiútelet(ed], *a.* escuteliforme.

scutiform [skiútiform], *a.* escutiforme.

scuttle [scútœl]. **I.** *s.* escotillón; trampa; barreno, agujero; carrera corta; paso acelerado; cubo, balde. **II.** *va.* barrenar, dar barreno; echar a pique. **III.** *vn.* apretar a correr. *V.* SCURRY.

scythe [sáiz]. **I.** *s.* guadaña, dalle. **II.** *va.* guadañar.—**scythed,** armado de guadaña.

Scythian [sízian], *a.* y *s.* escita.

'sdeath [šdez], *interj.* ¡vive Dios!

sea [sí]. **I.** *s.* mar; olaje, oleada, oleaje, marejada; ola grande; la mar, abundancia excesiva o vasta extensión de una cosa. **II.** *a.* de mar, marino, marítimo; naval.—**s. anchor,** ancla flotante.—**s. anemone,** anémone de mar.—**s. bank,** muralla de mar, rompeolas.—**s. bass,** pez marino de los E. U.—**s.-beat(en,** azotado por las olas.—**s. biscuit,** galleta.—**s. blue,** azul marino, verdemar.—**s. boat,** buque marinero.—**s.-born,** nacido en la mar; marino.—**s. breach,** irrupción de mar que rompe un dique.—**s. bream,** besuguete, chopa.—**s. breeze,** brisa de mar— **s. brief,** (mar.) carta de mar o marítima.—**s. cabbage, s. colewort, s. kale,** (bot.) berza marina.—**s. calf,** foca o becerro marino.—**s. caps,** cabrillas.—**s. captain,** capitán de buque de mar. —**s. card,** rosa náutica.—**s. chart,** carta de marear. —**s. cob,** gaviota.—**s. cock,** grifo de (comunicación con el) mar.—**s. compass,** brújula o aguja de marear.—**s. cow,** (ict.) manatí.—**s. dog,** (ict.) foca común; león marino; tiburón espinoso, perro de mar; (fam.) marinero viejo; pirata, filibustero. —**s. eagle,** (orn.) halieto.—**s. fan,** gorgona.—**s. foam,** espuma de mar.—**s. fowl,** aves marinas.— **s.-gate,** oleada larga; punto de salida al mar; compuerta de marea.—**s. goose,** barnacla, percebe.—**s. green,** verdemar, glauco.—**s. gull,** (orn.) gaviota.—**s. hedgehog,** apancora.—**s. hog,** cachalote.—**s. horse,** caballo marino o hipocampo; hipopótamo.—**s.-island cotton,** algodón sea-island.—**s. legs,** pie marino.—**s. letter,** patente de mar.—**s. level,** nivel del mar.—**s. line,** horizonte; sondaleza.—**s. lion,** león marino.—**s. mew,** gaviota.—**s. mile,** milla marina o geográfica.—**s. moss,** ova, alga.—**s. nettle,** ortiga de mar.—**s. nymph,** nereida.—**s. onion,** cebolla albarrana, escila marítima.—**s. ooze,** cieno de mar.—**s. otter,** lataz.—**s. pass**=s. LETTER.—**s. pen,** pluma de mar (pólipo).—**s. pike,** (ict.) espetón; róbalo; merluza.—**s. pilot,** piloto de altura.—**s. power,** potencia naval.—**s. risk,** riesgo o peligro de mar.— **s. room,** espacio para maniobrar sin peligro.—**s. rover,** pirata.—**s. serpent,** sierpe marina (monstruo que algunos han creído ver); (**S. S-**) (astr.) Hidra.—**s. snake,** (zool.) hidra=s. SERPENT.—**s. star,** =STARFISH.—**s. swine,** (ict.) marsopa o puerco marino.—**s. tortoise,** tortuga de mar.— **s.-tossed,** batido por el mar.—**s. trout,** (ict.) baila.—**s. turtle** = s. TORTOISE.—**s. unicorn,** narval.—**s. urchin,** erizo de mar.—**s. valve** = s. COCK.—**s. wall,** muro marítimo de contención.— **s. water,** agua de mar, agua salada.—**s. wolf,** trepador, león de mar.—**at s.,** en el mar; perplejo, confuso, perdido.—**beyond s., beyond seas,** o **beyond the s.,** allende el mar; fuera de aguas jurisdiccionales; fuera de la jurisdicción (de un país, estado, etc.)

seaboard [síbord]. **I.** *a.* costanero, litoral. **II.** *s.* costa, playa; litoral.

seacoast [sícóust], s. costa marítima, litoral.
seafarer [sífæːrœr], s. marino, navegante.
seafaring [sífæːring]. **I.** a. marino, marinero, navegante. **II.** s. vida del marino.
seagirt [sígœrt], a. rodeado o cercado por el mar.
seagoing [sígóing], a. marinero de altura; navegante.
seal [síl]. **I.** s. sello; sigilo, signáculo; timbre; precinto; selladura, sigilación; firma; autenticación, fianza; sacramento; (hidr.) obturación; líquido obturador; substencia o artefacto de cierre; (ict.) foca.—**s. ring,** sortija con sello.—**under the hand and s. of,** firmado y sellado por. **II.** va. sellar, poner el sello, sigilar, precintar; estampar; concluir, poner fin; afirmar, confirmar; cerrar una carta o un paquete (con lacre o goma); marchamar; (igl.) santiguar; bautizar, confirmar; guardar secreto; (mec.) tapar con chapaleta; obturar; tapar; (alb.) empotrar, encastrar.—**to s. up,** cerrar. **III.** vn. cazar focas.
sealed [síld], a. sellado o cerrado.—**s. orders,** instrucciones selladas.
sealer [sílœr], s. sellador; cazador de focas.
sealine [sílain], s. imitación de piel de foca hecha de pieles de conejo.
sealing [síling], a. de sellar; de tapar.—**s. liquid,** líquido obturador.—**s. wax,** lacre.
sealskin [sílskin], s. piel de foca.
seam [sím]. **I.** s. (cost.) costura; (fund.) rebaba; (cir.) sutura; (mec.) junta, costura (de un tubo, una caldera, etc.); grieta, hendedura; cicatriz; arruga; (geol. y min.) filón, vena, veta; capa delgada; yacimiento; (mar.) costura de los tablones. **II.** va. coser, juntar; señalar con cicatrices. **III.** vn. henderse, rajarse.
seamaid [síméid], s. sirena.
seaman [síman], s. marinero, marino, nauta.—**seamanlike** [-laik], a. de buen marinero, como de buen marino.—**seamanly** [-li], a. marino, marinesco.—**seamanship** [-ship], s. náutica, marina, marinería.
seamark [símárk], s. baliza, boya, señal.
seamless [símles], a. inconsútil, sin costura.—**s. tube,** tubo sin costura.
seamstress [símstres], s. costurera.
seamy [sími], a. con costuras; (fig.) lo peor.—**the s. side,** el lado peor.
sean [sín], s. = SEINE.
seance [séans], s. sesión de espiritistas.
seapiece [sípís], s. (pint.) marina.
seaplane [sípléin], s. hidroavión.—**s. carrier,** buque de hidroaviones.
seaport [síport], s. puerto de mar.
sear [sícr]. **I.** a. seco, marchito, agostado. **II.** s. (arm.) muelle real. **III.** va. agostar, secar, marchitar; tostar, chamuscar; cauterizar; endurecer, hacer insensible.
search [sœrch]. **I.** va. y vn. buscar, explorar, escudriñar, registrar (to search a house), registrar una casa); investigar, inquirir, indagar; (cir.) tentar.—**to s. after,** preguntar por; indagar, inquirir.—**to s. for,** buscar; solicitar, procurar.—**to s. into,** examinar, investigar.—**to s. out,** descubrir buscando. **II.** s. registro, visita, reconocimiento; pesquisa, indagación o investigación; busca, buscada.—**s. warrant,** auto que dispone que se haga un registro o reconocimiento.
searchable [sœrchæbœl], a. que puede buscarse o registrarse; investigable.
searcher [sœrchœr], s. investigador, buscador, explorador, escudriñador, indagador, registrador; vista, inspector; (arti.) gato de registro; (cir.) explorador, tienta; (ópt.) buscador.
searching [sœrching], a. penetrante, escrutador; completo, cabal, minucioso.
searchlight [sœrchláit], s. (elec.) proyector.
seashore [síshóœr], s. playa.
seaside [sísáid], s. playa, ribera, costa, orilla del mar.—**seaside pine,** pino bravo o negro, pinastro.
seasick [sísic], a. mareado.
seasickness [-nes], s. mareo, mareamiento.
seaside, s. V. SEASHORE.
season [síšn]. **I.** s. estación (del año); sazón; tiempo oportuno; temporada; época, mo-

mento.—**s. cracks,** grietas longitudinales (de tubos metálicos, etc.).—**s. ticket,** billete de abono o de temporada.—**in due s., in s.,** en tiempo oportuno.—**in s.,** en sazón; a su tiempo.—**in s. and out of s.,** a todas horas, en tiempo y a destiempo.—**out of s.,** fuera de sazón; intempestivo, a destiempo.—**to be in s.,** ser de la estación o del tiempo debido. **II.** va. sazonar; aliñar, condimentar; secar, curar (la madera); imbuir, persuadir, templar, moderar; aclimatar, habituar. **III.** vn. secarse, endurecerse, curarse (madera); sazonarse, madurarse, habituarse.
seasonable [síšnabœl], a. oportuno; a propósito; de estación.—**seasonableness** [-bœlnes], s. sazón, oportunidad, tempestividad.—**seasonably** [-bli], adv. en sazón, oportunamente, tempestivamente.
seasoncracking [-cráking], s. agrietamiento longitudinal.
seasoning [-ing], s. (coc.) condimento, aliño; chiste, salsa o sal (de un cuento, etc.); punto o madurez; aclimatación; desecación, cura (de la madera).
seat [sít]. **I.** s. asiento; silla, banco; escaño; fondillos de los calzones; nalga; sitio, paraje, lugar, situación, puesto; mansión, finca, quinta. —**s. back,** respaldo, espaldar.—**s. of a valve,** asiento de una válvula.—**s. of war,** teatro de la guerra. **II.** va. sentar, asentar; colocar en asientos; tener asientos para; ajustar (una válvula) en su asiento; fijar, afianzar; establecer; arraigar; poner asiento a (una silla, etc.); echar fondillos a (un pantalón). **III.** vn. asentar, ajustar en su asiento (una válvula, etc.).
seating [síting], s. acción de sentar o de sentarse; material para entapizar muebles; (mec.) lecho, base, asiento.—**s. capacity,** cabida (de personas sentadas), número de asientos.
seaward [síuard]. **I.** adv. hacia el mar. **II.** a. dirigido hacia el mar.
seaware [síuœar], s. algas arrojadas a la playa, que se usan para abono, etc.
seaway [síuéi], s. (mar.) mar gruesa o alborotada.
seaweed [síuíd], s. alga marina.
seaworthy [síuœrbi], a. marinero.—**seaworthiness** [-nes], s. buen estado de una embarcación.
sebaceous [sebéshus], a. sebáceo.
sebacic [sebésic], a. sebácico.
sebiferous [sebíferus], a. sebáceo; cerífero.
seborrhea [sebórría], s. seborrea, secreción excesiva de substancias sebáceas en la piel.
secant [sícant], a. y s. (geom.) secante.
secede [sesíd], vn. separarse.
seceder [sesídœr], s. separatista.
secession [seséshun], s. secesión.—**secessionism** [-ism], s. (pol.) separatismo.—**secessionist** [-ist], s. (pol.) separatista, secesionista.
seclude [seclúd], va. apartar, recluir o encerrar; alejarse de otros.—**secluded** [-ed], a. alejado o apartado; retirado, solitario.
seclusion [seclúžun], s. reclusión, aislamiento, soledad; retiro.
second [sécund]. **I.** a. segundo; secundario, subordinado; inferior; de segundos; para segundos.—**S. Advent,** segundo advenimiento de Jesucristo.—**S. Adventist,** sectario que cree que el segundo advenimiento será en sus días, o antes de pasada la generación viviente.—**s. best,** el mejor después del primero; accésit.—**s. cabin,** (mar.) segunda clase.—**s. cause,** causa secundaria.—**s.-class,** de segunda clase; de grado inferior.—**s. fiddle,** segundo violín (ú. fig. en la expresión to be, o to play, s. fiddle, desempeñar un papel secundario, obedecer, etc.).—**s. growth,** (agr.) bosque renacido.—**s.-hand, seconds hand,** segundero (de reloj).—**s.-hand** = SECONDHAND.—(at) **s. hand,** indirectamente, por conducto ajeno; de oídas.—**s. lieutenant,** subteniente, alférez.—**s. mark,** signo de segundos (″).—**s. moment,** momento de inercia.—**s.-rate** de segunda clase o categoría.—**s. sheet,** (com.) segunda página de una carta, gen. escrita en papel sin membrete; cuartilla para copia de carbón.—**s. sight,** conocimiento de lo futuro.—**seconds pendulum,** péndulo de segundos (cuyas oscilaciones son de 1 segundo).—**at s. hand,** indirectamente, por conducto ajeno; de oídas.—**on s. thought,** después de repensarlo; después de

pensarlo bien.—to be s. to none, no ser inferior a nadie o a ningún otro, no ir en zaga a nada o nadie. **II.** *s.* segundo; brazo derecho; ayudante; defensor, sostenedor; padrino (en un desafío); segundo (de tiempo), (mús.) segunda; (geom.) segundo. **III.** *va.* apoyar, apadrinar, ayudar, favorecer; secundar o apoyar (una proposición); segundar, asegundar.

secondarily [-erili], *adv.* secundariamente.

secondariness [-erines], *s.* calidad de secundario.

secondary [-eri]. **I.** *a.* (leng. ord., elec., geol. y fís.) secundario; subordinado, subalterno; subsecuente; resultante; accesorio.—**s. battery,** acumulador. **II.** *s.* lugarteniente, delegado, diputado, subalterno; (astr.) círculo secundario; planeta secundario; satélite; (orn.) pluma grande de la segunda articulación; (ent.) ala posterior; (elec.) secundario (circuito, bobina, etc.)

seconder [-œr], *s.* el que apoya o secunda una proposición.

secondhand [-jænd], *a.* de segunda mano, o usado; indirecto, por conducto ajeno o de oídas.

secondly [-li], *adv.* en segundo lugar.

secrecy [sícresi], *s.* secreto; reserva; clandestinidad; soledad, retiro.

secret [sícret]. **I.** *a.* secreto; callado, reservado; obsceno, vergonzoso.—**s. service,** policía secreta. **II.** *s.* secreto; clave.—*pl.* partes pudendas.

secretarial [sécretériæl], *a.* de secretario; de o para secretarios (escuela, etc.)

secretariat [-tériæt], *s.* secretaría (oficina); cuerpo de secretarios.—**secretariate** [-tériæt], secretaría (oficina).

secretary [-teri], *s.* secretario; amanuense; escritorio, pupitre, papelera.—**s. bird,** (orn.) serpentario.—**S. of State,** Secretario de Estado.—**S. of State for Air,** (Ing.) Ministro de Aviación.—**S. of the Interior,** Secretario de lo Interior o de Gobernación.—**S. of the Navy,** Secretario de Marina.— **S. of the Treasury,** Secretario de Hacienda o del Tesoro.—**S. of War,** Secretario de Guerra.

secretaryship [-teriship], *s.* secretaría (empleo).

secrete [[secrít], *va.* esconder, ocultar, encubrir; (fisiol.) secretar.

secretion [secríshun], *s.* (fisiol.) secreción; ocultación, escondimiento.

secretitious [secretíshus], *a.* segregado.

secretive [secrítiv], *a.* callado, reservado; (fisiol.) secretorio.

secretiveness [secrítivnes], *s.* inclinación a ocultar o esconder.

secretly [sécretli], *adv.* secretamente.

secretness [sícretnes], *s.* secreto, sigilo.

secretory [secrítori], *a.* secretorio.

sect [sect], *s.* secta; partido, pandilla.

sectarian [sectérian], *a.* y *s.* sectario.

sectarianism [-išm], *s.* sectarismo.

sectary [séctari], *s.* sectario.

sectile [séctil], *a.* sectil.

section [sécshun], *s.* sección, división; parte, porción; lámina, tajada muy delgada; subdivisión, departamento, negociado; compartimento; (E. U.) división de terreno de 1 milla en cuadro (259 hectáreas); (dib.) corte, sección (gen. se entiende la transversal); (impr.) párrafo, signo §. —**s. cutter,** instrumento de cortar secciones para el microscopio.

sectional [-al], *a.* regional, local; hecho de compartimentos.

sectionalism [-išm], *s.* regionalismo.

sector [séctœr], *s.* (geom. y mil.) sector; compas de proporción.

secular [sékiular]. **I.** *a.* secular; profano, mundano. **II.** *s.* seglar, lego.—**secularity** [-lériti], **secularness** [-larnes], *s.* mundanalidad.—**secularly** [-larli], *adv.* seglarmente.—**secularization** [-lariséshun], *s.* secularización.—**secularize** [-laraiš]. **I.** *va.* secularizar, exclaustrar. **II.** *vn.* aseglararse.

secularism [-larišm], *s.* secularismo, exclusión de la religión en las escuelas y otras instituciones; librepensamiento (en el sentido de antagonismo a la religión).—**secularist** [-ist], *s.* secularista, partidario del secularismo.

secund [sécund], *a.* (biol.) unilateral.

secundine [sécundain], *s.* secundina.

secure [sekiúœr]. **I.** *a.* seguro; tranquilo, confiado; descuidado; cierto, indubable; inexpugnable; firme, fuerte. **II.** *va.* asegurar, resguardar; salvar, proteger; asegurar, afianzar; garantizar; prender, coger; encerrar, aprisionar; procurarse, obtener, hacerse dueño de.

securely [-li], *adv.* seguramente, firmemente, fuertemente; sin riesgo; tranquilamente.

secureness [-nes], *s.* seguridad, calidad de seguro; falta de cuidado.

security [sekiúriti], *s.* seguridad; afianzamiento, aseguramiento; firmeza; protección o defensa; tranquilidad, confianza; descuido; fianza, garantía, caución, prenda; fiador.—*pl.* (com.) valores, obligaciones, títulos.

sedan [sedæn], *s.* silla de manos (se llama t. **s. chair**); (aut.) sedán.

sedate [sedéit], *a.* sentado, sosegado, serio.

sedately [-li], *adv.* sosegadamente.

sedateness [-nes], *s.* compostura, seriedad.

sedative [sédativ], *a.* y *s.* sedativo, calmante.—**s. salt,** ácido bórico.

sedentariness [sédentérines], *s.* vida sedentaria; calidad de sedentario.—**sedentary** [-teri], *a.* sedentario; inactivo; (zool.) sedentario.

sedge [sey], *s.* (bot.) juncia, junco, enea.—**s. warbler,** (orn.) curruca.

sedgy [séyi], *a.* abundante en juncias.

sediment [sédiment], *s.* sedimento, poso, asiento; borras; (geol.) sedimento.—**sedimental** [-méntal], **sedimentary** [sédiméntari], *a.* sedimentario.— **sedimentation** [-mentéishun], *s.* sedimentación.

sedition [sedíshun], *s.* sedición.—**seditious** [sedíshus], *a.* sedicioso.—**seditiously** [-li], *adv.* sediciosamente.—**seditiousness** [-nes], *s.* calidad de sedicioso.

seduce [sediús], *va.* seducir.—**seducement** [-mœnt], *s.* seducción.—**seducer** [-œr], *s.* seductor. —**seducible, seduceable** [-ibœl, -abœl], *a.* seducible.

seduction [sedúcshun], *s.* seducción.—**seductive** [-tiv], *a.* seductivo, atractivo; persuasivo.— **seductress** [-tres], *s.* seductora.

sedulity [sediúliti], *s.* diligencia, asiduidad o aplicación, ahinco.

seduious [sédiulus], *a.* asiduo, diligente, cuidadoso.—**sedulously** [-li], *adv.* diligentemente, asiduamente.—**sedulousness** [-nes], *s.* diligencia, asiduidad.

sedum [sídum], *s.* (bot.) género de las crasuláceas.

see [si], *va.* y *vn.* (*pret.* SAW; *pp.* SEEN) ver; acompañar (*I saw her to the steamer,* la acompañé al vapor).—*imp.* **see** (en citas) vide, véase. —**s.?** (fam.) ¿comprende? ¿sabe?—**to s. about,** pensar en; averiguar.—**to s. afar off,** ver de lejos, ver a lo lejos.—**to s. (a person) home,** acompañar (a una persona) a su casa.—**to s. into,** penetrar, ver en lo interior de.—**to s. (a person) off,** ir a despedir (a una persona).—**to s. red,** echar chispas, montar en cólera.—**to s. service,** estar en servicio durante la guerra; pasar por trabajo o uso rudo o fuerte.—**to s. stars,** (fam.) ver las estrellas.—**to s. the back of,** deshacerse, salir de.—**to s. the light,** comprender, despertarse (fig.); nacer; darse a luz, publicarse.—**to s. the point,** comprender, ver el sentido o aplicación de lo dicho.—**to s. through (a proposition)** comprender (una proposición).— **to s. through (a person),** leer (fig.), verle el juego (fig.), adivinar la intención o el pensamiento (a una persona).—**to s. (a person) through,** ayudar (a una persona) a salir del paso, o hasta lo último.—**to s. (a thing) through,** llevar (una cosa) hasta el cabo; estar (en una cosa) hasta el fin o hasta lo último.—**to s. through a millstone,** tener mucha penetración.—**to s. to,** atender a, tener cuidado de; cuidarse de.—**to s. to it that,** atender a que, ver que, hacer que.—**let me s., let us s.,** veamos, vamos a ver; déjeme pensar.

see, *s.* (igl.) silla, sede.

seed [sid]. **I.** *s.* semilla, simiente; pepita, cuesco; progenie, prole, generación.—**s. basket,** sembradera, cesto para grano.—**s. bud,** botón, germen.— **s. corn,** trigo o maíz para sembrar.—**s. drill,**

sembradora, máquina de sembrar.—s. lac, laca en grano.—s. pearl, aljófar, rostrillo.—s. plant, planta de semilla, que echa semillas.—s. plot, semillero.—s. vessel, (bot.) pericarpio. **II.** va. sembrar; despepitar. **III.** vn. hacer la siembra; granar, desgargolar.

seedcake [sídkéic], s. torta de semillas aromáticas.

seeder [sídœr], s. (agr.) sembradora, máquina de sembrar.

seediness [sídines], s. calidad de semilloso o de andrajoso.

seedling [sídling], s. planta de semilla; planta de semillero; árbol de pie; planta recién nacida o joven; grillo (tallo de semilla).

seedlip [sídlip], **seedlop** [-lop], s. sementero.

seedsman [sídsman], s. sembrador; tratante en semillas o simientes.

seedtime [sídtáim], s. sementera, siembra; tiempo de sembrar.

seedy [sídi], a. semilloso, que tiene muchas semillas; andrajoso, descamisado.

seeing [síing]. **I.** s. vista, visión. **II.** conj.—**s. that,** visto que, siendo así que, puesto que.

seek [sic]. **I.** va. buscar; tratar de, esforzarse por; explorar, escudriñar o registrar; pedir, exigir.—**to s. a person's life,** tratar de matar o querer matar a una persona. **II.** vn. buscar; investigar.—**to s. after,** buscar, tratar de obtener.—**to s. for,** buscar.

seeker [síkœr], s. buscador; investigador.—**s. after,** investigador de; buscador de.

seel [síl]. **I.** va. tapar o coser los ojos, cegar. **II.** vn. (mar.) tumbarse.

seem [sím], vn. parecer; parecerle a uno.—**it seems** parece, a lo que parece.—**it seems to me,** me parece.

seeming [síming]. **I.** s. apariencia, exterior; apariencia falsa. **II.** a. aparente.—**seemingly** [-li], adv. aparentemente.—**seemingness** [-nes], s. apariencia; plausibilidad.

seemliness [símlines], s. decoro, decencia; bien parecer; propiedad.

seemly [símli]. **I.** a. decente, decoroso, correcto; conveniente. **II.** adv. decentemente; de manera conveniente.

seen [sín], pp. de TO SEE.

seep [síp]. **I.** va. (E. U.) colar, pasar. **II.** vn. colarse, rezumarse, escurrirse.

seepage [sípey], s. coladura, escape; manadero (de petróleo, etc.)

seer [sír], s. profeta; adivinador, vidente; veedor.

seersucker [sírsúkœr], s. (tej.) sirsaca, carranclán.

seesaw [sísó]. **I.** s. vaivén, balance, vibración; balancín de sube y baja, columpio de balancín o de tabla. **II.** a. de vaivén, de balance. **III.** vn. balancear, columpiarse; jugar en el columpio de tabla.

seethe [síD]. **I.** va. (pp. SEETHED, y antiguamente SODDEN o SOD) hacer hervir; (farm.) elijar. **II.** vn. hervir, bullir; estar agitado.

seether [síDœr], s. caldera, marmita.

seggar [ségar], s. = SAGGAR.

segment [ségmœnt], s. segmento.

segmental [segméntal], **segmentary** [ségmenteri], a. segmentario.

segmentation [ségmentéiśhun], s. acción de dividir(se) en segmentos o partes; (biol.) segmentación.

segregate [ségregueit]. **I.** va. y vn. segregar(se). **II.** a. segregado, separado; selecto.—**segregation** [-guéiśhun], s. segregación, separación.

Seidlitz powders [sédlits páudœrs], s. (farm.) polvos de Seidlitz.

seignior [sínœr], s. (for.) señor.

seigniory [sínœri], s. señoría, señorío.

seignorage [sínorey], s. señoreaje; derecho de bráceaje.

seine [séin]. **I.** va. y vn. pescar con jábega o red barredera. **II.** s. jábega, red barredera.

seismic(al [sáismic(al], a. sísmico.

seismograph, seismometer [sáismograf, saismómetœr], s. sismógrafo, sismómetro.

seismologist [saismóloyist], s. sismólogo.

seismology [-yi], s. sismología.

seizable [sísabœl], a. expuesto a ser asido o embargado.

seize, seise [síś]. **I.** va. agarrar, coger; apoderarse de; aprovecharse de; comprender, darse cuenta de; secuestrar, embargar; sobrecoger.—**to be seized, o seised, of,** obtener posesión de.—**to be seized with,** sobrecogerse de. **II.** vn. (gen. con on o upon) agarrar, coger; apoderarse de.

seizer [síγœr], s. agarrador; secuestrador.

seizin, seisin [síśin], s. (for.) posesión (acto de poseer y cosa poseída); toma de posesión.

seizing [síśing], s. toma de posesión; (mar.) trinca, traba; ligadura, aferramiento.

seizure [síγœr], s. asimiento; aprehensión, prendimiento, prisión; captura, presa; (for.) embargo, secuestro, comiso.

sej(e)ant [síyant], a. (blas.) sentado.

Selachii [seléikiai], s. pl. (zool.) selacios.—**selachian** [-an], a. selacio.

seldom [séldum], adv. raramente, rara vez, por rareza.

select [seléct]. **I.** va. escoger, elegir, entresacar. **II.** a. selecto, escogido, florido, granado.

selection [-śhun], s. selección, elección, escogimiento.

selective [-tiv], a. escogedor, que tiene la facultad o el poder de escoger; (biol.) selectivo.—**s. call signal,** (tlf.) llamada ómnibus.—**s. telegraphy,** (radtlg.) sistema múltiplex alternativo.

selectman [-mæn], s. (E. U.) miembro del ayuntamiento, administrador municipal.

selectness [-nes], s. calidad de selecto o escogido.

selector [-œr], s. escogedor; (elec.) selector.

selenic [selénic], a. (quím.) selénico.

selenid [sélenid], **selenide** [-aid], s. selenuro.

selenite [sélenait], s. (min. y quím.) espejuelo, selenita; (S-) selenita, habitante de la luna.

selenium [selínium], s. (quím.) selenio.

selenographic(al [sélenográfic(al], a. selenográfico.

selenography [selenógrafi], s. selenografía.

self. I. a. mismo; por sí mismo; idéntico, propio (desusado excepto en el compuesto selfsame); puro, no mezclado (colores). **II.** s. (pl. SELVES) uno mismo, sí mismo; (en composición) por sí mismo.—**the s.,** el yo, el propio yo. Se une a los pronombres personales, a algunos adjetivos posesivos y al pronombre one para formar pronombres reflexivos o para dar más fuerza a la expresión: myself, yo mismo; me: himself, herself, itself, se: ourselves, yourselves, themselves, nos, os, se: one's self o oneself, sí mismo, se: my other self, mi otro yo. Véanse estos pronombres en sus respectivos lugares. Se separa a veces self del adjetivo posesivo, y entonces pueden traducirse por el pronombre sencillo respectivo: my wife and self, mi esposa y yo; my other self, mi otro yo. Antepuesto, self entra en muchas palabras con los significados de por sí mismo, a sí mismo, etc., y a menudo equivale al prefijo auto.—**s.-abased,** humillado por la conciencia de su propria falta o vergüenza.—**s.-abnegation,** abnegación.—**s.-acting,** automático.—**s.-assertive,** que se hace sentir; que hace sentir sus derechos o pretensiones.—**s.-binder,** máquina de segar con atador automático.—**s.-centered,** concentrado en sí mismo.—**s.-command,** dominio sobre sí mismo.—**s.-complacency,** complacencia en sí mismo.—**s.-conceit,** presunción, vanidad, arrogancia.—**s.-conceited,** presumido, arrogante, presuntuoso.—**s.-confidence,** confianza en sí mismo.—**s.-conscious,** consciente de sí mismo; concentrado en sí mismo, que obra con esfuerzo consciente y manifiesto por hacerlo bien; afectado, falto de naturalidad.—**s.-contained,** completo, que contiene en sí todos sus elementos o accesorios; moderado, dueño de sí mismo; callado, reservado.—**s.-contradiction,** contradicción manifiesta.—**s.-control,** imperio sobre sí mismo.—**s.-convicted,** convicto por confesión propia; que se condena a sí mismo.—**s.-deception, o delusion,** engaño de sí mismo, vana ilusión.—**s.-defeating,** contraproducente.—**s.-defense,** defensa propia.—**s.-denial,** abnegación.—**s.-denying,** abnegado, desinteresado.—**s.-determination,** autonomía, indepen-

---

Para la pronunciación de æ, œ, ᴅ, ś, śh, ᴜ, ȳ, ᴙ, ᴢ, véase la clave al principio del libro.

dencia.—s.-devotion, dedicación de una persona o sus deseos e intereses al servicio de una causa o de otra persona.—s.-esteem, amor propio.— s.-evident, patente, evidente por sí mismo.— s.-examination, examen de coɴciencia.—s.-excitation, (elec.) autoexcitación.—(to) s.-excite, (eléc.) autoexcitar.—s.-existent, existente por sí mismo, eterno.—s.-explaining, que se explica por sí mismo.—s.-feeder, de alimentación automática. —s.-government, imperio sobre sí mismo; (pol.) autonomía.—s.-help, ayuda propia o de sí mismo. —s.-identity, conciencia de la identidad del yo.— s.-importance, propia importancia.—s.-induction, (elec.) autoinducción.—s.-indulgence, complacencia excesiva para consigo mismo, falta de sobriedad, desenfreno.—s.-instructor, maestro de sí mismo.—s.-interest, propio interés.—s.-love, amor propio, amor de sí mismo.—s.-made, que se ha levantado por sus propios esfuerzos.— s.-moving, automotor.—s.-possession, sangre fría, serenidad.—s.-preservation, propia conservación.—s.-regulating, de regulación automática. —s.-reliance, confianza en sí mismo.—s.-reliant, confiado en sí mismo.—s.-respect, pundonor, dignidad, decoro, respeto de sí mismo.—s.-seeking, s. egoísmo; a. egoísta.—s.-sacrifice, abnegación.— s.-service, a. sin criados (apl. a ciertos restaurantes).—s.-starter, (mech.) de arranque automático.—s.-styled, que se apellida o titula, que a sí mismo se llama.—s.-sufficience, s.-sufficiency, presunción, confianza desmedida en sí mismo. —s.-sufficient, confiado en sí mismo; orgulloso, arrogante; que se basta a sí mismo.—s.-will, obstinación, terquedad, porfía.—s.-willed, obstinado, terco.—s.-winding, de cuerda automática (apl. a relojes a que da cuerda automáticamente un electromotor).

self-heal [sélf-jil], s. (bot.) sanícula.
selfhood [sélfjud], s. personalidad consciente.
selfial [sélfial], a. personal, particular.
selfish [sélfish], a. egoísta.—selfishly [-li], adv. por egoísmo.—selfishness [-nes], s. egoísmo.
selfsame [sélfséim], a. idéntico, mismísimo.
sell [sell, va. y vn. (pret. y pp. SOLD) vender; (fam.) convertir, convencer (ú. esp. en la voz pasiva to be sold to, estar convencido de, haberse convertido a).—to s. at auction, vender en pública subasta.—to s. for a mere song, vender por una bicoca.—to s. (for) cash, o for ready money, vender al contado.—to s. out, vender lo que queda antes de cerrar una tienda; vender sus bienes de un deudor para pagar; (fam.) venderse, hacer traición—to s. short, vender acciones o efectos que uno no tiene y que espera comprar a bajo precio antes de hacer la entrega.
seller [sélœr], s. vendedor.
selling [séling], I. s. venta, acción de vender. II. a. de venta; que vende.
selters, seltzer [sélters, séltsœr], s. agua de Seltz, agua carbónica.
selvage [sélvey], s. (tej.) hirma, orillo de paño; borde, orilla, lista, orla; (min.) salbanda.— selvages, (mar.) estrobos.
selves, pl. de SELF.
semantics [seméntics], s. semántica, estudio del desarrollo del significado de las palabras.
semaphore [sémafor], s. semáforo, telégrafo óptico; (f. c.) disco, telégrafo de señales.
semaphoric(al [semafóric(al], a. semafórico.
semasiology [semésióloyi], s. = SEMANTICS.— semasiologic(al [-siolóyic, -al], semántico.
semblance [sémblans], s. semejanza; exterior, apariencia; ademán, máscara, velo, imagen.
semen [sí-, sémen], s. semen; (bot.) simiente, semilla.
semester [seméstœr], s. semestre.
semi- [sémi], prefijo, semi, medio.
semiannual [-éniuœll, a. semestral, de cada seis meses.—semiannually [-i], adv. semestralmente.
semiannular [-éñular], a. semianular.
semiaxis [-éxis], s. semieje.
semibreve [-briv], semibrief [sémibrif], s. (mús.) semibreve.—s. rest, aspiración de semibreve.
semicircle [-sércœl], s. semicírculo.
semicircular [-sérkiular], a. semicircular.—s. canals, canales semicirculares (del oído).

semicircumference [-sœrcúmfœrœns], s. semicircunferencia.
semicolon [-cólun], s. punto y coma (;).
semidiameter [-daiémetœr], s. semidiámetro.
semidiurnal [-daiœrnal], a. semidiurno.
semidouble [-dúbœl]. I. a. (bot.) semidoble. II. s. (igl.) semidoble.
semifloret [-flóret], s. (bot.) semiflósculo.
semifloscular, semiflosculous [sémiflóskiular, -lus], a. (bot.) semifloscular.
semifluid [-flúid], a. semiflúido.
semiglobular [-glóbiular], a. semiesférico.
semilunar(y [-lúnar, -i], a. semilunar.
semilunation [-liunéishun], s. semilunio.
semimanufactured [-méniufæcchurd], a. a medio acabar.
semimonthly [-mónzli]. I. a. quincenal. II. s. publicación quincenal. III. adv. quincenalmente, dos veces por mes.
seminal [séminal], a. seminal, espermático; embrionario; elemental; (bot.) seminal, sementino.
seminar [seminár], s. estudio superior que hace un grupo de estudiantes; dicho grupo.
seminary [sémineri]. I. s. seminario; colegio; semillero, plantel. II. a. seminal; perteneciente a los seminarios.
semination [séminéshun], s. (ant.) sementera; diseminación, propagación.
seminific(al [séminífic(al], a. seminal, seminífero; sementino.
semiofficial [sémiofíshal], a. oficioso, semioficial.
semiordinate [-órdinet], s. (geom.) semiordenada.
semiporcelain [-pórcelen], s. porcelana falsa o imitada; loza de inferior calidad.
semiquadrate [-cuódret], s. (astr.) semicuadrado.
semiquartile [-cuórtil], s. (astr.) semicuadrado.
semiquaver [-cuéivœr], s. (mús.) semicorchea.
semiquintile [-cuíntil], s. (astr.) semiquintil.
semirigid [-ríyid]. I. a. (aer.) semirrígido. II. s. aeróstato semirrígido.
semisextile [-séxtil], s. (astr.) semisextil.
semispherical [-sférical], a. hemisférico.
semisteel [-stil], s. acero pudelado.
Semite [sémait], s. (hist.) semita.
Semitic [semític]. I. a. semítico. II. s. conjunto de las lenguas semíticas.—Semitics, s. estudio de los semitas.
semitone [sémitoun], s. (mús.) semitono.
semivocal [-vócal], a. semivocal.
semivowel [-váuel], s. letra semivocal.
semiweekly [-uíkli]. I. a. bisemanal. II. s. publicación bisemanal. III. adv. bisemanalmente.
semolina [semolína], s. sémola.
sempiternal [sémpitœrnal], a. sempiterno.
sempstress [sémstres], sf. costurera.
senary [sénari], a. senario.
senate [sénet], s. senado; junta directiva de algunas universidades; consejo, cuerpo legislativo; junta de personas venerables.—s. house, senado (sala).
senator [sénatœr], s. senador.
senatorial [-tórial], a. senatorio.
senatorship [-tœrship], s. senaduría.
senatus consultum [senéitus consúltum], senadoconsulto.
send. I. va. (pret. y pp. SENT) enviar, despachar, expedir, remesar; echar, lanzar, emitir, arrojar, producir; difundir, extender, propagar; conceder, dar.—to s. away, despedir, poner en la calle.—to s. back, devolver; enviar de vuelta, enviar otra vez.—to s. down, suspender (a un estudiante).—to s. forth, echar (retoños, etc.); despedir, exhalar (luz, vapores); enviar, despachar. —to s. in, hacer entrar; introducir.—to s. in one's papers, renunciar.—to s. off, despachar, expedir.—to s. one about one's business, echar o despachar a uno sin rodeos.—to s. up, (fam. E. U.) enviar arriba; mandar subir; izar; (fam. E. U.) enviar a la cárcel.—to s. word, mandar recado; avisar; enviar a decir. II. vn. enviar algún recado o recadero; (mar.) = SCEND.—to s. for, enviar a buscar, enviar por.

sender [séndœr], s. remitente; (elec.) transmisor·

send-off [sénd-off], s. (fam.) despedida afectuosa.

Senegalese [sénegælîs], s. y a. senegalés.

senescence [senésens], s. senectud.

senescent [senésent], a. que envejece.

seneschal [séneŝhal], s. senescal.

senile [sínil o sínail], a. senil, caduco.

senility [seníliti], s. senectud.

senior [sínior]. **I.** a. mayor, de mayor edad; más antiguo, decano; (E. U.) del último año en un colegio. **II.** s. señor mayor, anciano; decano; socio más antiguo o más caracterizado; (E. U.) escolar del último año en un colegio; (después de un nombre, en la forma abreviada **Sr.**) padre.

seniority [sinióriti], s. antigüedad; ancianidad; prioridad; reunión de estudiantes de último año.

senna [séna], s. (bot.) sen o sena.

sensation [senséiŝhun], s. sensación; excitación. —**sensational** [-al], a. relativo a la sensación; sensacional; escandaloso.—**sensationalism** [-îŝm], s. (filos.) sénsualismo.—**sensationalist** [-ist], sensualista.

sense [sens]. **I.** s. sentido; razón, juicio; sensación; sentimiento; (geom. y mec.) sentido, dirección (el primer término es el más propio y preciso).—**s. impression**, sensación, impresión sensual.—**s. organ**, órgano de los sentidos.—**s. perception**, percepción sensual.—**the senses**, los sentidos—**to be out of one's senses**, haber perdido el juicio. **II.** va. percibir por los sentidos; (fam.) sentir, inferir intuitivamente; sospechar.

senseless [sénsles], a. insensible, privado, sin conocimiento; sin sentido, absurdo; insensato, necio.—**senselessly** [-li], adv. insensatamente.—**senselessness** [-nes], s. tontería, insensatez.

sensibility [sénsibíliti], s. sensibilidad.

sensible [sénsibœl] **I.** a. cuerdo, razonable; sensato; perceptible, sensible; sensitivo.—**to be s. (of)**, hacerse cargo de, estar persuadido de. **II.** s. (mús.) sensible.—**sensibleness** [-nes], s. sensibilidad; cordura, sensatez.—**sensibly** [-ibli], adv. perceptiblemente, sensiblemente; cuerdamente.

sensitive [sénsitiv], a. sensitivo; sensible, impresionable; tierno, sentido; delicado; (fís., etc.) sensible (instrumento, etc.) (foto.) sensibilizado.—**s. plant**, (bot.) sensitiva, mimosa.—**sensitively** [-li], adv. sensiblemente.

sensitiveness [-nes], s. sensibilidad (de una persona, de un instrumento).

sensitization [sénsitiŝéiŝhun], s. (fot.) sensibilización.—**sensitize** [-aiŝ], va. sensibilizar.—**sensitized** [-aiŝd], a. sensibilizado.—**sensitizer** [-áiŝœr], s. sensibilizador.

sensorial [sensórial], a. sensorio.

sensorium [-um], s., **sensory** [sénsori], s. y a. sensorio.

sensual [sénŝhual], a. sensual, voluptuoso; carnal. —**sensualism** [-îŝm], s. sensualismo; sensualidad. —**sensualist** [-ist], s. sibarita; (filos.) sensualista.

sensuality [-éliti], s. sensualidad.

sensualize [-aiŝ], va. y vn. hacer sensual; volverse sensual.

sensually [-i], adv. sensual o voluptuosamente.

sensuous [sénŝhuus], a. sensorio o sensitivo; tierno, sensible, apasionado.

sensuousness [-nes], s. sensibilidad; afición a lo bello.

sent, pret. y pp. de TO SEND.

sentence [séntens]. **I.** s. (gram.) oración; (for.) sentencia, fallo; máxima, sentencia o dicho; (mús.) frase. **II.** va. sentenciar, condenar.

sentential [sénténŝhal], a. (gram.) de la oración. —**sententious** [-ŝhus], a. sentencioso, conceptuoso; lacónico.—**sententiously** [-li], adv. sentenciosamente.—**sententiousness** [-nes], s. estilo sentencioso.

sentience [sénŝhiens], s. conciencia, estado consciente; percepción; sensibilidad.—**sentient** [-ent]. **I.** a. consciente. **II.** a. ser consciente; conciencia, sensibilidad mental.

sentiment [séntimœnt], s. sentimiento; afecto, simpatía; modo de sentir o de pensar, opinión, concepto; sentido, significado.

sentimental [séntiméntal], a. sentimental.—**sentimentalism, sentimentality** [-méntalîŝm, mentǽliti], s. sentimentalismo.—**sentimentalist** [séntiméntalist], s. persona que se guía por sentimentalismo, sentimentalista.—**sentimentalize** [-méntalaiŝ], va. y vn. tratar u obrar sentimentalmente; atribuir sentimiento a.

sentimentally [-méntali], adv. sentimentalmente.

sentinel [séntinel], **sentry** [séntri], s. (mil.) centinela.—**sentry box**, garita de centinela.

sepal [sépal], s. (bot.) sépalo.

separability, separableness [séparabíliti, -bœlnes], s. calidad de separable; naturaleza separable.—**separable** [-bœl], a. separable.—**separably** [-bli], adv. separablemente.

separate [sépareit]. **I.** va. separar; apartar, alejar, divorciar. **II.** vn. separarse, desunirse. **III.** a. [séparet] separado, aparte; distinto, diferente; desunido, segregado.—**separately** [-li], adv. separadamente, por separado, uno a uno.—**separateness** [-nes], s. estado de separación.—**separation** [séparéiŝhun], s. separación.—**separatist** [séparatist], s. (pol.) separatista; (igl.) cismático.—**separative** [-tiv], a. separativo, distintivo.

separator [sépareitœr], s. separador.

separatory [séparatori], a. separativo.—**s.** (o **separating**) **funnel**, (quím.) embudo de separación.

sepia [sípia o sépia]. **I.** s. (pint.) sepia; dibujo a la sepia; (ict.) sepia, jibia; jibión. **II.** a. de sepia.

sepoy [sípoi], s. cipayo, soldado indio.

sepsis [sépsis], s. (med.) sepsis, putrefacción infecciosa.

sept, s. clan, tribu.

septa [sépta], s. pl. de SEPTUM.

September [septémbœr], s. septiembre.

septemia, septæmia [septímia], s. septicemia.

septenary [sépteneri]. **I.** a. septenario. **II.** s. septena; septenio.

septennial [septénial], a. sieteñal.

septet [septét], s. septena; (mús.) septeto.

septic(al [séptic(al], a. séptico.—**septicæmia, septicemia** [-símia], s. septicemia.—**septicemic** [-mic], a. septicémico.

septillion [septílion], s. septillón.

septuagenary [séptiuǽyeneri], a. septuagenario.—**septuagesima** [-ayésima], s. septuagésima.—**septuagesimal** [-mal], a. septuagésimo.

Septuagint [séptuayint], s. (bib.) versión de los Setenta.—**Septuaginal** [-æl], a. relativo a, o según, la versión de los Setenta.

septum [séptum], s. (anat.) séptum.

septuple [séptiupœl]. **I.** a. séptuplo. **II.** va. y vn. septuplicar, septuplicarse.

sepulchral [sepúlcral], a. sepulcral, fúnebre.

sepulcher, sepulchre [sépulkœr]. **I.** s. sepulcro, sepultura. **II.** va. sepultar, enterrar.

sepulture [sépulchur o -tiur], s. inhumación, sepultura, entierro.

sequacious [secuéiŝhus], a. secuaz; lógico.

sequel [sícuel], s. secuela, consecuencia, efecto; continuación.

sequela [sicuíla o secuéla], s. (med.) secuela, consecuencia.

sequence [sícuens], s. serie, orden de sucesión; arreglo; encadenamiento, ilación; efecto; séptima en los naipes, runfla de un palo; (mús.) modulación.

sequent [sícuent], a. siguiente, subsiguiente.

sequester [secuéstœr]. **I.** va. separar, retirar; (for.) secuestrar. **II.** vn. (for.) renunciar una viuda a toda intervención en la liquidación de la herencia de su marido.

sequestrable [secuéstrabœl], a. secuestrable.

sequestrate [secuéstret], va. (for.) confiscar, comisar; secuestrar.

sequestration [sécuestréŝhun], s. (for.) embargo, secuestración; reclusión, retiro.—**sequestrator** [-tréitœr], s. secuestrador.

sequestrum [secuéstrum], s. (cir.) secuestro.

sequin [sícuin], s. cequí o cequín.

Sequoia [secuóia], s. (bot.) árbol gigantesco de California.

seraglio [serállo], s. serrallo, harem.

seraph [séraf], *s.* (*pl.* -PHIM) serafín.—**seraphic-(al** [seráfic(al)], *a.* seráfico.—**seraphically** [-i], *adv.* seráficamente.

seraphine [sérafin], *s.* (mús.) serafina, organillo de salón.

Serb [sœrb], **Serbian** [-iæn], *s.* y *a* servio.—**Serbo-Croatian** [sœrbocroéishæn], *s.* servocroata (idioma y raza).

sere [sír], *a.* seco, marchito.

serenade [sérenéid]. **I.** *s.* (mús.) serenata. **II.** *va.* dar serenata a.

serene [serín], *a.* sereno, despejado; sosegado, tranquilo.—**most s.**, serenísimo.—**serenely** [-li], *adv.* serenamente.—**sereneness** [-nes], *s.* serenidad de ánimo, tranquilidad, calma.

serenity [seréniti], *s.* serenidad, bonanza; tranquilidad, calma; serenidad (título de algunos príncipes).

serf [sœrf], *s.* siervo.—**serfage** [-ey], **serfdom** [-dom], *s.* condición de siervo, servitud.

serge [sœry], *s.* (tej.) estameña, anascote

sergean(t)cy, *s.* = SERGEANTSHIP.

sergeant [sáryent], *s.* (mil.) sargento; (ant.) alguacil, ministril; escudero; (Ingl.) abogado de primera clase (llám. t. **s. at law**).—**s. at arms**, (en un cuerpo legislativo) oficial de orden, que hace guardar el orden.

sergeantship [sáryentship], *s.* sargentía; grado de sargento.

serial [sírial]. **I.** *a.* de serie, de orden (número, marca, etc.); consecutivo; formando serie; que se publica por entregas; sucesivo. **II.** *s.* obra que se publica por entregas.—**serially** [síriali], *adv.* en serie; por serie; por entregas.

sericate [sériket], *a.* sedoso; velludo.

sericeous [seríshus], *a.* sérico, sedoso.

sericultural [síricúlchural], *a.* sericícola.

sericulture [-chur], *a.* sericicultura.

series [siriis]. **I.** *s.* serie; (mat.) serie; progresión.—**in s.**, (elec.) en serie. **II.** *a.* en serie (arrollamiento, dínamo, etc.).—**s.-parallel**, (elec.) en serie-paralelo.—**s.-wound**, (elec.) arrollado en serie.

serin [sérin], *s.* (orn.) verderón.

seringa [seríngæ], *s.* (bot.) siringa, variedad del árbol del caucho; lila; (fam.) jeringuilla.

serio-comic(al [sírio-cómic(al], *a.* jocoserio.

serious [sírius], *a.* serio; grave; verdadero, sincero.—**seriously** [-li], *adv.* seriamente; gravemente.—**seriousness** [-nes], *s.* seriedad; gravedad.

serjeant, *s.* = SERGEANT.

sermon [sœrmun], *s.* sermón; sermoneo.—**S. on the Mount,** sermón del Monte.

sermonize [-ais], *va.* predicar; sermonear.

sermonizer [-aiscer], *s.* sermoneador.

serology [sérloyi], *s.* (med.) estudio de los sueros y sus efectos.

seron, seroon [serún], *s.* sera, serón.—**s. of cinnamon,** churla de canela.—**s. of cocoa,** sobornal de cacao.—**s. of indigo,** zurrón de añil.

serosity [serósiti], *s.* serosidad.

serotherapy [sírozéræpi], *s.* sueroterapia o seroterapia.

serotinous [serótinus], *a.* (bot.) serondo, serotino.

serous [sírus], *a.* seroso; icoroso.

serpent [sœrpent], *s.* serpiente o sierpe; (piro.) buscapiés; (mus.) serpentón; persona traidora; Satanás; (astr.) Serpiente.

serpentigenous [-tíyenus], *a.* nacido de una serpiente.

serpentine [-tin *o* -tain]. **I.** *a.* serpentino; caracoleado.—**s. marble**, serpentina (mármol). **II.** *s.* (min.) serpentina. **III.** *vn.* serpentear.

serpiginous [sœrpíyinus], *a.* serpiginoso.

serpigo [sœrpáigo], *s.* (med.) serpigo.

serrate(d [sérret(ed], *a.* dentellado; (bot.) serrado, endentado.

serration [serréishun], *s.* endentadura, recorte, recortadura.

serrature [sérrachur *o* -tiur], *s.* (biol.) estructura serrada, endentadura.

serried [sérrid], *a.* apretado.

serriform [-form], *a.* serrado, dentado.

serum [sírum], *s.* suero.—**s. sickness,** enfermedad causada por la inoculación de un suero.—**s. therapy,** sueroterapia, seroterapia.

servable [sœrvæbœl], *a.* servible.

servant [sœrvant], *s.* criado, sirviente; servidor.—**s. girl, s. maid,** criada.—**s. man,** criado.

serve [sœrv]. **I.** *va.* servir a, estar al servicio de; servir en, estar encargado de; servir de o para, ser de alguna utilidad para; escanciar (vino, etc.); manejar, hacer maniobrar o funcionar (un cañón, etc.); agasajar, obsequiar, divertir; abastecer, surtir; pagar, dar su merecido a; (for.) entregar (una citación o requerimiento); cumplir (una condena); (mar.) aforrar; recompensar; cubrir (el macho a la hembra).—**to s. an office,** desempeñar un cargo.—**to s. a warrant,** ejecutar un auto de prisión.—**to s. one a trick,** jugar a uno una mala partida.—**to s. one's self of,** servirse de, hacer uso de.—**to s. one's time,** acabar el tiempo de servicio.—**to s. one's turn,** bastar, ser suficiente.—**to s. notice (on),** avisar, notificar.—**to s. time,** cumplir una condena en presidio.—**it serves you right** (en tono de represión), bien se lo merece, la ha pagado Vd. como debía. **II.** *vn.* servir, ser criado; estar en sujeción; desempeñar los deberes de un empleo, servir a su país, en el ejército o en la marina; bastar, ser suficiente, útil o apto; (dep.) sacar o dar saque, servir la pelota; en ciertos juegos, servir con naipe del mismo palo.—**to s. for,** servir de.

server [sœrvœr], *s.* servidor; criado de mesa; acólito; bandeja; macho de cría (gallo, toro, etc.).

Servian [sœrviæn], *s.* y *a.* servio.

service [sœrvis]. **I.** *s.* servicio; servidumbre; desempeño; oficio; utilidad, ventaja; vajilla, servicio de mesa; (igl.) servicio; (for.) obligación de un criado o arrendatario; entrega legal de una citación; (mar.) forro de cable; cubrición; precio que se paga por la cubrición de un macho de cría; (bot.) verbal. **II.** *a.* de servicio: ordinario (uniforme, etc.).—**s. book,** misal; libro litúrgico.—**s. celling,** (aer.) techo utilizable, altura límite para una velocidad dada.—**s. pipe,** (hidr.) tubería de toma, tubería que va de la maestra a un edificio.—**s. station,** (aut.) taller de auxilio o de reparaciones urgentes.—**s. tree,** (bot.) verbal.—**at your s.,** a su disposición.—**it is of no s.,** no vale nada, de nada sirve.—**out of s.,** sin acomodo; sin conveniencia.—**to be of s.,** ser útil, servir.

serviceable [-abœl], *a.* servible, útil; duradero.—**serviceableness** [-abœlnes], *s.* calidad de servicial o duradero.—**serviceably** [-abli], *adv.* servicialmente, útilmente; duraderamente.

servient [sœrviœnt], *a.* (for.) subordinado.

servile [sœrvil]. **I.** *a.* servil; (gram.) que no pertenece a la raíz de la palabra. **II.** *s.* esclavo; letra o sílaba que no pertenece a la radical.

servilely [sœrvilli], *adv.* servilmente.

servileness [sœrvilnes], **servility** [sœrvíliti], *s.* servidumbre, esclavitud; bajeza, vileza.

serving [sœrving], *a.* sirviente; ministrante.—**s. maid,** criada, sirvienta.—**s. mallet,** (mar.) maceta de forrar.—**s. man,** sirviente, criado.

servitor[sœrvitœr], *s.* servidor; ayudante; seguidor, secuaz, partidario; (Ingl.) fámulo de colegio.—**servitorship** [-ship], *s.* famulato.

servitude [sœrvitiud], *s.* servidumbre; esclavitud; vasallaje, sujeción; trabajo forzado; servicio militar o naval (angloindio); (for.) servidumbre.

Servo-Croatian [sœrvocroéishæn], *s.* y *a.* servo-croata.

servomotor [-móutœr], *s.* servomotor, motor auxiliar; motor de dirección (de un torpedo).

sesame [sésame], *s.* (bot.) ajonjolí, sésamo, alegría.

sesamoid [sésamoid], *s.* y *a.* (anat.) sesamoide.

sesquioxide [sescuióxid], *s.* (quím.) sesquióxido.

sesquipedal [sescuípedal], **sesquipedalian** [séscuipedélian], *a.* sesquipedal.

sessile [sésil], *a.* (biol.) sesil, sentado.

session [séshun], *s.* sesión; tribunal inferior de la Iglesia presbiteriana; período escolar; (Ingl.) sala de justicia; término judicial.

sessional [-al], *a.* perteneciente a una sesión.

sesterce [séstœrs], *s.* sestercio.

sestet [séstet], *s.* las últimas seis líneas de un soneto; sextilla; (mús.) sexteto.

set [set], *va.* (*pret. y pp.* SET) poner; colocar; asentar; instalar, establecer; poner (una gallina) a empollar; meter, poner (fuego a una casa, etc.); fijar, inmovilizar, paralizar; embarazar, poner en aprietos; determinar, señalar; (con on) poner (la mente, la fe, el corazón, la esperanza) en resuelta, firme o anhelosamente; (a veces con **out**) plantar (un árbol); montar, engastar (un diamante); adornar, aderezar (con piedras preciosas, etc.); cuajar (leche); arreglar; preparar (insectos, etc.); ajustar; alistar, arreglar, poner (una herramienta, un reloj, etc.); afilar, amolar; (cir.) reducir, encasar (un hueso roto); (mec.) triscar (los dientes de una sierra); (impr.) parar (tipo); (constr.) depositar, colocar (piedras, etc.); (mar.) desplegar (velas); dar (la nota o la clave) (mús.); poner música a; apostar; (con *at*) apreciar (en), estimar (en), dar por; (con *on*) poner (precio, límite) a; apuntar, señalar, parar (la caza); dar (ejemplo, regla); mostrar, enseñar, **establecer**; armar, poner (una trampa), tender (lazos); (top.) establecer o poner (un instrumento) en estación.— **to s. afire**, poner fuego a, incendiar.— **to s. afloat**, poner a flote; esparcir, hacer circular.— **to s. against**, indisponer, malquistar con; oponer u oponerse; contraponer a.— **to s. agoing**, hacer ir; poner en juego o movimiento; echar (algo) a andar; dar impulso a.— **to s. apart**, poner aparte. — **to s. a price on**, fijar precio a; poner a precio, ofrecer premio por.— **to s. aside**, dar de mano; poner a un lado o aparte; apartar; ahorrar; hacer caso omiso de; desechar, rechazar; abrogar, anular.— **to s. a task**, imponer una tarea.— **to s. at defiance**, retar, desafiar; desconocer, no hacer caso de.— **to s. at ease**, tranquilizar.— **to s. at liberty**, poner en libertad.— **to s. at naught**, despreciar, tener en nada.— **to s. at odds**, desunir, malquistar.— **to s. at rest**, poner en reposo; poner fin a.— **to s. at variance**, desunir, poner en contradicción o antagonismo.— **to s. back**, hacer retroceder; hacer perder lo ganado.— **to s. before**, presentar a, exponer ante; poner a la vista de.— **to s. by**, hacer aprecio; poner a un lado; guardar.— **to s. by the ears**, hacer reñir, malquistar.— **to s. down**, poner, colocar; poner por escrito; imponer, determinar; establecer, sentar, enunciar; censurar o humillar.— **to s. eyes on**, ver; mirar; clavar los ojos a.— **to s. fast**, sujetar, consolidar; adelantar (un reloj).— **to s. fire to**, poner fuego a; incendiar; inflamar (las pasiones). —**to s. forth**, manifestar; exponer; promulgar; explicar; exhibir; ensalzar, alabar; publicar.— **to s. forward**, hacer adelantar o avanzar; promover, fomentar; empujar, impeler.— **to s. free**, poner en libertad.— **to s. great store by**, dar mucha importancia a.— **to s. in**, engastar.— **to s. in order**, arreglar, poner en orden.— **to s. light, o little, by**, menospreciar, dar poca importancia a.— **to s. milk**, poner leche a cuajar; cuajar leche.— **to s. off**, poner aparte, reservar, separar; comparar, contraponer; poner en relieve, hacer resaltar o destacarse; adornar, embellecer; disparar.— **to s. off against**, reemplazar por, dar como equivalente de. —**to s. on**, excitar, incitar, instigar contra; azuzar, echar (perros, etc.) a.— **to s. one's cap at, o for**, galantear, requebrar, tratar de insinuarse a (una mujer).— **to s. one's face**, estar resuelto.— **to s. one's hand**, o **one's hand and seal to**, poner su firma a, firmar; (fig.) aceptar, aprobar.— **to s. one's house in order**, poner su casa en orden, arreglar sus negocios; prepararse para la muerte.— **to s. one's mind on**, aplicarse a.— **to s. one's teeth**, apretar los dientes.— **to s. one's teeth on edge**, dar dentera.— **to s. one to work**, poner a uno a trabajar.— **to s. on fire**, pegar fuego a. — **to s. open**, abrir.— **to s. out**, exponer, manifestar; equipar, armar; publicar, promulgar; asignar, señalar; adornar, hermosear; (agr.) plantar, trasplantar.— **to s. over**, traspasar, ceder; dar la dirección o el mando de.— **to s. right**, colocar bien; enmendar, corregir, rectificar.— **to s. sail**, hacerse a la vela.— **to s. by**, dar valor o importancia a.— **to s. the watch**, rendir la guardia.— **to s. thinking**, hacer pensar.— **to s. to music**, poner en música.— **to s. to rights**, poner en orden.— **to s. to work**, poner a trabajar; emplear, ocupar.— **to s. up**, ensalzar, exaltar, elevar; erigir, fundar, instituir; sentar, levantar (tienda de campaña, etc.); enderezar, empinar; exponer y defender (una teoría, etc.); causar, producir, determinar; vender a subasta; (mec.) armar, montar; dar o pegar (un grito); establecer, abrir, poner (negocios, tienda, etc.); (impr.) poner en tipo; parar (tipo).— **to s. up a shop**, poner tienda. —**to s. up a tent**, levantar una tienda de campaña.— **to s. up the drinks**, (fam.) convidar (a beber).

set, *vn.* (astr.) ponerse (un astro); cuajarse, solidificarse; endurecerse; fraguar (el hormigón, etc.); fijarse; correr, moverse o fluir (una corriente); tender, inclinarse; aplicarse, dedicarse, ponerse a; cambiar, alterarse, deformarse; empezar a crecer o desarrollarse; convertirse en fruto o semilla; (danz.) situarse enfrente del compañero de baile; (fam.) empollar (lo correcto es *to sit*); (fam.) sentar, ajustar, caer bien (una prenda de vestir).— **to s. about**, emprender, comenzar.— **to s. forth**, avanzar, ponerse en marcha.— **to s. in**, comenzar, aparecer, sobrevenir; fluir (la marea).— **to s. off**, salir, partir.— **to s. on, o upon**, salir, partir; empezar; acometer, atacar.— **to s. out**, salir, partir; emprender un viaje o un negocio.— **to s. to**, aplicarse con vigor a; ponerse a (trabajar).— **to s. to work**, poner manos a la obra; emprender el trabajo.— **to s. up**, establecerse; principiar, aparecer.— **to s. up for**, pasar plaza de.

set. I. *a.* resuelto, determinado; obstinado, inflexible, inadaptable; fijo, invariable; establecido, prescrito; regular, arreglado, ajustado; formal; meditado, estudiado; puesto, sentado, colocado; rígido, yerto, inmóvil; hecho, trabajado, construído, fabricado; montado, engastado.—**s. form**, formulario.—**s. price**, precio fijo.—**s. screw**, tornillo de sujeción.—**s. square**, (dib.) escuadra. **II.** *s.* juego, surtido, colección, serie, grupo, clase; equipo; instrumento, etc., con sus accesorios; recado; compañía, camarilla, cuadrilla, banda, hato, pandilla; (joy.) terno, aderezo; (astr.) puesta; curso, movimiento, dirección, tendencia; encorvadura; porte; triscamiento de los dientes de ciertas sierras; deformación; asentamiento, cesación de cambio; (agr.) planta de trasplantar; bulbo; pie de árbol; fruto en estado rudimentario; (teat.) decoración; (sast.) V. FIT; (dep.) partida; (danz.) tanda; (tecn.) endurecimiento (de la cola, etc.); fraguado (del cemento, etc.).—**s. of books**, colección de libros; juego de libros.—**s. of chairs, juego de sillas**.—**s. of china**, servicio de porcelana.—**s. of diamonds**, aderezo de diamantes; terno.—**s. of horses**, tiro, tronco, pareja de caballos.—**s. of oars**, juego de remos.—**s. of stairs** = FLIGHT OF STAIRS.—**s. of teeth**, dentadura.

setaceous [setéśhus], *a.* cerdoso, cerdudo.

setback [sétbæc], *s.* retroceso, revés, contrariedad; contracorriente.

setbolt [sétbólt], *s.* (mar.) botador, perno de trabante.

set-down [-dáun], *s.* reprimenda; (fam.) peluca.

setiferous [setíferus], *a.* cerdoso.

setiform [sétiform], *a.* de forma de cerda.

set-off [-of], *s.* compensación; contrapeso; adorno; relieve, realce; saliente, vuelo; disminución progresiva; (for.) contrarreclamación; reconvención; (impr.) reprinte, tiznadura.

seton [sítun], *s.* (cir. y vet.) sedal, fuente.

setose [sítos], **setous** [sítus], *a.* cerdoso.

set-out [-áut], *s.* (fam.) arreglos y equipo para un viaje; boato, aparato.

settee [setí], *s.* banco, canapé.—**s. bed**, cama plegadiza en forma de canapé.

setter [sétœr], *s.* (en composición) el que monta, pone, coloca o fija; perro de ajeo, perdiguero; espión, espía; corchete, alguacil.

setting [séting], *s.* puesta de un astro, ocaso; (constr.) fraguado (del hormigón, etc.); (tea.) puesta en escena, decoraciones; (joy.) engaste, montadura; armadura, marco, guarnición; ajeo; (fam.) nidada.—**s. of the wind, o current**, (mar.) dirección del viento o la corriente.

settle [sétœl]. **I.** *va.* colocar, asentar; fijar, asegurar; arreglar; establecer, estatuir; dar una profesión o estado a; casar; colonizar, poblar; clarificar, quitar la hez; sosegar, calmar, decidir, determinar; poner fin a, acabar; señalar, fijar; ajustar, arreglar (cuentas); componer, redondear; saldar, liquidar, finiquitar; hacer firme y transitable (un camino).—**to s. on, o upon,** dar en dote, señalar, asignar. **II.** *vn.* posarse, reposarse, asentarse; hacer sedimiento; arraigar, establecerse, fijar su residencia; tomar estado; casarse; instalarse, poner casa; sosegarse, calmar; contraerse; decidirse, determinarse; liquidar con acreedores; saldar una cuenta.—**to s. down,** asentarse; fijarse; cobrar juicio; ponerse a. **III.** *s.* banco, escaño; escalón, grada de escalera.—**s. bed** = SETTEE BED.

settled [sétœld], *a.* fijo; establecido; arraigado, en orden; asentado; determinado, decidido; arreglado; saldado; poblado.

settlement [-mœnt], *s.* establecimiento, instalación; colonización; colonia; caserío, poblado, pueblo; (Ingl.) asiento, domicilio; (for.) dote que se da en arras a una mujer; poso, sedimento; asiento de un edificio; acomodo, empleo, destino; ajuste, convenio, arreglo; (com.) saldo, liquidación, finiquito; pago.

settler [sétlœr], *s.* poblador, colono; establecedor, fundador.—**s. of averages,** medidor de averías.

settling [sétling]. **I.** *s.* establecimiento, colonización; arreglo; instalación; asentamiento, hundimiento; ajustamiento.—*pl.* heces, zurrapas; sedimento, poso. **II.** *a.* de asentar; de sedimentación; de clarificación.

set-to [-tú], *s.* lucha, combate; disputa, debate.

set-up [-ʊp], *s.* talante, presencia; (metal.) máquina de comprimir para rebordear; (mec.) perno con extremo de pestaña; (fam.) invitación (a beber).

setwall [sétuol], *s.* (bot.) valeriana.

seven [sevn], *s.* y *a.* siete.—**the s. deadly sins,** los siete pecados capitales.—**the S. Hills,** las siete colinas (de Roma).—**the S. Seas,** todos los mares, el mundo entero.—**the S. Wise Men,** los siete sabios (de Grecia).—**the s. wonders,** las siete maravillas.

sevenfold [sévœnfold]. **I.** *a.* séptuplo. **II.** *adv.* siete veces.

sevenscore [sévœnscor], *s.* siete veintenas.

seventeen [sévœntín], *a.* y *s.* diecisiete.

seventeenth [-tinz]. **I.** *a.* decimoséptimo, diecisiete (ordinal). **II.** *s.* y *a.* diecisieteavo.

seventh [sévœnz]. **I.** *a.* séptimo. **II.** *s.* y *a.* (arit.) séptimo; (mús.) séptima.—**seventhly** [-li], *adv.* en séptimo lugar.

seventieth [-tiez]. **I.** *a.* septuagésimo, setenta (ordinal). **II.** *s.* y *a.* setentavo.

seventy [sévœnti], *a.* y *s.* setenta.

sever [sévœr]. **I.** *va.* separar, desunir, dividir; cortar, romper. **II.** *vn.* separarse, desunirse; entreabrirse; partirse.

several [sévœral]. **I.** *a.* varios; distinto, respectivo. **II.** *s.* varios, cada uno en particular.—**severally** [-i], *adv.* separadamente, distintamente, individualmente; a parte, cada uno de por sí.—**joint and s.,** solidario; solidariamente, in sólidum.

severalty [-ti], *s.* (for.) posesión privativa de un terreno.

severance [sévœrans], *s.* separación, partición.

severe [sevíœr], *a.* severo, riguroso; duro, cruel; rígido, estricto, austero; grave, serio; recio, fuerte; bravo.—**severely** [-li], *adv.* severamente, cruelmente; rigurosamente.

severeness [-nes], **severity** [sevériti], *s.* severidad, rigor, crueldad; rigidez, rigorismo, exactitud, austeridad; seriedad, gravedad.

sew [so], *va.* y *vn.* coser.

sewage [súey], *s.* aguas de albañal; alcantarillado (uso erróneo). *V.* SEWERAGE.

sewer [sóœr], *s.* (enc.) cosedor.

sewer [súœr], *s.* albañal, cloaca, alcantarilla.—**s. gas,** emanaciones de las cloacas.

sewerage [súœrey], *s.* alcantarillado; sistema de cloacas.

sewing [sóing]. **I.** *s.* costura. **II.** *a.* de coser; para coser.—**s. bee,** reunión de amigas para hacer costura.—**s. machine,** máquina de coser.—**s.-machine needle,** aguja de máquina de coser.—**s. press,** (enc.) telar.—**s. thread,** hilo de coser.

sex, *s.* sexo.—**the s.,** el bello sexo.

sexagenarian [séxayenérian], *s.* sesentón.

sexagenary [sexéyenœri], *a.* sexagenario.

Sexagesima [séxayésima], *s.* sexagésima.

sexagesimal [séxayésimal], *a.* sexagesimal.

sexennial [sexénial], *a.* que dura seis años, o acontece cada seis años.

sexless [séxles], *a.* neutro, sin sexo.

sext [sext], *s.* (igl.) sexta (una de las horas menores); sexto (libro de decretos canónicos).

sextain [séxtein], *s.* (poét.) sextilla.

sextant [séxtant], *s.* sextante (instrumento); (geom.) sextante.

sextet [séxtet], *s.* (mús.) sexteto.

sextile [séxtil], *s.* (astr.) sextil.

sextillion [sextíliun], *s.* sextillón.

sextodecimo [sextodésimo], *a.* y *s.* dieciseisavo.

sexton [séxton], *s.* (igl.) sacristán; muñidor, zacateca, enterrador; sepulturero.

sextuple [séxtiupœl], *a.* séxtuplo.

sexual [séxyual], *a.* sexual.—**s. intercourse,** cópula, coito; comercio sexual.

sexuality [sexyuéliti], *s.* sexualidad.

sexually [séxyuali], *adv.* sexualmente.

sgraffito [sgraffíto], *s.* (b. a.) obra esgrafiada.

shabbily [shǽbili], *adv.* zarrapastrosamente, andrajosamente; ruinmente, mezquinamente.

shabbiness [shǽbines], *s.* desaseo, desaliño, estado zarrapastroso; ruindad, mezquindad.

shabby [shǽbi], *a.* usado, gastado, raído; desaseado, andrajoso, zarrapastroso; ruin, vil.—**s. genteel,** cursi.

shack [shæc], *s.* choza, cabaña; pasto de bellotas.

shackle [shǽcœl]. **I.** *va.* encadenar, atar; poner esposas o grilletes a; trabar; poner obstáculos, estorbar; (elec.) poner un aislador en un corte de alambre. **II.** *s.* grillete, grillo, esposa; maneota, arropea, trabón; traba, impedimento; sujeción; (f. c.) cadena o perno de enganche.—**s. bolt,** cáncamo de grillete; perno de horquilla; gancho o eslabón de candado.

shad [shæd], *s.* (ict.) alosa, sábalo, trisa.

shaddock [shǽdoc], *s.* (bot.) pamplemusa; toronja.

shade [shéid]. **I.** *s.* sombra; umbría; retiro; matiz, tinte; ligera diferencia; un poco, cantidad pequeña; visillo, cortina, transparente; pantalla de lámpara; visera; sombraje, umbráculo, toldo; sombra, espectro, fantasma; ficción, ilusión, imagen.—*pl.* (**the shades,**) el báratro, el averno.—**s. tree,** árbol de sombra. **II.** *va.* sombrear, dar sombra; resguardar de la luz; esconder, amparar; (b. a.) sombrear; matizar, casar bien los colores; rasguear (las letras).

shadeless [-les], *a.* privado de sombra.

shadily [-dili], *adv.* con sombra, en la sombra; sospechosamente.

shadiness [-dines], *s.* calidad de sombreado.

shading [-ing], *s.* (b. a.) degradación, sombreado.

shadow [shǽdo]. **I.** *s.* sombra (proyectada por un objeto); obscuridad, sombrajo; imagen reflejada (en agua o espejo); sombra, aparecido; retiro, reclusión; (pint.) sombra, sombreado; vestigio, pizca (*not a shadow of doubt,* ni sombra de duda); (fig.) refugio, amparo. **II.** *va.* anublar, obscurecer, dar sombra, sombrear, (con **forth o out**) indicar, representar vagamente, simbolizar; espiar, seguir a uno como su sombra; (b. a.) sombrear, matizar. **III.** *vn.* anublarse, obscurecerse; cambiar gradualmente de color.

shadowgraph [-græf], *s.* = SKIAGRAPH.

shadowy [shǽdoi], *a.* umbroso, umbrío; obscuro, tenebroso; vago, indefinido; visionario; indicador, simbólico.

shady [shéidi], *a.* sombreado, umbroso; sospechoso; de dudosa moralidad; (fam.) obscuro, obscurito (de color—dicho de un mulato).—**on the s. side of,** pasado(s), más allá de (los cuarenta años, etc.).

shaft [shaft], s. flecha, dardo, saeta; (arq.) caña o fuste de columna; columna, obelisco; chapitel o aguja (de torre); (mec.) eje, árbol; cualquier mango largo; barra, humero, cañón de chimenea; (carr.) limón o limonera; varas de las sillas de manos; cañón o tubo de pluma; caja, pozo (de ascensor); caña (de un hueso); (min.) pozo; (fund.) vientre (de un alto horno); pozo de ventilación, respiradero (en edificios de varios pisos).—s. **furnace**, horno de alimentación superior o de carga por arriba.—s. **governor**, regulador axial (montado en el eje).—s. **horsepower**, potencia transmitida por el árbol de transmisión, potencia al freno.—s. **pump**, bomba de pozo.

shafted [shafted], a. provisto de eje o ejes.

shafting [shafting], s. (mec.) juego de ejes y correajes; sistema de ejes de transmisión; transmisión por eje o ejes.

shag [shæg], I. s. mechón, pelo áspero y lanudo; (tej.) felpa, (Amér.) tripe; jergón; cuervo marino. II. va. y vn. (pret. y pp. SHAGGED) hacer peludo, hacer escabroso, desigual.

shagbark [shǽgbark], s. = HICKORY.

shagged [shǽgued], a. peludo; achaparrado.

shagginess [shǽguines], s. calidad de peludo o afelpado.

shaggy [shǽgui], a. peludo, velludo, hirsuto; afelpado, lanudo; de somonte, áspero.

shagreen [shagrín], s. piel de zapa; lija; (ten.) marroquí.

shah [sha], s. chah.

shake [shéik]. I. va. (pret. SHOOK: pp. SHAKEN) sacudir o menear, blandir; hacer temblar; lanzar, despedir con ímpetu; debilitar; hacer vacilar o flaquear, desalentar; despertar, excitar, agitar; estrechar (la mano); (mús.) trinar (una nota); (fam. E. U.) desembarazarse o salir de, despedir.—to s. hands, estrechar la mano.—to s. hands with, dar o estrechar la mano a. El imp., shake hands with, se usa familiarmente para presentar una persona a otra, y puede checirse por "tengo el gusto de presentar a."—to s. in, o into, introducir una cosa en, sacudiéndola.—to s. off, sacudir; arrojar con una sacudida; zafarse o salir de.—to s. one's head, cabecear, mover la cabeza.—to s. to pieces, sacudir hasta hacer pedazos.—to s. up, sacudir, remover; agitar. II. vn. temblar; estremecerse; cimbrar; vacilar; titubear; (mús.) trinar; rajarse, agrietarse (dicho de la madera); (fam.) dar(se) la mano.—to s. with, temblar o estremecerse de.—to s. with laughter, desternillarse o reventar de risa. III. s. sacudida; sacudimiento, traqueteo; vibración; temblor de tierra; temblor; apretón de manos; tabla de ripia; un buen negocio; (fam.); periquete; instante; ganga; (ton.) duela; (mús.) trino; rajadura en una toza.—pl. escalofrío de la fiebre intermitente.

shakedown [-daun], s. cama improvisada sobre sillas, o de paja.

shaken [-œn], pp. de TO SHAKE; agitado; rajado o hendido (madero).

shaker [-œr], s. temblador, temblón; sacudidor; (E. U.) miembro de una secta religiosa.

Shakespearian [shéikspírian], a. perteneciente o relativo a Shakespeare.

shaking [shéiking]. I. s. sacudimiento, traqueteo; concusión; temblor o estremecimiento. II. a. temblante, temblón, tembloroso.

shako, shacko [shǽko], s. (mil.) chacó.

shaky [shéiki], a. trémulo; movedizo, vacilante, débil; (com.) falto de crédito o solvencia.

shale [shéil], s. esquisto; pizarra.—s. oil, aceite de esquistos.

shall [shæl], v. defec. (sin infinitivo, pretérito, participio ni imperativo). Como will, sirve para formar el futuro de otros verbos, conjugándose los dos en esta forma: para indicar simplemente una acción futura o probable, I shall, thou wilt, he will, we shall, you will, they will; para denotar propósito o determinación, mandato, permiso o amenaza, I will, thou shalt, he shall, we will, you shall, they shall. Así, por ejemplo: I shall die, moriré (tiempo futuro): I will die, quiero morir

(imperativo); he will die, él moriá (tiempo futuro); he shall die, morirá, que muera (imperativo).

shalloon [shalún], s. (tej.) chalón.

shallop [shǽlop], s. chalupa.

shallot [shǽlot], s. (bot.) chalote, ascalonia.

shallow [shǽlo]. I. a. bajo, somero, vadoso, poco profundo; superficial.—s.-bodied, (mar.) de poco calado.—s.-brained, (mar.) ligero de cascos, bobo. II. s. (mar.) bajío.

shallowness [-nes], s. poca profundidad; superficialidad.

shaly [shéili], a. pizarreño.

sham [shæm]. I. va. y vn. simular, fingir.—to s. Abra(ha)m, (mar.) fingirse enfermo.—s. fingimiento, bambolla, farsa. II. a. fingido, disimulado, supuesto; falso, postizo.—s. fight, (mil.) simulacro.—s. quarrel, contienda simulada.

shaman [shǽman], s. exorcista, hechicero.—shamanism [-ism], s. samanismo, religión que cree que los espíritus sobrenaturales se manifiestan por conducto de hechiceros.

shamble [shǽmbœl]. I. vn. andar bamboleándose, vacilar. II. s. bamboleo, paso vacilante.

shambles [shǽmbœls], s. pl. matadero, degolladero; carnicería, mercado.

shame [shéim]. I. s. vergüenza.—for s.! s. on you! ¡qué vergüenza! II. va. avergonzar, abochornar; afrentar, deshonrar; (con into o out of) impeler a, por un sentimiento de vergüenza.

shamefaced [-féist], a. tímido, vergonzoso; modesto, pudoroso.—shamefacedly [-li], adv. con rubor o modestia.—shamefacedness [-nes], s. timidez, vergüenza, rubor.

shameful [shéimful], a. vergonzoso.

shamefully [-i], adv. vergonzosamente.—shameless [shéimles], a. desvergonzado, sin vergüenza.—shamelessly [-li], adv. desvergonzadamente.—shamelessness [-nes], s. desvergüenza, impudencia.

shammer [shǽmœr], s. impostor, fingidor.

shammy, shamois [shǽmi], s. gamuza.—s. leather = CHAMOIS.

shampoo [shæmpú]. I. va. lavar y limpiar la cabeza; dar champú; sobar. II. s. champú; frotación, soba.

shamrock [shǽmroc], s. (bot.) trébol, trifolio; emblema de Irlanda.

shandygaff [shǽndigæf], s. bebida de cerveza y otro líquido.

shanghai [shǽngjai], va. (fam.) emborrachar o narcotizar y embarcar (a alguien contra su voluntad o su conocimiento); dormir (a uno) y llevárselo.

shank [shænc], s. caña o canilla de la pierna; zanca, pierna de las aves; (mec.) asta o ástil, mango, vástago. caña, espiga; (impr.) cuerpo del tipo; (zap.) fuste, caña; (zap.) enfranque de la suela; rabo o cola de botón; (bot.) pecíolo.—s. of an anchor, (mar.) caña de ancla.

shanked [shǽnct], a. que tiene caña, ástil o mango.

shan't, sha'n't [shant], (fam.) abreviación de SHALL NOT. V. SHALL.

shanty [shǽnti], s. (pl. SHANTIES) casucha choza, tabuquillo.

shapable, shapeable [shéipabœl], a. capaz de recibir una forma.

shape [shéip]. I. va. formar; dar forma a; determinar; adaptar; dirigir; regular. II. vn. (fam.) empezar; hacerlo, salir (bien o mal). III. s. forma, figura; (fam.) cuerpo, figura, hechura (de una persona); modelo; horma; molde; (fam.) condición, estado; (fam.) manera, modo; (ing.) barra de construcción (apl. a las que se denotan por su sección transversal, llamadas a veces perfiles o perfilados—barra de doble T, en U, etc.).

shapeless [shéiples], a. informe; disforme.

shapelessness [-es], s. deformidad, informidad.—shapeliness [shéiplines], s. belleza de forma, proporción.

shapely [shéipli], a. bien formado.

shaper [shéipœr], s. conformador; máquina de tallar o estampar.

shard [shard], s. (ant.) tiesto, casco.

share [s̄héær]. **I.** *va.* repartir; compartir, partir; (con **in**) participar de, tener o tomar parte en. **II.** *vn.* participar o tener parte.—**to s. alike**, repartir igualmente, tener una parte igual. **III.** *s.* parte, porción; cuota, cupo, escote; (com.) acción; interés, participación; (agr.) reja (del arado, etc.); (anat.) pubis.—**s. and s. alike**, por igual, por partes iguales.—**on shares**, con condición de tener una parte.

sharebone [-bóun], *s.* hueso del pubis.

shareholder [-jóuldœr], *s.* (com.) accionista.

sharer [s̄héærœr], *s.* partícipe, copartícipe.

shark [s̄hark]. **I.** *s.* (ict.) tiburón; escualo; pillastre, estafador. **II.** *va.* y *vn.* estafar, petardear, hurtar; (con **up**) reunir furtivamente.

sharker [s̄hárkœr], *s.* petardista, tahur.

sharp [s̄harp]. **I.** *a.* agudo; puntiagudo, aguzado; cortante, afilado; perspicaz, sagaz; listo, vivo, astuto; fino de oído; penetrante; acre, agrio; incisivo, mordaz, sarcástico; severo, rígido; violento, animado, acalorado; vigilante, atento; distinto, claro, bien delineado o definido; (mús.) sostenido; agudo, punzante (dolor); anguloso (fragmento, arena); fuerte, pronunciado (pendiente, curva, etc.\.—**s. features**, facciones enjutas. **II.** *s.* (mús.) sostenido (#); aguja de coser larga y delgada; estafador, fullero; (fam.) perito, experto. **III.** *adv.* = SHARPLY; (fam.) exactamente, en punto (apl. a ᴵa hora); (mús.) demasiado alto de tono.—**s.-edged**, afilado, aguzado.— **s.-eyed**, linceo, de vista penetrante.—**s.-nosed**, de nariz puntiaguda; de finísimo olfato.—**s.-pointed**, puntiagudo.—**s.-pointed pliers**, alicates de punta.—**s.-set**, ávido, ansioso.—**s.-sighted** = S.-EYED.—**s.-witted**, penetrante, perspicaz. **IV.** *va.* afilar, aguzar; (mús.) elevar medio tono: marcar con un sostenido. **V.** *vn.* (mús.) cantar o tocar más alto que el tono debido; engañar, trampear, petardear.

sharpen [s̄hárpœn]. **I.** *va.* afilar, aguzar, sacar punta a, amolar; adelgazar; (fig.) aguzar (el apetito, el ingenio, etc.); hacer más severo, intenso, acre, fogoso o ansioso. **II.** *vn.* aguzarse; afilarse; agriarse, acedarse.

sharpener [-nœr], *s.* amolador, aguzador, afilador.

sharper [-œr], *s.* tahur, fullero; petardista, estafador, caballero de industria.

sharply [-li], *adv.* (*v.* SHARP) con filo, corte o punta; prontamente; lacónicamente; brusca y mordazmente; severamente, rigorosamente; agudamente, vivamente; sutilmente, ingeniosamente.

sharpness [-nes], *s.* calidad de cortante, agudo, etc. (*v.* SHARP, *a.*); agudeza; sutileza, perspicacia, viveza; acrimonia, mordacidad; acritud, acidez; violencia, rigor; inclemencia.

sharpshooter [-s̄hútœr], *s.* tirador certero; tirador apostado.

shastra [s̄hǽstrœ], *s.* sastra, colección de los libros sagrados y filosóficos de la India.

shatter [s̄hǽtœr]. **I.** *va.* destrozar, hacer pedazos, astillas o añicos; estrellar, romper, trozar; quebrantar (la salud); frustrar (esperanzas). **II.** *vn.* hacerse pedazos, quebrarse, romperse; dar un estallido. **III.** *s.* fragmento, pedazo.—**into shatters**, en pedazos, en añicos (ú. esp. en **to break into shatters**, hacer pedazos o añicos).

shattery [s̄hǽtœri], *a.* desmenuzable, quebradizo.

shave [s̄héiv]. **I.** *va.* rasurar o afeitar; descañonar; (carp.) acepillar; desbastar; raspar; rozar, pasar rozando; rebanar; (ten.) descañonar; desollar a uno en un negocio, estafar. **II.** *vn.* afeitarse, hacerse la barba; llevarse la mejor parte en un trato. **III.** *s.* afeitada; cuchilla desbastadora de dos mangos; descuento exorbitante; (fam.) acción de pasar raspando o casi tocando (literal y figuradamente); escape, zafada (gen. en la expresión **to have a close s.**, escapar por casualidad, salvarse en una tabla).

shaveling [-ling], *s.* (despec.) hombre rapado; monje o fraile.

shaver [-œr], *s.* barbero; desollador (en los negocios), estafador; (fam.) jovencito, rapaz.

shaving [-ing]. **I.** *s.* afeitada, rasura; raspadura, acepilladura.—*pl.* **shavings (of wood)**, virutas,

alisaduras.—**shavings of hartshorn**, raeduras de cuerno de ciervo. **II.** *a.* de afeitar, para afeitar.— **s. brush**, brocha de afeitar.—**s. dish**, bacía.

shawl [s̄hol], *s.* chal, mantón.

shaws [s̄hos̄], *s. pl.* (fam.) hojas de hortaliza.

shay [s̄héi], *s.* = CHAISE.

she [s̄hij], *pron. fem.* ella; (delante de *who* o *that*) la, aquella (*she who speaks*, la que habla); hembra (en composición: **s.-ass**, borrica, burra.— **s.-cat**, gata.—**s.-devil**, diabla.—**s.-goat**, cabra.— **s.-mule**, mula).

sheaf [s̄hif]. **I.** *s.* (*pl.* SHEAVES) gavilla haz, garba, fajo, mostela; atado, paquete o lío; roldana. *V.* SHEAVE.—**s. of arrows**, haz de flechas. **II.** *va.* (agr.) agavillar, garbear.

sheal [s̄hil], *s.* vaina.

shealing [-ing], *s.* cabaña; cobertizo.

shear [s̄hiœr]. **I.** *va.* (*pret.* SHEARED o SHORE: *pp.* SHEARED o SHORN) tonsurar, rapar, esquilar, trasquilar; (tej.) tundir; cortar (gen. con tijeras o cizallas); (mec.) someter a esfuerzo constante; (a veces con *off*) romper por fuerza cortante o por deslizamiento. **II.** *vn.* romperse por deslizamiento o por esfuerzo cortante. **III.** *s.* esfuerzo cortante; fuerza cortante; deslizamiento, deformación debida al esfuerzo cortante.

shearer [-œr], *s.* esquilador, trasquilador.

shearing [-ing]. **I.** *s.* corte; esquileo, trasquila; deslizamiento; fractura por esfuerzo cortante. **II.** *a.* de deslizamiento; (mec.) cortante.— **s. machine**, esquiladora mecánica.—**s. strength**, resistencia al deslizamiento.—**s. stress**, esfuerzo cortante.

shears [s̄híærs̄], *s. pl.* tijeras grandes; (mec.) cizallas; correderas de un torno; grúa de tijeras, machina.

shearwater [s̄híæruótœr], *s.* (orn.) picotijera.

sheatfish [s̄hítfis̄h], *s.* (ict.) siluro.

sheath [s̄hiz], *s.* vaina; caja, manguito, funda, estuche, cubierta, envoltura.

sheathe [s̄hiz], *va.* envainar; poner vaina, forro o cubierta; (mar.) aforrar, embonar.

sheathing [s̄hízing], *s.* forro exterior, cubierta, aforro, embono.—**s. nails**, clavos de entablar.

sheathless [s̄híples], *a.* sin vaina.

sheave [s̄hív]. **I.** *s.* roldana; polea, garrucha, monopastos; (mec.) rueda excéntrica o su disco.—**s. holes**, (mar.) escoteras. **II.** *va.* (agr.) garbar, agavillar.

shed [s̄hed]. **I.** *va.* (*pret.* y *pp.* SHED) arrojar, quitarse; desprenderse de, largar; mudar; verter, derramar; esparcir, dejar caer; exhalar. —**to s. feathers**, pelechar. **II.** *vn.* mudar (los cuernos, la piel, las plumas.) **III.** *s.* vertiente; separación, reparto; cobertizo, tinglado; tejadillo, colgadizo, salidizo; sombraje, cabaña o barraca.

shedder [s̄hédœr], *s.* derramador; animal que muda la piel, las plumas, etc.

shedding [s̄héding], *s.* derramamiento, vertimiento; muda (de plumas, etc.)

sheen [s̄hin], *s.* resplandor, lustre, viso.

sheeny [s̄híni]. **I.** *a.* lustroso. **II.** *s.* (fam. desp.) judío.

sheep [s̄híp], *s.* (*sing.* y *pl.*) oveja, carnero; ovejas; rebaño; papanatas, simplón; (enc.) badana.— **s. botfly**, mosca de carnero.—**s. dip**, decocción insecticida para el lavado de los carneros antes de la esquila.—**s. dog**, perro de pastor.—**s. dung**, sirle o sirria.—**s. ranch**, hacienda de ovejas.— **run**, dehesa de ovejas, carneril.—**s.'s eye**, mirada al soslayo; ojeada modesta y amorosa.—**s.'s leather**, badana.—**s. tick**, garrapata.

sheepcote [s̄hípcout], **sheepfold** [-fold], *s.* redil, corral, aprisco.

sheephook [-júc], *s.* cayado, gayata.

sheepish [s̄hípis̄h], *a.* avergonzado, corrido; tímido, pusilánime.—**sheepishly** [-li], *adv.* tímidamente.—**sheepishness** [-nes], *s.* timidez, cortedad.

sheepmaster [-mǽster], *s.* ganadero.

sheepshank [-s̄hǽnk], *s.* pierna de un carnero; (mar.) margarita, catabre.

sheepshead [s̄hípsjed], *s.* (ict.) sargo.

sheepshearer [-ʃíærœr], s. esquilador.

sheepshearing [-ing], s. esquileo, trasquila.

sheepskin [-skin], s. badana.—**s. dressed with wool**, zalea.

sheepwalk [-uóc], s. dehesa de ovejas, carneril.

sheer [ʃíær]. **I.** a. puro, claro, consumado, cabal, completo; (tej.) ligero, fino, delgado; escarpado, enhiesto.—**s. hulk**, chata de arbola.—**s. legs** = SHEERS.—**s. rail**, escaño. **II.** adv. de un golpe, de una vez. **III.** s. (mar.) arrufo, arrufadura. **IV.** vn. (mar.) alargarse, desviarse; torcer, doblar.

sheers [ʃíærs], s. cabria de arbolar, machina, grúa de tijeras.

sheet [ʃít]. **I.** s. hoja, lámina, placa (de cualquier materia); sábana; pliego u hoja (de papel); diario; extensión de agua; (mar.) escota; (poét.) vela (de navío).—**s.** anchor, ancla de la esperanza, (fig.) áncora de salvación.—**s. bitts**, abitones.—**s. cable**, cable mayor.—**s. card**, cartulina en hojas.—**s. glass**, vidrio cilindrado o laminado.—**s. hole**, escotera.—**s. lightning**, fucilazos.—**s. metal (iron, steel,** etc.), metal (hierro, acero) en lámina o en planchas; palastro.—**s. pile**, tablestaca.—**s. piling**, tablestacas; construcción de tablestacas. **II.** va. ensabanar, envolver en sábanas; amortajar; extenderse en láminas u hojas.

sheeting [ʃíting], s. lencería para sábanas, (Méx.) manta, (Venez.) tocuyo ancho; (metal.) laminado; (hidr. y min.) encofrado.

sheik [ʃik o ʃéik], s. jeque.

shekel [ʃéccœl], s. siclo.—pl. (fam.) dinero.

sheldrake [ʃéldrek], s. (orn.) cataraña; mergánsar.

shelf [ʃelf], s. (pl. SHELVES) anaquel, estante, entrepaño; poyata; bajío, banco de arena; vuelo; capa horizontal (de roca) saliente; roca subyacente (de un depósito sedimentario)

shell [ʃel]. **I.** s. casco; cáscara (de nuez, de huevo, etc.); vaina, vainilla (de legumbres); (bot.) silicua; concha, carapacho; marisco; cubierta, corteza; armazón, esqueleto; cuerpo (de caldera); (fund.) camisa o revestimiento de horno; (arti.) bomba, granada; cápsula para cartuchos; bote largo y angosto para regatas; (poét.) lira; (mar.) casco o caja de motón; pieza acopada o ahuecada; (elec.) boquilla, caja (de portalámpara).—**s. gold**, oro de concha u oro molido para dorar.—**s. heap, s. mound**, montón de mariscos comestibles mezclados con utensilios y desperdicios.—**s.-lac**, laca.—**s. shock**, neurosis de guerra, desorden especial nervioso o mental causado por heridas, concusión del aire, temor, excitación mental, etc., en los campos de batalla. **II.** va. descascarar, descortezar, desvainar; encerrar en cáscara, vaina o cápsula; (arti.) bombardear; desgranar. **III.** vn. descascararse, desconcharse.

shellac [ʃélæc o ʃeláec]. **I.** s. laca. **II.** va. revestir de laca, barnizar con laca.

shellbark [ʃélbark], s. V. HICKORY.

sheller [-œr], s. desgranador; descascarador.

shellfire [ʃélfáiœr], s. (mil.) cañoneo con granadas; disparos de granadas.

shellfish [-fíʃ], s. mariscos.

shelling [-ing], s. descascaramiento; desgrane, desgranamiento; bombardeo.

shellproof [-prúf], a. a prueba de bomba.

shellwork [-uœrc], s. obra de concha.

shelly [-i], a. conchado o conchudo.

shelter [ʃéltœr]. **I.** s. resguardo, amparo, refugio, abrigo, asilo; guarida; protector, amparador. **II.** va. guarecer, abrigar, poner al abrigo o a cubierto, albergar, amparar, proteger, encubrir, ocultar, tapar.—**sheltered industries**, industrias no expuestas a la competencia extranjera. **III.** vn. refugiarse, guarecerse.

shelterless [ʃéltœrles], a. desamparado, sin asilo; desabrigado.

shelve [ʃelv]. **I.** va. poner sobre un estante o anaquel; (fig.) poner a un lado, dar carpetazo; proveer de estantes o anaqueles. **II.** vn. inclinarse, estar en declive.

shelves [ʃelvs], pl. de SHELF.

shelving [ʃélving]. **I.** a. inclinado. **II.** s. estantería, anaquelería; carpetazo; declive.

shelvy [ʃélvi], a. inclinado.

Sheol [ʃíol], s. báratro, infierno.

shepherd [ʃépœrd], s. pastor; zagal; (fig.) párroco, cura.—**s. dog**, perro de pastor.—**s.'s crook**, cayado.—**s.'s needle**, (bot.) aguja de pastor.—**s.'s purse** o **pouch**, (bot.) bolsa de pastor.—**s.'s watch**, hierba pajarera.

shepherdess [ʃépœrdes], s. pastora, zagala.

sherardize [ʃérardaiʃ], vt. galvanizar por el procedimiento Cowper-Coles (revestir de cinc por calentamiento con polvo de cinc en retortas cerradas; algunos usan sherardizar).

sherbet [ʃœrbet], s. sorbete, granizado.

sherd [ʃœrd], s. tiesto, casco, teioleta.

sherif [ʃerif o ʃérif], s. jerife.

sheriff [ʃérif], s. administrador ejecutivo de un condado.

sheriffalty, sheriffship, sheriffwick [ʃérifalti, -ʃhip, -uic], s. V. SHRIEVALTY.

sheriffdom [-dum], s. jurisdicción del sheriff.

sherry [ʃéri], s. vino de Jerez.—**s. cobbler**, refresco hecho con vino de Jerez.

sheth [ʃhez], s. dental del arado.

shew, shewed, shown, (ant.) V. SHOW.

shibboleth [ʃíbolez], s. palabra que sirve de santo y seña; lema; caballo de batalla (fig.)

shie [ʃhai], a. lanzar, arrojar.

shier [ʃháiœr], s. caballo asustadizo.

shield [ʃhíld]. **I.** s. escudo; broquel, tarja, rodela; egida, amparo; resguardo, reparo, defensa; protector, defensor; (blas.) escudo de armas.—**s.-bearer**, escudero. **II.** va. escudar, amparar, resguardar, defender, proteger.

shift [ʃhift]. **I.** va. cambiar; desviar; trasladar, transportar; mudar la ropa; (teat.) cambiar de decoración—**to s. a berth**, mudar fondo.—**to s. off**, diferir, aplazar: poner a un lado; librarse o salir de.—**to s. the cargo**, volver la estiva.—**to s. the helm**, cambiar el timón, poner el timón a la contra. **II.** vn. moverse, cambiar de puesto, mudarse; cambiar, variar, mudar; tergiversar, usar de frases equívocas.—**to s. about**, revolverse, girar.—**to s. for one's self**, valerse, darse maña, componérselas. **III.** s. cambio; sustitución, trastrueque; recurso, expediente; ardid, artificio; maña, subterfugio, fraude, evasión, excusa; camisa; tanda de obreros; revezo.

shiftable [ʃhíftabœl], a. mudable; revecero.

shifter [-œr], s. (mec.) desviador; (teat.) carpintero, tramoyista; zorrocloco.

shiftless [-les], a. inútil, incapaz; negligente, descuidado, perezoso; mal hecho, desaliñado.—**shiftlessly** [ʃhiftlesli], adv. negligentemente.—**shiftlessness**, [-nes], s. negligencia, pereza; inutilidad, incapacidad.

shillalah, shillelah [ʃhiléla], s. palo, cachiporra.

shilling [ʃhíling], s. (Ingl.) chelín; (E. U.) moneda antigua que variaba de valor en diversos estados. El término se usa aún en el sentido de 12½ centavos.

shilli-shalli, o **shilly-shally** [ʃhli-ʃhali]. **I.** vn., adv. y a. estar irresoluto, no saber qué hacer. **II.** s. vacilación, irresolución.

shim [ʃhim]. **I.** s. cuña o chaveta delgada; plancha o tira de relleno. **II.** va. cuñar; tapar, rellenar con una tira o tablilla.

shimmer [ʃhímœr]. **I.** vn. rielar. **II.** s. luz trémula; debil resplandor.

shimmy [ʃhími]. **I.** s. baile de movimientos temblorosos, baile nalgar; (fam.) camisa de mujer; (aut., fam.) zigzagueo de las ruedas y bamboleo del coche. **II.** vn. bailar el shimmy; (aut.) zigzaguear.

shin [ʃhin]. **I.** s. espinilla, camilla.—**s. bone**, (anat.) tibia. **II.** va. y vn. trepar.

shindy [ʃhíndi], s. (fam.) zacapela.

shine [ʃhain]. **I.** vn. (pret. y pp. SHONE) lucir, brillar, resplandecer; sobresalir, distinguirse; hacer buen tiempo; favorecer, ser propicio. **II.** va. reg. pulir, bruñir; dar lustre (a los zapatos), dar bola, embolar. **III.** s. resplandor, lustre, brillo;

buen tiempo, claridad; embolada (del calzado), emboladura.

shiner [sháincœr], s. el que o lo que brilla; (fam.) moneda de oro; pez plateado.

shingle [shíngœl]. **I.** va. cubrir con ripia; entejar con tejamaníes; cortar (el pelo) corto y en declive o en escalones; (metal.) cinglar, exprimir la escoria de. **II.** s. pelo corto en declive, o rebajado gradualmente; tabla de ripia, tejamaní, tajamaní; (E. U.) muestra o letrero de oficina; china, cascajo.—s. **nail,** abismal.

shingles [shíngœls], s. (med.) zoster, zona.

shining [sháining]. **I.** a. brillante, radiante, resplandeciente. **II.** s. lucimiento, esplendor, lustre; resplandor, brillo.

shiny [sháini], a. lustroso, brillante.

ship [ship]. **I.** s. buque, barco, nave, bajel, navío; aeróstato, dirigible, nave aérea—s. **biscuit,** galleta.—s. **boy,** paje de escoba, grumete.—s. **bread,** galleta.—s. **carpenter,** carpintero de ribera.—s. **chandler,** proveedor de buques.—s. **chandlery,** caballería, tienda de artículos de marina, jarcia, etc.—s. **fever,** tifo.—s. **money,** antiguo derecho sobre buques.—s. **of the line,** navío de alto bordo o de línea.—s. **of war,** buque de guerra.—s.-**plane,** avión de cubierta, que puede partir de o aterrizar en la cubierta de un buque.—s. **railway,** vía férrea para el transporte de embarcaciones.—s.'s **husband,** agente de un buque o empresa naviera.—s.'s **papers,** papeles o documentos legales de un buque.—s. **stores,** matalotaje.—s.'s **time,** hora local del buque.— s.'s **way,** andar del bajel.—s. **timber,** madera para construcciones navales. **II.** va. embarcar; (com.) enviar, despachar; (mar.) tripular, recibir a bordo la tripulación; embarcar (to ship a heavy sea, embarcar agua, encapillar un golpe de mar); armar, montar (mástiles, timón, remos).—to s. **oars,** armar los remos. **III.** vn. ir a bordo, embarcar; engancharse como marinero.

shipboard [shípbord], s. (mar.) bordo.—**on s.,** a bordo.

shipbuilder [-bíldœr], s. constructor de buques, arquitecto naval.

shipload [-lóud], s. cargamento que llena un buque; buque completamente cargado.

shipmaster [-mástœr], s. (mar.) patrón, capitán de buque.

shipmate [-méit], s. camarada de a bordo.

shipment [-mœnt], s. (com.) embarque; cargamento, partida; envío, despacho.

shipowner [-óunœr], s. naviero, armador.

shipper [-œr], s. (com.) embarcador; expedidor, remitente.

shipping [-ing]. **I.** s. buques; marina; (com.) embarque; envío, despacho. **II.** a. naval, marítimo, de marina mercante.—s. **agent,** consignatario de buques.—s. **articles,** contrata de marinero.— s. **bill,** factura de embarque.—s. **charges,** gastos de embarque.—s. **clerk,** (com.) dependiente de muelle.—s. **list** = s. **bill.**—s. **master,** oficial que contrata marineros.—s. **receipt,** recibo de embarque.

shipshape [-shéip], a. en buen orden, bien arreglado.

shipworm [-uœrm], s. broma, tiñuela.

shipwreck [-rec]. **I.** s. naufragio; desastre; desgracia, ruina. **II.** va. hacer naufragar o zozobrar, echar a pique.—**shipwrecked** [-d], a. naufragado.—**to be shipwrecked,** naufragar.

shipwright [-rait], s. carpintero de ribera o constructor de buques.

shipyard [-yard], s. astillero, varadero.

shire [shícœr o sháiœr], s. (Ingl.) condado.

shirk [shœrk]. **I.** s. el que se evade de hacer algo. **II.** va. y vn. evadir, eludir, evitar, esquivar, faltar a, desentenderse de, desatender.

shirr [shœr]. **I.** va. (cost.) fruncir, grandujar; (coc.) escalfar huevos en crema de leche. **II.** s. (cost.) frunce, fruncimiento; hilo de goma tejido en una tela para hacerla elástica.

shirred [shœrd], a. (cost.) fruncido; (tej.) elástico.—s. **eggs,** huevos escalfados en crema.

shirt [shœrt], s. camisa de hombre; (fund.) revestimiento (de horno).—s. **bosom, s. front,**

pechera de camisa.—s. **sleeve,** manga de camisa.— s. **waist,** corpiño de mujer; cuerpo de camisa.— **in one's s. sleeves,** en mangas de camisa.

shirting [shœrting], s. tela para camisas.

shist [shist], s. = SCHIST.

shiver [shívœr]. **I.** s. temblor, escalofrío, estremecimiento; brizna, astilla. **II.** vn. tiritar, temblar, calofriarse; cascarse, hacerse pedazos; estallar, estrellarse. **III.** va. estrellar, romper, hacer astillas o añicos; vibrar, sacudir; (mar.) flamear.—**shivering** [-ing], s. horripilación, calofrío, estremecimiento.—**shivery** [-i], a. trémulo, tembloroso; friolento, frío; friable, quebradizo.

shoal [shol]. **I.** s. bajo, bajío, alfaque, banco de arena; multitud, muchedumbre o manada; cardume, cardumen. **II.** a. poco profundo, bajo. **III.** va. y vn. disminuir en profundidad; reunirse en gran número.

shoaliness [shólines], s. falta de profundidad; calidad de somero.

shoaly [shóli], a. vadoso.

shoat, shote [shóut], s. cochinillo, gorrino; pelafustán, pelagatos.

shock [shoc]. **I.** s. choque; sacudida, sacudimiento; concusión, golpe; susto, sobresalto, emoción; conmoción; ofensa; desazón; (med.) postración nerviosa; (elec.) choque; (agr.) hacina, fascal, tresnal; pelo tupido, greñas; perro de lana. **II.** a. de choque; para choques; lanudo; desgreñado.—s. **absorber,** amortiguador.—s. **action,** (mil) carga en columna cerrada.—s. **dog,** perro de lanas.—s. **troops,** tropas escogidas. **III.** va. y vn. sacudir, dar una sacudida; chocar, ofender, disgustar; conmover; escandalizar, horrorizar; (agr.) hacinar.

shocking [shóking], a. espantoso, horrible; chocante, ofensivo.

shod [shod], part. y pret. de TO SHOE.

shoddy [shódi]. **I.** a. de lana artificial; falso, aparente. **II.** s. imitación de lana; paño burdo de lana artificial; (fam.) ostentación vulgar, impostura.

shoe [shu]. **I.** s. zapato; botín; calzado; herradura; suela de trineo; zapata (de ancla, de freno mecánico, de contacto eléctrico, etc.); galga de carruaje; (mar.) calzo, solera; tornapunta; contera, regatón; canal para conducir trigo o mineral a la tolva, etc.—s. **blacking,** bola, betún para zapatos.—s. **lace,** cordón o lazo de zapato.—s. **of a wheel,** llanta.—s. **peg,** (zap.) puntilla, estaquilla.—s. **polish,** lustre.—s. **store,** zapatería.—s. **string, s. tie** = s. LACE.—**to be in his** (their, etc.) **shoes,** estar en su pellejo. **II.** va. (pret. SHOD; pp. SHOD o SHODDEN) herrar (un caballo); calzar (el ancla, a una persona); poner regatón a, proveer de regatón; poner llantas a (una rueda).

shoeblack [shúblœc], s. limpiabotas.

shoehorn [-jórn], s. calzador.

shoeing [-ing]. **I.** s. acto de herrar o de calzar. **II.** a. de herrar; de calzar.—s.-**horn,** calzador.

shoemaker [-méikœr], s. zapatero.—s.'s **paring knife,** trinchete de zapatero.—s.'s **wax,** (zap.) cerapez, cerote.

shoemaking [-ing], s. fabricación de calzado, zapatería.

shoer [-œr], s. herrador.

shoful [shóful], s. (fam.) moneda falsa; (fam.) cabriolé.

shogun [shogún], s. general en jefe (del ejército japonés en tiempos pasados).

shole [shóul], s. (mar.) solera, tornapunta.

shone [shon], pret. de TO SHINE.

shoo [shú]. **I.** va. y vn. ahuyentar (aves domésticas) gritando: shoo! **II.** interj. ¡so! ¡fuera!

shook [shuk]. **I.** pret. de TO SHAKE. **II.** s. pl. shooks, paquete de duelas, bocoyes o barriles abatidos.

shoot [shút]. **I.** va. (pret. y pp. SHOT) herir o matar con arma de fuego; fusilar, pasar por las armas; disparar, tirar; descargar; vaciar; empujar, hacer salir; traspasar, atravesar rápidamente; vibrar, hacer saltar, dar barrena; ajustar (a una línea) cepillando.—to s. **a bolt,** echar, correr el pestillo.—to s. **off,** tirar, descargar (arma);

llevarse.—**to s. the rapids**, bajar por los rápidos (de un río).—**to s. the chute**, deslizarse en un tobogán de bote hacia el agua.—**to s. through**, atravesar, pasar de parte a parte.—**to s. up**, atacar a balazos (gen. en pandilla); entrar a (un pueblo) echando bala a diestra y siniestra. **II.** *vn.* tirar, disparar armas de fuego; pasar o correr rápidamente; salir, nacer, brotar, germinar; punzar (un dolor); sobresalir, destacarse.—**to s. at**, tirar a, hacer fuego o un tiro a.—**to s. forth**, lanzarse o abalanzarse.—**to s. out**, brotar, germinar.— **to s. over dogs**, cazar con perros.—**to s. up**, nacer, crecer; madurar. **III.** *s.* vástago, pimpollo, retoño, renuevo; recial de un río; artesa inclinada; tiro, certamen de tiradores, tiro al blanco; (arq.) refuerzo de arco o bóveda; gorrín, gorrino.

shooter [shútœr], *s.* tirador.

shooting shúting]. **I.** *s.* caza con escopeta; tiro; latido doloroso, punzada. **II.** *a.* de tiro; de tirar.—**s. match**, certamen de tiro al blanco.—**s. star**, estrella fugaz.—**s. stick**, (impr.) atacador.

shop [shop]. **I.** *s.* tienda o almacén; taller; fábrica. **II.** *a.* de tienda; de taller; de o relativo a gremios obreros (*shop committee*, comisión del gremio, o de los gremios; *shop deputy*, representante o delegado del gremio o de los gremios). **III.** *vn.* ir de tiendas; comprar, feriar.

shopboard [shópbórd], *s.* tabla de sastre.

shopboy [-bói], *s.* mancebo.

shopgirl [-gœrl], *s.* muchacha de tienda, dependienta.

shopkeeper [-kípœr], *s.* tendero.

shoplifter [-liftœr], *s.* ratero de tiendas.

shoplifting [-lifting], *s.* ratería en las tiendas.

shopman [-man], *s.* tendero; mercader; mancebo de tienda.

shopping [-ing], *s.* compras; acto de ir de tiendas.

shopwalker [-uócœr], *s.* vigilante (para impedir raterías en tienda o almacén).

shopwoman [-uman], *s.* tendera.

shorage [shórey], *s.* derecho de costa o ribera.

shore [shócœr]. **I.** *s.* costa, ribera, playa, orilla; puntal; costón; (mar.) escora, botante; (min.) entibo, adema.—**s. line**, contorno, borde de playa o ribera.—**s. of a pair of shears**, (mar.) puntal diagonal de cabria. **II.** *va.* apuntalar, acodalar; (mar.) escorar; llevar a tierra, a la orilla; circundar.

shoreless [shócœrles], *a.* sin costa ni playa.

shorn, *pp.* de TO SHEAR; mocho.

short [short]. **I.** *a.* corto; bajo, de escasa estatura; falto, escaso; breve, conciso; brusco, seco; insuficiente, deficiente; próximo, cercano; menguado, corto de alcances; (com.) falto de aquello que se vende y tiene que entregarse en cierto plazo; (pros.) breve; quebradizo.—**s. circuit**, (elec.) cortocircuito o corto circuito.—**s. circuit**, *va.* y *vn.* poner(se) en cortocircuito.—**s. column**, columna de compresión, pieza prismática o cilíndrica que no es de largo suficiente para romperse por pura flexión bajo la acción de una fuerza paralela al eje.—**s. cut**, atajo; método o modo abreviado o corto; picadura de tabaco.—**s. division**, (arit.) división sencilla rápida, en que se escriben sólo las cifras del cociente y los residuos parciales, determinados mentalmente, o sólo aquéllas. (El término es vago y se aplica gen. a la división por un dígito).—**s. money**, dinero prestado o para prestar a corto plazo (de pocos días). —**s. of**, lejos de; escaso de; inadecuado para; diferente de, sino, sólo (cambiando el giro: *nothing short of war*, sólo la guerra).—**S. Parliament**, (hist.) Parlamento Corto.—**s. rib**, (anat.) costilla falsa.—**s. sale**, venta de artículos que el vendedor no tiene aún.—**s. ton**, tonelada de 2000 libras (450 kg.).—**at s. notice** o **on S. NOTICE.**—**in a s. time**, o **while**, en un rato; en poco tiempo; dentro de poco.—**in s. order**, prontamente.—**on s. notice**, prontamente, con poca demora, con poco tiempo de aviso.—**to be s.**, estar escaso; para abreviar.— **to be s. of**, estar lejos de; no responder a; estar escaso de. **II.** *s.* resumen, compendio; (pros.) sílaba o vocal breve; (com.) déficit; venta de aquello que no se posee y debe entregarse en cierto plazo; persona que contrae dicho compromiso; en

baseball, puesto que ocupa el *shortstop*.—*pl.* salvado.—**for s.**, para abreviar, para mayor brevedad.—**in s.**, en suma, en resumen.—**the s. and the long of it**, en resumidas cuentas. **III.** *adv.* brevemente, breve.—**s.-bodied**, pequeño de estatura.—**s.-breathed**, asmático, corto de respiración, corto de resuello.—**s.-handed**, que carece de un número suficiente de operarios, marineros, etc.—**s.-nosed**, romo, chato, de nariz aplastada.— **s. of**, con excepción de, sin ir hasta.—**s.-stapled**, de hebra o fibra corta.—**s.-waisted**, corto de talle.—**s.-winded** = -BREATHED.

shortage [shórtey], *s.* déficit; merma.

shortcake [-kéic], *s.* torta de frutas.

shortcoming [-cúming], *s.* defecto; negligencia, omisión; falta, mengua.

shorten [shórtœn]. **I.** *va.* acortar; impedir, limitar, restringir; hacer tierna o deleznable (la pastelería) con mantequilla u otra grasa. **II.** *vn.* acortarse, abreviarse, disminuirse, encogerse.

shortening [shórtning], *s.* acortamiento; disminución; abreviación; manteca o mantequilla que se hacen hojaldres, etc.

shorthand [-jænd]. **I.** *s.* taquigrafía, estenografía. **II.** *a.* taquigráfico.

shortly [-li], *adv.* presto, luego, al instante; brevemente; en breve.

shortness [-nes], *s.* cortedad; pequeñez; brevedad; deficiencia.—**for s.**, para mayor brevedad.

shortsighted [-sáited], *a.* miope, cegato; falto de perspicacia.—**shortsightedness** [-nes], *s.* miopía; falta de perspicacia.

shortstop [-stop], *s.* en baseball, el jugador situado entre la segunda base y la tercera.

shot [shot]. **I.** *pret.* y *pp.* de TO SHOOT. **II.** *a.* (tej.) batido, tornasolado; relativo a o para perdigones.—**s. cartridge**, cartucho de perdigones.—**s. gage**, o **gauge**, vítola de calibrar proyectiles.—**s. locker**, (mar.) chillera.—**s. plug**, tapabalazo.— **s. pouch**, perdigonera.—**s. samples**, (metal.) muestras en forma de perdigones o pulverizadas vaciando en agua el metal fundido.—**s. silk**, seda tornasolada.—**s. tower**, torre para hacer perdigones. **III.** *va.* cargar con perdigones; limpiar botellas con perdigones. **IV.** *s.* perdigón; munición, perdigones; bala, proyectil; tiro, disparo; escopetazo; balazo; alcance (v. gr.: *within pistol shot*, a tiro de pistola); tirador; golpe, tirada, jugada (en el billar); escote; (min.) barreno.—**s. between wind and water**, balazo a flor del agua.—**not by a long s.**, (fam.) ni por asomo, ni por pienso.—**to have, o take, a shot at**, hacer un tiro a; echar una púa a.

shotgun [shótgún], *s.* escopeta.

should [shud], *subj.* de SHALL. Úsase como auxiliar para formar los modos condicionales de otros verbos, con la misma distinción respecto de *would*, que tiene *shall* respecto de *will* en la formación del futuro de indicativo (*v.* SHALL): vg.: *I said that I should go*, dije que iría: *would you go if I should go?* ¿Iría Vd. si yo fuese? Se usa muy frecuentemente como verbo defectivo con la significación de deber o haber de: *you should write to him at once*, debiera Vd. escribirle enseguida; *you should tell him*, Vd. debe (o debería) decirle; *the room should be kept open*, el cuarto debe mantenerse abierto. (No se cometa el error de creer que *should* equivale siempre a *debiera* o *debería*, pues a menudo equivale a *debe* o *deberá*).

shoulder [shóuldœr]. **I.** *s.* hombro; encuentro, espaldilla, paleta; pernil brazuelo o cuarto delantero; (carp.) can, pie de amigo; espaldón de espiga; sostén, soporte, parte saliente.—**s. belt**, tahalí.—**s. blade**, o **bone**, espaldilla, omoplato.— **s. knot**, (mil.) charretera mocha, capona.—**s. strap**, correón (de los aguadores) etc. (mil.) dragona.—**s. to s.** hombro a hombro.—**to put one's s. to the wheel**, meter su hombro. **II.** *va.* echarse a la espalda, cargar al hombro, llevar a hombros; (fig.) cargar con, asumir, tomar sobre sí; codear, meter el hombro.—**s. arms**, (mil.) armas al hombro.

shout [shaut]. **I.** *va.* y *vn.* vocear, gritar; vitorear, dar vivas.—**to s. one's self hoarse**, gritar hasta enronquecerse, desgañitarse. **II.** *s.* grito; aclamación.—**s. of applause**, viva.

shouter [sháutœr], *s.* gritador, baladrero.

shouting [shráik], s. orn.) pega reborda.

shouting [sháuting]. **I.** s. vocerío, gritería; aclamación. **II.** a. que vocea.

shove [shuv]. **I.** va. y vn. empujar, empellar, impeler.—**to s. along**, empujar; hacer avanzar.—**to s. away**, rechazar, alejar.—**to s. back**, hacer retroceder.—**to s. forward** = TO S. ALONG.—**to s. from**, empujar, rechazar a empujones.—**to s. off**, alejarse de, dejar.—**to s. out**, empujar hacia afuera, hacer salir. **II.** s. empellón, empujón, empuje, impulso.

shovel [shúvœl]. **I.** s. pala.—s. **hat**, sombrero de teja. **II.** va. traspalar.—**shovel(l)er** [-œr], s. palero, paleador.—**shovelful** [-ful], s. palada.—**shove(l)ling** [-ing], s. traspaleo.

shovelboard [-bord], s. tabla o mesa para jugar al tejo; juego de tejo.

show [sho]. **I.** va. (pret. SHOWED: pp. SHOWN o SHOWED) mostrar, enseñar; hacer ver, señalar; exponer, descubrir, manifestar; probar, demostrar; introducir, guiar, conducir.—**to s. a clear pair of heels**, o **the heels**, escaparse.—**to s. fight**, ofrecer resistencia, mostrarse resuelto a pelear.—**to s. forth**, exponer, mostrar; publicar, manifestar.—**to s. in**, introducir, hacer entrar (a una persona).—**to s. one's cards**, o **hand**, mostrar el juego (fig.), dejarse ver sus intenciones.—**to s. one's face**, presentarse, aparecerse.—**to s. one's teeth**, enseñar los dientes.—**to s. spirit**, mostrar buen ánimo.—**to s. the door to**, echar, despedir.—**to s. to the door**, acompañar a la puerta.—**to s. up**, hacer subir (a una persona); denunciar, descubrir, arrancar la careta a. **II.** vn. parecer, tener apariencia o señales de; aparecer, mostrarse, asomar, dar señal.—**to s. off**, alardear, fachendear.—**to s. up**, presentarse, parecer, ir. **III.** s. exhibición, exposición; espectáculo público; (teat.) función; ostentación, boato, prosopopeya; señal, indicación; apariencia, exterioridad; pretexto, máscara, velo; (fam. E. U.) oportunidad, suerte.—s. **bill**, cartel, cartelón.—s. **card**, tarjetón, letrero.—s. **case**, vitrina, aparador, caja de muestras.—s. **window**, ventana o escaparate de tienda.—**in open s.**, públicamente.

showbread [shóbréd], s. panes de proposición.

shower [sháuœr]. **I.** s. lluvia, chubasco, chaparrón; abundancia.—s. **bath**, baño de ducha o de regadera. **II.** va. regar, mojar; derramar con abundancia. **III.** vn. llover, caer un chubasco; caer con profusión.

shower [shóœr], s. mostrador, el que muestra.

showerless [sháuœrles], a. sin lluvia.

showery [-i], a. lluvioso.

showily [shóili], adv. ostentosamente, aparatosamente.—**showiness** [-nes], s. ostentación.

showman [shóuman], s. director de espectáculos; empresario de teatro, circo, museo, etc.

shown, pp. de TO SHOW.

showroom [shóurúm], s. cuarto de muestras (de mercancías).

showy [shóui], a. vistoso, aparatoso, ostentoso; chillon, charro.

shrank, pret. de TO SHRINK.

shrapnel [shrǽpnel], s. (arti.) granada de metralla.

shred [shred]. **I.** va. picar, desmenuzar, hacer tiras o trizas. **II.** s. triza, girón, tira, retazo; fragmento, pizca.

shredded [shréded], a. trojezado, desmenuzado, hecho trizas.

shrew [shru], s. arpía, mujer de mal genio; (zool.) musgaño, musaraña.

shrewd [shrud], a. perspicaz, sagaz; astuto, sutil, (ant.) solapado; agudo, cortante.—**shrewdly** [-li], adv. astutamente, sagazmente; solapadamente.—**shrewdness** [-nes], s. sagacidad, astucia, sutileza.

shrewish [shrúish], a. regañona.—**shrewishly** [-li], adv. de muy mal humor, a regaña dientes.—**shrewishness** [-nes], s. mal genio.

shrewmouse [shrúmáus], s. (zooi.) musgaño, musaraña.

shriek [shrík]. **I.** vn. chillar, gritar. **II.** s. chillido, grito agudo.

shrievalty [shrívalti], s. cargo o funciones de sheriff.

shrift [shrift], s. (igl.) confesión; absolución.

shrike [shráik]. s. (orn.) pega reborda.

shrill [shril]. **I.** a. agudo, penetrante. **II.** va. y vn. chillar.—**shrillness** [shrílnes], s. calidad de chillón.

shrimp [shrimp], s. camarón; (despec.) enano, hombre pequeño.

shrine [shráin]. **I.** s. relicario, urna, altar, sepulcro de santo; capilla, templete. **II.** va. = ENSHRINE.

shrink [shrink]. **I.** vn. (pret. SHRANK, SHRUNK; pp. SHRUNK, SHRUNKEN; (ant.) SHRINKED) encogerse, contraerse; disminuir, mermar; (con from) evadir, apartarse o huir de; retroceder; temblar, estremecerse; retir arse; apocarse.—**to s. away**, desaparecer por grados; sustraerse, huir.—**to s. back**, retirarse, retroceder.—**to s. up**, estrecharse; encogerse, arrugarse; temblar, estremecerse. **II.** va. encoger, contraer, reducir.—**to s. on**, montar en caliente (una llanta, una abrazadera, etc.).—**to s. up**. estrechar. **III.** s. encogimiento, acortamiento; contracción de nervios.

shrinkage [shrínkey], s. encogimiento o contracción; reducción, diminución; (com.) merma, pérdida.

shrinkingly [shrínkingli], adv. encogiéndose; retrocediendo.

shrive [shráiv], va. y vn. (pret. SHROVE o SHRIVED; pp. SHRIVEN o SHRIVED) (igl.) confesar; oír en confesión; confesarse.

shrivel [shrívœl]. **I.** va. arrugar, fruncir, doblar, encoger; estrechar; marchitar. **II.** vn. arrugarse, fruncirse, encogerse; avellanarse, acorcharse las frutas; encarrujarse, ensortijarse (el hilo, etc.).

shriven [shrívœn], pp. de TO SHRIVE.

shriver [shráivœr], s. confesor.

shroud [shráud]. **I.** s. mortaja; cubierta, carpeta, vestidura; corona (de una rueda); anillo de refuerzo (de una rueda dentada).—pl. (mar.) obenques; vientos o tirantes de la chimenea de un vapor. **II.** va. amortajar; cubrir, ocultar, abrigar. **III.** vn. guarecerse, refugiarse, encogerse.

shrove [shróuv], s. V. SHRIFT.—**Shrovetide**, **Shrove Tuesday**, martes de carnaval, martes de carnestolendas.

shrub [shrub], s. (bot.) arbusto.—**shrubbery** [shrúbœri], s. arbustos.—**shrubbiness** [shrúbines], s. abundancia de arbustos.—**shrubby** [shrúbi], a. cubierto de o abundante en arbustos; parecido a un arbusto; aparrado, fruticoso.

shrug [shrug]. **I.** va. encoger, contraer. **II.** vn. encogerse de hombros, o alzarse de hombros. **III.** s. encogimiento de hombros.

shrunk, **shrunken**, pret. y pp. de TO SHRINK.

shuck [shuc]. **I.** va. descascarar, descortezar, pelar; (E. U.) quitar la concha a una ostra. **II.** s. cáscara, vaina, hollejo; (E. U.) concha de marisco.—**not worth shucks**, (fam.) no valer tres cominos.

shudder [shúdœr]. **I.** vn. estremecerse, temblar. **II.** s. temblor, estremecimiento.

shuffle [shúfœl]. **I.** va. y vn. barajar; mezclar, revolver; pasar, traspasar; restregar; esquivar, evadir; desordenar.—**to s. along**, arrastrar los pies; ir tirando o pasando.—**to s. off**, soltar, echar a un lado, desprenderse o zafarse de.—**to s. up**, pergañar, hacer una cosa de mala manera. **II.** s. barajadura; evasiva, embuste, salida; restregamiento de pies en el suelo.

shuffleboard [-bórd], s. = SHOVELBOARD.

shuffler [shúflœr], s. embustero.

shun [shun], va. y vn. huir, rehuir, esquivar, evitar; retraerse, apartarse de.

shunt [shunt]. **I.** va. desviar; (f. c.) apartar; (elec.) poner en derivación; evadir, eludir; echar el muerto a uno. **II.** vn. desviarse; mudar de curso o de opinión. **III.** s. desviación; (elec.) derivación.—s. (-wound) dynamo, dínamo con excitación en derivación. **IV.** a. (elec.) en derivación; de derivación.—s. arc lamp, lámpara de arco en derivación.—s. box, caja de resistencias en derivación.—s. dynamo, dínamo de derivación, o dínamo shunt.—s. excitation, excitación en derivación.—s. ratio, relación de derivación.—s.-wound, de arrollamiento en derivación.

---

shunter [shúntœr], *s.* (Ingl. f. c.) guardagujas.

shut [shut]. **I.** *va.* (*pret.* y *pp.* SHUT) cerrar; encerrar; vedar, prohibir, impedir; negar la entrada; excluir; coger, agarrar (con algo que se cierra); plegar, doblar, cerrar (abanico, paraguas, etc.).—**to s. against,** cerrar a.—**to s. close,** cerrar.—**to s. from,** excluir.—**to s. off,** impedir la entrada, interceptar.—**to s. one's eyes to,** no hacer caso de; taparse los ojos (fig.).—**to s. out,** cerrar la puerta (a uno).—**to s. out rain,** impedir que entre la lluvia.—**to s. up,** cerrar; hacer callar; acabar, terminar; tapar; encerrar; acorralar, aprisionar.—**to s. up shop,** cerrar la tienda; terminar el trabajo o cesar en él; desistir de una empresa. **II.** *vn.* cerrarse.—**to s. close,** cerrarse bien.—**to s. down,** cesar (en el trabajo), parar.— **to s. down on,** (fam.) hacer cesar, suprimir, reprimir.—**to s. up,** callarse; agotarse. **III.** *s.* cierre; término, fin; juntura; (fig.) horizonte. **IV.** *a.* cerrado, entornado; sordo, poco sonoro; (gram.) sordo, cerrado.

shute [shut], *s.* trama de seda.

shutter [shútœr], *s.* cerrador; persiana; (foto.) obturador.

shuttle [shútœl], *s.* (tej.) lanzadera.

shuttlecock [shútœlcoc], *s.* volante, rehilete.

shy [shái]. **I.** *a.* tímido; asustadizo; cauteloso, prudente; esquivo, arisco; vergonzoso, recatado. **II.** *va.* (con **off** o **away**) hacer desviar, apartar; lanzar o arrojar. **III.** *vn.* respingar; asustarse. **IV.** *s.* sobresalto; respingo; lanzamiento; prueba, ensayo.

shyer [-œr], *s.* caballo asustadizo.

shyly [-li], *adv.* cautelosamente; tímidamente.

shyness [-nes], *s.* timidez; recato; reserva; esquivez.

shyster [sháistœr], *s.* (fam. E. U.) picapleitos, trapisondista.

si, *s.* (mús.) si, séptima nota.

sialagogic [sáiœlœgóyic], *a.* **sialagogue** [saiœlagog], *s.* sialagogo, que provoca la secreción de saliva.

Siamese [saiamís], *a.* y *s.* siamés.

Siberian [saibírian], *a.* siberiano.

sibilant [síbilant], *a.* sibilante.

sibilation [sibiléshun], *s.* silbido.

sibyl [síbil], *s.* sibila.—**sibylline** [síbilin *o* -lain], *a.* sibilino.

sic [sic], *adv.* *sic,* así dice.

sicamore, *s.* = SYCAMORE.

siccative [sícativ], *s.* y *a.* (pint.) secante, secativo.

Sicilian [sisílian], *a.* y *s.* siciliano.

sick. I. *a.* enfermo; (Ingl.) nauseado; (con **of**) cansado, disgustado, fastidiado, harto; impuro, viciado; dañado, malo, imperfecto.—**s. at heart,** afligido de corazón, angustiado.—**s. bed,** lecho de enfermo.—**s. flag,** (mar.) bandera amarilla.—**s. for,** deseoso de, suspirando por.—**s. headache,** jaqueca con náuseas.—**s. leave,** licencia por enfermedad.—**s. rate,** proporción de enfermos.—**s. room,** cuarto del enfermo.—**s. to death,** enfermo de peligro, de muerte.—**the S. Man of Europe,** la Turquía (en tiempo de los sultanes), el imperio turco.—**to be s. at one's stomach,** tener náuseas. **II.** *va.* buscar (ú en imperativo para azuzar a un perro); excitar, incitar.

sicken [sícœn]. **I.** *va.* enfermar; dar asco; apestar; debilitar, extenuar. **II.** *vn.* enfermarse; hartarse, fastidiarse, cansarse; nausear, tener asco; flaquear.

sickening [sícning], *a.* nauseabundo, repugnante, apestoso.

sickish [síkish], *a.* enfermizo, delicado; nauseabundo.

sickle [sícœl], *s.* hoz, segadera, segur.

sickliness [síclines], *s.* calidad de enfermizo; insalubridad.

sickly [sícli], *a.* enfermizo, achacoso; enclenque, endeble.

sickness [sícnes], *s.* enfermedad; náusea.

side [sáid]. **I.** *s.* lado, costado; cara (de un sólido); flanco; costado, orilla, margen; falda, ladera; facción, partido, bando, parte; lazo de parentesco; (mar.) costado, bordo, banda.—**s. by**

s., lado a lado; hombro a hombro, juntos.—**by the s. of,** al lado de; cerca de.—**on all sides,** o en every **s.,** por todos lados, por todas partes.—**on that s.,** a, de, en o por ese lado.—**on the other s.,** del o al otro lado; más allá; a la otra parte.—**on this s.,** a, de, en o por este lado; más acá. **II.** *a.* lateral; de lado; oblicuo; secundario, incidental; auxiliar.—**s. arms,** armas de cinto; espadas.—**s. car, carriage,** o **chair,** cochecillo lateral de remolque (de una motocicleta).—**s. chain,** (biol.) cadena lateral.—**s.-chain theory,** (biol.) teoría de las cadenas laterales.—**s. dish,** entremés.—**s. graftage,** o **grafting,** injerto de escudete.—**s. issue,** cuestión secundaria, incidente. —**s. light,** luz lateral; información o detalle incidental.—**s. show,** función o exhibición secundaria. —**s. table,** trinchero, bufete, aparador.—**s. wall,** pared lateral; pared.—**s.-wheel boat,** o **steamer, s.-wheeler,** vapor (buque) de ruedas laterales. **III.** *va.* y *vn.* (con **with**) tomar parte por, declararse por, unirse con, ser de la opinión de.

sideboard [-bord], *s.* aparador, copero.

sideface [-féis], *s.* perfil.

sidehill [-jil], *s.* ladera, falda.

sidelong [-long]. **I.** *a.* lateral, de lado. **II.** *adv.* lateralmente, de lado.

sidereal [saidíreal], **sideral** [sídœral], *a.* sideral.

siderite [sídœrait], *s.* (min.) siderosa o siderita.

siderostat [sídœrostœt], *s.* (astr.) sideróstato.

sidesaddle [-sǽdœl], *s.* silla de señora, silla de montar de lado, como solían las mujeres.

sideslip [-slíp]. **I.** *vn.* resbalar lateralmente. **II.** *s.* (aut.) resbalamiento o patinamiento lateral; (aer.) deslizamiento hacia adentro (en una curva).

sidestep [-stép]. **I.** *s.* paso lateral; paso a un lado. **II.** *vn.* dar un paso lateral; hacerse a un lado. **III.** *va.* (fam.) huir el cuerpo a; evitar, evadir.

sidetrack [-tréc]. **I.** *s.* (f. c.) apartadero, desviadero. **II.** *va.* (f. c.) meter en un apartadero (fam.) reducir a cosa secundaria, echar a un lado, arrinconar.

sidewalk [-uóc], *s.* acera.

sideward(s [-uord(s], *adv.* de lado, de costado.

sideways [-uéis], **sidewise** [-uais], *adv.* de lado, oblicuamente, al través.

siding [-ing], *s.* (f. c.) apartadero, desviadero; (carp.) costaneras, entablado de los costados; adhesión a un partido.

sidle [sáidœl], *vn.* bornear.

siege [siy], *s.* sitio, asedio, cerco.

sienite, *s.* = SYENITE.

sienna [siéna], *s.* tierra de siena.

siesta [siéstœ], *s.* siesta.

sieve [siv], *s.* cedazo, tamiz o criba; persona gárrula; canasto.

sift. I. *va.* cerner, cribar; examinar, escudriñar; dividir, separar, entresacar.—**to s. out,** investigar. **II.** *vn.* caer o pasar al través de un tamiz o cedazo.

sifter [síftœr], *s.* cernedor, cribador; garbillador; escudriñador; tamiz, harnero, cedazo, criba.

siftings [síftings], *s. pl.* granzas.

sigh [sái]. **I.** *vn.* suspirar; dar un quejido. **II.** *va.* (poét.) decir suspirando; lamentar. **III.** *s.* suspiro.

sighingly [sáingli], *adv.* suspirando.

sight [sáit]. **I.** *s.* vista; ojo; escena, cuadro, espectáculo; aspecto, facha; concepto, parecer, modo de ver; puntería; mira (de un cañón); pínula (de una brújula de agrimensor, etc.); agujero o abertura para mirar.—**a s. of,** (fam.) gran cantidad o número de.—**after s.,** (com.) a. . . . vista (*thirty days after sight,* a treinta días vista). —**at s.,** a la vista (giro, etc.); a primera vista; al ver, cuando se vea.—**to be a s.,** (fam.) parecer o estar como un adefesio; ser extraordinario o extraño; tener aspecto maltrecho. **II.** *a.* (com.) a la vista (*a sight draft,* una letra a la vista). **III.** *va.* ver, alcanzar con la vista; ver o descubrir con un instrumento; dirigir una visual; poner miras a un arma; apuntar; (com.) presentar (una letra) para su aceptación. **IV.** *vn.* apuntar; dirigir una visual.

sighted [-ed], *a.* provisto de mira.—**s. for,** con la mira puesta para.

sightless [-les], *a.* ciego; invisible.

sightliness [-lines], [*s.* elegancia o hermosura; apariencia vistosa.

sightly [-li], *a.* vistoso, hermoso.

sightseeing [-síing], *s.* acto de visitar objetos o puntos de interés.—**sightseer** [-síœr], *s.* persona que visita puntos u objetos de interés.

sigmoid(al [sígmoid, -æl], *a.* sigmoideo.

sign [sáin]. **I.** *s.* signo; señal; muestra, letrero, tablilla; firma, rúbrica; huella, vestigio, rastro. —**s. manual,** (Ingl.) firma del soberano; cualquier firma o rúbrica de propio puño.—**s. of the cross,** señal de la cruz.—**s. painter,** pintor de muestras o letreros.—**the signs of the times,** las indicaciones de la actualidad, el rumbo de los acontecimientos, las orientaciones de la época.— **the signs of the zodiac,** los signos del zodíaco. **I.** *va.* firmar; subscribir (un tratado, etc.); (con **off o away**) firmar la cesión o traspaso de; poner una marca o firma.

signal [sígnal]. **I.** *a.* señalado, notable; de o para señales.—**s. box,** garita de señales.—**s. code,** código de señales.—**s. corps,** (mil. E. U.) cuerpo de señales y comunicaciones (inclusas las telegráficas, telefónicas, etc.).—**s. failure,** fracaso completo, gran piña.—**s. light,** fanal.—**s. service** = SIGNAL CORPS; sistema o servicio de señales.—**s. telegraph,** telégrafo óptico.—**s. tower,** garita alta de señales. **II.** *s.* seña, señal. **III.** *va.* y *vn.* hacer señas, señalar, indicar.

signalize [-aiś], *va.* señalar, distinguir; singularizar, hacer notable.

signally [-i], *adv.* insignemente, grandemente; señaladamente.

signalman [-mæn], *s.* guardavía.

signalment [-ment], *s.* marca, acción de poner marcas de identificación (apl. esp. a los criminales).

signatory [sígnatori], *a.* y *s.* firmante, signatario.

signature [sígnachur], *s.* firma; rúbrica; (imp.) signatura; (mús.) signatura.

signboard [sáinbord], *s.* muestra de establecimiento; tablero de anuncios.

signer [sáinœr], *s.* firmante, signatario.

signet [sígnet], *s.* sello; signáculo; timbre.

significance, significancy [signíficans, -i], *s.* significación; significado.—**significant** [-ant], *a.* significativo.—**significantly** [-i], *adv.* significativamente.

signification [signifikéśhun], *s.* significación o significado.

significative [signíficativ], *a.* significativo; simbólico, emblemático.

signify [sígnifai], *va.* y *vn.* significar; importar.

signpost [sáinpost], *s.* poste o pilar de guía, que lleva letrero o señal; hito.

silage [sáiley], *s.* (agr.) ensilaje.

silence [sáilens]. **I.** *s.* silencio.—**s. gives consent,** quien calla otorga. **II.** *va.* imponer silencio, mandar o hacer callar; parar, acorralar; sosegar, aquietar; (mil.) apagar el fuego de (la artillería enemiga).

silencer [sáilensœr], *s.* (tecn.) silenciador, amortiguador de ruido.

silent [sáilent], *a.* silencioso; callado; muda (letra); tácito.—**s. partner,** (com.) socio comanditario.—**be s.,** calle Vd.

silentiary [sailénśhiari], *s.* silenciario.

silently [sáilentli], *adv.* silenciosamente, calladamente; tácitamente.

Silesian [silíśhæn], *s.* y *a.* silesio.

silex [sáilex], *s.* sílice, pedernal.

silhouette [siluét]. **I.** *va.* hacer aparecer en silueta. **II.** *s.* silueta.

silica [sílica], *s.* sílice, pedernal.

silicate [síliket], *s.* silicato.

silicic [silísic], *a.* silícico.

silicious [silíśhus], *a.* silíceo.—**s. earth,** tierra primitiva o sencilla de sílice o pedernal.

silicle [sílicœl], *s.* (bot.) silícula.

silicon [sílicon], *s.* (quím.) silicio.

siliqua [sílicua], *s.* silicua.

silique [silíc], *s.* (bot.) silicua.

siliquous [sílicuus], **siliquose** [sílicuous], *a.* siliçuoso.

silk [silc]. **I.** *s.* seda.—*pl.* silks, sedería, géneros de seda. **II.** *a.* de seda; sedero, perteneciente o relativo a la seda.—**s. cotton,** lana vegetal.— **s.-cotton tree,** (bot.) árbol bombáceo (apl. más esp. a la ceiba).—**s. culture,** sericultura.—**s. dyer,** tintorero de sedas.—**s. goods,** géneros de seda, sedería.—**s. hat,** sombrero de copa.—**s. mercer** = SILKMAN.—**s. plush,** felpa de seda.—**s. poplar,** pobo, álamo blanco.—**s. serge,** sarga.—**s. thrower** devanador o torcedor de seda.—**s. throwing,** torcedura de la seda.—**s. throwster** = s. THROWER —**s. weaver,** tejedor de seda.—**s. worm,** gusano de seda.

silkaline [sílkalin], *s.* silcalina (es nombre de fábrica), tela de algodón mercerizada muy semejante a la seda.

silken [sílkœn], *a.* de seda; sedoso; lujoso.

silkiness [sílkines], *s.* blandura, suavidad; molicie, afeminación.

silkman [sílkman], *s.* mercader de sedas, sedero.

silkweed [sílkuid], *s.* (bot.) asclepias.

silkworm [sílkuœrm], *s.* gusano de seda.

silky [sílki], *a.* asedado, sedoso, sedeño; de seda.

sill [sil], *s.* umbral de puerta; (carp.) solera, viga de carrera.

sillibub [sílibub], *s.* manjar de leche con vino o sidra.

sillily [sílili], *adv.* tontamente.

silliness [-nes], *s.* simpleza, tontería, necedad, mentecatada.

silly [síli], *a.* necio, tonto, mentecato; simple, inocente, cándido; disparatado.

silo [sáilo], *s.* (agr.) silo.

silt [silt]. **I.** *s.* cieno, sedimento, alución. **II.** *va.* y *vn.* (a veces con *up*) obstruir(se) con sedimentos. **III.** *vn.* infiltrarse; manar.

silundum [silúndum], *s.* silundo (nombre de fábrica), producto duro y refractario del horno eléctrico (carburo de silicio, a veces con oxígeno).

Silurian [silúrian], *s.* y *a.* siluriano.

Suridæ [silúridi], *s. pl.* silúridos.

silvan [sílvan], *a.* = SYLVAN.

silver [sílvœr]. **I.** *s.* plata; (com.) monedas de plata; vajilla de plata o plateada.—**s. beater,** batihoja, batidor de plata. **II.** *a.* de plata; argentino; plateado; blanco, cano.—**s. fir,** (bot.) abeto.—**s. fish,** (ict.) lepisma.—**s. foil,** hoja de plata.—**s. lace,** encaje o galón de plata.—**s. leaf,** hoja de plata.—**s. paper,** papel plateado; (fot.) papel sensibilizado con sales de plata; papel de seda para envolver artículos de plata.—**s. plate,** vajilla de plata o plateada.—**s.-plate,** *va.* platear. —**s.-plated,** plateado.—**s. print,** fotografía en papel de plata (sensibilizado con sales de plata).— **s. thistle,** (bot.) acanto.—**s. voice,** voz plateada. —**s. wedding,** bodas de plata (vigésimoquinto aniversario). **III.** *va.* platear; azogar, blanquear.

silvering [-ing], *s.* capa o baño de plata; plateado o azogamiento.

silversmith [-smiz], *s.* platero.—**s.'s roll,** cilindro de escarchar.—**s.'s shop,** platería.

silverware [-uéœr], *s.* plata labrada; vajilla de plata; artículos de plata.

silverweed [-uíd], *s.* (bot.) agrimonia.

silvery [sílvœri], *a.* plateado; argentino.

silvicultural [sílvicúlchuræl], *a.* de silvicultura, relativo a la silvicultura.—**silviculture** [-chur], *s.* silvicultura.—**silviculturist** [-ist], *s.* silvicultor.

simian [símian]. **I.** *s.* simio. **II.** *a.* símico.

similar [símilar], *a.* (leng. ord. y geom.), semejante.

similarity [simílæriti], *s.* semejanza.

similarly [símilarli], *adv.* semejantemente; análogamente, asimismo.

simile [símili], *s.* símil.

similitude [simílitiud], *s.* similitud, semejanza.

simious, simmious [símioid, símius], *a.* símico.

simitar [símitar], *s.* cimitarra.

simlin [simlin], *s.* (E. U.) calabaza.

simmer [símœr], *vn.* hervir a fuego lento.

simoniac [simóniæc], *s.* y *a.*, **simoniacal** [símonáícæl], *a.*, **simonist** [símonist], *s.* simoníaco.

simony [símoni], *s.* simonía.

Simonpure, Simon pure [sáimʊnpiúær], *a.* (fam.) verdadero, puro, genuino.

simoom, simoon [simún, -mún], *s.* simún.

simper [símpœr]. **I.** *vn.* sonreírse bobamente. **II.** *s.* sonrisa tonta.

simperingly [símpœringli], *adv.* sonriendo tontamente, con sonrisa necia.

simple [símpœl]. **I.** *a.* simple; puro; sencillo; llano; mero; ingenuo, inocente, cándido; mentecato, necio; poco importante, insignificante, ordinario.—**s. contract**, contrato oral, o escrito pero no perfeccionado.—**s. engine**, (m. v.) máquina de simple expansión.—**s. equation**, ecuación de primer grado.—**s.-hearted**, sencillo, ingenuo.— **s. interest**, interés simple.—**s. machines**, máquinas simples, mecanismos elementales—nombre que se da por costumbre a la palanca, el torno, el tornillo, la polea, la cuña y el plano inclinado.— **s.-minded**, cándido, confiado.—**s.-mindedness**, candor, sencillez.—**s. pendulum**, péndulo simple. **II.** *s.* simple, elemento.

simpler [símplœr], *s.* simplista; herbolario.

simpleton [símpœltʊn], *s.* simplón, gaznápiro, bobalicón, papanatas.

simplicity [simplísiti], **simpleness** [símpœlnes], *s.* sencillez; simplicidad; simpleza, bobería.

simplification [símplifikéishʊn], *s.* simplificación.—**simplify** [-fai], *va.* simplificar.

simply [símpli], *adv.* sencillamente; simplemente; únicamene, solamente; tontamente.

simulacrum [símuléicrʊm], *s.* simulacro; farsa, apariencia.

simulant [símiulant], *a.* que simula, imita o finge; de forma de.

simulate [símiuleit], *va.* simular, fingir.—**simulated contract**, contrato simulado.

simulation [-éishʊn], *s.* simulación, fingimiento, imitación.

simultaneity, simultaneousness [símʊltaníiti, símʊltéiniusnes], *s.* simultaneidad.

simultaneous [si- (*o* -sái) mʊltéinius], *a.* simultáneo.—**simultaneously** [-li], *adv.* simultáneamente.

sin. I. *s.* pecado, culpa.—**s.-born**, nacido de pecado.—**s. offering**, sacrificio o voto propiciatorio. **II.** *vn.* pecar.

Sinaic [sainéic], **Sinaitic** [sáinæític], *a.* sinaítico.

sinapism [sínæpism], *s.* sinapismo.

since [sins]. **I.** *adv.* hace (*four days since*, hace cuatro días); desde entonces.—**not long s.**, no hace mucho, hace poco. **II.** *prep.* desde (que), después (que). **III.** *conj.* (antes seguido de *that*), puesto que, como.

sincere [sinsíær], *a.* sincero.—**sincerely** [-li], *adv.* sinceramente.—**sincereness** [-nes], **sincerity** [sinsériti], *s.* sinceridad.

sinciput [sínsiput], *s.* sincipucio, coronilla.

sine [sáin], *s.* (mat.) seno.

sine [sáini], *prep.* (lat.) sin.—**s. die**, indefinidamente, hasta nueva orden.—**s. qua non**, condición esencial.

sinecure [sáinekiur], *s.* sinecura; prebenda, beneficio simple.

sinew [sínyu]. **I.** *va.* fortalecer. **II.** *s.* tendón; fibra, nervio, fortaleza.

sinewed [sínyud], **sinewy** [sínyui], *a.* nervoso, musculoso; fuerte, robusto.

sinful [sínful], *a.* pecaminoso; pecador.—**sinfully** [-l], *adv.* pecaminosa o pecadoramente, pecando.—**sinfulness** [-nes], perversidad, calidad de pecaminoso.

sing, *vn.* y *va.* (*pret.* SANG O SUNG) *pp.* SUNG) cantar; murmurar (el agua), gorjear (los pájaros), zumbar (los oídos).—**to s. a child to sleep**, arrullar a un niño.—**to s. out**, (fam.) vocear, anunciar gritando.—**to s. out of tune, o false**, desafinar.—**to s. the same song**, cantar la misma cantinela, repetir la misma cosa.

singe [sinʒ], *va.* chamuscar, socarrar, sollamar; (coc.) aperdigar un ave; dañar, perjudicar.—

singeing [-inʒ], *s.* socarra, chamusquina.—**singer** [-œr], *s.* el o lo que chamusca o sollama.

singer [sínɡœr], *s.* cantor; cantora, cantatriz.

Singhalese [síngælís], *s.* y *a.* cingalés.

singing [sínɡuing]. **I.** canto, música vocal. **II.** *a.* de canto; cantor; canoro.—**s. bird**, ave canora. —**s. book**, cuaderno de solfa, de canto.—**s. master**, maestro de canto.

single [sínɡœl]. **I.** *a.* único, solo; particular, individual; soltero; puro, incorrupto; (mar.) single.—**s.-acting**, (mec.) de simple efecto.—**s. block**, (mec.) motón sencillo.—**s.-breasted**, abierto, de faldellín al sego (saco).—**s. combat**, combate singular.—**s. entry**, partida simple.— **s.-entry**, por partida simple.—**s. file**, hilera; en hilera; por hileras, en desfilada.—**s.-handed**, solo, sin ayuda; manco.—**s.-hearted**, sencillo de corazón, ingenuo.—**s. life**, celibato.—**s. loader**, rifle de un solo cartucho.—**s.-minded**, concentrado en un solo propósito; ingenuo, sincero.— **s.-phase**, (elec.) monofásico.—**s.-phaser**, máquina monofásica.—**s.-plate clutch**, (aut.) embrague de disco único.—**s. shear**, esfuerzo cortante en un solo lado.—**s. state** = s. LIFE.—**s. tax**, (e. p.) impuesto único.—**s.-track**, de una sola vía. —**not a s.**, ni un, ni una. **II.** *va.* singularizar; particularizar; (con **out**) separar, retirar; escoger; señalar con especialidad. **III.** *s.* billete de un dólar

singleness [-nes], *s.* unidad; sencillez, llaneza; sinceridad, ingenuidad; soltería.

singlestick [-stic], *s.* (esgr.) bastón.

singly [sínɡli], *adv.* individualmente, de uno en uno, uno a uno, separadamente.

singsong [sínɡsóng], *s.* cadencia uniforme, sonsonete, tonillo.

singular [sínɡuiular]. **I.** *a.* singular; aislado aparte, peculiar; sencillo, simple; (ant.) único. **II.** *s.* (gram.) número singular.—**singularity** [-lǽriti], **singularness** [-larnes], *s.* singularidad, rareza.—**singularize** [-laraís], *va.* singularizar, particularizar.—**singularly** [-larli], *adv.* singularmente, particularmente.

Sinic [sínic], *s.* chinesco, chino.

sinister [sínistœr], *a.* siniestro.—**sinistrad** [-træd], *adv.* hacia el lado izquierdo del cuerpo.— **sinistral, sinistrorse** [-tral, -trors], *a.* siniestro, izquierdo.—**sinistrous** [-trus], *a.* siniestro.—**sinistrously** [-li], *adv.* siniestramente; hacia la izquierda.

sink [sinc]. **I.** *va.* (*pret.* SANK, SUNK: *pp.* SUNK, SUNKEN), hundir, sumergir; echar a pique; sumir, ahondar; cavar, abrir (un pozo); clavar en tierra; deprimir, abatir, humillar; disminuir, bajar, rebajar; abatir, hacer bajar; derrochar, malbaratar; suprimir, ocultar, hacer desaparecer; grabar. **II.** *vn.* hundirse, sumirse; naufragar, irse a pique; (arq.) sentarse, asentarse; introducirse, penetrar, caer; grabarse (en la memoria); descender, desaparecer; disminuir, menguar; debilitarse, sucumbir, perecer; dejarse caer, rendirse; abatirse, acoquinarse, amilanarse; (ant.) decaer, empeorar.—**to s. down**, caer por grados; penetrar profundamente.—**to s. into**, penetrar en, llegar a; caer en.—**to s. on one's knees**, caer de rodillas.—**to s. under**, atribularse en o con, anonadarse. **III.** *s.* sumidero; vertedero; fregadero; zahurda (fig.); cavidad; cauce, zanja.

sinkable [síncæbœl], *a.* hundible, sumergible.

sinker [síncœr], *s.* plomada de pescar.

sinking [síncing]. **I.** *s.* hundimiento; abertura (de un pozo, etc.); acción de hundir, hundirse, echar a pique, etc. (*v.* SINK). **II.** *a.* que hunde o que se hunde.—**s. fund**, fondo de amortización.

sinless [sínles], *a.* impecable; inmaculado.

sinlessness [sínlesnes], *s.* impecabilidad.

sinner [sínœr], *s.* pecador.

Sinn Fein [shin féin], *s.* Sinn Fein (asociación patriótica irlandesa).

sinologist [sinóloʒist], **sinolog(ue** [sínolog], *s.* sinólogo.—**sinology** [-i:], *s.* sinología.

sinople [sínopœl], *s.* (blas.) sinople.

sinter [síntœr], *s.* toba, incrustación.

sinuate [síñuet], **I.** *va.* formar oblicuidades, sinuosidades o senos. **II.** *a.* tortuoso, ondulado. —**sinuation** [-éishʊn], *s.* tortuosidad, corvadura.

sinuosity [siñuósiti], *s.* sinuosidad, tortuosidad. —**sinuous** [síñuvs], *a.* sinuoso, tortuoso.

sinus [sáinvs], *s.* seno, ensenada, bahía; cavidad, abertura, hueco; (anat.) seno.

sip. I. *va.* sorber, libar, chupar o churrupear. **II.** *s.* sorbo.

siphon [sáifvn]. **I.** *s.* sifón; cantimplora; probeta. **II.** *va.* y *vn.* sacar agua con sifón. **III.** *a.* de sifón.—**s. bottle,** sifón (botella), botella de sifón.—**s. pipe,** o **trap,** desagüe de sifón o en U.

siphonophore [sáifonofór], *s.* (zool.) sifonóforo.

sipper [sipœr], *s.* sorbedor.

sippet [sípet], *s.* sopita, sopilla, sopa.

sir [sœr], *s.* señor (*yes, sir,* sí, señor); (Ingl.) sir, título que se antepone al nombre de pila de los barones y caballeros de las órdenes militares.

sire [sáiær]. **I.** *s.* padre; progenitor; caballo padre: anciano; Señor, tratamiento del soberano. **II.** *va.* engendrar, producir (hablando de caballos).

siren [sáiren], *s.* sirena: mujer peligrosa y hechicera; cantatriz de mérito; (mar.) sirena de vapor.

Sirius [sírivs], *s.* (astr.) Sirio.

sirloin [sœrloin], *s.* solomillo.

sirocco [siróco], *s.* siroco, simún.

sirrah [sírra], *s.* (desp.) señoritingo, don Turuleque, u otra expresión despreciativa análoga.

sirup [sírup], *s.* jarabe.

sirupy [-i], *a.* semejante a jarabe.

sisal [sísæl, sisál], **s. grass, s. hemp,** henequén.

siskin [sískin], *s.* (orn.) verderón.

sismograph, etc. = SEISMOGRAPH, etc.

sissy [sísi]. **I.** *s.* (fam.) hermanita; ñiñita. **II.** *s.* y *a.* (fam.) afeminado, adamado.

sister [sístœr], *s.* hermana; (igl.) sor; monja.—**s.-in-law,** cuñada.

sisterhood [sístœrjud], *s.* hermandad, cofradía de mujeres; conjunto de hermanas.

sisterly [sístœrli], *a.* con hermandad, como corresponde a hermanas.

sistrum [sístrvm], *s.* sistro, cascabel músico de los antiguos egipcios.

sit [sit]. **I.** *va.* (pret. SAT, SATE; *pp.* SAT) sentar; dar asiento a; tener asientos o cabida para; cabalgar, sentarse en (un caballo, etc.).—**to s. out,** estarse (sentado) o aguantar (sentado) hasta el fin de, aguantar.—**to s. out a dance,** no bailar una pieza por sentarse a conversar. **II.** *vr.* sentarse. **III.** *vn.* sentarse; estar sentado; posarse; empollar (las aves); reunirse, celebrar junta o sesión; formar parte de un tribunal; sentar, venir (un vestido, etc.); montar, mantenerse a caballo; descansar, apoyarse.—**to s. at meat,** o **at table,** sentarse a la mesa, o a comer.—**to s. by,** sentarse o estar sentado cerca de, junto a o al lado de. —**to s. down,** sentarse; detenerse, parar; residir. —**to s. down before** (a city), poner sitio a, sitiar (una ciudad).—**to s. down on,** o **upon,** sentarse en; (fam.) reprimir; desairar, desechar.—**to s. for one's picture,** hacerse retratar.—**to s. on,** o **upon,** (fam.) hacer callar a, aplastar (fig.), dejar feo a.—**to s. tight,** (fam.) esperar sin decir nada, esperar la jugada del contrario (fig.), tenerse firme. —**to s. up,** incorporarse; sentarse (el enfermo, sea en la cama, sea en una silla); velar, estarse levantado, no acostarse.—**to s. up and take notice,** (fam.) abrir los ojos (fig.), despertar (fig.), poner cuidado.—**s. still,** estése quieto, no se mueva; conserve Vd. su asiento, no se levante Vd.

sitar [sitár], *s.* guitarra oriental.

site [sáit], *s.* asiento, solar; sitio, situación, local.

sited [sáited], *a.* situado, ubicado.

sith [siz] = SINCE.

sitter [sítœr], el que se sienta o está sentado; el que se hace retratar; el ave que empolla huevos.

sitting [síting]. **I.** *s.* acción o modo de sentarse; sentada delante de un retratista; sesión, junta; legislatura; sentada, ascutada; empolladura; nidada o cría. **II.** *a.* sentado; (bot.) sesil.—**s. room,** estancia.

situate [sítyueit]. **I.** *va.* situar; fijar sitio o lugar para. **II.** *a.* situado, sito, ubicado.

situation [-éishvn], *s.* situación; ubicación, posición; orientación, exposición; colocación, plaza, empleo; incidente, peripecia.—**out of a s.,** sin empleo, cesante.

situs [sáitvs], *s.* situación, posición, colocación.

six, *a.* y *s.* seis.—**at sixes and sevens,** a manga por hombro.

sixfold [síxfould], *a.* seis veces, seis veces más; de seis clases.

sixpence [síxpens], *s.* (Ingl.) moneda de plata (seis peniques, o medio chelín).

sixpenny [síxpeni], *a.* que vale o se vende por seis peniques; mezquino.

sixscore [síxcóœr], *s.* y *a.* seis ventenas.

sixteen [síxtín], *s.* y *a.* dieciséis.—**sixteenth** [-ínz], **I.** *a.* decimosexto; dieciséis (ordinal). **II.** *s.* y *a.* dieciseisavo.

sixth [sixz]. **I.** *a.* sexto; seis (del mes), **II.** *s.* sexto; (mús.) sexta.—**sixthly** [-li], *adv.* en sexto lugar.

sixtieth [síxtiez]. **I.** *a.* sexagésimo, sesenta. **II.** *s.* y *a.* sesentavo.

sixty [síxti], *a.* y *s.* sesenta

siz(e)able [sáisæbœl], *a.* de tamaño proporcionado; algo grande.

sizar [sáisar], *s.* (Ingl.) estudiante con beca; fámulo.

size [sáiš]. **I.** *s.* tamaño, medida, dimensiones; diámetro (de un tubo, alambre, etc.); cuerpo, talla, estatura; tipo de medida; cantidad especificada; (pap.) apresto; cola; sisa de doradores, cola de retazo; calibre, diámetro interior.— **s. stick,** (zap.) cartabón.—**to s.,** del tamaño debido o exacto; según medida. **II.** *va.* medir el tamaño de; calibrar; clasificar o separar según tamaño o estatura; valuar, justipreciar; dar el tamaño debido a, reducir al tamaño debido; (pap.) aprestar; (pint.) encolar; sisar; estofar, aparejar.—**to s. down,** disminuir gradualmente el tamaño de.— **to s. up,** (fam.) tomar las medidas a (fig.), justipreciar, juzgar.

sized [-d], *a.* dispuestos según tamaño o estatura; (precedido de adjetivo) de tamaño (*good-sized,* de buen tamaño; *large-sized,* de tamaño grande).

sizer [sáisœr], *s.* calibrador, pasabalas; encolador; aprestador.

siziness [sáisines], *s.* viscosidad.

sizing [sáising], *s.* encolado, aparejo, aderezo, estofo; calibradura; (pap.) apresto.

sizy [sáisi], *a.* viscoso, pegajoso.

sizz [siš], *vn.* silbar, chillar, chirriar.

sizzle [síscœl]. **I.** *va.* y *vn.* (fam.) quemar, chamuscar, quemarse o chamuscarse produciendo chirrido o siseo. **II.** *s.* (fam.) sonido como de siseo; calor excesivo.

skain [skéin]. **I.** *vn.* = SKEIN.

skate [skéit]. **I.** *vn.* patinar. **II.** *s.* patín (ict.) liza.—**skater** [-œr], *s.* patinador.

skating [-ing]. **I.** *s.* (el) patinar. **II.** *a.* de o para patinar.—**s. rink,** patinadero; sala de patinar.

skedaddle [skédædœl], *vn.* (fam.) tomar las de Villadiego; largarse.

skee [skí], *s.* SKI.

skeet [skít], *s.* (mar.) bañadera.

skein [skéin], *s.* madeja, cadejo.

skeletal [skéletal], *a.* de esqueleto; del esqueleto.

skeleton [skéleton]. **I.** *a.* en esqueleto o armazón; extenuado.—**s. key,** llave maestra. **II.** *s* esqueleto; armazón o armadura; esbozo, esquema.

skelp [skelp], *s.* tira o plancha metálica para tubos.

skeptic [sképtic], *s.* y *a.* escéptico.—**skeptical** [-al], *a.* escéptico.—**skeptically** [-cali], *adv.* escépticamente.—**skepticism** [-elsm], *s.* escepticismo.

sketch [skech]. **I.** *s.* diseño, esbozo, bosquejo, boceto, croquis; descripción a grandes rasgos; drama corto; (teat.) pieza corta o ligera. **II.** *va.* esquiciar, delinear, bosquejar, hacer un croquis de; describir a grandes rasgos.—**sketchily** [-li], *adv.* de modo abocetado.—**sketchiness** [-lnes], *s.* modo abocetado de una obra artística.—**sketchy** [-i], *a.* bosquejado, esquiciado; incompleto, fragmentario.

skew [skiú]. **I.** *a.* oblicuo, sesgado. **II.** *s.* movimiento, curso o posición oblicuos; mirada de soslayo. **III.** *va.* sesgar, poner al sesgo. **IV.** *vn.* andar o moverse sesgadamente; mirar de soslayo.

skewback [-bæc], *s.* (arq.) sotabanco.

skewer [-skiúœr]. **I.** *s.* (coc.) brocheta o broqueta. **II.** *va.* espetar.

ski [ski]. **I.** *s.* ski, patín largo noruego. **II.** *vn.* patinar con skis.

skiagraph [scáiægræf], *s.* = RADIOGRAPH.

skiascope [skáiascoup], *s.* = FLUOROSCOPE.

skid. I. *va.* proveer de varaderas; arrastrar sobre varaderas. **II.** *vn.* patinar (una rueda); (aut.) patinar o resbalar lateralmente. **III.** *s.* varadera; calzo; polín; rodillo; troza; tabla o madero inclinado de arrastre o deslizamiento; arrastradero; (aer.) patín.—**s.** road, arrastradero para trozas; camino con trozas transversales a intervalos.

skiff, *s.* esquife, botecillo, caique.

skilful [skieful], *a.* diestro, hábil, experto, ducho.— **skilfully** [-li], *adv.* diestramente.—**skilfulness** [-nes], *s.* habilidad, destreza.

skill [skil], *s.* habilidad, destreza, pericia, maña.

skilled [skild], *a.* práctico, instruído, experimentado, experto.—**skilless** [skil-les], *a.* inexperto.

skillet [skilet], *s.* cacerola o cazuela pequeña.

skim. I. *va.* desnatar; espumar; rasar, rastrear, tocar ligeramente; examinar superficialmente. —**to s. the ocean**, (mar.) peinar las olas. **II.** *vn.* deslizarse o pasar rasando.—**to s. over**, resbalar, rozar; hojear; tocar ligeramente una cuestión. **III.** *s.* acción de desnatar; nata; escoria, costra; desperdicios, inmundicias.—**s. milk**, leche desnatada; cosa insulsa.

skimmer [skímœr], *s.* espumadera.

skimming [skíming], *s.* despumación.

skimp. I. *va.* (fam.) escatimar; ejecutar con descuido. **II.** *vn.* ser tacaño; trabajar con descuido.

skin. I. *s.* piel (cutis, dermis, epidermis), pellejo, tegumento; (ten.) piel, cuero; odre, pellejo o cuero para vino, etc.; piel, pellejo o corteza de algunas frutas; forros (de un buque); cáscara, costra.—*pl.* pieles, corambre.—**s.-deep**, superficial.—**s. effect**, (elec.) efecto *skin*, efecto Kelvin. —**s. friction**, rozamiento entre el casco de un buque y el agua.—**s. game**, (fam.) fullería. — **s.-tight**, ajustado como un guante. **II.** *va.* desollar, despellejar; pelar, deshollejar; cubrir con piel; cubrir superficialmente. **III.** *vn.* cubrirse de pellejo o tegumento; cicatrizarse.—**to s. over**, cicatrizarse; hacerse costras.

skinflint [skínflint], *s.* avaro.

skink, *s.* (zool.) sequinco o estinco.

skinless [skínles], *a.* desprovisto de pellejo; de piel muy delgada.

skinner [skínœr], *s.* desollador; petardista, estafador; (ant.) pellejero; peletero.

skinniness [skínines], *s.* flacura.

skinny [skíni], *a.* flaco; pellejudo.

skip. I. *va.* saltar, omitir; saltar por encima de; hacer saltar rozando, como una piedra sobre el agua. **II.** *vn.* saltar, brincar, cabriolar, triscar. **III.** *s.* cabriola, salto, brinco; omisión.

skipper [skípœr], *s.* saltador, brincador; (ict.) escombresocio; gusanillo de queso; (mar.) patrón, mareante.—**s.'s daughter**, cabrilla de mar.

skipping [skíping], *s.* acción de saltar.—**s. rope**, cuerda con que saltan los niños.

skippingly [skípingli], *adv.* a saltos, a brincos.

skirmish [skœrmish], *s.* (mil.) escaramuza, refriega; zalagarda. **II.** *vn.* escaramuzar.

skirmisher [-œr], *s.* escaramuzador.

skirret [skírret], *s.* (bot.) chirivía.

skirt [skœrt]. **I.** *s.* falda, faldellín, saya, enaguas; (sast.) faldón; faldones de la silla de montar; orla, cenefa; orilla, margen, borde; (fam.) mujer, faldas (pl.).—**s. (board)** = BASEBOARD.— **s. dance**, (teat.) baile en que la bailarina hace graciosas posturas con su faldellín.—**skirts of a city**, contornos de una ciudad. **II.** *va.* poner enaguas a; proveer de borde, margen, etc.; seguir la orilla de;

costear; (cost.) orillar; poner canefa a. **III.** *vn.* (con *along*, *near*, etc.) moverse a lo largo de; costear; escoger la lana separando la de inferior calidad.

skirting [-ing], *s.* enaguas (consideradas como géneros); material para enaguas; BASEBOARD (llám. t. **s. board**).—*pl.* lana de inferior calidad.

skit, *s.* articulillo, suelto, pasquín; burla.

skittish [skítish], *a.* espantadizo; tímido; retozón; caprichudo, voluble.—**skittishly** [-li], *adv.* caprichosamente.—**skittishness** [-nes], *s.* desenvoltura; volubilidad.

skittle [skítœl], *s.* juego de bolos.

skive [skáiv]. **I.** *va.* (ten.) raspar, adelgazar; cortar en capas; (joy.) pulir. **II.** *s.* (joy.) disco para pulir el diamante.—**skiver** [-œr], *s.* cuero hendido con cuchillo; (enc.) cuero para pastas; cuchillo de adelgazar.

skulk [scʊlc], *vn.* remolonear; acechar; andar a sombra de tejado.

skulker [scúlcœr], *s.* socaire.

skull [scʊl], *s.* cráneo; calavera; remo para cinglar.

skullcap [-cæp], *s.* casquete (gorro); (anat.) sincipucio; (bot.) escutelaria.

skunk [skʊnk], *s.* (zool.) mofeta, (Am.) zorrino, zorrillo.—**s. cabbage**, (bot.) hierba fétida de la familia del yaro.

skurry, *v. y s.* = SCURRY.

sky [skái], *s.* cielo, firmamento.—**s. blue**, azul celeste, cerúleo.—**s.-clad**, (fam.) desnudo.— **s.-colored**, o **dyed**, azul celeste.—**s.-high**, tan alto como el cielo.—**s. pilot**, aviador; (fam.) clérigo.—**s. writing**, escritura aérea, formación de letreros o figuras con gases o vapores que se despiden de un avión.

skyey [skáii], *a.* etéreo.

skyed [skáid], **skyish** [skáiish], *a.* azulado.

skylark [skáilarc]. **I.** *s.* (orn.) alondra, calandria. **II.** *vn.* (fam.) chacotear, jaranear.— **skylarking**, [-ing], *s.* chacota, jarana.

skylight [-lait], *s.* claraboya, tragaluz.

skyman [-mæn], *s.* (fam.) aviador.

skyrocket [-róket], *s.* cohete, volador.

skysail [-seil, *s.* (mar.) periquito.

skyscraper [-scréipœr], *s.* (mar.) periquito; (fam.) rascacielos, edificio sumamente alto.

skyward(**s** [-ward(s], *adv.* hacia el cielo.

slab [slæb], *s.* costero; losa, plancha, tabla, laja. — **s. line**, (mar.) briol.

slabber [slæbœr], *vn.* babear, salivar.—**slabberer** [-œr], *s.* baboso.—**slabbering** [-ing], *s.* babeo.

slabby [slæbi], *a.* espeso, viscoso; mojado.

slack [slæc]. **I.** *a.* flojo, laxo; débil, poco firme; perezoso, negligente, tardo.—**s. ropes**, (mar.) cabos sueltos o en banda.—**s. water**, repunte de la marea; aguas represadas.—**s.-water navigation**, navegación por tramos. **II.** *s.* seno de un cabo; flojedad; polvo de carbón, cisco, carbón menudo.

slack, slacken [slæcœn]. **I.** *va.* aflojar, desapretar; retardar; disminuir; descuidar; eludir; apagar (la cal). **II.** *vn.* aflojarse; disminuir; (a veces con *up*) mermar, menguar; retardarse; descuidarse, flojear.

slacker [slæcœr], *s.* (fam.) el que elude el servicio militar en tiempo de guerra, cobarde.

slackly [slæcli], *adv.* flojamente.

slackness [slæcnes], *s.* flojedad.

slag [slæg], *s.* escoria.

slain [sléin], *pp.* DE TO SLAY.

slake [sléik]. **I.** *va.* apagar (apl. esp. a la cal); extinguir; remojar; desleír; calmar, moderar; aflojar. **II.** *vn.* apagarse (la cal).

slam [slæm]. **I.** *va.* cerrar de golpe; en los juegos de naipes, dar capote. **II.** *vn.* cerrarse de golpe y con estrépito. **III.** *s.* portazo; capote en el juego.

slander [slǽndœr]. **I.** *va.* calumniar. **II.** *s.* calumnia.—**slanderer** [-œr], *s.* calumniador.— **slandering** [-ing], *s.* columnia. **II.** *a.* calumnioso.—**slanderous** [-us], *a.* infamatorio, calumnioso.—**slanderously** [-li], *adv.* calumniosamente.

slang [slæng], *s.* (gram.) vulgarismo; jerga, jerigonza, caló.

slangy [slǽngui], *a.* vulgar en el lenguaje; que emplea vulgarismos o habla en caló.

slank [slænk], *pret.* de SLINK.

slant [slænt], *va.* y *vn.* oblicuar, sesgar; inclinarse, sesgarse.

slant(ing [slánt(ing]. **I.** *a.* sesgado, terciado, oblicuo; inclinado, en declive. **II.** *s.* oblicuidad, sesgo; inclinación; plano inclinado, declive; pulla, indirecta.

slantingly [-li], **slantwise** [slántuaís], *adv.* sesgadamente.

slap [slæp]. **I.** *va.* dar una palmada a (una persona) o en (la cara); poner o tirar violentamente. **II.** *s.* palmada; bofetada.—**a s. in the face,** bofetada; insulto. **III.** *adv.* de golpe y ꞏorrazo, de sopetón.

slapdash [slǽpdæsh], *a.* y *adv.* (fam.) de prisa, de una vez, de un golpe.

slash [slæsh]. **I.** *va.* acuchullar, dar cuchilladas. **II.** *vn.* tirar tajos y reveses. **III.** *s.* cuchillada; latigazo, azote; (sast.) [corte, cortadura, cuꞏchillo.

slat [slæt]. **I.** *va.* y *vn.* arrojar, tirar, lanzar. **II.** *s.* tablilla, loncha; (fam.) golpe.

slatch [slæch], *s.* (mar.) socaire; seno de un cabo.

slate [sléit]. **I.** *s.* pizarra, esquisto; pizarra para escribir; (E. U. pol.) lista de candidatos; programa de partido.—**s.-colored,** apizarrado. pizarreño.—**s. pencil,** pizarrín, pizarrete.—**s. quarry,** pizarral, cantera de pizarra. **II.** *va.* empizarrar; (ten.) quitar pelo a las pieles; (E. U. pol.) inscribir en una candidatura; redactar un programa de partido.

slater [sléitœr], *s.* pizarrero; raspador de pieles.

slattern [slǽtœrn]. **I.** *a.* puerco; desaliñado. **II.** *s.* mujer desaliñada.—**slatterliness** [-lines], *s.* desatavío; desaliño.—**slatternly** [-li]. **I.** *adv.* desaliñadamente. **II.** *a.* puerco, desaliñado.

slaty [sléiti], *a.* pizarreño.

slaughter [slótœr]. **I.** *s.* carnicería, matanza. **II.** *va.* matar; hacer una carnicería; destrozar.—**slaughterer, slaughterman** [-œr, mæn], *s.* matador; asesino; verdugo.—**slaughterous** [-us], *a.* mortífero, destructivo.

slaughterhouse [-jáus], *s.* matadero.

Slav ꞓslæv, *a.* y *s.* eslavo.

slave [sléiv]. **I.** *s.* esclavo.—**s. ant,** hormiga esclava.—**s. driver,** capataz de esclavos; persona opresiva o despótica.—**s.-making ant,** hormiga esclavizadora.—**s. trade,** trata de esclavos.—**s. trader,** negrero, traficante en esclavos. **II.** *vn.* trabajar como esclavo. **III.** *va.* esclavizar.

slaveborn [-born], *a.* nacido en la esclavitud.

slaveholder [-jóuldœr], *s.* amo o dueño de esclavos.

slaver [-œr], *s.* negrero.

slaver [slǽvœr]. **I.** *s.* baba. **II.** *vn.* babosear.

slaverbit [slǽvœrbit], *s.* sabores del freno.

slaverer [slǽvœrœr], *s.* baboso.

slavery [sléivœri], *s.* esclavitud.

Slavic [slǽvic], *a. V.* SLAVONIC.

slavish [sléivish], *a.* servil, abyecto; esclavizado.—**slavishly** [-li], *adv.* servilmente.—**slavishness** [-nes], *s.* servilismo.

Slavism [slávišm], *s.* eslavismo.

Slavonian [slavónian], *a.* y *s.* esclavón, eslavonio; eslavo.

Slavonic [slavónic], *a.* eslavo; esclavón.

slaw [slo], *s.* ensalada de col.

slay [sléi], *va.* (*pret.* SLEW) *pp.* SLAIN) matar.

slay, sley [sléi], *s.* (tej.) peine, cárcel.

slayer [sléœr], *s.* matador; asesino.

sleave [slív]. **I.** *s.* seda en rama, (llám. t. **s.,** o **sleaved,** silk). **II.** *va.* desenredar.

sleaziness [slésines], *s.* textura débil y ligera.

sleazy [slési], *a.* baladí, delgado, ligero.

sled. **I.** *va.* y *vn.* ir o llevar en trineo o narria. **II.** *s.* trineo, narria, rastra.

sledge [sley]. **I.** *va.* y *vn.* transportar o viajar en una narria. **II.** *s.* rastra, narria, trineo.—**s. hammer,** macho, mandarria, acotillo.

sleek [slíc]. **I.** *a.* liso, bruñido, alisado; suave, blando, zalamero. **II.** *va.* alisar, pulir, suavizar.

sleekly [slíkli], *adv.* lisamente; diestramente.

sleekness [slíknes], *s.* lisura.

sleeky [slíki], *a.* liso; taimado, mañoso.

sleep [slíp]. **I.** *va.* y *vn.* (*pret.* y *pp.* SLEPT) dormir (en toda acepción).—**to s. away,** disipar o malgastar el tiempo durmiendo.—**to s. in Jesus,** estar muerto, dormir en el Señor.—**to s. like a top,** dormir como un lirón.—**to s. off,** dormirla (la borrachera, etc.).—**to s. on,** seguir durmiendo.—**to s. on,** o **upon,** descuidarse o no hacer caso de; consultar con la almohada.—**to s. one's liquor away,** dormir la mona.—**to s. over,** consultar con la almohada.—**to s. soundly,** dormir profundamente. **II.** *s.* (leng. ord. y bot.) sueño.

sleeper [slípœr], *s.* (E. U. f. c.) coche dormitorio; (f. c.) traviesa, durmiente; animal aletargado; (mar.) carlinga, curva de yugo.

sleepily [-li], *adv.* con somnolencia, pesadez o torpeza.

sleepiness [-ines], *s.* somnolencia, sueño, modorra.

sleeping [slíping]. **I.** *s.* sueño. **II.** *a.* durmiente; dormido.—**s. bag,** especie de talego para envolverse por la noche cuando se duerme a la intemperie.—**s. car,** (f. c.) coche dormitorio.—**s. draft,** bebida calmante, narcótico.—**s. partner** = SILENT PARTNER.—**s. potion** = s. DRAFT.—**s. sickness,** encefalitis letárgica, letargo epidémico.

sleepless [-les], *a.* desvelado, insomne; de desvelo.—**sleeplessness** [-nes], *s.* insomnio.

sleepwalker [-uócœr], *s.* sonámbulo.—**sleepwalking** [-uóking], *s.* sonambulismo.

sleepy [-i], *a.* soñoliento, amodorrado; soporífero, soporoso; letárgico.

sleet [slít]. **I.** *s.* cellisca. **II.** *vn.* cellisquear.

sleetiness [slítines], *s.* estado del tiempo en que cellisquea.

sleety [slíti], *a.* cubierto de cellisca.

sleeve [slív], *s.* manga; (mec.) manguito; collar; (aer.) manguera.—**s. band,** (cost.) tira del puño, (sast.) vuelta de manga.—**s. buttons,** gemelos, mancuernas.—**s. coupling,** junta de manguito.—**s. links,** yugos.—**s. nut,** manguito de tuerca.

sleeveless [slívles], *a.* sin mangas.

sleigh [sléi], *s.* trineo.—**s. bell,** cascabel.—**s. ride,** paseo en trineo.

sleighing [sléing], *s.* paseo en trineo; estado de los caminos que permite ir en trineo.

sleight [sláit], *s.* habilidad, pericia, maña; ardid, artificio, estratagema.—**s. of hand,** juego de manos, prestidigitación.

slender [sléndœr], *a.* delgado; sutil, fino, ligero; flaco; delicado; escaso; pequeño, poco, corto, insuficiente; mediano.—**slenderly** [-li], *adv.* gadamente, sutilmente, ligeramente.—**slenderness** [-nes], *s.* delgadez, sutileza; debilidad; escasez; pequeñez.

slept, *pp.* y *pret.* de TO SLEEP.

sleuth [sluz]. **I.** *s.* pista, rastro; (fam.) detectivo, policía secreta particular. **II.** *va.* y *vn.* (fam.) espiar, acechar.

sleuthhound [-jáund], *s.* sabueso ventor; (fig.) agente de policía secreta.

slew, *pret.* de TO SLAY.

sley [sléi], *va.* y *s.* (tej.) *V.* SLAY.

slice [sláis]. **I.** *va.* rebanar, cortar en tajadas; tajar, cortar. **II.** *s.* rebanada, tajada, lonja; pala; espátula.—**s. bar,** hurgón, atizador.

slicer [-œr], *s.* rebanador; (joy.) sierra circular.

slick [slik]. **I.** *va.* alisar, pulir. **II.** *vn.* (gen. con *up*) componerse, acicalarse. **III.** *a.* liso, terso, lustroso; meloso, adulador; (fam.) diestro; mañoso. **IV.** *s.* lugar lustroso o aceitoso (en el agua); formón ancho de alisar (llám. t. **s. chisel**); punto liso y lustroso.

slide [sláid]. **I.** *vn.* (*pret.* SLID; *pp.* SLID o SLIDDEN) resbalar, deslizarse; patinar; escabullirse; salirse, escaparse; correr, pasar aprisa; pecar, cometer un desliz. **II.** *va.* hacer resbalar; meter o poner mañosa o suavemente; (con *let*) dejar correr, no hacer caso de. **III.** *s.* (fís.) tapa del chasis o portaplacas; platina (de microscopio o linterna májica); resbalón, resbaladura; resbaladero; plano inclinado; muesca, encaje (de un bastidor); (geol.) falla, dislocación;

desmoronamiento, alud; (mús.) ligado, portamento. **IV.** *a.* corredizo; de corredera.—**s. bar,** guía, barra de guía; barra corrediza.—**s. box,** (elec.) caja de resistencia con alambre de ontacto corredizo.—**s. rail,** (f. c.) aguja de cambi vía.—**s. rest,** (mec.) soporte de corredera; carrillo portaherramientas (de torno).—**s. rod,** vástago de la válvula de corredera.—**s. rule,** regla de cálculo.—**s. shaft** = **s. ROD.**—**s. valve,** válvula de corredera.—**s.-valve rod** = **s. ROD.**—**s. wire,** (elec.) alambre de contacto corredizo; brazo (del puente de Wheatstone) de contacto corredizo.

slider [sláidœr], *s.* resbalador, cursor.

sliding [sláiding]. **I.** *s.* deslizamiento. **II.** *a.* corredizo, corredero; resbaladizo, escurridizo.—**s. door,** puerta de corredera.—**s. friction,** rozamiento de resbalamiento.—**s. gear,** (aut.) cambio de velocidades con tren corredizo.—**s. knot,** nudo escurridizo.—**s. scale,** escala móvil, en la cual los impuestos, jornales, etc., varían según los precios de los artículos de consumo, o, en el caso de los obreros, según los precios corrientes de lo que producen.

slight [sláit]. **I.** *a.* ligero, leve; pequeño, corto, fútil, débil, flojo, delgado. **II.** *s.* desaire, desatención, feo, desprecio. **III.** *va.* menospreciar, despreciar, desairar; desatender, descuidar.

slightingly [-ingli], *adv.* con desprecio.

slightly [-li], *adv.* ligeramente; escasamente; descuidadamente.

slightness [-nes], *s* pequeñez, insignificancia; descuido, negligencia.

slim, *a.* delgado; sutil, tenue; poco lógico, débil, baladí; delicado; insuficiente, escaso.

slime [sláim]. **I.** *s.* limo, lama, légamo, cieno, fango; babaza; asfalto, chapapote. **II.** *va.* y *vn.* enfangar, enlodar, ensuciar con limo, lama, légamo o babaza; deslamar.

sliminess [-ines], *s.* viscosidad; mucosidad, limosidad.

slimy [-i], *a.* viscoso, limoso, legamoso; mucoso.

sling. I. *s.* honda; (cir.) cabestrillo; (mil.) charpa, portafusil; (E. U.) bebida alcohólica con azúcar y nuez moscada; (mar.) eslinga, balso.—**slings of the yard,** cruz de la vergas; estribos de las vergas. **II.** *va.* (*pret.* y *pp.* SLUNG) tirar con honda; tirar, arrojar; embalsar, embragar, izar, eslingar; poner en cabestrillo. **III.** *vn.* oscilar repentinamente; girar, dar vueltas.

slinger [slíngœr], *s.* hondero, pedrero.

slink, *vn.* (*pret.* y *pp.* SLUNK O SLANK) escabullirse, escaparse, escurrirse; (*pret.* y *pp.* SLINKED) (vet.) abortar, malparir.

slip. I. *va.* (*pret.* y *pp.* SLIPPED O SLIPT) deslizar; meter; sacar; llevarse cretamente; soltarse, zafarse, desprenderse de; soltar, desatar; (agr.) cortar esquejes de; (mar.) largar o soltar (un cable o cabo); malparir (la bestia); escaparse a, pasar inadvertido por; irse de (la memoria, etc.); descuidar, dejar pasar; dislocar (un hueso).—**to s. off,** quitarse de encima, soltar.—**to s. on,** ponerse (anillo, bata, etc.) de prisa.—**to s. the cable,** (mar.) soltar el cable por ojo. **II.** *vn.* resbalar, deslizarse; escurrirse, salirse de su sitio; cometer un desliz; errar o equivocarse; huirse; largarse; pasar sin ser visto; borrarse de la memoria.—**to s. away,** escabullirse, huirse.—**to s. down,** dejarse caer.—**to s. into,** introducirse, entrometerse; insinuarse.—**to s. out,** salir sin ser observado; dislocarse (un hueso); zafarse, soltarse; salirse.—**to s. up,** resbalar; (fam.) equivocarse; salir mal. **III.** *s.* resbalón; deslizamiento; resbalamiento (de una rueda, de la hélice); patinamiento; velocidad retrógrada del agua tras un buque; (elec.) resbalamiento, *slip* (del inducido, etc.); desliz, falta; platina (de microscopio, etc.); resbaladero; declive; falta; inadvertencia, lapso; (agr.) esqueje, estaca; escapada, huída; tira o pedazo; lengua de tierra; callejón; (E. U.) embarcadero; (geol.) falla, dislocación; (impr.) prueba, galerada; funda de almohada; bata o prenda de vestir holgada; mantillas de los niños; trailla de un perro; requesón de leche; légamo, limo.—**s. cover,** funda (de muebles, etc.).—**s. of the pen,** error de pluma.—**s. of the tongue,** lapsus linguæ.—**s. ring,** (elec.) anillo colector.—**s. stream,** (aer.) corriente retrógrada del aire.—**s. switch,** (f. c.) cruzamiento de (con) agujas; cruzamiento y cambiavías combinados.—**to give one the slip,** zafarse o salir de uno, sacarle le cuerpo.

slipboard [slípbórd], *s.* (mar.) corredera.

slipknot [slípnót], *s.* lazo o nudo corredizo.

slippage [slipey], *s.* resbalamiento; pérdida de velocidad debida al resbalamiento.

slipper [slípœr], *s.* chinela, babucha; zapatilla.

slippered [slípœrd], *a.* con zapatillas.

slipperiness [slíperines], *s.* calidad de resbaladizo; lubricidad; volubilidad.

slippery [slípœri], *a.* resbaladizo, resbaloso; evasivo, astuto, zorro; voluble, voltario.—**s. elm,** (bot.) variedad de olmo y su corteza medicinal.

slipshod [slípshód], *a.* en chancletas; desaseado.

slipslop [slípslóp], *s.* aguachirle; dislate.

slit. I. *va.* (*pret.* y *pp.* SLIT O SLITTED) rajar, hender, tajar; ranurar; cortar en tiras. **II.** *s.* raja; cortadura o cortada larga; hendedura; ranura.

slitting [-ing], *a.* de ranurar, de rajar; de cortar en tiras.—**s. file,** lima achaflanada.—**s. machine, s. mill,** máquina de cortar metal en tiras.—**s. saw,** sierra circular fina de cortar metales.

sliver [slívœr]. **I.** *va.* y *vn.* cortar en tiras; desgajar, desgajarse, romperse. **II.** *s.* brizna, astilla; lonja de pescado; torzal, mecha de fibras textiles; borde sin pulir de un tablón.

sloats [slóuts], *s. pl.* teleras de carro.

slob [slob], *s.* pantano, ciénaga; lodo; (fam.) sujeto despreciable o insignificante.

slobber [slóbœr]. **I.** *va.* babosear. **II.** *s.* baba.

sloe [slo], *s.* (bot.) endrino; endrina.

slogan [slógan], *s.* grito de combate.

sloop [slup], *s.* (mar.) balandra, chalupa.—**s. of war,** corbeta.

slop. I. *va.* y *vn.* verter, derramar; derramarse; mojar, ensuciar, enlodar. **II.** *s.* líquido derramado en el suelo; mojadura.—*pl.* agua sucia; aguachirle, lavazas, zupia; (despec.) atole, gachas; té o café flojo; (mar. y fam.) ropa mal hecha y barata.—**s. basin, s. bowl, s. bucket,** cubo o tina para agua sucia.—**s. jar,** tinaja de lavabo para aguas sucias.—**s. pail** = **s. BUCKET.**

slope [slóup]. **I.** *s.* (geol. y min.) buzamiento, inclinación; (f. c.) talud; declive, bajada; cuesta, falda, ladera; vertiente; (fort.) rampa; escarpa. **II.** *va.* sesgar, cortar o partir en sesgo; formar en declive; (cost.) escotar. **III.** *vn.* inclinarse, declinar, estar en declive; ir oblicuamente.—**sloping** [-ing], *a.* inclinado.—**slopingly** [-li], *adv.* sesgadamente, al sesgo; en declive.

sloppiness [slópines], *s.* calidad de mojado y sucio; estado cenagoso.

sloppy [slópi], *a.* mojado y sucio; lodoso, cenagoso; chapucero.

slopshop [slópshóp], *s.* bazar de ropa barata.

slopwork [-uœrc], *s.* chapucería.

slosh [slosh]. **I.** *va.* y *vn.* V. SPLASH. **II.** *s.* V. SLUSH.

slot, *s.* (mec.) muesca, ranura, canal, hendedura; pista, rastro; tira de madera, tablilla; pedazo; cerrojo.—**s. machine,** máquina de servicio automático, provista de una ranura por la cual se introduce una moneda, que la hace funcionar. **III.** *va.* ajustar en una ranura; acanalar, hacer una ranura en.

sloth [sloz], *s.* pereza; (zool.) perezoso.—**slothful** [slózful], *a.* perezoso.—**slothfully** [-i], *adv.* perezosamente, flojamente, haraganamente.—**slothfulness** [-nes], *s.* pereza.

slouch [sláuch]. **I.** *s.* mirada cabizbaja; inclinación del cuerpo; patán, rústico. **II.** *va.* y *vn.* estar cabizbajo o gacho; poner gacho.—**s. hat,** sombrero gacho.

slough [sláu], *s.* lodazal, cenagal o fangal; [slu] (E. U.) charca.

slough [sluf]. **I.** *va.* y *vn.* echar de sí una costra. **II.** *s.* piel o camisa que muda la serpiente; (med.) escara, tejido muerto.

sloughy [sláui], *a.* fangoso, pantanoso.

sloughly [slúfi], *a.* (med.) que tiene escara.

Slovak [slovǽc, slóvæc], *s.*, **Slovakian,** [slovǽki-æn, *o* = véikiæn], *s.* y *a.* eslovaco.

sloven [slǘvœn], *s.* persona desaseada.—**slovenliness** [-lines], *s.* desaliño, desaseo; suciedad, porquería; descuido, dejadez.—**slovenly** [-li]. **I.** *a.* desaliñado, puerco o sucio; dejado, descuidado. **II.** *adv.* desaliñadamente, suciamente.

slow [slóu]. **I.** *va.* y *vn.* (con **up** o **down**) retardar, aflojar (el paso), ir más despacio. **II.** *a.* lento, despacioso; pausado; tardo, tardío; atrasado (el reloj); calmoso, cachazudo; lerdo, estúpido.—**s. coach,** indolente, perezoso.—**s. fire,** fuego lento. **III.** *adv.* despacio, lentamente.—**s.-paced,** pesado en el andar.—**s.-witted,** torpe, estúpido.—**to go s.,** atrasar, estar atrasado (el reloj).

slowly [-li], *adv.* despacio, lentamente, pausadamente.

slowness [-nes], *s.* lentitud, morosidad; cachaza; pesadez, torpeza.

slowworm [-uǽrm], *s.* cecilia, culebra.

slub [slŭb]. **I.** *va.* torcer la lana. **II.** *s.* mechón.

slubber [slŭbœr], *s.* canillero; ovillador; mechón.

sludge [slŭy], *s.* lodo, cieno.

slue [slu]. **I.** *va.* (*pa.* SLUING: *pp.* SLUED) revirar, volver, girar. **II.** *s.* giro, vuelta.

slug [slŭg]. **I.** *s.* haragán, zángano; babosa, babaza; (arti.) posta; (impr.) lingote. **II.** *va.* (arti.) cargar con posta; (fam.) aporrear.

sluggard [slŭgard], *s.* haragán, holgazán.

sluggish [slŭguish], *a.* perezoso, tardo, pesado; inactivo.—**sluggishly** [-li], *adv.* perezosamente, lentamente.—**sluggishness** [-nes], *s.* lentitud, pesadez; inactividad.

sluice [slus]. **I.** *s.* acequia, saetín; compuerta; canal; (fig.) salida.—**s. gate,** compuerta.—**s. port,** brenca.—**s. valve,** compuerta; válvula compuerta, llave compuerta, llave de corredera. **II.** *va.* mojar, regar; (min.) lavar; soltar la presa de agua.

sluiceway [-uéi], *s.* saetín; canal, conducto; abertura de presa.

slum [slŭm]. **I.** *s.* barrio bajo, de gentes escuálidas o disolutas (ú. a menudo en *pl.*, y gen. denota barrios donde abunda la prostitución). **II.** *vn.* visitar los barrios bajos y lugares escuálidos o disolutos.—**slumdom** [slŭmdŭm], *s.* los barrios y lugares de la baja vida; la baja vida; el libertinaje.—**slumming** [slŭming], *s.* visita a los barrios de la baja vida.—**to go slumming,** recorrer los barrios o lugares de la baja vida.

slumber [slŭmbœr]. **I.** *va.* dormitar, estar medio dormido; dormir; dormirse o descuidarse. **II.** *s.* sueño ligero y tranquilo.

slumberous [-us], *a.* soñoliento, soporífero; dormido; tranquilo.

slump [slŭmp]. **I.** *vn.* hundirse el pie en una materia blanda; (fam.) quebrar; fracasar. **II.** *s.* asentamiento, hundimiento (rompiendo una costra); fracaso; quiebra; (com.) baja repentina en los valores.

slung, *pret.* y *pp.* de TO SLING.—**s. shot,** rompecabezas, arma ofensiva.

slunk, *pret.* y *pp.* de TO SLINK.

slur [slœr]. **I.** *va.* menospreciar, rebajar, desdorar; pasar por encima, suprimir, ocultar; farfullar, comerse sílabas o letras; (mús.) ligar las notas; manchar, ensuciar; (impr.) repintar. **II.** *s.* reparo, pulla, observación en desdoro; estigma; borrón o mancha ligera en la reputación; (mús.) ligadura (⌢ o ⌣); (impr.) trozo repintado.

slush [slŭsh]. **I.** *va.* ensebar, engrasar, embarrar; (con **up**) (alb.) rellenar; lavar echando agua. **II.** *s.* fango; agua nieve fangosa; grasa lubricante; pintura para evitar el enmohecimiento; desperdicios crasos de cocina; (fam.) tonterías sentimentales.—**s. fund,** (fam., pol.) fondos para corrupción política (puede llamarse caja de sobornos).

slushy [slŭshi], *a.* fangoso.

slut [slŭt], *s.* perra; mujer sucia.

sluttish [slŭtish], *a.* puerco, sucio, desaliñado.—**sluttishness** [-nes], *s.* porquería, suciedad.—**sluttishly** [-li], *adv.* asquerosamente.

sly [slái], *a.* astuto, taimado, socarrón, disimulado.—**on the s.,** a hurtadillas.

slyboots [sláibúts], *s.* camastrón, picarote.

slyly [-li], *adv.* astutamente, disimuladamente; a hurtadillas, callandito.

slyness [-nes], *s.* socarronería, astucia, disimulo.

smack [smæc]. **I.** *va.* y *vn.* hacer sonar un beso; rechuparse, saborear; saborearse. **II.** *vn.* (con *of*) saber (a), tener gusto, dejo (de); oler (a). **III.** *s.* sabor, gusto, gustillo; olor; tintura, conocimiento ligero o superficial; beso sonado; rechupete; manotada; chasquido de látigo; (mar.) queche.

smacker [smǽkœr], *s.* beso sonado.

small [smol]. **I.** *a.* pequeño, menudo, chico; menor; bajo de estatura; corto, exiguo; poco; insignificante; despreciable, mezquino; débil, flojo; tierno, blando; fino, delgado, de poco bulto o volumen; obscuro, bajo, vulgar, plebeyo.—**s. ale,** **s. beer,** cerveza débil o floja; vaso pequeño de cerveza; bagatela.—**s. arms,** armas ligeras o manuales (rifles, pistolas, espadas, etc.).—**s. cattle,** ganado menor.—**s. craft,** embarcaciones menores; cosas o personas de poca importancia.—**s. fry,** pececillos; gente menuda; cosas pequeñas.—**s. gross,** diez docenas.—**s. hours,** primeras horas (de la mañana).—**s. knees,** curvatones.—**s. letter,** letra minúscula.—**s. nettle,** ortiga menor, cania.—**s. pica,** lecturita (tipo de 11 puntos).—**s. potato,** (fam.) persona o cosa de poca monta.—**s. print,** letra menuda.—(**to**) **s. purpose,** (para) bien poco.—**s. sand,** arenilla, (Méx.) marmijita o margajita.—**s. talk,** chismografía, vulgaridades, frivolidades.—**s. voice,** vocecita, voz delgada.—**s. wares,** mercería, artículos menudos; pasamanería.—**s. wood,** brusca, verdasco, leña menuda. **II.** *s.* parte estrecha de cualquier cosa y en particular del lomo, canto o filo; cosa o cantidad pequeña. **III.** *adv.* en tono bajo o suave.

smallage [smólær], *s.* (bot.) apio silvestre.

smallclothes [smólclóubs], *s.* calzón.

smaller [smólœr], *a. comp.* de SMALL; menor, más chico, más pequeño, más bajo, más corto.—**smallest** [-est], *a. superl.* de SMALL; mínimo, menor, más chico, más pequeño, el másb ajo, más corto.—**smallish** [-ish], *a.* pequeñito.—**smallness** [-nes], *s.* pequeñez; bajeza, ruindad; exigüidad; insignificancia.

smallpox [smólpox], *s.* (med.) viruelas.

smalt [smolt], *s.* esmalte, esmaltín.

smart [smárt]. **I.** *a.* vivo, listo, hábil, ingenioso, activo; inteligente, talentoso; agudo, sutil; acerbo, punzante, mordaz; (Ingl.) elegante; de buen tono; galano; (E. U.) astuto, ladino. **II.** *s.* escozor; dolor, aflicción. **III.** *vn.* escocer, picar; requemar; mordicar; dolerse.

smarten [smártœn]. **I.** *va.* hermosear, embellecer. **II.** *vn.* escocer, picar.

smartly [smártli], *adv.* hábilmente; elegantemente; con despejo.—**smartness** [-nes], *s.* agudeza, vivacidad; habilidad, talento; astucia.—**smarty** [-i], *s.* (fam.) persona que se pasa de lista.

smash [smæsh]. **I.** *va.* y *vn.* romper, quebrar, aplastar, destrozar o hacer pedazos; (fam.) fracasar, quebrar, hacer bancarrota. **II.** *s.* rotura, destrozo; fracaso; ruina, quiebra; bebida de coñac, hierbabuena y azúcar.—**to go to s.,** arruinarse.

smash-up [-up], *s.* (fam.) desastre; desbarajuste; colisión desastrosa.

smatch [smæch], *s.* gusto, resabio; tintura.

smatter [smǽtœr]. **I.** *vn.* saber o hablar superficialmente. **II.** *s.* = SMATTERING.—**smatterer** [-œr], *s.* el que sabe una cosa superficialmente.—**smattering** [-ing], *s.* tintura, conocimiento superficial, barniz.

smear [smíœr]. **I.** *va.* untar, embarrar, tiznar; ensuciar. **II.** *s.* embarradura, mancha; (cerám.) media tapa.

smeary [smíœri], *a.* graso; lardoso.

smegma [smégma], *s.* (med.) esmegma.

smell [smel]. **I.** *va.* (*pret.* y *pp.* SMELLED o SMELT) oler.—**to s. a rat,** haber gato encerrado. **II.** *vn.* oler, exhalar fragancia o hedor.—**to s. of,** oler a. **III.** *s.* olfato; olor (bueno o malo); perfume o aroma; traza, vestigio.

smeller [smélœr], *s.* oledor, rastreador, husmeador.—*pl.* (fam.) narices.

smellfeast [smélfist], *s.* gorrista, mogollón.

smelling [sméling], *s.* husmeo, acción de oler.—**s. bottle,** vasito o redomilla para olores.—**s. salts,** sales aromáticas.

smell [smelt]. **I.** *pret.* y *pp.* de TO SMELL. **II.** *va.* y *vn.* fundir o beneficiar (minerales). **III.** *s.* (ict.) eperlano.

smelter [sméltœr], *s.* fundidor, apartador.

smeltery [smélteri], *s.* fundición.

smelting, *s.* fusión, fundición.—**s. furnace,** alto horno, horno de fundición.—**s. house,** fundición, apartado.—**s. pot,** cubilote.—**s. works** = S.HOUSE.

smew [smiú], *s.* (orn.) harla, mergo.

smift [smift], *s.* (min.) mecha.

smilax [smáilæx], *s.* (bot.) esmilace.

smile [smáil]. **I.** *vn.* sonreír, sonreírse; favorecer, ser propicio; (E. U. fam.) beber un trago.— **to s. at, on, upon,** sonreír a; favorecer. **II.** *va.* expresar con una sonrisa (*to smile assent,* consentir con una sonrisa; *to smile one's thanks,* dar las gracias con una sonrisa). **III.** *s.* sonrisa; aspecto agradable o risueño; disposición favorable o propicia; (E. U. fam.) trago.

smiling [smáiling], *a.* risueño, sonriente.

smilingly [-li], *adv.* con cara risueña, con sonrisa, sonriendo.

smirch [smœrch]. **I.** *va.* ensuciar, tiznar; mancillar, deslucir. **II.** *s.* tiznón, tiznadura.

smirk [smœrk]. **I.** *vn.* sonreírse estúpida o afectadamente. **II.** *s.* sonrisa boba o afectada; visaje. **III.** *a.* sonriente.

smite [smáit]. **I.** *va.* (*pret.* SMOTE o SMIT: *pp.* SMITTEN o SMIT) herir, golpear; afligir, castigar; asolar, azotar; encantar, robar el corazón; conmover, enternecer; apenar; aplanar, aplastar; (con **off o out**) cortar, partir o romper de un golpe; (ant.) matar de un golpe. **II.** *vn.* venir con fuerza repentina; chocar.

smith [smiz], *s.* forjador; en composición, artífice (v. gr.: *blacksmith, goldsmith, silversmith*). —**s. and farrier,** herrador, albéitar.—**s.'s parer,** pujavante.

smithereens [smídœrínz], *s. pl.* (fam.) añicos.

smithery [smídœri], *s.* herrería.

smithy [smízi], *s.* fragua, forja, hornaza.

smitten, *pp.* de TO SMITE; profundamente afectado; muy conmovido; muy enamorado.

smock [smoc], *s.* camisa de mujer.—**s.-faced,** de cara afeminada.—**s. frock,** blusa de obrero.

smoke [smóuk]. **I.** *s.* humo; sahumerio.—**s. arch,** (locom.) caja de humos.—**s. bell,** campana de lámpara.—**s. black,** negro de humo.—**s. box** = S. ARCH.—**s.-burner,** aparato fumívoro.— **s.-burning,** fumívoro.—**s. chamber,** o chest, = S. ARCH.—**s. condenser,** condensador o lavador de humo.—**s.-consumer,** = S. BURNER.—**s.-consuming** = S.BURNER.—**s.-dried,** curado o ahumado.—(**to**) **s.-dry,** curar, ahumar.—**s. helmet,** casco o careta de protección contra el humo.—**s. screen,** (mil.) cortina de humo, humo de protección.—**s.-tight,** a prueba de humo.—**s. tube,** (m. v.) tubo de humo.—**s.-tube boiler,** caldera de tubos de humo.—**s. washer** = S. CONDENSER.—**to end in s.,** volverse humo o agua de cerrajas. **II.** *va.* fumar; ahumar, curar al humo, sahumar; (con **out**) ahumar, ahogar con humo; hacer salir con humo; echar fuera.—**to s. the pipe of peace,** fumar la pipa de paz. **III.** *vn.* humear, echar humo; fumar.

smokehouse [-jáus], *s.* cuarto cerrado para ahumar o acecinar carnes, pieles, etc.

smokejack [-ʏéc], *s.* asador movido por el humo.

smokeless [-les], *a.* sin humo.—**s. powder,** pólvora sin humo.

smoker [-œr], *s.* fumador; sahumador; (api.) caja de ahumar abejas; (E. U., f. c.) vagón de fumar, fumadero; (fam.) tertulia en que se fuma.

smokestack [-stæc], *s.* chimenea.

smokiness [-ines], *s.* fumosidad.

smoking [-ing]. **I.** *s.* acción de fumar.—**no s. (allowed),** se prohíbe fumar. **II.** *a.* fumante, fumífero.—(E. U.) **s. car,** (Ingl.) **s. carriage,** (f. c.) vagón de fumar.—**s. jacket,** batín.—**s. room,** fumadero, cuarto de fumar.

smoky [-i], *a.* humeante; humoso; ahumado.

smolt [smóult], *s.* (ict.) murgón.

smolder, *vn.* = SMOULDER.

smooth [smuᴅ]. **I.** *a.* liso, pulido, alisado; parejo plano, igual; uniforme; fácil, suave, fluido; manso, tranquilo (agua, etc.); meloso, lisonjero; cortés, afable; (gram. griega) no aspirado; suave, que no rasca (v. gr. un licor).—**s.-faced,** barbilampiño, barbilucio; pulido, alisado; cariparejo.—**s.-grained,** de grano o veta lisa.—**s. muscle,** músculo no estriado.—**s.-paced,** que anda con paso igual.—**s.-shaven,** bien afeitado.— **s.-sliding,** que se desliza con suavidad e igualdad. —**s.-spoken, s.-tongued,** meloso, lisonjero o adulador. **II.** *va.* allanar, alisar, suavizar; (carp.) acepillar; lijar; facilitar; pacificar, aquietar; calmar, ablandar; (a veces con *away*) quitar; (gen. con *over*), zanjar, atenuar.

smoothbore [smúᴅbœr]. **I.** *a.* de ánima lisa. **II.** *s.* arma de ánima lisa.

smoother [smúᴅœr], *s.* alisador.

smoothing, *a.* de alisar, de allanar, de emparejar.—**s. iron,** plancha, alisador, raspa.—**s. plane,** cepillo corto.

smoothly [smúᴅli], *adv.* llanamente; fácilmente; blandamente; con halagos o afablemente.— **smoothness** [-nes], *s.* lisura, tersura; suavidad, blandura; dulzura.

smote [smóut], *pret.* de TO SMITE.

smother [smúᴅœr]. **I.** *va.* ahogar; asfixiar, sofocar; apagar; suprimir, ocultar, encubrir; embadurnar, embarrar; (coc.) estofar. **II.** *vn.* y *vr.* ahogar(se), asfixiar(se); estar latente, oculto o escondido. **III.** *s.* supresión, ocultación; ahoguío, sofocación; humareda, polvareda.

smothering [-ing], *a.* sofocante.—**smotheringly** [-li], *adv.* sofocantemente.

smo(u)lder [smóuldœr], *vn.* arder humeando, sin llama; arder en rescoldo; estar latente.

smudge [smᴕʏ]. **I.** *va.* tiznar, ensuciar; (E. U.) fumigar, ahumar. **II.** *s.* tiznajo, tiznadura, tiznón; (fumigación o ahumadura; (carr.) raspas de pintura y barniz.

smudgy [smᴕʏi], *a.* tiznado, holliniento, ensuciado; humeante.

smug [smᴕg], *a.* presumido, relamido.

smuggle [smᴕgœl]. **I.** *va.* pasar o meter de contrabando; alijar. **II.** *vn.* hacer contrabando.

smuggler [smᴕglœr], *s.* contrabandista.

smuggling [smᴕgling], *s.* contrabando.

smugly [smᴕgli], *adv.* pulidamente; afectadamente, con presunción.

smugness [smᴕgnes], *s.* afectación y nimiedad en el vestir; presunción.

smut [smᴕt]. **I.** *s.* tiznón, tiznadura, mancha; obscenidad, indecencia; (bot.) tizón, tizoncillo. **II.** *va.* tiznar, manchar; mancillar; (bot.) atizonar, añublar; destizonar; (fig.). **III.** *vn.* (bot.) añublarse, atizonarse.

smutch [smᴕch]. **I.** *va.* tiznar, manchar, ensuciar. **II.** *s.* mancha, tiznajo.

smuttily [smᴕtili], *adv.* suciamente.—**smuttiness** [-nes], *s.* suciedad; obscenidad, indecencia.— **smutty** [-ti], *a.* tiznado; humoso; (bot.) añublado, atizonado; obsceno, indecente, verde.

snack [snæc], *s.* (fam.) parte, porción; piscolabis. —**s. basket,** fiambrera.

snaffle [snǽfœl]. **I.** *s.* bridón del bocado (ll. t. **s. bit**). **II.** *va.* (equit.) refrenar; contener, reprimir; enganchar.

snag [snæg], *s.* (carp.) nudo en la madera; protuberancia; (dent.) raigón, sobrediente; pitón del asta del ciervo; (E. U.) tronco o tocón sumergido; obstáculo oculto ignorado.—**s. boat,** buque arrancatroncos.

snagged [snǽgued], *a.* lleno de sobredientes; nudoso.

snaggy [snǽgui], *a.* lleno de troncos o tocones; (carp.) nudoso, parecido a un tocón.

snail [snéil], *s.* caracol (de tierra); (E. U.) babosa; posma, persona roncera, lerda y pesada.— **s. clover,** alfalfa, mielga.—**s. pace,** paso de tortuga, de caracol.

snake [snéik]. **I.** *s.* culebra. **II.** *va.* (fam. E. U.) arrastrar tirando de una cosa; enrollar; (mar.) embutir, entrañar. **III.** *vn.* culebrear.

snakeroot [snéikrrút], *s.* (bot.) serpentaria.

snakeweed [snéicuíd], *s.* (bot.) bistorta.

snaky [snéiki], *a.* culebrino, serpentino, tortuoso; astuto, solapado; traidor; (E. U.) lleno de culebras.

snap [snæp]. **I.** *va.* chasquear, hacer estallar; dar, apretar o cerrar con golpe o estallido; romper con ruido y violencia; atrapar, arrebatar; interrumpir; (fam.) fotografiar instantáneamente; (E. U.) lanzar por el aire.—**to s. one's fingers**, castañetear con los dedos; (con *at*) burlarse de. **II.** *vn.* chasquear, dar un chasquido; estallar, romperse con estallido; romperse una cosa tirante; chispear (los ojos); levantar el gallo, hablar fuerte; fallar un tiro, hacer higa.—**to s. at**, querer morder, pegar una dentellada a.—**to s. off**, soltarse, saltar, abrirse de golpe. **III.** *s.* chasquido; castañeteo (con los dedos); estallido; cierre de resorte, corchete, cerrajita, garra; dentellada, mordiscón, mordedura; galletica; (fam.) vigor, energía; período corto (de frío); (fam.) ganga, cosa fácil (llám. t. **soft s.**). **IV.** hecho de repente, de golpe o instantáneamente; (fam.) ganga, cosa fácil, canonjía (llám. t. **soft s.**). **V.** *a.* hecho de repente, de golpe o instantáneamente.—**s. lock**, cerradura de resorte.—**s. switch**, (elec.) llave de interrupción, interruptor giratorio de resorte.

snapdragon [snǽpdrǽgun], *s.* (bot.) hierba becerra, antirrino; (vidr.) puntel.

snapper [snǽpœr], *s.* ratero, ladrón; punta del látigo; triquitraque, buscapiés; (ict.) pez comestible del golfo de México.—*pl.* castañuelas, castañetas.

snapping [snǽping]. **I.** *s.* acción del verbo TO SNAP. **II.** *a.* saltadizo.—**s. turtle**, gran tortuga voraz.

snappish [snǽpiŝh], *a.* respondón; regañón, agrio, arisco.—**snappishly** [-li], *adv.* mordazmente; agriamente, con aspereza.—**snappishness** [-nes], *s.* aspereza, sequedad.

snapshot [snǽpshót]. **I.** *s.* disparo rápido, sin apuntar; (foto.) instantánea. **II.** *va.* y *vn.* sacar una fotografía instantánea.

snappy [snǽpi], *a.* SNAPPISH; (fam.) vivo, enérgico; elegante, garboso.

snare [snéœr]. **I.** trampa, armadijo; garlito, celada, acechanza, artimaña, red; gatuperío, petardo; tirante para templar un tambor; (cir.) lazo.—**s. drum**, tambor con tirantes de cuerda. **II.** *va.* enredar, tender trampas o lazos a. **III.** *vn.* cazar con trampas o cepos.

snarl. **I.** *vn.* gruñir. **II.** *va.* y *vn.* enredar, enmarañar; embutir, estampar (artículos huecos de metal); enredarse, enmarañarse. **III.** *s.* gruñido; (fam.) contienda, riña; maraña, hilo enredado; cabellos desgreñados; complicación, enredo; (carp.) nudo en la madera.

snarler [snárlœr], *s.* regañón, perrenque.

snarly [snárli], *a.* enredoso, enredado; insidioso.

snatch [snǽch]. **I.** *va.* arrebatar; arrapar, agarrar, apercollar.—**to s. off**, arrebatar. **II.** *vn.* (con *at*) tratar de agarrar o arrebatar. **III.** *s.* arrebatamiento; arrebatiña; pedacito; bocado; ratito; sandez, salida de pie de banco.—**s. block**, (mar.) pasteca.—**by snatches**, a ratos.

snatcher [snǽchœr], *s.* arrebatador, ladrón.

snatchingly [snǽchingli], *adv.* arrebatadamente, precipitadamente.

snath(e [snep], (en Ingl.) **snead** [snid], *s.* mango de guadaña.

sneak [sník], *vn.* (con *in*), entrarse a hurtadillas; (con *out*) salirse a hurtadillas, escurrir el bulto; obrar solapadamente o con bajeza; arrastrarse; sisar, ratear.—**s. boat**, bote cubierto con ramas para cazar patos.—**s. thief**, ratero que se introduce en las casas sin ser visto.

sneak(er [sník(œr], *s.* sujeto ruin y solapado; (Ingl.) jarrito de ponche.

sneaking [sníking], *a.* servil, bajo, vil; secreto, oculto.—**s. fondness**, afición que se guarda secreta.—**sneakingly** [-li], *adv.* servilmente, con

bajeza; a hurtadillas.—**sneakingness** [-nes], *s.* bajeza, lisonja baja; vileza, ruindad.

sneck(et [snék(et], *s.* pasador, aldaba.

sneckdrawer [-drócœr], *s.* ladrón.

sneer [sníœr]. **I.** *vn.* (gen. con *at*) hacer un gesto de desprecio; echar una mirada despectiva. **II.** *va.* expresar o decir con un gesto de desprecio o escarnecedor. **III.** *s.* gesto, mirada o expresión de desprecio; mofa.—**sneerer** [-œr], *s.* mofador, fisgón, escarnecedor.—**sneering** [-ing]. **I.** *a.* burlón, despreciativo o escarnecedor. **II.** *s.* escarnio, gesto despreciativo, mofa.—**sneeringly** [-ingli], *adv.* despreciativamente; con mofa.

sneeze [sniŝ]. **I.** *vn.* estornudar.—**to s. at**, despreciar, menospreciar (gen. en la expresión, **not to be sneezed at**, no ser de despreciar, no ser un cualquiera). **II.** *s.* estornudo.—**s. gas**, gas estornudatorio.

sneezewort [sníŝuœrt], *s.* (bot.) cebadilla.

sneezing [sníŝing], *s.* estornudo.—**s. powder,** cebadilla, estornutatorio.

snell [snel], *s.* hilo corto de tripa, etc., de que están provistos algunos anzuelos, al cual se ata el sedal.

snick. **I.** *va.* cortar (con tijeras). **II.** *s.* (Ingl.) corte pequeño, tijeretada.—**s. and snee, s. or snee,** riña a navajazos o cuchilladas; (fam.) cuchillo.

snicker [sníkœr], **snigger** [snígœr]. **I.** *vn.* reírse tontamente. **II.** *s.* risita.

sniff. **I.** *va.* husmear, olfatear, oliscar, ventear; despreciar con resoplidos. **II.** *vn.* resollar, oler; sorberse los mocos. **III.** *s.* olfateo; cosa olfateada.

sniffy [snífi], *a.* (fam.) desdeñoso, estirado.

sniggle [snígœl], *va.* y *vn.* (Ingl.) pescar anguilas en presa; entrampar, enmarañar.

snip. **I.** *va.* tijeretear, dar tijeretadas; cortar con tijeras.—**to s. off**, cortar o recortar de un golpe. **II.** *s.* tijeretada; recorte, retazo, pedacito; parte; persona pequeña o insignificante.

snipe [snáip]. **I.** *s.* (orn.) agachadiza, becardón. **II.** *va.* y *vn.* cazar agachadizas; (mil.) hacer fuego o tirar de un apostadero (apl. a tiradores apostados).—**sniper** [-œr], *s.* = SHARPSHOOTER.

snippet [snípet], *s.* recorte, retacito.

snipsnap [snípsnæp], *s.* diálogo picante.

snivel [snívœl]. **I.** *s.* moquita. **II.** *vn.* moquear; llorar como una criatura; jeremiquear, hacer pucheros.—**snivel(l)er** [-œr], *s.* lloraduelos, llorón; mocoso.—**snivelly** [-i], *a.* mocoso; llorón.

snob [snob], *s.* fachendón, sujeto vulgar y fachendista, estirado con sus iguales e inferiores pero servil con sus superiores; rompehuelgas, esquirol, obrero que en las huelgas reemplaza a los huelguistas.—**snobbery** [snóbœri], fachenda, ínfulas.—**snobbish** [-ish], fachendoso, estirado.—**snobbishly** [-iŝhli], *adv.* fachendosamente, con vulgar presunción.—**snobbishness** [-iŝhnes], snobbism [-iŝm], *s.* = SNOBBERY. (Muchos emplean en español los términos ingleses snob, snobbism).

snood [snud], *s.* cintillo (emblema de virginidad).

snoop [snup]. **I.** *s.* entremetido; curioso. **II.** *vn.* entremeterse, husmear.—**snooper** [snúpœr], *s.* snoopy [snúpi], *a.* entremetido, curioso.

snooze [snuŝ]. **I.** *vn.* (fam.) dormitar, descabezar el sueño. **II.** *s.* (fam.) siestecita, sueño ligero.

snore [snóœr]. **I.** *va.* y *vn.* roncar. **II.** *s.* ronquido.

snorer [snórœr], *s.* roncador.

snoring [snóring], *s.* ronquido.

snort. **I.** *va.* y *vn.* resoplar, bufar. **II.** *s.* bufido, resoplido.

snot, *s.* (vulg.) moco.

snout [snáut]. **I.** *va.* proveer de hocico, boquerel o embocadura. **II.** *s.* hocico, morro, jeta; trompa de elefante; cañón de un fuelle, tobera; boquerel de manguera; embocadura de un cañón.—**s. beetle**, gorgojo.—**s. ring**, narigón para puercos.

snouted [snáuted], *s.* hocicudo.

snow [snóu]. **I.** *s.* nieve; nevada, nevasca.—**s.-blind**, cegado por el reflejo de la nieve.—**s.-blindness**, ceguera causada por el reflejo de la

nieve.—s.-bound, sitiado o detenido por .a nieve.
—s. bunting, (orn.) verderón de las nieves.—
s.-capped, coronado de nieve.—**s.-white,** níveo, blanco como la nieve. **II.** *vn.* nevar. **III.** *va.* (con **in, over, under,** o **up**) cubrir, obstruir, detener o aprisionar con nieve.

snowball [-ból], **I.** *va.* lanzar bolas de nieve a. **II.** *s.* pella o pelota de nieve.

snowbird [-bœrd], *s.* (orn.) pinzón de las nieves.

snowdrift [-dríft], *s.* ventisca, ventisquero.

snowdrop [-dróp], *s.* (bot.) campanilla blanca; flor de la leche.

snowfall [-fól], *s.* nevada, nevasca.

snowflake [-fléic], *s.* copo de nieve; (orn.) verderol de las nieves; (bot.) campanilla.

snowplow [-pláu], *s.* quitanieve; barredora ,de nieve.

snowshed [-shéd], *s.* guardaaludes.

snowshoe [-shú], *s.* raqueta reticular a la que se afirma el pie para andar sobre la nieve.

snowslide [-sláid], **snowslip** [-slíp], *s.* alud, avalancha de nieve.

snowstorm [-stórm], *s.* nevasca, nevada, tormenta de nieve.

snowy [snói], *a.* nevoso; cargado de nieve; níveo; puro, sin mancha.

snub [snʌb]. **I.** *va.* desairar, tratar con desprecio estudiado, con afectada arrogancia; (con **up**) parar de repente. **II.** *s.* desaire; nariz chata. **III.** *a.* romo, chato.—**s.-nosed,** chato.

snuff [snʌf]. **I.** *s.* moco o pavesa de candela; tufo; tabaco en polvo, rapé.—**s. taker,** tomador de rapé. **II.** *va.* olfatear, oliscar, oler, ventear; introducir una cosa en la nariz con el aliento; despabilar.—**to s. up,** tomar por la nariz. **III.** *vn.* aspirar.

snuffbox [-bóx], *s.* caja de rapé; tabaquera.

snuffer [snʌ́fœr], *s.* despabilador.—*pl.* despabiladeras.

snuffiness [snʌ́fines], *s.* tufo o suciedad causada por el rapé.

snuffle [snʌ́fœl]. **I.** *vn.* ganguear. **II.** *s.* gangueo.—*pl.* romadizo, catarro nasal.

snuffy [snʌ́fi], *a.* cubierto de rapé; tabacoso, que huele a rapé.

snug [snʌg]. **I.** *a.* cómodo, abrigado; bien dispuesto, bien aparejado; apañado, ajustado; acomodado.—**as s. as a bug in a rug,** (fam.) con toda comodidad. **II.** *s.* (mec.) tope, reborde. **III.** *va.* acomodar, aparejar, ajustar, apañar, alisar.

snuggery [snʌ́gœri], *s.* (fam.) aposento cómodo y bien arreglado.

snuggle [snʌ́gœl], *vn.* y *vr.* arrimar(se), apretar(se), poner(se) juntitos.

so [sóu]. **I.** *adv.* así (a veces en el sentido de "cierto", "verdad"): *that is so,* así es, eso es verdad; *that is not so,* eso no es cierto); pues bien, conque (usado expletivamente); tan; (fam.) muy, tan (*he is so good,* él es tan bueno, o muy bueno); más bien; sí, pues; (con *or*) poco más o menos, como (*ten years or so,* como diez años, poco más o menos diez años); (antes de adjetivo) así de, de este (antes de substantivo o adjetivo substantivado: *so wide,* así de ancho, de este ancho; *so big,* así de grande, de este tamaño); lo (*he is rich, but I am not so,* él es rico, pero yo no lo soy); también lo (*I am rich, and so is she,* soy rico, y ella también lo es).—**S.-and-S.,** Fulano, Fulano de tal.—**s. as to,** para, a fin de.—**s. be it,** amén, así sea.—**s.-called,** así llamado, llamado, según se llama (*the so-called hero,* el llamado héroe; *the new art, so called,* el llamado nuevo arte; el nuevo arte, según se llama).—**s. far,** hasta aquí, hasta ahí; hasta ahora.—**s. far as,** tan lejos como; hasta, hasta donde (a veces se cambia el giro: *so far as I know,* hasta donde yo sé, que yo sepa).—**s. fashion,** (fam.) así, de este modo.—**s. forth,** etcétera. —**s. many,** tantos.—**s. much,** tanto.—**s. much a,** tanto por.—**s. much as,** por mucho que, tanto como, siquiera, a lo menos.—**s. much for,** eso en cuanto a, eso basta en cuanto a.—**s. much the better,** tanto mejor.—**s. much the less,** tanto menos.—**s. much the worse,** tanto peor.—**s. s.,** así así, tal cual, medianamente.—**s. that,** de suerte que, de modo que; para que, a fin de que.—**s.**

then, así pues, conque, por tanto.—**s. to say, s. to speak,** por decirlo así.—**and s. forth,** etcétera; y así sucesivamente.—**be he ever, o never, s. powerful,** por poderoso que sea.—**how s.?** ¿cómo es eso? ¿cómo así?—**if ever s. little,** por poco que.—**if ever s.,** si así es, si lo fuere en tal caso.—**I hope s.,** I think s., así lo espero, lo creo.—**is that s.?** ¿así? ¿de veras? **II.** *conj.* con tal que, para que.

soak [sóuk]. **I.** *va.* empapar; remojar, (con **in** o **up**) chupar, embeber, absorber; beber con exceso. **II.** *vn.* estar en remojo; (con **in, into** o **through**) remojarse, esponjarse, calarse; beborrotear, empinar el codo. **III.** *s.* remojo, calada; líquido en que se empapa alguna cosa; (fam.) bebedor, borrachín; orgía.

soakage [sóukey], *s.* remojo; merma.

soaker [sóukœr], *s.* remojador; (fam.) borrachín.

soakingly [sóukingli], *adv.* empapando; por grados, paso a paso.

soaky [sóuki], *a.* empapado, calado.

soap [sóup]. **I.** *s.* jabón; (fam.) lisonja, adulación; dinero.—**s. bubble,** burbuja o pompa [de jabón.—**s. dish,** jabonera.—**s. earth,** esteatita, jaboncillo de sastre.—**s. house,** jabonería.—**s. maker,** jabonero.—**s. plant,** (bot.) amole. **II.** *va.* enjabonar, lavar con jabón; (fam.) adular.

soapbark [-bárc], *s.* quillay, cáscara de quillay.— **s. tree,** (bot.) quillay.

soapstone [-stóun], *s.* esteatita, jabón de sastre.

soapsuds [-súds], *s.* jabonaduras, bálago.

soapwort [-uœrt], *s.* (bot.) jabonera.

soapy [sóupi], *a.* jabonoso, saponáceo.

soar [sóœr]. **I.** *vn.* remontarse, cernerse; encumbrarse, aspirar; (aer.) deslizarse horizontalmente. **II.** *s.* vuelo o remonte.

sob. **I.** *s.* sollozo; suspiro (del viento). **II.** *vn.* sollozar. **III.** *va.* decir sollozando; expresar con sollozos.

sober [sóubœr]. **I.** *a.* cuerdo, sano; en su juicio, no borracho; sereno, tanquilo; de sangre fría; grave, serio, modesto; sobrio, templado, moderado; sombrío, de color apagado.—**s.-minded,** desapasionado; sereno.—**in s. earnest,** de veras, con seriedad, formalmente. **II.** *va.* desemborrachar, desembriagar; poner grave, serio, o pensativo. **III.** *vn.* volverse sobrio, cuerdo, moderado, sensato.—**to s. down,** serenar o serenarse; hacer volver o volverse cuerdo; sosegar, sosegarse.

soberly [-li], *adv.* sobriamente; juiciosamente.— **soberness** [-nes], **sobriety** [sobráieti], *s.* sobriedad; cordura; seriedad; calma.

sobriquet [sobriké], *s.* apodo.

sociable [sóshabœl], *a.* sociable.—**sociability** [-bíliti], *s.* sociabilidad.—**sociably** [-bli], *adv.* sociablemente.

social [sóshæl], *a.* social; sociable; (zool.) social, que vive en comunidad; (bot.) de agrupación densa; que ocupa grandes áreas.—**s. evil,** prostitución.—**s. service, s. work,** investigación y mejoramiento de la vida de las clases pobres y obreras (apl. esp. a la visitación de los hogares con el objeto de estudiar las condiciones existentes y ayudar a mejorarlas, sobre todo por instrucción y consejos; en algunos países se llama *previsión social;* puede también llamarse *auxilio social*).— **s. worker,** el que se consagra a *social work* (puede llamarse *auxiliador social*).

socialism [-ism], *s.* socialismo.—**socialist** [-ist], *a.* y *s.* socialista.—**socialistic** [-ístic], *a.* socialista.

sociality [soshiéliti], *s.* sociabilidad.

socialize [sóshalaís], *va.* socializar.

society [sosáieti], *s.* sociedad; círculos del buen tono; compañía, conversación o trato amenos.

Socinian [sosínian], *a.* sociniano.

Socinianism [-ism], *s.* socinianismo.

sociological [soshiolóyical], *a.* sociológico.

sociologist [soshióloyist], *s.* sociólogo.

sociology [soshióloyi], *s.* sociología.

sock [soc], *s.* calcetín, media corta; escarpín, zueco; comedia; reja de arado.

socket [sóket], *s.* cuenca, cubo, caja, encaje, cepo, ojo, casquillo, tubo de candelero, campana (de un tubo con junta de enchufe); (elec.) receptáculo, portalámpara; cualquier hueco en que encaja alguna cosa.—**s. of a tooth**, alvéolo de un diente.—**s. of the capstan**, (mar.) concha de cabrestante.—**s. of the eye**, cuenca del ojo.—**s. wrench**, llave de boca tubular.

socle [sócœl], *s.* (arq.) zócalo, rodapié.

Socratic(al [socrǽtic(al], *a.* socrático.

sod. I. *va.* (*pret.* SODDED: *ger.* SODDING) cubrir de césped. **II.** *s.* césped; témpano de tierra vegetal, turba, tepa.

soda [sóda], *s.* sosa, soda; carbonato u óxido de sodio; sal soda.—**s. ash**, carbonato sódico anhidro del comercio.—**s. fountain**, fuente de agua de soda.—**s. lime**, mezcla de cal y soda cáustica.—**s. water**, agua de soda, gaseosa.

sodality [sodǽliti], *s.* cofradía, hermandad.

sodden [sódœn]. **I.** *va.* mojar, empapar, saturar. **II.** *vn.* empaparse, mojarse; podrirse.

sodden. I. *pp.* de TO SEETHE. **II.** *a.* mojado, empapado, saturado.

sodium [sódiŭm], *s.* (quím.) sodio.

sodomite [sódomait], *s.* sodomita.

sodomy [sódomi], *s.* sodomía.

soever [soévœr], *adv.* por mucho o por más que sea (*how great soever*, por grande que sea).

sofa [sófa], *s.* sofá.

soffit [sófit], *s.* (arq.) sófito; paflón, intradós.

soft. I. *a.* blando, muelle; pastoso, plástico; dúctil, maleable, flexible; liso, suave al tacto; dulce, grato al oído; jugoso, mollar; blanducho, fofo; flojo (hilado); tierno, delicado; meloso, mimoso, almibarado; débil de carácter, condescendiente; de matices delicados o apagados; dulce (agua); (gram.) sibilante; sonante; (elec.) poco penetrante (apl. a ciertos rayos X).—**s.-boiled eggs**, huevos pasados por agua.—**s. brass**, latón recocido.—**s. bread**, mollete, pan tierno.—**s. coal**, hulla grasa, carbón bituminoso.—**s. drink**, bebida refrescante no alcohólica.—**s. iron**, hierro dulce o maleable.—**s.-shell**, de cáscara o carapacho blando.—**s. skin**, cutis suave.—**s. snap**, ganga, chiripa.—**s. soap**, jabón blando.—**s. solder**, soldadura débil o tierna (de baja temperatura).—**s. steel** = MILD STEEL.—**s. water**, agua no cruda.—**s. words**, palabras dulces o melosas. **II.** *interj.* ¡poco a poco! ¡sin ruido! ¡quedo! ¡callaos!

soften [sófœn], **I.** *va.* ablandar; reblandecer, molificar; mitigar, atemperar, calmar, amansar, suavizar; enternecer; endulzar; enervar, afeminar. **II.** *vn.* ablandarse; reblandecerse; templarse; amansarse; enternecerse.

soft(e)ner [-œr], *s.* ablandador o suavizador; (pint.) brocha ancha para amortiguar los colores.

softening [sófning]. **I.** *a.* suavizador, emoliente.—**s. iron**, (ten.) hierro de ablandar. **II.** *s.* reblandecimiento; ablandamiento; blandura; enternecimiento; suavidad.—**s. of the brain**, reblandecimiento cerebral.

softish [sóftish], *a.* blandito, blanducho.

softly [-li], *adv.* blandamente; callando; suavemente, sin ruido; lentamente, con lentitud, paso a paso.

softness [-nes], *s.* blandura; suavidad; pastosidad; (metal.) ductilidad, maleabilidad; dulzura, ternura; debilidad de carácter; delicadeza, molicie; (med.) morbidez.

soggy [sógui], *a.* empapado, mojado.

soho [sojó], *interj.* ¡hola! (voz de caza).

soil [sóil]. **I.** *va.* ensuciar, manchar, empañar; abonar; dar verde (al ganado); engordar o purgar con verde. **II.** *s.* terreno, tierra vegetal, suelo; país, región; suciedad, porquería; mancha; abono; pastura en que se refugia la caza.

soilage [-ey], **soiling** [-ing], *s.* (agric.) verdes; alimentación con verdes.

soirée [suaré], *s.* (fr.) tertulia, sarao.

sojourn [sóyœrn *o* soyœrn]. **I.** *vn.* residir, morar, permanecer. **II.** *s.* morada, permanencia, estancia.—**sojourner** [-œr], *s.* transeúnte.

sol [sol], *s.* sueldo, moneda de cobre de Francia; sol, moneda del Perú; (mús.) sol; (quím.) sol, coloide en suspensión.—(S-) el sol, Febo.

solace [sóles]. **I.** *s.* solaz. **II.** *va.* solazar.

Solanaceæ [sólænéisiĭ], *s. pl.* (bot.) solanáceas.—**solanaceous** [-shŭs], *a.* solanáceo.

solano [soláno], *s.* solano (viento).

Solanum [soléĭnŭm], *s.* (bot.) hierba mora.

solar [sólar], *a.* solar.—**s. attachment**, (top., astr.) anteojo solar (de un teodolito, tránsito o brújula).—**s. compass** (top.) brújula de (con) anteojo solar.—**s. cycle**, ciclo solar.—**s. lamp**, quinqué.—**s. microscope**, microscopio solar.—**s. plexus** (anat.) plexo solar.—**s. print**, (fot.) impresión solar o heliográfica.—**s. salt**, sal obtenida por evaporación al sol.—**s. spot**, mancha del sol.—**s. telegraph**, telégrafo solar, heliótropo, helióstato.—**s. transit**, tránsito (teodolito) de (con) anteojo solar.

solarium [solériŭm], *s.* apartamiento expuesto al sol (apl. esp. a los cuartos de convalescientes en los hospitales); SUN PARLOR.

sold [sóuld], *pret.* y *pp.* de TO SELL.—**to be s. to**, (fam.) estar convencido de, o convertido a.

soldan [sóldæn], *s.* soldán, sultán.

solder [sódœr]. **I.** *va.* soldar. **II.** *s.* soldadura.—**solderer** [-œr], *s.* soldador.—**soldering** [-ing]. **I.** *s.* soldadura. **II.** *a.* de soldar.—**s. iron**, soldador.

soldier [sólyœr], *s.* soldado.—*pl.* tropa.—**soldierlike** [-laic], **soldierly** [-li]. **I.** *a.* soldadesco, marcial, militar. **II.** *adv.* militarmente.—**soldiership** [-ship], *s.* soldadesca; milicia, talentos militares.—**soldiery** [-ri], *s.* soldadesca, tropa; servicio militar.

sole [sóul]. **I.** *va.* (zap.) solar, echar suelas a. **II.** *s.* planta (del pie); suela (del zapato); (ict.) lenguado; dado, tejuelo, base, fondo, suelo.—**s. leather**, (ten.) cuero de suela.—**s. of a guncarriage**, solera de cureña.—**s. of the rudder**, zapata del timón. **III.** *a.* único, solo; (for.) soltero; absoluto, exclusivo.—**s. agent**, único agente, agente exclusivo.

solecism [sólesism], *s.* solecismo; incongruencia.—**solecist** [-sist], *s.* el que comete solecismos.—**solecistic(al** [-sístic(al], *a.* incongruo o incongruente.—**solecize** [-saiś], *vn.* cometer solecismos.

solely [sóul-li], *adv.* únicamente, solamente.

solemn [sólemn], *a.* solemne.—**solemness** [-nes], *s.* solemnidad.—**solemnity** [solémniti], *s.* solemnidad.—**solemnization** [sólemniséishŭn], *s.* solemnización, celebración.—**solemnize** [-naiś], *va.* solemnizar, celebrar solemnemente.—**solemnly** [sólemli], *adv.* solemnemente; con todas las formalidades.

solenoid [sólenoid], *s.* (elec.) solenoide.

sol-fa [sol-fá]. **I.** *va.* y *vn.* (mús.) solfear. **II.** *s.* sol-fa; solfeo.

solfatara, *s.* (geol.) solfatara.

solfeggio [solféyio], *s.* (mús.) solfeo.

solicit [sólisit]. **I.** *va.* solicitar; importunar, rogar, implorar; inducir, incitar, tentar. **II.** *vn.* pedir, hacer una petición o solicitud.—**solicitation** [-éishŭn], *s.* solicitación, cuestación; incitación.—**solicitor** [-œr], *s.* procurador, agente, solicitador, diligenciero; pretendiente; abogado.—**S. General** (en los E. U.) subsecretario de justicia; (en Ing.) subfiscal de la corona.

solicitous [sólisitŭs], *a.* solícito.

solicitously [-li], *adv.* solícitamente.

solicitude [sólisitiud], *s.* solicitud, cuidado, afán, avidez.

solid [sólid]. **I.** *s.* sólido. **II.** *a.* sólido; compacto; puro (oro, plata, etc.); macizo; cúbico; unánime; (fam.) completo, verdadero.—**s. angle**, ángulo sólido.—**s. end**, cabeza cerrada (de una biela).—**s. for**, unánimemente en favor de.—**s. geometry**, geometría del espacio.—**s. tire**, (aut.) macizo, llanta maciza.—**to be, o stand, s. with**, (fam.) gozar de la entera confianza o el favor de; estar muy en gracia o valimiento con.

solidarity [sólidériti], *s.* solidaridad.

solidification [solidifikéishŭn], *s.* solidificación, consolidación.

solidify [sólidifai], *va.* y *vn.* solidificar(se).

solidity [sóliditi], **solidness** [sólidnes], *s.* solidez, consistencia, macicez.

solidly [sólidli], *adv.* sólidamente, firmemente.

solidungulate, solidungulous [solidúnguiulet, -lŭs], *a.* solípedo.

---

soliloquize, soliloquise [solílocuaiŝ], *vn.* soliloquiar, hablar a solas.

soliloquy [solílocui], *s.* soliloquio, monólogo.

soliped [sóliped], *s.* solípedo.

solitaire [sóliteær], *s.* (joy.) solitario; solitario (juego de una sola persona).

solitarily [-terili], *adv.* solitariamente.

solitariness [-terines], *s.* soledad, retiro.

solitary [-tæri]. **I.** *a.* solitario; solo, único, aislado; incomunicado; (zool. y bot.) solitario; simple, sencillo. **II.** *s.* solitario, ermitaño.

solitude [-tiud], *s.* soledad; vida solitaria.

sollar [sólar], *s.* (min.) descanso; (igl.) camarín.

solmization [sólmiŝéiŝhun], *s.* (mús.) solfa.

solo [sólo], *s.* (mús.) solo.

soloist [sóloist], *s.* (mús.) solista.

Solomon's seal [sólomœnŝ sil], *s.* (bot.) sello de Salomón.

solstice [sólstis], *s.* (astr.) solsticio.

solstitial [solstíŝhal], *a.* solsticial.

solubility [sólyubíliti], **solubleness** [sólyubœlnes], *s.* solubilidad.

soluble [sólyubœl], *a.* soluble.

solute [soliút], *s.* substancia disuelta.

solution [soliúŝhun], *s.* (quím.) solución, disolución; (mat.) solución (resultado, raíz de una ecuación, etc.); resolución (procedimiento).

solutive [sólyutiv], *a.* solutivo; soluble; laxativo, laxante.

solvability [sólvabíliti], **solvableness** [sólvabœlnes], *s.* solubilidad.

solvable [sólvabœl], *a.* disoluble; soluble.

solve [solv], *va.* resolver; desenredar, aclarar.

solvency [sólvensi], *s.* solvencia.

solvent [sólvent]. **I.** *a.* solvente, resolvente, disolutivo; (com.) solvente. **II.** *s.* disolvente, menstruo; (med.) disolvente.

somatic(al [sométic(al], *a.* corporal, corpóreo, físico.

somatology [somatóloyi], *s.* somatología.

somatome [sómatom], *s.* segmento teórico del cuerpo de un articulado.

somber, sombre [sómbœr], *a.* sombrío.

sombrero [sombrero], *s.* sombrero de fieltro de copa alta y alas anchas (el usado por los vaqueros mejicanos).

sombrous [sómbrus], *a.* (poét.) = SOMBER.

some [sum]. **I.** *a.* algo, de, un poco (cantidad indefinida); algún, alguno, alguna; unos pocos, ciertos, algunos, algunas, unos, unas (número indefinido). U. en leguaje fam. para indicar sumo grado, gran tamaño, excelencia, etc.: *some house, gran casa, buena casucha* (irón.); *he is some man,* es todo un hombre. Cuando es partitivo, se deja a menudo sin traducir: *give me some water,* déme agua.—**s. one,** alguien o alguno.—**s. . . . or other,** (fam.) alguno, uno . . . u otro (*for some reason or other,* por algún motivo, por un motivo u otro).—**s. people,** algunas personas, algunas gentes. **II.** *pron.* algunos; parte, una parte, una porción. **III.** *adv.* (fam.) cerca de, como, poco más o menos.

somebody [súmbódi], *s.* alguien, alguna persona; un personaje.—**s. else,** algún otro.

somehow [súmjáu], *adv.* de algún modo, de un modo u otro, por alguna razón.—**s. or other,** (fam.) = SOMEHOW.

somersault, somerset [súmœrsolt, -set], *s.* salto mortal.

something [súmzing]. **I.** *s.* alguna cosa, algo; cosa de importancia y suposición.—**s.** else, otra cosa; alguna otra cosa; algo más.—**s. or other,** (fam.) algo, alguna cosa. **II.** *adv.* algo, algún tanto.

sometime [-taim], *adv.* algún día, oportunamente, en algún tiempo.—**s. last week,** durante la semana pasada.

sometimes [-taims], *adv.* algunas veces, a veces.

somewhat [-juot]. **I.** *s.* alguna cosa, algo; un poco; sujeto o cosa de consecuencia. **II.** *adv.* algo, algún tanto, un poco.

somewhere [-juæær], *adv.* en alguna parte.—**s. else,** en alguna otra parte.

somite [sómait], *s.* = SOMATOME.

somnambulate [somnǽmbiuleit], *va.* y *vn.* andar o andar por en estado sonámbulo.—**somnambulist**], *s.* sonámbulo.—**somnambulism** [-liŝm], *s.* sonambulismo.

somniferous [somnífœrus], *a.* somnífero, soporífero.

somnific [somnífic], *a.* narcótico, soporífero.

somniloquism, somniloquence [somnílocuiŝm, -cuens], *s.* somnilocuencia.

somniloquist [somnílocuist], *s.* somnílocuo.

somnolence, somnolency [sómnolens, -i], *s.* somnolencia.—**somnolent** [-ent], *a.* soñoliento; soporífero, adormecedor.

son [sun], *s.* hijo (varón).—**s.-in-law,** yerno, hijo político.—**s. of a gun,** (fam.) camastrón, tuno, pillastre.—**S. of Man,** Hijo del Hombre.

sonant [sónant], *a.* (gram.) sonante; sonoro.

sonata [sonáta], *s.* (mús.) sonata.

song, *s.* canción, cantinela, canto, tonada; balada, poema lírico; poesía, verso; bagatela, nimiedad, poca cosa, bicoca.—**s. bird,** ave canora.—**the S. of Songs, the S. of Solomon,** (bib.) el Cantar de los Cantares.

songbook [sóngbúc], *s.* cancionero, libro de canciones.

songful [sóngful], *a.* melodioso.

songster [sóngstœr], *s.* cantor, cancionista, poeta; pájaro cantor.—**songstress** [sóngstres], *s.* cantora, cantadora, cantatriz.

soniferous [sonífœrus], **sonorific** [sonorífic], *a.* sonante, sonoro.

sonnet [sónet]. **I.** *va.* y *vn.* celebrar con sonetos; componer sonetos. **II.** *s.* (poét.) soneto.

sonneteer [sónetœr], *s.* compositor de sonetos.

sonometer [sonómetœr], *s.* sonómetro.

sonorous [sonórus], *a.* sonoro.—**sonorously** [-li], *adv.* sonoramente.—**sonorousness, sonority** [-nes, -iti], *s.* sonoridad.

sonship [súnship], *s.* filiación, calidad de hijo.

sonsy [sónsi], *a.* (fam.) dulce, placentero; en buen estado; alegre, feliz.

soon [sun]. **I.** *adv.* presto, pronto, prontamente. —**s. after,** poco después; poco después de.—**how s.?** ¿cuándo? ¿cuánto a más tardar? **II.** *s.* (E. U.) tempranero (el que indebidamente se anticipa a usar de un privilegio).

sooner [súnœr], *adv. comp.* de SOON: más pronto; antes; mejor.—**s. or later,** tarde o temprano.—**I would s. die,** antes la muerte; preferiría morir.—**the s. the better,** cuanto antes, o mientras más pronto, mejor.

soonest [-est], *adv. superl.* de SOON: más pronto (superl.); primero.—**at the s.,** no antes, no antes de, antes no.

soot [sut]. **I.** *va.* manchar o cubrir de hollín. **II.** *s.* hollín.—**sooted** [-ed], *a.* holliniento.

sooth [suz]. **I.** *a.* (ant.) agradable, delicioso; verdadero, real. **II.** *s.* verdad, realidad.

soothe [sud], *va.* calmar, aliviar, mitigar; ablandar, apaciguar; paliar, excusar.

soother [súdœr], *s.* consolador; aliviador; amansador, apaciguador; adulador.

soothing [súding], *a.* calmante; confortante, consolador.—**soothingly** [-li], *adv.* con dulzura, consoladoramente.

soothsayer [súzséiœr], *s.* adivino.

sootiness [sútines], *s.* fuliginosidad.

sooty [súti], *a.* holliniento; fuliginoso.

sop. **I.** *s.* sopa, pan o cualquier cosa empapada en un líquido; regalo, para sobornar o apaciguar a alguien. **II.** *va.* ensopar, empapar; (con *up*) absorber.

sophism [sófiŝm], *s.* sofisma.—**sophist** [sófist], *s.* sofista.—**sophister** [ŝófiŝtœr], *s.* (Ingl.) estudiante de último curso.—**sophistic(al** [sofístic(al], *a.* sofístico.—**sophistically** [-li], *adv.* sofisticamente.—**sophisticalness** [-nes], *s.* sofistería.

sophisticate [sofístikėt]. **I.** *va.* sofisticar; falsificar, alterar, adulterar; seducir, descarriar. **II.** *a.* adulterado, viciado, falsificado.—**sophisticated** [-kéited], *a.* corrido de mundo, falto de simplicidad, avezado a las cosas del mundo, sabido. —**sophistication** [-kéiŝhun], *s.* adulteración; falta de simplicidad.—**sophisticator** [-kéitœr], *s.* falsificador, adulterador.

sophistry [sófistri], *s.* sofistería.

sophomore [sófomoœr], *s.* estudiante de segundo año.

sopor [sópor], *s.* (med.) sopor, letargo.

soporiferous [sóporífœrus], *a.* soporífero.

soporiferousness [-nes], *s.* virtud o calidad soporífera.

soporific [soporífic]. **I.** *a.* soporífero, adormecedor. **II.** *s.* medicamento soporífero.

soppy [sópi], *a.* mojado, empapado.

soprano [sopráno], *a.* y *s.* tiple, soprano.

sorb, *s.* (bot.) serbo o serval.—**s. apple**, sorba o serba.

sorcerer [sórsœrœr], *s.* hechicero, brujo.

sorceress [sórsœres], *s.* hechicera, bruja.

sorcery [sórsœri], *s.* encantamiento, sortilegio, hechicería.

sordes [sórdiš], *s. pl.* sarro; pus o materia de las llagas.

sordet [sórdet], *s.* = SORDINE.

sordid [sórdid], *a.* mercenario, avariento, codicioso; vil, bajo; de color lodoso.—**sordidly** [-li], *adv.* codiciosamente, vilmente.—**sordidness** [-nes], *s.* codicia, avaricia; bajeza, vileza.

sordine [sórdin], *s.* (mús.) sordina.

sore [sóœr]. **I.** *s.* llaga o úlcera; lastimadura; matadura (del ganado); (Am.) encono; pena, espina, memoria dolorosa; disgusto. **II.** *a.* enconado, dolorido, sensible; apenado, apesarado; sentido, picado, resentido; doloroso, penoso; molesto; vehemente.—**s. ears**, mal de oídos.—**s. eyes**, mal de ojos.—**s. sight**, espectáculo doloroso.—**s. throat**, mal de garganta. **III.** *adv.* (ant.) muy penosamente.

sorely [-li], *adv.* penosamente; suma o urgentemente.

soreness [-nes], *s.* dolor, mal; calidad de dolorido, enconado o sensible; amargura de una pena.

sorghum [sórgum], *s.* (bot.) sorgo, zahina; (E. U.) melaza de sorgo.

sorites [soráitiš], *s.* sorites.

sororicide [sorórisaid], *s.* asesino (o asesinato) de una hermana.

sorority [-riti], *s.* club o hermandad de mujeres.

sorosis [sorósis], *s.* (bot.) fruto compuesto y mollar (como la piña); (E. U.) club de mujeres.

sorrel [sórrel]. **I.** *a.* alazán, roano. **II.** *s.* color alazán o roano; caballo (u otro animal) alazán; (bot.) acedera, acetosa, romaza.

sorrily [sórrili], *adv.* mal, malamente, pésimamente, lastimosamente.

sorrow [sórro]. **I.** *s.* pesar, dolor, pena; duelo, luto; desgracia, infortunio.—**s.-stricken**, agobiado de dolor.—**to my s.**, con gran sentimiento mío. **II.** *vn.* apesararse, sentir pena, afligirse.

sorrowful [-ful], *a.* pesaroso, afligido, desconsolado; triste, doloroso, lastimoso.—**sorrowfully** [-fuli], *adv.* dolorosamente, con pena; luctuosamente, lastimeramente.—**sorrowfulness** [-fulnes], *s.* pesar, tristeza, pesadumbre; calidad de triste o lastimoso.—**sorrowing** [-ing], *s.* aflicción, tristeza; lamentación.—**sorrowless** [-les], *a.* sin pena, sin pesar, libre de pesares.

sorry [sórri], *a.* apesadumbrado, pesaroso; arrepentido; triste, lamentable, lastimoso; malo, miserable, de inferior calidad; despreciable, ridículo.—**to be s.**, (fuera del significado literal) sentir, lamentar; arrepentirse; pesar (*you will be sorry*, le pesará).—**to be s. for**, sentir; compadecer.

sort [sort]. **I.** *s.* clase, especie; calaña; manera, modo, forma.—**s. of** = KIND OF.—**after a s., in a s.**, de cierto modo, hasta cierto punto.—**all sorts of**, toda clase de.—**in like s.**, de modo análogo.—**of sorts**, de varias clases; de mala muerte.—**of sorts**, indispuesto; malhumorado; triste; (impr.) falta de una fundición especial de letra o guarismos. **II.** *va.* (a veces con *over*) separar, dividir, distribuir en grupos, clasificar; (a veces con *out*) escoger, colocar, ordenar, arreglar. **III.** *vn.* corresponder, ajustar; estar de acuerdo; juntarse, rozarse; adaptarse.

sortable [sórtabœl], *a.* separable, clasificable; acomodado, conveniente, apto, oportuno.

sortie [sórti], *s.* (mil.) salida, surtida.

sortilege [sórtiley], *s.* sortilegio.

SOS, S. O. S. [es óu es], *s.* (rad.) SOS, llamada o señal de auxilio. (Las letras no son iniciales de nada; se escogieron arbitrariamente por facilidad de transmisión.)

sot. I. *s.* zaque, borrachín, tumbacuartillos, libertino. **II.** *va.* atontar, aturdir o atolondrar. **III.** *vn.* embriagarse.

soteriology [sotírióloyi], *s.* discurso o exposición acerca de la higiene; (teo.) doctrina de la salvación por Jesucristo.

sottish [sótiš], *a.* embotado, hecho una uva, embrutecido.—**sottishly** [-li], *adv.* torpemente.—**sottishness** [-nes], *s.* torpeza, embrutecimiento.

sotto voce [sóto vóche], *adv.* a sovoz.

sou [su], *s.* sueldo (moneda).

soubrette [subrét], *s.* (teat.) graciosa.

soubriquet [súbriqué], *s.* apodo.

souffle [sufl], *s.* (cir.) soplo, viento.

soufflé [sufléi], *s.* tortilla de claras y yemas de huevo batidas separadamente, o de claras solamente.

sough [suf o sáu]. **I.** *va.* y *vn.* suspirar, susurrar, murmurar. **II.** *s.* susurro, suspiro, murmullo.

sought [sot], *pret.* y *pp.* de TO SEEK.

soul [soul], *s.* alma; espíritu; corazón (en sentido metafórico).—**on**, o **upon my s.**, por vida mía, por mi vida. Con *soul* y algunos adjetivos y gerundios se forman varios compuestos, como *s.-sick*, *s.-thrilling*, etc. cuyo significado puede inferirse por el segundo elemento.

souled [sóuld], *s.* animado, con alma.

soulful [-ful], *a.* conmovedor, espiritual.—**soulfully** [-fuli], *adv.* de un modo que llega hasta el alma.—**soulfulness** [-fulnes], *s.* sensibilidad.

soulless [-les], *a.* desalmado; sin conciencia; sin conocimiento.

sound [sáund]. **I.** *a.* sano, bueno; ileso, incólume, entero; puro, ortodoxo; cierto, indubable; recto, justo; firme; bueno, completo; profundo, cabal; (com.) solvente.—**s. reasoning**, raciocinio sólido, seguro.—**s. sleep**, sueño profundo.—**of s. and disposing mind and memory**, (for.) de mente y memoria sanas, capaz de hacer testamento.—**of s. mind**, en su cabal juicio. **II.** *adv.* sanamente, vigorosamente. **III.** *s.* (geog.) estrecho; sonda, sondaleza; (cir.) tienta, sonda; son, sonido, tañido; ruido; vejiga natatoria (de los peces).—**s. board** = SOUNDING BOARD.—**s. post**, alma de violín.—**s. wave**, onda sonora. **IV.** *va.* sonar, tocar, tañer; dar el toque de; tañer; entonar, cantar; proclamar; celebrar; probar por el sonido; sondear; inquirir, rastrear, tantear; (cir.) sondar, tentar; (med.) auscultar.—**to s. a note**, dar señal, dar aviso; formular, enunciar (un plan, principio, regla, etc.). **V.** *vn.* sonar; resonar, esparcirse, divulgarse; dar toque de aviso o llamada.

sounder [-œr], *s.* (elec.) resonador; (mar.) sondeador; (cir.) tienta.

sounding [-ing]. **I.** *a.* sonante, sonable, sonoro; retumbante. **II.** *s.* (mar.) sondeo, braceaje, escandallada.—*pl.* sondas, cantidad de brazas; muestras sacadas del agua por el sondeador.—**s. balloon**, globo sonda, globo suelto de datos meteorológicos.—**s. board**, caja armónica (de un piano); secreto, cajón de los órganos; tornavoz, sombrero de púlpito.—**s. lead**, (mar.) escandallo.—**s. line**, sondaleza, bolina.

soundless [-les], *a.* sin sonido, sin ruido, silencioso; insondable.

soundly [-li], *adv.* sanamente, con salud; firmemente; verdaderamente, seguramente.—**to sleep s.**, dormir profundamente.

soundness [-nes], *s.* sanidad, salud; vigor; firmeza; verdad, rectitud, pureza; fuerza, validez; rectitud, justicia; pureza de la fe, ortodoxia.

soup [sup], *s.* sopa.—**s. kitchen**, cocina de carretilla, olla grande con fogón debajo montada en ruedas; dispensario de alimentos para los pobres.—**s. ladle**, cucharón.—**s. plate**, plato hondo o de sopero.—**s. tureen**, sopera.—**in the s.**, (vulg.) en apuros, en aprietos; caído, arrinconado.

Para la pronunciación de æ, œ, ᴅ, š, šh, ᴜ, ȳ, ʏ, z, véase la clave al principio del libro.

sour [sáuær]. **I.** *a.* agrio; acre, áspero, desabrido, huraño.—**s. apple,** manzana agria o verde.—**s. dock,** acedera.—**s. gourd,** (bot.) pan de mico.—**s. grapes!** ¡están verdes!—**s. grass,** acedera pequeña. **II.** *va.* agriar, acedar, avinagrar; desabrir, irritar, indisponer (los ánimos); descontentar, desagradar; macerar; hacer fermentar (la cal). **III.** *vn.* agriarse, avinagrarse; cortarse (la leche); revenirse, fermentar; irritarse, enojarse; corromperse, podrirse; (agr.) malearse (la tierra).

source [sors], *s.* fuente; nacimiento; origen, causa. —**to have,** o **to know, from a good s.,** saber de buena tinta.

sourcrout, sourkrout [-cráut], *s.* berza ácida; SAUERKRAUT.

sourish [-ish], *a.* agrillo, agrete, vinagroso.

sourly [-li], *adv.* agriamente.

sourness [-nes], *s.* agrio, agrura; acrimonia.

soursop [-sop], *s.* (bot.) guanábana; guanábano.

souse [sáus]. **I.** *s.* escabeche; cabeza, patas u orejas de cerdo adobadas; zambullida, chapuz; ataque repentino (del halcón). **II.** *adv.* zas, de cabeza. **III.** *va.* zabullir, chapuzar; arrojar, derramar, verter; (coc.) escabechar, adobar; arrojarse con violencia sobre. **IV.** *vn.* lanzarse de cabeza.

soutane [sutéin], *s.* sotana.

south [sáuz]. **I.** *s.* sud o sur; comarca o región situada al sur.—**the S.,** (E. U.), los estados del Sur. **II.** *a.* meridional, austral, del sur.—**S. African,** sudafricano.—**S. American,** sudamericano. —**S. Pole,** polo sur.—**s. wind,** viento del sur. **III.** *adv.* hacia el sur; del sur (viento).

southeast [-ist], *s.* y *a.* sudeste.—**s. by east,** sudeste cuarta al este.—**s. by south,** sudeste cuarta al sur.

southeaster [-ístœr], *s.* temporal o viento de sudeste.—**southeasterly** [-ístœrli], *a.* y *adv.* hacia el sudeste, al sudeste.—**southeastern** [-ístœrn], *a.* y *adv.* del sudeste.

souther [sáuðœr], *s.* viento o borrasca del sur.

southerly [súðœrli], *a.* meridional.

southern [súðœrn], *a.* meridional, austral, del sur; situado al sur.—**S. Cross,** Cruz del Sur.

southernmost [-móust], *a.* de más al sur, más meridional.

southernwood [súðœrnud], *s.* (bot.) abrótano, lombriguera, boja.

southing [sáuing]. **I.** *a.* que camina hacia el sur. **II.** *s.* diferencia de latitud sur.

southmost [-moust], *a.* más meridional (*superl.*).

southron [súðron], *s.* habitante del sur, meridional.

southward [sáuzuard]. **I.** *a.* situado hacia el sur. **II.** *adv.* hacia el mediodía.—**s. of the line,** al sur de la línea (ecuador).

southwest [-uést], *s.* y *a.* sudoeste.—**s. by south,** sudoeste cuarta al sur.—**s. by west,** sudoeste cuarta al oeste.

southwester [-uéstœr], *s.* vendabal del sudoeste; (mar.) chapona, sueste; sombrero de lona encerada.—**southwesterly** [-li], *a.* y *adv.* del sudoeste, hacia el sudoeste.—**southwestern** [-tœrn], del sudoeste.—**southwestward** [-tuard], *adv.* hacia el sudoeste.

souvenir [súvenir], *s.* memoria, prenda de recuerdo; estrena.

sovereign [sóvœren]. **I.** *s.* soberano; libra esterlina. **II.** *a.* soberano. **s. pontiff,** sumo pontífice.

sovereignly [-li], *adv.* soberanamente; supremamente.—**sovereignty** [-ti], *s.* soberanía.

soviet [sóviet]. **I.** *s.* sóviet. **II.** *a.* soviético, bolchevista.—**sovietdom** [-dum], *s.* los países soviéticos; bolchevismo.—**sovietism** [-ism], *s.* sovietismo, bolchevismo.—**sovietist** [-ist], *s.* sovietista, bolchevista.—**sovietize** [-aiš], *va.* y *vn.* sovietizar, convertir al sovietismo o bolchevismo; propagar el sovietismo.

sow [sáu], *s.* puerca, marrana; (fund.) goa, galápago.—, o **s. bug,** (ent.) cochinilla de tierra.—**s. pig,** lechona.—**s. thistle,** (bot.) cerraja, cardo ajonjero.

sow [so]. **I.** *vn.* y *vn.* (*pret.* SOWED; *pp.* SOWN o SOWED) (agr.) sembrar; desparramar, esparcir, diseminar.—**to s. one's wild oats,** correr sus mocedades, hacer travesuras juveniles.

sowbread [sáubred], *s.* (bot.) pamporcino.

sower [sóœr], *s.* sembrador; diseminador, desparramador; sembradera.

sowing [sóing]. **I.** *s.* sementera, siembra; sembradura, diseminación. **II.** *a.* de sembrar, sembrador.—**s. machine,** sembradera.—**s. time,** sementera, tiempo de sembrar.

sown [sóun], *pp.* de TO SOW.

soy [sói], **soya** [sóyæ], *s.* soja, soya, planta gramínea de China y de la India; salsa de soya; soya, fruto de la soya (llám. t. **s. bean** y **s. pea**).

spa, *s.* balneario; manantial de agua mineral; burga; caldas.

space [spéis]. **I.** *va.* espaciar; interlinear, regletear. **II.** *s.* (leng. ord., mús., impr.) *s.* espacio; extensión, trecho; distancia; lugar, cabida, campo; período, intervalo; rato; ocasión, tiempo, sazón, oportunidad; intersticio.—**S. band,** cuña o placa de espaciar.—**s. rule,** (impr.) raya fina.

spacer [spéisœr], *s.* espaciador; separador.

spacial [spéishal], *s.* = SPATIAL.

spacious [spéishus], *a.* espacioso, amplio, grande. —**spaciously** [-li], *adv.* espaciosamente.—**spaciousness** [-nes], *s.* espaciosidad, amplitud.

spade [spéid]. **I.** *s.* azada, pala; espada (en la baraja); (mil.) zapa.—**to call a s. a s.,** llamar al pan pan y al vino vino, hablar en plata. **II.** *va.* cavar o remover el suelo con la azada, azadonear.

spadeful [spéidful], *s.* palada.

spadiceous [spadíshus], *a.* (bot.) espadíceo.

spadix [spéidix], *s.* (bot.) espádice.

spaghetti [spaguéti], *s.* fideos largos, macarrones delgados.

spahee, spahi [spají], *s.* espahí, soldado de caballería turco o argeliano.

spake [spéik], *pret. ant.* de TO SPEAK.

spall [spol]. **I.** *s.* astilla. **II.** *va.* y *vn.* desastillar (se); descantillar(se); descascarar(se); desbastar, alisar toscamente.

spalt [spolt], *s.* (fund.) espalto.

span [spæn]. **I.** palmo; lapso, espacio, trecho; (arq.) tramo, luz; (aer.) envergadura, dimensión máxima transversal; ojo, apertura de arco o bóveda; (E. U.) pareja (de caballos); traba; (mar.) eslinga; amante, guía, braga, nervio.—**s. shackle,** zuncho, cepo o carlinga. **II.** *va.* medir a palmos; atravesar; abrazar, llegar de un lado a otro de; echar sobre, extenderse sobre; ligar, atar. **III.** *vn.* emparejarse (caballos); proceder por etapas o jornadas regulares.

span, *pret. ant.* de TO SPIN.

spandrel, spandril [spéndrel], *s.* (arq.) enjuta, embecadura, riñón.

spangle [spǽngœl]. **I.** *s.* lentejuela, bricho. **II.** *va.* adornar con lentejuelas.—**spangled skies,** cielo estrellado.

spaniard [spǽñard], *s.* español; (bot.) (nombre de un arbusto espinoso).

spaniel [spǽniel], *s.* perro de aguas.

Spanish [spǽnish], *s.* y *a.* español.—**S.-American,** hispanoamericano.—**S. bayonet,** (bot.) yuca —**S. black,** negro de España; corcho quemado.—**S. broom,** retama.—**S. cedar,** cedro rojo antillano. —**S. chalk,** esteatita de Aragón.—**S. fly,** cantárida.—**S. grass,** esparto.—**S. leather,** cordobán.— **S.-like,** españolado; a la española.—**S. mackerel,** (ict.) escombro.—**S. Main,** Tierra Firme; mar Caribe (apl. esp. a la parte meridional, que baña las costas de Tierra Firme).—**S. moss,** musgo negro o de Florida.—**S. oak,** roble español.—**S. puff,** buñuelo.—**S. sheep,** oveja merina.—**S. white,** blanco de España, yeso mate.

spank [spænk]. **I.** *va.* zurrar, dar una zurra, dar palmadas o nalgadas. **II.** *vn.* correr, ir de prisa. **III.** *s.* nalgada, palmada.

spanker [-œr], *s.* el o lo que da nalgadas; (mar.) maricangalla; (fam.) algo grande y hermoso; el que marcha velozmente.

spanking [-ing]. **I.** *a.* pronto, veloz; (fam.) extraordinariamente grande o hermoso. **II.** *s.* zurra, nalgadas.

spanless [spǽnles], *a.* que no se puede abarcar, medir, atravesar o colmar.

spanner [spǽnœr], *s.* (mec.) llave de tuercas; (ent.) oruga geómetra (llám. t. **spannerworm**).

spar. I. *s.* (min.) espato; (mar.) palo, mástil, verga; berlinga, percha, bordón; asna, cabrio, cabrial (de grúa o cabria); tranca, barra, cerreta; boxeo, pugilato; altercado, riña; pelea con espolones o las patas (gallos); (aer.) larguero.—*pl.* arboladura.—**s. buoy**, baliza.—**s. deck**, cubierta de guindaste. **II.** *vn.* boxear; pelear con espolones o con las patas; altercar. **III.** *va.* proveer de vergas o mástiles; mover o alzar por medio de mástiles y poleas.

sparable [spǽrabœl], *s.* (zap.) puntilla.

spare [spéœr]. **I.** *va.* ahorrar, economizar; escatimar; pasar o pasarse sin; perdonar; hacer gracia de; evitar.—**to have ... to spare**, tener de sobra. **II.** *vn.* abstenerse, detenerse, refrenarse, desistir; ser frugal, vivir con economía. **III.** *a.* disponible, sobrante; de repuesto; enjuto, descarnado; económico, mezquino; escaso; sobrio.—**s. bed**, cama de repuesto o de sobra.—**s.-built**, flaco, delgado.—**s. hours**, horas de recreo o de ocio.—**s. money**, dinero de reserva, ahorros.—**s. rigging**, (mar.) pertrechos o cordaje de respeto.—**s. room**, cuarto de sobra, cuarto para convidados.—**s. stores** = s. RIGGING.—**s. time**, tiempo desocupado, ratos de ocio.

spareness [-nes], *s.* magrura; escasez; ahorro; frugalidad.

sparerib [-rib], *s.* costilla de puerco casi descarnada.

sparger [spáryœr], *s.* regadera.

sparing [spéœring], *a.* escaso, limitado, poco; parco, frugal, económico.—**sparingly** [-li], *adv.* escasamente; parcamente; económicamente; rara vez; cautamente.—**sparingness** [-nes], *s.* ahorro; escasez; frugalidad, parsimonia.

spark [sparc]. **I.** *s.* chispa; (poét.) centella; (joy.) chispa, diamante pequeño; petimetre o pisaverde.—*pl.* (rad., fam.) radiotelegrafista.—**s. arrester, s. catcher**, (f. c.) chispero, sombrerete; (elec.) amortiguador de chispas, apagachispas.—**s. coil**, (elec.) bobina de inducción, bobina de chispas.—**s.-gap**, (elec.) distancia explosiva.—**s. micrometer**, (elec.) micrómetro de chispas.—**s. plug**, (m. comb. int.) bujía (de encendido). **II.** *va.* centellear; (fam.) galantear, enamorar. **III.** *vn.* chispear, echar chispas, centellear; (elec.) producir chispas; (fam.) enamorar.

sparker [spárcœr], *s.* (elec.) apagachispas, amortiguador de chispas.

sparking [-ing]. **I.** *s.* chispeo, chisporroteo; (elec.) producción de chispas. **II.** *a.* chispeante; (elec.) de chispas; que produce chispas.—**s. coil** = SPARK COIL. *V.* SPARK.—**s. distance**, (elec.) distancia explosiva máxima.—**s. plug** = SPARK PLUG, *V.* SPARK.—**s. tube**, (elec.) tubo de chispas.—**s. voltage**, (elec.) tensión (mínima) de descarga, o de chispas.

sparkle [spárkœl]. **I.** *s.* centelleo, destello. **II.** *vn.* chispear, rutilar, centellear, brillar; ser espumoso (ciertos vinos).

sparkler [spárklœr], *s.* (fam.) diamante.

sparkling [spárkling], *a.* centelleante, resplandeciente, rutilante; chispeante; espumoso.—**s. eyes**, ojos brillantes, chispeantes.—**s. wine**, vino espumoso.

sparklingly [-i], *adv.* con brillantez o brillo; con esplendor.

sparrow [spéro], *s.* (orn.) gorrión, pardal.

sparrowgrass [-grǽs], *s.* (vulg.) espárragos.

sparrowhawk [-jóc], *s.* gavilán, cernícalo.

sparry [spári], *a.* espático.

sparse [spars], *a.* esparcido, desparramado; claro, ralo.—**sparsely** [-li], *adv.* aquí y allá, a grandes trechos, no densamente.—**sparsity** [-siti], *s.* raleza; parquedad.

Spartan [spártan], *a.* y *s.* espartano.

spasm [spæsm], *s.* espasmo.—**spasmodic** [spæs-módic], *a.* espasmódico; irregular.—**spasmodically** [-cali], *adv.* espasmódicamente; a ratos, sin regularidad.

spastic [spǽstic], *a.* espástico, espasmódico.

spat [spæt]. **I.** *pret.* y *pp.* de TO SPIT. **II.** *va.* y *vn.* desovar los mariscos o moluscos; dar una pal-

madita; reñir ligeramente; batir (la lluvia). **III.** *s.* huevas de los mariscos; palmadita; manotada; sopapo, bofetada; gota grande de lluvia; salpicadura. (E. U.) riña, disputa.—*pl.* spats, botines, polainas cortas.

spathaceous [spæzéishus], **spathose, spathous** [spéizos], *a.* espatáceo.

spathe [speþ], *s.* (bot.) espata, espádice.

spathic [spǽzic], *a.* (min.) espático.

spatial [spéishal], *a.* del espacio, relativo al espacio, de espacio.

spatter [spǽtœr]. **I.** *va.* y *vn.* salpicar; manchar; regar, rociar, esparcir. **II.** *s.* salpicadura; rociamiento, rociada.

spatterdash [spǽtœrdæsh], *s. pl.* polaina.

spatterdock [spǽtœrdoc], *s.* núfar.

spattle [spǽtœl], *va.* (cerám.) motear la vajilla de loza.

spatula [spǽtiula], *s.* espátula.

spatulate [spǽtiulet], *a.* espatulado.

spavin [spǽvin], *s.* (vet.) esparaván.

spawn [spon]. **I.** *s.* (ict.) freza, huevas; pececillos; (despec.) producto, fruto, resultado. **II.** *va.* y *vn.* (ict.) desovar, frezar; (despec.) producir en abundancia.

spawner [spónœr], *s.* pez hembra.—**spawning** [-ing], *s.* freza, desove.—**s. time**, desove.

spay [spéi], *va.* castrar, sacar los ovarios a.

speak [spík], *va.* y *vn.* (*pret.* SPOKE y ant. SPAKE; *pp.* SPOKEN, ant. SPOKE) hablar; decir; comunicar(se); hablar de; recitar; producir con la palabra.—**to s. by the book**, hablar con detallada exactitud; hablar como un libro.—**to s. by the card**, hablar con pleno conocimiento de causa.—**to s. daggers**, desatarse en improperios, echar chispas.—**to s. for**, hablar en favor de; hablar en nombre de; ser señal de o recomendación para; solicitar; apalabrar, hacer guardar o reservar.—**to s. for itself**, hablar por sí mismo, ser evidente por sí mismo, ser claro y suficiente.—**to s. one's mind**, decir uno lo que piensa, hablar en plata.—**to s. out**, decir, hablar claro.—**to s. thick**, hablar con media lengua, hablar tartajoso.—**to s. through the nose**, ganguear, hablar gangoso.—**to s. to**, hablar a; (fam.) reprender.—**to s. to the point**, ir al grano, dejarse de rodeos.—**to s. up**, hablar en alta voz; interponer; decir claridades.—**to s. volumes**, encerrar muchísimo, ser de suma significación.

speakable [spíkabœl], *a.* decible.

speakeasy [-ísi], *s.* taberna clandestina.

speaker [spíkœr], *s.* el que habla; orador; preopinante; presidente de un cuerpo legislativo (en los E. U., de la cámara de representantes); (E. U.) libro de declamación.—**speakership** [-ship], *s.* presidencia (de cuerpo legislativo).

speaking [spíking]. **I.** *a.* parlante, hablante; para hablar.—**s. arc**, (elec.) arco cantante.—**s. likeness**, retrato que está hablando.—**s. machine**, máquina parlante (fonógrafo, etc.).—**s. rod**, (top.) mira parlante.—**s. trumpet**, bocina, portavoz.—**s. tube**, tubo acústico.—**to be on s. terms**, hablarse. **II.** *s.* habla, discurso, declamación; oratoria.

spear [spíœr]. **I.** *s.* lanza; venablo; arpón de pesca; (poét.) lancero; (bot.) brizna.—**s. box**, guarnición de bomba.—**s. grass**, (bot.) hierba de los prados. **II.** *va.* alancear. **III.** *vn.* brotar.

spearhead [-jéd], *s.* punta de lanza.

spearmint [-mint], *s.* (bot.) hierbabuena puntiaguda, menta verde.

spearwood [-ud], *s.* (bot.) eucalipto; acacia.

spearwort [-ucert], *s.* (bot.) ranúnculo.

special [spéshal]. **I.** *a.* especial; extraordinario, particular, privativo, peculiar; diferencial; hecho especialmente o a propósito.—**s. delivery**, entrega inmediata (de correo).—**s. steel**, acero de aleación.—**s. warrant**, (Ingl.) orden de arresto. **II.** *s.* persona o cosa especial; carta enviada para entrega inmediata; (ing., esp. hidr.) accesorio (apl. esp. a tubos cortos de unión).

specialism [-ism], *s.* consagración a una especialidad; carácter de especialista.—**specialist** [-ist], *s.* especialista.—**specialize, specialise** [-aiš], *va.* y *vn.* especializar, especializarse; tener por especialidad.—**specialization, -sation** [-iséiŝhʊn], s. especialización.—**specially** [-i], adv. especialmente; sobre todo.—**specialness** [-nes], s. especialidad.

speciality [speŝhiǽliti], s. especialidad, peculiaridad, rasgo característico.

specialty [spéŝhalti], s. especialidad; (for.) obligación firmada formalmente.

specie [spíŝhi], s. efectivo, metálico, numerario.

species [spíŝhiŝ], s. (sing. y pl.) (biol.) especie; (lóg.) especie; clase, género, suerte, variedad; forma, naturaleza; (farm.) polvos compuestos.

specific(al [spesífic(al]. **I.** a. específico, preciso; especificativo, determinado, distinto; peculiar; (med.) específico.—s. **gravity**, peso específico.—s. **heat**, calor específico.—s. **name**, nombre específico, el de la especie. **II.** s. (med.) específico.

specifically [-li], adv. específicamente; especificadamente.—**specific(al)ness** [-nes], s. calidad de específico.

specification [spésifikéiŝhʊn], s. especificación, mención.—pl. descripción detallada de un plan o aparato; presupuesto detallado; datos fundamentales; características; pliego de condiciones (muchos, sobre todo en América, usan *especificaciones* en este sentido).

specify [-fai], va. especificar; estipular, prescribir.

specimen [spéŝimen], s. muestra; ejemplar.—s. **book,** muestrario.

specious [spíŝhʊs], a. especioso, aparentemente plausible.—**speciously** [-li], adv. especiosamente.—**speciousness** [-nes], s. plausibilidad aparente.

speck, speckle [spéc, -œl]. **I.** s. manchita, mácula, motita; nube en un ojo; lunar, señal; punto, pizca. **II.** va. abigarrar, manchar, jaspear, espolvorear, motear.

spectacle [spéctacœl], s. espectáculo, ostentación, exhibición.—pl. (ópt.) espejuelos, gafas, anteojos, antiparras.

spectacled [-d], a. que lleva anteojos.

spectacular [spectǽkiular], a. de espectáculo; aparatoso.

spectator [spectéitœr], s. espectador.

spectra [-træ], s. pl. de SPECTRUM.

specter, spectre [spéctœr], s. espectro.

spectral [-tral], a. espectral.

spectrology [spectróloyi], s. (ópt.) espectrología.

spectroscope [spéctroscoup], s. (ópt.) espectroscopio.—**spectroscopic(al** [-cópic(al], a. espectroscópico.—**spectroscopy** [spectróscopi], s. espectroscopia.

spectrum [spéctrʊm], s. (ópt.) espectro; imagen o espectro ocular.—s. **analysis,** análisis espectral.

specular [spékiular], a. especular.—s. **iron,** hierro especular, hematites brillante.—s. **stone,** (min.) mica.

speculate [spékiuleit], va. y vn. especular, meditar; (com.) especular.—**speculation** [-léiŝhʊn], s. especulación, teoría; especulativa, teórica; meditación; (com.) especulación.

speculative [-lativ], a. especulativo, contemplativo; teórico; (com.) especulador.—**speculatively** [-li], adv. especulativamente; teóricamente; (com.) por especulación.—**speculativeness** [-nes], s. carácter especulativo.

speculator [spékiuléitœr], s. teórico; (com.) especulador; (teat.) revendedor de billetes.

speculum [spékiulʊm], s. (cir.) espéculum; (ópt.) espejo.

sped, pret. y pp. de TO SPEED.

speech [spích], s. palabra, habla, lenguaje; voz; discurso, arenga, alocución, perorata; disertación; (teat.) parlamento.—s. **from the throne,** discurso de la Corona.—**to make a s.,** pronunciar un discurso; echar perorata.

speechcraft [spíchcraft], s. arte de bien decir.

speechify [spíchifai], vn. (fam.) arengar, perorar.

speechless [spíchles], a. mudo; cortado, sobrecogido, sin habla.—**speechlessness** [-nes], s. mudez, falta de habla.

speechmaker [spíchméikœr],s. orador; perorador.

speed [spíd]. **I.** va. (pret. y pp. SPED O SPEEDED) ayudar, favorecer; acompañar, despedir; despachar, expedir; (gen. con *up*), acelerar, apresurar, dar prisa, avivar. **II.** vn. correr, apresurarse,

darse prisa; andar o moverse con presteza; (aut.) exceder la velocidad permitida; progresar, adelantar, prosperar, tener buen éxito. **III.** s. velocidad; rapidez; prontitud, presteza; progreso, éxito, suceso.—s. **counter,** (mec.) contador de vueltas (de una rueda), cuentavueltas.—s. **ga(u)ge, s. indicator,** s. **recorder,** cuentavueltas; (aut.) taquímetro, contador de velocidad.—s. **gear,** (aut.) cambio de velocidades.—s. **scout,** (aer. mil.) avión reconocedor rápido.—**at full s.,** a toda velocidad; a carrera tendida; a escape, a rienda suelta; a todo correr.—**with all s.,** a toda prisa, con toda la celeridad posible.

speeder [spídœr], s. el o lo que anda a gran velocidad o a revienta cinchas (apl. esp. al automovilista que excede la velocidad permitida).—**speeding** [-ing] s. (aut.) exceder la velocidad permitida, ir a revienta cinchas.

speedily [spídili], adv. rápidamente, velozmente; de prisa, pronto.—**speediness** [-nes], s. celeridad, rapidez; prontitud, prisa.

speedometer [spídómetœr], s. velocímetro.

speedway [spíduéi], pista pública.

speedwell [spíduel], s. (bot.) verónica.

speedy [spídi], a. veloz, rápido; pronto, vivo.

speiss [spáis], s. (fund.) compuesto de arseniuros y sulfuros de ciertos metales.

spell [spel]. **I.** s. hechizo, encanto; fascinación, arrobamiento; turno, tanda, revezo; (fam.) poco tiempo, rato, período, temporada; astilla; travesaño de silla.—s. **by spells,** por turnos; a ratos. **II.** va. (pret. y pp. SPELLED O SPELT) deletrear; descifrar; indicar, significar; estudiar (a veces con **over o out**); hechizar, encantar; revezar, relevar, reemplazar.—**to s. the watch,** llamar a la guardia. **III.** vn. deletrear.

spellbind [spélbaind], va. (pret. y pp. SPELLBOUND) conjurar, encantar.

speller [spélœr], s. deletreador; libro de deletrear.

spelling [spéling], s. deletreo.—s. **book,** cartilla de deletrear.

spelt [spelt]. **I.** pret. y pp. de TO SPELL. **II.** s. (bot.) escanda.

spelter [spéltœr], s. cinc del comercio, peltre.

Spencerian [spensíriæn], a. Spenceriano, de Spencer.—**Spencerism** [spénserism], s. spencerismo, filosofía de Spencer.

spend. I. va. (pret. y pp. SPENT) gastar, expender; consumir, agotar.—**to s. a mast,** (mar.) perder un palo. **II.** vn. gastar dinero, hacer gastos; gastarse, consumirse; echar o poner huevas.

spender [spéndœr], s. gastador.

spendthrift [-zrift], s. pródigo, manirroto.

Spenserian [spensíriæn], a. spenseriano, de Spenser.

spent [spent], pret. y pp. de TO SPEND.—s. **ball,** s. **bullet,** bala fría.

sperm [spœrm], s. esperma; esperma de ballena; aceite de ballena.— s. **duct,** espermiducto, conductos deferente y eyaculador juntos.—s. **oil,** aceite de ballena.—s. **sac,** vesícula seminal.—s. **whale,** cachalote.

spermaceti [spœrmasíti o séti], s. espermaceti o esperma de ballena.—s. **oil,** aceite de esperma.

spermary [spœrmæri], s. glándula espermática; testículo.

spermatheca [-zícæ], s. vesícula seminal.

spermatic(al [spœrmǽtic(al], a. espermático.—s. **cord,** cordón espermático.

spermatocyte [-tosait], s. espermatocito, célula generatriz de células espermáticas o espermatozoos.

spermatogenesis [-toyénesis], s. espermatogenia, espermatogénesis, desarrollo de los espermatozoides.

spermatogenesis [-tóyénesis] → **sperm(at)ology** [spœrm(at)óloyi], s. espermatología.

Spermatophyta [-tófitæ], s. pl. plantas que producen semillas.—**spermatophyte** [-tofáit], s. planta que produce semillas.

spermatorrhœa [-torría], s. espermatorrea.

spermatozoid [-tóŝoid]. **I.** s. espermatozoo. **II.** a. de carácter espermatozoo.

spermatozoon [-tośóon], *s.* espermatozoo, zoospermo.

spew [spiú], *va.* y *vn.* vomitar, arrojar.

spewer [spiúœr], *s.* el que vomita.

spewing [spiúing], *s.* espadañada.

sphacelate [sfǽselet],*va.* y *vn.* (med.) esfacelar(se).

sphacelus [sfǽselus], *s.* (med.) esfacelo.

sphagnous [sfǽgnus], *a.* esfagnoso, esfeñoso.

sphalerite [sfǽlœrait], *s.* (min.) esfalerita, blenda.

sphenoid [sfínoid]. **I.** *a.* esfenoidal. **II.** *s.* (anat.) esfenoides.

spheral [sfíral], *a.* esférico, redondeado, simétrico; armonioso.

sphere [sfïœr]. **I.** *s.* esfera; orbe; astro; esfera o círculo de acción. **II.** *va.* colocar en una esfera; redondear; rodear, abarcar.

spheric [sféric], *a.* celestial; exaltado; esférico.

spherical [sférical], *a.* esférico.

spherically [-li], *adv.* esféricamente.

sphericalness [sféricalnes], **sphericity** sferísiti], *s.* esfericidad.

spherics [sférics], *s.* teoría o estudio de las propiedades de la esfera.

spheroid [sfíroid], *s.* esferoide.

spheroidal [sfiróidal], *a.* esferoidal.

spherometer [sferómetœr], *s.* esferómetro.

spherule [sfériul], *s.* glóbulo.

sphincter [síinctœr], *s.* (anat.) esfínter.

sphinx [sfincs], *s.* esfinge; (ent.) esfinge.—**s. like**, (ent.) esfingido.

sphigmic [sfígmic], *a.* esfígmico; pulsátil.

sphygmograph [sfígmograf], *s.* esfigmógrafo.

sphygmomanometer [-mænómetœr], *s.* esfigmomanómetro, instrumento para medir la presión de la sangre arterial.

sphygmometer [sfígmómetœr], *s.* esfigmómetro.

spical, spicat(ed [spáical, spáiket(ed], *a.* (bot.) espigado, espiciforme; (orn.) espolonado.

spice [spáis]. **I.** *s.* especia; saborete, sainete, picante, interés; (poét.) aroma, fragancia.—**s. bag, churla.—spices**, especiería, especias.—**the s.**, (fig.) la flor y nata. **II.** *va.* (coc.) especiar, condimentar con especias; (fig.) dar gusto o picante a.

spicebush [-búśh], *s.* benjuí.

spicery [-œri], *s.* especiería; despensa; picante.— **spicily** [-ili], *adv.* de modo picante.

spick-and-span [spic-ænd-spæn], *a.* flamante, muy bien arregladito, fresco.—**s.-and-s. new**, flamante, nuevecito.

spicknel [spícnel], *s.* (bot.) tuero.

spicula [spíkiula], *s.* (bot.) espiguita.

spicular [spíkiular], *a.* agudo, puntiagudo; picante, mordaz.

spicule [spíkiul], *s.* espiguilla o espina; (zool.) púa; (bot.) espiguita, espiguilla.—*pl.* agujas de la escarcha o hielo.

spicy [spáisi], *a.* que contiene o sabe a especias; aromático, especiado; (fig.) sabroso, picante.

spider [spáidœr], *s.* (ent.) araña; arácnido; trébedes, cazo con pies; cubo y rayos (de una rueda).—**s.** (**crab**), meya, cangrejo marino.—**s. like**, parecido a una araña.—**s. line, s. thread**, hilo de tela de araña de un instrumento (llám. gen. *hilo*).—**s. web, s.'s web**, telaraña.

spiderwort [spáidœruœrt], *s.* (bot.) pasajera.

spiegel [spíguel], **spiegeleisen** [-áisen], *s.* (metal.) fundición especular (apl. hoy gen. a la manganica).

spigot [spígot], *s.* espiche, espita, canilla; tapón de espita; llave, grifo; macho, espiga (de un tubo).—**s.-and-faucet joint**, unión de espiga y campana, junta de enchufe.

spike [spáic]. **I.** *s.* (bot.) espiga de grano; alcayata, espigón, clavo largo, perno; (bot.) espiga de gramínea; alhucema, espliego. **II.** *va.* clavar con alcayatas, empernar, enclavijar; clavetear; (mil.) clavar (un cañón).

spikelet [spáiklet], *s. dim.* espiguita, espiguilla; espiga secundaria.

spikenard [spáicnard], *s.* (bot.) espicanardo, nardo; aceite vegetal.

spiker [spáicœr], *s.* clavador.

spiky [spáiki], *a.* erizado, puntiagudo; armado de púas; claveteado.

spile [spáil]. **I.** *va.* horadar un barril y ponerle espita, tapón o espiche; clavar estacas o pilotes. **II.** *s.* pilote (estaca); tarugo; clavija, espiche; (E. U.) llave de sangrar el arce azucarero.

spiling [spáiling], *s.* pilotaje.

spill [spil]. **I.** *s.* astilla, clavija; mecha, pajuela, fósforo de cartón; (fam.) vuelco; derramamiento. **II.** *va.* (*pret.* y *pp.* SPILLED O SPILT) derramar; desparramar, esparcir. **III.** *vn.* derramarse; rebosar.

spillway [spíluei], *s.* aliviadero (de una presa); vertedero, bocacaz.

spilt [spilt], *pret.* y *pp.* de TO SPILL.

spin. I. *vn.* (*pret.* SPUN, ant. SPAN; *pp.* SPUN) hilar; (con **out**) alargar, prolongar; retorcer, hacer girar (una peonza).—**to s. a yarn**, hilar; contar un cuento increíble. **II.** *vn.* hilar; girar, rodar; (aut.) girar sin avanzar. **III.** *s.* giro, vuelta; (fam.) paseo en coche o bicicleta; (aer.) barrena, picado muy pronunciado.

spinach, spinage [spínech], *s.* (bot.) espinaca.

spinal [spáinal], *a.* espinal.—**s. canal**, conducto vertebral.—**s. column**, espina dorsal o columna vertebral.—**s. cord**, medula espinal.

spindle [spíndœl]. **I.** *s.* huso, broca; (mec.) gorrón; eje; carretel; árbol; torno, ástil, aguja, peón.—**s. body**, (aut.) eje delantero.—**s.-legged**, zanquivano.—**s. of the capstan**, pinola [del cabrestante.—**s. of the steering wheel**, mazo de la rueda del timón.—**s. of the vane**, (mar.) huso, eje o fierro de la grímpola.—**s.-shanked** = **s.-LEGGED**. —**s.-shaped**, ahusado, fusiforme.—**s. tree**, (bot.) bonetero. **II.** *vn.* (bot.) crecer un tallo muy alto y delgado.

spindleshanks [-śhæncs], *s. pl.* zancas largas y flacas; (*sing.*) persona zanquivana.

spindling [-dling]. **I.** *a.* largo y delgado. **II.** *s.* persona o cosa larga y delgada.

spine [spáin], *s.* (anat.) espinazo, espina dorsal; (bot.) espina.

spinel [spínel], *s.* (joy.) espinela.—**s. ruby**, alabandina.

spinet [spínet], *s.* (mús.) espineta.

spiniferous [spainífœrus], *a.* espinoso.

spinnaker [spínakœr], *s.* (mar.) ala o arrastradera grande para yates de regata.

spinner [spínœr], *s.* hilador, hilandero; hiladora, máquina de hilar; araña de jardín.

spinneret [spíneret], *s.* órgano hilandero de las arañas y gusanos de seda, glándula de la seda.

spinning [-ing]. **I.** *s.* hilandería, arte de hilar; filatura; (aut.) rotación estacionaria de las ruedas. **II.** *a.* de hilar, hilador.—**s. frame**, hiladora continua de anillo.—**s. gland**, glándula hilandera o de la seda (del gusano).—**s. lathe**, torno de ahuecar metal en lámina.—**s. machine**, hiladora, máquina de hilar; (elec.) máquina para poner aislamiento al alambre.—**s. top**, trompo, peonza.—**s. wheel**, torno de hilar.

spinose [spáinos], *a.* espinoso.

spinosity [spainósiti], *s.* dificultad, cosa espinosa, perplejidad, enredo.

spinous [spáinus], *a.* espinoso, espíneo.

Spinozism [spínośism], *s.* (filos.) espinosismo.—**Spinozist** [-ist], *s.* y *a.* espinosista.

spinster [spínstœr], *s.* solterona; (ant.) hilandera.

spiny [spáini], *a.* espinoso; penoso, difícil.

spiracle [spíracœl], *s.* respiradero de un insecto o cetáceo; ventosa.

Spiræa [spairíæ], *s.* (bot.) género de las espíreas; (s-) espírea, reina de los prados.

spiral [spáiral]. **I.** *s.* espiral; (f. c.) curva de transición, curva de enlace entre una recta y una curva circular; (aer.) vuelo en espiral. **II.** *a.* espiral; en espiral; de caracol.—**s. curve**, (f. c.) =SPIRAL, *s.* **III.** *va.* poner a una curva circular una curva de transición. **IV.** *vn.* (f. c.) emplear curvas de transición; (aer.) volar en espiral.

spirally [spáirali], *adv.* espiralmente.

spirant [spáirant], *s.* consonante continua.

spire [spáiær]. **I.** *s.* (arq.) aguja, chapitel; brizna de hierba; cúspide, cima, ápice; espira, espiral, caracol. **II.** *va.* edificar con chapitel. **III.** *vn.* rematar en punta; germinar.

spirillum [spairílum], *s.* (biol.) espirilo, bacteria espiral.

spirit [spírit]. **I.** *s.* espíritu; aparecido, sombra, espectro; inclinación, vocación; humor, temple; espíritu de vino, alcohol; (farm.) espíritu; extracto, tintura; (ten.) solución usada como mordente.—*pl.* espíritus, vapores; humor (estado del ánimo).—**s. lamp,** lámpara de alcohol.—**s. level,** nivel de burbuja.—**s. of salt,** espíritu de sal, ácido muriático.—**s., o spirits, of wine,** espíritu de vino, alcohol.—**s. rapping,** (entre espiritistas) comunicación con los espíritus por medio de golpecillos o toques sobre una mesa.—**spirits of turpentine,** aceite de trementina, aguarrás.—**s. varnish,** barniz de alcohol. **II.** *va.* (con *away*) arrebatar, llevarse; sonsacar; (ant.) alentar, animar.

spirited [spírited], *a.* vivo, brioso; espiritoso, varonil, animoso.—**s. horse,** caballo fogoso.

spiritedly [-li], *adv.* animosamente, briosamente. —**spiritedness** [-nes], *s.* calor, vigor, energía; ardor; corazón, valor.

spiritism [-ism], *s.* espiritismo.—**spiritist** [-ist], *s.* espiritista.

spiritless [-les], *a.* abatido, amilanado; insípido; exánime, muerto.—**spiritlessly** [-li], *adv.* sin vigor, sin espíritu.—**spiritlessness** [-nes], *s.* abatimiento; falta de vigor.

spiritual [spírichual], *a.* espiritual; mental, intelectual; santo, puro; místico; eclesiástico; piadoso, religioso; (fil.) espiritualista.—**s. seance,** sesión espiritista.—**s. wife,** (entre los mormones), cualquiera esposa después de la primera.

spiritualism [-ism], *s.* espiritismo; espiritualismo.—**spiritualist** [-ist], *s.,* **spiritualistic** [-istic], *a.* espiritista; espiritualista.

spirituality [spírichuæliti], *s.* espiritualidad; bienes espirituales o eclesiásticos.

spiritualization [spírichualiséishun], *s.* acto de espiritualizar.—**spiritualize** [-aiš], *va.* espiritualizar.

spiritually [spírichuali], *adv.* espiritualmente.

spirituous [spírituius], *a.* espiritoso, espirituoso, destilado; embriagante, ardiente.—**s. liquors,** licores espirituosos, aguardientes.

spirituousness [-nes], *s.* calidad de espirituoso.

spirobacteria [spáirobactériæ], *s. pl.* de **spirobacterium** [-um], espirilo, bacteria espiral.

spirochete [-ket], *s.* (biol.) espiroqueta o espiroqueto.

spirometer [spairómetœr], *s.* espirómetro.

spirt [spœrt], *va.* y *s.* = SPURT.

spiry [spáiri], *a.* espiral, caracolado; piramidal, terminado en punta.

spit. **I.** *va.* (*pret.* y *pp.* SPIT, SPAT) escupir; esputar; (*pret.* y *pp.* SPITTED) (coc.) espetar; ensartar. **II.** *vn.* escupir; chisporrotear. **III.** *s.* asador, espetón; lengua de tierra; banco de arena; saliva; salivazo, escupitajo; espuma o huevos de varios insectos.

spitball [spítból], *s.* pelotilla de papel mascado.

spite [spáit]. **I.** *s.* rencor, despecho, ojeriza, mala voluntad.—**s. of, o in s. of,** a pesar de, a despecho de, no obstante.—**s. wall,** pared que por pique se levanta para obstruir la vista de un vecino. **II.** *va.* mostrar resentimiento, vejar, dar pique.

spiteful [spáitful], *a.* rencoroso; malicioso, malévolo.—**spitefully** [-i], *adv.* por despecho; con rencor, con tirria.—**spitefulness** [-nes], *s.* despecho; malevolencia, malicia, rencor.

spitfire [spítfaiœr], *s.* fierabrás.

spitter [spítœr], *s.* el que espeta; escupidor; gamezno.

spittle [spítcœl], *s.* saliva, salivazo.

spittoon [spítún], *s.* escupidera.

spitz [spits], *s.* perro de Pomerania.

splanchnic [splæncnic]. **I.** *a.* esplánico. **II.** *s.* nervio esplánico.

splanchnology [splæncnóloyi], *s.* (anat.) esplanología.

splash [splæsh]. **I.** *va.* salpicar, rociar, enlodar; chapotear, humedecer. **II.** *vn.* chapotear, chapalear. **III.** *s.* salpicadura, rociada; chapateo, chapaleo.—**s. lubrication,** lubricación por salpicadura.

splashboard [splæshbord], *s.* guardafango (de un carruaje).

splashy [splæshi], *a.* cenagoso, lodoso, sucio; húmedo.

splatter [splætœr], *va.* y *vn.* chapotear, guachapear, chapalear; chapurrear.

splay [spléi]. **I.** *va.* achaflanar, descantear; exponer a la vista, mostrar; (vet.) despaldar o despaldillar un caballo. **II.** *a.* extendido, desplegado, ancho; pesado. **III.** *s.* (arq.) alféizar, derrame; chaflán, bisel.

splayfoot, splayfooted [-fut, -fúted], *a.* que tiene los pies aplastados.

splaymouth [-mauz], *a.* boquiancho.

spleen [splín], *s.* (anat.) bazo; rencor; mal humor; tristeza, esplín.—**spleenful** [-ful], *a.* bilioso, irritable, adusto.

spleenwort [-uœrt], *s.* (bot.) escolopendra, culantrillo.

spleeny [-i], *a.* melancólico; bilioso; irritable, enfadadizo.

splendent [spléndent], *a.* esplendente; resplandeciente.

splendid [spléndid], *a.* espléndido; esplendente, brillante, resplandeciente; ilustre, glorioso; excelente.—**splendidly** [-li], *adv.* espléndidamente, brillantemente; excelentemente.

splendo(u)r [spléndor], *s.* esplendor; esplendidez.

splenetic [splenétic o splénetic], *a.* atrabiliario, atrabilioso, bilioso; rencoroso; regañón.

splenic [splénic], *a.* esplénico.

splenitis [splenáitis], *s.* esplenitis, inflamación del bazo.

splenius [splínius], *s.* (anat.) esplenio.

splenotomy [splenótomi], *s.* esplenotomía.

splice [spláis]. **I.** *va.* ayustar, empalmar; empotrar, unir, juntar; (fam.) casar. **II.** *s.* junta; ayuste; empalme; gaza.—**s. bar,** (f. c.) eclisa, placa de empalme.

splicing [spláising], *s.* ayuste, empalme.—**s. fid,** (mar.) pasador.

spline [spláin]. **I.** *s.* ranura para una junta de cuña; la cuña de tal junta; tira o faja flexible para dibujar curvas. **II.** *va.* ranurar.

splint. **I.** *va.* (cir.) entablillar. **II.** *s.* tira plana y delgada; astilla; (cir.) tablilla.—**s. bone,** sobrehueso.

splinter [splíntœr]. **I.** *va.* astillar, hacer astillas; (cir.) entablillar. **II.** *vn.* hacerse pedazos, romperse en astillas. **III.** *s.* astilla, esquirla, brizna; rancajo o astilla de madera clavada en la carne; astillazo.—**s. bar,** (carr.) balancín.

split. **I.** *va.* (*pret.* y *pp.* SPLIT o SPLITTED) hender, partir; rajar, cuartear, resquebrar, separar.— **to s. the difference,** partir la diferencia. **II.** *vn.* henderse, rajarse, romperse a lo largo, cuartearse, abrirse, resquebrajarse; estallar, reventar; dividirse.—**to s. upon a rock,** estrellarse contra una roca.—**to s. with laughing,** reventar de risa. **III.** *s.* hendidura, grieta, raja, cuarteadura; división, cisma, rompimiento. **IV.** *a.* hendido, partido, rajado, cuarteado; curado (pescado).—**s. infinitive,** (gram.) infinitivo partido, en que se interponen una o más palabras entre *to* y el verbo (*to clearly see,* en vez de *to see clearly*).—**s. key = s.** PIN.—**s. nut,** tuerca hendida o partida.—**s. pin,** chaveta hendida.—**s. pulley,** polea de dos piezas. —**s. ring,** (m. v.) anillo de empaquetadura (del émbolo).—**s. switch,** (f. c.) cambiavías de a gujas afiladas, o de recubrimiento.—**s. wheel,** rueda de dos piezas.—**s. wood,** leña rajada o en astillas.

splitsaw [splítsó], *s.* sierra para cortar madera longitudinalmente.

splotch [sploch]. **I.** *va.* manchar, salpicar. **II.** *s.* mancha, borrón.

splurge [splœry]. **I.** *vn.* fachendear. **II.** *s.* fachenda.

splutter [splútœr]. **I.** *va.* y *vn.* balbucear, farfullar. **II.** *s.* balbuceo; barullo.

spoil [spóil]. **I.** *va.* (*pp.* SPOILED, SPOILT) echar a perder; deteriorar, dañar, inutilizar; corromper, podrir; echar a perder conmimos; despojar, saquear. **II.** *vn.* inutilizarse, dañarse, echarse a perder; podrirse; ir al saqueo, robar. **III.** *s.* saqueo, robo; despojo, botín.—*pl.* (E. U.) gajes o beneficios de un cargo público; turrón.—**spoils system**, sistema de premiar servicios de partido con empleos públicos.

spoiled, *pp.* & *a.* dañado, inutilizado, echado a perder; podrido, rancio; vicioso, mimado (niño).

spoiler [spóiler], *s.* despojador, saqueador; ladrón; corruptor; consentidor.

spoilsman [spóilsman], *s.* (E. U. pol.) partidario del reparto de los empleos dentro del partido que gana en las elecciones.

spoke [spóuk]. **I.** *s.* rayo (de rueda); galga, retranca; escalón de escalera; (mar.) cabilla de la rueda del timón. **II.** *va.* (carr.) enrayar.

spoke, spoken, *pret.* y *pp.* de TO SPEAK.

spokeshave [-shéiv], *s.* rebajador de rayos.

spokesman [spócsman], *s.* interlocutor; el que habla en nombre de otro; el que lleva la palabra.

spoliation [spoliéishun], *s.* despojo, rapiña; (for.) expoliación.

spoliator [-éitœr], *s.* expoliador.

spondaic [spondéic], *a.* espondaico.

spondee [spóndi], *s.* (poét.) espondeo.

spondyl [spóndil], *s.* unión, articulación; (anat.) espóndilo, vértebra.

sponge [spunʏ]. **I.** *s.* esponja; (arti.) lanada, escobillón; mogollón, gorrista.—*s.* **cake**, bizcochuelo.—*s.* **tree**, cujé. **II.** *va.* mojar o limpiar con esponja; lavar(se) con esponja; borrar; esponjar; comer de gorra, chupar; escobillonar. **III.** *vn.* emberberse; pescar o recoger esponjas; vivir o comer de gorra.

spongelet [spúnʏlet], *s.* esponjita; (bot.)= SPONGIOLE.

sponger [-ʏœr], *s.* gorrista, sablista, pegote.

sponginess [-ʏines], *s.* esponjosidad.

sponging [spúnʏing], *s.* (acción de) limpiar o lavar con esponja, de pescar esponjas, de gorrear, etc. (*V.* SPONGE, *va.*).—*s.* o **sponging house**, (Ingl.) la casa de un alguacil donde quedaban detenidos provisionalmente los presos por deudas.

spongiole [-ʏiol], *s.* (bot.) espongiola.

spongy [-ʏi], **spongiose, spongious** [-ʏios, -ʏius] *a.* esponjoso, esponjado; fofo; empapado.

sponsion [spónshun], *s.* acto de salir fiador por otro.

sponson [spónson], *s.* barbeta lateral saliente de los buques de guerra.

sponsor [spónsor]. **I.** *s.* fiador; padrino o madrina; defensor, apadrinador, fomentador. **II.** *va.* apadrinar, ser padrino de; promover, fomentar.

spontaneity [spontaníiti], *s.* espontaneidad, voluntariedad.

spontaneous [spontáneus], *a.* espontáneo; natural, indígena, silvestre; esporádico.—*s.* **combustion**, combustión espontánea.—*s.* **generation**, generación espontánea.

spontaneously [-li], *adv.* espontáneamente.

spontaneousness [-nes], *s.* espontaneidad.

spontoon [spontún], *s.* (arm.) espontón.

spook [spuk], *s.* (fam.) fantasma, aparición.

spookish [-ish], **spooky** [-i], *a.* (fam.) que se parece a una fantasma; visitado por fantasmas; horripilante, de fantasmas o espantos.

spool [spul]. **I.** *s.* carrete, canilla, carretel.—*s.* **cotton**, hilo de algodón en carreteles. **II.** *va.* ovillar, encanillar, devanar.

spoon [spun], *s.* cuchara; anzuelo de cebo artificial (ll. t. **s. bait, s. hook**.) **II.** *va.* sacar con cuchara. **III.** *vn.* pescar con anzuelo de cebo artificial; (fam.) acariciarse, besarse.

spoonbill [spúnbil], *s.* (orn.) espátula.

spoondrift [-drift], *s.* (mar.) roció del mar.

spoonful [-ful], *s.* cucharada.

spoonwort [-uœrt], *s.* (bot.) coclearia.

spoony [-i]. **I.** *a.* (fam.) amartelado, acaramelado; besador. **II.** *s.* y *a.* galán meloso.

sporadic [sporǽdic], *a.* (med.) esporádico.

spore [spor], *s.* (bot. y biol.) espora; organismo diminuto, germen.—*s.* **case**, (biol.) esporangio.

sporiferous [sporíferus], *a.* esporífero, que produce esporas.

sporocarp [spórocarp], *s.* esporocarpio.—**sporocyte** [-sait], *s.* célula madre de las esporas.—**sporogenesis** [-ʏénesis], *s.* esporogénesis, reproducción por esporas; formación de esporas.—**sporogonium** [-gónium], *s.* esporogonio.—**sporophore** [-fœr], *s.* esporóforo, rama u órgano productor de esporas.—**sporophyl** [-fil], *s.* hoja generadora de esporas.—**Sporozoa** [-ʒoœ], *s. pl.* esporozoos.—**sporozoan** [-ʒoœn], *s.* y *a.* esporozoario.

sport [sport]. **I.** *s.* deporte; deportista; caballero, hidalgo, persona campechana o noble; burla, broma; hazmerreír; (biol.) individuo anormal; monstruo; (fam.) tahur. **II.** ostentar, hacer alarde de, lucir.—**to s. one's oak**, cerrar las puertas, no admitir visitas. **III.** *vn.* divertirse, jugar, holgar; bromear, chancearse; (biol.) variar espontáneamente del tipo normal. **IV.** *a.* deportivo.

sporting [spórting]. **I.** *s.* deportes. **II.** *a.* deportivo.—**s. goods**, artículos deportivos (de juegos, caza, pesca, etc.).—**s. house**, garito, casa de juego; burdel.—**s. man**, deportista; (fam. E. U.) tahur. —**s. woman**, deportista (mujer); (fam.) mujer de la vida airada.

sportive [-tiv], *a.* juguetón, retozón; aficionado a bromear.—**sportively** [-li], *adv.* de un modo retozón o festivo.—**sportiveness** [-nes], *s.* carácter retozón.

sportsman [spórtsmæn], *s.* SPORT (persona), SPORTING MAN.—**sportsmanlike** [-laic], *a.* deportivo, característico de los deportes; campechano.—**sportsmanship** [-ship], *s.* arte y pericia en el deporte.

sportswoman [-uman], *s.* deportista (mujer).

sporule [spórul], *s. dim.* esporo.

spot. I. *s.* sitio, lugar, paraje, puesto, punto; mancha, borrón, maca, tacha; palo (de baraja). —**s. cash**, dinero o pago al contado.—**s. welding**, soldadura eléctrica por puntos, o soldadura por el método Thomson-Harmatta.—**five-s., ten-s.**, etc. (fam.) billete de cinco, diez, etc., dólares; (baraja) cinco, diez, etc. (de un palo).—**in spots**, (fam.) en algunos respectos; aquí y allí.—**on o upon the s.**, ahí mismo, allí mismo, al punto, inmediatamente. **II.** *va.* abigarrar, motear; macular; manchar; (fam.) marcar, señalar, distinguir, observar, notar; poner (una bola de billar) en posición. **III.** *vn.* salir manchas; mancharse.

spotless [spótles], *a.* inmaculado, sin mancha.

spotlessness [-nes], *s.* calidad de inmaculado.

spotlight [spótláit], *s.* luz concentrada; (aut.) proyector, reflector móvil que va en el tablero o cerca de él.

spotted [spóted], *a.* manchado, moteado, pintado; apulgarado; esquizado (mármol).—**s. fever**, tabardillo pintado.

spotter [spótœr], *s.* vigilante mecánico.

spotty [spóti], *a.* cubierto de manchas.

spousal [spáušal]. **I.** *a.* (poét.) nupcial, conyugal. **II.** *s. pl.* nupcias, bodas.

spouse [spáuš], *s.* esposo, esposa.—**spouseless** [-les], *a.* soltero o viudo; sin esposo.

spout [spáut]. **I.** *s.* caño, pitón, conducto, surtidor; canilla de tonel, espita; gárgola, canalón; cuello de vasija; pico de cafetera o de tetera; chorro. **II.** *va.* y *vn.* arrojar o echar (un líquido); surgir, brotar, correr a chorro; (fam.) recitar, declamar.

sprain [spréin]. **I.** *va.* y *vn.* torcer(se). **II.** *s.* (med.) torcedura o torcimiento, relajación.

sprang, *pret.* de TO SPRING.

sprat [spræt], *s.* (ict.) sardineta.

sprawl [sprol]. **I.** *va.* y *vn.* tender o tenderse, caer o hacer caer o moverse con piernas o brazos extendidos; (agr.) desparramarse. **II.** *s.* acto de caer o tenderse abierto de brazos y piernas.

spray [spréi]. **I.** *va.* y *vn.* rociar, pulverizar un líquido. **II.** *s.* rociada, roció; espuma del mar; rociador, pulverizador; líquido o mixtura de rociar; ramaje.

sprayer [spréicœr], *s.* rociador, pulverizador.

spread [spred]. **I.** *va.* (*pret.* y *pp.* SPREAD) tender, extender, abrir, desplegar, desarrollar, desenvolver; desparramar, esparcir; divulgar; diseminar, propalar; untar con, dar una capa de; poner a la vista; exhibir; poner (la mesa), preparar; apartar, separar; (*impr.*) espaciar.—to s. abroad, esparcir, divulgar, propalar.—to s. one's self, (fam.) echar el resto.—to s. over, cubrir de o untar con. **II.** *vn.* extenderse, desplegarse; esparcirse; difundirse; desarrollarse, propagarse, cundir; apartarse, separarse; poner la mesa. **III.** *a.* extendido; (joy.) de poco brillo.—s.-eagle, (E. U. fig.) exageradamente patriótico (discurso).—s.-eagleism, oratoria patriotera, en que se extreman los alardes patrióticos. **IV.** *s.* extensión, amplitud; ancho; expansión; desarrollo; propagación, diseminación; cobertor de cama; tapete de mesa, mantel; (fam.) festín, banquete; (com.) = STRADDLE; (aer.) envergadura.

spreader [sprédœr], *s.* esparcidor; propagador; divulgador; separador; untador.

spree [sprí]. **I.** *vn.* ir de parranda; emborracharse. **II.** *s.* borrachera; holgorio, parranda.

sprig. **I.** *s.* ramita, mugrón, renuevo, pimpollo; vástago; puntilla, hita, espiga. **II.** *va.* adornar con ramitas; formar ramajes.

spriggy [sprígui], *a.* lleno de ramitas.

sprightliness [spráitlines], *s.* viveza, despejo, vivacidad, desenvoltura.—sprightly [-li], *a.* alegre, despejado, despierto, vivo.

spring. **I.** *va.* (*pret.* SPRANG O SPRUNG; *pp.* SPRUNG) soltar (un resorte o muelle); sacar o presentar de golpe; hacer volar o saltar (una mina); torcer, combar, encorvar; rendir un palo o verga; (arq.) arrancar o vaciar (un arco); insertar o meter doblando o forzando; saltar por encima de; pasar saltando; ojear (la caza); asegurar o montar con resortes.—to s. a leak, empezar a salirse o a hacer agua (un buque, una vasija).—to s. the luff, partir al puño. **II.** *vn.* saltar, brincar; salir, brotar, manar (un líquido); dimanar, provenir; presentarse súbitamente; alabearse, combarse, torcerse; nacer, brotar, crecer; levantarse, elevarse; arrancar (un arco, etc.).—to s. at, lanzarse sobre; saltar a.—to s. away, saltar a un lado; lanzarse de un salto.—to s. back, saltar hacia atrás; volver a su estado anterior bajo la acción de un resorte; recular.—to s. forth, brotar, crecer; salir; lanzarse, precipitarse.—to s. forward, abalanzarse, arrojarse, dispararse.—to s. up, nacer, brotar, crecer, desarrollarse; salir a luz, presentarse a la vista; subir, engrandecerse.—to s. upon = TO S. ON. **III.** *s.* muelle, resorte; ballesta; elasticidad, fuerza elástica; blandura o suavidad elástica; salto, brinco, corcovo, bote; vuelta a su posición anterior; motivo, móvil; primavera; fuente, manantial; origen, nacimiento; surtidor; alabeo, combadura. **IV.** *a.* primaveral, vernal, de primavera; de manantial; de resorte; para resortes.—s. back, lomo pegado (de un libro de cuentas, etc.).—s. balance, balanza de resorte.—s. catch, fiador de resorte.—s. latch, s. lock, picaporte, cerradura de golpe.—s. line, arranque, imposta (de un arco).—s. mattress, colchón de muelles.—s. steel, acero de (para) resortes.—s. switch, (f. c.) cambiavía automático de seguridad.—s. tide, aguas vivas.—s. valve, válvula de resorte.—s. water, agua de manantial.

springboard [spríngbórd], *s.* trampolín.

springe [sprinv], *s.* lazo, trampa (caza).

springer [sprínger], *s.* saltador, brincador; (arq.) imposta; sillar de arranque; perro ojeador.

springhalt [sprínghólt], *s.* cojera de caballo.

springiness [sprínguines], *s.* elasticidad, resorte, fuerza elástica.

springing [-ing]. **I.** *s.* acción del verbo TO SPRING; retoño, tallo; (arq.) línea de arranque. **II.** *pa.* de TO SPRING.—s. line = SPRING LINE.—s. wall, pared de arranque (de un arco).

springtide [spríngtáid], **springtime** [-táim], *s.* primavera.

springy [spríngui], *a.* muelle, elástico; lleno de manantiales; esponjoso.

sprinkle [sprínccel]. **I.** *va.* asperjar, rociar, esparcir; regar, desparramar; salpicar, polvorear o despolvorear; bautizar rociando. **II.** *vn.* (im-

pers.) llovizna (*tt sprinkles*, llovizna; *tt ts sprinkling*, está lloviznando). **III.** *s.* rocío, rociada; una pizca, un poco.

sprinkler [-klœr], *s.* rociador, irrigador, regadera; (igl.) aspersorio, hisopo; (arm.) mangual; carricuba, carro de riego.

sprinkling [-kling]. **I.** *s.* rociada, rociadura, aspersión; una pizca, un poco.—s. of rain, llovizna, cernidillo. **II.** *a.* de rociar, de riego.

sprint. **I.** *vn.* (dep.) apostar a correr, dar una carrera. **II.** *s.* corrida, carrera, cosetada.

sprinter [spríntœr], *s.* (dep.) el que corre velozmente.

sprit, *s.* (mar.) botavara.

sprite [spráit], *s.* duende, trasgo; hada.

spritsail [spritséil], *s.* (mar.) cebadera.

sprocket [spróket], *s.* diente de rueda de cadena.—s. gear, engranaje de rueda y cadena.—s. wheel, rueda dentada para cadena.

sprout [spráut]. **I.** *va.* hacer germinar o brotar; quitar los botones o vástagos. **II.** *vn.* (bot.) brotar o retoñar, echar botones o renuevos; crecer; ramificarse. **III.** *s.* (bot.) renuevo, retoño, grillo, serpollo, botón.—*pl.* bretones repolludos.

spruce [sprus]. **I.** *a.* garboso, apuesto, majo, pulido. **II.** *s.* (bot.) abeto, pícea.—s. beer, cerveza de abeto.—s. fir, (bot.) pinabete. **III.** *vn.* vestirse con esmero, ponerse majo.

sprucely [-li], *adv.* garbosamente.

spruceness [-nes], *s.* majeza, garbo.

sprue [spru], *s.* (fund.) mazarota; bebedero de molde.

sprung [sprung], *pret.* y *pp.* de TO SPRING.—s. mast, (mar.) palo rendido.

spry [sprái], *a.* vivo, listo, ágil, activo.

spryness [spráines], *s.* agilidad.

spud [spud], *s.* (agr.) laya, escarda; escoplo; (cir.) limpiaojos.

spue [spiú], *va.* y *vn.* = SPEW.

spume [spiúm]. **I.** *s.* espuma; espumarajo. **II.** *vn.* espumar, hacer espuma.

spumescent [spiumésent], *a.* espumescente.

spumous, spumy [spiúmus, -mi], *a.* espumoso, espumajoso, espumante.

spun [spun], *pret.* y *pp.* de TO SPIN.—s. yarn, (mar.) meollar.

spunge [spunv], *s.* esponja; (arti.) lanada.—*s.* y *v.* = SPONGE.

spunk [spunk], *s.* yesca; (fam.) corazón, genio (violento), coraje, valor; enojo.

spunky [spúnki], *a.* (fam.) vivo; valiente; enfadadizo, enojadizo.

spur [spœr]. **I.** *s.* espuela, acicate, aguijón, estímulo; excitación; corvejón, espolón del gallo; uña puntiaguda; pincho; (geog.) estribación, estribo; (arq.) riostra, contrafuerte, botarel, machón, puntal.—s. gear, rueda dentada; engranaje de ruedas dentadas (ll. t. s. gearing).—spurs of the beams, pernados de los baos.—spurs of the bitts, curvas de las bitas.—s. track, (f. c.) ramal corto.—s. wheel = s. GEAR.—on the s. of the moment, impulsivamente, sin pensarlo. **II.** *va.* y *vn.* espolear, picar con la espuela; incitar, estimular; calzar o ponerse las espuelas; apretar el paso.—to s. on, espolear, aguijar, estimular.

spurgall [spœrgol]. **I.** *va.* herir con la espuela. **II.** *s.* espoleadura.

spurge [spœry], *s.* (bot.) lechetrezna, titímalo, tártago.—s. laurel, lauréola.

spurious [spiúrius], *a.* espurio, (biol.) falso; (bot.) aparente.—spuriously [-li], *adv.* espuriamente.—spuriousness [-nes], *s.* falsedad, bastardía, calidad de espurio.

spurn [spœrn], *va.* y *vn.* despreciar, menospreciar; rechazar a puntapiés; cocear.

spurnwater [-uótœr], *s.* (mar.) guardaaguas.

spurred [spœrd], *a.* con espuelas; con espolones.—s. rye, centeno atizonado o afectado de cornezuelo.

spurrer [spœrœr], *s.* el que espolea.

spurrier [spœriœr], *s.* el que hace espuelas.

spurry [spœri], *s.* (bot.) espérgula.

spurt [spœrt]. **I.** *va.* y *vn.* arrojar o salir en chorro o chorros; espurriar; brotar, surgir; hacer un esfuerzo supremo. **II.** *s.* chorro; explosión de ira; esfuerzo supremo; rato, momento.

sputter [spútœr]. **I.** *va.* y *vn.* espurriar; chisporrotear; farfullar, barbotar. **II.** *s.* chisporroteo; chispeo de saliva; farfulla.—**sputterer** [-œr], *s.* escupidor, farfullador; el que chisporrotea saliva.

sputum [spiútŭm], *s.* (med.) esputo.

spy [spái]. **I.** *s.* espía.—**s. hole,** atisbadero. **II.** *va.* columbrar; espiar, observar; (con **out**) explorar, reconocer (un país).—**to s. out,** atisbar, divisar, columbrar. **III.** *vn.* espiar, atalayar; ser espía; meterse secretamente a averiguar.

spyboat [-bóut], *s.* barco explorador.

spyglass [-glǽs], *s.* anteojo de larga vista.

squab [scuób]. **I.** *a.* acabado de salir de la cáscara; implume; rechoncho o regordete. **II.** *s.* (orn.) pichón, pichoncillo; gordiflón; cojín, canapé, otomana. **III.** *adv.* de golpe y porrazo.

squabble [scuóbœl]. **I.** *va.* (impr.) empastelar. **II.** *vn.* reñir, disputar. **III.** *s.* pendencia, riña, disputa, contienda, trifulca.

squabbler [scuóblœr], *s.* pendenciero.

squad [scuod], *s.* (mil.) escuadra, patrulla, pelotón; partida.

squadrilla [scuódrilæ], *s.* (aer.) flotilla aérea.

squadron [scuódrŭn], *s.* (mar.) escuadra, armada, flota; (mil.) escuadrón; cuadro; soldados en formación; (aer.) = SQUADRILLA.

squalid [scuólid], *a.* escuálido.—**squalidness** [-nes], **squalidity** [scuolídití], *s.* = SQUALOR.

squall [scuól]. **I.** *va.* y *vn.* chillar, berrear. **II.** *v. ímpers.* haber borrasca. **III.** *s.* chillido, berrido; (mar.) racha, turbonada, chubasco.

squaller [scuólœr], *s.* chillador, chillón.

squally [scuóli], *a.* chubascoso; borrascoso.

squalor [scuólœr, scuéilœr], *s.* escualidez.

squama [scuéimæ], *s.* escama.—**squamaceous** [scuæméishŭs], **squamate** [scuéimet], *a.* escamoso, lamelar.—**squamation** [-méishŭn], *s.* carácter escamoso; disposición de las escamas.

squander [scuóndœr], *va.* y *vn.* malgastar, malrotar, despilfarrar, derrochar.—**squanderer** [-œr], *s.* derrochador, disipador, manirroto.

square [scuéær]. **I.** *a.* cuadrado; en cuadro (*two square feet,* dos pies cuadrados: *two feet square,* dos pies en cuadro); rectangular; a escuadra; perfecto, exacto, justo, cabal; íntegro, honrado, equitativo; (fam.) completo, abundante (*square meal,* comida completa); (com.) saldado, en paz; (mar.) en cruz; (mat.) elevado al cuadrado.—**s. bracket,** (impr.) paréntesis angular.—**s. dance,** contradanza, danza de figuras.—**s. deal, s. dealing,** buena fe, equidad, justicia, honradez.—**s. measure,** medida cuadrada o de superficie.—**s. plano,** piano de mesa.—**s. root,** (mat.) raíz cuadrada.—**s. rigged,** (mar.) aparejo de cruzamen.—**s. screw,** tornillo de filete cuadrado.—**s. timber,** madero escuadrado.—**to get s. with,** vengarse de, hacérselas pagar a. **II.** *s.* cuadrado; cuadro; (mat.) cuadrado, segunda potencia; plaza; (de pueblo o ciudad); cristal de ventana; casilla (de tablero de damas, etc.); (E. U.) manzana de casas; (dib.) escuadra, cartabón; (carp.) escuadra y proporción debida, orden; exactitud; honradez, equidad; (mil.) cuadro.—**on** (o **upon**) **the s.,** (fam.) honradamente, de buena fe; a escuadra.—**out of s.,** no en ángulo recto o a escuadra. **III.** *va.* cuadrar, formar en cuadro; escuadrar; (mat.) cuadrar, elevar al cuadrado; (geom.) reducir a un cuadrado equivalente; (b. a.) cuadricular; (carp.) cuadrar, escuadrar; (com.) saldar; pasar balance; ajustar, arreglar, justificar, conformar, poner de acuerdo; medir una superficie en metros, pies, etc. cuadrados; (mar.) bracear en cuadro. **IV.** *vn.* estar en ángulo recto; cuadrar, encajar, conformarse, ajustarse, convenir, concordarse, estar de acuerdo; (con **off**) tomar una actitud pugilística.

squared [scuéærd], *a.* cuadrado; escuadrado; (mat.) elevado al cuadrado; (dib.) cuadriculado (papel).—**s. stone,** mampuesto, piedra toscamente labrada y escuadrada.—**s. timber,** madera escuadrada.

squarely [-li], *adv.* en cuadro; perpendicularmente, a escuadra; honradamente, con toda equidad.

squareness [-nes], *a.* calidad de cuadrado; honradez, equidad, justicia.

squaring [-ing], *s.* cuadratura; escuadreo; escuadración; cuadriculación.—**s. shears,** cizallas de escuadrar.

squarrose, squarrous [scuéros o scuarrŭs], *a.* (biol.) áspero, escamoso.

squash [scuásh]. **I.** *s.* calabaza (apl. gen. a la de cuello corvo); cosa blanda o inmatura; pulpa; aplastamiento, despachurramiento.—**s. beetle, s. borer, s. bug,** nombres de insectos norteamericanos que atacan la calabaza.—**s. vine,** (bot.) cidracayote. **II.** *va.* aplastar, despachurrar.

squat [scuot]. **I.** *vn.* agacharse, agazaparse, sentarse en cuclillas; establecerse en un local sin derecho. **II.** *a.* agachado, puesto en cuclillas; rechoncho, cachigordete, rehecho. **III.** *s.* posición del que está en cuclillas.—**squatter** [-œr], *s.* advenedizo, intruso, colono usurpador.

squatty [-i], *a.* rechoncho, regordete.

squaw [scuó], *s.* india norteamericana.—**s. man,** hombre blanco casado con india.

squawk [scuoc]. **I.** *vn.* graznar. **II.** *s.* graznido.

squeak [scuíc]. **I.** *vn.* chirriar, rechinar; (fam.) delatar. **II.** *s.* chillido, chirrido.

squeal [scuíl]. **I.** *vn.* chillar, lanzar gritos agudos; (fam.) delatar. **II.** *s.* chilido, grito agudo.

squeamish [scuímish], *a.* delicado, escrupuloso, remilgado; asqueado.—**squeamishly** [-li], *adv.* remilgadamente, con asco.—**squeamishness** [-nes], *s.* remilgo, escrúpulo; asco, náusea.

squeegee [scuíyi], *va.* y *s.* = SQUILGEE.

squeeze [[scuís]. **I.** *va.* apretar, comprimir; estrechar; estrujar, exprimir, prensar, apachurrar; tupir, apretujar; acosar, agobiar; rebajar (jornales); (b. a.) recalcar.—**to s. in,** hacer entrar apretando.—**to s. out,** hacer salir, exprimir.—**to s. through,** forzar al través de.—**to s. to death,** (fam.) matar a apretones, apretar hasta matar. **II.** *vn.* pasar, entrar o salir apretando.—**to s. in,** meterse por lugar apretado o ponerse en sitio apretado.—**to s. through,** pasar apretadamente a través de, abrirse paso por. **II.** *s.* apretadura, apretón; facsímile recalcado de una moneda, etc.

squeezer [scuíscœr], *s.* exprimidera.

squelch [scuelch]. **I.** *va.* hacer callar, paralizar (fig.), aplastar (fig.), desconcertar; (con **out**) sofocar, derrotar, vencer. **II.** *vn.* ser vencido, desconcertado.—**squelcher** [-œr], *s.* cosa, persona o respuesta desconcertante.

squib [scuíb]. **I.** *s.* suelto o articulejo satírico; (piro.) buscapiés, carretilla. **II.** *va.* y *vn.* atacar con sátiras o pullas; soltar carretillas.

squid [scuíd], *s.* (ict.) calamar; cebo artificial.

squilgee [scuílyi]. **I.** *s.* rodillo o escobilla de goma para restregar y secar superficies mojadas. **II.** *va.* restregar con *squilgee.*

squill [scuil], *s.* (bot.) escila, albarrana; (ict.) esquila.

squinch [scuínch], *s.* (arq.) pechina.

squint [scuínt]. **I.** *s.* estrabismo; mirada bizca; mirada furtiva; tendencia indirecta. **II.** *va.* y *vn.* bizquear, mirar bizco; mirar de soslayo.—**squint(-eyed)** [(-áid], *a.* bizco, bisojo; avieso, torcido; ambiguo, obscuro.—**squinting** [-ing], *s.* (med.) estrabismo.

squire [scuáiœr]. **I.** *s.* escudero; (Ingl.) hacendado; (E. U.) alcalde, juez de paz.—**S. Brown,** señor Brown. *V.* ESQUIRE. **II.** *va.* acompañar.

squirm [scuœrm]. **I.** *vn.* retorcerse, serpear, serpentear; trepar; (con **out**) salir de un aprieto con trabajo. **II.** *s.* retorcimiento.

squirrel [scuérel], *s.* ardilla.—**s.-cage rotor,** (elec.) rotor de jaula.—**s.-cage winding,** arrollamiento de jaula o en cortocircuito.

squirt [scuœrt]. **I.** *va.* y *vn.* hacer salir o salir a chorros; esqurriar; jeringar. **II.** *s.* chorretada, chisguete, chorro; jeringazo.—**s. (gun),** jeringa.—**squirter** [-œr], *s.* el que jeringa.

St., *s.* abreviatura de **Saint,** San o Santo.

stab [stæb]. **I.** *va.* y *vn.* herir con arma blanca, dar de puñaladas. **II.** *s.* puñalada, estocada.

stabber [stǽbœr], *s.* heridor, apuñalador.

stability [stabíliti], *s.* estabilidad.
stabilize [stéibilais], *va.* estabilizar.—**stabilizer** [-láisœr], *s.* estabilizador.
stable [stéibœl]. **I.** *a.* estable. **II.** *s.* establo, caballeriza, cuadra; caballos de carrera de un particular. **III.** *va.* y *vn.* poner o estar colocado en establo.
stableboy [-bóy], **stableman** [-mæn], *s.* establero, mozo de caballos.
stableness [-nes], *s.* estabilidad.
stabling [-bling], *s.* estabulación; cabida de un establo.
staccato [stacáto], *a.* lacónico e incisivo; (mús.) staccato.
stack [stæc]. **I.** *s.* niara, rima o rimero, pila o hacina, montón; (mil.) pabellón de fusiles; cañón de chimenea; (fam.) copia, abundancia. **II.** *va.* hacinar, apilar, amontonar; poner las armas en pabellón.
stactometer [stæctómetœr], *s.* cuentagotas.
stadia [stéidiæ], *s. pl.* de STADIUM; (sing., top.) taquímetro, estadia.—**s. hairs** = s. WIRES.—**s. rod,** mira taquimétrica.—**s. surveying,** taquimetría. —**s. transit,** taquímetro.—**s. wires,** hilos taquimétricos.
stadiometer [-ómeter], *s.* estadiómetro, instrumento para medir líneas en un dibujo.
stadium [-diʊm], *s.* estadio; carrera (lugar para correr); grado de progreso o adelantamiento.
stadtholder [státjóldœr], *s.* estatúder.
staff [staf], *s.* (*pl.* STAVES o STAFFS) báculo, palo, cayado; apoyo, sostén, alivio, arrimo; palo, porra, garrote; vara, bastón de mando; percha, pértiga; vara de medir; jalón de mira; asta (de lanza, pica, bandera, etc.); (mil.) estado mayor, plana mayor; junta, cuerpo (*editorial staff*, cuerpo de redactores); (arq. y b. a.) cartón piedra; (mús.) pentagrama; (cir.) guía o sonda acanalada; (igl.) báculo pastoral.—**s. officer,** oficial de estado mayor.—**s. tree,** (bot.) alaterno.
staffwood [stáfud], *s.* madera para duelas.
stag [stæg], *s.* (zool.) ciervo, venado; (fam.) hombre, varón.—**s. beetle,** (ent.) ciervo volante.— **s. party,** (fam.) tertulia de hombres solos.
stage [stéiy]. **I.** *s.* (teat.) escenario, tablas; por extensión, teatro (arte y profesión); escena de acción, tablado, entarimado, plataforma, estrado; andamio; parada, descansadero, etapa, jornada; grado, estado; período (de una enfermedad); platina (de microscopio); (E. U.) diligencia, ómnibus; (arq.) escalón, paso de escalera; (mec.) grado (de una turbina de vapor, etc.).—**s. driver,** mayoral; cochero de ómnibus.—**s. forceps,** pinzas para microscopio.—**s. fright,** pánico oratorio, miedo de hablar en público.—**s. hand,** metesillas, tramoyista.—**s. manager,** (teat.) director de escena.—**s. micrometer,** micrómetro del portaobjetos.—**s. of growth,** grado de crecimiento.— **by short stages,** a pequeñas etapas, a cortas jornadas. **II.** *va.* (teat.) poner en escena; representar. **III.** *vn.* viajar en diligencia.
stagecoach [-cóuch], *s.* diligencia (vehículo).
stagecraft [-cræft], *s.* arte teatral; arte de escribir dramas o ponerlos en escena.
stager [stéyœr], *s.* caballo de diligencia.
stagger [stǽgœr]. **I.** *vn.* hacer eses, tambalear, bambolear; vacilar, titubear. **II.** *va.* causar vértigos o vahidos; asustar o azarar; hacer vacilar; hacer tambalear; disponer o arreglar (plantas, remaches, etc.) al tresbolillo; alternar; escalonar (escobillas en una dínamo, planos en un biplano). **III.** *s.* tambaleo, vacilación; (aer.) decalaje.
staggered [-d], *a.* al tresbolillo (remachado, plantas, etc.); escalonado, de planos escalonados (avión).—**s. wires,** (aer.) alambres entre los planos de un avión, paralelos al plano de simetría.
staggers [stǽgœrs], *s.* (vet.) vértigo de los caballos; vahido.
staghound [stégjáund], *s.* sabueso.
staging [stéiying], *s.* andamiaje; tráfico en diligencias y ómnibus.
Stagirite [stǽyirait], *s.* y *a.* estagirita.
stagnancy [stǽgnansi], *s.* estancación, estancamiento, paralización.—**stagnant** [-nant], *a.* estan-

cado.—**stagnate** [-net], *vn.* estancarse.—**stagnation** [-néishʊn], *s.* = STAGNANCY.
stagy [stéiyi], *a.* teatral.
staid [stéid], *a.* grave, serio, sosegado.
staid [stéid]. **I.** *pret.* y *pp.* de TO STAY. **II.** *a.* formal, sentado, juicioso.—**staidly** [-li], *adv.* juiciosamente.—**staidness** [-nes], *s.* juicio, seriedad.
stain [stéin]. **I.** *va.* y *vn.* manchar; colorar, teñir; descolorar; ensuciar; mancillar, desdorar; impregnar de materia colorante.—**stained glass,** vidrio de color. **II.** *s.* mancha, mácula; descoloramiento, descoloración; tinte, tintura; solución colorante.
stainer [stéinœr], *s.* pintor; tintorero.
stainless [stéinles], *a.* limpio; inmaculado.
stair [stéœr], *s.* escalón, peldaño.—*pl.* escalera.— **s. carpet,** alfombra de escalera.—**s. rod,** varilla para alfombra de escalera.
staircase [stéœrkéis], **stairway** [stéœruéi], *s.* escalera.
stake [stec]. **I.** *s.* estaca; piquete; (agr.) rodrigón; pira; (carr.) telero; tas, bigorneta; en los juegos, apuesta, posta o puesta; azar, riesgo; peligro, contingencia; premio (de contienda), (com.) interés, ganancia o pérdida contingente.—**s. boat,** bote anclado para marcar la dirección y distancias en las regatas.—**s. hedge,** cerca.—**at s.,** envuelto, comprometido, en peligro (*his honor was at stake*, su honor estaba comprometido, le iba en ello el honor). **II.** *va.* estacar; en los juegos, poner, apostar; aventurar, arriesgar, exponer.—**to s. all,** envidar el resto, aventurarlo todo.
stalactical [stalǽctical], **stalactitic** [stǽlæctític], *a.* estalactítico.
stalactite [stalǽctait], *s.* estalactita.
stalagmite [stalǽgmait], *s.* estalagmita.
stalagmitic [stǽlagmític], *a.* estalagmítico.
stalder [stóldœr], *s.* poíno.
stale [stéil]. **I.** *a.* añejo, viejo; rancio, pasado; gastado, anticuado.—**s. beer,** cerveza pasada.— **s. bread,** pan viejo.—**s. olive,** aceituna zapatera. —**s. wine,** vino picado. **II.** *va.* añejar, enranciar. **III.** *vn.* añejarse, enranciarse, picarse.
stalemate [stéilméit]. **I.** *s.* mate ahogado (en el ajedrez); estancación. **II.** *va.* dar mate ahogado a; estancar, paralizar.
staleness [stéilnes], *s.* rancidez; pasadez.
stalk [stok]. **I.** *va.* cazar al acecho. **II.** *vn.* andar con paso majestuoso, taconear; andar a hurtadillas.—**stalking-horse,** boezuelo para la caza; máscara, disfraz. **III.** *s.* (bot.) tallo, caña, agramiza, cabillo, pedúnculo, pecíolo; troncho de hortalizas; raspa de uva; pie de copa; paso majestuoso, taconeo.—**stalky** [stóki], *a.* tronchudo.
stall [stol]. **I.** *s.* pesebre, casilla de establo; puesto, parada, (Méx.) tenderete; tabanco; (teat.) luneta o butaca; (igl.) sitial de coro; (min.) galería, tajo de explotación.—**s.-fed,** cebado en establo.—**s.-feed,** *va.* cebar en establo. **II.** *va.* encerrar o meter en cuadra o establo; poner puestos o casillas; atascar, atollar; poner obstáculos. **III.** *vn.* estar atascado, atollado.
stallion [stǽliʊn], *s.* caballo padre, garañón.
stalwart [stóluart, stǽluart], *a.* fornido, forzudo, membrudo; (E. U. pol.) leal, fiel, firme.
stamen [stémen], *s.* (*pl.* STAMENS, rara vez STAMINA) (bot.) estambre.
stamina [stǽmina], *s.* nervio, fibra, vigor; sostén. —**staminal** [-al], *a.* estaminal; vital, esencial.
staminate [stǽminet], *a.* estaminífero.
stamineous [stamínius], *a.* estamíneo, estaminoso.
stammer [stǽmœr]. **I.** *va.* y *vn.* tartamudear; balbucear. **II.** *s.* tartamudeo; balbuceo.
stammerer [-œr], *s.* tartamudo, gago.
stamp [stæmp]. **I.** *va.* estampar; marcar, señalar; imprimir; estampillar; sellar; timbrar (papel, cartas); fijar el sello de correo; acuñar; patear, golpear con los pies; (min.) triturar, quebrantar, bocartear; apisonar; (fig.) marcar, infamar, estigmatizar.—**to s. out,** extirpar, suprimir. **II.** *vn.* patear, patalear, piafar. **III.** *s.* sello, estampilla (de correo); estampa, sigilación, impresión, marca; estampador, estampilla; cuño;

troquel; mano de mortero; (fig.) temple, **suerte**, clase; laya, calaña; (metal.) pisón, bocarte.—*pl.* **stamps**, timbres de impuesto; (fam.) dinero.—**s. act**, ley del timbre.—**s. duties**, derechos de papel sellado o del timbre.—**s. duty**, impuesto pagado en timbres puestos a ciertos artículos, timbres de contribución.—**s. mill**, molino de mineral, bocarte, molino de pisones.—**s. office**, oficina de timbres.

stamped [stæmpd], *a.* estampado; sellado.—**s. paper**, papel sellado.—**s. envelope**, sobre (cubierta) de sello estampado.—**s. weight**, peso marcado (por el contraste).

stampede [stæmpíd]. **I.** *va.* y *vn.* ahuyentar, espantar; huir con pavor; dispersarse en desorden; (pol.) obrar por común impulso, tomar de repente un acuerdo en una asamblea. **II.** *s.* estampida, desbocada, huída con terror pánico; tropel; determinación repentina y unánime.

stamper [stæmpœr], *s.* estampador; impresor; martinete de fragua; pilón, punzón de forja; bocarte, pisón; triturador de pólvora; mano de almirez.

stamping [-ing], *s.* timbrado, estampa, impresión, estampado; pataleo, pateo; trituración.—**s. machine**, estampador mecánico; máquina de perforar.—**s. mill**, bocarte, molino de pisones.

stanch. **I.** *va.* restañar; estancar. **II.** *a.* firme, fiel, adicto; constante; sano, fuerte, seguro.—**s. ship**, buque marinero. **III.** *s.* compuerta.

stanchion [stánshŭn], *s.* puntal, madrina, asnilla, pie derecho, montante, candelero.

stanchness [stánchnes], *s.* firmeza, constancia, lealtad.

stand [stænd], *va.* (*pret.* y *pp.* STOOD) poner derecho, colocar o poner de pie; resistir, hacer frente a; aguantar, sufrir, tolerar; someterse a, soportar, pasar por; importar, ser útil, ser de provecho; sostener, defender, conservar; (fam.) sufragar, pagar.—**to s. a chance**, o **a show**, tener probabilidad.—**to s. fire** (mil.) aguantar el fuego; (quím.) resistir al calor.—**to s. off**, tener a raya; contener; salir de.—**to s. on end**, poner de punta, asentar por un extremo.—**to s. one's ground**, resistir, defender su puesto o posición, mantenerse en su puesto.—**to s. the test**, pasar por la prueba, resistir la prueba.—**to s. treat**, (fam.) pagar la convidada.

stand, *vn.* estar; ponerse o estar de pie, tenerse derecho; sostenerse, resistir; quedarse; pararse, quedar suspenso; mantenerse, durar, perdurar; subsistir; tenerse, ponerse, estar en cierta postura; erguirse, levantarse, enderezarse; ocupar (buena o mala) posición, tener (buena o mala) reputación; poseer rectitud moral; estar situado, hallarse; persistir, perseverar; ser consecuente, acordar, convenir; quedar de acuerdo, quedar corrientes; navegar, correr, dirigirse, (*to stand on the same tack*, correr la misma bordada).—**to s. about**, rodear, cercar.—**to s. against**, resistir, hacer frente a.— **to s. alone**, estar solo; ser el único.—**to s. aloof (from)**, mantenerse apartado, retraerse (de).—**to s. aside**, hacerse a un lado, apartarse; estarse alejado.—**to s. back**, retroceder; quedarse atrás. —**to s. by**, sostener, favorecer,‖ ayudar, auxiliar; atenerse a, sostenerse en; someterse a; estar de mirón; estar cerca, quedarse allí; mantenerse listo. —**to s. far off**, mantenerse lejos.—**to s. fast**, no cejar o ceder.—**to s. for**, estar por, estar en lugar de, representar; significar, querer decir; tolerar, permitir; aprobar, favorecer; solicitar, pretender, presentarse como candidato u opositor; sostener, defender; apadrinar; mantener o sostener (una opinión); dirigirse o llevar rumbo a o hacia.— **to s. forth**, adelantarse, avanzar; presentarse.— **to s. from under**, alejarse de alguna cosa que está por caer.—**to s. in**, costar, montar, importar; estar en; sentir.—**to s. in bold relief**, resaltar vigorosamente.—**to s. in good stead**, servir, ser útil.—**to s. (one) in hand**, atañer, importar (a uno).—**to s. in need**, tener necesidad, necesitar. —**to s. in one's light**, taparle a uno la luz.—**to s. in with**, juntarse o estar aliado con.—**to s. in shore**, (mar.) correr hacia la tierra.—**to s. in the way**, cerrar el paso; estorbar, ser un obstáculo.—**to s. off**, mantenerse a distancia, apartarse; negar, denegar; desconvenir; no acer-

carse, mantenerse apartado.—**to s. off and on**, (mar.) bordear, barloventear.—**to s. on** o **upon**, estar colocado sobre, estar en; adherirse a; interesar, concernir, tocar, pertenecer; estimar, valuar; fijarse en; picarse de, tener su orgullo en; insistir en, gastar (ceremonia, etc.).—**to s. on end**, erizarse; mantenerse derecho; ponerse de punta.—**to s. on one's own feet**, o **legs**, valerse a sí mismo.— **to s. on tiptoe**, ponerse o estar de puntillas.—**to s. out**, mantenerse firme; resistir; separarse, apartarse; desconvenir; denegar; resalir, resaltar, destacarse, estar en relieve.—**to s. out of the way**, hacerse o estar a un lado, no estorbar.—**to s. out to sea**, llevar la proa al mar.—**to s. over**, aplazar; plantarse al lado de para vigilar o apurar.—**to s. pat**, (pol., fam.) plantarse, oponerse inflexiblemente a todo cambio, marcar el paso (fig.).—**to s. still**, no moverse; estarse quieto; estancarse.— **to s. to**, mantenerse al lado de, no abandonar; seguir usando o manejando.—**to s. together**, mantenerse unidos; mancomunarse.—**to s. to one's guns**, seguir haciendo fuego; mantenerse firme, no cejar.—**to s. to reason**, ser lógico; ser justo.—**to s. under**, sufrir, sostener; estar bajo.— **to s. up**, levantarse, alzarse; ponerse en pie.—**to s. up for**, defender, sostener, apoyar; personarse por, sacar la cara por.—**to s. up to**, cumplir con; hacer resueltamente frente a.—**to s. upon an end** =TO S. ON END.—**to s. upon ceremony**, gastar ceremonia, ser cumplimentero.—**to s. with**, convenirse; estar conforme con; disputar; irlas con.

stand, *s.* puesto, sitio, lugar, posición, situación, estación; tarima, estrado, plataforma; tribuna (de espectadores); mostrador, puesto en un mercado; velador, mesita, estante, pie, pedestal, alto; término; inactividad, estancamiento; atascamiento; oposición, resistencia; (mil.) armamento, equipo completo; (bot.) herbaje.

standard [stándard]. **I.** *s.* norma, tipo, pauta, medida, patrón, modelo, dechado, ley, marco, regla fija; (joy.) ley del oro o la plata; (mec.) soporte, poste, pilar, punta, madrina, pie, árbol; bandera, estandarte, pendón; (mar.) curva capuchina. **II.** *a.* normal, de ley; patrón (metro, yarda, libra, etc.); clásico.—**s. author**, autor clásico.—**s. bearer**, portaestandarte, portaguión. —**s. candle**, bujía normal.—**s. clock**, reloj magistral.—**s. gauge**, marca, medida o marco que sirve de norma; (f. c.) entrevía normal, anchura normal (56½ pulgadas).—**s. price**, precio corriente o regular.—**s. scale**, escala normal.—**s. solution**, (quím.) solución valorada.—**s. time**, tiempo normal; hora normal.—**s. weight**, peso legal, peso normal.—**s. work**, obra clásica.

standardize [-aiš], *va.* uniformar, normalizar.— **standardization** [-iséshŭn], uniformación, normalización; producción en serie.—**standardized production**, producción en serie.

stand-by [stǽnd-bai], *s.* adherente fiel; cosa o persona en que se puede confiar o con que se puede contar.

standing [-ing]. **I.** *a.* derecho o en pie; levantado, de pie; erecto; con pedestal, con pie; permanente, fijo, establecido; duradero, estable, constante; estancado, encharcado; (for.) vigente.—**s. army**, ejército permanente.—**s. collar**, cuello recto.—**s. committee**, comisión permanente.—**s. jib**, contrafoque.—**s. mast** = LOWER MAST.—**s. place**, **s. room**, sitio para estar de pie.—**s. timber**, árboles en pie.—**s. water**, agua estancada. **II.** *s.* posición, reputación, crédito; puesto, sitio, paraje; duración, antigüedad; alto, parada.

standish [-ish], *s.* escribanía.

standpatter [stándpétœr], *s.* (fam., pol.) el que se opone inflexiblemente a cambios. (*V.* STAND PAT *en* STAND, *vn.*).—**standpattism** [-išm]. *s.* oposición a cambio de política.

standpipe [-páip], *s.* columna o tubo vertical de depósito o de alimentación (de agua).

standpoint [-póint], *s.* punto de vista.

standstill [-stil], *s.* parada, detención; alto; pausa, descanso.

stand-up [-ŭp], *a.* recto, derecho, vertical; que se hace u ocupa de pie.

stanhope [stǽnjoup], *s.* cabriolé ligero.

stannary [stǽnari], *s.* mina de estaño.

stannic [stǽnic], *a.* estánnico.

stanniferous [stænífœrus], *a.* estannífero.

stanza [stǽnša], *s.* (poét.) estancia, estrofa.

stapes [stéipiš], *s.* (anat.) estribo.

staphylococcus [stǽfilocócus], (biol.) estafilococo.

staple [stéipœl]. **I.** *s.* artículo o producto principal; renglón de comercio; elemento o asunto principal; fibra, hebra o filamento; materia prima, materia bruta; emporio de comercio, mercado; (mec.) hembra de cerrojo, picolete, grapa, aro, argolla, armella; (mar.) cibica, grampa. **II.** *a.* (com.) corriente, de consumo o uso general; principal, prominente; establecido, admitido, reconocido; vendible.—**s. commodities**, artículos corrientes de consumo.—**s. ring**, argolla con espiga. **III.** *va.* asegurar con armellas; clasificar hebras textiles según su longitud.

stapler [stéiplœr], *s.* clasificador de lanas.

star [star]. **I.** *s.* estrella (astro, figura, hado, actor, mancha en la frente de un animal); cosa o persona principal; (impr.) asterisco; mancha brillante en una superficie metálica.—*s.* **apple**, (bot.) caimito.—**S. Chamber**, (Ingl.) antiguo tribunal criminal.—**s.-connected**, (elec.) con conexión de estrella.—**s. connection**, (elec.) conexión de estrella.—**s. contact**, (elec.) contacto de estrella.—**S. of Bethlehem**, (bot.) leche de gallina.—**s. polygon**, polígono estrellado.—**s.-shaped**, estelar.—**s.-spangled**, estrellado, tachonado de estrellas.—**s.-spangled banner**, bandera estrellada (nombre dado en los E. U. a la bandera nacional y a un himno patriótico).—**s. switch**, (elec.) estrella de interrupción, interruptor de estrella.—**s. wheel**, rueda catalina (de reloj).—**the stars and stripes**, las estrellas y listas (nombre de la bandera de los E. U.). **II.** *va.* adornar con estrellas; marcar con asterisco; dividir en líneas divergentes; (teat.) introducir como estrella. **III.** *vn.* ser estrella (de teatro); figurar como estrella o persona sobresaliente.

starboard [stárbord]. **I.** *s.* (mar.) estribor.—**s. side**, banda de estribor.—**s. watch**, guardia de estribor. **II.** *a.* y *adv.* a estribor.

starch [starch]. **I.** *s.* almidón, fécula; (fig.) entereza; rigidez, entonación. **II.** *va.* almidonar, atiesar.

starched [starcht], *a.* almidonado; tieso, serio, entonado.—**starcher** [-œr], *s.* almidonador.—**starchly** [-li], *adv.* almidonadamente, tiesamente.—**starchmaker** [-méikœr], *s.* almidonero.

starch(ed)ness [stárch(ed)nes], *s.* almidonamiento; tesura, gravedad.

starchy [stárchi], *a.* almidonado; tieso, entonado; de almidón; (med.) feculoso.

stare [stéœr]. **I.** *va.* clavar o fijar la vista en o a; encarar con; mirar de hito en hito o descaradamente.—**to s. one in the face**, dar en cara; estar cerca o a la vista; ser claro. **II.** *vn.* abrir grandes ojos; mirar con fijeza, asombro o insolencia; saltar a la vista; ser muy vivo o chillón (un color); erizarse (el pelo). **III.** *s.* mirada fija o de hito en hito; encaro.

starer [stéœrœr], *s.* el que mira fijamente.

starfish [stárfiš], *s.* estrella de mar.

stargazer [stárguéišœr], *s.* astrónomo; astrólogo.—**stargazing** [-šing], *s.* observación de las estrellas; distracción de ánimo; absorción en ideas quiméricas.

staring [stéœring], *a.* que mira fijamente; llamativo.—**s. colors**, colores llamativos, vivos, chillones.

stark. I. *a.* tieso, rígido; muerto; (fig.) inflexible, severo; completo, cabal; puro.—**s. and stiff**, rígido, muerto.—**s. madness**, locura completa.—**s. nonsense**, pura tontería. **II.** *adv.* completamente, enteramente.—**s. mad**, rematadamente loco.—**s. naked**, completamente desnudo o en cueros.

starkly [stárcli], *adv.* tiesamente, totalmente.

starless [stárles], *a.* sin estrellas.

starlight [stárláit]. **I.** *s.* luz de las estrellas. **II.** *a.* estrellado.—**s. night**, noche estrellada.

starlike [stárlaik], *a.* estrellado; brillante, radiante, rutilante.

starling [stárling], *s.* (orn.) estornino; estacada de protección.

starlit [stárlit], *a.* iluminado por las estrellas.

starred [stard], *a.* estrellado; afortunado.

starriness [stárines], *s.* abundancia de estrellas.

starry [stári], *a.* estrellado; centelleante, rutilante; estelífero, astrífero; sideral.

starwort [stárucœrt], *s.* (bot.) argamula.

start [start], *va.* principiar, comenzar; poner en marcha o en movimiento, dar impulso, hacer mover, andar o funcionar; (mec.) hacer arrancar; poner en marcha; levantar (la caza); dar la señal de partida; aflojar, dislocar; sacar un líquido de.—**to s. a train**, (f. c.) dar la señal de salida; poner el tren en marcha.—**to s. wine**, trasegar el vino.

start, *vn.* comenzar; partir, salir; arrancar (una máquina); sobresaltarse, asustarse; provenir, proceder, derivar; aflojarse; descoyuntarse; alabearse, combarse (como la madera).—**to s. aside**, echarse a un lado, ladearse.—**to s. after**, salir tras o en busca de; seguir a.—**to s. back**, dar un respingo; emprender el viaje de regreso.—**to s. for**, ponerse en camino hacia; presentarse como candidato para.—**to s. off**, partir, ponerse en marcha.—**to s. out**, principiar a.—**to s. up**, levantarse precipitadamente; salir de repente; ponerse en movimiento, empezar a funcionar, arrancar.

start, *s.* principio, comienzo; salida, partida; arranque (de una máquina); sobresalto, susto; respingo; ímpetu, arranque, pronto; estampida; ventaja, delantera; grieta, raja, abrimiento.—**by starts**, a saltos, por botes.—**by fits and starts**, a saltos y corcovos; a ratos.—**upon the s.**, al primer paso, al principio.

starter [stártœr], *s.* iniciador, arrancador, ojeador; principio, comienzo; cosa con que se principia; (m. v.) palanca de marcha; (aut.) arranque, mecanismo de arranque.

starting [-ing]. **I.** *s.* principio, comienzo; (acción de) comenzar, poner en marcha, etc. (V. START, *va.*); (aer.) lanzamiento. **II.** *a.* que inicia o principia; que pone en movimiento; de salida, de partida; (mec.) de puesta en marcha, de arranque; (aer.) de lanzamiento.—**s. course**, (aer.) pista de lanzamiento.—**s. crank**, (aut.) manubrio o manivela de arranque.—**s. engine**, máquina pequeña que mueve las partes de otra mayor que no está en acción regular, como para reparaciones, etc.—**s. handle** = S. CRANK.—**s. place**, lugar o punto de partida.—**s. point**, punto de partida.—**s. post**, poste de partida (en las carreras).—**s. run** = S. COURSE.

startle [stártœl], *va.* espantar, asustar, dar un susto; sobrecoger; alarmar.

starvation [starvéšhun], **I.** *a.* que causa hambre o inanición. **II.** *s.* hambre, inanición.

starve [starv]. **I.** *vn.* morir de hambre; hallarse en la inopia; (Ingl.) morir de frío. **II.** *va.* matar de hambre, hambrear; (Ingl.) hacer morir de frío; helar.—**to s. one's self**, dejarse morir de hambre.

starveling [-ling]. **I.** *s.* animal extenuado por el hambre. **II.** *a.* hambriento, muerto de hambre, famélico.

state [stéit]. **I.** *s.* estado, situación, condición; (pol.) estado; fausto, pompa, ceremonia; majestad; gobierno civil, en contraposición al eclesiástico.—**s.'s evidence**, testimonio aducido en una causa criminal; cómplice que declara por evitar el castigo.—**States General**, estados generales.—**s.'s rights, states' rights** = S. RIGHTS.—**in a s. of**, o to, en estado de.—**in S.**, con gran pompa, de gran ceremonia.—**the States**, los Estados Unidos. **II.** *a.* de estado; del estado; político, público; de lujo; de gala; perteneciente a los estados o a cada estado (de una república).—**s. affairs**, negocios o asuntos públicos o de estado.—**S. Department**, (E. U.) Ministerio de Estado.—**S. house**, (E. U.) edificio del Estado.—**S. paper**, documento de estado; pliego, documento o tratado político.—**S. prison**, penitenciaría del estado.—**s. rights**, derechos de los estados, soveranía de los estados. **III.** *va.* y *vn.* decir, expresar, declarar, afirmar; exponer, manifestar; enunciar, formular (un principio, ley, etc.); (mat., lóg.) enunciar, plantear.

statecraft [-craft], *s.* política, arte de gobernar.
stated [-ed], *a.* establecido, regular, fijo, periódico.
statehouse [-jáus], *s.* = STATE HOUSE. *V.* STATE *a.*
stateliness [-lines], *s.* grandeza, majestad, dignidad, pompa.
stately [-li], *a.* augusto, sublime, majestuoso, imponente, soberbio.
statement [stéitmœnt], *s.* declaración, exposición, presentación; manifestación; cuenta; relato, memoria, informe; enunciado (de problema, ley, etc.); proposición; (com.) estado de cuenta.
stater [-œr], *s.* moneda griega.
stateroom [-rum], *s.* (mar.) camarote; (f. c.) compartimiento, cámarote; salón de recepción de un palacio; pañol.
statesman [steitsman], *s.* estadista, hombre de Estado.—**statesmanlike** [-laik], *a.* de una manera propia de un estadista, como de estadista.
statesmanship [-ship], *s.* calidad de estadista; habilidad de estadista.
stateswoman [-úman], *s.* mujer de estado.
static [stǽtic], *s.* estática; (rad.) perturbación eléctrica atmosférica.
static(al [stǽtic(al], *a.* estático.
statics [stǽtics], *s.* estática.
station [stéshun]. **I.** *s.* estación (de f. c., de top.); sitio, situación, puesto; condición o posición social; (mar.) apostadero; (mil.) puesto militar, (igl.) estación.—**s. house**, cuartelillo de la policía; (f. c.) estación o paradero; caseta de salvamento en la costa. **II.** *va.* apostar, colocar, situar, alojar.
stationary [-eri], *a.* estacionario, estacional, estantío, fijo.—**s. engine**, máquina fija.
stationer [-œr], *s.* papelero.
stationery [-eri], *s.* papelería, efectos de escritorio.—**s. expenses**, gastos de escritorio.
statist [stéitist], *s.* estadístico.
statistic(al [statístic(al], *a.* estadístico.
statistician [stætistíshan], *s.* estadístico.
statistics [statístics], *s.* estadística; datos estadísticos.
statuary [stǽtiueri], *s.* estatuaria; estatuario, escultor.
statue [stǽtyu], *s.* estatua, imagen.
statuesque [stǽtyuésk], *a.* escultural.
statuette [stǽtyuét], *s.* figurilla.
stature [stǽtyur], *s.* estatura.
status [stéitus], *s.* estado legal; posición relativa.—**s. quo**, **s. in quo**, o **s. quo ante**, statu quo.
statute [stǽtyut], *s.* estatuto, ley, ordenanza, decreto, reglamento.—**s. law**, derecho escrito.—**s. mile**, milla ordinaria o terrestre (como 1609 m.), a distinción de la marina.
statutory [stǽtyutori], *a.* estatuído, establecido por la ley.
staunch [stanch], = STANCH.
stave [stéiv]. **I.** *va.* (*pret.* STAVED o STOVE) romper las duelas; abrir boquete, desfondar; quebrantar, destrozar; (ton.) poner duelas; (con **off**) rechazar, parar, detener, evitar; retardar, diferir.—**to s. and tail**, separar a dos que riñen; impedir. **II.** *vn.* desfondarse, romperse, hacerse pedazos.—**III.** *s.* duela de barril; ladera de un pozo; (mús.) pentagrama; (poét.) estrofa.—**staves and heading**, duelas y fondos.
staves [stéivs], *s. pl. reg.* de **stave**; [stavs] *pl. irreg.* de **staff**.
stavesacre [stéivsǽikœr], *s.* (bot.) estafisagra.
stay [stéi]. **I.** *va.* (*pret.* y *pp.* STAYED o STAID) parar, detener, impedir, poner freno; sostener, apoyar, reforzar; aplazar.—**to s. the stomach**, tomar un bocado. **II.** *vn.* quedarse, permanecer; estarse quieto; parar o pararse; tardar, detenerse; hospedarse.—**to s. away**, no volver.—**to s. in**, quedarse en casa, no salir.—**to s. out**, quedarse fuera, no entrar.—**to s. up**, velar, no acostarse. **III.** *s.* estancia, residencia; suspensión, espera, parada, detención; cesación temporal de un procedimiento judicial; freno, impedimento, obstáculo; refuerzo; sostén, soporte,

apoyo; puntal, entibo; (mec.) codal, contrete; atesador, fiador; (arq.) arbotante, apeo, estribo; tentemozo; ballena de corsé; (mar.) estay, nervio; estabilidad, fijeza; perseverancia, persistencia; inacción.—*pl.* corsé, cotilla. **IV.** *a.* de refuerzo, de sostén.—**s. bar**, montante de ventana.—**s. bolt** = STAYBOLT.—**s. rod**, tirante.—**s. tackle**, candeletón, estrinque.
stay-at-home [-at jóum], *s.* persona casera; persona que no sale a veranear; el que se está en su casa (a veces por cobardía, como en la guerra).
staybolt [-bóult], *s.* virotillo roscado, tornillo de separación y refuerzo.
staysail [-séil], *s.* vela de estay.
stead [sted], *s.* (precedido de **in**) lugar, sitio; las veces de; auxilio, ayuda.—**in his s.**, en su lugar.—**in s. of**, en lugar de, en vez de.
ste(a)dfast [stédfast], *a.* constante, inmutable; resuelto, determinado.—**steadfastly** [-li], *adv.* con constancia, con resolución.—**steadfastness** [-nes], *s.* inmutabilidad, constancia.
steadily [stédili], *adv.* constantemente; con constancia.
steadiness [-nes], *s.* estabilidad, firmeza; entereza, constancia.
steady [stédi]. **I.** *a.* firme, fijo, seguro, estable; juicioso, formal, asentado, constante, uniforme, continuo.—**s. flow**, flujo o corriente uniforme.—**s. load** = DEAD LOAD.—**s. pin**, clavija de fijación (de una polea). **II.** *va.* reforzar; hacer firme, impedir el movimiento de; calmar; fortalecer.
steak [stéik], *s.* (coc.) tajada para asar; biftec.
steal [stíl]. **I.** *va.* y *vn.* (*pret.* STOLE: *pp.* STOLEN) hurtar, robar; introducirse clandestinamente, pasar furtivamente, a hurtadillas; colarse, escabullirse, escapar sin ser visto.—**to s. along**, pasar en silencio, deslizarse sin ruido.—**to s. a march on**, ganar por la mano, sorprender.—**to s. away**, marcharse a hurtadillas; escabullirse.—**to s. down, forth, in, into**, descender, salir, penetrar furtivamente.—**to s. off** = TO S. AWAY.—**to s. over**, ganar insensiblemente.—**to s. up**, subir a ocultas.—**to s. upon**, aproximarse sin ruido a; sorprender.—**thou shalt not s.**, no hurtarás (en los mandamientos se prefiere en español la forma "no hurtar"). **II.** *s.* (fam.) hurto, robo.
stealing [stíling], *s.* hurto, robo.
stealingly [-li], *adv.* furtivamente, ocultamente, secretamente.
stealth [stelz], *s.* recato, cautela, reserva.—**by s.**, a hurtadillas, a escondidas.—**stealthily** [-ili], *adv.* clandestinamente.—**stealthy** [-i], *a.* furtivo, escondido, clandestino.
steam [stim]. **I.** *s.* vapor; vaho. **II.** *a.* de vapor; para vapor; por vapor.—**s. boiler**, caldera de vapor.—**s. chest**, caja o cámara de vapor.—**s. dome**, (m. v.) cúpula o cámara de distribución.—**s. drier** = S. TRAP.—**s. engine**, máquina de vapor.—**s. fitter**, montador de calderas y cañerías de vapor.—**s. ga(u)ge**, manómetro.—**s. hammer**, martinete de vapor.—**s. heat, s. heating**, calefacción por vapor.—**s. jacket**, camisa de vapor.—**s. pipe**, tubo o tubería de vapor.—**s. roller**, rodillo de vapor; (fam.) opinión, dictadura (de un partido, comité, etc.).—**s. port**, (m. v.) lumbrera de admisión.—**s. tight**, a prueba de vapor, hermético.—**s. trap**, purgador de agua de condensación.—**with all s. on**, a todo vapor. **III.** *va.* saturar de o limpiar con vapor; secar (ladrillos o adobes). **IV.** *vn.* generar vapor; emitir vaho o vapor; navegar o funcionar por vapor; evaporarse.
steamboat [stímbóut], *s.* buque de vapor (especialmente vapor de río).
steamer [stímœr], *s.* buque de vapor; bomba de vapor para incendios; marmita al vacío.
steamship [stímship], *s.* buque de vapor.
stearate [-et], *s.* estearato.
stearic [stiǽric], *a.* esteárico.
stearin [stíarin], *s.* (quím.) estearina.
steatite [stíatait], *s.* esteatita.
steed [stíd], *s.* caballo de regalo; corcel.
steel [stíl]. **I.** *s.* acero; arma blanca, espada, afilón, chaira; eslabón. **II.** *a.* de acero, acerino, acerado; duro; insensible.—**s. bronze**, bronce Uchatius (92% cobre, 8% estaño).—**s. clad**, cubierto o revestido de acero, acorazado.—**s. engrav-**

ing, grabado en acero.—s. wool, limaduras finas de acero. III. va. acerar, cubrir o armar de acero; acorazar; fortalecer; hacer insensible.

steeliness [stílines], s. dureza de acero.

steelworks [-stíluœrcs], s. fundición (fábrica) de acero.

steely [stíli], a. acerado, acerino, de acero; fuerte, inflexible, firme, duro.

steelyard [stílyard], s. romana.

steep [stíp]. I. a. empinado, pendiente; (fam.) excesivo, exorbitante. II. s. precipicio, despeñadero, derrumbadero. III. va. empapar, impregnar, remojar, macerar; poner en infusión; enriar.

steeper [stípœr], s. remojadero, pelambrera.

steeping [stíping], s. remojo, maceración.—s. trough, tub, o vat, cuba de remojar.

steeple [stípœl], s. espira, aguja, campanario.

steeplechase [-chéis], s. (dep.) carrera de obstáculos.

steepness [stípnes], s. calidad de empinado o pendiente; inclinación.

steepy [stípi], a. (poét.) enriscado.

steer [stíœr]. I. s. novillo, novillejo; buey. II. va. guiar, dirigir, conducir. III. vn. navegar, timonear; brujulear; gobernarse, conducirse, dirigirse; obedecer al timón.

steerage [stírey], s. (mar.) proa, rancho de la gente; entrepuente, alojamiento; gobierno, dirección.—s. passenger, pasajero de proa.

steerageway [-uéi], s. estela, surco de buque.

steering [stíœring]. I. s. dirección, gobierno (de buque, automóvil). II. a. de timonear; de dirección o gobierno.—s. column, (aut.) columna de dirección.—s. gear, (mecanismo de) dirección.—s. knuckle, (aut.) muñón de dirección.—s. wheel, (mar.) rueda del timón; (aut.) volante de dirección.

steersman [stíœrsman], s. (mar.) piloto, timonel, timonero.

steeve, steeving [stíving], s. (mar.) elevación angular del bauprés; grúa.

stein [stáin], s. pichel alemán para cerveza.

stellar [stélar], a. astral, estelar.

stellate [stélet], a. estrellado.

stelliferous [stclífœrus], a. estelífero.

stelliform [stéliform], a. estrellado.

stellular [stélular], a. estrellado; estelulado.

stellionate [stéliunet], s. (for.) estelonato.

stem. I. s. (bot.) tallo, tronco, vástago; pedúnculo; (mec. y carp.) vástago, caña, espiga, cabillo; pie (de copa); cañón de pluma; (gram.) raíz; rabo o rabito de una nota de música; (mar.) roda, tajamar, banque.—s. winder, reloj de remontoir.—s.-winding, de remontoir.—from s. to stern, de proa a popa. II. va. ir contra, hacer frente a, oponerse a, detener; embestir con la proa; represar, contener; tapar o enlodar (una junta); quitar los pedúnculos; desgranar (uvas, pasas); poner pedúnculos postizos (para hacer ramilletes).—to s. the tide, rendir la marea.

stemless [stémles], a. (bot.) acaule.

stempel, stemple [stémpœl], s. estemple, montante, asnado; travesaño.

stemson [stémsun], s. (mar.) contrabranque, contrarroda, sobrerroda.

stench, s. hedor, hediondez.

stencil [sténsil]. I. va. estarcir. II. s. patrón para estarcir, estarcidor; estarcido, marca.

stenciler [-œr], s. estarcidor.

stenograph [sténograf], s. escritura taquigráfica, maquinita para taquigrafiar.

stenographer [sténógrafœr], s. taquígrafo, estenógrafo.

stenographic(al [sténográfic, -al], taquigráfico, estenográfico.

stenography [sténógrafi], s. taquigrafía, estenografía.

stenosis [stenósis], s. (med.) estenosis.

stentor [sténtœr], s. estentor; persona de voz muy fuerte.

stentorian [stentórian], a. estentóreo.

step [step]. I. va. (pret. y pp. STEPPED O STEPT) poner, sentar, plantar (el pie); (con off) medir a

pasos); hacer dientes (en llaves); plantar (un mástil); (gen. con down) reducir, disminuir; escalonar; hacer escaleras en.—to s. down, (elec.) reducir (la tensión de una corriente; de donde.—s.-down transformer, transformador de reducción).—to s. up, elevar (la tensión de una corriente; de donde s.-up transformer, transformador elevador). II. vn. dar un paso; pisar, andar, caminar.—to s. after, seguir o ir detrás.—to s. aside, apartarse, hacerse a un lado.—to s. back, retroceder, volver atrás.—to s. down, bajar, descender.—to s. forth, avanzar.—to s. in, entrar.—to s. on, poner el pie sobre, pisar; andar sobre.—t. s. out, salir; apearse.—to s. over, atravesar.—to s. short, (mil.) acortar el paso.—to s. up, subir. III. s. paso; escalón; grada, peldaño (de escalera); barrote (de escalera de mano); estribo; umbral; grado; pisada, huella; medida, diligencia; comportamiento; (mús.) intervalo; pedestal de máquina; quicio de eje vertical; diente de una llave; (mar.) carlinga.—pl. medios, medidas, pasos, diligencias, gestiones; gradería, escalinata.—s. box, (mec.) rangua.—s. by s., paso a paso; punto por punto.—s. cure, vulcanización por presión creciente.—in s., de acorde; a compás; llevando el paso; (elec.) en fase.—out of s., desacuerdo; no llevando el paso; (elec.) in discordancia de fase.

stepbrother [-brótœr], s. medio hermano, o hermanastro.—stepchild [-cháild], s. hijastro, entenado.—stepdaughter [-dótœr], s. hijastra, entenada.—stepfather [-fáœr], s. padrastro.

stephanite [stéfanait], s. (min.) negrillo.

stepladder [-lédœr], s. escalera de mano.

stepmother [-múdœr], s. madrastra.—stepsister [-sístœr], s. media hermana, hermanastra.

steppe [step], s. estepa, llanura.

stepped [stept], a. escalonado.

stepping-stone [stéping-stóun], s. estriberón; piedra para apoyar el pie; escalón.

stercoraceous [stercoréshus], a. estercolizo.

stere [stíœr o stéœr], s. estéreo.

stereobate [stéreobet], s. (arq.) estereóbato.

stereographic(al [stereográfic(al], a. estereográfico.

stereography [stereógrafi], s. estereografía.

stereometer [stereómetœr], s. estereómetro.

stereometry [stereómetri], s. estereometría.

stereopticon [stereópticon], s. estereóptico, linterna mágica.

stereoscope [stéreoscoup], s. estereoscopio.

stereoscopic [stereoscópic], a. estereoscópico.

stereotomy [stereótomi], s. estereotomía.

stereotype [stéreotaip]. I. va. estereotipar. II. s. estereotipo, clisé.—s. plate, plancha estereotípica, clisé.—s. press, prensa o molde de estereotipar.

stereotyper [-táipœr], s. estereotipador.

stereotypic [-típic], a. estereotípico.

stereotyping [-táiping], s. estereotipia.

stereotypography [-taipógrafi], s. estereotipia.

steric [stéric], a. relativo al espacio.

sterile [stéril], a. estéril.—sterility [sterlíti], s. esterilidad.—sterilization [sterlíséishun], s. esterilización.—sterilize [-laís], va. y vn. (leng. ord. y med.) esterilizar.—sterilizer [-láísœr], s. esterilizador.

sterling [stœrling], a. esterlina; genuino, puro, verdadero.—s. silver, plata fina (de 0,925).

stern [stœrn]. I. a. austero, duro, torvo, severo; firme, decidido. II. s. (mar.) popa; (fam.) rabo, cola.—s. board, ciaboga, retroceso.—s. chase, caza en que la nave que persigue marcha en la estela de la otra.—s. chaser, guardatimón.—s.-fast, codera; tangidera.—s. frame, escudo, peto de popa.—s. port, porta de popa.—s. post=STERNPOST.—s. sheets, cámara de un bote.—s. timbers, gambotas de popa.—s.-wheeler, bote de rueda trasera, bote de vapor que tiene a popa una rueda de paletas.

sternly [-li], adv. severamente.

sternmost [-moust], a. popel.

sternness [-nes], s. severidad, rigor.

sternpost [-póust], s. (mar.) codaste, estambor; (aer.) codaste.

sternson [-sun], s. talón de quilla.

sternum [stǽrnʊm], *s.* (anat.) esternón.

sternutation [stǽrnutéishʊn], *s.* estornudo.

sternutatory [stǽrnútatori], *s.* estornutatorio.

sternway [stérnuéi], *s.* reculada, cía, retroceso.

stertor [stǽrtor], *s.* estertor.

stertorous [stǽrtœrus], *a.* estertoroso.

stethograph [stézograf], *s.* neumatógrafo.

stethoscope [stézoscoup], *s.* estetóscopo.

stethoscopic [stézoscópic], *a.* estetoscópico.

stethoscopy [stezóscopi], *s.* estetoscopia.

stevedore [stívedóœr], *s.* estibador.

stew [stiú]. **I.** *va.* y *vn.* (coc.) estofar. **II.** *s.* estofado, guisado; (fam.) ansiedad; agitación mental; (ant.) estufa.—*pl.* (ant.) burdel, lupanar.

steward [stiúard], *s.* administrador; mayordomo, senescal; despensero, ranchero; camarero (en los vapores).—**s.'s room,** despensa.—**stewardship** [-ship], *s.* mayordomía.—**stewardess** [-es], *s.* mayordoma; camarera de a bordo.

stewed [stiúd], *a.* estofado.—**s. meat,** estofado.

stewpan [-stiúpǽn], *s.* cazuela o cacerola.

stewpot [-pót], *s.* olla.

sthenia [szénia], *s.* (med.) estenia.

sthenic [szénic], *a.* esténico.

stibial [stíbial], *a.* antimonial.

stibin(e [stíbin], *s.* (quím.) estibina.

stibium [stíbium], *s.* estibio.

stich [stich], *s.* versículo, verso; HEMISTITCH; hilera de árboles.

stick. I. *s.* palo, estaca; garrote, porra; vara; bastón; varilla; palillo; barra, barrilla (de lacre, tinta china etc.); batuta; ristra; estique de escultor; arco de contrabajo; (mar.) palo, verga; hurgonazo, estocada, pinchazo; adhesión, pegadura; parada, demora; duda, escrúpulo, vacilación; (fam.) bodoque; (teat.) mal actor.—*pl.* **sticks,** támaras o rozo, leña menuda, chabasca.—**s. and stone,** todito, todito.—**s.-lac,** laca en palillos. **II.** *va.* (*pret.* y *pp.* STUCK) pegar; clavar, hincar; prender (con alfiler), fijar (con tachuelas, etc.); meter, introducir; matar o herir de una puñalada o cuchillada; picar, punzar; llenar de puntas; (fam.) confundir, aturrullar; embaucar, pegársela a uno; componer (tipo); (agr.) plantar (jalones).—**to s. out,** sacar, asomar, mostrar; perseverar hasta el fin en.—**to s. up,** saltear; parar para robar.—**to s. up one's nose at** (antes del nombre, si lo hay), hacer un gesto de desprecio, despreciar, hacer ascos. **III.** *vn.* estar clavado o prendido; (con **out, through, from**) salir, resaltar, sobresalir; pegarse, adherirse; permanecer fijo; permanecer, estarse; verse o estar parado o detenido; perseverar, ser constante; dudar, vacilar; atollarse.—**to s. at,** detenerse, sentir escrúpulo de.—**to s. at it,** (fam.) persistir.—**to s. at nothing,** (fam.) no pararse en nada.—**to s. by,** sostener, apoyar; pegarse (a alguno).—**to s. close,** mantenerse juntos.—**to s. fast,** pegarse, adherirse fuertemente.—**to s. in the mud,** atascarse en el fango, atollarse.—**to s. to,** pegarse o adherirse tenazmente a; perseverar, persistir en.—**he sticks at everything,** (fam.) se ahoga en poca agua.

stickiness [stíkines], *s.* calidad de pegajoso, glutinosidad.

sticking plaster [stíking plǽstœr], *s.* tafetán inglés, esparadrapo.

stickle [stícœl], *vn.* porfiar, disputar por menudencias.

stickleback [stícœlbǽc], *s.* (ict.) espino.

stickler [stíclœr], *s.* porfiador.

sticky [stíki], *a.* pegajoso.

stiff [stif]. **I.** *a.* tieso; duro, firme; envarado, entorpecido, embotado; yerto, aterido, rígido, inflexible; tenso, tendido; desmañado, chabacano; afectado, estirado, ceremonioso; almidonado; espeso; terco, persistente; difícil, severo; (com.) firme en los precios; (mar.) de aguante; fuerte, bravo (viento, etc.); (fam.) vigoroso, robusto; peliagudo, muy difícil; (com.) firme (mercado, precios); (fam.) subido, caro (precio); (mar.) de aguante.—**s.-backed,** testarudo, terco.—**s. collar,** cuello planchado.—**s.-hearted,** terco, testarudo.—**s. neck,** tortícolis.—**s.-necked,** obstinado, terco, testarudo; cuellierguido. **II.** *s.* apresto para en-

---

tiesar sombreros; (fam.) persona huraña o estirada; (fam.) cadáver.

stiffen [stífœn]. **I.** *va.* atiesar; endurecer; espesar; envarar, aterir o arrecir de frío; (elec.) aumentar la inductancia de. **II.** *vn.* atiesarse; endurecerse; enderezarse; espesarse; envararse, aterirse; obstinarse.

stiffener [stífnœr], *s.* contrafuerte; refuerzo, nervio.

stiffly [stífli], *adv.* tiesamente; obstinadamente, inflexiblemente.

stiffness [stífnes], *s.* tiesura, inflexibilidad; rigidez, envaramiento; (med.) rigor; terquedad, obstinación; dureza de estilo; espesura.

stifle [stáifœl]. **I.** *va.* sofocar, ahogar, asfixiar; apagar; suprimir, callar, ocultar. **II.** *vn.* ahogarse, sofocarse o asfixiarse. **III.** *s. s.* [joint], (vet.) articulación de la pata trasera que corresponde a la rodilla.

stigma, *s.* estigma, baldón, afrenta; (bot.) estigma; (anat. y zool.) marca o poro; (igl.) estigma; (med.) marca; cicatriz.

stigmatic [stigmǽtic], *a.* señalado, marcado; ignominioso; deforme.

stigmatize [stígmataiš], *va.* estigmatizar.

stile [stáil], *s.* portillo con escalones o con molinete; (carp.) larguero. *V.* STYLE.

stiletto [stiléto], *s.* estilete; ojeteador, punzón.

still [stil]. **I.** *va.* acallar, hacer callar; amortiguar; calmar, aquietar, apaciguar; parar, detener; (ant.) destilar. **II.** *adv.* todavía, aún; aun; no obstante, sin embargo, a pesar de eso. **III.** *a.* inmóvil; fijo; tranquilo, silencioso, quieto; apacible, sosegado; suave, sordo (ruido); no espumoso (vino); muerto, inanimado.—**s. life,** (pint.) naturaleza muerta.—**s.-life painting,** (pint.) bodegón.—**s. water,** agua tranquila. **IV.** *s.* silencio, quietud; alambique, destiladera.—**s. worm,** serpentín de alambique.

stillage [stíley], *s.* caballete.

stillborn [stílbórn], *s.* y *a.* nacido muerto.

still-hunt [stíl-jʊnt]. **I.** *va.* y *vn.* cazar al acecho; (pol.) solicitar votos clandestinamente. **II.** *s.* caza al acecho; conducta o método callados y cautos; (pol.) solicitación clandestina de votos.

stilling [stíling], *s.* poíno, codal.

stilly [stíli]. **I.** *a.* (poét.) tranquilo, silencioso. **II.** *adv.* quietamente.

stillness [stílnes], *s.* silencio, quietud, tranquilidad, calma.

stilt, *s.* zanco; muleta; soporte; esteva (del arado).

stilted [stílted], *a.* hinchado, altisonante.

stimulant [stímulant], *a.* y *s.* estimulante.—**stimulate** [stímiuleit]. **I.** *va.* estimular, excitar, incitar; avivar; (med.) estimular. **II.** *vn.* servir como estímulo o aguijón; ser estimulante; tomar estimulantes.—**stimulation** [-léishʊn], *s.* estímulo, aguijón o excitación; (med.) estimulación.—**stimulative** [-lativ]. **I.** *a.* estimulante. **II.** *s.* estímulo; excitación.—**stimulator** [-léitœr], *s.* irritador, acuciador.—**stimulus** [-lus], *s.* estímulo, aguijón; incentivo; (med.) estimulante; (bot.) guijón.

sting. I. *va.* y *vn.* (*pret.* y *pp.* STUNG) picar; pinchar, pungir; estimular, aguijonear; herir, atormentar; remorder la conciencia.—**to s. to the quick,** herir en lo vivo. **II.** *s.* aguijón; picadura, picada; picazón; (bot.) púa, aguijón; remordimiento de conciencia; estímulo.

stingily [stínyili], *adv.* cicatera o tacañamente.

stinginess [stínyines], *s.* tacañería, cicatería, mezquindad.

stingless [stíngles], *s.* sin aguijón; sin púa.

stingy [stínyi], *a.* mezquino, tacaño, cicatero; escaso, poco.

stink. I. *vn.* (*pret.* STANK O STUNK: *pp.* STUNK) heder. **II.** *s.* hedor, hediondez.—**stinkard** [-ard], ... persona hedionda.—**stinkball** [-bol], *s.* = STINKPOT.—**stinker** [-œr], *s.* cosa hedionda.—**stinking** [-ing], *a.* hediondo, apestoso.—**stinkingly** [-ingli], *adv.* hediondamente, con hediondez.—**stinkpot** [stínkpót], *s.* bomba asfixiante.

---

stint. **I.** *va.* restringir, escatimar; asignar una tarea. **II.** *vn.* ser económico o parco. **III.** *s.* cuota, tarea, destajo; límite, restricción.

stipe [stáip], *s.* (bot.) estipo.

stipend [stáipend], *s.* estipendio, sueldo.

stipendiary [staipéndieri], *a.* y *s.* estipendiario, soldadero.

stipple [stípœl]. **I.** *va.* (b. a.) picar, puntear. **II.** *s.* picado, punteado.—*s.* **graver,** graneador.

stippling [stípling], *s.* (b. a.) graneo.

stiptic(al [stíptic(al], *a.* estíptico.

stipulate [stípuleit]. **I.** *va.* estipular, especificar. **II.** *vn.* estipular, contratar, pactar. **III.** *a.* provisto de estípulas.

stipulation [-léishun], *s.* estipulación, condición; convenio, contrato, pacto.

stipule [stípiul], *s.* (bot.) estípula; (orn.) pluma reciente.

stir [stœr]. **I.** *va.* agitar, menear, batir; hurgar, remover, revolver; perturbar, excitar, irritar, suscita : animar, incitar; conmover; ventilar, discutir.—**to** *s.* **the fire,** atizar o avivar el fuego o la lumbre.—**to** *s.* **up,** conmover, excitar; aguijonear; poner en movimiento; revolver; despertar.—**to** *s.* **up a hornet's nest,** armar cisco.—**to** *s.* **up a storm =** TO RAISE A STORM. **II.** *vn.* moverse; menearse; rebullir. **III.** *s.* movimiento, conmoción, excitación, bullicio, alboroto.

stirrer [stœrcer], *s.* agitador; batidor, molinillo; mecedero (de vinos); meneador.

stirrup [stírup o stœrup], *s.* estribo; (zap.) tirapié; (mar.) estribo.—**s. leather,** ación.—**s. bone,** (anat.) estribo (del oído).—**s. cup,** trago o copa de despedida.

stitch [stich]. **I.** *va.* coser, embastar, bastear, hilvanar, unir, juntar.—**to** *s.* **up,** remendar; (cir.) dar puntos. **II.** *vn.* coser, bordar. **III.** *s.* (cost.) puntada; basta; punto; punzada, dolor punzante; (agr.) caballón, surco; distancia, jornada.

stitcher [stítchœr], *s.* cosedor, cosedora; ribeteadora; (enc.) cosedor.—**stitching** [-ing], *s.* puntos, puntadas; costura; pespunte, punto atrás.

stithy [stízi], *s.* (ant.) fragua; yunque.

stiver [stáivœr], *s.* stíver, moneda holandesa; bagatela, ardite.

stoat [stot], *s.* armiño.

stock. **I.** *s.* tronco, cepa; injerto; estirpe, linaje; (for.) línea directa de una familia; (com.) capital comercial; acciones; surtido (de mercancías); mercancías almacenadas, existencias; repuesto, provisión, cantidad de primeras materias; enseres; (muebles; (mec.) mango, manija, cubo, zoquete, leño, tajo; berbiquí de barrena; caja (de fusil, etc.); cepo (de ancla, yunque); grada de construcción, astillero; corbatín, alzacuello; colonia de abejas, colmena; baceta o monte de una baraja; ganado (=LIVE STOCK); (bot.) *pl.* V. STOCKS.—**s.-blind,** totalmente ciego.—**s. blocks,** (mar.) polines de la grada.—**s. company,** compañía o sociedad anónima.—**s. exchange,** bolsa, lonja (de acciones); asociación de corredores de bolsa.—**s. farmer,** ganadero.—**s. in hand,** mercancías en almacén, existencias.—**s. in trade,** artículos que se venden en una tienda; equipo, útiles (de un artesano, etc.); (fam.) caballo de batalla.—**s. rail,** riel fijo, contraaguja (de cambiavía).—**in** *s.,* en existencia.—**on the stocks,** (mar.) en vía de construcción; en preparación. **II.** *va.* proveer, abastecer, surtir; acumular, juntar, acopiar; encepar.

stockade [stokéid]. **I.** *va.* empalizar. **II.** *s.* empalizada, estacada, palanquera; vallado.

stockbroker [stóckbróucœr], *s.* corredor de bolsa, bolsista.

stockdove [-dúv], *s.* (orn.) paloma silvestre.

stockfish [-físh], *s.* (com.) bacalao seco pejepalo.

stockholder [-jóuldœr], *s.* accionista.

stockinet [stokinét], *s.* (tej.) elástica.

stocking [stóking], *s.* media, calceta.—**s. frame,** telar de medias.—**s. weaver,** tejedor de medias.

stockish [stókish], *a.* estúpido.

stockjobber [stócyóbœr], *s.* (Ingl.) agente de corredores de bolsa; (E. U.) corredor de bolsa (apl. esp. al agiotista).—**stockjobbing** [-ing], *s.* oficio del *stockjobber;* agiotista.

stocks, *s. pl.* de STOCK; cepo (castigo); valores, acciones; (mar.) astillero, gradas de construcción.

stocky [stóki], *a.* rechoncho.

stockyard [-yard], *s.* corral de ganado.

stodgy [stóyi], *a.* (fam.) pesado, indigesto; fangoso; pegajoso; regordete; hinchado.

stogy [stóugui], (fam.) bota burda o basta; cigarro tosco y barato.

stoic [stóic], *s.* y *a.,* **stoical** [-æl], *a.* estoico.—**stoically** [-i], *adv.* estoicamente.—**stoicism** [stóicism], *s.* estoicismo; estoicidad.

stoke [stóuk], *va.* y *vn.* atizar el fuego (m. v.).

stokehold [-jóuld], *s.* puesto de fogonero; cuarto de calderas.

stokehole [-jóul], *s.* (m. c.) boca del horno; sitio del fogonero; cuarto de claderas.

stoker [stóukœr], *s.* fogonero, paleador; alimentador de hogar.

stole [stóul], *s.* (igl.) estola.

stole, stolen, *pret.* y *pp.* de TO STEAL.

stolid [stólid], *a.* estólido; impasible.

stolidity [stolíditi], *s.* estolidez.

stolon [stólon], *s.* (bot.) estolón.

stoma [stóma], *s.* estoma.

stomach [stúmac]. **I.** *s.* estómago; vientre, barriga; apetito; deseo, afición, inclinación. **II.** *va.* tragar, digerir, sufrir, aguantar.

stomachal [-al], *a.* estomacal.—**stomacher** [-œr], *s.* peto, stomacher.

stomachic(al [stomékic(al]. **I.** *a.* estomacal, estomático. **II.** *s.* medicamento estomacal.

stomachless [stómacles], *a.* desganado.

stomata [stómætæ], *s. pl.* de STOMA.

stomatitis [stómátáitis], *s.* estomatitis.

stomatopod [stómætopód], *s.* y *a.* (zool.) estomápodo, estomatópodo.—**Stomatopoda** [stómætópodæ], *s. pl.* estomápodos, estomatópodos.—**stomatopodous** [-us], *a.* = STOMATOPOD.

stone [stóun]. **I.** *s.* piedra; piedra de molino, de amolar; piedra sepulcral; (joy.) piedra preciosa; (med.) piedra, cálculo; hueso, cuesco (de las frutas); (Ingl.) peso de 14 libras.—*s.* **age,** edad de piedra.—**s.-blind,** enteramente ciego.—**s. breaker,** bocarte, triturador.—**s.-cold,** frío como la piedra, frío helado.—**s. color,** gris azulado.—**s. crusher =** s. BREAKER.—**s.-dead,** muerto como una piedra.—**s.-deaf,** enteramente sordo.—**s.-dumb,** enteramente mudo.—**s. fruit,** fruta de hueso.—**s. hammer,** dolobre, almadana, marra.—**s. mason,** albañil.—**s. masonry,** mampostería (de piedra), cal y canto.—**s. parsley,** amomo, perejil perenne.—**s. pit,** *s.* **quarry,** pedrera, cantera.—**s.'s cast, s.'s throw,** tiro de piedra, corta distancia.—**s. trough,** pilón. **II.** *va.* apedrear; quitar los cuescos o huesos a las frutas; (alb.) revestir de piedras.

stonebreak [-bréik], *s.* (bot.) quebrantapiedras, saxífraga.

stonecrop [-cróp], *s.* (bot.) ombligo de Venus; cualquier planta crasulácea.

stonecutter [-cútœr], *s.* picapedrero, cantero.—**stonecutting** [-cúting], *s.* corte o labra de piedras.

stoner [-œr], *s.* apedreador; despepitador de frutas.

stoneware [-uéœr], *s.* cacharros; objetos de barro.

stonework [-uérc], *s.* obra de sillería.

stoneworks [-uércs], *s.* taller de cantería.

stoniness [-ines], *s.* calidad de pedregoso o pétreo; dureza.

stony [-i], *a.* pedregoso; (ant.) de piedra, pétreo; duro, insensible; petrificante.

stood [stud], *pret.* y *pp.* de TO STAND.

stool [stul]. **I.** *s.* banquillo, taburete, escabel; tarimilla, banqueta; inodoro, sillico; planta madre; vástago acodado; señuelo, añagaza.— *pl.* cámara, evacuación de vientre; (mar.) mesetas de los jardines.—**s. of repentance,** banquillo de la penitencia.—**s. pigeon,** cimbel, cimillo; persona empleada para embaucar. **II.** *va.* arar, cultivar; (fam.) atraer con añagazas o señuelos. **III.** *vn.* echar tallos, retoños, etc.; evacuar (el vientre); atraer con señuelos.

stoop [stup]. **I.** *vn.* agacharse, doblar o inclinar el cuerpo; ir encorvado, ser cargado de espaldas; encorvarse, combarse hacia adelante; humillarse, rebajarse; condescender; lanzarse, arrojarse sobre la presa. **II.** *va.* someter, abatir, hacer bajar. **III.** *s.* inclinación de hombros; descenso, caída; cimiento, declinación, abatimiento; (E. U.) gradería, escalinata de entrada.

stoop, stoup [stup], *s.* copa o frasco para beber; pila de agua bendita.

stoopingly [stúpingli], *adv.* con inclinación hacia abajo; servilmente.

stop. **I.** *va.* parar; detener, atajar, interceptar; suspender, paralizar, cesar o dejar de; contener, reprimir, refrenar; obstruir, atascar, tapar; estancar, represar.—**to s. one's mouth,** tapar la boca a uno, no dejarle que decir.—**to s. payment,** suspender el pago (de un cheque).—**to s. payments,** suspender pagos.—**to s. short,** detener brusca o repentinamente.—**to s. up,** tapar, cerrar, obstruir. **II.** *vn.* parar; pararse; detenerse, hacer alto; cesar; acabarse, terminar; (fam.) quedarse algún tiempo, alojarse; (mús.) cambiar el tono por medio de un agujero o un traste.—**to s. at,** detenerse en, reparar, pararse en.—**to s. short,** detenerse repentina o bruscamente. **III.** *s.* parada, detención; cesación; pausa, alto; interrupción; suspensión, paro (de trabajo); obstáculo, impedimento, obstrucción; represión; (mús.) tecla; llave; traste de guitarra; registro de órgano; (gram.) punto; (mec.) retén, fiador, seguro, leva, tope, paleta, lingüete, trinquete.—**s.-gap,** tapón, relleno; procedimiento o cosa de conveniencia; subterfugio, escapatoria.—**s.-over,** que permite detenerse en lugares intermedios (apl. a billetes de f. c.).—**s. valve,** válvula reguladora o de cierre.—**s. watch,** reloj de segundos muertos.

stopcock [stópcóc], *s.* llave, grifo, espita.

stope [stóup]. **I.** *va.* (min.) excavar en escalones. **II.** *s.* obra en escalones.

stoppage [stópey], *s.* cesación, interrupción; detención, interceptación; obstrucción, impedimento; represa; retención (sobre un pago); (med.) estrangulación.—**s. in transit,** (for.) embargo de mercancías durante su transporte, por insolvencia del comprador.

stopper [stópœr]. **I.** *va.* entaponar, tapar con tapón; (mar.) bozar. **II.** *s.* tapón; taco, tarugo; tapador, obturador; detenedor; (mar.) boza, estopor.—**s. bolts,** argollas de boza.

stopping [stóping]. **I.** *s.* parada; detención; interrupción. **II.** *a.* de detención, que detiene o para.—**s. place,** estadía, escala.

stopple [stópœl]. **I.** *va.* entaponar, atarugar. **II.** *s.* tapón, tarugo, taco, bitoque.

storage [stórey], *s.* almacenaje.—**s. battery,** (elec.) batería de acumuladores, o acumulador. —**s. reservoir,** depósito de abastecimiento; depósito de reserva.

storax [stórax], *s.* estoraque.—**s. tree,** (bot.) estoraque.

store [stóœr]. **I.** *s.* abundancia, acopio; provisión, repuesto; almacén, depósito; tienda.—*pl.* pertrechos, equipos; víveres, provisiones; municiones; bastimentos, provisiones de boca. **II.** *va.* proveer o abastecer; municionar o pertrechar; guardar, acumular; tener en reserva; almacenar.

storehouse [-jáus], *s.* almacén.

storekeeper [-kípœr], *s.* guardaalmacén; jefe de depósito; tendero, comerciante; (mar.) pañolero.

storeroom [-rúm], *s.* despensa; bodega, cilla; almacén, cuarto de almacenar; (mar.) pañol de víveres.

storeship [-shíp], *s.* (mar.) urca, navío almacén.

storied [stórid], *a.* historiado; de (tantos) pisos.

storiette [stóriét], *s.* cuentecillo, novela corta, historieta.

stork [storc], *s.* (orn.) cigüeña; (fam.) mensajero imaginario que trae los recién nacidos.—**s.'s bill,** (bot.) geranio.

storm [storm]. **I.** *s.* tempestad, temporal, tormenta o borrasca; vendaval; arrebato, frenesí; conmoción, tumulto; (mil.) ataque, asalto; turbonada.—**s. door,** guardapuertas, cancel.—**s. petrel,** petrel de la tempestad (así llamado porque diz

que la presagia).—**s. troops,** tropas escogidas.—**s. water,** (ing.) agua de lluvia.—**s.-water sewer,** alcantarilla para agua de lluvia. **II.** *va.* asaltar, tomar por asalto. **III.** *vn. impers.* haber tormenta; bramar o estallar de cólera.

stormbird [stórmbœrd], *s.* (orn.) procelaria.

storminess [stórmines], *s.* estado borrascoso, tempestuoso.

stormy [stórmi], *a.* tempestuoso, borrascoso; violento, turbulento.—**s. petrel** = STORM PETREL.

story [stóri]. **I.** *s.* historia; cuento, fábula, conseja; historieta; anécdota; (fam.) cuento de viejas, habilla; enredo, trama, argumento; (fam.) mentira, embuste; (fam.) artículo (escrito); (arq.) alto, piso.—**s. teller,** chismoso; embustero.—**as the s. goes,** según se dice, según cuenta la historia. **II.** *va.* historiar, narrar; colocar en pisos o rimeros.

stoup [stup], *s.* = STOUP.

stout [stáut]. **I.** *a.* fornido, forzudo; gordo, corpulento; fuerte, sólido, firme; resuelto, intrépido, animoso. **II.** *s.* cerveza fuerte.—**stoutly** [-li], *adv.* vigorosamente; recio; con resolución.—**stoutness** [-nes], *s.* corpulencia, gordura; solidez; fuerza; intrepidez.

stove [stóuv], *s.* estufa, hornillo; (Ingl.) invernadero; horno cerámico.

stove, *pret.* y *pp.* de TO STAVE.

stow [sto], *va.* aprensar, atestar, hacinar; colocar, meter, alojar; esconder, ocultar; (mar.) estibar, arrumar, abarrotar; arrizar.—**to s. the hold,** estibar, abarrotar.—**stowing quoins,** (mar.) abarrotes.

stowage [stóey], *s.* almacenaje; (mar.) estiba; arrumaje.

stowaway [stóeuéi], *s.* (mar.) polizón, llovido.

stower [stóœr], *s.* estibador.

strabismus [strabísmus], *s.* (med.) estrabismo.

strabotomy [strabótomi], *s.* estrabotomía.

straddle [strǽdœl]. **I.** *vn.* esparrancarse; montar a horcajadas; tener los extremos alternados o al tresbolillo; (fam.) no tomar partido. **II.** *va.* montar a horcajadas; montarse en; no tomar partido en; estar por ambas partes en (un partido, disputa). **III.** *s.* posición del que se esparranca o monta a horcajadas; operación de bolsa con opción de compra o venta.

straggle [strǽgœl], *vn.* extraviarse; rodar, andorrear; extenderse, desparramarse; estar esparcido o regado.

straggler [-glœr], *vn.* extraviarse; rodar, andorrear; extenderse, desparramarse; estar esparcido o regado.

straggler [-glœr], *s.* rezagado; vagamundo, tunante; rama extendida; objeto aislado.

straggling [-gling], *a.* rezagado; extraviado; disperso.—**s. branches,** ramas dispersas.—**s. soldier,** soldado rezagado.

straight [stréit]. **I.** *a.* derecho, recto; directo, en línea recta; lacio; erguido, derecho; justo, equitativo; íntegro, honrado; correcto, exacto; franco, o sin estorbos; seguido, no interrumpido.—**s. angle,** ángulo derecho, ángulo de lados colineares (180°).—**s. face,** cara seria.—**s. line,** línea recta.—**s.-line,** en línea recta; de movimiento en línea recta.—**s.-out,** sincero; firme, intransigente.—**s.-side tire,** (aut.) neumático sin talón. **II.** *adv.* directamente, en derechura, en línea recta; luego, al punto, inmediatamente. **III.** *s.* runfla de cinco naipes del mismo palo en el juego del *poker.*

straightedge [-ey], *s.* regla de (trazarlíneas).

straighten [stréitœn], *va.* enderezar; poner en orden, arreglar.—**straightener** [-œr], *s.* el que endereza o pone en orden.

straightforward (s [stréitfóruard(§]. **I.** *a.* recto, derecho; honrado, íntegro, sincero. **II.** *adv.* de frente.

straightly [-li], *adv.* en línea recta, directamente.

straightness [-nes], *s.* derechura, calidad de recto o derecho; rectitud.

straightway [-uéi], *adv.* inmediatamente, luego.

strain [stréin]. **I.** *va.* hacer fuerza a; poner tirante; poner, consagrar (la atención, etc.); forzar (la vista, los nervios, etc.); someter a esfuerzo; estirar; forzar; extremar; perjudicar por esfuerzo excesivo; colar, tamizar, cribar; apretar; agarrar; (mec.) someter a esfuerzo; (mec.)

deformar.—**to s. a point,** excederse; hacer una concesión; hacer violencia (a la lógica, a la conciencia, etc.). **II.** *vn.* hacer grande esfuerzo, esforzarse; resistir o estar sometido a esfuerzo; pasar o meterse por (un cedazo, una pared); infiltrarse.—**to s. at,** esforzarse o hacer grandes esfuerzos en o por. **III.** *s.* tensión, tirantez, esfuerzo fuerte o violento; lesión, relajación, torcedura, o cualquier otro daño debido a esfuerzo excesivo; (mec.) esfuerzo; (mec.) deformación (debe tenerse cuidado con estos dos últimos significados, pues los escritores técnicos no están acordes, aunque *esfuerzo* es el más común); huella, vena, indicio; (mús.) aire, melodía; acorde, acentos; parte distintiva de un poema, verso; estirpe, descendencia, raza, linaje; clase; genio o disposición heredada.

strainer [stréinœr], *s.* colador, coladera, coladero.

strait [stréit]. **I.** *a.* estrecho, angosto, ajustado, apretado.—**s.-jacket,** camisa de fuerza.—**s.-laced,** ceñido; estricto; mojigato. **II.** *s.* (geog.) estrecho; garganta, desfiladero, angostura o paso estrecho; apuro, aprieto, estrechez.

straiten [-œn], *va.* estrechar, angostar, contraer; constreñir, reducir.

straitly [-li], *adv.* estrechamente; estrictamente, rigorosamente.—**straitness** [-nes], *s.* estrechez, estrechura, angostura; aprieto, apuro; penuria.

strake [strec], *s.* (mar.) traca, hilada.

stramineous [stramíneus], *a.* (bot.) de color de paja; amarillo claro.

stramonium [stramónium], *s.* (bot. y farm.) estramonio.

strand [strænd]. **I.** *va.* y *vn.* encallar, embarrancar, vararse; quedarse desamparado; romper uno de los cabos de una cuerda; torcer, remendar, zurcir; (los cabos de un cordel). **II.** *s.* costa, marina, playa, ribera; cabo, hebra; ramal, cordón, torón (de cable); (aer.) cable de alambre con núcleo, formado arrollando varios alambres juntos al rededor de un alambre central.

stranded [-ed]. **I.** *pp.* de TO STRAND. **II.** *a.* de torones retorcidos (cable); varado.

stranding [-ing], *s.* encalladura, zaborda; retorcimiento.

strange [stréiny]. **I.** *a.* extraño, singular; forastero; ajeno; desconocido; retraído, reservado, esquivo.—**s. face,** cara desconocida.—**s. woman,** (bib.) ramera. **II.** *interj.* ¡cosa rara! ¡cáspita!

strangely [-li], *adv.* extrañamente; extraordinariamente.

strangeness [-nes], *s.* extranjería; extrañeza, rareza; reserva, esquivez; maravilla.

stranger [strényœr], *s.* extranjero, extraño, desconocido.—**he is a s. to me,** me es desconocido.—**to be a s. to,** desconocer, no conocer; ser desconocido.—**you are a s.,** se vende Vd. muy caro, no se le ve a Vd., milagro es verlo.

strangle [stréngœl]. **I.** *va.* estrangular; agarrotar, dar garrote; ahogar, sofocar. **II.** *vn.* morir estrangulado, estrangularse.

strangler [strénglœr], *s.* estrangulador.

strangles [stréngœlš], *s.* (vet.) estrangol.

strangulate(d [strénguiulcit(ed], *a.* (med.) estrangulado.

strangulation [-léišhun], *s.* estrangulación.

strangury [strénguiuri], *s.* estangurria.

strap [stræp]. **I.** *s.* correa; tira, faja, banda; abrazadera; precinta; gamarra; cabeza de biela; capona o charretera mocha; (sast.) trabilla de pantalón; (zap.) tirante, tirador; (carr.) correones, sopandas; (mar.) gaza. **II.** *va.* liar, atar o atar con correas; precintar; asentar (navajas de barba).

strappado [strapádo o péidi], *s.* (mil.) estrapada; tunda, azotaina.

strapper [strépœr], *s.* (fam.) objeto o persona alta y talluda.

strapping [stréping], *a.* (fam.) rollizo.—**s. girl, woman,** mocetona, mujerona.

strata [stréita], *s. pl.* de STRATUM.

stratagem [strétayem], *s.* estratagema.

strategic,al strategetic(al [stratéyic, tíyic; stræterétic(al], *a.* estratégico.—**strategics** [-tíyics], *s.* estrategia.—**strategist** [stréteyist], *s.* estratégico.—**strategy** [-yi], *s.* estrategia.

strath [stræz], *s.* (Esco.) valle extenso.

stratification [strétifikéishun], *s.* (geol.) estratificación.—**stratiform** [-form], *a.* estratiforme.—**stratify** [-fai], *va.* estratificar.—**stratigraphic(al** [-gréfic(al], *a.* estratigráfico.—**stratigraphy** [stratigrafi], *s.* estratigrafía.

stratocracy [stratócrasi], *s.* despotismo militar.

stratum [stréitum], *s.* estrato, lecho, capa, tonga, cama; (geol.) estrato; (anat.) capa de tejido.

stratus [stréitus], *s.* estrato.

straw [stró]. **I.** *s.* paja; bálago; sombrero de paja; bagatela, fruslería; indicio.—**not to care a s.,** no importarle a uno un comino, no dársele a uno un bledo.—**the last s.,** el golpe de gracia, el acabóse. **II.** *a.* de paja; pajizo; baladí; falso, ficticio.—**s. ball,** caución o fianza simulada.—**s. bed,** jergón de paja.—**s. bond,** bono o caución ficticios.—**s. color,** color pajizo.—**s.-color, s.-colored,** de color pajizo.—**s. hat,** sombrero de paja.—**s. man,** nulidad; títere.—**s. vote,** voto o votación no oficial, votos recogidos por persona o empresa particular (gen. un periódico) para determinar la opinión pública.

strawberry [-bérri], *s.* fresa.—**s. tree,** madroño.

strawboard [-bórd], *s.* cartón de paja.

straworm [-uœrm], *s.* gorgojo.

strawy [strói], *a.* pajizo; de paja.

stray [stréi]. **I.** *vn.* descarriarse, extraviarse. **II.** *a.* extraviado, descarriado, perdido. **III.** *s.* persona o animal descarriado o perdido; descarriamiento, descarrío.

streak [strík]. **I.** *s.* raya, lista, línea, faja, veta; reguero; rayo de luz; vena, rasgo de ingenio; traza, pizca; antojo, capricho; (min.) raspadura; (mar.) costura de tablas, traca, hilada. **II.** *va.* rayar, listar; abigarrar; gayar.

streaky [stríki], *a.* rayado, listado, veteado; bordado.

stream [strím]. **I.** *s.* corriente; arroyo; corriente de agua (término que comprende ríos y arroyos); flujo, chorro (de líquido gas, luz, etc.); curso.—**s. anchor,** anclote.—**s. tin,** estaño de aluvión, en grano.—**against the s.,** contra la corriente.—**down s., up s.,** agua abajo, agua arriba. **II.** *va.* y *vn.* correr, manar, fluir, brotar; salir a torrentes; derramar con abundancia; lavar en agua corriente; ondear, flotar, flamear, tremolar; pasar dejando un rastro de luz.

streamer [strímœr], *s.* flámula, gallardete, banderola, grímpola; aurora boreal.

streamlet [strímlet], *s.* arroyuelo.

streamline [strímlain]. **I.** *s.* trayectoria (de una corriente, esp. de las uniformes o que no tienen remolinos); línea de trabajo o trayectoria de la vena líquida. **II.** *a.* continuo y sin remolinos (movimiento); que permite o facilita flujo o corriente continuos, sin remolinos; (aut.) de tipo torpedo. **III.** *va.* dar forma que permita flujo continuo.

streamy [strími], *a.* surcado de arroyos; que mana a chorros; radiante.

street [strít], *s.* calle.—**s. car,** (coche de) tranvía.—**s. railway,** tranvía.—**s. sprinkler,** carricuba, carro de riego.

streetwalker [-uócœr], *s.* prostituta de calle, nocherniega.

strength [strengz], *s.* fuerza, vigor; potencia, pujanza, poder; validez, fuerza legal; (ing.) resistencia; fortaleza, firmeza, resistencia, solidez; intensidad; vehemencia; (quím.) concentración, grado de potencia o de concentración; cuerpo (del vino); seguridad, confianza; (mil.) número, magnitud (de soldados, de ejército, de fuerzas militares); (ant.) baluarte, plaza fuerte.—**s. of a current,** (elec.) intensidad de una corriente (gen. expresada en amperios).—**s. of a field,** intensidad de un campo (magnético, de atracción, etc.).—**s. of materials,** (ing.) resistencia de materiales.—**on the s.,** (fam.) en las listas, en el escalafón, en el servicio.—**on, o upon, the s. of,** fundándose en, confiando en.

strengthen [stréngzœn]. **I.** *va.* fortalecer, fortificar; confirmar, corroborar; reforzar; animar, alentar. **II.** *vn.* fortalecerse; reforzarse.

strengthener [-œr], *s.* refuerzo; confortador; corroborante.

strengthless [strénzles], a. débil.
strenuous [streñuus], a. estrenuo, fuerte; activo, enérgico; acérrimo, tenaz.
strenuously [-li], adv. vigorosamente, enérgicamente.—**strenuousness** [-nes], s. estrenuidad, energía, fortaleza.
streptococcus [stréptocócus], s. (biol.) estreptococo.
stress. I. s. fuerza, peso, importancia, entidad; (ing.) esfuerzo; violencia, tensión; compulsión, coacción; acento tónico, énfasis.—**s. of weather,** mal tiempo.—**by s. of weather,** (mar.) a causa de un temporal. **II.** va. someter a esfuerzo; dar importancia o énfasis a; poner en aprieto.
stretch [strech]. **I.** va. extender, alargar, tender; estirar, atesar; ensanchar, dilatar; violentar, forzar; exagerar, llevar al extremo; (mar.) hacer toda fuerza de vela.—**to s. a point,** excederse, pasarse de los justos límites.—**to s. forth,** alargar, extender.—**to s. one's self,** esperezarse, desperezarse.—**to s. out,** extender, estirar, alargar. **II.** vn. alargarse, extenderse, dar de sí, dilatarse. estirarse, desplegarse; (fig.) esforzarse; exagerar.—**to s. out,** extenderse, desplegarse, prolongarse.—**to s. out to sea,** (mar.) tirar a la mar. **III.** s. alargamiento; extensión, dilatación; tirantez, esfuerzo; violencia o interpretación forzada; alcance, trecho, distancia; lapso, tirada, intervalo; (mar.) bordada.—**s. of imagination,** esfuerzo de la imaginación.
stretcher [stréchœr], s. tendedor; estirador, dilatador, atesador, ensanchador; camilla, andas, parihuela; (alb.) soga; (carp.) viga, madero largo, tirante; (mar.) peana o pedestal de bote.
stretching [-ing], s. tendedura, alargamiento, estiramiento, entesamiento, tensión; acostamiento; esperezo.
strew [stru], va. (pp. STREWED o STREWN) regar, esparcir; sembrar, salpicar, espolvorear.
stria [stráia], s. (arq.) estría.—**striate** [stráieit], va. estriar.—**striate'd** [-eit, -eited], a. estriado.—**striation, striature** [-éishun, stráiatiur], s. estriación, estriadura.
stricken [stríkœn], pp. de TO STRIKE; herido (por un proyectil); atacado, agobiado; entrado en años.
strickle [stríkœl], s. (Ingl.) rasero.
strict, a. estricto, rígido; exacto, riguroso, escrupuloso; severo; áspero; estirado, tirante; (zool.) limitado, ceñido, estrecho.
strictly [-li], adv. estrictamente, exactamente, rigurosamente.—**s. private,** muy reservado.
strictness [-nes], s. exactitud, puntualidad; severidad, rigor; tirantez.
stricture [stríkchur], s. crítica severa, censura; (med.) estrechez, constricción.
stride [stráid]. **I.** s. paso largo, tranco, zancada. **II.** va. (pret. STRODE; pp. STRIDDEN, (ant.) STRID) cruzar a grandes trancos; montar a horcajadas. **III.** vn. andar a trancos.
strident [stráidœnt], a. estridente.
stridor [stráidor], s. estridor.
stridulate [strídiulet], vn. chirriar.
stridulation [strídiuléshun], s. chirrido.
stridulous [strídiulus], a. rechinante.
strife [stráif], s. contienda, lucha, refriega, rivalidad, porfía.
strigil [stríyil], s. cepillo fuerte, raspador; (arq.) ondulación.—**strigilation** [-éishun], (med.) estrigilación.
strike [stráic]. **I.** va. (pret. STRUCK; pp. STRUCK o STRICKEN, y ant. STROOK) golpear, pegar a, apuñear; herir; cutir o percutir; batir, tocar; chocar con, dar contra; encender (un fósforo); acuñar; (con off) cortar, quitar, cercenar; cerrar (un trato); (con out o off) borrar, tachar, testar; trazar, dibujar; dar (la hora); ocurrírle a uno (una idea); parecer, causar una impresión; descubrir, hallar, dar con, llegar a; asumir (una postura); arriar (una bandera); parar (el trabajo); allanar, nivelar; pasar o hacer (balance).—**to s. a jury,** elegir jurado.—**to s. a lead** (lid), (min.) hallar una veta.—**to s. an arc,** (elec.) hacer que se forme un arco.—**to s. an average,** formar el promedio,

tomar el término medio.—**to s. a snag,** dar contra un tronco sumergido; encontrar un obstáculo.—**to s. blind,** cegar o poner ciego de repente.—**to s. camp,** levantar el campo.—**to s. down,** arriar; derribar; matar.—**to s. dumb,** hacer mudo; pasmar, asombrar, dejar atónito.—**to s. fire,** sacar fuego del pedernal.—**to s. hands,** tocar la mano en señal de cerrar un contrato.—**to s. off,** (impr.) tirar, imprimir.—**to s. oil,** encontrar petróleo; hacerse rico de súbito; encontrarse un entierro (fig.).—**to s. out,** borrar, tachar, testar.—**to s. root,** echar raíces, arraigarse, acepar.—**to s. sail,** arriar una vela.—**to s. the tents,** plegar tiendas, levantar el campo.—**to s. through,** traspasar, atravesar; calar.—**to s. up,** tocar, tañer.—**to s. with admiration,** llenar de admiración.—**to s. work,** hallar trabajo; (rara vez) declararse en huelga. **II.** vn. golpear, dar golpes; tropezar, dar contra; batir; sonar (una campana); (mar.) varar, encallar, embarrancar; (con upon) suceder casualmente; encontrarse; ir adelante, avanzar; brotar, estallar, manifestar; declararse en huelga; rehusar, resistirse, plantarse; arriar el pabellón, rendirse; arraigar, echar raíces; (geol.) inclinarse, yacer; saturarse de sal (el pescado salado); (elec.) formar arco.—**to s. against,** chocar con, estrellarse contra.—**to s. at,** atacar, acometer.—**to s. back,** dar golpe por golpe.—**to s. for,** (fam.) dirigirse hacia; acometer.—**to s. home,** dar en el vivo.—**to s. in,** meterse; juntarse, unirse; interrumpir; conformarse con.—**to s. into,** comenzar de repente; penetrar.—**to s. on,** dar contra; descubrir.—**to s. out,** tomar una resolución; arrojarse, lanzarse.—**to s. upon**=TO S. AGAINST.—**to s. while the iron is hot,** hacer (uno) su agosto, aprovechar la ocasión; a hierro candente, batir de repente. **III.** s. golpe; huelga, paro del trabajo; descubrimiento de un filón; (fam.) buen éxito, ganga; rasero; medida. V. STRICKLE.—**s. breaker,** esquirol, obrero que reemplaza a los huelguistas.
strikeblock [-bloc], s. (carp.) cepillo bocel.
striker [-œr], s. golpeador, percusor; huelguista.
striking [-ing], a. sorprendente, notable; llamativo; que llama la atención; vívido; conspicuo; que está en huelga; percuciente.
string [string]. **I.** s. cuerda; cuerdecita, cordel, bramante; cuelga, ristra; cinta, presilla; hilera, fila; sarta (de mentiras, etc.); fibra, nervio, tendón; (mar.) durmiente del alcázar y castillo.—**s. beans,** (bot.) habichuelas, (Méx.) ejotes.—**s. instrument,** instrumento de cuerda. **II.** va. encordar; templar (un instrumento); ensartar, enhilar; encordelar; enhebrar; atar con bramante; tender (alambre, etc.); estirar, entesar; quitar las fibras.—**to s. out,** extender.—**to s. up,** (fam.) ahorcar. **III.** vn. extenderse en línea; parecer hebras o fibras.
stringed [stringd], a. encordado, encordelado; ensartado.—**s. instrument,** instrumento de cuerda.
stringency [strínyensi], s. aprieto, apuro, estrechez.—**stringent** [-yœnt], a. estricto, riguroso, severo; (com.) tirante.
stringer [stríngœr], s. (carp.) zanca; riostra; (f. c.) durmiente longitudinal; ensartador; encordador.
stringless [stríngles], a. sin cuerdas.
stringy [stríngui], a. fibroso, filamentoso; tenaz, duro, correoso.
strip. I. va. (pret. y pp. STRIPPED, STRIPT) desnudar; despojar, quitar; desvestir, desguarnecer; robar; descortezar; ordeñar hasta agotar; desgarrar o cortar en tiras.—**to s. a mast,** (mar.) desaparejar un palo.—**to s. off,** desnudar. **II.** s. tira, faja, listón, lista.
stripe [stráip]. **I.** va. rayar, gayar.—**striped and plaid,** rayado y listado. **II.** s. raya, lista, banda, franja, tira, galón, barra; cardenal (en el cuerpo); calaña, clase, género.—**striping** [-ing], s. listas, franjas.
stripling [strípling], s. mozalbete, mozuelo.
strive [stráiv], vn. (pret. STROVE; pp. STRIVEN) esforzarse, hacer lo posible; disputar; oponerse, contrarrestar; competir.
striver [stráivœr], s. competidor; luchador.
strobile [stróbil], s. (bot.) estróbilo.
strode [stróud], pret. de TO STRIDE.

stroke [stróuk]. **I.** *s.* golpe; (mec.) golpe (de émbolo), carrera (del émbolo); golpe del remo, boga, remada; toque, trazo, raya, rasgo, pincelada, plumada; ataque fulminante; rasgo de ingenio; golpe de mano; en el billar, tacada, jugada; proeza; éxito, feliz encuentro; caricia con la mano. —s. **oar**, bogavante, primer remero.—s. **of a pen** o **pencil**, plumada, pincelada.—s. **of fortune, of (good) luck,** golpe de fortuna.—s. **of wit,** chiste, gracia. **II.** *va.* pasar la mano por la espalda, acariciar; frotar suavemente; ranurar la piedra con cincel; (cost.) alisar un plegado.

strokesman [stróucsman], *s.* bogavante.

stroll [strol]. **I.** *vn.* vagar, callejear; pasearse. **II.** *s.* paseo.

stroller [strólœr], *s.* vagabundo; paseante, paseador; cómico ambulante.

stroma [stróumæ], *s.* (biol.) estroma.

strong [stróŋ], *a.* fuerte; concentrado, fuerte, espirituoso, de cuerpo (vino); capaz, hábil; violento, impetuoso; enérgico, eficaz; vivo, brillante; picante; celoso, acérrimo; marcado, pronunciado; numéricamente fuerte; (com.) pujante, con tendencia a la alza.—s. **box,** cofre fuerte, caja de caudales.—s.**-backed,** ancho de hombros. —s.**-bodied,** fornido, membrudo.—s.**-bodied wine,** vino de mucho cuerpo.—s.**-handed,** fuerte de manos y puños.—s.**-minded,** de espíritu vigoroso; de ideas ahombradas y hombrunas (apl. a mujeres).—s. **water,** agua fuerte.—**an army ten thousand s.,** un ejército de diez mil hombres.—**by,** o **with, the s. arm,** con mano de hierro, por la fuerza.

stronghold [stróŋgjould], *s.* plaza fuerte; fuerte, fortificación.

strongly [stróŋgli], *adv.* fuertemente; firmemente, sólidamente; acérrimamente; vehementemente.

strongyle [stróŋgyil], *s.* estróngilo, gusano parásito del hombre y los animales.—**strongylosis** [-lósis], *s.* estrongilosis, enfermedad causada por estróngilos.

strontia [n [strónšhia(n)], *s.* (min.) estronciana.

strontianite [-ait], *s.* (min.) estroncianita.

strontium [strónšhium], *s.* (quím.) estroncio.

strop. **I.** *va.* asentar (navajas). **II.** *s.* asentador de navajas; (mar.) estrovo.

strophe [strófi], *s.* (poét.) estrofa.

strove [strouv], *pret.* de TO STRIVE.

struck, *pret.* y *pp.* de TO STRIKE.—s. **jury,** jurado especial (escogido por procedimiento especial).— s. **measure,** medida al ras o rebajada (apl. a las de áridos cuando el contenido se empareja con los bordes superiores).

structural [strúcchuræl], *a.* de estructura; relativo a la estructura; (ing.) de construcción, de construcciones.—s. **iron,** hierro de construcciones; hierro en barras de construcción.—s. **resistance,** (aer.) resistencia pasiva.—s. **shape,** barra de construcción (apl. a las que se denotan por su sección transversal—barra en U, de doble T, escuadra, etc.).—s. **steel,** acero de construcciones; acero en barras de construcción.

structure [strúkchur], *s.* construcción (edificio, puente, etc.); estructura (disposición de las partes de un todo).

struggle [strúgœl]. **I.** *vn.* luchar, pugnar, bregar, forcejear; esforzarse; contender; agitarse. **II.** *s.* esfuerzo; disputa, contienda; pugna, forcejeo; lucha, conflicto.

strum [strum], *va.* y *vn.* arañar, tocar mal un instrumento de cuerda.

struma [strúma], *s.* lamparón, lamparones, tumores fríos.

strumous [strúmus], *a.* escrofuloso.

strumpet [strúmpet], *s.* ramera.

strung, *pret.* y *pp.* de TO STRING.

strut [strut]. **I.** *vn.* contonearse, pavonearse, farolear; inflarse, ensoberbecerse. **II.** *s.* contoneo, pavonada; (ing.) pieza de compresión, poste, puntal; columna; (carp.) riostra, jabalcón, tornapunta de caballete; (min.) adema; (cost.) plegadera.

struthious [strúzius], *a.* parecido o perteneciente a los avestruces.

strychnin(e, o **strychnia** [strícnin, strícnia], *s.* estricnina.

stub [stub]. **I.** *s.* (agr.) tocón, cepa; zoquete; fragmento, resto; cabo o colilla de tabaco; (E. U.) talón, matriz.—s. **bock,** libro talonario.—s. **iron,** hierro hecho de clavos viejos.—s. **nail,** puntilla, hita.—s. **pen,** pluma de escribir de punta mocha, pluma para letra redonda.—s. **twist,** hierro para cañones de fusil. **II.** *va.* (E. U.) tropezar contra una cosa baja; (agr.) rozar, desarraigar; reducir a tocón.

stubbed [stubd], *a.* a modo de tocón; lleno de tocones; fuerte, vigoroso; grosero.

stubbedness [stúbednes], *s.* forma parecida a un tocón.

stubble [stúbœl], *s.* (agr.) rastrojo.

stubborn [stúbœrn], *a.* cabezudo, testarudo o porfiado; inquebrantable, innegable.—**stubbornly** [-li], *adv.* inflexiblemente, tercamente.—**stubbornness** [-nes], *s.* obstinación, terquedad, porfía, tesonería.

stubby [stúbi], *a.* cachigordete; gordo, corto y tieso.

stucco [stúco], **I.** *a.* y *vn.* estucar. **II.** *s.* estuco. —s. **plasterer,** estucador, estuquista.—s. **work,** guarnecido, estuco.—s. **worker** = S. PLASTERER.

stuck [stuc], *pret.* y *pp.* de TO STICK.—**s.-up,** (fam.) presuntuoso, presumido.

stud [stud]. **I.** (carp.) poste de tabique, paral, pie derecho; perno, pasador; tachón, clavo de adorno; botón de camisa; refuerzo de eslabón; yeguada, caballada; caballeriza; (elec.) tornillo de contacto, borne, terminal.—s. **bolt,** perno trabado o de extremos roscados. **II.** *va.* tachonar.

studbook [stúdbúc], *s.* registro genealógico de caballos.

studding sails [-ing séils], *s. pl.* (mar.) alas o arrastraderas, rastreras.

student [stiúdent], *s.* estudiante; investigador; observador; persona que estudia o se ocupa en un asunto.—s. **lamp,** quinqué, lámpara Argand.

studhorse [stúdjórs], *s.* caballo padre.

studied [stúdid], *a.* estudiado, premeditado.

studio [stiúdio], *s.* estudio, taller.

studious [stiúdius], *a.* estudioso; asiduo, solícito; estudiado.—**studiously** [-li], *adv.* estudiosamente, asiduamente.—**studiousness** [-nes], *s.* estudiosidad, aplicación al estudio.

studwork [stúduœrc], *s.* (carp.) entramado.

study [stúdi]. **I.** *s.* estudio; asignatura, materia que se estudia; estudio, retrete, gabinete; meditación profunda; solicitud, cuidado; (mús.) estudio, ejercicio.—**to be in a brown s.,** pensar en las musarañas. **II.** *va.* estudiar; (con **out** o **up**) considerar, meditar; idear, proyectar. **III.** *vn.* estudiar; meditar.

stuff [stuf]. **I.** *s.* material, materia prima; materia, substancia, elemento fundamental; cosa, objeto; cachivaches, chismes, baratijas, muebla je; desechos, desperdicios; cosas, ideas o sentimientos sin valor; frusilería; género, paño, tela, estofa; jarope, mejunje, pócima; (mar.) betún; (carp.) tablas, tablillas. **II.** *interj.* ¡bagatela! ¡niñería! ¡frusilería! **III.** *va.* henchir, llenar; rellenar (un pavo, etc.), embutir; aforrar; hartar; atestar, empaquetar; disecar.—**to s. a ballot box,** (pol.) echar votos fraudulentos en una urna electoral. **IV.** *vn.* y *vr.* atracarse, hartarse, engullir.

stuffing [stúfing], *s.* material con que se atesta o rellena una cosa; atestadura, rehenchimiento; (mec.) empaquetado; (coc.) relleno.—s. **box,** (mec.) caja de empaquetado, prensaestopas.

stuffy [stúfi], *a.* que tupe; mal ventilado, sofocante.

stull [stul], (min.) entablado o andamio de protección contra piedras desprendidas.

stultification [stúltifikéshun], *s.* embobecimiento, aturdimiento.

stultify [stúltifai], *va.* embrutecer, atontar, embobecer; (for.) alegar locura o estupidez.

stum [stum]. **I.** *s.* mosto. **II.** *va.* echar mostaza al vino para que no fermente; azufrar un tonel.

stumble [stúmbœl]. **I.** *vn.* tropezar, dar un traspié; (con **on** o **upon**) encontrar o tropezar con. **II.** *s.* traspié, tropiezo, tropezón, desliz, desatino.

---

stumbler [stúmblœr], s. tropezador.

stumblingblock, stumblingstone [-blingblóc, -stóun], s. tropiezo, obstáculo.

stump [stʌmp]. **I.** s. tocón, cepa; troncho (de col); muñón (de brazo o pierna); raigón (de una muela); poste; (b. a.) esfumino; tope de cerradura; tribuna pública; (pol.) arenga electoral; (fam.) desafío, reto.—**to be up a s.**, (fam. E. U.) estar en un brete. **II.** a. parecido a un tocón; perteneciente a una arenga política.—**s. speaker,** orador callejero. **III.** va. recorrer haciendo discursos políticos; (fam.) desafiar; cachifollar, dejar patidifuso; tropezar; (b. a.) esfumar. **IV.** vn. renquear; andar sobre los muñones; (fam.) pronunciar discursos políticos.

stumpy [stúmpi], a. lleno de tocones; tozo, cachigordete.

stun [stʌn]. **I.** vn. aturdir, atontar; pasmar, privar; atronar, atolondrar, ensordecer, aturrullar. **II.** s. choque, golpe o sacudimiento que aturde; aturdimiento.

stung [stʌng], pret. y pp. de TO STING.

stunner [stúncœr], s. el o lo que aturde, atolondra o aturrulla; (fam.) cosa pasmosa.

stunning [-ing], a. (fam.) sorprendente; magnífico, excelente; elegante, hermoso.

stunt [stʌnt]. **I.** va. impedir el crecimiento o desarrollo de, no dejar medrar; (fam., E. U.) hacer ejercicios malabares o gimnásticos. **II.** s. falta de crecimiento o desarrollo; animal o planta achaparrados; (fam.) suerte, ejercicio o acción de habilidad o destreza; maniobra.

stupe [stiúp]. **I.** s. (med.) fomento, compresa. **II.** va. fomentar.

stupefacient [stiupeféishent],**stupefactive** [-fǽctiv], a. y s. estupefaciente, estupefactivo.

stupefaction [-fǽcshʌn], s. estupefacción, pasmo, estupor.—**stupefied** [-faid], a. estupefacto.—**stupefier** [-fáiœr], s. lo que produce estupor.—**stupefy** [-fai], va. causar estupor, dejar estupefacto, entorpecer, atolondrar; pasmar.

stupendous [stiupéndʌs], a. estupendo.

stupendously [-li], adv. estupendamente.

stupendousness [-nes], s. calidad de estupendo o maravilloso.

stupid [stiúpid], a. estúpido; estupefacto, turulato.

stupidity [stiupíditi], **stupidness** [stiúpidnes], s. estupidez; necedad, mentecatada.

stupidly [stiúpidli], adv. estúpidamente.

stupor [stiúpœr], s. estupor; atontamiento, estupidez.

sturdily [stœrdili], adv. robustamente, vigorosamente; tenazmente.—**sturdiness** [-ines], s. robustez, fuerza, vigor; tenacidad.

sturdy [stœrdi]. **I.** a. fuerte, robusto, vigoroso; firme, tenaz, porfiado. **II.** s. (vet.) modorra.

sturgeon [stœryʌn], s. (ict.) esturión, marón.

stutter [stútœr]. **I.** vn. tartamudear, tartalear. **II.** s. tartamudeo.—**stutterer** [-œr], s. tartamudo. —**stuttering** [-ing]. **I.** s. tartamudeo. **II.** a. tartamudo, tartajoso, balbuciente.

sty [stái], s. (pl. STIES) zahurda, pocilga; zaquizamí, tabuco, cuchitril; lupanar, burdel; (med.) orzuelo.

Stygian [stíryian], a. estigio.

style [stáil]. **I.** s. estilo, dicción, lenguaje; modo, uso, manera, moda, tono; género, escuela; (arq.) estilo; título, tratamiento; estilo, punzón para escribir; buril; estilo o gnomon del reloj de sol; (cir.) estilete; (zool.) pira; (bot.) estilo. **II.** va. intitular, nombrar, llamar.

stylet [-et], s. estilete, punzón; (zool.) púa.

stylish [-ish], a. elegante; a la moda.

stylist [-ist], s. estilista.

stylite [-ait], s. estilita.

stylobate [stáilobet], s. (arq.) estilóbato.

stylograph [-graf], s. estilógrafo.

stylographic [-grǽfic], a. estilográfico.—**s. pen,** pluma estilográfica.

styloid [stáiloid], a. estiloideo.

stylus [stáilʌs], s. punzón.

styptic [stíptic], a. y s. (med.) estíptico; astrictivo, astringente.

stypticity [stiptísiti], s. estipticidad.

styracaceous [stairakéishʊs], a. (bot.) estiracáceo.

styrax [stáirax], s. (bot.) estoraque.

Styx [stix], s. Estigia.

suable [siúabœl], a. que puede ser perseguido en justicia.

suasion [suéiyʊn], s. persuasión.—**moral s.,** influencia moral, medidas morales, sanción moral.

suasive [suéisiv], a. persuasivo, suasorio.

suave [suéiv], a. suave, afable.

suavity [suǽviti], s. suavidad; afabilidad, dulzura, blandura.

sub [sʌb], s. (fam.) subordinado; suplente, reemplazo; submarino.

subacid [sʌbásid], a. agrillo; (quím.) subácido.

subacrid [sʌbǽcrid], a. asperillo.

subaerial [sʌbeírial], a. subaéreo.

subagent [sʌbéyœnt], s. subejecutor, subagente.

subalpine [sʌbǽlpin], a. del límite superior de la vegetación forestal en las montañas.

subaltern [sʌbóltœrn, sʌbǽltœrn]. **I.** a. subalterno, subordinado, dependiente. **II.** s. oficial subalterno; alférez; teniente.

subalternant [sʌbǽltœrnant]. **I.** a. (lóg.) universal. **II.** s. proposición universal.

subalternate [-net], a. sucesivo; subalterno o subordinado.

subaqueous [sʌbéicuiʊs], a. subacuático.

subbase [sʌb-béis], s. (arq.) miembro más bajo de una base. V. SUBBASS.

subbass [sʌb-béis], s. (mús.) registro grave del pedal.

subcaliber [sʌbcélibœr], a. de menor calibre que el del cañón del arma (apl. a proyectiles).

subcarbonate [sʌbcárbonet], s. (quím.) subcarbonato.

subchanter [sʌbchántœr], s. sochantre.

subclavian [sʌbcléivian], a. (anat.) subclavio.— **s. artery,** arteria subclavia.—**s. vein,** vena subclavia.

subcommittee [sʌbcomíti], s. subcomisión.

subconscious [sʌbcónshʊs], a. subconsciente.

subconsciousness [-nes], s. subconsciencia.

subcontract [sʌbcóntræct], s. subcontrato.

subcontractor [sʌbcontrǽctœr], s. subcontratista.

subcutaneous [sʌbkiuténiʊs], a. subcutáneo, hipodérmico.

subdeacon [sʌbdícʊn], s. subdiácono.

subdeaconship [-ship], s. subdiaconato.

subdean [sʌbdín], s. subdecano o vicedecano.

subdelegate [sʌbdélegueit]. **I.** s. subdelegado. **II.** va. subdelegar.—**subdelegation** [-shʊn], s. subdelegación.

subdivide [sʌbdiváid], va. subdividir.

subdivision [sʌbdivíyʊn], s. subdivisión.

subdominant [sʌbdóminant], a. y s. (mús.) subdominante.

subduce [sʌbdiús], **subduct** [sʌbdúct], va. substraer, quitar, sacar.

subduction [sʌbdúcshʊn], s. substracción.

subdue [sʌbdiú], va. sojuzgar, someter, vencer, sujetar, dominar; domar o amansar; mejorar (tierras); extirpar (malas hierbas); suavizar.— **subdued tone,** tono sumiso; voz baja; color amortiguado.

subduer [sʌbdiúœr], s. sojuzgador, conquistador; domador, amansador.

subequatorial [-icuætórial], a. vecino al ecuador.

suberic [siubéric], a. subérico.

suberin [siúbœrin], s. suberina.

subexhaust [sʌbégsost], s. (máq. com. int.) escape auxiliar.

subfamily [sʌbfǽmili], s. (biol.) tribu, subfamilia.

subgenus [sʌbyínʊs], s. (biol.) subgénero.

subgrade [sʌbgréid], s. (f. c.) explanación o plataforma (de la vía).

subindex [sʌbíndex], s. (mat.) subíndice.

subjacent [sʌbyéisent], a. subyacente.

subject [sʌbyéct]. **I.** va. sujetar, someter; sojuzgar, subyugar; exponer, presentar; supeditar, subordinar. **II.** a. [sʌbyect] sujeto; expuesto, propenso; sometido, dominado, supeditado. **III.** *s.* súbdito; vasallo; materia, tópico, asunto, tema; (gram.) sujeto; (med.) individuo, sujeto; cadáver destinado a la disección.—**s. matter,** asunto, materia de que se trata.

subjection [subyécshun], *s.* sujeción; dependencia, servidumbre; sometimiento; ligadura.

subjective [-tiv], *a.* subjetivo.—**subjectively** [-li], *adv.* subjetivamente.—**subjectiveness** [-nes], *s.* subjetividad.— **subjectivism** [-ism], *s.* subjetivismo.—**subjectivist** [-ist], *s.* subjetivista.—**subjectivity** [subyectiviti], *s.* subjetividad.

subjoin [subyóin], *va.* añadir, adjuntar.

subjugate [súbyugueit], *va.* subyugar, sojuzgar, someter.—**subjugation** [-guéishun], *s.* sujeción, subyugación.

subjunctive [subyúnctiv], *a. y s.* subjuntivo.

subkingdom [subkḷgdum], *s.* subreino.

sublease [súblis]. **I.** *s.* subarriendo. **II.** *va.* [sublís], subarrendar.

sublet [sublét], *va.* subarrendar.—**subletting,** *s.* subarrendamiento.

sublimate [súblimet]. **I.** *s.* (quím.) sublimado. **II.** *va.* (quím.) sublimar; (fig.) refinar, purificar. —**sublimation** [-éishun], *s.* sublimación; refinamiento, perfección.

sublimatory [subláimatori], *a.* sublimatorio.

sublime [subláim]. **I.** *a.* sublime, excelso; supremo, extremo. **II.** *s.* lo sublime, sublimidad. **III.** *va. y vn.* sublimar, exaltar, ensalzar; (quím.) sublimar(se).—**sublimely** [-li], *adv.* sublimemente.—**sublimeness** [-nes], **sublimity** [sublímiti], *s.* sublimidad.

subliminal [sublíminæl], *a.* subconsciente.

sublingual [sublíngual], *a.* (anat.) sublingual.

sublunar [sublúnar], **sublunary** [súblunari], *a.* sublunar, terrestre.

submarine [súbmarin]. **I.** *s. y a.* submarino. **II.** *va. y vn.* hundir o atacar con un submarino; ser hundido por un submarino.—**s. armor,** traje de buzo.—**s. boat,** submarino (barco).—**s. chaser,** cazasubmarinos, buque antisubmarino, o contra submarinos.—**s. mine,** mina submarina.

submaxillary [submǽxilari], *a.* submaxilar.

submerge [submǽrv], *va. y vn.* sumergir(se).— **submergence** [-rens], **submersion** [-shun], *s.* sumersión, sumergimiento.

submersible [-sibœl], *s. y a.* sumergible; submarino.

submission [submíshun], *s.* sumisión, sometimiento; obediencia, deferencia; (for.) sometimiento a arbitraje.

submissive [-siv], *a.* sumiso, obediente; manso.

submissively [-li], *adv.* sumisamente, humildemente, rendidamente.

submissiveness [-nes], *s.* calidad de sumiso; obediencia, mansedumbre.

submit [submít]. **I.** *va.* someter, referir, dejar a la decisión (de); presentar, exponer como opinión propia, permitirse decir, proponer. **II.** *vr. y vn.* someterse, conformarse, resignarse.

submultiple [submúltipœl], *s.* submúltiplo.

subnormal [subnórmæl]. **I.** *a.* subnormal, deficiente. **II.** *s.* (mat.) subnormal.

suborder [subórdœr], *s.* (bot. y zool.) suborden; (arq.) orden subordinado.

subordinacy [subórdinasi], *s.* subordinación, sujeción.

subordinate [subórdinet]. **I.** *a. y s.* subalterno, subordinado, inferior, dependiente, secundario. **II.** *va.* subordinar, someter, sujetar.—**subordinately** [-li], *adv.* subordinadamente.—**subordination** [-éishun], *s.* subordinación, sujeción; menoría.

suborn [subórn], *va.* sobornar, cohechar.

subornation [subornéishun], *s.* soborno, cohecho.

suborner [subórnœr], *s.* sobornador, cohechador.

subpena, subpœna [subpína]. **I.** *s.* (for.) citación, comparendo. **II.** *va.* citar, emplazar.

subpolar [subpólar], *a.* subpolar.

subprefect [subprífect], *s.* subprefecto.

subprefecture [-chuœr], *s.* subprefectura.

subrogate [súbrogueit], *vt.* poner en lugar de otro, substituir.—**subrogation** [-éishun], *s.* substitución.

subscapular [subscǽpiular], *a.* (anat.) subescapular.

subscribe [subscráib], *va. y vn.* subscribir, firmar, rubricar; aprobar, consentir; subscribirse, abonarse.—**to s. for,** subscribirse a.—**subscriber** [-œr], *s.* infrascrito, firmante, el que subscribe; subscriptor, abonado.

subscription [subscrípshun], *s.* firma; subscripción, abono; cantidad subscrita.

subsection [subsécshun], *s.* subdivisión.

subsequence [súbsecuens], *s.* subsecuencia.

subsequent [-ent], *a.* subsecuente, subsiguiente.

subsequently [-li], *adv.* posteriormente, subsiguientemente.

subserve [subsœrv]. **I.** *va.* servir, ayudar. **II.** *vn.* servir como subordinado.—**subservience, subserviency** [-viens, -i], *s.* servicio, ayuda; subordinación.—**subservient** [-viœnt], *a.* útil o servicial; subordinado.—**subserviently** [-li], *adv.* subordinadamente; útilmente.

subside [subsáid], *vn.* apaciguarse, calmarse; bajar (un flúido); hundirse, irse a fondo.—**subsidence, subsidency** [-ens, -i], *s.* apaciguamiento, calma; desplome, sumersión, asiento.

subsidiary [subsídieri], *a.* subsidiario; secundario, incidental, auxiliar.

subsidize [súbsidáis], *va.* subvencionar.

subsidy [súbsidi], *s.* subvención, subsidio.

subsist [subsíst]. **I.** *vn.* subsistir, existir; permanecer, perdurar, conservarse; sustentarse, mantenerse. **II.** *va.* alimentar o mantener.

subsistence [-ens], *s.* existencia, subsistencia; sostenimiento o mantenimiento; cualidad inherente.—**s. department,** (E. U.) comisaría general.

subsistent [-ent], *a.* subsistente; inherente.

subsoil [subsóil]. **I.** *va.* arar, labrar la tierra. **II.** *s.* subsuelo.

substage [súbstéir], *s.* (fís.) disposición para los accesorios que van bajo la platina del microscopio; (geol.) subpiso, subdivisión de un sistema estratificado.

substance [súbstans], *s.* substancia; miga, enjundia, jugo, fuste; hacienda, caudal o bienes.

substantial [substǽnshal]. **I.** *a.* sólido, fuerte, resistente; importante, valioso; cuantioso, considerable; seguro; responsable; real, existente, verdadero; duradero; esencial; corpóreo, material; substancial, substancioso; enjundioso. **II.** *s.* realidad; parte esencial.

substantiality [substǽnshiǽliti], *s.* realidad; corporeidad.

substantially [-shali], *adv.* substancialmente; sólidamente.

substantialness [-nes], *s.* calidad de substancial; firmeza, fuerza, duración.

substantiate [substǽnshiéit], *va.* verificar, establecer, comprobar, justificar.

substantiation [-éishun], *s.* substanciación.

substantival [súbstantival], *a.* (gram.) substantivo.

substantive [súbstantiv]. **I.** *a.* substantivo; real, esencial, duradero; explícito; que tiene individualidad distinta, o recursos propios. —**s. dye,** tinte que no requiere mordente. **II.** *s.* (gram.) substantivo; el o lo que es independiente.

substantively [-li], *adv.* substancialmente, substantivamente.

substitute [súbstitiut]. **I.** *va.* substituir, reemplazar. **II.** *s.* substituto, suplente, reemplazo.

substitution [súbstitiúshun], *s.* substitución; reemplazo; delegación.

substratum [substrétum], *s.* capa inferior; substrato.

substructure [súbstrúkchur], *s.* subestructura.

subsume [subsiúm], *vt.* incluir.—**subsumption** [-súmpshun], *s.* inclusión; cosa o asunto incluidos; (lóg.) premisa menor.

subtangent [subtǽnyent], *s.* subtangente.

subtend [subténd], *va.* (geom.) subtender; (bot.) encerrar en la axila.

subtense [súbténs], *s.* (geom.) subtensa.

subterfuge [súbtœrfiur], *s.* subterfugio.

---

subterranean, subterraneous [súbterréinian, -niʊs], *a.* subterráneo.

subtile [sʊ́btil], *a.* sutil, delicado, tenue; refinado; penetrante.—**subtilely** [-li], *adv.* sutilmente.—**subtileness** [-nes], **subtility** [sʊbtíliti], *s.* sutileza, sutilidad; delgadez, tenuidad.—**subtilize** [-aiṡ], *va.* y *vn.* sutilizar, adelgazar, refinar.

subtilty [sʊ́btilti], *s.* sutileza, alambicamiento, agudeza, argucia.

subtitle [sʊbtáitœl], *s.* subtítulo; (tea.) título de escena cinematográfica.

subtle [sʊ́btœl], *a.* sutil, asuto, artero; perspicaz, penetrante; apto, perito; ingenioso, primoroso.

subtleness, subtlety [-nes, -ti], *s.* sutileza; astucia, artificio.

subtly [sʊ́tli], *adv.* sutilmente, delicadamente, artificiosamente.

subtract [sʊbtréct], *va.* substraer, quitar; (arit.) restar.—**subtraction** [-ṡhʊn], *s.* substracción; (arit.) resta, substracción.

subtrahend [súbtrajend], *s.* substraendo.

subtreasury [sʊbtréʸuri], *s.* (E. U.) subtesorería.

subtreasurer [sʊbtréʸurœr], *s.* subtesorero.

subtropic(al [sʊbtrópic(al], *a.* subtropical.

suburb [sʊ́bœrb], *s.* suburbio, arrabal.—*pl.* afueras, inmediaciones.—**suburban** [sʊbœ́rban], *s.* y *a.*, **suburbanite** [-ait], *s.* suburbano.

suburbicarian [sʊ́bœrbikéiriæn], *a.* suburbicario.

subvene [sʊbvín], *vn.* subvenir.

subvention [sʊbvénṡhʊn], *s.* subvención, subsidio, ayuda. *V.* SUBSIDY.

subversion [sʊbvœ́rṡhʊn], *s.* subversión, ruina, trastorno.—**subversive** [-siv], *a.* subversivo.—**subvert** [sʊbvœ́rt], *va.* subvertir, destruir, trastornar. —**subverter** [-œr], *s.* subversor, destructor, trastornador.—**subvertible** [-íbœl], *a.* subvertible, trastornaole, destruíble.

subway [sʊ́búéi], *s.* camino artificial subterráneo; mina; ferrocarril subterráneo.

succedaneous [sʊcsidéniʊs], *a.* sucedáneo.

succedaneum [-niʊm], *s.* substituto; (med.) sucedáneo.

succeed [sʊcsíd]. **I.** *va.* suceder o seguir a. **II.** *vn.* salir bien, tener buen éxito.—**to s. in**, tener buen éxito en; lograr.

succeeder [-œr], *s.* sucesor.—**succeeding** [-ing], *a.* subsiguiente, sucediente, futuro.

succentor [sʊcséntœr], *s.* sucentor, sochantre.

success [sʊcsés], *s.* buen éxito, buen resultado, triunfo; persona o asunto que tiene buen éxito. —**successful** [-ful], *a.* próspero, afortunado, airoso; fructuoso, productivo, satisfactorio.— **successfully** [-fulj], *adv.* con buen resultado, prósperamente, con buen éxito.—**successfulness** [-nes], *s.* feliz éxito, buen resultado.

succession [sʊcséṡhʊn], *s.* sucesión; seguida, continuación; linaje; herencia.

successive [-siv], *a.* sucesivo.—**successively** [-li], *adv.* sucesivamente.

successor [sʊcséscœr], *s.* sucesor; heredero.

succinate [sʊ́csineit], *s.* (quím.) succinato.

succinct [sʊcsínct], *a.* sucinto, breve; (ent.) enfaldado.—**succinctly** [-li], *adv.* sucintamente.— **succinctness** [-nes], *s.* brevedad, concisión.

succinic [sʊcsínic], *a.* succínico.

succinite [sʊ́csinait], *s.* (min.) succino, ámbar.

succory [sʊ́cori], *s.* (bot.) achicoria.

succotash [sʊ́cotæṡh], *s.* (E. U.) potaje de maíz tierno y habas.

succo(u)r [sʊ́cœr]. **I.** *va.* socorrer. **II.** *s.* socorro; (mil.) refuerzo; socorredor, auxiliador.

succubus [sʊ́kiubʊs], *s.* súcubo.

succulency [sʊ́kiulensi], *s.* suculencia.

succulent [-ent], *a.* suculento.

succumb [sʊcúm], *vn.* sucumbir.

succumbent [sʊcúmbœnt], *a.* sucumbiente.

succuss [sʊcús], *va.* sacudir.

succussion [sʊcúṡhʊn], *s.* sacudimiento.

such [sʊch]. **I.** *a.* tal; semejante; dicho, mencionado. Generalmente va seguido del *art. ind.* (*v.* A, *art. ind*) (*such a man*, tal hombre, semejante hombre; *such a case*, tal caso).—**s. a**, (fam.)

tan (*such a bad man*, un hombre tan malo).—**s. and s., o s. or s.**, tal o cual.—**s. . . . as**, como el que, de la clase del que; el . . . que (*such books as he reads*, libros como los que él lee, los libros que él lee; *I bought such a horse as I found*, compré el caballo que hallé). **II.** *pron.* tal.—**s. as**, los que, quienes (*such as come here*, los que vienen aquí; *such as wish to come*, los que, o quienes, deseen venir).

suck [sʊc]. **I.** *va.* y *vn.* chupar; mamar; amamantar.—**to s. in**, embeber, absorber, chupar.—**to s. out, o up**, chupar, extraer o sacar chupando o por succión. **II.** *s.* succión; chupada; mamada.— **to give s.**, amamantar, dar de mamar.

sucker [sʊ́cœr], *s.* lechón, gorrinillo; chupador; mamador; mamón, chupón, chupadera; (mec.) émbolo; tubo de aspiración; (bot.) pimpollo, vástago, retoño, serpollo, barbado; (ict.) rémora; liebre marina; (cir.) ventosa; (fam.) gorrista, gorrero; pelele, primo.

sucking [sʊ́king]. **I.** *s.* chupadura. **II.** *s.* mamante, chupadero; lechal, recental.—**s. fisb**, rémora.—**s. pig**, corzuelo, lechoncillo.

suckle [sʊ́cœl]. **I.** *va.* amamantar, dar de mamar, criar. **II.** *vn.* lactar, mamar.

suckling [sʊ́cling], *s.* mamón, mamantón, de teta, de cría.

sucrose [siúcros], *s.* sucrosa.

suction [sʊ́céṡhʊn], *s.* succión.—**s. hose**, manguera de alimentación.—**s. pipe**, tubo aspirante o de succión.—**s. pump**, bomba aspirante.

suctorial [sʊctórial], *a.* chupador, chupadero o chupón.

Sudanese, [sudanís *o* nís], *a.* y *s.* sudanés.

sudatory [siúdatori]. **I.** *a.* sudorífero. **II.** *s.* sudorífico; sudadero, estufa.

sudden [sʊ́dœn *o* súdn], *a.* repentino, súbito; apresurado, precipitado.—**all of a s., all on a s., of a s., on a s.**, de repente.

suddenly [-li], *adv.* de repente, repentinamente.

suddenness [-nes], *s.* calidad de repentino.

sudor [siúdœr], *s.* sudor.

sudoriferous [sudoríferʊs], *a.* sudorífero.

sudorific [siudorífic], *a.* y *s.* sudorífico.

Sudra [súdræ] *n.* zudra, cuarta casta de la India.

suds [sʊdṡ], *s. pl.* jabonaduras; espuma.—**in the s.**, (fam.) en apuros.

sue [siú], *va.* y *vn.* demandar, poner pleito, entablar juicio; (con **to** or **for**) rogar, pedir, suplicar, tratar de persuadir; (ant.) galantear.—**to s. for damages**, demandar por daños y perjuicios.

suet [siúet], *s.* sebo en rama; grasa.

suety [siúeti], *a.* seboso.

suffer [sʊ́fœr], *va.* y *vn.* sufrir, padecer, sentir; soportar, tolerar, conllevar; permitir, consentir, pasar.

sufferable [sʊ́fœrabœl], *a.* sufrible, soportable.

sufferably [-bli], *adv.* sufriblemente.

sufferance [sʊ́fœrans], *s.* tolerancia, consentimiento tácito; (ant.) sufrimiento; conformidad, resignación; (com.) permiso especial de la aduana.

sufferer [-œr], *s.* sufridor, paciente; víctima; el que tolera tácitamente.

suffering [-ing]. **I.** *s.* sufrimiento. **II.** *a.* paciente, doliente.—**s. humanity**, la doliente, o pobre, humanidad.

suffice [sufáis], *va.* y *vn.* bastar, ser suficiente.

sufficiency [sufíṡhensi], *s.* suficiencia; lo suficiente; eficacia; presunción.

sufficient [sufíṡhent], *a.* suficiente; apto, idóneo. —**sufficiently** [-li], *adv.* suficientemente; asaz, bastante.

suffix [sʊ́fix]. **I.** *va.* añadir como sufijo. **II.** *s.* [súfix] (gram.) sufijo.

suffocate [sʊ́fokeit]. **I.** *va.* sofocar, asfixiar, ahogar; apagar (un fuego). **II.** *vn.* sofocarse, asfixiarse, ahogarse.—**suffocating** [-ing], *a.* sofocante, asfixiante.—**suffocation** [-kéiṡhʊn], *s.* sofocación, asfixia.

suffocative [súfocativ], *a.* sofocante, sofocador.

suffragan [sʊ́fragan], *a.* y *s.* (igl.) sufragáneo.

suffrage [súfrey], s. sufragio; aprobación, consentimiento; (igl.) sufragio.—**suffragette** [súfrayét], s. sufragista (mujer).—**suffragist** [-yist], s. sufragista; votante.

suffruticose [svfrúticos], a. (bot.) leñoso y herbáceo.

suffuse [svfiús], va. difundir, bañar, cubrir.

suffusion [svfiúyʊn], s. difusión, baño; (med.) sufusión.

sufi [súfi], s. sufí o sofí.

sugar [shúgar]. **I.** s. azúcar; agasajo, lisonja.— **s. beet,** remolacha.—**s. bowl,** azucarero.—**s. cane,** caña de azúcar.—**s.-cane grinding,** molienda de caña de azúcar.—**s. candy,** azúcar canée. —**s.-coated,** confitado, garapiñado; azucarado.— **s.-coated pill,** píldora azucarada.—**s. loaf,** pan de azúcar.—**s. maple,** arce de azúcar.—**s. mill,** trapiche.—**s. of lead,** azúcar de plomo o sal de saturno.—**s. pill,** píldora de azúcar; píldora azucarada. —**s. plantation,** ingenio de azúcar.—**s. syrup,** miel, melado.—**s. tongs,** tenacillas para azúcar. **II.** va. azucarar, endulzar; confitar, garapiñar. **III.** vn. (E. U. y Canadá) hacer el azúcar de arce.

sugared [shúgard], a. azucarado, endulzado, dulce; garapiñado.

sugarplum [shúgarplʊm], s. confite, dulce.

sugary [shúgari], a. azucarado, dulce; meloso.

suggest [svyést], va. sugerir, insinuar, indicar.

suggestion [svyéschʊn], s. sugestión, insinuación, indicación.

suggestive [svyéstiv], a. sugestivo.

suicidal [siuisáidal], a. suicida.

suicide [siúisaid], s. suicidio; suicida.

sui generis [siúi yéneris], sui géneris.

sui juris [-yúris], de completa capacidad legal.

suing [siúing], s. solicitación, diligencia; galanteo.

suit [siút]. **I.** s. petición, súplica, solicitación; galanteo, cortejo; (for.) pleito, litigio; colección, serie, juego, surtido; flus, traje completo; (en la baraja) palo. **II.** va. y vn. cuadrar, convenir, acomodar, adaptar(se), ser apropiado o a propósito; ir o venir bien, sentar, encajar; agradar, contentar, satisfacer; ajustarse, acomodarse, casar, hermanarse.—**to s. one's self,** hacer uno lo que guste.

suitable [siútbœl], a. adecuado, apropiado, conveniente, satisfactorio, adaptable, a propósito.

suitability [-bíliti], **suitableness** [-bœlnes], s. adaptabilidad, conveniencia, adecuación.—**suitably** [-bli], adv. adecuada o convenientemente, propiamente, debidamente.

suitcase [siútkeis], s. maleta plana, maleta para trajes de hombre.

suite [suít], s. serie, juego; séquito, tren, acompañamiento, comitiva.—**s. of rooms,** serie de piezas, apartamento, crujía.

suitor [siútœr], s. (for.) demandante, parte actora; pretendiente, cortejo; suplicante, aspirante; postulante.

sulcate(d [súlket(ed], a. surcado, acanalado.

suleus [súlcus], s. (anat.) surco.

sulfate, sulfid, sulfur, sulfuric, etc. = SULPHATE, SULPHUR, etc.

sulk [sʊlk]. **I.** vn. amorrar. **II.** s. murria.

sulkiness [súlkines], s. ceño; murria.

sulky [súlki]. **I.** a. murrio, malhumorado; (bot.) achaparrado. **II.** s. (carr.) solitaria, calesín de un solo asiento.

sullage [súley], s. (fund.) escoria.

sullen [súlœn], a. hosco, adusto, murrio; lento; sombrío, tétrico.—**sullenly** [-li], adv. con murria, de mal humor.—**sullenness** [-nes], s. murria, mal humor; enfado, ceño.

sully [súli]. **I.** va. manchar, empañar; desdorar, mancillar. **II.** vn. empañarse. **III.** s. mancha; mancilla.

sulphacid [sʊlfæsid], s. sulfácido.

sulphate [súlfeit]. **I.** s. (quím.) sulfato. **II.** va. sulfatar.

sulphatize [súlfætaiš], va. convertir en sulfato.

sulphid(e [súlfid,-aid], s. sulfuro.

sulphite [súlfait], s. (quím.) sulfito; (fam.) persona original y despreocupada.—**sulphitic** [sʊl-

fític], a. (fam.) original, despreocupado, independiente.

sulphonal [súlfonal], s. sulfonal.

sulphonic [sʊlfónic], a. sulfónico.

sulphovinic [súlfovinic], a. sulfovínico.

sulphur [súlfœr]. **I.** s. azufre.—**s. dioxide,** anhídrido sulfuroso.—**s. trioxide,** anhídrido sulfúrico. **II.** va. azufrar.

sulphurate [sʊlfiuret]. **I.** va. sulfurar; azufrar. **II.** a. sulfúreo.

sulphuration [sʊlfiuréshun], s. sulfuración.

sulphurator [súlfiuréitor], s. sulfurador.

sulphuret [súlfiuret], s. (ant.) sulfuro.

sulphureous [sʊlfiúreus], **sulphurous** [súlfœrus], a. sulfúreo, azufroso, azufrado.

sulphureousness [-nes], s. calidad de sulfúreo.

sulphuric [sʊlfiúric], a. sulfúrico.

sulphurize [súlfiuraiš], va. sulfurar.

sulphurous [súlfiurus], a. sulfuroso.

sulphurwort [súlfœrucœrt], s. (bot.) servato.

sulphury [súlfœri], a. sulfúreo, azufroso.

sulphydrate [súlfjáidreit], s. sulfhidrato.

sulphydric [sʊlfjáidric], a. sulfhídrico.

sultan [súltan], s. sultán.

sultana [sʊltána], **sultaness** [súltanes], s. sultana.

sultriness [súltrines], s. bochorno.

sultry [súltri], a. bochornoso, sofocante.

sum [sʊm]. **I.** s. suma; substancia, esencia; cima, máximo, lo sumo; (fam.) problema de aritmética.—**s. and substance,** sustancia.— **s. total,** total.—**in s.,** en suma. **II.** va. y vn. sumar; (gen. con up) recapitular o resumir; (for.) presentar o exponer su alegato (un abogado).

sumac(h [súmæc, shúmæc], s. (bot.) zumaque.

sumless [súmles], a. innumerable.

summarily [súmarili], adv. sumariamente.

summarize [súmaraiš], va. epitomar, resumir.

summary [súmari]. **I.** a. breve, sucinto; pronto, sin demora. **II.** s. resumen.

summation [súméishun], s. (mat.) suma.

summer [súmœr]. **I.** a. estival, veraniego, de verano. **II.** s. verano, estío; (arq.) viga maestra; dintel; sotabanco; manto de chimenea.—**s. beam,** travesero de viga maestra.—**s. boarder,** veraneante.—**s. camp,** campo de verano, campo de tiendas en que se pasa el verano; colonia juvenil de verano, campo de verano para niños.—**s. solstice,** solsticio vernal o de verano.—**s. squash,** (bot.) cidracayote de verano.—**s. time,** estío, verano.— **s. wheat,** trigo candeal.—**to s.-fallow,** arar en verano y dejar en barbecho. **III.** vn. veranear, pasar el verano.

summerhouse [súmœrjáus], s. cenador, glorieta.

summersault, summerset [-solt, -set], s. salto mortal.

summertide [súmœrtaid], s. = SUMMER TIME. V. SUMMER.

summertree [súmœrtrí], s. = SUMMER BEAM. V. SUMMER.

summit [súmit], s. cima, cumbre, cúspide.

summon [súmʊn], va. citar, emplazar; llamar, convocar; mandar, requerir, intimar; (con up) espolear, aguijar, excitar.—**summoner** [-œr], s. emplazador.

summons [súmʊnš], s. (for.) citación, comparendo, emplazamiento, requerimiento; (mil.) intimación.

sump [sʊmp], s. (min.) sumidero; (máq. comb int.) colector de aceite.

sumpter [súmptœr], s. acémila.

sumption [súmpshun], s. premisa mayor.

sumptuary [súmpchueri], a. suntuario.—**s. laws,** leyes suntuarias.

sumptuous [súmpchuos], a. suntuoso, magnífico, espléndido.—**sumptuously** [-li], adv. suntuosamente.—**sumptuousness** [-nes], s. suntuosidad, pompa.

sun [sʊn], s. sol; luz de sol, solana.—**s. bath,** baño de sol, solana.—**s. dance,** danza del sol.— **s.-dried brick** = ADOBE.—**s. parlor, s. porch,** solana, carasol.—**s. spot,** mancha solar. **II.** va. asolear.—**to s. one's self,** tomar el sol.

sunbeam [súnbím], s. rayo de sol.

sunbeat [-bít], *a.* asoleado.
sunbonnet [-bónet], *s.* papalina.
sunbright [-brait], *a.* resplandeciente como el sol.
sunburn [-bœrn]. **I.** *va.* y *vn.* quemar(se) o tostar-(se) con el sol. **II.** *s.* quemadura de sol.—**sunburning** [-ing], *s.* quemadura del sol, solanera.
sunburnt [-bœrnt], *a.* quemado, tostado por el sol, requemado.
sundae [súndi], *s.* refresco de helado con frutas o nueces molidas.
Sunday [súndi]. **I.** *s.* domingo. **II.** *a.* dominical, del domingo, dominguero.—**S. clothes**, (fam.) trapitos de cristianar.—**S. law**, ley sobre la observancia del domingo.—**S. letter**, carta dominical.—**S. school**, escuela dominical de iglesia, doctrina dominical.
sunder [súndœr]. **I.** *s.* separación.—**in s.**, en dos. **II.** *va.* y *vn.* separar, apartar, dividir; romper o romperse; separarse.
sundew [-diu], *s.* (bot.) rosoli.
sundial [-dáiœl], *s.* reloj de sol, cuadrante solar.
sundown [-dáun], *s.* puesta del sol.
sundries [súndriš], *s. pl.* (com.) géneros varios.
sundry [súndri], *a.* varios, diversos.
sunfish [súnfiŝh], *s.* (ict.) rueda.
sunflower [-fláuœr], *s.* (bot.) girasol.
sung, *pret.* y *pp.* de TO SING.
sunglow [súngló], *s.* arrebol.
sunk, *pret.* y *pp.* de TO SINK.
sunken [súnkœn], *a.* sumido, hundido.
sunless [súnles], *a.* sombrío; sin luz; sin sol, nublado.
sunlight [-lait], *s.* luz del sol.
sunlike [-laik], *a.* semejante o parecido al sol; resplandeciente.
sunn [sʊn], **sunn hemp** [jemp], *s.* cáñamo de Bengala.
Sunna, Sunnah [súnæ], *s.* Zuna, cuerpo de tradiciones musulmanas.
Sunnite [-ait], *s.* zunita, miembro de cierta secta musulmana.
sunny [-i], *a.* de sol (día); asoleado, resolano; resplandeciente; alegre, risueño; halagüeño.—**s. side**, lado del sol; lado bueno, aspecto favorable.
sunproof [-prúf], *a.* a prueba del sol.
sunrise [-raiŝ], *s.* salida del sol, amanecer; (poét.) Oriente.
sunscald [-scóld], **sunscorch** [-scórch], *s.* (bot.) enfermedad causada por exceso de sol.
sunset [-set], *s.* puesta del sol; anochecida, oración.
sunshade [-ŝhéid], *s.* quitasol, parasol, sombrilla; sombrero; pantalla.
sunshine [-ŝhain], *s.* solana, luz del sol; claridad del sol; día.—**in the s.**, al sol.
sunshiny [-ŝháini], *a.* lleno de sol.
sunstroke [-stróuk], *s.* insolación.
sunstruck [-strʊc], *a.* atacado o herido de insolación.
sunup [-ʊp], *s.* (fam.) salida del sol.
sunward [-uard], *adv.* hacia el sol.
sunwise [-uaiŝ], *adv.* con el sol.
sup [sʊp]. **I.** *va.* sorber. **II.** *vn.* cenar. **III.** *s.* sorbo.
superable [siúpœrabœl], *a.* superable.
superableness [-nes], *s.* cualidad de superable.
superabound [siúpœrabáund], *vn.* superabundar.
superabundance [-abúndans], *s.* superabundancia, plétora; redundancia.—**superabundant** [-dant], *a.* superabundante.—**superabundantly** [-li], *adv.* superabundantemente.
superadd [-éd], *va.* sobreañadir, requintar.
superaddition [-adíŝhʊn], *s.* sobreañadidura.
superannuate [-éñuet], *va.* inhabilitar, imposibilitar; jubilar.—**superannuation** [-éíŝhʊn], *s.* inhabilitación; jubilación.
superb [siupœrb], *a.* soberbio, grandioso, magnífico, espléndido.—**superbly** [-li], *adv.* soberbiamente, grandiosamente.
supercargo [siúpercárgo], *s.* encomendero.
superciliary [-ŝílieri], *a.* superciliar.
supercilious [-ŝílivs], *a.* ceñudo; arrogante, altanero.—**superciliously** [-li], *adv.* arrogantemente.—**superciliousness** [-nes], *s.* arrogancia, altanería.

supercooling [-cúling], *s.* (quím.) sobrefusión.
superdominant [-dóminant], *s.* (mús.) superdominante.
superelevation [-élevéiŝhʊn], *s.* (f. c.) peralte (del riel exterior).
supereminence, supereminency [-éminens, -i], *s.* supereminencia.—**supereminent** [-éminent], *a.* supereminente, eminentísimo.
supererogate [-érogueit], *vn.* hacer más de lo obligatorio.—**supererogation** [-eroguéŝhʊn], *s.* supererogación.—**supererogatory** [-érogatori], *a.* supererogatorio.
superexcellent [-écselent], *a.* sobreexcelente, muy excelente.
superfetation [-fetéŝhʊn], *s.* superfetación.
superficial [-fiŝhal], *a.* superficial.
superficiality [-fiŝhiéliti], **superficialness** [siupœrfiŝhalnes], *s.* superficialidad.
superficially [-fíŝhali], *adv.* superficialmente.
superficiary [-fíŝhieri], *s.* (for.) superficiario.
superficies [-fíŝhiiŝ], *s.* superficie.
superfine [-fain], *a.* superfino, sobrefino, florete.
superfineness [-fáinnes], *s.* calidad de superfino.
superfluous [siupœrfluʊs], *a.* superfluo.
superfluousness [-nes], **superfluity** [siúpœrflúiti], *s.* superfluidad.
superfluously [-li], *adv.* superfluamente.
superheat [-jít], *va.* recalentar.—**superheated steam**, vapor recalentado.—**superheater** [-œr], *s.* recalentador (de vapor).—**superheating** [-ing], *s.* recalentamiento.
superheterodyne [-jéterodain], *a.* (rad.) superheterodino.
superhuman [siúpœrjiúmæn], *a.* sobrehumano.
superimpose [-impóuŝ], *va.* sobreponer.
superimposition [siúperímpoŝíŝhʊn], *s.* superposición.
superincumbent [-incúmbent], *a.* superyacente, sobrepuesto.
superinduce [-indiús], *va.* sobreañadir, promover.
superinduction [-indúcŝhʊn], *s.* sobreañadidura.
superintend [-inténd], *va.* superentender, vigilar, dirigir.—**superintendence, o superintendency** [-dens, -i], *s.* superintendencia, inspección, dirección.—**superintendent** [-dent], *s.* superintendente, inspector, interventor; capataz.
superior [siupíriœr], *a.* y *s.* superior (en todas sus acepciones).—**S. Court**, Audiencia.
superiority [siupiríriti], *s.* superioridad.
superlative [siupœrlativ], *a.* y *s.* superlativo.
superlatively [-li], *adv.* superlativamente, en sumo grado.—**superlativeness** [-nes], *s.* excelencia, grado superlativo.
superman [-mæn], *s.* superhombre.
supernal [siupœrnal], *a.* superno o supremo; celeste.
supernatant [siúpœrnéitænt], *a.* (quím.) (líquido) que queda después de formar un precipitado.
supernatural [-néchural]. **I.** *a.* sobrenatural. **II.** *s.* lo sobrenatural.—**supernaturally** [-i], *adv.* sobrenaturalmente.—**supernaturalism** [-iŝm], *s.* calidad de sobrenatural; creencia en lo sobrenatural.
supernumerary [-niúmœreri]. **I.** *a.* supernumerario, suplementario, agregado. **II.** *s.* supernumerario; (teat.) figurante, comparsa.
superphosphate [-fósfeit], *s.* superfosfato.
superpose [-póuŝ], *va.* sobreponer, superponer.
superposition [-poŝíŝhʊn], *s.* superposición.
superscribe [-scráib], *va.* sobrescribir, poner un sobrescrito a.—**superscription** [-scripŝhʊn], *s.* sobrescrito.
supersede [-síd], *va.* (for.) sobreseer; reemplazar; desalojar.
supersedeas [-sídeas], *s.* (for.) auto de sobreseimiento.
supersedure, supersession [-sídiur, -séŝhʊn], *s.* (for.) sobreseimiento.
superserviceable [-sœrvisabœl], *a.* demasiado servicial u oficioso.
superstition [-stíŝhʊn], *s.* superstición.
superstitious [-stíŝhʊs], *a.* supersticioso.

superstitiously [-li], *adv.* supersticiosamente.

superstructure [-strúkchœr], *s.* superestructura, parte superior de una construcción, o la obra propiamente, a distinción de los cimientos.

supertax [-tæx], *s.* impuesto adicional (impuesto sobre capitales o rentas que exceden cierto límite; puede lamarse *impuesto sobre riqueza excesiva*).

supervene [-vín], *vn.* sobrevenir, supervenir; suceder, acaecer.

supervenient [-vínient], *a.* superveniente.

supervention [-vénšhun], *s.* superveniencia, sobrevenida.

supervise [-váiš], *va.* superentender, inspeccionar, intervenir.—**supervision** [-viǯun], *s.* superintendencia, intervención o inspección.—**supervisor** [-váišœr], *s.* superintendente, inspector, interventor, sobrestante, veedor.

supination [siúpinéšhun], *s.* posición supina.

supine [siupáin]. **I.** *a.* supino, boca arriba; inclinado, pendiente; negligente, indolente, descuidado. **II.** *s.* [siúpain] (gram.) supino.—**supinely** [-li], *adv.* boca arriba; descuidadamente, con negligencia.—**supineness** [-nes], *s.* posición supina; descuido, negligencia, dejadez.

supper [súpœr], *s.* cena.—**s. time**, hora de cenar.

supperless [-les], *a.* sin cenar.

supplant [supplǽnt], *va.* suplantar, desbancar; reemplazar, desalojar.

supplanter [-œr], *s.* suplantador, el que suplanta a otro.

supplanting [-ing], *s.* suplantación.

supple [súpœl]. **I.** *a.* flexible; dócil, obediente, deferente; servil. **II.** *va.* y *vn.* hacer o volverse flexible, dócil u obediente.

supplement [súplemœnt]. **I.** *s.* suplemento; alcance; apéndice. **II.** *va.* completar; reforzar, ayudar.

supplemental, supplementary [-méntæl, -tari], *a.* suplementario, suplemental, supletorio.—**s. angles**, ángulos suplementarios.

suppleness [súpœlnes], *s.* flexibilidad; docilidad, condescendencia.

suppletory [súpletori], *a.* (for.) supletorio.

suppliance [súplians], *s.* ruego, súplica.

suppliant [súpliænt], **supplicant** [-plicænt], *s.* y *a.* suplicante.—**supplicate** [-plikeit], *va.* y *vn.* suplicar.—**supplication** [-plikéišhun], *s.* súplica; (igl.) preces, rogativa.—**supplicatory** [-cǽtori], *a.* suplicante.

supplier [supláicœr], *s.* suministrador.

supply [supláí]. **I.** *va.* surtir, abastecer, proveer; suministrar, proporcionar, habilitar; suplir, reemplazar. **II.** *s.* (*pl.* SUPPLIES) suministro, provisión, abastecimiento; substituto, suplente; (com.) abasto, oferta; repuesto, surtido.—*pl.* pertrechos; materiales, artículos, efectos; víveres, provisiones; enseres.—**s. and demand**, la oferta y la demanda.—**s. pipe**, (hidr.) caño o cañería de abastecimiento.—**s. price**, precio mínimo.

support [supórt]. **I.** *va.* sostener, aguantar, sustentar; mantener (a una persona, etc.), proveer para; sostener (un trato o diálogo); resistir, sufrir, tolerar; asistir, amparar; abogar por, apoyar; defender, atestiguar, probar, confirmar, justificar, vindicar; acompañar en público; (teatro) hacer un papel subordinado a otro; desempeñar un papel.—**to s. one's self**, mantenerse, ganarse la vida. **II.** *s.* sostén, apoyo, soporte; sustentación, sostenimiento; ayuda, protección; sufragio; prueba, justificación; sustento, manutención.—**in s. of**, en favor de, en apoyo de.

supportable [-abœl], *a.* soportable, llevadero; sostenible.—**supportably** [-bli], *adv.* soportable o llevaderamente.

supporter [supórtœr], *s.* mantenedor; defensor, sostenedor; partidario; sostén, soporte, sustentáculo; (arq.) atlante o telamón; (bl.) tenante.

supposable [supóusabœl], *a.* que puede suponerse.

suppose [supóuš], *va.* suponer.

supposedly [-edli], *adv.* supuestamente, que se supone (suponía, etc.).

supposer [-cer], *s.* suponedor.

supposition [súpošíšhun], *s.* suposición.

suppositional [-al], *a.* hipotético, supositivo.

supposititious [súpošítíšhus], *a.* supositicio, supuesto; falso, fingido.

suppositive [supóšitiv], *a.* supositivo.

suppository [supóšitori], *s.* supositorio, cala.

suppress [suprés], *va.* suprimir, sofocar, extinguir, acabar con; reprimir, contener; ocultar, omitir, eliminar; parar, detener.

suppressible [-sibœl], *a.* suprimible; reprimible.

suppression [-šhun], *s.* supresión, extinción, represión; (med.) suspensión.—**suppressive** [-siv], *a.* supresivo o represivo.—**suppressor** [-sœr], *s.* supresor.

suppurate [súpiuret], *va.* y *vn.* supurar.

suppuration [-éišhun], *s.* supuración; pus.

suppurative [-ativ], *a.* y *s.* supurativo.

supraliminal [siúpralíminæl], *a.* (psic.) mentalmente normal; relativo a la conciencia normal.

supramaxillary [siúpramǽxileri], *a.* y *s.* supramaxilar.

supramundane [-múndein], *a.* sobrenatural.

suprarenal [-rénal], *s.* suprarrenal.—**s. body, capsule**, o **gland**, cápsula suprarrenal.

supremacy [siuprémasi], *s.* supremacía.

supreme [siuprím], *a.* supremo.—**S. Being**, Ser Supremo.—**S. Court**, Corte Suprema, consejo o tribunal supremo.

supremely [-li], *adv.* supremamente; soberanamente, sumamente.

sural [siúral], *a.* sural.

surbase [sœrbéis], *s.* (arq.) cornisa de pedestal; moldura o vuelo en la parte superior.—**surbased** [-d], *a.* provisto de cornisa o moldura superior; rebajado (arco).

surcease [sœrsís], *vn.* cesar, acabarse.

surcharge [sœrchárγ]. **I.** *s.* sobrecarga, sobrepeso; recargo; resello. **II.** *va.* sobrecargar, recargar; resellar.

surcingle [sœrsingœl], *s.* sobrecincha; cíngulo, ceñidor.

surcoat [sœrcóut], *s.* (sast.) sobretodo, gabán; sobrevesta.

surd [sœrd]. **I.** *a.* (mat.) irracional; sordo (no sonoro). **II.** *s.* cantidad irracional; consonante sorda.

surdity [sœrditi], *s.* falta de sonoridad.

sure [šhúœr]. **I.** *a.* seguro, cierto, indudable, infalible; firme, sentado; certero; puntual; constante, estable.—**to be s.**, seguramente, sin duda; ya se ve. **II.** *adv.* (fam.) ciertamente, indudablemente, sin duda alguna.—**s. enough**, a buen seguro, con certeza.—**s.-footed**, de pie firme, seguro.

surely [-li], *adv.* ciertamente, seguramente, sin duda; indudablemente.

sureness [-nes], *s.* certeza, seguridad.

surety [šhúœrti], *s.* fiador, dita, garante; fianza, garantía, caución; seguridad, fieldad, certeza.—**of a s.**, de seguro, como cosa cierta.—**to be s. for**, ser fiador, salir garante de.

suretyship [-šhip], *s.* seguridad, fianza.

surf [sœrf], *s.* rompiente, resaca, marejada.

surface [sœrfes]. **I.** *va.* allanar, alisar, igualar. **II.** *s.* superficie, cara, sobrefaz.—**s. box**, (elec.) caja saliente.—**s. condenser**, condensador de superficie.—**s. feet**, pies de velocidad lineal por minuto.—**s. plate**, tabla rasa de comprobación de superficies planas.—**s. speed**, o **velocity**, velocidad superficial, o periférica.—**s. tension**, (fís.) tensión superficial.—**s. water**, agua superficial (a distinción de la subterránea).

surfacer [-œr], *s.* máquina de alisar o cepillar madera.

surfacing [-ing], *s.* alisamiento, aplanamiento; material de revestimiento o coronamiento; (min.) extracción (de mineral) cerca de la superficie; (f. c.) alineación (de los rieles entre sí).

surfeit [sœrfit]. **I.** *va.* ahitar, hartar, saciar, encebadar. **II.** *vn.* ahitarse, hartarse. **III.** *s.* ahito, empacho, indigestión; encebadamiento; empalagamiento; exceso.

surge [sœrγ]. **I.** *s.* oleaje, oleada. **II.** *vn.* agitarse o embravecerse (el mar); romper (las olas). **III.** *va.* hacer undular; (mar.) largar, lascar.

surgeon [sœ́rɹʊn], *s.* cirujano; (mil., mar.) médico (de ejército, de un buque).—**s. dentist**, cirujano dentista.—**s.-general**, (E. U.) médico mayor, jefe de sanidad militar o naval.

surgery [sœ́rɹœri], *s.* cirugía.

surgical [sœ́rɹical], *a.* quirúrgico.

surgy [sœ́rɹi], *a.* agitado, de leva.

surlily [sœ́rlili], *adv.* ásperamente, con mal humor, de mal modo.—**surliness** [-nes], *s.* mal genio, mal humor; murria.

surloin [sœ́rloin], *s.* solomillo.

surly [sœ́rli], *a.* áspero, rudo, insolente; furioso, tempestuoso.

surmise [sœrmáis]. **I.** *va.* conjeturar, suponer, presumir, barruntar. **II.** *s.* conjetura, suposición; barrunto.

surmount [sœrmáunt], *va.* vencer, superar; pasar; coronar, poner (algo) sobre.

surmountable [-abœl], *a.* vencible, superable.

surmullet [sœrmúlet], *s.* (ict.) mullo, salmonete.

surname [sœ́rnéim]. **I.** *s.* apellido, sobrenombre; apodo. **II.** *va.* apellidar, denominar, llamar.

surpass [sœrpás], *va.* sobrepujar, superar, aventajar.—**surpassing** [-ing], *a.* sobresaliente, superior, excelente.

surplice [sœ́rplis], *s.* (igl.) sobrepelliz.

surpliced [sœ́rplist], *a.* con sobrepelliz.

surplus, surplusage [sœ́rplʊs, -ex], *s.* sobrante, excedente, exceso, superávit.

surprise [sœrpráis]. **I.** *s.* sorpresa. **II.** *va.* sorprender.—**surprising** [-ing], *a.* sorprendente.—**surprisingly** [-ingli], *adv.* sorprendentemente.

surrebut [sœrrebʊ́t], *vn.* (for.) triplicar.

surrebutter [-œr], *s.* (for.) tríplica.

surrejoinder [-yóindœr], *s.* (for.) contrarréplica.

surrender [sʊrréndœr]. **I.** *va.* rendir, entregar; ceder, renunciar a, abandonar. **II.** *vn.* rendirse, entregarse. **III.** *s.* rendición, entrega; renuncia, dejación, abandono; sumisión; (for.) cesión.

surreptitious [sœrreptíshʊs], *a.* subrepticio.

surreptitiously [-li], *adv.* subrepticiamente.

surrey [súri], *s.* (E. U., carr.) especie de birlocho.

surrogate [súroguet]. **I.** *va.* subrogar, substituir, reemplazar. **II.** *s.* substituto; (igl.) vicario; (for.) juez de testamentarías.

surround [sʊrráund], *va.* circundar, cercar, rodear, ceñir, circuir.—**surrounding** [-ing]. **I.** *a.* circunstante, circunvecino, circumambiente. **II.** *s. pl.* alrededores, contornos, cercanías, inmediaciones; medio, circunstancias rodeantes.

surtax [sœ́rtæcs], *s.* impuesto adicional (sobre rentas que pasan de cierto límite).

surtout [sœrtút], *s.* (sast.) levitón, sobretodo.

surveillance [sœrvéilans], *s.* vigilancia.

survey [sœrvéi]. **I.** *va.* examinar, estudiar; reconocer, inspeccionar; (top.) levantar el plano de; medir (un terreno, etc.). **II.** *vn.* levantar planos; ejecutar operaciones topográficas. **III.** *s.* examen, estudio; distrito aduanero; (top.) medida, levantamiento de un plano (de un terreno).

surveying [-ing]. **I.** *s.* topografía, levantamiento de planos. **II.** *a.* de o para topografía.

surveyor [-œr], *s.* topógrafo; agrimensor; investigador, examinador; medidor de licores gravados (en la aduana); vista, inspector de aduana.—**s.'s chain**, cadena de agrimensor (gen. GUNTER'S CHAIN).—**s.'s compass**, brújula de agrimensor.—**s.'s level**, nivel de topografía.—**surveyorship** [-ship], *s.* empleo de topógrafo o inspector.

survival [sœrváival], *s.* supervivencia; sobreviviente; reliquia.—**s. of the fittest**, (biol.) supervivencia del más apto.

survive [sœrváiv], *va. y vn.* sobrevivir (a); salir o quedar vivo.—**surviver, survivor** [-œr], *s.* sobreviviente.—**survivorship** [-ship], *s.* supervivencia.

susceptance [sʊséptæns], *s.* (elect.) susceptancia.

susceptibility [sʊséptibíliti], *s.* susceptibilidad, delicadeza.—**susceptible** [-bœl], *a.* susceptible; sensible o delicado; capaz; impresionable; enamoradizo.—**susceptibly** [-bli], *adv.* de manera susceptible.—**susceptive** [-tiv], *a.* susceptivo.

suspect [sʊspéct]. **I.** *va. y vn.* sospechar, tener sospecha. **II.** *s.* persona sospechosa.

suspectedly [-edli] sospechosamente.

suspend [sʊspénd]. **I.** *va.* suspender; colgar; sospesar; mantener suspenso; interrumpir, descontinuar, aplazar. **II.** *vn.* (com.) suspender pagos; dejar de funcionar u obrar.

suspender [-œr], *s.* suspendedor.—*pl.* elásticos, tirantes del pantalón.

suspense [sʊspéns], *s.* suspensión, duda, incertidumbre; impaciencia; ansiedad; (for.) entredicho.

suspension [-shʊn], *s.* suspensión (en todas sus acepciones).—**s. bridge**, puente colgante.

suspensive [-siv], *a.* suspensivo.

suspensory [-sori], *a. y s.* suspensorio (ll. t. **s. bandage**).

suspicion [sʊspíshʊn], *s.* sospecha; (fam.) pizca, grano, átomo, sombra.

suspicious [sʊspíshʊs], *a.* sospechoso; suspicaz, desconfiado, malicioso.—**suspiciously** [-li], *adv.* sospechosamente; suspicazmente.

suspiciousness [-nes], *s.* recelo, desconfianza.

sustain [sʊstéin], *va.* sostener, aguantar, sustentar; tener, mantener; sufrir (como pérdida, desgracia, daño); (mús.) prolongar, sostener; apoyar, afianzar; animar, confortar; alimentar defender; establecer, probar.

sustainable [-abœl], *a.* sostenible; sustentable; defendible.

sustainer [-œr], *s.* sostenedor, defensor; protector, sustentador.

sustenance [sústenans], *s.* sustento, mantenimiento, subsistencia; alimentos.

sustentation [sústentéishʊn], *s.* sostenimiento, sustentación, sustentamiento, sustento.

sutler [sútlœr], *s.* vivandero.

Sutra [sútræ], *s.* sutra (precepto o colección de preceptos budistas o brahmanistas).

suttee [sʊtí], *s.* costumbre india de inmolar a la viuda en la hoguera funeraria de su marido; la viuda así inmolada.

suttle [sútœl], *a. y s.* neto; peso limpio.

sutural [siúchural], *a.* sutural.

suture [siúchur], *s.* (anat.) sutura, comisura; (bot.) rafe; (cir.) sutura, costura.

suzerain [siúseren], *s.* soberano.

suzerainty [siúserenti], *s.* soberanía.

swab [suób]. **I.** *s.* escobón, estropajo, fregajo; (cir.) esponja de hilas; (arti.) escobillón; (mar.) lampazo.—**s. wringer**, escurridor de lampazos. **II.** *va.* fregar, limpiar; (mar.) lampacear.

swabber [-œr], *s.* lampacero, galopín.

Swabian [suéibian], *s. y a.* suabo.

swaddle [suódœl], *va.* fajar, empañar.—**swaddling band**, o **cloth**, faja, pañal, envoltura de niños.

swag [suæg], *s.* (fam.) robo, hurto; (b. a.) guirnalda.—**swagbellied** [-bélid], *a.* ventrudo, panzudo.

swage [suéiy]. **I.** *s.* estampa, tas, yunque de estampar; herramienta o artificio para dar forma al metal al forjarlo.—**s. block**, matriz o bloque de estampar o modelar. **II.** *va.* forjar en estampa, estampar, dar forma a en el yunque de estampar.

swagger [suǽgœr]. **I.** *vn.* fanfarrear. **II.** *s.* fanfarria, baladronada.—**swaggerer** [-œr], *s.* jaque, baladrón, matasiete.

swain [suéin], *s.* zagal; enamorado.

swale [suéil], *s.* terreno pantanoso.

swallow [suólo]. **I.** *va.* tragar; tragarse; retractar, retirar, desdecir.—**to s. up**, tragar, tragarse; absorber. **II.** *s.* bocado, trago; deglución; tragadero, esófago; abismo, sima; sumidero; (orn.) golondrina; vencejo, avión.—**s. fish**, (ict.) golondrina.—**s.-tailed coat**, frac.

swallowtail [-téil], *s.* (carp.) cola de milano.

swallowwort [-uœrt], *s.* (bot.) asclepiada, celidonia.

swam [suæm], *pret.* de TO SWIM.

swamp [suomp]. **I.** *s.* pantano, marisma, ciénaga, fangal.—**s. oak**, (bot.) carrasco. **II.** *va.* sumergir, echar a pique, hacer zozobrar; empantanar, encenagar, encharcar; arruinar, hundir. **III.** *vn.* empantanarse; irse a pique, zozobrar.

swampy [suómpi], *a.* pantanoso, cenagoso.

swan [suon], *s.* (orn.) cisne.—**s.-like**, semejante al cisne; como de cisne.—**s.'s-down**, plumón de cisne; (tej.) moletón; paño de vicuña.—**s. song**, último canto del cisne moribundo; obra última.

swandown [-dáun], **swansdown** [-ŝdáun], *s.* = SWAN'S DOWN. *V.* SWAN.

swank [suænk]. **I.** *a.* delgado, flexible; ágil; alegre. **II.** *s.* (fam.) SWAGGER.

swanneck [suónnéc], *s.*nombre dado a varios artificios en que la parte más conspicua (brazos, soporte, etc.) tiene forma de U; (hidr.) pestaña saliente de paleta de una rueda.

swanskin [-skin], *s.* piel de cisne; lanilla, bayeta fina.

swap [suóp]. **I.** *va.* (fam.) cambiar, cambalachear, permutar. **II.** *vn.* hacer cambalaches o trueques. **III.** *s.* (fam.) cambalache, trueque, cambio. **IV.** *adv.* (Ingl.) de prisa, vivamente.

sward [suord]. **I.** *va.* encespedar. **II.** *vn.* cubrirse de hierbas. **III.** *s.* césped. *V.* TURF.

swarm [suórm]. **I.** *s.* enjambre. **II.** *va.* y *vn.* enjambrar, jabardear, desahijar; arrebozarse; pulular, hervir, bullir, hormiguear; (fam.) trepar.

swarmer [-œr], *s.* insecto que vive o anda en enjambres; tapón, pedazo de metal con que se llena una grieta.

swart [suórt], *a.* prieto, moreno, atezado.

swarthily [suórzili], *adv.* morenamente.

swarthiness [-nes], *s.* color moreno, atezamiento, tez morena.

swarthy [suórzi], *a.* atezado, prieto, moreno.

swash [suóŝh]. **I.** *s.* ruido o golpe de agua, chorretada; (mar.) canalizo.—**s. plate**, placa motriz. **II.** *va.* lanzar una chorretada. **III.** *vn.* batir o hacer ruido el agua; baladronear; meter bulla.—**swashbuckler** [-bûcloer], *s.* matasiete, espadachín, fanfarrón.—**swasher** [-œr], *s.* jaque, fanfarrón.—**swashing** [-ing], *a.* fanfarronesco; violento, abrumador.

swashy [suóŝhi], *a.* batiente.

swastika [suǽsticæ], *s.* svástica, signo simbólico en forma de cruz griega con los cuatro extremos volteados en ángulo recto en un mismo sentido.

swath [suóz], *s.* ringla o ringlera de mies segada; guadañada.

swathe [suéih]. **I.** *va.* fajar (una criatura). **II.** *s.* faja, pañal.

sway [suéi]. **I.** *va.* inclinar, ladear; influir en el ánimo de (alguno), inducir; blandir, cimbrar, mover; mandar, dominar, gobernar, regir; (mar.) izar, guindar.—**to s. up**, guindar. **II.** *vn.* ladearse, inclinarse, torcerse; oscilar, mecerse; tambalear, flaquear. **III.** *s.* poder, imperio, predominio, preponderancia, influjo; vaivén, oscilación, balanceo, bamboleo.

sweal [suîl], *vn.* derretirse, correrse.

swear [suéær], *va.* y *vn.* (*pret.* SWORE, y ant. SWARE: *pp.* SWORN) jurar; (gen. con **to**) declarar bajo juramento; renegar, echar votos o ternos; juramentar, tomar o prestar juramento.—**to s. by**,-jurar por; (fam.) poner confianza implícita en.—**to s. in**, juramentar, tomar juramento a.

swearer [suérœr], *s.* jurador, renegador.

sweat [suét]. **I.** *va.* y *vn.* (*pret.* y *pp.* SWEAT o SWEATED) sudar; trasudar; resudar; hacer sudar; arrancar informes o confesión a (un preso) con preguntas continuas, someter a interrogatorio persistente y minucioso; secar en horno; apelambrar; soldar; recortar o cercenar monedas. **II.** *s.* sudor; trabajo, fatiga; exudación. —**s. gland**, glándula sudorípara.

sweater [-œr], *s.* el que suda; patrón que impone trabajo excesivo por poco jornal; *swéter*, chaqueta elástica de punto de lana.

sweating [-ing], *s.* y *ger.* de TO SWEAT: transpiración, exudación.—**s. fever**, fiebre palúdica.—**s. iron**, raspador de sudor, cuchillo para raspar el sudor de los caballos.—**s. room**, sudadero, cuarto de sudar.—**s. sickness**, peste negra, muerte negra (de los siglos XV, XVI).—**s. system**, sistema opresivo que se aprovecha de la pobreza del obrero para forzarlo a trabajar sin tregua en cuartos apiñados (*v.* SWEATSHOP) por la mera subsistencia, y aun por menos. Practícanlo sobre todo los subcontratistas fabricantes de artículos baratos pagados a tanto por pieza. Puede llamarse *tlotismo industrial*.

sweatshop [suétŝhóp], *s.* taller donde se practica el *sweating system* (*v.* SWEATING), o sea donde se impone un trabajo excesivo por paga que escasamente alcanza para la vida.

sweaty [suéti], *s.* sudado, sudoso.

Swede [suíd], *s.* sueco; nabo sueco.

Swedish [-iŝh]. **I.** *a.* sueco. **II.** *s.* idioma sueco.

sweep [suíp]. **I.** *va.* (*pret.* y *pp.* SWEPT) barrer; arrastrar; repasar, pasar rápidamente por; recorrer, pasar la vista por; cubrir, abarcar.—**to s. away**, robar sin dejar nada; arrastrar con todo.—**to s. the bottom**, (mar.) rastrear, dragar. **II.** *vn.* barrer; pasar o deslizarse rápidamente; pasar arrasando; (a veces con *along*) pasar con paso o ademán majestuoso.—**to s. down**, descender precipitadamente. **III.** *s.* barredura, barrido; escobada; movimiento de abarque o comprensión (como ojeada, vistazo); alcance, abarque, extensión; curva, comba; barrendero; deshollinador; pieza de una máquina a lo largo de la cual se efectúa un rozamiento; remo largo y pesado; cigoñal de pozo; aspa de molino; guimbalete de bomba.—**s. net**, o **seine**, jábeca.—*pl.* barreduras.

sweeper [-œr], *s.* barrendero; barco barredor de minas; cable barredor.—**s. bar**, travesaño de la amoladera.

sweeping [-ing]. **I.** *a.* arrastrador, arrebatador; arrollador; absoluto, vasto, comprehensivo. **II.** *s.* barrido.—*pl.* barreduras, basura.

sweepstakes [stéiks], *s.* *sing.* y *pl.* (dep.) combinación en que una sola persona puede ganar todas las apuestas; carrera que decide todas las apuestas.

sweet [suít]. **I.** *a.* dulce; sabroso, rico, gustoso; oloroso, fragante; bello, bonito, lindo; amable, afable, agradable; fresco; (mec.) suave y sin ruido; (agr.) bueno, fértil (tierra).—**s. apple**, manzana dulce; anona, chirimoya.—**s. basil**, (bot.) albahaca.—**s. cicely**, perifollo (*v.* CICELY).—**s. corn**, variedad de maíz tierno cuyas mazorcas se cuecen para comer.—**s. fern**, helecho miriáceo.—**s. flag**, (bot.) cálamo aromático.—**s. gale** = s. WILLOW.—**s. gum**, ocozol.—**s. herbs**, (coc.) hierbas olorosas.—**s. oil**, aceite de oliva.—**s. pea**, guisante de olor.—**s. potato**, batata, patata dulce, (Amér.) camote, (Cuba) boniato.—**s. rush** = s. FLAG.—**s.-scented**, perfumado.—**s.-smelling**, odorífero, fragante, oloroso.—**s.-spoken**, melifluo. —**s.-tempered**, de carácter dulce, complaciente.—**s.-tongued**, melifluo, pico de oro.—(**to have a**) **s. tooth**, (tener) gusto por, o gustar de, dulces; (ser) goloso.—**s.-toothed**, goloso, aficionado a los dulces.—**s. william** (bot.) dianto, clavel barbado.—**s. willow**, mirto holandés. **II.** *s.* dulzura; deleite; persona querida.—*pl.* dulces, golosinas.

sweetbread [-bréd], *s.* lechecillas o mollejas de ternera.

sweetbrier [-bráicœr], *s.* (bot.) escaramujo oloroso, agavanzo.

sweeten [suítœn]. **I.** *va.* endulzar, dulcificar, azucarar, edulcorar; suavizar, mitigar, aplacar; embalsamar; purificar; hacer salubre. **II.** *vn.* endulzarse.—**sweetener** [-œr], *s.* dulcificante.

sweetheart [suítjart], *s.* dulce amiga; querida, amante; amador, galán, galanteador, cortejo.

sweeting [suíting], *s.* (bot.) camuesa.

sweetish [suítiŝh], *a.* algo dulce.

sweetly [suítli], *adv.* dulcemente.

sweetmeat [suítmít], *s.* dulce, confitura.

sweetness [suítnes], *s.* dulzura, melosidad, suavidad, delicadeza, apacibilidad, bondad.

sweetsop [-sóp], anona, chirimoya.

swell [suél]. **I.** *va.* (*pp.* SWELLED o SWOLLEN) hinchar, engrosar, inflar, entumecer, henchir, abultar, agravar; engreír, envanecer. **II.** *vn.* hincharse, engrosarse, entumecerse, abotagarse; henchirse; crecer, subir; dilatarse, esponjarse; hincharse, engreírse; embravecerse (el mar).—**to s. out**, arrojar (el árbol) sus hojas; espetarse, ampollarse, bufar. **III.** *a.* (fam.) elegante del buen tono; hinchado por una torcedura.—**to**

have a s. head, (fam.) estar engreído. **IV.** *s.* entumecencia, hinchazón, bulto; aumento de volumen; oleada, marejada; ondulación del terreno; prominencia, protuberancia; (mús.) unión de crescendo y diminuendo, y los signos (< >); pedal de expresión; (fam.) petimetre, persona que sigue las modas con exageración.—**s. box,** caja de expresión (de un órgano).—**s. organ,** órgano de expresión.— **s. pedal,** pedal de expresión.

swelling [suéling]. **I.** *s.* hinchazón, inflación; (med.) tumefacción, entumescencia, turgencia, abotagamiento; bulto, chichón, protuberancia. **II.** *a.* que se hincha o infla; turgente.—**s. breast,** seno agitado; pecho turgente.—**s. sea,** mar agitado.

swelter [suéltœr]. **I.** *va.* sofocar, achicharrar, abrumar de calor. **II.** *vn.* abrasarse, achicharrarse; sudar la gota gorda.

swept, *pret.* y *pp.* de TO SWEEP.

swerve [suœrv]. **I.** *va.* desviar, apartar, torcer. **II.** *vn.* desviarse, apartarse, extraviarse.

swift [sufft]. **I.** *va.* (mar.) tortorar. **II.** *a.* rápido, pronto, presto; veloz, volador; vivo, diligente, activo; sumarísimo, repentino; (mar.) velero. —**s.-footed, s. of foot,** de paso rápido, ligero, alípedo. **III.** *s.* (orn.) vencejo, arrejaque; lagartija; carrete, devanadera.

swifter [-œr], *s.* (mar.) tortor, andarivel; falso obenque.

swiftly [-li], *adv.*velozmente, prontamente, aprisa. —**swiftness** [-nes], *s.* velocidad, rapidez, prontitud.

swig [suíg]. **I.** *va.* y *vn.* beber a grandes tragos; (mar.) aballestar. **II.** *s.* (fam.) trago; mascavidrios; (mar.) aparejo.

swill [suíl]. **I.** *va.* emborrachar, embriagar. **II.** *vr.* emborracharse. **III.** *s.* bazofia; tragantada.— **s. milk,** leche de vacas alimentadas con bazofia o aguachirle.

swim [suím]. **I.** *vn.* (*pret.* SWAM O SWUM: *pp.* SWUM) nadar; flotar, sobrenadar; dejarse ir o llevar; resbalar o deslizarse suavemente; tener la cabeza ida o desvanecida; tener vértigo; padecer vahídos.—**to s. with the tide,** seguir la corriente o ir con la corriente. **II.** *va.* pasar a nado; hacer flotar. **III.** *s.* natación, nado; nadadera de pez; movimiento de deslizarse.

swimmer [suímœr], *s.* nadador; (vet.) esparaván.

swimming [suíming]. **I.** *a.* nadante, natatorio; aguado; lleno de lágrimas.—**s. bladder,** vejiga natatoria.—**s. place,** nadadero.—**s. pool,** piscina natatoria. **II.** *s.* natación, nado; vértigo, vahído. **III.** *adv.* rápidamente, fácilmente.

swimmingly [-li], *adv.* lisamente, sin tropiezo.

swindle [suíndœl]. **I.** *va.* petardear, estafar, timar. **II.** *s.* estafa, timo, petardo.—**swindler** [-dlœr], *s.* estafador, timador, trampeador.

swine [suáin], *s. sing.* y *pl.* marrano(s), puerco(s), cerdo(s).—**s. plague,** peste de los puercos.—**s. pox,** variedad de viruelas locas.—**s. thistle**=SOWTHISTLE.

swinebread [-bred], *s.* (bot.) trufa, criadilla de tierra; pan de puerco.

swineherd [-jérd], *s.* porquero, porquerizo.

swing [suíng]. **I.** *va.* (*pret.* y *pp.* SWUNG) columpiar, mecer, cunear, hacer oscilar; balancear, bambolear; blandir (arma); hacer girar; engoznar. **II.** *vn.* oscilar, columpiarse, mecerse, balancearse; girar, volverse, dar vueltas; (mar.) bornear.—**to s. about,** dar una vuelta.—**to s. clear,** evitar un choque. **III.** *s.* vibración, oscilación, vaivén, balanceo, bamboleo, balance; columpio, mecedor; libertad de acción, libre curso; (mec.) juego, carrera, movimiento, recorrido, alcance; respaldo de articulación (de cámara fotográfica). —**s. back,** respaldo de articulación de una cámara fotográfica.—**s. block,** (mec.) gorrón.—**s. bridge,** puente giratorio.—**s. door,** puerta giratoria de soporte central y varias alas.—**s. lamp,** lámpara colgante.—**s. plow,** arado de reja reversible.

swingbar [-bár], *s.* (carr.) balancín.

swinge [suiny], *va.* (metal.) soldar a martillo, forjar; azotar, castigar.

swingeing [suínying], *a.* (fam.) grande, pesado, extravagante.

swinger [suíngœr], *s.* columpiador.

swinging [suínguing]. **I.** *s.* oscilación, vibración; balanceo; borneo. **II.** *a.* oscilante, mecedor; colgante; giratorio.

swingle [suíngœl]. **I.** *va.* espadar o espadillar. **II.** *s.* espadilla; brazo corto del mayal; (carr.) = SWINGTREE.

swingletree [suíngœltri], **swingtree** [swíngtrí], *s.* (carr.) barra articulada de tiro.

swinish [suáiniâh], *a.* porcuno; cochino, grosero, sucio.—**swinishly** [-li], *adv.* cochinamente.— **swinishness** [-nes], *s.* calidad de cochino, marranada.

swipe [suáip]. **I.** *va.* (fam.) dar o golpear duro; robar. **II.** *s.* (fam.) golpe fuerte; cigüeñal de pozo.

swirl [suœrl]. **I.** *va.* y *vn.* arremolinar; arremolinarse. **II.** *s.* remolino, torbellino.

swish [suíâh]. **I.** *va.* y *vn.* blandir, dar un latigazo. **II.** *s.* movimiento o silbido del látigo al cortar el aire.

Swiss [suís], *a.* y *s.* suizo.

switch [suích]. **I.** *s.* (f. c.) desarrollo o construcción (de una vía inclinada) en zigzag. **II.** *a.* (f. c.) en zigzag, de desarrollo en zigzag.

switchboard [-bórd], *s.* (elec.) cuadro de distribución; (tlf.) cuadro conmutador.

switcher [-œr], *s.* (f. c.) guardagujas; locomotora de maniobra.

switchman [-man], *s.* (f. c.) guardagujas.

swivel [suívœl]. **I.** *va.* y *vn.* girar o hacer girar sobre un eje. **II.** *s.* alacrán, torniquete, eslabón giratorio; lanzadera (un telar de cintas; (arti.) pedrero, colisa (ll. t. **s. gun).**

swob, *s.* = SWAB.

swollen [suólœn]. **I.** *pp.* de TO SWELL. **II.** *a.* hinchado; henchido; crecido; turgente.—**s. with pride,** inflado, hinchado de orgullo.

swoon [suún]. **I.** *vn.* desmayarse, desvanecerse. **II.** *s.* desmayo, pasmo, síncope.

swoop [suúp]. **I.** *va.* descender y agarrar la presa al vuelo; coger, arrebatar. **II.** *vn.* caer, precipitarse sobre algo. **III.** *s.* descenso rápido y cogida al vuelo.

sword [sord], *s.* espada.—**s. arm,** brazo derecho. —**s. belt,** talabarte, biricú, cinturón.—**s. cane,** bastón de estoque.—**s. guard, s. hilt,** empuñadura, puño, guarda de la espada.—**s. law,** ley del más fuerte.—**s.-shaped,** ensiforme.

swordfish [sórdfish], *s.* (ict.) pez espada, jifia.

swordplay [-pléi], *s.* esgrima, manejo de la espada.

swordsman [sórdsman], *s.* (*pl.* SWORDSMEN) tirador, espada; militar.

swore, sworn, *pret.* y *pp.* de TO SWEAR.

swum, *pret.* y *pp.* de TO SWIM.

swung, *pret.* y *pp.* de TO SWING.

Sybarite [síbarait], *s.* sibarita.—**sybaritic(al** [-ritic(al], *a.* sibarítico.

sycamore [sícamor], *s.* (bot.) sicomoro; (E. U.) falso plátano.

syconium [saicónium], *s.* (bot.) siconio.

sycophancy [sícofansi], *s.* adulación, servilismo; parasitismo.—**sycophant** [-ant], *s.* adulador; parásito.—**sycophantic** [-ántic], *a.* adulatorio, lisonjero; chismoso, parlón.

syenite [sáienait], *s.* (min.) sienita.

syenitic [saienític], *a.* sienítico.

syllabary [sílaberi], *s.* silabario.

syllabic(al [siláebic(al], *a.* silábico.—**syllabically** [-cali], *adv.* por sílabas.—**syllabicate** [-keit], *va.* silabear.—**syllabication** [-kéiŝhun], *s.* silabeo.

syllable [sílabœl], *s.* (poét.) sílaba; pie.

syllabus [sílabʊs], *s.* sílabo, sumario, extracto, resumen, compendio.

syllepsis [silépsis], *s.* (gram. y ret.) silepsis.

sylleptic(al [-tic(al], *a.* que envuelve silepsis.

syllogism [síloyiȘm], *s.* silogismo.

syllogistic(al [síloyístic(al], *a.* silogístico.

syllogistically [-i], *adv.* silogísticamente.

syllogize [síloyaiȘ], *vn.* silogizar.

sylph [silf], *s.* silfo, sílfide; (orn.) colibrí.

sylva [sílva], *s.* selva.—**sylvan** [sílvan], *a.* selvático, silvático; rústico, rural.

sylvanite [-ait], *s.* (min.) telururo de oro y plata.

symbiosis [simbaiósis], *s.* (biol.) simbiosis.

symbol [símbol], *s.* símbolo; (teol.) credo.

symbolic(al [simbólic(al], *a.* simbólico.

symbolically [-i], *adv.* simbólicamente.

symbolics [-bólics], *s.* ciencia de los símbolos.

symbolism [símboliȘm], *s.* simbolismo.

symbolization [-iséishʊn], *s.* simbolización.

symbolize [-aiȘ], *va.* y *vn.* simbolizar.

symbology [simbóloyi], *s.* arte o tratado de los símbolos.

symmetalism [simétæliȘm], *s.* (e. p.) sistema monetario en que la moneda patrón consta de dos o más metales.

symmetrical [simétrical], *a.* simétrico.

symmetrically [-i], *adv.* simétricamente.

symmetrize [símetraiȘ], *va.* dar simetría a.

symmetry [símetri], *s.* simetría.

sympathetic(al [símpazétic(al], *a.* simpático; que simpatiza; afín.—*s.* **ink**, tinta simpática.—*s.* **nervous system**, (anat.) gran simpático.

sympathetically [-i], *adv.* simpáticamente, con simpatía, benévolamente.

sympathize [símpazaiȘ], *vn.* simpatizar, compadecerse, condolerse; doler, padecer o sentir por simpatía; convenir, armonizarse, ajustarse, congeniar.—**sympathizer** [-œr], *s.* aprobador, partidario, seguidor.

sympathy [símpazi], *s.* simpatía, afinidad; benevolencia; conmiseración, compasión, lástima; pésame; (med.) simpatía.

symphonic [simfónic], *a.* sinfónico; homónimo.

symphonious [-niʊs], *a.* armonioso.—**symphonist** [simfonist], *s.* sinfonista.—**symphony** [simfoni], *s.* sinfonía.

symphysis [símfisis], *s.* (anat.) sínfisis.

symposiac [simpósiac], *a.* perteneciente a los banquetes o convites.—**symposium** [-um], *s.* festín, banquete; colección de artículos o comentarios.

symptom [simptom, -tum], *s.* síntoma.

symptomatic(al [simptomǽtic(al], *a.* sintomático.

symptomatically [-i], *adv.* sintomáticamente.

symptomatology [-matóloyi], *s.* (med.) sintomatología.

synæresis [sinéresis], *s.* = SYNERESIS.

synagogue [sínagog], *s.* sinagoga.

synalepha [sinalífa], *s.* (gram.) sinalefa.

synalgia [sinælriæ], *s.* dolor proveniente de acción simpática.

synantherous [sinǽnzerʊs], *a.* (bot.) sinantéreo.

synarthrosis [sinarzrósis], *s.* (anat.) sinartrosis, articulación no movible.

synchronal [síncronal], *s.* sincrónico.—**synchronic(al** [sincrónic(al], *a.* sincrónico.

synchronism [síncroniȘm], *s.* sincronismo.

synchronization [-iséishʊn], *s.* sincronización.

synchronize [-aiȘ], *va.* y *vn.* sincronizar.

synchronizer [-aiȘœr], *s.* sincronizador.

synchronoscope [sincrónoscoup], *s.* sincronoscopio.

synchronous [síncronʊs], *a.* sincrónico.—**synchronously** [-i], *adv.* sincrónicamente.

synclinal [sincláinal], *a.* (geol.) sinclinal.

syncopate [síncopet], *va.* (gram., mús.) sincopar.

syncopation [-éishʊn], *s.* (gram. y mús.) síncopa.

syncope [síncope], *s.* (med.) síncope; (gram., mús.) síncopa.

syncretic [sincrétic], *a.* sincrético.

syncretism [síncretiȘm], *s.* sincretismo.—**syncretist** [-ist], *s.* sincretista.—**syncretize** [-aiȘ], *va.*

conciliar o tratar de conciliar o armonizar (doctrinas distintas).

syndactyl [sindǽctil], *s.* y *a.*, **syndactylous** [-ʊs], *a.* (zool.) sindáctilo, que tiene dos o más dedos soldados o unidos entre sí.

syndic [síndic], *s.* síndico.

syndicalism [síndicaliȘm], *s.* (e. p.) sindicalismo. —**syndicalist** [-ist], *s.* sindicalista.—**syndicalize** [-aiȘ], *va.* sindicalizar, poner bajo dominio sindicalista, u organizar según el sistema sindicalista.

syndicate [síndiket]. **I.** *va.* y *vn.* (com.) sindicar (se). **II.** *s.* (for.) sindicado; sindicatura; (com.) sindicato, asociación de capitalistas para emprender un negocio magno; (e. p.) sindicato, asociación de obreros.

syne [sáin], *adv.* (Esco.) tiempo atrás, tiempos de antaño.

synecdoche [sinécdoke], *s.* (ret.) sinécdoque.

syneresis [sinéresis], *s.* (gram.) sinéresis.

synergism [síneryiȘm], *s.* doctrina según la cual el alma coopera con la gracia divina.

synergy [sínœryi], *s.* (fís.) sinergia.

synesthesia [sineszíȳiæ], *s.* sensación en una parte del cuerpo diferente de la afectada directamente por el estímulo que la produce; sensación asociada o concomitante.

synod [sínod], *s.* sínodo.

synodal [sínodal], *s.*, **synodic(al** [sinódic(al], *a.* sinódico.

synonym [sínonim], *s.* sinónimo.

synonymize [sinónimaiȘ], *va.* usar sinónimos.

synonymous [-ʊs], *a.* sinónimo.

synonymy [sinónimi], *s.* sinonimia.

synopsis [sinópsis], *s.* sinopsis.

synoptic(al [sinóptical], *a.* sinóptico.

synovia [sinóvia], *s.* sinovia.—**synovial** [-l], *a.* sinovial.—**synovitis** [sinováitis], *s.* sinovitis.

syntactic(al [sintǽctical], *a.* sintáctico.

syntax [síntæcs], *s.* (gram.) sintaxis.

synthesis [sínzesis], *s.* síntesis; (cir.) reunión de partes divididas.

synthetic(al [sinzétic(al], *a.* sintético; fabricado.

synthetically [-li], *adv.* sintéticamente.

syntonic [sintónic], *a.* sintónico, sintonizado.

syntonization [síntoniséishʊn], *s.* (rad.) sintonización.—**syntonize** [-aiȘ], *va.* sintonizar.—**syntonizer** [-áiȘœr], *s.* sintonizador.—**syntony** [síntoni], *s.* sintonización.

syphilis [sífilis], *s.* sífilis.—**syphilitic** [-ític], *a.* sifilítico.—**syphilologist** [-lóyist], *s.* sifilógrafo.— **syphilology** [-lóyi], *s.* sifilografía.

syphon [sáifon], *s.* sifón.

syren [sáiren], *s.* = SIREN.

Syriac [síriæc], *a.* y *s.* siríaco.

Syrian [sírian], *s.* sirio.

syringa [sirínga], *s.* (bot.) jeringuilla; lila.

syringe [síriny]. **I.** *s.* jeringa, clister. **II.** *va.* jeringar, dar una lavativa o inyección.

syringotomy [siringótomi], *s.* (cir.) siringotomía.

syrtis [sœrtis], *s.* sirte, banco de arena.

syrup [sírup], *s.* jarabe.

system [sístem], *s.* sistema, método; clasificación ordenada; (fisiol. y biol.) sistema; (geol.) formación.

systematic(al [-ǽtic(al], *a.* sistemático.

systematically [-i], *adv.* sistemáticamente.

systematize [-ataiȘ], *va.* sistematizar; metodizar.

systemic [sistémic], *a.* sistemático; (fís.) relativo a todo el sistema o cuerpo.

systile [sístail], *s.* (arq.) sístilo.

systole [sístole], *s.* (fisiol.) sístole.

systolic [sistólic], *a.* sistólico.

syzygy [sísiyi], *s.* (astr.) sizigia.

T

t [ti], *s.* t.

T [ti]. **I.** *s.* objeto en forma de T; pieza (tubo, viga, etc.) en T. **II.** *a.* en T, de forma de T.— **T head**, (m. comb. int.) culata con válvulas opuestas.—**T iron**, hierro en T.—**T rail**, riel en T, o de hongo.—**T square**, (dib.) regla T.

Para la pronunciación de æ, œ, ᴅ, ş, ŝh, ʊ, ȳ, ɤ, z, véase la clave al principio del libro.

TAB   469   TAI

tab [tæb], *s.* proyección, apéndice; oreja de zapato; herrete de un cordón; cuenta.

tabard [tǽbard], *s.* tabardo.

Tabasco (sauce) [tæbǽsco (sos)], *s.* salsa de ají.

tabbinet [tǽbinet], *s.* (tej.) tabinete.

tabby [tǽbi]. **I.** *s.* (tej.) tabí; gato romano; gata. **II.** *a.* ondeado, moteado, mosqueado, que hace aguas.

tabefaction [tæbefǽcśhun], *s.* marasmo.

tabefy [tǽbefai], *vn.* extenuarse.

tabernacle [tæbœrnacœl], *s.* tabernáculo.

tabes [téibiş], *s.* (med.) tabes.

tabetic [tabétic]. **I.** *a.* tábido. **II.** *s.* tísico.

tabid [tǽbid], *a.* (ed.) tábido.

tablature [tǽblatiur], *s.* (anat.) pared del cráneo; pintura mural.

table [téibœl]. **I.** *s.* mesa; comida, manjares; tabla (matemática, de la ley, de materias, etc.), cuadro; losa, plancha; tarima; tablero; banco; meseta; (b. a.) tabla, pintura en tabla o piedra; (arq.) entablamento; palma de la mano; faceta superior de un diamante; piedra preciosa de dos facetas.—**t. beer,** cerveza floja, o de pasto.— **t. boarder,** pupilo, pensionista.—**t. cover,** carpeta, sobremesa, cubremesa.—**t. d'hôte,** mesa redonda de una fonda; comida de varios platos, o a la francesa.—**t. furniture** = TABLEWARE.—**t. knife,** cuchillo de mesa.—**t.-land,** altiplanicie, mesa, meseta.—**t. linen,** mantelería.—**t. of contents,** tabla de materias, índice.—**t. service,** o **set,** vajilla.—**t. wine,** vino de pasto o de mesa. **II.** *va.* y *vn.* dar carpetazo; poner (un naipe) sobre la mesa; (impr.) catalogar; poner índice; (carp.) ensamblar, acoplar.

tableau [tábló], *s.* (*pl.* TABLEAUX) cuadro al vivo.

tablecloth [téibœlclóz], *s.* mantel; tela para manteles, alemanisco.

tablespoon [téibœlspún], *s.* cuchara ordinaria de mesa.—**tablespoonful** [-ful], *s.* cucharada.

tablet [tǽblet], *s.* tabla, tableta, tablilla; bloc de papel; plancha, lápida; (farm.) tableta, pastilla.

tableware [téibœluǽr], *s.* servicio de mesa, artículos para la mesa.

tabloid [tǽbloid]. **I.** *s.* tabloid—nombre de fábrica de ciertas medicinas y otras preparaciones concentradas; periódico de noticias concisas o condensadas (apl. esp. a los chismosos y sensacionales). **II.** *a.* condensado, breve, conciso; de noticias breves (apl. esp. a periódicos populares ilustrados, sobre todo a los chismosos y sensacionales).

taboo, tabu [tabú]. **I.** *va.* declarar tabú; (fig.) prohibir, excluir, desterrar. **II.** *s.* tabú; preocupación, ostracismo.

tabo(u)r [téibœr], *s.* tamboril.—**taborer** [-œr], *s.* tamborilero.

tabo(u)ret [tǽburet], **tabret** [tǽbret], *s.* taborilete; taburete; bastidor de bordar.

tabourine [tǽburin], *s.* pandereta.

tabular [tǽbiular], *a.* tabular.—**tabulate** [-eit], *va.* poner o arreglar en forma de tabla.—**tabulated** [-ed], *a.* liso, plano.—**tabulation** [-éiśhun], *s.* reducción a forma tabular.—**tabulator** [-œr], *s.* constructor de tablas; tabulador (de máquina de escribir).

tacamahac [tǽcamajǽc], *s.* tacamaca; (bot.) álamo balsámico.

tacheometer [tækiómetœr], *s.* (top.) taquímetro; (hidr., med., etc.) contador de velocidad.

tachograph [tǽcograf], *s.* tacógrafo, registrador de velocidad.

tachometer [tæcómetœr], *s.* contador de velocidad.

tachygraphy [tækígrafi], *s.* taquigrafía.—**tachygrapher** [-œr], *s.* taquígrafo.—**tachygraphic(al)** [tækigráfic, -al], *a.* taquigráfico.—**tachygraphist** [tækígrafist], *s.* taquígrafo.

tachymeter [tækímetœr], *s.* contador de velocidad; (top.) taquímetro.—**tachymetric** [tækimétrie], *a.* taquimétrico.—**tachymetry** [tækímetri], *s.* (top.) taquimetría.

tacit [tǽsit], *a.* tácito.

tacitly [tǽsitli], *adv.* tácitamente.

taciturn [tǽsitœrn], *a.* taciturno.

taciturnity [tǽsitœrniti], *s.* taciturnidad.

tack [tæc]. **I.** *va.* clavar con tachuelas; puntear, pegar, coser, hilvanar; unir, añadir o anexar **II.** *vn.* virar, cambiar de bordada. **III.** *s.* tachuela, puntilla; hilván; (mar.) amura; bordada, virada; cambio de política; nuevo plan de acción.— **t. claw,** sacatachuelas.—**t. hammer,** martillo para tachuelas.—**t. tackle,** aparejo de amurar.

tackle [tǽcœl]. **I.** *va.* agarrar, asir; atacar (un problema, etc.), luchar con; (football) atajar a un adversario. **II.** *s.* (mar.) aparejo, poleame, maniobra, motonería, cuadernal, jarcia; equipo, avíos, enseres (vg. *fishing tackle,* avíos de pescar); (football) atajo y agarrada; atajador.—**t. block,** motón de aparejo.—**t. fall,** tira de aparejo.—**t. hooks,** ganchos de aparejos.

tact [tæct], *s.* tacto; tino, tiento.

tactic(al [tǽctic(al], *a.* táctico.

tactician [tæctíśhan], *s.* táctico.

tactics [tǽctics], *s.* *pl.* (mil.) táctica.

tactile [tǽctil], *a.* tangible, palpable; del tacto, relativo al tacto.

tactility [tæctíliti], *s.* calidad de tangible.

tactless [tǽctles], *a.* falto de tacto o de tino, impolítico.

tactual [tækchuǽl], *a.* relativo a, o causado por, el tacto.

tadpole [tǽdpoul], *s.* renacuajo.

ta'en [téin], *contr.* de TAKEN.

tænia, tenia [tínia], *s.* banda, faja, cinta; tenia, solitaria.

taffeta, taffety [tǽfeta, -ti], *s.* (tej.) tafetán.

taffrail [tǽfrel], *s.* (mar.) coronamiento.

taffy [tǽfi], *s.* melcocha, arropía; (E. U., fam.) lisonja, halago.

tag [tæg]. **I.** *s.* herrete; marbete, marca, rótulo, tejuelo; cartela; apéndice, extremo del rabo; tirador de una bota; pingajo, arrapiezo; muchedumbre, populacho; juego de muchachos.—**t. day,** *día de cartelas,* en que se solicitan en las calles contribuciones para obras de caridad, etc., colgando una cartelilla en el pecho o el ojal del contribuyente.—**the t. and rag,** o **the t., rag and bobtail,** el populacho, la canalla. **II.** *va.* clavetear o poner herretes; marcar con marbete o rótulo; pisar los talones, alcanzar y tocar.—**tagged lace,** agujeta.

Tagala, *s.* tagalo.

tagrag [tǽgræg], *s.* (fam.) chusma.

tagtail [tǽgteil], *s.* lombriz; gorrón.

Tahitian [tajítian], *s.* y *a.* tahitiano, de Tahití.

tail [téil]. **I.** *s.* cola, rabo; cabo, extremidad; apéndice; (astr.) cola (de cometa); (mús.) rabito de una nota; pie de página; reverso o cruz de una moneda; (sast.) faldón; (alb.) cola o entrega de un sillar; acompañamiento, escolta; fila o hilera de gente; (for.) limitación de propiedad; (aer.) planos de cola, planos estabilizadores traseros.—**t.-bay,** parte de una esclusa situada debajo de la compuerta inferior.—**t. coat,** saco de faldas sesgadas, (Colomb.) sacolevita; casaca.—**t. end,** extremo trasero, parte de atrás; lo último.—**t. fin,** (aer.) plano de deriva de cola.—**t. gate,** (f. c.) plano inclinado de un vagón a la vía; (hidr.) compuerta inferior de esclusa.—**t. lamp, t. light,** farol trasero.—**t. plane,** (aer.) plano fijo de cola, estabilizador de cola.—**t. rod,** (m. v.) prolongación del vástago del émbolo.—**t. unit,** (aer.) conjunto de cola.—**t. water,** agua de salida. **II.** *va.* añadir, agregar; cortar la cola; desrabotar; (con **on**) juntar, unir, empatar; tirar de.

tailage [téiley], *s.* derecho, tributo.

tailblock [téilblóc], *s.* (mar.) motón de rabiza.

tailed [téild], *a.* rabudo; de rabo.

tailing [-ing], *s.* (alb.) cola, entrega.—*pl.* restos, desechos.

tailor [téilœr], *s.* sastre.—**tailoress** [téilœres], *s.* sastra.—**tailoring** [-ing], *s.* sastrería (arte).

tailpiece [téilpís], *s.* apéndice; (impr.) florón, culo de lámpara; cola de violín o guitarra.

tailrace [téilreis], *s.* (hidr.) canal o conducto de salida o escape (del agua de una rueda); agua de salida.

taint [téint]. **I.** *va.* manchar, inficionar, corromper.—**II.** *vn.* inficionarse, corromperse, podrirse.—**III.** *s.* mácula, mancha, corrupción.—**taintless** [-les], *a.* incorrupto, puro.

take [téic], *va.* (*pret.* TOOK: *pp.* TAKEN) tomar; coger, asir, agarrar; recibir, aceptar; apropiarse, apoderarse de; percibir o cobrar; quitar, furtar. llevarse; llevar, conducir, acompañar; restar, deducir; prender, hacer prisionero; escoger; usar, emplear, adoptar; considerar, tener por; asumir, aceptar; admitir; adaptarse o hacerse a; tomar, emplear o necesitar (tiempo); coger, contraer (una enfermedad); coger, sorprender; sacar (un retrato, una copia); dar (un paseo); hacer (ejercicio); saltar (una barrera).—**to t. aback,** desconcertar.— **to t. a bite,** comer algo.—**to t. account of,** tener en cuenta, hacer caso de.—**to t. a different, o another, turn,** cambiar de aspecto.—**to t. advantage of,** aprovecharse de; abusar de.—**to t. advice,** aconsejarse, tomar consejo.—**to t. a fancy to,** prendarse de; antojarse de.—**to t. a header,** irse de cabeza.—**to t. aim,** apuntar, tomar puntería.—**to t. a journey,** hacer un viaje.—**to t. a leap,** dar un salto o brinco.—**to t. a liking to,** aficionarse a, coger cariño a.—**to t. a look at,** echar una ojeada a, mirar.—**to t. amiss,** tomar en mala parte, ofenderse de.—**to t. an oath,** prestar juramento.—**to t. a notion to,** aficionarse a; coger cariño a; metérsele a uno (algo) en la cabeza.—**to t. apart,** desarmar (una máquina).—**to t. asunder,** separar, desunir.—**to t. a shot at,** hacer un tiro a; echar una pulla a.—**to t. a step,** dar un paso; tomar una medida.—**to t. a turn, o a walk,** dar una vuelta, un paseo.—**to t. away,** quitar, sacar; llevarse.—**to t. back** (fam.) retractar, desdecirse de; recibir (algo) devuelto.—**to t. breath,** descansar; tomar aliento.—**to t. by storm,** tomar por asalto.—**to t. care,** tener cuidado.—**to t. care of,** cuidar de, atender a.—**to t. chances,** correr el riesgo, arriesgar; confiar en la suerte.—**to t. counsel,** deliberar; consultar.—**to t. down,** asentar, tomar nota de; bajar o poner más bajo; quitar los humos a; tragar; derribar.—**to t. effect,** surtir efecto; entrar en vigencia; poner en, o llevar a, efecto. —**to t. exception to,** oponerse a, no conceder o aceptar (una proposición, aserción, etc.).—**to t. fire,** encenderse; incendiarse.—**to t. for granted,** dar por sentado.—**to t. French leave,** despedirse a la francesa, escabullirse, irse callandito.—**to t. fright,** atemorizarse, sobresaltarse.—**to t. from,** despojar a, privar a, quitar a; restar o substraer de.—**to t. ground,** (mar.) varar, encallar.—**to t. heart,** tomar o cobrar aliento, no desalentar.—**to t. heed,** hacer caso, poner atención.—**to t. hold,** coger, agarrar; tomar posesión, apoderarse; encargarse; aprender, comprender, ponerse al corriente. —**to t. horse,** cabalgar, pasear a caballo; permitir la yegua que la cubra el caballo; (min.) ramificarse (una veta).—**to t. in,** hacer entrar, dar ingreso; admitir, recibir (en su casa, en la sociedad, etc.); acomodar; tomar; cobrar; recibir (dinero); entender; abarcar, comprender, incluir; observar, notar; contraer, encoger; cercar; (fam.) creer, tragar; estafar, embaucar, engañar.—**to t. in a reef,** tomar un rizo.—**to t. in hand,** emprender; tomar por su cuenta, hacerse cargo de.—**to t. into one's head,** metérsele a uno en la cabeza.—**to t. in tow,** tomar a remolque.—**to t. issue with,** oponerse a; disputar.—**to t. it out of,** desquitarse a costa de, hacer pagar el pato a.—**to t. leave,** despedirse.—**to t. leg bail,** tomar las de Villadiego.— **to t. note,** tomar nota, apuntar; notar, advertir. —**to t. notice,** darse por avisado; notar.—**to t. notice of,** hacer caso de; notar, observar; cuidarse de.—**to t. oath,** prestar juramento.—**to t. occasion,** aprovechar la oportunidad.—**to t. off,** separar, quitar; rebajar; cercenar, amputar; llevarse; arrebatar; causar la muerte a, matar; destruir; remedar, ridiculizar, copiar; despegar; embotar; quitarse (el sombrero, etc.); imitar.— **to t. offence,** ofenderse, darse por sentido.—**to t. offense at,** agraviarse u ofenderse de.—**to t. one down a peg,** bajarle a uno los humos.—**to t. one's breath, o one's breath away,** dejar a uno sin resuello, pasmado o turulato.—**to t. one's death of (cold, fever),** (fam.) exponerse a morir de (catarro, fiebre) [gen. es expresión hiperbólica que significa exponerse a (catarro, fiebre, etc.)].— **to t. one's life in one's hand,** arriesgar, o ju-

garse, la vida.—**to t. out,** llevar o poner fuera; sacar, obtener; omitir; quitar, arrebatar; arrancar; extraer.—**to t. over,** tomar posesión de; reportar.—**to t. (great) pains,** afanarse, empeñarse, esmerarse, darse la pena.—**to t. part with one,** tomar la defensa o el partido de uno.—**to t. pity on,** apiadarse o compadecerse de.—**to t. place,** suceder, ocurrir.—**to t. pot luck,** hacer penitencia. —**to t. root,** echar raíces, arraigarse.—**to t. sanctuary,** acogerse a sagrado.—**to t. sides,** tomar partido; (con *with*) ponerse de parte de, apoyar a.— **to t. soil,** empantanarse; refugiarse.—**to t. steps,** dar pasos, tomar medidas.—**to t. (account of) stock,** hacer inventario.—**to t. stock in,** creer; tener confianza en, dar importancia a.—**to t. the cake,** (fam.) llevarse la palma; ser el mejor (o el peor).—**to t. the chair,** presidir.—**to t. the floor,** tomar la palabra.—**to t. the heart out of,** (fam.) desalentar, quitar los bríos a.—**to t. the law in, o into, one's own hands,** hacerse justicia por sí mismo.—**to t. the wall,** tomar la acera; tomar la mayor parte.—**to t. to heart,** tomar a pecho.— **to t. to pieces,** hacer pedazos; desarmar; refutar punto por punto.—**to t. to task,** reprender, regañar; censurar, criticar.—**to t. up,** alzar, levantar; arrestar, poner preso; tomar, recibir, admitir; ocupar o llenar (espacio); comprender o incluir; quitar, rebajar o reducir; recoger; empezar o comenzar; atender a, emprender; dedicarse a; tomar posesión; (com.) pagar al vencimiento; aceptar; reprochar, censurar; (impr.) reunir; comprar o tomar al fiado; tomar prestado; (mec.) sostener, resistir (el peso, etc.); absorber, amortiguar.—**to t. up money,** tomar prestado.—**to t. upon one's self,** tomar a su cargo, encargarse de, asumir.—**to t. up quarters at,** alojarse en.—**to t. up the hatchet o to DIG UP THE HATCHET.—to t. warning,** estar alerta, tener cuidado.—**take my word for it,** créame Vd.; bajo mi palabra.—**take notice,** aviso, advertencia.—**to be taken with,** prendarse o estar prendado de.

take, *vn.* ser poseedor, adquirir propiedad; pegar bien, tener éxito, dar golpe, cuajar; prender (la vacuna, el fuego, etc.); hacer su efecto, ser eficaz; picar (el pez); sacar buen o mal retrato; pegar, adherirse; arraigar (las plantas).—**to t. after,** parecerse o salir a; imitar a, seguir el ejemplo de; ser como.—**to t. ill,** caer enfermo.—**to t. off,** partir, salir.—**to t. on,** echarse a morir, lamentarse con vehemencia; hacer grande alharaca. —**to t. on with,** juntarse con; prendarse de.—**to t. to,** dedicarse a; recurrir a; irse a; tomar afición a; ponerse a.—**to t. to one's heels,** apretar los talones, huir.—**to t. up with,** resignarse a; vivir o habitar con; adoptar, aceptar; arrogarse, atribuirse.

take, *s.* toma; cogida, redada; (impr.) tomada.— **t.-off,** sátira; caricatura; remedo; raya de donde se salta.—**t.-up,** atesador; (tej.) enjullo.

taken [téikœn], *pp.* de TO TAKE.—**to be t. ill,** o **sick,** caer enfermo, enfermar.—**to be t. off,** o **away,** morir.

taker [téikœr], *s.* tomador.

taking [téiking]. **I.** *a.* encantador, seductor, atractivo; (fam.) contagioso. **II.** *s.* toma, secuestro, embargo; afición, inclinación, afecto; (fam.) arrebato; brete, trance apurado.—*pl.* ingresos.

talaria [talé- o tálária], *s. pl.* talares.

Talbot [tólbot], *s.* perro de San Huberto.

talc [tælc]. **I.** *s.* talco.—**t. powder,** talco en polvo. **II.** *va.* tratar con talco, aplicar talco a.

talcose, talcous, talcky, talcoid [tælcos, -cus, -ki, -coid], *a.* talcoso.

talcum [tælcum], *s.* = TALC.

tale [téil], *s.* cuento; novela; narración, relato; fábula, conseja; embuste, filfa; habilla, chisme; cuenta, número.

talebearer [-béœrœr], **taleteller** [-télœr], *s.* soplón, chismoso.—**talebearing, taletelling-[-béœring, -téling], *s.* soplón, chismoso; habilla, chismografía.

talent [tælent], *s.* talento, capacidad, ingenio; aptitud; persona que tiene alguna habilidad; artista; talento (peso o valor de moneda).

talented [tælented], *a.* talentoso; hábil.

tales [téiliš], *s.* (for.) auto para la citación de jurados suplentes; lista de jurados suplentes.

talesman [-mæn], s. (pl. TALESMEN) jurado suplente.

taleteller [téiltélœr], s. enredador, chismoso, correvedile.

talion [tǽliʋn], s. talión.

talipes [tǽlipiš], s. pie de piña.—**taliped** [-ped], a. de pie de piña.

talipot [tǽlipot], s. talipata (es el nombre indígena), gran palma de Ceilán.

talisman [tǽlišman], s. talismán.

talismanic [tælismǽnic], a. talismánico.

talk [tok]. **I.** va. hablar o tratar de (to talk business, hablar de negocios); hablar (en) (they talk German, hablan (en) alemán); decir (he talks nonsense, dice disparates).—**to t. away**, malgastar (el tiempo) hablando; disipar con la palabra.—**to t. into**, convencer de, inducir a.—**to t. out of**, disuadir; sonsacar.—**to t. shop**, hablar de negocios o de la propia profesión sin necesidad o fuera de tiempo.—**to t. up**, alabar, ensalzar. **II.** vn. hablar; conversar, charlar.—**to t. away, to t. on**, hablar sin parar.—**to t. over**, discutir, conferenciar acerca de.—**to t. to**, hablar a; reprender.—**to t. to the purpose**, hablar al alma.—**to t. up**, hablar claro. **III.** s. plática, conversación; habla; discurso (apl. gen. al sencillo), plática; charla; voz común, fama, rumor; tema de una conversación.

talkative [tókativ], a. gárrulo, locuaz.

talkativeness [-nes], s. locuacidad, garrulidad.

talker [tóccœr], s. conversador, charlador; decidor; discursista; orador; charlatán, fanfarrón.

talking [tóking], a. parlante, hablante.—**t. doll**, muñeca parlante.—**t. machine**, máquina parlante (fonógrafo, etc.).

talking-to [-tu], s. represión, regaño, rapapolvo.

tall [tol], a. alto; grande; altisonante, exagerado.

tallage [tǽleʸ], s. alcabala; impuesto.

tallboy [tólboi], s. cajonería.

tallness [tólnes], s. altura, estatura, talla.

tallow [tǽlo]. **I.** va. ensebar. **II.** s. sebo.—**t. chandler**, velero.—**t.-chandler's shop**, velería.—**t. dip**, vela de sebo.—**t. tree**, (bot.) árbol del sebo.

tallowy [tǽloi], a. seboso, sebáceo.

tally [tǽli]. **I.** s. tarja, taja, tara, cuenta.—**t. stick**, tarja. **II.** va. tarjar, llevar la cuenta.—**to t. the sheets**, (mar.) cazar y atracar las escotas. **III.** vn. cuadrar, concordar, estar conforme.

tallyho [-jou]. **I.** interj. grito del cazador. **II.** s. coche de cuatro caballos.

tallyman [-mæn], s. tendero que vende a tarja.—**tallywoman** [-úman], s. tendera que vende a tarja.

Talmud [tǽlmʋd], s. Talmud.—**Talmudic(al** [tælmʋ́dic(al], a. talmúdico.—**Talmudist** [tǽlmʋdist], s. talmudista.

talon [tǽlʋn], s. garra; monte de la baraja; talón de hoja de espada.

talus [téilʋs], s. (anat.) astrágalo, tobillo; (arq.) talud.

tamable [téimabœl], a. domable, domesticable.

tamal(e [tamál(e], s. tamal.

tamandua [tæmǽnduæ], s. tamanduá, especie de oso hormiguero.

tamarack [tǽmaræc], s. (bot.) alerce.

tamarind [tǽmarind], s. tamarindo.

tamarisk [tǽmarisc], s. (bot.) tamarisco, taraje, taray.

tambac [tǽmbæc], s. = TOMBAC.

tambour [tǽmbur]. **I.** s. (mús.) tambor; (arq.) cancel; tambor.—**t. (frame)**, bastidor para bordar. **II.** va. bordar a tambor.

tambourine [tæmburín], s. pandero, pandereta.

tame [téim]. **I.** a. amansado, domado, domesticado; manso; dócil, tratable; sumiso; insubstancial, insípido; (fam.) moderado. **II.** vn. domar, domeñar, domesticar, amansar; avasallar, abatir; suavizar.—**tamely** [-li], adv. mansamente, dócilmente, sumisamente.—**tameness** [-nes], s. domesticidad; mansedumbre; sumisión; docilidad.—**tamer** [-œr], s. domador, amansador.

tamis [tǽmis], s. tamiz, cedazo.

tam o'shanter [tǽm o'šhǽntœr], s. boina escocesa.

tamkin [tǽmkin], s. (arti.) tapaboca.

tamp [tæmp], va. atacar (un barreno); apisonar.

tamper [tǽmpœr], vn. (con **with**) entremeterse en; tocar lo que no se debe, meterse en o con.

tampion [tǽmpiʋn], s. (arti.) tapaboca.

tampon [tǽmpon]. **I.** s. (cir.) tapón. **II.** va. taponar.

tam-tam [tǽm-tǽm], s. timbal.

tan [tæn]. **I.** va. (ten.) curtir, zurrar, adobar, aderezar; tostar, quemar. **II.** a. tostado, de color de canela. **III.** s. (ten.) corteza de curtir (ll. t. t. **bark, tanbark**); color de canela; tostadura del sol.—**t. liquor**, baño de casca.—**t. mill**, molino de corteza de roble.—**t. pit**, o **vat**, noque, tina de curtir.

tanager [tǽnaʸœr], s. (orn.) tángara.

tanbark [tǽnbárc], s. casca.

tandem [tǽndem]. **I.** a. tándem, con cilindros, planos, etc., uno tras otro (apl. a máquinas, aeroplanos, etc.); (elec.) de cascada. **II.** s. dos o más caballos enganchados uno tras otro; coche tirado en esa forma; tándem, bicicleta para dos ciclistas; (aer.) avión con alas en tándem (una tras otra). **III.** adv. en tándem, uno delante de otro; (elec.) en cascada.

tang [tæng]. **I.** s. dejo, gustillo, sabor; sonido, retintín; (mec.) cola, espiga, rabera. **II.** vn. hacer retiñir. **III.** vn. retiñir.

tangency [tǽnyensi], s. tangencia.

tangent [tǽnyent], s. (geom., trig.) tangente; (f. c.) recta, vía recta. **II.** a. tangente; tangencial; de tangentes.—**t. distance**, (f. c.) tangente (distancia de la intersección de dos tangentes al punto de tangencia).—**t. galvanometer**, galvanómetro de tangentes.—**t. point**, punto de tangencia.—**t. screw**, tornillo de aproximación (de un instrumento de precisión); (mec.) tornillo sin fin.—**t. spoke**, rayo tangencial, o tangente al cubo (de una rueda).—**t. wheel**, rueda de rayos tangenciales; rueda de engranaje con tornillo sin fin.

tangential [tænyénšhæl], a. tangencial.—**t. stress**, esfuerzo cortante.—**tangentially** [-l], adv. tangencialmente.

tangerine [tænyerin], a. y s. tangerino; naranja tangerina.

tangibility [tænyibíliti], s. calidad de tangible.

tangible [tǽnyibœl], a. tangible, palpable.

tangle [tǽngœl]. **I.** va. enredar; embrollar; confundir. **II.** vn. enredarse; confundirse. **III.** s. enredo, embrollo, maraña; confusión; alga marina.

tango [tǽngo], s. (danz.) tango.

tank [tænc]. **I.** s. tanque, depósito; aljibe; charco; (mil.) tanque, tractor blindado.—**t. car**, vagón tanque.—**t. engine, t. locomotive**, locomotora ténder, que lleva sus propios depósitos de agua y carbón.—**t. ship**, o **steamer**, (mar.) aljibe, barco tanque.—**t. tender**, (locom.) ténder para agua.—**t. valve**, (locom.) válvula de salida del tanque o depósito de agua. **II.** va. almacenar o poner en depósitos o tanques.

tankage [tǽnkeʸ], s. acto de poner en tanques; precio que se paga por guardar algo en tanques; cabida o capacidad de un tanque; residuo de las grasas.

tankard [tǽnkard], s. taza grande para beber.

tanker [tǽnccœr], s. barco tanque, aljibe.

tannate [tǽnet], s. (quím.) tanato.

tanned [tǽnd], pp. y a. curtido, curado; tostado del sol.

tanner [tǽnœr], s. curtidor, noquero.

tannery [tǽnœri], s. tenería o curtiduría.

tannic [tǽnic], a. (quím.) tánico.

tannin [tǽnin], s. tanino.

tanning [tǽning], s. curtimiento.

tansy [tǽnsi], s. (bot.) tanaceto, balsamita menor.

tantalize [tǽntalaiš], va. atormentar mostrando lo inasequible; atormentar, molestar.

tantalizing [-ing], a. atormentador.

tantalum [tǽntalúm], s. (quím.) tantalio.

Tantalus [-us], s. Tántalo.

tantamount [tǽntamaunt], a. equivalente.

tantivy [tæntívi], **I.** a. veloz, rápido. **II.** adv. velozmente.

tantrum [tǽntrʋm], s. berrinche, pataleta.

tanyard [tǽnyárd], *s.* tenería.

tap [tæp]. **I.** *va.* decentar (un barril); horadar (para sacar líquido); hacer incisión a un árbol (para extraer el jugo); unir o conectar con (para tomar agua, corriente); hacer una unión de toma o derivación en; tomar, sacar (agua, electricidad); sacar de, tomar de; roscar (tuerca o hembra de tornillo); (cir.) hacer una puntura en (un absceso); golpear ligeramente, dar una palmadita; taladrar, perforar; poner tacón a (un zapato.) **II.** *vn.* tocar o golpear ligeramente.—**to t. at the door,** llamar a la puerta. **III.** *s.* canilla, espita, tubo, o llave para sacar vino de un barril; tapón, tarugo; (mec.) macho de terraja; toma (de agua); (elec.) derivación; calidad o clase de vino; (fam.) mostrador de taberna; remiendo echado al talón de un zapato.—*pl.* (mil.) toque de apagar las luces.—**t. hole,** orificio de colada (de un alto horno).—**on t.,** sacado del barril, por vaso (cerveza, vino, etc.).

tape [téip], *s.* cinta, cintilla, galoncillo, trencilla, bocadillo ; cinta de papel o de metal; medida de ⅛ de pulg. (3,2 mm.); (top.) cinta.—**t. line, t. measure,** cinta para medir.

taper [téipœr]. **I.** *s.* bujía, cerilla, candela, vela pequeña; cirio (de iglesia); hacha, blandón; ahusamiento de un objeto. **II.** *a.* cónico, piramidal, ahusado. **III.** *va.* afilar, adelgazar, ahusar. **IV.** *vn.* rematar en punta, tener forma ahusada.

tapestry [tǽpestri]. **I.** *va.* entapizar; adornar con colgaduras. **II.** *s.* tapiz; tapicería, colgadura.

tapeworm [téipucœrm], *s.* tenia, solitaria.

tapioca [tæpióca], *s.* tapioca, mandioca.

tapir [téipœr], *s.* (zool.) tapir, danta.

tapis [téipis], *s.* tapete.—**on the t.,** sobre el tapete.

tapper [tǽpœr], *s.* el o lo que golpea; (tlg.) manipulador; (radtlg.) descohesor; (mec.) máquina de roscar tuercas o hembras de tornillo.

tappet [tǽpet], *s.* brazo, aleta; leva.—**t. gear,** (aut.) mando de levas.

tapping [tǽping], *s.* (cir.) paracentesis.

taproom [tǽprúm], *s.* taberna.

tapster [tǽpstœr], *s.* mozo de taberna.

tar. I. *s.* alquitrán, brea, pez líquida; (fam.) marinero.—**t. paper,** papel alquitranado.—**t. water,** agua de alquitrán. **II.** *vn.* alquitranar, brear, embrear, betunar.—**to t. and feather,** embrear y emplumar.

tarantella [tærantéla], *s.* tarantela.

tarantula [tæréntiula], *s.* tarántula.

tarbrush [tárbruśh], *s.* (mar.) escopero.

tardigrade, ó tardigradous [tárdigred, tardígradus], *a.* tardígrado, lento.

tardily [tárdili], *adv.* morosamente, tardíamente; fuera de tiempo.—**tardiness** [-nes], *s.* lentitud; tardanza; cachaza, flema.

tardo [tárdo], *a.* y *adv.* (mús.) lento; despacio.

tardy [tárdi], *a.* tardío, moroso, tardo, lento.

tare [téœr]. **I.** *s.* (bot.) cizaña; veza, lenteja; algarroba; vicia; (com.) tara, merma. **II.** *va.* destarar, restar la tara al pesar una cosa.

target [tárguet], *s.* blanco a que se tira, terrero; tablilla, corredera (de mira de nivelar); tarja, escudo o rodela.—**t. practice,** tiro al blanco.—**t. (leveling) rod,** mira de tablilla o de corredera (para nivelación).

tariff [tǽrif]. **I.** *s.* tarifa; arancel; impuesto; ley de impuestos (apl. esp. a los de aduana). **II.** *va.* hacer una tarifa (lista) de; afectar por razón de impuestos.

tarlatan, tarletan [tárlatan], *s.* (tej.) tarlatana.

tarn, *s.* lago pequeño entre montañas.

tarnish [tárniśh]. **I.** *va.* deslustrar, empañar; manchar, mancillar. **II.** *vn.* deslustrarse, perder el lustre; enmohecerse. **III.** *s.* deslustre, empañadura, mancha.

tarpaulin, tarpawling [tarpólin, -ling], *s.* lienzo empegado o alquitranado; encerado; sombrero encerado; (fam.) marinero.—**t. nails,** (mar.) estoperoles.

Tarpeian rock [tarpíyæn roc], roca Tarpeya.

tarragon [tǽragon], *s.* (bot.) estragón.

tarred [tard], *a.* embreado, alquitranado.

tarry [tǽri]. **I.** *vn.* tardar, demorarse, detenerse, quedarse. **II.** *a.* embreado, alquitranado; píceo. —**t.-fingered,** aficionado al hurto.

tarsal [társal], *a.* tarsal, del tarso.

tarsus [társus], *s.* (anat.) tarso.

tart. I. *a.* acre, ácido, picante; acedo, agridulce; mordaz. **II.** *s.* tarta, pastelillo de fruta.

tartan [tártan], *s.* (tej.) tartán; (mar. y carr.) tartana.

tartar [tártar], *s.* tártaro (*v.* ARGOL); (dent.) sarro, toba.—**t. emetic,** tártaro emético.

Tartar, *s.* y *a.* tártaro.—**to catch a T.,** hallar uno la horma de su zapato.

Tartarean [tartérean], *a.* tartáreo.

tartareous [tartéreus], *a.* compuesto de tártaro.

tartaric [tartéric], *a.* tártrico, tartárico.

tartarize [tártaraiś], *va.* tartarizar.

tartarous [tártarus], *a.* de tártaro.

Tartarus [tártœrus], *s.* el tártaro.

tartly [tártli], *adv.* agriamente.—**tartness** [-nes], *s.* acidez, agrura, acedía; acrimonia.

tartrate [tártret], *s.* tartrato.

tasco [tǽsco], *s.* talque.

task. I. *s.* tarea, faena, labor. **II.** *va.* atarear, señalar tarea.—**tasker** [-œr], **taskmaster** [-mæstœr], *s.* el que da o señala tareas.

taskwork [tǽscuœrc], *s.* destajo.

tassel [tǽsel]. **I.** *s.* borla, campanilla. **II.** *va.* adornar con borlas.—**tasselled** [-d], *a.* adornado con borlas o campanillas.

tasset [tǽset], *s.* escarcela; faldar.

tastable [téistabœl], *a.* sabroso, gustable.

taste [téist]. **I.** *va.* gustar; saborear, paladear; probar, catar; experimentar, ensayar. **II.** *vn.* (a menudo con **of**) saber a, tener sabor o gusto. **III.** *s.* gusto; sabor, gustadura; paladeo, saboreo; cata, sorbo, trago; ligera cantidad, un poco, muy poco; muestra, ejemplar; ensayo, prueba, experimento; gusto, discernimiento; afición, inclinación.—**in bad t.,** de mal gusto.—**in good t.,** de buen gusto.—**in poor t.** = IN BAD T.—**to have a t. for,** tener gusto por, gustar de.

tasteful [téistful], *a.* elegante, de buen gusto; (ant.) sabroso.—**tastefully** [-li], *adv.* elegantemente, con gusto.—**tastefulness** [-nes], *s.* gusto, discernimiento; gracia, elegancia.

tasteless [téistles], *a.* insípido, insulso; desabrido, falto de gracia; de mal gusto.—**tastelessly** [-li], *adv.* insípidamente; sin gusto, sin gracia.—**tastelessness** [-nes], *s.* insipidez, falta de gusto o de gracia.

taster [téistœr], *s.* catador, probador; probeta, catavino.

tasty [téisti], *a.* sabroso, embocado, gustoso.

tat [tæt], *va.* y *vn.* hacer encaje de frivolité.

Tatar [tátar], *s.* = TARTAR.

tatou [tatú], *s.* tato, tatú, armadillo grande americano.

tatter [tǽtœr], *s.* andrajo, pingajo, harapo, guiñapo, trapajo, jirón.

tatterdemalion [-deméliun], *s.* zarrapastrón.

tattered [-d], *a.* andrajoso, harapiento.

tatting [tǽting], *s.* encaje de hilo, frivolité.

tattle [tǽtœl]. **I.** *va.* charlar, chacharear. **II.** *vn.* chismear, comadrear. **III.** *s.* charla, cháchara; chismografía.—**tattler** [tǽtlœr], *s.* charlador, chacharero; chismoso; (orn.) agachadiza.

tattoo [tættú]. **I.** *s.* (mil.) retreta; tatú. **II.** *va.* tatuar.

Taube [táube], *s.* (aer.) taube, aeroplano taube.

taught [tot], *pret.* y *pp.* de TO TEACH.

taunt [tant o tont]. **I.** *va.* vilipendiar, vituperar. **II.** *s.* vituperio, dicterio.—**t.-masted,** (mar.) de mucha guinda.—**taunter** [-œr], *s.* vituperador.— **taunting** [-ing], *a.* insultante.—**tauntingly** [-li], *adv.* con vituperio; en tono insultante.

taupe [tóup], *s.* y *a.* gris oscuro.

tauriform [tóriform], *a.* de forma de toro; (astr.) referente a Tauro.

taurine [tórin o tórain], *a.* taurino, de toro; (astr.) relativo a Tauro.

Taurus [tórus], *s.* (astr.) Tauro.

taut [tot], *a.* (mar.) tieso, tirante, tenso; listo, preparado, en regla.—**to haul, o pull, t.,** tesar, atesar.

tauten [tótœn], *va.* (mar.) tesar, entesar.
tautness [tótnes], *s.* (mar.) calidad de tieso.
tautog [totóg], *s.* pez negruzco.
tautologic(al [totolóyic(al], *a.* tautológico.
tautologist [totóloyist], *s.* tautologista.
tautologize, tautologise [totóloyaiŝ], *vn.* repetir en diferentes palabras.
tautology [totóloyi], *s.* tautología.
tavern [tǽvœrn], *s.* taberna; mesón, posada, figón.—**t. keeper,** tabernero; posadero.
taw [to]. **I.** *va.* curtir (pieles en blanco).—**tawed leather** = ALUM LEATHER. **II.** *s.* bolita de mármol con que juegan los niños; línea desde donde se lanzan las bolas.
tawdrily [tódrili], *adv.* charramente.
tawdriness [-nes], *s.* charrería.
tawdry [tódri], *a.* charro, chillón.
tawer [tóœr], *s.* curtidor en blanco.
tawny [tóni], *a.* moreno, atezado, tostado.
tax [tæx]. **I.** *s.* impuesto, contribución, gabela; carga, exacción; esfuerzo.—**t. collector,** recaudador de contribuciones; exactor, alcabalero.—**t. list,** lista de cotribuyentes.—**t. rate,** cupo. **II.** *va.* imponer contribuciones a; (for.) tasar; acensuar; cargar, abrumar; abusar de; someter a esfuerzo o exigir esfuerzo de; (fam.) pedir como precio; (con **of** o **with**) acusar, tachar, imputar.
taxable [tǽxabœl], *a.* sujeto a impuesto o tributación; pechero.
Taxaceæ [tæxéisii], *s. pl.* (bot.) taxáceas, taxíneas.—**taxaceous** [-ŝhus], *a.* taxáceo.
taxation [tæxéiŝhun], *s.* tributación; imposición o repartimiento de contribuciones o impuestos.
taxer [tǽxœr], *s.* exactor; acusador.
taxgatherer [tǽxgædœrœr], *s.* = TAX COLLECTOR. *V.* TAX.
taxi [tǽxi]. **I.** *s.* (fam.) taxímetro (coche). **II.** *vn.* andar o ir en taxímetro; (aer.) correr por tierra o sobre el agua (un avión antes de elevarse o despegar).—**taxicab** [-cæb], *s.* taxímetro (coche).
taxidermal, taxidermic [tǽxidœrmal, -mic], *a.* taxidérmico.—**taxidermist** [-mist], *s.* disecador.—**taxidermy** [-miĵ, *s.* taxidermia.
taximeter [tǽximetœr], *s.* taxímetro (coche o instrumento).
taxonomy [tæxónomi], *s.* taxonomía.
taxpayer [tǽxpéiœr], *s.* contribuyente.
taxy [tǽxi], *s.* = TAXI.—**taxying,** *s,* (aer.) corrida.
Taylor's theorem [téilœrs źíorem], (mat.) serie de Taylor.
tazza [tatsa], *s.* (arq.) pila, tazón (receptáculo sostenido por un pie o pedestal).
Tcheka [chékæ], *s.* cheka, policía secreta rusa.
tea [ti], *s.* té; cualquier cocimiento, infusión o decocción medicinal; colación o refección de la tarde o prima noche; reunión en que se sirve té.—**t. ball,** bola perforada para hacer té.—**t. canister,** caja para té.—**t. rose,** o **t.-scented rose,** rosa té.—**t. set,** servicio para té.—**t. wagon,** mesa rodadiza para té.
teach [tích]. **I.** *va.* enseñar, instruir. **II.** *vn.* ejercer el magisterio, enseñar, ser maestro.
teachable [tíchabœl], *a.* dócil; susceptible de enseñanza, educable.
teache [tich], *s.* tacho, paila evaporadora.
teacher [tíchœr], *s.* maestro, maestra, preceptor, instructor.—**teachers' institute,** (E. U.) congreso pedagógico.
teaching [tíching]. **I.** *a.* docente. **II.** *s.* enseñanza, instrucción; doctrina.
teacup [tícup], *s.* taza para té.—**teacupful** [-ful], *s.* taza llena.
teak [tik], *s.* (bot.) teca.
teakettle [tíkétœl], *s.* marmita, olla de calentar agua.
teakwood [tíkud], *s.* teca.
teal [til], *s.* (orn.) cerceta; trullo.
team [tím]. **I.** *s.* tronco, pareja, par, yunta; atelaje; (dep.) equipo (grupo de jugadores); partido; manada de patos.—**t. work,** trabajo cooperativo, esfuerzos aunados. *V.* TEAMWORK. **II.** *va.* y *vm.* guiar un tronco o yunta; uncir, enganchar, enyugar.

teamster [tímstœr], *s.* tronquista.
teamwork [tímuœrk], *s.* trabajo aunado o colectivo, ejecutado por varias personas con cooperación mutua.
teapot [típót], *s.* tetera.
teapoy [típoi], *s.* mesita de adorno.
tear [tíœr], *s.* lágrima; gota; (fig.) llanto, aflicción.—**t. bomb,** (mil.) granada cargada con gas lacrimante.—**t. gas,** gas lacrimante, que afecta los ojos.—**t. shell** = T. BOMB.
tear [tᴇœr]. **I.** *va.* (pret. TORE, ant. TARE; pp. TORN) desgarrar, romper, rasgar, lacerar; rasguñar, arañar, arpar; arrancar, separar con violencia; atormentar.—**to t. asunder,** separar con violencia.—**to t. away,** arrancar; desmembrar.—**to t. down,** derribar, demoler.—**to t. in pieces,** despedazar, hacer añicos.—**to t. off** = TO T. AWAY.—**to t. one's hair,** arrancarse uno los cabellos.—**to t. one's self away,** arrancarse o desprenderse de un lugar, partir uno contra su voluntad.—**to t. to pieces** = TO T. IN PIECES.—**to t. to tatters,** hacer jirones.—**to t. up,** arrancar, desarraigar; deshacer, desbaratar. **II.** *vn.* rasgarse; andar precipitadamente.—**to t. away,** o **off,** irse precipitadamente. **III.** *s.* rasgón, rasgadura; desgarradura; precipitación; raja; (fam.) borrachera, jarana.
teardrop [tíœrdróp], *s.* lágrima.
tearful [tíœrful], *a.* lloroso, lagrimoso.
tearless [tíœrles], *a.* sin lágrimas.
tease [tiŝ]. **I.** *va.* molestar, atormentar, embromar, torear, cardar, rastrillar; (tej.) despinzar, carduzar; despedazar, desgarrar. **II.** *s.* atormentador; broma continua; (fam.) cócora.
teaser [tíŝœr], *s.* cócora, majadero; (elec.) excitador de una dínamo.
teaspoon [tíspun], *s.* cucharita, cucharilla de café.—**teaspoonful** [-ful], *s.* cucharadita.
teat [tit], *s.* pezón; teta, tetilla; ubre.
teazel [tíŝœl], *s.* cardencha, carda. **II.** *va.* cardar paño.—**teaz(e)ler** [tíŝlœr], *s.* pelaire; carda.
technical [técnical], *a.* técnico, tecnológico; literal, aparente.—**technicality** [-cǽliti], *s.* cosa técnica; argucia o sutileza; tecnicismo.—**technically** [-cali], *adv.* técnicamente.—**technicist** [-sist], *s.* técnico, experto.—**technics** [técnics], *s.* técnica; tecnicismo.
technique [tecník], *s.* (b. a.) técnica, ejecución, mecanismo.
technological [técnolóyical], *a.* tecnológico.
technologist [tecnóloyist], *s.* tecnólogo.
technology [-yi], *s.* tecnología.
techy [téchi], *a.* cosquilloso.
tectonic [tectónic], *a.* arquitectónico; (geol.) tectónico, relativo a la estructura.—**tectonics,** *s. sing.* y *pl.* arquitectura, arte de la construcción.
Te Deum [ti díum], *s.* (igl.) tedéum.
ted [ted], *va.* (agr.) henear.—**tedding** [-ing], *s.* henaje.
tedder [tédœr], *s.* heneador.
Teddy bear [tédi béœr], *s.* osito, juguete en forma de oso.
tedious [tídius], *a.* tedioso, fastidioso, pesado, aburridor.—**tediously** [-li], *adv.* tediosamente, aburridamente.—**tediousness** [-nes], *s.* **tedium** [tídium], *s.* tedio, aburrimiento, pesadez.
tee [tí]. **I.** *s.* (dep.) meta; en el golf, montoncillo donde se coloca la pelota que hay que lanzar; te, letra *t;* cosa en T (*v.* **T**): tubo en T; viga en T; barra atada por el centro a una cuerda o cadena. **II.** *va.* en golf, colocar la pelota en el *tee.*
teem [tím]. **I.** *va.* (ant.) parir; producir. **II.** *vn.* (gen. con **with**) rebosar (de), abundar (en); estar lleno (de).—**teeming** [-ing], *a.* prolífico, fecundo; lleno; abundante.
teens [tins], *s. pl.* los números cuyos nombres terminan en **-teen;** edad de trece a diecinueve años.
teepee [típi], *s.* = TEPEE.
teeter [títœr]. **I.** *vn.* balancearse, columpiarse. **II.** *s.* balanceo, vaivén.
teeth [tiŝ], *s. pl.* de TOOTH.—**in the t. of,** contra; en presencia de; a despecho de.—**to cast, to throw, in one's t.,** echar en cara a uno, arrojarle a la cara, en señal de insulto o desafío.
teeth(e [tíD], *vn.* endentecer, echar los dientes.

teething [-ing], s. dentición.

teetotal [títótàl], a. entero, completo, total; que se abstiene por completo de bebidas alcohólicas.—**teetotaler** [-œr], s. el que se abstiene por completo de bebidas alcohólicas.—**teetotalism** [-ĭŝm], s. abstinencia completa de bebidas alcohólicas.

teetotum [títótum], s. perinola.

tegmen [tégmen], s. (anat.) placa de hueso; (ento.) élitro; (bot.) túnica interior.

tegument [téguiumœnt], s. tegumento.

tegumentary [-méntari], a. tegumentario, que cubre.

teil(tree [tíl(tri], s. (bot.) tilo; alfónsigo, terebinto.

telamon [télamon], s. (arq.) talamón.

telautograph [telótograf], s. telautógrafo.

telautomatics [telótomǽtics], s. gobierno o mando (de un mecanismo) por ondas hertzianas.

telegram [télegram], s. telegrama.

telegraph [-grœf]. **I.** va. y vn. telegrafiar; enviar por telégrafo. **II.** s. telégrafo; tablero de noticias telegráficas, en el cual se escriben éstas para el público (Il. t. **t. board**).—**t. cable**, cable telegráfico.—**t. operator**, telegrafista.—**t. rope**, (mec.) cable sin fin (entre una grúa y la máquina que la mueve).—**t. wire**, alambre de telégrafos.

telegrapher, telegraphist [télegrafœr o telégrafœr, -fĭst], s. telegrafista.

telegraphic [-grǽfic], a. telegráfico.

telegraphically [-grǽficali], adv. telegráficamente.

telegraphone [telégrafoun], s. telegráfono, especie de telégrafo magnético.

telegraphy [telégrafi], s. telegrafía.

telemechanics [télemecǽnics], s. telemecánica.

telemeter [télemeter], s telémetro.—**telemetric** [télemétric], a. telemétrico.—**telemetry** [télemetri], s. telemetría.

telengiscope [telényiscoup], s. telengiscopio, combinación del telescopio y el microscopio.

teleologic(al [tĭleolóyic(al], a. teleológico.

teleology [teleóloyi], s. teleología.

Teleostomi [télióstomai], s. pl. teleósteos, peces de esqueleto completo.—**teleostome** [-toumi], s. teleósteo.

telepathy [telépæzi], s. telepatía.—**telepathic** [télepæzic], a. telepático.—**telepathically** [-ali], adv. telepáticamente.

telephone [télefoun]. **I.** va. y vn. telefonear. **II.** s. teléfono.—**t. exchange**, central telefónica.—**t. girl**, (fam.) chica telefonista.—**t. message**, telefonema.—**t. operator**, telefonista.

telephonic(al [telefónic(al], a. telefónico.

telephonist [telefonist], s. telefonista.

telephony [teléfoni], s. telefonía.

telephote [télefout], s. teléfoto, aparato para reproducir eléctricamente imágenes a distancia.

telephotograph [-fótogræf], s. telefotografía, imagen fotográfica hecha a distancia.—**telephotography** [-fotógrœfi], s. telefotografía, procedimiento de fotografiar a distancia.

telergy [télœryi], s. telepatía.

telescope [télescoup]. **I.** s. telescopio; catalejo; (top.) anteojo (de teodolito, nivel, etc.). **II.** va. y vn. enchufarse, meter(se) uno entre otro; meter(se) en.

telescopic(al [télescópic(al], a. telescópico; de larga vista; de enchufe, de secciones enchufadas.

telescribe [télescraib], s. fonógrafo registrador de telefonemas.

telespectroscope [télespéctroscoup], s. telespectroscopio, telescopio con espectroscopio; espectroscopio para telescopio.

telethermograph [télezœrmogrœf], s. teletermómetro registrador.

telethermometer [-zermómetœr], s. teletermómetro, instrumento para medir temperaturas a distancia.

television [téleví̄ʒun], s. televisión, formación eléctrica de imágenes a gran distancia.

Telford pavement [télford péivmœnt], pavimento Télford, compuesto de mezcla de piedras grandes y pequeñas y una capa superficial de

grava.—**telfordize** [-aĭŝ], va. y vn. poner o hacer pavimento Télford.

telic [télic], a. referente a un designio o intento.

tell [tel]. **I.** va. y vn. (pret. y pp. **TOLD**) decir; expresar; contar, relatar; explicar; descubrir, revelar; decidir, determinar; descifrar; adivinar, predecir; mandar, disponer, ordenar; contar, numerar.—**to t. off**, contar, reeontar; designar.—**to t. one's**, o **its, own tale**, contar por sí mismo el cuento, hacer ver por sí mismo lo que hay.—**to t. tales out of school**, revelar secretos.—**to t. volumes**, ser sumamente significativo.—**tell that to the marines**, a otro perro con ese hueso. **II.** vn. producir efecto; dejarse ver; (con **on**) delatar.

teller [télœr], s. relator, narrador; escrutador de votos; computista; pagador (de un banco).

telling [téling], a. eficaz, notable.

telltale [télteil], s. soplón, chismoso; indicador, contador, reloj de vigilancia; (mar.) axiómetro.

telluric [telúric], a. telúrico.

tellurid(e [télurid, -aid], s. telururo.

tellurion [telúrion], s. planetario.

tellurium [telúrium], s. (quím.) telurio.

tellurous [télurus], a. (quím.) teluroso.

telpherage [télfœrey], s. (elec.) transporte automático aéreo.

temerity [temériti], s. temeridad.

temper [témpœr]. **I.** va. moderar, mitigar, calmar; atemperar; mezclar, modificar, ajustar; temperar, ablandar; (metal.) templar. **II.** s. mal genio o carácter irascible; índole, humor o disposición; calma, ecuanimidad, sangre fría; (metal.) temple; punto (grado de densidad de una mezcla); cal de defecación (para el azúcar); (ant.) temperamento.—**to lose one's t.**, perder la paciencia, enojarse.

tempera [témpera], s. (pint.) templa.

temperament [témpœramœnt], s. temperamento; constitución, naturaleza; composición; disposición, genialidad; (mús.) temple.

temperamental [-al], a. complexional, genial.

temperamentally [-i], adv. por naturaleza, por índole, genialmente.

temperance [témpœrans], s. templanza, temperancia, sobriedad.—**temperate** [-et], a. sobrio, abstemio; templado, benigno; moderado.—**temperately** [-li], adv. sobriamente.—**temperateness** [-nes], s. templanza, moderación; serenidad.

temperature [témpœratiur], s. temperatura; (fam.) exceso de temperatura, fiebre.

tempered [témpœrd], a. templado; dispuesto, inclinado.

tempering [-ing]. **I.** a. atemperante, templador. **II.** s. temple; temperación; templadura.

tempest [témpest]. **I.** s. tempestad. **II.** va. agitar, conmover violentamente.

tempestuous [témpéschuus], a. tempestuoso, borrascoso; impetuoso.—**tempestuously** [-li], adv. tempestuosamente.—**tempestuousness** [-nes], s. calidad de tempestuoso.

Templar [témplar], s. Templario; (Ingl.) estudiante de leyes que habita en el Temple de Londres.

template [témplet], s. = TEMPLET.

temple [témpœl], s. templo; (anat.) sien; (tej.) encuentro, vara de telar.

templet [témplet], s. (tec.) plantilla, patrón, modelo; (mar.) gálibo; (constr.) solera, piedra o madero para distribuir la carga; cuña.

tempo [témpo], s. (mús.) tiempo, movimiento.

temporal [témporal]. **I.** a. temporal, secular; transitorio, pasajero; (anat.) temporal. **II.** s. (anat.) hueso temporal.

temporality [-éliti], s. temporalidad.—**temporally** [-ali], adv. temporalmente, transitoriamente.—**temporalty** [-alti], s. seglares.—**temporariness** [-erines], s. calidad de transitorio o provisional.—**temporary** [-eri], a. temporal, provisorio, interino.

temporize [témporaiŝ], vn. temporizar, contemporizar.

temporizer [-œr], s. temporizador, contemporizador.

---

tempt [temt], *va.* tentar, poner a prueba; provocar, desafiar.—**temptable** (-abœl], *a.* capaz de dejarse tentar.—**temptation** [témtéishun], *s.* tentación; solicitación; prueba; aliciente.—**tempter** [-œr], *s.* tentador.—**tempting** [-ing], *a.* tentador, atractivo.—**temptingly** [-li], *adv.* con tentación.—**temptress** [témtres], *s.* tentadora.

ten, *a.* y *s.* diez; (arit.) decena.—**t.-strike**, jugada en que se derriban los diez bolos con una sola bocha.

tenable [ténabœl], *a.* defensible.

tenacious [tenéshus], *a.* tenaz; pegajoso, adhesivo; porfiado; firme.—**tenaciously** [-li], *adv.* tenazmente, con firmeza.—**tenaciousness** [-nes], *s.* tenacidad; tesón, pertinacia.

tenacity [tenæsiti], *s.* tenacidad; tesón; terquedad, porfía.

tenaille [tenél], *s.* (fort.) tenaza.

tenaculum [tenækiulum], *s.* tenáculo.

tenancy [ténansi], *s.* tenencia, posesión, inquilinato.

tenant [ténant]. **I.** *s.* arrendatario, inquilino; residente, morador.—**t. for life**, residente, usufructuario o inquilino vitalicio. **II.** *vn.* tener en arriendo.

tenantable [-tabœl], *a.* habitable.

tenantless [-les], *a.* desarrendado, sin inquilinos; deshabitado.—**tenantry** [-tri], *s.* inquilinato; inquilinos en general.

tench [tench], *s.* (ict.) tenca.

tend [tend]. **I.** *va.* guardar, vigilar, cuidar; atender. **II.** *vn.* tender, propender; dirigirse; atender; propender; (con **on** o **upon**) asistir, servir a; estar atento a.

tendency [téndensi], *s.* tendencia o propensión; dirección, inclinación.

tender [téndœr]. **I.** *a.* tierno; delicado; muelle, mollar; benigno, benévolo, compasivo, sensible; adolorido; delicado; dulce, ameno.—**t.-hearted**, tierno de corazón, compasivo.—**t. of**, u **over**, cuidadoso de, solícito de los sentimientos de otros. **II.** *s.* oferta, ofrecimiento, propuesta; (for.) oferta formal de pago; lo que se ofrece en pago de una deuda; (mar.) escampavía, patache, falúa; guarda, servidor; (f. c.) ténder, servidor. **III.** *va.* ofrecer, presentar, proponer; (for.) ofrecer en pago sin condiciones; enternecer, ablandar. **IV.** *vn.* hacer una oferta o propuesta.

tenderfoot [-fut], *s.* (fam.) apodo que dan los mineros al recién llegado; inexperto, novato.

tenderling [-ling], *s.* pitón de asta de venado.

tenderloin [-lóin], *s.* filete.—**t.**, o **t. district**, barrio de Nueva York donde se vive la vida alegre.

tenderly [-li], *adv.* tiernamente.—**tenderness** [-nes], *s.* terneza, ternura; sensibilidad; delicadeza; benignidad, benevolencia.

tendinous [téndinus], *a.* tendinoso.

tendon [téndun], *s.* (anat.) tendón.

tendril [téndril], *s.* (bot.) zarcillo, tijeretas.

tenebrous [ténebrus], *a.* tenebroso.

tenement [ténemœnt], *s.* habitación, vivienda, alojamiento (apl. gen. a los de la gente pobre); (for.) heredamiento.—**t. (house)**, casa de vecindad.

tenementary [téneméntari], *a.* (for.) arrendable.

tenesmus [tenésmus], *s.* (med.) tenesmo, pujos.

tenet [ténet], *s.* dogma; principio; credo.

tenfold [ténfould]. **I.** *a.* décuplo. **II.** *adv.* diez veces.

tennis [ténis], *s.* tenis (juego).—**t. ball**, pelota de tenis.—**t. court**, cancha de tenis.

tenon [ténun]. **I.** *va.* (carp.) espigar, despatillar, desquijarar; juntar a espiga y mortaja. **II.** *s.* (carp.) espiga, almilla.—**t. saw**, sierra de ingletes.

tenonitis [-áitis], *s.* inflamación de un tendón.

tenor [ténœr]. **I.** *s.* tenor, curso, método; tendencia; texto, contenido, substancia de un escrito; (mús.) tenor; alto; viola. **II.** *a.* (mús.) de tenor.

tenotomy [tenótomi], *s.* tenotomía.

tenpenny [ténpeni], *a.* de diez peniques; clavo de cierto tamaño.

tenpins [ténpins], *s.* (E. U.) juego con diez bolos de madera.

tense [tens]. **I.** *a.* tieso, estirado, tenso, tirante. **II.** *s.* (gram.) tiempo (del verbo).

tenseness [ténsnes], *s.* tirantez.

tensibility [tensibíliti], *s.* facilidad en ponerse tenso.

tensible [ténsibœl], *a.* capaz de tensión.

tensile [ténsil], *a.* extensible; de tensión.—**t. strength**, resistencia de tensión, o a la tracción.—**t. stress**, esfuerzo de tensión o de tracción.

tensimeter [tensímetœr], *s.* manómetro.

tension [ténshun], *s.* tensión, tirantez; esfuerzo mental; (mec.) tensión, tracción; fuerza expansiva de un gas; regulador del hilo en una máquina de coser; (dipl.) tirantez de relaciones.

tensive [ténsiv], *a.* tirante, tenso.

tensor [ténsor], *s.* músculo extensor; (mat.) tensor.

tent. **I.** *s.* (mil.) tienda de campaña; pabellón, alfaneque; (cir.) lechino, tapón; tienta.—**t. bed**, catre de tijera.—**t. cloth**, terliz.—**t. pole**, mástil; montante de tienda. **II.** *vn.* acampar bajo tiendas. **III.** *va.* (cir.) tentar.

tentacle [téntacœl], *s.* (zool. y bot.) tentáculo.

tentacular [tentékiular], *a.* de tentáculo.

tentative [téntativ]. **I.** *a.* tentativo. **II.** *s.* tentativa, ensayo, prueba, tanteo.

tented [ténted], *a.* entoldado.

tenter [téntœr]. **I.** *s.* (tej.) tendedor. **II.** *va.* (tej.) estirar (el paño). **III.** *vn.* estirarse.

tenterhook [-júc], *s.* escarpia o alcayata; causa de ansiedad.

tenth [tenz]. **I.** *a.* décimo, deceno; diez (ordinal). **II.** *s.* décima parte, décimo; (igl.) diezmo.

tenthly [[ténzli], *adv.* en décimo lugar.

tentwort [téntucœrt], *s.* (bot.) culantrillo.

tenuirostral [ténuirróstral], *a.* tenuirrostro.

tenuity [teniúiti], *s.* tenuidad, raridad, delgadez; rarefacción.

tenuous [téniuus], *a.* tenue, delgado, sutil.

tenure [téniuœr], *s.* tenencia, posesión, pertenencia.

teocalli [tiocéli], *s.* (Méx.) teocalí.

tepee [típi], *s.* tienda o vivienda de los indios de los E. U.

tepefaction [tépefæcshun], *s.* templadura.

tepefy [-fai], *va.* y *vn.* entibiar; ponerse tibio.

tepid [tépid], *a.* tibio, templado.—**tepidity** [tepíditi], *s.* tibieza.—**tepidly** [tépidli], *adv.* tibiamente.

teratogeny [tératóyeni], *s.* teratogenia, producción de monstruos.—**teratoid** [-oid], *a.* monstruoso, anormal.—**teratologic** [-tolóyic], *a.* teratológico, relativo a la teratología.—**teratology** [-tóloyi], *s.* teratología, estudio de las monstruosidades.

terce [tœrs], *s.* tercerola.

tercentenary [tœrsénteneri]. **I.** *a.* de tres siglos. **II.** *s.* aniversario tricentésimo.

terebenthic [-bénzic], *a.* relativo a o del carácter de la trementina.

terebinth [térebinz], *s.* (bot.) terebinto.

terebinthine [-bínzin], *a.* terebintáceo.

teredo [terído], *s.* (ent.) broma.

terete [teríit], *a.* cilíndrico, redondo.

tergal [tœrgal], *a.* = DORSAL.

tergiversation [tœryivœrséishun], *s.* tergiversación, efugio, evasión.

tergiversate [-eit], *vn.* tergiversar.

term [tœrm]. **I.** *s.* término, vocablo, palabra; plazo; término, período; (for.) tiempo en que un tribunal está en sesión; límite, confín; fin; (lóg. y mat.) término.—pl. términos, palabras, expresiones; condiciones, estipulaciones; obligaciones impuestas; relaciones mutuas; precio.—**In set terms**, en términos escogidos.—**in terms of**, (mat.) en función de.—**not on any terms**, por ningún concepto, a ningún precio.—**to be on good terms with**, estar en buenas relaciones con.—**to bring to terms**, imponer condiciones a, hacer arreglos con.—**to come to terms**, arreglarse, convenirse.—**upon what terms?** ¿en qué términos? **II.** *va.* nombrar, llamar.

termagancy [tœrmagansi], *s.* carácter pendenciero.

termagant [-ant]. **I.** *a.* turbulento; pendenciero·
II. *s.* sierpe, fiera, arpía.

terminability [tœrmínæbíliti], *s.* terminabilidad.

terminable [-æbœl], *a.* terminable.—**terminably**
(-blí], *adv.* terminablemente.

terminal [tœrminal]. **I.** *a.* terminal, último, extremo, final. **II.** *s.* término, final; (arq.) término; (f. c.) estación terminal o extrema; (elec.)
terminal, borne.

terminate [tœrmineit], *va.* y *vn.* terminar.

termination [-éishun], *s.* terminación o fin;
(gram.) terminación, desinencia.

terminative [-etiv], *a.* terminativo.

terminator [-éitœr], *s.* el o lo que termina; (astr.)
límite de iluminación (de la luna o un planeta).

terminology [-óloyi], *s.* terminología.

terminus [tœrminus], *s.* término, fin; (f. c.) estación terminal; límite, mojón; (arq.) término,
remate; (**T-**, mit.) el dios Término.

termite [tœrmait], *s.* hormiga blanca.

terminer [tœrminœr], *s.* (for.) = OYER.

termless [tœrmles], *a.* ilimitado.

tern [tœrn]. **I.** *s.* terna, terno; (orn.) golondrina
de mar. **II.** *a.* ternario.

ternary [tœrnari]. **I.** *a.* ternario, trino. **II.** *s.*
terna, terno, trinca.

ternate [tœrnet], *a.* ternario.

terpene [tœrpin], *s.* (quím.) terpeno.—**terpin**
[tœrpin], *s.* (quím.) terpina.—**terpinol** [-ol], *s.*
(quím.) terpinol.

Terpsichorean [tœrpsicorían], *a.* de Terpsícore,
del baile.

terra [tœrra], *s.* tierra.—**t. alba**, tierra de pipa.—
t. cotta, terracota.—**t. cotta lumber**, objetos de
barro en que pueden clavarse clavos.—**t. firma**,
tierra firme.—**t. incognita**, tierra desconocida.

terrace [tœrres]. **I.** *va.* terraplenar. **II.** *s.* terraplén, bancal, balate, parata; terraza, terrero, terrado, azotea; balcón, galería abierta.

terrane, terrain [tœrren], *s.* (geol.) serie continua
de rocas; (mil.) campo, terreno.

terrapin [tœrrapin], *s.* emido (variedad de tortuga).

terraqueous [tœrrécuius], *a.* terráqueo.

terrazzo [tœrrátso], *s.* piso veneciano, pavimento
de cemento con astillas o fragmentos irregulares
de piedra ornamental (mármol, etc.).

terrene [tœrrín], *a.* térreo, terreno, terrenal.

terreplein [tœrplein], *s.* (fort.) plataforma.

terrestrial [tœrréstrial], *a.* terrestre, terreno.

terret [tœrret], *s.* portarriendas.

terre-tenant, ter-tenant [tœrtenænt], *s.* terrateniente.

terre-verte [tœær véært], *s.* (min.) tierra verde,
verdacho.

terrible [tœrríbœl], *a.* terrible o espantoso; tremendo.

terribleness [-nes], *s.* terríblez.—**terribly** [-blí],
adv. terriblemente, espantosamente.

terrier [tœrrίœr], *s.* perro de busca; (Ingl.) nutria
macho solitaria.

terrific [tœrrífic], *a.* terrífico, espantoso.

terrify [tœrrifai], *va.* aterrar, aterrorizar, espantar.

terrigenous [tœrríyenus], *a.* terrígeno.

territorial [tœrritórial], *a.* territorial.—**t. waters**,
aguas jurisdiccionales.

territoriality [tœrritoriéliti], *s.* territorialidad.

territory [tœrritori], *s.* territorio, región, distrito,
comarca; (geog.) territorio (división política).

terror [tœrrœr], *s.* espanto, terror.—**terrorism**
[-išm], *s.* terrorismo.—**terrorist** [-ist], *s.* terrorista,
partidario del terrorismo.—**terrorize** [-aiš], *va.* a-
terrorizar.—**terrorizer** [-aišœr], *s.* aterrorizador.

terse [tœrs], *a.* sucinto, breve, conciso; (ant.)
terso, liso, pulido.—**tersely** [-lí], *adv.* concisamente.
—**terseness** [-nes], *s.* concisión.

tertian [tœrshan]. **I.** *a.* tercianario. **II.** *s.* (med.)
terciana.

tertiary [tœrshieri]. **I.** *a.* terciario, tercero; (**T-**,
geol.) terciario. **II.** *s.* (**T-**, geol.) terreno terciario;
(orn.) pluma terciaria de un ave.

tertiate [tœrshiet], *va.* (arti.) medir el espesor de.

terzet [tœršet], *s.* (poét.) terceto.

terzetto [tertséto], *s.* (mús.) terceto.

tessellate [téseleit], *va.* taracear.

tessellate(d [téseleit(ed], *a.* teselado.

tessellation [-éishun], *s.* mosaico.

tessera [tésera], *s.* tesela; tésera.

tessitura [tesitúra], *s.* (mús.) tesitura.

test. I. *s.* prueba, ensayo, experimento; **examen**;
piedra de toque, criterio; (quím.) análisis; re-
saye; resultado de un análisis; reacción; reactivo;
(zool.) concha; (bot.) tegumento de una semilla.—
T. Act, (Ingl.) ley que imponía cierto juramento
de prueba a los empleados públicos.—**t. case**, (for.)
acción o causa de ensayo, para determinar la interpretación de una ley.—**t. meal**, comida de
prueba, para analizar el contenido o condición del
estómago.—**t. paper**, papel reactivo.—**t. tube**,
probeta, tubo de ensayos.—**t. types**, letras para
probar la vista.—**the acid t.**, la prueba suprema,
decisiva. **II.** *va.* probar, ensayar; hacer la prueba
de; poner a prueba; (for.) atestiguar.

testable [téstabœl], *a.* que puede probarse; que
puede legarse.

testacy [téstasi], *s.* estado o hecho de haber testado.

testaceous [téstéshus], *a.* testáceo.

testament [téstamœnt], *s.* testamento; (**T-**), el
Viejo y el Nuevo Testamento.—**testamental** [-al],
a. testamentario.—**testamentary** [-méntari], *a.*
testamentario.—**testate** [tésteit], *a.* testado.

testator [testéitœr], *s.* testador.—**testatrix**
[-trics], *s.* testadora.

tested [tésted], *a.* ensayado, probado.

tester [téstœr], *s.* probador, ensayador; (quím.)
reactivo; pabellón, baldaquín; (Ingl., fam.) medio chelín.

testes [téstis], *s. pl.* de TESTIS.

testicle [tésticœl], *s.* testículo.—**testicular** [tes-
tíkiular], *a.* testicular.—**testiculate** [testíkiulet], *a.*
en forma de testículo; que tiene testículos u órganos
parecidos a ellos.

testification [téstifikéshun], *s.* testificación.

testifier [-faiœr], *s.* testigo, testificador.

testify [-fai], *va.* y *vn.* (for.) testificar, atestiguar,
declarar, atestar.

testily [téstili], *adv.* impertinentemente.

testimonial [testimónial]. **I.** *a.* testimonial, testificativo. **II.** *s.* certificación o certificado, a-
testado, testimonios; recomendación; enco-
mio.

testimony [téstimoni], *s.* testimonio, atestación,
declaración; Tablas de la Ley, el decálogo; Libro
de la Ley, Antiguo Testamento.—**in t. whereof**,
en fe de lo cual.

testines [téstines], *s.* quisquillosidad, mal humor,
mal genio.

testis, *s.* (*pl.* TESTES) teste, testículo.

testudinal [testiúdinœl], *s.* testudíneo.

testudo [testiúdo], *s.* (mil.) testudo; (zool.) tortuga.

testy [tésti], *a.* enojadizo, quisquilloso.

tetanic [tetǽnic]. **I.** *a.* tetánico. **II.** *s.* droga o
substancia que causa tétano.

tetanus [tétanus], *s.* tétano, pasmo.

tetany [tétæni], *s.* tétano intermitente.

tête a tête [tet a tet], *s.* cara a cara, a solas; confidente (mueble).

tether [tédœr]. **I.** *s.* traba, maniota, correa, atadura. **II.** *va.* apersogar.

tetrachord [tétracord], *s.* (mús.) tetracordio.

tetracid [tetrǽsid], *a.* tetrácido.

tetrad [tétræd], *s.* grupo, de cuatro; (quím.) átomo o elemento tetravalente.

tetradynamous [tétrædínamus], *a.* (bot.) tetradínamo.

tetragonal [tetrǽgonal], *a.* tetrágono, cuadrangular.

tetragram [tétrægræm], *s.* tetragrama.

tetragrammaton [tétragrǽmæton], *s.* tetragrámaton.

tetrahedral [tetrajídral], *a.* tetraédrico.

tetrahedron [-jídron], *s.* tetraedro.

tetralogy [tetrǽloyi], *s.* tetralogía.

tetrameter [tetrǽmetœr], *s.* tetrámetro.

Tetrao [tétræo], *s.* (zool.) tetrao, género de gallináceas cuyo tipo es el urogallo.—**Tetraonidæ** [-ónidi], *s. pl.* (zool.) tetraónidas.

tetrarch [tétrarc], *s.* tetrarca.—**tetrarchate** [-et], **tetrarchy** [tétrarki], *s.* tetrarquía.

tetrasyllable [-síllæbœl], *s.*, **tetrasyllabic** [-silébic], *a.* tetrasílabo.

tetter [tétœr], *s.* herpe, empeine, serpigo, culebrilla.

Teuton [tiúton], *s.* teutón.—**Teutonic** [tiutónic]. I. *a.* teutónico.—**T. Knights,** Caballeros Teutónicos. II. *s.* tudesco.

tew [tiú], *va.* cascar, agramar, espadillar.

tewel [tiúel], *s.* tobera (de forja).

Texan [téxan], *a.* y *s.* tejano, de Tejas.

text, *s.* texto; lema, tema, tesis; (impr.) tipo.—**t. hand,** carácter de letra muy grueso.

textbook [téxtbúc], *s.* texto, libro de texto; libreto de ópera.

textile [téxtil]. I. *a.* textil, tejido, de tejer o de tejidos. II. *s.* tejido; material textil.

textual [téxtiual], *a.* textual.—**textualist** [-ist], *s.* textualista.—**textually** [-i], *adv.* textualmente.

texture [téxchur], *s.* textura, contextura; tejido, obra tejida; (biol.) tejido.

thalami [zǽlæmi], *s. pl.* de THALAMUS.

thalamus [zǽlæmUS], *s.* (bot.) tálamo; (anat.) tálamo óptico (ll. t. **optic t.**).

thalassography [zǽlæsógrafi], *s.* ciencia de la vida y otros fenómenos del mar.

thaler [tálœr], *s.* tálero (moneda).

thallic [zǽlic], *a.* tálico.

thallium [zǽlium], *s.* (quím.) talio.

Thallophyta [zælófitæ], *s. pl.* (bot.) talofitas.—**thallophyte** [zǽlofait], *s.*, **thallophytic** [-fític], *a.* talofita.—**thallus** [zǽlus], *s.* (bot.) talo, aparato vegetativo de la planta talofita.

than [ðæn], *conj.* que (comparativo: *I am taller than he,* soy más alto que él); de (cuando va delante de números: *fewer than ten,* menos de diez: *more than two,* más de dos: *more than once,* más de una vez). Las frases **t. whom, t. which** se traducen cambiando el giro: *Shakespeare, than whom there is no greater poet.* Shakespeare, que como poeta no tiene superior, o S., poeta de grandeza nunca sobrepasada. Lo mejor es traducir primero la expresión a manera de paréntesis, y luego darle forma más apropiada: Shakespeare (no hay poeta más grande que él); *this book, than which I know few more useful,* este libro (conozco pocos más útiles); este libro, cuya utilidad, que yo sepa, hay pocos que la sobrepasen.

thanage [-ey], *s.* dignidad o dominio del *thane.*

thane [zéin], *s.* caballero, gentilhombre.

thank [zænk]. I. *va.* agradecer, dar gracias.—**t. God,** a Dios gracias.—**t. you,** gracias. II. *s. pl.* **thanks,** gracias.—**t. to,** gracias a, debido a.

thankful [zǽnkfúl], *a.* agradecido.—**thankfully** *adv.* con agradecimiento.—**thankfulness** [-nes], *s.* agradecimiento, gratitud.—**thankless** [-zænkles], *a.* desagradecido; ingrato, infructuoso.—**thanklessness** [-nes], *s.* ingratitud.

thanksgiving [zæncsguíving], *s.* acción de gracias.—**T. Day,** día de acción de gracias.

thankworthy [zǽncuœrDi], *a.* digno de reconocimiento; meritorio.

that [ðæt]. I. *a.* (*pl.* THOSE [ðóuŝ]) ese, esa, aquel, aquella. II. *pron.* ése, ésa, eso; aquél, aquélla, aquello ; que, quien, el cual, la cual, lo cual; el, la (substantivado: *that of John,* el de Juan; *that of yesterday,* el de ayer).—**t. is,** o **t. is to say,** es decir.—**t. may be,** eso puede ser, es posible.—**t. way,** por aquel camino, por allí; de ese modo.—**t. which,** el que, la que, lo que.—**and all t.,** (fam.) y cosas por ese estilo.—**to put this and t. together,** atar cabos.—**upon t.,** sobre esto; luego. III. *conj.* que; para que, a fin de que, con el objeto de; cuando.—**not but t.,** no es decir que.—**save t.,** salvo que.—**so t.,** para que; con tal que; de modo que, de suerte que. IV. *adv.* (fam.) tan; tan . . . así, así de, de este tamaño, etc. (*that large,* tan grande así, así de grande, de este tamaño; *not that far,* no tan lejos).

thatch [zæch]. I. *s.* barda. II. *va.* bardar.

thatcher [zéchœr], *s.* bardador.

thaumaturge [zómatœry], *s.* taumaturgo, lagrero.—**thaumaturgic(-al** [-tœrvic, -œl], *a.* taumatúrgico.—**thaumaturgist** [-ist], *s.* taumaturgo.—**thaumaturgy** [-yi], *s.* taumaturgia.

thaw [zo]. I. *va.* y *vn.* deshelar, derretir(se).—**to t. out,** hacer(se) más tratable, menos reservado o ceremonioso, abrirse.—**it thaws,** deshiela. II. *s.* deshielo, derretimiento.

the [ði o ðæ]. I. *art.* el, la; lo; los, las. II. *adv.* Cuando precede a un comparativo, se traduce en español por **cuanto . . . tanto,** mientras más . . . tanto más, o expresiones análogas: *the more he spoke, the more we admired him,* mientras más hablaba más lo admirábamos; *the less you say, the better,* cuanto menos diga Vd., tanto mejor; *the sooner the better,* mientras más pronto, tanto mejor.

theater, theatre [zíætœr], *s.* teatro, coliseo; arte dramático; drama (literatura); teatro o escena de algún suceso.

theatric(al [ziǽtric(al]. I. *a.* teatral. II. *s. pl.* funciones teatrales.

theatrically [ziǽtricali], *adv.* teatralmente.

thee [ði], *pron.* caso oblicuo de THOU: te, a ti.

theft [zeft], *s.* hurto, robo, ladronicio.

thein(e [zíin], *s.* teína, alcaloide del té, idéntico a la cafeína.

their [ðéær], *pron. pos.* su, suyo, suya, de ellos, de ellas.—**theirs,** el suyo, la suya, los suyos, las suyas, de ellos o de ellas.

theism [zíism], *s.* teísmo.—**theist** [zíist], *s.*, **theistic(al** [zíístic(al], *a.* teísta.

them [ðem], *pron.* caso oblicuo de THEY: los, las, les, ellos, ellas.—**t. that, t. who** (despúes de preposición) los que, aquellos que, quienes (*this is for them who wish to learn,* esto es para los que, o para quienes, deseen aprender).

thematic [zimǽtic], *a.* temático.

theme [zim], *s.* tema, asunto; tesis, disertación; (mús.) tema, motivo.

themselves [ðemsélvŝ], *pron. pl.* ellos mismos, ellas mismas; sí mismos. Es el caso oblicuo del pronombre recíproco, y a veces se usa enfáticamente como nominativo. V. HIMSELF.

then [ðen]. I. *adv.* entonces, en aquel tiempo, a la sazón; luego, después, en seguida; en otro tiempo. II. *conj.* en tal caso, por consiguiente, pues, luego, por esta razón.—**now and t.,** de cuando en cuando; de vez en cuando.—**now . . . t . . . ,** ya . . . ya . . . .; ora . . . ora . . .—**now t.,** ahora bien; tenemos pues.—**what t.?** ¿qué más? ¿qué resultó, o qué resultará? ¿qué vendrá (vino) luego? ¿qué se hará (se hizo) luego?

thence [ðens], *adv.* (de lugar) de allí, desde allí; (de tiempo) desde entonces, desde aquel momento, de allí en adelante; (de modo) de ahí, por eso, por esa razón, por ese motivo.—**thenceforth** [-forz], *adv.* desde entonces, de allí en adelante.—**thenceforward** [-tóruard], *adv.* desde entonces; desde allí hacia adelante.

Theobroma [zíobrómæ], *s.* (bot.) teobroma, género cuyo tipo es el cacao.—**theobromin(e** [-min], *s.* teobromina.

theocracy [zíócrasi], *s.* teocracia.

theocratic(al [zíocrǽtic(al], *a.* teocrático.

theodicy [zíódici], *s.* teodicea.

theodolite [zíódolait], *s.* teodolito.

theogony [zíógoni], *s.* teogonía.

theologian [zíolóyian], *s.* teólogo.

theological [-yical], *a.* teológico; teologal.—**t. seminary,** seminario eclesiástico.—**t. virtues,** virtudes teologales.

theologically [-yicali], *adv.* teológicamente.—**theologize** [zíóloyaiŝ]. I. *va.* hacer teológico. II. *vn.* teologizar.—**theologue** [zíolog], *s.* seminarista.—**theology** [zíóloyi], *s.* teología.

theomachy [zíómaki], *s.* combate con los dioses.

theorbo [zíórbo], *s.* (mús.) tiorba.

theorem [zíorem], *s.* teorema; serie; ecuación. V. BINOMIAL THEOREM, TAYLOR'S THEOREM.

theoretic(al [zíorétic(al], *a.* teórico.—**theoretically** [-i], *adv.* teóricamente.—**theoric** [zióric]. I. *s.* teórica, especulativa. II. *a.* teórico, especulativo —**theorist** [zíorist], *s.* teórico.—**theorize** [-aiŝ], *vn.* exponer o formar teorías; teorizar.—**theory** [zíori] *s.* teoría; teórica.

theosophic(al [ziosófic(al], *a.* teosófico.
theosophism [zíosofiâm], *s.* teosofismo.
theosophist [ziósofist], *s.* teósofo.
theosophy [ziósofi], *s.* teosofía.
Therapeutæ [zérapiúti], *s. pl.* (hist.) terapeutas.
therapeutic(al [zérapiútic(al], *a.* terapéutico.
therapeutics [-tics], *s.* terapéutica.
therapeutist [-tist], *s.* terapeuta.
there [Déær]. **I.** *adv.* ahí, allí, allá; en eso, en cuanto a eso. Ú. como expletivo enfático, sobre todo antes del verbo cuando el sujeto va después: *there came a man,* vino un hombre; *lives there a man so cruel?* ¿vive hombre tan cruel?—**t. to be.** *V.* BE.—**t. you are,** (fam.) eso es todo; ahí nos (me, etc.) tiene; ahí está el busilis. **II.** *inter).* ¡eso es! ¡toma! ¡vaya! ¡mira!
thereabout(s [-abáuts], *adv.* por ahí, por allí, cerca; acerca de; aproximadamente.
thereafter [-æftœr]. **I.** tiempo después. **II.** *adv.* después de eso; conforme.
thereat [-æt], *adv.* en eso; entonces, en aquel punto o lugar.
thereby [-bái], *adv.* con eso, con lo cual; de tal modo, así; allí, por allí cerca; acerca de eso.
therefor [-for], *adv.* para eso, para esto.
therefore [-for o Dærfor], *adv.* y *conj.* por esto, por eso; luego, por tanto.
therefrom [-fróm], *adv.* de allí, de ahí; de eso.
therein [-ín], *adv.* allí dentro; en esto, en eso.—**thereinafter** [-æftœr], *adv.* (for.) posteriormente, después, adelante.—**thereinbefore** [-Defóær], *adv.* (for.) anteriormente, antes, más arriba.
thereinto [-intú], *adv.* dentro de eso o de esto.
thereof [-óf], *adv.* de esto, de eso.
thereon [-ón], *adv.* encima de él, ella, etc.; sobre él, etc.; encima.
thereout [-áut], *adv.* fuera de allí; fuera de eso o de esto.
thereto [-tú; (ant.) **thereunto** [-untú], *adv.* a eso, a ello; además.
theretofore [-tofóær], *adv.* antes de eso, hasta entonces.
thereunder [-úndœr], *adv.* debajo, debajo de eso, bajo eso.
thereupon [-upón], *adv.* sobre o encima de él, ella, etc.; por lo tanto, por consiguiente; sobre lo cual, luego, al punto.
therewith [-uíD], *adv.* con eso, con esto; luego, inmediatamente.
therewithal [-uiDól], *adv.* a más, además; con todo.
theriaca [ziráica], *s.* (farm.) triaca, teriaca.
theriac(al [-l], *a.* teriacal, triacal.
therm [zœrm], *s.* unidad térmica (el término se aplica a varias de ellas); (Ingl.) unidad térmica en función de la cual se expresa el coste del gas —equivale a 100,000 unidades térmicas británicas (B. T. U.).
thermæ [zérmi], *s. pl.* termas (de los romanos).
thermæsthesia, thermesthesia [zérmeszíỹiæ], *s.* sentido de la temperatura, capacidad de sentir cambios de temperatura.
thermal [zœrmal], *a.* termal, térmico.—**t. alarm,** alarma automática de calentamiento.—**t. unit,** unidad térmica.—**t. waters,** aguas termales.
thermic [zœrmic], *a.* termal, térmico.
thermion [zœrmion], *s.* termión, ión o electrón emitido por una substancia incandescente.
thermionic [zœrmiónic], *a.* (fís.) termiónico, relativo a los termiones.—**t. valve,** (rad.) tubo termiónico, lámpara termiónica.
thermit [zœrmit], *s.* termita.
thermocautery [zœrmocóteri], *s.* termocauterio.
thermochemical [-kémical], *a.* termoquímico.
thermochemistry [-kémistri], *s.* termoquímica.
thermocouple [-cúpœl], *s.* pila termoeléctrica.
thermodynamic [-dainámic], *a.* termodinámico. —**thermodynamics,** *s.* termodinámica.
thermoelectric [-eléctric], *a.* termoeléctrico.
thermoelectricity [-electrísiti], *s.* termoelectricidad.
thermogenesis [-yénesis], *s.* producción de calor (apl. esp. al de las funciones orgánicas).

thermograph [-græf], *s.* termógrafo, termómetro registrador.
thermometer [zœrmómetœr], *s.* termómetro.
thermometric(al [zœrmométric(al], *a.* termométrico.
thermometry [zœrmómetri], *s.* termometría.
thermopile [zœrmopáil], *s.* pila termoeléctrica.
thermos [zœrmos], **thermos bottle, thermos flask,** *s.* termos.
thermoscope [zœrmoscoup], *s.* termoscopio.
thermosiphon [zœrmosáifon], *s.* termosifón.
thermostat [zœrmostæt], *s.* termóstato.
thermotank [-tǽnc], *s.* caja de calefacción (o de enfriamiento), que contiene tubos por los cuales circula vapor, agua, etc. (puede llamarse *caja térmica).*
thesaurus [zesórus], *s.* tesauro.
these [Dîs]. **I.** *a. pl.* de THIS: estos, estas. **II.** *pron.* éstos, éstas.
thesis [zísis], *s.* tesis; disertación.
Thespian [zéspian], *a.* trágico, dramático.
Thessalian [zesSíliæn], *s.* y *a.* tesaliense.
Thessalonian [zésálóniæn], *s.* y *a.* tesalonicense.
theurgy [zíœrri], *s.* teurgia.
thew [ziú], *s.* tendón, músculo.—*pl.* fuerza muscular, vigor.
they [Déi], *pron. pl.* de HE, SHE o IT: ellos, ellas.
thick [zic]. **I.** *a.* grueso; espeso; tupido, denso; de espesor (2 *inches thick,* de 2 pulgadas de espesor); continuado, repetido; basto, grosero, tosco; nebuloso, brumoso, sombrío; estúpido, torpe; apagado, borroso; (fam.) íntimo.—**t.-and-thin,** cabal, a toda prueba.—**t. of hearing,** teniente de oído, duro de oído.—**t. stuff,** (mar.) tablones, palmejares. **II.** *s.* grueso, espesor; lo más denso, nutrido, tupido o recio.—**the t. of the fight,** lo más reñido del combate.—**through t. and thin,** por sobre todo; a toda costa, a despecho de todo. **III.** *adv.* frecuentemente, continuadamente; densa o tupidamente.—**t.-headed,** espeso, torpe.—**t.-lipped,** bezudo, jetudo.—**t.-necked,** cervigudo.— **t.-set,** rechoncho, grueso; plantado muy espeso.— **t.-skinned,** de pellejo espeso; sin vergüenza; indiferente; paquidermo.—**t.-skulled,** lerdo, torpe.
thicken [zícœn], *va.* y *vn.* espesar, condensar, engrosar, aumentar; reforzar; enturbiar(se); cerrarse; complicar(se).
thickening [-ing], *s.* espesamiento; espesativo.
thicket [zíket], *s.* maleza, soto, espesura, matorral, broza, manigua, fosca.
thickhead [zícjed], *s.* estúpido.
thickish [zíkish], *a.* algo espeso o denso.
thickly [zícli], *adv.* espesamente; densa o tupidamente; repetidamente.—**t. settled,** muy poblado.
thickness [zícnes], *s.* espesor; densidad; grueso, grosor; cuerpo, consistencia; capa (superpuesta); (fam.) estupidez.
thickskin [zícskin], *s.* persona sin vergüenza.
thickskull [-scúl], *s.* estúpido.
thief [zif], *s.* ladrón, estafador; moco de vela.—**t. tube,** pipeta, bombillo, catavinos.
thieve [ziv], *vn.* hurtar, robar.—**thievish** [-ish], *a.* rapaz.—**thievishly** [-li], *adv.* ladronamente, a modo de ladrones.—**thievishness** [-nes], *s.* latrocinio; rapacidad.
thigh [zái], *s.* muslo.—**t. bone,** fémur.
thill [zil], *s.* (carr.) limonera.
thimble [zímbœl], *s.* (cost.) dedal; (mec.) manguito; (mar.) guardacabo.
thimbleberry [-bérri], *s.* frambuesa negra.
thin [zin]. **I.** *a.* delgado, fino, tenue; flaco, descarnado; raro, ralo, claro; ligero, transparente; seroso, aguado; poco, corto, ligero, escaso; pequeño; (fam.) transparente, débil, artificial, inverosímil (apl. a excusas, etc.). **II.** *va.* enrarecer, poner ralo, adelgazar; (gen. con **out**) aclarar, entresacar. **III.** *vn.* enflaquecer, adelgazarse.
thine [Dáin], *pron.* y *a.* tuyo, el tuyo; tu, tus.
thing [zing], *s.cosa;* (desp.) tipo, quídam.—**above all things,** sobre todas las cosas, sobre todo, muy especialmente.—**as things stand,** como están las cosas.—**no such a t.,** no hay tal; nada de eso.— **poor (little) t.,** ¡pobrecito!—**the t.,** lo conve-

---

niente, lo que está de moda, lo necesario o lo que se desea.

think [zink]. **I.** *va.* y *vn.* pensar; proponerse, tener intención de; creer, juzgar, conjéturar. **II.** *vn.* (con **of, on** o **upon**) acordarse de, recordar; pensar en; reflexionar acerca de, meditar, considerar.—**to t. better of,** cambiar de opinión acerca de; formar mejor opinión de.—**to t. well (ill) of,** tener buen (mal) concepto de.—**as you t. fit,** como a Vd. le parezca mejor, como Vd. quiera.

thinker [zínkœr], *s.* pensador.

thinking [-ing], *s.* pensamiento, meditación, reflexión; juicio, concepto.—**to my t.,** en mi opinión, en mi concepto.—**to put on,** o **have on, one's thinking cap,** poner las mientes, avivar el seso.—**way of t.,** modo de pensar, opinión, parecer.

thinly [zínli], *adv.* delgadamente; esparcidamente; poco, en corto número.

thinness [zínnes], *s.* tenuidad, delgadez; flacura, magrez, escasez; raleza; raridad; poca consistencia.

thioaldehyde [záioældejaid], *s.* (quím.)aldehido sulfúrico.

thiogen [-yen], *s.* bacteria productora de azufre.

thionic [-ónic], *a.* (quím.) tiónico.

thiosulphuric [-sulfiúric], *a.* tiosulfúrico.

third [zœrd]. **I.** *a.* tercero.—**t. boiler,** meladora de azúcar.—**t. degree,** grado tres (en la masonería); (fam.) interrogatorio severo de un preso, gen. con crueldad o mal tratamiento.—**t. estate,** estado llano o común.—**t. eyelid,** (anat.) membrana nictitante.—**t. house,** (fam.) camarilla de cabilderos. —**t. member,** (aut.) eje de piñón cónico.—**t. person,** tercero; (gr.) tercera persona.—**t. rail,** (elec.) tercer riel, riel conductor.—**t.-rail,** *a.* de riel conductor.—**t. wire,** (elec.) conductor neutro (de un sistema trifilar). **II.** *s.* tercio, tercero.

thirdly [zérdli], *adv.* en tercer lugar.

thirst [zœrst]. **I.** *s.* sed; ansia, anhelo. **II.** *va.* y *vn.* tener o padecer sed; ansiar, anhelar.—**to t. for,** tener sed de; anhelar.

thirstiness [zérstines], *s.* sed; ansia.

thirsty [zérsti], *a.* sediento.—**to be t.,** tener sed.

thirteen [zértin], *s.* y *a.* trece.—**t. hundred,** mil trescientos.—**thirteenth** [-z]. **I.** *a.* décimotercio, trece (ordinal). **II.** *s.* y *a.* trezavo.

thirtieth [-tiez]. **I.** *a.* trigésimo, treinta (ordinal). **II.** *s.* y *a.* treintavo.

thirty [-ti], *s.* y *a.* treinta.

this [Dis]. **I.** *a.* (*pl.* THESE) este, esta. **II.** *pron.* éste, ésta, esto.

thistle [zísœl], *s.* (bot.) cardo; (mil.) abrojo.—**t. bird, t. finch,** jilguero.

thistledown [-dáun], *s.* papo de cardo.

thistly [zisli], *adv.* lleno de cardos.

thither [DíDœr], *adv.* allá, hacia allá; a ese fin, punto o resultado.

tho' [Do], *conj. contr.* de THOUGH.

thole [zóul], *s.* (mar.) tolete, escálamo, gavilán; asidero del mango de la guadaña; (arq.) tambor. —**tholepin** [-pin], *s.* tolete.

tholus [zólus], *s.* (arq.) tambor, cúpula.

Thomism [tómišm], *s.* tomismo.—**Thomist** [-ist], *s.* y *a.* tomista.

thong [zong], *s.* correa, correhüela, tira o tireta, guasca, zurriaga.

thoracic [zoræsic], *a.* torácico.

thorax [zóræx], *s.* tórax.

thoria [zóriæ], *s.* torina, óxido de torio.—**thorianite** [-nait], *a.* torianita, mineral de óxidos de torio, cerio, etc.—**thorite** [zórait], *s.* torita, mineral de silicato de torio.

thorium [zóriʊm], *s.* (quím.) torio.

thorn [zorn]. **I.** *va.* pinchar, traspasar o asegurar con una espina. **II.** *s.* (bot.) espina, púa; espino, abrojo.—**t. apple,** (bot.) estramonio.—**t. prickle,** abrojo.—**to be upon thorns,** estar en ascuas.

thornback [zórnbæc], *s.* (ict.) raya espinosa o lija raya.

thornless [zórnles], *a.* sin espinas.

thorny [zórni], *a.* espinoso; arduo.

thorough [zéro], *a.* cabal, completo, cumplido, acabado; consumado, perfecto; cuidadoso, con-

cienzudo.—**t. bass,** (mús.) contrapunto.—**t.-paced,** cabal, completo, perfecto.

thoroughbred [-bred], *a.* de pura raza, casta o sangre; bien nacido.

thoroughfare [-féær], *s.* vía pública.—**no t., n**e se pasa; calle cerrada.

thoroughgoing [-góing], *a.* cabal, completo, minucioso; pronunciado, intransigente.

thoroughly [-li], *adv.* enteramente, cabalmente; a fondo; concienzudamente.

thoroughness [-nes], *s.* entereza, calidad de cabal o completo; minuciosidad; escrupulosidad.

thoroughwax [-uéx], *s.* (bot.) perfoliada.

thoroughwort [-uért], *s.* (bot.) eupatorio.

thorp [zorp], *s.* lugar, villorrio, caserío.

those [Dóus]. **I.** *a. pl.* de THAT: aquellos, aquellas; esos, esas. **II.** *pron. pl.* ésos, ésas; aquellos, aquellas.—**t. that, t. which, t. who,** los que, aquellos que.

thou [Dáu]. **I.** *pron.* tú. **II.** *va.* y *vn.* tutear.

though [Do], *conj.* aunque, bien que, sin embargo, si bien, aun cuando.—**as t.,** como si.—**what t.,** aunque, ¿qué importa que . . .? En lenguaje familiar, ú. a menudo adverbialmente, sobre todo en oraciones de forma interrogativa, como expletivo enfático de encarecimiento: *isn't she pretty, though?* y qué bonita que es! *aren't you smart, though?* ¡qué vivo que eres!

thought [zot]. **I.** *pret.* y *pp.* de TO THINK.—**to be well t. of,** ser tenido en buen concepto, ser estimado. **II.** *s.* pensamiento; meditación, reflexión; consideración; idea; intención, propósito; memoria, recuerdo; cuidado, solicitud, atención; (fam.) poquito, migaja, pizca.—**to give (a) t. to,** pensar en, acordarse de.—**to take t. of,** o **for,** pensar en, proveer para.

thoughtful [zótful], *a.* pensativo, meditabundo; considerado; precavido.—**thoughtfully** [-li], *adv.* meditativamente, con reflexión, con previsión, con consideracion.—**thoughtfulness** [-nes], *s.* calidad de meditativo, preavido o considerado; cuidado, atención; previsión.

thoughtless [zótles], *a.* atolondrado, descuidado; irreflexivo; inconsiderado.—**thoughtlessly** [-li], *adv.* descuidadamente; irreflexivamente; sin consideración.—**thoughtlessness** [-nes], *s.* descuido o inadvertencia; ligereza o indiscreción; atolondramiento.

thousand [záusand]. **I.** *a.* mil. **II.** *s.* mil; millar. —**a t., one t.,** mil.—**by the t.,** por millar; por millares; por miles.

thousandth [záusandz]. **I.** *a.* milésimo. **II.** *s.* milésimo, milésima.

Thracian [zréshæn]. **I.** *s.* y *a.* traeio. **II.** **(t-)** *s.* gladiador vestido de tracio.

thrall [zrol], *s.* esclavo.—**t., thraldom** [-dʊm], *s.* esclavitud, servidumbre; dominación.

thrash [zræsh]. **I.** *va.* trillar, desgranar; batanear; batir; sacudir; (fam.) apalear, azotar, zurrar. **II.** *vn.* trillar el grano; arrojarse, agitarse; trabajar, afanarse; estar flojo, correrse en los cojinetes o bambolear (un eje).—**thrasher** [-œr], *s.* trillador, desgranador; trilladora mecánica, máquina trilladora; (orn.) malviz; (ict.) tiburón.

thrashing [-ing], *s.* trilla, trilladura, desgranamiento; (fam.) zurra, paliza.—**t. floor,** era.—**t. machine,** trillo, trilladora.

thrasonical [zrasónical], *a.* jactancioso, fachendoso.

thread [zred]. **I.** *s.* hilo; fibra, hebra; filete (de un tornillo).—**t. and thrum,** hilo e hilaza.—**t.-like,** filiforme.—**t. stockings,** medias de hilo. **II.** *va.* enhebrar, enhilar, ensartar; colarse a través de; roscar, labrar un filete en; pasar por. **III.** *vn.* brujulear.

threadbare [-béær], *a.* raído, muy usado; gastado; traqueado, viejo.

threadworm [-uérm], *s.* ombricilla filiforme, ascáride.

threat [zret], *s.* amenaza.—**threat**(en [zrétœn], *va.* amenazar; amagar.—**threatener** [zrétnœr], *s.* amenazador.—**threatening** [zrétning]. **I.** *s.* amenaza. **II.** *a.* amenazador, amenazante.—**threateningly** [-li], *adv.* con amenzas.

three [zri], _s._ y _a._ tres.—**t.-cleft**, (bot.) trífido.—**t.-color**, tricolor; tricromo (estampado).—**t.-cornered**, triangular; de tres picos.—**t.-decker**, navío de tres puentes.—**t. deep**, en tres hileras o filas.—**t.-leaved**, trifoliado.—**t.-legged**, de tres pies.—**t.-lobed**, trilobulado.—**t.-parted**, (bot.) tripartido.—**t.-phase**, trifásico.—**t.-ply**, triple; de tres capas.—**t. R.'s.** _V._ **R.**—**t.-square file**, lima triangular.—**t.-stringed**, de tres cuerdas.—**t.-toed**, de tres dedos (del pie.).—**t.-way cock**, llave o grifo de tres vías.—**t.-way switch**, interruptor de tres direcciones.—**t.-way valve**, válvula de paso triple.—**t.-wire**, (elec.) trifilar.

threefold [zrífould], triple.

threepense [zrípens, zrœpens], _s._ tres peniques.

threepenny [zrípeni o zrœpeni], _a._ barato, despreciable.

threepile [zrípail], _a._ terciopelo.

threescore [zríscœr], _a._ y _s._ tres veintenas, sesenta.—**t. and ten**, setenta.

threnody [zrénodi], _s._ treno.

thresh, _va._ = **THRASH**.

thresher [zréshœr], _s._ (ict.) tiburón. _V._ **THRASHER**.

threshold [zréshould], _s._ (arq.) umbral, tranco; entrada; comienzo.

threw, _pret._ de **TO THROW**.

thrice [zrais], _adv._ tres veces.

thrid [zrid], _vn._ colarse, pasar por.

thrift [zrift], _s._ economía, frugalidad; crecimiento, desarrollo.—**t. stamp**, (E. U.) pequeño bono de guerra en forma de estampilla emitido durante la guerra mundial.

thriftily [zríftili], _adv._ frugalmente, económicamente.—**thriftiness** [-nes], _s._ frugalidad, parsimonia.—**thriftless** [zríftles], _a._ manirroto, pródigo; extravagante.—**thrifty** [zríftii], _a._ frugal, económico; próspero, floreciente; vigoroso.

thrill [zril]. **I.** _va._ causar una emoción viva, hacer estremecerse. **II.** _vn._ estremecerse, conmoverse. **III.** _s._ emoción, estremecimiento.

thriller [zrílœr], _s._ (fam.) cosa o persona conmovedora, entusiasmadora, espeluznante, etc.

thrilling [zríling], _a._ conmovedor; espeluznante.

thrive [zráiv], _vn._ medrar, prosperar, adelantar, tener buen éxito.—**thriving** [-ing], _a._ próspero, floreciente.—**thrivingly** [-li], _adv._ prósperamente.

thro' [zru], _adv._ y _prep._ abrev. de **THROUGH**.

throat [zróut], _s._ garganta, cuello, gola, gaznate; paso, entrada, orificio.—**t. latch**, ahogadero (de la cabezada).

throatband [-bænd], _s._ ahogadero.

throating [zróuting], _s._ goterón.

throb [zrob]. **I.** _vn._ latir, palpitar; vibrar. **II.** _s._ latido, pulsación, palpitación.

throe [zro], _s._ angustia, dolor, agonía.

thrombosis [zrombósis], _s._ (med.) trombosis, coagulación en los vasos sanguíneos.—**thrombus** [-bus], _s._ coágulo que forma la trombosis.

throne [zróun]. **I.** _s._ trono.—**thrones**, _pl._ tronos. **II.** _va._ y _vn._ elevar al trono, exaltar.

throng [zrong]. **I.** _s._ tropel de gente, multitud, muchedumbre, caterva. **II.** _va._ apretar, atestar, llenar de bote en bote; estrujar. **III.** _vn._ venir en tropel, amontonarse, apiñarse.

throstle [zróscœl], _s._ (Ingl., orn.) zorzal, malvís; (tej.) telar continuo.

throttle [zrótœl]. **I.** _s._ gaznate, gorja, gargüero; traquiarteria; (mec.) gollete.—**t. valve**, (m. v.) válvula de estrangulación, válvula reguladora; (locom.) regulador; (aut.) acelerador. **II.** _va._ ahogar; estrangular (el vapor). **III.** _vn._ ahogarse, asfixiarse.

through [zru]. **I.** _a._ continuo, que va hasta el fin.—**t. bridge**, puente de tablero inferior.—**t. thicket**, (f. c.) billete para determinado punto pasando por varias líneas.—**t. train**, tren directo o terminal. **II.** _adv._ a través, de parte a parte, de un lado a otro; desde el principio hasta el fin; enteramente, completamente. **III.** _prep._ por; a través de; de un extremo (o de un lado) a otro de; por conducto o por medio de, por entre; por causa de, gracias a, por mediación de.

throughout [zruáut]. **I.** _prep._ por todo, en todo; a lo largo de; durante todo. **II.** _adv._ en todas partes; desde el principio hasta el fin; de parte a parte.

throve [zróuv], _pret._ de **TO THRIVE**.

throw [zróu]. **I.** _va._ y _vn._ (_pret._ **THREW**: _pp._ **THROWN**) arrojar, tirar, disparar, lanzar; echar (suertes, dados); derribar, echar por tierra; desmontar, apear; despojarse de; mudar (la piel); dirigir (la mirada); torcer (hilo); mover rápidamente; mover, dar vuelta a; parir (la coneja); perder con premeditación (una carrera, un juego); dar forma a los objetos de alfarería.—**to t. about**, esparcir.—**to t. aside**, desechar, poner de lado.—**to t. away**, arrojar; desperdiciar, malgastar; desechar, arrinconar.—**to t. back**, rechazar, devolver.—**to t. by**, arrinconar.—**to t. down**, derribar, echar por tierra; trastornar.—**to t. down the gauntlet**, echar el guante, retar.—**to t. in**, echar dentro; intercalar, insertar; añadir, dar de más, dar además de lo convenido.—**to t. off**, echar fuera; expeler, hacer salir; quitarse; sacudir; renunciar.—**to t. open**, abrir de par en par.—**to t. out**, proferir, hacer creer; expeler; excluir; esparcir, exhalar, despedir, emitir; insinuar.—**to t. overboard**, (mar.) echar a la mar, echar al agua; desechar, tirar.—**to t. silk**, torcer seda.—**to t. up**, echar al aire; elevar, levantar; renunciar a, abandonar; vomitar.—**to t. up the heels of**, echar a tierra de una zancadilla; frustrar.—**to t. up the sponge**, darse por vencido, desistir. **II.** _s._ tiro, echada, tirada; rato; (elec.) dirección (**two-t.**, **three-t.**, de dos, tres direcciones); desviación; (geol.) falla; (mec.) golpe o carrera; radio (de la excéntrica, manivela); lance de dados.—**within a stone's t.**, a tiro de piedra.

thrower [zróœr], _s._ tirador, lanzador, arrojador; torcedor.

throwster [zróstœr], _s._ torcedor de seda; jugador de dados.

thrum [zrum]. **I.** _s._ cadillos; hilo basto; borla; sonido de rascar una guitarra, etc. **II.** _va._ adornar con borlas; rascar las cuerdas de un instrumento.

thrush [zrush], _s._ (orn.) tordo, zorzal, malvís; (med.) afta; (vet.) higo.

thrust [zrust]. **I.** _vn._ (_pret._ y _pp._ **THRUST**) acometer, embestir (con espada, estoque, etc.); tirar una estocada; meterse, pasar abriéndose campo. **II.** _va._ meter; empujar, impeler; forzar; tirar una estocada con; atravesar; clavar, hincar; (_vr._ gen. con **on** o **upon**) entrometerse, meterse, tratar de hacerse recibir o aceptar; lanzarse.—**to t. aside**, rechazar; empujar a un lado.—**to t. forward**, empujar, echar adelante.—**to t. in**, meter, introducir.—**to t. on**, incitar, empujar.—**to t. out**, echar fuera; sacar.—**to t. the nose into**, entremeterse, meter las narices en, curiosear.—**to t. through**, apuñalar, atravesar de parte a parte.—**to t. upon**, imponer, hacer aceptar. **III.** _s._ empuje, empujón; pase, bote, estocada; lanzada; aguijonazo; arremetida, ataque; (mec., ing.) empuje, presión (de un eje, de un arco, etc.); (min.) derrumbe.—**t. bearing**, **t. block**, cojinete de empuje (apl. esp. al de anillos).—**t. collar**, anillo, de empuje.—**t. shaft**, (mar.) extremo del eje del motor provisto de anillos de empuje.

thud [zud]. **I.** _s._ baque, golpe o sonido de un objeto duro que choca con otro blando. **II.** _vn._ hacer ese ruido.

thug [zug], _s._ miembro de una secta de asesinos fanáticos de la India; por extensión, asesino; pícaro, bribón.

thumb [zum]. **I.** _s._ pulgar.—**t. nut**, tuerca con orejetas.—**t. tack**, chinche. **II.** _va._ manosear con poca destreza; emporcar con los dedos.

thumbscrew [zúmscrú], _s._ tornillo de mano (gen. de orejas); empulgueras (instrumento de tormento).

thumbstall [-stól], _s._ dedal, dedil.

thump [zump]. **I.** _s._ baque, porrazo, trastazo. **II.** _va._ y _vn._ aporrear, cascar, apuñear, acachetear.

thunder [zúndœr]. **I.** _s._ trueno; tronido, estruendo, estrépito. **II.** _va._ y _vn._ tronar; atronar, retumbar.—**it thunders**, truena.—**thunderbolt** [-boult], _s._ rayo, centella.—**thunderclap** [-clæp], _s._ trueno.—**thunderer** [-œr], _s._ tronador, fulminador.—**thundering** [-ing], _a._ atronador, tonante; (fam.) extraordinario.—**thunderous** [-us], _a._ tronador, atronador, tonante.—**thundershower**

[-sháuær], *s.* tronada con chubascos.—**thunderstorm** [-stórm], *s.* tronada.—**thunderstrike** [-stráic], *va.* fulminar, herir con rayo o centella; aturdir.—**thunderstruck** [-strŭc], *a.* estupefacto, turulato.

thuribel [ziúribœl], *s.* (igl.) turíbulo, incensario.—**thurifer** [-fœr], *s.* turibulario.—**thuriferous** [ziurífœrŭs], *a.* turífero.—**thurification** [ziúriñkéšhun], *s.* turificación.

Thursday [zœ̃rsdi], *s.* jueves.

thus [ðus]. **I.** *adv.* así, de este modo; en estos términos, *sic;* hasta ese punto, tanto; a ese grado; siendo así, en este caso.—**t. far**, hasta ahora; hasta aquí.—**t. it is**, así es que; así es como.—**t. much**, basta, no más, baste esto. **II.** *s.* [zus o zus] incienso.

thuya [ziúya], *s.* (bot.) tuya.

thwack [zuæc]. **I.** *va.* aporrear, pegar, zurrar; golpear. **II.** *s.* golpe, sequete, porrazo.

thwart [zuort]. **I.** *va.* impedir, desbaratar, frustrar. **II.** *a.* transversal, oblicuo, atravesado. **III.** *s.* banco de remeros, banco de bogar.

thy [ðái], *pron. pos.* tu, tus.

thyme [táim], *s.* (bot.) tomillo.

Thymelæaceæ [záimeliéisii], *s. pl.* (bot.) timeleáceas.—**thymelæaceous** [-šhus], *s.* timeleáceo.

thymol [táimol], *s.* (quím.) timol.

thymus [záimus], *s.* (anat.) timo.

thymy [táimi], *a.* oliente a tomillo.

thyroid [záiroid], *a.* en forma de escudo; tiroideo. **t. body, t. gland,** tiroides.—**t. cartilage,** nuez de la garganta; (en pájaros) cartílago laríngeo.

thyroiditis [-áitis], *s.* tiroiditis.

thyrse, thyrsus [zœrs, -sus], *s.* (bot.) tirso.

thyself [ðaisélf], *pron. recip.* tú mismo, tí mismo.—**love thy neighbor as t.,** ama a tu prójimo como a tí mismo.

tiara [taíera o tiára], *s.* tiara; diadema.

tibia [tíbia], *s.* (anat.) tibia; (ent.) cuarta articulación; (mús.) tibia.

tibial [tíbial], *a.* de la tibia.

tic, *s.* (med.) contracción nerviosa.

tick [tic]. **I.** *s.* tic tac, sonido acompasado; golpecito, palmadita; contramarca, contraseña; (ent.) garrapata, rezno, pito, ácaro; funda de colchón; (tej.) terliz, cotín; (fam.) crédito, fiado. **II.** *va.* sonar produciendo tic tac; marcar lo que se confronta. **III.** *vn.* hacer sonido de tic tac, batir; (fam.) vender o comprar al fiado.

tick(en [tík(en], **ticking** [ticking], *s.* (tej.) terliz, cotí.

ticker [tíkœr], *s.* indicador eléctrico automático de cotizaciones y noticias; reloj de bolsillo; (rad.) interruptor intermitente.—**t. coil,** (rad.) bobina de regeneración del audión.

ticket [tíket]. **I.** *s.* billete, (Méx.) boleto; pase, entrada; rótulo, marbete; marca; (E. U., pol.) balota; por extensión, candidatura.—**t. agent,** taquillero, (Méx.) boletero.—**t. holder,** tenedor de un billete.—**t. office,** taquilla o despacho de billetes; (teat.) taquilla.—**t. of leave,** licencia que se da a un penado para salir de la cárcel. **II.** *va.* rotular, marcar.

fickle [tícœl]. **I.** *va.* hacer cosquillas a; halagar, lisonjear, regalar los oídos; agradar; divertir.—**tickled to death,** (fam.) contentísimo. **II.** *vn.* hacer, tener o sentir cosquillas.—**tickler** [tíclœr], *s.* el que hace cosquillas; libro borrador o diario.—**tickling** [tícling], *s.* cosquillas.—**ticklish** [tícliš̆h], *a.* cosquilloso; inseguro, incierto; arduo, delicado, difícil.—**ticklishness** [-nes], *s.* calidad de cosquilloso o delicado.

ticktack [tíc-tác], *s.* tic tac; chaquete.

tidal [táidal], *a.* de marea; periódico.—**t. basin,** dique de marea.—**t. harbour,** puerto de grandes mareas.—**t. wave,** aguaje; gran conmoción, ola popular.

tidbit, *V.* TITBIT.

tide [táid]. **I.** *s.* marea; corriente; curso, marcha; flujo; tiempo, estación.—**t. gate,** compuerta de marea; angostura.—**t. wave** = TIDAL WAVE, *V.* TIDAL. **II.** *va.* llevar, conducir (la marea); (con **over**) superar una dificultad; aguardar la oportunidad. **III.** *vn.* navegar o flotar con la marea.—**tideless** [-les], *a.* sin marea.—**tidesman** [táidš̆man],

tidewaiter [-uéitœr], *s.* vista o empleado de aduanas.

tidily [táidili], *adv.* aseadamente.—**tidiness** [-nes], *s.* aseo, pulcritud.

tidings [táidingš̆], *s. pl.* nuevas, noticias.

tidewater [táiduótœr], *s.* agua afectada por la marea; costa del mar; (com.) puerto, embarcadero.

tideway [táiduéi], *s.* canal de marea.

tidy [táidi]. **I.** *a.* limpio, aseado; pulcro, ordenado. **II.** *s.* cubierta de respaldar. **III.** *va.* y *vn.* (fam.) asear, poner en orden.

tie [tái]. **I.** *va.* (*pret.* y *pp.* TIED; *pa.* TYING) atar, amarrar, liar; trincar; unir, enlazar, encadenar; restringir, limitar; empatar.—**to t. tight,** apretar.—**to t. up,** atar, amarrar, asegurar; recoger, levantar, impedir, obstruir; envolver. **II.** *s.* lazo, nudo, atadura, ligadura; vínculo; parentesco; apego, adhesión, unión; empate; corbata; (mús.) ligadura; (mar.) maroma, ostaga; (carp., ing.) tirante; (f. c.) traviesa.—*pl.* (E. U.) zapatos bajos.

tiebar [táibar], *s.* (ing.) tirante; (f. c.) barra transversal de las agujas de un cambio.

tiebeam [táibím], *s.* (arq.) tirante, viga de tensión (apl. esp. a la que sostiene la parte superior de una armadura).

tier [tíœr], *s.* fila, ringlera, tonga; (teat.) fila de palcos.—**t. of a cable,** andana; [táícœr] delantal de niño.

tierce [tíœrs], *s.* tercerola; (mús.) tercera; (igl.) tercia, hora canónica; (esgr.) tercia.

tiercet [tírset], *s.* (poét.) terceto.

tierod [táiród], *s.* (ing.) tirante.

tie-up [táiup], *s.* paralización (de la industria, el tráfico, etc.) debida a trastornos imprevistos, sobre todo a las huelgas; (mús.) ligadura; establo de ganado vacuno.

tiff [tif]. **I.** *s.* pique, disgusto; traguito, sorbo. **II.** *vn.* picarse, atufarse, reñir.

tiffany [tífani], *s.* gasa de seda.

tiffin(g [tífin(g], *s.* merienda.

tige [tiy], *s.* (arq.) fuste de columna.

tiger [táigœr], *s.* tigre; lacayuelo.—**t. beetle,** (ent.) cicindela.—**t. cat,** gato cerval o gato montés.—**t. lily,** (bot.) tigridia.

tigerish [táigœriš̆h], *a.* feroz; atigrado.

tight [táit], *a.* bien cerrado, hermético; (mar.) estanco; tirante, tieso; apretado, estrecho; muy ajustado; (com.) escaso, difícil de obtener; (fam.) embriagado, borracho.—**t. fit,** empalme muy ajustado.—**t.-fitting,** muy ajustado.—**t. lacing,** hábito de apretarse el corsé.—**t. rope,** cuerda tesa, cuerda de volatinero.—**t. squeeze,** (fam.) aprieto.

tighten [táitœn],*va.* y *vn.* estrechar, apretar; estirar, atesar.

tightly [-li], *adv.* estrechamente; apretadamente; ajustadamente.—**tightness** [-nes], *s.* tensión, tirantez; estrechez; impermeabilidad; (fam.) tacañería.

tights [táits], *s. pl.* calzas atacadas.

tigress [táigres], *s.* hembra del tigre.

tigrine [táigrin], *a.* atigrado.

tilbury [tílbœri], *s.* (carr.) tílburi.

tile [táil]. **I.** *s.* azulejo, losa, baldosa; teja; atanor; tubo de barro cocido u hormigón; (fam.) sombrero de copa, chistera.—**t. maker,** tejero.—**t. roof,** tejado de tejas. **II.** *va.* tejar, trastejar, losar; poner desagüe de atanores en; asegurar contra una intrusión; comprometer a guardar secreto.—**tiler** [-œr], *s.* trastejador; tejero; solador; tejera; portero de una sociedad secreta.

Tiliaceæ [tíliésii], *s. pl.* (bot.) tiliáceas.—**tiliaceous** [-šhus], *a.* tiliáceo.

tiling [-ing], *s.* trastejadura; azulejos, tejas en general; tejado.

till [til]. **I.** *s.* cajón o gaveta para guardar dinero. **II.** *prep.* hasta.—**t. further orders,** hasta nueva orden. **III.** *conj.* hasta que. **IV.** *va.* (agr.) cultivar, labrar.

tillable [tílabœl], *a.* labrantío.—**t. land,** tierra labrantía o de pan llevar.

tillage [tíley], *s.* labranza, labor, cultivo.

tiller [tílœr]. **I.** s. agricultor, labrador, cultivador; mango de sierra o de azadón; palanca; caña del timón; retoño, gamonito, vástago, renuevo.—**t. chain,** (mar.) guardín.—**t. hole,** limera.—**t. rope** = T. CHAIN. **II.** vn. echar retoños de la raíz.

tilt. I. s. inclinación, declive; justa, torneo; lanzada; toldillo, toldo, tendal.—**t. boat,** (mar.) carroza.—**t. hammer,** martinete de báscula. **II.** va. ladear, inclinar, volcar, voltear; martillar, forjar con martinete; dar una lanzada; entoldar. **III.** vn. inclinarse, reclinarse; ladearse; justar.

tilter [tíltœr], s. justador.

tilth [tilz], s. labranza, cultivo, labor; tierra cultivada; capa de cultivo del suelo.

tilting [tílting]. **I.** s. inclinación; vuelco, volteo; forjadura con martinete basculante. **II.** a. inclinado, ladeado; de vuelco, de volteo.—**t. car,** carro o vagón de vuelco.—**t. hammer,** martinete basculante.

timbal, tymbal [tímbal], s. timbal.

timber [tímbœr]. **I.** s. madera de construcción; palo, fuste, maderamen, maderaje; monte, bosque, árboles de monte; viga; madero; (mar.) cuaderna, miembro; armazón; mango de madera; materiales de construcción; cualidades.—**t. line,** límite de la vegetación selvática.—**t. merchant,** maderero.—**t. sow,** carcoma.—**t. yard,** astillero, taller de maderas. **II.** va. enmaderar.

timbered [tímbœrd], a. enmaderado; arbolado.

timberland [-lænd], s. tierras maderables.

timberwork [-uœrk], s. maderaje, maderamen.

timbre [tímbœr], s. timbre.

timbrel [tímbrel], s. adufe.

time [táim]. **I.** s. tiempo; época, edad; plazo; período, estación; vez, turno; intervalo; oportunidad o coyuntura; (com.) prórroga, respiro, espera; plazo; (mús.) compás, tiempo; (gram.) tiempo; hora (what time is it? ¿qué hora es? tell me the time, dígame la hora; my time has come, me ha llegado la hora).—**t. and tide,** oportunidad, tiempo y sazón.—**t. fuse,** espoleta graduada o de tiempo.—**t.-honored,** de antigua reputación, consagrado por el tiempo, tradicional.—**t. out of mind,** tiempo inmemorial.—**t. table,** horario, itinerario (de trenes).—**t. to come,** lo futuro, lo venidero.—**t. work,** trabajo a jornal o pagado por tiempo.—**any t.,** a cualquier hora; en cualquier tiempo u ocasión; cuando Vd. guste.—**at a t.,** a la vez.—**at no t.,** jamás.—**at this t.,** al presente, ahora.—**at this t. of day,** a la hora de ésta, a estas horas.—**at times,** a veces.—**behind t.,** atrasado, retardado.—**for the t. being,** por ahora, de momento; para entonces.—**from this t. forth,** desde ahora, de hoy en adelante, en lo futuro.—**from t. to t.,** de cuando en cuando.—**in an hour's t.,** en una hora.—**in old times, in times of yore,** antiguamente, en otros tiempos, en tiempos de Maricastaña.—**in t.,** a tiempo; con el tiempo.—**on t.,** a la hora debida, con puntualidad.—**this t. a twelvemonth,** de aquí a un año.—**to be on t.,** ser puntual; llegar con puntualidad. **II.** va. adaptar al tiempo, hacer con oportunidad; regular, poner a la hora; contar o medir el tiempo de; (mús.) llevar el compás.

timeful [táimful], a. oportuno.

timekeeper [-kípœr], s. reloj; cronómetro; marcador de tiempo.

timeless [-les], a. independiente del tiempo; intempestivo, inoportuno.

timeliness [-lines], s. oportunidad.

timely [-li]. **I.** adv. oportunamente. **II.** a. oportuno, conveniente.

timepiece [-pis], s. reloj.

timesaver [-séiver], s., **timesaving** [-ing], a. economizador de tiempo.

timeserver [-sœrvœr], s., **timeserving** [-ing], a., contemporizador, esclavo de las cosas del día, servil.

timeworn [-uórn], a. usado, gastado por el tiempo; traqueado, viejo.

timid [tímid], a. tímido.—**timidity** [timíditi], **timidness** [tímidnes], s. timidez.—**timidly** [tímidli], a. tímidamente.

timing [táiming]. **I.** a. de regulación de tiempo; registrador de tiempo; (m. comb. int.) de regulación o distribución del encendido.—**t. gear,** (m.

comb. int.) mecanismo del encendido. **II.** s. medida o cuenta del tiempo; (el) llevar cuenta del tiempo; (m. comb. int.) regulación o distribución del encendido.

timocracy [timócræsi], s. timocracia.—**timocratic** [timocrǽtic], a. timocrático.

timorous [tímorus], a. miedoso, timorato; tímido.—**timorously** [-li], adv. miedosamente; tímidamente.—**timorousness** [-nes], s. timidez; temor, miedo.

timothy [tímozi], s. (bot.) alfalfa.

tin. I. s. estaño; lata, hojalata; objeto de hojalatería; (fam.) dinero, moneda, plata.—**t. lata.—t. foil,** hoja de estaño.—**t. hat,** (fam.) yelmo de acero.—**t. plate,** hoja de lata.—**t. wedding,** décimo aniversario. **II.** va. estañar; cubrir con hoja de lata; envasar en lata; dar una capa (de soldadura, etc.) a.

tinamou [tínamú], s. (zool.) tinamú (inambú en guaraní).

tincal [tíncal], s. (com.) atíncar.

tinctorial [tinctórial], a. tintóreo.

tincture [tínkchur]. **I.** s. tintura, tinte; (farm.) tintura; (fig.) baño, gusto, gustillo.—**t. of iron, o of steel,** solución alcohólica de cloruro de hierro. **II.** va. teñir, colorar, tinturar.

tinder [tíndœr], s. yesca; mecha.

tinderbox [tíndœrbóx], s. yesquero.

tine [táin], s. púa, punta.

tinea [tínea], s. tínea; polilla; tiña.

ting. **I.** va. y vn. retiñir. **II.** s. retintín.

tinge [tiny]. **I.** va. colorar, teñir, matizar. **II.** s. tinte, matiz; gustillo, dejo.

tingle [tíngœl]. **I.** vn. y va. sentir o producir hormigueo o picazón. **II.** s. picazón, hormigueo, comezón; retintín.

tink, vn. V. TINKLE y CHINK.

tinker [tínkœr]. **I.** va. y vn. desabollar; chafallar, remendar chapuceramente. **II.** s. latonero; calderero remendón; desabollador.

tinkle [tínkœl], va. y vn. retiñir; zumbar los oídos.

tinkling [tínkling], s. retintín.

tinman [tínman], s. hojalatero.—**tinner** [-œr], s. hojalatero; envasador de latas.

tinny [tíni], a. de estaño.

tinsel [tínsel]. **I.** s. oropel, lentejuelas; lama de oro o plata, brocadillo, restaño; relumbrón. **II.** a. de oropel; de relumbrón. **III.** va. adornar con oropel.

tinsmith [tínsmiz], s. hojalatero.

tint. I. va. teñir, colorar, matizar. **II.** s. tinte, color, matiz; (b. a.) media tinta.

tintinnabulation [tíntinæbiuléishŭn], s. retintín, campanilleo.—**tintinnabulum** [-ŭm], s. campanilla.

tintype [tíntáip], s. (E. U., fot.) ferrotipo.

tinware [tínuéœr], s. efectos de hojalata.

tinwork [tínuœrc], s. hojalatería.

tiny [táini], a. chiquitico, menudo.

tip. **I.** s. punta, extremidad, cabo; casquillo, regatón, virola, agujeta; (zap.) puntera, bigotera; propina; informe dado por debajo de cuerda; palmadita, golpecito. **II.** va. ladear, inclinar, voltear; dar un golpecito a; dar propina a; informar por debajo de cuerda; guarnecer; poner regatón a.—**to t. the wink,** guiñar. **III.** vn. ladearse, inclinarse; dar propina.

tipcart [típcárt], s. carro de vuelco.

tippet [típet], s. palatina, esclavina.

tipple [típœl]. **I.** va. y vn. beber con exceso, empinar el codo; volcar, vaciar. **II.** s. bebida, licor; mecanismo de vuelco.—**tippling house,** taberna, bodegón.

tippler [típlœr], s. bebedor, mascavidrios.

tipsily [típsili], adv. como borracho.—**tipsiness** [-nes], s. calidad o estado de chispado.

tipstaff [típstaf], s. alguacil de vara, ministril; vara de justicia.

tipsy [típsi], a. chispado, calamocano; vacilante.

tiptoe [típtó], s. punta del pie.—**on t.,** en puntillas; ansioso.

tiptop [típtóp]. **I.** a. (fam.) lo mejor en su clase, excelente. **II.** s. cumbre, cima.

tirade [tiréid], s. diatriba, andanada, invectiva.

tire [táiœr]. **I.** *s.* (carr.) llanta, calce, loriga; diadema; (fam.) sensación de cansancio; (aut.) llanta, bandaje (el primer término es más correcto, pero el segundo es más claro y muy usado); neumático (es el sentido usual euando se trata de coches automóviles, no de camiones). **II.** *va.* cansar, fatigar; aburrir, fastidiar; (carr.) poner llantas.—**to t. out,** rendir de cansancio. **III.** *vn.* cansarse; aburrirse, fastidiarse.

tired [táiœrd], *pp.* y *a.* provisto de llantas; cansado, fatigado; aburrido.—**t. feeling,** lasitud, flojedad.—**t. out,** agotado, rendido de cansancio.

tiredness [-nes], *s.* cansancio, lasitud.

tireless [táiœrles], *a.* infatigable, incansable; sin llanta.—**tiresome** [-sʊm], *a.* tedioso, cansado, pesado.—**tiresomeness** [-sʊmnes], *s.* tedio, fastido, aburrimiento.

tirl [tœrl]. **I.** *va.* destejar; desvestir, desnudar; torcer, retorcer. **II.** *vn.* retemblar, retumbar; vibrar.

'tis [tiš], *abreviatura* de IT IS.

tisane [tišán], *s.* tisana.

tissue [tíšhu]. **I.** *s.* (biol.) tejido; (tej.) gasa, tisú, gloria, lama; serie conexa, encadenamiento.—**t. paper,** papel de seda. **II.** *va.* entretejer.

tit, *s.* (orn.) paro; jaca, caballito; golpecito.—**t. for tat,** taz a taz, taz por taz; tal para cual.

titanate [títæneit], *s.* (quím.) titanato.

titanic [taitænic], *a.* titánico; (quím.) titánico.

titanium [titéniʊm], *s.* (quím.) titanio.

titbit [títbit], *s.* bocado regalado, cotufo; trozo escogido.

titer, titre [táitœr], *s.* (quím.) concentración de una solución, determinada por análisis volumétrico.

tithable [táiɒæbœl], *a.* diezmable.—**tithe** [táiɒ]. **I.** *s.* diezmo; décima parte; pizca.—**t. free,** exento de diezmo. **II.** *va.* diezmar.—**tither** [-œr], *s.* diezmero.—**tithing** [-ing], *s.* diezmo; (Ingl.) decena de vecinos.—**tithingman** [-ingman], *s.* (Ingl.) cabeza del *tithing.*

titillate [títileit], *va.* titilar.

titillation [-éihʊn], *s.* titilación.

titlark [títlarc], *s.* (orn.) especie de alondra.

title [táitœl]. **I.** *s.* título; inscripción.—**t. by occupancy,** derecho del primer ocupante.—**t. page,** portada. **II.** *va.* titular, intitular; conferir título a; rotular.—**titled** [-d], *a.* de título, que tiene título.—**titleless** [táitles], *a.* sin título.

titling [títling], *s.* gorrión silvestre.

titmouse [títmaus], *s.* (orn.) paro.

titrate [táitreit], *va.* (quím.) graduar o determinar por análisis volumétrico; titular, dosificar.—**to t. against,** analizar volumétricamente, o dosificar, por comparación con.—**titration** [-éišhʊn], *s.* análisis volumétrico.

titter [títœr], *vn.* reír entre dientes.—**titter(ing** [-ing], *s.* risita entre dientes.—**titterer** [-œr], *s.* el que ríe entre dientes.

title [títœl], *s.* tilde, vírgula, ápice.

tittle-tattle [títœl-tætœl]. **I.** *a.* charla. **II.** *vn.* charlar.

tittle-tattler [-tætlœr], *s.* parlanchín.

titubation [titubéšhʊn], *s.* tropiezo; (pat.) tambaleo, inestabilidad.

titular [títiular]. **I.** *a.* titular; nominal. **II.** *s.* titular.—**titularly** [-li], *adv.* con sólo el título.—**titulary** [-i]. **I.** *a.* titular. **II.** *s.* el que tiene título o derecho a alguna cosa.

titup [títʊp]. **I.** *vn.* (fam.) andar inquieto, cabriolar. **II.** *s.* (fam.) cabriola brinco de contento.

tmesis [tmísis], *s.* (gram.) diácope.

TNT, T. N. T. [ti en ti], *s.* trinitrotolueno (poderoso explosivo).

to [tu]. **I,** *adv.* hacia el fin que se persigue; en la posición o dirección que conviene (*to lie to,* ponerse a la capa); en o al estado normal (*he came to,* volvió en sí).—**t. and fro,** de un lado a otro, de acá para allá.—**t.-and-fro motion,** vaivén. **II.** *prep.* a, en dirección a; hasta, hacia; para. Antepuesto al nombre o pronombre después de verbos de movimiento, dirección, unión, pertenencia, preferencia o atención, se traduce por

"a" (*give it to him,* dáselo a él: *I go to London,* voy a Londres; *it belongs to Peter,* pertenece a Pedro; *I prefer this book to mine,* prefiero este libro al mío). Cuando denota la intención o fin con que se ejecuta algo, o después de un participio pasivo o de un adjetivo, corresponde a "para," "por" o "a" en castellano (*he came only to see me,* vino sólo por verme, a verme, o para verme; *born to die,* nacido para morir; *ready to go out,* dispuesto para salir). Cuando expresa obligación o acción futura, se traduce por "que" (*I have to go,* tengo que irme: *he is to come,* tiene que venir). En otros casos se traduce de varios modos difíciles de clasificar, como en los siguientes ejemplos: *from door to door,* de puerta en puerta; *ten minutes to nine,* las nueve menos diez minutos; *he is a friend to the poor,* es amigo de los pobres; *King Philip II. was son* (o *successor*) *to Charles V.,* el rey Felipe II fué hijo (o sucesor) de Carlos V. **III.** partícula que sirve para indicar el infinitivo, y que no se traduce (*he wishes to go,* desea ir; *the verb "to go,"* el verbo "ir"; *to be or not to be,* ser o no ser).

toad [tóud], *s.* sapo, escuerzo.

toadeater [-tœr], *s.* pegote, parásito adulador y servil.—**toadeating** [-íting]. **I.** *s.* parasitismo servil. **II.** *a.* adulador servil y parásito.

toadflax [-flæx], *s.* (bot.) linaria, lino bastardo.—**toadstone** [-stóun], *s.* (min.) estelón.—**toadstool** [-stúl], *s.* (bot.) hongo; seta venenosa (gen. se usa en el segundo sentido).

toady [-i]. **I.** *va.* y *vn.* adular servilmente; ser zalamero. **II.** *a.* adulador, zalamero.

toast [tóust]. **I.** *va.* tostar; brindar por. **II.** *vn.* tostarse. **III.** tostada; tueste; brindis.—**t. water,** agua panada.

toaster [-œr], *s.* el que brinda; tostador; parrilla.

toasting [-ing], *a.* de tostar.—**t. fork,** horquilla de tostar; (fam.) espada.

toastmaster [-mæstœr], *s.* el que designa los brindis en un banquete.

tobacco [tobǽco], *s.* (bot.) tabaco.—**t. box,** tabaquera.—**t. field,** tabacal.—**t.-pipe clay,** tierra de pipa.—**t. plantation,** vega de tabaco, tabacal.—**t. pouch,** bolsa para tabaco.—**t. worm,** gusano del tabaco.

tobacconist [-nist], *s.* fabricante de tabaco; tabaquero, estanquero.

tobacconize [-naiš], *va.* fumigar con tabaco.

toboggan [tobógan]. **I.** *s.* (dep.) tobogán, trineo para deslizarse por una pendiente.—**t. slide,** tobogán, pendiente natural o artificial para deslizarse. **II.** *vn.* deslizarse en tobogán.

toby [tóubi], *s.* pichel, vaso grande, gen. en forma de hombre; cigarro tosco y barato.

tocsin [tócsin], *s.* toque de somatén.

today, to-day [tudéi], *s.* y *adv.* hoy.

toddle [tódœl]. **I.** *vn.* hacer pinitos. **II.** *s.* pinitos.—**toddler** [tódlœr], *s.* el que hace pinitos.

tod(dy [tód(i], *s.* ponche; vino de palmera.

to-do [tu-dú], *s.* (fam.) baraúnda; alharaca.

tody [tódi], *s.* (orn.) todi, pajarillo verde antillano.

toe [tóu]. **I.** *s.* dedo del pie; uña o pezuña; punta del pie (de media, del calzado); pie, base; saliente, brazo; puntas de las agujas, origen del cambio (en un cambiavía); extremo interior, de contacto con los rieles de unión, de un crucero de cambio.—**t. cap, o piece,** (zap.) puntera.—**toe-in,** convergencia (de una rueda).—**great t.,** dedo gordo del pie. **II.** *va.* tocar con la punta del pie; dar un puntapié; poner punteras; clavar oblicuamente; asegurar con clavos un puntal.—**to t. the mark,** estar o ponerse en la raya o punto de partida; obrar como se debe; hacerlo bien. **III.** *vn.* to **t. in,** andar con las puntas de los piés hacia adentro; (mec.) convergir (una rueda).

toenail [tóunéil], *s.* uña de los dedos del pie.

tog [tog], *va.* y *vn.* (gen. con **out** o **up**) acicalar (se), componer(se) majo, engalanar(se).

toga [tóga], *s.* toga.—**t. virilis,** toga viril.

togaed [tógad], *a.* togado.

together [tugéɒœr]. **I.** *adv.* juntamente; a un tiempo, simultáneamente; de continuo, de seguida, sin interrupción.—**t. with,** a una con, juntos; junto con. **II.** *a.* juntos.

toggle [tógœl], *s.* cazonete; palanca acodillada.— **t. bolt**, tornillo con fiador giratorio en T.—**t. joint**, junta de codillo.

toil [tóil]. **I.** *vn.* trabajar asiduamente, afanarse, atrafagar; moverse con dificultad. **II.** *s.* faena, trabajo; pena, fatiga, afán; obra laboriosa; (fig.) red, lazo.—**t. of a spider**, telaraña.

toilet [tóilet], *s.* acto de vestirse; tocado, vestido, atavío; tocador; (cir.) limpiadura de una herida; excusado, retrete.—**t. case**, neceser.—**t. paper**, papel para excusados.—**t. room**, retrete, lugar excusado.—**t. set**, juego de tocador.

toilful [tóilful], *a.* trabajoso.

toilsome [-sum], *a.* laborioso, trabajoso; penoso. —**toilsomely** [-li], *adv.* laboriosamente; fatigosamente.—**toilsomeness** [-nes], *s.* calidad de laborioso o fatigoso.

Tokay [tokéi], *s.* uva o vino de Tokay.

token [tóucœn], *s.* señal, muestra, prueba; prenda, recuerdo; medalla; tanto, ficha; tésera; distintivo, rasgo característico; (impr.) tirada de 250 impresiones.—**as a t. of**, en señal de.

told [tóuld], *pret.* y *pp.* de TO TELL.

tole [tóul], *va.* arrastrar, atraer, tirar.

Toledan [tolídan], *a.* toledano.

tolerable [tólœrabœl], *a.* tolerable; sufrible, llevadero; mediano.—**tolerableness** [-nes] *s.* calidad de tolerable o mediano.—**tolerably** [-bli], *adv.* tolerablemente, medianamente.

tolerance [-ans], *s.* tolerancia; (tecn.) tolerancia, discrepancia permitida.—**tolerant** [-ant], *a.* tolerante.—**tolerate** [-eit], *va.* tolerar.—**toleration** [-éišhun], *s.* tolerancia; tolerantismo.

tolidin(e [tólidin], *s.* (quím.) tolidina.

toll [tóul]. **I.** *s.* peaje, portazgo o pontazgo; derecho de molienda; tañido o doble de las campanas.—**t. bridge**, puente de peaje.—**t. collector** = TOLLMAN.—**t. corn**, maquila de molinero.—**t. gatherer** = TOLLMAN. **II.** *va., vn.* apagar o cobrar peaje o portazgo; tañer una campana; tocar o doblar (la campana); atraer; (for.) quitar, suprimir.—**to t. the hour**, dar la hora.

tollbooth [tóulbuz], *s.* (Ingl.) calabozo.

toller [tóulœr], *s.* campanero.

tollgate [tóulguéit], *s.* barrera de peaje.

tollhouse [tóljáus], *s.* oficina de portazgos.

tollman [tóulmæn], *s.* peajero, portazguero.

tolu [tolú], *s.* bálsamo de tolú.—**t. tree**, (bot.) árbol de tolú.

toluate [tólueit], *s.* (quím.) toluato.—**toluene** [-in], *s.* tolueno.—**toluic** [tolúic], *a.* tolúico (ácido). —**toluidin(e** [tolúidin], *s.* toluidina.

tom [tom], *s.* macho de algunos animales.

tomahawk [tómajoc]. **I.** *s.* (E. U.) hacha de guerra de los indios.—**to bury the t.**, envainar la espada (fig.), hacer la paz.— **to dig up the t.**, desenvainar la espada (fig.), declarar la guerra. **II.** *va.* herir con *tomahawk*.

tomato [tomáto, toméito], *s.* (bot.) tomate.—**t. plant**, tomatera.

tomb [tum], *s.* tumba.

tombac [tómbæc], *s.* tombac, latón de 90% de cobre y 10% de cinc.

tombless [túmles], *a.* sin sepulcro.

tomboy [tómbói], *s.* moza retozona.

tombstone [túmstoun], *s.* lápida o piedra sepulcral.

tomcat [tómcæt], *s.* gato (macho).

tomcod [tómcód], *s.* pez comestible.

tome [tóum], *s.* tomo, volumen.

tomentose, tomentous [tómentous, toméntus], *a.* (bot.) tomentoso.—**tomentum** [-méntum], *s.* (bot.) tomento.

tomfool [tómful], *s.* necio; payaso.—**tomfoolery** [-fúlœri], **tomfoolishness** [-fúlišhnes], *s.* mentecatada; payasada.

to-morrow, tomorrow [tu-móro], *s.* y *adv.* mañana.—**t. afternoon, morning, noon, night**, mañana por la tarde, por la mañana, al mediodía, por la noche.

tomtit [tómtit], *s.* (orn.) paro. *V.* TIT.

tompion [tómpion], *s.* (arti.) tapaboca; (impr.) tintero.

tomtom [tómtóm], *s.* tamtám, gongo.

ton [tun], *s.* tonelada.—**t.-mile**, tonelada-milla, transporte de . tonela a 1 milla de distancia.

tonal [tónal], *a.* (mús.) tonal.

tonality [tonéliti], *s.* tonalidad.

tone [tóun]. **I.** *s.* tono, sonido; (mús.) tono; timbre; entonación, tonillo, sonsonete; (gram.) acento, inflexión; (med.) tono; (pint.) tono.— **t. wheel**, (rad.) disco conmutador de audiofrecuencia. **II.** *va.* dar o modificar el tono, entonar; templar, afinar.—**to t. down**, (pint.) suavizar el tono; (mús.) amortiguar el sonido; modificar la expresión.—**to t. up**, vigorizar, robustecer; subir de tono. **III.** *vn.* corresponder en tono o matiz.

tongs [tongs], *s. pl.* tenazas, mordazas, pinzas, alicates.

tongue [tung]. **I.** *s.* (anat.) lengua; lenguaje, lengua, idioma; (mús.) lengüeta; (mec. y carp.) espiga; clavillo de hebilla; lengua de tierra; badajo de campana; (f. c.) carril movible (de un cambio); (elec.) tabique (de conducto eléctrico). —**t.-and-grove**, *va.* unir con junta machihembrada.—**t.-and-grove joint**, unión machihembrada.—**t.-and-lip joint**, empalme de espiga.— **t. grafting**, injerto de lengüeta.—**t.-tie**, hacer callar; frenillo.—**t.-tied**, con frenillo; que tiene impedimento en el habla.—**t. worm**, landrilla. **II.** *va.* (mús.) tomar la embocadura; (carp.) engargolar, machihembrar. **III.** *vn.* (mús.) tener embocadura; usar la lengua, hablar.

tongued [tungd], *a.* que tiene lengua o lengüeta.

tongueless [túngles], *a.* mudo, sin habla; deslenguado; turbado.

tonic [tónic]. **I.** *a.* (med. y mús.) tónico; tenso, rígido, tieso. **II.** *s.* (med.) tónico; (mús.) tónica o dominante.

tonicity [tonísiti], *s.* tonicidad.

tonight, to-night [tunáit], *adv.* y *s.* esta noche, a la noche.

toning [tóning], *s.* entonación.

tonka bean [tóncæ bin], *s.* sarapia; haba tonca (semilla de la sarapia).

tonnage [túnæy], *s.* tonelaje, porte o arqueo; (com.) derecho de tonelaje.

tonsil [tónsil], *s.* tonsila, amígdala.

tonsil(l)itis [-áitis o -ítis], *s.* (med.) amigdalitis.

tonsorial [tonsórial], *a.* barberil.

tonsure [tónshur], *s.* tonsura.

tontine [tóntin], *s.* tontina.

too [tú], *adv.* demasiado; además; también.—**t. many**, demasiados.—**t. much**, demasiado, excesivo.—**to be t. much for one**, no poder uno con; no poder aguantar más: ser el colmo; no entrale a uno, parecerle increíble. Como la frase "un poco demasiado" no es usual en español, **a little t., a little t. much**, etc., se traducen cambiando el giro: *he came a little too early*, vino un poco antes de lo que convenía, un poco anticipadamente, un poco temprano, etc.: *you went a little too far*, Vd. se pasó un poco, Vd. se excedió un poco, etc.: *he spoke a little too long*, habló un poco más de lo que convenía, su discurso se pasó un poco de largo, etc.

took [tuk], *pret.* de TO TAKE.

tool [tul]. **I.** *va.* y *vn.* labrar con herramienta; (enc.) relevar. **II.** *s.* herramienta, utensilio o instrumento; persona que sirve de instrumento a otra.—**t. bag, t. chest**, barjuleta, herramental. —**t. steel**, acero de herramientas.

toot [tut]. **I.** *va.* y *vn.* tocar el cuerno de caza, una bocina o un silbato. **II.** *s.* sonido de trompa, pitazo.

tooth [tuz]. **I.** *s.* (*pl.* TEETH) diente, muela; (mec.) diente de sierra o de rueda; leva, cama, púa: mella, melladura; gusto, paladar.—**t. and nail**, con todo tesón, con empeño.—**to have a sweet t.**, ser muy goloso, gustar de los dulces. **II.** *va.* dentar; mellar. **III.** *va.* y *vn.* (mec.) engranar.

toothache [túzéik], *s.* dolar de muelas.

toothbrush [-brúšh], *s.* cepillo de dientes.

toothed [tuzt], *a.* dentado, serrado, dentellado.— **t. wheel**, rueda dentada.

toothless [túzles], *a.* desdentado.

toothpick [túzpic], s. mondadientes, palillo.—**t. ease,** palillero.

toothshell [túzshel], s. dental, concha parecida a un diente.

toothsome [túzsʊm], a. sabroso.—**toothsomeness** [-nes], s. sabor agradable.

toothwort [túzʊœrt], s. (bot.) dentaria.

top. I. s. cima, cumbre, pico, ápice, cúspide; parte superior o parte de arriba; superficie; cabeza, remate, coronilla; coronamiento (de pared); copa (de árbol); punta; cielo, auge; primer puesto, último grado; copete, tupé; trompo, peonza; (carr.) fuelle; (aut.) capota; (mar.) cofa; tope. —**t.-armings,** o **armor,** empavesada de cofas —**t.-block,** motón de virador.—**t.-boots,** botas de campaña.—**t. cross,** cruzamiento de una raza inferior con una superior.—**t.-dress,** va. abonar la superficie del suelo.—**t.-dressing,** abono aplicado a la superficie.—**t. hat,** (fam.) sombrero de copa, chistera.—**t.-heavy,** demasiado pesado o grande por arriba.—**t. lantern,** farol de la cofa.—**t.-rails,** batayolas de las cofas.—**t.-rope,** amante del virador.—**t. tackle,** aparejo de virador.—**t.-timber,** barraganete.—**from t. to bottom,** de arriba abajo; completamente.—**from t. to toe,** de pies a cabeza, de alto abajo.—**on t. of,** encima de, sobre. —**over the t.,** (fam.) a la carga, al ataque, saliendo de las trincheras.—**the t. of the world,** (fam.) "el tejado del mundo," el polo. **II.** a. superior, más alto, primero, principal. **III.** va. descabezar, desmochar; cubrir, coronar, rematar; llegar a la cima de, coronar; sobrepujar, aventajar, exceder.—**to t. a yard,** (mar.) amantillar una verga.

topaz [tópæs], s. (joy.) topacio; (orn.) colibrí.

topcoat [tópcóut], s. saco; sobretodo, abrigo.

tope [tóup]. **I.** vn. excederse en la bebida. **II.** s. altar, bóveda budista.

topek [tóupec], s. cabaña de hojas y pieles de algunos indios norteamericanos y esquimales.

toper [tóupœr], s. borrachín, bebedor.

topfull [tópful], a. rebosando, lleno hasta los bordes.

topgallant [tópgælænt], s. juanete.

tophaceous [toféshʊs], a. arenoso, áspero.

tophus [tófʊs], s. (med.) tofo, nodo; (dent.) sarro; (min.) toba, tosca.

topic [tópic], s. asunto, materia, tema.—pl. (ret.) lugares comunes, tópicos.—**topic(al** [-al], a. tópico; local, limitado.—**topically** [-il], adv. localmente.

topknot [tópnót], s. moño alto, tupé, o copete.

toplofty [tóplófti], a. (fam.) elevado, prominente; pomposo, hinchado.

topman [tópman], s. aserrador de arriba; (mar.) gaviero.

topmast [tópmæst], s. mastelero.

topmost [tópmoust], a. de la cima o cumbre, de coronamiento.

topographer [topógrafœr], s. topógrafo.—**topographic(al** [tópográfic(al], a. topográfico.—**topographically** [-il], adv. topográficamente.—**topography** [topógrafi], s. topografía.

topping [tóping]. **I.** a. eminente, distinguido; empingorotado, empenachado, arrogante.—**t. lift,** perigallo. **II.** s. cubierta, mango, punta, extremidad, cabo.

topple [tópœl]. **I.** va. hacer caer, derribar, volcar. **II.** vn. volcarse, venirse abajo.

topsail [tópséil], s. gavia.—**t. sheets,** escotines.

topsoil [tópsóil]. **I.** s. capa superior del suelo (a distinción del subsuelo). **II.** va. quitar la capa superior.

topsy-turvy [tópsi-tœrvi], adv. trastornado, desbarajustado, patas arriba.

toque(t [tók(ét], s. cofia, toca.

tor, s. tormo.

Torah [tóræ], s. Tora, Libro de la Ley (entre los judíos)—es el Pentateuco.

torch, s. antorcha, hacha.—**t. holder,** tedero.— **t. thistle,** (bot.) céreo, cirio.—**torchbearer** [tórchbéærœr], s. hachero, portahachón.—**torchlight** [-láit], s. luz de antorcha.

tore [tóœr]. **I.** pret. de TO TEAR. **II.** s. (arq.) tondino; bocel; (mat.) toro.

toreador [tóriadór], s. toreador, torero.

torment [tormént]. **I.** va. atormentar, dar tormento; afligir. **II.** s. [tórment] tormento; pena, anguistia.

tormenter, o **tormentor** [torméntœr], s. atormentador.

tormentil [tórmentil], s. (bot.) tormentila.

torn, pp. de TO TEAR: roto, rasgado.

tornado [tornédo], s. tornado, huracán.

torpedo [torpído]. **I.** s. (pl. TORPEDOES) torpedo; (ict.) torpedo, tremielga, tembladera; (aut.) torpedo.—**t. boat,** torpedero.—**t.-boat destroyer,** cazatorpederos.—**t.-plane,** hidroavión torpedero.—**t.-tube,** tubo o cañón lanzatorpedos. **II.** va. torpedear. **III.** a. (aut.) torpedo (carrocería).

torpid [tórpid], a. entorpecido; adormecido, aletargado.—**torpidity** [torpíditi], **torpidness** [pidnes], s. entorpecimiento, embotamiento; apatía, pesadez.—**torpor** [tórpœr], s. entorpecimiento; adormecimiento; letargo, apatía, estupor.

torque [torc], s. collar; (fís., mec., elec.) momento de torsión; par de fuerzas.

torrefaction [tórefæcshʊn], s. (farm.) torrefacción.—**torrefy** [-fai], va. torrar, tostar.

torrent [tórrent], s. torrente.—**torrential** [torrénshal], a. torrencial.

torrid [tórrid], a. tórrido, tostado.—**t. zone,** zona tórrida.

torridness [tórridnes], a. **torridity** [torríditi], s. calidad de tórrido.

torsel [tórsel], s. torzal.

torsion [tórshʊn]. **I.** s. torcedura; torsión. **II.** a. de torsión.—**t. balance,** balanza de torsión.— **torsional** [-al], a. de torsión.

torso [tórso], s. torso.

tort, s. (for.) tuerto, agravio, sinrazón.

torticollis [tórticólis], s. tortícoli.

tortile [tórtil], a. torcido, doblado.

tortoise [tórtis], s. tortuga.—**t.-shell,** carey, concha de tortuga.

tortuosity [tortuósiti], **tortuousness** [tórtiuusnes], s. tortuosidad.—**tortuous** 'tórtiuus], a. tortuoso, sinuoso.

torture [tórchur]. **I.** s. tortura, tormento, suplicio. **II.** va. torturar, dar tormento, atormentar; torcer o tergiversar.—**torturer** [-œr], s. atormentador.

Torula [tórula], s. (bot.) musgo fungoideo.

torus [tórus], s. (arq.) torés; (mat.) toro.

Tory [tóri], s. (Ingl. pol.) tory, conservador.

Toryism [tóriism], s. credo político del partido tory en Inglaterra, torysmo.

toss [tos]. **I.** va. tirar, lanzar al aire; menear, agitar, mover, sacudir.—**to t. aside,** echar a un lado. —**to t. in a blanket,** mantear; discutir, repetir lo dicho.—**to t. oars,** arbolar los remos.—**to t. off,** tragar de golpe; = TO T. ASIDE. **II.** vn. ajetrearse; corcovear; mecerse, ondear.—**to t. for, to t. up,** jugar a cara o cruz. **III.** s. meneo, sacudimiento, sacudida; ajetreo; cara o cruz.—**t.-up,** cara o cruz.

tot, s. chiquitín, niño, niña.

total [tóutæl], s. y a. total.—**t. abstainer,** temperatísimo, el que se abstiene en absoluto de las bebidas alcohólicas.—**t. abstinence,** abstinencia absoluta de bebidas alcohólicas.

totality [tótélti], s. totalidad.

totalize [tóutalaiš], va. totalizar, hacer la suma de

totally [tótali], adv. totalmente.

tote [tóut], va. (fam., E. U. del Sud) cargar, llevar sobre los hombros.

totem [tótem], s. tótem, objeto o animal reverenciado por algunos salvajes como emblema o progenitor de la tribu.—**t. pole,** o **post,** pilar totémico, erigido por los indios de los E. U. y por otros pueblos primitivos con figuras totémicas pintadas y esculpidas.—**totemism** [totemišm], s. totemismo.

t'other [túðœr], abreviatura de THE OTHER, el otro.

totter [tótœr], vn. tambalear, temblar, vacilar.

tottering [-ing] **I** a. vacilante; derruído, ruinoso. **II.** s. bamboleo, tambaleo.—**totteringly** [-li], adv. de modo vacilante, tambaleando.

toucan [tucán], s. (orn.) tucán.

---

touch [tʊch]. **I.** *va.* tocar, tentar; palpar; alcanzar, herir; igualar, aproximarse a; ensayar, probar con la piedra de toque; (b. a.) delinear, esbozar; retocar; (mús.) tañer o tocar (un instrumento); mover, enternecer, conmover; irritar, aguijonear; afligir; tratar (un asunto); influir; tocar a; concernir, importar; (geom.) tocar, ser tangente a; aludir a, tratar por encima; afectar, desarreglar; (fam., a veces con **for**) pedir prestado a; robar a.—**to t. off,** descargar (arma); hacer o acabar de prisa; bosquejar.—**to t. up,** retocar; corregir. **II.** *vn.* tocar, tocarse; imponer las manos para curar.—**to t. and go,** (mar.) tocar y aparejar; tratar de un asunto ligeramente.—**to t. at a port,** hacer escala en un puerto.—**to t. on,** o **upon,** tocar en; tratar ligeramente de. **III.** *s.* tacto (sentido); toque; tocamiento, tiento; (b. a.) toque, ejecución, última mano, pincelada, rasgo; dolorcito, punzada; una sombra, un ápice; indirecta; ensayo ligero; (mús.) pulsacion; buena inteligencia, armonía o correspondencia; ensayo de metales con la piedra de toque; prueba, examen; corazonada.—**t. and go,** montado al pelo; precario, incierto; ligero de cascos.—**t. line,** línea de toque en la demarcación del cuadro de football.—**t. paper,** (piro.) papel de salitre para cebo.—**in t. with,** en comunicación o relaciones con; al corriente de.

touchable [tʊ́chabœl], *a.* tangible.
touchback [-bǽc], *s.*, **touchdown** [-dáun], *s.* diversos lances del juego de football.
touchhole [-jóul], *s.* fogón, oído del cañón.
touchily [-ili], *adv.* susceptiblemente.
touchiness [-ines], *s.* susceptibilidad, quisquillosidad.
touching [-ing]. **I.** *prep.* tocante a, en cuanto a, acerca de. **II.** *a.* patético, conmovedor. **III.** *s.* toque, palpamiento; tacto; contacto.—**touchingly** [-li], *adv.* patéticamente, tiernamente.
touch-me-not [-mí nót], *s.* (bot.) balsamina silvestre; (med.) nolimetángere.
touchstone [-stóun], *s.* piedra de toque; examen, prueba; criterio.
touchwood [-úd], *s.* yesca; hupe.
touchy [-i], *a.* quisquilloso, susceptible.
tough [tuf]. **I.** *a.* correoso, duro; vigoroso; resistente; flexible y fuerte; (fam.) difícil, penoso, arduo; rudo, vulgar.—**t. pitch,** (metal) composición y consistencia del cobre comercial; cobre comercial. **II.** *s.* (fam.) villano, malvado.
toughen [túfn], *va.* y *vn.* hacer(se) correoso; endurecer(se).
toughly [-li], *adv.* tenazmente.
toughness [-nes], *s.* tenacidad; endurecimiento; tesura, rigidez; flexibilidad, resistencia.
toupet [tupé], **toupee** [tupí], *s.* tupé.
tour [tur]. **I.** *s.* viaje, excursión, peregrinación; vuelta, circuito; turno.—**the grand t.,** viaje alrededor del mundo. **II.** *va.* viajar por, recorrer. **III.** *vn.* viajar por distracción.—**touring** [-ing], *a.* de turismo (apl. esp. a coches automóviles).—
tourist [-ist], *s.* turista.
tourmalin(e [túrmalin), *s.* turmalina, chorlo.
tournament [túrnamœnt], **tourney** [túrne]. **I.** *s.* torneo, justa. **II.** *vn.* justar.
tourniquet [túrniket], *s.* (cir.) torniquete.
tousle [táuscœl], *va.* (pp. TAUSL(E)D) despeinar.
tout [táut, tut]. **I.** *va.* y *vn.* espiar (apl. esp. a la observación clandestina de caballos de carrera, su manejo, etc.); solicitar parroquianos; seguir. **II.** *s.* espía, acecho (espía que obtiene informes relativos a carreras de caballos).
tow [to]. **I.** *s.* estopa; remolque; lo que va remolcado; atoaje.—**t.-head(ed,** pelirrojo.—**to take in t.,** atoar; encargarse de (algo o alguien), manejar. **II.** *va.* remolcar, atoar.
towage [tóey], *s.* remolque, atoaje; derechos de remolque.
toward(s [tóard(s̀], *prep.* hacia; con, para con; cosa de, alrededor de; tocante a.
toward, towardly [-li], *a.* dócil, complaciente, deferente.—**toward(l)ness** [-nes], *s.* docilidad, complacencia, deferencia.
towboat [tóbout], *s.* remolcador.
towel [táuœl], *s.* toalla, paño de manos.

towel(l)ing [-ling], *s.* género para toallas.
tower [táuœr]. **I.** *s.* torre; campanario; torreón; ciudadela, fortaleza. **II.** *vn.* elevarse, remontarse; descollar, sobresalir, destacarse.—**towered** [-d], **towery** [-i], *a.* torreado, guarnecido de torres.—**towering** [-ing], *a.* elevado; descollante, sobresaliente; dominante; violento.
towline [tóuláin], *s.* cable de remolque; sirga; estacha, arpón ballenero.
town [táun], *s.* ciudad; villa; pueblo, aldea, población; (E. U.) municipio; la ciudad, el pueblo (*he is in town,* está en la ciudad).—**t. clerk,** secretario de ayuntamiento.—**t. crier,** pregonero.—**t. hall, t. house,** casa consistorial, casa de ayuntamiento, concejo.
town(s)folk [táun(s)fóuc], *s.* vecinos de un pueblo.
township [-ship], *s.* (E. U.) municipio, sexmo; extensión de terrenos públicos de seis millas encuadro; (Ingl.) jurisdicción de una ciudad.
townsman [táunsman], *s.* vecino; conciudadano, paisano.
towntalk [-toc], *s.* hablillas de un pueblo.
towpath [tóupáz], *s.* camino de sirga.
towrope [tóurróup], *s.* = TOWLINE.
toxemia [toxímiœ], *s.* toxemia.
toxic(al [tóxic, -œl], *a.*, **toxicant** [-cœnt], *s.* y *a.* tóxico.—**toxication** [-kéiⁿun], *s.* toxicación, envenamiento.—**toxicity** [toxísiti], *s.* toxicidad.—**toxicological** [-colójical], *a.* toxicológico.—**toxicologist** [-cóloyist], *s.* toxicólogo.—**toxicology** [-cóloyi], *s.* toxicología.
toxin(e [tóxin], *s.* toxina.
toxophil [tóxofil], *a.* (bact.) toxófilo, que tiene afinidad por una toxina (apl. a ciertos microbios).
toy [tói]. **I.** *s.* juguete; retozo; perrillo diminuto (ll. t. **t. dog**).—**t. dealer,** juguetero.—**t. store,** juguetería (tienda). **II.** *a.* de juego; diminuto. **III.** *vn.* jugar, retozar, juguetear, estar de chacota.—**toyish** [tóish], *a.* menudo, de juguete.—**toyishness** [-nes], *s.* puerilidad, muchachada, fruslería, niñería.—**toyman** [-mœn], *s.* juguetero.—**toyshop** [-shóp], *s.* juguetería.
trace [tréis]. **I.** *s.* rastro, huella, pisada; vestigio, señal, indicio; tirante o tiradera.—*pl.* (quím.) indicios. **II.** *va.* trazar, delinear; calcar; rastrear, seguir la pista; trazar, señalar, plantear, indicar; reconstruir, determinar el origen o la forma primitiva de, investigar, descubrir, escudriñar; en jaezar, enganchar (caballo); galibar.—**to t. to,** derivar de; demostrar que (algo) proviene de; seguir, llevar o hacer remontar hasta.
traceable [-abœl], *a.* que se puede trazar, rastrear, o descubrir; atribuíble.
tracer [-œr], *s.* trazador; tiralíneas; calcador; puntero, punzón; cédula de investigación para averiguar el paradero de cartas o bultos extraviados.
tracery [-œri], *s.* (arq.) tracería.
trachea [tréikiœ], *s.* traquea, traquiarteria; (bot.) ducto.—**tracheal** [-al], *a.* traqueal.
tracheotomy [trekiótomi], *s.* traqueotomía.
trachoma [trœcómœ], *s.* tracoma.
trachyte [trékait], *s.* (min.) traquita.
trachytic [trakític], *a.* traquítico.
tracing [trésing]. **I.** *s.* trazo; calco; copia; vía, pista; acción de trazar, calcar, etc. *V.* TRACE, *va.* **II.** que traza; de trazar; de calcar.—**t. cloth,** tela de calcar.—**t. line,** (mar.) perigallo.—**t. paper,** papel tela.—**t. point,** aguja recorredora o estilete recorredor de un planímetro, etc.).
track [trœc]. **I.** *s.* vestigio, rastro, pista, huella, pisada, estampa; rodada, carril; rumbo, ruta; curso; camino trillado, senda, vereda; (f. c.) vía; rieles, carriles de la vía; (eq.) pista; (mar.) derrota, estela.—**t. ga(u)ge,** calibre de entrevía, gabarit.—**off the t.,** descarrilado; desviado, extraviado; (fam.) por los cerros de Ubeda.—**on the t.,** en la pista, en el rastro. **II.** *va.* rastrear, seguir la pista a; (mar.) sirgar.
trackage [trœ́key], *s.* remolque, sirgadura.
tracker [trœ́cœr], *s.* (mar.) sirguero.

tracklayer [-léiœr], _s._ tendedor o instalador de carriles.—**tracklaying** [-léiing], _s._ tendido, instalación o asiento de carriles.

trackless [-les], _a._ que no presenta ni deja rastro, ni huellas; sin caminos; cerrado; intransitado.

trackman [-mæn], **trackwalker** [-uócoer], _s._ recorredor de la vía.

trackwork [-uócrc], _s._ cálculo y construcción del sistema de carriles de las vías férreas.

tract [træct], _s._ trecho, tracto; región, comarca; terreno; (anat.) área, región; curso, serie; folleto, tratadico, opúsculo.

tractable [trǽctabœl], _a._ tratable, manejable, dócil.—**tractableness** [-nes], _s._ afabilidad; docilidad.—**tractably** [-abli], _adv._ afablemente; dócilmente.

tractate [trǽctet], _s._ opúsculo, ensayo.

traction [trǽcshun], _s._ tracción, arrastre; (fisiol.) contracción, fricción.—**t. engine,** máquina de arrastre.

tractive [-tiv], _a._ de tracción.

tractor [trǽctœr], _s._ tractor; máquina de arrastre; automóvil tractor; (aer.) aeroplano de tracción o de hélice delantera (Il. t. **t. airplane).**—**t. engine,** motor tractor o delantero.—**t. propeller,** o **screw,** (aer.) hélice de tracción, hélice delantera.

trade [tréid]. **I.** _s._ comercio; industria; oficio; contratación, negocio, trato; gremio; (E. U. pol.) convenio de mala ley; (Ingl.) servicio de submarinos.—**t. acceptance,** vale de, o giro aceptado, de compra, en que el vendedor gira contra el comprador, y el giro, aceptado, se convierte en papel negociable.—**t. agreement,** pacto entre patronos y gremios obreros.—**t.-mark,** marca de fábrica.—**t. name,** razón social; nombre comercial; nombre de fábrica (el especial o arbitrario dado por un fabricante a un producto).—**t. price,** precio con rebaja o descuento.—**t. school,** escuela de artes y oficios, escuela industrial.—**t.(s) -union,** gremio de obreros.—**t.(s)-unionism,** tradeunionismo, sistema de los gremios obreros.—**t.(s)-unionist,** tradeunionista, miembro de un gremio obrero; partidario de los gremios obreros.—**t. winds,** vientos alisios. **II.** _va._ y _vn._ negociar, comerciar, tratar, traficar; cambiar.—**to t. in,** negociar en.—**to t. on,**̣ (fam.) aprovecharse de.

trader [-œr], _s._ negociante, comerciante, traficante; buque mercante.

tradesfolk, tradespeople [treidsfóuc, -pípœl], _s. pl._ comerciantes; gentes del oficio.

tradesman [tréidsman], _s._ tendero, mercader; artesano, menestral.—**tradeswoman** [-úmęn, _s._ mujer comerciante, de negocios o versada en el comercio.

trading [tréiding]. **I.** _s._ comercio, trato.—**t. house,** factoría. **II.** _a._ mercantil, comercial; venal, corrompido, prostituido.—**t. post,** factoría.—**t. stamp,** billete de premio que se da al comprador como alciente.

tradition [tradíshun], _s._ tradición; (for.) tradición, entrega.—**traditional** [-al], _a._ tradicional. **traditionalism** [-alism], _s._ tradicionalismo. **traditionally** [-ali], _adv._ tradicionalmente.—**traditionary** [-eri]. **I.** _a._ tradicional. **II.** _s._ tradicionalista.

traduce [tradiús], _va._ calumniar.—**traducer** [œr], _s._ calumniador.

traducianism [trædiúshænism], _s._ doctrina según la cual tanto el alma como el cuerpo son engendrados por los padres.

traffic [trǽfic]. **I.** _s._ tráfico; comercio; transporte, acarreo; tránsito; movimiento; circulación; mercancías, artículos. **II.** _va._ y _vn._ negociar, comerciar, traficar.—**trafficker** [-œr], _s._ traficante.

tragacanth [trǽgacænȝ], _s._ tragacanto, adraganto, alquitira.

tragedian [travídian], _s._ trágico.—**tragedienne** [travedién, travídian], _s._ trágica.

tragedy [trǽvedi], _s._ tragedia.

tragic(al [trǽvic(al], _a._ trágico.—**tragically** [-li], _adv._ trágicamente.—**tragicalness** [-nes], _s._ calidad de trágico, carácter trágico.

tragicomedy [trǽvicómedi], _s._ tragicomedia.

tragicomic(al [-ic(al], _s._ tragicómico, jocoserio.

tragus [tréigus], _s._ (anat.) trago.

trail [tréil]. **I.** _va._ arrastrar; remolcar; traer, llevar (barro, etc.) en los pies, zapatos, etc; asentar (la yerba) con el andar, hasta formar vereda; rastrear, seguir el rastro o la pista; (E. U. f. c.) agregar (vagones) a un tren.—**to t. a switch,** (f. c.) tomar de talón el cambiavía, entrar en él por los talones o extremos fijos de las agujas. **II.** _vn._ arrastrar, iṛ arrastrando; dejar rastro; rezagarse, seguir el rastro o la pista; arrastrarse, trepar (una planta). **III.** _s._ rastro, pisada, pista; cola (de vestido, de cometa, etc.); trocha, sendero, vereda; indicio; (artl.) gualdera.—**t. bridge,** andarivel.—**t. rope,** (aer.) sonda, cuerda freno (cable colgante o de arrastre de un globo, que sirve de lastre variable para regular la altura).

trailer [tréilœr], _s._ el o lo que sigue el rastro o la pista; carro o coche remolcado.

trailing [tréiling], _a._ rastrero; remolcado; trasero. —**t. arbutus,** (bot.) gayuba.—**t. edge,** (aer.ͤ borde de salida.—**t. switch,** agujas (de cambiavías) tomadas de talón, o por sus extremos fijos.—**t. wheel,** rueda trasera.

train [tréin]. **I.** _va._ y _vn._ disciplinar, adiestrar, amaestrar; preparar, educar, enseñar; (dep.) entrenar; poner en espaldera; apuntar (un cañón). **II.** _s._ (f. c.) tren; séquito, comitiva; cabalgata; recua; reguero de pólvora; serie, sucesión, orden, curso; cola (de ave, de vestido, de cometa); (mec.) tren, juego, movimiento; artimaña; lazo, celada; trampa.—**t. dispatcher,** director del movimiento de trenes.—**t. mile,** tren-milla, milla por tren.—**t. mileage,** kilometraje por tren, total de tren-millas (tren-kilómetros).—**t. oil,** aceite de ballena o de pescado.—**t. tackle,** (art.) palanquines de retenida.

trainband [tréinbǽnd], _s._ milicia.

trainbearer [-bǽærœr], _s._ caudatorio.

trained [tréind], _a._ adiestrado, enseñado; educado, preparado.—**t. nurse,** enfermera o enfermero graduados.

trainer [-œr], _s._ domador, amaestrador; (dep.) entrenador; (agr.) espaldera.

training [-ing]. **I.** _s._ enseñanza, educación, instrucción, preparación; (dep.) entrenamiento. **II.** _a._ de instrucción; (dep.) de entrenamiento.—**t. school,** plantel, escuela práctica.

trainway [-uéi], _s._ plataforma de rieles para embarcar vagones ferroviarios en servicio.

trait [tréit], _s._ golpe, toque; rasgo.

traitor [tréitœr], _s._ traidor.—**traitorous** [-us], _a._ pérfido, aleve, traidor.—**traitorously** [-li], _adv._ alevosamente, pérfidamente.—**traitoroness** [-nes], _s._ alevosía, perfidia, traición.—**traitress** [-tres], _s._ traidora.

traject [travéct], _va._ tirar, arrojar.

trajection [travécshun], _s._ trayecto, travesía.

trajectory [travéctori], _s._ trayectoria.

tram [træm], _s._ (Ingl.) tranvía; carril, riel plano; (mec.) calibre de alineación.

tramcar [trǽmcár], _s._ carreta de carbón; coche de tranvía.

trammel [trǽmel]. **I.** _s._ impedimento, obstáculo, estorbo; traba, manea; llares, garabato de chimenea; compás de barra; calibre de alineación. **II.** _va._ trabar, poner trabas; estorbar, impedir.

tramontane [tramónten]. **I.** _a._ tramontano, ultramontano. **II.** _s._ extranjero.

tramp [træmp]. **I.** _va._ y _vn._ patullar, patear, pernear; pisar con fuerza; corretear, vagabundear. **II.** _s._ marcha pesada; ruido de pisadas; caminata, paseo largo; vago, vagabundo, guitón.—**t. steamer,** vapor volandero.

trample [trǽmpœl]. **I.** _va._ hollar, pisc tear, pisar. **II.** _vn._ patullar, pisar fuerte; (con oñ) ajar, atropellar, hollar, pisotear. **III.** _s._ pisoteo; atropello.

trampler [trǽmplœr], _s._ pisador.

tramroad [trǽmróud], **tramway** [-uei], _s._ tranvía.

trance [trans], _s._ rapto, arrobamiento; síncope, catalepsia; estado hipnótico.

tranquil [trǽncuil], _a._ tranquilo.—**tranquility** [trǽncuíliti], _s._ tranquilidad.—**tranquillize, tranquilise** [trǽncuilaiȝ], _va._ tranquilizar.—**tranquilly** [trǽncuili], _adv._ tranquilamente.

transact [trænsǽct], *va.* tramitar, hacer, ejecutar, despachar.

transaction [-sǽcǎhʊn], *s.* desempeño, gestión, negociación; transacción, negocio.—*pl.* trabajos de una sociedad docta; memorias; actas.

transactor [-sǽctœr], *s.* negociador, gestor.

transalpine [trænsǽlpin], *a.* transalpino.

transatlantic [trǽnsætlǽntic], *a.* transatlántico.

transcend [trænsénd]. **I.** *va.* sobrepujar, superar, propasar. **II.** *vn.* trascender.—**transcendence, transcendency** [-ens, -i], *s.* excelencia, superioridad; doctrina de que Dios es anterior al universo.—**transcendent** [-ent], *a.* sobresaliente, excelente; (filos.) incognoscible; no inmanente, sino anterior al universo.

transcendental [trǽnsendéntal], *a.* trascendental; eminente, sobresaliente; vago, indefinido; (mat.) trascendental, no algébrico; (fil.) transcendental.—**transcendentalism** [-ism], *s.* transcendentalismo.

transcendently [trænséndentli], *adv.* excelentemente.

transcontinental [trænscóntinéntal], *a.* transcontinental.

transcribe [trænscráib], *va.* transcribir, copiar, trasladar; (mús.) adaptar.—**transcriber** [-œr], *s.* copiador, copista; adaptador.

transcript [trénscript], *s.* trasunto, copia, traslado.

transcription [trænscrípǎhʊn], *s.* transcripción, trasunto, traslado.—**transcriptive** [-tiv], *a.* perteneciente al traslado.

transept [trénsept], *s.* (arq.) crucero.

transfer [trǽnsfœr]. **I.** *va.* transferir, trasladar, pasar, transbordar; (for.) transferir, traspasar. **II.** *s.* [trǽnsfœr] traspaso, transferencia; transbordo, traslado, transporte; (for.) traspaso, cesión.—**transferable** [trænsfœrabœl], *a.* transferible; convertible.—**transferee** [trénsfœrí], *s.* cesionario: persona transferida de un puesto o empleo a otro.—**transference** [trǽnsfœrens], *s.* transferencia.—**transferrer, transferror** [trænsfœrœr], *s.* (for.) transferidor, cesionista, cedente.

transfiguration [trænsfíguiuréiǎhʊn], *s.* transfiguración.—**transfigure** [-guiur], *va.* transfigurar.

transfix [trænsfíx], *va.* traspasar, atravesar.

transfixion [trænsfícǎhʊn], *s.* transfixión.

transform [trænsfórm], *va.* y *vn.* transformar(se).

transformable [-abœl], *a.* transformable.

transformation [trǽnsforméiǎhʊn], *s.* transformación.—**transformative** [trænsfórmative], *a.* transformativo.

transformer [trænsfórmœr], *s.* transformador; (elec.) transformador.

transformism [trænsfórmism], *s.* transformismo.

transfuse [trænsfiús], *va.* transfundir, transvasar, decantar.—**transfusion** [-ȳun], *s.* transfusión.

transgress [trænsgrés], *va.* y *vn.* transgredir, violar, quebrantar; propasarse, excederse; (geol.) translaparse.—**transgression** [-gréǎhʊn], *s.* transgresión; traspaso, extralimitación.—**transgressor** [-grésœr], *s.* transgresor, infractor.

tranship, *va.* = TRANSSHIP.

transience, transiency [trǽnǎhens, -i], *s.* calidad o estado de pasajero o transitorio.

transient [trénǎhœnt]. **I.** *a.* pasajero, transitorio; transeúnte. **II.** *s.* transeúnte.—**transiently** [-li], *adv.* temporalmente, de paso.—**transientness** [-nes], *s.* brevedad; naturaleza pasajera o transitoria.

transit [trénsit]. **I.** *s.* tránsito, paso, pasaje; trámite; (astr.) tránsito; (top.) tránsito, (teodolito de anteojo invertible sobre el ej e horizontal).—**t. instrument**, (top.) = TRANSIT; (astr.) anteojo meridiano. **II.** *va.* (astr., top.) pasar por; invertir (el anteojo del tránsito) en el plano vertical. **III.** *vn.* invertirase, ser invertido (el anteojo) en el plano vertical.

transition [trænsíǎhʊn], *s.* tránsito, paso, mudanza; transición; (mús.) transición.—**t. curve**, curva de transición, curva de enlace entre una circular y una vía recta.

transitional, transitionary [-al, -eri], *a.* transitorio.

transitive [trénsitiv], *a.* (gram.) transitivo.

transitively [-li], *adv.* transitivamente.

transitman [-mæn], *s.* (top., f. c.) encargado del tránsito (instrumento).

transitorily [-itorili], *adv.* transitoriamente; provisionalmente.

transitoriness [-nes], *s.* carácter transitorio.

transitory [-itori], *a.* transitorio, pasajero; provisional.

translatable [trænsléitabœl], *a.* traducible.

translate [trænsléit], *va.* traducir; descifrar, interpretar; (tlg.) transmitir por relevador; (igl.) trasladar de una silla episcopal a otra; transformar, cambiar.—**to t. from . . . into**, traducir del . . . al.

translation [-éiǎhʊn], *s.* translación; remoción; traducción, versión; (ret.) traslación.—**motion of t.**, movimiento de traslación.

translator [-éitœr], *s.* traductor; (elec.)repetidor.

transliterate [trænslíteret], *va.* representar las letras o sonidos de una lengua por las letras de otra.

translucency [trænslúsensi], *s.* translucidez.

translucent, translucid [-ent, -id], *a.* translúcido, trasluciente.

transmarine [trénsmarín], *a.* ultramarino o transmarino.

transmigrate [-migreit], *vn.* transmigrar.

transmigration [-éiǎhʊn], *s.* transmigración.

transmigrator [-migréitœr], *s.*, **transmigratory** [trænsmáigratori], *a.* transmigrador.

transmissibility [trænsmísibíliti], *s.* transmisibilidad.—**transmissible** [-bœl], *a.* transmisible.—**transmission** [-ǎhʊn], *s.* transmisión.—**transmissive** [-iv], *a.* transmisible; transmisor.

transmit [trænsmít], *va.* transmitir.—**transmittal** [-al], *s.* transmisión.—**transmitter** [-œr], *s.* remitente; (tlg., tlf.) (elec.) transmisor.

transmutability [trænsmiútabíliti], *s.* transmutabilidad.

transmutable [trænsmiútabœl], *a.* transmutable.

transmutably [-bli], *adv.* transmutablemente.

transmutation [trénsmiutéiǎhʊn], *s.* transmutación.

transmute [trænsmiút], *va.* transmutar.

transmuter [-œr], *s.* transmutador.

transom [trénsum], *s.* (carp.) travesaño; (arq.) montante, lumbre, claraboya; (carr.) telera; (mar.) yugo o peto de popa.

transpacific [trénspacífic], *a.* transpacífico, allende el Pacífico.

transpadane [-pǽdéin], *a.* transpadano.

transparency [trænspǽercensi], *s.* transparencia, diafanidad; transparente.—**transparent** [-œnt], *a.* transparente, franco, sincero.

transpiration [trénspiréiǎhʊn], *s.* transpiración.

transpire [trænspáiœr]. **I.** *va.* transpirar, exhalar, sudar. **II.** *vn.* rezumarse; translucirse; (común pero incorrecto) acontecer, suceder.

transplant [trænsplánt], *va.* trasplantar.

transplantation [trénsplæntéiǎhʊn], *s.* trasplante.

transport [trænspórt]. **I.** *va.* transportar, acarrear; deportar, desterrar; arrebatar, enajenar, conmover. **II.** *s.* [trénsport] transporte, acarreo; buque transporte; arrobamiento, rapto; paroxismo, acceso.

transportable [trénspórtabœl], *a.* transportable.

transportation [trénsportéiǎhʊn], *s.* transportación, transporte, acarreo; pasaje, billete; extrañamiento, deportación, destierro; coste del transporte.

transporter [trænspórtœr], *s.* transportador, porteador.

transporting [-ing], *a.* transportador, de transporte; arrobador, arrebatador.

transposal [trænspósal], *s.* transposición.

transpose [trænspóus], *va.* transponer; (mús.) transportar.

transposition [trénsposíǎhʊn], *s.* transposición.

transship [trænsǎhíp], *va.* transbordar.

transshipment [-mœnt], *s.* transbordo.

transubstantiate [trænsubstǽnṣhieit], *va.* transubstanciar.—**transubstantiation** [-éiṣhun], *s.* transubstanciación.

transudation [trænsiduéiṣhun], *s.* resudación, endosmosis.

transude [trænsiúd], *vn.* resudar, trazumarse.

transversal [trænsvœrsal]. **I.** *a.* transversal. **II.** *s.* (geom.) transversal.

transverse [-vœrs], *a.* transversal, transverso.

transversely [-li], *adv.* tranversalmente.

trap [træp]. **I.** *s.* trampa, armadijo; garlito, red, lazo; tranquilla; (mec.) sifón, tubo en U para obturación hidráulica; bombillo de retrete; (fam.) carruaje; juego del palo corvo.—*pl.* equipaje, bártulos, tarecos; escala de mano.—**t.** equipaje, bártulos, tarecos; escala de mano.—**t.** (**rock**), roca trapeana.—**t. shooting**, tiro al vuelo o a blanco que se mueve —**to be caught in the t.**, caer en el garlito, en la trampa o en la ratonera. **II.** *va.* coger con trampa; atrapar; hacer caer en el lazo o en el garlito; armar lazos o asechanzas; enjaezar, adornar.

trapdoor [trǽpdóœr], *s.* (teat.) escotillón, trampa; (min.) puerta de ventilación.

trapeze [trapíṣ], *s.* trapecio de gimnasia.

trapezing [-ing], *s.* ejercicio o suertes de trapecio.—**trapezist** [-ist], *s.* gimnasta de trapecio.

trapezium [trapíṣium], *s.* (geom.) trapezoide; (anat.) trapecio, hueso radial del carpo.

trapezoid [trǽpiṣóid], *s.* (geom.) trapecio.

trapezoidal [-al], *a.* trapecial.

trapline [trǽpláin], *s.* hilo de telaraña.

trappean [trǽpiæn, træpíæn], *a.* (min.) trapeano.

trapper [trǽpœr], *s.* el que pone trampas.

trappings [-pings], *s. pl.* jaeces, arreos, adornos.

Trappist [trǽpist], *s.* trapense.

trapstick [trǽpstic], *s.* pala o palo corvo.

trash [træṣh]. **I.** *s.* hojarasca, paja, basura; bagazo; cachivache, trasto, patarata; escamonda; quídam, un cualquiera; trabanco, trangallo. **II.** *va.* podar, escamondar; poner trabanco.

trashy [trǽṣhi], *a.* hojarascoso, baladí.

trauma [tróma *o* tráuma], *s.* lesión, herida.

traumatic [tromǽtic]. **I.** *a.* traumático. **II.** *s.* medicamento vulnerario.

traumatism [trómatiṣm], **traumatosis** [-tósis], *s.* traumatismo.

travail [trǽveil]. **I.** *vn.* trabajar, afanarse; estar de parto. **II.** *s.* afán, fatiga, trabajo; dolores de parto.

travel [trǽvœl]. **I.** *va.* y *vn.* viajar; navegar; andar, correr; recorrer. **II.** *s.* viaje; (mec.) golpe, curso, carrera, recorrido.—**t.-soiled, t.-stained**, manchado o sucio a causa del viaje.—**t.-worn**, fatigado por el viaje.

travel(l)er [-œr], *s.* viajero, viajador; (mar.) raca o arraca; artefacto movible, como carretilla, corredera, etc.

travel(l)ing [trǽveling], *a.* de viaje, para viajar.—**t. crane**, puente grúa.—**t. derrick**, grúa móvil (montada en carretilla).

travelog(ue [trǽvelog], *s.* descripción o representación de un viaje, o de objetos interesantes para viajeros.

traversable [trǽvœrsabœl], *a.* atravesable; negable, contestable.

traverse [trǽvœrs]. **I.** *a.* transversal, atravesado.—**t. board**, rosa de los pilotos.—**t. circle**, (art.) círculo en que se mueve la cureña.—**t. jury** = PETIT JURY.—**t. line**, (top.) poligonal, línea quebrada.—**t. survey**, (top.) trazado de una poligonal o línea quebrada.—**t. table**, (top.) tabla de coordenadas de latitud y longitud; (f. c.) plataforma corrediza con rieles para pasar vehículos de una vía a otra. **II.** *s.* (carp.) travesaño; travesero; cerco travesero; (fort.) través; (top.) trazado de una poligonal, o línea quebrada; línea transversal; viaje, pasaje; (for.) negación, contradicción, objeción legal; (mar.) bordada, ruta oblicua. **III.** *va.* atravesar, cruzar, recorrer; examinar o escudriñar con cuidado; mover lateral o transversalmente; cepillar de través; (for.) negar, oponerse; estorbar, impedir; contrariar, frustrar. **IV.** *vn.* atravesarse; hacer vaivén, moverse de un lado a

otro; dar vueltas, girar; (top.) trazar una poligonal, o línea quebrada.

travertin(e [trǽvœrtin], *s.* travertino.

travesty [trǽvesti]. **I.** *va.* disfrazar; parodiar. **II.** *s.* parodia.

trawl [trol]. **I.** *va.* arrastrar o rastrear (un arte de pesca). **II.** *vn.* pescar a la rastra o rastreando. **III.** *s.* cuerda larga y gruesa a la cual se atan otras provistas de anzuelos (llámase también **t. line**); TRAWLNET.

trawling [tróling], *s.* pesca a la rastra.

trawlnet [trólnét], *s.* especie de jábega o red barredera en forma de bolsa.

tray [tréi], *s.* bandeja; salvilla; batea; dornajo; artesa; platillo; cajón; cualquier vasija casi plana o de bordes bajos.

treacherous [tréchœrus], *a.* traidor, traicionero, alevoso, pérfido.—**t. memory**, memoria infiel.—**treacherously** [-li], *adv.* traidoramente, alevosamente.—**treacherousness** [-nes], *s.* calidad de traidor o pérfido; perfidia.

treachery [tréchœri], *s.* traición, felonía, perfidia.

treacle [tríccœl], *s.* melado, meladura; (farm.) triaca.

tread [tred]. **I.** *va.* y *vn.* (pret. TROD; pp. TRODDEN) pisar, hollar; andar, caminar; pisotear; patear, patalear; pisar (las aves); gallear, cubrir (el gallo a las gallinas).—**to t. back**, desandar, volver atrás.—**to t. in the footsteps of**, seguir las pisadas de, imitar.—**to t. on one's heels**, pisarle a uno los talones, seguirle de cerca. **II.** *s.* pisa; paso; pisada, huella, pisadura; escalón o peldaño de escalera; centro del torno; galladura, cicatrícula (del huevo); chalaza (del huevo); superficie de rodadura (de rueda, riel, etc.); distancia entre los centros de las superficies de rodadura de dos ruedas opuestas.

treadle [trédœl], *s.* cárcola, pedal; galladura (del huevo); chalaza (del huevo).

treadmill [trédmil], *s.* molino de rueda de andar; (fig.) tráfago.

treason [tríṣn], *s.* traición.—**treasonable** [-abœl], *a.* pérfido, desleal, traidor.—**treasonableness** [-nes], *s.* calidad de traidor; traición.—**treasonably** [-bli], *adv.* traidoramente.

treasure [tréyœr]. **I.** *s.* tesoro, caudal, riqueza; preciosidad.—**t.-house**, tesorería.—**t.-trove**, tesoro hallado. **II.** *va.* atesorar; acumular riquezas; guardar o recordar como un tesoro.

treasurer [-œr], *s.* tesorero.—**treasurership** [-ṣhip], *s.* dignidad o puesto de tesorero.

treasury [tréyuri], *s.* tesorería; erario, tesoro, hacienda; (T-) ministerio de hacienda o del tesoro (ll. t., **T. Department**).—**T. note**, bono (a la vista) de la tesorería.

treat [trít]. **I.** *va.* tratar; dar (buen o mal) trato; escribir o discurrir sobre alguna materia; (fam.) convidar, invitar. **II.** *vn.* tratar; negociar un tratado; (fam.) convidar. **III.** *s.* solaz, placer, deleite; obsequio, agasajo, convite; (fam.) convidada.

treatise [trítis], *s.* tratado (libro, escrito).

treatment [trítmœnt], *s.* trato; manera de tratar; (med., quím.) tratamiento.

treaty [tríti], *s.* tratado, pacto.—**t. port**, puerto o ciudad abiertos al comercio extranjero.

treble [trébœl]. **I.** *a.* triple, triplo; (mús.) atiplado, sobreagudo.—**t. block**, (mar.) cuadernal de tres ojos. **II.** *s.* (mús.) tiple. **III.** *va.* triplicar. **IV.** *vn.* triplicarse.

trebly [trébli], *adv.* triplicadamente.

trecentist [trechéntist], *s.* trecentista.—**trecento** [trechénto], *s.* el siglo XIV del arte y la literatura italianos.

tree [trí], *s.* árbol; palo, madero; horca; cruz.—**t. cactus**, pitahaya.—**t. fern**, helecho arborescente, helecho de árbo.—**t. frog**, rana arbórea.—**t. of life**, árbol de la vida, guayaco, palo santo.—**t. of the knowledge of good and evil**, árbol de la ciencia del bien y del mal.—**t. toad** = T. FROG.—**t. worship**, culto de los árboles.—**up a t.**, (fam.) puesto entre la espada y la pared; desinteresado, neutral.

treeless [tríles], *a.* pelado, sin árboles.

treenail [tríneil; fam. [trénel], s. (carp.) espiga, cabilla, clavija.

trefoil [trífoil], s. (bot.) trébol, trifolio.

treillage [tréiley], s. varaseto.

trek. I. vn. (pret. y pp. TREKKED) viajar en carromatos; emigrar; tirar de una carga. **II.** s. emigración; incursión; jornada.

trellis [trélis], s. enrejado; espaldera, arriate; varaseto.—**trelliswork** [-uœrc], enrejado, espaldera.

Trematoda [trémætóudæ], s. pl. (zool.) tremátodos.—**trematode** [-toud], s. y a. tremátodo.

tremble [trémbœl]. **I.** vn. temblar; estremecerse; tiritar; trinar. **II.** s. temblor, estremecimiento. —**trembler** [-blœr], s. el o lo que tiembla; (elec.) interruptor intermitente.—**trembling** [-bling], a. temblante, tembloroso, trémulo.—**t. poplar, t. tree,** álamo temblón.—**fremblingly** [-li], adv. trémulamente.

tremendous [treméndus], a. tremendo, formidable, terrible.—**tremendously** [-li], adv. tremendamente.

tremolo [trémolo], s. (mús.) trémolo.

tremor [trémœr], s. tremor, temblor, estremecimiento; vibración, trepidación.

tremulous [trémiulus], a. trémulo, tembloroso.

tremulously [-li], adv. trémulamente.

trench. I. va. y vn. surcar, hacer surcos; hacer zanjas o fosos; atrincherar.—**to t. the ballast,** (mar.) separar el lastre con mamparos. **II.** s. foso, zanja; tajo; agüera, presa; (mil.) trinchera.—**t. foot, t. feet,** enfermedad de los pies semejante a los sabañones, causada por el frío y la humedad, como en las trincheras.

trenchant [trénchant], a. afilado, cortante; mordaz, picante.

trencher [trénchœr], s. el que abre zanjas o fosos; trinchador; (coc.) trinchero, tajadero; viandas; comida; placeres de la mesa.—**trencherman** [-mæn], s. comedor; compañero de mesa.

trend. I. vn. dirigirse, tender, inclinarse. **II.** s. dirección, rumbo, curso, giro, tendencia.

trepan [trepán]. **I.** s. (cir.) trépano. **II.** va. (cir.) trepanar.—**trepanation** [-éishun], s. (cir.) trepanación.

trephine [trefáin o tréfin]. **I.** va. trepanar. **II.** s. trépano.

trepidation [trépidéishun], s. trepidación, azoramiento.

Treponema [tréponímæ], género de bacterias a que pertenece el espiroqueto, bacteria de la sífilis.

trespass [tréspas]. **I.** vn. (con **on** o **upon**) violar, quebrantar, infringir; invadir, rebasar o traspasar los límites; (con **against**) pecar, faltar.—**to t. on one's patience,** abusar de la paciencia de uno. **II.** s. transgresión, translimitación, invasión; infracción, violación; culpa, pecado; deuda (en el padrenuestro).

trespasser [-œr], s. transgresor, violador de una ley; pecador.

tress, s. trenza; rizo, bucle.—pl. cabellos abundantes.—**tressed** [trest], a. trenzado.

trestle [trésœl], s. bastidor; armadura; armazón de soporte o refuerzo; (ing.) caballete, viaducto sostenido por armaduras transversales reticuladas.—**t. bent,** palizada, armadura o armazón transversal (de un viaducto).—**t. horse,** borriquete.

trestletrees [-trís], s. (mar.) baos de los palos.

trestlework [-uœrc], **trestling** [-ing], s. (ing.) caballete, sistema (serie) de caballetes.

tret, s. (com.) deducción por merma, rebaja.

trevet [trévet], s. trípode.

trey [tréi], s. el tres (en dados o naipes).

triad [tráiæd]. **I.** s. terno, terna, trinca; (mús.) acorde. **II.** a. (quím.) trivalente.

triadic [tráiadic], a. y s. trino.

trial [tráial], s. prueba, esfuerzo, ensayo, experimento; toque, ensay; desgracia, aflicción; (for.) juicio, vista de una causa.—**t. by jury,** juicio por jurado.—**t. trip,** viaje de prueba.—**on t.,** a prueba.

triangle [tráiængœl], s. triángulo; (mús.) triángulo; (dib.) escuadra, cartabón; (fam.) con-

junto de tres cosas o personas; asunto en que están envueltos o en que participan tres cosas o personas (puede llamarse triada).

triangular [traiǽnguiular], **triangled** [traiǽngœld], a. triangular, triangulado; de tres (cosas. personas, etc.).—**triangularly** [-li], adv. triangularmente.

triangulate [traiǽnguiuleit], va. triangular.

triangulation [-éishun], s. triangulación.

Triassic [traiǽsic], a. y s. (geol.) triásico.

triatomic [tráiætómic], a. triatómico; trivalente.

tribal [tráibæl], a. tribal, de tribu, relativo a la tribu o a las tribus; descendiente de una misma hembra por la línea materna (apl. al ganado).

tribasic [traibéisic], a. tribásico.

tribe [traib], s. tribu; (bioi.) tribu, grupo.

tribesman [tráibsmæn], s. miembro de una tribu.

triblet [tríblet], s. (joy.) lastra.

tribrach [tráibræc], s. tribraquio.

tribulation [tríbiuléishun], s. tribulación, congoja.

tribunal [traibiúnal], (for.) sala, juzgado; tribunal; (igl.) confesionario.

tribune [tríbiun], s. tribuno, defensor del pueblo; tribuna.—**tribuneship** [-ship], s. tribunado.

tribunicial, tribunitial [-níshal], a. tribunicio.

tributary [tríbiuteri], a. y s. tributario (río, estado); subalterno, subordinado.

tribute [tríbiut], s. tributo; contribución.

trice [tráis]. **I.** s. momento, instante, tris.—**in a t.,** en un abrir y cerrar de ojos. **II.** va. (mar.) izar; amarrar, ligar.

tricennial [traisénial], a. tricenal.

triceps [tráiseps], s. (anat.) tríceps.

trichina [tricáina], s. triquina.

trichinization [tríkiniséishun], **trichinosis** [-nósis], s. triquinosis.—**trichinous** [-us], a. triquinoso; triquinado.

trichotomic [trícotómic], **trichotomous** [tricótomus], a. (biol., lóg.) tricótomo.

trichotomy [traicótomi], s. tricotomía.

trichroic [traicróic], a. tricroico.—**trichroism** [tráicroiŝm], s. tricroísmo.

trichromatic [tráicromǽtic], a. tricromático.—**trichromatism** [traicrómætiŝm], s. tricromatismo.

trick. I. s. treta, petardo, timo, engaño, socaliña; artería, ardid; trampa, tramoya, manganilla; juego de manos; chasco, burla; travesura; parchazo; destreza, maña; marrulla: costumbre, vicio, muletilla; baza, en el juego de naipes; (mar.) guardia del timonel. **II.** va. engañar, embaucar, timar; (con **out**) ataviar, componer, asear. **III.** vn. trampear, vivir de trampas.

tricker, trickster [trícœr, tríctsœr], s. trampista, embaucador, engañabobos.

trickery [trícœri], s. trampería, ardid.

trickish [tríkish], a. falso, trapacero; mañoso.

trickle [trícœl], vn. gotear; escurrir.

tricksy [trícsi], a. juguetón, retozón, travieso; artificioso, embustero; ilusorio.

tricky [tríki], a. falso, tramposo, marrullero; vicioso (el animal).

triclinium [traiclínium], s. triclinio.

tricolo(u)r [traicólor]. **I.** a. tricolor. **II.** s. bandera tricolor (apl. gen. a la francesa).

tricot [tríco], s. tejido de punto.

tricuspid [traicúspid], a. tricúspide.—**t. valve,** (anat.) válvula tricúspide.

tricycle [tráisicœl], s. triciclo.

trident [tráidœnt], s. tridente; arrejaque.

tridentate [tráidenteit], a. tridente.

Tridentine [traidéntin]. **I.** a. tridentino. **II.** s. católico romano.

tried [tráid], pp. y a. probado.

triennial [traiénial], a. trienal.—**triennium** [-um], s. trienio, período de tres años.

trier [tráiœr], s. experimentador, ensayador; juez, censor; examinador; ensayo, prueba.

trierarch [tráiœrarc], s. trierarca, capitán de trireme.

trifacial [triféishæl], s. y a. traifacial.—**t. nerve,** trigémino.

trifallow [tráifælo], va. (agr.) terciar.

trifid [tráifid], a. trífido.
trifle [tráifœl]. **I.** s. bagatela, fruslería, friolera; baratija, menudencia; crema aromatizada.—**a t.** (como adv.) un poco, un poquito. **II.** va. malgastar (el tiempo). **III.** vn. bromear, chancearse, guasearse; holgar; (con **with**) jugar; tratar sin seriedad; burlarse de, engañar.
trifler [tráiflœr], s. persona frívola.
trifling [-fling], a. frívolo; fútil, insignificante.
trifoliate(d [traifóliet(ed], a. trifoliáceo.
trifoliolate [traifóliolet], a. trifoliado.
triform [tráiform], a. triforme.
trifurcate(d [traifœrkeit(ed], a. trifurcado.
trifurcation [tráifœrkéishʊn], s. trifurcación.
trig. **I.** va. atar o trabar las ruedas. **II.** s. calzo, galga. **III.** a. peripuesto, acicalado; sano, firme.
trigeminal [traiʤéminæl], a. triple; relativo al trigémino.—**trigeminus** [-ʊs], s. (anat.) trigémino.
trigger [trígœr], s. (arm.) gatillo, disparador; pararruedas, calzo, galga.
triglyph [tráiglif], s. (arq.) triglifo.
trigon [tráigon], s. (geom., astr.), trígono.
trigonal [trígonal], a. triangular.
trigonometric(al [trígonométric(al], a. trigonométrico.—**t. function**, línea (mejor función, o razón) trigonométrica.—**trigonometrically** [-li], adv. trigonométricamente.
trigonometry [trígonómetri], s. trigonometría.
trihedral [traiídræl], a. triedro.—**t. angle**, triedro, ángulo triedro.—**trihedron** [-dron], s. triedro.
trilateral [trailǽtœral], a. trilátero, trilateral.
trilingual [trailíngual], a. trilingüe.
triliteral [trailítœral], a. trilítero.
trill [tril]. **I.** s. trino, gorjeo, gorgorito. **II.** vn. trinar, gorjear, gorgoritear; gotear.
trillion [tríliʊn], s. trillón (en Ingl. y Esp., la tercera potencia de un millón; en Fr. y E. U., un millón de millones).
trilobate(d [trailóubeite(ed], s. (pal.) trilobites. tres lobos.
trilobite [tráilobait], s. (pal.) trilobites.
trilocular [trailókiular], a. trilocular, de tres células o tres cavidades.
trilogy [tríloʏi], s. trilogía.
trim. **I.** a. ajustado, bien acondicionado; ataviado, acicalado. **II.** va. componer, arreglar, pulir, ajustar, adaptar; (carp.) alisar, desbastar, acepillar; podar, mondar; cortar ligeramente o un poco (cabellos, barba); despabilar (lámpara o vela); reponer (los carbones de una lámpara de arco); (cost.) adornar, guarnecer, franjear, pasamanar; afinar, igualar o equilibrar.—**to t. a ship**, (mar.) orientar un buque.—**to t. off**, recortar; atusar.—**to t. the hold**, abarrotar.—**to t. the sails**, orientar las velas.—**to t. up**, adornar, hermosear, componer. **III.** vn. vacilar, titubear entre dos partidos; nadar entre dos aguas; (mar.) estar bien equilibrado (buque). **IV.** s. atavío, adorno, aderezo, compostura; traje, vestido; estilo; condición, estado; buena condición, buen estado; guarnición, resguardo; disposición marinera de un buque, asiento.—**t. of the hold**, disposición de la estiva.—**t. of the sails**, (mar.) orientación de las velas.—**in (good) t.**, en buena condición, en buen estado; listo, preparado.
trimester [traiméstœr], s. trimestre.—**trimestr(i)al** [-tr(i)æl], trimestral.
trimeter [trímetœr], s. trímetro.
trimly [trím'li], adv. en regla.
trimmed [trimd], a. ataviado, adornado, guarnecido.
trimmer [trímœr], s. guarnecedor; contemporizador; (cost.) ribeteador; (min.) apilador de carbón, aparato para formar montones cónicos.
trimming [-ing], s. (cost.) guarnición, galón, alamar, franja, orla, adorno, pasamanería; desbastadura; ajuste; arreglo; poda.—pl. accesorios, piezas de adorno; arrequives.
trinal [tráinæl], a. trino.—**trine** [tráin]. **I.** a. triple; (astr.) trino. **II.** s. compuesto o reunión de tres elementos; (T-) Trinidad; (astr.) aspecto trino.
trinitarian [trinitérian], s. y a. trinitario.

trinitrocresol [traináitrocrísol], s. trinitrocresol.
—**trinitrophenol** [-fínol], s. ácido pícrico.—**trinitrotoluene** [-tóluin], **trinitrotoluol** [-ol], s. trinitrotolueno.
trinity [tríniti], s. trinidad.
tringle [tríngœl], s. vara de cortina; (arq.) listel.
trinket [trínket], s. dije, bujería, chuchería.
trinomial [trainómial]. **I.** a. (biol.) que tiene tres nombres; (álg.) trinomio. **II.** s. trinomio.
trio [trío, tráio], s. terno, terna; (mús.) trío, terceto.
triode [tráioud], s. (elec.) tubo de vacío con tres electrodos.
triones [traióniš], s. pl. (astr.) triones.
trioxid(e [traióxid, -aid], s. trióxido (apl. gen. a ciertos anhídridos: sulphur t., anhídrido sulfúrico).
trip. **I.** va. hacer caer a uno echándole la zancadilla; trompicar; armar un lazo o zancadilla; coger a uno en falta o cogerle un renuncio; bailar, mover los pies con ritmo; (mec.) soltar, disparar; desatar; (mar.) zarpar, levar anclas. **II.** vn. tropezar; equivocarse, cometer un desliz o descuido; (mar.) zarpar; correr, ir aprisa. **III.** s. viaje corto, excursión; tropiezo, traspié; desliz, paso falso; zancadilla; paso o movimiento ágil; (mar.) bordada.—**t. hammer**, martinete de fragua.
tripartite [trípartait o traipártait], a. tripartito.
tripe [traip], s. (coc.) tripas, callos, mondongo.
tripetalous [traipétalus], a. (bot.) tripétalo.
triphthong [trífzong], s. (gram.) triptongo.
triplane [traipléin], s. (aer.) triplano.
triple [trípœl]. **I.** a. triple, triplo. **II.** va. triplicar.—**t.-expansion**, de triple expansión.
triplet [tríplet], s. terno; cada uno de tres hermanos nacidos de un parto; (poét.) terceto, tercerilla; (mús.) tresillo.
triplex [tráiplex], a. tríplice.
triplicate [tríplikeit]. **I.** a. triplicado, triplo. **II.** s. tercera copia.
triplication [triplikéishʊn], s. acción de triplicar.
triplicity [traiplísiti], s. triplicidad.
triply [trípli], adv. por triplicado.
tripod [tráipod], s. trípode.
tripoli [trípoli], s. trípol (ll. t. t. stone).
Tripolitan [tripólitæn], s. y a. tripolitano.
tripper [trípœr], s. saltarín; disparador.
trippet [trípet], s. brazo, saliente, leva, uña.
tripping [tríping], s. tropezón, traspié; baile ligero.—**t. valve**, válvula de contacto.—**trippingly** [-li], adv. velozmente, con agilidad y ligereza.
triptych [tríptik], s. (b. a.) tríptico.
trireme [tráirrim], s. trirreme.
Trisagion [triséguion], s. trisagio.
trisect [traiséct], va. trisecar.
trisection [-sécshʊn], s. trisección.
trismus [trísmus], s. (med.) trismo, tétano de la mandíbula inferior.
trisulphid(e [traisúlfid, -aid], s. trisulfuro.
trisyllabic(al [traisilǽbic(al], a., **trisyllable** [traisílabœl o trisílabœl], s. trisílabo.
trite [tráit], a. traqueado, gastado, trillado; trivial vulgar.—**tritely** [-li], adv. vulgarmente; trilladamente.—**triteness** [-nes], s. vulgaridad, trivialidad, calidad de gastado o trillado.
tritheism [tráizeišm], s. triteísmo.
triton [tráiton], s. tritón; gasterópodo; lagartija acuática.
tritone [tráitoun], s. (mús.) trítono.
triturable [tritiurabœl], a. triturable.—**triturate** [-eit], va. triturar.—**trituration** [-éishʊn], s. trituración.
triumph [tráiʊmf]. **I.** s. triunfo, victoria. **II.** vn. triunfar; vencer, salir victorioso.
triumphal [traiʊmfal], a. triunfal.—**t. crown**, lauro.
triumphant [-ant], a. triunfante, victorioso.
triumphantly [-li], adv. triunfalmente, triunfantemente, en triunfo.
triumpher [tráiʊmfœr], s. triunfador.
triumvir [traiʊmvœr], s. triunviro.
triumvirate [-viret], s. triunvirato.
triune [tráiun], a. trino y uno.

trivet [trívet], *s.* trébedes, trípode.

trivial [trívial], *a.* trivial, frívolo.—**trivially** [-i], *adv.* frívola o trivialmente.—**triviality** [triviǽliti, **trivialness** [trívialnes], *s.* trivialidad.

trivium [trívium], *s.* trivio, las tres artes liberales.

triweekly [traiuíkli], *a.* que sucede tres veces por semana, o cada tres semanas.

trocar [trócar], *s.* (cir.) trocar.

trochaic(al [trokéic(al], *a.* trocaico.

trochanter [trociéntœr], *s.* (anat.) trocante; (ent.) segunda articulación de la pierna de un insecto.

troche [tróki], *s.* tablilla, trocisco.

trochee [tróki], *s.* (poét.) troqueo.

trochlea [tróclea], *s.* (anat.) troclea.

trochoid [trócoid]. **I.** *a.* que gira sobre su propio eje. **II.** *s.* trocoide.

trod, trodden, *pret. y pp.* de TO TREAD.—**trodden path,** camino trillado.

troglodyte [tróglodait], *s.* troglodita; mono antropoide; (orn.) troglodita.

trogon [trógon], *s.* (orn.) quetzal.

Trojan [tróyan], *a. y s.* troyano.

troll [tróul]. **I.** *va. y vn.* canturriar; pescar de un bote en movimiento, arrastrando el anzuelo; voltear, girar, rodar; andorrear, corretear. **II.** *s.* canción de varias estrofas; repetición, rutina; carrete de la caña de pescar; gnomo, enano.

trolley, trolly [tróli], *s.* (elec.) polea del trole; coche o tranvía de trole.—**t. car,** coche de tranvía de trole.—**t. line,** línea o sistema de tranvías de trole.—**t. pole,** trole; pértiga o vástago del trole (cuando, como sucede a menudo, *trole* se aplica al conjunto de vástago y polea).—**t. system,** sistema de trole.—**t. (wheel),** polea del trole.—**t. wire,** conductor o alimentador del trole; alambre de o para troles.

troll(e)yman [-mæn], *s.* conductor de tranvía de trole, motorista.

trolling [tróling], *s.* modo de pescar arrastrando el sedal y anzuelo casi a flor de agua desde un bote en movimiento.

trollop [trólop], *sf.* zangarilleja, gorrona.

trombone [trómboun], *s.* (mús.) trombón.

tromp(e [tromp], *s.* (fund.) trompa.

troop [trup]. **I.** *s.* tropa, cuadrilla; compañía (de actores); turba, caterva; (mil.) escuadrón de caballería.—*pl.* tropas, ejército. **II.** *vn.* atroparse, apiñarse, agavillarse, ir en tropel.—**to t. away,** o **off,** retirarse, marcharse en tropel.

trooper [trúpœr], *s.* soldado de caballería; corcel de guerra.

troopial [trúpial], *s.* (orn.) turpial, turicha.

Tropæolum [tropíolum], *s.,* **tropæolaceous** [-léi-shus], *a.* (bot.) tropéoleo.

trope [tróup], *s.* tropo, metáfora.

tropein(e [tropíin], *s.* (quím.) tropeína.

trophic(al [trófic, -æl], *a.* trófico, relativo a la nutrición.

trophied [trófid], *a.* adornado de trofeos.

trophy [trófi], *s.* trofeo.

tropic [trópic], *s.* trópico.

tropic(al [trópic(al], *a.* tropical; (ret.) trópico.

tropically [-i], *adv.* metafóricamente.

tropine [tróupin], *s.* (quím.) tropina.

tropism [tróupišm], *s.* (biol.) tropismo.

tropological [trópolóyical], *a.* tropológico.

tropology [tropóloyi], *s.* tropología.

trot. I. *va.* hacer trotar; pasar al trote. **II.** *vn.* trotar. **III.** *s.* trote; niñito.

troth [troz], *s.* verdad, fe, fidelidad; esponsales.—**in t.,** en verdad.

trotter [trótœr], *s.* trotón, trotador.

troubadour [trúbadur], *s.* trovador.

trouble [trúbœl]. **I.** *va.* turbar, perturbar; revolver, enturbiar; enfadar, hostigar, atribular; incomodar, molestar, importunar.—**to t. oneself,** molestarse, tomarse la molestia; inquietarse. **II.** *vn.* incomodarse, darse molestia, apurarse. **III.** *s.* turbación, perturbación, disturbio, inquietud; enfermedad, mal (*stomach trouble,* mal de estómago; *throat trouble,* enfermedad de la garganta); cuita, pena, congoja; disgusto, desavenencia; dificultad;

molestia, incomodidad, inconveniencia; impertinencia, engorro.—**to be in t.,** estar afligido; hallarse en un apuro.—**not to be worth the t.,** no valer la pena.

troubled [-d], *a.* afligido; inquieto, agitado; preocupado; en dificultades.—**t. waters,** aguas revueltas o agitadas.—**to be t. with,** sufrir de.

troubler [trúblœr], *s.* alborotador, perturbador.

troublesome [trúbœlsum], *a.* penoso, pesado, gravoso; importuno, enfadoso, impertinente; incómodo, fastidioso, dificultoso, molesto; querelloso, camorrero.

troublesomely [-li], *adv.* molestamente, enfadosamente.—**troublesomeness** [-nes], *s.* calidad de molesto, pesado, dificultoso.

troublous [trúblus], *a.* turbulento; confuso; inquieto, impaciente.

trough [trof], *s.* artesa, gamella, gamellón; dornajo, cubeta, batea; vivero; seno de dos olas; canal; canal invertida (para conductores eléctricos); (aer.) mínimo (de una depresión).

trounce [tráuns], *va.* (fam.) zurrar.

troupe [trup], *s.* (teat.) compañía.

trousers [tráušœrs], *s. pl.* pantalones.

trousering [tráušœring], *s.* géneros para pantalones.

trousseau [trusó], *s.* ajuar de novia.

trout [tráut], *s.* (ict.) trucha.

trover [tróuvœr], *s.* (for.) repetición.

trowel [tráuœl]. **I.** *s.* (alb.) llana, paleta; (agr.) desplantador. **II.** *va. y vn.* allanar, emparejar con la llana.

trowl [tróul], *v.* = TROLL.

troy [trói], **troy weight** [-uéit], *s.* peso troy, sistema de pesos cuya unidad es la libra de 5760 granos (0,37 kg.).

truancy [trúansi], *s.* briba, tuna.—**truant** [-ant] *s. y a.* novillero, tunante.

truce [trus], *s.* (mil.) tregua; suspensión.

truck [truc]. **I.** *va. y vn.* trocar, permutar, cambiar, traficar; acarrear, transportar en carretón. **II.** *s.* carro, carretón; camión; carretilla de mano; (f. c.) bogie, truck; (Ingl.) furgón de plataforma; (mar.) vertellos, bolas; efectos para vender o trocar; hortalizas para el mercado; (fam.) cosas sin valor, hojarasca, basura; cambio, permuta, trueque.—**t. mill** = FULLING MILL.

truckage [trúkey], *s.* carreteo, acarreo.

trucker [trúcœr], *s.* carretonero; verdulero.

truckle [trúcœl], *vn.* servir para ganar favores.

truckman [trúcman], *s.* carretero; verdulero; chamarilero.

truculence [trúkiulens], *s.* fiereza, crueldad.

truculent [-ent], *a.* truculento, feroz, cruel.

trudge [truy], *vn.* caminar con trabajo.

true [tru]. **I.** *a.* verdadero, cierto; ingenuo, sincero; verídico; exacto; justo, a plomo, a nivel, alineado, bien arreglado; genuino, puro, propio, natural; fiel, constante leal.—**t. bearing,** (top., mar.) rumbo relativo al meridiano astronómico.—**t. copy,** copia fiel.—**t. course,** (mar.) rumbo astronómico, o relativo al meridiano astronómico.—**t.-heartedness,** fidelidad, sinceridad.—**t. lover's knot,** nudo o lazo de perfecto amor.—**t. meridian,** meridiano astronómico (a distinción del magnético).—**t. time,** tiempo verdadero, tiempo solar verdadero.—**in t.,** alineado, exacto, bien arreglado.—**out of t.,** desarreglado, exacto, bien arreglado, desalineado, mal dispuesto. **II.** *adv.* exactamente, con verdad.—**t. blue,** leal, fiel.—**t.-born,** legítimo, verdadero; de nacimiento legítimo.—**t.-bred,** de casta o raza legítima.—**t.-hearted,** leal, sincero. **III.** *va.* (a veces con **up**) pulir, alisar, acabar; arreglar, corregir, rectificar.

trueness [trúnes], *s.* fidelidad; sinceridad; verdad; exactitud, arreglo perfecto.

truffle [trúfœl], *s.* (bot.) criadilla de tierra, trufa.

truism [trúišm], *s.* verdad trillada, vejez; (fam.) perogrullada.

trull [trul], *s.* perendeca, prostituta.

truly [trúli], *adv.* verdaderamente, en verdad; realmente, exactamente, con precisión; sinceramente, de buena fe.—**yours (very) t.,** su afectísimo, su seguro servidor.

trump [trʊmp]. **I.** *s.* triunfo, en juegos de naipes; (fam.) real mozo; birimbao.—**t. card,** naipe de triunfo (en el juego y fig.). **II.** *va.* (en los naipes) matar con un triunfo; engañar.—**to t. up,** forjar; inventar.

trumpery [trʊ́mpœri], *s.* hojarasca, oropel, relumbrón; cachivache, bujería, baratija; engaño, fraude.

trumpet [trʊ́mpet]. **I.** *s.* trompeta, clarín.—**t. blast,** trompetazo.—**t. creeper,** jazmín trompeta. —**t. honeysuckle,** madreselva.—**t. shell,** trompa o bocina marina.—**t.-tongued,** vocinglero.—**t. vine** = T. CREEPER. **II.** *va.* pregonar a son de trompeta, trompetear.

trumpeter [-œr], *s.* trompetero, trompeta; pregonero; (orn.) agamí; (ict.) trompa marina.

truncate [trʊ́nkeit], *va.* truncar.—**truncate(d** [-(ed], *a.* truncado.—**truncation** [-éiŝhʊn], *s.* truncamiento, tronca.

truncheon [trʊ́nchʊn o trʊ́nŝhʊn], *s.* tranca, garrote, porra, cachiporra, clava; bastón de mando; tronco sin ramas.

trundle [trʊ́ndœl]. **I.** *s.* rodaja.—**t.-bed,** carriola. **II.** *va.* y *vn.* rodar.

trundleshot [-ŝhót], *s.* (art.) palanquetas.

trundletail [téil], *s.* cola redonda.

trunk [trʊnk]. **I.** *s.* tronco (de árbol, del cuerpo, arterial); (ing.) línea principal (de un ferrocarril); tubería maestra o principal de abastecimiento, de alcantarillas, etc.), (en los dos últimos sentidos se dice gen. **t. line,** y en español se dice también *tronco* y *línea troncal*); baúl; (arq.) fuste (de columna); trompa (de elefante), pasaje; tolva; pozo, conducto (de ventilación, descarga, etc.); (m. v.) vástago anular de émbolo.—*pl.* calzones cortos de punto o de franela usados para baño, gimnasia, etc. (la Academia Española los llama *taparrabo*). **II.** *a.* troncal, del tronco; de la parte (vía, tubería, etc.) principal.—**t. engine,** (m. v.) máquina de vástago tubular.—**t. hose,** gregüescos. —**t. line.** *V.* TRUNK, s.—**t. sleeve,** manga corta ancha.

trunnel [trʊnel], *s.* = TREENAIL.

trunnion [trʊ́niʊn], *s.* (arti.) muñón.—**t. plates,** contramuñoneras.

truss [trʊs]. **I.** *s.* (cir.) braguero; armazón; armadura (de techo o tejado); viga de celosía o reticulada (de puente); (mar.) troza; (bot.) mazorca, racimo; haz, atado, lío, paquete; (Ingl.) 36 libras de paja o 60 de heno.—**t. beam,** viga armada o reforzada.—**t. bridge,** puente de vigas de celosía.—**t. girder,** viga de celosía. **II.** *va.* atirantar, apuntalar; armar; atrozar; (coc.) espetar.—**to t. up,** sofaldar; empaquetar, liar; ahorcar.

trussing [-ing], *s.* refuerzo, armadura; viga de celosía; piezas de una viga de celosía.

trusswork [-uœrc], *s.* entramado.

trust [trʊst]. **I.** *s.* confianza, fe (en una persona); (com.) crédito; (for.) fideicomiso, cargo, depósito; esperanza, expectación, creencia; (com.) trust, asociación de compañías industriales para fijar la producción, precio, etc., de un artículo, o para asumir la dirección y las ganancias de un negocio.—**T. Company,** banco de depósito.—**t. deed of sale,** (for.) escritura de venta condicionada.—**in t.,** en confianza; en depósito.—**on t.,** al fiado. **II.** *va.* y *vn.* confiar; tener confianza en o hacer confianza de; contar con; encargar y fiar; confiarse, fiarse; creer, dar crédito; vender al fiado; esperar.—**to t. to,** o **unto,** confiar en.

trustee [trʊstí], *s.* síndico, fideicomisario, fiduciario, depositario.

truster [trʊ́stœr], *s.* fiador.

trusteeship [trʊstíŝhip], *s.* cargo de fideicomisario.

trustful [trʊ́stful], *a.* confiado.—**trustfully** [-i], *adv.* confiadamente.—**trustfulness** [-nes], *s.* confianza plena.

trustily [trʊ́stili], *adv.* fielmente, lealmente, honradamente.—**trustiness** [-nes], *s.* fidelidad, probidad, integridad.

trustless [trʊ́stles], *a.* pérfido, que no merece confianza o crédito.

trustworthiness [trʊ́stuœrðines], *s.* confiabilidad, integridad, honradez.—**trustworthy** [-ði], *a.* fiable, confiable; fidedigno, seguro.

trusty [trʊ́sti], *a.* fiel, leal; íntegro; firme, fuerte, seguro.

truth [truz], *s.* verdad; fidelidad, constancia.—**of a t.,** o **in t.,** a la verdad, en verdad; en realidad, seriamente.

truthful [trʊ́zful], *a.* verídico, veraz; verdadero, exacto.—**truthfulness** [-nes], *s.* veracidad.

truthless [trʊ́zles], *a.* falso; fementido.

try [trái]. **I.** *va.* (*pret.* y *pp.* TRIED) probar, ensayar, tantear; procurar, tratar de, intentar; poner a prueba; exasperar, irritar; cansar; comprobar, (for.) procesar; ver (una causa o litigio); (metal.) purificar, refinar, afinar.—**to t. on,** probarse (ropa).—**to t. one's hand,** hacer uno la prueba.—**to t. one's luck,** probar fortuna.—**to t. out,** probar, someter a prueba. **II.** *vn.* probar, ensayar; procurar, hacer lo posible; (mar.) capear. **III.** *s.* prueba, ensayo.—**t. cock,** llave de purga.— **t.-square,** escuadra de comprobación.

trying [-ing], *a.* de prueba; molesto; exasperador, irritante; angustioso de tribulación, penoso.

tryout [-áut], *s.* prueba de la capacidad, eficacia o competencia de una persona o cosa.

trysail [-séil], *s.* vela mayor de capa.

tryst [trist o tráist]. **I.** *s.* cita o lugar de cita. **II.** *va.* y *vn.* dar una cita; acudir a una cita.

Tsar [sar], *s.* zar.

tsetse [tsétse], *s.* tsetsé.

tub [tʊb]. **I.** *s.* cuba, artesón, batea; tina; cubeta, tonel pequeño. **II.** *va.* encubar; entinar; bañar (a uno) en bañera. **III.** *vn.* bañarse en bañera.

tube [tiúb]. **I.** *s.* tubo; (anat.) conducto; tubo; túnel; ferrocarril subterráneo (ll. t. **t. railway).**— **t. saw,** sierra tubular. **II.** *va.* proveer de un tubo o de tubos.

tuber [tiúbœr], *s.* (bot.) tubérculo; (anat.) hinchazón, prominencia.

tubercle [tiúbœrcœl], *s.* tubérculo.

tubercular [tiubœrkiular], *a.*; **tuberculate** [-eit], *a.* tuberculoso.

tuberculation [-éiŝhʊn], *s.* tuberculización.

tuberculose [-lous], *a.* tuberculoso.

tuberculosis [tiubœrkiulósis], *s.* tuberculosis.

tuberculous [-lʊs], *a.* tuberculoso.

tuberose [tiúbœrous], *s.* (bot.) tuberosa.—**tuberosity** [-ósiti], *s.* tuberosidad.—**tuberous** [-ʊs], *a.* tuberoso.

tubiform [tiúbiform], *a.* tubiforme.

tubing [tiúbing], *s.* tubería; instalación de tubos, canalización; material para tubos.

tubular [tiúbiular], *a.* tubular.—**t. boiler,** caldera de tubos de humos, caldera multitubular.

tubulate [-leit], *va.* poner en tubos; dar forma de tubo a.—**tubulate(d** [-léit(ed], *a.* tubular.

tubule [tiúbiul], *s.* tubito.

tubuliflorous [-líflórʊs], *a.* (bot.) tubuliflоro.

tubulous [tiúbiulʊs], *a.* = TUBULATED.

tubulure [tiúbiuliúœr], *s.* tubo corto abierto de una retorta, recipiente, etc.

tuck [tʊc]. **I.** *s.* (cost.) alforza, recogido; (enc.) tapa con cartera; (mar.) falda, arca de popa. **II.** *va.* arremangar, recoger, asobarcar; arropar; (cost.) hacer alforzas.—**to t. up one's clothes,** arremangarse, sofaldar.

tucker [tʊ́cœr], *s.* (cost.) alforzador; camisolín, escote. **II.** *va.* (fam. E. U.) (con **out**) cansar, fatigar.

Tuesday [tiúŝde], *s.* martes.

tufa [tiúfa], *s.* tufa, toba.—**tufaceous** [tuféiŝhʊs], *a.* tobáceo.—**tuff** [tʊf], *s.* tufa.

tuft [tʊft]. **I.** *s.* copete, penacho, borla; manojo, ramillete; tupé, moño. **II.** *va.* empenachar; adornar con borlas.

tufted [tʊ́fted], *a.* copetudo, penachudo.

tufthunter [tʊ́ftjúnter], *s.* zalamero, adulón.

tufty [tʊ́fti], *a.* = TUFTED.

tug [tʊg]. **I.** *va.* tirar de; arrastrar; halar, remolcar. **II.** *vn.* luchar, esforzarse, tirar con fuerza. **III.** *s.* tirón, estirón.—**t. of war,** contienda de tiro de cuerda, en que los contincantes tiran de los extremos de una cuerda en direcciones opuestas; esfuerzo supremo.

tugboat [túgbóut], *s.* remolcador.

tugger [túgœr], *s.* el que da tirones.

tuille [tuíl], *s.* (arm.) faldar.

tuition [tuíshun], *s.* instrucción o enseñanza; precio de la enseñanza (gen. el que se paga por semestre, año, etc.).

tulip [tiúlip], *s.* (bot.) tulipán.—**t. tree**, (bot.) tulípero.

tulle [tul], *s.* (tej.) tul.

tumble [túmbœl]. **I.** *vn.* caer, dar en tierra; (gen. con **down**) desplomarse, venirse abajo; voltear, rodar, dar vueltas; dar saltos, brincar; volquearse, revolverse, revolcarse; (fam.) comprender, entender, caer en ello.—**to t. in** o **into bed**, (fam.) acostarse.—**to t. out**, (fam.) levantarse. **II.** *va.* revolver; tirar, arrojar (gen. con **over** o **about**) tumbar, derribar; volcar; desarreglar, trastornar; ajar o arrugar (la ropa); cazar al vuelo; pulir por fricción. **III.** *s.* tumbo, caída; vuelco, voltereta; desorden, confusión.

tumblebug [-búg], *s.* escarabajo pelotero.

tumble-down [-dáun], *a.* destartalado.

tumbler [túmblœr], *s.* vaso para beber; cortadillo; cubilete; volteador, saltabanco, titiritero; tentemozo, dominguillo; (mec.) tambor, tamborilete; (orn.) pichón volteador.—**t. of a lock**, rodete fiador (de cerradura).

tumbrel [túmbrel], *s.* (arti.) carro de artillería; chirrión, carreta.

tumefaction [tiúmefǽcshun], *s.* (med.) tumefacción, hinchazón.—**tumefy** [-fai], *va.* entumecer, hinchar.

tumid [tiúmid], *a.* túmido, hinchado; prominente, turgente; inflado.

tumidity, tumidness [tiumíditi, tiúmidnes], *s.* hinchazón; turgencia.

tumo(u)r [tiúmœr], *s.* (med.) tumor.

tumular [tiúmiular], *a.* abultado.

tumult [tiúmult], *s.* tumulto, alboroto, motín; conmoción; agitación.

tumultuarily [tiumúltiuarili], *adv.* tumultuariamente, desordenadamente.—**tumultuariness** [-nes], *s.* turbulencia.—**tumultuary** [-tiuari], *a.* tumultuario.

tumultuous [-tiuus], *a.* tumultuoso, alborotado.

tumultuously [-li], *adv.* tumultuosamente.

tumultuousness [-nes], *s.* turbulencia, tumulto.

tumulus [tiúmiulus], *s.* túmulo.

tun [tun], *s.* tonel, cuba; tanque de fermentación; cantidad de cerveza fermentada de una vez; tonelada (medida indeterminada).—**t. belly**, gran barriga. **II.** *va.* entonelar, envasar, embarrilar.

tuna [tiúnæ], *s.* (bot.) tuna, higo de tuna; (zool.) atún (ll. t. **t. fish**).

tunable [tiúnabœl], *a.* que se puede templar; cantable, armonioso, musical.

tune [tiún]. **I.** *s.* (mús.) tonada; tono; afinación, concordancia, armonía.—**in t.**, templado, afinado.—**out of t.**, destemplado, desafinado, desentonado. **II.** *va.* templar, afinar, acordar, entonar; ajustar, adaptar; (rad.) sintonizar.—**to t. out**, (rad.) excluir (señales, etc.) por sintonización apropiada, o sea, regulación debida del circuito receptor.—**to t. up**, (mec.) hacer funcionar por corto tiempo (una máquina, un automóvil) para poner en punto. **II.** *vn.* armonizar, modular; (rad.) (a veces con **in**) sintonizar el aparato receptor.

tuneful [-ful], *a.* armonioso, melodioso.

tuneless [-les], *a.* desentonado, disonante; mudo.

tuner [tiúnœr], *s.* afinador, templador.

tunic [tiúnic], *s.* túnica; túnico, blusa, ropón; (bot. y anat.) túnica.

Tunicata [tiunikéita], *s. pl.* tunicadas.

tunicate(d [-ed], *a.* (bot.) tunicado.

tunicle [tiúnicœl], *s.* túnica, tegumento; (igl.) tunicela.

tuning [tiúning]. **I.** *s.* afinación, templadura; (rad.) sintonización. **II.** *a.* de templar, de afinar; (rad.) sintonizador, de sintonización.—**t. coil**, (rad.) bobina de sintonización.—**t. fork**, diapasón.—**t. hammer, t. key**, llave de afinador.

tungstate [túngstet], *s.* tungstato.

tungsten [túngsten], *s.* (quím.) tungsteno, volframio.—**t. steel**, acero tungsténico.

tungstic [túnstic], *a.* (quím.) túngstico.

tungstite [-tait], *s.* (min.) tungstita, volframita.

tunnage [tœney], *s.* (Ingl.) tonelaje.

tunnel [túnel]. **I.** *s.* túnel; socavón; embudo; cañón de chimenea; (aer.) túnel de pruebas.—**t. net**, red abocinada. **II.** *va.* atravesar por túnel, construir un túnel a través de; horadar. **III.** *vn.* construir o abrir un túnel.—**tunnel(l)ing** [-ing], *s.* perforación; construcción de túneles o de un túnel o socavón.

tunny [túni], *s.* (ict.) atún.—**t. fishery**, almadraba.

tup [tup], *s.* morueco, carnero padre; cabeza del martinete.

tupelo [tiúpelo], *s.* (bot, E. U.) nisa.

Turanian [tiuréiniæn], *s.* y *a.* turanio.

turban [tœrban], *s.* turbante.

Turbelaria [tœrbelériæ], *s. pl.* (zool.) turbelarios.—**turbelarian** [-iæn], *a.* turbelario.

turbid [tœrbid], *a.* turbio, túrbido, espeso; zurrapiento; turbulento.

turbidity [tœrbíditi], **turbidness** [tœrbidnes], *s.* turbieza; turbulencia.

turbinal [tœrbinal], **turbinate(d** [-eit, -ted], *a.* en forma de peonza; espiral.

turbine [tœrbin], *s.* turbina (ll. t. **t. wheel**).

turbith [tœrbiz], *s.* = TURPETH.

turbot [tœrbot], *s.* (ict.) rodaballo.

turbulence, turbulency [tœrbiulens, -i], *s.* turbulencia.—**turbulent** [-ent], *a.* turbulento; levantisco, revoltoso.—**turbulently** [-li], *adv.* turbulentamente.

Turcoman, *s.* = TURKOMAN.

Turdidæ [tœrdidi], *s. pl.* (zool.) túrdidos.

Turdus [tœrdus], *s.* (orn.) género de los tordos.

tureen [tiurín], *s.* sopera, salsera.

turf [tœrf]. **I.** *s.* césped, tepe; turba; hipódromo; carreras de caballos, el hipódromo. **II.** *va.* encespedar.

turfiness [tœrfines], *s.* abundancia de césped o de turba.—**turfy** [-fi], *a.* encespedado; perteneciente a las carreras de caballos.—**t. ground**, cespedera.

turgescence, turgescency [tœryésens, -i], *s.* turgencia, hinchazón; engreimiento.

turgescent [-ent], *a.* turgente.

turgid [tœryid], *a.* turgente, hinchado; ampuloso, pomposo.—**turgidity** [tœryíditi], o **turgidness** [tœryídnes], *s.* turgencia, hinchazón.

Turk [tœrk], *s.* turco.—**T.'s head**, deshollinador.

turkey [tœrki], *s.* (orn.) pavo.—**t. buzzard**, aura, gallinazo.—**t. cock**, gallipavo.—**T. corn**, (bot.) maíz.—**t. gobbler**, pavo o guanajo.—**t. hen**, pava.—**t. millet**, alcandía.—**T. oak**, roble español.—**T. red**, carmesí.

Turkish [tœrkish], *a.* y *s.* turco.—**T. tobacco**, tabaco turco.—**T. towel(l)ing**, género de algodón grueso y velludo para toallas ásperas de baño.

turkois [tœrcois], *s.* = TURQUOISE

Turkoman [tœrkoman], *s.* turcomano.

turkscap [tœrcscæp], *s.* (bot.) martagón.

turmeric [tœrmeric], *s.* (bot.) cúrcuma.—**t. paper**, papel de cúrcuma.

turmoil [tœrmoil]. **I.** *s.* disturbio, tumulto, baraúnda, alboroto. **II.** *vn.* inquietarse, agitarse.

turn [tœrn], *va.* volver, voltear; dar vueltas a, hacer girar; marear; cambiar, transformar, convertir; tornear; volver del revés al derecho; revolver (en la mente); desviar; traducir; devolver, rechazar; doblar, dar la vuelta a; aplicar, destinar, adaptar; transferir; dar náusea.—**to t. a deaf ear to**, no dar oídos a, no hacer caso a o de.—**to t. adrift**, soltar o abandonar.—**to t. against**, predisponer en contra de; causar aversión a (contra).—**to t. an honest penny**, (fam.) ganar el dinero honradamente.—**to t. around**, volver, dar vuelta a.—**to t. (a person) around one's fingers**, tener (a una persona) de la ternilla, dominarla.—**to t. aside**, desviar; hacer a un lado.—**to t. away**, despedir, echar; desviar.—**to t. back**, volver atrás; devolver; restituir.—**to t. down**, piegar, doblar; poner boca abajo; bajar (el gas); (fam.) abandonar; rechazar; rehusar.—**to t. from**, desviar o alejar de.—**to t. in**, replegar; doblar hacia adentro; entregar.—**to t. into**, convertir en; cambiar en.—**to t. off**, despachar; desviar; cortar (el agua, el vapor); desconectar (el encendido, la lámpara, etc.); doblar; apartar; despedir; reducir torneando o en el torno; tornear.—**to t. off** (*the gas, water*), cerrar la llave (del gas, del agua).—**to t. off the light**, apagar la luz (volteando una llave).—**to t. on** (*water, steam*), abrir la llave (del agua, vapor); dar (vapor); echar (el agua); establecer (la corriente eléctrica); encender (la luz, volteando una llave).—**to t. one's back on**, voltear la espalda a. —**to t. one's coat**, cambiar de uniforme; pasarse al partido opuesto.—**to t. one's hand to**, dedicarse a, meter el hombro a.—**to t. out**, echar, expeler, arrojar; sacar hacia afuera; apagar; producir; volver al revés; doblar, torcer; echar al campo (los animales).—**to t. over**, transferir, pasar, trasladar; volver, invertir, volcar; revolver; doblar; abuñuelar (huevos).—**to t. over a new leaf**, enmendarse, empezar vida nueva.—**to t. tail**, volver la espalda, mostrar los talones.—**to t. the brain o the head of**, trastornar la cabeza o el juicio a; volver loco. —**to t. the cold shoulder to**, desairar, tratar con desprecio.—**to t. the flank of**, flanquear.—**to t. the scale**(s), cambiar el orden de cosas; determinar, decidir.—**to t. the stomach**, causar asco.—**to t. the tables**, cambiar la suerte; devolver la pelota.—**to t. to account, advantage, o profit**, sacar partido de, aprovechar.—**to t. up**, voltear, volver; levantar; cavar; arremangar.—**to t. up one's nose at**, mirar con desprecio, desdeñar.—**to t. up one's toes**, (fam.) lanzar el último suspiro, marcharse al otro mundo.—**to t. upside down**, trastornar; volver lo de arriba abajo; volcar.

turn, *vn.* girar, rodar, voltear, dar vueltas; torcer, seguir otra dirección; (mar.) virar; bornear; volverse, voltearse; convertirse en; hacerse, ponerse, volverse; mudar de posición, estado u opinión; desdecirse, cambiar de casaca; avinagrarse (vino), agriarse (leche).—**to t. about**, voltearse.—**to t. against**, volverse contra; coger aversión a.—**to t. aside**, desviarse, torcer.—**to t. away**, desviarse; alejarse.—**to t. back**, retroceder; volverse.—**to t. from**, apartarse de; huir de.—**to t. in**, guarecerse; entrar; llegar a casa.— **to t. into**, entrar en; transformarse, convertirse en.—**to t. off**, voltear, torcer; desviarse.—**to t. on**, depender de; volverse contra; acometer a.—**to t. out**, resultar; asistir; acudir; volverse o estar vuelto o dirigido hacia fuera; (fam.) salir de casa; levantarse.—**to t. over**, dar vueltas, revolverse; voltearse.—**to t. round**, cambiar de frente; voltearse, volverse; cambiar de opinión o partido.—**to t. short**, dar media vuelta.—**to t. to**, recurrir o acudir a; convertirse o transformarse en; redundar; dirigirse hacia.—**to t. turtle**, voltearse patas arriba.—**to t. up**, acontecer, suceder; aparecer.—**to t. upon**, estribar, depender de; recaer sobre.—**to t. upside down**, votearse patas arriba; zozobrar.— **my head turns (round)**, se me va la cabeza.— **please t. over (p. t. o.** en abreviatura), a la vuelta (de la página).

turn, *s.* vuelta, revolución; giro; rodeo, vuelta, recodo; turno, revezo, tanda; ocasión, oportunidad; fase, faz, aspecto; proceder, procedimiento, dirección; fase, faz, aspecto; proceder, procedimiento, comportamiento; partida o pasada (buena o mala) hecha a alguno; genio, inclinación o propensión, carácter; provecho, utilidad; forma, figura, hechura; giro de frase; vuelta, paseo corto, caminata. —**t. indicator**, (aer.) indicador de giro.—**t. of life**, menopausia.—**a friendly t.**, un favor.—**an ill t.**, una partida serrana.—**at every t.**, a cada instante, a cada momento.—**by turns**, por turnos. —**in t.**, a su turno, a su vez.—**to a t.**, exactamente, con absoluta perfección.—**to have a t. for**, ser aficionado a, tener aptitud para.—**to take turns**, turnarse.

turnbuckle [tǽrnbɔccœl], *s.* torniquete; tensor, templador; tarabilla.

turncoat [-cóut], *s.* (pol.) desertor, renegado, apóstata, tránsfuga.

turndown [-dáun], *a.* doblado hacia abajo, caído (cuello, etc.).

turner [-œr], *s.* tornero; gimnasta.—**t.'s lathe**, torno.

turnery [-œri], *s.* tornería.

turning [-ing]. **I.** *s.* vuelta, rodeo; recodo, ángulo; tornería; gimnasia.—*pl.* virutas que se hacen torneando. **II.** *a.* giratorio; de giro; de rotación.— **t. key**, llave de afinar.—**t. point**, punto decisivo, crisis; (top.) punto de cambio (en nivelación).—**t. radius**, radio de giro.

turnip [tǽrnip], *s.* (bot.) nabo.

turnkey [tǽrnki], *s.* llavero de una cárcel.

turnout [tǽrnaut], *s.* salida de personas a paseo; concurrencia; huelga de obreros; tren, séquito; carruaje de lujo; andén; (f. c.) apartadero, desviadero; producción de una fábrica en un tiempo determinado.

turnover [-óvœr]. **I.** *a.* doblado o vuelto hacia abajo. **II.** *s.* vuelco; vuelta, voltereta; pastelillo con repulgo; (coc.) estrelladera, pala; (e. p.) capital invertido transitoriamente, que debe reintegrarse antes de empezar a contar ganancias; cada una de las personas que se emplean durante períodos cortos para mantener un número constante de empleados; empleo parcial turnado.

turnpike [-páik], *s.* camino de portazgo; barrera de portazgo.—**t. road**, camino con portazgo.

turnplate [-pléit], *s.* = TURNTABLE.

turnscrew [tǽrnscrú], *s.* destornillador.

turnsole [-soul], *s.* heliotropo; girasol, mirasol.

turnspit [tǽrnspit], *s.* galopillo o perro que voltea el asador.

turnstile [tǽrnstail], *s.* torniquete.

turnstone [tǽrstoun], *s.* (orn.) revuelvepiedras.

turntable [tǽrntéibœl], *s.* (f. c.) placa giratoria; disco giratorio del microscopio.

turpentine [tǽrpentain], *s.* trementina.—**t. tree**, (bot.) terebinto.

turpeth [tǽrpez], *s.* turbit.—**t. mineral**, turbit mineral.

turpitude [tǽrpitiud], *s.* vileza, infamia; depravación.

turquoise [tœrcóis], *s.* turquesa.

turret [tǽrret], *s.* torrecilla; (mar.) torre blindada.

turreted [-ed], *a.* que tiene torre o figura de torre.

turtle [tǽrtœl], *s.* tortuga de mar; (impr.) bastidor cilindrado que sostiene el tipo en una prensa rotatoria.—**t. shell**, carey.

turtledove [-dúv], *s.* tórtola.

Tuscan [túscan], *a. y s.* toscano.

tush [tʌsh]. **I.** *s.* TUSK. **II.** *interj.* (ant.) ¡bah!

tusk [tʌsk], *s.* colmillo (de elefante, jabalí, foca)

tusked, tusky [-skt, -ki], *a.* colmilludo, que tiene colmillos.

tussis [túsis], *s.* tos.

tussle [tʌsœl]. **I.** *va. y vn.* (fam.) tener una agarrada. **II.** *s.* sarracina, agarrada, pelea.

tussock [tʌsoc], *s.* montecillo de hierbas crecientes; penacho, copete.

tut [tʌt], *interj.* ¡tate! ¡basta!

tutelage [tiútelœy], *s.* tutela, tutoría.

tutelar, tutelary [tiútelar, -leri], *a.* tutelar.—**t. angel**, ángel de la guardia.—**t. saint**, santo patrón.

tutor [tiútœr]. **I.** *s.* tutor, ayo, preceptor; (for.) curador. **II.** *va.* enseñar, instruir; (for.) ser curador de.

tutorage [-ey], *s.* tutoría, tutela; (for.) curaduría.

tutoress [-es], *s.* tutora, tutriz, aya.

tutti-frutti [túti frúti]. **I.** *s.* tutifruti, dulce o confitura de varias clases de frutas. **II.** *a.* compuesto de frutas de varias clases.

tutty [túti], *s.* tucía, atutía, cadmia.

tuwhit, tuwhoo [tujuít, tujú]. **I.** *vn.* gritar (el buho). **II.** *s.* grito del buho.

tuxedo [tʌxído], *s. smoking*, saco abierto de ceremonia.

tuyère [tuyéœr], *s.* alcribís, tobera.

twaddle [tuódœl]. **I.** *va. y vn.* charlar, parlotear. **II.** *s.* habladuría, charla; tonterías, disparates.

twain [tuéin]. **I.** *a.* dos. **II.** *s.* un par.

twang [tuéng]. **I.** *va. y vn.* producir un sonido vibrante; puntear las cuerdas de un instrumento; hablar por la nariz. **II.** *s.* punteato de una cuerda; tonillo nasal.

'twas [tuós], *contr.* de IT WAS, fué.

tweak [tuíc]. **I.** *va.* pellizcar retorciendo. **II.** *s.* pellizco retorcido.

tweed [tuíd]. **I.** *s.* (tej.) paño de lana de dos colores. **II.** *a.* hecho de este paño.

tweedle [tuídœl]. **I.** *va.* manosear, jugar con. **II.** *s.* sonido del violín.—**tweedledum** [-dŭm] **and tweedledee** [-dî], fo o fa.

'tween [tuín], *prep. contr.* de BETWEEN, entre.

tweeze, tweese [tuís], *s.* estuche de cirugía.—*pl.* pinzas.

tweezers [tuísœrs], *s. pl.* tenacillas, pinzas, despinzas.

twelfth [tuelfz]. **I.** *a.* duodécimo, doceno; doce (ordinal).—**T.-day** = TWELFTIDE.—**T.-night**, víspera del día de los Reyes. **II.** *s.* y *a.* dozavo; (mús.) duodécima.—**twelfthtide** [-táid], *s.* día de los Reyes, Epifanía.

twelve [tuélv], *a.* y *s.* doce.

twelvemo [tuélvmo], *a.* y *s.* (enc.) duodécimo.

twelvemonth [-monz], *s.* un año, o doce meses.

twentieth [tuéntiez]. **I.** *a.* vigésimo, veinte (ordinal). **II.** *s.* y *a.* veintavo.

twenty [tuénti], *a.* y *s.* veinte.

'twere [tuœr], *contr.* de IT WERE, fuese, estuviese, fuera, sería.

twibil [tuáibil], *s.* hacha de dos filos.

twice [tuáis], *adv.* dos veces; doble.—**t.-told**, repetido.

twiddle [tuídœl]. **I.** *va.* (fam.) jugar con; hacer girar. **II.** *vn.* girar. **III.** *s.* vuelta.

twig [tuíg]. **I.** *s.* ramita, vástago; varilla; (elec.) ramal, derivación. **II.** *va.* zurrar con una ramita.

twilight [tuáilait]. **I.** *s.* crepúsculo, nochecita.—**by t.**, entre dos luces. **II.** *a.* obscuro, sombrío, crepuscular.

twill [tuíl]. **I.** *va.* (tej.) cruzar, asargar.—**twilled silk**, tela cruzada de seda. **II.** *s.* tela cruzada o asargada.

twin [tuín]. **I.** *s.* y *a.* gemelo, mellizo.—**t. brother, sister**, hermano, hermana gemelos.—**T. Brothers**, o **Brethren**, Cástor y Pólux.—**t.-cylinder**, (m. v.) de cilindros gemelos.—**t. engine**, (m. v.) máquina de cilindros gemelos.—**Twins**, (astr.) Géminis.—**t.-screw**, de dos hélices (buque). —**t. tires**, (aut.) llantas gemelas. **II.** *vn.* nacer mellizo; aparearse; parir mellizos.

twinborn [-born], *a.* mellizo, gemelo.

twine [tuáin]. **I.** *va.* torcer; retorcer, enroscar; acordonar. **II.** *vn.* enroscarse, ensortijarse; caracolear.—**to t. about**, abrazar. **III.** *s.* hilo de bramante, guita; enroscadura, abrazo.

twinge [tuíny]. **I.** *va.* y *vn.* causar o sentir un dolor agudo; atormentar; sufrir. **II.** *s.* dolor agudo, punzada; remordimiento.

twinkle [tuínkœl], *va.* y *vn.* centellear, chispear, destellar, rutilar; parpadear, pestañear.

twinkle, twinkling [tuínkœl, -cling], *s.* titilación, centelleo; pestañeo, guiñada; momento, instante.—**in the twinkling of an eye**, en un abrir y cerrar de ojos.

twirl [tuœrl]. **I.** *va.* y *vn.* girar, hacer girar; dar vueltas. **II.** *s.* rotación, vuelta, giro; rasgueo.

twist [tuíst]. **I.** *va.* torcer, retorcer, enroscar, entrelazar, entretejer, arrollar, enrollar; virar, doblar, doblegar; trenzar; ceñir, bornear, rodear. **II.** *vn.* enroscarse, envolverse, torcerse; virarse; encarrujarse, ensortijarse; serpentear; caracolear. **III.** *s.* torsión, torcedura, enroscadura; tirón, sacudida; cordoncillo, torzal; peculiaridad, rasgo característico; contorsión, quiebro; rosca de pan; rollo de tabaco; en baseball, efecto dado a la pelota.—**t. drill**, barrena salomónica.

twister [-œr], *s.* torcedor; cordelero, soguero, cabestrero, guitero; torcedera; (mar.) torbellino, viento giratorio; (E. U.) ciclón; (dep.) pelota arrojada con efecto.

twit [tuít], *va.* machacar, remachar, reprender.

twitch [tuích]. **I.** *va.* tirar bruscamente. **II.** *vn.* crisparse, convelerse, contorcerse. **III.** *s.* crispatura; tirón, sacudida; contracción nerviosa; (equi.) acial.—**t. grass**, (bot.) cantinodia, sanguinaria.

twitter [tuítœr]. **I.** *vn.* gorjear los pájaros. **II.** *s.* gorjeo (de los pájaros); (fam.) agitación, inquietud.

'twixt [tuicst], *contr.* de BETWIXT.

two [tu]. **I.** *s.* y *a.* dos.—**t. and t.**, dos a dos.—**in t.**, en dos (partes o pedazos). **II.** *a.* de dos. En esta acepción modifica a muchos substantivos y adjetivos y participios derivados de substantivos, indicando siempre la existencia de dos de las partes que el substantivo denota, como en *two-volume*, de dos volúmenes; *two-cylinder*, de dos cilindros; *two-headed*, de dos cabezas; *two-centered*, de dos centros; *two-barreled*, de dos cañones.—**t.-beat valve**, válvula de campana.—**t.-cleft**, bífido, hendido en dos.—**t.-colo(u)r**, bicromático, relativo a la bicromía; de dos colores.—**t.-deck**, de dos puentes. —**t.-decker**, barco de dos puentes.—**t.-edged**, de dos filos.—**t.-faced**, de dos caras; doble, disimulado.—**t.-feeder**, (imp.) alimentada por dos personas (prensa).—**t.-foot rule**, regla de dos pies de largo.—**t.-handed**, de o para dos manos; ambidextro.—**t.-handed sword**, espadón.—**t.-horse**, de dos caballos.—**t.-legged**, de dos patas o pies; bípedo.—**t.-masted**, de dos palos o mástiles.—**t.-motor**, bimotor.—**t.-phase**, (elec.) bifásico.—**t.-ply**, de dos tramas; de dos capas; de dos hilos.—**t.-range transmission**, (aut.) cambio de marcha de doble reducción.—**t.-sided**, de dos lados; de dos caras, falso.—**t.-step**, galop, paso doble.—**t.-throw**, de dos direcciones (interruptor, etc.).—**t.-throw crankshaft**, cigüeñal de dos codos.—**t.-tongued**, falso, doble.—**t.-way valve**, válvula de dos direcciones o vías.—**t.-wire** (elec.) bifilar (sistema, distribución, etc.); de o para dos conductores.

twofold [túfould]. **I.** *a.* doble; duplicado; de dos clases o aspectos. **II.** *adv.* duplicadamente, al doble.

twopence [túpens], *s.* moneda de dos peniques.

twopenny [túpeni], *a.* del valor de dos peniques; despreciable.

tycoon [taicún], *s.* = SHOGUN.

tying [táiing], *gerund.* de TO TIE.

tympan [tímpan], *s.* (impr.) tímpano; (anat.) membrana; (arq.) tímpano.

tympanic [timpénic], *a.* (anat.) timpánico.—**t. membrane**, tímpano.

tympanites [tímpanáitis], *s.* timpanitis.

tympanum [tímpanum], *s.* (anat.) tímpano; (bot.) timpanillo; (arq.) tímpano, tímpano, faldón.

type [táip]. **I.** *s.* tipo; símbolo, signo, emblema; ejemplar distintivo; (impr.) tipo; (biol.) tipo, modelo.—**t. bar**, línea de tipos que se funde en una sola pieza.—**t. founder**, fundidor de letras de imprenta.—**t. foundry**, fundición de tipos.—**t. measure**, regla, tipómetro.—**t. metal**, metal de imprenta.—**t. wheel**, rueda tipográfica. **II.** *va.* y *vn.* mecanografiar, escribir en máquina.

typewrite [táiprráit], *va.* y *vn.* (*pp.* TYPEWRITTEN) mecanografiar escribir a máquina.

typewriter [táiprráitœr], *s.* mecanógrafo, escribiente a máquina; máquina de escribir.

typewriting [táiprráiting], *s.* arte de usar una máquina de escribir; trabajo hecho con dicha máquina.

typhoid [táifoid]. **I.** *a.* tifoideo.—**t. fever**, fiebre tifoidea. **II.** *s.* fiebre tifoidea.

typhoon [taifún], *s.* tifón.

typhous [táifus], *s.* tífico.

typhus [táifus], *s.* (med.) tifo (ll. t. **t. fever**).

typical [típical], *a.* típico; característico, regular.

typically [-i], *adv.* de modo típico o característico.

typicalness [-nes], *s.* representación figurativa o simbólica.

typify [típifai], *va.* representar, simbolizar, ser ejemplo de.

typist [táipist], *s.* mecanógrafo.

typographer [taipógrafœr], *s.* tipógrafo.

typographic(al [táipográfic(al], *a.* tipográfico.

typographically [-i], *adv.* tipográficamente.

typography [taipógrafi], *s.* tipografía.

typesetter [táipsétœr], *s.* máquina para componer tipos; (impr.) cajista.—**typesetting** [-ting], (imp.) composición (de tipo); tipografía.

Para la pronunciación de æ, œ, ḍ, ś, ŝh, u, ȳ, y, z, véase la clave al principio del libro.

typhlitis [tifláitis], s. tiflitis, inflamación del intestino ciego.

typhology [tifóloyi], s. (med.) ciencia de la ceguera.

typoscript [táiposcript], s. trabajo mecanográfico.

tyrannic(al [tairénic(al], **tyrannous** [tíranʊs], a. tiránico.—**tyrannically** [-i], **tyrannously** [-li], adv. tiránicamente.—**tyrannicide** [tairénisaid], s. tiranicidio; tiranicida.—**tyrannize** [tíranaiš], va. y vn. tiranizar.

tyranny [tírani], s. tiranía.

tyrant [táirant], s. tirano.

Tyrian [tírian], a. y s. tirio.—**T. dye,** púrpura de Tiro, múrice.

tyro [táiro], s. tirón, bisoño, novicio, novato.

Tyrolese [tírolis], **Tyrolian** [tirólian], a. y s. tirolés, del Tirol.

Tyrrhenian [tirínian], a. tirreno; etrusco.

tythe, s. y a. = TITHE.

Tzar, Tzarina, s. = CZAR, CZARINA.

tzetze, s. = TSETSE.

U

u [yu], s. u.

U [yu], **U-shaped** [-shéipt], a. en U, en forma de U (*U iron,* hierro en U; *U tube,* tubo en U; *U hanger,* barra de suspensión en U).—**U-boat,** submarino. (Llámase así a causa de la inicial *U* del nombre alemán).

ubiquitarian [yubícuitérian], a. y s. ubiquitario.

ubiquitous, ubiquitary [-tʊs, -teri]. **I.** a. ubicuo, omnipresente. **II.** s. ubiquitario.

ubiquity [-ti], s. ubicuidad, omnipresencia.

udder [údœr], s. ubre, teta.

udometer [yudómeter], s. udómetro o pluviómetro.

ugh! [yu], *interj.* ¡puf! ¡uf! ¡fo!

uglily [úglili], adv. feamente; perversamente; con mal genio.—**ugliness** [-nes], s. fealdad; fiereza; perversidad; (E. U.) mal genio.

ugly [úgli], a. feo, malparecido; asqueroso, repugnante; perverso, endiablado; fiero, feroz; malcarado, insolente, de mal genio, rudo.

uhlan [úlan], s. (mil.) ulano.

uintahite [yuíntæait], s. asfalto de Utah.

ukase [yukéis], s. ucase.

Ukrainian [yucréinian], s. y a. ucranio.

ulcer [úlscer], s. úlcera.—**ulcerate** [-eit], va. y vn. ulcerar(se).—**ulceration** [-éishʊn], s. ulceración.—**ulcerous** [-ʊs], a. ulceroso.

ulema [úlemá], s. concilio de los ulemas.

uliginous [yulíyinʊs], a. lagunero.

ullage [úley], s. merma de un tonel.

ulmaceous [ʊlméshʊs], a. (bot.) ulmáceo.

ulna [úlna], s. (anat.) cúbito.—**ulnar** [-ar], a. cubital.

ulster [úlstœr], s. levitón ruso.

ulterior [ʊltíriœr], a. ulterior.

ultima [última], s. última sílaba.

ultimate [últimeit], a. ultimo, final; fundamental, esencial; primario.—**ultimately** [-li], adv. últimamente, en su esencia; finalmente, al fin.

ultimatum [últiméitʊm], s. ultimátum.

ultimo [último], adv. del mes próximo pasado (abr. **ult.**).

ultimogeniture [últimoyénichœr], s. ultimogenitura, precedencia del hijo menor (opuesto a primogenitura).

ultra- [últra]. **I.** *prefijo* (lat.) mas allá o además. **II.** a. exagerado, extremo. **III.** s. *V.* ULTRAIST.

ultraism [últraišm], s. ultraísmo, exageración en las opiniones.

ultraist [últraist], s. ultraísta, exaltado, el que es exagerado en sus creencias.

ultramarine [últramarín]. **I.** a. ultramarino. **II.** s. azul formado del lapislázuli.

ultramicroscope [-máicroscoup], s. ultramicroscopio.

ultramicroscopic [-cópic], a. ultramicroscópico, invisible con el microscopio ordinario; relativo al ultramicroscopio.

Ultramontane [-móntein], s. y a. ultramontano; ultracatólico.—**Ultramontanism** [-móntanišm], s. ultramontanismo.

ultramundane [-múnden], a. ultramundano.

ultraudion [ʊltródion], s. (rad.) especie de regenerador o amplificador para grandes distancias.

ultraviolet [-váiolet], a. (fís.) ultraviolado.

ululant [úliulænt], a. ululante.—**ululate** [-eit], vn. ulular.—**ululation** [-éishʊn], s. ululato.

umbel [úmbœl], s. (bot.) umbela.

umbellate(d [-eit(ed], **umbelliferous** [-ífœrʊs], a. (bot.) umbelífero, aparasolado.

umber [úmbœr]. **I.** s. (pint.) tierra de sombra; sombra. **II.** a. pardo obscuro. **III.** va. sombrear.

umbilic [ʊmbílic]. **I.** a. umbilical. **II.** s. ombligo.

umbilical [-cal], a. umbilical; central; descendiente por parte de madre.

umbilicus [ʊmbiláicʊs], s. ombligo.

umbo [úmbo], s. cazoleta de broquel.

umbra [úmbra], s. (astr.) sombra.

umbrage [úmbrey], s. pique, resentimiento; sombra, umbría; sombrajo.

umbrageous [ʊmbréyʊs], a. sombrío, umbroso, umbrío, umbrático.—**umbrageousness** [-nes], s. umbría, sombra, umbrosidad.

umbrella [ʊmbrélæ], s. paraguas; parasol, sombrilla; (zool.) concha de los umbrélidos; (U-, zool.) umbrela.—**u. shell,** (zool.) umbrélido y su concha.—**u. stand,** paragüero.

umlaut [úmlaut], s. diéresis; cambio de sonido indicado por la diéresis.

umpirage [úmpirex], s. arbitraje, arbitramento, tercería.

umpire [úmpaiœr]. **I.** s. árbitro, arbitrador; tercero en discordia, compromisario o secuestro. **II.** va. y vn. arbitrar.

un- [ʊn], *prefijo* que denota negación, oposición, contrariedad o privación, y corresponde gen. a no, sin, des-, o in-. Anteponiéndolo a un infinitivo, participio, gerundio, substantivo, adjetivo o adverbio, se forman gran número de voces, muchas de las cuales no están en los diccionarios, por ser obvio su significado, dado el carácter negativo del prefijo.

unabased [-unabéist], a. no envilecido.

unabashed [unabǽsht], a. descocado.

unabated [unabéited], a. completo, cabal.

unabbreviated [unabríveieted], **unabridged** [unabríyd], a. íntegro, completo, sin abreviar.

unable [unéibœl], a. inhábil, incapaz, impotente; imposibilitado.—**to be u.,** no poder, serle a uno imposible.

unabsolved [unæbsólvd], a. no absuelto.

unaccented [unæccénted], a. sin acento.

unacceptable [unæcséptabœl], a. inaceptable.

unaccessible [unæcsésibœl], a. inaccesible.

unaccompanied [unæcúmpanid], a. solo, sin acompañamiento.

unaccomplished [unæcúmplisht], a. incompleto, no acabado; falto de prendas o gracias.

unaccountable [unæcáuntabœl], a. inexplicable, extraño; irresponsable.—**unaccountably** [-bli], adv. extraña o inexplicablemente; irresponsablemente.

unaccustomed [unæcústumd], a. desacostumbrado, insólito, inhabituado.

unacknowledged [unæcnóleyd], a. no reconocido; no declarado; por contestar.

unacquainted [unæcuéinted], a. desconocido, ignorado, extraño.—**to be u. with,** no conocer, ignorar.

unadjusted [unædyústed], a. no ajustado; no regulado o arreglado.

unadorned [unadórnd], a. llano, liso, simple, sin adorno.

unadulterated [unadúltereited], a. genuino, puro; natural, sin mezcla.

unadvisable [-adváisabœl], a. poco cuerdo, no prudente o conveniente.—**unadvised** [-váisd], a. inconsiderado; desatentado.—**unadvisedly** [-váisedli], adv. imprudentemente, desacordadamente.

---

unaffected [ʊnæfécted], *a.* inafectado, franco, natural; impasible.—**unaffectedly** [-li], *adv.* naturalmente, sin afectación.—**unaffectedness** [-nes], *s.* sencillez, lisura, naturalidad.

unaided [ʊnéided], *a.* sin ayuda.

unallowable [ʊnæláuabœl], *a.* inadmisible; no permisible.

unalloyed [ʊnælóid], *a.* puro, sin mezcla.

unalterable [ʊnóltœrabœl], *a.* inalterable; invariable, inmutable.—**unalterably** [-bli], *adv.* inalterablemente.

un-American [ʊn-américan], *a.* contrario al espíritu o a las instituciones norteamericanos.

unanimity [yúnanímiti], *s.* unanimidad.

unanimous [yunǽnimʊs], *a.* unánime.

unanimously [-li], *adv.* unánimemente.

unanimousness [-nes], *s.* unanimidad.

unannealed [ʊnæníld], *a.* no recocido.

unanswerable [ʊnǽnsœrabœl], *a.* incontrovertible, incontestable.

unanswerably [-bli], *adv.* indisputablemente.

unanswered [ʊnǽnscœrd], *a.* por contestar, no contestado; no correspondido.

unappealable [ʊnapílabœl], *a.* inapelable.

unapprehensive [ʊnaprejénsiv], *a.* incauto, sencillo; lerdo, torpe.

unapproachable [ʊnapróchabœl], *a.* inaccesible.

unapproachableness [-nes], *s.* inaccesibilidad.

unappropirate(d [ʊnaprópriet(ed], *a.* no concedido; libre; baldío.

unapproved [ʊnaprúvd], *a.* desaprobado.

unapt [ʊnǽpt], *a.* poco inclinado, poco propenso; inepto, inhábil; lerdo.—**unaptly** [-li], *adv.* ineptamente.—**unaptness** [-nes], *s.* ineptitud.

unarmed [ʊnármd], *a.* desarmado, indefenso; (zool. y bot.) inerme.

unartistic [ʊnartístic], *a.* inartístico.

unasked [ʊnáskt], *a.* no solicitado, espontáneo; no llamado; no convidado, sin convidar.

unaspirated [ʊnǽspireited], *a.* no aspirado.

unassailable [ʊnæséilabœl], *a.* inexpugnable.

unassignable [ʊnæsáinabœl], *a.* intransferible.

unassuming [ʊnæsiúming], *a.* modesto.

unattached [ʊnatǽcht], *a.* suelto, despegado; libre; (for.) no embargado; (mil.) de reemplazo.

unattainable [ʊnatéinabœl], *a.* inaseguible.

unattempted [ʊnatémpted], *a.* no experimentado, no ensayado, no intentado.

unattended [ʊnaténded], *a.* solo.

unattractive [ʊnatrǽctiv], *a.* inatractivo.

unau [yúno], *s.* (zool.) perezoso del Brasil.

unauthorized, unauthorised [ʊnózoraisd], *a.* no autorizado, desautorizado.

unavailable, unavailing [ʊnavéilabœl, -ling], *a.* inaprovechable, inadaptable; inútil, vano, ineficaz.

unavoidable [ʊnavóidabœl], *a.* inevitable.

unavoidableness [-nes], *s.* inevitabilidad.

unavoidably [-bli], *adv.* inevitablemente.

unaware [ʊnauéær], *a.* que ignora o no tiene conocimiento (de).

unaware(s [ʊnauéær(s], *adv.* inopinadamente, repentinamente, de improviso; sin pensar, inadvertidamente.

unbacked [ʊnbéct], *a.* sin ayuda, sin apoyo (rentístico); sin respaldo; cerril.

unbalance [ʊnbǽlæns], *va.* desequilibrar; trastornar.—**unbalanced** [-t], *a.* desequilibrado; chiflado, destornillado; (com.) no balanceado.

unballast [ʊnbǽlast], *va.* deslastrar.

unbaptized [ʊnbǽptaisd], *a.* no bautizado; no cristiano.

unbar [ʊnbár], *va.* desatrancar.

unbarrel [ʊnbérel], *va.* desembarrilar.

unbearable [ʊnbéærabœl], *a.* intolerable, insufrible, inaguantable.

unbeaten [ʊnbítœn], *a.* no pisado, no frecuentado; no batido; invicto.

unbecoming [ʊnbicúming], *a.* indecoroso; impropio; que sienta mal.—**unbecomingly** [-li], *adv.* indecorosamente; impropiamente.

unbeknown [ʊnbinóun]. **I.** *a.* (fam.) no conocido, no sabido. **II.** *adv.* (fam.) sin conocimiento (de otro), por o de sorpresa.

unbelief [ʊnbilíf], *s.* incredulidad, descreimiento; irreligión.

unbeliever [ʊnbilívœr], *s.* incrédulo, descreído.

unbend [ʊnbénd]. **I.** *va.* (prɛt. y *pp.* UNBENT o UNBENDED) enderezar, desencorvar; aflojar, zafar, soltar; descansar, solazarse; (mar.) desenvergar (las velas). **II.** *vn.* enderezarse; condescender, ceder; ponerse afable.

unbending [-ing], *a.* inflexible.

unbias(s)ed [ʊnbáiast], *a.* imparcial.

unbid(den [ʊnbíd(œn], *a.* no invitado; espontáneo, no pedido o solicitado.

unbind [ʊnbáind], *va.* (pret. y *pp.* UNBOUND) desligar, desatar, desamarrar; desvendar.

unbleached [ʊnblícht], *a.* crudo, sin blanquear.

unblemished [ʊnblémisht], *a.* puro, sin mancha.

unbolt [ʊnbóult], *va.* desbarretar, desempernar.—**unbolted** [-ed], *a.* desempernado; sin cerner.

unborn [ʊnbórn], *a.* innato; no nacido aún, venidero.

unbosom [ʊnbúsʊm], *va.* mostrar (uno) su corazón; desahogarse de, confesar.

unbottomed [ʊnbótʊmd], *a.* insondable; infundado; sin fondo.

unbound [ʊnbáund], *a.* no encuadernado; suelto, desatado.

unbounded [-ed], *a.* infinito, ilimitado.

unbrace [ʊnbrés], *va.* aflojar, soltar, desabrochar; desasegurar.

unbraid [ʊnbréid], *va.* destejer, destrenzar.

unbreakable [ʊnbréicabœl], *a.* irrompible; impenetrable.

unbreathed [ʊnbríꝺd], *a.* no comunicado a nadie.

unbred [ʊnbréd], *a.* malcriado.

unbridled [ʊnbráidœld], *a.* desenfrenado, licencioso, irrefrenable.

unbroken [ʊnbróukœn], *a.* intacto, entero; inviolado; parejo; no interrumpido; indómito, cerril.

unbuckle [ʊnbúcœl], *va.* deshebillar.

unburden [ʊnbérdœn], *va.* descargar; aliviar.

unburied [ʊnbérid], *a.* insepulto.

unburned, unburnt [ʊnbœrnt], *a.* no cocido; incombusto.—**u. brick,** adobe.

unbusinesslike [ʊnbísneslaik], *a.* contrario a la práctica mercantil; informal; inexperto en los negocios.

unbutton [ʊnbútœn], *va.* desabotonar, desabrochar.

uncalled [ʊncóld], *a.* no llamado, no pedido.—**u. for,** inmerecido, innecesario, gratuito.

uncancelled [ʊncænseld], *a.* sin cancelar; no anulado, no rescindido.

uncanny [ʊncǽni], *a.* misterioso, pavoroso; inhábil, incauto; poco seguro; severo.

uncap [ʊncǽp]. **I.** *va.* destapar; quitar el casquillo de un fusil. **II.** *vn.* descubrirse para saludar.

uncared [ʊnkéærd], *a.* (con **for**) desamparado, descuidado, abandonado.

uncase [ʊnkéis], *va.* desenvainar; (mil.) desplegar (la bandera); revelar.

unceasing [ʊnsísing], *a.* incesante.

unceasingly [-li], *adv.* sin cesar, incesantemente.

unceremonious [ʊnséremoniʊs], *a.* familiar, llano, de confianza, inceremonioso.

uncertain [ʊnsértœn], *a.* incierto; perplejo, irresoluto, indeciso.—**uncertainly** [-li], *adv.* inciertamente.—**uncertainty** [-ti], *s.* incertidumbre; (lo) incierto; irresolución; instabilidad, inseguridad.

unchain [ʊnchéin], *va.* desencadenar.

unchangeable [ʊnchéinyabœl], *a.* inalterable, invariable, inmutable· igual.—**unchangeableness** [-nes], *s.* inmutabilidad o invariabilidad.—**unchangeably** [-bli], *adv.* inmutablemente, invariablemente.—**unchanged** [ʊnchéinyd], *a.* inalterado.—**unchanging** [-ing], *a.* inalterable, inmutable, uniforme.

uncharitable [ʊnchǽritabœl], *a.* falto de benevolencia, duro.—**uncharitableness** [-nes], *s.* falto de benevolencia, dureza.—**uncharitably** [-bli], *adv.* sin benevolencia, duramente.

unchaste [ʊnchéist], *a.* incasto.—**unchastity** [ʊnchǽstiti], *s.* incontinencia, falta de castidad.

unchecked [ʊnchéct], *a.* desenfrenado; (com.) que no está confrontado.

unchristian [ʊncríschan], *a.* no cristiano; pagano, anticristiano.

unchurch [ʊnchǽrch], *va.* expulsar o excluir de la iglesia; excomulgar.—**unchurched** [-t], *a.* no perteneciente a, o miembro de, ninguna iglesia.

uncial [ʊnshal], *a.* uncial.

unciform [ʊnsiform], *s.* y *a.* unciforme.

Uncinaria [ʊnsinériæ], *s.* (zool.) uncinaria.

uncinariasis [-nœráiæsis], *s.* uncinariasis, anemia tropical.

uncircumcised [ʊnsǽrcʊmsáisd], *a.* y *s.* incircunciso.

uncivil [ʊnsívil], *a.* incivil, descortés.

uncivilly [-li], *adv.* incivilmente, descortésmente.

uncivilized [ʊnsívilaisd], *a.* incivilizado.

unclasp [ʊnclásp], *va.* desabrochar.

unclassifiable [ʊnclǽsifáiabœl], *a.* inclasificable.

uncle [ʊncœl], *s.* tío; anciano; (fam.) prestamista, usurero.—**U. Sam,** el tío Sam (los E. U.).

unclean [ʊnclín], *a.* sucio, inmundo; deseaseado; impuro; obsceno.

uncleanliness [ʊnclénlines], *s.* suciedad, desaseo, falta de limpieza.

uncleanly [ʊnclénli], *a.* sucio, desaseado, inmundo; impuro; indecente.

uncleanness [ʊnclínnes], *s.* suciedad; impureza, obscenidad.

uncloister [ʊnclóistœr], *va.* exclaustrar.

unclose [ʊnclóus], *va.* abrir; revelar.

unclouded [ʊncláuded], *a.* claro, despejado.

unco [ʊnco]. **I.** *a.* (Esco.) singular, raro. **II.** *adv.* extraordinariamente.

uncock [ʊncóc], *va.* (arm.) desmontar.

uncoil [ʊncóil], *va.* desarrollar, desenrollar.

uncoined [ʊncóind], *a.* no acuñado, sin acuñar.

uncollectable [ʊncoléctabœl], *a.* incobrable.

uncollected [-lécted], *a.* disperso, no cobrado.

uncolo(u)red [ʊncʊlœrd], *a.* descolorido; incoloro; imparcial.

uncombed [ʊncóumd], *a.* despeinado.

uncomfortable [ʊncʊmfœrtabœl], *a.* incómodo, penoso, desagradable, molesto; embarazado, intranquilo; indispuesto, con malestar.—**uncomfortableness** [-nes], *s.* incomodidad, penalidad; malestar; molestia, desagrado.—**uncomfortably** [-bli], *adv.* incómodamente; molestamente; penosamente.

uncommercial [ʊncomœ́rshal], *a.* poco versado o interesado en el comercio; impropio de un comerciantes o de los métodos comerciales.

uncommon [ʊncómʊn], *a.* poco común, excepcional, raro, extraño.

uncommonly [-li], *adv.* raramente; excepcionalmente.

uncompleted [ʊncomplíted], *a.* inacabado, incompleto.

uncomplimentary [ʊncómpliméntari], *a.* poco halagüeño; desfavorable, ofensivo.

uncompromising [ʊncómpromaísing], *a.* inflexible, firme; intransigente; irreconciliable.

unconcern [ʊnconsǽrn], *s.* indiferencia, frialdad.

unconcerned [-d], *a.* indiferente, frío, impasible.

unconcernedly [-nedli], *adv.* indiferentemente, sin inmutarse.

unconditional [ʊncondíshʊnal], *a.* absoluto, incondicional; a discreción.—**unconditionally** [-i], *adv.* incondicionalmente; a discreción.

unconditioned [ʊncondíshʊned], *a.* libre, exento de condiciones, no limitado ni restringido (filos.), incondicional, absoluto.

unconfined [ʊnconfáind], *a.* libre, ilimitado, sin trabas, sin obstáculos.

unconfirmed [ʊnconfǽrmd], *a.* no confirmado.

unconformability [ʊnconfórmabíliti], *s.* desconformidad; (geol.) discordancia.—**unconformable** [-bœl], *a.* desconforme, diferente; (geol.) discor-

dante.—**unconformity** [-miti], *s.* desconformidad; discordancia.

uncongenial [ʊnconyínial], *a.* incongenial, incompatible.—**uncongeniality** [-niæliti], *s.* incongenialidad, incompatibilidad.

unconnected [ʊnconnécted], *a.* inconexo, irrelacionado.

unconquerable [ʊncónkœrabœl], *a.* invencible, insuperable, inconquistable.

unconscionable [ʊncónshʊnabœl], *a.* desordenado, desmedido, injusto; sin conciencia.

unconscionably [-bli], *adv.* sin razón, sin conciencia.

unconscious [ʊncónshʊs], *a.* inconsciente; privado, insensible; no sabedor, que ignora; desconocido.—**unconsciously** [-li], *adv.* inconscientemente, sin saberlo.—**unconsciousness** [-nes], *s.* insensibilidad; falta de conocimiento, inconsciencia.

unconstitutional [ʊncónstitúshʊnal], *a.* inconstitucional.—**unconstitutionality** [-ǽliti], *s.* carácter inconstitucional.—**unconstitutionally** [-i], *adv.* inconstitucionalmente.

uncontrollable [ʊncontrólabœl], *a.* ingobernable; indomable, irrefrenable.

uncontrolled [ʊncontróuld], *a.* sin freno, libre.

unconventional [ʊnconvénshʊnal], *a.* despreocupado, informal, libre.—**unconventionality** [-ǽliti], *s.* despreocupación, informalidad, libertad de acción.

unconverted [ʊnconvǽrted], *a.* no convertido.

uncork [ʊncórk], *va.* destapar, descorchar.

uncorrected [ʊncorrécted], *a.* sin corregir, no corregido.

uncorrupted [ʊncorrúpted], *a.* incorrupto.

uncounted [ʊncáunted], *a.* no contado, sin contar; innumerable.

uncouple [ʊncúpœl], *va.* desconectar, desengranar, zafar, soltar.—**uncoupled,** suelto; soltero.

uncouth [ʊncúz], *a.* tosco, rústico; extraño.—**uncouthly** [-li], *adv.* rústicamente, toscamente, singularmente.—**uncouthness** [-nes], *s.* tosquedad, rusticidad; extrañeza, rareza.

uncover [ʊncʊ́vœr]. **I.** *va.* destapar, descubrir; desabrigar, desarropar; revelar, poner al descubierto. **II.** *vn.* descubrirse; desarrebozarse.

uncowl [ʊncául], *va.* quitar la capucha de.

uncreated [ʊncriéited], *a.* increado.

uncrown [ʊncráun], *va.* destronar.

unction [ʊnćshʊn], *s.* unción, ungimiento; untura, untamiento; ungüento; extremaunción; fervor, unción; divina gracia.

unctuous [ʊnćchuʊs], *a.* untuoso, craso; zalamero.—**unctuousness** [-nes], *s.* untuosidad.

uncultivated [ʊncúltiveited], *a.* yermo, baldío, inculto; rústico, grosero.

uncurl [ʊncœ́rl], *va.* y *vn.* desrizar, desencrespar, destorcer.

uncut [ʊncʊ́t], *a.* sin cortar; sin tallar, sin labrar (apl. a piedras preciosas).

undamaged [ʊndǽmeyd], *a.* ileso, indemne.

undaunted [ʊndánted], *a.* impávido, denodado; intrépido.—**undauntedly** [-li], *adv.* intrépidamente; impávidamente.—**undauntedness** [-nes], *s.* intrepidez; impavidez.

undecayed, undecaying [ʊndikéid, -kéing], *a.* inmarcesible, inalterable.

undeceive [ʊndisív] *va.* desengañar, desilusionar.

undecided [ʊndisáided], *a.* indeciso.

undecipherable [ʊndisáiførabœl], *a.* indescifrable.

undeclinable [ʊndicláinabœl], *a.* indeclinable.

undefiled [ʊndifáild], *a.* impoluto, puro, limpio, inmaculado.

undefinable [ʊndifáinabœl], *a.* indefinible.

undefined [ʊndifáind], *a.* indefinido.

undeniable [ʊndináiabœl], *a.* innegable.

undeniably [-bli], *adv.* innegablemente.

under [ʊndœr]. **I.** *a.* inferior; subalterno, subordinado; bajo (de tono).—**u. dog,** (fam.) el perdidoso; el más débil. **II.** *adv.* debajo; más abajo; menos. **III.** *prep.* debajo de, bajo, menos de o que; a (*under* sail, a la vela; *under steam,* al vapor); en; en tiempo de, en la época de;

conforme a, según.—**u. a cloud**, en aprietos.—**u. age**, menor de edad.—**u. arms**, bajo las armas.— **u. consideration**, en consideración.—**u. contract**, bajo contrato; conforme al contrato.—**u. cover**, al abrigo, a cubierto; dentro de un sobre.— **u. one's nose**, en las barbas de uno, en su presencia.—**u. pain of**, bajo o so pena de.—**u.-sea**, submarino. *V.* UNDERSEA.—**u. the care of**, al cuidado de.—**u. the circumstances**. en las circunstancias.—**u. the rose**, en secreto.—**u. way**, en camino; andando; principiando.—**to be u. an obligation**, deber favores. *Under* se usa en composición para denotar inferioridad de categoría o de lugar, o bien falta o escasez.

underbid [-bid], *va.* ofrecer menos que.

underbred [-bred], *a.* de raza impura; vulgar, sin urbanidad, rudo.

underbrush [-brúsh], *s.* maleza.

undercarriage [-cárriy], *s.* (aer.) tren de aterrizaje.—**u. skid**, patín de cola.

underclerk [úndœrclœrk], *s.* subsecretario, escribiente.

underclothes, underclothing [-clóuds, -clóuding], *s.* ropa interior.

undercurrent [-cœrœnt], *s.* corriente submarina; tendencia oculta.

undercut [-cút]. **I.** *va.* socavar; en pugilismo, dar una puñada de abajo arriba; formar (obra de relieve, etc.) con base adelgazada o rebajada (menor que la parte superior). **II.** *s.* socavadura; solomillo; puñada pugilística de abajo arriba; corte sesgado; muesca hecha en un árbol para que caiga por ella al cortarlo. **III.** de base rebajada o entallada, más angosto en la base que arriba.

underdo [-dú], *va.* (*pret.* UNDERDID; *pp.* UNDERDONE) (coc.) soasar, medio asar.—**underdone** [-dūn], *a.* soasado, a medio asar.

underdrain [-dréin], *s.* desagüe o avenamiento subterráneo.

underestimate [-éstimeit], *va.* menospreciar; apreciar en menos de lo que merece; no dar suficiente importancia a.

underfeed [-fíd], *va.* (*pret.* y *pp.* UNDERFED), *va.* desnutrir, no alimentar suficientemente.

underfeeding [-ing], *s.* desnutrición, alimentación deficiente.

underfilling [-fíling], *s.* cimiento de un edificio.

undergarment [-gárment], *s.* pieza de ropa interior.

undergo [-gó], *va.* (*pret.* UNDERWENT, *pp.* UNDERGONE) sufrir, padecer; aguantar, sobrellevar; pasar por, ser sometido a; arrostrar.

undergraduate [-grǽdiueit], *s.* estudiante no graduado aún.

underground [-gráund]. **I.** *a.* subterráneo; secreto.—**u. trolley**, tranvía de canalización subterránea. **II.** *s.* sótano, subterráneo; ferrocarril subterráneo. **III.** *adv.* bajo tierra; ocultamente.

undergrown [-gróun], *a.* achaparrado.

undergrowth [-gróuz], *s.* maleza, chamarasca; baja estatura.

underhand [-jǽnd]. **I.** *adv.* bajo mano, por bajo cuerda, clandestinamente. **II.** *a.* secreto, clandestino.

underhanded [-ed], *a.* disimulado, clandestino.

underlay [-léi]. **I.** *va.* reforzar; (impr.) calzar, realzar. **II.** *vn.* inclinarse (un filón). **III.** *s.* (impr.) calzo, realce; (min.) buzamiento.

underlease [-lís], *s.* subarriendo.

underlet [-lét], *va.* subarrendar.

underlie [-lái]. **I.** *va.* (*pret.* UNDERLAY, *pp.* UNDERLAIN) estar debajo de; ser la razón fundamental o sostén de; sustentar, sostener. **II.** *vn.* estar debajo.

underline [-láin], *va.* subrayar.

underling [úndœrling], *s.* subordinado; paniaguado, mequetrefe.

underlying [úndœrláiing], *a.* subyacente; fundamental.

undermine [-máin], *va.* socavar, minar, descalzar, zapar; trasminar.—**underminer** [-œr], *s.* minador, zapador; enemigo oculto.

undermost [-moust]. **I.** *a.* ínfimo, el más bajo. **II.** *adv.* debajo de todo.

underneath [-níz]. **I.** *adv.* debajo. **II.** *prep.* debajo de, bajo.

underpaid [-péid], *pp.* y *a.* mal pagado, insuficientemente retribuído.

underpay [-péi]. **I.** *va.* pagar insuficientemente. **II.** *s.* retribución insuficiente.

underpin [-pín], *va.* (alb.) socalzar, apuntalar, poner puntales.—**underpinning** [-ing], *s.* (arq.) apuntalamiento por la base.

underplot [-plót], *s.* acción secundaria en un poema; trama secreta.

underprize [-práiš], *va.* desapreciar, desestimar.

underproduction [-prodúcšhun], *s.* baja producción, producción insuficiente.

underprop [-próp], *va.* apuntalar.

underrate [-réit], *va.* menospreciar; adocenar, rebajar.

underrun [-rrún], *va.* correr por debajo de; (mar.) resacar; recorrer (los cables).

underscore [-scóœr]. **I.** *va.* subrayar. **II.** *s.* línea de subrayar o que subraya.

undersea, underseas [-sí, -síš], *adv.* bajo la superficie del mar.

undersecretary [-sécreteri], *s.* subsecretario.

undersell [-sél], *va.* vender a bajo precio, malbaratar; vender a menor precio que.

undershirt [-šhœrt], *s.* elástica, camiseta.

undershot [-šhót], *a.* (hidr.) de impulsión por abajo (apl. a ruedas).

undersign [-sáin], *va.* subscribir.—**the undersigned**, el infrascrito, el abajo firmado.

undersized [-saiśd], *a.* de tamaño o estatura menor que lo normal.

underskirt [-skœrt], *s.* enagua, (Cuba) sayuela; refajo.

underslung [-slúng], *a.* (aut.) aplícase a carrocerías suspendidas de las ballestas de tal modo que el bastidor del chasis queda más bajo que los ejes.

understand [-stǽnd], *va.* y *vn.* (*pret.* y *pp.* UNDERSTOOD) entender, comprender; saber, ser sabedor, tener conocimiento de, tener entendido; conocer, penetrar; sobrentender.

understanding [-stǽnding]. **I.** *s.* entendimiento, inteligencia; modo de ver, entender; comprensión; acuerdo, arreglo; armonía, mutua comprensión. **II.** *a.* entendedor, inteligente, perito.

understandingly [-li], *adv.* de manera inteligente, con conocimiento (de causa, de los hechos).

understate [-stéit], *va.* decir menos de lo que es.

understood [-stud], *pret.* y *pp.* de TO UNDERSTAND; sobrentendido, subentendido; convenido.—**to be u.**, sobrentenderse, subentenderse.— **be it u.**, entiéndase.—**it being u.**, bien entendido. —**that is u.**, está entendido; por supuesto, eso se entiende.

understratum [-stréitum], *s.* estrato subyacente.

understudy [-stúdi], *s.* (teat.) sobresaliente.

undertake [-téik], *va.* y *vn.* (*pret.* UNDERTOOK; *pp.* UNDERTAKEN) emprender, acometer, intentar; comprometerse a, responder de.

undertaker [-œr], *s.* empresario de pompas fúnebres, muñidor, zacateca; contratista.

undertaking [-ing], *s.* empresa: contratación; empresa funeraria; (for.) compromiso, promesa; empeño o garantía.

undertenant [-ténant], *s.* subarrendatario, subinquilino.

undertone [-tóun], *s.* voz baja; color apagado; doble sentido.

undertow [-tóu], *s.* resaca.

undervaluation [-vǽliuéšhun], *s.* menosprecio, estimación baja.

undervalue [-vǽliu], *va.* desapreciar, menospreciar, tasar en menos.

underwear [-ueœr], *s.* ropa interior.

underwent, *pret.* de TO UNDERGO.

underwood [-ud], *s.* maleza.

underwork [-œr], *s.* trabajar por menos jornal que otro. **II.** *vn.* trabajar menos de lo que se debe. **III.** *s.* trabajo de rutina.

underworld [-uǽrld], *s.* averno; mundo terrenal, la tierra; vida del vicio, clases depravadas.

underwrite [-ráit], *va.* (*pret.* UNDERWROTE: *pp.* UNDERWRITTEN) subscribir; (com.) asegurar (contra los riesgos del mar); obligarse a comprar todas las acciones de una nueva empresa que queden sin subscribir.—**underwritten**, infrascripto.

underwriter [-ráitœr], *s.* asegurador.

undeserved [ʊndeŝœ́rvd], *a.* inmerecido.

undeservedly [ʊndeŝœ́rvedli], *adv.* inmerecidamente, injustamente.—**undeserving** [-ing], *a.* desmerecedor, inmeritorio, indigno.

undesignedly [ʊndeŝáinedli], *adv.* involuntariamente, sin intención.—**undesigning** [-ning], *a.* sincero, sencillo; de buena fe.

undesirable [ʊndisáiærabœl], *a.* que no es de desearse; inconveniente, desventajoso; nocivo, pernicioso.

undetected [ʊndetected], *a.* no descubierto.

undetermined [ʊndetœ́rmind], *a.* indeterminado; indeciso, incierto.—**u. coefficients**, (mat.) coeficientes indeterminados.

undeveloped [ʊndevélopt], *a.* rudimentario, sin desarrollo.

undeviating [ʊndívieiting], *a.* regular, directo; sin rodeo, siempre igual.

undid [ʊndíd], *pret.* de TO UNDO.

undigested [ʊndiyésted], *a.* indigesto, no digerido; mal ordenado.

undignified [ʊndígnifaid], *a.* indecoroso, falto de dignidad; falto de seriedad o de gravedad.

undiminished [ʊndimíniŝht], *a.* sin diminución, sin merma, no disminuído.

Undine [ʊndín], *s.* Ondina.

undirected [ʊndirécted], *a.* sin dirección, sin señas.

undiscernible [ʊndiŝœ́rnibœl], *a.* invisible, imperceptible.

undisciplined [ʊndísiplind], *a.* indisciplinado, falto de corrección.

undiscovered [ʊndiscúvœrd], *a.* ignoto, oculto, por descubrir.

undisguised [ʊndisgáiŝd], *a.* sin disfraz; cándido, franco, abierto, sencillo.

undismayed [ʊndisméid], *a.* perseverante, que no ha perdido el ánimo o valor; firme.

undisputed [ʊndispiúted], *a.* que no se disputa.

undistinguishable [ʊndistíngüiŝhabœl], *a.* indistinguible.

undisturbed [ʊndistœ́rbd], *a.* imperturbado; imperturbable, impasible, sereno.

undivided [ʊndiváided], *a.* indiviso, íntegro.

undo [ʊndú], *va.* UNDID: *pp.* UNDONE) anular, desvirtuar, contrarrestar; reparar (un daño); arruinar, perder; causar pesadumbre a; deshacer; desatar, desliar; desarmar, desmontar.

undock [ʊndɔ́c], *va.* sacar del dique.

undoing [ʊndúing], *s.* desfacimiento; ruina, pérdida.

undone [ʊndún], *pp.* de TO UNDO; sin terminar; sin hacer.—**to be u.**, estar perdido o arruinado.— **to come u.**, deshacerse; desatarse.—**to leave nothing u.**, no dejar nada por hacer.

undoubted [ʊndáuted], *a.* indudable, seguro.

undoubtedly [-li], *adv.* indudablemente.

undraw [ʊndró], *va.* (*pp.* UNDRAWN) abrir, tirar hacia fuera.—**undrawn**, no sacado; no extraído; no sorteado (billete de lotería); (com.) no girado.

undreamed [ʊndrímd], *a.* no soñado.—**u. of**, inopinado.

undress [ʊndrés]. **I.** *va.* desnudar, desvestir, quitar la ropa; desvendar, quitar el vendaje. **II.** *vn.* desnudarse. **III.** *s.* [ʊndres] desabillé, paños menores; ropa de casa; traje de cuartel. —**to be in an u.**, estar de trapillo. **IV.** *a.* de trapillo; de confianza.

undressed [ʊndrést], *a.* desnudo; de trapillo; (com.) en rama o metido.—**u. sheepskins**, zaleas. —**u. skin**, cuero sin curtir o al pelo.

undried [ʊndráid], *a.* húmedo, sin secar; verde (frutos, etc.).

undue [ʊndiú], *a.* indebido, excesivo, desmedido; ilícito, injusto; (com.) por vencer.

undulate [ʊ́ndiuleit]. **I.** *vn.* undular, ondear, fluctuar. **II.** *va.* hacer ondear. **III.** *a.* ondeado, ondulado.—**undulating** [-ing], *a.* ondulante, undoso.—**undulation** [-éiŝhʊn], *s.* ondulación, onda, ondeo.

undulatory [ʊ́ndiulatori], *a.* undulatorio, undoso. —**u. theory**, (fís.) teoría de las ondulaciones.

unduly [ʊndiúli], *adv.* indebidamente; irregularmente, ilícitamente.

undutiful [ʊndiútiful], *a.* desobediente, que falta a sus deberes.—**undutifulness** [-nes], *s.* desobediencia; falta de respeto; falta de cumplimiento del deber.

undying [ʊndáiing], *a.* imperecedero.

unearned [ʊnœ́rnd], *a.* no ganado; inmerecido.

unearth [ʊnœ́rz], *va.* desenterrar.

unearthly [-li], *a.* sobrenatural; aterrador, espantoso.

uneasily [ʊníŝili], *adv.* inquietamente; incómodamente, penosamente.—**uneasiness** [-nes], *s.* inquietud, desasosiego, ansiedad; incomodidad, disgusto, malestar.—**uneasy** [ʊníŝi], *a.* inquieto, intranquilo, ansioso, desasosegado; molesto, incómodo; desgarbado; difícil, pesado.

uneducated [ʊnédyukeited], *a.* falto de educación, indocto, ignorante.

unemployed [ʊnemplóid], *a.* sin empleo, desocupado; ocioso, inactivo.—**unemployment** [-mœnt], *s.* falta de empleo, ociosidad.

unencumbered [ʊnencúmbœrd], *a.* libre de gravamen; saneado; sin trabas.

unending [ʊnénding], *a.* inacabable, sin fin, eterno.

unendowed [ʊnendáud], *a.* indotado.

unendurable [ʊnendiúrabœl], *a.* insufrible, inaguantable, insoportable.

unengaged [ʊnenguéyd], *a.* desocupado, libre, no comprometido.

unenviable [ʊnénviabœl], *a.* inenvidiable.

unenvied [ʊnénvid], *a.* no envidiado.

unequal [ʊnícual], *a.* desigual; ineficaz, insuficiente, inferior; desproporcionado; injusto, parcial; falto de uniformidad.—**unequalled** [-d], *a.* sin igual, sin par, incomparable.—**unequally** [-li], *adv.* desigualmente.

unequipped [ʊnecuípt], *a.* desprovisto, no preparado.

unequivocal [ʊnecuívocal], *a.* inequívoco.

unerring [ʊnœ́rring], *a.* infalible.—**unerringly** [-li], *adv.* infaliblemente.

unessayed [ʊneséd], *a.* no ensayado.

uneven [ʊnívn], *a.* desigual; escabroso, quebrado; irregular; non, impar.—**unevenly** [-li], *adv.* desigualmente.—**unevenness** [-nes], *a.* desigualdad; escabrosidad, aspereza; abolladura; desnivel; irregularidad, intercadencia.

uneventful [ʊnevéntful], *a.* exento de acontecimientos notables; tranquilo, quieto.

unexamined [ʊnegŝémind], *a.* no examinado.

unexampled [ʊnegŝémpœld], *a.* que no tiene igual, sin ejemplo, único.

unexceptionable [ʊnecsépŝhʊnabœl], *a.* intachable; irrecusable.—**unexceptional** [-al], *a.* ordinario, usual y corriente.

unexpected [ʊnexpécted], *a.* inesperado, impensado; repentino.—**unexpectedly** [-li], *adv.* de repente o inesperadamente.—**unexpectedness** [-nes], *s.* calidad de inesperado; (lo) inesperado.

unexperienced [ʊnexpírienst], *a.* inexperto.

unexplored [ʊnexplórd], *a.* inexplorado.

unexposed [ʊnexpóuŝd], *a.* (foto.) no expuesto.

unexpressive [ʊnexprésivj, *a.* sin expresión.

unfading [ʊnféding], *a.* inmarcesible.

unfailing [ʊnféiling], *a.* inagotable; indefectible; seguro, cierto, infalible.

unfair [ʊnféœr], *a.* doble, falso; injusto; leonino; de mala fe.—**unfairly** [-li], *adv.* de mala fe; injustamente; con doblez.—**unfairness** [-nes], *s.* falta de equidad; deslealtad, mala fe.

unfaithful [ʊnféizful], *a.* infiel, infidente; femtido, desleal; inexacto.—**the u.**, los infieles.—**unfaithfully** [-li], *adv.* infielmente, deslealmente.—**unfaithfulness** [-nes], *s.* infidelidad, perfidia, infidencia, deslealtad.

unfaltering [ʊnfólterinɡ], *a.* firme, resuelto, inquebrantable.—**unfalteringly** [ʊnfóltœrinɡli], *adv.* sin vacilar, resueltamente.

unfamiliar [ʊnfamíliar], *a.* poco familiar, poco común; no conocido; ignorante, poco conocedor.

unfasten [ʊnfásœn], *va.* desatar, desligar, desabrochar, desenganchar, desprender, soltar, aflojar, zafar.

unfathomable [ʊnfáðʊmabœl], *a.* insondable; sin fondo; impenetrable.

unfavo(u)rable [ʊnfévorabœl], *a.* desfavorable, desventajoso, adverso.—**unfavo(u)rably** [-blĭ], *adv.* desfavorablemente, desventajosamente.

unfed [ʊnféd], *a.* falto de alimento.

unfeeling [ʊnfíling], *a.* insensible, impasible, empedernido.—**unfeelingly** [-lĭ], *adv.* cruelmente; insensiblemente.

unfeigned [ʊnféind], *a.* verdadero, genuino; ingenuo.—**unfeignedly** [-edlĭ], *adv.* ingenuamente, sinceramente, sin fingimiento.

unfelt [ʊnfélt], *a.* no percibido, no sentido.

unfermented [ʊnfœrménted], *a.* no fermentado.

unfetter [ʊnfétœr], *va.* desmanear.

unfinished [ʊnfínisht], *a.* sin acabar.

unfit [ʊnfít]. **I.** *a.* inepto, incompetente; impropio, inoportuno; inadaptable, inadecuado, inservible. **II.** *va.* inhabilitar.—**unfitly** [-lĭ], *adv.* ineptamente; impropiamente.—**unfitness** [-nes], *s.* ineptitud, incompetencia; inadaptabilidad.

unfixed [ʊnfícst], *a.* suelto, desprendido; errante, voluble; desarreglado.

unflagging [ʊnflǽɡuinɡ], *a.* persistente, incansable.

unfledged [ʊnfléyd], *a.* sin empollar; inmaturo, novel.

unflinching [ʊnflínching], *a.* firme, resuelto.

unfold [ʊnfóuld]. **I.** *va.* desplegar, desdoblar, desenvolver, desarrollar, abrir; extender; descifrar, revelar, descubrir, poner en claro; manifestar, explicar. **II.** *vn.* abrirse, desenvolverse, desarrollarse.

unforeseen [ʊnfœrsín], *a.* imprevisto, impensado, inesperado.

unforgettable [ʊnforguétabœl], *a.* inolvidable.

unforgiving [ʊnforguíving], *a.* duro, inexorable, implacable, que no perdona.

unformed [ʊnfórmd], *a.* informe; embrionario; crudo.

unfounded [ʊnfáunded], *a.* infundado.

unfrequented [ʊnfricuénted], *a.* solitario.

unfrequently [ʊnfrícuentli], *adv.* rara vez.

unfriendliness [ʊnfréndlines], *s.* falta de amistad, hostilidad.—**unfriendly** [-lĭ], *a.* poco amistoso; enemigo; desfavorable, perjudicial; hostil.—**an u. act,** un acto hostil.

unfrock [ʊnfró‹], *va.* expulsar, deponer, degradar (a un monje, ministro del culto, etc.).

unfruitful [ʊnfrútful], *a.* estéril, infecundo; improductivo, infructuoso.—**unfruitfully** [-lĭ], *adv.* infructuosamente.—**unfruitfulness** [-nes], *s.* esterilidad, infecundidad; infructuosidad.

unfulfilled [ʊnfulfíld], *a.* incumplido.

unfurl [ʊnfœrl], *va.* desplegar, desdoblar, extender; (mar.) desaferrar.

unfurnished [ʊnfœrnisht], *a.* desamueblado; desprovisto.

ungainliness [ʊnguéinlines], *s.* falta de gracia, desgarbo, mala apariencia.—**ungainly** [ʊnguéinlĭ], *a.* desmañado, desgarbado, torpe.

ungear [ʊnguǽr], *va.* (mec.) desengranar.

ungenerous [-yénœrʊs], *a.* poco generoso, ajeno o contrario a la generosidad.—**ungenerously** [-lĭ], *adv.* sin generosidad; indignamente.

ungentlemanly, *o* **ungentlemanlike** [ʊnyéntœlmanli, -laic], *a.* indigno de un caballero.

ungird [ʊngœrd], *va.* desceñir, desfajar; descinchar.

unglazed [ʊnɡlésd], *a.* sin vidrios; sin vidriar; deslustrado; sin satinar (papel).

ungloved [ʊnglʊ́vd], *a.* sin guantes.

unglued [ʊnglúd], *pp.* despegado, desencolado.

ungodliness [ʊnɡódlines], *s.* impiedad, irreligión.

ungodly [-lĭ], *a.* impío, irreligioso; malvado, perverso.

ungovernable [ʊnɡʊ́vœrnabœl], *a.* indomable, ingobernable, díscolo.

ungraceful [ʊnɡréisful], *a.* desagraciado, desgarbado.

ungracefully [-lĭ], *adv.* sin gracia, deslucidamente.

ungracious [ʊnɡréishʊs], *a.* poco afable, desagradable, ofensivo.—**ungraciously** [-lĭ], *adv.* rudamente, ásperamente.—**ungraciousness** [-nes], *s.* aspereza, descortesía.

ungrammatical [ʊnɡræmǽtical], *a.* ingramatical, incorrecto.

ungrateful [ʊnɡréitful], *a.* desagradecido, ingrato; desagradable.—**ungratefully** [-lĭ], *adv.* ingratamente, desagradecidamente; desagradablemente, de mala gana.—**ungratefulness** [-nes], *s.* ingratitud, desagradecimiento.

ungratified [ʊnɡrǽtifaid], *a.* no satisfecho.

ungrounded [ʊnɡráunded], *a.* infundado, inmotivado, gratuito.

ungrudgingly [ʊnɡrʊ́yinɡli], *adv.* de buena gana, sin quejarse.

ungual [ʊ́nɡuæl], *s.* unguiculado.

unguarded [ʊnɡárded], *a.* desguarnecido, indefenso; descuidado, desprevenido; incauto, indiscreto.

unguent [ʊ́nɡüent], *s.* ungüento.

unguicular [ʊnɡüíkiular], *a.* unguiculado.

unguiculate [-eit], *a.* y *s.* (zool.) unguiculado.

unguided [ʊnɡáided], *a.* no dirigido, no gobernado, sin guía.

unguinous [ʊ́nɡüinʊs], *a.* oleoso, aceitoso.

ungula [ʊ́nɡuiulæ], *s.* = UNGUIS; (mat.) cilindro o cono cortados por un plano oblicuo a la base.

unguis [ʊ́nɡüis], *s.* uña, pezuña, garra, zarpa.

ungulate [ʊ́nɡuiulet], *a.* y *s.* ungulado.

ungum [ʊnɡʊ́m], *va.* desengomar.

unhair [ʊnjéær], *va.* (ten.) apelambrar.

unhallowed [ʊnjǽlod], *a.* profano, impío; profanado.

unhand [ʊnjǽnd], *va.* soltar; quitar las manos a.

unhandy [ʊnjǽndi], *a.* desmanotado, desmañado, torpe; incómodo.

unhang [ʊnjǽnɡ], *va.* (pret. y pp. UNHUNG) descolgar, desprender, desmontar, desarmar.

unhappily [ʊnjǽpili], *adv.* desgraciadamente, por desgracia.—**unhappiness** [-nes], *s.* infelicidad, desgracia, desdicha.—**unhappy** [ʊnjǽpi], *a.* infeliz, desdichado, desventurado; infausto, aciago, malhadado.

unharbo(u)red [ʊnjárbord], *a.* que no tiene puerto ni abrigo; desemboscado.

unharmed [ʊnjármd], *a.* ileso, incólume, sano y salvo; sin daño.

unharness [ʊnjárnes], *va.* desenjaezar, desguarnecer, desaparejar, desenganchar.

unhealthful [ʊnjélzful], *a.* malsano, insalubre.

unhealthfulness [-nes], *s.* insalubridad.

unhealthiness [ʊnjélzines], *s.* falta de salud.

unhealthy [ʊnjélzi], *a.* enfermizo, achacoso; insalubre, malsano.

unheard [ʊnjœrd], *a.* que no se ha oído; (con **of**) desconocido, obscuro; inaudito, extraño.

unheeded [ʊnjíded], *a.* desatendido, despreciado.

unheeding [ʊnjídinɡ], *a.* desatento, descuidado, distraído.

unhesitating [ʊnjésiteitinɡ], *a.* que no vacila; resuelto; pronto, listo.—**unhesitatingly** [-lĭ], *adv.* sin vacilar; prontamente.

unhewn [ʊnjiún], *a.* en bruto.

unhinge [ʊnjínɹ], *va.* desgoznar, desgonzar; desquiciar, sacar de quicio; desequilibrar, trastornar (el juicio).

unhitch [ʊnjích], va. descolgar, desatar; desenganchar, desaparejar.

unholily [ʊnjóulili], adv. impíamente.

unholiness [ʊnjóulines], s. impiedad.

unholy [ʊnjóuli], adv. profano, impío; pecaminoso.

unhono(u)red [ʊnɑ́óncœrd], a. despreciado.

unhook [ʊnjúk], va. desenganchar, desabrochar, desaferrar; descolgar.

unhoped-for [ʊnjóupd-for], a. inesperado; no esperado.

unhorse [ʊnjórs], va. desarzonar, desmontar.

unhung [ʊnjúng], pp. y pret. de TO UNHANG.

unhurt [ʊnjœrt], a. ileso; indemne.

uniaxial [yúniǽxial], a. uniaxial, de un solo eje.

unicellular [-séliular], a. unicelular.

unicolor [-cúlœr], a. unicolor.

unicorn [-corn], s. unicornio.

unidirectional [-dirécŝhʊnǽl], a. de una sola o misma dirección.—**u. current**, corriente continua de dirección constante.

unification [yúnifikéiŝhʊn], s. unificación.

unifilar [-fáilar], a. unifilar (magnetómetro, suspensión, etc.).

uniflorous [-flórʊs], a. unifloro.

uniflow [-flóu], a. (hidr.) de corrientes paralelas.

unifoliate [-fólieit], a. (bot.) unifoliado.

uniform [yúniform], I. a. uniforme; semejante; acorde, armonioso; consistente, constante. II. s. uniforme.—**in full u.**, de gran uniforme, de gala.

uniformity, uniformness [-fórmiti, -formnes], s. uniformidad.—**uniformly** [-formli], adv. uniformemente.

unify [yúnifai], va. unificar, unir.

unigenital [unijénitæl], a. unigénito.

unilateral [yúniɣáteral], a. unilateral.

unimaginable [ʊnimǽɣinabœl], a. inimaginable.

unimpaired [ʊnimpéærd], a. intacto, ileso, inalterado, incólume.

unimpeachable [ʊnimpíchabœl], a. intachable, irreprensible; irrecusable.

unimportant [ʊnimpórtant], a. de poca o ninguna importancia, insignificante.

unimproved [ʊnimprúvd], a. no adelantado; yermo, baldío, inculto; sin urbanizar.

uninflammable [ʊninflǽmabœl], a. no inflamable.

uninfluenced [ʊnínfluenst], a. no predispuesto, no afectado; exento de preocupaciones.

uninformed [ʊninfórmd], a. inculto, ignorante; mal informado.

uninhabitable [ʊninjǽbitabœl], a. inhabitable.

uninhabited [ʊninjǽbited], a. inhabitado.

uninjured [-ínɣcœrd], a. ileso, incólume; sin daño.

uninstructed [ʊninstrúcted], a. indocto; que no ha recibido aviso o instrucciones.

uninsured [ʊnínŝhúœrd], a. no asegurado.

unintelligible [ʊnintéliribœl], a. ininteligible.

unintelligibility [-bíliti], o **unintelligibleness** [-bœlnes], s. calidad de inintelligible.

unintelligibly [-ibli], adv. ininteligiblemente.

unintentional [ʊninténŝhʊnal], a. hecho sin intención, involuntario, no intencional.

unintentionally [-i], adv. sin intención, involuntariamente.

uninterested [ʊníntœrested], a. no interesado.

uninteresting [-ing], a. falto de interés, soso, insípido.

uninterrupted [ʊníntœrrúpted], a. continuo, no interrumpido.—**uninterruptedly** [-li], adv. sin interrupción, continuamente.

union [yúniʊn], I. s. unión; conformidad, concordia; mancomunidad, fusión; gremio obrero; estado matrimonial; proporción, simetría, armonía; emblema de una unión representado en un pabellón; (E. U.) las estrellas (de la bandera nacional).—**U. Jack**, pabellón militar de la Gran Bretaña.—**the U.**, (E. U.) la Unión Norteamericana. II. a. de o relativo al unionismo o a los gremios obreros; perteneciente a un gremio obrero.

unionism [-iŝm], s. unionismo.—**unionist** [-ist], s. unionista.

unionize [-aiŝ], va. reducir a gremio obrero; hacer entrar en un gremio, agremiar; establecer el sistema unionista en.

uniparous [yúnipaɾʊs], a. unípara.

unipersonal [yúnipœrsonal], a. unipersonal.

unipolar [-póular], a. (elec.) unipolar.

unique [yuníc], a. único en su género, singular, raro, original.

unisexual [yúniséxual], a. unisexual.

unison [yúnison], I. s. (mús.) unisonancia; unisón. II. a. unísono.—**unisonal** [yunísonæl], a. unísono.—**unisonous** [yunísonʊs], a. unísono; que suena solo.

unit [yúnit], I. s. unidad. II. a. unidad (en expresiones como unit force, fuerza unidad; unit volume, volumen unidad; unit pole, polo unidad); igual a la unidad; (arit.) de las unidades (unit figure, cifra de las unidades).

Unitarian [yúnitérian], s. unitario.

Unitarianism [-iŝm], s. unitarismo.

unite [yunáit], I. va. unir, juntar, reunir, enlazar; adunar, mancomunar; avenir, concordar. II. vn. unirse, juntarse; concertarse.

unitedly [yunáitedli], adv. unidamente, de acuerdo; a una.

unity [yúniti], s. unidad; unión, concordia; (mat.) la unidad.

univalent [yúnivéilœnt], a. (quím.) univalente.

univalve [yúnivalv], I. a. univalvo. II. s. molusco univalvo, gasterópodo.

univalvate, univalved [-vælvet, -vælvd], a. V. UNIVALVE.

universal [yúnivœrsal], a. universal.—**u. chuck**, mandril universal de torno.—**u. coupling, o joint**, junta universal; (aut.) cardán, junta cardánica.

Universalism [-iŝm], s. universalismo.—**Universalist** [-ist], s. universalista.

universality [-vœrséliti], a. universalidad, generalidad.—**universally** [-vœrsali], adv. universalmente, generalmente.

universe [yúnivœrs], s. universo, mundo.—**u. of discourse**, (lóg.) extensión de una idea o concepto, o conjunto de cosas o ideas que abarca.

university [yúnivœrsiti], s. universidad.

univocal [yunívocal], a. unívoco.—**univocally** [-i], adv. unívocamente.

unjointed [ʊnɣóinted], a. desunido; desencajado, desarticulado.

unjust [ʊnɣʌst], a. injusto; pecador.—**the just and the u.**, justos y pecadores.

unjustifiable [ʊnɣʌstífáiabœl], a. injustificable, inexcusable.—**unjustifiableness** [-nes], s. falta de justificación o razón.—**unjustifiably** [-bli], adv. injustificadamente.

unjustly [ʊnɣʌstli], adv. injustamente.

unkempt [ʊnkémpt], a. despeinado; desgreñado; desarreglado; desaseado; sin pulimento, tosco.

unkind [ʊnkáind], a. desprovisto de bondad o benevolencia, despiadado; duro, hiriente.

unkindliness [-lines], a. aspereza, dureza, falta de benevolencia.

unkindly [-li], adv. duramente, despiadadamente.

unkindness [-nes], s. falta de bondad, dureza; acción cruel, tratamiento duro o despiadado.

unknown [ʊnnóun], I. a. desconocido, ignoto.—**u. quantity**, (mat.) incógnita.—**u. to one**, sin saberlo uno. II. s. cosa o persona desconocida; (mat.) incógnita.

unlace [ʊnléis], va. desenlazar; desatar.

unlade [ʊnléid], va. (mar.) descargar.

unladylike [ʊnléidilaik], a. impropio de una dama; poco femenino.

unlaid [ʊnléid], a. y pp. de TO UNLAY.

unlawful [ʊnlóful], a. ilegal, ilícito, ilegítimo.—**u. interest**, usura.—**unlawfully** [-i], adv. ilegalmente, ilegítimamente, ilícitamente.—**u. born**, ilegítimo, bastardo.—**unlawfulness** [-nes], s. ilegalidad, ilegitimidad.

unlay [ʊnléi], va. destorcer.

unlearn [ʊnlœrn], va. desaprender, olvidar.

unlearned [ʊnlœrn(e)d], pp. y a. indocto, ignorante, ignaro; ignorado; no aprendido.

unleavened [ʊnlévœnd], a. ázimo.

---

unless [ʌnlés], *conj.* a menos que, a no ser que, como no sea, no siendo; salvo, con excepción de, excepto, si no, si no es.

unlevelled [ʌnléveld], *a.* desnivelado.

unlicensed [ʌnláisenst], *a.* no autorizado, sin permiso o licencia.

unlike [ʌnláic]. **I.** *a.* desemejante, diferente, distinto. **II.** *adv.* otramente, de otro modo; a diferencia de.—**unlikelihood, unlikeliness** [-lijud, -nes], *s.* improbabilidad, inverisimilitud.—**unlikely** [-lij]. **I.** *a.* inverosímil, improbable. **II.** *adv.* improbablemente.—**unlikeness** [-nes], *s.* disimilitud, desemejanza.

unlimber [ʌnlímbœr], *va.* (arti.) quitar el avantrén (a un cañón).

unlimited [ʌnlímited], *a.* ilimitado; sin restricción.

unlink [ʌnlínk], *va.* deseslabonar.

unliquidated [ʌnlícuideited], *a.* (com.) ilíquido, pendiente de pago.

unload [ʌnlóud]. **I.** *va.* descargar; exonerar, aligerar; (fam. E. U.) deshacerse de una mercancía. **II.** *vn.* descargar.

unlock [ʌnlóc], *va.* abrir (una cerradura, etc.); (impr.) desapretar (formas); dar libre acceso; revelar (secretos).

unlooked-for [ʌnlúct-for], *a.* inesperado, inopinado.

unloose [ʌnlús]. **I.** *va.* desatar, aflojar; desencadenar. **II.** *vn.* deshacerse, aflojarse.

unluckily [ʌnlúkili], *adv.* desgraciadamente, por desgracia.—**unluckiness** [-nes], *s.* mala suerte.

unlucky [ʌnlúki], *a.* de mala suerte; desgraciado, desafortunado; funesto, infausto, aciago, de mal agüero.

unmade [ʌnméid], *a.* increado; desarmado.

unmaidenly [ʌnméidœnli], *a.* impropio de una doncella.

unmake [ʌnméik], *va.* deshacer, destruir, aniquilar; deponer, destituir.

unman [ʌnmǽn], *va.* acobardar, desanimar; castrar, capar; (mil.) desguarnecer.

unmanageable [ʌnmǽneyabœl], *a.* inmanejable, ingobernable, indomable.

unmanlike, unmanly [ʌnmǽnlaic, -li], *a.* indigno de un hombre; afeminado, enervado.

unmannered [ʌnmǽnœrd], *a.* rudo, incivil, grosero.—**unmannerliness** [-lines], *s.* rudeza, grosería, mala crianza.—**unmannerly** [-li]. **I.** *a.* malcriado, mal educado, grosero. **II.** *adv.* descortésmente, groseramente.

unmarked [ʌnmárkd], *a.* sin marca; inadvertido.

unmarketable [ʌnmárketabœl], *a.* invendible, incomerciable.

unmarriageable [ʌnmǽriyabœl], *a.* incasable.

unmarried [ʌnmǽrid], *a.* soltero, soltera.

unmask [ʌnmásk], *va.* desenmascarar, quitar la careta; descubrir.

unmast [ʌnmǽst], *va.* desarbolar.

unmatched [ʌnmǽcht], *a.* único, sin par; desapareado, dispar.

unmeaning [ʌnmíning], *a.* sin significación, vacío o falto de sentido.

unmeasurable [ʌnméÿurabœl], *a.* ilimitado, inmensurable, inmenso.

unmeasured [-ÿurd], *a.* desmedido; infinito, ilimitado.

unmentionable [ʌnménshʌnabœl]. **I.** *a.* infando, que no debe mencionarse. **II.** *s. pl.* (fam.) calzones, pantalones.

unmerchantable [ʌnmérchantabœl], *a.* invendible, incomerciable.

unmerciful [ʌnmérsiful], *a.* inclemente, riguroso; cruel, despiadado.—**unmercifully** [-li], *adv.* cruelmente, desapiadadamente, sin misericordia.—**unmercifulness** [-nes], *s.* inclemencia, crueldad.

unmerited [ʌnmérited], *a.* desmerecido, inmerecido, inmérito.

unmindful [ʌnmáindful], *a.* olvidadizo, desatento, desentendido.—**to be u. of, o that,** olvidar, olvidar que; desconocer.

unmindfulness [-nes], *s.* desatención, descuido, negligencia.

unmistakable [ʌnmistéikabœl], *a.* inequívoco, inerrable, evidente.

unmitigated [ʌnmítiguéited], *a.* duro, no mitigado; redomado.

unmixed, unmixt [ʌnmícst], *a.* puro, sin mezcla; simple, sencillo.

unmolested [ʌnmolésted], *a.* quieto, tranquilo, sin ser molestado.

unmoor [ʌnmúœr], *va.* (mar.) desamarrar, desaferrar.

unmounted [ʌnmáunted], *a.* desmontado.

unmoved [ʌnmúvd], *a.* inmoble, inmovible, fijo; inmutable, impasible, frío; inflexible, inexorable.

unnamed [ʌnnéimd], *a.* innominado.

unnatural [ʌnnǽchural], *a.* contranatural, monstruoso, inhumano; desnaturalizado; forzado, artificial o afectado.—**unnaturally** [-i], *adv.* contra la naturaleza; afectada o forzadamente.—**unnaturalness** [-nes], *s.* calidad de desnaturalizado o afectado.

unnavigable [ʌnnǽvigabœl], *a.* innavegable.

unnecessarily [ʌnnéseserili], *adv.* sin necesidad, inútilmente.—**unnecessariness** [-nes], *s.* superfluidad; inutilidad.—**unnecessary** [ʌnnésœscri], *a.* innecesario.

unnerve [ʌnnérv], *va.* acobardar, quitar el valor, desalentar.

unnoticed [ʌnnóutist], *a.* desadvertido.

unobjectionable [ʌnobycˀˀshʌnabœl], *a.* exento de objeciones.

unobservant, o unobserving [ʌnobsœrvant, -ving], *a.* inobservante.

unobserved [ʌnobsœrvd], *a.* inadvertido.

unobstructed [ʌnobstrúcted], *a.* libre, no obstruido, despejado, raso.

unobtrusive [ʌnobtrúsiv], *a.* modesto, moderado, recatado.

unoccupied [ʌnókiupaid], *a.* desocupado o vacante.

unoffending [ʌnofénding], *a.* inofensivo.

unofficial [ʌnofíshal], *a.* no oficial.

unopened [ʌnóupœnd], *a.* cerrado, sin abrir.

unorganized [-órganaišd], *a.* inorganizado; inorgánico.

unostentatious [ʌnóstentéshus], *a.* sencillo, llano, modesto.—**unostentatiously** [-li], *adv.* sin ostentación.

unowned [ʌnóund], *a.* sin dueño; mostrenco.

unoxidizable, unoxidisable [ʌnócsidáisabœl], *a.* inoxidable.

unpack [ʌnpǽk], *va.* desempaquetar, desembalar, desenfardar; abrir, vaciar (un baúl, etc.), para sacar lo que en él se ha transportado).

unpaid [ʌnpéid], *a.* no pagado, sin pagar o por pagar.

unpalatable [ʌnpǽlatabœl], *a.* ingustable, de mal sabor.

unparalleled [ʌnpǽraleld], *a.* único, sin igual.

unpardonable [ʌnpárdœnabœl], *a.* imperdonable, inexcusable.

unpardonably [-bli], *adv.* imperdonablemente.

unparliamentary [ʌnpárlimÉntari], *a.* contrario a las reglas parlamentarias.

unpaved, unpaven [ʌnpéivd, ʌnpéivn], *a.* sin pavimentar, sin empedrar.

unpeg [ʌnpég], *va.* desenclavijar.

unpen [ʌnpén], *va.* soltar del redil.

unpeople [ʌnpípœl], *va.* despoblar.

unperceived [ʌnpœrsívd], *a.* inadvertido.

unpin [ʌnpín], *va.* quitar los alfileres, desprender; desenclavijar.

unpleasant [ʌnplésant], *a.* desagradable.

unpleasantly [-li], *adv.* desagradablemente.

unpleasantness [-nes], *s.* calidad de desagradable; (lo) desagradable; desagrado o desazón; (fam.) riña, desavenencia.

unpleasing [ʌnplíšing], *a.* desagradable.

unploughed, unplowed [ʌnpláud], *a.* inculto.—**u. land,** erial.

unpolished [ʌnpólisht]. c. áspero, tosco, sin pulir, mate; rudo, grosero, impolítico.—**u. diamond,** diamante en bruto.

unpolluted [ʌnpolúted], *a.* impoluto, puro, limpio; inmaculado, sin mancha.
unpopular [ʌnpópiular], *a.* impopular.
unpopularity [-lériti], *s.* impopularidad.
unpractical [ʌnpréctical], *a.* impráctico.
unpracticed, unpractised [-tist], *a.* inexperto, imperito; no practicado.
unprecedented [ʌnprésedénted], *a.* inaudito, sin precedente o sin ejemplar.
unprejudiced [ʌnpréyudist], *a.* imparcial.
unpremeditated [ʌnpreméditéited], *a.* impremeditado.—**umpremeditation** [-éiśhʌn], *s.* ausencia o falta de premeditación.
unprepared [ʌnprepéærd] *a.* desprevenido; desapercibido, desproveído.
unpreparedness [-ednes], *s.* falta de preparación.
unprepossessing [ʌnpripośésing], *a.* poco atractivo, poco insinuante.
unpretending [ʌnpreténding], *a.* modesto, sencillo, sin pretensiones.
unprincipled [ʌnprínsipœld], *a.* sin conciencia.
nnproductive [ʌnprodúctiv], *a.* improductivo.
unprofessional [ʌnproféśhʌnal], *a.* que no tiene profesión; extraño a una profesión o contrario a sus reglas.
unprofitable [ʌnprófitabœl], *a.* improductivo, inútil, infructuoso.—**unprofitableness** [-nes], *s.* inutilidad.—**unprofitably** [-bli], *adv.* inútilmente, sin provecho, sin beneficio.
unpromising [ʌnprómising], *a.* que no promete, que da poca esperanza.
unpronounceable [ʌnpronáunsabœl], *a.* impronunciable.
unpropitious [ʌnpropíśhʌs], *a.* desfavorable, impropicio.
unprosperous [ʌnpróspœrʌs], *a.* impróspero.
unprotected [ʌnprotécted], *a.* sin protección; sin defensa.
unproved, unproven [ʌnprúvd, ʌnprúvn], *a.* sin demostrar, no probado, no demostrado.
unprovided [ʌnprováided], *a.* desproveído, desprovisto, desabastecido; desprevenido.—**u. for,** (for.) no proveído.—**u. of, o with,** desprovisto de.
unprovoked [ʌnprovóuct], *a.* no provocado; sin motivo, sin provocación.
unpublished [ʌnpúbliśht], *a.* no publicado; inédito.
unpunished [ʌnpúniśht], *a.* impune.
unqualified [ʌncuólifaid], *a.* inhábil, inepto, incompetente; desautorizado; inhabilitado: absoluto, ilimitado, incondicional, omnímodo, sin restricción; completo, entero.
unquenchable [ʌncuénchabœl], *a.* inextinguible.
unquestionable [ʌncuéschᴜnabœl], *a.* incuestionable, indisputable.—**unquestionably** [-bli], *adv.* incuestionablemente, sin disputa.
unquestioned [ʌncuéschᴜnd], *a.* incontestable, indisputable; no examinado, no preguntado.
unquiet [ʌncuáiet], *a.* inquieto, desasosegado; agitado, turbado.—**unquietly** [-li], *adv.* inquietamente.—**unquietness** [-nes], *s.* inquietud, desasosiego.
unracked [ʌnréct], *a.* no trasegado.
unraked [ʌnréict], *a.* no trastrillado.
unravel [ʌnrévœl]. **I.** *va.* desenredar, desenmarañar; deshilar; desembrollar, aclarar; descifrar; desatar o desenredar el nudo de un drama. **II.** *vn.* desenredarse; desenlazarse.
unread [ʌnréd], *a.* no leído, sin leer; iliterato, indocto.
unreadiness [ʌnrédines], *s.* desprevención, falta de preparación; lentitud.—**unready** [-i], *a.* lento, lerdo; desprevenido.
unreal [ʌnrial], *a.* no real; quimérico, ilusorio, imaginario, inmaterial, incorpóreo; insincero.
unreasonable [ʌnríśnabœl], *a.* desrazonable.
unreasonableness [-nes], *s.* sinrazón, falta de razón.
unreasonably [-bli], *adv.* desrazonablemente.
unreclaimed [ʌnricléimd], *a.* incorregible; no reclamado; sin mejorar; no aprovechado.

unrecognizable [ʌnrécognáiśabœl], *a.* que no puede reconocerse.
unreconcilable [ʌnréconsáilabœl], *a.* incompatible; irreconciliable; intransigente (en pol. ú. a veces como *s.*).
unreconciled [ʌnréconsaild], *a.* no reconciliado, no resignado.
unrecoverable [ʌnricúvœerabœl], *a.* irrecuperable; irreparable; incurable.
unrecovered [ʌnricúvœrd], *a.* no recobrado.
unreeve [ʌnrív], *va.* (mar.) despasar.
unrefined [ʌnrifáind], *a.* no refinado, impuro; en bruto; inculto, rudo, grosero.
unregenerate [ʌnrᴇyénœret], *a.* irregenerado, no regenerado.
unreliable [ʌnreláiabœl], *a.* indigno de confianza; informal; incierto.
unrepentant, unrepented, unrepenting [ʌnrepéntant, -ted, -ting], *a.* impenitente.
unreserved [ʌnreśérvd], *a.* que no es reservado; sin restricción; franco; libre.—**unreservedly** [-vedli], *adv.* sin reserva; francamente.—**unreservedness** [-vednes], *s.* candor, franqueza, ingenuidad.
unresisted [ʌnreśísted], *a.* sin resistencia.
unresisting [-ing], *a.* que no ofrece resistencia.
unrespited [ʌnréspited], *a.* sin suspensión, remisión ni aplazamiento.
unrest [ʌnrést], *s.* inquietud, desasosiego.
unrestrained [ʌnrestréind], *a.* desenfrenado, licencioso; suelto, desembarazado; ilimitado.
unriddle [ʌnrídœl], *va.* descifrar, resolver.
unrifled [ʌnráifœld], *a.* no rayado, de ánima lisa; no pillado ni saqueado.
unrig [ʌnríg], *va.* (mar.) desaparejar.
unrighteous [ʌnráichᴜs], *a.* inicuo, malo, perverso; injusto.—**unrighteously** [-li], *adv.* inicuamente, perversamente.—**unrighteousness** [-nes], *s.* iniquidad, perversidad; injusticia.
unripe [ʌnráip], *a.* verde, agraz; crudo, prematuro.
unripeness [-nes], *s.* falta de madurez.
unrivalled [ʌnráivald], *a.* sin rival, sin igual.
unrivet [ʌnrívet], *va.* quitar los remaches.
unrobe [ʌnróub, *o* y *vn.* desnudar(se), desvestir(se).
unroll [ʌnróul]. **I.** *va.* desarrollar, desenrollar, desenvolver, desplegar. **II.** *vn.* abrirse, desarrollarse.
unroof [ʌnrúf], *va.* destechar.
unroot [ʌnrút], *va.* desarraigar, extirpar.
unruffled [ʌnrúfœld], *a.* tranquilo, sereno.
unruled [ʌnrúld], *a.* sin rayar (papel).
unruliness [ʌnrúlines], *s.* turbulencia, inquietud; desenfreno.
unruly [ʌnrúli], *a.* indócil, inmanejable; ingobernable; indómito; revoltoso, levantisco; intratable; desarreglado.
unsaddle [ʌnsádœl], *va.* desensillar; sacar de la silla, derribar.
unsafe [ʌnséif], *a.* peligroso, inseguro.—**unsafely** [-li], *adv.* peligrosamente.
unsaid [ʌnséd], *a.* no proferido, no dicho.
unsalable [ʌnséilabœl], *a.* invendible.
unsalted [ʌnsólted], *a.* no salado, sin salar; soso.
unsatisfactoriness [ʌnsétisfáctorines], *s.* calidad de insatisfactorio o defectuoso.
unsatisfactory [-tori], *a.* insatisfactorio, que no satisface; malo, inaceptable.
unsatisfied [ʌnsétisfaid], *a.* no satisfecho; descontento; no convencido; no saldado.
unsatisfying [-faing], *a.* que no satisface.
unsaturated [ʌnsétureited], *a.* no saturado.
unsavorily [ʌnséivorili], *adv.* desabridamente, con sabor soso.—**unsavoriness** [-nes], *s.* insipidez; mal sabor; mal olor.—**unsavo(u)ry** [-vori], *a.* insípido, soso; desabrido; hediondo; desagradable; de mala conducta.
unscathed [ʌnskéiᴅd], *a.* ileso; sin daño, incólume.

unscrew [ʊnscrú], va. desatornillar, destornillar; desenganchar, separar.

unscrupulous [ʊnscrúpiulʊs], a. inescrupuloso, falto de escrúpulo.

unscrupulously [-li], adv. sin escrúpulo, sin conciencia.

unseal [ʊnsíl], va. desellar, abrir.

unsearchable [ʊnsɛrchabœl], a. inescrutable.

unseasonable [ʊnsísnabœl], a. intempestivo, inoportuno; fuera de tiempo; prematuro; indebido, inconveniente.—**at u. hours,** a deshora.

unseasonableness [-nes], s. inoportunidad.

unseasonably [-bli], adv. intempestivamente, fuera de tiempo o sazón.

unseasoned [ʊnsísnd], a. sin sazonar, no sazonado; soso, insípido; verde (madera).

unseat [ʊnsít], va. quitar de un asiento; desarzonar; privar del derecho de tomar asiento (como legislador, etc.); echar abajo (a un ministerio).

unseaworthy [ʊnsíuɛrꝺi], a. innavegable, sin condiciones marineras.

unseemly [ʊnsímli], a. indecoroso, impropio, indigno.

unseen [ʊnsín], a. invisible.

unselfish [ʊnsélfish], a. desinteresado, generoso, desprendido.—**unselfishness** [-nes], s. desinterés, generosidad, abnegación.

unsensitized [ʊnsénsitaisd], a. (foto.) no sensibilizado, sin sensibilizar.

unserviceable [ʊnsɛrvisabœl], a. inútil o inservible.

unserviceableness [-nes], s. inutilidad.

unsettle [ʊnsétœl], va. alterar, perturbar, desarreglar, trastornar, conmover.

unsettled [ʊnsétœld], a. instable, variable, inconstante; desarreglado, descompuesto; no establecido, no instalado, vago, errante, sin residencia fija; indeciso; incierto; (com.) por pagar, no liquidado, pendiente; turbio, revuelto, inhabitado, despoblado; lunático.

unsex [ʊnséx], va. quitar (a una mujer) los atributos y condiciones propias de su sexo.

unsexual [ʊnséxyual], a. asexual.

unshackle [ʊnshǽcœl], va. destrabar, desencadenar, desaherrojar, libertar.

unshaken [ʊnshéikœn], a. firme, inmovible.

unshapen [ʊnshéipœn], a. disforme.

unshapely [ʊnshéipli], a. desproporcionado.

unshaven [ʊnshéivœn], a. sin afeitar.

unsheathe [ʊnshíꝺ], va. desenvainar.

unsheltered [ʊnshéltœrd], a. desabrigado; sin asilo, sin casa.

unship [ʊnshíp], va. desembarcar.—**to u. the oars,** desarmar los remos.—**to u. the rudder,** desmontar el timón.

unshod [ʊnshód], a. sin herrar, sin herraduras.

unshorn [ʊnshórn], a. intonso.—**u. sheep,** ovejas sin esquilar.

unsightliness [ʊnsáitlines], s. fealdad, deformidad.—**unsightly** [ʊnsáitli], a. feo, repugnante.

unsized [ʊnsáisd], a. desencolado; sin apresto (apl. al papel).

unskilful [ʊnskílful], o **unskilled** [ʊnskíld], a. inexperto, imperito.—**unskilfully** [-li], adv. sin arte, torpemente, sin pericia.—**unskilfulness** [-nes], s. impericia.

unsociable [ʊnsóshiabœl], a. insociable, intratable, huraño.—**unsociableness** [-nes], a. insociabilidad.—**unsociably** [-bli], adv. insociablemente.

unsold [ʊnsóuld], a. no vendido, sin vender.

unsolder [ʊnsódœr], vn. desoldar, desestañar.

unsoldierlike, unsoldierly [ʊnsóldʒerlaic, -li], a. indigno de un soldado, poco marcial.

unsolicited [ʊnsolísited], a. no solicitado, no buscado, sin solicitar.

unsophisticated [ʊnsofístikéited], a. puro, sin adulteración; sencillo, cándido; inexperto.

unsound [ʊnsáund], a. defectuoso; falto de vigor, de fuerza, de solidez; poco firme; falto de salud, enfermizo; erróneo, falso; heterodoxo; podrido; corrompido.

unsoundness [-nes], s. calidad de defectuoso; mal estado; heterodoxia; falta de solidez o de fuerza; corrupción.

unsparing [ʊnspǽɛring], a. liberal, generoso, pródigo; inhumano, cruel.—**unsparingly** [-li], adv. liberalmente, pródigamente; sin piedad.

unspeakable [ʊnspíkabœl], a. indecible; execrable, atroz.—**unspeakably** [-bli], adv. indeciblemente; execrablemente, atrozmente.

unspecialized [ʊnspéshalaisd], a. (biol.) no específico; general.

unspent [ʊnspént], a. inexhausto, no gastado.

unspotted [-póted], a. inmaculado, sin mancha.

unstable [ʊnstébœl], a. instable.

unstamped [ʊnstǽmpt], a. no sellado; no contrastado.—**u. letter,** carta sin sello o sin franquear.

unsteadily [ʊnstédili], adv. instablemente, inconstantemente.—**unsteadiness** [-nes], s. instabilidad, falta de firmeza, inconstancia.—**unsteady** [-i], a. instable, inseguro, no firme; inconstante, veleidoso.

unstinted [ʊnstínted], a. liberal.

unstop [ʊnstóp], va. destapar; abrir, dar paso.

unstratified [ʊnstrǽtifaid], a. no estratificado.

unstring [ʊnstríng], va. (pret. y pp. UNSTRUNG) desencordar; desensartar; desliar, desatar, aflojar; debilitar, trastornar (los nervios).

unstudied [ʊnstúdid], a. no estudiado; impensado, natural; desaplicado.

unsubstantial [ʊnsʊbstǽnshal], a. insubstancial, poco sólido; inconsistente.

unsuccessful [ʊnsʊcésful], a. infructuoso, sin éxito; desafortunado; que no logra buen éxito, impróspero.—**unsuccessfully** [-i], adv. sin buen éxito, infelizmente.—**unsuccessfulness** [-nes], s. falta de buen éxito.

unsuitable [ʊnsiútabœl], **unsuited** [ʊnsiúted], a. inapropiado, inadaptable; incompetente; impropio.

unsung [ʊnsúng], a. no cantado.

unsupported [ʊnsʊpórted], a. sin apoyo; sin sostén.

unsurpassed [ʊnsœrpást], a. excelente.

unsuspected [ʊnsʊspécted], a. no sospechado.

unsuspecting, unsuspicious [-ing, -píshʊs], a. confiado, cándido.

unsworn [ʊnsuórn], a. no juramentado.

unsymmetrical [ʊnsimétrical], a. asimétrico.

unsympathetic [ʊnsímpazétic], a. indiferente; falto de conmiseración.

unsystematic(al [ʊnsistemétic(al], a. falto de sistema, inmetódico.

untainted [ʊntéinted], a. incorrupto.

untamable [ʊntéimabœl], a. indomable.

untamed [ʊntéimd], a. indomado, bravío.

untarnished [ʊntárnisht], a. limpio, sin mancha.

untaught [ʊntót]. **I.** pret. y pp. de TO UNTEACH. **II.** a. no enseñado, sin enseñar.

unteach [ʊntích], va. (pret. y pp. UNTAUGHT) hacer desaprender; hacer olvidar o abandonar (una creencia, etc.)

untenable [ʊnténabœl], a. insostenible.

untenanted [-ténanted], a. desarrendado, desalquilado, vacío, desocupado.

unthankful [ʊnzénckful], a. ingrato; mal recibido.—**unthankfully** [-i], adv. ingratamente.—**unthankfulness** [-nes], s. ingratitud.

unthinking [ʊnzínking], a. descuidado, desatento, indiscreto; irreflexivo.

unthought-of [ʊnzót-ov], impensado, inesperado; olvidado.

unthread [ʊnzréd], va. desenhebrar, desensartar; deshilachar.

untidily [ʊntáidli], adv. desaseadamente; sin pulcritud.—**untidiness** [ʊntáidines], s. falta de pulcritud.—**untidy** [ʊntáidi], a. desaliñado, desarreglado, falto de pulcritud.

untie [ʊntái], va. desatar; desprender; desligar; deshacer (un nudo); aflojar, soltar, zafar.

until [ʊntíl]. **I.** prep. hasta. **II.** conj. hasta que.

untile [ʊntáil], va. destejar; desembaldosar.

untilled [ʊntíld], a. inculto, baldío.

untimely [untáimli]. **I.** *a.* intempestivo, extemporal, inoportuno, prematuro. **II.** *adv.* intempestivamente, sin sazón, abortivamente.

unto [úntu], *prep.* a, en, dentro; hacia.

untold [untóuld], *a.* nunca dicho, no narrado; sin decir; indecible, incalculable.

untouched [untúchd], *a.* intacto, ileso; insensible, impasible.

untoward [untóærd], *a.* enojoso, enfadoso, embarazoso; indócil, testarudo, refractario.

untowardness [-nes], *s.* calidad de enojoso o embarazoso; testarudez, terquedad.

untraceable [untrésabœl], *a.* que no se puede rastrear, inquirir o averiguar.

untrained [untréind], *a.* indisciplinado, indócil; inexperto, imperito.

untrammelled [untrémeld], *a.* libre, sin trabas; desembarazado.

untransferable [untrænsfœrabœl], *a.* intransferible, que no se puede traspasar o ceder.

untranslatable [-léitabœl], *a.* intraducible.

untravelled [untrévœld], *a.* inexplorado, intransitado; que no ha recorrido mundo, provinciano.

untried [untráid], *a.* no probado, no experimentado.

untrimmed [untrímd], *a.* sin adornos, sin guarniciones; sin cortar; sin arreglar; sin escuadrar (apl. al papel).

untrodden [untród(œn], *a.* no pisado ni hollado; no frecuentado.

untroubled [untrúbœld], *a.* quieto, tranquilo; claro, transparente.

untrue [untrú], *a.* falso; mendaz, falsario; engañoso, pérfido.—**untruly** [-li], *adv.* falsamente.

untrustworthiness [untrústuœrþines], *s.* calidad de indigno de confianza.

untrustworthy [-þi], *a.* indigno de confianza.

untrusty [untrústi], *a.* infiel, pérfido.

untruth [untrúz], *s.* falsedad, mentira; infidelidad, traición.

untutored [untiútord], *a.* inculto, que no ha recibido educación.

untwine [untuáin], **untwist** [untuíst], *va.* destorcer, desenrollar, desarrollar, desenroscar.

unused [uniúsd], *a.* inusitado, insólito; no usado, nuevo; desacostumbrado.

unusual [uniúyuæl], *a.* raro, extraordinario, untraño; excepcional; insólito, inusitado; desacostumbrado.—**unusually** [-i], *adv.* excepcionalmente; raramente.

unutterable [unútœrabœl], *a.* inenarrable, indecible.

unvalued [unvéliud], *a.* desestimado, menospreciado; inapreciable.

unvanquished [unvéncuišht], *a.* invicto.

unvarnished [unvárnišht], *a.* sin barnizar; sin adorno, sencillo.

unvarying [unvériing], *a.* invariable, constante, uniforme.

unveil [unvéil]. **I.** *va.* quitar el velo, descubrir. **II.** *vn.* descubrirse, quitarse el velo.

unventilated [unvéntileited], *a.* ahogado, falto de ventilación.

unwalled [unuóld], *a.* sin murallas, sin muros; abierto; sin paredes.

unwarily [unuérili], *adv.* incautamente, imprudentemente.—**unwariness** [-nes], *s.* imprevisión, falta de precaución.

unwarlike [unuórlaik], *a.* pacífico.

unwarned [unuórnd], *a.* desprevenido.

unwarrantable [unuórantabœl], *a.* indisculpable, injustificable, insostenible.

unwarrantably [-bli], *adv.* injustamente; injustificablemente, indefensiblemente.

unwarranted [unuóranted], *a.* injustificable, indefensible, inexcusable; sin garantía.

unwary [unuéri], *a.* incauto, imprudente, irreflexivo.

unwashed [unuóšht], *a.* sin lavar; puerco, sucio. —**the great u.**, (fam.) el populacho, la canalla.

unwavering [unuéivœring], *a.* firme, determinado, resuelto.

unwearied [unuírid], *a.* infatigable.

unweave [unuív], *va.* destejer, destramar.

unwed(ded [unuéd(ed], *a.* soltero.

unweeded [unuíded], *a.* no escardado, sin escardar; sin desherbar.

unwelcome [unuélcum], *a.* mal recibido, mal acogido; desagradable, incómodo, importuno.

unwell [unuél], *a.* indispuesto, enfermizo, malo; menstruante.

unwept [unuépt], *a.* no llorado, no lamentado; no vertidas (lágrimas).

unwholesome [unjóulsum], *a.* dañino, nocivo, malo para la salud; malsano, insalubre.

unwieldily [unuíldili], *adv.* pesadamente.

unwieldiness [-nes], *s.* pesadez, incomodidad.

unwieldy [unuíldi], *a.* pesado, ponderoso, difícil de manejar.

unwilling [unuíling], *a.* desinclinado, renuente, maldispuesto.—**unwillingly** [-li], *adv.* de mala gana o con repugnancia.—**unwillingness** [-nes], *s.* mala gana, repugnancia, renuencia.

unwind [unuáind]. **I.** *va.* (*pret. y pp.* UNWOUND) devanar (hilo, etc.); desenredar, desenmarañar, desenvolver. **II.** *vn.* devanarse, desarrollarse.

unwise [unuáis], *a.* imprudente, no cuerdo, indiscreto; ignorante, tonto.—**unwisely** [-li], *adv.* neciamente; imprudentemente, sin cordura.

unwitting [unuíting], *a.* inconsciente.

unwittingly [-li], *adv.* inconscientemente, sin saberlo.

unwomanly [unúmanli], *a.* indigno de una mujer.

unwonted [unuónted], *a.* no acostumbrado, poco común, inusitado.

unworkmanlike [unuœrkmanlaic], *a.* desmañado, sin maña, chapucero.

unworldly [unuœrldli], *a.* espiritual, no terrenal.

unworthily [unuœrþili], *adv.* indignamente.

unworthiness [-nes], *s.* indignidad, desmerecimiento.—**unworthy** [unuœrþi], *a.* indigno, desmerecedor.

unwounded [unúnded], *a.* ileso.

unwove(n, *pret. y pp.* de TO UNWEAVE.

unwrap [unrép], *va.* desenvolver.

unwrinkle [unrínkœl], *va.* desarrugar.

unwritten [unrítœn], *a.* no escrito; en blanco; tradicional.—**u. law**, derecho consuetudinario; derecho no escrito (apl. esp. a lo que muchos consideran el derecho natural de un cónyuge de vengar personalmente la afrenta del adulterio del otro).

unwrought [unrót], *a.* en bruto; no elaborado o manufacturado.—**u. wax**, cera virgen.

unyielding [unyílding], *a.* inflexible, inexorable, firme; reacio, terco.

unyoke [uyóuk]. **I.** *va.* desuncir; separar, desunir. **II.** *vn.* ser libertado de un yugo.

up [up]. **I.** *a.* que va hacia arriba; levantado (de la cama); empinado; erecto; ascendente.—**u. grade**, ascendente.—**u. in**, versado en. **II.** *s.* tierra elevada; prosperidad.—**ups and downs**, altibajos, vaivenes. **III.** *adv.* arriba, en lo alto, hacia arriba; en pie, derecho; de pie, levantado; (fam.) bien enterado, adelantado, competente, capaz, a la altura de, a la par de; llegado, acabado, concluido; enteramente, totalmente, completamente.—**u. and down**, *adv.* acá y allá; por todas partes; de arriba abajo; por todos lados; de un lado a otro.—**u.-and-down**, *a.* vertical, de vaivén (movimiento); (fam.) franco, claro, abierto.—**u. one's sleeve**, en secreto, para sí.—**u. the river** = UPSTREAM.—**up to**, hasta; capaz de; tramando, proyectando, haciendo (gen. algo reprensible); al corriente de, sabedor de.—**u. to anything**, dispuesto para cualquier travesura.—**u. to date**, hasta la fecha.—**u.-to-date**, *a.* moderno, al día. —**it is all u.**, todo se acabó.—**the hour is u.**, ha llegado la hora.—**time is u.**, ha expirado el plazo, se ha cumplido el tiempo; ha llegado la hora.—**to be u. against it**, (fam.) hallarse en apuros; tener que luchar con.—**to be u. in arms**, estar sublevado; haber tomado las armas; estar alborotado o excitado.—**to be u. to**

one, ser asunto de uno, tocarle a uno.—**what is u.?** ¿qué pasa? ¿de qué se trata?—El adverbio *up* se usa a menudo como expletivo enfático para indicar acción completa, y o no se traduce o se traduce cambiando algo el giro: *they ate up all they found,* se comieron cuanto encontraron (*puede agregarse:* sin dejar nada); *the enemy burned up the village,* el enemigo quemó la aldea por completo. **IV.** *prep.* hacia arriba de; a lo largo de;·en lo alto de. **V.** *interj.* ¡arriba! ¡aupa! ¡sus!—**u. there,** ¡alto ahí!—**u., u.!** ¡arriba, levántese Vd.!

upas [yúpas], *s.* (bot.) antiaro; ponzoña.

upbraid [ʌpbréid], *va.* echar en cara, vituperar, afear; reconvenir.

upburst [ʌpbǽrst], *s.* reventón, borbollón, erupción.

upcast [úpcæst]. **I.** *a.* tirado o arrojado a lo alto. **II.** *s.* tiro por alto; (min.) pozo de ventilación ascendente.

upcountry [úpcúntri]. **I.** *s.* tierra adentro, lo interior (de un país). **II.** *a.* de tierra adentro, del interior.

upgrowth [ʌpgróuz], *s.* crecimiento; lo que crece o ha crecido.

upheaval [ʌpjíval], *s.* solevantamiento; trastorno, cataclismo.

upheave [ʌpjív]. **I.** *va.* solevantar. **II.** *vn.* levantarse, alzarse.

uphill [úpjíl]. **I.** *adv.* cuesta arriba. **II.** *a* ascendente; penoso, dificultoso.

uphold [ʌpjóuld], *va.* (*pret. y pp.* UPHELD) sostener, apoyar; defender.—**upholder** [-œr], *s.* sostenedor; sustentáculo, apoyo.

upholster [ʌpjóulstœr], *va.* rellenar y cubrir muebles; tapizar o entapizar; poner colgaduras, cortinas, etc.—**upholsterer** [-œr], *s.* tapicero.—**upholstery** [-i], *s.* tapicería.

upkeep [úpkíp], *s.* conservación.

upland [úpländ]. **I.** *s.* terreno elevado, tierra alta. **II.** *a.* alto, elevado.—**u. cotton, uplands,** algodón superfino.—**u. rice,** arroz de secano o de montaña.—**uplander** [-œr], *s.* montañés.

uplift [ʌplíft]. **I.** *va.* levantar, elevar, alzar. **II.** *s.* levantamiento, elevación.

upmost [úpmoust], *a., super.,* de UP: lo más alto, elevado o último.

upon [ʌpón], *prep.* = ON, pero hay frases en que gen. se prefiere.—**u. my honor,** a fe mía, por mi (palabra de) honor.—**u. my word,** por mi palabra; (fam., *interj.*) ¡qué cosa! ¿habráse visto?

upper [úpœr]. **I.** *a.* superior, de encima o de arriba; alto.—**u. case,** (impr.) caja alta (mayúsculas y versalitas).—**U. Egypt,** Alto Egipto.—**u. hand,** ventaja, dominio.—**U. House,** cámara alta; senado.—**u. leather,** pala de zapato.—**u. transit,** (astr.) tránsito superior, culminación.—**u. works,** obra muerta.—**the u. regions,** las regiones etéreas.—**the u. ten, o ten thousand,** las clases de tono, la nata social. **II.** *s.* pala del zapato.—*pl.* botines.

uppercut [-cút], *s.* (dep.) golpe de abajo arriba con el brazo encogido.

uppermost [úpœrmoust]. **I.** *a.* más alto, supremo, más elevado, de encima de todo; principal, predominante. **II.** *adv.* en lo más alto; en primer lugar.

uppish [úpïsh], *a.* (fam.) arrogante.

uppishness [úpïshnes], *s.* altivez, arrogancia.

upright [úprrait]. **I.** *a.* derecho, vertical, recto, enhiesto; recto, probo, honrado, equitativo.— **u. piano,** piano recto o vertical.—**u. projection,** alzado, proyección vertical. **II.** *s.* montante, pieza vertical; soporte, apoyo.—**uprightly** [-li], *adv.* verticalmente; rectamente, con justicia.—**uprightness** [-nes], *s.* calidad de vertical; rectitud, probidad.

uprise [ʌprráiš], *vn.* levantarse.

uprising [ʌpráishing], *s.* levantamiento; solevantamiento; insurrección, sublevación; subida, cuesta, pendiente.

uproar [úprroœr], *s.* grita, bulla, alboroto, conmoción; rugido.—**uproarious** [-íus], *a.* ruidoso, tumultuoso; bullanguero.

uproot [ʌprrút], *va.* desarraigar, descuajar.

upset [ʌpsét]. **I.** *va.* trastornar, tumbar, turbar, desarreglar; volcar; (metal.) acortar a macha martillo; triscar los dientes de una sierra; (mar.) zozobrar. **II.** *vn.* volcarse. **III.** *a.* [ʌpset] propuesto.—**u. price,** precio mínimo fijado en una subasta. **IV.** *s.* vuelco; trastorno.

upsetter [-œr], *s.* prensa de acortar llantas.

upshot [úpšhot], *s.* resultado final, (fam.) total.

upside [úpsaid], *s.* parte superior, lo de arriba.— **u. down,** lo de arriba abajo, al revés; (fam.) patas arriba; en confusión.

upstairs [úpstǽrš]. **I.** *adv.* arriba, en el (o un) piso de arriba. **II.** *a.* de arriba (de las escaleras); alto (piso, etc.).

upstart [úpstart], *a.* y *s.* advenedizo; encumbrado; presuntuoso.

upstream [úpstrím], *adv.* río arriba.

uptake [úptéik], *s.* acción de alzar o levantar; tubo o conducto ascendente; (m. v.) canal de salida a la chimenea.

upthrow [úpzro], *s. V.* UPHEAVAL.

upthrust [úpzrúst], *s.* (geol.) solevantamiento.

uptown [úptáun]. **I.** *adv.* en o a la parte alta de la ciudad, arriba (hablando de dicha parte). **II.** *a.* de arriba, de la parte alta de la ciudad.

upturn [ʌptœrn], *va.* volver hacia arriba; trastornar; volcar.—**upturned** [-d], *a.* respingada (nariz).

upward [úpuard], *a.* vuelto hacia arriba; ascendente.

upward(s [úpuard(š], *adv.* hacia arriba; más; aproximadamente.—**u. and downwards,** por arriba y por abajo.—**u. of,** más de.

uranic [yuránic], *a.* celeste, astronómico; (quím.) uránico.

uraninite [yuréninait], *s.* (min.) uraninita, mineral de uranio que contiene helio, radio, etc.

uranium [yurénium], *s.* (min.) uranio.

uranometry [yuranómetri], *s.* uranometría.

Uranus [yúranus], *s.* (astr.) Urano.

urate [yúret], *s.* (quím.) urato.

urban [œrban], *a.* urbano.

urbane [œrbéin], *a.* fino, cortés.

urbanity [œrbǽniti], *s.* urbanidad, cultura.

urbanize [œrbænaiš], *va.* urbanizar.

urceolate [œrseolet], *a.* urceolado.

urchin [œrchin], *s.* rapacejo, granuja, pilluelo, golfillo, bribonzuelo; (zool.) erizo.

urea [yúria], *s.* (quím.) urea.

uredo [yurído], *s.* (med.) urticaria.

uremia [yurímia], *s.* uremia.—**uremic** [-ic], *a.* urémico.

ureter [yurítœr o yúretœr], *s.* uréter.

urethra [yurízræ], *s.* uretra.—**urethral** [-zral] *a.* uretíco, uretral.—**urethritis** [yurezráitis o zrítis], *s.* (med.) uretritis.—**urethroscope** [yurézroscoup], *s.* (cir.) uretroscopio.—**urethrotome** [-toum], *s.* (cir.) uretrótomo.—**urethrotomy** [yúrezrótomi], *s.* uretrotomía.

urge [œry]. **I.** *va.* impeler, empujar; incitar, impulsar; instar, apremiar; apresurar, acelerar; acosar, seguir de cerca; solicitar, importunar; pedir, recomendar con ahinco.—**to u. upon,** instigar; pedir o manifestar vehementemente a; empeñarse con, esforzarse por convencer a. **II.** *vn.* presentar argumentos o pretensiones; perorar; estimular, animar. **III.** *s.* impulso, instinto.

urgency [œrrensi], *s.* urgencia.—**urgent** [-œnt], *a.* urgente, apremiante.—**urgently** [-li], *adv.* urgentemente.

urger [œrœr], *s.* acuciador.

uric [yúric], *a.* úrico.

urim [yúrim], *s. pl.* adornos del pectoral del gran sacerdote de los judíos.

urinal [yúrinal], *s.* orinal; urinario, meadero, columna mingitoria.—**urinary** [-eri], *a.* urinario.— **urinate** [-cit], *vn.* orinar.—**urination** [-éišhun], *s.* micción.—**urinative** [-ativ], *a.* diurético.—**urinator** [-éitœr], *s.* (orn.) buzo, somormujador.

urine [yúrin], *s.* orina, orines.

uriniferous [-nífœrus], *a.* urinífero.

urinology [yúrinóloyi], *s.* parte de la medicina que trata de la orina.

urinoscopy [-óscopi], *s.* = UROSCOPY.
urinous [-ʊs], *a.* urinario; de orina.
urn [œrn], *s.* urna; jarrón.
urobilin [yúrobílin], *s.* (quím.) urobilina.
Urodela [-díliæ], *s. pl.* (zool.) uródelos.
urogenital [yúroɣénital], *a.* genitourinario.
urolith [-liz], *s.* urolito, cálculo urinario.
uropygium [yúropíɣiʊm], *s.* (orn.) rabadilla.
uroscopy [yuróscopi], *s.* uroscopia.
ursa [œrsa], *s.* (zool.) osa.—**U. Major,** (astr.) Osa Mayor.—**U. Minor,** Osa Menor.
Ursidæ [œrsidi], *s. pl.* (zool.) úrsidos.
ursiform [œrsiform], *a.* de figura de oso.
ursine [œrsin], *a.* ursino, propio del oso o relativo al oso.
Ursuline [œrsiulin], *a.* y *s.* ursulina.
Urticaceæ [œrtikéisii], *s. pl.* (bot.) urticáceas.
urticaceous [-ŝhʊs], *a.* urticáceo.
urticaria [œrtikéria], *s.* (med.) urticaria.
urticate [-eit], *va.* flagelar con ortigas.
urtication [-éiŝhʊn], *s.* flagelación con ortigas.
us [ʊs], *pron.* nos, a o para nosotros (caso oblícuo de WE).
us(e)able [yúŝabœl], *a.* que se puede usar.
usage [yúŝeɣ], *s.* trato, tratamiento; uso, usanza.
usance [yúŝans], *s.* (com.) usanza; (ant.) uso; interés; aprovechamiento, empleo.
use [yus]. **I.** *s.* uso; aplicación; servicio, utilidad, provecho, ventaja; necesidad; ocasión de usar; costumbre, uso.—**uses of the sea,** usos de la mar.—**in u.,** en uso; usándose.—**of no u.,** inútil.—**out of u.,** inusitado, olvidado o fuera de moda.—**to be of no u.,** no servir; ser inútil.—**to have no u. for,** no necesitar; no servirse de; (fam.) no tener muy buena opinión de; tener en poco, no tener en mucho. **II.** *va.* usar, emplear, gastar; hacer uso, servirse o valerse de; usar de; practicar; tratar; acostumbrar, habituar, (gen. en la voz pasiva **to be used,** estar acostumbrado).—**to u. one's (own) judgment,** obrar uno como le parezca.—**to u. one's (own) way,** obrar uno, o hacer (algo), a su modo.—**to u. up,** gastar, consumir, agotar; (fam.) rendir, agotar de cansancio o fatiga. **III.** *vn.* soler, acostumbrar. Ú. gen. en *pret.* para indicar acción, condición o costumbre pasadas y casi siempre equivale al pretérito imperfecto o de coexistencia con negación implícita, la cual puede hacerse explícita mediante un adverbio, como *antes: he used to come every day,* él solía venir todos los días, él venía todos los días; *the city used to be smaller,* antes (en otro tiempo) la ciudad era más pequeña; *slaves used to be sold,* antes (en otro tiempo) se vendían esclavos.
useful [yúsful], *a.* útil; provechoso.—**usefully** [-li], *adv.* útilmente; provechosamente.—**usefulness** [-nes], *s.* utilidad.
useless [yúsles], *a.* inútil; inservible; inepto.—**uselessly** [-li], *adv.* inútilmente.—**uselessness** [-nes], *s.* inutilidad.
user [yúŝœr], *s.* el que usa, se sirve o se vale de alguna cosa; consumidor, comprador; dueño.
usher [úŝhœr]. **I.** *s.* ujier, conserje, aposentador; (igl. y teat.) acomodador; (Ingl.) sotamaestro. **II.** *va.* (a menudo con **in**) introducir, aposentar, acomodar; anunciar.
ustion [ústiʊn], *s.* ustión, cauterización.
ustulation [ústiuléiŝhʊn], *s.* quemadura; canterización; (farm.) desecación o calcinación; (quím.) volatilización, expulsión por el calor.
usual [yúɣual], *a.* usual, acostumbrado, ordinario, común.—**usually** [-li], *adv.* usualmente, por lo general, por regla general, ordinariamente.—**usualness** [-nes], *s.* calidad de común u ordinario; (lo) común.
usucapt [yúŝiucæpt], *va.* (for.) usucapir.
usucap(t)ion [-képion, -cǽpŝhʊn], *s.* (for.) usucapión.
usufruct [-frʊct], *s.* usufructo.—**usufructuary** [-frúkchueri], *a.* y *s.* usufructuario.
usurer [yúɣurœr], *s.* usurero.
usurious [yuɣúriʊs], *a.* usurario.—**usuriously** [-li], *adv.* usurariamente.—**usuriousness** [-nes], *s* calidad de usurario.
usurp [yuŝœrp], *va.* usurpar; arrogarse

usurpation [yúŝœrpéŝhʊn], *s.* usurpación.
usurper [yuŝœrpœr], *s.*, **usurping** [-ing], *a.* usurpador.
usurpingly [-li], *adv.* por usurpación.
usury [yúɣuri], *s.* usura.
ut [ut], *s.* (mús.) ut, do.
utensil [yuténsil], *s.* utensilio.
uterine [yúterin], *a.* uterino.—**uteritis** [-áitis], *s.* metritis.—**uteromania** [yúteroméinia], *s.* ninfomanía.
uterus [yúterʊs], *s.* útero.
utilitarian [yutilitérian], *s.* y *a.* utilitario; (filos.) utilitarista.—**utilitarianism** [-iŝm], *s.* (filos.) utilitarismo.
utility [yutíliti], *s.* utilidad; servicio, (tea.) suplente.
utilizable [yútiláiŝabœl], *a.* utilizable, aprovechable.
utilize, utilise [-ais], *va.* utilizar, hacer uso de, aprovechar.
utmost [útmoust]. **I.** *a.* extremo, sumo; mayor, más grande; más posible; más distante; último, postrero. **II.** *s.* lo sumo, lo mayor, lo más.—**to do one's u.,** hacer uno lo sumo posible, cuanto pueda.
Utopia [yutópia], *s.* Utopía; (**u-**) utopía.
utopian [yutópian], *a.* utópico.
utricle [yútriccœl], *s.* (biol.) célula; (anat.) cavidad en el laberinto del oído; (bot.) utrículo.
utricular [yutríkiular], *a.* utricular.
utter [útœr]. **I.** *a.* total, entero, cabal, completo; absoluto, perentorio, terminante. **II.** *va.* proferir, pronunciar, articular; decir, expresar; dar (un grito, etc.); descubrir, publicar, revelar; engañar, defraudar con (moneda falsa); hacer pasar fraudulentamente; emitir, poner en circulación.
utterable [-abœl], *a.* articulable, decible.
utterance [-ans], *s.* prolación, pronunciación; expresión, lenguaje; aserción, declaración.
utterer [-œr], *s.* el que pronuncia o profiere; divulgador.
utterly [-li], *adv.* totalmente, completamente, enteramente, absolutamente.
uttermost [-moust], *a.* y *s.* = UTMOST.
utterness [-nes], *s.* extremidad; calidad de completo o absoluto.
uva [yúva], *s.* (bot.) grano de uva.
uvate [yúvet], *s.* (coc.) uvate.
uvea [yúvia], *s.* úvea, túnica del ojo.
uvula [yúviula], *s.* (anat.) úvula.—**uvular** [-ar], *a.* (anat.) uvular.
uxorial [uxórial], *a.* perteneciente a la esposa.
uxoricide [-said], *s.* uxoricida; uxoricidio.
uxorious [-uxórius], *a.* gurrumino.—**uxoriously** [-li], *adv.* con gurrumina.—**uxoriousness** [-nes], *s.* gurrumina.

V

v [vi], *s.* v.
V [vi] (ll. **capital vee,** ve mayúscula, cuando se desea especificar). **I.** *s.* (mec.) apoyo o guía en V; (fam.) billete de 5 dólares. **II.** *a.* en V, de forma de V; triangular.—**V engine** = V MOTOR.—**V gear,** rueda de dientes en hélice.—**V motor,** (aut.) motor de cilindros convergentes o en V.—**V thread,** filete triangular.—**V-threaded,** de filete triangular.—**V. tool,** cincel para ranuras triangulares.—**V-type engine** = V MOTOR.
vacancy [véicansi], *s.* vacuidad; vacío; vacancia, vacante, baja.—**vacant** [-ant], *a.* vacío, desocupado; descargado; libre, desembarazado; vacante; ocioso; vago; estúpido, estólido.
vacate [véikeit]. **I.** *va.* evacuar, dejar vacío; desocupar; abandonar; dejar vacante; anular, rescindir, revocar. **II.** *vn.* salir, irse, marcharse; vacar; desocupar.
vacation [vækéiŝhʊn], *s.* vacación, días feriados, asueto; (gi.) recle; (for.) anulación, revocación.—**vacationist** [-ist], *s.* persona que está de vacaciones (veraneante, si se trata del verano).
vaccinate [væcsineit], *va.* vacunar.—**vaccination** [-ŝhʊn], *s.* vacunación, inoculación.—**vaccinator** [-éitœr], *s.* vacunador.

vaccine [væcsin]. **I.** *a.* vacuno. **II.** *s.* (med.) vacuna.

vaccinia [væcsínia], *s.* vacuna.

vacillate [væsileit], *vn.* vacilar.

vacillation [-éishn], *s.* vacilación.

vacuity [vakiúiti], *s.* vacuidad, vacío; hueco, laguna; ociosidad; estupidez; inanidad.

vacuo [vækiuo], *s.* el vacío (en la expresión **in v.,** en el vacío).

vacuous [vækiuus], *a.* vacío, desocupado; fatuo, mentecato.

vacuum [vækiuum]. **I.** *s.* vacío. **II.** *a.* de vacío; aspirante.—**v. bottle,** termos; frasco Dewar de vacío.—**v. brake,** freno de vacío.—**v. cleaner,** limpiador aspirante o de vacío, aspirador de polvo, barredera aspirante.—**v. ga(u)ge,** vacuómetro, indicador de vacío.—**v. jacket,** envolvente de vacío.—**v. pan,** (azú.) tacho de vacío.—**v. pump,** bomba de vapor condensado, en que el vacío se hace por condensación de vapor.—**v. tube,** (elec.) tubo de vacío; (rad.) audión, tubo termiónico.—**v. valve,** (m. v.) válvula de admisión de aire; (rad.) = **v. tube.**—**in a v.,** en el vacío.

vade mecum [védi mícum], *s.* vademécum.

vagabond [vægabond]. **I.** *a.* vagabundo, vagamundo; fluctuante. **II.** *s.* vago, vagamundo, pelafustán.—**vagabondage, vagabondism** [-bóndev, -ísm], *s.* vagancia.—**vagabondize** [-aiš], *vn.* vagabundear, vagamundear.

vagary [vægéri], *s.* capricho, extravagancia, humorada, antojo.

vagina [væváinæ], *s.* (anat.) vagina; (bot.) vagínula; vaina.—**vaginal** [vævínæl *o* væváinæl], *a.* (anat.) vaginal; (bot.) relativo o semejante a vaginulas.—**v. process,** apófisis vaginal (del temporal).—**v. tunic,** túnica vaginal.—**vaginate** [vævineit], **vaginated** [-ed], *a.* vaginulado.—**vaginitis** [vævináitis], *s.* vaginitis, inflamación de la vagina.

vagitus [væváitus], *s.* primer grito de la criatura recién nacida.

vagrancy [véigransi], *s.* vagancia.—**vagrant** [-ant]. **I.** *a.* vagabundo, vagamundo, errante. **II.** *s.* vago, vagabundo.—**vagrantly** [-li], *adv.* vagarosamente.

vague [véig], *a.* vago, indefinido; incierto, dudoso. —**vaguely** [-li], *adv.* vagamente.—**vagueness** [-nes], *s.* vaguedad.

vail [véil]. **I.** *va.* y *s.* = VEIL. **II.** *s. pl.* (Ingl.) propina.

vain [véin], *a.* vano, vanidoso; suntuoso, llamativo; inútil, vano; fútil, hueco, insubstancial.—**in v.,** en vano.

vainglorious [-glórius], *a.* vanaglorioso, jactancioso.—**vaingloriously** [-li], *adv.* jactanciosamente. —**vainglory, vaingloriousness** [-glóri, -usnes], *s.* vanagloria, jactancia.

vainly [véinli], *adv.* vanamente, arrogantemente; inútilmente.—**vainness** [-nes], *s.* vanidad, envanecimiento; inutilidad.

vair [véær], *s.* (blas.) vero.

valance [vælans], *s.* cenefa, doselera, gotera del dosel; (tej.) damasco para muebles.

vale [véil], *s.* valle; cañada; canalizo.

vale [véli *o* vále], *interj.* (lat.) ¡adiós!

valediction [vælediCshun], *s.* vale, despedida.

valedictorian [-dictórian], *s.* alumno que hace el discurso de despedida a fin de curso.

valedictory [-díctori]. **I.** *a.* de despedida. **II.** *s.* discurso de despedida en los colegios.

valence [véilens], **valency** [-i], *s.* (quím.) valencia.

Valenciennes [valansiénš], *s.* puntas de Valenciennes.

valentine [vælentain], *s.* estrecho que un galán o una dama elige el día de San Valentín (14 de febrero); misiva o regalo anónimos y jocosos que suelen enviarse en dicho día; amante.

valerian [valírian], *s.* (bot.) valeriana.

Valerianaceæ [valriianéisii], *s. pl.* (bot.) valerianáceas.—**valerianaceous** [-éišhus], *a.* valerianáceo.—**valeric** [valéric], *a.* valeriánico.

valet [vælet], *s.* criado, camarero, paje, asistente; aguijón para adiestrar caballos.—**v. de chambre,** ayuda de cámara.

valetudinarian [væletiúdinérian], *a.* y *s.* valetudinario.—**valetudinary** [-eri], *a.* valetudinario, delicado, impedido.

Valhalla [valjála], *s.* Valhala (Campos Elíseos de los escandinavos); sala, cámara o templo de héroes.

valiant [væliant], *a.* valeroso, bravo.—**valiantly** [-li], *a. adv.* valerosamente.—**valiantness** [-nes], *s.* valentía, valor.

valid [vælid], *a.* válido, justo; valedero; fuerte.

validate [vælidet], *va.* validar.

validity [valíditi], **validness** [vælidnes], *s.* validez.

validly [vælidli], *adv.* válidamente.

valise [valís], *s.* maleta, saco de viaje.

valkyria, valkyrie [vælkíriæ, -kíri], *s.* valquiria.

valley [væle], *s.* valle; (arq.) lima hoya.

valo(u)r [vælœr], *s.* valor, valentía, ánimo, fortaleza.

valorization [-iséišhun], *s.* fijación arbitraria oficial de precios.—**valorize** [-aiš], *va.* y *vn.* fijar o tratar de fijar precios arbitrarios oficialmente.—**valorous** [-us], *a.* valeroso, valiente, intrépido.—**valorously** [-li], *adv.* valerosamente.

valuable [væliuabœl]. **I.** *a.* valioso; precioso, estimable, preciado. **II.** *s. pl.* joyas u otros objetos de valor.—**valuably** [-bli], *adv.* apreciadamente.—**valuation** [-éišhun], *s.* valía, tasa, tasación, valuación; avalúo.—**valuator** [-éitœr], *s.* tasador, avaluador.

value [væliu]. **I.** *s.* valor, mérito, valía; precio, justiprecio, valuación, monta; aprecio, estimación; entidad, importancia; (mús.) valor de una nota; (biol.) grado o lugar en una clasificación. **II.** *va.* valuar, valorar, tasar; preciar, apreciar, tener en mucho; considerar.—**valueless** [-les], *a.* sin valor, despreciable.—**valuer** [-œr], *s.* tasador, valuador, avaluador.

valval, valvar [vælval, -ar], *a.* valvar, relativo a las valvas.

valvate [vælvet], *a.* valvulado, valvular.

valve [vælv], *s.* válvula; ventalla; (anat.) válvula; (zool.) valva de los moluscos; (bot.) ventalla.— **v. box, v. chest,** (m. v.) caja de válvula.—**v. face,** cara, superficie de trabajo de la válvula.—**v. gear,** (m. v.) distribución, mecanismo de distribución.— **v. lift,** alza de la válvula; carrera de la válvula (si ésta es vertical de tubo).—**v. rod,** varilla de la válvula.—**v. seat,** asiento de la válvula.—**v. stem,** vástago de la válvula.—**v. travel,** carrera de la válvula.

valvular [vælviular], *a.* valvular.—**v. heart disease,** enfermedad orgánica de las válvulas del corazón.

valvule [vælviul], *s.* valvulilla.

vamose [vamús *o* vámos], *va.* y *vn.* marcharse, largarse; hacer ir.

vamp [væmp]. **I.** *s.* (zap.) empella; capellada; remiendo, remonta; (fam.) acompañamiento músico improvisado; (fam.) parásito, estafador, aventurero (apl. esp. a mujeres). **II.** *va.* (zap.) poner capellada; remontar, remendar; (fam., mús.) improvisar (acompañamiento); estafar, embaucar, timar.

vamper [væmpœr], *s.* remendón.

vampire [væmpair], *s.* vampiro; parásito; estafador, aventurero.

van [væn], *s.* carromato, galera, conductora de muebles; (Ingl., f. c.) furgón de equipajes; (mil.) vanguardia; jefes de una empresa; (ant.) aventador; bieldo; (min.) ensayo de arenas auríferas por el lavado.

vanadate [vénadet], *s.* (quím.) vanadiato.

vanadic [vanédic], *a.* vanádico.

vanadium [vanéidum], *s.* (quím.) vanadio.

vandal [vændal], *a.* y *s.* vándalo.—**vandalism** [-ísm], *s.* vandalismo.

Vandyke, Vandyck [vandáik]. **I.** *a.* de Van Dyck, a la Van Dyck.—**v. beard,** barba puntiaguda. **II.** *s.* (b. a.) cuadro pintado por Van Dyck; cuello ancho de lienzo y encaje.

vane [véin], *s.* veleta; (mar.) grímpola; aspa (de molino); paleta (de hélice); barba (de pluma); pínula (de instrumentos matemáticos).—**v. stock,**

armazón de grímpola.—**v. spindle**, huso o hierro de la grímpola.

vang [væng], *s*. (mar.) burra de mesana.

vanguard [vǽngard], *s*. vanguardia.

vanilla [vaníla], *s*. (bot.) vainilla.

vanillin [vænílin], *s*. (quím.) vanilina.

vanish [vǽniȟ], *vn*. desvanecerse, desaparecer.— **vanishing point**, (dib.) punto de la vista.

vanity [vǽniti], *s*. vanidad.—**v. bag, v. box, v. case, v. set**, neceser.

vanquish [vǽnkuiȟ], *va*. y *vn*. vencer.—**vanquishable** [-abœl], *a*. vencible.—**vanquisher** [-œr], *s*. vencedor.

vantage [vǽntey], *s*. ventaja, superioridad.—**v. ground**, posición ventajosa.

vapid [vǽpid], *a*. evaporado; insípido, soso, insulso.—**vapidity** [vapíditi], **vapidness** [vǽpidnes], *s*. insipidez.

vapo(u)r [véipœr]. **I.** *s*. vapor; niebla, bruma; vaho, exhalación; hálito; humo, cosa insubstancial; presunción, humos, fanfarronería; (med.) remedio inhalado.—*pl*. (ant.) vapores, melancolía. —**v. bath**, baño de vapor.—**v. galvanizing**, procedimiento de revestir de cinc en una atmósfera de vapor de este metal, sherardización. *V.* SHERARDIZE. **II.** *vn*. exhalar vapor, avahar; alardear, baladronear; (ant.) evaporarse. **III.** *va*. (ant.) evaporar; exhalar, avahar.

vaporer [véipœrœr], *s*. fanfarrón.

vaporise [-aiȟ], *va*. y *vn*. = VAPORIZE.

vaporish [-iȟ], *a*. vaporoso.—**vaporizable** [-áisabœl], *a*. vaporizable.—**vaporization** [-iȟéȟun], *s*. vaporización.—**vaporize** [-aiȟ], *va*. y *vn*. vaporizar(se).—**vaporizer** [-áiȟœr], *s*. vaporizador.

vaporous [-uȟ], *a*. vaporoso, nebuloso; hipocondríaco; vano, quimérico.—**vapory** [-ri], *a*. vaporoso; melancólico, hipocondríaco.

varanian [væréinisn], *s*. y *a*. (zool.) varánido.

Varanidæ [værǽnidi], *s. pl*. (zool.) varánidos.— **varanus** [værænuȟ], *s*. (zool.) varano, monitor.

variable [vériabœl], *s*. y *a*. (leng. ord., mec. y mat.) variable.—**v. gear**, (ing.) engranaje de relación de multiplicación variable.—**v.-speed gear**, (aut.) cambio de velocidades.

variableness [-nes], *s*. variabilidad, inconstancia. —**variably** [-bli], *adv*. variablemente.

variance [vérians], *s*. variación, cambio, mudanza; discordia, desavenencia, desacuerdo.—**to be at v.**, estar discordes, estar de punta.

variant [-ant]. **I.** *a*. variante, variable; inquieto, indeciso. **II.** *s*. sinónimo; (mat.) variante.

variation [-éȟun], *s*. variación; variedad; inflexión (gram.); (mús.) variación; (astr.) variación; (biol.) variación.

varicella [væriséla], *s*. varicela.

varicocele [vǽricosil], *s*. varicocele.

varicolored [véricúlœrd], *a*. abigarrado.

varicose [vǽricos], *a*. varicoso.

varied [vérid], *a*. variado, vario.

variegate [vériegueit], *va*. jaspear, vetear, varetear, matizar, gayar; (pint.) abigarrar, pintorrear, pintarrajar.—**variegated** [-ed], *a*. abigarrado, jaspeado, pintarrajado.—**variegation** [-éiȟun], *s*. jaspeadura; veteado, jaspeado.

variety [varáieti], *s*. variedad, diversidad.—**v. is the spice of life**, en la variedad está el placer.

variocoupler [vériocúplœr], *s*. (rad.) acoplamiento variable (apl. esp. al de conexión del receptor con la antena).

variola [varáiola], *s*. viruela.

varioloid [vérioloid *o* vǽrioloid], *s*. varioloide.

variolous [varáioluȟ], *a*. varioloso.

variometer [variómetœr], *s*. (rad.) variómetro.

variorum [-órum], *a*. anotado por varios críticos o expertos.

various [vériuȟ], *a*. varios; diverso, diferente; inconstante, mudable; desemejante; veteado, abigarrado.

variously [-li], *adv*. variamente.

varix [váricȟ], *s*. (med.) várice o variz.

varlet [várlet], *s*. lacayo; paje.

varletry [várletri], *s*. chusma, canalla.

varnish [várniȟ]. **I.** *s*. barniz; (cerá.) mogate. **II.** *va*. barnizar; (cerá.) vidriar; paliar, disimular, encubrir.—**varnisher** [-œr], *s*. barnizador; encubridor.

'varsity [vársiti], *s*. y *a*. (fam.) universidad (corruptela de UNIVERSITY).

vary [vέeri], *va*. y *vn*. variar, cambiar; desviar(se). —**varying** [-ing], *a*. variable

vas [væs], *s*. (anat.) conducto.—**v. deferens**, conducto deferente.

vascular [vǽskiular], *a*. vascular.—**vascularity** [-lǽriti], *s*. calidad de vascular.—**vasculose** [-lous], *a*. (bot.) vasculoso.

vase [véis *o* vaȟ], *s*. jarrón, vaso

vaseline [vǽselin], *s*. vaselina.

vasomotor [vǽsomótœr]. **I.** *a*. (anat.) vasomotor. **II.** *s*. (med.) estimulante que produce acción vascular.

vassal [vǽsal]. **I.** *s*. vasallo, siervo. **II.** *a*. tributario, servil.—**vassalage** [-ey], *s*. vasallaje.

vast [vast]. **I.** *a*. vasto, dilatado; inmenso, enorme, grandísimo. **II.** *s*. (poét.) inmensidad, infinito.—**vastly** [-li], *adv*. en sumo, grado, muy, muchísimo, sumamente.—**vastness** [-nes], *s*. vastedad, inmensidad.—**vasty** [-i], *a*. (poét.) vasto, inmenso.

vat [væt], *s*. tina, tanque; (ten.) noque

Vatican [vǽtican], *s*. Vaticano.

vaticide [vǽtisaid], *s*. asesino o asesinato de un profeta.

vaticinate [vatísineit], *vn*. y *va*. vaticinar.

vaticination [-éiȟun], *s*. vaticinio.

vaudeville [vódvil], *s*. (teat.) función de variedades; (ant.) jácara, romance, canción.

vault [volt]. **I.** *s*. bóveda; cúpula; cueva, bodega, subterráneo, sibil; tumba; (igl.) cripta; voltereta, salto. **II.** *va*. (arq.) abovedar. **III.** *va*. y *vn*. (dep.) voltear, saltar por encima con garrocha.

vaulted [vólted], *a*. abovedado, arqueado.

vaulter [vóltœr], *s*. volteador, saltador, volatín.

vaulting [-ing], *s*. abovedado, bóvedas; construcción de bóvedas.

vaunt [vant *o* vont]. **I.** *va*. y *vn*. ostentar, alardear, jactarse, vanagloriarse. **II.** *s*. jactancia, gala, fachenda.—**vaunter** [-œr], *s*. fanfarrón, fachendista.—**vaunting** [-ing], *a*. jactancioso.— **vauntingly** [-ingli], *adv*. con jactancia.

veal [vil], *s*. carne de ternera.—**v. cutlet**, coteleta de ternera.—**v. pie**, pastel de ternera.

vector [véctœr], *s*. (mat.) vector.—**v. quantity**, cantidad vectorial.—**vectorial** [vectórial], *a*. vectorial.

Veda [véda], *s*. Veda.

vedette [vedét], *s*. (mil.) centinela o escucha de caballería.

Vedic [vídic], *a*. védico, relativo a los Vedas, o de los Vedas.

veer [víœr]. **I.** *vn*. (mar.) virar, rolar, cambiar. **II.** *va*. virar, dirigir el buque a otro rumbo; arriar, aflojar, largar.—**to v. and haul**, lascar y halar; largar y escasear.—**to v. away the cable**, soltar cable.

veery [víri], *s*. (orn.) tordo canoro.

vegetable [véyetabœl]. **I.** *s*. planta, vegetal.—*pl*. verduras, hortalizas, legumbres. **II.** *a*. vegetable, vegetal; de hortalizas.—**v. garden**, huerta (de legumbres).—**v. ivory**, tagua.—**v. marrow**, medula vegetal.—**v. sulphur**, licopodio en polvo.

vegetal [véyetal], *a*. vegetal.

vegetarian [véyetérian], *a*., *s*. vegetariano, vegetalista.—**vegetarianism** [-iȟm], *s*. vegetarianismo.

vegetate [véyeteit], *vn*. vegetar.—**vegetation** [-éiȟun], *s*. vegetación.—**vegetative** [-ativ], *a*. vegetativo, vegetante.—**vegetativeness** [-nes], *s*. potencia vegetativa.

vehemence, vehemency [víjemens, -i], *s*. vehemencia.—**vehement** [-ent], *a*. vehemente, impetuoso, intensivo, extremoso.—**vehemently** [-li], *adv*. vehementemente, impetuosamente.

vehicle [víjicœl], *s*. vehículo, carruaje; medio; excipiente.

vehicular [vejíkiular], *a*. perteneciente o relativo al vehículo; de o para vehículos.

veil [véil]. **I.** *va*. velar, cubrir con velo; encubrir, disimular, disfrazar, tapar. **II.** *s*. velo; cortina; disfraz, máscara, pretexto.

vein [véin]. **I.** s. (anat.) vena; (ent.) nervio del ala de un insecto; (bot.) vena, nervio; (min.) vena, veta, capa, filón; (carp.) vena, hebra, trepa; humor, genio. **II.** va. jaspear, vetear.

veined [véind], a. venoso, que tiene venas; veteado, avetado.—**veinless** [-les], a. sin venas, desprovisto de venas.—**veinlet** [-let], s. venilla.

veinstone [-stóun], s. (min.) ganga.

veiny [-i], a. = VEINED.

veld, veldt [velt], s. veld, tierra abierta; sabanas, tierras ganaderas o de pastos.

vellicate [vélikeit], va. (med.) velicar.

vellication [-éishun], s. (med.) velicación.

vellum [vélum], s. vitela, pergamino.—**v. paper,** papel vitela.

velocimeter [vélosímetœr], s. velocímetro.

velocipede [velósipid], s. velocípedo.

velocity [velósiti], s. velocidad.

velodrome [vélodroum], s. velódromo, lugar de carreras (apl. esp. a las de bicicleta).

velours [velúœr], s. terciopelado.

velure [véliuœr]. **I.** s. terciopelado (tela); cepillo de pana. **II.** va. cepillar o limpiar con cepillo de pana; cubrir de terciopelado.

velvet [vélvet]. **I.** s. (tej.) terciopelo, velludo; (zool.) vello.—**v. like,** terciopelado.—**v. weaver,** terciopelero. **II.** a. de terciopelo, terciopelado.

velveteen [vélvetín], s. pana, velludillo.

velvety [vélveti], a. aterciopelado.

vena [vínæ], s. pl. **venæ** [vini] (anat., hidr.) vena. —**v. cava,** (anat.) vena cava.—**v. contracta,** (hidr.) contracción de la vena flúida.—**v. portæ,** (anat.) vena porta.

venal [vínal], a. venal, mercenario.

venality [venáliti], s. venalidad.

venatic [venátic], a. venatorio.

venation [venéishun], s. venación.

vend, va. vender (en carretón).

vendee [vendí], s. comprador.

vender [véndœr], s. vendedor ambulante, buhonero.

vendetta [vendéta], s. vendetta, venganza particular ejecutada por familias.

vendible [véndibœl]. **I.** a. vendible. **II.** s. géneros de venta.—**vendibleness** [-nes], s. calidad de vendible.

vendor [véndor], s. (for.) vendedor.

vendue [vendiú], s. venduta.

veneer [veníœr]. **I.** va. chapear, enchapar; revestir; tapar, ocultar, disfrazar. **II.** s. hoja para chapear, chapa; capa exterior, apariencia.

veneering [-ing], s. chapeado, enchapado; material para chapas.

venerability [vénerabíliti], s. venerabilidad.

venerable [vénœrabœl], a. venerable; venerando, sagrado.—**venerableness** [-nes], s. venerabilidad.—**venerably** [-bli], adv. venerablemente, con veneración o reverencia.—**venerate** [-eit], va. venerar, reverenciar.—**veneration** [-éishun], s. veneración, reverencia.—**venerator** [-éitœr], s. venerador.

venereal [veníreal], a. venéreo.

venery [véneri], s. venus, acto venéreo; (ant.) montería o caza mayor.

venesection [vínesécshun], s. flebotomía, sangría.

Venetian [veníshan], a. y s. veneciano.—**V. blinds,** persianas, celosías.—**V. chalk,** talco gráfico.—**V. window,** ventana trigeminada.

vengeance [vényæns], s. venganza.—**with a v.,** con violencia, con toda su alma; con creces, extremamente.

vengeful [vényful], a. vengativo.

venial [vínial], a. venial; perdonable.—**v. sin,** pecado venial.—**venially** [-li], adv. venialmente, levemente, ligeramente.—**veniality, venialness** [viniæliti, viniælnes], s. venialidad.

venire [venáire], s. (for.) auto de convocación del jurado.

venison [vénscen], s. carne de venado.

venom [vénum], s. veneno; tósigo, ponzoña; rencor.

venomous [-us], a. venenoso, ponzoñoso; dañoso; maligno.—**venomously** [-li], adv. venenosamente. —**venomousness** [-nes], s. venenosidad.

venous [vínus], a. venoso; veteado.—**v. blood,** sangre venosa.

vent. I. s. respiradero, resolladero, tronera, lumbrera, ventosa; salida, paso, abertura, pasaje; oído, fogón de arma de fuego; (fund.) bravera; ano; expresión; emisión; desahogo.—**v. searcher,** (arti.) gubio. **II.** va. expresar, desembuchar, desahogar, desfogar, dar salida.—**to v. one's spleen,** descargar uno la bilis.

ventail [vénteil], s. ventalla (de casco).

vental [véntal], a. del viento.

venter [[véntœr], s. vientre; cavidad; matriz.

venthole [véntjóul], s. orificio de escape; (arti.) oído, fogón; (ton.) venteo; atabe de cañería.

ventiduct [véntidúct, s. conducto de ventilación.

ventilate [véntileit], va. ventilar; proveer de respiradero; (ant.) aechar.—**ventilation** [-éishun], s. ventilación.—**ventilator** [-éitœr], s. ventilador.

ventose [véntos], a. ventoso, flatulento.

ventral [véntral], a. ventral, abdominal.—**v. hernia,** eventración, hernia abdominal.

ventricle [véntricœl], s. (anat.) ventrículo.

ventricular [ventríkiular], a. ventricular.

ventriloquism [-locuism], s. ventriloquia.—**ventriloquist** [-ist], s. ventrílocuo.—**ventriloquize** [-cuais], vn. hablar como ventrílocuo, ser ventrílocuo.—**ventriloquy** [-cui], s. = VENTRILOQUISM.

venture [vénchœr]. **I.** s. riesgo, ventura, albur; (com.) pacotilla, ancheta; operación o empresa arriesgada; especulación.—**at a v.,** a la ventura, al azar. **II.** va. aventurar, arriesgar. **III.** vn. osar, atreverse; aventurarse, arriesgarse.—**to v. abroad,** atreverse a salir, arriesgarse fuera.—**to v. at, o on,** probar ventura en.—**to v. out** = TO V. ABROAD. —**to v. upon** = TO V. AT.

venturer [vénchurœr], s. aventurero.

venturesome [-sum], a. atrevido, emprendedor; aventurado, azaroso.—**venturesomely** [-li], adv. atrevidamente.—**venturesomeness** [-nes], s. arrojo, temeridad, carácter aventurero.

Venturi meter, Venturi tube [ventúri mítœr, tiúb], s. (hidr.) medidor o tubo Venturi.

venturous [vénchœrus], a. osado, atrevido.—**venturously** [-li], adv. osadamente.—**venturousness** [-nes], s. arrojo, temeridad.

venue [véniu], s. (for.) jurisdicción en que se ha cometido un crimen o en que está sita la cosa litigiosa; (esgr.) pase.—**change of v.,** cambio de tribunal en un pleito.

venule [véniul], s. venilla.

Venus [vínus], s. Venus; (astr.) Venus.—**V.'s-comb,** (bot.) peine de pastor.—**V.'s-fan,** especie de zoófito.—**V.'s-flytrap,** (bot.) atrapamoscas.—**V.'s-looking-glass,** (bot.) campanilla.—**V.'s-navelwort,** (bot.) ombligo de Venus.

veracity [verásiti], s. veracidad.

veracious [veréshus], a. veraz, verídico.

veranda [verénda], s. pórtico, galería, balcón cubierto.

veratrin(e [vératrin], s. (quím.) veratrina.

veratrum [viréitrum], s. veratro, eléboro blanco.

verb [vœrb], s. (gram.) verbo.

verbal [vœrbal]. **I.** a. verbal; oral, de viva voz; literal; (gram.) verbal.—**v. contract,** contrato verbal, de palabra.—**v. noun,** substantivo verbal. **II.** s. substantivo verbal.

verbalism [-ism], s. expresión oral; palabrería.

verbally [-i], adv. verbalmente.

verbatim [vœrbéitim], adv. al pie de la letra, palabra por palabra.

verbena [vœrbína], s. (bot.) verbena.

Verbenaceæ [vœrbenéisii], s. pl. (bot.) verbenáceas.—**verbenaceous** [-shus], a. verbenáceo.

verbiage [vœrbiœy], s. verbosidad.

verbose [vœrbós], a. verboso, difuso, prolijo.

verboseness [-nes], **verbosity** [vœrbósiti], s. verbosidad, ampulosidad; palabrería.

verdancy [vœrdansi], s. verdor, verdín.

verdant [vœrdant], a. verde, verdoso, fresco; inocente, sencillo.

verd antique [vœrd æntíc], s. verde antiguo; pátina verde.

verdict [vœrdict], s. veredicto, fallo; opinión, dictamen.

verdigris [-digris], s. verdete, cardenillo, verdín.
verdin [vǽrdin], s. (Méx., orn.) paro.
verditer [vǽrditœr], s. (pint.) verdete.
verdure [vǽryur], s. verde, verdor, frondas.
verdurous [vǽryurus], a. verdoso.
Verein [feráin], s. sociedad, asociación.
verge [vœry]. **I.** s. borde, margen; vera, veril; círculo, anillo; alcance, esfera; vara, varilla, báculo; (alb.) boquilla; (arq.) fuste de columna; árbol de volante de un reloj; (Ingl., for.) jurisdicción del mayordomo de palacio.—**on**, o **upon, the v. of,** al borde de; a punto de, al, a dos dedos de. **II.** vn. acercarse a, tender.—**to v. on**, o **upon,** llegar casi hasta, acercarse a, rayar en.
verger [vǽrœr], s. alguacil de vara; macero; aposentador, pertiguero.
veridical [verídical], a. verídico.—**veridically** [-li], adv. verídicamente.
verifiable [vérifáiabœl], a. verificable.
verification [-fikéshun], s. verificación, comprobación.
verify [-fai], va. verificar, justificar, comprobar, demostrar; cerciorarse de; cumplir, ejecutar (una promesa); (for.) afirmar bajo juramento; acreditar.
verily [vérili], adv. en verdad.
verisimilar [vérisímilar], a. verosímil.
verisimilitude [-símilitud], s. verosimilitud.
veritable [véritabœl], a. verdadero.
verity [vériti], s. verdad, realidad; hecho; axioma.
verjuice [vǽryus], s. agraz; agrazada; aspereza, mordacidad.
vermeil [-mil], s. plata o bronce sobredorados; barniz transparente de agua; bermellón; granate rojo anaranjado.
vermicelli [vǽrmiséli o -chéli], s. fideos. (El s. inglés es siempre sing.).
vermicide [vǽrmisaid], s. vermífugo.
vermicular [vœrmíkiular], a. vermicular.—**v. work,** (arq.) ornamentación vermiforme.
vermiculate [-leit]. **I.** va. poner adornos vermiformes. **II.** a. vermiforme.—**vermiculation** [-élshun], s. movimiento vermicular de los intestinos.—**vermiculose, vermiculous** [-lous, -lus], a. vermicular.
vermiform [vǽrmiform], a. vermiforme; vermicular.—**v. appendix,** apéndice vermiforme.
vermifuge [vǽrmifiur], s. vermífugo.
vermillion [vœrmíliun]. **I.** s. bermellón, cinabrio. **II.** va. enrojar, teñir de rojo.
vermin [vǽrmin], s. (sing. y pl.) bichos asquerosos, sabandijas (gusanos, chinches, piojos, etc.)
vermination [-éishun], s. generación de bichos.
verminous [-us], a. (med.) verminoso.
vermivorous [vœrmívorus], a. vermívoro.
vermuth [vǽrmuz], s. vermut (licor).
vernacular [vœrnǽkiular]. **I.** a. vernáculo, nativo; local. **II.** s. idioma vernáculo.
vernacularism [-ism], s. modismo.
vernal [vǽrnal], a. vernal; primaveral.—**v. equinox,** equinoccio vernal.
vernier [vǽrniœr], s. nonio, vernier.
veronal [vǽronal], s. veronal (nombre de fábrica), especie de narcótico.
Veronese [veronís], a. y s. veronés.
veronica [virónicæ], s. lienzo de la Verónica.
verruca [verrúcæ], s. (med., hist. nat.) verruga.
verrucose, verrucous [vérrucous, -cus], a. verrugoso, cubierto de verrugas.
versatile [vǽrsatil], a. versátil; giratorio; inconstante, voluble.—**versatility** [-tíliti], s. versatilidad; veleidad, inconstancia; adaptabilidad; variedad de conocimientos.
verse [vœrs]. **I.** s. verso; estrofa, copla, poesía; versículo.—**v. maker,** versificador.—**v. making,** versificación. **II.** va. y vn. rimar, versificar, hacer versos.
versed [vœrst], a. versado, perito.
versed sine [sáin], s. (mat.) senoverso.
verseman [vǽrsman], s. poeta, versista.
versemonger [vǽrsmóngœr], s. poetastro.
versicle [vǽrsicœl], s. versículo.

versification [-fikéshun], s. versificación.—**versifier** [-fáiœr], s. versificador.—**versify** [-fai], va. y vn. versificar.
version [vǽrshun], s. versión; exposición, interpretación; traducción; (cir.) versión.
verso [vérso], s. reverso; (impr.) página par.
versus [vǽrsus], prep. (for.) contra.
vert [vœrt], s. (Ingl.) árbol o arbusto con hojas en un bosque; (for.) derecho de tala; (blas.) sinople.
vertebra [vǽrtebra], s. (pl. **vertebræ** [-bri]), vértebra.—**vertebral** [-al], a. vertebral; vertebrado.—**Vertebrata** [-bréitæ], s. pl. vertebrados.—**vertebrate** [-breit], s. y a. vertebrado.
vertex [vǽrtecs], s. vértice; cima, cumbre, cúspide, ápice.
vertical [vǽrtical], a. vertical.—**v. angles,** ángulos opuestos por el vértice.—**verticality** [-cáliti], s. verticalidad.—**vertically** [vǽrticali], adv. verticalmente.
vertices [-sis], s. pl. de VERTEX.
verticil [vǽrtisil], s. (biol.) verticilo.
verticillate [vœrtísilet], a. (bot.) verticilado.
verticity [vœrtísiti], s. verticidad, giro.
vertiginous [vœrtíyinus], a. vertiginoso.
vertigo [vǽrtigo], s. vértigo, vahido.
vervain [vǽrvein], s. (bot.) verbena.
verve [vœrv], s. vis, estro, numen.
very [véri]. **I.** a. mismo, idéntico; verdadero, real; mismísimo. **II.** adv. muy; mucho, muchísimo.—**v. much,** mucho, muchísimo; sumamente, muy (antes de un participio).—**v. many,** muchísimos.—**v. much so,** muy mucho, muchísimo, en sumo grado.
vesania [veséiniæ], s. (med.) vesania, locura.
vesica [vesáicæ], s. vejiga.—**v. piscis** [písis], (b. a.) aureola.
vesical [vésical], a. vesical.—**vesicant** [-ant]. **I.** a. vesicante. **II.** s. vejigatorio.—**vesicate** [-eit], va. avejigar.—**vesication** [-éishun], s. acción de producir vejigas o ampollas.—**vesicatory** [-atori], s. vejigatorio.—**vesicle** [-œl], s. vesícula, vejiguilla.
vesicula [vesíkulæ], s. vesícula.—**v. seminalis,** vesícula seminal.
vesicular [vesíkiular], a. vesicular, vesiculoso.
vesper [véspœr]. **I.** s. tarde, el anochecer; campana que llama a vísperas; véspero, estrella vespertina.—pl. (igl.) vísperas. **II.** a. vespertino.—**vespertine** [-tin], a. vespertino.
vespid [véspid], s. y a. (zool.) véspido.—**Vespidæ** [-di], s. pl. véspidos.
vessel [vésel], s. vasija, vaso; (anat.) vaso; (mar.) barco, buque, bajel, embarcación; (bot.) V. DUCT.—**vessels in ordinary,** (mar.) buques desarmados.
vest. **I.** s. chaleco, chaqueta antigua; elástica, camiseta interior; vestido, vestidura. **II.** va. revestir (de autoridad), investir; (for.) hacer entrega, dar posesión; vestir.—**to v. in,** revestir de, investir de, poner en posesión de.—**to v. with,** vestir de, revestir de. **III.** vn. vestirse; tener validez, ser válido.
vestal [véstal], s. y a. vestal; virgen.
vested [vésted], a. cabal y completo, absoluto; establecido o protegido por la ley.—**v. interests,** intereses creados.
vestibule [véstibiul], s. vertíbulo, portal, zaguán; salón de entrada (de un hotel, etc.); (anat.) vestíbulo (del oído); (f. c.) pasillo cubierto entre dos coches ferroviarios.—**v. car,** (f. c.) coche de un tren de pasillos cubiertos de comunicación (llamado **v. train**).
vestige [véstiy], s. vestigio.—**vestigial** [vestíyial], a. (biol.) atrofiado o degenerado.
vesting [vésting], s. corte de chaleco.
vestment [véstmœnt], s. prenda de vestir; ropa, vestidura; (igl.) vestimenta; sabanilla (de altar).
vestry [véstri], s. (igl.) vestuario, sacristía; junta que administra los asuntos de una iglesia episcopal protestante.—**vestryman** [-mæn], s. miembro de dicha junta.
vesture [véschur], s. vestido, vestuario; traje, hábito; (Ingl. for. ant.) todo lo que cubre el terreno excepto los árboles.

vetch [vech], *s.* (bot.) arveja, veza, yero, algarroba, almorta.

vetchling [véchling], *s.* arveja, áfaca.

veteran [vétœran], *s.* y *a.* veterano.

veterinarian [vétœrinérian], *s.* albéitar, veterinario.

veterinary [-neri], *a.* y *s.* veterinario.—**v. science**, veterinaria.—**v. surgeon**, albéitar.

veto [víto]. **I.** *va.* poner el veto; vedar, prohibir; rehusar la aprobación de. **II.** *s.* veto; prohibición hecha con autoridad.

vex [vecs], *va.* vejar, molestar, hostigar, irritar, enfadar; afligir, desazonar, acongojar; agitar, turbar, perturbar.—**to be vexed**, incomodarse, enojarse, picarse.

vexation [vecséishun], *s.* vejación, vejamen, molestia, maltrato; provocación, enojo, enfado; disgusto; chinchorrería.—**vexatious** [-shus], *a.* vejatorio, molesto, enfadoso; provocativo.—**vexatiously** [-li], *adv.* enfadosamente con molestia.—**vexatiousness** [-nes], *s.* vejamen, molestia, vejación.

vexed [vecst], *a.* discutido, debatido.—**v. question**, cuestión batallona.

via [váia o vía], *prep.* por la vía de, por.

viability [váiabíliti], *s.* viabilidad.

viable [váiabœl], *a.* viable.

viaduct [váiaduct], *s.* viaducto.

vial [váial], *s.* redoma, frasco, ampolleta.

viand [váiand], *s.* vianda, carne.—*pl.* comida, alimentos, provisiones, vitualla.

viatic [vaiétic], *a.* de viaje, de viático.

viaticum [vaiéticum], *s.* viático; (igl.) Viático.

vibrant [váibrant], *a.* vibrante.

vibrate [-breit]. **I.** *va.* vibrar, blandir. **II.** *vn.* vibrar, oscilar, cimbrar.—**vibratile** [-bratil], *a.* vibrátil, vibratorio.—**vibrating** [-bréiting], *a.* vibrante, oscilante, trepidante.—**vibration** [-bréishun], *s.* vibración, oscilación.—**vibrative** [-brœtiv], *a.* vibratorio.—**vibrator** [-bréitor], *s.* (elec.) interruptor intermitente, vibrador; (rad.) oscilador, interruptor de la bobina de inducción; (impr.) cilindro oscilante.—**vibratory** [-tori], *a.* = VIBRATIVE.

vibrio [víbrio], *s.* vibrión, especie de bacteria.

viburnum [vibœrnum], *s.* (bot.) viburno, mundillo.

vicar [vícar], *s.* vicario.—**v. forane**, vicario foráneo.—**v. general**, vicario general.—**vicarage** [vícarey], *s.* vicaría.—**vicarial** [vaikérial], *a.* vicarial.—**vicariate** [vaikériet]. **I.** *s.* vicariato. **II.** *a.* vicario.—**vicarious** [vaikérius], *a.* vicario; (fisiol.) substitutivo.—**vicarship** [vícarship], *s.* vicaría.

vice [váis], *s.* vicio, inmoralidad; defecto, falta; (eq.) vicio o resabio del caballo; substituto, suplente. *V.* VISE.

vice [váisi], *prep.* en lugar de, en vez de.—**V. L . . . , retired**, en lugar de L . . . , jubilado.

vice- [váis], *prefijo* que corresponde a "vice-" en español.—**v. admiral**, vicealmirante.—**v. admiralty**, vicealmirantazgo.—**v. chancellor**, vicecanciller, vicecancelario.—**v. consul**, vicecónsul.—**v. consulate, v. consulship**, viceconsulado.—**v. presidency**, vicepresidencia.—**v. president**, vicepresidente.

vicegerent [-yírent], *s.* y *a.* vicegerente, teniente, diputado, substituto.—**vicegerency** [-si], *s.* agencia, tenencia, substitución.

viceregal [vaisrígal], *a.* de virrey.

viceroy [váisroi], *s.* virrey.—**viceroyalty** [vaisróialti], **viceroyship** [-ship], *s.* virreinato.

vice versa [váisi vœrsa], *adv.* viceversa.

vicinage [vísiney], *s.* vecindad.—**vicinal** [-al], *a.* vecino, vecinal.

vicinity [visíniti], *s.* vecindad, cercanía.

vicious [víshus], *a.* vicioso, depravado; defectuoso, imperfecto; (eq.) resabioso; (fam.) maligno, rencoroso.—**v. circle**, círculo vicioso.—**viciously** [-li], *adv.* viciosamente.—**viciousness** [-nes], *s.* depravación; resabio, lacra.

vicissitude [visísitiud], *s.* vicisitud.

victim [víctim], *s.* víctima; (for.) interfecto.

victimize [víctimaiś], *va.* (fam.) hacer víctima; estafar, embaucar.

victor [víctor], *s.* vencedor, triunfador.

victoria [victória], *s.* (bot.) victoria, ninfea gigantea; (carr.) victoria.

Victorian [victórian], *a.* victoriano, perteneciente a la reina Victoria o a su época.

victorious [-us], *a.* victorioso.—**victoriously** [-li], *adv.* victoriosamente.—**victoriousness** [-nes], *s.* calidad de victorioso.

victory [víctori], *s.* victoria, triunfo.

victress [víctres], *s.* vencedora.

victual [vítœl]. **I.** *va.* abastecer, bastimentar, avituallar. **II.** *s. pl.* vitualla, víveres, provisiones.

victual(l)er [vítlœr], *s.* abastecedor, proveedor; comisario; hostelero.

vicugna, vicuña [vicúña], *s.* (zool.) vicuña.

vide [vaide], *v.* véase, véanse, *vide.*—**v. ante**, véase lo anterior.—**v. infra**, véase más abajo.—**v. supra**, véase más arriba.—**quod v.**, véase (esto, esta palabra, etc.).

videlicet [vidéliset], *adv.* a saber.

vie [vái], *va.* y *vn.* competir, rivalizar.

Viennese [vienís], *a.* y *s.* vienés.

view [viú]. **I.** *va.* mirar; ver; contemplar; examinar, inspeccionar, reconocer; considerar, especular. **II.** *s.* vista, mirada, inspección, contemplación; visión; escena, panorama, paisaje, perspectiva; alcance de la vista; modo de ver; opinión, parecer; fase, aspecto, mira, intención, propósito; apariencia, exterioridad; (for.) inspección judicial de una propiedad o paraje.—**at first v.**, a primera vista.—**at one v.**, de una ojeada, de una mirada.—**in v.**, en mira.—**in v. of**, en vista de; respecto de.—**on v.**, en exhibición.—**with a v. to**, a fin de, con el propósito de.—**with this v.**, con esta mira, con este intento.

viewer [viúœr], *s.* veedor, mirador.

viewless [viúles], *a.* invisible.

viewpoint [-póint], *s.* punto de vista.

vigesimal [vaiyésimal], *a.* vigésimo.

vigil [víyil], *s.* vela, velación, vigilia, desvelo; vigilancia; (igl.) vigilia.

vigilance, vigilancy [-ans, -i], *s.* desvelo, vigilancia, cuidado.—**v. committee**, junta de vigilancia.—**vigilant** [-ant], *a.* vigilante, atento, alerta.—**vigilante** [-ánti], *s.* vigilante, miembro de una junta vigilante.—**vigilantly** [-li], *adv.* vigilantemente, alertamente.

vignette [viñét]. **I.** *va.* (foto.) hacer un retrato en viñeta; aviñetar; adornar con viñetas. **II.** *s.* (arq.) ramaje; (impr.) viñeta, marmote o marmoseto; (foto. y grab.) viñeta.

vigo(u)r [vígœr], *s.* vigor; fuerza, tesón, energía; verdor, lozanía.—**vigorous** [-us], *a.* vigoroso o fuerte, robusto.—**vigorously** [-li], *adv.* vigorosamente, enérgicamente, con fuerza o con tesón.—**vigorousness** [-nes], *s.* vigorosidad; actividad.

viking [váiking], *s.* antiguo pirata escandinavo.

vilayet [vílayet], *s.* vilayato, provincia (de Turquía).

vile [váil], *a.* vil, bajo, soez, despreciable; malvado, ruin; (fam.) malísimo, detestable (dicho de las cosas).—**vilely** [-li], *adv.* vilmente, bajamente, ruinmente.—**vileness** [-nes], *s.* vileza, ruindad.

vilification [vilifikéishun], *s.* envilecimiento, vilipendio; difamación.

vilifier [víaiœr], *s.* difamador.—**vilify** [-fai], *va.* difamar, vilipendiar.

vilipend [vílipend], *va.* y *vn.* vilipendiar.

villa [víla], *s.* quinta, casa de campo.

village [víley], *s.* aldea, pueblo.—**villager** [-yœr], *s.* aldeano.

villain [vílæn], *s.* villano, bellaco, malvado; pechero.

villa(i)nous [vílænus], *a.* villano, bellaco, ruin; malvado; (fam.) asqueroso, repugnante.—**villainously** [-li], *adv.* vilmente, villanamente.—**villainousness** [-nes], *s.* ruindad, villanía.

villa(i)ny, villanage [vílani, -ney], *s.* villanía, vileza, infamia.

villanize [vílanaiś], *va.* avillanar.

villenage, villeinage [víleney], *s.* villanaje, servidumbre; feudo.

villose [vílous], **villous** [vílus], *a.* velludo o velloso; felpudo.

villosity [vilósiti], *s.* vellosidad.

villus [vílus], *s.* (anat.) vello.—*pl.* **villi**, (bot.) vellos.

vim, *s.* (fam.) fuerza, vigor; energía, espíritu.

viminal [víminal], **vimineous** [vimíneus], *a.* mimbroso.

vinaceous [vainéishus], *a.* vinario; vinoso.

vinaigrette [vínegrét], *s.* redomilla para esencia; (coc.) salsa de vinagre.

vincible [vínsibœl], *a.* vencible.

vinculum [vínkiulum], *s.* vínculo.

vindicable [víndicabœl], *a.* vindicable.

vindicate [víndikeit], *va.* vindicar.—**vindication** [-éishun], *s.* vindicación.—**vindicative** [-ketiv], *a.* vindicativo, justificativo.—**vindicator** [-kéiter], *s.* defensor, vindicador.—**vindicatory** [-catori], *a.* vindicatorio.

vindictive [vindíctiv], *a.* vengativo.—**vindictively** [-lil], *adv.* vengativamente, por venganza.—**vindictiveness** [-nes], *s.* carácter vengativo.

vine [váin], *s.* (bot.) enredadera; vid, parra.—**v. beetle**, (ent.) escarabajuelo.—**v. branch**, sarmiento.—**v. bud**, brota, bollón.—**v.-clad**, cubierto de enredaderas, de vides o de viñas.—**v. fretter, v. grub**, (ent.) pulgón, pulgón de las viñas, brugo revoltón.—**v. leaf**, hoja de vid o de parra.—**v.-like**, aparrado.—**v. pest**, filoxera.—**v. stock**, cepa.—**v. worm** = v. GRUB.

vinedresser [-dréscœr], *s.* viñador, deslechugador.

vinegar [vínegar], *s.* vinagre.—**v. aspect**, cara de vinagre.—**v. cruet**, vinagrera.

vinegarish, vinegary [-ish, -i], *a.* vinagroso, avinagrado, agrio.

vinery [váincœri], *s.* invernadero para las uvas; emparrado.

vineyard [víñard], *s.* viña, viñedo.

vinic [vínic], *a.* (quím.) vínico.

viniculture [víniculchœr], *s.* vinicultura.—**vinicultural** [-al], *a.* vinícola.—**viniculturist** [-ist], *s.* vinicultor.

viniferous [vinífeus], *a.* productor de vino.

vinification [vínifikéishun], *s.* vinificación.

vinous [váinus], **vinose** [váinous], *a.* vinoso; de color de vino.

vintage [víntey], *s.* vendimia.—**vintager** [-yœr], *s.* vendimiador, vinícola, vinariego.

vintner [víntner], *s.* vinatero, tabernero, tratante en vinos.

viny [váini], *a.* perteneciente a las vides, parras o enredaderas.

viol [váiol], *s.* (mús.) violón; (mar.) virador.—**double-base v.**, (mús.) contrabajo.

viola [váiola, vióla], *s.* (mús.) viola, alto; (V-), (bot.) género que incluye las violetas y los pensamientos.

violable [váiolabœl], *a.* violable.

Violaceæ [váioléisii], *s. pl.* (bot.) violáceas.—**violaceous** [-shus], *a.* violado, de color de violeta; (bot.) violáceo.

violate [váioleit], *va.* violar, infringir (una ley); violar o deshonrar (a una mujer).—**violation** [-éishun], *s.* violación, infracción (de una ley); violación, deshonra (de una mujer).—**violator** [-éitœr], *s.* violador.

violence [váiolens], *s.* violencia.—**violent** [-ent], *a.* violento.—**violently** [-lil], *adv.* violentamente.

violet [váiolet]. **I.** *s.* (bot.) violeta; color violado. **II.** *a.* violado.

violin [váiolín], *s.* violín; violinista.—**violinist** [-ist], *s.* violinista.

violoncellist [víolonchélist, váiolonsélist], *s.* violoncelista.—**violoncello** [-chélo, -sélo], *s.* violoncelo o violonchelo.

viper [váipœr], *s.* víbora.—**vipergrass** [-gras], *s.* (bot.) escorzonera.—**viperine, viperish, viperous** [-in, -ish, -us], *a.* viperino.

virago [vairégo], *s.* marimacho.

vireo [víreo], *s.* (orn.) víreo, virio.

virescent [virésent], *s.* verdoso.

Virgilian [vœrxílian], *a.* virgiliano.

virgin [vœrxin]. **I.** *s.* virgen, doncella; religiosa que ha hecho voto de virginidad; (V-), (astr.)

Virgo.—**the V.**, la Virgen. **II.** *a.* virginal, virgen.—**v. forest**, selva virgen.—**v. metal**, metal nativo.—**v. queen**, (Ingl.) la reina virgen (Isabel).—**v.'s bower**, (bot.) clemátide.—**v. soil**, tierra virgen.

virginal [vœrrinal]. **I.** *a.* virginal. **II.** *s.* (mús.) espineta.

virginity [vœrríniti], **virginhood** [vœrrinjud], *s.* virginidad.

Virgo [vœrgo], *s.* (astr.) Virgo.

viridescent [víridésent], *a.* verdoso.

viridity [viríditi], *s.* verdor.

virile [váiril *o* víril], *a.* viril.

virility [viríliti], *s.* virilidad.

virous [váirus], *a.* ponzoñoso.

virtu [virtú], *s.* curiosidad, rareza.—**objects**, o **articles, of v.**, objetos curiosos o raros.

virtual [vœrchuæl], *a.* virtual.—**v. amperes**, (elec.) amperaje efectivo, intensidad efectiva.—**v. axis**, (mec.) eje instantáneo de rotación.—**v. displacement**, (mec.) desalojamiento virtual, velocidad virtual.—**v. focus**, (fís.) foco virtual.—**v. image**, (fos.) imagen virtual.—**v. moment**, (mec.) momento virtual.—**v. velocity**, (mec.) velocidad virtual en la dirección de la fuerza.—**v. volts**, (elec.) voltaje efectivo.—**v. work**, (mec.) trabajo virtual.

virtuality [vœrchuéliti], *s.* virtualidad.

virtually [vœrchuali], *adv.* virtualmente.

virtue [vœrchu], *s.* virtud (en todas sus acepciones).—**virtues**, virtudes (quinto coro celestial).—**by o in v. of**, en virtud de.

virtuosity [virtuósiti], *s.* (b. a.) maestría, especialmente en la música.

virtuoso [virtuóso], *s.* artista eximio, músico muy hábil.

virtuous [vœrchuus], *a.* virtuoso; pura, casta (mujer); (ant.) eficaz.—**virtuously** [-lil], *adv.* virtuosamente.—**virtuousness** [-nes], *s.* virtud, calidad de virtuoso.

virulence [vírulens], *s.* virulencia; malignidad, acrimonia.—**virulent** [-ent], *a.* virulento, ponzoñoso; maligno, cáustico.—**virulently** [-lil], *adv.* virulentamente, malignamente.

virus [váirus], *s.* virus; virulencia.

vis [vis], *s.* (en frases) fuerza.—**v. a tergo**, fuerza impelente, agente extraño.—**v. inertiæ**, inercia fuerza de inercia.—**v. viva**, (mec.) fuerza viva.

vis-a-vis [vísaví]. **I.** *s.* (fr.) el que está enfrente **II.** *adv.* cara a cara.

visage [vísey], *s.* rostro, cara, semblante, faz, aspecto distintivo.

visaged [víseyd], *a.* de cara, de rostro, de semblante.

viscacha [viscácha], *s.* (zool.) vizcacha.

viscera [víscera], *s. pl.* de viscus: vísceras, entrañas.

visceral [vísceral], *a.* visceral; ventral, abdominal.

viscid [vísid], *a.* viscoso, pegajoso.—**viscidity** [vísiditi], **viscosity** [viscósiti], *s.* viscosidad.

viscount [váicaunt], *s.* vizconde.—**viscountess** [-es], *s.* vizcondesa.—**viscountship** [-ship], *s.* vizcondado.

viscous [víscus], *a.* viscoso, glutinoso, pegajoso.

viscus [víscus], *s.* víscera.—*pl.* **viscera**, vísceras, entrañas.

vise [váis], *s.* tornillo de carpintero.

visé [viséi]. **I.** *va.* (pret. VISÉD [viséid], pa. VISÉING [viséing]) visar, refrendar. **II.** *s.* visto bueno; refrendación, refrendo.

visibility [vísibíliti], **visibleness** [-ibœlnes], *s.* visibilidad.—**visible** [-bœl], *a.* visible, notorio; externo.—**visibly** [-bli], *adv.* visiblemente; manifiestamente.

Visigoth [vísigoz], *s.*, **Visigothic** [-ic], *a.* visigodo.

vision [víyun], *s.* visión, vista; fantasma; fantasía; revelación inspirada y profética; (cine.) representación de los pensamientos o sueños de un actor. (Podría llamarse *psicograma*.)

visionary [-eri]. **I.** *a.* visionario, imaginario, quimérico; impracticable, infactible. **II.** *s.* visionario, soñador.

visit [vísit]. **I.** *va.* visitar; hacer visita a; hacer un reconocimiento o registro de; (teol.) visitar. **II.** *vn.* visitarse; hacer visitas, ir de visita.

Para la pronunciación de æ, œ, ᴅ, ŝ, ŝh, ᴜ, Ῡ, ʏ, z, véase la clave al principio del libro.

III. *s.* visita, visitación; reconocimiento, registro, inspección; visita de médico; visitación de un obispo, etc.—**visitable** [-abœl], *a.* visitable, sujeto a inspección.

visitant [-ant], *s.* visitador, visitante.

visitation [-éishʊn], *s.* visitación, visita; inspección, registro, reconocimiento, gracia o castigo del cielo.—**visitatorial** [-atórial], *a.* perteneciente a la visitación.

visiting [-ing], *a.* visitador; de visita.

visitor [-œr], *s.* visita, visitador.

visor, visored = VIZOR, VIZORED.

vista [vísta], *s.* vista, perspectiva.

visual [víȝual], *a.* visual.—**v. angle, line,** ángulo, línea visual.

visuality [viȝuǽliti], *s.* calidad de visual; visibilidad.

visualization [víȝuæliséishʊn], *s.* representación, formación de una imagen mental clara; imagen mental; descripción vívida o gráfica.—**visualize** [-aiš], *va.* y *vn.* representar(se) vívidamente en la mente.

visually [víȝuali], *adv.* visualmente; visiblemente.

vital [váital], *a.* vital, cardinal, fundamental; fatal, mortal.—**v. statistics,** estadística demográfica.—**vitalism** [-išm], *s.* (biol.) vitalismo.—**vitalist** [-ist], *s.* vitalista.

vitality [vaitǽliti], *s.* vitalidad.

vitalize [váitalaiš], *va.* vivificar, dar vida; animar, reanimar.

vitally [váitali], *adv.,* vitalmente, fundamentalmente.

vitals [váitalš], *s. pl.* partes vitales.

vitamic [vitǽmic], *a.* = VITAMINIC.

vitamin(e [vítæmin], *s.* (quím.), vitamina.—**vitaminic** [vitæmínic], *a.* vitamínico.

vitel(l)ine [vítelin]. **I.** *a.* (bio.) vitelino. **II.** *s.* (quím.) vitalina.

vitellus [vitélʊs], *s.* vitelo, yema del huevo.

vitiate [víshieit], *va.* viciar; inficionar, infectar, corromper; (for.) viciar, invalidar.—**vitiation** [-éishʊn], *s.* depravación, corrupción; (for.) invalidación.

viticulture [vítícúlchœr o -tiur], *s.* viticultura.

viticultural [-al], *a.* vitícola.—**viticulturist** [-ist], *s.* viticultor, vitícola, vinador.

vitreous [vítreʊs], *a.* vítreo; vidrioso.—**v. body,** o **humor,** humor vítreo (del ojo).—**vitreousness** [-nes], *s.* vidriosidad.

vitrescent [vitrésent], *a.* vitrificable.

vitrifiable [vítrifáiabœl], *a.* vitrificable.

vitrification [-fikéishʊn], *s.* vitrificación.

vitriform [vítriform], *a.* vítreo.

vitrify [vítrifai]. **I.** *va.* y *vn.* vitrificar(se).

vitriol [vítriol], *s.* (quím.) vitriolo; ácido sulfúrico; sulfato.—**vitriolate(d** [-eit(ed], *a.* vitriolado.—**vitriolic** [vitriólic], *a.* vitriólico.

vituline [vítiulain o -lin], *a.* becerril.

vituperable [vitiúpœrabœl], *a.* vituperable.

vituperate [-eit], *va.* vituperar.—**vituperation** [-éihʊn], *s.* vituperación, vituperio.— **vituperator,** [-éitœr], *s.* vituperador.

viva voce [váiva vósi], *adv.* de viva voz, de palabra.

vivacious [vaivéishʊs], *a.* vivo, vivaracho, vivaz; (bot.) vivaz, perenne.

vivaciousness [-nes], **vivacity** [vaivǽsiti], *s.* vivacidad, viveza.

vivander [vívandiéi], *s.* vivandero.

vivandière [-diér], *s.* cantinera: vivandera.

vivarium [vaivériʊm], **vivary** [váivari, vívari], *s.* vivar, vivero.

Viverridæ [vivérridi], *s. pl.* (zool.) vivérridos.—**viverrin** [-in], *s.* y *a.* (zool.) vivérrido.

vives [váivš], *s. pl.* (vet.) adivas.

vivid [vívid], *a.* vivo, vívido, gráfico; intenso; subido, brillante (color); animado, enérgico, activo.—**vividly** [-li], *adv.* vivamente; vívidamente.—**vividness** [-nes], *s.* vivacidad; intensidad, fuerza, brillo.

vivification [vívifikéishʊn], *s.* vivificación.

vivify [vívifai], *va.* vivificar, dar vida.

viviparous [vaivíparʊs], *a.* (zool.) vivíparo.

vivisect [víviséct], *va.* y *vn.* disecar un animal vivo.

vivisection [-sécshʊn], *s.* vivisección.

vixen [víscœn], *s.* (zool.) zorra o raposa; mujer regañona o cólerica, arpía.

viz. *abrev.* de **videlicet** (se lee generalmente **namely** [néimli] o **to wit** [tu uit]), a saber).

vizcacha [viscácha], *s.* (zool.) vizcacha.

vizier, vizir [víšiær], *s.* visir.—**vizierate** [-et], **viziership** [-ship], *s.* visirato, oficio o dignidad de visir.

vizor [víšœr], *s.* visera.—**vizored** [-d], *a.* con visera, provisto de visera.

vocable [vócabœl], *s.* voz, vocablo.

vocabulary [vocǽbiuleri], *s.* vocabulario; nomenclador.

vocal [vócœl]. **I.** *a.* vocal; diptongo; consonante líquida (*l, r*). **II.** *a.* vocal; oral.—**v. bands** =v. CORDS.—**v. chink,** glotis.—**v. cords, v. lips,** cuerdas vocales.—**v. music,** canto.

vocalist [-ist], *s.* cantor, cantora, cantatriz.

vocality [vocéliti], *s.* calidad de vocal.

vocalization [vócalaiséshʊn], *s.* vocalización.

vocalize [-aiš], *va.* y *vn.* (mús.) vocalizar; marcar los puntos vocales en taquigrafía.

vocally [vócali], *adv.* vocalmente; verbalmente.

vocation [vokéishʊn], *s.* vocación; oficio, profesión.

vocational [-al], *a.* profesional; práctico; de artes y oficios.—**v. school,** escuela práctica (apl. esp. a las de artes y oficios).—**v. training,** instrucción práctica, enseñanza de oficios.

vocative [vócativ], *s.* y *a.* vocativo.

vociferate [vosífœreit], *vn.* vociferar.

vociferation [-éishʊn], *s.* vociferación.

vociferous [-fœrʊs], *a.* vocinglero.—**vociferously** [-li], *adv.* vocingleramente, a gritos.

vodka [vódcæ], *s.* vodca, bebida alcohólica rusa.

vogue [vog], *s.* moda.—**in v.,** en boga, de moda.

voice [vóis]. **I.** *s.* voz; habla, palabra; el que habla en nombre de otro; (gram.) voz (del verbo). **II.** *va.* expresar, proclamar, decir su parecer, interpretar, hacerse eco de; dar el tono; acordar o templar (un instrumento); (mús.) escribir la parte vocal de.

voiced [vóist], *a.* que tiene voz; dicho, expresado, hablado.

voiceless [vóisles], *a.* mudo; que no tiene voz ni voto.

void [vóid]. **I.** *a.* vacío, desocupado, hueco; vacante; (for.) nulo, inválido, írrito, sin valor ni fuerza; (con **of**) falto, privado, desprovisto; vano, ilusorio. **II.** *s.* vacuo, vacío; claro, laguna. **III.** *va.* anular, invalidar; vaciar, desocupar, evacuar.—**to v. out,** echar fuera, arrojar. **IV.** *vn.* vaciarse.

voidable [vóidabœl], *a.* anulable; que se puede evacuar o vaciar.—**voidance** [-ans], *s.* vaciamiento, evacuación; vacancia.—**voider** [-œr], *s.* vaciador; anulador; cestito para migajas.—**voidness** [-nes], *s.* vacío, vacuidad; invalidez.

voile [vóil, vual], *s.* (tej.) espumilla.

volant [vólant], *a.* volante; ligero.

Volapük [pron. franc.], *s.* volapuk, una de las lenguas artificiales universales.

volatile [vólatil], *a.* volátil; sutil, fugaz; voluble; pasajero, transitorio.—**v. oil,** aceite esencial o volátil.

volatileness [-nes], **volatility** [-tíliti], *s.* volatilidad; volatariedad, volubilidad.—**volatilization** [-tiliséishʊn], *s.* volatilización.—**volatilize** [-aiš], *va.* y *vn.* volatilizar(se).

vol-au-vent [vol o van], *s.* (coc.) una especie de fajardo.

volcanic [volcǽnic], *a.* volcánico.—**v. glass,** (min.) obsidiana.

volcano [volkéno], *s.* volcán.

vole [vol], *s.* ratón campestre.

volition [volíshʊn], *s.* voluntad; volición.

volitional [-al], **volitive** [vólitiv], *a.* volitivo.

volley [vóli]. **I.** *s.* descarga, andanada; salva; (dep.) voleo de la pelota. **II.** *va.* y *vn.* lanzar una descarga; (dep.) volear.

volplane [vólpléin], *vn.* (aer.) planear, deslizarse en aeroplano.

Volsci [vólsai], *s. pl.* (hist.) volscos.—**Volscian** [-8hæn], *s.* y *a.* volsco.

volt, *s.* voltio; (eq.) vuelta.—**v. ampere,** (en corriente continua) vatio; (en corriente alterna) voltamperio, vatio aparente.

voltage [vóltɛʏ], *s.* (elec.) voltaje.

voltaic [vóltaic], *a.* voltaico, galvánico.—**v. arc,** arco voltaico.—**v. battery,** pila voltaica.—**v. cell,** elemento de una pila.—**v. electricity,** electricidad dinámica.

Voltairian [voltérian], *a.* volteriano.

Voltairianism [-iȿm], *s.* volterianismo.

voltaism [vóltaiȿm], *s.* voltaísmo, galvanismo.

voltameter [vóltǽmetœr], *s.* voltámetro.

voltammeter [vóultǽmítœr], *s.* voltamperímetro (si se trata de corriente alterna); voltímetro (si de corriente continua).

voltmeter [vóultmítœr], *s.* voltímetro.

volubility [vóliubíliti], *s.* volubilidad; verbosidad.—**voluble** [-bœl], *a.* voluble.—**volubly** [-blі], *adv.* volublemente.

volume [vólium], *s.* tomo, volumen; rollo de vitela; volumen, bulto; caudal de río; importe, suma, gran cantidad; (mat. y mús.) volumen.

volumetric [vóliumétric], *a.* (fís.) volumétrico.

voluminous [voliúminʊs], *a.* voluminoso, abultado; prolijo, copioso.—**voluminously** [-li], *adv.* voluminosa o copiosamente.—**voluminousness** [-nes], *s.* calidad de voluminoso; prolijidad.

voluntarily [vólʊnterili], *adv.* voluntariamente.

voluntary [vólʊnteri]. **I.** *a.* voluntario. **II.** *s.* voluntario; (igl.) solo de órgano.

volunteer [vólʊntíœr]. **I.** *s.* voluntario. **II.** *va.* y *vn.* ofrecerse a hacer algo; contribuir voluntariamente; servir como voluntario.

voluptuary [volúpchueri], *s.* sibarita, voluptuoso.

voluptuous [volúpchuʊs], *a.* voluptuoso.

voluptuously [-li], *adv.* voluptuosamente.

voluptuousness [-nes], *s.* voluptuosidad.

volute [voliút], *s.* (arq.) voluta.—**v. spring,** resorte de espiral.

volvulus [vólviulʊs], *s.* (med.) miserere, íleo.

vomer [vómœr], *s.* (anat.) vómer.—**vomerine** [-in], *a.* del vómer.

vomica [vómica], *s.* vómica.

vomit [vómit]. **I.** *va.* y *vn.* vomitar, arrojar. **II.** *s.* vómito; vomitivo, emético.—**vomiting** [-ing], *s.* vómito.—**vomitive** [-tiv], *a.* vomitivo, emético.—**vomitory** [-tori]. **I.** *a.* y *s.* vomitivo. **II.** *s.* (arq.) vomitorio.

voodoo [vúdú]. **I.** *s.* vudú, brujería de los negros de los E. U. y las Antillas. **II.** *a.* vuduísta, relativo al vudú. **III.** *va.* hechizar, conjurar según las prácticas vuduístas.—**voodooism** [-iȿm], *s. vuduismo,* creencias y prácticas *vuduístas.*

voracious [voréȿhʊs], *a.* voraz, devorador; rapaz. —**voraciously** [-li], *adv.* vorazmente.—**voraciousness** [-nes], **voracity** [vorǽsiti], *s.* voracidad.

vortex [vórtecs], *s.* vórtice, vorágine, remolino, torbellino.

vortical [vórtical], **vortiginous** [vortíʏinʊs], *a.* vortiginoso.

votaress [vótares], *s.* mujer que ha hecho y cumple un voto.

votary [vótari]. **I.** *a.* votivo, consagrado al cumplimiento de un voto. **II.** *s.* el que se consagra a cumplir un voto; adorador; seguidor, partidario, adepto.

vote [vóut]. **I.** *s.* voto; votación.—**v. by show of hands,** votación que se efectúa levantando las manos. **II.** *va.* votar por; (fam.) dominar el voto de. **III.** *vn.* votar, dar voto.

voter [-œr], *s.* votante, voto, elector.

voting [-ing]. **I.** *s.* votación. **II.** *a.* de votación; de votar; electoral.—**v. precinct,** distrito electoral.

votive [vóutiv], *a.* votivo.—**v. mass** (igl.) misa votiva.—**v. offering,** exvoto, presentalla.—**v. tablet,** tablilla, exvoto.

vouch [váuch]. **I.** *va.* atestiguar, certificar, atestar, testificar; garantizar, responder de o por. **II.** *vn.* salir fiador; responder; atestiguar; afirmar.—**to v. for,** responder de; confirmar.

voucher [-œr]. **I.** *s.* comprobante, resguardo, recibo, descargo, cualquier documento justifica-

tivo; fiador. **II.** *va.* atestar, confirmar, certificar.

vouchsafe [-séif], *va.* conceder, permitir, otorgar.

voussoir [vusuár], *s.* (arq.) dovela, piedra de arco.

vow [váu]. **I.** *s.* voto, promesa solemne. **II.** *va.* hacer promesa solemne de, votar, hacer voto de, jurar. **III.** *vn.* hacer un voto.

vowel [váuel]. **I.** *a.* y *s.* vocal. **II.** *va.* poner vocales.

vox, *s.* (mús.) voz.—**v. humana,** registro del órgano que imita la voz humana.

voyage [vóiɛʏ]. **I.** *s.* viaje por mar, travesía; viaje redondo de un buque. **II.** *vn.* navegar, viajar. —**voyager** [-œr], *s.* viajero.

Vulcanian [vʊlkénian], *a.* vulcanio.

Vulcanism [vúlcaniȿm], *s.* vulcanismo.

Vulcanist [vúlcanist], *s.* vulcanista.

vulcanite [vúlcanait], *s.* vulcanita.

vulcanization [-iȿéiȿhʊn], *s.* vulcanización.

vulcanize [-áiȿ], *va.* y *vn.* vulcanizar.—**vulcanizer** [-áiȿœr], *s.* vulcanizador.—**vulcanizing** [-áiȿing]. **I.** *a.* vulcanizador, de vulcanizar. **II.** *s.* vulcanización.

vulgar [vúlgar]. **I.** *a.* vulgar; común, ordinario; vernáculo; público; generalmente sabido.—**v. fraction,** fracción común, quebrado. **II.** *s.* vulgo, plebe.

vulgarise [-aiȿ], *va.* y *vn.* = VULGARIZE.

vulgarism [-iȿm], *s.* vulgarismo.

vulgarity [vʊlgǽriti], *s.* vulgaridad.

vulgarization [vúlgariȿéiȿhʊn], *s.* vulgarización.

vulgarize [-aiȿ]. **I.** *va.* vulgarizar. **II.** *vn.* conducirse de un modo vulgar.

vulgarly [vúlgarli], *adv.* vulgarmente.

vulgarness [-nes], *s.* = VULGARITY.

Vulgate [vúlgueit], *s.* (igl.) Vulgata.

vulnerability [vúlnœrabíliti], *s.* vulnerabilidad. —**vulnerable** [-bœl], *a.* vulnerable.—**vulnerableness** [-neȿ], *s.* = VULNERABILITY.

vulnerary [vúlnœrǽri]. **I.** *a.* vulnerario. **II.** *s.* medicamento vulnerario.

vulpine [vúlpin], *a.* zorruno, raposuno, vulpino; astuto, ladino.

vulture [vúlchœr], *s.* (orn.) buitre.—**vulturine, vulturous** [-in, -ʊs], *a.* buitrero.

vulva [vúlva], *s.* (anat.) vulva.

vulvar [vúlvar], *a.* vulvario.

vying [váiing] (*ger.* de TO VIE), *a.* rival, emulador. —**vyingly** [-li], *adv.* con emulación, rivalizando.

W

w [dúbliu], *s.* w.

wabble [uóbœl]. **I.** *va.* y *vn.* balancear(se), tambalear, bambolear(se); vacilar. **II.** *s.* bamboleo, tambaleo.

wabbly [uóbli], *a.* que se bambolea; instable.

wacke [uǽke], *s.* roca parda terrosa.

wad [uod]. **I.** *s.* borra o pelote para rehenchir muebles; (cost.) huata; (arti.) taco; mineral de manganeso y cobalto.—**w. hook,** (arti.) sacatrapos, descargador. **II.** *va.* (cost.) acolchar, enhuatar; emborrar (muebles); (arti.) atacar.

wadding [uóding], *s.* (sast.) entretela, entreforro, relleno; huata o guata, algodón en hojas; pelotes; (arti.) taco.

waddle [uódœl]. **I.** *vn.* anadear. **II.** *s.* anadeo.

wade [uéid], *va.* y *vn.* vadear.—**wader** [-œr], *s.* el que vadea.—**w.,** o **wading bird,** (orn.) ave zancuda.

wadi, wady [uádi], *s.* uadi, valle (el primer término es árabe, y se aplica gen. a un valle atravesado por el cauce de un arroyo que se seca en tiempo seco).

wafer [uéifœr]. **I.** *va.* pegar o cerrar con oblea. **II.** *s.* oblea; hostia; (coc.) barquillo; (arti.) fulminante.—**w. iron,** (coc.) barquillero (molde).— **w. man,** obleero, barquillero.—**w. mold,** w. IRON.

waffle [uófœl], *s.* barquillo, suplicación; fruta de sartén.—**w. irons,** molde para hacer barquillos.

waft [uaft]. **I.** *va.* mecer, hacer flotar, sobrenadar, llevar por el aire. **II.** *s.* mecedura, fluctuación; bationdeo; ráfaga de aire o de olor; (mar.) señal hecha con bandera; banderín de señales.

waftage [uáftɐr], *s.* conducción por el aire o por el agua.

wafture [uáftyur], *s.* fluctuación.

wag [uæg]. **I.** *va.* sacudir, mover o menear ligeramente.—**to w. the tail**, rabear, colear. **II.** *vn.* oscilar, tambalear, balancearse; ir pasando, deslizarse; irse. **III.** *s.* coleada, coleo; movimiento de cabeza; burlador, matraquista, bromista.

wage [uéiɣ]. **I.** *va.* emprender, sostener, empeñar; (cerám.) hacer la masa.—**to w. war**, hacer guerra. **II.** *s.*ᵃ(gen. en *pl.*, **wages**) premio, galardón; (e. p.), *pl.* **wages**, paga, jornal, sueldo, salario. —**w. earner**, trabajador, obrero.

wager [uéiɣœr]. **I.** *va.* apostar, poner (apuesta). **II.** *s.* apuesta; gaje, palabra, empeño; prueba.— **w. of battle**, prueba del duelo, juicio de Dios determinado por el duelo.—**w. of law**, prueba de la compurgación, juicio de Dios determinado por el juramento del acusado y sus compurgadores.

waggery [uǽgœri], *s.* jocosidad, chocarrería, bufonada; travesura.—**waggish** [uǽguiŝh], *a.* chacotero, juguetón, retozón.—**waggishness** [-nes], *s.* retozo, chacota, chocarrería.

waggle [uǽgœl]. **I.** *va.* menear ligeramente. **II.** *vn.* anadear; menearse; bullir. **III.** *s.* meneo, anadeo, tambaleo.

Wagnerian [uægnírian], *a.* vagneriano.

wag(g)on [uǽgun], *s.* carro, carretón, carreta, carromato, galera; vehículo, coche; (Ingl., f. c.) furgón.—**w. maker** = WAGONWRIGHT.—**wag(g)-onage** [-ey], *s.* porte, carretaje.—**wag(g)oner** [-œr], *s.* carretero, carretonero, carromatero; (C-, astr.) Carro, Osa Mayor.—**wagonet(te** [-ét], *s.* carricoche, birlocho.—**wagonful** [-ful], **wagon-load** [-loud], *s.* galerada, carretada.—**wagon-wright** [-rait], *s.* carretero.

wagtail [uǽgteil], *s.* (orn.) aguzanieve, motacila; herreruelo; tipo, sujeto; meretriz.

waif [uéif], *s.* granuja; niño, animalito u objeto extraviado o abandonado; (for.) cosa robada y soltada por el ladrón; bienes mostrencos.

wail [uéil], *va.* y *vn.* deplorar, llorar, lamentar o lamentarse, gemir.—**wail(ing** [-ing], *s.* lamentación, lamento, gemido.

wainscot [uéinscot]. **I.** *s.* enmaderamiento, friso, alfarje, arrimadillo. **II.** *va.* entablar, enmaderar; poner friso de madera.—**wainscoting** [-ing], *s.* entablamento, entabladura, alfarje.

waist [uéist], *s.* cintura; talle; cinto, cinturón; (cost.) corpiño, corpecico, jubón; (mar.) combés de una nave.—**w. board**, (mar.) falca.—**w. rails**, varengas.

waistband [-bǽnd], *s.* pretina.

waistcloth [-clóɀ], *s.* pampanilla; (mar.) empavesada.

waistcoat [-cot *o* -cut], *s.* (sast.) chaleco; (ant.) chupa; (cost.) justillo, ajustador, monillo.

wait [uéit]. **I.** *va.* esperar, aguardar; dilatar, diferir. **II.** *vn.* estar aguardando o esperando, estar en expectativa; estar listo; servir; ser criado, sirviente o mozo (de fonda).—**to w. at table**, servir a la mesa.—**to w. for**, esperar.—**to w. on**, o **upon**, ir a ver o presentar sus respetos a; servir a; atender a, despachar (en una tienda); seguirse, inferirse; acompañar; poner cuidado en, velar sobre. **III.** *s.* espera; plantón; pausa, dilación, demora; (ant.) asechanza, celada.—*pl.* murga de nochebuena.

waiter [uéitœr], *s.* mozo de café o restaurante, sirviente, criado; azafate o bandeja.

waiting [-ing]. **I.** *s.* espera; servicio. **II.** *a.* que espera; que sirve; de espera.—**w. gentlewoman, w. maid**, doncella, camarera.—**w. room**, antesala; sala de espera.—**w. woman** = W. MAID.

Wai Wu Pu [uái uu pu], ministerio de relaciones exteriores (de China).

waitress [uéitres], *s.* criada, moza.

waive [uéiv], *va.* renunciar a; desistir de; repudiar.—**waiver** [-œr], *s.* renuncia (de un derecho, etc.); repudio.

wake [uéik]. **I.** *va.* despertar; resucitar; excitar; velar un muerto.—**to w. up**, llamar o despertar. **II.** *vn.* despertarse; velar, pasar la noche en vela; despabilarse; estar de velorio.—**to w. up**, despertar. **III.** *s.* vela o velación de un muerto, (Am.) velorio; (Ingl.) vela, fiesta nocturna o verbena; (mar.) estela, aguaje.

wakeful [-ful], *a.* vigilante, en vela, alerta; desvelado.—**wakefully** [-i], *adv.* desveladamente.—**wakefulness** [-nes], *s.* vigilia, desvelo, insomnio.

waken [-uéikn]. **I.** *va.* despertar. **II.** *vn.* despertar o despertarse; recordar.

wake-robin [-róbin], *s.* (bot.) aro o yaro; (E. U.) hierba liliácea.

waking [-ing]. **I.** *s.* vela, pervigilio. **II.** *a.* que despierta; despierto; de vela o vigilia.—**w. hours**, horas de vela.

Waldenses [uoldénsiŝ], *s. pl.* valdenses.—**Waldensian** [-ŝhæn], *s.* y *a.* valdense.

wale [uéil]. **I.** *va.* levantar roncha; azotar. **II.** *s.* roncha, cardenal, verdugo; (tej.) relieve; (mar.) cinta.

Walhalla [uoljélæ], *s.* = VALHALLA.

walk [uók]. **I.** *vn.* andar, caminar, marchar, ir a pie; pasear, pasearse; hablando de caballos, al paso; obrar, conducirse, portarse; aparecer (fantasmas, espectros o duendes); (fam.) liar el petate, ser despedido.—**to w. after**, seguir a, ir tras.—**to w. away**, irse, marcharse.—**to w. back**, volver atrás, regresar.—**to w. down**, bajar.—**to w. forth**, salir.—**to w. in**, entrar, pasar adelante; pasearse en; (bib.) vivir en.—**to w. out**, salir, irse. —**to w. over**, ir al paso (caballo); (fam.) ganar fácilmente; dominar a, abusar de.—**to w. up**, subir; acercarse.—**to w. up and down**, pasearse, ir y venir. **II.** *va.* hacer andar, pasear, sacar a pasear; recorrer, andar o pasar de una parte a otra de; andar por; hollar; conducir; hacer ir al paso (un caballo).—**to w. Spanish**, someterse, ceder.—**to w. the hospitals**, estudiar clínica en los hospitales.—**to w. the plank**, ser echado al mar (por los piratas, que hacían andar al acusado por una tabla oscilante haste volcarla); ser echado o despedido.—**to w. the streets**, andar por las calles, andorrear. **III.** *s.* paseo, caminata; modo de andar; paso del caballo; paseo, alameda; acera; carrera, oficio, empleo, estado, condición; método de vida, conducta, porte.

walker [uókœr], *s.* paseante, caminante; peatón.

walking [-uóking]. **I.** *s.* paseo; piso (estado de los caminos para andar). **II.** *a.* de andar, para andar; que anda.—**w. beam**, balancín (de máquina vertical de vapor).—**w. cane**, bastón.—**w. delegate**, visitador y representante o delegado de un gremio obrero.—**w. gentleman, w. lady**, (teat.) segundo galán, segunda dama.—**w. staff**, o **stick**, = W. CANE.—**to give one his w. papers**, o **ticket**, despedir a uno, darle calabazas.

walkout [uókáut], *s.* paro, huelga de obreros.

walkover [uókóvœr], *s.* triunfo fácil, ganga.

wall [uól]. **I.** *s.* pared; muro o tapia; (fort.) muralla; banca de roca natural.—**w. creeper**, (orn.) picomurario.—**w.-eyed**, ojizarco.—**w. fence**, tapia.—**w. fruit**, fruta de espalera o espaldera.—**w. louse**, chinche.—**w. paper**, papel de empapelar.— **w. pepper**, (bot.) siempreviva.—**w. piece**, cañón de muralla.—**w. plate**, (arq.) solera, viga de apoyo. —**w. rock**, (geol.) roca estéril, roca circundante de una veta.—**w. rue**, (bot.) ruda muraria.—**w. tree**, espaldera. **II.** *va.* emparedar, tapiar; murar, cercar; (fort.) amurallar.

wallaby [uólabi], *s.* especie de canguro.

Wallachian [uoléikiæn], *s.* y *a.* válaco.

wallet [uólet], *s.* cartera; bolsa de cuero; mochila; zurrón o alforia.

wallflower [-flúær], *s.* (bot.) alelí doble; (fam.) mujer que en un baile "come pavo."

Walloon [uolún], *s.* y *a.* valón.

wallop [uólup]. **I.** *vn.* bullir, hervir; bambolearse. **II.** *va.* (fam.) zurrar. **III.** *s.* golpe, tunda.

wallow [uólo]. **I.** *vn.* revolcarse, chapalear, estar encenagado en algún vicio.—**to w. in riches**, nadar en la opulencia. **II.** *s.* revuelco, revolcadura.

wallower [-œr], *s.* el que se revuelca en el fango.

wallwart [uólucœrt], *s.* (bot.) cañarroya.

walnut [uólnut], s. (bot.) nogal; nuez de nogal.—**w. tree**, nogal, noguera.

walrus [uólrus], s. morsa, vaca marina.

waltron [uóltrun], s. caballo marino.

waltz [uólts]. **I.** vn. valsar, bailar el vals. **II.** s. (mús. y danz.) vals.

waltzer [uóltscer], s. valsador, valsadora.

wampum [uómpum], s. cuentas o cañutillos de madreperla que usaban los indios americanos como dinero y como adorno; abalorio.

wan [uón], a. pálido, descolorido.

wand [uónd], s. vara; varita de virtudes; batuta.

wander [uóndœr], vn. errar ,vagar, rodar, andorrear; delirar; perderse, extraviarse; desviarse, apartarse.—**wanderer** [-œr], s. vagamundo, andorrero; persona errante o extraviada; transgresor.—**wandering** [-ing]. **I.** s. viaje; divagación; aberración; extravío; delirio. **II.** a. errante, errabundo; vago, vagamundo; descaminado, descarriado; delirante.—**W. Jew**, judío errante.—**w. kidney**, riñón flotante.

wanderlust [vándœrlúst], s. impulso hacia la vida errante, pasión de viajar.

wanderoo [uandœrú], s. (zool.) macaco con crin, mono grande.

wane [uéin]. **I.** vn. menguar, disminuir; decaer. **II.** s. mengua, diminución; decadencia, decremento, declinación; menguante (de la luna); (carp.) bisel.

wangle [uǽngœl], va. balancear, mecer; (fam.) sacar (dinero, etc.) con engañifas; ocultar, disimular.

wanigan [uónigæn], s. almacén, depósito; balsa con casilla.

wanness [uónnes], s. palidez; descaecimiento, languidez.

want [uónt]. **I.** va. necesitar, tener necesidad de; estar desprovisto de, carecer de; querer, desear; clamar, pedir con urgencia; exigir, requerir; dispensarse de, pasarse sin. **II.** vn. estar necesitado o indigente, carecer, pasar necesidades; faltar. **III.** s. necesidad, falta, carencia; privación, necesidad, indigencia; exigencia; solicitud, demanda.—**for w. of**, por falta de.—**to be in w.**, estar necesitado, sufrir necesidad.

wantage [uóntey], s. deficiencia, merma, déficit.

wanted [-ed], pp. de TO WANT. Ú. elípticamente en anuncios en el sentido de "se solicita," "se necesita," "se desea."

wanting [-ing], a. falto, defectuoso, deficiente; menguado; necesitado, escaso.—**to be w.**, faltar.

wanton [uóntun]. **I.** a. desenfrenado; protervo; juguetón, retozón, travieso; extravagante; suelto, libre; lascivo, salaz; licencioso, disoluto; desconsiderado; imperdonable; injustificable. **II.** s. libertino; ramera; persona frívola. **III.** va. malgastar; echar a perder. **IV.** vn. retozar, juguetear; hacer picardías; pasar el tiempo en liviandades.—**wantonly**, adv. desenfrenada o licenciosamente; protervamente.

wantonness [-nes], s. desenfreno, licencia; protervia; retozo; picardía; desgarro.

wapiti [uópiti], s. uapití, gran ciervo de la América del Norte.

war [uór]. **I.** s. guerra.—**w. bonnet**, (E. U.) casco de plumas que usan los indios cuando guerrean.—**w. bride**, novia (esposa reciente) de un soldado en servicio de guerra; (fam.) ganga de guerra; empresa industrial o comercial que prospera con la guerra.—**w. club**, maza.—**w. cry**, grito de guerra.—**w. dance**, danza bélica de los salvajes.—**W. Department**, ministerio de la guerra.—**w. flail**, mangual.—**w. horse**, corcel de guerra; veterano. **w. lord**, señor de los ejércitos; jefe guerrero.—**w. of secession**, (E. U.) guerra de secesión (de 1861 a 1865).—**w. paint**, pintura con que se embadurnan los indios para guerrear.—**w. tax**, impuesto de guerra.—**w. to the death**, **w. to the knife**, guerra a muerte.—**w. whoop**, alarido de guerra (de los indios americanos). **II.** vn. guerrear, estar en guerra.—**to w. on**, hacer la guerra a.

warble [uórbœl]. **I.** va. y vn. cantar con quiebras y trinos; trinar, gorjear; gargantear; murmurar (un arroyo). **II.** s. canto, gorjeo.—**warbler** [-blœr]

s. cantor, gorjeador; pájaro cantor; (orn.) cerrojillo.—**warbling** [-bling]. **I.** a. canoro, melodioso; susurrante. **II.** s. garganteo; canto, gorjeo.

ward [uord]. **I.** va. guardar, defender, proteger, poner a buen recaudo; (con **off**) parar, detener, evitar, desviar. **II.** s. pupilo o menor en tutela; barrio, cuartel o distrito de ciudad; sala, división, cuadra de hospital, etc.; pupilaje, tutela; guarda, custodia, protección; guarda de llave o cerradura; defensa, posición defensiva; guarda, guardián, conserje.

warden [uórdœn], s. custodio, guardián, celador, capataz; alcaide, carcelero; conserje, bedel; (en Ingl.) director de ciertos colegios; (igl.) V. CHURCHWARDEN.—**w. of a port**, capitán de un puerto.—pl. **wardens**, maestros o jurados en algún oficio.—**wardens and vestry**, mayordomos y junta parroquial.

wardenship [-ship], s. conserjería; bedelía; alcaidía.

warder [uórdœr], s. guarda, guardia.

wardrobe [uórdróub], s. guardarropa, armario, escaparate; ropería, guardarropía; vestuario, ropa.

wardroom [-rúm], s. (mar. mil.) cuarto de los oficiales; sala de reunión de un barrio.

wardship [uórdship], s. tutela, tutoría, pupilaje.

ware [uéœr], s. mercancías, mercaderías, efectos, géneros o artículos de comercio. (Hoy se usa la forma pl. **wares**).

warehouse [-jáus]. **I.** s. almacén, depósito.—**w. keeper**, guardaalmacén.—**w. rent**, almacenaje. **II.** va. almacenar.—**warehouseman** [-mæn], s. almacenero, almacenador.

warehousing system [-ing sístem], sistema de depósitos.

wareroom [uéœrrúm], s. pieza para almacenaje o venta de géneros.

warfare [uórfeær], s. guerra; milicia, arte militar; servicio militar; lucha, combate.

warily [uéœrili], adv. cautelosamente; astutamente.—**wariness** [-nes], s. cautela, precaución.

warlike [uórlaik], a. bélico, belicoso, marcial.

warlock [uórloc], s. (ant.) brujo; duende.

warm [uorm]. **I.** a. caloroso, cálido, caliente; ardiente, acalorado; fogoso, furioso, violento, celoso; conmovido, arrebatado, apasionado; afectuoso; (pintura) caliente, que tira a rojo o amarillo; reciente, fresco; cercano al objeto buscado; (fam.) molesto, fastidioso; peligroso.—**w.-blooded**, de sangre caliente; entusiasta, ardiente.—**w.-hearted**, de buen corazón; afectuoso; simpático.—**w. temper**, genio vivo, ardiente.—**to be w.**, tener calor; (con it por sujeto) hacer calor. **II.** va. calentar; caldear; abrigar; entusiasmar, encender, enfervorizar; (fam.) azotar, zurrar.—**to w. over**, calentar (comida fría). **III.** vn. calentarse; (gen. con **up**) entusiasmarse; acalorarse; tomar bríos.

warming [uórming]. **I.** s. calentamiento; calefacción. **II.** a. de calentar, para calentar; calentador.—**w. pan**, calentador de cama, mundillo.

warmly [uórmli], adv. acaloradamente; con entusiasmo, ardientemente; afectuosamente.

warmth [uormz], s. calor moderado; celo, entusiasmo, ardor; cordialidad; fantasía.

warn [uórn]. **I.** va. avisar, caucionar, prevenir, advertir; aconsejar, amonestar. **II.** vn. servir de escarmiento.—**warner** [uórnœr], s. amonestador.—**warning** [-ing], s. amonestación; advertencia, aviso, admonición; caución; lección, escarmiento.

warp [uórp]. **I.** s. torcedura, torcimiento, alabeo, comba; (tej.) urdimbre; (mar.) espía, calabrote, estacha, remolque.—**w. and woof**, trama y urdimbre.—**w. beam**, enjullo, plegador.—**w. thread**, lizo. **II.** va. torcer, retorcer; encorvar, empandar; combar, alabear; prevenir el ánimo; (tej.) urdir; (mar.) remolcar, espiar. **III.** vn. torcerse; combarse, alabearse; desviarse, alejarse, apartarse del camino recto; (tej.) urdir; (mar.) ir a remolque, espiarse.

warpath [uórpáz], s. senda que siguen los indios para atacar al enemigo.—**to be on the w.**, (fam.) estar en guerra; buscar pendencia, pelear.

warped [uórpd], *a.* con comba, adunco.—**w. surface,** (geom.) superficie alabeada.

warping [uórping], *pa.* y *s.* alabeo, combadura; (tej.) urdidura; (mar.) remolque, atoaje.—**w. machine,** o **mill,** urdidera.

warplane [uórpléin], *s.* avión de guerra.

warrant [uórrant]. **I.** *va.* garantir, garantizar; responder por; asegurar, fiar, certificar, aseverar; justificar; autorizar. **II.** *s.* (for.) auto, decreto, libramiento, mandamiento, cédula, patente, despacho; orden de prisión; autorización, poder; documento justificativo, comprobante, garantía; (com.) certificado de depósito; autoridad, apoyo, testimonio; sanción; justificación, apología, razón, motivo.

warrantable [-abœl], *a.* que se puede abonar, garantizar o justificar.—**warrantableness** [-nes], *s.* calidad de justificabe; certeza, seguridad.—**warrantably** [-bli], *adv.* justificadamente.

warrantee [uórranti], *s.* (for.) fiado.

warranter, warrantor [uórrantœr, -tor], *s.* (for.) garante, fiador.

warranty [uórranti], *s.* (for.) garantía; seguridad; autoridad, autorización.—**w. clause,** cláusula de evicción y saneamiento.

warren [uórren], *s.* conejera, conejar; vivar, vivero; vedado.—**warrener** [-œr], *s.* conejero.

warrior [uórriœr], *s.* guerrero.

warship [uórship], *s.* buque de guerra.

wart [uórt], *s.* verruga; espejuelos en la cuartilla del caballo; (bot.) verruga.—**w. hog,** facóquero, especie de jabalí sudafricano.—**wartwort** [-uœrt], *s.* (bot.) verrucaria.—**warty** [-i], *a.* verrugoso, averrugado.

warworn [uóruórn], *a.* agotado por el servicio militar.

wary [uéæri], *a.* cauto, cauteloso, prudente, avisado, precavido, astuto, sagaz.

was [uós], *pret.* del verbo TO BE.

wash [uósh]. **I.** *va.* lavar; bañar, regar; dar un baño o capa de metal; dar una mano o capa de color.—**to w. away, off,** o **out,** lavar, borrar, hacer desaparecer; quitar lavando; llevarse (el agua o un golpe de mar).—**to w. one's hands of,** lavarse las manos en cuanto a, no tomar parte en. **II.** *vn.* lavarse; lavar ropa, hacer la colada; (min.) lavar el mineral; (alb.) deslavar; (mar.) baldear; (fam.) no perder el color al lavarse, no desteñir; colar; gastarse por la acción del agua; mecerse. **III.** *s.* lavado, lavadura; colada; ropa lavada o para lavar (ropa sucia); lavación, ablución; lavatorio; loción, agua de tocador, cosmético; baño, capa; batiente del mar; chapaleo; aluvión, depósito; bazofia, lavazas, agua chirle; (mar.) pala de remo; (aer.) perturbación aerodinámica, conmoción del aire. **IV.** *a.* de o para lavar; lavable, que puede lavarse (apl. esp. a géneros que no destiñen).— **w. ball,** bola de jabón, jaboncillo de olor.—**w. leather,** gamuza.—**w.-off,** fugitivo, que se destiñe.

washbasin [-béisn], *s.* = WASHBOWL.

washboard [-bord], *s.* tablilla de lavandera; (carp.) rodapié; (mar.) falca, batemar, batidero.

washbowl [-bóul], *s.* jofaina, palangana.

washer [uóshœr], *s.* lavador; máquina de lavar; (mec.) arandela; alfardón, volandera, estornija, disco de cuero o de goma.

washerman [-mæn], *s.* lavandero.

washerwoman [-úman], *s.* lavandera.

washery [uósheri], *s.* (min.) lavadero (apl. esp. a los de hulla).

washhouse [-jaus], *s.* lavadero.

washin [uóshín], *s.* (aer.) alabeo que aumenta el ángulo de ataque; dicho aumento.

washing [uóshing], *s.* lavado, lavadura, lavamiento; ropa lavada o para el lavado; loción, lavatorio; blanqueadura; (mar.) baldeo; (min.) lave.—**w. machine,** máquina de lavar, lavadora mecánica.—**w. soda,** sosa para blanquear.

Washington orange [uóshingtun óreny], *s.* = NAVEL ORANGE.

washout [uósháut], *s.* hundimiento o derrumbe causado por el arrastre del agua; (aer.) alabeo que diminuye el ángulo de ataque; diminución del ángulo de ataque.

washpot [-pót], *s.* bacía; paila de lavar.

washstand [-stǽnd], *s.* palanganero, lavabo, aguamanil.

washtub [-túb], *s.* cuba de lavar o de colada; gamella, tina de lavar.

washy [uóshi], *a.* aguado; mojado; débil; flojo; insulso.

wasp [uósp], *s.* (ent.) avispa.

waspish [-ish], *a.* enojadizo, irascible; de cintura de avispa.—**waspishly** [-li], *adv.* ásperamente, con mal humor.—**waspishness** [-ness], *s.* mal genio, mal humor, irritabilidad.

wassail [uósel o uésel], *s.* francachela, gaudeamus, borrachera, orgía; bebida compuesta de vino, cerveza y especies; brindis.—**w. bowl,** ponchera.

wast [uóst], 2d *pers. sing. imperf.* de *ind.* de TO BE.

wastage [uéstey], *s.* merma, desgaste.

waste [uéist]. **I.** *va.* malgastar, derrochar, desperdiciar, malbaratar, disipar; gastar, consumir; comer, mermar, agotar; (ant.) desolar, arruinar, talar. **II.** *vn.* gastarse, consumirse; desgastarse, alterarse, dañarse.—**to w. away,** descaecer, consumirse; ir a menos, menguar. **III.** *a.* desechado, inútil; yermo, baldío, desierto, inculto; desolado; arruinado; superfluo, sobrante.—**w. paper,** papel de desecho.—**w. silk,** borra de seda. —**w. steam,** vapor de escape o de edución; vapor que se fuga. **IV.** *s.* despilfarro, derroche; decadencia, consunción; merma, pérdida; borra, restos, despojos, desperdicios; erial, desierto; extensión, inmensidad; disipación; estrago, devastación, destrozo, ruina; (min.) escombrera.—**w. pipe,** tubo de desagüe, desaguadero.

wastebasket [-bǽsket], *s.* cesto para papeles y desechos.

wasteful [uéistful], *a.* manirroto, malgastador, pródigo; destructivo, ruinoso; antieconómico.— **wastefully** [-i], *adv.* pródigamente, despilfarradamente; antieconómicamente.—**wastefulness** [-nes], *s.* prodigalidad; calidad de antieconómico; gasto inútil.

waster [uéistœr], *s.* disipador, gastador; devastador; desperfecto.

wasting [-ing]. **I.** *a.* que usa, agota o consume. **II.** *s.* derramamiento; desgaste; agotamiento; extenuación, consunción, marasmo.

wastrel [uéstrel], *s.* desperdicios; erial.

wasty [uéisti], *a.* yermo, baldío; desechado, sobrante.

watch [uóch]. **I.** *s.* reloj de bolsillo; vela, velación, desvelo o vigilia; vigilancia, cuidado, observación; centinela, vigía, atalaya, aguaita, guardia, sereno, vigilante; (mar.) cuarto, servicio, guardia.—**w. and ward,** patrulla, ronda.—**w. case,** caja de reloj, relojera.—**w. chain,** cadena o cinta de reloj, leontina.—**w. charm,** dije.—**w. dog,** perro de guarda o guardacasa.—**w. glass,** cristal de reloj; (mar.) ampolleta de media hora.— **w. guard** = **w.** CHAIN.—**w. house,** cuerpo de guardia.—**w. night,** víspera de año nuevo.—**w. spring,** muelle de reloj.—**w. stand,** porta-reloj. **to be upon the w.,** estar alerta o a quién vive. **II.** *va.* vigilar, observar; espiar, atisbar; cuidar, guardar; tener cuidado de o con. **III.** *vn.* vigilar, estar alerta; hacer centinela o guardia; velar.—**to w. for,** esperar; (a veces con **out**) buscar; tener cuidado con.—**to w. over,** guardar, vigilar; inspeccionar, superintender.

watcher [uóchœr], *s.* vigilante, velador; el que vela a un enfermo.

watchful [uóchful], *a.* despierto, vigilante, que está alerta; desvelado.—**w. waiting,** (pol.) espera vigilante, paciencia vigilante.

watchfully [-i], *adv.* desveladamente; atentamente, vigilando.—**watchfulness** [-nes], *s.* vigilancia, cuidado; desvelo.

watchmaker [uóchméikœr], *s.* relojero.—**w.'s shop,** relojería.

watchman [uóchman], *s.* sereno, guardián, vigilante, salvaguardia.

watchtower [uóchtáuœr], *s.* atalaya, torre; mirador, albarrana.

watchword [uóchuœrd], *s.* (mil.) santo y seña; nombre, consigna; lema.

Para la pronunciación de æ, œ, ɒ, š, šh, ᴜ, ȳ, ʏ, z, véase la clave al principio del libro.

watchwork [-uérk], *s.* mecanismo de un reloj de bolsillo.

water [uótœr], *s.* agua; cualquier extensión de agua (lago, río, mar); (fisiol.) linfa; orina, orines; (joy.) aguas (de las piedras preciosas); (tej.) viso (de los géneros); (com.) acciones emitidas sin aumento de capital que las represente. Se emplea en palabras compuestas y en frases para denotar que el segundo elemento crece en el agua, es movido por agua, la contiene o sirve para contenerla o ir por ella. Las frases más usuales se dan a continuación. Las palabras compuestas indivisas van en el lugar que les corresponde como tales.—**w. back,** caja de agua caliente en una estufa.—**w. ballast,** lastre de agua.—**w. bar,** (arq.) plancha o barra obturadora, para impedir la entrada del agua; (ing.) caballón, lomo de desviación.—**w. bath,** baño de María.—**w. battery,** (elec.) pila de agua.—**w. bearing,** cojinete lubricado por agua. —**w. bed,** (med.) colchón de agua (de cubierta impermeable inflado con agua).—**w. bird,** ave acuática.—**w. boatman** = **w.** BUG.—**w.-borne,** llevado por las aguas.—**w. bottle,** botella o bolsa para agua, calientapiés; vasija para recoger muestras acuáticas.—**w. brash,** acedía.—**w. bubble,** ampolla.—**w. buffalo,** carabao.—**w. bug,** (ent.) chinche de agua.—**w. butt,** bota de agua, pipa. **w. carriage,** transporte por agua; conducción de aguas por cañerías, etc.—**w. carrier,** aguador.— **w. cask** = **w.** BUTT.—**w. cell,** bolsa o celda de agua (del camello).—**w. clock,** reloj de agua.—**w. closet,** inodoro, excusado.—**w. cock,** grifo, espita. —**w. color,** (pint.) color para acuarela; acuarela.— **w. colorist,** acuarelista.—**w.-cool,** enfriar por agua.—**w.-cooled,** enfriado por agua.—**w. cooler,** cubilla refrigeradora de agua.—**w. cooling,** enfriamiento por agua.—**w. cress,** (bot.) berro.—**w. cure,** hidroterapia; tormento del agua consiste en repletar de agua el estómago de la víctima. —**w. curtain,** cortina de agua contra incendios. —**w. dog,** perro de aguas; (fam.) marinero viejo. —**w. engine,** máquina hidráulica; máquina de apagar incendios.—**w. front,** tierra ribereña.—**w. ga(u)ge,** indicador de nivel de agua.—**w. gas,** gas de agua.—**w. gate,** abertura para el agua; compuerta.—**w. gilding,** dorado al destemple.—**w. gland,** obturador hidráulico.—**w. glass,** vidrio soluble, silicato sodi-potásico; (m. v.) indicador de nivel.—**w. hammer,** (hidr.) golpe de ariete.—**w. head,** (hidr.) carga hidrostática, diferencia de nivel.—**w. hemlock,** (bot.) cicuta.—**w. ice,** sorbete.—**w. inch,** especie de paja de agua, cuyo valor varía, siendo poco más o menos 7 cuartos (*quarts*), o 6.6 litros, por minuto.—**w. jacket,** (m. v.) camisa de agua.—**w.-laid,** torcido hacia la izquierda (cable).—**w. level,** nivel de agua.—**w. leg,** (m. v.) placa de agua.—**w. lily,** (bot.) ninfea, nenúfar.— **w. line,** (mar.) línea de agua, línea de flotación.— **w.-logged,** anegado en agua.—**w. meter,** contador de agua.—**w. mill,** aceña, molino de agua.— **w. mint,** (bot.) hierbabuena acuática.—**w. mite,** (ent.) cresa de agua.—**w. nymph,** náyade.—**w. ordeal,** prueba del agua.—**w. pail,** cubo, balde.— **w. pipe,** cañería de abastecimiento o conducción de agua; caño o tubo para conducción de agua.— **w. pitcher,** jarro.—**w. plantain,** (bot.) alisma. —**w. power,** fuerza o energía hidráulica.—**w. purification,** (ing.) depuración de agua.—**w. rate,** cupo del consumo de agua.—**w. skater,** (ent.) tejedera.—**w. skipper,** (ent.) tejedor.—**w. snake,** culebra de agua.—**w. spider,** (ent.) esquila.—**w. spring,** manantial, ojo de agua.—**w. sprite,** ondina.—**w. supply,** abastecimiento de agua.—**w. table,** (arq.) retallo de derrame.—**w. tank,** tanque o depósito para agua.—**w. tax,** contribución de aguas.—**w.-tight,** hermético, estanco.—**w. tower,** torre de elevación de aguas; torre de agua para incendios.—**w. trough,** abrevadero.—**w. tube,** (m. v.) indicador de nivel.—**w.-tube boiler,** caldera acuatubular.—**w.** wave, onda de agua; especie de rizo u ondulación por vía húmeda, formado metiendo peinetas en el pelo humedecido.—**w. wheel,** rueda hidráulica.

water [uótœr]. **I.** *va.* regar; humedecer, mojar; aguar; bañar; echar agua a, diluir con agua; dar aguas o visos a (una tela).—**to w. cattle,** abrevar, dar de beber al ganado.—**to w. ships,** (mar.) hacer aguada.—**to w. the stock,** diluir o

aguar las acciones, aumentar su número sin aumentar el capital.—**to w. wine,** aguar o bautizar el vino. **II.** *vn.* chorrear agua o humedad; tomar agua (para una locomotora, etc.); beber agua. —**to make the mouth w.,** hacer la boca agua.

waterage [uótœrey], *s.* barcaje.

watercourse [-cors], *s.* corriente de agua; vaguada; río, arroyo; madre o lecho de un río; derecho de aguas.

watered [uótœrd], *a.* aguado, diluído; regado, abundante en agua.—**w. silk,** muaré.

waterer [uótœrœr], *s.* regador; aguador de noria; abrevador.

waterfall [-fol], *s.* cascada, catarata, caída de agua. Ú. gen. en pl.

waterfowl [-fául], *s. sing.* y *pl.* ave(s) acuática(s).

wateriness [-ines], *s.* acuosidad, humedad.

watering [-ing]. **I.** *s.* riego, regadura; irrigación; (mar.) aguada. **II.** *a.* de regar; de beber; de aguas.—**w. boat,** barco aguador.—**w. cart,** carro de regar.—**w. place,** aguadero o abrevadero; balneario, lugar de baños; fuentes de aguas minerales; (mar.) aguada.—**w. pot,** regadera, hurtagua.

waterish [-ish], *a.* ácueo, acuoso.

waterishness [-nes], *s.* raleza; acuosidad.

waterman [-mæn], *s.* barquero.

watermark [-márc], *s.* (pap.) marca de agua, corondel; nivel del agua.

watermelon [-mélœn], *s.* (bot.) sandía.

waterpot [-pót], *s.* aguamanil; regadera.

waterproof [-prúf]. **I.** *a.* a prueba de agua, impermeable. **II.** *va.* impermeabilizar, hacer impermeable.—**waterproofing** [-ing]. **I.** *s.* impermeabilización; material impermeable o de impermeabilizar. **II.** *a.* impermeable; de impermeabilizar.

watershed [-shéd], *s.* hoya, cuenca; vertiente.

waterside [-sáid], *s.* borde u orilla del agua.

waterspout [-spáut], *s.* manga o bomba marina, surtidor; remolino.

waterway [-uéi], *s.* vía de agua, canal o río navegable; (mar.) trancanil, canalón.

waterworks [-uércs], *s.* instalación de abastecimiento de agua.

watery [-i], *a.* acuoso, ácueo; seroso; claro, ralo; insípido, evaporado; lloroso.

watt [uót], *s.* (elec.) vatio.—**w. hour,** vatio-hora (se recomienda *vatihora*).—**w.-hour meter,** contador de vatio-horas (se recomienda *vatihorámetro*); contador de energía eléctrica.

wattage [uótœr], *s.* (elec.) vatiaje, potencia en vatios.

wattle [uótœl]. **I.** *s.* zarzo; sebe; barbas de gallo; barba de pez. **II.** *va.* enzarzar, tejer, entretejer, entrelazar.

wattless [uótles], *s.* (elec.) devatiada, avatia (corriente).

wattmeter [uótmítœr], *s.* vatímetro; (errónea pero frecuentemente) contador de vatio-horas.

waul [uól], *vn.* maullar.

wave [uéiv]. **I.** *s.* ola; onda, ondulación; movimiento de la mano, ademán; (tej. y joy.) aguas, visos.—**w. band,** (rad.) escala de longitudes de onda dentro de ciertos límites.—**w. crest,** cresta de la ola; (rad.) cresta de la onda.—**w. detector,** (rad.) detector de ondas.—**w. length,** (rad.) longitud de onda.—**w. meter,** (rad.) ondímetro.—**w. offering,** ofrenda de las primicias entre los judíos. —**w. train,** (rad.) tren de ondas, serie o sucesión de ondas.—**w. winding,** (elec.) arrollamiento ondulado. **II.** *va.* y *vn.* ondear, tremolar, blandir, agitar, flamear; hacer señas o señales.

waved [uéivd], *a.* ondeado, ondulado.

waveless [uéivles], *a.* sin olas, tranquilo, calmado; sin ondas.

wavelet [uéivlet], *s.* olita, cabrilla.

waver [uéivœr], *vn.* ondear, oscilar; tambalear, balancearse; vacilar, titubear.—**waverer** [-œr], *s.* veleta, persona mudable o irresoluta.—**wavering** [-ing]. **I.** *a.* irresoluto, inconstante. **II.** *s.* irresolución, vacilación, titubeo.—**waveringly** [-ingli], *adv.* con incertidumbre y vacilación.

wavy, waving [uéivi, -ing], *a.* ondeado, undoso, ondeante, ondulante.

wawl [uól], *vn.* = WAUL.

wax [uaecs]. **I.** *s.* cera. **II.** *a.* de cera.—**w. cake,** pan o marqueta de cera.—**w. candle,** vela de cera. —**w. chandler,** cerero.—**w. end,** (zap.) hilo encerado.—**w. etching,** electrotipia en cera.—**w. match,** cerilla, fósforo de cera.—**w. model(l)ing,** modelado en cera.—**w. painting,** encausto a la cera.—**w. paper,** papel encerado.—**w. plant,** (bot.) ceriflor.—**w. pocket,** cavidad secretora (de la abeja).—**w. process** = W. ETCHING.—**w. taper,** cirio, blandón, hacha de cera. **III.** *va.* encerar. **IV.** *vn.* hacerse, ponerse (*he waxed angry*, se puso colérico, se encolerizó; *I am waxing old*, me estoy haciendo viejo, me estoy envejeciendo.)

waxen [uǽcscœn], *a.* de cera; plástico.

waxflower [uǽcsfláuær], *s.* = WAX PLANT.

waxwing [uǽxuing], *s.* (orn.) picotera.

waxwork [uǽxucérk], *s.* objeto o figura de cera.— *pl.* figuras de cera.—**waxworker** [-œr], *s.* cerero; (zool.) abeja obrera.

waxy uǽcsi], *a.* ceroso; de cera; plástico; encerado.

way [uéi], *s.* vía; camino, senda; conducto, paso, pasaje; canal; distancia, espacio recorrido; rumbo, curso, dirección; ruta, rota, derrota; (mar.) marcha, andar, velocidad de un buque; modo, medio, manera, expediente: uso, costumbre, hábito; modo de obrar, sistema, línea de conducta, comportamiento; avance, progreso o adelantamiento; (fam.) estado (de salud).—*pl.* (mar.) anguilas de grada.—**w. in,** entrada.—**w. off,** muy lejos.—**w. out,** salida.—**w. station,** (f. c.) estación intermediaria.—**w. through,** pasaje.—**w. train,** tren de escala.—**ways and means,** medios y arbitrios.— **across the w.,** al otro lado, en el otro lado, en frente.—**any w.** (NO ANYWAY) de cualquier modo, de cualquiera manera, como se quiera.—**by w. of,** por la vía de, pasando por; por vía de, a modo de.— **by the w.,** entre paréntesis, de paso.—**by the w. of,** por la vía de.—**every w.,** por todas partes, de todos lados; de todos modos.—**no w.,** de ningún modo, de ninguna manera.—**on the w.,** en camino; de paso.—**on the w. to,** en camino de, con rumbo a.—**out of the w.,** fuera de camino; extraviado; escondido; fuera de orden; donde no estorba o estorbe; a un lado; poco común, extraordinario, original.—**over the w.** = ACROSS STHE W.—**that w.,** por ahí, por allí; de ese modo, así.—**this w.,** por aquí; de este modo, así.—**to be in the w.,** estar en el camino o en la vía; incomodar, estorbar.—**to have one's (own) w.,** hacer uno lo que quiera; salirse con la suya.—**under w.,** en camino, en marcha; empezado, haciéndose.

waybill [uéibil], *s.* hoja de ruta.

wayfarer [uéiféærœr], *s.* pasajero, viajador, viajante, caminante.

wayfaring [-ing], *a.* que va de viaje o de camino. —**w. man** = WAYFARER.—**w. tree,** (bot.) viburno.

waylay [uéiléi], *va.* insidiar, asechar para asaltar o robar.—**waylayer** [-œr], *s.* asechador, insidiador.

waymark [uéimárk], **waypost** [-póust], *s.* hito, mojón, poste indicador.

wayside [uéisáid]. **I.** *s.* orilla o borde del camino. **II.** *a.* junto al camino.

wayward [uéiuard], *a.* descarriado; díscolo, voluntarioso, avieso; vacilante.—**waywardly** [-li], *adv.* voluntariosa o aviesamente.—**waywardness**- [-nes], *s.* indocilidad, voluntariedad.

we [uí], *pron. pers.* (*pl.* de I) nosotros, nosotras.

weak [uíc], *a.* débil; frágil; poco fuerte, poco resistente; inseguro; ineficaz; impotente; escaso; (com.) flojo (precio o mercado); (gram. ingl.) regular (verbo o nombre) en sus desinencias o (adjetivo) en la formación del comparativo.—**w.- eyed,** de vista débil.—**w.-handed,** escaso de braceros; de manos débiles.—**w.-headed,** de inteligencia menguada.—**w.-kneed,** débil de rodillas; (fig.) falto de energía; servil.—**w.-minded,** pobre de espíritu; simple, mentecato, pusilánime.—**w. point, w. side,** el flaco, el lado débil.—**w.-sighted** = W.-EYED.

weaken [wícœn]. **I.** *va.* debilitar; enflaquecer; relajar; enervar; disminuir, atenuar. **II.** *vn.* debilitarse, flaquear, desfallecer; ahilarse.

weakfish [uícfish], *s.* (ict.) nombre de un pez norteamericano de boca muy delicada.

weakling [uícling], *a.* canijo, encajado.

weakly [uícli]. **I.** *adv.* débilmente, sin vigor, sin fuerzas. **II.** *a.* enfermizo, achacoso, enclenque, canijo.

weakness [uícnes], *s.* debilidad; decaimiento; poca consistencia; fragilidad; flaqueza, desliz; el flaco o lado débil; futilidad.

weal [uíl], *s.* bienandanza, bienestar o felicidad, prosperidad; cardenal, verdugón.

weald [uíld], *s.* campiña, campo abierto.

wealth [uelz], *s.* riqueza, abundancia.

wealthily [uélzili], *adv.* rica u opulentamente.

wealthiness [uélzines], *s.* riqueza; abundancia.

wealthy [uélzi], *a.* rico; abundante, exuberante.

wean [uín], *va.* destetar, deshijar; desbecerrar; descorderar; enajenar el afecto de.

weanling [uínling], *s.* niño o animal recién destetado; destetado.

weapon [uépṇn], *s.* arma.—*pl.* (biol.) púas, espinas; aguijones, garras, etc.; medios de defensa de vegetales y animales.—**weaponed** [-d], *a.* armado.—**weaponless** [-les], *a.* desarmado.

wear [uéær]. **I.** *va.* (*pret.* WORE; *pp.* WORN) usar; llevar o traer puesto (un traje, etc.); mostrar, tener aspecto o apariencia de, exhibir; gastar, consumir; desgastar, deteriorar; apurar, agotar; cansar, aburrir, enfadar; virar.—**to w. away,** gastar o consumir.—**to w. a youthful form,** tener aspecto juvenil.—**to w. down,** gastar, consumir; desgastar por rozamiento.—**to w. on,** llevar, tener puesto.—**to w. one's heart on one's sleeve,** andar con la cara descubierta, llevar el corazón en la mano.—**to w. out,** gastar, desgastar: acabar con, agotar; cansar, fastidiar.—**to w. the breeches,** o **the pants,** (fam.) llevar o haberse puesto los calzones, mandar. **II.** *vn.* gastarse, consumirse; durar, perdurar; pasar, correr (el tiempo); (mar.) virar.—**to w. away,** decaer; gastarse, consumirse. —**to w. off,** usarse, gastarse; borrarse; pasarse, disiparse, desaparecer.—**to w. on,** pasarse lentamente.—**to w. well,** durar largo tiempo, ser duradero. **III.** *s.* uso, gasto, deterioro; moda, boga.— **w. and tear,** uso; desgaste o deterioro natural (debido al uso).—**little the worse for w.,** casi nuevo, casi sin usar; como nuevo.

wearable [uéærabœl], *a.* que se puede llevar, usar o gastar.

wearer [-œr], *s.* el que lleva, gasta o usa algo.

wearied [uírid], *a.* cansado, fatigado; aburrido, fastidiado.—**weariness** [-nes], *s.* lasitud, cansancio; aburrimiento, fastidio.

wearing [uéæring]. **I.** *s.* uso; desgaste, deterioro; pérdida, decaimiento. **II.** *a.* de uso; desgastador; agotador, fatigoso.—**w. apparel,** ropa de uso.

wearisome [uírisum], *a.* tedioso, fastidioso, pesado, cansado, aburrido.—**wearisomely** [-li], *adv.* fatigosa o pesadamente.—**wearisomeness** [-nes], *s.* tedio, fastidio, cansancio, hastío.

weary [uíri]. **I.** *va.* cansar, fatigar, hastiar, aburrir, enfadar, molestar.—**to w. out,** moler, cansar la paciencia. **II.** *vn.* fatigarse, cansarse, aburrirse. **III.** *a.* cansado, fatigado, rendido, molido; aburrido, hastiado; tedioso, fastidioso.

weasand [uísand], *s.* (ant.) gaznate.

weasel [uíscœl], *s.* (zool.) comadreja.

weather [uépœr]. **I.** *s.* tiempo (estado atmosférico); vicisitudes de la suerte.—**to be bad, good w.** (con it por sujeto), hacer mal, buen tiempo. **II.** *a.* del tiempo, relativo al tiempo; (mar.) de barlovento, del lado del viento.—**w.-beaten,** trabajado por la tormenta; curtido por la intemperie.—**w.-bound,** detenido por el mal tiempo.—**W. Bureau,** (E. U.) Oficina Meteorológica (en el Ministerio de Agricultura de Wáshington).—**w. forecast,** predicción del tiempo.—**w. prophet,** pronosticador del tiempo.— **w. sheets,** escotas de barlovento.—**w. shore,** costa de barlovento.—**w. side,** costado de barlovento.—**w. signal,** señal (bandera, etc.) para indicar las variaciones del tiempo.—**w. strip,** burlete, gualdrín.—**w. vane,** veleta, giraldilla, grímpola. **III.** *va.* aguantar (el temporal); resistir a, sobrevivir a (la adversidad); orear, airear, poner al aire; secar al aire; (mar.) ganar (el barlovento); doblar o montar (un cabo).—**to w. a point,** ganar alguna ventaja.—**to w. out,** vencer (obstáculos). **IV.** *vn.* curtirse en la intemperie.

weatherboard [-bórd], s. (carp.) tabla solapada; (mar.) lado del viento.—**weatherboarding** [-ing], s. solapadura de tablas; (mar.) falsas.

weathercock [-cóc], s. veleta, giraldilla, cataviento; persona inconstante o mudable.

weatherglass [-glǽs], s. instrumento indicador del tiempo (barómetro, etc.).

weathering [-ing], s. desgaste o alteración debida a los agentes atmosféricos; (arq.) declive de derrame.

weatherly [-li], a. (mar.) de bolina, de barlovento.

weatherproof [-pruf], a. a prueba de mal tiempo, a prueba de intemperie, inatacable por los agentes atmosféricos.

weatherwise [-uáis], a. perito en pronosticar las mudanzas del tiempo.

weave [uív]. I. va. (pret. WOVE; pp. WOVEN, WOVE), tejer, tramar; trenzar; entrelazar; entretejer; urdir, forjar (cuentos). II. vn. tejer, trabajar en telar.

weaver [-œr], s. tejedor, tramador; araña tejedora. —**w. bird**, (orn.) tejedor.—**w.'s yarn**, hilaza.

weaving [uíving], s. tejido; textura.

weazen(ed, a. = WIZEN(ED.

web [uéb], s. tela, tejido, obra tejida; rollo de papel continuo; trama, lazo; artificio engañoso, trampa; (orn.) membrana que une los dedos de los palmípedos; tela de araña; barba o pelo de pluma; (ing.) alma (de viga, de riel); hoja de sierra o de espada.—**w.-footed**, palmado, palmípedo.

webbed [uébd], a. unido por una telilla o membrana; palmado, palmípedo.

webbing [uébing], s. cincha, pretal.

webfoot [uébfút], s. pie palmado.

wed [uéd]. I. va. casarse con; casar, unir en matrimonio. II. vn. casarse, contraer matrimonio.

wedded [uéded], pp. y a. casado.—**w. to**, empeñado en, declarado por, aferrado en.

wedding [uéding]. I. s. boda, nupcias, casamiento; unión, enlace. II. a. de boda, nupcial, de casamiento; de novia.—**w. cake**, torta o pan de boda.—**w. dress**, traje nupcial, o de boda.—**w. ring**, anillo nupcial, sortija de matrimonio.—**w. trip**, viaje de novios.

wedge [uéy]. I. s. cuña; calza o calce, alzaprima; (geom.) prisma triangular. II. va. acuñar, meter cuñas, calzar.

wedlock [uédloc], s. matrimonio, himeneo, connubio.

Wednesday [uénsdi], s. miércoles.

wee [uí], a. (fam.) pequeño, chiquito.

weed [uíd]. I. s. maleza, mala hierba, cizaña; lo que crece er abundancia dañosa o inútil; (fam.) tabaco; ropa o gasa de luto. II. va. desyerbar, sollar; (a veces con out) quitar, extirpar, suprimir; entresacar, segregar.—**weeder** [-œr], s. desyerbador, desmalezador; escarda.—**weedhook** [-júc], s. escarda.

weedy [-i], a. enmalezado; verboso; algoso.

week [uík], s. semana.—**w. day**, día de trabajo.— **w.-end**, fin de semana.—**this day w.**, de hoy en ocho días; hoy hace ocho días.

weekly [uícli]. I. a. semanal, hebdomadario.— **w. paper**, semanario, periódico semanal. II. adv. semanalmente, por semana.

ween [uín], vn. imaginar, pensar, creer.

weep [uíp], va. y vn. (pret. y pp. WEPT) llorar; deplorar, lamentar, condolerse de; (bot.) llorar, destilar; estar pendiente, inclinarse hacia el suelo.—**to w. for**, llorar a; llorar por; llorar de (tristeza, alegría, etc.).

weeper [uípœr], s. llorador, plañidero, floraduelos; llorón; gasa o seda de luto; velo de viuda; festón de musgo que pende de algunos árboles.

weeping [uíping]. I. s. llanto, lloro, lágrimas. II. a. plañidero, llorón.—**w. ash, w. willow**, fresno llorón, sauce llorón.

weepingly [-li], adv. llorosamente, con lágrimas, con llanto.

weevil [uívœl], s. (ent.) gorgojo; calapatillo, mordihuí; gusano del trigo.

weft [uéft], s. (tej.) trama. V. WOOF, WAIF, WAFT.

weigh [uéi]. I. va. pesar; alzar, levar (anclas); considerar, reflexionar acerca de; sobrecargar, agobiar, oprimir.—**to w. anchor**, (mar.) levar el ancla.—**to w. down**, exceder en peso; sobrepujar; agobiar, abrumar, oprimir.—**to w. out**, pesar, sacar o separar por peso. II. vn. pesar, ser pesado; ser digno de mucho aprecio, ser de importancia; (gen. con on) gravar, pesar sobre, ser opresivo o gravoso; (mar.) levar anclas; hacerse a la vela.— **to w. down**, hundirse por su propio peso.

weighable [uéiabœl], a. capaz de ser pesado o vendido al peso.

weighed [uéid], a. pesado; experimentado.

weigher [uéœr], s. pesador.—**public w.**, almotacén, pesador público.

weighing [uéing]. I. s. peso; pesada. II. a. de pesar, para pesar.—**w. machine, w. scale**, balanza; báscula.

weight [uéit]. I. va. cargar, gravar; aumentar el peso de; poner un peso o una pesa a. II. s. peso, pesantez; pesa; carga, gravamen; cargo, lastre. —**weights and measures**, pesas y medidas.—**by w.**, por peso.—**to be worth its w. in gold**, valer su peso en oro.

weightily [-tili], adv. pesadamente; con mucho peso, con gran fuerza.

weightiness [-tines], s. ponderosidad, pesadez; solidez, fuerza; importancia, momento.

weightless [uéitles], a. ligero, leve; sin peso; imponderable.

weighty [uéiti], a. ponderoso, pesado; grave, serio, importante; de peso.

weir [uíœr], s. (hidr.) vertedero, presa de aforo; presa. (El primer significado es el más usual.)

weird [uíœrd]. I. a. misterioso, horripilante, como del otro mundo, fantasmagórico.—**the W. Sisters**, las Parcas. II. s. destino; pronóstico; encantamiento.—**weirdness** [-nes], s. calidad de horripilante y misterioso.

welcome [uélcưm]. I. a. bienvenido, bien llegado; grato, agradable.—**you are w.**, sea Vd. bienvenido, no hay de qué (cuando se dan las gracias). **you are w. to it**, está a la disposición de Vd.; tengo mucho gusto en dárselo (prestárselo) a Vd.; (irónico) con gusto se lo dejo, buen provecho le haga. II. interj. ¡bien venido! III. s. bienvenida, buena acogida; parabién, enhorabuena. IV. va. dar la bienvenida a, recibir con agasajo.

welcomeness [-nes], s. calidad de ser bienvenido; buena acogida.—**welcomer** [-œr], s. el que acoge o da la bienvenida.

weld [uéld]. I. va. soldar; unir; unificar. II. vn. ser soldable, soldarse. III. s. soldadura (procedimiento y resultado).—**weldable** [-abœl], a. soldable.—**welder** [-œr], s. soldador; (elec.) transformador de soldar.—**welding** [-ing]. I. s. soldadura. II. a. de soldar, para soldar.

welfare [uélfœr], s. bienestar, bienandanza, felicidad; bien.

welkin [uélkin], s. (poét.) firmamento, cielo.—**to make the w. ring**, atronar el espacio.

well [uél]. I. va. verter, derramar. II. vn. manar, brotar, fluir. III. s. pozo (de agua, petróleo, etc.); fuente, manantial, ojo de agua; venero, origen; aljibe, cisterna; cavidad; vaso o copa de tintero; (arq.) caja o pozo de escalera; vivar de pesca; (mar.) caja de bombas o sentina.—**w. curb**, brocal (de pozo).—**w. of a ship**, (mar.) arca de bomba.—**w. of a fishing boat**, pozo de barco pescador.—**w. sweep**, cigüeñal o cigoñal de pozo.— **w. water**, agua de pozo.

well, a. bueno, bien, en buena salud o alentado; bien, satisfactorio; salvo, sano; grato, agradable o conveniente; ventajoso; bueno, provechoso; (ant.) valido, favorecido.—**w. and good**, enhorabuena, bien está.—**w.-being**, bienandanza, felicidad, bien, bienestar.—**w.-doer**, persona virtuosa; bienhechor; (fam.) persona acomodada.— **w.-doing**, benéfico; beneficencia, buenas obras; bienandanza, prosperidad.—**w.-wisher**, bienqueriente.

well, adv. bien; muy; favorablemente; suficientemente; convenientemente; con propiedad, razonablemente; con razón; en sumo grado, considerablemente.—**w.-accomplished**, lleno de dotes o buenas cualidades; bien educado.—**w.-affected**, bien intencionado.—**w.-appointed**, bien provisto; bien amueblado; bien equipado.—**w.-behaved**, de buena conducta; cortés.—**w.-born**, bien nacido.— **w.-bred**, bien criado o bien educado.—**w.-disposed**, bien dispuesto, favorable.—**w. done**, bien hecho; (coc.) bien cocido, bien asado.—**w. done!** ¡bravo! ¡bien hecho!—**w. enough**, bastante bien.— **w.-favored**, agradecido; bien parecido.—**w.-gowned**, bien vestida.—**w.-meaning**, bien intencionado; honrado, sincero.—**w.-meant**, hecho con buena intención.—**w.-nigh**, casi; poco menos que.—**w. off**, acomodado, bien de fortuna.— **w.-read**, leído, instruido, ilustrado.—**w.-spoken**, que habla bien; bien dicho; urbano.—**w.-spoken, of,** de buena reputación.—**w. then**, con que, pues bien.—**w.-thought of,** bien mirado.—**w.-timed**, oportuno.—**w.-to-do,** acomodado.—**w., w.!** ¡vaya, vaya! ¡qué cosa!

welladay [uéledéi], *interj.* ¡ay de mí!

wellhead [uéljed], *s.* fuente, manantial.

wellhole [-jóul], *s.* caja de escalera; boca de pozo.

wellspring [-spríng], *s.* manantial, fuente.

Welsh [uélsh]. **I.** *a.* galés, de Gales.—**W. rabbit,** tostada cubierta de queso derretido con cerveza. —the W., los galeses. **II.** *s.* idioma galés.

Welshman [uélshman], *s.* galés.

welt [uélt]. **I.** *s.* (cost.) ribete, vivo; (zap.) vira: (carp.) refuerzo; costurón, roncha, verdugo; (fam.) azotaina, tunda. **II.** *va.* (cost.) ribetear; (zap.) poner viras; azotar levantando ronchas.

welter [uéltœr]. **I.** *vn.* encenagarse; revolcarse en agua, cieno o lodo; hincharse las olas. **II.** *s.* oleaje; conmoción, agitación, tumulto; cenagal, revolcadero.

wen [uén], *s.* lobanillo, lupia.

wench [uénch]. *s.* (despec.) moza, criada.

wend [uénd]. **I.** *va.* dirigir, encaminar. **II.** *vn.* andar, ir, seguir camino, pasar.

wennish [uénish], *a.* que parece un lobanillo o lo tiene.

went [uent], *pret.* de TO GO.

wept [uept], *pret.* y *pp.* de TO WEEP.

were [uœr], *pret. pl.* de *indic.* y *sing.* y *pl.* de *subj.* de **to be**: *we were*, nosotros éramos o estábamos, fuimos o estuvimos: *if I were*, si yo fuera o fuese, estuviera o estuviese: *if they were*, si ellos fueran, fuesen, estuvieran o estuviesen; *there were*, había, hubo.—**as it w.**, por decirlo así: como si fuese.

wergild [uœrguíld], *s.* (hist.) multa o indemnización impuesta a un asesino y sus parientes entre los antiguos teutones.

wert [uœrt], 2a. *pers. sing. pret. indic.* y *subj.* del verbo TO BE.

werwolf [uœrulf], *s.* persona que, según la superstición, se convertía en lobo y devoraba a otras personas.

Wesleyan [uéslean], *a.* y *s.* wesleyano, de Wesley.

west [uést]. **I.** *s.* oeste, poniente, occidente, ocaso.—**w. northwest,** oesnorueste.—**w. southwest,** oessudueste. **II.** *a.* occidental, del oeste.—**W. End,** barrio aristocrático de Londres, al oeste de Charing Cross.—**W. Indies,** Antillas.—**W. Indian,** antillano.—**W. Pointer,** (E. U.) graduado de West Point (escuela militar nacional). **III.** *adv.* a poniente o hacia el poniente; hacia el occidente.

westerly [uéstœrli]. **I.** *a.* occidental; del oeste; al oeste; hacia el oeste. **II.** *adv.* hacia el oeste.

western [uéstœrn], *a.* occidental, ponentino.

westerner [-œr], *s.* natural o habitante del oeste.

westernmost [-moust], *a.* más occidental, del extremo occidental.

Westphalian [uéstféilian], *s.* y *a.* vestfaliano.

westward, *a.* que tiende o está al oeste.

westward(s, westwardly [uéstuard(s, -li)], *adv.* a poniente, hacia occidente, hacia el ocaso.

wet [uét]. **I.** *a.* mojado; húmedo; lluvioso; (fam., pol.) antiprohibicionista.—**w. blanket,** (fam.) aguafiestas, paño frío (fig.), el o lo que echa a perder o apaga el entusiasmo, la alegría, etc.—**w. bulb,** ampolla humedecida del psicrómetro.—**w.-bulb thermometer,** psicrómetro.—**w. goods,** líquidos envasados; (fam.) aguardiente, licor, vino. —**w.-nurse,** ama de leche, nodriza.—**w. plate,** (fot.) placa de colodión.—**w. process,** (quím.) vía

húmeda.—**w.-shod,** que tiene los zapatos mojados. **II.** *s.* humedad, agua; lluvia; (fam., pol.) antiprohibicionista, antineftalista. **III.** *va.* mojar, humedecer, humectar.—**to w. one's whistle,** (fam.) mojar el gaznate, beber.

wether [uéðœr], *s.* carnero castrado.

wetness [uétnes], *s.* humedad.

wetted [uéted], *pret.* y *pp.* del verbo TO WET.—**W. perimeter,** (hidr.) perímetro mojado.

wetting [uéting], *s.* mojada; mojadura, remojadura, remojo.—**w. machine,** (impr.) máquina para remojar el papel.

wey [uéi], *s.* (Ingl.) unidad de peso (82,56 kg.) y de medida (14,09 hectolitros).

whack [juæk]. **I.** *va.* (fam.) pegar, golpear, vapulear. **II.** *vn.* dar una tunda; (fam.) ajustar cuentas; participar de. **III.** *s.* golpe, trastazo; (fam.) participación; ganga.—**whacker** [-œr], *s.* vapuleador.—**whacking** [-ing], *a.* (fam.) grueso, desmesurado, enorme.

whale [juéil]. **I.** *va.* (fam.) vapulear, dar una tunda. **II.** *vn.* dedicarse a la pesca de la ballena. **III.** *s.*|(ict.) ballena; cachalote.—**w. oil,** grasa de ballena.

whaleback [-bæc], *s.* (mar.) buque de cubierta cerrada y redondeada que se usa en aguas turbulentas.—**whaleboat** [-bóut], *s.* buque ballenero. —**whalebone** [-bóun], *s.* ballena o barba de ballena.—**whalefin** [-fín], *s.* aleta de ballena.— **whaler** [-œr], *s.* ballenero, pescador de ballenas; buque ballenero.—**whaling** [-ing], *s.* pesca de ballenas; (fam.) tunda, zurra, vapuleo.

whang [juæng]. **I.** *va.* y *vn.* (fam.) dar tundas. **II.** *s.* cuero fuerte; tunda.

whap, whapper, *s.* = WHOP.

wharf [juórf], *s.* (*pl.* WHARFS o WHARVES) muelle, embarcadero, o desembarcadero; descargadero. —**wharfage** [juórfœr], *s.* muellaje.

wharfinger [juórfinyœr], *s.* fiel de muelle.

wharves [juórvs], *s. pl.* de WHARF.

what [juót]. **I.** *a.* qué.—**w. a,** qué (*v.* A, *art. indef.*) **II.** *pron.* qué, qué cosa; cuál; el que, lo que, aquello que.—**w. else?** ¿qué más?—**w. for?** ¿para qué?—**w. ho!** ¡hola!—**w. if,** qué será si, y si, qué se hará o sucederá si (en interrogaciones problemáticas: *what if he should refuse?* ¿y si él rehusa?) ; y qué importa que, aunque (*what if he is a doctor?* ¿y qué importa que él sea doctor? aunque sea doctor).— **w. of it?** ¿eso que qué importa?—**w. though?** aun cuando; ¿qué importa que?—**and w. not,** (fam.) y qué sé yo qué mas.—**but w.,** que no (*he is not so rich but what he needs assistance,* él no es tan rico que no necesite ayuda). **III.** *adv.* cuán, cuánto; cómo (*what do you call it?* ¿cómo se llama?).—**w. with,** tanto, sea, en parte, entre (*what with hunger and what with weariness,* parte por hambre, parte por cansancio; entre el hambre y el cansancio).

whatever [juotévœr], *pron.* cuanto, cualquier cosa que, todo lo que, sea lo que fuere, que sea.

whatnot [juótnót], *s.* rinconera, estante, juguetero; lo que Vd. guste; cualquier cosa.

whatsoever [juótsoévœr], *pron.* = WHATEVER.

wheal [juíl], *s.* cardenal, roncha.

wheat [juít], *s.* (bot.) trigo.—**w. field,** trigal, sembrado de trigo.

wheatear [juítiœr], *s.* (orn.) triguero.

wheaten [juítœn], *a.* de trigo.

Wheatstone bridge [juítstoun brix], *s.* (elec.) puente de Wheatstone.

wheedle [juídœl], *va.* halagar, engaitar, lagotear, sonsacar.

wheedler [-dlœr], *s.* engaitador, zalamero, lagotero.

wheel [juíl]. **I.** *s.* rueda; disco, roldana, rodete, rodaja; polea; bicicleta; rueda de fuegos artificiales; rueda del timón; (fig.) timón; muela o rodezno del molino; noria; rueda, instrumento de tortura.—**w. and axle,** torno.—**w. animal,** o **animalcule,** rotífero.—**w. barometer,** barómetro de cuadrante.—**w. base,** (f. c., aut.) distancia entre ejes.—**w. body,** cuerpo o plato de rueda.—**w. boss,** cubo de rueda.—**w. chair,** silla de ruedas.—**w. horse,** caballo de varas.—**w. rope,** galdrope. **II.** *va.* rodar o hacer rodar; acarrear, transportar o llevar sobre ruedas; volver, girar, hacer girar, dar

vueltas a; poner ruedas; labrar con rueda de alfarero. **III.** *vn.* rodar, girar, dar vueltas; ir en bicicleta; (a veces con **about**) cambiar de rumbo o de
opinión.

wheelbarrow [juílbáro], *s.* carretilla.

wheeler [juílœr], *s.* rodador, girador; caballo de
varas; ruedas; el o lo que rueda o da vueltas;
vapor de ruedas; aperador.

wheelhouse [-jáus], *s.* timonera.

wheeling [-ing], *s.* rodaje, transporte sobre
ruedas; paseo en bicicleta; estado de un camino
carretero; rotación; (mil.) vuelta.

wheelman [-man], *s.* (mar.) timonero, timonel;
(dep.) biciclista, ciclista.

wheelwright [-rait], *s.* carretero, aperador, carpintero de carretas.

wheelwork [-uérk], *s.* conjunto de ruedas de una
máquina.

wheeze [juís]. **I.** *vn.* resollar con dificultad y ronquera o ruido silbante. **II.** *s.* resuello difícil y
ronco (ll. t. **wheeziness, wheezing**).—**wheezy**
[-y], *a.* que resuella con dificultad y ronquera.

whelk [juélk], *s.* buccino, caracol de mar; barro,
granito; roncha, chichón, costurón.

whelky [juélki], *a.* granoso, granujiento.

whelm [juélm], *va.* sumergir, anegar; sobrepujar,
subyugar; destruir.

whelp [juélp]. **I.** *s.* cachorro, perrezno; (despec.)
mozalbete; (mar.) guardainfante; (mec.) diente
de engranaje. **II.** *vn.* parir (la hembra de animal carnívoro).

when [juén], *adv.* cuando, al tiempo que, o mientras que; desde que; que, en que; en cuanto, así
que, tan pronto como; y entonces: (*I waited till
noon, when I went home*, esperé hasta mediodía, y
{entonces me fui a casa).—*since* **w.?** ¿desde cuándo?
¿de cuando acá?

whence [juéns], *adv.* de donde o desde donde, de
que o quien; de qué causa; por eso es por lo que;
por consiguiente.

whencesoever [-soévœr], *adv.* de donde quiera, de
cualquier paraje que sea.

whene'er [juenéær], *contr.* de WHENEVER.

whenever, whensoever [juen(so)évœr], *adv.*
cuando quiera que, siempre que, en cualquier
teimpo que sea, todas las veces que.

where [juéær], *adv.* donde, dónde; en donde, por
donde, adonde.

whereabouts [-abáuts]. **I.** *s.* paradero. **II.** *adv.*
donde, en qué lugar.

whereas [jueæréés], *conj.* considerando; por cuanto, visto que, puesto que, siendo así que; mientras que, al paso que.

whereat [jueæærét], *adv.* a lo cual; en qué, por qué,
de qué.

whereby [jueærbái], *adv.* por lo cual, con lo cual,
por donde, de que; por medio del cual; ¿por
qué? ¿cómo?

where'er [jueréær], *contr.* de WHEREVER.

wherefore [juéæærfor]. **I.** *adv.* por lo cual; por qué;
por eso. **II.** *s.* (fam.) porqué, causa, motivo.

wherefrom [jueærfróm], *conj.* de donde.

wherein [jueærín], *adv.* donde, en donde, en lo
cual; en qué.

whereinto [jueæríntu], *adv.* en donde, dentro de
lo que o dentro de lo cual, en lo cual.

whereof [jueæróf], *adv.* de lo cual, de que; de
donde; cuyo; de qué.

whereon [jueærón], *adv.* en que; sobre lo cual,
sobre; en qué.

whereso'er, wheresoever [jueærsoé(v)œr], *adv.*
donde quiera, en cualquier parte que, en cualquier sitio que sea.

whereto, whereunto [jueær(ʊn)tú], *adv.* a lo
que, a que; donde, adonde.

whereupon [jueærʊpón], *adv.* sobre lo cual, después de lo cual, con lo cual; entonces; dónde.

wherever [-évœr], *adv.* dondequiera que o por
dondequiera que, adondequiera que.

wherewith [jueæruíþ], **wherewithal** [jueær-
uiþól]. **I.** *adv.* con que, con lo cual; ¿con qué?
II. *s.* dinero necesario, cumquibus.

wherry [juérri]. **I.** *s.* barquilla, chalana. **II.** *va.*
pasar en barco.—**wherryman** [-mæn], *s.* barquero.

whet [juét], *va.* afilar, amolar; (con **on**) agriar,
exasperar; aguzar o abrir el apetito.

whet(ting [-ing], *s.* afiladura, aguzadura, amoladura; aperitivo.

whether [juéþœr]. **I.** *conj.* si; sea, sea que, ora,
ya.—**w. or no,** o **w. or not,** de un modo u otro; sea
que . . . o que no . . .; tanto si . . . como si no
(*whether you will or not*, que quieras, que no quieras).
II. *pron.* (ant.) cual, cual de los dos.

whetstone [juétstóun], *s.* aguzadera, amoladera,
piedra de afilar.

whetter [juétœr], *s.* amolador.

whew [jiú], *interj.* ¡cáspita!

whey [juéi], *s.* suero

wheyey, wheyish [-i, -šh], *a.* seroso.

which [juích], *a.* y *pron. rel.* que, el cual, la cual,
lo cual, los cuales, las cuales; cuál.—**w. way?** ¿por
dónde? ¿por qué camino?—**all of w., all w.,** todo
lo cual.—**both of w.,** que . . . ambos, que (*the
book and the hat, ooth of which are on the table*, el
libro y el sombrero, que están [ambos] sobre la
mesa).—**the w.,** el cual, los cuales. lo cual.

whichever, whichsoever [juich(so)évœr], *pron.*
y *a.* cualquiera (que), cualesquiera; el que.

whidah bird [juída bœrd], *s.* (orn.) vidua, viuda.

whiff [juíf]. **I.** *s.* vaharada, fumada, fumarada,
bocanada, soplo de viento; (Ingl.) bote de vela.
II. *va.* soplar. **III.** *va.* y *vn.* echar bocanadas o
vaharadas.

whiffle [juífœl]. **I.** *va.* hacer bambolearse, sacudir; soplar, disipar, desvanecer; tremolar. **II.** *vn.*
vacilar, cambiar de rumbo o de opinión; echar
bocanadas.

whiffler [juífœr], *s.* fumador que echa bocanadas
de humo.

whiffletree [juífœltrí], *s.* (carr.) balancín, volea.
V. SWINGLETREE.

whig [juíg], *s.* (Ingl., pol.) partido liberal; liberal;
(E. U. pol.) partidario de la independencia en
1776; partido centralista, predecesor del actual
partido republicano.

whiggery [juígœri], **whiggism** [juíguišm], *s.* credo del partido *whig*.

while [juáil]. **I.** *s.* rato; tiempo.—**a little w.
ago,** hace poco rato, no hace mucho.—**all this w.,**
en todo este tiempo.—**all whiles,** a ratos; de cuando en cuando.—**a w. after,** poco después.—**a w.
ago,** hace poco rato.—**between whiles,** de cuando
en cuando, a intervalos.—**for a w.,** por algún tiempo.—**little w.,** ratito.—**the w.,** mientras tanto,
entre tanto.—**to be worth w.,** valer la pena.
II. *conj.* mientras, mientras que, al mismo tiempo
que; aun cuando, si bien. **III.** *va.* (gen. con **away**)
pasar, entretener (el tiempo).

whilom(e [juáilom]. **I.** *a.* (ant. o póet.) antiguo,
que fué. **II.** *adv.* antiguamente, en otro tiempo;
a veces.

whilst [juáilst], *conj.* mientras, mientras que.

whim [juím], **whims(e)y** [juímši], *s.* antojo, capricho, fantasía; (min.) malacate.—**w. gin,** cabria,
trucha.

whimper [juímpœr]. **I.** *vn.* sollozar, plañir, quejarse; lloriquear. **II.** *s.* plañido, quejido; lloriqueo.

whimsical [juímšical], *a.* caprichoso, caprichudo.

whimsicality [juímšicǽliti], *s.* extravagancia,
ridiculez.—**whimsically** [-cali], *adv.* caprichosamente, de un modo raro.—**whimsicalness** [-cal-
nes], *s.* rareza, singularidad, extravagancia.

whin [juín], *s.* (bot.) aliaga.

whine [juáin]. **I.** *vn.* gemir, plañir, quejarse, lamentarse; lloriquear. **II.** *s.* quejido, plañido,
lamento; lloriqueo.

whinny [juíni]. **I.** *vn.* relinchar. **II.** *s.* hin; relincho.

whip [juíp]. **I.** *va.* azotar, fustigar, flagelar;
zurrar, vapular, tundir; (con **away, in, off, on,**
etc.) asir, arrebatar, meter, sacar; (fam., E. U.)
vencer, batir, ganar a; (agr.) ribetear; batir
(huevos, crema); (cost.) sobrecoser; (mar.) envolver un cabo con cuerdecilla; izar con candeliza.—
to w. off, despachar prontamente. — **to w. out,**

arrebatar; sacar prontamente.—**to w. up,** agarrar, coger de repente; (mar.) izar con la candeliza. **II.** *vn.* echar a correr; obrar con ligereza; echar repetidas veces el anzuelo al agua.—**to w. down,** bajar corriendo o volando.—**to w. out,** zafarse, escaparse.—**to w. up,** subir corriendo. **III.** *s.* azote; látigo, zurriago; fuete, mayoral; (Ingl.) diputado encargado de velar por los intereses de su partido en el Parlamento; (mar.) amante, palanquín de estay.—**w. and spur,** a uña de caballo.—**w. graft, graftage, o grafting,** injerto machihembrado o de lengüeta.—**w. hand,** mano del látigo; mano derecha; (fig.) ventaja.—**w. money,** agujetas.

whipcord [juípcord], *s.* mecha, pajuela o tralla del látigo.

whipgraft [juípgraft], *va.* injertar a lengüeta y ranura, o por unión machihembrada.

whiplash [juíplǽsh], *s.* fusta del látigo.

whipper [juípœr], *s.* azotador; batidor.

whippersnapper [juípœrsnǽpœr], *s.* mequetrefe, ñiquiñaque.

whippet [juípet], *s.* especie de perro lebrero; (mil.) tanque ligero, tanque Renault (llámase t. **w. tank**).

whipping [juíping]. **I.** azotes, flagelación, vapuleo. **II.** *a.* de azotar, para azotar; azotador.— **w. post,** poste de flagelación, al cual se ata a los reos para azotarlos.—**w. top,** trompo, peonza.

whippletree [juípœltrí], *s.* (carr.) volea, balancín.

whippoorwill [juípuruíl], *s.* (orn.) chotacabra americana.

whipsaw [juípsó], *s.* sierra larga y angosta de bastidor para cortes longitudinales.

whipstaff [juípstaf], *s.* (mar.) pinzote; puño del látigo.

whipster [juípstœr], *s.* mequetrefe.

whipt [juípt], *pp.* de TO WHIP; ú. gen. como *a.*

whir(r [juœr]. **I.** *va.* y *vn.* girar; zumbar; rehilar. **II.** *s.* zumbido, aleteo.

whirl [juœrl]. **I.** *va.* y *vn.* girar, rodar, voltejear, dar vueltas, remolinar. **II.** *s.* giro, vuelta, rotación, volteo, remolino.

whirlbat [-bat], *s.* cesto; manopla de púgil.

whirlbone [-boun], *s.* rótula, choquezuela.

whirligig [juœrliguig], *s.* perinola; tiovivo; (ent.) girín.

whirlpool [-pul], *s.* vórtice, vorágine, remolino.

whirlwind [-uind], *s.* torbellino, remolino de viento, tifón.

whirr, *v.* y *s.* = WHIR.

whish [juísh], *s.* (fam.) zumbido de una varita que corta el aire.

whisk [juísk]. **I.** *s.* escobilla, cepillo; movimiento rápido; (coc.) batidor; manojo de heno o paja. **II.** *va.* cepillar, barrer, arrastrar; (con **away, off**) arrebatar, llevarse. **III.** *vn.* hopear, menear la cola; moverse con velocidad; marcharse de prisa.

whisker [juískœr], *s.* patilla; barba; bigotes del gato. Ú. gen. en *pl.*

whiskered [juískœrd], *a.* patilludo, barbudo.

whisk(e)y [juíski], *s.* whisky.

whisper [juíspœr]. **I.** *va.* y *vn.* cuchichear, secretear, decir al oído; murmurar, susurrar; apuntar, soplar o sugerir. **II.** *s.* cuchicheo; susurro, murmullo.—**whisperer** [-rœr], *s.* cuchicheador; susurrador.—**whispering** [-ing]. **I.** *s.* cuchicheo; susurro o murmullo. **II.** *a.* de cuchicheo, baja (la voz); murmurante, susurante.

whist [juíst]. **I.** *a.* silencioso, mudo, callado. **II.** *interj.* ¡chitón! ¡punto en boca! **III.** *s.* whist (juego de naipes).

whistle [juísœl]. **I.** *va.* y *vn.* silbar; chiflar.—**to w. for,** llamar silbando; (fam.) buscar en vano. **II.** *s.* silbo, silbido; chifla, rechifla; silbato, pito; silbido del viento; (fam.) gaznate.—**to pay (too) dear for one's w.,** pagar demasiado cara una chuchería.

whistler [juíslœr], *s.* silbador.

whit [juít], *s.* ápice, jota, punto, pizca.

white [juáit]. **I.** *a.* blanco; cano; puro, inmaculado; inocente; feliz, propicio; de plata; de vestiduras o hábitos blancos; (blas.) argén.—**w. alkali,** depósito blanco de sales de sodio y magnesio; (com.) carbonato sódico calcinado y refinado.—**w.**

ant, hormiga blanca, termita.—**w.-breasted,** pechiblanco.—**w. crop,** cereal (apl. esp. al ya maduro en la planta).—**w. damp,** gas venenoso de las minas de carbón (se cree ser óxido de carbono).— **w. elephant,** elefante blanco; carga, fardo, posesión estorbosa o gravosa (en este sentido se dice también *elefante blanco* en algunas partes).—**w.-eyed,** ojiblanco.—**w. flux,** castina blanca de carbonato potásico.—**w.-fronted,** cariblanco.—**w.-handed,** maniblanco; patiblanco; puro, inocente, de manos limpias (fig.).—**w. heat,** rojo blanco, candencia, incandescencia; fiebre (fig.), sumo acaloramiento, exacerbación.—**w.-hot,** calentado al (rojo) blanco.—**W. House,** Casa Blanca, palacio presidencial de los E. U.—**w. iron,** fundición blanca; hierro estañado, hojalata.—**w. lead,** albayalde, cerusa.—**w. lie,** mentirilla.—**w. lily,** azucena.—**w. list,** lista de gente favorecida, digna de confianza, etc.; (com., E. U.) lista de las transacciones de la bolsa.—**w.-livered,** cobarde; envidioso.—**w. magic,** magia blanca.—**w. matter,** substancia blanca (del cerebro).—**w. meat,** pechuga; manjar blanco, lacticinio.—**w. metal,** (met.) régulo como de 78% de cobre; (com., ind.) maillechort y otras aleaciones blancas semejantes.—**w. oak,** roble blanco.—**w. plague,** tisis.—**w. poplar** = SILVER POPLAR.—**w. slave,** víctima de la trata blanca, mujer forzada a vivir en la prostitución.—**w. slaver,** traficante en mujeres para la prostitución.—**w. slavery,** trata de blancas, tráfico en mujeres para la prostitución.—**w. sugar** = REFINED SUGAR.—**w. vitriol,** vitriolo blanco, sulfato de cinc. **II.** *s.* blanco (color); pintura blanca; persona blanca; blanco a que se tira; clara (del huevo); blanco de los ojos, esclerótica.—*pl.* **whites,** flores blancas, leucorrea; flor de harina.

whitebait [-beit], *s.* (ict.) boquerones pequeños.

whiteblies [-bains], *s.* (bot.) lúpulo.

whitecaps [-cæps], *s. pl.* (mar.) cabrillas; (E. U.) sociedad secreta de hombres enmascarados que castigan cruelmente a los vecinos que faltan a la moral.

whitefish [-fish], *s.* (ict.) pez parcido al salmón; albur, cadoce; merlán.

white(n [juáit)œn]. **I.** *va.* blanquear. **II.** *vn.* emblanquecerse.—**whitener** [-œr], *s.* blanqueador.

whiteness [juáitnes], *s.* blancura, albura; palidez; pureza, candor.

whitening [juáining], *s.* blanqueo; enjalbegadura, lechada.

whitewash [juáituósh]. **I.** *s.* (alb.) jalbegue, lechada, blanqueo; blanquete (afeite); informe en que se encubren las faltas de alguno.—**w. brush,** brochón. **II.** *va.* (alb.) blanquear, enlucir, encalar; encubrir (las faltas o defectos de alguno); (fam., Ingl.) poner a un deudor insolvente al abrigo de procedimientos ulteriores; (fam., E. U.) en el juego, dejar al contrario zapatero.

whitewasher [-œr], *s.* enjalbegador, blanqueador.

whitewashing [-ing], *s.* blanqueo, encaladura, jalbegue, enlucido.

whitewood [juáitud], *s.* (bot.) tulípero.

whither [juíðœr], *adv.* adonde; a que parte; dondequiera.—**whithersoever** [-soévœr], *adv.* adonde quiera.

whiting [juáiting], *s.* blanco de España, tiza; (ict.) fíce, romero, merlán.

whitish [juáitish], *a.* blanquizco, blanquecino.

whitishness [-nes], *s.* color blanquizco.

whitleather [juítleðœr], *s.* cuero baldés; ligamento de la nuca.

whitlow [juítlo], *s.* panadizo.

whitlowort [juítloucœrt], *s.* (bot.) nevadilla.

Whitsunday [juítsunde], *s.* domingo de Pentecostés.—**Whitsuntide** [-taid], *s.* pascua de Pentecostés.

whittle [juítœl]. **I.** *va.* cortar, tallar, cercenar, mondar; aguzar, sacar punta. **II.** *vn.* cortar un pedazo de madera con cuchillo. **III.** *s.* cuchillo, faca, navaja; (ant.) (**shawl**), manta.

whiz [juís]. **I.** *vn.* zumbar o silbar; rehilar. **II.** *s.* sonido entre zumbido y silbido.

who [ju], *pron. pers.* (interrogativo) ¿quién?; (relativo) quien, quienes, que, el que, la que, los que, las que.

whoa [juó], *interj.* ¡so! ¡cho o jo!

whoever [juévœr], *pron. pers.* quienquiera que, cualquiera que.

whole [jóul]. **I.** *a.* todo; entero; íntegro; intacto; enterizo, continuo; sano; ileso.—**w. brother, w. sister,** hermano, hermana carnal.—**w.-hearted,** sincero; enérgico, activo.—**w.-heartedly,** sinceramente, de todo corazón; con tesón.—**w. note,** (mús.) semibreve.—**w. number** (arit.) número entero.—**w. wheat,** morena, harina de trigo entero.—**w.-wheat bread,** pan íntegro, pan moreno de trigo entero.—**of w. cloth,** sin fundamento, por invención.—**the w.** (seguido de substantivo), todo el (*the whole country,* todo el país). **II.** *s.* total, totalidad, conjunto, todo.—**on, o upon, the w.,** en conjunto; en general.

wholeness [jóulnes], *s.* todo, integridad, totalidad; calidad de entero.

wholesale [jóuiséil]. **I.** *a.* (com.) al por mayor; en grande. **II.** *s.* venta o comercio al por mayor.—**by w.,** al por mayor.

wholesaler [-œr], *s.* comerciante al por mayor.

wholesome [jóulsum], *a.* sano, saludable, salutífero; edificante.—**wholesomely** [-li], *adv.* saludablemente.—**wholesomeness** [-nes], *s.* calidad de saludable, (lo) sano; sanidad, salubridad.

wholly [jóuli], *adv.* totalmente, enteramente.

whom [jum], *pron. pers.* (caso oblicuo de WHO) a quien, a quienes, que, al que o al cual, a la que o la cual, a los que o a los cuales, a las que o a las cuales.—**than w.** *V.* THAN.

whom(so)ever, *pron. pers.* (caso oblicuo de WHO-SOEVER) quienquiera, quienesquiera.

whoop [jup]. **I.** *s.* grito; alarido; estertor de la tos ferina; chillido del buho. **II.** *va.* insultar a gritos. **III.** *vn.* huchear, chiflar, gritar, vocear; respirar ruidosa y convulsivamente, como después de un paroxismo de tos; acometer.—**whooping cough,** tos ferina.

whop [juóp]. **I.** *va* (fam.) zurrar. **II.** *vn.* (E. U.) dejarse caer.

whopper [juópœr], *s.* (fam.) zurrador; mentira colosal; cosa extraordinaria, non plus ultra.

whore [jóœr]. **I.** *s.* prostituta, ramera. **II.** *va.* prostituir. **III.** *vn.* putear, putañear; (ant.) adorar dioses falsos.—**whoredom** [-dum], *s.* prostitución; clase de las prostitutas; (bib.) idolatría. —**whorish** [-iŝh], *a.* lascivo, putesco.

whorl [juœrl], *s.* contrapeso de la rueca; (bot.) verticilo; espiral del caracol marino.

whorled [juœrld], *a.* verticilado.

whortleberry [juœrtœlberi], *s.* (E. U.) = HUCKLE-BERRY; (Ingl.) = BILBERRY.

whose [juŝ], *pron.* (genitivo de WHO y WHICH) cuyo, cuya, cuyos, cuyas, de quién, de quienes, (*whose hat is this?* ¿de quién es este sombrero? *whose fault is it?* ¿de quién es la falta? ¿quién tiene la culpa? *whose book is it?* ¿de quién es el libro?)

whoso(ever [juso(évœr], *pron.* (ant.) *V.* WHOEVER.

why [juái]. **I.** *conj.* y *adv.* por qué; ¿por qué? por el cual, por la cual (vg.: *the reason why,* la razón por la cual). **II.** *interj.* ¡cómo! ¡toma! ¡qué! ¡ca! A veces se traduce por si: *why, I just saw it,* si lo acabo de ver; *why, he must be crazy,* si debe de estar loco. Se usa a menudo para dar énfasis, y no se traduce: *why, certainly,* por supuesto, ciertamente. **III.** *s.* el porqué, la causa.—**the w. and wherefore,** el porqué y la razón.

wich-hazel, *s.* (bot.) = WITCH-HAZEL.

wick [uic], *s.* mecha, pabilo.

wicked [uíked], *a.* malo, malvado, perverso, inicuo; travieso, picaresco.—**wickedly** [-li], *adv.* inicuamente, perversamente.—**wickedness** [-nes], *s.* maldad, iniquidad, perversidad; impiedad.

wicker [uíkœr]. **I.** *a.* mimbroso, tejido de mimbres. **II.** *s.* mimbre.—**wickerwork** [-uœrc], *s.* cestería, artículos de mimbre.

wicket [uíket], *s.* postigo, postigo, portezuela.

wide [uáid]. **I.** *a.* ancho; anchuroso; holgado; vasto, dilatado; extenso, amplio; del ancho de, de ancho (*five inches wide,* cinco pulgadas de ancho); remoto, apartado, lejano; liberal; comprensivo; muy abierto.—**w. ga(u)ge** = BROAD GA(U)GE. **II.** *adv.* lejos, a gran distancia; anchamente; extensamente; descaminadamente; fuera de

lugar o del caso.—**w.-awake,** muy despierto, vigilante.—**w.-mouthed,** boquiancho; abocardado o bocudo.—**w. open,** abierto de par en par.— **w.-spread,** esparcido, difuso.

widely [-li], *adv.* lejos, a gran distancia; extensivamente; muy, mucho; ancha u holgadamente.

widen [uáidœn]. **I.** *va.* ensanchar, extender, dilatar; abocardar. **II.** *vn.* ensancharse, dilatarse.

wideness [uáidnes], *s.* anchura.

widgeon [uíyun], *s.* (orn.) cerceta.

widow [uído]. **I.** *s.* viuda.—**w.'s weed,** luto de una viuda. **II.** *va.* dejar viuda; privar de una cosa muy útil.—**widower** [-œr], *s.* viudo.—**widowhood** [-jud], *s.* viudez.

width [uidz], *s.* anchura, ancho.

wield [uíld], *va.* esgrimir; manejar; mandar, gobernar.—**wieldy** [uíldi], *a.* manejable.

wife [uáif], *s.* (*pl.* WIVES) esposa; ama de casa.

wifehood [uáifjud], *s.* estado de la mujer casada.

wifeless [uáifles], *a.* sin mujer.

wifely [uáifli], *adv.* como mujer casada.

wig [uig], *s.* peluca; (Ingl., fam.) juez.

wigged [uigd], *a.* con peluca, de peluca.

wiggle [uígœl], *va.* y *vn.* (fam.) menear(se) rápidamente; culebrear.—**wiggler** [uíglœr], *s.* lo que culebrea; larva de mosquito.

wight [uáit], *s.* (despec.) tipo, sujeto.

wigmaker [uígméicœr], *s.* peluquero, fabricante de pelucas.

wigwag [uíguág]. **I.** *va.* y *vn.* mover(se) rápidamente de un lado a otro; menear(se); ondear; comunicar(se) por señales, banderolas, etc. **II.** *s.* comunicación por señales.

wigwam [uíguom], *s.* jacal de los indios norteamericanos; (fam., E. U.) gran edificio público para reuniones políticas, etc.

wild [uáild], *a.* silvestre; salvaje; montés; selvático, montaraz; cerril, indómito, fiero, feroz; cimarrón; inculto, desierto, despoblado; turbulento, alborotado; atronado, alocado; descabellado o disparatado; desenfrenado, libre, desarreglado o desordenado; extravagante, estrafalario o insensato; impetuoso, violento; borrascoso; fogoso.—**w. beast,** fiera.—**w. boar,** jabalí.—**w. carrot,** (bot.) dauco.—**w. goat,** cabra montés.—**w. goose,** (orn.) ganso silvestr.—**w.-goose chase,** (fig.) empresa quimérica.—**w. marjaram,** orégano.—**w. mustard,** ajenabo.—**w. oat,** avena loca o silvestre.— **w. oats,** (fig.) excesos de la juventud.—**w. olive,** acebuchina.—**w.-olive tree,** (bot.) oleastro, acebuche.—**w. rye,** (bot.) ballico.—**w. service,** (bot.) serbal silvestre.—**w. sow,** jabalina o puerca montés.—**w. swine,** jabalí.—**w. vine,** vid silvestre.

wildcat [uáildcæt], *s.* gato montés; atolondrado, descabellado, quimérico.—**w. bank,** (E. U.) banco que emite billetes sin valor.

wilder [uíldœr]. **I.** *va.* (poét.) despistar, confundir. **II.** *vn.* extraviarse.

wilderness [uíldœrness], *s.* desierto, yermo; soledad; tosquedad, selvatiquez; multitud confusa, mezcolanza; la inmensidad del mar.

wildfire [uáildfáiœr], *s.* (piro.) fuego griego; fuego fatuo; fucilazo; sarpullido.

wilding [uáildng]. **I.** *s.* planta silvestre. **II.** *a.* inculto; indómito.

wildly [uáildli], *adv.* sin cultivo; salvajemente; desatinadamente.

wildness [uáildnes], *s.* selvatiquez; tosquedad, rusticidad; rudeza, brutalidad, ferocidad; travesura; desvarío, locura.

wile [uáil]. **I.** *va.* engatusar, embaucar; (con away) pasar un rato. **II.** *s. pl.* ardid, fraude, engaño; astucia.

wilful [uílful], *a.* voluntarioso, testarudo; voluntario, premeditado.—**wilfully** [-li], *adv.* voluntariosamente; voluntariamente, intencionadamente.— **wilfulness** [-nes], *s.* terquedad, obstinación; intención, premeditación.

wilily [uáilili], *adv.* astutamente, arteramente, con astucia.—**wiliness** [-nes], *s.* artería, astucia.

will [uil], *va.* y *vn.* [Debe considerarse bajo tres aspectos: 1. *defectivo;* 2. *auxiliar;* 3. *regular.*—**1.**

Como defectivo, no tiene más tiempos que el indicativo presente (WILL en todas las personas, menos la 2a. del singular, que es WILT), el pretérito y el subjuntivo (WOULD para todas las personas menos la 2a. del singular, que es WOULDST), y significa desear: *what wilt thou?* ¿qué deseas? *come when you will,* venga Vd. cuando guste: *would God it were daylight,* plaguiera a Dios (u ojalá) que fuese de día.—2. Como auxiliar, tiene igualmente los tres tiempos citados, que se anteponen a un infinitivo (sin la partícula *to*) para formar el futuro de indicativo o de subjuntivo del segundo verbo, con la particularidad de que en las primeras personas significa determinación, voluntad, promesa, o amenaza, por parte del que habla, mientras que en las otras personas sólo indica tiempo futuro (véase SHALL): *I will go by all means,* iré a todo trance: *I suppose he will go too,* supongo que él irá también. A menudo el infinito se sobentiende: *he will not go, but she will* (go), él no irá, pero ella sí. A veces se usa enfáticamente en las segundas y terceras personas para denotar voluntad o determinación: *if you will go, then go,* si quieres ir, ve. Otras veces indica costumbre o persistencia: *he will sit for hours by the fire,* se pasa las horas junto a la lumbre. Ú. t. para indicar propiedades físicas: *platinum will not rust,* el platino no se enmohece. En preguntas de cortesía, se usa en el sentido de "¿me hace Vd. el favor?" etc.: *will you tell me the time?* ¿me hace Vd. el favor de decirme la hora?— 3. Como verbo regular (*pret.* y *pp.* WILLED, *ger.* WILLING; *pres. ind. I* WILL, *thou* WILT, *he* WILLS; *we, you, they,* WILL), significa querer, estar resuelto a, resolver; determinar, tener o determinar la voluntad; disponer, mandar, ordenar; (for.) legar, dejar en testamento; (neol.) sugestionar, hipnotizar. Cuando va seguido de infinitivo, éste retiene la partícula *to: I will to raise my arm, but cannot,* tengo la voluntad de levantar el brazo, pero no puedo; *I will my estate to be distributed,* dispongo que mis bienes se repartan.—**w. I, w. I;** w. he, w. he; w. ye, w. ye, quiera (queráis, etc.) o no quiera (queráis, etc.).

will, *s.* voluntad, facultad de querer; albedrío; discreción; volición; decisión; intención, resolución, determinación; (for.) testamento; (ant.) gana, inclinación, deseo; precepto, mandato.— **w.-o'-the-wisp,** fuego fatuo.—**w. power,** fuerza de voluntad.—**at w.,** a voluntad, a discreción.— **thy w. be done,** hágase tu voluntad.—**to have one's w.,** salirse uno con la suya; hacer lo que quiera.—**with a w.,** con toda el alma, con todo el corazón.

willing [uíling], *a.* gustoso, dispuesto, pronto, complaciente; espontáneo, voluntario.

willingly [-li], *adv.* voluntariamente; de buena gana, con gusto.—**willingness** [-nes], *s.* buena voluntad, buena gana, gusto, complacencia.

willow [uílo]. **I.** *s.* (bot.) sauce: mimbrera, bardaguera; (mec.) diablo, máquina para limpiar el algodón.—**w. oak,** (E. U.) roble con hojas parecidas a las del sauce.—**w. plot,** saucedal, salceda. **II.** *va.* limpiar (fibras).—**willowish** [-ish], *a.* parecido al sauce.—**willowy** [-i], *a.* mimbreño o sarguero; lleno de sauces; que se cimbrea, esbelto.

willy [uíli], *va.* limpiar (algodón, etc.)

willy-nilly [uíli-níli]. **I.** *a.* irresoluto. **II.** *adv.* velis nolis, de buen o mal grado.

wilt [uílt]. **I.** *va.* marchitar, ajar. **II.** *vn.* agostarse, marchitarse, secarse; descaecer; (fam.) amansarse; irse con el rabo entre piernas. **III.** *s.* (agr.) enfermedad hongosa que causa marchitamiento.

wilt, 2a. *pers. sing. pres. ind.* de WILL.

wily [uáili], *a.* astuto, marrullero.

wimble [uímbœl], *s.* barrena, taladro.

wimple [uímpœl], *s.* toca, grifón.

win [uín], *va.* y *vn.* (*pret.* y *pp.* WON) ganar, vencer; lograr, conquistar, obtener, alcanzar; persuadir, atraer, arrastrar tras sí; prevalecer.—**to w. one's spurs,** ganar la dignidad de caballero; llevarse la palma: hacerse a reputación.—**to w. out,** triunfar, salir bien, lograr buen éxito.

wince [uíns]. **I.** *vn.* retroceder, recular; respingar; tirar coces. **II.** *s.* respingo; devanadera de tintorero.

winch [uínch], *s.* (mec.) montacarga, malacate, torno; manubrio, cigüeña.

wind [uínd]. **I.** *s.* viento, aire; resuello, aliento, respiración; flatulencia, flato, ventosidad.—**w. aft,** viento en popa.—**w. ahead,** viento por la proa o a fil de roda.—**w.-bound,** detenido por vientos contrarios.—**w. ga(u)ge,** anemómetro.—**w. hatch,** (min.) pozo de extracción.—**w. instrument,** instrumento de viento.— **w. on end = w. AHEAD.—w. on the beam,** viento derrotero.—**w. tunnel,** (aer.) túnel de prueba, cámara de corriente de aire para probar aviones. **between w. and water,** a flor del agua.—**in the teeth of the w.,** in the w.'s eye, de cara al viento. —**something is in the w.,** se trama algo, algo pasa, algo se prepara.—**to get w. of,** husmear, descubrir.—**to have the w. up,** (fam.) estar ansioso, alarmado. **II.** *va.* ventear, husmear u olfatear; quitar el resuello a; recobrar el aliento; airear, orear. **III.** *va.* y *vn.* soplar, resoplar; echar aire; tocar un instrumento de viento.

wind [uáind]. **I.** *va.* (*pret.* y *pp.* WOUND [uóund] o WINDED [uáinded]) devanar, ovillar, encanillar; enrollar, arrollar; torcer, retorcer; dar cuerda a; manejar, dirigir, gobernar; perseguir, seguir las vueltas o los rodeos de; virar; (Ingl.) levantar o izar con torno; tejer.—**to w. a ship,** virar en redondo.—**to w. off,** devanar; desenrollar. —**to w. out,** desenmarañar, desenredar; salir de un enredo o laberinto.—**to w. up,** concluir, acabar, finalizar; devanar, ovillar; montar, excitar; dar cuerda a (un reloj). **II.** *vn.* enrollarse; arrollarse; (a veces con up) enroscarse; serpear, culebrear, serpentear, brujulear; rodear, ir con rodeos, insinuarse; torcerse, retorcerse, ensortijarse, retortijarse.—**to w. about,** enrollarse.—**to w. along,** serpentear, culebrar.—**to w. up,** terminar, acabar.

windage [uíndey], *s.* (arti.) viento o huelgo de la bala.

winder [uáindœr], *s.* argadillo, devanador, devanadera; (bot.) enredadera; carretel, canilla; (arq.) escalón de abanico.

windfall [uíndfól], *s.* fruta caída del árbol; ganga, ganancia inesperada.

windflower [uíndfláucœr], *s.* (bot.) anémone, anémona.

windgall [uíndgól], *s.* (vet.) aventadura.

windhover [uíndjœvœr], *s.* (orn.) cernícalo.

windiness [uíndines], *s.* ventolera; ventosidad, flatulencia, flato; hinchazón, verbosidad, vanidad, presunción.

winding [uáinding]. **I.** *s.* vuelta, revuelta, giro, rodeo; recodo, recoveco, tortuosidad; alabeo, comba, combadura; (elec.) arrollamiento; (min.) extracción del mineral; (mar.) pitazo del contramaestre.—**windings and turnings,** vueltas y revueltas, recovecos.—**w. up,** acto de dar cuerda (a un reloj); liquidación; conclusión; desenlace. **II.** *a.* sinuoso, tortuoso; serpentino; enrollado; en espiral; de caracol (escalera, etc.).—**w. sheet,** mortaja, sudario; ladrón de vela o bujía.—**w. tackle,** (mar.) aparejo de candeliza.

windlass [uíndlas], *s.* argüe, árgana o árgano; torno, cabria, montacarga; (min.) malacate; (mar.) cabrestante pequeño o molinete.

windless [uíndles], *a.* sin viento, encalmado; sin resuello.

windmill [uíndmil], *s.* molino de viento; (aer.) turbina de aire.

window [uíndo], *s.* ventana; vidriera.—**w. blind,** persiana.—**w. frame,** bastidor o marco de ventana. —**w. glass,** cristal o vidrio para ventanas.—**w. post,** jamba de ventana.—**w. sash,** marco de vidriera.—**w. seat,** asiento o banco interior al pie de una ventana.—**w. shade,** transparente, visillo.—**w. shutter = w.** BLIND.—**w. sill,** solera o repisa de ventana.—**w. stud,** montante o jamba de ventana.

windowed [uíndoud], *a.* fenestrado.

windpipe [uíndpaip], *s.* tráquea; gaznate.

windrow [uíndrró]. **I.** *s.* hilera de heno amontonado con el rastrillo; hilera doble de maíz para secar; hilera de árboles, yerba, etc., formada por el viento. **II.** *va.* arrollar (heno) en una hilera, rastrillar.

windsail [-séil], s. (mar.) manguera de viento.

windscreen [uíndscrín], **windshield** [-shíld], s. (aut.) parabrisa.—**w. wiper**, limpiavidrios para el parabrisa.

windstorm [-storm], s. huracán.

wind-up [uáindúp], s. conclusión, final, fin, desenlace.

windward [uínduard]. **I.** a. de barlovento.—**W. Islands**, Islas de Barlovento.—**w. tide**, marea contraria al viento. **II.** s. barlovento.—**to lie to w.**, barloventear. **III.** adv. a barlovento.

windy [uíndi], a. ventoso, ventiscoso; borrascoso; expuesto al viento; vano, hinchado, pomposo; flatulento.

wine [uáin]. **I.** s. vino; licor; holgorio o parranda en que se bebe; zumo fermentado de algunas frutas; (fam.) champaña.—**w. bag** = w. SKIN.—**w. bottle**, botella para vino.—**w. cellar**, bodega, cueva.—**w. cooler**, garapiñera.—**w. decanter**, garrafa para vino.—**w. grower**, vinariego, viñero, viticultor.—**w. industry**, industria vinícola.—**w. measure**, sistema de medidas para vino.—**w. palm**, palma de vino, de que se hace vino.—**w. press**, lagar, trujal, prensa de lagar.—**w. skin**, odre.—**w. vault**, candiotera, cueva, bodega.—**to be in w.**, estar ebrio. **II.** va. y vn. convidar u obsequiar con vino; beber vino.

winebibber [uáinbíbœr], s. borrachín, bebedor.—**winebibbing** [-bing]. **I.** s. beber en demasía, ser borracho. **II.** a. borracho, bebedor.

wineglass [uáingláes], s. copa para vino.

winery [uáinœri], s. candiotera.

winetaster [-téistœr], s. catavinos.

wing [uíng]. **I.** s. ala; vuelo; (mil. y arq.) ala, flanco; costado, lado; apéndice; (teat.) bastidor; (bot.) apéndice foliáceo; (aer.) ala.—**w. case**, **w. cover**, (ent.) élitro.—**w. flap**, (aer.) alerón engoznado.—**w. loading**, (aer.) intensidad de la carga, carga por unidad de superficie de sustentación.—**w. nut**, tuerca de orejas.—**w. rail**, (f.-c.) guardarriel.—**w. resistance**, (aer.) resistencia activa.—**w. screw** = w. NUT.—**w. transom**, (mar.) yugo principal.—**w.-transom knees**, curvas del yugo principal.—**w. wall**, (ing.) ala (de alcantarilla, etc.).—**on**, o **upon, the w.**, al vuelo; con un pie en el estribo; en marcha.—**to take w.**, alzar el vuelo, irse volando.—**under one's w.**, bajo la protección de uno. **II.** va. llevar, transportar sobre las alas; ejecutar por medio de las alas; hender (volando); dar o prestar alas a, impeler; añadir una ala (a un edificio, etc.); herir en el ala; dañar, incapacitar, inhabilitar. **III.** vn. alear, aletear; volar.

winged [uingd o uíngued], a. alado, alígero; que vuela; elevado.

wingless [uíngles], a. sin alas; áptero.

wink [uínk]. **I.** vn. pestañear, parpadear; guiñar; centellear, dar luz trémula; (con **at**) tolerar, disimular; hacer la vista gorda. **II.** s. pestañeo, parpadeo; un abrir y cerrar de ojos; guiño, guiñada; siestecita.—**to take forty winks**, (fam.) descabezar el sueño.—**not to sleep a w.**, no pegar o cerrar los ojos.

winker [uínkœr], s. guiñador; anteojera (de caballo); (fam.) párpado; músculo que produce el pestañeo.

winkle [uíukœl], s. caracol marino.

winner [uínœr], s. ganador, vencedor.

winning [uíning]. **I.** s. triunfo; ganancia, lucro. **II.** a. victorioso, triunfante; ganancioso; que gana; afortunado; atractivo, encantador; persuasivo.—**w. back**, desquite.—**w. post**, poste o pilar que marca el fin de una carrera.—**w. side**, partido triunfante.

winnow [uíno]. **I.** va. (agr.) aventar, aechar, ventilar; zarandar; cerner; analizar; entresacar, escoger; batir el aire (como con alas); soplar. **II.** vn. aechar el grano.

winnower [uínocœr], s. aventador.

winnowing [uínoing], s. aechadura, aecho, aventamiento, despajadura, zarandeo.—**w. fork**, bieldo.—**w. machine**, aventador mecánico.—**winnowings** [-ings], s. pl. tamo.

winrace [uínréis], s. velocidad máxima de trote de un caballo victorioso.

winsome [uínsum], a. atractivo, simpático.

winter [uíntœr]. **I.** s. invierno.—**w. beaten**, invernizo.—**w.'s bark**, (bot.) magnolia magallánica. **II.** a. hibernal, hiemal, de invierno.—**w. cherry**, (bot.) alquequenje.—**w. clothes**, ropa de invierno.—**w. quarters**, invernadero.—**w. season**, invierno, invernada.—**w. solstice**, solsticio de invierno.—**w. time**, invierno, tiempo de invierno.—**w. wheat**, trigo mocho. **III.** va. hacer invernar, guardar durante el invierno. **IV.** vn. invernar, pasar el invierno.

winterberry [-bérry], s. (bot.) apalachina.

wintergreen [-grín], s. (bot.) pirola; gualteria.

wintering [-ing], s. invernada.

winterish [-ish], a. invernizo.

winterless [-les], a. sin invierno.

wint(e)ry [uínt(œ)ri], a. invernal, invernizo; como de invierno.

wintriness [uíntrines], s. invernada.

winy [uáini], a. vinoso.

wipe [uáip]. **I.** va. limpiar frotando (con un trapo, etc.); enjugar, secar; frotar, restregar; cepillar; aplicar soldadura a; soldar.—**to w. away**, secar (frotando).—**to w. off**, borrar, cancelar; limpiar, lavar.—**to w. out**, borrar, cancelar, testar; destruir, extirpar. **II.** s. limpión, limpiadura; (fam.) revés, manotada.

wiper [uáipœr], s. persona que enjuga o restrega; limpiador, trapo, paño, toalla, (cualquier objeto que sirve para limpiar frotando); (mec.) leva, álabe.

wire [uáiœr]. **I.** s. alambre; hilo o cuerda metálica; cuerda de piano o arpa; telégrafo eléctrico; hilo (del retículo de un teodolito, etc.).—**w. cloth**, tela o gasa de alambre.—**w. coil**, carrete.—**w. edge**, filván (de una navaja, etc.).—**w. entanglement**, (mill.) alambrada, defensa de alambres trabados.—**w. fence**, alambrado, cerca de alambre.—**w. ga(u)ge** calibrador para alambre; escala de calibres o diámetros de alambre.—**w. gauze**, gasa de alambre, tela metálica.—**w. nail**, punta de París.—**w. plate**, hilera de estirar alambre.—**w. stretcher**, estirador de alambre.—**w. tapper**, quien forma subrepticiamente conexión con una línea telegráfica para interceptar mensajes u obtener informes. **II.** va. proveer de alambre; atar o liar con hilo metálico; (elec.) instalar conductores eléctricos en, hacer una canalización en; coger con lazo de alambre. **III.** va. y vn. (com.) telegrafiar.

wiredraw [uáiœrdró], va. (pret. WIREDREW; pp. -DRAWN) estirar (metal); alargar, prolongar; sutilizar; desfigurar; (m. v.) estrangular (el vapor).—**wiredrawer** [-œr], s. estirador de metales.

wireless [-less]. **I.** s. radiocomunicación; telégrafo o teléfono sin hilos. **II.** va. y vn. comunicar por radiotelegrafía o radiotelefonía (gen. lo primero). **III.** a. sin hilos (telégrafo, teléfono); de o por radiocomunicación.—**w. compass** = RADIO-COMPASS.—**w. telegraphy**, radiotelegrafía.—**w. telephony**, radiotelefonía.

wirepuller [-púlœr], s. titiritero; intrigante político.—**wirepulling** [-ing], s. maquinaciones secretas; intrigas políticas.

wirework [-uœrc], s. enrejado, alambrado.

wiring [uáiœring]. **I.** ger. de TO WIRE. **II.** s. (elec.) distribución (en, si el inglés va seguido de of); instalación de alambres de distribución; (cir.) costura con alambre; (aer.) alambrado.

wiry [uáiri], a. de alambre; semejante a un alambre; tieso, tenso; flaco pero fuerte y nervioso; débil (pulso).

wisdom [uísdum], s. sabiduría; sapiencia; discernimiento, juicio, buen criterio; cordura; sentido común; buena conducta; erudición; máxima, apotegma.—**w. tooth**, muela cordal o del juicio.

wise [uáis]. **I.** a. sabio, docto, ilustrado, erudito; cuerdo, juicioso, prudente, sensato, discreto.—**w. move**, paso acertado.—**the w. men**, los tres reyes magos; los siete sabios de Grecia.—**to put one w.**, advertir a uno lo que hay o lo que pasa, ponerlo al tanto. **II.** s. modo, manera.—**in any w.**, de cualquier modo.—**in no w.**, de ningún modo, absolutamente.

wiseacre [-éicœr], s. sabihondo, el que presume de sabio.

wisely [uáiŝli], *adv.* sabiamente; cuerdamente.

wish [uíŝh]. **I.** *va.* y *vn.* (a menudo con **for**) desear, querer. **II.** *s.* deseo; cosa deseada.—**to make a w.,** formar un deseo, pensar algo que se quiere.

wishbone [-bóun], *s.* espoleta de la pechuga de las aves.

wisher [uíŝhœr], *s.* persona que desea.

wishful [-ful], *a.* deseoso, ganoso; ansioso, anheloso; ávido.—**wishfully** [-i], *adv.* ansiosamente, ardientemente, con anhelo.

wishy-washy [uíŝhi-uóŝhi], *a.* (fam.) débil, ligero, diluído, aguado, flojo.

wisp [uísp]. **I.** *va.* cepillar; hacer un manojo. *V.* CRUMPLE. **II.** *s.* manojito, mechón, puñado; trozo; bandada de pájaros; escobilla; fuego fatuo; (vet.) enfermedad que ataca los pies del ganado.

wist [uíst], *pret.* de TO WIT.

wistaria, wisteria [uistériæ, -tiriæ], *s.* (bot.) vistaria.

wistful [uístful], *a.* anhelante, ansioso, ávido; pensativo.—**wistfully** [-i], *adv.* ansiosamente, ávidamente; pensativamente.—**wistfulness** [-nes], *s.* avidez, anhelo; estado pensativo.

wit [uít]. **I.** *va.* y *vn.* (*pret.* WIST) (ant.) saber, tener noticia.—**to w.,** a saber. **II.** *s.* rasgo de ingenio, agudeza, sal; ingenio, decidor; talento, ingenio; imaginación, inventiva.—*pl.* juicio, sentido, razón; industria.—**the five wits,** los cinco sentidos. —**to be at one's w.'s end,** no saber uno que hacer o decir; perder la chaveta.—**to be out of one's wits,** estar fuera de juicio o fuera de sí; no saber uno lo que hace.—**to live by one's wits,** vivir de gorra, ser caballero de industria.

witch [uích]. **I.** *s.* bruja, hechicera; vejarrona; mujer encantadora; niña traviesa. **II.** *va.* encantar, maleficiar, hechizar, embrujar.

witchcraft, witchery [-craft, -chœri], *s.* brujería, hechicería, sortilegio, aojadura; fascinación.

witch-elm [-élm], *s.* (bot.) = WYCH-ELM.

witch-hazel [-jéiŝœl], *s.* (bot.) hamamelis, carpe.

witching [-ing], *a.* encantador.

wite [uáit], *s.* pena, castigo; multa; reprensión; censura; falta.

with [uíɒ], *prep.* con; en compañía de; de (*to fill with*, llenar de; *to part with*, separarse de; *smitten with*, enamorado de; *a man with good sense*, un hombre de juicio; *the lady with the camellias*, la dama de las camelias; *the boy with a straw hat*, el niño del sombrero de paja). A veces queda mejor traducida por contra, en, entre, a, hacia, con respecto a, para con, concerniente (*with all speed*, a toda prisa; *to struggle with need*, luchar contra la necesidad; *deal not harshly with me*, no sea Vd. duro para conmigo; *this happens with students*, esto sucede entre estudiantes; *identical with*, idéntico a; *that country abounds with oil*, ese país abunda en petróleo).

withal [uiɒól], *adv.* además, a más de esto; también; por otra parte; con todo; al mismo tiempo.

withdraw [uiɒdró]. **I.** *va.* (*pret.* WITHDREW: *pp.* WITHDRAWN) retirar; apartar, separar, quitar, sacar, privar de; distraer, remover; desdotarse de, retractar o retractarse de. **II.** *vn.* retirarse, apartarse, separarse; irse, salir.

withdrawal [-al], *s.* retiro, retirada; recogida.

withdrawing-room [-ing-rum], *s.* retrete, gabinete.

withdrawn [-drón], *pp.* de TO WITHDRAW.

withdrew [uiɒdrú], *pret.* de TO WITHDRAW.

withe [uiz]. **I.** *s.* mimbre, junco; vencejo; (mec.) mango flexible; tabique divisorio en una chimenea. **II.** *va.* atar con juncos o mimbres.

wither [uíɒœr]. **I.** *va.* marchitar; ajar, deslucir; poner mustio; descarnar; debilitar; avergonzar, sonrojar. **II.** *vn.* (a veces con **away**) marchitarse, secarse. **III.** *s.* vencejo.—*pl.* cruz del caballo.— **w.-wrung,** herido en la cruz.

witherband [-bǽnd], *s.* pieza que sujeta los fustes de la silla de montar.

withered [uíɒœrd], *a.* mustio, marchito; seco. lacio, macilento.—**witheredness** [-nes], *s.* marchitez, marchitamiento, sequedad.

withhold [uiɒjóuld]. **I.** *va.* (*pret.* y *pp.* WITHHELD) detener, impedir; retener; apartar, con-

tener; negar, rehusar. **II.** *vn.* reprimirse, contenerse.

within [uiɒín]. **I.** *prep.* dentro de, en lo interior de; dentro de, en el espacio de; a la distancia de; al alcance de; a; a poco de; casi a, cerca de.— **w. an inch,** pulgada más o menos.—**w. a short distance,** a poca distancia.—**w. four months,** dentro de cuatro meses.—**w. hearing,** al alcance de la voz.—**he was w. a little of being killed,** por poco lo matan. **II.** *adv.* dentro, adentro, en el interior; dentro de uno, en el corazón o en la mente; en casa, en la habitación.—**from w.,** de adentro.

without [uiɒáut]. **I.** *prep.* sin; falto de; fuera de, mas allá de. **II.** *adv.* fuera, afuera, por fuera, hacia fuera, de la parte de afuera; exteriormente, en lo exterior. **III.** *conj.* (ant.) si no, a menos que.

withstand [uiɒstǽnd], *va.* (*pret.* y *pp.* WITHSTOOD) resistir; sufrir, soportar.

withy [uízi]. **I.** *a.* de mimbre; delgado; flexible. **II.** *s.* mimbre.

witless [uítles], *a.* necio, tonto.

witling [uítling], *s.* pelele.

witness [uítnes]. **I.** *s.* testigo; espectador; testimonio, atestación, prueba; (for.) testigo.—**in w. whereof,** en fe de lo cual.—**to be a w. of,** ser testigo de, presenciar. **II.** *va.* presenciar, ver, ser espectador de o concurrir a; (for.) atestar, atestiguar, testificar, declarar (como testigo); dar fe; mostrar.—**witnessed before me,** atestado ante mí. **III.** *vn.* dar testimonio; servir de testigo.

witted [uíted], *a.* ingenioso.

witticism [uítisism], *s.* rasgo de ingenio, dicho agudo, chiste, gracia, aticismo, epigrama.

wittily [uítili], *adv.* ingeniosamente, agudamente, donosamente.

wittiness [-nes], *s.* donosura, ingenio, sal, gracia.

wittingly [uítingli], *adv.* a sabiendas, exprofeso, adrede, de propósito.

witty [uíti], *a.* ingenioso, agudo; chistoso, gracioso, ocurrente; (ant.) satírico.—**w. saying,** chiste, agudeza.

wive [uáiv], *vn.* casarse, tomar esposa.

wives [uáivŝ], *s. pl.* de WIFE.

wizard [uíŝard]. **I.** *a.* hechicero, mágico. **II.** *s.* brujo, hechicero, mago, adivino.

wizen [uíŝœn]. **I.** *va.* y *vn.* marchitar(se), secar(se). **II.** *a.* marchito, mustio.

woad [uod], *s.* (bot., tint.) pastel, glasto, gualda.

woaded [uóded], *a.* teñido con glasto.

wobble, *vn.* = WABBLE.

woe [uó]. **I.** *s.* dolor, pena, angustia, pesar, calamidad, infortunio, miseria. **II.** *interj.* **w. is me!** ¡desgraciado de mí! ¡pobre de mí!

woe(e)begone [uóbigon], *a.* angustiado, desdichado, abrumado de pesares.

woe(e)ful [uóful], *a.* calamitoso, funesto; triste, afligido, angustiado; lastimero, doloroso; ruin, vituperable.—**wofully** [-i], *adv.* funestamente, desastrosamente; tristemente; ruinmente.

wold [uold], *s.* campiña undulada; bosque.

wolf [ulf], *s.* (*pl.* WOLVES) lobo; persona cruel o rapaz; larva destructora de varios escarabajos y mariposas nocturnas; (med.) = LUPUS.—**w. dog,** perro lobero o de cazar lobos; híbrido de perro y lobo.—**w. fish,** (ict.) lobo marino.—**w. hound,** mastín.—**w.'s milk,** (bot.) titímalo, lechetrezna.— **to cry w.,** gritar "¡el lobo!" dar falsa alarma.—**to have a w. by the ears,** ver las orejas al lobo.—**to have a w. in the stomach,** tener apetito voraz.

wolfish [úlfiŝh], *a.* lobero, lupino.

wolfram [uólfræm], *s.* (quím.) volframio, tungsteno.—**wolframite** [-ait], *s.* (min.) volframita.

wolfsbane [úlfsbéin], *s.* (bot.) acónito alpino, variedad de árnica.

wolverene, wolverine [úlvœrín], *s.* (zool.) especie de glotón.

wolves [úlvŝ], *s. pl.* de WOLF.

woman [úman], *s.* (*pl.* **women** [uímen]) mujer; las mujeres; criada, sirvienta. U. adjetivamente para denotar sexo femenino, v. gr: *woman writer*, escritora; *woman voter*, electora; *woman witness*, testigo mujer, o mujer testigo.—**w. hater,** aborrecedor de las mujeres.—**w. of the town,** dama

cortesana.—**w. of the world,** mujer de mundo.—
w. servant = SERVANT GIRL.
womanhood [-jud], s. estado o condición de mujer; sexo femenino.
womanish [-iṣh], a. mujeril, femenil, femenino, afeminado.
womankind [-káind], s. la mujer (en general), las mujeres; el sexo femenino.
womanliness [-lines], s. naturaleza o carácter femenil.
womanly, womanlike [-li, -laik]. **I.** a. mujeril; de mujer, femenil, femenino. **II.** adv. mujerilmente; femenilmente.
womb [um], s. útero, matriz; madre; caverna; seno, entrañas.
women [uímen], s. pl. de WOMAN.
won [uœn], pret. y pp. de TO WIN.
wonder [uóndœr]. **I.** va. desear saber, extrañarse; sorprenderse, maravillarse de; preguntarse (con una cláusula como complemento). Ú. a menudo para indicar incertidumbre o curiosidad, y puede traducirse por el futuro del verbo que le sigue: I wonder if it will rain tomorrow, ¿si lloverá mañana? I wonder what he wants, ¿qué querrá? **II.** vn. admirarse, asombrarse, pasmarse.—**to w. at,** extrañar, maravillarse de. **III.** s. admiración, pasmo; maravilla, prodigio, portento, milagro; enigma, misterio, cosa extraña o inexplicable.—**w.-worker,** fabricador de prodigios o milagros.—**no w.,** no es extraño, no es mucho.—**the seven wonders of the world,** las siete maravillas del mundo.
wonderer [-œr], s. el que hace prodigios o maravillas; el que se admira.
wonderful [-ful], a. maravilloso, portentoso, pasmoso, asombroso; admirable, excelente.
wonderfully [-i], adv. maravillosamente, prodigiosamente, a las mil maravillas; admirablemente, sumamente.
wonderland [-lænd], s. mundo fantástico; reino de las hadas o de los duendes.
wonderment [-mœnt], s. admiración, asombro, extrañeza, maravilla.
wonderstricken [-stríkœn], **wonderstruck** [-strʊ́k]. a. atónito, pasmado, asombrado.
wond(e)rous [uónd(œ)rʊs], a. extraño, maravilloso, pasmoso, asombroso.—**wondrously** [-li], adv. pasmosamente, maravillosamente.
wont [uʊ́nt]. **I.** a. acostumbrado, sólito.—**to be w.,** soler, tener la costumbre. **II.** vn. soler, acostumbrar. **III.** s. uso, costumbre, hábito. **IV.** va. habituar.
won't [uont o uʊ́nt], contr. (fam.) de **will not.**
wonted [uʊ́nted], a. acostumbrado, usual, habitual, ordinario.
woo [ú], va. y vn. cortejar, galantear, enamorar; pretender a una mujer.
wood [ud]. **I.** va. proveer de leña; cubrir con bosques; convertir en selva. **II.** vn. proveerse de leña. **III.** s. madera; leña; bosque, selva, monte (en este sentido ú. gen, en pl., **woods**); madero, palo.—**w. acid,** vinagre de madera, ácido pirolenoso, ácido acético.—**w. alcohol,** alcohol metílico.—**w. ant,** hormiga leonada.—**w.-block pavement,** pavimento de bloques de madera.—**w. borer,** xilófago, insecto u otro animal horadador (de los árboles y la madera); broma (molusco horadador).—**w. carving,** talla en madera.—**w. engraver,** grabador en madera.—**w. engraving,** grabado en madera.—**w. fiber,** fibra de la madera; célula de los tejidos vegetales; madera molida.—**w. ibis,** (zool.) tántalo, ave zancuda americana.—**w. lark,** (orn.) alondra, calandria.—**w. louse,** (ent.) porqueta; milpiés.—**w. nymph,** orea, napea.—**w. pigeon,** (orn.) paloma torcaz.—**w. pulp,** pulpa de madera (para papel).—**w. rasp,** escofina.—**w. screw,** tirafondo, tornillo de metal para madera (evítese el disparate "tornillo de madera").—**w. sorrel,** (bot.) aleluya, acederilla.—**w. thrush,** (orn.) tordo pardo.—**w. tick,** (ent.) carcoma.—**w. vinegar** = W. ACID.—**w. yard,** depósito de maderas, maderería.
woodbine [údbain], s. (bot.) madreselva; enredadera.
woodchopper [údchópœr], s. leñador.

woodchuck [údchʊ́c], s. (zool.) marmota.
woodcock [údcóc], s. (orn.) chocha, pitorra, chochaperdiz o becada.
woodcraft [údcráft], s. conocimientos relativos a los bosques.
woodcut [údcʊ́t], s. grabado en madera.
woodcutter [údcʊ́tœr], s. leñador; grabador en madera.
wooded [úded], a. provisto de madera; arbolado, plantado de árboles; cubierto de bosques.
wooden [údœn], a. de palo o madera; grosero, rudo; torpe, estúpido.—**w.-headed,** zote, zopenco, bolo.—**w. shoes,** zuecos, chanclos.—**w. wedding,** quinto aniversario.
woodhole [údjoul], s. = WOODSHED.
woodhouse [-jáus], s. leñera.
woodiness [ádines], s. calidad leñoso.
woodland [údlænd]. **I.** s. arbolado, monte, bosque, selva. **II.** a. de bosque, selvático.
woodless [údles], a. sin bosques.
woodman [údman], s. leñador; guardabosque; habitante de los bosques.
woodpecker [údpékœr], s. (orn.) picamaderos, pájaro carpintero.
woodpile [údpáil], s. pila de leña, tinada; hoguera.
woodruff [údrʊf], s. (bot.) aspérula.
woodshed [údshéd], s. leñera.
woodsman [údsman], s. leñador; guardabosque.
woodwork [úducérk], s. enmaderamiento, maderaje, maderamen; obra de carpintería.
woody [údi], a. leñoso; de madera; arbolado, selvoso.—**w. tissue,** tejido leñoso.
wooer [úœr], s. cortejador, pretendiente.
woof [uf], s. (tej.) trama; textura. V. WEFT.
wooing [úing], s. galanteo.
wool [ul]. **I.** s. lana; pasa (cabello de los negros). **II.** a. lanar, de lana; para lana; relativo o perteneciente a la lana.—**w. ball,** pelotón de lana.—**w.-bearing,** lanar.—**w. card,** carda.—**w. comber,** cardador.—**w. combing,** cardadura.—**w. fat, w. grease,** lanolina.—**w. stapler,** comerciante en lanas.—**w. winder,** velonero.
woold [uld], va. (mar.) trincar.
wooled [uld], a. que tiene lana, con lana.
wool(l)en [úlen]. **I.** a. de lana; lanoso, lanudo; lanero; rústico, vulgar.—**w. draper,** pañero, comerciante en paños.—**w. dyer,** tintorero de lana. **II.** s. paño o tejido de lana.
woolfell [úlfel], s. piel con su lana.
woolgathering [úlgǽdœring]. **I.** s. distracción. **II.** a. distraído, ensimismado, visionario.
woolgrower [úlgrócer], s. criador de ganado lanar.
woolgrowing [-ing], s. cría de ganado lanar.
woolliness [úlines], s. calidad de lanudo; lanosidad, vellosidad; pelaje.
woolly [úli], a. lanudo, lanoso; lanar, lanífero; de lana: coposo; crespo, pasudo (cabello); (b. a.) falto de detalles, vago y borroso; aborregado (cielo); (bot.) lanoso, lanuginoso, velludo.
woolman [úlman], s. lanero.
woolpack [úlpǽc], s. paca o fardo de lana; cúmulo (nube).
woolsack [úlsǽc], s. (ant.) asiento del gran canciller en la Cámara de los Lores; por extensión, dignidad de gran canciller.
woolsorter [úlsórtœr], s. escogedor de lana.
wooralli, woorari [úrali, -ri], s. curare.
wop [uóp], s. (fam.) jornalero extranjero (apl. esp. a los italianos).
word [uérd]. **I.** s. palabra; vocablo, voz; habla; conversación breve, dos palabras; dicho, sentencia, apotegma; aviso, recado, mensaje; noticia, noticias; santo y seña; voz de mando, orden, mandato.—pl. palabras mayores; disputa, contienda verbal.—**w. square,** cuadrado de palabras que pueden leerse en varios sentidos.—**by w. of mouth,** verbalmente, de palabra.—**in other words,** en otros términos.—**the W.,** (bib.) el Verbo. **II.** va. expresar; enunciar, formular; redactar; instar con palabras.
wordbook [uérdbúc], s. vocabulario.
wordiness [uérdines], s. verbosidad; palabrería.

wording [uǒrding], *s*. dicción, estilo; redacción, fraseología; expresión, términos.

wordless [uǒrdles], *a*. falto de palabras, mudo.

wordy [uǒrdi], *a*. verbal; verboso, difuso.

wore [uór], *pret*. de TO WEAR.

work [uǒrk]. **I.** *va*. trabajar; labrar, explotar (una mina, un privilegio, etc.); (cost.) bordar; tallar (una piedra); fabricar, elaborar, manufacturar; producir, preparar; formar, componer; obrar sobre, influir, impeler, excitar, inducir; investigar o resolver (un problema); hacer mover o andar, poner en movimiento; manejar, manipular; mover nerviosamente (los dedos); abrirse camino; hacer fermentar; (mar.) maniobrar; causar, efectuar, producir (algún efecto).—**to w. apump,** dar a una bomba.—**to w. down,** hacer bajar.—**to w. one's way,** abrirse camino.—**to w. out,** acabar a fuerza de trabajo; resolver (un problema); borrar o expiar (culpas, etc.); lograr o conseguir a fuerza de trabajo; ejecutar, llevar a cabo, efectuar; agotar (una mina); labrarse, determinar (su destino, etc.).—**to w. over,** alterar, rehacer.—**to w. through,** penetrar; atravesar a fuerza de trabajo.—**to w. up,** labrar, dar forma a; servirse de; amasar; agotar, consumir; excitar, inflamar.—**to w. water,** (m. v.) hacer o arrastrar espuma. **II.** *vn*. trabajar, estar empleado u ocupado; obrar, surtir efecto, tener buen éxito, ser eficaz; funcionar, marchar, ir (bien o mal); obrar u operar (un remedio); fermentar; (mec.) efectuar trabajo.—**to w. against,** trabajar contra; oponerse a.—**to w. at,** trabajar en; ocuparse en o de.—**to w. down,** descender, bajarse.—**to w. free,** aflojarse o soltarse con el movimiento o el uso.—**to w. in,** trabajar en; insinuarse en; entrar poco a poco.—**to w. into,** entrar en, penetrar en.—**to w. loose** = TO W. FREE. —**to w. out,** tener éxito (bueno o malo); surtir o no efecto; resultar.—**to w. round,** volverse lentamente y con esfuerzo.—**to w. to windward,** (mar.) barloventear, ceñir el viento.—**to w. upon,** obrar sobre; trabajar en, estar ocupado en; sublevar, excitar, mover a compasión. **II.** *s*. trabajo; faena, fajina; obra (construción, libro, producción, etc.); tarea; (cost.) labor, costura; bordado; obra, acción; empleo u ocupación; (mec.) trabajo (de una fuerza); obra (cosa en que se trabaja).—*pl*. fábrica, taller, establecimiento; rodaje, engranaje motor; mecanismo, maquinaria; (reloj.) movimiento.—**to be at w.,** estar ocupado; estar trabajando.—**to be hard at w.,** estar muy afanado o atareado.

workable [uǒrcabœl], *a*. (min.) explotable; practicable; trabajable, laborable, labradero; factible, viable; que puede trabajar, trabajarse o funcionar.—**workableness** [-nes], **workability** [-bíliti], *s*. aplicabilidad, practicabilidad; calidad de trabajable, explotable o manejable.

workaday [-adéi], *a*. laborioso.

workbag [uǒrcbǽg], *s*. saco de labor.

workbox [-bóx], *s*. caja o estuche de labor, costurero.

workday [-déi], *s*. día útil o de trabajo.

worker [-œr], *s*. trabajador; obrero; operario; abeja u hormiga obrera.

workfellow [-félŏ], *s*. compañero de trabajo; obrero.

workfolk(s [-fóuc$], *s*. = WORKPEOPLE.

workhouse [-jáus], *s*. hospicio, casa de misericordia; obrador, taller; casa de corrección; presidio.

working [-ing]. **I.** *s*. obra, trabajo; juego, funcionamiento, operación; (min.) explotación, laboreo; (mar.) maniobra, faena. **II.** *a*. que trabaja, laborante; obrero, trabajador; de trabajo; fundamental, que sirve de base, guía o regla.—**w. barrel,** cuerpo o cilindro (de bomba).— **w. capital,** capital circulante o de explotación.— **w. class,** clase obrera.—**w. cylinder,** (m. comb. int.) cilindro motor.—**w. day,** día de trabajo, día útil.—**w. drawing,** (ing.) plano, dibujo de guía.—**w. fluid,** fluido de trabajo.—**w. hypothesis,** postulado.—**w. load,** (ing.) carga (máxima) normal, carga de trabajo.—**w. model,** modelo de guía.—**w. plan,** W. DRAWING; plan, sistema.—**w. steam,** (m. v.) vapor vivo.—**w. strength,** coeficiente de trabajo.—**w. stress,** esfuerzo de trabajo.—**w. theory,** postulado.

workingman [-mæn], *s*. obrero, operario, jornalero, trabajador.

workman [-man], *sm*. trabajador, obrero, operario.

workmanlike, workmanly [-manlaik, -li]. **I.** *a*. primoroso, bien acabado. **II.** *adv*. primorosamente.

workmanship [-manŝhip], *s*. hechura, mano de obra.

workmaster [-mǽstœr], *s*. oficial.

workpeople [-pípœl], *s*. obreros, operarios.

workroom [-rúm], *s*. taller.

workshop [-ŝhop], *s*. taller, obrador.

workwoman [-uman], *s*. obrera.

world [uǒrld], *s*. mundo.—**w. power,** (pol. int.) gran potencia.—**w.'s end,** cabo del mundo.—**w. soul,** alma del universo.—**w. spirit,** espíritu del universo; Dios.—**W. War,** guerra mundial, gran guerra (la de 1914 a 1918).—**w.-weary,** cansado del mundo.—**w.-wide,** mundial.—**w. without end,** para siempre jamás; por los siglos de los siglos.—**for all the w.,** exactamente, cabalmente; bajo todos conceptos; por nada del mundo.—**the other w.,** el otro mundo, la vida futura.

worldliness [-lines], *s*. mundanalidad.

worldling [-ling], *s*. persona mundana.

worldly [-li]. **I.** *a*. mundano, mundanal, carnal, terreno o terrenal; seglar, profano. **II.** *adv*. mundana(l)mente, profanamente.—**w.-minded,** mundano, carnal, entregado a las cosas de este mundo.—**w.-mindedness,** mundanalidad, carnalidad.

worm [uǒrm]. **I.** *s*. gusano; lombriz; oruga; polilla, carcoma; coco, gorgojo; (fig.) gusano roedor, remordimiento; persona vil o despreciable; (mec.) tornillo sin fin; sacatrapos; (quím.) serpentín.—**w. and wheel,** engranaje de tornillo sin fin.—**w.-eaten,** carcomido, apolillado, abromado, picado o comido de gusanos.—**w. fence,** cercado en zigzag.—**w. gear,** rueda para tornillo sin fin.—**w. gear, w. gearing,** engranaje de tornillo sin fin.—**w. in the conscience,** gusano de la consciencia, remordimiento; por nada del mundo.—**w. tea,** tisana vermífuga.—**w. wheel,** rueda para engranaje de tornillo sin fin. **II.** *va*. insinuarse, introducirse o arrastrarse (como un gusano); sacar con sacatrapos; (fig.) arrancar mañosamente un secreto; quitar gusanos o lombrices.—**to w. a cable,** (mar.) embutir un cable. **III.** *vn*. trabajar u obrar lentamente y por bajo mano.

wormhole [-jóul], *s*. picadura de gusano.

wormlike [-laik], *a*. vermicular.

wormseed [uǒrmsid], *s*. (bot.) santónico.

wormwood [uǒrmud], *s*. (bot.) ajenjo.

wormy [uǒrmi], *a*. gusarapiento.

worn [uórn], *pp*. de TO WEAR.—**w. out,** gastado, raído; estropeado; cansado, rendido; agotado.

worried [uǒrried], *a*. angustiado; intranquilo, preocupado; vejado, incomodado.

worriment [uǒrrimœnt], *s*. = WORRY.

worrisome [-sum], *a*. angustioso, inquietante; molesto, vejatorio.

worry [uǒrri]. **I.** *va*. acosar; vejar; atormentar, angustiar; inquietar, preocupar; lacerar, desgarrar o matar mordiendo o sacudiendo. **II.** *vn*. estar intranquilo, inquietarse; morderse (los perros que riñen). **III.** *s*. cuidado, ansiedad, inquietud, zozobra; mordedura, desgarro, laceración.

worse [uǒrs]. **I.** *a. comp*. de BAD, ILL, EVIL: peor, más malo, inferior, en peor situación.—**w. and w.,** de mal en peor, peor que nunca; cada vez más malo (o peor).—**w. than ever,** peor que nunca.—**to be w. off,** estar en peores circunstancias, o quedar peor.—**to make, o render, w.,** empeorar. **II.** *adv*. peor; menos. **III.** *s*. peoría, menoscabo, detrimento; lo peor.—**for the w.,** en mal (gen. se tra. duce por *empeorar*, cambiando un poco el giro: *there has been a change for the worse,* la situación ha empeorado).—**to have the w. of it (of the fight,** etc.), llevar la peor parte, salir perdiendo.

worship [uǒrŝhip]. **I.** *s*. culto, adoración; reverencia, respeto.—**your w.,** usía; vuestra merced. **II.** *va*. adorar; reverenciar, honrar. **III.** *vn*. adorar; profesar culto o religión.—**worship(p)er** [-œr], *s*. adorador.

worshipful [-ful], *a.* adorable, venerable; (como tratamiento) honorable, respetable (*the worshipful president*, el respetable presidente.)—**w. master** [entre los francmasones], el Venerable.—**worshipfully** [-fuli], *adv.* venerablemente, con adoración.

worship(p)ing [-ing]. **I.** *s.* adoración, culto. **II.** *a.* adorador; venerador.

worst [uœrst]. **I.** *a. superl.* de BAD, ILL, EVIL: pésimo, malísimo, más malo, peor. **II.** *adv.* del peɔr modo posible; pésimamente. **III.** *s.* lo peor, lo más malo.—**at the w.**, en el peor estado posible; en las peores circunstancias.—**if (the) w. comes to the w.**, si sucede lo peor.—**to get the w. of**, llevar la peor parte en. **IV.** *va.* vencer, rendir o derrotar a; triunfar de.

worsted [uœrsted], *a.* vencido.

worsted [úrsted *o* ústed], *s.* estambre.—**w. stockings**, medias de estambre o de lana.—**w. work**, (cost.) labor hecha con estambre.—**w. yarn**, estambre.

wort [uœrt], *s.* planta, hierba (en composición: repollo; cerveza nueva que no ha fermentado.

worth [uœrʒ]. **I.** *s.* mérito; consideración, importancia, entidad; valor, valía; monta, precio; nobleza, excelencia, dignidad.—**a dollar's w. of**, un dólar de (lo que se compra). **II.** *a.* que vale o posee; equivalente a; de precio o valor de; (antes de gerundio) digno de, que vale la pena de, que merece (*he is a man worth knowing*, es hombre digno de conocerse; *the change is not worth making*, el cambio no vale la pena [de hacerse]); (ant.) digno, benemérito.—**to be w.**, valer, costar; merecer; (hablando de riqueza) tener (*Jones is worth a million dollars*, Jones tiene un millón de dólares).—**to be w. while**, valer la pena.

worthily [uœ́rðili], *adv.* dignamente, honorablemente.—**worthiness** [-nes], *s.* dignidad, mérito, valía.

worthless [uœ́rzles], *a.* inútil, inservible; sin valor; indigno, despreciable.—**worthlessness** [-nes], *s.* falta de mérito o de valor; inutilidad.

worthy [uœ́rði]. **I.** *a.* digno; apreciable, benemérito; merecedor, acreedor, meritorio.—**w. of notice**, digno de atención o de mención. **II.** *s.* notable, ilustre, benemérito.

would [ud], *pret. y subj.* de WILL. La distinción que se hace en el empleo de *would* y *should* es la misma que existe entre *will* y *shall*. (*V.* WILL, SHALL, SHOULD.) *Would* se usa a veces en el sentido de *querer* y equivale al presente, futuro o pretérito de subjuntivo, según las circunstancias: *those that would prosper*, los que quieran (o quisieren) prosperar; *I would I were there*, yo quisiera estar allá; *would God*, quiera (o quisiera) Dios, plegue (o pluguiera) a Dios.—**it w. seem**, parecería; parece, según parece.

would-be [úd-bi], *a.* pretendiente, aspirante, seudo, supuesto: *would-be poet*, presumido de poeta.

wound [uáund], *pret. y pp.* de WIND.

wound [und; (poét.) uáund]. **I.** *s.* herida; llaga, lesión; ofensa, golpe, daño. **II.** *va. y vn.* herir, llagar, lastimar; ofender, agraviar.

wounded [únded], *a.* herido; descalabrado.

woundwort [únducœrt], *s.* (bot.) vulneraria.

wove(n [uóv(œn], *pret. y pp.* de WEAVE.—**w. paper**, papel avitelado.

wrack [ræc], *s.* fuco, ova; naufragio, ruina; pecios; nubes sutiles, celajes.—**to go to w.**, arruinarse; correr a su perdición.

wraith [réiz], *s.* fantasma, espectro, aparecido, ánima en pena.

wrangle [rǽngœl]. **I.** *vn.* reñir; disputar, contender, altercar. **II.** *s.* pelotera, pendencia, riña; disputa, altercado.—**wrangler** [-glœr], *s.* pendenciero, camorrista; disputador, argumentador; (Ingl.) en la Universidad de Cambridge, graduado sobresaliente en matemáticas.

wrangling [-gling], *s.* camorra, reyerta, riña; disputa, altercación.

wrap [ræp]. **I.** *va.* (*pret. y pp.* WRAPPED *o* WRAPT) arrollar o enrollar; envolver.—**to w. up**, rollar, arrollar; envolver; apañar, arropar; embozar; cubrir, ocultar.—**to be wrapped up in**, estar envuelto o enrollado en; estar demasiado, pren-

dado de o embebido en. **II.** *s.* bata; abrigo.—*pl.* abrigos y mantas de viaje.

wrapper [ræpœr], *s.* envolvedor; funda, cubierta, cobertura, carpeta, papel; faja de periódico; capa de tabaco; bata, peinador, abrigo holgado; envoltura o pañal de niño; elástica, camiseta.

wrapping [-ing]. **I.** *a.* de envolver (apl. esp. al papel). **II.** *s.* envoltura, cubierta.

wraprascal [ræprrǽscœl], *s.* (ant.) abrigo holgado de paño burdo.

wrath [raz], *s.* ira, cólera.—**wrathful** [rázful], *a.* airado, colérico.—**wrathfully** [-li], *adv.* airada o coléricamente.

wreak [ríc], *va.* descargar (la cólera); tomar (venganza).

wreath [riz], *s.* corona, guirnalda; festón; trenza; espiral.

wreathe [ríð]. **I.** *va.* enroscar, entrelazar, tejer (coronas o guirnaldas), enguirnaldar; ceñir, rodear. **II.** *vn.* enroscarse, ensortijarse.

wreathy [ríði], *a.* coronado; enroscado, ensortijado; en espiral.

wreck [rec]. **I.** *s.* naufragio; ruina, destrozo, destrucción; buque naufragado, barco perdido; restos de un naufragio, pecios; (bot.) fuco, ova. **II.** *va.* hacer naufragar; arruinar, echar a pique; demoler, desbaratar. **III.** *vn.* naufragar, zozobrar, irse a pique; fracasar.

wreckage [rékey], *s.* naufragio; restos de naufragio, pecios.

wrecker [rékœr], *s.* raquero; destructor; demoledor.

wrecking [réking], *a.* de o relativo a naufragios; demoledor; que hace naufragar; ruinoso, desastroso.—**w. car**, (f. c.) furgón o carro de auxilio (en accidentes).

wren [ren], *s.* (orn.) reyezuelo, abadejo.

wrench [rench]. **I.** *va.* arrancar, arrebatar; torcer o retorcer; dislocar, desencajar, sacar de quicio.—**to w. one's foot**, torcerse el pie. **II.** *s.* arranque; tirón; torcedura, arrancamiento; (mec.) llave de tuerca; sistema compuesto de un par y una fuerza.

wrest [rest]. **I.** *va.* arrancar; torcer; desvirtuar, pervertir.—**to w. from**, arrebatar. **II.** *s.* violencia, torsión, torcimiento; dislocación; arranque; tergiversación, perversión; artificio, añagaza; llave de afinar.—**w. pin**, clavija de piano.

wrested [résted], *a.* torcido; forzado.

wrester [réstœr], *s.* violador, infractor.

wrestle [réscœl], *vn.* luchar a brazo partido; esforzarse; disputar.—**wrestler** [réslœr], *s.* luchador.—**wrestling** [réstling], *s.* lucha.

wretch [rech], *s.* infeliz, desventurado; ente vil, despreciable; miserable.

wretched [réched], *a.* infeliz, cuitado, desdichado, desgraciado; calamitoso, lastimero; vil, despreciable; perverso; mezquino; malísimo, detestable.—**wretchedly** [-li], *adv.* míseramente, desastradamente; ruinmente, vilmente.

wretchedness [-nes], *s.* desdicha, miseria, desgracia; escualidez, laceria; vileza, ruindad, bajeza.

wriggle [rígœl]. **I.** *va.* menear, retorcer, hacer colear. **II.** *vn.* colear, culebrear, serpentear, undular; retorcerse.—**to w. away**, escaparse culebreando.—**to w. into**, insinuarse en.—**to w. off**, escaparse culebreando o retorciéndose.—**to w. out**, escaparse, deslizarse.

wriggling [rígling], *s.* enroscadura, coleadura, ondulación, meneo serpentino.

wright [ráit], *s.* artífice, artesano, obrero.

wring [ring], *va.* (*pret. y pp.* WRUNG *o* WRINGED) torcer, retorcer; arrancar; estrujar, exprimir, escurrir; forzar; atormentar, aquejar.—**to w. off**, arrancar retorciendo.—**to w. out**, exprimir.

wringbolt [ríngboult], *s.* perno de atraca, clavija de apretar, argolla.

wringer [ríngœr], *s.* torcedor, torcedora; exprimidor (de ropa mojada).

wrinkle [rínccœl]. **I.** *s.* arruga, surco, buche; (fam.) capricho. **II.** *va.* arrugar, hacer arrugas.—**to w. one's brow**, fruncir o arrugar las cejas.—**to w. up**, arrugar, plegar. **III.** *vn.* arrugarse, encarrujarse.

wrinkled [rínccœld], *a.* arrugado; encarrujado; (cost.) fruncido, plegado.

wrinkly [ríncli], *a.* arrugado.

wrist [rist], *s.* (anat.) muñeca; (mec.) muñón; (m. comb. int.) muñón del pie de la biela, o eje del émbolo (ll. t. **w. pin**).; (m. v.) pasador de la cruceta.—**w. plate**, (m. v.) disco distribuidor.—**w. watch**, reloj de pulsera.

wristband [rístbænd], *s.* tirilla del puño de camisa.

wristdrop [-dróp], *s.* parálisis de los músculos de la mano debida a envenenamiento plúmbico.

wristlet [rístlet], *s.* manguito elástico.

writ [rit], *s.* escrito; escritura; orden; (for.) auto, mandamiento, decreto judicial, provisión, ejecutoria.—**w. of privilege**, auto de excarcelación. **Holy W.**, sagrada Escritura.

write [ráit]. **I.** *va.* (*pret.* WROTE: *pp.* WRITTEN) escribir; describir.—**to w. after,** copiar de.—**to w. a good hand,** hacer o tener buena letra.—**to w. down,** poner por escrito; redactar; apuntar; vilipendiar por escrito.—**to w. one's self,** calificarse, tomar algún título, calidad, honor, etc.—**to w. out,** redactar; copiar, trasladar, transcribir; escribir entero (sin abreviar).—**to w. over again,** volver a escribir.—**to w. up,** ensalzar por escrito, alabar; poner al día (el libro mayor). **II.** *vn.* escribir; tener correspondencia epistolar; ser escritor o autor.—**to w. back,** contestar a una carta.—**to w. on,** continuar escribiendo; escribir acerca de.

writer [ráitœr], *s.* escritor; autor; pendolista.— **the w.** (usado por modestia fingida para no decir *yo*) el que esto escribe; el infrascrito; nosotros (cambiando el verbo).

writhe [ráid]. **I.** *va.* torcer, retorcer. **II.** *vn.* contorcerse (por algún dolor).

writing [ráiting]. **I.** *s.* escritura; letra; escrito; el escribir, el arte de escribir. **II.** *a.* de o para escribir.—**w. book,** cuaderno de escritura.—**w. desk,** escritorio.—**w. machine,** máquina de escribir.—**w. master,** maestro de escritura.—**w. pad,** bloc de papel.—**w. paper,** papel de escribir (gen. se subentiende que es de cartas).—**w. set,** recado de escribir.—**in one's own w.**, de su puño y letra.

written, *pp.* de TO WRITE.

wrong [rong]. **I.** *s.* injuria, injusticia, agravio, tuerto, entuerto; mal (*knowledge of right and wrong,* conocimiento del bien y el mal); daño perjuicio; culpa, sinrazón; error, extravío; falsedad.—**to be in the w.**, no tener razón.—**to do w.**, obrar o hacer mal; hacer daño, causar perjuicio. **II.** *a.* injusto; desacertado; erróneo; incorrecto; falso; irregular; equivocado; inconveniente o inoportuno; mal hecho; mal escrito, etc.; que no es (era, etc.) (*he brought the wrong book,* trajo el libro que no era, u otro libro que el que debía haber traído, etc.).—**w.-headedness,** sinrazón, terquedad, obstinación.—**w. side,** envés, revés; lado malo.— **w. side out(ward),** al envés, al revés.—**to be w.**, ser malo; no ser justo; estar mal hecho (dicho, escrito, etc.); no tener razón. **III.** *adv.* mal; sin razón, sin causa; injustamente; al revés. **IV.** *va.* causar perjuicio a; hacer mal a; ofender; agraviar, injuriar; ser injusto con.

wrongdoer [róngdúœr], *s.* injuriador; malvado, perverso; pecador.—**wrongdoing** [-ing], *s.* maldad; perversidad, iniquidad.

wrongful [róngful], *a.* injusto; inicuo.

wrongfully [-i], *adv.* injustamente, sin razón, sin causa ni motivo.—**wrongly** [róngli], *adv.* injustamente; mal; equivocadamente.

wrongness [róngnes], *s.* injusticia, maldad, iniquidad; falsedad, error, inexactitud.

wrote [róut], *pret.* de TO WRITE.

wroth [roz], *a.* (ant.) airado, enojado.

wrought [rot]. **I.** *pret.* y *pp. irreg.* (ant.) de TO WORK. **II.** *a.* forjado; labrado.—**w. iron,** hierro forjado.—**w. up,** excitado; impelido.

wrung [rœng], *pret.* y *pp.* de TO WRING.—**W. mast,** (mar.) palo torcido.

wry [rái], *a.* torcido, doblado; pervertido, tergiversado.—**w. face,** gesto, visajes.—**w.-mouthed,** boquitorcido, boquituerto.—**wryed** [-d], *a.* sesgado, torcido.—**wryly** [-li], *adv.* torcidamente.

wryneck [-nec], *s.* (orn.) torcecuello; (med.) tortícoli.

wryness [-nes], *s.* torcedura.

wych-elm [uích-elm], *s.* olmo escocés.

wych-hazel, *s.* = WICH-HAZEL.

Wyclifite [uíclifait], *s.* y *a.* wiclefista, viclefista, seguidor de o relativo a Wiclef.

wye [uái]. **I.** *s.* la letra Y; horquilla, cualquier cosa en forma de Y. **II.** *a.* en Y, de forma de Y. (Gen. en vez de esta voz se escribe Y. *V.* Y.)

X

x [ecs], *s.* x.

X [ecs; *si quiere especificarse,* cǽpital ecs, *x mayúscula*]. **I.** *s.* cruz; cualquier cosa de forma de X. **II.** *a.* en cruz; en X, de forma de X.—**X ray,** rayo X.—**X-ray tube,** tubo de rayos X, tubo de vacío para la producción de rayos X.

xanthate [sænzeit], *s.* (quím.) xantato.

xanthein(e [sænzein], *s.* (quím.) xanteína.

xanthic [sænzic], *a.* xántico.

xanthin(e [sænzin], *s.* (quím.) xantina, jantina.

xanthochroi [sænzócroai], *s. pl.* caucasianos rubios.—**xanthochroid** [-croid], *a.* y *s.* rubio.

xanthophyl [sænzofil], *s.* (quím., bot.) jantófila, pigmento amarillo de las hojas.

xanthous [sænzus], *a.* mogol; rubio, blondo.

xanthoxylum [sænzócsilum], *s.* (bot.) jantóxilo; fresno espinoso.

xebec [síbec], *s.* (mar.) jabeque.

xenium [sí- (o sé-)nium], *s.* (*pl.* XENIA) golosina; (pint.) bodegón; presente o regalo que se da a un huésped o viajero eminente.

xenogamy [senógæmi], *s.* xenogamia, fecundación cruzada.

xenogenesis [sénoyénesis], *s.* producción de organismos distintos de los padres; (biol.) generación espontánea.

xenon [sínon], *s.* (quím.) xenon (cuerpo simple gaseoso).

xenophobia [sénofóubiæ], *s.* xenofobia, odio o antipatía hacia los extraños.

xerocollyrium [sirocolírium], *s.* (farm.) colirio seco.

xerophthalmia, xerophthalmy [serofzǽlmia, -mi], *s.* (med.) xeroftalmia.

xerophyte [sírofait], *s.* xerófita, planta de climas y suelos secos.

xerosis [serósis], *s.* (med.) xerodermia.

xiphias [sífias], *s.* (ict.) jifia.

xiphoid [sífoid], *a.* xifoideo, ensiforme.—**x. cartilage,** (anat.) xifoides.

Xmas [crísmas], *s.* (fam.) = CHRISTMAS.

xylene [sáilin], *s.* (quím.) xileno.—**xylic** [-ic], *a.* xílico.—**xylidin(e** [-din], *s.* xilidina.

xylocarpous [sailocárpus], *a.* de fruto duro y leñoso.

xylogen [sáiloyen], *s.* (quím.) xilógeno.

xylograph [sáilograf], *s.* xilografía, grabado en madera.—**xylographer** [sailógrafœr], *s.* grabador en madera.—**xylographic(al** [sáilogrǽfic(al], *a.* xilográfico.—**xylography** [sailógrafi], *s.* xilografía (arte).

xyloid [sáiloid], *a.* xiloide, semejante o relativo a la madera.

xylol [sáilol], *s.* (quím.) xyleno.

xylonite [-nait], *s.* celuloide.

xylophagous [sailófagus], *a.* xilófago.

xylophone [sáilofoun], *s.* (mús.) xilórgano o xilófono.

xyst [sist], *s.* pórtico, galería, terrado.

xyster [sístœr], *s.* (cir.) raspador de huesos.

Y

y [uái], *s.* y.

Y [uái; *si quiere especificarse,* cǽpital uái, *y mayúscula*]. **I.** *s.* horquilla; Y; cualquier cosa en forma de Y; (f. c.) cambio en Y, triángulo de cambio de marcha; (hidr.) tubo bifurcado, horquilla, tubo en Y. **II.** *a.* en Y, de forma de Y; de horquilla; bifurcado.—**Y box**, (elec.) caja bifurcada.—**Y connection**, (elec.) conexión de estrella. —**Y gun**, cañón doble antisubmarino en Y.—**Y level**, (tip.) nivel de apoyos en Y, nivel invertible en los apoyos (ll. a veces *nivel norteamericano*, por ser el más usado en los E. U.).—**Y track**, (f. c.) triángulo de inversión de marcha.

yacht [yot]. **I.** *s.* yate.—**y. race**, regata de yates. **II.** *vn.* ir, viajar o pasear en yate; manejar un yate.—**yachting** [yóting], *s.* deporte de los yates; paseo o navegación en yate.—**yachtsman** [-smæn], dueño o timonel de yate; deportista de yates.—**yachtsmanship** [-ship], *s.* arte del conductor de yates; habilidad en la conducción de yates.

yak [yæc], *s.* yac, especie de búfalo africano.

Yale lock [yéil lóc], cerradura Yale (es nombre de fábrica).

yam [yæm], *s.* (bot.) ñame.

yank [yænk]. **I.** *va.* (fam.) sacar de un tirón; dar un tirón. **II.** *vn.* (Ingl.) moverse rápidamente; farfullar, regañar. **III.** *s.* (fam.) tirón, estirón.

Yankee [yǽnki], *a.* y *s.* (fam.) yanqui, natural de la Nueva Inglaterra.—**Y. Doodle**, canción popular de los norteamericanos.—**Y. notions**, artículos de mercería.

yap [yæp]. **I.** *vn.* (fam.) ladrar; charlar. **II.** *s.* perro mostrenco; ladrido.

yard. I. *va.* acorralar, apriscar. **II.** *s.* corral; patio; cercado; yarda (medida); (mar.) verga.

yardarm [yárdarm], *s.* (mar.) penol de la verga.

yardstick, yardwand [yárdstic, -uond], *s.* yarda graduada de medir.

yarn, *s.* hilaza; hilo, hilado; (fam.) cuento largo e increíble, andaluzada.

yarrow [yǽro], *s.* (bot.) milenrama, milhojas.

yashmak [yǽsmæc], *s.* velo de las musulmanas.

yataghan [yǽtagæn], *s.* yatagán.

yaup [yop], *vn.* (fam.) *V.* YAP.

yaw [yo]. **I.** *s.* (mar.) guiñada; (aer.) derrape, desviación lateral con respecto a la línea regular de vuelo.—**y. guy**, (aer.) retenida de guiñada. **II.** *va.* y *vn.* (mar.) guiñar; (aer.) desviar(se) de la línea regular de vuelo por rotación alrededor del eje vertical.

yawing [-ing], *s.* (aer.) derrape, movimiento alrededor de eje vertical.

yawl [yol], *s.* (mar.) bote, yola; serení; balandra.

yawn [yon]. **I.** *vn.* bostezar; quedarse con la boca abierta; anhelar; abrirse. **II.** *s.* bostezo; abrimiento; abertura.—**yawner** [yóncœr], *s.* bostezador. —**yawning** [yóning]. **I.** *a.* bostezante; abierto. **II.** *s.* bostezo.

yaws [yoŝ], *s. pl.* tubérculos de una erupción cutánea y contagiosa en países tropicales.

ye [yi]. **I.** *pron.* (pl. de THOU) vosotros. **II.** (Di) *art.* (contr. ant. de THE), el, la, los, las.

yea [yéi]. **I.** *adv.* sí, ciertamente, verdaderamente; y aún, más aún, no solamente . . . sino. —**y. or nay**, sí o no. **II.** *s.* sí, voto afirmativo.— **the yeas and nays**, los votos en pro y en contra.

yean [yin], *vn.* parir la oveja.

yeanling [-ling], *s.* cordero o cabrito mamantón.

year [yíœr], *s.* año.—*pl.* años, edad; vejez.—**y.'s purchase**, renta anual.—**by the y.**, por año.—**in years**, de edad.—**of late years**, en los últimos años, en años recientes.—**once a y.**, una vez al año, cada año.—**to grow in years**, envejecer.

yearbook [yíærbúc], *s.* anuario.

yearling [yíærling], *s.* primal, añojo.—**y. lamb**, borro.

yearly [yíærli]. **I.** *a.* anual. **II.** *adv.* anualmente, cada año; una vez al año.

yearn [yœrn], *vn.* anhelar, desear vivamente, suspirar por.—**yearning** [-ing], *s.* anhelo.

yeast [yist], *s.* levadura, fermento; giste, espuma. —**y. cake**, pastilla o tortita de levadura.

yeasty [-i], *a.* de o semejante a levadura, espumoso; ligero; frívolo, trivial.

yeggman [yégmæn], *s.* (fam.) pícaro, ladrón.

yelk, *s.* (dialecto) *V.* YOLK.

yell [yel]. **I.** *va.* y *vn.* dar alaridos, vociferar, gritar, aullar; decir a gritos. **II.** *s.* alarido, grito,

aullido; grito salvaje o de guerra.—**college y.**, grito peculiar que sirve de distintivo a los estudiantes de cada colegio.

yellow [yelo]. **I.** *a.* amarillo; rubio; sensacional, escandaloso (periódico, etc.).—**y. berries**, bayas persas, semillas de cambrón.—**Y. Book**, Libro Amarillo (de Francia).—**y. brass**, latón ordinario. —**y. fever**, fiebre amarilla.—**y. flag**, (E. U.) bandera amarilla (la insignia de cuarentena).—**y. -hammer**, (orn.) verderol, verderón; picamaderos. —**Y. Jack**, (fam.) = Y. FEVER.—**y. jack**, (E. U.) bandera amarilla de cuarentena.—**y. jacket**, especie de avispa con pintas amarillas.—**y. lead**, albayalde calcinado.—**y. metal**, metal Muntz (aleación como de 60% de cobre y 40% de cinc.) —**y. ocher**, ocre amarillo.—**y. sapphire**, topacio oriental. — **y. spot**, mácula amarillenta en la retina de los vertebrados; (ent.) mariposa de mancha amarilla.—**y. water lily**, nenúfar amarillo. **II.** *s.* amarillo (color).

yellowbird [-bœrd], *s.* (orn.) jilguero, pintacilgo; cerrojillo; oropéndola.

yellowish [-ish], *a.* amarillento.—**yellowishness** [-ishnes], *s.* color amarillento.—**yellowness** [-nes], *s.* amarillez.

yellowwood [-úd], *s.* (bot.) fustete.

yelp. **I.** *vn.* latir, gañir, regañir (el perro). **II.** *s.* gañido del perro.—**yelping** [yélping], *s.* gañido.

yen, *s.* yen, moneda japonesa (como 2½ francos).

yeoman [yóman]. *s.* (pl. YEOMEN) hacendado, labrador acomodado; (mar.) pañolero; guardaalmacén.—**y. of the guard**, (Ingl.) alabardero de palacio.—**yeomanry** [-ri], *s.* burguesía; (Ingl.) cuerpo de guardia del rey.

yerk [yœrk], *va.* y *s.* = JERK.

yes [yes], *adv.* sí.

yesterday [-de], *s.* y *adv.* ayer.—**yesternight** [-nait], *s.* y *adv.* anoche, la noche pasada.

yet [yet]. **I.** *conj.* con todo, sin embargo, no obstante; mas, pero, empero; aun así. **II.** *adv.* aún, todavía, hasta ahora; a lo menos; más, además, más que; tanto como.—**as y.**, hasta ahora, hasta aquí, todavía.—**not y.**, todavía no, aún no.

yew [yu], *s.* (bot.) tejo.

yield [yíld]. **I.** *va.* producir; redituar, rendir, dar, dejar; dar de sí, ceder; deferir, condescender; devolver, restituir; admitir, pasar por, conceder; otorgar.—**to y. consent**, dar consentimiento, consentir.—**to y. up**, ceder, entregar; devolver, abandonar. **II.** *vn.* producir; dar utilidad; ceder, caer, sucumbir, rendirse o someterse; consentir; flaquear, ceder, doblegarse; mollearse, blandear.— **to y. to**, ceder a, rendirse a; acceder a , consentir en; someterse a. **III.** *s.* rendición; producción; rédito, rendimiento, renta, beneficio; cosecha.—**y. point**, (ing.) límite elástico aparente, esfuerzo mínimo de deformación permanente.

yielding [yílding], *a.* dócil, complaciente; flojo; condescendiente; dúctil.—**yieldingly** [-li], *adv.* libremente; flojamente.—**yieldingness** [-nes], *s.* facilidad en ceder o en condescender.

yodel [yódœl]. **I.** *va.* y *vn.* cantar modulando la voz rápidamente desde el tono natural al falsete, y viceversa. **II.** *s.* manera de cantar de los tiroleses.

yoke [yóuk]. **I.** *s.* yugo; horcajo, camella; horquilla; guía; tirante; culata (de imán); puente (de agujero de hombre); garra de fijación (de taladro); barra de timón; balancín o pinga (para llevar pesos); (cost.) hombrillo de la camisa; (aer.) palanca de mando.—*sing.* y *pl.* yunta de bueyes; par de otros animales.—**y. elm**, (bot.) carpe.—**y. of land**, yugada. **II.** *va.* uncir, acoyundar, acollarar, acoplar; sujuzgar, sujetar; oprimir.

yokefellow [-félou], **yokemate** [-méit], *s.* compañero de fatigas.

yokel [yócœl], *s.* campesino, patán.

yolk [yóuk o yóulk], *s.* yema (de huevo); exudación de las ovejas.

yon(der [yón(dœr]. **I.** *adv.* allí, allá, acullá. **II.** *a.* aquel, aquellos.

yore [yóœr], *s.* (poét.) otro tiempo; antaño.

Yorkshire bite [yórcŝhir báit], *s.* (fam.) embaucador, trampista; acción indigna, desvergonzada.

you [yu], *pron. pers. sing.* y *pl.* (nominativo y caso oblícuo) tú, usted, vosotros, ustedes; te, a ti, le, la, a usted, os, a vosotros, les, a ustedes. Se usa indefinidamente, y entonces se traduce por *uno* o haciendo refleja la construcción: *as you come near it, you see nothing,* cuando uno se acerca, no ve nada; *you cannot enter without permission,* no se puede entrar sin permiso.

young [yung]. **I.** *a.* joven; mozo; nuevo; tierno, verde; fresco, reciente; novicio, inexperto.—**y. face,** cara remozada.—**y. fellow,** joven, mozo.—**y. girl,** chica, mozuela (apl. gen. a jóvenes no mayores de 20 años).—**y. goat,** cabrito, chivo, choto.—**y. hare,** lebratillo.—**y. lady,** señorita.—**y. man,** joven (hombre).—**Y. Men's Christian Association,** Asociación de los Jóvenes Cristianos (más propiamente, Asociación Cristiana de los Jóvenes).—**y. one,** mozo; hijuelo; (fam.) niño, chiquillo.—**y. partridge,** perdigón.—**y. people,** los jóvenes.—**y. rabbit,** gazapillo, gazapo.—**y. woman,** joven, mujer joven.—**Y. Women's Christian Association,** Asociación de las Jóvenes Cristianas (es la expresión usual, aunque la traducción propia es Asociación Cristiana de las Jóvenes). **II.** *s. pl.* hijuelos, la cría de los animales. —**with y.,** preñada.

younger [yúngœr], *a.* más joven.—**y. brother,** hermano menor.—**to be the y. hand,** ser pie en el juego.

youngish [yúnguiśh], *a.* mozuelo, jovencillo, tierno.

youngling [yúngling], *s.* pequeñuelo.

youngster [yúngstœr], *s.* jovencito, mocito, mozalbete; (fam.) niño, chiquillo.

younker [yúnkœr], *s.* hacendado alemán; señorito.

your [yúœr], *pron.* (*sing.* y *pl.*) tu, tus, vuestro, vuestra, vuestros, vuestras; de usted(es.)

yours [yúœrs], *pron.* (*sing.* y *pl.*) el tuyo, la tuya, los tuyos, las tuyas; el vuestro, la vuestra, los vuestros, las vuestras; el, la, lo, los o las de usted o de ustedes; el suyo, la suya, los suyos, las suyas (de usted o de ustedes).—**y. affectionately,** su afectísimo.—**y. (very) cordially,** su afectísimo servidor.—**y. (very) faithfully,** su seguro servidor.—**y. sincerely** = Y. AFFECTIONATELY.— **y. (very) truly** = Y. FAITHFULLY. (Estas son formas convencionales de significado más o menos vago, y a veces se usan las unas por las otras.)

yourself [yursélf], *pron. pers.* tú mismo, Vd. mismo.—*pl.* **yourselves,** vosotros o Vds. mismos.

youth [yuz], *s.* juventud, mocedad; mozalbete, joven; la juventud, los jóvenes.

youthful [yúzful], *a.* juvenil; joven, mozo; fresco, vigoroso; juguetón.—**youthfully** [-i], *adv.* de un modo juvenil, como muchacho.—**youthfulness** [-nes], *s.* mocedad, juventud; frescura.

yowl [yául]. **I.** *vn.* (fam.) aullar, ladrar; gritar. **II.** *s.* aullido; alarido.

yperite [ípœrait], *s.* yperita, gas sofocante para granadas.

ytterbia [itœrbiæ], *s.* iterbia, óxido de iterbio.

ytterbium [-um], *s.* (quím.) iterbio.

yttria [ítria], *s.* (quím.) itria.

yttrium [ítrium], *s.* (quím.) itrio.

yucca [yuca], *s.* (bot.) yuca.

Yugoslav, etc. = JUGOSLAV, etc.

Yule [yul], **Yuletide** [-taid], *s.* pascua de Navidad.—**yule log,** nochebueno.

Z

z [âi o śed], *s.* z.

Z [śi]. **I.** *s.* hierro en Z; cosa de forma de Z. **II.** *a.* en Z, en forma de Z.—**Z bar,** barra en Z.—**Z beam,** viga en Z.—**Z column,** columna en Z.—**Z iron,** hierro en Z.

zaffer, zaffre [śéfœr], *s.* (min.) zafre.

zanana [śanána], *s.* V. ZENANA.

Zanthoxylum [sænzóxilum], *s.* (bot.) jantoxilo.

zany [śéini], *s.* bufón, truhán, simplón.

zeal [śil], *s.* celo; fervor; ardor; acucia.

zealot [śélot], *s.* entusiasta, partidario acérrimo, fanático.—**zealotry** [-tri], *s.* fanatismo.—**zealous**

[śélus], *a.* celoso, entusiasta.—**zealously** [-li], *adv.* apasionadamente, con pasión y celo; con ardor.

zebec [śíbec], *s.* V. XEBEC.

zebra [śíbra], *s.* (zool.) cebra.

zebu [śíbiu], *s.* (zool.) cebú.

zed [śed], *s.* ceta, nombre de la letra z.

zedoary [śédoœri], *s.* (bot.) cedoaria.

zeitgeist [tsáitgaist], *s.* espíritu u orientaciones de la época.

zemstvo [śémstfo], *s.* zemstvo, asamblea provincial rusa.

zenana [śenána], *s.* harén indio.

Zend [śend], *s.* zend.—**Z.-Avesta,** Zendavesta.

zenith [śíniz], *s.* cenit.—**z. distance,** distancia cenital.

Zep, Zepp [śep]. **I.** *s.* (fam.) Zepelín. **II.** *va.* (fam.) bombardear desde un Zepelín.

zephyr [śéfœr], *s.* céfiro, favonio; hilaza muy ligera para bordar.

Zeppelin [śépelin]. **I.** *s.* Zepelín. **II.** *va.* (**z-**) bombardear desde un Zepelín.

zero [śírou], *s.* cero.—**z. hour,** (mil.) hora de ataque: hora o momento críticos.—**z. lift,** (aer.) resistencia nula.—**z. weather,** tiempo de cero grados (de temperatura).

zest [śest]. **I.** *s.* deleite, gusto; sainete, sabor; luquete (que se echa a una bebida); bizna de la nuez. **II.** *va.* dar gusto o sabor.

zeugma [śiúgma], *s.* (ret.) zeugma.

Zeus [śiús], *s.* Júpiter griego.

zibeline [śíbelin, o -ain]. **I.** *a.* de marta; de piel de marta. **II.** *s.* piel de marta.

zibet [śíbet], *s.* (zool.) gato de algalia.

zigzag [śígsæg]. **I.** *va.* y *vn.* ir en zigzags, hacer zigzags, zigzaguear. **II.** *a.* serpentino, en zigzag. **III.** *s.* zigzag.

zinc [śinc]. **I.** *s.* (quím. y com.) cinc o zinc.—**z. blende,** blenda.—**z. bloom,** flor de cinc.—**z. white,** blanco u óxido de cinc. **II.** *va.* plaquear con cinc, galvanizar.

zincate [śínkeit], *s.* cincato.—**zincic** [śínkic], *a.* cíncico.—**zinciferous, zinkiferous** [śinkíferus], *a.* cincífero.—**zincite** [-ait], (min.) cincita, óxido natural de cinc.

zincograph [śíncogræf], *s.* cincograbado, grabado en cinc.—**zincography** [śincógrafi], cincografía, arte de grabar en cinc.

zincous [śíncus], *a.* cíncico, de cinc; del cinc, electropositivo (en una pila eléctrica).

Zion [śáion], *s.* Sion; cielo.—**Zionism** [-iśm], *s.* sionismo, movimiento en favor de reestablecer a los judíos en Palestina.—**Zionist** [-ist], *s.* y *a.* sionista.

zip [śip]. **I.** zumbido de, o como de, bala. **II.** *vn.* zumbar como una bala.

zircon [śércon], *s.* (min.) circón.

zirconium [śœrcónium], *s.* (quím.) circonio, zirconio.

zither(n [śízœr(n], *s.* (mús.) cítara.

zizyphus [śíśifus], *s.* (bot.) azufaifo.

zoanthropia [soanzrópia], *s.* (med.) zoantropia.

zocle [śócœl], *s.* = SOCLE.

zodiac [śódiæc], *s.* zodíaco; circuito.

zodiacal [śodáiacal], *a.* zodiacal.—**z. light,** luz zodiacal.

zoea [sofæ], *s.* zoe, forma larval de algunos crustáceos.

zoic [śóic], *a.* zoico; (geol.) fosilífero.

Zollverein [śólferain], *s.* unión aduanera.

zonal [śónal], *a.* perteneciente a una zona; que tiene bandas o zonas.

zone [śóun], *s.* zona; banda circular, faja; (poét.) cinturón o cíngulo.

zoned [śóund], *a.* que lleva cinturón; marcado con fajas.

zoneless [śóunles], *a.* que no tiene cinto.

zonule [śóniul], *s.* zona pequeña; faja, anillo, aro pequeño.

zoo [śu], *s.* (*contr.* de ZOOLOGICAL) (fam.) jardín zoológico.

zoochemistry [śookémistri], *s.* zooquímica, química biológica.

zoogeny [śoóyeni], *s.* zoogenia.

---

zoogloea [şooglía], *s.* aglomerado gelatinoso de bacterias.
zoographer [şoógrafer], *s.* zoógrafo.
zoographic(al [şoográfic(al], *a.* zoográfico.
zoography [şoógrafi], *s.* zoografía.
zooid [şóoid]. **I.** *a.* de carácter animal. **II.** *s.* (biol.) zooide.
zoolatry [şoólatri], *s.* zoolatría.
zoolatrous [-trus], *s.* zoólatra.
zoolite [şóolait], *s.* (geol.) zoolito.
zoological [şoolóyical], *a.* zoológico.
zoologist [şoóloyist], *s.* zoólogo.
zoology [şoóloyi], *s.* zoología.
zoom [şum], *vn.* (aer.) empinarse.
zoometry [şoómetri], *s.* zoometría.
zoomorphic [şóomórfic], *a.* zoomorfo, de forma de animal; que representa animales.—**zoomorphism** [-işm], *s.* representación de o por medio de animales; culto de animales.
zoonomy [şoónomi], *s.* zoonomía.
zoophagan [şoófagan], *s.* y *a.* carnívoro.
zoophagous [şoófagus], *a.* zoófago.
zoophyte [şóofait], *s.* zoófito.
zoophytic(al [şoofític(al], *a.* zoofítico.
zoosperm [şóospœrm], *s.* zoospora.
zoosporangium [-porényium], *s.* zoosporangio.
zoospore [-poœr], *s.* zoospora.
zootic [şoótic], *a.* (geol.) zoótico.
zootomist [şoótomist], *s.* zootómico.
zootomy [şoótomi], *s.* zootomía.

Zoroastrian [şóroæstrian], *a.* parsi, zoroástrico.
Zoroastrianism [-æstrianişm], *s.* zoroastrismo.
zoster [şóstœr], *s.* cíngulo; (med.) zóster, zona.
zouave [şuáv], *s.* (mil.) zuavo.
zounds [şáunds], *interj.* ¡voto al chápiro! ¡cáspita!
Zulu, Zooloo [şúlu], *a.* y *s.* zulú.
zwieback [tsvíbac, *gen.* suíbac], *s.* especie de pan retostado.
Zwinglian [şuínglißn]. **I.** *s.* zuingliano, partidario de Zwinglio. **II.** *a.* zwingliano, relativo a Zwinglio o a sus doctrinas.
zygoma [şaigómæ], *s.* arco cigomático; apófisis cigomática del temporal.
zygomatic [şáigomätic], *a.* (anat.) cigomático. —**z. bone**, hueso malar, pómulo.—**z. process**, apófisis cigomática del temporal.
zygomorphic, zygomorphous [-mórfic, -us], *a.* cigomorfo, en forma de yugo.—**zygomorphism** [-işm], *s.* cigomorfismo.
Zygophyllaceæ [-filéisii], *s. pl.* (bot.) cigofileas.— **zygophyllaceous** [-şhus], *a.* cigofileo.
zyme [şaim], *s.* (biol.) un fermento; germen de enfermedad cimótica.
zymic [şímic], *a.* címico.
zymogen [şáimoyen], *s.* (quím.) cimógeno; (bact.) organismo productor de fermentos
zymology [şaimóloyi], *s.* cimología.
zymosis [şaimósis], *s.* cimosis, fermentación morbífica; enfermedad cimótica.
zymotic [şaimótic], *a.* cimótico.

Para la pronunciación de æ, œ, ᴅ, ş, şh, ᴜ, ӯ, ʏ, z, véase la clave al principio del libro.

abraham lincoln
Andrew Johson
ulisses S. grant

Amvnistov esta acta restauraria
1881 tennesse The First of The socalled Jim crow lows
ride in separate railway
NAACP National Association for The
advancemet of colored People
Trabajo continuo y el progreso para privar
los derechos civiles
worbed through The courts disenfranchisement

APÉNDICE

NOMBRES GEOGRÁFICOS QUE SE ESCRIBEN DE DISTINTO MODO EN INGLÉS Y EN ESPAÑOL

A

Aachen [áken], Aquisgrán, Aix-la-Chapelle.
Abydos [æbáidos], Abidos.
Abyssinia [abisínia], Abisinia.
Achaia [akéia], **Achæa** [akía], Acaya.
Actium [ǽcshium], Accio.
Adelaide [ǽdeleid], Adelaida.
Admiralty Islands, Islas del Almirante.
Adrianople [éidrianópœl], Adrianópolis.
Adriatic [ædriǽtic] **Sea,** Mar Adriático.
Ægean [iyían], **Sea** Mar Egeo.
Ægina [eyáina], Egina.
Ægospotami [ígospótamai], Egos Pótamos.
Æolis [íolis], Eólida.
Ætna [étna], Etna.
Ætolia [etólia], Etolia.
Afghanistan [afgǽnistan], Afganistán.
Aix [ex], Ex.
Aix-la-Chapelle [ex-la-shapél], Aquisgrán.
Algeria [alyíriæ], Argelia.
Algiers [ǽlyicœrs], Argel.
Allegheny [ǽleguéini] **Mountains,** Montes Alleghanys.
Aleppo [alépo], Alepo.
Alessandria [alesándria], Alejandría.
Aleutian [aliúshan] **Islands,** Islas Aleutas o Aleutianas.
Alexandria [ælexǽndria], Alejandría (Egipto).
Alps [ælps], Alpes.
Alsace [alsás], Alsacia.
Alsace-Lorraine, Alsacia-Lorena.
Amazon [ǽmason], Amazonas.
Andalusia [ǽndalúshia], Andalucía.
Angouleme [angulém], Angulema.
Annam [ánám], Anam.
Antilles [æntíliš], Antillas.
Antioch [ǽntioc], Antioquía.
Antwerp [ǽntucœrp], Amberes.
Apennines [ǽpenainš], Apeninos.
Appalachian [ǽpalǽchian] **Mountains,** Montes Apalaches.
Aquitaine [ǽcuitén], Aquitania.
Arabia Deserta [aréibiæ desœ́rtæ], Arabia Desierta.—**A. Felix** [fílics], Arabia Feliz.—**A. Petræa** (petríæ], Arabia Petrea.
Archipelago [árkipélago], Archipiélago, Mar Egeo.
Ardennes [ardén], Ardenas.
Asia Minor [éiya máincœr], Asia Menor.
Assyria [asíriæ], Asiria.
Astrakhan [ǽstracǽn], Astracán.
Athens [ǽzenš], Atenas.
Attica [ǽticæ], Atica.
Austria-Hungary [óstriæ-júngari], Austria-Hungría.
Auvergne [ovœ́rñ], Auvernia.
Avignon [áviñón], Aviñón.

B

Babylon [bǽbilon], **Babylonia** [-lóniæ], Babilonia.

Bactra [bǽctræ], Bactria.—**Bactria** [-triæ], Bactriana.
Bagneres [bañér], Bañeras.
Baku [bakú], Bakú.
Balearic [bǽliǽrik] **Islands,** Islas Baleares.
Balkan [bólcœn] **Mountains,** Montes Balcanes.
Baltic [bóltic] **Sea,** Mar Báltico.
Baluchistan [balúchistǽn], Beluchistán, Baluchistán.
Banat [bǽnat], Banato.
Barbadoes [barbédoš], Barbada.
Barbary [bárbari], Berbería.
Basque [bæsc] **Provinces,** Provincias Vascongadas.
Bavaria [bavéria], Baviera.
Bayonne [bayón], Bayona.
Bayreuth [bairóit], Baireut.
Bearn [beár], Bearne.
Beaucaire [bokéær], Belcaire.
Bechuanaland [béchuǽnalǽnd], Bechuanalandia.
Beirut, Beyrout [béirut], Beirut.
Belgium [bélyium], Bélgica.
Belgrade [bélgréid], Belgrado.
Belize [belíš], Bélice.
Belleisle [beláil] **Strait of,** estrecho de Bella Isla.
Bengal [bengól], Bengala.
Bern o **Berne** [bern], Berna.
Bethany [bézæni], Betania.
Bethlehem [bézlijem], Belén.
Bethsaida [bezéida], Betsaida.
Bilboa [bilbóa], Bilbao.
Biscay [bíske], Vizcaya.
Bithynia [bizínia], Bitinia.
Black Sea, Mar Negro.
Bœotia [bióshiæ], Beocia.
Bois-le-duc [bua-le-dúc], Bolduque.
Bokhara [bokǽræ], Bojara, Bokhara.
Bologna [bolóña], Bolonia.
Bonn [bon], Bona.
Bordeaux [bórdó], Burdeos.
Bosporus, Bosphorus [bósporus], Bósforo.
Bothnia [bózniæ], Botnia.
Boulogne [bulón o bulóñ], Boloña.
Brabant [brabánt], Brabante.
Brandenburg [brándenburk], Brandeburgo.
Brazil [bræśil], Brasil.
Bremen [brémen], Brema.
Bretagne [bretáñ], **Brittany** [brítani], Bretaña.
British Columbia [colúmbiæ], Columbia Británica.
British Honduras [jondiúras], Belice, Beliza, Honduras Británica.
British Isles, Islas Británicas.
Bruges [brúyeš], Brujas.
Brussels [brúselš], Bruselas.
Bucharest [biúcarést], Bucarest.
Bukowina [búcovína], Bucovina.
Burgundy [bœrgundi], Borgoña.
Byzantium [baisǽnshum], Bizancio.

Para la pronunciación de æ, œ, ᴅ, ś, śh, ᴜ, ȳ, ʏ, z, véase la clave al principio del libro.

C

Cæsarea [sésaríæ], Cesarea.
Caffraria [cæfréria], Cafrería.
Calcutta [cælcúta], Calcuta.
Cambridge [kémbriʏ], Cambrigia.
Cameroon [cámerun], Camerón.
Campeachy [campíchi], Campeche.
Canaan [kéinæn], Canaán.
Canary Islands, Islas Canarias.
Canossa [kanósæ], Canosa.
Canterbury [cǽntœrbœri], Cantórbery.
Cape Breton [kéip bréton], **Island,** Isla Real o del Cabo Bretón.
Cape Colony, Colonia del Cabo.
Cape Haitien [jéitiæn], Cabo Haitiano.
Cape of Good Hope, Cabo de Buena Esperanza.
Capernaum [capœrnaʊm], Cafarná m.
Cape Verde [vœrdi] **Islands,** Islas del Cabo Verde.
Carcassonne [cárcasón], Carcasona.
Caribbean [cáribíæn], **Sea,** Mar Caribe, Mar de las Antillas.
Caroline [cárolain] **Islands,** Islas Carolinas.
Carpathian [carpézian] **Mountains,** Montes Carpacios.
Carthage [cárzeʏ], Cartago.
Caspian [cǽspian] **Sea,** Mar Caspio.
Castile [cæstíl], Castilla.
Catalonia [cǽtalóniæ], Cataluña.
Caucasus [cócasʊs], Cáucaso.
Cayenne [keién o caién], Cayena.
Ceylon [silón], Ceilán.
Chæronea [kéroniæ], Queronea.
Chalcedon [calsídʊn], Calcedonia.
Chaldea [caldíæ], Caldea.
Champagne [šhanpéin], Champaña.
Charente [šharánt], Carenta.
Chefoo [chífú], Chifú.
Cherbourg [šhérbúr], Cherburgo.
Chersonese [cœrsoniš], Quersoneso.
Chifu [chífú], Chifú.
China [cháinæ] **Sea,** Mar de la China.
Christiania [cristiániæ], Cristianía.
Circassia [sœrcáshæ], Circasia.
Coblenz [coblénts], Coblenza.
Coburg [cóburk], Coburgo.
Cochin China [cóchin cháinæ], Cochinchina.
Cologne [colóuñ], Colonia.
Compiègne [conpién], Compieña.
Constance [cónstans], **Lake of,** (lago de) Constanza.
Constantine [cónstǽntín], Constantina.
Constantinople [constǽntinópœl], Constantinopla.
Copenhagen [cópenjéiguen], Copenhague.
Corinth [córinz], Corinto.
Cornwall [córnuol], Cornualles.
Corsica [córsica], Córcega.
Corunna [corúna], Coruña.
Cracow [créco], Cracovia.
Crete [crit], Creta.
Croatia [croéišhiæ], Croacia.
Curaçao [cúrasáo], Curazao, Curasao.
Cyclades [cíklædiš], Cíclades.
Cydnus [sidnʊs], Cidno.
Cyprus [sáiprʊs], Chipre.
Czecho-Slovakia, Czechoslovakia [chékoslovákiæ], Checoeslovaquia.
Czernowitz [chœrnovits], Cernauti.

D

Damascus [damǽscʊs], Damasco.
Dalmatia [dalméišhiæ], Dalmacia.
Danube [dǽñub], Danubio.
Dardanelles [dárdanélš], Dardanelos.
Dauphiné [dofiné], Delfinado.
Dead Sea, Mar Muerto.
Deccan [décæn], Decán.
Delphi [délfai], Delfos.

Denmark [dénmark], Dinamarca.
Dieppe [diép], Diepe o Diepa.
Dnieper [nípœr], Niéper, Dniéper.
Dordogne [dordóñ], Dordoña.
Douro [dúro], Duero.
Dover, Dóver o Dovres.
Dover [dóvœr], **Strait of,** Paso de Calais.
Dresden [drésden], Dresde.
Dunkirk [dúnkœrk], Dunquerque.
Dvina [dviná], **Dwina** [duínæ], Duina.

E

Easter Island, Isla de Pascua, Rapanuí.
East Indies [índiš], Indias Orientales.
Edinburgh [édinbœro], Edimburgo.
Egypt [íʏipt], Egipto.
Elbe [élbe], Elba.
England [íngland], Inglaterra.
English Channel, Paso de Calais.
Ephesus [éfesʊs], Éfeso.
Epirus [epáirʊs], Epiro.
Escurial [eskiúrial], Escorial.
Esthonia [eszóniæ], Estonia.
Ethiopia [izíópiæ], Etiopía.
Eubœa [iubíæ], Eubea.
Euphrates [iufréitiš], Eufrates.
Europe [iúrʊp], Europa.

F

Finland [fínland], Finlandia.
Flanders [flǽnderš], Flandes.
Florence [flórens], Florencia.
Florida [flóridæ] **Keys,** Cayos de la Florida.
Flushing [flúšhing], Flesinga.
France [frans], Francia.
Franche-Comté [fransh-conté], Franco-Condado.
Franz Josef [frænts yósef] **Land,** Archipiélago o Tierra de Francisco José.
Freiburg, Friburg [fráiburk], Friburgo.
Friesland [frísland], Frisia.
Frontenac [frontenác], Frontiñac.
Frozen Sea, Mar Glacial.

G

Galilee [gǽlili], Galilea.
Gallipoli [gælípoli], Galípoli.
Garonne [garón], Garona.
Gascony [gǽsconi], Gascuña.
Gaul [gol], Galia.
Gelderland [guéldœrland], Güeldres.
Geneva [yeníva], Ginebra.
Genoa [yénoa], Génova.
Germany [yœrmani], Alemania; (hist. ant.) Germania.
Ghent [guent], Gante.
Gironde [yirónd], Gironda.
Giza [guísæ], Guidsé.
Glarus [glárus], Glaris.
Gold Coast, Costa de Oro.
Good Hope (Cape of), Cabo de Buena Esperanza.
Göteborg [gœteborg], Gotemburgo.
Göttingen [gœtinguen], Gotinga.
Græcia Magna [gríšhiæ mágnæ], Magna Grecia.
Granicus [granáicʊs], Gránico.
Great Britain [bríten], Gran Bretaña.
Greece [gris], Grecia.
Greenland [grínland], Groelandia.
Guadaloupe [godalúp], Guadalupe.
Guam [guám], Guaján, o Guam.
Guelderland [guéldœrland], Güeldres.
Guernsey [gœrnšé], Guernesey.
Guiana [guiǽnæ], Guayana.
Guienne [guién], Guiena.

H

Hague [jéig], **The,** La Haya.
Hainault [jenó], Henao.
Haiti [héiti], Haití.
Halicarnassus [hǽlicarnásus], Halicarnaso.
Hamburg [hǽmbœrg], Hamburgo.
Hankow [jáncóu], Hankao.
Hanse [jæns] **Towns, Hanseatic** [-siǽtic] **Towns,** ciudades hanseáticas.
Harbin [jarbín], Jarbín o Karbín.
Havana [javána], Habana.
Havre de Grace [jǽvœr de gras], Havre de Gracia.
Hawaii [jauái], Hawái, Hauái.
Hawaiian [jauáiyan] **Islands,** Islas Hawái.
Hayti, Haiti [jéiti], Haití.
Hebrides [jébridiš], Hébridas.
Hejaz [jeyáš], Heyaz.
Hellas [jélas], Hélada.
Herculaneum [jœrkiuléinium], Herculano.
Hindustan [jíndustǽn], Indostán.
Hispaniola [jíspæniólæ], la Española.
Holland [jóland], Holanda.
Holy Land, Tierra Santa.
Horn [jorn] **(Cape),** Cabo de Hornos.
Hungary [júngari], Hungría.
Hymettus [jaimétus], Himeto.

I

Iceland [áisland], Islandia.
Ilion [íliun], **Ilium** [-um], Ilión (Troya).
Illyria [ilíriæ], Iliria.
Illyricum [ilíricum], Ilírico.
Indian Ocean, Mar de las Indias.
Indus [índus], Indo.
Ionia [aióniæ], Jonia.
Ionian [aióniæn] **Sea,** Mar Jónico.
Ireland [áirland], Irlanda.
Iron Gates, Puertas de Hierro.
Issus [ísus], Iso.
Italy [ítali], Italia.
Ithaca [ízacæ], Itaca.
Ivory Coast, Costa del Marfil.

J

Japan [yapǽn], Japón.
Jeddo [yédo], Yedo.
Jericho [yérico], Jericó.
Jerusalem [yœrúsalem], Jerusalén.
Judah [yúda], Judá.
Jugoslavia [iúgosláviæ], Yugoeslavia.
Julian Alps [yúliæn alps], Alpes Julianos.
Jutland [yútland], Jutlandia.

K

Kaffraria [cafréiriæ], Cafrería.
Karelia [caríliæ], Carelia.
Kashmir [cǽšmir], Cachemira.
Key West, Cayohueso, Cayo Hueso.
Khartoum [cartúm], Jartum o Kartum.
Khiva [kívæ], Jiva.
Kiaochow [kiáuchóu], Kiao-Cheu.
Kronstadt [crónšhtat], Cronstadt.
Kurdistan [cúrdistǽn], Curdistán o Kurdistán.
Kurland [cúrlænd], Curlandia.

L

Lacedæmon [lǽsedemon], Lacedemonia.
Languedoc [languedóc], Langüedoc.
Lapland [lǽpland], Laponia.
Lassa [lásæ], Lasa.
Latium [léišhium], Lacio.
Lausanne [lošán], Lausana.
Lebanon [lébanon], Líbano.
Leeward Islands, Islas de Sotavento.
Leghorn [legjórn], Liorna.

Leningrad [léningræd], Leningrado.
Leyden [láiden], Leide, Leida.
Libya [líbiæ], Libia.
Liége [liéy], Lieja.
Lille [lil], Lila.
Limburg [límbœrg], Limburgo.
Limosin o **Limousin** [limuzǽn], Lemosín.
Lisbon [lísbun], Lisboa.
Lisle [lil], Lila.
Lithuania [liziuéiniæ], Lituania.
Loire [luár], Loira.
Lombardy [lómbardi], Lombardía.
London [lúndun], Londres.
Lorrain(e [lorén], Lerena.
Lothringen [lótringuen], Lorena, Lotaringia.
Louisiana [luišiǽna], Luisiana
Louvain [luvéin], Lovaina.
Low Countries, Países Bajos.
Lower California [cǽlifórniæ], Baja California.
Lower Egypt [íyipt], Bajo Egipto.
Lower Rhine [lóœr ráin], Bajo Rin.
Lucerne [lusǽrn], Lucerna.
Luxemburg [lúxembœrg], Luxemburgo.
Lyons [láiunš], Lion.

M

Macedon(ia [mǽsedon, -iæ], Macedonia.
Madeira [madéra], Madera.
Magellan [mayélan], **Strait of,** Estrecho de Magallanes.
Magna Græcia [mágnæ gríšhiæ], Magna Grecia.
Mainz [máinš]= **Mentz.**
Majorca [mayórca], Mallorca.
Malay [maléi, méilei] **Archipelago,** Malasia, Archipiélago Malayo.
Malay Peninsula, Península de Malaca.
Malay States, Federated, Estados Federados de Malaca.
Malines [malín], Malinas.
Marathon [mǽrazon], Maratón.
Marseilles [marsélš], Marsella.
Martinique [mártiníc], Martinica.
Maskat [mascǽt], Omán.
Mauritius [moríshius], Isla de Francia, o Mauricia.
Mayence [mayáns],= **Mentz.**
Mayenne [mayén], Mayena.
Mecca [mécæ], Meca.
Mediterranean [méditœréiniæn] **Sea,** Mar Mediterráneo.
Memphis [mémfis], Menfis.
Mentz [ments], Maguncia.
Metaurus [metórus], Metauro.
Meuse [mœs], Mosa.
Middleburg [mídœlbœrg], Midelburgo.
Milanese [milanís], Milanesado.
Minorca [minórca], Menorca.
Mississippi [misisípi], Misisipí.
Missouri [misúri], Misurí.
Mobile [mobíl], Mobila.
Mœsia [míšhiæ], Mesia.
Montpelier [monpelé], Mompeller.
Montserrat [montserrát], Monserrate.
Morocco [moróco], Marruecos.
Moscow [móscou], Moscú.
Moselle [mošél], Mosela.
Moukden [múkdén], Mukden.
Muscate [muscǽt], Omán.
Muscovy [múscovi], Moscovia.
Mycenæ [maisíni], Micenas.
Mysor [maisór], Maisur o Misora.

N

Naples [néipœlš], Nápoles.
Narbonne [narbón], Narbona.
Navarre [navár], Navarra.
Nazareth [nášarez], Nazaret.
Nejd [neyd], Neyed.

Netherlands [néᴅerlandŝ], Países Bajos, Holanda.
Neuburg [nóiburg], Neoburgo.
New Brunswick [brúnŝuic], Nuevo Brunswick.
New England [inglænd], Nueva Inglaterra.
Newfoundland [niúfundland], Terranova.
New Orleans [órleanŝ], Nueva Orleáns.
New South Wales [-uelŝ], Nueva Gales del Sur.
New York [yórk], Nueva York.
New Zealand [zíland], Nueva Zelandia.
Nicæa [náisiæ], Nicea.
Nice [nis], Niza.
Nile [náil], Nilo.
Nineveh [nínive], Nínive.
Nippon [nipón], Nipón, Nifón.
Normandy [nórmandi], Normandía.
North America [américæ], América del Norte.
North Carolina [cæroláinæ], Carolina del Norte.
North Sea, Mar del Norte.
Norway [nóruei], Noruega.
Nova Scotia [nóvæ skóŝhiæ], Nueva Escocia.
Nova Zembla [nóvæ ŝémblæ], Nueva Zembla.
Numantia [niumænŝhiæ], Numancia.
Nuremberg [niúrembrœg], Nuremberga.

O

Oceania [oshiǽniæ], **Oceanica** [-ǽnicæ], Oceanía.
Odessa [odésa], Odesa.
Old Castile [castíl], Castilla la Vieja.
Olives (Mount of), Olivet [ólivet], Monte Oliveto.
Olympia [olímpiæ], Olimpia.
Olympus [olímpus], Olimpo.
Olynthus [olínzus], Olinto.
Ophir [ófœr], Ofir.
Orange Free State [óranʏ fri stéit], Estado Libre de Orange.
Ostend [osténd], Ostende.
Ottoman [ótomæn] **Empire,** Imperio Otomano.
Oxus [óxus], Oxo.

P

Pacific Ocean, Océano Pacífico.
Palatinate [palǽtinet], Palatinado.
Palestine [pǽlestain], Palestina.
Palmyra [pælmáira], Palmira.
Pamphylia [pamfíliæ], Panfilia.
Parnassus [parnǽsus], Parnaso.
Parthia [párziæ], Partia.
Pekin [píking], Pekín.
Pella [pélæ], Pela.
Peloponnesus [péloponísus], Peloponeso.
Pennine Alps [pénain alps], Alpes Peninos.
Pennsylvania [pénsilvénia], Pensilvania.
Pensacola, Penzacola.
Pergamum [pœ́rgamum], Pérgamo.
Perpignan [pérpiñán], Perpiñán.
Persian Gulf, Golfo Pérsico.
Perugia [perúʏa], Perusa.
Petrograd [pétrogræd], Petrogrado.
Pharsalia [farséiliæ], Farsalia.
Philadelphia, Filadelfia.
Philippi [filípai], Filipos.
Philippines [fílipinŝ], Filipinas.
Philippopolis [filipópolis], Filipópolis.
Phocis [fósis], Fócide.
Phœnicia, Phenicia [feníŝhia], Fenicia.
Phrygia [fríʏia], Frigia.
Picardy [pícardi], Picardía.
Piedmont [pídmont], Piamonte.
Pillars of Hercules [jérkiuliŝ], Columnas de Hércules.
Piræus [pairíus], Pireo.
Placentia [plasénŝhia], Plasencia.
Platæa [plætíæ], Platea.
Poland [póuland], Polonia.
Polynesia [póliníŝhiæ], Polinesia.
Pompeii [pompéyi], Pompeya.
Pontus [póntus], Ponto.
Port Arthur [árᴅœr], Puerto Arturo.
Port-au-Prince [pórto-prǽns], Puerto Príncipe.
Port Mahon [majóun], Puerto Mahón.
Port of Spain [spéin], Puerto (de) España.
Porto Rico [pórto ríco], Puerto Rico.
Prague [préig], Praga.
Pressburg [présburg], Presburgo.
Prince Edward [éduard] **Island,** Isla del Príncipe Eduardo.
Provence [prováns], Provenza.
Providence [próvidens], Providencia.
Prussia [prúshiæ], Prusia.
Pyrenees [pirinís], Pirineos.

R

Rætia [ríŝhiæ], Retia.
Ratisbon [rǽtiŝbon], **Regensberg** [réguensbœrg], Ratisbona (ciudad de Alemania).
Red Sea, Mar Rojo.
Rheims [ræns], Reims.
Rhine [ráin], Rin o Rhin.
Rhineland [ráinlænd], Provincias Renanas.
Rhodes [róudŝ], Rodas.
Rhodesia [rodíŝhiæ], Rodesia.
Rhone [róun], Ródano.
Rif, Riff [rif], (el) Rif.
Rochelle (La) [róŝhél], La Rochela.
Rocky [róki] **Mountains,** Montes Rocosos o Rocallosos.
Romagna [romániæ], Romaña.
Rome [róum], Roma.
Rouen [rúen *o* ruán], Ruán.
Roumania [ruméinia], Rumania.
Roussillon [rúsillón], Rosellón.
Russia [rúŝhia], Rusia.

S

Saint-Nazaire [sǽn náŝeir], San Nazario.
Saint-Quentin [sǽn kántǽn], San Quintín.
Salamis [sálamis], Salamina.
Salonika [sáloníkæ], Salónica.
Salt Lake, Lago Salado.
Samothrace [sámozreis], Samotracia.
Sandwich Islands, Islas de Hauái.
Saragossa [særagósa], Zaragoza.
Sardinia [sardínia], Cerdeña.
Sarmatia [sarméiŝhiæ], Sarmacia.
St. Gothard [san gotár, sent gózard], San Gotardo.
St. Helena [sent jelínæ], Santa Elena.
St. Kitts [kits], San Kitts o San Cristóbal.
St. Lucia [lúŝhiæ], Santa Lucía.
St. Petersburg [pítœrsbœ́rg], San Petersburgo.
Savoy [savói], Saboya.
Saxe-Coburg [sacs kóbœrg], Sajonia-Coburgo.—**S.-Gotha** [gotæ], Sajonia-Gotha.—**S.-Weimar** [váimar], Sajonia-Wéimar.
Saxony [sǽxoni], Sajonia.
Scamander [scamǽndœr], Escamandro.
Scandinavia [scændinéiviæ], Escandinavia.
Scania [skéinia], Escania.
Schaffhausen [shafjáuŝen], Escafusa.
Scheldt [ŝhelt], Escalda.
Scotland, Escocia.
Scutari [skútari], Escutari.
Seine [séin], Sena.
Seoul [siúl], Seúl.
Serb-Croat-Slovene State [sœrb-cróat-slovín], Servia-Croacia-Eslovenia.
Serbia [sœ́rbiæ], (antes) **Servia,** Servia.
Severn [sévœrn], Severna.
Seville [sévil, sevíl], Sevilla.
Shantung [ŝhǽntúng], Chantung.
Sheba [shíbæ], Sabá.
Shetland [ŝhétland] **Islands,** Islas de Zetlandia.
Sicily [sísili], Sicilia.
Sienna [siéna], Sena.
Slavonia [slævóniæ], Eslavonia.
Slovakia [slovákiæ], Eslovaquia.

Slovenia [slovíniæ], Eslovenia.
Smyrna [smœrna], Esmirna.
Society Islands, Islas de la Sociedad, Tahití.
Soleure [solœr], Soleura.
Somaliland [somǽlilǽnd], Somalia.
Soudan [sudǽn], Sudán.
Sound [sáund], Sund.
South Africa, Union of, Unión Sudafricana.
South America [américæ], América del Sur, Sud-América.
South Carolina [cároláinæ], Carolina del Sur.
South Dakota [dakótæ], Dakota del Sur.
Spain [spéin], España.
Spanish America [américæ], Hispano-América, América Española.
Sparta [spárta], Esparta.
Spitzbergen [spitsbœrgœn], Espizberga.
Spoleto [spoléito], Espoleto.
Sporades [spóradiŝ], Espórades.
Stambul [stæmbúl], Estambul.
Stockholm [stócjoulm], Estocolmo.
Straits Settlements, Establecimientos del Estrecho (de Malaca).
Strasburg [strǽsbœrg], Estrasburgo.
Stromboli [strómboli], Estrómboli.
Styria [stíriæ], Estiria.
Sunda [súndæ] Isles, Islas de la Sonda.
Swabia [suéibia], Suabia o Suebia.
Sweden [suídœn], Suecia.
Switzerland [suítsœrland], Suiza.
Syracuse [sírakius], Siracusa.
Syria [síria], Siria.

T

Tagus [téigus], Tajo.
Tahiti [tæhiti], Tahití.
Tamatave [támatav], Tamatava.
Tanganyika [tængænyíkæ], Tangañica, Tanganyica.
Tangier [tangícœr], Tánger.
Tartary [tártari], Tatary [tátari], Tartaria.
Taurus [tórus], Tauro.
Texas [técsæs], Tejas.
Thames [temŝ], Támesis.
Thapsus [zápsus], Tapso.
Thebes [zibŝ], Tebas.
Thermopylæ [zœrmópili], Termópilas.
Thessalonica [zesálonica], Tesalónica.
Thessaly [zésali], Tesalia.
Thibet [tibét], Tibet.
Thrace [zres], Tracia.
Tiberias [taibírias], Tiberíades.
Ticino [tisíno], Tesino.
Tobago [tobéigo], Tabago.
Tokio, Tokyo, [tókio], Tokío.
Toulon [tulón], Tolón.
Toulouse [tulús], Tolosa.
Touraine [turén], Turena.
Tours [tur], Turs.
Trebizond [trébiŝónd], Trebisonda.
Trent, Trento.
Treves [trivŝ], Tréveris.
Triest [triést], Trieste.
Troy [troi], Troya.
Tunis [túnis], Túnez.
Turkestan [tœrkestǽn], Turquestán.

Turkey [tœrki], Turquía.
Tuscany [túscani], Toscana.
Tusculum [túskiulum], Túsculo.
Tyre [táiær], Tiro.
Tyrol [tírol], Tirol.
Tyrrhenian [tirrínian] Sea, Mar Tirreno.

U

Ukraine [iúkrein], Ucrania.
Ulm [ulm], Ulma.
United States of America, Estados Unidos de América.
Unterwalden [úntœrválden], Undervald.
Upper Egypt [íript], Alto Egipto.
Ural [iural] Mountains, Montes Urales.

V

Valenciennes [válansién], Valencienes.
Varennes [váren], Varenas.
Vauclus [voclúŝ], Valclusa.
Veii [víyai], Veyes.
Vendome [vandóm], Vandoma.
Venetia [veníŝhiæ], Véneto.
Venice [vénis], Venecia.
Versailles [versáll], Versalles.
Vesuvius [vesiúvius], Vesuvio.
Vienna [viéna], Viena.
Vienne [vién], Viena (de Francia).
Villefranche [vilfránŝh], Villafranca.
Vincennes [vinsénŝ o vænsén], Vincenas.
Virgin Islands, Islas Vírgenes.
Vosges [voŷ], Vosgos.

W

Wales [uéilŝ], Gales.
Wallachia [uoléikia], Valaquia.
Warsaw [uórso], Vɪ rsovia.
Wartburg [vártburk], Wartburgo.
Watling [uótling] Island, Isla de Guanahaní o San Salvador.
West Indies, Antillas.
Westphalia [uestféiliæ], Westfalia, Vestfalia.
West Virginia [vœryníæ], Virginia Occidental.
White Sea, Mar Blanco.
Windward Islands, Islas de Barlovento.
Wurtemburg [vúrtembœrg], Wurtemberg.

Y

Yannina [yáninæ], Janina.
Yeddo [yédo], Yedo.
Yellow River, Río Amarillo.
Yellow Sea, Mar Amarillo.
Yesso [yéso], Yeso.
Yugoslavia [iúgosláviæ], Yugoeslavia

Z

Zambesi [ŝambíŝi], Zambese, Zambeze.
Zanzibar [ŝánŝibár], Zanguébar (costa); Zanzibar (isla).
Zealand [ŝíland], Zelandia.
Zebu [zebú], Cebú.
Zululand [ŝúluland], Zululandia.

NOMBRES PROPIOS ORDINARIOS DE PERSONAS Y NOMBRES DE PERSONAJES NOTABLES

[Se dan sólo los que se escriben de distinto modo en inglés y en español.]

A

Abelard [ǽbelard], Abelardo.
Abraham [éibrajæm], Abrahán.
Absalom [ǽbsalom], Absalón.
Abu-Bekr [ábu békr], Abubéker.

Achilles [akíliŝ], Aquiles.
Adam [ǽdam], Adán.
Adela [ǽdela], Adela.
Adelaide [ǽdeleid], Adelaida.
Adeline [ǽdelain], Adelina.
Adolphus [adólfus], Adolfo.

Para la pronunciación de æ, œ, ᴅ, ŝ, ŝh, ᴜ, ŷ, ʏ, z, véase la clave al principio del libro.

Adrian [éidrian], Adriano.
Æmilius [imíliʊs], Emilio.
Æschilus [éskilʊs], Esquilo.
Æschines [éskiniŝ], Esquines.
Æschylus [éskilʊs], Esquilo.
Æsop [ísop], Esopo.
Agatha [ǽgaza], Águeda.
Agnes [ǽgnes], Inés.
Alan, Allen [ǽlan, ǽlen], Alano.
Alaric [ǽlaric], Alarico.
Albert [ǽlbœrt], Alberto
Albertus Magnus [ælbœ́rtʊs mǽgnus], Alberto
   Magno.
Alcæus [alsíʊs], Alceo.
Alexander [ǽlegŝǽndœr], Alejandro.
Alfred [ǽlfred], Alfredo.
Alice [ǽlis], Alicia.
Alphonso [ælfónŝo], Alfonso, Alonso, Ildefonso.
Alwin [ǽluin], Aluino.
Amadeus [ǽmadíʊs], Amadeo.
Ambrose [ǽmbrouŝ], Ambrosio.
Amy [éimi], Amata.
Anacreon [anákrion], Anacreonte.
Andrew [ǽndru], Andrés.
Ann, Anna [ána], Anne [æn], Ana.—Anne
   Boleyn [búlen], Ana Bolena.
Anselm [ǽnselm], Anselmo.
Antigonus [æntígonʊs], Antígono.
Antiochus [æntáiokʊs], Antíoco.
Antoninus [ǽntonáinʊs], Antonino.
Ant(h)ony [ǽntoni], Antonio.
Apuleius [æpiulíʊs], Apuleyo.
Archibald [árchibæld], Archibaldo.
Archimedes [árkimídiŝ], Arquimedes.
Aristophanes [ǽristófaniŝ], Aristófanes.
Aristotle [ǽristotœl], Aristóteles.
Arius [aráiʊs], Arrio.
Arnold [árnold], Arnaldo.
Arrian [ǽriæn], Arriano.
Artaxerxes ártæksœ́rksiŝ], Artajerjes.
Arthur [árzœr], Arturo.
Ashur-bani-pal [áshurbánipal], Asurbanipal.
Athanasius [œzanéiŝhiʊs], Atanasio.
Atilla [ǽtilæ], Atila.
Augustin [ógʊstin o (E. U.) ogústin], Austin
   [óstin], Augustín.
Augustus [ogústʊs], Augusto.
Aurelian [oríliæn], Aureliano.
Aurelius [oríliʊs], Aurelio.

B

Bede [bid], Bæda [bídæ], Beda.
Barnabas, Barnaby [bárnabæs, -bi], Bernabé.
Bartholomew [barzólomiu], Bartolomé.
Basil [bǽsil], Basilio.
Bayard [bayár], Bayardo.
Beatrice, Beatrix [bíatris, -trix], Beatriz.
Belisarius [béliséiriʊs], Belisario.
Benedict [bénedict], Benito.
Benedicta, Benita.
Bernard [bœ́rnard o bœrnár], Bernardo.
Bertha [bœ́rza], Berta.
Bertram [bœ́rtram], Beltrán.
Boccaccio [bokácho], Boccace [bokǽs], Bocacio,
   Boccaccio.
Bonaventura [bónaventúra], Buenaventura,
   Ventura.
Boniface [bónifes], Bonifacio.
Bourbon [búrbón], Borbón.
Bridget [bríyet], Brígida.
Brutus [brútʊs], Bruto.
Buddha [búdæ], Buda.

C

Cæsar [síŝœr], César.
Calvin [cálvin], Calvino.
Cambyses [cæmbáiseŝ], Cambises.
Camillus [camílʊs], Camilo.
Caracalla [cáracálæ], Caracala.

Caroline [cǽrolain], Carolina.
Cassandra [cæsǽndra], Casandra.
Cassius [caŝhiʊs], Casio.
Catharine [cǽzarin], Catherine [cǽzœrin], Ca-
   talina.
Catiline [cátilain], Catilina.
Cato [kéito], Catón.
Catullus [catúlʊs], Catulo.
Cecil [sésil], Cecilio.
Charlemagne [ŝhárleméin], Carlomagno.
Charles [charlŝ], Carlos.
Charlotte [ŝhárlot], Carlota.
Christ [cráist], Cristo.
Christian [críschan], Cristiano.
Christine [cristín], Cristina.
Christopher [crístofœr], Cristóbal.
Chrysostom [crísostom], Crisóstomo.
Ciceley [síseli], Cecilia.
Cicero [sísero], Cicerón.
Cincinnatus [sínsinéitʊs], Cincinato.
Claude [clod], Claudio.
Claudia [clódia], Claudia, Claudina.
Claudius [clódiʊs], Claudio.
Cleanthes [cliǽnzeŝ], Cleanto.
Clement [clémœnt], Clemente.
Cleobulus [clíobiúlʊs], Cleóbulo.
Clotilda [clotílda], Clotilde.
Clovis [clóvis], Clodoveo.
Columbus [colúmbʊs], Colón.
Commodus [cómodʊs], Cómodo.
Confucius [confiúŝhiʊs], Confucio.
Conrad [cónræd], Conrado.
Constance [cónstans], Constanza.
Constantine [cónstantain o -tin], Constantino.
Constantius [constǽnŝhiʊs], Constancio.
Cornelius [cornílʊs], Cornelio.
Crœsus [crísʊs], Creso.
Cyprian [síprian], Cipriano.
Cyril, Cyrillus [síril, sirílʊs], Cirilo.
Cyrus [sáirʊs], Ciro.

D

Dagobert [dágobert], Dagoberto.
Darius [daráiʊs], Darío.
Democritus [demócritʊs], Demócrito.
Demosthenes [demószeniŝ], Demóstenes.
Dennis [dénis], Dionisio.
Diogenes [daióyeniŝ], Diógenes.
Dionysius [dáioniŝhiʊs], Dionisio.
Dominic [dóminic], Domingo.
Domitian [domíŝhiæn], Domiciano.
Dorothy [dórozi], Dorotea.

E

Edmund [édmʊnd], Edmundo.
Edward [éduard], Eduardo.
Elagabalus [élagǽbalʊs], Elagábalo, Heliogábalo
   (hoy se prefiere el primero).
Eleanor, Elinor [élinœr], Leonor.
Elisha, Ellis [eláiŝha, élis], Eliseo.
Eliza [eláiŝa], Elisa.
Elizabeth [elíŝabez], Isabel.
Ellen [élen], Elena.
Elsa [élsa], Alicia.
Em(m)anuel [emmǽniuel], Manuel.
Emma, Ema o Manuela.
Emily [émili], Emilia.
Epictetus [épiktítʊs], Epicteto.
Epicurus [épikiúrʊs], Epicuro.
Erasmus [erǽsmʊs], Erasmo.
Eratosthenes [erátószeniŝ], Eratóstenes.
Ernest [œ́rnest], Ernesto.
Esther [éstœr], Ester.
Euclid [yúclid], Euclides.
Eugene [yuyín], Eugenio.
Eugenie [iúyéiní], Eugenia.
Euler [oílœr], Euler, Eulero.
Euphemia [yufímia], Eufemia.
Euphrosyne [yufrósine], Eufrosina.

Eusebius [yusíbiʊs], Eusebio.
Eustace [yústes], Eustaquio.
Eve [iv], Eva.
Ezechias [ésekáiæs], Ezequías.
Ezekiel [esíkiel], Ezequiel.

F

Fabius [féibiʊs], Fabio.
Felicia [felíshia], Felisa, Felicia.
Ferdinand [fœrdinænd], Fernando.
Florence [flórens], Florencio, Florencia
Frances [frænses], Francisca.
Francis [frænsis], Francisco.
Fredegonde [frédegónd], Fredegunda.
Frederica [frédœríca], Federica.
Frederic(k [frédœric], Federico.
Froyla, Froila o Fruela.

G

Gaius [guéiʊs], Gayo.
Galen [géilen], Galeno.
Gallienus [gæliénʊs], Galien(
Genseric [rénscœric], Genserico.
Geoffrey [réfre], Geofredo.
George [yory], Jorge.
Gerard [rerárd], Gerardo.
Germanicus [rœrménicʊs], Germánico.
Gertrude [gœrtrud], Gertrudis.
Gideon [guídion], Gedeón.
Gilbert [guílbœrt], Gilberto.
Giles [ráils], Gil.
Godfrey [gódfri], Godofredo.
Gracchii [grækiai], Gracos.
Gracchus [grækʊs], Graco.
Grace [gréis], Engracia.
Gregory [grégori], Gregorio.
Gustavus [gustéivʊs], Gustavo.
Guy [gái], Guido.

H

Hadrian [jéidriæn], Adriano.
Hannah [jæna], Ana.
Hannibal [jænibal], Aníbal.
Harold [jærold], Haraldo.
Helen [jélen], Elena.
Héloise [éiloís], Eloísa.
Helvetius [jelvíshiʊs], Helvecio.
Henrietta [jenriéta], Enriqueta.
Henry [jénri], Enrique.
Heraclitus [jéracláitʊs], Heráclito.
Herbert [jœrbœrt], Heriberto.
Herod [jérod], Herodes.
Herodotus [jeródotʊs], Herodoto.
Hesiod [jísiod], Hesíodo.
Hester [jéstœr], Ester.
Hezekiah [jésekáia], Ezequías.
Hiero [jáiiro], Herón.
Hieronymus [jáierónimʊs], Jerónimo.
Hilary [jílari], Hilario.
Hildebrand [jíldebrænd], Hildebrando.
Hipparchus [jipárcʊs], Hiparco.
Hippocrates [jipócratis], Hipócrates.
Hobart [jóbart], Huberto.
Homer [jómœr], Homero.
Honorius [jonóriʊs], Honorio.
Horace, Horatio [jóres, joréshio], Horacio.
Hortense [órtœns], Hortensia.
Hosea [josía], Oseas.
Hubert [jiúbœrt], Huberto.
Hugh [jiú], Hugo.—**H. Capet** [kéipet], Hugo Capeto.
Humbert [júmbœrt], Humberto.
Humphrey [júmfri], Hunfredo.

I

Ignatius [ignéshiʊs], Ignacio.
Innocent [ínosent], Inocencio.

Irenæus [áireníʊs], Ireneo.
Isabella [ísabéla], Isabel.
Isidore [ísidor], Isidro o Isidoro.

J

James [yeimŝ], Santiago, Jacobo, Jaime, Diego.
Jane [yéin], Juana.
Jansen, Jansenius [yænsen, sínius], Jansenio.
Jasper [yæspœr], Gaspar.
Jehovah [yijovæ], Jehová.
Jeremiah [yéremáia], **Jeremy** [yéremi], Jeremías.
Jerome [yeróum o yérom], Jerónimo.
Jesus Christ [yísʊs cráist], Jesucristo.
Joachim [yóakim], Joaquín.
Joan [yóan o yon], **Joanna** [yoéna], Juana.
Joan of Arc [yóun ov arc], Juana de Arco.
John [yon], Juan.
Jonah [yóna], Jonás.
Jonathan [yónazan] Jonatán, Jonatás.
Joseph [yóšef], José.
Josephine [yóšefin], Josefina.
Josephus [yosífʊs], Josefo.
Joshua [yóšhyua], Josué.
Josiah [yosáia], Josías.
Jovian [yóviæn], Joviano.
Judith [yúdiz], Judit.
Jugurtha [yugœrza], Yugurta.
Julia [yúlla], Julia.
Julian [yúllan], Julián; Juliano (emperador)
Juliet [yúliet], Julia.
Julius [yúliʊs], Julio.
Justinian [yʊstíniæn], Justiniano.
Justin Martyr [yústin mártœr], Justino Mártir.

K

Katharine, Katherine, Kathleen = CATHERINE.
Kempis, a [a kémpis], de Kempis.

L

Ladislas [lædislas], Ladislao.
Lætitia, Leticia.
Lambert [lémbœrt], Lamberto.
Lawrence, Laurence [lórens], Lorenzo.
Lazarus [læšarʊs], Lázaro.
Leander [liændœr], Leandro.
Leo [lío], León.
Leonard [lénard], Leonardo.
Leopold [líopould], Leopoldo.
Lepidus [lépidʊs], Lépido.
Letitia, Lettice [letíshia], Leticia.
Lewis [lúis], Luis.
Linnæus [liníʊs], Lineo.
Liutprand [liútprand], Liutprando.
Livy [lívi], Livio.
Longinus [lonyáinʊs], Longino.
Lothaire [lozéœr], Lotario.
Louis [lúis, lúi], Luis.
Louisa [luíša], **Louise** [luíŝ], Luisa, Eloísa.
Lucan [liúcœn], Lucano.
Lucia [liúshia], Lucía.
Lucian [liúshæn], Luciano.
Lucius [lúshiʊs], Lucio.
Lucretia [lucríshia], Lucrecia.
Lucretius [liucríshiʊs], Lucrecio.
Lucullus [liucúlʊs], Lúculo.
Lucy [lúsi], Lucía.
Luke [luk], Lucas.
Luther [lúzœr], Lutero.
Lycurgus [laicœrgʊs], Licurgo.
Lysander [laisændœr], Lisandro.
Lysias [lísiæs], Lisias.
Lysimachus [laisímacʊs], Lisímaco.
Lysippus [laisípʊs], Lisipo.

M

Mæcenas [mesínæs], Mecenas.
Magdalen [mǽgdalen], Magdalena.
Magellan [mayélæn], Magallanes.
Mahomet [majómet], Mahoma.
Malachi, Malachy [mǽlacai], Malaquías.
Marcel [marsél], **Marcellus** [-ʊs], Marcelo.
Margaret [márgaret], **Margery** [márvœri], Margarita.
Marian, Marion [mǽrian], Marjana.
Marius [máriʊs], Mario.
Marie Louise [marí luís], María Luisa.
Mark [mark], Marco, Marcos.
Martha [márzaį, Marta.
Martial [marshiæl], Marcial.
Mary [méri], María.
Masinissa [mǽsinísæ], Masinisa.
Matilda, Mathilda [matílda], Matilde.
Matthew [mǽziu], Mateo.
Matthias [mætzáias], Matías.
Maurice [móris], Mauricio.
Maximilian [mǽcsimílian], Maximiliano.
Messalina [mésalínæ], Mesalina.
Michael [máicael o máikel], Miguel.
Michelangelo [máikelǽnyelo], Miguel Ángel.
Miriam [míriam], María.
Mithridates [mízridéitiś], Mitrídates.
Mohammed [mojǽmed], Mahoma.
Moses [móuśeś], Moisés.

N

Napier [néipiœr], Néper, Nápier.
Nathan [nézan], Natán.
Nathanael, Nathaniel [nazǽn(a)iel], Nataniel.
Nebuchadnezzar [nébiucœdnéśar], Nabucodonosor.
Nehemiah [níjimáia], Nehemías.
Nepos [nípos], Népote.
Nero [níro], Nerón.
Nestorius [nestóriʊs], Nestorio.
Nicholas [nícolas], Nicolás.
Noah [nóa], Noé.

O

Octavius [octéiviʊs], Octavio.
Odoacer [ódoéisœr], Odoacro.
Oliver [ólivœr], Oliverio.
Origen [óriyen], Orígenes.
Osmond, Osmund [ósmʊnd], Osmundo
Othman [ózmæn], Otmán.
Otho [ózo], **Otto** [óto], Otón.
Ovid [óvid], Ovidio.

P

Patrick [pǽtric], Patricio.
Paul [pol], Pablo.
Paulina, Pauline [poláina, polína, polín], Paula, Paulina.
Pelaiah [peléya], Pelayo.
Pepin [pépin], Pepino.—**P. the Short,** Pepino el Breve.
Peregrine [péregrin], Peregrino, Peregrín.
Perseus [pœrsʊs, pœrsiʊs], Perseo.
Peter [pítœr], Pedro.
Phædrus [fídrʊs], Fedro.
Phineas [fínias], Fineas.
Philip [fílip], Felipe; Filipo (de Macedonia).
Philippa [filípa], Felipa.
Philippus [filípʊs], Filipo.
Philo Judæus [fáilo yudíʊs], Filo el Judío.
Phocion [fóshion], Foción.
Pindar [píndar], Píndaro.
Pius [páiʊs], Pío.
Plato [pléito], Platón.
Plautus [plótʊs], Plauto.
Pliny [plíni], Plinio.
Plotinus [plotáinʊs], Plótino.

Plutarch [plútarc], Plutarco.
Polybius [políbiʊs], Polibio.
Polycarp [pólicarp], Policarpo.
Polycletus [póliclitʊs], Policleto.
Polycrates [pólicratiś], Polícrates.
Pompey [pómpi], Pompeyo.
Praetorius [prǝtóriʊs], Pretorio.
Proclus [próclʊs], Proclo.
Procopius [procópiʊs], Procopio.
Prudence [prúdœns], Prudencia.
Ptolemy [tólemi], Tolomeo.
Pyrrhus [pírʊs], Pirro.
Pythagoras [pizǽgoræś], Pitágoras.

Q

Quintilian [cuintílian], Quintiliano.

R

Rachael [réchel], Raquel.
Ralph [rǽlf], Rodolfo.
Randall, Randolph [rǽndal, -olf], Randolfo.
Raphael [[rǽfael], Rafael.
Raymond [réimond], Raimundo, Ramón.
Rebecca, Rebekah [ribéca], Rebeca.
Reginald [révinald], Reinaldos, Reginaldo.
Regulus [réguiulʊs], Régulo.
René [rené], Renato.
Reuben [rúben], Rubén.
Reynold [rénold], Reinaldo.
Rhodes [rodś], Rodas.
Richard [ríchardį, Ricardo.
Robert [róbœrt], Roberto.
Roderic(k [róderic], Rodrigo.
Rodolphus [rodólfʊs], Rodolfo.
Roger [róyœr], Rogerio.
Rollo [rólo], Rollón, Rolón.
Romulus [rómyulʊs], Rómulo.
Ronald [rónald], Renaldo.
Rose [róuś], Rosa.
Roland, Rowland [róland], Rolando.
Rudolph [rúdolf], Rodolfo.
Rupert [rúpœrt], Ruperto.

S

Saladin [sǽladin], Saladino.
Sallust [sǽlust], Salustio.
Sam(p)son [sǽm(p)sʊn], Sansón.
Sardanapalus [sárdanapéilʊs], Sardanápalo.
Scaliger [scǽlivœr], Escalígero.
Scipio [sípio], Escipión.—**S. Africanus,** [ǽfrikéinʊs], Escipión el Africano.
Sennacherib [senǽkœrib], Senaquerib.
Sertorius [sœrtóriʊs], Sertorio.
Severus [sevírʊs], Severo.
Sigismund [sírismʊnd], Segismundo.
Silvanus, Silvan [silvénus, sílvan], Silvano.
Silvester, Sylvester [silvéstœr], Silvestre.
Solomon [sólomʊn], Salomón.
Solyman [sólimæn], Solimán.
Sophia [sofáia], Sofía.
Sophocles [sófocliś], Sófocles.
Spartacus [spártacʊs], Espartaco.
Stephen [stíven], Esteban.
Strabo [stréibo], Estrabón.
Stradivarius [strǽdivéiriʊs], Estradivario.
Suetonius [suetóniʊs], Suetonio.
Suleiman [súleimán], Solimán.
Sulla [súlæ], Sila.
Susan, Susanna [súsan, suśǽna], Susana.

T

Tacitus [tǽsitʊs], Tácito.
Tamerlane [tǽmœrlén], Tamerlán.
Terence [térens], Terencio.
Tertullian [tœrtúliæn], Tertuliano.
Thaddeus [zædíʊs o zǽdiʊs], Tadeo.
Thales [záliś], Tales.
Themistocles [zemístocliś], Temístocles.

Theobald [zíobald], Teobaldo.
Theocritus [zeócraitʊs], Teócrito.
Theodore [zíodor], Teodoro.
Theodoric [zíódoric], Teodorico.
Theodosius [ziodóshiʊs], Teodosio.
Theophilus [zíófilʊs], Teófilo.
Theophrastus [zíofræstʊs], Teofrasto
Theresa [tœrísa o terésa], Teresa.
Thomas [tómas], Tomás.
Thrasybulus [zræsibíɡlʊs], Trasíbulo
Thucydides [ziusídidiŝ], Tucídides.
Tiberius [taibírius], Tiberio.
Timothy [tímoʑi], Timoteo.
Timour [taimúr], Timur.
Titian [tíŝhæn], el Ticiano.
Titus [táitʊs], Tito.
Tobias [tobáiæŝ], Toby [tóubi], Tobías.
Trajan [tréiγæn], Trajano.
Tribonian [tribóniæn], Triboniano.
Turenne [túrén], Turena.
Tybald [tíbald], Teobaldo.

U

Ulpian [úlpiæn], Ulpiano.
Urban [œ́rban], Urbano.
Uriah [yuráia], Urías.

V

Valens [véilœnŝ], Valente.
Valentine [vǽlentain], Valentín.
Valentinian [vǽlentíniæn], Valentiniano.
Valerian [vælériæn], Valeriano.

Veremond [véremond], Bermudo, Veremundo.
Vergil [vœrryil], Virgilio.
Veronese [véironéise], el Veronés.
Vespasian [vespéiγiæn], Vespasiano.
Vespucci [vespúchi], Vespucio.
Vincent [vínsœnt], Vicente.
Virgil [vœrryil], Virgilio.
Vitruvius [vitrúvius], Vitruvio.

W

Walter [uóltœr], Gualterio.
Wilhelmina [uíljelmína], Guillermina
William [uíllam], Guillermo.

X

Xavier [ŝǽvicœr], Javier.
Xenocrates [ŝenócratiŝ], Jenócrates.
Xenophanes [ŝenófaniŝ], Jenófanes.
Xenophon [ŝénofʊn], Jenofonte.
Xerxes [ŝœrksiŝ], Jerjes.

Y

Yahveh [yáve], Jehová.

Z

Zachary [ŝǽcari], Zacarías.
Zeno [ŝíno], Zenón, Cenón.
Zoroaster [ŝóroœstœr], Zoroastro.
Zwingli [tsvíngle], Zuinglio.

NOMBRES DIMINUTIVOS Y ABREVIADOS DE PERSONAS USADOS FAMILIARMENTE EN INGLÉS

Al [æl] por Albert, Alfred o Alexander.
Aleck [ǽlec] por Alexander, Alejandro.

Bab [bæb] por Barbara, Barbarita.
Bat [bæt] por Bartholomew, Bartolo.
Bec, Becky [béki] por Rebecca, Rebeca.
Bel, Belle [bel] por Isabella, Bela, Belita.
Ben, Benny por Benjamin, Benjamín.
Bert, Bertie [bœrt, bœrti] por Herbert o Albert, Heriberto o Alberto.
Bess, Bet, Betsy, Bessy, Betty, Lizzie por Elizabeth, Belita, Belica.
Biddy por Bridget, Brígida.
Bob, Rob por Robert, Roberto.
Bill, Billy [bill, billi] por William, Guillermito.

Carrie [cǽrri] por Caroline, Carolina.
Charley, Charlie, Charly [chárli] por Charles, Carlitos.
Cis por Cicely, Cecilia.
Clare [cléær] por Clara, Clarita.

Dan [dæn] por Daniel, Daniel.
Davy [dévi] por David, David.
Dick, Dicky por Richard, Ricardito.
Dol, Dolly [dol, dóli] por Dorothy, Dorotea.
Dorick [dóric] por Theodoric, Teodorico.
Dy [dai] por Diana, Diana.

Ed, Eddy por Edward, Edwin, Edgar o Edmund.
Effie [éfi] por Euphemia, Eufemia.
Ellick por Alexander, Alejandro.
Etta [éta] por Henrietta, Enriqueta.

Fan, Fanny [fæn, fǽni] por Frances, Francisca, Frasquita, Paquita, Panchita, Currita, Paca, Farruca.
Fred por Frederick, Frederiquito.

Hal, Harry por Henry, Enriquito.
Harriet, Hatty, Hetty, Netty por Henrietta, Enriqueta.
Hodge [joγ] por Roger, Rogerio.

Jack por John, Juanito.
Jeff por Geoffrey o Jefferson.
Jem, Jemmy, Jim, Jimmie por James, Santiago, Jaimito, Jacobo.
Jerry por Jeremiah, Jerónimo, Geromo.
Jennie, Jenny por Jane, Juanita.
Joe, Josy [róu, róuŝi] por Joseph, Pepe, Pepito, Pepillo.
Johnny [róni] por John, Juanito, Juancho, Juanchito.
Josie [róuŝi] por Josephine, Pepa, Pepita, Pepilla.

Kate, Kitty por Catharine, Catuca, Catujita.
Kit por Christopher, Tobalito.

Larry, Laurie, Lawrie por Lawrence, Lorenzo.
Len por Leonard, Leonardo.
Letty por Letitia, Leticia.
Libby, Lib, Lizzie, Liz por Eliza, Elisa.
Lulu [lúlu] por Lucy y Louisa, Lucía, Luisita.

Madge, Maggie, Meg, Margery por Margaret, Margarita.
Magda por Magdalen.
Mae, May por Mary, Mariquita, Maruja.
Mat por Matthew, Mateo.
Mat, Mattie, Matty por Martha y Mathilda.
Maud [mod] por Mathilda, Matilde.
Mike [máik] por Michael, Miguelito.
Mol, Molly por Mary, Mariquita, Maruja.

Nan, Nancy por Ann, Anita.
Ned, Neddy por Edward o Edwin, Eduardo.

Para la pronunciación de æ, œ, ɒ, ŝ, ŝh, ʊ, ȳ, γ, ʑ, véase la clave al principio del libro.

Nel, Nelly por **Ellen** y **Eleanor,** Elenita y Leonorcita.
Netty por **Henrietta,** Enriqueta.
Nick por **Nicholas,** Nicolasito.

Pam por **Pamela,** Pamela.
Patty por **Martha,** Marta.
Peg, Peggy por **Margaret,** Margarita.
Pen por **Penelope,** Penélope.
Phil por **Philip,** Felipe.
Prue [pru] por **Prudence,** Prudencia.

Reta [ríta] por **Margaret,** Margarita.

Sal, Sally por **Sarah,** Sara.
Sam por **Samuel,** Samuel.

Sil por **Silvester,** Silvestre.
Sim por **Simon,** Simón, Simoncito.

Ted, Teddy, Theo por **Theodore,** Teodoro.
Tilda por **Mathilda,** Matilde.
Tim por **Timothy,** Timoteo.
Tom, Tommy por **Thomas,** Tomás.
Tony por **Anthony,** Toño, Toñico, Antoñito.
Tracy por **Theresa,** Teresita.

Val por **Valentine,** Valentín.
Vicky por **Victoria,** Victorina.
Vin por **Vincent,** Vicente.

Walt por **Walter,** Gualterio.
Will, Willie por **William,** Guillermito.

Zach [s̃æc] por **Zachary,** Zacarías.

ABREVIATURAS MÁS USUALES

[La abreviatura *sq.* significa *símbolo químico*]

A

A, *sq.* argon.
A. Academician; Academy; America; American; acre(s).
a. accepted; acre(s); alto; are(área); at.
aa. (med.) ana (de cada cosa).
A. A. S. American Association for the Advancement of Science.
A. A. C. *Anno ante Christum* (año a. de J. C.)
A. A. of A. Automobile Association of America.
A. B. Bachelor of Arts.
A. B. C. Argentina, Brazil, and Chile (el A. B. C.).
abs. re. *absente reo* (en la ausencia del acusado).
A. C. Alpine Club; alternating current; *Ante Christum.* (antes de J. C.); Army Corps.
acct., a/c. account (cuenta).
A. D. *Anno domini* (año de Cristo).
a. d. after date; *ante diem* (antes del día).
ad. advertisement (anuncio).
ad fin. *ad finem* (al fin).
ad inf. *ad infinitum* (hasta el infinito).
ad lib. *ad libitum* (a voluntad).
Adm. Admiral; Admiralty.
Adm. Co. Admiralty Court.
adv. ad valorem; *adversus* (contra); advertisement; advocate.
A. E. F. American Expeditionary Forces.
ae., aet., aetat. *œtatis* (de edad).
A. F. of L. American Federation of Labor.
Ag, *sq., argentum* (plata).
agt. agent.
Al, *sq.* aluminium.
Ala. Alabama.
Alas. Alaska.
a. m. *ante meridiem* (a. m., antes del mediodía).
A. M. *Anno mundi* (año del mundo); *artium magister* (bachiller en artes); *ante meridiem* (antes del mediodía); Ave Maria.
amt. amount.
an. *anno* (año); anonymous.
anon. anonymous.
ans. answer (repuesta; resultado—de un problema).
A. N. Z. A. C., *o* **Anzac.** Australian and New Zealand Army Corps (ll. gen. *Anzac,* como palabra completa).
app. appendix; appointed.
Apr. April.
aq., Aq. *aqua* (agua).
A. R. *Anno Regni* (año del reinado).
A. R. A. Associate of the Royal Academy.
arith. arithmetic.
Ariz. Arizona.

Ark. Arkansas.
A. R. R. *Anno regni Regis, Reginæ* (en el año del reinado del rey, de la reina).
art. article; artillery.
As, *sq.* arsenic.
A. S. C. E. American Society of Civil Engineers.
A. S. M. E. American Society of Mechanical Engineers.
A. S. P. C. A. American Society for the Prevention of Cruelty to Animals.
assn. association.
asst. assistant.
A. S. T. M. American Society for Testing Materials.
A. T. S. American Temperance Society; American Tract Society.
att., atty. attorney.
Att.-Gen. Attorney-General.
Au, *sq., aurum* (oro).
A. U. C. *ab urbe condita* (de la fundación de Roma).
Aug. August.
Auth. Ver. Authorized Version (de la Biblia).
a. v. *annos vixit* (vivió . . . años).
Av., ave. avenue.
av., avdp. avoirdupois.

B

B, *sq.* boron.
b. base; bass; book; born; brother.
B. British.
B. A. Bachelor of Arts; British Academy; British America.
Ba, *sq.* barium.
B. Agr. Bachelor of Agriculture.
bal. balance.
B. Arch. Bachelor of Architecture.
barr. barrister.
Bart., baronet.
bbl. (*pl.* **bbls.**) barrel(s).
B. C. before Christ; British Columbia.
B. C. E. Bachelor of Civil Engineering.
B. C. L. Bachelor of Civil Law.
bd. board; bond; bound.
bdl. (*pl.* **bdls.**) bundle(s).
bds. boards (pasta).
Be, *sq.* beryllium.
Bé. Baumé (grados Baumé).
b. e. bill of exchange.
bet. between.
b. h. p. brake horse power (potencia al freno).
Bi, *sq.* bismuth.
B. I. British India.

bl. (*pl.* **bls.**) bale(s); barrel(s).
B. L. Bachelor of Laws.
B/L. bill of lading.
b. l. bill of lading (conocimiento); breechloader; breechloading.
bldg. building (edificio).
B. L. E. Brotherhood of Locomotive Engineers.
b. m. board measure.
B. M. E. Bachelor of Mining Engineering.
B. O. T. Board of Trade.
b. p. below proof; bill of parcels; bills payable.—
B. P. O. E. Benevolent and Protective Order of Elks.
Br. Breton; British.
Br, *sq.* bromine.
Br. Am. British America.
b. rec. bills receivable.
Bros. brothers.
b. s. balance sheet; bill of sale.
B. S. Bachelor of Surgery.
B. Sc. Bachelor of Science.
Bt., bt. baronet; bought.
B. T. U. British thermal units.
bu., bus. bushel, bushels.
bx. box.

C

C, *sq.* carbon.
C. Cæsar; Caius; Cape; Catholic; centigrade; Chancellor; Chancery; Congress; Consul; Court.
c. cent; centime; chapter; cubic; current; center. —**c. to c.** center to center (de centro a centro).
Ca, *sq.* calcium.
C. A. Chartered Accountant; Chief Accountant; Confederate Army; Court of Appeal; Central America.
cal. calendar; calends; calorie.
Cal., Calif. California.
Cam., Camb. Cambridge.
Can. Canadá; Canadian.
cap. capital (mayúscula); capitalize; captain; *caput* (capítulo).
Capt. captain.
C. B. Cape Breton; Companion of the Bath; Common Bench.
Cb, *sq.* columbium.
cc., cc, c. c. cubic centimeter(s).
C. C. C. Christ's College, Cambridge; Corpus Christi College.
Cd, *sq.* cadmium.
Ce, *sq.* cerium.
C. E. Canada East; Civil Engineer; Church of England.
cent. centigrade; central; *centum* (ciento); century.
cert. certificate; certify
cf. *confer* (cotéjese).
c. f. & i. cost, freight, and insurance.
C. G. Consul-general; Captain-general; center of gravity.
cg. centigram(me.
C. G. S. *o* **c. g. s.** centimeter-gram-second (C. G. S., centímetro-gramo-segundo).
Ch. Chancery; Charles; China; Church.
ch. chapter; child, children; church.
chap. chapter.
Chas. Charles.
Chem. chemical, chemistry.
c. i. f. cost, insurance and freight (c. i. f., *o* c. s. f. costo, seguro y flete).
Cl, *sq.* chlorine.
cl. centiliter; clause; cloth (pasta de libros).
cm. centimeter.—**cm.²** square centimeter.—**cm.³** cubic centimeter.
c. m. circular measure (radianes).
Co, *sq.* cobalt.
Co. company; county.
c. o. care of; carried over.

C. O. D. collect (*o* cash) on delivery (cóbrese a la entrega).
Col. Colonel; Colorado; Colossians.
Colo. Colorado.
com. commentary; commerce; commercial.
Com. Commander; Commission; Commissioner; Committee; Commodore.
comp. comparative; compare; composer; compound.
Com. Ver. Common Version (de la Biblia).
con. conclusion; contra.
Cong. Congregational; Congress; Congressional.
Conn. Connecticut.
Cor. Corinthians; coroner.
cor. corpus; corrected; correction; correspondent.
cos cosine.
cot cotangent.
c. p. candle power; (gen. **C. P.**) chemically pure.
cp. compare (cotéjese, véase).
C. P. A. certified public accountant.
Cr, *sq.* chromium.
cr. credit.
cres., cresc. crescendo.
Cs, *sq.* cæsium.
C. S. Christian Science; Civil Service; Court of Sessions.
cs. cases (cajas).
C. S. A. Confederate States Army; Confederate States of America.
C. S. I. Companion of the Star of India.
Ct. Connecticut; court; Count.
ct. cent; county.
c. to c. center to center.
cts. cents; centimes.
Cu, *sq.*, *cuprum* (cobre).
cu., cub. cubic.
C. V. Common Version (versión corriente—de la Biblia).
C. W. Canada West.
c. w. o. cash with order.
cwt. hundredweight(s.

D

d. day; denarius (penique); died; dime; dollar.
d/a. days after acceptance.
D/A. deposit account.
Dan. Daniel; Danish.
D. A. R. Daughters of the American Revolution.
D. C. *da capo* (desde el principio); direct current; District of Columbia; District Court.
D. C. L. Doctor of Civil Law.
D. D. Doctor of Divinity.
d. d. days after date; day's date.
D. D. S. Doctor of Dental Surgery.
Dec. December.
deg. degree.
Del. Delaware.
Dep., Dept. department; deponent; deputy.
dft. defendant; draft.
D. G. *Dei gratia* (por la gracia de Dios); Director General.
dg. decigram.
dial. dialect, dialectical.
diam. diameter.
diff. difference; different; differs.
dim. diminuendo; diminutive.
dist. distance; district.
dkl. dekaliter(s).
Dkm. dekameter(s).
dl. deciliter.
D. L. O. Dead Letter Office.
dm. decimeter.
D. Mus. Doctor of Music.
D. O. Doctor of Osteopathy.
do. ditto (ídem, lo mismo).
dol., doll. (*pl.* **dols.**) dollar.
doz. dozen, dozens.
Dr. debtor; doctor.
dr. dram; drawer.

dram. pers. *dramatis personæ* (personajes dramáticos).
D. Sc. Doctor of Science.
D. V. *Deo volente* (Dios mediante).
D. V. M. Doctor of Veterinary Medicine.
dwt. pennyweight.
Dy, *sq.* dysprosium.
D. Z. Doctor of Zoology.

E

E. earl; earth; east; eastern; engineer; English.
ea. each.
E. & O. E. errors and omissions excepted.
E. C. Eastern Central (distrito postal de Londres); Established Church.
Eccl., Eccles. Ecclesiastes.
eccl., eccles. ecclesiastic.
ed. edition; editor (redactor).
Ed., Edin. Edinburgh.
edit. edited; edition.
E. E. Electrical Engineer; errors excepted.
E. E. & M. P. Envoy Extraordinary and Minister Plenipotentiary.
Eg. Egypt.
e. g., *exempli gratia* (v. g.).
E. I., E. Ind. East India; East Indies.
elec., elect. electrical; electricity.
Eliz. Elizabeth; Elizabethan.
E. lon., E. long. east longitude.
E. M. F. electromotive force.
E. N. E. east-northeast.
Eng. England; English.
eng., engin. engineer; engineering.
Erb, *sq.* erbium.
E. S. E. east-southeast.
esp., espec. especially.
Esq., Esqr. (*pl.* con **s**) esquire.
est., estab. established.
E. T., e. t. electric telegraph; English translation.
et al. *et alibi* (y en otra parte); *et alii* (y otros).
etc. et cetera.
et seq. *et sequentia* (y que sigue).
Eu, *sq.* europium.
Eur. Europe; European.
Ex., Exod. Exodus.
Exc. Excellency.
exc. excellent; except; excepted; exception.
Exch. exchange; exchequer.
ex. div. without dividend.
Exec., Exr. executor.
Execx., Exrx., Exx. executrix.
exp. export, exported; express.
Ezek. Ezekiel.

F

F, *sq.* fluorine.
F. Fahrenheit; Father; Fellow; Friday.
f. farthing; fathom; folio; forte (en la música); franc.
F. A. G. S. Fellow of the American Geographical Society.
Fah., Fahr. Fahrenheit.
F. A. M. Free and Accepted Masons.
far. farad; farthing.
F. A. S. Fellow of the Antiquarian Society.
F. B. S. Fellow of the Botanical Society.
fcp., fcap. foolscap.
F. D. Defender of the Faith.
Fe, *sq., ferrum* (hierro).
Feb. February.
ff. folios; following; fortissimo.
F. G. S. Fellow of the Geological Society.
fin. *ad finem* (al fin).
Fin. Sec. financial secretary.
Fla. Florida.
F. M. Field Marshal; Foreign Mission.
fo., folio.
f. o. b. free on board (libre a bordo).
fol. folio.

fol., foll. following.
f. o. r. free on rail (libre en la estación ferroviaria).
F. P. fire-plug.
Fr. France; Francis; French; Friday.
fr. fragments; francs; from.
F. R. A. S. Fellow of the Royal Astronomical Society.
F. R. C. P. Fellow of the Royal College of Physicians (Londres).
F. R. C. S. Fellow of the Royal College of Surgeons (Londres).
Fred., Fredk. Frederick.
F. R. G. S. Fellow of the Royal Geographical Society.
Fri. Friday.
F. R. I. B. A. Fellow of the Royal Institute of British Architects.
F. R. S. Fellow of the Royal Society.
F. S. A. Fellow of the Society of Antiquities (o of Atrs).
Ft. fort.—**ft.** feet, foot.
F. Z. S. Fellow of the Zoological Society.

G

G., German; Germany.
g. genitive; gram(me; guide.
Ga. Georgia.
Ga, *sq.* gallium.
Gal. Galatians; Galen.
gal., gall. (*pl.* **gals.**) gallon(s).
G. A. R. Grand Army of the Republic.
G. B. Great Britain.
G. B. & I. Great Britain and Ireland.
g. c. d. greatest common divisor.
g. c. m. greatest common measure.
G. C. S. I. Grand Commander of the Star of India.
Gd, *sq.* gadolinium.
G. D. Grand Duchess, Grand Duke.
Ge, *sq.* germanium.
gen. gender; general(ly; genus.
Gen. General; Genesis; Geneva.
Geo. George, Georgia.
Ger., Germ. German.
g. gr. great gross.
G. H. Q. General Headquarters.
Gl, *sq.* glucinum.
G. M. Grand Master.
G. M. T. Greenwich mean time.
Gov. Government; Governor.
Gov. Ptg. Off. Government Printing Office.
Govt. Government.
G. Ph. Graduate in Pharmacy.
G. P. O. General Post Office.
gr. grain; gram(me.
gs. guineas.
G. T. Good Templars; Grand Tiler.
gt. *gutta* (gota).—*pl.* **gtt.**
Gt. Br., Gt. Brit. Great Britain.
gu. guinea.

H

H, *sq.* hydrogen.
h. hardness; height; hour; hundred.
H. B. M. Her (*o* His) Britannic Majesty.
H. C. Herald's College; House of Commons.
h. c. f. highest common factor.
hdkf. handkerchief.
H. E. His Eminence; His Excellency; Hydraulic Engineer.
He, *sq.* helium.
hf. half.—**hf. cf.** half calf.
Hg, *sq., hydrargyrum* (mercurio).
hg. hektogram(me.
H. H. His (*o* Her) Highness; His Holiness.
hhd. hogshead.
H. I. Hawaiian Islands.
H. I. H. His (*o* Her) Imperial Highness.
H. I. M. His (*o* Her) Imperial Majesty.

H. L. House of Lords.
H. M. His (o Her) Majesty.
H. M. S. His (o Her) Majesty's service, ship o steamer.
Ho, sq. holmium.
Hon. Honorable.
hort., hortic. horticulture.
h. p. horse power; half pay.
H. Q. Headquarters.
H. R. Home Rule; House of Representatives.
hr. (pl. **hrs.**) hour(s).
H. R. H. His (o Her) Royal Highness.
H. T. Hawaii Territory.
ht. height

I

I, sq. iodine.
I. Idaho; island.
Ia., Iowa.
I. A. C. S. International Annealed Copper Standard.
ib., ibid. ibidem (ibídem).
Ice., Icel. Iceland, Icelandic.
id. idem. (ídem).
Ida. Idaho.
i. e. id est (esto es, es decir).
i. h. p. indicated horsepower.
Ill., Ills. Illinois.
imp. imperial; imported; importer.
in. inch(es).
In, sq. indium.
inc. including; incorporated.
incl. including.
incog. incognito.
incor. incorporated.
Ind. India; Indian; Indiana.
init. initio (al principio).
in. loc. cit. in the place cited.
I. N. R. I. Iesus Nazarenus, Rex Iudæorum (Inri—Jesús Nazareno, Rey de los Judíos).
ins. inches; insurance.
inst. instant; institute.
int. interest.
in trans. in transitu (en el tránsito).
inv. invented; inventor; invoice.
Io. Iowa.
I. O. O. F. Independent Order of Odd Fellows.
I. O. U. I owe you (abonaré).
i. q. idem quod (lo mismo que).
Ir, sq. iridium.
Is. Island, Isle.
Is., Isa. Isaiah.
Isl(s). Island(s).
It., Ital. Italian; Italic; Italy.
ital. italic (bastardilla).
I. W. Isle of Wight.
I. W. W. Industrial Workers of the World.

J

Jam. Jamaica.
Jan. January.
Jap. Japan, Japanese.
Jas. James.
J. C. Jesus Christ; Julius Cæsar; Justice Clerk.
J. D. Jurum Doctor (doctor en Jurisprudencia).
Jer. Jeremiah.
Jno. John.
Jon. Jonathan.
Jona. Jonathan.
Jos. Joseph.
Josh. Joshua.
J. P. Justice of the Peace.
Jr., junior.
Judg. Judges.
Jul. Julian; Julius; July; julep.
Jun. June; Junius, Junior.
Junc. junction (empalme, f. c.).
Junr. junior.

K

K. sq., Kalium (potasio).
K. King; Knight(s).
K., Ki. Kings (Libro de los Reyes).
K., Kal. Kalendæ, kalends.
Kan., Kans., Kas. Kansas.
K. B. King's Bench; Knight of the Bath.
K. C. King's Counsel; Knights of Columbus.
K. C. B. Knight Commander of the Bath.
Ken., Kentucky.
K. G. Knight of the Garter.
kg. keg; kilogram(s)—**kgs.,** kegs.
kilo., kilog. kilogram(me.
kilom. kilometer.
K. K. K. Ku-Klux-Klan.
km. kilometer(s).
km. kilometer(s)—**km.²** square kilometer(s).
Knt., Knight.
K. of C. Knights of Columbus.
Kr, sq. krypton.
Kt. Knight.
Ky. Kentucky.

L

L, sq. Lithium.
L. lady; lake; Latin; libra; London; Lord.
l. latitude; league; length; line; liter.
La. Louisiana.
La, sq. lanthanum.
Lab. Labrador.
Lat. Latin.—**lat.,** latitude.
lb. (**lbs.** pl.) libra, pound(s).
L. C. Lower Canada.
l. c. lower case; left center; letter of credit
L/C. Letter of Credit.
l. c. m. least common multiple.
Ld., ld. Lord; limited.
Leg., Legis. legislature; legislative.
Lev., Levit. Leviticus.
Li, sq. lithium.
L. G. Life Guards; Low German.
l. h. left hand.
lib. liber (libro).
Lieut. lieutenant.
Linn. Linnæus; Linnean.
liq. liquid; liquor.
Lit. D., Litt D. Literarum Doctor (doctor en letras).
LL. B. Legum Baccalaureus (bachiller en leyes).
LL. D. Legum Doctor (doctor en leyes).
loc. cit. loco citato.
log, logarithm.
lon., long. longitude.
Lond. London.
L. S. Linnean Society; locus sigilli (lugar del sello).—**l. s.** left side.
L. (o £) **s. d.** Libræ, solidi, denarii, pounds, shillings, pence.
Lt. Lieutenant.
L'd. limited.
Lu, sq. lutecium.

M

M. Monsieur; Member.
m. married; meridiem (mediodía); meter(s); mile; minim; month; moon.—**m.²** square meter(s). —**m.³** cubic meter(s).
M. A. Magister artium, Master of Arts.
Mad. Madam.
Maj. Major.
Mal. Malachi; Malayan.
man. manual (teclado).
Manit. Manitoba.
manuf. manufactory; manufacturer.
Mar. March.—**mar.** maritime.
M. Ar. Master of Architecture.
Mass. Massachusetts.
math. mathematics.

Matt. Matthew.
M. B. *Medicinæ baccalaureus,* Bachelor of Medicine.
M. C. Member of Congress; Member of Council; Master Commandant.
Mch. March.
M. D. *Medicinæ doctor,* Doctor of Medicine.
Md. Maryland.
Mdlle. Mademoiselle.
Mdm. Madam.
M. D. S. Master of Dental Surgery.
mdse. merchandise.
M. E. Methodist Episcopal; Mining Engineer; Mechanical Engineer.
Me. Maine.
meas. measure.
mech. mechanic; mechanical.
Med. medical; medicine; medieval.
mem. memorandum.
Messrs., MM. Messieurs.
metal., metall. metallurgy.
Meth. Methodist.
Mex. Mexican; Mexico.
mf. mezzo forte (algo fuerte).
mfd. manufactured.
mfg. manufacturing.
mfs. manufactures.
Mg, *sq.* magnesium.—**mg.** milligram.
mi. mile(s).
Mic. Micah.
M. I. C. E. Member Institute of Civil Engineers.
M. I. M. E. Member Institute Mining Engineers.
Mich. Michigan; Michaelmas.
mil., milit. military.
min. mining; minute.
Minn. Minnesota.
Min. Plen. Minister Plenipotentiary.
misc. miscellaneous; miscellany.
Miss. Mississippi; mission; missionary.
ml. millilitre.
mm. millimeter(s).—**m.²** square millimeter(s).
—**m.³** cubic millimeter(s).
Mme. (Mmes. *pl.*) Madame.
Mn, *sq.* manganese.
Mo, *sq.* molybdenum.
Mo. Missouri.
M. O. Money Order.
mo. (*pl.* **mos.**), month(s).
mod. moderato; modern.
Mon. Monday.
Mons. Monsieur.
Monsig. Monsignor.
Mont. Montana.
morn. morning.
M. P. Member of Parliament.
M. P. C. Member of Parliament, Canada.
m. p. h. miles per hour.
Mr. Mister, Master (señor).
Mrs. Mistress (señora).
MS. (*pl.* **MSS.**) manuscript(s).
M. S. Master of Science; Master of Surgery.
M. Sc. Master of Science.
m. s. l. mean sea level.
Mt. (**Mts.** *pl.*) mount, mountain.
Mus. Doc. Doctor of Music.
m. v. *mezza voce* (a media voz).
M. V. *Medicus Veterinarius* (médico veterinario).

N

N, *sq.* nitrogen.
N. north; Norse; Nero.
n. name; *natus* (nacido); neuter; noon, number.
Na, *sq., natrium* (sodio).
N. A. A. National Automobile Association.
N. A., N. Am. North America.
N. A. S. National Academy of Sciences.
naut. nautical.
nav. naval; navigation.
Nb, *sq.* niobium.

N. B. New Brunswick; North Britain; North British; *nota bene* (nótese bien).
N. C. North Carolina; New Church.
Nd, *sq.* neodymium.
n. d. no date.
N. Dak. North Dakota.
Ne, *sq.* neon.
N. E. northeast, northeastern.
N. E. New England.
Neb., Nebr. Nebraska.
n. e. i. *non est inventus* (no ha sido hallado).
nem. con. *nemine contradicente* (némine discrepante).
N. Eng., New England.
Neth. Netherlands.
Nev. Nevada.
New Test. New Testament.
N. F. Newfoundland.
N. G. National Guard; (fam.) no good (que no sirve para nada; malo).
Ng. Norwegian.—**n. g.** (fam.) no good (no sirve).
N. H. New Hampshire.
Ni, *sq.* nickel.
N. J. New Jersey.
N. l. north latitude.
N. M., N. Mex. New Mexico.
N. N. E. north-northeast.
N. N. W. north-northwest.
No. number (*pl.* **nos.**); north.
N. O. New Orleans.
nol. pros. *nolle prosequi.*
non seq. *non sequitur* (no sigue).
Norw. Norway, Norwegian.
Nos. numbers.
Nov. November.
N. P. New Providence; Notary Public.
N. S. Nova Scotia; New School (teol.); New Style.
n. s. not specified.
N/S not sufficient (funds).
N. S. W. New South Wales.
Nt, *sq.* niton.
N. T. New Testament; new translation.
n. u. name unknown.
Num., Numb. Numbers (Biblia).
N. V. New Version (de la Biblia).
N. W. northwest (N. O.)
N. Y. New York.
N. Z., N. Zeal. New Zealand.

O

O, *sq.* oxygen.
O. Ohio; Ossa.
o/a. on account (of).
ob. *obiit* (murió); *obiter* (de paso).
obdt., obt. obedient.
o. c. on centers (entre centros).
Oct. October.
O. D., o. d. outside diameter.
O. E. omissions excepted.
O. F. Odd Fellow; Old French.
O. K. all correct (visto bueno).
Okla. Oklahoma.
Old Test. Old Testament.
Ont. Ontario.
op. opposite; opus (obra).
Or. Oregon; Oriental.
ord. ordained; order; ordinance.
Ore., Oreg. Oregon.
Os, *sq.* osmium.
O. S. Old Saxon; Old School; Old Style (calendario); Old Series; Outside Sentinel.
O. T. Old Testament.
oz. (**oz.** *u* **ozs.** *pl.*). ounce.

P

P, *sq.* phosphorus.
p. page; part; particle; piano (suave); pint; pipe.
Pa. Pennsylvania.

P/A power of Attorney; private account.
Pat. Off. Patent Office.
paym't, payt. payment.
Pb, *sq., plumbum* (plomo).
P. B. British Pharmacopœia.
p. c. per cent.
p/c petty cash; prices current.
Pd, *sq.* palladium.
pd. paid.
P. E. Presiding Elder; Protestant Episcopal.
P. E. I. Prince Edward Island.
Penn. Pennsylvania.
per an., *per annum* (por año).
per ct. *per cent.*
pert. pertaining.
Peruv. Peruvian.
pf. perfect; preferred.
p. f. *più forte* (poco más fuerte).
Pg. Portugal; Portuguese.
Phar., Pharm. pharmacy; pharmacopeia; pharmaceutical.
Ph. C. Pharmaceutical Chemist.
Ph. D. Doctor of Philosophy.
Ph. G. Graduate in Pharmacy.
Phil., Phila. Philadelphia.
phot., photog. photographic; photography.
phys. physician; physics.
Phys. Sci. physical science.
P. I. Philippine Islands.
pil. *pilula* (píldora).
pkg. (pkgs. *pl.*) package(s).
pl. place; plate; plural.
plf., plff., pltff. plaintiff.
P. M. postmaster; *post meridiem* (tarde); paymaster; peculiar meter.—**pm.** premium.
P. O. post-office; Province of Ontario.
p. o. postal order; post office.
P. O. B. post-office box.
P. O. D. pay on delivery; Post-Office Department.
P. O. O. post-office order.
pop. population.
pp. pages; pianissimo.
p. p. i. policy proof of interest.
P. Q. Previous question; Province of Quebec.
Pr, *sq.* praseodymium.
Pr. preferred (stock).
pr. pair; price; pronoun; proper; present.
P. R. Porto Rico.
Pres. President; presidency.
prin. principal(ly); principles.
priv. Privative.
Prof. Professor.
Prot. Protestant.
pro tem. *pro tempore.*
Prov. Proverbs; province; provincial.
prox. proximo (el mes que viene).
Prs. printers.—**prs.** pairs.
Prus. Prussia; Prussian.
Ps., Psa. Psalm; Psalms.
P. S. postscript.
ps. pieces.
pt. part; payment; pint.
Pt, *sq.* platinum.
Pt. point; port.
P. T. O. please turn over.
pub. public; published; publisher.
Pub. Doc. public documents.
pwt. pennyweight.
P. X. please exchange.

Q

Q. Quebec; queen; Quintus.
q. quasi: query; quintal.
Q., question.
Q. B. Queen's Bench.
Q. C. Queen's Counsel.
Q. E. D. *quod erat demonstrandum* (L. C. D. D., lo cual debíamos demostrar).
Q. E. F. *quod erat faciendum* (que era lo que se trataba de hacer).

q. l. *quantum libet* (tanto como se desee).—**ql.** quintal.
q. s. *quantum sufficit* (lo que baste); quarter section.
qt. quantity; quart.—**qts.** quarts.
qu. question.
qu. query.
Que. Quebec.
ques. question.
q. v. *quantum vis* (cuanto se quiera); *quod vide* (véase).
qy. query.

R

R. Réaumur; radical; railway; recipe; river; republican; Royal.
r. rod; rood; rupee.
Ra, *sq.* radium.
R. A. Rear-admiral; right ascension; Royal Academy; Royal Arch.
Rad. Radical—**rad.** radix (raíz).
Rb, *sq.* rubidium.
R. C. Roman Catholic; Red Cross.
R. C. C., R. C. Ch. Roman Catholic Church.
rcpt., rec't., rect. receipt.
R. C. S. Royal College of Surgeons.
R. E. Reformed Episcopal; Right Excellent; Royal Engineers; Royal Exchange.
rec'd., recd. received.
Rec. Sec. recording secretary.
ref. reference; referred; reformed; reformer.
reg. registry; regular.—**Reg.,** *regina* (reina).
Reg., Regt. regent; regiment.
Rep. report; reporter; representative.
Rep., Repub. republic; republican.
Rev. Revelation (Apocalipsis); revenue; Reverend (**Revs.** *pl.*); review.
Rev. Stat. Revised Statutes.
Rev. Ver. Revised Version (de la Biblia).
R. F. A. Royal Field Artillery.
R. F. D. Rural Free Delivery.
R. G. S. Royal Geographical Society (Londres).
Rh, *sq.* rhodium.
R. H. Royal Highness.—**r. h.** right hand.
R. I. Rhode Island.
Rich., Rich'd. Richard.
R. I. P. *requiescat in pace* (en paz descanse).
R. M. S. Royal Mail Steamer.
R. N. Royal Navy.
R. N. R. Royal Naval Reserve.
Robt. Robert.
Rom. Cath. Roman Catholic.
R. P. Reformed Presbyterian; Regius Professor.
r. p. m. revolutions per minute.
r. p. s. revolutions per second.
R. R. railroad.
R. S. recording secretary; Revised Statutes.—**r. s.** right side.
R. S. V. P. *Répondez s'il vous plaît* (Sírvase contestar).
Rt. Hon. Right Honorable.
Rt. Rev. Right Reverend.
Ru, *sq.* ruthenium.
R. V. Revised Version (versión corregida—de la Biblia).
R. W., Rw., Ry. railway.

S

S, *sq.* Sulphur.
S. Saxon; Servius; Sextus; scribe; sign; society; south; Sunday; Sabbath.
s. second; section (**SS.,** *pl.*); series; shilling.
Sa, *sq.* samarium.
Sa., Saturday.
S. A. South Africa; South America; South Australia.
s. a. *secundum artem* (según arte); *sine anno* (sin fecha).
Sab. Sabbath.

S. Am. South America.
Sam., Saml. Samuel.
S. A. R. Sons of the American Revolution; South African Republic.
Sat. Saturday.
Sb, *sq. stibium* (antimonio).
S. B. Bachelor of Science.
Sc, *sq.* scandium.
S. C. South Carolina; Supreme Court.
s. c., s. caps., sm. caps. small capitals (versalitas).
sc. scene; *scilicet* (a saber).
Scot. Scotch; Scotland; Scottish.
scr. scruple (peso).
sculp., sculpt. *sculpsit* (lo esculpió); sculptor; sculptural; sculpture.
s. d. *sine die.*
S. D., s. d. sight draft.
S. D., S. Dak. South Dakota.
Se, *sq.* selenium.
S. E. southeast; southeastern.
sec secant.
Sec. secretary.—**sec.** second.
Sen. Senate; Senator.
Sen. Doc. senate document
sep. separate.
Sep., Sept. September.
Serg., Sergt. sergeant.
serv., servt. servant (= S. S. S.).
S. G. Solicitor-general.
s. g. specific gravity.
Sh., sh. shilling.
Shak., Shaks. Shakespeare.
Si, *sq.* silicon.
S. I. Staten Island; Sandwich Islands.
S. J. Society of Jesus.
S. l., S. lat. south latitude.
Sm, *sq.* samarium.
S. M. short meter; Sons of Malta.
Smith. Inst. Smithsonian Institution.
Sn, *sq., stannum* (estaño).
So. south.
Soc. Society; Socrates.
Soc. Isl. Society Islands.
sop. soprano.
sov. sovereign (moneda de oro).
S. P. C. A. Society for the Prevention of Cruelty to Animals.
S. P. C. C. Society for the Prevention of Cruelty to Children.
sp. gr. specific gravity.
spt. seaport.
sq. square; *sequentes-tia* (siguiente(s).
sqq. *sequentes* (siguientes).
Sr, *sq.* strontium.
Sr. senior; sir.
SS. saints.—**ss.** *scilicet* (es decir).
S. S. Sunday School; Sabbath School; Steamship.
s. s. screw steamer; steamship.
S. S. E. south-southeast.
S. S. W. south-southwest.
St. Saint; strait; street.
st. stanza; stet; strophe.
ster., stg. sterling.
str. steamer.
sub. subject; substitute; suburb; suburban.
Sun., Sund. Sunday.
sup., super. superior; superfine.
Sup., Supp. supplement.
Supt. superintendent.
Surg., surg. surgeon; surgery; surgical.
Surv. surveying; surveyor.
s. v. *sub verbo o voce* (en la palabra).
S. W. southwest; southwestern.

T

T. Territory; Testament; Titus; ton(s); Tuesday; Tullius.
t. tenor; ton; town; township; *tempore* (en el tiempo de).

Ta, *sq.* tantalum.
tan tangent.
Tb, *sq.* terbium.
Te, *sq.* tellurium.
te., teleg. telegram; telegraph.
Tenn. Tennessee.
Ter., Terr. Territory.
Test. Testament (Biblia).
Tex. Texas.
tf. till forbidden.
Th, *sq.* thorium.
Th. Thursday.
Tho., Thos. Thomas.
Thu., Thur., Thurs. Thursday.
Ti, *sq.* titanium.
t. i. d. *ter in die* (3 veces al día).
Tim. Timothy.
Tit. Titus.
Tl, *sq.* thallium.
Tm, *sq.* thulium.
t. o. telegraph office.
T. O. turn over; Telegraph Office.
tp. township.
Tr, *sq.* terbium.
tr. transpose; trill.
tr., trans. transitive; translation; translated; transaction; transportation.
treas. treasurer; treasury.
ts. till sale.
T. T. L. to take leave.
T. U. Trade-Union.
Tu., Tues. Tuesday.

U

U, *sq.* uranium
U. C. Upper Canada.
U. K. United Kingdom.
ult., ulto. último (el mes pasado).
um., unm. unmarried.
Unit. Unitarian.
Univ. Universalist; University.
U. S. United States.
U. S. A. United States of America; United States Army.
U. S. M. United States Mail; United States Marines.
U. S. M. A. United States Military Academy.
U. S. N. United States Navy.
U. S. N. A. United States Naval Academy.
U. S. P., U. S. Pharm. United States Pharmacopœia.
U. S. S. United States Senate; United States Steamer.
usu. usual, usually.
Ut. Utah.
ut sup. *ut supra* (como arriba o antes).
ux. *uxor* (esposa).

V

V, *sq.* vanadium.
V. venerable; Victoria; violin; volunteers.
v. verse; versus (contra); volume.
v. *vide* (véase).
Va. Virginia.
val. value.
Vat. Vatican.
Ven. Venerable.
vet., veter. veterinary.
Vet. Surg. veterinary surgeon.
v. g. *verbi gratia.*
Vice Pres. Vice President.
vid. *vide* (véa(n)se).
Vis., Visc., Visct. Viscount.
viz. *videlicet* (a saber).
vol. volume (*pl.* **vols.**); volunteer.
V. P. Vice President.
V. Rev. Very Reverend.
V. S. Veterinary Surgeon.

---

vs. *versus* (contra).
Vt. Vermont.
Vul., Vulg. Vulgate (Biblia).

W

W, *sq. Wolframium* (volframio, tungsteno).
W. warden; Welsh; west; western; William; Wednesday.
w. week; wife.
W. A. West Africa; West Australia.
W. Afr. West Africa.
Wash. Washington (Estado).
w. c. water-closet.
W. C. Western Central (distrito postal); Wesleyan Chapel; without charge.
W. C. T. U. Women's Christian Temperance Union.
We., Wed. Wednesday.
w. f., wf. wrong font.
w. g. wire gauge.
Whf. wharf.
W. I. West India; West Indies.
Wis., Wisc. Wisconsin.
Wisd. Wisdom (Biblia).
Wk. week.—**wk., w'k,** work.
W. lon. west longitude.
Wm. William.
W. N. W. west-northwest.
Wp. Worship.
Wpful. Worshipful.
W. S. W. west-southwest.
wt. weight.

W. Va. West Virginia.
Wy. Wyoming.

X

X, Xe, *sq.* xenon.
xcp. without coupon.
xd., xdiv. without dividend.
Xm., Xmas. Christmas.

Y

Y, *sq.* yttrium.
y. yard; year.
Yb, *sq.* ytterbium.
Y. B., Yr. B. Year-book.
yd. (*pl.* **yds.**) yard (medida).
Y. M. C. A. Young Men's Christian Association.
Y. M. Cath. A. Young Men's Catholic Association.
yn. then.—**yr.** their.—**ys.** this.—**yt.** that.
yr. (*pl.* **yrs.**) year; younger; your.
Y. W. C. A. Young Women's Christian Association.

Z

Zach. Zachary.
Zn, *sq.* zinc.
Zool. zoology; zoological.
Zr, *sq.* zirconium.

Para la pronunciación de æ, œ, ᴅ, ꜱ, ꜱ̌h, ᴜ, ȳ, ʏ, ᴢ, véase la clave al principio del libro.

SUPLEMENTO
DE LA PARTE INGLESA-ESPAÑOLA

Nota—Las palabras cuya pronunciación no se da aquí ocurren como encabezamientos, con su pronunciación, en el cuerpo del libro.

a. I. *art. indef.* Interpuesto entre el adjetivo *half* y un substantivo, no se traduce (*half a pound*, media libra· *half a month*, medio mes). **II.** *prep.*—**a.-maying** (*v.* MAY).

aardvark [árdvárc], *s.* oricteropo del Cabo, especie de mamífero hormiguero sudafricano.

aardwolf [árdúlf], *s.* prótel, hiena sudafricana.

aasvogel [ásfóugœl], *s.* buitre.

abalone [ǽbælóune], *s.* (zool.) haliotis, haliótide.

abaxial [æbǽxiœl], *a.* fuera del eje.

Abbaside [æbǽsaid], *s.* y *a.* abasida.

abdominous [æbdóminus], *a.* barrigón.

abductor [æbdúctœr]. **I.** *s.* secuestrador. **II.** *a.* (anat.) abductor (músculo).

abenteric [ǽbentéric], *a.* extraintestinal.

abirritant [æbírritænt], *s.* y *a.* contrairritante.

able-bodied seaman, marinero cabal. (Es nombre que se da como título de graduación o categoría a un marinero capaz de ejecutar todas las maniobras del oficio de marinero.)

abortient [æbórshent], *a.* =ABORTIFACIENT.

abortionist [æbórshunist], *s.* el que profesa la producción del aborto. (Puede llamarse *abortista* o *malpartista*).

about, *adv.* y *prep.*—**a.-face, a.-turn,** cambio de opinión o de conducta, cambio al partido contrario (a menudo con **make: to make an about-turn,** pasarse al partido opuesto, decir o hacer lo contrario, desdecirse).—**what a.** (*v.* WHAT).

above, *s.*—**the a.,** lo dicho, lo anterior, lo antedicho.

abovestairs [-stéærs], *adv.* = UPSTAIRS.

abradant [æbróidænt], *s.* y *a.* =ABRASIVE.

abrader [æbréidœr], *s.* material rayente.

absolute, *a.*—**a. alcohol,** alcohol absoluto, alcohol puro.—**a. ceiling,** (aer.) techo, altura máxima que un avión puede alcanzar en una atmósfera tipo.—**a. scale,** (fís.) escala termométrica absoluta, o de temperaturas absolutas.

absorbancy, absorbency [æbsórbænsi, -ensi], *s.* absorbencia.

absorptiometer [æbsórshiómetœr], *s.* absorciómetro.

absorption tube, (fís.) absorciómetro.

abstracted [æbstrǽcted], *a.* distraído, olvidadizo (=ABSENT-MINDED); separado, desligado.

abutment pier, estribo.

abyssal zone, la región profunda del mar.

academic, *a.* colegial, de colegio; convencional, tradicional, de usanza.

acardia [æcárdiœ], *s.* falta o carencia de corazón.

acariasis [æcæráiæsis], *s.* sarna, comezón.

Acarida [æcéridœ], *s.* (zool.) acáridos.

acatalepsia [æcǽtælépsiœ], *s.* (med.) incertidumbre del diagnóstico; inferioridad mental.

acatalepsy [-lepsi], *s.* (filos.) acatalepsia.

acaudal [æcódœl], *a.* acáudeo, sin cola.

Accadian [ækéidiæn], *s.* y *a.* acadio.

acceptance, *s.* giro aceptado.—**a. house,** casa de aceptación de giros, cuyo negocio principal es servir de librado a libradores de letras.

accession. I. *s.* ingreso, adquisición nueva (de libros en una biblioteca, etc.).—**a. book,** registro. **II.** *va.* registrar, apuntar.

accipiter [æcsípitœr], *s.* accípitre, ave de rapiña.

accolade, *s.* formalidad, ceremonia.

accoladed [écoléided], *a.* armado caballero; caballero titulado (que tiene el título de *Sir*).

accost, *va.* convidar a un acto de inmoralidad sexual.

account, *s.*—**a. rendered,** cuenta girada, o enviada.—**by all accounts,** según el decir, o la opinión, general.

accountant general, jefe de contabilidad.

accredited, *a.* acreditado; autorizado.

accrescent [æcrésent], *a.* creciente, que aumenta; (bot.) que sigue creciendo después de florecer.

accrual [æcrúœl], *s.* aumento, incremento; rédito; entrada (de mercancías, dinero, etc.).

accrue, *vn.* agregarse; acumularse; redituarse (interés); (for.) ser otorgado.—**to a. to,** agregarse a; venirle a; resultar para o resultarle a.

ace, *s.*—**within an ace of,** muy cerca de, por poco, en un tris (a veces hay que cambiar un poco el giro).—**a.-high,** (tenido) en grandísima estima, muy favorecido.

acedia [æsídiæ], *s.* acidia, pereza; (zool.) acedia, platija.

acephalia [æseféiliæ], *s.* acefalía, falta de cabeza.

acephalobrachia [æséfælobréikiæ], *s.* acéfalobraquia, falta de brazos y cabeza.

acetal [ǽsetæl], *s.* (quím.) acetal.

acetamide [æsétæmaid], *s.* (quím.) acetamida.

acetimetry [æsetímetri], *s.* acetimetría.

acetol [-tol], *s.* (quím.) acetol.

acetometer [-tómetœr], *s.* acetímetro.

acetyl [ǽsetil]. **I.** *s.* (quím.) acetilo. **II.** *a.* de acetilo.

acetylene, *a.* acetilénico, de acetileno.

achime [æcháim], *a. adv.* sonando, repicando (campanas).

achroma, achromia [æcrómæ, -iæ], *s.* acromia.

achromatopsia [æcrómætópsiæ], *s.* acromatopsia.

achy [éiki], *a.* adolorido, con dolor.

acid, *s.*—**a.-forming,** acidógeno, que produce gas.—**a. proof,** a prueba de ácidos, resistente a los ácidos.—**a. steel,** acero (hecho por el procedimiento) ácido.—**a. test,** prueba rigurosa decisiva.

acidimetry [ǽsidímetri], *s.* acidimetría.

acidosis [ǽsidóusis], *s.* (med.) asescencia, acidismo, exceso de acidez.

acme, *s.* non plus ultra, colmo.

acoustician [æcaustíshæn], *s.* acústico, versado en acústica.

Acrania [æcréiniæ], *s.* (zool.) acranianos.

acreage, *s.* tierras; extensión de tierra o de terreno, superficie.

acrobatics [æcrobǽtics], *s.* acrobatismo.

acrobatism [æcrobætísm], *s.* acrobatismo.

acromion [æcróumion], *s.* (anat.) acromio.

act. I. *va.*—**to a. out,** representar dramática o teatralmente.—**to a. the part of,** hacer el papel de; hacer las veces de; reemplazar. **II.** *vn.* (a veces con **up**) jaranear, travesear; fingir. **III.** *s.*—**a. of God,** (for.) caso fortuito, fuerza mayor.—**a. of grace,** acto de clemencia.

action, *s.* (b. a.) actitud, además.

activate, *va.* tratar (aguas inmundas) por aeración prolongada.—**activated sludge,** residuo lodoso de la aeración prolongada.

activator [ǽctiveitœr], *s.* (quím.) activador.

active, *a.*—**a. bond,** bono que devenga interés fijo desde que se emite.—**a. list,** lista de oficiales del servicio militar regular.

actualize [ǽkchuælaiś], *va.* realizar, dar realidad a, llevar a cabo.

acuminous [ækiúminus], *a.* =ACUMINATE.

ad [æd], *s.* anuncio, aviso.

Adam's fig, plátano.

Para la pronunciación de æ, œ, ᴅ, ŝ, ŝh, ᴜ, ȳ, ʏ, z, véase la clave al principio del libro

addax [ǽdæx], s. adax, variedad de antílope.
addict, s. adicto, aficionado; enviciado, morfinómano.
adding machine, s. sumadora, máquina de sumar.
addition, s.—**in a.,** además, fuera de esto.
Address to the Crown, contestación al discurso de la Corona.
addressing machine, s. =ADDRESSOGRAPH.
adduct [ædúct], va. (fisiol.) causar aducción.
adenia [ædíniæ], s. (med.) adenia, adenopatía.
adephagous [ædéfægʊs], a. adéfago, voraz.
adequacy [ǽdecuæsi], s. calidad de adecuado, suficiencia.
adhibit [ædjíbit], va. dejar entrar, admitir; aplicar, dar; unir, agregar.
ad hoc [æd joc], ad hoc.
ad hominem [-jóminem], ad hóminem.
adiantum [ædiǽntʊm], s. (bot.) adianto, culantrillo.
adiaphoresis [ædiǽforísis], s. adiaforesis, falta o insuficiencia de sudor.—**adiaphoretic** [-étic], s. y a. adiaforético (que impide el sudor).
ad infinitum [æd ínfináitʊm], adv. hasta el infinito, infinitamente.
ad interim [ínterim], adv. y a. interinamente, provisionalmente; interino, temporal.
ad libitum [líbitʊm], ad líbitum, a voluntad.
adminicle [ædmínicœl], s. adminículo, ayuda; (for.) prueba corroborante.
administer, vn. servir, auxiliar (=MINISTER).
admiralty alloy, brass, o **metal,** latón estañoso (contiene como 1% de estaño, y en el comercio se llama latón "admiralty").
admitted, a. aceptado, concedido, de validez reconocida.
adream [ædrím], a. y adv. soñando.
adulterator [ædúlteréitœr], s. adulterador.
advance, a. adelantado, anticipado.—**a. sheets,** pliegos sueltos impresos anticipados de un libro que se envían a los críticos, revistas, etc. antes de la publicación.
advantage, s.—**to a.,** ventajosamente, con provecho; en circunstancias o condiciones ventajosas.—**to one's a.,** con ventaja o provecho para uno.
Adventism, Adventist [ǽdventísm, -tist]. V. SECOND.
Aegean, Ægean [erĭæn], a. egeo, del mar Egeo.
aegis, ægis, s. protección, amparo.
Aeneid, Æneid [eníid], s. Eneida.
aerial torpedo, torpedo aéreo; granada de obús.
aerodynamic, a. aerodinámico.
aerogun [éicærogún], s. cañón antiaéreo.
aerophotography [-fotógrafi], s. aerofotografía.
aeroview [-viú], s. vista aérea, vista tomada desde un avión.
Aesculapian [éskiuléipiæn]. I. s. Esculapio, médico. II. a. esculapiano, de Esculapio; médico; medicinal.
Aesopian, Aesopic [esópiæn, -pic], a. esópico.
Aetolian [etóliæn], s. y a. etolio.
affair, s. cosa; (mil.) combate ligero.
afforce [æfórs], va. reforzar.
afforcement [-ment], s. refuerzo.
affreight [æfréit], va. fletar.
affy [æfái], va. desposarse con; unir estrechamente; declarar, atestiguar.
afield, adv. en el campo; al campo; lejos de casa; lejos del camino, descarriado; lejos del asunto.
a fortiori [ei fórshióri], a fortiori, con mayor razón.
African hair, fibra de miraguano.
Afro-American [ǽfroæméricæn], s. y a. afroamericano, negro americano.
after. I. a. posterior; siguiente; resultante, consiguiente; (mar.) de popa. II. adv. después que, después de que.
against time, (hacer algo) tratando de terminar (llegar, etc.) antes de cierto tiempo, o a tiempo.

agama [ǽgæmæ], s. (zool.) agama.
agami [ǽgæmi], s. (zool.) agamí.
agape [ǽgæpi], s. ágape, convite de fraternidad y caridad de los primeros cristianos.
age, va. dar su punto a, sazonar, perfeccionar (a veces dejando en reposo por algún tiempo, como con el vino y ciertas substancias químicas).
ageing [éiying]. I. ger. de TO AGE. II. s. envejecimiento; cambio debido a la acción del tiempo; acción de sazonar o llegar a su punto (a menudo tras permanecer en reposo por algún tiempo).
agent provocateur (se pronuncia como en francés), agente provocador, agente que secreta y fingidamente instiga a la ejecución de actos punibles, a fin de obtener pruebas de culpabilidad.
agger [ǽycœr], s. terraplén; camino.
agglutinant, aglutinate, s. aglutinante.
aging [éiying] =AGEING.
agist [æyíst], va. cuidar y alimentar o apacentar (ganado); gravar con impuesto.
agister, agistor [-œr], apacentador.
aglutition [æglutíshʊn], s. aglutición, incapacidad de tragar.
Agnus bell, toque (de campana) de agnusdéi.
agon [ǽgon], s. fiesta agonal.—pl. **agones** [ægónis], agonales (fiestas atléticas antiguas).
agonistics, s. agonística.
agony column, (fam.) columna o sección (de un periódico) de anuncios personales, sobre todo los relativos a personas desaparecidas.
agora [ǽgoræ], s. (hist. griega) ágora.
agoraphobia [-fóbiæ], s. (pat.) agorafobia.
agree, vn.—**to a. on,** o **to,** convenir en.
agriology [ægrióloyi], s. estudio de los pueblos no civilizados.
ahungered [æjúngœrd], a. hambriento.
air. I. s. aire, radiodifusión.—**to be on the air,** estar (hablando) en el radio; estar(se) transmitiendo por radio.—**to go on the a.,** hablar o dedicarse a hablar por radio para el público. II. a. —**a. base,** base de (operaciones de) aviación.—**a. casing,** cámara de aire aisladora.—**a. cleaner,** depurador del aire.—**a.-condition,** va. proveer de aire acondicionado.—**a.-conditioned,** de (con) aire acondicionado.—**a. conditioning,** acondicionamiento del aire.—**a.-cooled,** enfriado por aire.—**a. lane,** (aer.) vía aérea.—**a. line,** (aer.) línea de aviones, línea (empresa) aérea o de transporte aéreo.—**a. liner,** avión de una empresa de transporte aéreo.—**a. lock,** acumulación de aire, e interrupción que causa; cámara intermedia (de un cajón sumergido).—**a. mail,** correo aéreo.—**a. meter,** contador de aire o de gas.—**a. plant,** planta aerícola (que se alimenta de aire).—**a. pocket,** (aer.) =A. HOLE.—**a. sickness** = AERIAL SICKNESS.—**a. vesicle,** (anat.) vesícula aérea; (bot.) ampolla o vesícula de aire.—**a. view** = AEROVIEW.
aircraft, s. aerovehículo—**a. carrier,** portavión, buque de (para) aviones.
airfoil [éærfóil], s. (aer.) superficie de sustentación; ala.
airplane carrier = AIRCRAFT CARRIER.
airplanist [éærpléinist], s. aviador.
airport, s. estación o paradero de aviación. (Ú. t. en español aeropuerto).
airscape [éærskéip], s. (aer.) = AIR VIEW.
airsick [-síc], a. atacado, o que sufre, de mal de altura (v. AERIAL SICKNESS).—**airsickness** = AIR SICKNESS.
aitch [éich], s. hache (letra).
a la carte [a la cart], según lista (de comidas), según se pida. (En casi todas partes se dice a la carta, aunque esta expresión se tacha de galicismo.)
a la king, con salsa de hongos y pimientos.
alar [éilœr], a. del ala; alado; (bot., anat.) axilar.
Alaskan [ælǽscæn], s. y a. de Alaska.
Albigenses [ælbiyénsis], s. pl. albigenses.
Albigensian [-siæn], a. albigense.
albinic [ælbínic], a. albino.
albinism [ælbinísm], s. albinismo.
albuminate [ælbiúmineit], s. albuminato.—

albuminine (-minin), *s.* albuminina.—**albuminize** (-aiŝ), *va.* = ALBUMENIZE.—**albumose** (æĺbiumous), *s.* (quím.) albumosa.—**albumosuria** (æĺbiumosiúria), *s.* (med.) albumosuria.

alcoholometry [æĺcojolómetri], *s.* alcoholimetría.

alderwoman [óldœrúmæn], *s.* regidora.

aleurone.[æliúroun], *s.* (bot., quím.) aleurona.

algalia [algália], *s.* abelmosco.

algedonic [æĺredónic], *a.* algedónico.—**algedonics**, *s.* algédonica, ciencia del placer y el dolor.

algesia [æĺyíŝiœ], *s.* algesia, gran sensibilidad al dolor.

algorism [æĺgoriŝm], *s.* algoritmo.

alimentary, *a.* de nutrición, de alimentación.—**a. canal**, tubo digestivo.

alkaline earths, (quím.) tierras alcalinas.

all, *s.*—**a. one**, del mismo tenor; indiferente, igual, que no importa.—**a. told**, por todo; teniéndolo(s) todo(s) en cuenta.—**at a.**, absolutámente; de ninguna manera, en absoluto; siquiera algo, siquiera un poco [a menudo empleado enfática o expletivamente, y puede dejarse sin traducir; v. g. *has he any money at all?* ¿él tiene dinero? o, más explícitamente, ¿él tiene siquiera algún dinero? *was he there at all?*.¿él (siquiera) estuvo allí?].—**for a. I know**, quizá, posiblemente, eso no es imposible.—**If at a.** (*v.* IF).—**that is**, o **that's, a. there is to it**, eso es todo; no es, *o* no hay, más que eso; no hay más que hablar.

all, *a.*—**a.**-(seguido de *s.*), todo de (*all-steel*, todo de acero); de todo el (*an all-day task*, tarea de todo el día).—**a. day** (**night**, etc.), todo el día (toda la noche, etc.).—**A. fools' day** = APRILFOOL DAY.—**a. hours**, toda hora; altas horas de la noche, tarde por la noche.—**a. there**, (afirmativamente), listo, alerta, despierto; (**not to be a. there**, no estar en su juicio cabal, estar un poco chiflado).—**a. the way**, por, *o* en, todo el camino (o viaje, marcha, travesía, etc.); en todo, enteramente.—**a. the way** (a veces con **up** o **down**) **to**, hasta, o no se traduce [*he went all the way up to the roof*, subió hasta el tejado; *there are hats of several prices, all the way from two* (up) *to twenty dollars*, hay sombreros de varios precios, desde dos hasta veinte dólares].—**of a.** (seguido de *s.*) Esta frase se usa a menudo para expresar sorpresa, o sorpresa y desprecio, y puede traducirse, cambiando un poco el giro, por medio de *¡qué cosa! ¡quién lo creyera! ¿habráse visto? no faltaba más*, etc. (*they appointed John, of all people!* nombraron a Juan, ¡quién lo hubiera creído! *o* ¡qué cosa! *he asked me to marry him, of all things!* me propuso casamiento, ¿habráse visto? *o* no faltaba más).

all, *adv.* sólo, no, más, exclusivamente.—**a. at once**, repentinamente; de un golpe; a un tiempo.—**a. but**, casi, poco menos que.—**a.-inclusive**, omnímodo.—**a. off**, abandonado, frustado (viaje, plan, etc.).—**a. out**, completamente; agotado, rendido (= ALL IN); equivocado, confundido; resueltamente.—**a.-possessed**, maniático, destornillado, loco (fig.).—**a. right**, sin duda, ciertamente; (con lo **be**) satisfactorio, apropiado, aceptable, bueno (buen sujeto, buena persona), competente.—**a. the**, mucho; tanto más (**a. the better**, tanto mejor; **a. the worse**, tanto peor).—**a. the same**, a pesar de todo; sin embargo.—**a. too**, dəmasiado; muy; desgraciadamente (*it is all too true that my son did it*, desgraciadamente es verdad que mi hijo lo hizo).—**to be a. up with**, haber fracasado enteramente; estar de baja (fig.), haberlo perdid todo, estar caído por completo; estar desahuciado.

all, *conj.* aunque.

allegedly [æléyedli], *adv.* según se afirma, según se pretende (gen. insinuando que sin razón).

allergic [æĺœryic], *a.* alérgico.—**allergist** [æĺœr-yist), *s.* alergista, [especialista en alergia.—**allergy** [æĺœryi], *s.* alergia, especie de susceptibilidad anormal a los efectos de ciertas substancias que de ordinario son innocuas; cambio (gen. agravación) de susceptibilidad a una substancia causado por ella misma.

alliaceous [æliéiŝhus], *a.* aliáceo.

allogamy [æĺógœmi], *s.* alogamia (= CROSS-FERTILIZATION).

aloof, *adv.*—**to stand**, o **stay, a.**, no mezclarse, no tomar parte.

aloofness [æĺúfnes], *n.* alejamiento, aislamiento; no participación; indiferencia.

alpenglow [æĺpenglóu], *s.* resplandor de la puesta del sol.

alpenhorn, alphorn [æĺpenjórn, æĺpjórn], *a.* corneta alpestre.

Altaic [æltéic], *s.* y *a.* altaico.

Altar, *s.* (astr.) el Altar, Ara.

altar, *s.*—**a. boy**, acólito.—**a. bread**, pan eucarístico; hostias.

alternative. I. *s.* otra cosa (método, etc.) que puede escogerse o adoptarse. **II.** *a.* otro.

altigraph [æĺtigræf], *s.* altímetro registrador, aneroide registrador.

altiloquent [æĺtilocuent], *a.* altilocuente, grandílocuo.

altogether, *s.* (fam.) desnudo.—**in the a.**, enteramente desnudo, en cueros.

aluminate [æliúmineit], *s.* aluminato.

aluminite [-ait], *s.* (min.) aluminita.

amah [éimæ], *s.* criada; niñera; nodriza.

amanous [æmænus], *a.* sin manos.

amarylis, *s.* (bot.) amarilis.

amatol [æmœtol], *s.* amatol, explosivo compuesto de trinitrotolueno y nitrato de amonio.

ambary [æmbári], *s.* cáñamo de la India (ll. t. *gambo, bangue*).

ambassadorship [æmbǽsædœrship], *s.* embajada (cargo).

ambulacrum [æmbiuléicrum], *s.* (zool.) ambulacro.

ambulance, *va.* llevar en ambulancia.

amental [æméntæl], *a.* no mental; sin mente.

American, *a.*—A. cotton, algodón sea-island.—**A. tiger**, tigre americano, jaguar.

Americanese [æmérikæníŝ], *s.* inglés de los Estados Unidos. (Puede llamarse *lengua estadunidense*.)

amex [æméx], *s.* ejército norteamericano en Europa durante la guerra mundial (1917 a 1918).

amicrobic [æmicróbic], *a.* no micróbico.

amin(e [émin], *s.* (quím.) amina.

aminic [æmínic], *a.* amínico.

amnesty, *va.* indultar.

amoeboid, amoeboid [æmíboid], *a.* amiboideo.

amoralism [æmórælíŝm], *s.* amoralismo.

amorality [æmorélíti], *s.* amoralidad.

Ampère's stand, o **table**, *s.* (fís.) tabla o mesa de Ampère.

amphibion [æmfíbion], *s.* (aer.) = AMPHIBIAN.

amphipod [æmfipod], *s.* y *a.* anfípodo.—**Amphipoda** [æmfípodæ], *s. pl.* anfípodos.—**amphipodal** [-dœl], *a.* anfípodo.

amphitrite [æmfitrait], *s.* (zool.) anfitrite.

amphivorous [æmfívorus], *a.* carnívoro y herbívoro.

amplifier, *s.* (elec.) amplificador.—(rad.) altavoz, altoparlante.

ampoule [æmpúl], *s.* ampolleta o tubo de jeringa hipodérmica.

amputator [æmpiutéitœr], *s.* amputador, operador de una amputacin.—**amputee** [-tí], *s.* persona a quien se ha hecho amputación.

an, *conj.* si; y.—**a. if**, si.—**an'**, *conj.* (fam.) y.

an, *art. indef. V.* A.

anabasis [ænábasis], *s.* (pat. e hist.) anábasis; invasión.

anabatic, *a.* (med.) anabático.

anacanth [ænækænz], *s.* (zool.) anacanto, anacántino.—**Anacanthini** [ænækǽnzinai], *s.* (zool.) anacántinos.

anachronous [ænácronus], *a.* anacrónico.

anaerobe [ænéicœroub], *s.*, **anaerobic** [-óbic], *a.* anaerobio.

anamnesis [ænæmnísis], *s.* recuerdo; (med.) antecedentes de una enfermedad.

anaplastic [ænæplástic], *a.* anaplástico, relativo a la anaplastia.

anaplasty [-ti], *s.* (med.) anaplastia.

Anatolian [ǽnætóliæn], *s.* y *a.* anatolio.

anchor, *s.* riostra, tirante; soporte; artificio de sujeción o amarre; áncora (de reloj); áncora, amparo.—**a. drag,** (mar.) rastra.—**a. ice,** hielo esponjoso formado en el fondo del agua.—**a. mast,** (aer.) = MOORING MAST.

ancon [ǽncon], *s.* (anat.) codo; (arq.) ancón, ménsula.

and so forth, o **and so on,** etcétera; y así sucesivamente.

androecium, andrœcium [ændríshivm], *s.* (bot.) androceo.

androgyne [ǽndroyin], *s.* hermafrodita; hombre afeminado; mujer ahombrada; eunuco.

androphagous [ændrófægus], *a.* andrófago, antropófago.

androphobia [ændrofóbiæ], *s.* androfobia.

anecdotist [ænécdotist], *s.* anecdotista.

anesthesia, etc. *V.* ANÆSTHESIA, etc.

Angevin(e [ǽnyevin], *s.* y *a.* angevino.

angle, *s.*—**a. brick,** ladrillo de aristas oblicuas.—**a. of deflection,** (arti.) ángulo de elevación.—**a. of pitch,** (aer.) ángulo de cabeceo.—**a. of repose** = ANGLE OF FRICTION.—**a. of yaw,** (aer.) ángulo de derrape.—**a. plate,** plancha en ángulo, o angular.

Anglomania [ænglomériniæ], *s.* anglomanía.—**Anglophile** [-fáil], *s.* y *a.* anglófilo.—**Anglophobe** [-fóub], *s.* y *a.* anglófobo.—**Anglophobia** [-fóbiæ], *s.* anglofobia.

Angola cat, *s.* = ANGORA CAT.

angstrom [ǽngstrum], *s.* angstrom (un cienmillonésimo de centímetro).

angular, *a.*—**a. advance, a. lead,** (m. v.) ángulo de avance, o de calado (de la excéntrica).

anharmonic [ænjarmónic], *a.* anharmónico.

animal black, negro animal.

ankle strap, correflla de zapato que cruza el pie un poco arriba del empeine.

Annam [ǽnæm], *s.,* **Annamese** [-mís], *s.* y *a.,* **Annamite** [-ait], *s.* y *a.* anamita (pueblo, raza, lengua).

annates [ǽnæts], *s. pl.* anata.

announcer, *s.* (rad.) anunciador, noticiador, el que anuncia algo o da noticias por radio.

anorthite [ænórzait], *s.* (min.) anortita.

Anschluss [anshlús], *s.* unión. (Gen. se aplica a la unión de Alemania y Austria, y en este sentido se dice *Anschluss,* como en alemán).

Anser [ǽnsœr], *s.* (zool.) género de los ánsares.

answer, *vn.*—**to a. back,** replicar; responder, refunfuñar.—**to a. to the name of,** tener por nombre, llamarse; reconocer como nombre suyo.

ant, *s.*—**a. bird,** pájaro hormiguero.—**a. heap, a. hillock** = ANT HILL.

antechurch [ǽntichœrch], *s.* (arq.) anteiglesia.

antenna, *s.*—**a. grounding switch, a. switch,** (rad.), interruptor de conexión de la antena con tierra.—**a. resistance,** (rad.) resistencia del circuito de la antena.

anteprandial [ǽntipréndiæl], *a.* de antes de comer.

Anthesteria [ǽnzestíriæ], *s. pl.* antesterias, ciertas fiestas griegas.

anthill, *s.* = ANT HILL.

anthracene [ǽnzræsín], *s.* (quím.) antraceno.

antidiphtheritic [ǽntidifzerític], *s.* y *a.* antidiftérico.—**antifreeze** [-fríš], *s.* y *a.* anticongelante, que impide la congelación.—**antikamnia** [-kǽmniæ], *s.* antikamnia (es nombre de fábrica), especie de anodino.—**antiknock** [-nóc], *s.* antidetonante, substancia que impide la detonación.—**anti-Leaguer** [-lígœr], *s.* opuesto a la Sociedad de las Naciones.—**antinode** [-nóud], *s.* (fís.) sección ventral, o de entre nodos (de una cuerda que vibra).—**antiparallel** [-pérælel], *s.* y *a.* antiparalelo.—**antisubmarine** [-súbmærín], *a.* (de defensa) contra submarinos.—**antitank** [-tǽnc], *a.* (de defensa) contra tanques.—**antitrust** [-trúst], *a.* opuesto a los trusts; contra los trusts.

anurous [æniúrus], *a.* anurio, sin cola.

anvil block, yunque.

---

any, *adv.*—**a. more than,** más bien que, más que, más de lo que; ni tampoco.—**if a.** (*V.* IF.)—**not a. more,** no más; ya no.—**not a. too** (seguido de *a.* o *adv.*), no . . . ni con mucho, no . . . ni mucho menos (*that is not any too easy,* eso no es fácil, ni con mucho, *o,* eso no es tan fácil); no más de lo absolutamente necesario (*I did not come any too early,* no vine más temprano de lo absolutamente necesario, *o,* apenas tuve tiempo para llegar, *o,* llegué precisamente a tiempo); no más de lo que conviene, o de lo debido. (Gen., al traducir esta locución, es mejor cambiar el giro.)—**to be a. good,** servir para algo o en algo, valer algo (*nada* en oración negativa).

anything. I. *pron.*—**like a.** (*V.* LIKE.)—**to be a. but,** no ser absolutamente, o de ninguna manera, o ni con mucho (*he is anything but rich,* no es rico, ni con mucho). **II.** *adv.*—**not a.,** en nada, en absoluto, de ninguna manera.

anywhere near, siquiera aproximadamente.

anywheres, *adv.* = ANYWHERE.

Anzac [ǽnsac], *s.* ejército de Australia y Nueva Zelandia en la guerra mundial de 1914; soldado de este ejército.

apartment, *s.* apartamento, departamento.—**a. building** = A. HOUSE.—**a. hotel,** casa de apartamentos donde se sirven comidas.—**a. house,** casa de apartamentos, de departamentos o de pisos.

aperiodic [æpœríódic], *a.* aperiódico.

aphis [ǽfis], *s.* afidio.

aphrodite [ǽfrodáit], *s.* (zool.) afrodita.

aplenty [æplénti], *a.* y *adv.* en abundancia; mucho; muy.

Apodes [ǽpodîš], *s. pl.* (zool.) ápodos.

apothesine [æpózesin] (es nombre de fábrica), *s.* apotesina (un anestésico local).

appeal. I. *s.* halago, incentivo, estímulo.—**a. from the chair,** apelación de la resolución del presidente (o quien preside). **II.** *vn.* recomendarse.—**to a. from the chair,** apelar de la resolución o del fallo del presidente (o de quien preside).

appearer [æpfarœr], *s.* el que aparece; compareciente.

appellable [æpélæbœl], *a.* apelable.

appendectomy [æpendéctomi], *s.* apendicitomía, operación para extraer el apéndice vermiforme.

Appian [ǽpiæn], *a.* apio, de Apio, de los Apios.—**A. Way,** Vía Apia.

apprentice, *va.* alquilar o contratar como aprendiz.

appropriation, *s.* asignación (de una suma para fin determinado).

a priori [ei priórai], *a.* y *adv. a priori.*

apriorism [-išm], *s.* (filos.) apriorismo.—**apriorist** [-ist], (filos.) apriorista.

apron conveyor, transportador de cadena sin fin.

Aptera [ǽptœræ], *s. pl.* ápteros.

apteryx [-ix], *s.* (zool.) ápterix, ave australiana de alas rudimentarias.

Apulian [æpiúliæn], *s.* y *a.* apulio.

aquarelle [æcuærél], *s.* acuarela.

arbor. *s.*—**a. shaft** = CARDAN JOINT.—**a. vitæ,** (anat.) centro medular, árbol de la vida.

arbo(u)red [árbœrd], *a.* arbolado.

arc, *s.*—**a. weld,** soldura de arco (hecha con el arco eléctrico).—**a.-weld,** *va.* soldar con arco eléctrico.

architectonics [árkitectónics], *s.* (filos.) arquitectónica (término kantiano).

arctic fox, zorro azul.

arditi [ardíti], *s. pl.* arditos, soldados escogidos italianos.

area, *s.* región; comarca; terreno, tierra.

are n't, aren't [arnt], *contracción de* ARE NOT.

argala [árgælæ], *s.* (zool.) marabú; garza carroñera de la India.

argenteous [arréntius], *a.* argénteo, argentino.

argol [árgol], *s.* estiércol seco.

---

argyrol [árʏirol] (nombre de fábrica), *s.* argirol, argyrol, especie de antiséptico argentoso.

Arian, *s.* y *a.* (etnología) ario.

arm, *s.*—**a. band,** faja que ciñe la manga, en señal de luto, dignidad, etc.—**ln arms,** de pecho, de teta (niño).

Armageddon [ármæguédʊn], *s.* Armagedón; lucha suprema.

armo(u)r, *va.* reforzar, armar (hormigón).—**a. plate,** coraza.—**armo(u)red concrete,** hormigón armado.

around, *adv.* al lado y a lo largo de.—**the other way a.,** al contrario, viceversa, al revés.

arrantly, *adv.* vergonzosamente.

arrowheaded [érrojéded], *a.* lanciforme; cuneiforme.

arsphenamine [arsfenæmin], *s.* =SALVARSAN.

artificial manure, abono artificial.

as, *adv.* y *conj.*—**a. . . . a,** tan . . . como, a pesar de lo . . . que (*as weak as he was, he got up,* a pesar de lo débil que estaba, se levantó).—**a. . . . a. anything, a. . . . a. can be,** muy . . ., sumamente . . . (*as pretty as can be,* sumamente bonito).—**a. best I (he, we,** etc.**) can,** como mejor pueda (podamos, etc.).—**a. early a.** (antes de una expresión de tiempo), ya en, allá, remontando hasta (a veces cambiando un poco el giro).—**a. far as I know,** que yo sepa, hasta donde yo puedo juzgar, según se me alcanza.—**a. far a. it goes,** hasta donde va, en lo que contiene, etc. (subentendiéndose que hay alguna deficiencia; vg. *his plan is good as far as it goes, but lacks details,* su plan es bueno en lo que contiene, *o* en general, pero le faltan detalles; *his declaration was true as far as it went,* su declaración era verdadera en lo que contenía, *o* hasta donde él se extendió, *o* hasta donde él la llevó).—**a. far back a.** (antes de una expresión de tiempo) = AS EARLY AS.—**a. from** (antes de una expresión de tiempo), a partir de.—**a. if,** como (*as if jesting,* como bromeando).—**a. if to,** como para, como tratando de.—**a. it seems, looks, sounds,** etc., o **a. it may seem,** etc. (después de *a.*), aunque parece . . ., por . . . que parezca (*strange as it may seem,* por extraño que parezca).—**a. late a.** (antes de una expresión de tiempo). Esta locución significa literalmente *tan recientemente como;* indica que el tiempo de que se trata es comparativamente reciente, y se traduce por *no más, no hace más, apenas,* etc., cambiando el giro según las circunstancias; vg. *I saw her as late as last Friday,* no hace más que el viernes pasado que la vi; *as late as 1820, a woman was burned there as a witch,* aun en 1820 se quemó allí a una mujer por bruja; *Mr. Smith died as late as last year,* el señor Smith no murió hasta el año pasado.—**a. many a.,** tantos como; hasta.—**a. of** (antes de una expresión de tiempo). Esta locución envuelve a veces la idea de *según los datos, según los informes,* etc. (del tiempo en cuestión); mas por lo común es un mero expletivo que no hay que traducir; vg. *the balance, as of July 15, was $1000,* el saldo el 15 de julio era (según los datos) de $1000.—**a. such,** como tal.—**a. the case may be,** según el caso.—**a. well,** también; tanto como (*the men as well as the women,* tanto los hombres como las mujeres).—**(he, you,** etc.**) might, o may, as well** (seguido de infinitivo), lo mismo da que; es mejor que (*you might as well say you did it,* lo mismo da que usted diga que lo hizo; mejor es que usted diga que lo hizo).

ascaris [éskæris], *s.* (zool.) ascáride.

Ashantee, Ashanti [æshánti], *s.* y *a.* achanti, de Achanti (región del África occidental).

ashpan [éshpæn], **ashpit** [-pit], *s.* cenicero.

aside, *adv.*—**fooling, jesting,** o **joking, a.,** hablando en serio, dejándose de bromas.

ask, *vn.*—**to a. after,** preguntar por.

asocial [æsóshæl], *a.* asocial, insociable; concentrado en sí mismo, despreciador del cuerpo social.

assembly, *s.* montaje (de máquinas).—**a. room,** paraninfo, salón de reuniones generales; cuarto de montaje.

Associate Justice, (E. U.) magistrado de la corte suprema.

assorted, *a.* surtido, mezclado.

assurance, *s.* declaración, manifestación.

assure, *vn.*—**to a. of,** asegurar, manifestar.

Assyriologist [æsírióloʏist], *s.* asiriólogo.

Assyriology [-ʏi], *s.* asiriología.

astrakhan [éstrækæn], *s.* astracán (piel); tela astracán (imitación de la piel).

astrometry [æstrómetri], *s.* astrometría, parte de la astronomía que trata de la posición y dimensiones de los astros.

astrophotography [éstrofotógræfi], *s.* astrofotografía, fotografía de los astros.

astrophotometer [-tómetœr], *s.* astrofotómetro, instrumento para determinar la luminosidad de los astros.—**astrophotometry** [-tómetri], *s.* astrofotometría.

asymptotic [ésimtótic], *a.* asintótico.

ataman [étamæn], *s.* atamán, jefe cosaco.

atonic, *a.* (gram.) átono, sin acento prosódico.

atrabilious [étræbíliʊs], *a.* melancólico.

attaghan [éttægæn], *s.* yatagán.

audition, *s.* prueba de idoneidad, examen de prueba (a menudo en concurso) a que se somete a quien solicita un puesto como músico o para hablar en público.

auditorium, *s.* paraninfo; casa de reuniones y funciones públicas.

auspice, *s.*—**under the auspices of,** bajo los auspicios de, (Am.) auspiciado por.

autarchy, autarky [ótarki], *s.* autarquía, independencia económica (de un país), capacidad de un país de bastarse a sí mismo económicamente.

authority, *s.* junta, comisión, cuerpo directivo, departamento.

autobus, *s.* bus, autobús.

autodyne [ótodain], *a.* (rad.) autodino.

autogiro [-ʏáiro], *s.* (aer.) autogiro.

autographic(al, *a.* (tlg.) autoregistrador; que recibe o transmite en facsímile.

autogyro [-ʏáiro], *s.* (aer.) autogiro.

autoist [ótoist], *s.* (fam.) automovilista, conductor de automóvil.

automat [ótomæt], *s.* artificio o mecanismo automático; restaurante de servicio mecánico, en que los platos salen al echar el precio por una abertura.

Avars [aváɾs], *s. pl.* (hist.) ávaros.

avatar [évætáɾ], *s.* avatar (encarnación de Vichnú); encarnación; deificación, conversión en objeto de adoración o culto.

Averroism [éverroïsm], *s.* averroísmo.—**Averroistic** [-ístic], *a.* averroísta.

aviatress [éivietres], **aviatrix** [éiviéitriks], *s.* aviatriz.

avoidance [ævóidæns], *s.* evitación, acción de evitar o eludir.

awning, *s.* toldo voladizo (sobre puertas y ventanas); toldo de entrada, que va de la orilla de la acera a la puerta de una casa.

axon [ékson], *s.* (anat.) axon.

azolitmin [ésolítmin], *s.* azolitmina, una de las materias colorantes del tornasol.

azym [ésim], **azyme** [ésaim], *s.* pan ácimo, pan sin levadura.

B

baby, *a.* de, para o como nene; pequeño; de tierna edad; infantil.—**b. act,** acción infantil; ley de exculpación de menores.—**b. basket,** cesto de ajuar para nene.—**b. beef,** ternerillo para el matadero; su carne.—**b. blue,** azul muy claro brillante.—**b. bond,** bono de bajo valor nominal (gen. 50 ó 100 dólares).—**b. buggy, b. carriage,** cochecillo de nene.—**b. farm,** casa de crianza de niños, donde se los mantiene por paga (es el significado general); hospicio de niños desamparados. —**b. grand (piano),** piano de cola pequeño.—**b. pin,** imperdible.—**b. talk,** habla de nene o de chiquillo, tono infantil.

baccarat [békæræ], *s.* bacará (juego).

bachelordom [bǽchelordŭm], *s.* los solteros, el mundo de los solteros.

back. I. *s.* soporte; superficie de apoyo (*the back of the waves*, la superficie del mar, las olas); seguidores, secuaces; (arq.) trasdós (de un arco); (elec.) extremo de transmisión (de una dinamo); *pl.* (**backs**), cueros gruesos.—**in b. of**, detrás de.— **the b. of the mind**, la profunda interioridad del pensamiento.—**with one's b. to the wall**, acosado, a raya, en situación desesperada. **II.** *a.*—**b. door**, puerta falsa.—**b. draft**, explosión de gases de combustión; corriente de aire invertida.—**b. page**, página izquierda.—**b. pitch**, distancia entre dos hileras paralelas de remaches.—**b. seat**, asiento de atrás; posición inferior o de poca monta. —**b. stream**, remolino.—**b. street**, calle apartada o no central.—**b. talk**, respuesta insolente. **III.** *va.* —**to b. the wrong horse**, apostar por el mal caballo; apoyar el partido o bando que pierde; escoger mal.—**to b. water**, impulsar un barco hacia atrás; retractarse.

backfire [bǽcfáiær]. **I.** *s.* quema que se hace para detener otra; medida o acción defensiva; (m. comb. int.) explosión prematura en el cilindro; explosión en la parte de atrás de un arma de fuego. **II.** *vn.* hacer una quema para detener otra; (m. comb. int.) tener explosiones prematuras.

background, *s.* antecedentes; fundamento, raíz, base; medio, circunstancias rodeantes.

backlash [bǽclǽsh]. **I.** *s.* retroceso. **II.** *vn.* retroceder.

backling [bǽkling], *adv.* hacia atrás.

backswept [-suépt], *a.* (aer.) que tiene el borde delantero inclinado hacia el eje lateral del avión.

backwardation [bǽkuœrdéishŭn], *s.* (en la bolsa) aplazamiento de la entrega de acciones, con premio pagado por el vendedor por la demora; dicho premio.

backwash [bǽcuósh]. **I.** *s.* agua lanzada hacia atrás por remos, hélices, etc.; consecuencias, resultados. **II.** *va.* lanzar agua hacia atrás; quitar o agregar aceite a (la lana); limpiar (un filtro) invirtiendo la corriente.

baculiform [bækiúliform], *a.* derecho, recto.

bad. I. *s.*—**to the b.** (con **to be**), (estar o quedar) peor; perder o salir perdiendo. **II.** *a.*—**b. child** (**boy, girl**), niño travieso, pilluelo.—**b. form**, mal gusto, falta de formalidad o de etiqueta; cosa que no se mira bien.

baffle painting, pintura de disfraz (de un barco en tiempo de guerra).

bagman [bǽgmæn], *s.* agente viajero.

bail. I. *s.* anillo, aro; soporte arqueado de un toldo; pared exterior (de un castillo); patio; tabique de tablas suspendidas.—**on b.**, bajo fianza. **II.** *va.* afianzar, asegurar, zunchar con aros o fajas. —**to b. out**, achicar, sacar el agua de.—**to b. up**, zunchar; detener. **III.** *vn.*—**to b. out**, (aer.) descender en paracaídas.

baked on, *a.* aplicado en caliente.

baking soda, bicarbonato de sosa.

baksheesh, bakshish [bǽkshǐsh], *s.* propina.

balaam [béilæm], *s.* hojarasca, material sin valor para llenar una revista o periódico; cesto de manuscritos rechazados (lit. t. **b. box**).

balance, *va.* nivelar (el presupuesto, etc.)

balancing flap, (aer.) alerón.

Balanoglossus [bǽlænoglósŭs], (zool.) balanogloso.

balata [bǽlætæ], *s.* (bot.) balata; su jugo.

Balkan [bólkæn], **Balkanic** [bolkǽnic], *a.* balcánico.

bally [bǽli], vil, maldito.

ballyhoo [bǽlijú], *s.* alharaca; alharaquero.

balsa [bálsæ], *s.* balsa; (bot.) balso.

bam [bæm]. **I.** engaño, fraude. **II.** *va.* y *vn.* engañar, embaucar.

bambusaceous [bæmbuséishŭs], *a.* semejante al bambú, de la familia del bambú.

banana, *s.*—**b. flour**, o **meal**, harina de plátano. —**b. oil**, acetato de amilo.

band, *s.* (mec.) correa; (min.) veta o vena delgada; (rad.) = WAVE BAND.—**b. brake**, freno de cinta.—**b. saw**, sierra de cinta, sierra sin fin.—**b.**

wagon, carro de banda de música; (fam.) carro triunfal (fig.), partido o bando de la multitud (**to get into, u on, the b. wagon**, adherirse a la causa popular, seguir la corriente).

bandbox, *s.* caja redonda u ovalada para sombreros, gorras, etc.

bank, *s.* grupo; manada; serie, hilera; (elec.) batería (de lámparas).—**b. acceptance**, giro contra un banco aceptado por éste.—**B. for, u of, International Settlements**, Banco de Arreglos Internacionales.—**b. gravel**, cascajo al natural.— **b. guaranty**, seguro (de un depositante) contra quiebra (del banco).—**b. holiday**, día de fiesta para los bancos, en que éstos se cierran; período en que los bancos están cerrados.

banking indicator, (aer.) inclinómetro.

banner, *a.* excelente, sobresaliente; principal; conspicuo.—**b. cry**, grito de combate.

bar, *s.*—**b. magnet**, barra imanada.—**b. sight**, mira de atrás (de un cañón).—**b. winding**, (elec.) arrollamiento de barras.

barb wire = BARBED WIRE.

bargain, *s.*—**in**, o **into, the b.**, además, por añadidura.

bark, *s.*—**his b. is worse than his bite**, perro ladrador, poco mordedor.

barken [bárken], *va.* y *vn.* encostrar(se); curtir con cortezas.

barnstorm [bárnstórm], *va.* dar funciones de teatro o perorar en las aldeas o en el campo.

barnstormer [-œr], *s.* actorzuelo, actor de poca monta; actor de aldea, actor ambulante.

barrage balloon, globo de cortina contra aeroplanos, o de trampa, del cual van suspendidos alambres o redes.

barrel roll, (aer.) vuelta de un avión alrededor de su eje longitudinal.

barrister at law, abogado.

base, *s.* (elec.) casquillo (de lámpara).

baseboard, *s.* (arq.) zócalo, friso inferior.

bash [bæsh]. **I.** *s.* golpe fuerte. **II.** *va.* golpear fuertemente; despedazar, quebrar a golpes.

basket, *s.* (aer.) barquilla (de un dirigible).

basketball [bǽsketból], *s.* juego de balón y cesto. (En algunas partes se llama *baloncesto*, en otras *basketbol*.)

basking shark, tiburón gigante del Atlántico setentrional.

bat, *s.* (en baseball) voleador, palo de volear.

batch, *s.* (min.) solterón.

bate, *va.*—**to b. one's breath**, entrecortar el aliento, pasmarse (ú. gen. en la frase **with bated breath**, pasmado, con aliento entrecortado).

bather [béiœr], *s.* bañista.

batsman, *s.* voleador, el que volea la pelota en el juego de baseball.

battle cruiser, crucero de combate.

battleship, *s.* acorazado de línea.

be, *vn.* Seguido de infinitivo equivale a veces a: 1) *can, could*, vg. *how am I to know it?* ¿cómo puedo saberlo? *what were we to do?* ¿qué podíamos hacer? 2) *to be going to*, ir a, vg. *he was to speak that evening*, iba a hablar esa noche. Seguido de gerundio indica a veces un acto que acaba de ejecutarse o se piensa ejecutar pronto: *I am sending you the book under separate cover*, le envío el libro en otra cubierta; *we are not dining at home tonight*, esta noche no comemos (o comeremos) en casa. Seguido de *to be* y un participio en frases impersonales equivale a *ser* de seguido de infinitivo reflexivo: *it is to be regretted*, es de sentirse; *it is to be noted*, es de notarse.—**b. it so**, sea, así sea.—**to b. in**, estar adentro; estar en casa, en la oficina, etc. (en español se usa a menudo *estar* simplemente). —**to b. in with** (*v.* IN).—**to b. out**, haber terminado (*v.* t. OUT).—**to b. out with**, estar reñido con.

beacon, *s.* señal; señal luminosa, luz.

beam, *s.* ástil, cruz (de balanza).—**b. balance**, balanza de cruz.

bean, *s.* (vulg.) cabeza, testa.

bear, *va.*—**to b. interest**, devengar interés.

beautician [biutíshæn], *s.* embellecedor, persona que se ocupa en el trabajo de salones de belleza.

beauty salon, o **shop,** salón de belleza.

become, vn. pasar a ser.

bed of roses, ganga, canonjía, situación o puesto de holganza.

bedrock. I. s. roca firme; fundamento, base; lo peor, lo último, el límite. **II.** a. fundamental.

beef cattie, ganado vacuno de ceba, o de engorde.

befool, va. engañar, embaucar.

befuddle [bifúdœl], va. confundir, ofuscar.

beg, vn. suplicar, rogar.—**to b. off from,** rogar (uno) que se le exima de; excusarse de; evadir con súplicas; no desear, querer o pensar (ir, hacer algo, etc.)

begin, vn.—**not to b. to,** no . . . ni con mucho (he cannot begin to do what we need, él no puede hacer lo que necesitamos, ni con mucho; this does not begin to be enough, esto no es suficiente, ni con mucho).—**to b. with,** en primer lugar, para empezar.

begorra, begorry [bigórræ, -rri], interj. ¡caramba! ¡por Dios!

bell. I. s.—**b. hop** = B. BOY. **II.** va. acampanar; poner campana a.—**to b. the cat,** poner el cascabel al gato. **III.** vn. acampanarse; florecer.

belleric [beléric], s. (bot.) belérico, mirobalano.

belt. I. s. zona; estrecho; tira; (mar.) faja de la coraza en la línea de flotación; (fam.) golpe. —**b. course,** (arq.) faja o banda horizontal. **II.** va. poner correa a (una máquina); unir o conectar por correa; ceñir; rodear; golpear, herir.

beret [beréi], s. gorra vizcaína.

berth. I. s. (mar.) dársena, embarcadero, atracadero. **II.** va. atracar, llevar al puerto; dar camarote o pasaje a; dar anclaje a; entablar. **III.** vn. atracar, llegar a puerto.

beside the mark, o **the point,** impertinente, que no viene al caso; inconducente.

best. I. a.—**the b. part of,** la mayor parte de, casi todo (the best part of a month, casi todo un mes). **II.** adv.—**b. of all,** lo mejor de todo, lo mejor es que. **III.** va. aventajar, vencer, ganar a.

better. I. a.—**the b. part of** = THE BEST PART OF. **II.** adv. (fam.) = HAD BETTER.—**b. late than never,** más vale tarde que nunca.—**no b. and no worse,** ni mejor ni peor.

between, prep.—**b. the devil and the deep (blue) sea,** entre la espada y la pared.—**b. you and me,** entre usted y yo, entre nos. A veces se agregan palabras expletivas, que no se traducen; vg. **b. you and me and the lamppost.**

betwixt and between, a medias; así así; ni lo uno ni lo otro.

bewildering [biufídœring], a. perplejo, que pone a uno perplejo.

bicolor, bicolored [baicúlœr, -d], a. bicolor, de dos colores.

bifocal [baifóukæl], s. y a. bifocal, de lente dividida (dícese de los anteojos en que cada lente está dividida en dos, para distancias distintas).

big, a. noble, magnánimo.—**b. business,** negocio en grande escala; empresa o empresas comerciales dominadoras o acaparadoras.—**b. gun, b. shot,** persona de alto coturno.—**b. stick,** garrote, machete (fig.), poder de coacción.—**b. talk,** bravatas, roncas; lenguaje altisonante.—**b. toe,** dedo pulgar del pie.—**b. with,** preñado o lleno de, que encierra mucho o muchos (resultados, etc.).— **b. with child, b. with young,** preñada.

bike [báic], s. bicicleta.

bill, s.—**b. book,** cartera para billetes.—**b. form** = BILLHEAD.—**b. of particulars,** declaración o exposición detallada del demandante o demandado. —**b. rendered,** cuenta antes girada.

billposter, s. fijador de carteles; cartel.

bimotored [baimótœrd], a. de dos motores.

binder, s. capa interior, sobretripa (de cigarro).

biometry [baiómetri], s. cálculo de la duración probable de la vida; estadística biológica.

bird, s.—**b. bath,** alberquilla o pila de baño para pájaros.—**b. spider,** migala.

birdman [bœrdmæn], s. aviador.

birdwoman [-úmæn], s. aviatriz.

birefringence [báirefrínyens], s. birrefringencia, doble refracción.—**birefringent** [-yent], a. birrefringente, de doble refracción.

biretta [birétæ], s. (igl.) birreta.

bisexual, a. (psic.) que posee las características mentales de ambos sexos; movido sexualmente por ambos sexos.

bit, s.—**b. by b.,** a poquitos.—**to do one's b.,** ayudar uno en lo que pueda; servir uno a su patria.

bitter-ender [bítœréndœr], s. persona porfiada e intransigente.

bitulithic [bítiulízic], a. de piedra partida y asfalto. (Es término de fábrica. Puede adoptarse bitulítico.)

bizarre, a. caprichoso, fantástico.

black. I. s.—**in the b.,** del lado del haber, sin deudas. **II.** a.—**b. belt,** (E. U.) región de los negros.—**b. light,** rayos ultraviolados (del espectro).—**b. mass,** misa de difuntos.—**b. pope,** "papa negro," general de los jesuítas.—**B. Shirt,** camisanegra (fascista italiano). **III.** va.—**to b. out,** apagar las luces en (precaución contra bombardeo aéreo).—**to b. up,** pintarse de negro.

black-out, s. apagamiento de luces.

blank. I. a.—**b. assay** = BLANK ANALYSIS.—**b. check,** cheque en blanco; carta blanca.—**b. determination** = BLANK ANALYSIS.—**b. endorsement,** endoso al portador. **II.** va. (gen. con **out**), obstruir; borrar; sacar o cortar a punzón o a troquel.

blanket. I. s. capa, cubierta; manto, velo que oculta o cubre; (ing.) capa bituminosa.—**to throw a wet blanket on,** poner peros a. **II.** a. irrestricto, incondicional, absoluto. **III.** va. (rad.) paralizar (un radiorreceptor) por medio de fuertes señales o interferencia.

bleach, s. blanquimiento. *

bleacher, s. asiento o banco de bajo precio (ll. t. **bleacher seat**).

blear. I. s. impedimento de la vista, algo que la nubla. **II.** va. descarriar.

bleed, va.—**to b. white,** agotar; arrancar hasta el último céntimo a.

blesser [blésœr], s. bendecidor; bienhechor.

blighter [bláitœr], s. canalla.

blighty [bláiti]. **I.** s. Inglaterra; la tierra natal; ida del frente a casa o a la tierra natal o a otro lugar, con licencia o por causa de heridas o enfermedad (dicho de los soldados); causa de tal ida; soldado herido o enfermo que regresa del frente. **II.** a. inglés; que permite o exige que un soldado vuelva a casa o a su tierra (dícese de heridas, enfermedades, etc.).

blimp [blimp], s. (aer.) pequeño dirigible fláccido; (cine) caja silenciosa para una cámara fotográfica.

blind, a. de ciegos, para ciegos; ilegible, ininteligible; a ciegas.—**b. flying,** (aer.) vuelo a ciegas.—**b. snake,** (zool.) tiflope.—**b. spot,** (rad.) lugar donde la recepción es mala.

blinding [bláinding], a. que ciega; deslumbrador.

bloc, s.—**en b.,** en conjunto, global; enterizo, de una pieza.

block, s. caja (de polea).

blood, s.—**b. donor,** el que da su sangre para transfusión.—**b. pressure,** presión sanguínea, presión arterial.—**b. transfusion,** transfusión de sangre.

blow. I. s. fanfarronada; fanfarrón; holgorio, parranda; salida de gas; (ing.) rotura de una ataguía.—**at a (o one) b.,** de un golpe; repentinamente. **II.** va. convidar (a tomar algo); traicionar, denunciar; regar con agua (tabaco).—**to b. off steam,** dejar salir vapor; desfogarse, soltar la lengua.—**to b. through,** (m. v.) arrojar el aire por medio de una corriente de vapor.—**to b. one's horn,** o **trumpet,** alabarse.—**to b. the gaff,** revelar un secreto. **III.** vn. silbar; hincharse, abultarse (cemento, etc.); salir, escapar (un gas); quemarse (un fusible); ser llevado o levantado por el viento (polvo, etc.); irse, marcharse.—**to b. hot and cold,** estar entre sí y no, vacilar.—**to b. up,** frustarse; fracasar.—**to b. upon,** desacreditar; denunciar.

blowhole [blóujóul], *s.* respiradero; (fund.) escarabajo.

blowpipe, blowtube [blóutiúb], *s.* cerbatana.

blue. I. *s.* mujer pedante, doctora.—**the b.,** el cielo; el mar. **II.** *a.* erudita, sabida (mujer).—**b.-black,** azul muy obscuro.—**b. blood,** sangre azul. —**b.-blooded,** de sangre azul.—**b. fox,** zorro azul, raposo ferrero.—**b. lead,** (min.) galena.—**b. ointment,** ungüento mercurial.—**b. plate,** plato grande, gen. azul, dividido en compartimentos, en los cuales se sirven a un tiempo varios alimentos que forman una comida.—**b.-ribbon jury,** jurado especial escogido, compuesto de personas selectas. —**b. streak,** relámpago, rayo; cosa hecha con gran rapidez; como un relámpago, a la carrera (**to talk a b. streak,** hablar por los codos, soltar la tarabilla). **III.** *va.* lavar en agua de añil o azulada. **IV.** *vn.* ponerse azul.

blurb [blœrb], *s.* breve resumen encomiástico en que se describe a grandes rasgos el contenido de un libro; advertencia (gen. de los editores) que va en el forro del libro.

blush, *s.*—**at,** o **on, first b.,** a primera vista, al momento.

board of trustees, junta de síndicos.

boast, *vn.*—**nothing to b.,** o **speak, of,** no asciende a mucho, no es gran cosa.

bob. I. *s.* corcho (en la pesca con anzuelo); cebo que consiste en un manojo de trapos o lombrices. **II.** *va.* y *vn.* pescar con cebo de *bob;* golpear ligeramente; mover(se) de arriba abajo, subir y bajar.—**to b. up,** presentarse inesperadamente, surgir.

bobby [bóbi], *s.* policía (agente).

bobolink [bóbolink], *s.* =REEDBIRD.

Boche, boche [bosh], *s.* y *a.* alemán (es término francés despreciativo, que es mejor dejar en el original).

bock [boc], **bock beer** [bîær], cerveza extrafuerte.

body, *s.* cadáver.

bog, *va.* y *vn.* (a veces con **down**), hundir(se); atollar(se).—**to b. in,** emprender algo con vigor, echar el resto.

Bolivian [bolíviæn], *s.* y *a.* boliviano.

bolony [bolóuni], *s.* tonterías, hojarasca.

Bombacaceae [bombækéisii], *s.* (bot.) bombáceas.—**bombacaceous** [-shus], *a.* bombáceo.

bomber [bómœr], *s.* avión de bombardeo.

bonbonière [bónboniéær], *s.* bombonera.

bonded debt, deuda consolidada.

bonder [bóndœr], *s.* depositante de mercancías; (alb.) perpiaño.

bonehead [bóunjéd], *s.,* **boneheaded** [-jéded], *a.* mentecato, imbécil.

bonnet, *s.* (aut.) =HOOD.

boo [bu]. **I.** *s.* grita, rechifla. **II.** *va.* dar grita, rechiflar, silbar. **III.** *interj.* ¡fuera! ¡mira! ¡qué va!

boob [bub], *s.* bobo, zopenco.

booby, *s.* el que en un juego sale en zaga, o tiene el menor número de tantos.—**b. hatch,** cárcel; manicomio.—**b. prize,** premio que se da al peor jugador (al *booby*).

book. I. *s.*—**b. tile,** teja en forma de libro cerrado, con uno de los lados largos cóncavo y el otro convexo. **II.** *a.* de libros; para libros; en o según los libros (de contabilidad). **III.** *va.* apalabrar, hacer arreglos para (pasaje, cuartos, etc.).

booking [búking], *s.* registro; compra o venta de billetes.—**b. clerk,** dependiente encargado de la venta de billetes; taquillero.—**b. office,** oficina de venta de billetes; taquilla.

boom, *s.* cordón, cabeza (de puente).

booster battery, (rad.) batería de conservación del voltaje en el detector.

boozer [búsœr], *s.* bebedor, borrachín.

boozy [búsi], *a.* achispado, calamocano.

bore, *vn.*—**to b. from within,** crear descontento o causar defección en un gremio u otro cuerpo introduciendo en él como miembros agentes secretos de propaganda hostil; atacar desde adentro por traición.

born, *a.* de nacimiento, por naturaleza.—**b. to,** nacido en, o para.

bother, *vn.* molestarse.—**to b. about,** o **with,** molestarse o preocuparse con; hacer caso de.

bottleneck [bótœlnéc], *s.* estrechura; impedimento, obstáculo, dificultad.

bottom. I. *s.* tierra baja; vallecico (gen. en pl.); (f. c.) balasto.—**at (the) b.,** en el fondo, en realidad.—**to be at the b. of,** ser causa de; tener la culpa de. **II.** *a.* inferior, de abajo.—**b. ice**=ANCHOR ICE.—**b. side up,** patas arriba.

bounder [báundœr], *s.* persona mal vestida o sin modales.

bound up in, inseparable de; muy consagrado a; absorto en.

Bourdon [búrdón], *s.*—**B. ga(u)ge,** manómetro de Bourdon.—**B. tube,** tubo del manómetro de Bourdon.

bow [báu], *s.*—**to make one's b.,** presentarse, entrar; ser presentado.

box coat, sobretodo.

bracing, *s.* arriostramiento.

bracket. I. *s.* clase, grupo; categoría. **II.** *va.* poner entre paréntesis; unir, juntar; poner en una misma clase.

Brain Trust, (pol., E. U.) Trust de Sesos, o Trust de Sesudos, grupo de profesores que llamó como consejeros el presidente Franklin D. Roosevelt.

bran-new, *a.* nuevecito, enteramente nuevo.

brass. I. *s.* descaro, desfachatez.—**to get down to b. tacks,** entrar en materia, ir al grano. **II.** *va.* revestir de latón.—**to b. it**=TO BRAZEN IT OUT.

brassard [brǽsærd], *s.* brazal; faja que ciñe la manga.

brazing [bréising], *a.* de soldar, para soldar.—**b. metal,** latón de soldar, soldadura de latón.

breach, *s.*—**more honored in the b. than in the observance,** que descuella más por lo que se viola que por lo que se observa (precepto, principio, etc.).

breadboard [brédbórd], *s.* tabla para amasar o cortar pan.

break, *s.* oportunidad.—**an even b.,** oportunidad igual o justa; (salir, estar, etc.) sin ganar ni perder; empate, empatados (cambiando el giro).

breath, *s.*—**in the same b.,** al mismo tiempo, a renglón seguido.

breathe, *va.* decir (contar).

bridging [bríying], *s.* (arq.) puntales separadores.

brief, *s.*—**in b.** en resumen, concisamente.—**to hold no b. for,** no ser defensor de, no estar defendiendo.

brine, *va.* salar.

bring. I. *va.*—**to b. around,** ganarse a, convertir, persuadir; curar, sacar bien.—**to b. into play,** poner en juego.—**to b. off,** llevar a cabo, lograr el éxito de; librar; llevarse.—**to b. oneself to,** resolverse a. **II.** *vn.* producir.

briny [bráini], *a.* salado.

brittle star, (zool.) ofiuro.

broadcasting station, (rad.) difusora, emisora.

broadtail [bródtéil], *s.* carnero de Bujaria (o Bucaria); caracul (astracán de la mejor calidad).

bromidion [bromídiun], *s.* perogrullada.

bronchial pneumonia, bronchopneumonia [brónconiumónie], *s.* bronconeumonía.

broom brush, cepillo de escoba para ropa.

brown, *a.*—**b. coat,** (alb.) segunda capa de enlucido.—**b. mixture,** mixtura de orozuz y otros ingredientes muy usada para la tos.—**b. shirt,** camisaparda, nazi.

Brownian [bráuniæn], *a.* browniano.

Brumaire [brúméær], *s.* brumario (mes).

brush broom=BROOM BRUSH.

bryonin [bráionin], *s.* (quím.) brionina.

Bryozoa [bráiosóœ], *s. pl.* (zool.) briozoarios.

bryozoan [-sóœn], *s.* a. briozoario.

bubal [biúbæl], (zool.) búbalo.

bubbler, *s.* surtidor de beber agua.

bubly [búbli], *s.* muchacho, chicuelo.

buck, *s.* (fam.) dólar.

buckaroo [búkærú], s. vaquero; amansador.
buffing [búfing], a. de pulir, pulidor.
buff wheel, rueda de pulir.
bug, s. (fam.) microbio.
building tile, bloque hueco de hormigón o de arcilla.
built, a.—**b.-in,** como parte de la estructura, hecho en la estructura misma.—**b.-up,** compuesto de varias partes, piezas o capas.—**b.-up beam,** viga compuesta.—**b.-up roof,** tejado de capas superpuestas.
bulb, s. ensanche, protuberancia; (elec.) ampolla o bombilla (de lámpara); lámpara termiónica; (fís.) cubeta o bola (del termómetro); ampolla o pera (de jeringa).—**b. syringe,** jeringa de pera o de Crequy.
bulkhead, s. muro de contención ribereño.
bullyrag [búlirræg], va. molestar, atormentar; dar una broma a.
bump, va. y vn.—**to b. off,** matar, despachar; morirse.
bumper, a. lleno; excelente, magnífico; muy grande, numeroso o abundante.
bundle, vn. (gen. con **off**), liar y marcharse; liarlas; escabullirse, largarse.
Bunsen burner [búnsen bœrnœr], lámpara o mechero (de) Bunsen.
burn, vn.—**to b. out,** quemarse; apagarse.
burrow. I. s. cueva, madriguera. II. va. hacer cueva o cuevas en; hacer cavando o excavando.—**to b. oneself,** encuevarse, ocultarse. III. vn. hacer cueva o cuevas; encuevarse.
bus, s. (aut.) bus, autobús; chico o chica que sirven en un restaurante, sobre todo como ayudantes (llámanse t. **bus boy, bus girl**).
bushhammer [búshjémœr], s. pica, escoda.
business is business, la cuenta es cuenta.
bust, s. (cine) fotografía grande sacada a quemarropa (gen. de un detalle o de un actor).
but, conj. si.—**b. that,** que no; sino que; si no fuera porque.
butyl [biútil], s. (quím.) butilo.—**b. alcohol,** alcohol butílico (ll. t. **butylic alcohol**).
butylene [biútilin], s. (quím.) butileno.
butyrometer [biútirómetœr], s. butirómetro, medidor de la grasa de la leche.
by. I. prep. Antes de gerundio indica manera, y no se traduce (by studying, you will learn, estudiando, Vd. aprenderá). II. adv.—**b. and large,** de una manera general, como un todo.

C

cabaret, s. cabaret, cabaré.
cabinet, s. caja (de radio), mueble (término muy usado en vez de caja, pero que parece inapropiado).
caddy. I. s.=CADDIE. II. vn. ser o servir de muchacho de golf.
cahoot [cæhút]. I. s. compañía.—**to go cahoots,** formar compañía, asociarse. II. vn. ser o hacerse compañeros o socios.
caláboose [cælæbús], s. cárcel; calabozo.
call, va.—**to c. a bond,** avisar que un bono se pagará.—**to c. a halt,** detenerse, parar; (con **on**) detener, poner fin a.—**to c. attention to,** llamar la atención sobre.—**to c. it a day,** parar (en el trabajo).—**to c. it quits,** parar (en el trabajo); dejar la reyerta, dejar de reñir o de altercar.—**to c. to the bar,** recibir de abogado.—**to c. to the colors,** llamar al servicio militar.
calorics [kælórics], s. termología, ciencia del calor.
camaraderie [cámáráderí], s. compañerismo.
camion [cámión], s. autocamión militar.
camper [kémpœr], **camper-out** [-áut], s. persona que acampa o vive transitoriamente en tienda (toldo), choza rústica o campamento (gen. por placer).
campfire [kémpfáiœr], s. hoguera o fuego que se enciende en el campo o en un campamento, sea por placer, sea para cocinar; reunión.—**c. girl,** niña de la organización **Camp Fire Girls,** que es

semejante a la de las niñas exploradoras (girl scouts).
camp follower, acompañante civil, persona que, sin ser militar, acompaña a un ejército (criado, vendedor, etc.)
campanulate [cæmpæniuleit], a. acampanado.
canal rays, (fís.) rayos de Goldstein, rayos positivos.
cancan [cæncæn, cáncán], s. cancán.
Canis [kéinis], (zool.) género de los cánidos; (astr.) el Can.
cannily [cænili], adv. sagazmente; garbosamente; dignamente. (V. CANNY.)
cap, s. chapa (de la brújula).
capilliform [cæpíliform], a. capiliforme, de forma capilar o de pelo.
capital ship, acorazado mayor, de más de 10.000 toneladas inglesas.
captain, va. y vn. capitanear.
carbarn [cárbárn], **car barn,** s. cochera de tranvías.
carbo [carbo], s. residuo carbonoso de destilación.
carbon black = GAS BLACK.
carburetion [cárburéshʊn], s. carburación.
cardiology [cárdióloyi], s. cardiología, ciencia del corazón.
cardioscope [cárdioscoup], s. cardioscopio.
carillon [cárilon], carillón, conjunto de campanas acordadas; toque o sonido de ellas.
carmagnole [cármañóul], s. carmañola.
carpophagous [carpófægus], a. frugívoro.
carrac, carrack, s. (mar.) carraca; galeón.
carriage, s. cochecillo de niño.—**c. bolt,** perno de coche, perno grande de cuello cuadrado y cabeza de hongo.
carrier, s. agente transmisor o de propagación (de una enfermedad); empresa de transporte (gen. se aplica a los ferrocarriles); (rad.) onda de transmisión.
carry. I. va. ganar las elecciones en.—**to c. it,** ganar.—**to c. over,** guardar, tener para más tarde; aplazar, dar plazo a.—**to c. up to,** ajustar o amoldar a. II. vn. poderse transportar.—**to c. over,** continuar, persistir, durar.—**to c. through,** conducir a algo, ser eficaz.
carry-over, s. sobrante; reserva; (contabilidad) suma que viene o pasa de la cuenta o página anterior; saldo anterior.
cartel, s. (e. p.) sindicato o asociación comercial, trust; (pol.) convenio, acuerdo.—**cartelize** (cártelaiś), va. y vn. incorporar(se) en un sindicato.
cartogram [cártogræm], s. cuadro gráfico estadístico comparativo.
cascara sagrada [cæscáræ sægrádæ], cáscara sagrada.
cash. I. s.—**c. and carry,** pago al contado con transporte por el comprador. II. va. y vn.—**to c. in,** cambiar por dinero, hacer efectivo; sacar provecho (a veces con **on,** de).
casing, s. entubado de retención (en los pozos de petróleo, etc.).
casket, s. caja mortuoria.
cast, a.—**c.-shell tube,** tubo obtenido por estiramiento de un tubo vaciado.—**c. stone,** piedra artificial, hormigón prevaciado (ll. en algunas partes piedra reconstituida).
casual, a. indiferente, de paso, como de paso (a veces con fingimiento), parentético; advenedizo, extraño; (víctima) de accidente.
catalyst [cætelist], s. catalizador.
catapult, va. lanzar.
catchy [cæchi], a. atractivo; engañoso; irregular, interrumpido.
categorematic [cætegóremætic], a. (lóg.) categoremático.
catelectrode [cæteléctroud], s. electrodo negativo; cátodo.
cathedral chimes, tubos metálicos acordados que se tañen con un martillo e imitan las campanas.

cathode ray, rayo catódico.

cattle pest, morriña.

caveat, *s.* amonestación, advertencia.

ceiling, *s.* (aer.) techo; cima; límite superior; colmo.

cellophane [sélofein], *s.* celofano (es nombre de fábrica), tela transparente impermeable de envolver.

cement tile, baldosín o loseta de cemento, mosaico.

cenacle [sénækœl], *s.* cenáculo.

cenobium [senóbium], *s.* cenobio, monasterio.

Cephalochorda [séfælocórdæ], *s. pl.* (zool.) heptocardios o cefalocordatos.

Cephalopoda [séfælópodæ], *s. pl.* cefalópodos.—**cephalopodous** [-dus], *a.* cefalópodo.

cerargyrite [serárryrait], *s.* (min.) plata córnea.

certain. I. *s.* cierta suma (de dinero); cierto número.—**for c.,** con seguridad. **II.** *a.*—**to be c. to,** no poder dejar de; con toda seguridad (cambiando el giro: *this is certain to be useless,* esto será inútil con toda seguridad).

chain store, (en algunas partes) tienda múltiple. Puede también llamarse *tienda en serie.*

chairman, *s.* presidente, presidenta, persona que preside.

chancellery [chánseleri], **chancelry** [-selri], *s.* cancillería.

chancery, *s.* tribunal. (El nombre se aplica a tribunales de varias clases.)—**in c.,** en litigio; en aprietos; debajo del brazo del contrario (dícese de la cabeza de un boxeador).

chancy [chánsi], *a.* incierto, arriesgado; de buena suerte; que promete.

change, *va.*—**to c. face,** o **front,** cambiar de opinión o de conducta, desdecirse, virar de bordo (fig.)—**to c. one's tune,** cambiar de tono, cambiar de actitud.

change house, fonda, taberna.

chaperon, *s.* señora de compañía.

chauffeur, *s.* chofer.

cheat, *va.*—**to c. out of,** sacarle o quitarle (a uno) por engaño; privar de (gen. por engaño).

check. I. *s.* verificación, comprobación; comprobador, probador; grieta; grietecilla filiforme (en acero, hormigón, etc.); ensayo, prueba; marca.—**c. boy** (**girl**), mozo (moza) que recibe y guarda los sombreros, abrigos, etc. en restaurantes, etc. y da las contraseñas.—**c. mark,** marca.—**c.-off,** recaudación de contribuciones de los obreros a los gremios, haciendo que los patrones las rebajen de los salarios.—**c. room,** cuarto donde se deja algo a guardar, recibiendo una contraseña.—**c.-up,** examen, comprobación.—**c. writer,** máquina de estampar cheques, que arruga la parte del papel donde va escrito el importe del cheque. **II.** *va.* rajar, agrietar; dar a guardar (el sombrero, etc.), recibiendo una contraseña de reclamo.—**to c. up,** verificar, comprobar.—**to c. up on,** comprobar lo hecho por; seguir la pista a. **III.** *vn.* corresponder, estar conforme.

checking. I. *s.* agrietamiento. **II.** *a.*—**c. account,** cuenta corriente (en un banco).

checkroom [chécrúm], *s.* =CHECK ROOM.

cheek, *s.* **with (one's) tongue in (one's) c.,** fingidamente, irónicamente.

cheese. I. *s.* cosa o persona que vale (*that is the cheese,* ésa es la cosa, ése es el hombre). **II.** *va.*—**c. it,** calle, déjese de eso; márchese.

chef, *s.* maestro de cocina.

chela [chílæ], *s.* semiesclavo, esclavo que se cría con una familia; discípulo; novicio.

chenopodiaceous [kínopódiéishus], *a.* (bot.) quenopodiáceo.

chew, *va.*—**to c. the rag,** machacar, porfiar, dale que dale (cambiando un poco el giro).

chicken, *s.* (fam.) chica.

child, *a.* del niño, de (los) niños.—**c. labor,** trabajo de menores.—**c. welfare,** bien del niño.

chimera, *s.* (zool.) quimera, achagual.

chimney cap, capping, o **cope,** remate de chimenea.

chip, *s.* viruta.—**to carry a c. on one's shoulder,** ser belicoso, contencioso o pendenciero.

chippy [chípi], *s.* chica callejera.

chiropter [kiróptœr], *s.* (zool.) quiróptero. **Chiroptera** [-teræ], *s. pl.* quirópteros.

chisel, *va.* y *vn.* minar, socavar, atacar; engañar, embaucar.—**chiseler,** *s.* engañador; minador, socavador, el que ataca y quiere destruir o estorbar.

chiton [cáiton], *s.* túnica; (zool.) chitón.

chock, *s.* (mar.) cornamusa de guía.

choke, choke coil, (elec.) bobina de reactancia o de reducción.

chondrocranium [cóndrocréinium], *s.* (anat.) condrocráneo.

chord, *s.* cuerda; cordón; (aer.) cuerda; (ing.) cordón, cabeza (de un puente de celosía).

chorda dorsalis [córdæ dorséilis], (anat.) columna vertebral embrionaria.

choroid plexus, plexo coroideo.

chortle [chórtœl], *vn.* reírse.

Christology [cristóloyi], *s.* (teol.) cristología, parte de la teología que trata de la persona y atributos de Cristo; doctrina relativa a Cristo.

Christolatry [-lætri], *s.* cristolatría, adoración de Cristo.

Christophany [-fæni], *s.* aparición de Cristo.

chromatin [crómætin], *s.* (biol.) substancia protoplasmática del núcleo de las células, considerada como base de la herencia.

chrome steel, acero cromo, acero que contiene una pequeña contidad de cromo. (Muy común es la forma galicada *acero al cromo.*)

chromoplasm [-plæsm], *s.* =CHROMATIN.

chromosome [crómosoum], *s.* (boil.) partícula del protoplasma del núcleo de las células.

chronophotograph [cróunofótogræph], *s.* cada una de las fotografías que se sacan consecutivamente para el cinematógrafo.

chuck. I. *s.* pollo; muchacho, chico. **II.** *va.* sujetar o poner en el manguito portaherramienta.

chug. I. *s.* ruido sordo explosivo intermitente, traqueteo (ll. t. **chug-chug**). **II.** *vn.* traquear.

cinder, *s.* escoria; brasa; rescoldo; (gen. *pl.*) escarbillos, carbón a medio quemar; escoria volcánica.

cingulum [síngulum], *s.* cordón de fibras que une las circunvoluciones del cerebro.

cirque [sœrc], *s.* (geol.) cavidad de erosión glaciaria.

cistern, *s.* cubeta (de barómetro).

civvies [sívis], *s. pl.* de CIVVY; traje de paisano (a distinción del militar).

civvy [sívi], *s.* paisano (no militar).

class struggle, class war, lucha o guerra de clases (gen. se aplica a la entre el capital y el trabajo).

claustrophobia [clóstrofóubiæ], *s.* claustrofobia, temor anormal del encierro y de los lugares estrechos.

claw, *s.* (zool.) pinzas (del cangrejo, etc.)

clean. I. *a.* honesto; no endosado (bono, etc.); bien formado; con pocas correcciones o sin ellas (prueba de imprenta). **II.** *va.*—**to c. out,** sacarle hasta el último céntimo a. **III.** *vn.*—**to c. up after one,** limpiar lo que uno ha ensuciado, o después que uno ha acabado (de hacer algo).

clean-up, *s.* (clcc.) desaparición de los últimos vestigios de gas dentro de una lámpara eléctrica.

clear, *a.*—**c. of,** lejos de, a distancia de, sin tocar; separado de.

clearance sale, (venta de) realización.

cleat, *s.* tirilla de empalme; fiador, afianzador.

cleft, *s.* grieta, rajadura, fisura.

click, *va.* agarrar bruscamente, arrebatar; recibir o sufrir repentinamente.—**to c. it,** caer enfermo; caerle a uno un mal serio.

cling, *vn.* asirse.—**to c. to,** perseverar o persistir en; confiar en.

clinic, *s.* consultorio, dispensario.

clinic (al, *a.*—**c. chart,** gráfica de un enfermo, en que se representan gráficamente la temperatura, pulso, etc.—**c. thermometer,** termómetro clínico, o médico.

clip, *s.* celeridad, rapidez.

clock error, movimiento del reloj o del cronómetro (tiempo que el reloj pierde o gana por unidad de tiempo); estado del reloj o del cronómetro (error total en un momento dado). (Mejor es decir en todo caso *error del reloj,* o *del cronómetro,* expresión de significado obvio.)

close, *adv.*—**c. to,** muy cerca de; en relaciones muy íntimas con.—**c.-tongued,** callado, reservado.

closed chapter, asunto concluído.

clout, *va.* golpear, herir.

club car, (f. c.) coche club, arreglado como cuarto de club, con mesas de escribir, periódicos, etc.

clump, *vn.* andar torpemente con fuertes pisadas.

coaling [cóuling]. **I.** *s.* toma de carbón. **II.** *a.* de toma o aprovisionamiento de carbón.—**c. station,** puerto de toma de carbón.

cobalt blue, azul de cobalto.

cobwork [cóbuœrc], *s.* estructura de trozas horizontales.

cochin [cóuchin], *s.* y *a.* cochinchino (aplícase a las gallinas).

cockish [cókish], *a.* engreído, hinchado.

cockpit, *s.* parte baja de popa de la cubierta (de un yate).

cocky [coki] *a.* =COCKISH.

cocoa bean, grano de cacao; cacao en grano.

codefendant [cóudiféndænt], *s.* coacusado, acusado con otro u otros.

coed, co-ed [cóéd], *s.* alumna de un plantel de coeducación.

coeducation, *s.* coeducación.

coeducational [cóéyukéishunæl], coeducativo, de coeducación.

Coelenterata [seléntœréitæ], *s. pl.* (zool.) celenterados, celenterios.

coelenteron [seléntœron], *s.* celénteron, cavidad interna de los celenterados.

coercion, *s.* coacción.

colitis [coláitis], *s.* colitis, inflamación del colon.

collapse, *vn.* desplomarse, caerse.

color. I. *s.*—**c.-blind,** acromatopo, acromatópsico, que no distingue los colores.—**c. blindness,** acromatopsia, incapacidad de distinguir los colores. —**the colors,** el servicio militar. **II.** *va.* colorar, teñir.

colorful, *a.* dramático (fig.), pintoresco, interesantemente variado.

columnist [cólumnist], *s.* colaborador de un periódico encargado de una columna o sección permanente especial.

combine, *s.* (agric.) segadora con trituradora, máquina de segar provista de un mecanismo de trituración y limpia.

combustion chamber, (m. v.) cámara de combustión; (m. comb. int.) cámara de encendido.

come, *vn.*—**to c. across with,** entregar; pagar; desembolsar.—**to c. around** = TO COME ROUND.— **to c. down with,** enfermar de.—**to c. into one's own,** recobrar uno o hacer reconocer sus derechos; ser reconocido, hacerse sentir, hacer valer sus méritos.—**to c. one's way,** caerle a uno en suerte. —**to c. out at the small end of the horn,** salir perdiendo, llevarse lo peor.—**to c. through,** salir bien.—**to c. to,** tratarse de; anclar.—**to c. to grips with,** afrontar, atacar, habérselas con.—**to c. up,** presentarse, ocurrir.

come-at-able [cúmætæbœl], *a.* accesible; asequible, procurable.

comether [comézœr], *s.* asunto, cuestión; relaciones de amistad; compañerismo.—**to put the c. on,** inducir a, ganarse a, engatusar a.

comfort, *s.* confort.—**comfortable,** *a.* confortable.—**comfortably,** *adv.* confortablemente. (Estas voces se usan hoy muy comúnmente en todos los países de habla española.)

comfort station, lavatorio con excusado.

comic strip, hilera (en un periódico) de cuadros episódicos humorísticos; ilustración humorística en escenas.

comitia [comíshiæ], *s. pl.* comicios.

comitium [-shivum], *s.* lugar de reunión de los comicios.

comminate [cómineit], *va.* conminar; anatematizar.

commissionnaire [comísionéær], *s.* mensajero; (Ing.) soldado pensionado empleado como mensajero o en tareas sencillas.

commit, *va.* pasar, someter (a una comisión, etc.)

commodity money, (E. U.) moneda variable cuyo valor se fija en función del precio de los artículos de consumo de primera necesidad.

community, *s.* colectividad, cuerpo social.—**c. center,** centro social.—**c. garage,** garaje de compartimientos particulares.—**c. house,** centro social, casa o sala de reuniones de una población, asociación, etc.

communize [cómiunaís], *va.* comunizar, hacer común; hacer comunista.

compact, *s.* neceser, cajita o estuche de afeites (polvo y colorete para la cara).

companionate [compǽnionet] **marriage,** matrimonio de compañerismo, en que los cónyuges no tienen hijos, impidiendo la concepción, pueden divorciarse por mutuo consentimiento, y no tienen obligaciones pecuniarias mutuas.

company union, (E. U.) gremio interno, asociación de todos los obreros de una fábrica o compañía en forma de gremio particular, gen. controlado por los patronos para hacer oposición a los gremios o sindicatos generales.

compare. I. *va.*—**to c. notes,** comparar datos e informes; atar cabos (dos más personas).— **not to be compared to,** o **with,** no poder compararse con, ir muy en zaga a. **II.** *vn.*—**to c. well with** = TO COMPARE FAVORABLY WITH.—**to c. with,** poderse comparar con, ser comparable con; ser o valer por comparación o comparado con (*how does this house compare with mine?* ¿qué tal es esta casa comparada con la mía?)

complacence, complacency, *s.* serenidad, calma, impasibilidad.

complacent, *a.* satisfecho, impasible, tranquilo.

complex, *s.* (psicol.) complejo.

compound [cómpaund], *s.* palabra compuesta; recinto.

compression, *s.*—**c. bib, cock,** o **faucet,** grifo de decompresión.—**c. member,** pieza de compresión, o sometida a esfuerzo de compresión.—**c. ratio,** grado de compresión.—**c. tap** = COMPRESSION COCK.

comradeship [cómrædship], *s.* compañerismo, camaradería.

conation [conéishun], *s.* (psicol.) voluntad; (más recientemente) impulso mental.

conclusion, *s.*—**to a c,** hasta el fin, hasta llegar a un resultado definitivo.

concrete, *s.*—**c. block,** bloque hueco de hormigón.—**c. tile,** losa de hormigón; bloque pequeño hueco de hormigón.

concursus [concérsus], *s.* armonía entre la Causa Primaria y las causas secundarias; (igl.) concurso, examen de oposición.

condottiere [cóndotiére], *s.* condottiere, jefe de mercenarios; soldado mercenario; aventurero.

condottieri [-ri], *s. pl.* de CONDOTTIERE.

confarreate [confǽrieit], *a.* de confarreación.

confarreation [-riéishun], *s.* confarreación.

Confucian [confiúshan], *s.* y *a.* confuciano; partidario de Confucio.—**Confucianism** [-fiúshænism], *s.* confucianismo, doctrina de Confucio.

congratulate, *va.*—**to c. on,** felicitar por.

congress, *s.* (E. U., fam.) cámara de representantes.—**in c. assembled,** en sesión plenaria.

considering, *a.* (usado elípticamente) en vista de, o dadas, las circunstancias, el carácter, etc. de una persona o cosa.

consistent, *a.* armonizable.—**c. with,** compatible con; sin detrimento de.

consistently, *adv.* constantemente, sin cejar.

construction joint, empate.

consumptible [consúmptibœl]. **I.** *s.* cosa deteriorable o que se gasta. **II.** *a.* deteriorable, que se gasta con el uso o el tiempo.

container [contéinœr], *s.* recipiente, vasija; envase.

conte [cont], *s.* cuento; narración breve.

contestant, *s.* opositor.

continuity, *s.* (cine) =SCENARIO.

contraception, *s.* contraconcepción, prevención de la concepción o la preñez.

contraceptive [cóntræséptiv]. **I.** *a.* de contraconcepción, antipreñante, que impide la preñez. **II.** *s.* agente antipreñante, que impide la preñez.

contradictious [cóntrædícshus], *a.* contradictor, disputador; contradictorio.

contrary to, en oposición a; en violación de; al contrario de.

control. I. *s.* control; mecanismo de regulación o de gobierno; regulación; regulador; influencia predominante; (espiritismo) comunicante, agente que informa al médium. **II.** *a.* regulador; de gobierno; de comprobación.—**c. car,** (aer.) barquilla de gobierno o de dirección (de un dirigible). **III.** *va.* controlar; regular; verificar, comprobar.

convection, *s.* (fís.) convección, transmisión por circulación.

convention, *s.* costumbre, precedente; convencionalismo, formalismo.—**conventional,** *a.* convencional, formalista.—**conventionalism, conventionality,** *s.* formalismo, convencionalismo.

cooking [cúking], *s.* arte culinario.

cooperative, *s.* cooperativa (empresa, compañía, asociación cooperativa).

coopery [cúperi], *s.* latonería.

cootie [cúti], *s.* vaso o taza de madera; piojo.

copper, *s.* hierro de soldar, soldador con puntas de cobre.

coppersmith, *s.* artífice en cobre.

corbel. I. *s.* saliente, retallo; modillón; zapata de sustentación bajo una viga. **II.** *va.* apoyar por medio de zapatas; disponer en forma de saliente o retallo; proveer de zapatas o de salientes. **III.** *vn.* sobresalir.

corbie [córbil], *s.* cuervo.—**c. steps, corbiesteps,** (arq.) retallos o salientes escalonados.

core wall, muro central, corazón (de una presa).

coreligionary [corelíʸuneri], **coreligionis¿** [-ist], *s.* correligionario.

coreopsis [coriópsis], *s.* (bot.) coreopsis.

corkwood [córcúd], *s.* (bot.) balso.

Cornaceæ, Cornaceae [cornéisii], *s. pl.* (bot.) córneas.

cornaceous [-shus], *a.* (bot.) córneo.

corona, *s.*—**C. Australis,** Corona Austral.—**C. Borealis,** Corona Boreal.

corporate, *a.* corporativo; incorporado.—**c. name,** nombre de una corporación, compañía, etc.

corporation cock, stop, o **tap,** llave de toma.

corporative [córporéitiv], *a.* corporativo.

corpus, *s.*—**c. callosum,** (anat.) cuerpo calloso. —C. Christi, corpus.

corrie [córri], *s.* (geol.) = CIRQUE.

cosignatary [cosígnætæri], **cosignatory** [-tori], *s.* y *a.* cosignatario.

cost, *va.* calcular el coste de.—**costing** [cósting], *s.* cálculo de costes o gastos.

cotenancy [coténansi], *s.* coinquilinato.

cotenant [coténænt], *s.* coinquilino.

cotton, *a.* de algodón; del algodón; algodonero; para algodón; relativo al algodón.—**c. belt,** (E. U.) región algodonera.—**c. boll** = BOLL WEEVIL.—**c. press,** prensa o instalción de embalar algodón.—**c. weevil** = BOLL WEEVIL.

counsel, *s.*—**c. for the defense,** defensor.—**c. for the prosecution,** acusador; fiscal.

count, *va.*—**to c. out,** no contar; declarar vencido (a un pugilista que no se levanta tras contarle diez segundos).

counterbore [cáuntœrbóær]. **I.** *s.* ensanche de la boca (de un tubo, agujero, etc.); barreno de ensanchar. **II.** *va.* ensanchar la boca de.

countryfolk [cúntrifóuc], *s.* campesinos, labradores, gente del campo.

countryside [cúntrisáid], *s.* campo; distrito rural.

courlan [cúrlan], *s.* curlán, curlirí, especie de ave zancuda.

course, *s.* capa; hilera; cancha de golf.—**in due c.,** a su tiempo, oportunamente.

courser, *s.* corcel; cazador; (zool.) avefría; avestruz.

court, *s.*—**c. of record,** tribunal de actas perpetuas.—**to put out of c.,** demonstrar la falsedad de, invalidar.

Covenant of the League of Nations, pacto fundamental de la Sociedad de las Naciones.

cowl, cowling, *s.* (aer.) cubierta o tapa.

coxa [cócsæ], *s.* cadera.—**coxal** [cócsæl], coxal, de la cadera.—**coxalgia** [cocsælyia], *s.* coxalgia.— **coxalgic** [-yic], *a.* coxálgico.

crabby [cræbi], *a.* malhumorado, de mal genio.

cracked [cræct], *a.* destornillado, chiflado; pelado, sin un céntimo; (voz) desapacible.

cracking [cræking], *s.* destilación de separación, en que los elementos volátiles se separan variando la temperatura de acuerdo con el grado de volatilidad de cada uno.

crackpot [cræcpót], *s.* loco inofensivo; pobre diablo.

cracky [cræki], *a.* rajado; susceptible de rajarse; afable; lenguaz, locuaz.

craft, *s.*—**c. guild, c. union,** gremio de artesanos de un mismo oficio.—**the c.,** la masonería.

craftsmanship [cræftsmænship], *s.* habilidad en el oficio.

cram. I. *s.* apretura, apretujón; atestamiento, repleción; hartazgo; engullimiento, tragantona; persona que se aprende atropelladamente algo o se lo hace aprender a otra (dícese sobre todo de estudiantes y maestros); erudición a la violeta, o superficial; mentira, embuste, engaño. **II.** *va.* apretar, apretujar; apiñar; repletar, atestar; hartar; meterle (algo) en la cabeza a; preparar (a un estudiante) o aprender (un asunto) a la carrera. **III.** *vn.* hartarse, darse un atracón; leer o estudiar con empeño.

crammer [cræmœr], *s.* =CRAM (persona); mentira, engaño; (mec.) apretador, comprimidor.

cramming [cræming], *s. ger.* de TO CRAM, empleado substantivadamente.

crangon [crængon], *s.* (zool.) crangón.

crap [cræp]. **I.** *s.* horca; *pl.* sedimento; heces. **II.** *va.* ahorcar.

crash, *vn.* estrellarse.

crate. I. *s.* embalaje de tablas. **II.** *va.* entablar, embalar con tablas.

crawfish, crayfish, *s.* (zool.) cangrejo de río.

credit man, investigador de créditos, o de ventas al fiado, que averigua hasta dónde puede concederse crédito.

creosote. I. *s.*—**c. oil,** creosota cruda, sin refinar. **II.** *va.* creosotar.

crinkly [críncli], *a.* arrugado, áspero; ondulado.

crissum [crísum], *s.* (orn.) región anal; plumas anales.

crone, *vn.* hablar como viejo.

crony, *vn.* ser camarada o camaradas, amigarse íntimamente.

crop. I. *va.* (a veces con **off**) cortar, recortar; cultivar. **II.** *vn.* aflorar; dar frutos, producir mieses; (gen. con **forth, out, up**), descubrirse, dejarse ver.—**to c. out,** (min.) aflorar.

cropper, *s.* recortador, máquina recortadora; obrero recortador; caída de cabeza; SHARE CROPPER.—**to come, fall, get, a c.,** caer de cabeza; fracasar, salirle caro a uno.

cross, *a.*—**c. fire,** fuego o ataque por varios lados. —**c. hair** = CROSS WIRE.—**c. multiplication,** multiplicación en cruz.—**c.-word puzzle,** crucigrama, palabras cruzadas.

cross. I. *va.* cruzar; atravesar; (gen. con **off** o **out**) tachar, borrar con una raya; poner el trazo transversal a (una letra, gen. la *t*); pasar o mover de un lado a otro de; oponerse a, contrariar; marcar con una cruz; hacer frente a.—**to c. one's mind,** ocurrírsele a uno, pasarle a uno por la imaginación. **to c. one's self,** persignarse; santiguarse.—**to c. swords,** medir las armas, reñir, contender. **II.** *vn.* cruzar(se).—**to c. over,** pasar de un lado a otro, ir al otro lado.

crosscurrent [cróscœrrent], *s.* corriente contraria; tendencias o ideas encontradas.

crossroads [crósróuds], *s.* punto crítico, tiempo llegado de decidir.

croupous [crúpus], **croupy** [crúpi], *a.* cruposo, como de crup.—**c.** cough, tos perruna o cruposa.

crown. I. *s.* corona, parte visible de un diente; corona artificial (de un diente); (fort.) corona. —**c.** **wheel,** rueda coronaria, rueda de dientes perpendiculares a su plano.—**c.** **work,** (dentistería) corona artificial, trabajo en coronas artificiales; (fort.), corona, obra de corona o coronas.

crummy, *a.* bonita, linda; rolliza; desaseado, dejado, desgreñado.

crural, *a.* (anat.) femoral.—**c.** **canal,** conducto crural.

cubicle [kiúbikœl], *s.* cubículo, alcoba; compartimiento.

cuculliform [kiucúliform], *a.* de forma de capucha; CUCULLATED.

cully [cúli], *s.* compañero, camarada.

cultch [cúlch], *s.* basura; hueva de molusco.

cumbrous [cúmbrus], *a.* estorboso; pesado, molesto, difícil de manejar.

cumulo-cirrus [kiúmiulo sœrrus], *s.* (fís.) cirro, nubes que los marinos llaman *colas de gato.*— **cumulo-nimbus** [nímbus], *s.* nimbo, nube de lluvia.—**cumulo-stratus** [stréitus], estrato, masa nebulosa horizontal.

cumulus, *s.* masa, montón; cima, cúspide; (fís.) cúmulo, cierta clase de nube que los marinos llaman *balas de algodón.*

curie [kiúrí], *s.* (fís.) curie, unidad de masa de emanación de radio.

curricular [cœrríkiulær], *a.* del plan de estudios o relativo a él.

curtain call, aplauso de llamamiento, para que un actor se presente delante del telón después de bajado éste.

cushy [cúshi], *a.* fácil, descansado.

cut. I. *va.*—**to c. ice,** valer, ser de importancia. —**to c. one's throat,** cortarse el pescuezo (fig.), perderse.—**to c. out,** suprimir; (elec., mec.) desconectar. **II.** *a.* (fam.) achispado.—**c. gear,** (mec.) dientes tallados a máquina.—**c. thread,** filete tallado a máquina.

cut-out muffler, silenciador con válvula de escape libre en el tubo de escape.

cylinder block [*v.* BLOCK].

cystitis [sistáitis], *s.* cistitis,

cystocarp [sístocarp], *s.* (bot.) cistocarpo.— **cystocele** [-sil], *s.* cistocele, hernia de la vejiga.— **cystoscope** [-scoup], *s.* cistoscopio.

Czechoslovak [chécoslóvæc], *s.* y *a.* checoeslovaco.

D

da capo [da cápo], *adv.* desde el principio.

dalai lama [daláilæma], *s.* dalailama (sacerdote), primer lama o lama superior.

damn, *s.* (vulg.) ardite, pito (*that is not worth a damn,* eso no vale un pito).—**damn, damned,** *adv.* muy, como un diablo.

damned, *a.* maldito, del diablo; vil. Con el imperativo de *to be,* indica desprecio o indiferencia, y puede traducirse por *al diablo se lo doy, no me importa un pito, o que el diablo se lleve;* vg. *the people be damned,* llévese el diablo al pueblo, un pito me importa el pueblo, al diablo con el pueblo.

damping [dæmping], *s.* (elec.) amortiguación, disminución de la amplitud de las ondas.

dandify [dændifai], *va.* alechuguinar, acicalar.

dandy, *a.* excelente, magnífico, muy bueno.

darn, *va.* y *vn.* En lenguaje fam., úsase eufemísticamente en vez de DAMN en imprecaciones, reniegos, etc. V. DAMN, DAMNED.—**a darned sight,** (fam.) muchísimo.

dash, *s.* poquito, pequeña cantidad.

date line, línea de cambio de fecha.

davenport [dévenport], *s.* canapé; escritorio pequeño adornado.

day, *s.*—**d.** about, un día sí y otro no, cada dos días.—**d.** bed, sofá cama, sofá que de noche se convierte en cama.—**d.** letter, telegrama largo que se envía con ciertas restricciones por precio menor que el corriente.—**d.** of reckoning, día de ajustar cuentas (fig.), día de la justicia.—**d.** telegram = D. LETTER.

daylong [déilóng], *a.* de todo el día.

dead, *a.*—**d.** line, límite; línea vedada; fin del plazo, término.—**d.** load, carga fija.—**d.** stick, (aer.) hélice parada.—**d.** work, trabajo preliminar.

debunk [dibúnc], *va.* desenmascarar; quitar la basura a (fig.)

decastere [décæstíær], *s.* decastéreo, metro cúbico.

decelerate [diséleréit], *va.* y *vn.* retardar(se), disminuir la velocidad; mover(se) con movimiento retardado.

decidua [desídiuæ], *s.* membrana mucosa del útero que se desprende después de la menstruación o la preñez.

declutch [diclúch], *va.* desembragar.

decontrol [dícontróul]. **I.** *s.* terminación del control. **II.** *va.* terminar el control de.

default. I. *s.* incumplimiento de una obligación (sobre todo la de pagar), incumplimiento de pago, insolvencia.—**In d. of,** por falta de; por faltar. **II.** *va.* y *vn.* dejar de cumplir; no pagar.

defeatism [difítism], *s.* confesión de derrota o impotencia (algunos dicen *derrotismo*).—**defeatist** [-ist], *s.* y *a.* que, o el que, se declara vencido o impotente (algunos dicen *derrotista*).

defilade [défileid], *va.* (mil.) desenfilar, proteger contra fuego de enfilada.—**defilading** [-léiding], *s.* desenfilamiento, protección contra el fuego de enfilada.

deformable [dіfórmæbœl], *a.* deformable.

deformability [-bílity], *s.* deformabilidad.

defy, *va.* atreverse con.

degression [digréshun], *s.* decrecimiento; disminución progresiva.

degressive [-siv], *a.* decreciente; que disminuye progresivamente, o por grados.

dehydrogenize [díjáidroyenaiš], *va.* deshidrogenar, quitar el hidrógeno a.

delate [diléit], *va.* delatar; divulgar.

delegacy [délegæsi], *s.* delegación; carácter de delegado; cuerpo de delegados.

deliver, *va.* transmitir (energía, etc.)—**to d. the goods,** cumplir; hacer lo prometido o esperado.

demarche [demársh], *s.* proceder, medida; diligencia; cambio de proceder o de política.

demount [dimáunt], *va.* desmontar, desarmar (una máquina, un mueble, etc.)

dendrite, *s.* dendrita, planta fósil.

dendroid [déndroid], *a.* dendrítico.

dendrolite [-drolait], *s.* dendrita o rama fósil o petrificada.

de novo [de nóuvo], *adv.* de nuevo; desde el principio.

dentalium [dentéilium], *s.* (zool.) dentalio.

dent corn, maíz dentado o hendido, maíz ordinario de forraje.

dentiform [déntiform], *a.* denticular.

dentoid [déntoid], *a.* denticular.

deobstruent [dióbstruent], *s.* y *a.* desobstructivo, desobstruyente.

department, *s.* oficina, negociado.—**d. store,** tienda mixta, almacén de departamentos.

depend, *vn.*—**to d. on,** necesitar, tener por necesario; necesitar de; ser mantenido por.

dependability [dipéndæbílit], *s.* confiabilidad.

deportee [dipórtí], *s.* deportado, desterrado.

dermatitis [dœrmætáitis], s. (med.) dermitis, dermatitis, inflamación de la piel.

destructionist [distrʌcŝhʌnist], s. destructor; revolucionario, enemigo de las instituciones actuales.

detect, va. (rad.), rectificar.

detection, s. (rad.) rectificación.

detune [ditiún], va. (rad.) desintonizar, destemplar, poner fuera de sintonización.

deuton [diútʌn], s. (fís.) deutón.

devaluate [divǽlueit], va. depreciar.

devaluation [-éishʌn], s. depreciación.

devalue [divǽliu], va. depreciar.

develop, va. mejorar; ensanchar; urbanizar; establecer; realizar, efectuar.

development, s. mejora; ensanche; urbanización, caserío nuevo.

devil, s.—**d. worship,** adoración de espíritus malos; demonolatría.—**between the d. and the deep sea,** entre la espada y la pared.—**the d. take the hindmost,** quien se quede atrás, que pague el pato; quien se quede en zaga, con el diablo se las haya; el que venga atrás, que arree.

diabolism [daiǽbolism], s. perversidad, iniquidad; acción diabólica; hechicería, brujería; demonolatría; posesión demoníaca.

diagrammatic [dáiægræmǽtic], a. esquemático, gráfico.

diastrophism [daiǽstrofísm], s. dislocación; (geol.) deformación o transformación de la corteza terrestre.

diathermia [dáiæzœrmiæ], **diathermy** [-mi], s. (med.) diatermia, termopenetración eléctrica.

diatomaceous [dáiætoméíshʌs] **earth** =INFUSORIAL EARTH.

dick(e)y, a. dudoso, arriesgado; inseguro; mal de salud.

die-hard, diehard [dáijárd], s. reaccionario, oposicionista reacio.

dietician, dietitian [dáietíshæn], s. dietético, especialista o versado en dietética.

diffract [difrǽct], va. (fís.) difractar.

Digitigrada [dívitígreidæ], s. pl. (zool.) digitígrados.

dilution, s. reemplazo de obreros expertos por inexpertos.

dinette [dainét], s. comida ligera; comedorcillo.

dingo [díngo], s. dingo, perro salvaje australiano.

diosmose [daiósmous], **diosmosis** [dáiosmóusis], s. (fís.) ósmosis.

dipter [díptœr], s. (zool.) díptero.—**Diptera** [-æ], s. pl. dípteros.—**dipteran** [-æn], s. y a. díptero.—**dipterologist** [-óloγist], s. dipterólogo.—**dipterology** [-óloγi], s. dipterología.

diriment [díriment], a. dirimente.

dirt farmer, agricultor que se ocupa él mismo en el trabajo material de la labranza, o que labra la tierra con sus propias manos.

disappearing, a.—**d. bed,** cama escondida, cama engoznada que se oculta de día.—**d. gun,** cañón de cureña movible verticalmente, la cual baja y oculta el cañón después de la descarga.

disassemble [dísæsémbœl], va. desarmar, desmontar (un reloj, una máquina, etc.)

disassembly [-bli], s. desarme (de una máquina, etc.)

discant [dískænt], s. y verbo =DESCANT.

discharger, s. (fís.) excitador (de una botella de Leyden).

discount, va. dar poca importancia a, considerar exagerado.

discretion, s.—**in one's d.,** a juicio o voluntad de uno.

disease, a. de enfermedad; patógeno.—**d. germ,** microbio patógeno.

disembed [dísembéd], va. sacar, extraer.

disembellish [-bélish], va. desembellecer, quitar la belleza a.

disembroil [-bróil], va. desembrollar; restablecer el orden de o en.

disemploy [-emplóy], va. privar de empleo o de trabajo.

disorderly conduct, conducta escandalosa; desvergüenza.

disparage, va. condenar, atacar.

dispensation, s. designio divino; acto providencial; plan; don; ley divina; ley.

dispose, vn. disponer.—**to d. of,** disponer de; salir de; poner fin a.

disreputable, a. bajo, de mala fama; vergonzoso; desgarbado, dilapidado.

dissect, va. cortar en piezas o pedazos.

dissecting room, anfiteatro anatómico.

distinction, s.—**in d. from,** o **in d. to,** a distinción de.

distinctive, a. de distinción.

distinguish, va.—**as distinguished from,** a distinción de.

distinguishing, a. distintivo, que distingue.

Distoma [dístomæ], s. (zool.) dístomo.

distomatous [dístómætʌs], a., **distome** [dístoum], s. (zool.) dístomo, de dos bocas.

disulphate [daisúlfeit], s. bisulfato.

ditch, s.—**to the last d.,** hasta quemar el último cartucho, sin cejar.

dither [díðœr]. **I.** s. temblor. **II.** vn. temblar, tiritar; vibrar; molestarse.

divide, s. (geog.) divisoria.

diving, a.—**d. beetle,** escarabajo acuático.—**d. board,** trampolín o plataforma de saltar al agua.

do. I. va. Seguido de gerundio, equivale al tiempo correspondiente del verbo; to · do washing, lavar; she did sewing, ella cosía.—**to d. (up) brown,** hacer perfectamente; embaucar.—**to d. down,** ganar a; engañar, embaucar.—**to d. in,** pegarle a; despachar, matar; embaucar. **II.** vn. pasarlo; bandearse.—**what are you going to d. about it?** ¿qué piensa Vd. hacer? ¿qué puede Vd. hacer? haga Vd. lo que quiera.

dockage, s. impurezas; limpia.

dog, s.—**d.-cheap,** baratísimo, regalado.—**d. days,** días caniculares.—**d. fight,** pelea de perros; refriega; encuentro.—**d. fox,** zorro macho; zorro azul.—**every d. has his day,** a cada cual le llega su turno.

dogfight [dógfáit], s. =DOG FIGHT.

dolesome [dóulsʌm], a. triste; melancólico.

done, a. dado (decreto, etc.).—**d. for,** agotado, rendido; desahuciado; vencido, perdido, fuera de combate (fig.); muerto.

donkey, a. auxiliar, secundario.

dooryard [dóœryárd], s. patio de entrada, enfrente de la puerta principal.

dormer, s. gablete; ventana vertical de buhardilla de gablete, lumbrera (ll. t. **dormer window**).

doss [dos], s. dormidero, lugar donde dormir (gen. se entiende que es malo); cama; sueño.—**d. house,** posada de mala muerte, sobre todo para vagos.

dossier [dósiei], s. (for.) pieza de autos, expediente, documentos, papeles.

dot, s.—**on the d.,** en punto, a la hora exacta.—**to a d.,** perfectamente, absolutamente.

dotted line, línea para la firma.

double, a.—**d. bed,** cama ancha, para dos personas.—**d. eagle,** doble águila, moneda de oro de 20 dólares.—**d. house,** casa gemela, casa de familia separada de otra idéntica por una pared medianera.—**d.-throw switch,** interruptor, o conmutador, de dos direcciones.

doubt, s.—**when in d.,** en caso de duda.

dour [dáuœr], a. terco; difícil, trabajoso; ríguroso, fuerte; hosco.

douse. I. s. zabullida; golpe, tunda. **II.** va. meter en el agua; empapar; extinguir, apagar; quitar, quitarse. **III.** vn. caer en el agua.

down, adv.—**d. below,** allá abajo; más abajo.—**d. to date,** hasta la fecha, hasta nuestros días.

down-lead [dáunlíd], s. (rad.) =LEAD-IN.

downthrow [dáunzróu], s. derribo.

doxy [dóksi], s. amante (mujer); doctrina, creencia.

drab, a. monótono; seco, ordinario, sin atractivos.

draft, s. estiramiento.—**d. ga(u)ge,** indicador de tiro.

---

draftee [dræftí], *s.* reclutado.

drag. **I.** *s.* rastro, pista; fardo, impedimento; (fund.) marco o parte inferior de una caja de moldear.—**d. line,** (aer.) = GUIDE ROPE. **II.** *va.*—**to d. in,** traer por los cabellos. **III.** *vn.* atrasarse, ir en zaga; retrasarse; pasar con penosa lentitud, ser interminable (fig.)

dramshop [dræmshóp], *s.* cantina.

drawing account, cuenta corriente.

dreep [drip], *vn.* gotear; inclinarse; desalentarse, desanimarse.

drink, *va.* brindar por; beberse (su sueldo, etc.), gastar en beber.

dripstone [drípstóun], *s.* (arq.) alero, escurridero (cuando es de piedra).

drive. **I.** *s.* impulso, tendencia, anhelo. **II.** *va.* hincar.—**to d. to cover,** poner fin o coto a.

driveway, *s.* carretera; vía de entrada o de salida (de coches).

drivewell [dráivuél], *s.* = DRIVEN WELL.

drome [dróum], *s.* aeródromo.

drop, *s.* *y a.*—**d.-center rim,** llanta de canal.— **d. cover,** tapa caediza.—**d. valve,** válvula de cierre por gravedad.—**a.**, o **one, d. in the bucket,** una pizca no más, una nonada.—**at the d. of the hat,** por quítame allá esas pajas.

drumbeat [drúmbít], *s.* toque de tambor.

drumhead [drúmjéd], *s.* piel, cara o cabeza del tambor; (anat.) tambor, tímpano (del oído).— **d. courtmartial,** consejo de guerra de campaña, en el campamento o en la línea de batalla.

dry, *a.*—**d. cleaning,** limpia en seco (**to d.-clean,** limpiar en seco).—**as d. as dust,** sumamente árido o pesado.

dud [dud]. **I.** *s.* flojo, inútil (dicho de una persona); bomba o granada que no estalla; *pl.* **duds,** (fam.) trapos (ropa). ‖ **II.** *a.* que no estalla; (fam.) sin fibra, falto de energía.

duffer [dúfœr], *s.* estúpido; inútil, chambón; vendedor ambulante de artículos de imitación o de relumbrón; estafador, farsante; cosa que no vale nada, basura (fig.)

dugong [dúgong], *s.* (zool.) dugong, vaca marina.

dumb, *a.*—**d.-bell,** estúpido, imbécil.—**d.-waiter,** montaplatos (ll. así en algunas partes).

dummy, *s.* estúpido, imbécil; (en ciertos juegos) naipes que caen sobre la mesa.

dump, *s.* centro de allegamiento y distribución de pertrechos.

dumpy, *a.* melancólico; descontento, enfurruñado.

dunnage, *s.* equipaje.

dunny [dúni], *a.* medio sordo; estúpido.

duplex, *a.*—**d. house,** casa para dos familias.— **d. iron,** fundición recalentada en hormo eléctrico.

duralumin [diurǽliumin, diúrœliúmin] (nombre de fábrica), *s.* duraluminio, cuproaluminio, aleación de aluminio y cobre.

E

each, *pron.*—**e. and every,** todos.—**e. for himself,** cada cual por se cuenta, o por su lado.

eagle boat, especie de cazasubmarinos.

ear, *s.*—**to have one's e.,** tener influencia con uno, gozar de su confianza.

early. **I.** *a.*—**the e. part of,** el principio de. **II.** *adv.* antes de la hora.—**e. in,** a principios de.— **to be e.,** llegar temprano.

earmark, *va.* marcar.

ease. *va.* aflojar; facilitar.—**to e. of,** quitar por la fuerza; robar.

easily, *adv.* sobradamente.

East African, *s.* *y a.* del África oriental.

Easterner [ístœrnœr], *s.* (E. U.) oriental, habitante del este (de los E. U.)

ecclesia [eclíýiæ], *s.* (hist.) asamblea popular; iglesia, cuerpo de los fieles.

echidna [ekídnæ], *s.* (zool.) equidna (mamífero).

echo. **I.** *s.*—**to the e.,** estrepitosamente. **II.** *va.* repetir con aprobación; imitar; hacer eco a.

ectopia, *s.* (med.) ectopia.

edge, *s.* ventaja.—**to get,** o **have, the e. on,** llevar ventaja a.

edgeway, *adv.*—EDGEWISE.

editorialize [édítóriælaiš]. **I.** *va.* escribir críticamente acerca de, en estilo de editorial. **II.** *vn.* (con **about** o **on**) escribir un editorial acerca de.

effect, *s.*—**into e.,** en vigor.—**to the e. that,** de que, en el sentido de que.

effective, *a.* vigente, en vigor.

egocentric [ígoséntric], *s.* *y a.* egocéntrico.

ejecta [iyécta], *s.* *pl.* materias expelidas.

elbow. **I.** *s.*—**e. room,** lugar donde estar o moverse; libertad de acción.—**out at e.,** andrajoso.—**up to the elbows,** hasta los codos. **II.** *va.*—**to e. one's way,** abrirse paso codeando.

electric(al, *a.*—**e. cooker,** cocina eléctrica.—**e. eye,** tubo fotoeléctrico.—**e. horn,** bocina eléctrica. —**e. refrigerator,** nevera eléctrica, heladera automática.—**e. steel,** acero de horno eléctrico.—**e. varnish,** barniz aislador.

electron tube, (elec.) tubo de vacío; (rad.) tubo termiónico, válvula.

electrosteel [eléctrostíl], *s.* acero de horno eléctrico.

else, *a.* otro; más.—**anything e.,** algo más; cualquiera otra cosa.

empire cloth, tela barnizada aisladora.

enate [enéit], *s.* *y a.* pariente por descendencia materna común.—**enation** [enéišun], *s.* parentesco por madre.

encephalitis [enséfælǽitis], *s.* encefalitis, inflamación del cerebro.—**e. lethargica** [lezárýikæ], encefalitis letárgica o epidémica.

encirclement [ensœrcœlment], *s.* circunvalación; circunscripción; encerramiento, encierro, cerco, aislamiento.

enclave [énclaiv]. **I.** *s.* región enclavada en territorio extranjero; barrio o distrito habitado por extranjeros o destinado a un objeto especial; (anat.) órgano enclavado en otro. **II.** *va.* establecer dentro de territorio extranjero; encerrar dentro de territorio extranjero.

encyst [ensíst], *va.* *y vn.* enquistar(se).

end. **I.** *s.* división, parte (de un negocio, empresa, etc.).—**e. line,** línea de límite.—**e. point,** (quím.) punto de evaporación completa.—**e. reaction,** (quím.) reacción al final del procedimiento.—**in the e.,** al fin, a la larga, al fin y al cabo. **II.** *vn.*—**to e. up,** terminar, acabar; morirse.

endocrine, *s.* *y a.* endocrina (glándula).—**endocrinic** [éndocrínic], **endocrinous** [endócrinus], *a.* endocrino.—**endocrinology,** *s.* endocrinología.

endoparasite [éndopǽræsait], *s.* parásito interno.

endoscope [éndoscoup], *s.* endoscopio.

enforce, *va.* cumplimentar (una ley, etc.).

engineman [ényinmæn], *s.* maquinista.

enlightenment, *s.*—**the E.,** el renacimiento del siglo XVIII.

enologic(al [ínolóyic, -æl], *a.* enológico.—**enologist** [inóloyist], *s.* enólogo.—**enology** [inóloyi], *s.* enología.

entasis [éntæsis], *s.* (arq.) éntasis.

enteralgia [éntœrǽlyiæ], *s.* enteralgia, neuralgia intestinal.

entrance examination, examen de admisión, entrada o ingreso.

enzim [énšim], **enzyme** [énšaim, énšim], *s.* (igl.) pan de levadura; pan eucarístico (en la iglesia oriental); (quím.) fermento.

ephebe [éíb], *s.* (hist.) efebo, joven griego de entre 18 y 20 años, listo para alistarse en la tribu.

ephor [éfor], *s.* éforo (magistrado); superintendente de obras públicas.

epiphenomenon [épifenómenon], *s.* fenómeno secundario concomitante; (med.) epifenómeno.

episode, *s.* (cine) película o parte de un drama cinematográfico representado en una serie de funciones: en cada función se representa un *episode.*

epochal [épokæl], *a.* que forma época, trascendental, memorable.

ergosterin [œrgóstœrin], **ergosterol** [-oul], *s.* ergosterina.

escadrille, *s.* escuadrilla (aérea o naval).

et al [ei æl], y otros; etcétera.

ethicize [ézisaiŝ]. **I.** *va.* dar carácter ético a. **II.** *vn.* tratar de la ética; discurrir sobre la moral.

ethos [ízos], *s.* carácter, genio (de un pueblo, de una colectividad); rasgo distintivo.

eudemonic(al [iúdimónic, -æl], *a.* relativo a la felicidad; que tiene por fin la felicidad.

eudemonist [iudímonist], *s.* eudemonista, el que sostiene que la felicidad es el sumo bien.

eugenism [iúɣeniŝm], *s.* condiciones eugenésicas; eugenesia.—**eugenist** [-ist], *s.* persona versada en eugenesia.—**euthenics** [iuzénics], *s.*=EUGENICS.

evaginate [ivǽɣineit], *va.* volver al revés, de adentro afuera.

event, *s.*—**after the e.,** ya pasado, o ejecutado, el hecho.

ever, *adv.* en la (mi, su) vida. En oraciones interrogativas se emplea a veces como expletivo enfático para expresar sorpresa, dificultad, impaciencia, etc., y o no se traduce o se traduce introduciendo el verbo *poder* o el adverbio *nunca;* vg. *how did you ever do it?* ¿cómo lo hizo usted? o ¿cómo puede usted haberlo hecho? *are you ever going to finish?* ¿no terminará usted nunca?—**e. so much,** muchísimo (*I thank you ever so much,* muchísimas gracias, le agradezco muchísimo).— **for e. and a day,** interminablemente, eternamente.—**the best (prettiest,** etc.) **e.,** el mejor (más bonito, etc.) nunca visto, o que nunca se haya visto, o del mundo.

every, *adv.*—**e. so often,** cada cierto tiempo, a intervalos fijos.

everybody, everyone, *pron.*—**e. for himself,** cada cual por su cuenta; sálvese el que pueda.

ex [eks]. **I.** *a.* ex, que fué. **II.** *prep.* sin incluir; sin participación en; libre de cargo o gravamen hasta salir de.

excess, *va.* exigir como pago adicional a, hacer reargo a.

excess-profits tax, impuesto sobre ganancias excesivas, superiores al promedio durante cierto período de condiciones normales.

excise. I. *s.* impuesto sobre artículos de comercio interior; (Ing.) oficina de recaudación de impuestos interiores. **II.** *a.* de o relativo a impuestos interiores. **III.** *va.* cortar; extirpar; borrar; hacer una incisión en; gravar, someter a impuesto.

exclave [ékscleiv], *s.* parte de un país enclavada en otro, o situada dentro de otro.

exclusive of, exclusive, sin contar.

excreta [ekscrítæ], *s. pl.* excreciones.

excretal [-tæl], *a.* de excreción.

execute, *va.* (for.) formalizar.

exegetics [ékseɣétics], *s.* ciencia de la exégesis, sobre todo de la bíblica.

exercised, *a.* agitado, intranquilo, inquieto.

exhibitionism [égŝibíŝhuniŝm], *s.* (psic. y pat.) exhibicionismo, manía de poner al descubierto lo que no es modesto descubrir, sobre todo las partes pudendas.—**exhibitionist** [-ist], *s.* exhibicionista, que sufre de exhibicionismo.

expanded metal, metal desplegado.

expediential [ekspídiénshæl], *a.* de conveniencia, oportunista.

experiencial [ekspíriénshæl], *a.* experimental, de observación.—**experientially** [-li], *adv.* experimentalmente, por observación.

expressionism [ekspréŝhuniŝm], *s.* postimpresionismo, nuevo impresionismo.

extent, *s.* punto; límite.—**to that e.,** en tal grado, hasta ahí, hasta tal punto.

extrorse [ekstrórs], *a.* (hist. n.) extrorso, vuelto hacia afuera.

extroversion [ékstroɣœrshun], *s.* (psic.) tendencia a ocuparse más en el mundo exterior que en el interior; (med.) extroversión, extrofia.

extrovert. I. *s.* (psic.) persona que se ocupa más en el mundo exterior que en el interior. **II.** *vn.* ocuparse en el mundo exterior.

eyespot [áispót], *s.* ojo rudimentario; ojo embrionario.

eye-test chart, escala tipográfica oftalmométrica.

eyewash [áiuásh], *s.*=EYEWATER.

F

Fabaceae, Fabaceæ [fæbéisii], *s. pl.* (bot.) papilionáceas.—**fabaceous** [-shus], *a.* papilionáceo.

face. I. *s.* apariencias; prestigio.—**f. saving,** salvar las apariencias.—**in the f. of,** ante; luchando contra, a pesar de.—**on the f. of it,** según lo que se ve. **II.** *va.* afrontar; reconocer.

fact, *s.*—**the f. remains that,** a pesar de todo, es un hecho que.

faddish [fædish], *a.,* **faddist** [-ist], *s.* caprichoso; chiflado.

fag, *s.* (fam.) cigarrillo.—**f. end,** cabo (de tabaco, etc.)

failure to, el no, el dejar de, la falta de (seguido de *s.*) (*failure to pay,* el no pagar, el dejar de pagar, la falta de pago).

fair, *s.* feria; exposición; venta de caridad o en beneficio de una institución o persona (ll. *bazar* en algunas partes).

fall, *vn.*—**to f. across,** encontrarse con por casualidad.—**to f. for,** prendarse de; ser engañado por.—**to f. foul of**=TO FALL AFOUL OF.—**to f. from grace,** pecar; perder influencia, perder el favor del gobierno, etc.—**to f. heir to,** heredar.—**to f. in for**=TO COME IN FOR.—**to f. to,** caer en manos de, sucumbir ante.—**to f. to the ground,** caerse; desplomarse; fracasar.

Fallopian [fælópiæn] **tube,** (anat.) oviducto.

fallow, *s.* añojal (ll. t. **f. ground, f. land**).

false, *a.*—**f. face,** máscara.—**f. light (to place in a f. light,** poner mal, desacreditar).—**f. rib,** costilla falsa.

falsework [fólsuœrc], *s.* andamiaje.

fantasmagoria [fæntæsmægóriæ], *s.* fantasmagoría; (cine) figura que se acerca o que se aleja, figura proyectada en la pantalla que, aumentando o disminuyendo de tamaño, parece acercarse al auditorio o alejarse de él.

far. I. *a.*—**F. East,** Lejano Oriente. **II.** *adv.*— **f. and away,** en mucho.—**f. and near,** por todas partes.—**f.-flung,** vasto, extenso.—**f. into,** hasta muy adentro de; hasta muy tarde de (la noche, etc.), hasta muy avanzado (el verano, etc.).

farmerette [fármerét], *s.* agricultora, labradora.

farthermore [fárdœrmóœr], *adv.*=FURTHERMORE.

fascicle, *s.* (anat.) fascículo.

fashionmonger [fǽshunmóngœr], *s.* petimetre.

fastening, *s.* artefacto de afianzar, unir o trabar; afianzador; traba; clavazón.

fattling [fǽtling]. **I.** *s.* animal de ceba o de engorde. **II.** *a.* gordo; rollizo.

faultfinding [fóltfáinding]. **I.** *s.* crítica por manía; manía de criticar. **II.** *a.* criticón.

feather, *va.*—**to f. one's nest,** hacer para sí, cuidar de sí; sacar tajada.

feeble, *a.*—**f.-minded,** de inteligencia subnormal. —**f.-mindedness,** inteligencia subnormal.

feed, *vn.*—**to f. up on, o with,** hastiar u hostigar con, hartar de (gen. en la voz pasiva **to be fed up on, o with,** estar harto de).

feedhead, *s.* (fund.) canal de mazarota.

feel. I. *va.*—**to f. in one's bones,** tener uno fuerte presentimiento de, decírsele a uno el corazón.—**to f. one's way,** ir a tientas; proceder con tiento. **II.** *vn.* to f. bad, o badly, sentirse mal; estar triste, entristecerse; (con **about),** lamentar, sentir.—**to f. like,** tener gana de, querer (a veces se cambia el giro: *I feel like walking,* deseo andar; *I feel like a walk,* tengo gana de dar un paseo).—**to f. sorry,** sentir, estar apenado.—**to f. sorry for,** sentir; lamentar; compadecer, tener lástima a o de.

feeling, *s.* presentimiento, sospecha.

female, *s.* y *a.* (bot.) femenino.

fiat money, billetes sin respaldo ni garantía emitidos por un gobierno.

fibriform [fíbriform], *a.* fibroso o de aspecto fibroso.

fictionist [fícshunist], *s.* novelista.

fideicommissary [fáideaicómiseri], *s.* y *a.* (for.) fideicomisario.—**fiddeicomissum** [-comísum], *s.* (for.) fideicomiso.

fifty-fifty solder, soldadura de partes iguales de plomo y estaño.

fight. I. *va.* lidiar, sortear (toros); atacar; librar (una batalla).—**to f. out,** discutir, decidir por discusión; llevar la lucha hasta lo último, o hasta llegar a un resultado definitivo. **II.** *vn.*—**to f. shy of,** evadir.

figurant(e [fíguiurænt], *s.* (teat.) figurante (-ta).

figurer [fígiurœr], *s.* calculista; modelador.

filaria [failéiriæ], *s.* (zool.) filaria.

filariasis [fílæráiæsis], *s.* filariasis.

file. I. *s.* casillero (ll. t. **f. case**); protocolo (de notario, etc.). **II.** *a.* de archivo, de o para archivar. **III.** *va.* protocolar. **IV.** *vn.*—**to f. out,** salir en fila, desfilar.

filling, *s.* empaquetadura; rellenamiento (de tierra).

filling station, (aut.) estación (de toma) de gasolina. (Ll. t. *bomba de gasolina*).

film, filmize, *va.* (cine) hacer una película de, poner en la pantalla o en el cine. (En algunas partes dicen *filmar*.)

filter, *vn.*—**to f. in,** o **through,** infiltrarse; meterse, introducirse, colarse.

finalist [fáinælist], *s.* finalista, el que toma parte en el juego final o decisivo de un torneo deportivo.

finance. I. *s.* finanza, finanzas. **II.** *va.* financiar.—**financing,** *s.* financiación.

find, *va.*—**to f. favor with,** o **in the eyes of,** caer en gracia a, granjearse la buena voluntad de.—**to f. up,** descubrir; buscar.

fineness modulus, módulo de finura (del cemento, etc.)

finger, *s.* (mec.) uña.

finish. I. *s.* perdición.—**to a.,** o **the, f.,** hasta lo último, hasta el fin, hasta terminar. **II.** *va.* acabar con; abrumar, anonadar.—**to f. off,** completar, acabar.—**to f. up,** dar la última mano a; retocar; terminar.

fippence [fípens], *s.* cinco peniques.

fippenny [fípeni], *a.* (precio) de cinco peniques.

fire. I. *a.* de bomberos; de incendios; del servicio de incendios; refractario.—**f. house, f. station**=FIREHOUSE. **II.** *va.*—**to f. off,** descargar, disparar, hacer fuego con; apagar.—**to f. up,** encender. **III.** *vn.*—**to f. up,** enfurecerse.

firehouse [fáiœrjáus], *s.* estación de incendios o de bomberos.

firm, *vn.* ponerse firme, adquirir solidez.

first. I. *a.*—**f. aid,** primeros auxilios.—**f. lady of the land,** (E. U.) primera dama de la nación (título que se da a la esposa del presidente).—**f. officer,** primer piloto. **II.** *adv.* por primera vez, la primera vez.—**f. of all,** en primer lugar, ante todo.

fish, *s.*—**f. day,** día de vigilia.—**f. globe,** pecera.—**f. torpedo,** torpedo submarino pisciforme.—**neither f., flesh nor fowl,** ni carne ni pescado.

fissure, *s.* (anat.) cisura.

fit, *a.* en buena salud, bien.

fitting, *s.* tubo o pieza de unión o de conexión (en las tuberías).

flabellum [flæbélum], *s.* (igl.) flabelo.

flair [fléær]. **I.** *s.* olfato; sagacidad; aptitud. **II.** *va.* olfatear.

flame, *va.* tratar con la llama.

flare. I. *s.* ostentación, boato; ensanche. **II.** *va.* ensanchar, acampanar, abocinar.

flash, *s.* (cine) incidencia, incidente, proyección momentánea explicativa.

flashing over, flashover [fléshhóvœr], *s.* (elec.) formación de arco; descarga.

flat. I. *a.*—**f.-bed press,** prensa de platina. **II.** *adv.* completamente; abiertamente, decididamente; (com.) sin interés.

flatten, *va.* y *vn.*—**to f. out,** (aer.) enderezar(se).

flight, *s.* escuadrilla aérea.

fling, *s.*—**to take a f. at,** echar una pulla a.

flivver, *s.* fiasco, fracaso, pifia.

float, *s.* (alb.) llana de enlucir; (aer.) flotador.

floating dock, cajón sumergible para alzar un buque hundido.

floor tile, baldosín o loseta para pisos, mosaico.

flowage [flóiy], *s.* flujo, corriente; derramamiento; líquido que sale o se derrama; deformación (de un líquido) por deslizamiento interno de las moléculas.

flowers of sulphur, flor de azufre.

flu [flu], *s.* trancazo, influenza, gripe.

flubdub [flúbdúb]. **I.** *s.* tontería, dislate. **II.** *a.* tonto, inane.

flubdubbery [-beri], *s.*=FLUBDUB.

flunk [flunc]. **I.** *s.* fracasado, persona que fracasa. **II.** *va.* fracasar o salir mal en; hacer fracasar; despedir por incompetencia. **III.** *vn.* fracasar, salir mal; volverse atrás, desistir; ser despedido (de un colegio) por incompetencia.

flush valve, válvula de inodoro.

flying, *a.*—**f. ambulance,** (mil.) ambulancia volante.—**f. colors,** banderas desplegadas.—**f. fish,** volador, pez volante.—**f. fox,** murciélago frugívoro.—**f. machine,** avión.

follow-up, *a.* de refresco, de empuje, uno más (dícese especialmente de una nueva carta o diligencia para promover un negocio).

foodstuff [fúdstuf], *s.* producto o substancia alimenticia; *pl.* **foodstuffs,** víveres.

foot, *s.* peal (de media).—**f.-and-mouth disease,** fiebre aftosa, glosopeda, erupción vesicular que afecta sobre todo la boca y las patas del ganado.

footage [fútiy], *s.* número de pies, longitud en pies; (en las minas) trabajo por pie.

for, *prep.* Cuando significa *para*, es a veces mejor traducirlo por el dativo: *this is easy for me*, esto me es fácil; *lo this for me*, hágame esto. Seguido de *s.* o *pron.* y un infinitivo, se traduce cambiando el giro y poniendo el verbo en subjuntivo: *the plan is for John to go*, el plan es que Juan vaya.

forbear, *s.* antepasado.

force, *va.*—**to f. his (our,** etc.) **hand,** obligarlo (obligarnos, etc.) a hacer algo o a declarar su (nuestra, etc.) intención.—**to f. on,** imponer a.—**to f. the issue,** hacer que el asunto se discuta o decida pronto; hacer que se vaya al grano sin demora.

forced, *a.* forzado, fingido; forzado, forzoso, obligatorio.

forestage [fóœrstéiy], *s.* proscenio, parte anterior del escenario (gen. enfrente del telón).

forget, *va.*—**to f. all about it,** olvidarse de ello completamente.—**f. it,** no piense más en eso; no se preocupe.

forgettable [forgétæbœl], *a.* olvidable.

forgetter [-tœr], *s.* olvidadizo, olvidado.

forgiver [forguívœr], *s.* perdonador.—**forgiving** [-ving], *a.* perdonador, clemente, magnánimo.

former, *a.* ex, que fué (*former teacher*, ex maestro, maestro que fué).

fornix [fórniks], *s.* (anat.) fórnis; trígono cerebral.

forthright [fóœzráit]. **I.** *s.* vía recta o directa. **II.** *a.* directo, derecho. **III.** *adv.* directamente; en seguida, inmediatamente.

forum, *s.* reunión de debate, en que se discute un asunto.

founding [fáunding], *s.* fundición.

four, *s.*—**on all fours,** parejo; sin discordancia; en completa armonía; equivalente.

fourth arm, (mil.) fuerzas aéreas.

fraenum, frænum [frénum], *s.* frenillo (de la lengua).

frame. I. *s.* forma, sistema (de gobierno, etc.); tenor, alcance (de una ley, constitución, etc.); fotografía de una imagen transmitida por televisión; película de cine; FRAME-UP.—**f. of reference,** sistema de coordenadas. **II.** *a.* reticulado, de celosía (dícese de las construcciones); de tablas, de madera; de entramado (casa). **III.** *va.* (gen. con up) fabricar, inventar (algo contra alguno); arreglar clandestinamente de antemano (el resultado de un juego, etc.); acusar o hacer condenar con pruebas inventadas a propósito, formar un complot contra.

frame-up [fréim ʊp], *s.* complot; fraude.

framework, *s.* sistema, forma (de gobierno, etc.); tenor, alcance (de una ley, etc.)

frankfurter [frǽnkfœrtœr], *s.* salchicha' de Fráncford, especie de salchicha de carne de vaca y de puerco muy condimentada.

frat [fræt], *s.* (fam.) = FRATERNITY.

free, *a.*—**f. lance,** persona sin empleo regular, que sirve a cualquiera que solicita sus servicios (aplícase sobre todo a escritores y artistas).—**f. ship,** buque neutral.—**f. state,** (hist., E. U.), estado no esclavista, o sin esclavos.

frenum [frínʊm], *s.* = FRAENUM.

frenzied [frénsid], *a.* frenético.

fret, *vn.* estar inquieto.—**fretful,** *a.* inquieto.— **fretfulness,** *s.* inquietud, desasosiego.

fretty [fréti], *a.* inquieto; irritable, malhumorado; inflamado, apostemado.

friction, *s.* desavenencia, falta de armonía, antipatía.

frisk, *va.* registrarle los bolsillos y la ropa a; detener y registrar a (una persona) para robarle.

frost line, profundidad a que llegan las heladas.

frown, *vn.*—**to f. on,** o **upon,** mirar de mal ojo, desaprobar.

frozen, *a.* estancado, inutilizado (apl. a fondos, crédito, etc.)

fruit bat, murciélago frugívoro.

frumpish [frúmpiš], *a.* malhumorado, de mal genio.

frumps, *s.* ataque de mal humor, emberrinchamiento.

frumpy [frúmpi], *a.* = FRUMPISH.

frying, *a.*—**to fall out of the f. pan into the fire,** huir del fuego y dar en las brasas.

fulgurate [fúlguiureit], *vn.* fulgurar.—**fulgurating** [-éiting], *a.* fulgurante; (med.) lancinante.— **fulguration** [-éishun], *s.* fulguración.

full, *a.* y *adv.* ancho; puro, sin mezcla; (mar.) desplegada, llena (vela).—(at) **f. blast,** a plena capacidad; sin coto, hasta más no poder.—**f. blood,** sangre pura, raza pura; parentesco por ambos padres.—**f.-blooded,** sanguíneo; rubicundo; de sangre o raza pura; de raza (caballo).— **f.-dress,** de etiqueta; (mil.) de parada, de gala.— **f.-fashioned,** ajustado en todas sus partes.—**f.-length,** de cuerpo entero.—**f. sail,** (mar.) vela llena; con energía, resueltamente.—**f. scale, f. size,** tamaño natural.—**f.-size, f.-sized,** de tamaño natural.—**f. time,** tiempo o período completo, jornada completa, horas normales de trabajo. —**f. uniform,** uniforme de gala.

funeral, *a.*—**f. director,** empresario funerario.— **f. parlors,** funeraria.

funnel, *a.* abocinado.

funnies [fúniš], *s. pl.* láminas chistosas (de un periódico).

G

G., *a.* séptimo.—**G-man,** (E. U.) agente indagador, o detective, del Departamento de Justicia.

gaby [guéibi]. *s.* simplón, mentecato.

gad. I. *s.* taladro; barra aguzada; lingote. **II.** *va.* aguijonear; (min.) romper o volar (roca) con cuña o taladro.

gadget [gǽyet], *s.* artificio, cosa (que no se nombra); algo que no se recuerda.

gag, *a.* coartador, amordazante (fig.), de la mordaza (fig.) (aplícase a leyes, etc.)

ga(u)ge, *s.* espesor.—**g. board,** tabla de mezclar ingredientes.

Gallinae, Gallinæ [gælíni], *s. pl.* (zool.) gallináceas.

gallinule [gǽliniul], *s.* polla de agua.

gam. I. *s.* cardumen o banco (apl. sobre todo a las ballenas); visita. **II.** *vn.* reunirse en cardumen; visitarse.

gameness [guéimness], *s.* valor, resolución.

gamete [gǽmit], *s.* célula generadora.

gamma [gǽmæ], *s.* gama (letra griega).

gangsterism [gǽngstœrísm], *s.* bandolerismo organizado, pandillaje.

gas, *s.*—**g. buoy,** boya de gas.—**g. carbon,** carbón de retorta.—**g. concrete,** hormigón poroso. —**g. engine,** motor de combustion interna.—**g. helmet** = G. MASK.—**g. machine,** máquina generadora de gas.—**g. oil,** petróleo para gas.—**g. station,** estación de gasolina, puesto o instalación de gasolina, donde ésta se vende a los automovilistas. —**g. tube** = GASSY TUBE.

gaseous tube, (rad.) tubo o lámpara con exceso de gas, que estorba su funcionamiento.

gaskin [gǽskin], *s.* muslo (del caballo).

gasman [gǽsmæn], *s.* fabricante de gas; GAS FITTER.

gassing [gǽsing], *s.* tratamiento con gas; (mil.) ataque o asfixia con gas.

gastrin [gǽstrin], *s.* gastrina, hormona que causa la secreción del jugo gástrico.

gassy tube, (rad.) tubo o lámpara que contiene un poco de gas, pero no en demasía, y que puede usarse como detector.

gastric, *a.*—**g. fever,** fiebre biliosa remitente; dispepsia aguda.—**g. juice,** jugo gástrico.

gastroptosis [gǽstroptósis], *s.* (med.) prolapso del estómago.

gastrotomy [gæstrótomi], *s.* (cir.) gastrotomía, laparotomía.

gecko [guécol, *s.* (zool.) salamanquesa.

gene [yin], *s.* (biología) elemento determinante de la herencia, substancia, agente o factor generador determinante de los caracteres heredados.

genre [ȳanr], *s.* estilo o escrito costumbrista.

Germanophile [yœrmǽnofail], *s.* y *a.* germanófilo, partidario de los alemanes.

gerrymander [guérrimǽndœr], **I.** *va.* dividir (un estado, etc.) injusta o arbitrariamente en distritos electorales; tergiversar. **II.** *s.* división arbitraria injusta en distritos electorales; tergiversación, argucia.

get. I. *va.*—**to g. hold of,** posesionarse de; coger; aprender.—**to g. in,** allegar, proveerse de; lograr dar, meter, etc. (un golpe, una observación, etc.).—**to g. on,** ponerse (ropa).—**to g. one's goat,** serle a uno inaguantable, fastidiario.—**to g. up steam,** levantar vapor. **II.** *vn.*—**to g. around** = TO GET ABOUT, TO GET ROUND.—**to g. away with it,** salirse con la suya, llevar algo a cabo pasando por encima de todos o de todo.—**to g. busy,** moverse, menearse, poner manos a la obra.—**to g. out,** divulgarse.—**to g. to be,** llegar a ser; hacerse, ponerse (antes de *a.*).—**to g. together,** juntarse, reunirse; cooperar, obrar de común acuerdo.—**to tell one where to g. off,** decir a uno cuántas son cinco, ponerle en su puesto, cantárselas claras.

get-at-able [guétætæbœl], *a.* accesible, tratable; obtenible, asequible.

get-away, *s.* ida, partida; escape.

gibber. I. *s.* farfulla, tonterías. **II.** *a.* tonto, deshilvanado.

gimp, *s.* vigor, energía.

gimper [guímpœr], *s.* persona enérgica o emprendedora; persona hábil o diestra.

ginglymus [yínglimus], *s.* (anat.) ginglimo.

girlie [gœrli], *s.* (fam.) muchachita; chica.

give, *va.*—**to g. a thought to,** pensar en, acordarse de (gen. en oración negativa).—**to g. effect to,** poner en ejecución.—**to g. ground,** retirarse; ceder.—**to g. line,** o **rope,** dar rienda.—**to g. pause,** dar en qué pensar; hacer pensar; ser peliagudo.—**to g. points,** dar ventaja, dar tantos (en el juego); dar consejo, hacer indicaciones útiles.—**to g. tongue,** empezar a ladrar.—**to g. up the ghost,** morir; desistir, darse por vencido.—**to g. voice to,** decir, expresar.

glacial, *a.* (geol.) glaciario.

gladioli [glædáiolai], *s. pl.* de GLADIOLUS.

glass, *s.*—**g. sponge,** esponja silícea.—**g. wool,** tela de vidrio.

glaze, *s.* capa de hielo.

go, *vn.* resultar (bien, mal), tener (buen, mal) éxito; ponerse (loco, etc.); cuajar, surtir efecto; ser ley, no cambiarse, ser terminante; guiarse; rezar, decir; irse, desaparecer; consumirse, acabarse.—**to g. begging,** no tener demanda; no gustar.—**to g. by the board,** abandonarse; fracasar.—**to g. down,** pasar (a la historia, etc.); tragarse (cambiando el giro: *that does not go down with me,* eso no me lo trago yo).—**to g. in business,** emprender negocios.—**to g. in for,** tomar parte en; adherirse a; apoyar; dedicar algún tiempo a.—**to g. into,** ir o irse al.—**to g. into effect,** entrar en vigor.—**to g. on the air,** hablar o dedicarse a hablar por radio; transmitirse por radio.—**to g. past,** pasar, pasar de largo.—**to g. to war,** ir a la guerra; hacer guerra; (con **with**) hacer la guerra (a).—**to g. up the spout,** malograrse, fracasar.

godless, *a.* sin Dios, ateo.

God's acre, cementerio, camposanto.

go-getter [góugétœr], *s.* buscavida, sujeto emprendedor.

gold, *s.*—**g. dust,** (bot.) ombligo de Venus.—**g. point,** estado del cambio exterior en que los pagos pueden hacerse en oro no acuñado (oro en barras) sin perder.—**g. stick,** (Ing.) oficial de la corte.

golden, *a.*—**g. age,** siglo de oro, siglo dorado.—**g. mean,** justo medio; moderación, prudencia.

golf. I. *s.*—**g. course,** o **links,** cancha de golf. **II.** *vn.* jugar golf.

golfer [gólfœr], golfista, jugador de golf.

golliard [góliærd], *s.* bufón ambulante.

gomphosis [gomfósis], *s.* (anat.) gonfosis.

gone, *a.*—**to be g.,** haberse ido; faltar, haber desaparecido; haberse acabado.

gonof, gonoph [gónuf], *s.* cortabolsas, ratero.

good. I. *a.*—**g. book,** o **G. Book,** Sagrada Escritura, Biblia.—**g. cheer,** buen ánimo, confianza (**to be of g. cheer,** tener buen ánimo, tener aliento); fiesta, festividad, festín; buenas viandas, buena mesa.—**g. fellow,** campechano.—**g. graces,** favor, amistad, consideración. **II.** *adv.*—**g. and** (antes de *a.* o *adv.*), bien, muy.

goodwife [gúduáif], *s.* ama o señora de la casa.

grace, *s.*—**with a bad (good) g.,** de mala (buena) gana.

grade, *s.*—**down g.,** pendiente descendente; cuesta abajo.—**to make the g.,** lograr su propósito, vencer las dificultades.—**up g.,** pendiente ascendente; cuesta arriba.

grading, *s.* gradación, arreglo según tamaño, etc.

grain, *s.*—**against the g.,** contra la inclinación o el carácter de uno.—**with a g. of salt,** menos la tara (fig.)

grand, *s.* piano de cola; mil dólares.

grand stand, tendido, gradería de asientos.

granolite [grénolait], *s.* granolita, (cualquier) roca ígnea granosa.

grayfish [gréifish], *s.* (ict.) lija, cazón.

great, *a.*—**G. Scott!** ¡válgame Dios! ¡qué cosa! ¡Jesús!—**G. Wall,** Gran Muralla (de China).—**G. White Father,** Gran Padre Blanco, título que los indios dan al presidente de los E. U.

green, *a.*—**g. sand,** arena verde o húmeda.—**g. sickness,** clorosis.

greengrocery [gríngróseri], *s.* tienda de legumbres y frutas.

grill, grillroom, *s.* En casi todas partes, estas palabras se han adoptado en su forma inglesa, y no hay que traducirlas.

grind, *va.* esmerilar.

grinding. I. *s.* esmerilado. **II.** *a.* de pulir, de esmerilar; de amolar; de moler.—**g. balls,** bolillas moledoras o pulverizadoras.

grip car, coche o vagón de arrastre por cable.

grit, gritrock [grítróc], **gritstone** [grítstóun], *s.* asperón.

groceteria [grósetíriæ], *s.* especiería sin dependientes, donde los compradores entran, toman lo que quieren y pagan al salir.

ground. I. *s.* (rad.) tierra, objeto (tubería, calorífero, etc.) a que se ata el alambre de conexión con tierra. **II.** *a.* de tierra; de base, primero (capa, etc.); (elec.) de conexión con tierra.—**g. clamp,** (elec.) tira de conexión con tierra.—**g. detector,** (elec.) detector de tierras.—**g. ice** = ANCHOR ICE.—**g. lead** = G. WIRE.—**g. line,** (geom.) línea de (la) tierra.

gruel(l)ing [grúeling]. **I.** *s.* zurra, pega. **II.** *a.* agotador, en que uno tiene que poner todas sus fuerzas; abrumador.

guan [guán], *s.* (zool.) pava.

guarded [gárded], *a.* protegido, defendido; cauto, cauteloso.

guffaw [gufó] *vn.* reír a carcajadas.

gulp, *vn.* entrecortar el resuello; quedarse pasmado o turulato.

gumbo soil, (agr.) suelo pegajoso.

gumshoe [gúmshú]. **I.** *s.* zapato de goma. **II.** *a.* oculto, subrepticio; hecho con mucho tiento o muy cautelosamente.

gun. I. *va.* hacer fuego a; cañonear, atacar con cañones; proveer de cañones. **II.** *vn.* cazar con escopeta o rifle.

gunfire [gúnfáiær], *s.* fuego de artillería; fuego (de armas de fuego en general).

gunpower [gúnpáuœr], **gun power,** peso total de los proyectiles lanzados en una andanada por los cañones mayores de un barco de guerra.

gyp [yip]. **I.** *s.* sirviente, criado; timador, trampeador. **II.** *va.* y *vn.* timar, trampear, embaucar.

H

hafnium [jáfniúm], *s.* (quím.) hafnio.

hair, *s.*—**h.-check,** grietecilla (**to h.-check,** agrietarse finamente, con grietecillas filiformes).—**h.-checking,** agrietamiento filiforme.

hairsplitter [jéœrsplítœr], *s.* persona quisquillosa o pelillosa.

half, *a.*—**h.-heartedness,** frialdad, tibieza.—**h.-staff** = H.-MAST.

halitosis [jélitósis], *s.* mal aliento, aliento de mal olor.

hamal [jæmél], *s.* cargador; criado.

hamstring, *va.* incapacitar; mancar.

hamstrung [jæmstrúng], *pret.* y *pp.* de TO HAMSTRING.

hand. I. *s.*—**h. and seal,** firma.—**h. glass,** espejo de mano; lente de aumento.—**h. to hand,** cuerpo a cuerpo.—**on every h.,** por todas partes, por todos lados. **II.** *va.*—**to h. out,** entregar, dar.

handbag [jéndbæg], *s.* maleta; bolsa, saquillo.

handy man, hombre o mozo para tareas menudas varias.

hang-over [jéngóvœr], *s.* sobra, algo que queda; irritación o malestar que sigue a una borrachera.

happy medium, justo medio.

hard, *a.* y *adv.*—**h. boiled,** bien cocido, duro (huevo); terco, porfiado, (Am.) empecinado, petrificado.—**h.-fought,** reñido.—**h. liquor,** licor (a diferencia de la cerveza y el vino).—**h. on the heels of,** inmediatamente después de.—**h.-shell(ed,** con caparazón; porfiado, inflexible.—**h. usage,** mal trato, uso rudo.—**h.-worked,** trillado, rancio (fig.).—**h. worker,** trabajador muy asiduo.—**to be put h. to it,** verse en calzas prietas.

hardening, *s.* endurecimiento.—**h. of the arteries,** arterioesclerosis.

hardware, *s.* herraje, conjunto de accesorios metálicos.

have. I. *verbo.*—**to h. and to hold,** en propiedad, en dominio (es expletivo que no se traduce).—**to h. breakfast, lunch,** etc., desayunarse, almorzar, etc.—**to h. done (with),** haber terminado; no tener más que ver con.—**to h. got to,** tener que.—**to h. it in for,** tenérsela jurada a.—**to h. nothing on one,** no llevar ninguna ventaja a uno; no tener nada contra uno.—**to h. something on one,** llevar ventaja a uno; tener algo contra uno.—**to h. to do with,** tener que ver con; tratar de, versar sobre. **II.** *s.* el que tiene, el privilegiado (gen. en la frase **the haves and the have nots,** los que tienen y los desposeídos).

haw-haw [jojó]. **I.** *s.* carcajada. **II.** *vn.* reír a carcajadas.

hawk, *s.* (alb.) tabla portamezcla.

hazing, *s.* obligar a trabajar demasiado o en tareas desagradables; tunda, zurra.

head. I. *s.*—**h. resistance,** (aer.) resistencia de proa o al avance. **II.** *va.* formar cabeza en o a.

headline, *s.* encabezamiento.

headmaster [jédmǽstœr], *s.* director.

headmistress [jédmístres], *s.* directora.

headphone [jédfóun], *s.* (tlf.) boquilla auricular o receptor que se asegura en la cabeza con una cinta elástica.—**headset** [-sét], *s.* juego de *headphones*.

hear, *vn.*—**will not,** o **won't, h. of it,** no quiere (quiero, etc.) ni siquiera hablar de ello.

hearing, *s.*—**in one's h.,** que uno oye u oyó.

hearsay, *a.* de oídas.

heart, *s.*—**h. failure,** parálisis repentina del corazón.—**after one's own h.,** como a uno le gusta.—**to one's h.'s content,** a sus anchas, sin restricción.

heat, *s.*—**h. exchanger,** recipiente de intercambio térmico, compensador de temperatura. —**to be in h.,** estar en celo, (fam.) estar caliente (un animal).

heavy, *a.*—**h. artillery,** artillería mayor o de grueso calibre.—**h. duty,** servicio o trabajo fuerte (de una máquina).—**h. earth,** (min.) barita.—**h. seas,** mar bravo, borrascoso.—**h. water,** agua superhidrogenada (H_2H_2O).

hefty [jéfti], *a.* un poco pesado; vigoroso; riguroso.

hello, *interj.*—**h. there!** ¡hola! ¡oiga!—**h.-girl,** (chica) telefonista.

helm port, limera del timón.

help, helping, *s.* porción (de comida) que se sirve a uno o que uno se sirva de una vez. Conviene cambiar el giro: *I have had two helpings of rice,* me he servido (Vd. me ha servido, etc.) arroz dos veces

Hemichorda [jémicórdæ], *s. pl.* (zool.) hemicordios.—**hemichordate** [-deit], *s.* y *a.* hemicordio.

hemipter [jemíptœr], *s.* (zool.) hemíptero.— **Hemiptera** [jemípteræ], *s. pl.* hemípteros.— **hemipteral** [-æl], *a.,* **hemipteran** [-æn], *s.* y *a.,* hemíptero.

hemoptysis [jemóptisis], *s.* (med.) hemóptisis, hemorragia pulmonar.

hereinbefore [jíærínbifóær], *adv.* arriba, anteriormente, antes.

heterodyne. I. *s.* (rad.) generador heterodino. **II.** *a.* heterodino (receptor, sistema, etc.)

Hexapoda [jeksǽpodæ], *s. pl.* (zool.) hexápodos. —**hexapodous** [-dus], *a.* hexápodo.

hey, *interj.* ¡oiga! ¡digo!

hide. I. *s.* escondite. **II.** *vn.*—**to h. out,** esconderse, estarse escondido.

hideout [jáidáut], *s.* escondite.

hidrosis [jaidróusis], *s.* sudor; sudor excesivo o anormal; cualquier enfermedad cutánea acompañada de sudor excesivo.

hierocracy [jáierócræsi], *s.* supremacía eclesiástica, gobierno eclesiástico; jerarquía.

high. I. *a.* y *adv.*—**h.-blooded,** de noble alcurnia.—**h. blood pressure,** hipertensión arterial. —**h. command,** comando supremo, suprema comandancia.—**h. horse,** actitud arrogante, presunción.—**h. jinks,** retozo.—**h. life,** vida aristocrática.—**h. light,** (b. a.) toque de luz; cosa, acontecimiento o rasgo descollante.—**h.-proof,** de alta concentración.—**h. time,** tiempo de no esperar más, tiempo de decidirse o hacer algo; gran holgorio o parranda. **II.** *s.* alza, subida; escuela secundaria; (aut.) velocidad máxima.

highbred [jáibréd], *a.* de raza, de alcurnia pura; culto, bien educado.

higher brackets, clases superiores; gente de alta categoría.

highjacker, hijacker [jáiʏǽkœr], *s.* salteador (aplícase sobre todo al que roba a contrabandistas); ladrón de licores.

hike [jáic] **I.** *s.* caminata. **II.** *vn.* dar una caminata; andar, caminar.

hiker [jáikœr], *s.* caminador; andariego; el aficionado a las caminatas.

hindbrain [jáindbréin], *s.* cerebelo; parte posterior del encéfalo.

hinny, *s.* mulo nacido de caballo y burra.

hip joint, (anat.) articulación iliacofemoral; (ing.) nudo o articulación del extremo del cordón o cabeza superior de un puente y la pieza que apoya en el estribo.

hippocampus, *s.* (zool.) hipocampo, caballo de mar; (anat.) hipocampo (del cerebro).

hirdum-dirdum [jœrdum-dœrdum], *s.* gritería; alboroto, tumulto.

hirudo [jirúdo], *s.* (zool.) hirudo, sanguijuela.

histolysis [jistólisis], *s.* degeneración de los tejidos orgánicos.

hit. I. *va.*—**to h. it off,** avenirse, simpatizar. **II.** *vn.*—**to h. upon,** ocurrírsele a uno.

hitter [jítœr], *s.* golpeador.

hobble skirt, enagua apretada, ceñida o estrecha por abajo.

hobnob. I. *s.* charla amistosa. **II.** *adv.* a la diabla, a la ventura, al azar.

hod, *s.* (alb.) esparavel.

hog. I. *s.* (aer.) arqueo, comba vuelta hacia abajo. **II.** *va.* (agric.) echar cerdos a o en.

hoist bridge, puente levadizo.

hoister [jóistœr], *s.* elevador, levantador; grúa; ascensor.

hokey pokey [jókipóki], *s.* helado de inferior calidad vendido en las calles; HOCUS-POCUS.

hokum [jóucum], *s.* payasada; faramalla, farándula.

hold, *va.*—**to h. down,** conservar, no perder.— **to h. in,** contener, refrenar.—**to h. in affection, respect,** etc., tener cariño, etc. a.—**to h. one's ground,** o **one's own,** mantenerse firme; bandearse.—**to h. the bag,** o **the sac,** quedarse con las manos vacías; quedarse colgado.—**to h. up to,** exponer al (desprecio, etc.); poner en (ridículo).

hollyhock [jóliʏoc], *s.* (bot.) alcea rósea.

Holocephali [jóloséfælai], *s. pl.* (zool.) holocéfalos, quimeras (peces).—**holocephalan** [-læn], *a.* holocéfalo.

holophote [jólofout], *s.* reflector o faro de rayos concentrados.

homeland [jóumlænd], *s.* patria, tierra natal; (Ing.) Inglaterra (a distinción de las colonias).

homodyne [jómodain], *a.* (rad.) homodino.

Homoptera [jomópteræ], *s. pl.* (zool.) homópteros.

hone, *va.* pulir, esmerilar.

honk [jonc]. **I.** *s.* pitazo, sonido de la bocina de un automóvil; graznido. **II.** *va.* y *vn.* tocar o sonar la bocina; graznar.

hooch [juch], *s.* licor.

hoof-and-mouth disease =FOOT-AND-MOUTH DISEASE.

hookup, hook-up [júcup], *s.* (rad.) conexión o combinación de difusoras, transmisión por varias emisoras conectadas en circuito.

hooligan [júligæn]. **I.** *s.* rufián, truhán. **II.** *a* de rufianes, truhanesco.—**hooliganism** [-ism], *s.* truhanería, rufianismo.

hoosegow, hoosgow [júsgau], *s.* cárcel, prisión; encarcelamiento.

hop, *s. va.* salir o alzar el vuelo en (un avión), poner en marcha.

hopeless, *a.* desesperado; irremediable, irreparable; con que o con quien no se puede hacer nada, que no tiene entrada.

hormon(e [jórmoun], *s.* (quím.), hormón, hormona.

hormonic [jormónic], *a.* hormónico.

horn, *s.* miembro (de un dilema); (aer.) palanca de mando.—**at the small end of the h.,** llevándose lo peor, perdiendo.

---

hornswoggle [jórnsuógœl], *va.* engatusar, embaucar.

horny sponge, esponja córnea.

horse, *s.*—**h. tamer,** amansador de caballos.—**a h. of another color,** harina de otro costal, otra cosa, otro cantar.

hospitalization [jóspitæliséishʋn], *s.* hospitalización; tratamiento de hospital.

hospitalize [-aiš], *va.* convertir en hospital; hospitalizar, enviar al hospital.

hostess, *s.* maestra de ceremonias (en un cabaret, etc.); (aer.) mujer que atiende a los pasajeros.

hot, *a.*—**h. bulb,** (máq. comb. int.), tubo incandescente.—**h. dog**=FRANKFURTER.—**h. plate,** calorífero portátil de gas.—**h. pot, h. tube**=H. BULB.—**h.-wire ammeter,** (elec.) amperímetro térmico.

hotfoot [jótfút], *adv.* pronta o rápidamente.

hothead [-jéd], *s.* persona fogosa, arrebatada, turbulenta o de mal genio; agitador, alborotador, bochinchero.

house, *s.*—**h. of correction,** reformatorio.—**h. of ill fame,** o **repute,** burdel.—**h. surgeon,** cirujano residente.

how, *adv.* como.—**h. often,** cada cuánto (tiempo).

howler [jáuler], *s.* adefesio ridículo; aullador, mono aullador.

huddle. I. *s.* reunión, sobre todo de jugadores de futbol para recibir órdenes; junta o reunión secreta. **II.** *vn.* reunirse, juntarse.

hull, *s.* (aer.) flotador (de aeroplano); (aer.) armazón (de un dirigible rígido).

hummer [jǘmœr], *s.* (orn.) colibrí.

hunch, *s.* presentimiento.

hundred-per-center [júndred pœr séntœr], *s.* patriota de ciento por ciento, sin mezcla de influencias ni predilecciones extranjeras.

hunger. I. *s.*—**h. strike,** huelga del hambre, huelga de inanición. **II.** *vn.*—**to h. for,** tener sed de, anhelar.

hushboat, hush ship, barco armado disfrazado de barco mercante.

hydrochlorid(e [jáidroclóraid, -id], *s.* clorhidrato.

hydroid [jáidroid], *s.* y *a.* hidrozoario.

Hydroidea [jaidróidiæ], *s. pl.* hidrozoarios.

hydropath [jáidropæz], **hydropathist** [haidrópæzist], *s.* hidrópata.

hydrophone [jáidrofoun], *s.* hidrófono, instrumento que sirve para escuchar sonidos transmitidos por el agua.

Hydrozoa [jáidrośóæ], *s. pl.* hidrozoarios.

hyperope [jáipœroup], **hyperopia** [-ópia] = HYPERMETROPE, HYPERMETROPIA.

hyphenate [jáifeneit], *s.* ciudadano de dudosa ortografía, ciudadano norteamericano de origen extranjero. (El término, que es despectivo, alude al guión—*hyphen*—de la voz compuesta que indica las dos nacionalidades, como en *German-American*, ciudadano norteamericano de origen alemán.)

I

icterus [ícterʋs], *s.* (med.) ictericia.

ideate [aidíeit]. **I.** *s.* objeto correspondiente a una idea. **II.** *va.* concebir; pensar; recordar; idear. **III.** *vn.* formar ideas, pensar.

idler, *s.* rueda de guía (en un tractor).

if, *conj.* aunque. *If* introduce a veces una proposición de contraste numérico enfático, en el sentido de *cuando menos, ni uno menos;* vg. *she has fifty dollars, if she has one,* o, *if she has one cent,* ella tiene por lo menos cincuenta dólares, ella no tiene ni un centavo menos de, etc.

ignore, *va.* desentenderse o no hacer caso de; despreciar.

ill. I. *a.*—**i. repute**=ILL FAME. **II.** *adv.*—**i. at ease,** embarazado, confundido; inquieto, intranquilo.

illenium [ilíniʋm], *s.* (quím.) ilenio.

impact excitation, (rad.) excitación impulsiva.

implement. I. *s.* elemento, instrumento (de guerra, etc.). **II.** *va.* completar; llevar a cabo; (for.) cumplir.

impound, *va.* embalsar, rebalsar (aguas).

improve, *va.*—**to i. the opportunity,** aprovecharse de la oportunidad, hacer su agosto.

impulse excitation, (rad.) excitación impulsiva.

inbred, *a.* criado o nacido de padres de una misma raza o de razas muy semejantes.

inbreed, *va.* y *vn.* criar o producir sin mezcla de razas, o dentro de una misma raza.

incident wires=STAGGERING WIRES.

inclinometer [ínclinómetœr], *s.* (aer.) inclinómetro.

incorporate, *va.* comprender, encerrar.

incus [íncʋs], *s.* (anat.) yunque (uno de los huesecillos del oído).

indentation, *s.* hendedura, hueco, depresión.

independent seconds watch, reloj de segundos muertos, reloj cronográfico.

indexer [índecsœr], *s.* el que hace índice o índices.

indict, *va.* acusar, atacar.

indoor, *a.* interior, de casa; que se hace en la casa o bajo techo.

indoors, *adv.* bajo techo; en la casa, adentro.

industrialist [indústriælist], *s.* industrial.

ineluctable [ínelúctæbœl], *a.* ineluctable, inevitable; irresistible.—**ineluctably** [-bli], inevitablemente, ineluctablemente.

inescapable [íneskéipœbœl], *a.* ineludible.

inferno [infœrno], *s.* infierno.

infiltrate, *va.* y *vn.* penetrar, meter(se), introducir(se) en pequeño número por varias partes (dicho de los soldados en un ataque).

infiltration, *s.* (mil.) penetración de pequeñas fuerzas por varios puntos.

infusive [infúsiv], *a.* inspirador.

ingle [ingœl], *s.* llama; fuego; hogar.

ingrown [íngróun], *a.* que va penetrando en la carne a medida que crece (*v.* INGROWING); congénito, natural.

ingrowth [-óuz], *s.* crecimiento hacia adentro, lo que crece hacia adentro.

inguinal canal, conducto inguinal.

ingulf, *va.* tragarse.

inhalator [ínjæléitœr], *s.* (med.) inhalador.

initial, *va.* poner las iniciales a o en; firmar con iniciales.

in-law [inló], *s.* suegro, suegra; cuñado, cuñada. (Gen. se aplica a los suegros.)

in-patient [ínpéishent], *s.* enfermo residente en un hospital.

inquilin(e [ínkuilin, -lain], *s.* y *a.,* **inquilinous** [-láinʋs], *a.* Dícese del animal que vive en el nido de otro.

inside play, juego con señales secretas convenidas de antemano.

insightful [ínsáitful], perspicaz, clarividente.

instal(l)ment, *s.* cuota.—**i. plan,** pago por cuotas.—**on the i. plan,** con pago por cuotas.

institute, *s.* reunión de maestros.

instrumental, *a.*—**to be i. in,** contribuir a.

instrumentalism [ínstruméntælism], (fil.) pragmatismo.

instrumentality, *s.* medio, arbitrio.

inswept [ínsuépt], *a.* (aut.) más angosto adelante que atrás.

intaglio, *s.* obra de entalladura.

intelligence, *s.* conocimiento, informes; informador, indagador; indagación.—**i. bureau,** o **office,** oficina o departamento de indagación.—**i. officer,** oficial o agente de la oficina de indagación.—**i. quotient,** cociente intelectual, edad intelectual.

intelligentsia, *s. pl.* los intelectuales.

intensification [inténsifikéishʋn], *s.* acrecentamiento, aumento; avivamiento.

intensify, *va.* acrecentar; avivar.

interchurch [íntœrchœrch], *a.* relativo o común a varias iglesias o a las iglesias.

intercollegiate [íntœrcolíɣiet], *a.* intercolegiado, de entre universidades o estudiantes.

interest, *s.*—**the interests**, las grandes empresas, los intereses creados del comercio y la industria, los capitalistas.—**to one's (own) i.**, en bien o provecho de uno, que le conviene.

interested [ínterested], *a.* interesado.

interestingly [ínteréstingli], *adv.* interesantemente, amenamente.

interference, *s.* intromisión; (fís.) interferencia.

interlock, *s.* traba; trabazón; (cine) sincronización; (cine) sincronizador.

intermediacy [íntœrmídiasi], *s.* calidad de intermedio; intervención, mediación.

Internationale [æinternásionál], *s.* (la) Internacional (himno).

internationalism [íntœrnǽshunælísm], *s.* internacionalismo.—**internationality** [-næliti], *s.* internacionalidad.

interpose, *va.* (cine) reemplazar gradualmente una figura por otra, o cambiar la una en la otra.

interscholastic [íntœrscolǽstic], *a.* interescolar, de entre escuelas.

intersection, *s.* cruce (de calles, etc.)

intracoastal [íntræcóustæl], *a.* cercano a la costa.

intrigue, *va.* poner perplejo; atraer, interesar; despertar la curiosidad de.

introversion, *s.* (psic.) introversión.

introvert. I. *s.* y *a.* (psic.) introverso, que tiene la tendencia a concentrarse en sí mismo. **II.** *vn.* (psic.) concentrarse en sí mismo, ocuparse más en el mundo interior que en el exterior.

Invisible Empire = KU KLUX KLAN.

Iranian [airéiniæn], *s.* y *a.* iranio. (Hablando de la Irania moderna—Persia—puede traducirse por *persa*.)

iron lung, pulmón de hierro, activador pulmonar mecánico, caja de hierro con que se ciñe el cuerpo del enfermo, provista de un artificio que ayuda a la contracción y dilatación de los pulmones. (Puede adoptarse *pulmón de hierro*, que es la traducción literal del nombre dado al mecanismo por sus inventores.)

isba [ísba], *s.* (en Rusia) casa empajada de trozas.

island, *s.* zona (gen. plataforma o resalto) de seguridad o divisoria (en las calles y plazas).

isobar [áisobár], *s.* línea isobárica.

isochronize [aisócronais], *va.* hacer isócrono, poner en sincronismo.

isolationism [áisoléíshunísm], *s.* aislamientismo, prescindencia de otras naciones.—**isolationist** [-ist], *s.* aislamientista, partidario del aislamiento.

issuance [íshuœns], *s.* emisión; promulgación; publicación; distribución.

Istrian [ístriæn], *s.* y *a.* istrio.

it. *pron.* No se traduce cuando sigue a un *s.* y precede a un tiempo de *to be* seguido de infinitivo (*his duty it is to go*, su deber es ir).—**i. is . . . which**, o **that**, es lo que (*it is money that you need*, dinero es lo que Vd. necesita).—**is that i.?** ¿es eso? —**that is i.**, eso es.

J

jack, *va.* (gen. con **up**), soliviar con un cric.

jacket, *s.* forro; pellejo; cáscara; forro o envoltura metálica (de acero, etc.) de una bala de plomo.

jake [ɣéic], **jakey** [ɣéiki], *s.* gengibre de Jamaica, que se toma como licor.

jam. I. *s.* atoramiento, atascamiento; atascadero (fig.), situación peliaguda. **II.** *va.* y *vn.* atorar(se), trabar(se).—**III.** *va.* (rad.) enredar la transmisión de (una difusora), causar interferencia en, hacer ininteligible por ondas perturbadoras emitidas por otra difusora.

jammed, *a.* atorado, trabado; de bote en bote, repleto.

Jap [ɣæp], *s.* japonés.

jazz. I. *s.* baile con música de *jazz*. **II.** *va.* (a veces con **up**) convertir en *jazz*, o meter *jazz* en

(una pieza), *jazzificar*. **III.** *vn.* bailar o tocar *jazz*; hacer algo desordenadamente.

jazzy [ɣæsi], *a.* que tiene *jazz* o se parece al *jazz*.

jesting (ɣésting). **I.** *s.* (el) chancearse, uso de chanzas. **II.** *a.* chancero; de chanza.

jitter [ɣítœr], *vn.* estar nervioso, intranquilo, desasosegado.—**jitters** [ɣítœrs], *s. pl.* intranquilidad, desasosiego, inquietud.—**jittery** [-i], *a.* nervioso, intranquilo, inquieto.

job, *s.* obra o cosa que se está haciendo.—**on the j.**, en la tarea; en su puesto; (constr.) en el lugar de la obra.

jog trot, trote corto; pereza, lentitud.

joint, *a.* conjunto; de o por ambas cámaras (del congreso).

jollier [ɣólicr], candonguero; lisonjeador.

jollification [ɣólifikéishun], parranda, retozo, holgorio.

jolly. I. *a.* y *adv.* excelente, magnífico, de lo mejor; muy, sumamente. **II.** *va.* y *vn.* candonguear, engatusar con zalamerías; lisonjear, seguir el humor a).

juncture, *s.* momentos, circunstancias.

jungle, *s.* espesura, soto, breza, selva.

junior college, escuela semisuperior, en que se cursan sólo los dos primeros años de las escuelas superiores o universitarias; escuela de estudios universitarios de primero y segundo años.

just, *adv.*—**j. about**, poco más o menos; o poco menos (*this is just about right*, esto está bien, o poco menos).—**it is j. too bad**, es una gran lástima.

Justinian [ɣustíniæn], *a.* justinianeo.—**J. Code**, Código Justinianeo.

K

kaiserdom [káisœrdum], *s.* puesto, oficio o dominio de un káiser, o del káiser; kaiserismo. —**kaiserism** [-ism], *s.* kaiserismo.

kangaroo closure, (Ing.) limitación presidencial de la discusión de un proyecto a sus puntos principales.

kappa [kǽpæ], *s.* cappa, capa (letra griega).

karakul [cáracul], *s.* caracul, astracán de la mejor calidad.

keek [kic]. **I.** *s.* acción de asomarse; atisbo, husmeo; husmeador. **II.** *va.* y *vn.* atisbar, husmear; asomarse.—**keeker** [kíkœr]. *s.* atisbador; husmeador, averiguador de negocios ajenos.

keep, *va.*—**to k. body and soul together**, vivir, ir viviendo, no pasar hambre.—**to k. from**, mantener lejos de; impedir (cambiando el giro).—**to k. in mind**, recordar; tener en cuenta.—**to k. one's end up**, mantenerse en su puesto, no aflojar.—**to k. pace with**, correr parejas con.—**to k. up appearances**, salvar las apariencias.

keeper, *s.* armadura (de un imán).

keeping, *s.*—**in k. with**, por el mismo estilo que, al mismo tenor que.

kepi [képi], *s.* (mil.) quepis.

key. I. *s.* fundamento; persona o cosa principal; tono (de la voz); estilo; tabla, cuadro. **II.** *a.* principal; que sirve de clave o de guía; fundamental.

keynote, *a.* principal, fundamental.—**k. address**, o **speech**, discurso de apertura (de una convención política, etc.), declaración de principios y programa.

keynoter [kínóutœr], *s.* orador que pronuncia el discurso de apertura, en que se enuncia el programa del partido.

kibitzer [kíbitsœr], *s.* entremetido; equivoquista.

kick. I. *s.* (fam.) placer (**to get a k. out of**, hallar placer en); estímulo, aliento, impulso; reculada, retroceso (de un arma de fuego); fondo entrante (de botella).—**k. plate**, placa de protección. **II.** *vn.*—**to k. over the traces**, recelarse, abandonar o sacudir toda restricción.

kike [cáic], *s.* judío; KEEKER.

kill, *va.*—**to k. two birds with one stone**, hacer de un camino dos mandados.

Para la pronunciación de æ, œ, ᴅ, ŝ, ŝh, ᴜ, ȳ, y, z, véase la clave al principio del libro.

kind, s.—**nothing of the k.,** nada de eso; no hay tal.—**of a k.,** de una misma clase.—**of the k.,** semejante, tal.

kindergart(e)ner [kíndœrgárt(e)nœr), s. maestro de kindergarten.

kindly, adv. Se emplea mucho en el sentido de sírvase, ojalá me haga el favor, etc.

kink. I. s. carcajada; estertor. **II.** vn. reír a carcajadas.

Klansman [klǽnśmæn], s. miembro del KU KLUX KLAN.

knitting mill, fábrica de tejidos.

know. I. va.—**to k. a thing or two,** saber algo, o una que otra cosa; tener buen juicio.—**to k. how** (antes de infinitivo), saber.—**to k. one's place,** conocer uno la posición que ocupa, saber con quién habla.—**to k. the ropes,** conocer los detalles, estar al tanto, saber el juego (fig.).—**to k. what is what,** estar al corriente o al tanto.—**to k. where the shoe pinches,** saber dónde está el busilis, o la dificultad. **II.** vn.—**to k. better,** saber que no es así; saber lo que debe hacerse, o cómo debe portarse (uno). **III.** s. conocimiento.—**to be in the k.,** estar informado; estar en el secreto.

knuckle, vn.—**to k. down,** o to, consagrarse o emprender con vehemencia.—**to k. (under) to,** doblegarse ante; ceder a.

knurled, a. estriado.

kosher [cóśhœr], s. alimentos preparados de acuerdo con el ritual judío.

kotow. I. s. postración china de homenaje, con la frente en el suelo. **II.** vn. arrodillarse y tocar el suelo con la frente (homenaje chino); doblar la rodilla (fig.), portarse servilmente.

kowtow [coutáu], s. y v. = KOTOW.

K tube = HYDROPHONE.

kyack [káiæk], s. tercio (media carga).

kyke [cáic], s. = KEEK.

L

labia [léibiæ], s. pl. labios.

Laconian [læcóuniæn], s. y a. laconio.

ladrone [lædróun], s. soldado filipino insurgente; ladrón, bandido.

ladronism [ladrónîsm], s. pillaje, bandolerismo; (en las Filipinas) insurrección, levantamiento.

lag screw, tornillo grande para madera, con cabeza poligonal y movido con llave inglesa.

laky [léiki], a. transparente.

lambda [lǽmbdæ], s. lambda (letra griega).

lame duck, cesante, congresista o empleado público cesante, o que no ha sido reelegido; contratante insolvente.

landfall [lǽndfól], s. (aer.) aterrizaje.

landing, a.—**l. angle,** (aer.) ángulo de aterrizaje.—**l. stage,** plataforma flotante de embarcar y desembarcar.

land of the rising sun, tierra del sol naciente (el Japón).

lane, s. vía, ruta; paso, calle; zona (de tránsito).

lant [lænt], s. (industria de la lana) orines rancios.

large, a.—**l. bond,** bono mayor (de más de 1000 dólares).—**l. intestine,** intestino grueso.—**l. order,** empresa o tarea peliaguda.—**l.-scale,** en grande escala; de gran magnitud o alcance.—**in (the) l.,** en grande escala.

laryngeal sinus, seno laríngeo.

last, adv.—**at long l.,** al fin, al fin (repetición enfática).

laugh, va.—**to l. one out of countenance,** abochornar o confundir a uno a carcajadas.

laurustine [lórustin], **laurustinus** [-táinus], s. (bot.) durillo.

law, s.—**to be a l. unto one's self,** no tener uno ni rey ni roque, ser uno su propio juez, hacer lo que le da la gana.

lay, va.—**to l. low,** derribar; matar.

layoff [léióf], s. despido (de obreros).

lead [lid], s. (mec.) avance (a la admisión, etc.); (elec.) alambre aislado de conexión.

leader, s. cosa principal o sobresaliente; lo mejor.

lead-in [lídín]. **I.** s. (rad.) alambre de conexión de la antena con el receptor. **II.** a. (elec.) de entrada (a un instrumento o aparato).

leading article, editorial.

leafy [lífi], a. hojoso; de forma de hoja.

lean, a. deficiente, pobre (en el ingrediente principal); de carestía, de hambre.

leastways [lístuéiś], **leastwise** [-uaiś], adv. al menos, por lo menos.

leery [líœri], a. astuto; sospechoso, receloso.

left. I. s. (pol.) izquierda, izquierdas. **II.** a.—**l. over,** sobrante.—**l. wing,** (pol.) = LEFT, s.

left-hander [léftjǽndœr], s. zurdo (persona); zurdazo, golpe dado con la mano zurda.

leftist [léftist], s. (pol.) izquierdista.

leftover [léftóvœr], s. sobrante, sobra.

legionnaire [líyuneœr], s. legionario.

legitimate stage, s. las tablas (a distinción de la pantalla, el cine).

leitmotif [láitmotíf], s. (mús.) motivo.

lend, va.—**to l. countenance to,** apoyar.

length, lengths, s. extremo, punto.

lepas [lípas], s. (zool.) lepas, broma.

lepidopteran [lépídóptœræn], s. y a. (ent.) lepidóptero.

leprology [lepróloyi], s. ciencia de la lepra.

let, va.—**to l. blood,** sangrar.—**to l. down,** traicionar; abandonar; humillar.—**to l. good enough alone,** bueno está lo bueno (cambiando un poco el giro).—**to l. it go at that,** conformarse con eso; no hacer o decir más, dejar pasar.—**to l. one-self go,** desatarse, dejar la moderación.

level, vn.—**to l. off,** (aer.) enderezarse para aterrizar.

leveret [léveret], s. lebrato.

levy, vn. reclutar; imponer contribución.—**to l. on,** gravar, imponer contribución sobre.

liability, s. suma que una compañía de seguros está legalmente obligada a pagar.

liaison officer, oficial de intercomunicación y coordinación.

libertinism [líbœrtinîsm], s. abuso de la libertad del pensamiento; libertinaje.

Liberty, s. bono de la libertad.—**L. Bond,** bono de la libertad, nombre dado a los bonos emitidos por el gobierno de los E. U. durante la guerra mundial (1917 a 1919).—**L. Loan,** préstamo de la libertad, primera emisión de bonos de la libertad.—**at l.,** en libertad (**to be at l. to,** tener la libertad de).

lie, vn.—**to l. low,** ocultarse; no hacer ni decir nada, esperar; dejarse ver las intenciones.

life, s. duración.—**for l.,** vitalicio; para salvarse; hasta más no poder.—**for the l. of me,** a fe mía, en verdad.

lifeless, a. falto de vigor; agotado; falto de animación, sin vida, sin alma; inhabitado, sin ser viviente.

lifelessness [láiflesnes], s. falta de vida; falta de vigor o animación.

lift, s. alza, aumento; ida o viaje en un coche que pasa y cuyo dueño lleva a uno (gives one a lift).

light, s.—**l. pull,** tirador de lámpara, cadena o cuerda para encender y apagar una lámpara.—**l. wave,** onda luminosa.

lightning, s.—**l. beetle, l. bug,** cocuyo.—**l. switch,** (rad.) interruptor de conexión de la antena con tierra.

lignicoline [lignícolain], a. lignícula, que vive en la madera.—**lignification** [lignifikéiśhun], s. lignificación, conversión en madera.—**lignify** [-fai], va. y vn. lignificar(se), convertir(se) en madera.

Ligurian [liguiúriæn], s. y a. ligurio.

like. I. s. semejante, igual; (con **the**) cosa o persona tal o semejante. **II.** prep.—**l. anything,** o **everything,** muchísimo, hasta no más, hasta más no poder.

limulus [límiulus], s. (zool.) lémula.

linage [láiniy], s. número de líneas.

line. I. s. (com.) renglón, surtido, artículos.—**all along the l.,** en todos los ramos, abarcándolo todo.—**in l. with,** en línea recta con; en armonía o de acuerdo con. **II.** *va.* estar o ir a lo largo o en los bordes o las orillas de.—**to l. out,** marcar con rayas. —**to l. up,** alinear.

lingua franca [línguæ frǽnkæ], lengua franca.

linguiform [língüiform], *a.* lingüiforme, de forma de lengua.

Linnaean, Linnæan, Linnean [liníæn], *a.* lineano, de Lineo.

linter [líntœr], *s.* máquina desfibradora de algodón ya desmotado; *pl.* **linters,** fibra de residuo de algodón desmotado.

lip. I. *s.*—**l. service,** alabanza, defensa o apoyo fingidos, de labios afuera; homenaje de boca.— **l. stick,** (en algunas partes) lápiz labial. **II.** *va.* tocar con los labios; besar; lamer (como las olas).

lithotint [lízotint], *s.* cromolitografía, litografía en colores.

Lithuanian [líziuéiniæn], *s.* y *a.* lituano.

Little Entente, Pequeña Alianza.

Little Red Ridinghood [ráidingjúd], Caperucita Encarnada, Caperucita Roja.

liturgics [litœrvics], *s.* ciencia de la liturgia.— **liturgist** [-yist], *s.* docto en la ciencia de la liturgia; liturgista, partidario de la liturgia.

livable [lívæbœl], *a.* habitable.

live. I. *va.*—**to l. down,** vivir hasta que se olvide (una falta, un cargo, etc.) o hasta vindicarse de; ver desaparecer u olvidar con el tiempo.— **to l. out,** vivir hasta el fin de, sobrevivir a. **II.** *vn.* —**to l. fast,** vivir entregado a los placeres.—**to l. high,** darse buena vida; darse a los placeres de la mesa.—**to l. in,** vivir (uno) donde trabaja.—**to l. out,** no vivir en la casa donde sirve (apl. a los criados).

living, *a.* y *ger.*—**l. in,** *s.* vivir en el lugar donde se trabaja.—**l. out,** no vivir en la casa donde se sirve (apl. a los criados).—**l. room,** estancia, (en algunas pates) *living, living room.*

loading, *s.* (aer.) WING LOADING; (rad.) cambio de longitud de onda.—**l. coil, l. inductance,** bobina de inductancia que aumenta la longitud de onda.

lobe, *s.* (aer.) saco de gas; compartimiento.

lock, *s.* chaveta; cámara de aire comprimido.—**l. washer,** arandela de seguridad.

locular [lókiulær], *a.* locular, que tiene celdillas.

loculus [lókiulus], *s.* celdilla, cavidad.

log, *va.* cortar en trozas; cortar (madera) en trozas y transportar; arrastrar (madera); (mar.) apuntar en el cuaderno de bitácora; indicar (cierta velocidad) en la corredera.

log chip, (mar.) barquilla de la corredera.

logroll [lógróul], *v.* (pol., E. U.) entrar en o hacer por contubernio de ayuda recíproca (*v.* LOG-ROLLING).—**logroller** [-œr], *s.* el que forma contubernio u obra por contubernio de ayuda recíproca.—**logrolling** [-ing], *s.* contubernio de ayuda recíproca y trueque de votos, en que varios políticos convienen en apoyarse mutuamente, sobre todo en proyectos de ley propuestos en un cuerpo legislativo.

Lombard [lómbærd], *s.* y *a.* lombardo.

long. I. *a.*—**l. suit,** especialidad, fuerte (aquello en que uno sobresale). **II.** *adv.* durante mucho tiempo.—**l.-suffering,** doliente, afligido; sufrido, paciente en el sufrimiento.

longipennate [lónyipénet], *s.* y *a.* (zool.) longi-penne, de largas alas.—**Longipennes** [-niš], *s. pl.* (zool.) longipennes.—**longirostral** [-róstræl], *a.* longirostro, de largo pico.

longitudinal, *s.* (aer.) larguero.

looking, *a.*—**good (bad)-l.,** bien (mal) parecido, buen mozo (feo).

loony [lúni], *s.* y *a.* loco rematado.

lordosis [lordóusis], *s.* (med.) lordosis, encorvamiento de la columna vertebral.

lost, *pp.*—**not to be l. on,** o **upon,** no dejar de aprovechar a, no pasar inadvertido por.

lovesickness [lúvsícnes], *s.* mal de amores.

low. I. *s.* punto o lugar bajo; valor o precio mínimo; (aut.) primera velocidad. **II.** *a.*—**l.-carbon steel,** acero pobre en carbono.—**l.-waist,** de talle bajo. **III.** *adv.*—**l.-down,** *s.* información

confidencial o de primera mano, los hechos verdaderos; *a.* bajo, vil.

lowbrow [lóubráu], *s.* persona ajena a las cosas intelectuales.

loxodromics [lócsodrómics], *s.* arte loxodrómico.

lubrifaction [liúbrifǽcšhun], *s.* lubricación.— **lubritorium** [-tórium], **lubritory** [-tori], cuarto o estación de lubricación de automóviles.

lucarne [liucárn], *s.* ventanilla.

lump. I. *s.*—**in a l., in the l.,** todos juntos, sin distinción. **II.** *a.*—**l. coal,** carbón más grueso (el de mayores fragmentos que se produce).—**l. sum,** suma alzada, suma global o total.

lungmotor [lúngmotœr], *s.* =PULMOTOR.

luny [liúni], *s.* y *a.* loco; alocado.

Lycian [líšhiæn], *s.* y *a.* licio, de Licia.

lyddite [lídait], *s.* lidita (explosivo).

M

macaroni wheat, trigo para pastas.

machine, *s.*—**m.-gun,** *va.* ametrallar, atacar con ametralladoras.—**m. screw,** tornillo para metales.

macrograph [mǽcrogræf], *s.* dibujo o fotografía de un objeto como aparece a la simple vista.— **macrography** [mæcrógræfi], *s.* examen a la simple vista (a diferencia del microscópico).—**macrophysics** [mǽcrofíšics], macrofísica, estudio de los cuerpos que pueden observarse sin la ayuda del microscopio.

magic square, *s.* cuadrado mágico.

magnalium [mægnéilium], *s.* magnalio, aleación de aluminio y magnesio.

magnetograph [mægnétogræf], *s.* magnetómetro registrador.

magneton [mǽgneton], *s.* (fís.) magnetón.

mail. I. *s.*—**m. order,** pedido que se hace y se envía por correo.—**m.-order,** de envío de mercancías por correo. **II.** *va.* enviar por correo.

mailed fist, mano armada, espada desenvainada (fig.), fuerza bruta.

mailing list, *s.* lista de distribución (de personas a quienes se envía algo por correo).

mainspring [méinspring], *s.* móvil, motivo o causa principales; (rel.) muelle real.

major, *vn.*—**to m. in,** especializar en, estudiar como materia principal. (Apl. a estudios de escuela y superiores.)

make. I. *va.*—**to m. a fuss,** hacer alharaca, alharaquear.—**to m. a move,** moverse.—**to m. a shift** (*v.* TO MAKE SHIFT).—**to m. a wish,** desear, pensar en algo que se desea.—**to m. it a rule,** sentar por regla.—**to m. it one's business,** proponerse, empeñarse, tomar como cosa suya.—**to m. it right,** arreglar, pagar, compensar, indemnizar, resarcir, etc. (según las circunstancias).—**to m. known,** hacer saber; dar a conocer.—**to m. land** = TO M. THE LAND.—**to m. one's peace,** reconciliarse.—**to m. shift to,** esforzarse por, y lograr. —**to m. terms,** arreglarse.—**to m. the acquaintance of,** conocer a.—**to m. the worst of,** dar la peor apariencia a, menoscabar. **II.** *vn.*—**to m. as if,** o **as though,** fingir, fingirse.—**to m. bold,** atreverse; tomarse la libertad.—**to m. for,** contribuir o tender a.

makefast [méicfæst], *s.* amarradero.

making, *s.* fabricación; preparación.—**in the m.,** haciéndose o formándose, en vía de construcción o de formación.—**the m. of,** la causa o el medio del buen éxito de; lo que hace (hizo, etc.) a (una persona).

Malacopterygii [mælæcóptœríyiai], *s. pl.* malacopterigios.

Malacostraca [mælæcóstrækæ], *s. pl.* (zool.) malacostráceos.—**malacostracan** [-kæn], *s.* y *a.* malacostráceo.

mamba [mémbæ], *s.* (zool.) cobra surafricana muy venenosa.

man, *s.*—**m. power,** fuerzas asequibles, gente de combate.—**m. in the street,** el común de las gentes.—**the M. of Sorrows,** el Hombre de los Dolores, Jesucristo.—**the sick m. of Europe** el enfermo de Europa, Turquía, y el sultán de la Puerta Otomana.

managership [mǽneɪœrӡhip], *s.* gerencia.
maneuverability [mænúvœræbíliti], *s.* maniobrabilidad.—**maneuverable** [mænúvœræbœl], *a.* maniobrable.
manikin, *s.* mujer que se pone los trajes de venta para enseñarlos; pigmeo, enano.
manner, *s.*—**after the m. of**, como, a la manera de, (cambiando un poco el giro) a la, a lo.
march, *s.* frontera, lindero; (geog.) marca, provincia fronteriza.—**marchland** [márchlænd], *s.* región fronteriza, frontera.—**marchman** [-mæn], *s.* rayano, habitante de una frontera o de una marca.
marginalia [márvinéiliæ], *s. pl.* notas o anotaciones marginales.
margraviate [margréiviet], *s.* margraviato, dignidad y territorio de un margrave.
mark, *s.*—(**God**) **save the m.**! ¡caramba! ¡qué cosa!—**to be beside the m.**, no venir al caso.—**up to the m.**, enteramente satisfactorio, perfectamente bueno o bien.
marmite [mármít], *s.* marmita; bomba explosiva, granada.
Maronite [mǽronait], *s.* y *a.* maronita.
marriage lines, certificado de matrimonio.
marshmallow [márshmǽlo], *s.* (bot.) malvavisco, altea; bombón de altea.
martyred [mártœrd], *a.* mártir.
masher [mǽshœr], *s.* majador, moledor, pistadero; (fam.) galanteador.
masseur [mæsœr], *s.* masajista (hombre).—**masseuse** [-œ̃s], *s.* masajista (mujer).
mastaba, mastabah [mǽstæbæ], *s.* mastaba, especie de capilla mortuoria de los antiguos egipcios.
master-at-arms, *s.* especie de sargento de marina.
masthead, *s.* titulillo de un periódico, materia impresa en la parte superior de cada página (nombre del periódico, fecha, etc.)
masurium [mæsiúriʊm], *s.* (quím.) masurio, uno de los cuerpos simples.
matchmark [mǽchmárk]. **I.** *s.* = MATCH MARK (*v.* MATCH). **II.** *va.* marcar, poner marcas de apareamiento.
matter, *s.*—*pl.* **matters**, la situación, las cosas. —**in the m. of**, en cuanto a; en materia de.—**no m. how** (**good, safe**, etc.), por (muy, mucho) que (*no matter how far he goes*, por lejos que él vaya; *no matter how much you say*, por mucho que Vd. diga).—**to be something the m. with**, tener algún defecto, achaque, etc.; pasarle algo a.
mawkish, *a.* repugnante; fastidiosamente sentimental; hostigoso; insípido, sin alma (fig.)
Maya [máya], *s.* y *a.*, **Mayan** [-yan], *a.* maya (tribu, etc.)
mean, *va.* envolver, encerrar, traer o llevar consigo; decir de veras; estar resuelto.—**to m. business**, estar resuelto, proponerse hacer lo que se dice; hablar en serio.
meant, *pp.*—**to be m. for, to**, ser para; servir para; haber nacido para; tener por objeto, aplicarse a.
measure, *s.*—**for good m.**, para completar la cosa, de ñapa.—**to take the m. of**, apreciar en lo que vale, tomar las medidas a (fig.)
medical man, médico; médico general (que no es cirujano).
medula oblongata, bulbo raquídeo o medula oblongada.
meet, *s.* encuentro; reunión deportiva; concurso, torneo.
megafog [mégæfóg], *s.* aparato megafónico de transmisión de señales a barcos en tiempo brumoso.
mehari [mœjári], *s.* meharí, especie de camello del norte de África.
Melanesian [mélænís̄hæn], *s.* y *a.* melanesio.
melinite [mélinait], *s.* melinita (explosivo).
melting pot, *s.* amalgamación (de razas, etc.)
memorization [mémorís̄éis̄hʊn], *s.* aprendizaje de memoria.—**memorizer** [mémoráis̄œr], *s.* el que aprende de memoria; el que tiene buena memoria.

Mennonite [ménonait], *s.* y *a.* menonita.
menshevik [ménshevíc], *s.* menchevique, miembro (en Rusia) del partido radical moderado.—**menshevism** [-vism], *s.* menchevismo, mencheviquismo.—**menshevist** [-vist], *s.* menchevique, menchevista.
merge, *va.* y *vn.* unir(se), fusionar(se).
merger [mœryœr], *s.* fusion, unión, amalgamación comercial.
merit, *s.*—**on its** (**his,** etc.) **own merits**, por sí mismo.
metamorphy [métæmórfi], *s.* metamorfosis; (med.) metamorfosis anormal de los tejidos; (fisiol.) metabolismo.
metempiric(al [métempíric, -æl], *a.* (fil.) transcendental, que traspasa los límites de la experiencia.—**metempiricism** [-sism], *s.* metafísica, transcendentalismo.
metol [métol], *s.* (fot.) metol.
microphysics [máicrofísics], *s.* microfísica, ciencia de los átomos y las moléculas, física atómica.
middle. **I.** *a.*—**m. distance**, (pint.) segundo término.—**m. ground**, posición intermedia entre dos extremos; (pint.) segundo término.—**m. rail**, (elec.) riel central conductor.—**M. West**, (E. U.) estados centrales del norte. **II.** *s.*—**m. of the road**, posición intermedia, ni de un lado ni de otro.—**m.-of-the-road**, *a.* que no está ni de un lado ni del otro; indeciso, vacilante.
Midwest [míduést], *s.* = MIDDLE WEST.
migrant [máigrænt]. **I.** *s.* ave migratoria o de paso. **II.** *a.* MIGRATORY.
militarization [mílitæris̄éis̄hun], *s.* militarización.
militarize [-tæraiš], *va.* militarizar.
milk, *s.*—**m. bar**, puesto donde se sirven leche y sus productos.—**m. glass**, vidrio de criolita; ventosa de leche con que se extrae la leche de los pechos.—**m. of lime**, lechada de cal.—**m. station**, gota de leche.—**m. tooth**, diente de leche.
milker, *s.* máquina de ordeñar.
milo [máilou], *s.* especie de sorgo.
mimodrama [máimodrǽmæ], *s.* zarzuela pantomímica con baile.
minacious [minéis̄hʊs], *a.* amenazador.
mind, *s.*—**to have in m.**, pensar en.—**to have on one's m.**, tener mucho en las mientes, preocuparse con.
minor term, (lóg.) término menor (de un silogismo).
missing, *a.* desaparecido.—**m. link**, eslabón perdido o que falta.—**to be m.**, faltar; haber desaparecido.
mitis [máitis], *s.* hierro forjado alumínico colado, fundición maleable Wittenstrom-Ostberg.—**m. casting**, pieza vaciada de hierro forjado alumínico; procedimiento de fabricación de estas piezas.—**m. metal** = MITIS.
mix, *s.* mezcla de ingredientes; proporciones de los ingredientes de una mezcla; lío, confusión.
mixture, *s.* proporción de los ingredientes de una mezcla; mezcla, producto de ingredientes mezclados (hormigón, etc.)
mode, *s.* (estadística) valor que ocurre con la mayor frecuencia.
moderatorship [móderéitœrship], *s.* oficio y dignidad de MODERATOR.
molgula [mólguiulæ], *s.* (zool.) mólgula.
money maker, cosa con que se gana dinero; persona que gana y acumula dinero (gen. se usa en el sentido de persona metalizada).
monitor, *vn.* (rad.) probar un aparato transmisor escuchando en uno receptor.
monkey business, tonterías; tretas.
monocotyledon [mónocótilídun], *s.* (bot.) monocotiledóneo.
monopteral [monópteræl], *s.* y *a.* (arq.) monóptero.
monorail [mónoréil]. **I.** *s.* vía de un solo riel; grúa móvil de un solo riel o de monorrail. **II.** *a.* de un solo riel.

monument, *s.* (E. U.) parte del territorio del país reservada por el gobierno para usos nacionales.

moonlight school, escuela elemental nocturna para adultos analfabetos.

moonrise [múnráiŝ], *s.* salida de la luna.

moonset [-sét], *s.* puesta de la luna.

mooring harness, (aer.) bandas para los cables o cuerdas de amarre (de un dirigible).

moray [mórei], *s.* (ict.) morena.

moreover [móæróvœr], *adv.* además.

mother, *s.*—**m. hubbard** [júbærd], bata suelta.—**M.'s Day,** día de la madre, o de las madres.—**m.'s mark,** estigma, marca de nacimiento.

motor block = CYLINDER BLOCK.

motorcade [móutœrkeid], *s.* procesión de automóviles.

motorize [mótoraiŝ], *va.* motorizar, proveer de autovehículos, o motovehículos; reemplazar por autovehículos, o vehículos automóviles.

motor ship, barco de motor de combustión interna.

motor spirit, esencia, combustible para motores de combustión interna (apl. gen. a la gasolina).

mountaineer [máuntinfær], *s.* montañés.

mountainous [-nʊs], *a.* montañoso.

mounted [máunted], *a.* montado, a caballo, de a caballo.

moving, *a.* de mudanza (día, etc.).

much, *adv.*—**m. too,** demasiado.—**not so m. as,** no tanto como; ni siquiera.

muck, *vn.* trabajar con ahinco; haraganear.

muddle, *vn.*—**to m. through,** hacer algo malamente, salir del paso a duras penas.

mudhole [mʊ́djóul], *s.* hoyo lodoso; (m. v.) agujero de salida del lodo.

muffler, *s.* (mec.) silenciador.

multicolor [mʊ́lticúlœr], *a.* multicolor, de varios colores.

multitube [-tiúb], *a.* (rad.) de varias válvulas.

municipal building, casa consistorial

muraena [miurínæ], *s.* (ict.) morena.

mush, *s.* (rad.) ruido como de chisporroteo debido a irregularidades del aparato transmisor.

must, *a.* de carácter obligatorio, que obliga.

muttony [mʊ́tni], *a.* de sabor de carnero.

mycosis [maicósis], *s.* (med.) micosis.

myology [maióloyi], *s.* (anat.) miología.

myoma [maióumæ], *s.* (med.) mioma.

mystery boat, o **ship,** buque armado disfrazado de buque mercante indefenso.

N

naevus, nævus, [nívʊs], *s.* = NEVUS.

nail bed, asiento de la uña, dermis subungular.

napoo, napooh [næpú]. **I.** *a.* inútil, que no sirve; desaparecido, ido; muerto. **II.** *adv.* no más; bastante; nada. **III.** *va.* acabar con; matar. **IV.** *vn.* estar perdido; morirse.

Napoleonic [næpóuliónic], *a.* napoleónico.

national, *a.*—**N. Army,** (E. U.) ejército reclutado, parte del ejército formada por reclutamiento.—**n. monument,** (E. U.) terrenos nacionales reservados, parte del territorio del país reservada por el gobierno para usos nacionales.—**n. park,** (E. U.) vasta región de tierras nacionales, gen. con curiosidades naturales, reservada por el gobierno para el público.

natural features, aspecto físico, geografía física.

Nazi [nátsi], *s.* *y a.* nazi, nazista.

Natzism [nátsiŝm], *s.* nazismo.

near, *a.*—**N. East,** Levante.—**n. seal,** imitación de piel de foca.

necessarian [nésesériæn], *a.* determinista.—**necessarianism** [-iŝm], *s.* determinismo.

necktie, *s.* cabestro; cuerda; dogal.—**n. party,** o **sociable,** ahorcadura popular (extrajudicial), linchamiento en la horca.

necrophagous [necrófægʊs], *a.* necrófago, que se alimenta de cadáveres.

ne'er-do-good, ne'er-do-well, haragán, pelafustán.

negrophile [nígrofail], *s.* negrófilo, amigo o defensor de los negros.—**negrophobe** [-foub], *s.* *y a.* negrófobo, que teme u odia los negros.—**negrophobia** [-fóubiæ], *s.* negrofobia, temor u odio de los negros.

neolith [níoliŝ], *s.* herramienta u objeto neolíticos.

neutron [niútron], *s.* (fís.) neutrón.

nevus [nívʊs], *s.* estigma, marca de nacimiento.

new, *a.*—**N. Deal,** (pol., E. U.) *New Deal* (gen. se usa así la expresión, sin traducirla), política Roosevelt (del presidente F. D. Roosevelt).—**N.-Dealer,** partidario del *New Deal,* rooseveltista.—**N. Englander,** habitante de la Nueva Inglaterra (el extremo nordeste de los E. U.).—**n.-rich,** recién enriquecido.—**what is n.?** ¿qué hay de nuevo?

next to nothing, casi nada, poquísimo.

nice and, muy, bien.

nickel bronze, cuproníquel, aleación de cobre y níquel.

nifty [nifti], *a.* elegante; excelente.

niggling, *a.* remilgado; demasiado minucioso; molesto, fastidioso; bajo, mezquino.

night, *s.*—**n. blind,** hemerálope, que no ve bien de noche.—**n. blindness,** hemeralopia, defecto que consiste en la diminución de la visión durante la noche.

nipple, *s.* tubo roscado de unión.

Nipponese [níponíŝ], *s.* *y a.* nipón.

Nipponism [-íŝm], *s.* niponismo, japonismo.

nitrocotton [náitrocótn], *s.* algodón de pólvora.

nobody, *s.* nulidad, persona que no vale nada.

nomination, *s.*—**to put,** o **place, in n.,** proponer para candidato.

noncooperation, *s.* no cooperación con el gobierno, resistencia pasiva.

noneffective [nónefféctive], *a.* ineficaz; (mil.) no disponible, inhabilitado para el servicio activo. (En este último sentido, ú. t. como *s.*)

nonego [nónígo], *s.* (fil.) no yo.

nonfeasance [-fíŝæns], *s.* incumplimiento, falta de cumplimiento.

nonrestraint [-ristréint], *s.* no compulsión, suavidad (apl. al tratamiento de locos).

nonrigid [-ríyid], *a.* flexible; (aer.) fláccido (apl. a dirigibles).

nonskid [nónskíd], **nonskidding** [-ing], *a.* antideslizante.

nonslipping [nónslíping], *a.* no resbaladizo.

nonunion shop, taller o fábrica que no emplea obreros agremiados; taller o fábrica en que los gremios prohiben que sus miembros trabajen. (Ú. gen. en el primer sentido.)

nosebag [nóuŝbæg], *s.* morral, cebadera.

nothing, *s.*—**n. to boast,** o **speak, of,** poca cosa, no gran cosa.—**(there is) n. to,** o **in, it,** eso no vale nada, no asciende a nada.

notochord [nótocord], *s.* = CHORDA DORSALIS.

notorious, *a.* escandaloso, sensacional.

nowhere near, ni con mucho.

nub [nʊb], *s.* protuberancia; nudo; meollo.

nudist [niúdist], *s.* (b. a.) desnudista, partidario del desnudo.

nursery school = PLAY SCHOOL.

nut, *s.* chiflado, loco; maniático.—**nutty,** *a.* (Ing.) elegante, garboso; (E. U.) chiflado, loco.

O

ocarina [ócærínæ], *s.* (mús.) ocarina.

odds, *s.* diferencia; exceso; ventaja o tantos que se dan en un juego o apuesta.—**o. and ends,** sobras y picos.—**by all o.,** en todo; sin duda.

off, *adv.* *y prep.*—**to be o.,** salir, partir, ir saliendo o haber salido o partido; estar equivocado o despistado; haber abandonado (*England is off the gold standard,* Inglaterra ha abandonado el patrón oro).

offset, *a.* fuera de su lugar; desalineado; (mec.) no paralelo; no convergente; (imp.) de calcado en lámina de caucho (procedimiento en que se imprime primero en una lámina de caucho, y luego con ésta en el papel. En algunas partes se usa el término inglés *offset.*)

oger [óugœr], *s.* =OGRE.

oil, *s.*—**o. bird,** (orn.) guácharo.—**o. burner,** quemador de petróleo.—**o. field,** yacimiento petrolífero.

O. K. [o kei]. **I.** *a.* y *adv.* bueno, que sirve; que no está mal, pasadero; está bien. **II.** *va.* dar o poner el visto bueno a, aprobar.

okay [óukéi], *va.* =O. K., *va.*

old, *adv.* Antes de participio, indica antigüedad o largo tiempo (*old-established*, establecido o reconocido desde hace largo tiempo; *old-made*, hecho hace mucho tiempo).

Olympics, *s. pl.* juegos olímpicos.

Omnivora [omnívoræ], *s. pl.* omnívoros.

once, *adv.* una vez que, tan pronto como.—**o. a . . . always a . . .,** quien ha sido . . ., siempre lo será (*once a thief, always a thief*, quien ha sido ladrón, siempre lo será).—**o. too often,** una vez más de lo prudente; pasándose de los límites de la tolerancia.

once-over, *s.* ojeada, vistazo, examen rápido.

oncost [óncóst], *s.* (Ing., com.) =OVERHEAD.

ondograph [óndogræf], *s.* (elec.) ondógrafo, registrador de ondas.

ondometer [ondómetœr], *s.* (elec.) ondímetro.

one, *a.*—**o.-way,** de una sola dirección.—**at o. and the same time,** a un mismo tiempo.

oniscus [onískus], *s.* (zool.) onisco.

only, *adv.*—**o. too** =ALL TOO (*v.* ALL).—**if o.,** ojalá, si (cambiando el giro: *if only he would come!* ¡ojalá que él venga! ¡si él veniera!)

Onychophora [ónicóforæ], *s. pl.* onicóforos.

oogonium [óogóniʊm], *s.* (bot.) oogonio.

open, *a.*—**o. circuit,** (elec.) circuito de corriente intermitente.—**it is o. to you to,** Vd. puede, Vd. tiene la libertad de.

operability (óperæbfliti), *s.* (cir.) operabilidad, calidad de operable.—**operable** (-æbœl), operable.

ophiuran [ófiúræn], *s.* y *a.* ofiuro.

opt [opt], *va.* y *vn.* optar, escoger.

optic(al bench, (fís.) banco óptico.

order, *s.*—**o. blank,** hoja de pedidos.—**o. in council,** orden real, con anuencia del consejo del rey.—**a big, o large, o.,** una tarea pellaguda.—**on that o.,** de esa clase.—**to o.,** por encargo especial, según se pida, a la medida \(ropa que se manda hacer).

ornithopter [órnizóptœr], *s.* (aer.) ornitóptero.

orthocephalic [órzosefǽlic], *a.* ortocéfalo.

orthophyre [órzofáiær], *s.* (geol.) ortófido.

oscilate, *vn.* (elec.) producir corriente alterna.

otherness [óðœrnes], *s.* calidad de ser otro u otra cosa, existencia como cosa distinta de otras.

otter, *s.* (mar.) artificio dragaminas.

ounce, *s.* (farm.) onza de farmacia (31,1 g.]

out, *adv.*—**o. of commission,** fuera de servicio; desarreglado, que no funciona; fuera de combate.—**o. of date,** pasado, anticuado.—**o. of hand,** incontenible, irrepresible; desenfrenado.—**o. of pocket,** perdidoso, perdiendo.—**o. of reach,** inaccesible, inasequible.—**o. of season,** que no se da o se produce (en una estación o tiempo dado).—**o. of work,** sin trabajo.—**o. there,** en el frente, en los campos de batalla.

outbred [áutbréd], *a.* criado o producido por mezcla de razas.—**outbreed** [-bríd], *va.* criar o producir por mezcla de razas.—**outbreeding** [-ing], *s.* mezcla de razas.

out-Herod [áutjérod], *va.* sobrepasar o exceder en maldad; sobrepasar, aventajar.

outlook, *s.* actitud.

outmoded [áutmóuded], *a.* de moda pasada, anticuado.

outpatient [áutpéišhent], *s.* enfermo de fuera (de un hospital), que recibe tratamiento en el hospital pero no reside en él.

over. I. *prep.* a causa o por motivo de; durante. **II.** *adv.*—**o. against,** en frente de; en contraste o comparación con.

overhanging, *a.* voladizo, saledizo.

overhead. I. *s.* gastos generales (=OVERHEAD EXPENSES). **II.** *a.*—**o. railway,** ferrocarril aéreo o elevado.

overly [óuvœrli], *adv.* muy, mucho, demasiado.

overproduction, *s.* sobreproducción.

oxaluria [óxæliúriæ], *s.* (med.) exceso de oxalato cálcico en la orina.

oxidizer [óksidáišœr], *s.* oxidante.

P

pack. I. *s.* (med.) envoltura de sábanas o frazadas; material de envolver o embalar. **II.** *va.* hacer, formar o preparar fraudulentamente; hacer entrar en un complot; (med.) envolver en sábanas o frazadas. **III.** *vn.* conglomerarse.—**to p. up,** arreglar el equipaje.

packing effect, (fís.) pérdida de masa debida a pérdida de energía.

paddle, *va.*—**to p. one's own canoe,** bandearse por sí mismo, bastarse a sí mismo.

pagurus [pæguiúrus], *s.* paguro, cangrejo ermitaño.

pale, *vn.*—**to p. into insignificance,** ser insignificante.

pan, *s.* cuenca; depresión; hondonada.

pancake. I. *a.* plano. **II.** *vn.* (aer.) aumentar el ángulo de ataque al aterrizar.

panel, *s.* (ing.) recuadro, tramo (de puente); (aer.) pieza de tela de la envoltura (de un dirigible); (aer.) sección, cuadro (de un ala).—**p. length,** largo de los recuadros (de un puente).

panjandrum [pænyǽndrum], *s.* persona hinchada; gran personaje; hombre mayúsculo (ú. por lo común jocosa o satíricamente); ceremonia ridículamente exagerada, etiqueta hostigosa.

pantelephone [pæntélefoun], *s.* pantaléfono, microteléfono.

pantograph, *s.* (f. c. eléct.) soporte articulado del vástago del trole.

Papuan [pǽpuæn], *s.* y *a.* papú.

parent complex, (psic.) complejo Edipo.

parity, *s.* igualdad; (com.) paridad, cambio a la par.

park, *va.* estacionar, arrimar (un vehículo).

parking, *s.* estacionamiento (de un vehículo).

parotic [pærótic], *a.* de la región auricular.

parrot disease, psitacosis, sitacosis.

part, *s.* (for.) parte; pieza de repuesto.—**p. and parcel,** parte integrante.—**p. way,** en parte, hasta cierto punto.—**it is the p. of wisdom,** la prudencia aconseja.—**to meet p. way,** hacer algunas concesiones.

parted, *a.* partido, dividido, hendido; de dotes; ido, muerto.

Parthian [párziæn], *s.* y *a.* parto.

participating stock, acciones privilegiadas con participación en las ganancias, fuera del dividendo fijo que devengan.

parti-colored [párticúlœrd], *a.* multicolor.

particularism [partíkiulærísm], *s.* exclusivismo; (hist.) particularismo.

particularity, *s.* minuciosidad, escrupulosidad, quisquillosidad.

Passeres [pǽsœriš], *s.* (zool.) pájaros (división de las aves).

passive, *a.* (aer.) sin motor.

pat. I. *s.* torta (cosa de forma de torta). **II.** *va.* aplanar, aplastar; golpear ligeramente.—**to p. oneself on the back,** esponjarse, hincharse. **III.** *vn.* golpear ligeramente.

Patagonian [pétægóniæn], *s.* y *a.* patagón.

patch, *s.* (aer.) parche.

patchy [péchi], *a.* muy remendado; como de remiendos, deshilvanado; malhumorado, irritable.

path, *s.* callecilla, andador (en un jardín, etc.)

pathogene [pézoyín], *s.* microbio patógeno.

---

pathogeny [pæzóyeni], *s.* patogenia.
patrol wagon, ómnibus o diligencia de la policía.
paying teller, pagador (de un banco).
pedestrian, *s.* peatón.
peel, *vn.*—**to p. off** =TO PEEL.
peeve, *vn.* irritarse, ponerse o estar de mal humor.
peg. I. *va.* estabilizar, fijar o sostener el valor o precio de. **II.** *vn.* (gen. con **away**), afanarse; trabajar con ahinco.
pekin [pîkin], *s.* pequín (tela).
pelagrin [peléigrin], *s.*, **pelagrous** [-grᴜs], *a.* pelagroso.
Peloponnesian [péloponîshæn], *s.* y *a.* peloponense.
pen-pusher, escritor de (por) oficio.
perfuse [perfiúś], *va.* llenar; cubrir; vaciar; regar, rociar; forzar (un líquido) por, hacer entrar en.
perfusion [perfiúyᴜn], *s.* acción de cubrir, vaciar o regar; afusión; introducción de un líquido; líquido introducido; bautismo con agua rociada.
peripatus [perípætᴜs], *s.* (zool.) peripato, onicóforo.
Persian lamb =BROADTAIL.
persiflage [pêrsifláy], *s.* chulada, burla baladí.
petrous process, (anat.) peñasco (del temporal).
pharmacognosy [fármæcógnosi], *s.* farmacognosia, materia médica.
phi [fái], *s.* fi (letra griega).
Philistine, *s.* y *a.* reaccionario, ultraconservador; prosaico, positivista; inculto, vulgar.
Philistinism [filístinízm], *s.* convencionalismo, formalismo; falta de cultura, positivismo vulgar, aspiraciones bajas.
phonate [fóuneit], *va.* y *vn.* articular, enunciar.
phonautograph [fonótogræf], *s.* fonautógrafo.
phonetic spelling, escritura fonética, en que las palabras se escriben como se pronuncian, de acuerdo con reglas fijas para la pronunciación de cada letra.
phoney [fóuni], *a.* =PHONY.
phosphatize [fósfætáiś], *va.* fosfatar, tratar con o reducir a fosfato.
phosphaturia [-tiúriæ], *s.* fosfaturia, exceso de fosfatos en la orina.—**phosphaturic** [-tiúric], *s.* y *a.* que sufre de fosfaturia.
photoengrave [fótoengréiv], *va.* y *vn.* fotograbar.
photon [fóuton], *s.* (fís.) fotón.
photo process, procedimiento fotográfico.
phototherapy [fótozérapi], *s.* fototerapia.
phraseogram [fréisiogræm], **phraseograph** [-græf], *s.* combinación de signos taquigráficos que representa una frase.
phrenzied, phrenzy =FRENZIED, FRENZY.
Phylum [fáilᴜm], *s.* (h. nat.) tipo, división.
physical therapy, physiotherapy [físiozérapi], *s.* fisicoterapia, tratamiento de las enfermedades por agentes físicos (calor, electricidad, etc.)
pi [pái], *s.* pi (letra griega).
piano player, pianista; pianola, piano mecánico.
pickle. I. *va.* tratar con ácido por inmersión. **II.** *vn.* ratear, hurtar; comer poco.
picture, *s.*—**p. play,** drama de cine.—**to be in the p.,** figurar en el asunto.—**to be out of the p.,** no figurar ya en el asunto.
Piedmontese [pídmontîś], *s.* y *a.* piamontés.
pigeon English =PIDGEON ENGLISH.
pigeonhole, *va.* proveer de casillas; poner una casilla; archivar (fig.), relegar al olvido.
pike, *s.* carretera; peaje.
pileus [pílius], *s.* sombrero de fieltro sin ala; (bot.) sombrero u hongo.
pill box, pillbox, [pílbóks], *s.* caja para píldoras; (mil.) fortín armado de ametralladoras.
pilot chart, carta de marear.
pimento, *s.* =PIMENTO.
pincenez [pénsnéi], *s.* lentes o anteojos de nariz (sujetados en la nariz).
pindling [píndling], *a.* botarate; delicado, enfermizo; (Ingl.) enojadizo, irritable.
pinfold [pínfóuld]. **I.** *s.* corral, redil; ámbito. **II.** *va.* encerrar; encorralar.

pink, *s.*—**in the p. (of condition),** en el apogeo, en el mejor estado posible; que mejor no puede estar.
pinprick [pínpríc], *s.* pinchazo; molestia, irritación, antagonismo a poquitos.
pinworm, *s.* lombriz intestinal.
pioupiou [piúpiú], *s.* soldado (aplicábase sobre todo a los franceses).
pipe, *s.*—**p. cutter,** cortatubos.—**p. dream,** sueño, ilusión.
piping, *s.* (fund.) burbujas e impuerzas.
pipy [páipi], *a.* que tiene tubos; tubular; PIPING.
piperonal [píperonæl], *s.* (quím.) piperonal, heliotropina.
pique [pic]. **I.** *va.* (aer.) atacar picando, o de cabeza. **II.** *vn.* (aer.) picar, descender con grande inclinación hacia abajo.
pisciform [písiform], *a.* pisciforme, de forma de pez.
pit, *va.* deshuesar (una fruta).
pita flax, pita thread, pita (fibra).
pitapat. I. *s.* taque taque, golpeteo. **II.** *vn.* andar a la carrerita, o con pasitos rápidos; golpetear; latir violentamente (el corazón). **III.** *adv.* a la carrerita, a pasitos cortos rápidos; golpeteando, taque taque.
pitgame, pit-game fowl, gallo o gallos de pelea.
pitter-patter [pítœr-pǽtœr] =PITAPAT.
pitting [píting], *s.* picadura, picaduras (de un metal), corrosión diseminada.
pituitrin [pitiúitrin], *s.* pituitrina, substancia extraída de la glándula pituitaria.
pity, *s.*—**it is a p.,** es lástima, es de sentirse.
place, *s.* decimal (*five-place table*, tabla de cinco decimales).
placement [pléisment], *s.* colocación; empleo.—**p. agency, p. office,** agencia de colocaciones o de empleos, donde se suministran sirvientes u otros empleados.
plane. I. *s.* (aer.) plano, superficie de sustentación. **II.** *vn.* (aer.) volar, viajar en avión.
plastic surgery, anaplastia.
plate. I. *s.*—**p. battery,** (rad.) batería de alta tensión, batería del ánodo o placa (de un tubo termiónico).—**p. circuit,** (rad.) circuito de la placa y el filamento.—**p. current,** (rad.) corriente de entre el filamento y la placa.—**p. matter,** planchas electrotípicas vendidas a varios periódicos para la publicación simultánea de un escrito.—**p. ship** =TREASURE SHIP.—**p. voltage,** (rad.) tensión de la batería de la placa. **II.** *va.* revestir (un metal) con una capa (de otro metal); platear (si el metal de revestimiento es plata); dorar (si dicho metal es oro); (a veces con **out**) cultivar (bacterias) sobre una lámina; hacer una plancha electrotípica de (para imprimir).
plateau, *s.* altiplanicie, altiplano.
platinotype [plætinotáːp], *s.* (fot.) platinotipia; positiva platinotípica.
platoon school, escuela elemental dividida en dos grupos (*platoons*) de alumnos, que se turnan en el uso de las aulas, talleres, etc.
play. I. *s.*—**p. school,** escuela recreativa de chiquillos. **II.** *va.*—**to p. a joke on,** dar una broma a.—**to p. a (bad, dirty, mean) trick on,** hacer una mala jugada a.—**to p. both ends against the middle,** poner uno de punta entre sí a sus rivales, meter discordia entre ellos.—**to p. down,** hacer poco caso de. **III.** *vn.*—**to p. into the hands of,** dar entrada a, ayudar.
playground(**s,** *s.* campo de deportes.
playtime [pléitáim], *s.* tiempo de recreo o para recreo.
pleasure seeker, amante de los placeres; el que busca o anda tras los placeres.
plebiscitum [plébisáitᴜm], *s.* (hist.) plebiscito (ley).
pliotron [pláiotron], *s.* (elec.) pliotrón (es nombre de fábrica), tubo termiónico amplificador de tres electrodos.
plug, *s.*—**p. clip,** contacto o terminal de tapón o botón eléctrico.—**p. ga(u)ge,** calibre cilíndrico.—**p. key** =P. CLIP.

Para la pronunciación de æ, œ, ᴅ, ś, ŝh, ᴜ, ȳ, ʏ, z, véase la clave al principio del libro.

plumcot [plúmcot], *s.* injerto de ciruelo y albaricoque.

plunger, *s.* émbolo; cabeza del vástago (de ciertas válvulas).

plural, *a.*—**p. marriage,** poligamia.—**p. vote,** derecho de dar más de un voto o de votar en varias partes.

plus, *adv.* y más, con algo de sobra; más otras cosas (gastos, ganancia, etc.).—**to be, come out,** etc. **p. (something),** haber ganado, salir ganando (algo).

pluviometry [pluviómetri], *s.* pluviometría.

plyer [pláíær], *s.* (ing.) báscula (de un puente levadizo).

plywood [pláiúd], *s.* tabla multilaminar, compuesta de varias láminas superpuestas.

pneumatophore [niúmætofóær], *s.* (min.) respirador de seguridad, aparato que se emplea en lugares donde hay gases asfixiantes.

pocket. I. *s.* hoyo; hondonada, depresión; calle tapada o sin salida; tronera (de billar); (aer.) AIR POCKET.—**p. veto,** (E. U.) veto indirecto, o implícito, que consiste en no firmar el presidente una ley antes que el congreso se clausure, lo cual la invalida.

poetic(al justice, justicia ideal, justa distribución del premio y el castigo, armonía de la justicia.

poilu (pronunciación francesa, ó, más g., pualú), *s. poilu,* soldado francés.

point system, (imp.) "sistema de puntos," nombre que se da a un sistema especial de expresar el tamaño de tipos de imprenta; sistema de Braille o de signos en relieve para la lectura de los ciegos.

poison gas, gas tóxico.

polar star, pole star, estrella polar (ll. gen. *la polar).*

poliomyelitis [póliomáieláitis], *s.* poliomielitis, parálisis infantil.

pollution, *s.* contaminación, infección (del agua); mancilla, mancha; (med.) polución.

Pollyanna [póliǽnæ], nombre propio que se usa como *s.* en el sentido de *panglossismo* (voz derivada de *Pangloss*), optimismo excessivo, y como *a.* en el sentido de *panglossista, excessivamente optimista.*

pone [póun], *s.* torta o panecillo de maíz.

pontificalia [póntifikéiliæ], *s. pl.* (igl.) pontificales.

pontoon, *s.* flotador (de un aeroplano).

pop corn, maíz reventón de tostar o tostado.

porbeagle [pórbígœl], *s.* pez martillo.

porous plaster, emplasto o parche poroso.

porte cochère [port coshéær], puerta cochera.

portfolio, *s.*—**minister,** etc. **without p.,** ministro, etc. sin cartera, o sin departamento o ramo especial.

porthole [pórtjóul], *s.* portalón; tronera, abertura.

Portland cement, cemento pórtland.

position, *s.* situación; actitud; lo que uno sostiene.—**to be in (a) p. to,** estar en situación de, poder.

positron [pósitron], *s.* (fís.) positrón.

possibility, *s.* potencialidad; oportunidad.

postbellum [póstbélum], *a.* de despué de la guerra, posterior a la guerra.

post box, buzón.

postgraduate, *s.* y *a.* posgraduado; de posgraduados.

pot, *s.* (fund.) crisol (de horno).—**to go to p.,** arruinarse, desbaratarse, irse a pique (fig.).

potash bulbs, tubo de bolas.

potter. I. *va.* molestar, incomodar. **II.** *vn.* carecer de seriedad, ocuparse en fruslerías, ser frívolo; parlotear; haraganear, vagar.

pot-valiancy [pótvéliænsi], *s.* valor postizo, debido al licor, valor de borracho.—**pot-valiant** [-liænt], *a.* envalentonado por el licor.—**pot-valor** [vælœr], *s.* = POT-VALIANCY.

power, *s.*—**p. boat,** autobote, bote o barco de gasolina.—**p.-dive,** (aer.) *s.* picado (descenso)

rápido con el motor andando; *vn.* picar con el motor andando. (*V.* DIVE.)—**p. loading,** (aer.) carga normal por caballo de fuerza.—**p. tube,** (elec.) tubo generador, tubo de vacío generador de corriente alterna.—**the powers that be,** la autoridad, las autoridades.—**to the best of one's p. (and ability),** con todo empeño, hasta donde uno pueda, en lo sumo posible.

practical nurse, enfermera no graduada.

precool [prícúl], *va.* enfriar previamente; (com.) enfriar (frutas, etc.) antes de embarcar.

predicament, *s.* situación, circunstancias; dificultad.

preferentially [préferénshæli], *adv.* preferentemente.

prefigure [prifíguiuær], *va.* representar proféticamente; ver en lo futuro, representarse en la imaginación.

prefoliation [prifóuliéishun], *s.* (bot.) prefoliación.

pregnable [prégnæbœl], *a.* expugnable, vulnerable.

prejudice. *s.*—**without p.,** (for.) sin detrimento de derechos.

premaxilary [premǽxileri]. **I.** *s.* hueso intermaxilar. **II.** *a.* anteromaxilar, de enfrente de las mandíbulas.

premiere [premiéær], *s.* actriz protagonista; estreno (de un drama, etc.).

preoccupancy [prióikiupǽnsi], *s.* ocupación previa.

preparator [prepǽrætœr], *s.* preparador de ejemplares de historia natural.

preparatory to, como preparación, o preparándose, para; antes de.

prepotent [prepótent], *a.* prepotente.

preschool [príscúl], *a.* preescolar.

present, *a.* Cuando, al pasar lista para una votación, se enuncia el nombre de una persona que no quiere votar, ésta contesta: *present,* lo cual significa: no voto.—**p.-day,** actual.

presidium [presídium], *s.* (en Rusia) comité administrativo. (Puede usarse *presidio,* dando a la palabra este nuevo significado.)

press, *s.*—**p. agent,** agente de publicidad.—**p. conference,** entrevista con los periodistas.—**p. gang,** patrulla de reclutamiento.

pressgang [présgæng], *s* = PRESS GANG.

pressmark [présmárc]. **I.** *s.* marca de imprenta. **II.** *va.* poner marca de imprenta a.

pressure tube, (quím.) probeta cerrada para reacciones a alta presión.

preventorium [príventórium], *s.* hospital profiláctico, donde se trata a personas que han estado expuestas al contagio.

priestrid [prístríd], *a.* = PRIESTRIDDEN.

primp, *va.* y *vn.* (a veces con **up**) vestir(se) con afectación; acicalar(se); acicalar etc. afectadamente.

Prince Rupert's drops, lágrimas de Batavia.

principle, *s.*—**on general principles,** según, o de acuerdo con, principios generales; por sistema, según costumbre.

printer's proof, prueba de imprenta.

printery [prínteri], *s.* imprenta; taller de estampar géneros.

prison term, condena, período que por condena se pasa en una prisión.

privy purse, (Ing.) fondos para los gastos personales del rey; empleado que los maneja.

probate court, tribunal de testamentarías.

procedural [prosíyuræl], *a.* de procedimiento, tocante al procedimiento.

process. I. *s.*—**p. of law,** procedimiento legal.—**p. server,** portador de notificaciones oficiales. **II.** *va.* elaborar (dícese sobre todo de las materias primas que se elaboran o preparan para la industria o el mercado).

processal [prosésæl], *a.* procesal.

Progressivism [progresívism], *s.* (E. U.) progresismo, doctrinas del partido progresista (*Progressive party*).

---

project, s. construcción, obra, obras; tema, asunto.—**p. system,** sistema educativo en que al alumno se le asigna un tema completo para que lo trate, el cual gen. exige la lectura de obras de consulta.

proliferation [proliferéiŝhun], s. (bot.) multiplicación, reproducción.

proof plane, (elec.) plano de prueba.

propagandism [própægǽndiŝm], s. propagandismo, arte y práctica de la propaganda.

propagandize [-daiŝ]. **I.** va. hacer propaganda a o en. **II.** vn. hacer propaganda.

property line, línea de edificación.

proportioning, s. proporción, dosificación.

proration [proréiŝhun], s. prorrateo.

prospecting, s. (min.) cateo, exploración en busca de minas.

protem [protém], **protempore** [-pore], a. interino.

protester [protéstœr], s. el que protesta.

protestingly [protéstingli], adv. protestando, en tono de protesta.

provide, vn.—**to p. for,** tener en cuenta; dar disposiciones para o sobre; mantener.

providing [prováiding], conj. con tal que.

provision, s.—**to make p. for** =TO PROVIDE FOR.

prowl, vn. andar acechando.

psittacosis [sítæcóusis], s. (p)sitacosis.

psychoanalize, o **-lise** [sáicoǽnælaiŝ], va. someter a psicoanálisis, examinar psicoanalíticamente.

psychopath [-pæz], s. psicopático, el que sufre de enfermedad mental; psicópata, alienista.— **psychophysiology** [-fiŝhióloyi], s. psicofisiología, fisiología psicológica.

psychotic [saicótic]. **I.** s. y a. psicótico, psicopático, que sufre de enfermedad mental. **II.** a. psicótico, relativo a la psicosis.

publicize [públisaiŝ], va. dar publicidad a.

public law, derecho público; derecho internacional.

puerperium [puœrpírium], **puerpery** [puœrperi], s. puerperio, sobreparto.

pulmometer [pulmómetœr], s. espirómetro, instrumento para medir la capacidad de los pulmones.

pump priming, (pol., E. U.) "cebar la bomba," ayudar con fondos públicos para echar a andar las cosas (el comercio, la industria, etc.)

punctate(d [púncteit, -téfted], a. mosqueado.

purchasing power, valor mercantil (de la moneda), poder adquisitivo; capacidad consumidora o de comprar.

purebred [piúærbréd], **pure-breed** [-bríd], s. y a. (animal) de raza pura.

pursuit airplane, o **plane,** avión de combate.

pusher, s., **pusher airplane,** (aer.) avión propulsivo, el cual tiene la hélice detrás de las superficies de sustentación.

pussyfooter [púsifútœr], s. timorato, hombre de evasivas.—**pussyfooting** [-ting], s. subterfugio, evasiva; recurso a la evasión.

put, va.—**to p. (something) around,** cubrir o abrigar con (algo).—**to p. hard to it,** poner en dificultades (ú. gen. en la voz pasiva **to be put hard to it,** hallarse en calzas prietas, serle a uno muy difícil).—**to p. in a word for,** interceder por, hablar en favor de.—**to p. into effect,** poner en práctica; poner en vigor.—**to p. one's cards on the table,** jugar uno a cartas vistas, obrar franca y abiertamente.—**to p. on the spot,** poner en calzas prietas; matar.—**to p. over,** cubrir(se) con, echar(se) encima.—**to p. through,** meter al través de; atravesar; hacer ejecutar; someter a; dar curso a, hacer atender; hacer aceptar, lograr, llevar a cabo.

putsch [puch, putŝh], s. alzamiento, pronunciamiento.

puzzling [púŝling], a. confuso, nebuloso, que pone a uno perplejo.

puzzolan(a [pútsolæn(æ], s. puzolana.

pyramid, va. vn. aumentar(se), acumular(se).

pyrochemical [páirokémikæl], a. relativo a los fenómenos químicos a altas temperaturas.

pyroclastic [-clǽstic], a. (geol.) ígneo, volcánico.

Q

quadrennium [cuadrénium], **quadriennium** [cuádriénium], s. cuadrienio, cuatrienio.

quaky [kuéiki], a. tembloroso, gelatinoso.

quanta [cuántæ], s. (pl. de QUANTUM), cuantos, quántums. (Algunos dicen quanta, que no se recomienda.)

quantum [cuántum], **I.** s. (fís., mec.) cuanto, quántum, unidad elemental de energía. (Se aconseja la adopción de cuanto.) **II.** a. cuántico, relativo al cuanto o los cuantos.

quarrel, s.—**to have no q. with,** no reñir con; no oponerse a; no censurar.

quartz plate, (elec.) placa eléctrica de cuarzo; condensador de cuarzo.

Q-boat =MYSTERY BOAT.

queer, va. ridiculizar; echar a perder; desconcertar.

quintuplet [cuíntuplet], s. quintupleta, bicicleta de asientos en tándem para cinco personas; uno de cinco hermanos mellizos.

Q-ship =MYSTERY BOAT.

R

race, s.—**r. glass,** binóculo para carreras.—**r. ground,** hipódromo.

racial, a. racial, étnico, de (la) raza o de (las) razas.

racialism [réiŝhælîŝm], s. distinción de razas; odios de raza.

rack. I. a.—**r. rent,** alquiler exorbitante. **II.** va. estirar; mover con rueda y cremallera.—**to r. one's brains,** devanarse los sesos.

racket, s. fraude sistematizado; contubernio o pandilla de fraude sistematizado.

racketeer [rǽketíœr]. **I.** s. contrabandista; socaliñero intimidador, pícaro taimado que se vale de la intimidación, por lo común indirecta y más o menos encubierta, para sacar constantemente dinero a otras o a empresas comerciales amenazándolas con la violencia o con la ruina de sus intereses. **II.** vn. ser racketeer, valerse de la intimidación para la exacción.—**racketeering** [-ing], s. socaliña por intimidación.

rackrent, va. y vn. exigir arrendamiento exorbitante o usurario.

radial, o **radiant, engine,** motor de cilindros radiales.

radio. I. s. (rad.) radio (instrumento y transmisión).—**r. beacon** =RADIOPHARE.—**r. link,** circuito radiotelefónico intercalado en otro circuito. —**r. set,** radio (instrumento receptor o transmisor). —**r. tube** = ELECTRON TUBE. **II.** va. y vn. comunicar o transmitir por radio.

radiobroadcaster, s. (rad.) radiodifusor, perifoneador, persona que habla en una difusora.

radiology [réidióloyi], s. radiología, ciencia de la radiactividad.

radiophotography [-fotógræfi], s. radiofotografía, transmisión de fotografías por radio.

radioscope [-scoup], s. radioscopio.

radiovision [-víyun], s. radiovisión, transmisión de fotografías cinematográficas por radio.

rag. I. s. RAGTIME; RAGAMUFFIN; persona andrajosa; broma, fisga. **II.** va. rasgar; quebrantar, triturar; regañar, sermonear; embromar, fisgar; poner en música sincopada, o musiquilla. **III.** vn. tocar música sincopada o popular, tocar musiquilla; bailar.

ragweed [réguíd], s. (bot., E. U.) ambrosía; (bot., Ing.) zuzón.

rail, s. (orn.) rascón.

---

rake, _va._—**to r. over the coals,** echar un buen regaño a; criticar severamente, despedazar (fig.), despellejar (fig.)

rambunctious [ræmbúncŝhʊs], _a._ desaforado, ingobernable.

randan [rǽndæn], _s._ bote de tres remeros; acción de remar en estos botes; bochinche, algazara; bochinchero, alborotador.

range, _s._ límites; alcance; campo (de aplicación, etc.); excursión; cadena de montañas; dirección, línea; cocina de hierro.

ranging pole, (top.) jalón.

ranker [rǽnkœr], _s._ soldado; oficial que ha ascendido desde soldado raso.

rapid-firer, _s._ cañón de tiro rápido.

raspberry, _s._ crítica mordaz, desolladura; reprimenda, sermón.

raspy [rǽspi], _a._ =RASPING.

rataplan [rǽtæplǽn]. **I.** _s._ rataplán, sonido del tambor. **II.** _vn._ tamborear, tabalear.

rating, _s._ reprimenda, regaño, sermón.

ration _va._ poner a ración; racionar; distribuir en raciones.

raw, _s._ peladura, despellejadura; matadura; material en bruto; materia prima.

rayon [réion], _s._ rayón (fibra y tela).

razz [ræŝ]. **I.** _s._ crítica mordaz, desolladura; reprimenda, sermón. **II.** _va._ regañar, increpar sermonear.

read [red]. **I.** _pret._ y _pp._ de TO READ. **II.** _a._ leído, instruído.

realism, _s._ positivismo, espíritu práctico; reconocimiento o criterio de la realidad.—**realist,** _s._ positivista, hombre práctico o de realidades.— **realistic,** _a._ práctico, de acuerdo con la realidad.

rebate. I. _s._ reembolso. **II.** _va._ y _vn._ reembolsar; rebajar.

rebroadcast [ríbródkǽest], _va._ y _vn._ (rad.) redifundir, difundir de una difusora comunicaciones recibidas de otra.

receivable, _a._ (com.) por cobrar.

receiver, _s._ (tlf.), receptor, auricular.

receiving, _a._ receptor.—**r. set,** (rad.) radioreceptor.

receptionist [risépŝhʊnist], _s._ recibidor, empleado (gen. empleada) de una casa de negocios que recibe a los que van a ella.

recess, _s._ hueco.

recommender [récoméndœr], _s._ recomendante.

record, _s._—**of r.** =ON RECORD.

recountal [ricáuntœl], _s._ relato.

recruiter [recrútœr], _s._ reclutador.

red, _s._—**in the r.,** en el debe, endeudado, perdidoso.

redevelop [rídivélop], _va._ volver a desarrollar; (fot.) volver a revelar después de tratamiento químico.

redivivus [rídiváivʊs], _a._ revivido.

red light, luz roja empleada como señal de peligro, o, en los cruces de calles, para detener el tránsito.

red-light, _a._ de lupanar; de los lupanares; de mala vida.

redress, _va._ renovar, refaccionar.

redshirt, _s._ (pol.) camisarroja.

redtab [rédtæb], _s._ oficial del estado mayor.

referred to, mencionado; a que se hace referencia, a que uno se refiere.

reflex, _s._ (psic.) reflejo.

reforest [rífórest], _va._ restablecer el bosque o los bosques de o en.—**reforestation** [rífórestéishun], _s._ restablecimiento del bosque o de los bosques.

refringence o **refringency** [refrínyens, -yensi], _s._ poder de refractar.

refringent [-yent], _a._ refringente.

regard, _s._—**to have r. to,** tener en cuenta.

regardless, _adv._ prescindiendo de todo, a todo trance.

regiment, _va._ (mil.) regimentar; reglamentar; dominar oficialmente.

regimentation [réyimentéishun], _s._ (mil.) regimentación; reglamentación; dominio oficial.

regius [ríyiʊs] **professor,** real profesor (que ocupa una cátedra instituída por dádiva real).

regulatory [réguiulætori], _a._ regulador; reglamentario, que reglamenta.

Reich, _s._ Reich.—**Reichsmark** [réijsmárk], _s._ marco alemán, marco (unidad monetaria).

relay broadcast, difusión, por una difusora, de comunicaciones recibidas de otra; redifusión.

release, _va._ descargar (de una obligación).

relief, _s._—**on r.,** socorrido.—**to be on r.,** estar viviendo de socorro.

remodel, _va._ renovar, refaccionar.

render, _va._ (com.) enviar, girar (una cuenta).

rendrock [réndrróc], _s._ variedad de dinamita.

reorganizer [ríórgænáiŝœr], _s._ reorganizador.

report, _va._—(a veces con **out**), devolver (un proyecto de ley, etc.) con informe o dictamen.

repudiate, _va._ desconocer, rechazar, invalidar.— **repudiation,** _s._ desconocimiento, invalidación; infidencia.—**repudiator** [repiúdiéitoer], _s._ repudiador; desconocedor, invalidador; infidente.

reservation, _s._ (E. U.) tierras del gobierno, tierras nacionales reservadas por el gobierno (para indios, parques, escuelas, etc.)

resister [risístœr], _s._ resistidor, lo que o el que resiste.

resolved, _a._ resuelto, decidido; fundido, liquidado; separado, dividido.

resorcin [reŝórsin], _s._ (quím.) resorcina.

resorcinol [-nol], _s._ (quím.) resorcinol.

resort, _s._ lugar de temporada.

rest, _s._—**r. cure,** (med.) tratamiento del reposo, curación por el reposo y el sosiego, en que el enfermo se abstiene de esfuerzo físico y excitación mental.—**r. day,** día de descanso; domingo.

retentivity [rítentíviti], _s._ (magn.) retentividad.

retrocognition [rétrocogníŝhun], _s._ conocimiento supernormal (como el de los médiums) de lo pasado. (Puede llamarse _retrovidencia._)

reveal, _s._ (arq.) costado de vano de puerta o ventana; (aut.) borde de ventana.

revenue stamp, sello fiscal, sello de impuesto.

reversibility [rivœrsibíliti], _s._ reversibilidad, invertibilidad, calidad de poder invertirse; (for.) revocabilidad, carácter de revocable o anulable.

revision, _s._ corrección; enmienda.

revitalize [riváitælaiŝ], _va._ revivir, vivificar, dar un nuevo impulso a.

revolving fund, (E. U.) fondos públicos especiales para préstamos.

rhenium [rínium], _s._ (quím.) renio, rhenio.

rhesus [rísʊs], _s._ (zool.) macaco de la India.

Rhodian [róudiæn], _s._ y _a._ rodio; caballero de la orden de Rodas, o San Juan de Jerusalén.

rider, _s._ pilón, pesa corrediza (de una balanza).

ridge cap, cubierta de caballete.

rift. I. _s._ rompimiento, desacuerdo. **II.** _va._ rajar; rasgar. **III.** _vn._ rajarse, abrirse.

rig, _va._ (aer.) armar, arreglar (un avión o un dirigible); (gen. con **out**), vestir, acicalar.—**to r. the market,** manipular la lonja, tramar para cambiar los precios.

rigger, _s._ (aer.) montador aeronáutico.

right. I. _s._ (pol.) derecha, derechas, bando conservador o moderado.—**r. of assembly,** derecho de reunión.—**r. of way,** precedencia, prelación.—**by r., by rights,** de derecho, por derecho; propiamente, con razón.—**by r. of,** por razón de.—**in one's own r.,** por derecho propio de uno.—**to rights,** en orden. **II.** _a._ (pol.) derechista, de las derechas.—**r. cone, r. cylinder,** (geom.) cono, cilindro rectos.—**r. wing,** (pol.) derechas, las de derechas, las derechas.

rightist [ráitist], _s._ y _a._ (pol.) derechista.

ring, _s._ pandilla.

ringster [ríngstœr], _s._ miembro de una pandilla o de una camarilla.

rip, o **ripping, cord,** (aer.) cabo o cuerda de desgarre o de desinflación rápida (sirve para rasgar la faja de desgarre).

---

rip, o **ripping, panel,** o **strip,** (aer.) faja de desgarre, parche de desinflación rápida.

rising vote, votación en que los votantes se ponen de pie o permanecen sentados según que quieran dar voto afirmativo o negativo.

roaring, *s.* rugido, bramido.

robot [róbot], *s.* robot, hombre mecánico; autómata (persona).

rocking, *s.* (ing.) balasto de piedra; barra de giro o de vuelco del cenicero de un horno.

rodeo [rodéo], *s.* rodeo (de ganado); corral; función de vaqueros.

roller, *s.*—**r. bridge,** puente corredizo.—**r. coaster,** deslizador circular (en los lugares de diversión).—**r. mill,** molino de cilindros moledores (gen. para granos).

rolling kitchen, cocina de carretilla. (*V.* SOUP KITCHEN.)

roofless [rúfles], *a.* destechado, sin techo; sin amparo, sin hogar.

rookie, rooky, [rúki], *s.* recluta; novicio.

rooming house, casa donde se alquilan piezas de habitación.

root, *vn.* (a veces con **for**), aplaudir, alabar; gritar por el éxito de.

root and branch, por completo.

rope, *va.*—**to r. off,** cercar con cuerdas.

Rotarian [rotériæn], *s.* y *a.* rotario.

Rotary Club, Club Rotario.

rotor ship, barco de cilindros giratorios (*rotores*) movidos por el viento.

rough, *a.*—**r.-coat,** *va.* (alb.) dar la primera capa (de enlucido, etc.) a.—**r.-cut, r.-dressed,** a medio pulir, a medio labrar.—**r. going,** camino difícil o escabroso; cosa ardua.—**r. usage,** uso rudo, estropeo, maltrato.

roughing-in [rúfing in], *s.* primera capa de enlucido; aplicación de esta capa; colocación de las tuberías ocultas de un edificio.

roughneck [rúfnec], *s.* patán; rufián, truhán.

roughride [rúfráid], *va.* y *vn.* amansar; montar caballos indómitos; dominar, imponerse, dar la ley.

roughshod, *a.*—**to ride,** o **run, r. over,** andar u obrar sin hacer caso de dificultades; dominar, imponerse o dar la ley a; atropellar, tratar sin miramiento.

round, *va.*—**to r. up,** reunir; aprehender, coger.

round dance, baile de parejas (el baile común o corriente).

rounds, *s.* recorrido, demarcación (de un sereno, policía, etc.); jiras, idas y venidas, salidas de costumbre (como las de un médico, un sacerdote).—**to do,** o **go, one's r.,** hacer uno su ronda o su jira.

round-up [ráundúp], *s.* recogida, junta; apresamiento, aprehensión.

rube [rub], *s.* aldeano, campesino, rústico.

ruckus [rúcus], **ruction** [rúkshun], *s.* alboroto; alharaca.

rudder, *s.*—**r. plate,** pala del timón.—**r. post, r. stock,** madre del timón.

rumble, rumble seat, *s.* (aut.) asiento trasero descubierto.

rumbly [rúmbli], *s.* áspero, escabroso.

rumrunner [rúmrúncœr], *s.* importador de licor de contrabando; transportador de licor.

run. I. *va.* dejar correr o salir (agua de un grifo, etc.); mandar, dominar; tener o proponer como candidato.—**to r. a temperature,** tener fiebre.—**to r. out,** agotar; desperdiciar; echar.—**to r. over,** atropellar. **II.** *vn.* ser candidato; correrse (un color, etc.); extenderse, llegar (hasta).—**to r. away with,** llevarse la palma en, monopolizar (fig.), ser el protagonista en.—**to r. into,** pasar a, convertirse en; parar en; internarse en.—**to r. off,** huir; derramarse, fugarse (un líquido).—**to r. out,** expirar, terminar.—**to r. through,** ver, examinar, presentar, etc. a la ligera; hallarse o ser manifiesto en todo un escrito, plan, etc.—**to be running for,** ser, o estar de, candidato para.

run down, *a.* agotado, debilitado; ruinoso, maltrecho.

runoff [rúnóf]. **I.** *s.* agua de desagüe. **II.** *a.* final, decisivo; de desagüe.

rushlight [rúshláit], *s.* vela de junco; luz débil.

rust-proof [rústprúf], *a.* inoxidable.

rustless [rústles], *a.* sin herrumbre; inoxidable.

rut, *s.* bache, hoyo.

S

sabadilla [sábædílæ], *s.* (bot.) cebadilla, planta de Méjico y Centroamérica.

sabotage, *va.* y *vn.* cometer sabotaje (contra, en).

saccharization [sákæriśćishun], *s.* sacarificación; fermentación.

saccharize [sákæraiś], *va.* sacarificar, convertir en azúcar; fermentar.

sacral [séicræl], *a.* (anat.) sacro.

saddle, *s.*—**s. be in the s.,** llevar las riendas (fig.), estar en el poder, tener la superioridad; estar listo.

sadism [sædism], *s.* sadismo, crueldad sexual.—**sadist** [-ist], *s.* sadista.—**sadistic(al** [sædístic, -æl], *a.* sadista, sadístico.—**sadistically** [-æli], *adv.* sadista o sadísticamente.

safety, *s.*—**s. bolt,** cerrojo de seguridad, que no puede moverse desde el otro lado de la puerta.—**s. nut,** tuerca de seguridad.—**s. rail,** guardarriel.—**s. stop,** mecanismo de detención o de parada.—**s. zone,** zona de seguridad o de peatones, demarcación (en una calle) para el uso exclusivo de peatones.

saffranin(e [sáfrænin], **saffronine** [sáfronin], **saffron yellow,** *s.* (quím.), azafranina.

sagitta [sœyítæ], *s.* (anat.) sutura del parietal; (S-, astr.) Sagitario.

sagittate [sœyiteit], *a.* sagital.

salariat [saléiriæt], *s.* clases asalariadas no obreras (dependientes, profesionales, etc.).

salpa [sælpæ], *s.* (zool.) salpa.

salt, *s.*—**s. cup,** salero.—**s. horse,** carne salada.—**s. shaker,** salero de sacudir (frasco con tapa perforada).

salvage, *va.* salvar; recobrar.

Samoan [sæmóæn], *s.* y *a.* samoano, de las islas de Samoa (Archipiélago de los Navegantes).

sampan [sæmpæn], *s.* sampán (embarcación china).

sand, *va.* (gen. con **down**) alisar con papel de lija.

sand dollar, (zool.) especie de erizo pequeño de mar.

sapsucker [sæpsúkœr], *s.* especie de pájaro carpintero que destruye la albura de los árboles.

sartor [sártœr], *s.* remendón; sastre.

saturnism [sætœrnism], *s.* saturnismo, envenenamiento con plomo.

save, *va.*—**to s. appearances, to s.** (one's) **face,** salvar las apariencias, cubrir el expediente.

scaffolding, *s.* andamiaje.

scan, *vn.* (poet.) ajustarse a las reglas de la métrica, tener la medida propia.

scansion [skǽnshun], *s.* (poet.) escansión, acción de escandir; métrica.

scenic [sínic, sénic], *s.* paisaje cinematográfico.

schedule. I. *s.* suplemento, aditamento. **II.** *va.* fijar el tiempo para.

schoolroom [scúlrúm], *s.* aula, sala de clase.

scofflaw [scofló], *s.* burlador o violador de la ley.

scot-free, *a.*—**to go s.-f.,** salir enteramente libre, sin pena alguna.

Scotland Yard, cuartel de policía de Londres; la misma policía, especialmente el cuerpo de detectives.

scourings [scáurings], *s. pl.* ripic.

scrappy [scrǽpi], *a.* deshilvanado, incoherente, fragmentario; reñidor, pendenciero.

scrimshank [scrímshænk], *vn.* evadir (uno) su deber, zafarse de su obligación.

script, *s.* material escrito a máquina; sinopsis y argumento de un drama cinematográfico; manuscrito.

---

scroop [scrup]. **I.** *s.* chillido; chirrido. **II.** *vn.* chirriar; chillar.

sea, *s.*—**s. coal,** carbón mineral; (E. U.) hulla grasa.—**s. cucumber,** (zool.) holoturia, cohombro de mar.—**s. egg,** erizo de mar.—**s. hare,** (zool.) liebre marina, huevo de pulpo.—**s. squirt,** (zool.) ascidia.—**s. stores,** víveres para un viaje marítimo.—**the seven seas,** todos los mares.

seacraft [sícræft], *s.* barcos de mar; habilidad en la navegación.

Seanad Éireann [sǽnæd ǽrin], *s.* (en Irlanda) cámara alta, senado.

searchingly [sǽrchingli], *adv.* minuciosamente, penetrantemente, de modo escrutinador.

seasonal [síŝnæl], *a.* estacional.

seclusive [secliúsiv], *a.* retraído, amigo de la soledad.

see. I. *va.*—**to s. fit,** creer conveniente.—**to s. one's way (clear) to,** saber uno cómo pueda, o ver el modo de (hacer algo). **II.** *vn.*—**to s. eye to eye,** estar enteramente de acuerdo.

seedless [sídles], *a.* sin semillas; sin pepitas.

seep, *vn.* manar, brotar, salir.

seismogram [sáiŝmogræm], *s.* sismograma, registro sismográfico.—**seismographer** [saiŝmógræfœr], *s.* sismólogo.—**seismographic(al** [séiŝmográfic, -æl], sismográfico.

selection, *s.* trozo, pieza o escrito escogidos.

self, *s.* persona (*your good self,* su buena persona).—**s.-abuse,** censura de sí mismo; masturbación.—**s.-addressed envelope,** sobre con el nombre y dirección de uno.—**s.-affected,** amante de sí mismo.—**s.-assured** = SELF-RELIANT.—**s.-complacency,** satisfacción de sí mismo.—**s.-complacent,** satisfecho de sí mismo, engreído.—**s.-consistent,** consecuente consigo mismo.—**s.-expression,** modo de obrar según inclinación o carácter propios, expresión de la propia individualidad.—**s.-feeder,** (agr.) alimentador automático, aparato que automáticamente vacía alimentos (granos, etc.) en artesas, canales u otros comederos.—**s.-feeding,** de alimentación propia; (animal) criado o alimentado con alimentador automático.—**s.-governing,** autónomo.—**s.-heterodyne,** (rad.) autodino.—**s.-respecting,** digno, pundonoroso.—**s.-righteous,** pagado de su propia rectitud; farisaico.—**s.-righteousness,** vanagloria de la rectitud o virtud propia; fariseísmo.—**s.-same,** idéntico, mismísimo.

sell. I. *s.* broma; engaño, fraude. **II.** *va.* hacer aceptar o reconocer.—**to s.,** de venta, para la venta.—**to s. down the river,** traicionar.—**to s. out,** realizar, hacer venta de realización.

semicentennial [sémisenténiæl], *s.* y *a.* cincuentenario.

sensate [sénset], *a.* y *va.* percibido (percibir) por los sentidos.

sensationally [senséiŝhʊnæli], *adv.* sensacionalmente.

sensitivity [sénsitíviti], *s.* sensibilidad.

sepsis, *s.* infección séptica, infección causada por substancias pútridas.

septate [sépteit], *a.* tabicado, que tiene tabiques.

septic tank, foso séptico.

septum, *s.* septo, tabique.

serial, *s.* (cine) drama cinematográfico de varias películas, representado en uns serie de funciones; (Ing.) revista.

serpent, *s.* (aer.) sonda corta, cable corto de arrastre. (*V.* TRAIL ROPE.)

serpent star, (zool.) ofiuro.

serve, *va.* desempeñar (un puesto).—**to s. notice,** dar aviso, hacer saber, advertir.

server, *s.* mensajero, portador.

service. I. *s.*—**s. station,** (aut.) estación de servicio, taller de reparaciones urgentes. **II.** *va.* atender a; suministrar lo necesario a o para.

sestertium [sestérŝhiʊm], *s.* mil sestercios.

set, *va.*—**to s. store by,** dar valor o importancia a.—**to s. the pace,** dar el ejemplo.—**to s. the river, the Thames, the world, on fire,** hacer prodigios, ser el inventor de la pólvora (gen. en la forma negativa, *he will never set the world on fire,* él no es una maravilla, él no fué el inventor de

la pólvora).—**to s. up,** establecer (a una persona); instalar; poner de ejemplo o de modelo; (top.) poner en estación (un instrumento).

set screw, tornillo de sujeción; tornillo de presión.

setting, *s.* medio circundante, ambiente, concomitante.

settlement, *s.* centro de asistencia o servicio social.

seventy-five, *s.* cañón de 75 milímetros (ll. t. simplemente *setenta y cinco*).

severable [séveræbœl], *a.* separable; excluíble.

sewage. I. *s.* aguas fecales.—**s. disposal, s. purification,** depuración de aguas fecales. **II.** *va.* abonar o regar con aguas fecales.

sex appeal, incitación o provocación sexual, erotismo sensual.

shadowbox [ŝhǽdobóks], *vn.* **shadowboxing** [-ing], *s.* ejercitarse en el boxeo peleando con un contrario imaginario; luchar contra enemigos imaginarios.

shake. I. *s.* grieta, fisura.—**s.-up,** sacudida; reorganización o cambio de personal.—**the shakes,** calofrío; desasosiego; miedo (**to have the shakes,** temblar de miedo). **II.** *va.*—**to s. a leg,** bailar; menearse, darse prisa.—**to s. down,** hacer caer sacudiendo o rebullendo; robar o sacar dinero a.—**to s. up,** reorganizar; trastornar, cambiar bruscamente; regañar, sermonear. **III.** *vn.*—**to s. in one's shoes,** o **boots,** temblar de miedo.

shaker, *s.* espolvoreador.

shall. El tiempo futuro con *shall* se emplea a menudo, como el futuro en español, para indicar mandato, determinación, obligación o estipulación: *thou shalt not kill,* no matarás; *they shall not pass,* no pasarán; *the cement shall be Portland cement,* el cemento será cemento pórtland. También se usa como signo del subjuntivo: *when congress shall meet,* cuando el congreso se reúna.

shame, *s.*—**it is a s.,** es una vergüenza; es una lástima.

share crop, (agr.) cultivo de tierra ajena pagando al dueño con parte de lo producido.

share cropper, el que cultiva tierra ajena y paga alquiler con parte de los frutos.

shave. I. *s.* viruta; rebanada delgada; usurero; estafador. **II.** *va.* comprar (obligaciones comerciales) con descuento exorbitante.

sheathing, sheathing boards, tablas, enmaderado de un tejado o pared.

shebang [ŝhebǽng], *s.* tienda; cosa; madriguera, guarida, (Col.) jurgonera (taberna, casa de juego, etc.); casucha; pejiguera.

shebeen [ŝhebín], *s.* cantina de contrabando.

shed, *s.* hangar.

shelf, *s.*—**to put on the s.,** archivar (fig.), arrinconar, olvidar.

shell, *s.* cualquier pieza hueca de paredes delgadas.

shelve, *va.* archivar, arrinconar, olvidar.

shift, *vn.*—**to s. for oneself,** ingeniarse, bandearse.

shine, *vn.* alumbrar; hacer sol.

shinny [ŝhíni], *vn.* (gen. con **up**), trepar.

Shinto [ŝhínto], **Shintoism** [-iŝm], *s.* sintoísmo, religión primitiva del Japón.

ship, *s.*—**s. bread,** galleta de marineros.—**s. money,** (Ing.) impuesto de defensa naval, o para la armada.—**s. plane,** avión de cubierta o de portavión, que puede despegar de la cubierta de un portavión.

shogun, *s.* taicún.—**shogunate** [ŝhóguneit], *s.* taicunato, dignidad de taicún.

shoot, *va.*—**to s. down,** tumbar a balazos, derribar con armas de fuego.

shop steward = SHOP DEPUTY.

shop-worn, *a.* gastado, deteriorado con el trajín de la tienda.

shore leave, licencia para ir a tierra.

short. I. *s.*—**s. for,** forma abreviada de. **II.** *a.*—**s. story,** cuento. **III.** *va.* (elec.) poner en cortocircuito.

shorts, *s. pl.* calzones cortos flojos.

---

showdown [ŝhóudáun], *s.* declaración o acción perentoria o definitiva.

shrill, *a.* chillón.—**s.-tongued, s.-voiced,** de voz chillona.

shuffling, *a.* lerdo, pesado; embustero; evasivo, retrechero.

shunpike [ŝhúnpáic], *s.* atajo; vereda, camino apartado.

shut, *va.*—**to s. in,** encerrar.—**to s. off,** detener, cortar (el agua, etc.); interrumpir (a uno) en el teléfono, cortarle el circuito.—**to s. out,** excluir; ocultar, tapar.

shuttle. I. *s.* tren de traspaso (entre dos vías férreas); tren que va y viene entre dos lugares cercanos (ll. t. **s. train**); compuerta corrediza. **II.** *va.* y *vn.* mover(se) alternativamente de un lado a otro o de una parte o otra; ir y venir.

shy, *a.* difícil, obscuro; poco prolífico o fértil; falto, que falta (*I am shy a dollar*, me falta un dólar).

siderography [síderógræfi], *s.* grabado en acero blando.

sieve, *s.*—**s. cell**, (bot.) célula perforada.—**s. disk**, o **plate**, parte perforada de una célula.—**s. tissue**, tejido de células perforadas.—**s. tube, s. vessel** = s. CELL.

sight, *s.*—**in s.**, visible; cercano.—**in s. of**, a vista de.

sighted, *a.* (arma) con la mira arreglada para una distancia dada; que ve, que no es ciego.

sign, *vn.* firmar.—**to s. off**, (rad.) terminar, anunciar el fin de un programa o comunicación y cortar la transmisión.—**to s. on the dotted line**, firmar ciega y sumisamente.

siliceous [silíŝhus], *a.* = SILICIOUS.

silicide [sílisaid], *s.* (quím.) siliciuro.

silk-producing, *a.* (zool.) sericígeno.

Siluric [silúric], *a.* (geol.) silúrico.

silurid(an [siliúrid, -æn], *s.* y *a.* siluro.

simple, *s.* simplón, bobo; (med.) simple; (igl.) fiesta simple; persona de humilde alcurnia.—**the simples**, tontería, sandez.

sine curve, (geom.) sinusoide.

single, *a.* aislado; singular; sencillo (no doble, etc.).—**s. blessedness**, la (bendita) vida soltera.—**s.-pole**, unipolar.—**s.-screw**, de una hélice.—**s.-seater**, de un solo asiento.—**s.-throw**, de una dirección.—**s.-valued**, (mat.) de un solo valor (función, variable).

sink. I. *va.* liquidar; grabar en hueco. **II.** *vn.*—**to s. in**, ser comprendido, calar.

sinker, *s.* el que o lo que hunde; grabador en seco; soldado; buñuelo.

Sino- [sáino], *partícula*, chino- (*Sino-Japanese*, chinojaponés).

Sinophil(e [sáinofíl, -fail], *s.* sinófilo, chinófilo, amigo o partidario de China.

sinusoid [sáinusoid], *s.* sinusoide.

sinusoidal [-óidœl], *a.* sinusoidal.

siphonage [sáifuniy], *s.* desagüe o extracción por sifón; acción o funcionamiento del sifón.

sirdar [sœrdár], *s.* sirdar, jefe; mozo de palanquín, cargador; criado.

siriasis [siráiæsis], *s.* (med.) insolación; tratamiento por asoleo (puesta al sol).

sit. I. *va.*—**to s. out**, permanecer sentado durante; no tomar parte en. **II.** *vn.*—**to s. in**, asistir como miembro de, ser miembro, o participar en las deliberaciones, de; reunirse en.—**to s. over (a cup of coffee, their cigars**, etc.), hablar mientras (tomaban una taza de café, fumaban, etc.).

sit-down, *a.* que se hace (toma, etc.) sentado.—**s.-d. strike**, huelga de sentados, huelga pasiva, en que los huelguistas permanecen en el taller sin trabajar. (Ll. en algunas partes *huelga sentada*.)

skeg [skeg], *s.* (mar.) remate posterior de la quilla.

skeletonize [skéletunaiŝ], *va.* sacar el esqueleto a o de, reducir (un cuerpo mortal) a su estructura ósea; reducir a las partes esenciales; disminuir, reducir; bosquejar.

skelp. I. *s.* palmada. **II.** *va.* y *vn.* dar palmadas; dar fuertes coces.

sketch, *s.* drama o cuadro dramático de radio.

ski. I. *s.* esquí, patín largo de madera. **II.** *vn.* esquiar, deslizarse o andar en esquíes.

skin. I. *s.* avaro; petardista, estafador.—**by the s. of one's teeth**, por un tris, (salvarse) en una tabla, apenas, a duras penas.—**to be**, o **to get, under one's skin**, irritar o fastidiar a uno. **II.** *va.* agotar; sacar dinero a, pelar; aventajar, ganar. **III.** *vn.* ser embaucador o engañador; (gen. con **out**) escabullirse.

skitter [skítœr], *vn.* deslizarse saltando, ir saltando y rozando.

skookum [ŝkúcum], *a.* excelente, magnífico, de lo mejor.

skul(l)duggery [sculdúgœri], *s.* tretas, mañas.

skunk. I. *s.* marrano (fig.), canalla, persona ruin. **II.** *va.* ganar completamente a (en un juego) sin perder una jugada.

slash. I. *s.* entrada, abertura (en un bosque); (mil.) galón; *pl.* ramas; matorral pantanoso. **II.** *va.* cortar, hacer un corte largo en; azotar. **III.** *vn.* lanzarse, arrojarse.

slate, *s.*—**to have a clean s.**, tener las manos limpias (fig.), no tener mácula.—**to wipe the s. clean**, empezar de nuevo, abrirse un nuevo derrotero.

slater, *s.* crítico mordaz; (zool.) isópodo terrestre.—**slating** [sléiting], *s.* empizarrado; pizarras; líquido de empizarrar.

slaver [slévœr], *s.* idiota, imbécil; adulador, lavacaras.

sledder [slédœr], *s.* el que va en un trineo o lo arrastra; animal de trineo, que arrastra trineos.—**sledding** [-ding], *s.* ir en trineo o usarlo; marcha en trineo.

slicker [slíkœr], *s.* impermeable flojo; embaucador, farsante.

slide, *s.* (foto.) diapositiva.

slink. I. *s.* sujeto ruin o apocado; cobarde; animal nacido prematuramente. **II.** *a.* nacido antes de tiempo; inmaturo; flacucho; bajo, despreciable.

slip. I. *s.* mozuelo, mozalbete.—**there is many a s. between the cup and the lip**, entre el plato y la boca se pierde la sopa. **II.** *va.* deslizar, escapar de; (gen. con **in**), meter; (gen. con **out**) sacar. **III.** *vn.*—**to s. through one's fingers**, perder uno, o írsele a uno, repentinamente, o en un abrir y cerrar de ojos.

slipshod, *a.* descuidado; tosco, superficial, hecho a la diabla.

Slovene [slovín], *s.* y *a.* esloveno.

slump. I. *s.* aplastamiento, rebajamiento (de una masa húmeda por su propio peso). **II.** *va.* arrojar violentamente; hacer bajar (precios) súbitamente. **III.** *vn.* aplastarse, rebajarse; caer, bajar.

smacking. I. *s.* ruido agudo. **II.** *a.* chasqueador, que chasquea; bueno, medianamente fuerte (*smacking breeze*, buena brisa).—**s. noise**, o **sound**, chasquido.

small intestine, intestino delgado.

smart aleck [élic], *s.* tipo engreído o petulante.

Smilacaceae, Smilacaceæ [smálílækéisii], *s. pl.* (bot.) esmiláceas.

smilacaceous [-ŝhus], *a.* (bot.), esmiláceo.

snaphead [snǽpjéd], *s.* cabeza redonda.

snapheaded [-ed], *a.* de cabeza redonda.

sneakers, *s.* zapatos silenciosos (gen. con suela de caucho); zapatos de gimnasia.

sneakiness [sníkines], *s.* socarronería; husmeo; ruindad, bajeza.

sneaky [sníki], *a.* husmeador; socarrón, hipócrita; bajo, ruin.

sniperscope [snáipœrscoup], *s.* especie de periscopio de rifle, para uso en las trincheras.

snips, *s. pl.* tijeras de latonero.

snitch, *va.* enlazar, coger en un lazo; hurtar, ratear.

snow. I. *s.*—**s. broth**, agua con nieve; líquido muy frío.—**s. ice**, hielo de nieve conglomerada. **II.** *va.*—**to s. under**, derrotar por completo (como a un candidato).

snuff. I. *va.* (gen. con **out**), extinguir, apagar; destruir.—**to s. it,** morirse. **II.** *vn.* (con **out**) morirse.

so, *adv.* tanto, mucho; para que, a fin de que; con tal.—**s. far, s. good,** hasta aquí (ahí), muy bien; eso está bien.—**s. long,** hasta luego, abur; hasta aquí (ahí).—**s. l. as,** mientras que.—**s. or s.,** de un modo u otro.—**not s.,** no es así, eso no es verdad.—**or s.,** poco o menos.—**very much s.,** lo es (dijo, etc.) sin disputa o muy claramente.

soaky, *a.* afeminado, amujerado.

sober-mindedness [-máindednes], *s.* serenidad, espíritu desapasionado.

sob sister, escritora lacrimosa o de sentimentalismo cursi; repórter de lloriqueos.

sociable, *s.* tertulia; coche de asientos opuestos.

social. I. *s.* tertulia. **II.** *a.* socialista.—**s. democracy,** (pol. Alemania), democracia socialista.—**s. democrat,** (pol., Alemania) demócrata socialista.—**s. insurance,** seguro social.—**s. science,** ciencia política; sociología.—**s. service,** asistencia social (España, Colombia, etc.), servicio social (Perú, Argentina, Méjico, etc.), auxilio social. (Se recomienda la última forma).—**s. settlement,** centro de asistencia social.—**s. work** = S. SERVICE.

sociologically [sóshiolóyikæli], *adv.* sociológicamente.

soda, *s.* gaseosa; refresco de gaseosa.—**s. dispenser,** dependiente de fuente de gaseosa.—**s. fountain,** fuente de gaseosa.

soft, *a.* afeminado; apocado, de poco seso; meloso, besuqueador.—**s. palate,** velo del paladar. —**s. tube,** (elec.) tubo termiónico de vacío imperfecto.

soldering copper, soldador con puntas de cobre.

solid rock, roca firme; fundamento sólido.

solipsism [sólipsîsm], *s.* (fil.) doctrina que sostiene que el yo es lo único cognoscible o lo único existente.

solo, *s.* (aer.) vuelo de un aviador solo (ll. t. **solo flight).**

Solomonic [sólomónic], *a.* salomónico.

somatics [sométics], *s.* somatología.

something, *s.*—**to be s. of a,** tener algo de; ser de alguna magnitud o importancia, no ser pequeño, fácil, etc. (*he is something of an orator,* tiene algo de orador; *this is something of a problem,* éste no es problema fácil).

somnambulant [somnæmbiulænt], *a.* sonámbulo.

somniloquy [somnîlokui], *s.* somnilocuencia (apl. sobre todo a la hipnótica).

sooner, *adv.*—**no s. . . . than,** apenas . . ., tan pronto como . . . (*no sooner had John entered than she began to speak,* tan pronto como Juan hubo entrado, ella principió a hablar).

soothsaying [súzséiing], *s.* adivinación.

soundness, *s.* permanencia de peso (del cemento).

southpaw [sáuzpó], *s. a.* zurdo (apl. al que tira la pelota en el baseball).

sow [sóu], *vn.*—**to s. to,** sembrar de.—**who sows the wind reaps the whirlwind,** como sembráredes, cogeredes.

spaghetti, *s.* espaguetis; (elec.) tubería aisladora.

Spanish tile, teja española.

spare. I. *a.*—**s. parts,** repuestos, piezas de repuesto. **II.** *va.* no abusar de, compadecer, ahorrar trabajo o molestia a; usar con moderación; ahorrarle a, eximir de, escapar de (en la voz pasiva **to be spared:** *I was spared the labor,* fuí eximido del trabajo, o escapé del trabajo).—**to s. oneself,** cuidarse de sí mismo, ahorrarse trabajo, molestia, etc.—**and to s.,** y más, de sobra. **III.** *vn.* tener piedad o misericordia.

spark, *s.*—**s. gap,** (rad.) mecanismo de chispa.—**s. lead,** (m. comb. int.), avance al encendido.—**s. lever,** (aut.) manecilla de encendido.

sparrow, *s.*—**s. grass** (corrupción de *asparagus*), espárrago, espárragos.—**s. hawk,** gavilán pequeño.

spasticity [spæstísiti], *s.* calidad de espasmódico

spate [spéit], *s.* creciente, avenida; chaparrón, aguacero; tropel, montón.

speak, *vn.*—**to s. well for,** ser recomendación para, dar prestigio, honrar, demostrar el valor o el mérito de.

spearhead, *s.* vanguardia; ataque de vanguardia; arma de entrada (fig.), cosa con que se abre brecha (fig.) o se inicia algo.

spectrograph [spéctrogræf], *s.* (fís.) espectrógrafo, aparato para obtener una fotografía o representación de un espectro.—**spectrometer** [spectrómetœr], *s.* espectrómetro, refractómetro, instrumento para medir el índice de refracción.—**spectroscopically** [spéctroscópicæli], *adv.* espectroscópicamente.

speedster [spídstœr], *s.* (aut.) róadster rápido de dos asientos.

speed trap, (aut.) trampa de velocidad, para descubrir a los que exceden la velocidad permitada. Consiste en dos estaciones ocultas a lo largo de la vía, comunicadas por teléfono.

spellbinder [spélbáindœr], *s.* arengador, orador popular impetuoso y arrebatador.—**spellbound** [-báund], *a.* arrebatado, embelesado.

spelling bee, concurso o certamen de deletreo.

spermatocyst [spœrmætosîst], *s.* (anat.) vesícula seminal.

spermogonium [spœrmogónium], *s.* (bot.) esporangio de los hongos.

spiel [spil]. **I.** ejecución; obra, producción literaria; arenga. **II.** *vn.* arengar, hablar.

spiffy [spîfi], *a.* bien parecido, de buen talante; excelente, magnífico.

spike, *va.* anular, poner fin a.

spin, *va.* tornear.

spindlelegs [spíndœlégs], *s. pl.* = SPINDLESHANKS.

spineless [spáinles], *a.* invertebrado (literal y fig.); pusilánime, sin espinazo, sin energía, sin nervio; servil.

spinning, *s.*—**s. jenny,** hiladora, máquina de hilar.—**s. mill,** hilandería (fábrica).

spirit, *s.* ánimo, manera, intención, actitud (en expresiones como éstas: **in a friendly spirit,** de una manera amistosa; **in a spirit of friendship,** con ánimo amistoso, movido por un sentimiento de amistad).

spiritual, *s.* canto religioso de los negros del sur de los E. U.

splendiferous [splendíferus], *a.* espléndido; magnificentísimo.

splicer [spláiscœr], *s.* empalmador; (mar.) pasador.

splintery [splínteri], *a.* que puede desastillarse; astilloso, astillado.

split. I. *va.* descomponer (a veces con **off** o **up**); dividir, repartir; desunir, desamistar.—**to s. hairs,** pararse en pelillos, andarse con quisquillas. **II.** *vn.* disentir, estar en desacuerdo; revelar secretos, ser traidor.

split ballot, o **ticket,** papeleta de voto dividido, en que no se vota por todos los candidatos regulares de un partido.

splotchy [splóchi], *a.* manchado, salpicado, emborronado.

spokesman, *s.* vocero.

sponsor. I. *s.* persona responsable; patrocinador, patrono; (rad.) patrono, anunciante, quien costea un programa de radio que contiene un anuncio comercial. **II.** *va.* ser fiador o padrino de; ser responsable de; patrocinar; (rad.) presentar, costear (un programa con anuncios comerciales).

spoof [spúf]. **I.** *s.* timo. **II.** *va.* timar.

sporangium [sporényium], *s.* (bot.) esporangio.

sportsmanship, *s.* nobleza, magnanimidad.

sporty [spórti], *a.* deportivo; alegre, relajado, disipado.

spot. I. *a.* en existencia, listo para entregarse (dicho de mercancías).—**s. cash,** dinero contante; pago al contado. **II.** *s.*—**on the s.,** en calzas prietas.

spread, *s.* diferencia; anuncio con encabezamiento a través de dos páginas.

---

spring, s.—**s. gun,** pistola automática contra ladrones, disparada por un resorte.—**s. of action,** móvil, motivo determinante de la voluntad.

springbok [spríngbóc], s. (zool.) springbok, gacela del Cabo.

sprint, vn. correr a toda carrera.

squabbish [scuóbish], **squabby** [-bi], a. rechoncho.

square deal, juego limpio.

squilla [skuílæ], s. (zool.) esquila, camarón.

stabile [stéibil], a. fijo, sin moverse.

staff. I. s. personal; facultad; (constr.) yeso mezclado con fibra, cemento, etc. usado en construcciones temporales. **II.** va. proveer de funcionarios, nombrar funcionarios para.

stage. I. s. (rad.) elemento, unidad.—**s. coach,** diligencia, ómnibus.—**s. name,** nombre de teatro, nombre adoptado por un actor en su profesión. **II.** va. preparar; ejecutar; presentar.

stagger(ed biplane, biplano de alas escalonadas, en que el ala superior sobresale de la inferior.

stagger wires, (aer.) =STAGGERED WIRES.

stainless, a. que no se mancha.—**s. steel,** acero inoxidable.

stake, va.—**to s. off,** o **out,** (top.) demarcar con estacas.

stall. I. s. (aer.) caída de la velocidad de un avión más allá de la velocidad mínima de vuelo. **II.** vn. (aer.) bajar de la velocidad mínima de vuelo; hacerse ingobernable a causa de esta caída.

stand. I. va. **to s. against the wall,** fusilar.—**to s. . . . high,** tener . . . de alto (*the wall stands 20 feet high,* la pared tiene 20 pies de alto). **II.** vn.—**to s. by,** ser o permanecer fiel a; estar listo.—**to s. to,** tener probabilidad de.

standard. I. s.—**s. of living,** nivel normal de vida, vida normal. **II.** a.—**s. book,** o **work,** obra de autoridad reconocida; obra clásica.

standee [stændí], s. persona sin asiento, que asiste de pie a una función.

stand-off. I. s. empate, tablas (en el juego); indiferencia, frialdad; alejamiento; compensación, neutralización. **II.** a. reservado, retraído, frío.

stannate [stǽneit], s. (quím.) estannato.

stannous [-nus], a. (quím.) estannoso.

stapedius [stæpídius], s. (anat.) músculo estapedio, o del estribo.

star shower, caída de meteoritos.

starver [stárvœr], s. el que está muriendo de hambre; el que mata de hambre.

stasis [stéisis], s. (med.) éstasis, estancamiento de la sangre.

statoscope [stétoscoup], s. estatóscopo, aneroide de precisión.

steeplechaser [stípœlchéiscœr], s. caballo de carreras de obstáculos.

steer, vn.—**to s. clear of,** navegar a distancia prudente de, o evitando; evitar.

steering committee, comisión de iniciativas.

step. I. s. (rad.) elemento, unidad, parte. **II.** vn.—**to s. in,** intervenir; meterse, entrometerse.—**to s. on it,** o **to s. on the gas,** menearse, darse prisa.

Sterculiaceae, Sterculiaceæ [stérkiuliéisii], s. pl. (bot.) esterculias.

sterilize, va. paralizar, estancar.

stet [stet], va. (imp.) dejar como está, no cambiar.

stethometer [stezómetœr], s. estetómetro, instrumento para medir los movimientos del tórax.

stick, va.—**to s. up one's hands,** alzar uno las manos en señal de entrega o sumisión.

sticker [stíkœr], s. fijador de carteles; papel engomado por un lado (rótulo, cartel, etc.); cuestión batallona, cosa peliaguda; tapaboca, argumento incontestable; persona perseverante; persona que permanece fiel (a un partido, etc.); cosa que no se vende bien, que no tiene salida o demanda.

stick-up, s. salteamiento, robo por salteadores.

stiff, a. fuerte, obstinado (resistencia, etc.).—**to be frightened,** o **scared, s.,** casi morirse de miedo, quedarse yerto.

stillbirth [stílbœrz], s. parto muerto.

stinger [stíngœr], s. cosa o animal que punza o pica; aguijón de un insecto.

stinker, s. sujeto vil, tipo despreciable, canalla; (zool.) petrel grande que se alimenta de carroña.

stinkweed [stínkuíd], s. (bot.) estramonio.

stock, s. progenitor; raza; extracto; tablas, madera.—**s.-taking,** inventariar.—**s. yard,** corral de concentración (de ganado).

stockman [stócmæn], s. ganadero.

stock-still, a. enteramente quieto.

stomatology [stóumætólori], s. ciencia de la boca y sus enfermedades.

stone, s.—**s.-broke,** arrancado, sin un cuartillo. —**s. coal,** antracita.—**s.-still,** enteramente quieto.

stooge [stuy], s. preguntador apostado en el auditorio para que haga preguntas preparadas a un comediante, que las contesta chistosamente.

storm troops, tropas de asalto escogidas.

story teller, decidor de cuentos y anécdotas, narrador.

stovaine [stóuvæin] (nombre de fábrica), s. estovaína, especie de anestésico local.

stove, s. cocina o fogón de hierro.

stovepipe [stóuvpáip], s. tubería del fogón a la chimenea; chistera (ll. t. **stovepipe hat**).

straddler [strédlœr], s. el que no se decide, o está entre dos bandos opuestos inclinándose hacia ambos.

Stradivarius [strédivárius], s. estradivario, violín.

strafe [straf]. **I.** s. bombardeo violento. **II.** va. bombardear violentamente.

straight-out, a. franco, abierto, sin disfraz; intransigente, decidido.

straiten, va. embarazar, poner en calzas prietas; estorbar; apenar.—**straitened,** a. financieramente embarazado, en circunstancias apremiantes; necesitado, sin recursos.

strange, a.—**s. to say,** lo cual es extraño; (es) cosa extraña.

strangle hold, influencia o acción avasalladora o paralizadora; dominio completo.

strangulate, va. estrangular; (cir.) estrangular (cerrar u obstruir por compresión para cortar la circulación).

strap, s.—**s. brake,** freno de cinta.—**s. hinge,** bisagra de ramales.—**s. iron,** hierro en tiras; tira de hierro.—**s. oil,** tunda, felpa.

strategic, a. ventajoso, dominante.

stratosphere [stréitosffær], s. estratosfera, alta atmósfera.

straw poll, votación no oficial. (*V.* STRAW VOTE.)

streamer (headline), s. encabezamiento al través o del ancho de la página.

stretch, va.—**to s. a point,** hacer alguna concesión, ceder un poco.

strip, va. desvenar (tabaco).

striper [stráipœr], s. hombre de galones (apl. a los militares).

strips, strip tobacco, tabaco desvenado.

strobilaceous [stróbiléishus], a. conífero; de forma de cono.—**strobilation** [-léishun], s. reproducción asexual por división.

stroke, stroke oar, stroke oarsman, (mar.) bogavante.

strombus [strómbus], s. (zool.) estrombo.

strong, adv. fuertemente, enérgicamente; con entusiasmo.

struck, pp.—**to be s. by,** o **with,** llamar la atención a uno (cambiando el giro), parecerle a uno digno de notar.

structural, a. estructural.—**structurally,** a. estructuralmente, en cuanto a la estructura.

strummer [strúmœr], s. rascacuerdas, mal tocador.

stubby, a. cerdoso; cubierto de cepas.

stub iron =STUB TWIST.

Para la pronunciación de æ, œ, ᴅ, ŝ, ŝh, ᴜ, y̆, ɣ, z, véase la clave al principio del libro.

stuff, *s.* (imp.) manuscrito; blanca, dinero.

stumper [stúmpœr], **stump orator, stump speaker,** arengador político.

stung, *a.* burlado, chasqueado.

stunt. I. *s.* maniobra sensacional (sobre todo en el aire); (aer.) acrobacia. **II.** *vn.* hacer maniobras sensacionales; (aer.) hacer acrobacias.

stunted, *a.* mal desarrollado, atrofiado; achaparrado (árbol); enclenque, raquítico.

subchaser [súbchéiscœr], *s.* cazasubmarinos.

submachine gun, ametralladora de mano, arma de fuego automática que puede usarse ya como pistola, ya como fusil.

submaxila [súbmæksílæ], *s.* maxilar inferior.

submergible [sʌbmœrgibœl]. **I.** *s.* submarino. **II.** *a.* sumergible.

subreption [sʌbrrépshʊn], *s.* (for.) subrepción; juicio erróneo debido a subrepción.

sub rosa (sʌb róusæ], *adv.* muy confidencialmente, muy en secreto.

subsidiary. I. *s.* auxiliar; (com.) dependencia, compañía dependiente. **II.** *a.* dependiente, subordinado.

substantively, *adv.* substantivadamente.—**substantivize** [súbstæntivaiš], **substantize** [-taiš], *va.* substantivar.

substitute, *a.* substitutivo.

subtractive [sʌbtréctiv], *a.* substractivo; (mat.) negativo.

such, *a.*—**s. as it is** (**they are,** etc.), por poco(s), pequeño(s), etc. que sea(n) (*these advantages, such as they are,* estas ventajas, por pequeñas que sean; *his argument, such as it is,* su argumento, por débil que sea).—**no s. (a) thing,** no hay tal.— **there is s. (a) thing as,** hay algo que se llama, existe (*there is such a thing as honesty,* hay algo que se llama honradez, la honradez existe). A veces conviene cambiar el giro: *there is such a thing as losing patience,* hay casos en que se pierde la paciencia, la paciencia no es inagotable, o tiene sus límites.

sum, *s.*—**in s. and substance,** en resumen.

sun, *s.*—**s. bittern,** (orn.) alcaraván. **s.-god** = SUNGOD.—**s. valve,** válvula solar, actuada por el sol.—**in the s.,** al sol; en el mundo.—**to have a place in the s.,** ocupar su puesto en el mundo; hacerse conocer o sentir; tener importancia.— **under the s.,** en el mundo.

sundew, *s.* (bot.) rocío del sol, planta de la gota.

sungod [súngod], *s.* dios del sol.

super [siúpœr], *s.* cosa excelente; excelencia, alta calidad; SUPERNUMERARY; SUPERINTENDENT.

supercharged engine, (m. comb. int.) motor de alimentación adicional por presión.

supercharger [siúpœrchárycœr], *s.* (m. comb. int.) compresor para alimentación adicional forzada.

supernatant [-néitænt], *a.* flotante.—**superorganic** [-orgénic], *a.* sobreorgánico, fuera del organismo; mental; sobreindividual, superior al individuo.—**superphysical** [-físikæl], *a.* más allá de lo físico, inmaterial.—**supersensible** [-sénsibœl], **supersensual** [-sénshuæl], *a.* más allá de los sentidos, inaccesible a los sentidos; espiritual.— **supertax** [-tæks], *s.* impuesto sobre renta adicional (renta que excede un límite fijado por la ley).

supply, *va.*—**to s. with,** proveer de, suministrar.

sure. I. *a.*—**be s. and** (seguido de imperativo), no deje(n de, . . . sin falta (*be sure and come,* no deje de venir, venga sin falta). **II.** *adv.*—**s. enough,** efectivamente, en efecto, en realidad de verdad.—**for s.,** con seguridad, con certidumbre.

swamp, *va.* abrumar, recargar; inundar (fig.)

swanky [suǽnki], *a.* ágil, enérgico; ostencioso, jactancioso.

swaraj [suæráy, šhæráy], *s.* (India) autonomía, independencia.

swashbuckle [suóshbúkœl], *vn.* fanfarronear.

sweatband [suétbænd], *s.* tira de cuero del forro del sombrero.

sweatbox [suétbóks], *s.* tina de apelambrar; aparato secador.

sweep, *s.* cuerda dragaminas; SWEEPSTAKES.

swim, *s.* mundo, corriente de las cosas; sociedad, vida social; vida de tono; clases influyentes; (zool.) vejiga natatoria.—**to be in the s.,** estar en la corriente o la marcha de las cosas.

swing. I. *s.* autoridad, control.—**in full s.,** en su apogeo. **II.** *a.* giratorio; engoznado.

switch. I. *s.* sistema de trincheras de comunicación (ll. t. **switch line**). **II.** *va.* y *vn.* (a veces con **off**) desviar(se), cambiar(se).

swivel, *s.* articulación giratoria.

sword, *s.*—**to be at swords' points,** estar de punta, estar a matar, estar como perros y gatos.

syndicate. I. *s.* sindicato de manuscritos, empresa que compra artículos manuscritos y los vende para su publicación simultánea en varios periódicos o revistas. **II.** *va.* vender (manuscritos) a un sindicato de manuscritos.

syngenesis [sinyénesis], *s.* concurrencia de los gérmenes masculino y femenino en la formación del feto; generación o reproducción sexual.

synthesize [sínzesaiš], *va.* y *vn.* sintetizar; producir por síntesis.

syrinx [sírinks], *s.* (orn.) siringe, segunda laringe de las aves.

T

tabby, *s.* solterona chismosa.

tactful [tǽktful], *a.* cauto, mañoso.

tactfully [-i], *adv.* cautamente, mañosamente.

tactile, *a.* táctil, relativo al tacto.

tail, *s.*—**t. skid,** (aer.) patín de cola.—**t. spin,** (aer.) = SPIN.

tailless [téil-les], *a.* acaude, sin cola.

tailor. I. *a.* de sastre, hecho por un sastre (dícese también **tailor-made**). **II.** *va.* vestir, proveer de ropa. **III.** *vn.* ser sastre; ser (bueno o malo) para hacer ropa.

take, *va.*—**to t. a back seat,** ceder su puesto, perder influencia.—**to t. a bath,** bañarse.—**to t. a chance,** arriesgar; probar.—**to t. action,** actuar, hacer diligencia, tomar medidas.—**to t. a rest,** descansar.—**to t. arms,** tomar las armas; principiar la guerra.—**to t. back,** devolver; llevar a, o hacer pensar en (tiempos pasados, etc.).—**to t. breakfast,** desayunarse.—**to t. cold,** resfriarse.— **to t. into account,** o **consideration,** tener en cuenta.—**to t. it easy,** ir despacio, no afanarse; descansar.—**to t. it or leave it,** aceptar o rechazar sin discusión (gen. en forma imperativa, y puede traducirse por *si o no*).—**to t. it that,** entender que, inferir que.—**to t. lunch,** almorzar.—**to t. on,** asumir.—**to t. one at his word,** fiarse de la palabra de uno.—**to t. one's head off,** echar a uno un sermón, ponerlo como nuevo.—**to t. one's time,** ir despacio, no darse prisa.—**to t. the field,** entrar (en la cancha, etc.); salir a campaña.—**to t. the wind out of one's sails,** desarmar a uno (fig.), apagarle los fuegos (fig.)

takedown [téikdáun]. **I.** *a.* rifle desmontable; mecanismo de desmontar o desarmar. **II.** *a.* desarmable.

talkie [tóki], *s.* película de cine parlante; *pl.* **talkies,** cine parlante.

talking, *a.*—**t. picture,** película de cine parlante.—**t. point,** argumento, razón, aliciente (para inducir a la compra de algo).

tall hat, sombrero de copa, chistera.

tallish [tólish], *a.* un poco alto.

tamper, *s.* pisón.—**tamping bar, tamping iron,** pisón metálico.

taper, *vn.* (a veces con **off**), ahusarse; ir disminuyendo; cesar poco a poco.

tappoon [tæpún], *s.* (hidr.) tapa, compuerta de acequia.

target, *s.* (fís.) foco, o superficie de emisión, de rayos X.

Tasmanian [tæsméiniæn], *s.* y *a.* tasmanio.

tau [tau], *s.* tau (letra griega).

tearoom [tírrúm], *s.* salón de té; restaurante de comidas ligeras.

technician [tecníshæn], *s.* técnico.

teetee [títi], *s.* (zool.) tití.

telectroscope [teléctroscoup], *s.* telectroscopio, aparato para transmitir imágenes eléctricamente.

telega [telígæ], *s.* telega, especie de carro tosco usado en Rusia.

telelectric [télæléctric], *a.* teleléctrico, transmitido eléctricamente a distancia.

tell. I. *va.* distinguir, ver (la diferencia, etc.); saber, decidir.—**to t. the story,** contar el cuento, poner a las claras lo que hay. **II.** *vn.* saber, juzgar, predecir.—**to t. on,** descubrir, delatar a; dejarse ver en, afectar a.

telling, *s.* manera de decir o de contar.—**there is no t.,** no es posible decir, no puede preverse, ¡quién sabe!

tellurian. I. *s.* morador de la tierra. **II.** *a.* telúrico, terrestre.

telodynamic [télodainǽmic], *a.* teledinámico.

tenebræ [ténebri], *s. pl.* (ig.) tinieblas, matines del jueves, viernes y sábado santos.

tendrac, tenrec [téndræk, -rec], *s.* (zool.) tanrec, mamífero insectívoro de Madagascar.

terbium [tǽrbium], *s.* (quím.) terbio, uno de los cuerpos simples.

teredo, *s.* (ent.) teredo.

tergiversator [tǽryivœrséitœr], *s.* tergiversador.

termite, *s.* (zool.) termita, comején.

terne [tœrn]. **I.** *s.* aleación de estaño y plomo. **II.** *va.* revestir con esta aleación.—**terneplate** [-pléit], *s.* lámina con revestimiento de *terne.*

terrazzo, *s.* terrazo, cemento granítico.—**t. tile,** mosaico de terrazo, mosaico granítico.

tetrastyle [tétræstail]. **I.** *s.* (arq.) tetrastilo. **II.** *a.* de cuatro columnas o pilastras.

tetratomic [tétrætómic], *a.* (quím.) tetratómico.

tetrode [tétroud], *s.* (eléc.) tubo de vacío de cuatro electrodos.

textural [téckschuræl], *a.* de textura, relativo a la textura o contextura.

than, *conj.* de lo que; del que; de los que (*easier than you think,* más fácil de lo que Vd. cree).

that. I. *pron.* lo que.—**t. is how,** así es como se hace.—**t. is t.,** eso es lo que hay, es ¡asunto concluido, no hay más que hablar.—**at t.,** sin embargo; aunque. (*V.* t. LET.)—**for all t.,** a pesar de eso. **II.** *adv.*—**t. many,** tantos.—**t. much,** tanto. **III.** *conj.*—**in t.,** en que; a causa de que, por cuanto.

thatch. I. *s.* tejado de paja u hojas. **II.** *va.* empajar, techar con paja.—**thatcher** [-chœr], *s.* empajador.—**thatching,** *s.* (acción de) empajar; material de empajar.

theater, theatre, *s.* asunto o composición teatral, o para las tablas.

then, *adv.*—**but t.,** sin embargo, si bien es cierto que.

theocentric [zíoséntric], *a.* teocéntrico.

theologize [zíóloyaiŝ], *va.* y *vn.* teologizar.

thermionics [zœrmiónics], *s.* termiónica, ciencia de los fenómenos termiónicos.

thermit(e [zǽrmit] (nombre de fábrica), termita, mezcla de aluminio pulverizado y un óxido metálico, gen. de hierro.—**t. welding process,** soldadura con termita.

thermobattery [zǽrmobǽteri], *s.* pila termoeléctrica.

thermopenetration [-pénetréiŝhun], *s.* termopenetración.

thing. *s.* En lenguaje familiar, se aplica a veces a personas, sobre todo para expresar desprecio, compasión, etc.: *the young thing,* la chica, la pobre chica; *the mean thing,* el malvado, el ruin, el maldito, el sinvergüenza, el desconsiderado, etc. (Se escogerá el término que se adapte a las circunstancias).—**for one t.,** entre otras cosas.—**the t. in itself,** (filos.) las cosas en sí mismas, el mundo objetivo en sí mismo.

think. I. *va.*—**to t. it over,** pensarlo, meditarlo.—**to t. nothing of,** mirar con desprecio, tener en poco; creer fácil, considerar como cosa común y corriente, no dar importancia a. **II.** *vn.*—**to t. twice,** reflexionar mucho, andar con tiento.— **I don't t., I t. not,** creo que no.

thinkable [zínkæbœl], *a.* concebible.

third service, *s.* (E. U.) servicio de aviación, fuerzas aéreas.

thob [zob], *vn.* juzgar (uno) según sus deseos, creer en lo que le conviene.

threepence [zrípens], *s.* tres peniques; moneda de tres peniques.

through. I. *adv.*—**t. and t.,** enteramente; en todo; hasta los tuétanos.—**to be t.,** haber terminado.—**to be t. with,** haber terminado; no tener más que ver con; no ocuparse ya en.

throw, *va.*—**to t. light on,** esclarecer.—**to t. oneself away,** sacrificarse tontamente, rebajarse, echarse a pique.—**to t. out of gear,** desengranar, desconectar; trastornar.—**to t. to the wind(s),** descartar, no hacer caso de.—**to t. up the sponge,** rendirse, cantar el kirieleisón.

throwback [zróubæk], *s.* vuelta atrás, retroceso; (biol.) reversión; (cine) escena retrospectiva, que enseña acontecimientos pasados relacionados con el drama que se representa.

thulium [zúlium], *s.* (quím.) tulio.

Tibetan [tibétæn], *s.* y *a.* tibetano.

tie plate, placa de asiento del riel.

tie-up, *s.* paro.

tiger, *s.* rufián farandulero; un viva (vítor) más, el último viva.

tigerish [táigœriŝh], *a.* como de tigre; feroz.

tighten, *va.*—**to t. one's belt,** hacer economías o sacrificios, aguantar privaciones.

tigrish [táigriŝh], *a.* =TIGERISH.

tile, *s.* mosaico, baldosín; bloque hueco de hormigón o de arcilla.

timarau [táimaráu], *s.* timaráu, búfalo de Mindoro.

time, *s.*—**t. about,** alternadamente, por turnos.— **t. and again,** una vez y otra vez, repetidamente.— **t. switch,** interruptor horario. **t. was when,** en otro tiempo, tiempos hubo en que.—**at the t.,** en ese tiempo, entonces.—**behind the times,** atrasado.—**between times,** en los intervalos.—**for all t.,** para siempre, por siempre.—**in no t.,** en un instante, en un abrir y cerrar de ojos.—**the t. is not yet,** todavía no es tiempo, aún no ha llegado la hora.—**to have a good t.,** pasar un buen rato; pasar un día (unos días, una noche, etc.) agradable; divertirse.

tinned goods, conservas alimenticias en latas.

tippenny [típeni], *s.* dos peniques.

titer, titre, *s.* temperatura de solidificación.—**t. test,** determinación de la temperatura de solidificación.

titillate, *va.* cosquillear, hacer cosquillas; causar placer, dar gusto.—**titillation,** *s.* cosquilleo; sensación agradable.

titrimetry [taitrímetri], *s.* (quím.) análisis volumétrico.

toastmistress [tóustmístres], *s.* mujer que anuncia y presenta a los que proponen brindis.

tog, *s.* trapo, prenda de vestir; *pl.* **togs,** ropa, trapos.

toggery [tógœri], *s.* ropa, trapos; aperos, arreos.

token money, moneda divisionaria. (En los E. U., monedas inferiores al dólar).

tollage [tóuliy], *s.* peaje.

tomb, *s.*—**the Tombs,** la cárcel de Nueva York.

tonsillectomy [tónsiléctomi], **tonsillotomy** [-lótomi], *s.* (cir.) amigdalotomía, ablación de las amígdalas.

tonus [tóunus], *s.* tonicidad; (fisiol.) tono; (patol.) espasmo muscular.

too, *adv.*—**(it is) t. bad,** es lástima, es de sentirse.—**t. (funny, strange,** etc.) **for words,** inmensamente (chistoso, extraño, etc.), lo más ... del mundo.—**but t.,** desgraciadamente; muy, sumamente.—**none! t., not t.,** no muy, que a duras penas puede llamarse (bueno, eficaz, etc.).— **only t.** =BUT T. (*V.* t. ONLY.)

top. I. *s.* tabla (parte superior de una mesa). **II.** *a.* máximo.—**t. grafting,** modo de injertar en que el injerto se introduce en la copa o las ramas del patrón.—**t. hat,** sombrero de copa, chistera.— **t.-heavy,** mal proporcionado, organizado o distri-

buído; que tiene demasiado personal dirigente.
III. *va.*—**to t. off, out,** o **up,** rematar; terminar; preparar.

topping, *a.* excelente, magnífico.

tormenting [torménting], *a.* atormentador.

tormentingly [-li], *adv.* atormentadoramente, de modo atormentador.

tosh [tósh]. **I.** *s.* música celestial, tonterías; baño portátil. **II.** *vn.* bañarse.

totalitarian [totælitáriæn], *s.* y *a.* totalitario.— **totalitarianism** [-išm], *s.* totalitarismo.

tough. **I.** *s.* rufián, truhán. **II.** *a.* trabajable (metal); increíble, raro.

tracer, *s.* averiguación o averiguador de cosas perdidas (en los trenes, el correo, etc.); (artí.) artificio luminoso unido a un proyectil para determinar su trayectoria.

track, *s.* (dep.) concurso, torneo.

tract, *s.* (anat.) canal; sistema.

trail, *s.* carretera.—**t. car, trailer,** coche de habitación remolcado por un vehículo automóvil.

trainee [treiní], *s.* persona que se entrena o que se adiestra.

training ship, barco de instrucción marina.

trammel, *s.* red de pescar; red para coger pájaros.

trampolin(e [trémpolin]. **I.** *s.* función en que los personajes andan en zancos. **II.** *vn.* andar en zancos.

transgressible [trænsgrésibœl], *a.* violable.— **transgressing** [-grésing], *a.* transgresor.—**transgressingly** [-li], *adv.* transgresoramente, cometiendo transgresión.—**transgressive** [-grésiv], *a.* transgresor, culpable.

transient. **I.** *s.* viajero, persona de tránsito. **II.** *a.* de tránsito, que está de paso.

transmission, *s.* (aut.) cambio de velocidades (ll. t. transmission gear).

transmittance [trænsmítæns], *s.* transmisión.

transmitting set (rad.) radiotransmisor, aparato de transmisión.

transplanting, *s.* trasplante.

travel(l)ed [tréveld], *a.* que ha viajado; trillado, frecuentado (camino).

trawler [trólœr], *s.* pescador rastreador, que pesca a la rastra; barco rastreador, o de pesca a la rastra; barco dragaminas.

tray, *s.* (foto.) cubeta de revelar.

treasure ship, barco que lleva fondos o riquezas.

trench, *s.*—**t. back,** dolor de espalda acompañado de rigidez.—**t. fever,** especie de fiebre remitente, común en las trincheras, transmitida por los piojos.—**t. gun,** cañón de trinchera, usado en las trincheras.—**t. mouth,** inflamación de la boca; angina diftérica.—**t. nephritis,** nefritis aguda causada por la intemperie, como en las trincheras. —**t. warfare,** guerra de trincheras.

Trentine [tréntin], *s.* y *a.* tridentino.

trial. **I.** *s.* (for.) proceso.—**t. and error,** ensayo, experimento, prueba.—**t. jury,** jurado procesal.— **on t.,** (com.) a prueba; (for.) enjuiciado. **II.** *a.* de prueba; hecho por vía de experimento.—**t. balloon,** globo de prueba; artificio para probar la opinión pública, etc.

tribalism [tráibælišm], *s.* vida o sociedad tribal, o de tribu; espíritu tribal, o de tribu.

trick, *s.* artificio; problema (**to do the t.,** resolver el problema, dar en el busilis); arte; volada.

trolling [tróuling], *s.* pesca a la rastra con anzuelo, pesca desde un bote en movimiento, con el anzuelo arrastrando cerca de la superficie.

trooper, *s.* policía montado.

troopship [trúpship], *s.* buque de transporte de tropas.

tropic, *s.*—**T. of Cancer,** trópico de Cáncer.—**T. of Capricorn,** trópico de Capricornio.

troposphere [tróposfïær], *s.* troposfera, baja atmósfera, región de la atmósfera situada bajo la estratosfera.

trotol [trútol], **trotyl** [-til], *s.* (quím.) trinitrotolueno.

---

truck, *s.*—**t. system,** sistema de pago de salarios en especie.—**t. tractor,** camión remolcador que lleva parte del peso del remolque.

true, *a.*—**t. to life,** ajustado a la vida real, que pinta la vida al natural.

trupenny [trúpéni], *s.* sujeto honrado y confiable, buen sujeto.

trustification [trústifikéishun], *s.* trustificación, reducción a trust o incorporación en un trust.— **trustify** [-fai], *va.* reducir a trust, formar un trust de, *trustificar.*

truthfully [trúzfuli], *adv.* con verdad, con certeza.

try, *vn.*—**to t. and, to t. to,** tratar de, hacer lo posible por.

tube, *s.* (rad.) válvula, tubo termiónico.—**t. transmitter,** (rad.) radiotransmisor de tubos termiónicos.

tubulate, *a.* tubulado.—**t. retort,** retorta tubulada.

tubulose [tiúbiulous], *a.* tubuloso; tubular.

tulipwood [tiúlipúd], *s.* madera tulípera; árbol tulípero.

tumefacient [tiúmeféishent], **tumescent** [tiumésent], *a.* tumescente.

tundra [túndræ], *s.* tundra, llanura árida musgosa de las regiones árticas.

tuner, *s.* (rad.) circuito de sintonización.

tungstate, etc. (Por error, estas voces están después de TUNING en el cuerpo del Diccionario.)

turfman [tœrfmæn] *s.* aficionado a las carreras de caballos.

turn. **I.** *s.* aptitud; (tea.) pieza u acto cortos; (dep.) contienda, partido; (com.) transacción. **II.** *va.*—**to t. over in one's mind,** pensar con detenimiento, meditar sobre.—**to t. state's evidence,** confesar su delito y declarar contra sus cómplices (dicho de un reo).—**to t. thumbs down on,** condenar a; rechazar.

turnover, *s.* cambio; reorganización; número de transacciones comerciales; compras y ventas; período de venta y repuesto de un surtido de mercancías, o tiempo en que se les da salida o en que hay que reponerlas; número de empleados que se cambian o reemplazan en un tiempo dado.

tutorial [tiutóriæl], *a.* relativo a preceptores, curadores o curaduría.

tutorship [tiútœrship], *s.* curaduría, oficio de curador.

tweet [tuit]. **I.** *s.* gorjeo. **II.** *vn.* gorjear, piar.

twilight sleep, (med.) narcosis parcial obstétrica, producida para mitigar los dolores del parto.

two-way, *a.* de dos direcciones; de dos conductos; de tránsito en ambas direcciones (calle, vía).

tympanites [tímpænáitis], *s.* timpanitis, enfisema abdominal.

tympanitis [tímpænáitis], *s.* inflamación del tímpano; (a veces, incorrectamente) enfisema abdominal.

typescript [táipscript], *s.* material escrito a máquina; tipo de imprenta o de máquina de forma de letra de mano.

typhlops [tíflops], *s.* (zool.) tíflope.

U

uca [iúkæ], *s.* (zool.) =FIDDLER CRAB.

umbilical cord, cordón umbilical.

unassembled [únæsémbœld], *a.* desarmado, en piezas

unchecked, *a.* inestorbado.

uncommitted [úncomfted], *a.* no cometido; no cumplido, no hecho; no comprometido, sin compromiso.

uncompromisingly [uncómpromáísingli], *adv.* inflexiblemente, firmemente; de manera intransigente, sin concesión alguna.

under fire, en combate; bajo el fuego del enemigo, atacado por el enemigo.

Para la pronunciación de æ, œ, D, ŝ, sh, U, ў, Y, z, véase la clave al principio del libro.

underbuy [úndœrbái], va. comprar a menor precio que; pagar por (algo) menos de lo que vale.

undercharge [-chárʏ], va. cargar por (algo) menos de lo que conviene; cargar insuficientemente (un arma, etc.).

underfoot [-fút], adv. bajo los pies; en el piso, en el suelo. (A veces se cambia el giro: *it is wet underfoot*, el piso está húmedo, o mojado.)

underframe [úndœrfréim], s. armazón de sustentación.

undernourish [úndœrnœ́rish], va. = UNDERFEED.

undernourishment [-ment], s. = UNDERFEEDING.

understandable [-stǽndæbœl], a. comprensible.

understatement [-stéitment], s. proposición en que no se dice todo, en que se dice menos de lo que realmente hay; formulación ɔ exposición incompleta. (Gen. conviene cambiar un poco el giro.)

undertook [-túc], pret. de TO UNDERTAKE.

undisturbed, a. sin cambiar, sin mover, como está (estaba).

undulant [úndiulænt], a. undulante, ondulante.
—**u. fever**, fiebre de Malta o mediterránea.

unemployed, a. desempleado, parado.

unemployment, s. desempleo, paro forzoso.

unessential [únesénshæl], a. que no es esencial o indispensable; de poca importancia, que no importa.

Ungulata [únguiuléitæ], s. pl. ungulados.

union, s. (e. p.) sindicato, gremio de obreros.—**u. card**, matrícula gremial o de sindicato, expedida a los miembros de un gremio; certificado gremial o sindicalista, en que consta que un patrón o fábrica emplean sólo obreros agremiados.—**u.-made**, hecho por obreros agremiados.—**u. shop**, fábrica o taller que reconoce los derechos colectivos sindicalistas, o que emplea sólo obreros agremiados.—**u. suit**, traje interior de una sola pieza.

unionism, s. (e. p.) sindicalismo.

unionist, s. (e. p.) sindicalista.

unionize, va. (e. p.) sindicar.

unity, a. unitario.

unlimber, va. y vn. alistar(se), preparar(se).

unmoral [unmóral], a. amoral, ajeno a la moral o independiente de ella.

unprecedented, a. nunca visto.

unrelenting [unrilénting], a. inexorable, inflexible; tenaz.—**unrelentingly** [-li], adv. inexorablemente; sin tregua.

unsurmountable [unsœrmáuntæbœl], a. insuperable, invencible.

unto, prep. hasta; de; para.

untruthful [untrúzful], a. mendaz, inverídico, falto de veracidad; falso, no verdadero.—**untruthfully** [-li], adv. falsamente; mendazmente, faltando a la verdad.—**untruthfulness** [-nes], s. mendacidad, falta de veracidad; falsedad.

unutterably [unútœræbli], adv. indeciblemente, enormemente.

up, adv. para arriba (*from three dollars up*, de tres dólares para arriba).—**u. above**, arriba, más arriba.—**u.-and-doing**, a. que se menea, enérgico, emprendedor.—**u. and u.**, subiendo más y más; progresando.—**u. to the minute**, hasta este momento, hasta la fecha; enteramente al día.—**u.-to-the-minute**, a. que llega hasta el último momento o hasta la fecha; que está enteramente al día.

upheld [upjéld], pret. y pp. de TO UPHOLD.

upland cotton, algodón úpland.

upset, va. desconcertar; desbarajustar, desbaratar.—**upsetting**. I. s. acortamiento; vuelco; trastorno; desbarajuste. II. a. desconcertante.

urinanalysis [júrinænǽlisis], s. uroscopia, análisis urinario.

urochord [iúrocord], s. (zool.) urocordio.

Urochorda [iúrocórdæ], **Urochordata** [-cordéitæ], s. pl. (zool.) urocordios.

urology [yuróloʏi], s. = URINOLOGY.

use, s.—**no u.**, inútil.—**no u. of talking**, es inútil discutirlo, eso no tiene discusión; sin

duda, es claro que.—**what is the u.** (of)? ¿de qué sirve? ¿para qué? es inútil.

useful load, (aer.) carga útil.

usual, a.—**as u.**, como de costumbre, como siempre.

utility, s. empresa de servicio público.

V

vaccine point, lanceta o aguja de vacunar.

vactuphone [vǽctiufoun] (nombre de fábrica), s. vactúfono, instrumento empleado por los sordos para oír.

vagus [véigus], s. nervio neumogástrico.

valve, s. (rad.) válvula, tubo termiónico.

vamp, s. coqueta; bombero valuntario.

vane, s. (top.) tablilla, corredera (de una mira).

vanity, s. neceser, cajita de polvo y afeites.

variability [vériæbíliti], s. variabilidad.

variable, a.—**v. condenser**, (elec.) condensador de capacidad graduable continuamente.—**v. inductor**, (elec.) inductor de inductancia graduable continuamente.

vaudevillian [vodvíliæn], a. de, o relativo a, teatro de variedades.

veiled [véild], a. velado, encubierto, indirecto, disfrazado.

Velella [velélæ], s. (zool.) velela.

velum [vílum], s. (anat.) cubierta membranosa; velo del paladar.

venire [venáiæri], s. (for.) orden o requerimiento de comparecencia.

venireman [venáiærimæn], s. jurado (persona).

Vermes [vœrmis], s. pl. (zool.) vermes, gusanos.

vernier, s. (rad.) aparato o instrumento auxiliar de regulación o graduación.—**v. plate**, (top.) placa de los nonios.

versatile, a. de conocimientos muy variados; adaptable, que se adapta fácilmente a varias ocupaciones o situaciones.

vertical, a. por industrias, de cada industria por separado.

vibrion [víbrion], s. vibrión, especie de bacteria.

vicariously [vaikériusli], adv. substitutivamente, por substitución.

viewy [viúi], a. destornillado, visionario.

villi [vílai], s. (pl. de VILLUS), vellos.

virgin birth, (biol.) partenogénesis; (teo.) partc virginal de María, virginidad de María.

virginium [vœrýiniʊm], s. (quím.) virginio.

virtuosity [vœrtiuósiti], s. maestría, habilidad técnica; los maestros, los técnicos.

vis-a-vis, comparado, o por comparación, con; acerca de; en presencia de.

vision, s. clarividencia, perspicacia.

vitascope [váitæscoup], s. proyector cinematográfico.

vitriolic [vitriólic], a. vitriólico; mordaz, sumamente hiriente, feroz.

vocal, a. vocinglero, voceador.

voltaic pencil, buril eléctrico.

vote, va.—**to v. down**, rechazar por votación.

W

wade, vn. meterse en agua baja y andar en ella (como hacen los niños); (gen. con **in** o **through**), andar con dificultad en (el lodo, etc.); terminar con dificultad o con tedio.

wainscot, s. friso inferior.

wake, s.—**in the w. of**, tras; inmediatamente después de.

walk, s. andador, callecilla; plantación de árboles en hileras.—**w. of life**, clase social; oficio, ocupacion.

walkaway [uókœuéi], s. triunfo fácil, ganga.

wall, s.—**w. tile**, azulejo.—**to drive, push**, o **thrust, to the w.**, poner en calzas prietas, acosar.—**to go to the w.**, verse o hallarse acosado, o en calzas prietas; verse obligado a ceder.

wallboard [uólbórd], s. tabla de fibra comprimida para revestir paredes.

war, s.—**w. baby,** hijo natural de un soldado, engendrado en los campamentos; ganga debida a la guerra.—**w. head,** punta o cabeza de un torpedo, en la cual van los explosivos.

wardrobe trunk, baúl ropero, baúl cuelgarropa.

warmonger [uórmóngœr], s. atizador de la guerra.

washable [uóshæbœl], a. que puede lavarse.

washbasin, s. lavamanos.

wash sale, venta ficticia.

wastage, s. desperdicio; material desechado.

waste mold, molde transitorio, gen. de yeso, que se usa una vez y luego se rompe.

wastrel, s. botarate; holgazán; persona o animal enclenques.

watch, va.—**to w. one's step,** tener cuidado, andarse con tiento.

water. I. s.—**above w.,** fuera de la dificultad o del aprieto, salvo.—**in deep w.,** en dificultades, en aprietos. II. a. acuático; de agua; para agua; en el agua.—**w. bag,** redecilla, segundo estómago.— **w. carriage,** transporte por agua; conducción de agua; zanja de desagüe.—**w. carrier,** barco u otro artificio para transporte por agua; tubería o depósito de abastecimiento de agua.—**w. column,** columna de agua; indicador del nivel del agua; (f. c.) depósito de alimentación del ténder.—**w. heater,** calentador de agua; aparato de calefacción por agua.—**w. hole,** charco, charca; manantial (en el desierto).—**w. horse,** (zool.) hipocampo, caballo marino.—**w. line,** orilla del agua.—**w. plane,** (aer.) hidroavión.—**w. seal,** cierre hidráulico, agua de obturación.—**to be, o go, on the w. wagon,** abstenerse del licor, no beber.

watercraft [uótœrcræft], s. barcos, embarcaciones en general.

waterlogged [uótœrlógd], a. =WATER-LOGGED.

watertight [-táit], a. hermético, estanco.

way, s. situación, estado; razón, causa.—**all the w.,** en todo el camino; en todo; del todo; hasta el fin; (gen. con **in, out, to**) hasta.—**in the w. of,** para impedir o estorbar; que impide o estorba.— **the other w. around,** al contrario, al revés.

weather-worn, a. gastado o deteriorado por la intemperie, o por los agentes atmosféricos.

wedge, s.—**entering w.,** comienzo, entrada; (cambiando el giro) para abrir brecha.

weedy, a. flacucho; malparado, maltrecho; inservible, inútil.

week, s.—**w. end,** vacación del fin de semana.— **w.-end,** vn. pasar el fin de la semana; salir de vacación o ir a descansar durante el fin de la semana.—**w.-ender,** s. el que sale, o tiene costumbre de salir, de vacación durante el fin de la semana.

welding, a.—**w. blowpipe,** soplete de soldar.— **w. rod,** varilla de soldar, o de soldadura.—**w. torch,** lámpara de soldar; soplete de soldar.

well. I. s. receptáculo; cañón (de pluma fuente); canal (de llanta). II. adv.—**and w. he (we,** etc.) **may, o might (be),** y con razón.—**It is all very w. to** (antes de infinitivo), fácil es.

welsh, va. y vn. no cumplir; no pagar; alzarse con el santo y la limosna; engañar, estafar.—**welsher** [uélshœr], s. estafador, pícaro.

what. I. pron.—**w. about,** qué diremos de, qué opina Vd. de, qué le parece, qué hay de, qué hay en cuanto a, etc. (Gen. se cambia el giro.)—**w. about it?** ¿y eso qué importa?—**w. all, w. not,** qué sé yo qué más.—**w. is w.,** lo que hay; cuántas son cinco. II. a. lo, el, la, los, las.

wheeze, s. chiste viejo, cuento viejo.

whiffet [juffet], s. pelagatos, nulidad.

whip. I. s. latigazo; malacate o izador de caballos; caspiroleta, huevos batidos con leche; aspa de molino de viento; vibración; movimiento circular de vaivén; perrero, el encargado de mantener juntos los perros; exhortador, llamador. II. va. enrollar; reunir; mantener juntos.—**to w. in,** reunir, hacer juntar; mantener juntos.—**to w. into shape,** poner en debida forma o en forma final.

whisk broom, escobilla; cepillo de escoba.

white. I. s. monarquista; reaccionario, antirrevolucionario; centro del blanco (a que se tira); espacio en blanco. II. a. monarquista; antirrevolucionario.—**w. bronze,** bronce claro, rico en estaño.—**w. city,** lugar de diversiones.—**w. collar,** a. que no es obrero (dícese generalmente de los dependientes, empleados de oficina, agentes, etc.).—**w.-faced,** pálido; cariblanco.—**w. feather,** cobardía o señal de cobardía.—**w. gold,** aleación blanquizca de oro.—**w. paper,** informe oficial.

who, pron.—**as w. should say, as w. saith,** como quien dice.

whoopee [júpi], s. gran parranda, jolgorio; diversión.

wicking [uíking], s. mechas; material para mechas; material fibroso trenzado o torcido.

wielder [uíldœr], s. esgrimidor.

wildcat, s. pozo (de petróleo) de prueba o de exploración; locomotora sin vehículos.

willies [uíliş], s. pl. ataque de nervios; pavor, miedo pánico.

wind, s.—**w. brace,** contraviento, pieza de refuerzo contra el viento.—**w. bracing,** contravientos.

windshield, s. (aut.) guardabrisa, parabrisa.

winery, s. fábrica vinícola; bodega de vino.

wipe, va.—**to w. off the slate,** cancelar la cuenta; cancelar los planes o el programa anteriores para empezar de nuevo; mudar la hoja, cambiar de plan o de intento.—**to w. out,** suprimir; aniquilar; agotar.—**to w. the slate clean** = TO W. OFF THE SLATE.

wiper, s. (aut.) limpiavidrio del guardabrisa.

wire, s.—**w. glass,** vidrio armado con tela de alambre, la cual va encajada en el vidrio para reforzarlo e impedir que los fragmentos se caigan si el vidrio se rompe.—**w. rod,** varilla para alambre. —**w. rope,** cable de alambres.—**w. wheel,** pulidor o limpiador giratorio de alambre.

wireman [uáiœrmæn], **wirer** [uáiœrœr], s. (elec.) montador o tendedor de alambres de distribución; armador de trampas de alambre.

wisecrack [uáişcŕæk], s. agudeza, dicho u observación agudos.

wisecracker [-œr], s. decidor de agudezas.

wishful thinking, creencia deseada, o movida por el deseo, creer en lo que se desea, racionalización de la esperanza.

withheld [uiþjéld], pret. y pp. de TO WITHHOLD.

withstood [-stúd], pret. y pp. de TO WITHSTAND.

woman of the street, mujer de mala vida.

womenfolk [uímenfóuc], s. las mujeres.

wood. I. s.—**w. cement,** cola de alcohol (aglutinante disuelto en alcohol) para madera.—**w. turner,** torneador.—**w. turning,** arte de tornear. —**to be out of the wood(s),** haber salido de la dificultad, estar a salvo. II. a. de madera; para madera; de monte.

woodenhead [údenjéd], s. zopenco, imbécil.

woodworker [úduœrkœr], s. carpintero, ebanista; artífice que labra madera.

woodsy [údşi], a. selvático.

word, s.—**in so many words,** en esas mismas palabras, exactamente así; claramente, sin ambages.—**in the words of,** según las palabras de, como dice.—**in w.,** de palabra.—**the W.,** (bib.) el Verbo; la Escritura.—**to have words,** tener palabras, reñir de palabra.—**too . . . for words.** (V. TOO.)

work. I. s.—**at w.,** trabajando; funcionando.— **out of w.,** sin trabajo, sin empleo. II. va. pagar (por) con (en) trabajo.—**to w. in,** hacer entrar, meter.—**to w. it,** manejar las cosas, darse trazas.— **to w. one's way through,** pagar uno con su trabajo los gastos de.

workability, s. trabajabilidad; viabilidad.

workaday, a. ordinario, cuotidiano, de cada día; prosaico, árido, escueto.

worsen [uœrsen] va. y vn. empeorar(se).

worsening [-ing], s. empeoramiento.

worser [uœrsœr], a. y adv. peor.

worst, s.—**the w. is yet to come,** aún falta lo peor.—**the w. way,** muchísimo.

wowser [uáuŝœr], *s.* puritano quisquilloso; fariseo, formalista.

wrinkle, *s.* maña; idea, ocurrencia; indicio, insinuación.

write, *va.*—**to w. in,** o **into,** insertar o incorporar en.—**to w. off,** cancelar, saldar.—**to w. up,** narrar, relatar; describir.

write-up, *s.* bombo, escrito encomiástico.

writing, *s.*—**at the present,** o **at this, w.,** al tiempo que esto se escribe, ahora mismo.

wrong, *a.* censurable, represible; inicuo.

Y, Z

Y, *s.* Asociación Cristiana de los Jóvenes (erróneamente llamada Asociación de los Jóvenes Cristianos).

Yankeedom [yǽnkidum], *s.* tierra de los yanquis; los yanquis.—**Yankeeism** [-ism], yanquismo.—**Yankeeland,** *s.* Yanquilandia (apl. a la Nueva Inglaterra y a los E. U.).

yardstick, *s.* patrón, modelo; criterio.

yawmeter [yómítœr], *s.* (aer.) goniómetro de derrape, medidor de ángulos de derrape.

year of grace, year of our Lord, año de gracia.

yellow-dog money, moneda sin valor; billetes de un *wildcat bank.* (V. WILDCAT.)

yes-man [yésmæn], *s.* hombre servil, que obedece ciegamente.

yogi [yóugui], *s.* yogi, asceta de la India.

zebrass [ŝíbræss], *s.* híbrido nacido de cebra y burro.

zipper [ŝípoer], *s.* abrochador de corredera, apretador de corredera; bota o zapato que lo lleva. (Como éste es nombre de fábrica, puede adoptarse en español la forma *ziper*.)

zone. I. *s.* distrito, sección, territorio; zona, división, sección de una ciudad. **II.** *va.* dividir en zonas o secciones.

zoolater [ŝoólætœr], *s.,* **zoolatrous** [-trus], *a.* zoólatra.

zoolith [ŝóoliz], *s.* (geol.) zoolito.

zymogenesis [ŝáimoyénesis], *s.* (quím.) fermentación.

zymogenic [-nic], *a.* que produce fermentación.

Para la pronunciación de æ, œ, ᴅ, ŝ, ŝh, ᴜ, ȳ, ʏ, z, véase la clave al principio del libro.

APPLETON'S NEW

English-Spanish and Spanish-English

DICTIONARY

CONTAINING MORE THAN SIX THOUSAND MODERN WORDS AND TWENTY-
FIVE THOUSAND ACCEPTATIONS, IDIOMS AND TECHNICAL TERMS
NOT FOUND IN ANY OTHER SIMILAR WORK: WITH A PRO-
NOUNCING KEY AND THE FUNDAMENTAL TENSES
OF IRREGULAR VERBS

BY

ARTURO CUYÁS

Revised and enlarged

BY

ANTONIO LLANO

THIRD EDITION, WITH SUPPLEMENTS

D. APPLETON–CENTURY COMPANY

INCORPORATED

NEW YORK   LONDON

1942

PART II

SPANISH–ENGLISH

PARTE II

ESPAÑOL–INGLÉS

PART II
SPANISH-ENGLISH

PARTE II
ESPAÑOL-INGLÉS

PREFACE TO THE FIRST EDITION

In the compilation of this work the endeavor has been to produce in a compact volume that may be conveniently used by students, travelers, and business men a complete and accurate vocabulary of the Spanish language.

With this end in view, and for the purpose of including all the modern words with which the language has been enriched through a general advancement in human knowledge and activity, the thirteenth edition (1899) of the Dictionary of the Royal Spanish Academy—which is the latest and highest authority in Spanish lexicography—has been adopted as a groundwork, and every word, every acceptation, every idiom contained in that dictionary, with the exception of those that have become archaic, is defined in this volume.

Furthermore, many words and acceptations have been added which, while not purely Castilian, are in general use in Spanish-American countries and in the Philippine Islands, and also a great number of technical terms that are frequently used in commercial intercourse between Spanish- and English-speaking countries. Indeed, this rapidly increasing intercourse, and the ties that now bind to the United States several million people whose vernacular is the Spanish language, have been kept steadily in view during the preparation of the work, which is intended to be as helpful to the American or English student of Spanish as to the great number of Spaniards who are now studying English.

To accomplish this purpose, a radical departure has been made from the practice adopted in many dictionaries of giving long explanations in English of the meaning of a Spanish word, instead of supplying the student with the English equivalents. A bilingual dictionary, like a good rule, should work both ways, and to do this it should give equivalents rather than definitions.

Numberless examples might be cited here to show the laborious task implied in the search for correct equivalents, especially as regards technical terms, many of which are either omitted or erroneously translated in other dictionaries.

All the dictionaries of the Spanish and English languages, and especially those by Velázquez, Gray and Iribas, Lopes and Bensley, Ponce de León, Bustamante, Tolhausen, Wellesley and Gironés, have been frequently consulted and compared in the course of compilation, and acknowledgment is hereby made for valuable suggestions found in them.

Many new features, however, and thousands of words and acceptations not found in any similar work, have been introduced here, as any one may verify by careful comparison of a single page of this book with the corresponding page in any other dictionary. As illustrative examples of the exhaustiveness of this compilation, the reader is referred to such words as *a, de, con, por, que, le, se, nos, ese, uno; dar, hacer, coger, estar, correr, echar, ser, salir, seguir, poner, tirar, ver, venir; llave, medio, fuerza, ropa, tiro, título, viga, vida.*

One special feature will no doubt commend itself to students as a help toward the proper use of irregular verbs. The fundamental tenses of such verbs, from which other modes are formed, are given with each infinitive, as well as the literal mutations that some regular verbs undergo in some tenses.

In order to save space for more important matter, the pronunciation usually given for each word has been dispensed with, except in a few cases where some difficult word occurs; but as the Spanish pronunciation is simple, the few rules given in the following pages, explanatory of a comprehensive key placed at the foot of each page, should enable the student to pronounce any word correctly.

ARTURO CUYÁS.

NEW YORK, *July,* 1903.

PREFACE TO THE NEW EDITION

The main features distinguishing the new from the first edition are briefly stated below:

General Changes. In a great many respects, this edition is practically a new book. While, broadly speaking, the general plan of the author has been preserved, many important modifications, affecting both the form and the substance of the text, have been made. As was to be expected in the first edition of a work so arduous and comprehensive, requiring so much patient labor and scrupulous attention to minute and often very nice details, Cuyás fell into some errors and overlooked other defects, more or less serious, which the reviser has endeavored to correct. The large number of unusual English words and awkward expressions that the author no doubt took inadvertently from his predecessors have been replaced by forms that will look and sound more familiar and natural to the English-speaking reader. Many Spanish idiomatic phrases and sentences, which the author renders by bare explanations or long circumlocutions, have been translated by corresponding English idioms, where they exist. As examples, the following may be mentioned:

First edition	*New edition*
quemarse las cejas, to study with intense application.	**quemarse las cejas,** to burn the midnight oil.
meter su cuchara, (coll.) to join in other people's conversation.	**meter su cuchara,** (coll.) to put one's oar in, to butt in.
estar en capilla, to prepare for death, spoken of criminals.	**estar en capilla,** to be in the death house awaiting execution.

In the first edition, several nouns are given as adjectives, transitive verbs as intransitive, and vice versa. This oversight has been rectified. With regard to the grammatical functions of words, a convenient change has been made in the present edition: the equivalents of every word that can belong to more than one part of speech have been classed into corresponding groups headed by bold-faced Roman numerals. This facilitates considerably the work of locating any desired equivalent, as the numerals stand out conspicuously. Furthermore, all phrases beginning with a word that heads an article are given under the appropriate part of speech, and are, besides, arranged in alphabetical order. This order, although obviously natural, is seldom followed in

the first edition.   Care has been taken to give all the general meanings of each word taken by itself before giving the phrases, instead
of interspersing some of the phrases amidst the equivalents of the
single word, as is occasionally done in the first edition.   In order to
save space, only the initial of the chief word is given in the phrases.
This conforms to the method adopted in the leading dictionaries of the
English language.

To indicate the gender of nouns, a slight modification has been
introduced.   The notation *n.*, after a noun having but one ending,
indicates that the form given is used for both genders.   If the noun
has a special ending for the feminine, there can be, of course, no difficulty, since the feminine ending is always given after the masculine.

Many a Spanish word is used as both an adjective and a noun
(*n. & a.*).   In giving the English equivalent, the noun is given in
full, and the adjective often indicated by an appropriate ending, such
as "(-ing)."   Thus, "**creador,** *n. & a.* creator (-ing)" means that the
English adjective corresponding to the Spanish is *creating*.   In some
cases, an English noun is given as the equivalent of a Spanish adjective, but with the notation "(ú. a.)," which means "used adjectively,"
as most English nouns frequently are.

Authorities and sources of information. For the English, the
latest edition of the *New International Webster* (to call it "Webster's"
is to abuse the possessive) has been taken as a standard and guide,
specially as regards the writing of compound words.   But, naturally,
the *Standard*, the *Century*, the *Oxford* and other leading dictionaries
have been frequently consulted.   It may be well to remark that the
English-Spanish part of this edition contains many technical, colloquial, industrial and other words and phrases, as *balloon tire, shimmy*
(as used in automobilism and dancing), *death house, working capital,
wet process, mass formation, second sheet, motor oil, special* (as applied
to pipe fittings), *spot welding, butt in, up against it, nothing doing, clamshell bucket, cement gun, extruded metal*, that are not yet found even in
the monumental dictionaries just mentioned.

For the Spanish, the latest (1925) edition of the Dictionary of the
Spanish Academy has of course been constantly kept before the reviser's eyes during his work, and practically every new word it contains
has been incorporated in the new edition of the Cuyás.   This edition,
however, would have been a sorry production had that lexicon been
the only source of information used, and so, all the other leading Spanish dictionaries, the great Spanish encyclopedias, and many books on
special subjects—history, economics, engineering, physics, radio

transmission, biology, medicine, etc.—have been consulted. Besides, a large number of words have been added derived from the reviser's general experience as a reader, writer and translator.

The Spanish Academy is a very conservative institution; it is slow in admitting into the language words of foreign or popular origin; and, perhaps in order to keep the bulk of its Dictionary within prescribed limits, it excludes from that work an exceedingly large percentage of the technical terms used in the language by all writers on the corresponding subjects, and many of them even in the daily press and in ordinary conversation. A bilingual dictionary of the Spanish and any other language, as the two languages are actually spoken and written, would fall far short of its purpose if, following the Academy, it omitted such words and phrases as **acelerador,** *accelerator, throttle;* **aspirina,** *aspirin;* **audión,** *audion;* **baseball,** *baseball;* **boxear,** *to box;* **boxeo,** *boxing;* **cianuración,** *cyaniding;* **energía cinética,** *kinetic energy;* **football, futbol,** *football;* **fuselaje,** *fuselage;* **garaje,** *garage;* **hangar,** *hangar;* **kilometraje,** *mileage;* **kilovatio,** *kilowatt;* **parabrisa,** *windshield;* **psicanálisis,** *psychoanalysis;* **Sociedad de las Naciones,** *League of Nations;* **soviet, soviético,** *soviet;* **tenis,** *tennis;* **tobogán,** *toboggan;* **tubo termiónico,** *thermionic valve;* **volante de dirección,** *steering wheel;* **palanca de mando,** (aer.) *control stick;* **antropoide,** *anthropoid;* **pitecántropo,** *pithecanthropus;* **psicofisiología,** *physiological psychology,* and hundreds — perhaps thousands — of others.

One who would present the living, dynamic Spanish language of to-day must seek other sources of information. For the Spanish tongue *is* dynamic, and at the present time is evolving rapidly. When progress rides the swift airplane and the flitting ether wave, the language can no longer travel on the back of the medieval ox, whose hoof is no doubt sure, but whose pace is too tardy.

Addition of words. It need hardly be stated that, since the main reason for preparing a new edition has been to bring the work of Cuyás up to date, all important new words have been added that the progress of the intervening time has brought with it. The number of such words is exceedingly large, on account of the varied and rapid advances in science, industry, and commerce, of the conditions that arose during the War and have arisen since as effects of it, and because also of the universal social effervescence of recent years, which has profoundly affected politics, economics, customs, sociology, pedagogics, psychology, and even ethics and theology. Besides these terms, several thousand words and phrases have been added that were excluded by Cuyás, doubtless for the purpose of reducing the bulk of the work as much as possible, but which, being of very great importance, should be included.

Among the words added may be mentioned many that either are used exclusively in some Spanish-American countries or denote things or conditions found only in one or several of those countries; the principal technical terms that have come into existence since the issuing of the first edition, such as those relating to automobilism, aviation, and radio communication; and many important old technical terms omitted by Cuyás.

The number of geographical and other proper nouns is about twice as large in this edition as in the first, practically all important historical names being given.

A new feature that deserves special mention is the introduction of a large number of examples serving to make clear the meanings and applications of difficult words, especially of those in which the grammatical construction differs in the two languages. See, for instance, the articles **aquello, antojarse, caber, haber, lo, que, si, sí, se, ser.**

Omissions and condensation.   It would have been impossible to make the additions mentioned without either increasing too much the bulk of the work or omitting some of the material in the first edition.   Naturally, the *substance* of this material could not be reduced without seriously impairing the thoroughness of the book.   The difficulty has been obviated by leaving out an immense number of synonyms and half synonyms that the author often gives as equivalents of one Spanish word, and the agglomeration of which, besides occupying valuable space with superfluous redundancy, is more likely to confuse than to help the translator.   Another way in which space has been saved is the replacing of many explanations and circumlocutions by precise equivalent words and phrases, where such exist.   Cuyás's plan of giving equivalents rather than definitions is excellent, at least from the view point of space and economy.   But, although generally adhering to it, he often adopted the system of simply translating from the Academy's Dictionary the various meanings of the Spanish word, heedless of the obvious fact that all these meanings are covered by one English word, and that such translations were but unnecessary explanations of the different meanings of that word.   Not infrequently, while intent on giving these superfluous and sometimes redundant explanations, he overlooked the main English equivalent, which by itself would have been sufficient.   Thus, under **deber,** he left out *duty*—the most important meaning; under **débil,** he overlooked *weak;* under **bote** he omitted *boat,* and *suffering* under **sufrimiento.**

The following examples will convey a clear idea of the simplifications and condensation just referred to:

First edition	Second edition
armadura, skeleton, frame of a roof.	**armadura,** roof truss.
característica, (math.) logarithmic number preceding the period that divides the decimal fraction.	**característica,** (math.) characteristic (of a logarithm).
catedrático, professor in a university or any other literary establishment.	**catedrático,** professor.
contraproducente, *a.* thing [*sic*] alleged contrary to what it is designed to prove.	**contraproducente,** *a.* self-defeating.
contravidriera, second glass window, to keep off cold or heat.	**contravidriera,** storm window.
cruel, *a.* cruel, hard-hearted, intolerable, insufferable; hard, oppressive, bloody, violent, murderous, merciless, fierce, fiendlike.	**cruel,** *a.* cruel; severe, intense (pain, cold, etc.).
desguince, twist of the body to escape a thrust.	**desguince,** dodging, dodge.
desinflar, to let out the air or fluid with which anything is inflated.	**desinflar,** to deflate.
religión, religion; faith, belief, creed; devotion, piety, worship; any system of religion.	**religión,** religion.
verbo defectivo, any verb of which only a few modes are used.	**verbo defectivo,** defective verb.

The reviser would state that in pointing out the shortcomings of the first edition, it has not been his intention to belittle it. They are such small blemishes as invariably occur in first editions of even simpler works, and neither did nor could impair the reputation of the Cuyás Dictionary as by far the best book of its kind.

The editors and the reviser hope that, with the foregoing major changes and many minor changes that cannot be conveniently specified here, the new edition will have a reception even better than that justly accorded to the first.

ANTONIO LLANO.

NEW YORK.

SPANISH PRONUNCIATION

The only way of learning the exact sounds of the Spanish letters is by hearing them. Several of the English equivalents given below are only approximations.

VOWELS

The Spanish vowels are **a, e, i, o, u,** and occasionally **y.** Each vowel has but one sound.

The sound of **a** is full, open, as in *far, father, farm, alarm*.

The sound of **e** is intermediate between long *a* in *mate* and short *e* in *met*. Those not familiar with it may pronounce it like English *a* in *any, many*, or like long English *a* as pronounced by many Irish people, who omit the vanishing *ee*-sound.

The sound of **i** is the same as in *police, machine*.

The sound of **o** is as in *for, order, lord, form*.

Spanish **u** is pronounced like English *oo* in *moon, food*. It is silent in the syllables *que, qui;* also in the syllables *gue, gui*, unless marked with a dieresis (*güe, güi*).

With the exception of *u* in the cases stated, no Spanish vowel is ever silent.

CONSONANTS

B, b has a softer sound than in English, produced by joining the lips, without pressure.

C, c, before *a, o, u*, or before another consonant, has the sound of the English *k*, as in *carro* (car), *costo* (cost), *cubo* (cube), *clase* (class), *crema* (cream), *acto* (act).

C, c, before *e, i*, has the sound of English *th* in *theft, thin*, as in **cinc,** which is pronounced *theenk*. However, in many parts of Spain and in Spanish America, **c** in these cases, is pronounced like Spanish *s* (*seenk*).

Ch, ch, like English *ch* in *cheese, riches*. It never has the sound of *k*, nor of *ch* in *machine*.

D, d is softer than in English. It is sounded by touching the edge of the upper teeth with the tip of the tongue. Between two vowels (**todo,** *all*) and at the end of a word (**usted,** *you*) it has the sound of English *th* in *weather, with, although*.

F, f, the same as in English.

G, g, before *a, o, u,* or before a consonant, has the sound of English *g* in *gas, go, gun, grand, ignorant.* Before *e, i,* it has the sound of Spanish *j*.

H, h is *always* silent. There is absolutely no exception to this rule.

J, j has a sound similar to English *h*, but very much more strongly aspirated, like *ch* in the English *loch* or the German *ach*.

K, k, as in English.

L, l, as in English.

Ll, ll is a special letter, which sounds very much like English *ll* in *million, brilliant,* or, more exactly, like the combination *ll-y* in *all year*.

M, m, as in English.

N, n, as in English.

Ñ, ñ, like *ny* in *canyon, ronyon*.

P, p, as in English.

Q, q, as in English. With the exception of a few words taken from the Latin, this letter occurs only in the combinations *que, qui,* in which the *u* is always silent.

R, r, between two vowels, has a sound usually likened to that of English *r* in *very*, but which perhaps is more like that of English *d* in *caddy* when very rapidly pronounced.*

When it begins a word, or is preceded by *l, n, s,* or when doubled (**rr**), it has a rolling or trilling sound, produced by vibrating the tip of the tongue with a strong expulsion of breath.

S, s has the sound of English *s* in *sassafras,* and no other.

T, t differs from English *t* in that it is sounded by placing the tip of the tongue between the teeth.

V, v, as in English, although practically everybody pronounces it like Spanish *b*.

X, x sounds like *ks* or *gs*, never like *sh*. In *México, mexicano* (written *Méjico, mejicano* in nearly all places outside of Mexico) and a few other words of Mexican origin, it is pronounced like Spanish *j*.

Y, y, when a consonant, sounds like English *y* in *year, young.* When it stands alone as a conjunction (meaning *and*), or is at the end of a word, it is a vowel, and has the sound of Spanish *i*.

Z, z has the sound of English *th* in *thick, thatch, thought.* However, in some parts of Spain and throughout Spanish America it is pronounced like Spanish *s* (English *s* in *less*).

---

* It has been my experience with American beginners in Spanish that when such words as *cara, dinero, tiro* are dictated to them, they almost invariably write them *cada, dinedo, tido,* unless they have previously seen them written.—A. Ll.

Rules of Accentuation

The vowels *a, e, o* are called *strong vowels,* while *i* and *u* are called *weak vowels.*

1. When a word has a vowel with an orthographic accent, that vowel is the emphatic vowel of the word.

2. When a word ends in a vowel, in *n* or in *s,* and has no accent mark, the emphasis falls on the penult. It should be remembered that, for the application of this rule, any combination of a strong and a weak vowel, or of the two weak vowels, is regarded as one vowel. Thus, the penult of **nadie,** is *na-;* that of **cadmio,** *cad-;* that of **fraile,** *frai-* (emphasis on *a*); that of **reuma,** *reu-* (emphasis on *e*).

3. In words ending in a consonant other than *n* and *s* and having no accent mark, the emphatic syllable is the last.

4. With the exception of adverbs ending in *-mente,* no Spanish word has more than one emphatic vowel. In adverbs in *-mente,* the adjectives from which they are formed preserve their original emphatic syllable, and the first *e* of the ending is also emphasized. Thus, **tristemente** (from *triste*), **útilmente** (from *útil*), are accented thus: *tris'temen' te, u'tilmen'te.*

BEAR IN MIND —

1. That **ch, ll and ñ** are independent letters, coming after **c, l** and **n** respectively. Therefore, all words or syllables beginning with **ch** come after all words or syllables beginning with **c,** and similarly for words and syllables beginning with **ll** or **ñ.**

2. That the ending **-ces** generally indicates the plural of nouns or adjectives ending in *z.* Thus, the meanings of **rapaces, voces** are found under *rapaz, voz.*

3. That regular verbs whose radical ends in **c** change this letter to **qu** before **e.** Thus, the infinitive corresponding to **convoqué, convoquemos** is **convocar.**

4. That regular verbs whose radical ends in **z** change this letter to **c** before **e.** Thus, the infinitive corresponding to **alcé, alcemos** is **alzar.**

5. That in regular verbs ending in **-ger** or **-gir** the **g** of the radical is changed to **j** before **a** or **o.** Thus, the infinitives of **escojo, dirija** are respectively **escoger, dirigir.**

6. That in some parts of Spanish America, mainly in Chile, **i** is used instead of **y,** both as a conjunction (*and*) and at the end of words (**rei** for **rey, voi** for **voy**).

IRREGULAR VERBS

The fundamental forms of irregular verbs are given both with the respective infinitives and in the places where they alphabetically belong in the body of the dictionary. The orthographical changes made in some regular verbs to preserve the pronunciation of the radical (see 3 and 4, above) are given with the corresponding infinitives.

ABBREVIATIONS

a.	. . . . .	adjective.
adv.	. . . . .	adverb.
(aer.)	. . . .	aeronautics.
(agr.)	. . . .	agriculture.
(alg.)	. . . .	algebra.
(Am.)	. . . .	(Spanish) America(n).
(anat.)	. . . .	anatomy.
(api.)	. . . .	apiculture.
(app.)	. . . .	applied.
(arch.)	. . . .	architecture.
(archeol.)	. . .	archeology.
(Arg.)	. . . .	Argentina(-ine).
(arith.)	. . . .	arithmetic.
(arm.)	. . . .	armor.
art.	. . . . .	article.
(artil.)	. . . .	artillery.
(ast.)	. . . .	astronomy.
(astrol.)	. . .	astrology.
aug.	. . . .	augmentative.
(aut.)	. . . .	automobiles (-ism).
(bact.)	. . . .	bacteriology.
(b. b.)	. . . .	bookbinding.
(bib.)	. . . .	Biblical.
(biol.)	. . . .	biology.
(Bol.)	. . . .	Bolivia(n).
(bot.)	. . . .	botany.
(C. A.)	. . . .	Central America(n).
(car.)	. . . .	carriage building.
(carp.)	. . . .	carpentry.
cf.	. . . . .	confer (compare).
(Ch.)	. . . .	Chile.
(ch. constr.)	. . .	change(-ing) the construction.
(chem.)	. . . .	chemistry.
(chron.)	. . .	chronology.
(coll.)	. . . .	colloquial.
(Colomb.)	. . .	Colombia.
(com.)	. . . .	commerce.
comp.	. . . .	comparative.
conj.	. . . .	conjunction.
(contempt.)	. . .	contemptuous(ly).
contr.	. . . .	contraction.
(cook.)	. . . .	cookery.
(cut.)	. . . .	cutlery.
(danc.)	. . . .	dancing.
def.	. . . .	definite.
defect.	. . . .	defective.
(dent.)	. . . .	dentistry.
dim.	. . . .	diminutive.
(dipl.)	. . . .	diplomacy.
(Ec.)	. . . .	Ecuador.
(ecc.)	. . . .	ecclesiastical.
(elec.)	. . . .	electricity.
(eng.)	. . . .	engineering.
(ent.)	. . . .	entomology.
f.	. . . . .	feminine (noun).
(f. a.)	. . . .	fine arts.
(falc.)	. . . .	falconry.
(far.)	. . . .	farriery.
(fenc.)	. . . .	fencing.
(fig.)	. . . .	figurative(ly).
(fort.)	. . . .	fortifications.
(found.)	. . . .	foundry.
fut.	. . . .	future.
(gen.)	. . . .	generally.
(geog.)	. . . .	geography.
(geol.)	. . . .	geology.
(geom.)	. . . .	geometry.
(gl.)	. . . .	glass.
(gram.)	. . . .	grammar.

(hat.)	. . . .	hat making.
(her.)	. . . .	heraldry.
(hum.)	. . . .	humorous.
(hyd.)	. . . .	hydraulics.
(icht.)	. . . .	ichthyology, fishes.
imp.	. . . .	imperfect.
impers.	. . . .	impersonal.
ind.	. . . .	indicative.
indef.	. . . .	indefinite.
inf.	. . . .	infinitive.
(int. comb. eng.)	. .	internal-combustion gines.
(int. l.)	. . . .	international law.
interj.	. . . .	interjection.
interr.	. . . .	interrogative.
(iron.)	. . . .	ironically.
irr.	. . . .	irregular, irregularity
(jewel.)	. . . .	jewelry.
(journ.)	. . . .	journalism.
(Lat.)	. . . .	Latin.
(lith.)	. . . .	lithography.
(log.)	. . . .	logic.
m.	. . . . .	masculine.
(mach.)	. . . .	machinery (noun).
(mas.)	. . . .	masonry.
(math.)	. . . .	mathematics.
(mech.)	. . . .	mechanics.
(med.)	. . . .	medicine.
(met.)	. . . .	metaphorical.
(metal.)	. . . .	metallurgy.
(Mex.)	. . . .	Mexico.
(mil.)	. . . .	military.
(mill.)	. . . .	milling.
(min.)	. . . .	mining, mineralogy.
(mus.)	. . . .	music.
mut.	. . . .	mutation of letters.
(m. w.)	. . . .	metal work.
n.	. . . . .	noun.
(naut.)	. . . .	nautical.
neut.	. . . .	neuter.
(obs.)	. . . .	obsolete.
(opt.)	. . . .	optics.
(ordn.)	. . . .	ordnance.
(orn.)	. . . .	ornithology, birds.
(pal.)	. . . .	paleontology.
(pap.)	. . . .	paper making.
(p. e.)	. . . .	political economy.
pers.	. . . .	personal.
(pharm.)	. . . .	pharmacy.
(Philip.)	. . . .	Philippine Islands.
(philos.)	. . . .	philosophy.
(phot.)	. . . .	photography.
(phys.)	. . . .	physics.
(physiol.)	. . .	physiology.
(pict.)	. . . .	pictorial art.
pl.	. . . . .	plural.
(poet.)	. . . .	poetry.
(pol.)	. . . .	politics.
(P. R.)	. . . .	Porto Rico.
poss.	. . . .	possessive.
pp.	. . . . .	past participle.
prep.	. . . .	preposition.
pret.	. . . .	preterit.
(print.)	. . . .	printing.
pron.	. . . .	pronoun.
(prov.)	. . . .	provincial.
(pyr.)	. . . .	pyrotechnics.
(rad.)	. . . .	radio (communication).
(rept.)	. . . .	reptile.
(rop.)	. . . .	rope making.

xvi

(r. w.)	railways.	
S. A.	South America(n).	
(sad).	saddlery.	
(sew.)	sewing.	
(shoe.)	shoemaking.	
sing.	singular.	
(s. o.).	said of.	
(sp.)	specially.	
(spt.)	sport.	
(st. eng.) . . .	steam engines.	
subj.	subjunctive.	
(sug. man.) . . .	sugar manufacture.	
super.	superlative.	
(surg.)	surgery.	
(surv.)	surveying.	
(tail.).	tailoring.	
(tan.).	tannery.	
(tech.)	technology.	

(tel.)	telegraphy.	
(theat.)	theater.	
(theol.)	theology.	
(u.)	used.	
(u. a.)	used adjectively.	
V.	Vide, See.	
v.	vide, see; verb.	
va.	verb active (transitive).	
(Ven.)	Venezuela(n).	
Vd.	(usted) you.	
(vet.).	veterinary.	
vn.	verb neuter (intransitive).	
vr.	verb reflexive.	
(vulg.)	vulgar, low.	
(w.)	with.	
(W. I.)	West Indies.	
(zool.)	zoology.	

A NEW BILINGUAL DICTIONARY

OF THE

SPANISH AND ENGLISH LANGUAGES

SPANISH–ENGLISH PART

Abbreviations and proper names are given at the end.

a, *f.* a (letter *a*).—**a por a y be por be,** point by point, minutely.

a, *prep.* (1) to, before the indirect object; also, to indicate direction, end, purpose, objective, destination, interval, limit, approval, etc.; e.g.: *dí el libro a Juan,* I gave the book to John; *voy a Madrid,* I am going to Madrid; *él me enseñó a leer,* he taught me (how) to read; *vine a verle,* I came to see him; *de once a doce,* from eleven to twelve; *con el agua a la cintura,* with water (up) to the waist; *a mi gusto,* to my taste; *a mi pesar,* to my regret. (2) at, to indicate location, rate or quantitative state, request, time, distance, command, etc.: *a la puerta,* at the door; *a dos pesos por kilo,* at two dollars per kilo; *con el termómetro a 30°,* with the thermometer at 30°; *a solicitud mía,* at my request; *a instancias de Vd.,* at your request; *a las dos y media,* at half past two; *a la vista,* at sight; *a dos millas de Lima,* (at) two miles from Lima; *a su disposición,* at your disposal; *a voluntad,* at will. (3) by, to indicate manner, instrument or means, repetition in a series or process, etc.: *a mano,* by hand; *a máquina,* by machine; *a fuerza bruta,* by brute force; *a cañón,* by the cannon; *a pedazos,* by pieces; *a súplicas,* by entreaties; *paso a paso,* step by step; *poco a poco,* little by little. (4) on, to indicate coexistence, and in several idiomatic phrases: *a mi llegada,* on my arrival; *al entrar,* on entering; *a bordo,* on board, aboard; *a caballo,* on horseback; *a pie,* on foot.—It forms many idioms, which in this dictionary are given under the words serving as its object in them.—Followed by an infinitive, it forms implicitly negative phrases rendered by *if* and the subjunctive: *a estar él aquí,* if he were here, were he here. If, in such phrases, the infinitive is preceded by *no,* the translation may be made by using "but for": *a no venir Juan,* but for John's coming, had not John come; *a no ser por Vd.,* but for you.—Followed by nouns denoting a material or instrument with which something is made or done, it forms phrases translated by using the corresponding English nouns adjectively: *cuadro al óleo,* oil painting; *dibujo a lápiz,* pencil drawing. This construction is commonly but improperly applied to denote the natural agent moving a machine, or some characteristic feature of an apparatus or another object: *máquina a* (properly, *de*) *vapor,* steam engine; *tubo al* (properly, *de*) *vacío,* vacuum tube; *motor a* (properly, *de*) *ocho cilindros,* eight-cylinder motor. Before proper nouns, nouns denoting persons, and occasionally before other nouns, in the accusative case, *a* is a mere symbol of that case, and is not translated: *amo a mi madre,* I love my mother; *oigo a Juan,* I hear John; *veo a Nueva York,* I see New York; *esta línea encuentra a la otra,* this line meets the other.

aarónico, aaronita, *a.* Aaronic, relating to or descended from Aaron.

aba, *m.* aba, a coarse woolen fabric.

ababa, *f.* **ababol,** *m.* poppy (= AMAPOLA).

ab absurdo, *adv.* (mat. & log.) ad absurdum.

abacá, *m.* (bot.) abaca; manila hemp; manila-hemp fabric.

abacería, *f.* grocery.

abacero, ra, *n.* grocer.

abacial, *a.* abbatial.

ábaco, *m.* abacus, calculating frame; (arch). abacus; (min.) washing trough.

abacómite, *m.* one belonging to a ruler's train or retinue.

abad, *m.* abbot.

abada, *f.* rhinoceros.

abadanar, *m.* to dress or finish like sheepskin.

abadejo, *m.* codfish; pollack. *V.* BACALAO. Spanish fly or blistering beetle; (orn.) kinglet or golden-crested wren.

abadengo, ga, *a.* abbatial.

abadernar, *va.* (naut.) to fasten with short ropes.

abadesa, *f.* abbess.

abadía, *f.* abbey.

abadiato, *m.* abbotship.

abajadero, *m.* slope, incline.

abajador, *m.* (min.) stable man; helper.

abajeño, ña, *a.* (Amer.) lowlander.

abajo, *adv.* under, underneath, below, down.—**venirse a.,** to fall.—**¡a. N.!** down with N.! **venirse a.,** to fall.

abalanzar. I. *va.* (*pret.* ABALANCÉ: *subj.* ABALANCE) to balance; to dart; to impel. **II.** *vr.* to rush impetuously; to venture.

abalaustrado, da, *a.* = BALAUSTRADO.

abaleador, ra, *n.* grain cleaner or separator.

abalear, *va.* to clean or separate (grain) from chaff after winnowing.

abaleo, *m.* (agr.) cleaning or separating grain.

abalizar. I. *va.* (*pret.* ABALICÉ: *subj.* ABALICE) (naut.) to lay buoys in. **II.** *vr.* (naut.) to take bearings.

abalorio, *m.* glass bead; beadwork.

aballestar, *va.* (naut.) to haul a cable.

abámeas, *f. pl.* (bot.) Abama.

abanar, *va.* to ventilate with fans.

abanderado, *m.* standard-bearer.

abanderar, *va.* to register (a ship).

abanderizador, ra, *n.* ringleader.

For pronunciation, see the rules at the beginning of the book.

abanderizar. I. *va.* (*pret.* ABANDERICE: *subj.* ABANDERICE) to organize in bands. **II.** *vr.* to band together.

abandonado, da, *a.* negligent, shiftless; slovenly.

abandonamiento, *m.* forlornness; slovenliness; lewdness, debauchery.

abandonar. I. *va.* to leave; to forsake; to give up. **II.** *vr.* to despond; to give one's self up to.

abandono, *m.* = ABANDONAMIENTO.

abanicar, *va.* (*pret.* ABANIQUÉ: *subj.* ABANIQUE) to fan.

abanicazo, *m.* blow with a fan.

abanico, *m.* fan; anything fan-shaped; (coll.) sword; (naut.) derrick; crane.—**en a.,** fanshaped.

abaniqueo, *m.* fanning; swinging motion; excessive gesturing in speaking.

abaniquero, ra, *n.* fanmaker; fan dealer.

abano, *m.* fan; hanging fan; ventilator.

abanto, *m.* African vulture.

abaratar. I. *va.* to cheapen; to abate. **II.** *vr.* to fall in price.

abarca, *f.* sandal worn by peasants and muleteers.

abarcado, da, *a.* sandaled; embraced, contained.

abarcador, ra, *n.* clasper; monopolist.

abarcadura, *f.* **abarcamiento,** *m.* embracing, comprising.

abarcar, *va.* (*pret.* ABARQUÉ: *subj.* ABARQUE) to clasp, embrace, contain; to comprise; to monopolize.

abarcón, *m.* a pole-ring in carriages; large iron clamp.

abarloar, *va.* (naut.) to bring alongside a ship or wharf.

abarquero, ra, *n.* maker or seller of *abarcas*.

abarquillado, da, *a.* rolled up; curled up.

abarquillamiento, *m.* curling up into a roll.

abarquillar, *va.* to curl up; to form into a roll.

abarracarse, *vr.* to go into barracks.

abarraganarse, *vr.* to live in concubinage.

abarrancadero, *m.* heavy road; precipice; difficult business.

abarrancamiento, *m.* fall into a pit; embarrassment.

abarrancar. I. *va.* (*pret.* ABARRANQUÉ: *subj.* ABARRANQUE) to ditch; to form a ravine. **II.** *vr.* to fall into a pit; to become embarrassed.

abarredera, *f.* broom, carpet sweeper; anything that sweeps and cleans.

abarrotar, *va.* to bar; to strengthen with bars; (naut.) to stow; to overstock.

abarrote, *m.* (naut.) a small package for filling up; stop-gap; (Mex.) retail grocery.

abarrotero, ra, *n.* (Mex.) retail grocer.

abarse, *vr.* (*defective, used only in the imperative:* ÁBATE, ABAOS) to move aside; to get out of the way.

abastamiento, *m.* providing; supplying with provisions, stores, etc.

abastar, *va.* = ABASTECER.

abastecedor, ra, *n.* caterer, provider, purveyor.

abastecer, *va.* (*ind.* ABASTEZCO: *subj.* ABASTEZCA) to purvey; supply.

abastecimiento, *m.* providing; supply; provisions, supplies.

abastionar, *va.* (fort.) to protect or fortify with bastions.

abasto, *m.* supply of provisions; (met.) anything abundant; (com.) supply.

abatanar, *va.* to beat or full (cloth).

abate, *m.* abbé.

abatidamente, *adv.* dejectedly.

abatido, da, *a.* dejected; discouraged; crestfallen; abject, mean; (com.) depreciated, fallen in price or demand.

abatimiento, *m.* depression, low spirits; lowering, falling; taking apart; (naut., aer.) drift, leeway.

abatir. I. *va.* to throw down, overthrow, knock down; fold down; humble, debase; discourage, dishearten; lower, strike (a flag, etc.); to dismount, take apart. **II.** *vn.* to descend; stoop.

III. *vr.* to be disheartened or depressed; (naut.) to have leeway; (aer.) to drift.

abazón, *m.* cheek pouch.

abdicación, *f.* abdication.

abdicar, *va.* (*pret.* ABDIQUÉ: *subj.* ABDIQUE) to abdicate.

abdomen, *m.* abdomen.

abdominal, *a.* abdominal.

abducción, *f.* (log. & mat.) abduction.

abductor, *m.* (anat.) abducent muscle.

abecé, *m.* a-b-c, alphabet; rudiments.

abecedario, *m.* alphabet; primer.

abedul, *m.* birch.

abeja, *f.* bee.—**a. machiega, maesa,** *or* **maestra,** queen bee.—**a. neutra,** *or* **obrera,** working bee, worker.—**a. reina,** queen bee.

abejar, *m.* beehive. *V.* COLMENAR.

abejarrón, abejorro, *m.* bumblebee.

abejaruco, abejeruco, *m.* (orn.) bee eater.

abejera, *f.* beehive; balmmint or beewort.

abejero, *m.* beekeeper.

abejón, *m.* drone.

abejorro, *m.* bumblebee.

abejuno, na, *a.* relating to the bee.

abelmosco, *m.* (bot.) abelmosk.

abellacado, da, *a.* mean-spirited.

abellacarse, *vr.* to degrade one's self.

abellotado, da, *a.* acorn-shaped.

abencerraje, *n.* one of the Abencerrages.

aberenjenado, da, *a.* eggplant-shaped or -colored.

aberración, *f.* aberration, error, mania; (phys. & astr.) aberration.

aberrugado, da, *a.* warty.

abertal. I. *s.* crack; small opening. **II.** *a.* easily cracked or cleft.

abertura, *f.* aperture; opening; cleft, crevice, fissure; gap.

abestiado, da, *a.* beast-like.

abetal, *m.* fir wood or grove.

abete, *m.* hook for holding cloth while shearing it; (bot.) silver fir.

abetina, *f.* (chem.) abietin.

abetinote, *m.* fir-tree rosin.

abeto, *m.* (bot.) silver tree; yew-leaved fir; spruce; hemlock.

abetuna, *f.* fir-tree sprout.

abetunado, da, *a.* bitumen-like.

abetunar, *va.* = EMBETUNAR.

abey, *m.* jacaranda; (Cuba) a hard-wood tree.

abiertamente, *adv.* frankly, openly.

abierto, ta, *a.* open, clear; sincere, candid, frank, outspoken; full-blown.—*pp. irr.* of ABRIR.

abietina, *f.* = ABETINA.

abietíneas, *f. pl.* (bot.) plants forming the genus Abies (firs).

abigarrado, da, *a.* variegated, motley.

abigarrar, *va.* to paint with various ill-matched colours; to fleck.

abigeato, *m.* (law) cattle stealing.

abigeo, *m.* (law) cattle thief.

abigotado, da, *a.* having a heavy mustache.

abinicio, ab initio, from the beginning.

abintestato. I. *adv.* intestate. **II.** *a.* neglected, unprotected.

abintestato, *m.* legal adjudication of an intestate estate.

abiótico, ca, *a.* not life-producing or life-supporting.

abiselar, *va.* to bevel.

abisinio, a, *n.* & *a.* Abyssinian.

abismado, da, *a.* dejected, depressed; absorbed in profound meditation.

abismal. I. *a.* abyssal. **II.** *m.* clasp nail, shingle nail.

abismar. I. *va.* to depress, humble, destroy. **II.** *vr.* to think or feel deeply.

abismo, *m.* abyss; gulf; chasm; hell.

abitadura, *f.* (naut.) a turn of the cable around the bitts.

abitaque, *m.* joist.

abitar, *va.* (naut.) to bitt.
abitas, *m. pl.* (naut.) bitts.—**a. del molinete,** carrick bitts.
abitones, *m. pl.* topsail sheet bitts.
abizcochado, da, *a.* biscuit-shaped.
abjuración, *f.* abjuration, recantation.
abjurar, *va.* to abjure, retract under oath.
ablación, *f.* ablation.
ablactación, *f.* weaning.
ablactar, *va.* to wean.
ablandabrevas, *m. & f.* (coll.) good-for-nothing.
ablandador, ra, *m. & f.* mollifier.
ablandahigos, *m. & f.* (coll.) good-for-nothing.
ablandamiento, *m.* softening, mollification.
ablandar, *va. & vn.* to soften, mellow, relent; to loosen; to assuage, mitigate, melt, soothe.
ablandativo, va, *a.* mollifying.
ablanedo, *m.* hazel-nut or filbert plantation.
ablano, *m.* filbert.
ablativo, *m. & a.* (gram.) ablative.
ablepsia, *f.* ablepsia, lack of sight; loss of the mental powers.
ablución, *f.* ablution.
abnegación, *f.* abnegation, self-denial.
abnegar, *va.* (*ind.* ABNIEGO: *subj.* ABNIEGUE) to renounce, to deny one's self.
abobado, da, *a.* stultified, silly.
abobamiento, *m.* stupefaction, stupidity.
abobar. I. *va.* to stupefy. **II.** *vr.* to grow stupid.
abocado, *a.* mild, agreeable (s. o. wine).
abocamiento, *m.* approachment; meeting, interview.
abocar (*pret.* ABOQUÉ; *subj.* ABOQUE). **I.** *va.* to bring near; to draw in place (as cannon); to open the mouth of (a bag); to decant; to seize with the mouth. **II.** *vr.* to meet by appointment. **III.** *vn.* (man.) to occupy the mouth of, or enter, a channel, straight, etc.
abocardado, da, *a.* bell-mouthed.
abocardar, *va.* to widen or expand (a tube, hole, etc.); to ream.
abocardo, *m.* large drill.
abocetado, da, *a.* unfinished, rough (s. o. pictures).
abocinar, *va.* to shape like a trumpet.
abochornado, da, *a.* out of countenance, flushed, mortified.
abochornar. I. *va.* to overheat; to shame, to embarrass. **II.** *vr.* to blush, to become embarrassed; (agr.) to wilt or become diseased from excessive heat.
abofeteador, ra, *m. & f.* buffeter; one who insults or strikes.
abofetear, *va.* to slap; to insult.
abogacía, *f.* profession of a lawyer; law (as a subject or profession).
abogada, *f.* mediatrix; lawyer's wife.
abogado, *m.* lawyer, barrister; mediator.—**a. de secano,** quack lawyer; charlatan.
abogar, *vn.* (*pret.* ABOGUÉ: *subj.* ABOGUE) to advocate, plead; to intercede.
abolengo, *m.* ancestry, lineage; inheritance.
abolición, *f.* abolition, abrogation, extinction.
abolicionista, *m.* abolitionist.
abolir, *va. and defective (only those modes and persons are used having the letter i in their terminations)* to abolish; revoke, repeal.
abolsado, da, *a.* puckered, purse-shaped; having or forming pockets.
abollado, a. & m. = ALECHUGADO.
abolladura, *f.* unevenness, dent, embossment; bruise.
abollar, *va.* to emboss; to dent; to stun and confound; to bruise.
abollonar, *va.* to emboss.
abombar, *va.* to give a convex form to; to deafen, to confuse.
abominable, *a.* abominable, execrable.
abominación, *f.* abomination, detestation, execration.
abominar, *va.* to abominate, abhor.

abonado, da. I. *m. & f.* subscriber; commuter. **II.** *a.* reliable; apt, inclined; rich; fit.
abonador, ra, *m. & f.* (comm.) surety or security for a principal, person responsible for one who himself acts as surety; barrel maker's augur.
abonamiento, *m.* = ABONO; bail, security.
abonanzar, *vn.* (*impersonal verb: subj.* ABONANCE) to grow calm, clear up.
abonar. I. *va.* to bail; to improve; to guarantee, indorse, answer for; to manure; to give credit; (com.) to credit with, to put to the credit. (of a person). **II.** *vr.* to subscribe; to buy a season or commutation ticket. **III.** *vn.* = ABONANZAR.
abonaré, *m.* promissory note; due-bill.
abono, *m.* security, guarantee; subscription; allowance, discount; receipt, voucher; manure, fertilizer.
abordador, *m.* (naut.) boarder; intruder.
abordaje, *m.* (naut.) the act of boarding a ship.
abordar. I. *va.* (naut.) to board a ship; to run foul of a ship. **II.** *vn.* to put into a port.
abordo, *m.* = ABORDAJE.
aborigen. I. *a.* aboriginal. **II.** *m. pl.* (**aborígenes**) aborigines.
aborrascarse, *vr.* to become stormy.
aborrecedor, ra, *m. & f.* detester, hater.
aborrecer, *va.* (*ind.* ABORREZCO: *subj.* ABORREZCA) to hate, abhor; to desert (s. o. birds.)
aborrecible, *a.* hateful; abhorrent.
aborrecimiento, *m.* abhorrence, hate; dislike, grudge.
aborrezco. *V.* ABORRECER.
abortamiento, *m.* abortion.
abortar, *vn.* to miscarry, abort; to fail; (med.) to abort (a disease).
abortivamente, *adv.* abortively; inopportunely.
abortivo, va, *a.* abortive; producing abortion
aborto, *m.* miscarriage, abortion; monstrosity.
abortón, *m.* the abortion of a quadruped; unborn lamb's skin.
aborujar. I. *va.* to make lumps. **II.** *vr.* to muffle up.
abotagarse, *vr.* to become bloated.
abotinado, da, *a.* shaped like a gaiter.
abotonador, *m.* button-hook.
abotonar. I. *va.* to button. **II.** *vn.* to bud; germinate.
abovedado, da, *a.* arched, vaulted.
abovedar, *va.* to arch, to vault.
aboyado, da, *a.* with oxen.
aboyar, *va.* (naut.) to lay buoys.
abozalar, *va.* to muzzle.
abra, *f.* bay, haven; cove, creek; dale, valley; fissure, gorge.
abracadabra, *m.* abracadabra.
abracé. *V.* ABRAZAR.
abracijo, *m. dim.* (coll.) an embrace, a hug.
abrahonar, *va.* (coll.) to hold one fast by the garment.
abrasador, ra, *a.* burning, exceedingly hot.
abrasamiento, *m.* taking fire, burning; excess of passion.
abrasar. I. *va.* to burn; fire; to squander; to dry up; to provoke. **II.** *vr.* to glow; to be agitated by any violent passion.
abrasión, *f.* (geol. & med.) abrasion.
abrazadera. I. *f.* clasp, clamp, band, cleat; (print.) brace or bracket {. **II.** *a.* V. SIERRA ABRAZADERA.
abrazador, ra, *n.* embracer; bolster used in the Philippines.
abrazamiento, *m.* embracing.
abrazar, *va.* (*pret.* ABRACÉ: *subj.* ABRACE) to embrace, hug; to clasp, clamp, cleat; to contain, comprise; to surround; to accept, follow; to take charge of.
abrazo, *m.* hug, embrace.
ábrego, *m.* southwest wind.
abrenuncio, (Lat.) far be it from me; fie!
abrevadero, *m.* watering place for cattle, drinking trough.

abrevador, *m.* he who waters cattle; waterer.

abrevar, *va.* to water cattle; to irrigate; to soak skins.

abreviación, *f.* abbreviation; abridgment; shortening; contraction; reduction; acceleration; hastening.

abreviadamente, *adv.* briefly, summarily.

abreviador, ra. I. *m. & f.* one who abridges or shortens. **II.** *m.* (ecc.) abbreviator (Vatican officer).

abreviaduría, *f.* office of the pontifical abbreviator.

abreviador, ra, *m. & f.* abridger; abbreviator.

abreviamiento, *m.* = ABREVIACION.

abreviar, *va.* to abridge; abbreviate; hasten.

abreviatura, *f.* abbreviation; contraction; shorthand.—**en a.,** in abbreviation; (coll.) hastily.

abreviaturía, *f.* = ABREVIADURÍA.

abribonarse, *vr.* to become lazy, to loaf; to become a rascal.

abridero. I. *m.* a variety of freestone peach. **II.** *a.* easily opened; freestone, freeshell.

abridor, *m.* (bot.) nectarine, peach tree; opener; grafting knife; eardrop or wire to keep the ears pierced.—**a. de guantes,** glove stretcher.—**a. de láminas,** engraver.—**a. de latas,** can opener.— **a. en hueco,** die sinker.

abrigadero, *m.* sheltered place, shelter.

abrigaño, *m.* a place sheltered from the wind.

abrigar. I. *va.* to shelter, protect; to cover; to warm; to lodge; to patronize; (met.) to nourish; to cherish. **II.** *vr.* to take shelter; to cover one's self; to put on a wrap.

abrigo, *m.* shelter; protection; overcoat; wrap; aid, support; cover; (naut.) harbor, haven.— **al a. de,** sheltered from; under protection of, shielded by.

abril, *m.* April.—*pl.* (met.) years.—**estar hecho,** or **parecer, un a.,** to be dressed up, to look very smart, or very smartly dressed.—**los dieciséis abriles,** sweet sixteen.

abrileño, ña, *a.* April (u. a.), relating to, or like, April.

abrillantar, *va.* to cut a diamond into facets; to make sparkle; to impart brilliance; to glace, polish, brighten.

abrimiento, *m.* opening; cracking.

abrir. I. *va.* (*pp.* ABIERTO) to open, unlock, unfasten, uncover, unseal; to engrave; to expand, separate, distend; cut open, cleave; rend; dig.—**a. los cimientos,** to dig the foundation trenches. **II.** *vn.* to open; unfold; extend; display. **III.** *vr.* to open, expand; to chink, crack, cleave, yawn; (met.) to unbosom one's self.

abrochador, *m.* buttoner; buttonhook.

abrochadura, *f.,* **abrochamiento,** *m.* lacing, fastening, buttoning.

abrochar, *va.* to clasp, buckle, button, fasten with hooks and eyes.

abrogación, *f.* abrogation, repeal.

abrogar, *va.* (*pret.* ABROGUÉ: *subj.* ABROGUE) to abrogate, annul, repeal.

abrojal, *m.* thistly ground.

abrojín, *m.* purple shell.

abrojo, *m.* (bot.) thistle, thorn, prickle; (mil.) caltrop; crowfoot; thorny appendage to a scourge.—*pl.* hidden rocks in the sea.

abromado, da. I. (naut.) hazy, foggy; worm-eaten. **II.** *pp.* of ABROMARSE.

abromarse, *vr.* (naut.) to be worm-eaten.

abroquelar. I. *va.* (naut.) to boxhaul. **II.** *vr.* to shield one's self.

abrótano, *m.* (bot.) southernwood.

abrumador, ra, *a.* overwhelming, crushing; wearisome.

abrumar. I. *va.* to crush, overwhelm, oppress; to weary, annoy. **II.** *vr.* to become foggy; to worry.

abrupto, ta, *a.* abrupt; craggy, rugged.

abrutado, da, *a.* brutish, bestial.

abruzo, za, *a. & n.* Abruzzian.

absceso *m.* abscess.

abscisa, *f.* abscissa.

abscisión, *f.* (med.) incision.

absentismo, *m.* absenteeism.

ábside, *m.* or *f.* (arch.) presbytery.

absintina, *f.* (chem.) absinthin.—**absintismo,** *m.* (med.) absinthism.

absit, *interj.* (Lat.) God forbid!

absolución [ab-so-loo-the-on'], *f.* absolution; pardon, acquittal.—**a. de la demanda,** finding for the defendant.—**a. libre,** verdict of not guilty, acquittal.

absoluta, *f.* dogmatic assertion, ipse dixit, dictum.—**absolutamente,** *adv.* absolutely.

absolutismo, *m.* despotism, absolutism.

absolutista, *n.* absolutist.

absoluto, ta, *a.* absolute, unconditional; imperious, despotic.

absolutorio, a, *a.* absolutory, absolving.

absolver, *va.* (*pp.* ABSUELTO: *ind.* ABSUELVO: *subj.* ABSUELVA) to absolve; to acquit.

absorbción, *f.* absorption.

absorbencia, *f.* absorbing, absorption; absorbency.

absorbente, *m. & a.* absorbent (-ing).

absorber, *va.* (*pp.* ABSORBIDO, ABSORTO) to absorb; imbibe.

absorto, ta. I. *a.* amazed; absorbed in thought. **II.** *pp. irr.* de ABSORBER.

abstemio, mia, *a.* abstemious.

abstención, *f.* forbearance, abstention

abstenerse, *vr.* (*ind.* ME ABSTENGO: *pret.* ME ABSTUVE: *subj.* ME ABSTENGA) to abstain, forbear.—**a. de,** to abstain from, forbear.

abstergente, *a.* detergent; cleansing; abstergent.

absterger, *va.* to cleanse; to sterilize.

abstersión, *f.* abstersion, purification.

abstersivo, va, *f.* = ABSTERGENTE.

abstinencia *f.* abstinence, temperance; fasting.

abstinente, *a.* abstinent, abstemious.

abstracción [abs-trac-the-on'], *f.* abstraction; concentration.

abstractivo, va, *a.* abstractive.

abstracto, ta, *a.* abstract.—**en a.,** in the abstract.

abstraer. I. *va.* (*pp.* ABSTRAÍDO, ABSTRACTO; *ind.* ABSTRAIGO; *pret.* ABSTRAJE; *subj.* ABSTRAIGA) to abstract. **II.** *vn.* (with de) to do without; leave aside. **III.** *vr.* to be or become absorbed.

abstraído, da. I. *a.* retired; absent-minded. **II.** *pp.* of ABSTRAER.

abstraigo, yo abstraje, *V.* ABSTRAER.

abstruso, sa, *a.* abstruse, difficult.

absuelto, ta. I. *a.* acquitted. **II.** *pp.* of ABSOLVER.

absuelvo (*irr.* from ABSOLVER).

absurdidad, *f.* absurdity.

absurdo, da. I. *a.* absurd, nonsensical. **II.** *m.* absurdity, nonsense.—**reducción al a.,** reductio ad absurdum.

abubilla, *f.* (orn.) hoopoe.

abuela, *f.* grandmother.—**abuelo,** *m.* grandfather; elderly man; (gen. in the *pl.*) ancestor.

abulia, *f.* (med.) abulia.

abultado, da. I. *a.* bulky, massive, big. **II.** *pp.* of ABULTAR.

abultar. I. *va.* to augment; to enlarge. **II.** *vn.* to be bulky or large.

abundamiento, *m.* = ABUNDANCIA.—**a mayor a.,** furthermore; with greater reason.

abundancia, *f.* abundance.—**abundante,** *a.* abundant.—**abundantemente,** *adv.* abundantly.

abundar, *vn.* to abound.—**abundosamente,** *adv.* abundantly.—**abundoso, sa,** *a.* abundant.

abuñolado, da, abuñuelado, da, *a.* turned over (eggs); shaped like a fritter.

abuñuelar, *va.* to turn (eggs) over in frying; to shape like a fritter.

abur, *interj.* = AGUR.

aburar, *va.* to burn; scorch.

aburelado, da, *a.* dark red.

aburrición, *f.* = ABURRIMIENTO.

aburrido, da. I. *a.* weary; tiresome, boresome. **II.** *pp.* of ABURRIR.

aburrimiento, *m.* tediousness, weariness, ennui; annoyance.

aburrir. I. *va.* to vex, annoy; tire, weary, bore; to venture, hazard, spend. **II.** *vr.* to grow tired, weary; to be bored.

aburujado, da. I. *a.* pressed together; perplexed. **II.** *pp.* of ABURUJAR.

aburujar, *va.* & *vr.* to form lumps; to clot.—**aburujarse,** *vr.* to muffle up.

abusar, *vn.* to exceed, to go too far; to take undue advantage.—**a. de,** to abuse; to take undue advantage of; to impose upon.

abusión, *f.* abuse; superstition.

abusionero, ra, *a.* superstitious; fortune-telling.

abusivamente, *adv.* abusively.—**abusivo, va,** *a.* abusive.

abuso, *m.* misuse, abuse.

abyección, *f.* abjection, abjectness.

abyecto, ta, *a.* abject, servile, slavish.

acá, *adv.* here; hither.—**a. y acullá,** or **a. y allá,** here and there.—**¿de cuándo a.?** since when?—**para a.,** hither, here.—**por a.,** here, hereabouts; this way.

acabable, *a.* that can be finished; achievable.

acabadamente, *adv.* completely, perfectly.

acabado. I. *m.* finish. **II.** *a.* finished; perfect, faultless; consummate; wasted, emaciated; worn out; dilapidated. **III.** *pp.* of ACABAR.

acabador, ra, *m.* & *f.* finisher.

acabalar, *va.* to complete, to finish.

acaballadero, *m.* time and place at which horses cover mares.

acaballado, da. I. *a.* horselike. **II.** *pp.* of ACABALLAR.

acaballar, *va.* to cover (a mare).

acaballerado, da. I. *a.* gentlemanlike. **II.** *pp.* of ACABALLERAR.

acaballerar, *va.* to render genteel; to make a gentleman of.

acabamiento, *m.* completion, finishing; emaciation; death; end.

acabar. I. *va.* and *vn.* to finish; to complete; to end.—**a. con,** to finish, destroy; to get rid of, extirpate.—**a. de** (followed by *inf.*), to have just (followed by *pp.*): *él acaba de llegar,* he has just arrived. **II.** *vr.* to be finished; to end, terminate, be over; to grow feeble or wasted; (w. dative) to be or run out of; to become exhausted (ch. constr.: *se me acabó el pan,* I ran out of bread: *se me ha acabado la paciencia,* my patience is exhausted).

acabellado, da, *a.* light chestnut color.

acabestrillar, *vn.* to fowl with a stalking horse or ox.

acabildar, *va.* to unite persons by persuasion to do something.

acabóse, *m.* (coll.) end (usually tragic or disastrous).

acacia, *f.* acacia.

academia, *f.* academy; university; literary society.

académicamente, *adv.* academically.

académico, ca. I. *m.* academician. **II.** *a.,* academical.

acaecedero, ra, *a.* eventual, contingent.

acaecer, *vn. def.* (*subj.* ACAEZCA) to happen, to come to pass.

acaecimiento, *m.* event, incident.

acahual, *m.* (bot.) Mexican sunflower.

acal, *m.* (Mex.) canoe; craft, vessel.

acalabrotar, *va.* (naut.) to make a cable by intertwining three ropes containing each three strands.

acalefo, fa, *n.* & *a.* (zool.) acalephan.—*m. pl.* Acalephæ, Acalepha.

acalenturarse, *vr.* to become feverish.

acalia, *f.* (bot.) marshmallow.

acaloradamente, *adv.* heatedly, excitedly.

acalorado, da. I. *a.* heated, fiery, excited, angry. **II.** *pp.* of ACALORAR.

acaloramiento, *m.* ardor, heat, excitement.

acalorar. I. *va.* to warm; to inflame, excite; to move, to arouse enthusiasm in; to urge on; to further, promote. **II.** *vr.* to grow warm, excited.

acallar, *va.* to quiet, hush; to mitigate, assuage.

acamar, *va.* to lay plants flat.

acambrayado, da, *a.* cambric-like.

acamellado, da, *a.* camel-like.

acampamento, *m.* (mil.) encampment, camp.

acampanado, a, *a.* bell-shaped.

acampanar, *va.* to shape like a bell.

acampar, *va., vn.* & *vr.* to encamp.

acampo, *m.* common pasture.

ácana, *f.* a hard reddish Cuban wood.

acanalado, da. I. *a.* striated, fluted, corrugated, grooved. **II.** *pp.* of ACANALAR.—**acanalador,** *m.* (mech.) grooving plane.—**acanalados,** *m. pl.* ridge of a horse's back.

acanaladura, *f.* grove, stria, striation.

acanalar, *va.* to make a channel in; to flute, corrugate, groove.

acandilado, da, *a.* shaped like a three-cornered hat; dazzled.

acanelado, da, *a.* cinnamon-colored.

acanillado, da, *a.* ribbed, striped (cloth).

acantáceas, *f. pl.* (bot.) Acanthaceæ.—**acantáceo, a,** *a.* acanthaceous.

acantalear, *vn.* to hail large hailstones.

acantilado, da, *a.* bold; steep.

acanto, *m.* (bot.) prickly thistle; (arch.) acanthus leaf.

acantocéfalo, la, *n.* & *a.* (zool.) acanthocephalan.

acantonamiento, *m.* cantonment.—**acantonar,** *va.* to quarter (troops).

acantopterigio, gia, *n.* & *a.* (zool.) acanthopterygian.

acañaverear, *va.* to wound with sharp-pointed canes.

acañonear, *va.* to cannonade.

acaparador, ra, *n.* monopolizer.

acaparar, *va.* to monopolize; to corner, control (the market).

acaparrarse, *vr.* to close a bargain.

acaparrosado, da, *a.* copperas-hued.

acapizarse, *vr.* (coll.) to grapple; clinch.

acaponado, da, *a.* capon-like.

acaracolado, da, *a.* spiral-shaped, winding.

acaramelado, da. I. *a.* (coll.) overpolite, disgustingly attentive. **II.** *pp.* of ACARAMELAR.

acaramelar, *va.* to cover with caramel.

acarar, *va.* to confront; to face; to brave.

acardenalar. I. *va.* to beat black and blue. **II.** *vr.* to be covered with wales.

acareamiento, *m.* facing; confronting.

acarear, *va.* = ACARAR.

acariciador, ra, *m.* & *f.* one who fondles and caresses.

acariciar, *va.* to fondle, caress; to cherish.

acarnerado, da, *a.* having a sheeplike head.

ácaro, *m.* (zool.) acarus.—**a. de queso,** cheese mite.

acarralar, *va.* to skip a thread in weaving.

acarrarse, *vr.* to seek the shade (app. to sheep).

acarreadizo, za, *a.* portable.

acarreador, ra, *m.* & *f.* carrier; porter.

acarreamiento, *m.* carrying, transportation; cartage.—*pl.* supplies.

acarrear. I. *va.* to carry, cart, transport, convey; to occasion, cause. **II.** *vr.* to bring upon one's self.

acarreo, *m.* = ACARREAMIENTO.

acartonado, *a.* pasteboardlike.—**acartonar. I.** *va.* to give the appearance or consistence of pasteboard. **II.** *vr.* (coll.) to become dried up by age.

acasamatado, da, *a.* (fort.) having or resembling a casemate.

acaso. I. *m.* chance; accident. **II.** *adv.* by chance, by accident; maybe, perhaps.—**por si a.,** in case, if it should happen.

acastorado, da, *a.* beavered.

acatable, *a.* worthy of respect.

acatadamente, *adv.* respectfully.

acatalepsia, *f.* (med.) acatalepsy.

acataléptico, ca, *a.* acataleptic.

acatamiento, *m.* esteem, respect; obeisance.—**acatante. I.** *m.* & *f.* one who respects. **II.** *a.* respecting.—**acatar,** *va.* to hold in high esteem; to respect, revere, do homage to; to treat with great deference or respect.

acatarrarse, *vr.* to catch cold.

acato, *m.* = ACATAMIENTO.

acaudalado, da. I. *a.* rich, opulent, well-to-do. **II.** *pp.* of ACAUDALAR.

acaudalar, *va.* to hoard up riches; (met.) to acquire a reputation.

acaudillador, *m.* commander of troops; leader.

acaudillamiento, *m.* leading, command.

acaudillar, *va.* to command, lead.

acaule, *a.* (bot.) short-stemmed.

accedente, *a.* acceding.

acceder, *vn.* to accede, agree, consent.

accesible, *a.* accessible; attainable.

accesión, *f.* accession; accessory; (med.) paroxysm of fever.

acceso, *m.* access; carnal intercourse; accession; (med.) access.

accesoria, *f.* outbuilding.

accesoriamente, *adv.* accessorily.

accesorio, a, *a.* accessory, additional.

accessit, *m.* (Lat.) second prize or award.

accidentado, da. I. *a.* troubled, agitated; seized with a fit; undulating, rolling. **II.** *pp.* of ACCIDENTARSE.

accidental, *a.* accidental, contingent.

accidentalmente, *adv.* accidentally.

accidentarse, *vr.* to be seized with a fit.

accidente, *m.* accident; chance; sudden fit.—**a. del trabajo,** work accident, occupational accident.—**de,** or **por, accidente,** accidentally, by chance.

acción, *f.* action; feat; lawsuit; gesticulation, gesture; battle; action in drama, plot; (art) posture; (com.) stock, share.—**a. de gracias,** thanksgiving.—**a. de guerra,** battle.—**a. de presencia,** (chem.) catalysis.

accionar, *va.* to gesticulate; (mech.) to operate, to move.

accionista, *m.* stockholder, shareholder.

accípitre, *m.* bird of prey.—**accipitrino, na,** *a.* like a bird of prey, accipitral.

acebadamiento, *m.* disease of animals surfeited with barley.

acebadar, *va.* = ENCEBADAR.

acebal, *m.*, **acebeda,** *f.*, **acebedo,** *m.* plantation of holly trees.

acebo, *m.* (bot.) holly tree.

acebollado, da, *a.* damaged by *acebolladura.*

acebolladura, *f.* damage (to a tree) from separation of the woody layers.

acebuchal. I. *m.* grove or wood of wild olive trees. **II.** *a.* belonging to wild olives.—**acebuche,** *m.* (bot.) wild olive tree.—**acebucheno, na,** *a.* belonging to the wild olive.—**acebuchina,** *f.* wild olive.

acecinar. I. *va.* to salt and dry (meat). **II.** *vr.* to grow old, dry, withered.

acechador, ra, *m.* & *f.* ambusher; observer, lookout; intruder, prier.

acechar, *va.* to lie in ambush for; spy on.

acecho, *m.* waylaying, lying in ambush.—**al a.,** or **en a.,** *a.* in wait, in ambush.

acechón, na, *m.* & *f.* (coll.) = ACECHADOR.

acedamente, *adv.* sourly, bitterly.

acedar, *va.* to sour; to displease, vex.

acedera, *f.* (bot.) sorrel.

acederaque, *m.* (bot.) bead tree.

acederilla, *f.* (bot.) wood sorrel.

acederón, *m.* (bot.) a variety of sorrel.

acedia, *f.* acidity, heart-burn, sourness; roughness; asperity of address.

acedo, da, *a.* acid, sour; harsh, unpleasant.

acefalía, *f.* **acefalismo,** *m.* acephalism.

acéfalo, la, *a.* acephalous.—*pl.* ACEPHALI.

aceitada, *f.* oil spilled; cake kneaded with oil.

aceitar, *va.* to oil; to rub with oil.

aceitazo, *m.* *aug.* = ACEITÓN.

aceite, *m.* oil; essential oil.—**a. de ballena,** whale oil.—**a. de comer,** olive, sweet oil.—**a. de hígado de bacalao,** cod-liver oil.—**a. de palo,** balsam of copaiba.—**a. de vitriolo,** vitriol, oil of vitriol (sulphuric acid).—**a. lubricante,** lubricating oil.—**a. secante,** seccative oil.

aceitera, *f.* woman who sells oil; oil jar, oil cruet; oil can; (mech.) oil cup.—*pl.* **aceiteras,** casters.

aceitería, *f.* oil shop.

aceitero, ra, *m.* & *f.* oiler; oil seller.

aceitillo, *m.* (bot.) satinwood.

aceitón, *m.* lubricating olive oil.

aceitoso, sa, *a.* oily, greasy.

aceituna, *f.* olive.—**a. de la reina,** or **gordal,** queen olive.—**a. manzanilla,** manzanilla olive.—**a. picudilla** = A. ZORZALEÑA.—**a. zapatera,** stale olive.—**a. zofairón,** baby queen olive.—**a. zorzaleña,** crescent olive.

aceitunado, da, *a.* olive-colored.

aceitunero, ra, *n.* olive dealer.

aceituní, *m.* arabesque work.

aceitunil, *a.* olive-colored.

aceitunillo, *m.* (bot.) satinwood.

aceituno, *m.* (bot.) olive tree.

acelajado, da, *a.* showing clouds of various hues.

aceleración, *f.* acceleration; haste.

aceleradamente, *adv.* speedily, swiftly; hastily; acceleratedly.

acelerador, *m.* accelerator; (aut.) accelerator, foot throttle; (med.) accelerator.

acelerador, triz, *a.* accelerating.

aceleramiento, *m.* = ACELERACIÓN.

acelerar. I. *va.* to accelerate; to hasten, hurry, rush. **II.** *vr.* to move fast; to make haste.

aceleratriz, *f.* *a.* V. ACELERADOR, *a.*

acelerómetro, *m.* (aer.) accelerometer.

acelga, *f.* (bot.) salt-wort.

acémila, *f.* beast of burden.—**acemilar,** *a.* belonging to mules and muleteers.—**acemilería,** *f.* mule stable.—**acemilero, ra,** *m.* muleteer.

acemita, *f.* bran bread, Graham bread.

acemite, *m.* fine bran, middlings; pottage.

acendrado, da. I. *a.* purified, refined; unspotted, stainless. **II.** *pp.* of ACENDRAR.

acendrar, *va.* to purify or refine (metals); to free from stain or blemish.

acensuar, *va.* to tax (a property).

acento, *m.* accent.—**a. ortográfico,** graphic accent.—**a. prosódico,** or **tónico,** tonic accent, emphasis.—**acentuación,** *f.* accentuation.

acentuar, *va.* to accentuate; to emphasize.

aceña, *f.* water mill.—**aceñero,** *m.* water-mill keeper.

acepar, *vn.* to take root.

acepción, *f.* acceptation, meaning.

acepilladura, *f.* planing; wood shavings.

acepillar, *va.* to plane; to brush; to polish.

aceptabilidad, *f.* acceptability.—**aceptable,** *a.* acceptable, admissible.—**aceptablemente,** *adv.* acceptably.

aceptación, *f.* acceptation; approbation; (com.) acceptance.

aceptador, ra, *m.* & *f.* acceptor.

aceptante. I. *m.* & *f.* accepter. **II.** *a.* accepting.

aceptar, *va.* to accept; (com.) to accept or honor.

acepto, ta, *a.* acceptable, agreeable.

acequia, *f.* trench; drain; flume; channel.

acequiado, da. I. *a.* intersected by canals. **II.** *pp.* of ACEQUIAR.

acequiador, *m.* canal or dike maker.

acequiar, *va.* to construct ditches, channels, flumes in or for.

acequiero, *m.* canal or dike keeper.

ácer, *m.* (bot.) maple tree.

acera, *f.* sidewalk; row of houses on either side of a street.

acerado, da. I. *a.* made of steel. **II.** *pp.* of ACERAR.

acerar, *va.* to steel; to impregnate (liquids) with steel: to strengthen.

aceratosia, *f.* (vet.) aceratosis.

acerbamente, *adv.* cruelly, severely, harshly.— **acerbidad,** *f.* acerbity, harshness; rigor, cruelty.

acerbo, ba, *a.* tart; harsh, severe, cruel.

acerca de, *prep.* about, with regard to.

acercamiento, *m.* approximation, approaching; rapprochement.

acercar. I. *va.* (*pret.* ACERQUÉ: *subj.* ACERQUE) to bring or place near, or nearer. **II.** *vr.* (w. a) to draw near (to), approach.

ácere, *m.* maple tree.

acerico, acerillo, *m.* pincushion; small pillow.

aceríneo, a. I. *a.* (bot.) aceraceous. **II.** *f. pl.* Aceraceæ.

acerino, na, *a.* (poet.) steel-like; of steel.

acero, *m.* steel; sword; pointed or edged arm.— *pl.* (met.) arms; spirit, courage; appetite.— **a. colado,** or **fundido,** cast steel.

acerola, *f.* haw.

acerolo, *m.* (bot.) hawthorn.

acérrimamente, *adv.* vigorously; strongly.

acérrimo, ma, *a. sup.* very strong (taste, odor); very harsh; very vigorous; very stanch or stalwart.

acerrojar, *va.* to bolt; to lock.

acertadamente, *adv.* opportunely, fitly, wisely.

acertado, da. I. *a.* fit, proper; wise. **II.** *pp.* of ACERTAR.

acertador, ra, *m. & f.* good guesser.

acertar. I. *va.* (*ind.* ACIERTO: *subj.* ACIERTE) to hit the mark; to hit by chance; to succeed; to conjecture right. **II.** *vn.* to guess right; to suceed; (agr.) to thrive.—**a. a,** to happen.

acertijo, *m.* riddle, conundrum.

aceruelo, *m.* small packsaddle.

acervo, *m.* a heap; undivided estate.

acérvula, *f.* (anat.) acervulus cerebri.

acescencia, *f.* acescence.

acescente, *a.* acescent.

acetábulo, *m.* cruet; acetabulum (small cup); (anat.) acetabulum.

acetal, *m.* (chem.) acetal.

acetámida, *f.* (chem.) acetamide.

acetanilida, *f.* (chem.) acetanilide.

acetato, *m.* acetate.—**acético, ca,** *a.* acetic.

acetificar, *va.* to acetify.

acetileno, *m.* acetylene.

acetílico, ca, *a.* (chem.) acetylic.

acetilo, *m.* (chem.) acetyl.

acetímetro, *m.* acetimeter.

acetín, *m.* (bot.) satinwood.

acetina, *f.* (chem.) acetine.

acetol, *m.* (chem.) acetol.

acetolado, *m.* (pharm.) acetolatum.

acetona, *f.* acetone.

acetosa, *f.* (bot.) sorrel.

acetosidad, *f.* acetosity.

acetosilla, *f.* = ACEDERILLA.

acetoso, sa, *a.* acetous.

acetre, *m.* small bucket; holy-water pot.

acezar, *vn.* (*pret.* ACECÉ: *subj.* ACECE) to pant.— **acezo,** *m.* pant, panting.—**acezoso, sa,** *a.* panting.

aciago, ga, *a.* unfortunate, sad, fateful.

acial, *m.* barnacle, twitch.

aciano, *m.* (bot.) cornflower.

aciar, *m.* = ACIAL.

acíbar, *m.* aloes; aloe tree; bitterness; displeasure. —**acibarar,** *va.* to put aloes into; to embitter.

aciberar, *va.* to grind very fine.

acicalado. I. *m.* act of polishing any weapon; polish. **II.** *pp.* of ACICALAR (u. also as *a.*).

acicalador, ra. I. *a.* polishing; embellishing; attiring. **II.** *m.* burnishing tool.

acicaladura, *f.,* **acicalamiento,** *m.* burnishing; polish, glossiness; adornment; dressing.

acicalar. I. *va.* to polish, burnish; to dress, adorn, embellish. **II.** *vr.* (met.) to dress in style, to make an elaborate toilet.

acicate, *m.* long-pointed Moorish spur; inducement; goad.

acíclico, ca, *a.* (elec.) acyclic.

aciclo, cla, *a.* (bot.) acyclic.

acicular, *a.* aciculate; needle-shaped.

aciche, *m.* paving hammer; brick hammer.

acidez, *f.* acidity, tartness.

acidia, *f.* laziness; weakness.

acidificación, *f.* (chem.) acidification.

acidificar, *va.* to acidify.

acidimetría, *f.* acidimetry.

acidímetro, *m.* acidimeter.

acidioso, sa, *a.* lazy; weak; lax.

ácido, da. I. *m.* (chem.) acid. **II.** *a.* acid; sour, tart; harsh.

acidular, *va.* to acidulate.

acídulo, la, *a.* (chem.) acidulous, tart.

acierto, *m.* a good hit; ability; tact; knack; dexterity.

acierto, acierte. *V.* ACERTAR.

aciguatado, da. I. *a.* jaundiced. **II.** *pp.* of ACIGUATARSE.

aciguatarse, *vr.* to be seized with jaundice.

acijado, da, *a.* copper- or copperas-colored.

acije, *m.* copperas.

acijoso, sa, *a.* brownish.

acimboga, *f.* citron tree.

acimiforme, *a.* (bot.) acimiform.

ácimo, ma, *a.* = ÁZIMO.

acimut, *m.* azimuth.—**acimutal,** *a.* azimuthal, azimuth (u. a.)

acinesia, *f.* (med.) akinesia.

acino, *m.* (bot., anat.) acinus.

ación, '. stirrup strap.—**acionero,** *m.* maker of stirrup straps.

acipado, da, *a.* well-milled (woolens).

acirate, *m.* landmark, boundary.

acitara, *f.* pillter; partition wall; rail of bridge; chair or saddle cover.

acitrón, *m.* candied citron.

aclamación, *f.* acclamation.—**aclamador, ra,** *m. & f.* applauder.—**aclamar,** *va.* to shout, applaud, acclaim.

aclaración, *f.* explanation.—**aclarador, ra. I.** *a.* explanatory. **II.** *m.* comb in looms.—**aclarar. I.** *va.* to make clear; to explain; to thin; to clarify; to rinse. **II.** *vn.* to clear up; to recover brightness. —**aclaratorio, ria,** *a.* explanatory.

aclimatación, *f.* acclimatization.

aclimatar, *va. & vr.* to acclimatize.

aclocado, da. I. *a.* stretched. **II.** *pp.* of ACLOCARSE.

aclocar. I. *vn.* (*ind.* ACLUECO: *pret.* ACLOQUÉ: *subj.* ACLUEQUE) to brood, be broody. **II.** *vr.* to stretch one's self, lie down; to become broody.

acobardar, *va.* to daunt, intimidate, frighten.

acobijar, *va.* (agr.) to mulch.—**acobijo,** *m.* mulch.

acobrado, da, *a.* copper-hued.

acoceador, ra, *a.* that kicks, kicking.

acoceamiento, *m.* kicking.

acocear, *va.* to kick; wince, flinch; to oppress, ill-treat: debase.

acocotar, *va.* = ACOGOTAR.

acocote, *m.* long gourd used in Mexico for extracting the juice of the maguey.

acocharse, *vr.* to squat; stoop down.

acochinar, *va.* (coll.) to murder; to humble; to corner (a checker).

acodado, da, *a.* elbowed; cranked (axle); toggled.

acodadura, *f.* bending the elbow; (agr.) layering.

acodalamiento, *m.* (arch.) propping; staying.

acodalar, *va.* to prop; to shore; to stay.

acodar, *va.* to lean the elbow upon; to plant cuttings: to implant; (arch.) to prop, to stay; (carp.) to square (timber).

acoderamiento, *m.* (naut.) bringing the broadside to bear.

acoderar, va. (naut.) to put a spring on a cable; to bring the broadside to bear.

acodiciar. I. va. to long for, covet. **II.** vr. to become covetous.

acodillar. I. va. to bend into an elbow or angle. **II.** vr. to sink down under a burden.

acodo, m. (agr.) shoot, scion.

acogedizo, za, a. collected or gathered promiscuously.

aeogedor, ra, m. & f. harborer, protector.

acoger. I. va. (ind. ACOJO: subj. ACOJA) to receive; (met.) to protect, shelter. **II.** vr. (w. a) to take refuge (in); to resort (to).

acogeta, f. shelter, cover, place of safety.

acogida, f. reception; place of meeting, confluence: asylum.—**dar a. a una letra,** (com.) to honor a draft.—**tener buena, mala a.,** to be well, unfavorably received.

acogido. I. m. collection of breeding mares given to the owner of the principal steed, to keep them at a certain price; temporary admission of flocks into pasture ground. **II.** pp. of ACOGER.

acogimiento, m. = ACOGIDA.

acogollar. I. va. to cover up (plants). **II.** vn. to bud.

acogombradura, f. banking of plants.

acogombrar, va. to cover (plants) with earth, to bank. V. APORCAR.

acogotar, va. to kill by a blow on the neck.

acohombrar, va. (agr.) = APORCAR.

acojinamiento, m. (mech.) cushioning.

acojinar, va. to quilt; to cushion.

acolar, va. (her.) to unite (two coats of arms) under the same crown, shield, etc.

acolchar, acolchonar, va. to quilt; (naut.) to intertwine.

acolia, f. (med.) acholia.

acólito, m. acolyte, assistant.

acologia, f. (med.) acology.

acolladores, m. pl. (naut.) lanyards.

acollar, va. (ind. ACUELLO: subj. ACUELLE) (agr.) to cover with earth the base of a trunk; (naut.) to caulk.

acollarado, da, a. ring-necked.

acollarar, va. to yoke or harness (horses, oxen, etc.); to couple (hounds); to put a collar on.

acollonar, va. (col.) = ACOBARDAR.

acombar, va. to bend; to warp.

acomedirse, vr. to offer one's self, to volunteer.

acometedor, ra, n. & a. aggressor (-ive); enterpriser (-ing).

acometer, va. to attack; rush on, (coll.) go for; to undertake; to overtake.

acometida, f., **acometimiento,** m. attack, assault; branch or outlet (in a sewer).

acometividad, f. combativeness.

acomodable, a. easily arranged.—**acomodación,** f. accommodation.—**acomodadamente,** adv. commodiously, comfortably.—**acomodadizo, za,** a. accommodating.—**acomodado, da. I.** a. convenient, fit; well-to-do, wealthy; fond of comfort; moderate, reasonable. **II.** pp. of ACOMODAR. —**acomodador, ra,** n. one who accommodates; usher in a theatre.—**acomodamiento,** m. accommodation.

acomodar. I. va. to arrange, to accommodate; to set to rights; to place; to reconcile, compound, compromise; to furnish, supply; to take in, shelter, lodge. **II.** vn. to fit, to suit. **III.** vr. to condescend; to adapt one's self, to put up with; to settle, agree.

acomodaticio, cia, a. accommodating.

acomodo, m. employment, situation; lodgings.

acompañado, da. I. a. accompanied; frequented. **II.** n. assistant. **III.** pp. of ACOMPAÑAR.—**acompañador, ra, I.** n. chaperon, attendant; companion; (mus.) accompanist. **II.** a. accompanying.—**acompañamiento,** m. attendance; retinue; (mus.) accompaniment; supernumeraries in a theatre; (her.) ornament around an escutcheon.—**acompañante, ta,** n. & a. = ACOMPAÑADOR.

acompañar. I. va. to accompany; to attend, escort; to enclose; (mus.) to accompany. **II.** vr. to hold a consultation.

acompasadamente, adv. rhythmically, measuredly.

acompasado, da, a. measured, rhythmic; (coll.) monotonous and slow in tone; of fixed, regular habits.

acompasar, va. = COMPASAR.

acomplexionado, da, a. of good complexion.

acomunarse, vr. to unite, combine.

aconchabarse, vr. (coll.) = ACOMODARSE.

aconchar, va. to push to a place of shelter; (naut.) to run aground.

acondicionado, da. I. a. of good (or bad) disposition (persons); in good condition (things); of (good, bad) quality. **II.** pp. of ACONDICIONAR.

acondicionar. I. va. to prepare, to arrange; repair. **II.** vr. to acquire a quality or condition; to qualify.

acongojadamente, adv. sorrowfully, sadly.

acongojar. I. va. to afflict, grieve. **II.** vr. to become sad, to grieve.

aconitina, f. (chem.) aconitine.

acónito, m. (bot.) aconite.

aconsejable, a. advisable.

aconsejador, ra, n. adviser, counsellor.

aconsejar. I. va. to advise, to counsel. **II.** vr. (w. con) vr. to take advice, consult.

aconsonantar. I. va. to make (a word) rhyme with another; to use rhymes in prose. **II.** vn. to rhyme.

acontecedero, ra, a. possible, that may happen.

acontecer, v. impers. (subj. ACONTEZCA) to happen, come about.

acontecido, a. I. a. sad, despondent. **II.** pp. of ACONTECER.

acontecimiento, m. event, happening.

acontezca. V. ACONTECER.

acopado, da. I. a. cuplike, cupped. **II.** pp. of ACOPAR.

acopar, vn. to trim to shape; to cup, hollow.

acopetado, da, a. tufted.

acopiador, ra, n. one who stores or collects.

acopiamiento, m. gathering, collecting; collection; supply, stock.

acopiar, va. to gather, store, collect, garner.

acopio, m. gathering, storing; assortment; collection, quantity.

acoplado, da. I. a. fitted, adjusted; coupled; scarfed.—**a. directamente,** (mech.) direct-connected. **II.** pp. of ACOPLAR.

acopladura, f., acoplamiento, m. coupling; joint; scarfing.

acoplar. I. va. to couple, join, connect; to hitch, yoke; to frame (timber); to reconcile; to settle (differences); to pair, mate (animals). **II.** vr. to make up a difference; to settle, come to an agreement; (coll.) to become intimate.

acoquinamiento, m. intimidation.

acoquinar. I. va. to intimidate; frighten. **II.** vr. to be afraid.

acorar, va. to afflict, to cause grief.

acorazado, da. I. a. ironclad; shell (u. a., app. to transformers). **II.** m. armored ship, ironclad.

acorazamiento, m. armoring; armor.

acorazar, va. (pret. ACORACÉ: subj. ACORACE) to armor.

acorazonado, da, a. heart-shaped.

acorchamiento, m. shrivelling.

acorcharse, vr. to shrivel; to become stale (fruits); to become torpid.

acordada, f. (for.) resolution, decision.

acordadamente, adv. by common consent, jointly; with mature deliberation.

acordado, da. I. a. agreed; done with mature deliberation. **II.** pp. of ACORDAR.

acordar. I. va. (ind. ACUERDO: subj. ACUERDE) to resolve; to agree; to remind; to tune; to dispose (figures) in a picture; to make flush, level, smooth. **II.** *vn.* to agree. **III.** *vr.* (with **de**) to remember, recollect (*no me acuerdo de eso*, I do not remember that); to come to an agreement.—**si mal no me acuerdo**, if I remember well, if my memory does not fail me.

acorde. I. *a.* agreed; in tune; in agreement, in accord. **II.** *m.* chord; harmony of sounds or colors.

acordelar, *va.* to measure with a cord.

acordemente, *adv.* by common consent; harmoniously; consistently.

acordeón, *m.* accordion.

acordonado, da. I. *a.* surrounded; in the form of a cord. **II.** *pp.* of ACORDONAR.

acordonamiento, *m.* act of lacing; milling; cording; shirring.

acordonar, *va.* tc lace; to mill (a coin); to cord, shirr, twine; to surround.

acores, *m. pl.* (med.) achor, scald head.

acornar, acornear, *va.* to butt.

acorneador, ra, *n. & a.*; butter (-ing).

ácoro, *m.* (bot.) sweet flag.

acorralamiento, *m.* corralling.

acorralar, *va.* to corral; to surround; to intimidate; to silence.

acorrer. I. *va.* to help, succor. **II.** *vn.* to run to; hasten. **III.** *vr.* to take shelter.

acorrucarse, *vr.* = ACURRUCARSE.

acortamiento, *m.* shortening; (ast.) difference between the distance of the sun or a planet to the earth and the projection of that distance on the plane of the ecliptic.

acortar. I. *va.* to shorten; lessen; reduce; to obstruct.—**a. la vela,** (naut.) to shorten sail. **II.** *vr.* to shrivel; contract; shrink; to be bashful; to fall back.

acorullar, *va.* (naut.) to bridle (the oars).

acosador, ra, *n.* pursuer, persecutor.

acosamiento, *m.* relentless persecution.

acosar, *va.* to pursue relentlessly and pressingly; to vex, harass.

acosmismo, *m.* (philos.) acosmism.

acostado, da. I. *a.* stretched, laid down; in bed. **II.** *pp.* of ACOSTAR.—**acostamiento,** *m.* stretching or laying down; emolument.

acostar. I. *va.* (*ind.* ACUESTO: *subj.* ACUESTE) to lay down; to put to bed; to bring (a vessel) alongside the shore. **II.** *vn.* to tilt, to have a list. **III.** *vr.* to lie down; to go to bed.—**a. con las gallinas,** (coll.) to go to bed with the chickens.

acostumbradamente, *adv.* customarily.

acostumbrado, da, *a.* accustomed, used.

acostumbrar. I. *va.* to accustom. **II.** *vn.* to be accustomed, to be in the habit (*acostumbro comer temprano*, I am in the habit of dining early). **III.** *vr.* to get used, or become accustomed.

acotación, *f.,* **acotamiento,** *m.* boundary mark or monument; directions (for a [theatrical performance); marginal note; (surv.) elevation marked on a map.

acotar. I. *va.* to annotate; to accept; to select, pick out; to witness, vouch for; to cut off the top (of a tree); to set boundary marks or monuments to; to mark out; (surv.) to put the elevation figures on (a map). **II.** *vr.* to seek refuge outside the boundary line.

acotiledóneo, ea. I. *a.* (bot.) acotyledonous. **II.** *f. pl.* (bot.) Acotyledons.

acotillo, *m.* sledgehammer.

acoyundar, *va.* to yoke.

acre. I. *a.* sour; acrimonious; tart; hot; mordant; keen. **II.** *m.* acre.

acrecencia, *f.,* **acrecentamiento,** *m.* increase, augmentation, growth.

acrecentador, ra, *n. & a.* increaser (-ing).

acrecentar (*ind.* ACRECIENTO: *subj.* ACRECIENTE), **acrecer,** (*ind.* ACREZCO: *subj.* ACREZCA), *va.* to increase; to promote, advance.

acreditado, da. I. *a.* accredited; well reputed, of good repute. **II.** *pp.* of ACREDITAR.

acreditar, *va.* to assure, affirm; to verify, prove; (com.) to recommend, to answer for, to guarantee; to accredit, to authorize; prove.

acreedor, ra. I. *a.* meritorious, deserving.—**a. a,** deserving or worthy of. **II.** *n.* creditor.

acremente, *adv.* sourly, bitterly.

acrezca, co. *V.* ACRECER.

acribador, ra, *n. & a.* one who sifts; sifting.

acribadura, *f.* sifting.—*pl.* siftings.

acribar, *va.* to sift; to perforate like a sieve.

acribillar, *va.* to pierce like a sieve; torment; to cover with wounds.

acriminación, *f.* crimination, accusation.

acriminador, ra, *n.* accuser, informer.

acriminar, *va.* to accuse, to impeach, to charge; (law) to aggravate.

acrimonia, *f.* acrimony, sourness.

acrisoladamente, *adv.* honestly.—**acrisolado, da,** *a.* honest, virtuous, upright.

acrisolar, *va.* to assay; to refine; to purify, cleanse; to prove.

acristianar, *va.* (coll.) to baptize, to christen.

acritud, *f.* = ACRIMONIA.

acróbata, *n.* acrobat.—**acrobático, ca,** *a.* acrobatic.

acromático, ca, *a.* achromatic.—**acromatismo,** *m.* achromatism.—**acromatizar,** *va.* to achromatize.

acromatopsia, *f.* color blindness.

acromial, acromiano, na, *a.* (anat.) acromial.

acrómico, ca, *a.* achromic.

acromio, *m.* (anat.) acromion.

acrónico, ca, *a.* (astr.) acronycal.

acrópolis, *m.* (mil.) acropolis.

acróstico, ca, *a.* acrostic.

acrostolio, *m.* (naut.) acrostolium.

acrotera, *f.* (arch.) acroterium.

acta, *f.* act or record of proceedings; certificate of election.—*pl.* acts or records of communities, chapters, councils; proceedings; transactions, minutes; papers, file, etc.—**a. notarial,** notarial certificate.

actínico, ca, *a.* actinic.

actinio, *m.* actinium.

actinismo, *m.* actinism.

actinométrico, ca, *a.* (opt.) actinometric.

actinómetro, *m.* (opt.) actinometer.

actitud, *f.* attitude, position, posture.

activamente, *adv.* actively.

activar, *va.* to make active; to expedite, hasten.

actividad, *f.* activity, energy.—**en a.** in operation.

activo, va. I. *m.* (com.) assets. **II.** *a.* active.

acto, *m.* act, action; public function; commencement in colleges, etc.; act (of a play); thesis defended in universities; carnal intercourse.—**a. continuo,** immediately afterward.—**en el a.,** at once.

actor, a. I. *a.* acting, that acts.—**parte actora,** prosecution; plaintiff. **II.** *m.* actor, player; plaintiff, claimant.

actriz, *f.* actress.

actuación, *f.* actuation; action; moving.

actuado, da. I. *a.* actuated; skilled, experienced. **II.** *pp.* of ACTUAR.

actual, *a.* present, of the present time (not *actual*).

actualidad, *f.* present time (never *actuality*).—**en la a.,** at the present time, at present.

actualmente, *adv.* at present, at the present time (never *actually*).

actuante, *a.* defender of a thesis in colleges.

actuar. I. *vn.* to act; to perform judicial acts; to take the affirmative side in a university debate. **II.** *va.* to put in action, move.

actuario, *m.* clerk of a court of justice.—**a. de seguros,** actuary, one versed in the theory of insurance.

acuadrillar, *va.* to collect or head (a band of armed men).

acuantiar, *va.* to determine the quantity of.

acuapuntura, *f.* (med.) acupuncture.

acuarela, *f.* water-color painting.

acuarelista, *m.* water-color painter.

acuario, *m.* Aquarius (in zodiac); aquarium.

acuartelado, da. I. *a.* (her.) divided into quarters. **II.** *pp.* of ACUARTELAR.

acuartelamiento, *m.* quartering or billeting (of troops); troops; quarters.

acuartelar, *va.* to quarter, billet.—**a. las velas,** (naut.) to flat in the sails.

acuartillar, *vn.* to bend in the quarters under a heavy load (s. o. beasts of burden).

acuático, ca, acuátil, *a.* aquatic, water (u. as *a.*)

acuatizaje, *m.* (aer.) alighting on the water; place for alighting on the water.

acuatizar, *vn.* (aer.) to alight on the water.

acuatubular, *a.* water-tube (boiler).

acubado, da, *a.* resembling a pail or bucket.

acucia, *f.* zeal, diligence; longing.—**acuciamiento,** *m.* urging, hastening.—**acuciosamente,** *adv.* actively, diligently; eagerly.—**acuciar,** *va.* to urge, hasten; to covet.—**acucioso, sa,** *a.* zealous, hasty, eager.

acuclillado, da, *a.* cowering, squatting.

acuclillarse, *vr.* to crouch, squat.

acucharado, da, *a.* spoonlike.

acuchillado, da. I. *a.* slashed, stabbed, cut; schooled by experience; slashed (applied to garments). **II.** *pp.* of ACUCHILLAR.

acuchillador, ra, *n.* slasher; bully.

acuchillar. I. *va.* to cut, hack, slash, cut open. **II.** *vr.* to fight with knives or swords.

acudimiento, *m.* aid, assistance.

acudir, *vn.* to be present; to attend; to go, come; to respond; to go or come to the rescue; to resort; to apply.

acueducto, *m.* aqueduct.

acuello (*irr.* from ACOLLAR).

ácueo, a, *a.* watery; aqueous.

acuerdado, da, *a.* aligned.

acuerdo, *m.* resolution; determination; opinion; report, advice; remembrance, recollection; concurrence, accord; body of the members of a tribunal; harmony.—**de a.,** in agreement; unanimously; agreed, of the same opinion; complying, in accordance.—**de común a.,** unanimously; by mutual agreement.

acuerdo, yo acuerde. *V.* ACORDAR.

acuesto, yo acueste. *V* ACOSTAR.

acuitar. I. *va.* to afflict. **II.** *vr.* to grieve.

acular, *va.* (coll.) to make (a horse) back up.

aculebrinado, da, *a.* in the form of a culverin.

acúleo, a, *a.* (zool.) aculate, armed with a sting.

acullá, *adv.* on the other side, yonder; opposite.

acumen, *m.* acumen, quick discernment.

acuminado, da, *a.* acuminate.

acumulación, *f.* accumulation; gathering.

acumulador, ra, *n.* accumulator; (elec.) storage battery, accumulator.

acumular, *va.* to accumulate; to impute, to charge with; (law) to try or dispose of jointly.

acumulativamente, *adv.* cumulatively; (law) by way of prevention; by way of precaution; jointly.

acumulativo, va, *a.* cumulative; joint.

acuñación, *f.* coining, minting; wedging.

acuñador, ra, *n.* coiner; wedge; (print.) shooting stick.

acuñar, *va.* to coin, mint; to wedge; to key, lock; (print.) to quoin.

acuosidad, *f.* wateriness.

acuoso, sa, *a.* watery, aqueous.

acupuntura, *f.* (surg.) acupuncture.

acure, *m.* (Ven.) Guinea pig.

acurrucarse, *vr.* to huddle up.

acusación, *f.* accusation.—**acusado, da,** *n.* & *a.* defendant, accused.—**acusador, ra,** *n.* accuser; informer; prosecutor.—**acusante,** *a.* accusing, prosecuting.

acusar. I. *va.* to accuse; prosecute; indict; to acknowledge (receipt); at cards, to announce in due time that one holds certain cards that count so many points.—**a. las cuarenta,** to call out the forty honor points (at cards); (coll.) to give a piece of one's mind. **II.** *vr.* (w. de), to confess (to a confessor).

acusativo, *m.* & *a.* accusative.

acusatorio, ria, *a.* accusatory.

acuse, *m.* at cards, each of the cards duly announced in certain games. *V.* ACUSAR.—**a. de recibo,** acknowledgment of receipt.

acusiador, ra, *n.* & *a.* hastener (-ing), urger (-ing).

acusón, na, *a.* (coll.) telltale, talebearer.

acústica, *f.* acoustics.—**acústico, ca,** *a.* acoustic; speaking (tube).

acutángulo, *a.* (geom.) acute-angled.

acuté, *m.* (Arg.) agouti.

achacar, *va.* to impute.

achacosamente, *adv.* sickly.—**achacoso, sa,** *a.* sickly, ailing.

achaflanar, *va.* to chamfer, bevel.

achantarse, *vr.* (vulg.) to hide during danger.

achaparrado, da, *a.* shrub-sized tree.

achaque, *m.* habitual indisposition; monthly courses; pregnancy; subject matter; excuse, pretext; frequent lapse or failing.—*pl.* matters.

achaquiento, ta, *a.* = ACHACOSO.

acharolado, da, *a.* japanned; japanlike.

acharolar, *va.* to japan; enamel.

achatado, da, *a.* flattened.—**achatamiento,** *m.* flattening.—**achatar,** *va.* to flatten.

achicado, da. I. *a.* diminished; childish. **II.** *pp.* of ACHICAR.

achicador, ra, *m.* & *f.* diminisher; reducer; (naut.) scoop for baling boats.—**achicadura,** *f.* diminution; (naut.) baling.—**achicamiento,** *m.* = ACHICADURA.

achicar. I. *va.* to diminish, lessen; to humble; belittle; to bale, drain.—**a. el agua del navío,** to free the ship.—**a. un cabo,** to shorten a rope. **II.** *vr.* to humble one's self; to feel small.

achicoria, *f.* (bot.) chicory.

achicharrar, *va.* to fry too much; to overheat.

achichinque *m.* (min.) scooper.

achilenado, da, *a.* (Peru) pro-Chilean.

achinado, da, *a.* (Arg.) plebeian; of dark reddish color.

achinar, *va.* (coll.) to intimidate, frighten.

achinelado, da, *a.* slipper-shaped.

achiote, *m.* (bot.) arnotto tree; (com.) annatto.

achique, *m.* scooping, baling, draining.

achispado, da, *a.* tipsy.—**achispar. I.** *va.* (coll.) to make tipsy. **II.** *vr.* to get tipsy.

achocadura, *f.* knock against an object.

achocar, *va.* to throw one against the wall; to knock asunder; (coll.) to hoard money.

acholado, da, *a.* half Indian; half-breed.

achorizado, da, *a.* slashed; made into sausages.

achote, *m.* = ACHIOTE.

achubascarse, *vr.* (naut.) to become squally.

achucutarse, *vr.* (Am.) to become downhearted; to lose courage; to wither.

achuchar, *va.* (coll.) to crush with a blow; to thrust; push roughly; jostle.

achuchón, *m.* (coll.) push, squeeze.

achulado, da, *a.* (coll.) rough; tough.

achunchar, *va.* (Chile) to foil, frustrate.

achura, *f.* (Am.) gut (of cattle).

adafina, *f.* stew used by the Jews in Spain.

adagio, *m.* proverb, saying; (mus.) adagio.

adala, *f.* (naut.) pump dale.

adalid, *m.* chief, chieftain, leader.

adamado, da, *a.* effeminate, womanish.

adamantino, na, *a.* adamantine.

adamarse, *vr.* to become effeminate.

adamascado, da. I. *a.* damasklike. **II.** *pp.* of ADAMASCAR.—**adamascar,** *va.* to damask.

adámico, ca, *a.* Adamitic; (geol.) accumulated by the tide (s. o. sand and other deposits).—**adamita,** *m.* Adamite.

Adán, *m.* Adam; slovenly man.

adaptabilidad, *f.* adaptability, suitability.—**adaptable,** *a.* adaptable.—**adaptación,** *f.* adaptation.—**adaptado, da,** *a.* adapted, suited.—**adaptador, ra,** *n.* & *a.* adapter (-ing).

adaptante, *a.* adapting.

adaptar. I. *va.* to adapt, fit. **II.** *vr.* to adapt one's self.

adaraja, *f.* (arch.) toothing.

adarce, *m.* dry sea froth.

adarga, *f.* oval leather shield.

adargar, *va.* to shield, protect, defend.

adarguilla, *f.* small shield.

adarme, *m.* half a drachm, sixteenth part of an ounce (179 centigrams).

adarvar, *va.* to stun; to bewilder.

adarve, *m.* flat top of a wall.

adatar, *va.* to open an account; to credit.

adaza, *f.* (bot.) panic grass.

ad calendas græcas, at the time of the Greek kalends (never).

adecenamiento, *m.* formation with ten abreast.

adecenar, *va.* to form with ten abreast; to count by tens.

adecuación, *f.* fitness; adequateness.

adecuadamente, *adv.* adequately, fitly.

adecuado, da. I. *a.* adequate. **II.** *pp.* of ADE-CUAR.

adecuar, *va.* to fit, to adapt.

adefagia, *f.* voracity.—**adéfago, ga,** *a.* (zool.) adephagous.

adefesio, *m.* (coll.) nonsense, absurdity; blunder; queer person; ridiculous attire.

adefina, *f.* = ADAFINA.

adehala, *f.* gratuity, perquisite, tip.

adehesado. I. *m.* pasture land. **II.** *pp.* of ADEHESAR.—**adehesamiento,** *m.* pasturage; turning into pasture.—**adehesar,** *va.* to convert land into pasture.

adelantadamente, *adv.* beforehand.

adelantado, da. I. *m.* adelantado, governor of a province. **II.** *a.* anticipated; advanced; far ahead; proficient; precocious; bold, forward; fast (s. o. a watch); early (fruit, plants).—**por a.,** in advance. **III.** *pp.* of ADELANTAR.

adelantador, ra, *n.* one that advances, extends, or amplifies.

adelantamiento, *m.* progress; improvement, increase; furtherance; cultivation; anticipation; betterment, promotion.

adelantar. I. *va.* & *vn.* to progress, advance; to grow; to keep on; to anticipate; to pay beforehand; to improve; to go fast; to gain time, to be fast (s. o. a watch). **II.** *vr.* to take the lead; to come forward; (w. **a**) to excel, outdo.

adelante, *adv.* ahead; farther on; forward, onward.—**¡a!** forward! go on; come in.—**de a.,** ahead, in the front; forward, head (u. a.).—**de aquí en a., de hoy en a., o en a.,** henceforth, in future.—**más a.,** farther on.

adelanto, *m.* advance, progress; (com.) advanced payment.

adelfa, *f.* (bot.) rosebay.—**adelfal,** *m.* rosebay field.

adelgazado, da. I. *a.* made slender or thin. **II.** *pp.* of ADELGAZAR.

adelgazador, ra, *n.* one that makes thin or slender.

adelgazamiento, *m.* slenderness, thinness.

adelgazar. I. *va.* (pret. ADELGACÉ: subj. ADELGACE) to attenuate, to make thin, slender; to lessen; to taper; to split hairs. **II.** *vr.* to become thin or slender.

adema, *f.* (min.) shore; strut; prop.

ademador, ra, *n.* (min.) one who props.

ademán, *m.* gesture, look, manner; attitude.

ademar, *va.* (min.) to shore.

además, *adv.* moreover, furthermore, besides; exceedingly, too.—**a. de,** besides, in addition to.

ademe, *m.* = ADEMA.

adenia, *f.* (med.) adenia.

adenitis, *f.* adenitis.

adenoideo, *a.* adenoid.—**tumor a., vegetación a.,** adenoids.

adenología, *f.* (anat.) adenography.

adenoma, *m.* (med.) adenoma.

adenopatía, *f.* adenopathy.

adenosis, *f.* chronic adenosis.

adenoso, sa, *a.* glandular.

adentellar, *va.* to bite, to catch with the teeth.—**a. una pared,** to leave toothing stones or bricks in a wall to continue it.

adentro. I. *adv.* within, inside. **II.** *m.* (in the *pl.*) the innermost thoughts.

adepto, ta, *a.* adept; initiated.

aderezamiento, *m.* embellishment; dressing.

aderezar, *va.* (pret. ADERECÉ: subj. ADERECE) to dress, embellish, adorn; to prepare; to cook, season; dress; to clean; repair; to mix (drinks); to blend (wines); to gum (silk); to size (goods).

aderezo, *m.* dressing; adorning; finery; gum, starch, used to stiffen cloth with; set of jewelry; trappings of a saddle horse; furniture; hilt, hook, and other appendages of a sword.

aderra, *f.* rush rope.

adestrado, da. I. *a.* (her.) on the dexter side of the escutcheon. **II.** *pp.* of ADESTRAR.—**adestrador, ra,** *n.* teacher, trainer; censor, critic.—**adestramiento,** *m.* = ADIESTRAMIENTO.

adestrar. I. *va.* (ind. ADIESTRO: subj. ADIESTRE) to guide, lead; to teach, train. **II.** *vr.* to practice, train.

adeudado, da. I. *a.* indebted; in debt. **II.** *pp.* of ADEUDAR.

adeudar. I. *va.* to owe; to be dutiable; (com.) to charge, debit. **II.** *vr.* to run into debt.

adeudo, *m.* indebtedness; customhouse duty; (com.) debit; charge.

adherencia, *f.* adhesion, adherence; relationship; bond.

adherente. I. *a.* adhesive, adhering; attached. **II.** *n.* follower. **III.** *m.* (gen. *pl.*) accessory; equipment.

adherir, *va.* & *vr.* (ind. ADHIERO: subj. ADHIERA) to adhere; to stick.

adhesión, *f.* adhesion; following, adherence.

adhesivo, va, *a.* adhesive.

adhiero, yo adhiera. *V.* ADHERIR.

ad hoc, expressly.

adiabático, ca, *a.* adiabatic.

adiafa, *f.* tip given to seamen at end of a voyage.

adiamantado, da, *a.* adamantine.

adicción a díe, or **in díe,** (law) addictio in diem.

adición, *f.* addition; remark or note put to accounts.—**a. de la herencia,** acceptance of an inheritance.—**adicional,** *a.* additional.

adicionar, *va.* to make additions in, to add to; to extend, prolong.

adicto, ta, *n.* & *a.* addicted, devoted; follower supporter.

adiestrador, ra, *a.* = ADESTRADOR.

adiestrar, *va.* = ADESTRAR.

adiestro, adiestre. *V.* ADESTRAR.

adietar, *va.* to put on a diet.

adinamia, *f.* adynamia, debility, prostration.

adinerado, da, *a.* rich, wealthy.

adintelado, da, *a.* (arch.) falling from an arch gradually into a straight line.

ad ínterin, adinterim, provisional(ly), in the meantime.

adiós, *interj.* good-bye, adieu; hello (greeting).

adipocira, *f.* adipocere; soap from buried animals.

adiposidad, *f.* adiposity.—**adiposo, sa,** *a.* adipose.

adir, *va.* to accept (an inheritance).

aditamento, *m.* addition.

adiva, *f.* **adive,** *m.* jackal.—*pl.* **adivas,** (vet.) vives, fives.

adivinación, *f.* divination.—**adivinador, ra,** *n.* & *a.* diviner, soothsayer.—**adivinaja,** *f.* puzzle, conundrum.—**adivinanza,** *f.* prophecy, prediction; puzzle, riddle, conundrum; guess.

adivinar, *va.* to foretell, to soothsay; to divine, guess; to solve (a riddle).

adivino, na, *n.* soothsayer; fortune teller; wizard; guesser.

adjetivación, *f.* adjectival use or office; (gram.) agreement.—**adjetivadamente,** *adv.* adjectively.—**adjetival,** *a.* adjectival.

adjetivar, *va.* & *vr.* to use, or be used, adjectively; (gram.) to make agree.

adjetivo, va, *n.* & *a.* adjective.—**a. calificativo,** qualifying adjective.—**a. comparativo,** comparative adjective.—**a. determinativo,** limiting adjective.—**a. gentilicio,** proper adjective.

adjudicación, *f.* aajudgment, adjudication.

adjudicador, ra, *n.* & *a.* adjudicator (-ing).

adjudicar. I. *va.* to adjudge, adjudicate. **II.** *vr.* to appropriate.

adjudicativo, va, *a.* adjudicative.

adjudicatario, ria, *n.* grantee.

adjunción, *f.* (law) adjunction.

adjunta, *f.* (com.) letter inclosed in another.

adjunto, ta. I. *a.* joined, annexed, inclosed, attached, adjunct. **II.** *m.* adjective; addition.

adjutor, ra, *a.* & *n.* adjuvant; helper (-ing), assistant (-ing).

ad líbitum, at will, optional(ly).

adminicular, *va.* to strengthen, reinforce, corroborate.

adminículo, *m.* accessory.—*pl.* small things carried for emergencies.

administración, *f.* administration, management; office of an administrator.—**a. activa,** executive action.—**a. económica,** treasury department.—**a. militar,** commissariat.—**a. pública,** public administration.—**en a.,** in trust.—**por a.,** by the government; officially; by the management, company, firm, etc.

administrador, ra, *n.* administrator, manager; director, trustee.—**a. de aduanas,** collector of customs.—**a. de correos,** postmaster.

administrar, *va.* to administer.

administrativamente, *adv.* administratively.

administrativo, va, *a.* administrative; managerial.—**administratorio, ria,** *a.* (law) belonging to an administration or administrator.

admirable, *a.* admirable, excellent.

admirablemente, *adv.* admirably.

admiración, *f.* admiration, wonder; exclamation point (¡!).—**admirador, ra,** *n.* admirer.

admirar. I. *va.* to admire. **II.** *vr.* to wonder; to be surprised, amazed.—**a. de,** to be surprised at; to regard with admiration.

admirativamente, *adv.* admiringly.

admirativo, va, *a.* admiring; admirable; filled with admiration.

admisible, *a.* admissible.

admisión, *f.* admission, acceptance.

admitir, *va.* to receive; to admit, grant; to accept; to permit.

admonición, *f.* admonition, warning, advice.

admonitor, *m.* monitor, in some religious communities.

adnata, *f.* (anat.) adnata, the external white membrane of the eye.

adnato, ta, *a.* adnate.

adobado. I. *m.* pickled pork. **II.** *a.* pickled; curried, dressed. **III.** *pp.* of ADOBAR.

adobador, ra, *n.*dresser, preparer.

adobar, *va.* to dress, to prepare; to pickle (meat); cook; to tan or dress (hides).

adobe, *m.* adobe, unburnt sun-dried brick.

adobera, *f.* mould for adobe; brick-shaped cheese, and mould for it.

adobería, *f.* brickyard. *V.* TENERÍA.

adobío, *m.* front wall of a blast furnace.

adobo, *m.* repairing, mending; pickle sauce; dressing for seasoning; ingredients for dressing leather or cloth; pomade.

adocenado, da. I. *a.* common, ordinary, vulgar. **II.** *pp.* of ADOCENAR.

adocenar, *va.* to count or sell by dozens; to depreciate, underrate.

adoctrinar, *va.* to instruct. *V.* DOCTRINAR.

adolecente, *n.* sufferer; patient.

adolecer. I. *vn.* (ind. ADOLEZCO: *subj.* ADOLEZCA) to become ill; (w. **de**) to suffer or ail from; be subject to. **II.** *vr.* to condole.

adoleciente, *n.* & *a.* = ADOLECENTE.

adolescencia, *f.* adolescence.—**adolescente,** *n.* & *a.* adolescent.

adolezco. *V.* ADOLECER.

adolorido, da, *a.* *V.* DOLORIDO.

Adonaí, *n.* one of the names of Deity.

adonde (**adónde,** when interr.), *adv.* where, whither.

adondequiera, *adv.* wherever.

adopción, *f.* adoption.—**adopcionismo,** *m.* adoptionism, an ancient Spanish sect.—**adopcionista,** *a.* adoptionist.

adoptable, *a.* adoptable.—**adoptador, ra,** *n.* adopter.—**adoptante,** *n.* & *a.* adopter (-ing).—**adoptar,** *va.* to adopt; to embrace (an opinion).

adoptivo, va, *a.* adoptive.

adoquín, *m.* paving stone or tile.—**adoquinado,** *m.* pavement.—**adoquinar,** *va.* to pave.

ador, *m.* time for watering land, where water is officially distributed.

adorable, *a.* adorable.—**adoración,** *f.* adoration, worship.—**adorador, ra; adorante,** *n.* adorer or worshipper.

adorar, *va.* to adore, worship.

adoratorio, *m.* temples of idols in America; teocalli.

adormecedor, ra, *a.* soporiferous, soporific.

adormecer. I. *va.* (ind. ADORMEZCO: *subj.* ADORMEZCA) to cause drowsiness or sleep; to lull to sleep; to calm, lull. **II.** *vr.* to fall asleep; to grow benumbed; to persist in vice.

adormecido, da. I. *a.* mopish; sleepish, drowsy. **II.** *pp.* of ADORMECER.

adormecimiento, *m.* drowsiness, sleepiness, numbness.

adormezco. *V.* ADORMECER.

adormidera, *f.* (bot.) poppy.

adormir, adormirse. *V.* ADORMECER.

adormitarse, *vr.* to doze, drowse.

adornado, da, *a.* ornamented, adorned.

adornador, ra, *n.* adorner, decorator.

adornamiento, *m.* embellishment, decoration.

adornante, *n.* & *a.* adorner (-ing).

adornar, *va.* to adorn, embellish, decorate, ornament; to furnish, garnish; to be a gift or an accomplishment of.—**a. de,** to adorn with.

adornista, *m.* painter, decorator.

adorno, *m.* adornment; ornament; accomplishment.

adquiero, adquiera. *V.* ADQUIRIR.

adquirente, adquiriente, *n.* acquirer.

adquiridor, ra, *n.* acquirer.

adquirir, *va.* (ind. ADQUIERO; *subj.* ADQUIERA) to acquire, to obtain; to get.

adquisición, *f.* acquisition; attainment.

adquisidor, ra, *n.* = ADQUIRIDOR.

adquisitivo, va, *a.* acquisitive.

adra, *f.* turn; portion of the population of a town.

adraganto, *m.* tragacanth.

adrales, *m.* *pl.* hurdles, side boards (of a wagon).

adrazo, *m.* sea-water distiller.

adrede, adredemente, *adv.* purposely.

adrenalina, *f.* (chem.) adrenaline.

adrián, *m.* bunion: a magpie's nest.

adrizar, *va.* (naut.) to right.

adrubado, da, *a.* deformed.

adscribir, *va.* (*pp.* ADSCRIPTO) to inscribe; to add as an employee.

adscripción, *f.* inscription; appointment; adscription.

adscripto, ta, *irr.* *pp.* of ADSCRIBIR: adscript.

aduana, *f.* customhouse.

aduanar, *va.* to enter (goods) at the customhouse; to pay duty on.

aduanero, ra. I. *a.* customhouse, customs (u. as *a.*). **II.** *m.* customhouse officer; revenue officer.

aduar, *m.* Arab village or settlement; gipsy camp.

adúcar, *m.* coarse silk from outer part of cocoon; the stuff made from that silk.

aducción, *f.* adduction.

aducir, *va.* (ind. ADUZCO: *subj.* ADUZCA: *pret.* ADUJE) to adduce.

aductor, *m.* (anat.) adductor (muscle).

aduendado, da, *a.* fairylike.

adueñarse, *vr.* to take possession.

adufe, *m.* timbrel or tambourine.
adufero, ra, *n.* tambourine player.
adujadas, adujas, *f. pl.* (naut.) coil, coiled cable.
adujar, *va.* (naut.) to coil (a cable).
aduje, adujo. *V.* ADUCIR.
adula, *f.* = DULA.
adulación, *f.* fawning, adulation.
adulador, ra, *n.* fawner, adulator, cringer.
adular, *va. & vn.* to adulate, flatter fawningly; to cringe to, to fawn, creep, crouch, grovel.
adulatorio, ria, *a.* flattering, honey-mouthed.
adulero, *m.* = DULERO.
adulón, na, *n. & a.* toady, cringer (-ing).
adúltera, *f.* adulteress.
adulteración, *f.* adulteration.—**adulterado, da, I.** *a.* adulterated. **II.** *pp.* of ADULTERAR.—**adulterador, ra, adulterante,** *n. & a.* adulterator (-ing), adulterant; falsifier.
adulterar. I. *va.* to adulterate; to corrupt. **II.** *vn.* to commit adultery.
adulterinamente, *adv.* adulterously.
adulterino, na, *a.* adulterous; begotten in adultery; adulterated, falsified, forged.
adulterio, *m.* adultery.—**adúltero, ra,** *n.* adulterer (-ess).
adulto, ta, *n. & a.* adult.
adulzar, *va.* to render (metals) more ductile.
adumbración, *f.* adumbration, shade in a picture.
adunar, *va.* to unite, join; unify.
adunco, ca, *a.* aduncous; curved; warped.
adunia, *adv.* abundantly.
adusto, ta, *a.* austere, stern, sullen.
aduzco, aduzca, aduje. *V.* ADUCIR.
ad valórem, ad valorem.
advenedizo, za, *n. & a.* foreign (-er), newly-arrived, immigrant; upstart, parvenu.
advenimiento, *m.* arrival; advent.
advenir, *vn.* to come, to arrive.
adventicio, cia, *a.* adventitious, accidental; (law) acquired by industry.
adverbial, *a.* adverbial.—**adverbialmente,** *adv.* adverbially.—**adverbio,** *m.* adverb.
adversamente, *adv.* adversely.
adversario, *m.* adversary, opponent; foe.
adversativo, va, *a.* (gram.) adversative.
adversidad, *f.* adversity.—**adverso, sa,** *a.* adverse; calamitous; opposite, facing.
advertencia, *f.* admonition, warning; remark, notice; foreword.
advertidamente, *adv.* advisedly, deliberately.
advertido, da. I. *a.* noticed; skilful; intelligent; expert; clever. **II.** *pp.* of ADVERTIR.
advertir, *va.* (*ind.* ADVIERTO: *subj.* ADVIERTA: *pret.* ÉL ADVIRTIÓ) to take notice of, to observe; to instruct, advise, give notice or warning; to acquaint; to mark, to note.
adviento, *m.* Advent, the four weeks before Christmas.
advierto, advierta, advirtió. *V.* ADVERTIR.
advocación, *f.* appellation given to a church, chapel, or altar, dedicated to the Virgin or a saint.
adyacente, *a.* adjacent.
aechadero, *m.* place where grain is sifted.
aechador, ra, *n.* sifter; sieve.
aechaduras, *f. pl.* the refuse of grain, chaff.
aechar, *va.* to sift (grain).
aecho, *m.* sifting (of grain).
aeración, *f.* aeration, charging with gas or with air; (med.) action of atmospheric air in the treatment of disease.
aéreo, rea, *a.* aerial; aeronautic, air (u. as *a.*); (met.) airy, fantastic.
aerífero, a, *a.* aeriferous.
aerificar, *va.* to gasify, aerify.
aeriforme, *a.* aeriform.
aerobio, *n. & a.* aerobian.
aerobiosis, *f.* aerobiosis.
aerobús, *m.* aerobus.
aerodinámica, *f.* aerodynamics.
aeródromo, *m.* airdrome, aerodrome.

aerofobia, *f.* aerophobia, morbid dread of air.
aeróforo, a, *a.* aeriferous.
aerografía, *f.* aerography.
aerograma, *m.* wireless message.
aerolito, *m.* aerolite, meteoric stone.
aerología, *f.* aerology.
aeromancia, *f.* aeromancy.
aerometría, *f.* aerometry.
aerómetro, *m.* aerometer.
aeronauta, *m.* aeronaut.
aeronáutica, *f.* aeronautics.
aeronáutico, ca, *a.* aeronautic.
aeronave, *f.* airship, dirigible.
aeroplano, *m.* aeroplane, airplane.
aeroscopia, *f.* aeroscopy.
aerostación, *f.* aerostation, air navigation.
aerostática, *f.* aerostatics.
aerostático, ca, *a.* aerostatic.
aeróstato, *m.* aerostat, dirigible.
aeroterapia, *f.* aerotherapeutics.
aeta, *m.* tribe of mountaineers in the Philippines; their language.
afabilidad, *f.* affability.—**afable,** *a.* affable, pleasant, courteous.—**afablemente,** *adv.* affably.
áfaca, *f.* (bot.) yellow vetch.
afamado, da, *a.* celebrated, noted, famous.
afamar, *va.* to make famous, to give fame to.
afán, *m.* anxiety, solicitude, eagerness.
afanadamente, *adv.* ₁ anxiously, laboriously, eagerly.
afanador, ra, *n. & a.* eager; painstaker (-ing); hustler (-ing); hurrier (-ying); laborious, toilsome.
afanar. I. *va.* to press, urge, hurry. **II.** *vn. & vr.* to act or work eagerly or anxiously; to toil.
afaníptero, ra. I. *a.* (zool.) aphanipterous. **II.** *m. pl.* Aphaniptera, Siphonaptera.
afanita, *f.* = AFIBOLITA.
afanosamente, *adv.* = AFANADAMENTE.
afanoso, sa, *a.* solicitous; laborious, painstaking.
afarolarse, *vr.* (Am., coll.) to become unduly excited, (coll.) to make a fuss; to lose one's temper, (coll.) to get hot in the collar.
afarollonado, da, *a.* steep, cliffy.
afasia, *f.* aphasia.
afeador, *n. & a.* one who or that which deforms or makes ugly; deforming, distorting; that makes homely.
afeamiento, *m.* defacing; ugliness.
afear, *va.* to deform, deface; to make ugly or faulty; to impair, to decry, to condemn.
afeblecerse, *vr.* to grow feeble or delicate.
afección *f.* affection, fondness; (med.) affection.
afectación, *f.* affectation.—**afectadamente,** *adv.* affectedly.—**afectado, da. I.** *a.* affected. **II.** *pp.* of AFECTAR.—**afectador, ra,** *n.* one who acts affectedly.
afectar. I. *va.* to affect; (law) to charge, impose, encumber. **II.** *vr.* to be moved; to be shocked.
afectivo, va, *a.* affective.
afecto. I. *m.* affection, love,-fondness. **II.** *a.* affectionate; (w. **a**) fond (of), inclined; (law) subject to charge or encumbrance.
afectuosamente, *adv.* fondly, affectionately.
afectuosidad, *f.* fondness, affection.
afectuoso, sa, *a.* affectionate.
afeitada, *f.* shave, shaving.
afeitar. I. *va.* to shave; to beautify, embellish, make up; to trim (a tree, the tail and mane of a horse). **II.** *vr.* to shave (one's self); to paint (one's self).
afeite, *m.* paint, rouge, cosmetic; make-up.
afelio, *m.* (ast.) aphelion.
afelpado, da, *a.* plushlike or velvetlike.
afeminación, *f.* effeminacy; emasculation.
afeminadamente, *adv.* effeminately.
afeminado, da. I. *a.* effeminate. **II.** *pp.* of AFEMINAR.
afeminamiento, *m.* = AFEMINACIÓN.
afeminar, *va.* to effeminate, to unman.
aferente, *a.* afferent.

aféresis, *f.* (gram.) aphæresis.

aferrado, da. I. *a.* headstrong. **II.** *pp.* of AFERRAR.

aferrador, ra, *n.* one that grapples or grasps.

aferramiento, *m.* grasping, grappling, seizing or binding; obstinacy.—**a. de las velas,** (naut.) furling of the sails.

aferrar. I. *va.* to grasp, to seize; (naut.) to furl; to moor; to anchor. **II.** *vr.* to fasten to each other; to interlock; (w. **a**) to persist obstinately or persistently (in).

aferruzado, da, *a.* angry, irate.

afestonado, a, *a.* festooned.

afgano, na, *n. & a.* Afghan.

afianzamiento, *m.* security, guarantee, bail; prop, support; fastening, securing.

afianzar, *va.* (*pret.* AFIANCÉ: *subj.* AFIANCE) to become bail or security for; to guarantee; to prop; to make fast, clinch.

afición, *f.* affection, fondness; taste, inclination.

aficionadamente, *adv.* fondly; amateurishly.

aficionado, da. I. *n. & a.* amateur; (spt.) fan.— **a. a,** fond of, having a taste for. **II.** *pp.* of AFICIONAR.

aficionar. I. *va.* to cause or inspire affection, fondness or liking. **II.** *vr.* (w. **a**) to fancy; to become fond of.

afijo, ja, *n. & a.* (gram.) suffix (-ed).

afiladera, *f.* whetstone.

afilado. I. *pp.* of AFILAR. **II.** *a.* sharp, keen.

afiladura, *f.* sharpening, whetting.

afilamiento, *m.* slenderness of the face, nose, or fingers; AFILADURA.

afilar. I. *va.* to whet, grind, sharpen; to render keen. **II.** *vr.* to grow thin.

afiliado, *pp. & a.* affiliated; adopted.

afiliar. I. *va.* (w. **a**) to affiliate (with). **II.** *vr.* (w. **a**) to join, to affiliate one's self (with).

afiligranado, da, *a.* filigree, filigreed; slender, thin; delicate, neat.

afiligranar, *va.* to make filigree work; to polish, embellish.

áfilo, la, *a.* (bot.) leafless.

afilón, *m.* steel, knife sharpener; razor strop.

afilosofado, da, *a.* putting on airs of a philosopher.

afín. I. *a.* close by, contiguous; related. **II.** *m.* relation by affinity.

afinación, *f.* completion, finishing touch, refining; tuning.

afinadamente, *adv.* completely, perfectly.

afinado, da. I. *a.* well-finished, refined; well tuned. **II.** *pp.* of AFINAR.

afinador, ra, *n.* finisher; piano tuner; tuning key.

afinadura, *m.* = AFINACIÓN.

afinamiento, *m.* AFINACIÓN; refinement.

afinar. I. *va.* to complete; to polish; to refine (metals); to trim (binding); to tune. **II.** *vr.* to become polished.

afincar, *vn. & vr.* to acquire real estate.

afine, *a.* = AFÍN.

afinidad, *f.* analogy, resemblance; relationship; (chem.) affinity.

afino, *m.* refinement (of metals).

afirmación, *f.* affirmation.

afirmadamente, *adv.* firmly.

afirmador, ra, afirmante, *n. & a.* affirmer (-ing)

afirmar. I. *va.* to make fast, secure, fasten; to affirm, assert, contend. **II.** *vr.* to hold fast; to steady one's self or make one's self firm; to maintain firmly.

afirmativa, *f.* = AFIRMACIÓN.

afirmativamente, *adv.* affirmatively.

afirmativo, va, *a.* affirmative.

afistular, *va.* to render fistulous.

aflato, *m.* afflatus, inspiration.

aflechada, *a.* arrow-shaped (said of leaves).

aflicción, *f.* affliction, sorrow, grief.

aflictivo, va, *a.* afflictive, distressing.

aflicto, ta, *pp. irr.* of AFLIGIR.

afligidamente, *adv.* sorrowfully, sadly.

---

afligir. I. *va.* (*ind.* AFLIJO: *subj.* AFLIJA) to afflict, to cause pain. **II.** *vr.* to grieve, languish, repine, become despondent, lose heart.

aflijón, na, *a.* (Am., coll.) gloomy-tempered, ever-weeping.

aflojadura, *f.,* **aflojamiento,** *m.* relaxation; loosening, slackening.

aflojar. I. *va.* to loosen, slacken, relax, let loose; to relent, debilitate.—**a. los obenques,** (naut.) to ease the shrouds. **II.** *vn.* to grow weak, to abate. **III.** *vr.* to grow cool in fervor or zeal; to lose courage.

aflorado, *a.* V. FLOREADO.

afloramiento, *m.* (min.) outcrop.

aflorar, *vn.* to crop out.

afluencia, *f.* plenty, abundance; fluency.

afluente. I. *a.* affluent, copious, abundant; loquacious. **II.** *m.* affluent, tributary.

afluir, *vn.* (*ind.* AFLUYO: *subj.* AFLUYA) (w. **a**) to congregate, assemble (in): to flow (into).

aflujo, *m.* (med.) afflux, affluxion.

afofar, *va. & vr.* to make (become) spongy or light.

afogarar, *va.* = ASURAR.

afolador, ra. I. *n. & a.* calker (-ing). **II.** calking iron.

afolar, *va.* to calk, caulk.

afollar, *va.* to blow with bellows.

afondar, *va.* to put under water; (naut.) to sink, to founder.

afonía, *f.* (med.) aphonia.

afónico, ca, áfono, na, *a.* aphonic.

aforado, *a.* privileged, favored. **II.** *pp.* of AFORAR.

aforador, *m.* gauger; appraiser.

aforamiento, *m.* gauging; appraisement.

aforar, *va.* to gauge, measure; to appraise; to give privileges.

aforisma, *f.* (vet.) swelling in the arteries.

aforismo, *m.* aphorism, maxim.

aforístico, ca, *a.* aphoristical.

aforo, *m.* gauging; appraisement.

aforrador, ra, *n.* one who lines clothes.

aforrar. I. *va.* to line (clothes, vessels, tubes, etc.); (naut.) to sheathe.—**a. un cabo,** (naut.) to serve a cable. **II.** *vr.* to put on heavy underclothing; to gorge.

aforro, *m.* lining; (naut.) sheathing; (naut.) waist of a ship.

afortunadamente, *adv.* luckily, fortunately.

afortunado, da. I. *a.* fortunate, lucky. **II.** *pp.* of AFORTUNAR.—**afortunar,** *va.* to make happy.

afosarse, *vr.* (mil.) to entrench, "to dig in."

afoscarse, *vr.* to become hazy.

afrailar, *va.* (agr.) to trim (trees).

afrancesado, da, *a.* Frenchified, Frenchlike *pp.* of AFRANCESAR.

afrancesar. I. *va.* to Gallicize, to give a French termination to (words). **II.** *vr.* to be or become Frenchified; to be naturalized in France.

afrecho, *m.* bran.

afrenillar, *vn.* (naut.) to bridle (the oars).

afrenta, *f.* affront, outrage; disgrace.

afrentar. I. *va.* to affront, to insult. **II.** *vr.* to be ashamed, to blush.—**afrentosamente,** *adv.* ignominiously.—**afrentoso, sa,** *a.* ignominious.

afretar, *va.* to scrub and clean.

africano, na, *n. & a.* African.

áfrico, *m.* southwest wind. V. ÁBREGO.

afrodisia, *f.* aphrodisia.—**afrodisíaco, ca,** *n. & a.* aphrodisiac.

afrontar, *va.* to confront; to face.

afta, *f.* (med.) aphthæ, thrush.

aftoso, sa, *a.* (med.) aphthous.

afuera. I. *adv.* out; outside; in public.—**¡a.!** one side! clear the way! **II.** *f. pl.* suburbs, outskirts.

afuetear, *va.* (Am.) to horsewhip.

afufa, *f.* (coll.) flight.—**afufar,** *vn. & vr.* (coll.) to run away, to escape.

afusión, *f.* affusion, shower bath.

afuste, *m.* gun carriage.—**a. de mortero,** mortar bed.

---

agachadiza, *f.* (zool.) snipe.—**hacer la a.,** (coll.) to hide (one's self).

agachar. I. *va.* to lower, bow down. **II.** *vr.* to stoop, squat, crouch, cower.—**a. las orejas,** (coll.) to humble one's self, to bend the knee; to be dejected or crestfallen.

agalbanado, da, *a.* = GALBANOSO.

agalerar, *va.* (naut.) to tip (an awning).

agáloco, *m.* (bot.) aloes wood.

agalla, *f.* (bot.) gallnut; tonsils; windgalls of a horse; beaks of a shuttle; ear lobe (of a bird). —*pl.* (coll.) courage; cheek, gall.—**a. de ciprés,** cypress gall.

agallado, da, *a.* steeped in an infusion of gall.

agallato, *m.* gallate.—**agállico,** *a.* gallic.

agallón, *m.* large gallnut.—**agallones,** *pl.* strings of hollow silver beads; wooden beads used in rosaries.

agalludo, da, *a.* (Am.) stingy; cunning, foxy; brave.

agalluela, *f.* dim. of AGALLA.

ágamo, ma, *a.* (biol.) agamic, asexual.

agamuzado, da, *a.* chamois-colored.

agangrenarse, *vr.* to gangrene.

ágape, *m.* agape.

agarbado, da. I. *a.* = GARBOSO. **II.** *pp.* of AGARBARSE.

agarbarse, *vr.* to bend, stoop down, crouch.

agarbillar, *v.* = AGAVILLAR.

agareno, na, *a.* Mohammedan.

agárico, *m.* (bot.) agaric.

agarrada, *f.* (coll.) wrangle, scrap, scuffle.

agarradero, *m.* holder, handle; (coll.) protection, patronage; (naut.) anchorage.

agarrado, da. I. *a.* stingy, close-fisted. **II.** *pp.* of AGARRAR.

agarrador, ra, *n.* one that grasps or seizes. sadiron-holder; catch-pole; bailiff.

agarrafar, *va.* (coll.) to grab hard in a scuffle.

agarrama, *f.* = GARRAMA.

agarrar. I. *va.* to grasp, seize; (coll.) to obtain; to come upon. **II.** *vr.* to clinch, grapple, hold on.—**agarro,** *m.* grasp.

agarrochador, *m.* pricker, goader.

agarrochar, agarrochear, *va.* to prick with a pike or spear; to goad.

agarrotar, *va.* to compress with ropes; to garrote, to execute with the garrote.

agasajador, ra, *a.* kind, obliging.

agasajar, *va.* to receive and treat kindly; to fondle; to regale; to entertain.—**agasajo,** *m.* friendly treatment, kindness; consideration, regard; friendly present; afternoon refreshment or "tea."

ágata, *f.* agate.

agavanzo, *m.*, **agavanza,** *f.* = ESCARAMUJO.

agave, *m.* agave; (commonly but erroneously) pita. *V.* this last word.

agavillar. I. *va.* to bind or tie in sheaves. **II.** *vr.* (coll.) to associate with a gang of sharpers.

agazapar. I. *va.* (coll.) to nab a person. **II.** *vr.* to hide one's self; to crouch.

agencia, *f.* agency; ministration, commission; agent's bureau, office; diligence.

agenciar, *va.* to solicit, promote, negotiate.

agencioso, sa, *a.* diligent, active.

agenda, *f.* notebook, memorandum book.

agenesia, *f.* (med.) impotence, agennesis.

agente, *m.* agent; solicitor, attorney.—**a. de cambios,** bill broker.—**a. de negocios,** promoter. —**a. de policía,** policeman.—**a. fiscal,** assistant attorney.

agerasia, *f.* agerasia, green old age.

agérato, *m.* (bot.) sweet milfoil or maudlin.

agestado, da (bien, mal), *a.* (well-, ill-) featured.

agibílibus, *m.* (coll.) hustling; hustler.

agible, *a.* feasible, practicable.

agigantado, da, *a.* gigantic; extraordinary.

ágil, *a.* nimble, fast, light.—**agilidad,** *f.* agility, nimbleness, sprightliness.—**agilitar,** *va.* to render nimble; make active.—**ágilmente,** *adv.* nimbly, sprightly.

agio, agiotaje, *m.* (com.) exchange of paper money for coin, or coin for bills; premium; stockjobbing; usury; jobbing.

agiotador, ra; agiotista, *n.* money changer; bill broker; stockjobber; usurer.

agitable, *a.* agitable; that can be shaken.

agitación, *f.* agitation; excitement.

agitador, ra, *n.* & *a.* agitator (-ing), stirrer (-ing).

agitanado, da, *a.* gipsylike; bewitching.

agitar. I. *va.* to agitate; to stir, shake up; ruffle. **II.** *vr.* to flutter; to become excited.

aglobar, *va.* to pile, put together.

aglomeración, *f.* agglomeration.—**aglomerado,** *m.* coal brick, made with coal dust and tar.

aglomerar, *va.* to agglomerate.

aglutinación, *f.* agglutination.—**aglutinante. I.** *a.* agglutinating, cementing. **II.** *m.* cementing material; (med.) sticking plaster.

aglutinar, *va.* to stick, cement, agglutinate.

aglutinativo, va, *a.* agglutinative.

agnación, *f.* (law) agnation.—**agnado, da,** *n.* & *a.* agnate.—**agnaticio, cia,** *a.* agnatic.

agnición, *f.* (rhet.) recognition of a person in a poem or drama.

agnocasto, *m.* = SAUZGATILLO.

agnosticismo, *m.* agnosticism.

agnóstico, ca, *n.* & *a.* agnostic.

agnus, agnusdéi, *m.* Agnus Dei; ancient Spanish coin, of smallest value.

agobiar. I. *va.* to bend the body down; to overwhelm; to oppress, grind. **II.** *vr.* to bow; to couch.

agobio, *m.* bending down; oppression, burden.

agojía, *f.* water outlet in mines, drain.

agolar, *va.* (naut.) to furl (the sails).

agolpamiento, *m.* crowding, rush.

agolparse, *vr.* to crowd.

agonal, *a.* agonistic (app. sp. to the Janus games).

agonía, *f.* agony.

agonioso, sa, *a.* eager, persistent.

agonística, *f.* agonistics.

agonizante. I. *a.* dying. **II.** *m.* a monk who assists a dying person; in some universities, he who assists students in their examinations.

agonizar. I. *va.* to assist (a dying person); to annoy, to importune. **II.** *vn.* **estar agonizando,** to be dying.

ágora, *f.* agora, public place in Greek cities.

agorar, *va.* to divine, prognosticate.

agorero, ra, *n.* diviner, augur, fortune teller.

agorgojarse, *vr.* to be infested by grubs (app. to corn).

agostadero, *m.* summer pasture.

agostamiento, *m.* parching up.

agostar. I. *va.* to parch. **II.** *vn.* to pasture cattle on stubbles in summer.

agostero, *m.* harvestman; religious mendicant who begs corn in August.

agostizo, za, *a.* born in August; weak.

agosto, *m.* August; harvest time; harvest.— **hacer su a.,** to improve the opportunity, to strike while the iron is hot.

agotable, *a.* exhaustible.—**agotamiento,** *m.* exhaustion.

agotar. I. *va.* to drain off (water); to beat out one's brains; to run through (a fortune); to exhaust. **II.** *vr.* to become exhausted; to be out of print.

agracejo, *m.* unripened grape; unripe olive that falls; a kind of shrub.

agraceño, ña, *a.* resembling verjuice.

agracera. I. *f.* verjuice cruet. **II.** *a.* vine yielding unripening fruit.

agraciado, da. I. *a.* graceful, genteel. **II.** *pp.* of AGRACIAR. **III.** *m.* grantee.

agraciar, *va.* to adorn, embellish; to favor; to grace; to give employment to.

agracillo, *m. V.* AGRACEJO.

agradable, *a.* agreeable, pleasing, pleasant.

agradablemente, *adv.* agreeably, pleasantly.

agradar. I. *vn.* to be pleasing; to please, like (ch. const.: *esto le agrada*, this pleases him, he likes this. Here *le* is dative, not accusative.)

agradecer, *va.* (*ind.* AGRADEZCO: *subj.* AGRADEZCA); to thank for; be grateful for.—**agradecido, da. I.** *a.* grateful; thankful. **II.** *pp.* of AGRADECER.

agradecimiento, *m.* gratefulness, gratitude.

agradezco, agradezca. *V.* AGRADECER.

agrado, *m.* affability, agreeableness; pleasure, liking.—**esto no es de mi a.,** this does not please me.

agramadera, *f.* brake; scutch.

agramador, ra, *n.* flax or hemp breaker.

agramar, *va.* to dress (flax, hemp) with a brake.

agramilar, *va.* to point and color (a brick wall).

agramiza, *f.* the stalk of hemp; hemp, tow.

agrandamiento, *m.* enlargement.

agrandar, *va.* to enlarge, aggrandize, increase.

agranujado, da, *a.* grain-shaped; filled with grain.

agrario, ria, *a.* agrarian, rustic.

agravación, *f.* aggravation.—**agravador, ra,** *n.* aggravator; oppressor.—**agravamiento,** *m.* aggravating.—**agravantemente,** *adv.* aggravatingly; burdensomely.

agravar. I. *va.* to aggravate; to add to a burden; to oppress; to aggrieve; to exaggerate. **II.** *vr.* to become grave or worse.

agravatorio, ria, *a.* aggravating; (law) confirmatory and compulsory.

agraviadamente, *adv.* injuredly; in an offended manner.—**agraviador, ra,** *n.* injurer, offender.—**agraviamiento,** *m.* wrong, offense, injury.—**agraviante,** *a.* offending.

agraviar. I. *va.* to wrong, offend, injure, harm. **II.** *vr.* to be piqued, take offense.

agravio, *m.* offense, insult, affront; injury, damage, harm.—**agravioso, sa,** *a.* offensive, insulting; injurious.

agraz, *m.* unripe grape; grape verjuice; (coll.) displeasure; (bot.) red-berried mistletoe.—**en a.,** unseasonably.

agrazada, *f.* verjuice water with sugar.

agrazar. I. *vn.* to taste sour. **II.** *va.* to vex, annoy.

agrazón, *m.* wild grape; (bot.) gooseberry bush; (coll.) displeasure, resentment.

agrecillo, *m.* = AGRACILLO.

agredir, *va.* to attack, assault.

agregación, *f.* aggregation; aggregate, collection.

agregado, m. aggregate; congregation; assistant; supernumerary; attaché; farmhand living on another's farm or ranch; (eng.) aggregate (of concrete).

agregar, *va.* to add; to collect, gather, heap; to nominate, appoint.

agremiar, *va.* & *vr.* to form into a guild or union; to unionize.

agresión, *f.* aggression.—**agresivamente,** *adv.* aggressively.—**agresivo, va,** *a.* aggressive, offensive.—**agresor, ra,** *n.* aggressor, assaulter; (law) one who violates another's rights.

agreste, *a.* rustic, countrylike, wild; rude, uncultured, uncouth.

agrete, *a.* sourish, tartish.

agriamente, *adv.* sourly; harshly, tartly, bitterly, severely.

agriar. I. *va.* to make sour or tart; to irritate, exasperate. **II.** *vr.* to sour, turn acid.

agriaz, *m.* (bot.) bead tree.

agrícola, *a.* & *n.* agricultural; agriculturist.

agricultor, ra, *n.* husbandman, farmer, agriculturist.

agricultura, *f.* agriculture.

agridulce, *a.* bittersweet.

agrietado, da, *a.* cracked.

agrietarse, *vr.* to crack.

agrifolio, *m.* (bot.) holly tree.

agrilla, *f.* (bot.) = ACEDERA.

agrillarse, *vr.* = GRILLARSE.

agrillo, lla, *a.* *dim.* sourish, tartish.

agrimensor, *m.* land surveyor.

agrimensura, *f.* land surveying.

agrimonia, *f.* (bot.) agrimony, liverwort.

agrio, ria, *a.* sour, acrid; rough (app. to a surface); rude, disagreeable; brittle, unmalleable.—*pl.* **agrios,** sour-fruit trees.

agrión, *m.* (vet.) callosity in a horse's knee.

agrisado, da, *a.* grayish.

agrisetado, da, *a.* flowered (silk).

agronometría, *f.* (agr.) science of soils.

agronomía, *f.* theory of agriculture.

agrónomo, *m.* agronomist, agricultural scientist or engineer.

agropila, *m.* German bezoar.

agrupación, *f.* cluster; crowd; group; grouping; gathering.

agrupar, *va.* to group; to cluster.

agrura, *f.* acidity, acerbity; orchard of sour-fruit trees.

agua, *f.* water; liquid; rain; (chem.) liquor distilled from herbs, flowers, or fruit; lustre of diamonds; (naut.) leak; (arch.) slope (of a roof). *pl.* mineral waters in general; clouds (in silk, etc.); gloss (in feathers, stones, etc.); urine; tide.—**a. abajo,** downstream.—**a. arriba,** upstream; (fig.) uphill.—**a. bendita,** holy water.—**a. cruda,** hard water.—**a. de azahar,** orange-flower water.—**a. de cepas,** (coll.) wine.—**a. de cerrajas,** (coll.) worthless thing, truck, rubbish.—**a. de coco,** cocoanut milk.—**a. del pantoque,** (naut.) bilge water.—**a. del timón,** wake of a ship.—**a. de manantial,** spring water.—**a. de nafa,** orange-flower water; napha water.—**a. de nieve,** ice water.—**a. de olor,** perfume.—**a. de pozo,** well water.—**a. dulce,** fresh water.—**a. fresca,** cold water.—**a. fuerte,** aqua fortis, nitric acid.—**a. gorda,** hard water.—**a. llovediza,** rain water.—**a. nieve,** sleet.—**a. regia,** aqua regia.—**a. rica,** scented water.—**a. sal,** salt and water.—**a. termal,** hot-spring water.—**a. tofana,** aqua tofana.—**a. viento,** wind-and-rain storm.—**a. viva,** surface water, running water.—**¡hombre al a.!** ¡man overboard!—**aguas abajo,** downstream.—**aguas arriba,** upstream.—**aguas jurisdiccionales,** (int. l.) territorial waters.—**aguas madres,** (chem.) mother liquor.—**aguas mayores,** stools (evacuation).—**aguas menores,** urine; urinating.

aguacatal, *m.* avocado plantation or grove.

aguacate, *m.* avocado, alligator pear; pear-shaped emerald.

aguacatillo, *m.* (bot.) a variety of avocado.

aguacero, *m.* heavy shower.

aguacibera, *f.* ground sowed when dry and then irrigated; water used for such irrigation.

aguachar. I. *va.* (Am.) to tame, break (a horse); to win the good will of with gifts. **II.** *vr.* to fatten in idleness (app. to horses). **III.** *m.* pool, puddle.

aguachar, aguacharnar, *va.* = ENAGUACHAR.

aguachento, ta, *a.* (Am.) watery.

aguachinar, *va.* = ENAGUACHAR.

aguachirle, *f.* inferior wine; slipslop; any weak or stale liquor; trifle; frivolity.

aguada, *f.* watering station; flood in a mine; (naut.) water on board a ship; (art) water color.—**a la a.,** water color (picture).—**hacer a.,** to take water.

aguaderas, *f. pl.* frames for jars of water carried by horses.

aguadero, *m.* watering place; water station.

aguadija, *f.* water in pimples or sores.

aguado, da. I. *a.* watered; watery, thin; abstemious. **II.** *pp.* of AGUAR.

aguador, ra, *n.* water carrier; sprocket.—**a. del real,** (mil.) sutler.

aguaducho, *m.* water course; stall for selling water.

aguadura, *f.* surfeit of water (in cattle).

aguafiestas, *n.* (coll.) wet blanket.

aguafuerte, *f.* etching; etched plate.

aguagoma, *f.* gum water.

aguaitar, *va.* to spy, watch.—**aguaitamiento,** *m.* watching, spying, lying for some one.

aguajaque, *m.* fennel gum.

aguajas, *f. pl.* ulcers above the hoofs.

aguaje, *m.* tidal wave; (naut.) whirlpool or eddy at the rudder; sea current or stream; wake of a ship.

agualluvia, *f.* rain water.

aguamanil, *m.* water jug; washstand.

aguamanos, *m.* water for washing the hands; washstand.

aguamarina, *f.* aquamarine.

aguamelado, da, *a.* washed over with water and honey.

aguamiel, *f.* hydromel, honey and water, mead; unfermented juice of the maguey.

aguana, *f.* wood used in canoe making in South America.

aguanieve, *f.* magpie; sleet.

aguanosidad, *f.* aqueous substances.

aguanoso, sa, *a.* very wet; having much water, very watery.

aguantable, *a.* bearable, tolerable.

aguantar. I. *va.* to bear, endure; to resist; to maintain; (naut.) to carry a stiff sail. **II.** *vr.* to forbear.

aguante, *m.* strength, resistance; patience, tolerance.

aguañón, *m.* constructor of hydraulic works.

aguapié, *m.* small wine. *V.* AGUACHIRLE.

aguar. I. *va.* to dilute with water; to mar (pleasure). **II.** *vr.* to fill with water; to become thin (app. to liquids); (vet.) to become constipated from drinking water at the wrong time.

aguardar, *va.* to expect; to wait for; to grant time to.

aguardentado, da, *a.* containing aguardiente; tipsy, drunk.—**aguardentera,** *f.* liquor flask.—**aguardentería,** *f.* liquor shop; saloon.—**aguardentero, ra,** *n.* maker or seller of aguardiente.—**aguardentoso, sa,** *a.* mixed with aguardiente; harsh (app. to the voice).

aguardiente, *m.* aguardiente, spirituous liquor (app. sp. to liquor of inferior quality).—**a. de cabeza,** the first spirits drawn from the still.—**a. anisado,** anisette.—**a. de caña,** rum.

aguardo, *m.* lurking place for a hunter.

aguarrás, *m.* oil of turpentine.

aguatocha, *f.* pump.

aguaturma, *f.* (bot.) Jerusalem artichoke.

aguavientos, *m.* (bot.) yellow sage tree.

aguaza, *f.* aqueous humor; sap from trees.

aguazal, *m.* marsh, fen.

aguazarse, *vr.* to become marshy.

aguazo, painting in gouache.

aguazoso, sa, *a.* = AGUANOSO.

agudeza, *f.* sharpness; fineness; witty saying; repartee; wit.

agudo, da, *a.* sharp; sharp-pointed; keen-edged; high-pitched; witty; brisk, ready, active or lively; (med., geom.) acute.

agüera, *f.* trench for irrigation.

agüero, *m.* augury, prognostication; omen, sign, indication.

agüero, agüere. *V.* AGORAR.

aguerrido, da. I. *a.* inured to war; veteran. **II.** *pp.* of AGUERRIR.

aguerrir. I. *va.* & *vr.* (*defect.*) to accustom to war.

aguijada, *f.* spur, goad.

aguijador, ra, *n.* one that goads, spurs, or urges.

aguijadura, *f.* spurring, urging, egging on.

aguijar. I. *va.* to prick, spur, goad; to incite, egg on. **II.** *vn.* to march fast.

aguijatorio, ria, *a.* (law) re-mandatory.

aguijón, *m.* sting; prick; spur, goad.—**cocear,** or **dar coces, contra el a.,** to kick against the prick.

aguijonazo, *m.* thrust with a goad.

aguijoneador, ra, *n* one who pricks or goads.

aguijonear, *va.* to prick, goad; push, urge, egg on.

águila, *f.* eagle; eagle ray.—**a. barbuda,** lammergeir.—**a. blanca,** a variety of Andine vulture.—**a. cabdal,** or **caudal,** royal, or golden, eagle.—**a. de mar,** eagle ray.—**a. imperial,** imperial eagle.—**a. real** = A. CAUDAL.

aguileño, na, *a.* aquiline; hawknosed.

aguililla, *f. dim. V.* CABALLO AGUILILLA.

aguilón. I. *m.* boom of a crane. **II.** *n. aug.* of ÁGUILA.

aguilucho, *m.* young eagle, eaglet.

aguinaldo, *m.* New Year's gift, Christmas present; reed (Cuba).

aguja, *f.* needle; bodkin; hatpin; spire, steeple; needlefish, hornfish; needle shell; hand of a watch; style of a dial; needle, magnetic compass; (r. w.) switch rail; (r. w., gen. *pl.*) switch; spindle; pin (in typography and artillery); brad; graft.—*pl.* ribs of an animal; (r. w.) switch.—**a. capotera,** darning needle.—**a. colchonera,** tufting needle.—**a. de arria, a. de enjalmar,** packneedle.—**a. de marear,** binnacle, marine compass.—**a. espartera** = A. DE ENJALMAR.

agujazo, *m.* prick with a needle.

agujerear, *va.* to pierce, perforate.

agujero, *m.* hole; needlemaker; needle seller; dugout.

agujeta, *f.* lace, string or latchet tipped with ferrules.—*pl.* tip, gratuity; pains from fatigue.

agujetería, *f.* shop where *agujetas* are made or sold.

agujetero, ra, *n.* maker or seller of *agujetas*; pin or needle case or cushion.

agujón, *m. aug.* large needle.

agujuela, *f.* brad.

aguosidad, *f.* lymph.

aguoso, sa, *a.* aqueous, watery.

agur, *adv.* (coll.) adieu, farewell, good-bye.

agusanarse, *vr.* to become infested with worms.

agustiniano, na; agustino, na, *n.* & *a.* Augustinian (monk, nun).

agutí, *m.* agouti.

agúzadera, *f.* whetstone.

aguzadero, *m.* haunt of wild boars.

aguzado, da. I. *a.* sharp; keen. **II.** *pp.* AGUZAR.

aguzador, *n.* & *a.* sharpener (-ing).

aguzadura, *f.* whetting, sharpening.

aguzanieve, *f.* wagtail, a small bird.

aguzar, *va.* (*pret.* AGUCÉ: *subj.* AGUCE) to whet, sharpen; to urge, excite.—**a. el ingenio,** to sharpen the wit.—**a. las orejas,** to cock up the ears.—**a. la vista,** to sharpen the sight.

aguzonazo, *m.* = HURGONAZO.

¡ah!, *interj.* ah!

ahebrado, da, *a.* threadlike, fibrous.

ahelear. I. *va.* to gall, embitter. **II.** *vn.* to taste bitter.

aherrojamiento, *m.* putting in irons, shackling.

aherrojar, *va.* to chain, put in irons, shackle.

aherrumbrar. I. *va.* to impart the taste and color of iron to. **II.** *vr.* to have the taste and color of iron (as water); to become ferruginous; to rust.

ahervorarse, *vr.* to become heated.

ahí, *adv.* there; yonder.—**por a.,** somewhere around here; that way.—**por a., por a.,** about, more or less.

ahidalgado, da, *a.* gentlemanly.

ahijadero, *m.* sheep nursery, breeding place for sheep.

ahijado, da, *n.* godchild; protegé.

ahijador, ra, *n.* shepherd in charge of a sheep nursery.

ahijar. I. *va.* to adopt; to impute. **II.** *vn.* to bring forth young; to bud; shoot out.

ahilarse, *vr.* to become faint, weak; to grow sour; to grow thin.—**ahilo,** *m.* faintness, weakness.

ahinco, *m.* earnestness, eagerness, ardor.

ahitar, *va.* & *vr.* to surfeit, cloy, stuff.

ahitera, *f.* (coll.) violent or continued indigestion.

ahito, ta. I. *a.* gorged, surfeited; stuffed; full; disgusted, bored. **II.** *m.* indigestion; surfeit.

ahocicar, *vn.* (naut.) to pitch or plunge.

ahocinarse, *vr.* to run in deep and narrow ravines.

ahogadero, *m.* hangman's rope; stifling place; throatband, halter.

ahogadizo, za, *a.* easily drowned; harsh, rough (s. o. fruits); heavier than water, non-floating (s. o. wood).

ahogado, da. I. *a.* suffocated; drowned; close, unventilated.—**estar, or verse, a.,** to be overwhelmed or swamped. **II.** *pp.* of AHOGAR.

ahogador, ra, *n.* hangman.

ahogamiento, *m.* suffocation; drowning.

ahogar. I. *va.* (*pret.* AHOGUÉ: *subj.* AHOGUE) to drown; to choke, throttle, smother; to oppress; to quench, extinguish; to water (plants) to excess; (naut.) to founder. **II.** *vr.* to drown; to be suffocated.

ahogo, *m.* oppression, tightness (of the chest, etc.); suffocation; pain; severe affliction; embarrassment.

ahoguijo, *m.* (vet.) quinsy, swelled throat.

ahoguío, *m.* oppression in the chest.

ahombrado, da, *a.* (coll.) mannish.

ahondar. I. *va.* to deepen; to dig; to go deep into. **II.** *vn.* to go deep, penetrate; to advance in knowledge; to investigate.

ahonde, *m.* act of sinking or digging; depth to which a mine should reach to acquire title.

ahora. I. *adv.* now.—**a. mismo,** just now; at once.—**hasta a.,** hitherto, until now; so far.—**por a.,** for the present. **II.** *conj.* now; whether or (*ahora hable, ahora escriba, lo hace bien,* whether he speaks or writes, he does it well).—**a. bien,** now, now then.

ahorcadura, *f.* (act of) hanging.

ahorcajarse, *vr.* to sit astride.

ahorcar, *va.* (*pret.* AHORQUÉ: *subj.* AHORQUE) to hang (kill by hanging).

ahorita, *adv.* (coll.) just now.—**a. mismo,** just now, this very moment; right away, at once.

ahormar, *va.* to fit, shape, adjust; to break in (shoes); to bring to reason.

ahornagarse, *vr.* to become parched or burned.

ahornar. I. *va.* to put in an oven. **II.** *vr.* to be scorched in the oven without being baked.

ahorquillado, da. I. *a.* forked.—**ahorquillar. I.** *va.* to stay, prop up with forks. **II.** *vr.* to become forked.

ahorrado, da. I. *a.* unencumbered. **II.** *pp.* of AHORRAR.

ahorrador, ra. I. *n.* emancipator; saver, economizer. **II.** *a.* saving.—**ahorramiento,** *m.* emancipation, enfranchisement; saving.

ahorrar, *va.* to save, economize; to spare; to enfranchise, emancipate.—**no ahorrarse,** or **no ahorrárselas, con nadie,** to be afraid of nobody, not to mince words with anybody.

ahorrativa, *f.* (coll.) = AHORRO.

ahorrativo, va, *a.* frugal, thrifty, saving.

ahorro, *m.* economy.—*pl.* savings.

ahoyadura, *f.* hole; digging.

ahoyar, *vn.* to dig holes.

ahuate, *m.* (Mex.) prickly hair (of sugar cane, etc.).

ahuchador, ra, *n.* hoarder, miser.

ahuchar, *va.* to hoard.

ahuecamiento, *m.* hollowing.

ahuecar. I. *va.* (*pret.* AHUEQUÉ: *subj.* AHUEQUE) to make hollow; scoop out; to loosen; to give (to the voice) a tone of solemnity. **II.** *vr.* to become hollow; to puff up, swell, put on airs.

ahuehué, ahuehuete, *m.* a Mexican tree.

ahumado, da. I. *a.* smoky; smoked. **II.** *f.* smoke signal from the coast.

ahumar. I. *va.* to smoke; to cure in smoke. **II.** *vn.* to fume; to emit smoke. **III.** *vr.* to be smoked; to look smoky.

ahusado, da. I. *a.* spindle-shaped, tapered. **II.** *pp.* of AHUSAR.

ahusar, *va. & vr.* to taper.

ahuyentador, ra, *n.* one that drives or scares away; scarecrow.

ahuyentar, *va.* to drive away, put to flight; to frighten away; to overcome (a passion), banish (care).

aijada, *f.* goad.

aína, aínas, *adv.* soon; easily; almost.

aindiado, da, *a.* Indianlike.

airadamente, *adv.* angrily.—**airado, da,** *a.* angry, wrathful.—**airamiento,** *m.* wrath, anger.

airar. I. *va.* to anger, to irritate. **II.** *vr.* to grow angry.

aire, *m.* air; atmosphere; wind; briskness (of a horse); air, carriage, gait; aspect, countenance, look; musical composition; frivolity.—**a. colado,** cold draught.—**al aire libre,** in the open air, outdoors.—**en el a.,** in suspense, in the air.—**¿qué aires lo traen a Vd. por acá?** what good wind brings you here?—**tomar el a.,** to take a walk.

airear. I. *va.* to give air to, ventilate; to aerate; to charge with gas. **II.** *vr.* to take the air; to cool one's self.

airecico, llo, to, *m. dim.* gentle breeze.

airón, *m. aug.* violent gale; ornament of plumes; crest; crested heron; egret; deep Moorish well.

airosamente, *adv.* gracefully, lightly.

airosidad, *f.* graceful deportment.

airoso, sa, *a.* airy, windy; graceful, genteel; lively; successful.

aisladamente, *adv.* isolately, singly.

aislado, da, *a.* isolated; (elec., phys.) insulated.

aislador, ra, *n. & a.* isolator (-ing); (elec., phys.) insulator (-ing).

aislamiento, *m.* isolation; (elec., phys.) insulation; insulating material.

aislar. I. *va.* to isolate; (elec., phys.) to insulate. **II.** *vr.* to become isolated; to isolate or seclude one's self.

¡ajá! *interj.* aha!

ajada, *f.* garlic sauce.

ajado, da. I. *a.* garlicky. **II.** *pp.* of AJAR.

ajamiento, *m.* disfiguring; crumpling, rumpling.

ajaquecarse, *vr.* to have a headache.

ajar, *m.* garlic field.

ajar, *va.* to crumple, rumple.—**a. la vanidad a uno,** to pull down one's pride.

ajarafe, *m.* table-land; terrace; flat roof.

aje, *m.* chronic complaint.

ajea, *f.* brushwood for fuel.

ajear, *vn.* to cry (s. o. a pursued partridge).

ajedrea, *f.* (bot.) winter savory.

ajedrecista, *n.* chess player.

ajedrez, *m.* chess; (naut.) netting, grating.

ajedrezado, da, *a.* checkered.

ajedrista, *n.* chess player.

ajenabo, *m.* (bot.) wild mustard.

ajenable, *a.* alienable.

ajengibre, *m.* = JENGIBRE.

ajenjo, *m.* (bot.) wormwood; absinth.

ajeno, na, *a.* another's; foreign; abhorrent, contrary; ignorant; improper.—**a. a,** foreign to; free from.—**a. de,** devoid of, lacking; ignorant of; indifferent to.

ajenuz, *m.* (bot.) field fennel-flower.

ajeo, *m. V.* PERRO.

ajero, ra, *n.* garlic dealer or vender.

ajesuitado, da, *a.* Jesuitical, Jesuit-like.

ajete, *m.* young garlic; leek; garlic sauce.

ajetrearse, *vr.* to tire; to fidget.—**ajetreo,** *m.* fatigue; agitation.

ají, *m.* chili, capsicum; chili sauce.

ajiaceite, *m.* mixture of garlic and oil.

ajiaco, *m.* dish made of boiled meat and vegetables; chili sauce.

ajicola, *f.* glue made of kidskin boiled with garlic.

ajilimoje, ajilimójili, *m.* pepper-and-garlic sauce.

ajillo, *m.* tender young garlic.

ajimez, *m.* arched window with pillar in centre.

ajipuerro, *m.* leek. *V.* PUERRO.

ajironar, *va.* to put colored pieces in.

ajo, *m.* (bot.) garlic; garlic sauce; face paint; (coll.) oath, swear word; suspicious dealings, shady business.

ajobar, *va.* to carry on the back.

ajobilla, *f.* common sea shell.

ajobo, *m.* a heavy load or burden.

ajofaina, *f.* = ALJOFAINA.

For pronunciation, see the rules at the beginning of the book.

ajolote, *m.* axolotl, a Mexican amphibian.

ajomate, *m.* (bot.) a variety of seaweed.

ajonje, *m.* bird lime.

ajonjera, *f.*; **ajonjero,** *m.* (bot.) the low carline thistle.

ajonjolí, *m.* (bot.) benne, sesame.

ajoqueso, *m.* dish made of garlic and cheese.

ajorca, *f.* Moorish bracelet or anklets.

ajornalar, *va.* to hire by the day.

ajuagas, *f. pl.* malanders or ulcers over the hoofs.

ajuanetado, da, *a.* bunionlike.

ajuar, *m.* bridal apparel and furniture; trousseau; household furniture.

ajudiado, da, *a.* Jewish; Jewlike.

ajuiciado, da, *a.* wise, sensible.

ajuiciar, *vn. & vr.* to become wise; to reform, to mend one's ways.

ajustadamente, *adv.* tightly; justly, rightly.

ajustado, da. I. *a.* exact, right; stingy; adapted; tight; fitted. **II.** *pp.* of AJUSTAR.

ajustador, ra. I. *n* .fitter, adjuster. **II.** *m.* close waistcoat, jacket; (print.), justifier; (mech.) adapter; adjusting tool.

ajustamiento, *m.* agreement; fitting; settling of accounts; receipts.

ajustar. I. *va.* to regulate; to adapt, adjust, fit; to justify (type); to agree about; to settle (an account, a controversy, etc.); to reconcile; to press close, oppress; to size, make true; to trim; to engage, hire. **II.** *vr.* to settle; to conform; to engage one's self; to be engaged or hired.

ajuste, *m.* proportion of the constituent parts of a thing; adjustment, fitting; agreement, contract, covenant; engagement; settlement.—*pl.* couplings.

ajusticiar, *va.* to execute, put to death.

al (contraction of **a** and **el**) to the (followed by a masc. noun); used also with the infinitive of verbs to indicate coexistence or immediate anteriority, and often equivalent to "on" (followed by present participle), "about," "on the point of": *al llegar,* on arriving; *al amanecer,* at daybreak; *estoy al partir,* I am about to leave; *Juan estuvo al perder su empleo,* John was on the point of losing (*or,* came very near losing) his position.

ala, *f.* wing; row, file; (mil., aer.) wing; brim (of hat) (anat.) auricle; fin (of fish); leaf (of a door, table).—*pl.* **alas,** upper studding sails.—**a. de gavia,** maintop studding sail.—**a. de mesana,** (naut.) driver.—**a. de proa,** head of a ship.—**a. de sobremesana,** mizzentop studding sail.—**a. de velacho,** fore studding sail.—**cortar,** or **quebrantar, las alas a uno,** to discourage one, to throw a wet blanket on one's plans; to deprive one of means or elements; to clip one's wings.

Alá, *m.* Allah, Arabic name of God.

alabado. I. *m.* hymn in praise of the sacrament. **II.** *pp.* of ALABAR.—**alabador, ra,** *n.* praiser.—**alabamiento,** *m.* praise.—**alabancioso, sa,** *a.* (coll.) boastful, ostentatious.

alabanza, *f.* praise, commendation.

alabar, *va. & vr.* to praise, extol, commend. —**a. uno sus agujas,** (coll.) to blow one's own horn.

alabarda, *f.* halberd.—**alabardado, da,** *a.* halberd-shaped.—**alabardazo,** *m.* a blow with a halberd.—**alabardero,** *m.* halberdier; clapper hired to applaud in a theatre.

alabastrado, da, *a.* alabasterlike.

alabastrina, *f.* thin sheet of alabaster.

alabastrino, na, *a.* alabastrine.

alabastro, *m.* alabaster.

álabe, *m.* drooping branch of a tree; bucket (of a water wheel); mat used in carts; cam.

alabear, *va. & vr.* to warp.

alabega, *f.* (bot.) sweet basil.

alabeo, *m.* warping.

alabiado, da, *a.* lipped or ragged (coins).

alacena, *f.* cupboard; closet; (naut.) locker.

alaciar, *vn.* = ENLACIAR.

alacrán, *m.* scorpion; ring of the bit of a bridle; stop or hook in organ bellows; chain or link of a sleeve button; swivel.

alacranado, da, *a.* scorpion-bitten; vice- or disease-ridden.

alacranera, *f.* (bot.) scorpion grass.

alacranídeo, a; alacránido, da, *a.* scorpionlike.

alacranino, na, *a.* relating to the scorpion or to scorpions.

alacridad, *f.* alacrity.

alacha, alache, *f.* anchovy.

alada, *f.* fluttering of the wings.

aladares, *m. pl.* forelocks over the temples.

aladierna, *f.* = ALATERNO.

alado, da, *a.* winged.

aladrada, *f.* (prov.) furrow.

aladrar, *va.* to plow.—**aladro,** *m.* plow; plowed land.

aladroque, *m.* unsalted anchovy.

alafia, *f.*—**pedir a.,** (coll.) to beg pardon.

álaga, *f.* a species of yellow wheat.

alagar, *va.* to make ponds or lakes in.

alagartado, da, *a.* variegated, motley.

alajú, *m.* paste made of nuts and honey.

alamar, *m.* frog and braid trimming.

alambicadamente, *adv.* pedantically.

alambicado, da. I. *a.* distilled; pedantic, euphuistic; given with a sparing hand. **II.** *pp.* of ALAMBICAR.—**alambicamiento,** *m.* distillation; pedantry, affected language.

alambicar, *va.* to distil; to scrutinize.

alambique, *m.* still.—**por a.,** sparingly.

alambor, *m.* (arch.) face of a hewn stone; (fort.) inside slope.

alambrada, *f.* (mil.) wire entanglements.

alambrado, *m.* wire netting, wire screen; wire cover; electric wiring; wire fence; wire entanglements.

alambre, *m.* wire; (ant.) copper, bronze, brass; sheep bells.—**a. conejo,** rabbit wire (used for rabbit-catching nets).

alambrera, *f.* wire netting; wire screen; wire cover; (agr.) wire trellis.

alameda, *f.* poplar grove; public walk.

alamín, *m.* clerk appointed to inspect weights and measures; surveyor of buildings; (prov.) farmer appointed to superintend irrigation.

alamina, *f.* fine paid by potters.

alaminazgo, *m.* office of the *alamín.*

alamirré, *m.* musical chord.

álamo, *m.* (bot.) poplar.—**a. blanco,** white poplar.—**a. temblón,** aspen tree.

alampar, *va. & vr.* (coll.) to long for; to crave.

alamud, *m.* square bolt for a door.

alanceador, *m.* lancer.—**alancear,** *va.* to spear.

alandrearse, *vr.* to become dry, stiff, and blanched (*s. o.* silkworms).

alanés, *m.* a large Mexican deer.

alano, *m.* large mastiff.

alano, na, *a.* of or pertaining to the Alani.

alanzar, *va.* to spear.

alaqueca, *f.* bloodstone.

alar, *m.* overhanging roof (*v.* ALERO); snare made with horsehair.

alar, *va.* (naut.) to haul. *V.* HALAR.

alárabe, alarbe. I. *n. & a.* Arabian. **II.** *n* unmannerly person.

alarde, *m.* review of soldiers, parade; ostentation, boasting, vanity.—**hacer a.,** to boast, brag.

alardear, *vn.* to boast.—**alardoso, sa,** *a.* boastful, bragging.

alargadera, *f.* lengthening bar (of compasses, etc.); (chem.) adapter, lengthening tube.

alargador, ra, *n.* stretcher; one that lengthens or stretches.—**alargamiento,** *m.* lengthening; (eng.) elongation.

alargar. I. *va.* (*pret.* ALARGUÉ: *subj.* ALARGUE) to lengthen; to extend; to stretch; to protract, prolong; to increase; to hand (a thing to another).—**a. un cabo,** (naut.) to pay out a cable. **II.** *vr.* to be prolonged; to drag; to become longer.

alarguez, *m.* (bot.) dog-rose.

alaria, *f.* potters' finishing tool.

alarida, *f.* hue and cry.

alarido, *m.* howl, outcry, shout, scream.

alarije, *f.* name of a large grape. *V.* ARIJE.

alarma, *f.* alarm.—**alarmante,** *a.* alarming.— **alarmar. I.** *va.* to alarm. **II.** *vr.* to become alarmed.—**alarmista,** *n.* alarmist.

alastrar. I. *va.* to throw back the ears. *V.* AMUS-GAR; (naut.) to ballast. **II.** *vr.* to lie flat.

alátere, *n.* (fam.) constant companion, shadow (fig.)

alaterno, *m.* (bot.) mock privet.

alatinado, da, *a.* Latinlike, puristic (s. o. language).

alatrón, *m.* froth of saltpetre.

alavanco, *m.* = LAVANCO.

alavense, alavés, *a.* Alavese, of Alava.

alazán, na, *a.* sorrel-colored.

alazo, *m.* a stroke with the wings.

alazor, *m.* (bot.) bastard saffron.

alba, *f.* dawn of day; alb, white gown worn by priests.—**al a., al rayar del a.,** at daybreak.— **quebrar, rayar,** or **reír, el alba,** to dawn.

albacara, *f.* (fort.) round tower.

albacea. I. *m.* executor. **II.** *f.* executrix.

albaceazgo, *m.* executorship.

albacora, *f.* fish resembling a tunny; a large fig.

albada, *f.* ALBORADA; (Mex.) attack at daybreak.

albahaca, *f.* (bot.) sweet basil.

albahaquero, *m.* flowerpot; sweet-basil vender.

albahaquilla (de río), *f.* = PARIETARIA.

albaida, *f.* (bot.) the shrubby gypsophila.

albalá, *m.* or *f.* (obs.) royal letter patent; a public instrument.

albanega, *f.* hair net; net for catching partridges or rabbits.

albanés, esa, *n.* & *a.* Albanian.

albañal, albañar, *m.* common sewer; soiled-water sink.

albañil, *m.* mason, builder.

albañilería, *f.* masonry.

albaquía, *f.* remnant.

albar, *a.* white.

albarán, *m.* "to-let" sign; royal grant or cedula; letter patent.

albarazada, *f.* marble-colored grape.

albarazado, da, *a.* affected with white leprosy; pale, whitish; (Mex.) cross between Chinese and half-breed parents.

albarazo, *m.* white leprosy.

albarca, *f.* = ABARCA.

albarcoque, *m.* = ALBARICOQUE.

albarcoquero, *m.* apricot tree.

albarda, *f.* packsaddle.—**albardado, da. I.** *a.* different-colored skin at the loins. **II.** *pp.* of AL-BARDAR.—**albardar,** *va.* to put a packsaddle on; to lard (fowls).—**albardela,** *f.* small saddle.

albardería, *f.* packsaddle shop; packsaddle making.—**albardero, ra,** *n.* packsaddle maker.

albardilla, *f.* small packsaddle; coping; border of a garden bed; wool tuft; bard.

albardín, *m.* (bot.) matweed.

albardón, *m.* pannel; large packsaddle.

albardoncillo, *m.* *dim.* small packsaddle.

albarejo, *m.* a variety of wheat. *V.* TRIGO.

albareque, *m.* fishing net.

albaricoque, *m.* apricot.—**albaricoquero,** *m.* apricot tree.

albarillo, *m.* a tune on the guitar; white apricot.

albarino, *m.* white cosmetic.

albarrada, *f.* dry wall; earth fence; wall for defence.

albarranilla, *f.* blue-flowered onion.

albarraz, *m.* (bot.) ALBARAZO; lousewort.

albatoza, *f.* small covered boat.

albatros, *m.* albatross.

albayaldado, da, *a.* cerused.—**albayaldar,** *va.* & *vr.* to cover with white lead.

albayalde, *m.* white lead, ceruse.

albazano, na, *a.* of dark chestnut color.

albear, *va.* to whiten. *V.* BLANQUEAR.

albedrío, *m.* will; free will; impulsiveness, wilfullness; (law) precedent; judgment.—**al a. de uno,** to, or according to, one's judgment or pleasure; as one likes.

albéitar, *m.* veterinarian.—**albeitería,** *f.* veterinary science.

albellón, *m.* = ALBAÑAL.

albenda, *f.* ornamented white-linen hangings.

albendera, *f.* woman who makes hangings; gadding woman.

albengala, *f.* gauze worn in turbans.

albéntola, *f.* fine fishing net.

alberca, *f.* pool; reservoir, tank; pond.—**en a.,** roofless.

albérchiga, *f.*, **albérchigo,** *m.* a variety of peach.

alberchiguero, *m.* variety of peach tree.

albergador, ra, *n.* one who shelters.

albergar. I. *va.* (*pret.* ALBERGUÉ; *subj.* ALBER-GUE) to lodge, shelter, harbor; to keep (lodgers). **II.** *vr.* to lodge; to find shelter or lodging.

albergue, *m.* lodging; shelter; den; asylum.

alberguería, *f.* inn; poorhouse.

albericoque, *m.* apricot.

albero, *m.* whitish earth; dishcloth.

alberquero, *m.* tender of pools or tanks.

alberquilla, *f.* *dim.* little pool.

albicante, *a.* whitening, bleaching.

albicaudo, da, *a.* white-tailed.

albicaulo, la, *a.* (bot.) white-stemmed.

albiceps, *a.* white-headed, white-faced.

albiense, *n.* & *a.* (geol.) Albian.

albigense, *n.* & *a.* Albigensian.

albihar, *m.* (bot.) oxeye.

albilla, *f.*, **albillo,** *m.* early white grape.

albillo, *a.* wine of white grape.

albín, *m.* bloodstone; carmine pigment.

albina, *f.* salt-water marsh.

albino, na, *a.* albino.—**albinismo,** *m.* albinism.

Albión, *f.* Albion (England).

albita, *f.* (min.) albite, white feldspar.

albitana, *f.* fence to inclose plants; (naut.) an apron.—**a. del codaste,** (naut.) inner post.

albo, ba, *a.* snow white.

alboaire, *m.* glazed tile work.

albogalla, *f.* a kind of gallnut.

albogue, *m.* pastoral flute; martial music.

alboguero, ra, *n.* one that plays the *albogue* or makes *albogues*.

albohol, *m.* (bot.) red poppy.

albóndiga, *f.* ball of forced meat with eggs and spice.—**albondiguilla,** *f.* *dim.* small ball of forced meat.

albor, *m.* dawn; whiteness; beginning.—**a.,** or **albores, de la vida,** childhood, youth.

alborada, *f.* dawn; (mil.) battle at dawn; reveille; morning watch.

albórbola, *f.* shouting and yelling (gen. for joy or mirth).

alborear, *vn.* to dawn.

alborga, *f.* matweed sandal.

albornía, *f.* large glazed jug.

alborno, *m.* (bot.) alburnum.

albornoz, *m.* coarse woollen stuff; Moorish cloak; burnoose.

alboronía, *f.* dish of eggplant, tomatoes, pumpkins, and pimento.

alboroque, *m.* treat at the conclusion of a bargain.

alborotadamente, *adv.* noisily, confusedly.

alborotadizo, za; alborotado, da, *a.* restive; excitable; turbulent.

alborotador, ra, *n.* agitator, rioter.

alborotapueblos, *m.* rioter, agitator; (coll.) good-natured person; promoter of gaieties.

alborotar. I. *va.* to disturb, agitate, excite; to start (the game). **II.** *vr.* to become excited; fuss; riot.—**alboroto,** *m.* disturbance, tumult, riot; outcry, hubbub, fuss.

alborozador, ra, *n.* promoter of mirth.

alborozar, *va.* (*pret.* ALBOROCÉ: *subj.* ALBOROCE) to exhilarate, gladden.

alborozo, *m.* merriment, gaiety, joy.

---

albotín, *m.* = TEREBINTO.
albricias, *f. pl.* reward for good news; (Mex.) top holes in casting moulds.—¡albricias! joy! joy!
albudeca, *f.* (bot.) watermelon.
albufera, *f.* large lagoon by the sea.
albugíneo, a, *a.* entirely white; albuminous.
albugo, *m.* leucoma, a disease of the eye.
albuhera, *f.* lake or reservoir.
álbum, *m.* album.
albumen, *m.* albumen.—**albúmina,** *f.* albumin.
—**albuminoideo, a,** *adj.* albuminoid.
albuminoso, sa, albuminous.
albuminuria, *f.* (med.) albuminuria.
albur, *m.* dace, river fish; first draw at "monte"; risk, chance.—**correr un a.,** to venture, chance, risk.—*pl.* **albures,** a card game.
albura,— *f.* whiteness; (bot.) = ALBORNO.
alburero, *m.* *albures* player.
alburno, *m.* (bot.) = ALBORNO.
alca, *f.* razorbill (a bird).
alcabala, *f.* alcabala, tax on sales.—**a. del viento,** duty paid by a visiting merchant.—**alcabalatorio,** *m.* book of alcabala rates; tax register.—**alcabalero,** *m.* taxgatherer, revenue officer.
alcacel, alcacer, *m.* green barley.
alcachofa, *f.* (bot.) artichoke; instrument to stop blood; fluted mallets.—**alcachofado, da. I.** *a.* artichokelike. **II.** *m.* dish of artichokes.
alcachofal, *m.* artichoke bed.—**alcachofera,** *f.* artichoke plant.—**alcachofero, ra,** *a.* producing or selling artichokes.
alcahaz, *m.* large bird cage.—**alcahazada,** *f.* number of birds in a cage.—**alcahazar,** *va.* to cage (birds).
alcahuete, ta, *n.* pimp, procurer, bawd.
alcahuetear, *va. & vn.* to bawd, pander.
alcahuetería, *f.* bawdry, pandering; (coll.) dodge.
alcaicería, *f.* raw-silk exchange.
alcaico, *a.* (poet.) alcaic verse in Latin.
alcaide, *m.* governor of a castle; jailer, warden.
alcaidesa, *f.* wife of an *alcaide.*
alcaidía, *f.* office of a castle governor, warden, or jailer; duty on cattle.
alcalaíno, na, *n. & a.* (one) from Alcalá.
alcaldada, *f.* abusive action of an *alcalde.*
alcalde, *m.* mayor; justice of the peace; leader; name of a card game.—**a. de barrio,** selectman to whom the mayor delegates his function in a section of a city.—**alcaldear,** *vn.* (coll.) to play the *alcalde.*
—**alcaldesa,** *f.* wife of an *alcalde.*—**alcaldía,** *f.* office and jurisdiction of an *alcalde.*
alcalescencia, *f.* (chem.) alkalescence.
alcalescente, *a.* (chem.) alkalescent.
álcali, *m.* (chem.) alkali.—**alcalificable,** *a.* alkalifiable.—**alcalígeno, na,** *a.* alkaligenous.—**alcalimetría,** *f.* alkalimetry.—**alcalimétrico,** alkalimetric.—**alcalímetro,** *m.* alkalimeter.—**alcalinidad,** *f.* alkalinity.—**alcalino, na; alcalizado, da,** *a.* alkaline.—**alcalización,** *f.* (chem.) alkalization.—**alcalizar,** *va.* (pret. ALCALICÉ: subj. ALCALICE) (chem.) to render alkaline.—**alcaloide,** *m.* alkaloid.
alcaller, *m.* potter.
alcam, *m.* (bot.) bitter apple.
alcamonías. I. *f. pl.* various aromatic seeds for seasoning. **II.** *m.* = ALCAHUETE.
alcana, *f.* ALHEÑA.
alcance, *m.* reach; overtaking; balance; arm's length; scope, extent; range (of fire arms, etc.); capacity, ability; fathom; compass; supplement, extra edition; postscript; (print.) copy.—**irle a uno a, or en, los alcances,** to watch, or spy on, one.—**seguir los alcances a,** to pursue.
alcancía, *f.* bank, money box; earthen balls stuffed with flowers for missiles; (mil.) explosive bullet.
alcandía, *f.* (bot.) Turkey millet. *V.* ZAHINA.
alcandial, *m.* millet field.
alcandora, *f.* beacon; bonfire; white tunic.
alcanfor, *m.* camphor.—**alcanforada,** *f.* (bot.) a camphor-smelling plant.—**alcanforado, da,** *a.* camphorated.—**alcanforar,** *va.* to camphorate.—**alcanforero,** *m.* camphor tree.

alcántara, *f.* cover for velvet in the loom.
alcantarilla, *f.* small bridge; culvert; drain; sewer.—**alcantarillado,** *m.* sewage.
alcantarillar, *va.* to sewer.
alcanzadizo, za, *a.* easily reached or obtainable.
alcanzado, da. I. *a.* needy; in arrears; impecunious. **II.** *pp.* of ALCANZAR.
alcanzadura, *f.* (vet.) tumor in the pastern.
alcanzar. I. *va.* (pret. ALCANCÉ: subj. ALCANCE) to follow; overtake, come up to; to reach; to acquire, obtain, attain; to comprehend; to be creditor of a balance; to be contemporaneous. **II.** *vn.* to share; to suffice, to be enough; to reach. **III.** *vr.* to wound the pasterns with the feet (s. o. horses and cattle).
alcaparra, *f.* **alcaparro,** *m.* (bot.) caper bush; caper.—**alcaparrado, da,** *a.* dressed with capers.—**alcaparral,** *m.* caper field.—**alcaparrón,** *m.* *aug.* large caper.
alcaparrosa, *f.* = CAPARROSA.
alcaraván, *m.* (orn.) bittern.—**alcaravanero,** *m.* bittern hawk.
alcaravea, *f.* (bot.) caraway seed.
alcarceña, *f.* (bot.) bitter vetch.
alcarceñal, *m.* officinal tare field.
alcarracero, ra, *n.* potter; shelf for earthenware.
alcarraza, *f.* unglazed and porous jar.
alcartaz, *m.* = CUCURUCHO.
alcatifa, *f.* fine carpet or rug; layer of earth.
alcatraz, *m.* pelican. *V.* CUCURUCHO.
alcaucil, *m.* wild artichoke. *V.* ALCACHOFA.
alcayata, *f.* spike. *V.* ESCARPIA.
alcázar, *m.* castle; fortress; (naut.) quarterdeck.
alcazuz, *m.* licorice. *V.* OROZUZ.
alce, *m.* (zool.) elk; moose; cut (at cards).
alcino, *m.* (bot.) wild basil.
alción, *m.* Chinese swallow; MARTÍN PESCADOR.
alcista, *f.* bull (stock speculator).
alcoba, *f.* alcove; bedroom; case for the tongue of a balance; place for public weighing.
alcocarra, *f.* gesture, grimace.
alcohol, *m.* alcohol; antimony; galena; spirit of wine; cosmetic for pencilling eyebrows; liquor.
—**a. amílico,** amyl alcohol.—**a. metílico,** methyl alcohol, wood alcohol.
alcoholado, da. I. *a.* of a darker color around the eyes. **II.** *pp.* of ALCOHOLAR.—**alcoholador, ra,** *n.* rectifier of spirits.—**alcoholar,** *va.* to paint or dye with antimony; to distill alcohol from; to pulverize.—**alcoholato,** *m.* alcoholate.—**alcoholera,** *f.* vessel for antimony or alcohol.—**alcohólico, ca,** *a.* alcoholic.—**alcoholimetría,** *f.* alcoholometry.—**alcoholímetro,** *m.* alcoholimeter.—**alcoholismo,** *m.* alcoholism.—**alcoholización,** *f.* (chem.) alcoholization.—**alcoholizado, da,** *a.* affected by alcoholism.—**alcoholizar,** *va.* (pret. ALCOHOLICÉ: subj. ALCOHOLICE) to alcoholize.
alcor, *m.* hill.
Alcorán, *m.* Koran.—**alcoranista,** *m.* Koran expounder; Koran scholar.
alcornocal, *m.* plantation of cork trees.
alcornoque, *m.* (bot.) cork tree; blockhead.
alcornoqueño, ña, *a.* pertaining to the cork tree.
alcorque, *m.* corkwood clogs or soles; hollow for water around trees.
alcorza, *f.* sugar paste for frosting.
alcorzar, *va.* to frost with sugar.
alcotán, *m.* lanner, bird of prey.
alcotana, *f.* pickaxe.
alcotancillo, *m.* *dim.* young lanner.
alcrebite, *m.* sulphur.
alcribis, *m.* tuyere, tweer.
alcubilla, *f.* reservoir; basin, mill pond.
alcucero, ra. I. *n.* maker of tin oil bottles, cruets, etc. **II.** *a.* belonging to an oil bottle.
alcucilla, *f.* *dim.* small oil can.
alcuña, alcurnia, *f.* ancestry, lineage.
alcuza, *f.* oil bottle or cruet; oil can, oiler.
alcuzada, *f.* cruetful of oil.
alcuzcuz, *m.* balls of flour, water, and honey.
alcuzón, *m.* *aug.* large oil can.
aldaba, *f.* knocker, clapper (of a door); latch; sliding crossbar to secure doors and windows.

—**aldabada,** *f.* rap with the knocker; sudden fear; pangs of conscience.—**aldabazo, aldabonazo,** *m.* knocking.—**aldabear,** *vn.* to rap or knock at the door.

aldabía, *f.* horizontal crossbeam.—**aldabilla,** *f. dim.* small knocker; latch.—**aldabón,** *m. aug.* large knocker; iron trunk handle.

aldea, *f.* village, hamlet.

aldeanamente, *adv.* in village style, countrylike.

aldeaniego, ga, *a.* belonging to a hamlet.

aldeano, na. I. *n.* villager, peasant. **II.** *a.* rustic, uncultured.

Aldebarán, *m.* (ast.) Aldebaran, Bull's Eye.

aldehido, *m.* aldehyde.

aldehuela, aldeilla, *f. dim.* little village.

aldeorrio, *m.* small, insignificant village.

aldiza, *f.* small reed without knots.

aldrán, *m.* one who sells wine to shepherds.

aleación, *f.* alloying; alloy.—**alcador,** *m.* alloyer.

alear. I. *vn.* to flutter; to move the arms quickly up and down; to recover from sickness or fatigue. **II.** *va.* to alloy.

aleatorio, ria, *a.* relating to chance games; (law) aleatory, fortuitous.

alebrado, da. I. *a.* hare-hearted. **II.** *pp.* of ALEBRARSE.

alebrarse, *vr.* to squat; to cower.

alebrastarse, alebrestarse, *vr.* to cut capers; to become frightened or excited; to get puffed up.

alebronarse, *vr.* to lose heart.

aleccionamiento, *m.* instruction, coaching, lessons.—**aleccionar,** *va.* to teach, instruct, coach.

alece, *m.* ragout of fish liver.

alecrín, *m.* name of a Cuban fish.

alectórico, ca, *a.* pertaining to cocks; cocklike.

alechigar. I. *va.* to soften. **II.** *vr.* to turn milky.

alechugado, da. I. *a.* curled, wrinkled; fluted, plaited. **II.** *pp.* of ALECHUGAR.—**alechugar,** *va.* to curl like lettuce; to plait, flute.

aledaño, ña, *n.* & *a.* boundary (-ing), border.

alefanginas, *f. pl.* purgative pills from spices.

alefriz, alefriz, *m.* mortise, rabbet.

alefrizar, *va.* (pret. ALEFRICÉ: subj. ALEFRICE) to rabbet, mortise.

alegación, *f.* allegation, argument.

alegar, *va.* (pret. ALEGUÉ: subj. ALEGUE) to allege, affirm; quote; adduce.

alegato, *m.* (law) allegation, presentation, summing-up.

alegoría, *f.* allegory.—**alegóricamente,** *adv.* allegorically.—**alegórico, ca,** *a.* allegorical.—**alegorista,** *m.* allegorist.—**alegorizar,** *va.* (pret. ALEGORICÉ: subj. ALEGORICE) to turn into allegory.

alegrador, ra. I. *n.* & *a.* (one) causing merriment. **II.** *m.* paper cigar lighter; (mech.) reamer.

alegrar. I. *va.* to make merry, gladden, comfort, exhilarate; to enliven; to beautify; (mech.) to round, bore, ream, widen. **II.** *vr.* to rejoice; to be glad; to exult; to get tipsy.

alegre, *a.* merry, joyful; light-hearted, full of gaiety, lively; cheerful; funny, comic, facetious; gay; showy, fine; brilliant, pleasing (app. to colors); lucky, fortunate; (fam.) off-color (story); reckless, careless; optimistic; tipsy.—**a. de cascos,** featherbrained.

alegremente, *adv.* merrily, gaily; gladly, cheerfully; facetiously.

alegría, *f.* mirth, merriment, gaiety; rejoicing, joy; (bot.) sesamum; oily grain; paste of sesamum and honey.—*pl.* rejoicings, public festival.

alegrillo, *a.* sprightly, gay.

alegro, *m.* (mus.) allegro.

alegrón. I. *m.* (coll.) sudden, unexpected joy; a flash. **II. a., na,** *a.* tipsy; lively (from liquor).

alejamiento, *m.* removal to a distance; receding; retiring, withdrawal; estrangement.

alejandrino, na. I. *n.* & *a.* Alexandrian (from Alexandria). **II.** (-no) *n.* & *a.* Alexandrine (verse).

alejar. I. *va.* to remove to a distance; to separate; to withdraw; to estrange. **II.** *vr.* to recede, to draw or move away.

alejijas, *f. pl.* barley porridge.

alelarse, *vr.* to become stupified.

alelí, *m.* (bot.) winter gilliflower; violet.

aleluya, *f.* hallelujah; joy, merriment; Easter time; (bot.) wood-sorrel.—*pl.* small prints thrown among the people on Easter eve; dull, poor verses, doggerel.

alema, *f.* allotted quantity of irrigation water.

alemán, na, *n.* & *a.* German.

alemana, alemanda, *f.* ancient Spanish dance of German origin.

alemanisco, ca, *a.* Germanic; cloth made in Germany; huckaback; damask table linen.

alenguamiento, *m.* agreement relative to pasture lands.

alenguar, *va.* to pact about pasture lands or pasturage.

alentada, *f.* a long breath.

alentadamente, *adv.* bravely, gallantly.

alentado, da. I. *a.* spirited, courageous; well, in good health. **II.** *pp.* of ALENTAR.

alentador, ra. I. *n.* one who inspires courage. **II.** *a.* encouraging, cheering.

alentar. I. *vn.* (ind. ALIENTO: subj. ALIENTE) to breathe. **II.** *va.* to encourage, comfort, cheer.

aleaonado, da, *a.* lionlike; lion-colored.

alepín, *m.* a kind of bombazine.

alerce, *m.* (bot.) larch tree.

alero, *m.* projecting part of a roof; eaves; gable end, corona; hood moulding; water table; splashboard of a carriage.—*pl.* snares for partridges.

alerón, *m.* (aer.) aileron.

alerta, *f.* (mil.) watchword.

alerta, alertamente, *adv.* vigilantly, carefully.—**estar a.,** to be on the alert.

alertar, *va.* to render vigilant; to put on guard.

alerto, ta, *a.* vigilant, alert, guarded.

alesna, *f.* awl (= LESNA).—**alesnado, da,** *a.* awl-shaped, pointed.

aleta, *f. dim.* small wing; fin (of a fish); (arch.) alette; (mech.) leaf of a hinge; teeth of a pinion; blade (of a screw propeller).

aletada, *f.* motion of the wings.

aletargado, da. I. *a.* lethargic. **II.** *pp.* of ALETARGARSE.—**aletargamiento,** *m.* lethargy.

aletargarse, *vr.* to fall into a lethargy.

aletazo, *m.* blow with the wing; flapping.

aleteado, da, *a.* finlike, finned.

aletear, *vn.* to flutter, flap wings, flit.

aleteo, *m.* flapping of wings.

aleto, *m.* (orn.) (Peru) falcon. *V.* HALIETO.

aletón, *m. aug.* large wing.

aletría, *m.* vermicelli.

aleudarse, *vr.* to become fermented.

aleve, *a.* treacherous, perfidious.

alevilla, *a.* white moth resembling the silkworm's moth.

alevosa, *f.* (vet.) tumor under the tongue.

alevosamente, *adv.* treacherously.

alevosia, *f.* perfidy, treachery.

alevoso, sa, *a.* treacherous.

alexifármaco, ca, *a.* (med.) alexipharmic, antidotal.

alfa, *f.* alpha (Greek letter); beginning.

alfábega, *f. V.* ALBAHACA.

alfabéticamente, *adv.* alphabetically.

alfabético, ca, *a.* alphabetical.

alfabeto, *m.* alphabet.

alfaguara, *f.* copious stream.

alfajía, *f.* wood frame for windows and doors.

alfajor, *m.* = ALAJÚ.

alfalfa, *f.* (bot.) lucern, alfalfa.

alfalfal, alfalfar, *m.* alfalfa field.

alfalfe, *m.* = ALFALFA.

alfana, *f.* strong and spirited horse.

alfandoque, *m.* candy made with molasses, cheese and ginger, or of thickened brown-sugar syrup.

alfaneque, *m.* white eagle; tent, booth.

alfanjado, da, *a.* cutlass-shaped.—**alfanje,** *m.* hanger, cutlass.—**alfanjete,** *m. dim.* small cutlass.

For pronunciation, see the rules at the beginning of the book.

—**alfanjazo,** *m.* wound with a cutlass.—**alfanjón,** *m. aug.* large hanger or cutlass.—**alfanjonazo,** *m.* cut with a large hanger.

alfaque, *m.* shoal or bar.

alfaquí, *m.* alfaqui, a Mussulman expounder and teacher of the Koran.

alfar. I. *m.* pottery. *V.* ARCILLA. **II.** *a.* that raises the head too much (s. o. a horse). **III.** *vn.* to raise the head too much (s. o. a horse).

alfaraz, *a.* Moorish horse for light cavalry.

alfarda, *f.* tax paid for the irrigation of lands; light wooden beam.

alfardero, *m.* (prov.) collector of irrigation taxes.

alfardilla, *f.* galloon; tax for the cleaning of water-supply trenches.

alfardón, *m.* washer of a wheel; water tax.

alfarería, *f.* pottery.—**alfarero, ra,** *n.* potter.

alfarje, *m.* lower stone of an oil mill; ceiling adorned with carved work; wainscot.

alfarjía, *f.* = ALFAJÍA.

alféizar, *m.* splay of a door or window; embrasure.

alfeñicado, da, *a.* weakly, delicate.

alfeñicar, *va.* to frost with sugar.

alfeñicarse, *vr.* to become thin; (coll.) to affect delicateness.

alfeñique, *m.* sugar paste; delicate person.

alferecía, *f.* epilepsy.

alférez, *m.* ensign; second lieutenant.

alfil, *m.* bishop (in chess).

alfiler, *m.* pin; scarf-pin; jeweller's brooch.—*pl.* **alfileres,** pin money.—**a. de París,** wire nail.—**a. de seguridad,** safety pin (more generally called IMPERDIBLE).—**con todos sus alfileres,** or, **de veinticinco alfileres,** dressed up in high style.

alfilerazo, *m.* prick with a pin; large pin.

alfilerera, *f.* alfileria, seed of the geranium.

alfilerero, ra, *n.* maker or seller of pins.

alfiletero, *m.* pin case, needlecase; pincushion.

alfitete, *m.* paste made of coarse wheat flour.

alfolí, *m.* granary; salt depot.

alfoliero, alfolinero, *m.* keeper of a granary or depot.

alfombra, *f.* floor carpet; (med.) measles.

alfombrar, *va.* to carpet.—**alfombrero, ra,** *n.* carpet maker.—**alfombrilla,** *f.* small carpet, rug; (med.) measles.

alfóncigo, *m.* pistachio; pistachio tree.

alfonsearse, *vr.* (coll.) to mock, banter.

alfónsigo, *m.* = ALFÓNCIGO.

alfonsino, na, *a.* belonging to the Alphonsos (Spanish kings).

alfonsina, *f.* solemn act held in the Alphonsine college of Alcalá.

alforfón, *m.* buckwheat.

alforja, *f.* saddlebag; knapsack.

alforjero, *m.* maker or seller of saddlebags; lay brother who begs alms; one who carries the bag with provisions. *V.* PERRO A.

alforjilla, ita, uela, *f. dim.* small saddlebag; small knapsack.

alforza, *f.* plait, tuck.

alfoz, *m.* = ALHOZ.

alga, *f.* (bot.) alga.

aigadonera, *f.* (bot.) cudweed.

algaida, *f.* ridge of shifting sand; sand dune; jungle, brush.

algaído, da, *a.* (prov.) thatched.

algalaba, *f.* (bot.) white briony, wild hops.

algalia, *f.* civet, a perfume; catheter.

algaliar, *va.* to perfume with civet.

algara, *f.* skin (of an egg, onion, etc.); foraging party of cavalry.

algarabía, *f.* Arabic; (met.) gabble, jargon; din, clamor; (bot.) centaury.

algarada, *f.* loud cry; sudden attack; ancient battering ram.

algarero, ra, *a.* prating, chattering, talkative.

algarrada, *f.* driving bulls into the pen; bull baiting; battering ram.

algarroba, *f.* (bot.) carob bean; honey mesquit.

algarrobal, *m.* carob tree plantation or grove.

algarrobera, *f.*, **algarrobo** *m.* (bot.) carob tree.

algazara, *f.* huzza; din, clamor.

algazul, *m.* seaweed producing barilla.

álgebra, *f.* algebra; art of setting joints.

algebraico, ca; algébrico, ca, *a.* algebraic.

algebrista, *m.* algebraist; bonesetter.

algecireño, ña, *n. & a.* Algecirian, from, or pertaining to, Algeciras.

algidez, *f.* (med.) icy coldness.

álgido, da, *a.* algid, icy.

algo. I. *n.* some, something, aught.—**a. es a.,** or, **más vale algo que nada,** something is better than nothing; every little bit counts. **II.** *adv.* somewhat, a little, rather.

algodón, *m.* cotton; cotton plant.—**a. en rama,** raw cotton.—**algodones.** *V.* CENDALES.

algodonado, da, *a.* filled with cotton.

algodonal, *m.* cotton plantation.

algodonar, *va.* to cover or fill with cotton.

algodonería, *f.* cotton factory; cotton trade.

algodonero, *m.* cotton plant; cotton dealer; cottonwood poplar.

algodonoso, sa, *a.* cottony; covered with thick down; woolly; tasteless (s. o. fruits).

algonquín, na, *n. & a.* Algonquin.

algorín, *m.* place in oil mills for receiving olives.

algoritmo, *m.* algorithm; arithmetic.

algoso, sa, *a.* full of algæ.

alguacil, *m.* constable, peace officer, bumbailiff; short-legged spider.

alguacilazgo, *m.* office of an *alguacil.*

alguarín, *m.* storeroom; flour-mill bucket.

alguaza, *f.* (prov.) hinge.

alguien, *pro.* somebody, some one.

algún, *a. V.* ALGUNO.—**a. tanto,** a little, somewhat.

alguno, a. I. *a.* (**algún,** before *m. n.*) some, any. —**a. vez,** sometime; some times, now and then. **II.** *n.* somebody, some one.—*pl.* some, some people.

alhábega, *f.* (prov.) = ALBAHACA.

alhadida, *f.* (chem.) saffron or burnt copper.

alhaja, *f.* jewel, gem; showy furniture; (coll.) an excellent person; (ironic) a bad one, a tough one (s. o. persons, often in the form, ¡buena a.!)

alhajar, *va.* to adorn, to furnish, fit up.

alhajuela, *f. dim.* little jewel.

alhamel, *m.* (prov.) beast of burden; porter; muleteer.

alhana, *f.* alhanna, Tripoli earth.

alhandal, *m.* (pharm.) colocynth.

alharaca, *f.* clamor, fuss, ado.

alharaquiento, ta, fussy, clamorous, grumbling.

alhárgama, alharma, *f.* (bot.) wild rue.

alhasa, *f.* hydroa, a skin disease.

alhelí, *m.* gilliflower.

alheña, *f.* (bot.) privet; privet powder (*v.* AZÚMBAR); blasting of corn. *V.* ROYA.

alheñar. I. *va.* to dye with privet. **II.** *vr.* to become mildewed (app. to corn. *V.* ARROYARSE).

alhoja, *f.* a bird resembling a lark.

alholva, *f.* (bot.) fenugreek.

alhóndiga, *f.* public granary; wheat exchange.—**alhondiguero,** *m.* keeper of a public granary.

alhorma, *f.* Moorish camp or royal tent.

alhorre, *m.* meconium, first discharge from an infant's bowels; skin eruption.

alhoz, *m.* district, borough, neighboring district or dependence.

alhucema, *f.* (bot.) lavender.

alhumajo, *m.* pine needles.

aliabierto, ta, *a.* open-winged.

aliacán, *m.* jaundice.

aliacanado, da, *a.* jaundiced.

aliáceo, a, *a.* aliaceous, garliclike.

aliado, da. I. *a. & n.* ally, allied. **II.** *pp.* of ALIARSE.

aliaga, *f.* (bot.) furze, whin.—**aliagar,** *m.* furze field.

alianza, *f.* alliance; agreement, pact; (Bib.) covenant; alliance by marriage.

aliara, *f.* drinking horn.

aliaria, *f.* (bot.) garlic mustard.

aliarse, *vr.* to become allied, to form an alliance.

alias, *adv.* (Lat.) otherwise, alias.

alible, *a.* nutritive, nourishing.

alica, ta, *f. dim.* small wing.

álica, *f.* pottage of corn, wheat, and pulse.

alicaído, da, *a.* drooping, weak, extenuated; discouraged, depressed, downhearted.

alicántara, *f.*, **alicante,** *m.* name of a poisonous snake.

alicantina, *f.* (coll.) artifice, stratagem, trap.

alicantino, na, *n. & a.* (one) from Alicante.

alicatado, *m.* work inlaid with Dutch tiles.

alicates, *m. pl.* pliers.

aliciente, *m.* attraction, inducement.

alicuanta, *a.* aliquant.

alícuota, *f. a.* aliquot; proportional.—**partes alícuotas,** (arith.) aliquot parts.

alidada, *f.* alidade.

alienación, *f.* (law and med.) alienation.—**alienado, da,** *a.* insane.—**alienar,** *va.* = ENAJENAR.—**alienista,** *n.* alienist.

aliento, *m.* breath; vigor; bravery; enterprise, activity.—**dar a.,** to encourage; to further; to cheer.—**de un a.,** in a single breath; without stopping.—**sin a.,** out of breath.

aliento, aliente. *V.* ALENTAR.

alier, *m.* (naut.) rower; sailor on watch.

alifafe, *m.* callous tumor on a horse's hock; (coll.) chronic complaint.

alifar, *va.* (prov.) to polish, burnish.

alifara, *f.* (prov.) collation, luncheon.

alífero, ra, *a.* aliferous, winged.

aliforme, *a.* aliform, wing-shaped.

aligación, *f.* alligation; tying together.

aligamiento, *m.* alligation; binding together.

aligar, *va.* (*pret.* ALIGUÉ; *subj.* ALIGUE) = LIGAR.

aliger, *m.* cross guard (of a sword).

aligeramiento, *m.* alleviation, lightening.

aligerar, *va.* to lighten; to alleviate; to ease; to hasten; to shorten.

alígero, ra, *a.* (poet.) winged, fast, fleet.

alijador, ra, *n.* smuggler; (naut.) one who lightens; one who clears cotton of seeds.

alijar, *va.* (naut.) to lighten; to clear (cotton) of seeds, to gin; to smuggle.

alijar, *m.* waste, stony ground.

alijarar, *va.* to divide (waste lands) for cultivation.

alijarero, *m.* sharer of waste lands to till.

alijares, *m. pl.* royal pleasure resort in Granada.

alijariego, ga, *a.* relating to waste lands.

alijo, *m.* (naut.) lightening of a ship; alleviation; smuggled goods.

alilla, *f. dim.* small wing; fin of a fish.

alimaña, *f.* animal (gen. app. to destructive ones).

alimentación, *f.* feeding; meals, board; nutrition.—**de a.,** feeding, feed (u. a., as in *agua de alimentación,* feed water).

alimentar, *va.* to feed, nourish; to support, supply with the necessaries of life; to nurture, fondle, encourage, further; to cherish, have (hope).

alimentario, ria, *n.* one who enjoys a maintenance.

alimenticio, cia, *a.* nourishing; feeding, feed (u. a.).

alimentista, *n.* = ALIMENTARIO.

alimento, *m.* nourishment, food, nutriment; encouragement incentive.—*pl.* allowance, pension, alimony; meals, board.—**a. combustible,** carbohydrate or fat (s. o. food).—**a. plástico,** protein, nitrogenous food.—**a. respiratorio** = A. COMBUSTIBLE.

alimentoso, sa, *a.* nourishing, nutritious.

alimo, *m.* (bot.) *V.* ORZAGA.

alimoche, *m.* a bird of prey.

alimonarse, *vr.* to turn yellowish from disease (said of tree leaves).

alindado, da. **I.** *a.* affectedly nice or elegant.

alindar, *va.* to mark the limits of; to embellish.

alinde, *m.* (obs.) quicksilver for mirrors.

alineación, *f.* alinement.

alinear. **I.** *va.* to aline. **II.** *vr.* to aline itself; to fall in line; to form a line.

aliñador, ra, *n.* one who embellishes; one who seasons or dresses food.—**aliñar,** *va.* to adorn; to dress or season (food).—**aliño,** *m.* ornament, decoration; cleanliness; dressing or seasoning.—**aliñoso, sa,** *a.* dressed up, decked out; decorated.

alioli, *m.* (prov.) = AJIACEITE.

alionín, *m.* the blue-feathered duck.

alipata, *m.* a Philippine poison tree.

alípede, *a.* (poet.) winged, swift, nimble.

alípedo, da, *a.* (zool.) chiropterous.

aliquebrado, da, *a.* broken-winged; dejected.

alisador, ra, *n.* polisher, smoothing iron; silk stick; tool to shape wax candles.

alisadura, *f.* planing, smoothing, polishing.

alisaduras, *f. pl.* shavings, cuttings.

alisar, *va.* to plane, smooth, polish, burnish.

alisar, *m.* **aliseda,** *f.* alder-tree plantation.

alisios, *m. pl.* trade winds.

alisma, *f.* (bot.) water plantain.

aliso, *m.* (bot.) alder tree.

alistado, da. **I.** *a.* enlisted; striped.

alistador, ra, *n.* one who enrols or enlists.

alistamiento, *m.* enrolment; conscription, levy.

alistar, *va. & vr.* to enlist, enrol; to get or make ready.

aliteración, *f.* alliteration.

aliviador, ra, *n.* assistant; helper; spindle to raise or lower a running millstone.

aliviar, *va.* to lighten; to loosen; to alleviate, assuage, soothe, relieve; to hasten, speed up.

alivio, *m.* alleviation, easement; mitigation; relief; improvement, betterment.

alizace, *m.* foundation, trench.

alizar, *m.* dado or wainscotting of tiles.

aljaba, *f.* quiver.

aljafana, *f.* = ALJOFAINA.

aljama, *f.* assembly of Moors or Jews; synagogue.

aljamía, *f.* (obs.) corrupted Arabic spoken by the Moors; Moorish name of the Spanish language.

aljarafe, *m.* roof; terrace.

aljarfa, *f.*, **aljarfe,** *m.*, **aljerife,** *m.* tarred net with small meshes.

aljévena, *f.* (prov.) = ALJOFAINA.

aljez, *m.* gypsum; plaster of Paris.—**aljezar,** *m.* gypsum pit.—**aljezón,** *m.* = ALJEZ.

aljibe, *m.* cistern; reservoir, pool; (naut.) tank boat for supplying vessels with water.

aljibero, *m.* one who takes care of cisterns.

aljimerado, a, *a.* shaved, trimmed.

aljofaina, *f.* washbowl, basin.

aljófar, *m.* misshapen pearl; (poet.) water or dewdrops.—**aljofarado, da.** **I.** *a.* (poet.) full of little drops or pearls. **II.** *pp.* of ALJOFARAR.—**aljofarar,** *va.* to adorn with pearls.

aljofifa, *f.* mop.—**aljofifar,** *va.* to clean with a cloth, to mop.

aljonje, *m.* = AJONJE.—**aljonjera,** *f.* = AJONJERA.—**aljonjero,** *a.* AJONJERO.

aljonjolí, *m.* = AJONJOLÍ.

aljor, *m.* crude gypsum.

aljorozar, *va.* to level, render smooth; to plaster.

aljorra, *m.* (Cuba) a very small insect which, carried by the wind, destroys plantations.

aljuba, *f.* a Moorish garment.

alma, *f.* soul; ghost; phantom; human being; vigor, strength; substance, main point; staff; (mech.) attic ridge, scaffolding pole; web (of a beam, rail, etc.) (arm.) bore; core (of rope, of a casting); (naut.) body of a mast; sounding-post in a fiddle, etc.—**a. de cántaro,** fool.—**a. de Dios,** harmless, inofensive person; simple, kind-hearted person.—**a. en pena,** soul in purgatory.—**a. mía, mi a.,** my dearest; my love.—**con toda el a.,** with all one's heart and soul.—**dar, entregar, exhalar,** or **rendir, el alma,** to give up the ghost, to die.—**en el a.,** keenly, deeply; with all one's heart.—**tener el a. bien puesta,** to have courage and energy.

almacén, *m.* store, shop; warehouse; storage house, depot; magazine; naval arsenal, dock-

yard.—**a. de agua**, (naut.) water cask.—**a. de una bomba de agua**, (naut.) chamber of a pump.—
almacenado, da, *a.* stored, bonded.—**almacenador**, *m.* warehouseman.—**almacenaje**, *m.* storage.
—**almacenar**, *va.* to lay up, hoard; to store.—**almacenero**, *m.* shopkeeper.—**almacenista**, *m.* shop owner; salesman; (Cuba) wholesale grocer.
almáciga, *f.* mastic; tree nursery.
almacigado, da, *a.* perfumed with mastic.
almacigar, *va.* to perfume with mastic.
almácigo, *m.* tree nursery; mastic tree.
almaciguero, ra, *a.* relating to mastic.
almádana, almadaneta, *f.* almadena, stone-breaking hammer.
almadén, *m.* mine.
almadena, *f.* stone hammer.
almadía, *f.* canoe used in India; raft.
almadiero, *m.* a raft pilot.
almadraba, *f.* tunny fishery; tunny-fish net.
almadrabero, ra, *n.* tunny fisher.
almadreña, *f.* wooden shoes or sabots.
almaganeta, *f.* = ALMÁDANA.
almagesto, *m.* Almagest.
almagra, *f.* = ALMAGRE.
almagral, *m.* place abounding in ochre.
almagrar, *va.* to color with red ochre; (vulg.) to draw blood.
almagre, *m.* red ochre, red earth, Indian red.
almaizal, almaizar, *m.* gauze veil worn by Moors; sash worn by priests.
almajaneque, *m.* (mil.) battering ram.
almajara, *f.* (prov.) forcing bed, hotbed.
almajo, *m.* seaweed yielding barilla.
almaleque, *f.* long robe worn by Moors.
almanac, almanaque, *m.* almanac, calendar.—**hacer almanaques**, (met.) to muse, to be pensive.
almanaquero, ra, *n.* maker or vender of almanacs.
almancebe, *m.* fishing net.
almandina, *f.* (min.) red garnet; almandine.
almanguena, *f.* = ALMAGRE.
almanta, *f.* space between two rows of vines and olive trees; ridge between two furrows.
almarada, *f.* triangular poniard; needle for making rope sandals.
almarcha, *f.* town on marshy ground.
almarjal, *m.* glasswort field; marshy ground.
almarjo, *m.* (bot.) glasswort.
almaro, *m.* (bot.) common clary.
almarrá, *m.* cotton gin.
almarraja, almarraza, *f.* perforated glass bottle used for sprinkling or watering.
almártaga, almártega, almártiga, *f.* litharge; halter; massicot; (Colomb.) sluggard, good-for-nothing.
almartigón, *m.* rough halter.
almástiga, *f.* mastic.—**almastigado, da**, *a.* containing mastic.
almatrero, *m.* one fishing with shad nets.
almatriche, *m.* irrigation canal.
almazara, *f.* (prov.) oil mill.—**almazarero**, *m.* oil miller.
almazarrón, *m.* = ALMAGRE.
almea, *f.* Oriental poetess and dancer; bark of the storax tree; (bot.) star-headed water plantain.
almear, *m.* stack of hay, corn, or straw.
almeja, *f.* clam.—**almejar**, *m.* clam bed.
almejía, *f.* small cloak used by poor Moors.
almena, *f.* merlon of a battlement.
almenado, *m.* = ALMENAJE.
almenado, da. I. *a.* embattled. **II.** *pp.* of ALMENAR.
almenaje, *m.* series of merlons; battlement.
almenar, *va.* to crown with merlons.
almenar, *m.* cresset.
almenara, *f.* beacon; tailrace, outlet channel for irrigation water.
almendra, *f.* almond; kernel; bean; almond-shaped diamond; cut glass drop; fine cocoon.—**a. confitada**, praline.—**a. de cacao**, cocoa bean; chocolate nut.—**a. garapiñada**, sugar almond, praline.

almendrada, *f.* almond milk.—**almendrado, da. I.** *a.* almondlike. **II.** *m.* macaroon.
almendral, *m.* almond-tree plantation.
almendrera, *f.* **almendrero**, *m.* = ALMENDRO.
almendréro, ra, *a.* almond salver.
almendrilla, *f.* almond-shaped file.—**almendrillas**, almond-shaped diamond earrings.
almendro, *m.* almond tree.
almendrón, *m.* a Jamaica tree and its fruit.
almendruco, *m.* green almond.
almenilla, *f. dim.* small merlon; merlon-shaped fringe.
almete, *m.* helmet; soldier wearing a helmet.
almez, almezo, *m.* lotus tree.—**almeza**, *f.* fruit of the lotus tree.
almiar, *m.* haystack.
almíbar, *m.* sugar sirup.—**almíbares**, preserved fruit.—**almibarado, da. I.** *a.* (met.) soft, endearing; effeminate. **II.** *pp.* of ALMIBARAR.
almibarar, *va.* to preserve (fruit) in sugar; (met.) to conciliate with soft words.
almicantarada, *f.*, **almicantarat**, *f.* (ast.) almucantar, small circle parallel to the horizon.
almidón, *m.* starch; fecula.—**almidonado, da. I.** *a.* starched; (met.) dressed with affected nicety; spruce; stiff. **II.** *pp.* of ALMIDONAR.—**almidonar**, *va.* to starch.
almiforero, ra, *n.* horse thief.
almijara, *f.* oil tank (in the Almadén mines).
almijarero, *m.* keeper of oil tanks.
almilla, *f.* under waistcoat; short military jacket; tenon; breast of pork.
almimbar, *m.* pulpit of a mosque.
alminar, *m.* minaret, turret of a mosque.
almidonería, *f.* starch factory.
almiranta, *f.* (naut.) vice admiral's ship, flagship; admiral's wife.
almirantazgo, *m.* (naut.) board of admiralty; admiralty court; admiral's dues; admiralship.
almirante, *m.* admiral, commander of a fleet; headgear for women; swimming master; a kind of shell.
almirez, *m.* brass mortar; wood engraver's tool.
almirón, *m.* wild chicory.
almizclar, *va.* to perfume with musk.—**almizcle**, *m.* musk.—**almizcleña**, *f.* (bot.) musk, grape hyacinth.—**almizcleño, ña**, *a.* musky.
almizclera, *f.* muskrat.—**almizclero, ra. I.** *a.* musky. **II.** *m.* muskdeer.
almo, **ma**, *a.* creating, vivifying; venerable, holy.
almocadén, *m.* infantry commander (in ancient armies); cavalry officer commanding part of a platoon; delegated mayor of part of a city (in Morocco).
almocafrar, *va.* to dibble.—**almocafre**, *m.* gardener's hoe, dibble.
almocárabes, almocarbes, *m. pl.* (arch. and carp.) bow-shaped ornaments.
almocatracía, *f.* duty on broadcloths and woollens.
almoceda, *f.* tax on water for irrigation; right of irrigation upon fixed days.
almocela, *f.* ancient hood.
almocrate, *m.* sal ammoniac.
almocrí, *m.* reader of the Koran in a mosque.
almodí, *m.* = ALMUDÍ.
almodón, *m.* baking flour.
almodrote, *m.* sauce for eggplant; hodgepodge.
almófar, *m.* mail head cover under helmet.
almofía, *f.* = ALJOFAINA.
almofrej, almofrez, *m.* travelling bag for bedding.
almogama, *f.* (naut.) sternpost of a ship.
almogávar, *m.* soldier of raiding troops sent to enemy's territory; raider.—**almogavarear**, *va.* to raid.—**almogavaría, almogavería**, *f.* body of raiding troops.
almohada, *f.* pillow; bolster; pillowcase; (naut.) piece of timber on which the bowsprit rests.—**aconsejarse**, or **consultar**, **con la a.**, (coll.) to sleep on the matter, to think it over carefully.—

dar a., to raise to the nobility on the pillow (a ceremony in which the queen raises a lady to nobility by having her sit beside her on a pillow).

alóbroge, a. Allobrogic.—**alóbroges,** m. pl. Allobroges.

almohadilla, f. dim. small bolster or pillow; working case; sewing cushion; pads of a harness; projecting wall stone; callous excrescence on the back of mules.

almohadillado, da, a. cushioned.

almohadón, m. aug. large cushion or pillow.

almohatre, m. sal ammoniac.

almohaza, f. currycomb.

almohazador, m. groom.

almohazar, va. to curry with a currycomb.

almojábana, f. cake made of cheese and flour; cruller.

almojarifadgo, almojarifalgo, almojarifazgo, m. ancient duty on imports or exports.

almojarife, m. the king's taxgatherer; customhouse officer.

almojatre, m. sal ammoniac.

almojaya, f. putlog.

almona, f. public stores; shad fishery; soap manufactory.

almóndiga, almondiguilla, f. = ALBÓNDIGA, ALBONDIGUILLA.

almoneda, f. auction.—**almonedear,** va. to auction.

almoradux, m. (bot.) sweet marjoram.

almorávide, n. & a. Almoravide (name of an ancient Moorish tribe).

almorejo, m. a species of grass.

almorí, m. sweetmeat or cake.

almoronía, f. = ALBORONÍA.

almorranas, f. pl. (med.) piles.

almorraniento, ta, a. suffering from piles.

almorrefa, f. triangular tile.

almorta, f. (bot.) blue vetch.

almorzada, f. as much as can be held in the hollow of both hands; breakfast.

almorzado, da. I. a. having already breakfasted. **II.** pp. of ALMORZAR.

almorzar, va. (ind. ALMUERZO: pret. ALMORCÉ: subj. ALMUERCE) to breakfast; to lunch (gen. u. in latter sense, the verb applying to the mid-day meal).

almotacén, m. inspector of weights and measures; inspector's office.

almotacenazgo, m. office of an inspector.

almotacenía, f. fee paid to the market-clerk or inspector.

almozárabe, m. Christian subject to the Moors.

almud, m. a dry measure, about 0,8 of a liter.—
a. de tierra, about half an acre.—**almudada,** f. ground sufficient for one almud of seed.—**almudejo,** m. each of the weights kept by the almudero.
—**almudero,** m. keeper of dry measures.

almudí, almudín, m. (prov.) measure containing six cahices.

almuecín, almuédano, m. muezzin.

almuérdago, m. birdlime.

almuertas, f. pl. tax on cereals sold.

almuerza, f. double handful.

almuerzo, almuerce. V. ALMORZAR.

almuerzo, m. breakfast; lunch (gen. the latter, the term denoting the mid-day meal); breakfast cover.

almunia, f. orchard, vegetable garden.

almurí, m. = ALMORÍ.

almutazafe, m. (prov.) = ALMOTACÉN.

alnabi, m. Moorish prophet.

alnado, da, n. stepchild (= HIJASTRO).

alo, m. (Mex.) a large cockatoo.

aloaria, f. vault. V. PECHINA.

alobadado, da, a. bitten by a wolf; (vet.) laboring under morbid swellings.

alobunado, da, a. wolf-colored.

alocadamente, adv. rashly, recklessly.

alocado, da, a. half-witted; wild, reckless.

alocroísmo, m. property of being allochroic.

alocroíta, m. (min.) allochroite.

alocución, f. allocution, address, speech.

alodial, a. (law) allodial.—**alodio,** m. alodium.

áloe, m. (bot.) aloe tree, aloes.—**aloético, ca,** a. aloetic.—**aloína,** f. aloin, active principle of aloes.

aloja, f. metheglin, mead.

alojamiento, m. lodging; quartering of soldiers; (naut.) steerage.—pl. (mil.) camp, quarters.

alojar. I. va. to lodge; quarter (troops). **II.** vr. to take lodgings; to lodge; to dwell; to go (into), to be contained or to work (in).

alojería, f. metheglin shop.—**alojero, ra,** n. metheglin mixer and seller; box near the pit in theatres.

alomado, da, a. having a curved back.

alomar. I. va. to distribute equally (the load on a horse); to plow in furrows. **II.** vr. (far.) to become strong and vigorous.

alón, m. plucked wing of any fowl.

alondra, f. (orn.) lark.

alongadero, a. dilatory. V. LARGA.

alongamiento, m. delay.

alongar, va. to enlarge; to stretch, extend.

alópata, m. allopath.—**alopatía,** f. allopathy.—**alopático, ca,** a. allopathic.

alopecia, f. (med.) alopecia, baldness.

alopiado, da, a. opiate.

aloque, a. clear white (wine); red and white (wine).

aloquín, m. stone inclosure in a wax bleachery.

alosa, f. shad. V. SÁBALO.

alosna, f. (bot., prov.) wormwood.

alotar, va. (naut.) V. ARRIZAR.—**a. las anclas,** (naut.) to stow the anchors.

alotropia, f. (chem.) allotropy.

alotrópico, ca, a. (chem.) allotropic.

alpaca, alpaga, f. alpaca; fabric made from the wool of this animal; nickel silver.

alpañata, f. piece of chamois skin.

alpargata, f., **alpargate,** m. fiber sandal.

alpargatado, da, a. wearing alpargatas.

alpargatar, vn. to make alpargatas.

alpargatería, f. alpargata shop or factory.

alpargatero, ra, n. manufacturer of alpargatas.

alpargatilla, f. dim. small alpargata; crafty, designing fellow.

alpechín, m. juice oozing from a heap of olives.

alpende, m. shed for mining tools.

alpestre, a. Alpine.

alpícola, a. growing in the Alps.

alpicoz, m. (prov.) V. ALFICOZ.

alpinismo, m. mountain climbing.—**alpinista,** n. mountain climber, alpinist.

alpino, na, a. Alpine.

alpiste, m. birdseed.—**dejar a uno a.,** (fam.) to leave one out (of a business, etc.).—**quedarse a.,** (coll.) to be disappointed, to get left.

alpistela, alpistera, f. cake made of flour, eggs, sesamum, and honey.

alpistero, m. sieve for canary seed.

alquequenje, m. Barbadoes winter cherry, used as a diuretic.

alquería, f. farmhouse.

alquermes, m. kermes, a cordial; (pharm.) medicinal sirup.

alquerque, m. place in oil mills for laying the bruised olives.

alquez, m. wine measure containing twelve cántaras.

alquibla, f. point toward which Mohammedans look when praying.

alquicel, alquicer, m. Moorish cloak; cover for benches, tables, etc.

alquifol, m. (min.) alquifou, potter's ore.

alquiladizo, za, a. that can be let or hired.

alquilador, ra, n. hirer.—**alquilamiento,** m. hiring or letting.

alquilar. I. va. to let, rent; to hire; to fee. **II.** vr. to serve for wages, to hire.

alquilate, m. duty paid in Murcia on sales.

alquiler, m. wages; rent, rental; the act of hiring or letting.—**de a.,** for hire, for rent; that may be hired or rented.

alquilón, na, *a.* that can be let or hired.
alquilona, *f.* charwoman.
alquimia, *f.* alchemy —**alquímico, ca,** *a.* alchemistic.
alquimila, *f.* (bot.) ladies' mantle.
alquimista, *m.* alchemist.
alquinal, *m.* veil or headdress for women.
alquitara, *f. V.* ALAMBIQUE.
alquitarar, *va.* to distil.
alquitira, *f.* tragacanth.
alquitrán, *m.* tar, pitch; (naut.) stuff composed of pitch, grease, resin, and oil.—**a. mineral,** coal tar.—**alquitranado,** *m.* (naut.) tarpaulin, tarred cloth.—**alquitranar,** *va.* to tar.
alrededor, *adv.* around.—**a. de,** about, around.
alrededores, *m. pl.* environs, outskirts.
alrota, *f.* coarse tow. *V.* ARLOTA.
alsaciano, na, *n. & a.* Alsatian.
alsine, *m.* (bot.) scorpion grass.
alta, *f.* a kind of court dance; dancing exercise; fencing bout; certificate of discharge from a hospital, as being cured; (mil.) record or statement of the entrance of a man into active service: the man so entering.—**darse de a.,** to be admitted (in a profession, etc.), to join, become a member.
altabaque, *m.* needlework basket.
altabaquillo, *m.* (bot.) small bindweed.
altamente, *adv.* highly, exceedingly; (met.) in a distinguished manner.
altanería, *f.* haughtiness, loftiness, insolence; hawking.—**altanero, ra,** *a.* soaring, towering; haughty, arrogant, insolent.
altar, *m.* altar; the church; (st. eng.) bridge wall, bridge.—**a. mayor,** high altar.—**el A.,** (ast.) the Altar, Ara.
altarero, ra, *n.* altar maker or dresser.
altarreina, *f.* = MILENRAMA.
altavoz, *m.* (rad.) loudspeaker.
altea, *f.* (bot.) marsh mallow.
altearse, *vr.* (naut.) to rise above the surrounding land.
alterabilidad, *f.* alterability.—**alterable,** *a.* changeable, alterable.—**alteración,** *f.* alteration; unevenness of the pulse; strong emotion; tumult, commotion.—**alterado, da. I.** *a.* altered; disturbed, agitated. **II.** *pp.* of ALTERAR.—**alterador, ra,** *n. & a.* alterer (-ing), disturber (-ing).—**alterante,** *a.* (med.) alterative.
alterar. I. *va.* to alter, change, transform; to disturb, stir up. **II.** *vr.* to become altered, disturbed, agitated; to become angry.
alterativo, va, *a.* alterative.
altercación, *f.,* **altercado,** *m.* controversy, quarrel, wrangle.—**altercador, ra,** *n.* arguer, wrangler, quarreler.
altercar, *va.* to dispute obstinately, to quarrel, bicker, wrangle.
álter ago, alter ego, second self.
alternación, *f.* alternation.
alternadamente, *adv.* = ALTERNATIVAMENTE.
alternador, *m.* (elec.) alternator.
alternar, *va., vn. & vr.* to alternate.
alternativa, *f.* alternative; service by turn.
alternativamente, *adv.* alternatively.
alternativo, va., alterno, na, *a.* alternate, alternating.
alteza, *f.* elevation, sublimity, highness, height; (A-) Highness (title).
altibajo, *m.* embossed velvet; downright blow in fencing.—*pl.* uneven ground; vicissitudes.
altillo, lla. I. *a. dim.* rather high. **II.** *m.* hillock.
altilocuencia, *f.* grandiloquence.
altilocuente, *a.* (poet.) grandiloquent.
altimetría, *f.* altimetry; leveling.
altimétrico, ca., *a.* altimetric.
altímetro, tra. I. *a.* altimetric. **II.** *m.* altimeter, altitude indicator.
altísimo, ma. I. *a. aug.* exceedingly high, most high. **II.** *m.* (A-), Most High.
altisonante, altísono, na, *a.* high-sounding.
altitonante, *a.* (poet.) thundering.
altitud, *f.* altitude, elevation.
altivamente, *adv.* loftily, haughtily.

altivarse, *vr.* to put on airs.
altivez, altiveza, *f.* haughtiness, arrogance, insolence; pride.
altivo, va, *a.* haughty, proud, lofty; high-minded; overbearing, arrogant.
alto, ta. I. *a.* high; elevated; tall; arduous, difficult; eminent; enormous; deep.—**a. a bajo, (de)** downward; from the top down; from top to bottom. —**a. horno,** blast furnace.—**alta mar,** (naut.) high seas.—**a. relieve,** high relief.—**altas horas,** late hours.—**de a. bordo,** large sea-going (vessel). —**de lo a.,** from above.—**en a.,** up high. **II.** *m.* height, elevation; hill; story, floor; (naut.) depth or height of a ship; (mil.) halt; command to stop; place or time of rest.—**hacer a.,** to stop, to halt.— **pasar por a.,** to overlook, to forget. **III.** *interj.* halt!—**¡a. ahí!** halt! stop there!—**¡a. de aquí!** move off! **IV.** *adv.* loud, high.
altoparlante, *m.* (rad.) loudspeaker.
altozano, *m.* hillock, knoll; height; paved terrace or platform in front of a building (gen. a church).
altramuz, *m.* (bot.) lupine *altramuces;* black voting balls.
altruísmo, *m.* altruism.—**altruísta,** *n. & a.* altruist (-ic).
altura, *f.* height, altitude; tallness, stature; summit, top; (naut.) the latitude; (geom.) altitude (of a plane figure), height (of a solid).—*pl.* **alturas,** the heavens, Heaven.
alúa, *f.* (Arg.) glowworm.
alubia, *f.* (bot.) French bean.
aluciar, *va.* to polish, burnish, brighten.
alucinación, *f.,* **alucinamiento,** *m.* hallucination.—**alucinadamente,** *adv.* erroneously.
alucinar, *va. & vr.* to dazzle, fascinate, delude.
alucón, *m.* barn owl.
alud, *m.* avalanche.
aluda, *f.* (ent.) winged ant or emmet.
aludel, *m.* (chem.) sublimating pots.
aludir, *vn.* to allude, refer.
aludo, da, *a.* winged, large-winged.
aluengar, *va.* = ALONGAR.
alumbrado, da. I. *a.* aluminous, relating to alum; (coll.) flustered with wine, tipsy. **II.** *pp.* of ALUMBRAR. **III.** *m.* lighting.—*pl.* illuminati.— **de a.,** illuminating (gas, etc.).
alumbrador, ra, *n.* lighter; linkboy.
alumbramiento, *m.* supplying with light; childbirth.
alumbrar. I. *va.* to light, illuminate; to enlighten, instruct; to dip (cloth) into alum water; to dig about the roots of (vines). **II.** *vn.* to give, or shed, light; to be delivered (of a child), to have (give birth) to a child. **III.** *vr.* to get tipsy, to become lively (from liquor).
alumbre, *m.* alum.—**a. catino,** alkali from glasswort.—**a. de rasuras,** salt of tartar.—**a. sacarino,** alum whey.
alumbrera, *f.* alum mine.—**a. artificial,** alum works.
alumbroso, sa, *a.* containing alum.
alúmina, *f.* (chem.) alumina.
aluminado, da, *a.* (chem.) mixed with alum.
aluminato, *m.* aluminate.—**alumínico, ca,** *a.* aluminous.—**aluminífero, ra,** *a.* aluminiferous.
aluminio, *m.* aluminium, aluminum.
aluminita, *f.* aluminite.
aluminoso, sa, *a.* aluminous.
alumno, *na, n.* foster child; pupil, student.
alunado, da, *a.* lunatic; spasmodic, jerky from constipation (s. o. horses); long-tusked (boar); tainted (meat).
alunita, *f.* (min.) alunite.
alusión, *f.* allusion, reference, hint.
alusivamente, *adv.* allusively.
alusivo, va, *a.* allusive, hinting.
alustrar, *va.* to give luster to.
alutación, *f.* (min.) gold-dust-bearing stratum.
alutrado, da, *a.* otter-colored.
aluvial, *a.* alluvial.
aluvión, *f.* alluvium.
alveario, *m.* (anat.) alveary.

álveo, *m.* bed (of a river).

alveolar, *a.* alveolar.

alvéolo, *m.* alveolus, alveole, small cavity.

alverja, alverjana, *f.* (bot.) common vetch.

alvino, na, *a.* (med.) alvine.

alza, *f.* piece of leather put round the last to make the shoe wider; instrument used in ropewalks; advance, rise (in price); (typ.) overlay, frisket sheet; (artil.) front sight (gen. app. to the notched-slide sight).

alzacuello, *m.* neck stock.

alzada, *f.* height, stature (of horses); appeal.

alzadamente, *adv.* for a lump sum.

alzado. I. *m.* (arch.) front elevation; lump sum; fraudulent bankrupt. **II.** *pp.* of ALZAR.

alzadura, *f.* elevation.

alzamiento, *m.* lifting, raising; higher bid; rising (in arms) insurrection.

alzapaño, *m.* curtain holder.

alzapié, *m.* snare.

alzaprima, *f.* lever; wedge; (naut.) heaver.—**dar a.,** to ruin or damage by treacherous cunning.

alzaprimar, *va.* to raise with a lever; (naut.) to move with handspikes; to incite, spur on.

alzapuertas, *m.* dumb player; supernumerary.

alzar. I. *va.* (*pret.* ALCÉ: *subj.* ALCE) to raise (a load, price, siege, building, penalty); to lift, heave; to pick up; to carry off; to hide, lock up; to cut (the cards); to gather up and arrange in order (printed sheets) for the binder; to elevate (the host); (naut.) to heave.—**a. cabeza,** to recover from a calamity or disease.—**a. el codo,** to tope, to be a toper.—**a. la casa,** to break up house. —**a. velas,** (naut.) to set the sails; to raise camp (fig.), to move. **II.** *vr.* to rise in rebellion; to rise; to make a fraudulent bankruptcy; to appeal.—**a. con,** to run away with; to embezzle; to steal; to usurp.—**a. con el santo y la limosna,** to carry away, o appropriate, everything.

alzatirantes, *m. pl.* harness straps to suspend the traces.

allá, *adv.* there; thither, or to that place; (with a modifying *adv.*) far, beyond (*más allá,* farther; *muy allá,* much beyond, far beyond). Applied to time, it indicates remoteness, and either is not translated, or is rendered by "in the old times," "in times of old," "in the far-off time," etc.: *allá en mi niñez,* in the old times of my childhood; *allá en tiempo de Salomón,* in the far-off time of Solomon.—**por a.,** there, thereabouts, at that place.

allanador, *m.* leveller; gold-beater's book.

allanamiento, *m.* levelling; smoothing; acceptance of a judicial finding; affability, suavity.

allanar. I. *va.* to level, smooth; to flatten; to remove or overcome (difficulties); to pacify, subdue; to break into (a house). **II.** *vr.* to abide (by), acquiesce.

allegadizo, za, *a.* collected without choice.

allegado, da. I. *a.* near; related. **II.** *n.* friend; ally. **III.** *pp.* of ALLEGAR.

allegador, ra, *n.* reaper; gatherer; board for gathering thrashed wheat; poker.

allegamiento, *m.* collecting; reaping, gathering, close friendship; union; relationship.

allegar. I. *va.* (*pret.* ALLEGUÉ: *subj.* ALLEGUE) to gather, reap; to collect; to solicit, procure. **II.** *vr.* to come near, to approach.

allende, *adv.* beyond, on the other side of.—**a. el mar,** overseas.

allí, *adv.* there, in that place; thereto.—**de a.,** from there; thence.—**por a.,** that way; through there.

alloza, *f.* green almond. *V.* ALMENDRUCO.

allozo, *m.* (bot.) wild almond tree.

alludel, *m.* earthen water pipe. *V.* ALUDEL.

ama, *f.* mistress of the house; landlady; (woman) owner; housekeeper; wet nurse; (ant.) governess.—**a. de cría** = A. DE LECHE.—**a. de gobierno** = A. DE LLAVES.—**a. de leche,** wet nurse.—**a. de llaves,** housekeeper.

amabilidad, *f.* amiability, affability; kindness.

amable, *a.* amiable, affable; kind.

amablemente, *adv.* amiably; kindly; courteously.

amacayo, *m.* (Amer.) flower de luce.

amacena, *f.* (bot.) damson plum.

amaceno, na, *a.* Damascene.

amacollarse, *vr.* to throw out shoots.

amacrático, ca, *a.* amacratic.

amachetear, *va.* to strike with a machete.

amador, ra, *n. & a.* lover (-ing).

amadrigar. I. *va.* (*pret.* AMADRIGUÉ: *subj.* AMADRIGUE) to receive well, especially one not deserving. **II.** *vr.* to burrow; to seclude one's self.

amadrinar, *va.* to couple, yoke together; (naut.) to join (one thing to another); to act as godmother or bridesmaid to; to uphold.

amadroñado, da, *a.* resembling *madroños.*

amaestrado, da. I. *a.* taught, schooled; trained, experienced. **II.** *pp.* of AMAESTRAR.

amaestrar, *va.* to instruct, train, coach.

amagar. I. *va.* to threaten; to show signs of; to hint. **II.** *vn.* to threaten; to be impending; to feign. **III.** *vr.* (coll.) to hide.

amago, *m.* threatening; hint; empty promise; symptom of disease which does not follow.

ámago, *m.* bitter stuff found in some bee cells; nausea, loathing.

amainar. I. *va.* (naut.) to lower (the sails); to relax. **II.** *vn.* to subside, lessen, moderate. **III.** *vr.* to give in, yield, desist.

amaitinar, *va.* to observe attentively.

amajadar. I. *va.* to keep (sheep) in a field to fertilize it. **II.** *vr.* to be in, or go to, the fold (s. o. sheep, etc.)

amalecita, *n. & a.* Amalekite.

amalgama, *f.* amalgam.—**amalgamación,** *f.* amalgamation.—**amalgamar,** *va.* to amalgamate.

amamantar, *va.* to nurse, to suckle.

amán, *m.* amnesty.

amancebamiento, *m.* concubinage.

amancebarse, *vr.* to live in concubinage.

amancillar, *va.* to stain, pollute; to defame, to tarnish one's reputation.

amanecer, *vn. defect.* (*ind.* AMANEZCO: *subj.* AMANEZCA) to dawn; to arrive, be or appear at daybreak or in the morning (often ch. constr.: *amanecimos en la costa,* at dawn [or, in the morning] we were on shore, we reached the shore at daybreak, it was daybreak when we arrived at the shore: *amaneció la noticia en los periódicos,* the news appeared in the papers in the morning). Often used with *Dios* as subject: *amaneció Dios,* it dawned (literally, God sent forth the dawn). **II.** *m.* dawn, daybreak.

amanerado, da, *a.* full of mannerisms.

amanerarse, *vr.* to adopt mannerisms; to become affected.

amanojar, *va.* to gather by handfuls.

amansador, ra, *n.* tamer; horse breaker; soother, appeaser.—**amansamiento,** *m.* taming; breaking (s. o. horses).—**amansar,** *va.* to tame, domesticate; to break (a horse); to soften, pacify.

amantar, *va.* (coll.) to cloak.

amante, *n. & a.* lover (-ing); sweetheart.—*m. pl.* (naut.) ropes forming part of the running rigging.

amantillar, *va.* (naut.) to top the lifts.

amantillo, *m.* (naut.) lift.

amanuense, *m.* amanuensis, clerk.

amañar. I. *va.* to do cleverly. **II.** *vr.* to be handy, to adapt one's self.

amaño, *m.* cleverness, neatness.—*pl.* tools or implements; intrigue or machinations.

amapola, *f.* (bot.) poppy.

amar, *va.* to love.

amáraco, *m.* (bot.) marjoram. *V.* MEJORANA.

amarantáceo, a. I. *a.* (bot.) amaranthaceous. **II.** *f. pl.* (bot.) Amaranthaceæ.

amaranto, *m.* (bot.) amaranth.

amarar, *vn.* (aer.) to alight on the water.

amargado, da. I. *a.* embittered. **II.** *pp.* of AMARGAR.

amargaleja, *f.* bitter or wild plum.

amargamente, *adv.* bitterly.

amargar. I. *va.* (*pret.* AMARGUÉ: *subj.* AMARGUE) to make bitter; to exasperate, offend. **II.** *vn.* to be bitter. **III.** *vr.* to become bitter.

amargo, ga. I. *a.* bitter. **II.** *m.* bitterness; sweetmeat made of bitter almonds.—*pl.* bitters.

amargón, *m.* (bot.) dandelion.

amargor, *m.* bitterness.—**amargosamente,** *adv.* bitterly.—**amargoso, sa,** *a.* bitter.—**amarguillo, lla,** *a. dim.* somewhat bitter.—**amargura,** *f.* bitterness.

amaricado, a, *a.* (coll.) effeminate.

amarilídeo, a. I. *a.* (bot.) amarylidaceous. **II.** *f. pl.* (bot.) Amarylidaceæ.

amarilis, *f.* amaryllis.

amarilla, *f.* gold coin, especially the *onza;* vat; a liver disease of small cattle.

amarillazo, za, *a.* pale-yellow.—**amarillear,** *vn.* to incline to yellow.—**amarillejo, ja; amarillento, ta,** *a.* yellowish.—**amarillez,** *f.* yellowness. —**amarillito, ta,** *a. dim.* yellowish.

amarillo, lla. I. *a.* yellow. **II.** *m.* jaundice; a disease of silkworms.

amarinar, *va.* V. MARINAR.

amariposado, da, *a.* (bot.) papilionaceous; butterflylike.

amaro, *m.* (bot.) common clary.

amarra, *f.* cable; martingale.

amarradero, *m.* hitching post; tying or fastening place or object; (naut.) mooring berth.

amarraje, *m.* moorage (charge for mooring).

amarrar, *va.* to tie, fasten; lash, belay.

amarrazones, *pl.* (naut.) ground tackle.

amarre, *m.* tying; mooring; mooring line or cable. —**a. de retenida,** mooring guy (of a dirigible).

amarrido, da, *a.* dejected, gloomy.

amartelar. I. *va.* to court, make love to; to love devotedly. **II.** *vr.* to fall in love.

amartillar, *va.* to hammer; to cock (gun, pistol).

amasadera, *f.* kneading bowl.—**amasador, ra,** *n.* kneader.—**amasadura,** *f.* kneading.—**amasamiento,** *m.* uniting or joining; AMASADURA.

amasar, *va.* to knead; to mould; to arrange for a purpose.

amasijo, *m.* dough; (act of) kneading; quantity of mortar or plaster; medley; plot; place where dough is made.

amate, *m.* (Mex.) a fig tree the milky juice of which is used as a resolvent.

amatista, *f.* (min.) amethyst.

amatividad, *f.* amativeness.

amatorio, ria, *a.* amatory.

amaurosis, *f.* (med.) amaurosis.—**amaurótico, ca,** *n. & a.* amaurotic.

amauta, *m.* sage (among ancient Peruvians).

amayorazgado, da, *a.* entailed.—**amayorazgar,** *va.* to entail.

amazacotado, da, *a.* heavy, thick; jumbled, incoherent, clumsy (s. o. writings).

amazona, *f.* Amazon; amazon, mannish woman; a large parrot of Brazil; rider; riding habit.

amazónico, ca, *a.* Amazonian.

amba, *f.* (bot.) fruit of the mangrove.

ambages, *m. pl.* maze; circumlocutions, beating about the bush.—**sin a.,** in plain language, without mincing words.

ambagioso, sa, *a.* ambiguous.

ámbar, *m.* amber.—**a. griss,** ambergris.—**a. negro,** jet.—**a. pardillo** = **a.** GRIS.—**ambarar,** *va.* to scent with amber.

ambariba, *f.* (bot.) sweet centaury.

ambarilla, *f.* (bot.) amber seed.

ambarina, *f.* = ALGALIA.

ambarino, na, *a.* relating to amber; amberlike.

ambición, *f.* ambition; aspiration; covetousness.

ambicionar, *va.* to seek eagerly; to aspire to; to covet.

ambiciosamente, *adv.* ambitiously.

ambicioso, sa, *a.* ambitious, aspiring; covetous, greedy.

ambidextro, tra, *a.* ambidextrous.

ambiente, *m.* atmosphere, ambient air.

ambigú, *m.* luncheon, collation

ambiguamente, *adv.* ambiguously.

ambigüedad, *f.* ambiguity.

ambiguo, gua, *a.* ambiguous.

ámbito, *m.* contour, boundary line; limit; compass, scope.

amblar, *va.* to amble; to pace.

ambleo, *m.* short, thick wax candle; candlestick for the same.

ambliopía, *f.* (med.) ambliopia.

ambo, *m.* combination of two numbers in lotto.

ambón, *m.* pulpit on each side of the high altar.

ambos, bas, *a.* both.—**a. a dos,** both, or both together.

ambrosía, *f.* ambrosia; (met.) any delicious viand or liquor.—**a. campestre,** (bot.) buckthorn.

ambrosiano, na, *a.* Ambrosian.

ambuesta, *f.* V. ALMORZADA.

ambulancia, *f.* field hospital; ambulance.

ambulante, *a.* ambulant; shifting; roving.

ambulativo, va, *a.* of a roving turn; shifting; ambulatory.

ambulatorio, a, *a.* ambulatory.

ameba, *f.* = AMIBA.

amebeo, a, *a.* dialogue in verse.

amechar, *va.* to put a wick to or in.

amedrentador, ra, *n. & a.* threatener (-ing); discourager (-ing); frightener (-ing).

amedrentar, *va.* to frighten, discourage, intimidate.

amelga, *f.* ridge between two furrows.

amelgado. I. *m.* (prov.) boundary mound. **II.** *pp.* of AMELGAR.

amelgar, *va.* to open furrows in; to mark the boundaries of with mounds.

amelo, *m.* (bot.) golden starwort.

amelonado, da, *a.* melon-shaped.

amén, *m.* amen, so be it.—**a. de,** besides.—**llevarle a uno el amén,** to agree to, or approve, everything one says, to be one's echo.

amenaza, *f.* threat, menace.

amenazador, ra, *n. & a.* threatener (-ing).

amenazante, *a.* menacing, threatening.

amenazar, *va. & vn.* (*pret.* AMENACÉ; *subj.* AMENACE) to threaten, menace; be impending.

amencia, *f.* dementia.

amenguamiento, *m.* diminution, lessening, abatement.

amenguar, *va.* to diminish; to defame.

amenidad, *f.* amenity.

amenizar, *va.* (*pret.* AMENICÉ: *subj.* AMENICE) to render pleasant or agreeable.

ameno, na, *a.* pleasant, agreeable, pleasing.

amenorrea, *f.* amenorrhea.

amentáceo, cea, *a.* (bot.) amentaceous.

amentar, *va.* to lace (shoes).

amento, *m.* (bot.) ament. V. AMIENTO.

amerar. I. *va.* to mix (wine or liquor) with water. **II.** *vr.* to percolate; soak.

amerengado, da, *a.* like, or having, meringue; (coll.) prudish.

americana, *f.* sack coat.

americanismo, *m.* Americanism (in its broad sense).

americanista, *n.* **Americanist.**

americano, na, *a.* American (native of or belonging to America, not necessarily the U. S.).

amestizado, da, *a.* mestizolike.

ametalado, da, *a.* brass-colored.

ametista, *f.*, **ametisto,** *m.* = AMATISTA.

ametralladora, *f.* rapid-fire gun, machine gun.

ametrallar, *va.* to shoot with grapeshot.

amia, *f.* lamia, white shark.

amianto, *m.* (min.) amianthus; asbestos.

amiba, *f.* (zool.) amœba.—**amiboideo, a,** *a.* amœboid, amœbic.

amicísimo, ma, *a. sup.* most friendly, very good friend.

amida, *f.* (chem.) amide.—**amidina,** *f.* (chem.) amidine.

amidógeno, m. (chem.) amidogen.

amiento, m. leather strap to secure helmet; shoe lace; leather string.

amiga, f. female friend; schoolmistress; kindergarten; concubine, mistress.

amigable, a. friendly; fit, suitable.

amigablemente, adv. amicably.

amígdala, f. tonsil.

amigdaláceo, a. a. (bot.) amygdalaceous.—f. pl. Amygdalaceæ.

amigdalina, f. (chem.) amygdalin.

amigdalitis, f. tonsilitis.

amigdalotomía, f. (med.) tonsilotomy.

amigo, ga. I. n. friend.—**ser a. de,** to be a friend of; have a taste for. **II.** m. a man living in concubinage. **III.** a. friendly; fond.—**ser muy amigos,** to be very good friends.

amigote, m. aug. (coll.) dear old friend.

amiláceo, a. starchy.

amilanamiento, m. terror, abject fear, cowing.

amilanar. I. va. to frighten, terrify; stupefy; to cow. **II.** vr. to become terrified; to cower, quail; to flag.

amillaramiento, m. assessment of a tax.

amillarar, va. to assess a tax on.

amillonado, da. I. a. very rich. **II.** m. millionaire.

amimar, va. V. MIMAR.

amina, f. (chem.) amine.

aminorar, va. to lessen; to enfeeble.

amir, m. ameer.

amistad, f. friendship; concubinage.—**hacer amistad, or amistades,** to become acquainted, to make friends.—**hacer las amistades,** to make up, become reconciled.

amistar. I. va. to make (others) friends, to make acquainted. **II.** vr. to become acquainted; to become reconciled, to make up.

amistosamente, adv. amicably, in a friendly manner.

amistoso, sa, a. friendly, amicable.

amito, m. amice, part of a priest's garment.

amnesia, f. amnesia, loss of memory.

amnios, f. amnion, fœtal envelope.

amniótico, ca, a. amniotic.

amnistía, f. amnesty.

amnistiar. I. va. to grant pardon, to amnesty. **II.** vr. to receive amnesty.

amo, m. master, lord; proprietor, owner; foster father; overseer; (coll.) boss.

amoblar, va. = AMUEBLAR.

amodita, f. a horned serpent. V. ALICANTE.

amodorrado, da. I. a. drowsy, sleepy. **II.** pp. of AMODORRARSE.—**amodorrarse,** vr. to become drowsy.—**amodorrido, da,** a. = AMODORRADO.

amogotado, da, a. knoll-like.

amohecerse, vr. (ind. AMOHEZCO: subj. AMOHEZCA) to mould or rust.

amohinar, va. to irritate, annoy.

amojamado, da, a. tasting like tunny fish.

amojamar, va. to dry and smoke (tunny fish).

amojonador, m. one who sets landmarks.

amojonamiento, m. setting of landmarks.

amojonar, va. to set landmarks on.

amoladera, f. whetstone, grindstone.—**amolador,** n. & a. grinder (-ing); whetter (-ing); sharpener (-ing).—**amoladura,** f. whetting, grinding.

amolar, va. (ind. AMUELO: subj. AMUELE) to whet, grind, sharpen.

amoldar, va. to mould, fashion, figure; to adjust; to brand (cattle); to adapt.

amole, m. soap root.

amollador, ra, n. one who plays an inferior card, having a winning one.

amollar. I. va. (naut.) to ease off. **II.** vn. to play an inferior card, having a winning one.

amolletado, da, a. oblong, oval.

amomo, m. (bot.) grain of paradise.

amondongado, da, a. (coll.) coarse and fat.

amonedación, f. coining.—**amonedar,** va. to coin.

amonestación, f. admonition, warning; marriage banns.--**correr las amonestaciones,** to publish the banns.

amonestador, ra, n. & a. admonisher (-ing).

amonestar, va. to admonish, warn, advise; to publish (banns).

amoniacal, a. ammoniacal.

amoníaco, m. ammonia, ammoniac, gum resin.

amónico, ca, ammonic, ammonium (u. a.).

amonio, m. ammonium.

amonita. I. f. (zool.) ammonite.—**II.** n. & a. Ammonite.

amontarse, vr. to flee to the mountains.

amontonador, ra, n. heaper, accumulator.

amontonamiento, m. heaping, accumulating; hoarding; gathering; lodgment.

amontonar. I. va. to heap, pile up; accumulate; gather; to hoard, lay up. **II.** vr. (coll.) to accumulate; to pile up; to fly into a passion.

amor, m. love; the object of love.—pl. love affairs, amours.—**a. con a. se paga,** the payment should fit the debt.—**a. patrio,** love of country, patriotism.—**a. propio,** self-esteem, amour propre.—**por a. de,** for the sake of; on account of.—**de mil amores,** with all one's heart, with the greatest pleasure.

amoral, a. amoral.—**amoralismo,** m. amoralism.—**amoralidad,** f. amorality.

amoratado, da, a. livid.

amorcillo, m. dim. slight love, kindness.

amordazar, va. (pret. AMORDACÉ: subj. AMORDACE) to gag, muzzle; (naut.) to fasten with bitts.

amores, m. (bot.) red valerian.

amorfia, f. organic deformity.

amorfo, fa, a. amorphous.

amorgado, da, a. filled with morga or alpechín.

amorgar, va. to stupefy (fish) with morga or alpechín.

amoricones, m. pl. (coll.) love looks, flirtations.

amorío, m. love making; love, amour.

amoriscado, da, a. Moorlike.

amormado, da, a. having the glanders.

amorosamente, adv. lovingly, with love.

amoroso, sa, a. affectionate, loving; pleasing, gentle; mild.

amorrar. I. vn. (coll.) to be sullen; to muse. **II.** vr. to sulk.

amortajar, va. to shroud.

amortecer. I. va. (ind. AMORTEZCO: subj. AMORTEZCA) to deaden. **II.** vr. to faint, to swoon.

amortecimiento, m. swoon, fainting.

amortezco. V. AMORTECER.

amortiguación, f., **amortiguamiento,** m. softening, mitigation, lessening.

amortiguador, ra. I. n. & a. reducer (-ing), damper (-ing), softener (-ing). **II.** m. (mech.) dashpot; shock absorber.

amortiguar, va. to lessen, mitigate, deaden; to temper; to soften (colors); to absorb, take up (shocks).

amortizable, a. amortizable.

amortización, f. amortization.

amortizar, va. (pret. AMORTICÉ: subj. AMORTICE) to amortize; to recoup, recover; to abolish (offices, etc.); to refund.

amoscar. I. va. (pret. AMOSQUÉ: subj. AMOSQUE) to flap (flies). **II.** vr. to shake off the flies; to become peeved.

amosquilado, da, a. tormented with flies.

amostachado, a. wearing mustaches.

amostazar. I. va. (pret. AMOSTACÉ: subj. AMOSTACE) (coll.) to exasperate, provoke. **II.** vr. to be vexed, angry.

amotinadamente, adv. mutinously.

amotinado, da. I. a. mutinous. **II.** s. mutineer. **III.** pp. of AMOTINAR.

amotinador, ra, n. mutineer.

amotinamiento, m. mutiny.

amotinar. I. va. to excite to rebellion; to disorder (the mind). **II.** vr. to mutiny, rebel.

amover, va. to remove, to discharge.

amovibilidad, *f.* quality of being removed or revoked.

amovible, *a.* removable.

ampac, *m.* (bot.) champak.

ampara, *f.* (law) seizure of chattels.

amparador, ra, *n.* protector; shelterer.

amparar. I. *va.* to shelter; to protect, help, assist; to comply with the requirements for working (a mine). **II.** *vr.* to claim or enjoy protection; to defend one's self; to seek shelter.

amparo, *m.* favor, aid; protection; shelter, refuge, asylum.

ampelita, *f.* soft sandy slate.

ampelografía, *f.* viticulture, science of vine growing—**ampelográfico, ca,** relating to the science of viticulture.—**ampelógrafo, fa,** *n.* one versed in the science of viticulture.

amper, *s.* =AMPERIO.

amperaje, *m.* (elec.) amperage.

amperímetro, *m.* (electr.) amperemeter, ammeter.

amperio, *m.* (elec.) ampere.—**a.-hora,** amperehour.—**a.-vuelta,** ampere-turn.

amperómetro, *m.* = AMPERÍMETRO.

amplexicaulo, la, *a.* (bot.) amplexicaul.

amplexo, xa, *a.* (bot.) clasped by amplexicaul organs.

ampliación, *f.* enlargement.

ampliador, ra, *n.* & *a.* amplifier (-ying).

ampliamente, *adv.* largely, copiously, plentifully, amply.

ampliar, *va.* to amplify, enlarge, extend.

ampliativo, va, *a.* amplifying, enlarging.

amplificación, *f.* enlargement; (rhet.) amplification.

amplificador, ra, *n.* & *a.* amplifier (-ying), enlarger (-ing).

amplificar, *va.* to amplify, enlarge, extend, expand; to dilate, expatiate.

amplio, lia, *a.* ample, roomy, extensive, large; handsome; absolute.

amplitud, *f.* extent, largeness, fulness; (phys., astr.) amplitude.

ampo de la nieve, snow white. *V.* LAMPO.

ampolla, *f.* blister; decanter, cruet; water bubble; bulb (of a lamp).

ampoliar. I. *va.* to blister; to make hollow. **II.** *vr.* to bubble up.

ampollar, *a.* blisterlike, bubblelike.

ampolleta, *f. dim.* small vial; cruet; hourglass; bulb; (naut.) watch glass.

amprar, *vn.* (prov.) to borrow.

ampulosidad, *f.* verbosity.—**ampuloso, sa,** *a.* pompous, bombastic.

amputación, *f.* amputation.—**amputar,** *va.* to amputate.

amuchachado, da, *a.* boyish, childish.

amueblar, *va.* to furnish.

amueblo, amueble, *V.* AMOBLAR.

amuelo, amuele, etc. *V.* AMOLAR.

amugamiento, *m.* = AMOJONAMIENTO.

amugronador, ra, *a.* layer of vine shoots.

amugronar, *va.* to lay the shoot of a vine.

amujerado, da, *a.* effeminate.

amujeramiento, *m.* = AFEMINACIÓN.

amularse, *vr.* to become sterile (s. o. mares).

amulatado, da, *a.* mulattolike.

amuleto, *m.* amulet.

amunicionar, *va.* to supply with ammunition.

amuñecado, da, *a.* puppetlike.

amura, *f.* (naut.) beam of a ship at one-eighth of its length from the bow; part on each side of the ship that corresponds to that section; tack of a sail.

amurada, *f.* (naut.) interior side of a ship.

amurallar, *va.* to wall. *V.* MURAR.

amurar, *va.* (naut.) to haul (the tack) aboard.

amurcar, *va.* to gore with the horns.

amurco, *m.* blow with the horns.

amurillar, *va.* (agr.) to earth up.

amusco, ca, *a.* brown.

amusgar, *va.* to throw back (the ears); to contract (the eyes) to see better.

ana, *f.* ell; aune, a kind of fox.

anabaptismo, *m.* Anabaptism.

anabaptista, *n.* & *a.* Anabaptist.

anábasis, *f.* (med.) anabasis.

anacarado, da, *a.* like mother-of-pearl.

anacardina, *f.* anacardic preparation.

anacardino, na, *a.* anacardic.

anacardo, *m.* (bot.) cashew (tree or fruit).

anaco, *m.* dress of Indian women in Peru and Bolivia; in Ecuador, their hairdressing, a single braid.

anaconda, *f.* anaconda, a South-American boa.

anacoreta, *m.* anchorite, hermit.

anacorético, ca, *a.* anchoretical.

anacreóntico, ca, *a.* Anacreontic.

anacrónico, ca, *a.* anachronous.

anacronismo, *m.* anachronism.

ánade, *m.* & *f.* duck; by extension, goose.

anadear, *vn.* to waddle.

anadeja, *f. dim.* duckling.

anadino, na, *n.* young duck.

anadón, *m.* mallard.

anadoncillo, *m. dim.* duckling.

anaerobio, *n.* & *a.* (biol.) anaerobe (-ic).

anafalla, anafaya, *f.* thick corded silk.

anafe, *m.* portable furnace.

anáfora, *f.* anaphora.

anafre, *m.* portable furnace.

anafrodisia, *f.* anaphrodisia.

anafrodisíaco, ca, *a.* anaphrodisiac.

anafrodita, *n.* abstainer from sexual intercourse.

anáglifo, *m.* anaglyph.

anagnórisis, *f.* = AGNICIÓN.

anagoge, *m.,* **anagogia,** *f.* anagoge.

anagógico, ca, *a.* anagogical.

anagrama, *f.* anagram.

anagramatizador, ra, *n.* anagrammatist.

anal, *a.* anal.

analectas, *f. pl.* analects.

analéctico, ca, *a.* analectic.

analéptico, ca, *a.* (med.) restorative.

analepsia, *f.* (med.) analepsis.

anales, *m. pl.* annals.

analfabetismo, *m.* illiteracy.

analfabeto, ta, *n.* illiterate person.

analgesia, *f.* (med.) analgesia, insensibility to pain.—**analgésico, ca,** *n.* & *a.* anodyne.

analgesina, *f.* antipyrine.

análisis, *m.* or *f.* analysis; (gram.) parsing; (math.) analysis (gen. app. to infinitesimal calculus and the theory of functions).—**a. cualitativo,** qualitative analysis.—**a. cuantitativo,** quantitative analysis.—**a. espectral,** spectrum analysis.—**a. volumétrico,** volumetric analysis, titration (it is gen. u. in the latter sense).

analista, *m.* annalist.

analítica, *f.* (philos.) analytics; (math.) analytic geometry.

analíticamente, *adv.* analytically.

analítico, ca, *a.* analytical.

analizable, *a.* capable of analysis.

analizador, *m.* analyzer.

analizar, *va.* (*pret.* ANALICÉ: *subj.* ANALICE) to analyze; (gram.) to parse.

análogamente, *adv.* analogously; in like manner, likewise.

analogía, *f.* analogy; resemblance; (gram.) etymology.

analógicamente, *adv.* analogically.

analógico, ca; análogo, ga, *a.* analogous.

anamorfosis, *f.* anamorphosis.

ananá, ananás, *f.* (bot.) pine apple.

anapelo, *m.* (bot.) wolfsbane.

anapesto, *m.* anapæst, a Latin verse, $\smile \smile —$.

anaquel, *m.* shelf.

anaquelería, *f.* shelving, case of shelves.

anaranjado, da. I. *a.* orange-colored. II. *n.* orange (color).—**a. de metilo,** methyl orange.

anarquía, *f.* anarchy.—**anárquico, ca,** *a.* anarchical.—**anarquismo,** *m.* anarchism.

anarquista, *n. & a.* anarchist (-ic).
anasarca, *f.* (med.) general dropsy.
anascote, *m.* woollen stuff like serge.
anastasia, *f.* = ARTEMISA.
anastomosis, *f.* (anat.) anastomosis.
anástrofe, *m.* (rhet.) anastrophe, inversion of words.
anata, *f.* annats, yearly income.
anatema, anatematismo, anathema.
anatematizar, *va.* (pre. ANATEMATICÉ: *subj.* ANATEMATICE) to anathematize.
anatista, *m.* officer for the half-year's annats.
anatomía, *f.* anatomy; dissection.
anatómicamente, *adv.* anatomically.
anatómico, ca, *a.* anatomical.
anatomista, *m.* anatomist.
anatomizar, *va.* (pret. ANATOMICÉ: *subj.* ANATOMICE) to anatomize or dissect; (art) to draw or carve the bones and muscles of.
anavajado, da, *a.* knife-scarred.
anca, *f.* croup; (coll.) buttock.
ancado, *m.* (vet.) contraction of muscles of the hind legs.
ancianidad, *f.* old age; antiquity.
anciano, na, *n. & a.* old (man, woman), ancient.
ancla, *f.* anchor—**a. de la esperanza,** sheet anchor.—**echar anclas,** to anchor.—**sobre el a., sobre las anclas,** at anchor, anchored.
ancladero, *m.* (naut.) anchorage, anchoring place.
anclaje, *m.* casting anchor; anchoring ground.
anclar, *vn.* to anchor.
anclote, *m.* stream anchor, kedge.
anclotillo, *m.* kedge anchor.
ancón, *m.,* **anconada,** *f.* open road, bay.
áncora, *f.* = ANCLA.
ancoraje, *m.* = ANCLAJE.
ancorar, *vn.* = ANCLAR.
ancorca, *f.* yellow ochre.
ancorel, *m.* large stone to secure nets.
ancorería, *f.* anchor forge.
ancorero, *m.* anchor smith.
ancusa, *f.* (bot.) common alkanet.
anchamente, *adv.* widely, largely.
ancheta, *f.* small amount of goods ventured in trade; profit in a bargain.
anchicorto, ta, *a.* wider than long.
ancho, cha. I. *a.* broad, wide.—**ancha Castilla,** (coll.) as you please; without hindrance.—**a. de conciencia,** not overscrupulous, not too conscientious. **II.** *m.* width, breadth.—**a sus anchas,** with absolute freedom, unrestricted (ly), as one pleases.
anchoa, anchova, *f.* anchovy.
anchor, *m.* = ANCHURA.
anchuelo, la, *a. dim.* somewhat wide.
anchura, *f.* width, breadth; extent; laxity.
anchuroso, sa, *a.* large, spacious, extensive, vast, ample.
anchusa, *f.* (bot.) alkanet.
andábata, *m.* andabate.
andada, *f.* track, trail, pathway; thin, hard-baked cake.—*pl.* **andadas,** trail.—**volver a las andadas,** to backslide, to go back to one's old tricks.
andaderas, *f. pl.* gocart.
andadero, ra. I. *n.* runner. **II.** *m.* easy ground.
andado, *m.* stepchild. *V.* ALNADO.
andado, da. I. *a.* beaten, trodden; worse for use, threadbare; common, ordinary; elapsed. **II.** *pp.* of ANDAR.
andador, ra. I. *a.* fast walking or running, swift; that walks. **II.** *m.* messenger of a court; (naut.) fine sailer; leading string; garden walk.
andadura, *f.* gait; amble.
andaluz, za, *n. & a.* Andalusian.—**andaluzada,** *f.* boasting; exaggeration; (coll.) fish story, yarn.
andamiada, *f.,* **andamiaje,** *m.* scaffolding.
andamio, *m* scaffold, platform; (naut.) gang-board.
andana, *f.* row, line, tier.—**llamarse a.,** (coll.) not to fulfil a promise.

andanada, *f.* (naut.) broadside; grand stand for spectators; reproof, reprimand; tirade.
andaniño, *m.* gocart in which children learn to walk. *V.* POLLERA.
andante, *a.* walking; errant; (mus.) andante.
andantesco, ca, *a.* belonging to knights-errant.
andantino, *m.* (mus.) andantino.
andanza, *f.* (obs.) occurrence, event.—**buena** or **mala a.,** good or bad fortune.
andar, *va.* (pret. ANDUVE; *subj. imp.* 2d and 3d ANDUVIERA, ANDUVIESE; *fut.* ANDUVIERE) to walk, pace; to go, move (s. o. a person, a machine, watch, etc.); to act, behave; to elapse, pass; to run, function (as a machine); to be, get along; to be going (¿cómo anda el negocio? how is the business going?).—**a. en coche, automóvil,** etc., to go, ride in a carriage, automobile, etc.—**andarse por las ramas,** to beat about the bush. ¡anda! gracious! move on! get up! all right! go ahead! let it go!
andaraje, *m.* wheel of a wheel and axle; frame of a garden roller.
andariego, ga, *a.* restless, roving; fast walker, runner.
andarín, *m.* professional walker, runner.
andarina, *f.* = GOLONDRINA.
andarivel, *m.* ferry cable; (naut.) safety ropes.
andarrío, *m.* (orn.) white wagtail.
andas, *f. pl.* stretcher; litter; bier with shafts.
andén, *m.* horse path; sidewalk by a road, wharf, or bridge; platform (of a railway station).
andero, ra, *n.* litter bearer; bier bearer.
andesita, *f.* (geol.) andesite.
andilú, *m.* shoemaker's burnishing stick.
andino, na, *a.* Andean.
ándito, *m.* gallery or path around a building.
andolina, *f.* = GOLONDRINA.
andón, na, *a.* roving, that walks a great deal; ambling (s. o. horses).—**andonear,** *vn.* to amble.
andorga, *f.* (coll.) belly.—**llenar la a.,** to gorge, to stuff one's self.
andorina, *f.* = GOLONDRINA.
andorra, *f.* street walker.
andorrear, *vn.* to gad about.
andorrera, *f.* street walker.
andorrero, *m.* gadder, rover, tramp.
andosco, ca, *a.* two-year old (sheep).
andrajero, ra, *n.* ragpicker.
andrajo, *m.* rag, tatter; despicable person.
andrajosamente, *adv.* raggedly.
andrajoso, sa, *a.* ragged, in tatters.
andrina, *f.* sloe. *V.* ENDRINA.
andrino, *m.* (bot.) sloe tree, blackthorn.
androfobia, *f.* androphobia, dread of, or aversion to, men.
andrógino, *m.* androgyne.
androide, *m.* automaton shaped like a man.
andrómina, *f.* (coll.) trick, fraud, fib.
androsemo, *m.* (bot.) parkleaves.
andularios, *m. pl.* (coll.) long wide gown.
andullo, *m.* (naut.) canvas shield on harpings and blocks; plug tobacco.
andurriales, *m. pl.* byroads, lonely places.
anduve, anduviera, etc. *V.* ANDAR.
anea, *f.* (bot.) cattail. *V.* ESPADAÑA.
aneaje, *m.* alnage, ell measure.
anear, *va.* to measure by ells.
aneblar. I. *va.* (ind. ANIEBLO: *subj.* ANIEBLE) to cloud, darken. **II.** *vr.* to become cloudy.
anécdota, *f.* anecdote.—**anecdótico, ca,** *a* anecdotic.—**anecdotista,** *n.* anecdotist.
anegación, *f.* overflowing, inundation.
anegadizo, za, *a.* liable to be overflowed.
anegado, da. I. *a.* overflowed; wet, soaked. **II.** *pp.* of ANEGAR.
anegamiento, *m.* = ANEGACIÓN.
anegar. I. *va.* to inundate, flood; to submerge; to flush; to drown. **II.** *vr.* to drown, sink; to become wet or soaked; to be flooded.
anegociado, da, *a.* full of business.
anejín, anejir, *m.* popular proverb which can be sung.

anejo. I. *m.* church depending on another.
II. a., ja, *a.* annexed, joined. *V.* ANEXO, XA.
aneléctrico, ca, *a.* nonelectric.
anélido, da, *n. & a.* (zool.) annelid.—*m. pl.*
Annelida.
anemia, *f.* (med.) anæmia.—**a. tropical,** uncinariasis.
anémico, ca, *a.* anæmic.
anemografía, *f.* anemography.
anemográfico, ca, *a.* anemographic.
anemógrafo, *m.* one who studies anemography;
anemoscope.
anemometría, *f.* anemometry.
anemómetro, *m.* anemometer.
anemometrógrafo, *m.* anemometrograph.
anémona, anémone, *f.* (bot.) anemone, windflower.—**a. de mar,** sea anemone.
anemoscopio, *m.* anemoscope.
anepigráfico, ca, *a.* without title or inscription.
anequín.—a, or **de, a.,** at so much a head (in
shearing of sheep).
anerobio, a = ANAEROBIO, A.
aneroide, *a. & m.* aneroid (barometer).
anestesia, *f.* anæsthesia.—**anestesiar,** *va.* to
anæsthetize.—**anestésico, ca,** *m. & a.* anæsthetic.
aneurisma, *m. & f.* (med.) aneurism.
anexar, *va.* to annex.
anexidades, *f. pl.* annexes, appurtenances.
anexión, *f.* annexion; annexation.
anexionismo, *m.* annexationism.
anexionista, *m.* annexationist.
anexo, xa, *a. =* ANEJO, JA.
anfibio, a, *n. & a.* (zool. & aer.) amphibian
(-bious).
anfíbol, *m.* (min.) amphibole.—**anfibolita,** *f.*
(min.) amphibolite.
anfibología, *f.* amphibology.
anfibológicamente, *adv.* amphibologically.
anfibológico, ca, *a.* amphibological.
anfíbraco, *m.* (poet.) amphibrach, ‿ — ‿.
anficción, *m.* amphiction.—**anfictionía,** *f.* amphictyony.—**anfictiónico, ca,** *a.* amphictyonic.
anfímacro, *m.* (poet.) anphimacer, — ‿ —.
anfión, *m.* opium.
anfioxo, *m.* (zool.) amphioxus.
anfípodo, da, *n. & a.* amphipod.—*m. pl.* Amphipoda.
anfiprostilo, *m.* (arch.) amphiprostyle.
anfisbena, *f.* amphisbæna.
anfiscios, *m. pl.* amphiscii.
anfisbena, *f.* amphisbæna.
anfiteatro, *m.* amphitheatre.
anfitrión, *m.* host.
anfitrite, *f.* (poet. and zool.) amphitrite.
ánfora, *f.* amphora.—*pl.* cruets.
anfractuosidad, *f.* crookedness; anfractuosity.
anfractuoso, sa, *a.* anfractuous.
angaria, *f.* ancient servitude; forced delay in the
sailing of a ship.
angarillas, *f. pl.* handbarrow; panniers; cruet
stands. *V.* AGUADERAS.
angarillón, *m.* large wicker basket; large hand
barrow.
angaripola, *f.* calico.—*pl.* gaudy ornaments.
ángaro, *m.* beacon.
ángel, *m.* angel; a raylike fish.—**a. custodio,** or
de la guarda, guardian angel.
angélica, *f.* (bot.) garden angelica.—**a. carlina,**
(bot.) carline thistles.—**a. palustre**, wild angelica;
(pharm.) purgative mixture.
angelical, *a.* angelic.
angelicamente, *adv.* angelically.
angélico, ca, *a.* angelic.
angelico, ito, *m. dim.* little angel.
angelón, angelonazo, angelote, *m. aug.* large
figure of an angel placed on altars; fat child.
ángelus, *m.* Angelus.
angina, *f.* angina.—**a. de pecho,** angina pectoris.
angiología, *f.* angiology.
angiospermo, ma, *n. & a.* (bot.) angiosperm
(-ous).—*f.* Angiospermæ.
angla, *f.* cape (of land).

anglesita, *f.* (min.) anglesite.
anglicanismo, *m.* Anglicanism.
anglicano, na, *a.* Anglican.
anglicismo, *m.* Anglicism.
anglo, gla, *a.* Angle; English.
angloamericano, na, *n. & a.* Anglo-American.
anglomanía, *f.* Anglomania.
anglómano, na, *n.* Anglomaniac.
anglosajón, na, *a. & n.* Anglo-Saxon.
angolán, *m.* (bot.) alangium, East India tree.
angostamente, *adv.* narrowly.
angostar, *va. & vr.* to narrow, to contract.
angosto, ta, *a.* narrow, close; insufficient.
angostura, *f.* narrowness; strait; distress; narrows (in a river, etc.)
angra, *f.* small bay, cove.
angrelado, da, *a.* (her.) ingrailed, serrated.
anguarina, *f.* loose coat with long sleeves.
anguila, *f.* (zool.) eel.—**a. de cabo,** (naut.) rope
to flog sailors.—**anguilas,** launching ways.
anguilazo, *m.* stroke with a port rope.
anguilero, *a.* (basket) for eels.
anguina, *f.* (vet.) the vein of the groins.
angula, *f.* the brood of eels.
angular, *a.* angular.
angularmente, *adv.* angularly.
angulema, *f.* hemp stuff.—*pl.* (coll.) foolish
flattery. *V.* ZALAMERÍA.
ángulo, *m.* angle; angle iron.—**á. acimutal,** azimuth.—**á. de ataque,** (aer.) angle of attack.—**á.
de balance,** (aer.) angle of bank or of roll.—**á. de
contingencia,** (r. w.) (*interior*) intersection angle
(of two tangents).—**á. de resistencia nula,** (aer.)
angle of zero lift.—**á. entrante,** reëntrant angle,
convex angle.—**á. externo,** (geom.) exterior angle.
—**á. horario,** (astr.) hour angle.—**á. interno,**
(geom.) interior angle.—**á. recto,** right angle.—**á.
tangencial,** (r. w.) deflection angle (from a tangent to a curve).—**ángulos alternos externos,**
alternate exterior angles.—**ángulos correspondientes,** corresponding, or interior-exterior, angles.
—**ángulos opuestos por el vértice,** vertical
angles.
anguloso, sa, *a.* angular, cornered: sharp (s. o.
sand, etc.).
angustia, *f.* anguish, affliction, pang.
angustiadamente, *adv.* painfully.
angustiado, da. I. *a.* grieved, worried, sorrowful; anxious; narrow-minded. **II.** *pp.* of ANGUSTIAR.
angustiar, *va.* to cause anguish to, to afflict, worry,
distress.—**angustioso, sa,** *a.* full of anguish; causing anguish or worry.
anhelación, *f.* panting; longing.
anhelar, *vn.* to breathe with difficulty; to desire
anxiously, long for, covet.
anhélito, *m.* difficult respiration.
anhelo, *m.* vehement desire; eagerness.
anheloso, sa, *a.* anxiously desirous.
anhídrico, ca, *a. V.* ANHIDRO.
anhídrido, *m.* (chem.) anhydride.—**a. carbónico,** carbon dioxide, carbonic-acid gas.—**a. sulfúrico,** sulphur trioxide.
anhidrita, *f.* anhydrite.
anhidro, dra, *a.* anhydrous.
aní, *m.* (orn.) (S. A.) a pretty creeping bird.
anidar, *vn.* to nestle; (met.) to dwell, reside; to
cherish; to shelter.
anieblar, *va.* to darken, obscure; to mystify.
anilina, *f.* (chem.) aniline.
anilla, *f.* ring; curtain ring; hoop.
anillado, da, *a.* annulated.—*m. pl.* Annelida.
anillar, *va.* to form rings or hoops with; to fasten
with rings.
anillejo, anillete, *m. dim.* small ring.
anillo, *m.* small hoop; finger ring; circlet; ring of
a turbine; circular band; (naut.) hank or grommet; (arch.) astragal.—**venir como a. al dedo,**
to fit like a glove; to come in the nick of time.
ánima, *f.* soul (*v.* ALMA); (mech.) bore of a gun.
—**ánimas,** ringing of bells at sunset.
animable, *a.* susceptible of animation.
animación, *f.* animation, liveliness; bustle.

animado, da. I. *a.* lively, animated; manful. **II.** *pp.* of ANIMAR.

animador, ra, *n.* one who animates or enlivens.

animadversión, *f.* animadversion.

animal. I. *m.* animal; dunce, blockhead. **II.** *a.* animal; stupid.

animalización, *f.* animalization.

animalizar, *va.* to animalize.

animalote, *m. aug.* big animal.

animalejo, ico, illo, *m. dim.* small or little animal, animalcule.

animalucho, *m.* ugly, hideous animal.

animar. I. *va.* to animate, enliven, comfort; to revive; to incite, excite; to give power or vigor to. **II.** *vr.* to become lively; to feel encouraged, energetic; to take heart, cheer up.

anime, *f.* a myrrhlike resin.

animero, *m.* one who begs for the souls in purgatory.

animismo, *m.* animism.

ánimo, *m.* spirit, soul, mind; courage, valor, fortitude, manfulness; hardiness; mind, intention, will; thought; attention.

animosamente, *adv.* courageously.

animosidad, *f.* animosity; courage.

animoso, sa, *a.* brave, spirited, courageous.

aniñadamente, *adv.* childishly.—**aniñado, da,** *a.* childish.—**aniñarse,** *vr.* to become childish.

aniquilable, *a.* destructible.—**aniquilación,** *f.* annihilation.—**aniquilador, ra,** *n. & a.* annihilator (-ing).—**aniquilamiento,** *m.* destruction, annihilation; decay, wasting away.

aniquilar. I. *va.* to annihilate; to consume, waste away. **II.** *vr.* to decline; decay; to waste away, to become emaciated.

anís, *m.* (bot.) anise, aniseed; sugarcoated aniseed.

anisado, da. I. *a.* anisated; anislike. **II.** *m.* anisating; AGUARDIENTE ANISADO.

anisar. I. *va.* to tincture with anise. **II.** *m.* patch sowed with aniseed.

anisete, *m.* anisette.

anisidina, *f.* (chem.) anisidine.

anisilo, *m.* anisye.

aniversario, ria. I. *a.* annual, yearly. **II.** *m.* aniversary; holiday; annual funeral service.

anjeo, *m.* coarse linen.

ano, *m.* anus.

anoche, *adv.* last night.

anochecedor, ra, *n.* person who retires late at night; (coll.) night hawk.

anochecer. I. *vn.* (*ind.* ANOCHEZCO: *subj.* ANOCHEZCA) to grow dark (at the approach of night); to be or reach (somewhere) at nightfall (*anochecimos en París,* we reached Paris at nightfall. The construction of this verb is similar to that of AMANECER). **II.** *vr.* to become dark (at nightfall).

anochecida, *f.* dusk, nightfall.

anodinar, *va.* to use, or put under the influence of, anodynes.—**anodinia,** *f.* anodynia, absence of pain.

anodino, na, *n. & a.* (med.) anodyne.

ánodo, *m.* (elec.) anode.

anomalía, *f.* anomaly; (ast.) anomaly.

anómalo, la, *a.* anomalous.

anón, *m.* (bot.) custard apple tree.

anona, *f.* annona or custard apple; store of provisions.

anonáceo, a. I. *a.* (bot.) annonaceous. **II.** *m. pl.* Annonaceæ.

anonadación, *f.*; **anonadamiento,** *m.* annihilation; overwhelming, crushing.

anonadar. I. *va.* to annihilate; to diminish. **II.** *vr.* to humble one's self.

anónimamente, *adv.* anonymously.

anónimo, ma, *a.* anonymous.

anormal, *a.* abnormal.—**anormalmente,** *adv.* abnormally.

anortita, *f.* (min.) anorthite.

anotación, *f.* annotation, note.

anotador, ra, *n.* commentator.

anotar, *va.* to write notes; to comment, annotate.

anquera, *f.* (Mex.) round covering for the hind quarter of a horse.

anqueta.—estar de media a., to be uncomfortably seated.

anquialmendrado, da, *a.* having an almond-shaped croup.

anquiboyuno, na, *a.* having a croup like an ox.

anquilosis, *f.* (anat.) ankylosis.

anquirredondo, da, *a.* having a rounded croup.

anquiseco, ca, *a.* lean-crouped.

ansa, *f.* commercial bond among the free cities of Germany.

ánsar, *m.* goose.—**a. macho,** gander.—**ansarería,** *f.* goose farm.—**ansarero, ra,** *n.* gooseherd.—**ansarino, na. I.** *a.* (poet.) belonging to geese. **II.** *m.* gosling.

ansarón, *m.* = ÁNSAR.

anseático, ca, *a.* Hanseatic.

ansí, (obs.) = ASÍ.

ansia, *f.* anxiety; eagerness, ardent desire; longing, hankering; greediness.

ansiadamente, *adv.* anxiously; earnestly.

ansiar, *va.* to desire anxiously; to long for; to hanker for; to covet.

ansiedad, *f.* anxiety. V. ANSIA.

ansiosamente, *adv.* anxiously; eagerly.

ansioso, sa, *a.* anxious; eager; greedy; hot.

anta, *f.* elk; obelisk, needle.—*pl.* (arch.) antes, pillars of a building.

antagallas, *f. pl.* (naut.) spritsail reef bands.

antagónico, ca, *a.* antagonistic.

antagonismo, *m.* antagonism.—**antagonista,** *m.* antagonist, opponent; competitor.

antañazo, *adv.* (coll.) a long time since.

antaño, *adv.* long ago; yore.

antártico, ca, *a.* antarctic.

ante, *m.* elk; buffalo; buffalo skin; first dinner course; (Peru) name of a spicy drink consisting of wine, sugar, cinnamon, nutmeg, etc.

ante, *prep.* before; in the presence of.—**a. todo,** above all, first of all.

anteado, da, *a.* buff-colored.

antealtar, *m.* chancel.

anteanoche, *adv.* night before last.

anteayer, *adv.* day before yesterday.

antebrazo, *m.* fore arm.

antecama, *f.* carpet laid in front of a bed.

antecámara, *f.* antechamber; lobby; hall.

antecapilla, *f.* room before a chapel.

antecedente, *m.* antecedent.

antecedentemente, *adv.* previously, beforehand.

anteceder, *va.* to precede, go before.

antecesor, ra, *n.* predecessor, forefather.—*pl.* ancestors.

antecos, cas, *n. pl.* antiscii, antiscians.

antecoger, *va.* (*ind.* ANTECOJO: *subj.* ANTECOJA) to forereach; to gather in too soon.

antecolumna, *f.* (arch.) column of a porch.

antecoro, *m.* entrance leading to the choir.

Antecristo, *m.* Antichrist.

antedata, *f.* antedate.—**antedatar,** *va.* to antedate.

antedecir, *va.* (*for irr. v.* DECIR) to foretell.

antedicho, cha, *a.* aforesaid.

ante diem, (Lat.) the preceding day.

antediluviano, na, *a.* antediluvian.

antefirma, *f.* address before the signature.

anteiglesia, *f.* porch of a church; parochial church and district in Biscay.

antelación, *f.* precedence in order of time.

antemano.—de a., beforehand.

antemeridiano, na, *a.* of the forenoon (a. m.)

ante merídiem, in the forenoon (a. m.).

antemural, *m.* **antemuralla,** *f.*, **antemuro,** *m.* fort, rock or mountain serving for the defence of a fortress; safeguard.

antena, *f.* (naut.) lateen yard; (ent., aer.) antenna.—*pl.* antennæ.

antenallas, *f. pl.* pincers.

antenatal, *a.* prenatal.

antenoche, *adv.* night before last.

antenombre, *m.* title before a proper name.
anténula, *f.* antennule.
antenupcial, *a.* before marriage, prenuptial.
anteojera, *f.* spectacle case; eyeflap; blinker.
anteojero, ra. *n.* spectacle maker.
anteojo, *m.* spyglass; eyeglass; telescope (of a surveying instrument); opera glass.—*pl.* spectacles; goggles; winkers.—**a. de larga vista,** field glass.
antepagar, *va.* to pay beforehand.
antepasado, da. I. *a.* passed, elapsed. **II.** *n.* ancestor, predecessor.
antepecho, *m.* balcony, bridge rail, sill railing; breastwork, parapet, battlement; footstep of a coach; poitrel (harness); breast roller of a loom.
antepenúltimo, ma, *a.* antepenultimate.
anteponer, *va.* (*for irr. v.* PONER) to prefer; (w. a) to prefer; to place before.
anteportada, *f.* flyleaf bearing the title only of a book.
anteportal, antepórtico, *m.* vestibule, porch.
anteproyecto, *m.* preliminary plans for an architectural or engineering work.
antepuerta, *f.* portier; (fort.) anteport.
antepuerto, *m.* (naut.) anteport.
antera, *f.* (bot.) anther.
anterior, *a.* anterior; former; above, preceding.
anterioridad, *f.* anteriority; priority; preference.—**con a.,** previously, beforehand.
anteriormente, *adv.* previously.
antero, *m.* worker in buckskin.
antes, *adv.* before; formerly; first; rather; on the contrary.—**a. bien,** on the contrary.—**a. de,** before.—**a. de anoche** = ANTENOCHE.—**a. de ayer** = ANTEAYER.—**a. de que,** before.—**a. que,** before; rather than.
antesacristía, *f.* room before the sacristy.
antesala, *f.* antechamber.—**hacer a.,** to dance attendance in an antechamber.
antestatura, *f.* (mil.) small intrenchment of palisadoes and sandbags.
antetemplo, *m.* portico of a church.
antever, *va.* (*for irr. v.* VER) to foresee.
antevíspera, *f.* two days before.
antiafrodisíaco, a. anaphrodisiac.
antialcohólico, ca, *a.* antialcoholic.
antiapopléctico, ca, *a.* antiapoplectic.
antiapóstol, *m.* & *f.* antiapostle.
antiarina, *f.* (chem.) antiarin.
antiaro, *m.* upas tree.
antiartístico, ca, *a.* unartistic.
antiartrítico, ca, *a.* (med.) antiarthritic.
antiasmático, ca, *a.* (med.) antasthmatic.
antibaquio, *m.* antibacchic, poetic foot.
antibilioso, sa, *a.* antibilious.
anticiclón, *m.* anticyclone.
anticipación, *f.* anticipation; foretaste.
anticipada, *f.* (fenc.) unexpected thrust.
anticipadamente, *adv.* prematurely; in advance, beforehand.
anticipado, da, *a.* advanced (money); in advance (payment).
anticipador, ra, *n.* & *a.* anticipator (-ing).
anticipamiento, *m.* = ANTICIPACIÓN.
anticipante. I. *a.* (med.) anticipant. **II.** *m.* forestaller.
anticipar. I. *va.* to anticipate (in the sense of to do, bring to happen, etc. before the regular time); to advance (money, payment); to lend. **II.** *vr.* (w. a) to anticipate, act ahead of; to act or occur before the regular or expected time.
anticipo, *m.* advance; money lent; advance payment.
anticlerical, *a.* anticlerical.
anticlímax, *m.* or *f.* (rhet.) anticlimax.
anticlinal, *m.* (geol.) anticline.
anticonstitucional, *a.* unconstitutional.
anticosmético, ca, *a.* anticosmetic.
anticresis, *f.* (law) antichresis.
anticresista, *m.* the creditor in antichresis.
anticristiano, na, *a.* antichristian.
anticrítico, *m.* opponent to a critic.

anticuado, da. I. *a.* antiquated. **II.** *pp.* of ANTICUAR.
anticuar. I. *va.* to antiquate, outdate. **II.** *vr.* to become antiquated.
anticuario, ria, *n.* antiquarian.
antidisentérico, ca, *a.* antidysenteric.
antidoral, *a.* (law) = REMUNERATORIO.
antidotario, *m.* pharmacology; place in a pharmacy for antidotes.
antídoto, *m.* antidote.
antiemético, ca, *a.* (med.) antiemetic.
antiepiléptico, ca, *a.* (med.) antiepileptic.
antier, *adv.* day before yesterday.
antiesclavista, *a.* antislavery.
antiescorbútico, ca, *a.* antiscorbutic.
antiescrofuloso, sa, *a.* antiscrofulous.
antiespasmódico, ca, *a.* antispasmodic.
antifaz, *m.* veil that covers the face; mask.
antifebril, a. (med.) antifebrile.
antiflogístico, ca. I. *a.* (med.) antiphlogistic. **II.** *m.* antiphlogistic.
antífona, *f.* antiphony, anthem.
antifonal, antifonario, *m.* antiphonal.
antifonero, *m.* precentor.
antífrasis, *f.* antiphrasis.
antigramatical, *a.* ungrammatical.
antigualla, *f.* object of remote antiquity; antique; out-of-date custom or object.
antiguamente, *adv.* formerly, in antiquity.
antiguar, *vn.* to obtain seniority.
antigüedad, *f.* antiquity; ancient times; antique.
antiguo, gua. I. *a.* antique; ancient, old.—**A. Testamento,** Old Testament.—**a la antigua, a lo antiguo,** after the manner of the ancients, in an old-fashion manner.—**de antiguo,** from times of yore, since old times.—**lo antiguo,** ancient things; antiquity. **II.** *m.* aged member of a community; senior of a college.—**los antiguos,** the ancients.
antihelmíntico, ca, *a.* anthelminthic.
antiherpético, ca, *a.* (med.) antiherpetic.
antihistérico, ca. *a.* (med.) antihysteric.
antilogía, *f.* antilogy.
antilógico, ca, *a.* illogical.
antílope, *m.* antelope.
antillano, na, *n.* & *a.* West-Indian.
Antillas, *f. pl.* West Indies, Antilles.
antiministerial. I. *a.* opposed to the Administration. **II.** *n.* member of the opposition (to the government).
antimonárquico, ca, *a.* antimonarchical.
antimonial, *a.* antimonial.
antimoniato, *m.* antimonate.—**antimónico, ca,** *a.* antimonic.
antimonio, *m.* antimony.
antinacional, *a.* antinational.
antinatural, *a.* unnatural.
antinefrítico, ca, *a.* (med.) antinephritic.
antineurálgico, ca, *n.* & *a.* antineuralgic
antinomia, *f.* (law) antinomy.
antioqueno, *n.* & *a.* Antiochian.
antipalúdico, ca, *a.* antimalarial.
antipapa, *m.* antipope.—**antipapado,** *m.* antipapacy.—**antipapal,** *a.* antipapal.
antipara, *f.* screen; legging covering the front part of leg and foot.
antiparras, *f. pl.* (coll.) spectacles.
antipatía, *f.* antipathy; dislike, aversion.
antipático, ca, *a.* displeasing, disagreeable.—**antipatizar,** *vn.* not to be congenial.—**a. con,** to dislike, not to be congenial with.
antipatriótico, ca, *a.* unpatriotic.
antiperistáltico, ca, *a.* antiperistaltic.
antiperístasis, *f.* antiperistasis.
antiperistático, ca, *a.* antiperistatic.
antipestilencial, *a.* (med.) antipestilential.
antipirina, *f.* antipyrine.
antípoca, *f.* (law, prov.) agreement to lease.
antipocar, *va.* (law) to execute (a lease).
antípoda. I. *a.* antipodal. **II.** *m.* (in *pl.*) antipodes.
antipolítico, ca, *a.* impolitic.
antipútrido, da, *a.* antiseptic.

antiquísimo, ma, *a. sup.* very ancient.
antirreligioso, sa, *a.* irreligious.
antirrevolucionario, ria, *a.* antirevolutionary.
antirrino, *m.* (bot.) snapdragon.
antisemita I. *a.* anti-Semitic. **II.** *n.* anti-Semite.
antisepsia, *f.* (med.) antisepsy.
antiséptico, ca, *n.* & *a.* antiseptic.
antisifilítico, ca, *a.* antisyphilitic.
antisocial, *a.* antisocial, subversive of society.
antistrofa, *f.* antistrophe.
antítesis, *f.* antithesis.
antitético, ca, *a.* antithetical.
antitóxico, ca, *a.* antitoxic.
antitoxina, *f.* antitoxin.
antitrago, *m.* (anat.) antitragus.
antitrinitario, *m.* antitrinitarian.
antocarpo, *m.* (bot.) anthocarp, anthocarpous fruit.
antófago, ga, *a.* anthophagous.
antojadizo, za; antojado, da, *a.* capriciously desirous, having whimsical desires for trifles; wishing, or taking a notion to, everything (gen. said of children and women).
antojarse, *vr.* to be desired capriciously or on the spur of the moment, to arouse a whimsical desire, or a fancy [ch. constr.: *se me antojó ese sombrero,* I took a fancy to (buy) that hat, (coll.) I fell in love with that hat and longed for it; *no hago eso porque no se me antoja,* I don't do that because I don't want to, or, because I won't; *se nos antojó ir a Paris,* we took a notion to go to Paris]; to occur; to arouse suspicion (ch. const.: *se me antojó que Juan no sabía,* it occurred to me, or, I suspected, that John did not know).—*a.* **de,** to take a fancy to, to desire capriciously.
antojo, *m.* whim, capricious desire, fancy; will.—**a su a.,** as one pleases; arbitrarily.
antojuelo, *m. dim.* slight desire.
antología, *f.* anthology.
antonomasia, *f.* (rhet.) antonomasia.
antonomástico, ca, *a.* antonomastic.
antor, ra, *n.* (law) vender of stolen goods.
antorcha, *f.* torch, flambeau, taper; cresset.
antorchero, *m.* cresset.
antoría, *f.* (law, prov.) right against the seller of stolen goods.
antracita, *f.* anthracite coal.
ántrax, *m.* (med.) anthrax.
antro, *m.* cavern, grotto; (anat.) antrum.
antropofagía, *f.* anthropophagy.
antropófago, ga, *n.* & *a.* cannibal.
antropofobia, *f.* anthropophobia.
antropografía, *f.* anthropography.
antropoide, *n.* & *a.* anthropoid.
antropología, *f.* anthropology.
antropológico, ca, *a.* anthropological.
antropólogo, *m.* anthropologist.
antropómetra, *n.* anthropometrist.—**antropometría,** *f.* anthropometry.—**antropométrico, ca,** *a.* anthropometric.
antropomorfismo, *m.* anthropomorphism.
antropomorfita, *n.* anthropomorphite.
antropomorfo, fa, *a.* anthropomorphous.
antroposofía, *f.* anthroposophy.
antruejar, *va.* to play carnival tricks on.
antruejo, *m.* the three days of carnival before Ash Wednesday.
antuviada, *f.* (coll.) blow or stroke.
antuviar, *va.* to forestall, anticipate; to be first in striking or attacking.—**antuvión,** *m.* (coll.) sudden stroke or attack.—**de a.,** unexpectedly.
anual, *a.* annual, yearly.—**anualidad,** *f.* annual recurrence; annuity.—**anualmente,** *adv.* annually, yearly.
anuario, *m.* yearbook; trade directory.
anúbada, *f.* = ANÚTEBA.
anubarrado, da, *a.* clouded.
anublado, da, *a.* overcast, clouded, cloudy.
anublar. I. *va.* to cloud, darken; to obscure; **II.** *vr.* to be blasted, withered, mildewed; to fall through, fall off; to become cloudy.
anublo, *m.* = AÑUBLO.

anudar. I. *va.* to knot; to join, unite. **II.** *vn.* to wither, fade, pine away.—**anudarse la voz a uno,** (met.) to become speechless.
anuencia, *f.* compliance, consent.
anuente, *a.* condescending.
anulable, *a.* voidable.
anulación, *f.* abrogation, voiding, nullification.
anulador, ra, *n.* repealer.
anular, *va.* to annul, make void; to frustrate.
anular, *a.* ring-shaped. *V.* DEDO ANULAR.
anulativo, va, *a.* voiding.
anuloso, sa, *a.* annular.
anunciación, *f.* announcement; Annunciation.
anunciador, ra, I. *n.* & *a.* announcer (-ing); advertiser (-ing). **II.** *m.* (elec.) annunciator.
anunciante, *n.* announcer; advertiser.
anunciar, *va.* to announce, proclaim; to forebode; to advertise.
anuncio, *m.* announcement, notice; omen, forerunner; advertisement; (com.) advice.
anuo, nua, *a.* = ANUAL.
anuria, *f.* (med.) anuria.
anuro, *n.* (zool.) anuran.
anverso, *m.* obverse.
anvir, *m.* liquor from fermented tobacco leaves.
anzolero, *m.* fishhook maker or dealer.
anzuelo, *m.* fishhook; fritters.—**caer en el a.,** **tragar el a.,** to swallow the hook.
aña, *f.* hyena.
añacal, *m.* wheat carrier to mills; baker's board to carry bread.
añada, *f.* good or bad season in a year; moiety of arable land.
añadido, *m.* hair switch.
añadidura, *f.* addition, increase; extra, over.—**por a.,** in addition (often u. in the sense of "to make matters worse"); over, to boot.
añadir, *va.* to add, join; to exaggerate.
añafil, *m.* a Moorish musical pipe.
añafilero, *m.* player on the *añafil.*
añagaza, *f.* call, lure, or decoy; allurement, enticement.
añal. I. *a.* annual; one-year old. **II.** *m.* offering in memory of a person one year after his death.
añalejo, *m.* ecclesiastical almanac.
añascar, *va.* (pret. AÑASQUÉ: *subj.* AÑASQUE) (coll.) to collect (small trinkets).
añejar. I. *va.* to make old. **II.** *vr.* to grow old; to become stale.
añejo, ja, *a.* old; stale, musty.
añicos, *m. pl.* smithereens.—**hacer a.,** to break to smithereens.—**hacerse a.,** to take great pains, to exert one's self to the utmost.
añil, *m.* (bot.) indigo; indigo blue; ball blue.
añilar, *va.* to blue (clothes).—**añilería,** *f.* indigo farm.
añinero, *m.* dealer in lambskins.
añinos, *m. pl.* the fleecy skins of yearling lambs; lamb's wool.
año, *m.* year; cavalier; valentine drawn by lot on New Year's day; crop.—*pl.* birthday; long ago; old age.—**a. anomalístico,** anomalistic year.—**a. bisiesto,** leap-year.—**a. civil,** civil year.—**a. climatérico,** grand climacteric.—**a. económico,** fiscal year.—**a. intercalar,** leap-year.—**a. nuevo,** New Year.—**a. platónico,** Platonic year.—**a. sideral,** sidereal year.—**a. sinódico,** synodic period of the earth and another planet.—**a. tropical,** tropical or solar year.—**estar de buen a.,** to be in good health.—**por los años de . . .,** about the year . . .—**tener . . . años,** to be . . . years old (*tengo 20 años,* I am 20 years old; *¿cuántos años tiene Vd.?* how old are you?)
añojal, *m.* fallow land.
añojo, ja, *n.* yearling calf.
añoranza, *f.* homesickness.
añoso, sa, *a.* old, stricken in years.
añublado, da. I. *a.* blindfolded. **II.** *pp.* of AÑUBLAR.
añublar, añublarse, *V.* ANUBLAR.
añublo, *m.* mildew. *V.* TIZÓN.
añusgar, *vn.* to choke; to become angry.
aojador, ra, *n.* hoodoo, evil-eyed person.

aojadura, *f.* **aojamiento,** *m.* witchcraft, fascination, evil eye.

aojar, *va.* to charm, bewitch, hoodoo.

aojo, *m.* bewitching, fascination, evil eye.

aonio, nia, *a.* relating to the Muses.

aorta, *f.* (anat.) aorta.—**aórtico, ca,** *a.* aortic.

aovado, da, *a.* oviform, egg-shaped.

aovar, *vn.* to lay eggs.

aovillarse, *vr.* to crumple, shrink.

apabilar, *va.* to trim (a wick).

apabullar, *va.* (coll.) to flatten, crush.

apacentadero, *m.* pasture.

apacentador, *m.* herdsman.

apacentamiento, *m.* grazing; pasturage.

apacentar, *va.* (*ind.* APACIENTO: *subj.* APACIENTE) to graze (cattle); to graze (grass, etc.); to teach, instruct spiritually; to incite.

apacibilidad, *f.* peaceableness, mildness.

apacible, *a.* peaceable, peaceful, gentle, placid, calm.—**apaciblemente,** *adv.* peacefully, gently.

apaciento, apaciente. *V.* APACENTAR.

apaciguador, ra, *n.* & *a.* pacifier (-fying).

apaciguamiento, *m.* pacification.

apaciguar. I. *va.* to appease, pacify, calm. **II.** *vn.* (naut.) to abate. **III.** *vr.* to become calm, calm down.

apache, *m.* Apache.

apacheta, *f.* (Amer.) devotional heap of stones on hills.

apachurrar, *va.* (Am.) to crush, flatten.

apadrinador, ra, *n.* patron, defender, protector; second (in a duel).

apadrinar, *va.* to act as second of, in a duel; to act as godfather to; to uphold, approve, favor.

apagable, *a.* extinguishable, quenchable.

apagadizo, za, *a.* poorly burning, of difficult combustion.

apagado, da, *a.* humble-minded, submissive, pusillanimous; dull (color).

apagador, *m.* one that extinguishes; damper, extinguisher; damper (in pianos).

apagaincendios, *m.* fire engine; fire extinguisher.

apagamiento, *m.* extinguishment.

apagapenoles, *m. pl.* (naut.) leech ropes, leech lines.

apagar. I. *va.* (*pret.* APAGUÉ: *subj.* APAGUE) to quench, put out, extinguish; to efface, destroy; (art) to soften (colors); (mech.) to deaden.— **a. cal,** to slake lime.—**a. la voz,** to put a mute on musical instruments.—**a. los fuegos,** or **el fuego, del enemigo,** to silence the enemy's guns. **II.** *vr.* to become extinguished, go out, die out.

apagógico, ca, *a.* apagogical.

apainelado, da, *a.* elliptic (arch).

apaisado, da, *a.* elongated, having greater width than depth.

apalabrar, *va.* to make an engagement with; to speak about, discuss; to bespeak, speak for, engage.

apalancar, *va.* (*pret.* APALANQUÉ: *subj.* APALANQUE) to move with a lever.

apaleador, ra, *n.* cudgeller.—**apaleamiento,** *m.* drubbing, beating.—**apalear,** *va.* to cane, drub, cudgel; to horsewhip.

apaleo, *m.* moving or shovelling grain.

apanalado, da, *a.* honeycombed.

apancora, *f.* sea hedgehog.

apandar, *va.* (coll.) to pilfer, to steal.

apandillar, *va.* & *vr.* to form a gang or faction.

apanojado, da, *a.* (bot.) paniculate.

apantanar, *va.* to flood; to inundate.

apantuflado, da, *a.* slipper-shaped.

apañado, da, *a.* resembling woollen cloth in body; dexterous, skillful; (coll.) suitable.

apañador, ra, *n.* one that seizes; pilferer.

apañadura, *f.* act of seizing, snatching; trimming (on counterpanes).

apañamiento, *m.* = APAÑO.

apañar. I. *va.* to grasp, seize; to carry away; to pilfer; to dress, clothe; to fit close, wrap; to patch, mend. **II.** *vr.* (coll.) to be handy, to be skillful.

apaño, *m.* act of seizing or grasping; knack; patch, repair.

apañuscar, *va.* (*pret.* APAÑUSQUÉ: *subj.* APAÑUSQUE) to rumple, crush, crumple.

apapagayado, da, *a.* parrot like; aquiline nose.

aparador, *m.* sideboard, cupboard; workshop of an artisan; show window.

aparadura, *f.* (naut.) garbel, garboard plank.

aparar, *va.* to stretch out the hands or skirts for catching; (agr.) to dress (plants); (shoe.) to close (the uppers); to prepare, arrange; to dress with an adze, dub.—**a. un navío,** (naut.) to dub a ship.

aparasolado, da, *a.* (bot.) umbelliferous.

aparatado, da, *a.* prepared, disposed.

aparatero, ra, *a.* = APARATOSO.

aparato, *m.* apparatus; preparation; pomp, ostentation, show; circumstance; signs, symptoms; elaborate scenic display; collection of surgical instruments; system, associated organs.

aparatoso, sa, *a.* pompous, showy.

aparcería, *f.* partnership.—**aparcero, ra,** *n.* partner.

apareamiento, *m.* matching, mating, pairing.

aparear. I. *va.* to match, mate; to pair. **II.** *vr.* to be paired, matched, mated.

aparecer, *vn.* & *vr.* (*ind.* APAREZCO: *subj.* APAREZCA) to appear, show up, turn up.

aparecido. I. *m.* ghost. **II.** *pp.* of APARECER.

aparecimiento, *m.* apparition, appearing.

aparejado, da. I. *a.* fit; ready. **II.** *pp.* of APAREJAR.

aparejador, ra, *n.* one who prepares or gets ready; overseer of a building; (naut.) rigger.

aparejar. I. *va.* to get ready; to prepare; to saddle or harness; (naut.) to rig; to furnish; to size (work before painting or gilding); **II.** *vr.* to get ready; to equip.

aparejo, *m.* preparation, disposition; harness, gear; packsaddle; (mech.) tackle; (pict.) sizing canvas or board; (mas.) bond; (naut.) tackle and rigging on a ship; furniture.—*pl.* equipment, trappings.—**a. real,** main tackle.

aparentar, *va.* to feign, pretend.

aparente, *a.* apparent, not real; fit, suited; evident, manifest.

aparentemente, *adv.* apparently, outwardly.

aparición, *f.* apparition.

apariencia, *f.* appearance, aspect, looks; likeness, resemblance; vestige; outward show; pageant; probability, conjecture.—*pl.* scenic effects.

aparrado, da, *a.* shrubby, vinelike.

aparroquiado, da, *a.* established in a parish.

aparroquiar, *va.* to bring customers to.

apartadamente, *adv.* privately, apart.

apartadero, *m.* sidetrack, siding; free space (beside a road, etc.); sorting room.

apartadijo, *m.* small part, share, or portion.

apartadizo, *m.* recluse; small room; partition.

apartado, da. I. *a.* separated; distant, retired; distinct, different. **II.** *pp.* of APARTAR. **III.** *m.* retired room; smelting house; mail separated for early or special delivery; P. O. letter box; separation of cattle; board of cattle ranchers.

apartador, ra, *n.* one that divides or separates; sorter, separator.—**a. de metales,** smelter.

apartamiento, *m.* separation; retirement; secluded place; apartment, flat; waiver, relinquishment.

apartar. I. *va.* to part off; to separate, divide; to dissuade; to remove, to dislodge; to sort. **II.** *vr.* to withdraw, hold off; to desist.

aparte. I. *m.* paragraph; (theat.) aside. **II.** *adv.* separately; aside (on the stage).

aparvar, *va.* to heap (grain for thrashing).

apasionadamente, *adv.* passionately; unfairly, bigotedly.

apasionado, da. I. *a.* passionate; impassioned; intolerant; affected with pain; devoted, passionately fond. **II.** *pp.* of APASIONAR. **III.** *m.* admirer.

apasionamiento, *m.* passion.

apasionar. I. *va.* to impassion. **II.** *vr.* to become passionately fond.

apasturar, *va.* to pasture, forage.

apatán, *m.* (Philip.) a dry measure (.094 litre).

apatía, *f.* apathy.—**apático, ca,** *a.* apathetic.

apatusco, *m.* (coll.) ornament, dress.

apea, *f.* rope fetter for horses.

apeadero, *m.* landing, horseblock; railway station.

apeador, *m.* land surveyor.

apeamiento, *m.* = APEO.

apear. I. *va.* to dismount; to bring down; to survey; to set landmarks to; to fell; to block or scotch (a wheel); (arch.) to prop; (artil.) to dismount (a gun); to dissuade; to remove (difficulties); to shackle (a horse). **II.** *vr.* to alight.

apechugar, *va.* (*pret.* APECHUGUÉ: *subj.* APECHUGUE) to push with the breast; (met.) to undertake with spirit.

apedazar, *va.* (*pret.* APEDACÉ: *subj.* APEDACE) to patch, mend, repair.

apedernalado, da, *a.* flinty.

apedreado, da. I. *a.* stoned, pelted; variegated; pitted with the smallpox. **II.** *pp.* of APEDREAR.

apedreador, ra, *n.* stoner, stone thrower.

apedreamiento, *m.* lapidation, stoning.

apedrear. I. *va.* to stone; to kill with stones. **II.** *vn.* to hail. **III.** *vr.* to be injured by hail.

apedreo, *m.* stoning.

apegadamente, *adv.* devotedly.—**apegarse,** *vr.* to become attached.—**apego,** *m.* attachment, fondness.

apelable, *a.* appealable.

apelación, *f.* appeal; (fam.) consultation (of doctors); (fam.) remedy, help.

apelado, da. I. *a.* (law) successful in an appeal; of the same coat or color (s. o. horses). **II.** *pp.* of APELAR.

apelambrar, *va.* to steep (hides) in limewater.

apelante, *n.* & *a.* appellant.

apelar, *vn.* to appeal, have recourse to; to be of the same color, match (s. o. horses).

apeldar, *vn.* (coll.) to flee, run away.

apelde, *m.* (coll.) flight, escape.

apelmazado, da, *a.* compressed, compact.

apelmazamiento, *m.* compactness.

apelmazar, *va.* (*pret.* APELMACÉ: *subj.* APELMACE) to compress; to render less spongy.

apelotonar, *va.* & *vr.* to form into balls.

apellar, *va.* to dress (leather).

apellidado, da. I. *a.* named, by the name of. **II.** *pp.* of APELLIDAR.

apellidamiento, *m.* naming.

apellidar, *va.* to name; to proclaim; to call to arms.

apellido, *m.* surname, family name; nickname; forces called to arms.

apenar. I. *va.* to cause pain, sorrow. **II.** *vr.* to grieve.

apenas, *adv.* scarcely, hardly; with trouble; no sooner than, as soon as.

apencar, *vn.* (*pret.* APENQUÉ: *subj.* APENQUE) to accept with reluctance.

apéndice, *m.* appendix.—**a. cecal, vermicular,** or **vermiforme,** vermiform appendix.

apendicitis, *f.* appendicitis.

apendicular, *a.* appendicular.

apenino, na, *a.* Apennine.

apeo, *m.* survey; prop, propping.

apeonar, *va.* to walk or run swiftly (birds).

apepsia, *f.* (med.) apepsy, indigestion.

aperador, *m.* farmer; wheelwright; foreman.

aperar, *va.* to make, repair, equip.

apercibimiento, *m.* preparation, preparedness; order, advice, warning; summons.

apercibir, *va.* to provide; to get ready; to warn; advise; (law) to summon.

aperción, *f.* opening. V. ABERTURA.

apercollar, *va.* (coll.) to collar; to snatch.

aperdigar, *va.* = PERDIGAR.

apergaminado, da, *a.* parchmentlike.

aperitivo, va, *a.* aperitive.

apernador, *m.* dog that seizes game by the legs.

apernar, *va.* (*ind.* APIERNO: *subj.* APIERNE) to seize by the ham.

apero, *m.* farm implements; tools, equipment, outfit; sheepfold.

aperreado, da. I. *a.* harassed. **II.** *pp.* of APERREAR.—**aperreador, ra,** *n.* (coll.) importunate person, nuisance; intruder.—**aperrear. I.** *va.* to throw to the dogs; to annoy, bother. **II.** *vr.* to toil, overwork.

apersogar, *va.* (Mex.) to tether.

apersonarse, *vr.* (law) = COMPARECER.

apertura, *f.* opening (of a convention, etc.); reading (of a will).

apesadumbrado, da. I. *a.* sad, mournful, griefstricken. **II.** *pp.* of apesadumbrar, *va.* & *vr.* to grieve, to make (become) sad.

apesaradamente, *adv.* mournfully, sadly.

apesarar, *va.* & *vr.* = APESADUMBRAR.

apesgamiento, *m.* sinking under a burden.

apesgar. I. *va.* (*pret.* APESGUÉ: *subj.* APESGUE) to overwhelm with a load. **II.** *vr.* to be aggrieved.

apestado, da. I. *a.* pestered, annoyed; satiated; full, overstocked. **II.** *pp.* of APESTAR.

apestar. I. *va.* to infect with the plague; to corrupt, turn putrid; to annoy, bother; to sicken, nauseate. **II.** *vn.* to stink.

apestoso, sa, *a.* foul-smelling, sickening, nauseating, offensive.

apétalo, la, *a.* (bot.) apetalous.

apetecedor, ra, *n.* one that longs or desires.

apetecer, *va.* (*ind.* APETEZCO: *subj.* APETEZCA) to desire; to like.—**apetecible,** *a.* desirable.

apetencia, *f.* appetite, hunger; desire.

apetezco, ca, V. APETECER.

apetite, *m.* sauce, appetizer; inducement.

apetitivo, va, *a.* appetitive.

apetito, *m.* appetite.—**abrir el a.,** to make an appetite.

apetitoso, sa, *a.* appetizing, savory, palatable.

apezonado, da, *a.* nipple-shaped.

apezuñar, *vn.* to climb laboriously, sinking the edge of the hoof into the ground.

apiadarse, *vr.* (w. de) to pity, take pity (on).

apiaradero, *m.* shepherd's account of the sheep.

apiario, a, *a.* beelike.

apicarado, da, *a.* roguish, knavish; impudent.

apicararse, *vr.* to become roguish.

ápice, *m.* apex, summit, top, pinnacle; trifle; whit, iota; graphic accent; most intricate and pointed part of a question.

apículo, *m.* small, keen point.

apicultor, ra, *n.* apiculturist, beekeeper.

apicultura, *f.* apiculture, beekeeping.

ápidos, *m. pl.* (zool.) Apidæ.

apilador, *m.* piler of wool.

apilar, *va.* to heap, pile up.

apimpollarse, *vr.* to germinate.

apiñado, da. I. *a.* pyramidal, pine-shaped; crowded; congested; thick, close together. **II.** *pp.* of APIÑAR.

apiñadura, *f.*, **apiñamiento,** *m.* pressing together; crowd, jam, congestion.

apiñar. I. *va.* to press together, crowd. **II.** *vr.* to clog; to crowd.

apio, *m.* (bot.) celery.

apiolar, *va.* to gyve (a hawk); to tie by the legs; (col.) to seize, apprehend; to kill, murder.

apiparse, *vr.* (coll.) to gorge.

apirético, ca, *a.* apyretic.

apirexia, *f.* apyrexia.

apisonar, *va.* to tamp.

apitonamiento, *m.* putting forth the tenderlings; passion, anger.

apitonar. I. *vn.* to put forth the tenderlings; to bud, germinate. **II.** *va.* to break with bill or horn; to shell. **III.** *vr.* to abuse each other.

apizarrado, da, *a.* slate-colored.

aplacable, *a.* placable.—**aplacación,** *f.* appeasement.—**aplacamiento,** *m.* stay of execution.—**aplacador, ra,** *n.* & *a.* appeaser (-ing).

aplacar, *va.* (*pret.* APLAQUÉ: *subj.* APLAQUE) to appease, pacify, calm.

aplacer, *va.* to please.

aplacerado, da, *a.* (naut.) level and not very deep; (Am.) open, cleared of trees.

aplacible, *a.* pleasant.—**aplaciente,** *a.* pleasing, agreeable.—**aplacimiento,** *m.* pleasure.

aplanadera, *f.* levelling board, float; rammer.

aplanador, *m.* leveller; (mech.) battledore, brusher, riveter; ingot hammer; cylinder roller; (typ.) planer, planishing mallet.

aplanamiento, *m.* levelling.

aplanar. I. *va.* to smooth, make even; to terrify or astonish. **II.** *vr.* to tumble down; to weaken; to dismay.

aplanático, ca, *a.* aplanatic.

aplanchado, *m.* V. PLANCHADO.

aplanchadora, *f.* V. PLANCHADORA.

aplanchar, *va.* to iron (clothes).

aplantillar, *va.* to adjust or fit (stones).

aplastado, da. I. *a.* caked; dispirited. **II.** *pp.* of APLASTAR.

aplastar. I. *va.* to flatten, crush, smash; to floor (an opponent). **II.** *vr.* to become flat; to collapse.

aplaudidor, ra, *n.* & *a.* applauder (-ing).

aplaudir, *va.* to applaud.

aplauso, *m.* applause; approbation, praise.

aplayar, *vr.* to overflow the banks.

aplazamiento, *m.* convocation; summons; postponement.

aplazar, *va.* (*pret.* APLACÉ: *subj.* APLACE) to convene; to summon; to adjourn; to postpone.

aplebeyar. I. *va.* to make plebeian, to degrade. **II.** *vr.* to lower one's self, to become mean.

aplegar, *va.* (*pret.* APLEGUÉ: *subj.* APLEGUE) (prov.) to join, unite.

aplicable, *a.* applicable.—**aplicación,** *f.* application.—**aplicado, da. I.** *a.* studious, industrious, assiduous. **II.** *pp.* of APLICAR.

aplicar. I. *va.* (*pret.* APLIQUÉ: *subj.* APLIQUE) to apply; to clap; to attribute or impute; (law) to adjudge. **II.** *vr.* to apply one's self.

aplomado, da. I. *a.* lead-colored; heavy, dull, lazy. **II.** *pp.* of APLOMAR.

aplomar. I. *va.* to overload, crush. **II.** *vn.* to plumb. **III.** *vr.* to tumble, fall to the ground.

aplomo. I. *m.* tact, prudence, self-possession; (mus.) exactness in time; (pict.) due proportion. **II.** *a.* plumb, vertical.

apnea, *f.* apnea, want of respiration.

apocado, da. I. *a.* pusillanimous, mean-spirited, cowardly; of low extraction. **II.** *pp.* of APOCAR.

apocador, ra, *n.* lessener, diminisher.

Apocalipsis, *m.* Apocalypse, Revelation.

apocalíptico, ca, *a.* apocalyptical.

apocamiento, *m.* bashfulness; diffidence; pusillanimity, incapacity.

apocar. I. *va.* (*pret.* APOQUÉ: *subj.* APOQUE) to lessen; to cramp, contract. **II.** *vr.* to humble, belittle one's self.

apócema, apócima, *f.* (med.) apozem.

apocináceo, a. I. *a.* (bot.) apocynaceous. **II.** *f. pl.* Apocynaceæ.

apocopar, *va.* to apocopate.

apócope, *f.* (gram.) apocope; apocopation.

apócrifamente, *adv.* apocryphally.

apócrifo, fa, *a.* apocryphal.—**Apócrifos,** (Bib.) Apocrypha.

apocrisario, *m.* Byzantine envoy; (ecc.) apocrisarius.

apodador, *m.* wag, scoffer.

apodar, *va.* to give nicknames to, scoff.

apoderado, da. I. *a.* empowered, authorized. **II.** *pp.* of APODERAR. **III.** *m.* proxy; attorney.

apoderar. I. *va.* to empower; to grant power of attorney to. **II.** *vr.* to possess one's self, take possession.

apodíctico, ca, *a.* apodictic; indisputable.

apodo, *m.* nickname.

ápodo, da, *a.* (zool.) apodous, without feet.

apódosis, *f.* (rhet.) apodosis.

apofige, *f.* (arch.) apophyge.

apófise, apófisis, *f.* apophysis, process.

apoflegmático, ca, *a.* apophlegmatic.

apogamia, *f.* (bot.) apogamy.

apogeo, *m.* apogee; height (of fame, etc.)

apógrafo, *m.* apograph, transcript.

apolillado, da. I. *a.* moth-eaten, worm-eaten. **II.** *pp.* of APOLILLAR.

apolilladura, *f.* moth hole.

apolillar. I. *va.* to eat (clothes: s. o. moths). **II.** *vr.* to become moth-eaten.

apolinar, *a.* Apolline, belonging to Apollo.

apolinarista, *n.* & *a..* Apollinarian.

apolíneo, a, *a.* = APOLINAR.

apologético, ca, *a.* apologetic.

apología, *f.* apology, defence, eulogy.

apológico, ca, *a.* relating to apologues.

apologista, *n.* apologist.

apólogo, *m.* apologue, fable.

apoltronarse, *vr.* to grow lazy; to loiter.

apomazar, *va.* (*pret.* APOMACÉ: *subj.* APOMACE) to glaze; to burnish with pumice stone.

aponeurosis, *f.* (med.) aponeurosis.

aponeurótico, ca, *a.* aponeurotic.

apoplejía, *f.* apoplexy.

apoplético, ca, *a.* apoplectic.

aporcadura, *f.* hilling around plants.

aporcar, *va.* (*ind.* APUERCO: *pret.* APORQUÉ: *subj.* APUERQUE) to hill (plants).

aporisma, *m.* (surg.) ecchymosis.

aporismarse, *vr.* to become an ecchymosis.

aporracear, *va.* (prov.) to pommel.

aporrar. I. *vn.* (coll.) to stand mute. **II.** *vr.* (coll.) to become importunate.

aporreado, da. I. *a.* cudgelled; dragged along. **II.** *m.* name of a Cuban dish. **II.** *pp.* of APORREAR.

aporreamiento, *m.* beating or pommelling.

aporreante, *n.* (coll.) cudgeller.

aporrear. I. *va.* to beat, cudgel, knock, maul. **II.** *vr.* to study with intense application.

aporreo, *m.* beating, pommelling, cudgelling.

aporillarse, *vr.* to swell in the joints.

aportadera, *f.* pannier; large, long box for the side of a pack beast (they go in pairs); wooden tub with handles to carry grapes from the vineyard.

aportadero, *m.* stopping place.

aportar. I. *vn.* to make a port, to arrive; to reach an unexpected place. **II.** *va.* to cause, bring; (law) to contribute.

aportillar. I. *va.* to break down, break open. **II.** *vr.* to tumble down.

aposentador, ra, *n.* one that lets lodgings; usher.

aposentamiento, *m.* lodging.

aposentar. I. *va.* to lodge. **II.** *vr.* to take lodging.

aposento, *m.* room or apartment; temporary habitation; inn; (theat.) box.

aposesionar. I. *va.* to give possession. **II.** *vr.* to take possession.

aposición, *f.* (gram.) apposition.

apósito, *m.* external medicinal application.

aposta, apostadamente, *adv.* designedly, on purpose.

apostadero, *m.* station for soldiers; (naut.) naval station.

apostador, ra, *n.* better, one who bets.

apostal, *m.* good fishing place in a river.

apostáleos, *m. pl.* (naut.) thick planks for gun platforms.

apostar. I. *va.* (*ind.* APUESTO: *subj.* APUESTE) to bet, lay as a wager; to place (relays); to post (soldiers). **II.** *vr.* to place or station one's self.

apostasía, *f.* apostasy.—**apóstata,** *m.* apostate.—**apostatar,** *vn.* to apostatize.

apostema, *f.* abscess, tumor.

apostemación, *f.* (med.) formation of an abscess.

apostemar. I. *va.* to form an abscess in, to apostemate. **II.** *vr.* to become an abscess, to apostemate.

apostemilla, *f. dim.* small abscess, gumboil.
apostemoso, sa, *a.* apostematous.
aposteriori, *adv.* (philos.) a posteriori.
apostilla, *f.* marginal note, annotation.
apostillar. I. *va.* to annotate on the margin. **II.** *vr.* to break out in pimples.
apóstol, *m.* apostle.—*pl.* (naut.) hawse pieces.
apostolado, *m.* apostleship; the twelve Apostles.
apostólicamente, *adv.* apostolically.
apostólico, ca, *a.* apostolic.
apostrofar, *va.* to apostrophize.
apóstrofe, *f.* (rhet.) apostrophe.
apóstrofo, *m.* apostrophe.
apostura, *f.* gentleness, neatness.
apotegma, *m.* apothegm, maxim.
apoteosis, *f.* apotheosis, deification.
apotrerar, *va.* to take (horses) to pasture.
apoyadero, *m.* prop, support.
apoyadura, *f.* flow of milk in nursing.
apoyar. I. *va.* (w. **en**) to rest or support (on); to favor, advocate, support; to back, defend; to aid; to abet; to bear out, confirm; to droop or incline (the head—s. o. horses). **II.** *vn.* (w. **en** or **sobre**) to rest (on). **III.** *vr.* (w. **en**), to depend (on); to be based (on); to rest (on); to lean (on); to be supported (by).
apoyatura, *f.* (mus.) appoggiatura.
apoyo, *m.* prop, stay; support; fulcrum; protection, help, aid; approval, support, backing.
apreciable, *a.* appreciable, noticeable; worthy of esteem; (coll.) nice, fine; valuable; that can be priced; salable.
apreciación, *f.* estimation, valuation; appreciation; (tech.) least reading (of a vernier).
apreciadamente, *adv.* appreciatively.
apreciador, ra, *n.* estimator, appraiser.
apreciar, *va.* to appreciate; to appraise, estimate, price, value; to esteem.—**a. hasta,** to read to (s. o. an instrument).
apreciativo, va, *a.* appreciative.
aprecio, *m.* appraisement, valuation; esteem, regard, liking.
aprehender, *va.* to apprehend, seize; to conceive, think.—**aprehensión,** *f.* seizure, capture; apprehension, acuteness; fear.—**aprehensivo, va,** *a.* apprehensive.—**aprehensor, ra,** *n.* one that apprehends.
apremiador, ra, *n.* compeller.
apremiante, *a.* urgent, pressing.
apremiar, *va.* to press, urge; to compel, oblige.
apremio, *m.* pressure, constraint; (law) judicial compulsion.
aprendedor, ra, *n.* learner.
aprender, *va.* & *vn.* to learn.
aprendiz, za, *n.* apprentice.
aprendizaje, *m.* apprenticeship; (act of) learning.
aprensador, *m.* presser, calenderer.
aprensar, *va.* to dress, press, calender; to crush, oppress; (naut.) to stow.
aprensión, *f.* apprehension, scruple; fear; distrust, suspicion.
aprensivo, va, *a.* apprehensive, fearing.
apresador, *m.* privateer; captor.
apresamiento, *m.* capture; clutch, hold.
apresar, *va.* to seize, grasp; to capture.
aprestar, *va.* to prepare, make ready.
apresto, *m.* preparation; accoutrement.
apresuración, *f.* haste.—**apresuradamente,** *adv.* hastily.—**apresurado, da. I.** *a.* hasty, quick. **II.** *pp.* of APRESURAR.—**apresuramiento,** *m.* hastiness, quickness.
apresurar. I. *va.* to hasten. **II.** *vr.* to make haste.
apretadamente, *adv.* tightly, closely, fast.
apretadera, *f.* strap or rope to tie with.—*pl.* pressing remonstrances.—**apretadero,** *m.* truss for ruptures.—**apretadillo, lla,** *a. dim.* somewhat constrained; in danger.—**apretadizo, za,** *a.* easily compressible.—**apretado, da. I.** *a.* tight, compact; difficult, dangerous; stingy, tight, close-fisted. **II.** *pp.* of APRETAR.—**apretador,** *m.* one who presses; tightener; presser, rammer, quoin wedge; waistcoat; soft stays for children; broad bandage

for infants; hair net.—**apretadura,** *f.* compression. —**apretamiento,** *m.* tightening; crowding, jamming; conflict; closeness.
apretar. I. *va.* (*ind.* APRIETO: *subj.* APRIETE) to tighten; to press down, compress, compact; to squeeze; to vex, distress; to urge, press, drive. **II.** *vn.* to pinch (s. o. shoes, etc.).—**a. a** (followed by infinitive), to start to, to start (followed by present participle) with the implication of haste, effort, etc. (*apretamos a correr,* we started to run for all we were worth).—¡**aprieta!** gracious! nonsense!
apretón, *m.* pressure; struggle, conflict; short run.—**a. de manos,** handshake.
apretujar, *va.* (coll.) to squeeze, press hard.
apretujón, *m.* tight squeezing.
apretura, *f.* jamming, crush; narrowness; distress, anguish; straits, difficulties.
apriesa, *adv.* fast, rapidly.
aprieto, *m.* jamming, crush; stringency, scrape, difficulty; cramp, gripe.
aprieto, apriete. *V.* APRETAR.
apriori, a priori, *a.* & *adv.* a priori.
apriorismo, *m.* apriorism.—**apriorístico, ca,** *a.* aprioristic.
aprisa, *adv.* swiftly, promptly, fast.
apriscar, *va.* to gather (the sheep) in the fold.
aprisco, *m.* sheepfold.
aprisionar, *va.* to imprison.
aproar, *vn.* (naut.) to turn the prow.
aprobación, *f.* approval.—**aprobador, ra,** *n.* & *a.* approver (-ing).—**aprobante,** *n.* approver; examiner.
aprobar, *va.* (*ind.* APRUEBO: *subj.* APRUÉBE) to approve; to pass (in an examination).
aprobatorio, ria, *a.* approbative, approving.
aproches, *m. pl.* (mil., eng.) approaches.
aprontar, *va.* to prepare quickly; to deliver at once.
apropiación, *f.* appropriation, giving or taking possession; adaptation; (act of) fitting.
apropiadamente, *adv.* fitly, appropriately.
apropiado, da. I. *a.* appropriate, fit. **II.** *pp.* of APROPIAR.
apropiador, ra, *n.* appropriator.
apropiar. I. *va.* to give possession of; to apply, adapt, fit. **II.** *vr.* to appropriate, take possession of.
apropincuación, *f.* approach.—**apropincuarse,** *vr.* (coll.) to approach.
aprovechable, *a.* available; that can be used.
aprovechado, da. I. *a.* advanced, proficient; economical, saving. **II.** *pp.* of APROVECHAR.
aprovechamiento, *m.* utilization, use; exploitation, development; progress, proficiency.—**a. forestal,** forest products.
aprovechar. I. *vn.* to be useful, profitable o beneficial, to avail; to progress. **II.** *va.* to profit by; make use of. **III.** *vr.* to avail one's self.
aproximación, *f.* approximation.
aproximadamente, *adv.* approximately.
aproximado, da. I. *a.* approximate.—**a. hasta,** (arit.) approximate to. **II.** *pp.* of APROXIMAR.
aproximar, *va.* & *vr.* to approach; move near; to determine (be) approximately.
aproximativo, va, *a.* approximate; approaching.
apruebo, apruebe, *V.* APROBAR.
ápside, *m.* (arch.) apsis.
aptamente, *adv.* fitly, aptly.
áptero, ra, *a.* (ent.) apterous, wingless.
aptitud, *f.* aptitude, fitness, ability.
apto, ta, *a.* apt, fit, competent.
apuerco, apuerque. *V.* APORCAR.
apuesta, *f.* bet, wager.
apuesto, ta, *a.* elegant, genteel, spruce.
apuesto, apueste. *V.* APOSTAR.
apulgarar. I. *va.* to force with the thumb. **II.** *vr.* to become spotted by moisture (s. o. linen).
apulso, *m.* (astr.) passing of the edge of a celestial body over the vertical wire of the telescope. (This is the Academy's definition, although the term is often used in the sense of the English *appulse.*)
apunchar, *va.* to cut out the teeth of (a comb).

apuntación, *f.* note; memorandum; musical notation.

apuntado, da. I. *a.* pointed at both ends. **II.** *pp.* of APUNTAR.

apuntador, ra, *n.* observer; one that takes or keeps notes; prompter; (naut.) gunner.

apuntalamiento, *m.* propping.

apuntalar, *va.* to prop; to shore (a vessel).

apuntamiento, *m.* note, abstract, summary; judicial report.

apuntar. I. *va.* to aim, level; to point out, mark; to note, make a note of; to hint; to sketch; to stitch; to begin to appear; to sharpen; to prompt. **II.** *vr.* to begin to turn (s. o. wine).

apunte, *m. V.* APUNTAMIENTC; annotation, memorandum; rough sketch; prompt-book; stake (in games).

apuñadar, *va.* (prov.) to strike with the fist.

apuñalado, da, *a.* dagger-shaped.

apuñalar, *va.* to stab.

apuñar. I. *va.* to seize with the fist. **II.** *vn.* to tighten the fist.

apuñear, *va.* (coll.) to strike with the fist.

apuracabos, *m.* candle holder with a sharp point for the butt of the candle; save-all.

apuración, *f.* investigation; trouble, misfortune. **—apuradamente,** *adv.* punctually, exactly; with difficulty.**—apurado, da. I.** *a.* needy; exhausted; difficult; conscientious. **II.** *pp.* of APURAR.

apurador, *m.* refiner, purifier; APURACABOS.

apuramiento, *m.* research; exhaustion, consumption; pressing, urging; purification.

apurar. I. *va.* to purity; to clear up, verify, scrutinize; to consume, drain, exhaust; to push, hurry; to annoy. **II.** *vr.* to worry, fret, grieve; to exert one's self.

apurativo, *a.* (med.) detersive.

apuro, *m.* want, strait, difficulty, scrape; gripe.

aquejar, *va.* to grieve, sadden; to fatigue.

aquel (*f. sing.* **aquella;** *pl.* **aquellos, llas). I.** *a.* that, those, yonder. **II.** *pron.* he (*pl.* they, those, such as) (*aquellos que deseen venir,* those who, or such as, wish to come); those (ones); (**-él, -élla)** the former, the first mentioned.

aquello, *pron. neut.* that; the former, the first-mentioned (fact, statement, etc.); that thing, that matter, the matter we spoke about, etc. (used with reference to something known to the listener or reader but that it is not desired to mention).**—a. de (que),** the common saying, notion, belief, rule (that) (*no creo en aquello de que el comercio es la base del progreso,* I do not believe in the common saying that commerce is the foundation of progress).

aquello, lla. *V.* AQUEL.

aquellare, *m.* witches' Sabbath.

aquende, *adv.* on this side of.

aqueo, a, *n.* & *a.* Achæan.

aquerenciarse, *vr.* to become fond of.

aquese, *m.,* **aquesa,** *f.,* **aqueso,** *neut.* = ESE, etc.

aqueste, *m.,* **aqüesta,** *f.,* **aquesto,** *neut.* = ESTE, ESTA, etc.

aquí, *adv.* here; hither; then.**—de a.,** from here, from this place; hence.**—por a.,** here, hereabouts; this way, through here.

aquiescencia, *f.* (law) acquiescence, consent.

aquietar. I. *va.* to quiet, lull, pacify, hush, allay. **II.** *vr.* to become calm; to quiet down.

aquilatar, *va.* to assay; to examine closely.

aquilea, *f.* (bot.) milfoil, yarrow.

aquileña, *f.* (bot.) columbine.

aquilífero, *m.* Roman standard bearer.

aquilino, na, *a.* aquiline.

aquilón, *m.* north wind; north point.

aquilonal, aquilonar, *a.* northern, northerly.

aquillado, da, *a.* keel-shaped.

aquistar, *va.* to acquire.

ara, *f.* altar; communion table.

árabe, *n.* & *a.* Arab (-ic).**—arabesco,** *m.* arabesque, moresque work.**—arábico, ca,** *or* **go, ga,** *a.* Arabian, Arabic.**—arábiga,** *f.* a stone similar to spotted ivory.

arabismo, *m.* Arabism.**—arabista,** *n.* Arabist.

arácnido, da. I. *n.* & *a.* (zool.) arachnidian. **II.** *m. pl.* Arachnida.

aracnoides, *f.* (anat.) arachnoid membrane.

aracnoiditis, *f.* (med.) arachnitis.

arada, *f.* (agr.) plowed ground; husbandry.

arado, *m.* plow.**—arador,** *m.* plowman; (ent.) harvest mite.**—aradura,** *f.* plowing; land plowed in a day.

aragonés, esa, *n.* & *a.* Aragonese.

aragonita, *m.* (min.) aragonite.

arambel, *m.* rag, tatter.

arameo, a. *n.* & *a.* Aramean.

arana, *f.* imposition, trick; Cuban grass.

aranata, *f.* prairie dog.

arancel, *m.* tariff.**—a. de aduanas,** tariff.

arancelario, ria, *a.* tariff, customs (u. a.).

arandanedo, *m.* cranberry patch.

arándano, *m.* (bot.) cranberry.

arandela, *f.* the socket pan of a candlestick; (mech.) washer; axleguard; rivet plate, collar plate; guard around the staff of a lance; nave box of a gun carriage; (naut.) half-ports; glass candelabrum.

arrandillo, *m.* bird; (prov.) hip pad.

aranero, ra, *a.* deceitful, tricky.

aranzada, *f.* a land measure (a little less than .5 hectare).

araña, *f.* (ent.) spider; chandelier; (zool.) common weaver; (bot.) crowfoot.

arañador, ra, *n.* scratcher, scraper.

arañamiento, *m.* (act of) scratching.

arañar, *va.* to scratch; to scrape up (as money).

arañazo, *m. aug.* long, deep scratch.

araño, *m.* scratch, nipping.

arañuela, *f. dim.* small spider; a flower plant.

arañuelo, *m.* small spider; fold net.

arapende, *m.* ancient measure (120 sq. ft.).

arar, *va.* to plow, labor.

arar, *m.* an African coniferous tree.

araucano, na, *n.* & *a.* Araucanian.

araucaria, *f.* araucaria, a tall pine.

arauja, *f.* (Brazil) a creeping plant.

araza, *m.* a Uruguayan fruit tree.

arbalestrilla, *f.* an old surveying instrument.

arbellon, *m.* (prov.) gutter to drain roads.

arbitrable, *a.* arbitrable.**—arbitración,** *f.* arbitration.**—arbitrador, ra,** *n.* arbitrator; umpire, referee.

arbitraje, arbitramento, arbitramiento, *m.* arbitration, arbitrament.**—arbitral,** *a.* arbitral.

arbitrar, *va.* to arbitrate; to act unhampered; to contrive.

arbitrariamente, *adv.* arbitrarily.

arbitrariedad, *f.* arbitrariness; arbitrary act.

arbitrario, ria; arbitrativo, va, *a.* arbitrary; (law) arbitral; arbitrative.

arbitratorio, ria, *a.* arbitral.

arbitrio, *m.* free will; means, expedient; arbitration; bond, compromise; discretion, judgment. **—pl. arbitrios,** excise taxes.

arbitrista, *m.* schemer, contriver.

árbitro, *m.* arbitrator, arbiter.

árbol, *m.* (bot.) tree; (naut.) mast; in machines, upright post; (mech.) axle or shaft; arbor; spindle; drill; body of shirt; crown post of winding stairs.**—a. de Diana,** (chem.) arbor Dianæ.**—a de la ciencia del bien y del mal,** (Bib.) tree of the knowledge of good and evil.**—a. de la vida,** (Bib.) tree of life.**—a. del pan,** breadfruit tree.- **-a. de María,** tolu-balsam tree.**—a. de pie,** seed-grown tree.**—a. de Saturno,** (chem.) arbor Saturni.**—a. de transmisión,** transmission shaft, belt shaft.**—a. motor,** driving shaft or axle.

arbolado, da. I. *a.* wooded; masted. **II.** *pp.* of ARBOLAR. **III.** *m.* woodland.

arboladura, *f.* (naut.) masts and spars.

arbolar. I. *va.* to hoist; set upright.**—a. un navío,** (naut.) to mast a ship. **II.** *vr.* to rear on the hind feet.

arbolario, *m.* madcap.

arbolecico, arbolecillo, arbolico, arbolito, *m. dim.* arboret, small tree.

arboleda, *f.* grove.

arbolejo, *m. dim.* small tree.
arbolete, *m.* branch to fasten lime twigs on.
arbolillo, *m.* side of a blast furnace; small tree.
arbolista, *m.* arborist.
arbollón, *m.* floodgate, sluice, outlet.
arbóreo, rea, *a.* relating to trees.
arborescencia, *f.* arborescence.
arborescente, *a.* arborescent.
arboricultor, ra, *n.* arboriculturist.
arboricultura, *f.* arboriculture.
arboriforme, *a.* arboriform, tree-shaped.
arborizado, *a.* foliagelike.
arbotante, *m.* vault-supporting arch.
arbusto, *m.* shrub.—**arbustillo,** *m. dim.* small shrub.
arca, *f.* chest, coffer; reservoir, tank; ark; tempering oven for blown glass.—**a. cerrada,** extremely reticent person.—**a. de la Alianza,** Ark of the Covenant.
arcabucear, *va.* to shoot with a harquebus.
arcabucería, *f.* body of harquebusiers; number of harquebuses; fusillade of harquebuses; harquebus factory.—**arcabucero,** *m.* harquebus maker; harquebusier.
arcabuco, *m.* (Amer.) craggy spot.
arcabuz, *m.* harquebuse.—**arcabuzazo,** *m.* harquebus shot.
arcacil, *m.* (bot.) a species or variety of wild artichoke.
arcada, *f.* retching; (arch.) row of arches.
árcade, *a.* Arcadian.
arcadio, dia, *n. & a.* Arcadian.
arcaduz, *m.* conduit; bucket; means, way.
arcaico, ca, *a.* archaic.—**arcaísmo,** *m.* archaism.
arcaizar, *vr.* to use archaisms.
arcángel, *m.* archangel.
arcangélico, ca, *a.* archangelical.
arcano. I. *m.* arcanum. **II.** *a.* secret, recondite.
arcaza, *f. aug.* large chest.
arcazón, *m.* arbuscle, osier, willow plot.
arce, *m.* (bot.) maple tree.
arcedianato, *m.* archdeaconship.
arcediano, *m.* archdeacon.
arcedo, *m.* maple grove.
arcén, *m.* border, brim, edge.
arcilla, *f.* clay.—**arcilloso, sa,** *a.* clayey, argillaceous.
arciprestazgo, *m.* archpriesthood.
arcipreste, *m.* archpriest.
arco, *m.* arc; (arch.) arch; bow; fiddle bow; hoop (geom.) arc.—**a. iris,** rainbow.
arcón, *m. aug.* large chest; bin, bunker.
arcontado, *m.* archontate.—**arconte,** *m.* archon.
archicofradía, *f.* privileged brotherhood.
archidiácono, *m.* archdeacon.
archiducado, *m.* archdukedom, archduchy.
archiducal, *a.* archducal.—**archiduque,** *m.* archduke.—**archiduquesa,** *f.* archduchess.
archilaúd, *m.* large lute.
archimandrita, *m.* archimandrite.
archimillonario, ria, *a.* multimillionaire.
archipámpano, *m.* an imaginary dignity.
archipiélago, *m.* archipelago.
archivar, *va.* to file; deposit in an archive.
archivero, archivista, *m.* archivist.
archivo, *m.* archive, archives; file, files.
arda, *f.* squirrel.
ardalear, *va.* to make thin.
ardea, *f.* bittern.
ardentía, *f.* heat; phosphorescence; blink.
ardeola, *f.* small kind of heron.
arder, *vn.* to burn.
ardero, ra, *a.* squirrel dog.
ardid, *m.* stratagem, artifice, cunning.
ardido, da. I. *a.* heated; burning. **II.** *pp.* of ARDER.
ardiente, *a.* ardent, burning; passionate, fervent; fiery.—**ardientemente,** *adv.* ardently, fervidly; fearlessly.
ardilla, *f.* (zool.) squirrel.
ardimiento, *m.* conflagration; undaunted courage.

ardínculo, *m.* (vet.) inflamed swelling on the back.
ardite, *m.* ancient coin of little value; trifle; straw (fig.), farthing (fig.).—**no importar un a.,** not to matter a particle.—**no se me da un a.,** I don't care a straw, or a rap.—**no vaier un a.,** not to be worth a straw, not to amount to a hill of beans.
ardor, *m.* ardor; hotness, heat; dash, valor; fieriness.
ardoroso, sa, *a.* fiery, ardorous.
arduamente, *adv.* arduously.—**arduo, dua,** *a.* arduous.
área, *f.* area; are, square decameter.
areca, *f.* palm tree of the Philippine Islands.
arefacción, *f.* drying; extenuation.
arel, *m.* large sieve.—**arelar,** *va.* to sift.
arena, *f.* sand, grit; arena.—**arenáceo, ea,** *a.* arenaceous.—**arenal,** *m.* sandy ground, sand pit.—**arenalejo,** *m. dim.* small sandy place.—**arenar,** *va.* to sand; to rub with sand.
arenar, *va.* (*pret.* ARENQUÉ; *subj.* ARENQUE) to salt and dry (fish).
arencón, *m. aug.* large herring.
arenero, *m.* sand dealer; sand box.
arenga, *f.* harangue, speech.—**arengador, ra,** *n.* speech maker.—**arengar,** *vn.* (*pret.* ARENGUÉ; *subj.* ARENGUE) to harangue, deliver a speech.
arenilla, *f.* molding sand; powder to dry writing. —*pl.* granulated saltpeter.
arenisca, *f.* (miner.) sandstone.
arenisco, ca; arenoso, sa, *a.* sandy, gravelly, gritty; sand (u. a.).
arenque, *m.* herring.
aréola. *f.* areola, circle around the nipple.
areómetro, *m.* hydrometer.
areopagita, *m.* Areopagite.
areópago, *m.* Areopagus.
areóstilo, *m.* arœostyle.
areotectónica, *f.* areotectonics.
arepa, *f.* corn griddle cake.
arestín, *m.* (vet.) frush.
arestinado, da, *a.* afflicted with frush.
arete, *m.* eardrop, earring.
arfada, *f.* (naut.) pitching of a ship.
arfar, *vn.* (naut.) to pitch (s. o. a ship).
arfil, *m.* = ALFIL.
argadijo, argadillo, *m.* reel, bobbin, winder; blustering, noisy, restless person; large wicker basket.
argado, *m.* prank, trick.
argal, *m.* argol, crude tartar.
argalia, *f.* = ALGALIA.
argallera, *f.* saw for cutting grooves; forkstaff plane, reed plane.
argamandel. *m.* rag, tatter.
agamandijo, *m.* collection of trifling implements.
argamasa, *f.* mortar.—**argamasar. I.** *vn.* to make mortar. **II.** *va.* to cement with mortar.
argamasón, *m.* large dry piece of mortar.
argamula, *f.* (bot., prov.) golden starwort.
árgana, *f.* (mech.) crane.
árganas, *f. pl.* wicker baskets on a horse.
arganel, *m.* ring in an astrolabe.
arganeo, *m.* (naut.) anchor ring.
árgano, *m.* = ÁRGANA.
argel, *a.* (horse) whose right hind foot is white.
argelino, na, *a.* Algerine.
argema, argemón, *m.* (med.) argema.
argémone, *f.* (bot.) prickly or horned poppy.
argén, *m.* (her.) white or silver color, argent.
argentada, *f.* ladies' cosmetic.
argentado, da. I. *a.* silvered; silvery; slashed (shoes). **II.** *pp.* of ARGENTAR.
argentador, *n.* silversmith.
argentar, *va.* to plate, to adorn, with silver; polish like silver.
argentario, *m.* silversmith; master of the mint.
argénteo, a, *a.* silvery; silver-plated.
argentería, *f.* embroidery in gold or silver.
argentero, *m.* = ARGENTARIO.
argentífero, ra, *a.* silver-bearing.

argentina, *f.* (bot.) satin cinquefoil.
argentinismo, *m.* Argentinism, word or expression peculiar to Argentina.
argentino, na. I. *a.* silvery, argentine; Argentine, Argentinian. **II.** *m.* Argentine gold coin.
argento, *m.* (poet.) silver.
argentoso, sa, *a.* mixed with silver.
argila, argilla, *f.* clay.
argiritas, *m. pl.* marcasite, white pyrites.
argivo, va, *n.* & *a.* Argive.
argo, *m.* (chem.) argon.
argolla, *f.* ring; collar; staple; hoop; ring (in bowling); pillory.—**argolleta, ica, ita,** *f. dim.* small staple or ring.—**argollón,** *m. aug.* very large ring or staple.
árgoma, *f.* (bot.) furze.—**argomal,** *m.* furze plantation.—**argomón,** *m. aug.* large prickly furze, gorse.
argonauta, *m.* one of the Argonauts.
Argos, *m.* (myth.) Argus; very observant person.
argucia, *f.* subtilty, sophistry; trick, scheme.
argüe, *m.* windlass, capstan.
argüellarse, *vr.* (prov.) to become emaciated.
argüello, *m.* lack of health.
argüeñas, argüeñas, *f. pl.* = ANGARILLAS.
arguerita, *f.* (miner.) argyrite or argentite.
argüir. I. *vn.* (*ind.* ARGUYO: *subj.* ARGUYA) to argue, dispute. **II.** *va.* to infer, imply.
argumentación, *f.* argumentation.
argumentador, ra, *n.* arguer, reasoner.
argumentar, *vn.* to argue, dispute.
argumentativo, va, *a.* argumentative.
argumentillo, *m. dim.* argument of no account.
argumento, *m.* (theat., log., math.) argument; summary; indication, sign, token.
arguyente, *n.* arguer; opponent.
aria, *f.* (mus.) song for a single voice.
aribar, *va.* to reel into skeins.
aribo, *m.* reel for making skeins.
aricar, *va.* to plow across.
aridecer, *va.*, *vn.* & *vr.* (*ind.* ARIDEZCO: *subj.* ARIDEZCA) to render or become arid.
aridez, *f.* drought; barrenness, aridity.
árido, da. I. *a.* arid, dry, barren. **II.** *m. pl.* dry articles, sp. grains and vegetables, measured with dry measure.
Aries, *m.* Aries, sign of the zodiac.
arieta, *f. dim.* (mus.) arietta, short tune.
ariete, *m.* battering ram.—**a. hidráulico,** hydraulic ram.
arietino, na, *a.* resembling a ram's head.
arigue, *m.* Philippine timber.
arijo, ja, *a.* (agr.) light, easily tilled.
arillo, *m. dim.* earring; neck-stock frame.
arimez, *m.* projection in a building.
arindajo, *m.* (orn.) jay.
ario, ia, *n.* & *a.* Aryan.
arisblanco, ca, *a.* white-bearded wheat.
arisaro, *m.* (bot.) wake-robin.
arisco, ca, *a.* churlish, shy, cross, surly.
arisnegro, arisprieto, *a.* having blackish beard (s. o. wheat).
arista, *f.* beard or awn grains; (geom.) edge.—*pl.* (mil.) salient angles.
aristado, da, *a.* awned, bearded.
aristarco, ca, *n.* severe censurer.
aristocracia, *f.* aristocracy.—**aristócrata,** *m.* aristocrat.—**aristocrático, ca,** *a.* aristocratic.
aristoloquia, *f.* (bot.) birthwort.
aristoloquiáceo, a, *a.* (bot.) aristolochiaceous.—*f. pl.* Aristolochiaceæ.
aristón, *m.* (arch.) edge, corner; groin rib.
aristoso, sa, *a.* having many beards or awns.
aristotélico, ca, *a.* Aristotelian.
aristotelismo, *m.* Aristotelianism.
aritmancia, *f.* arithmancy.
aritmética, *f.* arithmetic.
aritméticamente, *adv.* arithmetically.
aritmético, *m.* arithmetician; accountant.
aritmético, ca, *a.* arithmetical.
aritmo, *a.* (med.) arrhythmic.
aritmómetro, *m.* calculating machine.

arjorán, *m.* (bot.) = CICLAMOR.
arlequín, *m.* harlequin, buffoon; mixed ice cream, Neapolitan.
arlequinada, *f.* harlequin's trick or joke.
arlo, *m.* (bot.) barberry.
arlota, *f.* tow of flax or hemp.
arma, *f.* weapon, arm; (mil.) technical division of military forces; (met.) means, power, reason.—*pl.* troops, armies; armorial ensigns, coat of arms.—**a. arrojadiza,** missile weapon.—**a. blanca,** steel arm.—**a. de caballería,** cavalry.—**a. de fuego,** firearm.—**a. de infantería,** infantry.—**a. de puño,** hand steel arm (sword, etc.).—**a. falsa,** trial, or test, attack.—**armas de agua,** (Mex.) waterproof skins for riding.—**¡a las armas!** to arms!—**de armas tomar,** resolute; capable.—**sobre las armas,** under arms.
armada, *f.* navy; fleet; squadron; armada.—**a. naval,** royal navy, royal fleet.
armadera, *f.* (naut.) main timber of a ship.
armadía, *f.* raft, float.
armadijo, *m.* trap, snare for game.
armadillo, *m.* (zool.) armadillo.
armado, da. I. *a.* armed; (mech.) mounted, assembled. **II.** *pp.* of ARMAR. **III.** *m.* man in armor in processions.
armador, *m.* outfitter, ship owner; privateer, cruiser; one who outfits whaleboats; (mech.) adjuster, fitter, assembler; jacket.
armadura, *f.* armor; framework, shell of a building; (mech.) setting, fitting; truss; (magn.) armature, yoke (of a magnet); framing, mounting; trestle.
armajal, *m.* moor, bog.
armamento, *m.* armament, equipment, accoutrements.
armar. I. *va.* to arm; to man; (carp.) to bind; to assemble, mount; (mech.) to adjust, set, frame, piece, mount, make true, rig up; (naut.) to equip, fit out, put in commission.—**a. caballero,** to knight.—**a. en corso,** to privateer.—**a. en guerra,** (naut.) to fit or equip (a ship) for war. **II.** *vr.* to prepare one's self; to arm one's self.—**armarse de,** to arm one's self with; put on.
armario, *m.* clothespress; cabinet; bookcase; wardrobe; closet.
armatoste, *m.* hulk; unwieldly machine; cumbersome piece of furniture; fat, clumsy fellow.
armazón, *f.* framework, skeleton, frame; hulk (of a ship)—*m.* skeleton of body.
armelina, *f.* ermine skin.
armella, *f.* staple, box staple, screw eye.
armelluela, *f. dim.* small staple or ring.
armenio, nia, *n.* & *a.* Armenian.
armería, *f.* armory, arsenal; gunsmith trade or shop.
armero, *m.* armorer, gunsmith; keeper of arms; (mil.) rack or stand for firearms.
armífero, ra; armígero, ra, *a.* warlike.
armilla, *f.* part of the base of a column.
armiñado, da, *a.* trimmed or lined with ermine fur; ermine-white.
armiño, *m.* (zool.) ermine.
armipotente, *a.* (poet.) mighty in war.
armisticio, *m.* armistice.
armoisín, *m.* thin silk or taffety.
armón, *m.* (ordn.) limber.
armonía, *f.* harmony.—**armónico, ca,** *a.* harmonious; musical, rhythmical; harmonic.
armonio, *m.* harmonium, reed organ.
armoniosamente, *adv.* harmoniously.
armonioso, sa, *a.* harmonious.
armonista, *f.* harmonist.
armonización, *f.* harmonization.
armonizar, *va.* (*pret.* ARMONICÉ: *subj.* ARMONICE) to harmonize.
armuelle, *m.* (bot.) orach.
arna, *f.* (prov.) beehive.
arnacho, *m.* (bot.) rest-harrow. *V.* GATUÑA.
arnés, *m.* harness; coat of mail, armor.—*pl.* harness, trappings; tools, outfit, equipment.
árnica, *f.* arnica.

arnilla, *f. dim.* (prov.) small beehive.
aro, *m.* hoop, rim; staple; hoop pole; (bot.) = YARO.—**entrar por el a.,** (coll.) to walk Spanish, to be forced to yield.
aroma. I. *f.* flower of the aromatic myrrh tree. **II.** *m.* aroma; perfume, fragrancy.
aromaticidad, *f.* aromatic quality, perfume.
aromático, ca, *a.* aromatic, fragrant.
aromatización, *f.* aromatization.
aromatizador, *m.* aromatizer, atomizer.
aromatizar, *va.* (*pret.* AROMATICÉ: *subj.* AROMATICE) to aromatize, perfume.
aromo, *m.* (bot.) aromatic myrrh tree.
aromoso, sa, *a.* aromatic, fragrant.
aroza, *m.* foreman in ironworks.
arpa, *f.* (mus.) harp.
arpado. I. *a.* serrated, toothed; (poet.) singing (bird). **II.** *pp.* of ARPAR.
arpadura, *f.* = ARAÑO.
arpar, *va.* to tear to pieces, rend, claw.
arpegio, *m.* (mus.) arpeggio.
arpella, *f.* (orn.) harpy.
arpeo, *m.* (naut.) grappling iron.
arpía, *f.* (poet.) harpy; fiend; ugly shrew.
arpillador, *m.* (Mex.) packer.
arpilladura, *f.* packing with sackcloth.
arpillar, *va.* (Mex.) to pack with sackcloth.
arpillera, *f.* sackcloth, burlap.
arpista, *m.* (mus.) harper, harpist.
arpón, *m.* harpoon.—**arponado, da,** *a.* harpoonlike.—**arponear,** *va.* to harpoon.—**arponero,** *m.* harpooner.
arqueada, *f.* stroke with the fiddle bow.
arqueador, *m.* ship gauger; wool beater.
arqueaje, *m.* gauging of a ship.
arqueamiento, *m.* = ARQUEO.
arquear, *va.* to arch; to beat (wool); to gauge (ships).
arqueo, *m.* arching; (naut.) tonnage; (com.) checking of money and papers in a safe.
arqueología, *f.* archæology.—**arquelógico, ca,** *a.* archæological.—**arqueólogo,** *m.* archæologist.
arquería, *f.* series of arches; (Mex.) aqueduct.
arquero, ra, *n.* treasurer, cashier; archer; bow maker.
arqueta, *f. dim.* small chest.
arquetipo, *m.* archetype.
arquetón, *m. aug.* large chest.
arquibanco, *m.* bench with drawers.
arquiepiscopal, *a.* archiepiscopal.
arquifilósofo, *m.* archphilosopher.
arquilla, ita, *f. dim.* little chest.
arquillo, *m. dim.* small bow.
arquimesa, *f.* (prov.) writing desk.
arquisinagogo, *m.* ruler of a synagogue.
arquitecto, *m.* architect.—**arquitectónico, ca,** *a.* architectural.—**arquitectura,** *f.* architecture.
arquitrabe, *m.* architrave.
arrabal, *m.* suburb.—*pl.* environs, outskirts.
arrabalero, ra, *a.* suburban; ill-bred.
arrabio, *m.* cast iron melted for making steel.
arracacha, *f.* arracacha.
arracada, *f.* earring with pendant.
arracimado, da. I. *a.* clustered. **II.** *pp.* of arracimarse, *vr.* to cluster.
arraclán, *m.* alder tree.
arráez, *m.* chief; captain or master of a ship.
arraigadamente, *adv.* fixedly, securely.
arraigadas, *f. pl.* (naut.) futtock shrouds.
arraigado, da, owning real estate; fixed, inveterate; rooted.
arraigar. I. *vn.* to take root. **II.** *vr.* to settle, to establish one's self; to take root, become rooted.
arraigo, *m.* settling in a place; landed property.
arralar, *vn.* = RALEAR.
arramblar, *va.* to cover with sand and gravel; to sweep away.
arrancaclavos, *m.* nail puller.
arrancada, *f.* (coll.) sudden departure, violent sally.
arrancadera, *f.* leading bell for cattle.

arrancadero, *m.* starting point; thickest part of a gun barrel.
arrancado, da. I. *a.* (coll.) broken, poor, penniless. **II.** *pp.* of ARRANCAR.
arrancador, ra, *n.* extirpator; extractor, puller.
arrancadura, *f.,* **arrancamiento,** *m.* extirpation; pulling out.
arrancapinos, *n.* small person, dwarf (fig.)
arrancar. I. *va.* (*pret.* ARRANQUÉ: *subj.* ARRANQUE) to root out, extirpate; to pull out, draw out, tear off. **II.** *vn.* to start; (naut.) to set sail.
arrancasiega, *f.* poor grain half mowed, half pulled up; quarrel, dispute.
arranciarse, *vr.* to grow or become rancid.
arrancharse, *vr.* to mess together.
arranque, *m.* extirpation; impulse, fit (of passion, charity, love, etc.); sudden start, sudden impulse; (arch.) springer (of an arch); (mech.) start; starter, starting gear.
arrapar, *va.* (low) to snatch away, carry off.
arrapiezo, arrapo, *m.* tatter, rag; worthless youngster.
arras, *f. pl.* consideration of a contract; coins the bridegroom gives to the bride at the wedding; dowry; earnest money, pledge.—**a. de la bodega,** (naut.) wings of the hold.
arrasado. I. *m.* satin-faced stuff. **II.** *pp.* of ARRASAR.—**arrasadura,** *f.* = RASADURA.
arrasamiento, *m.* razing, demolition.
arrasar. I. *va.* to level, raze, demolish; to obliterate; to fill up to the brim. **II.** *vn.,* *vr.* to clear up.
arrastradamente, *adv.* imperfectly; painfully, wretchedly.
arrastraderas, *f. pl.* (naut.) lower studding sails.
arrastradero, *m.* (naut.) careening place; log path, a path over which logs are dragged; spot whence dead bulls are carried off.
arrastrado, da. I. *a.* dragged along; rascally, knavish; destitute; (coll.) low, contemptible. **II.** *pp.* of ARRASTRAR.
arrastramiento, *m.* dragging.
arrastrante, *n.* applicant for a scholarship.
arrastrar. I. *va.* to drag; to drag down, degrade; to haul; to attract; to prompt, move, urge.—**a. bayeta,** to perform the ceremonies required of applicants for a scholarship.—**a. el ala a,** (coll.) to make up to, to make love to. **II.** *vn.* to touch the floor or ground (s. o. of something suspended); (in cards) to play a trump. **III.** *vr.* to crawl, creep (literally and fig.)
arrastre, *m.* dragging; haulage; drayage; leading a trump; slope or grade in a mining shaft; applicant for a scholarship; mining mill.
arrate, *m.* pound of sixteen ounces.
arratonado, *a.* gnawed by mice.
arrayán, *m.* (bot.) myrtle.
arrayanal, *m.* myrtle field or plantation.
¡arre! *interj.* gee, get up!
arreador, *m.* muleteer; driving whip.
arreala, *f.* herding the grazing flock.
arrear, *va.* to drive (horses, mules, etc.)
arrebañador, ra, *n.* gleaner, gatherer.
arrebañadura, *f.* gleaning, picking up.
arrebañar, *va.* to glean, gather.
arrebatadamente, *adv.* precipitately, headlong, recklessly; violently.—**arrebatado, da. I.** *a.* rapid, violent; precipitate, rash, impetuous. **II.** *pp.* of ARREBATAR.
arrebatador, ra. I. *n.* one that snatches or carries away. **II.** *a.* that snatches or carries away; captivating, charming; fiery, violent; stirring.
arrebatamiento, *m.* carrying away by violence; fury, rage; rapture; ecstasy.
arrebatar. I. *va.* to carry off; to snatch; to attract, to hold (the attention, etc.); to captivate, charm; to move, stir. **II.** *vr.* to be led away by passion.
arrebatiña, *f.* struggle, scramble, scuffle.
arrebato, *m.* surprise; sudden attack; fit, rage; rapture.
arrebol, *m.* red sky or clouds; rouge.

arrebolar. I. *va.* to paint red. **II.** *vr.* to rouge.

arrebolera, *f.* rouge box; rouge seller; (bot.) four-o'clock or marvel of Peru.

arrebollarse, *vr.* to precipitate; fall headlong.

arrebozar. I. *va.* (*pret.* ARREBOCÉ: *subj.* ARREBOCE) to overlay (meat) with jelly. **II.** *vr.* to muffle or wrap one's self up; to swarm.

arrebujadamente, *adv.* confusedly.

arrebujar. I. *va.* to jumble together; to huddle. **II.** *vr.* to wrap one's self up.

arreciar. I. *vn.* to increase in strength or intensity. **II.** *vr.* to become stronger.

arrecife, *m.* stone-paved road; (naut.) reef.

arrecirse, *vr.* to grow stiff with cold.

arrechucho, *m.* fit of anger; sudden and passing indisposition.

arredilar, *va.* to fold (sheep).

arredomado, da, *a.* = REDOMADO.

arredondar, arredondear, *va.* to round off.

arredramiento, *m.* removing to a greater distance; backing out; fear.

arredrar. I. *va.* to remove, separate; to terrify, scare. **II.** *vr.* to be or become afraid, to fear

arregazado, da. I. *a.* with the point turned up. **II.** *pp.* of ARREGAZAR.

arregazar, *va.* (*pret.* ARREGACÉ: *subj.* ARREGACE) to tuck up (the skirts).

arregladamente, *adv.* regularly, orderly.

arreglado, da. I. *a.* regular, moderate. **II.** *pp.* of ARREGLAR.

arreglador, *m.* (com.) surveyor, valuer (of averages).

arreglar. I. *va.* to regulate, guide; to frame; to arrange; to settle, adjust. **II.** *vr.* to conform; to settle, come to an agreement; to compromise.

arreglo, *m.* rule; order; disposition, arrangement; adjustment; (com.) agreement; compromise, settlement.—**con a. a,** according to.

arregostarse, *vr.* to relish.

arrejaca, *f.* = ARREJAQUE.

arrejacar, *va.* (*pret.* ARREJAQUÉ: *sub.* ARREJAQUE) to plow across for clearing weeds.

arrejaco, *m.* (orn.) swift, martin.

arrejada, *f.* (agr.) paddle of a plow.

arrejaque, *m.* fishing fork with three prongs.

arrejerar, *va.* (naut.) to make (a ship) fast by casting two anchors fore and one aft.

arrel, arrelde, *m.* weight of four pounds.

arrellanarse, *vr.* to sit at ease; to be satisfied with one's situation.

arremangado, da. I. *a.* turned upward. **II.** *pp.* of ARREMANGAR.

arremangar. I. *va.* (*pret.* ARREMANGUÉ: *subj.* ARREMANGUE) to tuck up (the sleeves, etc.) **II.** *vr.* to be determined.

arremango, *m.* tucking up.

arremetedero, *m.* place through which a fortress can be attacked.—**arremetedor, ra,** *m.* assailant, aggressor.

arremeter. I. *va.* to assail, attack. **II.** *vn.* to launch forth; to attack.—**arremetida,** *f.* attack, assault; start of horses.

arremolinado, da, *a.* whirling, in a whirl.

arremolinarse, *vr.* to form a crowd.

arrendable, *a.* rentable, farmable, tenantable.

arrendación, *f.* renting, lease.

arrendadero, *m.* ring to tie horses to.

arrendado, da. I. *a.* obedient to the reins; rented, leased. **II.** *pp.* of ARRENDAR.

arrendador, *m.* landlord; lessor; hirer; tenant, lessee, holder; farmer.

arrendadorcillo, *m.* *dim.* petty tenant.

arrendajo, *m.* mocking bird; (coll.) mimic.

arrendamiento, *m.* renting, letting; lease; rent, rental.—**arrendante,** *n.* lessor, renter.

arrendar, *va.* (*ind.* ARRIENDO: *subj.* ARRIENDE) to rent, let, lease, hire; to bridle; to tie (a horse); to train (a horse); to mimic.

arrendatario, ria, *n.* lessee, tenant.

arrentado, da, *a.* receiving a large rental.

arreo, *m.* dress, ornament, decoration.—*pl.* appurtenances, accessories; harness, trappings.

arreo, *adv.* successively, uninterruptedly.

arrepápalo, *m.* a kind of fritter.

arrepentido, da. I. *a.* repentant. **II.** *n.* penitent. **III.** *pp.* of ARREPENTIRSE.

arrepentimiento, *m.* repentance; lock of hair.

arrepentirse, *vr.* (*ind.* me ARREPIENTO; *subj.* me ARREPIENTA; *pret.* él se ARREPINTIÓ; *subj. imp.* me ARREPINTIERA, -SE, -RE) to repent.

arrepistar, *va.* to grind (rags) into pulp.

arrepisto, *m.* grinding or pounding (of rags).

arrepollado, da, *a.* cabbagelike.

arrepticio, cia, *a.* possessed by the devil.

arrequesonarse, *vr.* to curdle.

arrequife, *m.* singeing iron in cotton gins.

arrequives, *m. pl.* dress trimmings; ornaments; adornments; circumstances; requirements.

arrestado, da. I. *a.* bold, audacious. **II.** *pp.* of ARRESTAR.

arrestar. I. *va.* to arrest, imprison. **II.** *vr.* to be bold and enterprising; to dare.

arresto, *m.* detention; imprisonment, arrest; spirit, enterprise.

arretín, *m.* = FILIPICHÍN.

arretranca, *f.* (Am.) = RETRANCA.

arrevesado, da, *a.* = ENREVESADO, DA.

arrezafe, *m.* place full of brambles.

arrezagar, *va.* to raise. *V.* ARREMANGAR.

arria, *f.* drove of beasts. *V.* AGUJA DE ARRIA.

arriada, *f.* (prov.) flood, washout.

arrial, *m.* = ARRIAZ.

arrianismo, *m.* Arianism.—**arriano, na,** *n. & a.* Arian.

arriar. I. *va.* (naut.) to lower, to strike.—**a. la bandera,** to strike the colors. **II.** *vr.* to be flooded.

arriata, *f.* **arriate,** *m.* border, edge (in gardens); trellis; causeway.

arriaz, *m.* hilt-bar of a sword.

arriba, *adv.* above, high, on high, overhead; upstairs; (naut.) aloft.—**a. de,** above; higher up than; beyond (in an upward direction).—**de a. abajo,** from the top down; from top to bottom; from beginning to end; from head to foot.—**para a.,** up, upwards (e. g. *de cuatro pesos para arriba,* from four pesos up).

arribada, *f.* arrival.—**de a.,** (naut.) putting into a port by stress.—**arribaje,** *m.* (naut.) arrival.

arribar, *vn.* to arrive; (naut.) to put into a harbor in distress; to fall off to leeward; to reach; to recover, convalesce.

arribeño, ña, *n.* (Mex.) highlander.

arribo, *m.* arrival.

arricete, *m.* shoal, sand bank.

arricés, *m.* buckle of a stirrup strap.

arriendo, *m.* = ARRENDAMIENTO.

arriendo, arriende. *V.* ARRENDAR.

arrieraje, *m.* muleteers collectively; ARRIERÍA.

arriería, *f.* driving of mules.

arrierico, illo, ito, *m. dim.* of ARRIERO.

arriero, *m.* muleteer.

arriesgadamente, *adv.* dangerously, hazardously.

arriesgado, da, *a.* dangerous, risky; daring.

arriesgar. I. *va.* (*pret.* ARRIESGUÉ: *subj.* ARRIESGUE) to risk, hazard, jeopardize. **II.** *vr.* to expose one's self to danger; to dare.

arrimadero, *m.* support; stopping or landing place; shelter.

arrimadillo, *m.* mat, wainscot, dado.

arrimadizo, za, *a.* designed to be placed against or joined to a thing; parasitic, sycophantic, sponging.

arrimador, *m.* backlog in a fireplace.

arrimadura, *f.* act of ARRIMAR or ARRIMARSE.

arrimar. I. *va.* to place near; (naut.) to stow; to put beside or against; to put by; to give up, abandon; to lay down; to fling, dismiss; to discard.—**a. el hombro,** to work with a will; to lend a hand. **II.** *vr.* (w. a) to go near; to seek the protection of; to seek shelter in or under; to lean on or against; to join.

arrime, *m.* proximity to the goal (in bowling).

arrimo, *m.* putting near, beside or against (some person or thing); abandonment, relinquishment, giving up; support, protection; staff, cane, crutch; (ach.) idle wall, wall bearing no load.—**al a. de,** protected or shielded by.

arrimón, *m.* loafer, idler.—**estar de a.,** to keep watch.

arrinconado, da. I. *a.* distant, out of the way; neglected, put away, forgotten. **II.** *pp.* of ARRINCONAR.

arrinconar. I. *va.* to lay aside, put away; to re-move, dismiss; to neglect, forsake. **II.** *vr.* to live secluded.

arriñonado, da, *a.* kidney-shaped.

arriostrar, *va.* to brace, to stay.

arriscadamente, *adv.* boldly, audaciously.

arriscado, da. I. *a.* forward, bold; brisk, easy, free; craggy. **II.** *pp.* of ARRISCARSE.

arriscador, ra, *n.* (prov.) olive gleaner.

arriscar. I. *va.* (*pret.* ARRISQUÉ: *subj.* ARRIS-QUE) to risk. **II.** *vr.* to be vain, conceited; to plunge over a cliff (s. o. flocks).

arritranca, *f.* = RETRANCA.

arrizafa, *f.* = RUZAFA.

arrizar, *va.* (*pret.* ARRICÉ: *subj.* ARRICE) (naut.) to reef, stow, lash.

arroba, *f.* weight of twenty-five pounds (about 11½ kg.); name of a variable liquid measure.

arrobadizo, za, *a.* (coll.) feigning ecstasy.

arrobador, ra, *a.* enchanting, entrancing.

arrobamiento, *m.* ecstatic rapture, bliss, trance.

arrobarse, *vr.* to be enraptured, entranced.

arrobero, ra. I. *a.* weighing an arroba. **II.** baker for a community.

arrobo, *m.* = ARROBAMIENTO.

arrocabe, *m.* wooden frieze.

arrocero, ra, *n.* rice planter or dealer.

arrocinado, da. I. *a.* hacklike; jade, worn-out (horse). **II.** *pp.* of ARROCINARSE.

arrocinar. I. *va.* to brutify. **II.** *vr.* to become foolishly enamored; to become stupid.

arrodajarse, *vr.* (Costa Rica) to sit on the ground with the legs crossed.

arrodelado, da, *pp.* of ARRODELARSE: bearing a round shield or buckler.

arrodelarse, *vr.* to be armed with a buckler.

arrodilladura, *f.*, **arrodillamiento,** *m.* kneeling.

arrodillar. I. *va.* to make kneel down. **II.** *vr.* to kneel down.

arrodrigar, arrodrigonar, *va.* to prop (vines).

arrogación, *f.* arrogation; child adoption.

arrogador, ra, *n.* one who claims arrogantly.

arrogancia, *a.* arrogance; haughtiness; bravery, courage; stately carriage.—**arrogante,** *a.* arro-gant, overbearing; haughty, proud.

arrogantemente, *adv.* arrogantly; proudly.

arrogar. I. *va.* (*pret.* ARROGUÉ: *subj.* ARROGUE) to adopt; to arrogate. **II.** *vr.* to usurp.

arrojadamente, *adv.* audaciously, boldly.

arrojadizo, za, *a.* easily thrown or darted; mis-sile that can be, or is intended to be, thrown.

arrojado, da. I. *a.* rash, dashing, fearless. **II.** *pp.* of ARROJAR.

arrojador, ra, *n.* thrower, flinger.

arrojar. I. *va.* to throw, cast, dart, fling, hurl; to shed, emit; to bring forth, produce (shoots, sprouts); (naut.) to drive or cast on rocks; to make red-hot; to leave, show (a certain figure, as a balance, etc.); to turn away, dismiss. **II.** *vr.* to throw one's self; to venture.

arroje, *m.* man who drops as counterweight to raise the curtain in a theater.

arrojo, *m.* fearlessness, dash, boldness.

arrollador, ra. I. *a.* violent, sweeping; winding, that winds or serves to wind. **II.** *n.* one that winds.

arrollamiento, *m.* ARRULLO; (elec.) winding.

arrollar, *va.* to roll; to wrap; to twist; to carry off, sweep away; to defeat, rout, confound; to wind.

arromadizarse, *vr.* to catch cold.

arromar, *va.* to blunt; to dull.

arropado, da. I. *a.* mixed with must. **II.** *pp.* of ARROPAR.—**arropamiento,** *m.* wrapping, cover-ing; mixing with boiled wine.—**arropar,** *va.* to cover, wrap; to mix with boiled wine.—**arrope,** *m.* grape juice boiled to a sirup; boiled honey.

arropea, *f.* irons, fetters, shackles.

arropera, *f.* vessel for boiled must, etc.

arropia, *f.* taffy.—**arropiero, ra,** *n.* maker or seller of ARROPIA.

arrostrar. I. *va.* to set about dauntlessly; to defy, face. **II.** *vr.* to fight face to face.

arroyada, *f.*, **arroyadero,** *m.* channel of a stream; gully; flood, freshet.

arroyar, *vr.* to form, or run in, gullies; (agric.) to blight.

arroyuelo, *m. dim.* rill, brook.

arroyo, *m.* rivulet, small stream, brook.

arroz, *m.* rice.—**arrozal,** *m.* rice field.

arrozar (*pret.* ARROCÉ: *subj.* ARROCE), to ice.

arruar, *vn.* to grunt like a wild boar.

arrufadura, *f.* (naut.) sheer of a ship.

arrufaldado, da, *a.* with clothes tucked up.

arrufar. I. *va.* (naut.) to incurvate, to form the sheer. **II.** *vr.* to snarl.

arrufianado, da, *a.* ruffianly, impudent.

arrufo, *m.* = ARRUFADURA.

arruga, *f.* wrinkle; corrugation; rumple, fold, crease.

arrugación, *f.*, **arrugamiento,** *m.* corrugation, wrinkling, wrinkle.

arrugar, *va.* (*pret.* ARRUGUÉ: *subj.* ARRUGUE) to wrinkle, corrugate, crumple; to rumple, fold, gather, crease, pleat.—**a. el entrecejo,** to knit the brow.—**a. la frente,** to frown.

arrugia, *f.* (min.) gold mine.

arrugón, *m.* decoration of carved work.

arruinador, ra, *n.* & *a.* ruiner (-ing), demolisher (-ing), destroyer (-ing).—**arruinamiento,** *m.* de-struction, ruin.

arruinar, *va.* to demolish, ruin, destroy.

arrullador, ra, *n.* luller, rocker; flatterer.

arrullar, *va.* to lull; to court; to coo and bill.

arrullo, *m.* cooing and billing; lullaby.

arrumaco, *m.* caress, fondling.

arrumaje, *m.* (naut.) stowage.—**arrumar,** *va.* to stow.—**arrumazón,** *f.* (naut.) stowing; horizon overcast.

arrumbadas, *f. pl.* (naut.) wales of a row galley.

arrumbador, ra, *n.* heaper, piler; steersman.

arrumbamiento, *m.* (naut.) bearing.

arrumbar. I. *va.* to put away; to range (casks of wine) in a cellar; to silence; to remove from a trust; (naut.) to determine the direction of. **II.** *vn.*, *vr.* (naut.) to take bearings.

arrunflarse, *vr.* to have a flush of cards.

arrurruz, *m.* arrowroot.

arsáfraga, *f.* = BERRERA.

arsenal, *m.* shipyard, dockyard, navy yard; ar-senal.

arseniato, *m.* (chem.) arseniate.

arsenical, *a.* (chem.) arsenical.

arsénico. I. *m.* (chem.) arsenic; ratsbane. **II.** *a.* arsenic.—**arsenioso,** *a.* arsenious.—**arsenito,** *m.* arsenite.—**arseniuro,** *m.* arsenide.

arsolla, *f.* = ARZOLLA.

arta, *f.* (bot.) English plantain; ribwort.

artalejo, artalete, *m.* a sort of tart.

artanica, artanita, *f.* (bot.) sow bread

arte, *m.* or *f.* art; skill, craft, cunning; trade, pro-fession; artifice, device; intrigue; fishing net.—**a. bella,** one of the fine arts.—**artes y oficios,** arts and crafts.—**no tener a. ni parte en,** to have nothing to do with.

artefacto, *m.* manufacture, handiwork, contri-vance, appliance, device.

artejo, *m.* joint or knuckle of the fingers.

artemisa, artemisia, *f.* (bot.) mugwort.

artena, *f.* name of a water bird.

artera, *f.* iron bread stamp.

arteramente, *adv.* craftily, cunningly, artfully.

artería, *f.* cunning, trick, artfulness.

arteria, *f.* artery; (r. w., etc.) trunk line, main line; (elec.) feeder.—**arterial,** *a.* arterial.—**arterio-**

grafía, arteriography.—**arteriola,** *f.* arteriole, small artery.—**artereología,** arteriology.—**arteriosclerosis,** *f.* arteriosclerosis.—**arterioso, sa,** *a.* arterial; abounding in arteries.—**arteriotomía,** *f.* arteriotomy.—**arteritis,** *f.* arteritis.

artero, ra, *a.* cunning, artful.

artesa, *f.* trough; bowl; canoe.

artesano, na, *n.* artisan, mechanic.

artesiano, *a.* Artesian.

artesilla, *f.* trough.

artesón, *m.* kitchen tub; (arch.) carved panel on ceiling.

artesonado, da, *a.* panelled (ceiling).

artesuela, *f. dim.* small trough or bowl.

artético, ca, *a.* arthritic.

ártico, ca, *a.* arctic.

articulación, *f.* articulation, joint; pronunciation; (bot.) geniculation.

articuladamente, *adv.* distinctly, articulately.

articulado, da. I. *a.* articulate. **II.** *m.* (zool.) articulate.—*m. pl.* Articulata.

articular, *va.* to unite, join; to articulate; (law) to question, interrogate.

articular; articulario, ria, *a.* articular.

articulista, *n.* writer of articles.

artículo, *m.* article; plea; (bot.) geniculation; (anat.) joint.—*pl.* articles, things, goods, products.—**a. de fondo,** leader, editorial.

artífice, *n.* artificer, artisan, maker.

artificial, *a.* artificial.—**artificialmente,** *adv.* artificially.

artificio, *m.* workmanship, craft; artifice; cunning; trick, ruse; contrivance, device, appliance.

artificiosamente, *adv.* craftily, artfully.

artificioso, sa, *a.* skilful, ingenious; artful, crafty, cunning.

artiga, *f.* land newly broken up.

artigar, *va.* to break and level (land).

artillar, *va.* to mount (cannon).

artillería, *f.* gunnery, artillery; ordnance.—**a. de a lomo** = A. DE MONTAÑA.—**a. de avancarga,** muzzle-loading artillery.—**a. de campaña,** field artillery.—**a. de costa,** coast artillery.—**a. de montaña,** light mountain artillery.—**a. de plaza,** siege artillery.—**a. de retrocarga,** breech-loading artillery.

artillero, *m.* gunner, artilleryman.

artimaña, *f.* trap, snare, stratagem.

artimón, *m.* (naut.) mizzenmast.

artina, *f.* fruit of the boxthorn.

artista, *m.* artist.—**artísticamente,** *adv.* artistically.—**artístico, ca,** *a.* artistic.

artocárpeo, a, *a.* (bot.) artocarpous.

artolas, *f. pl.* set of two back-to-back seats.

artos, *m.* a kind of thistle; boxthorn.

artralgia, *f.* (med.) arthralgia.

artrítico, ca, *a.* arthritic.

artritis, *m.* (med.) arthritis, gout.—**artritismo,** *m.* arthritism.

artrografía, *f.* arthrography.

artrología, *f.* (anat.) arthrology.

artrópodo, da. I. *n.* & *a.* arthropod. **II.** *m. pl.* Arthropoda.

artrotomía, *f.* arthrotomy.

Arturo, *m.* (ast.) Arcturus.

arugas, *f.* (bot.) = MATRICARIA.

árula, *f. dim.* small altar.

aruñar, *va.*, **aruñazo,** *m.*, etc. = ARAÑAR, etc.

arúspice, *m.* augur, soothsayer.

aruspicina, *f.* auspicy.

arveja, *f.* (bot.) carob tree and its fruit; (S. A.) green pea.

arvejal, arvejar, *m.* field of carob trees; (S. A.) greenpea garden.

arvejo, *m.* (bot.) bastard chickpea.

arvejón, *m.* (bot.) chickling vetch.

arvejona, *f.* = ARVEJA.

arvense, *a.* growing in sown fields.

arza, *f.* (naut.) fall of a tackle.

arzobispado, *m.* archbishopric.—**arzobispal,** *a.* archiepiscopal.—**arzobispo,** *m.* archbishop.

arzolla, *f.* (bot.) lesser burdock; milk thistle.

arzón, *m.* saddletree.

as, *m.* (cards, dice, aer.) ace; Roman copper coin

asa, *f.* handle, haft; juice of certain plants.—**a. dulce,** gum benzoin.

asación, *f.* (pharm.) decoction.

asadero, ra. I. *a.* fit for roasting. **II.** *m.* (Mex.). small flat cheese.

asado, da. I. *a.* roasted; dressed. **II.** *m.* roast. **III.** *pp.* of ASAR.

asador, *m.* spit, roasting jack.

asadura, *f.* entrails, chitterlings.—**a. de puerco,** haslet.

asaeteador, *m.* archer, bowman.

asaetear, *va.* to attack, kill with arrows.

asaetinado, da, *a.* satinlike.

asafétida, *f.* asafœtida.

asainetado, da, *a.* farcical.

asalariado, da. I. *a.* salaried; hired. **II.** *n.* wage earner; hireling. **III.** *pp.* of ASALARIAR.

asalariar, *va.* to fix a salary to; to hire.

asalmonado, da, *a.* = SALMONADO.

asaltador, *m.* assailant, assaulter; highwayman.

asaltar, *va.* to assault, storm, assail; to surprise; to occur or come suddenly (to one).

asalto, *m.* assault; attack.—**a. de armas,** fencing bout.—**por a.,** by storm.

asamblea, *f.* assembly; legislature; meeting; junta; (mil.) assembly (bugle call).—**asambleísta,** *n.* assemblyman, member of an assembly.

asar. I. *va.* to roast. **II.** *vr.* to be roasting, to be very hot.

asarabácara, asáraca, *f.* (bot.) asarabacca.

asarero, *m.* (bot.) = ENDRINO.

asargado, da, *a.* sergelike, twilled.

asarina, *f.* (bot.) bastard asarum.

ásaro, *m.* (bot.) asarum.

asativo, va, *a.* (pharm.) dressed or boiled in its own juice.

asaz, *adv.* enough, abundantly.

asbestino, na, *a.* belonging to asbestos.

asbesto, *m.* asbestos.

ascalonia, *f.* (bot.) shallot.

ásear, *m.* army (in Morocco).—**áscari,** *m.* Moroccan infantryman.

ascárides, *f. pl.* ascarides.

ascendencia, *f.* line of ancestors; origin.

ascendente, *a.* ascendant, ascending.

ascender, *vn.* (ind. ASCENDIO: *subj.* ASCIENDA) to ascend, mount, climb; to be promoted.—**a. a,** to amount to.

ascendiente, *n.* ancestor; influence, power.

ascensión, *f.* ascension; exaltation.—**a. recta,** (astr.) right ascension.

ascensional, *a.* (ast.) ascensional.

ascenso, *m.* promotion.

ascensor, *m.* lift, elevator.

asceta, *m.* ascetic, hermit.—**asceticismo, ascetismo,** *m.* asceticism.—**ascético, ca,** *n.* & *a.* ascetic.

ascidia, *f.* (bot.) ascidium; (zool.) Ascidia, ascidian.—*pl.* (zool.) Ascidiaceæ.—**ascidiáceo, a,** *a.* ascidiaceous.

asciendo, ascienda. *V.* ASCENDER.

ascios, *m. pl.* (geog.) ascii.

asciro, *m.* (bot.) St. Andrew's cross.

ascitis, *f.* (med.) ascites.—**ascítico, ca,** *a.* ascitic.

asclepiada, *f.* (bot.) swallowwort.

asco, *m.* nausea, loathing; despicable thing.— **estar hecho un a.,** to be very dirty.—**hacer ascos,** to turn up one's nose.

ascoso, da, *a.* loathsomeness.—**ascoso, sa,** *a.* loathsome.

ascua, *f.* red-hot, or live, coal.—**¡ascuas!** how it pains! **en a.,** red hot.—**estar en ascuas,** to be greatly agitated.—**sacar el a. con la mano del gato,** or **con mano ajena,** (col.) to get some one to pull one's chestnuts out of the fire.

aseadamente, *adv.* cleanly, neatly.—**aseado, da. I.** *a.* clean, neat, tidy. **II.** *pp.* of ASEAR.— **asear,** *va.* to adorn, embellish, polish; to clean.

asechador, ra, *a.* insnarer, waylayer.

asechamiento, *m.*, **asechanza,** *f.* waylaying, snare, trap, stratagem.—**asechar,** *va.* to waylay;

For pronunciation, see the rules at the beginning of the book.

watch insidiously; to ambush.—**asechoso, sa,** *a.* waylaying; intriguing.

asedado, da. I. *a.* silky. **II.** *pp.* of ASEDAR.

asedar, *va.* to work (flax) soft as silk.

asediador, ra, *n.* besieger.—**asediar,** *va.* to besiege, blockade.—**asedio,** *m.* siege, blockade.

aseglararse, *vr.* to secularize himself.

asegundar, *va.* to repeat.

asegurable, *a.* insurable.—**aseguración,** *f.* insurance.

asegurado, da. I. *a.* assured, guaranteed; decided; fixed, anchored. **II.** *n.* person insured.

asegurador, ra, *n. & a.* insurer (-ing), underwriter (-ing).

aseguramiento, *m.* securing; security; insurance.

asegurar. I. *va.* to secure, fasten, fix; to affirm, assert; (com.) to insure. **II.** *vr.* to make sure; hold fast; get insured.

aseidad, *f.* self-existence.

asemejar. I. *va.* to make similar; to copy. **II.** *vr.* (w. **a**) to resemble.

asendereado, da. I. *a.* beaten; frequented; worn out by trouble. **II.** *pp.* of ASENDEREAR.

asenderear, *va.* to open a path in or through; to persecute.

asenso, *m.* assent, consent; credence.

asentada, *f.* session; sitting.

asentaderas, *f. pl.* buttocks. *V.* NALGAS.

asentadillas.—a a., *adv.* woman-fashion.

asentado, da. I. *a.* seated; settled; permanent. **II.** *pp.* of ASENTAR.

asentador, *m.* razor strop; turning chisel.

asentadura, *f.,* **asentamiento,** *m.* (law) possession of goods given by default; establishment, settlement.

asentar. I. *va.* (*ind.* ASIENTO: *subj.* ASIENTE) to place, fix, seat; to adjust; to stop at; to note down; to enter (an account, etc.); to strike; to found, establish; to hone; to estimate. **II.** *vn.* to fit; sit down; settle. **III.** *vr.* (arch.) to sink; settle.

asentimiento, *m.* assent.

asentir, *vn.* (*ind.* ASIENTO: *subj.* ASIENTE) to agree, to assent, acquiesce.

asentista, *m.* contractor.

aseo, *m.* cleanliness, neatness, tidiness.

asépalo, la, *a.* (bot.) without sepals.

asepsia, *f.* (med.) asepsis.—**aséptico, ca,** *a.* aseptic.

asequible, *a.* attainable, obtainable, available.

aserción, *f.* assertion, affirmation.

aserradero, *m.* sawmill; sawpit, sawhorse.

aserradizo, za, *a.* fit to be sawed.

aserrado, da. I. *a.* serrate, serrated, dented. **II.** *pp.* of ASERRAR.—**aserrador,** *m.* sawer or sawyer.—**aserradura,** *f.* sawing, kerf.—*pl.* sawdust.—**aserrar,** *va.* (*ind.* ASIERRO: *subj.* ASIERRE) to saw.

aserrín, *m.* sawdust.

asertivamente, *adv.* affirmatively.

asertivo, va, *a.* assertive.

aserto, *m.* assertion, affirmation.

asertorio, *a.* affirmatory.

asesar, *vn.* to become wise.

asesinar, *va.* to murder.—**asesinato,** *m.* murder. —**asesino, na,** *n.* assassin, murderer (-ess).

asesor, ra, *n.* assessor, adviser.—**asesorar. I.** *va.* to give legal advice to. **II.** *vr.* to take advice.— **asesoría,** *f.* office, pay and fees of an assessor.

asestador, *m.* gunner.—**asestadura,** *f.* taking aim.

asestar, *va.* to aim, point; to deal (a blow); to discharge, to fire.

aseveración, *f.* affirmation, assertion.

aseveradamente, *adv.* affirmatively.

aseverar, *va.* to asseverate, affirm, assert.

asfaltar, *va.* to asphalt.

asfáltico, ca, *a.* asphaltic; asphalt (u. a.); bituminous.

asfalto, *m.* asphalt, asphaltum.

asfíctico, ca, *a.* asphyxial.

asfixia, *f.* (med.) asphyxia.—**asfixiante,** *a.* asphyxiating.—**asfixiar. I.** *va.* to asphyxiate, suffocate. **II.** *vr.* to be asphyxiated.

asfódelo, *m.* asphodel, day lily.

asgo, yo asga. *V.* ASIR.

asi, *adv.* so, thus, in this manner; therefore. Followed by a verb in the subjunctive mood, it is translated by "would that".—**a., a., so so,** middling. —**a. como,** as soon as.—**a. como a.,** anyway, anyhow.—**a. que,** as soon as, after.

asiático, ca, *n. & a.* Asiatic.

asidera, *f.* (S. A.) = PEGUAL.

asidero, *m.* handle; occasion, pretext.—**asideros,** (naut.) towropes.

asido, da. I. *pp.* of ASIR. **II.** *a.* fastened, tied, attached.

asiduamente, *adv.* assiduously.—**asiduidad,** *f.* assiduity.—**asiduo, dua,** *a.* assiduous.

asiento, *m.* seat; site; solidity; settling; bottom; sediment, settlings; treaty; contract; entry; registry; judgment, wisdom; stability; permanence; mining district; list, roll; collar band; indigestion.

asiento, yo asienta. *V.* ASENTIR.

asiento, yo asiente. *V.* ASENTAR.

asierro, yo asierre. *V.* ASERRAR.

asignable, *a.* assignable.—**asignación,** *f.* assignation; distribution, partition; destination.

asignado. I. *m.* assignat. **II.** *pp.* of ASIGNAR.

asignar, *va.* to assign; to devote; to appoint; to ascribe attribute.

asignatura, *f.* subject (of study).

asilar, *va.* to shelter; to place in an asylum.

asilo, *m.* asylum, refuge; shelter.—**a. de huérfanos,** orphan asylum.—**a. de locos,** insane asylum.

asilla, *f. dim.* small handle; slight pretext; collar bone.

asimiento, *m.* grasp; attachment, affection.

asimilable, *a.* assimilable.—**asimilación,** *f.* assimilation.—**asimilar. I.** *vn.* to resemble. **II.** *va.* to assimilate.—**asimilativo, va,** *a.* assimilating.

asimismo, *adv.* likewise, so too, in like manner.

asimplado, da, *a.* like a simpleton.

asincrónico, ca, *a.* asynchronous.

asincronismo, *m.* asynchronism.

asíndeton, *m.* (rhet.) asyndeton.

asinino, na, *a.* asinine; asslike.

asíntota, *f.* (geom.) asymptote.

asir. I. *va. & vn.* (*ind.* ASGO: *subj.* ASGA) to grasp or seize; to hold; to take root. **II.** *vr.* (w. **de**); to avail one's self; to hold (to), to take hold (of); to take advantage (of); to dispute with each other. —**a. a las ramas,** to give foolish excuses.

asiriano, na; asirio, ria, *n. & a.* Assyrian.

asiriología, *f.* Assyriology.—**asiriólogo,** *n.* Assyriologist.

asistencia, *f.* attendance, presence; assistance, aid; reward; board, meals.—*pl.* allowance; alimony.

asistenta, *f.* handmaid; waiting maid; attendant.

asistente, *m.* assistant, helper; chief officer of justice at Seville; orderly.

asistir. I. *vn.* (w. **a**), to attend, be present (at); to follow suit. **II.** *va.* to lend; attend, take care of; to assist, help, serve; to accompany.

asma, *f.* asthma.—**asmático, ca,** *a.* asthmatic.

asna, *f.* she-ass, jenny.—*pl.* (carp.) rafters.

asnacho, *m.* (bot.) = GATUÑA.

asnada, *f.* foolish action.

asnado, *m.* side-wall timber in mines.

asnal, *a.* asinine, stupid, idiotic.

asnalmente, *adv.* foolishly, idiotically.

asnallo, m. (bot.) = GATUÑA.

asnería, *f.* stud of asses; idiotic action.

asnico, ca, *n. dim.* little ass.

asnilla, *f.* stanchion or prop.

asnillo, lla, *n. dim.* little ass; (zool.) field cricket.

asnino, na, *a.* asslike; asinine.

asno, *m.* donkey, ass.

asobarcar, *va.* (*pret.* ASOBARQUÉ: *subj.* ASOBARQUE) to take under the arm; to lift up (the skirts).

asocarronado, da, *a.* crafty, cunning.

asociación, *f.,* **asociamiento,** *m.* association; fellowship; partnership, union.

---

asociacionismo, *m.* associationism.

asociado, *m.* associate, partner.

asociar. I. *va.* to associate. **II.** *vr.* associate; to form a partnership; to join.

asolación, *f.* desolation, devastation.

asolador, ra, *n.* & *a.* destroyer (-ing), ruiner (-ing).

asoladura, *f.* = ASOLACIÓN.

asolamiento, *m.* destruction, havoc.

asolanar, *va.* to parch, dry up.

asolar. I. *va.* (*ind.* ASUELO: *subj.* ASUELE) to raze, devastate; to burn, parch (s. o. the sun). **II.** *vr.* to settle, get clear (wine); to become parched, dry up (s. o. the soil.)

asoldar, asoldadar, *va.* (*ind.* ASUELDO: *subj.* ASUELDE) to hire.

asolear. I. *va.* to sun. **II.** *vr.* to be sunburnt.

asomada, *f.* appearance; point from which something is first seen.

asomado, da. I. *a.* fuddled. **II.** *pp.* of ASOMAR.

asomar. I. *vn.* to begin to appear. **II.** *va.* to show, put out. **III.** *vr.* to become flustered with wine; to peep; (w. **a**) to look out of; to peep into.

asombradizo, za, *a.* timid, shy.—**asombrador, ra,** *a.* astonishing.

asombramiento, *m.* = ASOMBRO.

asombrar. I. *va.* to shade, darken; to frighten; to astonish, amaze. **II.** *vr.* (w. **de**) to wonder, be astonished (at).—**asombro,** *m.* dread, fear; amazement or astonishment.—**asombrosamente,** *adv.* amazingly, wonderfully.—**asombroso, sa,** *a.* wonderful, astonishing.

asomo, *m.* indication, sign; conjecture.

asonada, *f.* riotous crowd; mobbing, attack of a mob.

asonancia, *f.* consonance, harmony; (poet.) assonance.

asonantar, *va.* (poet.) to make assonant.

asonante, *n.* & *a.* assonant.

asonar, *vn.* (*ind.* ASUENO: *subj.* ASUENE) to be assonant; to accord.

asordar, *va.* to deafen.

asotanar, *va.* to excavate (the ground) for a cellar.

aspa, *f.* cross; reel; wings of a windmill; cross stud.—**aspadera,** *f.* (mech.) reel.—**aspado, da. I.** *a.* having both arms extended. **II.** *pp.* of ASPAR. —**aspador, ra. I.** *n.* reeler. **II.** *m.* reel.

aspalato, *m.* (bot.) rosewood.

aspalto, *m.* = ESPALTO.

aspar, *va.* to reel; to crucify; to vex.

aspaviento, *m.* exaggerated wonder or fear, fuss.

aspecto, *m.* aspect, look; (arch.) outlook; (ast.) aspect.

ásperamente, *adv.* rudely, harshly, gruffly.

asperear, *vn.* to taste acrid.

asperete, *m.* = ASPERILLO.

aspereza, *f.* asperity; roughness; keenness; harshness, snappishness; rough place.

asperges, *m.* aspersion, sprinkling.

asperidad, *f.* = ASPEREZA.

asperiego, ga, *a.* sour (pippin).

asperillo, *m.* sourish taste of unripe fruit.

asperillo, lla, *a. dim.* tart, sourish.

asperjar, *va.* to sprinkle.

áspero, ra, *a.* rough; knotty; harsh, gruff.

asperón, *m.* grindstone; flagstone.

aspérrimo, ma, *a. sup.* of ÁSPERO.

aspersión, *f.* aspersion; sprinkling.

aspersorio, *m.* water sprinkler.

áspid, áspide, *m.* asp, aspic.

aspillera, *f.* loophole, embrasure, crenel.

aspiración, *f.* aspiration; (mus.) short pause.

aspiradamente, *adv.* with aspiration.

aspirante, *n.* aspirant, neophyte.

aspirar. I. *va.* to inhale; to aspire; to covet; to aspirate; to suck. **II.** *vn.* to aspire; to draw breath in, inhale.

aspirina, *f.* aspirin.

asquear. I. *va.* to loathe. **II.** *vn.* to be nauseated.

asquerosamente, *adv.* loathsomely; basely.

asquerosidad, *f.* filthiness, foulness; vileness, baseness.

asqueroso, sa, *a.* filthy, loathsome; vile, base.

asta, *f.* lance; staff, pole, flagstaff; horn, antler; shank; shaft, spindle.—**a media a.,** at half mast.

ástaco, *m.* crawfish.

astado, astero, *m.* Roman pikeman.

astático, ca, *a.* astatic.

astenia, *f.* (med.) asthenia.

asténico, ca, *a.* (med.) asthenic.

asteria, *f.* starstone; cat's-eye.

asterisco, *m.* asterisk (*); (bot.) oxeye.

asteroide, *m.* asteroid.

asteroideo. I. *n.* & *a.* (zool.) asteroidean. **II.** *n. pl.* Asteroidea.

astigmatismo, *m.* astigmatism.

astigmómetro, *m.* astigmometer.

astil, handle; shaft; beam of a balance.

astilejos, *m. pl.* = ASTILLEJOS.

astilla, *f.* chip, splinter.—**astillar,** *va.* to chip.

astillazo, *m.* blow from a flying chip.

Astillejos, *m. pl.* (ast.) Castor and Pollux.

astillero, *m.* rack for lances, spears, pikes, etc.; shipyard, dockyard.

astilloso, sa, *a.* wood easily splintered.

astracán, *m.* astrakhan (cloth).

astrágalo, *m.* (arch.) astragal; (mil.) molding on a cannon; (bot.) milk vetch; (anat.) astragalus; round molding; beads.

astral, *a.* astral.

astrancia, *f.* (bot.) masterwort.

astricción, *f.* astriction.—**astrictivo, va,** *a.* astrictive, styptic.—**astricto, ta,** *a.* contracted; determined.

astrífero, ra, (poet.) starry.

astringencia, *f.* astringency.—**astringente,** *a.* astringent.—**astringir,** *va.* (*ind.* ASTRINJO: *subj.* ASTRINJA) to astringe, contract, compress.

astro, *m.* celestial body.

astrografía, *f.* astrography.

astroite, *m.* astroite, radiated fossil.

astrolabio, *m.* astrolabe.

astrólatra, *n.* astrolater.

astrolatría, *f.* astrolatry.

astrología, *f.* astrology.—**astrológico, ca,** *a.* astrological.—**astrólogo,** *m.* astrologer.

astrológicamente, *adv.* astrologically.

astronomía, *f.* astronomy.—**astronómicamente,** *adv.* astronomically.—**astronómico, ca,** *a.* astronomical.—**astrónomo,** *m.* astronomer.

astrosamente, *adv.* meanly, basely.

astroso, sa, *a.* vile, loathsome.

astucia, *f.* cunning, slyness.

astur, ra, asturiano, na, *n.* & *a.* Asturian.

asturión, *m.* pony; (zool.) SOLLO.

astutamente, *adv.* cunningly, craftily.

astuto, ta, *a.* astute, cunning, sly, crafty.

asueldo, yo asuelde *V.* ASOLDAR.

asuelo, yo asuele. *V.* ASOLAR.

asueno, yo asuene. *V.* ASONAR.

asueto, *m.* school holiday, vacation.

asumir, *va.* to assume; to raise, elevate.

asunción, *f.* assumption; elevation, ascent.

asunto, *m.* subject, matter; affair, business.

asuramiento, *m.* burning (s. o. cooking food).

asurarse, *vr.* to burn; to become parched.

asurcano, na, *a.* neighboring.

asurcar, *va.* (*pret.* ASURQUÉ: *subj.* ASURQUE) to furrow; to plow.

asustadizo, za, *a.* easily frightened; shy.

asustar. I. *va.* to frighten, scare. **II.** *vr.* to be frightened.

atabaca, *f.* (bot.) groundsel.

atabacado, da, *a.* tobacco-colored.

atabal, *m.* kettle-drum.—**atabalear,** *vn.* to clatter.

atabalero, ra, *n.* kettledrummer.

atabanado, da, *a.* spotted white.

atabardillado, da, *a.* of the nature of spotted fever.

atabe, *m.* small vent in water pipes.

atabillar, *va.* to fold (cloth) with selvages out.

atabladera, *f.* roller.—**atablar,** *va.* to level, roll.

atacadera, *f.* blaster's rammer.

atacado, da. I. *a.* (met.) irresolute, undecided; stingy, close. **II.** *pp.* of ATACAR.

atacador, *m.* aggressor; ramrod, rammer.

atacadura, *f.,* **atacamiento,** *m.* ramming.

atacamita, *f.* (min.) atacamite.

atacar, *va.* (*pret.* ATAQUÉ: *subj.* ATAQUE) to attack; to button; to fit; to ram; to corner.

atacir, *m.* (astrol.) division of the celestial arch into twelve parts.

ataderas, *f. pl.,* **ataderos,** *m. pl.* garters.

atadero, *m.* cord, rope; tying place or thing.

atadijo, ito, *m. dim.* (coll.) ill-shaped parcel.

atado. I. *m.* bundle, parcel. **II.** *a.* pusillanimous, good for nothing. **III.** *pp.* of ATAR.

atador, ra. I. *n.* tier, binder. **II.** *m.* bonnetstring.

atadura, *f.* fastening, binding; connection; knot.

atafagar, *va.* to stupefy; to tease.

atafetanado, da, *a.* taffetalike.

ataguía, *f.* cofferdam.

ataharre, *m.* broad crupper of a packsaddle.

atahorma, *f.* (orn.) osprey.

ataifor, *m.* deep dish; Moorish round table.

atairar, *va.* to mold (panels and frames).

ataire, *m.* molding in panels and frames.

atajadero, *m.* sluice gate.—**atajadizo,** *m.* partition.—**atajador,** *m.* one that stops or intercepts; (mil.) scout; (min.) lad who tends the horses.

atajar. I. *va.* to intercept, stop; to partition off. **II.** *vr.* to be confounded with shame or fear.

atajea, atajía, *f.* = ATARJEA.

atajo, *m.* short cut; interception, stopping.— **echar por el a.,** to escape through a loophole (fig.)

atalajar, *va.* to harness and hitch.

atalaje, *m.* breast harness; draft.

atalantar, = ATURDIR.

atalaya. I. *f.* watchtower; height. **II.** *m.* guard; lookout.—**atalayador, ra,** *n.* sentry, lookout; prier.—**atalayar,** *va.* to watch, guard; to spy or pry on.—**atalayero,** *m.* advance scout.

atalvina, *f.* = TALVINA.

atamiento, *m.* pusillanimity, meekness.

atanasia, *f.* (bot.) costmary or alecost; English type (14-point).

atanor, *m.* tile water pipe; tile (clay or concrete tube or pipe).

atanquía, *f.* depilatory; silk refuse.

atañer, *v. imp.* to belong, appertain, concern.

ataque, *m.* attack; (mil.) offensive works; (med.) fit (of illness); wrangle

ataquiza, *f.* laying (a vine).—**ataquizar,** *va.* to lay (a vine).

atar. I. *va.* to tie, bind; lace; to deprive of motion, stop.—**a. cabos,** to put two and two together, to draw one's own conclusions. **II.** *vr.* to become embarrassed.

ataracea, *f.* marquetry, inlaid work.

ataracear, *va.* to checker; inlay.

atarantado, da, *a.* bitten by a tarantula; restless; wild; astonished, amazed.

atarazana, *f.* arsenal; spinner's shed.

atarazar, *va.* to bite.

atareado, da. I. *a.* busy. **II.** *pp* of ATAREAR.

atarear. I. *va.* to give or assign work to. **II.** *vr.* to be exceedingly busy.

atarjea, *f.* culvert; conduit; drain pipe.

atarquinar. I. *va.* to cover with mud. **II.** *vr.* to be covered with mud.

atarraga, *f.* (bot.) = OLIVARDA.

atarrajar, *va.* = aterrajar.

atarraya, *f.* casting net.

atarugamiento, *m.* wedging; stuffing.

atarugar, *va.* (*pret.* ATARUGUÉ: *subj.* ATARUGUE) to fasten; to wedge, plug, bung; to stuff, fill; (coll.) to silence.

atasajado, da, *a.* stretched across a horse.

atasajar, *va.* to "jerk" (beef).

atascadero, atascamiento, *m.* deep miry place; obstruction; impediment.

atascar. I. *va.* (*pret.* ATASQUÉ: *subj.* ATASQUE) to stop (a leak); to obstruct. **II.** *vr.* to stick in mire; to get stopped up; to lose the thread; to be nonplussed, (coll.) to get stuck.

atasco, *m.* obstruction.

ataúd, *m.* coffin, casket; a grain measure.

ataujía, *f.* damaskeening.

ataujiado, da, *a.* damaskeened.

ataurique, *m.* (arch.) ornamented plasterwork.

ataviar, *va.* to dress out; deck; trim; adorn.

atávico, ca, *a.* atavistic.

atavío, *m.* dress; finery, gear.

atavismo, *m.* atavism.

ataxia, *f.* (med.) ataxia.—**atáxico, ca,** *a.* ataxic.

atediar. I. *va.* to bore, tire. **II.** *vr.* to be bored.

ateísmo, *m.* atheism.—**ateísta,** *n.* & *a.* atheist (-ic) (= ATEO).

ateje, *m.* a kind of hardwood tree (Cuba).

atelaje, *m.* ATALAJE; team.

atemorizar, *va.* (*pret.* ATEMORICÉ: *subj.* ATEMORICE) to cause fear to, to frighten.

atemperación, *f.* tempering.—**atemperante,** *a.* tempering, soothing, cooling.—**atemperar,** *va.* to temper, soften, assuage, cool; to accommodate.

atenacear, atenazar, *va.* to tear off the flesh of with nippers; to torture.

atención, *f.* attention; civility; kindness; deal in wool.—*pl.* affairs, business.—**en a. a,** considering, in view of.

atender. I. *vn.* (*pp.* ATENDIDO and ATENTO: *ind.* ATIENDO: *subj.* ATIENDA) to attend; to pay attention; to wait. **II.** *va.* to take care of (a person); to show courtesy to, to treat.

ateneo, *m.* athenæum.

atenerse, *vr.* (*ind.* me ATENGO: *pret.* me ATUVE; *sub.* me ATENGA) (w. **a**) to depend or rely (on); to abide (by).

ateniense, *n.* & *a.* Athenian.

atenta, *f.*—**su a.,** your favor.

atentación, *f.* (law) illegal procedure.

atentadamente, *adv.* contrary to law.

atentado, da. I. *a.* discreet, prudent, moderate; noiseless. **II.** *pp.* of ATENTAR. **III.** *m.* (law) transgression, offence, violation; crime.

atentamente, *adv.* attentively; politely.

atentar, *va.* (*ind.* ATIENTO: *subj.* ATIENTE) to attempt; to do or design illegally.

atentatorio, ria, *a.* unlawful.

atento, ta. I. *a.* attentive, heedful; polite, courteous. **II.** *pp. irr.* of ATENDER.

atenuación, *f.* extenuation, diminution; (rhet.) litotes.

atenuante, *a.* attenuating; extenuating (circumstances).

atenuar, *va.* to attenuate, extenuate, diminish, lessen; to emaciate, make lean.

ateo, a, *n.* & *a.* atheist (-ic).

atepocate, *m.* (Mex.) frog spawn.

atercianado, da, *a.* afflicted with tertian fever.

aterciopelado, da, *a.* velvety.

aterido, da, *a.* stiff with cold.

aterimiento, *m.* stiffness from cold.

aterino, *m.* atherine, sand smelt.

aterirse, *vr.* (*ind.* me ATIERO: *subj.* me ATIERA) to become stiff with cold.

atermal, *a.* cold (s. o. mineral waters).

atérmano, na, athermanous.

ateroma, *f.* atheroma.

atérmico, ca, *a.* = ATÉRMANO.

aterrador, ra, *a.* frightful, terrible, dreadful.

aterrajar, *va.* to thread, to tap (a screw).

aterramiento, *m.* ruin, destruction; terror; (naut.) landing place.

aterrar. I. *va.* (*ind.* ATIERRO: *subj.* ATIERRE) to destroy, pull down, demolish. **II.** *vn.* (aer.) to land. **III.** *vr.* (naut.) to stand inshore.

aterrar. I. *va.* (*this verb is regular in the following acceptations*) to terrify; to awe; to appal. **II.** *vr.* to be filled with terror, to be awed or appalled.

aterrizaje, aterrizamiento, *n.* (aer.) landing, alighting.

aterrizar, *vn.* (aer.) to land.

aterronar. I. *va.* to clod; to make bumpy. **II.** *vr.* to become lumpy; to cake.

aterrorizar, *va.* to frighten, terrify.

atesador, *m.* (mech.) stretcher, tightener; brace pin.

atesar, *va.* (*ind.* ATIESO: *subj.* ATIESE) to pull tight, to tighten; (naut.) to haul taut.

atesorador, ra, *n.* hoarder.

atesorar, *va.* to treasure, hoard up.

atestación, *f.* attestation, testimony, affidavit.

atestado, da, *a.* attested, witnessed.

atestados, *m. pl.* certificates, testimonials.

atestadura, *f.* cramming or stuffing; must for soaking casks.

atestamiento, *m.* cramming, stuffing.

atestar, *va.* (*ind.* ATIESTO: *subj.* ATIESTE) to attest, witness; to cram, stuff, crowd; to fill up wine casks.

atestiguación, *f.*, **atestiguamiento,** *m.* affidavit.

atestiguar, *va.* to depose, witness, attest; to give evidence, to prove.

atetado, da, *a.* mammiform.

atetar, *va.* to suckle.

atetillar, *va.* to trench around roots.

atezado, da. I. *a.* black. **II.** *pp.* of ATEZAR.

atezamiento, *m.* blackening.

atezar. I. *va.* (*pret.* ATECÉ: *subj.* ATECE) to blacken. **II.** *vr.* to become or get black.

atibar, *va.* to fill up.

atiborrar, *va.* to stuff with coarse wool.

aticismo, *m.* Atticism; witticism, joke.

ático, ca. I. *a.* Attic; elegant. **II.** *m.* Attic; (arch.) attic.

atiendo, yo atienda. *V.* ATENDER.

atiento, yo atiente. *V.* ATENTAR.

atierre, *m.* deals; caving in; run; (mining) attle, heap of waste ore.

atierro, yo atierre. *V.* ATERRAR.

atiesar, *va.* to stiffen.

atifle, *m.* potter's trevet.

atigrado, da, *a.* tiger-colored.

atildadura, *f.*, **atildamiento,** *m.* punctuation, censure; tidiness, nicety.

atildar, *va.* to put a dash or TILDE over; to censure; to adorn.

atinadamente, *adv.* cautiously; wisely; judiciously.

atinar, *vn.* to hit the mark; guess; find out.

atincar, *m.* tincal, borax.

atinconar, *va.* (min.) to prop the side walls of.

atiplar. I. *va.* to raise the pitch of. **II.** *vr.* to become very sharp.

atirantar, *va.* (arch.) to stay, brace with ties.

atiriciarse, *vr.* to become jaundiced.

atisbadero, *m.* peephole.—**atisbador, ra,** *n.* prier, observer.—**atisbadura,** *f.* prying, observing cautiously.—**atisbar,** *va.* to scrutinize; pry, watch. —**atisbo,** *m.* = ATISBADURA.

atisuado, da, *a.* tissuelike.

atizadero, *m.*, **atizador, ra,** *n.* inciter; poker; snuffer; feeder.

atizar, *va.* (*pret.* ATICÉ: *subj.* ATICE) to poke; snuff; dress; trim; rouse, stir.

atizonar. I. *va.* to bond (a wall) with headers; to embed (a beam in a wall). **II.** *vr.* (agr.) to become blighted.

atlantes, *m.* (arch.) atlantes or telamones.

Atlántico, *n.* & *a.* Atlantic.

atlas, *m.* atlas; (anat.) atlas; (com.) atlas (satin), rich satin.

atleta, *m.* athlete.—**atlético, ca,** *a.* athletic.— **atletismo,** *m.* athletics.

atmósfera, *f.* atmosphere; sphere of influence.

atmosférico, ca, *a.* atmospherical.

atoar, *va.* (naut.) to tow.

atocinado, da. I. *a.* fat, fleshy. **II.** *pp.* of ATOCINAR.

atocinar. I. *va.* to cut up (a pig); to convert into bacon; to assassinate. **II.** *vr.* to swell with anger; to fall desperately in love.

atocha, *f.* tough feather grass, bassweed.

atochal, atochar, *m.* bassweed field.

atochar, *va.* to fill with bassweed.

atochón, *m.* panicle of tough feather grass.

atol, atole, *m.* corn-flour gruel.—**atolería,** *f.* place where ATOLE is sold.—**atolero, ra,** *n.* maker and vender of ATOLE.

atolondrado, da. I. *a.* hare-brained, thoughtless, giddy, careless. **II.** *pp.* of ATOLONDRAR.

atolondramiento, *m.* confusion, perplexity, amazement; giddiness; recklessness.

atolondrar. I. *va.* to confound, amaze, perplex, rattle. **II.** *vr.* to become confused, rattled.

atolladero, *m.* deep miry place; difficulty, stumbling block.

atollar, *vn.* & *vr.* to fall into the mire; to stick in the mud; to be involved in difficulties, (coll.) to get stuck.

atomicidad, *f.* atomicity.—**atómico, ca,** *a.* atomic.—**atomismo,** *m.* atomism.—**atomista,** *m.* atomist.—**atomístico, ca,** *a.* atomistic.

átomo, *m.* atom.

atondar, *va.* to spur.

atonía, *f.* (med.) atony; debility.

atónito, ta, *a.* astonished, amazed, aghast.

átono, na, *a.* unaccented; atonic.

atontadamente, *adv.* foolishly, stupidly.

atontado, da. I. *a.* foolish, stupid; stunned. **II.** *pp.* of ATONTAR.

atontamiento, *m.* stupefaction, stunning.

atontar. I. *va.* to stun, stupefy; confound, confuse. **II.** *vr.* to become stupid, dull, stunned.

atorar. I. *va.* to obstruct; to jam; choke; to cut (wood). **II.** *vr.* to stick in the mire; fit the bore closely; choke.

atormentadamente, *adv.* anxiously, tormentingly.

atormentador, ra, *n.* & *a.* tormentor (-ing).

atormentar, *va.* to torment, torture.

atornillar, *va.* to screw.

atorozonarse, *vr.* to suffer gripes or colic.

atortolar. I. *va.* to confound; intimidate. **II.** *vr.* to be intimidated.

atortorar, *va.* (naut.) to frap (a ship).

atortujar, *va.* to squeeze, make flat.

atosigador, ra, *n.* & *a.* poisoner (-ing).

atosigamiento, *m.* poisoning.

atosigar, *va.* (*pret.* ATOSIGUÉ: *subj.* ATOSIGUE) to poison; to harass, press.

atóxicar, *va.* to poison.—**atóxico, ca,** *a.* not poisonous.

atrabancar, *va.* (*pret.* ATRABANQUÉ: *subj.* ATRA-BANQUE) to huddle; to perform in a hurry.

atrabanco, *m.* huddling, acting hurriedly.

atrabiliario, ria; atrabilioso, sa, *a.* atrabilarious.—**atrabilis,** *f.* black bile.

atracable, *a.* approachable.

atracadero, *m.* (naut.) landing place.

atracar. I. *va.* (*pret.* ATRAQUÉ: *subj.* ATRAQUE (naut.) to overtake; approach; to cram; pamper. **II.** *vn.* (naut.) to make the shore, to stop, moor. **III.** *vr.* to be pampered.

atracción, *f.* attraction.

atracón, *m.* overeating, gluttony; push.

atractivo, va. I. *a.* attractive. **II.** *m.* charm, grace; inducement.

atraer, *va.* (*ind.* ATRAIGO: *pret.* ATRAJE: *subj.* ATRAIGA) to attract; allure, charm.

atrafagado, da, *a.* very busy; laborious; fidgety.

atrafagar, *I.* *vn.* to toil, work hard. **II.** *vr.* to fidget, fuss.

atragantarse, *vr.* to choke; to become confused in conversation.

atraíble, *a.* attractable.

atraidorado, da, *a.* traitorlike, peculiar to traitors.

atraigo, atraje, atraiga. *V.* ATRAER.

atraillar, *va.* to leash; to follow (game) guided by a dog in leash.

atramento, *m.* black color.

atramparse, *vr.* to be trapped, snared; locked out; choked; blocked up; involved in difficulties.

atramuz, m. (bot.) lupine.

atrancar, va. (pret. ATRANQUÉ: subj. ATRANQUE) to bar (a door); to obstruct; to stride; to read hurriedly.

atrapamoscas, f. (bot.) Venus's flytrap.

atrapar, va. to overtake; to catch, grab; to trap, ensnare, deceive.

atrás, adv. backward, behind, back; past.—**a. de,** behind, back of.—**hacerse a.,** to fall back.

atrasado, da (pp. of ATRASAR), a. short of means, poor; backward; behind the times; late, tardy; slow (s. o. a watch).

atrasar. I. va. to retard, delay, detain. **II.** vn. to go or be slow (as a watch). **III.** vr. to remain behind; to lose time (s. o. a watch); to be in debt; to be late.

atraso, m. backwardness.—pl. arrears.

atravesado, da. I. a. squint-eyed; oblique; mestizo, crossbred, mongrel. **II.** pp. of ATRAVESAR.

atravesaño, m. crosstimber; crosspiece.

atravesar. I. va. (ind. ATRAVIESO: subj. ATRAVIESE) to place across, lay athwart; run through, pierce; cross; go through; wager; (naut.) to lie to. **II.** vr. (w. en) to be, come or lie across or in the way; to break in, interrupt, (coll.) butt in; to meddle; to spring up, arise (as an obstacle).

atravieso. V. ATRAVESAR.

atrayente, a. attractive.

atreguado, da, a. foolish; deranged; under truce.

atreguar. I. va. to give a truce to; to give an extension. **II.** vr. to agree to a truce.

atrenzo, m. conflict, difficulty.

atresia, f. (med.) atresia.

atresnalar, va. to collect into heaps.

atreverse, vr. to dare; to venture.

atrevidamente, adv. daringly, boldly.

atrevido, da. I. a. bold, daring, fearless; forward, insolent. **II.** pp. of ATREVERSE.

atrevimiento, m. boldness, audacity; effrontery, impudence.

atribución, f. attribution; attribution.

atribuir. I. va. (ind. ATRIBUYO: pret. él ATRIBUYÓ: subj. ATRIBUYA) to attribute, ascribe, impute. **II.** vr. to assume, take to one's self.

atribular. I. va. to grieve, afflict. **II.** vr. to be or become sad or despondent, to lose heart.

atributivo, va, a. attributive.

atributo, m. attribute; (log.) predicate.

atribuyo, ya. V. ATRIBUIR.

atrición, f. contrition; (vet.) contraction.

atril, m. lectern; music stand; easel.

atrillera, f. ornamental cover for a lectern.

atrincheramiento, m. intrenchment.

atrincherar, va. & vr. to intrench.

atrio, m. atrium; paved terrace or raised platform in front of a building (gen. a church).

atrípedo, da, a. (zool.) black-footed.

atrirrostro, tra, a. black-beaked.

atrito, ta, a. contrite.

atro, ra, a. (poet.) dark, black, obscure.

atrocidad, f. atrocity.

atrochar, vn. to go by cross-paths.

atrofia, f. atrophy.—**atrofiar,** va. & vr. to atrophy.—**atrófico, ca,** a. atrophic.

atrojarse, vr. (Mex., coll.) to be stumped.

atrompetado, da, a. trumpetlike.

atronadamente, adv. recklessly, hastily.

atronado, da, a. & n. reckless (person), thoughtless (person).

atronador, ra, n. & a. thunderer (-ing).

atronadura, f. crack or split; (vet.) tumor in the pastern.

atronamiento, m. thundering; stupefaction; (vet.) crepance.

atronar. I. va. (ind. ATRUENO: subj. ATRUENE) to deafen; stun, stupefy; stop (the ears of horses); kill (a bull). **II.** vr. to be thunderstruck.

atronerar, va. to make embrasures in.

atropar, va. to assemble in groups.

atropelladamente, adv. tumultuously, helter-skelter; unscrupulously.—**atropellado, da. I.** a. hasty; precipitate. **II.** pp. of ATROPELLAR.—**atropellador, ra,** n. trampler; transgressor, violator.—**atropellamiento,** m. trampling under foot; confusion.

atropellar. I. va. to trample under foot; knock down; push through; insult; violate. **II.** vr. to move or act hastily or recklessly.

atropello, m. trampling, upsetting; abuse, insult, outrage.

atropina, f. atropine.

atroz, a. atrocious; (fam.) huge, vast, enormous.

atrozar, va. (naut.) to truss (a yard).

atrozmente, adv. atrociously; enormously.

atruendo, m. pomp, ostentation.

atrueno, atruene. V. ATRONAR.

atruhanado, da, a. scurrilous, rascally.

atuendo, m. = ATRUENDO.

atufadamente, adv. peevishly.—**atufar. I.** va. to vex, irritate, plague. **II.** vr. to fret (liquors); to become angry.—**atufo,** m. vexation, annoyance.

atún, m. tunny fish.—**atunara,** f. place to catch tunny fish.—**atunera,** f. tunny-fish hook.

atunero, m. tunny fisherman or dealer.

aturar. I. va. to close tight. **II.** vr. to act wisely.

aturdido, da. I. a. harebrained, giddy, rattled. **II.** pp. of ATURDIR.—**aturdimiento,** m. bewilderment; confusion.

aturdir. I. va. to bewilder, amaze; rattle, perplex; stun. **II.** vr. to become dazed, bewildered, rattled, stunned.

aturrullar, va. to confound, perplex, bewilder.

atusador, ra, n. hairdresser; plant trimmer.

atusar. I. va. to trim; to comb and smooth (the hair). **II.** vr. to dress with too much care.

atutía, f. tutty.

auca, f. goose. V. OCA.

audacia, f. audacity, boldness.—**audaz,** a. bold, fearless, audacious.

audible, a. audible.

audiencia, f. audience, hearing; audience chamber; court of oyer and terminer; audiencia (a kind of high court and its jurisdiction).

audiofrecuencia, f. (rad.) audiofrequency.

audiómetro, m. audiometer.

audión, m. (rad.) audion.

auditivo, va, a. auditory.

auditor, m. judge.—**a. de guerra,** Judge Advocate (army).—**a. de la Rota,** member or auditor of the Rota.—**a. de marina,** Judge Advocate (navy).

auditoría, f. office of an AUDITOR.

auditorio, ria. I. a. auditory. **II.** m. audience.

auge, m. culmination, supreme height; (astr.) apogee.

augita, f. (min.) augite.

augur, m. augur, augurer.—**auguración,** f. auguration.—**augural,** a. augurial.—**augurar,** va. to augur.—**augurio,** m. = AGÜERO.

augusto, ta, a. august, magnificent.

aula, f. lecture hall; class room; (poet.) palace.

aulaga, f. furze, whin, gorse.

áulico, ca, a. aulic.

aulladero, m. place where animals howl.

aullador, ra, n. & a. howler (-ing).—**aullar,** vn. to howl, yell, cry.—**aullido, aúllo,** m. howl; cry of horror.

aumentable, a. that may be increased.

aumentación, f. increase; (rhet.) climax.

aumentado, da. I. a. increased, augmented; magnified.—**a. de,** or **en,** increased by. **II.** pp. of AUMENTAR.

aumentador, ra, n. & a. enlarger (-ing), amplifier (-ing).

aumentar, va. & vr. to augment, increase, enlarge, magnify.

aumentativo, va, a. increasing, enlarging; (gram.) augmentative.

aumento, m. augmentation, increase; enlargement; access, accession; growth.—pl. **aumentos,** promotion, advancement.

aun, adv. & conj. even; still; AÚN.—**a. cuando,** even if, even though, notwithstanding.

aún, *adv.* yet, still; as yet.—**a. no,** not yet, not as yet.—**más a.,** still more; nay; what is more; furthermore.

aunar. I. *va.* to unite, join; combine; assemble; unify. **II.** *vr.* to be united or confederated; to combine.

aunque, *conj.* though, notwithstanding, even if.

aúpa! *interj.* up, up! (to children).—**aupar,** *va.* to help (a child) get up.

aura, *f.* gentle breeze; (zool.) turkey buzzard; (med.) aura.—**a. popular,** popularity; popular acclamation.

auranciáceo, *a.* aurantiaceous, orangelike.

áureo, *m.* ancient gold coin; weight of four scruples.

áureo, rea, *a.* golden, gilt, gold.—**a. número,** golden number, the lunar cycle.

aureola, auréola, *f.* aureola.

auricalco, *m.* aurichalcum; brass.

aurícula, *f.* (anat.) auricle; (bot.) bear's-ear.

auricular, *a.* auricular.

auriculato, ta, *a.* auriculate.

aurífero, ra; *a.* auriferous, gold-bearing.

auriga, *m.* coachman; (ast.) Auriga, Charioteer.

aurígero, ra, *a.* = AURÍFERO.

aurista, *m.* aurist, specialist.

aurívoro, ra, *a.* avaricious of gold.

aurora, *f.* dawn; first appearance; beverage; roseate hue; (naut.) morning watch gun.—**a. austral,** aurora australis.—**a. boreal,** aurora borealis.

aurragado, da, *a.* badly tilled and cultivated.

auscultación, *f.* (med.) auscultation.

auscultar, *va.* (med.) to auscultate.

ausencia, *f.* absence.

ausentarse, *vr.* to absent one's self.

ausente, *a.* absent.—**ausentismo,** *m.* = ABSENTISMO.

auspicio, *m.* presage, prediction; protection, patronage; auspices.

austeramente, *adv.* austerely.—**austeridad,** *f.* austerity.—**austero, ra,** *a.* austere; astringent, acrid.

austral, *a.* austral.

australiano, na, *n.* & *a.* Australian.

austríaco, ca, *n.* & *a.* Austrian.

austrino, na, *a.* austral.

austro, *m.* south wind; notus.

auténtica, *f.* certificate, attestation.

autenticación, *f.* authentication.

auténticamente, *adv.* authentically.

autenticar, *va.* (*pret.* AUTENTIQUÉ: *subj.* AUTENTIQUE) to authenticate; attest.

autenticidad, *f.* authenticity.

auténtico, ca, *a.* authentic.

autillo, *m.* a particular decree of the Inquisition; (orn.) barn owl.

auto, *m.* judicial decree or sentence; writ, warrant; edict, ordinance.—*pl.* proceedings.—**a. de fe,** auto-da-fé.—**a. sacramental,** allegorical or religious play.—**en autos,** informed.

auto, *m.* (fam.) auto (automobile).

autobiografía, *f.* autobiography.

autobiográfico, ca, *a.* autobiographical.

autobús, *m.* autobus.

autocamión, *m.* autotruck.

autocracia, *f.* autocracy.

autócrata, *m.* autocrat.

autocrático, ca, *a.* autocratical.

autóctono, na, *a.* autochthonous.

autógamo, ma, *a.* (bot.) autogamous.

autogenesis, *f.* autogenesis, spontaneous generation.

autógeno, na, *a.* autogenous.

autografía, *f.* autography.

autográfico, ca, *a.* autographical.

autógrafo, *m.* autograph.

autoinducción, *f.* (elec.) self-induction.

autointoxicación, *f.* autointoxication, autotoxemia.

autómata, *m.* automaton.

automático, ca, *a.* automatic.

automotor, ra, triz, *n.* & *a.* automotor (-tive).

automóvil, *m.* automobile.—**automobilismo,** *m.* automobilism.—**automobilista. I.** *n.* automobilist, motorist, auto user. **II.** *a.* automotive, automobile (u. a.), motor-car (u. a.).

autonomía, *f.* autonomy; home rule; self-determination.—**autonómico, ca,** *a.* autonomic.—**autonomista,** *n.* autonomist.—**autónomo, ma,** *a.* autonomous.

autoplastia, *f.* (surg.) autoplasty.

autopsia, *f.* autopsy.

autópsido, da, *a.* having a metallic lustre.

autor, *m.* author; theatrical manager; (law) perpetrator or abettor of a crime.—**autores clásicos,** classics, classic authors.—**autora,** *f.* authoress.—**autorcillo,** *m.* *dim.* writer of no account.

autoría, *f.* business management of a theater.

autoridad, *f.* authority; ostentation, display.

autoritario, ria. I. *a.* authoritative; overbearing. **II.** *n.* & *a.* authoritarian.

autoritarismo, *m.* authoritarianism.

autoritarista, *n.* & *a.* authoritarian.

autoritativo, va, *a.* authoritative.

autorizable, *a.* that can be authorized.

autorización, *f.* authorization.

autorizadamente, *adv.* authoritatively, with authorization.

autorizado, da. I. *a.* respectable, responsible. **II.** *pp.* of AUTORIZAR.

autorizador, ra, *n.* & *a.* authorizer (-ing).

autorizamiento, *m.* = AUTORIZACIÓN.

autorizar, *va.* (*pret.* AUTORICÉ: *subj.* AUTORICE) to authorize, empower; to attest, legalize; prove by quotation; approve, exalt.

autorretrato, *m.* portrait of one's self.

autorzuelo, *m.* = AUTORCILLO.

autosugestión, *f.* autosuggestion.

autumnal, *a.* autumnal.

auxiliador, ra. I. *n.* & *a.* helper (-ing); abettor (-ing), saver (-ing).

auxiliante, *a.* helping, aiding.

auxiliar, *va.* to aid, help, assist; attend (a dying person).

auxiliar, *a.* auxiliary; helping; (gram.) auxiliary.

auxiliatorio, ria, *a.* (law) auxiliary.

auxilio, *m.* aid, help, assistance.

ava-ava, *f.* (bot.) kava.

avacado, da, *a.* cowlike.

avadarse, *vr.* to become fordable.

avahar. I. *va.* to warm with breath or vapor. **II.** *vn.* to fume, give out vapor.

aval, *m.* (com.) indorsement.

avalentado, da, *a.* bragging, boasting.

avalentonado, da, *n.* & *a.* braggart (-ing).

avalo, *m.* slight movement; earthquake.

avalorar, *va.* to estimate, value, price; to inspirit, encourage.

avaluación, *f.* valuation, appraisement.

avaluar, *va.* to value, appraise, estimate.

avalúo, *m.* valuation, appraisement.

avambrazo, *m.* armlet.

avampiés, *m.* spatterdashes.

avancarga, *f.* muzzle loading.

avance, *m.* advance; attack, assault; (com.) payment in advance; balance-sheet.

avantrén, *m.* limbers of a gun carriage.

avanzada, *f.* outpost, advance guard.

avanzado, da, *a.* advanced.

avanzar. I. *vn.* (*pret.* AVANCÉ: *subj.* AVANCE) to advance; (coll.) vomit; have a balance in one's favor. **II.** *va.* to advance, push forward.

avanzo, *m.* (com.) balance sheet.

avaramente, *adv.* avariciously.

avaricia, *f.* avarice.—**avariciosamente,** *adv.* greedily or covetously.—**avaricioso, sa,** *a.* = AVARIENTO.

avariento, ta, *a.* avaricious, miserly.

avaro, ra, *a.* = AVARIENTO.

avasallar. I. *va.* to subdue, subject, enslave. **II.** *vr.* to become a subject, vassal.

ave, *f.* bird; fowl.—**a. acuática,** water bird.—**a. del Paraíso,** bird of Paradise.—**a. de paso,** bird of passage, migratory bird.—**a. de rapiña,** bird of prey.—**a. lira,** lyre bird.—**a. pasajera** = A. DE PASO.—**a. rapaz** = A. DE RAPIÑA.

avecica, illa, ita, *f. dim.* little bird.

avecinar, *va.* & *vr.* to get near, approach.

avecindamiento, *m.* citizenship.

avecindar, *va.* & *vr.* to domicile (*vr.,*—one's self).

avechucho, *m.* ugly bird; sparrow hawk; ragamuffin.

avejentado, *a.* old in appearance.

avejentar, *va.* & *vr.* to make (or become) old looking.

avejigar, *va.* to produce pimples; blister.

avellana, *f.* filbert, hazelnut.

avellanado, da. I. *a.* nut-brown. **II.** *pp.* of AVELLANARSE.

avellanador, *m.* countersink bit, rose bit; rimer.

avellanal, avellanar, *m.* hazel plantation.

avellanar, *va.* to countersink.

avellanarse, *vr.* to shrivel.

avellaneda, *f.,* **avellanedo,** *m.* = AVELLANAL.

avellanera, *f.* = AVELLANO.

avellanero, ra, *n.* dealer in filberts.

avellanica, *f. dim.* small filbert.

avellano, *m.* hazelnut tree; filberttree.

avemaría, *f.* Hail Mary; rosary bead.—**al a.,** at dusk.—**en un a.,** in the twinkling of an eye.

¡Ave María! *interj.* gracious goodness!

avena, *f.* oats; (poet.) pastoral pipe.

avenáceo, a, *a.* oatlike.

avenado, da, *a.* relating to oats; lunatic.

avenal, *m.* oatfield.

avenamiento, *m.* draining, drainage.

avenar, *va.* to drain.

avenate, *m.* oatmeal gruel; fit of madness.

avenencia, *f.* agreement; compact; bargain; conformity; compromise.

avengo, yo avine. *V.* AVENIR.

aveníceo, cea, *a.* oaten.

avenida, *f.* flood, freshet; avenue; gathering; agreement; approaches, way of access.

avenidor, ra, *n.* mediator.

avenimiento, *m.* convention; agreement.

avenir. I. *va.* (*ind.* AVENGO: *pret.* AVINE: *subj.* AVENGA) to reconcile. **II.** *vr.* to settle differences; agree; compromise.

aventadero, *m.* winnowing place.

aventador, *m.* blowing fan; (arch.) scutcher; (gas) batwing; (agr.) winnower; pitchfork.

aventadura, *f.* (vet.) wind-gall.—**a. de estopa,** (naut.) leak.

aventajadamente, *adv.* advantageously; exceedingly well.

aventajado, da, *a.* advantageous; superior, excelling.

aventajar. I. *va.* to advance, raise, better; prefer; to be above or superior to. **II.** *vr.* (w. **a**) to be ahead (of); to advance, rise; to excel.

aventamiento, *m.* winnowing; fanning.

aventar. I. *va.* (*ind.* AVIENTO: *subj.* AVIENTE) to fan; air; winnow, expel. **II.** *vn.* to breathe hard. **III.** *vr.* to be inflated or puffed up; escape, run away; be tainted.

aventura, *f.* adventure; contingency, chance, event; risk.

aventurado, da, risky; uncertain.

aventurar, *va.* to venture, hazard, risk.

aventureramente, *adv.* adventurously.

aventurero, ra. I. *n.* (gen. *m.*) adventurer; knight-errant; free lance. **II.** *a.* adventurous; undisciplined.

avergonzar, avergoñar. I. *va.* (*ind.* AVERGÜENZO: *pret.* AVERGONCÉ: *subj.* AVERGÜENCE) to shame, abash, confound. **III.** *vr.* to be ashamed.

avería, *f.* aviary, poultry yard; damage; average. —**a. gruesa,** general average.

averiado, da. I. *a.* damaged. **II.** *pp.* of AVERIARSE.

averiarse, *vr.* to be damaged.

averiguable, *a.* investigable.—**averiguación,** *f.* investigation, inquiry, inquest.—**averiguada-**

mente, *adv.* certainly, surely.—**averiguador, ra,** *n.* & *a.* investigator (-ing), inquirer (-ing).

averiguar, *va.* to inquire, investigate, ascertain, find out.

averío, *m.* flock of birds; aviary.

averno, *m.* Avernus.

averroísmo, *m.* Averroism.—**averroísta,** *n.* & *a.* Averroist (-ic).

averrugado, da, *a.* having warts.

averrugarse, *vr.* to develop warts.

aversión, *f.* aversion, dislike, loathing.

Avesta, *m.* Avesta.

avestruz, *m.* (orn.) ostrich.

avetado, da, *a.* veined, streaked.

avezar, *va.* (*pret.* AVECÉ: *subj.* AVECE) to accustom, inure.

aviación, *f.* aviation.

aviado, *m.* (Am.) one supplied with money to work a mine.

aviador, *m.* provider; calking auger; one who supplies money to work mines; (aer.) aviator.

aviar. I. *va.* to equip; lend, advance money to; supply; prepare. **II.** *vr.* to prepare; equip one's self; to go, get on the way.

aviciar, *va.* to give bloom (to plants).

avicultor, ra, *n.* aviculturist.

avicultura, *f.* aviculture.

avidez, *f.* covetousness, avidity.

ávido, da, *a.* eager, anxious, covetous.

aviejarse, *vr.* to grow old.

aviento, *m.* pitchfork. *V.* BIELDO.

aviento, aviente. *V.* AVENTAR.

aviesamente, *adv.* perversely.—**avieso, sa,** *a.* crooked, irregular; mischievous, perverse.

avigorar, *va.* to invigorate; revive.

avilantez, avilanteza, *f.* forwardness, boldness, audacity; insolence.

avillanado, da, *a.* rustic; clownish; mean.

avillanar. I. *va.* to villanize; debase. **II.** *vr.* to become mean; degenerate.

avinado, da, *a.* wine-colored; bibulous.

avinagradamente, *adv.* harshly.—**avinagrado, da. I.** *a.* harsh, crabbed, peevish. **II.** *pp.* of AVINAGRAR.—**avinagrar. I.** *va.* to sour, acidulate. **II.** *vr.* to become sour.

avío, *m.* preparation, provision; money advanced. —*pl.* equipment.—**avíos de pescar,** fishing tackle. **¡al a.!** make ready! hurry up!

avión, *m.* (orn.) martin, martlet; (aer.) airplane. —**a. de cubierta,** ship plane.

avisadamente, *adv.* prudently.—**avisado, da., I.** *a.* cautious, sagacious, clear-sighted.—**mal a.** ill-advised. **II.** *pp.* of AVISAR.

avisador, ra, *n.,* adviser, admonisher; announcer, informer.

avisar, *va.* to inform, announce, give notice of; to warn, advise, counsel, admonish.

aviso, *m.* information, notice, announcement; advertisement; advice, warning; prudence, care, attention; (naut.) advice boat.—**andar,** or **estar, sobre a.,** to be prepared, to be warned and take precautions.

avispa, *f.* wasp.—**avispado, da,** *a.* lively, brisk, clever.—**avispar. I.** *va.* to spur, incite, rouse. **II.** *vr.* to fret, worry.—**avispero,** *m.* wasp's nest; (med.) carbuncle.—**avispón,** *m.* hornet.

avistar. I. *va.* to descry at a distance. **II.** *vr.* to have an interview.

avitar, *va.* (naut.) to bitt (the cable).

avitelado, *a.* vellumlike.

avituallar, *va.* (mil.) to victual.

avivadamente, *adv.* lively, briskly.

avivador, ra. I. *n.* enlivener; hastener. **II.** *m.* rabbet plane; fluting plane; perforated paper for raising silkworms; (arch.) quirk.

avivamiento, *m.* enlivening, quickness.

avivar. I. *va.* to quicken, enliven; sharpen; encourage; hasten; heat, inflame; vivify, revive; heighten (colors); rabbet.—**a. el ojo,** to be watchful. **II.** *vn.* to revive; cheer up.

avizor, *m.* one who watches.—**avizorador, ra,** *n.* & *a.* watcher (-ing).—**avizorar,** *va.* to watch; keep a sharp lookout; spy.

avocación, *f.*, **avocamiento,** *m.* (law) removing a lawsuit to a superior court.

avocar, *va.* (*pret.* AVOQUÉ: *subj.* AVOQUE) (law) to remove to a superior court.

avoceta, *f.* avocet, a wading bird.

avolcanado, da, *a.* volcanic.

avucasta, *f.* widgeon, wild duck.

avugo, *m.* very small early pear.

avuguero, *m.* a kind of pear tree.

avulsión, *f.* (surg.) forcible separation.

avutarda, *f.* bustard, wild turkey.

avutardado, da, *a.* bustardlike.

axial, *a.* axial.

axil. I. *a.* axial; (zool.) axillary. **II.** *m.* axil.

axila, *f.* armpit; (bot.) axilla.

axilar, *a.* axillar; (bot.) axillary.

axinita, *f.* axinite.

axioma, *m.* axiom; maxim.

axiomático, ca, *a.* axiomatic.

axiómetro, *m.* (naut.) axiometer.

axis, *m.* (anat.) axis, second vertebra; (zool.) axis deer.

axo, *m.* a woolen garment worn by the Peruvian Indians.

axoideo, a, *a.* (anat.) axoid, axoidean.

¡ay! *interj.* alas!—**¡a. de mí!** woe is me!

aya, *f.* governess, instructress.

ayate, *m.* cloth made of maguey fiber or sisal.

aye-aye, *m.* (zool.) aye-aye.

ayer, *adv.* yesterday.

¡aymé! *interj.* = ¡AY DE MÍ!

ayo, *m.* tutor or governor; teacher.

ayocote, (Mex.) kidney bean.

ayocuantoto, *m.* a Mexican mountain bird.

ayuda, *f.* help, aid, assistance, support; injection, enema, or clyster; syringe; (naut.) preventer rope.—**a. de cámara,** valet.—**a. de parroquia,** chapel of ease.

ayudador, ra, *n.* & *a.* helper (-ing).

ayudante, *m.* assistant; (mil.) adjutant, aide-de-camp.

ayudar, *va.* to aid, help, assist.

ayuga, *f.* (bot.) ground-pine.

ayunador, ra, ayunante, *n.* faster.

ayunar, *vn.* to fast.

ayunas—en a., fasting before breakfast; without knowledge.—**quedarse en a.,** not to understand, to be left at sea (fig.), to know nothing at all (about something).

ayuno, na. I. *a.* fasting, abstemious; uninformed. **II.** *m.* fast, abstinence.

ayunque, *m.* anvil.

ayuntable, *a.* joinable.

ayuntamiento, *m.* municipal government; sexual intercourse.

ayustar, *va.* (naut.) to splice.

ayuste, *m.* (naut.) splicing; scarf, scarfing.

azabachado, da, *a.* jetlike, jet-colored.

azabache, *m.* jet.—*pl.* jet trinkets.

azábara, *f.* common aloe.

azacán, *m.* water carrier.

azacaya, *f.* (prov.) water pipe.

azache, *a.* inferior (silk), from the outside of the cocoon.

azada, *f.* (agr.) hoe; spade.

azadica, illa, ita, *f.* *dim.* small hoe.

azadón, *m.* hoe.—**a. de peto,** or **de pico,** pickaxe.—**azadonada,** *f.* blow with a hoe.—**azadonar,** *va.* to hoe, to dig with a hoe.—**azadonazo,** *m.* stroke with a hoe.—**azadoncillo,** *m.* *dim.* small hoe.—**azadonero,** *m.* hoer.

azafata, *f.* lady of the queen's wardrobe.

azafate, *m.* low, flat basket; tray.

azafrán, *m.* (bot.) saffron; (naut.) afterpiece (of the rudder).—**azafranado, da. I.** *a.* saffronlike.—**azafranal,** *m.* saffron plantation.—**azafranar,** *va.* to dye with saffron.—**azafranero,** *m.* saffron dealer.

azagador, *m.* path for cattle.

azagaya, *f.* javelin, spear.—**azagayada,** *f.* cast of a javelin.

azahar, *m.* orange or lemon blossom.

azainadamente, *adv.* perfidiously.

azalá, *m.* Mohammedan prayer.

azalea, *f.* (bot.) azalea.

azamboa, *f.* a kind of citron.

azamboero, azamboo, *m.* zamboa tree.

azanahoriate, *m.* preserved carrot.

azanca, *f.* subterranean spring.

azanoria, *f.* carrot.

azar, *m.* unforeseen disaster; accident; disappointment; losing card or throw at dice; impediment; hazard, chance; cushion sides of a billiard pocket.

azarado, da, *a.* & *pp.* of AZARAR, confused, rattled.

azarar. I. *va.* to confuse, stagger, bewilder, rattle. **II.** *vr.* to get rattled, bewildered.

azarbe, *m.* irrigation trench.

azarbeta, *dim.* small irrigation trench.

azarcón, *m.* minium; orange (color).

azaría, *f.* a kind of coral.

azarja, *f.* instrument for winding raw silk.

azarolla, *f.* (bot.) = ACEROLA.

azarollo, *m.* true service tree.

azarosamente, *adv.* unfortunately.

azaroso, sa, *a.* unlucky, unfortunate.

ázcon, *m.* azcona, *f.* dart, javelin.

azenoria, *f.* carrot.

ázimo, ma, *a.* azymous, unleavened.

azimut, *m.* (ast.) azimuth.

azimutal, *a.* relating to the azimuth.

aznacho, aznallo, *m.* Scotch fir; a species of rest harrow.

azoado, da, *a.* nitrogenous.

azoar. I. *va.* to treat with nitrogen; make nitrogenous. **II.** *vr.* to absorb nitrogen; become nitrogenous.

azoato, *m.* nitrate.

ázoe, *m.* (chem.) nitrogen.

azofaifa, *f.* = AZUFAIFA.

azófar, *m.* brass, latten.

azogadamente, *adv.* quickly; restlessly.

azogado, da, *a.* restless; trembling.

azogamiento, *m.* overlaying with quicksilver; restlessness.

azogar. I. *va.* (*pret.* AZOGUÉ: *subj.* AZOGUE) to overlay, coat with quicksilver; to silver (a mirror, etc.); to slake (lime). **II.** *vr.* to be affected by mercury vapors; become agitated.

azogue, *m.* quicksilver; ship carrying quicksilver; market place.—**azoguejo,** *m.* small market place.—**azoguería,** *f.* amalgamation works.—**azoguero,** *m.* dealer in quicksilver; amalgamator.

azoico, ca, *a.* nitric; (geol.) azoic.

azolar, *va.* (*ind.* AZUELO: *subj.* AZUELE) to dress or hew (timber).

azolvar, *va.* to obstruct.—**azolvo,** *m.* obstruction.

azomar, *va.* to bait, madden.

azor, *m.* (orn.) goshawk.

azoramiento, *m.* confusion.—**azorar. I.** *va.* to terrify; confound; excite; prompt. **II.** *vr.* to become restless.

azorrado, da, *a.* drowsy, sleepy; (naut.) waterlogged.—**azorramiento,** *m.* heaviness of the head.—**azorrarse,** *vr.* to be drowsy from heaviness.

azotacalles, *m.* street lounger, idler.

azotado. I. *n.* criminal publicly whipped; penitent. **II.** *a.* variegated. **III.** *pp.* of AZOTAR.

azotador, ra, *n.* & *a.* whipper (-ing).

azotaina, *f.* drubbing, flogging, spanking.

azotalengua, *f.* goose grass.

azotamiento, *m.* whipping, flogging.

azotar, *va.* to whip; horsewhip; flagellate; strike repeatedly; scourge.

azotazo, *m.* *aug.* severe lash or spanking.

azote, *m.* whip; lash with a whip; spanking; scourge.—**el a. de Dios,** the Scourge of God (Attila).

azotea, *f.* flat roof.

azótico, *a.* (chem.) nitric.

azotina, *f.* = AZOTAINA.

azteca, *n.* & *a.* Aztec.

---

azúcar, *m.* sugar.—**a. blanco,** refined sugar (app. to the highest quality).—**a. candle,** or **candi,** rock candy.—**a. de nor** = A. BLANCO.—**a. de leche,** sugar of milk.—**a. de pilón,** loaf sugar.—**a. de plomo,** calcined sugar of lead.—**a. de Saturno,** sal Saturni.—**a. moscobado,** muscovado.—**a. moreno,** brown sugar.—**a. negro,** or **prieto,** coarse brown sugar.—**a. quebrado,** brown sugar. —**a. reflao** = A. BLANCO.—**a. terciado,** brown sugar.—**a. y canela,** sorrel gray.

azucarado, da. I. *a.* sugared; sugary; sugar-coated: affable, pleasing. **II.** *pp.* of AZUCARAR. **III.** *m.* cosmetic for ladies.

azucarar, *va.* to sugar; sweeten; soften; coat or ice with sugar.

azucarera, *f.* sugar bowl.

azucarería, *f.* retail sugar shop.

azucarero. I. *m.* sugar master; sugar bowl; sugar producer or dealer; confectioner. **II.** *a.* sugar (u. a.)

azucarillo, *m.* sweetmeat of egg white, sugar, and a flavor.

azucena, *f.* white lily.

azuche, *m.* pile shoe, pile ferrule.

azud, azuda, *f.* dam with a sluice; irrigation water wheel.

azuela, *f.* adze.—**a. curva,** hollow adze.—**a. de construcción,** shipwright's adze.

azufaifa, *f.* jujube or jujubes.

azufaifo, azufeifo, *m.* jujube tree.

azufrado, da. I. *a.* fumigated with sulphur; sulphureous; sulphur-hued. **II.** *pp.* of AZUFRAR.

azufrador, *m.* machine for drying linen; instrument for sulphuring vines.

azufral, *m.* = AZUFRERA.

azufrar, *va.* to bleach; to sulphur.

azufre, *m.* sulphur; brimstone.—**azufrera,** *f.* sulphur mine.—**azufrón,** *m.* pyrites powder.— **azufroso, sa,** *a.* sulphureous.

azul, *n.* & *a.* blue.—**a. celeste,** sky-blue.—**a. de mar,** or **marino,** navy blue.—**a. de Prusia,** Prussian blue.—**a. de ultramar,** or **ultramarino,** ultramarine.—**a. turquí,** indigo.

azulado, da, *a.* azure, bluish.—**azulaque,** *m.* = ZULAQUE.—**azular,** *va.* to dye or color blue.—**azular,** *vn.* to have a bluish cast.—**azulejado, da,** *a.* tiled.—**azulejo,** *m.* little bluebird; glazed tile; (bot.) blue-bottle.—**azulenco, ca,** *a.* = AZULADO. —**azulete,** *m.* blue lining.—**azulino, na,** *a.* bluish.

azumar, *va.* to dye (the hair).

azumbrado, da, *a.* measured by AZUMBRES; (coll.) tipsy.

azumbre, *f.* a liquid measure (about 2 liters).

azur, *a.* (her.) azure.

azurita, *f.* (min.) azurite.

azutero, *m.* sluice master.

azuzador, ra, *n.* & *a.* instigator (-ing).

azuzar, *va.* (*pret.* AZUCÉ: *subj.* AZUCE) to urge, set, sick (dogs); incite.

B

baba, *f.* drivel, slaver, spittle.

bababuí, *m.* mocking bird.

babada, *f.* = BABILLA.

babadero, babador, *m.* bib, chin cloth.

babaza, *f.* slime; limax, slug.

babazorro, *m.* clown, ill-bred man.

babear, *vn.* to drivel; slaver; court, woo with excessive demonstrations.

Babel, *f.* Babel, bedlam.

babeo, *m.* driveling, slavering.

babera, *f.* beaver of a helmet; bib.

babero, *m.* = BABADOR.

baberol, *m.* beaver. *V.* BABERA.

Babia, *f.*—**estar en B.,** to be absent-minded, or absorbed in other thoughts.

babieca, *m.* ignorant, stupid fellow; idiot.

babilla, *f.* muscles about the flank of a horse.

Babilonia, *f.* crowd, uproar, confusion, bedlam.

babilónico, ca, ‘or **onio, nia,** *a.* Babylonian.

babirusa, *f.* (zool.) babiroussa.

bable, *m.* Austrian dialect.

babor, *m.* (naut.) port, larboard.—**a b. todo,** head a-port.—**de b. a estribor,** athwart ship.

babosa, *f.* slug, limax; young onion.

babosear, *va.* to drivel, slaver.

babosilla, *f. dim.* small slug.

babosillo, illa, uelo, uela, *a. dim.* somewhat driveling or slavering; spoony.

baboso, sa, *a.* drivelling, slavering, silly; spoony, over-affectionate.

babucha, *f.* slipper, baboosh.

baca, *f.* top of a stagecoach; leather cover for a stagecoach.

bacalao *or* **bacallao,** *m.* codfish.

bacanales, *f. pl.* Bacchanalia.

bacante, *f.* bacchante.

bácara, bácaris, *f.* great fleabane.

bacelar, *m.* arbor with grapevines.

bacera, *f.* (vet.) swelling of the belly.

baceta, *f.* stock (card playing).

bacía, *f.* metal basin, washpot; shaving dish.

báciga, *f.* game played with three cards.

bacilar, *a.* (min.) of coarse fiber; (biol.) bacillar, bacillary.

bacilo, *m.* bacillus.

bacillar, *m.* new vineyard.

bacín, *m.* high chamber pot; despicable man.

bacina, *f.* poor box. *V.* BACÍA.

bacinada, *f.* filth thrown from a close-stool; despicable action.

bacinejo, *m. dim.* small chamber pot.

bacinero, ra, *n.* person who carries about the poor box in ʃ church.

bacineta, *f.* small poor box; pan (of a gun-lock).

bacinete, *m.* headpiece worn by warriors; cuirassier; (anat.) pelvis.

bacinica, *f.* small chamber pot.

bacinilla, *f.* chamber pot; alms basin.

baconiano, na, *a.* Baconian.

bacteria, *f.* bacterium.—**bacteriano, na,** *a.* bacterial.

bacteriológico, ca, *a.* bacteriological.

bacteriólogo, ga, *n.* bacteriologist.

báctris, *m.* bactris, a South-American palm.

báculo, *m.* walking stick, staff; support, relief, aid.—**b. pastoral,** bishop's crosier.

bache, *m.* deep hole, rut; sweating place for sheep.

bachiller, ra. I. *n.* bachelor (degree); babbler, prater. **II.** *a.* garrulous, loquacious.

bachilleramiento, *m.* conferring or obtaining the degree of bachelor.

bachillerar. I. *va.* to confer the degree of bachelor on. **II.** *vr.* to be graduated as a bachelor.

bachillerato, *m.* baccalaureate.

bachillerear, *vn.* to babble, prattle.

bachillerejo, ja, *n. dim.* talkative little person.

bachillería, *f.* babble, prattle.

badajada, *f.* stroke of a clapper; idle talk.

badajazo, *m. aug.* large clapper.

badajear, *vn.* to talk nonsense.

badajo, *m.* clapper of a bell; idle talker.

badajuelo, m. *dim.* small clapper.

badal, *m.* muzzle; shoulder and ribs of butcher's meat; (surg.) mouth opener.

badán, *m.* trunk of a body.

badana, *f.* dressed sheepskin.

badazas, *f. pl.* (naut.) keys of the bonnets.

badea, *f.* watermelon; insipid muskmelon; dull, insipid fellow.

badén, *m.* channel made by rainfall; catchwater conduit.

badiana, *f.* Indian aniseed, badiana.

badil, m., badila, *f.* fire shovel.

badina, *f.* puddle.

badomía, *f.* nonsense, absurdity.

badulacada, *f.* (Peru) = CALAVERADA.

badulaque, *m.* cosmetic; ragout of stewed livers; unreliable or good-for-nothing person.

baga, *f.* rope to tie burdens on the back of beasts; little head of flax.

---

bagaje, *m.* beast of burden; baggage of an army; horse appropriated by an army, or given to an officer.—**bagajero,** *m.* driver of military baggage.
bagar, *m.* to yield the seed (s. o. flax).
bagasa, *f.* prostitute, harlot.
bagatela, *f.* bagatelle, trifle.
bagazo, *m.* bagasse; oil cake.
bagre, *m.* name of a Spanish-American fish.
baguío, *m.* (Philip.) hurricane.
¡bah! *interj.* bah!
baharí, *m.* sparrow hawk.
bahía, *f.* bay, harbor.
bahorrina, *f.* slops; rabble.
bahuno, na, *a.* base, vile. *V.* BAJUNO.
baila, *f.* (icht.) sea trout.
bailable. I. *a.* danceable. **II.** *m.* ballet.
bailadero, *m.* public dancing place.
bailador, ra, *n.* dancer.
bailar, *vn.* to dance; spin.
bailarín, na, *n.* dancer; caperer.
baile, *m.* dance, ballet, ball; rout; bailiff.—**b. casero,** family, informal dance.—**b. de figuras,** square dance.—**b. de máscaras,** masquerade.—**b. de San Vito,** St. Vitus' dance.—**b. de trajes,** fancy-dress ball.—**b. serio,** formal dance.
bailete, *m.* short ballet.
bailía, *f.* **bailiazgo,** *m.* bailiwick.
bailiaje, *m.* commandery in the order of Malta.
bailío, *m.* knight commander of Malta.
bailotear, *vn.* (coll.) to dance frequently.
bailoteo, *m.* ungraceful dancing.
baivel, *m.* bevel with a curved leg.
bajá, *m.* pasha, bashaw.
baja, *f.* fall of price; casualty; vacancy.
bajada, *f.* descent; slope; inclination of an arch.
bajalato, *m.* office of a pasha.
bajamar, *f.* low water, low tide.
bajamente, *adv.* basely, meanly.
bajar. I. *vn.* to descend, come or go down; fall; drop, lessen, diminish. **II.** *va.* to lower, reduce; bring or take down; let down; humble. **III.** *vr.* to crouch, grovel; to alight, get down, dismount.
bajel, *m.* (naut.) ship, boat, vessel.
bajelero, *m.* owner or master of a vessel.
bajero, ra, *a.* lower, under (as, *sábana bajera,* under sheet).
bajete, *m.* *dim.* short person; (mus.) barytone; counterpoint exercise.
bajeza, *f.* meanness; lowliness; low action.
bajial, *m.* marsh.
bajillo, *m.* stand cask for wine.
bajío, *m.* shoal, sand bank, flat; obstacle.
bajista, *m.* (com.) bear (in stocks).
bajo. I. *adv.* underneath, below. **II.** *prep.* under.—**b. mano,** underhandedly, secretly. **III.** *m.* (mus.) bass (voice, score, singer, player and instrument); shoal; sand bank.—*pl.* under petticoats; hoofs.
bajo, ja, *a.* low; shallow; short; abject, despicable; common, humble; dull, faint; coarse, vulgar; downcast.—**b. relieve,** bas-relief.—**por lo b.,** on the sly, unobservedly.
bajoca, *f.* string bean; dead silkworm.
bajón, *m.* (mus.) bassoon; bassoon player.
bajoncillo, *m.* counter bass.
bajonista, *m.* bassoon player.
bajorrelieve, *m.* bas-relief.
bajovientre, *m.* hypogastrium.
bajuno, na, *a.* vile, low, contemptible.
bala, *f.* ball, bullet, shot; bale; wax ball; printer's inking ball.—**b. de cadena,** or **encadenada,** chain shot.—**b. enramada,** bar shot.—**b. fría,** spent bullet.—**b. perdida,** stray bullet.—**b. rasa,** solid cannonball.—**b. roja,** red-hot incendiary ball.
balada, *f.* ballad.
baladí, *a.* frivolous, trivial.
balador, ra, *n.* bleating animal.
baladrar, *vn.* to cry out, shout.
baladre, *m.* (bot.) rosebay.
baladrero, ra, *n.* shouter.—**baladro,** *m.* shout, outcry.

baladrón, na, *n.* boaster, bragger, bully.
baladronada, *f.* boast, bravado; rhodomontade.
baladronear, *vn.* to boast, brag, bully.
balagar, *m.* haystack, hayrick.—**bálago,** *m.* grain stalk, straw; soap ball.—**balaguero,** *m.* rick of straw.
balaj, *m.* balass, spinel ruby.
balance, *m.* oscillation, rolling, rocking, swinging; equilibrium; (com.) balancing; balance; balance sheet; (Cuba) rocking chair; (aer.) rolling.
balancear. I. *va.* to balance. **II.** *vn.* & *vr.* to roll, rock; to hesitate, waver.
balanceo, *m.* rocking, rolling; wabbling.
balancero, *m. V.* BALANZARIO.
balancín, *m.* splinter bar, swing bar; whippletree, singletree, whiffletree; (mech.) walking beam, balancebeam; minting mill; poy, a ropedancer's pole.—**balancines,** (naut.) lifts.—**balancines de la brújula,** (naut.) brass rings of the compass.
balandra, *f.* (naut.) bilander; sloop.
balandrán, *m.* cassock.
balandro, *m.* (Cuba) fishing smack.
balanitis, *f.* balanitis.
bálano, *m.* (anat.) balanus.
balante, *a.* (poet.) bleating.
balanza, *f.* scale; balance; comparative estimate, judgment.—**b. de comercio,** balance of trade.
balanzario, *m.* weighmaster (in the mint).
balanzon, *m.* (jewel.) cleaning pan.
balar, *vn.* to bleat.—**b. por,** to crave.
balastar, *va.* to ballast.
balasto, *m.* ballast.
balata, *f.* dancing song; ballad; (bot.) balata.
balate, *m.* terrace; border of a trench; slug.
balausta, -tra, *f.* varieties of pomegranate.
balaustrada, *f.* balustrade.
balaustrado, da, tral, *a.* balustered.
balaústre, *m.* baluster.
balaustrería, *f.* = BALAUSTRADA.
balay, *m.* wicker basket.
balazo, *m.* shot; bullet wound.
balbucear, *va.* & *vn.* to babble.—**balbucencia,** *f.* babbling.—**balbuciente,** *a.* babbling.
balbucir, *va.* & *vn.* = BALBUCEAR.
balcánico, ca, *n.* & *a.* Balkan.
balcón, *m.* balcony; porch.—**balconaje,** *m.,* **balconería,** *f.* range of balconies.
balconcillo, *m. dim.* small balcony.
balda, *f.* trifle.
baldadura, *f.,* **baldamiento,** *m.* disability.
baldaquín, baldaquino, *m.* canopy, daïs.
baldar, *va.* to cripple; trump; obstruct.
balde, *m.* bucket.
balde.—de b., gratis; idle; in vain.—**en b.,** in vain, with no result.
baldear, *vn.* (naut.) to wash (the deck).
baldeo, *m.* (naut.) washing the deck.
baldés, *m.* soft dressed skin for gloves, etc.
baldíamente, *adv.* vainly.
baldío, día, *a.* untilled, uncultivated; public (lands); idle, lazy; vagabond.—*m. pl.* public lands; commons.
baldón, *m.* affront, insult.
baldonar, baldonear, *va.* to insult, affront.
baldosa, *f.* ancient string instrument; paving tile; flat paving stone, flag.—**baldosado,** *m.* tile pavement.—**baldosín,** *m.* small square tile.
balduque, *m.* narrow red tape.
baleárico, ca; baleario, ia, *a.* Balearic.
baleo, *m.* round mat.
balería, *f.* (arti.) pile of balls or shot.
balero, *m.* ball mold.
baleta, *f. dim.* small bale of goods.
balido, *m.* bleating, bleat.
balín, *m.* small bullet.
balines, *m. pl.* mold shot, buckshot.
balista, *f.* ballista.
balística, *f.* (arti.) ballistics.
balitadera, *f.* call, a reed instrument for calling fawns.
baliza, *f.* buoy.

---

balneario, ria. I. *a.* pertaining to baths. **II.** *m.* bathing resort; watering place.

balompié, *m.* football.

balón, *m.* large football; game of football; large bale; bale of paper (24 reams); (aut.) balloon tire.

balota, *f.* ballot.

balotada, *f.* balotade, leap of a horse.

balotar, *vn.* to ballot.

balsa, *f.* pool; pond; (naut.) raft; half a butt of wine.

balsadera, *f.,* **balsadero,** *m.* ferry.

balsamera, *f.* flask for balsam.

balsamerita, *f.* small flask for balsam.

balsámico, ca, *a.* balsamic, balmy.

balsamina, *f.* (bot.) balsam apple.

balsamita mayor, (bot.) = ATANASIA.—**b. menor,** (bot.) maudlin, tansy.

bálsamo, *m.* balsam, balm; (med.) purest part of the blood.—**b. de copaiba,** balsam of copaiba.—**b. de calaba,** calaba balsam.—**b. de Judea,** or **de la Meca,** balsam of Mecca.—**b. del Canadá,** balsam of fir, Canada balsam.—**b. del Perú,** balsam of Peru.—**b. de María**= B. DE CALABA.—**b. de Tolú,** balsam of Tolu.

balsar, *m.* marshy ground with brambles.

balsear, *va.* to ferry on rafts.

balsero, ra, *n.* ferryman (-woman).

balso, *m.* rope with loops for raising men or goods on board ship; sling; a South-American tree having a very light wood, used for rafts.

balsopeto, *m.* large pouch carried near the breast; bosom.

bálteo, *m.* officer's belt.

báltico, ca, *a.* Baltic.

baluarte, *m.* bastion; bulwark; defence.

balumba, *f.* bulk of things put together.

balumbo, balume, *m.* bulky thing.

ballena, *f.* whale; train oil; whalebone; (**B-,** ast.) Whale, Cetus.

ballenato, *m.* young whale.

ballener, *m.* an ancient vessel.

ballesta, *f.* crossbow; ballista; spring (of a carriage).—**ballestada,** *f.* shot from a crossbow.

ballestazo, *m.* blow from a crossbow.

ballesteador, *m.* crossbowman, arbalister.

ballestear, *va.* to shoot with a crossbow.

ballestera, *f.* loopholes for crossbows.

ballestería, *f.* archery; number of crossbows or bowmen; armory for crossbows.

ballestero, *m.* archer, arbalister, crossbowman; crossbow maker; king's armorer; mace bearer; king's porter.

ballestilla, *f.* crossbow; small whiffletree; fleam; cross-staff; (naut.) forestaff.

ballestón, *m. aug.* large crossbow, arbalet.

ballestrinque, *m.* (naut.) clove hitch.

ballico, *m.* (bot.) rye grass.

ballueca, *f.* wild oats.

bambalear, *vn.* = BAMBOLEAR.

bambalina, *f.* fly in theatrical scenery.

bambarria, *m.* lucky stroke at billiards; fool, idiot.

bambochada, *f.* painting representing a spree.

bamboche, *n.* (coll.) plump, red-faced person.

bambolear, *vn. & vr.,* to swing, sway.

bamboleo, bamboneo, *m.* swinging, sway.

bambolla, *f.* (coll.) boast, humbug, sham.

bambú, bambuc, *m.* bamboo.

bambuco, *m.* a Colombian popular air.

banana, *f.,* **banano,** *m.* banana. *V.* CAMBUR.

banas, *f. pl.* (Mex.) matrimonial banns.

banasta, *f.* large basket.—**banastero,** *m.* basket maker or dealer.—**banasto,** *m.* large round basket.

banca, *f.* bench; stand; washing box; Philippine canoe; name of a card game; (com.) banking.

bancada, *f.* bench; portion of masonry.

bancal, *m.* oblong orchard or garden plot; terrace; bench cover.

bancalero, *m.* weaver of bench covers.

bancario, ria, *a.* banking; financial.

bancarrota, *f.* bankruptcy; failure.—**hacer b.,** to fail.

banco, *m.* form, bench; settee; pew; (mech.) bed, table, horse; planing bench; bench for rowers; cheeks (of the bit); pedestal; school of fish, shoal; (com.) bank.—**b. de ahorros,** savings bank. **b. de emisión,** bank of issue.—**b. de liquidación,** clearing-house.—**b. del tundidor,** shearing board.

banda, *f.* sash; scarf; ribbon; band, gang; party; crew; brass band; covey; bank, border, edge; side of a ship; felloe (of wheel); cushion (of a billiard table).

bandada, *f.* cover; flock of birds.

bandaje, *m.* (aut.) tire.

bandarria, *f.* (naut.) iron maul.

bandazo, *m.* (naut.) breaking of a wave on the side of a ship.

bandeado, da, *a.* striped.

bandear. I. *va.* to conduct. **II.** *vn.* to band. **III.** *vr.* to shift for one's self.

bandeja, *f.* tray.

bandera, *f.* flag, banner; colors; infantry.—**b. blanca, b. de paz,** white flag, flag of truce.—**b. de popa,** (naut.) ensign.—**b. de proa,** (naut.) jack.—**a,** or **con, banderas desplegadas,** with flying colors; openly, in broad daylight (fig.); freely.

bandereta, *f. dim.* banneret, small flag.—*pl.* (mil.) camp colors.

bandería, *f.* band, faction.

banderica, illa, *dim.* banneret, small flag.

banderilla, *f.* banderilla, a small dart with a bannerol for baiting bulls.—**poner a uno una b.,** to taunt or provoke one.

banderillear, *va.* to thrust banderillas in (a bull).

banderillero, *m.* banderillero, banderilla man.

banderín, *m.* camp colors; flag; railway signal; recruiting post.

banderizar, *va.* = ABANDERIZAR.

banderizo, za, *a.* that follows (a faction); fiery, excitable.

banderola, *f.* bannerol; camp colors; streamer, pennant; signal flag.

bandido, da, *n.* bandit.

bandín, *m.* (naut.) seat in a row galley.

bando, *m.* proclamation, edict; faction, party.

bandola, *f.* mandolin; (naut.) jury mast.

bandolera, *f.* bandoleer; bandit's wife; woman bandit.

bandolerismo, *m.* banditry, brigandage.

bandolero, *m.* highwayman, robber.

bandolín, *m.* = BANDOLA.

bandolina, *f.* bandoline.

bandolón, *m.* mandola.

bandullo, *m.* (vulg.) belly; the bowels.

bandurria, *f.* bandurria, bandore.

bánova, *f.* bedquilt, bedcover.

banquera, *f.* (prov.) open beehouse; frame for beehives.

banquero, ra, *n.* banker.

banqueta, *f.* three-legged stool; footstool; (mil.) banquette or footbank; sidewalk.—**b. de calafate,** (naut.) calking stool.—**b. de cureña,** (arti.) gun-carriage bed.

banquete, *m.* banquet.

banquetear, *vn.* to banquet, to feast.

banquillo, *m. dim.* little stool; prisoner's or defendant's seat.

banquito, *m. dim.* stool, footstool.

banzo, *m.* cheek of an embroidering frame.

bañadera, *f.* (naut.) skeet; bathtub.

bañadero, *m.* puddle; bathing place.

bañado. I. *m.* BACÍN. **II.** *pp.* of BAÑAR.

bañador, ra, *n.* one who bathes; (*m.*) dipping tub for candle makers.

bañar, *va.* to bathe, wash, lave; to water; dip; coat, apply a coating or layer to.

bañera, *f.* bathtub.

bañero, ra, *n.* bath owner; bath keeper.

bañil, *m.* pool in which cattle bathe.

bañista, *m.* bather.

baño, *m.* bath; bathing; bathing place; bathtub; bathroom; foot tub; coat, coating (of paint, etc.); (chem.) bath.—**b. de María,** water bath; double boiler.

bañueio, *m. dim.* little bath.

bao, *m.* (naut.) beam, cross timber.

baobab, *m.* (bot.) baobab.

baptisterio, *m.* baptistery.

baque, *m.* blow in falling; thud.

baqueta, *f.* ramrod; switch used in breaking in young horses.—*pl.* drumsticks; gantlet.—**a b., a la b.,** harshly, despotically, without consideration.

baquetazo, *m.* blow with a ramrod.

baqueteado, da. I. *a.* inured. **II.** *pp.* of BAQUETEAR.

baquetear, *va.* to inflict the punishment of the gantlet on; to vex.

baquía, *f.* familiarity with a region (app. sp. to roads, forests, etc.); skill.

baquiano, na. I. *n.* guide. **II.** *a.* skilful.

báquico, ca, *a.* Bacchic.

baquio, *m.* (poet.) a metrical foot.

baraja, *f.* pack of cards; game of cards.

barajadura, *f.* shuffling of cards; dispute.

barajar, *va.* to shuffle (the cards); to jumble together; entangle; to stop; to trick out of.

baranda, *f.* railing; banister; cushion (of a billiard table).—**barandado, barandaje,** *m.* balustrade.—**barandal,** *m.* upper and under piece of a balustrade; railing.—**barandilla,** *f. dim.* balustrade, railing.

barangay, *m.* barangay, balangay.

barangayán, *m.* = GUBÁN.

barata, *f.* barter; reduction sale; bargain.

baratador, ra, *n.* barterer.

baratar, *va.* to barter, traffic.

baratear, *va.* to sell cheap, to sell under price.

baratería, *f.* barratry, fraud, deception.

baratero, ra, *n.* one who exacts money from winning gamblers; one who sells cheap; haggler.

baratijas, *f. pl.* trifles, trinkets, notions.

baratillero, ra, *n.* peddler; seller of second-hand goods or articles.

baratillo, *m.* second-hand shop; cheap John; bargain counter; heap of trifling articles.

baratista, *n.* barterer, trafficker.

barato, ta. I. *a.* cheap.—**dar de b.,** to grant for the sake of argument.—**de b.,** gratis.—**lo b. es,** or **siempre es, caro,** cheap things are always dear. **II.** *m.* reduction sale; bargain sale; money given by winning gamblers to the bystanders. **III.** **(-o)** *adv.* cheaply.

báratro, *m.* (poet.) hell; abyss.

baratura, *f.* cheapness.

baraúnda, *f.* noise, hurly-burly, confusion.

barba, *f.* chin; beard; whiskers; wattle; first swarm of bees; top of beehive; player who acts old men's parts.—*pl.* head of a comet; slender roots; fibers; rough edges of paper; vanes of a quill. **—b. a b.,** face to face.—**b. cabruna,** (bot.) yellow goat's beard.—**b. cerrada,** heavy, thick beard.— **b. de Aarón,** (bot.) Aaron's beard.—**b. de ballena,** whalebone.—**en sus barbas,** to his face.—**por b.,** a head, apiece.—**tener pocas barbas,** to be young or inexperienced.

barbacana, *f.* (mil.) barbican; churchyard wall.

barbacoa, *f.* (Am.) barbecue.

barbada, *f.* jaw of a horse; bridle curb; dab, small flat fish.

barbadamente, *adv.* strongly, vigorously.

barbado, *m.* full-grown man; vine or tree transplanted; shoot; sucker.

barbado, da, *a.* bearded; barbed, barbated.

barbaja, *f.* (bot.) cut-leaved viper's grass.—*pl.* (agr.) first roots.

barbar, *vn.* to grow a beard; to rear bees; to strike root.

bárbaramente, *adv.* barbarously, savagely; atrociously; rudely, coarsely.

barbáricamente, *adv.* like barbarians.

barbárico, ca, *a.* barbarous, barbarian.

barbaridad, *f.* barbarity, barbarous deed, atrocity; cruelty; rashness; rudeness; wild statement or action; nonsense; blunder.

barbarie, *f.* barbarousness, barbary; barbarians; incivility, rusticity; cruelty.

barbarismo, *m.* barbarism; barbarousness; barbarous deed; barbarians.

barbarizar. I. *va.* (pret. BARBARICÉ: *subj.* BARBARICE) to barbarize. **II.** *vn.* to make wild statements.

bárbaro, ra. I. *a.* barbarous; barbarian; rude, unpolished. **II.** *n.* barbarian.

barbarote, *m. aug.* great barbarian.

barbato, ta, *a.* having the tail before the head (s. o. comets).

barbear, *va.* to reach with the chin; to be almost as high as; to fell (cattle) by twisting the neck; to shave.

barbechar, *va.* to fallow.—**barbechera,** *f.* series of plowings; fallowing season; plowing.

barbecho, *m.* fallow.

barbera, *f.* barber's wife.—**barbería,** *f.* barber's shop or trade.—**barberil,** *a.* pertaining to a barber; barberlike.

barbero, *m.* barber; mutton fish.

barbeta, *f.* (naut.) rackline, gasket; (arti.) barbette.—**a b.,** en barbette.

barbibermejo, ja, *a.* red-bearded.

barbiblanco, ca, *a.* gray or white-bearded.

barbicacho, *m.* ribbon tied under the chin.

barbicano, na, *a.* gray-bearded.

barbiespeso, sa, *a.* having a thick beard.

barbihecho, cha, *a.* fresh-shaved.

barbilampiño, ña, *a.* smooth-faced, beardless.

barbilindo, barbilucio, *a.* small, good looking (rather, pretty) and effeminate; dandy.

barbilla, *f.* point of the chin; (carp.) rabbet; (vet.) tumor under the tongue.

barbillera, *f.* tuft of tow; chin bandage.

barbinegro, gra, *a.* black-bearded.

barbiponiente, *a.* having the beard growing; apprenticed.

barbiquejo, *m.* bonnet string; guard ribbon for a hat; curb chain; (naut.) bobstay.

barbirrubio, bia, *a.* blond-bearded.

barbirrucio, cia, *a.* gray-bearded.

barbitaheño, ña, *a.* having a rough beard.

barbiteñido, da, *a.* having a dyed beard.

barbo, *m.* (zool.) barbel, a river fish.

barbón, *m.* long-bearded man; Carthusian lay brother; buck.

barboquejo, *m.* chin strap; hat guard.

barbotar, *vn.* to mumble, mutter.

barbote, *m.* beaver of a helmet.

barbudo, da. I. *a.* having a long beard. **II.** *m.* vine transplanted with the roots.

barbulla, *f.* loud prattling noise.

barbullar, *vn.* to talk loud and fast.

barbullón, na, *a.* loud, fast prattler.

barca, *f.* (naut.) boat, barge, bark.—**b. chata, b. de pasaje,** ferryboat.

barcada, *f.* passage in a ferryboat; boatload.

barcaje, *m.* ferriage.

barcal, *m.* wooden vessel.

barcarola, *f.* barcarolle.

barcaza, *f.* barge, lighter; privilege of loading and unloading.

barcelonés, sa, *a.* from, or of, Barcelona.

barceno, na, *a.* = BARCINO.

barceo, *m.* dry bass or sedge for mats, ropes, etc.

barcia, *f.* chaff.

barcina, *f.* grass net; large truss of straw.

barcinar, *va.* to load with sheaves.

barcino, na, *a.* ruddy, auburn.

barco, *m.* boat, barge, vessel, ship; bottom.

barcolongo, barcoluengo, *m.* oblong boat with a round bow.

barcón, barcote, *m. aug.* large boat.

barchilón, *m.* hospital nurse.

barda, *f.* bard, horse armor; thatch; reed.

bardado, da, *a.* barded, caparisoned.

bárdago, *m.* (naut.) pendant.

bardaguera, *f.* willow.

bardal, *m.* thatched wall or fence.

bardana, *f.* burdock.

bardar, *va.* to thatch (fences).

bardilla, *f. dim.* small brushwood.

bardiota, *m.* Byzantine soldier.

bardo, *m.* bard, poet.

bardoma, *f.* filth, mud.

bardomera, *f.* brush carried off by a stream.

bario, *m.* (chem.) barium.

barita, *f.* (chem.) baryta or barytes.

baritel, *m.* = MALACATE.

baritina, *f.* barium sulphate, heavy spar.

baríteno, m. (mus.) barytone.

barjuleta, *f.* knapsack, haversack; tool bag.

barloar, *va., vn. & vr.* (naut.) to grapple for the purpose of boarding; ABARLOAR.

barloas, *f. pl.* (naut.) relieving tackles.

barloventear, *vn.* (naut.) to ply to windward; beat about.

barlovento, *m.* (naut.) windward.—**ganar el b.,** to get to windward.

barnacla, *m.* barnacle, sea goose.

barniz, *m.* varnish; cosmetic; printer's ink.—**b. del Japón,** japan.

barnizador, ra, *n. & a.* varnisher (-ing).

barnizar, *va.* (*pret.* BARNICÉ: *subj.* BARNICE) to varnish.

barógrafo, *m.* barograph.

barología, *f.* barology.

barométrico, ca, *a.* barometric.

barómetro, *m.* barometer.

barometrógrafo, *m.* barometrograph.

barón, *m.* baron.—**barones del timón,** (naut.) rudder pendants and chains.—**baronesa,** *f.* baroness.—**baronía,** *f.* barony; baronage.

baroscopio, *m.* baroscope.

barotermógrafo, barotermómetro, *m.* barothermograph.

baroto, *m.* small boat in the Philippines.

barquear, *vn.* to go about in a boat.

barquero, *m.* bargeman, boatman, ferryman.

barqueta, *f.,* **barquete,** *m.,* **barquichuelo,** *m. dim.* small barge or boat.

barquilla, *f.* conical mold for wafers; little boat, wherry; (aer.) car, basket (of a dirigible).—**b. de la corredera,** (naut.) the log.

barquillero, ra. I. *n.* maker or seller of rolled wafers. **II.** *m.* wafer mold.

barquillo, *m.* cockboat; thin rolled wafer.

barquin, *m.,* **barquinera,** *f.* large bellows.

barquinazo, *m.* = BATACAZO.

barquinero, *m.* bellows maker.

barquino, *m.* wine bag. *V.* ODRE.

barra, *f.* (mech., eng.) bar, beam, rod; strip; sandbar; gross-spun thread in cloth; mold for small candles; chase bar; shaft of a carriage; thill; (her.) third part of a shield; a country game in Spain; railing in a court room; gallery (in a parliamentary hall, etc.); (naut.) spar.—*pl.* mining shares; stripes, bars (on a shield, etc.).—**b. colectora,** (elec.) busbar.—**b. de la excéntrica,** (st. eng.) eccentric rod.—**en barra,** or **en barras,** in bars, bar (u. a.).

Barrabás, *m.* devil (fig.).—**barrabasada,** *f.* serious mischief; bold action.

barraca, *f.* barrack, cabin, hut.

barraco, *m.* boar; spume of fermenting must; ancient ship gun; snag.

barrado, da. I. *a.* corded; ribbed; stripped; (her.) barred. **II.** *pp.* of BARRAR.

barragán, *m.* barracan, camlet; waterproof woollen stuff; waterproof overcoat.

barragana, *f.* concubine; morganatic wife.

barraganería, *f.* concubinage.

barraganete, *m.* (naut.) top-timber, futtock.

barral, *m.* demijohn containing about 25 pints.

barranca, *f.,* **barrancal,** *m.* deep hollow; gorge, ravine; cliff; precipice.

barranco, *m.* BARRANCA; cleft, gorge, ravine; cliff; great difficulty.

barrancoso, sa, *a.* uneven, rough.

barranquera, *f.* BARRANCA; obstruction, difficulty.

barraquillo, *m.* (artil.) short light gun.

barrar, *va.* to daub, smear; bar, barricade.

barrate, *m.* little joist or rafter.

barrear. I. *va.* to bar, barricade; to cancel, cross off. **II.** *vn.* to graze a knight's armor with a lance. **III.** *vr.* to intrench.

barrederas, *f. pl.* (naut.) studding sails.

barredero, ra. I. *a.* that drags along; sweeping. **II.** *f.* sweeper (machine), cleaner. **III.** *m.* baker's mop.

barredura, *f.* sweeping.—*pl.* sweepings, refuse, chaff.

barrena, *f.* drill; auger; gimlet; (aer.) spin; spinning dive.—**b. de diminución,** taper auger. —**b. de guía,** centerbit.—**b. de gusano,** wimble; rock drill.—**b. grande,** auger, borer.—**b. pequeña,** gimlet.

barrenado, da. I. *pp.* of BARRENAR. **II.** *a.* bored, drilled. **III.** *m.* boring, drilling.

barrenador, *m.* (naut.) auger or borer.

barrenar, *va.* to bore, drill; to foil.—**b. un navío,** (naut.) to scuttle a ship.—**b. una roca,** or **mina,** to blast a rock, or a mine.

barrendero, ra, *n.* sweeper, dustman (-woman).

barrenero, *m.* maker or seller of augers and drills; blaster, driller.

barrenillo, *m.* boring insect.

barreno, *m.* large borer, drill or auger; bored hole, blast hole; vanity.—**dar b.** (naut.) to sink (a ship).

barreña, *f.,* **barreño,** *m.* earthen pan; tub.

barrer, *va.* to sweep; (naut.) to rake.—**al b.** (com.) on an average.

barrera, *f.* barricade, barrier, parapet, fence; clay pit; mound of earth; cupboard for crockery; bar, tollgate, turnpike.

barrero, *m.* potter; marshy ground; salty soil.

barreta, *f.* small bar; shoe lining.

barretear, *va.* to fasten with bars; line (a shoe).

barretero, *m.* in mining, one who works with a crow, wedge, or pick.

barretón, *m.* miner's pickaxe, bede.

barriada, *f.* city ward, district, precinct, quarter.

barrial, *m.* mire.

barrica, *f.* cask containing about 60 gallons.

barricada, *f.* barricade.

barrido. I. *m.* sweep. **II.** *pp.* of BARRER.

barriga, *f.* belly; pregnancy.

barrigón, na, barrigudo, da, *a.* big-bellied.

barriguilla, *f. dim.* little belly.

barril, *m.* barrel; (naut.) water cask.

barrilame, *m.* stock of casks or barrels; barrel factory.

barrilejo, *m. dim.* rundlet, small barrel.

barrilería, *f.* = BARRILAME.

barrilero, ra, *n.* barrel maker, cooper.

barrilete, *m.* holdfast, dog, clamp; (naut.) mouse; (zool.) crab covered with prickles; keg; kite; piece of a clarinet.

barrilico, illo, ito, *m. dim.* keg, rundlet, small barrel, firkin.

barrilla, *f.* little bar; rod; (bot.) saltwort.

barrillar, *m.* barilla plantation; barilla pits.

barrio, *m.* city district, ward, precinct, quarter; suburb.

barrizal, *m.* clay pit; mire.

barro, *m.* clay; mud; earthenware; drinking vessel made of sugar clay.—*pl.* pimples in the face; (vet.) fleshy tumors.

barrocho, *m.* = BIRLOCHO.

barroso, sa, *a.* muddy, miry; pimpled; reddish.

barrote, *m.* short and thick iron bar; round rung (of a ladder); (carp.) brace.—**barrotes,** (naut.) battens, scantlings.

barrueco, *m.* pearl of irregular form.

barrumbada, *f.* extravagant expense; boast.

barruntador, ra, *n.* conjecturer.

barruntamiento, *m.* conjecturing, guessing.

barruntar, *va.* to conjecture, guess.

barrunto, *m.* conjecture.

bartola, *f.*—**a la b.,** carelessly.
bartolillo, *m.* three-cornered little meat pie.
bártulos, *m. pl.* household goods; tools.
baruca, *f.* cunning, deceit, trickery.
barulé, *m.* upper part of the stockings rolled over the knee.
barullo, *m.* confusion, disorder, tumult.
barzón, *m.* idle walk; ring of a yoke.
barzonear, *vn.* to loiter about.
basa, *f.* pedestal, base; basis.
basada, *f.* stocks for ship building.
basácula, *f.* locker of the thumb plate in a stocking frame.
basáltico, ca, *a.* basaltic.—**basalto,** *m.* basalt.
basamento, *m.* (arch.) base and pedestal.
basar. I. *va.* to support, give a base to; to base, found; (surv.) to refer (operation, etc.) to a base line. **II.** *vr.* (w. **en**) to base one's opinion (on), to have as one's reason.
basáride, *f.* (Mex.) bassaris, a species of racoon.
basca, *f.* squeamishness, nausea; swoon.
bascosidad, *f.* nastiness; filth.
báscula, *f.* platform scale.
base, *f.* base, basis; (mil., chem., alg., geom.) base; (surv.) base (line).
basicidad, *f.* (chem.) basicity.
básico, ca, *a.* basic.
basificar, *va.* (chem.) to basify.
basílica, *f.* royal palace; public hall; basilica, privileged church; (anat., arch.) basilica.
basilicón, *m.* (med.) basilicon, ointment.
basilio, lía, *n. & a.* Basilian (monk, nun).
basilisco, *m.* basilisk (animal, cannon).—**estar hecho un b.,** to be furious, (coll.) to be hot in the collar.
basquear, *vn.* to be squeamish or nauseated.
basquilla, *f.* a disease of sheep.
basquiña, *f.* upper skirt.
basta, *f.* coarse stitch; basting.
bastaje, *m.* porter; carrier.
bastante. I. *a.* sufficient, enough. **II.** *adv.* enough; rather, fairly, pretty.
bastantear, *va.* (law) to acknowledge the validity of (a power of attorney).
bastantemente, *adv.* sufficiently.
bastanteo, *m.* acknowledging a power of attorney.
bastantero, *m.* (law) officer who examines powers of attorney.
bastar, *vn.* to suffice; to be enough.—**¡basta!** that will do; stop.
bastarda, *f.* bastard file; piece of ordnance.
bastardear, *vn.* to degenerate; bastardize.
bastardelo, *m.* notary's draft book; blotter.
bastardía, *f.* bastardy; meanness.
bastardilla, *f.* a kind of flute; (print.) italic.
bastardo, da. I. *a.* bastard; (print.) bastard type. **II.** *n.* bastard. **III.** *m.* boa (snake); a kind of saddle; (naut.) parrel rope.
baste, *m.* stitch; saddle pad.
bastear, *va.* to baste.
bastero, *m.* maker or seller of packsaddles.
bastida, *f.* an ancient war engine.
bastidor, *m.* frame; easel; embroidery frame; stretcher for canvas; wing of stage scenery; window sash; frame of a screw propeller; (phot.) plate holder.—*pl.* (naut.) frames for canvas bulkheads.—**entre bastidores,** behind the scenes.
bastilla, *f.* hem.—**bastillar,** *va.* to hem.
bastimentar, *va.* to victual; to provision.
bastimento, *m.* supply of provisions; building, structure; mattress tufting; (naut.) vessel.
bastión. *m.* = BALUARTE.
basto, *m.* packsaddle; pad; ace of clubs.—*pl.* clubs (cards).
basto, ta, *a.* coarse; rude; gross; homespun.
bastón, *m.* walking cane; gad, truncheon; baton; roller of a silk frame.
bastonada, *f.,* **bastonazo,** *m.* bastinado.
bastoncillo, *m.* small cane or stick; narrow trimming lace.
bastonear, *va.* to cane.

bastonero, *m.* cane maker or seller; manager of a ball; cotillon leader; assistant jailer.
basura, *f.* sweepings, rubbish; ordure, refuse.
basurero, *m.* dustman; dustpan; dunghill.
basuriento, ta, *a.* full of rubbish.
bata, *f.* dressing gown; smoking jacket; wrapper; woman's frock; silk refuse.
bata, *n.* (Philip.) half-breed minor.
batacazo, *m.* violent contusion from a fall.
batahola, *f.* hurly-burly, bustle, hubbub.
batalla, *f.* battle; fencing bout; joust, tournament; (art.) battle piece.—**b. campal,** pitched battle.
batallador, ra, *n. & a.* battler (-ing), fighter (-ing).
batallar, *vn.* to battle, fight, struggle; fence.
batallola, *f.* (naut.) rail.
batallón, *m.* battalion.
batán, *m.* fulling mill.—*pl.* **batanes,** a boy's game.
batanar, *va.* to full (cloth).
batanear, *va.* to drub, thrash, beat.
batanero, *m.* fuller, clothier.
batanga, *f.* bamboo outrigger in boats (P. I.)
batata, *f.* sweet potato.—**batatal, batatar,** *m.* sweet-potato field.
bátavo, va, *a.* Batavian.
batayola, *f.* (naut.) rail.
batea, *f.* painted tray; foot tub; flat-bottomed boat, punt; large wash tray or trough.
batehuela, *f. dim.* small hamper or tray.
batel, *m.* small vessel.
batería, *f.* (artil., elec.) battery; (naut.) range of guns, broadside; repeated importunities; battering; (mus.) aggregate of percussion instruments in a band or orchestra.—**b. a rebote,** ricochet battery.—**b. cruzante,** cross battery.—**b. de acumuladores,** (elec.) storage battery.—**b. de cocina,** kitchen metal utensils.—**b. enterrada,** sunk battery.
batero, ra, *n.* mantua maker, dressmaker, ladies' tailor.
batey, *m.* (Cuba) sugar plant (factory).
batiborrillo, *m.* = BATURRILLO.
baticola, *f.* crupper.
batida, *f.* hunting party; battue.
batidera, *f.* beater (in masonry); stirrer (in glass-making); batlet; batting arm; scutcher; flap of a churn; instrument for cutting honeycombs.
batidero, *m.* continuous striking or beating; collision; craggy ground; (naut.) washboard.
batido, *m.* batter of flour, eggs, etc.
batido, da. I. *a.* shot, chatoyant (silks); beaten, trodden, as roads. **II.** *pp.* of BATIR.
batidor, *m.* beater; scout; ranger; lifeguard rider before a royal coach; outrider; leather beater; stirring rod; haircomb; hemp dresser.
batiente, *m.* jamb (of a door); leaf (of a door); port-sill; damper (of a piano); spot where the sea beats against the shore.—**b. de la bandera,** (naut.) fly of the ensign.—**b. de un dique,** apron of a dock.
batifulla, *m.,* **batihoja,** *m.* gold beater; sheet-metal worker; warp.
batimiento, *m.* beating.
batín, *m.* smoking jacket.
batintín, *m.* Chinese gong.
bationdeo, *m.* fluttering of a banner or curtain.
batiportar, *va.* (naut.) to house (a gun).
batiportes, *m. pl.* port-sills.
batir. I. *va.* to beat; dash, strike, clout; demolish, pull down; flap; pound; stir; comb; adjust (reams of paper); vanquish; reconnoiter; beat (a drum).—**b. banderas,** to salute with colors.—**b. el campo,** to reconnoiter the enemy's camp; to investigate.—**b. hoja,** to foliate.—**b. las olas,** to ply the seas.—**b. moneda,** to coin money.—**b. una catarata,** (med.) to couch a cataract. **II.** *vr.* to fight; engage in a duel; lose courage; decline in health.
batista, *f.* batiste, finest cambric.
bato, *m.* rustic, simpleton.
batojar, *va.* to beat down (the fruit of a tree).

batología, *f.* battology, needless repetition.

batómetro, *m.* bathometer, bathymeter, an instrument used for determining depths at sea.

batracio, cia. I. *n. & a.* batrachian. **II.** *m. pl.* Batrachia.

batuda, *f.* springboard jumping contest.

baturrillo, *m.* hodgepodge, mash, salmagundi; potpourri; medley.

batuta, *f.* conductor's wand; baton.—**llevar la b.,** to lead; preside; manage.

baúl, *m.* trunk, chest; belly.—**b. mundo,** Saratoga trunk.—**baulito,** *m. dim.* small trunk.

bauprés, *m.* (naut.) bowsprit.

bausán, na, *n.* manikin, effigy; fool, idiot.

bautismal, *a.* baptismal.

bautismo, *m.* baptism, christening.

bautista, *n.* baptizer; Baptist.—**el B.,** the Baptist (John).

bautisterio, *m.* baptistery.

bautizante, *n.* baptizer, christener.

bautizar, *va.* (*pret.* BAUTICÉ: *subj.* BAUTICE) to baptize, christen; name, call; mix (wine) with water.

bautizo, *m.* baptism; christening party.

bávaro, ra, *n. & a.* Bavarian.

baya, *f.* berry, any small globular fruit.

bayadera, *f.* Oriental dancer.

bayal. I. *a.* long-stem autumn flax. [**II.** *m.* lever used in raising millstones.

bayeta, *f.* baize, thick flannel; blanket (in typography).

bayetón, *m.* coating, cloth for coats; (Am.) long baize poncho.

bayo, ya. I. *a.* bay. **II.** *m.* silkworm moth used in angling.

bayoco, *m.* Italian copper coin; unripe or withered fig.

bayón, *m.* (Philip.) sack of matting for baling.

bayoneta, *f.* bayonet.—**bayonetazo,** *m.* bayonet thrust or wound.

bayoque, *m.* = BAYOCO.

bayuca, *f.* tippling house, tavern.

baza, *f.* trick (at cards).—**no dejar meter b.,** not to let one put in a single word.

bazar, *m.* bazaar, market place; department store.

bazo, *m.* (anat.) spleen.

bazo, za, *n. & a.* yellowish brown.

bazofia, *f.* offal, waste meat, refuse, remnants.

bazucar, *va.* (*pret.* BAZUQUÉ: *subj.* BAZUQUE) to stir (liquids) by shaking; to dash.

bazuqueo, *m.* shaking (a liquid); jumble.

be. I. *m.* baa, cry of sheep. **II.** *f.* b.

beata, *f.* woman engaged in works of charity; overpious woman, one that devotes much of her time to praying and church going (gen. u. in a bad sense, with the implication of prudery and bigotry).

beatería, *f.* affected piety; bigotry.

beaterio, *m.* pious women's house or institution.

beatificación, *f.* beatification.

beatíficamente, *adv.* beatifically.

beatificar, *va.* to beatify; to render respectable; to make happy.

beatífico, ca, *a.* (theol.) beatific.

beatilla, *f.* a kind of fine linen.

beatísimo, ma, *a. sup.* of BEATO.—**b. padre,** Most Holy Father (the Pope).

beatitud, *f.* beatitude, blessedness, holiness.

beato, ta. I. *a.* happy, blessed; beatified; devout; overpious, prudish, bigoted. **II.** *n.* pious person; one who lives in pious retirement; overpious, prudish person. *V.* BEATA.

beatón, na, *n.* hypocrite, bigot.

bebedero, *m.* drinking place or trough; spout; hole.—*pl.* strips for lining clothes; facing.

bebedero, ra; bebedizo, za, *a.* drinkable.

bebedizo, *m.* medicinal potion; draught; philter or love potion; poisonous draught.

bebedo, da, *a.* drunk.

bebedor, ra, *n.* tippler, toper.

beber, *va. & vn.* to drink; swallow; pledge, toast. —**b. a la salud de alguno,** to drink some one's health.—**b. como una cuba,** to drink like a fish.— **b. los pensamientos a alguno,** to anticipate one's thoughts.—**b. los vientos,** to solicit with much eagerness.

bebible, *a.* pleasant to drink, drinkable.

bebida, *f.* drink, beverage; potion; time allowed to workmen for drinks.

bebido, da. I. *pp.* of BEBER. **II.** *a.* intoxicated.

bebirina, *f.* (chem.) bebeerine.

bebistrajo, *m.* mixture of drinks.

beborrotear, *vn.* to sip often.

beca, *f.* collegian's sash worn over the gown; fellowship; pension; fellow, alumnus, collegian; tippet worn by dignitaries of the church.—*pl.* velvet or satin facings of cloaks.—**b. de merced,** scholarship.

becabunga, *f.* (bot.) brooklime.

becada, *f.* woodcock. *V.* CHOCHA.

becafigo, *m.* (orn.) figpecker.—**b. raro,** (orn.) red-headed linnet.

becardón, *m.* snipe.

becerra, *f.* (bot.) snapdragon.

becerril, *a.* bovine; calf (u. a.)

becerro, ra, *n.* yearling calf; calfskin; church register; book bound in calfskin.—**b. de oro,** golden calf; mammon, riches.—**b. marino,** sea calf, seal.

becoquín, *m.* cap tied under the chin.

becuadrado, *m.* first property in plain song, or Gregorian mode.—**becuadro,** *m.* (mus.) the sign ♮, denoting a natural tone.

bedel, *m.* beadle, warden.

bedelía, *f.* beadleship, wardenship.

bedelio, *m.* bdellium, an aromatic gum.

beduino, na, *a.* Bedouin; harsh, uncivil.

befa, *f.* jeer, scoff, mock, taunt.

befabemí, *m.* a musical sign.

befar. I. *va.* to mock, scoff, ridicule. **II.** *vn.* to move the lips trying to catch the chain of the bit (s. o. horses).

befo, *m.* lip of a beast; a kind of monkey.

befo, fa, *a.* blubber-lipped; knock-kneed.

begonia, *f.* begonia.—**begoniáceo, ea. I.** *a.* (bot.) begoniaceous. **II.** *f. pl.* Begoniaceæ.

behén, *m.* = BEN.

behetería, *f.* free, independent town; confusion, disorder.

bejín, *m.* (bot.) common puffball, fuzzball; whining, peevish child.

bejinero, *m.* one who extracts oil from the lees.

bejucal, *m.* place where BEJUCOS grow.

bejuco, *m.* large creeping or climbing wild plant; rattan.

bejuquillo, *m.* gold chain made in China; (bot.) ipecacuanha; thin BEJUCO.

belcho, *m.* (bot.) horsetail tree.

beldad, *f.* beauty, belle.

belemnita, *f.* belemnite.

belemnoide, belemnoideo, a, *a.* belemnoid.

Belén, *m.* Bethlehem; group of figures representing the birth of the infant Jesus for celebrating Christmas; confusion, bedlam.

beleño, *m.* (bot.) henbane, poison.

belérico, *m.* (bot.) a kind of myrobalan.

belez, *f.,* **belezo,** *m.* jar for oil or wine; furniture.

belfo, fa, *a.* blob-lipped or blubber-lipped.

belfo, *m.* thick underlip of a horse.

belga, *n. & a.* Belgian.—**bélgico, ca,** *a.* Belgian, Belgic.

bélico, ca, *a.* warlike, martial.—**belicosidad,** *f.* warlikeness.—**belicoso, sa,** *a.* warlike, bellicose; quarrelsome.

beligerancia, *f.* belligerency.

beligerante, *n. & a.* belligerent.

beligero, ra, *a.* (poet.) warlike, belligerent.

belísono, na, *a.* with martial, warlike sound.

belitre, *a.* low, mean, vile, vulgar; roguish.

bellacada, *f.* nest of rogues; knavish act.

bellacamente, *adv.* knavishly, roguishly.

bellaco, ca. I. *a.* artful, sly, cunning, roguish, deceitful. **II.** *m.* rogue, villain, knave.

bellacón, na; bellaconazo, za, *n. aug.* great knave, arrant rogue.

bellacuelo, *m. dim.* tricky, cunning little fellow.
belladama, belladona, *f.* (bot.) belladonna.
bellamente, *adv.* prettily, gracefully, fairly.
bellaquear, *vn.* to cheat, swindle; play knavish, roguish tricks.
bellaquería, *f.* knavery, roguery, cunning; vile act or expression.
belleza, *f.* beauty.
bello, lla, *a.* beautiful, fair.—**bello sexo,** fair sex.—**bellas artes,** fine arts.—**las bellas,** the fair ones.
bellorio, ria, *a.* mouse-colored.
bellorita, *f.* (bot.) primrose, cowslip.
bellota, *f.* acorn; carnation bud; perfume box.
bellote, *m.* large round-headed nail.
bellotear, *vn.* to feed on acorns.—**bellotera,** *f.* acorn season.—**bellotero, ra.** **I.** *n.* one who gathers or sells acorns **II.** *m.* oak tree.—**bellotica, lla, ita,** *f. dim.* small acorn.
bembo, ba. **I.** *n. & a.* negro; snouty, thick-lipped. **II.** *m.* thick lip, negro's lip.—**bembón, na,** *a.* snouty, thick-lipped, having lips like a negro's.
bemol, *m.* (mus.) flat.—**tener bemoles,** (coll.) to be very difficult, to be a tough job, or a big order.
bemolado, *a.* flat(ted), lowered a semitone.
bemolar, *va.* (mus.) to flat.
ben, *m.* behen, a small oil-producing fruit.
benarriza, *f.* (orn.) ortolan.
benceína, *f.* (chem.) benzein.—**bencilato,** *m.* a sak of benzilic acid.—**bencénico, ca,** *a.* benzene (u. a.).—**bencílico, ca,** *a.* benzilic.—**bencina,** *f.* benzine.
bendecidor, ra, *n. & a.* blesser (-ing).
bendecir, *va.* (*pp.* BENDITO and BENDECIDO: *ind.* BENDIGO: *pret.* BENDIJE: *imp.* BENDICE: *subj.* BENDIGA) to bless; consecrate.
bendición, *f.* benediction, blessing.—*pl.* marriage ceremony.
bendigo, bendije, bendiga. *V.* BENDECIR.
bendito, ta. **I.** *a.* sainted, blessed; simple, silly.—**es un b.,** he is a simpleton. **II.** *pp. irr.* of BENDECIR.
benedícite, *m.* (Lat.) permission solicited by ecclesiastics with this word.
benedicta, *f.* benedict, electuary.
benedictino, na, *a.* Benedictine.
benefactor, *m.* benefactor.
beneficencia, *f.* beneficence, charity.
beneficiación, *f.* benefaction.
beneficiado, *m.* curate; beneficiary.
beneficiador, ra, *n.* benefactor; improver, developer, exploiter (of a mine, etc.)
beneficial, *a.* relating to benefices or ecclesiastical livings.
beneficiar. **I.** *va.* to benefit; cultivate; develop, exploit; confer a sinecure on; purchase. **II.** *vr.* to profit.
beneficiario, ria, *n.* beneficiary.
beneficio, *m.* benefit; profits; favor, kindness, benefaction; benefit, ecclesiastical living; right belonging to one either by law or charter; working, development (of a mine).—**b. bruto,** gross profit.—**b. neto,** clear profit.—**b. simple,** sinecure.
beneficioso, sa, *a.* beneficial, profitable.
benéfico, ca, *a.* beneficent, kind, charitable.
benemérito, ta, *a.* meritorious, worthy.
beneplácito, *m.* approval, consent.
benevolencia, *f.* benevolence, kindness.
benévolo, la, *a.* benevolent, kind.
bengala, *f.* Bengal, thin slight stuff; cane.
bengalí, *n. & a.* Bengalese.
benignamente, *adv.* kindly, benevolently.
benignidad, *f.* benignity, kindness; mildness.
benigno, na, *a.* benign, kind; mild.
benito, ta, *n. & a.* Benedictine (friar or nun).
benjamita, *a.* descending from, or relative to, Benjamin or the tribe of Benjamin.
benjuí, *m.* benzoin.
benzoato, *m.* benzoate.—**benzoico, ca,** *a.* benzoic.—**benzol,** *m.* benzol.
beocio, cia, *n. & a.* Bœotian.

beodez, *f.* drunkenness.—**beodo, da,** *a.* drunk.
beorí, *m.* an American tapir.
beque, *m.* (naut.) head of the ship.
berberí, *n. & a.* Berber.
berberídeo, a. **I.** *a.* (bot.) berberidaceous. **II.** *m. pl.* Berberidaceæ.
berberina, *f.* (chem.) berberine.
berberís, *m.* (bot.) barberry, piperidge bush.
berberisco, ca, *n. & a.* Berber.
bérbero, *m.* barberry; a barberry confection.
berbí, *m.* a kind of woollen cloth.
berbiquí, *m.* drill brace, bitstock; wimble.
berquería, *f.* green market.
bercero, ra, *n.* greengrocer.
bereber = BERBERISCO.
berenjena, *f.* eggplant.—**berenjenado, da,** *a.* eggplant-colored.—**berenjenal,** *m.* bed of eggplants; difficulties, troubles.
bergamota, *m.* bergamot (fruit, essence, snuff).
bergamote, bergamoto, *m.* bergamot tree.
bergante, *m.* brazen-faced villain, ruffian, rascal.
bergantín, *m.* (naut.) brig, brigantine.
bergantinejo, *m. dim.* small brig.
bergantón, na, *n. aug.* brazen-faced person.
bergantonazo, *m. aug.* most impudent ruffian.
beriberi, *m.* beriberi.
berilo, *m.* beryl.
berlina, *f.* berlin (carriage); front compartment of a stagecoach or a railway carriage.
berlinés, sa, *a.* of or from Berlin.
berlinga, *f.* clothesline post; round timber.
berma, *f.* (mil.) berm, ground at the foot of a rampart.
bermejear, bermejecer, *vn.* to have a reddish color.
bermejizo, za, *a.* reddish.—**bermejo, ja,** *a.* bright reddish.—**bermejón, na,** *a.* reddish.—**bermejuela,** *f.* (zool.) red gurnard; (bot.) heather.—**bermejuelo, la,** *a. dim.* somewhat reddish.—**bermejura,** *f.* reddishness, ruddy color.
bermellón, bermillón, *m.* vermilion.
bermudiana, *f.* (bot.) grassflower.
bernardina, *f.* fanfaronade; boast.
bernardo, da, *n. & a.* Bernardine (monk, nun).
bernegal, *m.* cup with scalloped edges.
bernés, sa, *n. & a.* Bernese.
bernia, *f.* rug; cloak made of rug.
berra, *f.* strong watercress plant.
berraza, *f.* water parsnip.
berrear, *vn.* to cry like a calf, low, bellow.
berrenchín, *m.* foaming, grunting of a wild boar; cry of wayward children.
berrendearse, *vr.* to grow yellow (s. o. wheat).
berrendo, da, *a.* two-colored; spotted; dark brown (silkworm).
berrera, *f.* (bot.) = BERRAZA COMÚN.
berrido, *m.* bellowing.
berrín, *m.* child in a violent passion.
berrinche, *m.* anger, passion; sulkiness.
berrinchudo, *a.* irritable, sulky.
berrizal, *m.* place full of watercreses.
berro, *m.* (bot.) watercress.
berrocal, *m.* craggy or rocky place.
berrueco, *m.* rock; pin; a disease of the eye.
berza, *f.* (bot.) cabbage.—**b. común,** common cabbage.—**b. de perro,** dog's cabbage.—**b. lombarda,** red cabbage.
berzaza, *f. aug.* large head of cabbage.
besador, ra, *n. & a.* kisser (-ing).
besalamano, *m.* note with the abbreviation B. L. M. in the third person and unsigned.
besamanos, *m.* court day; salute with the hand.
besana, *f.* first furrow with a plow; series of parallel furrows.
besar. **I.** *va.* to kiss; to touch closely (s. o. inanimate things).—**b. la mano, or los pies,** expressions of courtesy and respect. **II.** *vr.* to strike heads or faces together accidentally.
besico, sillo, sito, *m. dim.* little kiss.—**besicos de monja,** (bot.) *V.* FAROLILLO.
beso, *m.* kiss; collision of persons or things; (among bakers) kissing crust.

bestezuela, *f. dim.* little beast.
bestia, *f.* beast, quadruped; (met.) dunce, idiot; ill-bred fellow.—**b. de carga,** beast of burden.
bestiaje, bestiame, *m.* group of beasts of burden.
bestial, *a.* bestial, brutal.—**bestialidad,** *f.* = BRUTALIDAD.—**bestialmente,** *adv.* bestially, brutally.—**bestiaza,** *m. aug.* great beast; big idiot.
bestiecica, cilla, cita; bestiezuela, *f. dim.* little beast; ignorant person.
bestión, *m. aug.* large beast.
béstola, *f.* paddle for cleaning the coulter of the plow.
besucador, ra, *n.* (coll.) kisser, spooner.
besucar. I. *va.* (*pret.* BESUQUÉ: *subj.* BESUQUE) to kiss repeatedly. **II.** *vn.* to spoon.
besucón, na, *n. & a.* spooner (-ing).
besugada, *f.* luncheon of sea breams.
besugo, *m.* (icht.) sea bream, red gilthead.
besuguera, *f.* pan for dressing BESUGOS.
besuguero, ra. I. *n.* fishmonger who sells breams. **II.** *m.* fishing tackle for breams.
besuguete, *m.* (zool.) red sea bream.
besuqueador, ra = BESUCADOR.—**besuquear,** *va. & vn.* = BESUCAR.—**besuqueo,** *m.*, (coll.) spooning.
beta, *f.* bit or line of thread, tape; beta, Greek letter.—**betas,** (naut.) pieces of cordage for all kinds of tackle.
betarraga, betarrata, *f.* (bot.) beet.
betel, *m.* betel, an Indian shrub.
bético, ca, *a.* Andalusian.
betlemita, *n. & a.* Bethlemite.—**betlemítico, ca,** *a.* from, or relating to, Bethlehem or the Bethlehemites.
betol, *m.* (chem.) betol.
betónica, *f.* (bot.) betony.
betuláceo, cea. I. *a.* (bot.) betulaceous. **II.** *f. pl.* Betulaceæ.
betulina, *f.* (chem.) betuline.
betún, *m.* bitumen, pitch; shoeblacking; coarse wax.—**b. judaico,** asphalt.—**betunar,** *va.* to pitch, tar.
beuna, *f.* a reddish wine made from a red grape of the same name.
bey, *m.* bey, Turkish governor.
bezaar, bezar, *m.* = BEZOAR.
bezante, *m.* (her.) bezant.
bezo, *m.* blubber lip; proud flesh in a wound.
bezoar, *m.* bezoar.—**b. occidental, b. oriental,** Occidental, Oriental bezoar.—**bezoárico, ca,** *a.* bezoardic.
bezote, *m.* ring worn by Indians in their under lip.
bezudo, da, *a.* blubber-lipped or blob-lipped.
biangular, *a.* biangulated, biangulous.
biazas, *f. pl.* saddlebags.
bíbaro, *m.* beaver.
bibero, *m.* a kind of linen from Galicia.
biberón, ra, *m.* nursing bottle.
Biblia, *f.* Bible.—**bíblico, ca,** *a.* Biblical.
bibliófilo, la, *n.* book lover, bibliophile.
bibliografía, *f.* bibliography.—**bibliográfico, ca,** *a.* bibliographical.
bibliógrafo, fa, *n.* bibliographer.
bibliomanía, *f.* bibliomania.—**bibliómano, na,** *n.* bibliomaniac.
biblioteca, *f.* library.
bibliotecario, ria, *n.* librarian.
bica, *f.* unleavened cake of maize.
bicapsular, *a.* (bot.) bicapsular.
bicarbonato, *m.* bicarbonate.
biceps, *m.* (anat.) biceps.
bicerra, *f.* wild or mountain goat.
bicicleta, *f.* bicycle.—**bicicletista, biciclista,** *n.* bicyclist.—**biciclo,** *m.* large bicycle.
bicípite, *a.* bicipital, two-headed.
bicoca, *f.* small fort; trifle, bagatelle.
bicolor, *a.* two-colored.
bicóncavo, va, *a.* biconcave, double-concave.
biconvexo, a, *a.* double-convex.
bicoquete, *m.* **bicoquín,** *m.* double-pointed skullcap.

bicorne, *a.* (poet.) bicornuous, bicorn.
bicorpóreo, rea, *a.* bicorporal.
bicos, *m. pl.* gold trimmings on skullcaps.
bicromato, *m.* bichromate.
bicromía, *f.* two-color print.
bicuento, *m.* (arith.) billion.
bicuadrado, da, *a.* raised to the fourth power; in the quadratic form (s. o. biquadratics having only even powers of *x*).
bicha, *f.* (arch.) fantastic caryatid.
bichero, *m.* (naut.) boathook.
bicho, *m.* small grubs or insects; (coll.) beast (often app. to bulls); ridiculous fellow.—*pl.* vermin.
bidé, *m.* bidet, washtub.
bidente. I. *a.* having two teeth or prongs. **II.** *m.* two-pronged spade.
biela, *f.* (mech.) connecting rod.
bielda, *f.* pitchfork with six or seven prongs, and a rack.—**bieldar,** *va.* to winnow corn with a BIELDO.—**bieldo, bielgo,** *m.* winnowing fork.
biempareciente, *a.* good-looking.
bien, *m.* good; dearest, darling (in the expression **mi b.,** my dearest, my darling).— *pl.* property; possessions; estate.—**bienes de fortuna,** worldly possessions.— **bienes dotales,** dower.— **bienes forales,** leasehold estate.— **bienes gananciales,** property acquired during married life.— **bienes inmuebles,** real estate (= BIENES RAÍCES).— **bienes monstrencos,** goods having no known owner.— **bienes muebles,** goods and chattels.— **bienes raíces,** real estate.— **bienes se**u**ientes,** real estate.— **bienes semovientes,** cattle.— **de b.,** honest.
bien, *adv.* well; right, uprightly; happily, prosperously; willingly, readily, heartily; very; perfectly, fully.—**b. a b.,** willingly.—**b. así como,** just as.—**b. que,** although.—**ahora b.,** now then.—**de b. en mejor,** better and better.—**más b.,** rather; somewhat.—**no b.,** as soon as, just as.— **por b.,** willingly.—**si b.,** while, though.—**y b.,** well, now then.—**¿y b.?** well? what of that?
bienal, *a.* biennial.
bienamado, *a.* dearly beloved.
bienandante, *a.* happy, prosperous.
bienandanza, *f.* happiness, welfare, prosperity.
bienaventuradamente, *adv.* luckily, happily.
bienaventurado, da, *a.* blessed; happy; fortunate; (iron.) simple, harmless.
bienaventuranza, *f.* beatitude; bliss; well-being. —*pl.* beatitudes.
bienestar, *m.* well-being, comfort.
bienfortunado, da, *a.* fortunate, successful.
biengranada, *f.* (bot.) curl-leaved goosefoot.
bienhablado, da, *a.* well and civilly spoken.
bienhadado, da, *a.* lucky, fortunate, happy.
bienhecho, cha, *a.* well-shaped, well-performed.
bienhechor, ra, *n.* benefactor.
bienintencionado, da, *a.* well-meaning.
bienio, *m.* term or space of two years.
bienmandado, da, *a.* obedient, submissive.
bienmesabe, *m.* meringue batter.
bienquerencia, *f.* good will, affection, esteem.
bienquerer. I. *va.* (*irr.* like QUERER) to esteem, to like. **II.** *m.* esteem, good will.
bienqueriente, *n.* well-wisher.
bienquistar, *va.* to reconcile.
bienquisto, ta. I. *a.* esteemed and respected. **II.** *pp.* of BIENQUISTAR.
bienteveo, *m.* = CANDELECHO.
bienvenida, *f.* safe arrival; welcome.
bienvenido, da, *a.* welcome.
bienvivir, *vn.* to live in comfort; live uprightly.
bifásico, ca, *a.* (elec.) two-phase.
bífido, da, *a.* (bot.) bifid.
bifilar, *a.* bifilar; (elec.) two-wire.
bil**oro, ra,** *a.* (bot.) biflorous.
biforme, *a.* biformed, biform.
bifronte, *a.* (poet.) double-fronted or double-faced.
biftec, *m.* beefsteak.
biftequera, *f.* (Chile) beefsteak broiler.

bifurcación, *f.* branch railroad; junction; bifurcation or forking.— **bifurcado, da,** *a.* forked or branched, bifurcate.—**bifurcarse,** *vr.* to branch off; to divide into two branches.

biga, *f.* (poet.) team; biga.

bigamia, *f.* bigamy.—**bígamo,** *m.* bigamist.

bigardear, *vn.* to live licentiously; to gad.

bigardía, *f.* jest; fiction; dissimulation.

bigardo, *m.* licentious friar; lubber.

bigarrado, da, *a.* = ABIGARRADO.

bígaro, bigarro, *m.* large sea snail.

bignoniáceo, cea. I. *a.* (bot.) bignoniaceous. **II.** *f. pl.* Bignoniaceæ.

bigorneta, *f. dim.* small anvil.

bigornia, *f.* anvil.

bigotazo, *m. aug.* large mustache.

bigote, *m.* mustache; block; (typ.) dash rule.

bigotera, *f.* leather cover for mustachios; ribbon ornament worn by women on the breast; folding seat in front of a chariot; bow compass.

bigotudo, *a.* having a large mustache.

bija, *f.* (bot.) arnotto tree; (com.) annatto.

bilateral, *a.* bilateral.

biliario, ria, *a.* biliary.

bilbaíno, na, *a.* of or from Bilbao.

bilingüe, *a.* bilingual.

bilioso, sa, *a.* bilious.

bilis, *f.* bile.

bilocarse, *vr.* (*pret.* BILOQUÉ: *subj.* BILOQUE) to be simultaneously in two different places.

biltrotear, *vn.* to gad.

biltrotera, *f.* gadder, gossiping woman.

billa, *f.* pocketing a ball after it has struck another.

billalda, billarda, *f.* a game of children.

billar, *m.* billiards; billiard table.

billarista, *n.* billiard player.

billete, *m.* an order of the king; note, brief letter; love letter; ticket.—**b. de banco,** bank-note.—**b. de abonado,** commutation ticket.—**b. de ida y vuelta,** round-trip ticket.—**b. kilométrico,** mileage ticket.

billetera, *f.* pocketbook, wallet.

billetico, *m. dim.* billet, love letter.

billón, *m.* billion (gen. one million millions).

billonésimo, ma, *n. & a.* billionth (gen. one millionth of one millionth).

bimano, na. I. *a.* bimanous. **II.** *m.* bimane. —*pl.* Bimana.

bimembre, *a.* having two members.

bimensual, *a.* occurring twice a month.

bimestral, *a.* bimonthly.—**bimestre. I.** *a.* bimonthly. **II.** *n.* bimonthly rent, salary, subscription, pension, etc.

bimetalismo, *m.* bimetallism.

bimetalista, *n.* bimetallist.

bimotor, ra, *a.* two-motor.

bina, *f.* second plowing or digging.—**binador,** *m.* he who digs the same ground again; weeding fork. —**binar,** *va.* to dig or plow the second time.

binario, ria, *a.* binary.

binazón, *f.* digging or plowing a second time.

binocular, *a.* binocular.

binóculo, *m.* binocle, dioptric telescope; marine or field glasses; opera glasses.

binomio, a. I. *a.* binomial. **II.** *m.* binomial.

binza, *f.* pellicle, lining of the shell of an egg; any thin membrane.

biodinámica, *f.* biodynamics.

biofísica, *f.* biophysics.

biogénesis, *f.* biogenesis.

biografía, *f.* biography.—**biográfico, ca,** *a.* biographical.—**biógrafo,** *m.* biographer.

biología, *f.* biology.—**biólogo, ga,** *n.* biologist.

biombo, *m.* screen.

bioquímica, *f.* biochemistry.

biótico, ca, *a.* biotic.

biotita, *f.* (min.) biotite.

bióxido, *m.* dioxide.

bipartido, da, *a.* (poet.) bipartite.

bipedal, *a.* bipedal.

bípede, bipedo, da, *n. & a.* biped.

bipétalo, la, *a.* (bot.) bipetalous.

biplano, *m.* (aer.) biplane.

bipolar, *a.* bipolar, two-pole.

biribís, *m.* = BISBÍS.

biricú, *m.* sword belt.

birimbao, *m.* (mus.) Jew's harp.

birla, *f., n.* **birlo,** *m.* bowling pin.—**birlador, ra,** *n.* one who bowls a second time from the place where the ball stopped the first time.—**birlar,** *va.* to bowl a second time from the same place; to knock down at one blow; to kill with one shot; to snatch away; to rob, pilfer.

birlibirloque, *m.*—**por arte de b.,** (coll.) by occult and extraordinary means.

birlocha, *f.* paper kite.

birlocho, *m.* two-seat light wagon without top.

birlón, *m.* jack pin (in bowling).

birlonga, *f.* name of a card game.—**a la b.,** carelessly.

birmano, na, *n. & a.* Burman.

birrectángulo, la, *a.* (geom.) birectangular, having two right angles.

birrefringencia, *f.* birefringence.

birrefringente, *a.* birefringent.

birreme, *n. & a.* bireme.

birreta, *f.* biretta.

birrete, *m.* cap.—**birretina,** *f.* grenadier's and hussar's cap; small cap.

bis, *bis,* Latin word used in the sense of "twice," "repeated" or "second."

bisabuela, *f.* great-grandmother.

bisabuelo, *m.* great-grandfather.

bisagra, *f.* hinge; shoemaker's boxwood polisher.

bisanuo, nua, *a.* (bot.) bisannual.

bisayo, ya, *a.* native of or pertaining to the Bisayas Islands in the Philippines.

bisbís, *m.,* a game resembling baccarat.

bisbisar, *va.* to mutter.—**bisbiseo,** *m.* muttering.

bisecar, *va.* to bisect.—**bisección,** *f.* bisection.

bisector, triz, *a.* (geom.) bisector.—**bisectriz,** *f.* bisector (of an angle).

bisel, *m.* bevel, bevel edge, chamfer; (coop.) sloping tool.—**biselado, da. I.** *a.* beveled. **II.** *m.* beveling; bevel.—**biselar,** *va.* to bevel.

bisextil, *a.* bissextile.

bisexual, *a.* (bot.) bisexual.

bisiesto, *a.* leap (year).

bisílabo, ba, *a.* disyllabic.

bislingua, *f.* (bot.) butcher's-broom.

bismuto, *m.* bismuth.

bisnieto, ta, *n. V.* BIZNIETO.

bisojo, ja, *a.* squint-eyed, cross-eyed.

bisonte, *m.* bison.

bisoñada, bisoñería, *f.* act of a novice or greenhorn.

bisoño, ña, *n. & a.* novice, tyro, greenhorn; inexperienced, new.

bispón, *m.* roll of oilcloth.

bístola, *f.* = BÉSTOLA.

bistorta, *f.* (bot.) great bistort, snakeweed.

bisturí, *m.* (surg.) bistoury, knife.

bisulco, ca, *a.* bisulcous, cloven-footed.

bisulfato, *m.* bisulphate.

bisulfuro, *m.* disulphide.

bisunto, ta, *a.* dirty, greasy.

bitácora, *f.* (naut.) binnacle.

bitadura, *f.* (naut.) cable bitt; a turn of the cable.

bitas, *f. pl.* (naut.) bitts.

bitones, *m. pl.* (naut.) pins of the capstan.

bitongo, ga, *a.* overgrown (s. o. children).

bitoque, *m.* bung, stopple.

bitor, *m.* (orn.) rail, king of the quails.

bituminoso, sa, *a.* bituminous.

bivalente, *a.* (chem.) bivalent.

bivalvo, va, *a.* bivalve, bivalvular.

biza, *f.* = BONITO.

bizantino, na, *a.* Byzantine.

bizarramente, *adv.* courageously, gallantly.

bizarrear, *vn.* to act spiritedly, gallantly.

bizarría, *f.* bravery, gallantry; generosity, magnanimity.—**bizarro, rra,** *a.* gallant, brave; generous, liberal.

For pronunciation, see the rules at the beginning of the book.

bizaza, *f.* saddle-bag.

bizcacha, *f.* viscacha, a South-Am. rodent.

bizcar, *vn.* (*pret.* BIZQUÉ: *subj.* BIZQUE) to squint.

bizco, ca, *a.* = BISOJO.

bizcochada, *f.* biscuit boiled in milk; long French roll.—**bizcochar,** *va.* to bake a second time.—**bizcochero,** *m.* biscuit cask; one who makes or sells biscuits.—**bizcochito,** *m. dim.* small biscuit.

bizcocho, *m.* biscuit; hard-tack; sponge cake; whiting made of old plaster; bisque.

bizcochuelo, *m. dim.* sponge cake.

bizcorneto, ta, *a.* (Am.) = BISOJO.

bizcotela, *f.* light biscuit with sugar icing.

bizma, *f.* poultice.—**bizmar,** *va.* to poultice.

bizna, *f.* zest, membrane which quarters the kernel of a walnut.

biznaga, *f.* (bot.) carrotlike ammi with sprigs used as toothpicks; useless, worthless thing.

biznieta, *f.* great-granddaughter.

biznieto, *m.* great-grandson.

bizquear, *vn.* to squint.

blanca, *f.* old copper coin; mite; (fam.) money, funds.—**b. morfea,** (vet.) alphos, white scurf, tetter, or ringworm.

blancazo, za, *a.* whitish.

blanco, ca. I. *a.* white; fair (s. o. to the complexion); (coll.) cowardly; light-colored. **II.** *n.* white person. **III.** *m.* white (color); white star or spot in horses; target; blank; gap left in writing; aim, goal; (print.) blank form; interlude, interval; white page; (her.) argent; sizing.—**b. de ballena,** spermaceti.—**b. de la uña,** half-moon of the nail.—**b. de plomo,** white lead.—**dar en el b.,** to hit the mark.—**en b.,** blank (space, book).—**quedarse en b.,** to be frustrated, disappointed.

blancor, *m.*, **blancura,** *f.* whiteness; fairness (of the skin).—**blancura del ojo,** (vet.) white film on the eye.

blancote, *n.* & *a.* (fam.) coward (-ly).

blancuzco, ca, *a.* whitish.

blandamente, *adv.* softly, mildly, smoothly.

blandeador, ra, *n.* & *a.* softener (-ing).

blandear. I. *va.* to soften, render mild; persuade, convince; brandish, flourish. **II.** *vn.* to slacken; yield, give in. **III.** *vr.* to soften, yield, change one's mind.

blandengue. I. *m.* Argentine lancer. **II.** *a.* exceedingly kind, bland.

blandiente, *a.* swaying, brandishing.

blandir, *va.* & *vr.* to brandish, flourish; sway, swing.

blando, da, *a.* soft; pliant; tender, kindly, mild, bland; delicate; pusillanimous, cowardly.

blandón, *m.* wax taper; large church candlestick.

blandoncillo, *m. dim.* small candlestick for wax tapers.

blanducho, cha, *a.* flabby, loose, soft.

blandura, *f.* softness; litheness, daintiness, delicacy; gentleness; emollient application; soft, endearing language; blandishing; white cosmetic; mild temperature.

blanqueación, *f.* blanching (metals); bleaching; whitewashing.

blanqueador, ra, *n.* blancher, whitener, whitewasher, kalsominer; bleacher.

blanqueadura, *f.,* or **blanqueamiento,** *m.* = BLANQUEO.

blanquear. I. *va.* to whiten, whitewash; blanch; bleach; to wax (the honeycomb) after winter to begin work (s. o. bees); to give coarse wax to bees in winter. **II.** *vn.* to show white, whiten.

blanquecedor, *m.* coin polisher (in the mint).

blanquecer, *va.* (*ind.* BLANQUEZCO: *subj.* BLANQUEZCA) to blanch (coin).

blanquecimiento, *m.* blanching.

blanquecino, na, *a.* whitish.

blanqueo, *m.* whitening, bleaching, whitewashing.

blanquería, *f.* bleaching place, bleach field

blanqueta, *f.* coarse blanket.

blanquete, *m.* whitewash; white paint for the face.

blanquición, *f.* blanching of metals.

blanquilla, *f.* doit, small coin; a long yellowish plum; white grape.

blanquillo, lla. I. *a. dim.* whitish. **II.** *m.* a South-American fish.

blanquimiento, *m.* bleaching solution.

blanquinoso, sa, *a.* = BLANQUECINO.

blanquizal, blanquizar, *m.* = GREDAL.

blanquizco, ca, *a.* whitish.

blao, *a.* (her.) azure.

blasfemador, ra, *n.* & *a.* blasphemer (-ing).

blasfemamente, *adv.* blasphemously.

blasfemante, *n.* & *a.* = BLASFEMADOR.

blasfemar, *vn.* to blaspheme; to curse.

blasfematorio, ria, *a.* blasphemous.

blasfemia, *f.* blasphemy; grave insult.

blasfemo, ma, *n.* & *a.* blasphemer (-ing).

blasón, *m.* heraldry, blazon, blazonry; armorial ensigns; honor, glory.—**blasonador, ra; blasonante,** *n.* & *a.* boaster (-ing).

blasonar. I. *va.* to design or emblazon (a heraldic shield). **II.** *vn.* to boast, brag.

blastema, *m.* (biol.) blastema.

blastodermo, *m.* (biol.) blastoderm.

blastogénesis, *f.* (biol.) blastogenesis.

blavo, va, *a.* yellowish gray and reddish.

bledo, *m.* (bot.) wild amaranth.—**no me importa un b.,** I don't care a straw.

blefaritis, *f.* (med.) blepharitis.

blefaroplastia, *f.* (med.) blepharoplasty.

blefaróstato, *m.* (surg.) blepharostat.

blenda, *f.* (min.) blende.

bleno, *m.* (zool.) hake, blenny.

blenorragia, *f.* (med.) blennorrhea.

blenorrea, *f.* (med.) chronic blennorrhea.

blinda, *f.,* **blindas,** *pl.* (fort.) blindage.

blindado, da, *n.* & *a.* iron-clad.

blindar, *va.* to armor; to protect with blindage.

blindaje, *m.* (mil.) blindage; (naut.) armor.

blino, *m.* = BLENO.

blocao, *m.* (mil.) portable blockhouse.

blonda, *f.* broad silk lace, blond lace.

blondina, *f.* narrow silk lace, narrow blond lace.

blondo, da, *a.* blond; flaxen, light.

bloque, *m.* block (of stone, etc.)

bloqueador, ra, *n.* & *a.* blockader (-ing).

bloquear, *va.* to blockade.

bloqueo, *m.* blockade.—**b. efectivo,** (int. l.) effective blockade.—**b. en el papel,** (int. l.) paper blockade.

blusa, *f.* blouse.

boa, *f.* (zool.) boa; tippet.

boardilla, *f.* = BUHARDILLA.

boato, *m.* ostentation, pomp; acclamation.

bobada, *m.* = BOBERÍA.

bobalías, *n.* very stupid person, dolt.

bobalicón, ona; bobazo, za, *n.* blockhead; simpleton.

bobamente, *adv.* foolishly, stupidly; easily, without any trouble.

bobarrón, na; bobatel, *n.* simpleton.

bobático, ca, *a.* silly, foolish, stupid.

bobear, *vn.* to act or talk foolishly; to dally, fribble.

bobería, *f.* foolish speech or action; trifle; folly, foolishness.—*pl.* idle conceits.

bóbilis,—de b. b., easily, with no effort; for nothing.

bobillo, illa, ito, ita, *n. dim.* little fool.

bobillo, *m.* big-bellied jug with one handle; modesty piece, a frill or lace formerly worn by women around the tucker.

bobina, *f.* bobbin; (elec.) coil.—**b. apagachispas,** blow-out coil.—**b. de inducción,** induction coil.—**b. de reacción,** or **de reactancia,** choking, kicking, or reactance, coil.—**b. de sintonización,** tuning coil.

bobo, ba, *n.* dolt, fool, simpleton, ninny; ruff formerly worn by women; (orn.) booby.—**b. de Coria,** great fool; fools in general.—**a bobas,** foolishly.

bobón, na, *n. aug.* big dolt, great fool.

bobote, ta, *n. aug.* great idiot or simpleton.

boca, *f.* mouth; entrance, opening; nozzle; muzzle; bunghole; pincers of crayfish; cutting part of edge tools; taste, flavor, relish; approaches (to a tunnel, etc.).—**b. abajo,** face downward, on one's stomach.—**b. a b.**= A B.—**b. arriba,** face upward, on one's back.—**b. de agua,** hydrant.—**b. de dragón,** (bot.) snap dragon.—**b. de fuego,** firearm (sp. artillery).—**b. del estómago,** pit of the stomach.—**b. de riego,** faucet (for a watering hose).—**a b.,** verbally, by word of mouth.—**a b. de,** at the beginning of.—**a b. de jarro,** drinking without measure; very near; at close range.—**a b. llena,** perspicuously, openly.—**andar de b. en b.,** to be the talk of the town.—**como b. de lobo,** pitch black.—**de b.,** A B.; boastingly.—**en b. cerrada no entra mosca,** (coll.) silence is golden, it pays to hold one's tongue.—**no decir esta b. es mía,** to keep a profound silence, not to say boo.

bocabarra, *f.* (naut.) barhole in a capstan.

bocacalle, *f.* opening of a street (into another); street intersection.

bocacaz, *m.* (hydr.) spillway.

bocací, bocacín, *m.* fine glazed buckram.

bocadear, *va.* to divide into bits or morsels.

bocadico, illo, ito, *m. dim.* morsel, bit.

bocadillo, *m.* thin, middling sort of linen; narrow ribbon or tape, gimp; morning luncheon given to laborers in the field; guava paste.

bocado, *m.* morsel, mouthful, bite, bit; modicum; bit of a bridle.—*pl.* preserved cut fruit.—**con el b. en la boca,** right after eating.—**no tener para un b.,** to be broken, to be in absolute destitution.

bocal, *m.* narrow-mouthed pitcher; mouthpiece; (naut.) narrows (of a harbor).

bocamanga, *f.* part of a sleeve near the wrist.

bocamina, *f.* entrance to a mine.

bocanada, *f.* mouthful (of liquor); whiff, puff (of smoke).—**b. de gente,** crowd, rush, jam.—**b. de viento,** sudden gust of wind.

bocarón, *m.* wind chest of an organ; wind trunk.

bocarte, *m.* ore crusher, stamp mill.

bocateja, *f.* front tile of each line of tiling.

bocatijera, *f.* socket for a carriage pole.

bocaza, *f. aug.* large wide mouth.

bocazo, *m.* fizzle (in blasting).

bocear, *va.* (vet.) = BOCEZAR.

bocel, *m.* (arch.) bowtel, solid cylindrical molding; tool for making bowtels.

bocelar, *va.* to make cylindrical moldings on.

bocelete, *m. dim.* small molding plane.

bocelón, *m. aug.* large molding plane.

bocera, *f.* something sticking to the lip after eating or drinking.

boceto, *m.* sketch.

bocezar, *vn.* (vet.) to move the lips from one side to another (s. o. horses).

bocín, *m.* round piece of bass mat put about the nave of a cart, as a cap of defence; feed pipe of an overshot wheel.

bocina, *f.* large trumpet, buglehorn, megaphone, foghorn, huntsman's horn; earpiece, receiver (of a telephone); horn (of a phonograph); speaking or hearing trumpet; a kind of shell; (B-, astr.) Ursa Minor; (mech.) bushing; wheel hoop.

bocinar, *vn.* to sound the trumpet or horn.

bocinero, *m.* trumpeter, hornblower.

bocón, na, *n.* wide-mouthed person; braggart.

bocoy, *m.* hogshead, large barrel or cask.—**bocoyes abatidos,** shooks of hogsheads.

bocudo, da, *a.* large-mouthed.

bocha, *f.* bowl, ball for playing at bowls; fold or bag in misfitting clothes.—**bochar,** *va.* to dislodge (a ball).—**bochazo,** *m.* stroke of one bowl against another.

boche, *m.* cherry pit, chuck hole; disappointment.

bochinche, *m.* (Am.) tumult, uproar, riot.

bochinchero, ra, *n.* (Am.) rioter; disturber.

bochista, *m.* good bowler.

bochorno, *m.* hot, sultry weather, scorching heat; rush of blood to the head; blush, flushing, humiliation, embarrassment.

bochornoso, sa, *a.* humiliating; embarrassing; sultry.

boda, *f.* nuptials, wedding.—**b. de negros,** (coll.) riotous carousal, orgy.—**bodas de diamante, de oro, de plata,** diamond, golden, silver wedding.

bode, *m.* (zool.) buck.

bodega, *f.* wine vault, cellar; abundant vintage; storeroom, warehouse; retail grocery; (naut.) hold of a ship.

bodegaje, *m.* (Am.) storage (charges).

bodegón, *m.* low-class chophouse; alehouse; painting representing still life, principally edibles.—**bodegoncillo,** *m. dim.* low-class chophouse.—**bodegonear,** *vn.* to run from one alehouse to another.—**bodegonero, ra,** *n.* one who keeps a low-class chophouse or alehouse.—**bodeguero, ra,** *n.* butler, one who has the care of a cellar; (Cuba) retail grocer.

bodeguilla, *f. dim.* small cellar or vault.

bodigo, *m.* manchet presented as an offering in the church.

bodijo, *m.* unequal match; hedge marriage with little ceremony.

bodocal, *n.* a kind of black grape.

bodocazo, *m.* stroke of a pellet shot from a crossbow.

bodollo, *m.* pruning knife, pruning hook.

bodoque, *m.* pellet, ball of clay shot from a crossbow; dunce, idiot.

bodoquera, *f.* blowgun; mold for clay pellets; cradle of a crossbow; pea-shooter.

bodoquillo, *m. dim.* clay pellet.

bodorrio, *m.* = BODIJO.

bodrio, *m.* soup formerly given to the poor; hodgepodge; mixture of hog's blood and onions for sausages.

bóer, *n.* & *a.* Boer.

boezuelo, *m.* stalking ox, which serves to screen fowlers.

bofe, *m.* lung, lights.

bófeta, *f.* thin, stiff cotton stuff.

bofetada, *f.* slap in the face, buffet.

bofetón, *m.* slap in the face, buffet; revolving-door trick.

boga. I. *f.* vogue, popularity; (zool.) ox-eyed cackerel, mendole; rowing; stroke; small two-edged knife. **II.** *m.* rower.—**bogada,** *f.* rowing stroke; bucking of clothes with lye.—**bogador,** *m.* rower.—**bogante,** *n.* & *a.* rower (-ing).—**bogar,** *vn.* (*pret.* BOGUÉ: *subj.* BOGUE) to row.

bogavante, *m.* (naut.) strokesman; large lobster.

bogotano, na, *a.* of or from Bogotá.

bohardilla, *f.* = BUHARDILLA.

bohemiano, na, *n.* & *a.* Bohemian.

bohémico, ca, *a.* Bohemian.

bohemio, mia; bohemo, ma. I. *n.* & *a.* Bohemian. **II.** *m.* short cloak formerly worn by the guard of archers. *V.* GITANO.

bohena, boheña, *f.* pork sausage.

bohío, *m.* (Sp. Am.) Indian hut, hovel, cabin.

bohordar, *vn.* to throw BOHORDOS in tournaments.—**bohordo,** *m.* short spear; dart used in tournaments; (bot.) scape.

boil, *m.* ox stall.

boina, *f.* flat, round woollen cap generally worn in Navarre and Biscay.

boj, *m.* box tree, boxwood; shoemaker's boxwood tool.

boja, *f.* southernwood. *V.* ABROTANO.

bojar, bojear. I. *va.* (naut.) to sail round and measure (an island or cape); scrape off the stains of (leather). **II.** *vn.* to measure.

bojedal, *m.* plantation of box trees.

bojeo, *m.* (naut.) sailing round and measuring an island or headland.

bojeta, *f.* a kind of herring.

bojiganga, *f.* company of strolling players.

bojo, *m.* = BOJEO.

bol, *m.* punch bowl; Armenian bole, red earth.

bola, *f.* ball; marble; bolus; game of bowling; (coll.) lie, falsehood, humbug, hoax, fib; (naut.) truck, ball for signals; shoe blacking.—**b. de jabón,** wash ball.—**dejar rodar la b.,** to let things run their natural course, to keep hands off; to look on with indifference.

bolada, *f.* stroke (in billiards).
bolado, *m. V.* AZUCARILLO.
bolandista, *n.* Bollandist.
bolazo, *m.* blow with a bowl.—**de b.,** hurriedly.
bolchevique, *n.* & *a.* Bolshevik (-vist).
bolchevismo, *m.* Bolshevism.
bolchevista, *n.* & *a.* = BOLCHEVIQUE.
boleadoras, *f. pl.* (Arg.) lariat with balls at one end, which are thrown to twist the lariat around an animal's legs.
bolear. I. *vn.* to play billiards for pleasure; to bowl; to boast, lie, fib. **II.** *va.* to throw; to throw the BOLEADORAS at, or catch with them; to confuse.
boleo, *m.* bowling; bowling green, place where balls are thrown.
bolera, *f.* bowling alley; dancer of BOLERO.
bolero, *m.* bolero, an Andalusian dance; bolero dancer.
bolero, ra, *a.* truant, fibbing, lying.
boleta, *f.* admission ticket; lodging billet; pay order; small package of tobacco.
boletar, *va.* to put up (tobacco) in packages.
boletero, ra, *n.* ticket agent.
boletín, *m.* pay warrant; pay bill; lodging billet; admission ticket; bulletin; (com.) price list; price current.
boleto, *m.* (Am.) ticket.
bolichada, *f.* game of BOLICHE; fish caught in a net.—**de una b.** at one throw, at the same time.
boliche, *m.* jack; small ball for bowling; small dragnet; small fish caught in a dragnet near the shore; furnace for lead smelting; toy called cup and ball.—*pl.* (naut.) foretop bowlines and top-gallant bowlines.
bolichero, ra, *n.* one who keeps a pigeonhole or trollmadam table.
bólido, *m.* shooting star.
bolilla, *f. dim.* small ball; marble (ball).
bolillo, *m.* bobbin for lace making; iron pin in the game of trucks; mold for stiffening lace cuffs; bone joined to skull of horses.—*pl.* paste nuts; starched lace cuffs.
bolín, *m.* jack; small bowl.—**de b., de bolán,** at random, carelessly.—**bolines,** (Am.) mold shot.
bolina, *f.* sounding line; punishment on ship-board; noise, turmoil; (naut.) bowline.—**echar de b.,** to boast.—**navegar de b.,** to sail with bowlines hauled.
bolinear, *va.* to sail with bowlines hauled.
bolisa, *f.* embers, hot cinders.
bolívar, *m.* bolivar, monetary unit of Venezuela (about 20 cents, or one franc).
boliviano, na. I. *n.* & *a.* Bolivian. **II.** *m.* boliviano, monetary unit of Bolivia (about 40 cents, or 2 francs).
bolo, *m.* one of the ninepins; cushion for lace making; axis or core of a winding staircase; dunce, blockhead; bolus, large pill; game of ninepins or tenpins; large knife, like a machete, used in the Philippines.
bolones, *m. pl.* (naut.) square bolts or mortar-bed pintles.
bolonio, *n.* & *a.* ignoramus, ignorant.
bolonés, esa, *a.* Bolognese; Bologna (u. a.)
bolsa, *f.* purse; money exchange; stock exchange; pouch, bag; (anat.) scrotum; (min.) pocket; (med.) sac.—**b. de pastor,** (bot.) shepherd's-purse.
bolsear, *vn.* to purse up, pucker.
bolsera, *f.* hair bag or net for ladies.
bolsería, *f.* purse or bag shop or factory.
bolsero, ra, *n.* manufacturer or seller of purses.
bolsica, ita, illa, *f. dim.* small purse.
bolsico, *m.* poke, pocket.
bolsicón, *m.* (Am.) baize skirt worn by poor women.
bolsillo, *m.* pocket; money.—**rascarse el b.,** to put one's hand in one's pocket (fig., in the sense of spending or paying), (slang) to come across.—**tener a una persona en el b.,** (coll.) to have a person in the palm of one's hand, or under one's thumb.

bolsín, *m.* gathering of brokers out of exchange hours.
bolsista, *m.* stockbroker; speculator.
bolso, *m.* purse of money, moneybag.
bolsón, *m. aug.* of BOLSO; large purse; large iron ring to hold braces of arches; board lining.
bolla, *f.* duty on woollens and silks formerly levied in Catalonia; tax on the manufacture of playing cards; in South America, great richness of an ore.
bolladura, *f.* = ABOLLADURA.
bollar, *va.* to mark (goods) with a lead seal; to emboss.
bollería, *f.* bakery, pastry shop.—**bollero, ra,** *n.* pastry cook; seller of sweet cakes.
bollico, ito, *m. dim.* small loaf or roll.
bollo, *m.* small loaf or roll, penny loaf; small biscuit or cake; puff in dress; tuft in upholstery; bruise made in metal; morbid swelling; lump; in Peru, bars of silver.—**bollos de relieve,** embossed or raised work.
bollón, *m.* brass-headed nail; bud on a plant; button earring.
bollonado, da, *a.* having brass-headed nails.
bolluelo, *m. dim.* of BOLLO.
bomba, *f.* pump; pumping engine; fire engine; shell, bombshell; carcass; piece of wind instruments; lamp globe; earthen jar or firkin for skimming oil from water; high hat.—**¡ b.!** listen! (calling attention to a toast).—**b. alimenticia,** feed pump.—**b. aspirante,** lift pump.—**b. aspirante-impelente,** lift-and-force pump.—**b. centrífuga,** centrifugal pump.—**b. de aire comprimido,** air lift.—**b. de alimentación** = B. ALIMENTICIA.—**b. de carena,** bilge pump.—**b. de doble efecto,** double-acting pump.—**b. de émbolo buzo,** plunger pump.—**b. impelente,** force pump.—**b. marina,** waterspout.—**b. rotatoria,** rotary pump.—**dar a la b.,** to pump.
bombáceo, a. I. *a.* (bot.) bombaceous. **II.** *f. pl.* Bombaceæ.
bombachas, *f. pl.* (Arg.) loose trousers fastened at the bottom.
bombacho, cha, *a.* loose, loose-fitting (s. o. trousers). *V.* PANTALÓN.
bombarda, *f.* bombard, ancient thick piece of ordnance; (naut.) bomb ketch or bomb vessel; ancient wind instrument; stop of a pipe organ.
bombardear, *va.* to bombard.—**bombardeo,** *m.* bombardment.—**bombardero,** *m.* bombardier.
bombasí, *m.* bombazine, dimity.
bombástico, ca, *a.* bombastic, high-sounding.
bombazo, *m.* report of a bursting bomb.
bombé, *m.* light two-wheeled carriage open in front.
bombear, *va.* to pump; to bomb, bombard; (Am.) to reconnoiter, watch, spy; to dismiss, (coll.) to fire; to praise, write up.
bombeo, *m.* pumping; curving, bulging.
bombero, *m.* fireman; pumper; howitzer.
bombilla, *f.* (Am.) small tube for drinking MATE; (naut.) hand lantern.
bombillo, *m.* lamp chimney; water-closet trap; small pump; sample or thief tube.
bombista, *n.* pump maker; lamp-chimney maker; praiser, writer of write-ups.
bombo, *m.* large drum; player on bass drum; (naut.) barge or lighter; leather pouch in billiards, for numbered balls.—**dar b.,** to praise excessively, to write up.
bombo, ba, *a.* astonished; (Am.) tepid.
bombón, *m.* bonbon, candy; vase or cup made of cane in the Philippines; carboy.
bombonaje, *m.* screw pine.
bombonera, *f.* box for bonbons.
bonachón, na, *a.* good-natured, kind
bonaerense, *a.* of or from Buenos Aires.
bonancible, *a.* moderate, calm, fair.
bonanza, *f.* fair weather; prosperity, success.—**ir en b.,** to be prosperous.
bonapartismo, *m.* Bonapartism.
bonapartista, *n.* & *a.* Bonapartist.
bonazo, za, *a.* good-natured, kind-hearted.

bondad, *f.* goodness, excellence; kindness, kindliness.—**bondadosamente,** *adv.* kindly.

bondadoso, sa, *a.* kind, good.

bonetada, *f.* salutation by taking off the hat.

bonetas, *f. pl.* (naut.) bonnets.

bonete, *m.* bonnet, college cap; secular clergyman; bonnet of a fortress; preserve jar; reticulum of ruminants.

bonetería, *f.* bonnet factory or shop.

bonetero, ra, *n.* bonnet maker or seller; (bot.) prickwood, gatheridge.

bonetillo, *m.* small cap or bonnet; a hair ornament.

bonga, *f.* a Philippine palm. *V.* ARECA.

bongo, *m.* a large, rough canoe or boat.

boniato, *m.* sweet potato.

bonicamente, *adv.* prettily, neatly, slyly.

bonico, ca, *a. dim.* fairly good.

bonificación, *f.* allowance, discount; bonus.

bonificar, *va.* (*pret.* BONIFIQUÉ: *subj.* BONIFIQUE) to credit; to improve.

bonina, *f.* (bot.) oxeye chamomile.

bonísimo, ma, *a. sup.* of BUENO: very good.

bonítalo, *m.* (ict.) = BONITO.

bonitamente, *adv.* prettily, neatly.

bonitillo, illa, *a. dim.* somewhat pretty.

bonito, *m.* striped tunny.

bonito, ta, *a.* pretty.

bonizal, *m.* cornfield.

bonizo, *m.* corn grown wild in Asturias.

bono, *m.* (com.) bond; certificate; duebill.

bonote, *m.* cocoanut fiber; (naut.) coir.

bonzo, *m.* bonze, a priest of Buddha.

boñiga, *f.* cow dung; casings.

boñigar, *a.* app. to a kind of round white fig.

Bootes, *m.* Bootes, a northern constellation.

boqueada, *f.* gasp, gasping.

boquear. **I.** *vn.* to gape, gasp; to breathe one's last; to end, terminate. **II.** *va.* to pronounce; to utter.

boquera, *f.* sluice in an irrigation canal; door; opening; cesspool; excoriation of the angles of the lips; (vet.) ulcer in the mouth.

boquerón, *m.* wide opening, large hole; (icht.) anchovy.

boquete, *m.* gap, narrow entrance.

boquiabierto, ta, *a.* open-mouthed; gaping.

boquiancho, cha, *a.* wide-mouthed.

boquiangosto, ta, *a.* narrow-mouthed.

boquiconejuno, na, *a.* rabbit-mouthed; hare-lipped (s. o. horses).

boquiduro, ra, *a.* hard-mouthed.

boquifresco, ca, *a.* fresh-mouthed (s. o. horses); frank, outspoken.

boquifruncido, da, *a.* pucker-mouthed.

boquihendido, da, *a.* large-mouthed, flewed.

boquihundido, da, *a.* having a sunken mouth.

boquilla, *f. dim.* little mouth; opening of breeches at the knees; opening in an irrigation canal; chisel for mortising; mouthpiece of a wind instrument; cigar-holder; (mas.) verge, course; (mech.) nozzle; bushing, bush; gas burner; mouth of a scabbard.

boquimuelle, *a.* tender-mouthed; unwary, easily imposed upon.

boquín, a kind of coarse baize.

boquinatural, *a.* well-mouthed.

boquinegro, gra. **I.** *a.* black-mouthed. **II.** *m.* or *f.* a blackish snail.

boquirrasgado, da, *a.* deep-mouthed.

boquirroto, ta, *a.* loquacious, garrulous.

boquirrubio, bia, *a.* simple, artless; conceited.

boquiseco, ca, *a.* dry-mouthed.

boquisumido, da, *a.* = BOQUIHUNDIDO.

boquita, *f. dim.* small or little mouth.

boquitorcido, da; boquituerto, ta, *a.* wry-mouthed, having a crooked mouth.

boquiverde, *a.* plain-spoken about off-color matters.

borácico, ca, *a.* boracic.—**boracita,** *f.* (min.) boracite.—**borato,** *m.* borate.

bórax, *m.* borax.

borbollar, *vn.* to bubble out, gush out.

borbollón, borbotón, *m.* bubbling, gushing up of water; flash.—**a borbollones,** impetuously.

borbollonear, *vn.* = BORBOLLAR.

borbónico, ca, *a.* Bourbonic.—**borbonismo,** *m.* Bourbonism.

borborigmo, *m.* rumbling in the bowels.

borbotar, *vn.* to gush out; to boil over.

borbotón, *m.* = BORBOLLÓN.—**a borbotones** = A BORBOLLONES.—**hablar a borbotones,** to speak in torrents.

borceguí, *m.* buskin, half-boot; lace shoe.

borceguinería, *f.* lace-shoe factory or shop.

borceguinero, ra, *n.* lace-shoe maker or retailer.

borcellar, *m.* brim of a vessel.

borda, *f.* hut, cottage; (naut.) gunwale.

bordada, *f.* (naut.) board, tack.—**dar una b.,** to tack; to promenade.

bordadillo, *m.* double-flowered taffeta.

bordado. **I.** *m.* embroidery. **II.** *pp.* of BORDAR.

bordador, ra, *n.* embroiderer.

bordadura, *f.* embroidery; (her.) border of an escutcheon.

bordaje, *m.* (naut.) side planks of a ship.

bordar, *va.* to embroider; to perform prettily and artistically.—**b. a tambor,** to tambour.

borde. **I.** *m.* border, edge, verge, fringe, ledge; hem of a garment; brim of a vessel; board, the side of a ship.—**b. de ataque,** (aer.) leading edge.—**b. de salida,** (aer.) trailing edge.—**a b.,** on the brink; on the eve. **II.** *a.* wild, savage, uncultivated; bastard.

bordear, *vn.* (naut.) to ply to windward.

bordelés, sa, *a.* of or from Bordeaux.

bordo, *m.* board, the side of a ship; border, outer edge; tack.—**a b.,** on board, aboard.—**al b.,** alongside the ship.—**dar bordos,** to tack.—**de alto b.,** sea-going, major (s. o. ships); (met.) of importance, of heavy caliber, first rank; high-up (s. o. persons).

bordón, *m.* Jacob's staff, pilgrim's staff; bass-string; bass of an organ; iteration of words; refrain, burden of a song; staff, guide, or support of another.—*pl.* (naut.) shores, outriggers.

bordoncico, illo, *m. dim.* small staff.

bordoneado, da, *a.* (her.) pommelled.

bordonear. **I.** *vn.* to try the ground with a staff or stick; to rove or wander about. **II.** *va.* to beat, club, cudgel.

bordonería, *f.* wandering idly about, on pretense of devotion.

bordonero, ra, *n.* vagabond, roamer, tramp.

bordura, *f.* (her.) = BORDADURA.

boreal, *a.* boreal, northern.

bóreas, *m.* Boreas, the north wind.

borgoña, *m.* Burgundy wine.

borgoñón, na, *a.* of or from Burgundy.—**a la borgoñona,** in Burgundy fashion.

borgoñota, *f.* a sort of ancient helmet.—**a la b.,** in the Burgundy fashion.

bórico, ca, *a.* boric.

borinqueño, ña, *n. & a.* Porto-Rican.

borla, *f.* tassel, tuft, lock, flaunt; in universities, doctor's bonnet; doctorship.—**tomar la b.,** to graduate.

borlica, illa, ita, *f. dim.* small tassel.

borlilla, *f.* (bot.) anther.

borlón, *m. aug.* large tassel; napped stuff, made of thread and cotton yarn.

borne, *m.* end of a lance; (bot.) cytissus; (elec.) binding post, binding screw; terminal.

borneadero, *m.* (naut.) berth of a ship at anchor; swinging berth.

borneadizo, za, *a.* pliant, easily warped.

bornear. **I.** *va.* to bend, turn, twist; (arch.) to model and cut (pillars); to hoist and place (building stones, etc.). **II.** *vn.* (naut.) to swing around the anchor. **III.** *vr.* to warp, bulge, curve.

borneo, *m.* turning or winding; swinging motion in dancing; (naut.) swinging round the anchor.

borneol, *m.* (chem.) borneol.

bornera, *a.* blackish millstone.

---

bornero, ra, *a.* ground by a BORNERA.

borní, *m.* (orn.) lanner, a kind of falcon.

boro, *m.* (chem.) boron.

borona, *f.* a grain resembling Indian corn; bread made from this grain.

boronía, *f.* = ALBORONÍA.

borra, *f.* yearling ewe; thick wool; goat's hair; nap; floss, burl; tax on sheep; lees, sediment, waste; idle talk; borax.—**b. de lana,** flock wool.—**b. de seda,** floss silk.

borracha, *f.* (coll.) borachio, a leather bottle for wine.

borrachear, *vn.* to drink habitually to excess, to be a drunkard.

borrachera, borrachería, *f.* drunkenness; carousal, drunken feast, orgy; drunken condition, (coll.) drunk; (met.) madness, great folly.

borrachero, *m.* a South American shrub, whose seed, ingested, causes delirium.

borrachez, *f.* intoxication; perturbation of the judgment or reason.

borrachín, *m.* drunkard.

borracho, cha. I. *n.* drunkard. **II.** *a.* drunk, intoxicated; violet-colored.—**borrachón, borrachonazo,** *m. aug.* great drunkard, tippler.

borrachuela, *f.* (bot.) bearded darnel.

borrachuelo, la, *n. dim.* little tippler.

borrador, *m.* rough draft; blotter.

borradura, *f.* erasure, scratch.

borragíneo. I. *a.* (bot.) boraginaceous. **II.** *f. pl.* Boraginaceæ.

borraj, *m. V.* ATÍNCAR and BÓRAX.

borraja, *f.* (bot.) borage.

borrajear, *vn.* to scribble, scrawl.

borrajo, *m.* = RESCOLDO.

borrar, *va.* to cross out, strike out; to efface, erase, rub out, obliterate; (met.) to cloud, darken, obscure.

borrasca, *f.* storm, tempest, squall; barren rock; (met.) hazard, danger; obstruction.—**b. deshecha,** violent tempest.

borrascoso, sa, *a.* stormy, tempestuous.

borrasquero, ra, *n. & a.* reveller (-ing).

borregada, *f.* large flock of sheep or lambs.

borrego, ga, *n.* lamb not yet a year old; (met.) simpleton.—**borreguero,** *m.* shepherd who tends lambs.—**borreguito,** *m. dim.* little lamb.

borrén, *m.* saddle-tree.

borrica, *f.* she-ass; ignorant woman.

borricada, *f.* drove of asses; cavalcade on asses; asinine word or action.

borrico, *m.* ass, donkey; (carp.) sawhorse.

borricón, borricote, *m. aug.* large jackass; plodder, laborious man; sawyer's horse.

borrilla, *f.* downy matter enveloping fruits.

borriqueño, ña, *a.* asinine.

borriquero, *m.* one who keeps or tends asses.

borriquete, *m.* (carp.) sawhorse.—**b. de proa,** fore-topmast.

borriquillo, illa, ito, ita, *n. dim.* little ass.

borriquillos, *m. pl.* crossbars of a table frame.

borro, *m.* wether not two years old; (coll.) dolt; duty on sheep.

borrón, *m.* blot; blur; rough draft; blemish, stigma, stain.

borroncillo, *m. dim.* small blot or stain.

barronear, *va.* to sketch; to waste (paper) by scribbling on it.

borroso, sa, *a.* full of dregs, thick, muddy.

borrufalla, *f.* empty sounds or words.

borrumbada, *f.* = BARRUMBADA.

boruca, *f.* noise, hubbub, uproar.

borujo, *m.* pack, bundle; bagasse of olive pits; oil cake.

borujón, *m.* = BURUJÓN.

borusca, *f.* withered leaf. *V.* SEROJA.

boscaje, *m.* cluster of trees, grove; (pict.) boscage, landscape.

Bósforo, *m.* Bosporus.

bosnio, nia, *n. & a.* Bosnian.

bosque, *m.* wood, forest; grove.

bosquecillo, *m. dim.* small wood, coppice.

bosquejar, *va.* to sketch; to plan, design; to explain in a rather obscure manner; to make a rough model of.

bosquejo, *m.* sketch; any unfinished work, writing or composition.—**en b.,** unfinished.

bosquete, *m.* wood; forest; artificial forest.

bosta, *f.* dung, manure.

bostezante, *a.* gaping, yawning.

bostezar, *vn.* (*pret.* BOSTECÉ: *subj.* BOSTECE) to yawn, gape.—**bostezo,** *m.* yawn, yawning.

bota, *f.* boot; small leather wine bag; butt or pipe for liquids; liquid measure equal to about 125 gallons; (naut.) water cask.—**b. de montar,** riding boot.—**ponerse las botas,** to become rich or prosperous, to strike oil (fig.).

botador, *m.* thrower, pitcher; punch; instrument for driving out nails; nail set; dentist's crow's bill or pelican; (naut.) starting pole, boat hook; (mech.) furnace bar, fire iron; bolt driver; (med.) refractor.

botafuego, *m.* linstock, match staff; irritable, quick-tempered person.

botagueña, *f.* pig-haslets sausage.

botalón, *m.* boom (of a crane or derrick).—**b. del foque,** jib-boom.

botamen, *m.* (naut.) all the water casks on board a ship; all the pots and jars in a drug store.

botana, *f.* plug; plaster on a wound; scar.

botánica, *f.* botany.—**botánico, ca,** *a.* botanical.

botánico, ca; botanista, *n.* botanist.

botanomancia, *f.* botanomancy, superstitious divination by herbs.

botantes, *m. pl.* (naut.) shores, outriggers.

botar. I. *va.* to cast, pitch, throw, fling, launch; (Am.) to squander, misspend; to throw away; (naut.) to shift (the helm).—**b. al agua,** (naut.) to launch. **II.** *vn.* to bound; rebound; to jump and kick, caper (s. o. an unbroken horse.). **III.** *vr.* = *vn.* in the last sense.

botaratada, *f.* rash, thoughtless action.

botarate, *m.* (coll.) madcap, thoughtless, blustering person; spendthrift.

botarel, *m.* (arch.) buttress, abutment, spur, counter pillar.

botarga, *f.* loose breeches, galligaskins; motley dress; harlequin, buffoon; a kind of large sausage. *V.* DOMINGUILLO.

botasilla, *f.* (mil.) bugle signal for the cavalry to saddle.

botavante, *m.* (naut.) boarding pike.

botavara. *f.* (naut.) small boom or pole, gaff, sprit; boat hook.—**b. de cangreja,** gaffsail boom.

bote, *m.* boat; thrust with a weapon; rebound; frolicsome bound of a horse; gallipot; toilet-box; pot or jar; chuck-farthing; (naut.) boat.—**b. de lastre,** ballast lighter.—**b. de tabaco,** snuff canister.—**b. salvavidas,** lifeboat.—**de b. y voleo,** instantly.—**de b. en b.,** crowded, jammed.

botecico, illo, ito, *m. dim.* canister; skiff.

botella, *f.* bottle.—**b. de Leiden,** Leyden jar.

botellazo, *m.* blow with a bottle.

botellón, *m.* demijohn.

botequín, *m.* (naut.) cog, scull.

botería, *f.* (naut.) collection of casks of wine.

botero, ra, *n.* one who makes leather bags and bottles for wine; boatman, ferryman (-woman).

botica, *f.* apothecary's shop, drug store; medicines. —**de todo, como en b.,** everything under the sun.

boticaria, *f.* apothecary's wife.

boticario, ria, *n.* apothecary.

botiga, *f.* (prov.) shop.—**botiguero,** *m.* shopkeeper.—**botiguilla,** *f. dim.* of BOTIGA.

botija, *f.* earthen round, short-necked jug; fat person.—**botijero,** *m.* one who makes or sells jars.—**botijilla, juela,** *f. dim.* small jar.

botijo, *m.* round earthen jar with a spout and handle; plump child.

botijón, *m. aug.* large earthen jar; fat child.

botilla, *f. dim.* small wine bag; woman's half-boot.

botiller, *m.* = BOTILLERO.

botillería, *f.* ice-cream parlor; (naut.) steward's room and stores.—**botiliero, ra,** *n.* one who prepares or sells ice cream and refreshments.

botillo, *m. dim.* small leather wine bag.

botín, *m.* buskin, half-boot; high shoe; spatterdash, leggings; booty, spoils of war.

botina, *f.* modern gaiter; a woman's boot.

botinero, ra. I. *a.* black-foot. **II.** *n.* shoemaker; soldier who took care of and sold the booty.

botinico, illo, ito, *m. dim.* little gaiter or spatterdash.

botiquín, *m.* medicine chest.

botito, *m.* gaiter with elastics or buttons.

botivoleo, *m.* recovering a ball at the rebound.

boto, ta. I. *a.* blunt; dull of understanding. **II.** *m.* wine skin; large gut filled with butter.

botón, *m.* button; sprout, bud; (fen.) tip of a foil; knob (of door or window); bead (in assaying); annulet of balusters, and of keys; piece of wood which fastens a fowling net; crankpin; dowel; handle.—**b. de fuego,** cautery in the form of a button.—**b. de oro,** (bot.) creeping double-flowered crowfoot.

botonadura, *f.* set of buttons.

botonazo, *m.* (fen.) thrust with a foil.

botoncito, *m. dim.* small button.

botonería, *f.* button maker's shop.

botonero, ra, *n.* button maker; button seller.

bototo, *m.* gourd or calabash for water.

botuto, *m.* stem of the papaw fruit; war trumpet of the Orinoco Indians.

bou, *m.* joint casting of a net by two boats.

bovaje, bovático, *m.* ancient duty on cattle.

bóveda, *f.* arch; vault; cave, cavern; vault for the dead.—**b. celeste,** firmament.—**b. craneal,** cranial cavity.—**b. palatina,** (anat.) palate.

bovedilla, *f.* (arch.) small vault, cove.—*pl.* (naut.) counters.

bóvido, da. I. *a.* (zool.) bovine. **II.** *m. pl.* Bovidæ.

bovino, na, *a.* bovine.

box, *m.* (bot.) = BOJ.

boxeador, ra, *n.* (spt.) boxer.—**boxear,** *vn.* to box.—**boxeo,** *m.* boxing.

bóxer, *m.* Boxer, a member of the Chinese Boxer Association.

boya, *f.* (naut.) beacon; buoy; net float.

boyada, *f.* drove of oxen.

boyal, *a.* relating to cattle.

boyante. I. *a.* buoyant, floating. **II.** *a.* (naut.) light, sailing well; prosperous, successful.

boyar, *vn.* (naut.) to buoy; to float.

boyazo, *m. aug.* large ox.

boyera, boyeriza, *f.* ox stall, cow house.

boyero, *m.* oxherd; ox driver; cowherd.

boyezuelo, *m. dim.* young or small ox.

boyuno, na, *a.* bovine.

boza, *f.* (naut.) rope with one end fast in a bolt ring.—**bozas,** (naut.) stoppers.

bozal. I. *m.* muzzle; bells on a harness. **II.** *a.* pure, unmixed (s. o. negroes); just-imported (s. o. negroes); novice, inexperienced, greenhorn; stupid, foolish; wild, not broken in, untamed.

bozalejo, *m.* small muzzle.

bozo, *m.* down that precedes the beard; mustache; mouth around the lips; headstall of a horse.

brabante, *m.* Brabant or Flemish linen.

brabantés, brabanzón, *n. & a.* Brabantine.

braceada, *f.* violent extension of the arms.

braceaje, *m.* coinage; beating the metal for coining; (naut.) bracing of the yards; depth of water.

bracear. I. *vn.* to move or swing the arms. **II.** *va.* (naut.) to brace; to fathom.

braceo, *m.* repeated swinging of the arms.

bracero. I. *m.* one who offers his arm to a lady; day laborer; strong-armed man. **II.** *a.* thrown with the hand (s. o. weapons).

bracete.—de b., arm in arm.

bracillo, *m.* branch of the mouth bit of a horse's bridle.

bracillo, ito, *m. dim.* little arm.

bracmán, *m.* Brahman.

bracmánico, ca, *a.* Brahmanic.

braco, ca, *a.* pug-nosed.

bráctea, *f.* (bot.) bract.

bractéola, *f.* bractlet.

bradipepsia, *f.* bradypepsia, slow digestion.

bradiuria, (med.) bradyuria.

brafonera, *f.* rerebrace; brassart.

braga, *f.* breeches, knickerbockers; child's clout, diaper; hoisting rope; (mil.) breeching, lashing rope.

bragada, *f.* flat of the thigh in beasts.

bragado, da, *a.* having the flanks of a different color from the rest of the body; (met.) ill-disposed, of depraved sentiments; energetic, firm.

bragadura, *f.* crotch; fork of a pair of breeches; flat of the thigh in beasts.

bragazas. I. *f. pl. aug.* wide breeches. **II.** *m.* man easily ruled, or henpecked.

braguero, *m.* truss, bandage for a rupture; brace; (Peru) martingale—**b. de cañón,** (arti.) breeching of a gun.

bragueta, *f.* front opening or flap of breeches.

braguetero. I. *m.* (low) lecher. **II.** *a.* lecherous.

braguillas, *f. pl. dim.* little breeches; child breeched for the first time; ugly, dwarfish person.

brahmán = BRACMÁN.

brahmanismo, *m.* Brahmanism.

brahmín = BRAHMÁN.

brahón, *m.* fold which, in ancient apparel, surrounded the upper part of the arm.

Brama, *f.* Brahma, deity of the Hindus.

brama, *f.* rut, mating season.

bramadera, *f.* rattle; horn call.

bramadero, *m.* rutting place.

bramador, ra, *n. & a.* roarer (-ing).

bramante. I. *m.* packthread, hempcord, twine; Brabant linen. **II.** *a.* roaring.

bramar, *vn.* to roar, bellow; to storm, bluster; to rage, cry.

bramido, *m.* cry uttered by wild beasts, howl; roaring of the elements.

bramil, *m.* chalkline used by sawyers.

bramín = BRACMÁN.

bran de Inglaterra, *m.* an old Spanish dance.

branca, *f.* point of a horn.—**b. ursina** = ACANTO.

brancada, *f.* dragnet or sweep net.

brancaursina, *f.* (bot.) bear's breech.

branchas, *f. pl.* gills of a fish.

brandal, *m.* (naut.) backstay, ladder rope.

brandís, *m.* greatcoat formerly worn.

brandy, *m.* brandy.

branque, *m.* (naut.) stem.

branquia, *f.* gill of a fish.

branquiado, da, *a.* branchiate.

branquial, *a.* branchial.

branquífero, ra, *a.* gill-bearing.

braña, *f.* summer pasture; brushwood.

braquial, *a.* brachial, belonging to the arm.

braquicéfalo, la, *a.* brachycephalous.

braquiópodo, da. I. *n. & a.* brachiopod. **II.** *m. pl.* Brachiopodæ.

braquiotomía, *f.* brachiotomy, amputation of the arms.

brasa, *f.* live coal; red-hot coal or wood.—**estar en brasas,** to be on pins and needles.—**estar hecho unas brasas,** to be red in the face, flushed.

braserito, *m. dim.* small pan to hold coals.

brasero, *m.* brazier, pan to hold coals; fire pan; place where criminals were burnt; (Mex.) hearth, fireplace.

brasil, *m.* (bot.) braziletto; brazilwood; rouge.

brasilado, da, *a.* of a red or brazilwood color; ruddy.

brasileño, ña, *n. & a.* Brazilian.

brasilete, *m.* Jamaica wood, braziletto.

brasilina, *f.* brazilin.

brasmología, *f.* science of the tides.

bravamente, *adv.* bravely, gallantly; cruelly; barbarously; finely, extremely well; plentifully, copiously.

bravata, *f.* bravado, boast, brag.

braveador, ra, *n.* bully, hector.

bravear, *vn.* to bully, hector, menace.

bravera, *f.* vent, chimney.

braveza, *f.* bravery; vigor; ferocity; fury.

bravilo, illa, *a. dim.* rather wild, not yet tamed.

bravío, vía. I. *a.* ferocious, wild, untamed; uncultivated; coarse, unpolished. **II.** *m.* fierceness.

bravo, va, *a.* brave, manly, fearless; bullying, hectoring; savage, wild, fierce; severe, untractable; rude, unpolished; sumptuous, expensive; excellent, fine.—¡**bravo!** bravo!

bravonel, *m.* brave; hector, braggart.

bravosidad, *f.* = GALLARDÍA.

bravucón, na, *n. & a.* boaster (-ing), braggart (-ing).

bravura, *f.* ferocity, fierceness; courage, manliness; bravado, boast, brag.

braza, *f.* fathom.

brazada, *f.* uplifting of the arms; armful.

brazado, *m.* armful.

brazaje, *m.* (naut.) depth of water.

brazal, *m.* bracer, brassart; bracelet; irrigation ditch from a river or canal; mourning band around the arm; (naut.) rail.

brazalete, *m.* armlet, bracelet. *V.* MANILLA, PULSERA.—*pl.* (naut.) brace pendants.

brazazo, *m. aug.* large or long arm.

brazo, *m.* arm (of the body, a chair, a lever, the sea); upper half of the arm; fore leg; branch (of a tree, a chandelier); bravery, energy, enterprise. —*pl.* hands, laborers; assistance, protection, backing; protectors, backers.—**b. a b.,** hand to hand. **b. de palanca,** lever arm.—**a b.,** by hand; swimming.—**a b. partido** = B. A B.—**con los brazos abiertos,** with open arms.—**con los brazos cruzados,** with crossed arms.—**de b.,** arm in arm.—**hecho un b. de mar,** gorgeously attired.—**ser el b. derecho de alguien,** to be somebody's right-hand man.

brazolas, *f. pl.* (naut.) coamings of the hatchways.

brazuelo, *m. dim.* small arm; shoulder or fore thigh of beasts; branch of the mouth bit of a bridle.

brea, *f.* pitch, tar; maltha; coarse canvas; sackcloth.

brear, *va.* to pitch, tar; to vex, plague; thwart; (met.) to play a joke on.

brebaje, *m.* beverage, potion; (naut.) grog.

breca, *f.* bleak or blay; a river fish. *V.* ALBUR.

brécol, *m.,* **brecolera,** *f.* (bot.) broccoli.

brecha, *f.* breach, opening; (met.) impression (on the mind).—**abrir b.,** to make a breach; to create an impression; to make progress.—**batir en b.,** (fort.) to batter, breach; to persecute.

brega, *f.* struggle; scrap, fight.—**andar a la b.,** to work hard.—**dar b.,** to be hard or laborious; (w. a) to play a trick or joke (on).

bregar. I. *vn.* (*pret.* BREGUÉ: *subj.* BREGUE) to contend, struggle. **II.** *va.* to work (dough) with a rolling pin.

bren, *m.* bran. *V.* SALVADO.

brenca, *f.* (bot.) maidenhair; sluice post.

brenga, *f.* filament, one of the three cristated anthers of saffron.

breña, *f.,* **breñal, breñar,** *m.* craggy and brambled ground.

breñoso, sa, *a.* craggy and brambled.

breque, *m.* (icht.) bleak.

bresca, *f.* honeycomb.

brescar, *va.* (*pret.* BRESQUÉ: *subj.* BRESQUE) to extract honeycombs from (a beehive).

bretador, *m.* call, whistle or pipe to call birds.

bretaña, *f.* fine linen made in Brittany; (bot.) hyacinth.

brete, *m.* fetters, shackles; perplexity, difficulties; (Philip.) a food made of leaves of betel.—**estar en un b.,** to be hard put to, to be in difficulties.

bretón, na. I. *n. & a.* Breton. **II.** *m.* (bot.) borecole, kale.

breva, *f.* early fruit of a fig tree; early large acorn; choice cigar, rather flat; (coll.) any valuable thing obtained easily, (coll.) snap, cinch.

breval, *m.* (bot.) early fig tree.

breve. I. *a.* apostolic brief. **II.** *f.* breve, longest note in music.

breve, *a.* brief, short, concise.—**en b.,** shortly, in a little while.

brevedad, *f.* briefness, conciseness.

brevemente, *adv.* briefly, concisely.

brevete, *m.* = MEMBRETE.

breviario, *m.* breviary; abridgement, epitome; brevier, small size of type.

brevipenne, *a.* (zool.) brevipennate.

brezal, *m.* heath, place planted with heaths.

brezo, *m.* (bot.) heath, heather.

briaga, *f.* bass-weed rope.

brial, *m.* rich silken skirt.

briba, *f.* truantship, idleness.

bribar, *vn.* to lead a vagabond life.

bribia, *f.* beggar's tale of woe.—**echar la b.,** to go a-begging.

bribón, na, *n.* vagrant; impostor; knave, scoundrel, rascal.—**bribonada,** *f.* knavery, petty villainy, mischief.—**bribonazo,** *m. aug.* great cheat, big rascal.—**briboncillo,** *m. dim.* little rascal.—**bribonear,** *vn.* to loiter about; to loaf.

bribonería, *f.* life of a vagabond; rascality.

bribonzuelo, *m. dim.* little rascal.

bricho, *m.* spangle, used in embroidery.

brida, *f.* bridle; rein; horsemanship; curb, restraint, check; rail coupling; fishplate; flange; clamp, staple (watchmaking).

bridecú, *m.* sword belt.

bridón, *m.* horseman riding a bur saddle; horse accoutred with a bur saddle; small bridle; (poet.) fine horse.

brigada, *f.* brigade; beasts of burden for an army. —**brigadero,** *m.* man who tends beasts of burden in the army.—**brigadier,** *m.* (mil.) brigadier general; navy officer commanding a division of a fleet.

brigola, *f.* (mil.) battering ram.

Briján, *m.*—**saber más que B.,** to be very wise and cautious.

brillador, ra, *a.* sparkling, glittering.

brillante. I. *a.* brilliant, bright; shining, sparkling, glittering; glossy, lustrous; excellent, magnificent. **II.** *m.* brilliant, diamond.

brillantemente, *adv.* brilliantly; brightly, resplendently; splendidly.

brillantez, *f.* brilliance. *V.* BRILLO.

brillar, *vn.* to shine, sparkle, glitter.

brillo, *m.* brillancy, brightness, lustre; splendor, magnificence.

brincador, ra, *n. & a.* leaper (-ing), jumper (-ing).

brincar, I. *vn.* (*pret.* BRINQUÉ: *subj.* BRINQUE) to leap, jump; frisk, skip, gambol; to fly into a passion, become excited, (coll.) kick. **II.** *va.* to omit, skip; to throw (a child) up and down.

brinco, *m.* leap, jump; hop, bounce; small jewel worn in the hair.

brindar. I. *vn.* (w. **por**) to drink a person's health; toast. **II.** *va.* to offer, present, afford.

brindis, *m.* drinking the health of another; toast.

brinqué. *V.* BRINCAR.

brinquillo, brinquiño, *m.* gewgaw, small trinket; sweetmeat from Portugal.

brinza, *f.* blade, slip, sprig, shoot.

brío, *m.* vigor, enterprise, courage.

briol, *m.* (naut.) bunt line.

briolín, *m.* (naut.) slab line.

brionia, *f.* (bot.) bryony.—**brionina,** *f.* (chem.) bryonin.

bríos.—¡**voto a b.!** *interj.* by the Almighty!

briosamente, *adv.* spiritedly, courageously, vigorously.

brioso, sa, *a.* vigorous, enterprising, courageous; lively, spirited.

brisa, *f.* breeze; bagasse of pressed grapes.

brisca, *f.* a card game.

briscado, da. I. *a.* mixed with silk (app. to gold and silver twist). **II.** *pp.* of BRISCAR.

briscar, *va.* to embroider with gold or silver twist.

brisera, *f.,* **brisero,** *m.* glass screen for a candle.

británica, *f.* (bot.) great water dock.

británico, ca, *a.* British.

britano, na., *n. & a.* Briton.

brizar, *va.* to rock (a cradle).

brizna, *f.* fragment; splinter or chip; filament, string (of beans, etc.).

briznoso, sa, *a.* full of fragments or scraps.

brizo, *m.* cradle.

broa, *f.* (P. I.) a kind of biscuit or cracker; (naut.) shallow cove.

broca, *f.* reel for twist, silk, or thread; conical drill for boring in iron; shoemaker's tack.

brocadillo, *m.* brocade of inferior quality.

brocado. I. *m.* gold or silver brocade. **II.** *a.* embroidered like brocade.

brocal, *m.* curbstone of a well; metal ring of the scabbard of a sword.—**b. de bota,** mouthpiece of a leathern wine bottle.

brocamantón, *m.* diamond brooch.

brocatel, *m.* stuff made of hemp and silk; white-streaked Spanish marble.

bróculi, *m.* broccoli, a sort of cabbage.

brocha, *f.* painter's brush; cogged dice.—**de b. gorda,** (painting) poorly done; (painter) of doors and windows; crude, badly done or written.

brochada, *f.* stroke of the brush.

brochado, da, *a.* relating to brocade.

brochadura, *f.* set of hooks and eyes.

brochazo, *m.* = BROCHADA.

broche, *m.* clasp; hook and eye; locket; hasp; brooch.

brocheta, *f.* (cook.) skewer.

brochón, *m. aug.* large brush; whitewash brush.

brochuela, *f. dim.* small brush.

brodio, *m.* = BODRIO.

brodista, *m.* poor student who comes for his portion of *bodrio* or hotchpotch.

broma, *f.* gaiety, merriment; noisy gathering; jest, joke; shipworm; teredo; oatmeal gruel; (mas.) riprap.

bromado, da, *a.* worm-eaten.

bromar, *va.* to bore (s. o. insects).

bromato, *m.* bromate.

bromatología, *f.* bromatology, science of foods.

bromear, *vn.* to joke, jest, make fun.

bromeliaceo, cea. I. *a.* (bot.) bromeliaceous. **II.** *f. pl.* Bromeliaceæ.

bromhidrato, *m.* hydrobromide.

bromhídrico, ca, *a.* hydrobromic.

bromhidrosis, *f.* osmidrosis, fetid sweating.

brómico, ca, *a.* (chem.) bromic.

bromista, *n..* merry person; practical joker.

bromo, *m.* (chem.) bromine; (bot.) brome grass.

bromurado, da, *a.* containing bromine; bromine (u. a., as in *agua bromurada*, bromine water).

bromuro, *m.* (chem.) bromide.

bronca, *f.* practical joke; wrangle, quarrel.

broncamente, *adv.* peevishly, morosely.

bronce, *m.* bronze; brass; (poet.) trumpet, bell, or cannon.—**b. de aluminio,** aluminum bronze.—**b. de campanas,** bell metal.—**b. de cañón,** gun metal.—**b. fosforado,** phosphor bronze.

bronceado, da. I. *a.* bronze-colored; tanned, sunburnt. **II.** *m.* bronze-color finish (-ing). **III.** *pp.* of BRONCEAR.

bronceadura, *f.* = BRONCEADO, *m.*

broncear, *va.* to bronze; to adorn with brass.

broncería, *f.* collection of bronzes.

broncíneo, a, *a.* bronzelike.

broncista, *n.* worker in bronze.

bronco, ca, *a.* rough, coarse, unpolished; crusty; sturdy; morose, crabbed; rude; hard; abrupt, harsh; hoarse.

bronconeumonía, *f.* broncho-pneumonia.

broncorrea, *f.* bronchorhea, excessive discharge of mucus from the bronchial tubes.

broncotomía, *f.* (surg.) bronchotomy.

broncha, *f.* short poniard; jewel; whitewashing brush.

bronquedad, *f.* harshness, roughness, rudeness; brittleness.

bronquial, *a.* (anat.) bronchial.

bronquina, *f.* dispute, quarrel, scrap.

bronquio, *m.* (anat.) bronchus, bronchial tube.

bronquíolo, *m.* (anat.) bronchiol.

bronquitis, *f.* bronchitis.

broquel, *m.* shield, buckler; support, protection.—**broquelazo,** *m. aug.* stroke with a shield or buckler; large shield or buckler.—**broquelero,** *m.* one who makes or wears shields or bucklers; wrangler, disputer.—**broquelete,** *m. dim.* small buckler.—**broquelillo,** *m. dim.* small shield; small earrings.

broqueta, *f.* skew. *V.* BROCHETA.

brosquil, *m.* sheepfold, sheepcote.

brota, *f.* vine bud. *V.* BROTE.

brotadura, *f.* budding.

brótano, *m.* (bot.) southernwood.

brotar. I. *vn.* to bud, germinate, put forth shoots; come out, gush, rush out; issue, break out, appear. **II.** *va.* to bring forth, produce.

brote, broto, *m.* germ of vines; bud of trees; fragment, crumb, bit.

brotón, *m.* large clasp; shoot, tender twig.

broza, *f.* rotten branches, leaves, etc., on the ground; weeds, underbrush; chaff, rubbish; (print.) brush.

brozar, *va.* (print.) to brush (type).

brozoso, sa, *a.* full of rubbish.

brucero, *m.* brush and broom maker or seller.

bruces.—a, or **de, b.,** forward, headlong; face downward; on one's stomach.

brucita, *f.* (min.) brucite.

brugo, *m.* vine grub, plant louse.

bruja, *f.* witch, hag; owl.—**brujear,** *vn.* to practice witchcraft.—**brujería,** *f.* witchcraft, sorcery.

brujidor, *m.* glaziers' nippers.

brujidura, *f.* bewitching, casting spells.

brujir, *va.* to pare off the corners and edges of.

brujo, *m.* sorcerer, conjurer, wizard.

brújula, *f.* magnetic needle; compass; sight, small hole to point a gun, peephole.

brujulear, *va.* at cards, to examine (one's cards) by slowly uncovering the tops; to discover by conjectures.

brujuleo, *m.* examining one's cards by slowly uncovering the tops; close examination; guess, conjecture.

brulote, *m.* fire ship; an ancient engine of war.

bruma, *f.* mist, fog.

brumador, ra, *a. V.* ABRUMADOR.

brumal, *a.* misty, foggy.

brumamiento, *m.* weariness, lassitude.

brumar, *va. V.* ABRUMAR.

brumario, *m.* Brumaire (month).

brumazón, *m.* thick fog or mist.

brumo, *m.* refined wax, for polishing tapers.

brumoso, sa, *a.* foggy, hazy, misty.

bruno, *m.* black plum; plum tree.

bruno, na, *a.* dark brown, blackish.

bruñido. I. *m.* polish, burnish. **II.** *pp.* of BRUÑIR.

bruñidor, ra. I. *n. & a.* burnisher (-ing); polisher (-ing). **II.** *m.* burnisher; collish.

bruñimiento, *m.* polishing, burnishing; polish.

bruñir, *va.* to burnish, polish; (coll.) to put on rouge; to fard.

brusca, *f.* (naut.) bevel, sweep, or rounding of masts; brushwood.

bruscamente, *adv.* rudely, harshly.

bruscate, *m.* stew made of milt and lambs' livers.

brusco, *m.* (bot.) kneeholly, butcher's broom; trifling remains; refuse shearings.

brusco, ca, *a.* rude, rough, rude.

brusela, *f.* (bot.) lesser periwinkle.

bruselense. I. *n.* native of Brussels. **II.** *a.* Brussels (u. a.)

brusquedad, *f.* rudensss; rude action or treatment.

brutal. I. *a.* brutal; brutish. **II.** *m.* brute.

brutalidad, *f.* brutality; brutishness; stupidity; brutal or stupid action.

brutalizar. I. *va.* to brutalize. **II.** *vr.* to become brutalized.

brutalmente, *adv.* brutally.

brutesco, ca, *a.* grotesque.

bruteza, *f.* roughness, want of polish; brutality.

bruto, *m.* brute, beast; ignoramus; blockhead.

bruto, ta, *a.* beastly; brutish, brutal; crude (ore, oil, etc.); gross (profits, etc.); unpolished, rough.—**en b.,** in a rough state, in the rough.

bruza, *f.* horse brush; stove brush; scrubbing brush; printer's brush.

bruzar, *va.* to brush.

bu, *m.* bugaboo, bugbear.—**hacer el b.,** to scare, frighten.

búa, *f.* pustule. *V.* BUBA.

buaro, buarillo, *m.* (orn.) buzzard.

buba, *f.* pustule, small tumor.—*pl.* buboes.

búbalo, *m.* African antelope.

bubático, ca, *a.* having buboes or glandular tumors.

bubilla, *f. dim.* small pustule, pimple.

bubón, *m.* bubo.

bubónico, ca, *a.* bubonic.

buboso, sa. *a.* having pustules or buboes.

bucal, *a.* relating to the mouth; buccal.

bucanero, *m.* buccaneer.

bucaral, *m.* plantation of BÚCARES.

bucarán, *m.* buckram. *V.* BOCACÍ.

búcare, *m.* a South American shade tree.

bucarito, *m. dim.* small earthen vessel of odoriferous earth.

búcaro, *m.* vessel made of an odoriferous earth of the same name; (Colomb.) BÚCARE.

buccino, *m.* buccinum, whelk.

buceador, ra, *n.* diver.—**bucear,** *vn.* to dive.

bucéfalo, *m.* bucephalus; blockhead, jackass.

bucentauro, *m.* bucentaur.

buceo, *m.* diving; searching under water.

bucero, ra, *a.* black-nosed (s. o. dogs).

bucle, *m.* ringlet, curl, lock of hair; loop.

buco, *m.* opening, aperture, gap; (zool.) buck.

bucólica, *f.* bucolic, pastoral poetry; food.

bucólico, ca, *a.* bucolic.

buchada, *f.* mouthful. *V.* BOCANADA.

buche, *m.* craw or crop; maw; belly; mouthful; young sucking ass; foal; bag, wrinkle, or pucker in clothes; bosom.

buchete, *m.* cheek puffed with wind.

buchón, ona, *a.* big-bellied.

budare, *m.* (Venez.) large baking pan.

búdico, ca, *a.* Buddhic, Buddhistic.

budín, *m.* pudding.

budión, *m.* (icht.) peacock fish.

budismo, *m.* Buddhism.—**budista,** *n.* & *a.* Buddhist(-ic).

buega, *f.* landmark.

buen, *a. contr.* of **bueno,** good. Used only before a masculine substantive, as *buen hombre,* good man, and before an infinitive used as a substantive, as *el buen decir,* correct speaking.

buenaboya, *m.* seaman who volunteered to serve on board a galley.

buenamente, *adv.* freely, spontaneously; conveniently, easily.

buenandanza, *f.* = BIENANDANZA.

buenaventura, *f.* fortune, good luck; fortune (as told by a fortune teller).

bueno [**buen** (*v.* BUEN)], **na. I.** *a.* good; kind; suited, fit; appropriate; well (*estoy bueno,* I am well); in good condition; great; high (excitement, fever, etc.); advisable, desirable; strange (often with *lo* in the expression **lo bueno es,** the strange thing is); simple, too good, (coll.) easy, soft.—**¡buena es ésa!** (coll.) that's strange; that is a pretty how-de-do, a pretty fix.—**bueno está lo bueno,** let good enough alone.—**buenas noches,** good night.—**buenas tardes,** good afternoon.—**buenos días,** good day, good morning.—**a buenas,** willingly, without compulsion.—**¿a dónde bueno?** where are you going?—**de buenas,** in good luck, lucky.—**de buenas a primeras,** all of a sudden, without warning.—**¿de dónde bueno?** where do you come from?—**por buenas, por las buenas** = A BUENAS. **II.** *adv.* well, very well, all right; that is enough.

buenparecer, *m.* good looks or appearance.

buera, *f.* pustule or pimple in the mouth.

buey, *m.* ox, bullock.—**b. de caza,** stalking ox.—**b. marino,** sea calf.—**bueyazo,** *m. aug.* big ox.—**bueyecillo, -zuelo,** *m. dim.* little ox.—**bueyuno, na,** *a.* bovine; oxlike.

bufado, da. I. *a.* blown (app. to glass drops blown very thin). **II.** *pp.* of BUFAR.

bufalino, na, *a.* belonging to buffaloes.

búfalo, *m.* buffalo.

bufanda, *f.* muffler.

bufar, *vn.* to puff and blow with anger; to snort.

bufete, *m.* desk or writing table; lawyer's office; bureau; sideboard.

bufetillo, *m. dim.* small desk or writing table.

bufido, *m.* bellow, roar, snort.

bufo, fa. I. *a.* comic, farcical. **II.** *n.* comic singer.

bufón, *m.* peddler, street vender; buffoon, merry andrew; fool, clown, jester.

bufón, na, *a.* funny, comical.—**bufonada,** *f.* buffoonery, jest.—**bufonazo,** *m. aug.* great buffoon.—**bufoncillo,** *m. dim.* little merry andrew.—**bufonearse,** *vr.* to jest.—**bufonería,** *f.* = BUFONADA.

bugada, *f.* = BOGADA.

bugalla, *f.* gallnut growing on oak leaves.

buglosa, *f.* (bot.) alkanet; bugloss.

buharda, *f.* dormer window; garret.

buhardilla, *f.* garret; skylight.

buharro, *m.* (orn.) eagle owl.

buhedera, *f.* embrasure, loophole.

buhedo, *m.* marl, a kind of calcareous earth.

buhero, ra, *n.* owl keeper.

buhío, *m.* = BOHÍO.

buho, *m.* (orn.) owl; (met.) unsociable person.

buhonería, *f.* peddler's box; peddlery.

buhonero, *m.* peddler, hawker.

buir, *va.* to polish, burnish.

buitre, *m.* vulture.—**buitrera,** *f.* place to catch vultures.—**buitrero,** *m.* vulture fowler.

buitrero, ra, *n.* vulturine.

buitrón, *m.* osier basket to catch fish; partridge net; furnace where silver ores are smelted; snare for game.

buja, *f.* chuck (in watchmaking).

bujarasol, *m.* fig with reddish pulp.

buje, *m.* axle box, bush box, iron ring; pillow of a shaft.

bujeda, *f.,* **bujedal, bujedo,** *m.* plantation of box trees.

bujería, *f.* gewgaw, bauble, toy, knickknack.

bujeta, *f.* boxwood box; perfume box; case for smelling bottle.

bujía, *f.* candle; candlestick; (fís.) candle, candlepower; (int. comb. eng.) spark plug (called also **b. del encendido**).—**b. normal,** standard candle.

bujiería, *f.* office where wax candles are kept.

bula, *f.* papal bull.

bulario, *m.* collection of papal bulls.

bulbo, *m.* (bot.) bulb.—**bulboso, sa,** *a.* bulbous.

buleto, *m.* brief granted by the Pope or by his legate.

bulevar, *m.* boulevard.

búlgaro, ra, *n.* & *a.* Bulgarian.

bulí, *m.* (Philip.) a palm tree. *V.* BURÍ.

bulimia, *f.* (med.) bulimia, excessive appetite.

bultito, *m. dim.* little lump; small bundle.

bulto, *m.* bulk, anything which appears bulky; form, object not clearly discerned; protuberance; tumor, swelling; massiness; bust; bundle, parcel, package; pillowcase.—**a b.,** wholesale; as a whole; broadly.—**de b.,** obvious, manifest, striking.—**escurrir, huir,** or **sacar, el b.,** to sneak out.

bululú, *m.* strolling player (actor).

bulla, *f.* noise, bustle, fuss; noisy stir, crowd, mob.—**bullaje,** *m.* noisy crowd.—**bullanga,** *f.* tumult, riot.—**bullanguero, ra,** *n.* rioter, turbulent person.

bullar, *va.* = BOLLAR.
bullebulle, *m.* busybody, bustler, hustler.
bullicio, *m.* bustle, noise, uproar; sedition; heat.
bulliciosamente, *adv.* noisily.
bullicioso, sa, noisy; lively, merry; turbulent, boisterous (s. o. the sea).
bullidor, ra, *a.* = BULLICIOSO.
bullir. I. *vn.* to boil, bubble up; move about, bustle, hustle. **II.** *va.* to move, stir.
bullón, *m.* dye bubbling up in a boiler; metallic ornament for large books; puff (in sewing).
bumerang, *m.* boomerang.
buneto, *m.* (orn.) hedge sparrow.
bungo, *m.* a Nicaraguan flatboat.
buniato, *m.* = BONIATO.
bunio, *m.* sort of earthnut or pignut.
buñolada, *f.* platter of buns or waffles; botch work.—**buñolería**, *f.* bun shop.—**buñolero, ra**, *n.* maker or seller of crullers or waffles.
buñuelo, *m.* fritter, bun, cruller; anything poorly done or spoiled; failure.
buque, *m.* vessel, ship; steamer; bulk, capacity (of a ship); hull (of a ship).—**b. de guerra**, man-of-war.—**b. de torres**, turreted man-of-war.—**b. de vapor**, steamer.—**b. de vela**, sailing vessel.—**b. mercante**, merchant vessel.
burato, *m.* Canton crêpe; cypress (fabric); transparent veil of light silk.
burba, *f.* an African coin of small value.
burbuja, *f.* bubble.—**burbujeo**, *m.* bubbling.
burbujear, *vn.* to bubble.
burchaca, *f.* = BURJACA.
burche, *m.* tower.
burda, *f.* (naut.) backstay.
burdégano, *m.* hinny, mule.
burdel. I. *m.* brothel. **II.** *a.* libidinous.
burdinalla, *f.* (naut.) sprit-topsail stay.
burdo, da, *a.* coarse; common, ordinary.
burel, *m.* (her.) bar, the ninth part of a shield; (naut.) marlinespike.—*pl.* **bureles**, (naut.) pointed wooden rollers.
burengue, *m.* mulatto slave.
bureo, *m.* court of justice; entertainment, amusement, diversion, spree.
bureta, *f.* burette.
burga, *f.* spa, hot springs.
burgalés, *m.* native of Burgos.
burgués, sa, *a.* bourgeois (*f.* bourgeoise).
burguesía, *f.* bourgeoisie.
buri, *m.* (bot.) buri, talipot palm.
buriel, *a.* reddish, dark red.
buriel, *m.* kersey, coarse cloth; ropewalk.
buril, *m.* burin, engraver's chisel; graver.
burilada, *f.* line or stroke of a burin; silver taken by an assayer for testing.
buriladura, *f.* engraving with a burin.
burilar, *va.* to engrave with a graver.
burjaca, *f.* pilgrim's leather bag.
burla, *f.* scoff, flout, mockery, sneer; jest, fun, trick; jeer, gibe; hoax, deceit, cheat.—**b. burlando**, in an easy way, without effort.—**b. pesada**, biting jest.—**burlas aparte**, joking aside.—**de burlas**, in jest.
burladero, *m.* refuge or covert in a bull ring.
burlador, ra. I. *n.* wag, jester, scoffer, practical joker; seducer. **II.** *m.* seducer, Don Juan; conjurer's cup.
burlar. I. *va.* to ridicule, mock, scoff; abuse; to deceive, frustrate, disappoint, evade. **II.** *vr.* (w. **de**) to mock, laugh at, make fun of; to gibe, banter.
burlería, *f.* fun, mockery, scoffing; drolling; fish story, yarn, fairy tale; deceit, illusion; derision, banter, ridicule.
burlescamente, *adv.* comically, ludicrously.
burlesco, ca, *a.* burlesque, jocular, ludicrous, comical, funny.
burleta, *f.* *dim.* little trick, fun, or joke.
burlete, *m.* weather strip.
burlón, na, *n.* & *a.* banterer (-ing), jester (-ing), scoffer (-ing).
buro, *m.* (prov.) chalk, marl.

buró, *m.* bureau; writing desk.
burocracia, *f.* bureaucracy.
burócrata, *f.* bureaucrat.
burocrático, *a.* bureaucratic.
burra, *f.* she-ass; ignorant, unrefined woman; industrious strong woman.
burrada, *f.* drove of asses; stupid or foolish action or expression; play contrary to rule in the game of BURRO.
burrajo, *m.* dry stable dung for fuel.
burrazo, za, *n.* *aug.* big ass.
burrero, *m.* ass keeper who sells asses' milk.
burrillo, *m.* (coll.) = AÑALEJO.
burrito, ta, *n.* *dim.* little ass.
burro, *m.* ass, donkey; sawyer's jack or horse; wheel of a reel; a game at cards; windlass.—**burros de la mesana**, (naut.) mizzen-bowlines.
burrumbada, *f.* = BARRUMBADA.
bursátil, *a.* relating to the bourse or exchange.
burujo, *m.* lump of pressed wool or other matter; parcel, package; bagasse.
burujón, *m.* lump, badly made parcel.
burujoncillo, *m.* *dim.* little lump or bundle.
busaca, *f.* (Am.) pocket (of a pool table); bag.
busardas, *f.* *pl.* (naut.) breasthooks, compass timbers.
busca, *f.* search, research; pursuit; terrier; hunting party.—*pl.* perquisites.
buscada, *f.* search, research.
buscador, ra. I. *n.* & *a.* searcher (-ing), investigator (-ing). **II.** *m.* finder (optical appliance).
buscaniguas, *m.* = BUSCAPIÉS.
buscapié, *m.* hint.
buscapiés, *m.* *sing.* squib cracker; serpent firecracker.
buscapleitos, *n.* quarrelsome person, trouble maker.
buscar. I. *va.* (*pret.* BUSQUÉ: *subj.* BUSQUE) to seek, look for.—**b. tres pies al gato**, to pick a quarrel. **II.** *vr.* to bring upon one's self.
buscarruidos, *n.* (coll.) quarrelsome person.
buscavidas, *n.* busybody, gossip monger; hustler; thrifty person.
busco, *m.* base of a sluice gate.
buscón, *na*, *n.* & *a.* searcher (-ing); cheat; pilferer (-ing), filcher (-ing).
busilis, *m.* (coll.) difficulty, difficult point.—**dar en el b.**, to hit the mark.
busqué. *V.* BUSCAR.
búsqueda, *f.* search.
busto, *m.* bust.
bustrófedon, *m.* boustrophedon, writing lines alternately from left to right and right to left.
butaca, *f.* armchair; easy-chair; orchestra chair in a theater.
butifarra, *f.* a sort of sausage made in Catalonia; gaskins, gallikins; (Peru) ham sandwich.
butifarrero, ra, *n.* maker and seller of BUTIFARRAS.
butilo, *m.* butyl.
butiondo, *a.* fetid; goatish; lustful.
butírico, ca, *a.* butyric.—**butírilo**, *m.* butyryl.—**butirina**, *f.* butyrin.
butomeo, a. I. *a.* (bot.) butomaceous. **II.** *f.* *pl.* Butomaceæ.
butrino, butrón, *m.* fowling net.
butuco, *m.* thick, stumpy plantain.
buyador, *m.* brazier.
buyo, *m.* (Philip.) chewing paste of bonga fruit and leaves, and lime.
buz, *m.* kiss of respect and reverent regard.—**hacer el b.**, to do homage or pay respect.
buzamiento, *m.* (geol.) dip of a stratum.
búzano, *m.* diver; a kind of culverin.
buzar, *va.* (geol.) to dip downward.
buzardas, *f.* *pl.* (naut.) breasthooks, forehooks.
buzcorona, *f.* blow on the head in fun while kissing the hand.
buzo, *m.* diver; an old kind of ship.
buzón, *m.* conduit, canal; letter drop, letter box, drop box; lid, cover; hook to take off the lids of melting pots; sluice of a mill.
buzonera, *f.* drain or gutter in a courtyard.

C

ca, *conj.* (obs.) because, for.

¡ca! *interj.* oh, no! no, indeed! *V.* ¡QUIÁ!

cabal, *a.* just, exact; perfect, complete, thorough; full; faultless, consummate.—**por sus cabales,** exactly, perfectly, according to rule and order.

cábala, *f.* cabala, superstitious divination; secret science of the Hebrew rabbis; cabal, intrigue, plot.

cabalgada, *f.* cavalcade; booty.

cabalgadero, *m.* mounting block.

cabalgador, ra. I. *n.* rider, horseman (-woman). **II.** *m.* horse block.

cabalgadura, *f.* sumpter, beast of burden.

cabalgar. I. *vn.* (*pret.* CABALGUÉ: *subj.* CABALGUE) to ride on horseback; to parade on horseback; to go in a cavalcade. **II.** *va.* to cover (a mare—s. o. a horse); to ride.

cabalgata, *f.* cavalcade.

cabalhuste, *m.* ancient saddle with high semicircular pommel and cantle.

cabalista, *m.* cabalist.

cabalístico, ca, *a.* cabalistic.

cabalmente, *adv.* exactly, completely, perfectly, fully, precisely.

caballa, *f.* horse mackerel.

caballaje, *m.* place where mares and she-asses are served by stallions or jackasses; money paid for that service.

caballar, *a.* belonging to or resembling horses, equine.

caballear, *vn.* to ride horseback.

caballejo, *m.* *dim.* little horse, nag; (vet.) shoeing-frame.

caballerato, *m.* ecclesiastical benefice granted by the Pope to a married layman; privilege of gentleman or esquire, in Catalonia.

caballerear, *vn.* to set up for a gentleman.

caballerescamente, *adv.* knightly, cavalierly.

caballeresco, ca, *a.* knightly, chivalrous; gentlemanly.

caballerete, *m.* *dim.* (coll.) spruce young gentleman.

caballería, *f.* riding beast; cavalry; art of riding, horsemanship; knight-errantry; chivalry; order of knights; knighthood; share of spoils given to a knight; (West Indies) a land measure (about 33 ½ acres).—**c. andante,** knight-errantry.—**c. mayor,** saddle horse or mule.—**c. menor,** ass.

caballerito, *m.* *dim.* young gentleman.

caballeriza, *f.* stable; number of horses, mules, etc., in a stable; stud of horses; staff of grooms, hostlers, etc.

caballerizo, *m.* head groom of a stable.—**c. del rey,** equerry to the king.—**c. mayor del rey,** master of the horse to the king.

caballero, *m.* knight; cavalier; gentleman; rider, horseman; a sort of fortification; old Spanish dance; (orn.) red-legged horseman; gambet.— **c. andante,** knight-errant.—**c. de industria,** defrauder, knave, one who lives by his wits, sponger. —**c. del hábito de Santiago,** knight of the military order of St. James.

caballero, ra, *a.* riding.

caballerosamente, *adv.* generously, nobly; like a gentleman.

caballerosidad, *f.* condition, quality of a gentleman; nobleness, knightly behavior.

caballeroso, sa, *a.* noble, generous; gentlemanlike, gentlemanly.

caballerote, *m.* (coll.) uncouth or unpolished gentleman.

caballeta, *f.* (ent.) field cricket.

caballete, *m.* ridge of a roof; carpenter's horse, trestle horse; trestle; easel; horse (instrument of torture); brake, for dressing hemp and flax; ridge between furrows; cap of a chimney; bridge of the nose; gallows of a printing press.—**c. de aserrar,** sawbuck, sawhorse.—**c. de colchar cabos,** (naut.) rope-laying truss, stakehead.

caballico, ito, *m.* *dim.* little horse, pony; hobbyhorse, rocking-horse.—**c. del diablo,** dragon fly.

caballista, *m.* horseman; good rider; horse connoisseur.

caballo, *m.* horse; (cards) knight—a figure on horseback, equivalent to the queen of English cards; (chess) knight; (med.) bubo.—*pl.* (mil.) horse, cavalry.—**c. aguililla,** (Am.), a very swift pacing horse.—**c. amaestrado,** horse completely broken in.—**c. blanco,** a person who finances a doubtful enterprise.—**c. castizo,** blood horse.—**c. de agua** = C. MARINO.—**c. de aldaba** = C. DE REGALO.—**c. de batalla,** battle horse, charger; hobby, favorite idea; specialty, forte; main or crucial point. —**c. de carga,** pack horse.—**c. de carrera,** or **corredor,** race horse.—**c. de caza,** hunter.—**c. de Frisia,** (mil.) chevaux-de-frise.—**c. de mar** = C. MARINO.—**c. de montar,** saddle horse.—**c. de palo,** any vessel fit for sea; rack for criminals; (tannery) tanner's beam.—**c. de posta,** post horse.—**c. de regalo,** gala horse, handsome horse kept for special occasions.—**c. de silla,** saddle horse.—**c. de tiro,** draught horse.—**c. de vapor,** horsepower.—**c. entero,** stallion.—**c. marino,** sea horse; river horse (hippopotamus).—**c. padre,** stallion.—**c. rabón,** docked horse.—**a c.,** on horseback.—**a c. regalado no hay que mirarle el diente, or no se le mira el colmillo,** you should not look a gift horse in the mouth.—**a mata c.,** at breakneck speed.

caballón, *m.* large, clumsy horse; ridge between two furrows.

caballuelo, *m.* *dim.* little horse.

caballuno, na, *a.* relating to horses; horselike.

cabaña, *f.* hut, cottage, cabin; hovel, mean dwelling; flock of ewes or breeding sheep; drove of mules; balk line in billiards.

cabañal. I. *a.* sheep-and-cattle (u. a.—s. o. roads). **II.** *m.* village or settlement of huts.

cabañera, *f.* a shepherd's rations for a week.

cabañero, ra. I. *a.* belonging to a CABAÑA in any of its acceptations. **II.** *n.* keeper of a CABAÑA.

cabañil. I. *a.* belonging to a shepherd's hut. **II.** *m.* man in charge of a drove of mules.

cabañuela, *f.* *dim.* small hut or cottage; weather prognostication made in August for the following year.—*pl.* festival of the Jews of Toledo.

cabe. I. *m.* stroke on a ball, in the game of ARGOLLA.—**dar un c. al bolsillo,** (met.) to hurt one in one's business, fortune, etc. **II.** *prep.* (poet.) near, nigh, by.

cabeceamiento, *m.* = CABECEO.

cabecear, *vn.* to nod; to shake the head in disapproval; to raise or lower the head (app. to horses); to incline to one side, to hang over (app. to a load); (naut.) to pitch; to lurch (s. o. carriages) —*va.* in writing, to give (the letters) a thick loop; among bookbinders, to put (the head-band) to (a book); to bind (cloth or rugs); to close by cauterization; to head (wine).

cabeceo, *m.* nod of the head; (naut.) pitching.

cabecera, *f.* beginning or principal part; upper end; head or head-board of a bed; seat of honor; headwaters; capital of a province, district, nation; fortified point of a bridge; head piece or vignette; each extremity of the back of a book; pillow or bolster.—**c. de puente,** bridgehead.

cabeciancho, cha, *a.* broad-headed.

cabecica, ita, *f.* *dim.* small head.

cabeciduro, ra, *a.* stubborn.

cabecilla, *m.* wrong-headed person; leader, ringleader.

cabellar, *vn.* to hair; to put on false hair.

cabellejo, *m.* *dim.* little hair.

cabellera, *f.* hair, head of hair; switch of hair; tail (of a comet).

cabello, *m.* hair of the head.—*pl.* hair of the head; large sinews (in mutton); corn silk.—**cabellos de ángel,** sweetmeat made with CIDRACAYOTE.—**asirse de un cabello,** to resort to trivial pretexts or flimsy arguments, to catch at trifles.—**traer por los cabellos,** to drag in irrelevantly, to resort to or introduce far-fetched (arguments, facts, etc.).

cabelludo, da, *a.* hairy; fibrous.

cabelluelo, *m.* *dim.* thin and short hair.

caber. I. *vn.* to go in or into (*la clavija no cabe en el agujero*, the peg does not go in the hole, the peg is too large for the hole); to have enough room, to be able to go through (often ch. constr.: *yo no quepo aquí*, I have not enough room here, this place is too small for me; *el elefante cabe por esta puerta*, the elephant can go through this door, this door is large enough for the elephant); to fall (to one), to befall, to have (often ch. constr.: *me ha cabido buena suerte*, good luck has befallen me, I have been fortunate; *me ha cabido el honor de ser nombrado*, the honor of being appointed has fallen to me, I have had the honor to be appointed); to be possible or natural (*todo cabe en la naturaleza*, in nature everything is possible); to be pertinent, appropriate or applicable.—**no cabe duda (de que)**, there is no doubt (that).—**no cabe más**, that is the worst (or the best), that is the limit.—**no c. de**, to overflow, to be filled, with.—**no c. en sí**, to be puffed up with conceit, (coll.) to have a big head.

cabero, *m.* maker of handles for tools.

cabestraje, *m.* halter; fee paid to a drover.

cabestrante, *m.* = CABRESTANTE.

cabestrar, *va.* to halter; to lead by the halter.

cabestrear, *vn.* to be led by a halter.

cabestrería, *f.* shop where halters and collars are made and sold.

cabestrero, ra. I. *a.* that can be led by a halter. **II.** *n.* maker or seller of horse collars and halters.

cabestrillo, *m.* sling; gold or silver chain.

cabestro, *m.* halter; leading ox.—**llevar, or traer, de cabestro,** to lead by the halter; (met.) to lead by the nose.

cabeza, *f.* head; chief, leader; understanding, mind, judgment, brains; beginning; end; big end; top or upper part; capital, seat (of a province, district, etc.); head of cattle.—**c. de chorlito,** harebrained.—**c. de puente,** bridgehead.—**c. mayor,** head of neat cattle.—**c. menor,** head of sheep, goats, etc.—**c. redonda,** blockhead.—**a la c.,** at the head.—**alzar c.,** to get better; to get on one's feet.—**de c.,** head first, headlong; *a.* brainy, smart.—**hacer c.,** to lead.—**levantar c.,** to retrieve one's health or fortune.—**no tener pies ni c.,** to have neither head nor tail.—**poner las cosas pies con c.,** to jumble things together; to put them topsy-turvy.

cabezada, *f.* headshake; stroke or butt given with the head, or on it; nod; headgear (of harness); headstall of a bridle; pitching of a ship; headband of a book; instep of a boot.—**dar cabezadas,** to nod.

cabezal, *m.* small pillow; (med.) compress; long round bolster; post of a door; fore part of a carriage; narrow mattress used by laborers.

cabezalejo, ico, illo, ito, *m. dim.* little pillow or bolster; small compress.

cabezalero, ra, *n.* executor of a will.

cabezazo, *m.* stroke with the head.

cabezo, *m.* summit; reef; collar band.

cabezón, na, *a.* big-headed; obstinate.—*m.* tax register; collar band; head; opening of a garment; cavesson or nose band, used in breaking in a horse.

cabezorro, *m. aug.* large, disproportioned head.

cabezota, *m. & f. aug.* (coll.) big-headed, clubheaded, obstinate person.

cabezudo, *m.* (icht.) chub, mullet.

cabezudo, da, *a.* large-headed; headstrong.

cabezuela, *f. dim.* small head; coarse flour; rose bud from which rose water is distilled; harebrained fellow, simpleton; (bot.) eryngo, ragwort-leaved centaury.

cabezuelo, *m. dim.* of CABEZA: little head.

cabida, *f.* content, capacity; space, room; influence.—**tener c.,** to be appropriate; to apply, be applicable.

cabila, *f.* (in Morocco) tribe.

cabildada, *f.* hasty, ill-advised proceeding.

cabildante, councilman, member of a CABILDO.

cabildear, *vn.* to lobby; to influence or win votes in a corporation.—**cabildeo,** *m.* lobbying.—**cabildero, ra,** *n.* lobbyist.

cabildo, *m.* chapter of a cathedral or collegiate church; meeting of a chapter; place where the meeting is held; municipal council.

cabilla, *f.* (naut.) dowel; treenail; belaying pin.

cabillejo, *m. dim.* (bot.) partial flower stalk.

cabillo. I. *m.* (bot.) stalk; stem; small end of a rope.

cabio, *m.* joist; breastsummer of a chimney; top or bottom piece of window or door frame.

cabito, *m. dim.* small end; butt.

cabizbajo, ja, *a.* crestfallen; thoughtful, pensive; melancholy.

cable, *m.* cable; cable's length, measure of 120 fathoms.—**c. de cizalla,** (aer.) shear wire (of a dirigible).

cablear, cablegrafiar, *va.* to cable.

cablegráfico, ca, *a.* pertaining to submarine telegraphy; cable (u. a.)

cablegrama, *m.* cablegram.

cabo, *m.* extreme, extremity; tip; bit; stub, stump; cape, headland, foreland; handle, haft, holder; rope, cord; thread; chief, leader; (mil.) corporal; end, termination, finish; parcel or package smaller than a bale.—*pl.* tail and mane (of a horse); loose pieces of apparel, as stockings, shoes, hats, etc.; divisions, sections, headings.—**c. de año,** anniversary funeral.—**c. de escuadra,** (mil.) corporal.—**c. de maestranza,** foreman of a workmen's brigade.—**c. de presa,** prizemaster.—**cabos negros,** black hair, eyes, and eye-brows.—**al c.,** at last.—**dar c. a,** to finish, end—**de c. a c.,** or **de c. a rabo,** from head to tail, from beginning to end.—**estar al c. de,** to be conversant with, or informed about.—**llevar a c.,** to carry out, to accomplish.—**llevar hasta el c.,** to carry to the end, to see (something) through.

cabotaje, *m.* (naut.) coasting trade; pilotage.

cabra, *f.* goat; engine formerly used to throw stones.—*pl.* small white clouds.

cabrahigadura, *f.* caprification.

cabrahigal, cabrahigar, *m.* wild-fig field.

cabrahigar, *va.* to caprificate.

cabrahigo, *m.* wild fig tree; its fruit.

cabrería, *f.* goat herd; goat's milk dairy.

cabreriza, *f.* goatherds' hut; woman goat tender.

cabrerizo, za. I. *a.* goatish, hircine. **II.** *n.* goatherd.

cabrero, ra, *n.* goatherd.

cabrestante, *m.* (naut.) capstan, winch.

cabria, *f.* crane; wheel and axle; winch; windlass; hoist; axletree; (naut.) sheers.

cabrilla, *f. dim.* little goat; (zool.) a kind of fish; sawhorse; sawbuck.—*pl.* (ast.) Pleiades; marks on the legs, produced by being continually too near the fire; (naut.) whitecaps.

cabrillear, *vn.* to form whitecaps.

cabrilleo, *m.* the lapping of the waves forming whitecaps.

cabrío, *m.* (carp.) joist.

cabrío. I. *a.* goatish, hircine. **II.** *m.* herd of goats.

cabriola, *f.* caper; gambol, skip; nimble leap.

cabriolar, *vn.* to caper or cut capers; to jump, curvet, frisk.

cabriolé, *m.* a kind of sleeveless cloak; cabriolet.

cabriolear, *vn.* = CABRIOLAR.

cabrita, *f. dim.* little she-kid.—**cabritero,** *m.* dealer in kids.—**cabritilla,** *f.* kid, dressed kidskin.—**cabritillo, cabrito,** *m. dim.* kid.

cabrón, *m.* buck, he-goat; cuckold.

cabronada, *f.* (low) infamous action which a man permits against his own honor; great annoyance or nuisance.

cabruno, na, *a.* goatish, goatlike, hircine.

cabruñar, *va.* to sharpen by hammering.

cabruño, *m.* sharpening the scythe.

cabujón, *m.* rough, unpolished ruby.

cabuya, *f.* (bot.) common American agave; sisal; sisal or hemp cord.—**dar c.,** to tie, to bind.—**ponerse en la c.,** to get the thread, to become informed.

cabuyero, *m.* (Am.) ship chandler.

cabuyería, *f.* (Am.) ship chandlery.

cacahual, *m.* cacao plantation.
cacahuate, cacahué, cacahuete, cacahuey, *m.* (bot.) peanut.
cacalote, *m.* (Mex.) raven.
cacao, *m.* (bot.) cacao; cacao tree, chocolate tree. **pedir c.,** (coll.) to beg for quarter, throw up the sponge.
cacaotal, *m.* cacao plantation.
cacaraña, *f.* pit caused by the smallpox.
cacarañado, da, *a.* pitted.
cacareador, ra, *n.* cackler; boaster, braggart.
cacarear, *vn.* to cackle; brag, boast.
cacareo, *m.,* cackling; boast, brag.
cacarizo, za, *a.* (Mex.) pock-marked.
cacatúa, *f.* (orn.) cockatoo.
cacaxtle, *m.* (Mex.) crate to carry fruit.
cacaxtlero, *m.* (Mex.) Indian who carries a CACAXTLE on his shoulders.
cacear, *va.* to stir with a dipper or ladle.
cacera, *f.* irrigating canal; channel, conduit.
cacería, *f.* hunt, hunting.
cacerilla, *f. dim.* small drain or canal.
cacerina, *f.* cartridge box or pouch.
cacerola, *f.* casserole.
caceta, *f. dim.* small pan.
cacica, *f.* wife or daughter of a cacique.
cacicato, cacicazgo, *m.* dignity and territory of a cacique.
cacillo, ito, *m. dim.* small dipper or ladle.
cacimba, *f.* hole dug on the sea shore for drinking water.
cacique, *m.* cacique, Indian chief; (coll.) boss; (orn.) cacique.
caciquil, *a.* relating to caciques; cacique-like; boss (u. a.)
caciquismo, *m.* caciquism, bossism.
cacle, *m.* (Mex.) leather sandal.
caco, *m.* pickpocket; coward; poltroon.
cacodilato, *m.* (chem.) cacodylate.
cacodílico, ca, *a.* (chem.) cacodylic.
cacodilo, *m.* (chem.) cacodyl.
cacófago, ga, *a.* cacophagous.
cacofonía, *f.* cacophony, harsh sound.
cacofónico, ca, *a.* cacophonous, ill-sounding.
cacografía, *f.* defective orthography.
cacomite, *m.* a Mexican flower plant.
cacomixtle, *m.* (Mex.) cacomistle.
cacoquimia, *f.* cacochymia.
cacoquímico, ca, *a.* cacochymical.
cacoquimio, *m.* one suffering from cacochymia.
cácteo, a, *a.* cactaceous.
cacto, *m.* (bot.) cactus.
cacumen, *m.* top, height; head, acumen.
cacha, *f.* each of the two leaves of a razor or knife handle; (Am., coll.) handle.—**hasta las cachas,** (coll.) up to the handle.
cachaco, *m.* (Am.) dandy, fop.
cachalote, *m.* sperm whale.
cachamarín, *n.* = CACHEMARÍN.
cachapa, *f.* (Ven.) corn bread with sugar.
cachar, *va.* to break in pieces; to split.
cacharpari, *m.* (Peru) farewell supper.
cacharrería, *f.* crockery store; collection or stock of earthen pots.
cacharrero, ra, *n.* maker or seller of crockery.
cacharro, *m.* coarse earthen pot, or a piece of it; useless, worthless thing, truck.
cachava, *f.* children's sport resembling hockey or golf; stick for driving the ball.
cachavazo, *m.* stroke with the CACHAVA.
cachaza, *f.* slowness, tardiness; forbearance; (Am.) rum; first froth on cane juice when boiled.
cachazudo, da, *a.* slow, calm, phlegmatic.
cache, *a.* (Arg.) uncouth.
cachemarín, *m.* = QUECHEMARÍN.
cachemir, *m.,* **cachemira,** *f.* cashmere.
cacheo, *m.* search for arms and weapons.
cachera, *f.* coarse shagged cloth or baize.
cachería, *f.* (Am.) small business; uncouthness.
cachetas, *f. pl.* teeth or wards in a lock.
cachete, *m.* blow on the face with the palm of the hand; cheek.

cachetero, *m.* short poniard; bullfighter who kills the bull with the poniard.
cachetina, *f.* hand-to-hand fight.
cachetudo, da, *a.* plump-cheeked, fleshy.
cachicamo, *m.* (Am.) armadillo.
cachicán, *m.* overseer of a farm; cunning, clever man.
cachicuerno, na, *a.* having a horn handle or haft.
cachidiablo, *m.* hobgoblin; one disguised in a devil's mask.
cachifo, fa, *n.* (Colomb., coll.) boy, girl.
cachifollar, *va.* (coll.) to disappoint; vex, humble, banter, sit upon.
cachigordete, eta, ito, ita, *a.* squat, plump.
cachillada, *f.* litter.
cachimba, *f.* **cachimbo,** *m.* (Amer.) smoking pipe.—**chupar c.,** (Venez.) to smoke a pipe; to suck one's thumb.
cachipolla, *f.* (ent.) dayfly or May fly.
cachiporra, *f.* stick with a big knob; bludgeon, billy.
cachiporrazo, *m.* blow with a bludgeon.
cachiporro, *m.* = CACHIPORRA.
cachirulo, *m.* earthen, glass, or tin pot for preserving liquor; head ornament formerly worn by women; (Mex.) lining of cloth or chamois for riding trousers; small three-masted vessel.
cachivache, *m.* pot, utensil; stuff, trash; broken crockery; trumpery; worthless fellow; (Am.) notion, trinket.
cachizo, *a.*—**madero c.,** log.
cacho, *m.* slice, piece; a card game; (icht.) surmullet; (Am.) horn.
cacho, cha, *a.* bent, crooked.
cachoias, *f. pl.* (naut.) cheeks of the masts.
cachón, *m.* breaker; small waterfall.
cachondez, *f.* sexual appetite.—**cachondo, da,** *a.* ruled by sexual appetite; in heat, rutting.
cachones, *m. pl.* breakers (waves).
cachopo, *m.* (naut.) gulf; dry trunk, stump.
cachorrillo, ito. I. *n.* little cub or whelp. **II.** *m.* pocket pistol.
cachorro, rra. I. *n.* whelp, puppy, cub. **II.** *m.* pocket pistol.
cachú, *m.* catechu, cutch.
cachúa, *f.* Indian dance in Peru, Bolivia, etc.
cachucha, *f.* rowboat; man's cloth or fur cap; Spanish dance in triple measure.
cachuchero, ra, *n.* maker or seller of caps; maker of seller of pin or needle cases.
cachucho, *m.* oil measure, containing the sixth part of a pound; pin or needle case; clumsy earthen pot.
cachuela, *f.* fricassee of rabbits' livers and lights; gizzard.
cachuelo, *m.* (icht.) small river fish resembling an anchovy.
cachulera, *f.* cavern; hiding place.
cachumbo, *m.* hard shell of cocoanut and other fruit.
cachunde, *f.* aromatic paste munched by the Chinese; cachou, cachunde.
cachupín, *m.* Spaniard who settles in Spanish America.
cada, *a.* every, each.—**c. cual,** each; every one, everybody.—**c. que** = C. VEZ QUE.—**c. uno** = C. CUAL.—**c. vez que, c. y cuando,** every time, whenever; as soon as.
cadahalso, *m.* shed, cabin, shanty.
cadalecho, *m.* bed made of branches of trees.
cadalso, *m.* platform, stage, stand; scaffold for capital punishment.
cadañal, ñego, ga, ñero, ra, *a.* annual, yearly.—**mujer c.,** woman who bears every year.
cadarzo, *m.* coarse, entangled silk which can not be spun; cover of the cocoon; narrow silk ribbon.
cádava, *f.* burnt stump of furze.
cadaval, *m.* place where many CADAVAS remain standing.
cadáver, *m.* corpse, cadaver.
cadavérico, ca, *a.* cadaverous.

cadejo, *m.* entangled hair; small skein; threads put together to make tassels.

cadena, *f.* chain; bond, tie; series; range (of mountains); malefactors chained together to be conducted to the galleys; imprisonment for life; (arch.) buttress.—**c. de puerto,** boom of a harbor.—**c. de rocas,** ledge or ridge of rocks.—**c. sin fin,** endless chain.

cadencia, *f.* cadence; fall of the voice; rhythm; measure; flow of verses or periods; in dancing, harmony of motion and music; (mus.) cadenza.

cadencioso, sa, *a.* rhythmical.

cadeneta, *f.* lace or needlework wrought in form of a chain; chain stitch; work put upon the heads of books to reinforce the sewing.

cadenilla, ita, *f. dim.* small chain; pearls of a certain size.

cadente, *a.* decaying, declining; going to ruin; rhythmical.

cadera, *f.* hip, the joint of the thigh.

caderillas, *f. pl.* bustle.

cadetada, *f.* injudicious, thoughtless action.

cadete, *m.* (mil.) cadet.

cadí, *m.* cadi, magistrate among Mohammedans.

cadillar, *m.* place where bur parsley grows.

cadillo, *m.* (bot.) great bur parsley; prickly bur weed; common burdock.

cadillos, *pl. m.* thrum; warp ends.

cadmía, *f.* calamine; tutty.

cadmio, *m.* (chem.) cadmium.

cado, *m.* ferret hole.

cadoso, cadozo, *m.* deep place in a river.

caducamente, *adv.* weakly, feebly.

caducante, *n.* & *a.* dotard (-ing).

caducar, *vn.* to dote; to be worn out by service; to fall into disuse; to become superannuated or extinct; (law, com.) to lapse.

caduceador, *m.* king at arms, who proclaims war and peace.

caduceo, *m.* caduceus, caduce.

caducidad, *f.* (law) caducity; decrepitude.

caduco, ca, *a.* worn out; senile; decrepit; perishable; frail.

caduquez, *f.* caducity; senility.

caedizo, za, *a.* ready to fall; (bot.) deciduous.

caedura, *f.* loose threads dropping from the loom.

caer. I. *vn.* (*ind.* CAIGO: *pret.* él CAYÓ: *subj.* CAIGA) to fall, drop, tumble down; lighten; fall off; hang down, droop; fit; become; deviate from the right path; fall due; decrease, decline, drop, fall; fall to one's lot; befall, happen to; come to pass; to understand, see; to become faint (s. o. color); to be included, fall (within certain limits, etc.).—**c. a,** to be (located) on (this or that side, etc.); to look down upon, overlook (*la ventana cae a la playa,* the window overlooks the beach).—**c. bien (mal),** to create a good (bad) impression, to be well (unfavorably) received; to fit (not to fit); to be (not to be) becoming.—**c. de,** to fall on (*caer de espaldas,* to fall on one's back, or backwards).—**c. de plano,** to fall flat (stretched).—**c. en cama, or enfermo,** to be taken ill.—**c. en la cuenta (de),** to notice, to think (of).—**c. en gracia,** to arouse liking, to become a subject of affection or esteem, to please.—**c. redondo,** to drop unconscious.—**al c. de la noche,** at nightfall. II. *vr.* **caerse,** to fall; to lose heart, to become downcast.—**c. de su peso, or c. de suyo,** to be self-evident, to be obvious; to fall, or fail, by itself.—**c. redondo** = CAER REDONDO.—**caércele a uno la cara de vergüenza,** to be deeply ashamed, to feel like hiding one's face.

café, *m.* coffee (tree, berry, beverage); coffeehouse: café.—**cafeína,** *f.* caffein.—**cafeona,** *f.* caffeol, the aromatic oil of coffee.—**cafetal,** *m.* coffee plantation.—**cafetera,** *f.* coffee pot; woman who gathers coffee berries; woman who makes and serves coffee.—**cafetero,** *m.* one who raises, makes or sells coffee; (bot.) coffee tree.—**cafetín,** *m.* small café.—**cafeto,** *m.* coffee tree.—**cafetucho,** *m.* small and untidy café.

cáfila, *m.* multitude, large number; caravan.

cafre, *n.* & *a.* Kaffrarian; savage, inhuman; rude, uncivil.

cagachín, *m.* small reddish mosquito.

cagafierro, *m.* scoria, dross of iron.

cagajón, *m.* horse dung; dung of mules or asses.

cagalaolla, *m.* masquerader who dances in processions.

cagarrache, *m.* one who washes the olive pits in an oil mill.

cagarria, *f.* St. George's-mushroom.

cagarropa, *m.* = CAGACHÍN.

cagarruta, *f.* dung of sheep, goats, and mice.

cagatinta, *m.* pettifogger; nickname given in contempt to attorney's clerks.

cahiz, *m.* nominal measure of twelve bushels.

cahizada, *f.* land sufficient for one CAHIZ of seed.

caída, *f.* fall; falling; tumble; downfall; lapse; drop; falling off; droop; diminution, drop; descent; (geol.) dip; landslip; interior gallery in houses of Manila, with views upon the courtyard.—*pl.* coarse wool cut off the skirts of a fleece; witty remarks, repartee; (sew.) reverse.—**c. de una vela,** depth or drop of a sail.—**a la c. de la tarde,** at the close of the afternoon.—**a la c. del sol,** at sunset.

caído, da. I. *a.* languid; downfallen. II. *pp.* of CAER.

caídos, *m. pl.* arrears of taxes or rents; slanting lines to show the proper slant in writing.

caigo, caiga. *V.* CAER.

caimacán, *m.* kaimakam, assistant grand vizier; (coll.) big gun, person of importance.

caimán, *m.* cayman, alligator; sharp, exploiter.

caimiento, *m.* fall, drop; droop, languidness.

caimito, caimo, *m.* star apple.

caique, *m.* (naut.) skiff, small boat.

cairel, *m.* false hair or wig worn by women to embellish their head dress; fringe trimming; silk threads to which the hair of wigs is fastened.

cairelar, *va.* to fringe.

caja, *f.* box; case; coffin; chest; cash box or safe; sheath; body (of a carriage, truck, etc.); stock (of firearm); cavity, hole; distributing or central post office; (com.) cash, funds; cashier's office; socket; frame; drum; printer's case; portable writing desk; well or cavity in which a staircase is raised; wooden case of an organ; (mil.) drum; drum case, or frame.—**c. alta,** (print.) upper case.—**c. baja,** (print.) lower case.—**c. capilla,** (naut.) chess for chapel ornaments.—**c. de ahorros,** savings bank.—**c. de amortización,** Department of Public Debts (an old branch of the Spanish administration); sinking fund.—**c. de las muelas,** (fam.) gums (of the mouth); mouth.—**c. del cuerpo,** thorax, thoracic cavity.—**c. de música,** music box.—**c. de reclutamiento,** (mil.) recruiting branch (of the army or navy).—**c. registradora,** cash register.—**con cajas destempladas,** roughly, without ceremony; coldly, slightingly.—**en c.,** cash, cash on hand (kept in the safe); (fig.) in good condition.

cajeras, *f. pl.* cavities in blocks which contain the sheaves.

cajero, ra. I. *n.* box maker; cashier. II. *m.* reservoir.

cajeta, *f.* little box; poor-box; (Mex.) box of jelly.

cajete, *m.* (Mex.) flat earthen pulque bowl.

cajetilla, *f.* package (of cigarettes).

cajetín, *m. dim.* very small box; (typ.) fount case, letter case.

cajilla, ita, *f. dim.* small box; (bot.) capsule.

cajiga, *f.,* **cajigal,** *m.* = QUEJIGO, QUEJIGAL.

cajista, *n.* compositor (in printing).

cajo, *m.* bookbinder's groove.

cajón, *m.* box, case, chest, drawer, till, locker, mold for casting; space between the shelves of a bookcase; wooden stand or shed for selling provisions; (Mex.) dry-goods store; crib, caisson.—**c. de sastre,** confused mass; odds and ends.—**ser de c.,** to be a matter of course, to go without saying.

cajonada, *f.* (naut.) lockers.

cajoncito, *m. dim.* small box or drawer.

cajonera, *f.* chest of drawers in a vestry.

cajonería, *f.* set of drawers; tallboy or chiffonier.

cajuela, *f. dim.* small box.

cal, *f.* lime.—**c. hidráulica,** hydraulic lime.—**c. muerta,** slaked lime.—**c. viva,** quicklime, unslaked lime.—**c. y canto** = CALICANTO.

cala, *f.* cove, small bay; fishing ground; sample slice cut out of a fruit to try its flavor; hole made in a wall to try its thickness; (med.) suppository; (naut.) hold; (bot.) calla lily.

calaba, *m.* calaba tree. *V.* CALAMBUCO.

calabacear, *va.* = DAR CALABAZAS.

calabacera, *f.* (bot.) pumpkin, gourd or squash plant. *V.* CALABAZA.

calabacero, ra. I. *n.* retailer of pumpkins. **II.** *m.* calabash tree.

calabacica, illa, ita, *f. dim.* small pumpkin.

calabacilla, *f.* core of gourd-shaped tassel; earring made of pearls in the shape of a gourd.

calabacín, *m.* small, young, tender pumpkin; dolt, silly person.

calabacinate, *m.* fried pumpkins.

calabacino, *m.* dry gourd, calabash bottle.

calabaza, *f.* (bot.) pumpkin; squash; gourd; (met.) stupid, ignorant person.—**c. confitera,** or **totanera,** pumpkin.—**c. vinatera,** bottle gourd, calabash.—**dar calabazas,** not to pass, in examination; to refuse (a lover), give the mitten.

calabazada, *f.* knock with the head against something.—**darse de calabazadas,** (met.) to labor in vain.

calabazar, *m.* pumpkin orchard.

calabazate, *m.* preserved pumpkin candied; piece of pumpkin steeped in honey.

calabazo, *m.* gourd.

calabazón, *m. aug.* large winter pumpkin.

calabobos, *m.* drizzle; mizzle.

calabocero, *m.* jailer; warden.

calabozaje, *m.* fee paid by prisoners to the jailer.

calabozo, *m.* dungeon; cell; calaboose; jail; curved pruning and weed-cutting knife.

calabrés, sa, *a.* Calabrian.

calabriada, *f.* mixture of different things; mixture of white and red wine; balderdash.

calabrote, *m.* (naut.) stream cable.

calacanto, *m.* (bot.) flea bane.

calacuerda, *f.* drum call to attack.

calada, *f.* soaking; wetting through; rapid flight of birds of prey; reprimand.

caladio, *m.* (bot.) caladium.

calado. I. *m.* open work in metal, stone, wood, or linen; fretwork; (naut.) draught of a vessel. —*pl.* **calados,** lace. **II.** *pp.* of CALAR.

calador, *m.* perforator; borer; one who makes open work; (naut.) calking iron; surgeon's office.

caladre, *f.* a bird of the lark family.

calafate, calafateador, *m.* calker.

calafateadura, *f.* calking.

calafatear, *va.* to calk.

calafateo, *m.,* **calafatería,** *f.* calking.

calafetear, *va.* = CALAFATEAR.

calafetín, *m.* calker's boy or mate.

calafraga, *f.* (bot.) saxifrage.

calagozo, *m.* bill or hedging hook.

calagraña, *f.* table grape, not fit for wine.

calaguala, *f.* (Peru, bot.) calaguala.

calahorra, *f.* public office where bread is distributed in times of scarcity.

calaíta, *f.* turquoise.

calaje, *m.* chest, trunk, coffer.

calaluz, *m.* (naut., Philip.) a kind of vessel.

calamaco, *m.* calamanco, a woollen fabric.

calamar, *m.* calamary, squid.

calambac, *m.* (bot.) calamba; eaglewood.

calambre, *m.* cramp.

calambuco. I. *m.* (bot.) calaba tree. **II.** *a.* (Cuba) pharisaical, hypocritical.

calamento, *m.* (bot.) mountain balm or calamint.

calamidad, *f.* calamity.

calamillera, *f.* pothook of a crane.

calamina, *f.* calamine.

calaminta, *f.* = CALAMENTO.

calamita, *f.* loadstone; magnetic needle.

calamite, *m.* a little green tree frog.

calamitosamente, *adv.* calamitously.

calamitoso, sa, *a.* calamitous, unfortunate.

cálamo, *m.* (bot.) sweetflag; (poet.) pen; ancient flute.

calamocano, *a.* fuddled; tipsy; unsteady.

calamoco, *m.* icicle.

calamón, *m.* (orn.) purple water hen or gallinule; round-headed nail; stay supporting the beam of an oil mill.

calamorra, *f.* (coll.) head, (vulg.) block.

calamorrada, *f.* butt of horned cattle.

calamorrar, *va.* to butt.

calandraca, *f.* (naut.) mess of hard-tack.

calandrajo, *m.* rag hanging from a garment: ragamuffin.

calandria, *f.* (orn.) bunting, calendar lark; calender; clothier's press; beetle mill; rolling press: mangle.

cálanis, *m.* (bot.) sweet flag.

calaña, *f.* pattern; sample; model, form; character; quality, kind, sort.

calañés, *a.* native of Calañas.—**sombrero c.,** Andalusian hat.

cálao, *m.* a large Philippine bird with serrated bill.

calapatillo, *m.* (zool.) weevil, or its grub.

calapé, *m.* turtle roasted in its shell.

calar. I *va.* to penetrate, soak through, permeate, drench; go through, pierce, perforate; to make open work in (metal, wood, linen, or paper; (mech.) to wedge; to let down (a drawbridge); to fix (the bayonet); to pull down (the hat); to pick (a pocket); to read through (a person), understand; to sample, take or cut out a sample of. **II.** *vn.* to draw (s. o. a ship). **III.** *vr.* to put on; to get drenched; to rush, dart down, descend (s. o. birds of prey); to get in, squeeze in; to sneak in, enter clandestinely.

calar, *a.* calcareous.

calato, ta, *a.* (Peru) nude, naked.

calavera, *f.* skull; madcap, hot-brained, wild fellow, daredevil.

calaverada, *f.* foolishness, tomfoolery.

calaverear, *vn.* to act foolishly and recklessly.

calaverilla, ita. I. *f. dim.* little skull. **II.** *m.* youth who sows his wild oats.

calaverón, *m. aug.* rake, debauchee.

calcado, *m.* tracing.

calcamar, *m.* a Brazilian sea bird.

calcáneo, *m.* (anat.) calcaneum.

calcañal, calcañar, *m.* heel, heel bone.

calcañuelo, *m.* a disease of bees.

calcar, *va.* (pret. CALQUÉ: subj. CALQUE) to trace; to trample on.

calcáreo, rea, *a.* calcareous.

calce, *m.* tire of a wheel; piece of iron or steel added to the coulter of a plow when it is worn; wedge; wheel shoe, a form of brake; (Am.) bottom (of a writing); (naut.) top.

calcedonia, *f.* chalcedony.

calcés, *m.* (naut.) masthead.

calceta, *f.* hose, stocking; fetters worn by criminals.—**hacer c.,** to knit.

calcetería, *f.* hosier's shop and trade; hosiery.

calcetero, ra, *n.* one who makes, mends, or sells thread stockings; hosier.

calcetín, *m.* sock.

calcetón, *m. aug.* cloth stocking worn under boots.

cálcico, ca, *a.* calcic.

calcídico, *m.* (archeol.) chalcidicum.

calcificación, *f.* calcification.

calcificar, *va.* to calcify.

calcímetro, *m.* lime meter, an instrument to determine the lime in soils.

calcina, *f.* mortar.

calcinación, *f.* (chem.) calcination.

calcinar, *va. & vr.* to calcine.

calcinatorio, *m.* calcinatory, calcining vessel.

calcio, *m.* calcium.

calcita, *f.* (min.) calcite.

calco, *m.* tracing.

calcografía, *f.* chalcography; place where engravings are engraved.

calcógrafo, *m.* engraver.

calcomanía, *f.* decalcomania.

calcopirita, *f.* chalcopyrite.

calculable, *a.* calculable.

calculador, ra. I. *n.* calculator, computer. **II.** *m.* calculating machine.

calcular, *va.* to calculate, compute; to estimate.

calculista, *n.* schemer; calculator, computer; designer.

cálculo, *m.* calculation, computation; estimate; conjecture; (math.) calculus (differential, integral, etc.); (med.) calculus.

calculoso, sa, *a.* calculose, calculous.

calcha, *f.* (Chile) workman's clothing and bedding.

calda, *f.* warming or heating.—**caldas,** hot mineral-water baths.—**dar calda a,** to heat, reheat.

caldaico, ca, *a.* = CALDEO.

caldario, *m.* calderium.

caldear, *va.* to warm, heat; to weld.

caldeo, a. I. *n.* & *a.* Chaldean, Chaldaic. **II.** *m.* heating.

caldera, *f.* caldron; sugar kettle; boiling pan; shell of kettle drum; (st. eng.) boiler.—**c. acuatubular,** water-tube boiler.—**c. de hogar interior,** flue boiler.—**c. de tubos de humos,** fire-tube boiler.—**c. de vapor,** steam boiler.—**c. fija,** stationary boiler.—**c. locomóvil,** portable boiler.—**c. marina,** or **marítima,** marine boiler.—**c. tubular,** tubular boiler.

calderada, *f.* caldronful.

calderería, *f.* brazier's or boiler maker's shop and trade.—**calderero,** *m.* brazier; coppersmith; boiler maker; tinker.

caldereta, *f. dim.* small caldron, kettle, pot; holy-water pot; fish stew; lamb stew; (Mex.) chocolate pot; (C. Am.) thunderstorm.

calderilla, *f.* holy-water pot; any copper coin.

caldero, *m.* semispherical caldron or boiler; a copper; caldronful; ladle.

calderón, *m.* large caldron or kettle; mark for a thousand (℈); (print.) paragraph (¶); (mus.) sign (⌒) denoting a pause; hold.

calderoniano, na, *a.* Calderonian, relating to, or like, Calderón or his style.

calderuela, *f. dim.* small kettle; dark lantern used to drive partridges into the net.

caldillo, caldito, *m.* sauce of a ragout or fricassee; light broth.

caldo, *m.* broth; beef tea; bouillon; salad dressing; sauce; gravy.—*pl.* (com.) wine, oil and liquors.—**c. alterado,** medicated broth.—**c. de carne,** consommé; beef tea.

caldoso, sa, *a.* having plenty of broth; thin.

calducho, *m.* ill-seasoned broth; hog wash.

calecer, *va.* to become heated.

calecico, *m. dim.* small chalice.

calefaciente, *a.* (med.) heating.

calefacción, *f.* heating.

calefactorio, *m.* calefactory (in covents).

caleidoscopio, *m.* = CALIDOSCOPIO.

calenda, *f.* part of the martyrology which treats of the acts of the saints of the day.—*pl.* **calendas,** calends.—**calendas griegas,** Greek calends (a time that will never come, as there were no Greek calends).

calendario, *m.* almanac; calendar.—**hacer calendarios,** (met.) to muse; to make hasty prophecies.

calendarista, *n.* calendar maker.

caléndula, *f.* (bot.) marigold.

calentador, *m.* heater; warming pan; (coll.) large, clumsy watch.

calentamiento, *m.* warming, heating; a horse disease.

calentano, na, *n.* (Am.) lowlander, native of a hot climate.

calentar. I. *va.* (*ind.* CALIENTO: *subj.* CALIENTE) to heat, warm; to heat and heat (a ball) in one's hand before it is played; to urge; press forward; despatch speedily. **II.** *vr.* to be in heat, rut; to get hot; become excited or angry.

calentón, *m.*—**darse un c.,** to take a bit of a warming.

calentura, *f.* fever.—**calenturiento, ta,** *a.* feverish.—**calenturilla,** *f. dim.* slight fever.—**calenturón,** *m. aug.* high fever.—**calenturoso, sa,** *a.* feverish.

calepino, *m.* (coll.) Latin dictionary.

calera, *f.* lime kiln; lime pit; fishing smack.

calería, *f.* place where lime is burnt and sold.

calero, ra. I. *a.* calcareous. **II.** *m.* lime burner, lime maker or seller.

calesa, *f.* two-wheeled calash, chaise.

calesera, *f.* bolero jacket.

calesero, *m.* driver of a calash.—**calesín,** *m.* light chaise.—**calesinero,** *m.* owner or driver of a light chaise.

caleta, *f.* (naut.) cove, creek, small bay or inlet; (Venez.) trade of carriers.

caletero, *m.* (Venez.) carrier.

caletre, *m.* (coll.) judgment, acumen, noddle.

calibeado, da, *a.* (med.) chalybean; chalybeate.

calibración, *f.* calibration; gaging.

calibrador, *m.* gage (instrument); calipers.

calibrar, *va.* to calibrate (a ball, a firearm); to gage, measure.

calibre, *m.* caliber; diameter, bore (of a cylinder, pipe, etc.); gage (instrument); calipers; gage, diameter (of wire).

calicanto, *m.* stone masonry; (bot.) allspice.—**de c.,** (fig.) strong, firm, solid.

calicata, *f.* (min.) trial pit.

caliciforme, *a.* chaliced, chalice-shaped.

calicó, *m.* = PERCAL.

calicud, *f.* silk stuff from India.

calicular, *a.* (bot.) calycular.

calículo, *m.* (bot.) calycle.

calicut, *f.* = CALICUD.

caliche, *m.* pebble burnt in a brick; crust of lime which flakes from a wall; (Peru and Chile) native saltpetre.

calidad, *f.* quality; grade; nobility; rank.—*pl.* conditions, terms, stipulations; personal qualifications; gifts, parts.—**en c. de,** as; in one's capacity as.

cálido, da, *a.* warm; hot; piquant; crafty, artful.

calidoscópico, ca, *a.* kaleidoscopic.

calidoscopio, *m.* kaleidoscope.

calientapiés, *m.* foot warmer.

calientaplatos, *m.* plate warmer.

caliente, *a.* warm, hot; fiery.—**en c.,** while hot; at once.—**estar c.,** to be in heat, rut.

caliento, yo caliente. *V.* CALENTAR.

califa, *m.* caliph.—**califato,** *m.* caliphate.

calificable, *a.* qualifiable.

calificación, *f.* qualification; judgment, censure; proof; mark (in an examination).

calificado, da. I. *a.* qualified, authorized, competent. **II.** *pp.* of CALIFICAR.

calificador, ra, *n.* qualifier; censor.

calificar. I. *va.* (*pret.* CALIFIQUÉ: *subj.* CALIFIQUE) to qualify; rate, class; pass on; judge; authorize; certify, attest; ennoble. **II.** *vr.* to prove one's noble birth and descent according to law.

calificativo, va, *a.* (gram.) qualifying.

califórnico, ca, *a.*; **californio, ia,** *n.* & *a.* Californian.

cáliga, *f.* caliga, a Roman soldier's sandal.

caligine, *f.* mist, obscurity, darkness.

caliginoso, sa, *a.* caliginous; dark; dim.

caligrafía, *f.* caligraphy, penmanship.

caligráfico, ca, *a.* caligraphic.

calígrafo, *m.* expert penman.

calilla, *f. dim.* a slight suppository.

calima, calina, *f.* thick vapor; light mist, haze.

calinda, *f.* (Cuba) a popular creole dance.

calinoso, sa, *a.* vapory, misty, hazy.

calípedes, *m.* slow-paced animal.

calípico, ca, *a.* (astr.) calippic.

calisaya, *f.* (bot.) calisaya.

calistenia, *f.* calisthenics.

cáliz, *m.* chalice; communion cup; bitter cup of grief and affliction; (bot.) calyx.

caliza, *f.* limestone (called also **piedra c.**).

calizo, za, *a.* calcareous; limy; calc (spar).

calma, *f.* calm; calmness, tranquillity; slowness; suspension of business; cessation of pain.—**c. chicha,** (naut.) dead calm.

calmadamente, *adv.* quietly, calmly.

calmado, da. I. *a.* quiet, calm, still. **II.** *pp.* of CALMAR.

calmante. I. *a.* mitigating; quieting, soothing. **II.** *m.* & *a.* (med.) narcotic, anodyne, sedative.

calmar. I. *va.* to calm, quiet, pacify; allay, mitigate, soothe. **II.** *vn.* to abate, to be becalmed. **III.** *vr.* to quiet down, to abate; to calm one's self, to be pacified.

calmo, ma, *a.* uncultivated, untilled; treeless; barren.

calmoso, sa, *a.* calm; slow, tardy; soothing.

calmuco, ca, *n.* & *a.* Kalmuck.

caló, *m.* cant; slang of gipsies and ruffians.

calocéfalo, la, *a.* having a beautiful head.

calofilo, la, *a.* having handsome leaves.

calofriado, da. I. *a.* chilly, shivering with cold. **II.** *pp.* of CALOFRIARSE.

calofriarse, *vr.* to have a chill.

calofrío, *m.* chill, shiver.

calomel, *m.*, **calomelanos,** *m. pl.* calomel.

caloña, *f.* fine or damages for slander.

calóptero, ra, *a.* handsome-winged.

calor, *m.* heat; glow; warmth, ardor; brunt of a battle; favor, kind reception.

caloría, *f.* calorie.

caloricidad, *f.* (physiol.) caloricity.

calórico, *m.* (chem.) caloric.

calorífero, *m.* heater, radiator.—**c. de aire,** hot-air register.—**c. de vapor,** steam radiator.

calorífero, ra, *a.* giving heat.

calorificación, *f.* calorification.

calorífico, ca, *a.* calorific.

calorífugo, ga, *a.* non-conductor of heat; fire-proof, non-combustible.

calorimetría, *f.* calorimetry.

calorimétrico, ca, *a.* calorimetric.

calorímetro, *m.* (chem.) calorimeter.

calorimotor, *m.* (phys.) calorimotor.

calorosamente, *adv.* = CALUROSAMENTE.

caloroso, sa, *a.* = CALUROSO.

calostro, *m.* colostrum.

caloyo, *m.* unborn lamb or kid.

calpamulo, la, *a.* (Mex.) half-breed.

calpisque, calpixque, calpizque, *m.* (Mex.) tax collector, steward.

calseco, ca, *a.* cured with lime.

calta, *f.* caltha, marsh marigold.

calumbarse, *vr.* to plunge, dive.

calumbo, *m.* plunge, diving.

calumnia, *f.* calumny, slander.

calumniador, ra, *n.* & *a.* slanderer (-ing).

calumniar, *va.* to slander.—**calumniosamente,** *adv.* slanderingly.—**calumnioso, sa,** *a.* calumnious, slanderous.

calurosamente, *adv.* warmly; ardently; hotly; passionately.

caluroso, sa, *a.* warm, hot; heating; excited; vehement, enthusiastic.

calva, *f.* bald head; bald pate; clearing, open space.—**c. de almete,** crest of a helmet.

calvar. I. *va.* to cheat, deceive. **II.** *vn.* to become bald.

calvario, *m.* Calvary; debts; tally; score.

calvatrueno, *m.* baldness of the whole head; a wild person.

calvaza, *f. aug.* large bald pate.

calverizo, za, *a.* having many barren or bare spots.

calvero, *m.* barren spot; clearing, open space.

calvete, *m. dim.* little bald pate, when only part of the head is bald.

calvez, calvicie, *f.* baldness.

calvijar, *m. V.* CALVERO.

calvilla, *f. dim.* little baldness.

calvinismo, *m.* Calvinism.—**calvinista,** *n.* & *a.* Calvinist (-ic).

calvo, va, *a.* bald; bare; barren.

calza, *f.* loose breeches; trousers; hose, stockings; garter or ribbon tied on some animals; wedge.—*pl.* fetters.—**c. de arena,** sandbag.—**calzas acuchilladas,** slashed trousers.—**echarle una c. a,** to size up (a person).—**en calzas prietas,** in an embarrassing or difficult position, in a tight fix.—**medias calzas,** stockings reaching to the knees.—**tomar las calzas de Villadiego,** to make a precipitate flight or escape, to bolt.

calzacalzón, *m.* galligaskins.

calzada, *f.* causeway; paved highway.

calzadera, *f.* hempen cord; net twine.

calzadillo, ito, *m. dim.* small shoe.

calzado, da, *a.* calceated, shod; with white feet (s. o. horses); having feathers on the legs and feet (s. o. birds).

calzado, *m.* footwear.

calzador, *m.* shoeing leather; shoehorn.

calzadura, *f.* act of putting on the shoes; tip for this service; felloe of a wheel.

calzar. I. *va.* (*pret.* CALCÉ: *subj.* CALCE) to put on (shoes, gloves, spurs, etc.); to scot or scotch (a wheel); to carry (a ball) of a certain size (s. o. firearms); to wedge, chock, key; (typ.) to overlay, raise, underlay; to shoe (an anchor); to put a steel edge on (an iron tool); to block (a wheel, carriage, to place something under the wheels to prevent sliding); to have (aptitudes, skill, ability, etc.). **II.** *vr.* to put on; to control, dominate; to get, to obtain.

calzo, *m.* (typ.) frisket sheet, overlay; (r. w.) block, brake shoe; (mech.) wedge, quoin; shoe of a felloe; (naut.) skid, chock, bed, shoe.

calzón, *m.* ombre, a game of cards; (Mex.) a disease of the sugar cane from lack of irrigation.—*pl.* breeches; trousers; (naut.) goosewing.—**c. corto,** knee breeches.

calzonarias, *f. pl.* (Colomb.) suspenders (for trousers).

calzonazos, *m. aug.* big breeches.—**ser un calzonazos,** to be a weak, soft fellow.

calzoncillos, *m. pl.* drawers, underdrawers.

calzoneras, *f. pl.* (Mex.) trousers buttoned down both sides.

calzorras, *m.* = CALZONAZOS.

callada, *f.* a dish of tripe; silence (u. only in certain phrases).—**a las calladas,** or **de callada,** privately, on the quiet.—**dar la c. por respuesta,** to answer by silence.

calladamente, *adv.* silently, secretly.

callado, da. I. *a.* silent; quiet; reticent. **II.** *pp.* of CALLAR.

callana, *f.* (Am.) an almost flat earthen bowl used as a baking griddle.

callandico, ito, *adv.* in a low voice; silently, without noise, slyly, softly.

callar, *vn.*, *va.* & *vr.* to keep silent; to stop talking (playing, singing, etc.); to shut up; to hush, conceal, keep from being known; to dissemble; (poet.) to abate, moderate, grow calm.—**c. su pico,** to hold one's tongue.—**¡calla! or ¡calle! you** don't mean it! is it possible?—**quien calla otorga,** silence gives consent.

calle. I. *f.* street; walk in a garden; passage, way.—**c. hita,** from house to house.—**abrir c.,** to clear the way.—**azotar las c.,** to loiter about, loaf.—**dejar en la c.,** to leave penniless, or in destitution.—**echar a la c.,** to put on the street, to put out of the house; to make public.—**hacer c.** = ABRIR C.—**llevar,** or **llevarse, de c.,** to sweep away; to overmaster; to confound, silence. **II.** *interj.* make way! move aside!

callear, *va.* to clear (walks) in a vineyard.

calleja, *f.* = CALLEJUELA.

callejear, *vn.* to walk or loiter about the streets; to gad; to ramble.

callejero, ra, *n.* loiterer, gadder.

callejo, *m.* pit into which game falls when pursued.

callejón, *m.* lane, alley.—**callejoncillo,** *m. dim.* little, narrow passage or lane.

callejuca, *f. dim.* small, narrow street.

callejuela, *f. dim.* small street, lane, or narrow passage; shift, subterfuge, evasion.

calleyo, *m.* = CALLEJO.

callialto, ta, *a.* horseshoe having swelling welts or borders.

callicida, *m.* corn exterminator.

callista, *n.* corn doctor, chiropodist.

callizo, *m.* V. CALLEJÓN and CALLEJUELA.

callo, *m.* corn, callousness on the feet; wen; (surg.) callus; extremity of a horseshoe.—*pl.* tripes.

callosidad, *f.* callosity, callousness.

calloso, sa, *a.* callous; corneous, horny.

cama, *f.* bed; couch; bed hangings and furniture; seat or couch of wild animals; floor or body of a cart; part of a plow that connects the share with the beam, the sheath; part of a melon resting on the ground; straw laid under animals or on plants; slice of meat put upon another when cooking; felloe of a wheel; check of a bridle; V-shaped piece in a cloak; garden bed; (mech.) cam; cog; catch; tooth; bed-plate; base; (geol.) layer, stratum.—**guardar, or hacer, c.,** to be confined to one's bed.—**hacer la c.,** to make the bed.—**hacerle la c. a uno,** to injure one secretly.

camada, *f.* brood of young animals, litter; band of thieves.

camafeo, *m.* cameo.

camal, *m.* hempen halter; camail.

camaleón, *m.* chameleon; person who changes his opinions to suit his interest.

Camaleopardo, *m.* (astr.) Cameleopard.

camalote, *m.* a South-Am. river plant resembling a floating island.

camama, *f.* (coll.) sham, humbug.

camamila, *f.* (bot.) common chamomile. V. MANZANILLA.

camándula, *f.* chaplet or rosary of one or three decades.—**tener muchas camándulas,** to be very tricky.

camandulense, *n.* & *a.* Camaldolite, order of Camandula or reformed Benedictines.

camandulería, *f.* hypocrisy, trickery.

camandulero, ra, *a.* & *n.* hypocrite (-ic), dissembler (-ing).

cámara, *f.* hall; parlor; chamber; each of the two houses of a legislative body; chamber (of a fire-arm, a mine); cabin of a ship; (aer.) cockpit; granary; mow; stool; evacuation by stool; laxity; (phot.) camera.—**c. alta,** senate; House of Lords, upper house .—**c. ardiente,** funeral chamber.—**c. baja,** House of Commons, lower house. chamber of deputies.—**c. clara,** camera lucida.—**c. de comercio,** chamber of commerce.—**c. lúcida,** camera lucida.—**c. mortuoria,** funeral chamber.—**c. obscura,** camera obscura.—**c. plegadiza,** folding camera.

camarada, *n.* comrade, companion, crony, pal, or chum.

camaraje, *m.* rent for a granary.

camaranchón, *m.* garret; attic.

camarera, *f.* head waiting maid; keeper of the queen's wardrobe; chambermaid; waitress.

camarería, *f.* employment of a waiting maid; ancient perquisite of the lord chamberlain.

camarero, *m.* chamberlain; steward or keeper of stores; waiter; valet.

camareta, *f. dim.* (naut.) small cabin; deck cabin; midshipman's cabin.

camariento, ta, *a.* having diarrhœa.

camarilla, *f. dim.* small room; coterie of private advisers of the king; coterie or ring of influential persons; clique.

camarín, *m.* place behind an altar where the images are dressed and the ornaments kept; closet; car (of elevator); (theat.) dressing room.

camarista. I. *m.* member of the supreme council; (Mex.) valet. **II.** *f.* maid of honor to the queen and princesses.

camarita, *f. dim.* small chamber or room.

camarlengo, *m.* lord of the bedchamber of the kings of Aragon; camerlengo.

cámaro, camarón, *m.* (zool.) shrimp.

camaronero, ra, *n.* shrimp seller.

camarote, *m.* (naut.) stateroom; berth.

camasquince, *n.* meddlesome person.

camastra, *n.* (Ch.) cunning, trickery.

camastrear, *vn.* (Ch.) to dissemble, act cunningly.

camastro, *m.* poor, miserable bed.

camastrón, na, *n.* sly, artful, cunning person.

camastronazo, *m. aug.* great impostor, humbug.

camastronería, *f.* cunning, humbug, trickery.

camatones, *m. pl.* (naut.) iron fastenings of the shrouds.

camba, *f.* check of a bridle; felloe; a V-shaped piece in garments.

cambalache, *m.* (coll.) barter.—**cambalachear,** *va.* to barter.—**cambalachero, ra,** *n.* barterer.

cambaleo, *m.* strolling troupe of players.

cámbaro, *m.* crawfish.

cambiable, *a.* fit to be bartered or exchanged; changing.

cambiador, ra, *n.* barterer; money changer.

cambial, *m.* bill of exchange.

cambiamano, *f.* railroad switch.

cambiamiento, *m.* change, alteration.

cambiante. I. *a.* bartering, exchanging; changing. **II.** *m.* banker, exchanger; iridescence; iridescent fabric.

cambiar. I. *va.* to change; to barter; to exchange. **II.** *vn.* to change, shift.

cambiavía, *m.* (r. w.) switch; switchman, switch tender.

cámbija, *f.* reservoir.

cambio, *m.* change; barter; exchange; premium paid or received for negotiating bills; rate of exchange (of money); rise and fall of the course of exchange; public or private bank; return of a favor; recompense.—**c. minuto,** small change.—**en c., in return; on the other hand.—en c. de,** in lieu of; instead of.

cambista, *m.* banker, money broker.

cambray, *m.* cambric, fine linen.—**cambrayado, da,** *a.* cambriclike.—**cambrayón,** *m.* coarse cambric.

cambriano, na; cámbrico, ca, *a.* (geol.) Cambrian.

cambrón, *m.* (bot.) buckthorn; bramble.

cambronal, *m.* brambled ground or place.

cambronera, *f.* (bot.) boxthorn.

cambuj, *m.* child's cap tied close to its head to keep it straight; mask.

cambujo, ja, *n.* & *a.* Indian mestizo; half-breed.

cambullón, *m.* (Peru) imposition, swindle.

cambur, *m.* a kind of plantain or banana.—**c. amarillo, or criollo,** yellow or Johnson banana.—**c. higo, or titiaro,** very small and fine variety of banana.—**c. manzano,** small banana with apple flavor.—**c. morado,** red banana.

cambuy, *m.* an American myrtle tree.

camedafne, *f.* (bot.) dwarf bay.

camedrio, camedris, *m.* (bot.) wall germander.

camelar, *va.* to flirt; court; woo; seduce, deceive.

cameica, *f.* (bot.) widowwail.

camelete, *m.* (obs.) a kind of large gun.

camelia, *f.* (bot.) camellia.

camelo, *m.* flirtation; courtship; joke, jest; disappointment; deceit.

camelote, *m.* camlet; (bot.) a tropical weed.

camelotillos, *m.* light or thin camlets.

camella, *f.* she-camel; ridge in plowed land; milk pail; yoke.

camellejo, *m. dim.* small camel.

camellería, *f.* stable or stand for camels; employment of a camel driver.

camellero, *m.* keeper or driver of camels.

camello, *m.* camel; an ancient gun; engine for setting ships afloat in shoal water.—**c. pardal,** camelopard.

camellón, *m.* ridge turned up by the plow or spade; drinking trough; carpenter's horse; bed of flowers; camlet.

camero, ra. I. *n.* upholsterer; one who lets beds. **II.** *a.* belonging or relating to beds.

camilla, *f. dim.* small bed, pallet, cot; litter, stretcher; clothes horse; shearer's frame.

caminador, ra, *n.* good walker.
caminante, *m.* traveler, walker.
caminar, *vn.* to walk, travel, go, move along.—**c. con pies de plomo,** to act cautiously, go slowly.—**c. derecho,** to act uprightly.
caminata, *f.* long walk for exercise; promenade; excursion, jaunt, outing.
camino, *m.* road; highway; path, pass; passage, trip, journey; profession, station, calling; way; manner, method; (min.) drift, gait; (naut.) ship's way, rate of sailing.—**c. carretero,** vehicle road, drive.—**c. cubierto,** (mil.) covert way.—**c. de herradura,** bridle road.—**c. de hierro,** railroad.—**c. de ruedas** = C. CARRETERO.—**c. de sirga,** tow path.—**c. real,** highway.—**c. trillado,** thoroughfare; routine; commonplace.—**c. vecinal,** municipal road, cared for by a municipality.—**abrir c.,** to open the way, find the means.—**de c.,** on the way; traveling (u. a.).—**fuera de c.,** off the road; unreasonable; astray.—**no llevar c.,** to be wrong, not to be cogent, not to lead anywhere.—**partir el c. con,** to meet half way.—**ponerse en c.,** to set off, start.—**traer a buen c.,** to disabuse to open the eyes of (one who is in error).
camión, *m.* dray, truck.—**c. automóvil,** auto-truck.—**camionaje,** *m.* truckage.
camisa, *f.* shirt; chemise; thin skin (of fruit); coat of whitewash; slough of a serpent; (mil.) chemise; (obs.) catamenia; jacket, case, casing; lining (of a furnace).—**c. alquitranada, embreada,** or **de fuego,** (naut.) fire chemise.—**c. de fuerza,** strait jacket.—**c. de una vela,** (naut.) body of a sail.—**c. de vapor,** steam jacket.—**meterse en c. de once varas,** to interfere in other people's affairs.—**no llegarle a uno la c. al cuerpo,** to be frightened; to be anxious.
camisería, *f.* shirt store, haberdashery.
camisero, ra, *n.* shirt maker, haberdasher.
camiseta, *f.* undershirt; short shirt with wide sleeves; chemisette.
camisilla, *f. dim.* small shirt.
camisola, *f.* ruffled shirt; dicky.
camisolín, *m.* shirt front; tucker; wimple.
camisón, *m. aug.* long and wide shirt; nightshirt; (Am.) gown; (Cuba) chemise.
camisote, *m.* ancient hauberk.
camita. **I.** *f. dim.* small bed, pallet, cot. **II.** *n.* & *a.* Hamite (-tic).—**camítico, ca,** *a.* Hamitic.
camomila, *f.* chamomile.
camón, *m. aug.* large bed; portable throne; glass partition; oriel window.—*pl.* round pieces forming the frame of a water wheel; oak tires of cart wheels; lath frame of an arch.
camoncillo, *m.* seat in a drawing-room.
camorra, *f.* quarrel.—**camorrear,** *vn.* to quarrel.
camorrista, *n.* noisy, quarrelsome person.
camote, *m.* (Am.) sweet potato; infatuation, love; lie, fib; lover; fool.—**tragar c.,** to hesitate in speaking, become confused, get rattled.
campal, *a.* field, camp (u. a.).
campamento, *m.* encampment; camp.
campana, *f.* bell; anything bell-shaped; (met.) parish church, parish; bell-shaped bottom of a well; (arch.) drum, corbel.—**c. de chimenea,** mantel of a chimney.—**c. de buzo,** diving bell.—**c. de rebato,** alarm bell.—**oir campanas y no saber dónde,** to have heard of a fact, but not to be well informed of its true nature.
campanada, *f.* stroke of a bell; scandal; sensational report.
campanario, *m.* belfry; noddle, head; rack (in looms).
campanear. **I.** *vn.* to ring the bells frequently. **II.** *va.* to divulge; noise about.
campanela, *f.* a fancy step in dancing.
campaneo, *m.* bell ringing; chime; gait, sway in walking.
campanero, *m.* bell founder; bellman; bell bird.
campaneta, *f. dim.* small bell.
campanil, *m.* small belfry.
campanilla, *f. dim.* small bell; hand bell; small bubble; (anat.) uvula; little tassel for ladies' gowns; (naut.) cabin bell; (bot.) bellflower.

campanillazo, *m.* violent ringing of a bell; signal given with a bell.
campanillear, *vn.* to ring a small bell often.
campanillero, *m.* bellman; public crier.
campanología, *f.* campanology.
campanólogo, ga, *n.* campanologist.
campante, *a.* surpassing; buoyant, cheerful.
campanudo, da, *a.* puffed up; bell-shaped; (bot.) campanulate; pompous, high-sounding.
campánula, *f.* (bot.) bellflower.
campanuláceo, a. **I.** *a.* (bot.) campanulaceous. **II.** *f. pl.* Campanulaceæ.
campanulado, da, *a.* campanulate, bell-shaped.
campaña, *f.* campaign; level country.—**c. naval,** (naut.) cruise.—**batir,** or **correr, la c.,** to reconnoiter.
campañola, *f.* water rat.
campar, *vn.* to excel; to encamp.
campeador, ra, *a.* surpassing in bravery.
campear, *vn.* to be in the field; to pasture; frisk about; crop out; grow; be prominent, excel.
campecico, illo, ito, *m. dim.* small field.
campechano, na. **I.** *a.* frank; hearty; cheerful; generous. **II.** *n.* & *a.* native of or belonging to Campeche.
campeche, *m.* campeche wood, logwood.
campeón, *m.* champion; combatant; defender.
campeonato, *m.* championship.
campero, ra. **I.** *a.* exposed to the weather in the open field; unsheltered, unhoused; good at farming; (Mex.) having a gait like gentle trotting; pacing. **II.** *m.* friar who superintends a farm; field guard.
campesino, na; campestre. **I.** *a.* rural; country (u. a.), rustic. **II.** *n.* countryman (-woman).
campilán, *m.* long, straight sabre used in the Philippines, broadening toward the point.
campillo, *m. dim.* small field.
campiña, *f.* flat tract of arable land; field; country; landscape.
campo, *m.* country; field; space, room; ground of silks and other stuffs; (mil.) field, camp; ground of a painting.—**c. de Agramonte,** bedlam.—**c. de batalla,** battle field.—**c. de labor,** cultivated ground; farm.—**c. del honor,** field of honor.—**c. de puna,** (Arg.) sandy, clayey grounds not suitable for cattle raising.—**c. magnético,** magnetic field.—**c. raso,** flat, open field (u. mainly in the phrase **a c. raso,** in the open air, in the open, without shelter).—**c. santo,** cemetery.—**c. visual,** field of vision.—**a c. traviesa,** or **travieso,** *adv.* cross-country.—**dar c. a la fantasía,** to give free range to one's fancy.—**quedar en el c.,** to be killed.—**salir al c.,** to go out to fight a duel.
camuatí, *m.* (Am.) hut, rough cabin.
camuesa, *f.* pippin (apple).
camueso, *m.* (bot.) pippin tree; dunce, fool.
camuñas, *f. pl.* all seeds, except wheat, barley, and rye.
camuza, *f.* chamois goat.
camuzón, *m. aug.* large chamois skin.
can, *m.* dog; (arch.) bracket; shoulder; modillion; corbel; trigger; an ancient piece of ordnance.—**C. Mayor,** (astr.) Canis Major.—**C. Menor,** (astr.) Canis Minor.—**el C.,** the Dog Star.
cana, *f.* gray hair; long measure, about two ells.—**echar una c. al aire,** to go on a lark.
canabíneo, a. **I.** *a.* (bot.) pertaining to the hemp family. **II.** *f. pl.* the hemp family.
canáceo, a. **I.** *a.* (bot.) cannaceous. **II.** *f. pl.* Cannaceæ.
canadense, canadiense, *n.* & *a.* Canadian.
canal. **I.** *m.* channel; strait; canal; duct. **II.** *f.* natural underground waterway; long and narrow dell; any open conduit; groove; gutter; carcass, body of an animal killed and dressed for food; comb of the loom; hemp once hackled; front edge of a book; drinking trough; crease, slot in metalwork; bed of a hot press; (tel.) copper pole; well (of the rim of a wheel).—**abrir en c.,** to cut from top to bottom.
canalado, da, *a.* = ACANALADO.
canaladura, *f.* (arch.) hollow molding; groove.

canaleja, *f. dim.* small drinking trough; mill spout; priest's hat.

canalera, *f.* roof gutter.

canalete, *m.* bladed paddle for canoeing.

canalita, *f. dim.* small channel, gutter or groove.

canalización, *f.* canalization; (elec.) wiring.

canalizar, *va.* to construct channels or canals in or for; to improve the channel of (a river, etc.); to canalize; (elec.) to wire.

canalizo, *m.* narrow channel.

canalón, *m. aug.* gutter, leader, spout; gargoyle.

canalla. I. *f.* rabble, canaille. **II.** *m.* mean, despicable fellow, cur.—**canallada,** *f.* base, despicable act.—**canallesco, ca,** *a.* base, currish.

canameño, *m.* (Am.) traveling hammock.

canana, *f.* cartridge belt.

cananeo, a, *n. & a.* Canaanite (-ish).

canapé, *m.* couch; settee; lounge.

canaria, *f.* female canary bird.

canariense; canario, ria, *n. & a.* of or belonging to the Canary Islands.

canario. I. *m.* canary bird; a dance introduced into Spain by natives of the Canaries; (naut.) a barge used in the Canary Islands. **II.** *interj.* zounds!

canasta, *f.* basket, hamper; crate.

canastero, ra, *n.* basket maker.

canastilla, *f. dim.* small basket; gift to ladies of the court; an infant's basket; wardrobe for a baby.

canastillo, *m.* small tray; pannier; small basket.

canasto, canastro, *m.* large basket.—¡**canastos!** *interj.* gracious! confound it!

cáncamo, *m.* a rare gum resembling myrrh; (naut.) ringbolt.—**c. de argolla,** ringbolt.—**c. de ojo,** eyebolt.

cancamurria, *f.* (coll.) sadness, melancholy.

cancamusa, *f.* (coll.) trick to deceive.

cancán, *m.* cancan (dance).

cáncana, *f.* cricket, stool for punishing children; a kind of spider.

cancanear, *vn.* to loiter about, loaf; (Am.) to stammer.

cancaneo, *m.* stammering.

cáncano, *m.* (coll.) louse.

cancel, *m.* wooden screen; glass case in chapel for the king.

cancela, *f.* front door grating or screen.

cancelación, canceladura, *f.* cancellation, expunging, obliteration.

cancelar, *va.* to annul; to dispel.

cancelaría, cancelería, *f.* papal chancery.

cancelario, *m.* chancellor in universities who grants degrees.

cáncer, *m.* cancer; (**C-,** astr.) Cancer.

cancerarse, *vr.* to develop a cancer; to become a cancer.

Cancerbero, *m.* (myth.) Cerberus; strict and incorruptible guard.

canceroso, sa, *a.* cancerous.

cancilla, *f.* wicker door or gate.

canciller, *m.* chancellor.

cancilleresco, ca, *a.* belonging to a chancelry; chancelrylike.

cancillería, *f.* chancelry.

canción, *f.* song, lay, ballad.

cancioncica, illa, ita, *f. dim.* canzonet.

cancionero, *m.* song book; song writer.

cancioneta, *f. dim.* little song, canzonet.

cancionista, *n.* author or singer of songs, songster, ballad singer.

cancriforme, *a.* cancriform.

cancrinita, *f.* cancrinite.

cancro, *m.* (bot.) sore spot in trees.

cancrófago, ga, *a.* crab-eating.

cancroide, *m.* cancroid tumor.

cancroideo, ea, *a.* cancroid, cancriform.

cancha, *f.* roasted corn or beans; cockpit; game grounds.

canchal, *m.* bouldery ground.

canchalagua, canchelagua, canchilagua, *f.* (Peru) a medicinal herb.

cancho, *m.* big boulder or rock.

candado, *m.* padlock; pendant; earring.—*pl.* cavities around the frog of a horse's feet.

candamo, *m.* an old rustic dance.

candar, *va.* to lock, shut.

cándara, *f.* sifting screen, sieve.

candela, *f.* fire; light; candle, taper; flower or blossom of the chestnut tree; inclination of the balance needle towards the thing weighed.—**en c.,** vertical (s. o. a mast).

candelabro, *m.* candelabrum; bracket.

candelada, *f.* = HOGUERA.

candelaria, *f.* Candlemas; (bot.) mullen.

candelecho, *m.* hut built on piles for watching a vineyard.

candelerazo, *m.* blow with a candlestick.

candelero, *m.* candlestick; student's lamp; fishing torch; (naut.) stanchions or crotches.—**estar en c.,** (met.) to be high in office; to hold an exalted station.

candelica, illa, ita, *f. dim.* small candle.

candelilla, *f.* (surg.) bougie, catheter; blossom; will-o'-the-wisp; catkin, ament.—**le hacen candelillas los ojos,** (coll.) his eyes sparkle with the fumes of wine.

candelizas, *f. pl.* (naut.) brails.

candelizo, *m.* (coll.) = CARÁMBANO.

candencia, *f.* incandescence.

candente, *a.* incandescent, red-hot.

cándidamente, *adv.* candidly.

candidato, *m.* candidate.

candidatura, *f.* candidacy; list of candidates; (U. S. pol.) slate.

candidez, *f.* candor, ingenuousness; whiteness.

cándido, da, *a.* candid, guileless; white, snowy.

candiel, *m.* sweetmeat of white wine, egg yolks, sugar, etc.

candil, *m.* kitchen or stable oil lamp; Greek lamp; (coll.) cock of a hat; (coll.) long irregular fold in petticoats; (Mex.) chandelier; top of a stag's horn.

candilada, *f.* (coll.) oil spilt from a lamp.

candileja, *f.* oil receptacle of a lamp.—*pl.* footlights of a theater; (bot.) willow-herb.

candilejo, *m. dim.* small kitchen lamp; (bot.) = LUCÉRNULA.

candilera, *f.* (bot.) lamp wick.

candilón, *m. aug.* large open lamp.

candiota. I. *n. & a.* of or belonging to the island of Candía. **II.** *f.* barrel; cake; large earthen jar for wine.

candiotera, *f.* wine cellar; storage place for casks.

candiotero, *m.* CANDIOTA maker.

candonga, *f.* (coll.) cunning; (coll.) merry, playful trick; practical joke; draught mule.—**candongo, ga,** *a.* (coll.) cunning, artful.—**candonguear,** *va.* (coll.) to joke with; play a joke on; (coll.) to shirk.—**candonguero, ra,** *n.* (coll.) joker.

candor, *m.* pure whiteness; candor.

candorosamente, *adv.* candidly.

candoroso, sa, *a.* candid, ingenuous.

cané, *m.* a card game of chance.

caneca, *f.* glazed stone bottle for liquor and cordials.

canecillo, *m.* (arch.) corbel, modillion; truss; cantilever; console.

canéfora, *f.* canephore.

canela, *f.* (bot.) cinnamon; (coll.) anything exquisitely fine; (Colomb.) vim, energy.

canelado, da, *a.* = ACANELADO.

canelo, la. I. *a.* cinnamon-colored. **II.** *m.* cinnamon tree.

canelón, *m.* gargoyle; CANALÓN; icicle; tubular fringe; cinnamon candy.—*pl.* end of a cat-o'-nine-tails.

canequí, *m.* = CANIQUÍ.

canesú, *m.* corset cover; yoke of a shirt.

caney, *m.* log cabin; (Cuba) bend of a river; bight.

canfol, *m.* Borneo camphor.—**canfolato,** *m.* (chem.) campholate.—**canfólico, ca,** *a.* (chem.) campholic.

canforato, *m.* (chem.) camphorate.

canfórico, ca, *a.* (chem.) camphoric.

cangilón, *m.* eartnen jar or pitcher; metal tankard for wine; bucket (of a water wheel); fold of a frilled collar.

cangrejal, *m.* place frequented by crabs or crawfish.—**cangrejero, ra,** *n.* crab seller.

cangrejo, *m.* (zool.) crab; crawfish.

cangrejuelo, *m. dim.* small crab.

cangrena, *f.* = GANGRENA.—**cangrenarse,** *vr.* = GANGRENARSE.—**caɪgrenoso, sa,** *a.* = GANGRENOSO.

canguelo, *m.* (coll.) fear.—**tener c.,** to show the white feather.

cangüeso, *m.* (zool.) a sea fish.

canguro, *m.* (zool.) kangaroo.

cania, *f.* (bot.) small nettle.

caníbal, *m.* cannibal, man-eater.

canibalismo, *m.* cannibalism.

canica, *f.* wild cinnamon.

canicie, *f.* whiteness of the hair.

canícula, *f.* dog days; (**C-,** astr.) Dog Star.

canicular, *a.* canicular.

caniculares, *m. pl.* dog days.

caniculario, *m.* beadle who drags dogs out of church.

canido, *m.* a kind of parrot.

cánidos, *m. pl.* (zool.) Canidæ, the dog family.

canijo, ja, *a.* (coll.) weak, infirm, sickly.

canil, *m.* coarse bread, dogs' bread.

canilla, *f.* long bone of either extremity; any of the principal bones of the wing of a fowl; stopcock, faucet; reel, bobbin, spool; unevenness of the woof in thickness or color.—**c. de la pierna,** shin bone.—**c. del brazo,** arm bone.

canillado, da, *a.* = ACANILLADO.

canillaire, *m.* = CANILLERO.

canillera, *f.* ancient armor; jambes; woman who makes reels; (Colomb.) fear.

canillero, *m.* small tap in a cask or vat; weaver's quill winder.

canime, *m.* (bot.) a Colombian tree producing a medicinal oil.

canina, *f.* excrement of dogs.

caninamente, *adv.* furiously, snarling.

caninero, *m.* one who gathers dogs' dung for tanyards.

caninez, *f.* inordinate appetite.

canino, na, *a.* canine.

caniquí, *m.* cannequin, Indian fine muslin.

canje, *m.* (mil., dipl., com., journ.) exchange.

canjeable, *a.* that can be exchanged.

canjear, *va.* to exchange (prisoners, treaties, credentials, newspapers).

cano, na, *a.* gray-haired; hoary, hoar; frosty; ancient; (poet.) white.

canoa, *f.* canoe.—**canoero,** *m.* canoeman.

canoi, *m.* (Am.) basket used by Indians in a fishing party.

canoíta, *m. dim.* small canoe.

canon, *m.* canon, rule, precept; catalogue of the books composing the Bible; catalogue, list; part of the mass; (law) fee paid in acknowledgment of superiority in a higher lord; (mus.) canon; (print.) canon type.—*pl.* canons, canonical law.

canonesa, *f.* canoness.

canónica, *f.* canonic life in a convent.

canonical, *a.* canonical, relating to canons.

canónicamente, *adv.* canonically.

canonicato, *m.* = CANONJÍA.

canónico, ca, *a.* canonical, canonic.

canóniga, *f.* (coll.) nap taken before dinner.

canónigo, *m.* canon, prebendary.

canonista, *m.* canonist.

canonizable, *a.* worthy of canonization.

canonización, *f.* canonization.

canonizar, *va.* to canonize; consecrate; (met.) to applaud or praise.

canonjía, *f.* canonship, canonicate; sinecure.

canoro, ra, *a.* canorous, musical, melodious.

canoso, sa, *a.* gray-haired, hoary, hoar, frosty.

canquén, *m.* (zool.) Chilean wild goose.

cansadamente, *adv.* botheringly, importunely.

cansado, da. I. tired; weary, wearied; tedious, tiresome, dry. **II.** *m.* bore. **III.** *pp.* of CANSAR.

cansancio, *m.* tiredness, weariness, fatigue.

cansar. I. *va.* to weary, tire, fatigue; to tease, harass; bore; (agr.) to exhaust (the soil). **II.** *vr.* to become tired or weary. **III.** *vn.* to tire, be tiresome.

cansera, *f.* (coll.) fatigue, weariness.

cansino, na, *a.* worn out by work (s. o. beasts).

cantable. I. *a.* tunable; that may be sung; (mus.) to be sung slowly. **II.** *m.* (mus.) a song with a slow tempo.

cantábrico, ca; cántabro, bra, *n.* & *a.* Cantabrian, of or from Cantabria.

cantada, *f.* cantata, musical composition.

cantador, *n.* singer (gen. of popular songs).

cantal, *m.* stone block.

cantaleta, *f.* charivari; tin-pan serenade.—**dar c.,** (coll.) to deride; laugh at; turn into ridicule; sermonize.

cantante, *n.* & *a.* singer (-ing).

cantar, *m.* song set to music.—**C. de los Cantares,** Song of Songs.—**cantares de gesta,** old legendary romances.—**ése,** or **eso, es otro c.,** (coll.) that is another story, that is a horse of another color.

cantar. I. *va.* to sing.—**cantarlas claras,** to speak in plain language, to speak without more bones, to call a spade a spade. **II.** *vn.* to sing; (coll.) to creak, make a harsh, grinding noise; (coll.) to divulge or give away a secret, to squeal; at cards, to call out the trump.—**c. de plano,** to make a full confession.

cántara, *f.* large, narrow-mouthed pitcher; a liquid measure (32 pints).

cantareico, illo, ito, *m. dim.* little song.

cantarera, *f.* shelf for jars, pitchers, etc.

cantarería, *f.* earthenware shop.

cantarero, ra, *n.* dealer in earthenware.

cantárida, *f.* Spanish fly; cantharides, Spanish fly blistering plaster; blister raised by the blistering plaster.

cantarillo, *m. dim.* small jar or pitcher.

cantarín, *m.* (coll.) songster; professional singer.

cantarina, *f.* songstress, (woman) singer.

cántaro, *m.* large, narrow-mouthed pitcher, and the liquid contained in it; a wine measure; vessel into which votes are put.—**llover a cántaros,** to rain pitchforks, to pour.

cantata, *f.* cantata.

cantatriz, *f.* (woman) singer.

canteles, *m. pl.* (naut.) ends of old ropes put under casks to keep them steady.

cantera, *f.* quarry; talent, genius.

cantería, *f.* art of hewing stone; building made of hewn stone; parcel of hewn stone.

cantero, *m.* stonecutter; extremity of a hard substance that can be easily separated from the rest.—**c. de heredad,** piece of ground.—**c. de pan,** crust of bread.

canticio, *m.* (coll.) constant or frequent singing.

cántico, *m.* canticle.

cantidad, *f.* quantity; amount; (gram.) time used in pronouncing a syllable; sum of money; large portion.—**c. de movimiento,** (mech.) momentum.

cantiga, *f.* poetical composition for a song.

cantil, *m.* steep rock.

cantilena, *f.* = CANTINELA.

cantimplora, *f.* siphon; water cooler.

cantina, *f.* wine cellar; bar room, saloon, public house; canteen; case used to cool wine on a journey.

cantinela, *f.* ballad; irksome repetition of a subject.

cantinera, *f.* vivandière.

cantinero, *m.* butler; sutler; saloon keeper, bartender.

cantiña, *f.* (coll.) a popular song.

cantizal, *m.* stony ground.

canto, *m.* singing; short heroic poem; canto, division of a long poem; chant or canticle; end, edge border; crust (of a loaf); thickness; back of a knife; front edge of a book; stone, pebble; game of throw.

ing the stone (duck on a rock); quarry stone, block; ashlar stone.—**c. rodado**, boulder.—**a c.**, very near.—**al c.**, by the side of.—**al c. del gallo,** at the cock's crow, at daybreak.—**con un c. a los pechos,** with pleasure; with alacrity.—**de c.,** on edge.

cantón, *m.* corner; canton, region.

cantonada, *f.* corner.—**dar c.,** to disappoint or evade.

cantonal, *a.* cantonal.

cantonalismo, *m.* (pol.) cantonalism.

cantonar, *va.* = ACANTONAR.

cantonearse, *vr.* = CANTONEARSE.

cantoneo, *m.* = CONTONEO.

cantonera, *f.* plate nailed to the corners of a chest, etc.; corner plate, clip; angle iron; corner bracket; wench; street walker

cantonero, ra, *n.* loafer.

cantor, ra. I. *n.* singer; minstrel; one who composes hymns or psalms; small singing bird. **II.** *a.* that sings.—**ave cantora,** song bird.

cantorcillo, *m. dim.* worthless singer.

cantorral, *m.* stony ground.

cantoso, sa, *a.* stony.

cantuariense, *a.* of or belonging to Canterbury.

cantueso, *m.* (bot.) French lavender, spike.

canturía, *f.* vocal music; musical composition; monotonous singing; method of performing musical compositions.

canturrear, canturriar, *va.* & *vn.* to hum, sing in a low voice.

cánula, *f.* (med.) canula.

canutero, *m.* = CAÑUTERO.

canutillo, *m.* = CAÑUTILLO.

canuto, *m.* = CAÑUTO.

caña, *f.* cane; reed; reed spear; stem, stalk; walking stick; bone of arm or leg; leg, upper part of boot or stocking; chase (of a gun); groove (for the barrel of a firearm); subterranean passage in mines; shaft of a column; marrow; (naut.) helm, tiller; drill; ratchet drill; a long and narrow wine tumbler; an Andalusian song; crack in a sword's blade; glass blower's pipe; (carp.) shank; reed of wind instruments.—**c. brava,** (Am.) bamboo.—**c. de azúcar,** sugar cane.—**c. de Bengala,** rattan.—**c. de cuentas,** (bot.) Indian shot, Indian reed.—**c. de Indias,** rattan.—**c. de la India** = C. DE CUENTAS.—**c. del pulmón,** (anat.) trachea.—**c. de pescar,** fishing pole or rod.—**c. de vaca,** bone of a cow's leg.—**c. dulce,** sugar cane.—**correr cañas,** to engage in equestrian exercises with reed spears.

cañacoro, *m.* (bot.) Indian shot, Indian reed.

cañada, *f.* dell, ravine; cattle path.

cañadilla, *f.* an edible mollusk, a variety of purple murex.

cañaduzal, *m.* = CAÑAMELAR.

cañafístula, *f.* cassia.

cañafístulo, *m.* (bot.) pudding-pipe tree; Cassia fistula.

cañaheja, cañaherla, *f.* (bot.) common fennel-giant.

cañahuate, *m.* a species of lignum-vitæ.

cañajelga, *f.* = CAÑAHEJA.

cañal, *m.* cane or reed plantation or field; weir or wear for fishing, made of canes or reeds; small sluice or channel, for catching fish.

cáñama, *f.* assessment of taxes.

cañamar, *m.* hemp field.

cañamazo, *m.* coarse canvas; canvas for embroidery; embroidered canvas; burlap.

cañamelar, *m.* sugar-cane plantation.

cañameño, ña, *a.* hempen, made of hemp.

cañamiel, *f.* (bot.) sugar cane.

cañamiza, *f.* hemp bagasse; bun.

cáñamo, *m.* (bot.) hemp; cloth made of hemp.—**c. en rama,** undressed hemp.

cañamón, *m.* hemp seed.

cañar, *m.* = CAÑAL.

cañareja, *f.* = CAÑAHEJA.

cañariego, ga, *a.*—**pellejos cañariegos,** skins of sheep that die on the road.

cañarroya, *f.* (bot.) pellitory, wallwort.

cañavera, *f.* (bot.) common reed grass.

cañaveral, *m.* cane or reed field; (Colomb.) bamboo field.

cañaverear, *va.* = ACAÑAVEREAR.

cañavería, *f.* place where reed grass, reeds or bamboo are sold.

cañaverero, ra, *n.* cane, reed or bamboo seller.

cañedo, *m.* = CAÑAVERAL.

cañería, *f.* conduit; aqueduct; water pipe line; piping.

cañero, ra, *n.* conduit maker; pipe layer; angler.

cañete, *m. dim.* small tube.

cañilavado, da, *a.* small-limbed.

cañilla, ita, *f. dim.* small cane or reed.

cañillera, *f.* ancient armor for the shinbone, jambes.

cañiza, *f.* coarse linen.

cañizal, cañizar, *m.* = CAÑAVERAL.

cañizo, *m.* hurdle, frame for rearing silkworms; hurdle used by hatters for shearing hats; (naut.) flake.

caño, *m.* tube, pipe; open sewer, ditch; gutter; spout; conduit; cellar or other place for cooling water; organ tube or pipe; (naut.) channel at the entrance to seaports.

cañón, *m.* any cylindrical tube or pipe; tube or pipe for blowing glass; quill; down, soft feathers; leg or sleeve of a garment; part of the beard next to the root; cannon, gun; (min.) gallery; (mech.) socket; gorge, ravine, canyon; bit of a bridle; flue (of a chimney); well (of a staircase).—**c. obús,** howitzer.—**c. rayado,** rifled gun.

cañonazo, *m.* cannon shot; report of a gun.

cañoncico, illo, ito, *m. dim.* small cannon; small tube or pipe.

cañonear. I. *va.* to cannonade, bombard. **II.** *vr.* to cannonade each other.—**cañoneo,** *m.* cannonade; bombardment.—**cañonera,** *f.* embrasure for cannon; large tent; holster; gunboat.—**cañonería,** *f.* set of organ pipes; (mil.) number of cannons collectively.—**cañonero, ra. I.** *a.* (naut.) carrying guns. **II.** *f.* gunboat.

cañota, *f.* (bot.) panicled sorghum.

cañuela, *f.* slender cane or reed.

cañuela, *f. dim.* small reed; (bot.) fescue grass.

cañutazo, *m.* (coll.) information, gossip, tale.

cañutería, *f.* set of organ pipes.

cañutillo, *m. dim.* small tube or pipe; bugle for fringes, tassels, etc.; quill of gold or silver twist for embroidery.

cañuto, *m.* internode of a cane; small pipe or tube; informer, talebearer.—**cañutos helados,** (Mex.) small ice-cream cylinders.

caoba, caobana, *f.* (bot.) mahogany.

caobo, *m.* (bot.) mahogany (tree).

caolín, *m.* kaolin.

caos, *m.* chaos.—**caótico, ca,** *a.* chaotic.

capa, *f.* cloak, mantle, cape; layer; coat, coating; lamina; cover; (met.) cloak, mask, cover; color of an animal; hider, harborer; property; fortune; (com.) primage; an American rodent; the spotted cavy; third mold used in casting bells; coat of paint; bed, stratum, vein, seam; (mas.) bed, course; wrapper for tobacco.—**c. del cielo,** canopy of heaven.—**c. del timón,** rudder coat.—**c. magna,** pontifical cope worn by officiating bishops.—**c. pluvial,** pluvial or choir cope.—**c. rota,** secret emissary.—**a c. y espada,** at any cost; through thick and thin.—**andar,** or **ir, de c. caída,** to be down in the mouth, seedy, crestfallen.—**de c. y gorra,** informal, informally.—**echar la c. al toro,** to risk all on a last effort, to play one's last trump.—**estar,** or **estarse, a la c.,** (naut.) to lie to.—**hacer de su c. un sayo,** to go one's way, to follow one's own judgment.

capá, *m.* capa, West-Indian tree used for building vessels.

capacete, *m.* helmet, casque.

capacidad, *f.* capacity; contents; ability, capability; talent.

capacitar, *va.* y *vr.* to enable, qualify, prepare; to commission, empower, delegate.

capacha, *f.* frail, hamper.

capachazo, *m.* blow with a basket.

For pronunciation, see the rules at the beginning of the book.

capachero, *m.* one who carries things in baskets.

capacho, *m.* frail, hamper, large basket; hempen pressing bag; (orn.) common owl, barn owl.—**c. de albañil**, bricklayer's hod.

capada, *f.* (coll.) anything carried in a person's cloak; cloakful.

capadocio, cia, *n.* & *a.* Cappadocian.

capador, *m.* gelder, castrator; whistle used by gelders.

capadura, *f.* castration scar which remains after castration; leaf of tobacco of the second cutting, used for filling or wrappers.

capar, *va.* to geld, castrate; (coll.) to curtail, cut down, reduce.

caparazón, *m.* caparison; saddle cover; oil-cloth carriage cover; piano cover; hempen feed bag, nose bag; carcass of a fowl; shell of insects and crustaceans.

caparídeo. I. *a.* (bot.) caparidaceous. **II.** *f. pl.* Caparidaceæ.

caparra, *f.* sheep louse.

caparrilla, *f. dim.* small tick that infests bees.

caparrós, *m.*, **caparrosa**, *f.* copperas.—**c. azul**, blue vitriol.—**c. blanca**, white vitriol.—**c. verde**, green vitriol.

capataz, *m.* overseer, foreman, steward, warden, conductor; leader.—**c. de cultivo**, practical agriculturist or forester.

capaz, *a.* capacious, ample, roomy, large; capable, able, competent.

capaza, *f.* (prov.) = CAPACHO.

capazmente, *adv.* capaciously, amply; ably.

capazo, *m.* large frail, hamper; esparto mat; blow with a cloak.

capazón, *m. aug.* very large esparto frail.

capciosamente, *adv.* insidiously, captiously, artfully, cunningly.

capcioso, sa, *a.* captious, insidious, artful.

capeador, *m.* bull fighter who challenges the bull with his cloak; cloak stealer.

capear, *va.* to strip or rob (one) of one's cloak; to challenge (a bull) with the cloak; (naut.) to lay to.

capeja, *f. dim.* small shabby cloak or cape.

capelina, *f.* (surg.) capeline.

capelo, *m.* dues received in ancient times by bishops from their clergy; cardinal's hat; cardinalate; (Am.) glass bell.

capellada, *f.* toe piece of a shoe.

capellán, *m.* chaplain; clergyman.—**c. castrense**, army chaplain.—**c. de altar**, priest who assists at the mass.—**c. de honor**, the king's private chaplain.—**c. de navío**, navy chaplain.—**c. mayor de los ejércitos**, vicar-general of the army.

capellanía, *f.* chaplaincy.

capellar, *m.* a Moorish cloak.

capellina, *f.* headpiece of a helmet or casque; hood worn by country people; trooper wearing a helmet; (surg.) capeline.

capeo, *m.* challenging a bull with a cloak.

capeón, *m.* young bull challenged with a cloak.

capero, *m.* priest who carries the cope, or pluvial, in churches; cloak rack.

caperuceta, illa, *f. dim.* small hood.

caperuza, *f.* pointed hood or cap; ulster cap.—**c. de chimenea**, chimney cap.—**dar en c.**, (coll.) to frustrate one's views and designs.

caperuzón, *m. aug.* large hood.

capeta, *f.* short cape.

capialzado, *a.* (arch.) arched cap piece; back (arch).

capibara, *m.* capybara, a large S.-A. rodent.

capichola, *f.* ribbed silk stuff.

capicholado, da, *a.* resembling CAPICHOLA.

capidengue, *m.* small cloak worn by women.

capigorrista; capigorrón, na, *n.* (coll.) vagabond; sloven person; student who never takes a high degree.

capilar, *n.* & *a.* capillary.

capilaridad, *f.* capillarity; capillary attraction.

capilla, *f.* hood; cowl; chapel; small church; priests and others employed in chapel service; choir (musicians and singers) of a church; chapter or assembly of collegians; (print.) author's proof sheet; (mil.) portable chapel; death house.—**c. ardiente**, chapelle ardente, a hall or chamber where a dead body lies in state.—**estar en c.**, to be in the death house, to be sentenced to death and awaiting execution; (coll.) to be on pins and needles.

capillada, *f.* hoodful; blow with a hood.

capilleja, ita, *f. dim.* small chapel.

capillejo, *m. dim.* small hood; skein of sewing silk.

capiller, capilero, *m.* clerk or sexton of a chapel; churchwarden.

capilleta, ita, *f. dim.* small chapel; chaplet; shrine; niche.

capillo, *m.* child's cap; christening fee; baptismal cap; ancient hood for women; bud of a rose; toe-piece lining; cap of a distaff; net for catching rabbits; colander for wax; silk cocoon; cloth that covered church offering; (anat.) prepuce.

capilludo, da, *a.* resembling a hood or cowl.

capincho, *m.* (zool.) carpincho, capybara.

capirotada, *f.* a batter made of herbs, eggs, etc.

capirotazo, *m.* blow on the nose with the finger; a fillip.

capirote. I. *a.* having the head of a different color from that of the body (s. o. cattle). **II.** *m.* hood; half-gown worn by collegians; sharp-pointed cap worn in processions; hood of a hawk.—**c. de colmena**, cover of a beehive.

capirotero, *a.* (hawk) used to carrying a hood.

capirucho, *m.* (coll.) = CAPIROTE.

capisayo, *m.* garment worn as a cloak; special vesture worn by bishops.

capiscol, *m.* precentor; subchanter.

capiscolía, *f.* office and dignity of a precentor.

capita, *f. dim.* small cloak.

capitación, *f.* capitation, imposition of taxes per head; poll tax.

capital. I. *m.* capital; estate of a husband at his marriage; principal (money placed at interest, invested, etc.); (com.) capital, capital stock; (mil.) capital of a bastion. **II.** *f.* capital city. **III.** *a.* capital, relating to the head; main, principal; leading; essential; great; excellent, unsurpassed.

capitalismo, *m.* capitalism.

capitalista, *n.* & *a.* capitalist (-ic).

capitalización, *f.* capitalization.

capitalizar, *va.* (*pret.* CAPITALICÉ: *subj.* CAPITALICE) to capitalize, add interest to principal.

capitalmente, *adv.* fatally; seriously.

capitán, *m.* captain; ringleader; leader, commander.—**c. de bandera**, (naut.) captain of the admiral's ship.—**c. de fragata**, navy officer ranking as lieutenant colonel.—**c. del puerto**, (naut.) port captain; harbor master.—**c. de navío**, navy officer ranking as a colonel.—**c. general**, captain general.—**c. general de ejército**, field marshal.—**c. general de provincia**, commander-in-chief of a military district.

capitana, *f.* admiral's ship; captain's wife.

capitanear, *va.* to command; to head, lead.

capitanía, *f.* captainship; captaincy; company commanded by a captain; tax paid to the port captain by ships anchored in the harbor.—**c. general**, captaincy general.

capitel, *m.* (arch.) capital of a column or pilaster; spire over the dome of a church.

capitolino, na, *a.* belonging to the capitol; Capitoline.

capitolio, *m.* capitol; any lofty or majestic public building.

capitón, *m.* (zool.) pollard, chub.

capítula, *f.* lesson, Bible passage read at divine service.

capitulación, *f.* capitulation; stipulation, agreement.—**c. de matrimonio**, articles of marriage.

capitulante, *n.* & *a.* capitulator (-ing).

capitular. I. *m.* capitular, member of a chapter. **II.** *a.* capitulary, belonging to a chapter.

capitular. I. *vn.* to enter into agreement; draw up the articles of a contract; compound; sing prayers at divine service; to capitulate. **II.** *va.* (law) to impeach.

capitulario, *m.* prayer book for divine service.

capitularmente, *adv.* according to the rules of a chapter.

capítulo, *m.* chapter; meeting of the prelates of religious orders, and place where they meet; meeting; charge, reproof, reprimand.—**capítulos matrimoniales,** articles of marriage.

capnomancia, *f.* capnomancy.

capolado, *n.* hash, minced meat.

capolar, *va.* to hash, mince, or chop; to behead.

capón, ona. I. *a.* castrated, gelded. **II.** *m.* eunuch; capon; (coll.) fillip on the head; fagot, bundle of brushwood; (naut.) anchor stopper at the cathead.

capona, *f.* epaulet without fringe.

caponado, da. I. *a.* tied together, as branches of vines. **II.** *pp.* of CAPONAR.

caponar, *va.* to tie up (the branches of vines).

caponera, *f.* coop, inclosure to fatten poultry; (coll.) place where one lives well at other people's expense; (coll.) jail; (mil.) caponier.

caporal, *m.* chief, ringleader; (Mex.) keeper of horned cattle.

capota, *f.* head of the teasel or fuller's thistle; light bonnet; leather top of some vehicles; cape without a hood.

capote, *m.* raglan or cloak with sleeves to keep off rain; short cloak of bright color, used by bullfighters; browbeating; (coll.) thick cloud or mist.—**dar c.,** to leave a guest without dinner, for coming late; to win all the tricks at cards.—**dije para mi c.,** I said to myself.

capotear, *va.* to trick (a bull) with a CAPOTE; to wheedle, bamboozle; to evade cleverly.

capotero, ra, *n.* cloak maker or dealer.

capotillo, *m.* cape, mantelet.—**c. de dos faldas,** a loose jacket.

capotín, *m. dim.* small cloak or CAPOTE.

capotudo, da, *a.* frowning.

caprario, ria, *a.* belonging to the goat.

Capricornio, *m.* (ast.) Capricorn.

capricho, *m.* whim, fancy; great desire; (mus.) caprice, capriccio; (art) original work that ignores accepted rules.

caprichosamente, *adv.* whimsically.

caprichoso, sa, *a.* capricious, whimsical.

caprichudo, da, *a.* stubborn; whimsical.

caprifoliáceo, a. I. (bot.) caprifoliaceous. **II.** *f. pl.* Caprifoliaceæ.

capriforme, *a.* capriform.

caprino, na, *a.* caprine.

caprípedo, da, *a.* (zool.) capriped, goat-footed.

cápsula, *f.* metal cap on bottles; cartridge shell; (bot., anat., chem., pharm.) capsule.

capsular, *a.* capsular, capsulary.

captar, *va.* to captivate, attract, win.

captura, *f.* (law) capture, seizure.

capturar, *va.* (law) to apprehend; to arrest.

capuana, *f.* (coll.) spanking.

capucha, *f.* hood; cowl; capuche; (print.) circumflex accent.

capuchina, *f.* Capuchin nun; (bot.) nasturtium; small lamp with extinguisher; confection of egg yolks.—*pl.* (naut.) crotches and knees.

capuchino, na, *n.* & *a.* Capuchin.

capucho, *m.* cowl, hood, capuche.

capuchón, *m. aug.* of CAPUCHO; lady's cloak with hood; short domino.

capulí, capulín, *m.* capulin, a kind of cherry.

capullito, *m. dim.* small cocoon; small bud.

capullo, *m.* cocoon; flax knotted at the end; (com.) bunch of boiled flax; germ or bud of flowers; coarse stuff of spun silk; cup of an acorn; bur of a chestnut; prepuce.

capuz, *m.* ducking (of a person); ancient hooded cloak.

capuzar, *va.* (naut.) to sink (a ship) by the head.

caquéctico, ca, *a.* cachectic.—**caquexia,** *f.* cachexia.

caqui, *n.* & *a.* khaki.

car, *m.* (naut.) larger end of the mizzenyard and mizzen.

cara, *f.* face; visage, mien, countenance; base of a sugar loaf; façade, front, surface, facing.—**c. a c.,** face to face.—**c. apedreada** = C. EMPEDRADA.—**c. de acelga,** pale, sallow face.—**c. de aleluya** = C. DE PASCUA.—**c. de bronce,** brazen face.—**c. de cartón,** wrinkled face.—**c. de hereje,** harried face. —**c. de Pascua,** smiling, cheerful face.—**c. de perro,** ugly (angry) face, bearish face.—**c. de pocos amigos,** churlish look, froward countenance.— **c. de vaqueta** = C. DE BRONCE.—**c. de viernes,** sad, lean, meagre face.—**c. empedrada,** face pitted by the smallpox.—**c. y cruz,** heads or tails.— **a c. descubierta,** openly.—**buena c.,** good appearance; promising or encouraging appearance.—**de c.,** opposite, facing.—**dar a uno con las puertas en la c.,** to shut the door in one's face.—**dar el sol de c.,** to have the sun in one's face.—**dar en c.,** to call to task, to throw in one's face.—**decírselo en su c.,** to tell one to one's face.—**de dos caras,** double-faced, false.—**no volver la c. atrás,** not to flinch.

carabao, *m.* (zool.) carabao.

cárabe, *m.* amber.

carabela, *f.* (naut.) caravel; large basket or tray for provisions.

carabelón, *m.* (naut.) brig, brigantine.

carabido, da. I. *a.* (zool.) carabideous. **II.** *m. pl.* Carabidæ.

carabina, *f.* fowling piece; carbine.—**c. rayada,** rifle carbine.—**la c. de Ambrosio,** a harmless weapon; a worthless thing; bluff.

carabinazo, *m.* report or firing of a carbine; carbine wound.

carabinero, ra, *n.* carabineer; internal-revenue guard.

cárabo, *m.* a small Moorish vessel; (zool.) a kind of crab or cockle; (orn.) large horned owl.

carabú, *m.* a handsome tree of India.

caracoa, *f.* (Philip.) small row barge.

caracol, *m.* (zool.) snail; winding staircase; prancing of a horse; nightdress used by women in Mexico; cochlea of the ear.—**c. marino,** periwinkle.—¡caracoles! *interj.* = ¡CARAMBA!

caracla, *f.* small snail with a whitish shell; shell used as a horn.

caracolear, *vn.* to caracole, wind.—**caracolejo,** *m. dim.* small snail or snail shell.—**caracoleo,** *m.* caracoling.—**caracolero, ra,** *n.* snail gatherer or dealer.

caracolilla, *f. dim.* small snail shell.

caracolillo, *m. dim.* small snail; (bot.) snail-flowered kidney bean; veined mahogany.—*pl.* trimmings, fringes.—**café c.,** pea-bean coffee.

caracolito, *m. dim.* small snail.

carácter, *m.* character; brand on cattle; temper, nature, disposition; loftiness of soul, firmness, energy; style of speaking or writing.—**caracteres de imprenta,** printing types.

característica, *f.* characteristic: actress who plays the part of old ladies; feature, fundamental property; (math.) characteristic.

ca.racterísticamente, *adv.* characteristically.

característico, ca, *a.* characteristic, typical, distinctive, distinguishing.

caracterizado, da, *a.* characterized, distinguished; apt, competent; reliable, responsible.

caracterizar, *va.* (*pret.* CARACTERICÉ: *subj.* CARACTERICE) to characterize, distinguish by peculiar qualities; to confer a distinguished employment, dignity, or office on; to mark, point out; to act (a part) properly.

caracha, *f.,* **carache,** *m.* itch, mange, scab of the llamas.

caracho, cha, *a.* violet-colored.

caraguata, *f.* a kind of Paraguayan sisal.

caraja, *f.* sail used by Vera Cruz fishermen.

caramanchel, *m.* fixed or movable shed over the hatchways of ships.

caramanchón, *m.* garret; CAMARANCHÓN.

caramba. I. *interj.* (coll.) gracious! confound it! **II.** *f.* ancient headgear for women.

carámbano, *m.* icicle, a shoot of ice.

carambanado, da, *a.* forming icicles.

carambillo, *m.* (bot.) saltwort.

carambola, *f.* carom, in billiards; a method of playing the card game called *revesino;* (coll.) device or trick to cheat or deceive; (bot.) fruit of the carambola tree.—**por c.,** (coll.) indirectly.

carambolo, *m.* (bot.) carambola tree.

carambolear, *va.* to carom.

carambolero, *m.* carom player; *revesino* player.

carambú, *m.* (bot.) willow herb.

caramel, *m.* (icht.) a kind of pilchard or sardine.

caramelización, *f.* caramelization.

caramelizar, *va.* to caramelize.

caramelo, *m.* caramel; (P. I.) AZUCARILLO.

caramente, *adv.* dearly; exceedingly, highly; rigorously.

caramiello, *m.* a kind of hat worn by women.

caramillar, *vn.* saltwort field.

caramillera, *f. pl.* pothook.

caramillo, *m.* flageolet; small flute; (bot.) saltwort; confused heap of things; deceit; trick; gossip; tale-carrying.

caramuzal, *m.* vessel used by the Moors.

caranga, *f.,* **carangue,** *m.* a W. I. flat fish.

carantamaula, *f.* (coll.) hideous mask or visor; ugly, hard-featured person.

carantoña, *f.* (coll.) ugly old woman who paints and dresses in style.—*pl.* caresses, soft words and acts of endearment.—**carantoñera,** *f.* coquette.—**carantoñero,** *m.* flatterer, cajoler.

caraña, *f.* a kind of resinous American gum.

caráota, *f.* (Ven.) bean.

carapa, *f.* carapa, carap.

carapacho, *m.* shell.

carapato, *m.* castor oil.

caraqueño, ña, *a.* Caracas (u. a.).

carasol, *m.* sun parlor, solarium.

carate, *m.* brown spots on the skin, similar to "liver spots"—common in the lowlands of S. A.

carátula, *f.* pasteboard or wire mask; title page of a book; (met.) the histrionic art.

caratulero, ra, *n.* mask maker or dealer.

carava, *f.* holiday meeting of country people.

caravana, *f.* caravan; company of traders, pilgrims, etc.

caray. I. *m.* tortoise shell. **II.** *interj.* (Am.) =CARAMBA.

caraza, *f. aug.* big face.

cárbaso, *m.* a kind of fine flax; (poet.) sail of a ship; an ancient tunic.

carbinol, *m.* (chem.) carbinol.

carbólico, ca, *a.* carbolic.

carbolíneo, *m.* (chem.) carbolineum.

carbón, *m.* coal; charcoal; carbon (of an arc lamp).—**c. animal,** bone black, animal charcoal. —**c. de arranque,** root charcoal (made from roots).—**c. de leña,** charcoal.—**c. de piedra, or mineral,** coal.—**c. vegetal** = C. DE LEÑA.

carbonada, *f.* coal charge of a furnace; broiled chop or steak; grillade; a kind of pancake.

carbonario, *m.* Carbonaro.

carbonarismo, *m.* Carbonarism.

carbonatado, da, *a.* carbonated.

carbonatar, *va.* (chem.) to carbonate.

carbonato, *m.* (chem.) carbonate.

carboncillo, *m. dim.* small coal; black crayon; carbon pencil.

carbonear, *vn. & va.* to make charcoal (of).

carboneo, *m.* carbonization; charring.

carbonera, *f.* wood prepared for burning into charcoal; place where charcoal is made; coalhouse, coal hole, coal cellar, coal bin; coal pit, colliery, coal mine; woman who sells charcoal.

carbonería, *f.* coal yard, coal shed; coal mine.

carbonero, ra. I. *a.* relating to coal or charcoal. **II.** *m.* charcoal maker; collier, coal miner; coal merchant; (naut.) coal ship, collier.

carbónico, ca, *a.* (chem.) carbonic.

carbónidos, *m. pl.* (chem.) carbon and its compounds.

carbonífero, ra, *a.* carboniferous.

carbonita, *f.* carbonite.

carbonización, *f.* carbonization.

carbonizado, da, *a.* carbonized.

carbonizar, *va.* (*pret.* CARBONICÉ: *subj.* CARBONICE) to carbonize; char.

carbono, *m.* (chem.) carbon.

carbonoso, sa, *a.* carbonaceous, coaly, charry.

carborundo, *m.* carborundum.

carboxilo, *m.* (chem.) carboxyl.

carbuncal, *a.* carbuncular.

carbunclo, carbunco, *m.* carbuncle; precious stone; gangrenous tumor.

carbuncoso, sa, *a.* = CARBUNCAL.

carbúnculo, *m.* = RUBÍ.

carburación, *f.* carburation.

carburador, *m.* (int. comb. eng.) carburetor.

carburante, *n. & a.* carburetant (-ing).

carburar, carburizar, *va.* to carburize, carburet.

carburo, *m.* (chem.) carbide.

carcaj, *m.* = CARCAX.

carcajada, *f.* outburst of laughter.

carcajear(se), *vn. & vr.* to laugh boisterously or heartily.

carcamal, *n.* (coll.) old, decrepit person.

carcamán, *m.* tub; heavy, unseaworthy vessel.

cárcamo, *m.* (Am.) riffle, a cleated trough.

carcañal, carcañar, *m.* heel bone, calcaneum.

cárcava, *f.* gully; (mil.) inclosure; mound; hedge; ditch; grave.

carcavina, *f.* = CÁRCAVA.

cárcavo, *m.* hollow in which a water wheel turns.

carcavón, *m.* large and deep ditch.

carcavuezo, *m.* deep pit.

carcax, *m.,* **carcaza,** *f.* quiver; sash with a case in which the cross is borne in a procession; (Am.) leathern case for a rifle at the saddle bow; Moorish anklet.

cárcel, *f.* jail; prison; groove of a sluice gate; (carp.) clamp, clasp, cramp; (mech.) holder; cheek; collar; (print.) cheek of a printing press; (weav.) reed of a loom.

carcelaje, *m.* jailer's fees.

carcelario, ria, *a.* relating to a jail.

carcelería, *f.* imprisonment; bail given for the appearance of a prisoner.

carcelero, ra. I. *a.* = CARCELARIO. **II.** *m.* jailer, warden.

carceraje, *m.* = CARCELAJE.

carcinoma, *m.* (med.) carcinoma.

carcinomatoso, sa, *a.* (med.) carcinomatous.

cárcola, *f.* treadle of a loom.

carcoma, *f.* wood borer; woodlouse; wood tick; gribble; dust made by the wood borer; grief, anxiety; spendthrift; (med.) caries.

carcomer. I. *va.* to gnaw; to destroy (s. o. wood borers); to consume or impair by degrees, to undermine. **II.** *vr.* to decay, decline; become worm- or insect-eaten.

carcomido, da, *a.* worm-eaten; consumed; decayed; impaired.

carda, *f.* act of carding; teasel; card; hatter's jack; severe reprimand or censure; (naut.) a small vessel like a galley.

cardador, ra, *n.* carder, comber; (ent.) myriapod.

cardadura, *f.* carding, combing (wool).

cardamomo, *m.* (bot.) cardamomum.

cardar, *va.* to card or comb (wool); to raise (the nap on cloth) with a teasel.

cardelina, *f.* (orn.) goldfinch, thistle finch.

cardenal, *m.* cardinal; (orn.) Virginian nightingale; cardinal bird, redbird; wale.

cardenalato, *m.* cardinalate, cardinalship.

cardenalicio, cia, *a.* belonging to a cardinal.

cardencha, *f.* (bot.) teasel; card, comb.—**c. cardadora,** fuller's teasel.—**c. silvestre,** wild teasel.

cardenchal, *m.* place where teasels grow.

cardenillo, *m.* verdigris; (painting) verditer, Paris green.

cárdeno, na, *a.* livid.

cardería, *f.* cardery.

cardero, ra, *n.* card maker.

cardíaca, *f.* (bot.) common motherwort.

cardíáceo, a, *a.* heart-shaped.

cardíaco, ca, *a.* (med.) cardiac, cardiacal.

cardialgia, *f.* (med.) cardialgia, heartburn.

cardiálgico, ca, *a.* belonging to cardialgy.

cardias, *m.* cardiac orifice of the stomach.

cardillo, illo, ito, *m. dim.* small thistle.

cardíaco, ca, *a.* cardiac, relating to the heart.

cardillo, *m.* (bot.) golden thistle.

cardinal, *a.* cardinal (point); main, fundamental.

cardiografía, *f.* cardiography.

cardiógrafo, *m.* cardiograph.

cardiología, *f.* cardiology.

cardiópata, *n.* (med.) cardiopathic person, one suffering from heart disease.

cardiopatía, *f.* cardiopathy.

cardioscopio, *m.* cardiometer.

carditis, *f.* (med.) carditis.

carduzal, *m.* land covered with thistles and weeds.

cardo, *m.* (bot.) thistle.—**c. alcachofero,** garden artichoke.—**c. aljonjero,** stemless, carline thistle. —**c. arrocife,** cardoon artichoke.—**c. bendito,** blessed thistle, centaury, holy thistle.—**c. borriqueño,** (bot.) spear-plume thistle.—**c. corredor,** sea holly, field eringo.—**c. de comer, c. hortense** = C. ARROCIFE.—**c. huso,** wooly carthamus.—**c. lechero, or mariano,** milk thistle.—**c. santo** = C. BENDITO.—**c. setero** = C. CORREDOR.—**c. silvestre** = C. BORRIQUEÑO.

cardón, *m.* act and effect of carding; (bot.) CARDENCHA.

Cardona, *m.*.—**más listo que C.,** very smart, clever fellow, sharp as a needle.

cardoncillo, *m.* (bot.) mountain carthamus.

carducha, *f.* large iron comb for wool.

cardume, cardumen, *m.* shoal of fishes.

carduzador, *m.* carder.

carduzal, *m.* = CARDIZAL.

carduzar, *va.* (*pret.* CARDUCÉ: *subj.* CARDUCE) to card or comb (wool.).

carear, *va.* (law) to confront (criminals); (coll.) to compare; to tend (cattle, sheep).—*vr.* to assemble or meet; to meet face to face.

carecer, *vn.* (*ind.* CAREZCO: *subj.* CAREZCA) (w. de) to lack, not to have.

carena, *f.* (naut.) careening, repairing; (poet.) ship.—**dar c.,** (coll.) to reprimand in a jocular way; to banter.

carenar, *va.* to careen.

carencia, *f.* lack; scarcity.

carenero, *m.* careening place.

careo, *m.* (law) confrontation of criminals or witnesses; comparison; act of placing or meeting face to face; (fort.) front of a bastion or fortress.

carero, ra, *a.* (coll.) selling things dear.

carestía, *f.* scarcity, dearth; lack; famine, famishment; dearness, high price.

careta, *f.* mask.—**quitar la c.,** to tear off the mask, to unmask.

careto, ta, *a.* having the forehead marked with a white spot or stripe (s. o. horses).

carey, *m.* (zool.) tortoise, shell turtle; tortoise shell.

carezco, carezca. *V.* CARECER.

carga, *f.* load; burden; freight, cargo; loading; charge (of a cannon, furnace, etc.); nozzle of the flask which measures the powder for a charge; corn measure containing 4 FANEGAS; a preparation to cure sprains and inflammation in horses and mules; impost, duty, tax; (hydr.) head; (mil.) charge, attack.—**c. concejil,** municipal obligatory service.—**c. de rotura, c. de fractura,** breaking load.—**c. fija,** (eng.) dead load.—**c. hidrostática,** (hydr.) head.—**c. móvil,** (eng.) live load.—**c. personal,** obligatory personal service.—**a cargas,** abundantly, in great plenty.—**volver a la c.,** to insist; to harp on a subject; to keep at it.

cargadas, *f. pl.* a card game.

cargadera, *f.* (naut.) downhauls, brails.—*pl.* (Colomb.) suspenders.

cargadero, *m.* place where goods are loaded or unloaded; freight station.

cargadilla, *f.* (coll.) increase of a debt newly contracted.

cargado, *m.* Spanish step in dancing.

cargado, da, *a.* loaded, full; fraught.—**c. de espaldas,** round-shouldered, stooping.—**c. de vino,** full, tipsy.

cargador, *m.* shipper; freighter; expressman, carrier; porter; rammer, ramrod; large pitchfork for straw; (arch.) post put in a doorway or window; (naut.) tackle; plate used in gilding.

cargamento, *m.* (naut.) cargo; shipment.

cargar. I. *va. & vn.* (*pret.* CARGUÉ: *subj.* CARGUE) to load; burden; to carry (a load); to charge (a furnace, battery, etc.); to attack; to ship; to overload, overburden; to clog; to lay in, collect; to charge in account; to book; to impose or lay (taxes); to impute, charge (one) with; to crowd; (coll.) to vex, annoy, pester; in cards, to take (a card with a higher one); (gram.) to put more stress or inflection on one letter or syllable.—**c. la mano,** to pursue with eagerness; to reproach with severity; to overcharge; to be too exacting. **II.** *vn.* to incline, tip; (w. en or sobre) to rest (on), be supported (by), lean (against); to bear abundantly (s. o. trees); (w. con) to assume (responsibility); bear (the blame); carry away; (w. sobre) to urge, press. **III.** *vr.* (w. sobre) to rest (on); (w. contra) to lean (against, on); to gather, become denser, heavier or darker (s. o. the clouds, the sky); (w. de) to have or obtain in large number or quantity; to load one's self (with); to become tired, peeved or vexed; to trouble one's self.

cargaréme, *m.* receipt, voucher.

cargazón, *f.* cargo; abundance; clumsy, badly-made thing.—**c. de cabeza,** heaviness of the head. —**c. de tiempo,** cloudy, thick weather.

cargo, *m.* act of loading; burden, load, weight; load of stones weighing 40 *arrobas* (1000 lb.); number of baskets piled one on the other and put in the oil press; load of pressed grapes to be repressed; total amount of what has been received, in a general account; post, dignity, office, ministry; charge, keeping, care; duty, obligation; command or management; fault or inefficiency in the performance of duty; charge, accusation; (law) count. —**c. concejil,** compulsory public office or function.—**c. de conciencia,** remorse, sense of guilt.— **c. y data,** (com.) creditor and debtor (Cr. and Dr.). —**hacer c. a uno de,** to charge one with.—**hacerse c. de,** to take into consideration; to make one's self acquainted with; to understand.

cargoso, sa, *a.* burdensome, onerous.

carguero, ra. I. *a.* of burden (s. o. animals); freight-carrying, freight (u. a.) **II.** *n.* beast of burden.

carguío, *m.* cargo, freight; load.

cariacontecido, da, *a.* sad, mournful.

cariacuchillado, da, *a.* having the face marked with cuts or gashes.

cariado, da, *a.* carious, rotten.

cariadura, *f.* (med.) caries, bone ulcer.

cariaguileño, ña, *a.* (coll.) aquiline-nosed and pointed-faced.

carialegre, *a.* smiling, cheerful.

cariampollado, da, *or* **cariampollar,** *a.* round-faced, plump-cheeked.

cariancho, cha, *a.* broad-faced, chubby, chub-faced, bull-faced.

cariarse, *vr.* (med.) to become carious.

cariátide, *f.* (arch.) caryatides.

caribe, *m.* cannibal, man-eater, savage; Carib, Indian of the Antilles.

caribito, *m.* a river fish of the bream species.

cariblanco, ca. I. *a.* white-faced. **II.** *m.* a Central American small wild boar.

caribobo, ba, *a.* stupid- or dumb-looking.

caribú, *m.* (zool.) caribou.

carica, *f.* a kind of spotted kidney bean.

caricatura, *f.* caricature.—**caricaturar,** *va.* to caricature.—**caricaturesco, ca,** *a.* caricaturish.— **caricaturista,** *m.* caricaturist.—**caricaturizar,** *va.* = CARICATURAR.

caricia, *f.* caress; petting; endearing expression.

cariciosamente, *adv.* fondlingly, caressingly.

caricioso, sa, *a.* fondling, endearing, caressing.

caricuerdo, da, *a.* wise-looking.

caridad, *f.* charity, charitableness; refreshment given to travelers at the church door.—**la c. empieza por uno mismo,** charity begins at home.

caridelantero, ra, *a.* (coll.) brazen-faced, bold-looking.

caridoliente, *a.* mournful-looking.

caries, *f.* (med.) caries.

carifruncido, da, *a.* (coll.) wrinkle-faced; frowning, cross-looking.

carigordo, da, *a.* (coll.) full-faced.

cariharto, ta, *a.* round-faced.

carilampiño, ña, *a.* smooth-faced, beardless.

carilargo, ga, *a.* long-visaged.

carilucio, cia, *a.* (coll.) having a shining face.

carilla, *f. dim.* little or small face; face guard; silver coin in Aragon worth eighteen CINEROS, or deniers; page (of a book).

carilleno, na, *a.* (coll.) plump-faced.

carillo, lla, *a. dim.* rather dear or expensive.

carimba, *f.* (Peru) brand on slaves.

carincho, *m.* a dish resembling chile con carne.

carinegro, gra, *a.* of a swarthy complexion; black-faced.

cariñana, *f.* ancient headdress like a nun's veil.

cariño, *m.* love, fondness, affection; endearing expression; pet.—**cariñosamente,** *adv.* fondly, affectionately, kindly.—**cariñoso, sa,** *a.* affable, affectionate, endearing, loving.

cariofileo, a. I. (bot.) caryophyllaceous. **II.** *f. pl.* Caryophyllaceæ.

cariofilina, *f.* (chem.) cariophyllene.

cariópsida, *f.* (bot.) caryopsis.

cariparejo, ja, *a.* (coll.) having an impassive countenance.

carirraído, da, *a.* (coll.) brazen-faced, impudent.

carirredondo, da, *a.* round-faced.

carisma, *m.* divine gift or favor, charism.

carita, *f. dim.* little or small face.

caritán, *m.* (Philip.) gatherer of tuba.

caritativamente, *adv.* charitably.

caritativo, va, *a.* charitable.

cariucho, *m.* (Ec.) an Indian national dish.

cariz, *m.* aspect.

carlán, *m.* a person having certain rights and jurisdiction in a district.

carlanca, *f.* mastiff's collar.—**tener muchas carlancas,** to be very cunning or crafty.

carlancón, *m.* (coll.) very sharp or crafty person.

carlanía, *f.* dignity and district of a CARLÁN.

carlear, *vn.* to pant.

carlín, *m.* an ancient silver coin.

carlina, *f.* (bot.) carline thistle.

carlinga, *f.* (naut.) step of a mast.

carlismo, *m.* Carlism.—**carlista,** *n., a.* Carlist.

carlita, *f.* reading eyeglasses.

carlovingio, gia, *a.* Carlovingian.

carmañola, *f.* carmagnola.

carmelita. I. *n. & a. f.* Carmelite. **II.** *f.* flower of the great Indian cress.

carmelitano, na, *a.* Carmelite.

carmen, *m.* country house and garden; villa; Carmelite order; verse; poem.

carmenador, *m.* teasler (man or machine).

carmenadura, *f.* teaseling (woolen cloth, etc.)

carmenar, *va.* to teasel; to disentangle, unravel; to comb (the hair); (coll.) to pull (the hair); to cheat.

carmes, *m.* kermes, the cochineal insect.

carmesí. I. *m.* cochineal powder. **II.** *n. & a.* crimson, bright red.

carmín, *m.* coloring matter of cochineal; carmine color; (bot.) pokeweed, phytolacca.—**c. bajo,** pale rose color.

carminativo, *m.* (med.) carminative.

carnada, *f.* bait.

carnaje, *m.* salt beef.

carnal. I. *a.* carnal, sensual; related by blood; full (as in *hermano carnal,* full brother). **II.** *m.* time of the year when meat may be eaten (opposed to Lent and other fast days).

carnalidad, *f.* carnality, lustfulness.

carnalmente, *adv.* carnally, sensually.

carnaval, *m.* carnival.—**carnavalesco, ca,** *a.* belonging to or resembling a carnival.

carnaza, *f.* fleshy side of a hide or skin; (coll.) abundance of meat; bait.

carne, *f.* flesh; meat (flesh meat, pap or meat of fruit); flesh, one of the evil temptations; kin; name of a children's game with a hollow bone.—**c. ahogadiza,** meat from a drowned animal.—**c. asada en horno,** baked meat.—**c. asada en parrillas,** broiled meat.—**c. bien cocida,** well-done meat.—**c. cediza,** tainted meat.—**c. de cañón,** cannon fodder; inferior person or people.—**c. de gallina,** (met.) goose flesh, goose skin.—**c. de membrillo,** preserved quinces.—**c. de pelo,** meat of small quadrupeds (hares, rabbits, etc.).—**c. de pluma,** flesh of fowls.—**c. fiambre,** cold meat.—**c. magra, c. mollar,** lean meat.—**c. momia,** (coll.) choice meat without bones.—**c. sin hueso,** (met.) much profit and little trouble.—**c. viva,** quick or raw flesh in a wound.—**c. y hueso,** flesh and blood.—**c. y sangre,** flesh and blood, near kindred.—**cobrar carnes,** to recover one's flesh or weight, to pick up.—**echar carnes,** (coll.) to grow fat, put on flesh.—**en carnes,** naked.—**en c. viva,** raw, with the flesh exposed.—**envuelto en carnes,** fleshy, fat.—**ni c. ni pescado,** neither flesh nor fish; nondescript; insipid.—**ser c. y hueso de,** to be flesh and blood of, to be part and parcel of.—**ser uña y carne,** (met.) to be hand and glove, to be one, to be intimate.

carnecilla, *f.* small excrescence in some part of the body; caruncle.

carnerada, *f.* flock of sheep.

carneraje, *m.* tax or duty on sheep.

carnerario, *m.* (prov.) charnel house.

carnereamiento, *m.* poundage, penalty for the trespass of sheep.

carnerear, *va.* to fine for damage done by sheep.

carnerero, ra, *n.* shepherd (-ess).

carneril, *m.* sheepwalk; pasture for sheep.

carnero, *m.* sheep; mutton; sheepskin; family vault, burying place; charnel house.—**c. ahogado,** stewed mutton.—**c. ciclán,** ridgil or ridgeling.—**c. de simiente,** ram kept for breeding.—**c. manso para guía,** bellwether.—**c. marino,** seal.—**no hay tales carneros,** (coll.) there is no such a thing.

carneruno, na, *a.* sheeplike; relating or belonging to sheep.

carnestolendas, *f. pl.* carnival (the three carnival days before Ash Wednesday).

carnet, *m.* bank book; memorandum book.

carnicería, *f.* meat market, butcher's shop; slaughter house; carnage, slaughter.

carnicero, *m.* butcher.

carnicero, ra, *a.* carnivorous; bloodthirsty, sanguinary; fattening (s. o. pasture grounds); (coll.) meat fiend (s. o. one who eats much meat); belonging to shambles.

carnicol, *m.* hoof of cloven-footed animals.

carnificación, *f.* carnification.

carnificarse, *vr.* to carnify.

carnina, *f.* (chem.) carnine.

carnívoro, ra. I. *n. & a.* carnivore (-vorous). **II.** *m. pl.* Carnivora

carniza, *f.* (coll.) refuse of meat; cat or dog meat; decayed flesh.

carnosidad, *f.* carnosity, proud flesh; fatness, fleshiness.

carnoso, sa, *a.* fleshy, carnous; full of marrow; meaty, pulpous (app. to fruit).

carnudo, da, *a.* = CARNOSO.

carnuza, *f.* disgusting coarse or heaped meat.

caro, *adv.* dearly, at a high price or cost.

caro, ra, *a.* dear, costly; dear, beloved.—**c. mitad,** better half.

caroca, *f.* decoration in public festivities; farcical piece; (coll.) caress, endearing action or expression made with a selfish purpose.

carocha, *f.* = CARROCHA.

carochar, *va.* = CARROCHAR.

carolingio, a, *n. & a.* Carolingian, Carlovingian.

cárolus, *m.* an ancient Flemish coin.

caromomia, *f.* the dry flesh of a mummy.

carona, *f.* padding of the saddle next to the animal's back; part of the animal's back on which the saddle lies.

caroñoso, sa, *a.* old, galled, and cast off.

caroquero, ra. I. *n.* wheedler, flatterer. **II.** *a.* honey-worded, fondling.

carosis, *f.* complete stupor.

carótida, *f.* & *a.* (anat.) carotid.

carozo, *m.* core of an apple, pear, etc.; corn cob.

carpa, *f.* (icht.) carp; part of a bunch of grapes which is torn off; (Peru) canvas tent.

carpanel, *m.* (arch.) basket-handle arch.

carpanta, *f.* (coll.) keen appetite, hunger.

carpe, *m.* common hornbeam tree; witch-hazel.

carpedal, *m.* hornbeam plantation.

carpelo, *m.* (bot.) carpel.

carpeta, *f.* table cover; portfolio, letter file, case or envelope for filing documents; docket; writing desk; small curtain or screen before the door of a tavern.

carpetazo, *m.* blow or stroke with a CARPETA.—**dar c.,** to lay by; lay on the table; pigeonhole.

carpintear, *vn.* to do carpenter's work.

carpintería, *f.* carpentry; carpenter's shop.

carpintero, *m.* carpenter, joiner; woodpecker.—**c. de blanco,** joiner.—**c. de carretas,** cartwright.—**c. de navío,** shipwright.—**c. de obras de afuera,** carpenter who timbers or roofs houses.—**c. de prieto** = c. DE CARRETAS.—**c. de ribera** = c. DE NAVÍO.—**c. real,** ivory-billed woodpecker.

carpir, *vn.* to quarrel, wrangle; to scratch.

carpo, *m.* (anat.) carpus, wrist.

carpobálsamo, *m.* carpobalsamum.

carpóforo, *m.* (bot.) carpophore.

carpología, *f.* (bot.) carpology.

carquesa, *f.* in glassworks, annealing furnace.

carquexia, *f.* (bot.) a species of broom plant.

carraca, *f.* carack, large and slow-sailing ship; rattle; ratchet brace; the Cadiz navy yard.

carraco, ca, *a.* old, withered, decrepit.

carral, *m.* barrel, vat.

carraleja, *f.* black beetle with yellow stripes; oil beetle; Spanish blistering beetle.

carralero, *m.* cooper.

carranque, *m.* a Peruvian cranelike bird.

carrañón, *m.* short-stemmed wheat.

carrasca, *f.,* **carrasco,** *m.* (bot.) pin oak, swamp oak.—**carrascal, carrascalejo,** *m.* pin-oak field.—**carrascón,** *m.* *aug.* large pin oak.

carraspada, *f.* negus (beverage).

carraspera, *f.* (coll.) hoarseness; frog-in-the-throat; sore throat.

carraspique, *m.* (bot.) candytuft.

carrasposo, sa, *a.* suffering from chronic hoarseness or sore throat; (Colomb., Ven.) rough (to the touch).

carrasqueño, ña, *a.* belonging to the pin oak; harsh, sharp.

carrera, *f.* run; race; course; racetrack; highroad; avenue, broad street; row; stroke (of a piston); travel (of a valve); range of iron teeth in combing cards· line, parting of the hair; girder, joist; broken stitch in a stocking; course and duration of life; career; course, method of life; conduct, mode of action; route of a line of steamers; coach or stage line; Spanish step in dancing.—**c. de baquetas,** gantlet, a military punishment.—**c. de Indias,** trade from Spain to South America.—**a c. abierta,** at full speed.—**a la c., de c.,** hastily, hurriedly.—**no poder hacer c. con,** not to be able to bring (one) to reason.—**partir de c.,** to act in a rash and inconsiderate manner.—**poner en c.,** to give employment (to), to procure employment for.

carrerilla, ta, *f.* *dim.* small race, sprint or course; rapid motion in a Spanish dance; (mus.) rise or fall of an octave.

carrerista, *n.* race fan.

carrero, *m.* = CARRETERO.

carreta, *f.* long narrow cart, wagon.

carretada, *f.* cartful, cart load; (Mex.) measure for lime, equivalent to 3,000 pounds.—*pl.* great quantity.—**a carretadas,** (coll.) copiously, in abundance, in heaps.

carretaje, *m.* cartage; trade with carts.

carretal, *m.* rough, ragged ashlar.

carrete, *m.* spool, bobbin, reel; reel of a fishing rod; (elec.) bobbin, coil.

carretear. I. *va.* to cart, to convey in a cart or wagon; to drive (a cart). **II.** *vr.* to draw unevenly (s. o. oxen or mules).

carretel, *m.* spool, reel, bobbin; fishing reel, line reel; (naut.) log reel; spunyarn winch; ropewalk reel.—**c. de carpintero,** carpenter's marking line.

carretela, *f.* calèche, calash.

carretera, *f.* wheel or vehicle road; drive.

carretería, *f.* number of carts; trade of a carman; cartwright's yard; wheelwright's shop.

carretero, a. I. *a.* for vehicles, vehicle (u. a.) **II.** *m.* cartwright; carter, driver, truckman.

carretil, *a.* belonging to a cart or truck.

carretilla, *f.* *dim.* small cart; wheelbarrow, pushcart, trolley cart, handcart; (r. w.) truck; gocart; squib, firecracker; small wheel.—**c. de equipaje,** baggage truck or car.—**de c.,** mechanically, unconsciously, by rote.

carretón, *m.* cart; truck; gocart.—**c. de lámpara,** pulley for raising or lowering lamps.

carretonada, *f.* wagonload, truckload.

carretoncillo, *m.* *dim.* small go-cart.

carretonero, *m.* truckman, truck driver.

carricoche, *m.* ancient cart with a coachlike body; wagonette; muck cart, dung cart.

carricuba, *m.* watering or sprinkling cart.

carricureña, *f.* (mil.) carriage of a light gun.

carriego, *m.* osier fishing basket; rough basket for bleaching flax yarn.

carriel, *m.* (C. A.) traveling bag for papers and money; (Colomb.) GUARNIEL.

carril, *m.* rut, cartway, cart-rut; narrow road; furrow; (r. w.) rail.

carrillada, *f.* oily or medullar substance of a hog.

carrillera, *f.* jaw; chin stay, chin strap.

carrillo, *m.* *dim.* small cart; cheek; (naut.) hoisting tackle.

carrilludo, da, *a.* plump or round-cheeked.

carriola, *f.* trundle bed; small chariot, curricle.

carrizal, *m.* reed-grass.

carrizo, *m.* (bot.) common reed-grass field.

carro, *m.* cart; car; running gear of a carriage without the body; (**C-,** ast.) Great Bear, Dipper; (naut.) manufactory for cables and other ship cordage; measure for wood; cartload; bed of a printing press.—**c. de colchar,** rope maker's sledge.—**c. de riego,** sprinkling car.—**c. de volteo,** tip car, tilt car, dump car.—**C. Mayor,** Great Bear.—**C. Menor,** Little Bear, Ursa Minor.—**c. tranvía,** or **urbano,** street car.—**untar el c.,** (met.) to grease the hand, to bribe.

carrocería, *f.* shop where carriages are made, repaired or sold; (aut.) body.

carrocilla, *f.* *dim.* small carriage.

carrocín, *m.* chaise, curricle.

carrocha, *f.* seminal substance of insects; eggs.

carrochar, *vn.* to lay eggs (s. o. insects).

carromatero, *m.* carter; charioteer; carman.

carromato, *m.* long, narrow cart with two wheels and tilt.

carronada, *f.* (arti.) short gun of large calibre.

carroña, *f.* carrion, putrid flesh.

carroñar, *va.* to infect (sheep) with the scab.

carroño, ña, *a.* putrefied, putrid, rotten.

carroza, *f.* large coach; superb state coach; caroche; (naut.) awning.

carruaje, *m.* vehicle; carriage; car.

carruajero, *m.* carter, wagon driver, coach driver.

carruco, *m.* small cart used in mountains.

carrucha, *f.* = GARRUCHA.

carrujado, da, *a.* corrugated, wrinkled.

carta, *f.* letter, epistle; royal ordinance; map, chart; playing card; written constitution, charter.—**c. blanca,** carte blanche, full powers.—**c. certificada,** registered letter.—**c. credencial,** credentials.—**c. cuenta,** bill or account of sale.—**c. de arapaco,** safe-conduct.—**c. de contramarca,** letter of reprisal (against those having letters of marque).—**c. de crédito,** letter of credit.—**c. de**

creencia = C. CREDENCIAL.—**c. de dote,** articles of marriage.—**c. de encomienda,** letter of safe-conduct.—**c. de espera,** (law) moratory permit, moratorium.—**c. de examen,** license to practice a trade or profession.—**c. de fletamento,** (com.) charter party.—**c. de guía,** safe-conduct, passport.—**c. de horro,** letter of enfranchisement.—**c. de libre,** (law) guardian's discharge.—**c. de marear,** sea chart.—**c. de moratoria** = C. DE ESPERA. —**c. de naturaleza,** naturalization papers.—**c. de pago,** acquittance, receipt, discharge in full.—**c. de presentación, c. de recomendación,** letter of introduction.—**c. de sanidad,** bill of health.—**c. de seguridad,** safe-conduct.—**c. de Urías,** trap, snare. traitorous scheme.—**c. de vecindad,** burgher brief.—**c. de venta,** bill of sale.—**c. de vuelta,** dead letter.—**c. en lista,** letter "to be kept till called for"; general-delivery letter.—**c. orden,** mandatory letter.—**c. receptoria,** warrant, voucher.—**c. requisitoria,** letter requisitorial.—**c. viva,** messenger who delivers his message verbally.—**a c. cabal,** thorough, in every respect, every inch.—**enseñar las cartas,** to show one's hand.—**pecar por c. de más o de menos,** to have either too much or too little—**tomar cartas,** to take part; to be (in something); to take sides.

cartabón, *m.* carpenter's square; drawing triangle; rule; shoemaker's slide, size stick; quadrant, gunner's square.

cartagenero, ra, *a.* of or from Cartagena.

cartaginense; cartaginés, esa, *n.* & *a.* Carthaginian.

cártama, *f.,* **cártamo,** *m.* (bot.) = ALAZOR.

cartapacio, *m.* memorandum book; student's notebook; book satchel; batch or pile of papers.

cartapel, *m.* memorandum filled with useless matter.

cartear. I. *vn.* to play low cards as feelers. **II.** *va.* & *vn.* (naut.) to steer by the chart. **III.** *vr.* to write to each other; to correspond (write).

cartel, *m.* placard, handbill, poster; cartel.

cartela, *f.* slip of paper, piece of wood, or other materials on which a memorandum is made; (arch.) modillion, console, bracket; iron stay supporting a balcony.

cartelera, *f.* billboard.

cartelón, *m. aug.* long edict; show bill.

carteo, *m.* intercourse by letters.

cartera, *f.* portfolio; writing case; pocketbook; wallet; notebook; letter case, letter box; portfolio, office of a cabinet minister; pocket flap.

cartería, *f.* employment of letter carrier; sorting room in a post office.

carterista, *m.* pickpocket.

cartero, *m.* letter carrier, postman.

cartesianismo, *m.* Cartesianism.

cartesiano, na, *n.* & *a.* Cartesian.

carteta, *f.* a card game.

cartica, ita, *f.* short letter, note.

cartilagíneo, a; cartilaginoso, sa, *a.* (zool.) cartilaginous.

cartílago, *m.* (anat.) cartilage; parchment.

cartilla, *f. dim.* short letter, note; primer; certificate of a clergyman duly ordained.—**leerle a uno la c.** (met.) to give one a lecture.—**no saber la c.,** to be extremely ignorant, to know nothing.

cartografía, *f.* chartography.—**cartográfico, ca,** *a.* chartographic.—**cartógrafo,** *m.* chartographer.

cartomancia, *f.* cartomancy, fortune telling by cards.

cartómetro, *m.* curvometer.

cartón, *m.* pasteboard; binders' board; metal ornament imitating the leaves of plants; cartoon, painting, or drawing on strong paper.—**c. piedra,** (art) staff; papier-maché.

cartonero, ra, *n.* pasteboard maker.

cartuchera, *f.* cartridge box or pouch.

cartucho, *m.* cartouch; cartridge; metallic cartridge; roll of coins; (Am.) paper cornet.

cartuja, *f.* Carthusian order.—**cartujano, na,** *a.* Carthusian.—**cartujo,** *m.* Carthusian monk; (coll.) taciturn man; recluse.

cartulario, *m.* archives or registry; archivist; coucher, register book in monasteries.

cartulina, *f.* bristol board, cardboard.—**c. común,** millboard.—**c. de porcelana,** enamelled card.—**c. en hojas,** sheet card.

carúncula, *f.* caruncle.—**c. lagrimal,** lachrymal caruncle.

caruto, *m.* (bot.) caruto. genipap.

carvajal, carvallar, carvalledo, *m.* oak field.

carvajo, carvallo, *m.* (bot.) common British oak.

carvi, *m.* (bot.) common caraway; caraway seed.

casa, *f.* house; dwelling; home; household; family residing in a house; firm, commercial house; square of a chess or draught board.—**c. consistorial, c. de ayuntamiento,** city hall, town hall. —**c. de banca,** banking house.—**c. de beneficencia,** asylum, poorhouse.—**c. de campo,** country house.—**c. de comercio,** commercial house, firm. **c. de Dios,** house of God, church.—**c. de empeño,** pawnshop.—**c. de expósitos,** foundling home.—**c. de huéspedes,** boarding house.—**c. de juego,** gambling house.—**c. de locos,** madhouse; noisy place, bedlam.—**c. de maternidad,** lying-in hospital, maternity hospital.—**c. de moneda,** mint.— **c. de orates,** madhouse.—**c. de placer** = C. DE CAMPO.—**c. de posada, c. de pupilos** = C. DE HUÉSPEDES.—**c. de sanidad,** health office.—**c. de socorro,** emergency hospital.—**c. de tía,** (coll.) jail.—**c. de tócame Roque,** a house where many live, not well directed, and in consequent disorder. —**c. de vacas,** dairy farm.—**c. de vecindad,** tenement house.—**c. mortuoria,** house of the deceased.—**c. real,** royal palace.—**c. solar,** or **solariega,** manor, old homestead, ancient mansion of a family.—**en c.,** at home.—**no tener c. ni hogar,** to have neither house nor home.—**su c.** (often abbreviated to **s. c.**), a polite form of giving one's address, saying "your house" instead of 'my house," the implication being that "my house" is yours or at your disposal: it simply means "my address is."

casabe, *m.* cassava.

casaca, *f.* dress coat; (coll.) marriage, wedding. —**volver c.,** to become a turncoat.

casación, *f.* (law) cassation, abrogation, repeal.

casacón, *m.* greatcoat; cassock.

casadero, ra, *a.* marriageable.

casado, da. I. *a.* married. **II.** *m.* (print.) imposition. **III.** *pp.* of CASAR.

casalicio, *m.* house, edifice.

casamata, *f.* (mil.) casemate.

casamentero, ra, *n.* match or marriage maker; marriage broker.

casamiento, *m.* marriage, matrimony; wedding.

casamuro, *m.* (mil.) single wall without a terreplein.

casapuerta, *f.* vestibule, entrance hall.

casaquilla, *f.* short jacket.

casar. I. *vn.* & *vr.* to marry; get married.—**c. con,** to marry, be married to (Shakespeare says "to marry *with*," as in Spanish).—**antes que te cases, mira lo que haces,** look ere you leap. **II.** *va.* to marry, join in wedlock; couple, pair; to match; to suit; (law) to repeal, annul; (paint.) to blend; (typ.) to impose.

casar, *m.* hamlet, small village.

casarón, *m. aug.* large old house.

casatienda, *f.* tradesman's shop and dwelling combined.

casca, *f.* grape skins; tanning bark; a kind of fruit cake.

cascabel, *m.* bell, jingle; rattle; cascabel, knob at the end of the breech of a cannon.—**poner el c. al gato,** to undertake a risky thing, to dare, venture. —**ser un c.,** to be a rattlebrain.

cascabelada, *f.* jingling with small bells; (coll.) thoughtless or indiscreet speech or action, break.

cascabelear. I. *va.* to feed with vain hopes; to bamboozle. **II.** *vn.* to act with levity or recklessly.

cascabeleo, *m.* jingling of bells.

cascabelero, ra, *a.* light-witted.

cascabelillo, *m. dim.* small black plum.

cascabillo, *m.* bee's bell; glume of cereals, chaff, husk; cup of an acorn.

cascaciruelas, *n.* (coll.) mean, base person.

cascada, *f.* waterfall, cataract, cascade.

cascado, da. I. *a.* broken, burst; decayed; infirm; crazy. **II.** *pp.* of CASCAR.

cascadura, *f.* bursting or breaking asunder.

cascajal, cascajar, *m.* gravel pit; gravelly place; place where grape husks are thrown.

cascajero, *m.* (Colomb.) CASCAJAL; old mine still containing some ore.

cascajo, *m.* gravel; fragments; rubbish; (coll.) old and useless furniture, junk; dry fruit.—**estar hecho un c.,** to be old and infirm, to be a total wreck.

cascajoso, sa, *a.* gravelly.

cascamajar, *va.* to break, crush, or pound slightly.

cascamiento, *m.* breaking, bruising.

cascanueces, *m.* nutcracker.

cascapiñones, *m.* one who shells hot pine nuts and cleans the seed; pine-nut cracker.

cascar. I. *va.* (*pret.* CASQUÉ: *subj.* CASQUE) to crack, burst, break into pieces; crunch; (coll.) to lick, beat, strike. **II.** *vn.* (coll.) to talk too much. **III.** *vr.* to break open.

cáscara, *f.* rind, peel, shell, hull, husk; shell; bark (of trees); lansquenet, a card game.—**c. sagrada,** (med.) cascara sagrada, bark of the Californian buckthorn.—**de la c. amarga,** mischievous; rash; sporty; ultraradical, extremist.

cáscaras! *interj.* goodness gracious! by Jove!

cascarela, *f.* lansquenet card game.

cascarilla, *f. dim.* small thin shell, skin or bark; Peruvian bark; thin metal shell; powdered egg shell for cosmetic.

cascarillero, ra, *n.* gatherer of Peruvian bark.

cascarón, *m. aug.* eggshell; (arch.) arch, vault; calotte; niche for the sacrament; trick in lansquenet; (Mex.) cascaron, eggshell filled with confetti.

cascarrabias, *com.* (coll.) testy, irritable person.

cascarrón, na, *a.* (coll.) rough, harsh, rude.

cascarudo, da, *a.* hully, thick-rinded or shelled.

cascaruleta, *f.* (coll.) noise made by the teeth when chucked under the chin.

casco, *m.* skull, cranium; potsherd; fragments of an earthen vessel; quarter of a fruit; coat or tegument (of an onion); crown (of a hat); helmet; hull (of a ship); head (of a barrel); casque, headpiece; tree of a saddle; (com.) cask, pipe, vat, tank; printers' inking ball; sheepskin stripped of the wool; hoof.—*pl.* heads of sheep or bullocks without the tongues and brains.—**c. y quilla,** bottomry.

cascol, *m.* resin of a Guayaquil tree.

cascolote, *m.* (Mex.) thick bark of a tree.

cascote, *m.* rubbish, debris.

cascudo, da, *a.* large-hoofed.

caseación, *f.* coagulation of milk to make cheese.

caseato, *m.* (chem.) caseate.

caseico, ca, *a.* (chem.) lactic.

caseificar, *va.* (chem.) to change into casein; to separate the casein from (milk).

caseína, *f.* casein.

caseoso, sa, *a.* caseous, cheesy.

casera, *f.* housekeeper.

caseramente, *adv.* informally.

casería, *f.* manor's lodge; outbuilding for farm hands.

caserío, *m.* group of houses; small village, settlement.

caserna, *f.* (mil.) casern; barracks.

casero, ra. I. *n.* landlord (-lady); house agent; caretaker. **II.** *a.* domestic; homemade; house (u. a.); familiar; housekeeping.

caserón, *m. aug.* big house.

caseta, *f. dim.* small house, cottage, hut.—**c. de baños,** bathing house.

casi, *adv.* almost, nearly.—**c. que,** or **c. c.,** very nearly.

casia, *f.* (bot.) bastard cinnamon, cassia.

casica, illa, ita, *f. dim.* small house, cabin.

casicontrato, *m.* (law) = CUASICONTRATO.

casilla, *f.* ticket office; hut of a railway guard or flagman; cabin; booth; keeper's lodge;

pigeonhole; square (of chessboard).—*pl.* ruled columns in accounts; points of a backgammon table.—**sacar a uno de sus casillas,** (coll.) to make one change one's habits; to vex one beyond patience.—**salir de sus casillas,** to forget one's self.

casiller, ra, *n.* servant who empties slops etc.

casillero, *m.* desk or board with pigeonholes.

casillo, *m. dim.* trifling or slight case.

casimbas, *f. pl.* (naut.) buckets for baling.

casimir, m., casimira, f., casimiro, m. cassimere, kerseymere.

casino, *m.* casino, dancing hall, public resort, clubhouse; social or political club.

Casiopea, *f.* (ast.) Cassiopeia.

casiterita, *f.* (min.) cassiterite.

caso, *m.* case; occurrence, event; (law, med. gram.) case.—**c. que,** in case.—**dado c.,** or **demos c.,** supposing that.—**de c. pensado,** deliberately.—**en c. de que** = c. QUE.—**en tal c.,** in such a case.—**en todo c.,** at all events, anyway.—**hacer c.,** to mind, obey.—**hacer c. de,** to take notice of; to mind; to take into account; to esteem.—**no hacer, or no venir, al c.,** to be irrelevant, to have nothing to do with the case.—**poner por c.,** to assume, suppose.—**vamos al c.,** let us come to the point.

casón, *m. aug.* large house.

casorio, *m.* (coll.) hasty or unwise marriage; informal wedding.

caspa, *f.* dandruff, scurf.

caspera, *f.* fine comb for dandruff.

caspia, *f.* core of an apple.

caspio, ia, *a.* Caspian.

caspiroleta, *f.* (Am.) eggnog.

¡cáspita! *interj.* gracious! confound it! by Jove!

casposo, sa, *a.* full of dandruff; lentiginous.

casquetazo, *m.* blow with the head.

casquete, *m.* helmet, skullcap, cap; skull; wig, periwig; (mech.) cap; (arch.) calotte; helmet shell; plaster to remove the scurf.

casquiacopado, da, *a.* cup-hoofed (horse).

casquiblando, da, *a.* soft-hoofed.

casquiderramado, da, *a.* wide-hoofed.

casquijo, *m.* gravel; ballasting material.

casquilla, *f.* cell of the queen bee.

casquillo, *m. dim.* little helm; tip, cap; ferrule; socket; iron arrowhead; (Am.) horseshoe.

casquimuleño, ña, *a.* having narrow hoofs like a mule (s. o. horses).

casquito, *m. dimin.* of CASCO.—**casquitos de guayaba,** guava preserve.

casquivano, na, *a.* feather-brained; ridiculously conceited.

casta, *f.* caste, race, breed; clan; offspring; kind or quality.—**hacer c.,** to get a particular breed.

Castálidas, *f. pl.* the Muses.

castalio, ia, *a.* belonging or relating to Castalia.

castamente, *adv.* chastely.

castaña, *f.* (bot.) chestnut; bottle, jug, jar; club of hair, chignon; abandoned mine; (Mex.) valise, satchel.—**c. apilada,** or **pilonga,** dried chestnut.—**c. regoldana,** wild or horse-chestnut.—**dar a uno la c.,** to play a trick on one.

castañal, m., castañar., m., castañeda, f., castañedo, *m.* chestnut grove or plantation.

castañera, *f.* country abounding with chestnut trees.

castañero, ra, *n.* chestnut dealer or seller.

castañeta, *f.* castanet; snapping of the fingers.

castañetazo, *m.* blow with a castanet; cracking a chestnut in the fire; cracking of the joints.

castañete, *m. dim.* small chestnut tree.

castañeteado, *m.* sound of castanets.

castañetear, *vn.* to rattle the castanets; to clatter the teeth; to crackle, clack the knees; to cry (app. to partridges).

castañeteo, *m.* sound of castanets; rattling the castanets; clattering; rattling noise.

castaño, *m.* (bot.) common chestnut tree; chestnut wood.—**c. de Indias,** horse-chestnut tree.—**c. regoldana,** wild chestnut tree.—**pasar de c. oscuro,** (coll.) to be beyond reason or endurance.

castaño, ña, *a.* hazel, brown.

castañola, *f.* a large Mediterranean sea fish.

---

castañuela, *f.* castanet; (bot.) round tuberous-rooted cyperus.—*pl.* (naut.) cleats fastened to the yardarms.—**estar como_unas castañuelas,** (coll.) to be very gay.

castañuelo, la, *a. dim.* of a light chestnut color.

castellán, *m.* castellan, governor or warden of a castle.—**castellana,** *f.* mistress of a castle; stanza in old Spanish poetry.—**castellanía,** *f.* castellany, district belonging to a castle.

castellanizar, *va.* to make (a word) Spanish.

castellano, *m.* Spanish language; ancient Spanish coin, fiftieth part of a gold mark; castellan, lord or warden of a castle.

castellano, na, *a.* Castilian; Spanish (language, grammar, etc.).

castellar, *m.* (bot.) St. John's-wort, tutsan.

casticidad, *f.* correctness, quality of being good Spanish.

castidad, *f.* chastity.

castigación, *f.* castigation, punishment; revision and correction.

castigadera, *f.* strap or rope for tying the clapper of a wether's bell; small cord with which the ring of a stirrup is tied to the girth.

castigador, ra, *n. & a.* punisher (-ing), chastiser (-ing), castigator (-ing).

castigar, *va.* (*pret.* CASTIGUÉ: *subj.* CASTIGUE) to chastise, punish, castigate; to afflict, put to pain, grieve; to revise and correct (proof sheets or writings).

castigo, *m.* chastisement, punishment; penalty; penance; censure, animadversion, reproach; alteration or correction.

castillaje, *m.* castle toll. *V.* CASTILLERÍA.

castillejo, *m.* small castle; gocart; scaffolding.

castillería, *f.* transit toll over castle property.

castillo, *m.* castle; wooden tower on the back of an elephant; mounting of a velvet loom; cell of the queen bee.—**c. de fuego,** fireworks.—**c. de naipes,** flimsy structure; air castles.—**c. de proa,** (naut.) forecastle.—**c. roquero,** castle built on a rock.—**hacer castillos en el aire,** to build air castles.

castilluelo, *m. dim.* castlet, small castle.

castina, *f.* (chem. and metal.) flux.

castizo, za, *a.* of noble descent; of good breed; pure-blooded; pure, correct (language).

casto, ta, *a.* chaste.

castor, *m.* (zool.) beaver; beaver cloth; (Mex.) fine red baize.

Cástor, *m.* (ast.) Castor (a star).—**C. y Pólux,** (naut.) corposant, St. Elmo's fire.

castorcillo, *m.* a kind of rough sergelike cloth.

castoreño, ña, *a.* made of beaver.

castóreo, *m.* castoreum.

castorina, *f.* a kind of cloth similar to castor cloth; (chem.) castorin.

castra, *f.* pruning; pruning season.

castración, *f.* castration, gelding.

castradera, *f.* iron instrument with which honey is taken from a hive.

castrado, m. eunuch.—**castrador, ra,** *n.* gelder, castrator.—**castradura,** *f.* castration; scar remaining after castration.

castrametación, *f.* (mil.) castrametation, encamping.

castrapuercas, *m.* sowgelder's whistle.

castrar, *va.* to geld, castrate; to cut away the proud flesh of (a wound); to prune; to cut the honeycombs from (beehives).

castrazón, *f.* act of cutting honeycombs out of hives; season when it is done.

castrense, *a.* military.

castro, *m.* game played by boys; act of taking honeycombs out of hives; headland; hilltop with castle in ruins.

castrón, *m.* castrated goat.

casual, *a.* casual, accidental, occasional.

casualidad, *f.* chance; chance event; hazard; accident; coincidence.—**por c.,** by chance.

casualmente, *adv.* accidentally; by chance.

casuáridos, *m. pl.* (zool.) family of the cassowaries.

casuario, *m.* (zool.) cassowary.

casuca, casucha, *f.*; **casucho,** *m.* (coll.) miserable hut or cottage; crib.

casuísta, *n.* casuist.—**casuística,** *f.* casuistry.

casuístico, ca, *a.* casuistical.

casulla, *f.* chasuble, vestment worn by priests.

casullero, ra, *n.* one who makes chasubles and other vestments for priests.

casus belli, casus belli, cause for war.

cata, *f.* act of trying a thing by the taste; sample, trial; plummet for measuring heights; (Am.) buried treasure; trial excavation (of prospective mine); hidden thing (sp. if valuable).

catabre, *m.* (naut.) sheep-shank.

catacaldos, *m.* taster of wine, soup, etc.; sampler.

cataclismo, *m.* cataclysm; catastrophe.

catacresis, *f.* (rhet.) catachresis.

catacumbas, *f. pl.* catacombs.

catacústica, *f.* catacoustics.

catadióptrica, *f.* (phys.) catadioptrics.

catadióptrico, ca, *a.* (phys.) catadioptric.

catador, *m.* taster, sampler.—**catadura,** *f.* act of tasting; (coll.) gesture, face, countenance.

catafalco, *m.* catafalque.

catalán, na, *n. & a.* Catalan, Catalonian.

cataléctico, ca; catalecto, ta, *a.* (poet.) catalectic.

catalejo, *m.* telescope.

catalepsia, *f.* (med.) catalepsis.—**cataléptico, ca,** *a.* cataleptic.

catalicón, *m.* catholicon, panacea.

catalina, *f.* *V.* RUEDA CATALINA.

catálisis, *f.* (chem.) catalysis.—**catalítico, ca,** *a.* catalytic.—**catalizador,** *m.* catalyser; catalytic.

catalogar, *va.* to catalogue, list.

catálogo, *m.* catalogue, table, list.

catalpa, *f.* (bot.) catalpa.

catalufa, *f.* a kind of floor carpet.

catán, *m.* Indian sabre or cutlass.

catante, *n.* one who tastes or looks.

cataplasma, *f.* cataplasm, poultice.

cataplexia, *f.* cataplexy; apoplexy; (vet.) cataplepsis.

catapulta, *f.* catapult.

catar, *va.* to taste, sample, try by the taste; to investigate, examine; to judge, pass on; to esteem, respect; to bear in mind; to cut the combs out of (beehives).

cataraña, *f.* (orn.) sheldrake.

catarata, *f.* cataract, waterfall, cascade; cataract of the eye.—**abrirse las cataratas del cielo,** to rain heavily, to pour.—**tener cataratas,** (coll.) not to understand clearly.

catarral, *a.* catarrhal.

catarribera, *m.* falconer; (joc.) lawyer appointed to examine into the proceedings of magistrates.

catarro, *m.* catarrh.—**c. epidémico,** influenza.

catarroso, sa, *a.* catarrhal; subject to or troubled with a cold.

catártico, ca, *a.* (med.) cathartic.

catastral, *a.* relating to the census.

catastro, *m.* royal tax formerly imposed on real estate; census or list of real property of a county or state.

catástrofe, *f.* catastrophe; dénouement, winding up (sp. when sad or tragic).

cataviento, *m.* (naut.) dogvane; weathercock.

catavino, *m.* small jug or cup for tasting wine; small hole at the top of wine vessels for tasting the wine; rounder of taverns.

catavinos, *m.* winetaster, expert sampler.

cate, *m.* a weight, common in the Philippine Islands, equivalent to 0.633 kg.

catecismo, *m.* catechism.

catecú, *m.* catechu. *V.* CATO.

catecuménico, ca, *a.* catechumenical.

catecúmeno, na, *n.* catechumen.

cátedra, *f.* seat or chair of a professor; professorship; subject taught by a professor; lecture room in a university.—**c. del Espíritu Santo,** pulpit.—**c. de San Pedro,** Holy See.

catedral, *n. & a.* cathedral.

For pronunciation, see the rules at the beginning of the book.

catedralidad, *f.* dignity of a cathedral church.

catedrático, *m.* professor; contribution paid to bishops and prelates.

catedrilla, *f. dim.* small or poor professor's chair; in some universities, lecture by an aspirant to a professorship.

categorema, *f.* (log.) quality of being assignable to a category.

categoría, *f.* (phil.) category; class, condition; character, quality.—**de c.,** of importance; of high rank, prominent.

categóricamente, *adv.* categorically.

categórico, ca, *a.* categorical, categoric.

catenaria, *n.* & *a.* catenary.

catequesis, *f.* catechesis.

catequismo, *m.* catechizing, religious instruction; art of teaching by questions and answers.

catequista, *m.* catechist.

catequístico, ca, *a.* catechetical, catechetic.

catequizante, *n.* & *a.* catechiser (-ing).

catequizar, *va.* (*pret.* CATEQUICÉ; *subj.* CATEQUICE) to catechise; to instruct in the Christian faith; to peasuade, induce.

caterético, ca, *a.* (med.) erosive, catheretic.

caterva, *f.* multitude; throng, crowd.

catéter, *m.* (surg.) catheter.—**cateterismo,** *m. m.* catheterism.—**cateterizar,** *va.* to catheterize.

cateto, *m.* (arch.) cathetus; (geom.) leg (of a right-angled triangle).

catetómetro, *m.* cathetometer.

catilinaria, *f.* one of Cicero's orations against Catiline; severe criticism or denunciation.

catín, *m.* copper-refining crucible.

catinga, *f.* (Am.) bad smell (sp. that of negroes); SOBAQUINA.

catingoso, sa, catingudo, da, *a.* (Am.) ill-smelling.

catire, *n.* & *a.* (Am.) blond, light-haired.

catirrino, na. I. *n.* & *a.* (zool.) catarrhine. **II.** *m. pl.* Catarrhina, a division of the primates.

catite, *m.* loaf of the best refined sugar.

cato, *m.* Japan earth. *V.* CATECÚ, CACHÚ.

catoche, *m.* (Mex. coll.) bad humor.

catódico, ca, *a.* (elec.) cathodic.

cátodo, *m.* cathode.

católicamente, *adv.* in a catholic manner.

catolicismo, *m.* Catholicism.

católico, ca. I. *a.* catholic, general or universal; true, infallible. **II.** *n.* & *a.* (Roman) Catholic. **no estar muy c.,** (coll.) to feel under the weather. **III.** *m.* chemical furnace.

catolicón, *m.* catholicon; panacea.

catón, *m.* reading book for children.

catoniano, na, *a.* Catonian.

catóptrica, *f.* catoptrics.

catóptrico, ca, *a.* catoptrical.

catorce, *n.* & *a.* fourteen; fourteenth.

catorcena, *f.* group of fourteen.

catorceno, na, *a.* fourteenth. *V.* PAÑO.

catorzavo, va, *n.* & *a.* fourteenth.

catre, *m.* small bedstead; cot.—**c. de mar,** hammock or cot.—**c. de tijera,** field bed.

catrecillo, *m.* camp canvass chair.

catricofre, *m.* folding bed, bed lounge.

caucálide, *m.* (bot.) = CADILLO.

caucáseo, a; caucásico, ca, *a.* Caucasian.

cauce, *m.* bed of a river; trench, ditch.

caución, *f.* caution, precaution; security, pledge, surety, guarantee; (law) bailbond.—**c. juratoria,** parole.

caucionar, *va.* (law) to guard against an evil or loss; to bail.

cauchal, *m.* rubber plantation or patch.

cauchero, ra. I. *a.* (India) rubber (u. a.). **II,** *n.* rubber man, one engaged in the rubber industry or trade.

cauchil, *m.* small basin or reservoir of water.

caucho, *m.* India rubber, caoutchouc, gum elastic.

cauda, *f.* train or tail of a bishop's robe.

caudal, *f.* fortune, wealth, means; volume (of water); plenty, abundance.—**hacer c. de,** to value highly.

caudal, *a.* (zool.) caudal.

caudalejo, *m. dim.* middling fortune.

caudalosamente, *adv.* copiously, abundantly.

caudaloso, sa, *a.* of great volume, carrying much water; copious, abundant; rich, wealthy.

caudatario, *m.* clergyman who carries the train of an officiating bishop's robe.

caudato, ta, *a.* having a tail (s. o. a comet); bearded, hairy.

caudatrémula, *f.* (orn.) wagtail.

caudillaje, *m.* leadership; tyranny; bossism.

caudillo, *m.* commander, chief, leader.

caudimano, na, *a.* (zool.) having a prehensile or a working tail.

caudón, *m.* a bird of prey.

caulescente, *a.* (bot.) caulescent.

caulícolo, caulículo, *m.* (arch.) ornament of the capital of columns.

caulífero, a, *a.* (bor.) cauliferous.

cauro, *m.* northwest wind.

causa, *f.* cause; motive, reason; lawsuit, case; trial (at law).—**c. célebre,** famous (criminal) case, cause célèbre.—**c. final,** (phil.) final cause.—**c. primaria,** or **primera,** first cause.—**c. pública,** public welfare, common weal.—**a,** or **por, c. de,** on account of, because, due to.

causador, a, *n.* originator.

causal, *a.* causal.—**causalidad,** *f.* causality.

causante. I. *a.* causing, originating, causative. **II.** *n.* originator; (law) the person from whom a right is derived; constituent, principal.

causar, *va.* to cause, occasion; to sue.

causídico, ca. I. *n.* advocate, counsellor. **II.** *a.* (law) causidical, forensic.

causón, *m.* burning fever of short duration.

causticidad, *f.* causticity.

cáustico, ca. I. *a.* caustic, burning; biting, aggressive. **II.** *m.* (med.) caustic.

cautamente, *adv.* cautiously.

cautela, *f.* caution, prudence; craft, cunning.

cautelar, *va.* & *vr.* (w. **de**) to guard against.

cautelosamente, *adv.* cautiously, warily.

cauteloso, sa, *a.* cautious, wary.

cauterio, *m.* (med.) cautery.—**c. actual,** actual cautery, burning with hot iron.—**c. potencial,** potential cautery, produced by chemicals.

cauterización, *f.* cauterization, cauterizing.

cauterizador, *m.* he who or that which cauterizes.

cauterizante, *a.* cauterizing.

cauterizar, *va.* (*pret.* CAUTERICÉ; *subj.* CAUTERICE) to cauterize; to reproach with severity; to blame.

cautivar, *va.* to take prisoner, carry into captivity; to captivate, charm.

cautiverio, *m.,* **cautividad,** *f.* captivity.

cautivo, va, *n.* captive.

cauto, ta, *a.* cautious, wary, prudent.

cava, *f.* digging and earthing of vines; wine cellar in the royal palace.

cavacote, *m.* mound made with the hoe.

cavadiza, *a.* dug out of a pit (as sand).

cavador, ra, *n.* digger.

cavadura, *f.* digging.

caván, *m.* a measure used in the Philippine Islands, equivalent to seventy-five quarts.

cavar. I. *va.* to dig, excavate; to paw (s. o. horses). **II.** *vn.* to dig; to think carefully or intently; to go to the bottom (of a subject, etc.)

cavatina, *f.* (mus.) cavatina.

cavazón, *f.* digging.

cávea, *f.* (archeol.) cavea (cage or cave).

caverna, *f.* cavern, cave; hollow or depth of a wound.

cavernilla, *f. dim.* small cavern.

cavernoso, sa, *a.* cavernous, caverned.

caveto, *m.* (arch.) cavetto.

caví, *m.* oca, a South-American tuber.

cavia, *f.* circular excavation at the foot of a tree to collect water.

cavial, caviar, *m.* caviar.

cavicornio, nia. I. *a.* (zool.) cavicorn. **II.** *m. pl.* Cavicornia.

cavidad, f. cavity.

cavilación, f. cavilling.—**cavilar,** va. to cavil; to criticize.—**cavilosamente,** adv. captiously.—**cavilosidad,** f. captiousness, cavilling.—**caviloso, sa,** a. captious, overparticular; faultfinding.

cayada, f., **cayado,** m. shepherd's hook, crook; crozier of a bishop; walking staff.

cayán, m. awning of matting in some Philippine boats.

cayente, a. falling.

cayeputi, m. cajuput tree; cajuput oil.

cayo, m. rock, shoal, islet; key.

cayote, m. (bot.) = CIDRACAYOTE.

cayuco, m. (Ven.) a small fishing boat.

caz, m. trench, ditch; mill race, flume.

caza, f. hunting, chase; game; pursuit.—**c. mayor,** big game.—**c. menor,** small game.—**andar a c. de,** to be, or go, hunting for, or in search of.—**dar c.,** to pursue.

cazabe, m. (bot.) manioc, cassava; flour of the cassava plant; bread made with it.

cazadero, m. chase; hunting grounds.

cazador, ra. I. a. hunting. **II.** n. hunter.—**c. de alforja,** one who sports with dogs, snares, and other devices **III.** f. huntress; hunting jacket.

cazamoscas, m. (orn.) flycatcher.

cazar, va. (pret. CACÉ: subj. CACE) to chase, hunt; (coll.) to attain by skill; (coll.) to charm and captivate by caresses and deceitful tricks; to chase, pursue.—**c. una vela,** (naut.) to tally a sail; haul the sheet aft.

cazatorpedero, m. torpedo-boat destroyer.

cazcalear, vn. (coll.) to fidget and fuss.

cazcarria, f. splashings of mud on clothes; (Am.) sheep dung.

cazcarriento, ta, a. (coll.) splashed, bemired.

cazo, m. dipper, ladle; founders' scoop; size kettle; glue pot; melting pan.

cazoleja, eta, f. dim. small saucepan; pan of a musket lock; perfuming pan.

cazolero, m. (coll.) man who does women's work in the kitchen.

cazoleta, f. pan of a musket lock; boss or defence of a shield; hand guard or languet of a sword; a kind of perfume.

cazolón, m. aug. large earthen pot or stewpan.

cazón, m. (icht.) dogfish or small shark.

cazonal, m. tackle for shark fishing.

cazonete, m. (naut.) toggle.

cazudo, da, a. having a thick back (s. o. knives).

cazuela, f. earthen cooking pan; stewing pan, crock; meat dressed in an earthen pan; (theat.) gallery reserved for women.

cazumbrar, va. to join (staves) with hempen cords.

cazumbre, m. hempen cord to join staves.

cazumbrón, m. cooper.

cazurro, ra, a. (coll.) taciturn, sulky, sullen.

cazuz, m. (bot.) ivy.

ce I. f. cee, name of the letter c—**c. por be,** or **c. por c.,** minutely, circumstantially.—**por c. o por be,** somehow or other. **II.** interj. hark! hear! come here! see here!

cea, f. thigh bone.

ceanoto, m. (bot.) New Jersey tea, redroot.

ceática, f. (med.) sciatica.—**ceático, ca,** a. (med.) sciatical.

ceba, f. fattening of domestic animals.

cebada, f. barley.—**c. perlada,** pearl barley.

cebadal, m. barley field.

cebadazo, za, a. belonging to barley.

cebadera, f. nose bag; barley bin; (naut.) spritsail; (metal.) furnace charger.

cebadería, f. barley market.

cebadero, m. place where game or fowls are fed; breeder and feeder of hawks; mule carrying the feed; bell mule; (metal.) mouth for feeding a furnace; barley dealer.

cebadilla, f. (bot.) Indian caustic barley; (bot.) sneeze-wort; (bot., prov.) prickly oxeye; hellebore snuff.

cebado, da, a. (her.) ravening; haunting a particular place (s. o. animals haunting a place where they find food or prey).

cebador, m. one who fattens animals; priming horn, powder horn.

cebadura, f. fattening of domestic animals.

cebar. I. va. & vn. to fatten (animals); to stuff, cram; to feed (a furnace, fire, lamp); to prime (a firearm); to start (a machine or apparatus); to light (a rocket or pyrotechnic piece); to remagnetize; to excite and cherish (a passion); to bait (a fishhook). **II.** vn. to penetrate; take hold of; stick fast. **III.** vr. to be firmly bent upon a thing; to prey upon; gloat over (a victim).

cebellina, f. (zool.) sable; sable fur.

cebero, m. feed bag, nose bag.

cébido, da. I. n. & a. (zool.) cebid. **II.** m. pl. Cebidæ.

cebo, m. food given to animals, fodder; fattening of animals; bait; incentive; a kind of monkey; (arti.) priming of guns.—**c. fulminante,** percussion cap.

cebolla, f. (bot.) onion; bulb of the onion; any bulbous root; oil receptacle of a lamp; spherical screen in a water pipe—**c. albarrana,** (bot.) squill.—**c. ascalonia,** (bot.) shallot garlic.

cebollana, f. (bot.) three-toothed globularia; chives.

cebollar, m. onion patch.—**cebollero, ra,** n onion seller.—**cebolleta,** f. dim. tender onion.—**cebollino,** m. young onion fit to be transplanted; onion seeds; (bot.) chive, cive.—**cebollón,** m. aug. large onion.—**cebolludo, da,** a. bulbous, having a big bulb.

cebón, m. fattened bullock or hog.

ceboncillo, m. dim. fatling.

cebra, f. (zool.) zebra.—**cebrado, da,** a. having stripes like the zebra.

cebratana, f. = CERBATANA.

cebruno, na, a. deer-colored.

cebú, m. (zool.) zebu; (Arg.) a variety of monkey.

ceca, f. mint (for coining).—m. (**C-**) name of the mosque that the Arabs had in Cordova, the most venerated after Mecca.—**de C. en Meca,** or **de la C. a la Meca,** to and fro, hither and thither, from place to place.

cecear. I. vn. to pronounce s like c. **II.** va. to call, hail; to lisp.

ceceo, m. lisping, lisp; calling, hailing.

ceceoso, sa. I. a. lisping. **II.** n. lisper.

cecial, m. fish cured and dried.

cecina, f. corned beef, dried beef, jerked beef, hung beef.

cecografía, f. writing of the blind.

cecógrafo, m. cecograph, an apparatus for the blind to write.

ceda, f. zee, last letter of the alphabet.

cedacería, f. shop where sieves or cribs are made or sold.—**cedacero,** m. maker or seller of sieves, cribs, etc.—**cedacillo, ito,** m. dim. small sieve.

cedazo, m. sieve, screen, strainer.

cedazuelo, m. dim. small sieve or strainer.

cedente. I. a. ceding, granting. **II.** n. conveyer, assigner, transferrer.

ceder. I. va. to transfer, cede, convey, yield; deliver up. **II.** vn. to yield, submit, comply, give in; to give out, slacken, fail; to happen, turn out ill or well; to abate, diminish.

cedilla, f. cedilla.

cedizo, za, a. tainted.

cedoaria, f. (herb.) zedoary.

cedral, m. cedar field or forest.

cedras, f. pl. skin saddlebags.

cedria, f. cedrium, resin from the cedar.

cédride, f. fruit of the cedar tree.

cedrino, na, a. cedrine, cedarn.

cedrio, m. = CÉDRIDE.

cedro, m. (bot.) cedar; Spanish juniper.—**c. colorado,** red cedar.—**c. de la India,** deodar.—**c. de las Antillas,** Spanish cedar.—**c. del Líbano,** cedar of Lebanon.—**c. de Misiones,** an Argentine cedar, producing fine wood and a valuable febrifuge.—**c. dulce,** red cedar.

cédula, *f.* cedula, slip of parchment or paper written or to write upon; order, bill, decree; cedule, a scroll or writing.—**c. ante diem,** secretary's summons of meeting to the members of a society.—**c. de abono,** order to remit a task.—**c. de aduana,** permit.—**c. de cambio,** (com.) draft. —**c. personal,** or **de vecindad,** official document declaring the name, occupation, domicile, etc. of the bearer, and to serve for identification.—**c. real,** royal letter patent.—**echar cédulas,** (coll.) to draw or cast lots.

cedulaje, *m.* fees or dues paid for a cedula.

cedulilla, ita, *f. dim.* small slip of paper.

cedulón, *m. aug.* large bill; long edict; proclamation; public notice.

cefalalgia, *f.* (med.) cephalalgia, headache.

cefalea, *f.* violent headache, migraine.

cefálico, ca, *a.* cephalic.

cefalitis, *f.* cephalitis, phrenitis.

céfalo, *m.* (zool.) mullet, a kind of perch.

cefalópodo, da. I. *n.* & *a.* (zool.) cephalopod. **II.** *m. pl.* Cephalopoda.

cefalotomía, *f.* cephalotomy.

cefalotórax, *m.* (anat.) cephalothorax.

Cefeo, *m.* Cepheus, a constellation.

céfiro, *m.* zephyr.

cefo, *m.* a large African monkey.

cegajo, *m.* two-year-old he-goat.

cegajoso, sa, *a.* blear-eyed.

cegar. I. *vn.* (*ind.* CIEGO: *pret.* CEGUÉ: *subj.* CIEGUE) to grow blind. **II.** *va.* to blind; to wall up (a door or window); to close up (a well); to stop up, close (a channel, road).—**c. una vía de agua,** (naut.) to fother a leak. **III.** *vr.* to become or be blinded (by passion, etc.)

cegarra, *a.* (coll.) CEGATO.

cegarrita, *n.* (coll.) one who contracts the eye to see at a distance.

cegato, ta, *a.* (coll.) short-sighted.

cegatoso, sa, *a.* = CEGAJOSO.

cegesimal, *a.* (phys.) C. G. S. (app. to the system of units in which the fundamental units are the centimeter, gram and second).

ceguecillo, lla, *n. dim.* little blind person.

ceguedad, *f.* blindness; ignorance, intellectual darkness; obfuscation.

ceguera, *f.* disorder in the eye; absolute blindness; obfuscation.

ceguezuelo, la, *n.*=CEGUECILLO.

ceiba, f., ceibo, *m.* (bot.) ceiba, God tree, W. I. silkcotton tree; (**ceiba**) sea moss, alga.

ceja, *f.* eyebrow: edging of clothes; projecting part, as in the binding of books; bridge of a string instrument; summit; circle of clouds round a hill; cloud cap; (arch.) weather molding; rim; (carp.) rabbet; (naut.) opening in the clouds.— **dar entre ceja y ceja,** to tell one unpleasant truths to one's face.—**hasta las cejas,** to the utmost, to the extreme.—**quemarse las cejas,** to burn the midnight oil.—**tener entre c. y c.,** to dislike, have a grudge against; to have on one's brain, to think constantly about.

cejadero, *m.* hold-back strap of a harness.

cejar, *vn.* to go backward; hold back; to hesitate; to slacken, relax.

cejijunto, ta, *a.* having eyebrows that meet.

cejo, *m.* fog from rivers; esparto cord tied around a bundle of esparto grass.

cejudo, da, *a.* having heavy and long eyebrows.

cejuela, *f. dim.* small eyebrow.

celada, *f.* sallet; helmet without visor; ambuscade, ambush; snare; lurch; artful trick; part of the key of the crossbow; horse soldier with helmet.—**c. borgoñota,** visorless helmet.

celadilla, *f. dim.* small helmet.

celador, ra, *n.* watchman (-woman), caretaker; curator; monitor in a school; warden.

celaje, *m.* aspect of the sky with clouds of varied hues; cloud scenery; cloud effect; painting representing the rays of the sun breaking through clouds; presage, prognostic; skylight; sky of a picture.—*pl.* light, swiftly moving clouds; scud.

celandés, sa, *n.* & *a.* New Zealander.

celar, *vn.* & *va.* to fulfil (duties) with care; to watch (any person's motions) from fear; to cover, conceal; to engrave; to carve.

celda, *f.* cell (in a convent, beehive, prison).

celdica, illa, ita, *f. dim.* cellule.

celdilla, *f.* cell in beehives; (bot.) cell; capsule.

celebérrimo, ma, *a. sup.* most (very) famous.

celebración, *f.* celebration; praise, applause.

celebrador, ra, *n.* applauder, praiser, approver; celebrator.

celebrante, *n.* & *a.* celebrator (-ing); celebrant (officiating).

celebrar, *va.* to celebrate; praise, applaud, approve; to revere, respect, venerate; to be glad of, rejoice at; to say (mass).

célebre, *a.* famous, renowned; (coll.) facetious, witty, funny.

célebremente, *adv.* with celebrity; facetiously, humorously.

celebridad, *f.* celebrity, renown, fame; pomp, magnificence; public demonstration, celebration, pageant.

celebro, *m.* skull; brain; fancy, imagination, prudence.

celemín, *m.* a dry measure (about a peck).

celeminada, *f.* quantity contained in a CELEMÍN.

celenteriado, da; celenterio, ria. I. *n.* & *a.* (zool.) coelenterate. **II.** *m. pl.* Coelenterata.

célere. I. *a.* quick, rapid. **II.** *m.* one of the select three hundred knights of ancient Roman nobility.

celeridad, *f.* celerity, quickness.

celerífero, ra, *a.* rapid-transit, of rapid transportation.

celerímetro, *m.* speedometer, speed gage.

celeste, *a.* celestial, heavenly; sky-blue.

celestial, *a.* celestial, heavenly; agreeable, delightful, excellent; (iron.) silly, sottish.

celestialmente, *adv.* celestially, heavenly.

celestina, *f.* (min.) celestite; procuress.

celfo, *m.* = CEFO.

celia, *f.* a beverage made from wheat; a kind of beer.

celíaca, *f.* (med.) coeliac artery; coeliac passion.

celíaco, ca, *a.* (med.) coeliac, relating to the coeliac passion; afflicted with the coeliac passion.

celibato, *m.* celibacy; (coll.) bachelor, single man.—**célibe,** *n.* unmarried person.

célico, ca, *a.* celestial, heavenly.

celidonia, *f.* (bot.) common celandine, swallowwort.

celindrate, *m.* ragout made with coriander seed.

celo, *m.* zeal, ardor, fervour; piety, devotion; heat, rut.—*pl.* jealousy; suspicions.—**dar celos,** to excite suspicions.

celosamente, *adv.* with zeal; jealously.

celosía, *f.* lattice; Venetian blind; jealousy.

celoso, sa, *a.* zealous; jealous; suspicious; (naut.) light and swift-sailing.

celotipia, *f.* jealousy.

celsitud, *f.* celsitude, elevation, grandeur; (obs.) highness, a title, now expressed by **alteza.**

celta, *n.* & *a.* Celt(ic).

celtibérico, ca; celtiberio, ria; celtíbero, ra, *n.* & *a.* Celtiberian.

celticismo, *m.* Celticism.

céltico, ca, *a.* Celtic.

celtista, *n.* Celtist.

celtohispánico, ca; celtohispano, na, *a.* Celtic-Spanish. Celto-Spanish (s. o. remains of the old Celtic civilization in Spain).

célula, *f.* cell.—**celular, celulario, ia,** *a.* cellular.

celulilla, *f. dim.* very small cell or cavity.

celuloide, *m.* celluloid.

celulosa, *f.* cellulose, woody fibre.

celuloso, sa, *a.* cellulose, containing cells.

cellenco, ca, *a.* (coll.) decrepit.

cellisca, *f.* fine rain, snow, or sleet driven by a heavy wind.

cellisquear, *vn.* to sleet, to be squally with fine snow or rain.

cello, *m.* hoop used in cooperage.

cementación, *f.* cementation.

cementar, *va.* (metal.) to cement; convert; to subject to the process of cementation.

cementerio, *m.* cemetery, graveyard.

cemento, *m.* cement; (metal.) cement, substance used in converting metals; cementing material. —**c. armado,** reinforced concrete.—**c. de Pórtland** (more commonly **c. pórtland**), Portland cement.

cementoso, sa, *a.* cementing; cementlike.

cena, *f.* supper; by extension, the Last Supper.

cenaaoscuras, *n.* recluse; miser.

cenáculo, *m.* cenacle.

cenacho, *m.* basket for fruit and greens.

cenadero, *m.* supper room; summerhouse.

cenador, *m.* one fond of suppers; summerhouse in a garden; arbor, bower; gallery around a courtyard.

cenagal, *m.* slough, quagmire; arduous, unpleasant affair.

cenagoso, sa, *a.* muddy, miry, marshy.

cenar, *va.* to sup.

cenceño, ña, *a.* lean, thin, slender.

cencerra, *f.* = CENCERRO.

cencerrada, *f.* charivari; tin-pan serenade.

cencerrear, *vn.* to jingle continually; to play on an untuned guitar; to make a din or rattling noise.

cencerreo, *m.* noise made by mule or cow bells.

cencerro, *m.* bell worn by the leading wether or cow; ill-tuned guitar; (ora.) wood crow.—**c. zumbón,** bell borne by the leading horse or mule.—**a cencerros tapados,** on the sly, quietly, by stealth.

cencerrón, *m.* small bunch of grapes remaining ungathered.

cencido, da, *a.* untilled, uncultivated.

cencro, *m.* a Brazilian serpent.

cendal, *m.* light thin stuff made of silk or thread; gauze; scarf used by priests in consecrating the host; barbs of a feather.—*pl.* cotton for an inkstand.

cendea, *f.* (prov.) in Navarre, municipal borough composed of several villages.

cendra, cendrada, *f.* bone-dust paste used for cupels. —**ser una c.,** (met.) to be lively as a cricket.

cenefa, *f.* border; band or stripe on the edge of a stuff; middle piece of a priest's chasuble; rim, hangings, flounce, trimming; (naut.) top rim; paddle-box rim; awning.

cení, *m.* fine brass or bronze.

cenia, *f.* water-elevating machine; well wheel and axle; garden watered from a well with a wheel and axle.

cenicero, *m.* ash hole, ash pit, ash pan.

cenicienta, *f.* thing or person unjustly despised or ill treated.—**la C.,** Cinderella.

ceniciento, ta, *a.* ash-color red.

cenicilla, *f.* (bot.) oidium.

cenit, *m.* (ast.) zenith.—**cenital,** *a.* zenith. (u. a.)

ceniza, *f.* ashes, cinders.—**cenizas azules,** blue paint; lapis lazuli.—**cenizas de estaño,** putty. —**cenizas de vegetales,** potash.—**cenizas graveladas,** weed ashes.

cenizal, *m.* heap of ashes.

cenizo, *m.* (bot.) white goosefoot.

cenizo, za, *a.* ash-colored.

cenizoso, sa, *a.* ashy; covered with ashes.

cenobial, *a.* cenobial.—**cenobio,** *m.* cenoby.

cenobita, *m.* Cenobite, monk.

cenobítico, ca, *a.* cenobitical.

cenojil, *m.* garter.

cenopegias, *f. pl.* the feast of tabernacles among the Jews.

cenotafio, *m.* cenotaph.

cenote, *m.* cenote, a water reservoir in a cave.

cenozoico, ca, *a.* (geol.) Cenozoic.

censal, *n.* & *a.* V. CENSO and CENSUAL.

censalista, *m.* = CENSUALISTA.

censatario, ria ; censero, ra, *n.* one who pays an annuity out of his estate; lessee.

censo, *m.* census; agreement for settling an annuity on a person; annual rent; lease; rental;

income; polltax among the Romans.—**c. al quitar, or redimible,** quit rent or annuity that can be paid at once by a certain sum.—**c. de agua,** water tax.—**c. de por vida,** life annuity.

censontli, censontle, *m.* (Mex.) mocking bird.

censor, *m.* censor, critic; censorious person.

censorio, ria, *a.* censorian.

censual, *a.* belonging to a lease, annuity, or rent; rental; belonging to lawful interest.

censualista, *m.* lessor, annuitant.

censura, *f.* censorship; office of a censor, and act of censoring; review (of a book); censure, blame, reproach; gossiping; censure, spiritual punishment.

censurable, *a.* blamable, reprehensible, blameworthy.

censurador, ra ; censurante, *n.* & *a.* critic (-al); faultfinder (-ing), censor (-ing).

censurar, *va.* to review, criticise, judge; to censure, blame; to accuse, reprehend; to find fault with.

centaura, centaurea, *f.* (bot.) centaury.—**c. mayor,** great centaury.—**c. menor,** common erythræa.

centauro, *m.* (myth.) centaur; (C-, ast.) Centaur.

centavo, *m.* hundredth (part); cent.

centella, *f.* lightning; thunderbolt; flash of a flint struck with steel; flake of fire; remaining spark of passion, smoldering fire (fig.).

centellador, ra, *a.* brilliant, flashing.

centellante, *a.* sparkling, flashing.

centellar, or centellear, *vn.* to sparkle, to flash; to twinkle.

centelleo, *m.* sparkling, glittering; twinkling.

centellica, ita, *f. dim.* small flash or spark.

centellón, *m. aug.* large spark or flash.

centén, *m.* an old Spanish gold coin worth about 25 pesetas.

centena, *f.* hundred.

centenadas.—a c., by hundreds.

centenal, *m.* rye field; hundred.

centenar, *m.* hundred; rye field.—**a centenares,** by hundreds.

centenario, ria. I. *a.* centenary; secular. **II.** *m.* centennial.

centenazo, za, *a.* belonging to rye.

centenero, ra, *a.* good for rye (s. o. land, soil).

centeno, *m.* (bot.) rye.

centeno, na, *a.* hundredth.

centenoso, sa, *a.* mixed with rye.

centesimal, *a.* centesimal; between one and one hundred.

centésimo, ma, *n.* & *a.* hundredth.

centiárea, *f.* centiare (square metre).

centigrado, da, *a.* centigrade.

centigramo, *m.* centigram.

centilitro, *m.* centiliter.

centiloquio, *m.* centiloquy, a work divided into a hundred parts.

centímano, na, *a.* (poet.) hundred-handed, having a hundred hands.

centímetro, *m.* centimeter.

céntimo. I. *m.* centime; hundredth part of a monetary unit. **II.** *n.* & *a.* hundredth.

centinela, *com.* (mil.) sentry, sentinel; person on watch.—**c. a caballo,** vidette, sentinel on horseback.—**c. avanzado,** advance guard.—**c. de vista,** prisoner's guard.—**c. perdida,** forlorn hope.— **estar de c.,** or **hacer c.,** to stand sentry, to be on guard.

centinodia, *f.* (bot.) knot grass, persicaria.

centípedo, *m.* centipede.

centiplicado, da, *a.* centuple, hundredfold.

centola, centolla, *f.* center fish, a marine crab with spotted scales.

centón, *m.* crazy quilt; coarse covering of war engine in old times; cento, a literary composition.

centrado, da, *a.* centered.

central, *a.* central, centric.

centralismo, *m.* centralism.

centralista, *n.* & *a.* centralist (-ic).

centralización, *f.* centralization.
centralizar, *va.* (*pret.* CENTRALICÉ: *subj.* CEN-TRALICE) to centralize.
centralmente, *adv.* centrally.
centrar, *va.* to center.
céntrico, ca, *a.* central.
centrífugo, ga. I. *a.* centrifugal. **II.** *f.* centrifugal machine.
centrípeto, ta, *a.* centripetal.
centro, *m.* center; middle, midst; innermost part, core; (mil.) center of an army; height and depth of a thing; main office, headquarters; (pol.) center; principal object of desire and exertion; social circle in which a person moves; (bot.) disk of flowers; short flannel dress worn by Indian women in Ecuador.—**c. de gravedad,** center of gravity.—**centros nerviosos,** nervous centers.—**estar en su c.,** to be satisfied.
centroamericano, na, *n.* & *a.* Central-American.
centrobárico, ca, *a.* centrobaric.
centunviral, *a.* centumviral.—**centunvirato,** *m.* centumvirate.—**centunviro,** *m.* centumvir.
centuplicar, *va.* to centuplicate.
céntuplo, pla, *a.* centuple.
centuria, *f.* century (period of time; division of Roman army).
centurión, *m.* centurion.
centurionazgo, *m.* office of a centurion.
cenzalino, na, *a.* pertaining to mosquitoes.
vénzalo, *m.* (ent.) mosquito.
ceñido, da. I. *a.* moderate in pleasure or expense; narrow-waisted; beelike-waisted. **II.** *pp.* of CEÑIR.
ceñidor, *m.* belt, girdle, cest, sash.
ceñidura, *f.* act of girding.
ceñiglo, *m.* (bot.) white goosefoot, summer cypress.
ceñir. I. *va.* (*ind.* CIÑO: *subj.* CIÑA) to gird, surround, girdle; to hem in; to condense, abbreviate.—**c. el viento,** (naut.) to haul the wind.—**c. espada,** to wear a sword. **II.** *vr.* to reduce one's expenses; to confine or limit one's self.
ceño, *m.* frown; browbeating; supercilious look; ring, hoop, band; (vet.) circle round the upper part of a horse's hoof; (poet.) gloomy aspect.
ceñoso, sa; ceñudo, da, *a.* frowning; browbeating; supercilious; grim, gruff.
ceo, *m.* (zool.) doree, dory.
cepa, *f.* underground butt end of a tree stem; stump, stub; vinestock; stock or origin of a family; bud or root of the horns and tails of animals; (arch.) pier of an arch; (agr.) sole of a plow; (car.) tongue of a pole.—**de buena c.,** of acknowledged good quality; on good authority.
cepacaballo, *m.* (bot.) cardoon.
cepeda, *f.* land overgrown with heath.
cepejón, *m.* butt end of a branch torn from the trunk.
cepellón, *m.* ball left around the roots of a plant for transplanting.
cepera, *f.* inflammation of the hoofs; CEPEDA.
cepilladura, *f.* = ACEPILLADURA.
cepillar, *va.* = ACEPILLAR.
cepillo, *m.* brush; (carp.) plane; charity box, poor-box corban.—**c. bocel,** fluting plane; modelling plane.—**c. de dientes,** toothbrush.—**c. de ropa,** clothesbrush.—**c. para la cabeza,** hairbrush.—**c. para ropa,** clothesbrush.
cepo, *m.* bough or branch off a tree; stock of an anvil; stocks, for punishment; (naut.) bilboes; stock (of an anchor); reel for winding silk; trap, snare; charity box; (mil.) stocks of a gun carriage; (mech.) block; socket; clasp, clamp; joining press; shoemaker's horse; (zool.) = CEPO.—*pl.* notch cleats.—**c. colombiano,** or **c. de campaña,** (Am.) an old form of military punishment in which the thumbs were tied together, the knees put between the arms, and one or two rifles placed on the arms between these and the legs.—**c. de maniguetes,** (naut.) crosspiece of the kevel.—**c. de molinete,** (naut.) knighthead of the windlass.—**¡cepos quedos!** keep still! keep quiet! cut it out!
cepón, *m. aug.* large stub of a tree or vinestock.

ceporro, *m.* old vine pulled up for fuel.
cequí, *m.* an ancient gold coin.
cequión, *m.* (Ch.) large ditch or channel.
cera, *f.* wax; beeswax; wax tapers and candles.—*pl.* honeycomb.—**c. aleda,** propolis, bee glue.—**c. de dorar,** gold size.—**c. de higos,** drum of figs.—**c. de los oídos,** earwax, cerumen.—**c. virgen,** virgin wax.—**no hay más e. que la que arde,** there is nothing more than what you see.—**ser como una c., ser una c., estar hecho de c.,** to be very condescending, very docile, very "easy."
ceráceo, ea, *a.* ceraceous.
cerachates, *f. pl.* wax stones.
cerafolio, *m.* (bot.) common chervil.
cerambícido, da. I. *n.* & *a.* (zool.) cerambycid. **II.** *m. pl.* Cerambycidæ.
cerámica, *f.* ceramic art; ceramics.
cerámico, ca, *a.* ceramic, relating to pottery.
ceramista, *m.* ceramist.
ceramita, *f.* a precious stone; a kind of brick of exceedingly high strength.
cerapez, *f.* cerate, plaster of wax and pitch.
cerasina, *f.* cerasin.
cerasta, *f.,* **ceraste, cerastes,** *m.* cerastes, a horned serpent.
cerastio de granada, *m.* (bot.) white mouse-ear chickweed.
ceratias, *m.* double-tailed comet.
cerato, *m.* (pharm.) cerate.
cerbatana, *f.* blowgun, popgun, pea-shooter; ear trumpet for the deaf; small culverin.
cerbero, *m.* = CANCERBERO.
cerca, *f.* fence; hedge.
cerca, *adv.* near, close by, nigh. Preceding a noun, pronoun, or adverb, it requires **de**) *cerca de París,* near Paris; *cerca de aquí,* near here (but *aquí cerca,* near here).—**c. de** (when not used as explained), nearly, about.—**de c.,** closely.—**por aquí c.,** near here, somewhere near here.
cercado, da. I. *a.* inclosed, fenced in, walled in. **II.** *m.* garden or field fenced in; inclosure; fence; lock. **III.** *pp.* of CERCAR.
cercador, *m.* hedger, fencer; iron graver; marking iron; blunt chisel for repoussé work.
cercanamente, *adv.* near, nearly.
cercanía, *f.* proximity; (gen. *pl.*) neighborhood, vicinity, surroundings.
cercano, na (w. **de** before noun, etc.) *a.* near, neighboring; close.
cercar, *va.* (*pret.* CERQUÉ: *subj.* CERQUE) to hem, circle, compass, gird; to surround; to fence in, hedge in, wall in; to pale; (mil.) to invest, lay siege to; to crowd about.
cercén.—a c., all around.
cercenadamente, *adv.* with retrenchment.
cercenadera, *f.* clipping knife used by waxchandlers.—**cercenador,** *m.* clipper.—**cercenadura,** *f.* clipping, retrenchment.—*pl.* cuttings.
cercenar, *va.* to pare, clip; to lop off the ends or extremities of; to lessen, reduce, curtail, cut down.
cercera, *f.* air tube of a vault.
cerceta, *f.* (orn.) widgeon, garganey, a species of duck.—*pl.* first growth of a deer's antlers.
cercillo, *m.* tendril of a vine.
cerciorar. I. *va.* to assure, affirm. **II.** *vr.* to make sure.
cerco, *m.* fence; hoop, ring; rim, border, edge; halo; (mil.) blockade, siege; circular motion; circle of people; frame or case of a door or window.—**alzar,** or **levantar, el c.,** to raise a blockade.—**poner c. a,** to lay siege to, to blockade.
cercopiteco, *m.* (zool.) cercopithecus, an African monkey.
cercha, *f.* flexible wooden rule for measuring curved objects; (arch.) form or center for building arches; (carp.) segment of a rim.
cerchar, *va.* = ACODAR.
cerchón, *m.* = CIMBRA.
cerda, *f.* horse's hair; bristle; (zool.) sow; newmown cereals; bundle of flax broken but not yet hackled.—*pl.* snares for birds.—**c. de puerco,** hog's bristle.

cerdamen, _m._ bristles prepared for brushes.

cerdear, _vn._ to be weak in the fore quarter; to emit a harsh and inharmonious sound; (coll.) to decline a request or demand; to look for excuses.

cerdito, _m. dim._ little pig.

cerdo, _m._ hog.—**c. de muerte,** pig old enough to be slaughtered.—**c. de vida,** pig not old enough to be slaughtered.

cerdoso, sa; cerdudo, da, _a._ bristly; hairy.

cereal, _n._ & _a._ cereal.

cerebelitis, _f._ cerebellitis, inflamation of the cerebellum.

cerebelo, _m._ (anat.) cerebellum.

cerebral, _a._ cerebral.

cerebrina, _f._ (chem.) cerebrin.

cerebritis, _f._ cerebritis, inflamation of the cerebrum.

cerebro, _m._ cerebrum; brain.

cerebroespinal, _a._ cerebrospinal.

cereceda, _f._ = CEREZAL.

cerecilla, _f. dim._ = GUINDILLA.

cerecita, _f. dim._ small.cherry.

ceremonia, _f._ ceremony; pomp, display; formality; ceremoniousness; compliment.—**de c.,** with all due ceremony; formal; full, evening (u. a.—s. o. dress).—**guardar c.,** to comply with the formalities; to be formal.—**por c.,** simply as a matter of form or of etiquette.

ceremonial. I. _m._ book of ceremonies for public occasions. **II.** _a._ ceremonial, ceremonious.

ceremonialmente, _adv._ with all ceremony.

ceremoniáticamente, _adv._ ceremoniously.

ceremoniático, ca, _a._ ceremonious.

ceremoniosamente, _adv._ ceremoniously.

ceremonioso, sa, _a._ ceremonious, formal.

céreo, _m._ (bot.) torch thistle.

cereolita, _f._ soft, waxlike lava.

cerería, _f._ wax chandler's shop; chandlery in the royal palace.

cerero, ra, _n._ wax chandler.—**c. mayor,** royal chandler.

cereza, _f._ cherry.—**c. garrafal,** large white-heart cherry, bigaroon.

cerezal, _m._ cherry orchard.

cerezo, _m._ (bot.) cherry tree; cherry wood.—**c. silvestre,** dog-cherry tree.

cergazo, _m._ (bot.) rockrose, cistus.

cérico, ca, _a._ ceric, relating to cerium.

céridos, _m. pl._ (chem.) cerium metals.

cerífero, ra, _a._ ceriferous.

ceriflor, _f._ (bot.) honeywort, honeyflower.

cerilla, _f._ wax taper in rolls; wax match; a kind of cosmetic; cold cream; wax tablet; earwax.

cerillera, _f._ lamplighter with a taper.

cerillo, _m._ (Mex.) wax match.

cerina, _f._ a variety of wax or waxlike material extracted from the cork tree.

cerinto, _m._ (bot.) wax flower, honeywort.

cerio, _m._ (chem.) cerium.

cerita, _f._ (min.) cerite.

cermeña, _f._ small early pear; muscadine.

cermeño, _m._ (bot.) muscadine pear tree.

cernada, _f._ cinder; leached ashes; size on canvas for painting; (vet.) plaster of ashes and other ingredients.

cernadero, _m._ coarse linen strainer for lye; an old linen or silk-and-linen fabric for collars.

cernedero, _m._ apron worn in sifting flour; place for sifting flour.—**cernedor,** _m._ sifter.

cerneja, _f._ fetlock of a horse.

cernejudo, da, _a._ having large fetlocks.

cerner. I. _va._ (_ind._ CIERNO: _subj._ CIERNA) to sift; to bolt. **II.** _vn._ to bud and blossom; to drizzle; to mizzle. **III.** _vr._ to waggle, wiggle, waddle; to soar.

cernícalo, _m._ (orn.) kestrel; sparrow-hawk; person of scanty abilities.—**coger,** or **pillar, un c.,** (coll.) to get drunk.

cernidillo, _m._ drizzle; short and waddling gait.

cernido. I. _n._ sifting; the flour sifted. **II.** _pp._ of CERNER.

cernidura, _f._ sifting.

cernir, _va._ = CERNER.

cero, _m._ zero; cipher; naught.—**ser un c.,** or **un c. a la izquierda,** to be a mere cipher, to be insignificant or of no account, not to count.

ceroferario, _m._ acolyte bearing a candelabrum.

cerografía, _f._ cerography.

cerógrafo, _m._ (arch.) wax seal used by the Romans.

ceroleína, _f._ cerolein, a constituent of beeswax.

cerollo, lla, _a._ reaped when green and soft.

ceroma, _m._ ceroma, an unguent used by Roman athletes.

ceromancía, _f._ ceromancy.

ceromiel, _m._ ceromel.

cerón, _m._ dross of wax.

ceroplástica, _f._ ceroplastics.

cerotato, _m._ (chem.) cerotate.

cerótico, ca, _a._ cerotic.

cerote, _m._ shoemaker's wax; shoeblacking; (coll.) panic; fear.

ceroto, _m._ (pharm.) soft cerate of oil and wax.

cerquillo, _m. dim._ small circle or hoop; seam or welt of a shoe; ring of hair or tonsure; hair bangs.

cerquita. I. _f. dim._ small fence or inclosure. **II.** _adv._ at a small distance; very near.—**aquí c.,** close by, very near here.

cerrada, _f._ hide or skin covering the backbone.

cerradera, _f._, **cerradero,** _m._ bolt staple; catch of a lock; catch, clasp; purse strings.—**echar la cerradera,** to lend a deaf ear; to refuse point-blank.

cerradero, ra, _n._ & _a._ applied to the place locked, and to the thing with which it is locked.

cerradizo, za, _a._ that may be locked or fastened.

cerrado, _m._ = CERCADO.

cerrado, da. I. _a._ incomprehensible, obscure; close, reserved; dissembling; secreted, concealed; obstinate; inflexible; cloudy, overcast; stupid, thick; dense. **II.** _pp._ of CERRAR.

cerrador, _m._ shutter; locker; lock; any contrivance that shuts or locks.

cerradura, _f._ lock; closure; act of shutting or locking.—**c. de golpe,** or **de muelle,** spring lock. —**c. embutida,** mortise lock.

cerraja, _f._ lock of a door; bolt; (bot.) common sow-thistle.

cerrajear, _vn._ to work as, or to be, a locksmith.

cerrajería, _f._ trade of a locksmith; locksmith's shop or forge.

cerrajero, _m._ locksmith.

cerrajón, _m._ steep, craggy cliff.

cerramiento, _m._ closure, occlusion; act of shutting or locking; costiveness; inclosure; (arch.) roof; (mas.) partition wall.

cerrar. I. _va._ & _vn._ (_ind._ CIERRO: _subj._ CIERRE) to close, shut, fasten, lock; stop up; obstruct; block up; blind; inclose, include, contain; fence in; to fold and seal (a letter).—**c. la boca,** to be silent, shut up.—**c. los oídos,** to turn a deaf ear. —**c. los ojos,** to close one's eyes; die; sleep; to be stubborn.—**al c. del día,** at the close of day, at nightfall. **II.** _vr._ to close; to remain firm in one's opinion; to become cloudy and overcast; to close up, get close to each other.—**cerrársele a uno todas las puertas,** to find all avenues closed.

cerrazón, _f._ dark and cloudy weather preceding a storm.

cerrejón, _m._ hillock.

cerrero, ra, _a._ wild; untamed; unbroken (s. o. horses).

cerreta, _f._ (naut.) spar; rough tree.

cerril, _a._ mountainous; rough, uneven; wild, untamed, unbroken; (coll.) unpolished, rough, boorish.

cerrilla, _f._ die for milling.—**cerrillar,** _va._ to mill (coined metal).—**cerrillo,** _m. dim._ little eminence. —_pl._ dies for milling.

cerrión, _m._ icicle.

cerro, _m._ hill; peak; neck of an animal; backbone; hackled and cleaned flax or hemp.—**c. enriscado,** steep, rugged hill.—**en c.,** bareback; nakedly, without the proper or usual trappings.—**por los cerros de Ubeda,** (coll.) foreign to the purpose, irrelevant, (coll.) off the track.

cérrojillo, *m.* (orn.) wagtail, warbler; small bolt or latch.

cerrojo, *m.* bolt, latch.

cerrón, *m.* a kind of coarse fabric made in Galicia.

cerruma, *f.* weak or defective quarter in horses.

certamen, *m.* literary contest; disputation; competition; (obs.) duel, battle.

certero, ra, *a.* well-aimed; good shot (shooter); sure; well-informed; skillful.

certeza, *f.* certainty, assurance.

certidumbre, *f.* certainty, conviction.

certificación, *f.* certificate, affidavit.

certificado, *n.* certificate, attestation, testimonial.

certificador, ra, *n.* & *a.* certifier (-ying).

certificar, *va.* (*pret.* CERTIFIQUÉ: *subj.* CERTIFIQUE) to certify, attest; to register (a letter); (law) to prove by a public instrument.

certificatorio, ria, *a.* that certifies or serves to certify.

certísimo, *a. sup.* of CIERTO: most certain.

cerúleo, lea, *a.* cerulean, sky-blue.

ceruma, *f.* (vet.) = CERRUMA.

cerumen, *m.* earwax, cerumen.

cerusa, *f.* ceruse, white lead.

cerval, *a.* belonging to deer.

cervantesco, ca; cervántico, ca; cervantino, na, *a.* like, or in the style of, Cervantes; relating or peculiar to Cervantes.

cervantista, *n.* expert in matters relating to Cervantes (may be called *Cervantian, Cervantist,* or *Cervantes scholar*).

cervario, ria, *a.* = CERVAL.

cervatica, *f.* = LANGOSTÓN.

cervatico, illo, *m. dim.* small deer.

cervato, *m.* fawn.

cervecería, *f.* brewhouse, brewery; alehouse, beer-saloon.—**cervecero, ra,** *n.* brewer; beer seller.

cerveza, *f.* beer, ale.

cervicabra, *f.* gazelle.

cervical; cérvico, ca, *a.* (anat.) cervical.

cérvido, da. I. *a.* (zoöl.) cervine, relating to deer or cervids. **II.** *n.* cervid. **III.** *m. pl.* Cervidæ.

cervigudo, da, *a.* high- or thick-necked.

cerviguillo, *m.* thick nape of the neck.

cervillera, *f.* helmet.

cervino, na, *a.* deerlike.

cerviz, *f.* cervix, nape of the neck.—**bajar,** or **doblar, la c.,** to humble one's self.—**levantar la c.,** to be elated, to grow proud.—**ser de dura c.,** to be incorrigible or stubborn.

cervuno, na, *a.* resembling or belonging to deer; deer-colored.

cesación, *f.,* **cesamiento,** *m.* cessation, discontinuance, stopping, pause.—**c. a divinis,** suspension from religious functions.

cesante. I. *n.* dismissed public officer, in some cases with a pension; retired official. **II.** *a.* ceasing.

cesantía, *f.* state of a retired official; the pension he receives.

cesar, *vn.* to cease, stop; to desist; to retire; to leave a post or employment.

cesáreo, rea, cesariano, na, *a.* Cæsarean.—**cesarismo,** *m.* Cæsarism.—**cesarista, n.** & *a.* Cæsarist (-ic).

cese, *m.* cease; stop of pension.

cesible, *a.* (law) transferable.

cesio, (chem.) cæsium.

cesión, *f.* cession, transfer, conveyance; resignation; concession.—**c. de bienes,** surrender of property.

cesionario, ria, *n.* cessionary, grantee, assignee, transferree.

cesionista, *n.* transferrer, assigner, grantor.

cesonario, ria, *n.*=CESIONARIO.

césped, céspede, *m.* turf, sod, clod, sward, grass; grass plot, lawn; rind of a vine where it has been pruned.

cespedera, *f.* field where green sods are cut.

cespitar, *vn.* to hesitate.

cesta, *f.* basket, pannier, hamper; scoop or racket fastened to the arm for playing ball.—**cestada,** *f.* basketful.—**cestería,** *f.* basket factory or shop.—**cestero, ra,** *n..* basket maker or seller.

cestiaro, *m.* Roman pugilist who fought with the cestus.

cestica, illa, ita, *f. dim.;* **cestico, illo, ito,** *m. dim.* small basket; hand basket.

cesto, *m.* hand basket, maund, hutch; cestus used by Roman boxers.—**coger agua en c.,** to labor in vain.—**estar hecho un c.,** (coll.) to be overcome by sleep or liquor.—**quien hace un c. hará ciento,** he that steals a pin will steal a pound.—**ser un c.,** (coll.) to be ignorant and rude.

céstodo. I. *n.* & *a.* (zoöl.) cestode. **II.** *m. pl.* Cestoda.

cestón, *m. aug.* large pannier or basket; (mil.) gabion.—*pl.* corbeils.

cestonada, *f.* range of gabions.

cesura, *f.* cæsura, pause in poetry.

cetáceo, cea. I. *n.* & *a.* cetacean. **II.** *m. pl.* Cetaceæ.

cetilo, *m.* (chem.) cetyl.

cetina, *f.* whale oil, sperm oil.

cetís, *m.* an old Portuguese coin.

cetra, *f.* leather shield formerly used.

cetre, *m.* assistant acolyte.

cetrería, *f.* falconry, hawking; fowling with falcons.

cetrero, *m.* verger, falconer; sportsman.

cetrino, na, *a.* citrine, lemon-colored; jaundiced, melancholy; belonging to citron.

cetro, *m.* sceptre; reign of a prince; verge borne by canons on solemn occasions; wand or staff; perch or roost for birds.—**empuñar el c.,** to ascend the throne, to begin to reign.

ceugma, *f.* (rhet.) zeugma.

cía, *f.* hip bone, huckle bone.

ciaboga, *f.* (naut.) putting a row galley about with the oars.—**hacer c.,** to turn the back, to flee.

cianato, *m.* (chem.) cyanate.—**ciánico, ca,** *a.* cyanic.

cianhídrico, ca, *a.* hydrocyanic.

ciánico, ca, *a.* cyanic.

cianógeno, m. cyanogen.

cianosis, *f.* cyanosis.

cianuración, *f.* (metal.) cyaniding.

cianuro, *m.* (chem.) cyanide.

ciar, *vn.* to back up, retrograde; (naut.) to hold water, to back off, to go astern; to slacken, slow down.

ciática, *f.* (med.) sciatica.

ciático, ca, *a.* sciatic, sciatical.

ciato, *m.* (bot.) a tropical tree fern.

cibario, ria, *a.* cibarious, relating to food.

cibéleo, lea, *a.* belonging to the goddess Cybele.

cibera, *f.* quantity of wheat put at once in the hopper; all seeds or grains fit for food; bagasse of grain, fruit, husks, etc.; hopper in a cornmill.

cibica, *f.* clout; hurter of a wooden axle tree; (naut.) staple, cramp.

cibicón, *m.* large kind of clout.

cíbolo, la, *n.* bison.

cibui, *m.* (Peru) a variety of cedar.

cicadáceo, a; cicádido, da. I. *n.* & *a.* (bot.) cycad. **II.** *f. pl.* Cycadaceæ.

cicatear, *vn.* (coll.) to be sordidly parsimonious.

cicatería, *f.* niggardliness, stinginess.

cicatero, ra, *a.* niggardly, stingy.

cicateruelo, la, *n. dim.* stingy little person; little miser; curmudgeon.

cicatricera, *f.* a woman who used to follow troops and tend the wounded.

cicatricilla, *f. dim.* small scar.

cicatriz, *f.* cicatrice, scar.—**cicatrización,** *f.* cicatrization.—**cicatrizal,** *a.* cicatricial.—**cicatrizante,** *n.* & *a.* cicatrisant.

cicatrizar, *va.* & *vn.* (*pret.* CICATRICÉ: *subj.* CICATRICE) to cicatrize; to heal.

cicatrizativo, va, *a.* cicatrisive.

cicércula, cicercha, *f.* = ALMORTA.

cícero, *m.* (print.) pica; (print.) unit of measurement for type bodies, equivalent to 12 points.

cicerone, n. cicerone, guide.

ciceroniano, na, a. Ciceronian.

ciclamor, m. an ornamental tree.

ciclatón, m. tunic formerly worn by women.

cíclico, ca, a. cyclical.

ciclismo, m. wheeling as a sport.

ciclista, n. cyclist, rider on a bicycle.

ciclo, m. cycle.

cicloidal, cycloidal.—**cicloide,** f. cycloid.

ciclometría, f. cyclometry.

ciclométrico, ca, a. cyclometric.

ciclómetro, m. cyclometer.

ciclón, m. cyclone.

Cíclope, m. Cyclops.—**ciclópeo, a,** a. Cyclopean.

ciclorama, m. cyclorama.

ciclóstilo, m. cyclostyle.

ciclóstomas, m. pl. (zoöl.) Cylostomata.

cicuta (bot.) hemlock, cicuta; water hemlock; spotted cowbane.

cid, m. leader, chief.—**el C.,** or **el C. Campeador,** El Cid, a title of the Spanish hero Rodrigo Díaz de Vivar.

cidra, f. (bot.) citron.

cidracayote, f. (bot.) American gourd or calabash.

cidrada, f. preserve made with citrons.

cidral, m. plantation of citron trees.

cidria, m. = CEDRIA.

cidro, m. (bot.) citron tree.

cidronela, f. citronella, common balm.

ciegamente, adv. blindly.

ciegayernos, m. showy but wortniess thing; humbug.

ciego, ga. I. a. blind; choked or closed; blinded.—**c. de,** blind with, blinded by.—**a ciegas,** blindly, in the dark; thoughtlessly. II. n. blind person; (anat.) cæcum or blind gut; large black pudding.

ciego, ciegue. V. CEGAR.

cieguecico, ica; illo, illa; ito, ita; cieguezuelo, ela, n. dim. little blind person.

cielito, m. S. A. tune and dance; darling, dearest, dearie.

cielo, m. sky, firmament; heaven(s); atmosphere, climate; ceiling; glory, felicity; paradise; roof; cover; canopy (of a bed).—**c. raso,** flat ceiling; clear sky.—**c. de la boca,** roof of the palate.—**a c. descubierto,** in the open air; in the open, openly.—**a c. raso,** in the open air.—**escupir al c.,** to do bad deeds that turn against the doer, to throw a boomerang (fig.).—**estar hecho un c.,** to be splendid, brilliant.—**llovido del c.,** godsend.—**poner en,** or **por, el c.,** to praise to the utmost, to lionize.—**tomar el c. con las manos,** to be carried away with joy, grief, etc.—**un c. alegre,** a clear, beautiful sky.—**venirse el c. abajo,** to pour, rain pitchforks.—**ver el c. abierto,** to find an unforeseen opportunity.—**ver el c. por embudo,** not to know the world.

ciempiés, m. centipede; mediocre literary work.

cien, a. one hundred (used before nouns instead of ciento, as, cien hombres, a hundred men; cien mujeres, a hundred women). V. CIENTO.

ciénaga, f. marsh, moor, miry place.

ciencia, f. science; knowledge; certainty.—**ciencias exactas,** exact sciences.—**ciencias naturales,** natural science.—**a c. cierta,** with certainty, knowingly.—**a c. y paciencia de,** with the knowledge and connivance of.

cienmilésimo, ma, n. & a. hundred-thousandth.

cienmilmillonésimo, ma, n. & a. hundred-thousand millionth.

cienmillonésimo, ma, n., a. hundred-millionth.

cieno, m. mud, mire, slime; slough, bog.

científicamente, adv. scientifically.

científico, ca. I. a. scientific. II. n. scientist.

ciento. I. a. (v. CIEN) one hundred; one hundredth (calle ciento, One-hundredth Street). II. m. a hundred. (Gen. without the article: tengo ciento, I have a hundred; somos ciento, we are a hundred. When used with the article before a noun, it is followed by de: un ciento de libros, a hundred books).—pl. tax assessed at so much per cent.; piquet, a card game.—**por c.,** per cent; by

the hundred.—**por cientos,** by hundreds, by the hundred; in large number.

cientopiés, m. (zoöl.) centipede.

cierna, f. the staminate blossom of vines, corn, and some other plants.

cierne,—en c., in blossom; in its infancy.

cierno, cierne. V. CERNER.

¡cierra España! interj. war cry of the ancient Spaniards.

cierre, m. act and mode of closing; shutting, locking, fastening; snap; clasp; plug of a valve.—**c. hidráulico,** hydraulic seal, water seal.

cierro, m. inclosure.—**c. de cristales,** glass-covered balcony or veranda.

cierro, cierre. V. CERRAR.

ciertamente, adv. certainly, surely.

cierto, ta. I. a. certain, doubtless; sure, positive; true. When used indefinitely, it does not gen. take the article: cierto lugar, a certain place.—**de c.,** certainly, surely; in earnest.—**no por c.,** certainly not.—**por c., sí por c.,** certainly, surely, yes indeed. II. adv. certainly.

cierva, f. hind, female stag.—**ciervo,** m. deer, hart, stag.—**c. volante,** stag beetle.

cierzo, m. cold northerly wind.

cifosis, f. (med.) outward bending of the spine.

cifra, f. figure, number, numerical character; cipher, code, cryptogram; monogram, device, emblem; sum total; contraction, abbreviation; music written with numbers.—**en c.,** secretly, mysteriously; briefly, concisely.

cifrar, va. to write in cipher; to abridge.—**c. en,** to place (one's hopes, etc.) on; to make (a thing) depend on.

cigarra, f. (ent.) cicada, harvest fly.

cigarral, m. in Toledo, orchard or fruit garden.

cigarrera, f. cigar cabinet or showcase; pocket cigarcase.

cigarrero, ra, n. cigar maker or dealer.

cigarrería, f. cigar shop.

cigarrillo, m. cigarette.

cigarrista, n. hard smoker.

cigarro, m. cigar; (in some places) cigarette.—**c. de papel,** cigarette.—**c. puro,** cigar.

cigarrón, m. aug. large cicada.

cigomático, ca, a. zygomatic.

cigoñal, m. well sweep.

cigoñino, m. (orn.) young stork.

cigoñuela, f. (orn.) small storklike bird.

cigua, f. (bot.) a tropical tree.

ciguatarse, vr. = ACIGUATARSE.

ciguatera, f. (Mex.) a kind of jaundice, from eating diseased fish.

ciguato, ta, a. suffering from CIGUATERA.

cigüeña, f. (orn.) white stork; crane; bell crank; (mach.) crank, winch.

cigüeñal, m. CIGOÑAL; (int. comb. eng.) crankshaft.

cigüeñuela, f. dim. small crank or winch.—**c. de la caña del timón,** (naut.) gooseneck of the tiller.

cigüete, f. a variety of white grape.

cija, f. building for sheltering sheep; dungeon; granary.

cilanco, m. pool left by a river on the shore.

cilantro, m. (bot.) coriander.

ciliado, da, a. ciliated.—**ciliar, a.** ciliary.

cilicio, m. haircloth; hair shirt.

cilindrado, a. rolled; calendered.

cilindrar, va. to roll; calender; bore; rebore.

cilindricidad, f. cylindricity.

cilíndrico, ca, a. cylindrical.

cilindro, m. cylinder; roller; press roll; chamber.

cilindroeje, m. (anat.) axis cylinder, axon.

cilindroide, m. (geom.) cylindroid.

cilindroideo, a, a. cylindroid, cylinderlike.

cilla, f. granary; tithe.

cillazgo, m. storehouse fees paid on tithes.

cillerero, m. cellarist or butler of a convent.

cilleriza, f. nun who directs the domestic affairs of a convent.

cillerizo, za, n. keeper of a granary.

cillero, *m.* keeper of a granary or storehouse for tithes; granary; vault; cellar; storeroom.

cima, *f.* summit, peak; top; cap, head; finish, completion; heart and tender sprouts of cardoons.—**dar c.,** to conclude happily.—**por c.,** in the uppermost part, at the very top.

cimacio, *m.* (arch.) cymatium, gola, ogee.

cimarrón, na. I. *a.* (Amer.) wild, unruly. **II.** *n.* runaway slave; maroon; (Arg.) black maté; (naut.) lazy sailor.

cimarronear, *vn.* (Am.) to run away; to drink black maté.

cimbalaria, *f.* (bot.) ivywort.

cimbalillo, *m. dim.* small bell.

címbalo, *m.* small bell; cymbal.

cimbanillo, *m.* = CIMBALILLO.

címbara, *f.* large sickle.

cimbel, *m.* decoy pigeon; rope used to tie decoy pigeons.

cimborio, cimborrio, *m.* (arch.) dome.

cimbra, *f.* (carp.) form. center (for an arch, etc.); (naut.) curvature; bending of a board.

cimbrado. I. *m.* quick bending movement in a Spanish dance. **II.** *pp.* of CIMBRAR.

cimbrar. I. *va.* to brandish; to shake, to sway, to bend; (carp.) to place cradlings in; (arch.) to arch; (coll.) to give a drubbing to. **II.** *vr.* to bend; vibrate.

cimbre, *m.* subterranean gallery or passage.

cimbrear, *va. & vr.* = CIMBRAR.

cimbreño, ña, *a.* pliant, flexible.

cimbreo, *m.* act of bending, brandishing, swaying, vibrating.

címbrico, ca, *a.* Cimbrian.

cimbro, bra, *n. & a.* Cimbrian.

cimbronazo, *m.* stroke with the flat of a sword (*v.* CINTARAZO); (Am.) jerk, sudden shaking.

cimentación, *f.* foundation; laying of a foundation.

cimentado, *m.* refining of gold.

cimentador, *m.* one that lays the foundation.

cimentar, *va.* (*ind.* CIMIENTO: *subj.* CIMIENTE) to lay the foundation of; to found; to ground; to establish the fundamental principles of; to refine (metals).

cimenterio, *m.* = CEMENTERIO.

cimento, *m.* cement. *V.* CEMENTO.

cimera, *f.* crest of a helmet or coat of arms.

cimerio, ria, *a.* Cimmerian.

cimero, ra, *a.* placed at the height of some elevated spot; apical.

cimiento, *m.* foundation; groundwork, bed; base; root, origin.

cimiento, cimiente. *V.* CIMENTAR.

cimillo, *m.* flexible twig on which a decoy pigeon is tied.

cimitarra, *f.* scimitar, falchion.

cimófana, *f.* cymofane, cat's-eye.

cimorra, *f.* (vet.) glanders.

cinabrio, *m.* cinnabar; vermilion.

cinamato, *m.* (chem.) cinnamate.

cinámico, *a.* (chem.) cinnamic.

cinamomo, *m.* (bot.) bead tree; (P. I.) privet.

cinc, *m.* zinc.

cinca, *f.* infraction of the rules of the game of ninepins (tenpins).

cincel, *m.* chisel; engraver; scorper; burin; drove. —**cincelador,** *m.* engraver; sculptor; stonecutter.

cincelar, *va.* to chisel, engrave, carve.

cincelito, *m. dim.* small chisel.

cinco, *n. & a.* five; fifth (app. specially to dates); five-spot card; (Ven.) five-string guitar.—**decir cuántas son c.,** to threaten with reproof or punishment; to tell (one) what is what.—**no saber cuántas son c.,** (coll.) not to know beans.

cincoenrama, *f.* (bot.) common cinquefoil.

cincograbado, *m.* zinc etching.

cincografía, *f.* zincography.

cincomesino, na, *a.* five-month old.

cincona, *f.* (bot.) cinchona.—**cinconina,** *f.* (chem.) cinchonine.

cincuenta, *n. & a.* fifty; fiftieth (*calle cincuenta,* Fiftieth Street).

cincuentavo, *n. & a.* fiftieth.

cincuentén, *m.* piece of timber fifty palms in length (50 x 3 x 2).

cincuentena, *f.* group of fifty.—**una c. de,** fifty.

cincuenteno, na, *a.* fiftieth.

cincuentón, na. I. *a.* fifty-year-old. **II.** *n.* fifty-year old person.

cincha, *f.* girth, cinch.—**cinchadura,** *f.* cinching, girthing.—**cinchar,** *va.* to girt, cinch up.— **cinchera,** *f.* girth place; (vet.) sore in the part where mules are girted.

cincho, *m.* belt, girdle, sash or bellyband; iron hoop; tire of a wheel; cheese mold; (Mex.) cinch; (arch.) transverse rib; (vet.) a growth in the hoofs of horses.

cinchón, *m. aug.* broad cinch or girth.

cinchuela, *f. dim.* small cinch or girth; narrow ribbon.

cine, *m.,* **cinema,** *m.* (coll.) cinema (moving picture, "movie").

cinegética, *f.* cynegetics, art of hunting with dogs.

cinegético, ca, *a.* cynegetic.

cinemática, *f.* kinematics.

cinemático, ca, *a.* kinematic.

cinematográfico, ca, *a.* cinematographic.

cinematografía, *f.* cinematography.

cinematógrafo, *m.* cinematograph; moving-picture play.

cineración, = INCINERACIÓN.

cinerario, ia, *a.* cinerary.

cinéreo, a; cinericio, cia, *a.* ashy; ash-colored.

cinética, *f.* kinetics.—**cinético, ca,** *a.* kinetic.

cingalés, sa, *n. & a.* Singhalese.

cíngaro, ra, *n.* gipsy.

cinglar, *va.* (metal.) to shingle, expell impurities of (iron) by hammering.

cinglador, *m.* (metal.) shingler.

cingleta, *f.* rope with a cork to buoy up a net.

cíngulo, *m.* cingulum, girdle, cordon; ancient military badge.

cínicamente, *adv.* cynically.

cínico, ca. I. *a.* cynic, cynical; satirical; impudent, barefaced. **II.** *n.* cynic.

cínife, *m.* mosquito.

cinismo, *m.* cynicisim; shamelessness, barefacedness, impudence.

cinocéfalo, *m.* (zoöl.) cynocephalus.

cinógeno, *m.* (aut.) starter.

cinoglosa, *f.* (bot.) hound's-tongue.

Cinosura, *f.* (ast.) Cynosure, Little Bear.

cinquén, *m.* an ancient Spanish coin.

cinqueño, cinquillo, *m.* game of ombre, played by five persons.

cinta, *f.* ribbon; tape, band, strip, sash; (surv.) tape; strong net for tunny fishing; lowest part of the pastern of a horse; (arch.) fillet, belt; scroll; sidewalk curb; first course of floor tiles; moving-picture film (called also **c. cinematográfica**).—**cintas de navío,** (naut.) wales.—**cintas gallmas,** bow wales or harpings.—**en c.,** under subjection.

cintadero, *m.* part of a crossbow to which the string is fastened.

cintagorda, *f.* coarse fishing net.

cintajos, *m. pl.* knot or bunch of tumbled ribbons; tawdry ornaments in female dress.

cintarazo, *m.* slap with a sword or something flat.

cintarear, *va.* (coll.) to slap with a sword.

cinteado, da, *a.* adorned with ribbons.

cintería, *f.* ribbon trade; ribbon shop; collection or heap of ribbons.—**cintero, ra. I.** *n.* ribbon weaver or dealer. **II.** *m.* belt, girdle; hoisting rope.

cintilla, *f. dim.* small ribbon, narrow tape.

cintillo, *m.* hatband; ring set with precious stones.

cinto, *m.* belt, girdle.

cintra, *f.* (arch.) curvature (of an arch).

cintrel, *m.* (arch.) guide rule or line for arching.

cintura, *f.* waist; girdle, belt; throat of a chimney.—**meter en c.,** (coll.) to keep in a state of subjection or control.

cinturica, illa, ita, *f. dim.* small girdle; small or delicate waist.

cinturón, *m. aug.* large waist; belt, girdle, cest; that which encircles or surrounds.

ciño, ciña, ciñé, ciñera. *V.* CEÑIR.

cipariso, *m.* (poet.) cypress.

cipayo, *m.* Sepoy.

ciperáceo, a. **I.** *a.* (bot.) cyperaceous. **II.** *f. pl.* Cyperaceæ.

cipo, *m.* cippus, short stone pillar.

cipolino, na, *a.* cipoline.

ciprés, *m.* cypress.—**cipresal,** *m.* cypress grove.

cipresino, na, *a.* resembling or belonging to cypress.

ciprino, na; ciprio, ia, *n.* & *a.* Cyprian.

ciquiricata, *f.* (coll.) caress; flattery.

circasiano, na, *n.* & *a.* Circassian.

circe, *f.* Circe; artful, deceitful woman.

circense, *a.* Circensian.

circo, *m.* circus; amphitheatre; moor buzzard.

circón, *m.* zircon.—**circonia,** *f.* zirconium oxide.

circonio, *m.* zirconium.

circuición, *f.* act of surrounding or encircling.

circuir, *va.* (ind. CIRCUYO: *subj.* CIRCUYA) to surround, compass, encircle.

circuito, *m.* circuit; contour, periphery; enclosure, field.

circulación, *f.* circulation; currency; traffic; movement.

circulante, *a.* circulatory, circulating.

circular, *vn.* to circulate; travel, move, run (s. o. vehicles, traffic, etc.).

circular, *a.* circular; circulatory; circling.

circularmente, *adv.* circularly.

circulatorio, ria, *a.* circulatory.

círculo, *m.* circle; circumference; ring; circuit, district; social circle, club, casino.—**c. acimutal,** (naut.) azimuth circle.—**c. horario,** (ast.) hour circle.—**c. mamario,** (anat.) areola of the nipple.—**c. máximo,** (geom.) great circle.—**c. polar,** (ast.) polar circle.—**c. repetidor,** (surv., etc.) repeating circle.—**c. vicioso,** vicious circle, reasoning in a circle.

circumambiente, *a.* surrounding.

circumcirca, *adv.* about, thereabout; almost.

circumpolar, *a.* circumpolar.

circuncidante, *n.* & *a.* circumciser (-ing).

circuncidar, *va.* to circumcise; to diminish, curtail, clip.

circuncisión, *f.* circumcision.

circunciso, sa, *a.* circumcised.

circundar, *va.* to surround, circle, compass.

circunferencia, *f.* circumference.

circunferencial, *a.* circumferential.

circunferencialmente, *adv.* in a circular manner.

circunflejo, ja, *a.* circumflex.

circunlocución, *f.*, **circunloquio,** *m.* circumlocution.

circunnavegación, *f.* circumnavigation.

circunnavegar, *va.* to circumnavigate, to sail round.

circunscribir, *va.* (pp. CIRCUNSCRIPTO and CIRCUNSCRITO) to circumscribe; enclose, encircle.

circunscripción, *f.* circumscription.

circunscriptible, *a.* circumscribable.

circunscriptivo, va, *a.* circumscribing, limiting.

circunscripto, ta; circunscrito, ta, *a.* circumscribed.

circunspeción, *f.* circumspection, prudence; decorum, dignity.

circunspectamente, *adv.* circumspectly.

circunspecto, ta, *a.* circumspect, cautious.

circunstancia, *f.* circumstance, incident; condition, state; particular, detail.—**c. agravante,** aggravating circumstance.—**c. atenuante,** extenuating circumstance.—**en las circunstancias presentes,** in, or under, the circumstances.

circunstanciadamente, *adv.* circumstantially, minutely, in detail.

circunstanciado, da. **I.** *a.* with all particulars, in detail. **II.** *pp.* CIRCUNSTANCIAR.

circunstancial, *a.* circumstantial.

circunstante. **I.** *a.* surrounding; present, attending. **II.** *m. pl.* bystanders, persons present; audience.

circunvalación, *f.* circumvallation.

circunvalar, *va.* to surround, encircle; (mil.) to circumvallate, surround with trenches.

circunvecino, na, *a.* neighboring, adjacent, contiguous, surrounding.

circunvolución, *f.* convolution.

cirial, *m.* processional candleholder.

cirigaña, *f.* flattery.

cirineo, *m.* (coll.) mate, assistant.

cirio, *m.* thick and long wax taper.—**c. pascual,** paschal candle.

cirolero, *m.* plum tree.

cirro, *m.* (med.) schirrus; (bot.) short rootlets of creepers; (meteor.) cirrus.

cirrosis, *f.* cirrhosis.

cirroso, sa, *a.* scirrhous, fibrous, cirrhose.

ciruela, *f.* plum; prune.—**c. de fraile,** long green plum.—**c. de yema,** yellow plum.—**c. pasa,** dried plum, prune.—**c. verdal,** green gage.

ciruelar, *m.* plantation of plum trees.

ciruelica, illa, ita, *f. dim.* small plum.

ciruelico, illo, ito, *m. dim.* dwarf plum tree.

ciruelo, *m.* (bot.) plum tree.

cirugía, *f.* surgery.

cirujano, na, *n.* surgeon.

cisalpino, na, *a.* cisalpine.

cisca, *f.* reed for roofing huts and cottages.

ciscar. **I.** *va.* (pret. CISQUÉ: *subj.* CISQUE) (coll.) to besmear, to dirty. **II.** *vr.* to ease nature.

cisco, *m.* coal dust, culm, slack; breeze; (coll.) noisy wrangle, hubbub, hue and cry.

cisión, *f.* incision.

cisípedo, da, *a.* finger-footed.

cisma, *m.* schism; disturbance in a community; discord.

cismático, ca, *n.* & *a.* schismatic; disturber (-ing).

cismontano, na, *a.* from or on this side of the mountains.

cisne, *m.* (orn.) swan; (C-, ast.) Cygnus, Swan; good poet or musician.

cispadano, na, *a.* cispadane.

cisquero, *m.* coal-dust seller; pounce bag.

cistel, cister, *m.* Cistercian order of St. Bernard.

cisterciense, *n.* & *a.* Cistercian.

cisterna, *f.* cistern; reservoir; water tank.

cístico, *a.* (surg.) cystic.—**cistitis,** *f.* cystitis

cisto, *m.* (bot.) cistus, rockrose.

cistoscopio, *m.* cystoscope.

cistotomía, *f.* (surg.) cystotomy.

cisura, *f.* incision.

cita, *f.* appointment engagement; summons; citation, quotation.

citable, *a.* worthy of being cited, quotable.

citación, *f.* citation, quotation; summons judicial notice.

Citano, na, *n.* = ZUTANO.

citar, *va.* to make an appointment with; to convoke, convene; to quote; to summon; to give judicial notice.—**c. a juata,** to call a meeting.

cítara, *f.* cithara, zither musical instrument; (mas.) partition wall of the thickness of a brick.

citarilla, *f. dim.* small zither; (mas.) thin partition wall.

citarista, *n.* zither player.

citatorio, ria, *a.* (law) citatory (app. to a summons).

citerior, *a.* hither, nearer, toward this part.—**España c.,** the higher or northeastern part of Spain.

citiso, *m.* (bot.) shrub trefoil, cytisus.

cítola, *f.* in corn mills, clack or clapper.

citolegia, *f.* primer.

citoplasma, *m.* (biol.) cytoplasm.

citote, *m.* (coll.) summons, citation.

citramontano, na, *a.* from, or located on, this side the mountains.

citrato, *m.* (chem.) citrate.

---

cítrico, ca, *a.* (chem.) citric.

citrina, *f.* lemon oil.

citrón, *m.* lemon; (P. R., bot.) lime.

ciudad, *f.* city; civic body.

ciudadanía, *f.* citizenship.

ciudadano, na. **I.** *a.* of or belonging to a city; civil; citylike. **II.** *n.* citizen.

ciudadela, *f.* (mil.) citadel, fortress; (Am.) tenement house.

civeta, *f.* civet cat.

civeto, *m.* civet, the perfume.

cívico, ca, *a.* civic. *V.* DOMÉSTICO.

civil, *a.* civil; polite, courteous; (law) civil, not criminal.

civilidad, *f.* civility, politeness, urbanity.

civilista, *n.* attorney skilled in the civil law, especially the Roman law; (Am.) partisan of civil government, opponent of militarism.

civilización, *f.* civilization.

civilizador, ra, *a.* civilizing.

civilizar, *va.* (*pret.* CIVILICÉ: *subj.* CIVILICE) to civilize.

cívilmente, *adv.* civilly, courteously, politely; according to the civil law.

civismo, *m.* civism; patriotism.

cizalla, *f.* shears, plateshears; filings, metal clippings.

cizallar, *va.* to shear.

cizaña, *f.* (bot.) darnel; weed; corrupting vice; discord, disagreement; pollution.

cizañador, ra, *n.* one who sows discord or enmity, trouble maker.

cizañar, *vn.* to sow discord, to provoke enmity.

cizañero, ra, *n.* = CIZAÑADOR.

clac, *m.* collapsible hat.

clamar, *vn.* to utter loud outcries; to whine; to clamor, vociferate; (w. **por**) to want, require, demand.

clámide, *f.* short cape, the chlamys of the Greeks.

clamor, *m.* clamor, outcry; whine, plaint; toll of bells, knell.

clamoreada, *f.* outcry, clamor; whine, plaint.

clamorear, *vn.* to clamor; implore assistance, to appeal; to toll.

clamoreo, *m.* repeated or prolonged clamor; knell; (coll.) importunate appeal.

clamorosamente, *adv.* clamorously.

clamoroso, sa, *a.* clamorous, loud, noisy.

clan, *m.* clan.

clandestinamente, *adv.* clandestinely.

clandestinidad, *f.* clandestinity, secrecy.

clandestino, na, *a.* clandestine, secret.

clanga, *f.* = PLANGA.

clangor, *m.* (poet.) sound of a trumpet.

clara, *f.* white of an egg; piece of ill-woven cloth; bald spot; (coll.) short interval of fair weather on a rainy day.

claraboya, *f.* skylight; bull's-eye; transom.

claramente, *adv.* clearly; openly.

clarar, *va.* = ACLARAR.

clarea, *f.* mulled wine, mulse.

clarear. **I.** *va.* to give light to. **II.** *vn.* to dawn, to grow light, to clear up. **III.** *vr.* to be transparent, translucent; to give one's self away.

clarecer, *vn.* (*subj.* CLAREZCA) to dawn, to grow or become light.

clarete, *m.* claret.

claridad, *f.* brightness, splendor, light; clearness, distinctness; glory of the blessed; celebrity, fame.—*pl.* plain truths, plain language.

clarificación, *f.* clarification, refining.

clarificadora, *f.* clarifying pan, evaporator.

clarificar, *va.* (*pret.* CLARIFIQUÉ: *subj.* CLARIFIQUE) to brighten, to illuminate; to clarify, purify, refine.

clarificativo, va, *a.* purificative or purificatory.

clarilla, *f.* lye of ashes.

clarimente, *m.* an ancient lotion used by women.

clarín, *m.* bugle, clarion; organ stop; bugler; fine cambric; (orn.) an American song bird.

clarinada, *f.* (coll.) uncalled-for, tart remark.

clarinado, da, *a.* (her.) bell-bearing.

clarinero, *m.* bugler.

clarinete, *m.* clarinet; clarinet player.

clarión, *m.* white crayon, chalk.

clarisa, *f.* Clare, nun of the order of St. Clare.

clarísimo, ma, *a.* (*sup.* of CLARO) very clear, perfectly clear; most illustrious.

clarividencia, *f.* clairvoyance; clear-sightedness.

clarividente, *a.* clairvoyant; clear-sighted, sagacious.

claro, *m.* skylight; break in a discourse; gap, lacuna, interval; bald spot; glade; clearing; light spot; (arch.) space between columns; (naut.) clear spot in the sky.—**de c. en c.,** evidently, manifestly.—**pasar la noche de c.,** or **en c.,** not to sleep a wink.—**poner en c.,** to make plain.—**por lo c.,** clearly, manifestly, conspicuously.—**sacar en c.** = PONER EN C.; to conclude, arrive at a conclusion.

claro, *adv.* = CLARAMENTE.

claro, ra, *a.* clear; bright, light, nitid; neat; thin, rare, sparse; cloudless, fair; light, not deeply tinged; plain, clear; obvious, evident, indisputable; open, frank, ingenuous; celebrated, illustrious; sagacious, quick of thought.—**c. está, of course**; evidently.—**c. intervalo,** remission of madness; lucid interval.—**c. oscuro,** chiaroscuro.—**a la clara, a las claras,** in the open, openly.

claror, *m.* = RESPLENDOR.

claroscuro, *m.* combination of fine and heavy strokes in penmanship; monochrome, painting in one color; chiaroscuro, light and shade.

clarucho, cha, *a.* (coll.) too watery, too thin.

clase, *f.* class; class in school; lecture; order; classis; kind, kin.

clásicamente, *adv.* classically.

clasicismo, *m.* classic style, classicism.

clásico, ca, *a.* classical, classic; principal; remarkable.

clasificación, *f.* classification.

clasificar, *va.* (*pret.* CLASIFIQUÉ: *subj.* CLASIFIQUE) to classify, to class.

claudicación, *f.* claudication; halting or limping; crookedness.

claudicante, *a.* claudicant, claudicating; halting, limping.

claudicar, *vn.* (*pret.* CLAUDIQUÉ: *subj.* CLAUDIQUE) to claudicate, halt, limp; to proceed in a bungling manner, without rule or order.

claustral, *a.* claustral, cloistral.

claustro, *m.* cloister; piazza; gallery around a court; faculty of a university; monastic state.

cláusula, *f.* (gram.) period, sentence; clause of a discourse; (law) clause, article.

clausulado, da, *a.* (rhet.) written in short sentences.

clausular, *va.* to close (a period), terminate (a speech).

clausulilla, *f.* dim. short or little clause.

clausura, *f.* cloister; inner recess of a convent, sanctum; clausure, confinement, retirement; cloture, closure.—**vivir en c.,** to lead a monastic or retired life.

clava, *f.* club, cudgel; (naut.) scupper.

clavadizo, za, *a.* adorned with nails.

clavado, da. **I.** *a.* nailed, adorned with nails, hobnailed; exact, precise.—**venir c.,** to fit exactly. **II.** *pp.* of CLAVAR.

clavador, *m.* nail driver.

clavadura, *f.* nailing, driving a nail to the quick in horseshoeing.

clavar, *va.* to nail, fasten with nails; to fasten in, drive in, stick in, force in; to stick, prick, gore, pin, pierce; to set in gold or silver; (coll.) to cheat, to deceive.—**c. a un caballo,** to prick a horse in shoeing.—**c. la artillería,** to spike, to nail up the guns.—**c. las armas,** to ground the arms. **c. los ojos,** or **la vista, en,** to stare or look with fixed eyes at.

clavaria, *f.* = CLAVERA.

clavario, *m.* = CLAVERO.

clavazón, *f.* set of nails.

clave. I. *m.* clavichord. **II.** *f.* key or code; (arch.) keystone of an arch; (mus.) clef.—**echar la c.**, to close (a speech, an affair).

clavel, *m.* (bot.) pink, carnation.—**c. reventón,** large carnation.

clavelito, *m. dim.* (bot.) a plant bearing a small variety of pink.

clavelón, *m. aug.* (bot.) marigold.

clavellina, *f.* (bot.) pink, carnation; (mil.) vent stopple.

claveque, *m.* rock crystal cut like a diamond.

clavera, *f.* nail mold; heading stamp; nail hole; nail bore; screw hole; boundary where landmarks are set up.

clavería, *f.* office and dignity of the keybearer in military orders; (Mex.) treasury of a cathedral.

clavero, ra, *n.* keeper of the keys; treasurer, cashier; key bearer of some military orders; (*m.*) aromatic clove tree.

clavete, *m. dim.* tack, small nail.

clavetear, *va.* to nail; to garnish with nails; to point or tag (a lace).

clavicordio, *m.* clavichord, harpsichord.

clavicornio, nia. I. *n. & a.* (zoöl.) clavicorn. **II.** *m. pl.* Clavicornia.

clavícula, *f.* (anat.) clavicle, collar bone.

clavicular, *a.* (anat.) clavicular.

clavija, *f.* pin, peg; treenail, pintle, peg of a string instrument.—**c. maestra,** fore-axletree pintle.—**apretar las clavijas,** to push home an argument; put on the screws.

clavijera, *f.* water hole in walls.

clavijero, *m.* bridge of a clavichord.

clavillo, ito, *m. dim.* small nail, spill, brad, tack, pin.—**c. de hebilla,** rivet of a buckle.—*pl.* cloves.

claviórgano, *m.* clavichord, instrument having strings and pipes.

clavo, *m.* nail; spike; (naut.) rudder of a ship; severe grief or pain; (vet.) tumor between the hair and the hoof of a horse; (min.) bunch of rich ore; corn (on the feet); (surg.) lint; tent.—**c. de especia,** clove.—**c. de gota de sebo,** semispherical-headed nail.—**c. de herradura,** hobnail.—**c. de rosca,** screw nail.—**c. romano,** (Am.) curtain knob, picture nail.—**c. tachuela,** tack.—**c. trabadero,** keyed bolt.—**c. trabal,** clasp nail.—**dar en el c.,** to hit the nail on the head.—**de c. pasado,** self-evident, well-known; easy (a "cinch").—**sacarse el c.,** to get even.—**un c. saca otro c.,** one grief cures another.

clazol, *m.* (Mex.) bagasse.

clemátide, *f.* (bot.) traveller's-joy, virgin's-bower, clematis.

clemencia, *f.* mercy, forbearance.—**clemente,** *a.* merciful.—**clementemente,** *adv.* mercifully.

clementísimo, ma, *a. sup.* of CLEMENTE.

clepsidra, *f.* clepsydra, water clock.

cleptomanía, *f.* kleptomania.

cleptomaníaco, ca; cleptómano, na, *n. & a.* kleptomaniac.

clerecía, *f.* clergy.

clerical. I. *a.* clerical, relating to the clergy. **II.** *n.* (pol.) Clerical, belonging to the Clerical party.

clericalismo, *m.* clericalism.

clericalmente, *adv.* in a clerical manner.

clericato, *m.* state and dignity of a clergyman.

clericatura, *f.* clergy, ecclesiastical state.

clérigo, *m.* clergyman.—**c. de misa,** presbyter.—**c. de misa y olla,** ignorant priest.

cleriguillo, *m. dim.* petty clergyman (a term of contempt.)

clerizón, *m.* chorister.

clerizonte, *m.* layman who wears a clerical dress; ill-dressed or ill-mannered clergyman.

clero, *m.* clergy.

cliente, *n.* client.

clientela, *f.* protection or patronage; following, clientele; clientship, condition of a client.

clima, *m.* climate, clime.—**climatérico, ca,** *a.* climacteric, climacterical; (coll.) ill-humored.

climatología, *f.* climatology.—**climatológico, ca,** *a.* climatological.

clímax, *m.* (rhet.) climax.

clin, *f.* = CRIN.

clínica, *f.* clinic; clinic wards of hospitals.

clínico, ca, *a.* clinic, clinical.

clínico, *m.* (eccl.) clinic.

clinométrico, ca, *a.* clinometric.

clinómetro, *m.* clinometer.

clinopodio, *m.* (bot.) calamint.

clíper, *m.* (naut.) clipper.

clisado, *m.* stereotyping.

clisar, *va.* to stereotype; to make a cliché or stereotype plate of.

clisé, *m.* stereotype plate; (print.) cut.

clistel, clister, *m.* clyster.

clitómetro, *m.* (surv.) clinometer.

clitoris, *m.* (anat.) clitoris.

clivoso, sa, *a.* (poet.) sloping.

clo, clo, *m.* cackle of a hen.

cloaca, *f.* sewer; (zool.) cloaca, large intestine of fowls.

clocar, *va.* to cluck.

cloque, *m.* (naut.) grapnel; grappling iron, harpoon.

cloquear. I. *vn.* to cluck, to cackle. **II.** *va.* to angle.

cloqueo, *m.* cluck, chuck, cackle.

cloquera, *f.* broodiness.

cloquero, *m.* tunny harpooner.

cloral, *m.* chloral.

clorato, *m.* chlorate.

clorhidrato, *m.* hydrochlorate.

clorhídrico, *m.* hydrochloric.

clórico, *a.* chloric.

cloris, *f.* (orn.) greenfinch.

clorita, *f.* (min.) chlorite.

cloro, *m.* chlorine.

clorófila, *f.* chlorophyll, green coloring-matter of plants.

clorofílico, ca, *a.* chlorophyllaceous, chlorophyllian.

cloroformico, ca, *a.* chloroformic.

cloroformización, *f.* chloroformization.

cloroformizar, *va.* (pret. CLOROFORMICÉ: subj. CLOROFORMICE) to chloroform.

cloroformo, *m.* chloroform.

clorosis, *f.* (med.) chlorosis, greensickness.

cloroso, sa, *a.* chlorous.

clorótico, ca, *a.* chlorotic.

cloruro, *m.* chloride.

club, *m.* club, social or political association.

clueco, ca. I. *a.* broody; (coll.) decrepit. **II.** *f.* brooding hen.

coa, *f.* sharp stick used by Indians to till the land; (Mex.) a kind of hoe.

coacción, *f.* coaction; compulsion.

coacervar, *va.* to heap together.

coactivo, va, *a.* coactive, coercive, compulsory.

coacusar, *va.* (for.) to accuse jointly.

coadjutor, *m.* coadjutor, assistant, associate, coworker.

coadjutora, *f.* coadjutrix.

coadjutoría, *f.* coadjuvancy, help, assistance; coadjutorship.

coadministrador, *m.* coadministrator.

coadunación, *f.,* **coadunamiento,** *m.* coadunition.—**coadunar,** *va.* to join closely together.

coadunar, *va.* to join closely together.

coadyutor, *m.* = COADJUTOR.

coadyutorio, ria, *a.* cooperative.

coadyuvador, *m.* fellow helper, assistant.

coadyuvante. I. *n.* coadjuvant, helper, assistant. **II.** *a.* cooperative, auxiliary.

coadyuvar, *va.* to help, assist, aid.

coagente, *m.* coagent, associate.

coagulable, *a.* coagulable.—**coagulación,** *f.* coagulation.—**coagulador, ra,** *n. & a.* coagulator (-ing, -ive).

coagulante, *n. & a.* coagulant.

coagular. I. *va.* to coagulate, to curd. **II.** *vr.* to coagulate, condense, clod, curdle.

coagulativo, va, *a.* coagulative.

coágulo, *m.* coagulated blood, clot; coagulation; body formed by coagulation.

coairón, *m.* piece of timber.

coalescencia, *f.* (med.) coalescence.

coalescente, *a.* coalescent.

coalición, *f.* coalition.

coalla, *f.* (orn.) woodcock.

coapóstol, *m.* co-apostle.

coaptación, *f.* (surg.) coaptation.

coarmador, *m.* part owner of a vessel.

coarrendador, *m.* joint lessor.

coarrendatario, ria, *n.* joint tenant.

coartación, *f.* limitation, restriction; obligation to be ordained within a certain time.

coartada, *f.* alibi.—**probar la c.,** to prove an alibi.

coartado, da, *a.* (slave) who has paid his master a partial sum to obtain freedom.

coartar, *va.* to limit, restrain.

coate, ta, *a.* (Mex.) = CUATE.

coatí, *m.* (zool.) coati.

coautor, ra, *n.* coauthor, joint author.

coba, *f.* (coll.) funny yarn.

cobaltífero, ra, *a.* cobalt-bearing, cobaltiferous.

cobaltina, *f.* (min.) cobaltite.

cobalto, *m.* cobalt.

cobarde, *a.* cowardly; faint-hearted.—**cobardear,** *vn.* to be a coward; to be faint-hearted.—**cobardemente,** *adv.* cowardly.

cobardía, *f.* cowardice.

cobertera, *f.* cover, potlid; bawd; procuress; white water lily.—*pl.* the two middle feathers of a hawk's tail.

cobertizo, *m.* shed, hut.

cobertor, *m.* coverlet, bedspread, quilt.

cobertura, *f.* cover, wrapper, covering, coverlet; act of a grandee of Spain covering himself the first time he is presented to the king.

cobija, *f.* imbrex tile; short mantilla; fine feather; cover; blanket; (Mex.) shawl.—*pl.* (Mex.) bed-clothes.

cobijador, ra, *a.* covering, protective.

cobijamiento, *m.* act of covering; lodging.

cobijar, *va.* to cover; shelter, protect; lodge.

cobijo, *m.* = COBIJAMIENTO.

cobra, *f.* rope for yoking oxen; a number of mares (not less than five) for treading out the corn; (zool.) cobra.

cobrable, *a.* collectable.

cobradero, ra, *a.* that may be recovered or collected.

cobracapelo, *f.* (zool.) cobra.

cobrador, *m.* collector, receiving teller; (r. w.) conductor.

cobranza, *f.* recovery or collection of money; retrieval of game.

cobrar. I. *va.* to collect, receive (what is due); recover (something lost); to retrieve, recuperate, regain; to gain; to charge (price, fee); to pull, draw in; to win, obtain.—**c. ánimo,** or **corazón,** to take courage.—**c. carnes,** to become fat, put on flesh.—**c. fuerzas,** to gather strength. **II.** *vr.* to recover; to come to.

cobratorio, ia, *a.* belonging to collection of money; collectible.

cobre, *m.* copper; kitchen brass utensils; (mus.) brass instruments of an orchestra.—**c. de cecial,** pair of dried hake or haddock.—**c. quemado,** copper sulphate.—**c. verde,** malachite.—**batir el c.,** to pursue with spirit and vigor, to hustle.

cobreño, ña, *a.* made of copper.

cobrizo, za, *a.* coppery, cupreous; copper-colored.

cobro, *m.* COBRANZA; receptacle; place of safety.

coca, *f.* (bot.) coca; coca leaves; juice from coca leaves, coca tea; (prov.) bugbear; (naut.) a sort of small vessel; side hair of women put back from the face; (coll.) head; (coll.) rap with the knuckles on the head; cake.—**c. de Levante,** moonseed yielding the India fishberries.

cocada, *f.* coconut candy or preserve.

cocador, ra, *a.* wheedling, coaxing, flattering.

cocaína, *f.* cocaine.

cocal, *m.* coconut field or plantation.

cocán, *m.* (Peru) breast of a fowl.

cocar, *va.* (coll.) to coax; to gain by wheedling and flattering; to flirt with; make faces at.

cocarar, *va.* to supply coca leaves to.

cocaví, *m.* coca and other provisions for a journey.

coccíneo, nea, *a.* of a purple color.

cocción, *f.* coction, baking, calcining.

cóccix, *m.* (anat.) coccyx.

coceador, ra, *n.* & *a.* kicker (-ing).

coceadura, *f.,* **coceamiento,** *m.* kicking.

cocear, *va.* & *vn.* to kick.—**c. contra el aguijón,** to kick against the prick.

cocedero, ra. I. *a.* easily boiled. **II.** *m.* place where anything is cooked or baked.

cocedizo, za, *a.* = COCEDERO.

cocedura, *f.* act of boiling; coction.

cocer. I. *va.* (ind. CUEZO: *subj.* CUEZA) to boil; to cook; to burn, bake, calcine (brick, etc.); to digest. **II.** *vn.* to boil, cook, ferment; to seethe, ferment without fire, as wine. **III.** *vr.* to suffer intense and continued pain.

cocido, da. I. *a.* & *pp.* of COCER. boiled, baked, cooked; skilled, experienced. **II.** *m.* a Spanish dish of boiled meat and vegetables.

cociente, *m.* quotient.

cocimiento, *m.* coction, decoction; bath or mordant for dyeing.

cocina, *f.* kitchen; cuisine, cookery; pottage of greens.—**c. económica,** cooking range.

cocinar, *va.* & *vn.* to cook; (coll.) to meddle in other people's affairs.

cocinero, ra, *n.* cook; chef.

cocinilla, ita, *f.* *dim.* small kitchen; cooking stove; fireplace.

cóclea, *f.* ancient machine for raising water; endless screw.

coclearia, *f.* (bot.) common scurvy grass.

coco, *m.* (bot.) coconut tree; coconut; coconut shell; vessel made of coconut shell; worm or grub of seeds and fruit; coccus; scale insect; coccus (bacterium); bugbear; phantasm; cocos, India berries from which rosaries are made; gesture, grimace; flattering gesture.—**c. avellanado,** dry coconut.—**c. de embarque,** select coconut.—**c. nacido,** sprout.—**c. pequeño,** cull.—**c. vano,** dry.—**c. zarazo,** rot.—**hacer cocos,** (coll.) to flatter, wheedle; to flirt.

cocobacilo, *m.* bubonic-plague bacillus.

cocobálsamo, *m.* fruit of the balm of Gilead.

cocobolo, *m.* (bot.) a hardwood tree; cocobolo.

cocodrillo, *m.* crocodile.

cocol, *m.* (Mex.) (bread) roll.—**cocolero, ra,** *n.* roll baker.

cocoliste, *m.* (Mex.) an epidemic fever.

cócora, *f.* annoying person, bore.

cocoso, sa, *a.* worm-eaten; gnawed by grubs.

cocotal, *m.* clump of coconut trees; coconut plantation or field.

cocote, *m.* occiput.

cocotero, *m.* (bot.) coconut tree.

cocuyo, *m.* glowworm.

cocha, *f.* (min.) small water reservoir.

cochambre, *m.* (coll.) greasy, dirty thing.

cochambrería, *f.* (coll.) heap of filthy things.

cochambrero, ra; cochambroso, sa, *a.* (coll.) nasty, filthy, stinking.

cocharro, *m.* wooden or stone dish, cup, platter.

cochastro, *m.* little, sucking wild boar.

coche, *m.* carriage, coach; car.—**c. comedor,** dining car.—**c. de alquiler,** hack or hackney coach.—**c. de plaza,** or **de punto,** hack licensed at a customary stand.—**c. de tranvía,** street car.—**c. dormitorio,** sleeping car.—**c. parado,** balcony.—**c. salón,** parlor car.—**c. simón** = C. DE ALQUILER.

cochear, *vn.* to drive a carriage.

cochera, *f.* carriage house; (r. w.) car house, roundhouse, barn; garage; coachman's wife.—**puerta c.,** carriage porch; porte-cochère.

cocheril, *a.* (coll.) relating to coachmen.

cochero. I. *m.* coachman. **II.** *a.* easily boiled.

cocherón, *m. aug.* large coach house; engine house; roundhouse.

cochevira, *f.* lard.

cochevís, *m.* crested shore lark.

cochifrito, *m.* fricassee of lamb, mutton, etc.

cochigato, *m.* a Mexican bird.

cochina, *f.* sow.

cochinada, *f.* herd of swine; (coll.) hoggishness; mean, dirty action, dirty trick.

cochinamente, *adv.* hoggishly, filthily; meanly, basely.

cochinata, *f.* (naut.) rider.

cochinería, *f.* foulness, filthiness; meanness, niggardliness, baseness.

cochinero, ra, *a.* for hogs (s. o. fruit of poor quality given to hogs).

cochinilla, *f.* woodlouse; cochineal.

cochinillo, illa, *n. dim.* pig.—**c. de Indias,** guinea pig.—**c. de leche,** sucking pig.

cochino, na, *n. & a.* dirty, filthy, vile (person).

cochino, na, *n.* hog.

cochiquera, *f.* (coll.) hogsty, pigpen; small and filthy room.

cochite hervite, (coll.) helter-skelter.

cochitril, *m.* (coll.) pigsty; filthy room.

cochura, *f.* coction; boiling; dough for a batch of bread.

coda, *f.* tail; (mus.) coda, ending, finale.

codadura, *f.* layer of an old vine.

codal, *m.* elbow piece of ancient armor; short and thick wax candle; shoot of vine; frame of a handsaw; carpenter's square; prop, shore, stay, strut; stay bolt.

codal, *a.* one cubit long.

codaste, *m.* (naut, aer.) sternpost.

codazo, *m.* blow with the elbow; hunch.

codear. I. *vn.* to elbow. **II.** *va.* to nudge.

codeína, *f.* codein.

codelincuencia, *f.* joint delinquency, complicity.

codelincuente, *n.* associate, partner in crime, accomplice.

codera, *f.* itch or scabbiness on the elbow; piece reinforcing the elbows of jackets; elbow rail; (naut.) breastfast.

codesera, *f.* spot grown over with hairy Cytisus.

codeso, *m.* (bot.) hairy Cytisus.

codeudor, ra, *n.* joint debtor.

códice, *m.* old manuscript; codex.

codicia, *f.* covetousness, cupidity, greediness.— **la c. rompe el saco,** covetousness is self-defeating.

codiciable, *a.* covetable.—**codiciador, ra,** *n. & a.* coveter (-ing).

codiciante, *a.* coveting.

codiciar, *va. & vn.* to covet.

codicilar, *a.* pertaining to a codicil.

codicilo, *m.* codicil.

codiciosamente, *adv.* covetously, greedily.

codicioso, sa, *a.* greedy, covetous, grasping; ambitious; (coll.) diligent; laborious; thrifty.

codificar, *va.* (*pret.* CODIFIQUÉ: *subj.* CODIFIQUE) to codify.

código, *m.* code (of laws).—**c. del honor,** code of honor.—**c. de minas,** mining code.—**c. de señales,** signal code.—**c. mercantil,** mercantile, or commerce, code.—**c. militar,** military law.—**c. penal,** penal, or criminal, code.

codillera, *f.* (farr.) tumor on the knee of a horse.

codillo, *m.* knee of quadrupeds; bend; elbow; knee; breech; angle; codille, a term at ombre; part of a branch of a tree which joins the trunk; foot rule; stirrup of a saddle.—**codillos,** file used by silversmiths.

codo, *m.* elbow; cubit; (mech.) angle, elbow, knee; foot rule.—**c. real,** royal cubit.—**alzar el c.,** to drink too much.—**comerse los codos de hambre,** to be starving to death.—**hablar por los codos,** to chatter, to be a chatterbox.—**levantar el c. =** ALZAR EL CODO.

codón, *m.* leather dock of a horse's tail.

codorniz, *f.* (orn.) quail.

coeducación, *f.* coeducation.

coeducar, *va.* to coeducate.

coeficiencia, *f.* coefficiency.

coeficiente, *a.* coefficient.—**c. de seguridad,** safety factor.—**c. de trabajo,** working stress.

coepíscopo, *m.* contemporary bishop.

coercer, *va.* (ind. COERZO: *subj.* COERZA) to coerce, check, restrain.—**coercibilidad,** *f.* coercibility, liability to restraint.—**coercible,** *a.* coercible, subject to check.

coerción, *f.* coercion, restraint, check.

coercitivo, va, *a.* coercive, restraining.

coetáneo, a, *a.* coetaneous, contemporary.

coeterno, na, *a.* coeternal.

coevo, va, *a.* coeval.

coexistencia, *f.* coexistence.

coexistente, *a.* coexistent.

coexistir, *vn.* to coexist.

coextenderse, *vr.* to be coextensive.

cofa, *f.* (naut.) top of the lower masts.

cofia, *f.* hair net, cowl, headdress, coif; die case in coining.

cofiezuela, *f. dim.* small hair net or coif.

cofín, *m.* small basket for fruit; fruit box.

cofosis, *f.* complete deafness.

cofrade, *n.* member (of a confraternity or brotherhood).

cofradía, *f.* confraternity, brotherhood, sisterhood; trades union; association.

cofre, *m.* trunk for clothes; coffer; box, case; (print.) coffin of the imposing stone.

cofrecico, illo, ito, *m. dim.* small trunk or box.

cofrero, ra, *n.* trunk maker or seller.

cofto, ta, *a. =* COPTO.

cogedera, *f.* rod for gathering grass hemp; box for catching swarming bees; pole for gathering fruit; handle.

cogedero, ra. I. *a.* ready to be gathered. **II.** *n.* handle.

cogedizo, za, *a.* that can be easily collected or gathered.

cogedor, *m.* collector, gatherer; dust box or dust pan; coal or ash shovel; box for the woven velvet.

cogedura, *f.* act of gathering or collecting.

coger. I. *va.* (*ind.* COJO: *subj.* COJA) to catch; to seize, grasp, take hold of; to fetch, gather, collect, take; to imbibe, soak; to have room or capacity for; to occupy, take up; to find, procure; to surprise, catch; attack unexpectedly; to intercept, obstruct.—**c. la delantera,** to get the start. **II.** *vn.* to fit, have room, reach.

cogida, *f.* (coll.) gathering or harvesting of fruits; (coll.) yield of fruits; (coll.) act of the bull's catching the bullfighter; (fish.) catch.

cogido, da. I. *a. & pp.* of COGER. **II.** *m.* gather, fold in clothing, curtains, etc.

cogitabundo, da, *a.* pensive, thoughtful.

cogitación, *f.* (obs.) meditation, cogitation.

cogitativo, va, *a.* cogitative; given to meditation.

cognación, *f.* cognation; kindred, relationship.

cognado, da, *a.* cognate; related by blood.

cognaticio, ia, *a.* cognatic.

cognición, *f.* cognition.

cognomento, *m.* cognomination, surname.

cognoscible, *a.* knowable..

cognoscitivo, va, *a.* cognitive.

cogollico, ito, *m. dim.* small heart of garden plants.

cogollo, *m.* heart of garden plants; shoot of a plant; top, summit.

cogombro, *m. =* COHOMBRO.

cogón, *m.* (bot.) bamboo used in the Philippines for thatching.

cogonal, *m.* COGÓN plantation.

cogotazo, *m.* slap on the back of the neck.

cogote, *m.* occiput, back of the neck; crest at the back of the helmet.—**ser tieso de c.,** (coll.) to be haughty, conceited, airy, stiff.

cogotudo, da, *a.* thicknecked.

cogucho, *m.* sugar of coarse quality.

cogujada, *f.* (orn.) crested lark.

cogujón, *m.* corner of a mattress or bolster.

cogujonero, ra, *a.* pointed, as the corners of mattresses or bolsters.

cogulla, *f.* cowl, monk's habit.

cogullada, *f.* = PAPADA DE PUERCO.

cohabitación, *f.* cohabitation.

cohabitar, *vn.* to cohabit.

cohecha, *f.* (agr.) last tillage before sowing the crop.

cohechador, *m.* briber, suborner.

cohechar, *va.* to bribe, suborn; (agr.) to plow the last time before sowing.

cohecho, *m.* bribery; (agr.) plowing season.

cohén, *n.* soothsayer; procurer, pimp.

coheredera, *f.* coheiress, joint heiress.

coheredero, *m.* coheir, joint heir.

coherencia, *f.* coherence; connection.

coherente, *a.* coherent; connected; consistent; cohesive.

coherentemente, *adv.* cohesively; connectedly: **cohesión,** *f.* cohesion.—**cohesivo, va,** *a.* cohesive.

cohesor, *m.* (rad.) coherer.

cohete, *m.* skyrocket.—**cohetería,** *f.* fireworks shop.

cohetero, *m.* maker or seller of fireworks.

cohibición, *f.* cohibition, prohibition.

cohibir, *va.* to cohibit, prohibit, restrain.

cohobación, *f.* (chem.) cohobation.

cohobar, *va.* to redistil, cohobate.

cohombral, *m.* cucumber bed.

cohombrillo, *m.* *dim.* gherkin.

cohombro, *m.* cucumber; fritter cut into pieces like a cucumber.

cohonestar, *va.* to give an honest appearance to (an action).

cohorte, *f.* cohort.

coima, *f.* perquisite received by the keeper of a gaming table.

coime, coimero, *m.* keeper of a gaming table; scorer at billiards.

coincidencia, *f.* coincidence.

coincidente, *a.* coincident.

coincidir, *vn.* to coincide.

coinquinarse, *vr.* to become stained.

cointeresado, da. **I.** *a.* jointly interested. **II.** *n.* joint party in interest.

coipo, coipú, *m.* coypu, a S.-A. amphibious mammal similar to the beaver.

coirón, *m.* (S. A.) a kind of thatching grass

coironal, *m.* COIRÓN field.

coito, *m.* coition, carnal copulation.

coja, *f.* (coll.) lewd woman.

cojear, *vn.* to limp, hobble; to deviate from virtue.—**c. de,** to limp with; to have the defect of.

cojera, *f.* lameness, hobble, limp.

cojijo, *m.* complaint of some slight injury; grub or insect.

cojijoso, sa, *a.* peevish, irritable.

cojín, *m.* cushion, pillow; saddle pad.

cojinete, *m.* *dim.* cushionet, small cushion, small pillow, pad; rail chair; (mech.) journal bearing, shaft bearing; pillow block.

cojitranco, ca, *a.* an epithet applied to evil-disposed lame persons.

cojo, ja, *n.* & *a.* lame, cripple, halt.

cojudo, da, *a.* entire, not gelt or castrated.

cojuelo, ela, *a.* *dim.* a small cripple.

cok, *m.* coke.

col, *f.* cabbage (this name is given to several varieties).—**c. común,** Savoy cabbage.

cola, *f.* tail; cue; tail end; hind portion of anything; extremity; appendage; line of people awaiting turn; end seat in a row; lowest place in a school class; (arch.) inside joint; (sew.) train of a gown; (mus.) prolonged note at the end of a song. —**c. de caballo,** (bot.) horsetail.—**c. de golondrino,** (fort.) hornwork.—**(a) c. de milano,** tongue-and-groove, dovetailed.—**de c.,** rear, last. —**hacer c.,** to stand in line.—**tener,** or **traer, c.,** (coll.) to be followed by serious consequences.

cola, *f.* glue.—**c. clara,** transparent glue.—**c. de boca,** lip glue.—**c. de pescado,** isinglass.—**c. de retazo,** or **retal,** size used by painters.

colaboración, *f.* collaboration, working together; contribution (to a periodical, etc.).

colaborador, ra, *n.* collaborator, coworker; contributor (to a periodical, etc.)

colaborar, *vn.* to collaborate; to contribute.

colación, *f.* collation, critical comparison; act of bestowing an ecclesiastical benefice, or conferring degrees in universities; conference on spiritual affairs; slight repast, luncheon; sweetmeats given to servants on Christmas eve; precinct or district of a parish.—**sacar a c.,** to make mention of.—**traer a c.,** (coll.) to produce proofs or reasons; to introduce, in conversation, something irrelevant.

colacionar, *va.* to collate.

colactáneo, a, *n.* foster brother or sister.

colada, *f.* wash, buck, bucking; common, an open ground; road for cattle over a common; tap (of a furnace); (coll.) good sword.

coladera, *f.* strainer, colander; wax-chandler's sieve; (Mex.) perforated sink cover.

coladero, *m.* colander, strainer, drainer, filtering bag; narrow passage; (min.) hole for dumping ore.

colador, *m.* colander; collator; (print.) leach tub.

coladora, *f.* woman who bucks clothes.

coladura, *f.* colation, straining, filtration.—*pl.* wax dregs.

colagogo, ga, *a.* bile-producing, stimulating bile secretion.

colaire, *m.* place through which a current of air passes.

colambre, *f.* (tan.) = CORAMBRE.

colanilla, *f.* small sliding bolt; sash bolt.

colaña, *f.* low partition in stairs or granaries; joist about twenty palms long and six inches broad.

colapez, colapiscis, *f.* isinglass. *V.* COLA DE PESCADO.

colapso, *m.* (med.) collapse, prostration.

colar. **I.** *va.* & *vn.* (*ind.* CUELO: *subj.* CUELE) to strain, drain, pass through, percolate, filter; to bleach clothing after washing; to collate; (coll.) to spread false news; to pass counterfeit money; to pass through a narrow place; (coll.) to drink wine. **II.** *vr.* to strain, be filtered; to steal or squeeze into a place; (coll.) to be displeased with a jest.

colateral, *a.* collateral.

colateralmente, *adv.* collaterally.

colativo, va, *a.* collative; filtering.

colbac, *m.* calpack, Turkish cap.

colcótar, *m.* (chem.) colcothar; rouge; jewellers' red.

colcha, *f.* coverlet, quilt, bedspread.

colchadura, *f.* quilting; (naut.) laying or twisting ropes.

colchar, *va.* to quilt. *V.* ACOLCHAR.—**c. cabos,** (naut.) to lay or twist ropes.

colchero, ra, *n.* quilt maker.

cólchico, *m.* (bot.) colchicum, meadow saffron.

colchón, *m.* mattress.—**c. de muelles,** spring mattress.—**c. de pluma,** feather bed.—**c. de viento,** air cushion, air bed.

colchoncillo, illo, ito, *m.* *dim.* small mattress.

colchonero, ra, *n.* mattress maker.

colchoneta, *f.* quilted covering for a lounge.

coleada, *f.* wag of the tail; (S. Am.) act of felling a bull by a twist of the tail.

coleadura, *f.* wagging of the tail; wriggling.

coleador, *m.* (S. Am.) man who fells a bull by twisting its tail.

colear. **I.** *vn.* to wag, wriggle, wiggle-waggle. **II.** *va.* (Mex.) in bullfights, to take (the bull) by the tail, while on horseback, and, by suddenly starting the horse, to overturn him; (S. Am.) to fell (cattle) by the tail.

colección, *f.* collection, aggregation, accumulation; set; array; gathering.

coleccionador, ra, *n.* collector (of stamps, birds, etc.).

coleccionar, *va.* to collect, form a collection of.

coleccionista, *n.* = COLECCIONADOR.

colecta, *f.* assessment; collect, a prayer; collection of voluntary offerings.

colectación, *f.* levy; collecting rents, taxes, etc.

colectar, *va.* to collect (taxes, etc.).

colecticio, cia, *a.* untrained; new (s. o. soldiers); compilatory, of the nature of a compilation.

colectivamente, *adv.* collectively.

colectividad, *f.* collectivity; mass of people; community.

colectivismo, *m.* collectivism.

colectivista, *n. & a.* collectivist (-ic).

colectivo, va, *a.* aggregated, collective; (gram.) collective.

colector, *m.* collector, gatherer; tax or rent collector; water conduit; (elec.) commutator.

colecturía, *f.* collectorship; office of the collector; tax office.

colega, *m.* colleague; contemporary (newspaper).

colegatario, ra, *n.* collegatary, colegatee.

colegiado, *a.* collegiate.

colegial. I. *m.* collegian, collegiate. **II.** *a.* college (u. a.)

colegiala, *f.* college woman.

colegia mente, *adv.* in a collegial manner.

colegiarse, *vr.* to form an association.

colegiata, *f.* collegiate church.

colegiatura, *f.* fellowship in a college.

colegio, *m.* college; school, academy, seminary; body of students, students collectively; association; college, body of dignitaries, electors, etc.

colegir, *va.* (*ind.* COLIJO: *pret.* el COLIGIÓ: *subj.* COLIJA) to collect or gather; to deduce, infer, conclude.

colegislador, ra, *a.* colegislative (body).

coleo, *m.* = COLEADURA.

coleóptero, ra. I. *a.* coleopterous. **II.** *m. pl.* Coleoptera.

coleorriza, *f.* (bot.) coleorhiza.

cólera. I. *f.* anger, rage, fury. **II.** *m.* cholera.—**c. asiático,** Asiatic cholera.—**c. morbo,** cholera morbus.

colera, *f.* ornament for the tail of a horse.

coléricamente, *adv.* angrily, wrathfully.

colérico, ca, *a.* angry, wrathful; irascible, irritable.

coleriforme, *a.* choleriform.

colerina, *f.* cholerine.

coleta, *f.* cue or queue of the hair; (coll.) short addition to a discourse or writing; postscript; (Am.) burlap.—**cortarse la c.,** to quit the (bull) ring.

coletero, ra, *n.* maker or seller of buff doublets and breeches.

coletilla, *f. dim.* small cue.

coletillo, *m. dim.* small buff doublet.

coleto, *m.* buff doublet or jacket; (coll.) body of a man; interior of a person.—**decir para su c.,** to say to one's self.—**echarse al c.,** (coll.) to read through; to eat or drink.

colgadero, *m.* hook or peg to hang things upon; hat or coat rack; hanger.

colgadero, ra, *a.* fit to be hung up.

colgadizo, *m.* shed; shed roof; brick bake.

colgadizo, za, *a.* hanging, suspended.

colgado, da, *a.* suspended; (coll.) disappointed, left (u. in the expressions **dejar c.,** to disappoint, to fail; **quedarse c.,** to be foiled, to get left).

colgador, *m.* (print.) peel hanger; y-lintel.

colgadura, *f.* tapestry, hanging or drapery; bunting.—**c. de cama,** bed hangings.

colgajo, *m.* tatter or rag hanging from clothes; bunch of grapes or fruit hung up to be preserved.—*pl.* the fleshy tissues left in some amputations.

coigandejo, *m.* (Colomb.) = COLGAJO.

colgandero, ra, *a.* = COLGANTE.

colgante. I. *a.* hanging, pending, clinging. **II.** *m.* (arch.) drop, pendent; (mech.) hanger; (carp.) king-post.

colgar. I. *va.* (*ind.* CUELGO: *pret.* COLGUÉ: *subj.* CUELGUE) to hang up, suspend; to adorn with hangings; (coll.) to kill by hanging.—**c. los hábi-**

tos, to doff the cassock. **II.** *vn.* to hang, be suspended; dangle; flag, hover, droop.

colibacilo, *m.* intestinal microbe.

coliblanca, *f.* (orn.) white-tailed S.-A. eagle.

coliblanco, ca, *a.* white-tailed.

colibre, colibrí, *m.* (orn.) humming bird.

cólica, *f.* colic.

colicano, na, *a.* gray-tailed.

cólico, ca. I. *a.* (med.) belonging to the colon. **II.** *m.* colic.—**c. hepático,** hepatic colic.—**c. miserere,** ileus.—**c. nefrítico,** or **c. renal,** renal colic.

colicuación, *f.* colliquation.—**colicuante,** *a.* colliquant; colliquative.—**colicuar. I.** *va.* to colliquate, melt, dissolve. **II.** *vr.* to colliquate; to become liquid.—**colicuativo, va,** *a.* colliquative.

colicuecer, *va.* (*ind.* COLICUEZCO: *subj.* COLICUEZCA) to fuse or melt.

coliflor, *f.* (bot.) cauliflower.

coligación, *f.* colligation; binding of things together; connection, union; alliance.

coligado, da. I. *n.* leaguer, convenanter. **II.** *a.* allied, associate, associated. **III.** *pp.* of COLIGARSE.

coligadura, *f.,* **coligamiento,** *m.* = COLIGACIÓN.

coligarse, *vr.* to colligate, colleague, confederate, unite, become allies.

coligió, colijo, colija. *V.* COLEGIR.

colilla, *f. dim.* small tail; stub of a cigar or cigarette.

colillero, ra, *n.* person who gathers cigar stubs for a trade.

colimación, *f.* collimation.

colimador, *m.* collimator.

colín, *a.* short-tailed horse.

colina, *f.* hill, hillock, knoll; seed of cabbage.

colinabo, *m.* (bot.) turnip; young cabbage.

colindante, *a.* contiguous, adjacent, abutting.

colindar, *vn.* (w. **con**) to be contiguous, or adjacent (to), to abut (on).

colino, *m.* small cabbage not transplanted.

colirio, *m.* collyrium, eyewash.

colirrábano, *m.* (bot.) kohlrabi.

colisa, *f.* (arti.) swivel gun.

coliseo, *m.* theatre, opera house, playhouse; colosseum.

colisión, *f.* collision, crush, clash; bruise, chafe, soreness from rubbing; opposition, clash of ideas.

colitigante, *m.* co-litigant, one who carries on a lawsuit with another.

colitis, *f.* colitis.

colmadamente, *adv.* abundantly, plentifully.

colmado, da. I. *a.* filled, full, heaped; (w. **de**) having in abundance. **II.** *m.* specialty eating house (gen. the specialty is sea food). **III.** *pp.* of COLMAR.

colmar, *va.* to heap up, fill to the brim; to fulfil, make up; to bestow liberally; (w. **de**) to bestow in abundance, to give in plenty.

colmena, *f.* beehive.—**colmenar,** *f.* apiary.

colmenero, ra, *n.* beekeeper, beemaster.

colmenilla, *f.* (bot.) morel, an edible mushroom.

colmillada, *f.* attack, or wound, with tusks or fangs.

colmillar, *a.* belonging to an eyetooth, fang or tusk.

colmillazo, *m. aug.* large eyetooth; COLMILLADA.

colmillejo, *m. dim.* small eyetooth, fang or tusk.

colmillo, *m.* eyetooth, canine tooth; fang; tusk.—**escupir por el c.,** (coll.) to brag, boast.—**mostrar los colmillos,** (coll.) to show spirit and resolution.—**tener colmillos,** (coll.) to be quicksighted, not easily imposed upon.

colmilludo, da, *a.* having long eyeteeth, fangs, or tusks; sagacious, quick-sighted.

colmo, *m.* heap; finishing, completion, crowning; overmeasure; fill; thatched roof; height.—**a c.,** abundantly, plentifully.—**llegar a c.,** to reach perfection.—**ser el c.,** (coll.) to be the limit.

colmo, ma, *a.* heaping full.

colocación, *f.* place, situation, position, employment; laying, putting in place; distribution of parts.

colocar, *va.* (*pret.* COLOQUÉ: *subj.* COLOQUE) to arrange, put in due place or order; to place, provide with a situation or employment.

colocasia, *f.* (bot.) Egyptian bean.

colocolo, *m.* a handsome S.-A. wild cat; (Ch.) an imaginary monster hatched from a rotten egg.

colocutor, ra, *n.* collocutor.

colodión, *m.* collodion.

eolodra, *f.* milk pail; kit; pailful; wooden can for measuring wine; drinking can with a handle; drinking horn with a cork bottom; whetstone case.—**ser una c.,** (coll.) to be a toper.

colodrazgo, *m.* tax on wine sold at retail.

colodrillo, *m.* occiput, nape of the neck.

colofón, *m.* (print.) colophon.

colofonia, *f.* colophony; resin.

colofonita, *f.* garnet of a light green or rosy red color.

coloidal, *a.* (chem.) colloidal.—**coloide,** *m.* colloid.

coloideo, a, *a.* (chem.) colloidal.

colombiano, na, *n.* & *a.* Colombian.

colombino, na, *a.* Columbian, relating to Columbus.

colon, *m.* (anat.) colon; (gram.) principal part or member of a period.

colonato, *m.* system of colonization.

colonche, *m.* (Mex.) an intoxicating drink from the sap of the cactus and sugar.

colonia, *f.* colony; plantation; silk ribbon two fingers wide.

colonial, *a.* colonial.

colonización, *f.* colonization.

colonizador, ra, *n.* & *a.* colonizer (-ing).

colonizar, *va.* (*pret.* COLONICÉ: *subj.* COLONICE) to colonize; settle.

colono, *m.* colonist, settler; planter, farmer.

coloño, *m.* load of wood carried on the back.

coloquíntida, *f.* (bot.) colocynth; bitter apple or gourd.

coloquio, *m.* colloquy, talk.

color, *m.* color; dye; paint; rouge; pretext, pretence, false show or appearance; coloring, tint; complexion; flush, blush; aspect.—**c. muerto,** or **quebrado,** wan or faded color.—**c. vivo,** bright color.—**de c.,** colored.—**sacarle los colores a uno,** to make one blush.—**so c.,** on pretense, under pretext.

coloración, *f.* coloring, coloration, painting.

colorado, da. **I.** *a.* ruddy; red; indelicate, smutty; colored; specious.—**poner a uno c.,** to put one to the blush.—**ponerse c.,** to blush. **II.** *pp.* of COLORAR.

colorante, *a.* coloring.

colorar, *va.* to dye; paint, stain, tint, color.

colorativo, va, *a.* coloring.

colorear. **I.** *va.* to make plausible, palliate, excuse. **II.** *vn.* to redden, grow red.

colorete, *m.* rouge.

colorido, *m.* coloring or color; pretext, pretense.

colorido, da. **I.** *a.* colored. **II.** *pp.* of COLORIR.

coloridor, ra, *n.* = COLORISTA.

colorimetría, *f.* colorimetry.

colorimétrico, ca, colorimetric.

colorímetro, *m.* colorimeter.

colorín, *m.* (orn.) linnet; bright, vivid, loud color.

colorir, *va.* to color artistically; make plausible.

colorista, *m.* colorist.

colosal, *a.* colossal, huge, gigantic.

colosense, *n.* & *a.* Colossian.

coloso, *m.* colossus.

colotipia, *f.* collotype; collotypy.

colpa, *f.* whitish sort of copperas; a flux.

colpotomía, *f.* (surg.) colpotomy, incision of the vagina.

cólquico, *m.* colchicum, meadow saffron.

columbino, na, *a.* dovelike, innocent, candid.

columbio, *m.* (chem.) columbium, niobium.

columbrar, *va.* to spy, perceive, discern at a distance; to trace by conjectures.

columelar, *m.* incisor.

columna, *f.* (arch., eng., mil., print.) column; supporter, protector; pile of things; column of air or water.—**c. dorsal,** spine.—**c. miliaria,** milestone.—**c. salomónica,** (arch.) twisted column.—**c. vertebral,** spine.

columnario, ria, *a.* columnar (app. to money coined in Spanish America, with the impression of two columns).

columnata, *f.* colonnade.

columpiar. **I.** *va.* to swing. **II.** *vr.* to swing; (coll.) to waddle.

columpio, *m.* swing; seesaw.

coluna, *f.* = COLUMNA.

colunita, *f. dim.* small column.

colurión, *m.* (orn.) lesser butcher bird, flusher.

coluro, *m.* (ast.) colure.

colusión, *f.* collusion.—**colusoriamente,** *adv.* collusively, fraudulently.

colusorio, ria, *a.* collusory, collusive.

colutorio, *m.* (pharm.) gargle.

coluvie, *f.* gang of rascals; sewer, sink.

colza, *f.* (bot.) colza, summer rape.

colla, *f.* collet, piece of ancient armor; (P. I.) continuous squalls preceding the monsoons; channel of an auger; last oakum placed in a seam.

collado, *m.* height, fell, hillock.

collar, *m.* necklace; chain or cord from which hang certain insignia of honor; collar, collet.

collarcito, *m. dim.,* **collarejo,** *m. dim.* small collar or necklace.

collarín, *m.* black neck stock edged with white, worn by the Roman Catholic clergy; collar of a coat.

collarino, *m.* (arch.) half round, torus.

collazo, *m.* plowman, farmhand, laborer.

colleja, *f.* (bot.) lamb's-lettuce or corn salad.—*pl.* slender nerves in a sheep's neck.

collera, *f.* collar, breast harness for draught cattle; horse collar; (naut.) stay of the dead blocks.

collerón, *m.* harness collar, hame.

colleta, (bot.) a kind of small cabbage.

collón, *m.* (coll.) coward, poltroon, base fellow.

collonada, *f.,* **collonería,** *f.* (coll.) cowardice.

coma, *f.* comma (,); (mus.) each of the parts into which a tone is divided.

coma, *m.* (med.) coma, profound insensibility.

comadre, *f.* midwife; mother or godmother with respect to each other; (coll.) gossip; pal, intimate friend; go-between.

comadrear, *vn.* to gossip, tattle.

comadreja, *f.* weasel.

comadreo, *m.* **comadrería,** *f.* gossip, gossipping.

comadrero, ra, *n.* & *a.* gossip (person), gossipping (person).

comadrón, *m.* man midwife, accoucheur.

comal, *m.* (Mex.) flat earthenware pan for cooking maize cake.

comalía, comalición, *f.* an epizoötic disease of sheep.

comandado, da, *a.* (mil.) officered.

comandancia, *f.* command; office of a commander; province or district of a commander.—**C. general de Marina,** High Court of Admiralty.

comandanta, *f.* commander's wife.

comandante, *n.* commander, commandant, leader; major, (Colomb.) lieutenant colonel.

comandar, *va.* (mil.) to command, govern.

comandita, *f.* (com.) silent partnership.

comanditario, a. **I.** *a.* (com.) belonging or relating to a silent partnership; silent (partner, partnership). **II.** *n.* (com.) silent partner.

comando, *m.* (mil.) command.

comarca, *f.* territory, region; border, boundary, limit.

comarcano, na, *a.* neighboring, near, bordering.

comarcar. **I.** *va.* (*pret.* COMARQUÉ: *subj.* COMARQUE) to plant (trees) in a straight line, so as to form walks. **II.** *vn.* to border, to abut (on).

comatoso, sa, *a.* (med.) comatose.

comba, *f.* curvature, warp, bend, bulge; game of jumping or skipping rope; skipping rope.

combadura, *f.* bending, bend, bulging, belly; sag.

combar. I. *va.* to bend, to curve. **II.** *vr.* to warp, bulge, sag.

combate, *m.* combat, fight, battle; agitation of the mind; struggle.

combatible, *a.* combatable, conquerable.

combatidor, ra, *n.* combatant.

combatiente, *n.* & *a.* combatant, fighter (-ing).

combatir, *va.* & *vn.* to combat, fight; to contest, attack, oppose; to struggle.

combatividad, *f.* (phren.) combativeness.

combeneficiado, *m.* prebendary of the same church as another.

combés, *m.* open space; (naut.) waist of a ship; upper deck.

combinable, *a.* combinable.

combinación, *f.* combination; aggregate of words beginning with the same syllable; concurrence; (chem.) combination; compound.

combinar, *va.* & *vr.* to combine, join, unite.

combinatorio, ria, *a.* combining, uniting; combinative; (math.) combinatorial.

combleza, *f.* concubine of a married man.

comblezo, *m.* one who lives in concubinage with a married woman.

combo, ba. I. *a.* bent, crooked, warped. **II.** *m.* stand or frame for casks.

comburente, *a.* producing combustion.

combustibilidad, *f.* combustibility.

combustible. I. *a.* combustible. **II.** *m.* fuel.

combustión, *f.* combustion.

combusto, ta, *a.* burnt.

comedero, ra. I. *a.* eatable, edible. **II.** *m.* feeding trough; dining room, eating place.

comedia, *f.* comedy; play, drama; farce; theater. **—c. de capa y espada,** costume play of the seventeenth century.—**c. de costumbres,** modern-society play.—**c. de enredo,** play with a complicated plot.—**c. togada,** ancient Latin play; Grecian or Roman costume play.

comedianta, *f.* comedienne.

comediante, *m.* player, actor, comedian.—**c. de la legua,** strolling player.

comediar, *va.* to divide into equal shares or parts, to average.

comedidamente, *adv.* courteously, civilly; with moderation.

comedido, da. I. *a.* civil, polite, courteous; prudent, moderate. **II.** *pp.* of COMEDIRSE.

comedimiento, *m.* civility, politeness, kindness; moderation, prudency.

comedio, *m.* center of a realm or place; intermediate time between epochs.

comedión, *m.* long and tedious comedy.

comedirse, *vr.* (*ind.* me COMIDO: *subj.* me COMIDA) to govern one's self; to be moderate, civil, obliging, kind.

comedor, ra. I. *n.* & *a.* eater (-ing), feeder (-ing). **II.** *m.* dining room.

comején, *m.* a kind of wood borer.

comejonera, *f.* nest of COMEJÉN; (Ven.) disreputable resort.

comendador, *m.* knight commander of a military order; prefect of religious houses.

comendadora, *f.* superior of a nunnery.

comendatario, *m.* commendatary.

comendaticio, cia, *a.* commendatory (letter).

comendatorio, ria, *a.* relating to letters of introduction or recommendation.

comendero, *m.* commendator, beneficiary of the crown.

comensal, *n.* commensal; member of a household; table companion.

comensalía, *f.* fellowship of house and table.

comentador, ra, *n.* commentator.—**comentar,** *va.* to comment.—**comentario,** *m.* commentary.—**comentarista,** *n.* commentator.—**comento,** *m.* comment.

comenzante, *n.* & *a.* beginner (-ing).

comenzar, *va.* & *vn.* (*ind.* COMIENZO: *pret.* COMENCÉ: *subj.* COMIENCE) to commence, begin.

comer. I. *vn.* to eat; to feed; to dine.—**c. a dos carrillos,** to enjoy two places or benefices at the same time.—**c. como un sabañón,** (coll.) to eat excessively, to stuff oneself.—**c. de mogollón,** to live at other people's expense; to sponge.—**c.,** or **comerse, vivo,** to devour (fig.), to scalp (fig.); to be very painful or troublesome.—**tener que c.,** to have a competence. **II.** *va.* to eat; to have (an income); to spend, waste, exhaust; to corrode, consume; to take (a piece or checker in a game). **III.** *vr.* to omit, skip; to eat.—**comerse a uno con los ojos,** to look daggers at one.—**comerse los codos de hambre,** (coll.) to be starved to death.—**comerse unos a otros,** to live like cats and dogs. **IV.** *m.* eating.—**ganar de c.,** to earn a livelihood.

comerciable, *a.* merchantable, marketable; sociable, social, affable.—**comercial,** *a.* commercial, mercantile.—**comercialmente,** *adv.* commercially.

comerciante, *n.* trader, merchant.—**c. comisionista,** commission merchant.

comerciar, *vn.* to trade, deal; to commerce, have intercourse.

comercio, *m.* trade, commerce, communication, intercourse; unlawful sexual intercourse; tradesmen, body of merchants; business section of a town; store, shop; a card game.—**c. exterior,** foreign trade.—**c. interior,** domestic commerce.

comestible. I. *a.* eatable, comestible. **II.** *m. pl.* victuals, provisions.

cometa. I. *m.* (ast.) comet.—**c. crinito,** long-bearded comet. **II.** *f.* kite; a card game.

cometedor, ra, *n.* offender, perpetrator.

cometer, *va.* to commit, charge, intrust; to commit, perpetrate; (com.) to order.

cometido, *m.* commission; charge, trust; task, duty.

comezón, *f.* itch, itching; longing desire.

cómicamente, *adv.* comically.

comicastro, tra, *n.* mediocrer actor, actor of no account.

comicial, *a.* comitial.

comicios, *m. pl.* comitia; (pol.) primaries, district assemblies.

cómico, ca. I. *a.* comic, dramatic, relating to the stage; comical, ludicrous, funny. **II.** *n.* player, actor (-tress); writer of comedies.

comida, *f.* eating; food, dressed victuals; dinner; meal, fare; feed.

comidilla, *f. dim.* slight repast; peculiar fancy, fad, or favorite amusement.

comido, da, *a.* fed; having eaten.—**c. por servido,** hand-to-mouth wages.

comienzo, *m.* beginning, initiation, start.

comienzo, comience. *V.* COMENZAR.

comilitón, *m.* parasite. *V.* CONMILITÓN.

comilitona, comilona, *f.* (coll.) splendid and plentiful repast.

comilón, na, *n.* great eater, glutton.

comilla, *f. dim.* of COMA.—*pl.* quotation marks (" ").

cominear, *vn.* (coll.) to indulge in trifles or occupations belonging to women.

cominero. I. *a.* meddlesome, officious. **II.** *n.* cotquean.

cominillo, *m.* darnel. *V.* JOYO.

comino, *m.* (bot.) cumin plant, cumin seed; a Colombian tree producing very valuable construction and cabinet wood.—**no valer un c.,** not to be worth a rush.

comisar, *va.* to confiscate, sequestrate, attach.

comisaría, *f.,* **comisariato,** *m.* commissaryship, commissariat.

comisario, *m.* commissary; delegate, deputy; manager.—**c. de barrio,** or **cuartel,** justice of the peace of a ward.—**c. de entradas,** in hospitals, the person that keeps an account of the patients who enter.—**c. de guerra,** (mil.) reviewing officer. —**c. ordenador,** (mil.) assistant quartermaster.

comisión, *f.* trust; commission; mandate, charge; precept, order; ministration, ministry; commission, perpetration.

comisionado, da. I. *a.* commissional or commissionary; commissioned, deputed, empowered. **II.** *n.* commissioner; (com.) agent; proxy, attorney. **III.** *pp.* of COMISIONAR.

For pronunciation, see the rules at the beginning of the book.

comisionar, va. to commission, depute, empower, appoint.

comisionista, m. commissioner; commission merchant; commission agent.

eomiso, m.(law) confiscation of prohibited goods; the goods when confiscated; (com.) seizure, attachment.

comisorio, ria, a. obligatory for a time or valid for a fixed day.

comistión, f. = CONMISTIÓN.

comistrajo, m. (coll.) hodge-podge, mess.

comisura, f. (anat.) commissure; suture.

comital, a. = CONDAL.

comité, m. committee; commission.

comitente, n. & a. constituent.

comitiva, f. suite, retinue, followers.

cómitre, m. (naut.) boatswain on board a galley; sea captain under orders of the admiral of the fleet.

comiza, f. (icht.) a kind of barbel.

como (interr. **cómo**). **I.** adv. how; in what manner; to what degree; as; like; if; as soon as; in the same manner as; so that; such as; that; inasmuch as.—¿cómo? what is it? what did you say?—¿cómo así? how? how so?—¿cómo no? why not? of course, naturally. **II.** interj. why, is it possible?

cómoda, f. chest of drawers; bureau.

comodable, a. that can be lent or borrowed.

cómodamente, adv. conveniently; comfortably.

comodante, n. (for.) one who lends gratuitously for a limited time.

comodatario, ria, n. borrower; pawnbroker.

comodato, m. loan; contract of loan and restitution.

comodidad, f. comfort, convenience; ease, freedom from want; leisure; opportunity; profit, interest, advantage.

comodín, m. (coll.) something of general utility; in cards, a card that has different values.

cómodo, m. utility, profit, convenience.

cómodo, da, a. convenient, handy, suitable; comfortable.

comodoro, m. (naut.) commodore.

compacto, ta, a. compact, close, dense.

compadecer. I. va. (ind. COMPADEZCO: subj. COMPADEZCA) to pity; sympathize with. **II.** vr. to agree with each other, accord, conform; (w. de) to pity, sympathize (with).

compadraje, m. confederacy or alliance for mutual protection and advancement (gen. used in a bad sense); ring, clique.

compadrar, vn. to become a godfather or mother; to contract a spiritual affinity.

compadrazgo, m. COMPADRAJE; condition or state of COMPADRES.

compadre, m. godfather and father of a child, each with respect to the other; protector, benefactor; (coll.) friend, old chap (an expression of familiarity).

compadrear, vn. (coll.) to be on familiar terms.

compadrería, f. friendship between COMPADRES, companions, pals.

compaginación, f. arrangement, connection.

compaginador, ra, n. arranger, adjuster.

compaginar, va. to arrange in proper order; to unite, join.

companage, compango, m. cold lunch, cold cuts.

compaña, f. (obs.) family; company.

compañerismo, m. good fellowship, comradeship.

compañero, ra, n. companion, friend, pal, comrade, chum; fellow member; partner or associate; one of a pair, mate.

compañía, f. company; society; partnership; company; (mil.) company; theatrical company.—c. de Jesús, Society of Jesus.—c. de la legua, strolling company of players.—c. de seguros, insurance company. (For c. anónima, c. comanditaria, etc. v. SOCIEDAD.)

comparable, a. comparable.

comparación, f. comparison.

comparador, m. comparing rule; comparer.

comparar, va. to compare; confront, collate.

comparativamente, adv. comparatively.

comparativo, va, a. comparative.

comparecencia, f. appearance (before a judge, etc.)

comparecer, vn. (ind. COMPAREZCO: subj. COMPAREZCA) to appear (before a judge, etc.)

compareciente, n. & a. (one) that appears (before a judge, etc.)

comparendo, m. summons, citation.

comparición, f. (law) appearance.

comparsa, f. retinue of personages represented on the stage; masquerade in carnival.—n. figurant on the stage.

comparte, n. (law) joint party; accomplice.

compartimiento, m. compartment; division of a whole into parts; inclosure, department; (aer.) curtain (of a dirigible).

compartir, va. to divide into equal parts; to share.

compás, m. compasses; dividers; calipers; territory and district assigned to a monastery; (mus.) measure, time, motion of the baton of a conductor; space on the staff between two bars; size, compass; rule of life, standard, pattern; springs of a coach roof.—c. de barra, beam compass.—c. de calibres, calipers.—c. de división, dividers.—c. de espesores, or de gruesos, spring calipers; thickness gage.—c. de mar, or de marear, mariner's compass.—c. de proporción, proportional dividers.—c. de puntas secas, or de punta fija, dividers.—c. de regla = c. DE BARRA.—a c., in right musical time.—llevar el c., (mus.) to keep time.

compasadamente, adv. by rule and measure.

compasar, va. to measure with a rule and compass; to arrange properly; (mus.) to divide (a score) into equal parts.—c. la carta de marear, (naut.) to prick the chart.

compasible, a. pitiful; compassionate.

compasillo, m. (mus.) quadruple, or ⁴⁄₄ measure.

compasión, f. compassion, pity, sympathy.

compasivamente, adv. compassionately.

compasivo, va, a. compassionate, merciful, tender-hearted.

compaternidad, f. = COMPADRAZGO.

compatibilidad, f. compatibility.

compatible, a. compatible, suitable, consistent (with).

compatricio, cia; compatriota, n. countryman (countrywoman), compatriot, fellow citizen.

compatrón, m. = COMPATRONO.

compatronato, m. common right of patronage.

compatrono, na, n. fellow patron or patroness, joint patron.

compeler, va. to compel, force, constrain.

compendiador, ra, n. epitomizer, abridger.

compendiar, va. to abridge, condense.

compendiariamente, adv. briefly.

compendio, m. compendium, epitome, abridgment, summary, abstract.

compendiosamente, adv. briefly, concisely.

compendioso, sa, a. brief; abridged, concise; compact.

compendizar, va. = COMPENDIAR.

compenetración, f. compenetration.

compenetrarse, vr. to compenetrate, pervade, intermix.

compensable, a. compensable.

compensación, f. compensation; recompense, reward.—de c., compensating.

compensador, ra. I. a. compensated; balanced. **II.** m. compensator; compensating pendulum.

compensar, va. & vn. to compensate, recompense; to counterbalance; to balance, equilibrate; to make amends for, indemnify.

compensativo, va. I. a. compensating. **II.** m. (chem.) compensation.

compensatorio, ria, a. compensating.

competencia, f. competition, rivalry; competence; cognizance.—a c., vyingly.

competente, *a.* competent, apt, able; consistent (with); applicable (to); adequate.

competentemente, *adv.* competently.

competer, *vn.* to be one's business or concern, to be incumbent on.

competición, *f.* competition.

competidor, ra. I. *n.* competitor, rival, opponent. **II.** *a.* competing.

competir, *vn.* (*ind.* COMPITO: *subj.* COMPITA) to vie, contest, contend, compete; to be on a level or par with another.

compilación, *f.* compilation; compilement.

compilador, ra, *n.* compiler; collector.

compilar, *va.* to compile.

compinche, *m.* (coll.) bosom friend, comrade, chum, crony, pal.

compito, compita. *V.* COMPETIR.

complacedero, ra, *a.* = COMPLACIENTE.

complacencia, *f.* pleasure, satisfaction; complacency, compliance, condescension.

complacer. I. *va.* (*ind.* COMPLAZCO: *subj.* COMPLAZCA) to please, humor, accommodate. **II.** *vr.* (w. en) to be pleased (with or to), to delight (in), to take pleasure (in).

complaciente, *a.* pleasing, accommodating, kind, agreeable.

complazco, complazca. *V.* COMPLACER.

complejo, ja, *a.* = COMPLEXO.

complejidad, *f.* = COMPLEXIDAD.

complementario, ia, *a.* complementary; completing, perfecting.

complemento, *m.* complement; perfection; completion; (gram.) object.

completamente, *adv.* completely, entirely; absolutely.

completar, *va.* to complete, perfect, finish.

completas, *f. pl.* completory, compline.

completivamente, *adv.* completively.

completivo, va, *a.* completive, completing, finishing.

completo, ta, *a.* complete, perfect; finished, completed; full, absolute.

complexidad, *f.* complexity, intricacy.

complexión, *f.* constitution, temperament of the body, habit, nature.

complexionado, da, *a.* constituted.—**bien, mal c.,** of a good, bad, constitution.

complexional, *a.* constitutional, temperamental.

complexo. I. *a.* complex; intricate, arduous, difficult. **II.** *m.* complex.

complicación, *f.* complication.

complicadamente, *adv.* complicatedly.

complicado, da, *a.* complicated.

complicar, *va.* (*pret.* COMPLIQUÉ: *subj.* COMPLIQUE) to complicate; to jumble together.

cómplice, *com.* accomplice.

complicidad, *f.* complicity.

complot, *m.* plot, conspiracy.

complutense, *n.* & *a.* Complutensian.

compluvio, *m.* (archeol.) compluvium.

componedor, ra. I. *n.* compositor, typesetter; writer, author; composer; contriver; mender, repairer; arbitrator. **II.** *m.* (print.) composing stick.

componenda, *f.* fees paid for bulls and licenses; arbitration; compromise; settlement.

componente, *n.* & *a.* component.

componer. I. *va.* (*pp.* COMPUESTO: *ind.* COMPONGO: *pret.* COMPUSE: *subj.* COMPONGA) to compose; compound; construct; prepare; amount to; devise, invent; to mend, repair; heal, restore; to strengthen, brace, fortify; to trim, fit up, garnish; to compose (differences), reconcile, adjust, settle; to ward off; to compose (music); to write (poetry, etc.); (print.) to compose.—**c. el semblante,** to put on a calm appearance.—**c. tanto de renta,** to have so much a year. **II.** *vr.* to arrange one's clothes, hair, etc.; to compose, calm, quiet one's self.—**componérselas,** to shift for one's self.

componible, *a.* mendable, capable of repair; adjustable, that may be settled or compounded.

comporta, *f.* large basket for grape gathering.

comportable, *a.* bearable, endurable.

comportamiento, *m.* behavior, deportment.

comportar. I. *va.* to suffer, tolerate. **II.** *vr.* to comport, deport or behave one's self.

comporte, *m.* behaviour, conduct; air, manner, carriage.

comportería, *f.* trade and shop of a COMPORTERO.

comportero, ra, *n.* maker or seller of COMPORTAS.

comportilla, *f. dim.* small basket.

composición, *f.* composition; repair, mending; making up, compromise, adjustment; (print.) composition; (met.) composure; calm, modest, or sedate appearance.

compositivo, va, *a.* compositive, synthetic.

compositor, ra, *n.* musical composer.

compostura, *f.* composure; mending, repair, repairing; cleanliness, neatness of dress; adjustment, settlement, compromise; modesty, circumspection, sedateness; adulterating compound.

compota, *f.* preserves, sweetmeats.

compotera, *f.* compotier.

compound, *a.* (st. eng., elec.) compound.

compra, *f.* purchase; buying, shopping.—**hacer compras,** to make purchases, to shop.

comprable; compradero, ra; compradizo, za, *a.* purchasable.

comprado, compradillo, *m.* play in the game of ombre.

comprador, ra; comprante, *n.* buyer; purchaser; shopper; caterer.

comprar, *va.* to buy, purchase; to shop.

compraventa. *V.* CONTRATO DE COMPRAVENTA.

comprehensivo, va, *a.* comprehensive.

comprendedor, ra, *n.* one who comprehends or understands.

comprender, *va.* to embrace, comprise, include, cover; to understand, comprehend.

comprensibilidad, *f.* intelligibility, comprehensibility.

comprensible, *a.* comprehensible, understandable.

comprensión, *f.* comprehension, understanding; comprehensiveness; act of comprising or containing.

comprensivo, va, *a.* comprehensive; capable of understanding; comprising, containing.

comprensor, ra, *n.* one that understands, attains or embraces; (theol.) blessed one.

compresa, *f.* (surg.) compress.

compresbítero, *m.* fellow presbyter or priest.

compresibilidad, *f.* compressibility.

compresible, *a.* compressible.

compresión, *f.* compression; (gram.) SINÉRESIS.

compresivamente, *adv.* compressibly, contractedly.

compresivo, va, *a.* compressive, compressing, reducing, compacting.

comprimente, *a.* compressing; restraining.

comprimible, *a.* compressible; repressible.

comprimir. I. *va.* to compress, compact, condense; to repress, restrain. **II.** *vr.* to become compact; to control one's self.

comprobación, *f.* verification, checking; proof, substantiation; (print.) checking up of proof corrections.

comprobante. I. *a.* proving, evidential. **II.** *m.* proof, evidence; voucher.

comprobar, *va.* (*ind.* COMPRUEBO: *subj.* COMPRUEBE) to verify, confirm, check; to corroborate, compare; to prove, substantiate, evidence.

comprofesor, *m.* colleague, member of the same profession.

comprometedor, ra. I. *a.* compromising, jeopardizing. **II.** *n.* one that jeopardizes.

comprometer. I. *va.* to compromise, arbitrate; to engage, bind; to render accountable or answerable; to expose, jeopardize, endanger. **II.** *vr.* to commit one's self; to become liable; to bind one's self; to expose one's self; to become engaged, betrothed; to become involved or implicated.

comprometimiento, *m.* pledge, promise; adjustment; jeopardy, embarrassment, predicament.

compromisario, ria, *n.* arbitrator, umpire, referee; presidential elector.

compromiso, *m.* compromise, arbitration; pledge, obligation; commitment; jeopardy, embarrassment, predicament; engagement, betrothal; engagement, appointment.

compropietario, ia, *n.* joint owner.

comprovincial, *a.* comprovincial, of the same metropolitan church.

comprovinciano, na, *a.* from the same province.

compruebo, compruebe. *V.* COMPROBAR.

compuerta, *f.* hatch or half-door; lock, sluice, floodgate; door curtain of an old-fashioned coach; piece of cloth bearing a knight's badge. —**c. de marea,** (naut.) tide gate, tiderace.

compuestamente, *adv.* regularly, orderly.

compuesto, a. I. *a.* compound; composed, consisting, made up; repaired; arranged. **II.** *m.* compound, preparation, mixture. **III.** *pp.* of COMPONER.

compulsa, *f.* (law) authentic or attested copy of an instrument or writing duly compared.

compulsar, *va.* (law) to make an authentic copy or transcript of; to compare, collate.

compulsión, *f.* compulsion.

compulsivo, va, *a.* compulsive.

compulsorio, ria, *n.* compulsory decree of a court, ordering an authentic copy to be made.

compunción, *f.* compunction, repentance.

compungido, da, *a.* compunctious, repentant.

compungirse, *vr.* (*ind.* COMPUNJO: *subj.* COMPUNJA) to feel compunction or remorse.

compungivo, va, *a.* pricking, stinging.

compurgación, *f.* compurgation.

compurgador, ra, *n.* compurgator.

compurgar, *va.* to prove (one's veracity or innocence) by the oath of another.

computación, *f.* computation, calculation.

computador, ra, *n.* computer.

computar, *va.* to compute, calculate.

computista, *m.* computist, computer.

cómputo, *m.* computation, calculation.

comulación, *f.* cumulation.

comulgante, *n.* (ecc.) communicant.

comulgar. I. *va.* (*pret.* COMULGUÉ: *subj.* COMULGUE) to administer communion.—**c. con ruedas de molino,** to fool, bamboozle, humbug. **II.** *vn.* to commune, communicate; to take communion.

comulgatorio, *m.* communion altar.

común. I. *a.* common, public; common, usual, customary, ordinary, generally or extensively used; current; vulgar, mean, low.—**c. de dos,** (gram.) that applies to both genders.—**c. de tres,** that applies to masculine, feminine, and neuter.—**en c.,** in common.—**por lo c.,** in general, generally. **II.** *m.* community; watercloset.—**c. de las gentes,** the general public, the average person, the man in the street.

comuna, *f.* main irrigation channel; Commune (of Paris); (Am.) municipality.

comunal. I. *m.* commonalty, common people. **II.** *a.* common, commonable.

comunero, ra. I. *a.* popular, common, pleasing to the people. **II.** *n.* commoner, one of the common people; joint holder of a tenure of lands; member of the party that upheld liberty against the encroachments of Charles V.; (Colomb.) member of the body of first patriots that rose against Spanish rule.

comunicabilidad. *f.* communicability.

comunicable, *a.* communicable; communicative.

comunicación, *f.* communication, intercourse; communiqué, official statement.—*pl.* means of communication.

comunicado, *m.* article of a personal nature sent to a periodical for publication.

comunicante, *n.* communicant.

comunicar. I. *va.* (*pret.* COMUNIQUÉ: *subj.* COMUNIQUE) to communicate, impart, make known; to announce; to transmit, send. **II.** *vr.* to communicate; to connect.—**c. entre sí,** to communicate with each other; to correspond, exchange correspondence; to be in mutual communication.

comunicativo, va, *a.* communicative; unreserved, informative.

comunidad, *f.* commonness; commonalty, the common people; community; corporation, guild, society.—*pl.* the cities of Castile which rose in support of Spanish liberty against the government of Charles V.—**de c.,** conjointly.

comunión, *f.* communion; fellowship; familiar intercourse; congregation; political party.

comunismo, *m.* communism.

comunista, *n.* & *a.* communist (-ic).

comúnmente, *adv.* commonly, usually, generally; frequently, often.

comuña, *f.* mixed wheat and rye, maslin, or meslin.—**comuñas,** seeds.

con, *prep.* with; by (when followed by infinitive: *con confesar se salvó*, by confessing, he saved himself); in other infinitive phrases, it simply indicates action, and the phrase is translated by the English gerund or infinitive (*con escribir basta*, writing is enough); notwithstanding, despite (also in infinitive phrases: *con ser muy enérgico, nada pudo hacer*, notwithstanding his being very energetic, he could do nothing); in (*con dolor*, in pain). With the pronouns *mí, sí, tí*, it forms the single words **conmigo,** with me, **consigo,** with himself, **contigo,** with thee.—**c. tal que,** provided that.—**c. que,** and so, then, so then.—**c. todo,** nevertheless, notwithstanding.

conato, *m.* endeavour, effort, exertion; (law) crime attempted but not committed, attempt.

concadenar, *va.* to concatenate; to chain or link together.

concambio, *m.* exchange.

concanónigo, *m.* fellow canon.

concatedralidad, *f.* union of two cathedral churches.

concatenación, *f.* concatenation.

concausa, *f.* concause, joint cause.

cóncava, concavidad, *f.* concavity, hollowness; hollow, cavity.

cóncavo, va. I. *a.* concave. **II.** *m.* concavity.

concebible, *a.* conceivable.

concebir, *va.* & *vn.* (*ind.* CONCIBO: *subj.* CONCIBA) to conceive, become pregnant; to conceive, have an idea of; to comprehend, understand.

concedente, *n.*, *a.* granter (-ing), conceder (-ing).

conceder, *va.* to give, bestow, grant; concede, admit.

concedido, da, *a.* conceded, granted.

concejal, *m.* councilman.

concejil, *a.* relating to the municipal council; common, public, belonging to the public.

concejo, *m.* civic body of a small town; municipal council; town hall; in Asturias, a district composed of several parishes with one common jurisdiction; foundling.

concento, *m.* concert of voices, harmony.

concentración, *f.* concentration.

concentrado, da. I. *a.* concentered, concentrate. **II.** *pp.* of CONCENTRAR.

concentrar. I. *va.* to concentrate; concenter. **II.** *vr.* = RECONCENTRARSE.

concéntrico, ca, *a.* concentric.

concepción, *f.* conception, act of conceiving; idea; immaculate conception of the Virgin; feast of the Immaculate Conception; Madonna, picture of the Virgin.

conceptear, *vn.* to give smart repartees.

conceptible, *a.* conceivable.

conceptismo, *m.* affected or exaggerated witticism.

conceptista, *m.* one who affects or overdoes witticism.

concepto, *m.* concept, thought, idea; pithy sentence, epigram, flash of wit; judgment, opinion; expression of opinion.

conceptualismo, *m.* conceptualism.

conceptualista, *a.* conceptualist.

conceptuar, *va.* to conceive; judge, think, form an opinion of.

conceptuosamente, *adv.* ingeniously, wittily, pithily.

For pronunciation, see the rules at the beginning of the book.

conceptuoso, sa, *a.* witty, sententious, epigrammatic.

concernencia, *f.* respect, concernment, relation.

concerniente, *a.* (w. **a**) concerning, relating (to); applicable.—**en lo c. a,** with regard to, as for.—**lo c.,** (u. by itself) what concerns the matter, the proper action, consideration, etc.

concernir, *v. def.* (*ind.* ello CONCIERNE: *subj.* ello CONCIERNA) (w. **a**) to concern, belong, appertain, be the business (of).

concertadamente, *adv.* regularly, orderly, methodically, concertedly; by agreement or appointment.

concertado, da, *a. V.* MAMPOSTERÍA.

concertador, *m.* regulator, adjuster, expediter.

concertante, *a.* (mus.) concerted, arranged for two or more voices or instruments.

concertar. I. *va.* (*ind.* CONCIERTO: *subj.* CONCIERTE) to arrange by agreement, adjust, harmonize, to agree on; to bargain, covenant, conclude (an agreement); close (a deal); (mus.) to harmonize (musical instruments); to compare, estimate the relative qualities of; to start or rouse (the game). **II.** *vn.* to agree, accord, suit one another. **III.** *vr.* to go hand in hand; to covenant; to contrive, design.

concertina, *f.* concertina, a musical instrument similar to the accordion.

concertista, *n.* person who manages or performs in concerts.

concesible, *a.* grantable.

concesión, *f.* concession, grant.

concesionario, *m.* (law) grantee, concessionary.

concesivo, va, *a.* that may be granted.

concia, *f.* prohibited part of a forest.

concibo, conciba. *V.* CONCEBIR.

conciencia, *f.* conscience; conscientiousness; consciousness.—**a c.,** conscientiously.—**en c.,** in good earnest, in truth.

concienzudamente, *adv.* conscientiously, scrupulously, thoroughly.

concienzudo, da, *a.* conscientious, scrupulous, thorough.

concierto, *m.* good order and arrangement; concert; bargain; agreement; contract; act of beating the wood with hounds to start the game; musical concert; concerto, a musical composition. —**de c.,** by agreement.

concierto, concierte. *V.* CONCERTAR.

conciliable, *a.* reconcilable, capable of conciliation.

conciliábulo, *m.* conventicle: unlawful assembly or meeting.

conciliación, *f.* conciliation; settlement (of disputes); affinity; winning (esteem, friendship, favor).

conciliador, ra, *n. & a.* conciliator (-ing), peacemaker (-ing), reconciler (-ing).

conciliar, *va.* to conciliate, compose, reconcile; to gain, win (affection, esteem).—**c. el sueño,** to induce sleep.—**c. las amistades,** to make friends.

conciliar. I. *a.* conciliar, relating to councils. **II.** *n.* member of a council.

conciliativo, va, *a.* conciliatory.

concilio, *m.* council; collection of decrees.

concisamente, *adv.* concisely.—**concisión,** *f.* conciseness.—**conciso, sa,** *a.* concise.

concitación, *f.* instigation, stirring up.

concitador, ra, *n.* instigator, incitor, agitator.

concitar, *va.* to excite, stir up, agitate.

concitativo, va, *a.* inciting; stirring.

conciudadano, *m.* fellow citizen, countryman.

conclave, cónclave, *m.* conclave; place in which a conclave is held; meeting, convention.

conclavista, *m.* conclavist; domestic of a cardinal.

concluir, *va.* (*ind.* CONCLUYO: *subj.* CONCLUYA) to conclude, end, finish, close; to convince with reason, make evident, silence by argument; to decide finally, determine; to infer, deduce; to close (judicial proceedings); to submit to a final decision; (fenc.) to disarm (an adversary) by engaging the guard of his sword.

conclusión, *f.* conclusion, end; winding up, denouement; close or closure; date; issue; conclusion of the proceedings in a lawsuit; conclusion, inference, deduction, consequence; thesis in schools. —**en c.,** finally, in conclusion; in closing.

conclusivo, va, *a.* conclusive, final.

concluso, sa, *a.* concluded, closed, terminated.

concluyente, *a.* concluding, conclusive; irrefutable, unanswerable.

concluyentemente, *adv.* conclusively.

concluyo, conluya. *V.* CONCLUIR.

concofrade, *m.* fellow member, brother (of a brotherhood).

concoide, *f.* (geom.) conchoid.

concoideo, a, *a.* conchoidal, shell-like.

concolega, *m.* fellow collegian.

concomerse, *vr.* (coll.) to shrug the shoulders.

concomido, concomimiento, *m.* (coll.) shrugging of the shoulders.

concomitancia, *f.* concomitance.

concomitante, *a.* concomitant, accompanying.

concomitar, *va.* to accompany, be a concomitant of, go with.

concordable, *a.* concordant, conformable, agreeable, consistent.

concordación, *f.* coördination, conformity.

concordador, ra, *n.* conciliator, peacemaker, moderator.

concordancia, *f.* concordance, conformity; harmony, concord of sounds; concordance of text or words; (gram.) concord, agreement.—*pl.* concordance (of a book, an author).

concordante, *a.* concordant, agreeing.

concordar. I. *va.* (*ind.* CONCUERDO: *subj.* CONCUERDE) to accord, regulate; to make agree. **II.** *vn.* to accord, agree, tally, to be congenial; be in accord; (gram.) to agree.

concordata, *f.,* **concordato,** *m.* concordat, covenant made by a government with the Pope.

concorde, *a.* concordant, agreeing, tallying, in agreement.

concordemente, *adv.* with one accord, in agreement, concordably.

concordia, *f.* concord, conformity, harmony; agreement, settlement out of court; peace, good will.—**de c.,** jointly, by common consent.

concorpóreo, rea, *a.* concorporeal, of the same body.

concreción, *f.* concretion.

concrecionar, *vn. & vr.* to form concretions.

concrescencia, *f.* (phys.) concrescence.

concretamente, *adv.* concretely.

concretar. I. *va.* to unite, harmonize, bring into conformity; to reduce to its simplest form. **II.** *vr.* to limit or confine one's self (to a subject).

concreto, ta. I. *a.* concrete, not abstract.—**en c.,** in the concrete; in brief, summing up. **II.** *m.* concretion; (erroneously but commonly) concrete (building material).

concubina, *f.* concubine, mistress.

concubinario, *m.* one who keeps a mistress.

concubinato, *m.* concubinage.

concúbito, *m.* coition.

concuerdo, concuerde. *V.* CONCORDAR.

conculcación, *f.* violation (of rights).

conculcador, ra, *n.* violator (of rights), oppressor.

conculcar, *va.* (*pret.* CONCULQUÉ: *subj.* CONCULQUE) to trample under foot; to violate, infringe.

concuñado, da, *n.* brother or sister-in-law, term confined to persons who are married to two brothers or sisters.

concupiscencia, *f.* concupiscence, lust, cupidity.

concupiscible, *a.* concupiscible, exciting desire.

concurrencia, *f.* audience; attendance; concurrence, coincidence; competition.

concurrente, *a.* concurrent; coincident.

concurrido, da. I. *pp.* of CONCURRIR. **II.** *a.* frequented; attended (s. o. a function, meeting, etc.)

concurrir, *vn.* to concur; to meet in one point, time, or place; to attend; to contribute; to coincide, agree; to compete (in an examination, etc.)

concursar, *va.* (law) to declare insolvent.

concurso, *m.* concourse, confluence of persons; conflux, crowd, congregation, assembly; aid, assistance; competitive contest between candidates for a professorship, curacy, etc.—**c. de acreedores,** meeting of creditors.

concusión, *f.* concussion, shaking, shock; exaction, extortion.

concusionario, ia. I. *a.* concussive, shaking. **II.** *n.* extortioner.

concha, *f.* shell, case, carapace; mollusk, shellfish; tortoise shell; any object that has the shape of a shell; prompter's box; bay in the shape of a horseshoe; basin; fixed grindstone in mills; ancient copper coin, worth about three farthings; (arch.) volute; conch; the external ear; shell of a dagger or cutlass; shell-shaped covering of the spike of Indian corn.—**c. de cabrestante,** (naut.) socket of the capstan.—**c. de nácar,** mother-of-pearl shell.—**conchas de escobenes,** (naut.) navel woods or navel hoods.—**meterse en su c.,** to become a recluse; to shut up like a clam.—**tener muchas conchas,** to be very reserved, artful, cunning.

conchabanza, *f.* manner of making one's self easy and comfortable; (coll.) plotting, conspiracy.

conchabar. I. *va.* to join, unite; to mix (inferior wool with superior). **II.** *vr.* to unite for some evil purpose; to plot, conspire.

conchado, da, *a.* scaly, shelly.

conchal, *a.* V. SEDA CONCHAL.

conchífero, ra, *a.* conchiferous, shell-bearing.

conchil, *m.* rock shell; murex.

conchilla, ita, *f. dim.* small shell.

conchudo, da, *a.* shelly, scaly; cunning, crafty, reserved.

conchuela, *f. dim.* = CONCHILLA.

condado, *m.* earldom, county; dignity of a count or earl.—**condal,** *a.* relating to the dignity of an earl or count.

conde, *m.* earl, count; overseer; elected head or chief of the gipsies.

condecente, *a.* convenient, fit, proper.

condecoración, *f.* decoration, embellishing or decorating; jewelled insignia of knighthood; medal; badge.

condecorar, *va.* to decorate, adorn, embellish; to bestow honors on; to bestow a medal or insignia on; to knight.

condena, *f.* the clerk of the court's attestation of the sentence of a condemned criminal; sentence, term of imprisonment, penalty.

condenable, *a.* condemnable, blamable, damnable.

condenación, *f.* condemnation; sentence to penalty; conviction (of a criminal); punishment; damnation.

condenado, da, *a.* damned, condemned to eternal punishment; condemned; convicted.

condenador, ra, *n. & a.* condemner (-ing), blamer (-ing), incriminator (-ing).

condenar. I. *va.* to prove, find or declare guilty, convict; to sentence; to damn; to condemn, censure, blame; to disapprove; to nail or wall up (a door, window, passage); to condemn as unsafe. **II.** *vr.* to condemn one's self, acknowledge one's fault; to be damned (to hell).

condenatorio, ria, *a.* condemnatory, damnatory.

condensabilidad, *f.* condensability.

condensable, *a.* condensable.

condensación, *f.* condensation.

condensador, ra. I. *a.* condensing. **II.** *m.* (st. eng., elec.) condenser.—**c. de chorro,** (st. eng.) jet condenser.—**c. de mezcla,** (st. eng.) mixing condenser.—**c. de placas,** (elec.) plate condenser.—**c. de superficie,** (st. eng.) surface condenser.

condensante, *a.* condensing.

condensar. I. *va.* to thicken, condense, compress. **II.** *vr.* to be condensed; to gather.

condensativo, va, *a.* condensative.

condesa, *f.* countess.

condescendencia, *f.* condescension, condescending, compliance, complacency.

condescender, *vn.* (ind. CONDESCIENDO: *subj.* CONDESCIENDA) to condescend, yield, submit, comply.

condescendiente, *a.* condescending, agreeable, complacent.

condesciendo, condescienda. V. CONDESCENDER.

condesita, *f. dim.* little or young countess.

condesito, *m. dim.* little earl; little count.

condesil, *a.* (coll.) belonging or relating to counts or countesses. V. CONDAL.

condestable, *m.* constable; lord high constable; (naut.) master gunner.

condestablía, *f.* constableship.

condición, *f.* condition, quality, state; footing; habit, disposition, temper; constitution; quality; rank, class; fashion; clause, stipulation, specification.—**c. callada,** tacit condition, condition understood.—**c. imposible de derecho,** provision or stipulation contrary to the law.—**c. imposible de hecho,** physically impossible provision, provision impossible per se, or de facto.—**c. sine qua non,** condition sine qua non, or absolutely indispensable.—**a c. de que,** or **con la c. de que,** on condition that.—**estar en condiciones de,** to be in condition to.—**tener c.,** to have a bad temper.

condicionado, da. I. *a.* conditioned; conditional. **II.** *pp.* of CONDICIONAR.

condicional, *a.* conditional.

condicionalmente, *adv.* conditionally; hypothetically.

condicionar, *vn.* to agree, accord; to impose conditions.

condicioncilla, ita, *f. dim.* hasty temper; small clause or stipulation.

condignamente, *adv.* condignly, deservedly, duly.

condigno, na, *a.* condign, suitable, deserved, due, merited.

cóndilo, *m.* (anat.) condyle.

condimentar, *va.* to dress or season (victuals).

condimento, *m.* condiment, seasoning.

condiscípulo, *m.* schoolfellow, schoolmate, fellow student.

condolerse, *vr.* (ind. CONDUELO: *subj.* CONDUELA) (w. de) to condole (with), to be sorry (for), to sympathize (with), to regret.

condominio, *m.* joint ownership.

condómino, *m.* joint owner.

condonación, *f.* condonation, pardoning.

condonar, *va.* to pardon, forgive, remit.

condonante, *a.* condoning, forgiving, remitting.

cóndor, *m.* Chilean and Colombian gold coin worth ten dollars; (orn.) condor.

condotiero, condottiere, *m.* condottiere. (English *pl.* condottieri, as in Italian.)

condrila, *f.* (bot.) common gum succory.

condrín, *m.* weight for precious metals in the Philippines = 0.3768 gramme, or about one-fourth a pennyweight.

condrografía, *f.* description of cartilages.

condrográfico, ca, *a.* chondrographic.

condrología, *f.* chondrology.

condropterigio, gia. I. *n. & a.* (ich.) chondropterygian. **II.** *m. pl.* Chondropterygii.

conducción, *f.,* **conducencia,** *f.* conveyance; carriage; cartage, transportation; act of conveying or conducting, leading, guiding; conduct; stipulated rate or charge for transportation; (aut.) driving.

conducente, *a.* conducive, conducent; official.

conducir. I. *va. & vn.* (ind. CONDUZCO: *pret.* CONDUJE: *subj.* CONDUZCA) to convey, carry; take, accompany; guide, direct, lead; to direct, manage, conduct; (aut.) to drive. **II.** *vn.* to conduce, contribute, favor; be fitted for; lead to. **III.** *vr.* to behave, act, conduct one's self.

conducta, *f.* conduct, behavior; conveyance, convoy; property conveyed; conduct, government, command, direction, management; party of recruits conducted to the regiment; contract made by a town or village with a physician to attend its sick.

conductero, *m.* one in charge of a convoy.

conductibilidad, *f.* conductibility.

conductible, *a.* conveyable, conductible.

conductividad, *f.* conductivity.

conductivo, va, *a.* conductive, conducting.

conducto, *m.* duct, conduit; channel through which any business is conducted or managed; means; mediator; person through whom anything is accomplished.—**por c. de,** by means of; through.

conductor, *m.* conductor; leader; usher; guide, conveyer; (phys.) conductor; (aut.) driver, motorist.

conductor, ra. I. conducting. **II.** *f.* conductress, directress; moving van.

conduelo, conduela. *V.* CONDOLER.

condueño, *m.* (com.) joint owner.

condumio, *m.* (coll.) meat dressed to be eaten with bread; plenty of food.

conduplicación, *f.* (rhet.) reduplication.

condutal, *m.* (mas.) leader; gutter.

conduzco, conduzca. *V.* CONDUCIR.

conectador, ra. I. *a.* connecting. **II.** *m.* connector.

conectar, *va.* to connect.

conceja, *f.* female rabbit.

concejal, conejar, *m.* rabbit warren.

conejera, *f.* warren for breeding rabbits; burrow; brothel; (coll.) den or cavern inhabited by poor people or frequented by bad characters, joint.

conejero. I. *m.* warrener, keeper of a rabbit warren. **II.** *a.* rabbit (u. a.), for rabbits.

conejillo, lla; conejito, ta, *n. dim.* little rabbit. —**c. de Indias,** guinea pig.

conejo, ja, *n.* (zool.) rabbit.—**conejuna,** *f.* rabbit down or fur.— **conejuno, na,** *a.* relating to rabbits, rabbit (u. a.).

conexidades, *f. pl.* rights annexed to the principal.

conexión, *f.* connection, union, joint, coherence. —*pl.* connections (social, commercial).

conexionarse, *vr.* to make (social, commercial) connections, to get in touch.

conexivo, va, *a.* connective.

conexo, xa, *a.* connected, united.

confabulación, *f.* confabulation, easy conversation, chat; leaguing, conspiracy, plot, collusion.

confabulador, ra, *n.* story teller, gossip; schemer, plotter.

confabular. I. *vn.* to confabulate; talk informally, chat. **II.** *vr.* to league, enter into conspiracy.

confalón, *m.* gonfalon, standard, ensign.

confalonier, confaloniero, *m.* gonfalonier, chief standard-bearer.

confarreación, *f.* confarreation.

confección, *f.* any handwork, fancy work, ready made article; (pharm.) confection, compound remedy, concoction.

confeccionador, ra, *n.* one who makes articles of dress or any handwork.

confeccionar, *va.* to make, prepare; put together; to compound, put up (medicines, prescriptions).

confederación, *f.* confederacy, confederation, federation, coalition; international treaty or convention.

confederado, da. I. *n.* & *a.* confederate, covenanter (-ing), associate. **II.** *pp.* of CONFEDERAR.

confederar, *va.* & *vr.* to confederate, join, form a confederacy.

conferencia, *f.* conference, meeting, conversation, interview; congress; daily lecture in universities; public lecture.

conferenciante, *n.* lecturer.

conferenciar, *vn.* to confer, consult together, hold an interview; to lecture.

conferir. I. *va.* (*ind.* CONFIERO: *subj.* CONFIERA) to confer; to give, bestow, award; to compare. **II.** *vn.* to confer; to lecture.

confesa, *f.* nun who was a widow.

confesado, da. I. *a.* & *pp.* of CONFESAR; confessed. **II.** *n.* (coll.) penitent.

confesante, *n.* one who confesses before a judge.

confesar. I. *va.* (*pp.* CONFESADO and CONFESO: *ind.* CONFIESO: *subj.* CONFIESE) to confess, acknowledge, own, avow, grant; to confess, hear or receive confessions; to confess to a priest.—**c. de plano,** to confess plainly or openly. **II.** *vr.* to confess or make confession; to shrive.

confesión, *f.* confession, avowal, acknowledgment; confession to a priest.—**c. auricular,** auricular confession.

confesionario, *m.* treatise with rules for confessing; confessional.

confesionista, *n.* Lutheran.

confeso, sa. I. *n.* (law) one who confesses a crime; converted Jew. **II.** *m.* lay-brother.

confesonario, *m.* confessional.

confesor, *m.* father confessor; title given to holy men by the Roman Catholic Church.

confetti, *m. pl.* confetti.

confiable, *a.* trusty, reliable.

confiadamente, *adv.* trustingly, with confidence.

confiado, da. I. *a.* confident, unsuspicious, trusting; presumptuous, arrogant or forward. **II.** *pp.* of CONFIAR.

confiador, *m.* (law) joint surety, fellow bondsman.

confianza, *f.* confidence, trust, reliance, faith; courage, firmness of opinion; presumptuousness, forwardness, assurance; familiarity, intimacy.— **de c.,** informal, unceremonious.—**en c.,** confidentially.

confiar. I. *vn.* (w. en) to rely (on), to trust (in). **II.** *va.* to confide, intrust, credit; commit to the care of another.

confidencia, *f.* trust, confidence; secret or confidential information.—**confidencial,** *a.* confidential.—**confidencialmente,** *adv.* confidentially.

confidente. I. *n.* confident, intimate, counsellor; detective, informer, secret agent, spy; settee for two persons, tête-à-tête. **II.** *a.* true, faithful, trusty.

confidentemente, *adv.* confidently, faithfully.

confiero, confiera. *V.* CONFERIR.

confieso, confiese. *V.* CONFESAR.

configuración, *f.* configuration.

configurar, *va.* to form, shape.

confín, *m.* limit, boundary, confine, border.

confín, confinante, *a.* bordering, abutting, conterminous; limiting, boundary (u. a.).

confinación, *f.* = CONFINAMIENTO.

confinado, da, *n.* one confined to a place or region under surveillance.

confinamiento, *m.* confinement, exile; (law) confinement within certain bounds under surveillance.

confinar, *va.* & *vn.* to banish, exile; to confine, imprison or immure; to border upon, abut.— **c. con,** to abut on, be bounded by.

confingir, *va.* (*ind.* CONFINJO: *subj.* CONFINJA) (pharm.) to mix into one mass.

confirmación, *f.* confirmation, corroboration, attestation; (eccl.) confirmation.

confirmadamente, *adv.* firmly, assuredly.

confirmador, ra, *n.* confirmator, attester, confirmer.

confirmante, *n.* & *a.* confirmer (-ing).

confirmar, *va.* to confirm, corroborate, verify; to strengthen, support, ratify; (ecc.) to confirm.

confirmativamente, *adv.* confirmingly.

confirmatorio, ria, *a.* confirmatory, confirmative.

confiscable, *a.* confiscable, forfeitable.

confiscación, *f.* confiscation, forfeiture.

confiscado, da, *a.* confiscate, confiscated.

confiscar, *va.* (*pret.* CONFISQUÉ: *subj.* CONFISQUE) to confiscate.

confitar, *va.* to confect, to candy with melted sugar; to make into sweetmeats or into preserves; to dulcify, to sweeten.

confite, *m.* comfit, sugarplum.—**confites,** dainties, sugarplums, bonbons.—**morder en un c.,** to be hand and glove, to be intimate.

confitente, *a.* = CONFESO.

confíteor, *m.* (ecc.) confiteor.

confitera, *f.* vessel for comfits; box for candies.

confitería, *f.* confectionery; confectioner's shop.

confitero, ra, *n.* confectioner; tray for sweetmeats.

confítico, illo, ito, *m.* *dim.* small comfit; caraway comfit.—*pl.* ornaments in the shape of comfits wrought on coverlets.

confitura, *f.* confection, sweetmeat.

conflación, *f.* fusion, melting of metals, smelting.

conflagración, *f.* conflagration; sudden and violent perturbation of towns and nations.

conflátil, *a.* fusible.

conflicto, *m.* conflict, struggle, strife, combat; (met.) agony, pang.

confluencia, *f.* confluence.—**confluente,** *a.* confluent.

confluir, *vn.* (*ind.* él CONFLUYE: *pret.* CONFLUYÓ: *subj.* CONFLUYA) to join or meet (app. to rivers and sea currents); to assemble or concur in one place.

conformación, *f.* conformation.

conformador, *m.* shaper; hat conformator; boot crimper.

conformar. I. *va.* to conform, adjust, fit. **II.** *vn.* to suit, fit, conform; cohere; level. **III.** *vr.* to comply, to agree; to yield, submit; to resign one's self.

conforme. *a.* alike, corresponding, suitable, congruent, consonant, accordant; correct, acceptable, O. K.; consistent; compliant, resigned.—**c. a,** consistent with, agreeable to.

conforme, *adv.* in due proportion; agreeably, according to.

conformemente, *adv.* conformably, unanimously; correctly; agreeably.

conformidad, *f.* resemblance, likeness; conformity; agreement, consistence, consonance, congruence; concord, concordance; symmetry; close attachment of one person to another; affinity; submission, patience, resignation.—**de c.,** by common consent; correctly.—**en c.,** agreeably, suitably, according to.

conformismo, *n.* conformism.

conformista, *m.* conformist.

confortación, *f.* comfort, consolation; encouragement.

confortador, ra, *n.* & *a.* comforter (-ing), consoler (-ing), strengthener (-ing).

confortamiento, *m.* comfort, consolation; encouragement.

confortante. I. *a.* comforting, soothing. **II.** *m.* calmative, stomachic.—*pl.* mitts.

confortar, *va.* to comfort, strengthen, enliven, invigorate; to encourage, console, cheer, solace.

confortativo, va, *a.* comfortable, cordial; encouraging, cheering, strengthening.

conforte, *m.* = CONFORTACIÓN.

confracción, *f.* fracture, breaking.

confraternidad, *f.* confraternity, brotherhood.

confricación, *f.* rubbing, friction.

confricar, *va.* to rub.

confrontación, *f.* confrontation, confronting; comparison, comparing; sympathy, natural conformity.

confrontante, *n.* & *a.* confronter (-ing).

confrontar. I. *va.* to collate, confront; to compare. **II.** *vn.* to agree in sentiments and opinion; (w. **con**) to border upon.

confucianismo, *m.* Confucianism.

confuciano, na; confucionista, *n.* & *a.* Confucian.

confundir. I. *va.* (*pp.* CONFUNDIDO and CONFUSO) to confound, jumble; to perplex, confuse, darken, throw into disorder; to confute by argu-

ment; to abase, humiliate. **II.** *vr.* to be bewildered, perplexed, confounded, rattled, mixed up; to be ashamed and humbled.

confusamente, *adv.* confusedly; helter-skelter.

confusión, *f.* confusion, disorder; perplexity, perturbation, entanglement, confusedness; obscurity; humiliation, shame, ignominy.

confuso, sa, *a.* confused, mixed, confounded, jumbled together; obscure, doubtful, unintelligible; blurred, indistinct; fearful, timorous, perplexed.—**en c.,** confusedly.

confutación, *f.* confutation, disproof.

confutar, *va.* to confute, disprove, refute.

congelable, *a.* congealable.—**congelación,** *f.* solidification, freezing, congealing; congealment.—**congelador,** *m.* freezer.—**congelamiento,** *m.* = CONGELACIÓN.—**congelar,** *va.* & *vr.* to congeal, freeze.—**congelativo, va,** *a.* having the power of congealing.

congénere, congenérico, ca. *a.* congeneric, of like kind.

congenial, *a.* congenial; analogous.

congeniar, *vn.* to be congenial.

congénito, *a.* congenital, connate.

congerie, *f.* congeries, heap, mass.

congestión, *f.* (med.) congestion.

congestionar. I. *va.* to congest. **II.** *vr.* to accumulate (s. o. the blood).

congiario, *m.* congiary.

congio, *m.* congius, an ancient liquid measure.

conglobación, *f.* conglobation, acquired sphericity; mixture and union of immaterial things; (rhet.) accumulation of proofs.

conglobar, *va.* to conglobate, heap together.

conglomeración, *f.* conglomeration, heterogeneous mixture.

conglomerado, da, *n.* & *a.* conglomerate.

conglomerar, *va.* to conglomerate.

conglutinación, *f.* conglutination, glutination; cementing, sticking.

conglutinar. I. *va.* to conglutinate, cement, unite. **II.** *vr.* to conglutinate, stick together.

conglutinativo, va; conglutinoso, sa, *a.* viscous, glutinous, cementing.

congoja, *f.* anguish, dismay, anxiety, grief, sorrow.—**congojar,** *va.* to afflict, grieve.

congojosamente, *adv.* anxiously, sorrowfully.—**congojoso, sa,** *a.* afflictive, distressing; afflicted.

congoleño, ña, *a.* of or relating to the Congo.

congosto, *m.* narrow pass, canyon.

congraciador, ra, *n.* flatterer, fawner, wheedler, congratulator.

congraciamiento, *m.* flattery, fawning.

congraciar. I. *va.* to adulate, flatter. **II.** *vr.* to get into one's good graces.

congratulación, *f.* congratulation.

congratular. I. *va.* to congratulate, compliment. **II.** *vr.* to congratulate one's self, rejoice.

congratulatorio, ria, *a.* congratulatory, congratulating.

congregación, *f.* congregation; meeting, assembly; fraternity, brotherhood.

congregacionalismo, *m.* Congregationalism.

congregacionalista, *n.* & *a.* Congregationalist.

congregante, ta, *n.* member of a congregation, fraternity, or brotherhood.

congregar, *va.* & *vr.* (*pret.* CONGREGUÉ: *subj.* CONGREGUE) to assemble, meet, congregate, gather.

congresista, *n.* congressman (-woman).

congreso, *m.* congress, consistory, convention, assembly; sexual intercourse.—**C. de los Diputados,** in Spain and some Spanish American republics, House of Representatives.

congrio, *m.* (zool.) conger eel, sea eel.

congrua, *f.* competent sustenance to one who is to be ordained a priest.

congruamente, *adv.* conveniently; becomingly.

congruencia, *f.* convenience; fitness; congruence.

congruente, *a.* congruent, agreeing, corresponding.

congruentemente, *adv.* suitably, congruously.

congruísmo, *m.* congruism, a religious doctrine.

congruísta, *n.* supporter of congruism.

congruo, grua, *a.* congruous, apt, fit, suitable.

cónica, *f.* (math.) conic, conic section.

conicidad, *f.* conicity.

cónico, ca, *a.* conical, conic.

conífero, ra. I. *a.* (bot.) coniferous. **II.** *f. pl.* Coniferæ.

conidio, *m.* (bot.) conidium.

coniforme, *a.* coniform.

conivalvo, va, *a.* (zool.) having a conical shell.

coniza, *f.* (bot.) great fleabane.

conjetura, *f.* conjecture, surmise, guess.

conjeturable, *a.* conjecturable.

conjeturador, ra, *n.* conjecturer, guesser.

conjetural, *a.* conjectural.

conjeturalmente, *adv.* conjecturally, guessingly.

conjeturar, *va.* to conjecture, to guess.

conjuez, *m.* cojudge.

conjugación, *f.* conjugation.

conjugado, da. I. *a.* (math.) conjugate. **II.** *pp.* of CONJUGAR.

conjugar, *va.* (*pret.* CONJUGUÉ: *subj.* CONJUGUE) (gram.) to conjugate.

conjunción, *f.* conjunction, union, association, league; conjugation; copulation; act of coupling or joining together; consolidation; (gram., ast.) conjunction.

conjuntamente, *adv.* in all, all together, jointly.

conjuntiva, *f.* (anat.) conjunctiva.

conjuntivo, va, *a.* conjunctive.

conjuntivitis, *f.* (med.) conjunctivitis.

conjunto, ta. I. *a.* united, connected; contiguous; allied by kindred or friendship; mixed or incorporated with another thing. **II.** *m.* whole, aggregate, entirety.—**en c.,** as a whole; in all, totally.

conjura, conjuración, *f.* conspiracy, conjuration, plot, machination.

conjurado, da. I. *n.* conspirator. **II.** *pp.* of CONJURAR.

conjurador, ra, *n.* conspirator; conjurer, exorcist.

conjuramentar. I. *va.* to take an oath to, to swear in. **II.** *vr.* to bind one's self by oath, to take an oath.

conjurante, *a.* conjuring; conspiring.

conjurar. I. *vn.* to conjure; conspire, plot; to join in a conspiracy. **II.** *va.* to exorcise; to conjure; to entreat, implore; avert, ward off.

conjuro, *m.* conjuration; exorcism, incantation; entreaty.

conllevador, ra, *n.* helper, assistant.

conllevar, *va.* to aid or assist; to bear.

conmemoración, *f.* remembrance; commemoration; anniversary.—**conmemorar,** *va.* to commemorate.—**conmemorativo, va,** *a.* commemorative.

conmemoratorio, ria, *a.* commemoratory.

conmensal, *m.* messmate, fellow boarder.

conmensalía, *f.* commensality.

conmensurabilidad, *f.* commensurability.

conmensurable, *a.* commensurable.

conmensuración, *f.* commensuration.

conmensurar, *va.* to commensurate.

conmensurativo, va, *a.* commensurable.

conmigo, with me, with myself. *V.* CON.

conmilitón, *m.* comrade, companion; fellow soldier.

conminación, *f.* commination, threat.

conminar, *va.* to threaten; (law) to denounce punishment.

conminatorio, ria, *a.* comminatory, denunciatory, threatening.

conminuta, *a.* (surg.) comminuted.

conmiseración, *f.* commiseration, pity, sympathy.

conmistión, *f.* commixion.

conmisto, ta, *a.* mixed, mingled, incorporated.

conmistura, *f.* = CONMISTIÓN.

conmixto, ta, *a.* = CONMISTO.

conmoción, *f.* commotion, excitement, stirring up, flurry, disturbance.

conmonitorio, *m.* written narrative of an event; (law) reminder from a superior to an inferior judge.

conmovedor, ra. I. *a.* touching; sad, pathetic; exciting, stirring. **II.** *n.* disturber, agitator.

conmover, *va.* (*ind.* CONMUEVO: *subj.* CONMUEVA) to touch, appeal to; to disturb, agitate, stir up.

conmutabilidad, *f.* commutability.

conmutable, *a.* commutable.

conmutación, *f.* commutation, exchange.

conmutador, *m.* electric switch; telegraph key.

conmutar, *va.* to exchange, barter.

conmutativo, va, *a.* commutative.

connatural, *a.* connatural, inborn.

connaturalización, *f.* naturalization, adaptation to new conditions, acclimatization.

connaturalizarse, *vr.* to accustom one's self; to become inured or acclimated.

connaturalmente, *adv.* connaturally.

connivencia, *f.* connivance; plotting.

connotación, *f.* connotation; distant relationship.

connotado, *n.* remote relationship.

connotante, *a.* connotative.

connotar, *va.* to connote, imply.

connotativo, va, *a.* (gram.) connotative, connotive.

connovicio, cia, *n.* fellow novice.

connubial, *a.* connubial, matrimonial, conjugal.

connubio, *m.* matrimony, marriage, wedlock.

connumerar, *va.* to enumerate, include in a number.

cono, *m.* (geom.) cone; (bot.) cone, fruit of the pine family.

conocedor, ra. I. *a.* (w. **de**) familiar (with), expert (in). **II.** *n.* connoisseur, expert; chief herdsman.

conocer. I. *va.* (*ind.* CONOZCO: *subj.* CONOZCA) to know; to experience, observe, perceive, comprehend; to be acquainted with; to know carnally. **II.** *vn.* to know.—**c. de una causa,** or **pleito,** (law) to try a case (app. to a judge). **III.** *vr.* to know each other; to know one's self.

conocible, *a.* cognoscible, knowable.

conocidamente, *adv.* in a known manner.

conocido, da. I. *n.* acquaintance. **II.** *a.* prominent, well known. **III.** *pp.* of CONOCER.

conocimiento, *m.* knowledge, understanding, cognition; consciousness; skill, ability; acquaintance, slight friendship; (com.) bill of lading; note of identification, voucher; (Am.) check for baggage.—*pl.* learning, erudition.—**venir en c. de,** to learn of.

conoidal, *a.* conoidal.—**conoide,** *f.* conoid.

conopial, conopio, *m.* (arch.) ogee arch.

conozco, conozca. *V.* CONOCER.

conque. I. *conj.* so then; now then; and so; well then. **II.** *m.* (coll.) wherewithal.

conquiforme, *a.* conchiform.

conquiliología, *f.* (zool.) conchology.

conquista, *f.* conquest, subjugation; conquered territory or thing; winning another's affections.

conquistable, *a.* conquerable; attainable, accessible.

conquistador, ra, *n. & a.* conqueror (-ing).

conquistar, *va.* to conquer, overcome, subdue; to win (another's affections).

conrear, *va.* to grease (wool); (agr.) to hoe.

conregnante, *a.* reigning with another.

conreinar, *vn.* to reign with another.

consabido, da. I. *a.* already known, alluded to, in question, before-mentioned, aforesaid. **II.** *pp.* of CONSABER.

consabidor, ra, *n.* one who possesses knowledge jointly with others.

consagración, *f.* consecration.

consagrado, da. I. *a.* consecrated, sacred; devoted, given (to study, sports, etc.). **II.** *pp.* of CONSAGRAR.

consagrante, *n.* consecrator.

consagrar. I. *va.* to consecrate, hallow, make sacred; to deify; to consecrate, devote, dedicate; to erect (a monument). **II.** *vr.* to devote or give one's self (to study, work, etc.)

consanguíneo, nea, *a.* consanguineous, cognate, kindred.

consanguinidad, *f.* consanguinity.

consciente, *a.* conscious; of sound mind, sane; (law) compos mentis.

conscientemente, *adv.* consciously.

conscripción, *f.* (mil.) conscription.

conscripto, *a. V.* PADRE.

consectario. I. *m.* corollary. **II.** *a.* consequent; annexed.

consecución, *f.* attainment, obtaining, acquisition.

consecuencia, *f.* consequence, conclusion, inference; issue; consistence, firmness, coherence; consequence, importance, moment, concern.—**en c.,** consequently, therefore.—**guardar c.,** to be consistent.—**por c.** = EN C.—**ser de c.,** to be important.—**traer a c.,** to adduce, bring to bear, or as corroborative evidence.

consecuente. I. *m.* effect, issue, consequence; (math.) consequent. **II.** *a.* consequent, following; consistent, logical.

consecuentemente, *adv.* consequently.

consecutivamente, *adv.* consecutively.

consecutivo, va, *a.* consecutive.

conseguimiento, *m.* attainment, obtainment, acquisition.

conseguir, *va.* (*ind.* CONSIGO: *subj.* CONSIGA) to attain, get, obtain.

conseja, *f.* story, fairy tale, fable.

consejera, *f.* counsellor's wife; woman adviser.

consejero, *m.* counsellor, member of a council; adviser; anything that gives warning.—**c. de la corona,** crown minister.

consejo, *m.* counsel, advice; council, court, assembly of magistrates, advisory board, consulting body; council house.—**c. de guerra,** court-martial; council of war.—**c. de ministros,** cabinet.

consenciente, *a.* consenting; conniving.

consenso, *m.* general assent; agreement of opinion, consensus.

consensual, *a.* (law) consensual.

consentido, da. I. *a.* spoiled (child), coddled. **II.** *pp.* of CONSENTIR.

consentidor, ra, *n.* complier, conniver; coddler.

consentimiento, *m.* consent; coddler, compliance, acquiescence; (med.) consent.

consentir. I. *va.* (*ind.* CONSIENTO: *subj.* CONSIENTA) to allow, permit, tolerate, acquiesce in, condescend to; to believe; to accept, admit; to coddle, spoil, overindulge. **II.** *vn.* (mech.) to flag, give way, weaken, become loose. **III.** *vr.* to spring, crack, begin to break.

conserje, *m.* keeper or warden of a royal palace, castle, or public building; janitor, concierge.

conserjería, *f.* wardenship of a royal palace or castle; warden's dwelling; janitor's office, conciergerie.

conserva, *f.* conserve, preserve, jam; pickles; fleet of merchantmen under convoy of a ship of war.—**c. trojezada,** preserve of minced fruit.—**conservas alimenticias,** canned goods.

conservación, *f.* conservation; maintenance, upkeep.

conservador, ra. I. *n.* conservator, preserver; curator. **II.** *n. & a.* conserver (-ing); (pol.) Conservative.

conservaduría, *f.* dignity in the order of Malta.

conservante, *n. & a.* conserver (-ing).

conservar, *va.* to conserve, maintain, preserve, keep; to guard; to preserve or pickle (fruit), to can.

conservativo, va, *a.* conservative, preservative.

conservatoría, *f.* place and office of a JUEZ CONSERVADO; grant to communities to choose their own conservators.—*pl.* letters patent granted by conservatory judges.

conservatorio, *m.* conservatory; place for instruction in the fine arts.

conservatorio, ria, *a.* conservatory; having a preservative quality.

conservero, ra, *n.* conserver, preparer of conserves.

considerable, *a.* considerable, great, large.

considerablemente, *adv.* considerably.

consideración, *f.* consideration, regard, notice, sake, account; reflection, contemplation, meditation; importance; urbanity, respect.—**en c.,** considering, in consideration, in proportion.—**ser de c.,** to be of importance or moment.

consideradamente, *adv* considerately; calmly.

considerado, *a.* prudent; considerate; esteemed, respected, distinguished.

considerador, ra, *n.* considerer, considerator.

considerando. I. *ger.* of CONSIDERAR. **II.** *conj.* whereas (as used in enumerating reasons or circumstances in legal language). **III.** *m.* introductory clause, clause introduced with "whereas."

considerante, *a.* considering.

considerar, *va.* to consider, meditate, think over; to treat with urbanity, show consideration or kindness to.

consiento, consienta. *V.* CONSENTIR.

consiervo, *m.* fellow serf.

consigna, *f.* (mil.) watchword, countersign.

consignación, *f.* consignation, assignation, apportionment; (com.) consignment, shipment.

consignador, ra, *n.* (com.) consignor.

consignar, *va.* to consign, assign, make over; to set apart, devote; to yield, intrust; to state in writing; to lay by, to deposit; (com.) to consign (goods); (law) to deposit in trust.

consignatario, *m.* trustee; (law) mortgagee who enjoys the property mortgaged until the debt be paid out of the proceeds; (com.) consignee.

consigo, with one's self, with himself, herself, themselves, yourself, or yourselves. *V.* CON.—**c. mismo, c. propio,** or **c. solo,** alone, by one's self.

consigo, consiga. *V.* CONSEGUIR.

consiguiente. I. *m.* consequence, result, effect. —**de c., por c., por el c.,** consequently, therefore. **II.** *a.* consequent, resulting, following; consistent, logical.

consiguientemente, *adv.* consequently.

consiliario, *m.* counsellor; assistant to head of a corporation.

consintiente, *a.* consenting, agreeing.

consistencia, *f.* consistence, consistency; stability; duration; coherence; conformity; firmness, solidity.

consistente, *a.* consistent, firm, solid.

consistir, *vn.* to consist, subsist, continue fixed; to be comprised, contained.—**c. en,** to lie, to consist in (*never* to consist *of*, in the sense of "to be composed of").

consistorial, *a.* consistorial, belonging or relating to an ecclesiastical court.

consistorialmente, *adv.* in or by a consistory.

consistorio, *m.* consistory, ecclesiastical court; pontifical senate; in some Spanish towns, the municipal council and the townhouse or town hall.—**c. divino,** tribunal of God.

consocio, *m.* partner, associate; companion, fellow, comrade.

consol, *m.* (Peru) = CONSOLA.

consola, *f.* console, pier table; bracket shelf.

consolable, *a.* consolable, relievable.

consolablemente, *adv.* consolably, comfortingly.

consolación, *f.* consolation, comfort; (in some card games) forfeit.

consolado, da. I. *a.* consoled, comforted. **II.** *pp.* of CONSOLAR.

consolador, ra, *n. & a.* comforter (-ing), consoler (-ing), soother (-ing).

consolante, *a.* comforting, consoling, soothing.

consolar, *va.* (*ind.* CONSUELO: *subj.* CONSUELE) to console, comfort, cheer, soothe.

consolativo, va; consolatorio, ria, *a.* consolatory, consoling, comforting.

consólida, *f.* (bot.) = CONSUELDA.—**c. real,** larkspur.

consolidación, *f.* consolidation.

consolidado, da, *a.* consolidated; funded (s. o. debts).—*pl.* consolidated annuities, consols, government securities.

consolidar. I. *va.* to consolidate, compact; to harden, strengthen; to fund (debts). **II.** *vr.* to consolidate, grow firm, hard, or solid; (law) to unite.

consolidativo, va, *a.* consolidant, consolidative.

consonancia, *f.* consonance, harmony, rime; consistency, congruence; consent; conformity.

consonante. I. *m.* riming word, rime; (mus.) consonous or corresponding sound. **II.** *f. & a.* (gram.) consonant. **III.** *a.* consonant, consistent, concordant.

consonantemente, *adv.* consonantly, fittingly.

consonar, *vn.* (ind. CONSUENO: subj. CONSUENE) (mus.) to make harmonious sounds; (poet.) to rime; to agree, harmonize, become, fit.

cónsones, *m. pl.* (mus.) concordant sounds, chords.

cónsono, na, *a.* consonous, harmonious, consonant.

consorcio, *m.* consortium, partnership, society; martial union; friendly intercourse; mutual affection.

consorte, *n.* consort; companion, partner, mate; one who enters or defends an action jointly with another.

conspicuo, cua, *a.* conspicuous; prominent, distinguished.

conspiración, *f.* conspiracy, plot.

conspirado, da; conspirador, ra; conspirante, *n. & a.* conspirator (-ing).

conspirar, *vn.* to conspire, plot; to agree together, coöperate, combine.

constancia, *f.* constancy, steadiness.

constante. I. *a.* constant; continual, uninterrupted; firm, unalterable, immutable; loyal, constant; manifest, apparent, clear; composed, consisting. **II.** *f. & a.* (math.) constant.

constantemente, *adv.* constantly; firmly, unalterably; evidently, undoubtedly.

constantinopolitano, na, *a.* of or belonging to Constantinople.

constar, *v. imp.* to be clear, evident, certain; to be of record, registered; to be composed (of), to consist (of); of verses, to have the proper measure and accent.

constelación, *f.* constellation; climate, temperature; epidemic.

consternación, *f.* consternation, distress; horror, panic.

consternar, *va.* to terrify, strike with horror or amazement; to cause a panic to or in; to distress, grieve.

constipación, *f.* constipation; cold in the head.

constipado, da. I. *a.* constipated; having, or suffering from, a cold. **II.** *m.* cold in the head. **III.** *pp.* of CONSTIPAR.

constipante, *a.* constipating, binding.

constipar. I. *va.* to constipate, bind; to cause a cold. **II.** *vr.* to become costive; to catch cold.

constipativo, va, *a.* = CONSTIPANTE.

constitución, *f.* constitution (in all its meanings); rules and by-laws.

constitucional. I. *m.* constitutionalist, constitutionist. **II.** *a.* constitutional.

constitucionalidad, *f.* constitutionality.

constitucionalismo, *m.* constitutionalism.

constitucionalmente, *adv.* constitutionally.

constituir. I. *va.* (ind. CONSTITUYO: subj. CONSTITUYA) to constitute; erect, establish, make, create; appoint, depute. **II.** *vr.* **constituirse en obligación de,** to bind one's self to perform.

constitutivo, va. I. *a.* constitutive, essential. **II.** *n.* constituent.

constituyente, *n. & a.* constituent.

constreñidamente, *adv.* compulsively.

constreñimiento, *m.* constraint, compulsion.

constreñir, *va.* (ind. CONSTRIÑO: subj. CONSTRIÑA) to constrain, compel, force; (med.) to bind or make costive; to contract.

constricción, *f.* contraction.

constrictivo, va, *a.* binding, constricting, astringent; compelling, forcing.

constrictor, ra, *a.* constrictor.

constringente, *a.* constringent.

constriño, constriña. *V.* CONSTREÑIR.

construcción, *f.* construction; act and art of constructing; architecture; structure; building; (gram.) construction.—**de c.,** *a.* building, structural.

constructor, ra, *n.* builder; maker.—**c. de buques,** shipbuilder.

construir, *va.* (ind. CONSTRUYO: subj. CONSTRUYA) to form, build, construct; to translate literally; (gram.) to construct.

constuprador, *m.* debaucher, defiler, corrupter.

constuprar, *va.* to defile, debauch, corrupt.

consubstanciación, *f.* consubstantiation.

consubstancial, *a.* (theol.) consubstantial.

consubstancialidad, *f.* consubstantiality.

consuegrar, *vn.* to become joint fathers- or mothers-in-law.

consuegro, gra, *n.* parent-in-law with respect to the parent of his son- or daughter-in-law.

consuelda, *f.* (bot.) comfrey.

consuelo, *m.* consolation, comfort; joy, merriment.—**sin c.,** (coll.) out of rule or measure, to excess.

consuelo, consuele. *V.* CONSOLAR.

consueno, consuene. *V.* CONSONAR.

consueta, *n.* stage prompter; (prov.) directory for divine service.—*pl.* short prayers.

consuetudinario, ria, *a.* customary, generally practised; common (law) (theol.) in the habit of sinning.

cónsul, *n.* consul.—**c. general,** consul general.

consulado, *m.* consulate; consulship; tribunal or court of commerce.—**c. general,** consulate general.

consular, *a.* consular.

consulta, *f.* question proposed, or the answer given in writing; consultation, conference, meeting for deliberation; report made and advice given to the king in council.

consultable, *a.* worthy or necessary to be deliberated upon.

consultación, *f.* consultation, conference, meeting.

consultante, *n. & a.* consulter (-ing).

consultar, *va.* to consult, ask advice of; to advise; to deliberate about, discuss.—**c. con la almohada,** (coll.) to sleep over, think over.

consultivo, va, *a.* consultative, conciliary, advisory.

consultor, ra, *n. & a.* consulter (-ing), adviser (-ing), counsel, counsellor.

consultorio, *m.* bureau of information; (med.) consulting institution, clinic.

consumación, *f.* consummation, end, completion; destruction, suppression, total extinction.—**c. de los siglos,** end of the world.

consumadamente, *adv.* perfectly, completely, consummately.

consumado, da. I. *a.* consummate, complete, perfect. **II.** *pp.* of CONSUMAR. **III.** *m.* jelly broth, consommé.

consumador, ra, *n.* finisher; one who consummates, perfects, or finishes.

consumar, *va.* to consummate, finish, perfect, complete.

consumativo, va, *a.* consummate; that consummates or completes (s. o. the sacrament).

consumido, da, *a.* (coll.) thin, exhausted, emaciated, wasted away; easily afflicted.

consumidor, ra, *n. & a.* consumer (-ing).

consumimiento, *m.* consumption.

consumir. I. *va.* (pp. CONSUMIDO and CONSUNTO) to consume; to waste away; to destroy, extirpate; to wear out, exhaust; to aflict, grieve; to take (the Eucharist) in the mass (used also as *vn.*). **II.** *vr.* to be spent, exhausted; to fret; to be uneasy, vexed; to waste away, pine, languish.—**c. de,** to be consumed by, or with.

consumo, *m.* consumption (of provisions, fuel, merchandise).—*pl.* excise tax.

consunción, *f.* consumption, waste, decline; (med.) consumption, tuberculosis.

consuno, na.—de c., jointly, together, in accord.

consuntivo, va, *a.* consuming.

consustanciación, *f.* = CONSUBSTANCIACIÓN.

consustancial, *a.* = CONSUBSTANCIAL.

contabilidad, *f.* bookkeeping, accounting; calculability.

contabilista, *n.* bookkeeper, accountant.

contacto, *m.* contact; (elec.) contact; terminal, binding post.

contadero, ra. I. *a.* countable, numerable. **II.** *m.* narrow passage where sheep or cattle are counted.—**entrar, or salir, por c.,** to go in or out through a narrow passage.

contado, da, *a.* scarce, rare, uncommon.—**al c.,** (for) cash.—**de c.,** cash; instantly, immediately; in hand.—**por de c.,** of course, as a matter of course.

contador, ra, *n.* purser, paymaster, cashier; computer; accountant; numberer, numerator, automatic counter; telltale; meter for gas, water, or electricity; cash register, counter; table or bench in a business office, desk; (law) auditor; receiver.

contaduría, *f.* accountant's or auditor's office at the exchequer; auditorship; office of a cashier, paymaster or treasurer; box office, in a theater.

contagiar. I. *va.* to infect, communicate, spread by contagion; to corrupt, pervert. **II.** *vr.* (w. de) to become infected, take by contagion.

contagio, *m.* contagion; contagious disease; corruption of morals.

contagión, *f.* progressive malignity of a disease, as cancer; propagation of vice and evil habits.

contagiosidad, *f.* contagiousness.

contagioso, sa, *a.* contagious; perverting.

contal, *m.* string of beads for counting.

contaminación, *f.* contamination, pollution; defilement; stain, blot.

contaminado, da. I. *pp.* of CONTAMINAR. **II.** *a.* contaminated, corrupted, polluted.

contaminar, *va.* to contaminate, defile, pollute; pervert, corrupt; to infect by contagion; to corrupt, vitiate, or destroy the integrity of (a text or original); to profane.

contante.—dinero c., or **dinero c. y sonante,** ready money, cash.

contar. I. *va.* (*ind.* CUENTO: *subj.* CUENTE) to count, reckon, number; to relate, tell; to book; to place to account; to class; to rate; to consider, look upon. **II.** *vn.* to compute, figure.—**c. con,** to depend on, rely on; to reckon with, take into account.

contemperar, *va.* to temper, moderate.

contemplación, *f.* contemplation, meditation; compliance, complaisance.

contemplador, ra, *n.* contemplator.

contemplar, *va.* to contemplate, examine, study; to view, behold, look upon; to meditate, muse over; to be lenient or condescending with; to coddle, overindulge, spoil (a child).

contemplativamente, *adv.* attentively, thoughtfully, contemplatively.

contemplativo, va. I. *a.* contemplative; studious; lenient; condescending. **II.** *m.* contemplator; pious devotee.

contemporáneamente, *adv.* contemporaneously, simultaneously.

contemporaneidad, *f.* contemporaneousness.

contemporáneo, nea, *n.* & *a.* contemporary, coetaneous, coeval.

contemporización, *f.* temporizing, compliance.

contemporizador, ra, *n.* temporizer; complier.

contemporizar, *vn.* (*pret.* CONTEMPORICÉ: *subj.* CONTEMPORICE) to temporize; to comply.

contención, *f.* contention; emulation; contest, dispute, strife.

contencioso, sa, *a.* contentious; quarrelsome, disputatious; (law) being the object of strife or dispute; litigious.

contendedor, *m.* = CONTENDOR.

contender, *vn.* (*ind.* CONTIENDO: *subj.* CONTIENDA) to fight, combat; contend, debate; dispute; litigate; to argue, discuss, expostulate.

contendiente, *n.* & *a.* fighter (-ing), disputant, litigant.

contendor, *m.* fighter, contender, antagonist, opponent.

contenedor, ra, *n.* holder, tenant.

contenencia, *f.* suspension in the flight of birds; a peculiar movement in Spanish dancing; (law) demurrer.

contener. I. *va.* (*ind.* CONTENGO: *pret.* CONTUVE: *subj.* CONTENGA) to contain, hold; to comprise, include, embrace; to check, curb, restrain, stop. **II.** *vr.* to control one's self, to refrain.

contenido, da. I. *a.* moderate, prudent, temperate, modest. **II.** *pp.* of CONTENER. **III.** *m.* contents; inclosure.

conteniente, *a.* containing, comprising.

contenta, *f.* (com.) indorsement (*v.* ENDOSO); satisfactory treat or present; (mil.) certificate of good conduct.

contentadizo, za, *a.* (sometimes preceded by **bien**) easily pleased.—**mal c.,** hard to please.

contentamiento, *m.* contentment, joy, satisfaction, content.

contentar. I. *va.* to satisfy, gratify, please; (com.) to indorse. *V.* ENDOSAR.—**ser de buen (mal) c.,** to be easy (hard) to please. **II.** *vr.* to be contented, pleased, or satisfied.

contentible, *a.* contemptible.

contentivo, va, *a.* containing, comprising.

contento, ta. I. *a.* glad, pleased, contented, satisfied, content. **II.** *m.* contentment, joy, satisfaction, mirth; (law) release, discharge.—**a c.,** to one's satisfaction.

contera, *f.* shoe (of cane, umbrella, etc.); chape of a scabbard; button of the cascabel of a gun; refrain of a song.—**por c.,** at the end, as a finish.

contérmino, na, *a.* contiguous, abutting.

conterráneo, nea, *n.* countryman (-woman), fellow citizen.

contertuliano, na; contertulio, lia, *a.* belonging to the same social circle, of the same set.

contestable, *a.* contestable, disputable.

contestación, *f.* answer, reply; contestation, the act of contesting; debate, altercation, dispute.

contestar. I. *va.* to answer, reply; to confirm (the deposition of another); to prove; to attest. **II.** *vn.* to agree, to accord.

conteste, *a.* (law) confirmation of the evidence of another.

contexto, *m.* intertexture; context.

contextuar, *va.* to prove by quoting authorities.

contextura, *f.* contexture, texture; context; frame and structure of the human body.

conticinio, *m.* dead of night.

contienda, *f.* contest, dispute, debate; strife, fray, struggle.

contiendo, contienda. *V.* CONTENDER.

contignación, *f.* (arch.) contignation.

contigo, with thee. *V.* CON.

contiguamente, *adv.* contiguously, closely.

contiguidad, *f.* contiguity, closeness.

contiguo, gua, *a.* contiguous, close, adjacent.

continencia, *f.* continence, self-control; abstinence, moderation; graceful bow in a dance; act of containing.—**c. de la causa,** (law) unity which should exist in every judgment or sentence.

continental, *a.* continental.

continente. I. *m.* continent; container; countenance, mien. **II.** *a.* continent, abstemious, sober, moderate.

continentemente, *adv.* moderately, abstemiously, chastely.

For pronunciation, see the rules at the beginning of the book.

contingencia, *f.* contingency, emergency, possibility, risk.

contingente. I. *a.* contingent, fortuitous, accidental. **II.** *m.* contingent, share.

contingentemente, *adv.* casually, accidentally, contingently.

contingible, *a.* that may happen, possible.

continuación, *f.* continuation; prolongation, lengthening; continuance, stay.

continuadamente, *adv.* continuedly.

continuador, ra, *n.* continuer, continuator.

continuamente, *adv.* continually; continuously.

continuar, *va.* & *vn.* to continue, pursue, carry on; to remain in the same state, hold; to last, endure; to prolong.

continuativo, va, *a.* continuative.

continuidad, *f.* continuity.

continuo, nua. I. *a.* continuous, uninterrupted; prolonged; continual, constant, lasting; assiduous, steady, persevering; (mech.) endless.—**a la continua,** or **de continuo,** continually, constantly. **II.** *m.* continuous whole; yeoman of the crown; (math., phil.) continuum.

contonearse, *vr.* to walk with an affected air or manner. to strut.—**contoneo,** *m.* affected gait or manner of walking, strut.

contorcerse, *vr.* (*ind.* CONTUERZO: *subj.* CONTUERZA) to distort, twist one's body, writhe.

contorción, *f.* contortion.

contornado, *a.* (her.) turned toward the left side of the shield (s. o. heads of animals).

contornar, contornear, *va.* to trace the contour or outline of.

contorneo, *m.* = RODEO.

contorno, *m.* environs or vicinity of a place; contour, outline.—**en c.,** round about.

contorsión, *f.* contortion, twist, wry motion, grotesque gesture.

contra. I. *prep.* against, across, athwart, in opposition to, counter, contrary to, opposite to; (in composition, gen.) counter. **II.** *m.* opposite sense; opposite opinion; pedal of an organ.—*pl.* (mus.) organ pipes forming the lowest bass.—**el pro y el c.,** the pros and cons. **III.** *f.* difficulty, obstacle; counter, in fencing; (Am.) extra, something thrown in, ÑAPA.—**en c., en c. de,** against.—**hacer la c., llevar la c.,** to oppose, to contradict.

contraabertura, *f.* (surg.) contrafissure.

contraábside, *n.* western absis.

contraaletas, *f. pl.* (naut.) counter-fashion pieces.

contraalmirante, *m.* rear admiral.

contraamantillos, *f. pl.* (naut.) preventer lifts, counterbraces.

contraamura, *f.* (naut.) preventer tack.

contraaproches, *m. pl.* (fort.) counterapproaches.

contraarmiños, *m. pl.* (her.) black field and white spots.

contraataque, *m.* (mil.) counter attack.—*pl.* fortified lines of defense.

contrabajo, *m.* (mus.) contrabass; contrabass viol; contrabassist, contrabasso.

contrabalancear, *va.* to counterbalance, counterpoise.

contrabalanza, *f. V.* CONTRAPESO and CONTRAPOSICIÓN.

contrabandear, *vn.* to smuggle.

contrabandista, *m.* smuggler, contrabandist.

contrabando, *m.* contraband; smuggling; unlawful action.—**c. de guerra,** contraband of war. —**ir,** or **venir, de c.,** to go, or come, by stealth; to sneak out, or in.

contrabarrado, da, *a.* (her.) counterbarred.

contrabarrera, *f.* inner barrier in a bull ring.

contrabasa, *f.* (arch.) = PEDESTAL.

contrabatería, *f.* counterbattery.

contrabatir, *va.* to fire upon (the enemy's artillery).

contrabitas, *f. pl.* (naut.) standards of the bitts.

contrabolina, *f.* (naut.) preventer bowline.

contrabovedilla, *f.* (naut.) second counter, upper counter.

contrabracear, *va.* (naut.) to counterbrace.

contrabraceo, *m.* (naut.) counterbracing.

contrabranque, *m.* (naut.) stemson, apron.

contrabraza, *f.* (naut.) preventer brace.

contrabrazola, *f.* (naut.) headledge.

contracalcar, *va.* to trace from the back, so as to obtain a back view of the original drawing.

contracambiada, *f.* changing of the fore foot by a horse.

contracambio, *m.* (com.) re-exchange; (met.) = EQUIVALENTE.

contracanal, *m.* counterchannel.

contracandela, *f.* (Am.) back fire, fire made to create a gap between part of a burning field and the rest, in order to prevent the spread of the conflagration.

contracarril, *m.* check rail, guard rail, safety rail; wing rail.

contracción, *f.* contraction, shrinking, shriveling; corrugation; abbreviation; abridgment.

contracebadera, *f.* (naut.) sprit-topsail.

contracédula, *f.* counterdecree.

contracifra, *f.* countercipher.

contraclave, *f.* (arch.) voussoir next to the keystone.

contracodaste interior, *m.* (naut.) inner sternpost.—**c. exterior,** (naut.) back of the stern-post.

contracorriente, *f.* countercurrent, reverse current; stopwater.

contracosta, *f.* coast opposite another.

contráctil, *a.* contractile, contractible.

contractilidad, *f.* contractility, contractibility.

contracto, ta, *a.* contracted.

contractual, *a.* contractual.

contractura, *f.* (med.) contracture.

contracuartelado, da, *a.* (her.) having the quarters opposed in metal or color.

contracuerdas, *f. pl.* (naut.) outward deck planks or platforms.

contracurva, *f.* (r. w.) reversed curve.

contradancista, *m.* leader of a cotillon.

contradanza, *f.* quadrille, cotillon.

contradecir, *va.* (*pp.* CONTRADICHO: *ind.* CONTRADIGO: *pret.* CONTRADIJE: *fut.* CONTRADIRÉ: *subj.* CONTRADIGA) to contradict, gainsay.

contradicción, *f.* contradiction; opposition; gainsaying.

contradicho, cha, *pp. irr.* of CONTRADECIR.

contradictor, ra, *n.* contradictor, gainsayer.

contradictoria, *f.* (log.) contradictory.

contradictoriamente, *adv.* contradictorily, inconsistently.

contradictorio, ria, *a.* contradictory.

contradigo, contradije, contradiga. *V.* CONTRADECIR.

contradique, *m.* counterdock, counterdike.

contradriza, *f.* (naut.) second halliard.

contradurmente, condtradurmiente, *m.* (naut.) clamp.

contraeje, *m.* countershaft.

contraelectromotriz, *a.* (elec.) counter electromotive.

contraemboscada, *f.* counterambuscade.

contraemergente, *a.* (her.) countersalient.

contraempuñadura, *f.* (naut.) preventer earring.

contraendosar, *va.* to reindorse, indorse back.

contraer. I. *va.* & *vn.* (*pp.* CONTRAÍDO and CONTRACTO: *ind.* CONTRAIGO: *pret.* CONTRAJE: *subj.* CONTRAIGA) to contract (an obligation, a disease); tighten, join, unite; to incur; acquire; to reduce.—**c. matrimonio,** to marry (get married). **II.** *vr.* to contract, diminish; to shrink.

contraescarpa, *f.* (mil.) counterscarp.

contraescota, *f.* (naut.) preventer sheet.

contraescotín, *m.* (naut.) preventer topsail sheet.

contraescritura, *f.* counterdeed.

contraestay, *m.* (naut.) preventer stay.

contrafajado, da, *a.* (her.) having faces opposed in metal or color (s. o. shields).

contrafallar, *va.* at cards, to trump after another.

contrafallo, *m.* trumping after another, at cards.

contrafianza, *f.* indemnity bond.

contrafigura, *f.* person or dummy that imitates a personage in the theater.

contrafilo, *m.* (arm.) back edge (near the point).

contraflorado, da, *a.* (her.) having flowers opposed in color and metal.

contrafoque, *m.* (naut.) foretop stay sail.

contrafoso, *m.* (fort.) avantfosse or outer ditch.

contrafuero, *m.* infringement or violation of a charter or privilege.

contrafuerte, *m.* strap of leather to secure the girths on a saddletree; spur, counterfort (of a mountain); stiffener of a shoe; (fort.) counterfort; (arch.) abutment, buttress, spur.

contragolpe, *m.* (med.) counterstroke (contrecoup); (eng.) back or reverse stroke (of a piston).

contraguardia, *f.* (fort.) counterguard.

contraguía, *f.* in a team, the near or left-hand animal.

contrahacedor, ra, *n.* imitator, impersonator.

contrahacer, *va.* (*pp.* CONTRAHECHO: *ind.* CONTRAHAGO: *pret.* CONTRAHICE: *subj.* CONTRAHAGA) to counterfeit, falsify, forge; to imitate, copy; to pirate (the works of an author); to mimic, impersonate.

contrahaz, *m.* wrong side (of cloth).

contrahecho, 'cha. I. *a.* humpbacked, deformed; counterfeit, counterfeited; spurious, fictitious. **II.** *pp.* of CONTRAHACER.

contrahierba, *f.* (bot.) contrayerva, a South American medicinal plant; antidote.

contrahilera, *f.* line of defense that defends another.

contrahilo, *m.*—**a c.,** across the grain.

contrahoradar, *va.* to bore on the opposite side.

contrahuella, *f.* (arch.) riser of a stair.

contraigo, contraje, contraiga. *V.* CONTRAER.

contraindicación, *f.* (med.) contraindication.

contraindicante, *m.* (med.) contraindicant.

contraindicar, *va.* (*pret.* CONTRAINDIQUÉ: *subj.* CONTRAINDIQUE) (med.) to contraindicate.

contralecho, *m.*—**a c.,** (arch.) crossbond.

contralizo, *m.* (weav.) back leash.

contralmirante, *m.* rear admiral.

contralor, *m.* comptroller, inspector.

contraloría, *f.* comptrollership.

contralto, *m.* contralto.

contraluz, *f.* counterlight.

contramaestre, *m.* overseer, foreman; (naut.) boatswain.

contramalla, contramalladura, *f.* double net for catching fish.—**contramallar,** *va.* to make (nets) with double meshes.

contramandar, *va.* to countermand.

contramangas, *f. pl.* oversleeves.

contramaniobra, *f.* countermanœuvre.

contramarca, *f.* countermark; duty to be paid on goods which have no customhouse mark.

contramarcar, *va.* (*pret.* CONTRAMARQUÉ: *subj.* CONTRAMARQUE) to countermark.

contramarco, *m.* (carp.) counterframe.

contramarcha, *f.* countermarch, retrocession; part of a weaver's loom; (mil. and naut.) evolution.—**de c.,** reverse (lever, etc.).

contramarchar, *vn.* to countermarch; to go backwards.

contramarea, *f.* (naut.) countertide.

contramesana, *f.* (naut.) mizzenmast.

contramina, *f.* countermine; (min.) driftway, heading.—**contraminar,** *va.* to countermine, to counterwork.

contramolde, *m.* countermold.

contramotivo, *m.* (mus.) countersubject.

contramuelle, *m.* (mech.) duplicate spring.

contramuralla, *f.,* **contramuro,** *m.* (mil.) countermure, low rampart.

contranatural, *a.* counternatural, contranatural, unnatural.

contraorden, *f.* countermand.

contrapalanquín, *m.* (naut.) preventer clew garnet.

contrapares, *m. pl.* (arch.) counterrafters.

contraparte, *f.* counterpart, duplicate copy of a deed.

contrapartida, *f.* (in bookkeeping) emendatory or corrective entry.

contrapás, *m.* a step in dancing.

contrapasamiento, *m.* act and effect of passing to the opposite side or party.

contrapasar, *vn.* to join the opposite party.

contrapaso, *m.* back step; (mus.) counternote.

contrapelo.—a c., *adv.* against the grain.

contrapesar, *va.* to counterbalance; to countervail, offset.

contrapeso, *m.* counterweight; counterpoise, counterbalance, countervail; plummet; balancing weight; ropedancer's pole; equipollence, equivalence of power; makeweight, something of inferior quality thrown to complete the weight of meat, fish, etc.

contrapeste, *m.* remedy against pestilence or epidemic.

contrapilastra, *f.* (arch.) counterpilaster; (carp.) doorstrip.

contrapolicía, *f.* police that secretly watches the ordinary police.

contrapóliza, *f.* insurance policy that annuls a previous one.

contraponedor, ra, *n.* one who compares.

contraponer, *va.* (*pp.* CONTRAPUESTO: *ind.* CONTRAPONGO: *pret.* CONTRAPUSE: *subj.* CONTRAPONGA) to oppose; to compare.

contraposición, *f.* contraposition; counterview; contrast.

contrapozo, *m.* (fort.) counterblast.

contrapresión, *f.* back pressure.

contraprincipio, *m.* opposite principle, statement contrary to a principle known as such.

contraproducente, contraproducéntem, *a.* self-defeating, producing the opposite of the desired effect.

contrapromesa, *f.* withdrawal of a promise; promise opposed to another.

contraproposición, *f.* counterproposition.

contrapropósito, *m.* change of purpose; purpose opposed to another.

contraprueba, *f.* (print.) counterproof, second proof; counterdrawing.

contrapuerta, *f.* inner large door after the street door.

contrapuesto, ta, *a.* & *pp. irr.* of CONTRAPONER; (w. a) compared, contrasted (with); opposed (to).

contrapuntante, *n.* counterpoint singer.

contrapuntear. I. *va.* (mus.) to sing in counterpoint; to taunt; to revile. **II.** *vr.* to abuse one another; to wrangle, dispute.

contrapuntista, *m.* (mus.) contrapuntist, one skilled in counterpoint.

contrapunto, *m.* (mus.) counterpoint, harmony.

contrapunzón, *m.* puncheon for driving in a nail; counterpunch; gunsmith's countermark on guns.

contraquerella, *f.* cross-complaint.

contraquilla, *f.* (naut.) false keel.

contrariamente, *adv.* contrarily.

contrariar, *va.* to contradict, oppose, counteract, thwart, run counter; to disappoint; vex, upset.

contrariedad, *f.* contrariety, contrariness; opposition, contradiction; disappointment, impediment, obstacle; trouble, vexation.

contrario, *m.* opponent, antagonist, competitor, rival.

contrario, ria, *a.* contrary, opposite, contradictory; opposed, adverse; abhorrent; unfavorable, antagonistic; mischievous.—**al e.,** on the contrary.—**en c.,** against, in opposition to.—**llevar la contraria,** to contradict; to oppose.—**por el c., or por lo c.,** on the contrary.

contrarregistro, *m.* control register.

contrarreguera, *f.* lateral drain.

contrarréplica, *f.* rejoinder, reply to an answer; rebutter.

contrarrestar, *va.* to resist, oppose, check; to counteract, offset; to strike back (a ball); to counterbuff.

contrarresto, *m.* check; opposition, contradiction; player who strikes back the ball.

contrarrevolución, *f.* counter-revolution.

contrarrevolucionario, ria, *n.* & *a.* counter-revolutionist, counter-revolutionary.

contrarriel, *m.* (r. w.) guard rail, wing rail.

contrarroda, *f.* (naut.) stemson.

contrarronda, *f.* (mil.) counterround.

contrarrotura, *f.* (vet.) plaster or poultice applied to fractures or wounds.

contrasalida, *f.* countersally.

contrasalva, *f.* (mil.) countersalute.

contraseguro, *m.* a contract by which an underwriter agrees to return to the insured, under specified conditions, all premiums previously paid.

contrasellar, *va.* to counterseal.

contrasello, *m.* counterseal, small seal superimposed on another seal.

contrasentido, *m.* countersense, opposite sense; conclusion contrary to premises; nonsense.

contraseña, *f.* countersign, countermark; (mil.) watchword.—**c. de salida,** (theat.) check (to readmit one who goes out).

contrasol, *m.* sunshade.

contrastable, *a.* contrastable.

contrastar. I. *va.* to contrast, place in opposition, oppose; to resist; contradict; to assay and stamp (metals); to examine, inspect (weights and measures). **II.** *vn.* to contrast, be different.

contraste, *m.* contrast; opposition; strife, contest; assayer of the mint; assayer's office; assay; mark of assay; inspector of weights and measures; public office where raw silk is weighed: (naut.) sudden change of the wind, by which it becomes foul or contrary.

contrata, *f.* contract.

contratación, *f.* trade, commerce; enterprise, undertaking; business transaction.

contratante, *n.* & *a.* contractor (-ing).

contratar, *va.* to enter into an agreement about; to contract for; to engage, hire; to make a deal or bargain about.

contratela, *f.* among hunters, second inclosure of canvas to shut up game.

contratiempo, *m.* disappointment; misfortune, mishap.

contratista, *m.* contractor; lessee; patentee; grantee; covenanter.

contrato, *m.* contract.—**c. a la gruesa,** or **a riesgo marítimo,** respondentia.—**c. aleatorio,** aleatory contract.—**c. consensual,** consensual contract.—**c. de compraventa,** or **de compra y venta,** contract of bargain and sale.—**c. de locación y conducción,** agreement to let one enjoy the use of property for a price or service.—**c. de retrovendendo,** reversion clause of bargain and sale.—**c. enfitéutico,** emphyteusis.—**c. perfecto,** contract of record.

contratorpedero, *m.* torpedo-boat destroyer.

contratrancaniles, *m. pl.* (naut.) inner waterways.

contratreta, *f.* counterplot.

contratrinchera, *f.* (mil.) countertrench.

contratuerca, *f.* check nut, lock nut.

contravalación, *f.* (mil.) contravallation.

contravalar, *va.* to form a line of contravallation about.

contravalor, *m.* (com.) countervalue, equivalent.

contravapor, *m.* (st. eng.) back steam.

contravención, *f.* contravention, violation (of a law).

contraveneno, *m.* counterpoison, antidote; precaution taken to avoid some infamy or mischief.

contravenir, *va.* (*ind.* CONTRAVENGO: *pret.* CONTRAVINE: *subj.* CONTRAVENGA) to contravene, transgress, violate; to oppose, obstruct, baffle; countermine.

contraventana, *f.* window shutter.

contraventor, ra, *n.* transgressor, offender.

contravidriera, *f.* storm window.

contravisita, *f.* second visit, made to verify the results of a previous one.

contravoluta, *f.* (arch.) inner volute.

contray, *m.* a sort of fine cloth.

contrayente, *a.* engaged, contracting (app. to persons betrothed).

contrecho, cha, *a.* crippled, maimed.

contrete, *m.* (naut.) breastshore; crochet; angle iron; stay; gusset, face wheel in watches.

contribución, *f.* contribution; tax, impost.—**c. de sangre,** military service.—**c. territorial,** land tax.

contribuidor, ra, *n.* & *a.* contributor (-ing).

contribuir, *va.* & *vn.* (*ind.* CONTRIBUYO: *subj.* CONTRIBUYA) to contribute.

contribulado, da, *a.* grieved, afflicted.

contributario, *m.* contributor, taxpayer.

contribuyente. I. *a.* contributing; contributory. **II.** *n.* contributor; taxpayer.

contrición, *f.* contrition, compunction, repentance.

contrín, *m.* weight used in the Philippines (0.39 gramme, or 6½ grains).

contrincante, *m.* competitor, rival, opponent.

contristar, *va.* to sadden, grieve.

contrito, ta, *a.* contrite, repentant, penitent.

control, *m.* (not correct, but common) control.

controlar, *va.* (not considered correct, but widely used, sp. in technical language) to control.

contróler, *m.* (elec.) controller (sp. that on an electric car or locomotive—more properly called COMBINADOR).

controversia, *f.* controversy, debate.

controversista, *m.* controversialist, debater.

controvertible, *a.* controvertible, disputable.

controvertir, *va.* (*ind.* CONTROVIERTO: *subj.* CONTROVIERTA) to controvert, dispute, argue against.

contubernio, *m.* cohabitation, concubinage; base or infamous alliance.

contumacia, *f.* obstinacy, stubbornness; (law) contumacy, non-appearance, contempt of court; default.

contumaz, *a.* obstinate, stubborn; contumacious, disobedient; guilty of contempt of court.

contumazmente, *adv.* contumaciously; obstinately, stubbornly.

contumelia, *f.* contumely, reproach, abuse; contumeliousness.

contumeliosamente, *adv.* contumeliously, reproachfully.

contumelioso, sa, *a.* contumelious, reproachful, sarcastic.

contundente, *a.* producing contusion (s. o. weapons); impressing the mind deeply, forceful.

contundir, *va.* to contuse, bruise, pound.

conturbación, *f.* perturbation, uneasiness, anxiety.

conturbado, da. I. *a.* turbulent, troublesome. **II.** *pp.* of CONTURBAR.

conturbador, *m.* perturber, disturber.

conturbar. I. *va.* to perturb, disquiet, disturb, trouble. **II.** *vr.* to become uneasy, agitated, anxious.

conturbativo, va, *a.* disquieting, disturbing.

contusión, *f.* contusion, bruise.

contuso, sa, *a.* bruised.

contutor, *m.* assistant tutor, fellow tutor.

conuco, conusco, *m.* (Am.) patch of ground given to slaves; maize field.

convalecencia, *f.* convalescence.

convalecer, *vn.* (*ind.* CONVALEZCO: *subj.* CONVALEZCA) to recover from sickness; to recover lost prosperity, influence, etc.; (coll.) to come back.

convaleciente, *n.* & *a.* convalescent.

convalidar, *va.* (law) to confirm.

convecino, na, *a.* neighboring.

For pronunciation, see the rules at the beginning of the book.

convelerse, *vr.* (med.) to twitch; to be contracted.

convencedor, ra, *n.* & *a.* convincer (-ing).

convencer. I. *va.* (*pp.* CONVENCIDO and CONVICTO: *ind.* CONVENZO: *subj.* CONVENZA) to convince; to prove irrefutably to (a person). **II.** *vr.* to become convinced.

convencible, *a.* convincible.

convencido, da. I. *a.* convinced. **II.** *pp.* of CONVENCER.

convencimiento, *m.* conviction, belief; (act of) convincing.—**en el c. de que,** being convinced that, believing that.

convención, *f.* convention; contract, agreement, pact; conformity.—**convencional,** *a.* conventional.

convencionalismo, *m.* conventionalism, conventionality.

convencionalmente, *adv.* conventionally.

convengo, convenga. *V.* CONVENIR.

convenible, *a.* docile, tractable, compliant.

convenido, da. I. *pp.* de CONVENIR. **II.** *a.* settled by consent; agreed.

conveniencia, *f.* conformity, congruity, consistence; suitability, fitness; desirability, expedience, advantage; agreement, adjustment; employ, service; servant's place in a house or family; convenience, ease.—*pl.* emoluments, perquisites; income, property.

conveniente, *a.* useful, advantageous, good; accordant, conformable; fit, suitable; desirable, advisable; expedient, opportune, timely; decent, discreet.

convenientemente, *adv.* fitly, appropriately, suitably; expediently.

convenio, *m.* convention, agreement, pact; consent; contrivance.

convenir. I. *vn.* (*ind.* CONVENGO: *pret.* CONVINE: *subj.* CONVENGA) to agree; coincide, cohere; to fit, harmonize, comport, suit; to correspond, belong; to assemble, convene; to be wise, advisable, desirable or advantageous.—**c. en,** to agree to. **II.** *v. imp.* to suit, to be to the purpose, to be meet.—**conviene, a saber,** namely, to wit. **III.** *vr.* to agree, make a deal; suit one's interest.

conventazo, *m.* *aug.* large convent.

conventico, illo, ito, *m.* *dim.* (coll.) tenement inhabited by persons of ill repute.

conventícula, *f.,* **conventículo,** *m.* conventicle.

convento, *m.* convent; monastery; nunnery; community of religious men or women.

conventual. I. *a.* conventual, monastic. **II.** *m.* conventual, a monk; Conventual, a member of the Conventual Franciscan order.

conventualidad, *f.* state of living in a convent or monastery; assignment of a monk to a convent.

conventualmente, *adv.* monastically.

convenzo, convenza. *V.* CONVENCER.

convergencia, *f.* convergence.

convergente, *a.* convergent, converging.

converger, convergir, *vn.* to converge; to agree in opinion.

conversable, *a.* sociable, tractable.

conversación, *f.* conversation, talk; conference; commerce, intercourse, society, company; illicit intercourse.

conversar, *vn.* to converse, talk; to chat; to live in the company of others; to have social intercourse; (mil.) to change front, wheel.

conversión, *f.* conversion; change, transformation; (rhet.) apostrophe; (mil.) wheel, wheeling.

conversivo, va, *a.* having the power of converting or changing.

converso. I. *m.* convert; lay brother. **II.** *pp. irr.* of CONVERTIR.

convertibilidad, *f.* convertibility.

convertible, *a.* convertible; movable, transferable.

convertido, da. I. *pp.* of CONVERTIR. **II.** *n.* & *a.* (one) converted.

convertidor, *m.* (elec., metal.) converter.

convertir. I. *va.* (*pp.* CONVERTIDO and CONVERSO: *ind.* CONVIERTO: *subj.* CONVIERTA) to convert; reform; change; transform. **II.** *vr.* to be converted, reformed.

convexidad, *f.* convexity.

convexo, xa, *a.* convex.

convicción, *f.* conviction, certainty, certitude.

convicto, ta, *pp. irr.* of CONVENCER; (law) convicted, guilty.

convictor, *m.* (prov.) boarder; person living in a college without being a member or student.

convictorio, *m.* among the Jesuits, living quarters of students.

convidada, *f.* invitation to drink, treat.

convidante, *n.* inviter, one who invites; host.

convidado, da. I. *a.* & *pp.* of CONVIDAR; invited. **II.** *n.* invited guest.

convidador, ra, *n.* inviter.

convidar. I. *va.* to invite; to treat; to allure, entice, induce. **II.** *vr.* to offer one's services spontaneously; to invite one's self, come uninvited.

convierto, convierta. *V.* CONVERTIR.

convincente, *a.* convincing; convincible.

convincentemente, *adv.* convincingly.

convite, *m.* invitation; feast to which persons are invited; treat.

convivencia, *f.* act of living together.

conviviente, *a.* living together.

convocación, *f.* convocation, calling.

convocador, ra, *n.* convener, convoker.

convocar, *va.* (*pret.* CONVOQUÉ: *subj.* CONVOQUE) to convene, convoke, call together, summon; to acclaim.

convocatoria, *f.* letter of convocation, edict, summons; notice of meeting.

convocatorio, ria, *a.* that convokes.

convóluto, ta, *a.* convolute.

convolvuláceo, cea, *a.* convolvulaceous.

convólvulo, *m.* (zool.) vine inchworm; (bot.) convolvulus.

convoy, *m.* convoy, conduct, escort, guard; property under convoy; (coll.) retinue; railway train.

convoyante, *a.* convoying.

convoyar, *va.* to convoy, escort, guard.

convulsión, *f.* convulsion.

convulsivamente, *adv.* convulsively.

convulsivo, va, *a.* convulsive.

convulso, sa, *a.* convulsed.

conyugal, *a.* conjugal, connubial.

conyugalmente, *adv.* conjugally, matrimonially.

cónyuge, *n.* spouse, husband or wife.

coñac, *m.* cognac, brandy.

cooperación, *f.* coöperation.

cooperador, ra; cooperante, *n.* & *a.* coöperator (-ing, -ive); contributor (-ing).

cooperar, *vn.* to coöperate.

cooperario, ria, *n.* = COOPERADOR.

cooperativamente, *adv.* coöperatively, coöperatingly.

cooperativo, va. I. *a.* coöperative, coöperating. **II.** *f.* coöperative association or society.

coopositor, *m.* one who is a candidate with another for a professorship, etc., to be obtained by competition.

coordenado, a. I. *a.* coördinate. **II.** *f.* (math.) coördinate.—**c. cartesiana,** Cartesian coördinate. —**c. polar,** polar coördinate.

coordinación, *f.* coördination.

coordinadamente, *adv.* coördinately.

coordinado, da. I. *a.* coördinate. **II.** *pp.* of COORDINAR.

coordinamiento, *m.* = COORDINACIÓN.

coordinar, *va.* to coördinate.

copa, *f.* goblet, wineglass, cup; liquid contained in a glass; drink (of liquor); treetop; bower; crown of a hat; brasier, fire pan; roof or vault of an oven or furnace; gill, liquid measure; teacupful; (in cards) spot corresponding to a heart.—*pl.* hearts, one of the four suits at cards; bosses of a bridle.

copada, *f.* = COGUJADA.

copado, da. I. *a.* tufted, copped, abundant in foliage. **II.** *pp.* of COPAR.

copaiba, *f.* (bot.) copaiba.

copal, *m.* copal, a transparent resin.

copaljocol, *m.* a Mexican tree resembling a cherry tree.

copanete, cópano, *m.* an ancient small boat.

copaquira, *f.* (Am.) copperas.

copar, *va.* in monte, to put on a card a sum equal to what there is in the bank; (coll.) to corner; (mil.) to surprise; cut off the retreat of; to corner; to grab.

copartícipe, *n.* participant, copartner.

copayero, *m.* copaiba tree.

copaza, *f. aug.* large cup or glass with a stem.

copazo, *m. aug.* large fleece of wool; large flake of snow.

copec, *m.* kopeck (Russian coin).

copela, *f.* (metal.) cupel.—**copelación,** *f.* cupellation.—**copelar,** *va.* to cupel, refine by cupellation.

copépodo. I. *n.* & *a.* (zool.) copepod. **II.** *m. pl.* Copepoda.

copera, *f.* cupboard, sideboard; china closet.

coperillo, *m. dim.* little cupbearer.

copernicano, na, *a.* Copernican.

copero, *m.* cupbearer; sideboard, buffet; glass rack.

copeta, *f. dim.* small cup or drinking vessel.

copete, *m.* toupee, tuft, pompadour, aigret; forelock of a horse; crownwork of a piece of furniture; top of the shoe that rises over the buckle; top, summit; projecting top or cop of sherbet or ice cream.—**asir la ocasión por el c.,** to profit by, or improve, the opportunity.—**de c.,** or **de alto c.,** of (the) blood, of the nobility; aristocratic, high-rank.—**tener mucho c.,** to put on airs, to be haughty or stuck up.

copetudo, da, *a.* copped, tufted; rising to a top or head; high, lofty.

copey, *m.* an American tree of excellent wood for engraving; bitumen found in Ecuador.

copia, *f.* copiousness, plenty, abundance; fertility; copy (of a letter, picture, etc.); imitation; taking up; rate or valuation of tithe; (gram.) list of nouns and verbs, and the cases they govern; (poet.) couple.—**c. verbal,** literal, verbatim copy.

copiador, *m.* copyist, copier, transcriber.—**c. de cartas,** (copying) letter book.

copiante, *n.* copyist; imitator.

copiar, *va.* to copy; to imitate; to mimic, take up; ape: (poet.) to describe, depict.—**c. del natural,** to copy from life.

copilador, *m.* compiler, collector.

copilar, *va.* to compile, collect.

copilla, *f. dim.* of COPA; cigarlighter.

copín, *m.* in Asturias, a grain measure equal to half a CELEMÍN.

copina, *f.* (Mex.) skin taken off whole.

copinar, *va.* to remove (a skin) entire.

copiosamente, *adv.* copiously, abundantly.

copiosidad, *f.* copiousness, abundance.

copioso, sa, *a.* copious, abundant.

copista. I. *m.* copyist, transcriber. **II.** *m.* copying machine.

copita, *f. dim.* small glass or cup.

copito, *m. dim.* small fleece or flake.

copla, *f.* couplet; popular song, ballad; sarcastic hint or remark; lampoon.

coplear, *vn.* to compose or sing ballads.

copleja, *f. dim.* little ballad.

coplero, ra, *n.* ballad seller; poetaster.

coplica, illa, ita, *f. dim.* little ballad.

coplista, *n.* = COPLERO.

coplón, *m. aug.* low, vile poetry (gen. used in the plural, **coplones**).

copo, *m.* small bundle of cotton, hemp, flax, or silk, put on the distaff to be spun; snowflake; bottom of a purse seine; hauling with a purse seine; cornering, surprise; grab; (Am.) treetop (properly COPA).

copón, *m. ang.* large cup or drinking vessel; ciborium.

coposo, sa, *a.* V. COPADO.

copra, *f.* copra, dried kernel of the coconut.

coprolito, *m.* (pal.) coprolite; (med.) intestinal calculus.

copropietario, ia, *n.* joint owner, coproprietor.

cóptico, ca, *a.* Coptic.

copto, *m.* Coptic, the language of the Copts.

copudo, da, *a.* tufted, bushy, thick-topped (tree).

cópula, *f.* joining, coupling two things together; connection; copulation, carnal union; (arch.) cupola; (log.) copula.

copularse, *vr.* to copulate.

copulativamente, *adv.* jointly.

copulativo, va, *a.* joining or uniting together; (gram.) copulative.

coque, *m.* coke.

coquera, *f.* head or handle of a top; small concavity in a stone; coke scuttle or box; (Am.) a place for coca.

coquero, ra, *n.* dealer in coconuts.

coqueta, *f.* coquette, flirt; feruling, or blow with a ferule on the hand by a schoolmaster; small loaf or roll.

coquetear, *vn.* to flirt, coquet.

coqueteo, *m.* coquetting, flirting; flirtation.

coquetería, *f.* coquetry; flirtation; affectation.

coquetón, *m.* male flirt, lady-killer.

coquimbo, *m.* (Am.) burrowing owl.

coquina, *f.* cockle, an edible bivalve; shell of a cockle; soft shelly stone.

coquinero, ra, *n.* cockleseller.

coquito, *m. dim.* small coconut; grimace to amuse children; turtledove of Mexico; a tall Chilean palm tree.

coráceo, a, *a.* = CORIÁCEO.

coracero, *m.* cuirassier; (coll.) poor cigar.

coracilla, *f. dim.* small coat of mail.

coracina, *f.* small breastplate.

coracora, *f.* (Philip.) coasting vessel.

coracha, *f.* leather bag.

corachín, *m. dim.* small leather bag.

coraje, *m.* courage, bravery; fortitude, mettle; anger, passion.—**corajoso, sa,** *a.* brave, dashing.—**corajudo, da,** *a.* angry, ill-tempered.

coral. I. *m.* coral; (Ven., Colomb.) a white-and-red poisonous snake.—*pl.* string of corals. **II.** *a.* choral, belonging to the choir.

coralero, ra, *n.* worker or dealer in corals.

coralífero, ra, *a.* coral-bearing.

coralillo, *m.* a venomous coral-color snake.

coralina, *f.* coral insect, sea coralline; any sea animal resembling coral.

coralino, na, *a.* coralline, of or resembling coral.

corambre, *f.* hides, skins, dressed or undressed; pelts.

corambrero, *m.* dealer in hides and skins.

Corán, *m.* Koran.—**coránico, ca,** *a.* Koranic.

coranvobis, *m.* (coll.) corpulent person strutting about with affected gravity.

coraza, *f.* cuirass, armor plating; shell or carapace of a turtle, etc.; armor (of a vessel, cable, etc.)

coraznada, *f.* pith of a pine tree; fricassee of the hearts of animals.

corazón, *m.* heart; core, pith; love, benevolence, affection; spirit, courage, will, mind; middle or centre of anything; in a loom, cam.—**c. de un cabo,** (naut.) heart strand.—**anunciar,** or **decir, el c.,** to have a presentiment.—**arrancársele a uno el c.,** to be heartbroken, to bleed at the heart (ch. constr.: *se me arranca el corazón al ver su desgracia,* my heart bleeds at his misfortune).—**de c.,** heartily, sincerely; courageous, enterprising.—**llevar,** or **traer, el c. en la mano,** to wear one's heart upon one's sleeve.

corazonada, *f.* impulse of the heart; presentiment, foreboding; (coll.) entrails.

corazonazo, *m. aug.* great heart.

corazoncico, illo, ito, *m. dim.* little heart; fainthearted person.

corazoncillo, *m.* (bot.) perforated St.-John's-wort.

corbachada, *f.* lash with a CORBACHO.

corbacho, *m.* cowhide whip.

corbata. I. *f.* cravat, necktie; scarf, neckcloth; sash or ribbon badge tied to banners; ribbon, insignia of an order. **II.** *m.* magistrate not brought up to the law.

corbatería, *f.* necktie shop.

corbatero, ra, *n.* necktie maker or dealer.

corbatín, *m.* cravat, tie; stock.

corbato, *m.* cooler, worm tub of a still.

corbatón, *m.* small knee, bracket.

corbe, *m.* an ancient measure for baskets.

corbeta, *f.* (naut.) corvette.—**c. de guerra,** sloop of war.

corcel, *m.* steady horse, charger.

corcesca, *f.* ancient barbed spear.

corcino, *m.* small deer.

corcova, *f.* hump, crooked back; hunch, protuberance, curvature.

corcovado, da. I. *a.* humpbacked, gibbous; crooked. **II.** *pp.* of CORCOVAR.

corcovar, *va.* to crook.

corcovear, *vn.* to curvet, cut capers.

corcoveta, *f. dim.* small hump; (coll.) crook-backed person.

corcovo, *m.* spring, curvet made by a horse on the point of leaping; (coll.) crookedness, wrong step, unfair proceeding.

corcusido, da. I. *a.* clumsily mended or sewed on. **II.** *pp.* of CORCUSIR.

corcusir, *va.* (coll.) to darn clumsily.

corcha, *f.* cork bark; wine cooler; (naut.) laying of a rope.

corchar, *va.* (naut.) to lay (strands of ropes).

corche, *m.* cork-soled sandal or clog.

corchea, *f.* (mus.) quaver, an eighth note.

corchear, *va.* to grain (leather) with a cork.

corchera, *f.* wine cooler made of cork.

corcheta, *f.* eye of a hook or clasp; (carp.) rabbet in a door or window frame.

corchete, *m.* clasp, hook, hook and eye (*pl.* **corchetes,** hooks and eyes); crotch; snaplock, catch; (coll.) constable; brace to connect lines in writing or printing (⁓); (carp.) bench hook.

corcho, *m.* cork; bark of the cork tree; wine cooler; beehive; cork box for carrying eatables; cork mat; cork-soled sandal or clog; float of a fishing line; (mil.) tampion.

corchoso, sa, *a.* corklike.

corda, *f.*—**estar a la c.,** (naut.) to be close-hauled or lying to.

cordaje, *m.* rigging; cordage.

cordal, *m.* double tooth; string bar at the bottom of stringed instruments.—*pl.* **cordales,** grinders.

cordato, ta, *a.* prudent, discreet, judicious.

cordel, *m.* cord, small rope; (naut.) line; length of five steps; land measure in Cuba equal to about 1 sq. ch.—**c. de corredera,** log line.—**a c.,** in a straight line.

cordelado, da, *a.* twisted silk for ribbons or garters.

cordelazo, *m.* stroke or lash with a rope.

cordelejo, *m. dim.* small rope; fun, jest.—**dar c.,** to banter.

cordelería, *f.* cordage; ropewalk; (naut.) rigging.

cordelero, ra, *n.* ropemaker, cordmaker.

cordelito, *m. dim.* small rope, cord, or line.

cordellate, *m.* grogram, a kind of fabric.

cordera, *f.* ewe lamb; meek, gentle, or mild woman.

cordería, *f.* cordage; place where cordage is kept.

corderica, illa, ita, *f. dim.* little ewe lamb.

corderico, illo, ito, *m. dim.* little lamb.

corderillo, *m.* lambskin dressed with the fleece.

corderina, *f.* lambskin.

corderino, na, *a.* of the lamb kind, belonging to lambs.

cordero, *m.* lamb; dressed lambskin; meek, gentle, or mild man.—**c. añal,** yearling lamb.—**c. de Dios,** Lamb of God (Christ).—**c. pascual,** paschal lamb.—**c. recental,** suckling lamb.

corderuela, *f. dim.* little ewe lamb.

corderuelo, *m. dim.* little or young lamb.

corderuna, *f.* lambskin.

cordeta, *f.* small bassweed rope.

cordezuela, *f. dim.* small rope.

cordíaco, ca, *a.* = CARDÍACO.

cordial. I. *a.* cordial, hearty, affectionate; sincere; invigorating, reviving. **II.** *m.* cordial; tonic.

cordialidad, *f.* cordiality, heartiness, sincerity.

cordialmente, *adv.* cordially, sincerely, affectionately, heartily.

cordiforme, *a.* heart-shaped.

cordila, *f.* spawn of tunny fish.

cordilo, *m.* an amphibious animal resembling a crocodile.

cordilla, *f.* guts of sheep given to cats to eat.

cordillera, *f.* cordillera, mountain range.

cordita, *f.* cordite (explosive).

corditis, *f.* inflammation of the vocal cords.

cordobán, *m.* cordovan, Spanish leather; tanned goatskin.

cordobana, *f.* nakedness, nudity.—**andar a la c.,** to go stark naked.

cordobanero, ra, *n.* cordovan tanner.

cordobés, sa, *f.* of or belonging to Cordova.

cordón, *m.* cord, round cord, twine; girdle with which monks tie their habits; (mil.) cordon; strand of a cable or rope; (arch.) torus moulding; string course; milled edge of a coin.—*pl.* (mil.) aglets or aiguillettes; harness cords of a velvet loom.—**c. umbilical,** umbilical cord.

cordonazo, *m. aug.* large cord; stroke with a cord or rope.—**c. de San Francisco,** first storm in October.

cordoncico, illo, ito, *m. dim.* small cord.

cordoncillo, *m.* twisted cord; round lace, lacing, braid; milling on edge of a coin.

cordonería, *f.* work of twisters or lace makers; lace maker's shop.

cordonero, ra, *n.* lace maker, laceman or woman; ropemaker.

cordula, *f.* = CORDILO.

cordura, *f.* prudence, practical wisdom, sanity.

corea, *f.* dance accompanied with a chorus; (med.) chorea, St. Vitus's dance.

corear, *vn.* to compose chorus music.

corecico, illo, *m. dim.* of CUERO.

coreo, *m.* foot in Latin verse; trochee; connected harmony of a chorus.

coreografía, *f.* art of dancing; choregraphy, writing dance music.—**coreográfico, ca,** *a.* choregraphic.—**coreógrafo,** *m.* choreograph.

corezuelo, *m. dim.* small hide; sucking pig; small roasted pig.

cori, *m.* Montpellier coris, St.-John's-wort.

coriáceo, a, *a.* coriaceous, leathery.

coriámbico, ca, *n. & a.;* **coriambo,** *m.* choriambic.

coriandro, *m.* (bot.) coriander.

coribante, *m.* Corybantes, priest of Cybele.

coribantismo, *m.* corybantiasm, a kind of frenzy accompanied by many contortions.

Corífero, *m.* coryphæus, leader of the ancient dramatic chorus; leader of a sect or party.

corimbo, *m.* (bot.) corymb.

corindón, *m.* corundum.

corintio, tia, *n. & a.* Corinthian.

corión, *m.* (anat.) chorion.

corista, *n.* chorister, chorus singer.

corito, ta. I. *a.* naked; timid, pusillanimous. **II.** *n.* person who treads grapes in the wine-press.

coriza, *f.* leather sandal worn by peasants in some parts of Spain; (med.) coryza, rhinitis.

corladura, *f.* gold varnish.

corlar, corlear, *va.* to cover with gold varnish.

corma, *f.* stocks; trouble, uneasiness.

cornac, cornaca, *m.* keeper of domesticated elephants.

cornada, *f.* thrust with the horns; upward thrust with a foil, in fencing.

cornadillo, *m. dim.* small coin.

cornado, *m.* an old copper coin mixed with some silver.

For pronunciation, see the rules at the beginning of the book.

cornadura, *f.* horns.

cornal, *m.* strap or thong with which oxen are tied to the yoke by the horns.

cornalina, *f.* (min.) cornelian, carnelian.

cornamenta, *f.* horns of any animal.

cornamusa, *f.* cornemuse, a sort of bagpipe; (mus.) a sort of brass horn; (naut.) belaying cleat.

cornatillo, *m.* a kind of olive.

córnea, *f.* (anat.) cornea.—**c. opaca,** sclerotic.

corneador, ra, *n. & a.* butting animal.

cornear, *va.* = ACORNEAR.

cornecico, illo, ito, *m. dim.* cornicle, small horn.

corneja, *f.* (orn.) crow; fetlock; dow.

cornejal, *m.* dogwood field.

cornejalejo, *m.* (bot.) pod.

cornejo, *m.* (bot.) hound tree or cornel tree, dogwood.

cornelina, *f.* = CORNALINA.

córneo, a, *a.* horny, corny, callous.

cornerina, *f.* = CORNALINA.

cornero, *m.* crust.

corneta. I. *f.* bugle; horn used by swineherds; cornet, ensign of horse; flag carried by horse troops; troop of horse; (naut.) broad pennant; rear admiral's flag.—**c. de llaves,** cornet.—**c. de monte,** huntsman's horn.—**c. de posta,** post's horn. **II.** *n.* bugler.

cornete, *m. dim.* small bugle horn.

cornetín, *m.* cornet; cornettist.

cornezuelo, *m.* ergot of rye; (vet.) instrument for bleeding horses; (bot.) CORNICABRA.

corniabierto, ta, *a.* having wide-spread horns.

cornial, *a.* horn-shaped.

corniapretado, da, *a.* having horns close-set.

cornicabra, *f.* (bot.) turpentine tree, pistachio tree, wild fig tree; a kind of crescent olive.

cornidelantero, ra, *a.* having the corns directed forwards.

corniforme, *a.* horn-shaped.

cornigacho, cha, *a.* having the horns turned slightly downward.

cornigero, ra, *a.* (poet.) horned, cornigerous.

cornija, *f.* (arch.) cornice.

cornijal, *m.* angle or corner of a mattress, building, etc.

cornijamento, cornijamiento, *m.* (arch.) = CORNISAMENTO.

cornijón, *m.* (arch.) entablature; street corner of a building.

cornil, *m.* = CORNAL.

corniola, *f.* = CORNALINA.

cornisa, *f.* (arch.) cornice.

cornisamento, cornisamiento, *m.* (arch.) entablature.

cornisica, illa, ita, *f. dim.* small cornice.

cornisón, *m.* = CORNIJÓN.

corniveleto, ta, *a.* having horns turned strongly upward.

cornizo, corno, *m.* = CORNEJO.

cornucopia, *f.* cornucopia; sconce; pier glass.

cornudo, da. I. *a.* horned. **II.** *m.* cuckold.

cornúpeta, *a.* (poet.) attacking with the horns.

coro, *m.* choir; chorus; singing chorus; assembly unanimous in sentiment; choir loft; choir of angels; memory.—**de c.,** from memory, by rote.—**hablar a coros,** to speak alternately.—**hacer c. a,** to follow, support; to play second fiddle to.

corocha, *f.* vine fretter or vine grub; an ancient loose coat.

corografía, *f.* chorography.

corográficamente, *adv.* chorographically.

corográfico, ca, *a.* chorographical.

corógrafo, fa, *n.* chorographer.

coroideo, a, *a.* choroid.

coroides, *f.* (anat.) choroid, choroid coat of the eye.

corojo, *m.* a tropical palm bearing an oily nut; the nut itself.

corola, *f.* (bot.) corolla.

corolario, *m.* corollary.

corolifloro, ra. I. *a.* (bot.) corollifloral. **II.** *f. pl.* Corolliflóræ.

corología, *f.* chorology, science of the distribution of organisms on the earth's surface.

corona, *f.* crown; wreath, garland; halo, aureola; coronet; top of the head; clerical tonsure; an old Spanish gold-and-silver coin; crown, English silver coin; Portuguese coin; reward, distinction, honor; splendor, ornament, decoration; end or crowning of a work; glory, triumph; rosary of seven decades; (ast.) corona; (naut.) pendant; (bot.) corona, crown; (mil.) crown-work; (arch.) corona, crown; (vet.) pastern of horses.—**c. circular,** (geom.) circular ring, space between two concentric circles.—**c. de fraile,** three-toothed globularia.—**c. de rey,** (bot.) melilot.—**c. real,** (bot.) annual sunflower.

coronación, *f.* coronation; crowning, completion; (arch.) crown.

coronado, *m.* tonsured Catholic clergyman.

coronador, ra, *n.* crowner, finisher.

coronal. I. *m.* (anat.) frontal bone. **II.** *a.* belonging to the frontal bone; frontal, relating to the forehead.

coronamiento, *m.* end of a work; (arch.) top ornament; capping; (naut.) taffrail.

coronar, *va.* to crown; to cap, to top; to complete, perfect; to decorate the top of; to crowd on a roof or on the top of a hill.

coronaria, *f.* crown wheel of a watch.

coronario, ria, *a.* coronary; (bot.) coronary; extremely refined (gold).

corondel, *m.* (print.) column rule; reglet; watermark in paper.

coronel, *m.* colonel; top molding; (her.) crown.

coronela. I. *f.* colonel's wife. **II.** *a.* applied to the company, flag, etc., supposed to belong to the colonel of a regiment.

coronelato, m., coronelía, *f.* colonelship.

coronilla, *f. dim.* small crown; top of the head; coxcomb; cap; chaplet; ear of a bell; (bot.) coronilla.—**c. de fraile,** French daisy.—**c. de rey,** nine-leaved coronilla.—**c. juncal,** rush coronilla.

coroza, *f.* cone hood of pasteboard worn as a mark of infamy; straw cape or cloak worn by farmers.

corozal, *m.* corozo field or plantation. *V.* COROZO.

corozo, *m.* = COROJO.

corpanchón, corpazo, *m. aug.* very big body or carcass.—**c. de ave,** carcass of a fowl.

corpecico, illo, ito; corpezuelo, *m. dim.* little or small body, or carcass; underdoublet; waist; corset cover.

corpiño, corpiñejo, *m. dim.* small body; under doublet; waist; corset cover.

corporación, *f.* corporation, guild; community; institution, organization.

corporal. I. *a.* corporal, bodily, belonging to the body. **II.** *m.* (eccl.) corporal cloth.

corporalidad, *f.* corporality; any corporeal substance.

corporalmente, *adv.* corporally, bodily.

corporativo, va, *a.* corporate.

corpóreo, rea, *a.* corporeal, corporeous.

corpudo, da, *a.* corpulent, bulky.

corpulencia, *f.* corpulence, corpulency.

corpulento, ta, *a.* corpulent, fleshy, fat.

Corpus, *m.* Corpus Christi, religious festival and procession.

corpuscular, *a.* corpuscular.

corpusculista, *n.* atomist.

corpúsculo, *m.* corpuscle.

corpus delicti, (law.) corpus delicti.

corral, *m.* corral; yard; poultry yard; fold, stockyard; fishpond; ancient playhouse; blank left by students in writing the lectures.—**c. de madera,** timber yard.

corralera, *f.* an Andalusian song and dance; brazen-faced, impudent woman.

corralero, *m.* keeper of a dung yard.

corralillo, ito, *m. dim.* small corral or yard.

corraliza, *f.* yard, corral, court.

corralón, *m. aug.* large corral or yard.

correa, *f.* leather strap; tether; leash; toughness, flexibility; (mech.) belt, belting; hand strap.—*pl.* duster made of straps.—**c. de zapatos,** shoe string, lace, latchet.—**besar la c.,** (coll.) to be obliged to humble one's self to another.—**tener c.,** to bear wit or raillery without irritation; to be strong and hardy.

correaje, *m.* heap of leather straps'or thongs; belting.

correal, *m.* reddish dressed deerskin.

correar, *va.* to draw out (wool) and prepare for use.

correazo, *m.* blow with a strap.

correcalles, *n.* loiterer.

corrección, *f.* correction; adjustment (of an instrument); correctness; proper demeanor; decorum.

correccional, *a.* correctional, corrective.

correccionalismo, *m.* system of eliminating criminal tendencies by education and correctional treatment in adequate institutions.

correccionalista, *n.* follower of, or believer in, CORRECCIONALISMO.

correccionalmente, *adv.* correctively.

correctamente, *adv.* correctly.

correctivo, va. I. *a.* corrective. **II.** *m.* corrective, corrective agent or measure.

correcto, ta, *a.* correct; conformable to the rules; irreproachable.

corrector, *m.* corrector, amender; (print.) proofreader; superior, or abbot, in the convent of St. Francis of Paula.

corredentor, ra, *n.* one who redeems from captivity jointly with another.

corredera, *f.* race ground; small wicket or back door; runner or upper grinding stone in a corn mill; street; procuress; (naut.) log or log line; roller, metal cylinder for rolling plate glass; cockroach; (st. eng.) slide valve; (print.) track, slide, rail; (mech.) tongue, rail, guide (of piston rod, etc.), runner; (mint) milling machine.

corredizo, za, *a.* running; sliding; easy to be untied, like a running knot.

corredor, ra. I. *m.* runner; race horse; corridor, gallery; (fort.) covert way; (mil.) scout, forerunner; broker.—**c. de aduana,** customhouse broker.—**c. de cambios, or de oreja,** exchange broker; (coll.) talebearer; procurer, procuress. **II.** *a.* running; (zool.) ratite, flightless, non-flying (s. o. birds that do not fly, like the ostrich). **III.** *f. pl.* (zool.) Ratitæ, flightless birds.

corredorcillo, *m. dim.* small corridor; petty broker.

corredura, *f.* overflowing.

correduría, *f.* broker's office; brokerage.

correería, *f.* trade and shop of a strap-maker.

correero, ra, *n.* strap maker or seller.

corregencia, *f.* coregency.

corregente, *m.* coregent.

corregibilidad, *f.* corrigibility.

corregible, *a.* corrigible.

corregidor, *m.* corrector; corregidor, Spanish magistrate; mayor.

corregidora, *f.* wife of a CORREGIDOR.

corregimiento, *m.* office or district of a CORREGIDOR.

corregir. I. *va.* (*ind.* CORRIJO: *subj.* CORRIJA) to correct; to adjust (an instrument); to remove, destroy; remedy; to reprehend, admonish; to punish; to temper, mitigate.—**c. el cuerpo,** (coll.) to go to stool.—**c. pruebas,** (print.) to read proofs. **II.** *vr.* to mend, reform.

corregüela, correhüela, *f. dim.* small strap; child's play with stick and strap; (bot.) bindweed.

correinante, *a.* reigning with another.

correjel, *m.* sole leather.

correlación, correlation.

correlativamente, *adv.* correlatively.

correlativo, va, *a.* correlative.

correligionario, ia. I. *a.* of the same religion or politics. **II.** *n.* coreligionist; one of the same party.

correncia, *f.* (coll.) looseness, diarrhœa.

correndilla, *f.* (coll.) short run.

correntía, *f.* artificial irrigation of stubbly ground.

correntiar, *va.* to irrigate (stubble ground).

correntío, tía, *a.* current; running; (coll.) light, free, unembarrassed.

correntón. na. I. *n.* gadder, man about town. **II.** *a.* gay, pleasant, cheerful.

correntoso, sa, *a.* swift, rapid, having a strong current (s. o. streams).

correo, *m.* post; mail; courier; letter carrier; post office; accomplice.—**c. marítimo,** packet boat.

correón, *m. aug.* large leather strap.

correoso, sa, *a.* flexible, easily bent; tough, leathery.

correr. I. *vn.* to run; to race; to flow; to blow; to pass away; to take the proper course; to extend, expand; to arrive; become due; to go on, continue; to prevail, be current or common; to pass, be accepted or admitted, be. current; to be said, be common talk; (followed by **con**) to charge one's self with a matter, take care of.—**c. a rienda suelta,** to ride full speed; to give loose reign to passion. —**c. la voz,** to be reported, to be said or rumored.—**c. por cuenta de uno,** to be one's affair.—**a más c., a todo c.,** at full speed; swiftly. **II.** *va.* to cause to run or move swiftly; to race (a horse); to pursue; to move, push, draw aside, draw, slide; to meet with; to go over, travel; to sell at auction; (coll.) to snatch away; to disconcert, rattle, make blush.—**c. baquetas,** to run the gantlet.—**c. el gallo,** (Mex.) to pass the night carousing in the streets.—**correrla,** to go on a spree.—**c. la cortina,** to draw the curtain; to discover anything; to conceal, quash.—**c. monte,** to go hunting.—**c. mundo,** to travel.—**c. un velo,** to draw a veil. **III.** *vr.* to file right or left; to slide, go through easily; to slide, slip; to spread itself; to melt, run out, run over; (coll.) to be very generous; to become confused; to run away, to flee.

correría, *f.* hostile incursion, foray, raid; pleasure trip, excursion; leather strap.—*pl.* youthful escapades; travels.

correspondencia, *f.* correspondence, relation, fitness, agreement; commerce, intercourse; correspondence (mail, writing); friendship, interchange, requital; consentaneousness; consent.

corresponder. I. *vn.* (w. **a**) to return (a favor, love); to correspond; fit, suit; belong, regard, concern; to agree. **II.** *vr.* to correspond, keep up intercourse by mail; to respect or esteem each other.

correspondiente. I. *a.* corresponding, respective; conformable, agreeable, suitable. **II.** *m.* correspondent.

correspondientemente, *adv.* correspondingly.

corresponsal, *m.* correspondent; agent; corresponding clerk.

corretaje, *m.* brokerage.

corretear, *vn.* to walk the streets, rove, ramble.

corretora, *f.* nun who directs the choir.

correvedile, correveidile, *m.* (coll.) talebearer; mischief maker; procurer, go-between.

correverás, *m.* spring or mechanical toy.

corrida, *f.* course, run, sprint, race; career; (aer.) taxying.—**c. de toros,** bull baiting, bullfight.—**de c.,** at full speed, swiftly; in haste; fast, without stopping.

corridamente, *adv.* currently, plainly; easily.

corrido, da. I. *a.* exceeding in weight or measure; expert, experienced; abashed, confused, ashamed; continuous, unbroken.—**de c.** = DE CORRIDA. **II.** *pp.* of CORRER. **III.** *m.* shed along the walls of a corral.

corriente. I. *a.* current; running, flowing; present (month or year), instant; plain, easy; generally received, admitted; ordinary, common, general; regular, standard; fluent (app. to style); marketable, merchantable; correct, acceptable.—**al c.,** posted, informed; punctually. **II.** *f.* current (of a river, of electricity, etc.); tendency; course.—**c. alterna, or alternativa,** alternating current.—**c. avatía, or devatíada,** (elec.) watless current.—**c. continua,** (elec.) direct current.—**c. de aire,**

air draught.—**c. del Golfo,** Gulf Stream.—**contra la c.,** against the tide (fig.).—**dejarse llevar de la c.,** to follow the current, follow the crowd. **III.** *adv.* all right.

corrientemente, *adv.* currently.

corrijo, corrija. *V.* CORREGIR.

corrigendo, da, *n.* inmate of a reformatory.

corriflero, *m.* idler, lounger, loafer.

corrillo, *m.* group of talkers (gen. app. to gossips or loungers).

corrimiento, *m.* act of running; melting; (med.) running sore; gumboil; landslide; shyness.

corrincho, *m.* meeting of low, vulgar people.

corrivación, *f.* impounding of brooks and streams.

corro, *m.* group of gossipers or spectators; circular space.—**hacer c.,** to clear the way.

corroboración, *f.* corroboration.

corroborante, *n.* & *a.* corroborator (-ing, -ive).

corroborar, *va.* to corroborate.

corroborativo, va, *a.* corroborative.

corrobra, *f.* treat to close a bargain.

corroer, *va.* to corrode.

corrompedor, ra, *n.* & *a.* corrupter (-ing).

corromper. I. *va.* (*pp.* CORROMPIDO and CO-RRUPTO) to corrupt; vitiate, mar; seduce, debauch; to bribe. **II.** *vn.* to stink. **III.** *vr.* to rot, become putrid; to become corrupt or corrupted.

corrompidamente, *adv.* corruptly.

corrompido, da. I. *a.* corrupt; spoiled, unsound; depraved, degenerate. **II.** *pp.* of CO-RROMPER.

corrosible, *a.* corrosible.

corrosión, *f.* corrosion.

corrosivo, va, *a.* corrosive.

corroyente, *a.* corroding, corrosive; abrasive.

corroyera, *f.* a kind of sumac used in tanning.

corrugación, *f.* corrugation, contraction into wrinkles.

corrugador, *m.* (anat.) corrugator.

corrulla, *f.* (naut.) room under deck in a row galley.

corrumpente, a. corrupting, vitiating; (coll.) teasing, vexatious, wayward.

corrupción, *f.* corruption, putrefaction; decay; pollution, filth; stench; corruptness; perversion, distortion (of a writing); depravity, immorality.

corruptamente, *adv.* corruptly.

corruptela, *f.* corruption; depravation, corruptness; (law) bad habit or practice contrary to law; abuse.—**corruptibilidad,** *f.* corruptibility.—**corruptible,** *a.* corruptible.—**corruptivo, va,** *a.* corruptive.—**corrupto, ta,** *a.* corrupt.

corruptor, ra, *n.* & *a.* corrupter (-ing).

corrusco, *m.* (coll.) broken bread.

corsario, ria, *n.* & *a.* privateer; corsair, pirate.

corsé, corset.

corsear, *vn.* to cruise against the enemy.

corsetería, *f.* corset factory or shop.

corsetero, ra, *n.* corset maker or dealer.

corso, *m.* privateering.—**a c.,** posthaste, with post horses.

corso, sa, *n.* & *a.* Corsican.

corta, *f.* felling of wood; cutting.

cortabolsas, *n.* (coll.) pickpocket, filcher.

cortacallos, *m.* corn cutter.

cortacigarros, *m.* cigar cutter.

cortacircuitos, *m.* (elec.) circuit breaker.

cortada, *f.* (Am.) cutting off the retreat; attack from the rear; troops engaged in these operations.

cortadera, *f.* chisel for cutting hot iron; knife used by beekeepers.

cortadero, ra, *a.* cutting readily; easily cut.

cortadillo, *m.* small drinking glass; a liquid measure, about a gill; clipped piece of money.—**echar cortadillos,** to speak in an affected manner; to drink wine.

cortado, da. I. *pp.* of CORTAR. **II.** *a.* adapted, proportioned, fit, exact; (her.) parted in the middle; confused, abashed; written in short sentences. **III.** *m.* (danc.) caper, cabriole.

cortador, ra. I. *n.* cutter; that which cuts; splitter. **II.** *m.* butcher; slicing machine, cutter; (tel.) interrupter; (zool.) scissorbill.—*pl.* incisor teeth.

cortadora, *f.* cutting board in a velvet loom.

cortadura, *f.* cut, cutting, incision; slit, slash; (fort.) parapet with embrasures and merlons; work raised in narrow passes.—*pl.* shreds.

cortafrío, *m.* cold chisel; cutting iron.

cortafuego, *m.* (agr.) clear space to prevent fire from spreading; (arch.) fire wall.

cortalápiz, *m.* pencil sharpener.

cortamente, *adv.* sparingly, scantily; curtly.

cortante. I. *a.* cutting, sharp. **II.** *m.* butcher.

cortapapel, *m.* paper cutter, paper knife.

cortapiés, *m.* (coll.) thrust at the legs in fencing.

cortapisa, *f.* obstacle, hindrance; elegance and grace in speaking; restriction with which a thing is given, "strings."

cortaplumas, *m.* penknife, pocketknife.

cortapuros, *m.* cigar cutter.

cortar. I. *va.* to cut, cut up, cut off, cut out; curtail; to disjoin, separate, hew, cleave, chop, hack, carve, fell; whittle; to shut or cut off (steam, water, etc.); dock; pare, prune; interrupt, stop, cut short; to abridge; to take a short cut; to suspend, restrain, keep back; to pronounce or enunciate; to read; to arbitrate or decide.—**c. a uno,** (met.) to put one to the blush.—**c. la corriente,** (elec.) to break the circuit, cut off the current. **II.** *vr.* to be daunted, ashamed, confused; to curdle; to chap; to fret; to fray; (geom.) to intersect, cut each other.

cortavapor, *m.* cut-off of a steam engine.

cortavidrios, *m.* glazier's diamond.

cortaviento, *m.* wind shield.

corte. I. *m.* cutting edge; cutting; cut; felling of trees; arbitration, compromise or settlement; measure, expedient, step; notch, hack, slot; in tailoring, cut, fit, also the stuff necessary for a garment (*un corte de chaleco*), a vest pattern; *un corte de pantalón,* the stuff required for a pair of trousers); edge of a book; (min.) shaft; cross opening; (in drawing) section, sectional view. **II.** *f.* (royal) court; levee; retinue, suit; yard; courtship; civility, politeness; stable for cattle; sheepfold; ancient tribunal of chancery.—*pl.* Cortes, Spanish parliament. —**c. celestial,** heaven.—**c. suprema,** Supreme Court.

cortedad, *f.* smallness, littleness, minuteness; dulness, stupidity; pusillanimity; timidity, bashfulness.—**c. de medios,** poverty, indigence.

cortejador, *m.* wooer.

cortejante. I. *a.* courting. **II.** *m.* gallant, beau.

cortejar, *va.* to accompany, escort, attend; to court, woo, make love to.

cortejo, *m.* court; homage paid to another; courtship; gift, present; gallant, beau; lover, sweetheart; paramour.

cortés, *a.* courteous, civil, gracious, polite.

cortesanamente, *adv.* courteously, politely.

cortesanazo, za, *a.* *aug.* awkwardly or fulsomely polite.

cortesanía, *f.* courtesy, civility, politeness.

cortesano, na. I. *a.* courtlike; courteous, obliging; courtly. **II.** *n.* courtier.

cortesía, *f.* courtesy; civility or courteousness; compliment; attention; gift, present; days of grace for payment; mercy, favor.

cortésmente, *adv.* courteously, politely.

corteza, *f.* bark of a tree; peel, skin, rind, crust of bread, pies, etc.; a wild fowl of the family of widgeons; outward appearance; rusticity, want of politeness, crustiness.

cortezón, *m.* *aug.* thick bark, rind, or crust.

cortezudo, da, *a.* corticose, barky; rustic, unmannerly, unpolished.

cortezuela, *f.* *dim.* thin bark, skin, or rind.

cortical, *a.* cortical.

cortijada, *f.* collection of houses about a grange.

cortijo, *m.* farmhouse, grange, manse.—**alborotar el c.,** (coll.) to cause excitement, to stir up hornets' nest.

cortil, _m._ = CORRAL.

cortina, _f._ curtain; shade; portière; (fort.) curtain; (bot.) cortina.

cortinaje, _m._ curtains, hangings.

cortinal, _m._ fenced-in land near a village or farmhouse.

cortinilla, _f._ small screen, shade; carriage curtain.

cortinón, _m. aug._ large heavy curtain.

cortiña, _f._ garden plot.

corto, ta, _a._ short; dull, stupid; pusillanimous; shy, bashful, backward; imperfect, defective.— **c. circuito,** (elec.) short circuit.—**c. de alcances,** stupid.—**c. de genio,** diffident.—**c. de oído,** hard of hearing.—**c. de vista,** shortsighted.—**a la corta o a la larga,** sooner or later.

cortocircuito, _m._ (elec.) short circuit.

cortón, _m._ mantis, an orthopterous insect.

corulla, _f._ in galleys, place for the stoppers of cables.

corundo, _m._ corundum.

coruñés, sa, _a._ of or belonging to Corunna.

coruscación, _f._ coruscation, brillancy, flashing.

coruscante, _a._ coruscant, glittering, brilliant.

coruscar, _va._ (poet.) to shine.

corusco, ca, _a._ = CORUSCANTE.

corva, _f._ bend of the knee, ham, hock; (vet.) curb.

corvadura, _f._ curvature, crookedness, bend; gibbousness; (arch.) bend of an arch or vault.

corvato, _m._ young crow or rook.

corvaza, _f._ (vet.) curb.

corvecito, _m. dim._ little crow or rook.

corvejón, _m._ gambrel, hock; spur of a cock;(zool.) cormorant.

corvejo, _m._ hock joint of a quadruped.

corveta, _f._ curvet, corvetto; leap or bound of a horse.

corvetear, _vn._ to curvet, bound, leap.

córvidos, _m. pl._ (zool.) Corvidæ.

corvillo, _m._ hooked bill; pruning knife; shoemaker's paring knife; small sickle in velvet looms.

corvina, _f._ a variety of conger eel in the Mediterranean; corvina, a Californian fish.

corvino, na, _a._ corvine, rooklike; belonging or relating to rooks.

corvo, _m._ (zool.) a variety of mullet; pothook.

corvo, va, _a._ bent, crooked; arched; stingy, mean.

corzo, za, _n._ roe deer, fallow deer.

corzuelo, _m._ wheat left in the husks by the thrashers.

cosa, _f._ thing.—**c. de,** about, more or less.—**c. del otro jueves,** (coll.) a marvellous thing; something out of date.—**c. de oír,** a thing worth hearing.—**c. de risa,** laughable thing, a thing to laugh at.—**c. de ver,** a thing worth seeing.—**c. no vista,** or **nunca vista,** unheard-of thing.—**c. rara,** a strange thing; strange to say.—**c. hecha,** surely, as good as done (ch. constr.).—**cada c. para su c.,** everything in its place, or where it belongs.—**como quien no quiere la c.,** unconcernedly, in a go-as-you please way.—**como si tal c.,** as if nothing had happened.—**cosas de,** doings, or tricks of (ch. constr.: _esas son cosas de Juan,_ that is one of John's tricks; that is just like John).—**cosas del otro jueves,** something very unusual.—**fuerte c.,** nuisance.—**no es c.,** it is nothing, it is but a trifle; no matter.—**no hay tal c.,** no such thing.—**no ser,** or **no valer, c.,** not to be worth a rush.—**no ser gran c.,** not to amount to much.—**poquita c.,** (coll.) a pusillanimous person.—**¿qué c.?** (coll.) how goes it? what's the news?

cosaco, ca, _n. & a._ Cossack.

cosario, _m._ carrier, expressman; huntsman, hunter.

cosario, ria, _a._ belonging or relating to carriers; frequented, having much traffic (s. o. roads).

coscarana, _f._ (prov.) cracknel, crisp cake.

coscarse, _vr._ (coll.) = CONCOMERSE.

coscoja, _f._ (bot.) kermes, or scarlet, oak; dry leaves of the kermes oak; ring or knob on the bit of a bridle.

coscojal, coscojar, _m._ plantation or field of kermes.

coscojo, _m._ kermes berry.—_pl._ chain of a horse's bridle.

coscomate, _m._ (Mex.) corn barn.

coscón, na, _a._ crafty, sly.

coscoroba, _f._ a South-American variety of swan.

coscorrón, _m._ contusion; bump on the head.

cosecante, _m._ (geom.) cosecant.

cosecha, _f._ harvest, crop; yield; harvest time; harvest gathering; reaping; aggregate of immaterial things, as virtues, vices, etc.—**c. de vino,** vintage.—**de su c.,** of one's own invention.

cosechar, _va._ to reap, gather (the harvest).

cosechero, ra, _n._ owner or reaper of a crop or harvest, harvester.

coselete, _m._ corselet, ancient coat of armor; pikeman; thorax of insects.

coseno, _m._ (math.) cosine.—**c. verso,** coversed sine.

coser, _va._ to sew; to join, unite; to rivet (as a boiler); (naut.) to lash, nail, fix, frap, seize.— **c. a puñaladas,** (coll.) to stab repeatedly.—**c. un motón,** (naut.) to lash a block.—**c. y cantar,** to offer no difficulties; to be a cinch, a walkover, etc.—**coserse con la pared,** to stick close to a wall.—**coserse la boca,** not to speak a word, to shut up like a clam.

cosera, _f._ piece of land that can be irrigated at once.

cosetada, _f._ race, quick run, sprint.

cosible, _a._ that may be sewed.

cosita, _f.dim._ small thing, trifle; (Cuba) luncheon.

cosicosa, _f._ = QUISICOSA.

cosido, da. I. _a._ (w. **a**) devoted (to), wedded (to). **II.** _m._ sewing; needlework.—**c. de cama,** quilt and blankets stitched together. **III.** _pp._ of COSER.

cosiduras, _f. pl._ (naut.) lashings.

cosmético, _m._ cosmetic.

cósmico, ca, _a._ cosmic.

cosmogonía, _f._ cosmogony.

cosmogónico, ca, _a._ cosmogonic.

cosmografía, _f._ cosmography, descriptive astronomy.

cosmográfico, ca, _a._ cosmographical.

cosmógrafo, fa, _n._ cosmographer.

cosmología, _f._ cosmology.

cosmológico, ca, _a._ cosmological.

cosmopolita, _n. & a._ cosmopolite, cosmopolitan.

cosmopolitismo, _m._ cosmopolitism.

cosmorama, _m._ cosmorama.

cosmos, _m._ cosmos.

coso, _m._ place or enclosure for bullfights or other public spectacles; timber worm; main street.

cospel, _m._ coin blank, in the mint.

cospillo, _m._ bagasse of the olive.

cosquillas, _f. pl._ tickling; ticklishness.—**buscarle a uno las c.,** (coll.) to tease and irritate one. —**hacer c.,** to tickle; to excite, disturb; to incite.— **tener c.,** to be ticklish.—**tener malas c.,** (coll.) to be easily offended; to be ill-tempered; to be overparticular.

cosquillejas, _f. pl. dim._ little tickling.

cosquilleo, _m._ tickling sensation.

cosquilloso, sa, _a._ ticklish; susceptible, easily offended.

costa, _f._ cost, price, charge; expense, expensiveness; fatigue; coast; shore, beach; seashore, seaboard; strand; heel shiner; sole polisher.—_pl._ costs of a lawsuit.—**c. de barlovento,** weather shore.—**a c. de,** at the expense of.—**a mi c.,** at my expense.—**a toda c.,** at all hazards; at any price.— **condenar en c.,** to sentence to pay the costs.— **dar a la c.,** (naut.) to be blown or driven to shore, to be beached.

costado, _m._ side; (mil.) flank.—_pl._ race, lineage, succession of ancestors.—**c. de barlovento,** (naut.) weather side.

costal. I. _m._ sack or large bag; brace of frame for making adobe walls. **II.** _a._ costal, belonging to the ribs.

costalada, _f._, **costalazo,** _m._ blow on one falling flat on the ground.

costalejo, _m. dim._ small sack.

costalero, *m.* porter who carries goods.

costalito, *m. dim.* small sack.

costanera, *f.* slope.—*pl.* (carp.) rafters.

costanero, ra, *a.* belonging to a coast; declivous, sloping.—**buque c.,** coaster, coasting vessel.

costanilla, *f. dim.* gentle slope; steep street.

costar, *vn.* (*ind.* CUESTO: *subj.* CUESTE) to cost; to cause or occasion detriment or loss.—**c. la torta un pan,** (coll.) to pay dear for one's whistle.

costarricense; costarriqueño, ña, *n.* & *a.* Costa-Rican.

coste, *m.* cost, expense, price.—**a c. y costas,** at cost.

costear. I. *va.* to pay the cost of. **II.** *vr.* to pay; to produce sufficient to repay its cost; (naut.) to coast.

costeño, ña, *a.* from, or relating to, the coast or seashore; coasting (vessel).

costera, *f.* side of a bale of goods; surmullet, fishing season; outside quire of a ream; slope of a hill.

costero, *m.* first plank cut from a pine tree.

costero, ra, *a.* belonging to the coast; outward.

costezuela, *f. dim.* slight declivity or slope.

costilla, *f.* rib; chop; cutlet; (coll.) wife, better half; rung of a chair; stave of a barrel; (carp.) fur; (arch.) rib of a cupola; springer; (coll.) property, wealth; (bot.) rib of a leaf.—*pl.* (coll.) shoulders, back; (agr.) wooden strips to which horses are tied in plowing; (mech.) cramp-irons, chimney ties.—**c. falsa,** false rib.—**c. flotante,** floating rib.—**costillas de un navío,** (naut.) ribs of a ship.—**medirle a uno las costillas,** to cudgel one.

costillaje, costillar, *m.* (anat.) the ribs, or rib system; (naut.) frame of a ship.

costilludo, da, *a.* (coll.) broad-shouldered.

costino, na, *a.* belonging to the costus root; (Ch., Arg.) COSTEÑO.

costo, *m.* cost, price; charges, expense; labor, fatigue; (bot.) sweet and bitter costus; costus root.—**a c. y costas,** at cost.

costosamente, *adv.* expensively, extravagantly.

costoso, sa, *a.* costly, dear, expensive; difficult to be obtained; sad, grievous.

costra, *f.* crust, scab; broken biscuit; incrusted part of a wick; crust of casting.

costrada, *f.* candied seedcake.

costroso, sa, *a.* crusty, having crusts or scabs.

costumbre, *f.* custom; habit; catamenia, courses. —*pl.* customs, ways.

costumbrista, *n.* genre writer, one who portrays everyday life and prevailing customs.

costura, *f.* sewing, needlework; seam, stitching; (surg.) suture; (mech.) crease, ridge; joint; riveting; (naut.) splicing of a rope; (carp.) joint. —**c. sobrecargada,** felting.—**sin c.,** seamless (sp. app. to tubes).

costurera, *f.* seamstress.

costurero, *m.* lady's workbox or worktable; sewing room.

costurón, *m. aug.* big seam; coarse suture; large scar.

cota, *f.* coat of mail (called also **c. de malla**); coat of arms, tabard coat; (top.) number indicating the elevation of a point above datum; quota, share; back and callous part of a boar's hide.

cotana, *f.* mortise, mortise hole.

cotangente, *f.* (geom.) cotangent.

cotanza, *f.* a kind of medium-fine linen.

cotarrera, *f.* (coll.) gadding woman.

cotarro, *m.* charity hut to shelter beggars; side of a pit.—**alborotar el c.,** to cause disturbance.— **andar de cotarro en c.,** to go sauntering about.

cotejar, *va.* to compare, confront.

cotejo, *m.* comparison, collation.

cotense, *m.* (Mex.) coarse brown linen wrapper.

coterráneo, *a.* = CONTERRÁNEO.

cotí, *m.* ticking for mattresses.

cotidianamente, *adv.* daily.

cotidiano, na, *a.* daily, everyday; quotidian.

cotiledón, *m.* (bot.) cotyledon.

cotiledóneo, ea, *a.* cotyledonous.

cotilla, *f.* stays, corsets.

cotillero, ra, *n.* stay maker.

cotillo, *m.* face or flat surface of a hammer.

cotillón, *m.* cotillon.

cotín, *m.* back stroke given to a ball.

cotiza, *f.* (her.) cotise; (mech.) dents for the warp; (S. A.) an Indian sandal.

cotizable, *a.* quotable; valued (at).

cotización, *f.* (com.) quotation; price current, price list.

cotizado, da, *a.* (com.) quoted, listed; (her.) cotised.

cotizar, *va.* (*pret.* COTICÉ: *subj.* COTICE) to quote (prices); to cry out (current prices) in the exchange.

coto, *m.* inclosure of pasture grounds; landmark, boundary; combination among merchants: measure of a handbreadth; billiard contest; fine or mulct; chub; rate or price limitation; (med.) goiter.—**poner c. a,** to put a stop to, to check.

cotobelo, *m.* opening in the branch of a bridle.

cotón, *m.* printed cotton.

cotona, *f.* (Mex.) chamois jacket.

cotonada, *f.* cottonade; print, printed cloth.

cotoncillo, *m.* button of a maulstick or painter's staff.

cotonía, *f.* dimity, fine fustian.

cotorra, *f.* a kind of parrot; magpie; (coll.) loquacious woman.—**cotorrear,** *vn.* to chatter; to gossip.—**cotorreo,** *m.* chattering; gossiping.

cotorrera, *f.* hen parrot; (coll.) prattling woman.

cotorrón, ona. I. *a.* affecting youth, or acting sillily like young people (s. o. old persons). **II.** *m.* (Am.) bachelor.

cotral, *m.* old worn-out ox turned out to graze.

cotudo, da, *a.* hairy, cottony; having a goiter.

cotufa, *f.* (bot.) Jerusalem artichoke; tidbits; delicate food.—**pedir cotufas en el golfo,** to expect impossibilities.

cotufero, ra, *a.* producing tidbits or delicate food.

cotunto, *m.* (Cuba) a kind of night bird.

coturno, *m.* cothurnus, buskin.

covacha, *f.* small cave or hollow underground; grot or grotto.

covachuela, *f. dim.* small cave or grotto; (coll.) office of a crown minister, formerly in the vaulted corridors of the royal palace.

covachuelista *or* **covachuelo,** *m.* (coll.) clerk in one of the COVACHUELAS.

covadera, *f.* (Peru) guano bed.

covanilla, *f..* **covanillo,** *m. dim.* basket for gathering grapes.

covezuela, *f. dim.* small cave.

coxal, *a.* hip (u. a.), relating to the hip or hip joint.

coxalgia, *f.* hip-joint disease, coxalgia.

coxcojilla, ita, *f.* children's play; hopscotch.— **a c.,** lamely, haltingly, hippety-hoppety.

coxis, *m.* (anat.) coccyx.

coy, *m.* (naut.) hammock, cot, sailor's bed.— **afuera coys,** all hammocks up.

coya, *f.* (Peru) queen, wife and sister of the Inca.

coyabra = CUYABRA.

coyote. I. *a.* (Am.) native, domestic. **II.** *m.* (Mex.) coyote; (coll.) curbstone broker.

coyunda, *f.* strap for yoking oxen; shoestring; dominion, tyranny; matrimonial union.

coyuntura, *f.* joint, articulation; occasion, juncture, opportunity; nick of time.

coz, *f.* kick; drawback; recoil of a gun; flowing back of a flood; butt of a pistol; (coll.) churlishness, unprovoked brusqueness.—**c. de mastelero,** (naut.) heel of a mast.—**dar coces,** to kick.—**dar coces contra el aguijón,** to kick against the prick.—**soltar una c.,** to answer rudely.—**tirar coces,** to kick.

cozcojilla, *f.* = COXCOJILLA.

crabrón, *m.* hornet.

crac, *m.* failure, bankruptcy.

crameria, *f.* krameria, rhatany.

cran, *m.* (print.) nick of a type.

craneal; craneano, na, *a.* cranial.

---

cráneo, *m.* skull, cranium.
craneología, *f.* craniology.
craneometría, *f.* craniometry.
craneómetro, *m.* craniometer.
craneoscopía, *f.* cranioscopy.
craniano, na, *a.* cranial.
crápula, *f.* intoxication; crapulence, debauchery.
crapuloso, sa, *a.* drunken; gluttonous; dissolute, dissipated.
crasamente, *adv.* grossly; rudely.
crascitar, *vn.* to crow; to croak.
crasiento, ta, *a.* greasy.
crasitud, *f.* fatness, corpulency, obesity; ignorance, stupidity, dulness.
craso, sa, *a.* fat, greasy; thick, gross, crass.
crasuláceo, a. I. *a.* (bot.) crasulaceous. **II.** *f. pl.* Crasulaceæ.
cráter, *m.* crater of a volcano.
crátera, *f.* (archeol.) crater.
cratícula, *f.* small wicket through which nuns receive the communion.
craza, *f.* crucible.
crea, *f.* a kind of linen stuff.
creable, *a.* creatable.
creación, *f.* creation.
creado, da. I. *a.* created, begotten, made. **II.** *pp.* of CREAR.
Creador, *m.* Creator.
creador, ra, *n. & a.* creator (-ing, -ive); originator (-ing).
crear, *va.* to create; to institute, establish; to appoint, be made.
crébol, *m.* (bot.) holly tree.
crecedero, ra, *a.* able to grow; increasable.
crecer. I. *vn.* (*ind.* CREZCO: *subj.* CREZCA) to grow; to bud forth; to increase; to swell; to augment in extrinsic value (s. o. money).—**c. como la mala hierba,** to grow like weeds. **II.** *vr.* to swell with pride or with authority.
creces, *f. pl.* augmentation, increase, excess; additional quantity of corn paid by a farmer to a public granary, besides what he borrowed from it.—**con c.,** amply.
crecida, *f.* freshet.
crecidamente, *adv.* plentifully, copiously, abundantly.
crecidito, ta, *a. dim.* somewhat grown.
crecido, da. I. *a.* grown, increased; grave, important; large, swollen. **II.** *pp.* of CRECER.
crecidos, *m. pl.* widening stitches in knitting.
creciente. I. *a.* growing, increasing; crescent; susceptible of increase. **II.** *m.* (her.) half-moon with points upward. **III.** *f.* swell, freshet of waters; leaven; crescent (of the moon).—**c. de la marea,** (naut.) flood tide, flow, flowing.
crecimiento, *m.* growth; growing; increase, increment.—**c. de la marejada,** (naut.) swell of the sea.
credencia, *f.* sideboard of an altar.
credencial, *f.* credential, accreditation.—*pl.* credentials.
credibilidad, *f.* credibility.
crédito, *m.* credit; acquiescence, assent; belief, faith; reputation, character, name, standing; note, bill, order for payment.—**créditos activos,** assets.—**créditos pasivos,** liabilities.—**a c.,** on credit.—**dar c.,** to believe; to give credit.
credo, *m.* creed, articles of faith.—**c. político,** political creed, platform.—**en un c.,** in a trice.
crédulamente, *adv.* credulously, unsuspectingly.
credulidad, *f.* credulity.
crédulo, la, *a.* credulous.
creedero, ra, *a.* credible.—**tener buenas creederas,** to be easy of belief.
creedor, ra, *a.* credulous.
creencia, *f.* belief; creed, persuasion.
creer, *va.* (*pret.* él CREYÓ) to believe; to credit; to think, think it probable.—**creerse del aire,** to be credulous.—**ver y c.,** seeing before believing.—**ya lo creo,** (coll.) of course, undoubtedly.
crehuela, *f.* Osnaburg, a sort of linen.
creíble, *a.* credible, likely, believable.

creíblemente, *adv.* credibly, possibly.
crema, *f.* cream of milk; custard; diæresis; cream, select society; cold cream; cosmetic.
cremación, *f.* cremation, incineration.
cremallera, *f.* ratch, rack; toothed bar.
cremar, *va.* to cremate.
crematística, *f.* science of acquiring and preserving wealth.
cremat ólogo, ga, *n.* political economist.
crematología, *f.* political economy.
crematológico, ca, *a.* economical, relating to political economy.
cremómetro, *m.* creamometer.
cremonés, sa, *a.* of or relating to Cremona.
crémor, *m.*—**c. tártaro,** cream of tartar.
crencha, *f.* parting of the hair into two parts; each of these parts.
creosota, *f.,* **creosoto,** *m.* creosote.
crepitación, *f.* crepitation, crackling; (surg.) crepitus of fractures.
crepitante, *a.* crackling, crepitant.
crepitar, *vn.* to crackle, crepitate.
crepuscular; crepusculino, na, *a.* crepuscular.
crepúsculo, *m.* crepuscule, twilight; dawn; dusk.
cresa, *f.* egg or larva of the queen bee; flyblow, egg of a fly; maggot.
crescendo, *m.* (mus.) crescendo.
crespilla, *f.* agaric.
crespina, *f.* hair net.
crespo, pa. I. *a.* curly; crispy; (bot.) crispleaved; obscure and bombastic; (Am.); angry, displeased, vexed. **II.** *m.* (Am.) curl.
crespón, *m.* crape.
cresta, *f.* comb (of a bird); cockscomb, aigrette, tuft; crest of a helmet; wave crest; top, brow; crest or summit of a mountain; (min.) crop; (mill.) cramp iron.—**c. de la explanada,** (fort.) crest of the glacis.—**alzar,** or **levantar, la c.,** to be elated with pride.
crestado, da, *a.* crested.
crestería, *f.* (arch.) cresting; (fort.) battlement.
crestomatía, *f.* chrestomathy.
crestón, *m. aug.* large crest; crest of a helmet; (min.) outcrop.
creta, *f.* chalk.
cretáceo, cea, *a.* cretaceous; chalky.
cretense; crético, ca, *n. & a.* Cretan.
crético, *m.* verse of three syllables.
cretinismo, *m.* cretinism.
cretino, na, *n. & a.* cretin.
cretona, *f.* cretonne.
creyente, *n. & a.* believer (-ing).
creyón, *m.* crayon; charcoal pencil; black chalk.
crezneja, *f.* braid of hair; streak of bleached bassweed.
cría, *f.* act of nursing; breeding; rearing, bringing up; keeping (as bees); brood of animals; suckling; (coll.) child reared by a nurse.
criada, *f.* female servant; maid, maid servant.—**c. de mano,** (Cuba) housemaid; wash bat.
criadero, *m.* nursery, plantation of young trees; breeding place; fish hatchery; (min.) seam; cocoon bed; hotbed.
criadero, ra, *a.* fruitful, prolific.
criadilla, *f.* testicle of an animal; lamb fry; mountain oyster; small loaf or roll; potato; (bot.) truffle.
criado, *m.* servant, menial, groom, valet.
criado, da. I. *a.* bred. **II.** *pp.* of CRIAR.
criador, ra. I. *a.* creating, creative; fruitful, fecund. **II.** *n.* rearer, raiser, breeder, keeper (as of bees); creator. **III.** *f.* wet nurse.
criaduelo, la, *n. dim.* little or young servant.
criamiento, *m.* renovation and preservation.
criandera, *f.* (Am.) wet nurse.
crianza, *f.* nursing; lactation; breeding; manners, education; nursery.—**dar c.,** to breed; to rear, educate, bring up.
criar, *va.* to create; to breed, procreate; to raise, rear, bring up; to nurse, nourish; to fatten (animals).—**c. carnes,** to grow fat.—**c. molleja,** to grow lazy.

criatura, *f.* creature; fœtus; baby, infant; child; being, man.—**es una c.,** he is but an infant, or like an infant

criba, *f.* cribble, sieve, crib, screen.

cribado, da, *a.* sifted, screened.

cribador, ra, *n.* sifter.

cribar, *va.* to sift, sieve, screen.

cribo, *m.* = CRIBA.

cric, *m.* jackscrew, lifting jack. *V.* GATO.

crica, *f.* trench, fissure; (med.) female pudenda.

crimen, *m.* crime; (theol.) mortal sin.

criminación, *f.* incrimination.

criminal, *n.* & *a.* criminal.

criminalidad, *f.* criminality, guilt.

criminalista, *m.* criminalist.

criminalmente, *adv.* criminally.

criminar, *va.* to accuse, incriminate.

criminología, *f.* criminology.

criminoso, sa. I. *n.* delinquent, criminal. **II.** *a.* criminal, guilty.

crimno, *m.* coarse flour meal.

crin, *f.* mane, horsehair.

crinado, da, *a.* crinite, maned, having long hair.

crinífero, ra, *a.* mane-bearing.

crinito, ta, *a.* = CRINADO.

crinolina, *f.* crinoline.

crío, *m.* nursing baby.

criolita, *f.* (min.) cryolite.

criollo, lla. I. *n.* creole. **II.** *a.* indigenous, domestic.

cripta, *f.* crypt.

criptógamo, ma. I. *a.* (bot.) cryptogamous. **II.** *f. pl.* Cryptogamia.

criptografía, *f.* cryptography.

criptograma, *m.* cryptogram, a writing in cipher.

cris, *m.* creese or kris, a Malayan dagger.

crisálida, *f.* (ent.) pupa, chrysalis.

crisantema, *f.*, **crisantemo,** *m.* (bot.) chrysanthemum.

crisis, *f.* crisis; judgment passed after mature deliberation; criterion; decisive moment.—**c. ministerial,** resignation or dismissal of the cabinet.

crisma. I. *m.* chrism. **II.** *f.* (coll.) head, "block."

crismera, *f.* chrismatory.

crisneja, *f.* = CRIZNEJA.

crisoberilo, *m.* chrysoberyl.

crisocola, *f.* chrysocola.

crisol, *m.* crucible; croslet or crosslet; cruset; hearth of a furnace.

crisolada, *f.* charge of a crucible.

crisolito, *m.* (min.) chrysolite.—**c. oriental,** yellow topaz.

crisopacio, *m.* = CRISOPRASA.

crisopeya, *f.* alchemy.

crisoprasa, *f.* (min.) chrysoprase.

crispamiento, *m.* contraction, twitching.

crispar. I. *va.* to cause (muscles) to contract convulsively. **II.** *vn.* to twitch.

crispatura, *f.* crispation, spasmodic contraction.

crispir, *va.* to marble, marbleize.

crista, *f.* (her.) crest.

cristal, *m.* (min. and chem.) crystal; flint glass; looking-glass; a fine shiny woollen stuff.—**c. de roca,** rock crystal.—**c. tallado,** cut glass.—**c. tártaro,** cream of tartar.

cristalería, *f.* glassware; glass store.

cristalino, na. I. *a.* crystalline, clear. **II.** *m.* (anat.) crystalline of the eye.

cristalizable, *a.* crystallizable.

cristalización, *f.* crystallization.

cristalizador, *m.* (chem.) vessel in which crystals are made.

cristalizar, *va.* & *vr.* (*pret.* CRISTALICÉ: *subj.* CRISTALICE) to crystallize.

cristalografía, *f.* crystallography.

cristalográfico, ca, *a.* crystallographical.

cristaloide, *m.* (chem.) crystaloid.

cristel, *m.* clyster.

cristianamente, *adv.* Christianly.

cristianar, *va.* (coll.) to baptize, to christen.

cristiandad, *f.* Christendom; observance of the law of Christ; missionary's flock.

cristianesco, ca, *a.* applied to Moorish forms which imitate the Christian manner.

cristianillo, illa, *n.* contemptible Christian; (app. to Spaniards by the Moors).

cristianísimo, *a. sup.* most Christian (app. to certain sovereigns as a title).

cristianismo, *m.* Christianity; the body of Christians; christening.

cristianizar, *va.* (*pret.* CRISTIANICÉ: *subj.* CRISTIANICE) to christianize.

cristiano, na. I. *a.* Christian. **II.** *n.* Christian; (coll.) the Spanish language, opposed to Arabic or other foreign tongues; (coll.) living soul, person; (coll.) watered wine.

cristino, na, *a.* supporting the Queen Regent María Cristina against the pretender Don Carlos.

Cristo, *m.* Christ; image of Christ crucified.—**haber la de Dios es C.,** to have a grand dispute or quarrel.—**ni por un C.,** by no means, not for the world.—**poner como un c.,** to abuse, ill-treat.

cristofué, *m.* (Ven.) a bird.

cristus, *m.* christcross, a cross formerly printed at the beginning of the alphabet; the alphabet.—**estar en el c.,** to be in the rudiments, or learning the A B C.—**no saber el c.,** to be very ignorant, not to know one's A B C.

crisuela, *f.* dripping pan of a lamp.

criterio, *m.* criterion; judgment, discernment.

crítica, *f.* criticism, critique, critical examination; censure.

criticable, *a.* that may be criticised; blameworthy.

criticador, ra, *n.* & *a.* critic (-izing).

criticar, *va.* (*pret.* CRITIQUÉ: *subj.* CRITIQUE) to criticise; to judge; to blame, find fault with.

criticastro, *m.* criticaster.

criticismo, *m.* critical, or Kantian, philosophy.

crítico, ca, *n.* critic, criticiser; (coll.) affected writer or speaker; censurer, faultfinder.

crítico, ca, *a.* critical, critic, decisive; hypercritical; (med.) critical.

criticón, *m.* = CRITICASTRO.

critiquizar, *va.* to overcriticise, criticize for the sake of criticizing.

crizneja, *f.* braid of hair; trace or rope of osiers or rushes.

croar, *vn.* to croak like a frog.

croata, *n.* & *a.* Croatian.

crocante, *m.* almond or peanut brittle.

crocino, na, *a.* of crocus, saffron.

crocitar, *vn.* to crow.

crocodilo, *m.* crocodile.

crochet, *m.* crochet.

cromático, ca, *a.* (mus. and opt.) chromatic.

cromatismo, *m.* chromatic aberration.

cromato, *m.* chromate.

cromatología, *f.* chromatology, the science of colors.

crómico, ca, *a.* chromic.

cromo, *m.* chromium; chromo, a chromolithograph.

cromolitografía, *f.* chromolithograph, colored lithograph; chromolithography.

cromolitografiar, *va.* to chromolithograph.

cromolitográfico, ca, *a.* chromolithographic; lithographed in colors.

cromolitógrafo, fa, *n.* chromolithographer.

cromoso, sa, *a.* chromous.

cromosfera, *f.* (astr.) chromosphere.

cromotipia, *f.* color printing.

cromotipografía, *f.* chromotypography.

crónica, *f.* chronicle.

crónico, ca, *a.* chronic.

cronicón, *m.* brief chronicle.

cronista, *m.* chronicler, annalist.

crónlech, *m.* (archeol.) cromlech.

cronografía, *f.* chronography.

cronógrafo, *m.* annalist.

cronograma, *f.* chronogram.

cronología, *f.* chronology.

cronológicamente, *adv.* chronologically.

cronológico, ca, *a.* chronological, chronologic.
cronologista; cronólogo, ga, *n.* chronologist.
cronometría, *f.* chronometry.—**cronométrico, ca,** *a.* chronometric.—**cronometrista,** *n.* chronometer maker.
cronómetro, *m.* chronometer.
croqueta, *f.* croquette, fritter.
croquis, *m.* sketch, rough draft.
croscitar, *vn.* to crow.
crótalo, *m.* castanet; rattlesnake (crotalus).
croton, crotontiglio, *m.* castor-oil plant.
crotorar, *vn.* to cry like a crane or stork.
cruce, *m.* crossing; crossroads.
crucera, *f.* withers of a horse.—*pl.* bolting pins.
crucería, *f.* Gothic architecture.
crucero, *m.* crucifer, cross-bearer; crossing of two streets or roads; railway crossing; (arch.) transept; (print.) crossbar of a chase; (carp.) crosspiece; binding beam; (naut.) cruising station; cruiser; (ast.) Cross, a constellation; (min.) cleavage plane.
cruceta, *f.* crosspiece; headstick; crosshead (of connecting rod); crosstail; (naut.) crosstree; trelliswork.
cruciata, *f.* (bot.) crosswort.
cruciferario, *m.* crucifer, cross-bearer.
crucífero, *m.* crucifer, cross-bearer; crutched friar.
crucífero, ra. I. *a.* cruciferous; cross-shaped; bearing a cross; (bot.) cruciate. **II.** *f. pl.* (bot.) Cruciferæ.
crucificado, da. I. crucified.—**el C.,** the Crucified, Jesus Christ. **II.** *pp.* of CRUCIFICAR.
crucificar, *va.* (*pret.* CRUCIFIQUÉ: *subj.* CRUCIFIQUE) to crucify; to vex, torment, torture; to sacrifice; to ruin.
crucifijo, *m.* crucifix.
crucifixión, *f.* crucifixion.
cruciforme, *a.* cruciform.
crucífero, ra, *a.* cruciferous.
crucillo, *m.* pushpin, a game.
crudamente, *adv.* rudely, crudely.
crudelísimo, ma, *a. superl.* most cruel.
crudeza, *f.* crudity, crudeness; unripeness; rawness; hardness (s. o. water); rudeness; severity, rigor; (coll.) vapor, vain boasting.—**crudezas del estómago,** undigested food.
crudo, da, *a.* raw; crude; green, unripe; rude; cruel, pitiless; rough, unfinished; immature; hard of digestion; blustering, hectoring person; hard (s. o. water); (med.) unripe, not mature.
cruel, *a.* cruel.—**crueldad,** *f.* cruelty; cruel action or treatment.
cruelmente, *adv.* cruelly, with cruelty.
cruentamente, *adv.* bloodily, with effusion of blood; cruelly.
cruento, ta, *a.* bloody; cruel, inhuman.
crujía, *f.* (naut.) midship gangway of a galley; large open hall, corridor or passage in a building, with rooms on either side; great hall of a hospital; aisle of a ward; in cathedrals, passage between rails from choir to altar.—**c. de piezas,** suite of rooms.—**pasar c.,** to run the gantlet; to suffer great troubles.
crujidero, ra, *a.* creaking, crackling, rustling.
crujido, *m.* crack, creak, crackling, creaking; rustle; (metal.) flaw in a blade.
crujidor, ra. I. *a.* cracking, creaking. **II.** *n.* glass trimmer.
crujiente, *a.* cracking, creaking; rustling.
crujir, *vn.* to crackle, creak; rustle.
cruor, *m.* cruor, blood clog; coloring matter of the blood; blood globules.
cruórico, ca, *a.* bloody.
crup, *m.* (med.) croup, membranous or true croup.
crupal, *a.* (med.) croupal, croupous.
crural, *a.* crural, belonging to the leg.
crustáceo, cea. I. *n. & a.* crustacean (-ceous). **II.** *m. pl.* Crustacea.
crústula, *f.* = CORTEZUELA.
cruz, *f.* cross; tail (of a coin); upper end of a tree trunk, where the branches begin; (vet.) withers;

(print.) dagger, obelisk.—*pl.* wings of a reel.—**c. ancorada,** or **de Jerusalén,** anchor cross.—**c. de las bitas,** (naut.) crosstree of the bitts.—**C. del Sur,** (ast.) Southern Cross.—**c. de Malta,** Maltese cross.—**c. de San Andrés,** St. Andrew's cross.—**c. gamada,** swastika.—**c. griega,** Greek cross.—**c. latina,** Latin cross.—**c. potenzada,** potent cross.—**c. trebolada,** trefoil cross.—**c. y raya,** no more of this.—**de la c. a la fecha,** from beginning to end.—**en c.,** crosswise, crossing each other; cross-shaped.
cruzada, *f.* crusade; tribunal of the crusade; crossroads.
cruzado, da. I. *a.* crossed; cross (breed, etc.); crosswise, transverse, twilled.—**estarse con los brazos cruzados,** to be idle. **II.** *m.* an old Spanish coin; Portuguese coin; crusader; knight of a military order; manner of playing on the guitar; figure in dancing.
cruzamen, *m.* (naut.) square or width (of a sail).
cruzamiento, *m.* crossing.
cruzar. I. *va.* (*pret.* CRUCÉ: *subj.* CRUCE) to cross; to lay, place, pass, or go across; to honor with a cross or medal; to cruise; to cross (the breed); to twill.—**c. la cara a uno,** to hack one's face. **II.** *vr.* to be knighted; to cross each other; to accumulate.
cu, *m.* name of the letter *q*; ancient Mexican temple.
cuaderna, *f.* double fours, in background; fourth part of anything; (naut.) frame.—**c. maestra,** (naut.) midship frame.
cuadernal, *m.* (naut.) block, tackle.
cuadernalete, *m.* (naut.) short double block.
cuadernillo, *m.* quire of paper; clerical directory.
cuaderno, *m.* writing book, memorandum book, composition book; (print.) four printed sheets placed within each other; an ancient form of punishment for students; pack of cards.—**c. de bitácora,** (naut.) log book.
cuadra, *f.* large hall; stable; ward in hospital, barracks, or prison; quarter of a mile; (Am.) block of houses; (naut.) quarter of a ship.
cuadradamente, *adv.* exactly, completely.
cuadradillo, *m. dim.* little cube; block of sugar; cross-section paper, plotting paper.
cuadrado, da. I. *a.* square; perfect. **II.** *pp.* of CUADRAR. **III.** *m.* square; square ruler; clock, in stockings; gusset of a shirt sleeve; die; (arith., alg.) square; (ast.) quadrate; (carp.) square; (print.) quadrat, quad.—**de c.,** face to face; perfectly.
cuadragenario, ria, *a.* forty-year old.
cuadragésima, *f.* Lent.
cuadragesimal, *a.* Lenten.
cuadragésimo, ma, *a.* fortieth.
cuadral, *m.* (carp.) angle brace, truss; shoulder tie.
cuadrangular, *a.* quadrangular.
cuadrángulo, *m. & a.* quadrangle (-gular).
cuadrantal, *a.* (math.) quadrantal.
cuadrante, *m.* (geom.) quadrant; (ast.) quadrant; sundial; clock face; face of a watch; (law) fourth part of an inheritance; ancient copper coin.
cuadrar. I. *va. & vn.* to square; to form into or reduce to a square; (arith.) to square; (pict.) CUADRICULAR; to square, fit, suit, adjust; to please. **II.** *vr.* (mil.) to stand at attention; (coll.) to assume a very serious attitude.
cuadratín, *m.* (print.) quadrat.
cuadratura, *f.* squaring, square; (math., ast.) quadrature.
cuadrete, *m. dim.* small square.
cuadricenal, *a.* done every forty years.
cuadrícula, *f.* quadricle; quadrille.
cuadriculado, da, *a.* cross-section, squared (paper).
cuadricular, *va.* (pict.) to graticule.
cuadricular, *a.* squared, in squares.
cuadrienal, *a.* quadrennial, comprising four years.
cuadrienio, *m.* time and space of four years.

cuadrífido. da, *a.* (bot.) quadrifid.
cuadrifoliado, da, *a.* (bot.) quadrifoliated.
cuadriforme, *a.* four-faced.
cuadriga, *f.* quadriga.
cuadril, *m.* haunch bone; haunch; hip.
cuadriliteral, *a.* consisting of four letters.
cuadrilátero, ra. I. *a.* quadrilateral, four-sided.
II. *m.* (geom.) quadrilateral.
cuadrilongo, ga. I. *a.* rectangular. **II.** *m.* rectangle; (mil.) rectangular formation.
cuadrilla, *f.* meeting of four or more persons; gang; party; crew; herd; troop; band of armed men; patrol of the Inquisition.
cuadrillero, *m.* chief of a band; patrolman of the Inquisition; (Philip.) rural guard.
cuadrillo, *m. dim.* small square; Moorish dart.
cuadrimestre, *m.* period of four months.
cuadringentésimo, ma, *a.* four-hundredth.
cuadrinieto, ta, *n.* great-grandchild.
cuadripartido, *a.* quadripartite, divided in four.
cuadriplicado, da, *a.* quadrupled.
cuadrisílabo, ba, *a.* quadrisyllable.
cuadrivio, *m.* a quadrivial place; quadrivium, in the Pythagorean system.
cuadrivista, *m.* expert in the quadrivium.
cuadríyugo, *m.* cart with four horses; quadriga.
cuadro, *m.* square; picture, painting; picture frame; window frame; flower bed; (mil.) square body of troops; (print.) platen; scene, tableau, division of a play; impressive spectacle; vivid description.—**c. de distribución,** (elec.) switchboard.—**c. de servicio,** (r. w.) train schedule.—**cuadros de costumbres,** genre writings, on everyday life.—**en c.,** on each side, square (*tres pies en cuadro,* three feet square).—**estar, or quedarse, en c.,** to be bereft of either relatives or means; (mil.) to be reduced to the officers (s. o. a body of troops having lost its soldiers).
cuadrúmano, na. I. *a.* quadrumanous, four-handed. **II.** *m. pl.* Quadrumana.
cuadrupedal, *a.* quadruped.
cuadrupedante, *a.* (poet.) quadrupedant.
cuadrúpede, cuadrúpedo, da, *n.* & *a.* quadruped.
cuádruple, *a.* quadruple, fourfold.
cuádruplex, *a.* (tel.) quadruplex.
cuadruplicación, *f.* quadruplication.
cuadruplicar, *va.* to quadruplicate.
cuádruplo, pla, *a.* quadruple, fourfold.—**al c.,** quadruply.
cuaga, *m.* (zool.) quagga, a South-African wild ass, similar to the zebra.
cuajada, *f.* curd of the milk separated from the whey.
cuajadillo, *m.* a sort of silk gauze with flowers.
cuajado. I. *m.* a sort of mince pie. **II.** *a.* dumfounded.
cuajaleche, *f.* (bot.) yellow bedstraw; cheese rennet.
cuajamiento, *m.* coagulation.
cuajar. I. *va.* to coagulate, curd, curdle; to ornament or decorate with too many ornaments. **II.** *vn.* (coll.) to succeed, take; to please, be well received. **III.** *vr.* to coagulate; to curdle; to fill, become full.
cuajar, *m.* rennet bag, maw; stomach of a sucking animal; crop of a fowl; the fourth stomach, or abomasum, of a ruminant.
cuajarón, *m.* grume, clot, gore.
cuajo, *m.* rennet, runnet, maw; curdling, bonny-clabber; concretion, coagulation.—**arrancar de c.,** to eradicate, to tear up by the roots.—**tener buen c.,** to be too dull and patient.
cuakerismo, *m.* Quakerism.
cuákero, ra, *n.* & *a.* Quaker.
cual (*pl.* **cuales**). **I.** *rel. pron.* which, such as, as.—**cada c.** *V.* CADA.—**el c., la c., los cuales, las cuales,** which, who.—**lo c.,** which.—**por lo c.,** for which reason, for that reason, whence. **II.** *adv.* as, like. **III.** (**cuál**) *interr. pron.* which, what.—**a c. más,** vyingly. **IV.** (**cuál**) *interjectional pron.* how. **V.** (**cuál**) *distributive or disjunctive pron.* some (*cuál más, cuál menos,* some more, some less).

cualesquier, *pl.* of CUALQUIER.
cualesquiera, *pl.* of CUALQUIERA.
cualidad, *f.* quality.
cualitativo, va, *a.* qualitative.
cualquier, *a.* any.
cualquiera. I. *a.* any. **II.** *pron.* any one, some one, either one or the other, whichsoever, whoever.—**ser un c.,** to be of no account.
cuan, *adv. contr.* of CUANTO, how, as: used only before adjectives and adverbs.
cuando (*interr.* **cuándo**), *adv.* when, in case that, if; though, although, even; sometimes.—**c. más, or c. mucho,** at most, at best.—**c. menos,** at least.—**c. quiera (que),** when you please; whenever.—**de c. en c.,** from time to time, now and then.—**¿hasta c.?** when shall I see you again?
cuantía, *f.* amount, quantity; rank, distinction, importance, degree.
cuantiar, *va.* to estimate; appraise.
cuantidad, *f.* quantity.
cuantimás, (coll.) = CUANTO MÁS.
cuantiosamente, *adv.* copiously.
cuantioso, sa, *a.* numerous, copious, abundant.
cuantitativo, va, *a.* quantitative.
cuanto. I. *neutral pron.* all (that), as much as (*cuanto Vd. quiera,* all you wish).—**en c. a,** with regard to.—**II.** *adv.* as, the more (*cuanto más habla, menos dice,* the more he speaks the less he says).—**c. antes,** immediately, without delay.—**c. más (que),** the more; all the more because.—**por c.,** inasmuch as.—**en c.,** as soon as. **III.** (**cuánto**) *interr. pron.* how much; how long; how far. **IV.** (**cuánto**) *interjectional adv.* how.
cuanto, cuanta. I. *a.* as much as, all the (in the *pl.,* as many as, all the: *cuantos libros halle,* all the books, or as many books as, you find). **II.** *pron.* all that, all who. **III.** (**cuánto, ta**) *interr.* & *interjectional a.* & *pron.* how much (in the *pl.,* how many).
cuaquerismo, *m.* Quakerism.
cuáquero, ra, *a.* Quaker.
cuarango, *m.* Peruvian-bark tree.
cuarcita, *f.,* (min.) quartzite.
cuarenta, *n.* & *a.* forty; fortieth.
cuarentavo, va, *n.* & *a.* fortieth.
cuarentena, *f.* quarantine; period of forty days, months, or years; fortieth part; Lent; suspension of assent to anything; the number 40 in general, two score.—**hacer c.,** to be in quarantine.
cuarentón, na, *n.* & *a.* (person) forty years old.
cuaresma, *f.* Lent; collection of Lent sermons.
cuaresmal, *a.* Lenten.
cuarta, *f.* fourth, fourth part, quarter; quadrant, fourth part of a circle; (naut.) quarter, point of the compass; quart, sequence of four cards in piquet; (fen.) carte; span (of the hand); a lineal measure (¼ vara); quart, liquid measure; (mil.) quarter of a company of soldiers; (mus.) fourth; (carp.) square timber; section; (prov.) guide mule; (Mex.) short whip.
cuartago, *m.* nag, pony, hack.
cuartal, *m.* bread weighing one quarter of a loaf; quarter, dry measure, fourth part of a fanega.
cuartán, *m.* grain measure (18 litres 8 centiliters); oil measure (4 litres 15 centiliters).
cuartana, *f.* quartan, an ague recurring every four days.
cuartanal, *a.* quartan.
cuartanario, ria, *a.* laboring under a quartan.
cuartar, *va.* to plow for the fourth time.
cuartazo, *m. aug.* large room; (Mex.) blow with a whip.—*pl.* coarse, corpulent person.
cuartear. I. *va.* to quarter, divide into four equal parts; to bid a fourth more on, at public sales; to make a fourth person at (a game); to zigzag up steep places; (Mex.) to whip. **II.** *vr.* to split, crack, rift.
cuartel, *m.* quarter, fourth part; district; ward of a city; barracks; duty imposed on villages for the quartering of soldiers; (coll.) dwelling, habitation; quarter, remission of life granted by victorious troops; flower bed; (poet.) quatrain; (her.) quarter; (naut.) hatch.—**c. de la salud,** safe place,

shelter.—**c. general,** general headquarters.—**c. maestre general,** (mil.) quartermaster-general.—**estar de c.,** to be off active service with reduced pay.

cuartelada, *f.* military coup d'état, sedition of soldiers to carry out a coup d'état.

cuartelar, *va.* (her.) to quarter.

cuartelero, *m.* (mil.) soldier who keeps the ward clean.

cuarteo, *m.* act of dodging; crack, rift, fissure.

cuartera, *f.* dry measure (about 70 liters); land measure (about 36 acres); square timber.

cuarterada, *f.* land measure (about 7 sq. me. ters).

cuartero, ra, *n.* collector of grain taxes.

cuarterola, *f.* quarter cask.

cuarterón, *m.* quartern, quarter, fourth part; quarter of a pound; upper shutter of windows; (carp.) door or wainscot panel.

cuarterón, na, *n.* & *a.* quadroon.

cuarteta, *f.* (poet.) quatrain.

cuartete, cuarteto, *m.* (poet.) quatrain; (mus.) quartet.

cuartilla, *f.* fourth part of an ARROBA; grain measure (about 1.38 liters); liquid measure (quarter of a CÁNTARA); fourth part of a large sheet of paper; sheet of paper; (print.) sheet of copy; pastern of horses.

cuartillo, *m.* pint, fourth part of a pottle in liquid measure; fourth part of a peck in dry measure; fourth part of a REAL.

cuartilludo, da, *a.* (horse) having long pasterns.

cuartito, *m. dim.* small room, hall room.

cuarto, ta. I. *n.* & *a.* fourth, fourth part, quarter. **II.** *m.* room, chamber, hall; copper coin worth four MARAVEDIS; series of paternal or maternal ancestors; crack in horses' hoofs; quarter of clothes; quarter of animals or of criminals whose body is quartered; quarter of an hour; (ast.) quarter (of the moon); service in the royal palace.—*pl.* cash, money; well-proportioned members of an animal's body.—**c. a c.,** in a mean, stingy manner.—**c. bocel,** astragal.—**c. de baño,** bathroom.—**c. de conversión,** quarter wheeling.—**c. de costura,** sewing room.—**c. de dormir,** bedroom.—**de tres al c.,** of little moment.—**en c.,** (print.) quarto.—**no tener un c.,** not to be worth a farthing.—**tener cuartos,** or **cuatro cuartos,** to be well off, to have money.

cuartogénito, ta, *a.* fourth-born.

cuartón, *m.* quarter; large joist or girder; beam sixteen feet long; oblong patch of farming land; a liquid measure.

cuarzo, *m.* quartz.—**c. citrino,** Occidental topaz.

cuarzoso, sa, *a.* quartzose.

cuasi, *adv.* almost.

cuasia, *f.* (bot.) quassia.

cuasicontrato, *m.* (law) quasi contract.

cuasidelito, *m.* unintentional wrong.

cuasimodo, *m.* Quasimodo, first Sunday after Easter.

cuate, *m.* (Mex.) twin.—**eso no tiene c.,** (coll.) that has no match.

cuaterna, *f.* union of four things; four points in the game of lotto.

cuaternario, ria, *a.* quaternary.

cuaternidad, *f.* quaternity, quaternary.

cuaternio, *m.* (math.) quarternion.

cuaterno, na, *a.* consisting of four numbers.

cuatezón, na, *a.* (Mex.) hornless ox or sheep.

cuatí, *m.* a South-American monkey.

cuatralbo, ba. I. *a.* having four white feet. **II.** *m.* commander of four galleys.

cuatratuo, tua, *a.* quadroon.

cuatrero, *m.* horse thief, cattle thief.

cuatriduano, na, *a.* lasting four days.

cuatrienio, *m.* = CUADRIENIO.

cuatrillo, *m.* a card game.

cuatrillón, *m.* quadrillion.

cuatrimestre. I. *a.* lasting four months. **II.** *m.* period of four months.

cuatrín, *m.* an ancient small coin.—*pl.* (coll.) cash in general.

cuatrinca, *f.* union of four persons or things; four cards of a kind.

cuadrisílabo, ba, *a.* = CUADRISÍLABO.

cuatro. I. *n.* & *a.* four; fourth.—**c. letras,** a few lines.—**más de c.,** (coll.) a great many. **II.** *m.* figure 4; one who votes for four absent persons; (mus.) quatuor, quartet; four, four-spot card. **III.** *pl. f.* **las cuatro,** four o'clock.

cuatrocientos, tas, *n.* & *a.* four hundred.

cuatrodoblar, *va.* to quadruple.

cuatropea, *f.* duty on horse sales.

cuatropeado, *m.* step in dancing.

cuatrotanto, *m.* (coll.) quadruple.

cuba, *f.* cask; big-bellied person; (coll.) toper, drunkard; tub, coop, vat, trough.

cubano, na, *n.* & *a.* Cuban.

cubeba, *f.* (bot.) cubeb.

cubería, *f.* cooperage, cooper's shop.

cubero, *m.* cooper.

cubertura, *f.* cover, covering.

cubeta, *f. dim.* of CUBA; small barrel or cask, keg; tub, pail, bucket; trough; basin, cup or cistern (of a barometer).

cubetilla, ita, *f. dim.* small bucket.

cubeto, *m. dim.* of CUBO; small pail, tub, or vessel.

cúbica, *f.* cubica, fine worsted fabric.

cubicación, *f.* measurement of solids; calculation of volumes; cubing.

cúbicamente, *adv.* cubically.

cubicar, *va.* (math.) to cube; to determine the volume of.

cubichete, *m.* (naut.) waterboards or weatherboards; (mil.) gun apron.

cúbico, ca, *a.* cubical, cubic.

cubiculario, *m.* groom, valet-de-chambre.

cubierta, *f.* cover, covering; envelope; book cover; casing; coat, facing; roof; top of a carriage; pretext, pretence; deck (of ship).—**c. del motor,** (aut.) hood.

cubiertamente, *adv.* secretly, under cover.

cubierto, ta. I. *pp. irr.* of CUBRIR. **II.** *m.* cover, place for one at the table; roof; shed; covert, coverture, cover; allowance of a soldier; dinner; refreshment tray or plate.

cubil, *m.* lair or couch of wild beasts.

cubilar, *vn.* to take shelter.

cubilete, *m.* copper pan or mold for kitchen use; pastry made in it; dicebox, juggler's goblet; tumbler, mug; (Colomb., fam.) high hat.

cubiletero, *m.* juggler; paste mold.

cubilote, *m.* cupola smelting furnace; smelting pot.

cubilla, *f.,* **cubillo,** *m.* Spanish fly, blister-beetle; water cooler; small box near the stage; (naut.) socket for flagpole; bucket or scoop of a waterraising wheel.

cubital, *a.* cubital.

cúbito, *m.* (anat.) ulna.

cubo, *m.* (geom. & alg.) cube; wooden pail, bucket; tub, vat; mill pond; barrel of a watch or clock; fort, small tower; nave or hub of a wheel; bayonet socket; (mas.) hodful of mixed mortar; (mech.) tongue way, socket, shaft case; (carp.) stock; (arch.) dado, die.

cuboide, *m.* (anat.) cuboid bone.

cubrecama, *f.* coverlet, counterpane, bedspread.

cubrecorsé, *m.* corset cover.

cubrepán, *m.* fire shovel used by shepherds.

cubreplatos, *m.* wire-net cover for food in dishes.

cubriente, *a.* covering, hiding.

cubrimiento, *m.* covering; roofing.

cubrir. I. *va.* (*pp.* CUBIERTO) to cover; spread over; face; coat; envelop; veil; shroud; screen, hide, palliate; disguise, mask, dissemble, cloak; hood, drape, clothe; box up; case, incase; (mil.) to cover or protect; (arch.) to roof; to fertilize, fecundate; (com.) to meet (a draft); to cover (a shortage or expenses); to compensate; to include, comprise. —**c. la cuenta,** to balance an account.—**c. la mesa,** to lay the table.—**c. los gastos,** to pay expenses. **II.** *vr.* to cover one's self; to protect one's self against loss, damage or attack; to hedge; to be covered; to put on one's hat; in fencing, to be well guarded.—**cubrírsele a uno el corazón,** to feel deep grief.

cuca, *f.* root tubercle of a sedge; a Peruvian plant; coca; sort of caterpillar; (coll.) gambling woman.—**c. y matacán,** a card game.—**mala ɣ.,** (coll.) wicked person.

cucamonas, *f. pl.* (coll.) = CARANTOÑAS.

cucaña, *f.* greased pole to climb for a prize; the sport itself; anything acquired with little trouble at other people's expense.

cucañero, *m.* (coll.) parasite, hanger-on.

cucaracha, *f.* cockroach, croton bug; cochineal; hazel-colored snuff.—**cucarachera,** *f.* cockroach nest.

cucarda, *f.* = ESCARAPELA.

cucarrón, *m.* (Colomb.) beetle.

cuclillas.—en c., in a crouching or squatting position.—**sentarse en c.,** to squat.

cuclillo, *m.* (orn.) cuckoo.

cuco, ca. I. *a.* (coll.) prim, dainty; cunning, crafty, astute; alert for one's own advantage. **II.** *m.* a kind of caterpillar; cuckoo; a card game; (coll.) gambler.

cucuiza, *f.* (Am.) thread of the agave.

cuculí, *m.* a handsome South-American wild pigeon.

cucuma, *f.* bread made in Colombia from a root like yucca.

cuculla, *f.* cowl, old-fashioned hood.

cucúrbita, *f.* distilling retort.

cucurbitáceo, a. I. *a.* (bot.) cucurbitaceous. **II.** *f. pl.* Cucurbitaceæ.

cucurucho, *m.* paper cone; cornucopia.

cucuy, cucuyo, *m.* = COCUYO.

cucha, *f.* (Peru) = LAGUNA.

cuchar, *va.* to fertilize with CUCHO.

cuchar, *f.* spoon; ancient corn measure, twelfth part of a peck; tax or duty on grain.—**c. herrera,** iron spoon.

cuchara, *f.* spoon; ladle, dipper; (mas.) trowel; (naut.) pitch ladle; (mil.) gunner's ladle;(naut.) scoop for baling boats; bucket, scoop (of dredging machine, excavator, etc.).—**c. cafetera,** teaspoon.—**meter c.,** or **su c.,** to meddle, intrude; to put in one's oar, "butt in."

cucharada, I. *f.* spoonful; ladleful.—**meter c.,** or **su c.** = METER CUCHARA. *V.* CUCHARA.

cucharadita, *f.* teaspoonful.

cucharal, *m.* spoon bag used by shepherds.

cucharero, ra, *n.* spoon maker or dealer.

cuchareta, *f. dim.* small spoon; a variety of wheat; inflammation of the liver in sheep.

cucharetear, *vn.* (coll.) to stir with a spoon; to busy one's self with other people's affairs.

cucharetero, *m.* maker or retailer of wooden spoons; spoon rack; petticoat fringe.

cucharilla, *f.* liver disease in swine; (surg.) scoop. —**c. de barrenero,** (min.) scraper.

cucharita, illa, *f. dim.* small spoon, teaspoon, coffee spoon.

cucharón, *m. aug.* large spoon; soup ladle, kitchen ladle, dipper; scoop, bucket (of a dredge, excavator, etc.)

cucharro, *m.* (naut.) harping; watering vessel made from a gourd.

cuchi, cuchí, *m.* (Am.) hog.

cuchichear, *vn.* to whisper.

cuchicheo, *m.* whisper, whispering.

cuchichiar, *vn.* to call like a partridge.

cuchilla, *f.* large chopping knife; cleaver; any knife; blade of a knife or sword; ancient poniard; (poet.) sword; mountain ridge; knife edge.

cuchillada, *f.* cut or slash with a knife; gash, deep wound.—**dar c.,** to win the preference of the public (s. o. competing actors).

cuchillar, *a.* belonging or relating to knives.

cuchilleja, cuchillejo, *m. dim.* small knife; paring knife used by horseshoers.

cuchillera, *f.* knife case or scabbard.

cuchillería, *f.* cutler's shop; cutlery.

cuchillero, *m.* cutler.

cuchillo, *m.* knife; knife edge; gore, triangular piece in a garment; right of governing; any object or place ending in a point or acute angle; (arch.) gable frame; (naut.) cant piece; triangular sail; goring of a sail; (carp.) beam, girder.—*pl.* chief feathers in a hawk's wing.—**c. de monte,** hunter's cutlass.

cuchillón, *m. aug.* large knife.

cuchipanda, *f.* (coll.) cheerful dinner shared by several persons.

cuchitril, *m.* narrow hole or corner; very small room, "den"; hut.

cucho, *m.* fertilizer of manure and vegetable matter.

cuchuchear, *vn.* = CUCHICHEAR.

cuchufleta, *f.* joke, jest, fun.

cuchufletero, ra, *n.* jester, tease.

cuchuvo, *m.* (Am.) saddle bag.

cudria, *f.* flat woven bast rope.

cudú, koodoo, an African antelope.

cuébano, = CUÉVANO.

cuélebre, *m.* = DRAGÓN.

cuelga, *f.* bunch of grapes or other fruit hung up for use; (coll.) birthday present.—**c. de cebollas,** bunch of onions.

cuelgacapas, *m.* cloak hanger, rack.

cuelgo, cuelgue. *V.* COLGAR.

cuelmo, *m.* candlewood.

cuelo, cuele. *V.* COLAR.

cuellicorto, ta, *a.* short-necked.

cuellierguido, da, *a.* stiffnecked; swelled up with pride.

cuellilargo, ga, *a.* long-necked.

cuello, *m.* neck; throat; collar (of garments); neck of a bottle; neck stock; small end of a wax candle; thinnest part of a mast, pole, cane, etc.; collar of a beam in oil mills.—**levantar el c.,** to be prosperous.

cuenca, *f.* wooden bowl; socket of the eye; basin of a river; deep valley.

cuenco, *m.* earthen bowl; sifting basket.

cuenda, *f.* end of packthread; tie of a skein; end of a skein.

cuenta. I. *f.* computation, calculation, count, reckoning; account; bill; note; statement (of accounts); narrative, report; obligation, care, duty; bead (of a rosary, etc.); accountability; reason, satisfaction; consideration, merit, importance.—**c. corriente,** (com.) account current.—**c. de venta,** (com.) account sales.—**c. en participación,** joint account.—**c. pendiente,** unsettled account.—**c. simulada,** pro forma account.—**c. y mitad,** (com.) joint account.—**cuentas del Gran Capitán,** account overcharged.—**a c.,** or **a buena c.,** on account, in part payment.—**a esa c.,** at that rate.—**caer en la c.,** to notice, to see (fig.).—**dar c.,** to answer, report, give an account.—**dar de algo,** (coll., iron.) to waste, destroy.—**de c. y riesgo de,** for account and risk of.—**en resumidas cuentas,** (coll.) in short, in a word; after all.—**estemos a cuentas,** let us settle this, let us come to an understanding.—**hacer cuentas,** to figure, reckon.—**hacer cuentas alegres,** or **galanas,** to build air castles.—**hacer la c.,** to figure out.—**hacer,** or **hacerse, la c.,** to imagine, take for granted.—**la c. es c.,** business is business.—**llevar c.,** or **la c.,** to keep account; to count, reckon.—**por c. y mitad,** joint account.—**tener c.,** to answer the purpose; be profitable or advantageous; (w. **con**) to be concerned (with), have a part (in).—**tener en c.,** to take into account, remember, bear in mind.—**tomar por su c.,** to take upon one's self.—**vamos a cuentas** = ESTEMOS A CUENTAS. **II.** *interj.* take care, look out!

cuentadante, *m.* one who renders an account of moneys received.

cuentagotas, *m.* dropper (for counting or measuring drops).

cuentahilos, *m.* thread counter; linen prover; weaver's glass.

cuentapasos, *m.* odometer.

cuentero, ra, *n. & a.* = CUENTISTA.

cuentezuela, *f. dim.* small account.

cuentista, *m.* talebearer, informer.

cuento, *m.* tale, story; narrative; fable, fairy tale; gossip; million; million of millions; articulation of the wing; account; number; ferrule of a pike, cane, or tool; prop, shore, support.—**c. de viejas**, old women's stories, notion, supersittion.—**andar en cuentos**, to be at loggerheads; to carry tales; to gossip.—**dejarse de cuentos**, to stop beating about the bush, to come to the point.—**estar en el c.**, to be informed, to be on the inside.—**sin c.**, numberless.—**traer a c.**, to bring to bear upon the subject; to drag into the subject.—**venir a c.**, to be pertinent, to be to the point.

cuento, cuente. *V.* CONTAR.

cuentón, na, *n.* story-teller, talebearer.

cuera, *f.* leather jacket.

cuerda, *f.* cord, rope, string; (fishing) line; string for musical instruments; compass of a voice; (geom.) chord; match for firing a gun; chain of a watch or clock; a West-Indian land measure (3.93 centiares); number of galley slaves tied together.—*pl.* human nerves.—**c. floja**, or **tesa**, tight rope, ropedancing rope.—**cuerdas de las cubiertas**, (naut.) deck streaks or strakes.—**cuerdas vocales**, vocal chords.—**bajo c.**, or **por debajo de c.**, underhandedly, deceitfully.—**dar c. a**, to wind up (a watch, clock).

cuerdamente, *adv.* prudently, wisely.

cuerdecica, illa, ita, *or* **cuerdezuela**, *f. dim.* funicle, small cord.

cuerdo, da, *a.* prudent, discreet, sensible, wise, judicious; in his senses, not mad.

cuerecico, ito, *m. dim.* small hide or skin.

cuerezuelo, *m.* sucking pig.

cuerna, *f.* horn vessel; stag's or deer's horn; sportsman's horn.

cuernecico, illo, ito, *m.* cornicle, small horn.

cuernezuelo, *m. dim.* cornicle, small horn; farrier's paring knife.

cuerno, *m.* horn; feeler, antenna of insect; horn of the moon; button of a manuscript roll; huntsman's horn; (bot.) horn; (naut.) outrigger; (farr.) a disease of horses; callosity.—**c. de abundancia**, horn of plenty.

cuero, *m.* pelt, fell, rawhide; tanned skin, leather; goatskin dressed entire, which serves as a bag to carry wine or oil; toper, drinker.—*pl.* hangings or drapery of gilded or painted leather.—**c. cabelludo**, scalp.—**c. de suela**, sole leather.—**c. exterior**, cuticle.—**c. interior**, skin.—**cueros al pelo**, raw hides, undressed hides.—**de cuero**, leathern, leather (u. a.).—**en cueros**, or **en cueros vivos**, stark naked.—**entre c. y carne**, between the skin and the flesh.

cuerpecico, illo, ito; cuerpezuelo, *m. dim.* small body; small carcass.

cuerpo, *m.* body, matter (opposed to spirit); (chem.) body, element; body of an animal; also, more narrowly, the trunk; figure and build of a person; corpse; body, assembly, corporation, guild; (geom.) body, solid; body, thickness (of oil, etc.); (arch.) entire part of a building up to a cornice or entablature; volume, book, whole of a book, except preface and index; (law) body, collection of laws; degree of thickness of silks, woollens, or cottons; strength, thickness of liquids; collective mass; body in several other senses, as a body of a musical instrument, of one, of scientific or diplomatic persons, etc.—**c. a c.**, hand to hand; in single combat.—**c. de batalla de una escuadra**, the entire division of a fleet.—**c. de bomba**, barrel of a pump.—**c. de caldera**, boiler shell.—**c. de ejército**, army corps. —**c. de guardia**, guard; guarded place, post of a guard.—**c. del cabrestante**, (naut.) barrel of the capstan.—**c. del delito**, corpus delicti.—**c. sin alma**, dull person.—**c. tiroides**, (anat.) thyroid gland.—**c. volante**, (mil.) flying column.—**a c. de rey**, royally, like a king.—**a c. descubierto**, without cover or shelter; manifestly.—**de c. entero**, full-length (picture).—**en c.**, without cloak or wrap.—**en c. de camisa**, in shirt sleeves.—**en c. y alma**, (coll.) body and soul, wholly.—**estar de c. presente**, to be actually present; to lie in state. —**hacer del c.**, to go to stool.—**tomar c.**, to increase, enlarge, grow.

cuerria, *f.* circular space fenced in where chestnuts are thrown to ripen.

cuerva, *f.* (orn.) crow, rook.

cuervecico, illo, ito, *m. dim.* little rook.

cuervo, *m.* (orn.) raven; crow; rook.—**c. marino**, cormorant; (**C-**, ast.) Corvus, a southern constellation.

cuesco, *m.* stone (of fruit); millstone of an oil mill; wind from behind.

cuesquillo, *m. dim.* small stone of fruit.

cuesta, *f.* slope, grade; petition or collection of money for charitable or pious purposes.—**c. abajo**, down hill.—**c. arriba**, up hill; painfully, with great trouble and difficulty.—**a cuestas**, on one's shoulders or back; to one's charge or care.

cuestación, *f.* petition, solicitation or collection for a charitable purpose.

cuestero, ra, *n.* alms collector.

cuestezuela, *f. dim.* easy slope, light grade.

cuestión, *f.* question, dispute, quarrel; matter, problem, affair, business.—**c. batallona**, much-debated, or vexed, question.—**c. candente**, burning question.—**c. de gabinete**, state affair that may cause a change in the cabinet; serious matter.

cuestionable, *a.* questionable, doubtful.

cuestionar, *va.* to dispute, discuss, argue.

cuestionario, *m.* questionnaire.

cuestor, *m.* questor; solicitor of alms.

cuesto, cueste. *V.* COSTAR.

cuestuario, ria; cuestuoso, sa, *a.* lucrative, productive.

cuestura, *f.* questorship.

cuete, *m.* firecracker.

cueto, *m.* (fort.) rocky peak; defended tor.

cuetzale, *m.* (orn.) quetzal, a large Mexican bird of golden green plumage.

cueva, *f.* cave, grotto; cellar.—**c. de fieras**, den of wild beasts.—**c. de ladrones**, nest of thieves.

cuévano, *m.* basket, hamper; (min.) sump basket.

cuevero, *m.* maker of caves and grottoes.

cueza, *f.*, **cuezo**, *m.* mortar hod.

cuezo, cueza. *V.* COCER.

cugujada, *f.* (orn.) common field lark, skylark.

cugulla, *f.* cowl.

cuicacoche, *f.* a Mexican song bird.

cuida, *f.* in ladies' seminaries, young lady who takes care of a young girl.

cuidado. I. *m.* care, solicitude; attention, heed; keeping, custody, charge, trust; carefulness, caution; fear, apprehension, anxiety.—**estar con c.**, to be anxious or apprehensive.—**estar de c.**, to be seriously ill.—**no hay c. (de que)**, there is no danger (that).—**no pasar c.**, not to worry.— **tener cuidado**, to be careful; to be worried or anxious. **II.** *interj.* look out! beware!

cuidadosamente, *adv.* carefully.

cuidadoso, sa, *a.* careful; solicitous; painstaking; curious, observing.

cuidante, *n.* caretaker.

cuidar. I. *va.* to care for, look after, keep; to execute with care, diligence, and attention; take care of. **II.** *vn.* **c. de**, to take care of. **III.** *vr.* to take care of one's self.—**c. de**, to look out for, to be on guard against; to avoid; to pay attention to.

cuido, *m.* caretaking.

cuita, *f.* care, grief, affliction, trouble.—**contar sus cuitas**, to tell one's troubles.

cuitadamente, *adv.* afflictedly, sorrowfully.

cuitado, da, *a.* unfortunate, wretched; timid.

cuitamiento, *m.* bashfulness, timidity.

cuja, *f.* lance bucket; bedstead.

cuje, *m.* withe; pole supported by two vertical ones for hanging tobacco.—*pl.* hop poles.

cují, *m.* (bot.) sponge tree.

cujisal, *m.* plantation of sponge trees.

culantrillo, *m.* (bot.) maidenhair fern.

culantro, *m.* (bot.) coriander.

culata, *f.* buttock, haunch; butt of a firearm; screw pin which fastens the breech of a gun to the stock; rear part; (int. comb. eng.) cylinder head; (elec.) yoke (of an electromagnet).

culatada, *f.* kick; recoil of a firearm.

culatazo, *m.* recoil of a gun; blow with the butt of a firearm.

culcusido, *m.* botch work.

culebra, *f.* snake; trick, fun, joke; hazing; distil worm; cock of a firearm; sudden disorder in a peaceful assembly.—**c. de cascabel,** rattlesnake.—**saber más que las culebras,** (coll.) to be very crafty and cunning.

culebrazo, *m. aug.* big snake; whipping given by jail prisoners to newcomers; hazing.

culebrear, *vn.* to wriggle (as a snake); to wind (as a rivulet).

culebrilla, *f.* tetter, ringworm; a skin disease; rocking staff of a loom; fissure in a gun barrel.

culebrina, *f.* (mil.) culverin; ondulated meteor.

culebrino, na, *a.* snaky.

culebrón, na, *n. aug.* big snake; crafty fellow, double-dealer; intriguing woman.

culera, *f.* stain of urine in swaddling clothes; patch on the seat of trousers.

culero, *m.* clout, diaper, breechcloth.

culero, ra, *a.* slothful, lazy.

culinario, ia, *a.* culinary.

culminación, *f.* culmination; high tide.

culminante, *a.* culminating.

culminar, *vn.* to culminate.

culo, *m.* breech, backside, rump, buttock; bottom; socket; anus; bottom of anything.

culombio, *m.* (elec.) coulomb.

culón, *m.* (coll.) retired soldier.

culpa, *f.* fault; guilt; sin.—**echar la c. a,** to blame.—**tener la c. de,** to be to blame, or responsible, for.

culpabilidad, *f.* culpability, guilt.

culpabilísimo, ma, *a. super.* guilty or culpable in the highest degree.

culpable, *a.* culpable, guilty; blamable, blameworthy.

culpablemente, *adv.* culpably.

culpación, *f.* inculpation, blame.

culpadamente, *adv.* culpably.

culpado, da. I. *a.* guilty. II. *pp.* of CULPAR.

culpar, *va.* to blame, accuse; condemn.

cultamente, *adv.* neatly, politely, in a refined manner; affectedly, in a showy manner.

cultedad, *f.* (hum.) affected elegance and purity of style; fustian.

culteranismo, *m.* high-flown style; fustian.

culterano, na. I. *n.* purist with affectation; fustianist. II. *a.* relating to fustian.

cultero, ra, *a.* (hum.) using high-flown style.

cultiparlar, *vn.* to speak with affected elegance.

cultiparlista, *a.* speaking with affected elegance and correctness.

cultipicaño, ña, *a.* (hum.) speaking with affected elegance and in a jeering manner.

cultivable, *a.* cultivable, arable.

cultivación, *f.* cultivation, culture.

cultivador, *m.* cultivator, tiller; husbandman, planter; light plow; hand cultivator.

cultivadora, *f.* cultiva.ing machine.

cultivar, *va.* to cultivate; to farm, develop, husband, till; to dress (a garden); to nurse (a plant); to preserve.

cultivo, *m.* cultivation; farming, tillage; culture of the mind; elegance of manners; (bact.) culture.

culto, *m.* worship; religion; cult; respect or veneration for superior men; homage to lofty ideals.—**c. divino,** public worship in churches.—**c. externo,** external religious ceremonies.

culto, ta, *a.* improved, cultivated; nursed (plants); pure, elegant, correct (style and language); cultured, educated; enlightened, civilized.

cultura, *f.* cultivation of the soil or of the mind; urbanity, politeness; culture.

cultural, *a.* cultural.

culturar, *va.* to cultivate.

cuma, *f.* (S. A.) godmother; crony.

cumárico, ca, *a.* (chem.) coumaric.

cumarina, *f.* (chem.) coumarin.

cumarú, *m.* Tonka bean, coumaron.

cumbé, *m.* a negro dance.

cumbre, cumbrera, *f.* top, summit, crest; peak of a mountain; acme; greatest height of favor,

fortune, science, etc.; (carp.) ridgepole, tie-beam, rooftree.

cúmplase, *m.* be it carried out—a term used by the executive of Spanish-American republics over his signature in approving an act of Congress; also, as a confirmation of an appointment.

cumpleaños, *m.* birthday.

cumplidamente, *adv.* completely.

cumplidero, ra, *a.* that must be fulfilled or executed; convenient, fit, suitable; accomplishable.

cumplido, da. I. *a.* full, complete, thorough; accomplished, perfect; large; plentiful, ample; fulfilled, lapsed, passed; due; polished, courteous. II. *pp.* of CUMPLIR. III. *m.* compliment; attention, courtesy; present; ceremony, formality.

cumplidor, ra. I. *n.* one who executes a commission or trust. II. *a.* true to his (her) word, reliable.

cumplimentar, *va.* to compliment, congratulate; to show courtesy to; to fulfil, carry out.

cumplimentero, ra, *a.* (coll.) full of compliments; excessively courteous or formal; officious; ceremonious.

cumplimiento, *m.* completion, performance, fulfilment; lapse, expiration; compliment; civility, courtesy; formality, ceremony; complement.—**con c., con cumplimientos,** formally, ceremoniously. —**de cumplimiento,** formal.

cumplir. I. *va.* to execute, discharge, perform, obey, fulfil; keep (a promise).—**c. años,** to reach one's birthday (*hoy cumplo veinte años,* I am twenty years old to-day). II. *vn.* to perform one's duty; to fulfil a social engagement; to perform a duty in the name of another; to have served the time required in the militia; to mature, expire, fall due; to behoove; to be fit.—**c. con,** to fulfil, do, perform. —**c. por otro,** to perform in another's name.—**por c.,** as a matter of form. III. *vr.* to be realized or fulfilled; to come true; to expire, be up (s. o. a period of time).

cumquibus, *m.* (coll.) money, boodle, wherewith.

cumulador, m. = ACUMULADOR.

cumular, *va.* to accumulate.

cumulativamente, *adv.* cumulatively.

cumulativo, va, *a.* cumulative.

cúmulo, *m.* heap, pile; congeries; large quantity or number, lot; cumulus (clouds).

cuna, *f.* cradle; foundling hospital; place of birth; family, lineage; origin, source.

cunasiri, *m.* a Peruvian aromatic tree.

cuncuna, *f.,* a Chilean caterpillar; (Colomb.) wild pigeon.

cunchos, *m. pl.* an indigenous independent race in Chile.

cundido, *m.* provision of oil, vinegar, and salt given to shepherds; honey or cheese given to boys.

cundir, *vn.* to spread, applied to liquids or news; to yield abundantly; to grow, expand, propagate.

cunear. I. *va.* to rock (a cradle). II. *vr.* to swing; to rock.

cuneiforme, *a.* cuneiform, wedge-shaped.

cúneo, *m.* (mil.) triangular formation of troops; space between the passages in ancient theatres.

cuneo, m. rocking motion; (naut.) rolling, pitching.

cunera, *f.* cradle rocker, woman appointed to rock the infantas in the royal palace.

cunero, ra, *n.* foundling.

cuneta, *f.* (mil.) small trench; side ditch; gutter, road drain.

cuña, *f.* wedge, quoin; paving stone.

cuñadía, *f.* kindred by affinity.

cuñado, da, *n.* brother- (sister-) in-law.

cuñar, va. = ACUÑAR.

cuñete, *m.* keg; firkin.

cuño, *m.* coin; die for stamping money; the device stamped; mark on silver; (mil.) triangular formation of troops.

cuociente, *m.* quotient.

cuodlibetal, cuodlibético, ca, *a.* quodlibetic.

cuodlibeto, *m.* argument; debatable point; thesis; subtilty; pungent saying.

cuota, *f.* quota, share.

cupano, *m.* (P. I.) a large tree, the bark yielding a dyestuff and the wood being used for building.

cupé, *m.* coupé, cab; banquette of a coach.

cupido, *m.* gallant, lover.

cupitel.—tirar de c., to throw a bowl archwise.

cupo, *m.* quota, share; tax rate.

cupón, *m.* (com.) coupon.

cupresino, na, *a.* (poet.) made of or belonging to the cypress tree.

cúprico, ca, *a.* cupric.

cuprífero, ra, *a.* cupriferous.

cuproso, sa, *a.* cuprous.

cúpula, *f.* cupola, dome, vault; turret of a monitor; (bot.) cupule, cup.

cupulifero, ra, *a.* cupuliferous, cup-bearing.

cupulino, *m.* (arch.) sky lantern.

cuquillo, *m.* (orn.) cuckoo.

cura. I. *m.* parish priest, rector, curate; any clergyman. **II.** *f.* cure, healing; curing, seasoning (of timber, etc.); parsonage.—**c. de almas,** cure, or care, of souls.

curable, *a.* curable.

curaca, *m.* (Peru) governor, potentate; master, boss.

curación, *f.* cure, healing.

curadero, *m.* bleaching place.

curadillo, *m.* (icht.) codfish, ling fish.

curado, da, *a.* & *pp.* of CURAR; cured, strengthened, restored to health; hardened, tanned; cured, seasoned; salted.

curador, *m.* overseer, caretaker; healer; (law) guardian, curator, administrator.—**c. de bacalao,** cod salter.—**c. de lienzo,** bleacher of linen cloth.

curadora, *f.* curatrix, woman guardian; woman doctor.

curaduría, *f.* guardianship.

curandero, *m.* quack, medicaster.

curar. I. *vn.* & *vr.* to recover from sickness; (**cura de**), to take care of. **II.** *va.* to cure, heal, restore to health; to administer (medicines); prescribe; to salt, cure, preserve; to bleach (fabrics); to cure, season (timber); to soothe, subdue.

curare, *m.* curare.—**curarina,** *f.* curarine.

curasao, *m.* curaçoa, curaçao.

curatela, *f.* (law) = CURADURÍA.

curativo, va, *a.* curative.

curato, *m.* curacy, parish.

curazao, *m.* curaçao.

curbaril, *m.* (bot.) W.-I. locust tree; courbaril.

curculiónido, da, *a.* curculionid.

cúrcuma, *f.* (bot.) curcuma, turmeric.

curcusilla, *f.* = RABADILLA.

curdo, da, *n.* & *a.* KURD (-ish).

cureña, *f.* gun carriage; stay of a crossbow; gunstock in the rough.—**a c. rasa,** (mil.) without a parapet or breastwork; (coll.) without shelter or defence.

cureñaje, *m.* aggregate of gun carriages.

curesca, *f.* shear wool from the cloth.

curí, *m.* (Am.) guinea pig; (bot.) a South-American coniferous tree, whose cones are used as food.

curia, *f.* ecclesiastical tribunal; bar, the legal profession; care, skill, nice attention; (old Roman) curia.—**c. romana,** pontifical court, aggregate of tribunals and congregations forming the Pope's court.

curial. I. *a.* curial. **II.** *m.* curialistic agent; officer of a court; attorney; (Roman) curial, member of a curia.

curialesco, ca, *a.* clerical, priestlike.

curiana, *f.* cockroach.

curiara, *f.* (Am.) a long canoe.

curiel, *m.* (Cuba) guinea pig.

curiosamente, *adv.* curiously; neatly, cleanly; in a diligent, careful manner.

curiosear, *vn.* to pry into others' affairs; (coll.) to be a busybody.

curiosidad, *f.* curiosity, inquisitiveness; neatness, cleanliness; curious thing; rare object or person; curio.

curioso, sa, *a.* curious, inquisitive, prying; neat, clean; careful, attentive, diligent; odd, quaint, rare.

curricán, *m.* spinning tackle.

curro, rra, *a.* (coll.) showy, tawdry, loud; (coll.) native of Cadiz.

curruca, *f.* (orn.) linnet, babbling warbler.

currutaco, ca. I. *a.* ultra-fashionable, dudish, exquisite. **II.** *n.* dude, fop, dandy.

cursado, da. I. *a.* accustomed, habituated, inured. **II.** *pp.* of CURSAR.

cursante. I. *a.* frequenting; assiduous. **II.** *n.* student, pupil.

cursar, *va.* to frequent, to do repeatedly; to study; to take action on, attend to.

cursi, *a.* vulgar, shoddy, in bad taste; awkward, clumsy.

cursillo, *m. dim.* short course of lectures in a university.

cursivo, va, *a.* (print.) cursive, script.

curso, *m.* course, direction, career, progress; run, route, current; course of study; term of tuition in schools; collection of the principal treatises used in instruction in some branch; lapse; succession; (com.) current rate.—*pl.* laxity or looseness of the body.—**c. de la corriente,** (naut.) current's way.

cursor, *m.* (mech.) slider, slide.

curtación, *f.* (ast.) curtation.

curtido, da. I. *pp.* of CURTIR. **II.** *a.* tanned, curried; accustomed, expert; weather-beaten. **III.** *m.* leather; tanning. **IV.** *m. pl.* tanned leather.

curtidor, *m.* tanner, currier, leather dresser.

curtiduría, *f.* tanyard; tannery.

curtiente, *n.* tanning material or substance.

curtimiento, *m.* tanning.

curtir. I. *va.* to tan (hides, the complexion); to inure to hardships, to harden.—**estar curtido,** (coll.) to be used or inured. **II.** *vr.* to become tanned or sun-burned.

curto, ta, *a.* short, dock-tailed.

curú, *m.* (Peru) a clothes moth.

curuca, *f.* (orn.) eagle owl.

curucucú, *m.* a disease caused by the bite of a South-American snake.

curuja, *f.* (orn.) eagle owl.

curul, *a.* curule; edile.

curva, *f.* curve; curvature; bend; (naut.) knee.—**c. de bao,** (naut.) spur.—**c. de enlace,** (r. w.) connecting curve.—**c. de nivel,** (surv.) contour line.

curvatón, *m.* (naut.) small knee, bracket.

curvatura, *f.* curvature; curving.

curvilíneo, a, *a.* (geom.) curvilinear.

curvímetro, *m.* curvometer.

curvo, va. I. *a.* curve, curved; crooked, bent. **II.** *m.* inclosed pasture ground.

cusculia, *f.* = COSCOJA.

cuscurro, *m.* end piece of bread.

cuscuta, *f.* (bot.) common dodder.

cusir, *va.* (coll.) to sew clumsily.

cúspide, *f.* cusp, apex, top, summit, peak.

cuspídeo, dea, *a.* (bot.) cuspidate.

custodia, *f.* custody, safe-keeping; monstrance; custodia; shrine; guard, keeper, guardian, custodian; tabernacle.

custodiar, *va.* to guard; to convoy; take care of.

custodio, *m.* guard, watchman; custodian.

cutáneo, nea, *a.* cutaneous, of the skin.

cúter, *m.* (naut.) cutter.

cuti, *m.* bedticking, crash.

cutícula, *f.* pellicle, cuticle, epidermis.

cuticular, *a.* cuticular.

cutio, *m.* labor, work.

cutir, *va.* to knock, strike, pound, beat, hammer.

cutis, *m.* or *f.* skin of the human body (esp. that of the face); complexion.

cutó, *m.* (naut.) dirk.

cutral, *n.* old worn-out ox or cow.

cutre, *m.* miser.

cuyabra, *f.* (Colomb.) bowl or receptacle formed by halving a gourd lengthwise.

cuyo, *m.* (coll.) beau, lover, wooer, sweetheart.

cuyo, ya, (*pl.* **cuyos, cuyas**), *pron. pos.* of which, of whom, whose, whereof.

cuzma, *f.* sleeveless shirt.

czar, *m.*; **czarevitz,** *m.*; **czariano, na,** *a.*; **czarina,** *f.*= ZAR, ZAREVITZ, etc.

CH

cha, *f.* (Philip.) tea.

chabacanamente, *adv.* bunglingly, clumsily.

chabacanería, *f.* bungle, muddle; vulgar expression or action.

chabacano, na. I. *a.* awkward, clumsy. **II.** *m.* (Mex.) a variety of apricot.

chacal, *m.* jackal.

chácara, *f.* = CHACRA.

chacarero, ra, *n.* (S. A.) field laborer.

chacarrachaca, *f.* loud wrangle.

chacina, *f.* pork seasoned with spice for sausages and balls.

chacó, *m.* shako, military cap.

chacolí, *m.* chacoli, a light red wine made in Vizcaya, Spain.

chacolotear, *vn.* to clatter (s. o. a loose horseshoe).

chacoloteo, *m.* clapping of a loose horseshoe.

chacón, *m.* (Philip.) a large lizard.

chacona, *f.* chaconne, an old Spanish dance.

chaconada, *f.* jaconet.

chacota, *f.* noisy mirth.—**echar a ch.,** (coll.) to carry off with a joke.—**hacer ch. de,** (coll.) to turn into ridicule, make fun of.

chacotear, *vn.* to indulge in noisy mirth.

chacotero, ra, *a.* (coll.) waggish, acting the merry-andrew.

chacra, *f.* (Am.) a small isolated farm.

chacuaco. I. *m.* (Mex., min.) small smelting furnace. **II.** *a.* (coll.) rustic, boorish.

chachalaca. I. *f.* (Mex.) a gallinaceous bird that cries continually while flying; (coll.) chatterbox. **II.** *a.* chattering, talkative.

cháchara, *f.* (coll.) prate, chitchat, idle talk.

chacharear, *vn.* (coll.) to prate, chatter, prattle.

chacharero, ra; chacharón, na, *n. & a.* prater (-ing), prattler (-ing).

chacho, *m.* (coll.) little boy (short for MUCHACHO); stake at the game of ombre.

chafaldetes, *m.* (naut.) clew lines.

chafaldita, *f.* (coll.) chaff, raillery, banter.

chafalditero, ra, *n.* (coll.) chaffer, person given to banter.

chafalmejas, *n.* (coll.) dauber.

chafalonía, *f.* (Peru) old plate.

chafallar, *va.* to botch, to mend clumsily.

chafallo, *m.* coarse patch, botch, clumsy mending.

chafallón, na, *n.* (coll.) botcher.

chafar, *va.* to flatten; to crease, rumple, crumple; (coll.) to cut short.

chafarote, *m.* cutlass; (coll.) broadsword; (fig.) sword, military force.

chafarrinada, *f.* blot, spot, stain.

chafarrinar, *va.* to blot, stain.

chafarrinón, *m.* blot, stain.—**echar un ch. a,** (coll.) to disgrace; to defame, throw mud at.

chaflán, *m.* bevel, chamfer.

chaflanar, *va.* to bevel, chamfer; (carp.) to cant.

chagra, *m.* a rustic in Ecuador.

chagrín, *m.* grained morocco.

chaguarama, *f.* a Central-American palm.

chair, *m.* (tan.) inner side of a skin.

chaira, *f.* steel for sharpening knives, etc.

chal, *m.* shawl.

chala, *f.* (Peru) green corn husk.

chalado, da, *a.* addle-pated, light-witted.

chalán, na, *n.* hawker, huckster; horsedealer; horse breaker.

chalana, *f.* scow, lighter, wherry.

chalanear. I. *va.* to buy or sell dexterously; to break (horses). **II.** *vn.* to deal in horses.

chalanería, *f.* artifice and cunning used by dealers in buying and selling.

chalate, *m.* (Mex.) small, lean horse.

chaleco, *m.* waistcoat, vest.

chalequero, ra, *n.* vest maker.

chalet, *m.* chalet, hut; cottage in the style of the Swiss chalets.

chalí, *m.* mohair; challis, shalli; delaine.

chalina, *f.* cravat, scarf.

chalote, *m.* (bot.) shallot.

chalupa, *f.* (naut.) sloop, shallop, launch, small light vessel; long boat; (Mex.) a small canoe; (Mex.) corn pancake.

chalupero, *m.* boatman, canoeman.

chalma, *f.* (low) barter, trade.

chamada, *f.* chips, brushwood, brush fire.

chamagoso, sa, *a.* (Mex.) greasy, filthy; ill-performed; low, vulgar.

chamar, *va.* (vulg.) to barter, trade off.

chamarasca, *f.* brushwood, brush fire.

chamarillero, ra, *n.* gambler; dealer in second-hand goods.

chamarillón, *m.* bad player at cards.

chamariz, *m.* (orn.) blue titmouse.

chamarón, *m.* (orn.) long-tailed titmouse.

chamarra, *f.* a garment of very coarse frieze.

chamarreta, *f.* a short, loose jacket.

chamba, *f.* CHIRIPA; (Colomb.) wide, deep ditch.

chambelán, *m.* chamberlain.

chamberga, *f.* long and wide cassock.

chambergo, ga. I. *a.* belonging or relating to the Chamberga regiment, serving as a guard to Charles II. of Spain.

chambilla, *f.* stone wall surmounted by an iron railing.

chambón, na. I. *a.* (coll.) awkward, unhandy; bungling. **II.** *n.* botcher, bungler, greenhorn.

chambonada, *f.* (coll.) blunder.

chambra, *f.* dressing sack; matinée.

chambrana, *f.* doorcase, jamb dressing.

chamelote, *m.* camlet.—**ch. de aguas,** clouded camlet.

chamelotón, *m.* coarse camlet.

chamicera, *f.* half-burnt woodland.

chamicero, ra, *a.* belonging to scorched wood.

chamiza, *f.* (bot.) chamiso; brush used as kindling wood.—**chamizal,** *m.* chamiso thicket.—**chamizo,** *m.* half-burnt log or stick of kindling wood.

chamorra, *f.* (coll.) a shorn head.

chamorro, ra, *a.* shorn, with hair cropped.

champán, *m.* (naut.) pink stern; sampan.

champaña, *m.* champagne.

champola, *f.* (Cuba) refreshment made from GUANÁBANA.

champú, *m.* shampoo.

champurrado. I. *m.* mixture of liquors; (Mex.) chocolate made with ATOLE instead of water. **II.** *pp.* of CHAMPURRAR.

champurrar, *va.* (coll.) to mix (liquors).

chamuchina, *f.* (Peru) populace, rabble.

chamuscado, da. I. *a.* (coll.) tipsy; addicted to vice; singed, scorched. **II.** *pp.* of CHAMUSCAR.

chamuscar, *va.* (*pret.* CHAMUSQUÉ: *subj.* CHAMUSQUE) to singe or scorch; to sear.

chamusco, *m.* = CHAMUSQUINA.

chamuscón, *m. aug.* large singe or scorch.

chamusquina, *f.* scorching or singeing; (coll.) scolding, wrangling, high words.—**oler a ch., to** look like (show signs of) a fight.

chanada, *f.* (coll.) trick, joke; deceit.

chanate, *m.* (Mex.) blackbird.

chancaco, ca, *a.* brown.

chancear, *vn. & vr.* to jest, joke, fool.

chancero, ra, *a.* jocose, sportful, merry.

chanciller, *m.* chancellor.

chancillería, f. chancery; right and fees of a chancellor.

chancla, f. old shoe with worn-down heel.

chancleta, f. slipper.—**en ch.,** having no back (s. o. shoes).—**chancletear,** vn. to go slipshod.

chancleteo, m. clatter of slippers.

chanclo, m. patten; clog, galosh, overshoe.

chancro, m. chancre.

chanchira, f. (Colomb.) rag, ragged clothes.

chanchiriento, ta, a. (Colomb.) ragged.

chancho, cha. I. a. (Am.) dirty, unclean; mean; stingy. **II.** n. dirty person; hog.—**ch. de monte,** (Perú) agouti.

chanchullero, ra, n. trickster, sharper; smuggler.

chanchullo, m. unlawful or disorderly conduct; sharp practice, vile trick; (Am.) contraband.

chanfaina, f. ragout of livers and lights.

chanflón, na. I. a. awkward, coarse, gawky. **II.** m. copper coin beaten out.

changa, f. (Cuba) jest.

changador, m. (S. A.) porter, carrier.

changamé, m. (orn.) thrush of Panama.

chango, a, n. (Am.) monkey.

changote, m. (metal.) bloom, billet.

changuear, vn. to be sporty or jesting.

changuí, m. (coll.) jest, trick (used with DAR); (Cuba) a country dance.

changuito, ta, n. dim. little monkey.

chantado, m. wall or fence of upright flags.

chantaje, m. blackmail; blackmailing.

chantajista, n. blackmailer.

chantar. I. va. to put on; to tell to one's face; to give a piece of one's mind to (ch. constr.); to build (a fence) with upright flagstones; to pave with flagstones. **II.** vr. to put on.

chanto, m. flagstone.

chantre, m. precentor.

chantría, f. precentorship.

chanza, f. joke, jest, fun.—**ch. pesada,** offensive or serious joke.

chanzoneta, f. ballad, chansonette; (coll.) joke, jest; little merry song.

chanzonetero, ra, n. ballad writer; petty poet.

chapa, f. veneer; plate, sheet (of metal); foil; cap; leather chape; rosy spot on the cheek, flush; rouge; transom and trunnion plates in gun-carriages; judgment, good sense.—pl. game of tossing up coins.

chapado, da, a. having red cheeks.—**ch. a la antigua,** old-fashioned.

chapalear, vn. = CHAPOTEAR; CHACOLOTEAR.

chapaleo, m. splash, splatter.

chapaleta, f. flap valve, clack valve; cap; clapper.

chapaleteo, m. continuous splashing of the waters on the shore.

chapapote, m. (Cuba) mineral tar, variety of asphalt.

chaparra, f. a kind of oak; ancient low-roofed carriage; bramble bush.

chaparrada, f. shower.

chaparral, m. (Am.) chaparral; plantation of evergreen oaks.

chaparrear, vn. to shower, to pour.

chaparreras, f. pl. chaps, chaparejos.

chaparro, m. (bot.) evergreen oak.

chaparrón, m. violent shower, downpour.

chapatal, m. mire; muddy place.

chapear. I. va. to veneer; inlay; cover with metal plate. **II.** vn. to splash, splatter.

chapelete, m. an ancient cover for the head.

chapeo, m. hat.

chapera, f. inclined plane.

chapería, f. ornament of metal plates.

chaperón, m. chaperon (ancient hood or cap).

chapeta, f. small metal plate; red spot on the cheek.

chapetón, na. I. n. & a. (Am.) Spaniard, Spanish. **II.** m. CHAPETONADA; (Mex.) silver plate on a riding harness.

chapetonada, f. (Peru) disease of Europeans due to change of climate; act or conduct worthy of a CHAPETÓN.

chapín, m. woman's clog with a cork sole.

chapinazo, m. blow with a clog or patten.

chapinería, f. shop where clogs and pattens are made and sold; art of making them.

chapinero, ra, n. clog maker or seller.

chápiro, m. a word used only in the phrases, ¡por vida del chápiro verde! good gracious! ¡voto al chápiro! by Jove! by thunder!

chapitel, m. (arch.) spire; capital of a column; (naut.) agate socket of the needle.

chaple, m. graver.

chapó, m. four-handed billiard game.

chapodar, va. to lop.

chapodo, m. lopping; branch lopped off.

chapón, m. large blot of ink.

chapona, f. = CHAMBRA.

chapote, m. black wax for cleaning the teeth.

chapotear. I. va. to wet with a sponge or wet cloth. **II.** vn. to paddle in the water, to dabble.

chapoteo, m. splash, splatter.

chapucear, va. to botch, bungle, cobble.

chapuceramente, adv. fumblingly, clumsily, bunglingly.

chapucería, f. bungle, botch; clumsy fib.

chapucero, ra. I. a. rough, unpolished; clumsy, bungling; rude. **II.** m. blacksmith who makes nails, trivets, shovels, etc.; nailer; junk dealer.

chapurrar, chapurrear, va. to splatter or jabber (a language); to speak brokenly; to mix (app. to liquors).

chapurrear, va. to jabber (a language).

chapuz, m. ducking; clumsy performance.—pl. chapuces, (naut.) mast spars.

chapuzar. I. va. (pret. CHAPUCÉ: subj. CHAPUCE) to duck. **II.** vn. & vr. to dive, draggle, duck.

chaqué, m. cut-away coat.

chaqueta, f. jacket; sack coat; (mech.) case, casing, jacket.

chaquete, m. game of checkers.

chaquetear, vn. (Cuba) to run away with fright.

chaquetón, m. aug. pea-jacket; (Cuba) overcoat.

chaquira, f. (Peru) fine mock pearl or glass colored bead; (Colomb.) bead.

charada, f. word charade.

charadrio, m. (orn.) common roller.

charal, m. (Mex.) a lake fish.

charamusca, f. (Mex.) twisted candy; (Peru) brushwood.

charamusquero, ra, n. (Mex.) seller of twisted candy.

charanga, f. military brass band; fanfare.

charango, m. (Peru) a kind of bandore or small guitar.

charanguero, ra. I. a. clumsy, unpolished. **II.** m. bungler, botcher; peddler, hawker; small coast-trading ship.

charca, f. pool, basin, pond.

charco, m. pool, puddle.—**pasar el ch.,** (coll.) to cross the big pond (the sea).

charla, f. prattle, chat, talk; loquaciousness; (orn.) Bohemian chatterer, silktail.

charlador, ra, n. & a. prater (-ing), talker (-ative), chatterbox.

charladuría, f. garrulity, gossip, prattle.

charlante, n. gabbler, chatterer.

charlantín, m. (orn.) mean prattler, gossip.

charlar, vn. to chat, prattle, prate.

charlatán, na, n. prater, babbler; charlatan, quack, humbug.

charlatanear, vn. = CHARLAR.

charlatanería, f. garrulity, verbosity; charlatanry, quackery, humbug.

charlatanismo, m. charlatanry, quackery; verbosity, loquaciousness.

charneca, f. (bot.) mastic tree.

charnecal, m. plantation of mastic trees.

charnela, f. hinge, chape of a buckle, hinge joint, knuckle.

charneta, f. (coll.) hinge joint.

charol, m. varnish, japan; patent leather.—**darse ch.,** to blow one's own horn, to brag.

charolar, *va.* to varnish, polish, enamel; japan.

charolista, *n.* gilder, varnisher.

charpa, *f.* leather belt with compartments for pistols; sling for a broken arm; (naut.) sling.

charpar, *va.* to scarf; to lap.

charque, *m.* jerked beef.

charquear, *va.* to jerk or dry (beef).

charqueo, *m.* (min.) cleaning of the drains; cleaning holy-water fonts.

charquí, *m.* = CHARQUE.

charquillo, *m. dim.* small pool or puddle.

charrada, *f.* speech or action of a peasant; country dance; (coll.) tawdriness, tinsel, gaudiness.

charramente, *adv.* tawdrily, gaudily, tastelessly.

charrán, *a.* rascally, knavish.—**charranada,** *f.* knavish, roguish action.—**charranear,** *vn.* to play the knave.—**charranería,** *f.* rascality, knavery, roguery.

charrasca, *f.* folding knife; (coll., hum.) dangling sword.

charrería, *f.* tawdriness, gaudiness.

charretera, *f.* strap on the bottom of trousers; the buckle of the strap; (mil.) the lower part of trousers to fasten them with a buckle; the buckle; epaulet.—**ch. mocha,** shoulder knot; (coll.) shoulder pad for carrying loads.

charro, ra. **I.** *n.* churl; coarse, ill-bred person. **II.** *a.* tawdry, showy, flashy, loud.

chascar, *vn.* to crackle, crack, sputter.

chascarrillo, *m.* (coll.) spicy anecdote.

chasco, *m.* practical joke, jest, trick; failure, disappointment.—**dar ch.,** to disappoint.—**dar un ch.,** to play a merry trick.—**llevarse ch.,** to be disappointed, to get left.

chasí, *m.* photographic plate holder.

chasis, *m.* (aut.) chassis.

chasponazo, *m.* mark made by a spent bullet.

chasquear. **I.** *va.* to crack or snap (a whip); to fool; to play a waggish trick on; to disappoint, fail; cheat. **II.** *vn.* to crack, snap; crepitate.

chasqui, *m.* (Peru) postboy, foot messenger.

chasquido, *m.* crack of a whip or lash; crack, noise made by timber when it breaks or splits.

chata, *f.* bedpan; (naut.) flat-bottomed boat.—**ch. alijadora,** lighter.—**ch. de arbolar,** sheer-hulk.—**ch. de carenar,** careening hulk.

chatedad, *f.* flatness.

chato, ta, *a.* flat; flat-nosed; flattened.

chatón, *m.* bezel holding a gem; large gem set in.

chatre, *a.* (Ecuador) richly decked out.

chaúl, *m.* blue Chinese silk.

chauvinismo, *m.* chauvinism.

chauvinista, *n. & a.* chauvinist (-ic).

chaval, la, *n.* lad, lass.

chaveta, *f.* bolt, forelock, pin, key, wedge.—**perder la ch.,** to become rattled.

chaya, *f.* (Ch.) amusement consisting in throwing water on passers-by during carnivals; confetti; spray of a watering pot.

chayote, *m.* (Mex.) pear-shaped fruit with a large stone.

chayotera, *f.* (Mex.) a climbing plant yielding the CHAYOTE.

chaza, *f.* point where the ball is driven back or where it stops, in the game of PELOTA; mark where the ball stops; (naut.) space between ports.—**hacer chazas,** to walk on the hind feet (s. o. horses).

chazador, *m.* person employed to stop the ball and mark the game.

chazar, *va.* to stop (the ball) before it reaches the winning point; to mark the point whence the ball was driven back.

checo, ca, *n. & a.* Czech.

checoeslovaco, ca, *n. & a.* Czecho-Slovak, Czecho-Slovakian.

chécheres, *m. pl.* (Colomb.) small things, notions.

cheira, *f.* = CHAIRA.

chelín, *m.* shilling.

chepa, *f.* (coll.) hump, hunch.

cheque, *m.* (com.) check, sight draft.

cherna, *f.* (zool.) ruffle, a salmonlike fish.

cherva, *f.* (bot.) castor-oil plant.

cheurón, *m.* (her.) chevron.

chía, *f.* short black mantle, cowl; white medicinal earth; (bot.) lime-leaved sage.

chibalete, *m.* (print.) cabinet, composing frame.

chibcha. **I.** *m.* Chibcha, one of the aborigines of the Bogota (Colomb.) plateau. **II.** *a.* Chibcha, relating or belonging to the Chibchas.

chibuquí, *m.* Turkish chibouk.

chicada, *f.* herd of sickly kids; childish action.

chicalote, *m.* Mexican argemone.

chicana, *f.* chicanery.

chicanero, ra, *a.* tricky, cunning.

chicle, *m.* chicle.

chico, ca. **I.** *a.* little, small. **II.** *n.* little boy or lad, little chap; little girl or lass; dear lad, dear fellow; dear lass; (coll.) boy, old chap (as a term of familiarity).

chicolear, *va.* (coll.) to pay compliments to (a woman).

chicoleo, *m.* (coll.) flattering compliment.

chicoria, *f.* = ACHICORIA.

chicorrotico, ca, llo, lla, to, ta, *a. dim.* (coll.) very little or small, tiny (child).

chicorrotín, *a.* (coll.) very small, tiny.

chicotazo, *m.* (Mex.) blow with a whip.

chicote, ta. **I.** *n.* (coll.) fat strong boy or girl. **II.** *m.* (naut.) end of a rope or cable; junk; (Mex.) whip; (coll.) cigar.

chicotear, *va.* (Mex.) to whip.

chicozapote, *m.* (bot.) sapodilla.

chicuelo, la, *n. dim.* little boy; little girl.

chicha, *f.* chicha, a popular fermented beverage, variously made from either maize, pineapple, etc.; meat, flesh.

chícharo, *f.* (bot.) pea.

chicharra, *f.* harvest fly, jarfly, cicada; talkative woman; kazoo, a plaything.—**cantar la ch.,** (coll.) to be scorching hot.

chicharrar, *va.* = ACHICHARRAR.

chicharrear, *vn.* to creak; to chirp (said of the cicada).

chicharrero, ra. **I.** *n.* maker or seller of kazoos. **II.** *m.* (coll.) very hot place or climate.

chicharro, *m.* young tunny fish; horse-mackerel.

chicharrón, *m.* crackling, fried scrap, cracknel; overroasted meat; (coll.) person sunburnt or tanned

chiche, *m.* (Am.) potted and devilled fish.

chichear, *va.* to hiss as a sign of displeasure.

chicheo, *m.* act of hissing.

chichería, *f.* tavern where CHICHA is sold.

chichero, ra, *n.* seller or drinker of CHICHA.

chichigua, *f.* (Mex., vulg.) wet nurse.

chichimeco, ca, *n. & a.* Chichimec (-an).

chichisbeador, *m.* gallant, wooer.

chichisbear, *va.* to woo, court.

chichisbeo, *m.* court paid to a lady; cicisbeo, gallant who dangles after a married woman.

chichón, *m.* bump; bruise.

chichoncillo, cito, *m. dim.* small bump.

chichonera, *f.* tumbling cap; wadded hood worn by children.

chichota, *f.*—**sin faltar ch.,** without lacking one iota.

chifla, *f.* whistling, hissing; paring knife.

chiflacayote, *m.* a large kind of pumpkin.

chifladera, *f.* whistle.

chifladura, *f.* hissing, whistling; (coll.) crankiness; whim, fad; hobby, mania.

chiflar. **I.** *va.* to pare (leather); to hiss; (coll.) to tipple. **II.** *vn.* to whistle. **III.** *vr.* (coll.) to become mentally unbalanced; to lose one's head.

chiflato, *m.* whistle.—**chifle,** *m.* whistle, call; instrument to decoy birds; (naut.) priming horn; powderflask.—**chiflete,** *m.* whistle.—**chiflido,** *m.* shrill whistling sound.—**chiflo,** *m.* whistling.

chiflón, *m.* (Am.) air draught; (Mex.) water spout; (min.) caving of loose stone.

chilaba, *f.* Moorish hooded garment.

chilacayote, *m.* (bot.) bottle gourd.
chilanco, *m.* = CILANCO.
chilar, *m.* field planted with chillies.
chile, *f.* (bot.) chilli, red pepper.
chileno, na; chileño, ña, *n.* & *a.* Chilean.
chilindrina, *f.* (coll.) trifle, thing of little value; (coll.) joke, fun, witticism, anecdote.
chilindrinero, ra, *n.* & *a.* (coll.) trifler (-ing).
chilidrón, *m.* a card game.
chilote, *m.* (Mex.) = JILOTE.
chiltipiquín, *m.* (Mex.) small hot chilli.
chilla, *f.* call for foxes, hares, or rabbits; (carp.) clapboard.
chillado, *m.* roof of clapboards.
chillador, ra, *n.* & *a.* screamer (-ing); screecher (-ing); creaking.
chillante, *a.* shrieking, screeching.
chillar, *vn.* to screech, scream, shriek; to crackle, creak; to imitate the notes of birds; to hiss, sizz, (s. o. something frying).
chilleras, *f. pl.* (naut.) shot lockers for balls; rowlocks.
chillido, *m.* screech, scream, shriek, shrill sound; bawling of a woman or child.—**dar un ch.,** to utter a scream.
chillo, *m.* call.
chillón, *m.* lath nail.—**ch. real,** spike.
chillón, na. **I.** *n.* (coll.) screamer, bawler; whiner. **II.** *a.* whining; screechy, shrill, harsh; showy, tawdry, loud.
chimachima, chimango, *m.* (Ch., Peru,) a species of caracara.
chimenea, *f.* chimney, smokestack; hearth, fireplace; kitchen range, cooking stove.—**ch. francesa,** fireplace.
chimpancé, *m.* chimpanzee.
china, *f.* pebble, small stone; (bot.) Chinaroot; porcelain; China silk or cotton stuff; game of shutting the hands, and guessing which contains the pebble; (P. Rico) sweet orange.
china, *f.* (Am.) maid servant; (C. A.) children's nurse; (Colomb.) little or young girl; (Colomb.) spinning top.
chinampa, *f.* small garden tract in lakes near Mexico.
chinampero, *m.* tiller of a CHINAMPA.
chinanta, *f.* (Philip.) a unit of weight (about 13¾ lbs.).
chinarro, *m.* large pebble.
chinateado, *m.* stratum or layer of pebbles.
chinazo, *m.* aug. blow with a pebble.
chinacharrazo, *m.* (coll.) = CINTARAZO.
chinacharrero, *m.* place swarming with bedbugs; fishing smack.
chinche, *m.* or *f.* bedbug; thumb tack; (coll.) tedious person, bore.
chinchero, *m.* bug trap made of twigs; place full of bedbugs.
chinchilla, *f.* chinchilla, a South-American rodent, and its fur.
chinchín, *m.* (Cuba) drizzling rain.
chinchorrería, *f.* (coll.) nuisance, vexation; (coll.) mischievous tale.
chinchorrero, ra, *n.* insidious and pestering taleteller.
chinchorro, *m.* small dragnet; smallest rowboat on board a ship.
chinchoso, sa, *a.* (coll.) querulous, tiresome.
chinela, *f.* slipper; pattens, chopines, or clogs worn by women in bad weather.
chinero, *m.* china closet, cupboard.
chinesco, ca, *a.* Chinese.—*m. pl.* (mus.) bell tree.
chinito, ta, *n.* (Am.) dearie, dearest.
chino, na. **I.** *a.* Chinese. **II.** *n.* Chinaman, Chinawoman. **III.** *m.* Chinese (language); (Colomb.) boy (sp. a newsboy, gamin, etc.); (Am.) crossbred (app. to the offspring of non-white parents).
chinquirito, *m.* (Mex.) rum from lees of sugar.
chipichipi, *m.* (Mex.) mist; drizzle.
chipirón, *m.* calamary.

chiprio, pria; chipriota, chipriote, *n.* & *a.* Cyprian (from Cyprus).
chiqueadores, *m. pl.* disks of tortoise shell formerly used in Mexico as a feminine ornament; small plasters for headache.
chiquero, *m.* pigpen; hut for goats; place where bulls are shut up.
chiquichaque, *m.* (coll.) sawyer; noise of things rubbing against each other.
chiquichuite, *m.* (Mex.) willow basket.
chiquilicuatro, *m.* (coll.) dabbler, meddler.
chiquillada, *f.* childish speech or action.
chiquillería, *f.* (coll.) a great number of small children.
chiquillo, illa, *n.* small child, little one.
chiquirritico, ica, illo, illa, ito, ita, *a. dim.* very small, tiny.
chiquirritín, na, *n.* (coll.) baby boy; baby girl; very little child.
chiquítico, ca; llo, lla, *a. dim.* very small, tiny.
chiquitín, na, *n.* = CHIQUIRRITÍN.
chiquito, ta. **I.** *a.* small, little; very small, very little, tiny.—**andarse en chiquitas,** to be lenient condescending.—**hacerse ch.,** to be modest, to conceal one's accomplishments. **II.** *n.* little boy (girl), little one.
chiribitas, *f. pl.* (coll.) particles that float in the eyes and obscure the sight.
chiribitil, *m.* crib, narrow and low hole or corner; small room, "den."
chirigaita, *f.* a kind of gourd.
chirigota, *f.* (coll.) jest, joke, fun.
chirimbolos, *m. pl.* (coll.) odds and ends; utensils, traps.
chirimía. **I.** *f.* (mus.) flageolet. **II.** *n.* flageolet player.
chirimoya, *f.* (bot.) cherimoya, a tropical fruit.
chirimoyo, *m.* cherimoya tree.
chirinola, *f.* bowling, boys' game; trifle.—**estar de ch.** (coll.) to be in good spirits.
chiripa, *f.* in billiards, fluke; (coll.) stroke of good luck; chance or unexpected event.—**de ch.,** by chance, unexpectedly.
chiripear, *vn.* to make flukes at billiards.
chiripero, ra, *n.* poor player who wins by fluke; lucky person.
chirivía, *f.* (bot.) parsnip; (orn.) wagtail.
chirla, *f.* mussel.
chirlador, ra, *n.* (coll.) clamorous prattler.
chirlar, *vn.* to talk fast and loud.
chirle. **I.** *a.* (coll.) insipid, tasteless. **II.** *m.* dung of sheep and goats.
chirlo, *m.* large wound in the face and the scar it leaves.
chirona, *f.* (coll.) prison.
chirriadero, ra; chirriador, ra, *a.* hissing; sizzling, when frying; creaking, as a hinge; chirping.
chirriar, *vn.* to hiss; sizz; creak, squeak; (coll.) to sing out of tune or time.
chirrido, *m.* chirping of birds; chattering; creaking; any shrill sound.
chirrío, *m.* creaking noise made by carts.
chirrión, *m.* tumbrel, creaking muck or dung cart.
chirrionero, *m.* scavenger, dung-cart driver.
chirumen, *m.* (coll.) common sense.
¡chis! *interj.* hush! silence!
chisgarabís, *n.* (coll.) meddler, dabbler; insignificant, noisy person.
chisguete, *m.* (coll.) small draft of wine; small spout of any liquid, squirt.—**echar un ch.,** to drink.
chisme, *m.* tale of a gossip monger; gossip; (coll.) jigger, any household utensil or trifle.
chismear, *va.* to tattle, gossip.
chismero, ra, *n.* & *a.* talebearer (-ing), gossip (-ing).
chismografía, *f.* (coll.) gossip, tattle.
chismoso, sa, *n.* & *a.* = CHISMERO, RA.
chispa, *f.* spark; ember; sparkle; flake; very small diamond; small particle; state of drunkenness; cleverness, wit; rumor.—**coger una ch..**

(coll.) to get drunk.—**de ch.,** flintlock.—**echar chispas,** (coll.) to rave, be in a passion.—**ser ch.,** to be all life and spirits.

chisparse, *vr.* (Am.) to get tipsy.

¡chispas! *interj.* fire and tow! blazes!

chispazo, *m.* flying off of a spark; damage it does; (coll.) tale mischievously circulated.

chispeante, *a.* sparking, sparkling.

chispear, *vn.* to spark; sparkle; to scintillate; to rain gently.

chispero, *m.* blacksmith; spark catcher; (coll.) Madrilenian ruffian.

chispero, ra, *a.* sparkling.

chispo. I. *a.* (coll.) tipsy. **II.** *m.* short drink.

chisporrotear, *vn.* (coll.) to sputter sparks.

chisporroteo, *m.* (coll.) sputtering sparks.

chisposo, sa, *a.* sputtering, sparkling.

chistar, *vn.* to mumble, mutter; answer back.

chiste, *m.* witty saying; joke, jest.—**dar en el ch.,** to guess right.

chistera, *f.* hand fish basket; (coll.) silk hat.

chistosamente, *adv.* facetiously, humorously.

chistoso, sa, *a.* funny, witty.

chita, *f.* ankle bone in sheep and bullocks; a game with this bone.—**a la ch. callando,** on the quiet, by stealth.

chiticalla, *m.* (coll.) discreet person; secret.

chiticallando, *adv.* (coll.) quietly, on the quiet. —**a la ch.,** noiselessly, quietly.—**andar,** or **ir, ch.,** to go on tiptoes, to go very quietly.

chito, *m.* piece of wood or bone on which money is put in the game of CHITA.—**irse a chitos,** (coll.) to lead a debauched life, to go to the dogs.

¡chito! ¡chitón! *interj.* hush! not a word!

chitón, *m.* molusk with coat-of-mail shell.

chiva, *f.* kid; female goat.

chivata, *f.* shepherd's staff.

chivato, *m.* kid between six and twelve months old; (Colomb.) rascal, knave.

chivero, *m.* (Am.) puma.

chivetero, chivital, chivitil, *m.* fold for kids.

chivo, va. I. *n.* kid; goat. **II.** *m.* pit for the lees of oil; (Colomb.) anger, angry spell.

¡cho! *interj.* whoa!

choca, *f.* part of the game given to a hawk; soap-boiler's paddle.

chocador, ra. I. *n. & a.* provoker (-ing). **II.** *a.* repulsive, disagreeable.

chocante, *a.* provoking; disagreeable; strange, surprising.

chocar. I. *vn.* (*pret.* CHOQUÉ: *subj.* CHOQUE) to strike, collide, hit, clash; to meet, fight, combat. **II.** *va.* to provoke; to displease, be disliked; to surprise.

chocarrear, *vn.* to joke, act the buffoon.

chocarrería, *f.* buffoonery, coarse jest.

chocarrero, ra, *a.* scurrilous, vulgar.

chocilla, *f. dim.* hut, low cottage.

choclar, *vn.* in the game of ARGOLLA, to drive the ball through the rings.

choclo, *m.* clog, galosh; (Am.) green ear of maize.

choclón, *m.* in the game of ARGOLLA, the driving of a ball through the rings.

choco, *m.* small cuttlefish.

chocolate, *m.* chocolate.

chocolatera, *f.* chocolate pot; woman who makes or sells chocolate.

chocolatería, *f.* shop where chocolate is sold.

chocolatero, ra. I. *a.* fond of chocolate. **II.** *n.* chocolate maker or dealer. **III.** *m.* (Mex.) stiff north wind.

chocolatear, *vn.* = CHOCOLOTEAR.

chocha, chochaperdiz, *f.* (orn.) woodcock.

chochear, *vn.* to dote.

chochera, chochez, *f.* dotage.

chocho, cha. I. *n. & a.* dotard (-ing). **II.** *m.* (bot.) lupine; cinnamon candy stick.—*pl.* sweetmeats, dainties.

chofer, chófer, *n.* chauffeur.

chofes, *m. pl.* livers and lights; lungs.

chofeta, *f.* chafing dish; fire pan; foot stove.

choflista, *n.* one living on livers and lights.

cholo, la, *n.* (Am.) a term applied by whites to Indians and servants; half-breed.

cholla, *f.* (coll.) skull, head, noddle; faculty.

chonta, *f.* a hardwood palm tree.

chontal, *m.* CHONTA field or grove; Chontal, one of the Chontal tribe of Nicaragua; (coll.) uncivilized Indian; uncultured person.

chopa, *f.* (icht.) a kind of sea bream; (naut.) topgallant poop.

chopera, *f.* black-poplar grove.

chopo, *m.* (bot.) black poplar tree; (coll.) musket, gun.

choque, *m.* impact; collision; clash; (mil.) skirmish; (naut.) chock, fur, rush.

choquezuela, *f.* (anat.) kneepan.

chordón, *m.* raspberry jam.

choricera, *f.* woman who makes or sells sausages; (mech.) sausage stuffer.

choricería, *f.* = SALCHICHERÍA.

choricero, ra, *n.* sausage maker or seller.

chorillo, *m.* (Peru) mill for coarse fabrics.

chorizo, *m.* pork sausage; counterweight.

chorlito, *m.* (orn.) curlew or gray plover; (orn.) red shank.

chorlo, *m.* schorl, tourmalin.

chorote, *m.* (Ven.) poor-quality chocolate.

chorreado, da. I. *a.* striped. **II.** *pp.* of CHO-RREAR.

chorreadura, *f.* dripping, welling; stain from drippings.

chorrear, *vn.* to spout, to outpour; to drip; to be dripping wet; to come out one by one.

chorreo, *m.* spouting, dripping.

chorrera, *f.* spout or place whence liquids drip; mark left by dripping or running water; ornament formerly appended to badges; shirt frill; (coll.) string (of things), stream (of things, people), lot (in the sense of great quantity or number).

chorretada, *f.* (coll.) squirt, spurt, jet.

chorrillo, *m. dim.* small spout; (coll.) continual coming in and outgoing of money.

chorrito, *m. dim.* small spout.

chorro, *m.* jet, spurt; stream; anything issuing, entering, flowing, or passing.—**ch. de voz,** voice of large volume.—**a chorros,** (coll.) abundantly.—**de ch.,** jet (u. a.)

chorroborro, *m.* (coll.) flood, inundation.

chorrón, *m.* dressed hemp.

chortal, *m.* fountain or spring.

chota, *f.* sucking kid; heifer calf.

chotacabras, *f.* (orn.) goat-sucker, churn owl.

chote, *m.* (Cuba) = CHAYOTE.

chotear, *va.* (Cuba, coll.) to banter, gibe.

choteo, *m.* (Cuba, coll.) chaffing, jeering.

choto, *m.* sucking kid, calf.

chotuno, na, *a.* sucking (young goats or kids); poor, starved (lambs); goatish.—**oler a ch.,** to smell like a goat.

chova, *f.* (orn.) jay, chough; jackdaw, crow.

choz, *f.* stroke, blow; suddenness.

choza, *f.* hut, hovel, cabin, shanty.

chozno, na, *n. f.* great-grandson (-daughter).

chozo, *m.* small hut or cabin.

chozpar, *vn.* to gambol, caper.—**chozpo,** *m.* gambol, leap.—**chozpón, na,** *a.* frisky, capering.

chozuela, *f. dim.* small hut or shanty.

chual, *m.* (bot.) pigweed or goosefoot.

chualar, *m.* place abounding in pigweed.

chubarba, *f.* (bot.) stonecrop.

chubasco, *m.* squall, shower.

chubascoso, sa, *a.* squally, gusty.

chúcaro, ra, *a.* (Am.) shy (s. o. horses); wild (s. o. cattle).

chucero, *m.* (mil.) pikeman.

chucha, *f.* female dog; (S. A.) opossum.

chuchear. I. *va.* to fowl with calls, gins, and nets. **II.** *vn.* to whisper.

chuchería, *f.* gewgaw, trinket, notion, titbit; fowling with calls, gins, and nets; trifle.

chuchero, ra, *n.* birdcatcher; (Cuba) switch tender.

chucho, *m.* (coll.) dog; (Cuba) whip; (Cuba) railway switch; (Ch., Arg.) chill; malaria.

chuchumeco, *m.* contemptible little fellow.

chueca, *f.* head of a bone; hockey; small ball for playing hockey; (coll.) joke, trick; soap maker's paddle.

chuecazo, *m.* stroke given to a ball at hockey.

chufa, *f.* (bot.) chufa, edible tuber of a sedge.

chufar, *vn. & vr.* to mock, to scoff.

chufería, *f.* place where chufa orgeat and sherbet are made or served.

chufero, ra, *n.* seller of chufas.

chufeta, *f.* (coll.) jest; chafing dish; fire pan.

chufleta, *f.* (coll.) taunt, scoff.

chufletear, *vn.* (coll.) show contempt.

chufletero, ra, *a.* (coll.) taunting, sneering.

chulada, *f.* droll speech or action; pleasant conversation; breach of manners.

chulear, *va.* to jest with, to poke fun at; (Mex.) to court, make love to.

chulería, *f.* pleasing manner.

chuleta, *f.* chop; cutlet; (carp.) chips for filling joints; (coll.) slap, blow with the fist.

chulillo, illa, ito, ita, *m. & f. dim.* little wag.

chulo, la. I. *n.* punster, jester; funny person; sly, deceitful person. **II.** *m.* rascal, knave; pimp, man kept by a woman; bullfighter's assistant; butcher's mate. **III.** *f.* woman of low class loud in dress and manners. **IV.** *a.* (Am.) pretty, nice, graceful, attractive.

chulla, *f.* slice of bacon.

chumacera, *f.* (mech.) journal bearing; (naut.) rowlock.

chumbe, *m.* (Am.) band or cord to hold the dress at the waist.

chumbera, *f.* (bot.) opuntia, prickly pear.

chumbo, prickly pear, Indian fig.

chumpipe, *m.* (C. A.) turkey.

chuncaca, *f.* (C. A.) = CHANCACA.

chunga, *f.* (coll.) jest, fun, banter.—**estar de ch.,** to be in good humor.

chungón, ona, *n.* jester.

chunguearse, *vr.* (coll.) to chaff, gibe, jest.

chupa, *f.* waistcoat; undercoat with sleeves; (Philip.) liquid measure (0.735 liter); dry measure (0.37 liter).—**poner a uno como ch. de dómine,** (coll.) to wipe the floor with one.

chupada, *f.* suck, suction.

chupaderito, *m. dim.*—**andarse con,** or **en, chupaderitos;** to use ineffective means for difficult tasks.

chupadero, ra, dor, ra. I. *a.* sucking, absorbent. **II.** *m.* baby's coral or teething ring; (mech.) suction tube; (Am.) tippler.

chupado, da, *a.* (coll.) lean, emaciated.

chupadorcito, *m. dim.* of CHUPADOR; CHUPADERITO.

chupadura, *f.* act and effect of sucking.

chupaflores, *m.* (orn.) humming bird.

chupalandero, *m.* snail that lives on plants.

chupamiel, chupamirtos, *m.* humming bird.

chupar, *va.* to suck; to draw, sip; to absorb; to imbibe; (coll.) to hang upon (others) for subsistence; to fool.—**ch. la sangre** (coll.) to stick like a leech.—**chuparse los dedos,** to eat with pleasure; to be overjoyed.

chupativo, va, *a.* of a sucking nature.

chupeta, *f.* (naut.) roundhouse.

chupeta, illa, ita, *f. dim.* short waistcoat.

chupetear, *va.* to suck gently and by starts.

chupeteo, *m.* gentle sucking.

chupetín, *m.* man's inner garment.

chupetón, *m.* violent suction.

chupón, na. I. *n. & a.* (coll.) sponge, parasite. **II.** *m.* (bot.) sucker, shoot; (mech.) sucker, plunger piston, valve bucket.

churdón, *m.* raspberry jam.

churla, *f.,* **churlo,** *m.* seroon, spicebag.

churra, *f.* little pin-tailed grouse; heifer one year old.

churrasco, *m.* (Am.) piece of broiled meat.

churrascón, *m.* scorching.

churre, *m.* (coll.) thick, dirty, oozing or dripping grease; anything dirty and greasy.

churrea, *f.* Californian grouse.

churriburri, *m.* = ZURRIBURRI.

churriento, ta, *a.* greasy.

churrigueresco, ca, *a.* (arch.) overloaded, tawdry, loud.

churreguerismo, *m.* (arch.) overornamentation, tawdriness.

churro, ra. I. *a.* coarse; having coarse wool (s. o. sheep). **II.** *m.* a sort of fritter.

churrullero, ra, *n.* tattler, gossip.

churrupear, *vn.* to sip wine.

churruscarse, *vr.* to be scorched.

churrusco, *m.* bread toasted too much.

churumbela, *f.* reed instrument resembling a flageolet; (Am.) small cup for maté.

churumen, *m.* = CHIRUMEN.

churumo, *m.* (coll.) juice or substance.

chus ni mus.—(coll.) **no decir chus ni mus,** not to say a word, not to say boo, not to open one's mouth.

chuscada, *f.* pleasantry, joke.

chuscamente, *adv.* in a droll manner.

chusco, ca, *a.* droll, merry, funny.

chusma, *f.* crew and slaves of a row galley; rabble, mob, crowd.

chuspa, *f.* (Am.) bag.

chute, *m.* (C. A.) prick.

chuza, *f.* (Mex.) stroke at billiards knocking all the pins with one ball.

chuzar, *va.* (Colomb.) to prick.

chuzazo, *m.* large pike; prick; thrust with a prick or pointed weapon.

chuzo, *m.* pike; prick; anything pointed; (naut.) boarding pike.—*a.* **chuzos,** abundantly, impetuously.—**echar chuzos,** (coll.) to brag.

chuzón, na. I. *n.* crafty, artful person; wag, punster, jester. **II.** *m. aug.* = CHUZAZO.

D

dable, *a.* possible, practicable.

daca (word formed by the verb **da** and the adv. **acá**), give me, give it me.

da capo, (mus.) da capos.

dacio, cia. I. *n. & a.* Dacian. **II.** *m.* tribute, tax.

dación, *f.* (law) dedition, yielding or giving up; delivery.

dactílico, ca, *a.* dactylic.—**dáctilo,** *m.* dactyl.

dactilografía, *f.* typewriting.

dactilografista, *n.* typewriter, typist.

dactilógrafo, *m.* typewriter (machine); typist.

dactilología, *f.* dactylology.

dactiloscopia, *f.* dactyloscopy, study of finger prints.

dactiloscópico, ca, *a.* dactyloscopic, relating to finger prints.

dádiva, *f.* gift, gratification, grant, keepsake.

dadivosamente, *adv.* liberally, bountifully.

dadivosidad, *f.* liberality, bounty.

dadivoso, sa, *a.* bountiful, liberal.

dado. I. *m.* die; block, bushing; pivot collar; coin; (arch.) dado.—*pl.* (naut.) case or grapeshot.—**d. falso,** false die.—**dados de las velas,** (naut.) tablings of the bowling cringles.—**correr el d.,** (coll.) to be in good luck.—**estar como un d.,** to fit exactly. **II.** *a. & pp.* of DAR.—**d. que,** provided; so long as; assuming that.

dador, ra. *n.* giver; (com.) drawer of a bill of exchange; bearer (of a letter).

daga, *f.* dagger; line of bricks in a kiln.—**llegar a las dagas,** (coll.) to reach the most difficult point.

dagoba, *f.* (arch.) dagoba, an East-Indian shrine.

dagón, *m. aug.* large dagger.

daguerrotipar, *va.* to daguerreotype.

daguerrotipia, *f.* making daguerreotypes.

daguerrotipo, *m.* daguerreotype.

daguilla, *f. dim.* small dagger.

daifa, *f.* mistress, concubine.

dala, *f.* (naut.) pump dale of a ship.

¡dale! *interj.* expressive of displeasure at obstinacy.

dalia, *f.* (bot.) dahlia.

dálmata; dalmático, ca, *n.* & *a.* Dalmatian.

dalmática, *f.* dalmatica, wide-sleeve tunic.

daltoniano, na, *a.* color-blind.

daltonismo, *m.* color blindness, daltonism.

dallador, *m.* grass mower.

dallar, *va.* to mow.

dalle, *m.* scythe, sickle.

dama, *f.* lady, dame; noble or distinguished woman; lady courted by a gentleman; lady of honor at court; mistress or concubine; king in checkers; an old Spanish dance; (metal.) dam of a blast furnace.—**d. cortesana,** courtesan.—**soplar la d.,** to huff a king in the game of draughts; (coll.) to carry off and marry a woman who was courted by another man.

damajuana, *f.* demijohn.

damascado, da, *a.* = ADAMASCADO.

damascena, *f.* damson, plum.

damasceno, na, *a.* Damascene.

damasco, *m.* damask, figured silk stuff; Brussels apricot; damson, plum.

damasina, *f.* silk stuff resembling damask.

damasquillo, *m.* silk or woollen stuff resembling damask; apricot.

damasquinado, da, *a.* damaskeened.

damasquino, na, *a.* damaskeened; Damascene. **—a la d.,** Damascus fashion.

damería, *f.* excessive nicety in conduct, prudery.

damisela, *f.* young woman; (coll.) courtesan.

damnificar, *va.* (*pret.* DAMNIFIQUÉ: *subj.* DAMNIFIQUE) to hurt, to damage, to injure.

danchado, da, *a.* (her.) dentate, indented.

danés, sa. I. *a.* Danish. **II.** *n.* Dane. **III.** *m.* Danish (language).

dánico, ca, *a.* Dane, Danish.

dango, *m.* (orn.) a species of eagle.

danta, *f.* (zool.) tapir.

dante. I. *a.* giving. **II.** *n.* giver.

dantellado, da, *a.* dentated, serrated.

dantesco, ca, *a.* Dantesque.

danubiano, na, *a.* Danubian.

danza, *f.* dance; set or number of dancers; entangled affair; (Cuba and P. Rico) a slow dance and its tune.—**d. de espadas,** (coll.) quarrel, fight. **—meter en la d.,** (coll.) to draw into the fray, to involve.

danzador, ra, *n.* dancer.

danzante, ta, *n.* dancer; (coll.) active person, hustler; (coll.) fickle, airy person.

danzar, *vn.* (*pret.* DANCÉ: *subj.* DANCE) to dance; to whirl; (coll.) to introduce one's self into any business.

danzarín, na, *n.* dancer; (coll.) giddy, meddling person.

danzón, *m.* (Cuba) slow dance and its tune.

dañable, *a.* prejudicial, condemnable.

dañado, da. I. *a.* spoiled, tainted, bad, wicked; damned. **II.** *pp.* of DAÑAR.

dañador, ra. I. *a.* injurious. **II.** *n.* one who hurts or harms.

dañar. I. *va.* to hurt, damage, impair; to harm, injure; to spoil; to weaken. **II.** *vr.* to spoil; to be damaged.

dañino, na, *a.* mischievous, destructive; harmful, hurtful, injurious.

daño, *m.* damage, hurt, loss, nuisance, hindrance. **—d. emergente,** (law) damage caused by non-payment.—**daños y perjuicios,** damages.—**en daño de,** with damage to, to the injury of, to the detriment of.

dañosamente, *adv.* harmfully, injuriously; mischievously.

dañoso, sa, *a.* harmful, noxious, injurious.

dar, *va.* (*ind.* DOY: *pret.* DI: *subj.* DÉ) to give; to hand, to deliver; to confer, grant; to inspire, suggest; to represent (as a play); to emit (as heat, light); to return, to render (as thanks); to proffer, to extend (as the hand); to suppose, to as-

sume, to consider; to allow, admit, concede (a proposition); yield (as fruit, crops, income, etc.); to surrender, submit; to excite, to cause (as pain, sorrow); to strike (the hour); to hold, maintain; to deal (cards); to manifest, show (as signals); to enable, to allow; to apply, put on (as paint, a coating). When joined to some nouns, it expresses the action implied by the noun, as *dar saltos,* to jump; *dar golpes,* to strike (blows).—**d. a conocer,** to make known.—**d. a entender,** to insinuate.—**d. a luz,** to be delivered of, give birth to; to issue, publish.— **d. caza,** to chase, pursue.—**d. calle,** to clear the way.—**d. cuenta de,** to account for.—**d. culadas,** (naut.) to strike repeatedly.—**d. de baja,** to dismiss from the army, muster out.—**d. de barato,** to grant, take for granted.—**d. de mano,** to depreciate or despise.—**d. diente con diente,** to shiver with cold.—**d. el espíritu,** to give up the ghost.—**d. el nombre,** or **el santo,** (mil.) to give the watchword.—**d. el sí,** to grant; to consent to marry.—**d. en cara,** or **en rostro,** to reproach, upbraid, throw in one's face.—**d. fiado,** to give on credit.—**d. fiador,** or **fianza,** to find bail, give security.—**d. fin a,** to complete, finish.—**d. fin de,** to destroy.—**d. fondo,** (naut.) to cast anchor.— **d. fruto,** to yield fruit.—**d. gana,** to excite a desire, to make one feel like (doing something); to have a mind to.—**d. garrote,** to garrote, strangle with the garrote.—**d. golpe,** to astonish; to create a sensation, make a hit.—**d. grima,** to strike with despair, terror, pity.—**d. guerra,** to wage war; torment.—**d. higa,** to miss fire.—**d. la cara por,** to go to the defense of.—**d. largas,** to prolong an affair.—**d. los buenos días,** to say good-day, pass the time of day.—**d. los días a uno,** to congratulate one on one's birthday.—**d. memorias,** to give regards.—**d. parte** (often w. de) to report, communicate; to announce.—**d. poder,** to empower, authorize; give power of attorney.—**d. por** (followed by *pp.*) to take for, to consider as.—**d. prestado,** to lend.—**d. punto,** (com.) to become insolvent.—**d. que decir,** to give occasion for censure or criticism.—**d. que hacer,** to give trouble.— **d. que pensar,** to arouse suspicions.—**d. que sentir,** to hurt others' feelings; to give occasion for regret.—**d. razón de,** to give information about.— **d. un abrazo,** to embrace.—**d. un grito,** to scream.—**d. voces,** to call or scream.—**d. zapatetas,** to leap with joy.—**darla de,** (coll.) to brag of being, to set up for.—**no d. pie con bola,** not to do a thing right, to make a mess of it.

dar, *vn.* to give; to yield, stretch; to set in, come on (ch. constr.: *me dió fiebre,* I was taken with fever; *me dió catarro,* I took cold, or was taken with a cold).—**d. a,** to overlook, open on (*mi ventana da al parque,* my window overlooks the park). **—d. a la bomba,** to pump.—**d. al traste** (often w. **con**), to give up; to spoil, destroy; to set aside, ignore.—**d. con,** to meet, to find (*por fin di con él,* at last I found him).—**d. contra,** to knock or hit against.—**d. de,** to fall down, to fall on (*dar de espaladas,* to fall on one's back); to offer, to serve (*dar de comer,* to feed; to serve meals).—**d. de codo,** to elbow; to treat with contempt.—**d. de sí,** to give, stretch, extend.—**d. en,** to persist in; to fall into (as an error); to contract, acquire (as a custom); to guess, find out (as a joke, puzzle); to hit, to strike.—**d. en el clavo,** to hit the mark.—**d. en que pensar,** to arouse suspicion; to set one to thinking.—**d. en un bajío,** (naut.) to strike ground, to get on shore.—**d. en vacío,** or **en vago,** to fail.—**d. mal,** to have poor luck at cards.—**d. sobre,** to rush on, to attack.—**d. tras,** to pursue, follow with hostility.—**dé donde diere,** inconsiderately, heedlessly.

dar, *vr.* (**darse**) to yield, surrender, submit; to devote one's self.—**d. a la vela,** to set sail.—**d. a merced,** to surrender at discretion; (hunting), to halt exhausted.—**d. la mano,** or **las manos,** to shake hands.—**d. maña,** to manage ably.—**d. por** (followed by *pp.*), to consider one's self as.—**d. por sentido,** to show resentment, to take offense. **—d. por vencido,** to acknowledge defeat; to surrender; to give up.—**d. priesa,** or **prisa,** to make haste.—**d. una panzada,** (coll.) to eat to satiety, to stuff one's self.—**no se me da nada,** I don't care.—**no se me da un bledo,** I don't care a straw.

dardabasí, *m.* (orn.) hawk, kite.
dardada, *f.* blow of a dart.
dárdano, na, *a.* Trojan, Dardanian.
dardo, *m.* dart, arrow; light lance; fresh-water fish, dartfish, dace.—**d. de pescador,** fishgig, harpoon.
dares y tomares, *m. pl.* (coll.) give and take; disputes.—**andar en dares y tomares,** to dispute, to dill-dally.
dársena, *f.* inner harbor; dock.
dartros, *m. pl.* (med.) dartre.—**dartroso, sa,** *a.* dartrous.
darviniano, na; darwiniano, na, *n.* & *a.* Darwinian.
darvinismo, darwinismo, *m.* Darwinism.
darvinista, darwinista, *n.* & *a.* Darwinian.
dasocracia, *f.* forestry.
dasocrático, ca, *a.* forest (u. a.), relating to forestry.
dasonomía, *f.* = DASOCRACIA.
dasonómico, ca, *a.* = DASOCRÁTICO.
data, *f.* date, specified day of a month and year; item in an account; outlet of a reservoir.—**estar de mala d.,** to be in bad humor.
datar. I. *va.* to date; (com.) to credit on account. **II.** *vn.* to take origin, date.
dataria, *f.* dataria.
datario, *m.* datary, a papal officer.
dátil, *m.* (bot.) date; (zool.) date shell.
datilado, da, *a.* datelike.
datilera, *f.* common date palm.
datilillo, *m.* *dim.* small date.
datismo, *m.* (rhet.) use of redundant synonyms.
dativo, *m.* & *a.* (gram.) dative.
dato, *m.* datum; title of high dignity in Oriental countries.—*pl.* data.
daturina, *f.* daturine.
dauco, *m.* (bot.) wild carrot.
davalar, *vn.* (naut.) to drift.
davídico, ca, *a.* Davidic, of David.
daza, *f.* (bot.) lucern; (bot.) panic grass.
de, *prep.* of; from (*soy de Boston,* I am from Boston; *confesó de miedo,* he confessed from fear); for, to (*hora de partir,* time to leave; *tiempo de arar,* time for plowing); with (*la dama de las camelias,* the lady with the camellias; *el señor de los guantes,* the gentleman with the gloves; *casa de tres pisos,* three-story house; *ríe de alegría,* he laughs with joy); on, at (*la casa de la derecha,* the house on the right); in (*dos pies de diámetro,* two feet in diameter). Sign of possessive: *la ley de Dios,* the law of God; *la casa de mi padre,* my father's house. Denotes the manner in which a thing is done: *comer de pie,* to eat standing; *se vistió de prisa,* he dressed in haste. Denotes the object or purpose to which a thing is put: *escopeta de caza,* fowling gun; *cuarto de fumar,* smoking room; *máquina de coser,* sewing machine. Indicates the material of which a thing is made: *vaso de plata,* silver cup. Is used by women before their husbands' family name: *doña Isabel Pérez de González,* Mrs. Isabel Pérez-González (née Pérez.) Before **un, uno, una,** denotes rapid action: *se bebió el vino de un trago,* he drank the wine at a gulp. Indicates the moving power or agent of a machine: *máquina de vapor,* steam engine; *molino de viento,* windmill. Sometimes used as an emphatic expletive after an adjective: *el pícaro del muchacho,* the rogue of a boy.
dé, *irr. imp.* & *subj.* of DAR.
dea, *f.* (poet.) goddess.
deán, *m.* dean.
deanato, deanazgo, *m.* deanship.
debajo, *adv.* beneath, underneath.—**d. de,** under, beneath.
debate, *m.* debate; altercation.
debatir, *va.* to argue, discuss, debate.
debe, *m.* (com.) debtor side of an account, debit (Dr. in bookkeeping).
debelación, *f.* conquering in war; conquest.
debelador, ra, *n.* conqueror, victor.
debelar, *va.* to conquer; subdue, put down.
deber, *va.* to owe; must, ought, have to. When used with **de,** it indicates supposition or belief: *él*

debe de haber salido, he must have (I think he has) gone out.
deber, *m.* duty, obligation.
debidamente, *adv.* justly, duly, exactly.
debido a, owing to, on account of.
debiente. I. *a.* owing. **II.** *n.* debtor.
débil. *a.* weak; feeble.
debilidad, *f.* weakness.
debilitación, *f.* debilitation, weakness.
debilitadamente, *adv.* feebly, weakly.
debilitante, *a.* weakening, debilitating.
debilitar. I. *va.* to weaken; to debilitate, enfeeble, enervate. **II.** *vr.* to become feeble.
débilmente, *adv.* weakly, lamely.
débito, *m.* debt.—**d.,** or **d. conyugal,** conjugal duty.
debitorio, *m.* contract of bargain and sale upon credit, by virtue of a partial payment.
debó, *m.* scraper (for skins).
debutante, *n.* debutant, debutante.
debutar, *vn.* to make one's debut.
década, *f.* decade, ten.
decadencia, *f.* decadence, decay, decline.—**ir en d.,** to be on the decline.
decadente, *a.* decaying, declining, decadent.
decaedro, *m.* (geom.) decahedron.
decaer, *vn.* (ind. DECAIGO: subj. DECAIGA) to decay, fail, languish, fade; (naut.) to fall to leeward.
decágono, *m.* (geom.) decagon.
decagramo, *m.* decagram.
decagrama, *m.* decagram.
decaimiento, *m.* decay, decline; weakness.
decalaje, *m.* (aer.) stagger.
decalitro, *m.* decaliter.
decálogo, *m.* decalogue.
decámetro, *m.* decameter.
decampar, *vn.* to decamp.
decanato, *m.* deanship; deanery.
decano, *m.* senior, dean; oldest member of a community or corporation.
decantación, *f.* pouring off, decantation.
decantado, da, *a.* boasted, exalted.
decantar, *va.* to cry up, to exaggerate, to puff; to decant, to draw off.
decapitación, *f.* beheading.
decapitar, *va.* to behead, decapitate.
decápodo, da. I. *n.* & *a.* (zool.) decapod. **II.** *m. pl.* Decapoda.
decárea, *f.* decare, ten ares.
decasílabo, *a.* ten-syllable.
decena, *f.* ten; (mus.) tenth; (arith.) ten (figure in second place from the right).
decenal, *a.* decennial, lasting ten years.
decenar, *m.* group of ten.
decenario, ria. I. *a.* decennary, decennial. **II.** *m.* ten-bead rosary; decennial.
decencia, *f.* decency, propriety; cleanliness, tidiness; honesty, modesty.
decenio, *m.* decade, ten years, decennial.
deceno, na, *a.* tenth.
decentar. I. *va.* (ind. DECIENTO: subj. DECIENTE) to cut off the first slice of; to begin to lose, as the health. **II.** *vr.* to have bedsores.
decente, *a.* decent; honest; kind, "nice"; tidy; well-behaved.
decentemente, *adv.* decently; fairly, honorably; modestly, comely; (iron.) excessively.
decenvirato, *m.* decemvirate.
decenviro, *m.* decemvir.
decepción, *f.* disappointment, disillusionment; humbug.
deciárea, *f.* deciare, one-tenth of an are.
decible, *a.* that may be expressed, speakable.
decidero, ra, *a.* that may be said without difficulty or impropriety.
decididamente, *adv.* decidedly.
decidido, da, *a.* decided, professed, devoted.
decidir. I. *va.* to decide, determine, resolve. **II.** *vr.* to decide, to be determined.
decidor, ra. I. *n.* one who speaks with fluency and elegance; a wit. **II.** *a.* of pleasant speech, being a good talker.

deciento, deciente. *V.* DECENTAR.

decigramo, *m.* decigram.

decilitro, *m.* deciliter.

décima, *f.* (poet.) ten-line stanza; tenth stanza.

decimal. I. *a.* decimal; pertaining to tithes. **II.** *n.* decimal.

décimanovena, *f.* one of the registers of a pipe-organ.

decímetro, *m.* decimeter.

décimo, ma, *n. & a.* tenth.

décimoctavo, va, *a.* eighteenth.

décimocuarto, ta, *a.* fourteenth.

décimonono, na, *a.* nineteenth.

décimonoveno, na, *a.* nineteenth.

décimoquinto, ta, *a.* fifteenth.

décimoséptimo, ma, *a.* seventeenth.

décimosexto, ta, *a.* sixteenth.

décimotercero, ra, *a.* thirteenth.

décimotercio, cia, *a.* thirteenth.

deciocheno, na, *n. & a.* eighteenth.

decir, *va. & vn.* (gerund, DICIENDO: *pp.* DICHO: *ind.* DIGO: *pret.* DIJE: *fut.* DIRÉ: *subj.* DIGA) to say, tell; speak; to name, call; to denote, bespeak, indicate, show, be a sign of.—**d. bien,** to be right, to speak true.—**d. mal,** to misspeak; to be mistaken.—**d. por d.,** to talk for the sake of talking —**d. para sí,** or **para su capote,** to say to oneself. —**como quien dice,** as who should say, as if to say, as if meaning.—**como quien no dice nada,** unconcernedly; and this is, or which is, no small matter.—**¡digo!** I say! hark! hear!—**el qué dirán,** what people will say.—**ello dirá,** we shall see, time will tell.—**es d.,** that is to say, that is.—**por mejor d.,** more properly speaking; rather.—**se dice,** they say, it is said.

decir, *m.* a saw, proverbial or familiar saying; witty remark; language.—**el bien d.,** elegant style of language.—**el d. de las gentes,** the opinion of the people.—**es un d.,** it is a mere saying.

decisión, *f.* decision, determination, resolution, issue; decision, judgment by court of justice; verdict by a jury.

decisivamente, *adv.* decisively.

decisivo, va, *a.* decisive, final, conclusive.

declamación, *f.* declamation, harangue, oration, speech; oratorical invective; reading, recitation; delivery in reciting.

declamador, ra, *n.* orator; reciter.

declamar, *vn.* to declaim; recite; harangue; rant.

declamatorio, ria, *a.* declamatory.

declaración, *f.* declaration; statement; interpretation, exposition; avowal; manifestation; account; overture, proposal; (law) deposition.

declaradamente, *adv.* declaredly, avowedly.

declarado, da, *a.* declared; stanch.

declarador, ra, *n. & a.* declarer (-ing); deponent.

declarante. I. *a.* declaring, expounding. **II.** *n.* declarer, deponent; witness.

declarar. I. *va.* to declare, manifest, make known, state; to expound, explain; (law) to determine and decide, to find; (law) to depose upon oath. **II.** *vr.* to declare one's opinion, to explain one's mind; (coll.) to make a declaration of love.

declarativo, va, *a.* declarative, assertive.

declaratorio, ria, *a.* declaratory, explanatory.

declinable, *a.* (gram.) declinable.

declinación, *f.* declination, descent, decay, fall, decline, falling; (gram.) declension, inflection; (ast.) declination; (arch.) deviation.—**d. de la aguja,** magnetic declination.

declinante, *a.* declining; bending down.

declinar. I. *vn.* to decline; to lean downward or to either side, to bend, slope; to descend; abate, diminish (s. o. diseases); to approach the end; (naut.) to vary from the true magnetic meridian. **II.** *va.* (gram.) to decline; (law) to challenge (a judge); to transfer to another tribunal.

declinatoria, *f.* (law) plea that questions the competency of a judge.

declinatorio, *m.* declinator (instrument).

declive, *m.* declivity, dip; descent, slope, fall; (r. w.) gradient, grade.—**en d.,** slanting, sloping.

declividad, *f.* declivity.

declivio, *m.* = DECLIVE.

decocción, *f.* decoction.

decomisar, *va.* to confiscate, seize, forfeit.

decomiso, *m.* confiscation, forfeiture, seizure.

decoración, *f.* decoration; ornament; theatrical scenery; act of committing to memory.

decorado, *m.* decoration, ornamentation; thing committed to memory.

decorador, ra, *n. & a.* decorator (-ing).

decorar, *va.* to decorate; adorn, embellish; to exalt; to learn by heart; to recite; to repeat.

decorativo, va, *a.* decorative.

decoro, *m.* honor, respect, reverence due to any person; circumspection, gravity; integrity, purity, honesty; decorum, decency, civility; fitness, propriety.

decorosamente, *adv.* decently, decorously.

decoroso, sa, *a.* decorous, decent.

decorticación, *f.* decortication.

decrecer, *vn.* (ind. DECREZCO: *subj.* DECREZCA) to decrease, diminish.

decreciente, *a.* diminishing, decreasing.

decremento, *m.* decrement, decrease.

decrepitación, *f.* (chem.) decrepitation.

decrepitante, *a.* (chem.) decrepitant.

decrepitar. I. *va.* to decrepitate, to expose to a high heat. **II.** *vn.* to decrepitate, to crackle.

decrépito, ta, *a.* decrepit.—**decrepitud,** *f.* decrepitude.

decretal, *f. & a.* decretal.

decretalista, *m.* decretist.

decretar, *va.* to decree, resolve; decide.

decretero, *m.* list of the names and offences of criminals; decretal, collection of decrees.

decretista, *m.* decretist.

decreto, *m.* decree; judicial decree or decision.

decretorio, ria, *a.* (med.) decretory, critical, determining.

decúbito, *m.* (med.) decubitus.

decuplar, decuplicar, *va.* to multiply by ten.

décuplo, pla, *n. & a.* decuple, tenfold.

decuria, *f.* decury; class of ten students.

decuriato, *m.* student belonging to a class of ten.

decurión, *m.* decurion, commander of a decury; in schools, monitor having the care of ten pupils.

decursas, *f. pl.* (law) arrears of rent.

decurrente, *a.* (bot.) decurrent.

decurso, *m.* course, lapse of time.

decusado, da, *a.* (bot.) decussate, decussated.

dechado, *m.* model; sample, pattern, standard; linen on which young girls perform several sorts of nedlework.

dedada, *f.* portion of some substance, like honey, that can be taken up with the tip of the finger. —**dar una d. de miel,** (met.) to feed one's hopes.

dedal, *m.* thimble; leather finger stall used by calkers.

dedalera, *f.* (bot.) foxglove.

dédalo, *m.* labyrinth; entanglement.

dedicación, *f.* dedication; consecration; inscription.

dedicante, *n. & a.* dedicator (-ing).

dedicar. I. *va.* (pret. DEDIQUÉ: *subj.* DEDIQUE) to dedicate, devote; to inscribe (a literary work). **II.** *vr.* (w. a) to devote one's self (to), to make a specialty (of), to interest one's self (in).

dedicativo, va, *a.* = DEDICATORIO.

dedicatoria, *f.* dedication, inscription of a book or work of art.

dedicatorio, ria, *a.* dedicatory.

dedición, *f.* unconditional surrender.

dedil, *m.* thumbstall of rubber, linen, or leather.

dedillo, ito, *m. dim.* little finger.—**saber al d.,** to have at one's finger tips.

dedo, *m.* finger; toe; forty-eighth part of a Spanish vara; finger's breadth, small bit.—**d. anular,** ring, or fourth, finger.—**d. auricular** = DEDO MEÑIQUE.—**d. del corazón, cordial,** or **de enmedio,** middle finger.—**d. gordo, d. grande,** thumb; big toe.—**d. índice,** index finger, forefinger.—**d. meñi-**

que, little finger; little toe.—**d. pulgar,** thumb: big toe.—**d. saludador** = D. ÍNDICE.—**a dos dedos,** within an inch (fig.).—**alzar el d.,** to raise one's hand (in taking an oath, etc.).

deducción, *f.* derivation, origin; deduction, inference, conclusion; (mus.) natural progression of sounds; (math.) derivation (of a formula).

deducible, *a.* deducible, inferable.

deduciente, *a.* deducing, inferring.

deducir, *va.* (*ind.* DEDUZCO: *pret.* DEDUJE: *sub.* DEDUZCA) to deduce, infer; to fetch, to devise, to draw; (law) to allege in pleading, to offer as a plea; (com.) to subtract, deduct; (math.) to derive (a formula).

deductivo, va, *a.* deducive.

defácile, *adv.* easily.

defacto, *adv.* de facto.

defalcar, *va.* = DESFALCAR.

defecación, *f.* defecation, purification; voiding of excrement.

defecadora, *f.* defecator (in sugar refining).

defecar. I. *va.* (*pret.* DEFEQUÉ: *subj.* DEFEQUE) to defecate, purify, clarify. **II.** *vn.* to defecate, void excrement; to defecate, remove impurities.

defección, *f.* defection, apostasy, desertion.

defectible, *a.* that may be faulty or lacking.

defectillo, *m. dim.* slight fault or defect.

defectivo, va, *a.* defective, imperfect; (gram.) defective.

defecto, *m.* defect, fault, blemish, imperfection. —*pl.* (print.) sheets lacking, after a day's work, to complete the full number.

defectuosamente, *adv.* defectively, faultily.

defectuoso, sa, *a.* defective, imperfect, faulty.

defendedero, ra, *a.* defensible.

defendedor, ra, *a. & n.* = DEFENSOR.

defender, *va.* (*ind.* DEFIENDO: *subj.* DEFIENDA) to defend; protect; to prohibit, forbid; to prevent, retard, delay.

defendible, *a.* defensible.

defenecer, *va.* to close (an account).

defenecimiento, *m.* (com.) settlement.

defensa, *f.* defense.—*pl.* (fort.) defenses, fortifications; (naut.) skids or skeeds, fenders;(mech.) fender, guard, pad.

defensión, *f.* safeguard, defense.

defensiva, *f.* defensive.—**estar, ponerse, a la d.,** to be or stand on the defensive.

defensivo, va. I. *a.* defensive, justificatory, defensory. **II.** *m.* defense, safeguard, preservative; (med.) compress.

defensor, ra, *n.* defender; supporter; (law), counsel for the defense, defender.

defensoría, *f.* duty and office of a defender.

defensorio, *m.* plea, defense.

deferencia, *f.* deference, condescension.

deferente, *a.* assenting, deferring to the opinion of another, deferential.

deferir. I. *vn.* (*ind.* DEFIERO: *subj.* DEFIERA) to yield, submit. **II.** *va.* to communicate; to share in jurisdiction or power.

deficiencia, *f.* deficiency.

deficiente, *a.* deficient, faulty.

déficit, *m.* deficit, shortage.

defiendo, defienda. *V.* DEFENDER.

defiero, yo defiera. *V.* DEFERIR.

definible, *a.* definable.

definición, *f.* definition; decision, determination. —*pl.* statutes of military orders.

definido, da. I. *a.* definite. **II.** *pp.* of DEFINIR.

definidor, ra. I. *n. & a.* definer (-ing). **II.** *m.* in some religious orders, member of the governing committee.

definir, *va.* to define; to establish, determine.

definitivamente, *adv.* definitively.

definitivo, va, *a.* definitive.—**en definitiva,** in conclusion; in short.

definitorio, *m.* governing chapter or assembly of a religious order; house or hall where such a chapter is held.

deflagración, *f.* deflagration, sudden burning.

deflagrador, *m.* deflagrator, ignitor.

deflagrar, *va.* to deflagrate.

deflegmar, *va.* (chem.) to dephlegmate.

defoliación, *f.* defoliation, shedding of leaves.

deformación, *f.* deformation; defacing.

deformador, ra, *n. & a.* deformer (-ing); defacer (-ing).

deformar. I. *va.* to deform, disfigure, misshape. **II.** *vr.* to become deformed, lose or change its shape.

deformatorio, ria, *a.* deforming, disfiguring.

deforme, *a.* deformed, disfigured; hideous.

deformemente, *adv.* deformedly.

deformidad, *f.* deformity; hideousness, ugliness; gross error.

defraudación, *f.* defrauding, defalcation; fraud, deceit.

defraudador, ra, *n.* defrauder, defaulter.

defraudar, *va.* to defraud; to rob of; to intercept (light); to disturb (sleep).

defuera, *adv.* externally, outwardly, on the outside.—**por d.,** outwardly.

defunción, *f.* death, demise.

degeneración, *f.* degeneration, degeneracy.

degenerado, da, *n. & a.* degenerate.

degenerar, *vn.* to degenerate.

deglución, *f.* (med.) deglutition, swallowing.

deglutir, *va.* to swallow.

degollación, *f.* decollation, beheading.

degolladero, *m.* throttle, windpipe; shambles, slaughterhouse; stand with block where people were beheaded; in ancient theatres, board that partitioned the pit.

degollado, *m.* low neck cut in a waist.

degollador, *m.* headsman, executioner.

degolladura, *f.* cutting of the throat; (mas.) joint; (carp.) slender part of balusters; low neck cut in a waist.

degollante, *n.* (coll.) bore, nuisance.

degollar, *va.* (*ind.* DEGÜELLO: *subj.* DEGÜELLE) to behead, decapitate; to cut (a waist) low in the neck; to destroy, ruin; (coll.) to importune.

degollina, *f.* (coll.) slaughter, butchery.

degradación, *f.* degradation, humiliation, debasement; depravity, baseness, degeneracy; (art.) degradation, diminution, blending.

degradante, *a.* degrading.

degrador. I. *va.* to degrade, debase; humiliate, revile. **II.** *vr.* to degrade or lower one's self.

degu, *m.* a ratlike Chilean rodent.

degüello, degüelle. *V.* DEGOLLAR.

degüello, *m.* decollation, act of beheading or cutting the throat; neck or narrow part of many things; destruction, ruin; putting to the sword; attack without quarter.—**tirar al d.,** to endeavor to harm or ruin a person.

degustación, *f.* act of tasting.

dehesa, *f.* pasture ground.

dehesar, *va.* to turn into pasture ground.

dehesero, *m.* keeper of a pasture ground.

dehiscencia, *f.* (bot.) dehiscence.

deicida, *m.* deicide, slayer of a god.

deicidio, *m.* deicide, murder of a god; slaying of Jesus.

deidad, *f.* deity, divinity; god, goddess.

deificación, *f.* deification.

deificar, *va.* (*pret.* DEIFIQUÉ: *subj.* DEIFIQUE) to deify; to exalt or praise extravagantly, lionize.

deífico, *a.* deific, deifical, divine.

deiforme, *a.* deiform, godlike.

Deípara, *f.* Deipara, the Mother of God (app. to the Virgin Mary).

deísmo, *m.* deism.—**deísta,** *n. & a.* deist (-ic).

deja, *f.* prominence between two fissures or notches.

dejación, *f.* abandonment, relinquishment, giving up; (law) assignment.

dejada, *f.* relinquishment.

dejadez, *f.* slovenliness, neglect.

dejado, da. I. *a.* slovenly; indolent, negligent; dejected, low-spirited. **II.** *pp.* of DEJAR.

dejamiento, *m.* act of leaving, relinquishing, or giving up; indolence, carelessness; languor, depression of spirits; abdication, resignation; coolness, indifference, estrangement.

dejar. I. *va.* to leave; to let; let go, relinquish; to permit, consent, allow; to leave, abandon; forsake, desert; to yield, produce, bring (as income, profit); to commit, give in charge, intrust; to deliver, deposit (as money); to fling up, to give up; to lay away.—**d. cargado,** to debit.—**d. dicho,** to leave word or orders.—**d. en cueros,** to strip (one) of one's money or property.—**d. escrito,** to leave in writing.—**d. fresco,** to frustrate, to baffle. **II.** *vr.* not to take care of one's self; to let or allow one's self (to die, be robbed, etc.); to become languid; to abandon one's self.—**d. caer** (w. **con** before noun or phrase) to insinuate, bring up as if casually; to drop in, appear unexpectedly; to give up.—**d. de,** to stop, set aside, leave off.—**d. ver,** to be seen, to be easy to see; to be seen, or appear, in public, at friends' homes, etc. **III.** *vn.* (w. **de** and *inf.*) to cease, stop (followed by present participle); to fail to.—**d. de ser,** to cease to be, disappear, die, be no longer.—**no d. de ser,** (w. *a.*) to be, to be rather.—**no d. de tener,** not to be without, not to lack.

dejativo, va, *a.* lazy, slovenly, indolent.

dejillo, *m. dim.* slight relish or taste which remains after eating or drinking.

dejo, *m.* abandonment, relinquishment; end, termination; negligence, slovenliness; relish or taste which remains after eating or drinking; effect; peculiar inflection or accent in speaking.

de jure, de jure.

del, *contraction of* DE *and* EL: of the.

delación, *f.* accusation, information.

delantal, *m.* apron; dashboard of a carriage.

delante, *adv.* before, ahead, in front.—**d. de,** *prep.* before, in front of, in the presence of.

delantera, *f.* front, fore end, fore part; front seats in theaters, etc.; fore skirt, fore part of garments; boundary line of a town, village, property; lead, advance, advantage.

delantero, ra. I. *a.* foremost, first; front (u. a.) **II.** *m.* postilion.

delatable, *a.* accusable, blamable.

delatante, *n.* informer, accuser.

delatar, va. to inform against, accuse, denounce.

delator, ra, *n.* accuser, informer, denouncer.

dele, *m.* (print.) dele, mark of deletion, delete (δ).

delectación, *f.* delectation, pleasure, delight.

delegación, *f.* delegation; power conferred; proxy; office of a delegate.

delegado, da, *n.* delegate, proxy.

delegante, *n.* constituent, one that delegates.

delegar, va. (DELEGUÉ; DELEGUE) to delegate.

deleitabilísimo, ma, *a. sup.* most delightful.

deleitable, *a.* delectable, delightful.

deleitablemente, *adv.* delightfully.

deleitación, *f.,* **deleitamiento,** *m.* delectation, pleasure, delight.

deleitante, *a.* delighting, delightful.

deleitar. I. *va.* to delight, please. **II.** *vr.* to delight, take delight or pleasure.

deleite, *m.* pleasure, delight, gratification; lust, carnal appetite.

deleitosamente, *adv.* delightfully; cheerfully.

deleitoso, sa, *a.* delightful, pleasing.

deletéreo, sa, *a.* deleterious, poisonous.

deletreador, *m.* speller.

deletrear, va. to spell, to read by spelling; to decipher or interpret.

deletreo, *m.* spelling; reading by spelling.

deleznable, *a.* crumbly; fragile, frail, perishable; smooth, slippery.

délfico, ca, *a.* Delphian, of Delphi.

delfín, *m.* (icht.) dolphin; (ast.) Dolphin, a northern constellation; dauphin, formerly the eldest son of the King of France.

delfina, *f.* dauphiness.

delgadamente, *adv.* thinly, delicately; acutely, sharply, finely.

delgadez, *f.* thinness, tenuity; acuteness, ingenuity; slenderness, leanness.

delgado, da. I. *a.* thin; lean; lank, slender, slim; light, delicate, tenuous; acute, fine, ingenious, sharp; (agr.) poor, exhausted. **II.** *m.* (naut.) dead rise; flank of an animal.

delgaducho, cha, *a.* thinnish, lanky.

deliberación, *f.* deliberation.

deliberadamente, *adv.* deliberately.

deliberante, *a.* deliberating, deliberative.

deliberar. I. *vn.* to deliberate, ponder; to consult or take counsel together. **II.** *va.* to determine after mature consideration.

deliberativo, va, *a.* deliberative.

delicadamente, *adv.* delicately.

delicadez, *f.* delicateness, weakness of constitution; prudery; overscrupulosity.

delicadeza, *f.* delicacy, fineness, refinement; sensitiveness; daintiness, tenderness, softness; scrupulosity, susceptibility; subtlety, dexterity; acuteness of understanding, refinement of wit; perspicacity.

delicado, da, *a.* delicate; gentle, refined; effeminate, finical, ladylike; sensitive, susceptible; delicate, exquisite, delicious; thin, slender; subtile; fastidious, prudish; scrupulous, honest, upright; arduous, difficult; captious, suspicious.

delicia, *f.* delight, satisfaction; sensual pleasure.

deliciosamente, *adv.* deliciously, delightfully.

delicioso, sa, *a.* delicious, delightful.

delictivo, va, *a.* relating to crime or guilt.

delicuescencia, *f.* (chem.) deliquescence.

delicuescente, *a.* (chem.) deliquescent.

delimitación, delimitar = DEMARCACIÓN, DEMARCAR.

delincuencia, *f.* delinquency, guilt.

delincuente. I. *n.* delinquent, offender. **II.** *a.* delinquent, guilty.

delineación, *f.* delineation, draft, sketch.

delineador, ra, *n.* delineator, draftsman, designer.

delineam(i)ento, *m.* = DELINEACIÓN.

delineante. I. *a.* designing. **II.** *n.* draftsman.

delinear, va. to delineate, draw, sketch, design.

delinquimiento, *m.* delinquency, guilt.

delinquir, *vn.* (*inf.* DELINCO: *subj.* DELINCA) to transgress, to offend, to be guilty.

delio, *m.* Delian, from or of Delos.

deliquio, *m.* swoon, faint; ecstasy, rapture.

delirante, *a.* delirious.

delirar, *vn.* to be delirious; to rave; to rant, talk nonsense.

delirio, *m.* delirium; frenzied rapture; rant, nonsense.

delírium tremens, *m.* delirium tremens.

delito, *m.* delict, transgression of a law; crime.

delta. I. *f.* delta (Δ), fourth letter of the Greek alphabet. **II.** *m.* delta (of a river).

deltoideo, a, *a.* deltoid, triangular.

deltoides. I. *a.* deltaic, deltoid. **II.** *m.* (anat.) deltoid.

delusivo, va, *a.* delusive, fallacious.

delusoriamente, *adv.* delusively, deceitfully.

delusorio, ria, *a.* deceitful, fallacious.

demacración, *f.* (med.) emaciation, marasmus.

demacrar. I. *va.* to cause wasting of. **II.** *vr.* to waste away.

demagogia, *f.* demagogism; demagogy.

demagógico, ca, *a.* demagogical.

demagogo, ga, *n.* demagogue.

demanda, *f.* demand, claim, complaint; request; petition, the act of asking charity; gathering, charity-box; image carried about by beggars of alms; question, inquiry; enterprise, endeavor; (com.) demand, call; (law) claim; (naut.) lookout.

demandadero, ra, *n.* messenger to do errands in convents or prisons.

demandado, da. I. *n.* (law) defendant. **II.** *pp.* of DEMANDAR.

demandador, ra, *n.* one who claims, asks, or begs; one who solicits charity for pious uses; (law) complainant, plaintiff.

demandante, *n.* (law) complainant, plaintiff.

demandar, va. to demand, ask, solicit; to wish for, desire; (law) to enter an action against.

demarcación, f. demarcation.

demarcador, m. boundary surveyor.

demarcar, va. to demarcate, demark, limit.

demás, a. other.—**los d., las d.,** others; the others.—**lo d.,** the rest.—**por lo d.,** aside from this; as to the rest. **II.** adv. besides, moreover.—**estar d.,** to be useless or superfluous; to be unwelcome, not wanted.

demasía, f. excess, surplus, superabundance; boldness, audacity, insolence; badness, iniquity; guilt; outrage; affront; (min.) space between two claims.—**en d.,** excessively.

demasiadamente, adv. excessively; too.

demasiado, adv. too, excessively; too much.

demasiado, da, a. too, excessive; too much, too many.

demencia, f. dementia, insanity.

dementar. I. va. to render demented or insane. **II.** vr. to become demented.

demente, a. demented, mad, insane.

demérito, m. demerit, ill desert; act of demeriting.

demeritorio, ria, a. without merit, undeserving.

demisión, f. submission, humility.

democracia, f. democracy.

demócrata, m. democrat.

democráticamente, adv. democratically.

democrático, ca, a. democratic.

democratizar, va. to democratize.

demografía, f. demography.—**demográfico, ca,** a. demographic.

demógrafo, fa, n. demographist.

demoledor, ra, n. & a. demolisher (-ing).

demoler, va. (ind. DEMUELO: subj. DEMUELA) to demolish, tear down, dismantle.

demolición, f. demolition, destruction.

demonche, m. (coll.) little devil.

demoníaco, ca, a. demoniacal, devilish.

demonio. I. m. demon; evil spirit; (the) devil. **II.** interj. the deuce!

demonolatría, f. demonolatry (sp. worship of the devil).

demonología, f. demonology.

demonomancia, f. divination with the assistance of demons.

demontre. I. m. devil. **II.** interj. the deuce!

demoñejo, demoñuelo, m. dim. little demon or devil, imp.

demora, f. delay, procrastination; (naut.) bearing; (com.) demurrage; (Am.) period of eight months in which Indians are obliged to work in the mines.

demorar. I. va. to delay. **II.** vn. to delay, tarry; (naut.) to bear (la costa demora norte, the coast bears north). **III.** vr. to delay; tarry, stop (on the way).

demostino, na, a. Demosthenic, like, or relating to, Demosthenes.

demostrable, a. demonstrable.

demostrablemente, adv. demonstrably.

demostración, f. demonstration, proof; (mil.) demonstration.

demostrador, ra, n. & a. demonstrator (-ing); teacher.

demostrar, va. (ind. DEMUESTRO: subj. DEMUESTRE) to demonstrate, prove; to teach.

demostrativamente, adv. demonstratively.

demostrativo, va, a. demonstrative.

demótico, ca, a. demotic (s. o. Egyptian writing).

demudación, f. change, alteration.

demudar. I. va. to alter, change, vary; to cloak, disguise. **II.** vr. to be changed; to change color suddenly, or the expression of countenance.

demuelo, yo demuela. V. DEMOLER.

demuestro, yo demuestre. V. DEMOSTRAR.

demulcente, a. & m. demulcent, emollient.

denante, denantes, adv. (obs.) V. ANTES.

denario, ria. I. a. denary. **II.** m. denarius.

dende, prep. (obs. or prov.) since.

dendrita, f. (min.) dendrite.

dendrítico, ca, a. dendritic.

dendrografía, f. dendrology.

dendrómetro, m. (math.) dendrometer.

denegación, f. denial, refusal, denegation.

denegar, va. (ind. DENIEGO: pret. DENEGUÉ: subj. DENIEGUE) to deny, refuse, denegate.

denegrecer, va. (ind. DENEGREZCO: subj. DENEGREZCA) to blacken, darken.

denegrir, va. = DENEGRECER.

dengoso, sa, a. finicky, fastidious, overnice.

dengue, m. fastidiousness, prudery; a woman's cape with long points; boat used in the sardine fishery; dengue, or breakbone fever; influenza; affectation.

denguero, ra, a. prudish, affected.

deniego, yo deniegue. V. DENEGAR.

denigración, f. defamation, stigma, disgrace.

denigrar, va. to denigrate, revile, defame.

denigrativamente, adv. revilingly, insultingly.

denigrativo, va, a. reviling; soiling; blackening.

denodadamente, adv. bravely, resolutely.

denodado, da, a. brave, daring, intrepid.

denominación, f. denomination.

denominadamente, adv. distinctly, markedly.

denominador, m. (arith.) denominator.—**quitar, or hacer desaparecer, los denominadores,** (alg.) to clear of fractions.

denominar, va. to call, give a name to.

denominativo, va, a. denominative.

denostadamente, adv. ignominiously, insultingly.

denostador, ra, n. & a. vilifier (-ing) or reviler (-ing).

denostar, va. (ind. DENUESTO: subj. DENUESTE) to insult, to revile, abuse.

denotación, f. designation, denotation.

denotar, va. to denote, express; to explain.

denotativo, va, a. denoting, denotative.

densamente, adv. closely, densely.

densidad, f. density; closeness, compactness; specific gravity; obscurity, darkness; confusion. —**d. de población,** density of population, population per unit of area.

densímetro, m. densimeter.

denso, sa, a. dense, thick; close, compact.

dentado, da. I. a. having teeth; denticulated, dentated, serrated, toothed; crenated, indented; cogged, pronged. **II.** pp. of DENTAR.

dentadura, f. set of teeth, false cr natural.

dental. I. a. dental, belonging to the teeth or to dentistry; (gram.) dental. **II.** m. bed to which the plowshare is fixed; (agr.) teeth of a rake; fork used to separate the straw from corn.

dentar. I. va. (ind. DIENTO: subj. DIENTE) to tooth; to furnish with teeth, clogs, or prongs; to indent; to cut into teeth. **II.** vn. to teeth, cut teeth.

dentaria, f. (bot.) toothwort.

dentecillo, m. dim. small tooth.

dentejón, m. yoke for oxen.

dentellada, f. gnashing of teeth; bite, nip, seizure with the teeth; mark made by the teeth.—**a dentelladas,** with the teeth.

dentellado, da. I. a. denticulate, dented, serrated; bitten or wounded with the teeth. **II.** pp. of DENTELLAR.

dentellar, vn. to chatter (s. o. the teeth).

dentellear, va. to bite; to bite on or into.

dentellón, m. piece of a door lock; (arch.) dentil.

dentera, f. tooth edge; (coll.) envy.—**dar d.,** to set the teeth on edge; to cause great desire or longing, make one's mouth water.

dentezuelo, m. dim. little tooth.

dentición, f. dentition, teething.

denticular, a. dentiform, toothlike; denticulate, toothed.

dentículo, m. (arch.) denticle, dentil.

dentífrico, ca, a. dentifrice.

dentirrostros, m. pl. (zool.) Dentirostres.

dentista, m. dentist.

dentistería, f. dentistry.

dentívano, na, *a.* having long and large teeth (s. o. horses).

dentolabial, *a.* (gram.) dentilabial.

dentón, na. I. *a.* (coll.) having large uneven teeth. **II.** *m.* a sea fish of the Sparus genus.

dentrambos, contraction of DE ENTRAMBOS, of both, from both.

dentro, *adv.* inside, within.—**d. de,** inside of.—**d. del año,** in the course of the year.—**d. de poco,** shortly.—**d. en,** in the interior of.—**a d.,** inside.—**de d.,** from inside.—**hacia d.,** towarts the interior, inwards.—**por d.,** inside, on the inside.

dentudo, da, *a.* having large uneven teeth.

denudación, *f.* (geol.) denudation.

denudar, *va.* (geol.) to denude.

denuedo, *m.* daring, bravery, intrepidity.

denuesto, *m.* affront, insult, abuse.

denuesto, denueste. *V.* DENOSTAR.

denuncia, *f.* denunciation, arraignment, accusation; announcement, declaration, proclamation; (min.) denouncement.

denunciable, *a.* that may be denounced.

denunciación, *f.* denunciation, denouncement.

denunciador, ra, *n.* denunciator, accuser; announcer; denouncer.

denunciante, *n. & a.* denouncer (-ing); informer (-ing); accuser (-ing).

denunciar, *va.* to advise, give notice; to denounce; to prognosticate, foretell; to pronounce, proclaim, publish solemnly; (min.) to denounce.

denunciatorio, ria, *a.* denunciatory.

denuncio, *m.* (min.) denouncement.

Deo gracias, *m.* Deo gratias (thanked be God), a form of greeting; submissive, humble attitude.

deontología, *f.* deontology.

Deo volente, God willing.

deparar, *va.* to offer, afford, furnish, present.

departmental, *a.* departmental.

departamento, *m.* department; compartment; section; extent of country under the jurisdiction of the admiral commanding in chief any of the four arsenals in Spain.

departidor, ra, *n.* converser, interlocutor.

departir, *vn.* to chat, talk, converse.

depauperar, *va.* to depauperate, impoverish; (med.) to weaken, exhaust.

dependencia, *f.* dependence, dependency; subordination; branch office; business, affair; trust, charge; dependence, relation; (arch.) outbuildings; relation by consanguinity or affinity.—*pl.* accessories.

depender, *vn.* (w. **de**) to depend, to rely (on).

dependiente. I. *a.* dependent, subordinate. **II.** *m.* clerk.

dependientemente, *adv.* dependently.

depilatorio, a, *a.* depilatory.

deplorable, *a.* deplorable, lamentable, pitiful.

deplorablemente, *adv.* deplorably, sadly.

deplorar, *va.* to deplore, lament, regret.

deponente, *n. & a.* deposer (-ing), deponent; (gram.) deponent.

deponer. I. *va.* (*pp.* DEPUESTO: *ind.* DEPONGO: *pret.* DEPUSE: *fut.* DEPONDRÉ: *subj.* DEPONGA) to lay by, put aside; to depose, remove from office; (law) to attest, depose; to take down, remove. **II.** *vn.* to evacuate the bowels; (law) to depose, testify.

depopulador, ra, *n. & a.* depopulator (-ing); devastator (-ing).

deportación, *f.* deportation, banishment.

deportar, *va.* to deport, exile, banish.

deporte, *m.* sport; amusement, recreation.

deportismo, *m.* sports, sporting.

deportista, *n.* sportsman (-woman).

deportivo, va, *a.* sporting, sport (u. a.)

deposición, *f.* assertion, affirmation; deposition; degradation from dignity or station; (law) deposition, testimony; evacuation (of the bowels).

depositador, ra, *n.* depositor.

depositante, *n. & a.* depositor (-ing).

depositar. I. *va.* to deposit; to intrust, confide; to put (a person) in safety, to bring (a person) out of danger of violence or intimidation; to inclose; to place (a corpse) in a receiving vault; to lay aside, put away. **II.** *vr.* (chem.) to settle.

depositaria, *f.* depository; subtreasury; dignity and office of a depositary; trust.

depositario, ria. I. *a.* relating to a depository. **II.** *n.* depositary, trustee, receiver.

depósito, *m.* deposit, trust, depository; (com.) store, warehouse, depot; (mech.) chamber; (chem.) deposit, precipitate, sediment; (geol.) deposition.—**d. de agua,** tank, reservoir.—**en d.,** deposited; in bond.

depravación, *f.* depravation, depravity.

depravadamente, *adv.* depravedly.

depravado, da, *a.* depraved, lewd.

depravador, ra, *n.* depraver, corrupter.

depravar, *va.* to deprave, corrupt.

deprecación, *f.* petition, prayer, entreaty.

deprecante, *a.* supplicating, pleading.

deprecar, *va.* (*pret.* DEPREQUÉ: *subj.* DEPREQUE) to entreat, implore.

deprecativo, va; deprecatorio, ria, *a.* = DEPRECANTE.

depreciación, *f.* depreciation.

depreciar. I. *va.* to depreciate, to reduce the price of; to undervalue. **II.** *vr.* to depreciate.

depredación, *f.* depredation, plundering; malversation committed by guardians or trustees.

depredador, ra, *n. & a.* depradator (-ing), marauder (-ing).

depredar, *va.* to depredate, maraude, pillage.

depresión, *f.* depression, pressing down; (ast. and naut.) depression, dip; (com.) dulness, decline.—**d. de horizonte,** (naut.) dip of the horizon.

depresivo, va, *a.* depressive, depressing.

depresor, ra, *n. & a.* depressor (-ing); oppressor (-ing).

deprimente, *a.* = DEPRESIVO.

deprimir. I. *va.* to depress, compress; to humiliate; to belittle, make light of. **II.** *vr.* to become depressed or compressed; to be or seem lower.

de profundis, *m.* De Profundis, the 130th psalm, sung at funerals.

depuesto, *pp. irr.* of DEPONER.

depurable, *a.* purifiable.

depuración, *f.* purification.

depurar, *va.* to depurate, purify.

depurativo, va. I. *a.* purifying. **II.** *m.* (med.) depurative.

deputar, *va.* = DIPUTAR.

deque, *adv.* (coll.) since.

derecera, *f.* straight way or road.

derecha, *f.* right hand; right side; (pol.) right, moderate or conservative party.—**a la d.,** to the right, on the right-hand side; (mil.) right about.—**a. derechas,** or **las derechas,** right, well done; honestly, rightly, justly.—**a tuertas o derechas,** right or wrong; inconsiderately.

derechamente, *adv.* directly, straight; wisely; honestly, justly.

derechera, *f.* direct or straight road; short cut.

derechero, *m.* clerk who collects fees.

derecho, *m.* right; law; equity; exemption, frank, grant, privilege; road, path; right side (of cloth, etc.).—*pl.* fees, dues, taxes, duties.—**d. administrativo,** administrative law; collection of ordinances, regulations, etc.—**d. canónico,** canon law.—**d. civil,** or **común,** civil law.—**d. consuetudinario,** common law, law established by custom and precedent.—**d. de gentes,** international law; jus gentium (among the Romans).—**d. de visita,** right of search.—**d. diferencial de bandera,** differential duties.—**d. divino,** right divine.—**d. internacional,** international law.—**d. mercantil,** commercial law.—**d. municipal,** municipal law.—**d. natural,** natural right.—**d. no escrito** = D. CONSUETUDINARIO.—**d. penal,** criminal law.—**d. positivo,** positive law.—**de d.,** de jure.—**derechos consulares,** consular fees.—**derechos de aduana,** custom-house duties.—**derechos de almacenaje,** storage

—**derechos de anclaje,** anchorage dues.—**derechos de depósito** = DERECHOS DE ALMACENAJE.—**derechos de entrada,** import duties.—**derechos de muelle,** wharfage, pierage.—**derechos de puerto,** harbor dues, port dues.—**derechos de remolque,** towage.—**derechos reales,** inheritance tax; duty on transfer of real estate.

derecho, *adv.* = DERECHAMENTE.

derecho, cha, *a.* straight; right, (opposite to left); right-handed; just, lawful, reasonable, legitimate; (mech.) standing, upright.—**d. la caña,** (naut.) right the helm.—**hecho y d.,** perfect, complete; in all respects; grown up; true, certain; without doubt.

derechuelo, *m.* first seams taught to little girls.

derechura, *f.* straightness.—**en d.,** by the most direct road; as the crow flies.

deriva, *f.* (naut.) ship's course; deviation, drift; (aer.) drift; drifting.

derivación, *f.* derivation, descent; deduction, inference; draining of water, turning of its course; (gram.) derivation; (elec.) branch, tap (of a wire, current, etc.); shunt.—**en d.,** (elec.) shunt (u. a.); shunted.

derivada, *f.* (math.) derivative.

derivado, da, *a.* (gram.) derivative.

derivar. I. *vn.* & *vr.* to derive, proceed, descend **II.** *vn.* (naut., aer.) to drift. **III.** *va.* to guide, lead, conduct; to derive, trace to its origin; (elec.) to tap; to shunt.

derivativo, va, *a.* derivative.

derivómetro, *m.* (aer.) drift meter.

dermalgia, *f.* neuralgia of the skin.

dermatitis, *f.* dermatitis.

dermatología, *f.* dermatology.

dermatológico, ca, *a.* dermatological.

dermatólogo, ga, *n.* dermatologist.

dermatosis, *f.* dermatosis.

dermesto, *m.* (zool.) larder beetle.

dermis, *f.* derm, dermis, skin.

derogación, *f.* derogation, repeal; deterioration, diminution.

derogar, *va.* (*pret.* DEROGUÉ: *subj.* DEROGUE) to derogate, annul, revoke, repeal; to reform; to remove.

derogatorio, ria, *a.* annulling, repealing.

derrabadura, *f.* wound made in docking the tail of an animal.

derrabar, *va.* to dock the tail of.

derrama, *f.* apportionment of an assessment, tax, or contribution.

derramadamente, *adv.* profusely, lavishly; disorderly, confusedly.

derramadero, ra, *a.* = VERTEDERO.

derramado, da; derramador, ra, *a.* prodigal, extravagant.

derramamiento, *m.* pouring out; spilling, shedding; overflow; dispersion, scattering; lavishing, wasting.—**d. de sangre,** bloodshed.

derramar. I. *va.* to pour out; to spill; shed; scatter; to apportion (taxes); to publish, spread; to lavish, give freely; to waste. **II.** *vr.* to overflow, run over; to be scattered or spread; to fly abroad.

derrame, *m.* overflow, running over; spread, scattering; shedding; portion of liquor or seed lost in measuring; leakage; waste; (arch.) chamfering, splay; declivity, slope; (naut.) draft of a sail; outlet of a ravine, driftway; (med.) effusion, discharge.

derramo, *m.* (arch.) chamfering, splay, flare, bevel, flanging of a door or window.

derrape, *m.* (aer.) yawing.

derraspado, *a.* beardless (wheat).

derredor, *m.* circumference, circuit.—**al d.,** or **en d.,** round about.—**al d. de, en d. de,** about, around.

derrelicto, a. I. *a.* abandoned, forsaken; derelict. **II.** *m.* (naut.) derelict.

derrelinquir, *va.* (*pp.* DERRELICTO: *ind.* DERRELINCO: *subj.* DERRELINCA) to abandon, forsake.

derrenegar, *vn.* (*for. irr. v.* NEGAR).—**d. de,** (coll.) to hate, detest, loathe, abhor.

derrengada, *f.* (prov.) a step in dancing.

derrengado, da. I. *a.* bent, crooked; lame, crippled. **II.** *pp.* of DERRENGAR.

derrengadura, *f.* dislocation of the hip; lameness.

derrengar, *va.* (*ind.* DERRIENGO: *subj.* DERRIENGUE) to sprain or dislocate the hip of; to break or injure the spine of; to cripple; to bend, make crooked; to knock (the fruit) off a tree.

derrengo, *m.* stick with which fruits are knocked down.

derreniego, *m.* (coll.) V. RENIEGO.

derretido, da. I. *a.* enamored, deeply in love; melted. **II.** *pp.* of DERRETIR.

derretimiento, *m.* thaw, liquefaction, fusion, melting; consuming love or passion.

derretir. I. *va.* (*ind.* DERRITO; *subj.* DERRITA) to liquefy, melt, fuse; (coll.) to change (money); to consume, expend, waste, exhaust. **II.** *vr.* to fuse, melt, thaw; to be deeply in love; to fall in love very easily; to grow tender or loving, to be very impatient.

derribado, da. I. *a.* having round and low buttocks (s. o. horses). **II.** *pp.* of DERRIBAR.

derribador, *m.* feller of beeves at abattoirs.

derribar. I. *va.* to throw down, knock down; overthrow; fell; to demolish, tear down; to strike down (a bull) with a pike on horseback; to subdue (a passion). **II.** *vr.* to tumble down, to throw one's self on the ground.

derribo, *m.* demolition, pulling down; debris, ruins.

derriengo, yo derriengue. V. DERRENGAR.

derrito, derrita. V. DERRETIR.

derrocadero, *m.* rocky precipice.

derrocamiento, *m.* throwing down, overthrow.

derrocar, *va.* to precipitate or fling down from a rock; to pull down, demolish; to pull down (from office, position, etc.), put down; to oust; to dethrone, overthrow.

derrochador, ra, *n.* prodigal, spendthrift, squanderer.

derrochar, *va.* to waste, squander.

derroche, *m.* waste, squandering.

derrota, *f.* defeat, rout; overthrow; route, road, path, track; (naut.) ship's course;

derrotar, *va.* to defeat; to waste away, wear away; to ruin; (naut.) to cause to drift.

derrote, *m.* thrust of a bull's horn.

derrotero, *m.* (naut.) collection of seacharts; ship's course; navigation track or route; course, way or plan of life, conduct, or action.

derrubiar, *va.* to undermine or wash away.

derrubio, *m.* alluvion, alluvium.

derruir, *va.* (*ind.* DERRUYO: *subj.* DERRUYA) to demolish, tear down, raze, destroy.

derrumbadero, *m.* precipice; craggy, steep, and broken ground; arduous affair.

derrumbamiento, *m.* landslide; collapse; downfall.

derrumbar. I. *va.* to throw down headlong. **II.** *vr.* to throw one's self headlong; to sink down, crumble away, tumble down.

derrumbe, *m.* tumbling down, collapse; landslide.

derviche, *m.* dervish.

desabarrancar, *va.* (*for mut. v.* ABARRANCAR) to drag, draw, or pull out of a ditch; to disentangle, extricate.

desabastecer, *va.* (*for mut. v.* ABASTECER) not to supply with provisions.

desabejar, *va.* to remove bees from.

desabillé, *m.* dishabille; house or morning gown.

desabitar, *va.* (naut.) to unbitt.

desabollador, *m.* an instrument used by tinworkers; tinker, planisher.

desabollar, *va.* to tinker.

desabonarse, *vr.* to discontinue a subscription.

desabono, *m.* discontinuance of a subscription; prejudice, injury.

desabor, *m.* inspidity, want of taste.

desabordarse, *vr.* (naut.) to get clear of a ship which has run foul of one's vessel.

desaborido, da, *a.* tasteless, insipid; without substance; (coll.) dull, witless.

desabotonar. I. *va.* to unbutton. **II.** *vn.* to blow, bloom, blossom.

desabozar, *va.* (naut.) to unstopper.

desabridamente, *adv.* without taste or flavor; rudely, disagreeably.

desabrido, da, *a.* tasteless, insipid; rude, disagreeable, peevish; kicking (gun); bleak, sharp.

desabrigadamente, *adv.* without covering; without shelter.

desabrigado, da, *a.* uncovered; shelterless; harborless; without support.

desabrigar, *va.* (*for mut. v.* ABRIGAR) to uncover; to strip; to deprive of shelter or harbor.

desabrigo, *m.* lack of covering, clothing, shelter or harbor; destitution.

desabrillantar, *va.* & *vr.* to disluster.

desabrimiento, *m.* insipidity, flatness; rudeness, disagreeableness; despondency, lowness of spirits; recoil of firearms.

desabrir, *va.* to impart a bad taste to; to vex, plague, torment, harass.

desabrochar. I. *va.* to unclasp, unbutton, unfasten; burst open. **II.** *vr.* to unbosom, to open one's heart.

desacalorarse, *vr.* to cool off.

desacatadamente, *adv.* disrespectfully.

desacatado, da. I. *a.* disrespectful. **II.** *pp.* of DESACATAR.

desacatador, ra, *n.* irreverent, uncivil, or disrespectful person.

desacatamiento, *m.* disrespect.

desacatar, *va.* to treat disrespectfully; to desecrate, profane; dishonor.

desacato, *m.* disrespect, incivility; lack of reverence; desecration, profanation.

desaceitado, da, *a.* lacking oil.

desaceitar, *va.* to take off oil or grease from.

desacerar, *va.* to unsteel.

desacerbar, *va.* to temper, sweeten, take away harshness and bitterness from.

desacertadamente, *adv.* unwisely; wrongly or erroneously.

desacertado, da, *a.* wrong, mistaken; unwise.

desacertar, *vnr.* (*for irr. v.* ACERTAR) to err, make a mistake, act unwisely.

desacidificar, *va.* to remove acidity from; to neutralize (an acid).

desacierto, *m.* error, mistake, blunder.

desacobardar, *va.* to remove fear from; to encourage, reassure.

desacollar, *va.* (*for irr. v.* ACOLLAR) to dig up the ground about (vines).

desacomodadamente, *adv.* incommodiously, inconveniently.

desacomodado, da. I. *a.* destitute of conveniences; out of employment; out of service; troublesome. **II.** *pp.* of DESACOMODAR.

desacomodamiento, *m.* inconvenience, trouble.

desacomodar. I. *va.* to inconvenience; to trouble, discommode; to discharge, dismiss. **II.** *vr.* to lose one's place (s. o. servants).

desacomodo, *m.* discharge; loss of a place or position.

desacompañamiento, *m.* lack of company or society.

desacompañar, *va.* to leave the company of.

desaconsejado, da. I. *a.* ill-advised, imprudent. **II.** *pp.* of DESACONSEJAR.

desaconsejar, *va.* to dissuade.

desacoplar, *va.* to unfasten, disconnect.

desacordadamente, *adv.* unwisely, unadvisedly.

desacordado, da; desacordante, *a.* discordant.

desacordar. I. *va.* (*for irr. v.* ACORDAR) to untune. **II.** *vr.* to be forgetful.

desacorde, *a.* discordant; inharmonious, incongruous.

desacorralar, *va.* to let out of the corral or penfold; to bring (a bull) into the ring or open field.

desacostumbradamente, *adv.* unusually.

desacostumbrado, da. I. *a.* unaccustomed, not used; unusual. **II.** *pp.* of DESACOSTUMBRAR.

desacostumbrar, *va.* to disaccustom, break of a habit.

desacotar, *va.* to lay open (a pasture); to take down (fences); to raise or withdraw (a prohibition); to withdraw from (an agreement); among boys, to play without conditions or rules; to reject, refuse.

desacoto, *m.* taking fences off a pasture-ground; raising a prohibition.

desacreditar, *va.* to discredit; bring discredit on, injure the credit or reputation of.

desacuerdo, *m.* discordance, disagreement; error, mistake, blunder; forgetfulness; mental derangement.

desacuerdo, yo desacuerde. *V.* DESACORDAR.

desacuñador, *m.* (print.) shooting stick.

desacuñar, *va.* (print.) to unwedge, loosen.

desaderezar, *va.* to ruffle, disarrange.

desadeudar, *va.* & *vr.* to free from debt.

desadorar, *va.* to cease to worship or love.

desadormecer, *va.* (*for irr. v.* ADORMECER) to wake, to rouse.

desadornar, *va.* to divest of ornaments.

desadorno, *m.* want of embellishments and charms.

desadvertidamente, *adv.* inadvertently.

desadvertido, da. I. *a.* unwise, imprudent; unnoticed. **II.** *pp.* of DESADVERTIR.

desadvertimiento, *m.* unwisdom; lack of reflection, thoughtlessness.

desadvertir, *va.* (*for irr. v.* ADVERTIR) to give no heed to, not to notice.

desafear, *va.* to remove or lessen the blemishes of.

desafección, *f.* disaffection.

desafecto, ta. I. *a.* disaffected; opposed. **II.** *m.* disaffection, discontent.

desaferrar, *va.* (naut.) to loosen, unfasten; unmoor, heave out; to convince, bring to a change of opinion.

desafiadero, *m.* private dwelling ground.

desafiador, ra, *n.* challenger, duellist; one who dares or defies.

desafianzador, ra, *n.* one who withdraws security.

desafiar, *va.* to challenge, dare; to defy; to rival, oppose, compete with.

desafición, *f.* disaffection.

desaficionar, *va.* & *vr.* to destroy or lose the desire, wish, or affection of.

desafijar, *va.* to disown as a son.

desafinación, *f.* discordance, being out of tune.

desafinadamente, *adv.* dissonantly or discordantly.

desafinar. I. *vn.* to be inharmonious, to be out of tune; to speak irrelevantly. **II.** *vr.* to get out of tune.

desafío, *m.* challenge; duel; struggle, contest, rivalry, competition.

desaforadamente, *adv.* disorderly, excessively, outrageously, impudently.

desaforado, da. I. *a.* disorderly, lawless; impudent, outrageous; huge, uncommonly large. **II.** *pp.* of DESAFORAR.

desaforar. I. *va.* to encroach upon the rights of; (mil.) to cashier. **II.** *vr.* to be outrageous or disorderly.

desaforrar, *va.* to take off the lining of; (naut.) to unserve, unsheath.

desafortunado, da, *a.* unfortunate, unlucky.

desafuero, *m.* excess, outrage, open violence.

desagarrar, *va.* (coll.) to unfasten, loosen.

desagitadera, *f.* instrument used in removing honey-comb.

desagitar, *va.* to remove honeycombs from.

desagraciado, da, *a.* ungraceful.

desagraciar, *va.* to disfigure, make ungraceful.

desagradable, *a.* disagreeable, unpleasant, uncomfortable.

desagradablemente, *adv.* disagreeably.

desagradar, *va.* to displease, offend.

desagradecer, *va.* (*for irr. v.* AGRADECER) to be ungrateful.

desagradecidamente, *adv.* ungratefully.

desagradecido, da, *a.* ungrateful.

desagradecimiento, *n.* ingratitude.

desagrado, *m.* discontent, displeasure.

desagraviar, *va.* to right a wrong to, to apologize to; to indemnify.

desagravio, *m.* satisfaction for an injury; compensation for damages; vindication.

desagregación, *f.* disintegration, segregation.

desagregar, *va.* (*for mut. v.* AGREGAR) to disjoin, separate, disintegrate, segregate.

desaguadero, *m.* drain, waste pipe, outlet; drain of money.

desaguador, *m.* small drain for irrigation.

desaguar. I. *va.* to drain, empty; to squander, waste. **II.** *vn.* to flow, disembogue. **III.** *vr.* to discharge by vomit or stools.

desaguazar, *va.* to drain.

desagüe, *m.* drainage; drain, outlet; waste.

desaguisado, da. I. *a.* lawless, illegal, unjust. **II.** *m.* offence, injury, wrong, outrage.

desaherrojar, *va.* to unchain, unshackle.

desahijar. I. *va.* to wean; to separate (the young) from the dams. **II.** *vr.* to breed swarms (s. o. bees).

desahitarse, *vr.* to relieve indigestion.

desahogadamente, *adv.* comfortably, easily; freely, unobstructedly; in a brazen-faced or unconcerned manner, brazenly.

desahogado, da. I. *a.* petulant, impudent, brazen-faced; clear, free, unencumbered; in comfortable circumstances; (naut.) having sea room. **II.** *pp.* of DESAHOGAR.

desahogar. I. *va.* (*for mut. v.* AHOGAR) to ease the pain of, alleviate, relieve. **II.** *vr.* to recover from fatigue or disease; to unbosom, to disclose one's grief; to give a piece of one's mind; to express one's feelings; to extricate one's self from debt.

desahogo, *m.* ease, relief from pain, work, or affliction; unbosoming or disclosing one's troubles or grief; laxity; comfort, ease; comfortable circumstances.

desahuciadamente, *adv.* hopelessly.

desahuciado, da. I. *a.* despaired of, hopeless. **II.** *pp.* of DESAHUCIAR.

desahuciar, *va.* to take away all hope from; to give over; to declare (a patient) past recovery; to dispossess or oust (a tenant).

desahucio, *m.* dispossession of a tenant.

desahumado, da. I. *a.* mild, faded, vapid (liquor). **II.** *pp.* of DESAHUMAR.

desahumar, *va.* to free from smoke.

desainadura, *f.* a disease of horses caused by melting of their fat from overwork.

desainar. I. *va.* to remove the fat of (an animal); to lessen or diminish the thickness or substance of. **II.** *vr.* to lose fat.

desairadamente, *adv.* unhandsomely, clumsily, gracelessly.

desairado, da. I. *a.* unhandsome, graceless; disregarded, slighted, unrewarded, unsuccessful **II.** *pp.* of DESAIRAR.

desairar, *va.* to disregard, to slight, to ignore; to treat with disrespect; to rebuff.

desaire, *m.* slight, rebuff, disdain, disrespect; awkwardness, clumsiness.

desaislarse, *vr.* to cease to be insulated or isolated; to leave one's seclusion.

desajustar. I. *va.* to disarrange, disadjust. **II.** *vr.* to disagree, to withdraw from an agreement; to get out of order or adjustment.

desajuste, *m.* disarrangement, lack of adjustment; disagreement.

desalabanza, *f.* vituperation, disparagement.

desalabar, *va.* to dispraise, belittle, disparage.

desalabear, *va.* (carp.) to straighten.

desalabeo, *m.* (carp.) straightening.

desaladamente, *adv.* anxiously, swiftly, eagerly; greedily; hurriedly.

desalado, da, *a.* hasty, impatient, disordinate.

desaladura, *f.* (chem.) = DESALAZÁN.

desalar. I. *va.* to cut off the wings of; to remove the salt from. **II.** *vr.* to run or walk swiftly; to be in great haste; to long for, to crave; to lose its salt (s. o. of fish, meat, etc.)

desalazón, *f.* (chem.) removing the salt from a liquid.

desalbardar, *va.* to take off the packsaddle from.

desalentadamente, *adv.* faintly, feebly.

desalentador, ra, *a.* dispiriting, discouraging.

desalentar. I. *va.* (*for irr. v.* ALENTAR) to put out of breath by labor; to discourage, to dismay. **II.** *vr.* to jade.

desalfombrar, *va.* to take up the carpets from.

desalforjar. I. *va.* to take out of a saddlebag. **II.** *vr.* (coll.) to loosen one's garments; to make one's self easy.

desalhajar, *va.* to strip of fine furniture.

desaliento, *m.* dismay, depression of spirits, discouragement, dejection; faintness, languor.

desaliento, yo desaliente. *V.* DESALENTAR.

desalineación, *f.* lack of alinement; getting or putting out of alinement.

desalinear, *va.* to throw out of alinement.

desaliñadamente, *adv.* slovenly, uncleanly.

desaliñar, *va.* & *vr.* to disarrange, disorder, ruffle; to make slovenly or dirty.

desaliño, *m.* slovenliness, negligence of dress; disarray; neglect.—*pl.* very long earrings.

desalivación, *f.* salivation.

desalivar, *vn.* to salivate.

desalmadamente, *adv.* soullessly, inhumanly.

desalmado, da. I. *a.* soulless, inhuman, merciless; impious, profligate. **II.** *pp.* of DESALMAR.

desalmamiento, *m.* inhumanity; perversity.

desalmar, *va.* & *vr.* to long for eagerly, to crave.

desalmenado, da, *a.* stripped of battlements or merlons.

desalmidonar, *va.* to take the starch out of.

desalojamiento, *m.* dislodging; displacing.

desalojar. I. *va.* to dislodge, dispossess, oust, evict, eject; to displace. **II.** *vn.* to quit one's lodgings; to move out.

desalquilado, da, *a.* unrented, vacant.

desalquilar, *va.* & *vr.* to leave or cause to leave (a rented room or house); to become vacant.

desalterar, *va.* to allay, assuage, calm down.

desalumbradamente, *adv.* blindly, erroneously.

desalumbrado, da, *a.* dazzled, rattled, dazed; groping in the dark.

desalumbramiento, *m.* blindness, want of judgment, foresight, or knowledge.

desamable, *a.* unlovable.

desamador, ra, *n.* one who has ceased loving; one who dislikes persons or things.

desamar, *va.* to love no more; to dislike, hate.

desamarrar. I. *va.* to untie, unbind, unlash; to separate; (naut.) to unmoor; to unbend (a rope). **II.** *vr.* to get loose; to part.

desamasado, da, *a.* dissolved, disunited.

desamigado, da, *a.* unfriendly; estranged.

desamistarse, *vr.* to fall out, to quarrel.

desamoblar, *va.* = DESAMUEBLAR.

desamoldar, *va.* to change the form, proportion, or symmetry of; to disfigure.

desamor, *m.* disaffection; lack of sentiment and love; enmity, hatred.

desamorado, da. I. *a.* loveless, cold-hearted. **II.** *pp.* of DESAMORAR.

desamorar. I. *va.* to extinguish the love of. **II.** *vr.* to cease loving.

desamoroso, sa, *a.* unloving.

desamorrar, *va.* (coll.) to make lively, make (a person) talk.

desamortajar, *va.* to disenshroud.

desamortización, *f.* disentail.

desamortizador, ra, *a.* disentailing.

desamortizar, *va.* (AMORTIZAR) to disentail.

desamotinarse, *vr.* to withdraw from mutiny.

desamparadamente, *adv.* helplessly.

desamparado, da, I. *pp.* of DESAMPARAR. **II.** *a.* forsaken; needy, helpless.

desamparador, ra, *n.* & *a.* forsaker (-ing).

desamparar, *va.* to forsake, abandon, leave; to quit; (naut.) to dismantle, dismast.

desamparo, *m.* abandonment, desertion; want of protection, helplessness, neediness; dereliction.

desamueblado, da, *a.* unfurnished.

desamueblar, *va.* to strip of furniture.

desanclar, desancorar, *va.* (naut.) to weigh the anchor of.

desandadura, *f.* going back over the same road.

desandar, *va.* (*pret.* DESANDUVE) to retrace.—**d. lo andado,** to undo what has been done.

desandrajado, da, *a.* ragged, in tatters.

desangramiento, *m.* bleeding to excess.

desangrar. I. *va.* to bleed to excess; to draw a large quantity of water from; to exhaust the means of, to make poor. **II.** *vr.* to lose blood, to bleed.

desanidar. I. *vn.* to leave the nest. **II.** *va.* to dislodge from a post.

desanimación, *f.* lifelessness, dullness.

desanimadamente, *adv.* spiritlessly, faintly, with discouragement.

desanimado, da, *a.* (com.) dull, flat; discouraged, disheartened.

desanimar. I. *va.* to dishearten, discourage; to damp, pall, daunt. **II.** *vr.* to jade.

desánimo, *m.* discouragement, downheartedness.

desanublar. I. *va.* & *vr.* to calm down, cool off. **II.** *va.* to elucidate, make clear.

desanudar, *va.* to untie, loosen; to extricate, disentangle.

desanudadura, *f.* untying; disentanglement.

desañudar, *va.* = DESANUDAR.

desaojadera, *f.* woman supposed to dispel charms.

desaojar, *va.* to cure of the effects of the evil eye.

desapacibilidad, *f.* disagreeableness.

desapacible, *a.* disagreeable, unpleasant.

desapaciblemente, *adv.* disagreeably.

desapadrinar, *va.* to disapprove, disavow.

desaparear, *va.* to separate (two of a pair).

desaparecer. I. *va.* (*for irr. v.* APARECER) to cause to disappear. **II.** *vn.* & *vr.* to disappear.

desaparecimiento, *m.* disappearance.

desaparejar, *va.* to unharness, unhitch; (naut.) to unrig (a ship).

desaparición, *f.* disappearance; (ast.) occultation.

desaparroquiar. I. *va.* to remove from a parish. **II.** *vr.* to remove from one parish to another; (com.) to cease to be a customer.

desapasionadamente, *adv.* dispassionately.

desapasionarse, *vr.* to root out love or fondness.

desapegarse, *vr.* to lose liking or love (for a person or thing).

desapego, *m.* loss of love, affection, or liking; coolness; impartiality, disinterestedness; indifference.

desapercibidamente, *adv.* inadvertently, unpreparedly.

desapercibido, da, *a.* unprovided; unprepared, unguarded.

desapercibimiento, *m.* unpreparedness.

desapestar, *va.* to disinfect.

desapiadadamente, *adv.* unmercifully.

desapiadado, da, *a.* merciless.

desaplicación, *f.* lack of application.

desaplicadamente, *adv.* indolently, without application.

desaplicado, da, *a.* indolent, careless, neglectful.

desaplomar, *va.* to put out of plumb.

desapoderadamente, *adv.* hastily, impetuously.

desapoderado, da. I. *a.* impetuous, unruly. **II.** *pp.* of DESAPODERAR.

desapoderamiento, *m.* seizure of another's possessions; depriving of power or authority.

desapoderar, *va.* to dispossess; to rob; to repeal or revoke the power of attorney of.

desapolillar. I. *va.* to free and clear of moths. **II.** *vr.* (coll.) to take the air when it is cold or after a long confinement.

desaporcar, *va.* (*for changes v.* APORCAR) to take away (from plants) earth which had been heaped about them.

desaposentar, *va.* to dispossess, oust, evict; to drive from one's mind.

desaposesionar, *va.* to deprive of holdings.

desapoyar, *va.* to withdraw support of or from.

desapreciar, *va.* to undervalue, belittle.

desaprecio, *m.* depreciation, belittling, undervaluation.

desaprender, *va.* to unlearn.

desaprensar. I. *va.* to take away the gloss of (clothes). **II.** *vr.* to extricate one's self.

desapretar, *va.* (*for irr. v.* APRETAR) to slacken, loosen, loose; to ease, free from anxiety.

desaprisionar. I. *va.* to release, to set at liberty. **II.** *vr.* to extricate one's self.

desaprobación, *f.* disapprobation, disapproval.

desaprobar, *va.* (*for irr. v.* APROBAR) to disapprove, condemn; to negative.

desapropiamiento, *m.* = DESAPROPIO.

desapropiarse, *vr.* (w. **de**) to surrender (one's property), to renounce, transfer.

desapropio, *m.* surrender or transfer of property.

desaprovechadamente, *adv.* unprofitably.

desaprovechado, da, *a.* unprofitable; unimproved; backward.—**desaprovechamiento,** *m.* unimprovement; backwardness.

desaprovechar. I. *va.* to waste, misspend, make no use of. **II.** *vn.* to be backward, to make little or no progress.

desapruebo, yo desapruebe. *V.* DESAPROBAR.

desapuntalar, *va.* to take away the props or supports of or from.

desapuntar, *va.* to unstitch, rip up; to lose the aim of (a gun).

desaquellarse, *vr.* to become disheartened.

desarbolar, *va.* (naut.) to unmast (a ship); (agr.) to cut down trees in, to clear of trees.

desarbolo, *m.* unmasting a ship or laying her up in ordinary.

desarenar, *va.* to clear of sand.

desareno, *m.* clearing of sand.

desarmado, da, *a.* unarmed.

desarmador, *m.* hammer of a gun.

desarmadura, *f.,* **desarmamiento,** *m.* disarming, disarmament.

desarmar, *va.* to disarm; to prohibit the carrying of arms to; to undo, dismount, take apart; to disband; to make (a bull) butt in the air; (naut.) to lay up.

desarme, *m.* disarming, disarmament.

desarraigar, *va.* (*for mut. v.* ARRAIGAR) to eradicate, root out; to dig up (a tree); to extirpate, exterminate; to expel.

desarraigo, *m.* eradication; expulsion.

desarrancarse, *vr.* to desert, to separate from a body or association.

desarrapado, da, *a.* ragged.

desarrebozadamente, *adv.* frankly, clearly.

desarrebozar, *va.* & *vr.* to unmuffle; to lay open, manifest, uncover.

desarrebujar, *va.* to disentangle; to unfold, spread out; to uncover; to explain, clear up.

desarregladamente, *adv.* disorderly.

desarreglado, da, *a.* immoderate, intemperate; extravagant, excessive; slovenly, disordered, disarranged; lawless, unruly.

desarreglar, *va.* to disarrange, derange, disorder.

desarreglo, *m.* disarrangement, disorder, confusion; derangement; licentiousness.

For pronunciation, see the rules at the beginning of the book.

desarrendar. I. *va.* to break up the lease of; to unbridle (a horse). **II.** *vr.* to shake off the bridle (s. o. horses).

desarrimar, *va.* to remove, separate; to dissuade.

desarrimo, *m.* want of props or support.

desarrinconar, *va.* to bring out, unearth.

desarrollable, *a.* developable.

desarrollar. I. *va.* to develop; to unroll, unfold, unwind, unfurl; to promote, improve; to explain, expound; to work out; (math.) to develop (a surface), to rectify (a curve), to develop or expand (a power, a function); (r. w.) to develop (a line) (*v.* DESARROLLO). **II.** *vr.* to develop; evolve; to unwind, unfold.

desarrollo, *m.* development; unfolding; unwinding; (math.) development (of a surface, a curve); rectification, calculation of the length (of a curve); expansion, development (of a power, a function); (r. w.) development, lengthening of the line by curves to obtain the appropriate grade.

desarropar, *va.* to uncover, to undress.

desarrugadura, *f.* taking out wrinkles.

desarrugar, *va.* (*for mut. v.* ARRUGAR) to take wrinkles out of, to smooth out.

desarrumar, *va.* (naut.) to break out (the hold).

desarticulación, *f.* disarticulation.

desarticular, *va. & vr.* to disarticulate; (naut.) to loose, disconnect.

desartillar, *va.* to take the guns out of.

desarzonar, *va.* to throw from the saddle, unhorse.

desasado, da, *a.* without handles.

desaseadamente, *adv.* untidily, slovenly.

desaseado, da, *a.* slovenly, not clean.

desasear, *va.* to make dirty or unclean; to disarrange, to disorder.

desasegurar. I. *va.* to loosen, unbrace, make unsteady. **II.** *vr.* (Am.) to cancel an insurance.

desasentar. I. *va.* (*for irr. v.* SENTAR) to displace, move, remove. **II.** *vn.* to be unbecoming; to be disliked, to displease. **III.** *vr.* to stand up.

desaseo, *m.* uncleanliness, untidiness, slovenliness.

desasimiento, *m.* loosening or letting loose; alienation of affection; lack of interest.

desasimilación, *f.* (physiol.) katabolism.

desasir. I. *va.* (*for irr. v.* ASIR) to loosen, let go, give up. **II.** *vr.* (w. de) to disengage or rid one's self (of); to give away, give up.

desasistir, *va.* to abandon, forsake.

desasnar. I. *va.* (coll.) to polish (one's manners). **II.** *vr.* to grow clever; to become polite.

desasociable, *a.* unsociable.

desasosegadamente, *adv.* uneasily, anxiously.

desasosegar, *va.* (*for irr. v.* SOSEGAR) to disquiet, disturb, make uneasy or anxious.

desasosiego, *m.* restlessness, uneasiness.

desastradamente, *adv.* calamitously, unhappily. **—desastrado, da,** *a.* wretched, unfortunate; shabby, ragged.

desastre, *m.* disaster, catastrophe.

desastrosamente, *adv.* disastrously.

desastroso, sa, *a.* unfortunate, disastrous.

desatacar. I. *va.* (*for changes v.* ATACAR) to loosen, untie, unfasten; to draw (the ramrod from). **II.** *vr.* to unfasten one's trousers.

desatadamente, *adv.* loosely, freely.

desatado, da. I. *a.* loose, untied. **II.** *pp.* of DESATAR.

desatador, ra, *n.* one that unties or unfastens.

desatadura, *f.* untying, loosening.

desatalantado, da, *a.* unwise, injudicious.

desatancar, *va.* (*pret.* DESATANQUÉ: *subj.* DESATANQUE) to clear of obstructions.

desatar. I. *va.* to untie, undo (a knot), unfasten, unhitch, loose, loosen, unbind; to separate, detach; to let loose; to liquefy, dissolve; to unriddle, solve, find out, unravel. **II.** *vr.* to give a loose rein to one's tongue; to lose all reserve, fear, or bashfulness; to break loose, break out (as a storm).**—d. en.** to break out into, to let out, to pour out (insult, etc.).

desatascar, *va.* (*for. changes v.* ATASCAR) to pull or draw out of the mud; to remove an obstruction from; to extricate from difficulties.

desataviar, *va.* to strip of ornaments.

desatavío, *m.* uncleanliness, disarray.

desate, *m.* glibness, excessive talk; disorderly proceeding.**—d. de vientre,** looseness of the bowels.

desatención, *f.* inattention; absent-mindedness; disrespect, slight, discourtesy.

desatender, *va.* (*for irr. v.* ATENDER) to pay no attention to; to be unheedful or unmindful of; to disregard, slight, neglect; to take no notice of.

desatentadamente, *adv.* unwisely, injudiciously.

desatentado, da. I. *a.* unwise, injudicious; excessive, rigorous; disordered. **II.** *pp.* of DESATENTAR.

desatentamente, *adv.* discourteously.

desatentar, *va.* (*for irr. v.* ATENTAR) to perturb the mind of, to perplex, confuse, derange.

desatento, ta, *a.* inattentive, careless, heedless, thoughtless; unmannerly, discourteous.

desaterrar, *va.* (Am.) to free (a mine) from rubbish and debris; to remove obstructive earth or mud from.

desatesorar, *va.* to spend the treasure of.

desatiendo, yo desatienda. *V.* DESATENDER.

desatibar, *va.* (min.) = DESATORAR.

desatiento, *m.* lack of the sense of touch; restlessness, uneasiness, worry.

desatierre, *m.* (min.) dumping ground; cleaning-up, removal of debris, etc.

desatinadamente, *adv.* unwisely, foolishly, bunglingly; extravagantly, disproportionately.

desatinado, da. I. *a.* unwise, ill-advised, foolish, wild. **II.** *pp.* of DESATINAR. **III.** *n.* idiot, fool, madcap.

desatinar. I. *va.* to rattle, to confuse, bewilder. **II.** *vn.* to act or talk foolishly; to get rattled or bewildered; to lose one's bearings.

desatino, *m.* lack of tact, adroitness, or address; unwisdom; foolish act or expression; irrelevancy; nonsense, folly, blunder.

desatolondrar. I. *va.* to bring (a person) to his senses. **II.** *vr.* to recover one's senses, to wake up (fig.), open one's eyes.

desatollar, *va.* = DESATASCAR.

desatontarse, *vr.* to recover from stupefaction.

desatorar, *va.* (naut.) to break out (the hold); (min.) to clear from rubbish.

desatornillar, *va.* to unscrew.

desatracar, *va.* (*for changes v.* ATRACAR) (naut.) to sheer off, to bear away.

desatraer, *va.* (*for changes v.* TRAER) to disjoin, separate.

desatraillar, *va.* to uncouple (hounds).

desatrampar, *va.* to clear, remove the obstructions from. *V.* DESATASCAR.

desatrancar, *va.* (*for changes v.* ATRANCAR) to unbar; to clear, remove the obstructions from.

desatufarse, *vr.* to go out from a close room; to become calm, to calm down, cool off.

desaturdir, *va.* to rouse from dizziness or stupor.

desautoridad, *f.* want of authority.

desautorización, *f.* withdrawal of authority.

desautorizadamente, *adv.* without authority.

desautorizado, da, *a.* unauthorized; discredited.

desautorizar, *va.* (*for mut. v.* AUTORIZAR) to take authority from, to deprive of authority.

desavahado, da, *a.* clear (weather), free from vapor; bold.**—desavahamiento,** *m.* uncovering a hot thing to let it cool.**—desavahar. I.** *va.* to expose to the air, to let cool off; to air, ventilate. **II.** *vr.* to become, or get, lively or sprightly.

desavecindado, da. I. *a.* deserted, unpeopled. **II.** *pp.* of DESAVECINDARSE.

desavecindarse, *vr.* to change one's domicile.

desavenencia, *f.* discord, disagreement, misunderstanding; quarrel.

desavengo, yo desavenga. *V.* DESAVENIR.

desavenido, da. I. *a.* discordant, disagreeing. **II.** *pp.* of DESAVENIR.

desavenir. I. *va.* (*for irr. v.* VENIR) to disturb, unsettle. **II.** *vr.* to disagree, to quarrel.

desaventajadamente, *adv.* disadvantageously.

desaventajado, da, *a.* disadvantageous; inferior.

desaviar. I. *va.* to mislead, lead astray; to strip of necessaries or conveniences. **II.** *vr.* to go astray; to lose the means of acquiring necessaries.—**desavío,** *m.* leading or going astray; want of necessary means.

desavisado, da. I. *a.* ill-advised, unadvised, misguided. **II.** *pp.* of DESAVISAR.

desavisar, *va.* to contradict (previous advice, news or reports); to countermand.

desayudar, *va.* to prevent from being aided.

desayunado, da. I. *a.* having breakfasted. **II.** *pp.* of DESAYUNAR.

desayunarse. *vr.* to breakfast; to have first intelligence; to be aware of something.

desayuno, *m.* light breakfast, morning meal (usually coffee or chocolate and rolls or bread).

desazogar. I. *va* (*for. mut. v.* AZOGAR) to take off the quicksilver from (a looking-glass). **II.** *vr.* (Peru) to become restless.

desazón, *f.* insipidity, want of taste or flavor; displeasure, vexation; uneasiness, restlessness; unfitness of a soil for agricultural purposes.

desazonado, da, *a.* (agr.) unfit for cultivation; peevish, ill-humored; indisposed.

desazonar. I. *va.* to render tasteless; to vex, ruffle. **II.** *vr.* to become indisposed.

desbabar, *vn.* to drivel, to slaver.

desbagar. *va.* (*pret.* DESBAGUÉ: *subj.* DESBAGUE) to extract (the flaxseed) from the capsule.

desbancar, *va.* (*pret.* DESBANQUÉ: *subj.* DESBANQUE) to clear (a room) of benches, etc.; to win the bank from, to break the bank (ch. const.); to cut out, supplant in the affection of another.

desbandada, *f.* disbandment.—**a la d.,** in great disorder, helter-skelter.

desbandar. I. *va.* to disband. **II.** *vr.* (mil.) to disband; to desert the colors.

desbarahustar, desbarajustar. I. *va.* to disorder, confuse, disarrange. **II.** *vr.* to get out of order, break down.

desbarahuste, desbarajuste, *m.* disorder, confused medley.

desbaratadamente, *adv.* brokenly, dispersedly.

desbaratado, da. I. *a.* (coll.) debauched, corrupted. **II.** *pp.* of DESBARTAR.

desbaratador, ra, *n.* destroyer, confounder, disturber; debaucher.

desbaratamiento, *m.* perturbation, commotion, disarrangement, ruin, downfall.

desbaratar. I. *va.* to destroy, break to pieces, smash, ruin; to waste, misspend, squander; to cross, impede, prevent, thwart; (mil.) to disperse, rout, break up. **II.** *vn.* to talk nonsense. **III.** *vr.* to be unbalanced; to get out of order; to fall to pieces; to become, or get, undone.

desbarate, desbarato, *m.* smash, breakage, destruction; (mil.) rout, defeat; waste, squandering.—**d. de vientre,** loose bowels.

desbarbado, da, *a.* beardless.

desbarbar, *va.* to trim, to cut off filaments from; (coll.) to shave.

desbarbillar, *va.* (agr.) to cut out (from young vines) the roots which spring from the stems.

desbardar, *va.* to remove thatch from.

desbarnizar, *va.* to remove the varnish from.

desbarrancadero, *m.* (Am.) precipice.

desbarrar, *vn.* to throw an iron bar without taking aim; to sneak, steal away; to act foolishly; to talk nonsense.

desbarretar, *va.* to unbar, unbolt.

desbarrigado, da, *a.* small-bellied.

desbarrigar, *va.* (*for mut. v.* ABRIGAR) (coll.) to rip open the belly of.

desbarro, *m.* foolish action; nonsensical talk; aimless throw of the bar (sports).

desbastador, *m.* dressing chisel, paring tool, hewer.

desbastadura, *f.* planing, trimming, hewing.

desbastar, *va.* to hew, pare, dress, trim, plane, smooth; to waste, consume, weaken; to educate and polish.

desbaste, *m.* hewing, rough dressing, trimming.

desbastecido, da, *a.* unprovided.

desbautizarse, *vr.* (coll.) to lose one's temper, fly into a passion; (coll.) to break one's neck or fracture one's head.

desbazadero, *m.* humid, slippery place.

desbeber, *va.* (coll.) to urinate.

desbecerrar, *va.* to wean (young animals).

desblanquecido, da; desblanquiñado, da, *a.* blanched, bleached.

desbocadamente, *adv.* impudently, shamelessly, without restraint.

desbocado, da, *a.* (arti.) wide-mouthed (s. o. cannon); runaway (horse); broken-lipped or mouthed (as a jar); broken-faced (as a tool); foul-mouthed, indecent.

desbocamiento, *m.* impertinence, impudence; act of running away (s. o. a horse).

desbocar. I. *va.* (*pret.* DESBOQUÉ: *subj.* DESBOQUE) to break the mouth or spout of. **II.** *vn.* to disembogue. **III.** *vr.* to run away; (coll.) to use abusive language, unloosen one's tongue.

desbonetarse, *vr.* (coll.) to take off one's cap.

desboquillar, *va.* to break or remove the mouthpiece or stem of (a pipe, etc.); to break or remove the nozzle of.

desbordamiento, *m.* inundation, overflowing.

desbordar, *vn.* & *vr.* to overflow; to lose one's temper or self-control; to give free rein to one's tongue or passions.

desbornizar, *va.* to take the cork from (the tree).

desborrar, *va.* to burl; to lop off the shoots of.

desbragado, da, *a.* (coll.) breechless; shabby.

desbravador, *m.* mustang breaker.

desbravar. I. *va.* to tame, to break in (horses). **II.** *vn.* to become less fierce; to diminish in force, to moderate, abate.

desbrazarse, *vr.* to stretch out the arms violently.

desbrevarse, *vr.* to evaporate, lose body and strength (s. o. wine).

desbridamiento, *m.* (surg.) separation of fibrous tissues with an instrument.

desbridar, *va.* (surg.) to open up, separate the tissues of.

desbriznar, *va.* to chop or mince (meat); to cut or divide into small parts; to pluck the stamens, the filaments of.

desbroce, *m.* clippings, cuttings from pruning trees; clearing of lands or trenches.

desbrozar, *va.* (*for changes v.* ROZAR) to clear away rubbish from.—**desbrozo,** *m.* = DESBROCE.

desbruar, *va.* to clean (cloth) of grease; to put (cloth) in the fulling mill.

desbrujar, *va.* = DESMORONAR.

desbuchar, *va.* to disclose (one's secrets); to ease (the stomach) (s. o. birds).

desbulla, *f.* oyster shell.—**desbullar,** *va.* to extract (an oyster) from its shell.

desca, *f.* (naut.) tar pot.

descabal, *a.* imperfect, incomplete.

descabalamiento, *f.* diminution, impairment.

descabalar, *va.* to take away a part of; to chop off, impair, damage, maim, cripple; to pilfer.

descabalgadura, *f.* dismounting or alighting from a horse.

descabalgar. I. *vn.* (*for mut. v.* CABALGAR) to dismount, to alight from a horse. **II.** *va.* to dismount (a gun).

descabelladamente, *adv.* wildly, haphazard, thoughtlessly.

descabellado, da. I. *a.* dishevelled, disordered, disarranged; out of all reason, illogical, preposterous, absurd. **II.** *pp.* of DESCABELLAR.

descabelladura, *f.* tossing or dishevelling of the hair.—**descabellamiento,** *m.* = DESPROPÓSITO.

descabellar. I. *va.* & *vr.* to disorder and undress (the hair). **II.** *va.* to kill (the bull) by pricking it in the back of the neck with the sword.

descabello, *m.* killing the bull properly. **V.** DESCABELLAR.

descabestrar, *va.* to unhalter.

descabezadamente, *adv.* wildly, thoughtlessly.

descabezado, da. I. *a.* beheaded; light-headed, injudicious, wild, rash. **II.** *pp.* of DESCABEZAR.

descabezamiento, *m.* act of beheading; quandary, puzzling predicament.

descabezar. I. *va.* (*pret.* DESCABECÉ: *subj.* DESCABECE) to behead; to revoke (an assessment); to cut the upper parts or points of; to head, to top; to poll; to lop off; to overcome; (naut.) to break (a mast) through its neck.—**d. el sueño,** to take a nap. **II.** *vn.* to terminate, to abut. **III.** *vr.* (coll.) to screw one's wits, to batter one's brains; to shed the grain (s. o. cereals).

descabritar, *va.* to wean (goats).

descabullirse, *vr.* to sneak off, to steal away, to scamper; to elude the strength of an argument.

descacilar, *va.* to trim (bricks).

descachar, *va.* (Ch.) to cut off the horns of.

descachazar, *va.* to skim (sugar-cane juice).

descaderar, *va.* to hip, to sprain or dislocate the hip of.

descadillador, ra, *n.* one who cuts off the fag-end of the warp.—**descadillar,** *va.* to cut off the loose threads or fag-end of (the warp).

descaecer, *vn.* (*for irr. v.* ACAECER) to decline, droop, languish; decrease; (naut.) to edge away.

descaecido, da. I. *a.* weak, feeble, languishing. **II.** *pp.* of DESCAECER.

descaecimiento, *m.* weakness, debility; despondency, dejection, languor.

descaezco. *V.* DESCAECER.

descaimiento, *m.* = DESCAECIMIENTO.

descalabazarse, *vr.* (coll.) to puzzle one's brains, to screw one's wits.

descalabrado, da, *a.* & *pp.* of DESCALABRAR; injured; wounded on the head.—**salir d.,** to be a loser, to fail, be worsted.

descalabradura, *f.* slight wound in the head; scar remaining after such wound.

descalabrar. I. *va.* to wound slightly in the head; to attack or impeach the character of; to hurt, to injure; (naut.) to cause (a ship) considerable damage; to occasion losses to. **II.** *vr.* to fracture one's skull; (Peru) to become ruined or be violently destroyed.

descalabro, *m.* calamity; great loss; misfortune.

descalandrajar, *va.* to rend or tear into rags.

descalar, *va.* (naut.) to unship (the helm); to unhang (the rudder).

descalcador, *m.* (carp.) ripping iron, claw; (naut.) ravehook.

descalcar, *va.* (*for mut. v.* CALCAR) (naut.) to extract oakum from (seams).

descalce, *m.* undermining, unwedging.

descalcez, *f.* lack of shoes, barefootedness.

descalificación, *f.* disqualification, withdrawal of authority.

descalificar, *va.* to disqualify, to take the power of authority from.

descalostrado, da, *a.* having passed the days of the first milk.

descalzadero, *m.* little door of a pigeonhole.

descalzador, *m.*, bootjack; crowbar.

descalzar. I. *va.* (*for mut. v.* CALZAR) to pull off the shoes and stockings from or of; to take off wedges or chocks from; to undermine. **II.** *vr.* to pull off one's shoes and stockings; to lose a shoe (s. o. horses).—**d. los guantes,** to pull off, or take off, one's gloves.

descalzo, za, *a.* barefoot, barefooted, shoeless; barefooted (s. o. certain friars and nuns).

descamación, *f.* (med.) desquamation.

descambiar, *va.* to cancel an exchange or barter.

descaminadamente, *adv.* absurdly, unreasonably, foolishly.

descaminado, da, *a.* & *pp.* of DESCAMINAR; ill-advised, misguided, mistaken.

descaminar. I. *va.* to misguide, mislead, lead astray; to seize as contraband; declare contraband; punish for smuggling. **II.** *vr.* to go astray, to lose one's way.

descamino, *m.* leading or going astray; seizure of smuggled goods; the goods thus seized; error, blindness; deviation from justice, truth, reason.

descamisado, da. I. *a.* shirtless, naked, ragged. **II.** *m.* (coll.) ragamuffin.

descampado, da, *a.* disengaged, free, open, clear.—**en d.,** in the open air.

descansadamente, *adv.* easily, without toil or fatigue, leisurely.

descansadero, *m.* resting place.

descansado, da. I. *a.* rested, refreshed. **II.** *pp.* of DESCANSAR.

descansar. I. *vn.* to rest, take repose; to be quiet; to rest, lean upon; to be satisfied; to trust or place confidence (in a person); to lie at rest (as lands which lie fallow); to sleep in death. **II.** *va.* to aid or alleviate; to place or set down on a support or base.

descansillo, *m.* landing of a stairway.

descanso, *m.* rest, repose, quiet; relief, aid, help; sleep; landing of stairs; (mech.) seat, bench, support; (mil.) parade rest.

descantar, *va.* to clear from stones.

descantear, *va.* to smooth angles or corners in; to splay, chamfer, edge.

descanterar, *vn.* to take off the corners or ends of.

descantillar, *va.* to pare off, to chip; to subtract from.

descantillón, *m.* = ESCANTILLÓN.

descantonar, *va.* = DESCANTILLAR.

descañonar, *va.* to pluck out the feathers of; to shave close; (coll.) to trick (one) out of his money.

descaperuzar, *va.* & *vr.* to unhood, uncowl.

descaperuzo, *m.* taking off the cowl, hood, cap.

descapillar, *va.* to take the hood off.

descapirotar, *va.* to take off the CAPIROTE.

descaradamente, *adv.* impudently, barefacedly.

descarado, da. I. *a.* impudent, barefaced, saucy. **II.** *pp.* of DESCARARSE.

descaramiento, *m.* = DESCARO.

descararse, *vr.* to behave in an impudent or insolent manner, to be saucy.

descarburación, *f.* decarbonization.

descarburar, *va.* to decarbonize.

descarcañalar, *va.* & *vr.* to run down (s. o. the heel of a shoe).

descarga, *f.* unburdening, unloading; (mil.) volley, round, discharge; (mas.) easement of a wall; (elec.) discharge.

descargadero, *m.* wharf, unloading place.

descargador, *m.* unloader, lighterman; wad hook.

descargadura, *f.* bone that a butcher takes out of meat.

descargar. I. *va.* (*for mut. v.* CARGAR) to unload, disburden; to ease, lighten; to empty, dump; to free or relieve; to take off the flap and bones of (meat); (mil.) to fire, to discharge (firearms); to unload (fire arms), to draw out the charge of powder and ball from; (naut.) to brace (a lee), to clear (the sails or yards); (elec.) to discharge; to deal, give, inflict (as blows); to acquit, clear from a charge, exonerate; to free or release from a charge, obligation, or debt. **II.** *vn.* to disembogue or disgorge; to vent fury, to burst, to strike with violence (as a storm). **III.** *vr.* (w. de) to resign (one's place or employment); to shirk duty by transferring it to another; to shake off, rid one's self of; (law) to clear or vindicate one's self.

descargo, *m.* unloading, unburdening; exoneration, discharge, acquittal; (com.) acquittance, receipt, release, discharge, voucher; (law) plea or answer to an impeachment or action.

descargue, *m.* unloading; license to unload vessels.

descariñarse, *vr.* to withdraw or lose love or affection; to become cool.

descariño, *m.* coolness, indifference.

descarnada, *f.*—**la d.,** death.

descarnadamente, *adv.* plainly, without trimmings; with effrontery.

descarnado, da, *a.* thin, lean; bare, unadorned.

descarnador, *m.* (dent.) scraper; (tan.) hide scraper.

descarnadura, *f.* divesting of flesh.

descarnar. I. *va.* to excarnate, clear from flesh; to take or eat away; to corrode, wash away, abrade, denudate; (tan.) to flesh, to scrape; to remove from earthly things. **II.** *vr.* to lose flesh, become emaciated.

descaro, *m.* impudence, barefacedness, effrontery, sauciness, assurance.

descarriamiento, *m.* going or leading astray.

descarriar. I. *va.* to lead astray, misguide, mislead; to separate (cattle). **II.** *vr.* to be separated; to deviate from justice or reason; to go astray; to lead a dissipated life.

descarrilamiento, *m.* derailment.

descarrilar. I. *va.* to derail. **II.** *vn.* & *vr.* to run off the track, be derailed.

descarrilladura, *f.* act of breaking the jaws.

descarrillar, *va.* to break the jaws of.

descarrío, *m.* going astray, losing the way.

descartar. I. *va.* to discard, fling away, lay away. **II.** *vr.* to discard (at cards); to excuse one's self; to shirk.

descarte, *m.* cards discarded; act of discarding; act of shirking; evasion, subterfuge.

descasamiento, *m.* unmarrying.

descasar, *va.* to unmarry; to annul the marriage of; to separate, put asunder; (print.) to alter the position of (the pages of a sheet).

descascar. I. *va.* (*for mut. v.* CASCAR) to decorticate; to rodomontade; to bluster; to mumble. **II.** *vr.* to break into pieces.

descascarador, ra, *n.* huller, husker, sheller.—**d. de café,** coffee pulper.

descascarar. I. *va.* to peel, decorticate, flay; to shell, hull, husk. **II.** *vr.* to peel off, shell off.

descascarillar, *va.* to decorticate; to take off the powder from (the face).

descaspar, *va.* to take dandruff from; (tan.) to scrape (a half-dressed hide).

descasque, *m.* decortication, (particularly of the cork tree).

descastado, da, *a.* showing little natural affection to whom it is due.

descastar, *va.* to deprive of caste; to exterminate.

descatolizar, *va.* to cause to abandon Catholicism.

descaudalado, da, *a.* ruined, penniless.

descebar, *va.* to unprime (firearms).

descendencia, *f.* descent, origin; offspring.

descendente, *a.* descending.

descender. I. *vn.* (*pp.* DESCENDIDO: *ind.* DESCIENDO: *subj.* DESCIENDA) to descend; get or go down; to flow or run, as liquids; to descend, be descended, derive; to stoop, lower one's self. **II.** *va.* to let down, lower; to bring down.

descendiente. I. *a.* descending. **II.** *m.* descendant, offspring.

descendimiento, *m.* descent, lowering.

descensión, *f.* descension, descent.

descenso, *m.* descent; lowering; fall, degradation; (med.) hernia, rupture; prolapse of the womb.

descentrado, da, *a.* out of center; out of plumb.

descentralización, *f.* decentralization.

descentralizador, ra, *n.* & *a.* decentralizer (-ing).

descentralizar, *va.* (*for mut. v.* CENTRALIZAR) to decentralize; to grant local autonomy to.

descentrar. I. *va.* to uncenter. **II.** *vr.* to get out of center or out of plumb.

desceñidura, *f.* ungirding or loosening a belt.

desceñir, *va.* (*for irr. v.* CEÑIR) to ungird, to loosen or take off (as a belt, a crown).

descepar, *va.* to eradicate, to pull up by the roots; to extirpate; (naut.) to remove the stocks from (an anchor).

descerar, *va.* to take the empty combs from (a beehive).

descercado, da. I. *a.* open, unfenced, undefended. **II.** *pp.* of DESCERCAR.

descercador, *m.* one who forces the enemy to raise a siege.

descercar, *va.* (*for mut. v.* CERCAR) to destroy or pull down a wall, a fence, etc. of; to raise the siege of; to oblige (the enemy) to raise a siege.

descerco, *m.* the act of raising a siege.

descerezar, *va.* to pulp (the coffee berry).

descerrajado, da, *a.* (coll.) corrupt, wicked, ill-disposed.

descerrajadura, *f.* taking off locks or bolts.

descerrajar, *va.* to take the lock off; to discharge (firearms).

descerrumarse, *vr.* (vet.) to be wrenched or distorted at the joints.

descervigamiento, *m.* act of twisting the neck.

descervigar, *va.* to twist the neck of; humiliate.

desciendo, yo descienda. *V.* DESCENDER.

descifrable, *a.* decipherable.—**descifrador, ra,** *m.* decipherer.—**descifrar,** *va.* to decipher.

descimbramiento, *m.* (arch.) removing the centers.

descimbrar, *va.* (arch.) to remove the centers of.

descimentar, *va.* to demolish the foundations of.

descinchar, *va.* to ungirt.

descivilizar. I. *va.* to uncivilize. **II.** *vr.* to become uncivilized.

desclavador, *m.* carpenter's chisel; nail puller, claw wrench.

desclavar, *va.* to draw out the nails from, unnail, unpeg.

descoagulable, *a.* that may be redissolved after coagulation.

descoagulación, *f.* solution, of a clot or curd.

descoagulante, *a.* that liquefies a clot or curd, clot-dissolving.

descoagular, *va.* to liquefy, dissolve (a clot).

descobajar, *va.* to pull the stem from (a grape).

descobijar, *va.* to uncover.

descocadamente, *adv.* impudently, boldly, brazen-facedly.

descocado, da. I. *a.* (coll.) bold, excessively free and forward. **II.** *pp.* of DESCOCAR.

descocar. I. *va.* (*for mut. v.* CHOCAR) to clean, to clear (trees) from insects. **II.** *vr.* (coll.) to be impudent, saucy, or petulant.

descocedura, *f.* digestion.

descocer, *va.* (*for irr. v.* COCER) to digest.

descoco, *m.* barefacedness, impudence, sauciness.

descodar, *va.* to rip, to unstitch.

descoger, *va.* (*for. irr. v.* COGER) to unfold, extend, spread, expand.

descogollar, *va.* to strip (a tree) of shoots; to take out the heart of (vegetables).

descogotado, da, *pp.* & *a.* (coll.) low-necked.

descogotar, *va.* to cut off the horns of (a stag).

descolada, *f.* (Mex.) slight, discourtesy.

descolar, *va.* (*for irr. v.* COLAR) to dock or crop the tail of; to cut off the fag end of (a piece of cloth); (carp.) to unglue; (Mex.) to ignore, slight; (C. A.) to dismiss, "to fire."

descolchar, *va.* (naut.) to untwist (a cable).

descolgar. I. *va.* (*for irr. v.* COLGAR) to take down, to let down. **II.** *vr.* to come down gently, to slip down (by a rope, etc.); to descend; (w. **con**) to make an unexpected remark or sally; to come on suddenly (as a cold snap).

descoligado, da, *a.* not belonging to a league, non-union.

descolmar, *va.* to strike off (the heaping corn in a measure); to diminish.

descolmillar, *va.* to pull out or break the fangs or eyeteeth of.

descoloramiento, *m.* discoloration.

descolorante, *m.* & *a.* discolorer (-ing).

---

descolorar, *va.* & *vr.* to discolor, pale, lose its color, fade.

descolorido, da. I. *a.* discolored, pale, colorless. **II.** *pp.* of DESCOLORIR.

descolorimiento, *m.* discoloration, fading.

descolorir, *va.* & *vr.* to discolor, pale, bleach, fade.

descolladamente, *adv.* loftily, haughtily.

descollamiento, *m.* =DESCUELLO.

descollar, *vn.* & *vr.* (*for irr. v.* ACOLLAR) to tower, stand out, be prominent or conspicuous, excel.

descombrar, *va.* to disencumber, to clear of obstacles, débris, etc.

descombro, *m.* disencumbrance.

descomedidamente, *adv.* rudely, disagreeably; excessively, immoderately.

descomedido, da. I. *a.* excessive, disproportionate, immoderate; rude, disagreeable, disobliging. **II.** *pp.* of DESCOMEDIRSE.

descomedimiento, *m.* rudeness, incivility.

descomedirse, *vr.* (*for irr. v.* MEDIR) to forget one's self; to be rude or disrespectful.

descomer, *vn.* (coll.) to ease nature.

descomido, me descomida. *V.* DESCOMEDIRSE.

descomodidad, *f.* inconvenience, discomfort.

descompadrar. I. *va.* (coll.) to cause estrangement of. **II.** *vn.* (coll.) to disagree, to fall out.

descompaginar, *va.* to disarrange, upset.

descompás, *m.* excess, redundancy, want of measure or proportion.

descompasadamente, *adv.* DESCOMEDIDAMENTE.

descompasado, da. I. *a.* excessive, extravagant, disproportionate; out of tune or time. **II.** *pp.* of DESCOMPASARSE.

descompasarse, *vr.* to exceed all rule and measure; be out of tune or time; forget one's self.

descomponer. I. *va.* (*for irr. v.* COMPONER) to disarrange, unsettle, upset, disturb; to disable; to destroy the harmony of, set at odds; to decompound; (chem.) to decompose; (mech.) to resolve (forces). **II.** *vr.* to decompose, spoil, rot; to get out of order; to forget one's self, lose one's temper; to change for the worse; to become stale.

descompongo. *V.* DESCOMPONER.

descomposición, *f.* discomposure, disagreement; disarrangement; disorder, confusion; decomposition, putrefaction, rotting; (chem.) decomposition, separation of elements; (mech.) resolution (of forces).

descompostura, *f.* disarrangement; disadjustment; slovenliness, uncleanliness, untidiness; forwardness, want of modesty; disrespectful conduct, impudence.

descompuestamente, *adv.* impudently, insolently.

descompuesto, ta. I. *a.* impudent, insolent; out of temper; immodest; out of order. **II.** *pp. irr.* of DESCOMPONER.

descomulgado, da. I. *a.* perverse, nefarious, wicked. **II.** *pp.* of DESCOMULGAR.

descomulgador, *m.* excommunicator.

descomulgar, *va.* (*for mut. v.* COMULGAR) to excommunicate.

descomunal, *a.* extraordinary, monstrous, enormous, huge, colossal.

descomunalmente, *adv.* immensely, enormously, extraordinarily.

descomunión, *f.* excommunication.

desconceptuar, *va.* & *vr.* = DESACREDITAR.

desconcertadamente, *adv.* disorderly, confusedly, disconcertedly.

desconcertado, da, *pp.* & *a.* disorderly, slovenly; disconnected; disconcerted, baffled.

desconcertador, ra, *n.* disturber, disconcerter.

desconcertadura, *f.* disturbance; confusion.

desconcertante, *a.* disconcerting, baffling.

desconcertar. I. *va.* (*for irr. v.* CONCERTAR) to disarrange, disturb, confuse; to disconcert, thwart, baffle; to disjoint, dislocate. **II.** *vr.* to disagree; to act or speak thoughtlessly or recklessly; to become disarranged; to be or to become disjointed (s. o. bones).

desconcierto, *m.* disconcert, disagreement; disorder, confusion; disarrangement (as of machinery); want of prudence and circumspection; maladministration, mismanagement; flux or looseness of the body.

desconcierto. *V.* DESCONCERTAR.

desconcordia, *f.* discord, disagreement, disunion.

desconchabar, *va.* (Am.) to disarrange, upset.

desconchadura, *f.* removal of varnish, stucco, etc.; peeling, scaling.

desconchar. I. *va.* to strip off a surface (varnish, stucco, plaster, etc.). **II.** *vr.* to peel off, scale off.

desconectar. I. *va.* to disconnect. **II.** *vr.* to become disconnected.

desconfiadamente, *adv.* diffidently; distrustfully, suspiciously.

desconfiado, da. I. *a.* diffident, distrustful; mistrustful, jealous. **II.** *pp.* of DESCONFIAR.

desconfianza, *f.* diffidence; distrust; jealousy, suspicious fear.

desconfiar, *vn.* (w. **de**) to distrust, to have no confidence in; to suspect, doubt; to have little hope.

desconformar. I. *vn.* to dissent, disagree, differ in opinion. **II.** *vr.* to disagree; not to fit or suit each other.—**desconforme,** *a.* discordant, disagreeing, contrary.—**desconformidad,** *f.* disagreement, opposition, nonconformity; inequality, unlikeness, disparity.

descongestión, *f.* ceasing or removal of congestion.

descongestionar, *va.* to remove the congestion of.

desconocer, *va.* (*for irr. v.* CONOCER) to fail to recognise; to disregard, ignore; to forget; to deny, disown, disavow; to be unacquainted with; to be ungrateful for.

desconocidamente, *adv.* ignorantly, unknowingly; ungratefully.

desconocido, da. I. *a.* ungrateful, unthankful; unknown. **II.** *pp.* of DESCONOCER. **III.** *n.* unknown person, stranger.

desconocimiento, *m.* ungratefulness, ingratitude; ignorance; disregard.

desconozco. *V.* DESCONOCER.

desconsentir, *va.* (*for irr. v.* CONSENTIR) not to acquiesce in, to disapprove.

desconsideradamente, *adv.* inconsiderately; rashly, recklessly.

desconsiderado, da, *a.* inconsiderate; imprudent, thoughtless, rash.

desconsiento. *V.* DESCONSENTIR.

desconsolación, *f.* disconsolateness, grief.

desconsoladamente, *adv.* disconsolately.

desconsolado, da. I. *a.* disconsolate, griefstricken, dejected, downhearted. **II.** *pp.* of DESCONSOLAR.

desconsolador, ra, *a.* discouraging; lamentable.

desconsolar. I. *va.* (*for irr. v.* CONSOLAR) to afflict; to treat rudely. **II.** *vr.* to lose one's cheerfulness; to become low-spirited or afflicted.

desconsuelo, *m.* affliction, disconsolateness; disorder in the stomach.

desconsuelo. *V.* DESCONSOLAR.

descontagiar, *va.* to purify, to disinfect.

descontar. I. *va.* (*for irr. v.* CONTAR) to discount, deduct, allow, take off; to abate, lessen, diminish; to detract from merit of; to take for granted. **II.** *vr.* to miscount.

descontentadizo, za, *a.* fastidious, hard to please, overparticular; easily displeased, squeamish.

descontentamiento, *m.* discontentment, displeasure; grief.

descontentar, *va.* to dissatisfy, displease.

descontento, ta. I. *a.* discontented, dissatisfied, displeased; uneasy. **II.** *m.* discontent; uneasiness, dissatisfaction.

descontinuación, *f.* discontinuance, cessation.

descontinuar, *va.* to discontinue, leave off, cease.

descontinuo, nua, *a.* disjoined, discontinued; discontinuous.

desconvenible, *a.* discordant, disparate, opposed.

desconveniencia, *f.* inconvenience, disadvantage.—**desconveniente,** *a.* inconvenient; discordant, incongruous.

desconvenir, *vn.* (*for irr. v.* CONVENIR) to disagree; to be unlike or dissimilar; not to suit, match, or mate.

desconversable, *a.* unsociable, retiring.

desconvidar, *va.* to recall (as an invitation or a promise).

descopar, *va.* to lop off the top of (a tree).

descorazonadamente, *adv.* dejectedly, spiritlessly, with dismay.—**descorazonamiento,** *m.* lowness of spirits, depression, dejection.

descorazonar, *va.* to tear out the heart of; to dishearten, discourage.

descorchador, *m.* uncorker, cork drawer.

descorchar, *va.* to decorticate (a cork tree); to uncork; to break (a beehive) to steal the honey; to break open.

descordar, *va.* to uncord (an instrument).

descorderar, *va.* to wean (lambs).

descornar. **I.** *va.* to dishorn, to knock off the horns of. **II.** *vr.* to break one's skull by a fall.

descoronar, *va.* to take off the top or crown of.

descorrear, *vn. & vr.* to loosen the skin that covers the tenderlings of a deer.

descorregido, da, *a.* incorrect, disarranged.

descorrer. **I.** *va.* to run back over (the same ground); to draw (as a curtain). **II.** *vn.* to flow.

descorrimiento, *m.* flow.

descortés, *a.* impolite, uncivil, discourteous.

descortesía, *f.* incivility, discourtesy.

descortésmente, *adv.* discourteously, rudely.

descortezador, *m.* one who strips off the bark; decorticator.

descortezadura, *f.,* **descortezamiento,** *m.* decortication, excortication; bark taken off.

descortezar. **I.** *va.* (*pret.* DESCORTECÉ: *subj.* DESCORTECE) to decorticate; to flay; take off the crust or; strip off the bark of; to hull, shell (as fruits); to rough-hew; to polish or civilize. **II.** *vr.* to become polished.

descortinar, *va.* (fort.) to demolish or destroy (a curtain).

descosedura, *f.* ripping, unseaming.

descoser. **I.** *va.* to rip, unseam, unstitch; to separate, disjoin; (naut.) to unlash.—**no d. los labios,** to keep a profound silence; **II.** *vr.* to loose one's tongue.

descosidamente, *adv.* immoderately.

descosido, da. I. *a. & pp.* of DESCOSER; ripped, unseamed, unstitched; disjointed, disconnected; deranged. **II.** *n.* babbler, teller of secrets.—**comer** or **beber como un d.,** to eat or drink immoderately.

descostarse, *vr.* to draw away from an object or a coast.

descostillar. I. *va.* to strike or hit in the ribs; to take out the ribs of; to break the ribs of. **II.** *vr.* to fall flat on the ground.

descostrar, *va.* to take off the crust of.

descotar. I. *va.* to remove a restriction from. **II.** *vr.* to expose the neck and shoulders.

descote, *m.* exposure of the neck and shoulders; low cut of a waist.

descoyuntado. da. I. *a.* disjointed, disconnected, out of gear. **II.** *pp.* of DESCOYUNTAR.

descoyuntamiento, *m.* luxation, dislocation, derangement; pain or tiredness from overexertion.

descoyuntar. I. *va.* to luxate or disjoint; to vex, displease; to upset, disarrange. **II.** *vr.* to become disjointed, get out of joint.—**d. de risa,** to split one's sides with laughter.

descoyunto, *m.* = DESCOYUNTAMIENTO.

descrecencia, *f.* decrement, decreasing.

descrecer, *va. & vn.* (*for irr. v.* CRECER) to decrease, diminish; to fall, to subside (tides and rivers); to grow short (days).

descrecimiento, *m.* decrease, diminution.

descrédito, *m.* discredit, loss of reputation.

descreer, *va.* to disbelieve; to deny due credit to; to disown or abjure.

descreídamente, *adv.* incredulously.

descreído, da. I. *n. & a.* unbeliever (-ing); infidel. **II.** *pp.* of DESCREER.

descreimiento, *m.* unbelief, lack of faith.

descrestar, *va.* to take off the crest or comb of; (Am., coll.) to impose upon; to swindle.

descriarse, *vr.* to weaken; to pine with desire or anxiety.

describir, *va.* (*pp.* DESCRITO) to describe; to sketch, delineate; to relate minutely.

descripción, *f.* description; sketch, delineation; (law) inventory, schedule.

descriptible, *a.* describable.

descriptivo, va, *a.* descriptive.

descriptor, ra, *n. & a.* describer (-ing).

descrismar. I. *va.* to remove the chrism from; (coll.) to give one a blow on the head. **II.** *vr.* (coll.) to lose patience, to lose one's temper.

descristianar, *va.* = DESCRISMAR.

descristianizar, *va.* to dechristianize.

descrito, ta, *pp. irr.* of DESCRIBIR; described.

descruzar, *va.* (*for mut. v.* CRUZAR) to uncross.

descuadernar. I. *va.* to unbind (books); to disarrange, disconcert, disorder. **II.** *vr.* to get disjointed, loose.

descuadrillado, da. I. *pp. & a.* separated from the rank or lines. **II.** *m.* (vet.) sprain in the haunch.—**descuadrillarse,** *vr.* to be sprained in the haunches.

descuajado, da. I. *a.* dispirited, disheartened; liquefied. **II.** *pp.* of DESCUAJAR.

descuajar, *va.* to dissolve, liquefy; to eradicate, to grub; to extirpate, uproot; to dishearten.

descuajaringarse, *vr.* (coll.) to be broken down by excessive fatigue; to fall to pieces.

descuaje, descuajo, *m.* (agr.) grubbing up weeds; clearing ground of underbrush.

descuartelar, *va.* to remove from winter quarters; to undo the quartering of (the sails).

descuartizamiento, *m.* quartering; breaking or cutting in pieces; carving.

descuartizar, *va.* (*for mut. v.* ATIZAR) to quarter; to carve.

descubierta, *f.* pie without an upper crust; (mil.) reconnoitering; (naut.) scanning of the horizon at sunrise and sunset.—**a la d.,** openly, in the open.

descubiertamente, *adv.* manifestly, openly.

descubierto, ta. I. *a.* patent, manifest, exposed, unveiled; bareheaded. **II.** *m.* solemn exposition of the sacrament; shortage, deficiency, overdraft.—**al d.,** openly, manifestly.—**en d.,** (com.) uncovered; overdrawn; owing a balance.—**estar, quedar, en d.,** (com.) to owe a balance; to have overdrawn a bank account. **III.** *f.* DESTAPADA. **IV.** *pp.* of DESCUBRIR.

descubretalles, *m.* small fan.

descubridero, *m.* eminence commanding an extensive view; lookout.

descubridor, ra, *n.* discoverer; finder, descrier; (mil.) scout, spy; vessel on a voyage of discovery.

descubrimiento, *m.* discovery; find; disclosure; country or thing discovered.

descubrir. I. *va.* (*pp.* DESCUBIERTO) to discover; disclose, show, bring to light; to uncover, make visible, expose to view, lay open; to reveal, communicate, make known; (ecc.) to expose (the sacrament); (mil.) to reconnoiter; to overlook.—**d. la tierra,** (naut.) to make the land.—**d. por la popa** or **por la proa,** (naut.) to descry astern or ahead. **II.** *vr.* to uncover one's self, to take off one's hat.

descuelgo, yo descuelgue. *V.* DESCOLGAR.

descuello, yo descuelle. *V.* DESCOLLAR.

descuello, *m.* excessive height or tallness; prominence, superiority; loftiness, haughtiness.

descuento, *m.* discount; deduction, rebate, allowance; diminution, decrease.

descuento, descuente. *V.* DESCONTAR.

descuernacabras, *m.* cold north wind.

---

descuerno, *m.* (coll.) slight, affront.

descuidadamente, *adv.* carelessly, negligently.

descuidado, da. I. *a.* careless, negligent or thoughtless; unprepared, unaware; slovenly, unclean. **II.** *pp.* of DESCUIDAR.

descuidar. I. *va.* to neglect, forget, overlook; to relieve from care; to divert the attention of. **II.** *vn.* to lack attention or diligence; to be careless or neglectful; to make one's self easy, not to trouble one's self. **III.** *vr.* to be forgetful of duty, to become negligent.

descuido, *m.* carelessness, indolence, negligence, forgetfulness, absent-mindedness; oversight, slip; lack of attention; incivility, coldness; improper or disgraceful action; imprudence; immodesty.—al d., unobserved, on the sly.—al d., or al d. y con cuidado, with studied carelessness or naturalness.

descuitado, da, *a.* living without trouble or care.

descular, *va.* to break the bottom of (as of a jar).

deschuponar, *va.* (agr.) to strip (a tree) of its shoots or suckers.

desdar, *va.* to turn in the opposite direction so as to untwist or loosen.

desde, *prep.* since, from, after.—**d. entonces,** since then, ever since.—**d. luego,** immediately, whereupon; doubtless, of course.—**d. niño,** from a child, ever since one's childhood.—**d. que,** since, ever since.

desdecir. I. *vn. (for irr. v.* DECIR) (w. **de**) to degenerate, to fall from its kind; to differ, to disagree; to be unworthy (of) or unbecoming (to); to detract (from), to impair. **II.** *vr.* to retract, recant.

desdén, *m.* disdain, slight, scorn, contempt.—**al d.,** affectedly careless.

desdentado, da. I. *a.* toothless. **II.** *m. pl.* (zool.) edentates. **III.** *pp.* of DESDENTAR.

desdentar, *va.* to draw teeth from.

desdeñable, *a.* contemptible, despicable.

desdeñadamente, *adv.* disdainfully, scornfully.

desdeñador, ra, *n. & a.* scorner (-ing), disdainer (-ing, -ful).

desdeñar. I. *va.* to disdain, scorn. **II.** *vr.* to be disdainful; (w. **de**) to loathe.

desdeñosamente, *adv.* disdainfully.

desdeñoso, sa, *a.* disdainful, contemptuous.

desdevanar, *va.* to unwind or unravel (a clue).

desdibujado, da, *a.* (art) badly drawn.

desdibujo, *m.* faulty drawing.

desdicha, *f.* misfortune, ill-luck, misery.

desdichadamente, *adv.* unfortunately, unhappily.

desdichado, da. I. *a.* unfortunate; unhappy, unlucky, wretched. **II.** *n.* wretch, unfortunate one; good-for-nothing, insignificant person.

desdicho, *pp. irr.* of DESDECIR.

desdigo, yo desdiga. *V.* DESDECIR.

desdinerar, *va.* to impoverish.

desdoblar, *va.* to unfold, to spread open.

desdorar, *va. & vr.* to take off the gilding of; to lose its guilding; to tarnish or sully the reputation of.

desdoro, *m.* dishonor, blemish, blot, stigma.

deseable, *a.* desirable.—**deseablemente,** *adv.* desirably.—**deseador, ra,** *n.* desirer, wisher.

desear, *va.* to desire, wish.

desecación, *f.* desiccation, exsiccation

desecado, da, *a.* dry, desiccated.

desecador, *m.* drying room; dryer.

desecamiento, *m.* desiccation.

desecante, *a. & n.* dryer (-ing), desiccant, desiccative.

desecar, *va. (for mut. v.* SECAR) to dry; to desiccate; to drain, to draw.

desecativo, va. I. *a.* desiccative, exsiccant. **II.** *m.* healing plaster.

desechadamente, *adv.* vilely, despicably.

desechado, da, *a. & pp.* of DESECHAR; refused, excluded, expelled, rejected; outcast.

desechar, *va.* to reject; to exclude; to depreciate, undervalue; decline, refuse; to put aside, lay aside; cast off; to vote down.

desecho, *m.* residue, surplus, remainder; débris, rubbish, refuse, offal; rejection; disregard, contempt.—**de d.,** cast off, discarded; scrap (iron, etc.)

desedificación, *f.* scandal, bad example.

desedificar, *va. (for mut. v.* EDIFICAR) to disedify.

deseguida, *a.* lewd (woman).

deselectrización, *f.* diselectrification.

deselectrizar, *va.* to diselectrify.

deselladura, *f.* unsealing or taking off the seals.

desellar, *va.* to unseal, to take off the seals of.

desembalaje, *m.* unpacking, opening of bales.

desembalar, *va.* to unpack, open.

desembaldosar, *va.* to take up the flagstones or tiles of; to unpave.

desemballestar, *vn.* (falc.) to get ready to come down (s. o. a falcon).

desembanastar. I. *va.* to take out of a basket; (coll.) to draw (the sword). **II.** *vn.* to talk much and without sense. **III.** *vr.* to break out or break loose; (coll.) to alight from a carriage.

desembarazadamente, *adv.* freely, without embarrassment.

desembarazado, da, *a.* free, disengaged; clear, open; unrestrained, unencumbered.

desembarazar. I. *va. (for mut. v.* EMBARAZAR) to disembarrass, free, ease; to remove an impediment or encumbrance from; to clear; to unburden, disencumber, expedite. **II.** *vr.* to rid one's self of difficulties or hindrances.

desembarazo, *m.* disembarrassment, disencumbrance; disengagement; freedom, lack of restraint or hindrances; ease, naturalness.

desembarcadero, *m.* landing place; wharf, pier.

desembarcar. I. *va. (for mut. v.* EMBARCAR) to unload, put ashore, debark. **II.** *vn.* to land, debark, go ashore; (coll.) to alight (from a vehicle); (coll.) to be delivered of a child; to end (as a staircase).

desembarco, *m.* landing, debarkation, unloading; landing place at the top of stairs.

desembargadamente, *adv.* freely.

desembargador, *m.* chief magistrate and privy councillor in Portugal.

desembargar, *va. (for mut. v.* EMBARGAR) to remove impediments from; (law) to disembargo.

desembargo, *m.* (law) raising of an embargo.

desembarque, *m.* landing or debarkation; unloading.

desembarrancar, *va.* = DESABARRANCAR.

desembarrar, *va.* to clear of mud.

desembaular, *va.* to take out of a trunk; to empty; (coll.) to speak (one's mind) freely; to disclose (one's thoughts).

desembebecerse, *vr. (for irr. v.* EMBEBECER) to recover one's senses, to come to.

desembelesarse, *vr.* to recover from amazement or abstraction.

desembocadero, *m.,* **desembocadura,** *f.* exit, outlet; mouth (of a river, canal, etc.)

desembocar, *vn.* (w. **en**) *(for mut. v.* EMBOCAR) to disembogue, to flow (into); to end (at), lead (to).

desembojadera, *f.* woman who takes the cocoons of silkworms from the southern-wood.

desembojar, *va.* to remove (silk-cocoons) from the southern-wood.

desembolsar, *va.* to empty from, or out of, a purse; to disburse.

desembolso, *m.* disbursement, expenditure.

desemboque, *m.* = DESEMBOCADERO.

desemborrachar. I. *va.* to sober, to make sober, to cure of intoxication. **II.** *vr.* to become sober, get over one's intoxication.

desemboscarse, *vr.* to get out of the woods; to get clear of an ambuscade.

desembotar, *va.* to remove dulness from (a cutting edge); to sharpen (as wits).

desembozar, *va. & vr. (for mut. v.* EMBOZAR) to unmuffle or uncover; to unmask, show one's self in one's true colors (or others in theirs).

desembozo, *m.* uncovering or unmuffling the face.

For pronunciation, see the rules at the beginning of the book.

desembragar, *va.* (*for mut. v.* BRAGAR) to unbind from the cable; (mech.) to ungear, disengage, disconnect.

desembravecer, *va.* (*for. irr. v.* EMBRAVECER) to tame, domesticate; to calm, pacify.

desembravecimiento, *m.* taming or reclaiming from wildness.

desembrazar, *va.* (*for mut. v.* ABRAZAR) to take (something) off the arms; to dart or throw (weapons); to throw from the arms.

desembriagar. I. *va.* (*for mut. v.* EMBRIAGAR) to sober, to cure from intoxication. **II.** *vr.* to become sober, to recover from drunkenness.

desembridar, *va.* to unbridle.

desembrollar, *va.* to unravel, disentangle, clear, extricate.

desembrozar, *va.* = DESBROZAR.

desembuchar, *va.* to disgorge, to turn out of the maw (birds); (coll.) to unbosom.

desemejante, *a.* dissimilar, unlike.

desemejantemente, *adv.* dissimilarly.

desemejanza, *f.* unlikeness, dissimilarity.

desemejar. I. *vn.* to be dissimilar or unlike. **II.** *va.* = DESFIGURAR.

desempacar. I. *va.* (*for mut. v.* EMPACAR) to unpack. **II.** *vr.* (coll.) to grow calm, to be appeased, cool off.

desempachar. I. *va.* to make (the stomach) discharge undigested food. **II.** *vr.* (coll.) to grow bold, to lose all bashfulness.

desempacho, *m.* ease; forwardness, unconcern.

desempalagar. I. *va.* & *vr.* (*for mut. v.* EMPALAGAR) to remove nausea or loathing (from); to restore the appetite (to). **II.** *va.* to clear (a mill) of stagnant water.

desempanar, *va.* to clean (a glass); to take off the clouts and swaddling clothes from (children).

desempapelar, *va.* to unwrap, take out of a package; to take (paper hangings) off a wall, to take off the paper of.

desempaque, *m.* act of unpacking.

desempaquetar, *va.* to unpack.

desemparejar, *va.* to unmatch, make unequal or uneven.

desemparentado, da, *a.* without relatives.

desemparvar, *va.* to gather in heaps.

desempastado, da, *a.* unbound (s. o. books).

desempastar, *va.* to take the cover off (a book); to take the filling out of (a tooth).

desempastelar, *va.* (print.) to distribute (mixed letters).

desempatar, *va.* to disjoint, disunite; to make unequal or uneven; to decide (a tie vote); to run, play, or shoot off a tie.

desempedrador, *m.* one who unpaves.

desempedrar, *va.* (*for irr. v.* EMPEDRAR) to unpave.—**ir desempedrando la calle,** (coll.) to go very rapidly.

desempegar, *va.* (*for mut. v.* PEGAR) to unglue; to take the pitch off.

desempeñado, da. I. *a.* free or clear of debt. **II.** *pp.* of DESEMPEÑAR.

desempeñar. I. *va.* to redeem, to recover (what was pledged), to take out of pawn; to clear or extricate from debt; to perform, discharge (a duty); to fill (an office, a function, a part); to transact; to accomplish, carry out (an undertaking); to act (a part in a play); to acquit, free from an obligation: to disengage from a difficulty. **II.** *vr.* to extricate one's self from debt; in bull fighting, to disengage one's self from the attack of a bull.—**desempeñarse de la tierra,** or **costa,** (naut.) to claw off, to stand off shore.

desempeño, *m.* the act of redeeming a pledge; performance of an obligation or promise; fulfilment, discharge; acting of a part.

desempeorarse, *vr.* to recover from sickness, to regain health.

desemperezar, *vn.* & *vr.* (*for mut. v.* EMPEREZAR) to relinquish habits of laziness and indolence; to shake off laziness.

desempernar, *va.* to take the bolts out of.

desemplomar, *va.* to remove the leaden seal from.

desemplumar, *va.* = DESPLUMAR.

desempobrecer. I. *va.* (*for irr. v.* EMPOBRECER) to relieve from poverty. **II.** *vr.* to extricate one's self from poverty.

desempolvar, *va.* to remove dust or powder from, to dust.

desempolvoradura, *f.* dusting.

desempolvorar, *va.* to dust.

desemponzoñar, *va.* to heal from the effects of poison; to free from poison.

desempotrar, *va.* to remove the support of; to take out.

desempulgadura, *f.* unbending of a bow.

desempulgar, *va.* (*for mut. v.* COMULGAR) to unbend (a bow).

desenalbardar, *va.* to take a packsaddle off (an animal).

desenamorar. I. *va.* to destroy the love or affection of. **II.** *vr.* to lose love or affection.

desenastar, *va.* to remove the handle or haft from.

desencabalgar, *va.* (*for mut. v.* CABALGAR) (mil.) to dismount (cannon).

desencabestradura, *f.* disentangling of a beast from the halter.

desencabestrar, *va.* to disentangle the feet of (a beast) from the halter.

desencadenar. I. *va.* to unchain; to free, liberate. **II.** *vr.* to break loose, free one's self from chains; to become infuriated, lose one's self-control; to break out with fury (s. o. a storm); to come down in torrents (s. o. rain).

desencajado, da. I. *a.* run down, looking bad, rickety; out of kilter; out of joint. **II.** *pp.* of DESENCAJAR.

desencajadura, *f.* disjointedness, disconnection.

desencajamiento, *m.* = DESENCAJE.

desencajar. I. *va.* to disjoint, unjoin, disconnect, throw out of gear; to disarticulate; to luxate. **II.** *vr.* to become rickety; to get disjointed, disconnected, out of gear.

desencajonar, *va.* to unpack, take out of a box.

desencaje, *m.* disjointednes; broken-down appearance; rickety appearance.

desencalabrinar, *va.* to remove dizziness from; to free from stupidity; to remove wrong impressions from.

desencalcar, *va.* (*for mut. v.* CALCAR) to loosen or dissolve (what was caked or close pressed).

desencallar, *va.* (naut.) to set (a stranded ship) afloat again.

desencaminar, *va.* to mislead, lead astray.

desencantamiento, *m.* = DESENCANTO.

desencantar, *va.* to disenchant; disillusion.

desencantaración, *f.* act and effect of drawing lots or of balloting.

desencantarar, *va.* to draw (lots) for candidates out of a CÁNTARO; to withdraw (a name).

desencanto, *m.* disenchantment, disillusion.

desencapillar, *va.* (naut.) to unrig, to take off the rigging of.

desencapotadura, *f.* stripping off a cloak or a greatcoat.

desencapotar. I. *va.* to strip (one) of his cloak or greatcoat; (coll.) to uncover, to make manifest; to raise and keep up the head of (a horse). **II.** *vr.* to clear up (s. o. the sky); to put away anger, to smooth one's brow, put on a pleasing countenance.

desencaprichar. I. *va.* to dissuade from error or prejudice; to disabuse, to cure of conceit. **II.** *vr.* to desist, yield, get over a whim, give up a hobby or mania.

desencarcelar, *va.* to disincarcerate, to set at liberty.

desencarecer, *va.* (*for irr. v.* CARECER) to reduce, to lower the price of.

desencarnar, *va.* to prevent (dogs) from eating game; to lose affection, liking for; to divert the mind from.

desencastillar, va. to expel or drive out of a castle; to manifest, make appear, reveal.

desencepar, va. (naut.) to clear (the anchor).

desencerrar, va. (for irr. v. CERRAR) to free from confinement; to open, to unclose; to disclose, make known.

desencintar, va. to ribbon off (a person or thing); to remove the curb of (a sidewalk).

desenclavar, va. to draw out nails from; to put (one) violently out of one's place.

desenclavijar, va. to take the pins or pegs out of.

desencoger. I. va. (for irr. v. COGER) to unfold, to spread open. **II.** vr. to lay aside bashfulness or reserve, to grow bold.

desencogimiento, m. ease, naturalness.

desencoladura, f. act or effect of ungluing.

desencolar, va. to unglue, to unsize.

desencolerizarse, vr. to grow calm, to cool off.

desenconamiento, m. act and effect of allaying an inflammation or appeasing anger.

desenconar. I. va. to allay (an inflammation); to calm, appease; to make mild and benign. **II.** vr. to become milder; to be appeased, to quiet down, cool off.

desencono, m. mitigation of anger or passion.

desencordar, va. (for irr. v. ACORDAR) to unstring (a musical instrument).

desencordelar, va. to loosen, to untie or take away strings or cords from.

desencorvar, va. to straighten.

desencrespar, va. to uncurl, unfrizzle.

desencrudecer, va. (for irr. v. ENCRUDECER) to prepare (silk or thread) for receiving the dye; to clean (fabrics) with lye.

desencrudecimiento, m. cleansing with lye.

desencuadernar, va. to unbind, to take off the binding of (a book).

desendemoniar, desendiablar, va. to drive an evil spirit out of.

desendiosar, va. to humble the vanity of.

desenfadadamente, adv. without embarrassment, boldly, unconcernedly.

desenfadaderas, f. pl.—**tener d.,** (coll.) to be resourceful.

desenfadado, da. I. a. unencumbered, free; ample, spacious; bold. **II.** pp. of DESENFADAR.

desenfadar. I. va. to appease, pacify. **II.** vr. to calm down, become calm, cool off.

desenfado, m. freedom, ease, naturalness; relaxation, diversion, entertainment.

desenfaldar, va. to let fall the train of (a gown).

desenfangar, va. to clean the mud out of.

desenfardar, desenfardelar, va. to unpack (bales of goods).

desenfilada. I. a. (mil.) under cover from fire. **II.** f. (fort.) defilading.

desenfilar, va. to put under cover from flank fire; (fort.) to defilade.

desenfrailar, vn. to leave the monastic life, become secularized; (coll.) to come out from subjection; to rest from business for a time.

desenfrenadamente, adv. ungovernably, licentiously.

desenfrenado, da. I. a. ungoverned, unbridled, outrageous, wanton. **II.** pp. of DESENFRENAR.

desenfrenamiento, m. unruliness, rashness, wantonness, licentiousness, boundless liberty or license; libidinousness.

desenfrenar. I. va. to unbridle. **II.** vr. to give loose rein to one's passions and desires; to fly into a violent passion; to be mad or wild.

desenfreno, m. = DESENFRENAMIENTO.—**d. de vientre,** diarrhea.

desenfundar, va. to take out of a bag, bolster, pillowcase, sheath, etc.

desenfurecerse, vr to become calm or appeased.

desengalanar, va. to remove trappings or adornments from.

desenganchar, va. to unhook, unclasp, unpin, unfasten; to uncouple; to disengage; to unhitch, unharness.

desengañadamente, adv. truly, clearly, ingenuously; awkwardly, carelessly, scurvily.

desengañado, da. I. a. undeceived, disabused, schooled by experience; despicable; ill-executed. **II.** pp. of DESENGAÑAR.

desengañador, ra, n. undeceiver, disabuser.

desengañar, va. to undeceive, free from error, disabuse, set right.

desengañilar, va. to free or disengage (a person or animal held by the throat).

desengaño, m. detection or discovery of an error; undeceiving; disillusion, disappointment; censure, reproof, reproach, upbraiding.—pl. sad lessons of experience.

desengarrafar, va. to unfasten or disengage from claws or clinched fingers.

desengarzar, va. to take out of a setting; to loosen from clasps, links or hooks.

desengastar, va. to take out of its setting.

desengomar, va. to ungum; to unsize (silk).

desengoznar, va. to unhinge; to disjoint.

desengranar. I. va. to uncouple; to disengage. **II.** vr. to get out of gear.

desengrane, m. disengaging of gear.

desengrasador, m. wringing machine; scourer; wiping clout.

desengrasar, va. to clean from grease; to scour.

desengrase, m. removal of grease; cleaning, scouring.

desengraso, m. (Ch.) dessert.

desengrosar, va. (for irr. v. ENGROSAR) to extenuate, make lean, weaken; to make thin or fine.

desengrudamiento, m. removal of sticking paste.

desengrudar, va. to scrape or rub off paste from.

desengrueso. V. DESENGROSAR.

desenguantarse, vr. to take off one's gloves.

desenhebrar, va. to unthread.

desenhornar, va. to take out of the oven.

desenjaezar, va. (for mut. v. ENJAEZAR) to unharness; to unsaddle.

desenjalmar, va. to take off a packsaddle from.

desenjaular, va. to uncage; (coll.) to remove from or let out of jail.

desenlabonar, va. to unlink.

desenlace, m. denouement, winding up; conclusion, end.

desenladrillar, va. to take off the tiles or bricks of.

desenlazar, va. (for mut. v. ENLAZAR) to unlace, untie, loose; to unravel (a dramatic plot)

desenlodar, va. to remove, clean off, mud from.

desenlosar, va. to take up the flagstones of; to unpave.

desenlutar, va. & vr. to take off mourning (from); to banish sorrow.

desenmallar, va. to take (fish) out of the net.

desenmarañar, va. to disentangle; to sleave (as a skein); straighten up; unravel, make clear.

desenmascarar, va. to unmask.

desenmohecer, va. (for irr. v. ENMOHECER) to clear of rust.

desenmudecer. I. va. (for irr. v. ENMUDECER) to remove an impediment of speech from. **II.** vn. & vr. to break a long silence.

desenojar. I. va. & vr. to appease, pacify, calm, allay the passion of. **II.** vr. to amuse one's self.

desenojo, m. appeasement, getting over anger.

desenojoso, sa, a. appeasing, reconciling.

desenredar. I. va. to disentangle; to unravel; to extricate, loose; to clear. **II.** vr. to extricate one's self from difficulties.

desenredo, m. disentanglement; denouement.

desenrollar, va. to unroll, unwind.

desenronar, va. to remove débris from.

desenronquecer, va. to free from hoarseness.

desenroscar, va. (for mut. v. ENROSCAR) to untwine, untwist; to unscrew.

desensabanar, va. (coll.) to change or take off the sheets of.

desensamblar, va. to disjoint, separate.

desensañar, va. to appease, pacify.

desensartar, va. to unthread, unstring.

desensebar. I. *va.* to strip of fat. **II.** *vn.* to change occupation or exercise in order to render one's work more endurable; to draw breath; to take away the taste of fat (with an olive or sweets).

desenseñado, da, *a.* untaught.

desenseñar, *va.* to unteach.

desensillar, *va.* to unsaddle.

desensoberbecer. I. *va.* (*for irr. v.* ENSOBERBECER) to humble. **II.** *vr.* to become humble, to control one's pride.

desensortijado, da, *a.* dislocated, displaced.

desentablar, *va.* to rip up or off planks or boards from; to disturb, disarrange, confuse; to embroil; to break off (a bargain); to estrange.

desentalingar, *va.* (naut.) to unbend (a cable).

desentarimar, *va.* to remove a platform or stand from.

desentarquinar, *va.* to free from mud.

desentejar, *va.* to untile, take off the tiles of.

desentenderse, *vr.* (*for irr. v.* ENTENDER) (w. **de**) to feign not to understand; to ignore; to pay no attention (to); to shirk.

desentendido, da. I. *a.* unmindful, showing or feigning ignorance.—**hacerse el d.,** or **darse por d.,** (coll.) to wink at a thing; to pretend not to have noticed. **II.** *pp.* of DESENTENDERSE.

desenterrador, *m.* one that disinters or digs up.

desenterramiento, *m.* disinterment.

desenterrar, *va.* (*for irr. v.* ENTERRAR) to disinter, unbury, dig up, unearth; to recall.

desentiendo. *V.* DESENTENDERSE.

desentierramuertos, *m.* (coll.) calumniator or abuser of the dead.

desentierro. *V.* DESENTERRAR.

desentoldar, *va.* to take off an awning from; to strip of ornaments.

desentonación, *f.* dissonance.

desentonadamente, *adv.* unharmoniously.

desentonado, da, *a.* & *pp.* of DESENTONAR; out of tune; inharmonious, discordant.

desentonamiento, *m.* dissonance.

desentonar. I. *va.* to humble; to wound the pride of. **II.** *vn.* to be out of tune; to be inharmonious. **III.** *vr.* to be rude or uncouth; to raise the voice in disrespect.

desentono, *m.* harsh, rude tone of voice; musical discord; false note.

desentornillar, *va.* to unscrew.

desentorpecer. I. *va.* (*for irr. v.* ENTORPECER) to free from torpor; to restore motion to (torpid limbs). **II.** *vr.* to be freed from torpor; to be restored from numbness; to become lively, smart, or pert.

desentrampar, *va.* to free from debts.

desentrañamiento, *m.* giving away one's belongings as a proof of love.

desentrañar. I. *va.* to eviscerate, disembowel; to penetrate or dive into; to bring out, reveal, dig out; (naut.) to remove loops, twists, from (ropes). **II.** *vr.* to give away one's all out of love.

desentristecer, *va.* (*for irr. v.* ENTRISTECER) to soothe the sadness of, to cheer, comfort.

desentronizar, *va.* (*for mut. v.* ENTRONIZAR) to dethrone; to deprive of power or authority.

desentumecer, desentumir. I. *vr.* to be freed from numbness. **II.** *va.* to free from torpor.

desenvainar, *va.* to unsheath (as a sword); (coll.) to expose, uncover; to take out, show (the claws or talons).

desenvelejar, *va.* (naut.) to strip of sails.

desenvendar, *va.* to take off fillets or bands from.

desenvenenar, *va.* to extract, remove poison from; to destroy the poison of, or in.

desenvergar, *va.* (*for mut. v.* ENVERGAR) (naut.) to unbend (a sail).

desenviolar, *va.* to bless or purify (a holy place which has been desecrated).

desenvoltura, *f.* sprightliness, ease; impudence; effrontery; lewd posture or gesture in women; graceful and easy delivery in conversation or acting.

desenvolvedor, ra, *n.* unfolder, investigator.

desenvolver. I. *va.* (*for irr. v.* ENVOLVER) to unfold, unroll; unwrap; to decipher, discover, unravel; to develop (as a theme); to evolve. **II.** *vr.* to be forward, to behave with too much assurance; to unfold, unroll.

desenvolvimiento, *m.* unfolding, development.

desenvueltamente, *adv.* in a free and easy manner; expeditiously.

desenvuelto, ta, *pp.* & *a.* forward; free, easy.

desenvuelvo. *V.* DESENVOLVER.

desenyesar. I. *va.* to remove plaster from. **II.** *vr.* to scale off (s. o. a plastered surface).

desenzarzar, *va.* & *vr.* to disentangle from brambles; to appease, reconcile.

deseo, *m.* desire, wish.—**tener d. de, venir en d. de,** to desire.

deseoso, sa, *a.* desirous.

desequido, da, *a.* dry.

desequilibrado, da. I. *a.* unbalanced, unpoised; of an unbalanced mind; reckless, thoughtless. **II.** *pp.* of DESEQUILIBRAR.

desequilibrar, *va.* to unbalance.

desequilibrio, *m.* lack of equilibrium; an unbalanced condition; disorder, disturbance, confusion.

deserción, *f.* desertion; (law) abandonment of a suit by plaintiff.

deserrado, da, *a.* free from error.

desertar. I. *va.* to desert; to abandon. **II.** *vr.* (w. **de**) to desert.—**d. a,** to go over to.

desertor, ra, *n.* deserter; forsaker.

deservicio, *m.* disservice; fault committed against a person who has a claim to services.

deservidor, *m.* he who fails in serving another.

deservir, *va.* (*for irr. v.* SERVIR) not to perform one's duty to; to disserve.

desescamar, *va.* to scale; to remove scales from.

desescombrar, *va.* to clear of rubbish.

deseslabonar, *va.* to cut the links of; to unlink.

desespaldar, *va.* to wound in the shoulder.

desespaldillar. I. *va.* to wound in the shoulder blade. **II.** *vr.* to receive a lesion in the shoulder blade.

desesperación, *f.* despondency, despair, desperation; anger, passion, fury.—**es una d.,** (coll.) it is unbearable.

desesperadamente, *adv.* despairingly, hopelessly; desperately, furiously, madly.

desesperado, da. I. *a.* desperate, hopeless; furious, raving mad. **II.** *pp.* of DESESPERAR.

desesperante, *a.* causing despair, maddening; hopeless.

desesperanzar. I. *va.* (*for mut. v.* ESPERANZAR) to deprive of hope, to discourage. **II.** *vr.* to lose hope, to despair, become discouraged.

desesperar. I. *vn.* to lose hope, to despair. **II.** *va.* to make (one) despair, to discourage hope. **III.** *vr.* to despair, to despond; to fret, to be grievously vexed.

desespigar, *va.* (*v.* ESPIGAR) to thrash (grain).

desesponjarse, *vr.* to lose sponginess.

desestancar, *va.* (*for mut. v.* ESTANCAR) to take away (a monopoly) from; to declare open to trade, raise the monopoly on.

desestañar, *va.* & *vr.* to unsolder.

desester, *va.* to take the matting off.

desestero, *m.* act and season of taking off the mats.

desestima, desestimación, *f.* disesteem, disrespect; crying down, rejection.

desestimador, ra, *n.* & *a.* contemner (-ing), despiser (-ing).

desestimar, *va.* to disregard, contemn, undervalue; to reject, deny.

desfacedor, *m.* (obs.) destroyer.—**d. de entuertos,** undoer of injuries, righter of wrongs.

desfacer, *va.* (*for irr. v.* HACER) (obs.) = DESHACER.—**d. agravios,** or **d. entuertos,** to right wrongs.

desfacimiento, *m.* (obs.) destruction, undoing.

desfachatadamente, *adv.* impudently, with effrontery, brazenly.

---

desfachatado, da, *a.* (coll.) impudent, saucy, "nervy," "cheeky," brazen.

desfachatez, *f.* (coll.) impudence, assurance, effrontery, barefacedness, "nerve," "cheek."

desfajar, *va.* to ungird.

desfalcador, ra, *n.* embezzler, defaulter.

desfalcar, *va.* (*for mut. v.* CALCAR) to take away part of; to cut off, to lop; to defalcate, embezzle.

desfalco, *m.* diminution, diminishing, detracting; defalcation, embezzlement, peculation.

desfallecer. I. *vn.* (*for irr. v.* FALLECER) to pine, to fall away, to grow weak; to swoon, faint. **II.** *va.* to weaken, debilitate.

desfalleciente, *a.* pining, languishing.

desfallecimiento, *m.* languor; dejection; swoon, fainting fit.

desfallezco. *V.* DESFALLECER.

desfavorable, *a.* unfavorable, contrary.

desfavorablemente, *adv.* unfavorably.

desfavorecedor, ra, *n.* disfavorer, contemner.

desfavorecer, *va.* (*for irr. v.* FAVORECER) to disfavor, to discountenance; to despise, contemn; to injure, hurt; to contradict, oppose.

desfibrar, *va.* to rid of fibers; to extract the fiber from.

desfiguración, *f.*, **desfiguramiento,** *m.* deformation, disfigurement.

desfigurar. I. *va.* to disfigure, deform; misshape; to disguise (as the voice); to misrepresent, misstate, distort; to cloud, to darken. **II.** *vr.* to become disfigured.

desfijar, *va.* to take off, pull off, remove.

desfilachar, *va.* = DESHILACHAR.

desfilada, *f.* (mil.) single file.

desfiladero, *m.* defile, narrow passage; road at the side of a precipice.

desfilar, *vn.* (mil.) to defile, to march off by files, to file off; to march in review.

desfile, *m.* defiling, marching by files.

desflecar, *va.* (*for mut. v.* SECAR) to remove the flakes of (wool) or frettings of (cloth).

desflegmación, *f.* dephlegmation.

desflemar, *va.* to dephlegmate.

desflocar, *va.* = DESFLECAR.

desfloración, *f.* defloration.

desfloramiento, *m.* violation, ravishment.

desflorar, *va.* to tarnish, to disluster; to ruffle, discompose; to violate, deflower; to treat superficially, touch upon.

desflorecer, *vn.* & *vr.* to lose the flowers.

desflorecimiento, *m.* falling of flowers.

desflueco. *V.* DESFLOCAR.

desfogar. I. *va.* (*for mut. v.* AHOGAR) to vent, to make an opening in for fire; to give loose rein to (a horse). **II.** *vr.* to vent one's anger.

desfogonadura, *f.* erosion of a cannon.

desfogonar, *va.* to widen or burst the vent of (a cannon).

desfogue, *m.* venting or foaming out of passion.

desfollonar, *va.* to strip useless leaves off.

desfondar, *va.* to break or take off the bottom of; (naut.) to penetrate the bottom of (a ship); (agr.) to cultivate or dig (the soil) to a great depth.

desformar, *va.* to disfigure, deform.

desfortalecer, desfortificar, *va.* (*for irr. v.* FORTALECER, FORTIFICAR) (mil.) to dismantle, to demolish.

desforzarse, *vr.* to take revenge.

desfosforar, *va.* to dephosphorize.

desfrenar, *va.* to unbridle.

desfrutar, *va.* to take the green fruit off (a tree).

desgaire, *m.* graceless mien or deportment; slovenliness; affected carelessness in dress; contemptuous gesture.—**al d.,** affectedly careless; disdainfully.

desgajadura, *f.* disruption, tearing off the branch of a tree.

desgajar. I. *va.* to tear off the branches of; to break or tear off. **II.** *vr.* to be separated or disjointed; to be torn off; to fall off.

desgaje, *m.* act of breaking or tearing off.

desgalgadero, *m.* rugged declivitous place.

desgalgado, da, *a.* & *pp.* precipitated.

desgalgar, *va.* & *vr.* (*for mut. v.* APAGAR) to precipitate, to throw headlong.

desgalichado, da, *a.* (coll.) ungainly, ungraceful.

desgana, *f.* lack of appetite; unwillingness, reluctance.—**desganado, da,** having no appetite.

desganar. I. *va.* to discourage. **II.** *vr.* to lose one's appetite; to lose interest; to become reluctant or unwilling.

desganchar, *va.* to lop off the branches of.

desgano, *m.* = DESGANA.

desgañifarse, desgañitarse, *vr.* to shriek, to scream to the top of one's voice.

desgarbado, da, *a.* ungraceful, uncouth, ungainly, gawky.

desgargantarse, *vr.* (coll.) to get hoarse from bawling or screaming, to shout one's self hoarse.

desgargolar, *va.* to ripple (as flax or hemp); to take (a board) out of a groove.

desgaritar. I. *vn.* (naut.) to lose the course. **II.** *vr.* to go astray from a fold (s. o. sheep); to give up a plan or undertaking.

desgarradamente, *adv.* impudently, barefacedly, shamelessly.

desgarrado, da, *pp.* & *a.* licentious, dissolute; impudent, shameless, bold.

desgarrador, ra. I. *n.* tearer. **II.** *a.* tearing; heart-breaking, heart-rending.

desgarradura, *f.* rent, laceration, break.

desgarrar. I. *va.* to rend, tear; to claw; (Cuba) to expectorate, cough up (phlegm). **II.** *vr.* to withdraw from another's company; to tear one's self away.

desgarro, *m.* laceration, rent, break, breach; impudence, effrontery; looseness, criminal levity; idle boast, brag.

desgarrón, *m. aug.* large rent or hole; piece of cloth torn off.

desgastamiento, *m.* prodigality, extravagance.

desgastar. I. *va.* to wear away, abrade, consume, waste by degrees; to corrode, gnaw, eat away. **II.** *vr.* to lose strength and vigor; to debilitate one's self; to wear down or away.

desgaste, *m.* slow waste; attrition, abrasion; wear and tear; erosion, fray.

desgatar, *va.* (agr.) to root out the rest-harrow from.

desgaznatarse, *vr.* = DESGAÑITARSE.

desglosar, *va.* to blot out marginal notes from; to take off; to separate sheets from (a book).

desglose, *m.* act of blotting out a comment or gloss.

desgobernado, da. I. *a.* ill-governed or ungovernable person. **II.** *pp.* of DESGOBERNAR.

desgobernadura, *f.* (vet.) confining of a vein.

desgobernar. I. *va.* (*for irr. v.* GOBERNAR) to disturb or overset the government of; to misgovern; to dislocate or disjoint (as bones); (vet.) to bar (a vein) on a horse's leg; (naut.) to neglect, not handle right. **II.** *vr.* to affect ridiculous motions in dancing.

desgobierno, *m.* mismanagement; misgovernment; misrule; maladministration; (vet.) barring a vein on a horse's leg.

desgolletar, *va.* to break off the neck of (a bottle or other vessel); to uncover the neck of.

desgomar, *va.* to ungum, to unsize (silk).

desgonzar, *va.* = DESGOZNAR.

desgorrarse, *vr.* to pull off one's hat, cap, etc.

desgoznar. I. *va.* to unhinge, disjoint. **II.** *vr.* to be dislocated or disjointed; to be torn in pieces; to distort the body with violent motions.

desgracia, *f.* misfortune, mishap; affliction, sorrow, grief, bereavement; enmity, unfriendly attitude; disgrace, state of being out of favor; lack of grace, ungracefulness; unpleasantness, rudeness of language and address.—**caer en d.,** to lose favor.—**correr d.,** to fail.—**por d.,** unfortunately.

desgraciadamente, *adv.* unfortunately.

desgraciado, da. I. *a.* unfortunate, unhappy, unlucky: misadventured, luckless, hapless; out of work; disagreeable, ungrateful. **II.** *n.* wretch, unfortunate or God-forsaken person. **III.** *pp.* of DESGRACIAR.

desgraciar. I. *va.* to displease; maim; to spoil. **II.** *vr.* to disgrace, to lose favor; to fall out (with a person); to become a cripple; to lose the perfection formerly possessed; to degenerate; to die young: to fail, fall through (as a project).

desgramar, *va.* to pull up the grass of.

desgranadera, *f.* grape picker.

desgranador, ra, *n.* sheller, thrasher; flail.

desgranamiento, *m.* (agr.) shaking or beating out grain; thrashing, shelling; (mil.) grooves that the powder forms on the inner orifice of the venthole.

desgranar. I. *va.* to beat or shake out the grain from (cereals); to thrash, flail; to shell (as peas). **II.** *vr.* to shed the grains; to scatter about (as beads); (mil.) to wear away (app. to the vent of firearms).

desgrane, *m.* shelling; act of the grain becoming loose; scattering of grain or beads.

desgranzar, *va.* to separate the husks or chaff from; (pict.) to give the first grinding to (colors).

desgrasar, *va.* to remove the grease from.

desgrase, *m.* removal of grease.

desgreñar. I. *va.* to dishevel. **II.** *vr.* to quarrel: to pull each other's hair.

desguace, *m.* rough dressing (of lumber).

desguarnecer, *va.* (*for irr. v.* GUARNECER) to strip of trimmings and ornaments; to deprive of strength; to strip of all accessories; to disgarnish; to disgarrison; to disarm; to unharness.

desguarnezco. *V.* DESGUARNECER.

desguarnir, *va.* (naut.) to unrig (the capstan).

desguazar, *va.* to rough-dress (timber) with the ax; (naut.) to take (a ship) to pieces; to unbuild, break up.

desguince, *m.* knife that cuts rags in paper-mills; dodging, dodge.

desguindar. I. *va.* (naut.) to take and bring down. **II.** *vr.* to slide down a rope.

desguinzar, *va.* to cut (cloth or rags) in paper mills.

deshabitado, da. I. *a.* uninhabited, untenanted, deserted. **II.** *pp.* of DESHABITAR.

deshabitar, *va.* to quit, move out of; to unpeople, to depopulate.

deshabituación, *f.* disuse, disusage, desuetude.

deshabituar, *va.* to disaccustom.

deshacedor, m..—d. de agravios, undoer of injuries, righter of wrongs.

deshacer. I. *va.* (*for irr. v.* HACER) to undo; to destroy; take apart; to undo, untie, open (as a parcel); to consume, to diminish; to cancel, blot or scratch out; to efface; to cut to pieces, destroy; to put to flight; to melt, dissolve, liquefy; to cut up, divide; to violate (a treaty or agreement); (mil.) to discharge from service.—**d. agravios,** to right wrongs. **II.** *vr.* to be wasted, consumed, destroyed; to grieve, mourn; to disappear, vanish; to do anything with vehemence: to grow feeble or meagre; to be crippled, grievously maltreated.—**deshacerse de,** to get rid, or rid one's self, of; to part with.—**deshacerse en lágrimas** to burst into tears.

deshago, deshice, deshaga. *V.* DESHACER).

deshaldo, *m.* = MARCEO.

deshambrido, da, *a.* exceedingly hungry, famished, starving.

desharrapado, da. *a.* shabby, ragged, in tatters.

desharrapamiento, *m.* misery, meanness.

deshebillar, *va.* to unbuckle.

deshebrar, *va.* to unthread, to ravel into threads to separate into filaments.

deshecha, *f.* simulation, evasion, shift; polite farewell: a step in a Spanish dance.—**a la d.,** dissemblingly; deceitfully.—**hacer la d.,** to dissemble, feign, pretend.

deshechizar, *va.* to disenchant; break a spell in.

deshechizo, *m.* disenchantment, breaking of a magic spell.

deshecho, cha, *a.* & *pp.* of DESHACER; undone, destroyed, wasted; melted; in pieces; perfectly mixed (app. to colors).

deshelar. I. *va.* & *vr.* (*for irr. v.* HELAR) to thaw; to melt. **II.** *v. imp.* to thaw.

desherbar, *va.* (*for irr. v.* HERBAR) to pluck up or extirpate herbs from; to weed.

desheredación, *f.,* **desheredamiento,** *m.* disinheriting, disinheritance.

desheredar. I. *va.* to disinherit; to cut out from an hereditary right. **II.** *vr.* to degenerate.

deshermanar. I. *va.* to unmatch. **II.** *vr.* to violate the love due to a brother.

desherradura, *f.* (vet.) surbating.

desherrar, *va.* (*for irr. v.* HERRAR) to unchain; to rip off the shoes of (horses).

desherrumbrar, *va.* to clean of rust.

deshidratación, *f.* dehydration.

deshidratar, *va.* to dehydrate.

deshidrogenar, *va.* to dehydrogenize.

deshielo, *m.* thaw, thawing.

deshielo, deshiele. *V.* DESHELAR.

deshilachar. I. *va.* to ravel, to uncord. **II.** *vr.* to fuzz, to ravel.

deshiladiz, *m.* = FILADIZ.

deshilado, *m.* openwork, drawn work.

deshilado, da, *pp.* & *a.* marching in a file.—**a la d.,** in file, one after another; stealthily; deceitfully, dissemblingly.

deshiladura, *f.* ripping, ravelling out.

deshilar. I. *va.* to ravel; to scrape (lint); to distract (bees); to carve (a fowl) in thin strips. **II.** *vr.* to grow thin; to fuzz.

deshilo, *m.* obstructing the communication of bees, to get them into a new hive.

deshilvanado, da, *pp.* & *a.* disjointed, disconnected; without sequence.

deshilvanar, *va.* to remove the basting threads from.

deshincadura, *f.* act of drawing out anything nailed or fixed.

deshincar, *va.* to draw out, pull out, remove.

deshinchadura, *f.* act of abating a swelling.

deshinchar. I. *va.* to reduce the swelling of, to deflate; to appease the anger or annoyance of. **II.** *vr.* to contract, decrease, shrink, shrivel (app. to anything swollen or puffed); (coll.) to abate presumption, to give up airs.

deshojador, *m.* stripper of leaves.

deshojadura, *f.* stripping a tree of its leaves.

deshojar, *va.* to strip off the leaves of.

deshoje, *m.* falling off of leaves.

deshollejar, *va.* to peel, pare, skin (as grapes); to shell (as beans).

deshollinadera, *f.* chimney-sweeping broom.

deshollinador, *m.* chimney sweeper; any device used for sweeping chimneys; (coll.) one that examines and inspects minutely and curiously.

deshollinar, *va.* to sweep or clean (chimneys); to clean (ceilings and walls) with a turk's head; (coll.) to view and examine minutely.

deshonestamente, *adv.* dishonorably, disgracefully; lewdly, lustily, immodestly.

deshonestarse, *vr.* to be indecorous or lewd.

deshonestidad, *f.* immodesty; indecency; dishonesty; lewdness.

deshonesto, ta, *a.* immodest; lewd, unchaste, lustful; dishonest, crooked.

deshonor, *m.* dishonor, disgrace; insult, affront.

deshonorar, *va.* to dishonor, disgrace; to deprive of office or employ.

deshonra, *f.* dishonor, disgrace; seduction or violation (of a woman).—**tener a d.,** to consider dishonorable or disgraceful.

deshonrabuenos, *n.* calumniator; degenerate.

deshonradamente, *adv.* dishonorably, shamefully, disgracefully.

deshonrador, ra, *n.* dishonorer, disgracer.

deshonrar, *va.* to affront, insult, defame; to dishonor, disgrace; to scorn, to despise; to seduce or ruin (a woman).

deshonrible, *a.* (coll.) shameless, despicable.

---

deshonroso, sa, *a.* dishonorable, disgraceful.
deshora, *f.* unseasonable or inconvenient time.—
a d., or **a deshoras,** untimely, unseasonably; extemporary.
deshornar, *va.* to take out of the oven.
deshospedamiento, *m.* inhospitality, act of refusing strangers a lodging.
deshuesar, *va.* to bone (an animal); to take the pits out of (fruits).
deshumanizar, *va.* to dehumanize.
deshumano, na, *a.* inhuman.
deshumedecer. I. *va.* (*for mut. v.* HUMEDECER) to exsiccate, to deprive of humidity. **II.** *vr.* to dry, become dry.
desiderable, *a.* desirable.
desiderativo, va, *a.* desirous.
desiderátum, *m.* desideratum.
desidia, *f.* laziness, indolence.
desidiosamente, *adv.* indolently, lazily.
desidioso, sa, *a.* lazy, indolent.
desierto, ta. I. *a.* deserted, uninhabited, lonely.
II. *m.* desert, waste, wilderness.
designación, *f.* designation.
designar, *va.* to purpose, intend; to designate, name, appoint.
designio, *m.* design, purpose, intention.
desigual, *a.* unequal, unlike; uneven, unlevel, rough, broken, craggy; arduous, difficult; perilous; changeable; abrupt; excessive, extreme.
desigualar. I. *va.* to make unequal or dissimilar; to mismatch. **II.** *vr.* to excel, to surpass.
desigualdad, *f.* inequality, difference; changeableness, inconstancy; wrong, injury, injustice; knottiness; unevenness, roughness, cragginess.
desigualmente, *adv.* unequally, unevenly.
desilusión, *f.* disillusion, disillusionment.
desilusionar. I. *va.* to disillusion, disenchant; to undeceive. **II.** *vr.* to lose an illusion; to be disabused, undeceived; to become disillusioned.
desimaginar, *va.* to blot out or obliterate in the mind.
desimanación, *f.* = DESIMANACIÓN.
desimanar. I. *va.* to demagnetize. **II.** *vr.* to become demagnetized, lose its magnetism.
desimantación, *f.* = DESIMANACIÓN.
desimantar, *va.* & *vr.* = DESIMANAR.
desimpresionar, *va.* to undeceive.
desinclinar, *va.* to disincline.
desincorporación, *f.* disincorporation, end of corporate existence.
desincorporar, *va.* & *vr.* to disincorporate.
desincrustante. I. *a.* scale-removing. **II.** *n.* disincrustant, boiler compound.
desincrustar, *va.* to remove incrustations from.
desinencia, *f.* (gram.) declension, inflection, desinence; (rhet.) ending of a sentence.
desinfección, *f.* disinfection; disinfecting.
desinfectante, *n.* & *a.* disinfectant (-ing).
desinfectar, *va.* to disinfect; to sterilize.
desinficionamiento, *m.* disinfection.
desinficionar, *va.* to free from infection; to disinfect.
desinflamar, *va.* to remove the inflammation of.
desinflar, *va.* to deflate.
desinsaculación, *f.* act of drawing lots.
desinsacular, *va.* to draw lots or names from an urn or balloting box.
desinterés, *m.* disinterestedness.
desinteresadamente, *adv.* disinterestedly.
desinteresado, da, *a.* disinterested, impartial.
desinvernar, *vn.* (mil.) to leave winter quarters.
desirvo. *V.* DESERVIR.
desistencia, *f.,* **desistimiento,** *m.* desisting, act of desisting.
desistir, *vn.* (w. **de**) to desist, cease, give up; to flinch (from); (for.) to waive (a right).
desjarretadera, *f.* hooked knife for hocking or hamstringing cattle.
desjarretar, *va.* to hock, to hamstring; (coll.) to weaken, to debilitate (as by bleeding a patient).
desjarrete, *m.* act of hamstringing or hocking.

desjugar, *va.* (*for mut. v.* ENJUGAR) to extract the juice from.
desjuiciado, da, *a.* lacking sense or judgment.
desjuntamiento, *m.* separation, disjunction.
desjuntar, *va.* & *vr.* to disjoint, divide; to separate, to part.
deslabonar. I. *va.* to unlink, to disjoin; to destroy. **II.** *vr.* to withdraw, to retire.
desladrillar, *va.* = DESENLADRILLAR.
deslamar, *va.* to clear of mud.
deslastrar, *va.* to unballast.
deslatar, *va.* to take off the laths from.
deslavado, da, *pp.* & *a.* impudent, barefaced.
deslavadura, *f.* washing, rinsing.
deslavar, *va.* to wash or cleanse superficially, to rinse; to wet, spoil by wetting; to take away the color, force, or vigor of.
deslavazar, *va.* = DESLAVAR.
deslazamiento, *m.* disjunction, dissolution.
deslazar, *va.* to unlace, untie.
desleal, *a.* disloyal; perfidious, faithless.
deslealmente, *adv.* disloyally, treacherously.
deslealtad, *f.* disloyalty, treachery, faithlessness.
deslechar, *va.* to remove the leaves and dirt from (silkworms).
deslecho, *m.* act of cleansing silkworms.
deslechugador, *m.* vinedresser, pruner.
deslechugar, deslechuguillar, *va.* (agr.) to cut and prune the branches of (vines).
desleidura, *f.,* **desleimiento,** *m.* dilution; making thin or weak.
desleír, *va.* (ind. DESLÍO: pret. él DESLIÓ: subj. yo DESLÍA) to dilute; dissolve; to make thin or weak.
deslendrar, *va.* to clean (the hair) of nits.
deslenguado, da, *pp.* & *a.* loquacious, impudent, foul-mouthed, scurrilous.
deslenguamiento, *m.* loquacity, impudence.
deslenguar. I. *va.* to cut out the tongue of. **II.** *vr.* to speak impudently or recklessly, to unloosen one's tongue.
desliar, *va.* to untie, loose, unpack.
desligadura, *f.,* **desligamiento,** *m.* disjunction, untying.
desligar. I. *va.* (*for mut. v.* LIGAR) to loosen, untie, unbind; to disentangle, extricate, unravel; to absolve from ecclesiastical censure; excuse from an obligation; to remove (from a ship) part of its knees or futtock-timbers, or the spikes holding them; (med.) to unfasten (bandages or ligatures); (mus.) to play or sing staccato. **II.** *vr.* to get loose, to give way.
deslindable, *a.* capable of demarcation.
deslindador, *m.* one who sets boundaries.
deslindamiento, *m.* demarcation, determination of boundaries.
deslindar, *va.* to mark the boundaries of; to clear up, to define, circumscribe.
deslinde, *m.* = DESLINDAMIENTO.
desliñar, *va.* to clean (fulled cloth) before sending to the press.
desliz, *m.* slip; act of slipping or sliding; false step; frailty, slight fault; (min.) mercury that escapes in smelting silver ore.
deslizable, *a.* that can slip or slide.
deslizadero. I. *m.* slippery place. **II.** *a.* = DESLIZADIZO.
deslizadero, ra; deslizadizo, za, *a.* slippery.
deslizador, *m.* (aer.) glider.
deslizamiento, *m.* slip, slipping; skidding.
deslizar. I. *vn.* & *vr.* (pret. DESLICÉ: subj. DESLICE) to slip; to slide; to act or speak carelessly. **II.** *vr.* to shirk, to evade; to skid; to glide.
deslomadura, *f.* act of breaking the back; (vet.) a disease of the muscles of the loins.
deslomar, *va.* to break the back of; to distort or strain the loins of, to chine.
deslucidamente, *adv.* ungracefully, inelegantly; poorly, badly, unsuccessfully.
deslucido, da, *pp.* & *a.* unadorned; ungraceful, awkward; useless, fruitless.—**quedar,** or **salir, d.,** to fail, make or be a failure, to make or be a fizzle.

deslucimiento, *m.* failure, lack of success; awkwardness, uncouthness.

deslucir. I. *va.* (*for irr. v.* LUCIR) to tarnish or impair the lustre and splendor of; to discredit, impair the reputation of. **II.** *vr.* to do poorly or badly, to be a failure, to be or make a fizzle; to obscure one's merit.

deslumbrador, ra, *a.* dazzling, glaring.

deslumbramiento, *m.* glare, overpowering lustre, dazzling; confusion of sight or mind, hallucination.

deslumbrante, *a.* dazzling.

deslumbrar, *va.* to dazzle; to puzzle, to leave in doubt and uncertainty.

deslustrador, ra, *n. & a.* tarnisher (-ing).

deslustrar, *va.* to tarnish, to take away the lustre of, to dim; to unglaze; to sponge; to make less beautiful or illustrious; to soil, stain, (reputation, etc.)

deslustre, *m.* spot or stain; dimness, dulness; disgrace, ignominy, stigma.

deslustroso, sa, *a.* unbecoming, ugly.

desmadejamiento, *m.* languishment, languidness.

desmadejar. I. *va.* to enervate, to produce languor in. **II.** *vr.* to languish, to be enervated and weak.

desmadrado, da, *a.* separated from the mother (s. o. animals).—**desmadrar,** *va.* to separate (an animal) from the mother.

desmagnetizar, *va.* to demagnetize.

desmajolar, *va.* to pull up (vines) by the roots; to loosen or untie.

desmalezar, *va.* to weed.

desmallador, ra, *n.* one who breaks or cuts meshes.

desmalladura, *f.* act of ripping up or breaking meshes.

desmallar, *va.* to cut and destroy the meshes of.

desmamar, *va.* = DESTETAR.

desmamonar, *va.* to cut off the young shoots of.

desmán, *m.* misbehavior; excess in actions or words; misfortune, mishap, calamity.

desmanarse, *vr.* to stray from a flock or herd.

desmandado, da, *pp. & a.* impuden*t*; unbridled, lawless, unruly; disobedient.

desmandamiento, *m.* countermanding of an order; sauciness, impudence.

desmandar. I. *va.* to repeal (an order), to countermand; to revoke. **II.** *vr.* to transgress the bounds of justice and reason; to be impudent; to lose moderation or self-control; to stray from the flock; to go astray.

desmanear, *va.* to unfetter, to take off fetters or shackles from (horses, mules, etc.).

desmangar, *va.* to take off the handle of.

desmanotado, da, *a.* unhandy, awkward.

desmantecar, *va.* to take butter or lard out of.

desmantelado, da, *a. & pp.* of DESMANTELAR; dismantled, ruinous, dilapidated.

desmantelar, *va.* to dismantle; to abandon, desert, forsake; (naut.) to unmast.

desmaña, *f.* awkwardness, clumsiness; laziness.

desmañado, da, *a.* unhandy, clumsy, awkward; lazy, indolent.

desmarañar, *va.* to disentangle.

desmarcar, *va.* (*for mut. v.* MARCAR) to remove, efface, obliterate (marks).

desmarojador, ra, *n.* one who rids the trees of dead leaves or branches.

desmarojar, *va.* to take dry leaves or branches off (a tree).

desmarrido, da, *a.* sad, dejected; exhausted.

desmatar, *adv.* = DESCUAJAR.

desmayadamente, *adv.* weakly, dejectedly.

desmayado, da, *a. & pp.* of DESMAYAR; pale, wan, faint of lustre; dismayed, discouraged.

desmayar. I. *vn.* to be dispirited, faint-hearted, discouraged. **II.** *va.* to dismay, depress, discourage. **III.** *vr.* to faint, swoon.

desmayo, *m.* swoon, fainting fit; lowering of vigor or strength; dismay, discouragement.

desmazalado, da, *a.* weak, dejected, faint-hearted, spiritless.

desmechado, da, *a.* (Am.) disheveled.

desmedidamente, *adv.* disproportionately, excessively.

desmedido, da. I. *a.* excessive, out of proportion or measure. **II.** *pp.* of DESMEDIRSE.

desmedirse, *vr.* to forget one's self, to be impudent or saucy; to lose self-control.

desmedrar. I. *vn.* to decrease, decay. **II.** *va.* to impair, deteriorate.

desmedro, *m.* diminution, detriment.

desmedular, *va.* to remove the marrow from.

desmejora, *f.* deterioration, depreciation, impairment; diminution, loss.

desmejorar. I. *va.* to debase, to make worse, impair. **II.** *vn. & vr.* to decline, become worse; to deteriorate.

desmelancolizar, *va.* to cheer, enliven, gladden.

desmelar, *va.* to take the honey from (a hive).

desmelenar, *va.* to dishevel, to disarrange or muss the hair of.

desmembración, *f.* dismemberment, amputation, division.

desmembrador, ra, *n.* divider; one who dismembers or divides.

desmembrar, *va.* (*for irr. v.* SEMBRAR) to dismember, to tear asunder; to curtail; (surg.) to amputate; to separate, divide.

desmemoria, *f.* forgetfulness; lack of memory.

desmemoriado, da. I. *a.* forgetful; devoid of memory. **II.** *pp.* of DESMEMORIARSE.

desmemoriarse, *vr.* to become forgetful, to forget; to lose memory.

desmenguar, *va.* to lessen; to diminish.

desmentida, *f.* act of giving the lie.

desmentidor, ra. I. *a.* that gives the lie, disproving. **II.** *n.* one who gives the lie; disprover.

desmentir. I. *va.* (*for irr. v.* MENTIR) to give the lie to; to convince of a falsehood; to contradict; to counterfeit, conceal, dissemble; to do things unworthy of (one's birth, character, profession). **II.** *vn.* to deviate from the right line. **III.** *vr.* to recant, retract.

desmenuzable, *a.* crisp, crumbly, crimp, easily crumbled.

desmenuzador, ra, *n.* one who crumbles; investigator; purifier.

desmenuzamiento, *m.* crumbling, breaking into small pieces.

desmenuzar. I. *va.* (*pret.* DESMENUCÉ: *subj.* DESMENUCE) to crumble, crumb; to shred; to break or tear into bits; to chip, mill, fritter; to sift, examine minutely. **II.** *vr.* to crumble, to fall into small pieces.

desmeollamiento, *m.* taking out the marrow.

desmeollar, *va.* to take the marrow or pith from.

desmerecedor, ra, *a.* unworthy, undeserving.

desmerecer. I. *va.* (*for irr. v.* MERECER) to become unworthy or undeserving of. **II.** *vn.* to lose worth; to deteriorate; to be comparatively inferior, to compare unfavorably.

desmerecimiento, *m.* demerit, unworthiness.

desmesura, *f.* excess, lack of measure.

desmesuradamente, *adv.* disproportionately, excessively.

desmesurado, da. I. *a.* disproportionate, excessive. **II.** *pp.* of DESMESURAR.

desmesurar. I. *va.* to disorder, disarrange, disturb. **II.** *vr.* to be forward, impudent, saucy.

desmiembro. *V.* DESMEMBRAR.

desmiento. *V.* DESMENTIR.

desmigajar. I. *va.* to crumble; to comminute (as bread). **II.** *vr.* to crumble.

desmigar, *va.* (*pret.* DESMIGUÉ: *subj.* DESMIGUE) to crumble (bread).

desmineralización, *f.* (med.) abnormal loss of mineral substances.

desmirriado, da, *a.* (coll.) lean, emaciated, exhausted; melancholy.

desmocha, desmochadura, *f.* lopping or cutting off; diminution or destruction of part of a thing.

desmochar, *va.* to lop or cut off the top of (a tree, etc.); to unhorn.

desmoche, *m.* = DESMOCHA.

desmocho, *m.* heap of things lopped or cut off.

desmogar, *vn.* to cast the horns, as deer.

desmogue, *m.* act of casting the horns.

desmografía, *f.* desmography.

desmolado, da, *a.* having no molars or grinders.

desmoldamiento, *m.* removal of a casting from the mold.

desmoldar, *va.* to remove from the mold, to "strike the frame."

desmolde, *m.* = DESMOLDAMIENTO.

desmología, *f.* desmology.

desmonetización, *f.* demonetization; conversion of coins into bullion.

desmonetizar, *va.* to convert (money) into bullion; to demonetize.

desmonta, *f.* = DESMONTE.

desmontado, da. **I.** *a.* unmounted, dismounted; (mech.) knocked down. **II.** *pp.* of DESMONTAR.

desmontador, ra, *n.* one who fells wood; dismounter.—**desmontadura,** *f.* felling timber, clearing of shrubbery.

desmontar. **I.** *va.* to clear (a wood); to remove (dirt or rubbish); to grub, to fallow; to uncock (firearms); to take apart (as a machine); to dismount (a troop of horse); to dismount (cannon).— **d. el timón,** (naut.) to unhang the rudder. **II.** *vn., vr.* to dismount, to alight from a horse, mule, etc.

desmonte, *m.* grubbing or clearing of trees and undergrowth; timber remaining on the spot.

desmoñar, *va.* (coll.) to undo the hairknot).

desmoralización, *f.* demoralization; corruption.

desmoralizado, da, *a.* & *pp.* of DESMORALIZAR; demoralized, depraved, corrupted.

desmoralizar. **I.** *va.* (for mut. v. MORALIZAR) to demoralize, corrupt, deprave. **II.** *vr.* to become demoralized; (mil.) to lose the morale, to flag in morale.

desmoronadizo, za, *a.* easily crumbled, crumbly; lacking solidity or permanence.

desmoronamiento, *m.* crumbling.

desmoronar. **I.** *va.* to abrade, to destroy by little and little, to ruin by insensible degrees. **II.** *vr.* to fall, decay, crumble.

desmostar. **I.** *va.* to separate the must from (grapes). **II.** *vn.* to ferment.

desmotadera, *f.* woman who burls cloth; burling iron.

desmotador, ra. **I.** *n.* & *a.* burler (-ing). **II.** *f.* cotton opener; (Am.) cotton gin.

desmotar, *va.* to burl; to gin.

desmullir, *va.* to disarrange or impair the softness of.

desmurador, *m.* mouser (cat).

desmurar, *va.* to exterminate rats from.

desnarigado, da, *a.* & *pp.* noseless.

desnarigar, *va.* to cut off the nose of.

desnatar, *va.* to skim; to take off the flower or choicest part of.

desnaturalización, *f.* expatriation, denaturalization, denationalization.

desnaturalizado, da. **I.** *a.* denaturalized; denatured; low, base, conscienceless. **II.** *pp.* of DESNATURALIZAR.

desnaturalizar. **I.** *va.* (for mut. v. NATURALIZAR) to denaturalize, denationalize; to banish, exile, expatriate; to disfigure, pervert (as a fact); to denature. **II.** *vr.* to abandon one's country.

desnegamiento, *m.* denial; contradiction; retraction, retractation.

desnegar. **I.** *va.* (for irr. v. NEGAR) to deny, gainsay, contradict. **II.** *vr.* to retract, recant.

desnervar, *va.* to enervate.

desnevado, da. **I.** *a.* free from snow. **II.** *pp.* of DESNEVAR.

desnevar, *va.* (for irr. v. NEVAR) to thaw, dissolve.

desnivel, *m.,* **desnivelación,** *f.* unevenness, difference of elevation, drop.

desnivelado, da, *pp.* & *a.* unlevel, uneven.

desnivelar. **I.** *va.* to unlevel, make uneven. **II.** *vr.* to lose its level.

desnucamiento, *m.* breaking the neck.

desnucar. **I.** *va.* (pret. DESNUQUÉ: subj. DESNUQUE) to break the neck of; to kill by a blow on the nape. **II.** *vr.* to break one's neck.

desnudador, ra, *n.* one that denudes.

desnudamente, *adv.* nakedly; evidently.

desnudar. **I.** *va.* to strip, undress, denude, uncover; to fleece; (naut.) to unrig. **II.** *vr.* to undress, to strip, to deprive one's self of; to rid one's self of.

desnudez, *f.* nudity, nakedness.

desnudo, da. **I.** *a.* nude, naked; bare, uncovered; ill-clothed; plain, evident; empty-handed; destitute of merit, interest, etc. **II.** *m.* nude figure in art.

desnutrición, *f.* malnutrition, underfeeding.

desobedecer, *va.* & *vn.* (for irr. v. OBEDECER) to disobey.

desobedezco. *V.* DESOBEDECER.

desobediencia, *f.* disobedience.

desobediente, *a.* disobedient.

desobedientemente, *adv.* disobediently.

desobligar, *va.* (for mut. v. OBLIGAR) to release from an obligation; to disoblige; to offend; to alienate the good will of.

desobstrucción, *f.* clearing, removal of obstructions or obstacles.

desobstruir, *va.* (for irr. v. OBSTRUIR) to remove obstructions from, to clear; (med.) to deobstruct.

desocupación, *f.* leisure, want of occupation.

desocupadamente, *adv.* deliberately, leisurely.

desocupado, da. **I.** *a.* idle, without occupation; vacant, unoccupied. **II.** *pp.* of DESOCUPAR.

desocupar. **I.** *va.* to vacate; to evacuate; to empty. **II.** *vr.* to disengage one's self from a business or occupation.

desodorante, *n.* & *a.* deodorant.

desoir, *va.* to pretend not to hear; not to heed.

desojar. **I.** *va.* & *vr.* to break or burst the eye of (as of a needle). **II.** *vr.* to strain one's sight; to look intently.

desolación, *f.* desolation, destruction, havoc; fall; intense grief or affliction.

desolado, da. **I.** *a.* desolate; disconsolate. **II.** *pp.* of DESOLAR.

desolar. **I.** *va.* (for irr. v. ASOLAR) to desolate, lay waste; to harass. **II.** *vr.* to suffer great grief.

desoldar. **I.** *va.* to unsolder. **II.** *vr.* to come unsoldered, break apart (s. o. soldered pieces).

desolladamente, *adv.* (coll.) impudently, petulantly.

desolladero, *m.* abattoir, slaughterhouse.

desollado, da. **I.** *a.* (coll.) forward, impudent, insolent. **II.** *pp.* of DESOLLAR.

desollador, ra. **I.** *n.* flayer, extortioner. **II.** *m.* butcher bird.

desolladura, *f.* act and effect of flaying or skinning; excoriation; extortion.

desollar, *va.* (for irr. v. RESOLLAR) to flay, to skin; to excoriate; to fleece; to cause great harm or injury to.—**d. vivo,** (coll.) to extort an immoderate price from, to soak, stick; to roast, speak ill of.

desollón, *m.* = DESOLLADURA.

desonce, *m.* discount of a certain number of ounces in each pound.

desonzar, *va.* to discount or deduct a certain number of ounces per pound of; to insult, to defame, revile.

desopilar, *va.* to clear, remove obstructions from.

desopilativo, va, *a.* deobstruent.

desopinado, da. **I.** *a.* having lost reputation. **II.** *pp.* of DESOPINAR.

desopinar, *va.* to defame.

desoprimir, *va.* to free from oppression.

desorden, *m.* disorder, confusion; lawlessness, license, excess; turmoil, disturbance, riot.

desordenadamente, *adv.* disorderly, irregularly, confusedly.

desordenado, da. I. *a.* disorderly, irregular, disordered; orderless; lawless, licentious. **II.** *pp.* of DESORDENAR.

desordenar. I. *va.* to disorder, disarrange. **II.** *vr.* to exceed or go beyond all rule; to be out of order, to be irregular; to get unruly, be unmanageable (as a horse).

desorejado, da, *a.* (coll.) licentious, dissolute, degraded.

desorejador, ra, *n.* one who crops off the ears.

desorejamiento, *m.* cropping off the ears.

desorejar, *va.* to crop off the ears of.

desorganización, *f.* disorganization.

desorganizador, ra, *n.* & *a.* disorganizer (-ing).

desorganizar. I. *va.* (*for mut. v.* ORGANIZAR) to disorganize; to break up, disperse; (chem.) to decompose; (mil.) to disband. **II.** *vr.* to become disorganized; to disband, disperse; (med.) to be altered, disorganized.

desorientar, *va.* & *vr.* to disorient; to lose or cause to lose one's bearings; to lose the way; to confuse, to lead into error.

desorillar, *va.* to cut off the selvage of (cloth); to cut the border off.

desortijado, da. I. *a.* (vet.) sprained. **II.** *pp.* of DESORTIJAR.

desortijar, *va.* to hoe or weed the first time.

desosar, *va.* (*ind.* DESHUESO: *subj.* DESHUESE) to bone. *V.* DESHUESAR.

desovar, *vn.* to spawn.

desove, *m.* spawning; spawning season.

desovillar, *va.* to unwind; to unclew, unravel, disentangle.

desoxidable, *a.* deoxidizable.—**desoxidación,** *f.* deoxidation.—**desoxidante,** *n.* & *a.* deoxidizer (-ing).

desoxigenante, *n.* & *a.* = DESOXIDANTE.

desoxidar, *va.* to deoxidize.

desoxigenación, *f.* deoxidation.

desoxigenar, *va.* to deoxidize.

despabiladeras, *f. pl.* snuffers.

despabilado, da, *a.* & *pp.* snuffed (candles); watchful, vigilant; lively, active, smart.

despabilador, ra. I. *n.* & *a.* snuffer (-ing). **II.** *m.* candle snuffer.

despabiladura, *f.* snuff of the candle.

despabilar. I. *va.* to trim or snuff (a candle); to trim, cut off from; to finish briefly or quickly (as a dinner or a fortune); to rouse, to enliven; (coll.) to rob, to plunder: (coll.) to kill.—**d. el ingenio,** to sharpen the wits.—**d. los ojos,** to keep a sharp lookout. **II.** *vr.* to wake up.

despacio. I. *adv.* slowly; deliberately. **II.** *interj.* softly, gently.

despacioso, sa, *a.* slow, phlegmatic, sluggish.

despacito, *adv.* (coll.) very slowly, gently, softly.

despachaderas, *f. pl.* (coll.) surly rejoinder; quickness, resourcefulness.

despachado, da. I. *a.* (coll.) impudent, boldfaced, brazen. **II.** *pp.* of DESPACHAR.

despachador, ra, *n.* sender, one who despatches.

despachar. I. *va.* to despatch; to expedite, abridge, facilitate; to send; to ship, to express; to perform with despatch; to get out, write and send, attend to (correspondence) ; to dismiss, discharge.—**d. géneros,** or **mercaderías, en la aduana,** to clear or take out goods or merchandise at the customhouse.—**d. un barco,** (com.) to clear a vessel at the customhouse. **II.** *vr.* to make haste. **III.** *vn.* in offices, to carry papers drawn up for the signature of the principal; (com.) to expend, to let goods go for money or barter; (coll.) to wait on customers.

despacho, *m.* expedient, determination; despatch, expedition; shipping, shipment, sending; custom, application from buyers; cabinet, department; office, bureau; countinghouse; depot; sale of goods; trade; demand; commission, warrant, patent; official communication or despatch.—**d. de**

aduana, clearance.—**d. de billetes,** or **boletos,** ticket office.—**d. de localidades,** box office.—**d. telegráfico,** cablegram, telegram.—**d. universal,** state department.—**tener buen d.,** to be quick, to be energetic and prompt.

despachurrado, da. I. *a.* smashed, squashed, crushed.—**dejar a uno d.,** (coll.) to leave one dumfounded. **II.** *pp.* of DESPACHURRAR.

despachurrar, *va.* (coll.) to squash, smash, crush; (coll.) to make a jumble of (an explanation).—**d. el cuento,** to interrupt a story and prevent its conclusion.

despajador, ra, *n.* & *a.* winnower (-ing).

despajadura, *f.* winnowing.

despajar, *va.* to winnow or separate (grain from chaff).

despajo, *m.* winnowing or cleaning.

despaldar, *va.* & *vr.* to dislocate or break the shoulder of.—**despaldilladura,** *f.* breaking or dislocation of an animal's shoulder.

despaldillar, *va.* to remove the stems from (raisins); to strip (tobacco, etc.)

despalmador, *m.* (naut.) careening place, dockyard; hoof-paring knife.

despalmadura, *f.* calking, paying the bottom.

despalmar, *va.* (naut.) to grave, to calk; to pare off (a horse's hoof).

despalme, *m.* = DESPALMADURA.

despampanador, *m.* pruner of vines.

despampanadura, *f.* act of pruning vines.

despampanar. I. *va.* to prune (vines); (coll.) to astound by a piece of news. **II.** *vn.* (coll.) to unbosom, to give vent to one's feelings. **III.** *vr.* (coll.) to be injured by a fall.

despamplonador, ra, *n.* one who separates (vine) stems.

despamplonar. I. *va.* to separate the shoots of. **II.** *vr.* to sprain the hand.

despanar, *va.* to remove from the field.

despancijar, despanzurrar, *va.* (coll.) to burst the belly of.

despapar, *vn.* to carry the head too high (s. o. a horse).

desparecer, *vn.* to disappear. *V.* DESAPARECER.

desparedar, *va.* to take down the walls of.

desparejar, *va.* to break a pair of, to separate from a pair.

desparpajado, da, *a.* & *pp.* of DESPARPAJAR; pert, petulant, garrulous.

desparpajar. I. *va.* to undo in a disorderly manner. **II.** *vn.* & *vr.* (coll.) to rant, to prattle.

desparpajo, *m.* (coll.) pertness of speech or of manner.

desparramado, da. I. *a.* wide open; spread, scattered. **II.** *pp.* of DESPARRAMAR.

desparramador, ra, *n.* disperser; dilapidator; prodigal, waster, spendthrift.

desparramamiento, *m.* spreading, scattering; squandering, extravagance, dissipation.

desparramar. I. *va.* & *vr.* to scatter, disseminate, spread; to squander, dissipate, lavish. **II.** *vr.* to amuse one's self; to be dissipated.

despartidor, *m.* one who separates or divides.

despartimiento, *m.* separation, or division.

despartir, *va.* to part, separate, divide; to reconcile, make peace between.

desparvar, *va.* to undo the sheaves and spread the stalks of (grain) on the floor.

despasar, *va.* (naut.) to unsling, unreeve, shift.

despatarrada, *f.* (coll.) split of the legs; a certain change or movement in a Spanish dance. — **hacer la d.,** (coll.) to pretend disease or pain; to feign death.

despatarrarse, *vr.* (coll.) to straddle; to fall with split legs; to make a split; to be stupefied or dumfounded; to remain motionless.

despatillar. I. *va.* to tenon; (naut.) to break off the arm of (an anchor). **II.** *vr.* (coll.) to shave off one's whiskers.

despavesaderas, *f. pl.* = DESPABILADERAS.

despavesadura, *f.* act of snuffing a candle.

despavesar, *va.* to snuff (a candle).

despavoridamente, *adv.* terrifiedly, aghast.

despavorido, da, *a.* terrified, aghast.

despavorir, *vn.* & *vr.* (*def.*: it has only the moods and persons having the letter **i**) to be terrified, to be frightened, to be aghast.

despeadura, *f.*, **despeamiento,** *m.* bruising the feet with travel; (vet.) surbating.

despearse, *vr.* to bruise the feet (or hoofs) or make them sore by much walking.

despectivo, va, *a.* depreciatory; contemptuous.

despechadamente, *adv.* angrily, spitefully.

despechar. I. *va.* to enrage, to excite indignation in; (coll.) to wean. **II.** *vr.* to fret; to despair; to be spiteful.

despecho, *m.* spite; despair; grudge.—**a d. de,** despite, in spite of, in defiance of.

despechugadura, *f.* cutting off the breast of a fowl; uncovering one's breast.

despechugar. I. *va.* (*for mut. v.* APECHUGAR) to cut off the breast of (a fowl). **II.** *vr.* (coll.) to uncover the breast; to walk with bare breast.

despedazador, ra, *n.* & *a.* dissector (-ing); tearer (-ing); lacerator (-ing); mangler (-ing).

despedazamiento, *m.* laceration, dissection, cutting to pieces; mangling.

despedazar. I. *va.* (*for mut. v.* APEDAZAR) to cut into bits, to tear into pieces; to cut asunder; to limb, to claw; to lacerate, mangle; to torment, to harrow (as the feelings). **II.** *vr.* to break or fall to pieces.—**d. de risa,** to hold one's sides with laughter.

despedida, *f.* leave-taking, farewell, leave; seeing a person off; discharge, dismissal.

despedimiento, *m.* = DESPEDIDA.

despedir. I. *va.* (*for irr. v.* PEDIR) to emit, discharge, dart, fling, throw off; to dismiss, discharge; to see (a person) off on a journey; to escort (a guest) to the door; to dismiss (as from the mind). **II.** *vr.* (w. **de**) to take leave (of), to say good-bye (to); to quit; to renounce; to go out from service, to leave one's occupation.—**d. a la francesa,** to take French leave; to sneak away.

despedregar, *va.* to clear of stones.

despegable, *a.* that may be unglued or disjoined.

despegadamente, *adv.* unconcernedly, unaffectionately.

despegado, da. I. *a.* unglued; (coll.) sour of temper; unpleasant, harsh; distant, indifferent; unaffectionate, unfeeling. **II.** *pp.* of DESPEGAR.

despegador, ra, *a.* that unglues or detaches.

despegadura, *f.* ungluing, detaching, separating.

despegamiento, *m.* = DESAPEGO.

despegar. I. *va.* (*for mut. v.* PEGAR) to unglue, detach, separate, disjoin.—**d. los labios, la boca,** to speak. **II.** *vr.* to come off; to withdraw one's affection; to become indifferent. **III.** *vn.* (aer.) to rise, to take off.

despego, *m.* asperity; aversion; coolness, indifference, lack of affection.

despeinado, da, *a.* uncombed, unkempt.

despeinar, *va.* to disarrange the hair of.

despejadamente, *adv.* expeditiously, readily, smartly, neatly.

despejado, da. I. *a.* sprightly, smart, vivacious; clear, cloudless; unobstructed, clear. **II.** *pp.* of DESPEJAR.

despejar. I. *va.* to remove impediments from, clear; (math.) to solve for, find the value of. **II.** *vr.* to become bright and smart; to amuse one's self; to be relieved of pain (**s. o.** a patient); to clear up (s. o. the weather, sky, etc.)

despejo, *m.* removal of obstacles, clearing; sprightliness, smartness, briskness; grace, ease.

despelotar, *va.* to dishevel.

despeluzamiento, *m.* entanglement or disarrangement of the hair; making the hair stand on end; horripilation.

despeluzar, *va.* & *vr.* to make (the hair) stand on end; to be horrified.

despeluznante, *a.* making the hair stand on end; horrifying.

despeluznar, *va.* & *vr.* = DESPELUZAR.

despellejadura, *f.* scratch, slight wound; skinning.—**despellejar,** *va.* to flay, to skin, to strip, to uncase.

despenador, ra, *n.* one that relieves pain.

despenar, *va.* to relieve from pain; (coll.) to kill.

despendedor, ra, *n.* spendthrift, prodigal, lavisher, waster.

despender, *va.* to spend; to waste, squander.

despensa, *f.* pantry, larder; store of provisions for a journey; butlership; provisions for daily use; marketing; contract for a yearly supply of fodder; (naut.) steward's room.

despensería, *f.* office of steward.

despensero, ra, *n.* butler; caterer, dispenser, distributer; (naut.) steward.

despeñadamente, *adv.* precipitately.

despeñadero, ra. I. *a.* steep, precipitous, headlong. **II.** *m.* precipice, crag; dangerous undertaking.—**despeñadizo, za,** *a.* steep, precipitous; glib, slippery.—**despeñamiento,** *m.* = DESPEÑO.

despeñar. I. *va.* to precipitate, to fling down a precipice. **II.** *vr.* to throw one's self headlong; to lead a riotous life.

despeño, *m.* precipitate fall; loss of fortune and character; diarrhœa.

despepitador, *m.* stoner, corer (for fruit).

despepitadora, *f.* stoner, corer; seed separator.—**d. de algodón,** cotton gin.

despepitar. I. *va.* to remove the seeds from; to gin. **II.** *vr.* to loosen one's tongue; to vociferate; to speak or act rashly or heedlessly.—**d. por,** to long for, to be dying or itching to.

despercudir, *va.* to clean or wash.

desperdiciadamente, *adv.* profusely, wastefully.

desperdiciado, da, *a.* & *pp.* of DESPERDICIAR; wasted, destroyed, squandered.

desperdiciador, ra, *n.* spendthrift, squanderer.

desperdiciar, *va.* to waste; to squander, misspend; not to avail one's self of, not to utilize, to lose, miss (an opportunity, etc.).

desperdicio, *m.* waste; prodigality, profusion; (gen. *pl.*) refuse, offal, remains, garbage.

desperdigamiento, *m.* spreading, scattering.

desperdigar, *va.* to separate, disjoin; to scatter.

desperecerse, *vr.* to crave, to long, to desire eagerly.

desperezarse, *vr.* to stretch one's limbs; to shake off sloth.

desperezo, *m.* = ESPEREZO.

desperfecto, *m.* deterioration, wear and tear; slight injury or damage, blemish, imperfection, flaw.

desperfilar, *va.* (pict.) to soften the lines of.

despernada, *f.* a movement in dancing.

despernado, da. I. *a.* weary, fatigued, tired **II.** *pp.* of DESPERNAR.

despernar. I. *va.* (*for irr. v.* APERNAR) to injure or cut off the legs of. **II.** *vr.* to injure or lose one's legs.

despertador, ra. I. *n.* awakener. **II.** *m.* alarm bell in clocks; alarm clock; warning, admonition, hint that causes worriment.

despertamiento, *m.* awakening.

despertar. I. *va.* & *vr.* (*pp.* DESPERTADO, DESPIERTO: *ind.* DESPIERTO: *subj.* DESPIERTE) to awaken; to enliven; to remind, recall; to excite, sharpen (as the appetite). **II.** *vr.* to awake, wake up; to revive.

despesar, *m.* displeasure, aversion, dislike.

despestañar. I. *va.* to pluck out the eyelashes of. **II.** *vr.* to look intently, to study hard.

despezar, *va.* to bevel; to taper.

despezo, *m.* taper; bevel.—*pl.* (arch.) beveled faces of a stone at the joints.

despezonar. I. *va.* to cut off the nipple or stem of; to divide, to separate. **II.** *vr.* to break off (as the stalk of fruit or the arm of an axletree).

despezuñar. I. *va.* to cut off the hoof of. **II.** *vr.* (Am.) to rush at breakneck speed.—**d. por,** to long for; to hustle for, set one's heart on.

despiadadamente, *adv.* unmercifully, pitilessly.

despiadado, da, *a.* unmerciful, pitiless.

---

despicar. I. va. (for mut. v. PICAR) to satisfy, to gratify. **II.** vr. (w. **de** or **con**) to take revenge (of), get square (with).

despicarazar, va. to pick (the figs) (said of birds)

despichar. I. va. to expel or discharge; to pick; (Am.) to crush, smash. **II.** vn. (coll.) to die.

despidida, f. gutter, passage for water.

despidiente, m. board between a hanging scaffold and the wall.—**d. de agua,** (arch.) flashing.

despido. V. DESPEDIR.

despierno. V. DESPERNAR.

despiertamente, adv. ingeniously, cleverly.

despierto, ta, a. awake; vigilant, watchful; diligent; sprighty, lively, smart; clear-sighted.

despierto, despierte. V. DESPERTAR.

despiezo, m. (arch.) = DESPEZO.

despilar, va. (min.) to take away the pillars of.

despilfarradamente, adv. wastefully; slovenly.

despilfarrado, da. I. a. ragged, shabby, in tatters; prodigal, wasteful. **II.** pp. of DES-PILFARRAR.

despilfarrador, ra, a. spendthrift, wasteful.

despilfarrar, va. to waste, squander.

despilfarro, m. slovenlines, uncleanliness; waste, lavishness, squandering, extravagance; misgovernment, maladministration.

despimpollar, va. to prune away the useless stems of.

despinces, m. pl. tweezers. V. DESPINZAS.

despintar. I. va. to blot or efface; to disfigure; to mislead. **II.** vn. to degenerate. **III.** vr. to fade, wash off, lose color; to forget.

despinzadera, f. woman that burls —pl. burling iron.—**despinzar,** va. (pret. DESPINCÉ: subj. DES-PINCE) to burl.

despinzas, f. pl. burling iron.

despiojar, va. & vr. to cleanse from lice; (coll.) to relieve from misery.

despique, m. vengeance, revenge.

despistar, va. to turn from the right trail.

despizcar. I. va. (for mut. v. PIZCAR) to triturate, crush; break or cut into small bits. **II.** vr. to exert one's self to the utmost.

desplacer. I. va. (for irr. v. PLACER) to displease. **II.** m. displeasure.

desplanchar, va. to wrinkle, rumple, muss

desplantación, f. eradication, uprooting.

desplantador, ra. I. n. eradicator, one who pulls up plants. **II.** m. trowel, scoop trowel.

desplantar. I. vr. to lose one's erect posture in fencing or dancing. **II.** va. to uproot; to deviate from the vertical.

desplante, m. oblique posture in fencing; injudicious action or speech.

desplatar, va. to separate silver from.

desplate, m. act of separating silver from other metals.

desplayar, vn. to recede from the shore (as the tide).

desplazamiento, m. displacement.

desplazar, va. (naut.) to displace, have a displacement of.

desplazco. V. DESPLACER.

desplegadura, f. unfolding, spreading out; elucidation, explanation.

desplegar. I. va. (for irr. v. PLEGAR) to unfold, display; to spread, lay out; to explain, elucidate; (naut.) to unfurl.—**d. la bandera,** to hoist the flag. **II.** vr. to open, unfold (as flowers); to spread out, deploy (as troops).

despleguetear, va. (agr.) to remove the folds from the tendrils of (vines).

despliegue, m. unfurling, unfolding; spreading out; (mil.) deployment.

desplomar. I. va. to put out of vertical, to cause to lean (s. o. a wall, etc.). **II.** vr. to get out of plumb, to lean over; to tumble down, collapse, topple over.

desplome, m. leaning, lack of verticality; collapse, tumbling down, downfall.

desplomo, m. deviation from the vertical.

desplumadura, f. deplumation.

desplumar. I. va. & vr. to deplume, to pluck; (coll.) to despoil or strip of property. **II.** vr. to moult.

despoblación, f. depopulation.

despoblado, m. uninhabited place; wilderness.

despoblado, da, a. & pp. depopulated.

despoblador, ra, n. & a. depopulator (-ing).

despoblar. I. va. to depopulate; to despoil or desolate. **II.** vr. to become depopulated.

despojador, ra, n. & a. despoiler (-ing), spoiler (-ing).

despojar. I. va. to despoil, strip of property; to deprive of, to cut off from, judicially; to dismiss, turn out of a place or employment. **II.** vr. (w. **de**) to undress, to strip; (w. **de**) to relinquish; to forsake, to divest one's self.

despojo, m. spoliation; plunder, spoils; slough, cast-off skin of a serpent; head, pluck, and feet of slaughtered animals.—pl. leavings, scraps of the table; giblets of fowls; débris; second-hand building materials.

despolarización, f. depolarization.

despolarizador, ra, n. & a. depolarizer (-ing).

despolarizar, va. (for mut. v. POLARIZAR) to depolarize.

despolvar, va. to dust.

despolvorear, va. to dust; to cast away, scatter, dissipate; (coll.) to sprinkle.

despopularizar, va. & vr. (for mut. v. POPULARI-ZAR) to make or become unpopular.

desportillar, va. to chip off the corners or edges of; break the neck of (a bottle, pot, etc.); (arch.) to splay.

desposado, da. I. a. newly married; handcuffed. **II.** pp. of DESPOSAR.

desposando, da, n. person newly married or about to be married; bride; bridegroom.

desposar. I. va. to marry (to perform the marriage ceremony for) **II.** vr. to be betrothed, engaged or married.

desposeer, va. to dispossess, oust.

desposeimiento, m. dispossession.

desposorio, m. betrothal; (gen. pl.) mutual promise to contract marriage, engagement.

déspota, m. despot, tyrant.—**despóticamente,** adv. despotically.—**despótico, ca,** despotic.—**despotismo,** m. despotism.—**despotizar,** va. & vn. to tyrannize, to oppress.

despotricar, vn. & vr. (coll.) to talk without restraint.

despreciable, a. contemptible, despicable; inappreciable, negligible.

despreciador, ra, n. & a. despiser (-ing), scorner (-ing), contemner (-ing).

despreciar, va. to despise, scorn, contemn; to reject, lay aside; to neglect.

despreciativo, va, a. depreciative, depreciatory; contemptuous.

desprecio, m. scorn, contempt; slight; neglect; dispraise.

desprender. I. va to unfasten, loose, separate; to emit, give out. **II.** vr. (gen. w. **de**) to give way, to fall down; to issue (from), come out (of); to extricate one's self (from); to dispossess one's self (of), give away; to follow, be a consequence (of); to part (with): to rid one's self (of).

desprendido, da, pp. & a. disinterested, generous; unfastened, loose

desprendimiento, m. act of loosening; disinterestedness; indifference; landslide, landslip.

desprensar, va. to remove from the press.

despreocupación, f. freedom from bias, openmindedness; unconventionality.

despreocupado, da, a. & pp. unprejudiced; unconventional; freethinking.

despreocupar. I. va. to unbias, free from prejudice. **II.** vr. to become unbiased, to shake off prejudice; (w. **de**) to ignore; to discard, set aside; to pay no attention (to).

desprestigiado, da. I. a. having a bad reputation, in bad repute, unpopular. **II.** pp. of DES-PRESTIGIAR.

desprestigiar. I. *va.* to bring into disrepute, to impair the reputation of. **II.** *vr.* to lose reputation or prestige.

desprestigio, *m.* loss of reputation of prestige, unpopularity.

desprevención, *f.* improvidence, want of caution.

desprevenidamente, *adv.* improvidently.

desprevenido, da, *a.* unprovided; unprepared.

desproporción, *f.* disproportion; disparity.

desproporcionadamente, *adv.* disproportionately.

desproporcionado, da, *a.* & *pp.* of DESPROPORCIONAR; disproportionate; disproportioned; unsuitable, unbecoming.

desproporcionar, *va.* to disproportion, to mismatch, to misproportion.

despropositado, da, *a.* absurd.

despropósito, *m.* absurdity, nonsense.

desproveer, *va.* (*pp.* DESPROVEÍDO, DESPROVISTO) to deprive of provisions or the necessaries of life.

desproveídamente, *adv.* improvidently.

desproveído, da. I. *a.* unprovided; unprepared. **II.** *pp.* of DESPROVEER.

desprovisto, ta, *a.* & *pp.* *irr.* of DESPROVEER; (w. de) unprovided, lacking.

despueble, despueblo, *m.* depopulation.

despueblo, yo DESPUEBLE. *V.* DESPOBLAR.

después, *adv.* after, afterward, next, then, later. —**d. de,** after; next to.—**d. de que, d. que,** after.

despulir, *va.* to tarnish; to frost, grind (glass).

despulsarse, *vr.* to be violently affected with any passion; (w. **por**) to desire eagerly.

despumación, *f.* despumation, skimming.

despumadera, *f.* = ESPUMADERA.

despumar, *va.* = ESPUMAR.

despuntador, *m.* (min.) ore separator; hammer for breaking ore.

despuntadura, *f.* blunting, taking off the point.

despuntar. I. *va.* to blunt, to crop, cut off, wear out the point of; to cut away the dry combs of (a beehive); (naut.) to double (a cape). **II.** *vn.* to advance or make progress in knowledge; to manifest wit and genius; to begin to sprout or bud; to surpass, excel, morally; to dawn (in such expressions as **d. el día, d. el alba, d. la aurora,** all of which mean to dawn).

desquejar, *va.* to pluck up a shoot near the root of (a plant).—**desqueje,** *m.* pulling up a shoot near the root of a plant.

desquerer, *va.* to lose affection or liking for, to cease to love or like.

desquiciamiento, *m.* unhinging, disjoining; downfall.

desquiciador, ra, *n.* he who or that which unhinges, unsettles or overthrows.

desquiciar. I. *va.* to unhinge, to disjoint; to unsettle, disorder; to deprive of favor or protection; to undermine; to overthrow. **II.** *vr.* to become unhinged; to lose support or backing; to fall down.

desquijaramiento, *m.* act of breaking the jaws.

desquijarar, *va.* to break the jaws of; (naut.) to break the cheek of (a block).

desquijerar, *va.* (carp.) to tenon.

desquilatar, *va.* to diminish the intrinsic value of (gold).

desquitar. I. *va.* to retrieve (a loss). **II.** *vr.* (w. de) to win one's money back; to retaliate, take revenge, get even, get square.

desquite, *m.* compensation, recovery of a loss; revenge, satisfaction, retaliation.

desrabotar, *va.* to cut off the tail of.

desramar, *va.* to strip of branches.

desramillar, *va.* (agr.) = DESLECHUGAR.

desrancharse, *vr.* to withdraw from a mess.

desrastrojar, *va.* to remove the stubble from.

desrayadura, *f.* last furrow of tillage; deep boundary furrow.—**desrayar,** *va.* to open furrows in for irrigation; to make a boundary furrow in.

desrazonable, *a.* unreasonable.

desregladamente, *adv.*, **desreglado, da,** *a.*, **desreglarse,** *vr.* = DESARREGLADAMENTE, etc.

desrelingar, *va.* (naut.) to take away the bolt-ropes from (the sails).

desreputación, *f.* (coll.) dishonor, disrepute.

desrizar, *va.* (*for mut. v.* RIZAR) to uncurl.

desroblar, *va.* to take the rivets out of.

desroñar, *va.* to lop off decayed branches from.

destacamento, *m.* detachment; station; military post.—**destacar,** *va.* (*for mut. v.* ATACAR) (mil.) to detach.

destaconar, *va.* to wear out the heels of.

destajador, *m.* smith's hammer.

destajar, *va.* to contract for (a job); to do as taskwork; to cut (the cards); to bring out, make stand out. **II.** *vr.* to stand out; to tower, be conspicuous; to project.

destajero, ra, destajista, *n.* person who does taskwork.

destajo, *m.* job, taskwork.—**a d.,** by the job, by the lump; earnestly, diligently.

destalonar, *va.* to break or wear out the heels of; to take off coupons from; (vet.) to level the hoofs of.

destallar, *va.* to prune useless branches from.

destapada, *f.* pie without an upper crust.

destapar. I. *va.* to uncover. **II.** *vr.* to become or get uncovered.

destapiado, *m.* place where mud walls have been torn down.

destapiar, *va.* to pull down the mud walls of.

destaponar, *va.* to remove the stopper from.

destarar, *va.* (com.) to diminish the tare of.

destartalado, da, *a.* huddled, jumbled; scantily and poorly furnished.

destazador, ra, *n.* one who cuts up slaughtered animals.

destazar, *va.* to cut up (a carcass).

deste, ta, to, contraction formerly used for **de este, de esta, de esto.**

destechadura, *f.* unroofing.

destechar, *va.* to unroof.

destejar, *va.* to untile; to leave defenceless.

destejer, *va.* to unweave, ravel, unknit, unbraid.

destellar. I. *vn.* to twinkle, beam, sparkle, flash. **II.** *va.* to give forth, emit.

destello, *m.* sparkle, beam, flash, scintillation.

destempladamente, *adv.* intemperately; discordantly, inharmoniously.

destemplado, da. I. *a.* inharmonious; out of tune; intemperate; (art) inharmonious, incongruous. **II.** *pp.* of DESTEMPLAR.

destemplanza, *f.* unsteadiness of the weather; disorder, intemperance; excess, abuse; (med.) indisposition, distemper; want of moderation.

destemplar. I. *va.* to distemper, alter, disconcert, derange; to put to confusion; to untune. **II.** *vr.* to be ruffled, discomposed; to be out of order; to be irregular or abnormal; to get out of tune; to act improperly or rashly; to lose moderation; to lose its temper (s. o. metals).

destemple, *m.* discordance, disharmony; being out of tune; discomposure, disorder; intemperance, lack of moderation; distemper, slight indisposition; untempering, lack of temper (s. o. metals).

destentar, *va.* to lead out of temptation.

desteñir, *va.* & *vr.* (*for irr. v.* TEÑIR) to discolor, to change from the natural hue.

desternillarse, *vr.* to break one's cartilage or gristle.—**d. de risa,** (coll.) to split one's sides with laughter.

desterradero, *m.* retired part of the town.

desterrado, da. I. *a.* & *pp.* of DESTERRAR; banished, outcast. **II.** *n.* exile, outcast.

desterrar, *va.* (*ind.* DESTIERRO: *subj.* DESTIERRE) to banish, exile; to lay or put aside; to take the earth off the roots of.

desterronador, ra, *n.* clod crusher, stubble plow.

desterronar, *va.* & *vr.* to break the clods of.

destetadera, *f.* pointed instrument placed on the teats of cows to prevent the calves from sucking.

destetar. I. *va.* to wean. **II.** *vr.* to wean one's self from an evil habit or custom.

destete, *m.* weaning.
desteto, *m.* number of weanlings; place where newly-weaned mules are kept.
destiempo, *adv.* —**a d.,** unseasonably, untimely.
destiento, *m.* surprise; commotion in the mind.
destierre, *m.* removal of dirt from ore, cleaning.
destierro, *m.* exile, banishment; place where the exile lives; any remote and solitary place.
destierro, yo destierre. *V.* DESTERRAR.
destilable, *a.* distillable.
destilación, *f.* distillation; filtration; flow of humors.—**d. seca,** destructive distillation.
destiladera, *f.* still, alembic, distilling vessel; filter.
destilador, ra. I. *n.* & *a.* distiller (-ing). **II.** *m.* filtering stone; alembic, still.
destilar. I. *va.* to distil; to filter through a stone. **II.** *vn.* to distil, to drop, to fall in drops.
destilatorio, ria. I. *a.* distillatory, distilling. **II.** *m.* distillery; still, alembic.
destilería, *f.* distillery.
destinación, *f.* destination; assignment.
destinar, *va.* to destine; to appoint; to designate; to allot, assign; (naut.) to station (ships).
destinatario, ria, *n.* addressee; consignee.
destino, *m.* destiny, fate; destination; appointment, office, employment; piece of unfinished dry honeycomb; (naut.) station.—**con d. a,** bound for, going to.
destiño, él destiñó. *V.* DESTEÑIR.
destiranizado, da, *a.* freed from tyranny.
destitución, *f.* dismissal from an employment, office, or charge; destitution, dereliction, abandonment.
destituible, *a.* dismissable, removable.
destituido, da, *a.* & *pp.* of DESTITUIR; destitute, forsaken, friendless, helpless.
destituir, *va.* (*for mut. v.* HUIR) to deprive; to make destitute; to dismiss from office.
destocar, *va.* (*for mut. v.* TOCAR) to uncoif, to pull off the cap or headdress from.
destorcedura, *f.* untwisting; uncurling.
destorcer. I. *va.* (*for irr. v.* TORCER) to undo, untwist, uncurl; to rectify, to straighten out. **II.** *vr.* to become untwisted; to bend, warp; to feaze, to unlay; to deviate; to drift.
destorgar, *va.* (prov.) to break off the branches of (evergreen oaks) when taking off their acorns.
destornillado, da. I. *a.* reckless, heedless, rash. **II.** *pp.* of DESTORNILLAR.
destornillador, *m.* unscrewer; screwdriver.
destornillamiento, *m.* unscrewing; recklessness, rashness, wildness.
destornillar. I. *va.* to unscrew. **II.** *vr.* to act recklessly, or wildly.
destoserse, *vr.* to feign a cough.
destostarse, *vr.* to lose gradually the tanning of the skin by the sun.
destotro, tra, *a.* (obs.) contraction of **de este otro, de esto otro, de esta otra.**
destrabar, *va.* to unfetter, unbind, to untie, loosen, separate; to break the barriers of.
destraillar, *va.* to unleash.
destral, *m.* small axe or hatchet.
destraleja, *f.* very small hatchet.
destralero, ra, *n.* axe maker.
destramar, *va.* to unweave, to undo the warp of.
destrejar, *vn.* to work or act with expertness.
destrenzar, *va.* (*for mut. v.* TRENZAR) to unplait, unbraid, undo a tress of.
destreza, *f.* dexterity, skill; nimbleness.
destrincar, *va.* & *vr.* (naut.) to loose, to unlash.
destripacuentos, *n.* one who interrupts often the person who is talking, butter-in.
destripamiento, *m.* disembowlment; crushing.
destripar, *va.* to disembowel, gut, eviscerate; to crush, smash; to draw out the inside of; (coll.) to interrupt and spoil (a story).
destripaterrones, *m.* (coll.) harrower, clodbeater; uncultured person.

destripular, *va.* to discharge the crew of.
destrísimo, ma, *a.* *super.* very dexterous or skillful.
destriunfar, *va.* (cards) to draw out the trumps from (the other players).
destrizar. I. *va.* (*for mut. v.* RIZAR) to mince, crumble, break in pieces; to tear in strips. **II.** *vr.* to be heart-broken, to languish with grief.
destrocar, *va.* to return (a thing bartered).
destrón, *m.* blind man's guide.
destronamiento, *m.* dethronement.
destronar, *va.* to dethrone, overthrow.
destroncamiento, *m.* detruncation, amputation, lopping of trees; ruination.
destroncar, *va.* (*for mut. v.* RONCAR) to detruncate, lop, cut short; to maim, dislocate; to cut in pieces; to ruin, destroy.
destrozador, ra, *n.* destroyer; mangler.
destrozar, *va.* (*pret.* DESTROCÉ: *subj.* DESTROCE) to destroy, to shatter, to mangle, to break or cut to pieces; to annihilate; to waste, squander.
destrozo, *m.* destruction, havoc, ruin; rout, defeat; massacre.
destrozón, na, *a.* destructive of wearing apparel, shoes, etc.
destrucción, *f.* destruction.
destructibilidad, *f.* destructibility.
destructible, *a.* destructible.
destructivamente, *adv.* destructively.
destructividad, *f.* destructiveness.
destructivo, va, *a.* destructive.
destructor, ra, *n.* & *a.* destructor, destroyer (-ive, -ing).
destrueco, destrueque, *m.* mutual restitution of things bartered.
destrueco, destrueque. *V.* DESTROCAR.
destruible, *a.* destructible.
destruidor, ra, = DESTRUCTOR, RA.
destruir. I. *va.* (*for irr. v.* HUIR) to destroy; to ruin; to demolish; to squander; to baffle, thwart; to prevent from earning a living. **II.** *vr.* to destroy one another; (math.) to cancel.
destruyente, *a.* destroying, destructive.
destuerzo. *V.* DESTORCER.
desubstanciar, *va.* = DESUSTANCIAR.
desucación, *f.* act of extracting the juice.
desudar, *va.* to wipe off the sweat from.
desuellacaras, *m.* (coll.) bad barber; (coll.) impudent, shameless person.
desuello, *m.* act of flaying, fleecing, or skinning; forwardness, impudence, insolence; (coll.) extortion.
desuelo, desuele. *V.* DESOLAR.
desuello, desuelle. *V.* DESOLLAR.
desulfuración, *f.* desulphurization.
desulfurar, *va.* to desulphurize.
desuncir, *va.* (*for mut. v.* UNCIR) to unyoke.
desunidamente, *adv.* separately, severally; disunitedly.
desunión, *f.* separation, disunion, disjunction; discord, disunion, feud.
desunir. I. *va.* to separate, disunite; to occasion discord between; to estrange. **II.** *vr.* to loosen, to fall or break apart; to become separated.
desuno, *adv.* (obs.) jointly.
desuñar. I. *va.* to tear off the nails of; to pull out the roots of. **II.** *vr.* to plunge into vice and dissipation.
desurcar, *va.* (*for mut. v.* SURCAR) to remove or undo furrows in.
desurdir, *va.* to unweave; to upset, nip in the bud, stop, frustrate.
desusadamente, *adv.* unusually, contrary to custom.
desusado, da, *a.* & *pp.* of DESUSAR; obsolete, out of date, archaic.
desusar. I. *va.* to disuse, to discontinue the use of. **II.** *vr.* to become obsolete; to go out of date.
desuso, *m.* disuse, obsoleteness, desuetude.
desustanciación, *f.* enervation, sapping of vigor.

desustanciar, *va.* to enervate, deprive of strength and substance.

desvahar, *va.* (agr.) to take away the dry or withered part of (a plant).

desvaído, da, *a.* tall and graceless, gaunt; dull (s. o. colors).

desvainadura, *f.* act of shelling.

desvainar, *va.* to shell, to husk.

desvalido, da, *a.* helpless, destitute, unprotected.

desvalijador, *m.* highwayman.

desvalijamiento, *m.* act of robbing the contents of a valise; robbery.

desvalijar, *va.* to take out the contents of (a valise or gripsack); to rob.

desvalimiento, *m.* dereliction or abandonment; want of favor or protection; want, neediness.

desván, *m.* garret, loft.—**d. gatero,** cockloft, room over the garret.

desvanecer. I. *va.* (ind. DESVANEZCO: subj. DESVANEZCA) to disintegrate, spread, or divide into minute parts; to cause to evanesce or disappear; to take away from the sight; to undo, to remove. **II.** *vr.* to pall, to grow vapid, to become insipid; to vanish, evanesce; to swell with presumption or pride; to faint, swoon.

desvanecidamente, *adv.* haughtily, proudly.

desvanecimiento, *m.* pride, haughtiness, loftiness; giddiness, dizziness.

desvaporizadero, *m.* place for evaporating.

desvarar, *va., vn.* & *vr.* (v. RESBALAR); (naut.) to set afloat a ship that was aground.

desvariadamente, *adv.* ravingly, foolishly or madly, stupidly.

desvariado, da. I. *a.* delirious, raving; disorderly, irregular; nonsensical; long, crooked (as branches of trees). **II.** *pp.* of DESVARIAR.

desvariar, *vn.* to rave, rant; to dote; to make extravagant demands.

desvarío, *m.* extravagant action or speech; delirium, raving; inconstancy; caprice, whim; monstrousness, extravagancy; derangement, disunion.

desvedado, da, *pp.* & *a.* unprohibited, free.

desvedar, *va.* to raise the prohibition of.

desveladamente, *adv.* watchfully, vigilantly.

desvelado, da. I. *a.* watchful, vigilant, careful. **II.** *pp.* of DESVELAR.

desvelamiento, *m.* watchfulness.

desvelar. I. *va.* to keep awake. **II.** *vr.* to go without sleep; to pass a sleepless night; be watchful or vigilant.

desvelo, *m.* watching, want or privation of sleep; watchfulness, vigilance; anxiety, uneasiness.

desvenar, *va.* to separate or clear the veins of; to extract from the veins of (mines) or the filaments of (plants); to raise the bit of (a bridle), so as to form an arch.

desvencijado, da, *a.* rickety, loose-jointed.

desvencijar. I. *va.* to disunite, weaken, divide, break. **II.** *vr.* to be ruptured, disjointed, loose, relaxed; (coll.) to be exhausted.

desvendar, *va.* to take off a bandage from, to unbandage.

desveno, *m.* arch of a bit.

desventaja, *f.* disadvantage.

desventajosamente, *adv.* disadvantageously, unprofitably.

desventajoso, sa, *a.* disadvantageous, unfavorable, unprofitable, detrimental.

desventar, *va.* to vent, to let out the air of.

desventura, *f.* misfortune, mishap; misery.

desventuradamente, *adv.* unhappily, unfortunately.

desventurado, da, *a.* unfortunate, unlucky, wretched; chicken-hearted, pusillanimous.

desvergonzadamente, *adv.* shamelessly.

desvergonzado, da, *a.* impudent; shameless.

desvergonzarse, *vr.* (for irr. v. AVERGONZAR) to speak or act in an impudent or insolent manner.

desvergüenza, *f.* impudence, effrontery, assurance; shamelessness; shame, disgrace.

desvergüenzo. *V.* DESVERGONZARSE.

desvestir, *va.* & *vr.* to undress.

desvezar, *va.* (agr.) to cut the young shoots of (vines) near the roots.

desviación, *f.* deviation, deflection; oblique direction; (med.) vicious direction of some parts of the body (as the bones); extravassation of fluids; (ast.) deviation from the meridian; variation of the magnetic needle.

desviadero, *m.* railway switch, siding, side-track.

desviado, da. I. *a.* devious, out of the common track, askew. **II.** *pp.* of DESVIAR.

desviar. I. *va.* to deviate, deflect, sway; to dissuade; put by; (fen.) to ward off; (r. w.) to switch. **II.** *vr.* to deviate, to wander; to turn off; to swerve.

desviejar, *va.* among shepherds, to separate the old ewes or rams from (the flock).

desvío, *m.* deviation, turning away; going astray; deflection; aversion, displeasure; coldness, indifference; (f. c.) siding, side track; (mas.) steadying board (of a suspended platform).

desvirar, *va.* to pare off the fore part of (a sole); (b. b.) to trim (a book); (naut.) to reverse (the capstan).

desvirgar, *va.* (low) to deflower.

desvirtuar, *va.* to lessen the value, strength or merit of; to detract from.

desvitrificación, *f.* devitrification.

desvitrificar, *va.* devitrify.

desvivirse, *vr.* (w. por) to love excessively; to desire anxiously; to long (for), be dying (for, to).

desvolvedor, *m.* nut wrench.

desvolver, *va.* (for irr. v. VOLVER) to alter the shape of; to plow, till.

desvuelto, *pp.* irr. of DESVOLVER.

desyemar, *va.* (agr.) to remove buds from; to separate the yolk from the white of (an egg).

desyerbador, ra, *n.* grubber, weeder.

desyerbar, *va.* to weed, grub.

deszocar, *va.* to disable the foot of.

deszumar, *va.* to extract the juice or substance from.

detallar, *va.* to detail, relate minutely, particularize; to specify; to retail.

detalle, *m.* detail, particular; retail.

detallista, *n.* detailer.

detasa, *f.* (r. w.) rebate.

detective; detectivo, va, *n.* detective.

detector, *m.* (elec.) detector.

detención, *f.* delay, stop, stay, halt, standstill, deadlock; (naut.) demurrage, arrest, embargo (of a ship).

detenedor, ra, *n.* detainer, stopper; check, arrester, catch.

detener. I. *va.* (for irr. v. TENER) to stop, detain, check, arrest; (naut.) to capture, to embargo; to keep back; to retain, reserve. **II.** *vr.* to tarry, stay, stop over; to stop, halt; to pause.

detengo, detenga. *V.* DETENER.

detenidamente, *adv.* dilatorily; carefully, painstakingly, thoroughly.

detenido, da. I. *a.* sparing, niggardly, parsimonious; dilatory; careful, thorough, conscientious. **II.** *pp.* of DETENER.

detenimiento, *m.* care, thoroughness.

detentación, *f.* (law) deforcement.

detentador, *m.* deforciant.

detentar, *va.* to deforce (law), to retain or keep unlawfully.

detergente, *a.* (med.) detergent, detersive.

deterger, *va.* (med.) to absterge.

deterioración, *f.* = DETERIORO.—**deteriorar,** *va.* & *vr.* to deteriorate, impair, damage, wear out.—**deterioro,** *m.* deterioration, impairment, damage, wear and tear.

determinable, *a.* determinable, ascertainable.

determinación, *f.* determination, resolution; conclusion or final decision; firmness.

determinadamente, *adv.* determinately; resolutely; definitely; expressly, especially.

determinado, da. I. *a.* determinate, determined, decided; fixed, resolute; settled, definite; (math.) determinate. **II.** *pp.* of DETERMINAR.

determinante. I. *a.* determining, determinate, determinative. **II.** *m.* (gram.) determining verb. **III.** *m.* or *f.* (math.) determinant.

determinar. I. *va.* to determine; to limit; to specify; to distinguish, discern; to appoint, to assign (as time and place); to decide, resolve; to conclude (as a lawsuit). **II.** *vr.* to determine, resolve; to make up one's mind.

determinativo, va, *a.* determinative.

determinismo, *m.* (philos.) determinism.

determinista, *n.* & *a.* (philos.) determinist.

detersión, *f.* (med.) detersion; cleansing.

detersivo, va; detersorio, ria, *a.* detersive, cleansing, detergent.

detestable, *a.* detestable; hateful.

detestablemente, *adv.* detestably; hatefully.

detestación, *f.* detestation, abhorrence, abomination.

detestar, *va.* to detest, abhor, abominate.

detienebuey, *m.* (bot.) common rest-harrow.

detonación, *f.* detonation, report.

detonante, *a.* detonating.

detonar, *vn.* to detonate; to flash, to explode.

detorsión, *f.* (med.) distortion.

detracción, *f.* detraction, defamation, obloquy; detraction, withdrawing, taking away.

detractar, *va.* to detract, defame, to slander.

detractor, ra, *n.* & *a.* detractor (-ing), slanderer (-ing, -ous).

detraer, *va.* (*for irr. v.* TRAER) to detract, remove, take away; to defame, slander, villify.

detrás, *adv.* behind, after; back; in the rear.—**d. de,** behind, back of.—**por d.,** from the rear, from behind; behind one's back.

detrimento. *m.* detriment, damage, harm.—**con (sin) d. de,** with (without) detriment to.

detrítico, ca, *a.* detrital, detritic.

detritus, *m.* detritus.

deuda, *f.* debt; fault, offence; indebtedness; public debt.—**d. consolidada,** funded debt.—**d. exterior,** foreign debt.—**d. flotante,** floating debt.—**d. interior,** internal debt.—**d. pendiente,** unpaid balance.—**deudas activas,** assets.—**deudas pasivas,** liabilities.

deudo, da, *n.* relative, kindred.

deudor, ra, *n.* & *a.* debtor; indebted.

Deuteronomio, *m.* Deuteronomy.

deutóxido, *m.* (chem.) deutoxide, dioxide.

devalar, *vn.* (naut.) to deviate; to drift.

devanadera, *f.* reel, spool, bobbin, winding frame.—**d. de golpe,** clock reel, snap reel; (naut.) log reel.

devanador, ra, *n.* winder, spool, reel; anything on which another is wound.—**d. de lanzadera,** shuttle winder.

devanar, *va.* to reel, spool, wind.—**devanarse los sesos,** to screw one's wits.

devanear, *vn.* to rave, talk nonsense; to dote.

devaneo, *m.* delirium, alienation of mind, giddiness; frenzy; idle or mad pursuit; dissipation.

devantal, *m.* apron.

devastación, *f.* devastation, destruction, havoc.

devastador, ra, *n.* & *a.* desolator (-ing), devastator (-ing).

devastar, *va.* to devastate, lay waste, ruin.

devengar, *va.* (*for mut. v.* VENGAR) to earn, draw (as salary, interest, etc.).

devenir, *vn.* to happen; to become, be transformed into.

deviación, *f.* = DESVIACIÓN.

devoción, *f.* piety, devoutness; prayer; devotion, strong affection, constant and faithful attachment.

devocionario, *m.* prayer book.

devocionero, ra, *a.* devotional.

devolución, *f.* (law) devolution, restitution.—**d. de derechos,** (com.) drawback; debenture.

devolutivo, *a.* (law) returnable, restorable.

devolver, *va.* (*for irr. v.* VOLVER) to return; to restore; to refund, pay back.

devoniano, na; devónico, ca, *a.* Devonian.

devorador, ra. I. *n.* devourer. **II.** *a.* devouring, intense, ravenous.

devorante, *a.* = DEVORADOR.

devorar, *va.* to devour, swallow up, consume ravenously, gobble.

devotamente, *adv.* devoutly, piously.

devotería, *f.* false devoutness, overreligiosity.

devoto, ta, *a.* devout, pious; strongly attached, devoted.

devuelto, ta, *pp. irr.* of DEVOLVER.

devuelvo, devuelva. *V.* DEVOLVER.

dexiocardia, *f.* dexiocardia.

dextrina, *f.* dextrine.

dextro, *m.* area around a church.

dextrógiro, *m.* (phys.) dextrorotatory

dextrórsum, *adv.* towards the right.

dextrosa, *f.* (chem.) dextrose.

dey, *m.* dey (ruler).

deyección, *f.* (geol.) débris; (med.) dejection.

dezmable, *a.* tithable.

dezmar, *va.* = DIEZMAR.

dezmatorio, *m.* place where tithes are collected; tithing.

dezmeño, ña; dezmero, ra. I. *a.* belonging to tithes. **II.** *m.* tither.

dezmería, *f.* tithe land.

di, *pret. irr.* of DAR: *imperat. irr.* of DECIR.

día, *m.* day; daylight, sunshine.—**d. artificial,** ordinary day, from sunrise to sunset.—**d. de año nuevo,** New Year's day.—**d. de cumpleaños.** = D. DE AÑOS.—**d. de abstinencia** = D. DE AYUNO.—**d. de años,** birthday.—**d. de ayuno,** fast day, fasting day.—**d. de besamanos,** court day.—**d. de carne,** meat day.—**d. de cutio,** work day.—**d. de descanso,** day of rest, Sabbath.—**d. de fiesta,** holiday.—**d. de gala,** court day; holiday; gala day.—**d. de huelga,** day off (when no work is done); (med.) intercalary day.—**d. del juicio,** doomsday.—**d. de los difuntos,** All-Soul's Day.—**d. de los Inocentes,** Innocents' Day.—**d. de pescado** = D. DE VIGILIA.—**d. de recibo,** reception day, at-home day.—**d. de trabajo,** working day.—**d. de viernes,** Meager Day.—**d. de vigilia** = D. DE AYUNO.—**d. entre semana,** working day, week day.—**d. festivo** = D. DE FIESTA.—**d. diado,** appointed day.—**d. intercalar,** intercalary day of February.—**d. laborable** = D. DE TRABAJO.—**d. medio,** mean day.—**d. natural** = D. ARTIFICIAL.—**d. onomástico,** a person's saint's day.—**d. pesado,** gloomy day.—**d. por medio,** every other day.—**d. quebrado,** half holiday.—**d. sidéreo,** sidereal day.—**d. útil** = D. DE TRABAJO.—**días caniculares,** dog days.—**días de gracia,** (com.) days of grace.—**días ha,** it is a long time since.—**a días,** at times, once in a while.—**al d.,** up to date; per day.—**al otro d.,** on the following day.—**buenos días,** good morning.—**cada tercer d.** = UN D. SÍ Y OTRO NO.—**dar los días,** to send birthday congratulations.—**de d.,** by day.—**de d. en d.,** or **de un d. para otro,** from day to day.—**de hoy en ocho días,** this day week.—**el d. de hoy,** or **hoy en d.,** the present day.—**el d. menos pensado,** one of these days, when one least expects.—**el mejor d.,** some fine day.—**el otro d.,** the other day.—**en días de Dios, en los días de la vida,** never.—**en su d.,** at the proper time.—**entre d.,** in the daytime.—**hasta el d. de hoy,** to this day.—**los días de uno,** one's saint's day or birthday.—**ser persona de días,** or **tener días,** to be in years, to be of advanced age.—**un día sí y otro no,** day about, every other day.

diabasa, *f.* diorite (diabase).

diabetes, *f.* diabetes.

diabético, ca, *a.* diabetic.

diabla, *f.* (coll.) she-devil.—**a la d.,** carelessly, roughly.—**cosido a la d.,** (b.b.) bound in paper.

diablazo, *m.* *aug.* great devil.

diablear, *vn.* (coll.) to commit deviltries, play pranks.

diablejo, *m.* little devil, imp.

diablesa, *f.* (coll.) she-devil.

diablillo, *m.* *dim.* deviling, devilkin, little devil, imp; (coll.) smart, clever, mischievous fellow.—

d. cartesiano, or **de Descartes,** (phys.) Cartesian diver.

diablo, *m.* devil, Satan; devil, a perverse, cunning, subtle or hideous person.—**d. cojuelo,** artful devil.—**¡cómo diablos!**—(coll.) how the deuce.—**como un d.,** (coll.) like the deuce, like the devil.—**eso es el d.,** (coll.) that is the trouble.—**haber la de todos los diablos,** there to be (that is, *there* followed by the appropriate tense of *to be*) a great row or commotion.—**llevarse el d.,** to be ruined, fall through, be a fizzle.—**no valer un d.,** (coll.) to be good for nothing.—**¡qué d.!** or **¡un d.!** (coll.) the devil!—**ser de la piel del d.,** to be a limb of the devil.

diablura, *f.* diabolical undertaking; deviltry, mischief, wild prank.

diabólicamente, *adv.* diabolically, devilishly.

diabólico, ca, *a.* diabolical, devilish.

diábolo, *m.* diabolo, an old game.

diacatalicón, *m.* diacatholicon.

diacitrón, *m.* lemon peel preserved in sugar.

diaconado, *m.* deaconship.

diaconal, *a.* diaconal.—**diaconato,** *m.* deaconship.—**diaconía,** *f.* deaconry.

diaconisa, *f.* deaconess.—**diácono,** *m.* deacon.

diacrítico, ca, *a.* (gram.) diacritical; (med.) diagnostic.

diacústica, *f.* diacoustics.

diadelfo, fa, *a.* (bot.) diadelphous.

diadema, *f.* diadem, crown; glory, halo.

diademado, da, *a.* (her.) diademed.

diafanidad, *f.* diaphaneity, transparency.

diáfano, na, *a.* transparent, clear, diaphanous.

diáfisis, *f.* (anat.) diaphysis.

diaforesis, *f.* (med.) diaphoresis, perspiration.

diaforético, ca, *a.* (med.) diaphoretic.

diafragma, *m.* (anat., mech., etc.) diaphragm.

diafragmático, ca, *a.* diaphragmatic.

diagnosis, *f.* (med.) diagnostics.

diagnosticar, *va.* (*pret.* DIAGNOSTIQUÉ: *subj.* DIAGNOSTIQUE) to diagnose.

diagnóstico, ca. I. *a.* (med.) diagnostic. **II.** *m.* diagnosis.

diagonal. I. *a.* diagonal; oblique. **II.** *f.* (geom.) diagonal.

diagonalmente, *adv.* diagonally, obliquely.

diágrafo, *m.* diagraph.

diagrama, *f.* diagram.

diálaga, *f.* (min.) diallage.

diálisis, *f.* (chem.) dialysis.

dialectal, *a.* dialect (u. a.), relating to dialects.

dialéctica, *f.* dialectics.

dialéctico, ca. I. *a.* dialectic, dialectical. **II.** *n.* dialectician, logician.

dialecto, *m.* dialect, a variety of a language; derived language.

dialectología, *f.* dialectology, science or study of dialects.

dializador, ra, *m.* & *a.* (chem.) dialyzer (-ing).

dializar, *va.* (chem.) to dialyze.

dialogal, *a.* colloquial, dialogic, dialogical.

dialogar, *vn.* to dialogize; to chat, converse.

dialogismo, *m.* (rhet.) dialogism.

dialogístico, ca, *a.* colloquial, dialogistic.

dialogizar, *vn.* = DIALOGAR.

diálogo, *m.* dialogue.

dialoguista, *m.* dialogist.

dialtea, *f.* marsh-mallow ointment.

diamagnético, ca, *a.* (phys.) diamagnetic.

diamantado, da, *a.* diamondlike.

diamante, *m.* diamond; adamant.—**d. en bruto,** rough or uncut diamond; (coll.) an uncultured person of sterling qualities.

diamantífero, ra, *a.* diamantiferous, diamond-bearing.

diamantino, na, *a.* adamantine, diamantine.

diamantista, *m.* diamond cutter; jeweller.

diametral, *a.* diametrical.

diametralmente, *adv.* diametrically.

diámetro, *m.* diameter.

diana, *f.* (mil.) reveille; (poet.) the moon.

dianche, *m.* & *interj.* (coll.) the deuce, the devil.

diandro, dra, *a.* (bot.) diandrous.

diantre, *m.* (coll.) = DIANCHE.

diapasón, *m.* (mus.) tuning fork; diapason; pitch, accord; regular octave.—**d. normal,** standard pitch.

diapédesis, *f.* (phys.) diapedesis.

diapente, *m.* (mus.) perfect fifth.

diaplejía, *f.* (med.) general paralysis.

diapositiva, *f.* (phot.) diapositive; lantern slide.

diaprea, *f.* a sort of round plum.

diaquilón, *m.* diachylon, diachylum.

diariamente, *adv.* daily.

diario, ria. I. *a.* daily. **II.** *m.* journal, diary; daily newspaper; daily household expense.—**d. de navegación,** log book.

diarista, *n.* journalist, diarist.

diarrea, *f.* diarrhœa.

diarreico, ca; diárrico, ca, *a.* diarrheic.

diartrosis, *f.* (anat.) diarthrosis.

diascordio, *m.* (pharm.) diascordium.

diáspero, *m.* jasper.

diásporo, *m.* (min.) diaspore.

diastasa, *f.* (chem.) diastase.

diastasis, *f.* (surg.) diastasis.

diástilo, *a.* (arch.) diastyle.

diástole, *m.* (anat. and rhet.) diastole.

diatérmano, na; diatérmico, ca, *f.* diathermanous.

diatesarón, *m.* (mus.) diatessaron.

diatésico, ca, *a.* (med.) diathetic.

diátesis, *f.* (med.) diathesis.

diatómico, ca, *a.* (chem.) diatomic.

diatónicamente, *adv.* diatonically.

diatónico, a. (mus.) diatonic.

diatriba, *f.* diatribe.

dibujador, ra, *n.* draftsman (-woman).

dibujante, *m.* **I.** *a.* sketching. **II.** *m.* draftsman.

dibujar. I. *va.* to draw, make a drawing of; to depict, describe vividly. **II.** *vr.* to throw a shadow upon a surface.

dibujo, *m.* drawing; sketch; portrayal, description.—**d. a pulso,** freehand drawing.—**d. del natural,** drawing from life or from nature.—**d. lineal,** instrumental drawing.

dicacidad, *f.* pertness, sauciness, banter.

dicaz, *a.* keen, biting (s. o. speech).

dicción, *f.* diction, style, language.

diccionario, *m.* dictionary.

diccionarista, *n.* lexicographer.

diciembre, *m.* December.

dicente, diciente, *a.* saying, talking.

diclinismo, *n.* (bot.) diclinism.

diclino, na, *a.* (bot.) diclinous.

dicotiledón; dicotiledóneo, a. I. *a.* (bot.) dicotyledonous. **II.** *n.* dicotyledon. **III.** *f. pl.* Dicotyledones.

dicotomía, *f.* dichotomy.

dicotómico, ca; dicótomo, ma, *a.* dichotomic, dichotomous.

dicroico, ca, *a.* (phys.) dichroic.

dicroísmo, *n.* (phys.) dichroism.

dictado, *m.* title of dignity or honor; dictation.—*pl.* dictates, promptings.

dictador, ra, *n.* dictator.

dictadura, *f.* dictatorship.

dictamen, *m.* opinion, judgment; suggestion, insinuation, advice.

dictaminar, *vn.* to express an opinion, pass judgment.

dictamo, *m.* (bot.) dittany.—**d. bastardo,** shrubby white horehound.—**d. blanco,** or **real,** white flaxinella.—**d. crético,** marjoram.

dictar, *va.* to dictate; to command, prescribe, direct; to inspire, suggest, prompt.

dictatorial, *a.* dictatorial.

dictatorialmente, *adv.* dictatorially.

dictatorio, ria, *a.* dictatorial.

dicterio, *m.* taunt, keen reproach; insult.

dicha, *f.* happiness, good, luck, good fortune.—**a d.,** or **por d.,** *adv.* by chance.

dicharachero, ra, *a.* (coll.) that uses slang.

dicharacho, *m.* (coll.) vulgar, low, or slang expression.

dichero, ra, *a.* witty.

dicho, cha. I. *m.* saying, saw, proverb; expression, sentence; statement; witty remark, repartee; declaration, deposition; promise of marriage.—**d. de las gentes,** gossip; rumor.—**del d. al hecho hay gran trecho,** it is a long way from saying to doing; it is one thing to say, and quite another thing to do. **II.** *a. & pp.* of DECIR.—**d. y hecho,** no sooner said than done; sure enough, as expected.—**lo d. d.,** I mean what I say, I have said it; it's agreed.

dichosamente, *adv.* happily, fortunately.

dichoso, sa, *a.* happy; fortunate, lucky.

didáctica, *f.* didactics.

didácticamente, *adv.* didactically.

didáctico, ca; didascálico, ca, *a.* didactic, didactical.

didelfo, fa, *n. & a.* (zool.) didelprian (as the kangaroo or the opossum).

didimio, *m.* (chem.) didymium.

dídimo, ma, *a.* (bot.) didymous.

diecinueve, *n. & a.* nineteen; nineteenth.

diecinueveavo, va, *n. & a.* nineteenth.

dieciochavo, va, *n. & a.* eighteenth.

dieciocheno, na. I. *a.* eighteenth. **II.** *m.* a kind of cloth.

dieciocho, *n. & a.* eighteen; eighteenth.

dieciseis, *n. & a.* sixteen; sixteenth.

dieciseisavo, va, *n. & a.* sixteenth.

dieciseiseno, na, *a.* sixteenth.

diecisiete, *n. & a.* seventeen; seventeenth.

diecisieteavo, va, *n. & a.* seventeenth.

diedro, dra. I. *a.* dihedral. **II.** *m.* dihedral angle.

dieléctrico, ca, *a.* dielectric.

diente, *m.* tooth; fang or tusk of wild boars or elephants; tooth (of a saw, comb, rake, file); cog (of a wheel or pinion); tine or prong (of a fork); tongue (of a buckle); clove (of garlic).—*pl.* indented edges of tools or ornaments, indentations.—**d. de león,** (bot.) dandelion or lion's tooth.—**d. de lobo,** burnisher, spike.—**d. de perro,** sculptor's dented chisel; (bot.) dog-tooth violet.—**d. incisivo,** incisor, cutting tooth, foretooth.—**d. molar,** molar tooth, back tooth.—**dientes caninos,** eye teeth, canine teeth.—**dientes postizos,** artificial teeth.—**aguzar los dientes,** to whet the appetite.—**a regaña dientes,** *adv.* most unwillingly.—**decir,** or **hablar, entre dientes,** to mumble, to mutter.—**dar d. con d.,** to shiver with cold or fear, to be with teeth chattering.—**de dientes afuera,** without sincerity, as mere lip service.—**tener buen d.,** to be a good eater.

dientecico, illo, ito, *m. dim.* little tooth.

diéresis, *f.* diæresis.

diesi, *f.* (mus.) diesis; a sharp.

diestra, *f.* right hand; favor, support.

diestramente, *adv.* skilfully, cleverly, neatly.

diestro, tra. I. *a.* right; dexterous, able, skilful, handy; dexter; sagacious, wise; sly, artful, cunning; favorable, propitious.—**a d. y siniestro,** recklessly; right and left. **II.** *m.* skilful fencer; bullfighter; halter or bridle.

dieta, *f.* diet, prescribed or regulated meals; diet, legislative assembly; (law) one day's journey of ten leagues by land; daily salary of judges and other officers of the law; daily fees paid to a physician.—*pl.* (naut.) provisions for the sick and wounded.

dietario, *m.* family account book; record book, book where notable events are registered.

dietética, *f.* (med.) dietetics.

dietético, ca, *a.* dietetic, dietetical.

diez, *m. & a.* ten; tenth.—**d. de bolos,** pin standing alone in front of the ninepins.—*pl. f.* **las diez,** ten o'clock.

diezmador, *m.* = DIEZMERO.

diezmal, *a.* decimal.

diezmar, *va.* to decimate; to tithe; (mil.) to punish one in ten of.

diezmero, *m.* tither.

diezmesino, na, *a.* ten months old.

diezmilésimo, ma, *n. & a.* ten-thousandth.

diezmilímetro, *m.* ten-thousandth of a meter.

diezmillonésimo, ma, *n. & a.* ten-millionth.

diezmo, *m.* tithe; tenth part; duty of ten per cent; decimation.

difamación, *f.* defamation.—**difamador, ra,** *n. & a.* defamer (-ing).—**difamar,** *va.* to defame, to discredit.—**difamatorio, ria,** *a.* defamatory.

difarreación, *f.* (obs.) diffarreation.

diferencia, *f.* difference, dissimilarity; disagreement; (math.) difference.—**a d. de,** unlike; as distinguished from.

diferenciación, *f.* (biol., math., etc.) differentiation.

diferencial. I. *a.* differential. **II.** *f.* (math.) differential.

diferenciar. I. *va.* to differentiate; to change or alter the use or destination of. **II.** *vn.* to differ, dissent, disagree. **III.** *vr.* to differ, to be different; to distinguish one's self.

diferente, *a.* different.

diferentemente, *adv.* differently.

diferir. I. *va.* (*ind.* DIFIERO: *subj.* DIFIERA) to defer, postpone, put off; to adjourn, suspend; to protract, prolong, extend. **II.** *vn.* to differ, be different; (naut.) to remove the gaskets of a sail.

difícil, *a.* difficult, hard.

difícilmente, *adv.* with difficulty; hardly.

dificultad, *f.* difficulty; objection.

dificultador, ra. I. *n.* one who raises difficulties. **II.** *a.* causing difficulties.

dificultar, *va.* to make difficult; to impede.

dificultosamente, *adv.* with difficulty.

dificultoso, sa, *a.* difficult, hard; (coll.) ugly, homely.

difidación, *f.* declaration of war.

difidencia, *f.* diffidence, distrust.

difidente, *a.* distrustful, diffident.

difiero, difiera. *V.* DIFERIR.

difilo, la, *a.* (bot.) two-leaf.

difluencia, *f.* diffluence.—**difluente,** *a.* diffluent.

difluir, *vn.* (*for mut. v.* HUIR) to be diffused or spread out.

difracción, *f.* diffraction.

difringente, *a.* diffractive.

difteria, *f.* (med.) diphtheria.

diftérico, ca, *a.* diphtheritic.

difteritis, *f.* (med.) diphtheritic inflammation.

difundido, da, *a. & pp.* of DIFUNDIR; diffuse, diffused, scattered.

difundir, *va.* to diffuse, outspread; to divulge, publish; (rad.) to broadcast.

difunto, ta. I. *a.* defunct, deceased, dead; late; decayed, withered. **II.** *m. & f.* corpse.

difusamente, *adv.* diffusely, diffusedly.

difusible, *a.* diffusible.

difusión, *f.* diffusion; diffusiveness, dispersion; exuberance of style; (rad.) broadcasting.

difusivo, va, *a.* diffusive.

difuso, sa, *a.* diffuse; wordy, diffused, widespread.

difusor, ra. I. *a.* difusing, defusive; (rad.) broadcasting. **II.** *m.* (sug. man.) diffuser.

digástrico, ca, *a.* digastric.

digerible, *a.* digestible.

digerir, *va.* (*ind.* DIGIERO: *subj.* DIGIERA) to digest; to bear; to put up with; (chem.) to digest.

digestible, *a.* digestible.

digestión, *f.* (physiol. and chem.) digestion.

digestivo, va. I. *a.* digestive. **II.** *m.* (surg.) suppurative.

digesto, *m.* (law) digest, systematic compilation of laws.

digestor, *m.* digester (apparatus).

digiero, digiera. *V.* DIGERIR.

digitación, *f.* fingering.

digitado, da, *a.* (bot. and zool.) digitate.

digital. I. *a.* digital. **II.** *f.* (bot.) digitalis, foxglove.

digitalina, *f.* (chem.) digitalin.

digitígrado, da, *a.* digitigrade.

For pronunciation, see the rules at the beginning of the book.

dígito, ta. I. *a.* digital. **II.** *m.* (ast., arith.) digit.

dignación, *f.* condescension, accommodation.

dignamente, *adv.* worthily; with dignity.

dignarse, *vr.* to condescend, deign, vouchsafe.

dignatario, *m.* dignitary.

dignidad, *f.* dignity, high rank, office or position; honor, greatness; dignified bearing; archbishop or bishop.

dignificante, *a.* (theol.) dignifying.

dignificar, *va.* to dignify.

digno, na, *a.* meritorious, worthy, deserving; suitable, fit, fitting, appropriate.

digo, diga. *V.* DECIR.

digresión, *f.* digression; (ast.) digression.

digresivamente, *adv.* digressively.

digresivo, va, *a.* digressive.

dihueñe, dihueñi, *m.* (Ch.) an edible fungus growing on trees.

dij, dije. *m.* amulet, charm; trinket; watchcharm; any small piece of jewellery; (coll.) person of sterling qualities; one gorgeously attired.

dije, dijo. *V.* DECIR.

dilaceración, *f.* dilaceration.

dilacerar, *va.* to dilacerate, tear asunder.

dilación, *f.* delay, procrastination.

dilapidación, *f.* dilapidation.—**dilapidador, ra,** *n.* dilapidator.—**dilapidar,** *va.* to dilapidate.

dilatable, *a.* dilatable, expansible.

dilatación, *f.* dilatation, expansion, distention; prolongation; enlargement; diffuseness, prolixity; calmness, serenity in sorrow; (phys., st. eng.) expansion.—**d. lineal,** linear expansion.

dilatadamente, *adv.* dilatedly; with delay or procrastination.

dilatado, da, *a.* & *pp.* of DILATAR; large, extended, extensive, vast; prolix, drawn out.

dilatador, ra. I. *a.* dilating, expanding; retarding, causing delay. **II.** *m.* (surg.) dilator.

dilatar. I. *va.* to dilate, widen, expand, enlarge, lengthen, prolong; to swell, spread out; to defer, retard, delay, put off, protract; (met.) to comfort, to cheer up. **II.** *vr.* to be diffuse, to extend, expatiate; to expand.

dilatativo, va, *a.* dilative.

dilatoria, *f.* delay, waste of time.

dilatorio, ria, *a.* dilatory, delaying, long.

dilección, *f.* dilection, love, affection.

dilecto, ta, *a.* loved, beloved.

dilema, *m.* dilemma.

dilemático, ca, *a.* dilemmatic.

diligencia, *f.* diligence, assiduity, industriousness; speediness, activity, briskness; diligence, stage-coach; (coll.) affair, business, errand; (law) judicial proceeding.—**hacer d.,** or **la d.,** to endeavor, try.—**hacer una d.,** to do an errand; to attend, or go on, some business.

diligenciar, *va.* to conduct, to carry out; to further.

diligenciero, *m.* agent, attorney.

diligente, *a.* diligent, assiduous; prompt, swift.

diligentemente, *adv.* diligently, assiduously.

dilogía, *f.* ambiguity, double sense.

dilucidación, *f.* elucidation, explanation.

dilucidador, ra, *n.* elucidator.

dilucidar, *va.* to elucidate, explain, discuss.

dilucidario, *m.* explanatory writing.

dilución, *f.* dilution.—**diluente,** *a.* diluent.

diluir, *va.* & *vr.* (*for mut. v.* HUIR) to dilute; to weaken.

diluvial, *a.* (geol.) diluvial.—**diluviano,** *a.* diluvian.

diluviar, *vn. impers.* to rain heavily.

diluvio, *m.* flood, deluge; overflow, inundation; (coll.) vast abundance, a lot, lots.

dimanación, *f.* springing or issuing.

dimanante, *a.* springing, originating.

dimanar, *vn.* (w. **de**) to spring or proceed (from); to originate (in); to be due (to); to follow (from).

dimensión, *f.* dimension; extent, capacity, magnitude, size.

dimensional, *a.* dimensional.

dimes, *pl. m.*—**andar en d. y diretes,** to higgle, chaffer, quibble, argue.

dimidiar, *va.* to dimidiate, to halve.

diminución, *f.* diminution.—**ir en d.,** to taper (as a pole); to be diminishing or becoming less or lower.

diminuir, *va., vn.* & *vr.*=DISMINUIR.

diminutamente, *adv.* diminutively; minutely; by retail.

diminutivamente, *adv.* (gram.) diminutively.

diminutivo, va. I. *a.* diminishing; diminutive. **II.** *m.* (gram.) diminutive.

diminuto, ta, *a.* diminutive, very little or small.

dimisión, *f.* resignation (of membership, office).

dimisorias, *f. pl.* letters dimissory; (coll.) dismissal or discharge, "firing", "passports."

dimitir, *va.* to resign, give up, relinquish.

dimorfismo, *m.* (min.) dimorphism.

dimorfo, fa, *a.* (min.) dimorphous.

din, *m.* (coll.) money, boodle.

dina, *f.* (phys.) dyne.

dinamarques, sa, *n.* & *a.* Dane, Danish.

dinamia, *f.* kilogrammeter per unit of time (a unit of power).

dinámica, *f.* dynamics.—**dinámico, ca,** *a.* dynamic.

dinamismo, *m.* dynamism.

dinamista, *n.* & *a.* dynamist (-ic).

dinamita, *f.* dynamite.

dinamitero, ra, *n.* dynamiter.

dínamo, *f.* (gen. *m.* in Am.) dynamo.

dinamoeléctrico, ca, *a.* dynamo-electric.

dinamométrico, ca, *a.* dynamometric.

dinamómetro, *m.* dynamometer.

dinasta, *m.* dynast, sovereign, monarch.

dinastía, *f.* dynasty.

dinástico, ca, *a.* dynastic, dynastical.

dinastismo, *m.* fealty to a dynasty.

dinerada, *f.* large sum of money.

dineral, *m.* large sum of money; formerly, a set of weights for gold and silver.

dinerillo, *m.* small copper coin; (coll.) small sum of money.

dinero, *m.* money; currency, coin; gold, coinage; ancient Spanish silver coin; standard of silver, 24 grains; Peruvian silver coin; wealth, fortune.—**d. contante,** or **efectivo,** ready money, cash.—**persona de d.,** person of means, or well off.

dineroso, sa, *a.* moneyed, rich.

dineruelo, *m. dim.* small coin; a little money, some money.

dinornis, *m.* (pal.) dinornis, moa.

dinosauro, *m.* (pal.) dinosaur.—*pl.* Dinosauria.

dinoterio, *m.* (pal.) dinothere, dinotherium.

dintel, *m.* (arch.) lintel, doorhead.

dintelar, *va.* to provide with lintels.

dintorno, *m.* (art.) within the contour.

diocesano, na. I. *a.* diocesan. **II.** *m.* diocesan, bishop.

diócesi, diócesis, *f.* diocese.

dioico, ca, *a.* (bot.) diœcious.

dionisia, *f.* bloodstone; hematite.

dionisíaco, ca, *a.* Dionysiac, Bacchic.

dioptra, *f.* diopter.

dióptrica, *f.* dioptrics.

dióptrico, ca, *a.* dioptric.

diorama, *m.* diorama.

diorámico, ca, *a.* dioramic.

diorita, *f.* diorite.

dios, *m.* god; (**D-**) God.—**D. es D.,** as sure as God lives; by Jupiter!—**D. le guarde,** God be with you.—**D. lo haga,** or **lo quiera,** God grant.—**D. los hace y ellos se juntan,** birds of a feather flock together.—**¡D. mío!** my God! goodness me! oh my!—**anda con D.,** farewell, adieu.—**la,** or **las, de D. es Cristo,** turmoil, bedlam, row.—**mediante D.,** God willing.—**no lo quiera D.,** God forbid.—**plegue a D.,** or **quiera D.,** God grant.—**¡por D.!** for God's sake! by God! goodness!—**sea como D. quiera,** be it as God wishes.—**¡válgame D.!** bless me!—**¡válgate D.!** God preserve, or bless, you!—**vaya Vd. con D.,** good-bye; go on; off with you, be gone.—**¡vive D.!** as sure as God lives; by God! by heaven!

diosa, *f.* goddess.

diostedé, *m.* a South-American bird, similar to the toucan.

diploma, *m.* diploma; bull, patent, license; title, credential.

diplomacia, *f.* diplomacy.

diplomática, *f.* diplomacy; (archæol.) diplomatics.

diplomático, ca. I. *a.* diplomatic, diplomatical; (archæol.) diplomatic. **II.** *m.* diplomatist, diplomat.

diplopia, *f.* (med.) diplopia.

dipsáceo, a. I. *a.* (bot.) dipsacaceous. **II.** *f. pl.* Dipsacaceæ.

dipsomanía, *f.* dipsomania, excessive craving for liquor.

díptero, ra. I. *a.* (arch.) having two wings or a double colonnade; (ento.) dipterous. **II.** *m. pl.* Diptera.

dipterocárpeo, a. I. *a.* (bot.) dipterocarpaceous. **II.** *f. pl.* Dipterocarpaceæ.

díptica, *f.*, **díptico,** *m.* diptych.

diptongación, *f.* (gram.) diphthongization.

diptongar, *va.* to diphthongize.

diptongo, *m.* diphthong.

diputación, *f.* deputation; object of a deputation.

diputado. I. *m.* deputy, representative, delegate; (com.) assignee.—**d. a Cortes,** congressman. —**d. cunero,** (coll.) congressman who owes his election to the influence of the government. **II.** *pp.* of DIPUTAR.

diputador, ra, *n. & a.* constituent.

diputar, *va.* to depute, delegate, commission; to constitute, empower.

dique, *m.* dike, dam, mole, jetty; (naut.) dry dock; check, bar, stop; (min.) crop.

dirección, *f.* direction, course, tendency, trend, turn; direction, management, administration; order, command, instruction; address (for letters, etc.); board of directors, executive board; editorship of a newspaper; managership of a theater; office of a director.

directamente, *adv.* directly, in a direct manner.

directivo, va. I. *a.* directive, managing. **II.** *f.* governing board, board of directors, management.

directo, ta, *a.* direct; straight.

director, ra. I. *n. & a.* director (-ing). **II.** *n.* director, manager; chief; editor (of a newspaper); principal (of a college).—**d. de escena,** stage manager.—**d. de orquesta,** conductor, leader of an orchestra.—**d. espiritual,** father confessor.

directorial, *a.* directorial.

directorio, ria. I. *a.* directive, directorial. **II.** *m.* directory; body of directors, directorate.

directriz, *f.* (grom.) directrix.

dirigente, *a.* directing, leading; ruling.

dirigible. I. *a.* dirigible; manageable; (aer.) dirigible. **II.** *m.* (aer.) dirigible.

dirigir. I. *va.* (ind. DIRIJO: subj. DIRIJA) to direct; to dedicate (a work); to address (a letter, etc.); to command, lead, head; to govern, control, manage; (naut.) to steer. **II.** *vr.* (w. **a**) to address; to apply, resort (to); to go (to or toward).

dirimente, *a.* breaking off, dissolving.

dirimible, *a.* that may be broken off.

dirimir, *va.* to dissolve, disjoin, separate; to annul, to declare void; to adjust, reconcile.

dirruir, *va.* to ruin, destroy.

disanto, *m.* holy day.

discantar, *va.* to chant, sing; to comment; to descant, discourse much about; (mus.) to sing in counterpoint.

discante, *m.* small guitar; concert, especially of string instruments.

disceptación, *f.* argument, controversy.

disceptar, *vn.* to dispute, argue.

discernidor, ra, *n. & a.* discerner (-ing).

discerniente, *a.* discerning.

discernimiento, *m.* discernment, judgment, discrimination; (law) appointment of a guardian.

discernir, *va.* (ind. DISCIERNO: subj. DISCIERNA) to discern, judge, discriminate; (law) to appoint (a guardian).

disciplina, *f.* discipline; education, instruction; systematic training; any art or science taught; rule of conduct, order.—*pl.* scourge, cat-of-nine-tails; flagellation.

disciplinable, *a.* disciplinable.

disciplinadamente, *adv.* with discipline.

disciplinado, da. I. *a.* disciplined, trained; marbled, variegated (as flowers). **II.** *pp.* of DISCIPLINAR.

disciplinal, *a.* disciplinal, disciplinary.

disciplinante. I. *a.* disciplinary; Disciplinant. **II.** *n.* Disciplinant.

disciplinar. I. *va.* to discipline, educate, instruct, train; (mil.) to drill. **II.** *vr.* to scourge one's self as penance.

disciplinario, ria, *a.* disciplinary.

disciplinazo, *m.* lash.

discipulado, *m.* discipleship; education, instruction; number of pupils.

discipular, *a.* belonging to a disciple or pupil.

discípulo, la, *n.* disciple; follower; pupil, student.

disco, *m.* disk; a quoit; solid wheel; circular plate (glass, metal, etc.); discus; (astr.) disk.—**d. de señales,** (r. w.) signal disk; semaphore.

discóbolo, *m.* discobolus, discus thrower.

discoidal, discoide, discoideo, a, *a.* disk-like, flat and round.

díscolo, la, *a.* ungovernable; wayward, froward.

discoloro, ra, *a.* (bot.) colorless.

disconforme, -midad = DESCONFORME, etc.

discontinuación, *f.* discontinuation.

discontinuar, *va.* to discontinue, to stop.

discontinuo, a, *a.* discontinuous.

disconveniencia, -niente, -nir, = DESCONVENIENCIA, -NIENTE, -NIR.

discordancia, *f.* disagreement, discordance.

discordante, *a.* dissonant, discordant.

discordar, *vn.* to discord, disagree.

discorde, *a.* discordant; (mus.) dissonant.

discordia, *f.* discord, disagreement, discordance, opposition, clash.

discrasia, *f.* (med.) cacochymia.

discreción, *f.* discretion, prudence, judgment; acuteness of mind, sagacity; liberty of action and decision.—**a d.,** optional; (mil.) at discretion, unconditionally.

discrecional, *a.* optional, discretionary.

discrecionalmente, *adv.* optionally, discretionarily.

discrepancia, *f.* discrepancy.

discrepante, *a.* disagreeing, discrepant.

discrepar, *vn.* to differ, to disagree.

discretamente, *adv.* discreetly.

discretear, *vn.* to affect discretion.

discreteo, *m.* affected discretion.

discreto, ta, *a.* discreet, circumspect, prudent; ingenious, sharp, witty; (math.) discrete (s. o. quantity); (med.) distinct, segregate (as in smallpox).

discrimen, *m.* hazard, risk, peril; difference.

discriminador, ra, *n. & a.* (Am.) discriminator (-ing, -ive).

discriminar, *va.* (Am.) to discriminate.

disculpa, *f.* apology, excuse; exculpation.

disculpabilidad, *f.* excusability; pardonableness.

disculpable, *a.* excusable; pardonable.

disculpablemente, *adv.* pardonably, excusably.

disculpadamente, *adv.* excusably.

disculpar, *va. & vr.* to exculpate; to excuse; to apologize.

discurrir. I. *vn.* to roam, ramble about; to flow (as a river); to reflect, think; to reason; to discourse. **II.** *va.* to invent, plan, contrive; to conjecture, infer.

discursante, *n.* discourser, lecturer.

discursar, *vn.* (w. **sobre** or **acerca de**) to discourse (on); treat (of); to lecture (on).

discursear, *vn.* (coll. and contempt.) to harangue, to make a speech.

---

discursista, *m.* speech maker.
discursivo, va, *a.* discursive; thoughtful, meditative, cogitative.
discurso, *m.* discourse; cogitation, ratiocination, reasoning; speech, lecture, oration; dissertation; treatise, tract; conversation, talk; space of time.
discusión, *f.* discussion.
discutible, *a.* controvertible, disputable.
discutidor, ra, *n. & a.* arguer (-ing).
discutir, *va. & vn.* to discuss.
disecación, *f.* dissection, anatomy.
disecador, ra, *n.* dissector; taxidermist.
disecar, *va.* (*for mut. v.* SECAR) to dissect; to make an autopsy of; to stuff (dead animals).
disección, *f.* dissection, anatomy.
disector, ra, *n.* dissector.
diseminación, *f.* dissemination; scattering, spreading.—**diseminador, ra,** *n. & a.* disseminator (-ing); spreader (-ing).
diseminar, *va.* to disseminate; spread, scatter.
disensión, *f.* dissent; contest, strife.
disenso, *m.* dissent, disagreement.
disentería, *f.* (med.) dysentery.
disentérico, ca, *a.* dysenteric.
disentimiento, *m.* dissent, disagreement.
disentir, *vn.* (*for irr. v.* SENTIR) to dissent, to disagree, to differ.
diseñador, ra, *n.* designer, delineator.
diseñar, *va.* to draw; to sketch, outline.
diseño, *m.* sketch, plan, outline; portrayal, description.
disertación, *f.* dissertation, disquisition.
disertador, ra; disertante, *n. & a.* discourser (-ing), expounder (-ing).
disertar, *vn.* (w. **sobre** or **acerca de**) to discourse (on), treat (of), discuss.
diserto, ta, *a.* eloquent, fluent.
disfagia, *f.* (med.) dysphagia.
disfamación, *f.* defamation.—**disfamador, ra,** *n. & a.* defamer (-ing).—**disfamar,** *va.* to defame. —**disfamatorio, ria,** *a.* defamatory.
disfasia, *f.* (med.) dysphasia.
disfavor, *m.* disregard, disfavor.
disforme, *a.* deformed, hideous; huge, big.
disformidad, *f.* deformity; excessive bigness.
disfraz, *m.* mask, costume, disguise; dissimulation, dissembling.
disfrazar. I. *va.* (*for mut. v.* ABRAZAR) to disguise; to misrepresent. **II.** *vr.* to masquerade, to travesty.
disfrutar. I. *va.* to benefit by; to have the benefit of; to enjoy (good health, etc.). **II.** *vn.* **d. de,** to enjoy, to have.
disfrute, *m.* use, enjoyment, benefit.
disgregable, *a.* separable.
disgregación, *f.* separation, disjunction; disintegration, dissociation.
disgregar, *va.* (*for mut. v.* AGREGAR) to separate, disjoin, disperse.
disgregativo, va, *a.* disjunctive.
disgustadamente, *adv.* with displeasure.
disgustar. I. *va.* to displease; to dislike (ch. constr.: *esto me disgusta,* I dislike this); to offend; to anger. **II.** *vr.* to be (get) displeased or angry; to fall out (with each other).
disgustillo, *m. dim.* displeasure, slight unpleasantness or difference.
disgusto, *m.* disgust, loathing; ill humor; displeasure; unpleasantness, quarrel; vexation, annoyance; grief, sorrow.—**a d.,** against one's will.
disidencia, *f.* dissidence, nonconformity.
disidente, *a. & n.* dissident, dissenter (-ing), nonconformist.
disidir, *vn.* to dissent, disagree.
disílabo, ba, *a.* dissyllable.
disimetría, *f.* dissymmetry, lack of symmetry.
disimétrico, ca, *a.* unsymmetric.
disímil, disimilar, *a.* dissimilar.
disimilitud, *f.* unlikeness.
disimulable, *a.* that may be dissembled; excusable.
disimulación, *f.* dissimulation, dissembling.

disimuladamente, *adv.* dissemblingly, on the sly, on the quiet.
disimulado, da. I. *a.* dissembling; reserved, sullen; sly, cunning.—**hacer la d.,** (coll.) to feign ignorance. **II.** *pp.* of DISIMULAR.
disimulador, ra, *n. & a.* dissembler (-ing).
disimular, *va.* to dissimulate, dissemble; to feign, pretend; to tolerate, overlook, let pass; to color, to misrepresent.
disimulo, *m.* dissimulation; tolerance.
disipable, *a.* easily scattered; capable of being dissipated.
disipación, *f.* dissipation; dispersion, scattering; evanescence; extravagance, waste.
disipado, da. I. *a.* dissipated; prodigal; dissolute. **II.** *pp.* of DISIPAR.
disipador, ra, *n. & a.* squanderer (-ing); spendthrift.
disipar. I. *va. & vr.* to dissipate, to disperse, to scatter (as clouds). **II.** *va.* to squander, misspend, lavish; to drive away, put to flight.
dislate, *m.* nonsense, absurdity.
dislocación, dislocadura, *f.* dislocation; sprain; (min.) slide.
dislocar, *va. & vr.* (*for mut. v.* COLOCAR); to dislocate, displace, sprain, disjoint.
dismembración, *f.* = DESMEMBRACIÓN.
dismenorrea, *f.* dysmenorrhœa.
disminución, *f.* DIMINUCIÓN; (vet.) a disease in horses' hoofs.
disminuir. I. *va.* (*for mut. v.* HUIR) to diminish, lessen, lower, decrease; to detract from. **II.** *vr.* to diminish, decrease.
disnea, *f.* dyspnœa.—**disneico, ca,** *a.* dyspnœic.
disociación, *f.* separation, dissociation.
disociar, *va.* to dissociate, separate.
disolubilidad, *f.* dissolubility; solubility.
disoluble, *a.* dissoluble.
disolución, *f.* dissolution, disintegration; (chem.) dissolution; solution; dissoluteness, dissipation. —**d. de sociedad,** dissolution of partnership.
disolutamente, *adv.* dissolutely, licentiously.
disolutivo, va, *a.* solvent.
disoluto, ta, *a.* dissolute, loose, dissipated.
disolvente, *m.* dissolvent, dissolver.
disolver. I. *va.* (*for irr. v.* ABSOLVER) to loosen, untie; to dissolve (as a meeting); to separate, disunite; (phys. and chem.) to dissolve. **II.** *vr.* to dissolve.
disón, *m.* (mus.) discord.
disonancia, *f.* harsh sound; disagreement, discord; (mus.) dissonance.
disonante, *a.* dissonant, inharmonious; discordant, unsuitable.
disonar, *vn.* (*for irr. v.* SONAR) to disagree in sound, to be inharmonious; to be discordant, to disagree.
dísono, na, *a.* dissonant, inharmonious.
dispar, *a.* unlike, unequal, unmatched.
disparada, *f.* (Am.) sudden and hasty start; flight.—**a la d.,** at full speed; hurriedly and recklessly.—**de una d.,** promptly; at once.
disparadamente, *adv.* hurriedly.
disparador, *m.* shooter; trigger; ratchet or ratchet wheel, in clockwork; (naut.) anchor tripper.
disparar. I. *va. & vn.* to shoot, discharge, fire; let off; to cast or throw with violence. **II.** *vn.* (coll.) to talk nonsense, to blunder. **III.** *vr.* to run headlong, to rush; to run away (as a horse); (naut.) to turn violently (as the capstan); to go off (as a gun).
disparatadamente, *adv.* blunderingly; absurdly; nonsensically.
disparatado, da, *pp. & a.* absurd, foolish, nonsensical.
disparatador, ra, *n.* nonsensical talker.
disparatar, *vn.* to act absurdly; to talk nonsense; to blunder.
disparate, *m.* blunder, mistake; absurdity, nonsense.
disparatorio, *m.* nonsensical or blundering act, speech or writing.

disparejo, ja, a. uneven.

disparidad, f. disparity, inequality.

disparo, m. discharge, explosion; nonsense, absurdity.

dispendio, m. excessive expense; excessive waste.

dispendiosamente, adv. expensively.

dispendioso, sa, a. costly, expensive.

dispensa, f. dispense, privilege, exemption, dispensation; document granting a dispensation.

dispensable, a. dispensable; excusable.

dispensación, f. dispensation, exemption.

dispensador, ra, a. granting a dispensation; dispensing, distributing.

dispensar, va. to dispense, deal out, distribute; to exempt; to acquit, absolve; to excuse, pardon.

dispepsia, f. (med.) dyspepsia.

dispéptico, ca, a. dyspeptic.

dispersar, va. to disperse, scatter, put to flight; to dissipate.—**dispersión,** f. dispersion.

disperso, sa, a. dispersed, separated; scattered.

dispertador, ra, = DESPERTADOR.

dispertar, va. & vn. = DESPERTAR.

displacer, va. & vn. = DESPLACER.

displicencia, f. disagreeableness; lukewarmness.

displicente, a. disagreeable, unpleasant; peevish, fretful.

disponedor, ra, n. & a. disposer (-ing), distributer (-ing).

disponente, a. disposing.

disponer. I. va. & vn. (for irr. v. PONER) to dispose; arrange, prepare, lay out; to resolve, direct, order, command. **II.** vr. to prepare one's self, to get ready; to make one's will.

dispongo, disponga. V. DISPONER.

disponible, a. disposable, available.

disposición, f. disposition, arrangement; disposal; aptitude, inclination, natural fitness, capacity; state of health; condition, circumstances; elegance of carriage: temper; ability, expediency; proportion, symmetry, measure; resolution, order, command: specification, requirement; provision, proviso, prescription; power, authority; (naut.) trim of a ship.—**a la d. de usted,** I am (or it is) at your disposal.

dispositivamente, adv. dispositively.

dispositivo, va, a. dispositive.

dispuesto, ta. I. a. disposed, ready; comely, genteel, graceful.—**bien d.,** quite well; favorably disposed or inclined.—**mal d.,** indisposed, ill; unfavorably disposed. **II.** pp. irr. of DISPONER.

dispuse, dispuso. V. DISPONER.

disputa, f. dispute, controversy; contest; debate. —**sin d.,** undoubtedly, indisputably.

disputable, a. disputable; contestable.

disputador, ra, n. disputant, disputer.

disputar, va. vn. to dispute, controvert, contend, debate, contest; to question; to debate, argue; to fight for.

disputativamente, adv. disputingly.

disquisición, f. disquisition.

distancia, f. distance, interval of time or place; range; difference, disparity.—**a d.,** at a distance, far.—**distanciar,** va. to place at a distance; to separate, put farther apart.

distante, a. distant, far, remote; (naut.) off.

distantemente, adv. distantly.

distar, vn. to be distant; to be different.—**d. de,** to be far from; to be (a specified distance) from.

distender, va. (for irr. v. TENDER) (med.) to distend, to swell.

distensión, f. distention, expansion.

dístico, m. (poet.) distich, couplet.

distinción, f. distinction; difference, diversity; prerogative, privilege; honorable note of superiority; order, precision.—**a d. de,** in contradistinction with, as distinguished from; unlike.

distingo, m. restriction, qualification; (log.) distinction.

distinguible, a. distinguishable.

distinguido, da, a. & pp. of DISTINGUIR; distinguished, conspicuous, prominent.

distinguir. I. va. (for mut. v. EXTINGUIR) to distinguish, discriminate; to see clearly and at a

distance; to esteem, show regard for; to clear up, explain. **II.** vr. to distinguish one's self, to excel; (w. **de**) to differ, be distinguished (from).

distintamente, adv. distinctly; differently.

distintivo, va. I. a. distinctive. **II.** m. distinctive mark; distinguishing or peculiar feature or fact.

distinto, ta, a. distinct; plain, clear; different (a very common meaning).

distocia, f. (surg.) dystocia.—**distócico, ca,** a. dystocial.

distracción, f. heedlessness, absent-mindedness; oversight; diversion, amusement, pastime; licentiousness, want of constraint.—**por d.,** for amusement, as a diversion; through an oversight.

distraer. I. va. (for irr. v. TRAER) to distract, to harass the mind; to perplex, bewilder, confuse; to divert, amuse, entertain; to lead astray. **II.** vr. to be absent-minded; to be inattentive; to amuse or enjoy one's self.

distraídamente, adv. absent-mindedly, without thinking.

distraído, da, pp. & a. inattentive, heedless; absent-minded; dissolute, licentious.

distraigo, distraiga. V. DISTRAER.

distraimiento, m. = DISTRACCIÓN.

distraje, distrajo. V. DISTRAER.

distribución, f. distribution; division, apportionment; (print.) distribution of type.

distribuidor, ra. I. n. & a. distributer (-ing). **II.** m. (hydr.) guides, guide system (of a turbine); (st. eng.) slide valve; valve gear.

distribuir, va. (for mut. v. HUIR) to distribute, divide, deal out; to sort (as mail matter); (print.) to distribute (type).

distributivo, va, a. distributive, dissuading.

distribuitor, ra; distribuyente, n. & a. distributer (-ing).

distrito, m. district, ward, precinct, region.

disturbar, va. to disturb.

disturbio, m. disturbance, outbreak.

disuadir, va. to dissuade, deter.

disuasión, f. dissuasion, determent.

disuasivo, va, a. dissuasive, dissuading.

disuelvo, disuelva. V. DISOLVER.

disuelto, ta, a. & pp. irr. of DISOLVER: dissolved.

disuria, f. (med.) dysuria.

disyunción, f. disjunction, separation; (gram.) disjunctive particle.

disyunta, f. (mus.) change of the voice.

disyuntivamente, adv. disjunctively; singly.

disyuntivo, va. I. a. disjunctive. **II.** f. disjunctive proposition; dilemma.

disyuntor, m. (elec.) circuit breaker.

dita, f. surety, bondsman; security, bond.

ditá, m. (bot.) dita, a Philippine tree that yields ditamine.

ditaína, f., ditamine, a febrifuge extracted from dita bark.

diteísmo, m. ditheism.—**diteísta,** n. & a. ditheist (-ic).

ditirámbico, ca, a. dithyrambical.

ditirambo, m. dithyramb.

dítono, m. (mus.) ditone.

diuresis, f. (med.) diuresis, excess of urine.

diurético, ca, a. & m. diuretic.

diurno, na. I. a. diurnal. **II.** m. diurnal, prayerbook.—f. pl. butterflies, Lepidoptera.—m. pl. dayflies.

diuturnidad, f. diuturnity, long duration.

diuturno, na, a. diuturnal, lasting.

diva, f. goddess; diva, great singer.

divagación, f. wandering, digression.

divagador, ra, n. & a. roamer (-ing), rambler (-ing); digressor (-ing).

divagar, vn. (for mut. v. VAGAR) to roam, to ramble; to digress.

diván, m. divan, supreme council among the Turks; place at its meetings; divan, low cushioned sofa; collection of Oriental poems.

divergencia, f. divergence, divergency.

divergente, a. divergent; dissenting.

---

divergir, *vn.* to diverge; to dissent.
diversamente, *adv.* diversely, differently.
diversidad, *f.* diversity, unlikeness; variety, abundance, plenty.
diversificar, *va.* to diversify, vary.
diversiforme, *a.* diversiform, of varied forms.
diversión, *f.* entertainment, amusement.
diversivo, va, *a.* (med.) divertive.
diverso, sa, *a.* diverse, different; various, several.
divertido, da, *a. & pp.* amusing, entertaining; humorous, funny.
divertimiento, *m.* diversion, amusement.
divertir. I. *va.* (*for irr. v.* VERTIR) to turn aside, divert; to amuse, entertain; (mil.) to divert (the enemy). **II.** *vr.* to amuse one's self, to have a good time.
dividendo, *m.* (arith., & com.) dividend.
divididero, ra, *a.* divisible.
dividir. I. *va. & vn.* to divide. **II.** *vr.* to divide; to split; to be divided; (w. **de**) to separate (from), part company (with).
dividivi, *m.* (bot.) dividivi, a tropical-American tree yielding valuable dyeing and tanning products.
dividuo, dua, *a.* (law) divisible.
divierto, divierta. *V.* DIVERTIR.
divieso, *m.* (med.) furuncle, boil.
divinal, *a.* (poet.) = DIVINO.
divinamente, *adv.* divinely; admirably.
divinatorio, ria, *a.* divinatory.
divinidad, *f.* divinity; god; woman of great beauty.—**la D.,** the Deity.
divinización, *f.* deification.
divinizar, *va.* (*for mut. v.* AMENIZAR) to deify; (met.) to sanctify.
divino, na. I. *a.* divine; excellent, admirable; most beautiful. **II.** *n.* diviner.
divirtió. *V.* DIVERTIR.
divisa, *f.* badge, emblem, impress; (law) devise.
divisar, *va.* to descry at a distance, to perceive indistinctly; (her.) to vary.
divisibilidad, *f.* divisibility.
divisible, *a.* divisible.
división, *f.* division; distribution; section, quarter, ward, compartment; disunion, discord; hyphen; (mil.) division; (math. and other sciences) division.
divisional, *a.* divisional.
divisivo, va, *a.* divisible, divisive.
diviso, sa, *a.* divided, disunited.
divisor, ra. I. *n. & a.* divider (-ing). **II.** *m.* (math.) divisor.
divisorio, ria. I. *a.* dividing. **II.** *m.* (print.) copyholder. **III.** *f.* (geol.) divide.
divo, va. I. *a.* (poet.) divine, godlike. **II.** *m.* god.
divorciar. I. *va.* to divorce; to separate, part, divide. **II.** *vr.* to be divorced.
divorcio, *m.* divorce; disunion; breach.
divulgable, *a.* that may be divulged.
divulgación, *f.* divulgation, publication.
divulgador, ra, *n. & a.* divulger (-ing).
divulgar, *va.* (*for mut. v.* COMULGAR) to publish, divulge, spread, give out, reveal; to popularize.
diz (contr. of DÍCESE), it is said.
dizque. I. = DIZ QUE. *V.* DIZ. **II.** *m.* objection, muttering; rumor.
do, *m.* (mus.) C, first note of the scale.
do, dó, *adv.* (poet.) DONDE, DÓNDE.
dobla, *f.* an ancient Spanish gold coin.
dobladamente, *adv.* doubly; deceitfully, artfully.
dobladilla, *f.* an ancient game of cards.—**a la d.,** doubly, repeatedly.
dobladillo, *m.* (sew.) hem, border; strong knitting thread.
doblado, da. I. *a.* strong, robust, thick-set; deceitful, dissembling. **II.** *pp.* of DOBLAR. **III.** *m.* measure of the fold in cloth.
doblador, ra, *n.* doubler, bender, folder.
dobladura, *f.* fold, crease.
doblamiento, *m.* doubling, bending, folding.

doblar. I. *va.* to double, make double; to fold; to crease; to bend; to subdue; to induce or influence.—**d. un cabo,** (naut.) to double or round a cape. **II.** *vn.* to toll the passing bell. **III.** *vr.* to bend; bow, stoop; submit, acquiesce, give in, yield.
doble. I. *a.* double, twofold, duplicate; thick, heavy (as cloth); thick-set, robust, strong; double-faced, deceitful; (chem.) binary.—**al d.,** doubly. **II.** *m.* fold, crease; toll of the passing bell; step in a Spanish dance.
doblegable, *a.* pliable, pliant; easily folded.
doblegadizo, za, *a.* easily bent or folded.
doblegar. I. *va.* (*for mut. v.* ENTREGAR) to fold; twist; bend; to gain by persuasion, to dissuade. **II.** *vr.* to bend; to yield, submit, acquiesce.
doblemente, *adv.* doubly; deceitfully, artfully.
doblero, *m.* (carp.) piece of timber.
doblete. I. *a.* of medium thickness. **II.** *m.* doublet (gem); a stroke in billiards.
doblez. I. *m.* crease, ply, fold; duplication. **II.** *f.* duplicity, double-dealing.
doblón, *m.* doubloon, an old Spanish gold coin.
doblonada, *f.* heap of doubloons or money.— **echar doblonadas,** (coll.) to exaggerate one's income.
doce, I. *n. & a.* twelve; twelfth. **II.** *f. pl.* **las doce,** twelve o'clock.
doceañista, *n.* maker or follower of the 1812 Spanish Constitution.
docena, *f.* dozen.—**d. de fraile,** baker's dozen.— **a docenas,** abundantly, in great quantities.
docenal, *a.* sold by dozens.
docenario, ria, *a.* containing a dozen.
docente, *a.* educational; teaching.
doceno, na. I. *a.* twelfth. **II.** *n. & a.* (cloth) of twelve hundred threads.
docientos, *a.* = DOSCIENTOS.
dócil, *a.* docile, yielding, tractable; obedient; pliable, flexible, soft.
docilidad, *f.* docility, gentleness, meekness; flexibility; manageableness; tractableness.
dócilmente, *adv.* mildly, meekly.
docimasia, docimástica, *f.* docimacy.
docimástico, ca, *a.* docimastic.
doctamente, *adv.* learnedly.
docto, ta, *a.* learned.
doctor, ra. I. *n.* doctor; teacher of any art or science; (coll.) physician. **II.** *f.* (coll.) a bluestocking; (coll.) wife of a doctor.
doctorado, *m.* doctorate, doctorship.
doctoral, *a.* doctoral.
doctoramiento, *m.* act of conferring or taking the degree of doctor.
doctorando, *m.* one about to graduate as a doctor.
doctorar, *va.* to confer the degree of doctor on.
doctorcillo, *m. dim.* (coll.) insignificant doctor; quack, petty physician.
doctrina, *f.* doctrine; preaching of the Gospel; Sunday school; catechism; (Am.) curacy.
doctrinador, ra, *n.* instructor, teacher.
doctrinal. I. *m.* catechism. **II.** *a.* doctrinal.
doctrinante, *a.* instructor.—**doctrinar,** *va.* to teach, to instruct.—**doctrinario, ria,** *a.* doctrinarian.—**doctrinario, a. I.** *a.* doctrinal; party (u. a.); relating to, or following, doctrinairism. **II.** *n.* doctrinaire.
doctrinarismo, *m.* doctrinairism.
doctrinero, *m.* teacher of Christian doctrine; (Am.) curate, parish priest.
doctrino, na, *n.* charity pupil.
documentación, *f.* documentation; documents.
documentado, da, *a.* having the necessary documents or vouchers.
documental, *a.* documentary.
documentalmente, *adv.* with proper documents.
documento, *m.* document; instruction, advice to avoid evil; (com.) collateral security.
dodecaedro, *m.* dodecahedron.
dodecágono, *m.* dodecagon.
dodecasílabo, ba, *a.* having twelve syllables.

dogal, *m.* halter, noose, slipknot; hangman's rope.
dogma, *m.* dogma.—**dogmáticamente,** *adv.* dogmatically.—**dogmático, ca. I.** *a.* dogmatical or dogmatic. **II.** *n.* dogmatist.—**dogmatismo,** *m.* dogmatism.—**dogmatista,** *n.* dogmatist.
dogmatizador, dogmatizante, *m.* dogmatizer, dogmatist.
dogmatizar, *va.* to dogmatize.
dogo, ga, *n.* bulldog.
dogre, *m.* dogger, Dutch boat.
doladera, *n.* cooper's adze.
dolador, *m.* joiner; stonecutter.
doladura, *f.* shavings, splinters, chips.
dolaje, *m.* wine imbibed by pipestaves.
dolamas, *f. pl.,* **dolames,** *m. pl.,* (vet.) hidden vices and defects (of horses).
dolar, *va.* to hew (wood or stone).
dólar, *m.* dollar (U. S. money).
dolencia, *f.* aching, ache; disease, ailment.
doler. I. *vn.* (*ind.* DUELO: *subj.* DUELA) to pain, ache; to hurt; to cause regret or grief. **II.** *vr.* (gen. w. **de**) to repent; to regret; to be moved (by), take pity (on), condole (with), feel or express sympathy (for), to complain (of).
dolicocéfalo, la, *a.* dolichocephalous, dolichocephalic.
doliente. I. *a.* aching, suffering; sorrowful; sick. **II.** *m.* mourner; patient (sick person).
dolmen, *m.* (archæol.) dolmen.
dolo, *m.* fraud, deceit, guile.
dolobre, *m.* stone hammer.
dolomía, *f.* (min.) dolomite.
dolomítico, ca, *a.* dolomitic.
dolor, *m.* pain, aching, ache; sorrow, affliction, grief; regret, repentance, contrition.—*pl.* throes of childbirth.—**d. de corazón,** heartache; repentance.—**d. de costado,** pneumonia.—**d. latente,** dull pain, constant but not severe pain.—**dolores del parto,** labor pains.—**estar con dolores,** to be in labor.
dolora, *f.* a short sentimental and philosophic poem.
dolorcillo, ito, *m. dim.* slight pain.
dolorido, da. I. *a.* doleful, afflicted; painful, aching; sore, tender; heartsick. **II.** *m.* chief mourner.
dolorosamente, *adv.* painfully; sorrowfully, regrettably, lamentably, pitifully.
Dolorosa, *f.* (art.) Mater Dolorosa, Sorrowing Mary.
doloroso, sa, *a.* painful; regrettable; pitiful.
dolosamente, *adv.* deceitfully.
doloso, sa, *a.* deceitful; fraudulent.
doma, *f.* breaking of a horse.
domable, *a.* tamable; conquerable.
domador, ra, *n.* tamer; horsebreaker.
domadura, *f.* act of taming or subduing.
domar, *va.* to tame; to break in; to subdue, overcome, master, conquer.
dombo, *m.* dome, cupola.
domeñar, *va.* to reclaim, to make tractable; to tame, domesticate; to master, subdue.
domesticable, *a.* tamable, capable of domestication.
domesticación, *f.* domestication.
domésticamente, *adv.* domestically.
domesticar. I. *va.* (for *mut. v.* DEDICAR) to domesticate. **II.** *vr.* to become tame.
domesticidad, *f.* domesticity; domestication.
doméstico, ca. I. *a.* domestic; domesticated, tamed. **II.** *n.* family servant.
domestiquez, *f.* tameness.
domiciliado, da, *a. & pp.* of DOMICILIARSE; domiciled, residing.
domiciliar, *va. & vr.* to domicile, domiciliate.
domiciliario, ria, *a.* domiciliary.
domicilio, *m.* domicile; home, dwelling house.
dominación, *f.* dominion, domination, authority, rule, command, power; (mil.) commanding ground.—*pl.* dominations, angelic beings.
dominador, ra. I. *a.* dominating, controlling; overbearing. **II.** *n.* dominator.

dominante, *a.* domineering, dictatorial, overbearing; prevailing; excelling; commanding, towering; (mus.) dominant.
dominar. I. *va.* to dominate, govern, rule; to control; to master (a subject, language, etc.); to subdue, repress. **II.** *vr.* to control one's self.
dominativo, va, *a.* == DOMINANTE.
dómine, *m.* dominie, teacher; puffed-up fool, pompous, empty-headed fellow.
domingada, *f.* Sunday festival or function.
domingo, *m.* Sunday.—**D. de Cuasimodo,** Low Sunday.—**D. de Ramos,** Palm Sunday.—**D. de Resurrección,** Easter Sunday.
dominguero, ra, *a.* done on Sunday; Sunday (u. a.), for, or relating to, Sunday.
dominguillo, *m.* tumbler (a toy).
dominica, *f.* the Sabbath.
dominical. I. *a.* dominical, Sunday (u. a.) **II.** *f.* Sunday function in universities.
dominicano, na; dominico, ca, *n. & a.* Dominican.
dominico, *m.* Jacobin friar.
dominicatura, *f.* duty of vassalage.
dominio, *m.* dominion; domination, rule, authority; domain; (law) fee.—**d. absoluto,** (law) fee simple absolute.—**d. directo,** (law) dominium directum.—**d. eminente,** (law) eminent domain.—**d. público,** public or general knowledge; (law) public domain, government or state property.—**d. útil,** (law) dominium utile.
dómino, *m.* game of dominoes.
dominó, *m.* domino, a hooded robe; game of dominoes.
dompedro, *m.* (bot.) morning-glory.
don, *m.* Don, title for a gentleman, equivalent to Mr. or Esq. in English, but used only before Christian names, as *Don Juan, Don Alfonso;* gift, present, donation; ability, natural gift, faculty, knack.—**d. de acierto,** tact.—**d. de errar,** (coll.) knack for doing things wrong.—**d. de gentes,** winning manners.
dona, *f.* woman, dame; (Ch.) legacy.—*pl.* wedding presents given by the bridegroom to the bride.
donación, *f.* donation, gift, grant.—**d. piadosa,** donary, pious donation.
donadío, *m.* property derived from royal grants.
donado, da. *n.* lay brother (sister).
donador, ra, *n.* donor, bestower, giver.
donaire, *m.* gracefulness, gentility; witticism.
donairosamente, *adv.* gracefully.
donairoso, sa, *a.* graceful, elegant; witty.
donante, *n. & a.* giver (-ing).
donar, *va.* to give, bestow, contribute.
donatario, ria, *n.* donee, grantee.
donatista, *n. & a.* Donatist.
donativo, *m.* donative, donation, gift.
doncel. I. *m.* king's page; virgin man. **II.** *a.* mild, mellow in flavor (as wine).
doncella, *f.* maid, servant; virgin; maiden, lass; lady's maid, waiting maid; (icht.) snakefish.
doncelleja, *f. dim.* little maid.
doncellez, *f.* maidenhood.
doncellica, ita, *f. dim.* young maid, girl.
doncellueca, *f.* (coll.) old maid.
doncelluela, *f. dim.* young maid.
donde (*interr.* **dónde**) *adv.* where; wherein; in which; wherever; (Am.) to, or at, the house, shop, etc. of [*voy donde Juan,* I am going to John's (house); *esto se vende donde Macy,* this is sold at Macy's].—**d. no,** otherwise.—**a d.,** where, whereto.—**¿por dónde?** whereabouts? by what way or road? by what reason or cause?
dondequiera, *adv.* anywhere; wherever.—**por d.,** everywhere, in every place.
dondiego, dondiego de día, (bot.) morning-glory.—**dondiego de noche,** *m.* (bot.) jalap, marvel of Peru.
dongón, *m.* (Philip.) a tree of very hard wood used in shipbuilding.
donillero, *m.* roper-in, decoy.
donjuán, *m.* (bot.) = DONDIEGO.
donosamente, *adv.* gracefully, pleasingly.

---

donosidad, *f.* gracefulness; wittiness.
donoso, sa, *a.* gay, witty; graceful.
donosura, *f.* gracefulness, elegance; wittiness.
doña, *f.* title given to a lady, equivalent to the English Mrs. or Miss, but used only before Christian names, as *Doña Isabel;* formerly, a duenna or a nun.—*pl.* present made every year to the miners in the iron mines in Spain.
doñear, *vn.* (coll.) to converse much with women.
doñegal, doñigal, *a.* a variety of fig.
doquier, doquiera, *adv.* = DONDEQUIERA.
dorada, doradilla, *f.* (icht.) gilthead, giltpoll.
doradilla, *f.* (bot.) common ceterach.
doradillo, *m.* fine brass wire; (orn.) wagtail; satinwood.
dorado, da. I. *pp.* & *a.* gilt, gilded. **II.** *m.* (act or operation of) gilding.
dorador, ra, *n.* gilder.—**doradura,** *f.* gilding.
doral, *m.* (orn.) flycatcher.
dorar, *va.* to gild; to palliate, excuse; (poet.) to illume (as sunshine).
dórico, ca, *a.* Doric.
dorio, ria, *n.* & *a.* Dorian.
dormán, *m.* dolman, huzzar's jacket.
dormida, *f.* sleep of the silkworm; place where animals repose; (Am.) alcove; bed.
dormidera, *f.* (bot.) garden poppy.—*pl.* (coll.) readiness to sleep.
dormidero, ra. I. *a.* soporiferous, narcotic. **II.** *m.* place where cattle repose.
dormiente, = DURMIENTE.
dormilón, na. I. *n.* (coll.) sleepy head. **II.** *f. pl.* screw earrings.
dormir. I. *vn.* (ind. DUERMO: *pret.* el DURMIÓ: *subj.* DUERMA) to sleep; (naut.) to be calm or still.—**d. a pierna suelta,** (coll.) to be fast asleep; to sleep soundly and peacefully. **II.** *vr.* to go to sleep, fall asleep.
dormirlas, *m.* hide and seek.
dormitar, *vn.* to dose, nap.
dormitivo, *m.* dormitive.
dormitorio, *m.* dormitory; bedroom.
dornajo, *m.* small trough; tray; pan.
dornillo, *m.* small trough, wooden bowl.
dorsal, *a.* dorsal, belonging to the back.
dorso, *m.* spine, back; dorsum.
dos. I. *n.* & *a.* two; second (of the month); deuce.—**d. a d.,** two to two, or two by two.—**a d. por tres,** suddenly.— **de d. en d.,** two abreast; by twos, in pairs.—**en un d. por tres,** in a twinkling.—**las d.,** two o'clock.—**para entre los d.,** between you and me.
desalbo, ba, *a.* having two white stockings (s. o. horses).
dosañal, *a.* biennial, of two years.
doscientos, tas, *n.* & *a.* two hundred; two-hundredth.
dosel, *m.* canopy, dais; portière.
doselera, *f.* valance, drapery of a canopy.
dosificación, *f.* proportioning; determination of the quantity of a substance; (med.) dosage.
dosificar, *va.* to measure out the doses of (a medicine); to proportion (ingredients, etc.); to determine the quantity of; to analyse.
dosimetría, *f.* (med.) dosimetric system.
dosimétrico, ca, *a.* dosimetric.
dosis, *f.* dose (of medicine); quantity.
dotación, *f.* dotation, endowment, foundation; settlement, dowry; equipment; (naut.) complement of a crew; (mil.) munition and garrison of a fortress; (Cuba) workmen on a plantation.
dotado, da, *a.* & *pp.* of DOTAR; dowered, portioned.—**d. de,** endowed with, gifted with.
dotador, ra, *n.* endower, donor.
dotal, *a.* dotal, relating to a dowry.
dotar, *va.* to portion; to endow; to give a dowry to; to gift, to endow with powers or talents.
dote, *m.* & *f.* dowery, dowry; stock of counters to play with.—*f. pl.* gifts, talents received from nature; endowments.
dovela, *f.* (arch.) voussoir, stone of an arch.
dovelaje, *m.* voussoirs of an arch.

dovelar, *va.* to hew (a stone) for an arch.
doy. *V.* DAR.
dozayado, da, *a.* twelve-sided.
dozavo, va, *n.* & *a.* twelfth.
dracma, *f.* (pharm.) drachm; Greek silver coin.
draconiano, na, *a.* Draconian.
draga, *f.* dredge.—**dragado,** *m.* dredging.
dragaminas, *m.* mine sweeper.
dragar, *va.* (*for mut. v.* TRAGAR) to dredge.
dragante, *m.* (naut.) bowsprit pillow.
drago, *m.* (bot.) dragon tree.
dragomán, *m.* = TRUJAMÁN.
dragón, *m.* dragon; (zool.) dragon; (bot.) dragon; (metal.) feeding opening of a furnace; (mil.) dragoon, a soldier; (vet.) white spots in the pupils of horses' eyes; a kind of exhalation or vapor; (D-, ast.) Dragon, Draco.
dragona, *f.* (mil.) shoulder knot; female dragon.
dragoncillo, *m.* drake, ancient gun; little dragon or dragoon.
dragonear, *vn.* (w. de) to pass one's self for, to pretend to be, play the.
dragontea, dragontía, *f.* (bot.) common dragon.
dragontino, na, *a.* dragonish.
drama, *m.* drama.—**dramática,** *f.* dramatic art.
dramáticamente, *adv.* dramatically.
dramático, ca, *a.* dramatic.
dramatismo, *m.* quality of being dramatic.
dramatizable, *a.* dramatizable.
dramatizar, *va.* & *vn.* to dramatize.
dramaturgia, *f.* dramatic art.
dramaturgo, ga, *n.* playwright.
drástico, ca, *a.* (med.) drastic.
drecera, *f.* straight row of houses, trees, etc.
drenaje, *m.* drainage.
dríada, dríade, *f.* dryad.
dril, *m.* drilling, strong cloth, drill.
drino, *m.* a kind of poisonous serpent.
driza, *f.* (naut.) halyard.
drizar, *va.* (naut.) to hoist up (the yards).
droga, *f.* drug; medicine; fib; stratagem, artifice, deceit; nuisance.
drogmán, *m.* = DRAGOMÁN.
droguería, *f.* drug store; drug trade.
droguero, ra, *n.* druggist.
droguete, *m.* drugget.
droguista, *n.* druggist; cheat, humbug, impostor.
dromedario, *m.* dromedary; unwieldy animal.
drope, *m.* (coll.) vile, despicable man.
druida, *m.* Druid.—**druídico, ca,** *a.* Druidic.
druidismo, *m.* druidism.
drupa, *f.* (bot.) drupe, stone fruit.
drusa, *f.* (min.) geode, vug.
dúa, *f.* (min.) gang of workmen.
dual. I. *a.* (gram.) dual. **II.** *m.* incisor.
dualidad, *f.* duality.—**dualismo,** *m.* (philos.) dualism.—**dualista,** *n.* & *a.* dualist (-ic).
dubio, *m.* (law) doubt.
dubitable, *a.* doubtful, dubious.
dubitación, *f.* dubitation, doubt.
dubitativo, va, *a.* (gram.) doubtful, dubious.
ducado, *m.* duchy, dukedom; ducat.
ducal, *a.* ducal.
ducentésimo, ma, *a.* two-hundredth.
dúctil, *a.* ductile; yielding.
ductilidad, *f.* ductility.
ductivo, va, *a.* conducive.
ductor, *m.* guide, conductor; (surg.) probe.
ductriz, *f.* conductress.
ducha, *f.* douche, shower bath; stripe (in cloth); straight piece of land reaped.
ducho, cha, skilful, expert.
duda, *f.* doubt.—**sin d.,** or **sin d. alguna,** no doubt, doubtless.
dudable, *a.* dubious, doubtful.
dudar, *vn.* & *va.* to doubt.—**d. de,** to doubt; to distrust.
dudosamente, *adv.* doubtfully, dubiously.
dudoso, sa, *a.* doubtful, dubious; hazardous.
duela, *f.* (coop.) stave.
duelaje, *m.* = DOLAJE.

duelista, *m.* duellist.

duelo, *m.* sorrow, grief, affliction; mourning; mourners; condolement; bereavement; duel.— **duelos y quebrantos,** giblets and haslets, formerly eaten on Saturday.—**sin d.,** abundantly.

duelo, duela. *V.* DOLER.

duende, *m.* elf, hobgoblin, ghost.

duendecillo, *m. dim.* little elf.

duendo, da, *a.* tame (as doves).

dueña, *f.* owner, proprietress, mistress, landlady; duenna; married lady.

dueñesco, ca, *a.* duennalike.

dueño, ña, owner, proprietor, landlord (-lady); master (to a servant).—**d. de sí mismo,** self-controlled.—**hacerse dueño de,** to appropriate to one's self, take possession of; to become familiar with, to master (a subject, a theory, etc.).—**ser d. de,** to own, be master of; to be at liberty to(do, etc.)

duermo, yo duerma. *V.* DORMIR.

duermevela, *m.* (coll.) dozing, light sleep.

duerna, *f.*, **duerno,** *m.* = ARTESA.

düerno, *m.* (print.) double sheet.

düeto, *m.* duet.

dugongo, *m.* (zool.) dugong.

dula, *f.* common pasture ground.

dulcamara, *f.* (bot.) bittersweet; (pharm.) dulcamara; nightshade.

dulce. I. *a.* sweet; fresh (as water); comfortable, pleasing, pleasant, agreeable; soft, ductile (as metals). **II.** *m.* comfiture, sweetmeat, confection, bonbon.—**d. de almíbar,** preserves.

dulcecillo, illa, ito, ita. I. *a. dim.* sweetish, somewhat sweet. **II.** *m.* bonbon, candy.

dulcedumbre, *f.* sweetness.

dulcémele, *m.* (mus.) dulcimer.

dulcemente, *adv.* sweetly.

dulcera, *f.* preserve dish, compotier.

dulcería, *f.* confectionery shop.

dulcero, ra. I. *a.* fond of sweets. **II.** *n.* confectioner.

dulcificación, *f.* dulcification.

dulcificante, *a.* dulcifying; sweetening.

dulcificar, *va.* to sweeten, dulcify.

Dulcinea, *f.* (coll.) Dulcinea, sweetheart, beloved one.

dulcísono, na, *a.* sweet-toned.

dulía, *f.* dulia, saint worship.

dulimán, *m.* long Turkish robe.

dulzaina, *f.* (mus.) flageolet; (coll.) quantity of sweetmeats.

dulzainero, *m.* flageolet player.

dulzaino, na, *a.* (coll.) too sweet or rich.

dulzamara, *f.* (bot.) = DULCAMARA.

dulzarrón, na, *a.* (coll.) sickening, too sweet.

dulzura, *f.* sweetness; meekness; gentleness; comfort, pleasure; forbearance; pleasing manner, kindliness.

dulzurar, *va.* (chem.) to dulcify, unsalt.

duma, *f.* duma, douma.

duna, *f.* (geol.) dune.

dúo, *m.* (mus.) duo, duet.

duodecimal, *a.* (arith.) duodecimal.

duodécimo, ma, *a.* twelfth.

duodécuplo, pla, *a.* duodecuple.

duodenal, *a.* duodenal.

duodenario, ria, *a.* lasting twelve days.

duodenitis, *f.* (med.) duodenitis.

duodeno, na. I. *a.* twelfth. **II.** *m.* (anat.) duodenum.

duomesino, na, *a.* of two months.

dupla, *f.* in colleges, extra dish.

duplex, dúplex, *a.* (tel.) dúplex.

dúplica, *f.* (law) answer.

duplicación, *f.* duplication, doubling.

duplicadamente, *adv.* doubly.

duplicado. I. *m.* duplicate; counterpart.—**por d.,** in duplicate. **II.** *a.* & *pp.* of DUPLICAR; duplicate, doubled.

duplicador, *m.* duplicator.

duplicar, *va.* (*for mut. v.* APLICAR) to double, duplicate; to repeat.

duplicatura, *f.* = DOBLADURA.

dúplice, *a.* double.

duplicidad, *f.* duplicity, deceit, foul dealing.

duplo, *m.* double, twice as much; duple.

duque, *m.* duke; fold in mantillas.

duquecito, *m. dim.* young or little duke.

duquesa, *f.* duchess.

dura, *f.* (coll.) duration, continuance.

durabilidad, *f.* durability, permanence.

durable, *a.* durable, lasting.

duración, *f.* duration; life.

duraderamente, *adv.* durably, lastingly.

duradero, ra, *a.* lasting, durable.

duramadre, duramáter, *f.* (anat.) dura mater.

duramen, *m.* (bot.) duramen.

duramente, *adv.* rigorously, harshly.

durante, *prep.* during.

durar, *vn.* to last; to endure; to wear (s. o. clothes).

duraznero, *m.* (bot.) peach tree.

duraznilla, *f.* a variety of peach.

durazno, *m.* (bot.) peach; peach tree.

dureza, *f.* hardness, solidity, firmness; sharpness of temper, obduracy; harshness, hardness of heart, cruelty; steadiness, perseverance; obstinacy; (art.) crudeness; (med.) tumor or callosity.—**d. de vientre,** costiveness.

durillo, lla. I. *a. dim.* rather hard. **II.** *m.* (bot.) common laurestine; (vet.) callosity.

durmiente. I. *a.* sleeping, dormant. **II.** *m.* (arch.) dormant or dormer; girder, stringer; (r. w.) crosstie, sleeper; (naut.) clamp, shelf.

duro, ra. I. *a.* hard; solid, firm; vexatious, unbearable; unjust, unkind; oppressive, rigorous, cruel; stubborn, obstinate; avaricious, stingy; rude, harsh, rough; (naut.) carrying a stiff sail; (art) harsh, crude; (mus.) harsh, inharmonious.— **a duras penas,** with difficulty; hardly, scarcely. **II.** *m.* dollar, peso; (Am.) low, rough saddle. **III.** *adv.* hard, forcibly, violently.

duunvir, *m.* duumvir.—**duunviral,** *a.* duumviral.—**duunvirato,** *m.* duumvirate.

duunviro, *m.* duumvir.

dux, *m.* doge.

E

e, *conj.* and (used only before words that begin with *i* or *hi* not followed by *e*).

¡ea! *interj.* (used to attract attention or as an encouragement.)

ebanista, *m.* cabinetmaker.

ebanistería, *f.* cabinetwork or cabinetmaking; cabinetmaker's shop.

ébano, *m.* (bot.) ebony.

ebenáceo, a. I. *a.* (bot.) ebenaceous. **II.** *f. pl.* Ebanaceæ.

ebionita, *n.* & *a.* Ebionite.

ebonita, *f.* ebonite, hard rubber.

ebriedad, *f.* ebriety.

ebrio, bria; ebrioso, sa, *a.* intoxicated, drunk.

ebulición, ebullición, *f.* ebullition; boiling.

ebúrneo, a, *a.* eburneous, ivorylike.

ecarté, *m.* game of cards.

Eccehomo, *m.* Ecce Homo; wretched, pity-inspiring person.

eclampsia, *f.* (med.) eclampsia.

eclecticismo, *m.* eclecticism.

ecléctico, ca, *n.* & *a.* eclectic.

Eclesiastés, *m.* Ecclesiastes (one of the books of the Old Testament).

eclesiásticamente, *adv.* ecclesiastically.

eclesiástico, ca. I. *a.* ecclesiastical. **II.** *m.* clergyman, ecclesiastic, priest, minister; Ecclesiasticus.

eclesiastizar, *va.* = ESPIRITUALIZAR.

eclímetro, *m.* clinometer.

eclipsable, *a.* that may be eclipsed.

eclipsar. I. *va.* (ast.) to eclipse; to outshine. **II.** *vr.* (ast.) to be eclipsed.

eclipse, *m.* (ast.) eclipse.

eclipsis, *f.* (gram.) ellipsis.

eclíptica, *f.* ecliptic.

eclisa, *f.* (r. w.) fishplate, shin.

écloga, *f.* eclogue.

eco, *m.* echo; distant sound (as of a drum); repetition of words.—**hacer e.,** to fit, correspond; to become important or famous; to create an impression; to be noised about.

ecoico, ca, *a.* echoic.

ecometría, *f.* (arch.) echometry.

ecómetro, *m.* echometer.

economato, *m.* guardianship, trusteeship.

economía, *f.* economy.—**e. animal,** animal economy.—**e. política,** political economy, economics.

económicamente, *adv.* economically.

económico, ca, *a.* economical, economic; saving, thrifty; frugal; miserly, niggardly.

economista, *m.* economist.

economizar, *va.* to economize; to save.

ecónomo, *m.* curator or guardian; trustee; ecclesiastical administrator.

ecrena, *f.* (med.) vesicular eczema.

éctasis, *f.* (gram.) ectasis.

ectoblasto, ectodermo, *m.* (biol.) ectoblast, ectoderm.

ectopia, *f.* (med.) ectopia.

ectropión, *m.* (med.) ectropion.

ecuable, *a.* equitable; uniform (motion).

ecuación, *f.* equation.—**e. de tiempo,** (ast.) equation of time.

ecuador, *m.* equator.

ecuanimidad, *f.* equanimity.

ecuatorial. I. *a.* equatorial. **II.** *f.* equatorial telescope.

ecuatoriano, na, *n.* & *a.* Ecuadorian.

ecuestre, *a.* equestrian.

ecuménico, ca, *a.* œcumenical.

ecuóreo, rea, *a.* (poet.) belonging to the sea.

echacantos, *m.* (coll.) rattle-brained fellow.

echacorvear, *vn.* (coll.) to pimp; to procure.

echacorvería, *f.* (coll.) profession of a pimp or procurer.

echacuervos, *m.* (coll.) pimp; procurer; cheat, impostor; a nickname given to some preachers.

echada, *f.* cast, throw; (sport) man's length.

echadero, *m.* place of rest or repose.

echadillo, *m.* foundling.

echadizo, za, *a.* spying; artfully spread (s. o. propaganda); foundling; rejected, discarded.

echador, ra, *n.* thrower.

echadura, *f.* brooding, hatching; winnowing.

echamiento, *m.* cast, throw; casting or throwing; rejection; ejection, expulsion.

echapellas, *m.* wool soaker.

echar. I. *va.* to cast, throw, fling, hurl, pitch, toss, dart; to turn or drive away, eject, throw out, expel; to discharge, dismiss, (coll.) fire; to emit, give out (as sparks); to pour (as wine); to put (in, into); to jet (as cargo); to put on (as a cloak); to turn (as a key); to begin to have or grow (as teeth, hair, etc.); to put forth, produce, bear (shoots, fruit); to put on, to apply; to lay on or impose (as a tax); to play (as a game); to lean toward; to move, push; to set (aside); to tell (a fortune); to couple, mate (male and female animals for procreating); to impute, to ascribe; to perform for a wager; to deal out, to distribute; to publish, give out, issue; (with the words **rayos, centellas, chispas, fuego,** etc.) to show much annoyance, to be very angry; (with the name of a punishment) to condemn to.—**e. abajo,** to overthrow, throw down; to tear down, demolish.—**e. a fondo,** or **a pique,** (naut.) to sink; to ruin, spoil, wreck.—**e. a la cara** = E. EN CARA.—**e. al mundo,** to create; to bring forth.—**e. a pasear,** or **a paseo,** = E. CON CAJAS DESTEMPLADAS.—**e. a perder,** to spoil, ruin.— **e. baladronadas,** to boast, brag.—**e. bando,** to publish something through a crier; (coll.) to sermonize, lecture.—**e. boca,** to sharpen; to even the tip of.—**e. bravatas** = E. BALADRONADAS.—**e. carnes,** to put on flesh, gain weight.—**e. carrillos,** to grow plump in the cheeks.—**e. chufas,** to act the bully.—**e. con cajas destempladas,** or **enhoramala,** to dismiss contemptuously; to turn away in a harsh manner.—**e. coche,** to set up a coach.—**e.**

de menos, to miss.—**e. de ver,** to notice, to observe.—**e. el bofe,** to work very hard; to solicit anxiously.—**e. el cuerpo fuera,** to withdraw from an affair.—**e. el escandallo,** (naut.) to take soundings.—**e. el guante,** to arrest.—**e. en cara,** or **en la cara,** to throw in one's face.—**e. en tierra** = E. ABAJO.—**e. la carga a otro,** to throw the blame upon another; to pass the buck.—**e. la corredera,** (naut.) to heave the log.—**e. los bofes** = E. EL BOFE.—**e. los hígados,** to be exhausted or dead tired.—**e. los hígados por,** (coll.) to desire anxiously, to itch for (or to).—**e. plantas** = E. BALADRONADAS.—**e. por el suelo,** or **por tierra** = E. ABAJO.—**e. por en medio, e. por la calle de en medio,** to rush recklessly; to take a final resolution. —**e. raíces,** to take root.—**e. suertes,** to draw lots.—**e. tierra a,** to bury (fig.); to hush up.—**e. todo a rodar,** to spoil everything, to make a fizzle. —**e. un remiendo** (a), to put a patch (on).—**e. un remiendo a la vida,** (coll.) to take a little refreshment.—**echarla de,** to pretend or claim to be, to boast of being, to pass one's self off as. **II.** *vn.*— **e. a** (followed by infinitive), to begin to, to start (followed by participle: *echar a correr,* to start running).—**e. de baranda,** to exaggerate, boast.—**e. en tierra,** (naut.) to land, to disembark.—**e. por,** to go by, take to, take the way of. **III.** *vr.* to lie down; to stretch one's self at full length; to throw one's self down; to apply one's self; to sit (s. o. a hen or any other bird).—**e. a morir,** to give up in despair; to worry one's self to death.—**e. a perder,** to spoil; to become stale; to become ruined or destroyed; to go down (in prestige, virtue, etc.)—**e. en brazos de,** to throw one's self in the arms of; to trust in; to resort to.

echazón, *f.* (law) jetson or jettison.

edad, *f.* age; epoch, era, time.—**e. crítica,** critical age, change of life (in women).—**e. madura,** mature age, maturity.—**e. media,** Middle Ages.— **e. provecta** = E. MADURA.—**de e.,** advanced in years, of mature age.

edecán, *m.* (mil.) aide-de-camp.

edema, *f.* œdema.

edematoso, sa, *a.* œdematous, edematose.

Edén, *m.* Eden, paradise.

edición, *f.* edition, issue; publication.—**e. príncipe,** first edition.

edicto, *m.* edict, proclamation, placard.

edificación, *f.* construction, building; edification.

edificador, n. & *a.* edifier (-ying); constructor (-ing), builder (-ing).

edificante, *a.* edifying; erecting.

edificar, *va.* & *vn.* (*for mut. v.* APLICAR) to edify; to build, construct, erect.

edificativo, va, *a.* edifying.—**edificatorio, ria,** *a.* relating to building or making.

edificio, *m.* edifice, building, structure.

edil, *m.* edile, a Roman magistrate.

edilidad, *f.* edileship.

editar, *va.* to publish.

editor, ra, *n.* & *a.* publisher (-ing).

editorial. I. *n.* & *a.* editorial. **II.** *a.* publishing.

edredón, *m.* eider down; feather pillow.

educable, *a.* educable.

educación, *f.* education; good breeding, politeness.—**e. física,** physical culture.

educador, ra, *m.* & *a.* educator (-ing).

educando, da, *n.* pupil, student.

educar, *va.* (*pret.* EDUQUÉ: *subj.* EDUQUE) to educate, instruct, raise, train.

educativo, va, *a.* educational.

educción, *f.* deduction; eduction; (st. eng.) exhaust.

educir, *va.* to educe, extract, bring out.

edulcoración, *f.* edulcoration.

edulcorar, *va.* (chem.) to sweeten.

efe, *f.* Spanish name of the letter *f.*

efectismo, *m.* (art) striving after effect.

efectista, *a.* (art) sensational.

efectivamente, *adv.* effectually; really, actually.

efectivo, va. I. *a.* effective; real, actual.—**hacer e.,** to cash (a check, etc.). **II.** *m.* (com.) cash, specie.—**e. en caja,** cash on hand.—**en e.,** in cash, in coin.

efecto, *m.* effect; end, purpose, meaning; general intent; (in billiards) English.—*pl.* assets; merchandise, chattels, goods, movables; (com.) drafts.—**efectos a pagar,** bills payable.—**efectos a recibir,** bills receivable.—**efectos en cartera,** securities in hand.—**efectos públicos,** public securities.—**con,** or **en, e.,** in fact, actually; (math., log.) for (in introducing the proof of a proposition).

efectuación, *f.* accomplishment.

efectuar, *va.* to effect, carry out, do, make.

efemérides, *f. pl.* ephemeris.

efémera, *a.*—**fiebre e.,** (med.) ephemera, a fever lasting one day.

efémero, *m.* (bot.) iris.

efendi, *m.* effendi (Turkish title).

eferente, *a.* efferent.

efervescencia, *f.* effervescence; ardor, fervor.

efesio, sia, *n. & a.* Ephesian.

eficacia, *f.* efficacy, efficiency.

eficaz, *a.* efficacious, effective.

eficazmente, *adv.* efficaciously, effectively.

eficiencia, *f.* efficiency, effectiveness.

eficiente, *a.* efficient, effective.

eficientemente, *adv.* efficiently.

efigie, *f.* effigy, image.

efímera, *f.* (med.) ephemera; (ent.) dayfly or May fly.

efímero, ra, *a.* ephemeral.

eflorescerse, *vr.* to effloresce.—**eflorescencia,** *f.* efflorescence.—**eflorescente,** *a.* efflorescent.

efluvio, *m.* effluvium or effluvia; exhalation, emanation.

efod, *m.* ephod (a Jewish garment).

éforo, *m.* ephor (a Greek magistrate).

efugio, *m.* subterfuge, evasion, shift.

efundir, *va.* to effuse, pour out, spill.

efusión, *f.* effusion, shedding, efflux; confidential disclosure of sentiments.—**e. de sangre,** bloodshed.

efuso, sa, *a.* effused.

égida, egis; protection, defence.

egílope, *f.* (bot.) wild bastard oat.

egipcíaco, ca; egipciano, na; egipcio, cia; egiptano, na, *n. & a.* Egyptian.

egiptología, *f.* Egyptology.

egiptólogo, *m.* Egyptologist.

égira, *f.* hegira.

égloga, *f.* eclogue, pastoral poem.

egoísmo, *m.* selfishness, self-love, egoism.

egoísta. I. *a.* selfish, egoistic. **II.** *m.* egoist.

egotismo, *m.* egotism.—**egotista,** *n. & a.* egotist (-ic).

egregiamente, *adv.* egregiously.

egregio, gia, *a.* egregious, eminent.

egrena, *f.* iron clamp.

egreso, *m.* expense, debit.—*pl.* discharge.

egrisador, *m.* box for diamond dust.

egrisar, *va.* to polish (diamonds).

¡eh! *interj.* eh! here!

eje, *m.* axis; axletree, axle; shaft, spindle, arbor.—**e. auxiliar,** countershaft.—**e. conjugado,** minor axis (of an ellipse).—**e. coordenado,** coördinate axis.—**e. de (las) abscisas,** axis of abscissæ.—**e. de (las) coordenadas** = E. COORDENADO.—**e. delantero,** front axle (of a vehicle).—**e. de las x, de las y,** *x*-axis, *y*-axis.—**e. de ordenadas,** axis of ordinates.—**e. secundario,** countershaft.—**e. trasero,** rear axle (of a vehicle).

ejecución, *f.* execution, performance; execution, capital punishment; (law) attachment; (mus.) technique.

ejecutable, *a.* feasible, practicable.

ejecutante, *n.* performer; (law) one who compels another to pay a debt by legal execution.

ejecutar, *va.* to execute, perform, make, do, carry out; to execute (a criminal); to impel, urge, importune, incite; (law) to attach the property of.

ejecutivamente, *adv.* executively; promptly.

ejecutivo, va. I. *a.* executive; active; executory. **II.** *m.* executive.

ejecutor, ra, *n.* executor; executer; (law) officer who attaches property.—**e. de la justicia,** executioner.

ejecutoria, *f.* sentence, judgment; letters patent of nobility, pedigree; executorship.

ejecutoria, *f.* office of an attacher or other executive officer.

ejecutorial, *a.* (law) applied to the execution of the sentence of an ecclesiastical tribunal.

ejecutoriar, *va.* to obtain (a judgment) in one's favor; to establish the truth of.

ejecutorio, ria, *a.* (law) executory.

ejemplar. I. *a.* exemplary. **II.** *m.* pattern, model; precedent, example; specimen, sample; copy of a work; example, warning.—**sin e.,** without precedent; exceptional and not a precedent.

ejemplarmente, *adv.* exemplarily; edifyingly.

ejemplificación, *f.* exemplification, illustration.

ejemplificar, *va.* to exemplify, to illustrate.

ejemplo, *m.* example, instance; pattern, copy; exemplar.—**dar e.,** to set an example.—**sin e.,** without precedent or parallel, unheard-of.

ejercer, *va.* (ind. EJERZO: subj. EJERZA) to exercise, practise; perform, ply; to exert.

ejercicio, *m.* exercise, exertion; employment, office, task; ministry; practice; fiscal year; military drill.—**e. espiritual,** spiritual retreat.—**hacer e.,** to exercise; (mil.) to drill.

ejercitación, *f.* exercise, practice.

ejercitante. I. *n.* one who is in a spiritual retreat; exerciser. **II.** *m.* exercising, training.

ejercitar. I. *va.* to exercise, to put into practice; to drill (troops); to train. **II.** *vr.* to practise.

ejercitativo, va, *a.* that may be exercised.

ejército, *m.* army.

ejido, *m.* common, public land.

ejión, *m.* (arch.) corbel piece, purlin, bracket.

ejotes, *m. pl.* (Mex.) string beans.

el, *art. masc. sing. (pl.* **los)** the.

él, *pron. masc. sing. (pl.* **ellos)** he.

elaboración, *f.* elaboration.

elaborado, da. I. *a.* elaborate; manufactured, wrought. **II.** *pp.* of ELABORAR.

elaborador, ra, *n. & a.* elaborator (-ing); manufacturer (-ing).

elaborar, *va.* to elaborate; to manufacture.

elación, *f.* elation, haughtiness, pride; magnanimity, generosity; inflation of style.

elamita, *n. & a.* Elamite (-ic).

elasticidad, *f.* elasticity.

elástico, ca. I. *a.* elastic. **II.** *f.* undershirt. **III.** *m.* an elastic (webbing); wire spring.—*m pl.* suspenders.

elaterina, *f.* (chem.) elaterin.

elaterio, *m.* (bot.) elaterium.

elche, *m.* apostate, renegade.

ele, *f.* Spanish name of the letter *l.*

eleagnáceo, a. I. *a.* (bot.) elæagnaceous. **II.** *f. pl.* Elæagnaceæ.

eleático, ca, *n. & a.* (philos.) Eleatic.

eleatismo, *m.* (philos.) Eleaticism.

elebor, eléboro, *m.* (bot.) hellebore.

elección, *f.* election; choice, selection.

electivo, va, *a.* elective.

electo, ta. I. *a. & pp.* or ELEGIR; elect, chosen. **II.** *n.* elect, person chosen or appointed.

elector, ra. I. *n. & a.* elector (-ing). **II.** *m.* elector, German prince.

electorado, *m.* electorate.

electoral, *a.* electoral.

electricidad, *f.* electricity.

electricista, *m.* electrician.

eléctrico, ca, *a.* electric, electrical.

electrificación, *f.* electrification.

electrificar, *va.* to electrify.

electriz, *f.* electress.

electrización, *f.* electrification, electrization.

electrizador, ra; electrizante, *n. & a.* electrifier (-ying).

electrizar. I. *va. (pret.* ELECTRICÉ: *subj.* ELECTRICE) to electrify. **II.** *vr.* to become electrified.

electro, *m.* amber; electrum.

electrocución, *f.* electrocution.
electrocutar, *va.* to electrocute.
electrodinámica, *f.* electrodynamics.
electrodinámico, ca, *a.* electrodynamic.
electrodinamómetro, *m.* electrodynamometer.
electrodo, *m.* electrode.
electrofisiología, *f.* electrophysiology.
electróforo, *m.* electrophorus.
electroimán, *m.* electromagnet.
electrólisis, *f.* electrolysis.
electrólito, *m.* electrolyte.
electrolizable, *a.* electrolyzable.
electrolización, *f.* electrolyzation.
electrolizar, *va.* to electrolyze.
electromagnetismo, *m.* electromagnetism.
electrometalurgia, *f.* electrometallurgy.
electrometría, *f.* electrometry.
electrométrico, ca, *a.* electrometric.
electrómetro, *m.* electrometer.
electromotor, ra. I. *a.* electromotor. **II.** *m.*
  electric motor.
electromotriz, *a.* electromotive (force).
electrón, *m.* (phys.) electron.
electronegativo, va, *a.* electronegative.
electropositivo, va, electropositive.
electropuntura, *f.* electropuncturation.
electroquímica, *f.* electrochemistry.
electroquímuco, ca, *a.* electrochemical.
electroscopio, *m.* electroscope.
electrostática, *f.* electrostatics.
electrotecnia, *f.* electrotechnics, electrical engineering.
electroterapia, *f.* electrotherapeutics.
electrotipia, *f.* electrotyping.
electrotípico, ca, *a.* electrotypic.
electuario, *m.* electuary.
elefancía, *f.* (med.) elephantiasis.
elefancíaco, ca, *a.* elephantiac.
elefante, ta, *m.* elephant.
elefantíasis, *f.* elephantiasis.
elefantino, na, *a.* elephantine.
elegancia, *f.* elegance, gracefulness; neatness.
elegante, *a.* elegant, stylish, tasteful, graceful.
elegantemente, *adv.* elegantly, tastefully.
elegía, *f.* elegy.
elegiaco, ca, *a.* elegiac, mournful.
elegibilidad, *f.* elegibility.
elegible, *a.* eligible.
elegido, da. *a.* & *pp.* elect, chosen.
elegir, *va.* (*pp.* ELEGIDO, ELECTO: *ind.* ELIJO: *subj.*
  ELIJA) to elect; choose, select, prefer.
élego, ga, *a.* mournful, plaintive.
emental, *a.* elementary; fundamental.
elementalmente, *adv.* elementarily.
elementar, *a.* elementary.
elemento, *m.* element; constituent, ingredient;
  (elec.) element.—*pl.* elements, rudiments.
elemí, *m.* elemi, gum resin.
elenco, *m.* catalogue, list, table, index.
eleusino, na, *a.* Eleusinian.
elevación, *f.* elevation; height; rise, ascent; exaltation, dignity; advancement; exaltation of
  mind, ecstasy, rapture; haughtiness, pride.
elevadamente, *adv.* with elevation, loftily.
elevado, da. I. *a.* elevated; high; exalted, grand,
  lofty. **II.** *pp.* of ELEVAR.
elevador, *m.* elevator, hoist, lift.
elevamiento, *m.* elevation; ecstasy, rapture.
elevar. I. *va.* to raise, elevate, heave, lift, hoist;
  exalt. **II.** *vr.* to rise, ascend, soar; to be enraptured; to be elated.
elidir, *va.* to weaken; (gram.) to elide.
elijo, yo elija. *V.* ELEGIR.
elijable, *a.* (pharm.) that may be seethed.
elijación, *f.* (pharm.) seething.
elijar, *va.* (pharm.) to seethe.
eliminación, *f.* elimination.
eliminador, ra, *n.* & *a.* eliminator (-ing).
eliminar, *va.* to eliminate.
elipse, *f.* (geom.) ellipse.
elipsis, *f.* (gram.) ellipsis.

elipsoidal, (geom.) ellipsoidal.
elipsoide, *m.* (geom.) ellipsoid.
elípticamente, *adv.* elliptically.
elipticidad, *f.* ellipticity.
elíptico, ca, *a.* elliptic, elliptical.
Elíseos, Elisios (Campos), *m. pl.* Elysian (fields)
elisión, *f.* (gram.) elision.
élitro, *m.* (ent.) elytron.
elixir, elíxir, *m.* elixir.
elocución, *f.* elocution; effective diction, style.
elocuencia, *f.* eloquence.—**elocuente,** *a.* eloquent.—**elocuentemente,** *adv.* eloquently.
elogiador, ra, *n.* eulogist, encomiast.
elogiar, *va.* to praise, extol, eulogize, laud.
elogio, *m.* eulogy, praise.
elongación, *f.* (astr.) elongation.
elote, *m.* (Mex.) ear of green corn.
elucidación, *f.* elucidation.
elucidar, *va.* to elucidate.
eludible, *a.* eludible, avoidable.
eludir, *va.* to elude, to evade, avoid.
elzeviriano, na, *a.* Elzevir.
ella, *pron. fem. sing.* (*pl.* **ellas**) she.
elle, *f.* name of the letter *ll.*
ello, *pron. neuter sing.* it.—**e. dirá,** the event will
  tell.—**e. es que,** the fact is that (often used as an
  expletive).
ellos, ellas, *pron. m.* & *f. pl.* they.
emaciación, *f.* (med.) emaciation, emaceration.
emanación, *f.* emanation; effluvium.
emanante, *a.* emanating, issuing.
emanantismo, *m.* (philos.) emanationism, theory of creation by emanation.
emanar, *vn.* to emanate, issue; to follow, arise
  (from).
emancipación, *f.* emancipation.
emancipador, ra, *n.* & *a.* emancipator (-ing).
emancipar. I. *va.* to emancipate. **II.** *vr.* to free
  one's self; to become free or independent.
embabiamiento, *m.* (coll.) gape-gazing.
embachar, *va.* to pen (sheep to be shorn).
embadurnador, ra, *n.* & *a.* dauber (-ing).
embadurnar, *va.* to besmear, to bedaub.
embaidor, ra, *n.* & *a.* swindler (-ing).
embaimiento, *m.* delusion, illusion; deceit, imposition, imposture.
embair, *va.* and defective (*only those modes and*
  persons are used that have **i** *in the ending*) to impose upon, deceive, humbug.
embajada, *f.* embassy, legation; (coll.) message,
  errand.
embajador, *m.* ambassador.—**e. cerca de,** ambassador to.
embajadora, embajatriz, *f.* ambassadress; ambassador's wife.
embalador, *m.* packer.
embalaje, *m.* packing, baling.
embalar, *va.* to bale, pack.
embaldosado, *m.* tile floor; pavement.
embaldosar, *va.* to pave with tiles or flags.
embalsadero, *m.* morass, swamp, marsh.
embalsamador, ra, *m.* embalmer.
embalsamamiento, *m.* embalming.
embalsamar, *va.* to embalm; to perfume.
embalsar, *va.* to put on a raft; to dam; (naut.) to
  sling or hoist.
embalse, *m.* act of putting into a pond or on a
  raft; (naut.) slinging.
embalumar. I. *va.* to load unequally. **II.** *vr.* to
  embarrass one's self with business.
emballenador, ra, *n.* stay maker.
emballenar, *va.* to stiffen with whalebones.
emballestado, da. I. *a.* & *pp.* of EMBALLESTARSE. **II.** *m.* (vet.) contraction of the nerves
  in the feet.
emballestarse, *vr.* to get ready to discharge a
  crossbow.
embanastar, *va.* to put into a basket.
embancarse, *vr.* (metal.) to stick to the walls of
  the furnace.
embanderar, *va.* to decorate with banners.

embaquetar, *va.* (Mex.) to build sidewalks for (a street).

embarazada, *a. f.* pregnant.

embarazadamente, *adv.* with embarrassment.

embarazador, ra, *n. & a.* embarrasser (-ing).

embarazar, *va.* (*for mut. v.* ABRAZAR) to embarrass; (coll.) to impregnate.

embarazo, *m.* impediment; embarrassment, confusion, awkwardness; perplexity; pregnancy.

embarazosamente, *adv.* cumbersomely; embarrassingly.

embarazoso, sa, *a.* difficult, entangled, cumbersome; vexatious, embarrassing.

embarbascado, da, *pp. & a.* difficult, intricate, involved.

embarbascar. I. *a.* to stupefy (fish) by throwing hellebore, mullein, etc., into the water; to perplex, confound, embarrass. **II.** *vr.* to become entangled among roots (s. o. a plow).

enbarbecer, *vn.* (*ind.* EMBARBEZCO: *subj.* EMBARBEZCA) to have a beard appearing.

embarbillar, *va.* (carp.) to join.

embarcación, *f.* vessel, ship, craft; embarkation; navigation.—**e. de alijo,** (naut.) lighter.—**e. menor,** small craft.

embarcadero, *m.* wharf, quay, pier, ferry; (r. w.) freight station.

embarcador, ra, *m.* shipper.

embarcar. I. *va.* (*for mut. v.* ABARCAR) to embark, to ship; to embark or engage in an enterprise.—**e. agua,** (naut.) to ship a sea. **II.** *vr.* to embark, to go on shipboard.

embarco, *m.* embarkation (of persons).

embardar, *va.* to thatch.

embargador, ra, *n.* one who lays an embargo.

embargante, *a.* arresting, impeding, restraining. —**no e.,** nothwithstanding, nevertheless.

embargar, *va.* (*for mut. v.* ALARGAR) to impede, restrain, suspend; (law) to embargo, to seize, to attach.

embargo, *m.* indigestion; (law) embargo, sequestration, seizure, attachment.—**sin e.,** notwithstanding, however.

embarnizadura, *f.* varnishing.

embarnizar, *va.* to varnish.

embarque, *m.* shipment (of goods).

embarrador, ra, *n.* plasterer, dauber; fibber, mischief maker.

embarradura, *f.* smear, plastering; mud stain.

embarrancar. I. *vn. & vr.* to run aground. **II.** *vr.* to stick in the mud.

embarrar. I. *va.* to plaster roughly; to stain or smear with mud; to bedaub. **II.** *vr.* to collect or mount upon trees (as partridges).

embarrilador, *m.* packer in barrels.

embarrilar, *va.* to barrel.

embarrotar, *va.* = ABARROTAR.

embarrullador, ra, *n.* muddler, one who makes a mess of things.

embarullar, *va.* (coll.) to muddle, make a mess of; to do carelessly or disorderly.

embasamiento, *m.* (arch.) foundation.

embastar, *va.* to baste, to stitch.

embaste, *m.* basting.

embastecer. I. *vn.* (*for irr. v.* ABASTECER) to grow fleshy. **II.** *vr.* to become gross or coarse.

embate, *m.* dashing of the waves; sudden impetuous attack.—**embates de la fortuna,** sudden reverses of fortune.

embaucador, *m.* sharper, impostor.

embaucamiento, *m.* deception, humbug.

embaucar, *va.* (*for mut. v.* CADUCAR) to deceive, trick, humbug.

embaular, *va.* to pack in a trunk; (coll.) to cram with food.

embausamiento, *m.* amazement, astonishment.

embazador, *m.* one who or that which dyes a thing brown.

embazadura, *f.* brown dye or tinge; (met.) amazement, astonishment.

embazar. I. *va.* (*for mut. v.* CAZAR) to dye, tinge, or shade brown; to astonish; to embarrass.

II. *vn.* to be dumfounded. **III.** *vr.* to become tired, disgusted, or satiated.

embebecer. I. *va.* (*ind.* EMBEBEZCO: *subj.* EMBEBEZCA) to entertain, amuse. **II.** *vr.* to be struck with amazement.

embebecidamente, *adv.* amazedly.

embebecimiento, *m.* amazement, astonishment.

embebedor, ra, *n. & a.* imbiber (-ing).

embeber. I. *va.* to imbibe, drink in, absorb; to soak, saturate; to contain, include; to sink in, enchase, introduce, insert; to incorporate; to shrink, shorten, reduce, squeeze. **II.** *vn.* to shrink, to contract. **III.** *vr.* to be enraptured or ravished; to be absorbed in thought; to learn thoroughly, to master.

embecadura, *f.* (arch.) spandrel.

embelecador, ra, *n.* impostor, sharper.

embelecar, *va.* (*for mut. v.* AHUECAR) to impose upon, deceive, humbug.

embeleco, *m.* fraud, imposition, humbug.

embeleñado, da, *a. & pp.* of EMBELEÑAR; enraptured, ravished; stupefied, besotted.

embeleñar, *va.* to narcotize with henbane; to charm, fascinate.

embelesamiento, *m.* rapture, ecstasy.

embelesar. I. *va.* to charm, enchant, fascinate. **II.** *vr.* to be charmed, ravished, or delighted.

embeleso, *m.* rapture, ecstasy, fascination, ravishment; charm.

embellaquecerse, *vr.* to become a knave.

embellecer, *va.* (*ind.* EMBELLEZCO: *subj.* EMBELLEZCA) to beautify, embellish.

embellecimiento, *m.* embellishment or beautifying.

embermejar, embermejecer. I. *va.* (*ind.* EMBERMEJEZCO: *subj.* EMBERMEJEZCA) to dye red; to put to blush, to shame. **II.** *vn.* to blush; to turn red.

emberrenchinarse, emberrincharse, *vr.* (coll.) to fly into a violent passion (as children).

embestida, *f.* assault, violent attack, onset, drive; (coll.) importunate demand.

embestidor, ra. I. *n. & a.* rusher (-ing). **II.** *n.* importunate solicitor or beggar.

embestidura, *f.* attack, assault, onset.

embestir. I. *va.* (*ind.* EMBISTO: *subj.* EMBISTA) to assail, attack, rush against; (coll.) to importune with unreasonable demands; (mil.) to attack, make a drive on. **II.** *vn.* to attack, rush.

embetunar, *va.* to bituminate; to black.

embicar, *va.* (*pret.* EMBIQUÉ: *subj.* EMBIQUE) (naut.) to top (the yards).

embijar, *va.* to paint with minium.

embisto, yo embista. *V.* EMBESTIR.

embizcar. I. *va.* to make cross-eyed. **II.** *vn. & vr.* to become cross-eyed.

emblandecer. I. *va.* (*ind.* EMBLANDEZCO: *subj.* EMBLANDEZCA) to soften, to mollify. **II.** *vr.* to soften, become soft; to be moved to pity.

emblanquecer. I. *va.* (*ind.* EMBLANQUEZCO: *subj.* EMBLANQUEZCA) to bleach or whiten. **II.** *vr.* to become white.

emblanquecimiento, *m.* whitening, bleaching.

emblema, *m.* emblem, symbol.

emblemáticamente, *adv.* emblematically.

emblemático, ca, *a.* emblematic.

embobamiento, *m.* astonishment, enchantment, gape-gazing.

embobar. I. *va.* to amuse, entertain; to enchant, fascinate. **II.** *vr.* to be struck with astonishment, to stand aghast.

embobecer. I. *va.* (*ind.* EMBOBEZCO: *subj.* EMBOBEZCA) to stultify, make foolish, stupefy. **II.** *vr.* to become stupefied or foolish.

embobecimiento, *m.* stultification.

embocadero, *m.* mouth of a channel.

embocado, da, *pp. & a.* tasty (wine).

embocador, *m.* = EMBOCADERO.

embocadura, *f.* entrance by a narrow passage (mus.) embouchure, mouthpiece; mouthpiece of a bridle; taste (of wine); mouth (of a river); (arch.) proscenium arch.

embocar, *va.* (*pret.* EMBOQUÉ: *subj.* EMBOQUE) to put into the mouth; to put through a narrow passage; (coll.) to swallow in haste, to cram; to hoax.

embocinado, da, *a =* ABOCINADO.

embochinchar, *vn.* to raise a row or a riot.

embodegar, *va.* to store.

embojar, *va.* to prepare sheds for (silkworms).

embojo, *m.* shed for silkworms.

embolada, *f.* piston stroke.

embolar, *va.* to put balls on the tips of (bulls' horns); to apply the gilding size to; to shine, polish (shoes).

embolia, *f.* (med.) embolism.

embolismador, ra, *n. & a.* detractor (-ing).

embolismal, *a.* embolismic (year).

embolismar, *vn.* (coll.) to gossip, to carry tales.

embolismático, ca, *a.* confused, muddled.

embolismo, *m.* embolism, intercalation; confusion, disorder, maze; (coll.) falsehood.

émbolo, *m.* (mech.) piston; (med.) embolus.—**e. buzo,** plunger (of a pump).

embolsar, *va.* to put into a purse; to reimburse.

embolso, *m.* act of putting (money) into a purse.

embonar, *va.* to make good, improve, repair; (naut.) to sheathe.

embono, *m.* (naut.) doubling, lining, stiffening, sheathing.

emboñigar, *va.* to plaster with cow dung.

emboque, *m.* passage through the mouth or a narrow place (as a ring or a channel); (coll.) deception, cheat, fraud.

emboquillar, *va.* to put a tip on (a cigarette); (min.) to make the entrance of (a shaft); to prepare the mouth of (a drill) for blasting.

embornal, *m.* (naut.) scupper hole.

emborrachador, ra, *a.* intoxicating.

emborrachamiento, *m.* (coll.) intoxication.

emborrachar. I. *va.* to intoxicate. **II.** *vr.* to become intoxicated, to get drunk.

emborrar, *va.* to stuff, wad, pad; to card a second time; (coll.) to cram (food).

emborrazamiento, *m.* basting a roasting fowl.

emborrazar, *va.* (*pret.* EMBORRACÉ: *subj.* EMBORRACE) to tie pieces of pork to (a fowl) for basting.

emborricarse, *vr.* (coll.) to become a jackass.

emborrizar, *va.* (*pret.* EMBORRICÉ: *subj.* EMBORRICE) to give the first combing to (wool).

emborronar. I. *va.* to blot. **II.** *va. & vn.* to scribble.

emborrullarse, *vr.* (coll.) to dispute noisily.

emboscada, *f.*, **emboscadura,** *f.* ambush, ambuscade.

emboscar. I. *va.* (*pret.* EMBOSQUÉ: *subj.* EMBOSQUE) (mil.) to place in ambush. **II.** *vr.* to retire into a forest; to lie in ambush.

embosquecer, *vn. & vr.* to become wooded.

embotado, da, *pp. & a.* blunt, dull.

embotador, ra, *n.* one who blunts the points or edges of swords, etc.

embotadura, *f.* bluntness or dulness (app. to weapons).

embotamiento, *m.* blunting of weapons; bluntness, obtuseness, dulness.

embotar. I. *va.* to blunt, to dull (an edge or point); to enervate, debilitate; to dull, stupefy; to place (tobacco) in a jar. **II.** *vr.* to become dull; (coll.) to put on the boots.

embotellador, ra, *n. & a.* bottler (-ing).

embotellar, *va.* to bottle; to bottle up.

embotijar. I. *va.* to set jars under (a tile floor) for draining; to put into jars or bottles. **II.** *vr.* (coll.) to swell, to expand; to be in a passion.

embovedar, *va. =* ABOVEDAR.

emboza, *f.* inequalities in the bottom of barrels.

embozadamente, *adv.* dissemblingly.

embozado, da. I. *a.* muffled, with face covered or concealed (sp. with a cloak). **II.** *pp.* of EMBOZAR. **III.** one with muffled or concealed face.

embozar. I. *va.* (*pret.* EMBOCÉ: *subj.* EMBOCE) to muffle; to cloak, to dissemble; to muzzle. **II.** *vr.* to muffle one's self up.

embozo, *m.* muffler; fold in upper part of bedclothing; artful way of expressing one's thoughts. —**quitarse el e.,** to take off one's mask, to show one's real intention, lay one's cards on the table.

embrace, *m.* curtain clasp.

embracilado, da, *a.* (coll.) carried about in the arms, as children.

embragar, *va.* (*for mut. v.* BRAGAR) to put the clutch on; (naut.) to sling.

embrague, *m.* clutch; coupling.

embravecer. I. *va.* (*ind.* EMBRAVEZCO: *subj.* EMBRAVEZCA) to enrage, to irritate. **II.** *vn.* to become strong (s. o. plants). **III.** *vr.* to become angry; to be enraged; to swell (s. o. the sea).

embravecimiento, *m.* fury, rage, passion.

embrazadura, *f.* clasp of a shield or buckler; grasp, clasping, embracing.

embrazar. I. *va.* (*pret.* EMBRACÉ: *subj.* EMBRACE) to clasp (a shield); to grasp, buckle. **II.** *vn.* to gear, engage.

embreado, *m.*, **embreadura,** *f.* (naut.) paying with pitch, tarring.

embrear, *va.* (naut.) to pay with pitch.

embregarse, *vr.* to quarrel, wrangle.

embreñarse, *vr.* to hide among brambles.

embriagado, da, *a. & pp.* of EMBRIAGAR; intoxicated, drunk.

embriagar. I. *va.* (*pret.* EMBRIAGUÉ: *subj.* EMBRIAGUE) to intoxicate; to transport, enrapture. **II.** *vr.* to get drunk.

embriaguez, *f.* intoxication, drunkenness; rapture.

embridar, *va.* to bridle; to govern, check.

embriogenia, *f.* (biol.) embryogeny.—**embriogénico, ca,** *a.* (biol.) embryogenic.—**embriología,** *f.* embryology.—**embriológico, ca,** *a.* embryologic.—**embriólogo, ga,** *n.* embryologist.

embrión, *m.* embryo.

embrionario, ria, *a.* embryonal, embryonic.

embroca, embrocación, *f.* (med.) embrocation.

embrocar, *va.* (*pret.* EMBROQUÉ: *subj.* EMBROQUE) to pour out of one vessel into another by joining the mouths; to place upside down; (med.) to embrocate; to wind on a bobbin or quill; (shoe.) to tack to the last; to toss between the horns.

embrochado, da, *a.* embroidered.

embrochalar, *va.* (carp.) to support (a beam) by a crosspiece or a stay.

embrolla, *f.* (coll.) = EMBROLLO.

embrolladamente, *adv.* tanglingly.

embrollador, ra, *n. & a.* entangler (-ing), troublemaker (-ing).

embrollar, *va.* to entangle, twist, muddle, to insnare, embroil.—**e. la bandera,** (naut.) to waft the ensign.

embrollo, *m.* tangle, confusion, jumble; trickery, deception; embroiling; involved plot or story.

embrollón, na, *n.* liar, talebearer; mischief-maker; entangler.—**embrolloso, sa,** *a.* tangled.

embromado, da. I. *a* vexed, annoyed; (naut.) misty, hazy, foggy. **II.** *pp.* of EMBROMAR.

embromador, ra, *n.* one who is tumultuously merry; banterer, chaffer; wheedler; trickster.

embromar, *va.* to cajole, to wheedle; to chaff, banter; to vex, annoy; to detain, delay; to injure, harm.

embroquelarse, *vr. =* ABROQUELARSE.

embroquetar, *va.* to skewer the legs of.

embrosquillar, *va.* to put (cattle) into a fold.

embrujar, *va.* to bewitch.

embrutecer. I. *va.* (*ind.* EMBRUTEZCO: *subj.* EMBRUTEZCA) to brutify, make irrational. **II.** *vr.* to become brutified or irrational.

embrutecimiento, *m.* brutification.

embuchado, *m.* a kind of sausage.

embuchar, *va.* to stuff with minced meat; to cram the maw of (animals); (coll.) to swallow without chewing.

embudador, *m.* filler (with a funnel).

embudar, *va.* to put a funnel into: to trick; to scheme, to insnare.

embudista, *m.* trickster, intriguer.

embudito, *m. dim.* little funnel.

embudo, *m.* funnel; wax candle mold; water-closet basin; trick; fraud.

embullarse, *vr.* (Cuba) to get ready for a ball, sport, etc.; to revel, to be gay.

embullo, *m.* (Cuba) excitement, anticipation; gaiety, revelry.

emburujar, *va.* (coll.) to jumble, muddle.

embuste, *m.* fib, lie; trick, fraud.—*pl.* gew-gaws, baubles, trinkets.

embustear, *vn.* to fib, lie; impose upon, gab.

embustería, *f.* deceit, imposture, trick.

embustero, ra, *n.* liar; talebearer; trickster, cheat; hypocrite; (coll.) cajoler.

embusterón, na, *n. aug.* big liar.

embusteruelo, la, *n. dim.* little liar, fibber.

embutidera, *f.* rivet knob.

embutido, da. I. *pp.* of EMBUTIR. **II.** *m.* inlaid work, marquetry; sausage.

embutidor, *m.* rivet set, punch.

embutidura, *f.* (naut.) worming.

embutir, *va.* to inlay, to enchase; to insert; to stuff; to pack tight; to force; to imbed; (coll.) to cram, to eat much; (naut.) to worm.

eme, *f.* Spanish name of the letter *m.*

emenagogo, *m.* (med.) emmenagogue.

emendable, *a.* amendable.

emendación, *f.* emendation, amendment, correction; satisfaction, amends.

emendador, *m.* emendator.

emendar, *va.* = ENMENDAR.

emergencia, *f.* act of emerging; emergency, accident; (opt.) emergence.

emergente, *a.* emergent, resulting, issuing.

emérito, *a.* emeritus.

emersión, *f.* (ast.) emersion.

emético, ca. I. *n.* & *a.* emetic. **II.** *m.* tartar emetic.

emetocatártico, ca, *n.* & *a.* emetocathartic.

emetropia, *f.* (med.) emmetropia, normal vision.

emienda, *f.* = ENMIENDA.

emigración, *f.* emigration; number of emigrants; periodical migration of animals.

emigrado, da. I. *n.* & *a.* emigrant. **II.** *pp.* of EMIGRAR.

emigrante, *n.* & *a.* emigrant.

emigrar, *vn.* to emigrate.

eminencia, *f.* eminence, prominence; height, hill; eminence, title given to cardinals.—**con e.,** eminently.

eminencial, *a.* eminential.

eminencialmente, *adv.* eminently.

eminente, *a.* eminent, prominent; high, lofty.

eminentemente, *adv.* eminently.

eminentísimo, ma, *a.* most eminent.

emir, *m.* emir, ameer.

emisario, *m.* emissary; spy; outlet, discharge; (med.) emunctory.

emisión, *f.* emission, vent; issue (of paper money, bonds, etc.); (med.) emission.

emisor, ra. I. *a.* emitting; (rad.) broadcasting. **II.** *m.* (rad.) transmitter; broadcasting apparatus or instrument.

emitir, *va.* to emit, send forth; to issue (as bonds, etc.); to utter, express; (rad.) to broadcast.

emoción, *f.* emotion.

emocional, *a.* emotive; emotional.

emocionante, *a.* touching, causing emotion.

emocionar, *va.* to touch, move, shock, arouse emotion in.

emoliente, *m.* & *a.* emollient.

emolumento, *m.* emolument, fee, perquisite.

emotivo, va, *a.* emotive, relative to emotion.

empacar. I. *va.* (*pret.* EMPAQUÉ: *subj.* EMPAQUE) to pack, to bale. **II.** *vr.* to persist, act stubbornly; to become confused or rattled; to balk.

empacón, *a.* (Am.) obstinate, stubborn; balky.

empachado, da, *a.* & *pp.* of EMPACHAR; awkward, timid, bashful; surfeited, glutted; (naut.) overloaded.

empachar. I. *va.* to impede, embarrass; to overload, cram, encumber; to cause indigestion; to disguise. **II.** *vr.* to be ashamed, embarrassed, bashful; to surfeit.

empacho, *m.* bashfulness, timidity; embarrassment; obstacle; surfeit, indigestion.—**sin e.,** without ceremony; without blushing; unconcernedly.

empachoso, sa, *a.* embarrassing; disgraceful.

empadronador, *m.* census taker.

empadronamiento, *m.* census; tax list.

empadronar, *va.* to take the census of; to register (taxpayers).

empajada, *f.* hay with bran for horses.

empajar, *va.* to cover or stuff with straw: thatch.

empalagamiento, *m.* surfeit, cloying; boring.

empalagar, *va.* (*pret.* EMPALAGUÉ: *subj.* EMPALAGUE) to pall, cloy; surfeit; to vex, bother.

empalago, *m.* = EMPALAGAMIENTO.

empalagoso, sa, *a.* cloying, too rich or sweet; sickening; wearisome, annoying, boresome.

empalamiento, *m.* empalement, empaling.

empalar, *va.* to empale.

empaliada, *f.* hangings of bunting.

empaliar, *va.* to adorn with hangings.

empalizada, *f.* palisade, stockade, pale fence.

empalizar, *va.* to palisade, to stockade.

empalmadura, *f.* joint; coupling; splicing.

empalmar. I. *va.* to couple, join; to splice. **II.** *vn.* (r. w.) to branch, to join.

empalme, *m.* scarf, joint, connection; splicing; (r. w.) junction.

empalomado, *m.* (hydr.) loose-stone damming wall.

empalomar, *va.* (naut.) to sew (the boltrope).

empalletado, *m.* (naut.) mattress barricade.

empamparse, *vr.* (Am.) to get lost in a pampa.

empanada, *f.* meat pie; fraudulent muddle or concealment.

empanadilla, *f. dim.* small pie; movable footstep in carriages.

empanado, da. I. *a.* room receiving light from another room. **II.** *pp.* of EMPANAR.

empanar. I. *va.* to bake in paste; to sow (grain). **II.** *vr.* (agr.) to be choked by too much seed.

empandar, *va.* to bend, to sag; to warp.

empandillar, *va.* (coll.) to cheat at cards.

empantanar, *va.* to submerge; to swamp; to bemire; to embarrass; to obstruct.

empañadura, *f.* swaddling of children; stain; tarnishing.

empañar, *va.* to swaddle; to dim, blur, tarnish; to soil, sully.

empañetar, *va.* (Am.) to plaster.

empañicar, *va.* (naut.) to hand or furl.

empapar. I. *va.* to imbibe, saturate, soak, drench. **II.** *vr.* (w. en) to imbibe; to be soaked; to absorb; to enter into the spirit (of); (coll.) to surfeit.

empapelado, *m.* papering, paper hanging; paper (on a wall); paper lining.

empapelador, ra, *n.* paperhanger.

empapelar, *va.* to wrap up in paper; to paper.

empapirotar, *va.* (coll.) to adorn, to deck.

empapujar, *va.* (coll.) to make (one) eat too much, to stuff.

empaque, *m.* packing; mien, appearance, looks.

empaquetador, ra, *n.* packer.

empaquetadura, *f.* packing, gasket.

empaquetar, *va.* to pack; to stuff.

emparamado, da, (Am.) *pp.* & *a.* shivering with cold; frozen (fig.).

emparamarse, *vr.* (Am.) to freeze to death; to shiver with cold.

emparamentar, *va.* to adorn, to bedeck.

emparchar, *va.* to cover with plasters.

emparedado, da. I. *n.* recluse. **II.** *m.* sandwich. **III.** *pp.* of EMPAREDAR.

emparedamiento, *m.* confinement, religious retirement; cloister.

---

emparedar, *va.* to immure, to shut up between walls.

emparejador, ra, *n.* smoother, matcher, fitter.

emparejadura, *f.,* **emparejamiento,** *m.* matching; smoothing; evening up.

emparejar, *va. & vn.* to level, make even, smooth; to match, to fit; to put abreast.

emparentar, *vn. & vr.* to become related by marriage.

emparentado, da, *a. & pp.* of EMPARENTAR; related by marriage.

emparrado, *pp. & m.* vine arbor or bower.

emparrar, *va.* to embower.

emparrillado, *m.* (eng.) grillage; grate.

emparrillar, *va.* to broil on the gridiron.

emparvar, *va.* to lay (grain) for thrashing.

empastado, da, *a.* (b. b.) bound with a stiff cover (cloth, calf, etc.).

empastador, ra. **I.** *a.* painter who impastes. **II.** *m.* paste brush. **III.** *n.* bookbinder.

empastar, *va.* to fill (a tooth); to paste; to clam; (art) to impaste; (b. b.) to bind with a stiff cover (cloth, leather, etc.).

empaste, *m.* filling (of a tooth); binding; (art) impasto.

empastelar, *va. & vr.* (coll.) to compound, compromise; (print.) to pie.

empatadera, *f.* (coll.) checking, impeding.

empatar, *va.* to equal; to be a tie (as in voting); to hinder, obstruct; to join.

empate, *m.* tie, equal number of votes; hindrance, stopping, checking; joint; joining.

empavesada, *f.* (naut.) waistclothes; armings; hammock cloth; boat's cloth.—**empavesadas de las cofas,** top armor.

empavesado, da. **I.** *a.* covered with a large shield. **II.** *m.* soldier with large shield; dressing of a ship. **III.** *pp.* of EMPAVESAR.

empavesar, *va.* (naut.) to dress (ships); (naut.) to spread (waistclothes).

empavonar, *va.* = PAVONAR.

empecatado, da, *a.* very wily, evil-minded, incorrigible; ill-starred, unlucky.

empecer. **I.** *va.* (*ind.* EMPEZCO: *subj.* EMPEZCA) to hurt, offend, injure. **II.** *vn.* to prevent.

empecimiento, *m.* damage; obstacle.

empecinado, *m.* PEGUERO; (Am.) stubborn, incorrigible.

empecinarse, *vr.* (w. en) (Am.) to persist (in), be stubborn (about), or bound (to).

empechar, *va.* to prevent, hinder.

empedernido, da, *a.* hard-hearted.

empedernir. **I.** *va.* (*def.: only those modes are used that have i in their termination*) to indurate, to harden. **II.** *vr.* to be petrified; to become hard-hearted.

empedrado, da. **I.** *a.* spotted with clouds (s. o. the sky); pitted from smallpox (s. o. the face). **II.** *pp.* of EMPEDRAR. **III.** *m.* stone pavement.

empedrador, *m.* stone paver.

empedramiento, *m.* stone paving.

empedrar, *va.* to pave with stones.

empega, *f.* pitch varnish; mark with pitch.

empegado, *m.* tarpaulin.

empegadura, *f.* coat of pitch.

empegar, *va.* (*for mut. v.* PEGAR) to pay with pitch; to mark (sheep) with pitch.

empego, *m.* marking sheep with pitch; (Am.) pitchy taste.

empeguntar, *va.* to mark (sheep) with pitch.

empeine, *m.* groin; instep; hoof; tetter, ringworm; cotton flower.

empeinoso, sa, *a.* full of ringworms.

empelar, *vn.* to grow hair.

empelazgarse, *vr.* (coll.) to become involved.

empelechar, *va.* to cover or line with marble.

empelotarse, *vr.* to get into a wrangle; to take off all one's clothes.

empeltre, *m.* small shoot or sapling.

empella, *f.* vamp of a shoe.

empellar, *va.* to push, shove, jostle.

empellejar, *va.* to cover or line with skins.

empeller, *va.* = EMPELLER.

empellón, *m.* push, shove.—**a empellones,** pushing, by pushing rudely.

empenachado, da, *a.* plumed.

empenachar, *va.* to adorn with plumes.

empenta, *f.* prop, stay, shore.

empeñadamente, *adv.* strenuously; hard; insistently.

empeñado, da. **I.** *a.* determined, persisting. **II.** *pp.* of EMPEÑAR.

empeñar. **I.** *va.* to pawn; to pledge, gage; to engage, to oblige. **II.** *vr.* to bind one's self; to persist; to intercede, to mediate; (mil.) to begin (s. o. a battle).

empeñero, ra, *n.* (Mex.) pawnbroker.

empeño, *m.* pledge, pawn; engagement, contract; earnest desire; determination, firmness; protection, favor, recommendation; recommender.—**con c.,** eagerly, persistently.

empeoramiento, *m.* deterioration; making matters worse; becoming worse.

empeorar. **I.** *va.* to impair, to deteriorate; make worse. **II.** *vn. & vr.* to grow worse.

empequeñecer, *va.* (*ind.* EMPEQUEÑEZCO: *subj.* EMPEQUEÑEZCA) to make smaller, diminish; belittle.

emperador, *m.* emperor.—**emperatriz,** *f.* empress.

emperchado, *m.* fence formed with interwoven green trees.

emperchar, *va.* to hang on a perch.

emperdigar, *va.* = PERDIGAR.

emperejilar, *va. & vr.* to dress elaborately.

emperezar. **I.** *vn. & vr.* to be lazy, indolent. **II.** *va.* to retard, delay, obstruct.

emperifollar, *va. & vr.* = EMPEREJILAR.

empergaminado, da, *a.* bound in parchment.

empernar, *va.* to bolt, nail, spike, peg.

empero, *conj.* yet, however, notwithstanding.

emperrada, *f.* a card game.

emperramiento, *m.* obstinacy.

emperrarse, *vr.* (w. en) (coll.) to be obstinate or stubborn (about); to persist (in).

empesador, *m.* warp evener.

empetro, *m.* (bot.) crowberry.

empezar, *va. & vn.* (*ind.* EMPIEZO: *pret.* EMPECÉ: *subj.* EMPIECE) to begin.

empicarse, *vr.* to become too fond or infatuated.

empicotadura, *f.* act of pilloring.

empicotar, *va.* to pillory; to picket.

empiedro, empiedre. *V.* EMPEDRAR.

empiema, *f.* (med.) empyema.

empiezo, yo empiece. *V.* EMPEZAR.

empilonar, *va.* (Cuba) to pile up (tobacco leaves).

empinada, *f.* (aer.) zooming.

empinado, da, *a.* steep; high, lofty.

empinador, *n.* (coll.) toper.

empinadura, *f.,* **empinamiento,** *m.* erection, elevation, rising.

empinar. **I.** *va.* to raise; to exalt; to tip, incline.—**e. el codo,** to be a toper, to drink much. **II.** *vr.* to stand on tiptoe; to stand on the hind legs; to tower, rise high; (aer.) to zoom.

empingorotado, da, *pp. & a.* haughty, stuck up.

empingorotar, *va.* (coll.) to raise with a wedge or support.

empino, *m.* (arch.) summit of a curve.

empiolar, *va.* = APIOLAR.

empíreo, a. **I.** *a.* empyreal; celestial, divine. **II.** *m.* empyrean.

empireuma, *f.* (chem.) empyreuma.

empireumático, ca, *a.* (chem.) empyreumatic.

empíricamente, *adv.* empirically

empírico, ca. **I.** *a.* empirical. **II.** *m.* quack, empiric.

empirismo, *m.* empiricism; quackery.

empizarrado, *m.* slate roof.

empizarrar, *va.* to roof with slate.

emplastadura, *f.,* **emplastamiento,** *m.* plastering, putting plasters on; applying paint or cosmetics (to the face).

emplastar. I. *va.* to apply plasters to; to paint the face of; (coll.) to stop, check, obstruct. **II.** *vr.* to get smeared.

emplastecer, *va.* (art) to smooth for painting.

emplástico, ca, *a.* glutinous, sticky.

emplasto, *m.* plaster, poultice.

emplástrico, ca, *a.* glutinous, sticky; (med.) suppurative, dissolving.

emplazador, ra, *n.* (law) summoner.

emplazamiento, *m.* (law) summons.

emplazar, *va.* (*pret.* EMPLACÉ: *subj.* EMPLACE) (law) to summon; (sport) to set (the hunting party).

empleado, da. I. *n.* employee; officeholder. **II.** *pp.* of EMPLEAR.

emplear. I. *va.* to employ; give occupation to; to engage, hire; to appoint; to invest, to spend (as money); to use. **II.** *vr.* to be employed, to follow business.

empleita, *f.* = PLEITA.

empleitero, ra, *n.* one who plaits and sells bassweed.

emplenta, *f.* section of mud wall made at once.

empleo, *m.* employ, employment, occupation; public office; calling, profession; aim or object of desire; investment.

empleomanía, *f.* (coll.) mania for public office.

emplomado, *pp.* & *m.* roof covered with lead.

emplomador, ra, *n.* one who leads (covers, lines, etc. with lead.)

emplomadura, *f.* leading (covering, filling, etc., with lead); lead covering, lining, etc.

emplomar, *va.* to lead; to line with sheet lead; to put lead seals to.

emplumar. I. *va.* to feather; to adorn with plumes; to tar and feather. **II.** *vn.* to mew; to moult.

emplumecer, *vn.* (*ind.* EMPLUMEZCO: *subj.* EMPLUMEZCA) to fledge.

empobrecer. I. *va.* (*ind.* EMPOBREZCO: *subj.* EMPOBREZCA) to impoverish. **II.** *vn.* to become poor.—**empobrecimiento,** *m.* impoverishment.

empolvar, *va.. vr.* to cover with dust; to powder.

empolvoramiento, *m.* covering with dust or powder.

empolvorar, empolvorizar, *va.* = EMPOLVAR.

empollador, ra. I. *n.* hatcher. **II.** *m.* incubator.

empolladura, *f.* brood of bees.

empollar. I. *va.* to brood, to hatch. **II.** *vn.* to breed (s. o. bees).

emponchado, da, *a.* (Am.) covered with, or wearing, a poncho.

emponzoñador, ra, *n.* & *a.* poisoner (-ing, -ous).

emponzoñamiento, *m.* poisoning.

emponzoñar, *va.* to poison; to corrupt.

empopar, *va.* (naut.) to poop.

emporcar, *va.* (*ind.* EMPUERCO: *pret.* EMPORQUÉ: *subj.* EMPUERQUE) to soil, dirty, foul.

emporio, *m.* emporium, mart.

empotramiento, *m.* (arch.) embedding.

empotrar, *va.* (arch.) to embed, to fix in a wall; to scarf, to splice; to put (beehives) in a pit; (naut.) to fasten (cannon).

empotrerar, *va.* (Am.) to convert into pasture; to put (cattle) in a pasture.

empozar. I. *va.* (*pret.* EMPOCÉ: *subj.* EMPOCE) to throw into a well; to soak (flax). **II.** *vr.* (coll.) to be pigeonholed.

empradizar. I. *va.* to turn into a meadow; (Colomb.) to weed. **II.** *vr.* to become a meadow.

emprendedor, *n.* & *a.* enterpriser (-ing).

emprender, *va.* to undertake, to engage in.—**e. a,** or **con,** to address, accost.

empreñar, *va.* to impregnate; to beget.

empresa, *f.* enterprise, undertaking; device, motto; intention, purpose; management of a theater.

empresario, *m.* one who undertakes; contractor; theatrical manager; impresario.

empréstito, *m.* loan.—**c. público,** government loan.

emprima, *f.* = PRIMICIA.

emprimado, *pp.* & *m.* last combing to wool.

emprimar, *va.* to give the last combing to (wool); (coll.) to deceive.

empringar, *va.* = PRINGAR.

empuchar, *va.* to buck (skeins of thread).

empuerco, empuerque. *V.* EMPORCAR.

empuesta.—de e., from the rear, from behind.

empujar, *va.* to push, impel, shove.

empuje, empujo, *m.* push, pressure; energy, enterprise; (eng.) thrust.

empujón, *m.* push, violent shove.—**a empujones,** pushing, jostling.

empulgadura, *f.* drawing the string of a crossbow.—**empulgar,** *va.* to draw the string of (a crossbow).—**empulgueras,** *f.* *pl.* wings of a crossbow; thumbscrews.

empuñador, ra, *n.* grasper.

empuñadura, *f.* hilt (of a sword); beginning (of a story).

empuñar, *va.* to clinch, clutch, gripe, hold tightly with the fist.

empuñidura, *f.* (naut.) earing.

emulación, *f.* emulation; envy, jealousy.

emulador, ra, *m.* emulator, rival.

emular, *va.* to emulate, rival, contest with.

emulgente, *a.* emulgent.

émulo, la, *n.* competitor, rival, emulator.

emulsión, *f.* emulsion.—**emulsionar,** *va.* to emulsify.—**emulsivo, va,** *a.* emulsive, emulsifying.—**emulsor,** *m.* grease mixer.

emunción, *f.* (med.) excretion.

emuntorio, *m.* emunctory.—*pl.* emunctory glands in armpits, groins, and back of the ears.

en, *prep.* in; at; on, upon (*en la mesa,* on the table; *en domingo,* on Sunday; *en la pared,* on the wall; *en esa ocasión,* on that occasion); to; into (*convertir en gas,* to convert into a gas; *convertirse en polvo,* to turn to dust); (before gerund) on, upon, immediately after (*en llegando,* on arriving; *en acabando esta carta,* immediately, or right, after finishing this letter). Before adjectives it gives them adverbial signification (*en alto,* on high).

enaceitarse, *vr.* to become oily or rancid.

enaguachar, *va.* to load with water.

enagua, *f.* gen. in the *pl.,* **enaguas,** underskirt, petticoat; skirt.

enaguazar, *va.* to flood.

enagüillas, *f.* *pl.* short skirt or petticoat; kilt.

enajenable, *a.* alienable.

enajenación, *f.,* **enajenamiento,** *m.* alienation (of property); absence of mind; rapture, overjoy.— **e. mental,** mental derangement.

enajenar. I. *va.* to alienate, to transfer (property); to transport, enrapture. **II.** *vr.* to be enraptured, ravished.

enálage, *f.* (gram.) enallage.

enalbardar, *va.* to saddle (beasts of burden); to cover with a batter; to bread.

enalmagrado, da, *a.* & *pp.* of ENALMAGRAR; colored with ochre; vile, despicable.

enalmagrar, *va.* to cover with ochre.

enalmenar, *va.* to provide with battlements.

enaltecer, *va.* = ENSALZAR.

enamarillecer, *va.* & *vr.* to dye yellow.

enamoradamente, *adv.* lovingly, wooingly.

enamoradizo, za, *a.* inclined to fall in love.

enamorado, da. I. *a.* fond of love making; in love, enamored, lovesick. **II.** *pp.* of ENAMORAR. **III.** *n.* lover; sweetheart.

enamorador, ra, *n.* & *a.* courter (-ing), wooer (-ing); lovemaker (-ing).

enamoramiento, *m.* love, being in love; courting, lovemaking.

enamorar. I. *va.* to inspire love in; to make love to, woo, enamor. **II.** *vr.* (w. de) to fall in love (with).

enamoricarse, *vr.* (coll.) to be slightly in love.

enanchar, *va.* (coll.) to widen, enlarge.

enangostar, *va.* = ANGOSTAR.

enanito, ita. I. *a., dim.* little, minute. **II.** *n.* little dwarf; midget.

enano, na. I. *a.* dwarfish, small, little. **II.** *n.* dwarf.

enante, *m.* (bot.) water dropwort.

enantes, *a.* (low) = ANTES.

enarbolar. I. *va.* to hoist, raise high, hang out. **II.** *vr.* = ENCABRITARSE.

enarcar, *va.* to arch; to hoop (barrels).

enardecer. I. *va.* (*ind.* ENARDEZCO: *subj.* ENARDEZCA) to fire with passion, to inflame. **II.** *vr.* to be kindled, inflamed (with passion).

enardecimiento, *m.* act of inflaming or state of being inflamed with passion; being or becoming fiery or impassioned.

enarenación, *f.* plastering a wall before painting.

enarenar. I. *va.* to sand; to gravel. **II.** *vr.* (naut.) to ground.

enarmonar. I. *va.* to raise, to rear. **II.** *vr.* to rise on the hind feet.

enarmónico, ca, *a.* enharmonic.

enartrosis, *f.* (anat.) enarthrosis.

enastado, da, *a.* horned.

enastar, *va.* to put a haft or handle on.

encabalgamiento, *m.* gun carriage.

encabalgar. I. *vn.* (*pret.* ENCABALGUÉ: *subj.* ENCABALGUE) to rest upon (as a beam on a joist). **II.** *va.* to provide horses for.

encaballadura, *f.* (mas.) lapping over.

encaballar, *va.* to lap over, to imbricate (as tiles).

encabar, *va.* to put a handle to.

encabellecerse, *vr.* to grow hair.

encabestrar. I. *va.* to halter; to force to obedience. **II.** *vr.* to become entangled in the halter.

encabezador, *m.* header, reaping machine.

encabezadura, *f.* scarfing, heading.

encabezamiento, *m.* headline, heading, title; census taking; tax roll; act of enrolling tax-payers; tax rate.—e. de factura, billhead.

encabezar. I. *va.* to draw up (a tax roll); to put a heading or title to; to head, lead; to strengthen (wine) with alcohol; (carp.) to scarf, to join. **II.** *vr.* to compound for taxes; to compound, to compromise.

encabezonamiento, *m.* = ENCABEZAMIENTO.

encabezonar, *va.* = ENCABEZAR.

encabillar, *va.* (naut.) to scotch, pin, bolt.

encabrahigar, *va.* = CABRAHIGAR.

encabriar, *va.* (arch.) to place the rafters of.

encabritarse, *vr.* to rise on the hind feet.

encabuyar, *va.* (Am.) to tie with cabuya.

encachado, *m.* (hyd.) concrete lining.

encachar, *va.* (hyd.) to line with concrete.

encadenación, encadenadura, *f.*, **encadenamiento,** *m.* chaining, enchainment; concatenation, linking, connection.

encadenar, *va.* to chain, fetter, shackle; to enslave; to concatenate, connect, link together (as thoughts); to captivate; to paralyze.

encajador, *m.* one who chases or inserts; chasing tool.—encajadura, *f.* act of chasing, inserting or joining; socket, groove.

encajar. I. *va.* to chase, drive in, fit in, insert; to push or force in; (carp.) to rabbet, join; (mech.) to gear; to fit closely (as a lid); to put in (a remark); to tell (a story); to throw out (a hint); to fire off; to throw, hurl (as a missile); to administer (as a scolding); to pass off (as a spurious coin). **II.** *vn.* to fit. **III.** *vr.* to thrust one's self into some narrow place; to intrude, to butt in.

encaje, *m.* act of adjusting or fitting; socket, cavity, groove; enchasing; joining; lace; inlaid work, mosaic; looks, appearance.

encajera, *f.* woman who makes lace.

encajerado, da, *a.* (naut.) fouled on the sheave.

encajetillar, *va.* to packet (cigarettes, tobacco).

encajonado, da. I. *a.* narrow, flanked by steep inclines (s. o. rivers). **II.** *pp.* of ENCAJONAR. **III.** *m.* (mas.) packed work; cofferdam.

encajonamiento, *m.* packing in boxes or cases; narrowing between steep banks (s. o. rivers).

encajonar, *va.* to box; to case; to narrow.

encalabozar, *va.* (coll.) to put into a dungeon.

encalabrinado, da. I. *a.* headstrong, stubborn, obstinate. **II.** *pp.* of ENCALABRINAR.

encalabrinar. I. *va.* to affect the head of with some unpleasant smell or vapor. **II.** *vr.* (coll.) to become stubborn.

encalada, *f.* metal piece of a harness.

encalador, *m.* lime pit or vat.

encaladura, *f.* whitewashing.

encalar, *va.* to whitewash; to lime.

encalmadura, *f.* (vet.) a disease of horses caused by overheating.—encalmarse, *vr.* (vet.) to be overheated; (naut.) to be becalmed.

encalostrarse, *vr.* to become sick by sucking the first milk.

encalvecer, *vn.* (*ind.* ENCALVEZCO: *subj.* ENCALVEZCA) to become bald.

encalladero, *m.* (naut.) shoal, sand bank.

encalladura, *f.* (naut.) grounding, stranding.

encallar, *vn.* (naut.) to run aground; to fail.

encallecer. I. *vn.* (*ind.* ENCALLEZCO: *subj.* ENCALLEZCA) to get corns or callosities. **II.** *vr.* to become hardened or callous.

encallecido, a. & pp. of ENCALLECER; hardened; hard-hearted; callous.

encallejonar, *va.* to put in, or force into, an alley.

encamación, *f.* (min.) stull.

encamarar, *va.* to store (grain).

encamarse, *vr.* (coll.) to keep one's self in bed; to lie down (game); to be lodged by rain, wind, etc. (as corn).

encambijar, *va.* to conduct (water).

encambrar, *va.* = ENCAMARAR.

encambronar, *va.* to hedge with brambles; to strengthen with iron.

encaminadura, *f.*, **encaminamiento,** *m.* act of putting on the right road.

encaminar. I. *va.* to guide, to put on the right road; to direct, to manage; to forward. **II.** *vr.* (w. to) to take the road (to); to be on the way (to); to be intended (for; to).

encamisada, *f.* (mil.) camisado; an ancient night masquerade.

encamisar. I. *va.* to put a shirt or a cover on. **II.** *vr.* to put a shirt over one's clothes for a camisado.

encampanado, da, *a.* bell-shaped.

encanalar, encanalizar, *va.* to convey through pipes or conduits.

encanallarse, *vr.* to associate with ruffians; to become a ruffian.

encanarse, *vr.* to stiffen from rage (s. o. infants).

encanastar, *va.* to put in baskets.

encancerarse, *vr.* = CANCERARSE.

encandecer, *va.* to make incandescent.

encandelar, *vn.* (agr.) to bud (s. o. trees).

encandiladera, *f.* (coll.) procuress, bawd.

encandilado, da. I. *a.* high-cocked (s. o. hats). **II.** *pp.* of ENCANDILAR.

encandiladora, *f.* = ENCANDILADERA.

encandilar. I. *va.* to dazzle; to daze, bewilder; (coll.) to stir (the fire). **II.** *vr.* to have blood-shot eyes, as from drink; to be dazzled.

encanecer, *vn.* (*ind.* ENCANEZCO: *subj.* ENCANEZCA) to grow gray-haired; to mould; to grow old.

encanijamiento, *m.* weakness, emaciation.

encanijar. I. *va.* to weaken (a baby) by poor nursing. **II.** *vr.* to pine, be emaciated.

encanillar, *va.* to wind on a quill or spool.

encantación, *f.* incantation.

encantado, da, *a.* absent-minded; haunted; enchanted, charmed. **II.** *pp.* of ENCANTAR.

encantador, ra. I. *n.* enchanter, sorcerer; charmer. **II.** *a.* charming, delightful.

encantamiento, *m.* enchantment.

encantar, *va.* to enchant, charm; bewitch; to fascinate; to delight.

encantarar, *va.* to put into a jar or ballot box.

encante, *m.* auction, public sale.

encanto, *m.* enchantment, charm, spell; fascination; delight.

encantorio, *m.* (coll.) enchantment.

encantusar, *va.* (coll.) to coax, wheedle.

encañada, *f.* gorge, notch.

For pronunciation, see the rules at the beginning of the book.

encañado, *pp.* & *m.* conduit for water, pipe line; hedge or trellis of reeds.

encanador, ra, *n.* spool winder.

encañar. I. *va.* to hedge with reeds; to convey (water) through pipes; to drain; to wind (silk). **II.** *vn.* to form stalks (s. o. cereals).

encañizada, *f.* (fish.) weir.

encañonar. I. *va.* to put into pipes; to plait; to fold; to wind on quills. **II.** *vn.* to fledge out.

encañutar, *va.* to flute.

encapacetado, da, *a.* wearing a helmet.

encapachadura, *f.* number of bags of olives to be pressed.

encapachar, *va.* to put into a frail; (agr.) to protect (grapes) with the shoots.

encapado, da, *a.* cloaked.

encapazar, *va.* to collect into a basket.

encaperuzado, da, *a.* hooded.

encaperuzarse, *vr.* to put on a hood.

encapillado, *pp.* & *n.* clothes on one's back.

encapilladura, *f.* (naut.) top rigging.

encapillar. I. *va.* (naut.) to rig (the yards); (min.) to start a new gallery in. **II.** *vr.* to put on clothes over the head.

encapirotado, da, *pp.* & *a.* wearing a hood.

encapotadura, *f.*, **encapotamiento,** *m.* frown.

encapotar. I. *va.* & *vr.* to cloak; to muffle. **II.** *vr.* to become cloudy; to lower the head too much (s. o. horses).

encapricharse, *vr.* to indulge in whims; to become stubborn; (coll.) to be enamored or infatuated.

encapuchar, *va.* to cover with a hood.

encapuzar, *va.* to cover with a cowl.

encarado, da, *pp.* & *a.* faced; haughty.—**bien or mal e.,** well or ill faced.

encaramar, *va.* & *vr.* to raise; to elevate; to extol; to climb; to reach a high post.

encaramiento, *m.* act of facing or aiming.

encarar. I. *vn.* to face. **II.** *va.* to aim, to point. **III.** *vr.* (w. con) to face.

encaratularse, *vr.* to mask.

encarcelación, *f.* incarceration.

encarcelar, *va.* to imprison; (carp.) to clamp, to jam; (mas.) to embed with mortar; (naut.) to woold.

encarecedor, ra, *n.* & *a.* praiser (-ing), extoller (-ing).

encarecer, *va.*, *vn.* & *vr.* (ind. ENCAREZCO: *subj.* ENCAREZCA) to raise the price; to overrate; to extol; to enhance; to recommend.

encarecidamente, *adv.* exceedingly, highly; eagerly, earnestly.

encarecimiento, *m.* enhancement, exaggeration.—**con e.,** ardently, earnestly.

encargado, da. I. *a.* in charge. **II.** *pp.* of ENCARGAR. **III.** *n.* person in charge; agent, representative.— **e. de negocios,** chargé d'affairs; (Mex.) agent, attorney.

encargar. I. *va.* (pret. ENCARGUÉ: subj. ENCARGUE) to entrust, put under the care (of a person); to advise, warn; to order (goods, etc.); to ask, request. **II.** *vr.* to take charge.

encargo, *m.* charge, commission, request; office, place, employ; (com.) order.

encariñar. I. *va.* to inspire affection, fondness, or love. **II.** *vr.* (w. con) to become fond of.

encarna, *f.* giving entrails of game to dogs.

encarnación, *f.* incarnation; carnation, flesh color; adhesive cement; (surg.) incarnation.

encarnadino, na, *a.* incarnadine.

encarnado, da, *a.* & *pp.* of ENCARNAR; incarnate; flesh-colored; red.

encarnadura, *f.* (surg.) natural state of flesh; effect produced by an edged weapon on the flesh.

encarnamiento, *m.* (surg.) incarnation.

encarnar. I. *vn.* to incarnate; to penetrate, or lodge in, the flesh; (med.) to granulate (as a wound); to make a strong impression upon the mind. **II.** *va.* to incarnate; to embody; to flesh (hunting dogs); to bait (a fishhook); to paint or

make flesh-colored; to cause or produce granulation in (a wound). **III.** *vr.* to unite, mix (with one another).

encarnativo, *m.* & *a.* (surg.) incarnative.

encarne, *m.* entrails given to dogs.

encarnecer, *vn.* to grow fleshy, put on flesh.

encarnizado, da. I. *a.* blood-, or flesh-, colored; cruel, pitiless; bloody, hard-fought. **II.** *pp.* of ENCARNIZAR.

encarnizamiento, *m.* act of fleshing (dogs); cruelty, rage, fury.

encarnizar. I. *va.* (pret. ENCARNICÉ: subj. ENCARNICE) to flesh; to provoke, irritate. **II.** *vr.* to be or become fond of flesh (s. o. dogs); to be cruelly bent, to gloat on the infliction of pain or revenge.

encaro, *m.* stare; blunderbuss; aim; levelling a musket.

encarpetar, *va.* (Am.) to put or keep in a file or portfolio; to lay (a motion, bill, etc.) on the table.

encarrilar, encarrillar. I. *va.* to put in the right track; to set right. **II.** *vr.* (naut.) to be fouled on the sheave.

encarroñar. I. *va.* to infect, corrupt. **II.** *vr.* to be infected or corrupted.

encarrujado, da. I. *pp.* & *a.* curled; corrugated; fluted. **II.** *m.* fluting, shirring, gathering.

encarrujarse, *va.* & *vr.* to curl, twist, coil, kink.

encartación, *f.* enrolment under a charter; vassalage, tenure at will; village under vassalage.—*pl.* charter lands, especially those adjoining the province of Vizcaya.

encartamiento, *m.* outlawry, proscription; sentence on an absent defendant; charter.

encartar. I. *va.* to ban; to summon; to proscribe; to enrol; to register in a tax list; to serve (in card games). **II.** *vr.* to be unable to discard (in card games).

encarte, *m.* fortuitous order in which the cards remain at the close of a hand.

encartonador, ra, *n.* (b. b.) one who applies boards.

encartonar, *va.* to bind in, or cover with, boards.

encasar, *va.* (surg.) to set (a bone).

encascabelado, da, *a.* adorned with bells.

encasillado, *m.* set of pigeonholes.

encasillar, *va.* to put in pigeonholes; to distribute, assign; to make a list of (candidates).

encasquetar. I. *va.* & *vr.* to clap on (one's hat) close to the head. **II.** *va.* to convince. **III.** *vr.* to persist in, to be headstrong about; to get a notion.

encasquillador, *m.* (Am.) farrier.

encasquillar, *va.* to shoe (horses).

encastar. I. *va.* to improve (a race of) by crossing. **II.** *vn.* to breed.

encastillado, da, *pp.* & *a.* lofty, haughty.

encastillador, ra, *n.* one who shuts himself up in a castle; headstrong person.

encastillamiento, *m.* act of shutting up in a castle or steadfastly adhering to an opinion.

encastillar. I. *va.* to fortify with castles. **II.** *vn.* to make the cell of the queen bee in beehives. **III.** *vr.* to shut one's self up in a castle; to be unyielding or headstrong.

encastrar, *va.* to chase, embed.

encastre, *m.* fitting in; groove; socket.

encatarrado, da, *a.* having a cold.

encatusar, *va.* = ENGATUSAR.

encauchado, *m.* India-rubber poncho.

encauchar, *va.* to cover with rubber.

encausar, *va.* to prosecute, indict, sue.

encauste, *m.* = ENCAUSTO.

encáustico, ca, *a.* encaustic.

encausto, *m.* (art) encaustic painting.

encauzamiento, *m.* channeling; direction.

encauzar, *va.* to channel; to conduct through channels; to guide, lead, direct.

encavarse, *vr.* to hide in a cave.

encebadamiento, *m.* (vet.) surfeit.

encebadar. I. *va.* (vet.) to surfeit. **II.** *vr.* to be surfeited (s. o. horses).

encebollado, *m.* beef stew with onions.

encefálico, ca, *a.* encephalic.

encefalitis, *f.* (med.) encephalitis.

encéfalo, *m.* encephalon, brain.

encelamiento, *m.* jealousy.

encelar. I. *va.* to excite jealousy in, make jealous. **II.** *vr.* to become jealous.

encella, *f.* cheese basket or mold.

encellar, *va.* to mold (curds or cheese).

encenagado, da. I. *a.* mixed or filled with mud. **II.** *pp.* of ENCENAGARSE.

encenagamiento, *m.* wallowing in dirt or vice.

encenagar. I. *va.* (*pret.* ENCENAGUÉ: *subj.* ENCENAGUE) to mud, to mire. **II.** *vr.* to wallow in dirt, mire, or vice.

encendedor, ra. I. *n.* & *a.* lighter (ing). **II.** *m.* lighter.

encencerrado, da, *a.* carrying a weatherbell.

encender. I. *va.* (*ind.* ENCIENDO: *subj.* ENCIENDA) to kindle, light; to inflame, inspirit, incite. **II.** *vr.* to take fire; to burn.—e. en, to burn with (anger, etc.); to become excited with.

encendidamente, *adv.* ardently.

encendido, da. I. *a.* & *pp.* of ENCENDER; inflamed; red. **II.** *m.* (int. comb. eng.) ignition.

encendimiento, *m.* kindling, lighting; incandescence, glow; ardor, eagerness.

encenizar, *va.* to cover with ashes.

encentador, *m.* one who begins to use things.

encentadura, *f.,* **encentamiento,** *m.* act of beginning the use of a thing.

encentar. I. *va.* to begin the use of. **II.** *vr.* to develop bedsores.

encepador, *m.* stocker, gunstocker.

encepadura, *f.* (carp.) tie joint.

encepar. I. *va.* to put in the stocks; to stock (a gun); (naut.) to stock (the anchor); (carp.) to join with ties. **II.** *vr.* to take root; (naut.) to foul (s. o. the anchor).

encepe, *m.* (agr.) taking firm root.

encerado, da. I. *pp.* of ENCERAR. **II.** *a.* wax-colored; like wax; thick; hard (as a boiled egg). **III.** *m.* oilcloth, oilskin; (naut.) tarpaulin; sticking plaster; blackboard in schools.

enceramiento, *m.* act and effect of waxing.

encerar, *va.* to wax; to inspissate (lime).

encernadar, *va.* = ACERNADAR.

encerotar, *va.* to wax (thread).

encerradero, *m.* sheepfold; pen.

encerrador, ra, *n.* one who locks up; driver of black cattle.

encerradura, *f.,* **encerramiento,** *m.* act of locking up; cloister, retreat; prison, jail, dungeon.

encerrar. I. *va.* (*ind.* ENCIERRO: *subj.* ENCIERRE) to lock or shut up; to confine; to include, embrace, contain, involve. **II.** *vr.* to live in seclusion; to be locked up; to be closeted.

encerrona, *f.* (coll.) voluntary retreat.

encespedar, *va.* to cover with sod.

encestar, *va.* to put in a basket.

encía, *f.* gum (of the mouth).

enciclico, ca. I. *a.* encyclic. **II.** *f.* encyclical.

enciclopedia, *f.* encyclopædia, cyclopædia.

enciclopédico, ca, *a.* encyclopedic.

enciclopedismo, *m.* Encyclopedism.

enciclopedista, *a.* & *n.* encyclopedist.

enciendo, encienda. V. ENCENDER.

encierro, *m.* act of closing or locking up; confinement; inclosure; cloister, religious retreat; prison, lockup; folding (of cattle).

encierro, encierre. V. ENCERRAR.

encima. I. *adv.* above; at the top; overhead; over and above, besides.—e. de, on, upon.—por e. superficially, hastily.—por e. de, over; regardless of. **II.** *f.* (Am.) boot, something added.

encimar. I. *va.* to place on top; to raise high; to throw in, give to boot. **II.** *vr.* to rise above.

encina, *f.* (bot.) evergreen oak, holm oak.

encinal, encinar, *m.* holm-oak grove.

encinta, *a.* pregnant.

encintado, *m.* curb (of a side walk, etc.)

encintar, *va.* to ribbon.

encismar, *va.* (coll.) to sow discord among.

encisto, *m.* encysted tumor.

encizañar, *va.* = CIZAÑAR.

enclaustración, *f.* cloistering.

enclaustrar, *va.* to cloister.

enclavación, *f.* nailing or fixing.

enclavadura, *f.* (carp.) groove; embedding.

enclavar, *va.* to nail; to embed; (vet.) to prick (horses) in shoeing; to pierce through.

enclavijar, *va.* to join, pin; to peg (a guitar).

enclenque, *a.* weak, feeble, sickly.

enclítico, ca, *n.* & *a.* (gram.) enclitic.

enclocar, encloquecer, *vn.* & *vr.* to become broody.

encobar, *vn.* & *vr.* to hatch eggs; to sit (on eggs).

encobijar, *va.* = COBIJAR.

encobrado, da, *a.* containing copper; copper-colored.

encoclar = ENCLOCAR.

encocorar, *va.* (coll.) to vex, annoy.

encofrado, *m.* (min.) plank lining, timbering.

encofrar, *va.* (min.) to plank; to timber.

encoger. I. *va.* (*ind.* ENCOJO: *subj.* ENCOJA) to contract, shorten, shrink; to discourage. **II.** *vr.* to be low-spirited, dismayed, or bashful; to shrink, to shrivel.—e. de hombros, to shrug the shoulders.

encogidamente, *adv.* abjectly; bashfully, awkwardly.

encogido, da, *pp.* & *a.* bashful, timid.

encogimiento, *m.* contraction, shrinkage; pusillanimity; bashfulness; awkwardness.

encojar. I. *va.* to cripple, to lame. **II.** *vr.* to become lame; (coll.) to feign sickness.

encolado, *m.,* **encoladura,** *f.,* **encolamiento,** *m.,* gluing; priming, sizing.

encolar, *va.* to glue; to stick.

encolerizar. I. *va.* (*pret.* ENCOLERICÉ: *subj.* ENCOLERICE) to anger. **II.** *vr.* to become angry.

encomendable, *a.* commendable.

encomendado, da. I. *pp.* of ENCOMENDAR. **II.** *n.* one under a knight commander.

encomendamiento, *m.* = ENCOMIENDA.

encomendar. I. *va.* (*ind.* ENCOMIENDO: *subj.* ENCOMIENDE) to recommend, commend; to entrust; to knight. **II.** *vn.* to hold a knight commandery. **III.** *vr.* to commit one's self to another's protection; to put one's self in the hands of; to send compliments.

encomendero, *m.* agent; commissionaire.

encomiador, ra, *n.* & *a.* praiser (-ing).

encomiar, *va.* to praise, eulogize, extol.

encomiasta, *m.* eulogizer, panegyrist.

encomiástico, ca, *a.* encomiastic, complimentary.

encomienda, *f.* commission, charge; message, compliment sent; encomienda (certain estates assigned or granted by the Spanish kings); knight commandery; land or rent belonging to a commandery; badge of a knight commander; patronage, protection, recommendation; compliments, respects; (Am.) parcel-post parcel.

encomio, *m.* praise, encomium, eulogy.

encompadrar, *vn.* (coll.) to become a COMPADRE; to be close friends.

enconamiento, *m.* inflammation, soreness; infection; animadversion, anger.

enconar. I. *va.* to inflame, irritate, provoke; to increase the inflammation or soreness of; to infect. **II.** *vr.* to rankle, to fester.

enconcharse, *vr.* (Am.) to withdraw one's self from society or the public; to retire into one's shell.

encono, *m.* rancor, ill-will; soreness; sore spot, sore.

enconoso, sa, *a.* easily festered or infected; rancorous, resentful.

enconrear, *va.* to oil (wool) before carding.

encontradamente, *adv.* contrarily.

encontradizo, za, *a.* that may be met on the way.

encontrado, da. I. *a.* opposite; in front; hostile, opposed. **II.** *pp.* of ENCONTRAR.

encontrar. I. *va.* to find; to meet. **II.** *vn.* to meet; to collide. **III.** *vr.* to meet; to collide; to be, find one's self, feel (apl. to health); to oppose, or be opposed to, each other; to conflict; to find; (w. **con**) to meet, come across or upon.

encontrón, *m.* collision, clash, shock.

encopetado, da. I. *a.* presumptuous, haughty, stuck up; of high social standing or noble descent. **II.** *pp.* of ENCOPETAR.

encopetar, *va.* to raise (the hair), as in a toupee.

encorachar, *va.* to put in a leather bag.

encorajar. I. *va.* to encourage; to inflame. **II.** *vr.* to be furious, in a rage.

encorar. I. *va.* (*ind.* ENCUERO: *subj.* ENCUERE) to cover with or wrap up in leather; to cause or help the formation of skin in (a wound). **II.** *vn.* & *vr.* to heal, develop skin (s. o. a wound).

encorazado, da, *a.* covered with a cuirass; covered with leather.

encorchar, *va.* to hive (bees); to cork (bottles).

encorchetar, *va.* to put on hooks or clasps; to hook, to clasp.

encordar, *va.* (*ind.* ENCUERDO: *subj.* ENCUERDE) (mus.) to string (instruments); to lash or bind with ropes.

encordelar, *va.* to string; to bind with strings.

encordonado, da. I. *a.* corded; adorned with cords. **II.** *pp.* of ENCORDONAR.

encordonar, *va.* to cord; to tie with cords.

encorecer. I. *va.* (*ind.* ENCOREZCO: *subj.* ENCOREZCA) to cause the formation of skin in (a wound). **II.** *vn.* & *vr.* = ENCORAR.

encoriación, *f.* healing a wound.

encornado, da, *a.* horned.

encornadura, *f.* disposition of the horns.

encornudar, *vn.* to begin to grow horns.

encorozar, *va.* to put a COROZA on the head of (a criminal).

encorralar, *va.* to corral.

encorrear, *va.* to strap (cattle).

encorsetar, *va.* & *vr.* to put a corset on.

encortinar, *va.* to provide with curtains, put up curtains on or in.

encorvada, *f.* act of bending the body; grotesque manner of dancing; (bot.) hatchet wetch coronilla.—**hacer la e.,** to feign sickness.

encorvadura, *f.*, **encorvamiento,** *m.* bending; curvature, crookedness.

encorvar, *va.* & *vr.* to bend, curve.

encostillado, *m.* timbering; lathing.

encostradura, *f.* incrustation, crust.

encostrar. I. *va.* to crust, to incrust. **II.** *vr.* to become crusty; to develop a crust or a scab.

encovadura, *f.* act of placing in a cellar.

encovar. I. *va.* (*ind.* ENCUEVO: *subj.* ENCUEVE) to put in a cellar; to keep, lock up, conceal. **II.** *vr.* to hide one's self.

encrasar, *va.* to fatten; to thicken.

encrespador, *m.* crisping iron, curling tongs.

encrespadura, *f.* act of curling the hair.

encrespamiento, *m.* curling; erection, standing on end (s. o. the hair); fury, roughness (of the sea, the waves, etc.)

encrespar. I. *va.* to curl; to set (the hair) on end; to ruffle (the feathers). **II.** *vr.* (naut.) to become rough and boisterous (s. o. the sea); to be agitated (by passion); to wrangle; to become entangled (s. o. affairs).

encrestado, da, *a.* & *pp.* of ENCRESTARSE; adorned with a crest or comb; haughty, lofty.

encrestarse, *vr.* to stiffen the crest or comb (as a cock); to be proud or haughty.

encrucijada, *f.* street or road intersection; ambush; opportunity to do harm to another.

encrudecer. I. *va.* (*ind.* ENCRUDEZCO: *subj.* ENCRUDEZCA) to make (a wound) worse or raw; to exasperate, irritate. **II.** *vr.* to be enraged.

encruelecer. I. *va.* (*ind.* ENCRUELEZCO: *subj.* ENCRUELEZCA) to excite to cruelty. **II.** *vr.* to become cruel.

encuadernación, *f.* (b. b.) binding.

encuadernador, ra, *n.* bookbinder.

encuadernar, *va.* (b. b.) to bind; to reconcile.—**sin e.,** unbound.

encuarte, *m.* extra horse to draw a coach uphill.

encubar, *va.* to cask (liquids); to put (a criminal) into a butt.

encubertar. I. *va.* (*ind.* ENCUBIERTO: *subj.* ENCUBIERTA) to caparison, trap (as a horse). **II.** *vr.* to put on armor.

encubierta, *f.* fraud, deceit, imposition.

encubiertamente, *adv.* hiddenly, secretly; deceitfully, fraudulently.

encubierto, ta, *a.* & *pp. irr.* of ENCUBRIR (*also irr. ind.* from ENCUBERTAR).

encubridor, ra, *n.* & *a.* concealer (-ing).

encubrimiento, *m.* concealment.

encubrir, *va.* (*pp.* ENCUBIERTO) to hide, conceal, cloak, mask, palliate.

encuentro, *m.* encounter, meeting; collision, clash; find, finding; (mil.) encounter, fight; joint (in fowls); in quadrupeds, points of the shoulder blades; (arch.) angle, nook, corner.—*pl.* temples of a loom.—**salir al e. de,** to go to meet; to encounter.

encuentro, encuentre. *V.* ENCONTRAR.

encuerdo, encuerde. *V.* ENCORDAR.

encuitarse, *vr.* to grieve.

enculatar, *va.* to cover (a beehive).

encumbrado, da. I. *a.* high, elevated; lofty, stately. **II.** *pp.* of ENCUMBRAR.

encumbramiento, *m.* act of raising or elevating; height, eminence.

encumbrar. I. *va.* to raise, elevate. **II.** *vn.* to ascend. **III.** *vr.* to rise; to be proud, to rate one's self high.

encunar, *va.* to put in the cradle; to catch between the horns.

encureñado, da, *a.* (gun) put on the carriage.

encurtido, *m.* pickle.—**encurtir,** *va.* to pickle.

enchabetar, *va.* (naut.) to forelock.

enchancletar, *va.* to put slippers on.

enchapado, *m.* veneer; plates or sheets forming a cover or lining.

enchapar, *va.* to veneer; to cover with metal plates or sheets.

enchapinado, da, *a.* built upon a vault.

encharcada, *f.* pool of water, puddle.

encharcarse, *vr.* to form puddles.

enchicharse, *vr.* (Am.) to drink chicha to excess; to become angry, flare up.

enchilada, *f.* (Mex.) pancake of maize with chilli.

enchilar, *va.* (Am.) to put chilli on or in; to anger.

enchiquerar, *va.* to shut (the bull) in the CHIQUERO; (coll.) to imprison.

enchivarse, *vr.* (Colomb.) to get angry.

enchuchar, *va.* (Cuba) (r. w.) to switch.

enchufar, *va.* & *vr.* to fit (a tube) into another; to telescope.

enchufe, *m.* socket joint; telescoping, sliding of one thing into another.

ende.—por e., therefore, consequently.

endeble, *a.* feeble, weak, frail; flimsy.

endeblez, *f.* feebleness; flimsiness.

endecasílabo, ba, *a.* hendecasyllable.

endecha, *f.* dirge, doleful ditty.

endechadera, *f.* = PLAÑIDERA.

endechar. I. *va.* to sing funeral songs to. **II.** *vr.* to grieve, mourn.

endehesar, *va.* to put (cattle) in the pasture.

endemia, *f.* (med.) endemia.

endémico, ca, *a.* (med.) endemic.

endemoniado, da, *pp.* & *a.* possessed with the devil; devilish, fiendish, perverse.

endemoniar, *va.* to possess with a devil; (coll.) to irritate, provoke, enrage.

endentado, da, *a.* (her.) serrated.

endentar, *va.* & *vn.* (*ind.* ENDIENTA: *subj.* ENDIENTE) to gear, engage, mesh.

endentecer, *vn.* (*ind.* ENDENTEZCO: *subj.* ENDENTEZCA) to cut teeth, to teeth.

enderezadamente, *adv.* rightly.

enderezado, da. I. *a.* fit, appropriate. **II.** *pp.* of ENDEREZAR.

enderezador, ra, *n.* good manager; righter; straightener.

enderezamiento, *m.* straightening; setting right.

enderezar. I. *va.* (*pret.* ENDERECÉ: *subj.* ENDERECE) to straighten; to right, set right; to address, dedicate; to manage well. **II.** *vn.* to take the direct road. **III.** *vr.* to straighten up; to set one's self, prepare for an undertaking.

endeudarse, *vr.* to contract debts.

endevotado, da, *a.* pious; devoted, fond.

endiablada, *f.* boisterous masquerade.

endiabladamente, *adv.* devilishly; horribly.

endiablado, da, *a.* & *pp.* devilish, diabolical; ugly, deformed; perverse, wicked.

endiablar. I. *va.* to pervert, corrupt. **II.** *vr.* to be furious.

endíadis, *f.* (rhet.) hendiadys.

endibia, *f.* (bot.) endive, succory.

endilgador, ra, *n.* (coll.) pander.

endilgar, *va.* to direct, guide; to assist; to thrust (a weapon, an insult), to deal (a blow); to spring (something) on (a person).

endiosamiento, *m.* haughtiness, pride; ecstasy, abstraction; deification.

endiosar. I. *va.* to deify. **II.** *vr.* to be elated with pride; to be devoutly abstracted.

endoblasto, *m.* (biol.) endoblast, hypoblast.

endocardio, *m.* (anat.) endocardium.

endocarditis, *f.* (med.) endocarditis.

endocarpo, *m.* (bot.) endocarp.

endodermo, *m.* (biol.) endoderm.

endogénesis, *f.* (biol.) endogeny.

endolinfa, *f.* (anat.) endolymph, liquid that fills the labyrinth of the ear.

endorsar, *va.* to indorse (as a draft); to transfer.

endorso, *m.* (com.) indorsement.

endosador, endosante, *m.* indorser.

endosar, *va.* to indorse (a draft, etc.).

endosatario, ria, *n.* indorsee.

endose, *m.* indorsement (of a draft, etc.).

endoselar, *va.* to hang; to provide with a dais.

endósmosis, *f.* endosmosis.

endoso, *m.* = ENDOSE.

endotérmico, ca, *a.* (chem.) endothermic.

endriago, *m.* fabulous monster.

endrina, *f.* sloe, fruit of the sloe tree.

endrino, *m.* (bot.) blackthorn, sloe tree.

endrino, na, *a.* sloe-colored.

endulzadura, *f.* sweetening.

endulzar, *va.* (*pret.* ENDULCÉ: *subj.* ENDULCE) to sweeten; to soften, soothe; (art) to soften, tone down.

endurador, ra, *a.* parsimonious, niggardly.

endurar, *va.* to harden; to save; to endure, bear; to delay, put off.

endurecer, *va.* & *vr.* (*ind.* ENDUREZCO: *subj.* ENDUREZCA) to harden; to inure; to exasperate, irritate.

endurecidamente, *adv.* obstinately; harshly.

endurecido, da, *a.* & *pp.* of ENDURECER; hard, hardy; indurated, hardened; obdurate; tutored by experience, inured.

endurecimiento, *m.* hardness; hardening; obstinacy; tenaciousness; hard-heartedness.

ene, *f.* Spanish name of the letter *n.*

enea, *f.* (bot.) cat's-tail, reed mace, rush.

enebral, *m.* plantation of juniper trees.

enebrina, *f.* fruit of the juniper tree.

enebro, *m.* (bot.) common juniper.

enejar, *va.* to put an axle on.

eneldo, *m.* (bot.) common dill.

enema, *f.* enema, injection, clyster.

enemiga, *f.* enmity, hatred, ill-will.

enemigamente, *adv.* inimically.

enemigo, ga. I. *a.* (w. **de**) inimical, hostile (to); opposed, adverse (to). **II.** *n.* enemy, foe; devil. (In the latter sense, and in military language, the noun is *m.*).—**e. capital,** mortal enemy.—**e. jurado,** sworn enemy.—**el e. malo,** the devil.

enemistad, *f.* enmity, hatred.

enemistar. I. *va.* to make enemies of. **II.** *vr.* (w. **con**) to become an enemy (of); to fall out (with).

éneo, ea, *a.* (poet.) brazen, brass (u. a.).

energía, *f.* energy; (mechanical) power.— **e. cinética,** kinetic energy.—**e. potencial,** potential energy.—**transmisión de e.,** power transmission.

enérgicamente, *adv.* energetically.

enérgico, ca, *a.* energetic, lively.

energúmeno, na, *n.* person possessed with a devil; violent, impulsive person.

enero, *m.* January.

enervación, *f.* enervation.

enervar. I. *va.* to enervate, unnerve; to weaken. **II.** *vr.* to become weak.

enfadadizo, za, *a.* irritable, irascible, peevish.

enfadar. I. *va.* to vex, incense, anger. **II.** *vr.* to fret, become angry.—**enfado,** *m.* vexation, anger; trouble, drudgery.—**enfadosamente,** *adv.* vexatiously.—**enfadoso, sa,** *a.* vexatious, annoying.

enfaldar. I. *va.* (agr.) to lop off the lower branches of. **II.** *vr.* to tuck up (the skirts).

enfaldo, *m.* act of tucking up one's clothes.

enfangar. I. *va.* (*pret.* ENFANGUÉ: *subj.* ENFANGUE) to soil with mud. **II.** *vr.* (naut.) to ground in the mud; (coll.) to soil one's reputation; to sink (into vice, etc.).

enfardar, *va.* to pack, bale, fardel.

enfardelador, *m.* packer.—**enfardeladura,** *f.* packing, baling.

enfardelar, *va.* to bale, pack, fardel.

énfasis, *m.* emphasis.—**enfáticamente,** *adv.* emphatically.—**enfático, ca,** *a.* emphatic.

enfermar. I. *vn.* to fall ill. **II.** *va.* to make sick.

enfermedad, *f.* illness, sickness.

enfermería, *f.* infirmary, sanitarium.

enfermero, ra, *n.* nurse (for the sick).

enfermizo, za, *a.* infirm, sickly; unwholesome, unhealthful.

enfermo, ma. I. *a.* ill, sick; sickly. **II.** *n.* patient.

enfermoso, sa, *a.* (Am.) = ENFERMIZO; indisposed, ailing somewhat.

enfervorizar. I. *va.* to heat, inflame, incite. **II.** *vr.* to become fervorous or heated.

enfeudación, *f.* infeudation, enfeoffment.

enfeudar, *va.* to feoff, to enfeoff.

enfielar, *va.* to put in a balance.

enfilar, *va.* to place in a row or line; to pierce or string in a line; (mil.) to enfilade.—**e. el curso,** (naut.) to direct the course, to bear.

enfisema, *m.* (med.) emphysema.

enfistolarse, *vr.* to become a fistula.

enfiteusis, *m.* & *f.* (law) emphyteusis.

enfiteuta, *m.* (law) emphyteuta.

enfitéutico, ca, *a.* emphyteutic.

enflaquecer. I. *va.* (*ind.* ENFLAQUEZCO: *subj.* ENFLAQUEZCA) *va.* to make thin or lean; to extenuate, to fade. **II.** *vn.* & *vr.* to become thin, lose weight. **III.** *vn.* to weaken.

enflaquecimiento, *m.* loss of flesh, emaciation.

enflautada, da, *a.* (coll.) inflated.

enflautador, ra, *n.* (coll.) procurer.

enflautar, *va.* (coll.) to procure; (coll.) to deceive, cheat, humbug.

enflechado, da, *a.* ready to discharge.

enfocar, *va.* to focus.

enfoscar. I. *va.* (*pret.* ENFOSQUÉ: *subj.* ENFOSQUE) (mas.) to fill up (holes). **II.** *vr.* to be ill-humored; to be deep in a business; to be cloudy.

enfrailar. I. *va.* to make (one) a monk or friar. **II.** *vr.* to become a friar.

enfranquecer, *va.* to frank, to free.

enfrascamiento, *m.* entanglement.

enfrascar. I. *va.* (*pret.* ENFRASQUÉ: *subj.* ENFRASQUE) to bottle. **II.** *vr.* to be entangled or involved; to be deeply engaged in work.

enfrenador, ra, *n.* & *a.* bridler (-ing), restrainer (-ing).

enfrenamiento, *m.* bridling; checking, curbing.

enfrenar, *va.* to bridle; to govern by the bridle; to curb, to restrain; to put the brake on.

enfrentar. I. *va.* to confront, put face to face; to face. **II.** *vr.* (w. **con**) to face; to oppose.

enfrente, *adv.* opposite, in front.—**e. de,** opposite.

enfriadera, *f.* bottle cooler, refrigerator.

enfriador, enfriador, *m.* cooling place; refrigerator; cold storage.

enfriamiento, *m.* refrigeration; cooling; cold, chill.

enfriar. I. *va.* to cool. **II.** *vr.* to cool; to cool off or down.

enfullar, *va. & vn.* (coll.) to cheat at cards.

enfundadura, *f.* casing; putting into cases.

enfundar, *va.* to case, to put into a case (as a pillow); to fill up, to stuff.

enfurecer. I. *va.* (*ind.* ENFUREZCO: *subj.* ENFUREZCA) to enrage, make furious. **II.** *vr.* to rage, to become furious or stormy.

enfurruñarse, *vr.* (coll.) to get angry; sulk.

enfurtir, *va.* to full (cloth); to felt.

engabanado, da, *a.* wearing an overcoat.

engace, *m.* catenation, connection.

engafar, *va.* to bend (a crossbow); to hook; to set (a gun) at half cock.

engaitador, ra, *n.* (coll.) wheedler.

engaitar, *va.* (coll.) to coax, to wheedle.

engalanar, *va.* to adorn, deck; (naut.) to dress.

engalgar, *va.* to pursue closely; to scotch (a wheel); (naut.) to back (an anchor).

engallado, da, *a.* erect, upright; haughty.

engallador, *m.* martingale.

engalladura, *f.* = GALLADURA.

engallarse, *vr.* to draw one's self up arrogantly; to keep the head near the chest (s. o. horses).

enganchador, *m.* hooker.

enganchamiento, *m.* hooking; enlisting in the army; decoying.

enganchar. I. *va.* to hook, hitch, couple, connect; to entrap; to decoy into the military service. **II.** *vr.* to engage; to enlist in the army; to be caught on a hook.

enganche, *m.* = ENGANCHAMIENTO.

engandujo, *m.* twisted thread of a fringe.

engañabobos, *m.* (coll.) trickster; fool trap.

engañadizo, za, *a.* easily deceived.

engañado, da. I. *a.* mistaken; deceived. **II.** *pp.* of ENGAÑAR.

engañador, ra, *n. & a.* deceiver (-ing).

engañapastor, *m.* (orn.) wagtail.

engañar. I. *va.* to deceive; cheat; fool, hoax; to wile away (as time). **II.** *vr.* to deceive one's self; to make a mistake.

engañifa, *f.* (coll.) deceit, trick, catchpenny.

engaño, *m.* deceit, fraud; hoax, lure; mistake, misunderstanding, misapprehension.

engañosamente, *adv.* deceitfully, guilefully; deceivingly, misleadingly.

engañoso, sa, *a.* deceitful, artful, false; deceiving, misleading.

engarabatar. I. *va.* (coll.) to hook. **II.** *vr.* to become crooked.

engarabitarse, *vr.* (coll.) to climb, ascend.

engarbarse, *vr.* to perch high on a tree.

engarbullar, *va.* (coll.) to entangle, involve; to make a mess of.

engarce, *m.* union, connection; hooking; chasing of jewellery.

engargantar. I. *va.* to put into the throat. **II.** *vn.* to thrust the foot into the stirrup; to gear, to mesh, to interlock.

engargolar, *va.* to join (pipes).

engaritar, *va.* to fortify, to adorn with sentry boxes; (coll.) to trick, fool.

engarrafador, *m.* grappler.

engarrafar, *va.* (coll.) to grapple.

engarrotar. I. *va.* to garrote; to make numb (with cold). **II.** *vr.* to become numb with cold; to be very cold, frozen (fig.).

engarzador, ra, *n.* one who hooks or enchains; stringer of beads.

engarzar, *va.* (*pret.* ENGARCÉ: *subj.* ENGARCE) to join, to link, to hook; to curl.

engastador, *m.* enchaser, setter.

engastar, *va.* to set (as diamonds); to enchase.

engaste, *m.* setting (of stones); enchasing; pearl flat on one side.

engatado, da. I. *n.* petty robber, pilferer. **II.** *pp.* of ENGATAR.

engatar, *va.* (coll.) to cheat; wheedle.

engatillado, da. I. *a.* thick, high-necked (horses and bulls). **II.** *pp.* of ENGATILLAR.

engatillar, *va.* (arch.) to bind with a cramp iron.

engatusador, ra, *n. & a.* coaxer (-ing), wheedler (-ing).

engatusamiento, *m.* (coll.) wheedling, coaxing.

engatusar, *va.* (coll.) to inveigle, wheedle.

engavillar, *va.* = AGAVILLAR.

engazador, ra, *n.* = ENGARZADOR.

engazamiento, *m.* = ENGARCE.

engazar, *va.* to link; (naut.) to strap (blocks); to dye in the cloth.

engendrable, *a.* that may be engendered.

engendramiento, *m.* begetting, generating.

engendrador, ra, *n. & a.* generator (-ing); engenderer (-ing).

engendrar, *va.* to beget, engender, generate; to produce, bear; to create; (math.) to generate.

engendro, *m.* fœtus, shapeless embryo; bungling, badly-made thing; poor work; (coll.) show.—**mal e.,** perverse youth.

englobar, *va.* to englobe, inclose, include.

englobado, da, *a.* collared.

engolfar. I. *vn.* (naut.) to enter a gulf or deep bay. **II.** *vr.* to be deeply engaged or absorbed.

engolillado, da, *a.* wearing the GOLILLA.

engolondrinarse, *vr.* (coll.) to be elated with pride; to fall in love.

engolosinar. I. *va.* to allure. **II.** *vr.* to become fond of.

engolletado, da. I. *a.* (coll.) conceited, haughty. **II.** *pp.* of ENGOLLETARSE.

engolletarse, *vr.* (coll.) to be conceited.

engomadura, *f.* first gumming; coat which bees lay over their hives.

engomar, *va.* to gum, to size; to glue.

engorar, *va.* to addle. *V.* ENHUERAR.

engorda, *f.* (Am.) ENGORDE; number of animals fattened together or at a time.

engordadero, *m.* sty to fatten hogs.

engordador, ra, *a.* fattening; pampering.

engordar. I. *va.* to pamper, fatten, lard. **II.** *vn.* to become fat; to become rich.

engorde, *m.* fattening (hogs, etc.).

engorro, *m.* embarrassment, nuisance.

engorroso, sa, *a.* troublesome, annoying.

engoznar, *va.* to hinge; to put hinges on.

engranaje, *m.* (mech.) gear, gearing.

engranar, *vn.* to gear, to interlock.

engrandar, *va.* = AGRANDAR.

engrandecer, *va.* (*ind.* ENGRANDEZCO: *subj.* ENGRANDEZCA) to augment, aggrandize; to enlarge; to exalt, extol; to exaggerate, magnify.

engrandecimiento, *m.* increase, enlargement; aggrandizement, exaltation; exaggeration.

engranerar, *va.* to store (grain).

engranujarse, *vr.* to become covered with pimples; to become a knave.

engrapar, *va.* (mas. and carp.) to cramp.

engrasación, *f.* lubrication, oiling, greasing.

engrasador, *m.* oiler, lubricator.

engrasar, *va.* to grease, oil, lubricate; to stain with grease; to dress (cloth); to manure.

engredar, *va.* to clay, to chalk; to full.

engreído, da, *a. & pp.* of ENGREIR; conceited.

engreimiento, *m.* conceit, presumption, vanity.

engreír. I. *va.* (*ind.* ENGRÍO: *subj.* ENGRÍA) to encourage the conceit of, to make vain; to elate. **II.** *vr.* to become vain or conceited.

engrescar, *va. & vr.* to pick a quarrel; to make (one) join in merriment.

engrifar, *va. & vr.* to curl, crisp, crimp; to make (the hair) stand on end (from fright).

engringarse, *vr.* (coll.) to follow foreign customs, to act like foreigners.

---

engrosar. I. *va.* (*ind.* ENGRUESO: *subj.* ENGRUE-SE) to swell, enlarge; increase; to thicken, broaden. **II.** *vn.* & *vr.* to become strong or corpulent; to increase.

engrudador, *m.* paster.—**engrudamiento,** *m.* pasting.—**engrudar,** *va.* to paste.—**engrudo,** *m.* paste.

engrueso, engruese. *V.* ENGROSAR.

engruesar, *va.* = ENGROSAR.

engrumecerse, *vr.* to clot, to curdle.

engualdrapar, *va.* to caparison.

enguantado, da, *pp.* & *a.* wearing gloves.

enguantarse, *vr.* to put gloves on.

enguedejado, da, *a.* wearing long hair.

enguijarrar, *va.* to pave with pebbles.

enguillar, *va.* (naut.) to wind (a thin rope around a thicker one).

enguirnaldado, da, *a.* garlanded.

enguirnaldar, *va.* to garland.

enguizgar, *va.* to incite, prompt, stimulate.

engullidor, ra, *n.* devourer, gobbler, glutton.

engullir, *va.* to devour, gobble.

engurrio, *m.* sadness, melancholy.

engurruñarse, *vr.* (coll.) to become melancholy.

enharinar, *va.* to cover with flour.

enhastiar, *va.* to annoy, cloy, bore.

enhastillar, *va.* to put arrows in (a quiver).

enhatijar, *va.* to cover (hives) with bassweed.

enhebrar, *va.* to thread; to string.

enhenar, *va.* to cover with hay.

enherbolar, *va.* to poison with herbs.

enhestador, ra, *n.* one who raises or hoists.

enhestadura, *f.* erection, raising, hoisting.

enhestar. I. *va.* (*ind.* ENHIESTO: *subj.* ENHIESTE) to erect; to raise, to hoist; to set upright. **II.** *vr.* to rise upright.

enhielar, *va.* to mix with gall or bile.

enhiesto, ta, *a.* erect, upright; lofty.

enhilado, da. I. *a.* well-arranged, in good order, in line. **II.** *pp.* of ENHILAR.

enhilar, *va.* to thread; to direct; to line.

enhorabuena. I. *f.* congratulation, felicitation. **II.** *adv.* well and good; all right.

enhoramala, *adv.* in an evil hour.—**vete e.,** (coll.) go to blazes!

enhornar, *va.* to put into an oven.

enhuecar, *va.* = AHUECAR.

enhuerar, *va.*, *vn.* & *vr.* to addle.

enigma, *m.* enigma.—**enigmáticamente,** *adv.* enigmatically.—**enigmático, ca,** *a.* enigmatical.

enigmatista, *m.* enigmatist.

enjabonadura, *f.* = JABONADURA.

enjabonar, *va.* to soap; to wash with soap; (coll.) to soft-soap.

enjaezar, *va.* (*pret.* ENJAECÉ: *subj.* ENJAECE) to trap, harness.

enjaguar, *va.* = ENJUAGAR.

enjagüe, *m.* adjudication required by the creditors of a ship.

enjalbegador, ra, *n.* whitewasher.

enjalbegadura, *f.* whitewashing.

enjalbegar, *va.* to whitewash; to paint (the face).

enjalma, *f.* packsaddle.—**enjalmar. I.** *va.* to packsaddle. **II.** *vn.* to make packsaddles.

enjalmero, *m.* packsaddle maker.

enjambradera, *f.* queen bee. *V.* CASQUILLA.

enjambradero, *m.* place where bees form hives.

enjambrar. I. *va.* to hive (bees). **II.** *vn.* to breed a new hive; to produce abundantly.

enjambrazón, *f.* swarming of bees.

enjambre, *m.* swarm; crowd.

enjarciadura, *f.* (act of) rigging.

enjarciar, *va.* to rig (a ship).

enjardinar, *va.* to trim and arrange (trees) as in gardens.

enjaretado, *m.* grating, lattice work.

enjaretar, *va.* to run a string through (a hem); (coll.) to speak or act hurriedly and thoughtlessly.

enjaular, *va.* to cage; to imprison, confine.

enjebar, *va.* to steep in lye, to buck.

enjebe, *m.* lye; (act of) bucking.

enjergar, *va.* (coll.) to start and direct.

enjertación, *f.* grafting; insertion; inoculation; budding.

enjertal, *m.* nursery of grafted fruit trees.

enjertar, *va.* = INJERTAR.

enjerto. I. *m.* INJERTO; mixture. **II.** *pp. irr.* of ENJERTAR.

enjorguinar. I. *va.* to smear with soot. **II.** *vr.* to be blackened with soot.

enjoyar, *va.* to adorn with jewels; to set with precious stones; to adorn, embellish.

enjoyelado, da, *a.* worked into jewels; covered with jewels, bejeweled.

enjoyelador, *m.* setter, jeweler.

enjuagadientes, *m.* (coll.) mouth wash.

enjuagadura, *f.* rinsing the mouth.

enjuagar, *va.* to rinse (mouth, cups, etc.).

enjuagatorio, enjuague, *m.* act of rinsing; mouth wash; finger bowl.—**enjuague,** plot, scheme.

enjugador, ra. I. *n.* drier. **II.** *m.* drum for the drying of linen.

enjugar. I. *va.* (*pret.* ENJUGUÉ: *subj.* ENJUGUE) to dry; to wipe off moisture from. **II.** *vr.* to become lean.

enjuiciamiento, *m.* (law) act of instituting and prosecuting a judicial proceeding; suit.

enjuiciar, *va.* (law) to bring a suit or action against; to try, carry on (a case); to indict; to pass judgment on.

enjulio, enjullo, *m.* cloth beam of a loom; warp rod.

enjundia, *f.* fat in the ovary of fowls; grease or fat of any animal; substance, force.

enjundioso, sa, *a.* fat, fatty; substantial.

enjunque, *m.* (naut.) heavy ballast or cargo; kentledge.

enjuta, *f.* (arch.) spandrel.

enjutar, *va.* (mas.) to dry (plaster, etc.).

enjutez, *f.* dryness, aridity.

enjuto, ta. I. *a.* & *pp. irr.* of ENJUTAR; dried; lean, skinny; austere. **II.** *m. pl.* brushwood; titbits to excite thirst.

enlabiador, ra, *n.* wheedler.

enlabiar, *va.* to wheedle, cajole, entice.

enlabio, *m.* enticement, alluring by soft words.

enlace, *m.* connection, coherence, interlocking; link, lacing; wedding; relationship; affinity.

enlaciar. I. *va.* to render lax or languid. **II.** *vr.* to wither, to decay.

enladrillado, *m.* brick pavement.

enladrillador, *m.* bricklayer.

enladrilladura, *f.* brickwork.

enladrillar, *va.* to pave with bricks.

enlagunar, *va.* to flood, to turn into a pond.

enlajar, *va.* (Ven.) to pave with tiles or flags.

enlamar, *va.* to cover with slime.

enlanado, da, *a.* covered with wool.

enlardar, *va.* to baste. *V.* LARDAR.

enlargues, *m. pl.* (naut.) rope ends.

enlatar, *va.* to cover (a roof) with tin; to can.

enlazable, *a.* that can be joined.

enlazador, ra, *n.* binder, uniter.

enlazadura, *f.,* **enlazamiento,** *m.* connection, binding, uniting, linking, coupling; lacing.

enlazar. I. *va.* (*pret.* ENLACÉ: *subj.* ENLACE) to lace, bind, join, unite, connect. **II.** *vr.* to become joined in wedlock; to become related by marriage; to interlock; to join or be linked or connected.

enlechuguillado, da, *a.* wearing a ruff round the neck.

enlegajar, *va.* to sort or arrange (papers) into a batch or parcel.

enlejiar, *va.* to buck (clothes); to make into lye.

enlenzar, *va.* to strengthen with adhesive strips.

enligarse, *vr.* to be caught with birdlime.

enlistonado, *m.* (carp., mas.) lathing, lath work.

enlistonar, *va.* to lath, lay lath work on.

enlizar, *va.* to provide (a loom) with leashes.

enlodadura, *f.* act of soiling with mud.

---

enlodar, *va.* to bemire, to soil with mud; to throw mud at; to lute.

enloquecedor, ra, *a.* maddening.

enloquecer. I. *va.* (*ind.* ENLOQUEZCO: *subj.* EN-LOQUEZCA) to madden, render insane; to distract. **II.** *vn. & vr.* to become insane; to be vexed, annoyed or in despair; (*agr.*) to become barren (s. o. trees).

enloquecimiento, *m.* madness, insanity.

enlosado. I. *m.* pavement; tile floor; paving, tiling. **II.** *pp.* of ENLOSAR.—**enlosador, ra,** *n.* tile layer, paver.

enlosar, *va.* to pave or cover with flags, tile or slabs.

enlozanarse, *vr.* to make a show of vigor and strength.

enlucido. I. *m.* (coat of) plaster; plastering. **II.** *pp.* of ENLUCIR.

enlucidor, *m.* (mas.) plasterer.

enlucimiento, *m.* polishing; (mas.) plastering.

enlucir, *va.* (*ind.* ENLUZCO: *subj.* ENLUZCA) to polish (plate); (mas.) to plaster.

enlustrecer, *va.* to clean, brighten, polish.

enlutar, *va.* to put in mourning, put crape or mourning on, to crape; to veil; to darken.

enllantar, *va.* to rim, to shoe (a wheel).

enllentecer, *va.* to soften, blandish.

enmaderación, *f.,* **enmaderamiento,** *m.,* woodwork; wainscoting.

enmaderar, *va.* to plank, board; to roof with timber; to floor with boards.

enmagrecer, *vn.* to become lean or skinny.

enmalezarse, *vr.* to become weedy.

enmallarse, *vr.* to be caught in the meshes.

enmangar, *va.* to put a handle on.

enmantar. I. *va.* to cover with a blanket. **II.** *vr.* to become melancholy.

enmarañamiento, *m.* entanglement, intricacy.

enmarañar, *va.* to tangle (as hair, etc.); to entangle, perplex, involve in difficulties; to puzzle, confound.

enmararse, *vr.* (naut.) to take sea room.

enmaridar, *vn. & vr.* to get a husband, marry.

enmarillecerse, *vr.* to become yellow.

enmaromar, *va.* to tie with a rope.

enmascarar. I. *va.* to mask. **II.** *vr.* to masquerade, put on a mask.

enmasillar, *va.* to putty, cement.

enmatarse, *vr.* to hide among the plants.

enmelar, *va.* to bedaub with honey; to sweeten.

enmendación, *f.* emendation, correction.

enmendadamente, *adv.* accurately, exactly.

enmendador, ra, *n.* corrector, emendator, reviser.

enmendadura, *f.* = ENMIENDA.

enmendar. I. *va.* (*ind.* ENMIENDO: *subj.* EN-MIENDE) to amend, correct; to repair; to reform; to indemnify. **II.** *vr.* to mend, reform, lead a new life.

enmienda, *f.* emendation, correction; reward, premium; (law) satisfaction, indemnity.

enmohecer, *va. & vr.* (*ind.* ENMOHEZCO: *subj.* EN-MOHEZCA) to mold, mildew; to rust.

enmohecido, da, *pp. & a.* rusty, moldy, mildewed.—**enmohecimiento,** *m.* rusting, molding.

enmollecer, *va.* to soften, mollify.

enmondar, *va.* to clear (cloth) from knots.

enmontarse, *vr.* (Colomb.) to become overgrown with weeds and trees.

enmordazar, *va.* to gag, muzzle.

enmudecer. I. *va.* (*ind.* ENMUDEZCO: *subj.* EN-MUDEZCA) to hush, to silence. **II.** *vn.* to become dumb; to be silent.

enmugrar, *va.* to soil, cover with dirt.

ennegrecer, *va.* (*ind.* ENNEGREZCO: *subj.* ENNE-GREZCA) to blacken; to darken, to obscure.

ennegrecimiento, *m.* blackening.

ennoblecedor, ra, *a.* ennobling, noble.

ennoblecer, *va.* (*ind.* ENNOBLEZCO: *subj.* ENNO-BLEZCA) to ennoble; to adorn, embellish.

ennoblecimiento, *m.* ennoblement.

ennudecer, *vn.* = ANUDARSE.

enodio, *m.* fawn, young deer.

enojada, *f.* (coll.) outburst of anger; getting angry.

enojadizo, za, *a.* fretful, peevish, ill-tempered.

enojado, da, *a. & pp.* angry, cross.

enojar. I. *va.* to make angry, vex, irritate; to annoy. **II.** *vr.* to become angry, to get cross; to become violent, furious (s. o. the elements).

enojo, *m.* anger; (gen. *pl.*) trouble, suffering; annoyance.

enojosamente, *adv.* angrily; troublesomely.

enojoso, sa, *a.* vexatious, troublesome; irritating.

enojuelo, *m. dim.* slight peevishness.

enología, *f.* œnology, art of wine making.

enológico, ca, *a.* œnological.

enometría, *f.* wine alcoholometry.

enómetro, *m.* wine alcoholometer.

enorgullecer. I. *va.* (*ind.* ENORGULLEZCO: *subj.* ENORGULLEZCA) to make proud. **II.** *vr.* to be proud; to swell with pride.

enorgullecimiento, *m.* pride; haughtiness.

enorgullecido, da. I. *a.* haughty, proud. **II.** *pp.* of ENORGULLECER.

enorme, *a.* enormous; horrible, wicked, heinous.

enormemente, *adv.* enormously; horridly.

enormidad, *f.* enormity, enormousness, horridness; atrocity.

enormísimo, ma, *a.* most horrid.

enotecnia, *f.* practical œnology, or art of wine making.

enotécnico, ca, *a.* relating to wine making.

enquiciar, *va.* to put (a door, window) in place; to put in order; to make firm or stable.

enquillotrarse, *vr.* to become conceited; (coll.) to fall in love.

enquiridión, *m.* enchiridion, handbook, manual.

enrabiar, *va.* to anger, enrage.

enraizar, *vn.* to take root.

enramada, *f.* bower, arbor; grove.

enramar, *va.* to embower or decorate with tree branches.

enramblar, *va.* to tenter (cloth).

enrame, *m.* act of embowering.

enranciarse, *vr.* to become rancid or stale.

enrarecer. I. *va.* (*ind.* ENRAREZCO: *subj.* EN-RAREZCA) to thin, rarefy. **II.** *vr.* to become thin or rarefied.

enrarecimiento, *m.* rarefaction.

enrasar, *va.* (mas.) to make even or level, to flush.—**enrase,** *m.* (mas.) levelling course.

enrastrar, *va.* to string (silk cocoons).

enrayar, *va.* to put spokes on (a wheel).

enredadera. I. *a.* climbing, twining (s. o. plants). **II.** *f.* (bot.) climber; vine; bindweed, bellbind.

enredado, da. I. *pp.* of ENREDAR. **II.** *a.* entangled, matted, involved, intricate.

enredador, ra, *n.* entangler; tattler, busybody, intermeddler.

enredar. I. *va.* to entangle; to confound, puzzle; to involve in difficulties; to catch in the net; to lay, set (snares, nets); to sow discord among or between. **II.** *vn.* to fumble; to be frisky (as boys). **III.** *vr.* to become entangled; (naut.) to foul (s. o. the anchor).

enredo, *m.* tangle, entanglement; perplexity, puzzle; intricacy; falsehood, mischievous lie; plot (of a play, etc.).

enredoso, sa, entangled, intricate; beset with difficulties.

enrehojar, *va.* to bleach (wax leaves).

enrejado, *pp. & m.* railing, grating; trellis, lattice; grillwork, openwork.

enrejar, *va.* to range bricks in crisscross tiers.

enrejar, *va.* to fence with railing or grating; to put a grating to; to make a trellis for; to grate, lattice; to attach the plowshare to (the plow); to wound (cattle's feet) with a plowshare.

enrevesado, da, frisky; difficult; nonsensical.

enriado, *m.* retting of flax or hemp.

enriador, ra, *n.* one who rets flax or hemp.

enriar, *va.* to ret (hemp, flax).

---

enrielar, *va.* to make ingots or rails from; to put on the track; to guide, start in the right direction.

enripiar, *va.* (mas.) to fill with riprap.

enriquecedor, ra, *n. & a.* enricher (-ing), wealth producer (-ing).

enriquecer. I. *va.* (*ind.* ENRIQUEZCO: *subj.* ENRIQUEZCA) to enrich; to adorn. **II.** *vr.* to become rich.

enriscado, da. I. *a.* mountainous, craggy; full of cliffs. **II.** *pp.* of ENRISCAR.

enriscamiento, *m.* raising; taking refuge among rocks.

enriscar. I. *va.* to lift, to raise. **II.** *vr.* to take refuge among rocks.

enristrar, *va.* to couch (the lance); to string (onions, etc.); to go direct to (a place); to overcome (a difficulty).

enristre, *m.* act of couching a lance.

enrocar, *va.* at chess, to castle (the king); to place (flax or wool) on the distaff.

enrodelado, da, *a.* armed with a shield.

enrodrigonar, *va.* to prop or train with stakes.

enrojar, enrojecer. I. *va.* (*ind.* ENROJEZCO: *subj.* ENROJEZCA) to redden; to make red-hot; to put to the blush. **II.** *vr.* to blush; turn red.

enrollar, *va.* to roll, coil, wind, wrap.

enromar, *va.* to blunt, dull.

enrona, *f.* rubbish, refuse, débris.

enronar, *va.* to throw rubbish in (a place).

enronquecer. I. *va.* (*ind.* ENRONQUEZCO: *subj.* ENRONQUEZCA) to make hoarse. **II.** *vn. & vr.* to become hoarse.

enronquecimiento, *m.* hoarseness.

enroñar, *va.* to fill with scabs or scurf.

enroscadamente, *adv.* curlingly.

enroscadura, *f.* act of twisting; convolution, sinuosity, twist, curlicue.

enroscar. I. *va.* (*pret.* ENROSQUÉ: *subj.* ENROSQUE) to twine, to twist. **II.** *vr.* to curl or twist itself; to coil.

enrubiador, ra, *a.* that turns the hair blond.

enrubiar, *va.* to dye (the hair) blond, bleach.

enrubio, *m.* dyeing blond; the dye used.

enrudecer. I. *va.* (*ind.* ENRUDEZCO: *subj.* ENRUDEZCA) to make dull. **II.** *vr.* to become dull.

enruinecer, *vn. & vr.* to become vile.

ensabanar, *va.* to wrap up in sheets.

ensacador, ra, *n.* sacker, bagger.

ensacar, *va.* (*for mut. v.* SACAR) to sack, bag.

ensaimada, *f.* light coffee cake.

ensalada, *f.* salad; hodge podge, medley.

ensaladera, *f.* salad dish or bowl.

ensaladilla, *f.* assortment of dry sweetmeats; jewel made up of different precious stones.

ensalmador, ra, *n.* bonesetter; quack.

ensalmar, *va.* to set (bones); to enchant; to cure by spells.

ensalmo, *m.* enchantment, spell, charm.—**como por e.,** or **por e.,** as if miraculously, suddenly and unexpectedly.

ensalobrarse, *vr.* to become salty.

ensalzador, ra, *n.* exalter, praiser, extoller.

ensalzamiento, *m.* exaltation, praise.

ensalzar, *va.* (*pret.* ENSALCÉ: *subj.* ENSALCE) to extol, exalt, praise.

ensamblador, *m.* joiner.

ensambladura, *f.* joinery; act of joining; joint.

ensamblaje, *m.* joining, coupling.

ensamblar, *va.* to join, couple; connect.

ensamble, *m.* = ENSAMBLAJE.

ensancha, *f.* extension, enlargement.

ensanchador, ra. I. *a.* stretching, expanding. **II.** *m.* stretcher, expander, reamer; glove stretcher.

ensanchamiento, *m.* widening, enlargement, dilation, expansion, stretch.

ensanchar. I. *va.* to widen, extend, enlarge; to stretch.—**e. el corazón,** to cheer up. **II.** *vr.* to assume an air of importance; to expand, enlarge.

ensanche, *m.* dilatation, enlargement, widening, extension, expansion, stretch; material turned in in seams of garments.

ensandecer, *vr.* to become stupid; to turn mad.

ensangrentamiento, *m.* covering with blood.

ensangrentar. I. *va. & vr.* (*ind.* ENSANGRIENTO: *subj.* ENSANGRIENTE) to stain with blood. **II.** *vr.* to become heated or fiery; to cover one's self with blood.

ensañamiento, *m.* ferocity, cruelty.

ensañar. I. *va.* to irritate, enrage. **II.** *vr.* to gloat; to vent one's fury; to be merciless.

ensarnecerse, *vr.* to get the itch.

ensartar, *va.* to string (as beads); to thread; to link; to tell disconnectedly, to rattle off.

ensay, *m.* assay, trial, proof.

ensayador, ra, *n.* assayer; rehearser.

ensayar. I. *va.* to try, practise, rehearse; to test; to assay. **II.** *vr.* to exercise one's self, to train, to practise.

ensaye, *m.* assay, test (of metals).

ensayista, *n.* essayist, essay writer; (Ch.) assayer.

ensayo, *m.* test; essay; trial, examination, experiment; rehearsal; exercise, preparatory practice; (com.) sample, test, trial.

ensebar, *va.* to grease, tallow.

enselvado, da, *pp. & a.* wooded.

enselvar. I. *va.* to place in a wood. **II.** *vr.* to hide in, or retire to, the woods; to become wooded.

ensenada, *f.* cove, inlet, small bay.

ensenado, da. I. *a.* having the form of a cove or inlet. **II.** *pp.* of ENSENAR.

ensenar. I. *va.* to put in one's bosom. **II.** *vr.* (naut.) to embay.

enseña, *f.* standard, colors, ensign.

enseñable, *a.* teachable.

enseñado, da. I. *pp.* of ENSEÑAR. **II.** *a.* accustomed; trained.

enseñador, ra, *n.* teacher, instructor.

enseñamiento, *m.*, **enseñanza,** *f.* teaching; instruction, education.

enseñar. I. *va.* to teach; to train; to show, point out. **II.** *vr.* to school one's self; to become accustomed, inured.

enseño, *m.* (coll.) education.

enseñoreador, *m.* one who domineers.

enseñorear. I. *va.* to lord, to domineer. **II.** *vr.* to possess one's self (of a thing).

enserar, *va.* to cover with matting.

enseres, *m. pl.* chattels; fixtures, accessories; implements; household goods.

enseriarse, *vr.* (Am.) to become serious.

ensiforme, *a.* ensiform, sword-shaped.

ensilaje, *m.* ensilage.—**ensilar,** *va.* to ensilage.

ensillado, da. I. *a.* saddle-backed (horses). **II.** *pp.* of ENSILLAR.

ensilladura, *f.* part of a horse on which the saddle is placed.

ensillar, *va.* to saddle.

ensimismarse, *vr.* to become absorbed in thought.

ensoberbecer. I. *va.* (*ind.* ENSOBERBEZCO: *subj.* ENSOBERBEZCA) to make proud. **II.** *vr.* to become proud and haughty; to become boisterous (s. o. the elements).

ensoberbecimiento, *m.* excessive pride.

ensogar, *va.* to fasten with a rope.

ensolerar, *va.* to fix stools to (beehives).

ensolver, *va.* (*pp.* ENSUELTO: *ind.* ENSUELVO: *subj.* ENSUELVA) to inclose, include; to condense, abridge; (med.) to resolve.

ensopar, *va.* to make sops of; to steep, soak; to drench.

ensordecedor, ra, *a.* deafening.

ensordecer. I. *va.* (*ind.* ENSORDEZCO: *subj.* ENSORDEZCA) to deafen. **II.** *vn. & vr.* to become deaf; to become silent.

ensordecimiento, *m.* deafness.

ensortijamiento, *m.* curling, crimping, crisping; ringlet, curlicue, kink.

ensortijar, *va. & vr.* to curl, to form ringlets; to kink; to put on rings.

ensotarse, *vr.* to go into a thicket.

ensuciador, ra, *n.* & *a.* stainer (-ing), soiler (-ing).

ensuciamiento, *m.* staining, soiling, polluting.

ensuciar. **I.** *va.* to stain, soil, smear; to sully, foul, defile, pollute. **II.** *vr.* to soil one's bed, clothes, etc.; (coll.) to be dishonest; to lower one's self.

ensueño, *m.* dream; illusion, fantasy.

entablación, *f.* act of flooring or boarding up; register in churches.

entablado, da. **I.** *pp.* of ENTABLAR. **II.** *m.* boarded or parqueted floor.

entabladura, *f.* act of flooring or boarding up; planking, timbering.

entablamento, *m.* (arch.) entablature.

entablar. **I.** *va.* to cover with boards; to board up; to plank; to initiate, start, begin (as a negotiation); to bring (a suit or action); to place (the men) on a chessboard; (surg.) to splint. **II.** *vr.* to settle (as the wind); to establish one's self.

entable, *m.* position of men on a chessboard; position, employment; business, business position or circumstance.

entablillar, *va.* (surg.) to splint.

entalamadura, *f.* awning of a cart, etc.

entalamar, *va.* to cover with an awning.

entalegar, *va.* (com.) to put in a bag.

entalingar, *va.* (naut.) to clinch (the cable).

entallable, *a.* capable of being carved.

entallador, *m.* sculptor, cutter in wood or stone; engraver; carver.

entalladura, *f.*, entallamiento, *m.* sculpture, carving; (carp.) mortise, groove, notch.

entallar. **I.** *va.* to notch; to make a cut in, to sculpture, to carve; to engrave. **II.** *vn.* to fit to the body (as a waist).

entallecer, *vn.* (agr.) to shoot, to sprout.

entapizar, *va.* to hang tapestry on.

entarascar, *va.* (coll.) to overdress.

entarimado, da. **I.** *pp.* of ENTARIMAR. **II.** *m.* parquetry, inlaid floor.

entarimar, *va.* to floor with boards.

entarquinamiento, *m.* fertilizing with slime.

entarquinar, *va.* to manure with slime; to bemire; to reclaim (swamp lands).

éntasis, *m.* (arch.) entasis.

ente, *m.* entity, being; (coll.) guy.

entecado, da; enteco, ca, *a.* sickly, weak, thin.

entejar, *va.* to tile.

entelequia, *f.* (phil.) entelechy.

entelerido, da, *a.* numb or shivering with cold; seized with fright; (Am.) sick-looking, thin, frail.

entena, *f.* (naut.) lateen yard.

entenado, da, *n.* stepson (-daughter).

entenallas, *f. pl.* (mech.) pincers; handvise.

entendederas, *f. pl.* (coll.) understanding, brain, noddle.

entendedor, ra, *n.* one who understands.

entender. **I.** *va.* & *vn.* (*ind.* ENTIENDO: *subj.* ENTIENDA) to understand.—e. de, to be familiar with, to know.—e. en, to be in charge of, to deal with, attend to; to have authority to pass on or enquire into. **II.** *vr.* to be understood; to be meant.—e. con, to belong with, to be included in; to have to do with; to deal with. **III.** *m.* understanding, opinion.—a mi e., según mi e., in my opinion, according to my understanding (of the matter).

entendidamente, *adv.* knowingly.

entendido, da, *a.* able; posted; prudent.—darse por e., to take notice, to pay attention.—no darse por e., not to take notice, to ignore.

entendimiento, *m.* intellect, mind, understanding; comprehension.

entenebrecer, *va.* to obscure, darken.

enterado, da, *a.* & *pp.* of ENTERAR; informed, posted.

enteramente, *adv.* entirely, fully; quite.

enterar, *va.* to inform, report, acquaint, advise.

entereza, *f.* entirety, completeness; integrity, uprightness; perfection; fortitude, firmness; presence of mind.—e. virginal, virginity.

entérico, ca, *a.* (med.) enteric.

enterísimo, ma, *a.* most complete.

enteritis, *f.* (med.) enteritis.

enterizo, za, *a.* of, or in, one piece; whole.

enternecedor, ra, *a.* pitiful, touching.

enternecer. **I.** *va.* (*ind.* ENTERNEZCO: *subj.* ENTERNEZCA) to soften; to touch, move to pity. **II.** *vr.* to be moved to pity, to be affected.

enternecidamente, *adv.* compassionately.

enternecimiento, *m.* compassion, pity.

entero, ra. **I.** *a.* entire, whole; sound, perfect; honest, upright; pure, uncorrupted; strong, robust, vigorous; informed, instructed; uncastrated; strong, thick (dry goods); (arith.) whole, integral.—por e., entirely, fully. **II.** *m.* (arith.) integer.—los enteros, (arith.) the integral part (of a decimal).

enterocele, *m.* (med.) enterocele, intestinal hernial tumor.

enterocolitis, *f.* (med.) enterocolitis.

enterorragia, *f.* (med.) enterorrhagia, intestinal hemorrhage.

enterotomía, *f.* (surg.) enterotomy, intestinal incision.

enterrador, *m.* gravedigger; sexton.

enterramiento, *m.* interment, burial, funeral.

enterrar, *va.* (*ind.* ENTIERRO: *subj.* ENTIERRE) to inter, bury; to survive.

enterronar, *va.* to cover with clods.

entesamiento, *m.* stretching, making taut.

entesar, *va.* to stretch, make taut.

entestado, da, *a.* obstinate, stubborn.

entibador, *m.* one who shores up mines.

entibar. **I.** *vn.* to rest, to lean upon. **II.** *va.* to prop, to shore up.

entibiadero, *m.* cooling room or bath.

entibiar. **I.** *va.* to make lukewarm; to cool; to temper, moderate. **II.** *vr.* to cool down; to slacken.

entibo, *m.* stay, prop; foundation.

entidad, *f.* entity; value, consequence, moment, importance.

entiendo, entienda. *V.* ENTENDER.

entierro, *m.* burial, interment, funeral; grave.

entierro, entierre. *V.* ENTERRAR.

entigrecerse, *vr.* (coll.) to become furious as a tiger.

entimema, *f.* (log.) enthymeme.

entinar, *va.* to put into the dyeing vat.

entintar, *va.* to ink, ink in (a drawing); to stain with ink; to tinge or dye.

entiznar, *va.* to stain; to revile, defame.

entoldado, *pp.* & *m.* tent or group of tents; covering with tents or awnings.

entoldamiento, *m.* covering with tents or with awnings.

entoldar. **I.** *va.* to cover with an awning; to adorn with hangings. **II.** *vr.* to dress gorgeously; to swell with pride; to become cloudy.

entomizar, *va.* to tie bass cords around (posts or laths), that the plaster may stick.

entomología, *f.* entomology.

entomológicamente, *adv.* entomologically.

entomológico, ca, *a.* entomological.

entomólogo, *m.* entomologist.

entonación, *f.* modulation; intonation; blowing the bellows of an organ.

entonadera, *f.* blow lever of an organ.

entonado, *m.* (phot.) process of toning.

entonado, da, *a.* (fig.) haughty, stuck up.

entonador, ra. **I.** *n.* one who sings in tune; (phot.) one that tones. **II.** *m.* organ blower.

entonamiento, *m.* intonation.

entonar. **I.** *va.* to modulate, intonate; to sing in tune; (art) to harmonize (colors); (phot.) to tone (prints); to blow (the bellows of an organ); (med.) to tone up. **II.** *vr.* to put on grand airs.

entonatorio, *m.* book of sacred music.

entonces. **I.** *adv.* then. **II.** *m.* time.

entonelar, *va.* to put in casks or barrels.

entono, *m.* act of intoning; arrogance, haughtiness, airs.

For pronunciation, see the rules at the beginning of the book.

entontecer. I. *va.* (*ind.* ENTONTEZCO: *subj.* ENTONTEZCA) to mope, make foolish; to confuse. **II.** *vn.* & *vr.* to become foolish.

entontecimiento, *m.* act of becoming foolish; state of foolishness.

entorchado, *m.* bullion fringe; bullion embroidery on the uniform of generals; (mus.) bass strings.

entorchar, *va.* to make a torch by twisting (candles); (mus.) to cover with wire.

entorilar, *va.* to stall (the bull).

entornar, *va.* to half-close; to set ajar.

entornillar, *va.* to form a screw or spiral of, to thread.

entorpecer, *va.* (*ind.* ENTORPEZCO: *subj.* ENTORPEZCA) to benumb; to stupefy; to clog, obstruct, delay.

entorpecimiento, *m.* torpor, numbness, stupefaction; dulness, stupidity; obstruction, delay.

entortadura, *f.* crookedness.

entortar, *va.* to bend; to make crooked; to make blind of one eye.

entosigar, *va.* to poison.

entozoario, *m.* entozoan.

entrada, *f.* entrance, door, gate; admission; entry; arrival; number of people in a theater, (*entrada llena,* full house); beginning (of a book, speech, etc.); familiar access, intimacy; good hand at cards; entrée (course at dinner); commencement (of a season, etc.); (com.) entry (in a book); cash receipts.—*pl.* temples (of the head).—**entradas y salidas,** collusion.

entrado, da, *pp.* of ENTRAR.—**e. en años,** advanced in years.

entrador, ra, *a.* (Am.) energetic, hustling; (Ch.) intruding, intrusive, fond of butting in.

entramado, *m.* (carp.) framework, studwork, baywork.

entramar, *va.* (carp.) to provide with studwork or framework.

entrambos, bas, *a.* & *pron. pl.* both.

entrampar. I. *va.* to entrap, insnare; to trick, deceive; to entangle; to encumber. **II.** *vr.* (coll.) to become indebted; to be involved in difficulties.

entrante, *a.* entering; coming, next (*el mes entrante,* next month).

entraña, *f.* entrail.—*pl.* entrails, bowels; humaneness, kindness; heart (fig.); affection; disposition; idiosyncrasy; the inmost recess of anything.

entrañable, *a.* most affectionate; deep, profound (affection).

entrañablemente, *adv.* dearly; deeply.

entrañar. I. *va.* to penetrate to the core; to contain, involve, carry within. **II.** *vr.* to contract intimacy and familiarity.

entrapada, *f.* coarse crimson cloth.

entrapajar, *va.* to bandage with rags.

entrapar. I. *va.* to powder (the hair) for a dry shampoo; (agr.) to manure with rags. **II.** *vr.* to become as dirty as a rag.

entrar. I. *vn.* (w. **a, en, por**) (the English equivalent is often transitive) to go in, come in, enter; to go (into); to flow (into); to attack, fight; to be admitted or have free entrance (to); to join; to begin; to be one of, be counted with; to be believable or understandable (to one); to be taken with (fear, etc.); to enter or go into (an agreement, etc.); to attack; to influence, convince. **II.** *va.* to introduce, put in; to enter, take by force. **III.** *vr.* to enter; to squeeze or sneak in; to break in.

entre, *prep.* between, among, amongst, amidst; within.—**e. manos,** in hand.—**e. mí,** within myself.—**e. tanto,** in the meantime; meanwhile.

entreabierto, ta. I. *pp. irr.* of ENTREABRIR. **II.** *a.* half-opened, ajar.

entreabrir, *va.* (*pp.* ENTREABIERTO) to half-open, to set ajar.

entreacto, *m.* intermission; small cigar.

entreancho, cha, *a.* neither wide nor narrow.

entrecalle, *m.* (arch.) clear between two consecutive moldings.

entrecanal, *f.* (arch.) fillet between flutes.

entrecano, na, *a.* grayish (hair or beard).

entrecasco, *m.* = ENTRECORTEZA.

entrecava, *f.* very shallow digging.

entrecavar, *va.* to dig shallow.

entrecejo, *m.* space between eyebrows; frowning.

entrecerca, *f.* space between inclosures.

entreclaro, ra, *a.* slightly clear.

entrecogedura, *f.* act of catching.

entrecoger, *va.* (*for mut. v.* COGER) to catch; to intercept; to compel by arguments or threats.

entrecoro, *m.* chancel.

entrecortado, da, *a.* confused, hesitating.

entrecortadura, *f.* cut that does not sever.

entrecortar, *va.* to cut without severing.

entrecorteza, *f.* imperfection in timbers.

entrecriarse, *vr.* to grow among other plants.

entrecruzar, *va.* (*subj.* ENTRECRUCE) to intercross; interlace, interweave.

entrecubiertas, *f. pl.* (naut.) between decks.

entrecuesto, *m.* backbone.

entrechocarse, *vr.* to collide, impinge on each other.

entredicho, *m.* interdiction, prohibition.

entredoble, *a.* of medium thickness.

entredós, *m.* insertion; (print.) long primer.

entrefino, na, *a.* middling fine.

entrega, *f.* delivery, conveyance; fascicle of a publication; surrender.

entregadero, ra, *a.* (com.) deliverable.

entregador, ra, *n.* deliverer; executor.

entregamiento, *m.* delivery.

entregar. I. *va.* (*pret.* ENTREGUÉ: *subj.* ENTREGUE) to deliver; to give up, surrender; (com.) to transfer, to pay; to insert, introduce, embed.—**a e.,** (com.) to be supplied or delivered. **II.** *vr.* to deliver one's self up, to surrender, submit.—**e. a,** to abandon or devote one's self to.—**e. de,** to receive, to take charge or possession of.

entrejuntar, *va.* (carp.) to join (the panels of a door) to the frame.

entrelazar, *va.* (*for mut. v.* LAZAR) to interlace, interweave, braid, entwine.

entreliño, *m.* (agr.) space between rows of trees.

entrelistado, da, *a.* striped or variegated.

entrelucir, *vn.* & *vr.* (*for irr. v.* LUCIR) to show through.

entremedias, *adv.* in the meantime; halfway.—**e. de,** between; among.

entremés, *m.* interlude, farce; side dish.

entremesear, *va.* to act in a farce; to throw into one's talk, bring up.

entremesista, *a.* writer or player of farces.

entremeter. I. *va.* to place between; to insert **II.** *vr.* to intrude, obtrude; intermeddle; meddle; interpose officiously.

entremetido, da. I. *pp.* of ENTREMETER. **II.** *n.* meddler, intruder, intermeddler; busybody; go-between. **III.** *a.* meddlesome; officious.

entremetimiento, *m.* intrusion, intermeddling, meddlesomeness; interposition.

entremezcladura, *f.* intermixture.

entremezclar, *va.* to intermingle, intermix.

entremiche, *m.* (naut.) capstan, chock.

entremorir, *vn.* to flicker (as a flame).

entrenador, ra, *n.* trainer.

entrenar, *va.* & *vn.* to train.

entrencar, *va.* to put rods in (a beehive).

entrenzar, *va.* (*v.* TRENZAR) to plait (the hair).

entreoir, *va.* (*for irr. v.* OIR) to hear indistinctly.

entreordinario, ria, *a.* middling.

entrepalmadura, *f.* (vet.) a hoof disease.

entrepanes, *m. pl.* pieces of unsown ground.

entrepañado, da, *a.* composed of panels.

entrepaño, *m.* (arch.) intercolumniation: pier; (carp.) panel; shelf.

entreparecerse, *vr.* to show through.

entrepaso, *m.* rack pace (of horses).

entrepechuga, *f.* flesh within the wishbone.

entrepeines, *m. pl.* comb wool.

entrepelado, da, *a.* pied; variegated.

entrepelar, *va.* to variegate (hair).

entrepernar, *vn.* to put the legs between those of others.

entrepiernas, *f. pl.* inner surface of the thighs; pieces put into the fork of breeches.

entrepiso, *m.* (min.) space between galleries.

entreplano, (aer.) gap.

entrepretado, da, *a.* (vet.) weak in the breast or shoulder.

entrepuentes, *m. pl.* (naut.) between decks.

entrepunzadura, *f.* pricking pain.

entrepunzar, *va.* to prick slightly.

entrerrenglón, *m.* interline.

entrerrenglonadura, *f.* interlineation.

entrerrenglonar, *va.* to interline.

entresaca, entresacadura, *f.* thinning of wood; pruning of branches; sorting; picking out.

entresacar, *va.* (*for mut. v.* SACAR) to pick out or choose; to sift, cull; to thin out.

entresijo, *m.* mesentery; anything hidden.

entresuelo, *m.* entresol, mezzanine.

entresurco, *m.* space between furrows.

entretalla, entretalladura, *f.* bas-relief.

entretallar, *va.* to carve in bas-relief; to engrave; to make openwork on; to intercept.

entretanto, *adv.* meanwhile.

entretejedor, ra, *a.* interweaver.

entretejedura, *f.* intertexture, interweaving.

entretejer, *va.* to interweave, intermix, intertwine; to tissue, to variegate; to insert, mix, mingle.

entretejimiento, *m.* intertexture, interweaving; variegation.

entretela, *f.* (sew.) interlining.

entretelar, *va.* to insert an interlining in.

entretenedor, ra, *n. & a.* entertainer (-ing).

entretener. I. *va.* (*for irr. v.* TENER) to amuse, to entertain; to keep in hope or expectation; to allay (pain), to make less troublesome; to delay, put off, postpone. II. *vr.* to amuse one's self.

entretenida.—dar con la e., or dar la e., to give excuses (to), dismiss with empty talk and vain promises or evasions.

entretenido, da. I. *a. & pp.* of ENTRETENER; entertaining, pleasant, amusing. II. *m.* aspirant to an office.

entretenimiento, *m.* amusement, entertainment, sport, pastime.

entretiempo, *m.* spring or autumn.

entreuntar, *va.* to anoint or paint slightly.

entrevenarse, *vr.* to diffuse through the veins.

entreventana, *f.* (arch.) window pier.

entrever, *va.* to see imperfectly.

entreverado, da. I. *pp.* of ENTREVERAR. II. *a.* intermingled, intermixed.

entreverar, *va.* to intermix, intermingle.

entrevía, *f.* (r. w.) gauge or gage.

entrevista, *f.* interview, meeting, conference.

entrevistar, *va.* to interview.

entripado, da. I. *a.* contained in the intestines; not yet cleaned (s. o. a dead animal). II. *m.* (coll.) anger or displeasure.

entristecedor, ra, *a.* sad, saddening.

entristecer. I. *va.* (ind. ENTRISTEZCO: *subj.* ENTRISTEZCA) to sadden, grieve. II. *vr.* to grieve, to become sad.

entristecimiento, *m.* sadness; fretting.

entrojar, *va.* to garner (grain).

entrometer, *va. & vr.* = ENTREMETER.

entrometimiento, *m.* intermeddling, intrusion.

entronar, *va.* to enthrone.

entroncar, *vn.* to be descended from the same stock; to have relationship; be connected (u. also as *vr.*); (r. w.) to make a junction (u. also as *vr.*).

entronerar, *va.* to pocket (a ball).

entronización, *f.* enthronement.

entronizar. I. *va.* (*pret.* ENTRONICÉ: *subj.* ENTRONICE) to enthrone; to exalt. II. *vr.* to be elated or puffed up with pride.

entronque, *m.* cognation; connection; relationship; railway junction.

entropía, *f.* (phys.) entropy.

entropión, *m.* (med.) entropion, inversion of the eyelids.

entruchada, *f.*, entruchado, *m.* (coll.) plot, intrigue.

entruchar, *va.* (coll.) to decoy, lure, entice.

entruchón, na, *n.* decoyer, plotter.

entrujar, *va.* to store up; (coll.) to reimburse.

entuerto, *m.* wrong, injustice.—*pl.* afterpains.

entullecer. I. *va.* (ind. ENTULLEZCO: *subj.* ENTULLEZCA) to stop, check, obstruct. II. *vn.* to be crippled or maimed.

entumecer. I. *va.* (ind. ENTUMEZCO: *subj.* ENTUMEZCA) to benumb. II. *vr.* to become numb or asleep (s. o. limbs); to swell, to surge.

entumecimiento, *m.* torpor, deadness; numbness; swelling.

entumirse, *vr.* to become numb.

entunicar, *va.* to plaster for fresco painting.

entupir, *va.* to obstruct, block up; to compress.

enturbiar. I. *va.* to muddle, to make muddy or turbid; to obscure, confuse. II. *vr.* to become muddy; to get disordered or deranged.

entusiasmado, da, *a. & pp.* of ENTUSIASMAR; enthusiastic.—entusiasmar. I. *va.* to enrapture, make enthusiastic. II. *vr.* to become enthusiastic. —entusiasmo, *m.* enthusiasm.—entusiasta, *n.* enthusiast.—entusiástico, ca, *a.* enthusiastic.

énula campana, *f.* (bot.) elecampane.

enumerable, *a.* numerable.—enumeración, *f.* enumeration.—enumerar, *va.* to enumerate.

enumerativo, va, *a.* enumerative.

enunciación, *f.*, enunciado, *m.* statement.

enunciar, *va.* to state.

enunciativo, va, *a.* enunciative.

envainador, ra, *a.* sheathing.

envainar, *va.* to sheathe (as a sword).

envalentonamiento, *m.* encouragement.

envalentonar. I. *va.* to encourage, to inspirit; to make bold. II. *vr.* to become courageous.

envalijar, *va.* to pack or put in a valise.

envanecer. I. *va.* (ind. ENVANEZCO: *subj.* ENVANEZCA) to make vain. II. *vr.* to become vain.

envanecimiento, *m.* conceit.

envarado, da, *a. & pp.* stiff, benumbed.

envaramiento, *m.* stiffness, numbness.

envarar, *va.* to benumb, stiffen.

envasador, *m.* filler, packer; funnel.

envasar, *va.* to tun, cask, barrel; to bottle; to put into any container; to drink (liquor) to excess; to sack (grain); to run through the body with.

envase, *m.* filling, bottling; container; packing.

envedijarse, *vr.* to get entangled; (coll.) to wrangle.

envejecer. I. *va.* (ind. ENVEJEZCO: *subj.* ENVEJEZCA) to make old; to make look old. II. *vn.* to become old. III. *vr.* to become old or old-fashioned; to hold out a long time.

envejecido, da, *a. & pp.* grown old, old-looking; accustomed, habituated.

envejecimiento, *m.* oldness, age; aging.

envenenador, ra, *n. & a.* poisoner (-ing).

envenenamiento, *m.* poisoning.

envenenar, *va.* to envenom, to poison.

enverar, *vn.* to look ripe.

enverdecer, *vn. & vr.* to become green.

envergadura, *f.* breadth of the sails; breadth of a spread bird, from tip to tip; (aer.) span.

envergar, *va.* (naut.) to bend (the sails).

envergues, *m. pl.* (naut.) ropebands.

envero, *m.* color of ripe grape.

envés, *m.* wrong or back side; back, shoulders.

envesado, *m.* fleshy part of hides.

envestidura, *f.* investiture.

envestir, *va.* to invest.

enviada, *f.* sending, shipment.

enviadizo, za, *a.* missive.

enviado, *m.* envoy; messenger.—e. extraordinario, envoy extraordinary.

enviador, ra, *n. & a.* sender (-ing).

enviajado, da, *a.* (arch.) oblique, sloped.

enviar, *va.* to send; to ship; dispatch.—**e. a uno a pasear,** (coll.) to send one about his business; to give one his walking ticket.—**e. enhoramala,** (coll.) to send to the devil.

enviciar. **I.** *va.* to corrupt, teach bad habits to.—**II.** *vn.* to have luxurious foliage and little fruit. **III.** *vr.* (w. **en**) to acquire bad habits; to acquire the habit (of); to take to (drinking, etc.).

envidador, *m.* challenger at cards.
envidar, *va.* to stake a sum against.
envidia, *f.* envy.—**envidiable,** *a.* enviable.—**envidiar,** *vn.* to envy.—**envidiosamente,** *adv.* enviously.—**envidioso, sa,** *a.* envious.

envilecedor, ra, *a.* degrading, debasing.
envilecer. **I.** *va.* (*ind.* ENVILEZCO: *subj.* ENVILEZCA) to vilify, debase. **II.** *vr.* to degrade one's self.
envilecimiento, *m.* vilification, debasement.
envinagrar, *va.* to put vinegar into.
envinar, *va.* to put wine to (water).
envío, *m.* (com.) remittance; consignment of goods, shipment.
envión, *m.* push, shove.
envirotado, da, *a.* airy, stuck up.
enviscamiento, *m.* daubing with birdlime.
enviscar. **I.** *va.* (*pret.* ENVISQUÉ: *subj.* ENVISQUE) to daub with birdlime; to irritate, to anger. **II.** *vr.* to be glued with birdlime.
envite, *m.* stake at cards; invitation; offer; push, **al primer e.,** at once, right off; at the start.
enviudar, *vn.* to become a widower or widow.
envoltorio, *m.* bundle; defective woof.
envoltura, *f.* swaddling clothes; cover, wrapper, envelope, sheath; covering, wrapping.
envolvedero, envolvedor, *m.* wrapper, wrapping, envelope, cover.
envolver. **I.** *va.* (*pp.* ENVUELTO: *ind.* ENVUELVO: *subj.* ENVUELVA) to wrap, to bundle, make up into a package; to swaddle; to floor (an opponent); to imply, mean; to contain, carry with it; (mil.) to surround. **II.** *vr.* to be implicated; to be unlawfully connected (with women); to be mixed with a crowd.
envolvimiento, *m.* envelopment; wrapping.
envuelto, ta, *pp. irr.* of ENVOLVER.
enyerbar. **I.** *va.* (Cuba) to sod. **II.** *vr.* to become covered or overgrown with grass.
enyesado, *m.* plasterwork; plaster; plastering.
enyesadura, *f.* plastering.
enyesar, *va.* to plaster; to chalk; to whitewash.
enyugar, *va.* to yoke.
enzainarse, *vr.* to look askance; (coll.) to become insidious.
enzamarrado, da, *a.* having on a shepherd's jacket of undressed sheepskin; wearing chaps.
enzarzar. **I.** *va.* to throw among brambles; to sow discord among or between; to put hurdles for (silkworms). **II.** *vr.* to be entangled among brambles; to become involved in difficulties; to squabble, to wrangle.
enzootia, *f.* epizootic.
enzunchar, *va.* to bind with iron bands or hoops.
enzurdecer, *vn. & vr.* to become left-handed.
enzurronar, *va.* to bag; (coll.) to inclose.
eñe, *f.* name of the letter ñ.
eoceno, na, *n. & a.* Eocene.
eólico, ca; eolio, lia, *a.* Æolian, Æolic.
epacta, *f.* (ast.) epact.
epactilla, *f.* annual devotional calendar.
epéndimo, *m.* (anat.) ependyma.
epéntesis, *f.* (gram.) epenthesis.
eperlano, *m.* (icht.) smelt, a small fish.
épica, *f.* epic poetry.—**épicamente,** *adv.* epically.
epicarpo, *m.* (bot.) epicarp.
epicedio, *m.* epicedium, elegy.
epiceno, na, *a.* (gram.) epicene.
epicentro, *m.* (geol.) epicentre, portion of the earth overlying a seismic focus.
epicíclico, ca, *a.* epicyclic.
epiciclo, *m.* epicycle.
epicicloide, *f.* epicycloid.

épico, ca, *a.* (poet.) epic, heroic.
epicráneo, *m.* (anat.) epicranium.
epicureísmo, *m.* epicurism; Epicureanism.
epicúreo, rea, *n. & a.* epicurean.
epidemia, *f.* (med.) epidemic.
epidemial; epidémico, ca, epidemic.
epidérmico, ca, *a.* epidermic.
epidermis, *f.* epidermis, scarfskin.
epidota, epidoto, *m.* (min.) epidote.
epifanía, *f.* Epiphany; twelfth night.
epifisis, *f.* (anat.) epiphysis.
epifito, ta. **I.** *a.* (bot.) epiphytic. **II.** *f.* (bot.) epiphyte.
epifonema, *f.* (rhet.) epiphonema.
epigástrico, rea, *a.* epigastric.
epigastrio, *m.* epigastrium.
epiglosis, *f.* (zool.) epiglottis; epipharynx (of insects).
epiglotis, *f.* epiglottis.
epígrafe, *m.* epigraph.—**epigrafía,** *f.* epigraphy.
epigráfico, ca, *a.* epigraphic.
epigrafista, *n.* epigrapher.
epigrama, *m.* epigram; witticism; inscription.
epigramatario, ria, *n.* epigrammatist; collection of epigrams.
epigramáticamente, *adv.* epigrammatically.
epigramático, ca, *a.* epigrammatic.
epigramatista, epigramista, *n.* epigrammatist.
epilepsia, *f.* (med.) epilepsy.
epiléptico, ca, *n. & a.* epileptic.
epileptiforme, *a.* epileptoid.
epilogación, *f.* = EPÍLOGO.
epilogal, *a.* epilogistic, compendious.
epilogar, *va.* (*pret.* EPILOGUÉ: *subj.* EPILOGUE) to epilogize, recapitulate, sum up.
epilogismo, *m.* (ast.) epilogism, computation.
epílogo, *m.* epilogue; summing up.
epinicio, *m.* epinicion, triumphal ode.
epiplón, epíploon, *m.* (anat.) omentum.
epiquerema, *m.* (log.) epicheirema.
epiqueya, *f.* mild and prudent interpretation of the law.
epirota, *n. & a.,* epirótico, ca, *a.* Epirote (from Epirus).
episcopado, *m.* episcopacy; episcopate; bishopric.
episcopal, *a.* episcopal; Episcopal.
episcopalismo, *m.* episcopalism; Episcopalianism.
episcopologio, *m.* chronological list of bishops.
episódico, ca, *a.* episodic, episodical.
episodio, *m.* episode; digression.
epispástico, ca, *a.* epispastic, blistering.
epistaxis, *f.* (med.) epistaxis, nosebleed.
epístola, *f.* epistle, letter; epistle, part of the mass.—**epistolar,** *a.* epistolary.
epistolario, *m.* epistolary; volume of letters.
epistolero, ra, *n.* epistler.
epístrofe, *f.* (rhet.) epistrophe.
epitafio, *m.* epitaph.
epitalámico, ca, *a.* epithalamic.
epitalamio, *m.* epithalamium, nuptial song.
epitasis, *f.* epitasis.
epitelial, *a.* epithelial.
epitelio, *m.* (naut.) epithelium.
epitelioma, *m.* (med.) epithelioma.
epitema, *m.* epithem.
epíteto, *m.* (gram.) epithet.
epitima, *f.* = EPITEMA.
epitimar, *va.* to apply an epithem to.
epitimo, *m.* (bot.) lesser dodder.
epitomadamente, *adv.* concisely.
epitomador, ra, *a.* epitomizer.—**epitomar,** *va.* to epitomize, abstract, summarize.—**epítome,** *m.* epitome, abstract, summary.
epizoario, a, *a.* (zool.) epizoic, epizoan.
epizootia, *f.* (vet.) epizooty, epidemic influenza.—**epizoótico, ca,** *a.* epizootic.
época, *f.* epoch, age, era; time.
epoda, *f.,* epodo, *m.* (poet.) epode.
epónimo, *m.* eponym.
epopeya, *f.* epopee, epic poem.

epsomita, *f.* Epsom salts.

epulón, *m.* epicure, great eater.

equiángulo, la, *a.* (geom.) equiangular.

equidad, *f.* equity, equitableness; impartiality, justice.

equidiferencia, *f.* (mat.) equidifference, arithmetical progression.

equidistancia, *f.* equidistance.—**equidistante,** *a.* equidistant.—**equidistar,** *vn.* to be equidistant.

equilátero, ra, *a.* (geom.) equilateral.

equilibrar, *va.* to equilibrate, balance; to counterpoise, counterbalance.

equilibre, *a.* balanced, equilibrious.

equilibrio, *m.* equilibrium, balance, equipoise.—**e. europeo,** European balance of power.

equilibrista, *m.* balancer, equilibrist.

equimosis, *m.* (med.) ecchymosis.

equino, na. I. *a.* equine. II. *m.* (zool.) echinus; (arch.) echinus.

equinoccial, *a.* equinoctial.

equinoccio, *m.* equinox.

equinococo, *m.* (med.) echinococcus.

equinodermo, ma. I. *n.* & *a.* (zool.) echinoderm. II. *m.* *pl.* Echinodermata.

equipaje, *m.* baggage or luggage; equipment; (naut.) crew; (mil.) baggage train.

equipar, *va.* to fit out, equip, furnish.

equiparación, *f.* comparison, collation.

equiparar, *va.* to compare, to match.

equipo, *m.* equipment; (mil.) fitting out; accoutrement, equipment, trappings.

equipolencia, *f.* (log.) equipollence.

equipolente, *a.* equivalent, equipollent.

equiponderante, *a.* equiponderant.

equiponderar, *vn.* to equiponderate.

equis, *f.* name of the letter *x*.

equisetáceo, a, *a.* (bot.) equisetaceous.

equitación, *f.* horsemanship, riding.

equitativamente, *adv.* equitably.

equitativo, va, *a.* equitable, fair, just.

equivalencia, *f.* compensation; equivalence.

equivalente, *a.* equivalent, tantamount; compensatory, compensative.

equivalentemente, *adv.* equivalently.

equivaler, *vn.* (for *irr. v.* VALER) to be equivalent.

equivocación, *f.* mistake, error; equivocation.

equivocadamente, *adv.* mistakenly, by mistake.

equivocado, da. I. *a.* mistaken. II. *pp.* of EQUIVOCAR.

equívocamente, *adv.* equivocally.

equivocar. I. *va.* (pret. EQUIVOQUÉ: subj. EQUIVOQUE) to mistake. II. *vr.* to be mistaken, to make a mistake.

equívoco, ca. I. *a.* equivocal, ambiguous. II. *m.* equivocation, quibble, pun.

equivoquista, *n.* dim. quibbler, punster.

era, *f.* era, age; thrashing floor; vegetable patch; garden bed.—**e. común, cristiana,** or **vulgar,** Christian era.

era, *verbal form.* V. SER.

eraje, *m.* virgin honey.

eral, *m.* two-year-old ox.

erar, *va.* to lay out (a garden).

erario, *m.* exchequer, public treasury.

erbio, *m.* (chem.) erbium.

ere, *f.* name of the letter *r*.

erección, *f.* erection, raising; erectness, elevation; foundation, establishment.

eréctil, *a.* erectile.—**erectilidad,** *f.* erectility.

erector, ra, *n.* erector, founder.

eremita, *m.* hermit, recluse.

eremítico, ca, *a.* hermitical, solitary.

eremitorio, *m.* place with one or more hermitages.

eretismo, *m.* (med.) erethism.

erg, *m.* (phys.) = ERGIO.

ergástula, *f.,* **ergástulo,** *m.* ergastulum.

ergio, *m.* (phys.) erg (a unit of energy).

ergotina, *f.* (med.) ergotin.

ergotismo, *m.* (med.) ergotism; sophistry.

ergotista, *m.* debater, sophist.

ergotizar, *vn.* to ergotize; to argue fallaciously.

erguimiento, *m.* straightening up.

erídano, *m.* (ast.) Eridanus.

erguir. I. *va.* (ind. IRGO or YERGO: pret. él IRGUIÓ: subj. IRGA or YERGA: gerund, IRGUIENDO) to erect, to set up straight. II. *vr.* to straighten up; to stand or sit erect; to swell with pride.

erial, eriazo, za. I. *a.* unplowed, untilled, uncultivated. II. *m.* unimproved land.

erica, *f.* (bot.) heath, heather.

ericáceo, cea, *a.* (bot.) ericaceous.

Erídano, *m.* (astr.) Eridanus.

erigir, *va.* (ind. ERIJO: subj. ERIJA) to erect, raise, build; to found, establish.

eringe, *f.* (bot.) field eringo.

erío, ría, *a.* untilled, uncultivated.

erisipela, *f.* (med.) erysipelas.—**erisipelar,** *va.* to cause erysipelas to.—**erisipelatoso, sa,** *a.* (med.) erysipelatous.

erístico, ca, *a.* eristic, disputatious.

eritema, *f.* (med.) erythema.

Eritreo, a, *a.* Erythræan (app. to the Red Sea).

eritrina, *f.* (chem.) erythrin.

eritrosina, *f.* (chem.) erythrosin.

eritroxíleo, lea. I. *a.* (bot.) erythroxylaceous. II. *f.* *pl.* Erythroxylaceæ.

erizado, da, *pp.* & *a.* covered with bristles.—**e. de.,** beset with (difficulties, etc.); covered with, abounding in; bristling with.

erizamiento, *m.* setting on end, as the hair; bristling up.

erizar. I. *va.* (pret. ERICÉ: subj. ERICE) to set on end, to bristle. II. *vr.* to bristle; to stand on end (s. o. the hair).

erizo, *m.* (zool.) hedgehog; sea-urchin; prickly husk of a chestnut, etc.; (mech.) urchin, carding roller; sprocket wheel, rag wheel, spartoothed wheel.

ermita, *f.* hermitage.—**ermitaño,** *m.* hermit.

ermitorio, *m.* = EREMITORIO.

ermunio, *a.* exempt from tribute and service.

erogación, *f.* expense.

erogar, *va.* (pret. EROGUÉ: subj. EROGUE) to lay out, spend.

erogatorio, *m.* pipe through which liquor is drawn.

erosión, *f.* erosion, wearing away.

erotema, *f.* (rhet.) interrogation.

eróticamente, *adv.* erotically.—**erótico, ca,** *a.* erotical, erotic.—**erotismo,** *m.* eroticism.

erotomanía, *f.* erotomania, love madness.

errabundo, da, *a.* wandering.

errada, *f.* miscue, in billiards.

erradamente, *adv.* erroneously, mistakenly.

erradicación, *f.* eradication.

erradicar, *va.* to eradicate.

erradizo, za, *a.* wandering to and fro.

errado, da. I. *a.* mistaken, in error; erroneous. II. *pp.* of ERRAR.

erraj, *m.* fine coal made from the stones of olives.

errante, *a.* errant; roving, wandering, nomadic.

errar. I. *va.* (ind. YERRO: subj. YERRE) to miss (the target, blow, etc.); to fail in one's duty to, to offend. II. *vn.* to wander, roam, to err. III. *vn.* & *vr.* to be mistaken, to commit an error.

errata, *f.* erratum, typographical error.—**erratas,** or **fe de erratas,** errata, list of errata.

errático, ca, *a.* wandering, vagabond; erratic.

errátil, *a.* (coll.) wavering, not firm or steady.

erre, *f.* name of the double letter *rr*, and of *r* when it has the same sound.—**e. que e.,** pertinaciously, obstinately.

erróneamente, *adv.* erroneously, mistakenly.

erróneo, nea, *a.* erroneous, mistaken.

erronía, *f.* opposition, dislike, grudge.

error, *m.* error, mistake.—**e. clásico, e. craso,** gross error.

erubescencia, *f.* erubescence, blush.

eructación, *f.* eructation, belching.

eructar, *vn.* to belch, eructate.

eructo, *m.* belching, eructation.

erudición, *f.* erudition, learning.

eruditamente, *adv.* learnedly.
erudito, ta. I. *a.* erudite, learned. **II.** *n.* erudite, person of great learning, scholar.
eruginoso, sa, *a.* rusty, musty.
erupción, *f.* eruption, bursting forth; (med.) eruption, rash.
eruptivo, va, *a.* eruptive.
erutación, *f.,* **erutar,** *vn.,* **eruto,** *m.* = ERUCTA-CIÓN, etc.
ervato, *m.* (bot.) sea sulphurwort.
ervilla, *f.* (bot.) bitter vetch-seed.
es, *irr. form of* SER.
esa, *a. & pron., f. form of* ESE. Sometimes used colloquially in the sense of "one," "that," "that thing," "that story," "that situation," etc.: *ésa es buena,* that is a good one, that is a strange thing; *ésa no la creo,* I don't believe that, I can't go that one; *no venga con ésa,* don't come with that stuff; you don't say! don't tell me that.
esbatimentar. I. *va.* (art) to delineate (a shadow). **II.** *vn.* to cast a shadow.
esbatimento, *m.* shade (in a picture).
esbeltez, esbelteza, *f.* tall and elegant stature.
esbelto, ta, *a.* tall, slender and well built.
esbirro, *m.* bailiff, apparitor; myrmidon.
esbozar, *va.* to s'ketch.
esbozo, *m.* sketch, outline; rough draught.
escabechar, *va.* to souse, pickle; (coll.) to stab and kill.
escabeche, *m.* souse, pickle; pickled fish.
escabel, *m.* footstool; small seat; bench.
escabiosa, *f.* (bot.) field scabious.
escabioso, sa, *a.* (med.) scabious.
escabro, *m.* scab, itch, or mange in sheep; roughness on the bark of trees.
escabrosamente, *adv.* roughly, ruggedly.
escabrosidad, *f.* inequality, unevenness, roughness; cragginess; hardness, asperity.
escabroso, sa, *a.* rough, uneven; craggy, rugged, clifted; rude, unpolished.
escabullimiento, *m.* evasion, slipping away.
escabullirse, *vr.* to escape, to evade; to slip or sneak away.
escacado, da, *a.* (her.) checkered.
escafandro, *m.* scaphander, diving dress.
escafilar, *va.* to trim (a brick or tile).
escafoides, *a.* (anat.) scaphoid (bone).
escala, *f.* ladder, stepladder; scale; graduated rule or instrument; seaport, stopping place; (mus.) scale; (mil.) military register.—**e. franca,** free port.—**a e. vista,** openly.—**hacer e. en,** to touch, or stop, at (a port).
escalada, *f.* (mil.) escalade, scalado.
escalado, da. I. *a.* cut open (fish) to be salted or cured. **II.** *pp. of* ESCALAR.
escalador, ra, *n. & a.* climber (-ing), scaler (-ing).
escalafón, *m.* army register.
escalamiento, *m.* (mil.) scaling.
escálamo, *m.* (naut.) thole, tholepin; rowlock.
escalar, *va.* (mil.) to scale; to enter surreptitiously.
escaldada, *f.* loose and lewd woman.
escaldado, da. I. *a.* cautious, suspicious, wary. **II.** *pp. of* ESCALDAR.
escaldar, *va.* to burn, scald; to make red-hot.
escaleno, *a.* (geom.) scalene.
escalentamiento, *m.* (vet.) inflammation of the feet.
escalera, *f.* staircase; stair; ladder; sloats of a cart.—**e. de caracol,** winding stair.—**e. de costado,** (naut.) quarter-deck ladder.—**e. de desahogo** = E. EXCUSADA.—**e. de mano,** ladder.—**e. de servicio,** service stairs.—**e. excusada,** or **falsa,** stairs leading to bedrooms or family apartments.—**e. real** = E. DE COSTADO.
escalereja, *f.* *dim.* small ladder; stepladder; (mech.) rack; drenching instrument.—**en e.,** in degrees; stepped.
escalerón, *m.* *aug.* large staircase.
escalerilla, *f.* = ESCALEREJA.
escaleta, *f.* frame for raising carriages.
escalfado, da, *pp. & a.* blistered; poached (eggs).

escalfador, *m.* barber's pan; water heater; chafing dish.
escalfar, *va.* to poach (eggs).
escalfarote, *m.* wide boot lined with hay.
escalfeta, *f.* small pan for live coals; chafing dish; dish warmer.
escalinata, *f.* (arch.) perron, high stoop.
escalio, *m.* land abandoned for tillage.
escalmo, *m.* barlock, rowlock.
escalo, *m.* breaking a way into or out of a place.
escalofriado, da, *a.* shivering, chilled.
escalofrío, *m.* chill.
escalón, *m.* step of a stair; stepping stone; rank, degree of dignity; (mil.) echelon.
escalonar, *va.* (mil.) to form in echelon; to step.
escaloña, *f.* (bot.) eschalot, shalot, scallion.
escalpar, *va.* to scalp.
escalpelo, *m.* (surg.) scalpel, dissecting knife.
escalplo, *m.* currier's or tanner's knife.
escama, *f.* fish scale; small scaly piece in ancient armors; scale (any scalelike formation or exfoliation); resentment, grudge.
escamada, *f.* embroidery in the shape of scales.
escamado, da. I. *a. & pp.* tutored by painful experience. **II.** *m.* work in the shape of scales.
escamadura, *f.* scaling (a fish); arousing suspicion.
escamar. I. *va.* to scale (fish); (coll.) to cause suspicion. **II.** *vn.* to embroider scale or shell fashion. **III.** *vr.* to be tutored or made wise by painful experience.
escamel, *m.* sword-maker's anvil.
escamochear, *vn.* to breed bees.
escamocho, *m.* remnants of a meal; (api.) after-swarm.
escamonda, *f.* (agr.) pruning.
escamondadura, *f.* pruned branches.
escamondar, *va.* to prune, lop; to trim.
escamondo, *m.* pruning or clearing of trees.
escamonea, *f.* (bot.) scammony.
escamoneado, da. I. *a.* relating to scammony. **II.** *pp. of* ESCAMONEARSE.
escamonearse, *vr.* (coll.) to be suspicious.
escamoso, sa, *a.* scaly, squamous.
escamotar, *va.* in jugglery, to palm; to rob by artful means, to play for a sucker.
escamoteador, ra, *n.* juggler, prestidigitator, conjurer; sharp, swindler.
escamotear, *va.* = ESCAMOTAR.
escamoteo, *m.* jugglery, sleight of hand; exploitation, getting money from others by artful means, swindling.
escampada, *f.* stampede.
escampado, da, *pp. & a.* open, clear.
escampar. I. *vn.* to stop raining; to clear up (s. o. the sky); to leave off working. **II.** *va.* to clear out.
escampavía, *f.* (naut.) tender; revenue cutter.
escampo, *m.* clearing out; clearing up, cessation of rain.
escamudo, da, *a.* full of scales.
escamujar, *va.* to prune.—**escamujo,** *m.* lopped-off olive branch; time of pruning olive trees.
escancia, *f.* pouring or serving wine.
escanciador, ra, *n.* cupbearer.
escanciar, *va.* to pour, serve, or drink (wine).
escanda, *f.* (bot.) spelt-wheat.
escandalar, *m.* (naut.) room for the compass.
escandalizador, ra, *n. & a.* scandalizer (-ing).
escandalizar. I. *va.* (*pret.* ESCANDALICÉ: *subj.* ESCANDALICE) to scandalize. **II.** *vr.* to be scandalized; to be irritated.
escandalizativo, va, *a.* scandalous.
escándalo, *m.* scandal; licentiousness; tumult, commotion; astonishment.
escandalosa, *f.* (naut.) gaff sail.
escandalosamente, *adv.* scandalously, shamefully.—**escandaloso, sa,** *a.* scandalous, shameful; turbulent.
escandallar, *va.* (naut.) to sound.
escandallo, *m.* (naut.) deep-sea lead; proof, trial, experiment.

escandia, *f.* (bot.) Cienfuegos wheat.

escandina, *f.* (min.) scandia, scandium oxide.

escandinavo, va, *n. & a.* Scandinavian.

escandio, *m.* (chem.) scandium, a rare metal.

escandir, *va.* (poet.) to scan.

escanilla, *f.* cradle.

escantillar, *va.* to gauge; to measure from a point or line; to measure off, lay off; to hew by patterns.

escantillón, *m.* pattern, templet; rule.

escaña, *f.* (bot.) St. Peter's corn.

escañero, *m.* seat keeper.

escaño, *m.* bench with a back; (naut.) sheer-rail.

escañuelo, *m.* footstool.

escapada, *f.,* **escapamiento,** *m.* escape, flight, escapade.

escapar. I. *va.* to drive (a horse) at great speed. **II.** *vn. & vr.* to escape, to flee; to run away; to make one's escape.—**e. en una tabla,** to have a narrow escape.

escaparate, *m.* press, glass case, cupboard, cabinet, wardrobe; show window.

escaparatico, *m. dim.* little cupboard, cabinet or wardrobe.

escapatoria, *f.* escape, flying, flight; excuse, evasion, subterfuge, loophole.

escape, *m.* escape, flight; subterfuge, evasion; escapement (of a watch); (st. eng., etc.) exhaust.—**a. e.,** or **a todo e.,** at full speed.—**de e.,** (st. eng.) exhaust (u. a.).

escapo, *m.* (arch.) shaft of a column.

escápula, *f.* (anat.) scapula, shoulder blade.

escapular. I. *a.* scapular. **II.** *va.* (naut.) to double or clear (a cape).

escapulario, *m.* scapulary.

escaque, *m.* any of the squares of a chessboard; (her.) any of the squares of a coat of arms.—*pl.* chess.

escaqueado, da, *a.* checkered.

escara, *f.* (surg.) eschar, scab, slough.

escarabajear. I. *vn.* to crawl to and fro like insects; to scrawl, scribble. **II.** *va.* (coll.) to worry, harass.

escarabajo, *m.* (ent.) black beetle; short, ill-shaped person; flaw in a cast; scarab, scarabæus (of the Egyptians).—*pl.* scrawl.

escarabajuelo, *m. dim.* (ent.) vine beetle.

escarabídeo, a. I. *a. & n.* scarabæid. **II.** *m. pl.* Scarabæidæ.

escaramucear, *vn.* to skirmish.

escaramujo, *m.* (bot.) dog-rose, hep tree; hep; (zool.) goose barnacle.

escaramuza, *f.* (mil.) skirmish; dispute, quarrel.

escaramuzador, ra, *n.* skirmisher; disputer.

escaramuzar, *vn.* to skirmish.

escarapela, *f.* cockade, badge; quarrel ending in blows.

escarapelar. I. *vn. & vr.* to dispute, wrangle, quarrel (s. o. women). **II.** *vr.* (Am.) to have the hair stand on end.

escarbadero, *m.* scratching place.

escarbadientes, *m.* toothpick.

escarbador, ra, *n.* scratcher, scraper.

escarbadura, *f.* scratching.

escarbaorejas, *m.* earpick.

escarbar, *va.* to scrape or scratch (as fowls); to dig, dibble; to poke (the fire); to dig into, to investigate.

escarbo, *m.* scraping, scratching.

escarcela, *f.* large pouch; game bag; cuish; kind of headdress for women.

escarceo, *m.* small broken waves occasioned by currents.—*pl.* bounds and windings of spirited horses.

escarcina, *f.* a kind of cutlass.

escarcuñar, *va.* = ESCUDRIÑAR.

escarcha, *f.* white frost, rime; frostwork.

escarchada, *f.* (bot.) ice plant, fig marigold.

escarchado, da. I. *a. & pp.* of ESCARCHAR; frosted. **II.** *m.* gold or silver embroidery; frosting upon cakes.

escarchador, *m.* freezing tool.

escarchar. I. *vn.* to freeze, frost. **II.** *va.* to put frosting on; to dilute (potter's clay) with water.

escarcho, *m.* (icht.) red surmullet.

escarda, *f.* weedhook, rubbing hoe; weeding.

escardadera, *f.* woman weeder; gardener's hoe.

escardador, ra, *n. & a.* weeder (-ing).

escardadura, *f.,* **escardamiento,** *m.* weeding.

escardar, escardillar, *va.* to weed; to weed out, root out.

escardillo, lla, *n.* small weedhook; gardener's hoe; thistledown.

escariador, *m.* reamer.—**escariar,** *va.* to ream.

escarificación, *f.* (surg.) scarification.

escarificador, *m.* (agr.) scarifier, harrow, cultivator; (surg.) scarificator.

escarificar, *va.* (surg. and agr.) to scarify.

escarioso, sa, *a.* (bot.) scarious.

escarizar, *va.* (surg.) to clean by taking away the scurf or scab.

escarlador, *m.* comb polisher.

escarlata, *f.* scarlet, red; cloth of a scarlet color; (med.) scarlet fever.

escarlatina, *f.,* (com.) red or crimson woollen fabric; (med.) scarlatina.

escarmenador, *m.* comb for wool, etc.

escarmenar, *va.* to comb (wool, silk, etc.); to disentangle; to cheat.

escarmentado, da, *a.* taught by punishment or painful experience.

escarmentar. I. *vn.* (ind. ESCARMIENTO: *subj.* ESCARMIENTE) to be tutored by experience, to take warning. **II.** *va.* to correct severely, to inflict an exemplary punishment on.

escarmiento, *m.* warning, lesson, punishment.

escarnecedor, ra, *n. & a.* scoffer (-ing), scorner (-ing).

escarnecer, *va.* (ind. ESCARNEZCO: *subj.* ESCARNEZCA) to scoff, mock, ridicule, jeer, gibe.

escarnecidamente, *adv.* scornfully.

escarnecimiento, *m.* scoffing, derision.

escarnio, *m.* scoff, gibe, jeer, mock.

escaro, *m.* (icht.) a kind of mutton fish.

escaro, ra, *a.* having crooked feet.

escarola, *f.* (bot.) endive; ruff, frill.

escarolado, da, *pp. & a.* curled, frilled.

escarolar, *va.* to frill, ruffle.

escarótico, ca, *a.* (surg.) escharotic, caustic.

escarpa, *f.* declivity, slope, bluff, cliff; (mil.) scarp.

escarpado, da. I. *a.* steep, craggy, rugged. **II.** *pp.* of ESCARPAR.

escarpadura, *f.* escarpment; bluff, cliff.

escarpar, *va.* to rasp (works of sculpture); (mil.) to escarp.

escarpe, *m.* escarpment; (arch.) scarf of a wall; scarf joint.

escarpelo, *m.* rasp; (surg.) scalpel.

escarpia, *f.* tenterhook, meat hook; spike.

escarpiador, *m.* clamp, fastener; ESCARPIDOR.

escarpidor, *m.* large-toothed comb.

escarpín, *m.* thin-soled shoe; dancing pumps; woollen slippers.

escarpión.—en e., in the form of a tenterhook.

escarza, *f.* (farr.) sore in the hoofs.

escarzano, na, *a.*—**arco e.,** (arch.) segment arch.

escarzar, *va.* (api.) to remove honeycombs from (a hive).

escarzo, *n.* (api.) black comb without honey; operation and time of removing honey from a hive; floss silk.

escarzo, za, *a.* (farr.) lame from hoof sores.

escasamente, *adv.* scantily, sparingly; hardly, scarcely.

escasear. I. *va.* to give sparingly; to spare, to husband. **II.** *vn.* to be scarce; to diminish.

escasez, *f.* scarcity, scantiness; poverty, want.

escaso, sa, *a.* small, limited; little; sparing, parsimonious, niggardly; scarce, scanty.

escatimado, da, *pp. & a.* little, scanty.

escatimar, *va.* to curtail, lessen; to misconstrue.
escatimosamente, *adv.* maliciously.
escatimoso, sa, *a.* cunning, malicious.
escatófago, ga, *a.* scatophagous.
escatología, *f.* scatology; eschatology, doctrine of last things.
escatológico, ca, *a.* scatologic; eschatologic.
escaupil, *m.* (Mex.) ancient padded armor.
escavanar, *va.* (agr.) to loosen and weed (the ground) with a grub hoe.
escayola, *f.* stucco parget, scagliola.
escena, *f.* stage; scenery; scene; sight, view; incident, episode.
escenario, *m.* stage, boards.
escénico, ca, *a.* scenic, belonging to the stage.
escenografía, *f.* scenography.
escenográficamente, *adv.* scenographically.
escenográfico, ca, *a.* scenographic.
escenógrafo, *m.* scenographer.
escépticamente, *adv.* skeptically.
escepticismo, *m.* skepticism.
escéptico, ca, *n.* & *a.* skeptic.
esciagrafia, *f.* skiagraphy.
esciágrafo, *m.* skiagraph.
escinco, *m.* (zool.) skink, a lizard.
escila, *f.* (bot.) squill.
escirro, *m.* (med.) scirrhus.
escirroso, sa, *a.* (med.) scirrhous.
escisión, *f.* division; schism.
escita, *n.* & *a.*; **escítico, ca,** *a.* Scythian.
esclarecedor, ra, *n.* & *a.* enlightener (-ing).
esclarecer. I. *va.* to lighten, illuminate; to enlighten; elucidate; ennoble. **II.** *vn.* to dawn.
esclarecidamente, *adv.* illustriously.
esclarecido, da, *pp.* & *a.* illustrious, prominent.
esclarecimiento, *m.* enlightening; elucidation; dawn; ennoblement; merit, worth.
esclavina, *f.* pilgrim's cloak; collar worn by priests; tippet; cape.
esclavista, *a.* proslavery.
esclavitud, *f.* slavery.
esclavizar, *va.* (*pret.* ESCLAVICÉ: *subj.* ESCLAVICE) to enslave.
esclavo, va, *n.* slave.—**e. ladino,** formerly, one who had been a slave for a year.
esclavón, ona; esclavonio, nia, *n.* & *a.* Slavonian, Slavonic.
escleroftalmia, *f.* (med.) sclerophthalmia.
escleroma, *m.* (med.) scleroma.
esclerosis, *f.* (med.) sclerosis.
esclerótica, *f.* sclerotic.
esclusa, *f.* lock; sluice; floodgate; milldam.
escoa, *f.* (naut.) bend of a ship's rib.
escoba, *f.* broom; (bot.) Spanish broom.
escobada, *f.* sweep, sweeping.
escobadera, *f.* woman sweeper.
escobajo, *m.* old broom; stalk of a bunch of grapes.
escobar. I. *va.* to sweep with a broom. **II.** *m.* broom field.
escobazar, *va.* to sprinkle with a broom.
escobazo, *m.* stroke or blow with a broom.— **echar a escobazos,** to dismiss harshly or roughly, to kick out (fig.).
escobén, *m.* (naut.) hawse hole.
escobera, *f.* (bot.) Spanish broom.—**escobero, ra,** *n.* broom maker or seller.—**escobeta,** *f.* small brush.
escobilla, *f.* brush; whisk, small broom; (bot.) bur of the teasel; gold or silver sweepings; (elec.) brush (of a dynamo).
escobillón, *m.* (mil.) merkin; swab.
escobina, *f.* chips cut in boring; filings.
escobo, *m.* brushwood, briers, brambles.
escobón, *m.* *aug.* large broom; Turk's head; scrubbing brush; swab.
escocedura, *f.* burning pain.
escocer. I. *vn.* (*ind.* ESCUECE: *subj.* ESCUEZA) to feel a sharp, burning pain; to smart. **II.** *vr.* to smart; to chafe.
escocés, sa, *n.* & *a.* Scotch.
escocia, *f.* (arch.) scotia; (com.) codfish.

escocimiento, *m.* smart, pungent pain.
escoda, *f.* stonecutter's hammer.
escodar, *va.* to hew or cut (stones).
escofia, *f.* coif, headtire.
escofiar, *va.* to dress with a coif.
escofieta, *f.* = ESCOFIA.
escofina, *f.* rasp, file; wood rasp.
escofinar, *va.* to rasp.
escogedor, ra, *n.* & *a.* chooser (-ing).
escoger, *va.* (*ind.* ESCOJO: *subj.* ESCOJA) to choose, select, pick out, sort; elect.
escogidamente, *adv.* choicely, selectly; nicely.
escogido, da, *pp.* & *a.* chosen, choice, select.
escogimiento, *m.* selection, choice, choosing; sorting, separation.
escolar. I. *n.* pupil, student. **II.** *a.* scholastic, school (u. a.)
escolásticamente, *adv.* scholastically.
escolasticismo, *m.* scholasticism.
escolástico, ca. I. *a.* scholastic, scholastical; school (u. a.). **II.** *n.* Scholastic, Schoolman.
escoliador, ra, *n.* scholiast.
escoliar, *va.* to gloss, explain, comment.
escoliasta, *n.* = ESCOLIADOR.
escolimado, da, *a.* (coll.) weak, delicate.
escolimoso, sa, *a.* (coll.) fastidious, hard to please, fussy.
escolio, *m.* scholium; gloss, commentary.
escoliosis, *f.* (med.) scoliosis.
escolopendra, *f.* (ent.) scolopendra, centipede; a marine worm; (bot.) spleenwort.
escolta, *f.* escort, convoy, guard.
escoltar, *va.* to escort, convoy, guard.
escollera, *f.* breakwater, jetty; cliff.
escollo, *m.* reef; difficulty, danger.
escombra, *f.* clearing, removal of obstacles.
escombrar, *va.* to clear of rubbish; to clean.
escombro, *m.* rubbish, débris; riprap; a small raisin; (icht.) mackerel.
escomerse, *vr.* to wear out.
esconce, *m.* corner, angle.
escondedero, *m.* hiding or lurking place.
esconder. I. *va.* to hide, conceal; to include, contain. **II.** *vr.* to hide; to skulk.
escondidamente, *adv.* secretly, hiddenly.
escondidas, escondidillas.—a e., on the sly, hiddenly.
escondimiento, *m.* concealment.
escondite, *m.*, **escondrijo,** *m.* lurking place; hiding place.—**jugar al e.,** to play hide and seek.
esconzado, da, *a.* angular, oblique.
escopeta, *f.* shotgun, fowling piece.—**e. de dos cañones,** double-barrel gun.—**e. de viento,** air gun.
escopetar, *va.* to dig out (gold mines).
escopetazo, *m.* gunshot; gunshot wound.
escopetear, *va.* to shoot at with a shotgun; to compliment, pay compliments to.
escopeteo, *m.* gunshot fire.
escopetería, *f.* infantry armed with guns; repeated gunshots.
escopetero, *m.* gunner, musketeer; gunsmith.
escopetilla, *f.* *dim.* small gun.
escopetón, *m.* *aug.* large fowling piece.
escopladura, escopleadura, *f.* mortise hole, chisel cut.
escoplear, *va.* to chisel, mortise, notch.
escoplillo, ito, *m.* *dim.* small chisel.
escoplo, *m.* chisel.
escora, *f.* (naut.) stanchion, bilge head, prop, outrigger; (naut.) central line of a vessel; (naut.) tilt.—**e. lateral,** (car.) rolling.
escorar. I. *va.* (naut.) to prop, to shore up. **II.** *vn.* (naut.) to list, to heel.
escorbútico, ca, *a.* scorbutic, scorbutical.
escorbuto, *m.* (med.) scurvy.
escorchapín, *m.* passage boat, ferry.
escorchar, *va.* to flay, to skin.
escordio, *m.* (bot.) water germander.
escoria, *f.* dross, slag, scoria; lee; mean or worthless thing.—*pl.* scoriæ, volcanic ashes.
escoriáceo, cea, *a.* scoriaceous.

escoriación, *f.* = EXCORIACIÓN.
escorial, *m.* dumping place for dross; slag heap.
escoriar, *va.* = EXCORIAR.
escorificación, *f.* (chem.) scorification.
escorificar, *va.* (chem.) to scorify, reduce to scoria or slag.
escorpena, escorpina, *f.* (icht.) grouper.
escorpioide, *f.* (bot.) = ALACRANERA.
escorpión, *m.* (ent.) scorpion; (icht.) fish resembling a grouper; ancient ballister; (E-, ast.) Scorpion; cat-o'-nine-tails with metal points.
escorpiónideos, *m. pl.* (zool.) Scorpionida, the scorpion family.
escorrozo, *m.* (coll.) pleasure, enjoyment.
escorzado, *pp.* & *m.* (art) foreshortening.
escorzar, *va.* (art) to foreshorten.
escorzo, *m.* (art) foreshortening.
escorzón, *m.* toad.
escorzonera, *f.* (bot.) viper root or garden viper grass.
escota, *f.* stonecutter's hammer; (naut.) sheet.
escotado, *pp.* & *m.* = ESCOTADURA.
escotadura, *f.* low cut in the neck (of a dress); armhole in armor; large trapdoor of a stage.
escotar, *va.* to cut (a dress) low in the neck; to club, contribute to a common expense; to draw (water) by a trench.
escote, *m.* low neck, decolleté; tucker; share, quota.
escotera, *f.* (naut.) sheet hole.
escotero, ra, *a.* free, disengaged, unburdened.
escotilla, *f.* (naut.) hatchway.
escotillón, *m.* scuttle, trapdoor; stage trap.
escotín, *m.* (naut.) topsail sheet.
escotismo, *m.* Scotism (doctrines of Scotus).
escotista, *n.* Scotist.
escoznete, *m.* (prov.) nut pick.
escozor, *m.* smart pungent pain, burning, smarting; grief, affliction.
escriba, *m.* scribe, among the Hebrews.
escribanía, *f.* office or employment of an actuary or scrivener; escritoire, scrutoire; portable writing case; ornamental inkstand.
escribano, *m.* actuary, scrivener.—**e. de cámara,** clerk of a high court of justice.—**e. del agua,** (ent.) water skater.—**e. de número, or del número,** one of a certain number of notaries public.
escribido, *pp. reg.* of ESCRIBIR, used only in the idiom leído y escribido, (coll.) would-be learned, posing as learned.
escribiente, *m.* amanuensis, clerk.
escribir. I. *va.* (*pp. irr.* ESCRITO) to write. **II.** *vr.* to enroll one's self; to carry on correspondence with each other.
escriño, *m.* straw hamper; jewel box, casket.
escrita, *f.* (icht.) spotted skate fish.
escritillas, *f. pl.* lamb's fries.
escrito, ta. I. *pp. irr.* of escribir. **II.** *m.* writing; manuscript; literary composition; (law) writ; brief.
escritor, ra, *n.* writer.—**escritorcillo, lla,** *n.* *dim.* petty writer, writer of no account.
escritorillo, *m. dim.* small writing desk.
escritorio, *m.* writing desk; countinghouse; office, study.
escritorzuelo, la, *n. dim.* writer of no account.
escritura, *f.* writing, handwriting, penmanship; deed, indenture, instrument; (E-) Scripture.—**e. de seguro,** insurance policy.
escriturar. I. *va.* (law) to bind by deed; to indenture; to engage (as an artist). **II.** *vr.* to sign articles.
escriturario, ria. I. *a.* (law) scriptory, scriptorian; scriptural. **II.** *n.* scripturist.
escrófula, *f.* (med.) scrofula.
escrofularia, *f.* (bot.) figwort.
escrofulariáceo, cea, *a.* scrophulariaceous.
escrofulismo, *m.* (med.) scrofulism.
escrofuloso, sa, *a.* scrofulous.
escroto, *m.* scrotum.
escrupulillo, *m. dim.* slight scruple; jinglet.
escrupulizar, *vn.* to scruple, doubt, hesitate.

escrúpulo, *m.* scruple, hesitation; scrupulosity, conscientiousness; (pharm.) scruple, a small weight (20 gr.).
escrupulosamente, *adv.* scrupulously; precisely, minutely, thoroughly.
escrupulosidad, *f.* scrupulosity, conscientiousness; exactness, nicety, thoroughness.
escrupuloso, sa, *a.* scrupulous, conscientious; nice, exact, thorough; hypercritical, squeamish.
escrutador, ra, *n.* examiner, inquirer, searcher; inspector of an election.
escrutar, *va.* to count (votes); to scrutinize.
escrutinio, *m.* scrutiny, investigation; election returns.
escrutiñador, *m.* scrutator, censor.
escuadra, *f.* carpenter's square; drawing triangle; angle iron; knee, angle brace; (mil.) squad; (naut.) squadron, fleet.—**e. de agrimensor,** (surv.) cross-staff.—**e. sutil,** light coastguard fleet.—**a e.,** square, at right angles.—**falsa e.,** bevel square.—**fuera de e.,** out of square, at an oblique angle.
escuadración, *f.* squaring.
escuadrador, *m.* squaring tool; groover.
escuadrar, *va.* (carp.) to square.
escuadreo, *m.* squaring, quadrature.
escuadría, *f.* scantling of timber; square.
escuadro, *m.* = ESCRITA.
escuadrón, *m.* (mil.) squadron, troop of horse.—**e. volante,** (mil.) flying column.
escuadronar, *va.* to form in squadrons.
escuadroncillo, cete, *m. dim.* small troop.
escuadronista, *m.* (mil.) tactician.
escualidez, *f.* squalor, wretchedness.
escuálido, da, *a.* weak, languid; squalid, filthy.
escualo, *m.* (icht.) spotted dogfish; shark.
escualor, *m.* squalor, filthiness.
escucha, *f.* (mil.) scout; vedette; sentinel, sentry; in convents, a chaperon; listening hole.
escuchador, ra; escuchante, *n.* listener.
escuchar. I. *va.* to listen, hearken; to mind, heed. **II.** *vr.* to hear one's self with complacency.
escudar, *va.* to shield, protect, defend.
escuderaje, *m.* service of a page or footman.
escuderear, *va.* to serve as a page or squire to.
escudería, *f.* service of a page or squire.
escuderil, *a.* belonging to a page or squire.
escuderilmente, *adv.* in the style of a page.
escudero, *m.* shield bearer, squire, page; gentleman of illustrious ancestry; shield maker.
escuderón, *m.* conceited squire.
escudete, *m.* escutcheon; gusset; rain stain on olives; (bot.) white water lily.
escudilla, *f.* bowl, large cup.
escudillar, *va.* to pour into bowls; to lord, domineer.
escudillita, *f. dim.* small bowl.
escudillo, ito, *m. dim.* small shield; a gold coin.
escudo, *m.* shield, buckler, escutcheon, coat of arms; escutcheon of a lock or knocker; shield, protection; coin of different values; bandage used in bleeding; sideplate of a gun; (naut.) backboard of a boat.—**e. de armas,** arms (on a flag, etc.).—**e. de popa,** (naut.) stern escutcheon.
escudriñable, *a.* investigable.
escudriñador, ra, *n.* & *a.* prier (-ying); scrutinizer (-ing), searcher (-ing); scrutator (-ing).
escudriñamiento, *m.* investigation, scrutiny.
escudriñar, *va.* to scrutinize, search, pry into.
escuela, *f.* school; schoolhouse; (art) school, style; experience.—**e. normal,** normal school.—**e. primaria,** primary and grammar school.—**e. secundaria,** high school.—**e. superior,** institution of higher learning, or of professional studies (university, college, etc.).
escuerzo, *m.* (zool.) toad; (coll.) flabby person.
escueto, ta, *a.* disengaged, free from encumbrances; solitary, uninhabited.
escueznar, *va.* to extract the kernel of.
escuezno, *m.* soft kernel of a nut.
esculcar, *va.* to spy, to watch; to search; (Am.) to search the pockets of.

---

esculpidor, ra, *n.* engraver.
esculpir, *va. & vn.* to sculpture; to engrave.
escultor, *m.* sculptor.—**escultora,** *f.* sculptress.
escultórico, ca, *a.* sculptural.
escultura, *f.* sculpture; carved work.
escultural, *a.* sculptural.
escullador, *m.* dipper for oil.
escupidera, *f.* spittoon, cuspidor.
escupidero, *m.* spitting place; disgraceful situation.
escupido, da. I. *pp.* of ESCUPIR. **II.** *m.* spittle.
escupidor, ra, *n.* great spitter.
escupidura, *f.* spitting, spittle; fever sore.
escupir, *va. & vn.* to spit; to break out in the skin; to dart, fling, throw, cast away; to work out, throw off.
escupitajo, *m.,* **escupitina,** *f.,* **escupitinajo,** *m.* (coll.) spit.
escurar, *va.* to scout (cloth) before milling.
escurialense, *a.* belonging to, or like, the Escorial (a famous Spanish monastery).
escurreplatos, *m.* dish-draining rack.
escurribanda, *f.* (coll.) evasion, subterfuge; diarrhœa; scuffle, bustle.
escurrida, *a.* wearing tight-fitting skirts; having narrow hips.
escurridero, *m.* drain pipe or conduit (in mines); draining or wringing place.
escurridizo, za, *a.* slippery; difficult to hold.
escurridor, *m.* colander; ESCURREPLATOS.
escurriduras, escurrimbres, *f. pl.* rinsings (as of wine); lees, dregs.
escurrimiento, *m.* dripping, running off; sneaking out.
escurrir. I. *va.* to drain off a vessel; to wring (as clothes).—**e. el bulto,** to sneak away. **II.** *vr.* to drop, drip, ooze, leak, trickle; to slip, slide, glide; to escape, slip out, sneak away.
escuyer, *m.* purveyor of meat to the palace.
esdrújulo, la, *a.* (gram.) (word) accented on the antepenultimate syllable.
ese, *f.* name of the letter *s*; link of a chain of the figure of this letter.—*pl.* **eses,** reeling of a drunken man (gen. in the phrase **hacer eses,** to reel).
ese, *m.,* **esa,** *f.* (*pl.* **esos, esas),** *a.* that (*pl.* those), as *ese hombre,* that man: *esas mujeres,* those women.
ése, *m.,* **ésa,** *f.* (*pl.* **ésos, ésas),** *dem. pron.* that (one) (*pl.,* those), as *tengo ése,* I have that one; *dame ésas,* give me those. *V.* ESA.
esecilla, *f. dim.* small link of a chain.
esencia, *f.* essence, being; (chem.) essence, perfume.
esencial, *a.* essential.
esencialmente, *adv.* essentially, principally.
eseniano, na; esenio, nia, *n. & a.* Essene (-ian).
esfenoidal, *a.* (anat.) sphenoidal.
esfenoides, *m.* (anat.) sphenoid bone.
esfera, *f.* sphere; clock dial; quality, condition, rank; (poet.) heaven.—**e. armilar,** armillary sphere.—**e. celeste,** celestial sphere.—**e. de actividad,** sphere of action.—**e. paralela,** (astr.) parallel sphere.—**e. recta,** (astr.) right sphere.
esferal, *a.* = ESFÉRICO.—**esféricamente,** *adv.* spherically.—**esfericidad,** *f.* sphericity.—**esférico, ca,** *a.* spherical.—**esferoidal,** *a.* spheroidal.— **esferoide,** *f.* spheroid.
esferómetro, *m.* spherometer.
esfigmógrafo, *m.* sphygmograph.
esfigmómetro, *m.* sphygmometer.
esfinge, *f.* sphinx.—**esfingido, da,** *a.* sphinxlike.
esfínter, *m.* (anat.) sphincter.
esforrocinar, *va.* to remove the ESFORROCINOS from.
esforrocino, *m.* sprig shooting from the trunk of a vine.
esforzadamente, *adv.* vigorously; bravely.
esforzado, da. I. *a.* strong, vigorous; brave; enterprising. **II.** *pp.* of ESFORZAR.
esforzador, ra, *n. & a.* encourager (-ing).
esforzar. I. *va.* (ind. ESFUERZO: *pret.* ESFORCÉ: *subj.* ESFUERCE) to strengthen, invigorate; to

encourage. II. *vr.* to exert one's self, to make efforts, to try hard.
esfuerzo, *m.* courage, spirit, vigor; effort, strong endeavor; (eng.) stress.—**e. cortante,** (eng.) shear, shearing stress.
esfumado, da, *pp. & a.* (art) sfumato.
esfumar, *va.* (art) to stump.
esfumino, *m.* (art) stump (for shading).
esgarrar, *va. & vn.* to raise phlegm; to clear one's throat.
esgrafiado, *m.* (art) graffito.
esgrafiar, *va.* to decorate with graffito; to scratch on with a graffito tool or graver.
esgrima, *f.* fencing (the art).—**esgrimidor,** *m.* fencer or fencing master.—**esgrimidura,** *f.* fencing (the act).—**esgrimir,** *va.* to wield.
esgrimista, *n.* fencer; (ch.) sponger.
esguazable, *a.* fordable.—**esguazar,** *va.* to ford (as a river).—**esguazo,** *m.* fording.
esgucio, *m.* (arch.) quarter-round molding.
esguín, *m.* young salmon before entering the sea.
esguince, *m.* dodging, dodge; frown; twist or sprain of a joint.
esguízaro, ra, *n. & a.* Swiss; ragamuffin.
eslabón, *m.* link of a chain; steel for striking fire with a flint; table steel; name of a very poisonous scorpion.
eslabonador, *m.* chain maker.
eslabonamiento, *m.* linking, uniting; connection, sequence, concatenation.
eslabonar, *va.* to link, interlink; to join, unite; to connect, concatenate.
eslavo, va, *n. & a.* Slav.
eslinga, *f.* (naut.) sling, span.
eslingar, *va.* (naut.) to sling up, hoist.
eslora, *f.* (naut.) length of a ship.—*pl.* binding strakes of the deck.
eslovaco, ca, *n. & a.* Slovakian.
esloveno, na, *n. & a.* Slovene.
esmaltador, ra, *n.* enameller.
esmaltadura, *f.* enamelling; enamel work.
esmaltar, *va.* to enamel; to adorn, embellish.
esmalte, *m.* enamel; enamel work; smalt.
esmaltín, *m.* smalt.
esmaltina, *f.* (min.) smaltite.
esmeradamente, *adv.* carefully, conscientiously, thoroughly.
esmerado, da. I. *a.* careful, painstaking, carefully done. **II.** *pp.* of ESMERAR.
esmeralda, *f.* emerald.
esmeraldina, *f.* (min.) emeraldine.
esmeraldino, na, *a.* emeraldlike.
esmerar. I. *va.* to polish, to brighten. **II.** *vr.* (w. con or en) to do one's best, to take pains.
esmerejón, *m.* (orn.) merlin; small-caliber gun.
esmeril, *m.* emery; small-caliber gun.
esmerilar, *va.* to burnish, to polish with emery, to grind.
esmero, *m.* careful attention, painstaking.
esmoladera, *f.* whetstone.
esmuciarse, *vr.* to slip from the hands.
esnón, (naut.) spencer mast, trysail mast.
eso, *dem. pron. neut.* that (that thing, fact, etc.). —**e. de** = AQUELLO DE.—**e. es,** that is it.—**e. mismo,** the very thing.—**a e. de,** toward, about.—**no es e.,** it is not that.
esofágico, ca, *a.* esophageal.
esófago, *m.* (anat.) esophagus, gullet.
esotérico, ca, *a.* esoteric; confidential, secret.
esotro, m., esotra, *f., dem. pron.* this or that other.—*pl.* **esotros,** *m.,* **esotras,** *f.,* those others.
espabiladeras, *f. pl.* snuffers.
espabilar, *va.* to snuff (a candle).
espaciar. I. *va.* to space; diffuse, expand, dilate, spread; (print.) to lead; to space. **II.** *vr.* to walk to and fro; to amuse one's self; to cheer up; to expatiate.
espacio, *m.* space; room, capacity; slowness, delay, procrastination; (mus.) interval.
espaciosamente, *adv.* deliberately; spaciously.
espaciosidad, *f.* spaciousness, capacity.

espacioso, sa, *a.* spacious, roomy, ample; slow, deliberate.

espada, *f.* sword; blade, rapier; swordsman; (cards) spade; (icht.) swordfish; matador, bullfighter who kills the bull.—**entre la e. y la pared,** between the devil and the deep sea.

espadachín, *m.* dexterous swordsman; bully, hackster.

espadadero, *m.* braking floor.

espadador, *m.* hemp beater.

espadaña, *f.* (bot.) reed mace; belfry.

espadañada, *f.* regurgitation; spewing.

espadañal, *m.* place where reed mace grows.

espadañar, *va.* to spread out (the tail feathers).

espadar, *va.* to brake, scutch, swingle.

espadarte, *m.* (icht.) swordfish.

espadería, *f.* sword cutler's shop.

espadero, *m.* sword cutler, bladesmith.

espádice, *m.* (bot.) spadix.

espadilla, *f.* red insignia of the order of Santiago; swingle, hemp brake; (naut.) scull, oar used as helm; ace of spades; hair bodkin; (bot.) corn flag.

espadillar, *va.* to brake, scutch, swingle.

espadillazo, *m.* adverse fortune at cards.

espadín, *m.* small gala sword; rapier.

espadita, *f.* *dim.* small sword.

espadón, *m.* *aug.* spadone, large sword, broadsword; eunuch.

espadrapo, *m.* = ESPARADRAPO.

espagírica, *f.* metallurgy.

espagírico, ca, *a.* metallurgic.

espaí, *m.* (mil.) spahi.

espalda, *f.* (anat.) back, shoulders; (fort.) shoulder of a bastion.—*pl.* back or back part; (mil.) rearguard.—*a.* **espaldas, or a espaldas vueltas,** treacherously.—**hablar por las espaldas de uno,** to talk behind one's back.

espaldar, *m.* backplate of a cuirass; back of a seat; espalier in gardens.—*pl.* tapestry hangings against which chairs lean.

espaldarazo, *m.* accolade; light blow on the back.

espaldarcete, *m.* palette in ancient armor.

espaldarón, *m.* backplate in armor.

espaldear, *va.* (naut.) to dash against the poop of.

espalder, *m.* stern rower in a galley.

espaldera, *f.* espalier, trelliswork.

espaldilla, *f.* scapula, shoulder blade; hind quarter of a waistcoat or jacket.

espalditendido, da, *a.* (coll.) stretched on one's back.

espaldón, *m.* (carp.) tenon; (fort.) intrenchment, barrier; (naut.) a hawse piece.

espaldudo, da, *a.* broad-shouldered.

espalera, *f.* espalier, trelliswork.

espalmadura, *f.* (farr.) parings of hoofs.

espalmar, *va.* = DESPALMAR.

espalto, *m.* dark-colored paint; spalt.

espantable, *a.* frightful, horrid, terrible.

espantablemente, *adv.* horribly, frightfully.

espantada, *f.* stampede, running away; giving up from fear, (coll.) cold feet.

espantadizo, za, *a.* timid, skittish, shy.

espantador, ra, *n.* bugbear, frightener.

espantajo, *m.* scarecrow; fright.

espantaiobos, *m.* (bot.) bladder or bastard senna.

espantamoscas, *m.* fly net; flyflap.

espantanublados, *m.* rake, vagabond.

espantapájaros, *m.* scarecrow.

espantar. I. *va.* to scare, frighten, daunt; to chase or drive away. **II.** *vr.* to be astonished, to marvel.

espantavillanos, *m.* gaudy stuff or trinket.

espanto, *m.* fright, dread, terror; horror; threat; wonder; hideousness, grimness.

espantosamente, *adv.* dreadfully.

espantoso, sa, *a.* frightful, dreadful; fearful; wonderful.

español, la. I. *n.* & *a.* Spanish. **II.** *n.* Spaniard (*f.* Spanish woman).

españolado, da. I. *a.* Spanishlike; Spaniolized. **II.** *pp.* of ESPAÑOLAR.

españolar, *va.* (coll.) = ESPAÑOLIZAR.

españoleta, *f.* ancient Spanish dance.

españolismo, *m.* love, devotion to Spain; Hispanicism.

españolizar. I. *va.* to Hispaniolize. **II.** *vr.* to adopt the customs and manners of Spain.

esparadrapo, *m.* court-plaster.

esparaván, *m.* (vet.) spavin; (orn.) sparrow hawk.—**e. de garbanzuelo** = E. SECO.—**e. huesoso,** bone spavin.—**e. seco,** swimmer.

esparavel, *m.* casting net.

esparciata, *a.* Spartan.

esparcidamente, *adv.* separately, scatteredly.

esparcido, da. I. *a.* scattered; merry, festive, gay. **II.** *pp.* of ESPARCIR.

esparcidor, ra, *n.* & *a.* scatterer (-ing), spreader (-ing).

esparcimiento, *m.* scattering, dissemination; amusement, recreation, diversion, relaxation; frankness, openness.

esparcir. I. *va.* (*ind.* ESPARZO: *subj.* ESPARZA) to scatter, spread; disseminate; divulge. **II.** *vr.* to amuse one's self, to make merry.

esparragado, *m.* dish of asparagus.

esparragador, ra, *n.* asparagus grower.

esparragamiento, *m.* cultivation of asparagus.

esparragar, *vn.* to grow asparagus.

espárrago, *m.* (bot.) asparagus; pole of an awning; (min.) peg ladder.

esparragón, *m.* corded silk stuff.

esparraguera, *f.* asparagus plant; asparagus bed.

esparraguero, ra, *n.* asparagus seller.

esparraguina, *f.* (min.) asparagin.

esparrancado, da. I. *a.* wide-legged, divaricated. **II.** *pp.* of ESPARRANCARSE.

esparrancarse, *vr.* (coll.) to spread the legs wide apart.

espartal, *m.* matweed field.

espartano, na, *n.* & *a.* Spartan.

esparteína, *f.* (chem.) sparteine.

esparteña, *f.* rope-sole sandal.

espartería, *f.* mat-work factory or shop.

espartero, ra, *n.* maker and seller of mat-work.

espartilla, *f.* mop of esparto grass.

espartizal, *m.* esparto field.

esparto, *m.* (bot.) esparto grass, matweed.

espasmo, *m.* (med.) spasm.

espasmódico, ca, *a.* spasmodic, convulsive.

espata, *f.* (bot.) spathe.

espatarrada, *f.* = DESPATARRADA.

espatarrarse, *vr.* = DESPATARRARSE.

espático, ca, *a.* (min.) spathic.

espato, *m.* (min.) spar.—**e. calizo,** calcite, calc spar.—**e. de Islandia,** Iceland spar.—**e. flúor,** fluorspar.—**e. pesado,** barite, heavy spar.

espátula, *f.* spatula; (art) palette knife.

espaviento, *m.* = ASPAVIENTO.

espavorido, da, *a.* = DESPAVORIDO.

especería, *f.* = ESPECIERÍA.

especia, *f.* spice.—*pl.* medicinal drugs.

especial, *a.* special, particular.—**en e.,** specially, in particular.

especialidad, *f.* specialty; course, subject (of study).

especialista, *n.* specialist.

especialización, *f.* specialization; specializing.

especializar. I. *va.* to specialize; to limit, confine. **II.** *vr.* (w. en) to specialize (in).

especialmente, *adv.* especially.

especiar, *va.* to spice, season.

especie, *f.* species; kind, sort; event, incident; case, affair, business; piece of news; statement; pretext, show.—**en e.,** in kind.

especiería, *f.* grocery shop.

especiero, *m.* grocer.

especificación, *f.* specification.

especificadamente, *adv.* in a specified manner.

especificar, va. (*pret.* ESPECIFIQUÉ: *subj.* ESPECIFIQUE) to specify, particularize, itemize.

especificativo, va, *a.* specifical, specifying.

For pronunciation, see the rules at the beginning of the book.

específico, ca. I. *a.* specific, specifical. **II.** *m.* (med.) specific.

espécimen, *m.* specimen, sample.

especioso, sa, *a.* neat, beautiful; apparent, specious, deceiving.

especiota, *f.* (coll.) hoax, fake news.

espectáculo, *m.* spectacle, show, pageant.

espectador, ra, *n.* spectator, look-on.

espectral, *a.* (phys.) spectral, spectrum (u. a.).

espectro, *m.* spectre, phantom, hobgoblin; (opt.) spectrum.

espectroscopia, *f.* (opt.) spectroscopy.

espectroscópico, ca, *a.* spectroscopic.

espectroscopio, *m.* (opt.) spectroscope.

especulación, speculation, contemplation; (com.) venture.

especulador, ra, *m.* & *a.* speculator (-ing).

especular. I. *va.* to behold, view, inspect; to speculate, meditate about. **II.** *vn.* to speculate; (com.) to speculate, dabble in stocks, etc.

especulativa, *f.* understanding.

especulativamente, *adv.* speculatively.

especulativo, va, *a.* speculative; thoughtful.

espéculo, *m.* speculum.

espejado, da, *a.* mirrorlike.

espejear, *vn.* to shine.

espejeo, *m.* = ESPEJISMO.

espejería, *f.* mirror factory or shop.

espejero, ra, *n.* mirror maker or seller.

espejico, illo, ito, *m.* *dim.* small mirror.

espejismo, *m.* mirage; illusion.

espejo, *m.* looking-glass, mirror; (naut.) stern; frame.—**e. de cuerpo entero,** full-length glass, pier glass.—**e. ustorio,** burning glass.

espejuela, *f.* curve of the bit.—**e. abierta,** snaffle.

espejuelo, *m.* *dim.* small looking-glass; specular stone, selenite; leaf of mica; lark mirror; candied citron; (vet.) wart on pastern.—*pl.* spectacles, eyeglasses.

espelta, *f.* (bot.) spelt, a cereal.

espélteo, a, *a.* belonging to spelt.

espelunca, *f.* dark, gloomy cave.

espeluzar, *va.* = DESPELUZAR.

espeluznante, *a.* (coll.) setting the hair on end, dreadful, horrifying.

espeluznar, *va.* & *vr.* to dishevel the hair; to set the hair on end (from fright).

espeque, *m.* handspike; pump brake; strut, prop; lever.

espera, *f.* waiting; stay, pause; (mus.) stop, interval; restraint, prudence; (law) respite, adjournment; ancient piece of ordnance; (carp.) notch.—**en e.,** waiting.—**en e. de,** waiting for, awaiting; expecting.

esperador, ra, *a.* expectant.

esperantista, *n.* Esperantist.

esperanto, *m.* Esperanto.

esperanza, *f.* hope; (often *pl.*) prospects.—**dar e.,** or **esperanzas,** to give encouragement; to promise, to bid fair.—**no hay e.,** there is no hope, or no chance, the case is hopeless.

esperanzar, *va.* to give hope to.

esperar. I. *va.* to hope; to expect; to wait for, await, look for; to fear. **II.** *vn.* to wait; to hope. —**quien espera desespera,** long hoping ends in despair, or in hopelessness. **III.** *vr.* to wait, stay.

esperezarse, *vr.* to stretch one's self.

esperezo, *m.* stretching one's arms and legs.

esperma, *f.* sperm.—**e. de ballena,** spermaceti.

espermaceti, *m.* (com.) spermaceti.

espermático, ca, *a.* spermatic, seminal.

espermatorrea, *f.* spermatorrhœa.

espermatozoario, espermatozoide, espermatozoo, *m.* spermatozoon.

espernada, *f.* split end link of a chain.

espernancarse, *vr.* = ESPARRANCARSE.

esperón, *m.* *aug.* long wait; (naut.) = ESPOLÓN.

esperpento, *m.* horrible or hideous thing or person; absurdity, nonsense.

espesar. I. *va.* to thicken, inspissate, coagulate, curdle; to mass, assemble; to make closer (as

knitting). **II.** *vr.* to condense; to thicken, become thicker.

espesativo, va, *a.* thickening.

espeso, sa, *a.* thick, dense; curdy; frequent, often repeated; slovenly, dirty; dull, heavy.

espesor, *m.* thickness.

espesura, *f.* thickness, density, closeness; thicket, close wood; abundant head of hair; slovenliness.

espetaperro, espetaperros.—a e., at breakneck speed, precipitately.

espetar. I. *va.* to spit, to skewer; to pierce, run through; (coll.) to spring (something) on (one). **II.** *vr.* to be stiff with pride; (coll.) to thrust one's self into place.

espetera, *f.* kitchen rack, scullery.

espetón, *m.* spit, poker, rake, iron prong, large pin; (zool.) sea-pike.

espía, *n.* spy; (naut.) warp, chest rope.

espiar. I. *va.* to spy, to watch, to lie in wait for. **II.** *vr.* (naut.) to warp.

espibia, *f.*, **espibio, espibión,** *m.* (vet.) dislocation in the nape of the neck.

espicanardi, espicanardo, *f.* (bot.) spikenard.

espiciforme, *a.* (bot.) spicate.

espícula, *f.* (zool.) spicule.

espichar. I. *va.* to prick. **II.** *vn.* (coll.) to give up the ghost, to die.

espiche, *m.* sharp-pointed weapon; meatspit; spile, spigot.

espichón, *m.* wound with a pointed weapon.

espiga, *f.* (bot.) tassel (as of corn); (carp.) tenon, dowel, peg; (mech.) pin, tongue, shank, tree-nail, stem; tang of a sword; brad, headless nail; (ordn.) fuse of a bomb or shell; (naut.) masthead.

espigadera, *f.* gleaner, leaser.

espigado, da. I. *a.* tall, grown; (agr.) eared, ripe. **II.** *pp.* of ESPIGAR.

espigadora, *f.* = ESPIGADERA.

espigar. I. *vn.* (*pret.* ESPIGUÉ: *subj.* ESPIGUE) to glean; (carp.) to tenon. **II.** *vn.* (agr.) to tassel (as corn); to grow tall.

espigón, *m.* sting (as of bees); point of a sharp tool or dart; bearded spike; ear of corn; peak; breakwater or pier.

espiguilla, ta, *f.* *dim.* spikelet; small edging of lace, tape, or inkle.

espina, *f.* thorn; fishbone; spine, backbone; splinter; scruple, doubt, suspicion.—**e. blanca,** (bot.) woolly-cotton thistle.—**e. dorsal,** vertebral or spinal column, spine.—**dar mala e.,** to cause suspicion or anxiety.—**estar en espinas,** to be anxious, to be on pins and needles.—**sacarse la e.,** to get even, to retrieve one's losses.

espinaca, *f.* (bot.) spinach.

espinadura, *f.* pricking with a thorn.

espinal, *a.* spinal, dorsal.

espinar, *va.* to prick with thorns; to surround (trees) with thorn bushes; to nettle, provoke.

espinar, *m.* place full of thorn bushes; dangerous undertaking, arduous enterprise.

espinazo, *m.* spine, backbone.

espinel, *m.* fishing line with many hooks.

espinela, *f.* (poet.) ten-line stanza; spinel ruby.

espíneo, ea, *a.* made or full of thorns.

espinera, *f.* (bot.) = ESPINO.

espineta, *f.* (mus.) spinet.

espingarda, *f.* a small cannon; long Moorish shotgun.

espingardada, *f.* wound from an ESPINGARDA.

espinica, ita, illa, *f.* *dim.* small thorn.

espinilla, *f.* shin bone; blackhead, comedo.

espinillera, *f.* (arm.) greave, jambe.

espino, *m.* (bot.) hawthorn, buckthorn.

espinosismo, *m.* Spinozism.

espinosista, *n.* & *a.* Spinozist (-ic).

espinoso, sa, *a.* thorny; arduous; dangerous.

espinzar, *va.* to burl. *V.* DESPINZAR.

espiocha, *f.* pickaxe.

espión, *m.* spy.

espionaje, *m.* espionage, spying.

espira, *f.* spiral line, helix; spire, steeple; turn (of a winding); (arch.) surbase of a column.

espiración, *f.* expiration, respiration.
espirador, ra, *n.* one who expires or breathes.
espiral. I. *a.* spiral, winding. **II.** *f.* (math.) spiral.
espiralmente, *adv.* spirally.
espirante, *a.* expiring, respiring.
espirar. I. *va.* to expire, breathe, exhale; to move, animate; to infuse a divine spirit in. **II.** *vn.* to expire, breathe.
espirativo, va, *a.* that infuses spirit.
espiritado, da, *a.* (coll.) extremely thin.
espiritar. I. *va.* = ENDEMONIAR. **II.** *vr.* (coll.) to be agitated, to fret.
espiritismo, *m.* spiritism.
espiritista, *n.* & *a.* spiritist (-ic).
espiritosamente, *adv.* spiritedly.
espiritoso, sa, *a.* spirituous, spirited, lively.
espíritu, *m.* spirit; soul; genius; ardor, courage; inclination, turn of mind; spirit, liquor.—*pl.* spirits, demons, hobgoblins; (chem.) spirits, ether.—**e. de contradicción,** contradictory temper, mania of contradicting.—**e. de sal,** spirit of salt (hydrochloric acid).—**e. de vino,** spirits of wine, rectified spirit.—**e. Inmundo, e. maligno,** the devil.—**E. Santo,** Holy Ghost.
espiritual, *a.* spiritual; ghostly.
espiritualidad, *f.* spirituality; incorporality.
espiritualismo, *m.* (philos.) spiritualism (as opposed to materialism).
espiritualista. *m.* spiritualist (-ic) [as opposed to materialist (-ic)].
espiritualización, *f.* spiritualization.
espiritualizar, *va.* to spiritualize.
espiritualmente, *adv.* spiritually.
espirituoso, sa, *a.* spirituous; ardent; spirited.
espirómetro, *m.* spirometer.
espiroqueta, *m.,* **espiroqueto,** *m.* (bact.) spirochete.
espita. *f.* faucet, stopcock, spigot, spout; tap; (coll.) tippler, drunkard.
espitar, *va.* to put a faucet on; to tap.
espito, *m.* (print.) peel, hanger.
esplancnico, ca, *a.* (anat.) splanchnic.
esplendente, *a.* (poet.) shining, resplendent.
esplender, *vn.* (poet.) to shine, glitter.
espléndidamente, *adv.* splendidly, magnificently.—**esplendidez,** *f.* splendor, grandeur; abundance; liberality.
espléndido, da, *a.* splendid, magnificent, grand; liberal; resplendent.
esplendor, *m.* splendor, magnificence, grandeur; fulgency, radiance; nobleness.
esplendorosamente, *adv.* with splendor.
esplendoroso, sa, *a.* splendid, radiant.
esplenético, ca; esplénico, ca, *a.* splenic.
esplenio, *m.* (anat.) splenium.
esplenitis, *f.* (med.) splenitis.
espliego, *m.* (bot.) lavender.
esplín, *m.* (coll.) spleen, melancholia, the blues.
esplique, *m.* bird snare.
espolada, *f.* prick with a spur.—**e. de vino,** (coll.) large draught of wine.
espolazo, *m.* violent prick with a spur.
espoleadura, *f.* wound made with a spur.
espolear, *va.* to spur; to instigate, incite.
espoleta, *f.* fuse (of a bomb); wishbone.
espolín, *m.* *dim.* small goad spur; shuttle for brocading or flowering; silk brocade.
espolinado, da, *pp.* & *a.* flowered; brocaded.
espolinar, *va.* to brocade; to flower.
espolio, *m.* (ecc.) spolium.
espolique, *m.* running footman.
espolista, *m.* running footman; one who farms a spolium.
espolón, *m.* cock's spur; ridge, crag of a mountain; (arch.) spur, buttress; (eng.) mole, breakwater, jetty, groin, starling; (naut.) ram of a man-of-war; (naut.) fender-beam.
espolonada, *f.* sudden onset of horsemen.
espolvorear, espolvorizar, *va.* to sprinkle with powder.
espondaico, ca, *a.* (poet.) spondaic.

espondeo, *m.* (poet.) spondee.
espondil, *m.* (anat.) spondyl, vertebra.
espondilitis, *f.* (med.) spondylitis.
esponja, *f.* sponge; (coll.) sponger.
esponjado, da. I. *a.* puffed up. **II.** *pp.* of ESPONJAR. **III.** *m.* = AZUCARILLO.
esponjadura, *f.,* **esponjamiento,** *m.* sponging; flaw in cast metal; puffing up.
esponjar. I. *va.* to sponge, soak, imbibe. **II.** *vr.* to swell; to puff up; (coll.) to glow with health.
esponjera, *f.* sponge holder.
esponjilla, ita, uela, *f.* *dim.* small sponge.
esponjosidad, *f.* sponginess.
esponjoso, sa, *a.* spongy, porous.
esponsales, *m. pl.* betrothal, engagement.
esponsalicio, cia, *a.* nuptial, spousal.
espontáneamente, *adv.* spontaneously.
espontanearse, *vr.* to avow or declare spontaneously or of one's own accord.
espontaneidad, *f.* spontaneity, spontaneousness.
espontáneo, nea, *a.* spontaneous; willing.
espontón, *m.* spontoon, half-pike.
espontonada, *f.* salute or blow with a spontoon.
espora, *f.,* (bot.) spore.
esporádico, ca, *a.* sporadic, isolated.
esporangio, *m.* (bot.) sporangium.
esporidio, *m.* (bot.) sporidium.
esporífero, ra, *a.* (bot.) sporiferous.
esporo, *m.* (bot.) spore.
esporocarpio, *m.* (bot.) sporocarp.
esporogonio, *m.* (bot.) sporogonium.
esporozoario, esporozoo. I. *n.* & *a.* (zool.) sporozoan. **II.** *m. pl.* Sporozoa.
esportada, *f.* frailful, basketful.—**esportear,** *va.* to carry in frails, panniers, or baskets.—**esportilla,** *f.* *'im.* small frail.—**esportillero,** *m.* porter, carrier.—**esportillo,** *m.* pannier, frail, basket.—**esportón,** *m.* *aug.* large pannier or frail.
esposa, *f.* spouse, wife.—*pl.* manacles, handcuffs, fetters, shackles.
esposar, *va.* to shackle, fetter, handcuff.
esposo, *m.* spouse, husband, consort.
espuela, *f.* spur, rowel; stimulus, incitement.—**e. de caballero,** (bot.) larkspur.
espuenda, *f.* bank of a canal.
espuerta, *f.* two-handled frail.—**a espuertas,** abundantly.
espulgadero, *m.* place where beggars clean themselves from fleas.—**espulgador, ra,** *n.* one who cleans off lice or fleas.—**espulgar,** *va.* (pret. ESPULGUÉ: subj. ESPULGUE) to clean from lice or fleas; to examine closely.—**espulgo,** *m.* act of cleaning from lice or fleas.
espuma, *f.* froth, lather, foam, scum.—**e. de la sal,** sea froth.—**e. de mar,** meerschaum.—**e. de nitro,** aphronitrum.—**e. de plata,** litharge of silver.
espumadera, *f.* skimmer, colander.
espumador, ra, *n.* & *a.* skimmer (-ing).
espumajear, *vn.* to froth at the mouth.
espumajo, *m.* froth.—**espumajoso, sa,** *a.* foamy, frothy.—**espumante,** *a.* foaming, frothing, lathering; sparkling (s. o. wine).
espumar. I. *va.* to skim, to scum. **II.** *vn.* to froth, foam.—**espumarajo,** *m.* foam or froth from the mouth.—**espumero,** *m.* place where salt water crystallizes.—**espumescente,** *a.* spumescent.
espumilla, *f.* Oriental crape, gauzy fabric.
espumillón, *m.* heavy silk crape.
espumosidad, *f.* frothiness, foaminess.
espumoso, sa, *a.* foamy, spumous, frothy, sparkling (as wine).
espundia, *f.* (vet.) cancerous ulcer.
espurio, ria, *a.* spurious, adulterated; bastard.
espurrear, espurriar, *va.* to sprinkle with water or another liquid held in the mouth.
espurrir, *va.* to stretch out (as the feet).
esputar, *va.* & *vn.* to expectorate.
esputo, *m.* spittle, saliva; sputum.
esquebrajar, *va.* = RESQUEBRAJAR.
esqueje, *m.* (agr.) cutting, slip.
esquela, *f.* billet, note.
esqueletado, da, *a.* very thin, emaciated.

For pronunciation, see the rules at the beginning of the book.

esquelético, ca, *a.* skeletal; thin, wasted.
esqueleto, *m.* skeleton; very thin person; (naut.) carcass, framework of a ship; (aut.) carcass (of a tire); (Am.) form, blank (as bill forms, application blanks, etc.); (Ch.) outline, rough draft.—**en e.,** unfinished.
esqueíita, *f. dim.* small note, billet.
esquema, *m.* symbol; scheme, plan.
esquemáticamente, *adv.* schematically.
esquemático, ca, *a.* schematic.
esquematismo, *m.* schematism.
esquematizar, *va.* to sketch, outline.
esquena, *f.* spine of fishes.
esquero, *m.* leather bag or pouch.
esquiciar, *va.* to sketch, outline, delineate.
esquicio, *m.* sketch, outline.
esquifada, *f.* skiff or boat load; vault of a cistern.
esquifar, *va.* (naut.) to fit out (a ship).
esquifazón, *f.* (naut.) boat's crew.
esquife, *m.* skiff, small boat; (arch.) cylindrical vault.
esquila, *f.* small bell; cattle bell; sheepshearing; (icht.) prawn; (ent.) waterspider; (bot.) squill.
esquiladero, *m.* shearing place.
esquilador, *m.* sheepshearer, clipper.
esquilar, *va.* to shear, crop, clip; to fleece.—**e. la carona,** to shear the back of a mule.—**sin e.,** unshorn.
esquileo, *m.* shearing.
esquilimoso, sa, *a.* (coll.) fastidious, overnice.
esquilmar, *va.* to harvest; to impoverish; to cheat, to swindle, to exploit.
esquilmeño, ña, *a.* fruitful, productive.
esquilmo, *m.* harvest; farm production.
esquilón, *m.* large call or cattle bell.
esquimal, *n.* & *a.* Eskimo.
esquina, *f.* corner, nook, angle.
esquinado, da, *pp.* & *a.* cornered, angled; intractable, unsociable.
esquinal, *m.* corner plate; angle iron; iron knee.
esquinante, to, *m.* (bot.) aromatic rush.
esquinar. I. *va.* to form a corner with, meet forming a corner; to square (timber, etc.); to estrange, cause to quarrel, set against. **II.** *vr.* to quarrel, to fall out.
esquinazo, *m.* corner; (Ch.) serenade.—**dar e.,** to dodge, to evade, get out of the sight of (one that follows), shake off; to abandon, leave in the lurch.
esquinco, *m.* skink, lizard.
esquinela, *f.* (arm.) greave, jambe.
esquinzador, *m.* rag room in paper mills; rag engine.
esquinzar, *va.* to cut (rags) in paper mills.
esquirla, *f.* (surg.) splinter of a bone.
esquirol, *m.* (coll.) strike breaker, scab; (prov.) = ARDILLA.
esquisto, *m.* (min.) schist; slate.
esquistoso, sa, *a.* laminated; schistose, slaty.
esquitar, *va.* to pardon, to remit (a debt).
esquite, *m.* (Mex.) popped corn.
esquivar. I. *va.* to shun, elude, avoid, evade, escape. **II.** *vr.* to disdain, withdraw, coy.
esquivez, *f.* disdain, asperity, coldness.
esquivo, va, *a.* elusive, evading; shy, reserved, coyish, cold.
esquizado, da, *a.* mottled (as marble).
estabilidad, *f.* stability.
estabilísimo, *adv. sup.* very stable or firm.
estable, *a.* stable, steady, firm, fast.
establear, *va.* to tame, accustom to the stable.
establecedor, ra, *n.* founder.
establecer. I. *va.* (ind. ESTABLEZCO: *subj.* ESTABLEZCA) to establish, found; to decree, enact. **II.** *vr.* to establish or settle one's self.
estableciente, *n.* & *a.* establisher (-ing).
establecimiento, *m.* establishment; statute, law, ordinance, decree; establishment, founding; institution.
establemente, *adv.* stably, firmly.
establero, *m.* hostler, groom, horsekeeper.
establo, *m.* stable; cattle barn.
estabulación, *f.* stabling.

estaca, *f.* stake, picket, pile, pole; stick, cudgel, bludgeon; (agr.) grafting twig; cutting; (carp.) clamp nail.
estacada, *f.* (mil.) palisade, stockade; paling, fence work; pile pier; place for a duel.
estacar. I. *va.* (*pret.* ESTAQUÉ: *subj.* ESTAQUE) to stake; to fence with stakes; to tie to a stake. **II.** *vr.* to remain stiff as a pole.
estación, *f.* state, condition, position; season (of the year); hour, moment, time; (r. w.) station, depot; devotional visit to a church; stay, stop; telegraph or police station; party of persons posted at some place; (astr.) stationary point; (ecc.) station; (surv.) station.
estacional, *a.* seasonal; (ast.) stationary.
estacionamiento, *m.* stationing, settling.
estacionario, ria, *a.* stationary.
estacionarse, *vr.* to remain stationary.
estacionero, ra, *n.* one who prays before stations in church.
estacón, *m. aug.* large stake.
estacte, *m.* oil of myrrh.
estacha, *f.* (naut.) towline, hawser; harpoon rope.
estada, *f.* stay, sojourn.
estadal, *m.* a linear measure of about 10 ft. 9 in.; blessed ribbon worn around the neck.
estadía, *f.* (surv.) stadia, stadia transit.
estadía, *f.* (com. and naut.) stay, detention; demurrage; cost of such stay.
estadio, *m.* race course; stadium (road measure).
estadista, *m.* statesman.
estadística, *f.* statistics.
estadístico, ca, *a.* statistical.
estadizo, za, *a.* stagnant (as water).
estado. I. *m.* state; condition (of persons or things, (as, *eso llegó en mal estado,* that came in bad condition); estate, class, rank; profession; state, condition (whether single, married, or widowed); state, nation, commonwealth; statement, account, report; a measure of length (1.85 yds.).—*pl.* States, legislature (*los Estados Generales,* the States-General) (ch. constr.: *declarar una ciudad en estado de guerra,* to declare a city in a state of martial law, to put it under martial law).—**e. general,** or **e. llano,** the commons, the common state (as distinguished from the nobility, etc.).—**e. mayor,** (mil.) staff.—**e. mayor general,** (mil.) general staff. **II.** *pp.* of ESTAR.
estadojo, estadonio, *m.* stake of a cart.
estafa, *f.* swindle, trick, deceit; stirrup.
estafador, ra, *n.* swindler.
estafar, *va.* to swindle, defraud.
estafermo, *m.* movable wooden figure of an armed man; idle fellow.
estafeta, *f.* courier, post, express; post office; general-delivery office or department (of post office); post-office branch.
estafetero, *m.* postmaster; post-office clerk.
estafetil, *a.* belonging to a courier or post.
estafilocacia, *f.* (bact.) infection due to staphylococci.
estafilococo, *m.* (bact.) staphylococcus.
estafiloma, *m.* (med.) staphyloma.
estafisagra, *f.* (bot.) stavesacre, lousewort.
estagirita, *n.* & *a.* Stagirite.
estala, *f.* seaport, stopping place.
estalación, *f.* class, rank, order.
estalactita, *f.* stalactite.
estalagmita, *f.* stalagmite.
estallante, *a.* bursting, exploding.
estallar, *vn.* to explode, burst.
estallido, estallo, *m.* crack, crackling, crashing, crash, snap, outburst; report (as of firearms).
estambor, *m.* (naut.) sternpost.
estambrado, *m.* worsted cloth.
estambrar, *va.* to spin (worsted).
estambre, *m.* worsted, woollen yarn; (bot.) stamen.
estamenara, *f.* (naut.) futtock.
estamento, *m.* one of the estates composing the Cortes in Aragon (clergy, nobility, commons).

estameña, *f.* tammy cloth, serge.

estameñete, *m.* a kind of serge.

estamíneo, nea, *a.* made of worsted.

estaminífero, ra, *a.* (bot.) staminate.

estampa. I. *f.* print, stamp, cut; engraving; first sketch; printing, press; track, impression, footstep.—**estampas iluminadas,** colored plates.—**la e. de la herejía,** (coll.) a hideous face. **II.** *m.* impression, stamping.

estampado, *m.* cotton print, calico; impression, stamping; cloth printing.

estampador, *m.* stamper; stamp, puncheon.

estampar, *va.* to print, stamp, emboss; to imprint, give (as a kiss); to impress, fix (as in the mind).

estampería, *f.* office for printing or selling prints.

estampero, ra, *n.* stamp or print maker or seller.

estampida, *f.* stampede.—**dar una e.,** (coll.) to run away in debt.

estampido, *m.* report of a gun; crack, crash.

estampilla, *f.* *dim.* small print; rubber stamp; signet, seal; postage stamp.

estampillado, *m.* stamping.

estampillar, *va.* to stamp.

estampita, *f.* *dim.* small print or stamp.

estancación, *f.*, **estancamiento,** *m.* stagnation.

estancar. I. *va.* (*pret.* ESTANQUÉ; *subj.* ESTANQUE) to stanch, check, stem; (naut.) to fother (a leak); (com.) to corner, to monopolize; to interdict, suspend. **II.** *vr.* to stagnate, become stagnant.

estancia, *f.* stay, sojourn; dwelling, habitation; sitting room, living room; (poet.) stanza; (Am.) small farm.

estanciero, ra, *n..* small farmer.

estanco, ca. I. *a.* water-tight. **II.** *m.* monopoly; store for monopolized goods; repository, archives, files.

estandarte, *m.* standard, flag, banner, colors.

estangurria, *f.* strangury; catheter.

estannato, *m.* (chem.) stannate.

estánnico, ca, *a.* (chem.) stannic.

estannoso, sa, *a.* (chem.) stannous.

estanque, *m.* pond, reservoir, pool.

estanquero, ra, *n.* reservoir keeper; retailer of monopoly goods; tobacconist.—**estanquillero, ra,** *n.* tobacconist.—**estanquillo,** *m.* cigar store.

estanquito, *m.* *dim.* small pond, pool.

estantal, *m.* (arch.) buttress.

estante. I. *a.* existing, extant; fixed, permanent. **II.** *m.* shelf; bookcase; (print.) cabinet.—*pl.* (naut.) props of the crossbeams.

estantería, *f.* shelving.

estantigua, *f.* phantom, vision, hobgoblin; (coll.) tall, skinny, uncouth person, fright.

estantío, tía, *a.* standing still, stationary; dull, slow.

estañador, *m.* tinner, tinman.—**estañadura,** *f.* tinning.—**estañar,** *va.* to tin, blanch; to solder.—**estañero,** *m.* tinner; seller of tinware.

estaño, *m.* (chem.) tin.

estaquero, *m.* year-old buck or doe.

estaquilla, ita, *f.* (shoe.) peg; wooden pin; spike, long nail.

estaquillador, *m.* (shoe.) pegging awl.

estaquillar, *va.* to peg, to fasten with pegs.

estar. I. *vn.* (*ind.* ESTOY; *pret.* ESTUVE; *subj.* ESTÉ) to be. When followed by the gerund of a reflexive verb, it sometimes takes the reflexive pronoun from that verb (*estarse vistiendo,* instead of *estar vistiéndose,* to be dressing). When preceded by a dative case, "for" is used in English before the corresponding objective case (*este sombrero me está demasiado grande,* this hat is too large for me; *eso no me es posible,* that is not possible for me).—**e. a,** to sell at (so much) apiece.—**e. al,** to be on the point of.—**e. bien,** to be well; to be all right, acceptable, suitable.—**e. con,** to live in company with; to be engaged or talking with; to have (a disease), to be ill with; to be in a state of (anxiety, anger, etc.).—**e. de,** to be in the condition or doing the act indicated by the following noun (*estoy de mudanza,* I am moving; *estoy de prisa,* I am in haste; *estoy de vaca-*

ciones, I am on my vacation; *Juan está de cónsul,* John is now consul).—**e. en,** to understand, comprehend (*estoy en lo que Vd. me dice,* I understand what you say); to be of opinion; to stand, to cost (*este sombrero me está en seis pesos,* this hat costs me six dollars); to depend (*en eso está,* it depends on that); to lie, consist.—**e. en grande,** to live in luxury.—**e. en sí,** to know what one is doing.—**e. para,** to be about to; to be in a mood or in condition to or for (*no estoy para eso,* I am in no mood for that).—**e. por,** to be for, in favor of; (followed by *infin.*) to remain to be, not to have been (followed by *pp.*); to have a mind to, to have a notion or a desire to.—**e. por ver,** to remain to be seen.—**e. sobre sí,** to be cautious or wary; to be puffed up with conceit.—**¿a cómo estamos? ¿a cuántos estamos?** what date (of the month) is it? what is the date?—**¡dónde estás!** what have we come to! what a thing!—an expression of admiration or disgust at what is seen or heard.—**está escrito,** it is written.—**¿estamos?** is it agreed? do you understand?—**estamos a** (followed by the day, date), this is, it is (*estamos a lunes,* this is Monday; *estamos a cinco,* this is the fifth).—**¿está Vd.?** do you understand? do you see the point? **II.** *vr.* to be, to keep; to stay, to remain (*Juan nunca se está callado,* John is never silent, or, never keeps silent; *debemos estarnos aquí,* we must remain here).

estarcido, *m.* pounced drawing; stencil.

estarcir, *va.* to stencil.

estarna, *f.* (orn.) small partridge.

estática, *f.* (mech.) statics.

estático, ca, *a.* static, statical.

estator, *m.* (mech., elec.) stator.

estatua, *f.* statue.—**quedarse hecho una e.,** to stand aghast, to be rooted to the ground.

estatuar, *va.* to adorn with statues.—**estatuaria,** *f.* (art) statuary, sculpture.—**estatuario, ria. I.** *a.* belonging to statuary. **II.** *m.* statuary; sculptor.

estatúder, *m.* stadtholder.

estatuderato, *m.* stadtholdership.

estatuir, *va.* to establish, ordain, enact.

estatura, *f.* stature, height of a person.

estatuto, *m.* statute, law, ordinance.

estay, *m.* (naut.) stay.

este, *m.* east, orient.

este, *m.,* **esta,** *f.,* *a.* this.—*pl.* **estos, estas,** these.

éste, *m.,* **ésta,** *f.* *pron. dem.* this, this one; the latter.—*pl.* **éstos,** *m.,* **éstas,** *f.,* these; the latter.

esté. *V.* ESTAR.

esteárico, ca, *a.* stearic.—**estearina,** *f.* stearine.

esteatita, *f.* (min.) steatite, soapstone.

esteba, *f.* prickly plant growing in swamps; stevedore's pole.

estebar, *va.* to put (cloth) in the dye kettle.

estela, *f.* (naut.) wake, track of a ship; (arch.) stela.

estelar, *a.* sidereal, stellar.

estelaria, *f.* (bot.) silvery lady's-mantle.

estelárido, da. I. *n.* & *a.* (zool.) asteroidean. **II.** *m. pl.* Asteroidea, starfishes.

estelífero, ra, *a.* (poet.) stelliferous, starry.

esteliforme, *a.* stelliform, star-shaped.

estelión, *m.* (zool.) stellion; toadstone.

estelionato, *m.* (law) stellionate.

estelón, *m.* toadstone.

estelulado, da, *a.* stellular, star-shaped.

estemple, *m.* (min.) stemple.

estenografía, *f.* stenography, shorthand.

estenografiar, *va.* to stenograph, take down in shorthand.

estenográficamente, *adv.* stenographically.

estenográfico, ca, *a.* stenographic.

estenógrafo, fa, *n.* stenographer.

estenosis, *f.* (med.) stenosis, narrowing.

estentóreo, a, *a.* stentorian.

estepa, *f.* (bot.) rockrose; steppe, barren plain.

estepar, *m.* rockrose field.

estepilla, *f.* (bot.) white-leaved rockrose

éster, *m.* (chem.) ester.

estera, *f.* mat, matting.

esterar. I. *va.* to cover with matting. **II.** *vn.* (coll.) to wear winter clothes before time.

estercoladura, f., **estercolamiento,** m. manuring.—**estercolar. I.** va. to dung, muck, manure. **II.** vn. to void the excrements.—**estercolero,** m. driver of a muck cart; dung hill, dung heap.

estercolizo, za; estercóreo, a, a. stercoraceous.

estercuelo, m. stercoration, manuring.

estéreo, m. stere (one cubic metre).

estereocromía, f. stereochromy.

estereografía, f. stereogaphy.

estereográfico, ca, a. stereographic.

esterógrafo, m. stereographer.

estereometría, f. stereometry.

estereómetro, m. stereometer.

estereoscopio, m. stereoscope.

estereotipa, f. = ESTEREOTIPIA.

estereotipador, m. stereotyper.

estereotipar, va. to stereotype; to print from stereotypes.

estereotipia, f. stereotypography, stereotyping; place where stereotypes are made.

estereotípico, ca, a. stereotypic.

estereotomía, f. stereotomy.

esterería, f. matting factory or shop.

esterero, ra, n.. matting maker or seller.

estéril, a. sterile, barren; unfruitful, fruitless.

esterilidad, f. sterility, barrenness; scarcity, want of crops.

esterilizador, ra, n. & a. sterilizer (-ing).

esterilizar, va. to sterilize.

esterilla, f. dim. small mat; straw plait; narrow gold or silver braid.

estérilmente, adv. barrenly, fruitlessly.

esterlín, m. = BOCACÍ.

esterlina, a. sterling (pound).

esternón, m. (anat.) sternum, breastbone.

estero, m. inlet, estuary; matting, covering with matting; matting season.

esterquilinio, m. dunghill, dung heap.

estertor, m. rattle in the throat; stertor.

estertoroso, sa, a. stertorous.

esteta, n. æsthetician; sodomite.

estética, f. æsthetics.—**estéticamente,** adv. æsthetically.—**estético, ca,** a. æsthetic.

estetoscopia, f. (med.) stethoscopy.

estetoscopio, m. (med.) stethoscope.

esteva, f. plow handle; reach of a carriage.

estevado, da, a. bow-legged.

estevón, m. = ESTEVA.

estezado, m. = CORREAL.

estiaje, m. low-water mark.

estiba, f. rammer; place where wool is compressed; (naut.) stowage.

estibador, m. stevedore, longshoreman.

estibar, va. to compress (wool); (naut.) to stow.

estibia, f. (vet.) luxation. V. ESPIBIA.

estibio, m. antimony, stibium.

estibina, f. (min.) stibine.

estiércol, m. dung, manure.

estigio, gia, a. Stygian.

estigma, m. birthmark; stigma, brand, mark of infamy; affront, disgrace; (bot.) stigma.

estigmatizador, ra, n. & a. stigmatizer (-ing).

estigmatizar, va. to stigmatize; to affront.

estilar. I. va. to use, be in the habit of using; to draw up (a document). **II.** vr. to be in style.

estilicidio, m. stillicide, dropping, eavesdrop.

estilista, n. stylist, master of style.

estilita, a. stylite, pillarist; (E-), Stylites (St. Simeon).

estilo, m. style (writing instrument); gnomon or style of a dial; (arch. and lit.) style; use, custom, fashion; (bot.) style.—**e. antiguo,** (chron.) old style.—**e. familiar,** colloquial style.—**e. nuevo,** (chron.) new style.—**por e.,** or **por ese e.,** of that kind, like that.

estilóbato, m. (arch.) stylobate, pedestal.

estilográfico, ca. I. a. **pluma,** f. fountain pen. **II.** f. fountain pen.

estima, f. esteem; (naut.) dead reckoning.

estimabilidad, f. estimableness; worth.

estimabilísimo, ma, a. sup. most estimable.

estimable, a. estimable, worthy, excellent; computable.

estimación, f. esteem, regard; estimate, valuation.—**e. propia,** self-respect.

estimador, ra, n. esteemer; estimator.

estimar, va. to estimate, value; to esteem, respect, honor; to judge; to thank.

estimativa, f. power of judging; instinct.

estimulante. I. a. stimulating, exciting. **II.** m. stimulant.

estimular, va. to stimulate; to goad, incite, encourage.

estímulo, m. stimulus; inducement; incitement; stimulation; encouragement.

estinco, m. skink, a kind of lizard.

estío, m. summer.

estiomenar, va. (med.) to corrode, mortify.

estiómeno, m. (med.) mortification, gangrene.

estipendiar, va. to give a stipend to.

estipendiario, m. stipendiary.

estipendio, m. stipend, salary, pay, wages, fee.

estípite, m. (arch.) pilaster in the form of an inverted pyramid.

estipticar, va. (med.) to apply a styptic to.

estipticidad, f. (med.) stypticity.

estíptico, ca, a. styptic, astringent; costive; (met.) miserly, stingy.

estiptiquez, f. stypticity.

estípula, f. (bot.) stipule.

estipulación, f. stipulation, proviso, specification, requirement.

estipulante, n. & a. stipulator (-ing).

estipular, va. to stipulate, covenant, specify.

estira, f. knife used by curriers.

estiracáceo, a. styracaceous.

estiradamente, adv. scarcely; with difficulty; violently, forcibly.

estirado, da. I. pp. & a. extended, stretched; stiff, stuck up; drawn.—**e. en frío,** hard-drawn (s. o. metals). **II.** m. stretching; drawing.

estirador, ra, n. stretcher; drawing frame.

estirajar, va. (coll.) = ESTIRAR.

estirajón, m. (coll.) = ESTIRÓN.

estiramiento, m. stretching, pulling; drawing (of metals).

estirar. I. va. to stretch, lengthen; to pull; to draw (metals).—**e. en frío,** to hard-draw. **II.** vr. to stretch; to become airy, to put on airs.

estirazar, va. (coll.)=ESTIRAR.

estirón, m. strong pull; pluck, haul or hauling; rapid growth.

estirpe, f. stock, lineage, pedigree.

estítico, ca, a. = ESTÍPTICO.

estivada, f. burning of undergrowth.

estival, vo, va, a. summer (u. a.).

esto, pron. dem. neut. this.—**e. es,** that is; that is so.—**a e.,** hereto, hereunto.—**con e.,** herewith.—**en e.,** at this juncture; at once, right away; herein, hereinto.—**por e.,** hereby; that is why; for this reason.—**sobre e.,** hereon, hereupon.

estocada, f. stab, thrust, tilt, lunge.

estocafís, m. (com.) stockfish.

estofa, f. quilted silk stuff; quality, condition.

estofado, da. I. pp. & a. quilted; ornamented; stewed. **II.** m. stew.

estofador, m. quilter.

estofar, va. to quilt; to paint on a gilt ground; to size before gilding; to stew.

estofo, m. quilting; painting on gilt; sizing.

estoicamente, adv. stoically.—**estoicidad,** f. imperturbability.—**estoicismo,** m. stoicism.—**estoico, ca,** n. & a. stoic (-al).

estola, f. stole, worn by priests.

estolidez, f. stupidity, incapacity.

estólido, da, a. stupid, foolish.

estolón, m. aug. large stole; (bot.) stolon.

estoma, m. (bot.) stoma.

estomacal, a. stomachic.

estomagar, vn. & va. (pret. ESTOMAGUÉ: subj. ESTOMAGUE) to bore; to annoy, make angry.

estómago, *m.* stomach.—**tener buen e.,** or **mucho e.,** to ignore slights and offences, to be thick-skinned; to have an elastic conscience.

estomaguero, *m.* stomacher.—**estomatical,** *a.* stomachic.—**estomaticón,** *m.* stomach plaster.

estomatitis, *f.* stomatitis.

estopa, *f.* tow; burlap; oakum.

estopada, *f.* quantity of tow for spinning.

estopear, *va.* to calk with oakum.

estopeño, ña, *a.* tow (u. a.).

estoperol, *m.* (naut.) scupper nail; tow wick.

estopilla, *f.* finest part of hemp or flax; lawn, batiste, cheesecloth.

estopín, *m.* (arti.) priming tube; quick match.

estopón, *m.* coarse tow.

estopor, *m.* (naut.) stopper.

estoposo, sa, *a.* towlike, filaceous.

estoque, *m.* estoc, rapier; (bot.) corn flag.

estoqueador, *m.* matador (bull fighter).

estoquear, *va.* to make a thrust at with a rapier.

estoqueo, *m.* thrusting or stabbing.

estoraque, *m.* (bot.) officinal storax; gum of the storax tree.

estorbador, ra, *n.* & *a.* hinderer (-ing), obstructor (-ing).

estorbar, *va.* to hinder; obstruct; be in the way.

estorbo, *m.* hindrance, obstruction, nuisance.

estorboso, sa, *a.* hindering, in the way.

estornija, *f.* linchpin; washer; a boys' play.

estornino, *m.* (orn.) starling.

estornudar, *vn.* to sneeze.—**estornudo,** *m.* sneeze.—**estornutatorio,** *m.* sternutatory.

estotro, tra, compound pronoun of ESTO and OTRO, this other.

estovar, *va.* = REHOGAR.

estoy. *V.* ESTAR.

estrabismo, *m.* (med.) strabismus, squint.

estracilla, *f.* small rag; coarse brown paper; blotting paper.

estrada, *f.* causeway, paved road.—**e. encubierta,** (mil.) covert way.

estradiota, *f.* riding with long stirrups and stiff legs; a kind of lance.

estradiote, *m.* estradiot, Greek horseman.

estrado, *m.* drawing room; drawing-room furniture; dais for a throne; baker's table; lecturing platform.—*pl.* court rooms.

estrafalariamente, *adv.* (coll.) carelessly, slovenly; wildly, queerly, strangely.

estrafalario, ria, *a.* (coll.) slovenly; wild; odd, queer, eccentric.

estragadamente, *adv.* depravedly.

estragador, ra, *a.* corrupting, destroying.

estragamiento, *m.* disorder, depravation.

estragar, *va.* (pret. ESTRAGUÉ: subj. ESTRAGUE) to deprave, vitiate, corrupt, spoil.

estrago, *m.* ravage, ruin, havoc; wickedness.

estragón, *m.* (bot.) tarragon wormwood.

estrambote, *m.* burden of a song.

estrambóticamente, *adv.* oddly, queerly.

estrambótico, ca, *a.* odd, queer, eccentric.

estramonio, *m.* (bot.) common thorn apple.

estrangol, *m.* inflammation in a horse's tongue.

estrangul, *m.* (mus.) mouthpiece.

estrangulación, *f.* strangling, choking; strangulation; (st. eng.) throttling; (hyd.) stoppage.

estrangulador, ra, *n.* & *a.* strangler (-ing).

estrangular, *va.* to strangle, choke, throttle; (med.) to strangulate; (st. eng.) to throttle.

estratagema, *f.* stratagem; trick, artful deception; craftiness; finesse; fetch.

estrategia, *f.* (mil.) strategy.

estratégicamente, *adv.* strategically.

estratégico, ca. I. *a.* (mil.) strategic. **II.** *n.* strategist.

estratego, ga, *n.* strategist.

estratificación, *f.* (min.) stratification.

estratificar, *va.* & *vr.* (min.) to stratify.

estratiforme, *a.* stratiform.

estratigrafía, *f.* stratigraphy.

estratigráfico, ca, *a.* stratigraphical.

estrato, *m.* stratum, layer; stratus (cloud).

estrave, *m.* (naut.) stem knee.

estraza, *f.* rag, fragment of cloth.

estrechamente, *adv.* narrowly; tightly, closely; intimately; nearly, hardly; exactly, punctually; strongly, forcibly; strictly, rigorously; scantily, penuriously.

estrechamiento, *m.* tightening; narrowing.

estrechar. I. *va.* to tighten; to narrow, reduce, contract; to constrain, compel; to press; to follow closely.—**e. la mano,** to shake hands; to greet; to send regards or good wishes. **II.** *vr.* to narrow; to bind one's self strictly; reduce one's expenses; become related or intimate; to act in concert.

estrechez. I. *f.* narrowness; tightness; compactness, closeness; intimacy; austerity; penury, poverty. **II.** *m.* strait, pass, narrow passage; peril, danger, risk.

estrecho, cha. I. *a.* narrow; tight; intimate, close; rigid, austere; exact, punctual; narrowminded, illiberal, mean-spirited; poor, indigent, penurious; stingy, close.—**e. de conciencia,** over-scrupulous, narrow-minded. **II.** *m.* Valentine; predicament, fix; (geog.) strait, channel.—**al e.,** by force, by compulsion.—**poner en e.,** to force.

estrechón, *m.* (naut.) = SOCOLLADA.—**e. de manos,** handshaking.

estrechura, *f.* narrowness, straitness; narrow passage, narrows; austerity; distress, predicament, straits; intimate familiarity.

estregadera, *f.* scrubbing brush, mop.

estregadero, *m.* object on which beasts rub themselves; washing place for clothes.

estregadura, *f.,* **estregamiento,** *m.* rubbing; scrubbing.

estregar, *va.* (ind. ESTRIEGO: pret. ESTREGUÉ: subj. ESTRIEGUE) to rub; scour, scrub; scratch (as matches).

estregón, *m.* aug. rough rubbing.

estrella, *f.* star; star wheel; star (on a horse's forehead); (mil.) star fort.—**e. de mar,** starfish.—**e. de rabo,** comet.—**e. fija,** fixed star.—**e. fugaz,** shooting star.—**e. polar,** polestar, Polaris.—**con estrellas,** after night, before sunrise.—**poner por las estrellas,** to lionize, to overpraise.—**ver. estrellas,** to feel racking pain; to see stars (fig.).

estrellada, *f.* (bot.) ladies' mantle.

estrelladera, *f.* (cook.) egg slice, turnover.

estrelladero, *m.* pan for candied yolks.

estrellado, da, *pp.* & *a.* starry; scar-faced (s. o. horses); fried (eggs).

estrellamar, *f.* (bot.) buckthorn plantain; (icht.) starfish.

estrellar. I. *va.* (coll.) to dash to pieces, shatter; to fry (eggs). **II.** *vr.* to fail; (w. contra) to butt (against), dash (against), be shattered (by)—gen. with the implication of failure, damage or destruction.

estrellar, *a.* stellated, starry.

estrellera, *f.* (naut.) foretackle; burton.

estrellero, ra, *a.* that throws up his head (s. o horses).

estrellica, ita, uela, *f.* dim. little star.

estrellón, *m.* aug. large star; star-shaped piece in fireworks.

estremecedor, ra, *a.* frightful, terrifying.

estremecer. I. *va.* (ind. ESTREMEZCO: subj. ESTREMEZCA) to shake, to make tremble. **II.** *vr.* to shake, tremble, shudder.

estremecimiento, *m.* trembling, shaking; shudder, shuddering

estrena, *f.* gift; love offering, remembrance; first use of a thing; inauguration; début.

estrenar. I. *va.* to handsel, to use or to do by the first time; to commence, begin, inaugurate. **II.** *vr.* to begin to act in some capacity; (theat.) to make one's début; to appear for the first time.

estreno, *m.* commencement, handsel, inauguration; (theat.) first performance; début.

estrenque, *m.* stout esparto rope.

estrenuidad, *f.* vigor, energy, enterprise.

estrenuo, nua, *a.* strong, vigorous; enterprising.

estreñido, da, *pp.* & *a.* costive; stingy.

estreñimiento, *m.* costiveness.
estreñir. I. *va.* (*ind.* ESTRIÑO: *subj.* ESTRIÑA) to bind, constipate. **II.** *vr.* to become costive.
estrepada, *f.* (naut.) a pull in unison.
estrépito, *m.* crash, din, deafening noise.
estrepitosamente, *adv.* noisily, obstreperously.
estrepitoso, sa, *a.* noisy, deafening; boisterous, obstreperous.
estreptococia, *f.* (med.) infection by streptococci.
estreptococo, *m.* (bact.) Streptococcus.
estría, *f.* (arch.) fluting, stria, groove.
estriadura, *f.* (arch.) fluting, grooving.
estriar. I. *va.* (arch.) to flute, to gutter. **II.** *vr.* to become grooved, striated.
estribación, *f.* (geog. and arch.) counterfort.
estribadero, *m.* prop, stay.
estribar, *vn.* (w. **en**) to rest (on); to be based (on), to lie (in).
estribera, *f.* stirrup (of a saddle or an arbalist).
estribería, *f.* stirrup factory or shop.
estriberón, *m.* stepping stone; (mil.) temporary road.
estribillo, *m.* burden or refrain of a song.
estribo, *m.* stirrup; step or footboard of a coach; (mech.) brace, stay, stirrup bolt; clasp of the felloes; (arch.) buttress, abutment; (met.) rest, support, basis; (carp.) cross prop, main brace; (geog.) counterfort.—**perder los estribos,** to talk nonsense; to lose one's head.
estribor, *m.* (naut.) starboard.
estricnina, *f.* (med.) strychnine.
estricote.—al e., without rule or order.
estrictamente, *adv.* strictly.—**estrictez,** *f.*(Am.) strictness.—**estricto, ta,** *a.* strict.
estridente, *a.* obstreperous; strident.
estridor, *m.* noise, creak, screech.
estrige, *f.* (orn.) screech owl; vampire.
estrigilación, *f.* (med.) strigilation, vigorous rubbing or brushing.
estro, *m.* (poet.) afflatus, inspiration.
estróbilo, *m.* (bot.) strobile, cone.
estrobo, *m.* loop formed with a short rope or cable; (aer.) grummet.
estrofa, *f.* (poet.) stanza.
estroma, *m.* (anat.) stroma.
estronciana, *f.* (chem.) strontia.
estroncianita, *f.* (min.) strontianite.
estroncio, *m.* (chem.) strontium.
estropajear, *va.* (mas.) to rub; to scrub.
estropajeo, *m.* (mas.) rubbing, scrubbing.
estropajo, *m.* mop; swab, dishclout; esparto scrubbing broom; worthless thing.
estropajosamente, *adv.* stammeringly.
estropajoso, sa, *a.* (coll.) ragged, slovenly; (coll.) tough (meat); (coll.) stammering.
estropeado, da, *pp.* & *a.* lame, crippled; damaged; fatigued.
estropear, *va.* to maim, cripple; to damage or spoil by rough usage; to spoil, ruin (a thing, plan, etc.); (mas.) to stir (mortar).
estropeo, *m.* rough usage; injury or damage; fatigue, weariness.
estropicio, *m.* (coll.) breakage, crash (of table service, etc.); needless turmoil.
estrovo, *m.* (naut.) strap for blocks.
estructura, *f.* structure; order, method.
estructural, *a.* structural.
estruendo, *m.* din, clangor, clamor, clatter; confusion, turmoil; pomp, ostentation.
estruendosamente, *adv.* noisily, obstreperously.
estruendoso, sa, *a.* obstreperous, noisy, loud.
estrujadura, *f.,* **estrujamiento,** *m.* pressing, squeezing, crushing, rumpling.
estrujar, *va.* to press, squeeze, crush, rumple, mash, jam, bruise.
estrujón, *m.* last pressing of grapes; crush, squeeze, pressure, jam.
estrupador, *m.,* **estrupar,** *va.,* **estrupo,** *m.* = ESTUPRADOR, ESTUPRAR, ESTUPRO.
estuación, *f.* flow of the tide.
estuante, *a.* hot, boiling, glowing.
estuario, *m.* estuary, inlet.

estucador, *m.* stucco plasterer.
estucar, *va.* & *vn.* (mas.) to stucco.
estuco, *m.* stucco; plaster, scagliola.
estuche, *m.* case (as for jewelry, etc.); box, casket; étui, sheath (for scissors, etc.); cabinet; small comb; in card games, certain combination of cards; a clever, handy fellow.
estudiador, ra, *a.* (coll.) very studious.
estudiante, *m.* student.
estudiantil, *a.* (coll.) scholastic, student (u. a.), college (u. a.), of students.
estudiantillo, lla, *n. dim.* little student.
estudiantina, *f.* students; strolling band of students.
estudiantino, na, *a.* (coll.) belonging to students.—**a la e.,** (coll.) in the manner of students.
estudiantón, *m. aug.* assiduous but slow student.
estudiar, *va.* to study; (art) to copy.
estudio, *m.* study; investigation; discussion, paper (article, writing); college, school; library, reading room; studio.—*pl.* sciences, letters.—**estudios mayores,** higher studies.
estudiosamente, *adv.* studiously.
estudiosidad, *f.* studiousness.
estudioso, sa, *a.* studious.
estufa, *f.* stove; heater; hothouse; drying chamber, dry bath; sweating room, sudatory; small brasier.
estufador, *m.* stewpan.
estufero, estufista, *m.* stove maker.
estufilla, *f.* hand muff; foot stove; chafer.
estultamente, *adv.* foolishly.
estulticia, *f.* foolishness, silliness.
estulto, ta, *a.* foolish, silly.
estuosidad, *f.* burning, heat, glow.
estuoso, sa, *a.* hot, ardent, glowing.
estupefacción, *f.* stupefaction, numbness.
estupefactivo, va, *a.* stupefying.
estupefacto, *a.* motionless, stupefied.
estupendamente, *adv.* stupendously.
estupendo, da, *a.* stupendous, wonderful.
estúpidamente, *adv.* stupidly.—**estupidez,** *f.* stupidity.—**estúpido, da,** *a.* stupid.
estupor, *m.* (med.) stupor; amazement.
estuprador, *m.* ravisher, violator.
estuprar, *va.* to ravish, violate.
estupro, *m.* ravishment, rape, constupration.
estuque, *m.* stucco.—**estuquería,** *f.* stuccoing; stucco work.—**estuquista,** *n.* stuccoer.
esturar, *va.* to dry by fire; overcook.
esturgar, *va.* to polish (delft ware).
esturión, *m.* (icht.) sturgeon.
estuve, estuvo. *V.* ESTAR.
ésula, *f.* (bot.) leafy-branched spurge.
esviaje, *m.* (arch.) obliquity.
etalaje, *m.* bosh (of a blast furnace).
etapa, *f.* (mil.) ration given to troops in the field; stage; station, stop.
etcétera, *f.* et cætera.
éter, *m.* (phys., chem.) ether; (poet.) the sky.
etéreo, rea, *a.* ethereal; (poet.) heavenly.
eterificación, *f.* (chem.) etherification.
eterificar, *va.* (chem.) to etherify, convert into ether.
eterismo, *m.* etherism, effect of excessive ether.
eterización, *f.* (med.) etherization.
eterizar, *va.* (med.) to etherize.
eternal, *a.* eternal.—**eternalmente, eternamente,** *adv.* eternally; everlastingly.
eternidad, *f.* eternity.—**eternizar. I.** *va.* (*pret.* ETERNICÉ: *subj.* ETERNICE) to eternize, perpetuate; to prolong indefinitely. **II.** *vr.* to be everlasting, to be exceedingly slow, to stay forever (fig.).—**eterno, na,** *a.* eternal, everlasting.
eteromanía, *f.* ether habit.
eterómano, na, *n.* one afflicted with the ether habit, ether fiend.
etesio, *a.* etesian, recurring yearly.
ética, *f.* ethics.—**éticamente,** *adv.* ethically.
ético, ca. I. *a.* ethical, moral; (med.) hectic, consumptive. **II.** *n.* ethicist.
etileno, *m.* (chem.) ethylene.

etílico, ca, *a.* (chem.) ethylic.
etilo, *m.* (chem.) ethyl.
etimología, *f.* etymology.
etimológicamente, *adv.* etymologically.
etimológico, ca, *a.* etymological.
etimologista, *m.* etymologist.
etimologizar, *va.* to etymologize.
etimólogo, ga, *n.* etymologist.
etiología, *f.* (philos. and med.) etiology.
etíope: etiópico, ca; etiopio, a, *n.* & *a.* Ethiopian (-ic).
etiópide, *f.* (bot.) clary, Ethiopian mullein.
etiqueta, *f.* etiquette, ceremony, formality; (com.) label.—de e., ceremonious, formal.—estar de e., to be distant, cool to each other.
etiquetero, ra, *a.* ceremonious, formal.
etiquez, *f.* = HETIQUEZ.
etites, *f.* (min.) eaglestone, ætites.
etmoides, *m.* (anat.) ethmoid.
etnarca, *m.* ethnarch.—etnarquía, *f.* ethnarchy.
étnico, ca, ethnic.
etnografía, *f.* ethnography.—etnográfico, ca, *a.* ethnographic.—etnógrafo, ethnographer.
etnología, *f.* ethnology.—etnológico, ca, *a.* ethnologic.—etnólogo, *m.* ethnologist.
etrusco, ca, *n.* & *a.* Etruscan.
eubeo, a; euboico, ca, *n.* & *a.* Eubœan, Euboic.
eubolia, *f.* discretion in speech.
eucalipto, *m.* (bot.) eucalyptus.
eucaliptol, *m.* eucalyptus oil.
eucaristía, *f.* Eucharist.—eucarístico, ca, *a.* eucharistic.
eucologio, *m.* (eccl.) euchologion.
eucrasia, *f.* (med.) eucrasy, sound health.
eucrático, ca, *a.* (med.) euchratical.
eudiómetro, *m.* (chem.) eudiometer.
eufemismo, *m.* (rhet.) euphemism.
eufonía, *f.* euphony.
eufónico, ca, *a.* euphonic, euphonious.
euforbiáceo, a. I. *a.* (bot.) euphorbiaceous. II. *f. pl.* Euphorbiaceæ.
euforbio, *m.* (bot.) officinal spurge.
euforia, *f.* resistance to disease; (med.) euphory, feeling well, sense of good health.
eufótida, *f.* (geol.) euphotide.
eufrasia, *f.* (bot.) eyebright.
eugenesia, *f.* eugenics.
eugenol, *m.* (chem.) eugenol.
eunuco, *m.* eunuch.
eupatorio, *m.* (bot.) eupatorium.
eupepsia, *f.* eupepsy, normal digestion.
eupéptico, ca, *n.* & *a.* digestive.
euritmia, *f.* (arch.) eurythmy.
eurítmico, ca, *a.* having eurythmy.
euro, *m.* eurus, east wind.—e. austro, or noto, southeast wind.
europeo, a, *n.* & *a.* European.
éuscaro, ra; éusquero, ra, *n.* & *a.* Basque; Basque language.
éustilo, *m.* (arch.) eustyle.
eutanasia, *f.* euthanasia.
eutiquianismo, *m.* Eutychianism.
eutiquiano, na, *a.* Eutychian.
eutrapelia, eutropelia, *f.* moderation in pleasures; pastime, sport.
eutrapélico, ca; eutropélico, ca, *a.* moderate, temperate.
evacuación, *f.* evacuation; exhaustion.
evacuante, *a.* evacuant, evacuating.
evacuar, *va.* to empty, evacuate; to quit, vacate, leave.—e. un negocio, or una diligencia, to transact a business; to do an errand.
evacuativo, va, torio, a, *a.* evacuative.
evadir. I. *va.* to evade, elude, avoid. II. *vr.* to escape, sneak away.
evaluación, *f.*, evaluar, *va.* = VALUACIÓN, etc.
evangeliario, *m.* evangelistary.
evangélicamente, *adv.* evangelically.
evangélico, ca, *a.* evangelical.
evangelio, *m.* gospel.—pl. gospel relic booklet worn by children around the neck.
evangelismo, *m.* evangelism.

evangelista, *m.* evangelist; gospel chanter.
evangelizador, ra, *n.* & *a.* evangelizer (-ing).
evangelizar, *va.* to evangelize.
evaporable, *a.* evaporable.—evaporación, *f.* evaporation.—evaporador, ra. I. *a.* evaporating. II. *n.* evaporator.
evaporar, *va.* & *vr.* to evaporate.
evaporizar, *va.* & *vr.* (pret. EVAPORICÉ: subj. EVAPORICE) to vaporize.
evasión, *f.*, evasiva, *f.* evasion; escape.
evasivamente, *adv.* evasively.
evasivo, va, *a.* evasive, elusive.
evección, *f.* (ast.) evection.
evento, *m.* event, contingency.
eventración, *f.* (med.) ventral hernia.
eventual, *a.* eventual, fortuitous.
eventualidad, *f.* contingency.
eventualmente, *adv.* eventually.
eversión, *f.* eversion, destruction, ruin.
evicción, *f.* eviction.
evidencia, *f.* evidence, proof; obviousness.
evidenciar, *va.* to prove, make evident.
evidente, *a.* evident.
evidentemente, *adv.* evidently.
evitable, *a.* avoidable.—evitación, *f.* avoidance.
evitar, *va.* to avoid; to shun; to spare.
eviterno, na, *a.* imperishable, lasting.
evo, *m.* age, long time, æon; eternity.
evocación, *f.* evocation, evoking.
evocar, *va.* (pret. EVOQUÉ: subj. EVOQUE) to call out, evoke.
evolución, *f.* evolution; change (of conduct, policy, etc.); (mil. and naut.) evolution, manœuvre.
evolucionar, *vn.* to change one's conduct, policy, etc., (mil. and naut.) to perform evolutions or manœuvres; (biol., philos.) to evolve.
evolucionismo, *m.* evolutionism.
evolucionista. I. *a.* evolutionary, evolution (u. a.). II. *n.* evolutionist.
evolutivo, va, *a.* evolutionary, evolution (u. a.).
ex, *prep.* prefix, ex, out, out of, off; formerly.
ex abrupto, *adv.* abruptly, violently.
exacción, *f.* exaction; impost, tax, contribution, levy.
exacerbación, *f.* exasperation; exacerbation.
exacerbar, *va.* to irritate, exasperate; exacerbate.
exactamente, *adv.* exactly.
exactitud, *f.* exactness; punctuality; accuracy; correctness.
exacto, ta, *a.* exact; accurate; precise; punctual; assiduous.
exactor, *m.* taxgatherer.
exaedro, *m.* (geom.) hexahedron.
exageración, *f.* exaggeration.—exagerador, ra, *n.* & *a.* exaggerator (-ing).—exagerante, *a.* exaggerating.
exagerar, *va.* to exaggerate.
exagerativamente, *adv.* exaggeratively.
exagerativo, va, *a.* exaggerating.
exagonal, *a.* hexagonal.
exágono, na. I. *a.* hexagonal. II. *m.* hexagon.
exaltación, *f.* exaltation, elevation; (chem.) sublimation.
exaltado, da, *a.* hot-headed; ultra-radical.
exaltamiento, *m.* exaltation; ultra-radicalism.
exaltar. I. *va.* to exalt, elevate, lift; to praise, extol. II. *vr.* to become excited.
examen, *m.* examination; inquiry; interrogatory; inspection, investigation, search; exploration, survey.
exámetro, *m.* = HEXÁMETRO.
examinador, ra, *n.* & *a.* examiner (-ing).
examinando, *m.* examinant.
examinante, *a.* examining.
examinar, *va.* to examine; to question; to investigate, inspect, go over, search.
exangüe, *a.* exsanguine, anæmic; weak.
exanimación, *f.* exanimation.
exánime, *a.* spiritless, weak, lifeless.
exantema, *f.* exanthema.
exantemático, ca, *a.* exanthematous.

exarca, *m.* exarch.—**exarcado,** *m.* exarchate.

exarco, *m.*=EXARCA.

exasperación, *f.* exasperation.—**exasperador, ra; exasperante,** *a.* exasperating.—**exasperar,** *va.* to exasperate.

excandecencia, *f.* anger, passion.

excandecer. I. *va.* (*ind.* EXCANDEZCO: *subj.* EXCANDEZCA) to irritate, provoke, enrage. **II.** *vr.* to become angry.

excarcelación, *f.* setting (a prisoner) free.

excarcelar, *va.* to set (a prisoner) free.

ex cáthedra, *adv.* ex cathedra.

excava, *f.* (agr.) pit around the root of a plant.

excavación, *f.* excavation.—**excavar,** *va.* to excavate.

excedente. I. *a.* exceeding. **II.** *m.* (com.) surplus.

exceder. I *va.* to exceed, surpass; to overstep. **II.** *vr.* to go too far; to forget one's self; to overstep one's authority.

excelencia, *f.* excellence, superiority; excellency (title).—**por e.,** par excellence.

excelente. I. *a.* excellent, first-rate. **II.** *m.* an ancient gold coin.

excelentemente, *adv.* excellently.

excelentísimo, ma, *a. superl.* most excellent.

excelsamente, *adv.* sublimely.—**excelsitud,** *f.* excelsitude, loftiness.—**excelso, sa,** *a.* elevated, sublime, lofty.—**el E.,** the Most High.

excéntricamente, *adv.* eccentrically.

excentricidad, *f.* eccentricity.

excéntrico, ca. I. *a.* eccentric, eccentrical; odd, queer. **II.** *f.* (mech.) eccentric.

excepción, *f.* exception; (civil law) plea in defense, denying cause for action.

excepcional, *a.* exceptional, unusual.

excepcionalmente, *adv.* exceptionally.

excepcionar, *va.* (law) to deny the validity of or ground for (a legal action).

exceptivo, va, *a.* exceptive.

excepto, *adv.* excepting, except, with the exception of.

exceptuar, *va.* to except.

excerta, *f.* excerpt, extract, citation.

excesivamente, *adv.* excessively.

excesivo, va, *a.* excessive.

exceso, *m.* excess; (com.) surplus.—**e. de equipaje, or de peso,** baggage excess.—**en e.,** in excess; excessively, to excess.

excipiente, *m.* (pharm.) excipient.

excitabilidad, *f.* excitability.

excitable, *a.* excitable.

excitación, *f.* excitation, exciting; excitement.

excitador, *m.* (elec.) exciter.

excitante, *a.* exciting, excitant.

excitar. I. *va.* to excite, move, stir up, rouse; (elec.) to excite, energize. **II.** *vr.* to become excited, lose one's equanimity.

excitativo, va, *a.* exciting, excitative.

excitatriz, *f.* (elec.) exciter, exciting dynamo.

exclamación, *f.* exclamation.

exclamar, *vn.* to exclaim.

exclamativo, va; torio, ria, *a.* exclamatory.

exclaustración, *f.* secularization of monks.

exclaustrado, *m.* secularized monk.

exclaustrar, *va.* to secularize (monks).

excluir, *va.* (*ind.* EXCLUYO: *subj.* EXCLUYA) to exclude; to bar out, debar.

exclusión, *f.* exclusion, shutting out, debarring.

exclusiva, *f.* refusal; rejection, exclusion; sole right or agency.

exclusivamente, *adv.* exclusively.

exclusive, *adv.* exclusively; exclusive, excluded.

exclusivismo, *m.* exclusivism.

exclusivista, *n.* & *a.* exclusivist (-ic), exclusive (s. o. persons).

exclusivo, va, *a.* exclusive.

excluso, *pp. irr.* of EXCLUIR.

excogitable, *a.* imaginable, reasonable.

excogitar, *va.* to excogitate, meditate; find, invent, devise.

excomulgado, da, *pp. n.* & *a.* excommunicated; wicked, perverse.

excomulgador, ra, *n.* excommunicator.

excomulgar, *va.* (*for mut. v.* COMULGAR) to excommunicate; to anathematize, accurse.

excomunión, *f.* excommunication.—**e. mayor,** anathema.

excoriación, *f.* excoriation, flaying.

excoriar, *vn.* (med.) to excoriate, flay.

excrecencia, *f.* excrescence, excrescency.

excreción, *f.* excretion.

excremental, *a.* = EXCREMENTICIO.

excrementar, *va.* to void by stool.

excrementicio, cia, *a.* excrementitious.

excremento, *m.* excrement; excretion.

excrementoso, sa, *a.* excrementitious.

excretar, *vn.* to excrete; eject the excrements

excreto, ta, *a.* excreted, ejected.

excretorio, ria, *a.* excretory, excretive.

excrex, *m.* (*pl.* **excrez**) (law) increase of dower.

exculpación, *f.* exculpation, exoneration.

exculpar, *va.* & *vr.* to exculpate, exonerate.

excursión, *f.* excursion, trip, tour; (law) excussion, liquidation.

excursionista, *n.* excursionist.

excusa, *f.* excuse.

excusabaraja, *f.* basket with a cover.

excusable, *a.* excusable.

excusadamente, *adv.* unnecessarily.

excusado, da. I. *pp.* & *a.* exempted, privileged; unnecessary; reserved, set apart. **II.** *m.* ancient privilege of exemption from the payment of tithes; water-closet.

excusador, ra. I. *a.* excusing. **II.** *n.* excuser; substitute, vicar.

excusalí, *m.* small apron.

excusar. I. *va.* to excuse; to exempt; to prevent, avoid, shun. **II.** *vr.* to excuse one's self; to apologize.

excusión, *f.* (law) excussion, attachment.

execrable, *a.* execrable.—**execrablemente,** *adv.* execrably.—**execración,** *f.* execration.

execrador, ra, *n.* & *a.* execrater (-ing.)

execrando, da, *a.* execrable.—**execrar,** *va.* to execrate.—**execratorio, ria,** *a.* execratory.

exedra, *f.* (arch.) exedra.

exégesis, *f.* exegesis.—**exégeta,** *m.* exegete.

exegético, ca, *a.* exegetic, explanatory.

exención, *f.* exemption.

exentado, da, *pp.* & *a.* exempt, exempted.

exentamente, *adv.* freely; frankly, clearly, simply, sincerely.

exentar. I. *va.* to exempt; to excuse. **II.** *vr.* to except one's self.

exento, ta. I. *a.* exempt; free, freed, disengaged; clear, open, unobstructed. **II.** *pp. irr. of* EXIMIR. **III.** *m.* officer in the Spanish lifeguards.

exequátur, *m.* exequatur.

exequias, *f. pl.* exequies, obsequies.

exequible, *a.* attainable.

exéresis, *f.* (surg.) ablation, removal.

exergo, *m.* exergue.

exfoliación, *f.* exfoliation, scaling or peeling off.

exfoliar. I. *va.* to exfoliate. **II.** *vr.* to scale off.

exhalación, *f.* exhalation; bolt of lightning; shooting star; effluvium, fume, vapor, emanation.

exhalador, ra, *n.* & *a.* exhaler (-ing.)

exhalar. I. *va.* to exhale, breathe forth, emit. **II.** *vr.* to exhale, evaporate; to be exhausted by violent exercise.

exhausto, ta, *a.* exhausted.

exheredación, *f.* disinheritance.

exheredar, *va.* to disinherit.

exhibición, *f.* exhibition, exposition.

exhibir, *va.* to exhibit, expose, display; to show.

exhortación, *f.* exhortation, admonition.

exhortador, ra, *n.* & *a.* exhorter (-ing).

exhortar, *va.* to exhort, admonish.

exhortatorio, ria, *a.* exhortatory.

exhorto, *m.* (law) letters requisitorial.

exhumación, *f.* exhumation, disinterment.

exhumar, *va.* to exhume, unbury.

---

exigencia, *f.* exigency; requirement; demand.

exigente, *a.* exacting.

exigible; exigidero, ra, *a.* exigible, requirable.

exigir, *va.* (*ind.* EXIJO: *subj.* EXIJA) to require; exact, demand; need; to urge.

exigüidad, *f.* exiguousness, scantiness, smallness.

exiguo, gua, *a.* exiguous, small, scanty.

eximente, *a.* exempting.

eximio, mia, *a.* eximious; famous, worthiest, most excellent.

eximir, *va.* to exempt, excuse, except.

exinanición, *f.* inanition; debility.

exinanido, da, *a.* debilitated, very weak.

existencia, *f.* existence; life, being.—*pl.* (com.) stock in hand, goods.—**en e.,** (com.) in stock.

existente, *a.* existing, extant, existent; (com.) on hand, in stock.

existimación, *f.* estimation, opinion.

existimar, *va.* to form an opinion of, to judge.

existir, *vn.* to exist, to be.

éxito, *m.* issue, result, end; success.

ex libris, (print.) ex libris.

Éxodo, *m.* Exodus; (é-) exodus, emigration.

exoneración, *f.* exoneration.—**exonerar,** *va.* to exonerate.

exorable, *a.* exorable.

exorar, *va.* to exorate, beg, entreat.

exorbitancia, *f.* exorbitance.—**exorbitante,** *a.* exorbitant, excessive.

exorbitantemente, *adv.* exorbitantly.

exorcismo, *m.* exorcism.—**exorcista,** *n.* exorciser, exorcist.—**exorcizante,** *n.* & *a.* exorciser (-ing).—**exorcizar,** *va.* to exorcise.

exordio, *m.* exordium.

exornación, *f.* (rhet.) exornation.

exornar, *va.* to adorn, embellish.

exosmosis, *f.* (phys.) exosmose.

exotérico, ca, *a.* exoteric, public, common.

exotérmico, ca, *a.* (chem.) exothermic, heat-evolving.

exótico, ca, *a.* exotic, foreign, extraneous.

expansibilidad, *f.* expansibility.

expansible, *a.* expansible.

expansión, *f.* expansion, extension.

expansivo, va, *a.* expansive; sociable, communicative.

expatriación, *f.* expatriation.

expatriar. I. *va.* to expatriate. **II.** *vr.* to emigrate, leave one's country.

expectable, *a.* conspicuous, eminent.

expectación, *f.* expectation, expectancy.

expectante, *a.* expectant.

expectativa, *f.* expectation, expectancy, hope; (law) expectancy, abeyance.

expectoración, *f.* expectoration; sputum.

expectorante, I. *a.* expectorating. **II.** *m.*(med.) expectorant.

expectorar, *va.* & *vn.* to expectorate.

expedición, *f.* expedition; despatch, speed, nimbleness, facility; pontifical brevet or bull; (mil.) expedition; excursion, jaunt, journey.

expedicionario, ria, *a.* expeditionary.

expedicionero, *m.* expeditioner.

expedidor, ra, *n.* (com.) forwarding merchant, agent, shipper, sender, despatcher.

expediente, *m.* (law) action, proceedings; file of papers bearing on a case; despatch, course of business; expedient, measure, resource, means to an end; facility in the management of affairs; reason, motive, pretext; supply, provision.—**cubrir el e.,** to pretend, show the appearance of doing something; keep up appearances; save one's face.

expedienteo, *m.* procedure, taking action on the papers or documents in the case; (coll.) entangling and confusing matters; red tape.

expedir, *va.* (*ind.* EXPIDO: *subj.* EXPIDA) to expedite, facilitate; to issue; to draw out; to ship, send.

expeditamente, *adv.* expeditiously, easily.

expeditivo, va, *a.* expeditious, speedy, quick.

expedito, ta, *a.* prompt, expeditious, quick.

expelente, *a.* expellant, expelling.

expeler, *va.* to expel, eject, throw out.

expendedor, ra. I. *a.* spending. **II.** *n.* dealer, retailer, agent, seller; (law) distributor of counterfeit money.

expendeduría, *f.* shop where officially monopolized goods are sold.

expender, *va.* to expend, spend, lay out; to sell at retail, to deal in; (com.) to sell on commission; (law) to pass (counterfeit money or stolen goods)

expendición, *f.* retail selling; commission selling.

expendio, *m.* expense, outlay; consumption; (Am.) EXPENDICIÓN; (Mex.) EXPENDIDURÍA.

expensar, *va.* (Am.) to defray the expense of.

expensas, *f. pl.* expenses, charges, costs.—**a. expensas de uno,** at one's expense.

experiencia, *f.* experience; experiment, trial.

experimentado, da, *pp.* & *a.* experienced.

experimentador, ra, *n.* experimenter.

experimental, *a.* experimental.

experimentalmente, *adv.* experimentally.

experimentar, *va.* to experience; to experiment, test, try.

experimento, *m.* experiment, test, trial.

expertamente, *adv.* expertly.

experto, ta, *n.* & *a.* expert.

expiación, *f.* expiation, atonement; purification.

expiar, *va.* to expiate, atone for, make amends for; to purify.—**expiativo, va,** *a.* expiational.

expiatorio, ria, *a.* expiatory.

expillo, *m.* (bot.) = MATRICARIA.

expiración, *f.* expiration.—**expirante,** *a.* expiring.—**expirar,** *vn.* to expire.

explanación, *f.* explanation, elucidation; (r. w.) roadbed.

explanada, *f.* lawn; (fort.) esplanade, glacis; (arti.) platform.

explanar, *va.* to level, grade; explain, elucidate.

explayamiento, *m.* dilating, dwelling upon a subject; outing.

explayar. I. *va.* to extend, dilate, enlarge. **II.** *vr.* to dwell upon a subject; to be extended; to enjoy an outing.

expletivo, va, *n.* & *a.* expletive.

explicable, *a.* explicable, explainable.

explicación, *f.* explanation.

explicadera, *f. pl.* (coll.) facility of explaining.

explicar. I. *va.* (*pret.* EXPLIQUÉ: *subj.* EXPLIQUE) to explain, expound, construe. **II.** *vr.* to explain one's self.

explicativo, va, *a.* explicative, explanatory.

explícitamente, *adv.* explicitly.

explícito, ta, *f.* explicit.

exploración, *f.* exploration.

explorador, ra, *n.* & *a.* explorer (-ing).

explorar, *va.* to explore; investigate, search into, examine; (mil.) to scout.

exploratorio, ria, *a.* exploratory, exploring.

explosión, *f.* explosion; outburst; (min.) blast.

explosivo, va, *n.* & *a.* explosive.

explosor, *m.* exploder; (rad.) exploder, oscillator.

explotable, *a.* workable; (min.) workable.

explotación, *f.*, exploitation; development, working (of a mine, etc.); plant, works; operation, running (of a factory, railroad, etc.).

explotador, ra, *n.* & *a.* exploiter (-ing).

explotar, *va.* to exploit; to work (a mine, etc.); to develop (mines, lands, etc.); to operate, run (a business, a railroad, etc.).

expoliación, *f.* spoliation —**expoliador, ra,** *n.* & *a.* spoliator (-ing).

expoliar, *va.* to spoliate, despoil.

exponencial, *f.* & *a.* (math.) exponential.

exponente. I. *n.* & *a.* exponent. **II.** *m.* (math.) exponent.

exponer. I. *va.* (*for irr. v.* PONER) to expose, show, lay bare; to expound, explain; to expose, put in danger, jeopardize; to expose, abandon (a child). **II.** *vr.* to expose one's self, run a risk.

exportable, *a.* exportable.

exportación, *f.* exportation, export.—**de e.,** export (u. a., as in *derechos de exportación,* export duties).—**exportador, ra,** . & *an.* exporter (-ing).

exportar, *va.* to export.

exposición, *f.* exposition, statement; peril, risk, jeopardy; petition, claim; exposition, exhibition, fair; (drama) exposition; (arch.) situation, orientation.

expositivo, va, *a.* explanatory, expositive.

expósito, ta, *n.* & *a.* foundling.

expositor, ra, *n.* & *a.* expounder (-ing), exponent; exhibitor (-ing).

expremijo, *m.* cheese vat.

expresado, da, *a.* before-mentioned, aforesaid.

expresamente, *adv.* expressly; clearly.

expresar. I. *va.* (*pp.* EXPRESADO, EXPRESO) to express, state, tell; (art) to delineate, design. **II.** *vr.* to express one's self, to speak.

expresión, *f.* expression; declaration, statement; form; phrase, utterance; present, gift; expression, squeezing, pressing out (of oils, etc.).

expresivamente, *adv.* expressively.

expresivo, va, *a.* expressive; affectionate, kind.

expreso, sa. I. *a.* expressed; express, clear; express, fast (train, etc.). **II.** *m.* express (train).

exprimidera, *f.*, **exprimidero,** *m.*, squeezer.

exprimido, da, *pp.* & *a.* squeezed; dry.

exprimir, *va.* to squeeze, press out; to express (one's thoughts) vividly.

ex profeso, *adv.* on purpose, expressly.

expropiación, *f.* expropriation.

expropiar, *va.* to expropriate.

expuesto, ta, *a.* & *pp. irr.* of EXPONER; exposed, liable; displayed; in danger.

expugnable, *a.* expugnable.—**expugnación,** *f.* (mil.) expugnation.—**expugnador, ra,** *n.* (mil.) expugner.—**expugnar,** *va.* (mil.) to take by storm.

expulsar, *va.* (*pp.* EXPULSADO, EXPULSO) to expel, eject, drive out.—**expulsión,** *f.* expulsion, expelling, ejection.—**expulsivo, va,** *a.* expelling.—**expulso, sa,** *a.* & *pp. irr.* of EXPELER and EXPULSAR; driven out, expelled; outcast.—**expulsor, ra,** *n.* & *a.* expeller (-ing), ejector (-ing).

expurgación, *f.* expurgation.

expurgar, *va.* (*for mut. v.* PURGAR) to expurgate, expunge, purge away, cleanse, purify.

expurgatorio, ria, *a.* expurgatory. *V.* ÍNDICE.

expurgo, *m.* expurgation, purification.

exquisitamente, *adv.* exquisitely.

exquisito, ta, *a.* exquisite, delicious.

éxtasi, éxtasis, *m.* ecstasy.—**extasiar,** *va.* & *vr.* to delight; to enrapture.—**extático, ca,** *a.* ecstatic.

extemporal; extemporáneo, a, *a.* untimely.

extemporáneamente, *adv.* untimely, inopportunely.

extender. I. *va.* & *vr.* (*pp.* EXTENDIDO, EXTENSO: *ind.* EXTIENDO: *subj.* EXTIENDA) to extend, enlarge, prolong, spread, expand, outstretch; to unfold, unfurl; to draw up (a document); (com.) to extend, prolong. **II.** *vr.* to extend, reach; to stretch out; to enlarge upon, expatiate; to spread, become general or popular.

extendidamente, *adv.* extensively.

extendido, da, *pp.* & *a.* extended, stretched out; spacious; general, widely spread.

extensamente, *adv.* extensively.

extensión, *f.* extension; extent, length; expanse; extensiveness; space, capacity; (log.) extension.

extensivamente, *adv.* by extension.

extensivo, va, *a.* ample.

extenso, sa, *pp. irr.* of EXTENDER, and *a.* extended, extensive, spacious.—**por e.,** at length, with full particulars.

extensor, ra. I. *a.* extending. **II.** *m.* (med.) extensor.

extenuación, *f.* attenuation; emaciation.

extenuado, da, *pp.* & *a.* emaciated, wasted.

extenuar. I. *va.* to emaciate, weaken. **II.** *vr.* to languish, waste away.

extenuativo, va, *a.* weakening, emaciating.

exterior. I. *a.* exterior; external, outside, outward; foreign (commerce, debt, etc.).—**lo e.,** the outside; outside things or matters; foreign affairs. **II.** *m.* outside; personal appearance; foreign countries.

exterioridad, *f.* exteriority; outward appearance; demeanor; show, pomp.

exteriorizar. I. *va.* to externalize, make manifest. **II.** *vr.* to unbosom one's self.

exteriormente, *adv.* externally, outwardly.

exterminador, ra, *n.* & *a.* exterminator (-ing).

exterminar, *va.* to exterminate; to raze.

exterminio, *m.* extermination, ruin, destruction.

externado, *m.* day-student school or college.

externamente, *adv.* externally.

externo, na. I. *a.* external, outward; exterior (angle, etc.). **II.** *n.* day pupil.

ex testamento, by will or testament.

extiendo, extienda. *V.* EXTENDER.

extinción, *f.* extinction; extinguishment; suppression, abolition; obliteration.

extinguible, *a.* extinguishable.

extinguir, *va.* (*pp.* EXTINGUIDO, EXTINTO: *ind.* EXTINGO: *subj.* EXTINGA) to quench, extinguish, put out; to suppress, destroy.

extintivo, va, *a.* (law) extinguishing.

extinto, ta, *a.* extinguished, extinct.

extintor, *m.* fire extinguisher.

extirpación, *f.* extirpation, eradication.

extirpador, ra. I. *n.* & *a.* extirpator (-ing). **II.** *m.* (agr.) cultivator.

extirpar, *va.* to extirpate, root out, eradicate.

extorsión, *f.* extortion; overcharge.

extra, *n.* & *a.* (coll.) extra.—**e. de,** besides, in addition to.

extracción, *f.* extraction; exportation; drawing numbers in the lottery.

extracta, *f.* (law) true copy, extract.

extractador, ra, *n.* abstractor.

extractar, *va.* to abstract, epitomize, abridge.

extracto, *m.* abstract, summary; (pharm.) extract.—**e. de saturno,** white lead.

extractor, ra, *n.* & *a.* extractor (-ing).

extradición, *f.* extradition.

extradós, *m.* (arch.) extrados.

extraente, *n.* & *a.* extractor (-ing).

extraer, *va.* (*for irr. v.* TRAER) to extract, draw out, remove; to export; (math.) to extract (a root); (law) to take a copy of; (chem.) to extract.

extraigo, extraje, etc. *V.* EXTRAER.

extrajudicial, *a.* extrajudicial.

extrajudicialmente, *adv.* extrajudicially.

extralimitarse, *vr.* to overstep one's power or authority.

extramuros, *adv.* outside (a town), without.

extranjería, *f.* alienship.

extranjerismo, *m.* foreignism.

extranjerizar. I. *vn.* to introduce foreign customs. **II.** *vr.* to act like a foreigner, adopt foreign ways.

extranjero, ra, *a.* & *n.* foreign (-er), alien.—**el e.,** foreign countries, abroad (ch. constr.: **está en el extranjero,** he is abroad).

extranjía, *f.* (coll.) alienship.

extranjis.—de e., (coll.) foreign; strange, unexpected.

extrañación, *f.*, **extrañamiento,** *m.* alienation; expulsion, exile; emigration.

extrañamente, *adv.* strangely.

extrañar, *va.* to banish; to cut, ignore (a person); to estrange; wonder at, find it strange; to miss.

extrañeza, *f.* oddity, queerness; surprise, wonderment; estrangement.

extraño, ña. I. *a.* strange; foreign; extraneous. **II.** *n.* stranger; foreigner.

extraoficial, *a.* extraofficial, non-official.

extraordinariamente, *adv.* extraordinarily.

extraordinario, a. I. *a.* extraordinary. **II.** *m.* extra dish at dinner; special courier.

extraterritorial, *a.* extraterritorial.

extraterritorialidad, *f.* extraterritoriality.

extravagancia, *f.* oddness, folly, freak.

extravagante. I. *a.* eccentric; freakish, queer, odd, grotesque. **II.** *f. pl.* (eccl.) extravagants.

extravagantemente, oddly, grotesquely.

extravasación, *f.* (med.) extravasation.

extravasarse, *vr.* to extravasate, exude.

extravenado, da, *pp. & a.* extravenate.

extravenarse, *vr.* to exude through the veins.

extraviado, da, *pp. & a.* stray, gone astray; mislaid, missing; unbalanced, of unsound mind.

extraviar. I. *va.* to mislead, misguide; to misplace, mislay; to embezzle. **II.** *vr.* to go astray; to miscarry (as a letter); to deviate, to err.

extravío, *m.* deviation; aberration; misconduct; misplacement.

extremadamente, *adv.* extremely.

extremadas, *f. pl.* time for making cheese.

extremado, da, *pp. & a.* extreme; consummate (in good or bad).

extremamente, *adv.* extremely, exceedingly.

extremar. I. *va.* to carry to an extreme. **II.** *vr.* to exert one's self to the utmost, to take special pains.

extremaunción, *f.* extreme unction.

extremeño, ña, *a.* Estremenian.

extremidad, *f.* extremity; end; edge, brink, border, brim; extreme or remotest part; (anat.) extremity.

extremista, *n. & a.* extremist.

extremo, ma. I. *a.* extreme, last, terminal; furthest; greatest, of the highest degree, utmost. **II.** *m.* extreme, utmost point, highest degree; apex; furthest end, extremity; greatest care.—**con e.,** extremely, in the utmost degree.—**de e. a. e.,** from one end to the other.—**en e.** = CON E.—**hacer extremos,** to express one's feelings with vehemence, to gush.—**por e.** = CON E.

extremoso, sa, *a.* extreme, vehement; very affectionate.

extrínsecamente, *adv.* extrinsically.

extrínseco, ca, *a.* extrinsic.

exuberancia, *f.* exuberance.—**exuberante,** *a.* exuberant, overabundant, luxuriant.

exudación, *f.* exudation.

exudar, *vn. & va.* to exude; to ooze out.

exulceración, *f.* (med.) exulceration.

exulcerar. I. *va.* (med.) to exulcerate, ulcerate. **II.** *vr.* to become ulcerated.

exultación, *f.* exultation, great joy.

exutorio, *m.* (med.) exutory, issue.

exvoto, *m.* votive offering.

F

fa, *m.* (mus.) fa, F.

fabada, *f.* in Asturias, pork and beans.

fábrica, *f.* fabrication; structure, building, pile; factory, works, mill, manufactory.

fabricación, *f.* manufacturing; manufacture, make.—**fabricador, ra.** *n. & a.* fabricator (ing); schemer (ing).

fabricante, *n. & a.* maker (-ing), manufacturer (-ing).

fabricar, *va.* (*pret.* FABRIQUÉ: *subj.* FABRIQUE) to build, construct, frame; to manufacture, make; to fabricate, contrive, devise.

fabril, *a.* manufacturing.

fabriquero, ra, *n.* manufacturer; church warden.

fabuco, *m.* (bot.) beech mast.

fábula, *f.* fable, fiction, legend, tale; rumor, report, common talk; story, falsehood.—**f. milesia,** Milesian tale.

fabulador, *m.* fabulist, author of fables.

fabulilla, ita, *f. dim.* little fable.

fabulista, *n.* fabulist, writer of fables.

fabulosamente, *adv.* fabulously.

fabuloso, sa, *a.* fabulous; marvellous.

faca, *f.* jackknife used by seamen.

facción, *f.* faction, turbulent party; (mil.) battle; any act of military service.—*pl.* features, lineaments, physiognomy.—**f. de testamento,** (law) faculty of testating.

faccionario, ria, *a.* factionary.

faccioso, sa. I. *a.* factious. **II.** *n.* rebel.

facer, *va.* (obs.) = HACER.

faceta, *f.* (jewel) facet of a gem.

facial, *a.* facial; intuitive.

facialmente, *adv.* intuitively.

facies, *f.* (med. & biol.) facies, characteristic appearance.

fácil, *a.* easy, convenient; probable, likely; pliant, docile, handy; easily pursuaded or seduced.—**f. de** (followed by *inf.*), easy to.

facilidad, *f.* ease, easiness, facility; ready compliance, convenience; opportunity.

facilillo, illa, ito, ita, *a. dim.* rather easy.

facilitación, *f.* facilitation.

facilitar, *va.* to facilitate, expedite; to supply, deliver, afford.

facilitón, na, *n.* (coll.) one who assumes to make everything easy.

fácilmente, *adv.* easily, without difficulty.

facineroso, sa. I. *a.* wicked, villainous. **II.** *n.* habitual criminal; villain, rascal.

facistol, *m.* chorister's desk; lectern.

facóquero, ra, *n.* wart hog.

facsímil, facsímile, *m.* facsimile.

factible, *a.* feasible, practicable.

facticio, cia, *a.* factitious, artificial.

factor, *m.* factor, element, cause; (com.) factor, agent, commissioner; (mil.) victualler; (r. w.) baggagemaster; (math.) factor.

factoraje, *m.*, **factoría,** *f.* factorage; agency; factory; trading in a foreign country; entrepôt.

factorial, *n.* (math.) factorial.

factótum, *m.* factotum, man of all work; busybody.

factura, *f.* (com.) invoice, bill; (art) handling.—**f. consular,** consular invoice.—**f. simulada, proforma,** invoice.

facturar, *va.* (com.) to invoice, to bill; (r. w.) to check (baggage).

fácula, *f.* (ast.) facula.

facultad, *f.* faculty; power, authority; science, art; faculty (in a university); graduates or alumni taken collectively; (med.) physiological power or ability; license, permission.—*pl.* fortune, wealth.—**facultades del alma,** mental faculties or powers.

facultar, *va.* to empower, authorize.

facultativamente, *adv.* facultatively.

facultativo, va. I. *a.* facultative; optional; belonging to a faculty. **II.** *n.* physician.

facundia, *f.* facundity, eloquence.

facundo, da, *a.* eloquent, fluent.

facha, *f.* (coll.) appearance, look, mien, face.—**f. a f.,** face to face.—**en f.** (naut.) lying to.

fachada, *f.* (arch.) façade; frontispiece of a book; (coll.) figure, build (of a person).—**hacer f. a,** to face, be in front of.

fachenda. I. *f.* (coll.) vanity, conceit. **II.** *n.* (coll.) vain, conceited person.

fachendear, *vn.* (coll.) to brag, boast.

fachendista, dón, na, doso, sa, *a.* conceited, vain, bluffing.

fachoso, sa, *a.* ill-favored, of ridiculous mien; (Mex.) conceited, bluffing.

fada, *f.* fairy, enchantress, witch; (bot.) small pippin apple.

faena, *f.* work, labor, task, toil.—*pl.* business affairs.

faenero, ra, *n.* (Am.) farm hand.

faetón, *m.* phaeton.

fagocito, *m.* (biol.) phagocyte.

fagot, *m.* (mus.) bassoon, fagotto.

faisán, na, *n.* (orn.) pheasant.

faja, *f.* band, bandage, roller, fillet; swathing band; sash; girdle; border; (geog.) zone; newspaper wrapper; (arch.) fascia, belt, fillet; (naut.) reef band.

fajadura, *f.* swathing, swaddling; (naut.) band round a rope.

fajamiento, *m.* rolling or swathing.

fajar, *va.* to swathe, swaddle; to band, belt, girdle.—**f. con,** (coll.) to fall on, to attack.

fajardo, *m.* meat pie, patty; vol-au-vent.

fajeado, da, *a.* banded, fasciated.

fajero, *m.* crochet swaddling band.

fajín, *m. dim.* small band or sash; general's sash.

fajina, *f.* toil, task, work; (agr.) shock, stook, rick of sheaves; fagot of brushwood; (mil.) bugle call; (fort.) fascine.

fajinada, *f.* (fort.) fascine work or revetment.

fajo, *m.* bundle; sheaf.—*pl.* swaddling clothes.

fajón, *m. aug.* large band, roller, or sash; plaster border.

fajuela, *f. dim.* small bandage or roller.

falacia, *f.* deceit; deceitfulness; perfidy.

falange, *f.* (mil. & anat.) phalanx.—*pl.* phalanges.

falangeta, *f.* (anat.) third phalanx.

falangia, *f.*, **falangio,** *m.* (ent.) phalangium, or daddy longlegs.

falangiano, na, *a.* (anat.) phalangeal.

falangio, *m.* V. FALANGIA.

falansterio, *m.* phalanstery.

falárica, *f.* phalaric, fire dart.

fálaris, *f.* (orn.) coot, scoter.

falaz, *a.* deceitful, treacherous.

falazmente, *adv.* deceitfully, treacherously.

falbalá, *m.* flounce, furbelow; flap on the skirt of a coat.

falca, *f.* small wedge; (naut.) washboard.

falcado, da. I. *pp.* & *a.* hooked, falcated. **II.** *m.* scythed chariot.

falcario, *m.* soldier armed with a falchion.

falce, *f.* sickle, reaping hook; falchion.

falcidia, *f.* (law) Falcidian.

falcinelo, *m.* (orn.) glossy ibis.

falcón, *m.* ancient small cannon; falcon.

falconete, *m.* falconet, small cannon.

falcónido, da. I. *a.* (zool.) belonging to the falcon family. **II.** *m. pl.* Falconidæ.

falda, *f.* skirt, flap; the lap; incline, slope; loin (of beef, etc.); tasset, tuilles, in armor.—*pl.* skirts (fig.), women.

faldamenta, faldamento, *m.* skirt.

faldar, *m.* tasset, tuille, in armor.

faldear, *va.* to skirt (a hill).

faldellín, *m.* overskirt; underskirt.

falderillo, illa, *a. dim.* little lap dog.

faldero, ra, *a.* belonging to the lap; fond of women.

faldeta, *f. dim.* small skirt; covering cloth or canvas.

faldicorto, ta, *a.* having short skirts.

faldillas, *f. dim. pl.* skirts; coat tails.

faldistorio, *m.* fold for bishop's stool.

faldón, *m. aug.* long flowing skirt, flap; coat tail; shirt tail; hanging drapery; flap of a saddle; top millstone; (arch.) gable; tympanum.

faldriquera, *f.* pocket.

falencia, *f.* misstatement, mistake.

falibilidad, *f.* fallibility.

falible, *a.* fallible.

falimiento, *m.* untruth, deceit, falsehood.

falo, *m.* (anat. & bot.) phallus.

falordía, *f.* story, fairy tale, fable.

falsa, *f.* garret; guide lines; (mus.) dissonance.

falsaamarra, *f.* (naut.) preventer rope.

falsabraga, *f.* (fort.) low rampart.

falsada, *f.* irregular flight of birds.

falsamente, *adv.* falsely, untruly.

falsario, ria. I. *a.* falsifying, forging, counterfeiting. **II.** *n.* forger, counterfeiter, falsifier.

falsarregla, *f.* bevel square, bevel rule.

falseador, ra, *n.* forger, counterfeiter, falsifier.

falsear. I. *va.* to adulterate, counterfeit, forge; to pierce; (carp.) to bevel. **II.** *vn.* to slacken; (mus.) to be false (s. o. a string).

falsedad, *f.* falsehood, untruth; deceit, guile; perfidy, duplicity.

falseo, *m.* (mas. and carp.) bevelling.

falsete, *m.* spigot; small door; (mus.) falsetto voice.

falsía, *f.* = FALSEDAD.

falsificación, *f.* falsification, forgery.

falsificador, ra, *n.* falsifier, counterfeiter, forger.

falsificar, *va.* (*pret.* FALSIFIQUÉ: *subj.* FALSIFIQUE) to falsify, counterfeit, forge, adulterate.

falsilla, *f.* guide lines for writing.

falsío, *m.* (cook.) a kind of stuffing.

falso, sa. I. *a.* false, untrue; incorrect; deceitful, perfidious; spurious, forged, counterfeit; mock, sham; vicious (horses or mules); defective, false (weights or honeycombs); (mech.) temporary; unsubstantial.—**f. flete,** dead freight.—**f. posición,** (arith.) position (an old method of solution). —**f. testimonio,** false testimony; slander, libel; imposture.—**de f., en f.,** deceitfully, misleadingly; without proper safety or strength (in this sense, **sobre falso** also used). **II.** *m.* (sew.) facing, skirt binding.

falta, *f.* lack, want, absence, deficiency, shortage; fault; defect; flaw; failing; shortcoming; offence, misdeed, misbehavior; deficiency in the weight of coin; (law) default; stoppage of the catamenia in pregnant women.—**f. de aceptación, de pago,** (com.) nonacceptance, nonpayment.—**a f. de,** in want of or for want of.—**hacer f.,** to be necessary; to be missing; to be missed (ch. contr.: *Vd. me hace mucha falta,* I miss you very much).—**sin f.,** without fail; without fault.

faltante, *a.* wanting, lacking.

faltar, *vn.* to be wanting; to fall short; to fail, falter, flinch; not to fulfil one's promise, not to perform one's engagement; to need, lack, be in want of (ch. constr.: *me faltan dos pesos,* I lack, *or* need, *or* am short, two dollars); to offend; to sin; to be absent or missing; to die; (naut.) to break, part, give way.—**f. a.,** to offend against, to break; to be unfaithful to.—**f. a la verdad,** to speak untruthfully, to lie.—**f. al respeto a,** to treat disrespectfully.—**f. para** (used impersonally), to lack to (or for), to be . . . to (*falta un cuarto para las dos,* it is a quarter to two; *falta una semana para vencerse la letra,* it lacks a week for the draft to be due).—**f. poco para,** not to be long before; come near (ch. constr.: *falta poco para terminar,* it will not be long before the end; *poco faltó para que la matasen,* she came near being killed).—**¡no faltaba más!** (coll.) that is the limit! the idea!

falto, ta, *a.* devoid; short; deficient, defective.

faltrero, ra, *n.* pickpocket, petty thief.

faltriquera, *f.* pocket.

falúa, *f.* (naut.) small boat, tender.

falucho, *m.* (naut.) felucca, lateener.

falla, *f.* fault, failure; fallal, sort of head covering; (Philip.) fine paid by Indians for leaving work; (naut.) defect, deficiency; (geol.) fault, break, slide.

fallar. I. *va.* (law) to give sentence, to pass judgment or render a verdict on; to ruff (at cards). **II.** *vn.* to fail, be deficient or wanting.

falleba, *f.* shutter bolt.

fallecer, *vn.* (*ind.* FALLEZCO: *subj.* FALLEZCA) to die; to fail, run out, expire.

fallecimiento, *m.* decease, death, demise.

fallido, da, *a.* deceived, disappointed, frustrated; (com.) bankrupt.

fallo, lla. I. *a.* at cards, lacking a card of the suit played. **II.** *m.* (law) verdict, judgment, decision; lack of a card of the suit played.

fama, *f.* fame; report, rumor.—**es f.,** it is said.

famélico, ca, *a.* hungry, ravenous.

familia, *f.* family; household.

familiar. I. *a.* familiar; domestic; common, frequent; plain, homelike, unceremonious. **II.** *m.* domestic member of the household; servant, especially of the clergy; college servitor; bosom friend; officer of the Inquisition; demon, familiar spirit.—*pl.* attendants, suite.

familiaridad, *f.* familiarity.

familiarizar. I. *va.* (*pret.* FAMILIARICÉ: *subj.* FAMILIARICE) to make well known, to make popular; familiarize. **II.** *vr.* to accustom, habituate one's self; to become familiar.

familiarmente, *adv.* familiarly.

familión, *m. augm.* large family.

famosamente, *adv.* famously.

famoso, sa, *a.* famous; (coll.) great, excellent.

fámula, *f.* (coll.) maidservant.

famular, *a.* famular, domestic.

famulato, famulicio, *m.* servantship.

fámulo, *m.* famulus; (coll.) servant.

fanal, *m.* lighthouse; lantern; bell glass; candle screen.

fanáticamente, *adv.* fanatically.—**fanático, ca,** *n. & a.* fanatic.—**fanatismo,** *m.* fanaticism.

fanatizador, ra, *n.* one who spreads fanaticism.

fanatizar, *va.* to make fanatical.

fandango, *m.* fandango.

fandanguero, ra, *a.* frequenter of balls.

faneca, *f.* (icht.) pout, whiting pout.

fanega, *f.* grain measure (about 1.60 bu.).—**f. de cacao,** 116 lbs. of cocoa.—**f. de sembradura,** ground necessary to sow a FANEGA of seed.—**f. de tierra,** a land measure (about 1.59 acres).

fanegada, *f.* = FANEGA DE TIERRA.—**a fanegadas,** in great plenty or abundance.

fanerógamo, ma, *a.* (bot.) flowering.

fanfarrear, *vn.* to bully, brag, swagger.

fanfarria, *f.* (coll.) swagger, bluster.

fanfarrón, na, *n.* (coll.) blusterer, swaggerer, braggart; boaster, bully.

fanfarronada, *f.* fanfaronade, boast, brag, bluff.

fanfarronear, *vn.* to brag, boast.

fanfarronería, *f.* fanfaronade, bragging.

fanfarronesca, *f.* swagger, fanfaronading.

fanfurriña, *f.* (coll.) fit of the sulks.

fangal, fangar, *m.* slough, marsh, quagmire.

fango, *m.* mire, mud.—**fangoso, sa,** *a.* muddy, miry.

fantasear, *vn.* to fancy, to imagine.

fantasía, *f.* fantasy, fancy, imagination; caprice, whim, conceit; (coll.) vanity, conceit; (naut.) dead reckoning; (mus.) fantasia.—*pl.* string of pearls.

fantasioso, sa, *a.* (coll.) conceited, vain.

fantasma. I. *m.* phantom, ghost, apparition; vain, conceited person. **II.** *f.* scarecrow.

fantasmagoría, *f.* phantasmagoria.

fantasmagórico, ca, *a.* phantasmagoric.

fantasmón, na. I. *a. aug.* (coll.) supinely conceited. **II.** *m.* presumptuous coxcomb.

fantásticamente, *adv.* fantastically.

fantástico, ca, *a.* fantastic, fanciful; conceited.

fantoche, *m.* = TÍTERE.

fañado, da, *a.* one year old.

faquín, *m.* porter, carrier, laborer.

faquir, *m.* fakir.

fara, *f.* (zool.) an African serpent.

farachar, *va.* to beat (hemp).

farad, faradio, *m.* (elec.) farad.

faradización, *f.* (med.) faradization.

faradizar, *va.* (med.) to faradize.

faralá, *m.* flounce, rufflet, frill.

farallón, *m.* headland; cliff.

faramalla. I. *f.* (coll.) cajolery. **II.** *n.* (coll.) cajoler.—**faramallero, ra, llón, na,** *n.* (coll.) cajoling tattler.

farandola, *f.* farandole (a dance).

farándula, *f.* profession of a low comedian; strolling troupe of players; (coll.) cajolement; show, conceit, ostentation.

farandulero, ra, *n.* comedian, player; (coll.) cajoler; boaster, vain person.

farandúlico, ca, *a.* relating to the strollers.

Faraón, *m.* Pharoah; (f-); faro (card game).

faraónico, ca, *a.* Pharaonic.

faraute, *n.* trusted messenger; player who recites the prologue; (coll.) meddling person, busybody, butter-in.

farda, *f.* ancient tax; bundle of clothing; (carp.) notch.

fardacho, *m.* (zool.) lizard.

fardaje, *m.* fardage, dunnage.

fardar, *va.* to furnish or supply with clothes.

fardel, *m.* bag, knapsack; parcel, bundle.

fardelillo, lejo, *m. dim.* small bundle.

fardería, *f.* collection of packages, luggage.

fardo, *m.* bale, parcel, bundle; burden, load.

farellón, *m.* rocky headland, cliff.

farfalá, *f.* flounce, furbelow.

farfalloso, sa, *n. & a.* stutterer (-ing).

farfante; farfantón, na, *n.* (coll.) boasting babbler.

farfantonada, farfantonería, *f.* idle boast.

fárfara, *f.* (bot.) colt's-foot; shell membrane (of an egg).—**en f.,** immature, as an egg without a shell; unfinished, half done.

farfulla. I. *f.* (coll.) gibberish, gabble, jabber. **II.** *n.* (coll.) jabberer, gabbler.

farfulladamente, *adv.* hurriedly and recklessly.

farfullador, ra, *n. & a.* (coll.) jabberer (-ing).

farfullar, *vn.* (coll.) to gabble, to jabber, to gibber; (coll.) to act hurriedly.

farfullero, ra, *n.* gabbler, jabberer.

fargallón, na. I. *n.* (coll.) bungler, botcher. **II.** *a.* slovenly, untidy.

farillón, *m.* = FARALLÓN.

farináceo, cea, *a.* farinaceous.

farinetas, *f. pl.* (prov.) porridge.

faringe, *f.* (anat.) pharynx.—**faríngeo, a,** *a.* pharyngeal.—**faringitis,** *f.* pharyngitis.

farisaicamente, *adv.* pharisaically.

farisaico, ca, *a.* pharisaical, pharisaic.

farisaísmo, fariseísmo, *m.* pharisaism.

fariseo, *m.* Pharisee; hypocrite; (coll.) tall, lean, ugly person.

farmacéutico, ca. I. *a.* pharmaceutical. **II.** *m.* pharmacist, apothecary, druggist.

farmacia, *f.* pharmacy; drugstore, apothecary's.

farmacología, *f.* pharmacology.

farmacológico, ca, *a.* pharmacological.

farmacopea, *f.* pharmacopœia.

farmacópola, *n.* apothecary, pharmacist, druggist, chemist.

farmacopólico, ca, *a.* pharmaceutical.

faro, *m.* lighthouse; beacon.

farol, *m.* lantern, light; street lamp; cresset; conceited fellow.—**faroles de señales,** (naut.) signal lanterns.

farola, *f.* street light with several arms; big lantern; lighthouse.

farolear, *vn.* (coll.) to boast, brag.

farolería, farolón, *f.* boast, bragging, show.

farolero, ra, *n.* lantern maker; lamplighter; (coll.) strutting coxcomb.

farolico, ito, illo, *m. dim.* small lantern.—**f. de jardín,** (bot.) Indian heartseed.

farolón, *n. & a.* boaster (-ing), braggart (-ing); (coll.) coxcomb, boaster; large lantern.

farota, *f.* brazen-faced woman.

farotón, na, *a.* (coll.) brazen-faced, cheeky.

farpa, *f.* pointed scallop on the edge of draperies.

farpado, da, *a.* scalloped, notched.

farra, *f.* (icht.) a kind of salmon.

fárrago, farrago, *m.* farrago, medley.

farragoso, sa, *a.* full of confused ideas; full of confusion.

farraguista, *n.* person having the head full of confused ideas or half-digested knowledge, pedantic scholar.

farro, *m.* peeled barley; spelt wheat.

farsa, *f.* farce; company of players; a badly constructed play; sham, humbug.

farsanta, *f.* farce actress.

farsante, *m.* pretender, humbug, fraud; (obs.) player.

farseto, *m.* quilted jacket.

farsista, *n.* writer of farces.

fas.—por f. o por nefas, justly or unjustly.

fascal, *m.* (agr.) shock, stook, rick.

fasces, *f. pl.* fasces.

fascículo, *m.* fascicle (part of a book).

fascinación, *f.* fascination, enchantment.

fascinador, ra, *n. & a.* fascinator (-ing), charmer (-ing).—**fascinante,** *a.* fascinating, charming.

fascinar, *va.* to fascinate, bewitch, enchant; to deceive, allure.

fase, *f.* phase, aspect; (astr., elec.) phase.

fásoles, *m. pl.* (bot.) beans.

fastial, *m.* (arch.) crowning pyramid.

fastidiar. I. *va.* to sicken; vex, annoy, bother, bore; to disappoint. **II.** *vr.* to weary; to become vexed, bored or displeased.

fastidio, *m.* squeamishness; dislike; weariness, ennui; nuisance, bother.

fastidiosamente, *adv.* squeamishly.

fastidioso, sa, *a.* squeamish, sickening; vexing, annoying; tedious, tiresome; displeased, annoyed.

fastigio, *m.* (arch.) fastigium; pinnacle, apex, top.

fasto, ta. I. *a.* happy (day or event). **II.** *m.* pomp, pageantry, show.—*pl.* fasti; annals.

fastosamente, fastuosamente, *adv.* pompously, gaudily, magnificently.

fastoso, sa; fastuoso, sa, *a.* pompous, ostentatious.

fatal, *a.* fatal, unavoidable; unfortunate, fated.

fatalidad, *f.* fatality, necessity (both in the philosophic sense); destiny; ill fate, calamity.

fatalismo, *n.* fatalism, determinism.

fatalista, *n.* & *a.* fatalist (-ic), determinist (-ic).

fatalmente, *adv.* fatedly, fatefully; necessarily, unavoidably; calamitously, unluckily; exceedingly bad, wretchedly.

fatídicamente, *adv.* fatidically.

fatídico, ca, *a.* fatidical, oracular.

fatiga, *f.* fatigue, tiredness, weariness; hardship; anguish, anxiety; hard breathing.

fatigadamente, *adv.* with difficulty, with toil.

fatigador, ra, *a.* annoying; tiring.

fatigar. I. *va.* (*pret.* FATIGUÉ: *subj.* FATIGUE) to fatigue, tire; vex, annoy. **II.** *vr.* to tire, become fatigued.

fatigosamente, *adv.* painfully, wearisomely.

fatigoso, sa, *a.* tiring; tiresome, boresome; tired, fatigued.

fatimí, fatimita, *n.* Fatimite.

fatuidad, *f.* fatuity, foolishness; stupidity; conceit, vanity.

fatuo, tua, *a.* fatuous, stupid; foppish, vain.

fauces, *f. pl.* (anat.) fauces, gullet.

fauna, *f.* fauna.

fauno, *m.* faun.

fausto, ta. I. *a.* happy, fortunate. **II.** *m.* pomp, ostentation; great luxury.

faustoso, sa, *a.* = FASTUOSO, SA.

fautor, ra, *n.* abetter, helper, supporter.

fautoría, *f.* aid, assistance.

favilla, *f.* (poet.) ashes of an extinguished fire.

favonio, *m.* westerly wind, zephyr.

favor, *m.* favor; help, aid, service; gift, grace; compliment; love token.—**a f. de,** in behalf of; on account of; taking advantage of, aided by.

favorable, *a.* favorable.

favorablemente, *adv.* favorably.

favorcillo, *m. dim.* small favor.

favorecedor, ra, *a.* favorer; helper; client, customer.

favorecer, *va.* (*ind.* FAVOREZCO: *subj.* FAVOREZCA) to favor; to help, befriend; to abet.

favoritismo, *m.* favoritism.

favorito, ta, *n.* & *a.* favorite.

faz, *f.* face; (arch.) front.—**f. a f.,** face to face.

fe, *f.* faith; faithfulness; testimony; credit, credence; promise given; assertion, asseveration; certificate, testimonial.—**f. de erratas,** (print.) errata; list or table of errata.—**f. púnica,** Punic faith, *Punica fides.*—**a buena f.,** doubtless.—**a f.,** in truth, in good earnest.—**a f. mía,** by my faith.—**dar f.,** to give credit, to attest, to certify, to witness.—**de buena f.,** in good faith.—**de mala f.,** in bad faith.—**en f.,** consequently.—**en f. de lo cual,** in witness whereof.—**por mi f.,** by my faith.—**tener f. a,** to have faith in.

fealdad, *f.* ugliness, homeliness; deformity; hideousness; turpitude, foulness.

feamente, *adv.* uglily, deformedly; unworthily, indecorously; brutally, inordinately.

febeo, bea, *a.* Phœbean.

feble. I. *a.* weak, feeble; (jewel) deficient in weight or quality. **II.** *m.* light coin.

feblemente, *adv.* feebly, weakly.

Febo, *m.* (poet.) Phœbus.

febrero, *m.* February.

febricitante, *a.* (med.) slightly feverish.

febrífugo, ga, *a.* & *m.* (med.) febrifuge.

febril, *a.* (med.) febrile, feverish.

febroniano, na, *a.* Febronian.

fecal, *a.* (med.) fæcal.

fecí, *n.* & *a.* Fezan (from Fez).

fecial, *m.* fecialis, one of the fetiales.

fécula, *f.* fecula; starch.—**feculencia,** *f.* feculence, dregs.—**feculento, ta,** *a.* containing fecula; feculent, foul.

fecundable, *a.* capable of fecundation.

fecundación, *f.* fecundation, fertilization.

fecundamente, *adv.* fruitfully.

fecundante, *a.* fecundating.

fecundar, *va.* to fertilize, fecundate.

fecundativo, va, *a.* fecundating, fertilizing.

fecundidad, *f.* fecundity, fertility, fruitfulness.

fecundizar, *va.* to fecundate, fertilize.

fecundo, da, *a.* fecund, fruitful, fertile, prolific; abundant, copious.

fecha, *f.* date; standing.—**de la cruz a la f.,** from the beginning to the end.

fechador, *m.* dater; (Am.) post-office cancelling stamp.

fechar, *va.* to date (a letter, etc.).

fecho, cha, (obs.) *pp. irr.* of FACER (= HACER): used only in official documents, meaning done, issued, or executed.

fechoría, *f.* misdeed, villainy.

federación, *f.* federation, confederation.

federal. I. *a.* federal. **II.** *m.* federalist.

federalismo, *m.* federalism.

federativo, va, *a.* federative.

fehaciente, *a.* (law) authentic.

feldespático, ca, *a.* (min.) feldspathic.

feldespato, *m.* (min.) feldspar.

felice, *a.* (poet.) happy.

felicidad, *f.* felicity, happiness; good luck, good fortune.

felicitación, *f.* congratulation, felicitation.

felicitar, *va.* to congratulate, felicitate.

félido, da. I. *n.* & *a.* (zool.) feline. **II.** *m. pl.* Felidæ.

feligrés, sa, *n.* parishioner.

feligresía, *f.* parish, parishioners.

felino, na, *n.* & *a.* feline.

feliz, *a.* happy, fortunate, felicitous.

felizmente, *adv.* happily, felicitous'y.

felón, na, *n.* (law) felon, criminal.

felonía, *f.* treachery, disloyalty, felony.

felpa, *f.* plush; (coll.) reprimand, drubbing.

felpado, da, *a.* plushy, shaggy, villous.

felpilla, *f.* chenille.

felposo, sa, *a.* felted; plush-covered.

felpudo, da. I. *a.* plushy. **II.** *m.* doormat.

femenil, *a.* feminine, womanish.

femenilmente, *adv.* effeminately, womanishly.

femenino, na, *a.* feminine; female.

fementidamente, *adv.* perfidiously.

fementido, da, *a.* false, unfaithful.

femineidad, *f.* (law) quality of belonging to a woman.

feminismo, *m.* feminism, doctrine of the social and political equality of woman.

feminista, *n.* feminist, follower of feminism. (*V.* FEMINISMO).

femoral, *a.* (anat.) femoral.

fémur, *m.* (anat.) femur.

fenacetina, *f.* phenacetin.

fenaquistoscopio, *m.* (phys.) phenakistoscope.

fenda, *f.* crack in the bark of trees.

fendiente, *m.* gash, deep cut or wound.

fenecer. I. *va.* (*ind.* FENEZCO: *subj.* FENEZCA) to finish, conclude, close. **II.** *vn.* to die; to end.

fenecimiento, *m.* finish, termination, end; death.

fenestrado, da, *a.* fenestrate.

fenianismo, *m.* Fenianism.

feniano, na, *n.* & *a.* Fenian.

fenicar, *va.* to carbolize, put carbolic acid in or to.

fenicio, cia, *n.* & *a.* Phœnician.
fénico, ca, *a.* carbolic.
fenilamina, *f.* (chem.) phenylamine.
fénix, *m.,* phœnix; model; king (in the sense of excellent or highest person).
fenogreco, *m.* (bot.) fenugreek.
fenol, *n.* phenol.
fenolftaleína, *f.* phenolphthalein.
fenomenial, *a.* phenomenal.
fenómeno, *m.* phenomenon.—*pl.* phenomena.
feo, ea. I. *a.* ugly, homely; improper; heinous; serious, alarming.—**dejar f.,** to slight. **II.** *m.* slight, affront.
feote, ta; feotón, na, *a. aug.* exceedingly homely.
feracidad, *f.* feracity, fruitfulness, fertility.
feral, *a.* cruel, bloodthirsty.
feraz, *a.* fertile, fruitful; abundant, plentiful.
féretro, *m.* bier, coffin.
feria, *f.* market, fair, bazaar; (eccl.) any week day (excepting Saturday or a feast day); holiday; rest, repose.
feriado, da, *pp.* & *a.*—**día f.,** day when courts are not open; holiday.
ferial. I. *a.* ferial. **II.** *m.* market, fair.
feriante, *n.* trader at fairs.
feriar. I. *va.* to trade, barter; to purchase at a fair; to give fairings. **II.** *vn.* to suspend work; to keep holidays.
ferino, na, *a.* ferine, wild, savage, ferocious.
fermata, *f.* (mus.) pause or hold (⌢).
fermentable, *a.* fermentable.
fermentación, *f.* fermentation.
fermentante, *a.* fermenting.
fermentar, *vn.* & *va.* to ferment.
fermentativo, va, *a.* fermentative.
fermento, *m.* ferment, leaven, leavening.
fernambuco, *m.* Pernambuco wood.
fernandina, *f.* a kind of linen stuff.
feroce, *a.* (poet.) ferocious.
ferocidad, *f.* ferocity.
feróstico, ca, *a.* (coll.) irritable, wayward.
feroz, *a.* ferocious, fell, fierce; ravenous.
ferozmente, *adv.* ferociously.
ferra, *f.* a variety of salmon. *V.* FARRA.
ferrada, *f.* iron-knobbed club.
ferrado, da. I. *a.* ferrate, iron-bound. **II.** *m.* a corn measure between 13 and 16 liters; a land measure (between 4 and 6 acres).
ferrar, *va.* to garnish with iron.
férreo, rea, *a.* ferrous; iron (u. a.), made of iron; harsh, stern, severe.—**vía férrea,** railroad.
ferrería, *f.* ironworks, foundry.
ferreruelo, *m.* short cloak without cape.
ferrete, *m.* sulphate of copper used to color glass; (gl.) ferret; marking iron.
ferretear, *va.* to bind, mark, or work with iron.
ferretería, *f.* hardware; hardware shop.
ferriciánogeno, *m.* ferricyanogen.
ferricianuro, *m.* ferricyanide.
férrico, ca, *a.* containing iron; (chem.) ferric.
ferrífero, ra, *a.* ferriferous, iron-bearing.
ferrificarse, *vr.* to be converted into iron.
ferrizo, za, *a.* ferreous, iron (u. a.), of iron.
ferro, *m.* (naut.) anchor.
ferrocarril, *m.* railroad, railway.—**f. aéreo,** elevated railroad.—**f. de cable,** cable railway.—**f. de circunvalación,** belt, or girdle, railway.—**f. de cremallera,** rack railroad.—**f. de sangre,** animal-power railroad; horse tramway.—**f. de vapor,** stream railroad.—**f. eléctrico,** electric railroad.—**f. elevado,** elevated railroad.—**f. funicular,** cable railroad; ropeway.—**f. subterráneo,** underground railroad.—**f. urbano,** street railroad.
ferrocarrilero, ra, *a.* (Am.) = FERROVIARIO.
ferrociánogeno, *m.* ferrocyanogen.
ferrocianuro, *m.* ferrocyanide.
ferrón, *m.* workman in ironworks.
ferroso, sa, *a.* ferrous.
ferrovía, *f.* railway.
ferrovial, ferroviario, ria, *a.* railroad (u. a.), pertaining to railroads.
ferrugiento, ta, *a.* containing iron.

ferrugíneo, nea; ferruginoso, sa, *a.* ferruginous.
fértil, *a.* fertile, fruitful; copious, plentiful.
fertilidad, *f.* fertility; fruitfulness; abundance, plenty.
fertilizador, ra, *a.* fertilizing.
fertilizante, *n.* & *a.* fertilizer (-ing).
fertilizar, *va.* (*pret.* FERTILICÉ: *subj.* FERTILICE) to fertilize, enrich, make fruitful.
fértilmente, *adv.* fruitfully.
férula, *f.* ferule; rule, yoke, authority; (surg.) splint; (bot.) ferula.
feruláceo, ea, *a.* ferulaceous.
ferventísimo, ma, *a. sup.* very fervent or pious.
férvido, da, *a.* fervid, ardent.
ferviente, *a.* = FERVOROSO.
fervor, *m.* intense heat; fervor.
fervorcillo, *m. dim.* slight and brief fervor.
fervorizar, *va.* to heat, inflame, incite.
fervorosamente, *adv.* fervently.
fervoroso, sa, *a.* fervent; active, efficient.
festejador, ra, *n.* & *a.* entertainer (-ing).
festejante, *a.* feasting, entertaining; wooing.
festejar, *va.* to entertain, to feast; to court, to woo, to make love to; to celebrate.
festejo, *m.* feast, entertainment; obsequiousness; courtship.
festero, ra, *n.* director of church music.
festín, *m.* feast, banquet.
festinación, *f.* speed, haste, hurry.
festinar, *va.* to hasten.
festival, *m.* festival.
festivamente, *adv.* festively.
festividad, *f.* festivity; rejoicing, gaiety, merry-making; holiday; witticism.
festivo, va, *a.* festive, gay; festival, festal.
festón, *m.* garland, wreath, festoon.
festonar, festonear, *va.* to festoon.
fetal, *a.* fetal, fœtal.
feticida. I. *n.* one committing feticide. **II.** *a.* feticidal.
feticidio, *m.* feticide.
fetiche, *m.* fetich.—**fetichismo,** *m.* fetichism
fetichista. I. *a.* fetichistic. **II.** *n.* fetichist.
fetidez, *f.* fetidity.—**fétido, da,** *a.* fetid.
feto, *m.* fetus, fœtus.
fetor, *m.* = FETIDEZ.
feúco, ca, cho, cha, *a.* ugly, repulsive.
feudal, *a.* feudal.—**feudalidad,** *f.,* **feudalismo,** *m.* feudalism.—**feudatario, ria,** *a.* & *n.* feudatory.
feudista, *m.* (law) feudist.
feudo, *m.* fief, feud, feod.
fez, *m.* fez, Turkish cap.
fiable, *a.* trustworthy, responsible.
fiado, da, *a.* & *pp.* of FIAR; on trust.—**al f.,** on trust, on credit.—**en f.,** on bail.
fiador, ra. I. *n.* bondsman, guarantor, surety, bail.—**f. carcelero,** one who is bail or surety for a person.—**dar f.,** io give surety.—**salir f.,** to go surety. **II.** *m.* fastener; (mech.) stop, catch, pawl, click, trigger; tumbler of a lock; (falc.) creance.
fiambrar, *va.* to cook for cold cuts or lunch.
fiambre. I. *a.* cold-served (as victuals). **II.** *m.* cold victuals, cold lunch; (coll.) old joke or piece of news, "chestnut."
fiambrera, *f.* lunch basket; dinner pail.
fiancilla, *f.* (car.) binding ring.
fianza, *f.* surety, bail, bond, caution, guarantee, security; suretyship.—**f. de aduana,** customhouse bond.—**f. juratoria** = CAUCIÓN JURATORIA.
fiar. I. *va.* to answer or go surety for; to bail; to sell on trust, give credit for; to intrust, confide. **II.** *vn.* to confide; to sell on trust, give credit.
fiasco, *m.* failure.
fiat, *m.* consent; (law) fiat.
fibra, *f.* fibre, filament, staple; energy, stamina, vigor; (min.) vein of ore.
fibrina, *f.* (chem.) fibrin, fibrine.
fibroideo, a, *a.* fibroid.
fibroma, *m.* (surg.) fibroma.
fibroso, sa, *a.* fibrous.
ficción, *f.* fiction, invention; tale, story.

fice *m.* (icht.) whiting.
ficoideo, a. I. *n.* & *a.* (bot.) ficoid (-al). **II.** *f.* *pl.* Ficoideæ, Aizoaceæ.
ficticio, cia, *a.* fictitious.
ficto, ta, *a.* feigned, counterfeited, artificial.
ficha, *f.* chip, counter, marker; domino (man).— **mala f.,** bad character (s. o. a person).
fidedigno, na, *a.* trustworthy, creditable.
fideero, ra, *n.* maker of Italian paste.
fideicomisario, *m.* fideicommissioner.
fideicomiso, *m.* trust; feoffment to use.
fideísmo, *m.* (philos.) fideism, acceptance of faith as the foundation of truth.
fidelidad, *f.* fidelity, faithfulness; honor; fealty, loyalty.
fidelísimo, ma, *a. sup.* of FIEL.
fideos, *m. pl.* vermicelli; spaghetti.
fiduciario, ria, *n.* & *a.* fiduciary.
fiebre, *f.* fever; intense excitement, heat of passion.— **f. amarilla,** yellow fever.— **f. héctica,** hectic fever.— **f. intermitente,** intermittent fever.
—**f. láctea,** milk fever, lacteal fever.— **f. miliar,** miliary fever.— **f. palúdica,** malaria.— **f. perniciosa,** pernicious intermittent fever.— **f. puerperal,** puerperal fever.— **f. remitente,** remittent fever.— **f tifoidea,** typhoid fever.
fiebrecilla, *f. dim.* slight fever.
fiel. I. *a.* faithful, loyal, devoted; true, exact, accurate. **II.** *m.* public inspector, especially of weights and measures; pointer of a balance or steelyard; pin of the scissors.— **f. contraste,** official who weighs and stamps metals.— **f. de muelle,** wharfinger.— **f. de romana,** official inspector of meat weighing in slaughter houses.— **f. medidor,** inspector of measures.— **en f.,** equal weight, even balance.
fielato, fielazgo, *m.* office of the FIEL; octroi at a city's gates.
fieldad, *f.* public inspectorship; surety, security, guarantee.
fielmente, *adv.* faithfully.
fieltro, *m.* felt; felt hat, overcoat or rug.
fiemo, *m.* (prov.) dung, manure.
fiera, *f.* wild beast; fierce, violent person; (coll.) exceedingly able, shrewd or cunning person; person strenuously or habitually given or devoted to something, "fiend."
fierabrás, *m.* (coll.) bully, blusterer; wayward forward child.
fieramente, *adv.* fiercely, ferociously; haughtily.
fiereza, *f.* fierceness, ferocity; deformity.
fiero, ra. I. *a.* fierce, cruel; ferocious; ugly, deformed; rough, rude; haughty; huge, enormous; furious, terrible; wild, savage. **II.** *m. pl.* fierce threats and bravadoes.
fierro, *m.* iron; brand.
fiesta, *f.* feast, entertainment, merriment; festivity, festival, holiday; caress, act of endearment; holy day.—*pl.* holidays, vacation.—**f. de guardar,** or **de precepto,** holy day, Mass day.—**f. fija,** or **inmoble,** immovable feast.—**f. movible,** movable feast.—**aguar la f.,** to mar one's pleasure.—**hacer f.,** to quit work, to take a holiday.—**hacer fiestas,** to caress; to wheedle, to fawn to.—**se acabó la f.,** (coll.) it's all over; drop it, let's drop it.
figle, *m.* (mus.) ophicleide.
figón, *m.* eating house, chophouse.
figonero, ra, *n.* keeper of an eating house.
figulino, na, *a.* terra cotta (u. a.)
figura. I. *f.* figure; shape; build; mien, looks; ill-shaped person, guy; face card or court card; (law) form, mode; (mus.) musical note; (gram., rhet., geom.) figure.—**f. de bulto,** figure in sculpture; high relief.—**f. de retórica,** figure of speech. **II.** *m.* stiffly pompous person.
figurable, *a.* imaginable.
figuración, *f.* figuration.
figuradamente, *adv.* figuratively.
figurado, da, *pp.* & *a.* figurative; rhetorical, ornate, florid.
figurante, ta. I. *m.* figurant. **II.** *f.* figurante.
figurar. I. *va.* to shape, fashion; to draw, sketch; to represent; to feign. **II.** *vn.* to figure, be

conspicuous. **III.** *vr.* to fancy, imagine to occur, come to one's mind; to seem.
figurativamente, *adv.* figuratively.
figurativo, va, *a.* figurative, typical; symbolical, emblematic.
figurería, *f.* grimace, affected gesture.
figurero, ra, *n.* (coll.) one who makes grimaces or affected gestures; maker of statuettes.
figurilla, ita, *f. dim.* (coll.) little insignificant person; (art) figurine, statuette.
figurín, *m.* fashion plate; lay figure.
figurón, *m. aug.* huge figure having a ridiculous appearance; (coll.) pretentious nobody.—**f. de proa,** (naut.) figurehead.
fija, *f.* door hinge; (mas.) trowel.
fijación, *f.* stability, firmness; billposting; fixing; locking, immobilizing.
fijador, ra. I. *n.* & *a.* fixer (-ing); fastener (-ing). **II.** *m.* (mas.) pointer, workman that points the joints; (carp.) door and window setter; (phot. and art) fixing liquid.
fijamente, *adv.* firmly, assuredly; intensely, attentively; fixedly, steadfastly.
fijar. I. *va.* (*pp.* FIJADO, FIJO) to fix, fasten; to make fast, firm, or stable; to determine, settle, establish; clinch; to post (as bills); to fix (the eyes, the attention, etc.); (phot., art) to fix; to set (a date). **II.** *vr.* (w. en) to settle (in); to determine, resolve; to rivet one's attention (on); to take notice (of), pay attention (to).
fijeza, *f.* firmness, stability; steadfastness.
fijo, ja, *a.* fixed, firm; settled, permanent; (mech.) stationary.
fil, *m.*—**f. derecho,** leapfrog.—**f. de roda,** (naut.) right ahead.—**estar en f.,** to be in line.
fila, *f.* tier, row, line, range; (mil.) rank.—**en f.,** in a line, in a row; (mil.) abreast.
filacteria, *f.* phylactery.
filadelfo, fa. I. *n.* & *a.* (bot.) (plant) belonging to the genus Philadelphus (mock orange, syringa, etc.). **II.** *f. pl.* family of these plants.
filadiz, *m.* floss silk, ferret.
filagrama, *f.* wire mould for a watermark.
filamento, *m.* filament, fibre, thread.
filamentoso, sa, *a.* filamentous, fibrous.
filandria, *f.* filander, backworm.
filantropía, *f.* philanthropy.
filantrópicamente, *adv.* philanthropically.
filantrópico, ca, *a.* philanthropic.
filántropo, pa, *n.* philanthropist.
filarete, *m.* (naut.) waist netting.
filaria, *f.* (zool.) filaria, a parasitic nematode worm.
filariasis, filariosis, *f.* (med.) filariosis, infection with filariæ.
filarmonía, *f.* love of music.
filarmónico, ca, *a.* philharmonic.
filástica, *f.* (naut.) rope yarn.
filatelia, *f.* philately.—**filatélico, ca,** *a.* philatelic.—**filatelista, n.** philatelist.
filatería, *f.* verbosity.
filatero, ra, *n.* verbose speaker.
filatura, *f.* spinning.
filbán, *m.* rough edge of a tool.
filderretor, *m.* superfine camlet.
filelí, *m.* superfine flannel.
fileno, na, *a.* (coll.) delicate, small.
filete, *m.* (arch.) fillet, listel; (sew.) narrow hem; small spit for roasting; welt of a shoe; snaffle bit; (mech.) edge, border, ring, rim; thread (of a screw); (print.) ornamental line; tenderloin, loin of beef.
filetear, *va.* to fillet; to crease; to tool.
filetón, *m. aug.* (arch.) large fillet or listel; heavy bullion for embroidering.
filfa, *f.* (coll.) fib, hoax, false.
filiación, *f.* filiation; connection, relationship; personal description; (mil.) regimental register.
filial, *a.* filial.—**filialmente,** *adv.* filially.
filiar. I. *va.* to register the pedigree and description of. **II.** *vr.* to enrol.
filibote, *m.* flyboat, light vessel.

filibusterismo, *m.* filibusterism.

filibustero, *m.* filibuster.

filicida, *n.* filicide, one who kills his child.

filicidio, *n.* filicide, killing a son or daughter.

filiforme, *a.* filiform.

filigrana, *f.* filigree, filigrane; spun work; watermark in paper; delicate, fanciful thing.

filili, *m.* (coll.) fineness, neatness, delicacy.

filipéndula, *f.* (bot.) dropwort spiræa.

filipense, *n.* & *a.* Philippian.

filípica, *f.* Philippic; invective.

filipichin, *m.* moreen, woollen cloth.

filipino, na, *n.* & *a.* Philippine.

filis, *m.* knack; trinket, charm.

filisteo, tea. I. *n.* & *a.* Philistine. **II.** *n.* (coll.) very tall and corpulent person.

filo, *m.* cutting edge; dividing line; ridge; (arch.) arris.

filocartista, *n.* collector of postal cards.

filófago, ga, *a.* (ent.) phyllophagous.

filología, filológica, *f.* philology.—**filológico, ca,** *a.* philological.—**filólogo, ga,** *n.* philologist.

filomanía, *f.* (bot.) phyllomania.

filomela, filomena, *f.* nightingale, philomel.

filón, *m.* (geol.) vein, lode.

filonio, *m.* philonium, a kind of eyesalve with opium.

filopos, *m. pl.* pieces of linen used to drive game.

filoseda, *f.* vesting; silk and worsted or cotton cloth.

filosofador, ra, *n.* & *a.* philosophizer (-ing).

filosofar, *vn.* to philosophize.

filosofastro, *m.* philosophaster.

filosofía, *f.* philosophy.

filosóficamente, *adv.* philosophically.

filosófico, ca, *a.* philosophical, philosophic.

filosofismo, *m.* philosophism.

filosofista, *m.* philosophist.

filósofo, fa, *n.* philosopher.

filoxera, *f.* phylloxera.

filtración, *f.* filtration.—**filtrador, ra. I.** *n.* & *a.* filterer (-ing). **II.** *m.* filter.

filtrar. I. *va.* & *vn.* to filter. **I.** *vn.* to percolate, filter. **III.** *vr.* to leak out; disappear; to filter through.

filtro, *m.* filter; philter, love potion.—**f. de vacío,** vacuum filter.—**f. prensa,** filter press for refining sugar.

fillo, *m.* a sort of fritter.

fimbria, *f.* border of a skirt.

fimo, *m.* dung, manure.

fimosis, *f.* (med.) phimosis.

fin, *m.* end, ending, conclusion; end, object, purpose.—**a f. de que,** so that.—**a fines de,** towards the end of. late in (the week, etc.).—**al f.,** at last.—**al f. y a la postre, or al f. y al cabo,** at last; lastly; after all.—**en f.,** finally, lastly; in fine; well (used as an expletive: *en fin, veremos,* well, we shall see).—**por f.,** at last.—**sin f.,** endless; numberless.

finado, da. I. *pp.* & *a.* dead, deceased; late (recently deceased). **II.** *n.* deceased, person dead.

final. I. *a.* final; ultimate; conclusive. **II.** *m.* end, termination, conclusion.

finalidad, *f.* finality; end pursued or attained.

finalista, *n.* follower of the doctrine of final causes.

finalizar. I. *va.* to finish, conclude. **II.** *vn.* to end, to be finished or concluded.

finalmente, *adv.* finally, lastly.

finamente, *adv.* finely, nicely, delicately.

finamiento, *m.* death, decease, demise.

financiero, ra. I. *a.* financial. **II.** *m.* financier.

finar. I. *vn.* to die. **II.** *vr.* to long.

finca, *f.* real estate, land, house property; country property, farm, ranch.

fincar, *vn.* & *vr.* (*pret.* FINQUÉ: *subj.* FINQUE) to buy real estate.

finchado, da, *a.* swelling with pride.

finés, sa, *a.* Finnic, Finnish.

fineza, *f.* fineness; goodness, purity; kindness, expression of regard, courtesy; friendly influence or assistance; keepsake, gift, favor.

fingidamente, *adv.* feignedly; hypocritically.

fingido, da, *pp.* & *a.* feigned, dissembled.

fingidor, ra, *n.* & *a.* dissembler (-ing), feigner (-ing).

fingimiento, *m.* simulation, deceit, pretence.

fingir, *va.* & *vr.* (*pp.* FINGIDO, FICTO: *ind.* FINJO: *subj.* FINJA) to feign, dissemble, pretend, affect, sham; to fancy, imagine.

finible, *a.* capable of being finished.

finiquitar, *va.* to settle and close (an account).

finiquito, *m.* settlement of accounts; adjustment, release, quittance.

finítimo, ma, *a.* bordering, contiguous, near.

finito, ta, *a.* finite.

finlandés, sa, *a.* Finnish.

fino, na, *a.* fine; perfect, pure; thin, slender, subtle; delicate, nice; affectionate, true; sagacious, cunning, shrewd; sharp (as a point); courteous, polite; refined (as gold); (naut.) sharp.

finta, *f.* an ancient tax; feint in fencing.

finura, *f.* fineness; purity; politeness; courtesy.

fiñana, *m.* black-bearded wheat.

fiordo, *m.* fiord.

fique, *m.* = CABUYA.

firma, *f.* signature; sign manual, hand (as hand and seal); subscription; act of signing; (com.) firm name.—**f. en blanco,** blank signature; full powers.—**buena f.,** reliable firm or house.—**dar, or llevar, la f.,** to empower or be empowered to sign the firm name.

firmamento, *m.* firmament, sky.

firmán, *m.* firman.

firmante, *n.* signer, subscriber.

firmar, *va.*, *vn.* & *vr.* to sign.—**f. en blanco,** to give a blank signature.

firme. I. *a.* firm, stable, solid; hard, compact; unswerving, stanch, unyielding.—**estar en lo f.,** to be certain or positive. **II.** *m.* groundwork, bed, foundation; ballast or gravel bed on a road; roadbed.—**de f.,** steadily; solidly; violently, strongly.—**en f.,** definitive, final, in final form. **III.** *adv.* firmly, strongly.

firmemente, *adv.* firmly.

firmeza, *f.* firmness, stability; hardness, compactness.

firmón, na, *n.* one who signs another's work.

fiscal. I. *a.* fiscal. **II.** *m.* attorney-general; district attorney, prosecutor; (coll.) intermeddler, prier.

fiscalía, *f.* office and business of a FISCAL.

fiscalización, *f.* discharge of a FISCAL's duties.

fiscalizador, ra. I. *a.* acting as a FISCAL. **II.** *n.* prier, censurer, fault finder.

fiscalizar, *va.* (*pret.* FISCALICÉ: *subj.* FISCALICE) to prosecute; to criticise, censure.

fisco, *m.* national treasury, exchequer.

fisga, *f.* fishgig; raillery, banter, chaff; grain of spelt wheat; bread of spelt wheat.

fisgador, ra, *n.* harpooner; banterer.

fisgar, *vn.* to chaff, banter; to fish with a fishgig; to peep, to pry.

fisgón, na, *n.* banterer, chaffer, jester; prier.

fisgonear, *vn.* to pry habitually.

fisgoneo, *m.* habitual or frequent prying.

física, *f.* physics.—**físicamente,** *adv.* physically.

físico, ca. I. *a.* physical. **II.** *n.* physicist; physician; military or naval surgeon; physique; (coll.) face.

fisieoquímico, ca, *a.* physicochemical.

fisil, *a.* fissile.

fisiocracia, *f.* physiocracy.

fisiócrata, *n.* physiocrat.

fisiología, *f.* physiology.—**fisiológicamente,** *adv.* physiologically.—**fisiológico, ca,** *a.* physiological.—**fisiologista, fisiólogo,** *m.* physiologist.

fisionomía, *f.* physiognomy, appearance, looks, features.

fisioterapia, *f.* treatment of disease by natural agents (fresh air, sunlight, etc.).

fisiparidad, *f.* (biol.) fissiparity.

fisíparo, ra, *a.* (biol.) fissiparous.

fisonomía, *f.* = FISIONOMÍA.

fisonómico, ca, *a.* physiognomical.

fisonomista, fisónomo, *m.* physiognomist.

fistol, *m.* crafty person; shrewd gambler; (Mex.) scarf pin.

fístola, fístula, *f.* water pipe or conduit; (mus.) reed or pipe; (surg.) fistula.

fistular, *a.* (med.) fistular, fistulous.

fistuloso, sa, *a.* fistulous.

fisura, *f.* (geol.) fissure, cleft; (surg.) fissure of bone, or "green-stick" fracture; (surg.) fissure in the anus.

fitófago, ga, *a.* phytophagous.

fitografía, *f.* phytography.—**fitográfico, ca,** *a.* phytographic.—**fitógrafo,** *m.* phytographer.

fitología, *f.* phytology, botany.

fitonisa, *f.* = PITONISA.

fitotomía, *f.* (bot.) phytotomy.

flabelicornio, *a.* having flabellate antennæ.

flabelífero, ra, *a.* flabellum carrier.

flabeliforme, *a.* flabelliform.

flacamente, *adv.* languidly, weakly, feebly.

fláccido, da, *a.* flaccid, limber, lax, soft.

flaccidez, *f.* (med.) flaccidity, laxity, limberness.

flaco, ca. I. *a.* thin, lean; feeble, languid; frail, weak of resolution.—**f. de memoria,** short of memory. **II.** *m.* weak point, weakness.

flacucho, cha, *a.* rather thin or lank.

flacura, *f.* thinness, lack of flesh, leanness.

flagelación, *f.* flagellation, scourging.

flagelador, ra, *n.* flagellator.—**flagelante,** *n.* & *a.* flagellant (-ing).—**flagelar,** *va.* to scourge, flagellate, whip.—**flagelo,** *m.* lash, scourge; flagellum.

flagrancia, *f.* flagrancy.

flagrante, *a.* resplendent; present.—**en f.,** flagrante delicto, in the very act.

flagrar, *vn.* (poet.) to burn, glow, shine.

flama, *f.* flame, excessive ardor.

flamante, *a.* flaming, bright, resplendent; brand-new, fresh, spick and span.

flamear, *vn.* to flame, blaze; (naut.) to shiver, to flutter (s. o. sails).

flamen, *m.* flamen.—**f. dial,** flamen Dialis.—**f. marcial,** flamen Martialis.—**f. quirinal,** flamen quirinalis.

flamenco, *m.* (orn.) flamingo.

flamenco, ca, *n.* & *a.* Flemish.

flamenquilla, *f.* small platter; (bot.) marigold.

flámeo, *m.* ancient bridal veil.

flamero, *m.* torch holder.

flamígero, ra, *a.* (poet.) flammiferous.

flámula, *f.* (naut.) streamer, pennon.

flan, *m.* flawn, rich custard.

flanco, *m.* side; (mil. and fort.) flank.

flanela, *f.* = FRANELA.

flanqueado, da. I. *a.* with both flanks protected. **II.** *pp.* of FLANQUEAR.

flanqueante, *a.* flanking.

flanquear, *va.* (mil. and fort.) to flank.

flanqueo, *m.* (mil.) flank attack, flanking.

flaquear, *vn.* to flag, weaken; to become weak; to threaten ruin or downfall.

flaqueza, *f.* leanness, thinness, emaciation; feebleness, weakness; frailty, foible; flagginess.

flato, *m.* flatus, windiness.

flatoso, sa, *a.* flatuous, windy.

flatulencia, *f.* flatulency, windiness.

flatulento, ta, *a.* flatulent, windy.

flatuoso, sa, *a.* flatuous, windy.

flauta, *f.* (mus.) flute.—**f. travesera,** German flute.

flautado, da. I. *a.* flutelike. **II.** *m.* flute stop in an organ.

flauteado, da, *a.* flutelike, soft and sweet (s. o. the voice).—**flautero, ra,** *n.* flute maker.

flautillo, *m.* = CARAMILLO.

flautín, *m.* (mus.) octave flute, piccolo.

flautista, *n.* flute player.

flébil, *a.* deplorable, lamentable.

flebitis, *f.* phlebitis, inflammation of a vein.

flebotomía, *f.* phlebotomy, bloodletting.

flebotomiano, na, *n.* phlebotomist.

fleco, *m.* fringe, purl, flounce.

flecha, *f.* arrow, dart; (fort.) work of two faces and two sides; (naut.) front piece of the cutwater; (eng., arch.) maximum ordinate; deflection (as of a beam).

flechador, *m.* archer.

flechaduras, *f. pl.* (naut.) ratlines.

flechar. I. *va.* to dart, to shoot (an arrow or dart); to strike with an arrow; (coll.) to inspire sudden love; (Mex.) to point out, without fear, in gambling. **II.** *vn.* to make a bow ready to shoot.

flechaste, *m.* (naut.) ratline.

flechazo, *m.* stroke with a dart or arrow.

flechera, *f.* (Am.) long, sharp canoe.

flechería, *f.* shower of arrows.

flechero, ra, *n.* archer, bowman; arrow maker.

flegmasia, *f.* (med.) phlegmasia.

fleje, *m.* iron hoop or strap.—**flejes para aros,** hoop poles.

flema, *f.* phlegm.—**flemático, ca,** *a.* phlegmatic.

fleme, *f.* (vet.) fleam.

flemón, *m.* phlegmon; gumboil.

flemonoso, sa, *a.* phlegmonous.

flemoso, sa, *a.* mucous, phlegmy.

flemudo, da, *a.* phlegmatic.

flequezuelo, *m. dim.* narrow fringe.

fletador, ra, *n.* (com.) freighter, charterer.

fletamento, *m.* (com.) charter, charterage, charter party.

fletar, *va.* to freight or charter (a ship).

flete, *m.* freight, freightage.

flexibilidad, *f.* flexibility.—**flexible,** *a.* flexible; lithe; supple; manageable, docile.

flexión, *f.* flexion, flexure.

flexor, ra. I. *a.* bending. **II.** *m.* bender; (anat.) flexor.

flexuoso, sa, *a.* (bot.) flexuose.

flictena, *f.* (med.) phlyctena, small blister.

flin, *m.* (cut.) polishing stone.

flocadura, *f.* (sew.) fringe trimming.

flogístico, ca, *a.* phlogistic.

flogisto, *m.* phlogiston.

flogosis, *f.* inflammation, phlegmasia.

flojamente, *adv.* slowly, carelessly, laxly.

flojear, *vn.* to slacken, to grow weak.

flojedad, *f.* weakness, feebleness, laxity; sloth, laziness, negligence.

flojel, *m.* wool shorn from cloth; down, soft feathers.

flojera, *f.* (coll.) weakness. *V.* FLOJEDAD.

flojo, ja, *a.* loose, lax, slack; weak; flaccid; lazy; (Colomb.) timorous, cowardly.

floqueado, da, *a.* fringed.

flor, *f.* flower; blossom; down of fruits newly gathered; prime; film on the surface of liquors; (chem.) flower, powder; compliment; grain, outside of tanned leather; cheating trick of gamblers; (gen. *pl.*) flowers, menstruation.—**f. compuesta,** (bot.) compound flower.—**f. de la edad,** youth; prime of life.—**f. de lis,** fleur-de-lis, iris.—**f. del sol** (bot.) = CORONA REAL.—**f. de mano,** artificial flower.—**f. y nata,** flower, élite.—**flores blancas,** leucorrhœa.—**flores de cantueso,** trifle, small matter.—**a f. de,** flush with; (naut.) awash.—**decir,** or **echar, flores,** to pay compliments, to flatter.

flora, *f.* (bot.) flora.

floración, *f.* (bot.) flowering, florescence.

florada, *f.* season of flowers with beemasters.

floral, *a.* (bot.) floral.

florales, *a. pl.* Floralia, floral feasts or games.

florar, *vn.* to flower, blossom, bloom.

flordelisado, da, *pp.* & *a.* (her.) fleuretté.

flordelisar, *va.* (her.) to flourish with irises.

floreado, da, *a.* & *pp.* flowered, figured (goods); made of the finest flour.

florear, *va.* to flower; to bolt (flour); to flourish, brandish; (mus.) to flourish on the guitar; to pay compliments to.

florecer. I. *vn.* (*ind.* FLOREZCO: *subj.* FLOREZCA) to flower, bloom, blossom; to flourish, thrive, prosper. **II.** *vr.* to mould, become mouldy.

florecica, illa, ita, *f. dim.* floweret, small flower.

floreciente, *pa. & a.* flourishing, flowering.

florentín, tino, tina, *n. & a.* Florentine.

florentísimo, ma, *a. sup.* very prosperous.

floreo, *m.* witty but idle talk; compliment; (fenc.) flourish; (mus.) flourish; cross caper, in dancing.

florero, ra. I. *a.* flattering. **II.** *n.* florist. **III.** *m.* flowerpot; flower vase; flower stand, jardinière; (art) flower piece. **IV.** *f.* flower girl.

florescencia, *f.* (bot.) florescence, flowering.

floresta, *f.* wooded field; delightful rural place; collection of fine, pleasing things.

florestero, *m.* forester, forest keeper or guard.

floreta, *f.* leather border on the edge of a girth.

florete. I. *a.* (com.) first quality, superfine. **II.** *m.* fencing foil.

floretear, *va.* to garnish with flowers.

floretista, *m.* fencer.

floricultor, ra, *n.* floriculturist.

floricultura, *f.* floriculture.

floridamente, *adv.* flowerily; flourishingly.

floridano, na, *n. & a.* Floridian (from Florida), Florida (u. a.).

floridez, *f.* floridity, floridness.

florido, da, *a.* flowery; full of flowers; choice, select. *V.* PASCUA FLORIDA.

florífero, ra, florígero, ra, *a.* floriferous.

florilegio, *m.* florilegium, anthology.

florín, *m.* florin (coin).

floripondio, *m.* (bot.) floripondio.

florisar, *va.* = FLORDELISAR.

florista, *n.* maker of artificial flowers.

florón, *m. aug.* large flower; (arch.) fleuron, rosette.

flósculo, *m.* (bot.) floscule, floret.

flota, *f.* (naut.) fleet of merchant ships; (obs.) squadron.

flotable, *a.* floatable; navigable.

flotación, *f.* flotation, flotage, floating.

flotador, ra. I. *n. & a.* floater (-ing). **II.** *m.* float.

flotadura, *f.,* **flotamiento,** *m.* flotation, flotage; floating.—**flotante,** *a.* floating.—**flotar,** *vn.* to float (on a liquid or in the air).—**flote,** *m.* floating. —**a f.,** afloat.

flotilla, *f. dim.* flotilla; small fleet.

fluctuación, *f.* fluctuation; wavering.

fluctuante, *a.* fluctuating.

fluctuar, *vn.* to fluctuate; waver, oscillate; to be in danger; to hesitate, vacillate.

fluctuoso, sa, *a.* fluctuant, wavering.

fluente, *a.* fluent, flowing.

fluidez, *f.* fluidity, fluidness; fluency.

flúido, da. I. *a.* fluid; fluent (as speech). **II.** *m.* fluid.

fluir, *vn.* (gerund, FLUYENDO: *ind.* FLUYO: *subj.* FLUYA) *vn.* to flow; to issue, ooze, run out.

flujo, *m.* flux, flow, flowing· (med.) flux, hæmorrhage; (naut.) flow, rising tide; (chem.) flux.— **f. blanco,** the whites.—**f. de palabras,** flow of words, volubility.—**f. de reir,** habit of laughing.— **f. de risa,** fit of laughter.—**f. de sangre,** hæmorrhage.—**f. de vientre,** diarrhœa.

fluminense, *a.* from Rio de Janeiro.

flúor, *m.* (chem.) fluorine; (chem.) flux.

fluorescencia, *f.* (phys.) fluorescence.

fluorescente, *a.* fluorescent.

fluorhídrico, ca, *a.* hydrofluoric.

fluórico, ca, *a.* (chem.) fluoric.

fluorina, fluorita, *f.* fluor spar, fluorite.

fluvial, *a.* fluvial, river (u. a.).

fluviógrafo, fluviómetro, *m.* fluviograph, an instrument for registering the rise and fall of a river.

flux, *m.* (Am.) suit (of clothes); flush, at cards.— **hacer f.,** (coll.) to spend one's whole fortune without paying a debt.

fluxión, *f.* (med.) fluxion; cold in the head.

foca, *f.* (zool.) fur-bearing seal.

focal, *a.* (anat. and phys.) focal.

foceifiza, *f.* a kind of Arabian mosaic.

focino, *m.* goad for elephants.

foco, *m.* focus; center, source; (med.) core or center of an abscess; (mil.) touchhole of a gun. —**f. de luz eléctrica,** bunch of electric lights.

fóculo, *m.* small fireplace.

fodolí, *a.* meddlesome, intrusive.

fofo, fa, *a.* spongy, soft; empty, trashy (s. o. style).

fogaje, *m.* hearth money.

fogarada, *f.* blaze, bonfire.

fogaril, *m.* cresset, moon, cage.

fogarín, *m.* common hearth for field hands.

fogarizar, *va.* to build bonfires in.

fogata, *f.* bonfire, blaze; fougade.

fogón, *m.* hearth, fireside; cooking place, cooking stove, kitchen range; vent or touchhole of a gun; (naut.) caboose, cuddy.

fogonadura, *f.* (naut.) mast hole.

fogonazo, *m.* powder flash; flash in a pan.

fogonero, *m.* fireman, stoker.

fogosidad, *f.* fieriness, heat, vehemence.

fogoso, sa, *a.* fiery, vehement, impetuous; spirited (as a horse).

fogote, *m.* fagot, bundle of twigs.

fogueación, *f.* numbering of hearths or fires.

foguear, *va.* to accustom to the discharge (noise) of firearms; (arti.) to scale (a gun).

foguezuelo, *m. dim.* small fire.

foja, *f.* (law) leaf of manuscript or folio; (orn.) coot, scoter.

fole, *m.* leather bag, especially of the bagpipe.

folgo, *m.* foot muff or warming bag.

folías, *f. pl.* a kind of merry dance.

foliáceo, *a.* (bot.) foliaceous.

foliación, *f.* foliation, numbering the pages of a book; (bot.) foliation.

foliar, *va.* to page, to folio.

foliatura, *f.* paging (of a book).

folículo, *m.* (bot.) follicle, pericarp; (anat.) follicle, membranous sac.

folijones, *m. pl.* an ancient Castilian dance.

folio, *m.* folio, leaf of a book; size of a bookleaf.— **f. de Descartes,** (geom.) folium of Descartes.—**f. índico,** (bot.) Indian leaf.—**al primer f.,** at first sight.—**de a f.,** (coll.) very great, monumental (truth, fact, etc.); egregious (blunder, etc.).

foliolo, *m.* (bot.) foliole of a compound flower.

folión, *m.* (prov.) fireworks.

folklore, *m.* folklore.—**folklórico, ca,** *a.* folkloric, relating to folklore.—**folklorista,** *n.* folklorist, one versed in folklore.

foluz, *f.* an ancient small copper coin.

folla, *f.* irregular conflict in a tournament; medley, variety show.

follada, *f.* puff-paste patty.

follaje, *m.* foliage; leafage; gaudy ornament; superabundance of figures of speech; fustian.

follar, *va.* to blow with bellows; to form into leaves.

follero, folletero, *m.* bellows maker or seller.

folletín, *m.* feuilleton, serial story in a newspaper.

folletinista, *n.* writer of FOLLETINES.

folletista, *n.* pamphleteer.

folleto, *m.* pamphlet, booklet.

follón, na. I. *a.* lazy, indolent; cowardly. **II.** *m.* coward; rogue, knave; conceited fellow; noiseless rocket.

fomentación, *f.* (med.) fomentation.

fomentador, ra, *n. & a.* fomenter (-ing), promoter (-ing).

fomentar, *va.* to foment, to warm; to promote, further, encourage; to prompt; (med.) to foment; (agr.) to improve.

fomento, *m.* fomentation; warmth, fuel; fostering, furtherance, promotion; improvement, development; (med.) fomentation, lotion.

fomes, *m.* (med.) fomes; cause of excitement.

fonación, *f.* phonation, emission of the voice; pronunciation.

fonas, *f. pl.* (sew.) gores, gussets.

fonda, *f.* inn; eating house.

fondable, *a.* fit for anchoring.

fondado, da, *a.* (coop.) reinforced in the heads

fondeadero, *m.* (naut.) anchoring ground; haven.

fondear. I. *va.* (naut.) to sound; to raise from the bottom of water; to search (a ship); to examine closely. **II.** *vn.* to cast anchor.

fondeo, *m.* (naut.) search; casting anchor.

fondillón, *m.* dregs and lees of a cask of liquor; old Alicante wine.

fondillos, *m. pl.* seat of trousers.

fondista, *n.* innkeeper, hotel keeper.

fondo, *m.* bottom; depth; rear part, furthest end; ground (of stuffs); head (of a boiler, cylinder, etc.); substance; (art) background; thickness of a diamond; extent of a man's capacity; disposition, nature (of a person); principal or essential part of a thing; stock, quantity, store (of virtues, vices, etc.); fund, capital; (mil.) space occupied by a rank; (mech.) bed, bottom plate, foundation; (coop.) head; (naut.) bottom.—*pl.* funds, resources. —**f. de amortización,** sinking fund.—**f. de reserva,** reserve fund.—**fondos públicos,** or **del Erario,** public funds.—**fondos vitalicios,** life annuities.—**a f.,** perfectly, thoroughly.—**dar f.,** to cast anchor.—**de f.,** abreast; editorial (article).— **echar a f.,** to sink.—**en f.,** abreast.—**en el f.,** at bottom, in substance.—**irse a f.,** (naut.) to founder; (fenc.) to thrust.—**limpiar los fondos,** (naut.) to hog a ship's bottom.

fondón, *m.* FONDILLÓN; ground of silk or velvet; brocade; (min.) fondon.

foneidoscopio, *m.* phoneidoscope.

fonética, *f.* phonetics.—**fonético, ca,** *a.* phonetic.—**fonetismo,** *m.* phonetism.

fónico, ca, *a.* phonic, acoustic.

fonil, *m.* (naut.) wooden funnel.

fonje, *a.* bland, soft, spongy.

fonografía, *f.* phonography.—**fonográfico, ca,** *a.* phonographic.—**fonógrafo,** *m.* phonograph.— **fonograma,** *m.* phonogram, phonograph record.

fonolita, *f.* (min.) clinkstone, phonolite.

fonología, *f.* phonology.—**fonológico, ca,** *a.* phonologic.—**fonólogo, ga,** *n.* phonologist.

fonsadera, *f.* an ancient war tax.

fonsado, *m.* (fort.) foss or ditch.

fontal, *a.* fontal; original, main.

fontana, *f.* (poet.) fountain, spring, water jet.

fontanal. I. *a.* fontal, relating to fountains 'or springs. **II.** *m.* source or spring of water; place abounding in springs.

fontanar, *m.* water spring.

fontanela, *f.* (anat.) fontanel; (surg.) seton needle.

fontanería, *f.* pipe laying; water-pipe system, pipe line.

fontanero, ra, *n.* pipe layer.

fontezuela, *f. dim.* small fountain.

fontegí, *m.* a variety of wheat.

fontículo, *m.* (surg.) fonticulus, issue.

football, *m.* football.

foque, *m.* (naut.) jib.—**f. de caza,** or **f. mayor,** standing jib.—**f. segundo,** forestay sail.

forajido, da, *n.* outlaw, fugitive from justice.

foral, *a.* (law) statutory.

foralmente, *adv.* judicially.

foramen, *m.* (mill.) hole in the nether stone.

foráneo, nea, *a.* foreign.

forastero, ra. I. *a.* foreign; exotic. **II.** *n.* stranger.

forcejar, forcejear, *vn.* to struggle, strive, labor; contest, contend.

forcejo, *m.* struggle, strife.

forcejón, *m.* violent effort or struggle.

forcejudo, da, *a.* strong, robust.

forceps, *m.* (surg.) forceps.

forchina, *f.* (mil.) forklike weapon.

forense, *a.* (law) forensic.

forero, ra. I. *a.* conformable to the statue law of a country. **II.** *m.* owner of leasehold estate; lessee.

forestal, *a.* forestal.

forillo, *m.* backing, in theatrical scenery.

forja, *f.* smelting furnace; chafery; bloomery, smithy; forge; forging; (mas.) mortar.

forjado, da. I. *a.* wrought (s. o. metals); forged. **II.** *pp.* of FORJAR.

forjador, *m.* forger; ironmaster, smith, blacksmith; goldbeater.

forjadura, *f.* forging.

forjar, *va.* to forge, hammer or stamp into shape; to frame, form, fabricate; to counterfeit, falsify; to invent, concoct (as a falsehood).

forlón, *m.* an ancient two-seat chaise.

forma, *f.* form, shape; frame, make; method, order; manner; hand, form or cast of writing; pattern, mold, matrix; (print.) form, format; (hat.) block; (eccl.) host for the communion of the laity.—*pl.* build, figure (s. o. persons).—**dar f. a,** to give form to, shape; to put in order, arrange.— **de f. que,** so as, so that.—**en debida f.,** or **en f.,** in due form, properly.—**en f., en toda f.,** in due form or manner; thoroughly, in a thorough and proper manner.—**tomar f.,** to develop, to become realized, to materialize.

formable, *a.* that may be formed.

formación, *f.* formation, forming; form, shape; twisted cord for gold embroidery; (geol.) formation, system; (mil.) formation, array.

formador, ra, *n.* & *a.* former (-ing).

formaje, *m.* cheese vat; cheese.

formal, *a.* formal, regular, methodical; proper, genuine; serious, grave, steady, sedate; truthful, reliable; well-behaved.

formaldehido, *m.* formaldehyde.

formalidad, *f.* formality; exactness, punctuality; gravity, seriousness, solemnity; requisite, requirement; red tape; established practice; legal precedent.—**con f.,** in earnest.

formalina, *f.* (chem.) formalin.

formalismo, *m.* formalism.

formalista, *n.* formalist.

formalizar. I. *va.* to put in final form; to execute, legalize (a deed, etc.); to make explicit, to formulate. **II.** *vr.* to become serious or earnest.

formalmente, *adv.* formally; seriously.

formar. I. *va.* to form; shape, fashion; (mil.) to combine, arrange. **II.** *vn.* to adjust the edges of embroidery work; (mil.) to draw up. **III.** *vr.* to form, take form, grow, develop.

formativo, va, *a.* formative.

formato, *m.* (Am.) format (of a book).

formatriz, *f. a.* = FORMADORA.

formejar, *va.* (naut.) to clear (the ship); to trim (the hold).

formero, *m.* (arch.) side arch of a vault.

formiato, *m.* (chem.) formate.

formicante, *a.* (med.) formicant (pulse).

fórmico, *m.* (chem.) formic (acid or ether).

formidable, *a.* formidable; immense, huge.

formidablemente, *adv.* formidably.

formidoloso, sa, *a.* timorous, timid; dreadful, frightful, horrible.

formillón, *m.* hat block, hat form.

formón, *m.* chisel; punching press for cutting wafers.

fórmula, *f.* formula; recipe, prescription; (eccl.) profession of faith.

formular, *va.* to formulate.

formulario, *m.* formulary.

formulismo, *m.* formulism; red tape.

formulista, *n.* & *a.* formulist (-ic).

fornáceo, cea, *a.* (poet.) furnacelike.

fornelo, *m.* portable little oven or furnace.

fornicación, *f.* fornication.—**fornicador, ra,** *n.* & *a.* fornicator (-ing).—**fornicar,** *va.* to fornicate. —**fornicario, ria,** *a.* relating or addicted to fornication.

fornicio, *m.* fornication.

fornido, da, *a.* robust, lusty, stout.

fornitura, *f.* (mil.) furniture; (print.) types cast to complete sorts.

foro, *m.* forum; court of justice; bar, the legal profession; back, in stage scenery; leasehold; rental.—**por tal f.,** on such conditions.

forrado, *pp.* & *a.* lined, doubled.

forraje, *m.* forage, fodder; foraging; (coll.) trifles.

forrajeador, ra, *n.* forager, fodderer.
forrajear, *vn.* to gather forage or fodder.
forrajera, *f.* (mil.) shako guard.
forrar, *va.* to line (as clothes); to cover (as a book or an umbrella); (anat.) to sheathe, to fur.
forro, *m.* lining, doubling, inside, backing; (naut.) furring, planking, sheathing; cover of a book.— **f. de cabos,** (naut.) service, serving ropes.—**f. sobrepuesto de cable,** (naut.) keckling, rounding.
fortachón, na, *a.* (coll.) powerfully strong.
fortalecedor, ra, *n.* & *a.* fortifier (-fying).
fortalecer, *va.* (*ind.* FORTALEZCO: *subj.* FORTALEZCA) to fortify, strengthen, corroborate; to fortify (a place); to aid, encourage, support.
fortalecimiento, *m.* fortifying, strengthening; fortification, defences.
fortaleza, *f.* fortitude; firmness; courage, strength vigor; stronghold, fortress, fort.
¡forte! I. *interj.* (naut.) avast! II. *a.* (mus.) loud.
fortepiano, *m.* (mus., obs.) pianoforte.
fortezuelo, la. I. *a. dim.* not very strong. II. *m.* small fort.
fortificable, *a.* fortifiable.
fortificación, *f.* fortification; fort; military architecture.—**f. de campaña,** field fortification.
fortificador, ra, *n.* & *a.* fortifier (-fying)
fortificante, *a.* fortifying.
fortificar, *va.* (*pret.* FORTIFIQUÉ: *subj.* FORTIFIQUE) to strengthen, invigorate; (mil.) to fortify.
fortín, *m. dim.* fortin, fortlet, small fort.
fortitud, *f.* fortitude.
fortuitamente, *adv.* fortuitously.
fortuito, ta, *a.* fortuitous, accidental.
fortuna, *f.* fortune, chance, fate; good luck; wealth, resources; storm, tempest; accident of the sea.—**por f.,** fortunately, luckily.
fortunón, *m. aug.* great stroke of fortune; immense fortune (wealth).
forúnculo, *m.* (med.) boil.
forzadamente, *adv.* forcibly, violently.
forzado, da. I. *pp.* & *a.* forced, compelled. II. *n.* criminal sentenced to the galleys.
forzador, *m.* ravisher; forcer.
forzal, *m.* solid part of a comb.
forzamiento, *m.* act of forcing or violating.
forzar, *va.* (*ind.* FUERZO: *pret.* FORCÉ: *subj.* FUERCE) to force, break in (as a door); to compel, force; to subdue by force; to ravish.
forzosa, *f.* decisive move at the game of draughts; compulsion.—**hacer la f. a uno,** (coll.) to compel one to act against one's will.
forzosamente, *adv.* necessarily; by force, forcedly, violently.
forzoso, sa, *a.* necessary, unavoidable; obligatory, compulsory.
forzudamente, *adv.* with great power and force.
forzudo, da, *a.* strong, vigorous, lusty.
fosa, *f.* grave; (anat.) fossa.
fosar, *va.* to dig a pit or trench around.
fosca, *f.* haze; thicket, jungle.
fosco, ca, *a.* frowning, cross.
fosfático, ca, *a.* (chem.) phosphatic.
fosfato, *m.* (chem.) phosphate.
fosfaturia, *f.* (med.) phosphaturia.
fosfeno, *m.* (physiol.) phosphene.
fosfina, *f.* (chem.) phosphine.
fosfito, *m.* phosphite.
fosforado, da, *a.* phosphated.—**bronce f.,** phosphor bronze.
fosforera, *f.* match box.
fosforero, ra, *n.* vender of matches.
fosforescencia, *f.* phosphorescence.
fosforescente, *a.* phosphorescent.
fosforescer, *vn.* (*ind.* FOSFOREZCO: *subj.* FOSFOREZCA) to phosphoresce.
fosfórico, ca, *a.* phosphoric.
fosforita, *f.* (min.) phosphorite.
fósforo, *m.* phosphorus; friction match; morning star.
fosforoscopio, *m.* (phys.) phosphoroscope.
fosforoso, sa, *a.* phosphorous.

fosfuro, *m.* phosphide, phosphuret.
fósil, *n.* & *a.* fossil.—**fosilífero, ra,** *a.* fossiliferous.—**fosilización,** *f.* fossilization.
fosilizarse, *vr.* to fossilize, become fossil.
foso, *m.* pit, hole in the ground; (theat.) cellar under the stage; (fort.) moat, ditch, foss.
fotocromía, *f.* photochromy, color photography.
fotoeléctrico, ca, *a.* photoelectric.
fotofobia, *f.* (med.) photophobia.
fotófobo, ba, *a.* suffering from photophobia.
fotófono, *m.* (phys.) photophone.
fotogénico, ca, *a.* photogenic.
fotoglíptico, ca, *a.* photoglyptic.
fotograbado, *m.* photoengraving, photogravure.
fotograbar, *va.* & *vn.* to photoengrave.
fotografía, *f.* photography; photograph.
fotografiar, *va.* to photograph.
fotográficamente, *adv.* photographically.
fotográfico, ca, *a.* photographic.
fotógrafo, *m.* photographer.
fotolitografía, *f.* photolithography; photolithograph.—**fotolitografiar,** *va.* to photolithograph.
fotolitográficamente, *adv.* photolithographically.—**fotolitográfico, ca,** *a.* photolithographic.
fotología, *f.* photology, optics.
fotometría, *f.* photometry.—**fotométrico, ca,** *a.* photometric.—**fotómetro,** *m.* photometer.
fotomicrografía, *f.* photomicrography.
fotoquímica, *f.* photochemistry.
fotosfera, *f.* (ast.) photosphere.
fototerapia, *f.* (med.) phototherapeutics.
fototerápico, ca, *a.* phototherapeutical.
fototipia, *f.* = FOTOLITOGRAFÍA.
fototípico, ca = FOTOLITOGRÁFICO.
fototipografía, *f.* phototypography.
fototipográfico, ca, *a.* phototypographic.
fótula, *f.* (Am.) cockroach.
fotuto, *m.* (Cuba) whistle; trumpet, horn.
foya, *f.* oven full of charcoal.
frac, *m.* dress coat.
fracasar, *vn.* to fail, come to naught; (naut.) to crumble, to break in pieces.
fracaso, *m.* downfall, ruin; calamity; failure.
fracción, *f.* fraction, breaking into parts; (math.) fraction.—**f. continua,** continued fraction.—**f. decimal periódica,** repeating decimal.
fraccionado, da. I. *a.* fractional. II. *pp.* of FRACCIONAR.
fraccionamiento, *m.* division into fractions.
fraccionar, *va.* to divide into fractions.
fraccionario, ria, *a.* fractional.
fractura, *f.* fracture, breaking; (surg.) fracture.
fracturar, *va.* to fracture, break, rupture.
fraga, *f.* a kind of raspberry; thicket of brambles.
fragancia, *f.* fragrance, scent; good name or reputation.
fragante, *a.* fragrant; flagrant, notorious.—**en f.** = EN FLAGRANTE.
fragaria, *f.* (bot.) strawberry.
fragata, *f.* (naut.) frigate.—**f. de aviso,** packet boat.—**f. ligera,** light fast-sailing vessel.
frágil, *a.* brittle, breakable, fragile; frail, weak.
fragilidad, *f.* fragility, brittleness; frailty.
frágilmente, *adv.* in a frail way.
fragmentario, ria, *a.* fragmentary.
fragmento, *m.* fragment.
fragor, *m.* noise, clamor, crash.
fragoroso, sa, *a.* (poet.) noisy, obstreperous, thundering, roaring.
fragosidad, *f.* roughness; impenetrability, thickness (of a forest); craggedness, cragginess.
fragoso, sa, *a.* craggy, rough, uneven; full of brambles and briers; noisy, roaring.
fragrancia, fragrante, *a., f.* = FRAGANCIA, etc.
fragua, *f.* forge, as for iron; blacksmith's shop.
fraguado, *m.* setting, hardening.
fraguador, ra, *n.* schemer.
fraguar. I. *va.* to forge; to plan, plot, brew, scheme, concoct. II. *vn.* (mas.) to set (s. o. concrete, etc.).
fragura, *f.* = FRAGOSIDAD.

frailada, _f._ (coll.) rude or unbecoming action of a monk.

fraile, _m._ friar, monk; fold turned up at bottom of a skirt; priest; (arch.) hood over a hearth; (print.) friar, badly inked spot; (b.b.) fold in a leaf; upright post of a floodgate; (Cuba) bagasse.

frailear, _va._ (agr.) to prune close to the trunk.

frailecico, cillo, _m._ _dim._ little friar; (orn.) lapwing; wedge securing the spindle of a silk reel.

frailengo, ga, leño, ña, _a._ = FRAILESCO.

frailería, _f._ (coll.) monks in general; priests in general; body of monks or priests.

frailero, ra, _a._ very fond of priests.

frailesco, ca, _a._ monkish, friary; priestlike.

frailía, _f._ monkery; regular clergy.

frailote, _m._ _aug._ big and coarse friar.

frailuco, _m._ despicable friar.

frailuno, na, _a._ (coll.) friarlike; priestlike.

frambuesa, _f._ (bot.) raspberry.

frambueso, _m._ (bot.) raspberry bush.

frámea, _f._ javelin, dart.

francachela, _f._ = COMILONA.

francalete, _m._ leather strap with a buckle.

francamente, _adv._ frankly, openly.

francés, sa. I. _a._ French.—**a la francesa,** after the French fashion.—**despedirse a la f.,** (coll.) to take French leave. **II.** _n._ Frenchman (-woman). **III.** _m._ French language.

francesada, _f._ anything characteristic of the French; French invasion (of Spain in 1808).

francesilla, _f._ (bot.) common yard crowfoot.

franciscano, na, _a._ Franciscan; gray-colored.

francisco, ca, _a._ Franciscan.

francmasón, _m._ Freemason, mason.

francmasonería, _f._ Freemasonry.

franco, _m._ Frank; franc (French coin); fair time, when merchandise is sold free of duty.

franco, ca, _a._ frank, open; free, clear, disengaged; exempt, privileged; Frankish; (com.) duty free; in compound words, French, as _francoamericano_, Franco-American.—**f. a bordo,** free on board, f. o. b.—**f. de porte,** postpaid.

francófilo, _n._ & _a._ Francophil, admirer of or friendly to the French.

francolín, _m._ (orn.) francolin.

francote, ta, _a._ _aug._ (coll.) frank, open-hearted.

franchipán, _m._ franchipane, a perfume.

franchote, franchute, _n._ (contempt.) Frenchy.

franela, _f._ flannel.

frange, _m._ (her.) division of the field of a shield.

frangente. I. _a._ frangent, fracturing. **II.** _m._ accident, disaster, mishap.

frangible, _a._ brittle, frangible, breakable.

frangir, _va._ to break into pieces.

frangollar, _va._ (coll.) to do hurriedly.

frangollo, _m._ pottage of wheat and milk; (Am.) poorly-made stew.

frangote, _m._ (com.) bale of goods.

frángula, _f._ (bot.) berry-bearing alder.

franja, _f._ (sew.) fringe, trimming, band, braid, border; stripe.

franjar, franjear, _va._ (sew.) to trim with braids, bands, or stripes; to border.

franjón, _m._ _aug._ wide braid trimming.

franjuela, _f._ _dim._ narrow braid trimming.

franqueamiento, _m._ = FRANQUEO.

franquear. I. _va._ to exempt, to grant immunity to; enfranchise; to prepay; to make liberal grants or gifts; to open, clear; to free (a slave). **II.** _vr._ to yield easily to the desire of others; unbosom one's self; (naut.) to be ready for sailing.

franqueo, _m._ postage; liberating a slave.

franqueza, _f._ frankness; freedom, liberty, exemption.—**con f.,** frankly.

franquía, _f._ (naut.) sea room, offing.—**en f.,** ready.

franquicia, _f._ exemption from taxes; franchise, privilege, grant.

frasca, _f._ small branches.

frasco, _m._ flask, vial, bottle; powder flask.

frase, _f._ phrase; idiom, epigram; style of a writer —**f. hecha,** proverb, saying, saw.—**f. musical,** (mus.) phrase.—**f. sacramental, standard form.**—**hacer frases,** to speak much saying little.

frasear, _va._ to phrase; (mus.) to phrase.

fraseología, _f._ phraseology; style of a writer; verbosity, pomposity.

frasquera, _f._ bottle case, liquor case.—**f. de fuego,** (naut.) fire case or fire chest.

frasquerilla, ita, _f._ _dim._ small bottle case.

frasqueta, _f._ (print.) frisket.

frasquete, frasquillo, ito, _m._ _dim._ small flask.

fratás, _m._ plastering trowel.

fratasar, _va._ to trowel, smooth with the trowel.

fraterna, _f._ (coll.) severe reprimand, lecture.

fraternal, _a._ fraternal, brotherly.

fraternalmente, _adv._ fraternally.

fraternidad, _f._ fraternity, brotherhood.

fraternizar, _vn._ to fraternize.

fraterno, na, _a._ fraternal, brotherly.

fratricida, _n._ fratricide (murderer).

fratricidio, _m._ fratricide (murder).

fraude, _m._, **fraudulencia,** _f._ fraud.

fraudulentamente, _adv._ fraudulently.

fraudulento, ta, _a._ fraudulent; deceitful, artful.

fray, _m._ _contr. of_ FRAILE, used as a title before the names of clergymen belonging to certain religious orders, as _Fray Luis de Granada_.

frazada, _f._ blanket.

frazadilla, _f._ _dim._ small or light blanket.

frecuencia, _f._ frequency.

frecuentación, _f._ frequenting.

frecuentador, ra, _n._ & _a._ frequenter (-ing).

frecuentar, _va._ to frequent; to repeat.

frecuentativo, _a._ (gram.) frequentative.

frecuente, _a._ frequent.

frecuentemente, _adv._ frequently, often.

fregadero, _m._ scullery, sink.

fregado, _pp._ & _m._ scouring or scrubbing; (coll.) complicated affair.

fregador, ra. I. _n._ & _a._ washer (-ing). **II.** _m._ scullery; dishclout, mop, scrubbing brush.

fregadura, _f._ rubbing, scrubbing, scouring.

fregajo, _m._ mop, swab (= ESTROPAJO).

fregamiento, _m._ = FRICACIÓN.

fregar, _va._ (ind. FRIEGO: _pret._ FREGUÉ: _subj._ FRIEGUE) to rub; to scrub, mop, swab, scour; to wash (dishes); (Am.) to annoy, bother.

fregatriz, fregona, _f._ kitchenmaid; dishwasher.

fregonil, _a._ (coll.) wenchlike.

fregonzuela, _f._ _dim._ little kitchen girl.

freidura, _f._ frying or dressing in a pan.

freila, _f._ (eccl.) lay sister.

freile, _m._ knight or priest of a military order.

freír, _va._ (_pp._ FREÍDO, FRITO: _gerund_, FRIENDO: _ind._ FRÍO: _pret._ él FRIÓ: _subj._ FRÍA) to fry or dress in a frying pan.—**freírse de calor,** to be excessively hot, to be baking.—**freírsela a uno,** (coll.) to deceive one premeditatedly.—**al f. será el reír,** he laughs well who laughs last.

freje, _m._ (prov.) = FLEJE.

fréjol, frejol, _m._ (bot.) kidney bean.

frémito, _m._ roar.

frenar, _va._ to bridle, to govern by the bridle; to brake, apply the brake to.

frenería, _f._ bridle making; harness shop.

frenero, _m._ bridle maker or seller; (r. w.) brakeman.

frenesí, _m._ frenzy, fury, madness; folly.

frenéticamente, _adv._ frantically, madly.

frenético, ca, _a._ mad, frantic, frenzied.

frenillar, _va._ (naut.) to bridle (the oars).

frenillo, _m._ (anat.) frenum; (naut.) bridle, fox, ratline.—**no tener f. en la lengua,** to be outspoken, not to mince one's words.

freno, _m._ bridle or bit of the bridle; (car.) brake (for wheel); (mech.) check, stop, brake; curb, restraint, control.—**f. al vacío,** or (more properly) **de vacío,** vacuum brake.

frenología, _f._ phrenology.—**frenológico, ca,** _a._ phrenological.—**frenólogo,** _m._ phrenologist.

frenópata, _m._ phrenopathist.

frenopatía, _f._ phrenopathy, mental disease.

frenopatología, *f.* alienism, science of mental diseases.

frente. I. *f.* forehead; countenance, mien; intellect.—**II.** *adv.* in front, opposite, across the way.—**III.** *m.* (mil.) front; (fort.) face of a bastion; front, fore part, face, façade; obverse (of coins, etc.).—**f. a f.,** face to face.—**f. por f.,** directly opposite.—**a f.,** straight ahead.—**al f.,** opposite; (com.) carried forward.—**de f.,** from the front, front (u. a.); (mil.) facing; abreast.—**del f.,** brought forward.—**en f.** = F. POR F.

frentero, *m.* pad to protect a child's forehead.

frentón, ona, *a.* having a large forehead.

freo, *m.* (naut.) narrow channel, strait, fretum.

fresa, *f.* (bot.) strawberry; (mech.) drill, bit, milling tool.

fresada, *f.* an ancient dish of flour, milk and butter.

fresadora, *f.* (mech.) milling machine.

fresal, *m.* strawberry patch.

fresar, *va.* (mech.) to mill; to drill; to machine.

fresca, *f.* cool air, fresh air; piece of one's mind, biting remark.—**decir cuatro frescas a uno,** to rebuke one without mincing words.—**tomar la f.,** to take the air.

frescachón, na, *a.* robust and fresh-looking; (naut.) brisk (s. o. the wind).

frescal, *a.* (fish) not entirely fresh, but preserved with little salt.

frescamente, *adv.* recently, lately, of late; coolly; bluntly.

fresco, ca. I. *a.* fresh; cool; recent, newly come; just made, finished, or gathered; latest; fresh, buxom, ruddy; calm, cool; bold, forward; unconcerned, unabashed, unmoved.—**estar, o quedar, f.,** to be disappointed, to fail.—**quedarse f.,** to act coolly, to show no scruple or concern. **II.** *m.* cool air, fresh air; (art) fresco; (Peru) a pineapple refreshment.—**al f.,** in the open air; in the night air; (art) fresco (painting).—**tomar el f.,** to take some fresh air, to go out for some fresh air.

frescor, *m.* cool, refreshing air; freshness; (art) flesh-color.

frescote, ta, *a. aug.* (coll.) fresh, ruddy, youthful.

frescura, *f.* freshness; coolness; luxuriant verdure or foliage; frankness, openness; freedom of manner, ease; tranquillity, coolness, unconcern.

fresero, ra. I. *n.* strawberry vender. **II.** *f.* (bot.) strawberry plant.

fresnal, *m.* belonging to the ash tree.

fresneda, *f.* plantation of ash trees.

fresnillo, *m.* (bot.) white fraxinella.

fresno, *m.* ash tree; (com.) ash wood.—**f. americano,** white ash.—**f. húngaro,** Hungarian ash.

fresón, *m.* (bot.) Chile strawberry.

fresquecito, ita. I. *a. dim.* (coll.) little cool; nice and fresh. **II.** *n.* cool breeze.

fresquera, *f.* meat safe.

fresquería, *f.* (Am.) ice-cream parlor.

fresquero, ra, *n.* vender of fresh fish.

fresquillo, lla, *a.* = FRESQUESITO, TA.

fresquista, *m.* fresco painter.

fresquito, ta. I. *a. dim.* cool, coolish; fresh, just made, gathered, etc. **II.** *m.* cool, fresh air. **III.** *adv.* freshly made, recent, latest.

frey, *m. contr.* of FREILE; used as a title before the name of a clergyman belonging to a military order.

frez [freth], *f.* dung.

freza, *f.* dung, excrement; spawning; trail of fish in spawning; spawn, roe; time when silkworms eat; hole dug by an animal.

frezada, *f.* blanket.

frezar. I. *vn.* (*pret.* FRECÉ: *subj.* FRECE) to eject excrements; to eject the droppings of grubs from hives. **II.** *va.* to nibble (the leaves) (s. o. silkworms); to spawn; to rub in order to spawn; to root (as hogs); to scratch (the ground) (as dogs).

friabilidad, *f.* friability, brittleness.

friable, *a.* friable, fragile, brittle.

frialdad, *f.* coldness; unconcern, coolness; nonsense; (med.) impotence.

fríamente, *adv.* coldly, frigidly, coolly; flatly.

friático, ca, *a.* foolish, graceless, silly.

fricación, *f.* friction, frication.

fricandó, *m.* (cook.) fricandeau.

fricar, *va.* to rub together.

fricasé, *m.* (cook.) fricassee.

fricción, *f.* friction, rubbing.

friccionar, *va.* to rub.

friega, *f.* friction, rubbing.

friego, yo friegue. *V.* FREGAR.

friera, *f.* chilblain on the heel.

frigidez, *f.* frigidity.—**frígido, da,** *a.* frigid.

frigio, gia, *n. & a.* Phrygian.

frigorífico, ca. I. *a.* frigorific, refrigerating. **II.** *m.* cold-storage house or room; packing house.

friísimo, ma, *a. sup.* extremely cold.

frijol, fríjol, *m.* kidney bean.

frimario, *m.* Frimaire, third month of the French-Revolution calendar.

fringílago, *m.* (orn.) titmouse.

fringílido, da. I. *n. & a.* (zool.) fringilline. **II.** *m. pl.* Fringillidæ.

frío, ía. I. *a.* cold; impotent; indifferent, unmoved, unemotional; dull, graceless, witless. **II.** *m.* cold.—*pl.* (Am.) malaria.

friolento, ta, *a.* chilly; very sensible to cold.

friolera, *f.* trifle, bauble, gewgaw.

friolero, ra, *a.* = FRIOLENTO.

frisa, *f.* frieze; (fort.) palisade.

frisado, *pp. & m.* curly silk plush or shag.

frisador, ra, *n.* frizzler.—**frisadura,** *f.* frizzling, shagging.—**frisar. I.** *va.* to frizzle or frizz (cloth); to rub; (naut.) to line, to pack. **II.** *vn.* to resemble; to approach, to be near.

friso, *m.* (arch.) frieze; wainscot, dado, mopboard.

frisol, frísol, *m.* (bot.) kidney bean.

frisón, na. I. *n. & a.* Frisian. **II.** *m.* large draught horse.

frisuelo, *m.* kidney bean.—*pl.* fritters.

frita, *f.* (gl.) frit, ferretto.

fritada, *f.* fry; dish of anything fried.

fritillas, *f. pl.* fritters, pancakes.

frito, ta. I. *a. & pp. irr.* of FREÍR, fried. **II.** *m.* fry.

fritura, *f.* fry, fritter.

frívolamente, *adv.* frivolously.

frivolidad, *f.* frivolity; frivolousness.

frívolo, la, *a.* frivolous.

frivolité, *f.* tatting, fancywork.

fronda, *f.* (bot.) leaf; frond; (surg.) a sling-shaped bandage.—*pl.* frondage, foliage, verdure.

fronde, *m.* (bot.) frond, fern leaf.

frondosidad, *f.* frondage, leafy foliage.

frondoso, sa, *a.* leafy, luxuriant.

frontal. I. *a.* frontal, relating to the forehead. **II.** *m.* (eccl.) frontal, altar hanging; (anat.) frontal bone.

frontalera, *f.* brow band (of a bridle); brow pad under a yoke; (eccl.) trimmings of an altar frontal; place where frontals are kept.

frontera, *f.* frontier, boundary, border; binder of a frail basket; (arch.) façade; side of a soft-brick mold.

fronterizo, za, *a.* frontier (u. a.); facing, opposite.

frontero, ra. I. *a.* opposite, facing. **II.** *m.* governor or commander of frontier forces; frontlet or brow pad for children. **III.** *adv.* in front.

frontil, *m.* yoke pad for draught oxen.

frontino, na, *a.* marked in the face.

frontis, *m.* (arch.) frontispiece, façade.

frontispicio, *m.* front; title page; (arch.) frontispiece, façade; (coll.) face.

frontón, *m.* main wall of a handball court; fives court; (arch.) pediment.

frontudo, da, *a.* broad-faced; (s. o. animals); having a large forehead.

frontura, *f.* front of a stocking frame.

frotación, *f.* rubbing.

frotador, ra, *n.* one who or that which rubs.

frotadura, *f.* rubbing.

frotamiento, *m.*, **frotante,** *a.* rubbing.

frotar, *va.* to rub.

frote, *m.* friction, rubbing; attrition.

fructidor, *m.* Fructidor, twelfth month of the French-Revolution calendar.

fructíferamente, *adv.* fruitfully.

fructífero, ra, *a.* fructiferous, fruit-bearing; fruitful.

fructificación, *f.* (bot.) fructification.

fructificador, ra, *n.* & *a.* fertilizer (-ing).

fructificar, *vn.* (*pret.* FRUCTIFIQUÉ: *subj.* FRUCTIFIQUE) to fructify, bear fruit; to yield profit.

fructuario, ria, *a.* (law) usufructuary.

fructuosamente, *adv.* fruitfully, profitably.

fructuoso, sa, *a.* fruitful, profitable.

fruente, *a.* enjoying.

frugal, *a.* frugal, parsimonious, thrifty.

frugalidad, *f.* frugality, thrift.

frugalmente, *adv.* frugally, thriftily.

frugívoro, ra, *a.* frugivorous.

fruición, *f.* fruition, enjoyment, gratification.

fruir, *vn.* (*for irr. v.* HUIR) to enjoy what has been hoped for:

fruitivo, va, *a.* fruitive, enjoyable.

frumentario, ria; frumenticio, cia, *a.* (bot.) frumentaceous.

frunce, *m.* (sew.) shirr, shirring, gather.

fruncido, da, *pp.* & *a.* shirred; gathered; contracted.

fruncidor, *m.* (sew.) gatherer.

fruncimiento, *m.* shirring, gathering; humbug, deceit, imposture.

fruncir. I. *va.* (*ind.* FRUNZO: *subj.* FRUNZA) (sew.) to gather, shirr; to pucker; to contract, reduce; to conceal or disguise (the truth).— **f. las cejas,** to knit the eyebrows.—**f. los labios,** to curl or pucker the lips. **II.** *vr.* to affect modesty; to be shocked.

fruslera, *f.* brass turnings or clippings.

fruslería, *f.* trifle, bauble, tidbit.

fruslero, ra, *a.* trifling, frivolous, futile.

frustráneo, nea, *a.* vain, useless, nugatory.

frustrar. I. *va.* to frustrate, defeat, thwart. **II.** *vr.* to miscarry, to fail, to fall through, to be a failure.

frustratorio, ria, *a.* frustrative, defeating.

fruta, *f.* fruit; fruitage.—*pl.* fruit (edible, specially table, tree fruits).—**f. del tiempo,** fruit eaten in season; anything incident or peculiar to a season. —**f. de sartén,** pancake, fritter.—**f. nueva,** something new, novelty.

frutaje, *m.* (art) painting of fruits and flowers.

frutal. I. *a.* (bot.) fruit-bearing, fruit (u. a.). **II.** *m.* fruit tree.

frutar, *vn.* to bear or yield fruit.

frutería, *f.* fruitery, fruit store.

frutero, ra. I. *n.* fruiterer; fruit basket, fruit dish. **II.** *m.* napkin or doily over a fruit dish; (art) painting representing fruit; ornamental piece of artificial fruit.

frutescente, *a.* frutescent; shrublike, shrubby.

frútice, *m.* perennial shrub.

fruticoso, sa, *a.* (bot.) fruticose.

frutilla, *f. dim.* small fruit; (Am.) strawberry; bead for rosaries.

frutillar, *m.* (Am.) strawberry bed.

fruto, *m.* fruit; any useful produce of the earth; any product of man's intellect or labor; benefice, profit.—*pl.* (com.) produce, commodities. —**f. de bendición,** child lawfully begotten.—**sacar f. de,** or **con,** to derive benefit from, succeed in.

ftaleína, *f.* (chem.) phthalein.—**ftálico, ca,** *a.* phthalic.—**ftatilo,** *m.* phthatyl.

fu, *interj.* of disgust; sound imitating the snarling of a cat.

fúcar, *m.* rich, opulent man; nabob.

fucilar, *vn.* (poet.) to flash, to lighten.

fucilazo, *m.* heat lightning.

fucsia, *f.* (bot.) fuchsia.

fucsina, *f.* (chem.) fuchsine.

fuego. I. *m.* fire; conflagration; beacon fire; bonfire, watch fire; skin eruption, rash; firing of firearms; hearth, fireplace; ardor, heat of an action; hearth: house; (vet.) cautery.—*pl.* lights, lighthouse; (mil.) fire, firing.—**f. de San Telmo,** (naut.) Castor and Pollux.—**f. fatuo,** jack-o'-lantern, will-o'-the wisp, ignis fatuus.—**f. graneado,** (mil.) continued firing, drumfire.—**f. griego,** Greek or wild fire.—**f. nutrido** = F. GRANEADO.—**f. sacro,** St. Anthony's fire, erysipelas.—**fuegos artificiales,** fireworks.—**a f. y sangre,** by fire and sword.—**dar f. a un navío,** (naut.) to bream a ship. **II.** (¡fuego!) *interj.* (mil.) fire!—¡f! ¡f. de Cristo! ¡f. de Dios! blazes! confound it!

fueguecillo, cito, zuelo, *m. dim.* small fire.

fueguino, na, *a.* & *n.* Fuegian.

fuellar, *m.* bright talcum ornament on wax tapers.

fuelle, *m.* bellows; blower; (car.) hood, top; clouds over mountains; (sew.) puckers in clothes; (coll.) talebearer.

fuente, *f.* water spring; fountain; source; (often *pl.*) headwaters, source (of a river); dish, platter; (surg.) seton, issue.—**beber en buenas fuentes,** to be well-informed.

fuentecica, cilla, cita, zuela, *f. dim.* small or little fountain.

fuer, *m. contr. of* FUERO.—**a f. de,** *adv.* as a, in the manner of (*a fuer de caballero,* as a gentleman).

fuera. I. *adv.* out, without, outside.—**f. de,** out of; besides, in addition to.—**f. de quicio,** unhinged; out of order, out of joint.—**f. de sí,** out of oneself; aghast.—**de f.,** from the outside.—**hacia f.,** outward.—**por f.,** on the outside. **II.** (¡fuera!) *interj.* out! away! put him out! get out!

fuerarropa.—hacer f., a command used in the galleys for the rabble to undress.

fuero, *m.* statute law; jurisdiction, judicial power; privilege or exemption granted to a province; compilation of laws.—**f. de la conciencia,** tribunal of conscience; heart of hearts.—**f. exterior,** or **externo,** statute law; legal tribunals.—**f. interior,** or **interno,** = F. DE LA CONCIENCIA.—**a f.,** according to law or custom.—**de f.,** de jure; according to law.

fuerte. I. *a.* strong; powerful; intense, severe; secure, fast, impregnable; firm, compact; efficacious; thick, heavy; proficient, surpassing; loud; manly, determined, unswerving; hard, not malleable; terrible; grave; excessive; having excess of weight.—**es f. cosa,** it is very hard. **II.** *m.* fort, fortress; strong point, forte; (mus.) forte, loud (marked *f*). **III.** *adv.* strongly, hard, copiously, abundantly, excessively.

fuertecico, cito, cillo, zuelo, *m. dim.* small fortress, blockhouse.

fuertemente, *adv.* strongly, firmly, fast; powerfully; vehemently.

fuerza, *f.* force; strength; stress; violence; firmness, stanchness; efficacy; fortitude, courage; virtue, efficiency; mental power; (mech.) power; (mil., gen. *pl.*) force(s); (fort.) fortress, a strong place; strongest part of a thing; proneness, strong propensity; the third of a sword next the hilt; (sew.) stiffening piece in garments.—**f. animal,** animal power.—**f. atractriz,** attractive force.—**f. bruta,** brute force.—**f. centrífuga,** centrifugal force.—**f. centrípeta,** centripetal force.—**f. contraelectromotriz,** counterelectromotive force.—**f. de agua,** water power.—**f. de sangre** = F. ANIMAL.—**f. de vapor,** steam power.—**f. electromotriz,** electromotive force.—**f. mayor,** (law & com.) superior force, force majeure.—**f. motriz,** moving force; power.—**f. viva,** (mech.) vis viva (twice the kinetic energy).—**fuerzas conspirantes,** conspiring powers.—**fuerzas de mar y de tierra,** naval and land forces.—**a f. de,** by dint of, by force of.—**a la f.** = POR F.—**a viva f.,** by main force; with the utmost effort.—**de por f.,** by force, forcibly; necessarily.—**en f. de,** on account of.—**hacer f. de remos,** (naut.) to pull hard at the oars.—**hacer f. de velas,** (naut.) to crowd sail, to carry a press of sail; to make a strenuous effort.—**por f., por la f.** = DE POR F.—**ser f.,** to be necessary.

fuerzo, yo fuerce. *V.* FORZAR.

fuetazo, *m.* (Am.) blow with a whip.—*pl.* horse-whipping.—**dar,** or **pegar, fuetazos,** *m.* (Am.) to horsewhip.

fuete, *m.* (Am.) horsewhip.

fufú, *m.* (Am.) mass made of yam, plantain, etc., and pounded.

fuga, *f.* flight; escape; runaway; elopement; leak, leakage; (mus.) fugue.—**f. deshecha,** precipitate flight.—**f. precipitada,** stampede.—**poner en f.,** to put to flight, rout.

fugacidad, *f.* fugacity, brevity.

fugar, *vr.* (*pret.* me FUGUÉ: *subj.* me FUGUE) to flee, to run away; to escape, leak out.

fugaz, *a.* fugacious; fugitive, running away; brief, fleeting.

fugazmente, *adv.* fleetingly.

fugitivo, va. I. *n.* & *a.* fugitive, runaway. **II.** *a.* brief, perishable, unsteady, unstable.

fuina, *f.* =GARDUÑA.

fulanito, ta; fulano, na, *n.* so-and-so.—**F. de tal,** John Doe, so-and-so.—**F., Sutano y Mengano,** Tom, Dick and Harry.

fulcro, *m.* (mech.) fulcrum.

fulgente, *a.* (poet.) refulgent, brilliant.

fúlgido, da, *a.* bright, resplendent.

fulgor, *m.* fulgency, brilliancy.

fulguración, *f.* flash; flashing; (med.) lightning stroke.

fulgurante, *a.* resplendent, shining.

fulgurar, *vn.* to flash, shine with brilliancy.

fulgurita, *f.* (geol.) fulgurite.

fulguroso, sa, *a.* fulgurous.

fúlica, *f.* (orn.) fulica, coot.

fuliginoso, sa, *a.* fuliginous, dark, sooty.

fulminación, *f.* fulmination, thundering.

fulminado, *pp.* & *a.* struck by lightning.

fulminador, ra, *n.* & *a.* thunderer (-ing); fulminator (-ing).

fulminante. I. *pa.* & *a.* fulminating, thunder-ing; exploding, explosive; (med.) violent, deadly. **II.** *m.* (arti.) cap, percussion cap.

fulminar, *va.* to fulminate; to discharge, flash out (lightning); to cause to explode; to throw out as an object of terror; to thunder, utter wrathfully.

fulminato, *m.* (chem.) fulminate.

fulminatriz, *a.* (*fem.*) fulminating.

fulmíneo, nea, *a.* fulmineous.

fulmínico, a. (chem.) fulminic (acid).

fulminoso, sa, *a.* fulminatory.

fulleresco, ca, *a.* belonging to sharpers.

fullería, *f.* cheating at play; guile, cunning.

fullero, ra, *n.* sharper; cheat.

fullingue, *a.* (Ch.) of bad quality; sickly, lifeless.

fullona, *f.* (coll.) dispute, quarrel, wrangle.

fumable, *a.* smokeable, good to smoke.

fumada, *f.* puff, whiff (of smoke).—**fumadero,** *m.* smoking room.—**fumador, ra. I.** *n.* smoker. **II.** *a.* addicted to smoking.—**fumante,** *a.* smok-ing, fuming.

fumar, *va.* & *vn.* to smoke (cigars, etc.).

fumarada, *f.* puff, whiff, or blast of smoke; pipe-ful of tobacco.

fumaria, *f.* (bot.) fumitory.

fumarola, *f.* (geol.) fumarole.

fumífero, ra, *a.* (poet.) smoking.

fumífugo, ga, *a.* smoke-dispersing.

fumigación, *f.* fumigation.—**fumigador, ra,** *n.* & *a.* fumigator (-ing).—**fumigar,** *va.* (*pret.* FUMI-GUÉ: *subj.* FUMIGUE) to fumigate.—**fumigatorio, ria. I.** *a.* fumigatory. **II.** *m.* perfuming pan.

fumista, *n.* stove worker or plumber.

fumistería, *f.* stove works or shop.

fumívoro, ra, *a.* smokeless.

fumorola, *f.* = FUMAROLA.

fumosidad, *f.* smokiness.

fumoso, sa, *a.* fumy, smoky.

funámbulo, la, *n.* funambulist, rope dancer.

función, *f.* function; functioning, operation, working; religious ceremony, public demonstra-tion; (theat.) performance, play; (math., physi-ol.) function; (mil.) fight, engagement, battle.

funcional, *a.* (math., physiol.) functional.

funcionamiento, *m.* (mech.) functioning, work-ing, running, performance.—**de f.,** operating.

funcionar, *vn.* to function; to work, run (s. o. machines).

funcionario, *m.* functionary, public official.

funda, *f.* case, sheath, cover, envelope, slip.—**f. de almohada,** pillowcase.

fundación, *f.* foundation; founding, establish-ing; erection, raising, building; basis; rise, be-ginning, origin; endowment, foundation, en-dowed institution; (arch.) foundation, base, groundwork.

fundadamente, *adv.* with good reason, with good evidence or proof.

fundador, ra, *n.* founder.

fundamental, *a.* fundamental.

fundamentalmente, *adv.* fundamentally.

fundamentar, *va.* to found; to establish on a basis; to ground; to base; to set firm.

fundamento, *m.* foundation, groundwork; basis; reason, fundamental principle; source, origin, root; good behavior, orderliness (s. o. children); (weav.) weft, woof.

fundar. I. *va.* to found; to raise, erect, build; to establish, institute; to base, ground. **II.** *vr.* (w. en) to base one's opinion (on).

fundente. I. *a.* (chem.) fusing, melting, smelt-ing. **II.** *m.* (chem.) flux; (med.) dissolvent.

fundería, *f.* foundry; smelting work.

fundible, *a.* fusible.

fundibulario, *m.* Roman soldier armed with a sling—**fundíbulo,** *m.* ancient war engine for throwing stones.

fundición, *f.* fusion, melting, casting; foundry, smeltery; cast; cast iron; (print.) font.

fundidor, *m.* melter, smelter.

fundir. I. *va.* to fuse or melt; to smelt; to cast. **II.** *vr.* to fuse, melt; to merge, blend, unite.

fundo, *m.* (law) fundus; rural property.

fúnebre, *a.* funereal, mournful, sad; funeral; dark, lugubrious.

fúnebremente, *adv.* mournfully, sorrowfully.

funeral, *n.* & *a.* funeral (as a *n.*, often *pl.*).

funerala.—a la f., (mil.) inverted (arms).

funerario, ria, *a.* funeral.

fúnereo, rea, *a.* mournful, sad, funereal.

funestamente, *adv.* sadly, dolefully.

funestar, *va.* to blot, tarnish, stain, profane.

funesto, ta, *a.* regrettable, untoward; mournful, sad, dismal.

fungiforme, *a.* fungiform.

fungible, *a.* consumable, fungible.

fungir, *vn.* (Am.) to act in some capacity.

fungo, *m.* (surg.) fungus.

fungosidad, *f.* (surg.) fungosity, excrescence.

fungoso, sa, *a.* fungous, excrescent, spongy.

funicular, *a.* funicular.

funículo, *m.* (bot.) funicle or funiculus.

fuñique, *a.* awkward; timorous, pusillanimous.

furente, *a.* furious, raging, frantic.

furgón, *m.* wagon; car.

furia, *f.* fury; rage; fit of madness; ill-tempered person; hurry, hustling; zeal, ardor.—**a toda f.,** with utmost speed.

furibundo, da, *a.* furious, enraged, frantic.

furiente, *a.* = FURENTE.

furierismo, *m.* Fourierism.

furierista, *n.* & *a.* Fourierist (-ic).

furiosamente, *adv.* furiously.

furioso, sa, *a.* furious; very great, excessive.

furlón, *m.* = FORLÓN.

furo, ra. I. *a.* shy, unsociable, reserved; un-tamed, wild. **II.** *m.* (Cuba) orifice of the sugar mold.—**hacer f.,** to conceal a thing with the de-sign of keeping it.

furor, *m.* furor, fury, madness, rage, anger; enthu-siasm, exaltation of fancy.—**f. uterino,** (med.) nymphomania.

furriel, furrier, *m.* (mil.) quartermaster; clerk of the king's mews.

furriela, furriera, *f.* place of keeper of the keys of the king's palace.

For pronunciation, see the rules at the beginning of the book.

furrusca, *f.* (Colomb.) row, brawl.
furtivamente, *adv.* by stealth, clandestinely.
furtivo, va, *a.* furtive, clandestine.
furúnculo, *m.* (surg.) furuncle, boil.
furunculoso, sa, *a.* furunculose.
fusa, *f.* (mus.) demisemiquaver.
fusado, da, *a.* (her.) charged with fusils or spindles.
fusca, *f.* (orn.) a dark-colored duck.
fusco, ca, *a.* fuscous, brown, dark.
fuselado, da, *a.* = FUSADO, DA.
fuselaje, *m.* (aer.) fuselage.
fusente, *a.* receding (tide).
fusibilidad, *f.* fusibility.
fusible. I. *a.* fusible. **II.** *m.* (elec.) fuse.
fusiforme, *a.* fusiform, spindle-shaped.
fusil, *m.* rifle, gun, musket.—**f. de aguja,** needle gun.—**f. de chispa,** flintlock musket.—**f. de percusión,** or **de pistón,** musket.—**f. de retrocarga,** breechloader.—**f. rayado,** rifle.
fusilamiento, *m.* execution by shooting.
fusilar, *va.* to shoot, execute by shooting.
fusilazo, *m.* musket shot, rifle shot.
fusilería, *f.* (mil.) musketry; body of fusileers or musketeers.
fusilero, *m.* fusileer, musketeer.
fusión, *f.* fusion, melting; alliance, union.
fusionar, *va.* to unite, bring together, merge.
fusionista, *n.* fusionist.
fusique, *m.* bottle-shaped snuffbox.
fusor, *m.* smelting ladle or vessel.
fusta, *f.* brushwood; woollen stuff; whiplash; (naut.) lateen-rigged lighter.
fustán, *m.* fustian; (Am.) petticoat.
fustanero, *m.* fustian manufacturer.
fuste, *m.* wood, timber; tree and bows of a saddle; (poet.) saddle; shaft of a lance; foundation of anything not material; substance, importance; (arch.) fust, shaft of a column.
fustero, ra. I. *a.* belonging to a fust, foundation, etc. **II.** *m.* turner or carpenter.
fustete, *m.* (bot.) Venetian sumac; fustic, yellowwood.
fustigante, *a.* fustigating.
fustigar, *va.* to lash, fustigate.
fustina, *f.* place for fusing metals.
futesa, *f.* trifle, bagatelle, bauble, gewgaw.
fútil, *a.* trifling, flimsy, trivial.
futilidad, *f.* worthlessness, triviality.
futre, *m.* (Ch.) dude, fop, coxcomb.
futura, *f.* acquired right to an office or employment before its vacancy; (coll.) betrothed, intended bride.
futurismo, *m.* (art) futurism.
futurista, *n.* & *a.* (art) futurist (-ic).
futuro, ra. I. *a.* future. **II.** *m.* betrothed, future husband; future, futurity; (gram.) future.—**en lo f.,** in future, hereafter.

G

gabacho, cha, *a.* applied to the natives of some places at the foot of the Pyrenees, and also in derision to the French; (coll.) Frenchified.
gabán, *m.* (tail.) greatcoat, overcoat.
gabaonita, *n.* & *a.* Gabaonite.
gabarda, *f.* (bot.) wild rose.
gabardina, *f.* gabardine.
gabarit, *m.* (r. w.) track gauge.
gabarra, *f.* (naut.) lighter, barge, gabbard.
gabarrero, *m.* (naut.) lighterman.
gabarro, *m.* flaw or defect in goods; error, mistake; drudgery, burdensome obligation; (mas. and art) badigeon, filling; (vet.) swelling on the pastern of horses; pip (disease of fowls).
gabarrón, *m.* *aug.* (naut.) large barge.
gabasa, *f.* = BAGASA.
gábata, *f.* bowl for mess on galleys.
gabazo, *m.* bagasse.
gabela, *f.* gabel, tax; duty, burden.

gabinete, *m.* cabinet (ministers of state and privy councillors); private room where the cabinet meets; reception room, sitting room; private parlor; library, study; studio; ladies' boudoir or dressing room; laboratory.—**g. de lectura,** reading room.—**de g.,** theoretical, parlor (u. a., and applied to one whose knowledge is purely theoretical or bookish).
gablete, *m.* (arch.) gable.
gabote, *m.* (prov.) shuttlecock.
gacel, *m.,* **gacela,** *f.* gazelle.
gaceta, *f.* gazette; record (a publication); newspaper.—**mentir mas que la g.,** to be an inveterate liar.
gacetera, *f.* woman who sells newspapers.
gacetero, *m.* news writer; seller of newspapers.
gacetilla, *f.* personal-news column; town talk, gossip; newspaper squib; newsmonger.
gacetillero, *m.* newspaper reporter; paragrapher; wretched writer, penny-a-liner.
gacetista, *n.* one who delights in reading newspapers; newsmonger, gossip.
gacha, *f.* very thin watery mass; (Cuba) unglazed crock.—*pl.* porridge; pap; caresses, pettings.—**hacerse unas gachas,** to be too soft or affectionate.
gaché, *m.* (prov.) fellow, guy.
gacheta, *f.* spring lever of a latch; tooth of a latch; sticking paste.
gacho, cha, *a.* turned down, bent downward; having horns curved downward (s. o. cattle); slouching (as hats).—**a gachas,** (coll.) on allfours.
gachón, na. I. *a.* (coll.) graceful, sweet, attractive, bright. **II.** *n.* pampered, spoiled, petted child.
gachonada, gachonería, *f.* (coll.) gracefulness, cunningness, brightness, piquancy.
gachuela, *f.* *dim.* of GACHA.
gachumbo, *m.* (Am.) shell of various fruits, from which cups and other vessels are made.
gachupín, *m.* = CACHUPÍN.
gaditano, na, *a.* of or belonging to Cadiz.
gaélico, ca, *a.* Gaelic.
gafa, *f.* hook for bending a crossbow.—*pl.* (naut.) can hooks, grapple hooks; spectacles; spectacle bows.
gafar, *va.* to hook, to claw, to catch with a hook or with the nails.
gafedad, *f.* (med.) claw hand.
gafete, *m.* clasp, hook and eye.
gafo, fa, *a.* suffering from claw hand.
gago, ga, *n.* stammerer, stutterer.
gaguear, *vn.* (Am.) to stutter.
gaguera, *f.* (Am.) stuttering.
gaita, *f.* flageolet; hurdy-gurdy; (coll.) neck.—**g. gallega,** bagpipe; hornpipe.—**estar de g.,** (coll.) to be very merry.
gaitería, *f.* gay and gaudy dress.
gaitero, ra. I. *a.* (coll.) unbecomingly sportive and gay; (coll.) gaudy, showy, flamboyant. **II.** *n.* piper, one who plays the bagpipe.
gaje, *m.* salary, pay, wages.—*pl.* perquisites, fees.
gajo, *m.* branch (of a tree); part of a bunch of grapes torn off; pyramidal raceme of any fruit; each division of an orange, pomegranate, etc.; prong or tine of pitchforks, etc.; spur of a mountain ridge.
gajoso, sa, *a.* composed of GAJOS.
gala, *f.* gala; full, or court, dress; graceful, pleasing address; parade, ostentation; choicest part; (Am.) prize.—*pl.* regalia, finery, trappings, paraphernalia.—**galas de novia,** bridal trousseau.—**de g.,** full-dress (uniform).—**hacer g. de,** to glory in, boast of.
galabardera, *f.* (bot.) wild rose.
galactita, galactites, *f.* fuller's earth.
galactómetro, *m.* galactometer, lactometer.
galactosa, *f.* (chem.) galactose.
galafate, *m.* artful thief, cunning rogue.
galaico, ca, *n.* & *a.* = GALLEGO.
galamero, ra, *a.* dainty, sweet-mouthed.

galán, *m.* spruce, well-made man; gallant, courtier; lover, wooer; ladies' man; (theat.) leading man or woman.

galanamente, *adv.* elegantly, smartly, gracefully.

galancete, *m. dim.* spruce little man or lad; (theat.) juvenile leading man.

galanga, *f.* (bot.) officinal galangal.

galano, na, *a.* smartly dressed; tasteful; elegant, pleasing (s. o. literary style); beautiful, fresh (as flowers); (Cuba) mottled, party-colored.

galante, *a.* gallant, polished, attentive to ladies.

galanteador, *m.* wooer, lover; flatterer.

galantear, *va.* to court, woo, pay attention to.

galantemente, *adv.* gallantly, politely, attentively.

galanteo, *m.* gallantry, courtship, wooing.

galantería, *f.* gallantry, courtesy, politeness; grace, elegance; compliment to a lady; liberality, generosity.

galanura, *f.* prettiness, gorgeousness, elegance.

galapagar, *m.* place where tortoises abound.

galápago, *m.* fresh-water tortoise; (agr.) bed of plowshare; (arm.) frame for boring guns; mold for convex tiles; (found.) pig, ingot; (mas.) small centering frame; (surg.) strip with ends forked or deeply notched; (sad.) English saddle; (Am.) sidesaddle; (mil.) shed formed with shields joined together; mantelet, vinea, cat castle, sow; (vet.) scratch.

galapaguera, *f.* aquarium for tortoises.

galapo, *m.* (rop.) laying top.

galardón, *m.* guerdon, reward, prize.

galardonador, ra, *n. & a.* rewarder (-ing).

galardonar, *va.* to reward, recompense, requite.

gálata, *n. & a.* Galatian.

galato, *m.* (chem.) gallate.

galatites, *f.* fuller's earth.

galaxia, *f.* soapstone, steatite; (ast.) Galaxy, Milky Way.

galayo, *m.* cliff.

galbana, *f.* sloth, laziness, indolence.

galbanado, da, *a.* galbanum-colored.

galbanero, ra, *a.* (coll.) lazy, indolent.

gálbano, *m.* (pharm.) galbanum.

galbanoso, sa, *a.* indolent, lazy, shiftless.

gálbulo, *m.* nut of the cypress tree.

galdrope, *m.* (naut.) wheel rope.

galdrufa, *f.* spinning top.

gálea, *f.* galea, ancient helmet.

galeato, ta, *a.* preface in answer to actual or probable criticism.

galeaza, *f.* (naut.) galleas.

galega, *f.* (bot.) officinal goat's-rue.

galena, *f.* (min.) galena.

galénico, ca, *a.* Galenic.—**galenismo,** *m.* Galenism.—**galenista,** *n.* Galenist.

galeno, na, *a.* (naut.) moderate, soft (wind).

gáleo, *m.* (icht.) swordfish.

galeón, *m.* (naut.) galleon.

galeota, *f.* (naut.) galliot.

galeote, *m.* galley slave.

galera, *f.* (naut.) galley; wagon, van; house of correction for women; extra line of beds in a hospital ward; (print.) galley; (arith.) fraction line; (carp.) smooth plane, organ-builder's plane; furnace for distilling sulphur.

galerada, *f.* carload, van load; (print.) galley; galley proof.

galerero, *m.* wagoner, van driver.

galería, *f.* gallery, lobby, corridor; art museum; collection of paintings; (fort.) narrow covered passage across a moat; (min.) gallery, driftway, heading.—**g. de popa,** (naut.) stern gallery or balcony.

galerilla, *f. dim.* small gallery.

galerín, *m. dim.* (print.) wooden galley.

galerita, *f.* (orn.) crested lark.

galerna, *f.*, **galerno,** *m.* (naut.) stormy northwest wind.

galerón, *m.* (Mex.) large room serving as jail or prison; (Am.) a kind of popular air and dance.

galés, sa, *n. & a.* Welsh.

galfarro, *m.* rogue, loafer, idler; (orn.) hawk.

galga, *f.* rolling stone; (mill) stone wheel that grinds olives; (zool.) greyhound bitch; a kind of eruption or rash; bier or stretcher in which poor people are taken to be buried; drag, Scotch brake for a wheel; (naut.) back of an anchor.—*pl.* long shoe laces for women's slippers.

galgo, *m.* greyhound.

galgo, ga, *a.* (Am.) hungry; eager.

galgueño, ña, *a.* resembling, or relating to, greyhounds.

gálgulo, *m.* (orn.) roller.

galianos, *m. pl.* shepherd's meal.

galibar, *va.* (naut.) to trace, to mould.

gálibo, *m.* templet; (r. w.) gauge for the width and height of an open freight car (to determine whether there will be enough clearance in tunnels, etc.).

galicado, da, *a.* French in construction or form (s. o. words, style, etc.).—**galicano, na,** *n. & a.* Gallican.—**galicismo,** *m.* Gallicism.—**galicista,** *n.* Gallicizer, user of gallicisms.

gálico, *m.* venereal disease; syphilis.

galicoso, sa, *a.* (coll.) infected with syphilis.

galilea, *f.* (arch.) galilee porch or chapel.

galileo, a, *n. & a.* Galilean.

galillo, *m.* uvula, hanging palate.

galimatías, *m.* gibberish, galimatias.

galio, *m.* (bot.) cheese-rennet bedstraw; (chem.) galium.

galiopsis, *f.* (bot.) common hedge-nettle.

galiparlista, *n.* = GALICISTA.

galipodio, *m.* white frankincense; galipot.

galizabra, *f.* lateen-rigged vessel.

galo, la, *n. & a.* Gaul (-ic).

galocha, *f.* galosh, clog, patten.

galón, *m.* galloon, tape, braid, binding lace; bullion, gold or silver galloons used on uniforms; stripe; gallon, liquid measure.—*pl.* (naut.) sheer rails.

galonazo, *m. aug.* large galloon; ornament.

galoneador, ra, *n.* one who binds with braid or galloons.

galoneadura, *f.* (sew.) trimming.

galonear, *va.* (sew.) to bind, to trim with galloons.

galonero, ra, *n.* braid or galloon maker.

galonista, *m.* (coll.) pupil of a military college wearing corporal stripes as a reward.

galop, *m.* (danc.) galop.

galopar, *vn.* to gallop.

galope, *m.* gallop; haste, speed.—**a g.,** or **de g.,** hurriedly, speedily.

galopeado, da. I. *pp. & a.* (coll.) hastily done. **II.** *m.* (coll.) whipping, flogging.

galopear, *vn.* = GALOPAR.

galopillo, *m. dim.* scullion, kitchen boy.

galopín, *m.* ragamuffin; rascal, rogue; shrewd fellow; clever knave; (naut.) swabber, cabin boy; scullion.

galopinada, *f.* roguish act, knavery.

galopo, *m.* rascal, rogue.

galpito, *m.* weak, sickly chicken.

galpón, *m.* (Am.) slaves' quarters (in old times); shed.

Galván, *m.*—**eso no lo entenderá G.,** (coll.) that is a puzzle, that is a hard nut to crack.

galvánico, ca, *a.* galvanic.

galvanismo, *m.* (phys.) galvanism.

galvanización, *f.* (phys.) galvanization.

galvanizar, *va.* (pret. GALVANICÉ: subj. GALVANICE) to galvanize; to electroplate.

galvanocauterio, *m.* (med.) galvanocautery.

galvanómetro, *m.* galvanometer.

galvanoplastia, galvanoplástica, *f.* galvanoplasty, electrotypy.

galvanoplástico, ca, *a.* galvanoplastic.

galladura, *f.* cicatricula, tread of an egg.

gallar, *va.* to tread (as a cock).

gallarda, *f.* a Spanish dance and its music; (print.) type of a size between minion and brevier.

gallardamente, *adv.* elegantly, gracefully.

gallardear, *vn.* to act with grace or elegance.

gallardete, *m.* (naut.) pennant, streamer.

gallardetón, *m.* (naut.) broad pennant.

gallardía, *f.* gracefulness; gallantry, bravery, nobleness; activity, briskness.

gallardo, da, *a.* graceful, elegant; magnanimous, generous; lively; brave, gallant.

gallareta, *f.* (orn.) widgeon.

gallarón, *m.* (orn.) a kind of bustard.

gallaruza, *f.* hooded garment.

gallear. I. *va.* to tread (as cocks). **II.** *vn.* to surpass, excel; to assume an air of importance; to raise the voice in anger; to crow; to bully; (found.) to have flaws.

gallegada, *f.* a group of GALLEGOS; peculiar action or speech of a GALLEGO; a Galician dance and its tune.

gallego, ga. I. *n.* & *a.* Galician, belonging to the province of Galicia. **II.** *m.* northwest wind.

galleo, *m.* (found.) flaw in a casting.

gallera, *f.* cockpit.

galleta, *f.* ship biscuit, hardtack; small vessel or pan.

galletica, *f.* small cracker or biscuit.

gallillo, *m.* uvula.

gallina. I. *f.* hen.—**g. de Guinea,** Guinea hen. **II.** *n.* coward, chicken-hearted person.—**g. ciega,** blindman's buff.

gallináceo, a. I. *n.* & *a.* (zool.) gallinacean (-ceous). **II.** *f. pl.* Gallinaceæ, Gallinæ.

gallinaza, *f.* hen dung; (orn.) GALLINAZO.

gallinazo, *m.* (zool.) gallinazo, turkey buzzard.

gallinejas, *f. pl.* fried chicken tripes.

gallinería, *f.* poulterer's shop; hencoop or henhouse; cowardice, pusillanimity.

gallinero, ra. I. *a.* chicken-eating. **II.** *n.* poulterer, poultry dealer. **III.** *m.* poultry yard; hencoop, henroost, henhouse; basket for carrying poultry; ladies' club or bee; (coll., theat.) nigger heaven, top gallery.

gallineta, *f.* (orn.) sandpiper; ruffed grouse.

gallipato, *m.* (orn.) merganser.

gallipava, *f.* a large variety of hen.

gallipavo, *m.* (orn.) turkey; (coll.) false, unpleasant note in singing.

gallipuente, *m.* bridge without rails.

gallístico, ca, *a.* gamecock (u. a.); cockfight (u. a.); relating to gamecocks or cockfights.

gallito, *m. dim.* small cock; beau, coxcomb; cock of the walk, bully.

gallo [gahl'-lyo], *m.* (orn.) cock, rooster; (icht.) dory, sea fish; boss, chief, leader; cork float for fishing; (carp.) wall board of the roof; false note in singing.—**g. de pelea,** or **inglés,** gamecock.—**alzar el g.,** to speak loud and arrogantly.—**hacerse el g.,** to become the ruler in any meeting, body, etc.—**otro g. le cantara,** he would be better (or worse) off, he would have fared differently.—**salir con una pata de g.,** to give a foolish or irrelevant answer.—**ser el g.** = HACERSE EL G.—**tener mucho g.,** to be very arrogant and overbearing.

gallocresta, *f.* (bot.) annual clary sage.

gallofa, *f.* food given to pilgrims; greens for salad and pottage; idle tale; French roll; directory of divine service.

gallofar, gallofear, *vn.* to loaf about as a beggar.

gallofero, ra; gallofo, fa. I. *a.* idle, lazy, vagabond. **II.** *n.* tramp.

gallón, *m.* green sod, turf; (arch.) echinus.

gallonada, *f.* wall made of sods.

gama, *f.* (zool.) doe; (mus.) gamut.

gamarra, *f.* (sad.) martingale, check, strap.

gamarza, *f.* (bot.) wild Syrian rue.

gambaj, *m.* acton.

gámbaro, *m.* = CÁMBARO.

gambax, *m.* = GAMBAJ.

gamberra, *f.* prostitute, strumpet.

gambesina, *f.,* **gambesón,** *m.* acton.

gambeta, *f.* (danc.) crosscaper; prance.

gambetear, *vn.* to caper like a horse.

gambeto, *m.* quilted greatcoat; cap for a newborn child.

gambito, *m.* (chess) gambit.

---

gamboa, *f.* (bot.) a variety of quincy.

gambota, *m.* (naut.) counter timber, arched timber.

gamella, *f.* bow (of yoke); large wooden trough or tub; washtub; boundary mound.

gamelleja, *f. dim.* small trough or tub.

gamellón, *m. aug.* large yoke bow; large tub; trough in which grapes are trodden.

gamezno, *m.* little young fallow deer.

gamo, *m.* buck of the fallow deer.

gamón, *m.* (bot.) asphodel.

gamonal, *m.* asphodel field or patch; (Am.) boss.

gamonalismo, *m.* (Am.) bossism.

gamonito, *m.* shoot, tiller, sucker.

gamonoso, sa, *a.* abounding in asphodels.

gamopétalo, la, *a.* (bot.) gamopetalous.

gamosépalo, la, *a.* gamosepalous.

gamuno, na, *a.* chamois (u. a.), shammy.

gamuza, *f.* (zool.) chamois; chamois, shammy skin.

gamuzado, da, *a.* chamois-colored.

gamuzón, *m. aug.* large chamois.

gana, *f.* appetite, hunger; desire; mind.—**dar g.,** or **ganas, de** (followed by *inf.*) to arouse desire to, to make (one) feel like (followed by present participle); to feel like.—**de buena g.,** willingly.—**de g.,** energetically, in earnest.—**de mala g.,** unwillingly.—**no me da la g.,** I don't want to, I won't.—**tener g.,** or **ganas, de,** to desire; to wish to; to have a mind to.—**tenerle g.,** or **ganas, a,** to desire; to wish to have a fight with.

ganable, *a.* that may be gained or won, gainable.

ganadería, *f.* cattle raising; cattle ranch; stock farm; live stock; cattle brand.

ganadero, ra. I. *a.* belonging to cattle. **II.** *n.* grazier, owner of cattle; stock farmer; dealer in cattle; drover.

ganado, *m.* live stock; cattle; herd, flock, drove; (coll.) rabble.—**g. caballar,** horses.—**g. de cerda** = G. MORENO.—**g. de pata hendida,** oxen, cows, sheep, goats.—**g. mayor,** cattle (including horses, asses, mules).—**g. menor,** sheep.—**g. moreno,** swine, hogs.—**g. ovejuno,** sheep.—**g. vacuno,** (bovine) cattle.

ganador, ra, *n.* & *a.* gainer (-ing), winner (-ing).

ganancia, *f.* gain, profit, advantage.—**g. bruta,** gross profit.—**g. líquida,** net profit.—**ganancias y pérdidas,** (com.) profit and loss.

ganancial, *a.* relating to earnings or profit.

ganancioso, sa, *a.* lucrative, profitable; gaining.

ganapán, *m.* drudge; common laborer; rude, coarse man.

ganapierde, *m.* give-away, losing game.

ganar, *va.* to gain; to win; to earn; to clear, to make (money); to attain, obtain, acquire; to surpass, be superior to; to draw (interest).

ganchero, *m.* conductor of a raft of timber.

ganchillo, ito, *m. dim.* little hook or crotch.

gancho, *m.* hook; crook, crotch; hairpin; shepherd's crook; sheephook; (coll.) allurer, roper-in; pimp; procurer, pander; (coll.) attractiveness, especially of a woman.—**echar el g. a,** to catch; to hook, land (fig.).

ganchoso, sa, *a.* hooked, curved.

ganchuelo, *m. dim.* = GANCHILLO.

gándara, *f.* low jungle.

gandaya, *f.* laziness, idleness; a kind of coif.—**andar a la g.,** to gad, loaf, lounge.

gandido, da, *a.* (Am.) gluttonous.

gandinga, *f.* (min.) washed fine ore; (Cuba) liver stew.

gandir, *va.* to eat.

gandujado, *pp.* & *m.* accordion plaiting.

gandujar, *va.* (sew) to plait, shirr, fold.

gandul, la, *n.* (coll.) idler, loafer, tramp.

gandulear, *vn.* to loaf, lounge, gad.

gandulería, *f.* idleness, laziness, lounging.

ganeta, *f.* (zool.) = GINETA.

ganforro, ra, *n.* (coll.) rogue, rascal.

ganga, *f.* (orn.) little pin-tailed grouse; (min.) gangue, veinstone; (coll.) snap, cinch.

gangarilla, *f.* company of strolling players.

gangliforme, *a.* gangliform.

---

ganglio, *m.* (anat.) ganglion.

ganglionar, *a.* (anat.) gangplionic.

gangoso, sa, *a.* snuffling, speaking with a twang.

gangrena, *f.* (med.) gangrene, blood poisoning.

gangrenarse, *vr.* to gangrene, become gangrenous or infected.

gangrenoso, sa, *a.* gangrenous.

ganguear, *vn.* to snuffle, to speak with a twang.

ganguero, *a.* (coll.) cinch-seeking, running after easy jobs.

gánguil, *m.* (naut.) fishing barge; dump scow.

ganoideo, a. **I.** *n.* & *a.* (zool.) ganoid. **II.** *m. pl.* Ganoidei.

ganoso, sa, *a.* desirous, wishing.

gansada, *f.* (coll.) stupidity.

gansarón, *m.* (orn.) gosling; tall, thin, gawky man.

ganso, sa, *n.* (orn.) gander, goose; slow, lazy person; silly person, ninny.—**g. bravo,** wild goose

gante, *m.* linen manufactured in Ghent.

gantés, esa, *a.* from, or relating to, Ghent; Ghent (u. a.).

ganzúa, *f.* picklock, false key, skeleton key; picklock, burglar.

gañán, *m.* day laborer; farm hand; rustic.

gañanía, *f.* gang of laborers; lodge for the same.

gañido, *pp.* & *m.* yelping, howling.

gañiles, *m. pl.* cartilaginous larynx; gills of the tunny fish.

gañir, *va.* to yelp or howl (as a dog); to croak, cackle, crow; (coll.) to talk hoarsely.

gañón, gañote, *m.* (coll.) throat; a kind of fritter.

gaón, *m.* (naut.) substitute for the oar in Indian vessels.

garabatada, *f.* (coll.) hooking.

garabatear. **I.** *vn.* to throw a hook at, or for, something; to scrawl, scribble; (coll.) to beat about the bush. **II.** *va.* to hook.

garabateo, *m.* hooking; scribbling, scrawling.

garabatillo, *m. dim.* small hook.

garabato, *m.* hook; pothook; grapple, grapnel, creeper, claw bar, hand bale hook; meathook or gambrel; scrawl, scribble; muzzle; winsome ways.—*pl.* scrawling; hand gestures.

garabatoso, sa, *a.* full of scrawls; charming, attractive.

garabito, *m.* market stall.

garaje, (improperly) **garage,** *m.* garage.

garambaina, *f.* gaudiness; (coll.) ridiculous affectation or mannerism; illegible scrawl.

garante. **I.** *a.* responsible. **II.** *n.* (com. and law) warranter, guarantor, surety; bondsman, bail.

garantía, *f.* guarantee; (com. and law), warranty, guaranty, security; indorsement; collateral; bail.

garantir, *va. def.* (*only those modes and persons are used that have the letter* i *in their endings*) to guarantee.

garantizar, *va.* (*pret.* GARANTICÉ: *subj.* GARANTICE) to guarantee; to indorse, answer or vouch for.

garanón, *m.* stallion jackass; male breeding camel.

garapacho, *m.* tortoise.

garapiña, *f.* congealed particles of any liquid; scalloped galloon or lace; (Cuba) fermented pineapple juice.

garapiñado, da, *pp.* & *a.* candied, sugarcoated; (jew.) frosted.

garapiñar, *va.* to ice, to freeze (cream, sirup, etc.); to candy.

garapiñera, *f.* ice-cream freezer; wine cooler.

garapita, *f.* net for small fish.

garapito, *m.* small insect, like a tick.

garapullo, *m.* paper dart; shuttlecock.

garatura, *f.* (tan.) scraper.

garatusa, *f.* a card game; (coll.) caress.

garay, *m.* (Philip.) an ancient sailboat.

garba, *f.* sheaf, as of wheat.

garbanzal, *m.* ground sown with chickpeas.

garbanzo, *m.* (bot.) chickpea.

garbanzuelo, *m. dim.* small chickpea; (vet.) a disease in horses' feet. *V.* ESPARAVÁN.

garbar, *va.* (agr.) to sheaf or sheave.

garbear. **I.** *va.* (agr.) to sheaf. **II.** *vn.* to affect an air of dignity and grandeur.

garbera, *f.* (agr.) shock of sheaves.

garbías, *m. pl.* omelet of herbs, cheese and flour.

garbillador, ra, *n.* sifter; riddler; garbler.

garbillar, *va.* (agr.) to sift; (min.) to riddle; to garble.—**garbillo,** *m.* coarse sieve for grain; (min.) riddle; riddled ore.

garbín, *m.* coif made of network.

garbino, *m.* southwest wind.

garbo, *m.* gracefulness, gentility, elegant carriage; knack; frankness, nobleness, generosity.

garbosamente, *adv.* gracefully; nobly.

garbón, *m.* (orn.) male partridge.

garboso, sa, *a.* natty, spruce, graceful, sprightly; noble, generous.

garbullo, *m.* garboil, mêlée of children.

garcero, ra, *a.* (orn.) heron hawk.

garceta, *f.* (orn.) little egret; side locks of hair.— *pl.* tenderlings.

gardenia, *f.* (bot.) gardenia.

garduja, *f.* barren stone in quicksilver mines.

garduña, *f.* (zool.) marten.

gadruño, ña, *a.* (coll.) filcher, petty thief.

garete, *m.*.—**al g.,** (naut.) adrift.

garfa, *f.* claw of a beast or bird; hand, in contempt: ancient tax.—**echar la g.,** to claw or seize anything with the nails.

garfada, *f.* clawing or seizing with the nails.

garfear, *vn.* to hook, to seize with a hook.

garfiada, *f.* = GARFADA.

garfio, *m.* hook, drag hook; gaff.

gargajeada, *f.* ejection of phlegm.—**gargajear,** *vn.* to expectorate phlegm.—**gargajeo,** *m.* = GARGAJEADA.—**gargajiento, ta,** *a.* that expectorates phlegm.—**gargajo,** *m.* phlegm.—**gargajoso, sa,** *a.* = GARGAJIENTO.

garganchón, *m. V.* GARGÜERO.

garganta, *f.* throat; gullet; instep; gorge, notch; (agr.) sheath of a plow; (arch.) shaft of a column or balustrade; (mech.) neck, throat, gullet, waist, groove of a sheave.—**tener buena g.,** to be a good singer.

gargantada, *f.* liquid or blood ejected from the throat.

gargantear, *vn.* to quaver, to warble; (naut.) to strap a deadeye.

garganteo, *m.* quavering, warbling.

gargantil, *m.* cut in barbers' basins.

gargantilla, *f.* necklace; (Philip.) water jug.

gárgara, *f.* gargle, gargling.—**hacer gárgaras,** to gargle.

gargarismo, *m.* gargle; gargling.

gargarizar, *vn.* to gargle, gargarize.

gárgol. **I.** *a.* empty, addle (eggs). **II.** *m.* (mech.) groove, furrow, mortise.

gárgola, *f.* (arch.) gargoyle; linseed.

gargüero, garguero, *m.* gullet; windpipe.

garifalte, *m.* (orn.) = GERIFALTE.

garifo, fa, *a.* = JARIFO.

gariofilea, *f.* (bot.) common avens or herb bennet.

garita, *f.* sentry box; porter's lodge; watercloset; privy.

garitero, *m.* master of a gaming house; gamester, gambler.

garito, *m.* gaming house; watchman's house; gambling den; profits of gambling.

garla, *f.* (coll.) talk, chatter.

garlador, ra; garlante, *n.* & *a.* (coll.) babbler (-ing), prater (-ing).

garlar, *vn.* (coll.) to babble, prattle, chatter.

garlito, *m.* fish trap; snare, trap, or gin.—**caer en el g.,** (coll.) to fall into a trap.—**coger en el g.,** to detect in wrong-doing.

garlocha, *f.* goad stick.

garlopa, *f.* (carp.) jack plane, long plane.

garma, *f.* steep slope.

garnacha, *f.* judge's robe or gown; a variety of purple grape, and the wine made from it; company of strolling players.

garniel, *m.* muleteer's girdle.

garo, *m.* an ancient Roman dish.

garra, *f.* claw of a wild beats, talon of a bird of prey; clutch; hand (in contempt); (mech.) catch, claw, hook, fang, clutch.—**caer en las garras de,** to fall into the clutches of.—**echarle a uno la g.,** (coll.) to grasp, arrest, imprison one.—**sacar de las garras de,** to free from.

garrafa, *f.* carafe, decanter.

garrafal, *a.* specially large and sweet (s. o. cherries); great, huge.

garrafilla, *f. dim.* small carafe.

garrafiñar, *va.* (coll.) to grapple, snatch away.

garrafón, *m. aug.* large carafe; demijohn, carboy.

garrama, *f.* tax paid by Mohammedans; imposition, fraud, robbery.

garramar, *va.* to rob, to plunder and pillage.

garranar, *va.* to rob, to plunder and pillage.

garrancha, *f.* (coll.) sword.

garrancho, *m.* branch broken off a tree.

garrapata, *f.* sheep and cattle tick; (mil.) disabled horse.

garrapatear, *vn.* to scribble, to scrawl.

garrapatilla, *f. dim.* small tick.

garrapato, *m.* pothook, scrawl.

garrar, *vn.* (naut.) to drag.

garrasí, *m.* side-buttoned breeches worn by Venezuelan plainsmen.

garrear, *vn.* = GARRAR.

garridamente, *adv.* gracefully, neatly.

garrideza, *f.* elegance, gracefulness.

garrido, da *a.* handsome, graceful.

garroba, *f.* carob bean.—**garrobal,** *m.* plantation of carob trees.—**garrobilla,** *f.* (tan.) chips of carob trees for staining.

garrocha, *f.* a sort of alpenstock; goad stick.

garrochada, *f.*, **garrochazo,** *m.* prick or blow with a goad stick.—**garrocheador, ra,** *n.* goader, pricker. —**garrochear,** *va.* = AGARROCHAR.—**garrochón,** *m. aug.* spear or goad stick used by bullfighters on horseback.

garrofa, *f.* carob bean.

garrofal, *m.* = GARROBAL.

garrón, *m.* spur of cocks and birds; talon of a bird of prey; paw of rabbits, etc.

garrotal, *m.* plantation of olive trees, made with cuttings.

garrotazo, *m.* blow with a cudgel.

garrote, *m.* club, bludgeon, truncheon, cudgel; garrote (for capital punishment); hazel basket or panier; (naut.) turning fid.—**dar g.,** to garrote. execute with the garrote.

garrotear, *va.* (Am.) = APALEAR.

garrotillo, *m.* (med.) croup.

garrubia, *f.* carob bean. *V.* ALGARROBA.

garrucha, *f.* pulley.—**g. combinada,** sheave, block.—**g. fija,** fast pulley.—**g. movible,** movable pulley.—**g. simple,** single pulley.

garrucho, *m.* (naut.) cringle, mast hoop.

garruchuela, *f. dim.* small pulley.

garrudo, da, *a.* muscular, brawny, strong.

garrulador, ra, *a.* garrulous.—**garrulería,** *f.* prattle, chatter.—**garrulidad,** *f.* garrulity.

gárrulo, la, *a.* chirping, as birds; chattering, prattling; garrulous.

garúa, *f.* (Am.) drizzle.—**garuar,** *vn.* to drizzle.

garujo, *m.* concrete. *V.* HORMIGÓN.

garulla, *f.* loose grapes; (coll.) rabble.

garullada, *f.* gang of rogues.

garvier, *m.* small pouch.

garza, *f.* (orn.) heron; (Colomb.) stork.—**g. real,** purple heron.

garzo, za. I. *a.* blue; blue-eyed. **II.** *m.* agaric, mushroom.

garzón, *m.* lad, boy; waiter; stripling; adjutant in the life guards.

garzota, *f.* (orn.) night heron; plumage, aigrette; crest of a helmet.

garzul, *m.* a kind of wheat.

gas, *m.* gas; vapor, emanation, fume; (coll.) **gas** light.—**g. del alumbrado,** illuminating gas.—**g. pobre,** producer gas.

gasa, *f.* gauze.

gascón, na; nés nesa, *n.* & *a.* Gascon.

gasconada, *f.* gasconade, boast, bravado.

gaseiforme, *a.* gasiform, gaseous.

gaseosa, *f.* soda water.—**gaseoso, sa,** *a.* gaseous. —**gasificable,** *a.* gasifiable.—**gasificación,** *f.* gasification.—**gasificar,** *va.* to gasify.

gasista, *n.* gas fitter.

gasógeno, *m.* gazogene; mixture of benzine and alcohol used for lamps and for cleaning.

gasolina, *f.*, **gasoleno,** *m.*, gasoline.

gasometría, *f.* gasometry.

gasómetro, *m.* gasometer; gas meter.

gasón, *m.* YESÓN; large clods of unbroken earth; sod.

gastable, *a.* that may be spent or worn out.

gastadero, *m.* (coll.) place where anything is wasted or spent; wasting; spending.

gastado, da, *pp.* & *a.* worn-out, useless; blasé.

gastador, ra. I. *a.* lavish, prodigal, extravagant. **II.** *n.* spender, spendthrift; (mil.) pioneer, sapper; criminal sentenced to hard labor.

gastamiento, *m.* consumption; wearing out.

gastar. I. *va.* to spend, expend; to waste, use, consume, wear out, fret; to have or wear habitually; to own, disport, keep (as carriages, etc.); to plunder, pillage, sack; to digest.—**g. frases y rodeos,** (coll.) to beat around the bush.—**gastarlas,** (coll.) to act, behave, conduct one's self.—**g. salud,** to enjoy good health. **II.** *vr.* to become old or useless; to waste away, wear out; to fray.

gasterópodo, da, *a.* (zool.) gasteropod.

gasto, *m.* expenditure, expense; consumption; spending, consuming; waste, use, wear and tear; (hydr.) discharge.—**gastos de escritorio,** stationery expenses (in an office).—**gastos de explotación,** operating, running or working expenses. —**gastos de representación,** incidental expenses (of a public functionary); allowance for incidental expenses.

gastoso, sa, *a.* = GASTADOR.

gastralgia, *f.* (med.) gastralgia.

gástrico, ca, *a.* gastric.

gastritis, *f.* (med.) gastritis.

gastrocele, *m.* (med.) gastrocele.—**gastrocolitis,** *f.* (med.) gastrocolitis.—**gastroenteritis,** *f.* (med.) gastroenteritis.—**gastrointestinal,** *a.* gastrointestinal.

gastromanía, *f.* gluttony.

gastrómano, na, *n.* & *a.* glutton (-ous).

gastronomía, *f.* gastronomy, epicurism.

gastronómico, ca, *a.* gastronomic.

gastrónomo, *m.* epicure, gastronomer.

gastrorrafia, *f.* (surg.) gastrorraphy.

gastrorragia, *f.* gastrorrhagia.

gastrotomía, *f.* (surg.) gastrotomy.

gástrula, *f.* (biol.) gastrula.

gata, *f.* she-cat; (coll.) Madrid woman; (bot.) GATUÑA; (mil.) cat castle; (naut.) cathead.—**g. del ancla,** (naut.) cat tackle.—**a gatas,** on all fours.

gatada, *f.* cat trick; clawing; turn of a hare when closely pursued; (coll.) artful dodge, scurvy trick.

gatallón, *m.* (coll.) rogue, cheat, scamp.

gatatumba, *f.* (coll.) affected civility or submission; dissembling, pretence.

gatazo, *m. aug.* large cat; (coll.) artful trick, cheat, deception.

gateado, da. I. *pp.* & *a.* feline, catlike. **II.** *m.* a very compact American striped wood.

gateamiento, *m.* scratching; clambering; going on all fours.

gatear. I. *vn.* to creep (s. o. children); to climb up, clamber; to go upon all fours. **II.** *va.* (coll.) to scratch or claw; to steal, to rob.

gatera, *f.* cat's hole; (bot.) common catmint; (naut.) cathole.

gatería, *f.* number of cats together; (coll.) gang of toughs or ill-bred boys; (coll.) simulation, cunning, trick.

gatero, ra, *a.* frequented by cats.

gatesco, ca, *a.* (coll.) feline, catlike.

gatica, illa, ita, *f. dim.* little she-cat, pussy.

gaticida, *m.* (coll.) cat killer.

gatico, ito, *m. dim.* little cat, pussy.

gatillazo, *m.* noise made by a trigger at firing.

gatillo, *m. dim.* little cat; pelican, dentist's forceps; (arti.) trigger; nape of a bull or ox; (arch.) cramp iron; filcher, petty thief.

gato, *m.* cat, tomcat; moneybag and the money kept in it; (coop.) hooping tong; (mech.) jack, lifting jack, screw jack; (arti.) gun searcher; (coll.) pickpocket, petty thief, filcher; (coll.) shrewd fellow; (coll.) native of Madrid.—**g. cornaquí,** (naut.) jackscrew.—**g. de algalia,** (zool.) civet cat.—**g. encerrado,** (coll.) nigger in the woodpile. —**g. montés,** wildcat.—**dar, meter,** or **vender, g. por liebre,** (coll.) to cheat, to fool, to give chalk for cheese.

gatuna, gatuña, *f.* (bot.) rest-harrow, cammock.

gatunero, ra, *n.* seller of smuggled meat.

gatuno, na, *a.* catlike, feline.

gatuperio, *m.* hotchpotch; (coll.) fraud, snare.

gauchada, *f.* (Am.) artifice; act of a Gaucho.

gauchaje, *m.* meeting or body of Gauchos.

gauchesco, ca, *a.* relating to the Gauchos; Gaucho-like.

gaucho, cha. **I.** *n.* Gaucho, Argentine pampas man (woman); good horseman. **II.** *a.* GAUCHESCO; knavish, rascally, tricky; rude, unpolished, vulgar.

gaudeamus, *m.* (coll.) feast, entertainment or merrymaking.

gavanza, *f.* flower of the dog-rose.

gavanzo, *m.* (bot.) dog-rose.

gaveta, *f.* drawer, till, locker.

gavetilla, *f. dim.* small desk drawer.

gavia, *f.* (naut.) main topsail; top (in galleys); mad man's cage; ditch; (min.) gang of basket passers; (orn.) GAVIOTA.—*pl.* (naut.) topsails of the main and fore mast.

gavial, *m.* gavial, an East-Indian crocodile.

gaviero, *m.* (naut.) topman, mastman.

gavieta, *f.* (naut.) scuttle, bowsprit bee.

gaviete, *m.* (naut.) davit in a longboat.

gavilán, *m.* (orn.) sparrow hawk; fine hair stroke in penmanship; nib of a pen; (arm.) quillon of a sword; brad or pin of a goad stick; (naut.) iron hook; (bot.) thistle flower; (naut.) tholes.

gavilancillo, *m. dim.* young hawk; incurvated point of an artichoke leaf.

gavilla, *f.* (agr.) gavel or sheaf of grain; bundle of vine shoots; gang of thugs.

gavillero, *m.* (agr.) place where gavels of grain are collected.

gavina, *f.* (orn.) = GAVIOTA.

gavión, *m.* (mil.) gabion; (coll.) large hat.

gaviota, *f.* (orn.) gull, sea gull.

gavitel, *m.* (naut.) small buoy.

gavota, *f.* gavot, a French dance.

gaya, *f.* stripe on stuffs, etc.; badge given to victors in Roman games; (orn.) magpie.

gayado, da, *pp.* & *a.* motley, striped.

gayadura, *f.* garniture, party-colored trimming.

gayar, *va.* to streak, stripe; to trim with ribbons of various colors; to variegate.

gayata, *f.* crook, sheephook.

gayo, ya, *a.* gay, festive, merry; showy.—**gaya ciencia,** poesy, minstrelsy, art of poetry.

gayola, *f.* (naut.) cage; (coll.) jail; (prov.) raised hut for watching vineyards.

gayomba, *f.* (bot.) white single-seed broom.

gayuba, *f.* (bot.) red-berried arbutus.

gayubal, *m.* GAYUBA field.

gaza, *f.* loop of a bow; (naut.) strap, loop, collar, splice, noose.

gazafatón, *m.* nonsense, foolish talk, balderdash.

gazapa, *f.* lie, fib, falsehood.

gazapatón, *m.* = GAZAFATÓN.

gazapera, *f.* warren for rabbits; (coll.) den where suspicious characters meet; (coll.) brawl, row.

gazapico, illo, ito, *m. dim.* little rabbit, bunny.

gazapina, *f.* assembly of ruffians; brawl, row.

gazapo, *m.* cony, young rabbit; shrewd, artful fellow; (coll.) great lie; blunder, mistake.

gazapón, *m. aug.* = GARITO.

gazmiar. **I.** *va.* to steal and eat tidbits. **II.** *vr.* (coll.) to complain; to resent.

gazmol, *m.* a kind of growth on the tongue of birds of prey.

gazmoñada, gazmoñería, *f.* prudery.

gazmoñero, ra; gazmoño, ña, *a.* prude, priggish.

gaznápiro, ra, *n.* churl, simpleton, booby.

gaznar, *vn.* = GRAZNAR.

gaznatada, *f.* blow on the throttle; BOFETADA.

gaznate, *m.* throttle, windpipe; a kind of fritter.

gaznatón, *m.* GAZNATADA; pancake, fritter.

gazofia, *f.* = BAZOFIA.

gazofilacio, *m.* gazophylacium, treasury of the temple of Jerusalem.

gazpachero, ra, *n.* maker of GAZPACHO.

gazpacho, *m.* Andalusian dish made of biscuit, oil, vinegar, onions, and garlic; crumbs of bread fried in a pan.

gazuza, *f.* (coll.) keen appetite, hunger.

ge, *f.* Spanish name of the letter *g*.

gea, *f.* mineral or inorganic constituents of a region, and the work describing it.

geato, *m.* (chem.) geate or humate.

gehena, *m.* Gehenna, hell.

geico, ca, *a.* (chem.) geic.

géiser, *m.* geyser.

gelatina, *f.* gelatine; jelly.

gelatiniforme, *a.* gelatiniform, gelatinelike.

gelatinoso, sa, *a.* gelatinous.

gelatinudo, da, *a.* (Am.) gelatinous; phlegmatic, lazy. slow.

gelfe, *m.* black slave.

gélido, da, *a.* (poet.) gelid, frigid.

gema, *f.* (jew.) gem; (carp.) slab, flitch; (bot.) bud.

gemación, *f.* (bot.) gemmation.

gemela, *f.* (bot.) Arabian jasmine.

gemelífloro, ra, *a.* (bot.) geminiflorous.

gemelo, la. **I.** *n.* twin. **II.** *m. pl.* binocular telescope; opera glasses; field or marine glasses; cuff buttons.—**Gemelos,** (astr.) Gemini.

gemido, *pp.* & *m.* lamentation, moan; howl

gemidor, ra, *n.* & *a.* lamenter (-ing); howler (-ing), moaner (-ing).

geminífloro, ra, *a.* geminiflorous.

géminis, *m.* (pharm.) a kind of plaster; (G-, astr.) Gemini.

gemíparo, ra, *a.* (biol.) gemmiparous.

gemir, *vn.* to groan, moan; to grieve; to howl; to roar, whistle (as the sea or wind); to grunt.

genciana, *f.* (bot.) gentian.

gencianáceo, a. **I.** *n.* & *a.* (bot.) gentian (-aceous). **II.** *f. pl.* Gentianaceæ.

gencianeo, ea, *a.* gentianaceous.

gendarme, *m.* gendarme.

gendarmería, *f.* (mil.) gendarmerie.

genealogía, *f.* genealogy.—**genealógico, ca,** *a.* genealogical.—**genealogista,** *n.* genealogist.

geneático, ca, *a.* genethliacal.

geneo, *m.* a Peruvian banana.

generable, *a.* generable.

generación, *f.* generation; succession, lineage.

generador, ra. I. *n.* & *a.* generator (-ing). **II.** *m.* (mech. and elec.) generator. *V.* GENERATRIZ.

general. I. *a.* general; common, usual.—**en g., por lo g.,** in general, generally. **II.** *m.* (mil.) general; (eccl.) superior of a religious order; lecture hall in a university; (prov.) customhouse.

generala, *f.* (mil.) the general (a roll of the drum); wife of a general.

generalato, *m.* (eccl. and mil.) generalship.

generalero, *m.* = ADUANERO.

generalidad, *f.* generality; (prov.) community, corporation; (prov.) custom duties.

generalísimo, *m.* generalissimo.

generalización, *f.* generalization.

generalizador, ra, *n.* & *a.* generalizer (-ing).
generalizar. I. *va.* (*pret.* GENERALICÉ: *subj.* GENERALICE) to generalize. **II.** *vr.* to become general, usual, or popular; to spread.
generalmente, *adv.* generally.
generar, *va.* to generate, produce.
generativo, va, *a.* generative.
generatriz, *n.* & *a.* (math.) generator (-ing.).
genéricamente, *adv.* generically.
genérico, ca, *a.* generic.
género, *m.* genus; class; kind; kin; manner, way, sort; cloth, stuff, material; (gram.) gender.—*pl.* dry goods; (com.) goods, merchandise, commodities.—**g. humano,** mankind.—**de g.,** (art.) genre.
generosamente, *adv.* generously.
generosidad, *f.* generosity; hereditary nobility; bravery, fortitude.
generoso, sa, *a.* generous; noble, magnanimous; excellent, choice (said mainly of wine).
genesíaco, ca, *a.* genesiacal.
genésico, ca, *a.* genesial.
génesis. I. *m.* (**G-**) Genesis. **II.** *f.* origin, beginning; cause; genesis.
genetlíaca, *f.* genethliacs, astrology.
genetlíaco, ca. I. *a.* genethliacal. **II.** *m.* genethliac.
gengibre, *m.* = JENGIBRE.
genial, *a.* temperamental; pleasant, cheerful.
genialidad, *f.* temperament.
genialmente, *adv.* genially.
geniazo, *m.* *aug.* strong temper.
genio, *m.* genius; temperament, nature, disposition, temper; character, genius, peculiarities (as of a language); representative type, embodiment; angel, spirit.—**g. del mal,** evil spirit.—**buen g.,** good nature, equable temper.—**de buen (mal) g.,** good- (evil-) tempered.—**mal g.,** bad, or ill, temper.
genista, *f.* (bot.) Genista. *V.* RETAMA.
genital. I. *a.* genital. **II.** *m.* TESTÍCULO.
genitivo, va. I. *a.* generative. **II.** *m.* (gram.) genitive or possessive case.
genízaro, ra. I. *a.* composed of different species; (Mex.) half-breed. **II.** *m.* Janizary.
genol, *m.* (naut.) futtock.
genovés, sa. I. *n.* & *a.* Genoese. **II.** *n.* (formerly) banker.
gente, *f.* people, folk, crowd, any number of persons; army, troops; gang; retinue; gens, clan, race, nation; (coll.), family, folks.—**g. baja,** lower classes; rabble, mob.—**g. común,** common folk.—**g. de bien,** honest people.—**g. de capa parda,** villagers, countrymen, rustics.—**g. de color,** colored people.—**g. de la cuchilla,** butchers.—**g. de la garra,** thieves, pickpockets.—**g. de la vida airada,** the underworld, libertines.—**g. del bronce,** merry crowd.—**g. de paz,** a friend, or friends.—**g. de pelo,** or **de pelusa,** people of property.—**g. de trato,** tradesmen, dealers.—**g. de traza,** well-behaved people.—**g. fina,** cultured people.—**g. menuda,** children.—**g. perdida,** vagrants, vagabonds.—**g. principal,** the nobility or gentry.—**g. vulgar** = G. COMÚN.—**de g. en g.,** from one to another, from generation to generation.
gentecilla, *f.* low, contemptible people.
gentil. I. *a.* Gentile; genteel, graceful, handsome; excellent, exquisite. **II.** *n.* gentile, pagan, heathen.
gentileza, *f.* gentility, gracefulness; easiness, sprightliness; nattiness; ostentation, pageantry; courtesy, politeness.
gentilhombre, *m.* fine fellow; my good man; gentleman, the servant who waits about the person of a man of rank; person sent to the king with important despatches.—**g. de cámara,** lord of the bedchamber.—**g. de manga,** nobleman who attends the princes of Spain while children.
gentilicio, ia, *a.* gentilitious; national, tribal; hereditary.
gentílico, ca, *a.* heathen, gentile, pagan.
gentilidad, *f.* gentilism, heathenism, paganism; the body of heathens or gentiles.

gentilismo, *m.* = GENTILIDAD.
gentilizar, *vn.* to observe the rites of gentiles or heathens.
gentilmente, *adv.* gently, politely; heathenishly.
gentío, *m.* crowd, multitude.
gentualla, gentuza, *f.* rabble, mob; people of no account.
genuflexión, *f.* genuflexion.
genuino, na, *a.* genuine.
geocéntrico, *a.* geocentric.
geoda, *f.* (geol.) geode.
geodesia, *f.* geodesy.
geodésico, ca, *a.* geodetical.
geófago, ga, *a.* geophagous, earth-eating.
geodesta, *m.* geodesist.
geodinámica, *f.* geodynamics.
geogenia, *f.* (geol.) geogeny.
geogénico, ca, *a.* geogenic.
geognosia, *f.* (geol.) geognosy.
geognosta, *m.* geognost, geologist.
geognóstico, ca, *a.* geognostic.
geogonía, *f.* = GEOGENIA.
geogónico, ca, *a.* geogonic.
geografía, *f.* geography.
geográficamente, *adv.* geographically
geográfico, ca, *a.* geographical.
geógrafo, fa, *n.* geographer.
geología, *f.* geology.
geológico, ca, *a.* geological.
geólogo, ga, *n.* geologist.
geomancia, *f.* geomancy.
geomántico, ca. I. *a.* geomatic. **II.** *m.* geomancer.
geómetra, *n.* geometer, geometrician.
geometría, *f.* geometry.—**g. analítica,** analytic geometry.—**g. del espacio,** solid geometry.—**g. descriptiva,** descriptive geometry.—**g. no euclidiana,** non-Euclidean geometry.—**g. plana,** plane geometry.
geométricamente, *adv.* geometrically.
geométrico, ca, *a.* geometrical, geometric.
geomorfía, *f.* (geol.) geomorphy.
geonomía, *f.* (geol.) geonomy.
geonómico, ca, *a.* geonomic.
geoponia, geopónica, *f.* geoponics, agriculture; gardening.
geopónico, ca, *a.* geoponic, agricultural.
georama, *f.* georama.
georgiano, na, *a.* Georgian, relating to Georgia.
geórgica, *f.* georgic, poem on husbandry.
geotropismo, *m.* (bot.) geotropism.
geraniáceo, cea, *a.* (bot.) geraniaceous.
geranio, *m.* (bot.) crane's-bill; geranium.—**g. de rosa,** rose geranium.
gerbo, *m.* (zool.) jerboa.
gerencia, *f.* (com.) managership, management.
gerente, *m.* (com.) manager.
gericaya, *f.* (Mex., cook.) custard.
gerifalco, gerifalte, *m.* (orn.) gerfalcon.
germanesco, ca, *a.* belonging to the jargon of the gipsies.
germanía, *f.* jargon or cant of the gipsies, thieves, etc.; slang; concubinage; a faction in Valencia during the days of Charles V.
germánico, ca, *a.* Germanic, German.
germanio, *m.* (chem.) germanium.
germanismo, *m.* Germanism, German form employed in another language.
germano, na, *n.* & *a.* German (-ic) (used only with reference to Germania, or ancient Germany); full (brother, sister.)
germanófilo, la, *n.* & *a.* Germanophilist (-ic); pro-German.
germen, *m.* germ; gem; spring, source.
germinación, *f.* (bot.) germination.
germinal. I. *a.* germinal, **II.** *m.* Germinal, seventh month of the French revolutionists.
germinar, *vn.* to germinate.
germinativo, va, *a.* germinative.
gerundense, *a.* of or belonging to Gerona.
gerundiada, *f.* (coll.) pompous and unmeaning expression.

gerundiano, na, *a.* pompous, empty (style or phrase).

gerundio, *m.* (gram.) gerund; (coll.) pompous, bombastic speaker.

gesolreút, *m.* (mus.) first of the signs which serves as a clef to music; G or soprano clef.

gesta, *f.* gest, a narrative of a person's deeds; romance.

gestación, *f.* (med.) gestation; exercise among the Romans for the health.

gestatorio, ria, *a.* gestatory, portable.

gestear, *vn.* to gesticulate, make grimaces.

gestero; ra, *n. & a.* (one) that makes grimaces or faces; making grimaces; gesticulator (-ing).

gesticulación, *f.* gesticulation, gesture.

gesticular. I. *vn.* to gesticulate, make gestures or grimaces. **II.** *a.* gesticulatory.

gestión, *f.* conduct; exertion, effort, action, measure, step; negotiation, management.

gestionar, *va.* to conduct, manage; to take steps to attain or carry out.

gesto, *m.* face, visage; grimace; gesture.—**estar de buen g.,** to be in good humor.—**hacer gestos,** to make wry faces or grimaces; to gesticulate.

gestor, *m.* (com.) superintendent, manager, agent, promotor, representative, attorney.

gestudo, da, *a.* (coll.) ill-humored, cross.

giba, *f.* hump, crooked back, hunch, gibbosity; (coll.) nuisance, annoyance.

gibado, da, *pp. & a.* hunchbacked.

gibar, *va.* corvar; (coll.) to molest, annoy, vex.

gibelino, na, *n. & a.* Ghibelline.

gibón, *m.* (zool.) gibbon.

giboso, sa, *a.* gibbous, humpbacked.

gibraltareño, ña, *a.* Gibraltar (u. a.).

gícama, *f.* (Mex.) a root resembling yucca.

giganta, *f.* giantess; (bot.) sunflower.

gigantazo, za, *n. aug.* huge giant.

gigante. I. *a.* gigantic. **II.** *m.* giant.

gigantea, *f.* (bot.) sunflower.

giganteo, a; gigantesco, ca, *a.* gigantic.

gigantez, *f.* gigantic stature or size.

gigantilla, *f.* large-headed figure.

gigantismo, *m.* (med.) giantism.

gigantón, na, *n. aug.* giant of enormous size.— **gigantones,** gigantic figures of pasteboard.— **echar los gigantones a,** (coll.) to reprehend severely, to give a dressing down.

gijonense; gijonés, sa, *a.* of or belonging to Gijón.

gilí, *a.* (coll.) foolish, stupid.

gilvo, va, *a.* honey-colored or pinky.

gimelga, *f.* (naut.) fish, paunch.

gimnasia, *f.* = gimnástica.—**gimnasio,** *m.* gymnasium; school, academy.—**gimnasta,** *m.* gymnast.—**gimnástica,** *f.* gymnastics.

gimnástico, ca, *a.* gymnastic, gymnastical.

gímnico, ca, *a.* gymnastical.

gimnosofista, *m.* gymnosophist.

gimnoto, *m.* (zool.) gymnotus, electric eel.

gimo, yo gima. *V.* gemir.

gimotear, *vn.* (coll.) to whine.—**gimoteo,** *m.* whining.

ginebra, *f.* Moorish rattle; gin (liquor); confusion, bedlam; a card game.

ginebrada, *f.* a kind of puff-paste tart.

ginebrés, sa; ginebrino, na, *n. & a.* Genevan.

ginceeo, *m.* gynceeum.

ginecocracia, *f.* gynecocracy, gynarchy.

ginecología, *f.* (med.) gynecology.

ginecológico, ca, *a.* gynecological.

ginecólogo, ga, *n.* gynecologist.

ginesta, *f.* genista. *V.* hiniesta.

gineta, *f.* genet, a kind of weasel.

gingidio, *m.* (bot.) wild spinach.

gingival, *a.* (anat.) gingival, relating to the gums. —**gingivitis,** *f.* gingivitis, inflammation of the gums.

ginglimo, *m.* (anat.) ginglymus.

ginsén, ginseng, *m.* (bot., pharm.) ginseng.

girada, *f.* (danc.) gyration; pirouette.

girado, *m.* (com.) drawee.

girador, girante, *m.* (com.) drawer.

giralda, *f.* vane or weathercock in the form of a statue (from that on the spire of the cathedral of Seville); **(G-)** name of this tower.

giraldete, *m.* surplice without sleeves.

giraldilla, *f. dim.* small vane or weathercock; a popular dance in Asturias.

girándula, *f.* (pyr. and hyd.) girandole.

girar, *vn.* to revolve, rotate, turn; (com.) to draw (a check, draft).—**g. contra,** or **a cargo de,** to draw on.

girasol, *m.* (bot.) sunflower.

giratorio, ria, *a.* revolving, rotary, turning.

girifalte, *m.* (orn.) = gerifalte.

girino, *m.* embryo of a frog.

giro, *m.* turn; revolution, rotation; gyration; course or turn of affairs; bend, tendency; bias, trend; turn of a sentence; threat, bravado; (com.) draft; circulation; bulk of business; line of business, specialty.—**g. postal,** money order.— **tomar otro g.,** to take another course; to change one's mind.

girondino, na, *n. & a.* Girondist, Girondin.

giroscópico, ca, *a.* gyroscopic.

giroscopio, *m.* gyroscope.

giróvago, ga, *a.* = vagabundo.

gis, *m.* crayon.

gitanada, *f.* mean, contemptible trick; blandishment, wheedling, caress, flattery.

gitanamente, *adv.* in a sly, winning manner

gitanear, *va.* to flatter, wheedle, cajole.

gitanería, *f.* wheedling, flattery, cajolery.

gitanesco, ca, *a.* gipsylike, gipsy (u. a.).

gitanillo, lla, *n. dim.* little gipsy.

gitanismo, *m.* gipsyism, gipsy life.

gitano, na. I. *a.* gipsylike; gipsy; sly, artful, honey-mouthed. **II.** *n.* gipsy.

glabro, bra, *a.* bald; beardless.

glacial, *a.* glacial.

glacialmente, *adv.* glacially.

glacis, *m.* (fort.) glacis.

gladiador, gladiator, *m.* gladiator.

gladiatorio, ria, *a.* gladiatorial, gladiatory.

gladio, gladiolo, *m.* (bot.) gladiolus.

glande, *m.* (anat.) glans penis.

glandífero, ra; glandígero, ra, *a.* glandiferous.

glándula, *f.* gland.—**g. pineal,** pineal body, pineal gland.—**g. pituitaria,** pituitary gland.

glandular, *a.* glandular.—**glandulilla,** *f. dim.* glandule, small gland.—**glanduloso, sa,** *a.* glandulous, glandular.

glasé, *m.* glacé or glacé silk.

glaseado, da, *a.* glossy, glacélike.

glasear, *va.* to calender (paper).

glasto, *m.* (bot.) woad or dyers' weed.

glauberita, *f.* glauberite.

glaucio, *m.* (bot.) celandine.

glauco, ca, *a.* (bot.) glaucous.

glauco, *m.* (zool.) a mollusk of the Glaucus genus.

glaucoma, *m.* (med.) glaucoma.

gleba, *f.* lump or clod turned up by the plow.

glera, *f.* = cascajar.

glicerato, *m.* (chem.) glycerate.

glicerido, *m.* (chem.) glyceride.

glicerina, *f.* glycerine.

glicocola, *f.* (chem.) glycocoll.

glicol, *m.* (chem.) glycol.

glicosuria, *f.* (med.) glycosuria.

glíptica, *f.* glyptics, stone engraving.

gliptodonte, *m.* (pal.) glyptodon.

gliptografía, *f.* glyptography.

globo, *m.* globe, sphere; the earth; globular lampshade.—**g. aerostático,** air balloon.—**g. cautivo,** captive balloon.—**g. celeste,** (astr.) celestial globe. —**g. cometa,** (aer.) kite baloon.—**g. dirigible,** dirigible balloon, airship.—**g. nodriza,** (aer.) nurse balloon.—**g. sonda,** (aer.) sounding balloon, captive balloon with recording instruments.—**g. terráqueo,** or **terrestre,** (the) globe, (the) earth.— **en g.,** as a whole; without details; in bulk.

globoso, sa, *a.* globe-shaped.

globular, *a.* globular.

globulariáceo, a, *a.* (bot.) globulariaceous.

glóbulo, *m. dim.* small globe; (biol.) globule.

globulillo, *m. dim.* globulet, globule; homeopathic pill.

globulina, *f.* (chem.) globulin.

globuloso, sa, *a.* globulous, globulose.

gloria. I. *f.* glory; heavenly state, bliss, blessedness; pride, boast; transparent gauze, gossamer, tissue; a kind of cream tart or cake; (art) opening in the sky representing angels, splendors, etc. **II.** *m.* (eccl.) gloria, doxology.

gloriarse, *vr.* (w. **de** or **en**) to boast (of), be proud (of), take delight (in).

glorieta, *f.* summerhouse, bower, arbor; circle or square at intersection of streets.

glorificación, *f.* glorification; praise.

glorificador, ra; glorificante, *n. & a.* glorifier (-fying).

glorificar. I. *va.* (*pret.* GLORIFIQUÉ: *subj.* GLORIFIQUE) to glorify, adore, worship; to exalt; to praise, honor, extol. **II.** *vr.* = GLORIARSE.

gloriosamente, *adv.* gloriously.

glorioso, sa, *a.* glorious; enjoying the bliss of heaven, blessed; boastful, ostentatious.

glosa, *f.* gloss, scholium; comment, commentary, note; (com. and law) explanatory annotation in accounts; (poet.) a kind of rondelet; (mus.) variation of a theme.

glosador, ra, *n.* commentator, glosser, gl. *t.*rist; (com.) auditor.

glosalgia, *f.* (med.) glosalgia.

glosar, *va.* to gloss, annotate, comment; (com.) to audit; (poet.) to compose (rondelets); (mus.) to vary (a theme).

glosario, *m.* glossary.

glose, *m.* glossing, commenting.

glosilla, *f. dim.* short gloss, comment, or note; (print.) minion type, 7-point.

glositis, *f.* (med.) glossitis.

glótico, ca, *a.* glottic, relating to the glottis.

glotis, *f.* (anat.) glottis.

glotón, na. I. *a.* gluttonous. **II.** *n.* glutton, gormandizer.

glotonamente, *adv.* gluttonously.—**glotonazo, za,** *n. aug.* great glutton; gormandizer.—**glotonear,** *vn.* to be a glutton, gormandize.—**glotonería,** *f.* gluttony.

glucina, *f.* (chem.) glucina.

glucinio, *m.* (chem.) glucinum, beryllium.

glucogenia, *f.* (physiol.) glycogeny (esp. of the liver).

glucómetro, *m.* glucometer, hydrometer for determining the quantity of sugar in a liquid.

glucosa, *f.* (chem.) glucose.

glucósido, *m.* (chem.) glucoside.

glucosuria, *f.* (med.) glucosuria.

gluma, *f.* (bot.) glume.

gluten, *m.* gluten; gliadin, glutin; glue.

glúteo, tea, *a.* gluteal.

glutinosidad, *f.* glutinousness, viscosity.

glutinoso, sa, *a.* glutinous, viscous.

gneis, *m.* (geol.) gneiss.

gnetáceo, a, *a.* (bot.) gnetaceous.

gnómico, ca, *a.* gnomic.

gnomo, *m.* gnome, fabulous being.

gnomon, *m.* gnomon, sundial; square.—**g. movible,** bevel square.

gnomónica, *f.* gnomonics, science of dialing.

gnomónico, ca, *a.* gnomonic, gnomonical.

gnosticismo, *m.* gnosticism.—**gnóstico,** *n. & a.* gnostic.

goa, *f.* pig-iron bloom.

gobernación, *f.* government; governor's office or official house.

gobernador, ra. I. *a.* governing. **II.** *n.* governor; ruler. **III.** *f.* governor's wife; female ruler.

gobernadorcillo, *m.* (Philip) justice of the peace.

gobernalle, *m.* (naut.) rudder, helm.

gobernante. I. *n. & a.* ruler (-ing). **II.** *n.* (coll.) self-appointed manager or leader.

gobernar. I. *va. & vn.* (*ind.* GOBIERNO: *subj.* GOBIERNE) to govern, rule; to command, lead, direct; to manage, run; to control, steer, helm. **II.** *vn.* (naut.) to obey the helm.

gobernativo, va, *a.* = GUBERNATIVO.

gobernoso, sa, *a.* (coll.) methodical, tidy.

gobierna, *f.* weather vane.

gobiernista. I. *a.* gubernatorial, government (u. a.); that supports the government. **II.** *n.* supporter of the government.

gobierno, *m.* government; ministers composing a cabinet; dignity, office, and term of a government; district or province under a governor; guidance, management, direction; control (of a business, an automobile, an airplane); (naut.) helm, rudder; steering, conning.—**g. de casa,** household.—**de g.,** controlling (lever, etc.), control (u. a.); of the State.—**para su g.,** for your guidance.—**servir de g.,** to be a guide or norm; to be a warning or a lesson.

gobierno, yo gobierne. *V.* GOBERNAR.

gobio, *m.* (icht.) gudgeon.

goce, *m.* enjoyment; fruition; possession.

gocete, *m.* neck guards in ancient armor.

gociano, na, *a.* Gothic.

gocha, *f.* (coll.) sow.—**gocho,** *m.* (coll.) hog.

godesco, ca, *or* **godible,** *a.* joyful, cheerful.

godo, da, *n. & a.* Goth (-ic); (Colomb., pol.) conservative.—**ser g.,** (Spain, fam.) to be of noble blood.

goflo, *m.* (Cuba) roasted corn meal or maize.

gofo, fa, *a.* stupid, ignorant; (art) dwarf figure.

gofrador, *m.* leaf marker, florist's tool.

gofrar, *va.* to mark (leaves) for artificial flowers.

gola, *f.* gullet, throat; gorget in ancient armor; (mil.) gorget, crescent-shaped insignia of duty; (fort.) gorge; (arch.) cyma, ogee.—**g. inversa, or reversa,** (arch.) cyma reversa.

goldre, *m.* quiver for shafts or arrows.

goleta, *f.* (naut.) schooner.

golf, *m.* golf.

golfán, *m.* (bot.) water lily.

golfillo, *m. dim.* small gulf; urchin.

golfín, *m.* (icht.) dolphin.

golfo, *m.* (geog.) gulf; sea, main; (poet.) gulf, abyss; faro (game); (Madrid) ragamuffin.

golilla. I. *f.* (sew.) gorget, ruff; collar worn by some magistrates in Spain; (mas.) short joining pipe; flange of a pipe. **II.** *m.* (coll.) magistrate wearing a GOLILLA.

golillero, ra, *n.* collar maker.

golmajo, ja, *n.* (prov.) gormandizer.

golondrina, *f.* (orn.) swallow; (icht.) flying gurnard, swallow fish.—**g. de mar,** (orn.) tern.

golondrinera, *f.* (bot.) swallowwort, celandine.

golondrino, *m.* (orn.) male swallow; vagrant, deserter; (med.) large tumor in the armpit.

golondro, *m.* (coll.) desire, longing.—**andar en golondros,** (coll.) to feed on vain hopes.—**campar de g.,** (coll.) to live at another's expense, to sponge.

golosamente, *adv.* eagerly; inordinately.

golosear, *va.* = GOLOSINAR.

golosina, *f.* dainty, delicacy, sweet morsel, titbit; daintiness, sweet tooth; inordinate desire or appetite; trifle.

golosinar, golosinear, golosmear, *vn.* to look for and eat tidbits, dainties, or sweetmeats; to taste and relish nice things.

goloso, sa, *a.* having a sweet tooth, fond of dainties, niceties, or sweetmeats.

golpazo, *m. aug.* heavy blow, stroke, or knock.

golpe, *m.* blow; stroke, hit, knock; wound, hurt; shock, clash; attack, spell; action, push, act; crowd, throng of people; abundance; heart beat; spring bolt of a lock; (sew.) passementerie trimming; pocket flap (of a coat); attack in fencing; astonishment, surprise; witty sally or remark; hole for planting; number of cuts planted in one hole; (mech.) stroke (of piston); travel (of a valve); (naut.) sweep; (mus.) touch, act of striking a key, etc.—**g. de arco,** bowing of a violin.—**g. de cuartel,** military coup.—**g. de estado,** coup d'etat.—**g. de fortuna,** stroke of good fortune.—**g. de gracia,** finishing stroke, coup de grâce.—**g. del reloj,** tick of the watch or clock.—**g. de mar**

(naut.) surge, heavy sea.—**g. de remo,** oar stroke.
—**g. seco,** sharp, quick blow or stroke.—**dar g.,** to
cause surprise; to create a sensation.—**de g., suddenly,** all at once.—**de g. y porrazo,** unexpectedly,
unawares.—**de un g.,** at one blow; all at once.

golpeadero, *m.* place much beaten; repeated
blows.

golpeador, ra, *n.* & *a.* striker (-ing), beater
(-ing), hitter (-ing).

golpeadura, *f.* percussion; act of beating, hammering, or striking.

golpear. I. *va.* to strike, hit, hammer; to bruise.
II. *vn.* to beat; to knock, pound (as a piston); to
tick (as a watch).

golpecico, illo, ito, *m. dim.* slight blow.

golpeo, *m.* repeated striking, beating or knocking.

golpete, *m.* door catch (to keep it open).

golpetear, *va.* & *vn.* to strike or pound continually; to rattle.

golpeteo, *m.* continued striking; constant hammering; knocking, pounding; rattling.

gollería, golloría, *f.* dainty; delicious morsel;
(coll.) delicacy, superfluity, excess.

gollete, *m.* throttle, upper part of the throat;
neck of a bottle; neckband of some religious
habits.—**estar hasta el g.,** (coll.) to be full; to be
in difficulties; to have lost patience.

gollizo, *m.* narrow passage of mountains or rivers.

goma, *f.* gum; India rubber; rubber band; rubber
eraser; (surg.) gumma, a kind of syphilitic
tumor.—*pl.* (Am.) overshoes, rubbers.—**g. adra-
gante,** gum tragacanth.—**g. arábiga,** gum arabic.
—**g. de borrar,** rubber eraser.—**g. elástica,** India
rubber.—**g. laca,** lac.—**g. tragacanta =** G. ADRA-
GANTE.

gomecillo, *m.* = LAZARILLO.

gomero, ra. I. *a.* relating to gums or to rubber.
II. *m.* rubber man, one engaged in the rubber
business or in the extraction of rubber.

gomía, *f.* bugbear; (coll.) glutton.—**g. del caudal,** spendthrift.

gomífero, ra, *a.* gummiferous.

gomorresina, *f.* gum resin.

gomosidad, *f.* gumminess, viscosity.

gomoso, sa. I. *a.* gummy; gum-producing; full
of viscous matter. **II.** *m.* dude, dandy.

gonce, *m.* hinge.

góndola, *f.* gondola; omnibus, stage, carry-all.

gondolero, ra, *n.* gondolier.

gonela, *f.* skirt formerly worn in Aragon.

gonfalón, *m.* banner, gonfalon, pennant.

gonfalonier, niero, *n.* = CONFALONIER.

gongórico, ca; gongorino, na, *a.* euphuistic.

gongorismo, *m.* euphuism.—**gongorista,** *n.*
(poet.) euphuist.—**gongorizar,** *vn.* to write eu-
phuistically.

goniometría, *f.* goniometry.—**goniométrico,**
ca, *a.* goniometric.—**goniómetro,** *m.* goniometer.

gonococo, *m.* (biol.) gonococcus.

gonorrea, *f.* (med.) gonorrhœa.

gonorreico, ca, *a.* gonorrhœal.

gorbión, *m.* = GURBIÓN.

gordal, *a.* fat, big, fleshy.

gordana, *f.* oil extracted from oxen's testicles.

gordazo, za, *a. aug.* very fat and big.

gordico, ica, illo, illa, ito, ita, *a. dim.* fattish,
rather plump.

gordiflón, na; gordinflón, na, *a.* (coll.) chubby,
flabby, fat.

gordo, da. I. *a.* fat, corpulent, fleshy, stout;
fat, rich, oily; great, large, big. **II.** *m.* fat, suet.

gordolobo, *m.* (bot.) great mullein.

gordón, na, dote, ta, *a. aug.* (coll.) very fat.

gordura, *f.* grease, fat; fatness, stoutness.

gorfe, *m.* a deep hole in a river forming a whirlpool or eddy.

gorga, *f.* hawk food; whirlpool.

gorgojarse, *vr.* = AGORGOJARSE.

gorgojo, *m.* grub, weevil; (coll.) dwarfish person.

gorgojoso, sa, *a.* infested by grubs or weevils.

gogona, *f.* gorgonia, sea fan, a zoophyte.

gorgóneo, a, *a.* Gorgonian.

gorgorán, *m.* a sort of silk grogram.

gorgorita, *f.* rain bubble.—*pl.* trill, shake.

gorgoritear, *vn.* (coll.) to warble, trill.

gorgorito, *m.* (coll.) trill, shake.

gorgorotada, *f.* swallow (as of water).

gorgoteo, *m.* gurgle, gurgling sound.

gorgotero, ra, *n.* peddler, hawker.

gorguera, *f.* (sew.) gorgeret, ruff; (arm.) gorget.

gorguerín, *f. dim.* small neck ruff or frill.

gorguz, *m.* javelin, shaft.

gorigori, *m.* (coll.) chant at funerals.

gorila, *m.* (zool.) gorilla.

gorja, *f.* throat, throttle; rejoicing, merrymaking;
(naut.) head of the keel.

gorjal, *m.* collar of a doublet; (arm.) gorget.

gorjeador, ra, *n.* & *a.* warbler (-ing), modulator
(-ing).

gorjear. I. *vn.* to warble, trill, quaver, sing.
II. *vr.* to gabble (as a child).

gorjeo, *m.* warble, trilling; gabble of a child.

gormar, *va.* to vomit.

gorra. I. *f.* cap, bonnet; woman's hat; hunting
cap; (mil.) bearskin cap; (coll.) intrusion at
feats without invitation; (coll.) sponging.—**g. de
señora,** lady's hat or bonnet.—**de g.,** (Colomb.,
coll.) at other people's expense, sponging, as a
sponge. **II.** *m.* parasite, sponger.

gorrada, *f.* = GORRETADA.

gorrería, *f.* bonnet and cap factory or shop.

gorrero, ra, *n.* cap maker; parasite, sponger,
deadhead.

gorretada, *f.* salute with a cap.

gorrete, *m. dim.*; **gorrica, illa, ita,** *f. dim.*;
gorrico, illo, ito, *m. dim.* small cap.

gorrín, *m.* small pig, sucking pig.

gorrinada, *f.* (coll.) dirty, hoggish action.

gorrinera, *f.* pigsty, pig's pen.

gorrinillo, ito, *m. dim.* little pig.

gorrino, na, *n.* small pig, sucking pig.

gorrión, *m.* (orn.) sparrow.

gorrioncillo, *m. dim.* small sparrow.

gorrionera, *f.* (coll.) den of rogues.

gorrista, *n.* parasite, sponger.

gorro, *m.* cap, coif.—**g. de dormir,** nightcap.—
g. frigio, Phrygian cap, cap of liberty.

gorrón, na. I. *n.* sponger, parasite; libertine.
II. *m.* round smooth pebble; (mech.) journal;
spindle; pivot or gudgeon of a gate or door;
pillow, swing block; lazy, unhealthy silkworm.

gorronal, *m.* place full of pebbles or gravel.

gorronazo, m. *aug.* great lecher or rake.

gorullo, *m.* lump or ball (as of wool).

gorupo, *m.* (naut.) granny's bend.

gosipino, na, *a.* having a cottony surface.

gota, *f.* drop of liquid; (med.) gout; (arch.) gutta.
—**g. a g.,** drop by drop.—**g. caduca,** or **coral,**
(med.) epilepsy, falling sickness.—**g. serena,**
(med.) amaurosis.—**gotas amargas,** bitters.

goteado, da, *pp.* & *a.* spotted, speckled.

gotear, *vn.* to drop, drip, dribble, leak; to measure by drops; to give by dribblets.

gotera, *f.* leak, leakage; drip, dripping; (arch.)
gutter; valance of a canopy or tester; (agr.) disease of trees caused by infiltration; chronic
ailing.

goterón, *m.* large raindrop; (arch.) throating.

gotica, illa, ita, *f. dim.* droplet, small drop.

gótico, ca, *a.* Gothic.—**gotón, na,** *n.* & *a.* Goth.

gotoso, sa, *a.* gouty.

goyesco, ca, *a.* relating to, or like, Goya or his
style, Goya (v. a.).

gozador, ra, *n.* enjoyer.

gozante, *n.* & *a.* enjoyer (-ing).

gozar. I. *va.* to enjoy; to have possession or
fruition of. **II.** *vn.* (w. de), to enjoy, have. **III.** *vr.*
to rejoice.

gozne, *m.* hinge.

gozo, *m.* joy, pleasure, glee, mirth, gladness; sudden blaze of dry chips of wood.—*pl.* couplets
with a burden, in praise of the Virgin.—**¡el g. al
pozo!** all has come to naught!—**no caber de g.,** or
saltar de g., to be in high spirits, to be very happy.

gozosamente, *adv.* joyfully, cheerfully.

gozoso, sa, *a.* joyful, cheerful, glad, merry.

gozque, *m.* a cur dog.

gozquejo, *m. dim.* small cur.

grabado. I. *pp. & a.* engraved, carved, cut. **II.** *m.* engraving; art of engraving; cut, picture, illustration.—**g. al agua fuerte,** etching.—**g. al agua tinta,** aquatint, aquatinta.—**g. al humo,** mezzotint.—**g. al barniz blando,** soft-ground etching.—**g. a media tinta =** G. AL AGUA TINTA.— **g. a puntos,** stipple engraving, stipple.—**g. en fondo,** or **en hueco,** punch or die sinking.—**g. en madera,** wood engraving, wood carving.—**g. en negro =** G. AL HUMO.—**g. punteado =** G. A PUNTOS.

grabador, ra, *n.* engraver, carver; cutter, sinker.

grabadura, *f.* act of engraving; sculpture.

grabar, *va.* to engrave; to cut, carve; to impress upon the mind.—**g. al agua fuerte,** to etch.—**g. en hueco, en blanco,** or **relieve,** to emboss.

grabazón, *f.* engraving, sculpture.

gracejar, *vn.* to write or speak wittily.

gracejo, *m.* graceful, winsome way.

gracia, *f.* grace; gracefulness; cleverness; free gift, benefaction, kindness; graciousness, condescension; benevolence, courtesy, pleasing manners; pardon, mercy; remission of a debt; witty saying or expression; joke, jest; humor, facetiousness; comicalness; brightness, cuteness of a child; (coll.) name (of a person).—*pl.* thanks; accomplishments; (myth., **G-**) (the Three) Graces.—**G. y Justicia,** *V.* MINISTERIO.—**gracias,** thanks, thank you.—**gracias a,** thanks to.—**gracias a Dios.** thank God.—**caer de la gracia de,** to lose the favor or good will of.—**caer en g.,** to please, to be liked.—**dar gracias,** to thank, to give thanks.— **decir dos gracias,** to tell home truths.—**de g.,** gratis, for nothing.—**en g.,** in favor.—**en g. de,** for the sake of, out of regard for; in consideration of.—**hacer g. de,** to excuse from; to free from.

graciable, *a.* good-natured; affable, amiable; easily granted.

grácil, *a.* gracile, slender, small.

graciola, *f.* (bot.) hedge hyssop.

graciosamente, *adv.* gracefully; graciously or kindly; gratuitously; facetiously.

graciosidad, *f.* gracefulnss, beauty, excellence.

gracioso, sa. I. *a.* graceful, pleasing, accomplished; facetious, witty, funny; liberal, gracious; gratuitous, free. **II.** *m.* (theat.) low comedian, fool. **III.** *f.* (theat.) soubrette, chambermaid.

grada, *f.* step of a staircase; gradin (as of an amphitheatre); stand or gallery having gradins; superaltar; (eccl.) locutory; (agr.) harrow, brake.—*pl.* (arch.) perron, gradatory.—**g. de astillero,** (naut.) altar.—**g. de cota,** brush-harrow. —**g. de dientes,** harrow with teeth.—**g. de dique,** (naut.) altar.

gradación, *f.* (mus.) gradation; (rhet.) climax.

gradado, da, *pp. & a.* having gradins or steps.

gradar, *va.* (agr.) to harrow.

gradeo, *m.* harrowing.

gradería, *f.* series of steps, gradins or superaltars.

gradilla, *f. dim.* tile or brick mold; small step-ladder.

gradinar, *va.* (art) to chisel with a gradine.

gradino, *m.* gradine, sculptor's chisel.

gradiolo, *m.* (bot.) = GLADIOLO.

grado, *m.* step of a staircase; degree (of kindred); degree, academical title; (mil.) rank; (math., geog.) degree; (com.) grade, class, graduation of value or quality; (gram.) degree (of comparison); (law) stage of proceedings; (met.) will, pleasure.— *pl.* minor orders.—**de g.,** willingly, with pleasure.— **de g. en g.,** gradually, by degrees.—**de mal g.,** unwillingly.—**de su g. =** DE G.—**en g. superlativo,** or **en sumo g.,** in the highest degree.—**mal de mi g.,** against my wishes, much to my regret, unwillingly.

graduable, *a.* that may be graduated; adjustable.

graduación, *f.* graduation; (mil.) rank.

graduado, da. I. *pp. & a.* (mil.) brevet; graduated. **II.** *m.* graduate.

graduador, *m.* graduator, gauge.

gradual. I. *a.* gradual. **II.** *m.* (eccl.) response sung at mass.—**gradualmente,** *adv.* gradually.

graduando, *m.* one recently, or about to be, graduated.

graduar. I. *va.* to compare, grade, classify; to graduate; to give military rank to; (com.) to gauge, to appraise; to adjust. **II.** *vr.* to graduate, be graduated, take a degree.

gráficamente, *adv.* graphically.

gráfico, ca. I. *a.* graphic, graphical; clear, vivid. **II.** *m.* or *f.* graph, diagram.

gráfila, *f.* milled edge of coin.

grafio, *m.* graver for graffito or scratchwork.

grafioles, *m. pl.* biscuits in the form of an S.

grafito, *m.* (min.) graphite.

grafófono, *m.* graphophone.

grafolita, *f.* grapholite.

grafología, *f.* graphology.

grafomanía, *f.* graphomania, mania for writing (books, articles) for publication.

grafómano, na, *n.* graphomaniac.

grafómetro, *m.* (surv.) graphometer.

grafostática, *f.* graphic statics.

gragea, *f.* minute colored bonbons.

graja, *f.* (orn.) female jackdaw; jay.

grajal, *a.* belonging to crows, ravens, or magpies.

grajear, *vn.* to caw, as crows; to chatter, as magpies.

grajero, ra, *a.* abounding in, or frequented by, jackdaws.

grajo, *m.* (orn.) jackdaw.

grajuelo, *m. dim.* small jackdaw.

grama, *f.* (bot.) creeping cynodon; couch grass, dog's grass, grama grass.

gramal, *m.* couch grass or dog's grass field.

gramalla, *f.* long scarlet gown formerly worn in Aragon; coat of mail.

gramallera, *f.* pothanger.

gramar, *va.* to knead.

gramática, *f.* grammar; study of the Latin language.—**g. parda,** (coll.) horsesense, shrewdness.

gramatical, *a.* grammatical.

gramaticalmente, *adv.* grammatically.

gramático, ca. I. *a.* grammatical. **II.** *n.* grammarian.—**gramatiquear,** *vn.* (contempt.) to grammatize, to talk grammar.

gramatiquería, *f.* (coll. & contempt.) things grammatical, grammatical stuff.

gramil, *m.* (carp.) joiner's marking gauge.

gramilla, *f.* bed of the hemp brake.

gramíneo, ea, *a.* (bot.) gramineous.

graminívoro, ra, *a.* graminivorous.

gramo, *m.* gramme, gram.

gramófono, *m.* gramophone; phonograph.

gramómetro, *m.* (print.) type gauge.

gramoso, sa, *a.* covered with couch grass; belonging to couch grass.

grampa, *f.* staple, clamp, cramp.

gran, *a. contr.* of GRANDE (*used only in sing. and before m. or f. nouns*), large, big; grand, great.— **g. bestia,** tapir, elk.—**g. mogol,** Grand Mogul or Great Mogul.

grana, *f.* (agr.) act of seeding; seeding time; (ent.) cochineal; kermes; kermes berry; scarlet grain; scarlet color; fine scarlet cloth; fresh red color of the lips and cheeks; small seed of some plants.— **g. del paraíso,** (bot.) = CARDAMOMO.

granada, *f.* (bot.) pomegranate; (mil.) grenade, shell.—**g. de mano,** hand grenade.

granadera, *f.* (mil.) grenadier's pouch.

granadero, *m.* (mil.) grenadier; (coll.) very tall person.

granadilla, *f.* (bot.) passion flower, granadilla.

granadillo, *m.* (bot.) West-India red ebony.

granadino, na. I. *a.* native of or belonging to Granada (Spain), or New Granada (now Colombia). **II.** *m.* flower of the pomegranate tree.

granado, da. I. *pp. & a.* remarkable, noted, illustrious; select, choice, seedy. **II.** *m.* (bot.) pomegranate tree.

granador, *m.* (pyr.) granulating sieve; spot destined for this operation.

granalla, *f.* (found.) granulated metal.

granar. I. *vn.* (agr.) to seed, to kern, to ear out. **II.** *va.* (pry.) to grain, granulate.

granate, *m.* garnet.

granatín, *m.* a kind of ancient cloth.

granazón, *f.* seeding, shedding the seed.

grancé, *a.* madder-colored.

grande. I. *a.* large, big; great; grand.—**en g.,** on a large scale. **II.** *n.* grandee.—*pl.* grandees; great men.—**grandecico, ica, illo, illa, ito, ita,** *a.* pretty large.—**grandemente,** *adv.* greatly; very well; extremely; grandly.

grandevo, va, *a.* (poet.) of advanced age.

grandeza, *f.* greatness; grandeur, magnificence; grandeeship; grandees collectively; bigness; quantity; size, magnitude.

grandezuelo, la, *a. dim.* = GRANDECICO.

grandilocuencia, *f.* grandiloquence.

grandilocuente; grandílocuo, cua, *a.* grandiloquent.

grandillón, na, *a. aug.* excessively large or big.

grandiosamente, *adv.* magnificently, grandly.

grandiosidad, *f.* greatness; grandeur; abundance.

grandioso, sa, *a* grandiose, grand, magnificent.

grandor, *m.* size.

grandote, ta, *a. aug.* (coll.) very big.

grandullón, na, *a.* overgrown.

graneado, da, *pp.* & *a.* grained, spotted, granulous; (Peru) select, choice. *V.* FUEGO GRANEADO.

graneador, *m.* (art) stipple graver.

granear, *va.* (agr.) to sow (grain); (art) to stipple; to grain (a lithographic stone).

granel, *m.* heap of grain.—**a g.,** in a heap; (com.) in bulk.

granelar, *va.* (tan.) to grain (leather).

graneo, *m.* (agr.) act of shedding or sowing seed; (art) stippling.

granero, *m.* granary, barn; grange; cornloft; grain-producing country.

granete, *m.* (mech.) countersink, punch.

granévano, *m.* (bot.) goat's-thorn.

granguardia, *f.* (mil.) grand guard.

gránico, *m. dim.* granule, small grain.

granilla, *f.* nap on wrong side of cloth.

granillo, *m. dim.* granule, small grain; gain or profit frequently obtained; pimple on the rump of canary birds and linnets.

granilloso, sa, *a.* granulous, granular.

granítico, ca, *a.* granitic.

granito, *m. dim.* small grain; small pimple; (min.) granite; (pharm.) granule; small egg of a silk-worm.

granívoro, ra, *a.* granivorous.

granizada, *f.* hailstorm; deluge (fig.), great number (of things, facts, etc.); water ice.

granizar, *vn.* to hail; to pour down with violence.

granizo, *m.* hail; hailstorm; cloud or web in the eyes.

granja, *f.* grange, farm, farmhouse.—**g. modelo,** model farm.

granjear. I. *va.* to gain, earn, profit. **II.** *va.* & *vr.* to get, obtain, win (as the goodwill of another).

granjeo, *m.* act of getting or acquiring; gain, profit, advancement.

granjería, *f.* gain, profit, advantage.

granjero, ra, *n.* farmer, husbandman; dealer in profitable commodities.

grano, *m.* grain; cereal; each single seed; (pharm.) grain (20 make an English scruple, and 24 a Spanish scruple); (arti.) bushing (or bouching) of a cannon; pimple; (jew.) unit of weight (.05 g.). —*pl.* (com.) cereals, corn, breadstuffs.—**granos del paraíso,** (bot.) = AMOMO.—**ir al g.,** (coll.) to come to the point, to get down to brass tacks.

granoso, sa, *a.* granulous, grainy, granular, granulated (as leather).

granuja. I. *f.* loose berries of grapes; grapestone; group of roving boys. **II.** *m.* (coll.) little rogue, waif, gamin, urchin.

granujado, da, *a.* = AGRANUJADO.

granujiento, ta, *a.* full of pimples.

granujo, *m.* (coll.) pimple or tumor in the flesh.

granujoso, sa, *a.* full of pimples.

granulación, *f.* (chem. and med.) granulation.

granulador, ra, *m.* or *f.* granulating machine.

granular. I. *va.* to granulate. **II.** *vr.* to become covered with granules or pimples.

granular, *a.* granular; full of pimples.

gránulo, *m. dim.* granule; pellet.

granulosidad, *f.* granularity.

granuloso, sa, *a.* granulous, granular.

granza, *f.* (bot.) madder; garancine.—*pl.* siftings, chaff; dross of metals.

granzón, *m.* ore screenings.—*pl.* refuse of straw left by cattle.

granzoso, sa, *a.* full of chaff or screenings.

grañón, *m.* pap made of boiled wheat; boiled grain of wheat.

grao, *m.* strand, shore.

grapa, *f.* clamp, clasp, clutch, cramp iron; (carp.) holdfast; (vet.) mangy ulcers in the joints.

grapón, *m. aug.* (mech.) brace, hook, ram, iron dog.

grasa, *f.* grease; fat; suet; oil; gum of juniper trees; pounce; (naut.) slush; slag of metals; base of an ointment or pomade.—**g. de ballena,** whale oil, blubber.—**g. de pescado,** fish oil.

grasera, *f.* vessel for fat or grease; slushtub; dripping pan.—**grasería,** *f.* tallow chandler's shop. —**grasero,** *m.* (min.) slag dumper.—**graseza,** *f.* quality of fat or grease.—**grasiento, ta,** *a.* greasy, oily; filthy.—**grasilla,** *f.* pounce.

graso, sa. I. *a.* fat, oily, unctuous, lardy. **II.** *m.* fat, grease.

grasones, *m. pl.* wheat porridge.

grasoso, sa, *a.* = GRASIENTO.

grasura, *f.* = GROSURA.

grata, grataguja, *f.* burnisher, smoothing chisel; wire brush; rasp.

gratamente, *adv.* gratefully; agreeably.

gratar, *va.* to brush or burnish.

gratificación, *f.* gratification; reward; gratuity; tip; fee.

gratificador, ra, *n.* & *a.* gratifier (-ing); rewarder (-ing); tipper (-ing).

gratificar, *va.* (pret. GRATIFIQUÉ: subj. GRATIFIQUE) to reward, recompense; to tip, fee; to gratify, please.

gratil, *m.* (naut.) edge of a sail; luff, leech.

gratis, *adv.* gratis, free, for nothing.

gratisdato, ta, *a.* gratuitous, given away.

gratitud, *f.* gratitude, gratefulness.

grato, ta, *a.* pleasing, pleasant; acceptable; grateful; gratuitous.—**su grata (carta),** (com.) your favor.

gratonada, *f.* chicken ragout or fricassee.

gratuitamente, *adv.* gratuitously.

gratuito, ta, *a.* gratuitous, gratis; unfounded; uncalled-for.

gratulación, *f.* congratulation.

gratular. I. *vn.* to congratulate. **II.** *vr.* to rejoice.

gratulatorio, ria, *a.* congratulatory.

grava, *f.* gravel; broken stone.

gravamen, *m.* tax; charge, obligation, hardship, burden, inconvenience, nuisance; encumbrance; (law) mortgage, lien.

gravar, *va.* to burden, oppress; to fatigue; to tax; (law) to encumber.

gravativo, va, *a.* injurious; burdensome.

grave, *a.* weighty, ponderous, heavy; grave, serious; circumspect; troublesome, vexatious; arduous, difficult; (mus.) grave (tone); (gram.) grave (accent); (word) having the inflection on the penultimate syllable.

gravear, *vn.* to weigh, gravitate, sink.

gravedad, *f.* gravity, graveness, seriousness; (phys.) gravity.—**de g.,** serious; seriously, dangerously.

gravedoso, sa, *a.* haughty, self-important.

gravemente, *adv.* gravely; seriously, dangerously.

gravidez, *f.* pregnancy.

grávido, da, *a.* (poet.) gravid, pregnant.

gravimétrico, ca, *a.* gravimetric.
gravímetro, *m.* (phys.) gravimeter.
gravitación, *f.* (phys.) gravitation.
gravitar, *vn.* to gravitate; to rest, press (on).
gravoso, sa, *a.* costly; onerous; vexatious.
graznador, ra, *a.* croaking; cawing; cackling.
graznar, *vn.* to croak, caw, cackle.
graznido, *m.* croak, caw, cackle; croaking.
greba, *f.* (arm.) greave(s) or jambe(s).
greca, *f.* Grecian fret.
greciano, na; grecisco, ca, *a.* Grecian.
grecismo, *m.* Grecism, Hellenism.
grecizante, *a.* Grecianizing, Hellenizing.
grecizar, *va.* & *vn.* to Grecize.
greco, ca. I. *a.* Grecian. **II.** *n.* Greek.
grecolatino, na, *a.* Greco-Latin.
grecorromano, na, *a.* Greco-Roman.
greda, *f.* clay, chalk, marl, potter's clay.
gredal. I. *m.* clay pit, marlpit, loam pit. **II.** *a.* clayey, loamy.
gredoso, sa, *a.* clayey, marly.
grefier, *m.* registrar in the house of Burgundy.
gregal. I. *m.* northeast wind in the Mediterranean. **II.** *a.* gregarious, going in flocks.
gregario, ria, *a.* gregarian; dull, stupid.
gregoriano, na, *a.* Gregorian.
gregorillo, *m.* neckcloth formerly worn by women.
gregorito, *m.* (Mex.) disappointment; practical joke.
greguería, *f.* outcry, clamor, hubbub.
gregüescos, *m. pl.* Grecian wide breeches.
greguisco, ca, *a.* Grecian.
gregüizar, *va.* to Grecize.
gremial. I. *a.* belonging to a guild or trade-union, union (u. a.). **II.** *m.* member of a guild; union man; (eccl.) lapcloth used by bishops at divine service.
gremio, *m.* lap; body, society, company, guild, corporation; fraternity; trades-union.
grenchudo, da, *a.* having a long mane.
greña, *f.* long entangled or matted hair; anything entangled; (prov.) heap of grain to be thrashed; (prov.) first leaves of a vine shoot.—**andar a la g.,** to pull each other's hair (s. o. women); to argue excitedly.—**en g.,** (Mex.) raw (s. o. silk, etc.).
greñudo, da. I. *a.* dishevelled; shy (horse). **II.** *m.* shy horse.
greñuela, *f.* first shoots of a vine.
gres, *m.* pottery material consisting of clay and quartzose sand.
gresca, *f.* carousal, revelling, clatter; wrangle, quarrel, row.
grey, *f.* flock, herd; congregation of the faithful; people, race, nation.
grial, *m.* grail, legendary holy chalice.
griego, ga. I. *a.* Greek, Grecian. **II.** *m.* the Greek language; (coll.) cheating gambler; unintelligible language, Greek (fig.).
grieta, *f.* crevice, crack, cleft; chink, fissure, cranny, flaw; split, vein, shake, rent; scratch or fissure in the skin.—**grietas en las manos,** chapping of the hands.
grietado, da, *a.* fissured, cracked, showing flaws.
grietarse, *vr.* to crack, split; to part in clefts or fissures; to become chapped.
grietecilla, *f. dim.* small fissure or scratch.
grietoso, sa, *a.* cracked; crannied, flawy.
grifa, *f.* (print.) script.
grifado, da, *a.* script (type).
grifalto, *m.* a kind of small culverin.
grifo, fa. I. *a.* (print.) script; kinky, entangled (as hair). **II.** *m.* griffin or griffon, a fabled animal; (Am.) child of a negro and an Indian; (mech.) faucet, cock.—*pl.,* frizzled hair.
grifón, *m. aug.* fountain faucet.
grigallo, *m.* (orn.) a variety of francolin.
grilla, *f.* female cricket.—**ésa es g.,** (coll.) that is a fake.
grillarse, *vr.* to shoot, to sprout.
grillera, *f.* cricket hole; cricket cage.

grillero, *m.* he who puts on and takes off the irons of prisoners.
grillete, *m. dim.* shackle, fetter.
grillo, *m.* (ent.) cricket; (bot.) shoot, sprout.—*pl.* fetters, irons, gyves, shackles.—**andar a grillos,** to waste one's time in trifles.
grima, *f.* fright, horror; disgust.—**dar g.,** to disgust; to cause discouragement or fear.
grimoso, sa, *a.* horrible; repulsive, disgusting.
grímpola, *f.* (naut.) pennant, streamer.
grinalde, *m.* ancient form of grenade.
gringo, ga, *n.* (Am.) foreigner (sp. app. to Englishmen and Americans).
griñón, *m.* wimple worn by nuns; apricot ingrafted in a peach tree.
gripal, *a.* (med.) relating to la grippe.
gripe, *f.* (med.) grip, grippe, influenza.
gripo, *m.* an ancient merchant vessel.
gris. I. *a.* gray. **II.** *m.* (zool.) minever, Siberian squirrel and its fur; (coll.) cold, sharp air or weather.
grisalla, *f.* (art) grisaille, camaieu.
grisáceo, a; gríseo, a, *a.* grayish.
griseta, *f.* flowered silk stuff; (agr.) disease of trees caused by infiltration; French grisette.
grisú, *m.* (min.) fire damp.
grita, *f.* clamor, outcry, uproar; screaming, halloo, shouting; hooting, catcall.—**g. foral,** (law) summons, citation.
gritador, ra, *n.* & *a.* clamorer (-ing), shouter (-ing), screamer (-ing).
gritar, *vn.* to shout, cry out, scream, shriek; to hoot, catcall.
gritería, *f.* outcry, uproar, shouting.
grito, *m.* cry, scream, howl, shriek, shout; hoot, whoop.—**a g. herido,** in a loud voice, with a clamorous cry.—**alzar el g.,** to talk loud and haughtily.—**estar en un g.,** to be in continual pain.—**levantar el g.** = ALZAR EL G.—**poner el g. en el cielo,** to cry to heaven, to complain loudly, (coll.) to make a great fuss, to howl.
gritón, na, *a.* (coll.) vociferous, clamorous.
gro, *m.* grosgrain, twilled silk frabric.
groelandés, sa; groenlandés, sa, *n.* & *a.* Greenlander (-ish), Greenland (u. a.).
groera, *f.* (naut.) rope hole.
grog, *m.* grog (drink).
gromo, *m.* (bot.) leafy bud, young shoot.
gropos, *m. pl.* cotton put in inkstands.
gros, *m.* an ancient coin of small value.
grosamente, *adv.* grossly.
grosella, *f.* (bot.) berry of the red currant.—**g. blanca,** gooseberry.
grosellero, *m.* (bot.) currant bush.
groseramente, *adv.* grossly, coarsely, roughly; rudely, in an unmannerly way.
grosería, *f.* rudeness, ill-breeding; rusticity; discourtesy; coarseness, clumsiness; ignorance.
grosero, ra, *a.* coarse, rough; plain, homespun, not fine; thick, fat, bulky; rude, unpolished; discourteous, churlish, uncivil.
grosezuelo, la, *a. dim.* rather stout.
grosísimo, ma, *super. of* GRUESO: exceedingly stout; very bulky.
groso, *m.* coarse snuff, badly powdered.
grosor, *m.* thickness.
grosularia, *f.* (min.) grossularite.
grosulárieo, a, *a.* (bot.) grossulaceous.
grosulina, *f.* (chem.) grossulin.
grosura, *f.* fat, suet, tallow; meat diet, in opposition to fasting.
grotescamente, *adv.* grotesquely.
grotesco, ca, *a.* grotesque.
grúa, *f.* crane, derrick, hoisting machine; an ancient war engine; (naut.) bend.—**g. corredera,** traveling crane.—**g. de caballete,** gantry crane.—**g. de la cuaderna maestra,** midship bend.—**g. fija,** stationary crane.—**g. flotante,** crane ship; floating crane.—**a la g.,** in and out.
gruero, ra, *a.* trained to pursue cranes (app. to birds of prey).
gruesa, *f.* gross, twelve dozen; (eccl.) chief part of a prebend; (law) bottomry.

gruesamente, *adv.* grossly, coarsely.

grueso, sa. I. thick; bulky, corpulent; fleshy, stout; (coll.) pregnant; big; coarse, homespun, dense, thick, heavy; large around (as a post, etc.); heavy, black (s. o. type); heavy, dull, stupid, slow. **II.** *m.* thickness; bulk, corpulence; density, heaviness; main part, main body of an army; down stroke in penmanship.—**en g.,** (com.) in gross, in the gross, in bulk, by wholesale.

gruir, *vn.* (*for irr. v.* HUIR) to cry like a crane.

grujidor, *m.* glazier's nippers.

grujir, *va.* (gl.) to trim or pare with a GRUJIDOR.

grulla, *f.* (orn.) crane.

grullada, *f.* (coll.) gang or crowd of idlers; (coll.) patrol of constables or police officers.

grullero, ra, *a.* crane (u. a.—s. o. falcons), crane-hunting.

grumete, *m.* (naut.) cabin boy, ship boy.

grumillo, *m.* *dim.* small grume, clot, or curd.

grumo, *m.* grume, clot; cluster, bunch; (agr.) bud of trees; tip of a fowl's wing.—**g. de leche,** curd.

grumoso, sa, *a.* grumous, clotty.

gruñido, *pp.* & *m.* grunt.—**gruñidor, ra,** *n.* & *a.* grunter (-ing), growler (-ing).—**gruñimiento,** *m.* grunting, growling, grumbling.

gruñir, *vn.* to grunt; to creak (as doors, hinges, etc.); to grumble, growl, snarl.

gruñón, na, *n.* & *a.* (coll.) = GRUÑIDOR.

grupa, *f.* croup, rump of a horse.

grupada, *f.* squall, burst of wind and rain.

grupera, *f.* cushion at the back of a saddle for carrying a satchel, etc.; (sad.) crupper.

grupo, *m.* group; set; clump, cluster.

gruta, *f.* cavern, grotto, grot.—*pl.* crypts, vaults, subterranean galleries.

grutesco, ca, *a.* (art) grotesque, bizarre.

¡gua! *interj.* (Am.) gracious! horrors!

guabina, *f.* (Colomb.) a popular peasant air.

guaca, *f.* Indian grave, sp. one containing treasure; (Am.) buried treasure; (Am.) hole in the ground where gathered fruit is put to ripen.

guacamaya, guacamayo, *m.* (orn.) macao or macaw.

guacamole, *m.* (Cuba) salad of alligator pear.

guacia, *f.* (bot.) acacia; acacin, gum arabic.

guaco, *m.* (bot.) guaco, birthwort; (orn.) curassow.

guachapear. I. *va.* (coll.) to splatter (water) with the feet; (coll.) to make a botch of. **II.** *vn.* to clap, as horses' shoes when loose; to clatter.

guachapelí, *m.* solid strong wood used for ships in Guayaquil.

guacharaca, *f.* (orn.) = CHACHALACA.

guácharo, ra. I. *a.* sickly; dropsical. **II.** *m.* birdling, especially of a sparrow; (orn.) oil-bird, guacharo.

guachinango, ga, *a.* (Cuba) Mexican; (Mex.) artful, cunning.

guacho, cha. I. (Am.) orphan, foundling; solitary, forlorn. **II.** *m.* birdling of a sparrow.

guadañones, *m. pl.* hopple, fetterlock.

guadalajareño, ña, *a.* of or belonging to Guadalajara.

guadamací, cil, *m.* = GUADAMECÍ.

guadamacilería, *f.* embossed-leather factory.

guadamacilero, *m.* manufacturer of embossed leather.—**guadamecí, guadamecil,** *m.* embossed or printed leather.—**g. brocado,** gilt or silvered embossed leather.

guadameco, *m.* ornament worn by women.

guadaña, *f.* (agr.) scythe.—**guadañar,** *va.* (agr.) to scythe, to mow.—**guadañero,** *m.* scytheman; (Cuba) owner of a GUADAÑO.

guadañil, *m.* mower of hay.

guadaño, *m.* (Cuba) small boat in the port of Havana; transport vessl.

guadapero, *m.* (bot.) wild common pear; boy who carries victuals to reapers or mowers.

guadarnés, *m.* harness room or locker; harness keeper; officer of the king's mews.

guadijeño. I. *m.* poniard, stiletto, knife. **II.** *a.* belonging to Guadix.

guadramaña, *f.* trick, deceit, imposition.

guadua, *f.* (Am.) a variety of large, thorny bamboo.

guadual, *m.* GUADUA field.

guagua. I. *m.* & *f.* (Peru) baby. **II.** *m.* (Mex.) insect that destroys fruit. **III.** *f.* (Cuba) omnibus, street car.—**de g.,** free, gratis.

guagüero, ra, *n.* (Cuba) bargain driver; deadhead.

guaicán, *m.* (icht.) = RÉMORA.

guainambí, *m.* (Mex., C. A.) humming bird.

guaira, *f.* (Am.) smelting furnace; (naut.) leg-of-mutton sail.

guairo, *m.* (Am.) small two-masted coaster.

guaita, *f.* (mil.) night watch or sentinel.

guajada, *f.* (Mex.) nonsense, frivolity.

guajalote, *m.* (Mex.) turkey.

guajamón, na, *a.* (Cuba) orange-colored.

guájar, *m.* & *f.*, **guájaras,** *f. pl.* fastnesses, roughest part of a mountain.

guaje, *m.* (Mex.) calabash for learning to swim.

guájete por guájete, *idiom.* tit for tat.

guajira, *f.* a Cuban popular song.

guajiro, ra, *n.* & *a.* (Cuba) rustic, rural; rude, boorish.

guajolo'e, *m.* = GUAJALOTE.

¡gualá! *interj.* assuredly; by God!

gualatina, *f.* dish made of boiled apples, milk of almonds, and broth, beaten up with spice and rose water.

gualda, *f.* (bot.) weld, wild woad, dyer's weed, reseda.

gualdado, da, *a.* weld-colored, yellowish.

gualdera, *f.* (arti.) trail, bracket; (carp.) stringboard; (naut.) whelp, check.

gualdo, da, *a.* weld, yellow or gold-colored.

gualdrapa, *f.* horse trappings, housing; (coll.) tatter, rag hanging from clothes.

gualdrapazo, *m.* (naut.) flap of a sail; jerk.

gualdrapear. I. *va.* to put end to head, or in consecutive order (as pins with the point of each on the head of the next). **II.** *vn.* (naut.) to flap (as sails).

gualdrapeo, *m.* flapping of the sails.

gualdrapero, *m.* ragamuffin, ragged fellow.

gualdrín, *m.* weather strip.

guamá, *m.* guamá, a West-Indian tree much used for shade.

guama, *f.* fruit of the guamo.

guamo, *m.* guamo, a large fruit tree.

guanábana, *f.* bullock's-heart, custard apple.

guanábano, *m.* (bot.) custard apple (tree).

guanaco, *m.* guanaco, a kind of llama.

guanajo, *m.* (Cuba) turkey; (coll.) simpleton.

guancoche, *m.* (Mex., C. A.) burlap.

guanche, *n.* ancient inhabitant of the Canaries.

guando, *m.* (Am.) stretcher, litter.

guanera, *f.* place abounding in guano.

guanina, *f.* (bot.) (Am.) a leguminous plant.

guano, *m.* any palm tree; palm leaves used for thatching; guano, seabirds' dung used as fertilizer.

guantada, *f.*, **guantazo,** *m.* slap.

guante, *m.* glove; collection for charity.—*pl.* extra pay, fee, or tip.—**guantes de ante,** buff gloves.—**guantes de cabritilla,** kid gloves.—**echar el g. a,** to challenge; (coll.) to seize, grasp; to imprison.—**echar un g.,** to take a collection for charitable purposes.—**poner como un g.,** to render as pliable as a glove; (coll.) to abuse, dress down.—**salvo el g.,** (coll.) excuse my glove.

guantelete, *m.* gauntlet.

guantería, *f.* glove factory or shop; glove making.—**guantero, ra,** *n.* glover, glove maker.

guañín, *a.* base gold.

guañir, *vn.* to grunt like pigs.

guao, *m.* (Mex., S. Am.) a terebinthine tree whose seeds are used as hog feed and whose wood is used for charcoal; (West Indies) guao, a poisonous tree.

guapamente, *adv.* (coll.) bravely, courageously.

guapear, *vn.* (coll.) to boast of courage; (coll.) to take pride in fine dress.

guapetón, na, *a. aug.* brave, daring, bold.

guapeza, *f.* (coll.) bravery; ostentation in dress; good looks, handsomeness.

guapinal, *m.* (C. A.) a resin-yielding tree.

guapo, pa. I. *a.* (coll.) brave, daring; enterprising; good-looking or handsome; spruce, neat; ostentatious, vain; gay, sprightly. **II.** *m.* gallant, beau, lovemaker; brawler, quarrelsome person.

guapote, ta, *a.* (coll.) good-natured; good-looking, handsome.

guaquero, *m.* vessel for drinking chicha found in ancient Peruvian tombs.

guaracha, *f.* a Spanish clog dance; a Cuban song; (Mex.) sandal.

guaraná, *f.* (bot.) guarana, a Brazilian yielding astringent and nerve-stimulating substances.

guarango, ga. I. *a.* (Ch., Arg.) ill-bred, unmannerly. **II.** *m.* (Peru, Ec.) a species of wild prosopis; (Ven.) dividivi.

guaraní. I. *a.* Guaranian. **II.** *m.* Guarani.

guarapo, *m.* juice of the sugar cane; fermented cane liquor.

guarda. I. *n.* guard; keeper.—**g. de cota,** gamekeeper.—**g. de la aduana,** officer of the customhouse. **II.** *f.* custody; trust, wardship, safe-keeping; observance of a law or ordinance; nun who accompanies men through convents; outside rib or guard of a fan; (b. b.) flyleaf, blank sheet; ward of a lock or of a key; (mech.) guard plate, shoe; sheath of a pruning knife.—**g. bauprés,** (naut.) knight-heads, bollard timbers. **III.** *interj.* take care! beware! look out!

guardaaguas, *m.* (naut.) spurn water; (carp.) flashing board; (car) splash leather.

guardaagujas, *m.* (r. w.) switchman.

guardaalmacén, *m.* storekeeper.

guardamigo, *m.* prop placed under the chin of criminals while they are flogged.

guardabanderas, *m.* (naut.) yeoman of signals.

guardabarrera, *m.* (r. w.) gatekeeper.

guardabosque, *m.* forest keeper, gamekeeper.

guardabrazo, *m.* (arm.) brassard.

guardabrisa, *f.* glass shade for candles; (aut.) windshield.

guardacabras, *m.* goatherd.

guardacalada, *f.* opening in eaves.

guardacamisa, *f.* (Ven.) undershirt.

guardacantón, *m.* spurstone, checkstone.

guardacartuchos, *m.* (naut.) cartridge case.

guardacostas, *m.* (naut.) revenue cutter.

guardacuños, *m.* keeper of the dies in the mint.

guardadamas, *m.* officer who escorted ladies of the court.

guardadamente, *adv.* guardedly.

guardado, da, *pp. & a.* guarded, reserved.

guardador, ra. I. *a.* very thrifty and provident; law-abiding; stingy, miserly. **II.** *m.* guardian; (mil.) keeper of the spoils.

guardafrenos, *m.* (r. w.) brakeman.

guardafuego, *m.* (naut.) breaming board.

guardaguas, *m.* = GUARDAAGUAS.

guardahumo, *m.* (naut.) smoke sail.

guardainfante, *m.* farthingale, ladies' hoop.—*pl.* (naut.) capstan whelp.

guardaja, *f.* = GUEDEJA.

guardajoyas, *m.* keeper of the crown jewels; place where the crown jewels are kept.

guardalado, *m.* battlement of a bridge.

guardalmacén, *n.* = GUARDAALMACÉN.

guardalobo, *m.* (bot.) poet's cassia.

guardamalleta, *f.* lambrequin.

guardamancebo, *m.* (naut.) manrope.

guardamano, *f.* guard of a sword.

guardamateriales, *m.* buyer of bullion and other necessaries for a mint.

guardamigo, *m.* = GUARDAAMIGO.

guardamonte, *m.* (arti.) guard of a gunlock; forester, keeper of a forest.

guardamuebles, *m.* storeroom for furniture; guard over the furniture of a palace.

guardamujer, *f.* servant of the queen.

guardapapo, *m.* (arm.) gusset.

guardapelo, *m.* locket.

guardapesca, *n.* boat that inspects and guards fisheries.

guardapiés, *m.* skirt.

guardapolvo, *m.* dust guard; dust wrapper; cover; inner lid of a watch; projection over a window or door to carry off the water.

guardapuerta, *f.* storm door.

guardar. I. *va.* to keep; to guard, protect, watch over; to lay up, store, lay by, reserve; to observe, respect; to fulfil (one's duty).—**g. la cara,** to hide, to dissemble.—**g. miramientos,** to show regard or consideration.—**guardársela a uno, to** bide one's time to take revenge on. **II.** *vr.* (w. **de)** to guard (against), avoid, beware (of).

guardarraya, *f.* (Cuba) path in cane or coffee plantations; (min.) boundary of a drill hole.

guardarrío, *m.* (or a.) kingfisher.

guardarropa. I. *f.* wardroom, coat room. **II.** *m.* keeper of a wardrobe; wardrobe, clothespress; (bot.) lavender cotton.

guardarropía, *f.* (theat.) wardrobe.

guardarruedas, *m.* = GUARDACANTÓN.

guardasellos, *m.* seal keeper.

guardasol, *m.* = QUITASOL.

guardatimón, *m.* (naut.) stern chaser.

guardavajilla, *f.* room for keeping the (royal) plate or table service.

guardavía, *m.* (r. w.) signalman; lineman.

guardavientos, *m.* (agr.) protection from the wind.

guardera, *f.* female keeper.

guardería, *f.* keepership.

guardia. I. *f.* guard (body of armed men); defence, custody, protection; (naut.) watch; turn of persons in watching or of officers on duty; (fenc.) guard.—**g. civil,** body of rural police in Spain.—**g. de babor,** larboard watch.—**g. de corps,** life guard.—**g. de estribor,** starboard watch.—**g. del tope,** masthead lookout.—**g. municipal,** city police.—**g. valona,** Walloon guard.— **en g.,** on guard.—**estar de g.,** (mil.) to be on guard duty.—**montar la g.,** to mount guard.— **mudar la g.,** to relieve the guard.—**salir de g.,** to come off guard. **II.** *m.* soldier belonging to the guards, guardsman.—**g. civil,** a member of the rural police in Spain.—**g. marina,** midshipman.— **g. municipal,** policeman.

guardián, na. I. *n.* keeper, guardian, warden; watchman. **II.** *m.* local superior of convents of the order of St. Francis; (naut.) boatswain's mate; quarterman; gunner's yeoman; (naut.) strong hawser.

guardianía, *f.* guardianship of a convent and the district assigned to it.

guardilla, *f.* garret, attic; (sew.) guard, welt; each of the two extreme thick teeth of a comb.

guardín, *m.* (naut.) tiller rope, tiller chain; (naut.) port lanyard.

guardoso, sa, *a.* frugal, parsimonious; niggardly, stingy.

guarecer. I. *va.* (*ind.* GUAREZCO: *subj.* GUAREZCA) to shelter, protect, preserve; to cure. **II.** *vr.* to take refuge or shelter.

guarentigio, gia, *a.* (law) (contract) containing a warranty clause.

guarida, *f.* den, cave, lair of a wild beast; shelter; lurking place, cover, haunt.

guarimán, *m.* (bot.) (Am.) tree of the magnolia family, with aromatic bark used as spice.

guarín, *m.* suckling pig.

guarismo, *m.* (arith.) figure, digit; number.

guarne, *m.* (naut.) turn (of a cable or tackle).

guarnecedor, ra, *n. & a.* garnisher (-ing), furnisher (-ing), trimmer (-ing).

guarnecer, *va.* (*ind.* GUARNEZCO: *subj.* GUARNEZCA) to garnish, adorn, embellish, decorate, furbish; (sew.) to trim, bind, edge, face, border, line, welt; (jew.) set in gold, silver, etc.; (mas.) to plaster; (arm.) to put a guard on; to harness; (mil.) to garrison.

guarnecido. I. *pp.* of GUARNECER. **II.** *m.* (mas.) plastering; stucco work.

guarnés, *m.* harness room.

guarnición, *f.* (sew.) trimming, binding, edging, welt, flounce, furbelow, garniture, garnish, any ornamental hem, lace, or border; (jew.) setting; (mech.) packing; (arm.) guard of a sword; (mil.) garrison.—*pl.* gears or traces of mules and horses; harness; fixtures, fittings (for gas, electric lamps, etc.); accessories.

guarnicionar, *va.* (mil.) to garrison.

guarnicionería, *f.* harness maker's shop.

guarnicionero, *m.* harness maker.

guarniel, *m.* leather pouch with divisions or pockets, strapped accross the back and chest over one shoulder; (Mex.) powderflask.

guarnigón, *m.* (orn.) young quail.

guarnimiento, *m.* (naut.) lines or ropes for reeving.

guarnir, *va.* GUARNECER; (naut.) to reeve; to rig.

guaro, *m.* a very talkative small parrot; (C. A.) sugar-cane fire water.

guarra, *f.* sow.—**guarrillo,** *m. dim.* small pig.—**guarro,** *m.* hog.

¡guarte! *interj.* take care! beware! look out!

guaruba, *f.* (orn.) a red-necked American parrot; howling monkey.

guasa, *f.* (coll.) jest, fun, joke; dulness; (W. I.) (icht.) jewfish.

guasanga, *f.* (Cuba) noisy mirth.

guasanguero, ra, *a.* (Cuba) jolly, merry, noisy.

guasca, *f.* (Peru) piece of cord or rawhide; (Colomb.) strip of raw fiber, fibrous bark, etc., to tie with.—**dar g.,** to whip.

guaso, *m.* Gaucho; lasso.

guasón, na, *a.* (coll.) jocose, witty; dull, uninteresting.

guasquear, *va.* (Am.) to whip, to scourge.

guataca, *f.* (Cuba) spade; (coll.) large ear.

guataquear, *va.* (Cuba) to spade.

guatemalteco, ca, *n. & a.* Guatemalan.

guateque, *m.* (Cuba) country dance.

guatequear, *va.* (Cuba) to dance (as in the country).

guatiní, *m.* (Cuba) = TOCORORO.

guau, *m.* bowwow, the bark of a dog.

guavina, *f.* = GUABINA.

¡guay! *interj.* alas! alack!

guaya, *f.* grief, sorrow, affliction.

guayaba, *f.* fruit of the guava tree.

guayabal, *m.* guava-tree orchard or field.

guayabo, *m.* (bot.) guava tree.

guayacán, *m.* (bot.) lignum-vitæ, guaiacum.

guayacana, *f.* (bot.) date-plum.

guayaco, *m.* = GUAYACÁN.

guayacol, *m.* (chem.) guaiacol.

guayapil, guayapín, *m.* = HUIPIL.

guayaquileño, ña. I. *n.* Guayaquil man (woman). **II.** *a.* from, or relating to, Guayaquil.

guazubirá, *m.* an Argentine deer.

gubán, *m.* (Philip.) a large clinker-built canoe.

gubernamental, *a.* governmental.

gubernativamente, *adv.* by act of the government.

gubernativo, va, *a.* administrative, governmental, gubernatorial.

gubia, *f.* (carp.) gouge, centering chisel; (arti.) vent searcher.

gubiadura, *f.* notch, channel.

guedeja, *f.* long lock of hair; forelock; lion's mane.—**guedejilla,** *f. dim.* small lock of hair.

guedejón, na, joso, sa, judo, da, *a.* long-haired.

güeldo, *m.* shrimps, clams, etc., used as bait.

güelfo, fa, *n. & a.* Guelph.

guelte, gueltre, *m.* money, cash; wealth.

güemul, *m.* guemul, an Andean variety of deer.

güepil, *m.* (Mex.) = HUIPIL.

güérmeces, *m.* morbid swelling in the throat of birds of prey.

guerra, *f.* war, warfare.—**g. a muerte,** war without quarter, war to the death.—**g. de bolas, g. de**

palos, two different games of billiards.—**dar g.,** to cause annoyance or trouble.

guerreador, ra, *n. & a.* warrior (-ing), fighter (-ing).

guerreante, *n. & a.* warrior (-ing).

guerrear, *vn.* to war, wage war, fight.

guerreramente, *adv.* warlike.

guerrero, ra. I. *a.* martial, warlike. **II.** *m.* warrior, fighter, soldier, military man.

guerrilla, *f. dim.* guerrilla; body of partisans, skirmishers, or light horsemen; skirmish, light engagement; a card game.

guerrillear, *vn.* to engage in guerrilla warfare.

guerrillero, *m.* (mil.) guerrilla man.

guía. I. *n.* guide, cicerone; leader, director, adviser.—**g. de forasteros,** court guide. **II.** *m.* (mil.) guide. **III.** *f.* guide, guide sign; guidebook; directory; (mech.) guide, rule, guide bar, guide pin, guide screw, guide tube, etc.; (com.) customhouse permit, cocket; driving shaft of a noria; (agr.) young shoot left on a vine or tree for training others; young shoot or sucker of a vine; (naut.) guy, leader, span, hauling-line, preventer-rope; (min.) leader; handlebar of a bicycle; guard of a fan; leader, foremost horse; (pyr.) fuse.—*pl.* guide lines, reins for controlling the leader horses.—**a guías,** driving four-in-hand.

guiadera, *f.* guide or conductor in mills; upright guide in oil mills, lifts, etc.

guiado, da, *pp. & a.* guided; having a guide or a permit.

guiador, ra, *n.* guide, director, leader.

guiar. I. *va.* to guide, lead; to drive; to pilot; (agr.) to train (a plant). **II.** *vr.* (w. **por**) to go or be governed (by), to follow.

guiguí, *m.* (Philip.) (zool.) flying squirrel.

guija, *f.* pebble; gravel; (bot.) ALMORTA.—*pl.* (coll.) strength, force, vigor.

guijarral, *m.* place abounding in pebbles.

guijarrazo, *m.* blow with a pebble or a cobble.

guijarreño, ña, *a.* pebbly, gravelly; hardy, strong.

guijarrillo, ito, *m. dim.* small pebble.

guijarro, *m.* pebble, cobble

guijarroso, sa, *a.* pebbly.

guijeño, ña, *a.* belonging to or resembling pebbles; hard, relentless.

guijo, *m.* gravel.

guijón, *m.* = NEGUIJÓN.

guijoso, sa, *a.* gravelly, pebbly.

guilalo, *m.* (Philip.) coasting vessel with sails of matting.

guilla, *f.* plentiful harvest.

guillame, *m.* joiner's rabbeting plane.

guillote, *m.* husbandman who enjoys the produce of a farm; (naut.) treenail or iron pin; vagrant, sponger; idle fellow; novice gambler.

guillotina, *f.* guillotine; cardboard-cutting machine.—**de g.,** sliding.

guillotinar, *va.* to guillotine.

guimbalete, *m.* pump brake, pump handle.

guimbarda, *f.* an ancient dance; (carp.) grooving plane.

guinchar, *va.* to prick, goad.

guincho, *m.* goad, pike; (Cuba) sea gull.

guinda, *f.* (bot.) berry of the mazard; (naut.) height of the masts (and top-masts).—**echar guindas a la tarasca,** (coll.) to be very easy.

guindado, da, *pp. & a.* hoisted, set up; garnished with mazard berries.

guindajos, *m. pl.* (Cuba) hangings, fringe, tassels.

guindal, *m.* (bot.) mazard tree.

guindalera, *f.* plantation of mazard trees.

guindaleta, *f.* crank rope; fulcrum of a balance.

guindaleza, *f.* (naut.) hawser.

guindamaina, *f.* salute by dipping the flag.

guindar. I. *va.* to hang on high; (coll.) to obtain or procure in competition with others; (coll.) to hang (a person). **II.** *vn.* to be suspended, to hang.

guindaste, *m.* (mech.) horse, frame; (naut.) timber head jeer, knighthead of the jeers.

---

guindilla, *f. dim.* pod of the red pepper.

guindillo de Indias, *m.* (bot.) shrub of the capsicum family; red pepper.

guindo, *m.* (bot.) mazard tree.—**g. griego,** large mazard cherry tree.

guindola, *f.* (naut.) triangular hanging stage; life buoy.

guinea, *f.* guinea, English gold coin.

guineo, a. I. *a.* Guinea, of Guinea.—**g. manzano,** (Cuba) = CAMBRIR.—**gallina g.,** Guinea hen. **II.** *m.* a negro dance; (Cuba) banana.

guinga, *f.* gingham.

guinja, *f.* **guinjo,** *m.* jujube.

guinjo, guinjolero, *m.* (bot.) jujube tree.

guiñada, *f.* wink; (naut.) yaw, lurch.

guiñador, ra, *n.* & *a.* winker (-ing).

giñadura, *f.* = GUIÑADA.

guiñapiento, ta; guiñaposo, sa, *a.* ragged, tattered, torn.—**guiñapo,** *m.* tatter, rag; ragamuffin, tatterdemalion.

guiñar, *va.* to wink; (naut.) to yaw, to lurch.

guiño, *m.* = GUIÑADA.

guión, *m.* cross, standard carried before prelates and corporations; gonfalon in processions; royal standard; master of ceremonies; leader of a dance; hyphen; explanatory text or reference table; (mil.) guidon; (mus.) repeat; (naut.) loom of an oar.

guionaje, *m.* office of guide or conductor.

guipar, *va.* (coll. and vulgar) to see.

güipil, *m.* (Mex.) = HUIPIL.

guipuzcoano, na. I. *n.* & *a.* native of or belonging to the province of Guipúzcoa. **II.** *m.* one of the Basque dialects.

guira, *f.* (bot.) calabash tree.

guirgüiesco, ca, *a.* = GREGÜISCO.

guiri, *n.* anti-Carlist; Liberal.

guirigay, *m.* (coll.) gibberish; jargon.

guirindola, *f.* frill of a shirt.

guirlache, *m.* roast almond caramel; brittle.

guirlanda, guirnalda, *f.* garland, wreath; (naut.) puddening; (mil.) light ball.

guirnaldeta, *f. dim.* small garland.

güiro, *m.* bottle gourd, fruit of the calabash tree; (Cuba) gourd used as an instrument to accompany dance music; (Arg., etc.) green corn stalk.

guirre, *m.* (prov. Canaries) vulture.

guisa, *f.* manner, fashion.—**a g. de,** like, in the manner of.

guisado, *pp.* & *m.* stew; ragout, fricassee.

guisador, ra; guisandero, ra, *n.* cook.

guisantal, *m.* pea patch.

guisante, *m.* (bot.) pea.—**g. de olor,** sweet pea.

guisar, *va.* to cook or dress (victuals); to arrange, prepare, adjust.

guiso, *m.* cooked dish; seasoning, condiment.

guisopillo, *m.* = HISOPILLO.

guisote, *m.* poorly cooked dish.

guita, *f.* packthread, twine; (coll.) money.

guitar, *va.* to sew with packthread.

guitarra, *f.* (mus.) guitar; (mas.) muller for pulverizing gypsum.—**guitarrazo,** *m.* blow with a guitar.—**guitarrear,** *vn.* to play the guitar.—**guitarrero, ra,** *n.* guitar maker; guitar player.—**guitarresco, ca,** *a.* (coll.) belonging to the guitar.—**guitarrillo,** *m.*; **lla,** *f. dim.* small guitar.

guitarrista, *n.* guitar player.—**guitarro,** *m.* (mus.) small four-string guitar.—**guitarrón,** *m. aug.* large guitar; (coll.) cunning knave.

guitero, ra, *n.* twine maker.

guito, ta, *a.* treacherous, vicious (as a mule).

guitón, na. I. *n.* mendicant, vagrant, vagabond, tramp. **II.** *m.* an ancient coin.

guitonear, *vn.* to loiter, loaf, idle about.

guitonería, *f.* idleness; vagabond life.

guizazo, *m.* (Cuba) (bot.) a kind of weed.

guizgar, *va.* to excite, invite.

guizque, *m.* hook of a hanging lamp.

guja, *f.* (arm.) vouge or voulge.

gula, *f.* gluttony, inordinate appetite.

gules, *m. pl.* (her.) gules, red.

guloso, sa, *a.* gluttonous; greedy.

gulusmear, *vn.* (coll.) = GOLOSINEAR.

gullería, *f.* dainty.

gulloría, *f.* (orn.) a kind of lark. *V.* GOLLERÍA.

gúmena, *f.* (naut.) cable.—**gumeneta,** *f. dim.* (naut.) small cable.

gumía, *f.* a kind of dagger or poniard.

gumífero, ra, *a.* gum-producing, gummiferous.

gura, *f.* (orn.) (Philip.) a crested wild pigeon.

gurbión, *m.* coarse twisted silk; heavy-yarn silk cloth; spurge gum resin.

gurdo, da, *a.* silly, simple, nonsensical.

gurriato, *m.* nestling sparrow.

gurrufero, *m.* (coll.) deformed and vicious nag.

gurrumina, *f.* (coll.) uxoriousness, unbecoming submission to a wife.

gurrumino, na. I. *a.* mean, contemptible. **II.** *n.* (C. A.) boy, girl, child. **III.** *f.* (C. A.) trifle. **IV.** *m.* (coll.) henpecked husband.

gurullada, *f.* (coll.) = GRULLADA.

gurullo, *m.* lump or knot.

gurullón, *m.* a knot of wool in cloths.

gurumete, *m.* ship's boy. *V.* GRUMETE.

gurupa, *f.* croup of a horse. *V.* GRUPA.

gurupera, *f.* crupper. *V.* GRUPERA.

gurupetín, *m. dim.* small crupper.

gurvio, a, *a.* curved (s. o. tools).

gurvión, *m.* = GURBIÓN.

gusanear, *vn.* to itch. *V.* HORMIGUEAR.

gusanera, *f.* place where worms or microbes are bred; (coll.) ruling passion.

gusanico, ito, *m. dim.* small worm.

gusaniento, ta, *a.* grubby, full of vermin, maggoty, worm-eaten.

gusanillo, *m. dim.* small worm or grub; (sew.) gold, silver, or silk twist; twist-stitch embroidery; (mech.) bit of a gimlet or auger.

gusano, *m.* (zool.) worm, grub, caterpillar; threadworm, pinworm; meek, dejected person; distemper of sheep.—**g. de la conciencia,** worm of conscience, remorse.—**g. de luz** = LUCIÉRNAGA. —**g. de San Antón,** gray grub.—**g. de seda,** silkworm.—**g. revoltón,** vine inchworm.

gusarapiento, ta, *a.* wormy, grubby; filthy; rotten.

gusarapillo, ito, *m. dim.* small water worm.

gusarapo, *m.* water worm; any annelid found in liquids, especially vinegar.

gustable, *a.* tastable, gustable.

gustadura, *f.* gustation, tasting.

gustar. I. *va.* to taste; to try. **II.** *vn.* to be pleasing, to cause pleasure. Gen. this verb is rendered by "to like," but changing the construction: *esto me gusta,* I like this; *¿le gusta a Vd. la música?* do you like music? *la comida nos gustó mucho,* we liked the dinner very much; *como Vd. guste,* as you like, as you will.—**g. de,** to like, to have a liking for.

gustativo, *a.* lingual (as a nerve).

gustazo, *m. aug.* (coll.) great pleasure.

gustillo, *m. dim.* peculiar flavor, or relish.

gusto, *m.* taste; tasting; pleasure; liking; will, determination; choice; discernment; caprice, fancy, whim; diversion.—**a g.,** at will, to one's taste or judgment.—**con mucho g.,** with great pleasure.—**cosa de g.,** tasty, fancy article.—**dar g.,** to gratify, to please.—**darse g.,** to indulge in pleasure, to have a good time; to live well.—**de buen (mal) g.,** in good (bad) taste.—**de mí g.,** to my taste.—**el g. del día,** prevailing taste or fashion.—**tener g. en,** to take pleasure in, to be glad to.—**tener g. por,** to have a taste for, to like.

gustosamente, *adv.* tastefully; fain, gladly.

gustoso, sa, *a.* savory, palatable; tasty; cheerful, merry, joyful; pleasing, pleasant; willing, ready.

gutagamba, *m.* gamboge.

gutapercha, *f.* gutta-percha.

gutiámbar, *m.* gamboge.

gutífero, ra, *a.* guttiferous, gum-yielding.

gutural, *a.* guttural.

guturalmente, *adv.* gutturally.

guzmán, *m.* nobleman who formerly served as midshipman or cadet.

H

ha, *verbal form.* V. HABER.

¡ha! [ah], *interj.* ah! alas!

haba, *f.* broad bean or horse bean; bean; kernel; ballot (ball); (vet.) tumor in the palate of horses; (min.) prill.—**h. común caballar,** (bot.) horse bean.—**h. de Egipto,** Egyptian bean.—**h. de las Indias,** sweet pea.—**h. de San Ignacio,** St. Ignatius' bean.—**h. marina,** navelwort, kidneywort.—**h. tonca,** Tonca bean.—**esas son habas contadas,** that is a sure thing; that is as clear as daylight.

habado, da, *a.* (vet.) having HABAS; dappled (as a horse).

habanera, *f.* (mus.) a Cuban air and dance tune.

habanero, ra, *a.* Havanese, of Havana.

habano. I. *a.* Havana (u. a.). **II.** *m.* Havana cigar.

habar, *m.* bean field.

habascón, *m.* (S. Am.) a parsniplike root.

hábeas corpus, *m.* habeas corpus.

háber, *m.* doctor of the law among the Jews.

haber. I. *va.* (ind. HE: pret. HUBE, él HUBO: fut. HABRÉ: subj. HAYA) to have, own, possess; (gen. passive) to catch, lay hands on; to get (*el ladrón no pudo ser habido,* the thief could not be caught; *el niño lee cuantos libros puede haber,* the boy reads all the books he can get). **II.** *v. auxil.* to have (*haber hablado,* to have spoken: *habiendo hablado,* having spoken; *yo he hablado,* I have spoken). **III.** *vn.* (w. de) to have to, must (*hemos de salir,* we have to, or must, go out; *ha de saber Vd.,* you must know). **IV.** *v. imp.* there to be (that is, "there" followed by the appropriate form of "to be"), to take place. In this sense, the third person of the indicative is **hay,** and only the third person singular is used in all modes and tenses, for the verb has no subject: the word or phrase which in English is the subject of the equivalent "to be" is in Spanish the accusative, not the subject, of "haber" (*hay peligro,* there is danger; *aqui hay un buen teatro,* there is a good theater here; *en Colombia hay muchas minas,* there are many mines in Colombia; *ayer hubo dos accidentes,* there were two accidents yesterday; *mañana no habrá escuela,* there will be no school tomorrow). The form **ha,** applied to time, has the adverbial value of "ago" (*dos años ha,* two years ago).—**h. que,** (3rd. pers. pres. ind., hay) to be necessary, must (ch. constr.: *hay que ir,* it is necessary to go; *hay que escribir una carta,* it is necessary to write a letter, a letter must be written).—**no hay de qué,** you are welcome.—**no hay más que,** there is nothing more to; there is nothing but; it is enough, it suffices. V. *vr.* **habérselas con,** to deal with; to face, to cope with.

haber, *m.* in bookkeeping, credit, Cr.; (gen. *pl. haberes*) property, possessions, estate.—**h. monedado,** coin, specie.

haberio, *m.* beast of burden.

habichuela, *f.* (bot.) French bean **or** kidney bean.—**h. verde,** string bean.

habiente, *a.* (law) having, possessing.

hábil, *a.* capable, skillful.

habilidad, *f.* ability, skill; talent.—*pl.* accomplishments.

habilidoso, sa, *a.* skillful, able.

habilitación, *f.* habilitation, qualification; outfit, equipment; (mil.) office and bureau of a paymaster.—**h. de bandera,** concession to a foreign vessel to engage in the coasting trade.

habilitado, da. I. *pp.* & *a.* qualified; competent. **II.** *m.* paymaster.

habilitador, ra, *n.* qualifier; outfitter.

habilitar, *va.* to qualify, enable; to provide, supply with, fit out, equip.

hábilmente, *adv.* ably, skillfully.

habitabilidad, *f.* habitability, habitableness.

habitable, *a.* habitable.

habitación, *f.* dwelling, residence, habitation, abode, lodging; room, chamber, suite of rooms, apartment; (law) caretaking; habitat.

habitáculo, *m.* dwelling, residence, abode.

habitador, ra, *n.* inhabitant, resident, dweller.

habitante. I. *a.* inhabiting. **II.** *n.* inhabitant; dweller, resident.

habitar, *va.* to inhabit, live, dwell, reside.

hábito, *m.* dress, habit, habiliment, garment; habit, custom.—*pl.* dress of ecclesiastics; robes of the military orders.

habituación, *f.* habit, custom.

habitual, *a.* habitual, usual, customary.

habitualmente, *adv.* customarily, usually.

habituar. I. *va.* to accustom, habituate, inure. **II.** *vr.* to become accustomed, accustom one's self, get used.

habitud, *f.* relation, connection.

habla, *f.* speech; language, tongue; dialect; conversation, talk.—**al h.** (naut.) within speaking distance.—**estar en h.,** to talk.—**estar sin h.,** or **perder el h.,** to lose or become speechless.—**negar,** or **quitar, el h.,** to cease speaking to, to cut.

hablado, da, *pp.* & *a.*—**bien h.,** using choice language.—**mal h.,** using vile or vulgar language.

hablador, ra. I. *a.* talkative. **II.** *n.* talker, gabbler, prattler, chatterbox; gossip.

habladorcillo, lla, *n. dim.* babbling dandiprat.

habladuría, *f.* impertinent speech; gossip, empty talk.

hablante, *a.* speaking, talking.

hablanchín, na; hablantín, na, *n.* (coll.) talkative person.

hablar. I. *vn.* to speak; to talk, converse.—**h. a,** to speak to; to hail (a ship).—**h. a chorros,** to speak fast.—**h. a destajo,** (coll.) to talk much and at random.—**h. a gritos,** to shout.—**h. al alma,** to speak things that touch the quick.—**h. alto,** to speak loud.—**h. a tontas y a locas,** to speak recklessly or disconnectedly.—**h. claro,** to speak in plain language, to call a spade a spade.—**h. con,** to speak with; to court, to woo.—**h. de,** to speak, or talk, of or about.—**h. de chanza,** to joke, to speak in jest.—**h. en griego,** or **en gringo,** to talk gibberish, to talk Greek (fig.).—**h. en plata** = H. CLARO.—**h. entre dientes,** to mutter, to mumble.—**h. gordo,** to bully, to bluff.—**h. por boca de ganso,** to speak from hearsay; to be a mouthpiece.—**h. por h.,** to talk for the sake of talking.—**h. por los codos,** to talk incessantly, to chatter.—**estar hablando,** to be perfect; to be manifest. **II.** *va.* to speak, utter, say.—**h. disparates,** to talk nonsense. **III.** *vr.* to speak to each other; to be on speaking terms.

hablilla, *f.* rumor, gossip, report, little tale.

hablista, *n.* scholar, scholarly writer.

hablistán, *n.* (coll.) prattler, chatterer.

habón, *m. aug.* wheat, whelk.

haca, *f.* pony, pad, small horse.

hacán, *m.* learned man among the Jews.

hacanea, *f.* nag, small horse.

hacecico, illo, ito, *m. dim.* small sheaf; fascicle.—**h. de rayos luminosos,** pencil of luminous rays.

hacedero, ra, *a.* feasible, practicable.

hacedor, *m.* maker; steward, manager of a farm.—**el H.,** the Creator, the Maker.

hacendado, da. I. *a.* & *pp.* acred, landed, owning real estate. **II.** *m.* landholder, farmer, planter, rancher.

hacendar. I. *va.* to transfer or make over. **II.** *vr.* to purchase real estate.

hacendeja, *f. dim.* small farm or ranch.

hacendera, *f.* public work at which all the neighborhood assists.

hacendero, ra, *a.* industrious, sedulous.

hacendilla, duela, *f. dim.* small farm or ranch.

hacendista, *m.* (pol.) economist; financier.

hacendoso, sa, *a.* assiduous, industrious.

hacer, *va.* (pp. HECHO: ind. yo HAGO, él HACE: pret. yo HICE, él HIZO: fut. HARÉ: subj. HAGA) to make; to produce, form; to prepare; conceive, devise, compose; deliver, utter (as a plan, a poem, a speech); to arrange, make (a bed), pack (a trunk, valise); to shed, cast, project (as a shadow); to raise, produce (as dust, smoke); to do; to gain, earn; to accustom, inure; to assemble, convoke; to act, perform (as a play, a part); to do, execute, carry out; to suppose, think (*yo hacía a Juan en*

Paris, I thought John was in Paris; *le haciamos muy rico*, we supposed he was very rich); to hold in, feel, have (*hacer estimación*, or *aprecio*, to hold in esteem, to have regard for); (followed by *inf.*), to order, have (followed by *pp.*: *Juan hizo construir la casa*, John had the house built; *Juan hizo nombrar a Pedro*, John had Peter appointed); (followed by *inf.*) to make, compel (*la haremos confesar*, we shall make her confess; *lo hice firmar*, I made him sign).—**h. agua,** (naut.) to leak.—**h. alarde,** to boast.—**h. ánimo,** to mean, to purpose.—**h. antesala,** to dance attendance, to be kept waiting.—**h. bancarrota,** to fail, to become bankrupt. —**h. bola,** to play hookey; to stay away.—**h. buen tercio,** to do a good turn.—**h. cara, h. cara a,** to face, resist, oppose.—**h. con,** to supply, provide, furnish (*te haré con dinero*, I will provide thee with money).—**h. caso,** to mind, pay attention.—**h. caso de,** to take into account, pay attention to.— **h. corrales** = H. BOLA.—**h. cuentas,** to figure, reckon; to estimate.—**h. chacota** (w. de) to ridicule, to turn into ridicule.—**h. daño a,** to hurt, harm; not to agree with (s. o. effect of food on persons).—**h. de** = H. CON.—**h. de las suyas,** to play one's tricks, to run true to type.—**h. de tripas corazón,** to pluck up courage or heart.—**h. diligencia,** to try, to endeavor, to take measures.—**h. el favor,** to do the favor (*hágame el favor*, do me the favor, please).—**h. fiesta,** to take a holiday.—**h. fiestas a,** to fondle, caress; cajole; fawn to.—**h. frente** = H. CARA.—**h. fuego,** (mil.) to fire.—**h. fuerza,** to struggle; to exert force; to carry weight, exert influence, appeal.—**h. fuerza a,** to do violence to; to impress, convince.—**h. fuerza de vela,** (naut.) to crowd sail.—**h. gasto,** to spend.— **h. h.,** to have made, cause to be made, order to be made.—**h. juego,** to be well matched.—**hacerla,** to act unworthily; to fall below expectations; to act (with modifying word indicating the character of the action—usually bad).—**h. la barba,** to shave; (Mex.) to flatter.—**h. la corte,** to court, to woo; to pay court in palace.—**h. la cuenta,** to figure out.—**h. la cuenta sin la huéspeda,** to reckon without the host.—**h. la guerra,** to war, to wage or make war.—**h. las amistades,** to become reconciled, make up.—**h. la vista gorda,** to wink at, to connive at.—**h. limosna,** to give alms.— **hacerlo bien (mal),** to perform, or acquit one's self, well (badly).—**h. mal,** to do wrong, harm; to act wrongly; to be injurious.—**h. mal de ojo,** to fascinate.—**h. memoria de,** to remember.—**h. milagros,** to do wonders.—**h. mofa de,** to mock, scoff.—**h. morisquetas,** to play pranks.—**h. papel,** to cut a figure; to play a part.—**h. pedazos,** to break or tear into pieces; to break (as the heart). **h. presente,** to remind of, call attention to.—**h. que,** to pretend, feign; to have, order (ch. constr.: *hace que escribe*, he pretends to be writing; *haga que lo traigan*, have it brought).—**h. saber,** to make known; to inform, notify.—**h. señas,** to motion.—**h. su agosto,** to make hay while the sun shines.—**h. su apacheta,** to have made a fortune; to make one's pile.—**h. vela,** (naut.) to set sail.— **h. ver,** to show, demonstrate.—**¿qué hace?** a form of greeting) how do you do? how are you?

hacer, *vn.* to matter, signify; to be pertinent, or to the purpose (*¿qué le hace?* what does it matter? *eso no hace al caso*, that has nothing to do with the case); to agree, accord, match (*esto no hace con eso*, this does not agree with (or match) that).—**h. como que, h. como si,** to act as if.—**h. de,** to act as (*hacer de notario*, to act as a notary; *hago de carpintero*, I am doing a carpenter's work). —**h. del** (*f.* **de la**) to pretend to be, to play the (*hacer del bobo*, to play the idiot).—**h. del cuerpo,** to go to stool.—**h. el** (*f.* **la**) = H. DEL.—**h. para, h. por,** to endeavor, to try, make an effort, do one's best to (*haré por venir*, I will endeavor to come; *hacer por*, or *para, salvarse*, to strive to save one's self).—**h. por h.,** to act to no purpose.—**h. por la vida,** to eat something.

hacer, *v. impers.* (referring to the state of the weather and followed by a noun) to be (with "it" as subject: *hace mal tiempo*, it is bad weather; *hace buen día*, it is a good day), or to be (with "it" as subject and followed by the corresponding English adjective: *hace calor*, it is warm; *hace viento*, it is windy). Applied to a lapse of time, it is rendered by "to be," with "it" as subject, or by "ago" (*hace un año*, it is now one year, or a year ago; *ayer hizo un mes*, a month ago yesterday, or it was a month yesterday).

hacer, *vr.* (**hacerse**) to become, to grow; to move, shift, recede, draw aside; to inflict upon one's self (as a wound, a scratch); to pretend to be, pass one's self off for.—**h. a,** to become accustomed or inured to; to come by, acquire.—**h. a la vela,** (naut.) to set sail.—**h. añicos,** to break to smithereens.—**h. chiquito,** to pretend to be modest; to conceal one's knowledge.—**hacérsele a uno,** to be . . . to one, to seem . . . to one (*eso se me hace misterioso*, that seems mysterious to me). —**h. de miel,** to be sweet, lenient, or obliging.— **h. de rogar,** to like to be coaxed.—**h. pedazos,** to break into, or to, pieces.—**h. tarde,** to grow late.— **h. tortilla,** to fall down flat.

hacera, *f.* sidewalk.

hacezuelo, *m. dim.* of HAZ.

hacia, *prep.* toward, in a direction to; near, about.—**h. acá,** hither.—**h. adelante,** forward.— **h. allá,** thither.—**h. atrás,** backward.—**h. casa,** homeward.—**h. dónde,** whither, toward which (what) place, where.—**h. el cielo,** heavenward.— **h. el mar,** seaward.—**h. popa,** (naut.) abaft.— **h. proa,** (naut.) afore.

hacienda, *f.* landed property; plantation; farm; ranch; estate, fortune, wealth; finance.—*pl.* domestic work, household duties.—**h. de beneficio** (Mex., min.) reduction works.—**h. pública,** public treasury; public funds; public finances.—**real h.,** public treasury, public funds (in a monarchy).

hacina, *f.* (agr.) shock, stack; pile, heap.

hacinador, ra, *n.* (agr.) stack maker.

hacinamiento, *m.* accumulation; heaping or stacking.

hacinar, *va.* (agr.) to stack; to pile, heap; accumulate; to hoard.

hacha, *f.* axe; large taper with four wicks; an ancient Spanish dance; (naut.) link.—**h. de armas,** battle axe, twibill.—**h. de viento,** flambeau, torch.

hachazo, *m.* blow or stroke with an axe.

hache, *f.* name of the letter *h*.

hachear. I. *va.* to cut with an axe; to hew. **II.** *vn.* to strike with an axe.

hachero, *m.* torch stand; (mil.) axeman; woodman, woodcutter, lumberman.

hacheta, *f. dim.* small axe or hatchet; small torch or link.

hacho, *m.* torch or link; beacon hill.

hachón, *m.* large torch or link; cresset.

hachote, *m. aug.* large axe.

hachuela, *f. dim.* small hatchet or axe; hand axe, adze.

hada, *f.* fairy.

hadar, *va.* to divine, foretell; to enchant.

hado, *m.* fate, destiny, doom.

hagiografía, *f.* (eccl.) hagiography.

hagiógrafo, *m.* hagiographer.

hago, haga. *V.* HACER.

haitiano, na, *n.* & *a.* Haitian.

¡hala! *interj.* (naut.) pull! haul!

halagador, ra. I. *a.* promising, rosy; flattering; coaxing. **II.** *n.* flatterer, cajoler, coaxer.

halagar, *va.* (*pret.* HALAGUÉ: *subj.* HALAGUE) to cajole, to flatter; to coax, allure, wheedle; to fondle, treat with tenderness.

halago, *m.* cajolery, flattery; caress, cooing.

halagüeñamente, *adv.* endearingly, flatteringly; promisingly, alluringly.

halagüeño, ña, *a.* endearing; attractive, alluring, promising, bright; fawning, flattering.

halar, **I.** *va.* (naut.) to haul, pull, tow. **II.** *vn.* to pull ahead.

halcón, *m.* (orn.) falcon.—**halconado, da,** *a.* falconlike.—**halconcico, illo, ito,** *m. dim.* jashawk.—**halconear,** *va.* (coll.) to inveigle, allure.— **halconera,** *f.* place where falcons are kept.— **halconería,** *f.* falconry.—**halconero,** *m.* falconer, hawk trainer.

halda, *f.* skirt (*v.* FALDA); a lapful; packing bag.—**haldas en cinta,** (coll.) disposed and ready for anything.—**de haldas o de mangas,** (coll.) justly or unjustly, with good or ill will, in any way.—**haldada,** *f.* skirtfull.—**haldear,** *vn.* to run along with the skirts flying loose.—**haldica, illa, ita,** *f. dim.* small skirt.—**halduda, da,** *a.* full-skirted.

haleche, *m.* (icht.) anchovy.

halieto, *m.* (orn.) sea eagle.

haliéutico, ca, *f.* halieutic, relating to fishing.

hálito, *m.* breath; vapor, effluvium; breeze.

halo, *m.* (ast.) halo.

halófilo, la, *a.* (bot.) halophilous.

halógeno, na, *a.* (chem.) halogen.

halografía, *f.* (chem.) halography.

haloideo, a, *a.* (chem.) haloid.

halón, *m.* (ast.) halo.

haloque, *m.* (naut.) an ancient small vessel.

haloza, *f.* wooden shoe.

hallado, da, *pp.* & *a.* found.—**bien h.,** welcome; easy, contented.—**mal h.,** uneasy, constrained.

hallador, ra, *n.* finder, discoverer.

hallar. I. *va.* to find; come across; to find out; to discover; to detect, catch; to understand, solve, interpret, decipher. **II.** *vr.* to be (in a place); to reside; to feel (as to health), to fare; to be pleased or content in a place.

hallazgo, *m.* act of finding; find, thing found; recovering anything lost; reward.

hallulla, *f.* **hallullo,** *m.* cake baked on or under cinders.

hamaca, *f.* hammock; hammock carriage.

hamaquero, *m.* hammock maker; hammock bearer; hammock hook.

hambre, *f.* hunger; appetite; famine; greediness; eagerness, longing, desire.—**h. canina,** canine appetite, inordinate hunger.—**h. y valentía,** pride and poverty.—**tener h.,** to be hungry.

hambrear. I. *va.* to hunger, starve, famish; to subdue by famine. **II.** *vn.* to hunger, to be hungry.

hambrientamente, *adv.* hungrily.

hambriento, ta, *a.* hungry; starved; greedy, covetous; longing; (Colomb., coll.) stingy.

hambrón, na, *n.* (coll.) hungry person.

hamburgués, sa, *a.* from or relative to Hamburg, Hamburg (u. a.)

hamez, *f.* distemper in falcons that makes them lose their feathers.

hamo, *m.* fishhook.

hampa, *f.* life of a company of rogues and vagabonds formerly in Andalusia.

hampesco, ca, *a.* vagabond, villainous.

hampo, hampón, *m.* rowdy, bully.

hanega, *f.* a dry measure. *V.* FANEGA.

hanegada, *f.* land ‸sown with a FANEGA of corn.

han(n)overiano, na, *n.* & *a.* Hanoverian.

hansa, *f.* Hanse, Hanseatic League.

hanseático, ca, *a.* Hanseatic.

haragán, na. I. *n.* idler, loiterer, loafer; idle, lazy person. **II.** *a.* idle, slothful, indolent.

haraganamente, *adv.* idly, lazily, slothfully.

haraganear, *vn.* to lead an idle life; to be lazy, to act the truant; to lounge, idle, loiter.

haraganería, *f.* idleness, laziness, sloth.

harapo, *m.* tatter, rag.—**harapiento, ta; haraposo, sa,** *a.* ragged, tattered.

harca, *f.* military expedition; expeditionary forces.

harem, harén, *m.* harem.

harija, *f.* mill dust, stive.

harina, *f.* flour, meal; farina; breadstuffs; powder, dust.

harinado, *m.* flour dissolved in water.

harinero, ra. I. *a.* made of or relating to flour. **II.** *m.* mealman, flour dealer; flour chest.

harinoso, sa, *a.* mealy; farinaceous; flourlike.

harmonía, harmonio, harmonioso, etc. = ARMONÍA, ARMONIO, etc.

harnerico, illo, ito, *m. dim.* small sieve.

harnero, *m.* sieve, sifter.—**estar hecho un h.,** to be covered with wounds.

harón, na, *a.* slow, sluggish; balky.—**haronear,** *vn.* to dawdle, move sluggishly; to be tardy or slow; to balk.—**haronía,** *f.* sluggishness, laziness.

harpa, harpado = ARPA, ARPADO.

harpía, *f.* harpy.

harpillera, *f.* burlap; sackcloth.

hartada, *f.* = HARTAZGO.

hartar, *va.* & *vr.* (*pp.* HARTADO and HARTO) to glut, stuff, gorge: to sate, satiate, gratify desire; to satisfy, cloy, fill to excess.

hartazgo, hartazón, *m.* satiety, glut, fill.

harto, ta. I. *a.* satiate, satiated, glutted, full; sufficient, full, complete. **II.** *adv.* enough or sufficiently.

hartura, *f.* satiety, glut, fill; plethora, superabundance; full gratification.

hasta. I. *prep.* till, until; up to, down to; as far as.—**h. ahora,** heretofore, hitherto.—**h. aquí,** heretofore; thus far, up to here.—**h. después, h. luego,** good-bye, so long.—**h. no más,** to the utmost. **II.** *conj.* also even.

hastial, *m.* (arch.) gable wall; coarse, rude man; (min.) side face of a gallery.

hastiar, *va.* to loathe, disgust; cloy, sate.

hastío, *m.* loathing, disgust; wearisomeness.

hataca, *f.* large wooden ladle; rolling pin.

hatajar, *va.* to divide (cattle) into flocks or herds.

hatajo, *m.* small herd or flock; (coll.) lot, multitude, lots.

hatear, *vn.* to collect one's traps when travelling; to supply shepherds with provisions.

hatería, *f.* allowance of provisions and clothes for shepherds.

hatero, ra. I. *a.* (animals) that carry a shepherd's baggage. **II.** *m.* carrier of provisions to shepherds; (Cuba) cowboy; cattle herder.

hatijo, *m.* covering of straw or feather grass over beehives.

hatillo, *m. dim.* small bundle; a few clothes; (Colomb.) a sort of telescoping rawhide hamper.—**coger el h.,** (coll.) to quit, to pack and go.—**echar el h. al mar,** (coll.) to lose one's temper.—**tomar su h.** = COGER EL H.

hato, *m.* herd of cattle; flock of sheep; (Am.) farm or cattle ranch; shepherds' lodge; provisions for shepherds; clothes, wearing apparel; heap, lot, cluster; gang, band or meeting of suspicious people.

haxix, *m.* hasheesh.

hay, *impers. irr. form* of HABER: there is, there are.

haya, *verbal form. V.* HABER.

haya, *f.* (bot.) beech tree.

hayal, hayedo, *m.* beech forest or field.

hayo, *m.* (Am.) (bot.) coca; coca leaves prepared for chewing.

hayuco, *m.* beech mast, fruit of the beech.

haz [abth‸]. **I.** *m.* fagot, fascine, bundle, bunch; (agr.) gavel, sheaf; (mil.) file of soldiers, also troops arranged in divisions; pencil (of rays). **II.** *f.* face, visage; surface; right side or outside of cloth; (arch.) facing, façade.—*pl.* fasces.—**a sobre h.,** apparently, at first sight.—**ser de dos haces,** to be double-faced.—**sobre la h. de la tierra,** upon the face of the earth. **III.** *imp.* of HACER.

haza, *f.* piece of tillable land.

hazalefa, *f.* towel.

hazaña, *f.* feat, exploit, heroic deed.

hazañería, *f.* affected fear or admiration.

hazañero, ra, *a.* prudish, affectedly grave and scrupulous.

hazañosamente, *adv.* valorously, bravely.

hazañoso, sa, *a.* gallant, courageous, heroic.

hazmerreír, *m.* laughing stock.

he, *interj.* generally followed by the adverbs **aquí** or **allí,** or by a pronoun, to introduce or call attention to: *he aquí,* here is, here you have; lo! lo and behold! *heme aquí,* here I am: *helos allí,* there they are. *V. irr. forms of* HABER.

hebdómada, *f.* hebdomad, week; seven years.

hebdomadario, ria. I. *a.* weekly. **II.** *n.* (eccl.) hebdomadary.

hebén. I. *n.* white grapes like muscatels. **II.** *a.* insignificant, of no account.

hebetado, da, *a.* (Am.) brutified, sottish.

hebilla, *f.* buckle, clasp.—**hebillaje,** *m.* set of buckles.—**hebillero, ra,** *n.* buckle maker or seller —**hebilleta, hebilluela,** *f.* *dim.* small buckle.— **no faltar h.,** to be complete.—**hebillón,** *m.* *aug.* large buckle.

hebra, *f.* fibre, thread, filament; string; staple; grain (of wood); needleful of thread; pistil of the blossom of saffron; (min.) vein, layer, stratum. —*pl.* (poet.) hair.—**ser,** or **estar, de buena h.,** to be strong and robust.

hebraico, ca, *a.* Hebrew.—**hebraísmo,** *m.* Hebraism.—**hebraísta, hebraizante,** *n.* Hebraist.

hebreo, a, *n.* & *a.* Hebrew; (coll.) pawnbroker; (coll.) usurer (-ious).

hebrero, *m.* esophagus of ruminants.

hebrica, illa, ita, *f.* *dim.* small needleful of thread.

hebroso, sa, *a.* fibrous, stringy.

hecatombe, *f.* hecatomb.

hectárea, *f.* hectare.

héctico, ca, *a.* hectic.

hectiquez, *f.* (med.) phthisis.

hectógrafo, *m.* hectograph, copygraph

hectogramo, *m.* hectogram.

hectolitro, *m.* hectoliter.

hectómetro, *m.* hectometer.

hectóreo, ea, *a.* belonging to Hector.

hectovatio, *m.* hectowatt, 100 watts.

hecha, *f.* (obs.) date; irrigation tax.—**de esta h.,** from this time.

hechiceresco, ca, *a.* relating to witchcraft.

hechicería, *f.* witchcraft, witchery, enchantment; charm, fascination.

hechicero, ra. I. *n.* witch, wizard; hag; charmer, enchanter, bewitcher. **II.** *a.* entrancing, charming, bewitching, fascinating.

hechizar, *va.* (*pret.* HECHICÉ: *subj.* HECHICE) to bewitch, enchant, entrance; to charm, to fascinate.

hechizo, *m.* bewitchment, fascination; trance, enchantment; delight, bliss.

hechizo, za, *a.* artificial, feigned; made to order; portable, easily mounted.

hecho, cha. I. *pp.* *irr.* of HACER. **II.** *a.* made; done; ready-made; finished; fully matured, ripe or developed; accustomed, inured, used.—**h. un león,** like a lion, furiously; angry.—**h. y derecho,** in every respect; true, real; perfect, complete.—**a lo h., pecho,** we must make a clean breast of it, or the best of it.—**bien h.,** well done or made; all right; right (in a moral sense).—**mal h.,** wrong, unrighteous; badly done or made. **III.** *m.* fact; event; act, action, deed; point at issue.—**de h.,** in fact, actually; in earnest; de facto.—**de h. y de derecho,** de facto and de jure.—**en h. de verdad,** in truth.

hechura, *f.* making, make; workmanship; form; build (of a person); work done and price paid for it; creature, henchman.—**no tener h.,** to be impracticable or not feasible.

hedentina, *f.* stench, stink.

heder, *vn.* (*ind.* HIEDO: *subj.* HIEDA) to stink; to vex, annoy, bore.

hediondamente, *adv.* stinkingly.

hediondez, *f.* stench, stink.

hediondo, da, *a.* stinking, fetid; annoying, wearisome; dirty, repulsive; lewd, obscene.

hedor, *m.* stench, stink.

hegelianismo, *m.* Hegelianism.

hegeliano, na, *n.* & *a.* Hegelian.

hegemonía, *f.* (pol.) hegemony.

héjira, héjira, *f.* Hegira.

helable, *a.* congealable.

helada, *f.* frost; nip.—**h. blanca,** hoarfrost.

heladería, *f.* (Am.) ice-cream parlor or shop.

heladero, ra, *n.* (Ch.) ice-cream maker or seller.

heladizo, za, *a.* easily congealed.

helado, da. I. *a.* & *pp.* frigid; frozen, congealed; frost-bitten; cold, indifferent; astonished, astounded. **II.** *m.* ice cream; water ice.

helamiento, *m.* congelation, freezing, frost.

helar. I. *va.* & *vn.* (*ind.* HIELO: *subj.* HIELE) to congeal, to freeze; astonish, amaze; dispirit, discourage, dissuade. **II.** *v.* *impers.* to freeze (*aquí hiela frecuentemente,* it freezes often here). **III.** *vr.* to freeze, to congeal, to be coagulated; to grow motionless, to be stupefied, dispirited.—**se me heló la sangre,** my blood curdled.

hele, hétele, aquí, *interj.* behold it! *V.* н½.

helechal, *m.* fern field.—**helecho,** *m.* fern.

helena, *f.* (naut.) jack-with-a-lantern.

helénico, ca, *a.* Helenic.

helenio, *m.* (bot.) sneezeweed.

helenismo, *m.* Hellenism; Greek idiom.

helenista, *m.* Hellenist.—**heleno, na,** *a.* Hellenic.

helera, *f.* pip, disease of fowls.

helero, *m.* snowcap on mountains; (geol.) glacier.

helgado, da, *a.* jag-toothed.

helgadura, *f.* space between, or irregularity of, the teeth.

helíaco, ca, *a.* (ast.) heliacal.

heliantemo, *m.* (bot.) a helianthaceous plant.

heliantina, *f.* (chem.) methyl orange.

helianto, *m.* (bot.) helianthus, sunflower.

hélice, *f.* (**H-,** ast.) Ursa Major; (geom.) helix; (naut., aer.) screw propeller.

helicoidal, *a.* helicoidal.

helicoide, *m.* (geom.) helicoid.

helicónides, *f.* *pl.* (myth.) the Muses.

heliconio, nia, *a.* (myth.) Heliconian.

helicóptero, *m.* (aer.) helicopter.

helio, *m.* (chem.) helium.

heliocéntrico, ca, *a.* heliocentric.

heliograbado, *m.* heliogravure.

heliografía, *f.* blue print.

heliógrafo, *m.* heliograph.

heliómetro, *m.* heliometer.

helioscopio, *m.* helioscope.

helióstato, *m.* heliostat.

helioterapia, *f.* (med.) heliotherapy.

heliotropina, *f.* (chem.) piperonal.

heliotropo, *m.* (bot.) heliotrope; (min.) blood-sone; (ast.) heliotrope, an instrument.

heliotropismo, *m.* (bot.) heliotropism.

heliotropo, *m.* = HELIOTROPIO.

helizoario, *m.* (zool.) heliozoan.

helmintiasis, *f.* (med.) helminthiasis.

helminto. I. *n.* & *a.* helminthic. **II.** *m.* *pl.* Helminthes.

helmintología, *f.* (med.) helminthology.

helvecio, cia; helvético, ca, *a.* Helvetic, Swiss.

hematemesis, *f.* (med.) hæmatemesis, blood vomiting.

hematidrosis, *f.* (med.) hæmatidrosis.

hematites, *f.* (min.) hematite.

hematología, *f.* (med.) hæmatology.

hematómetro, *m.* (med.) hæmatometer.

hematoscopio, *m.* hæmoscope.

hematosis, *f.* (physiol.) hæmatosis.

hematuria, *f.* (med.) hæmaturia.

hembra, *f.* female; (coll. or vulg.) woman; (sew.) eye of a hook; (mech.) nut of a screw; bolt clasp, staple.—**h. del timón,** (naut.) gudgeon of the rudder.

hembraje, *m.* (S. Am.) female cattle.

hembrear, *vn.* to be inclined to females; to generate or produce females only, or chiefly.

hembrica, illa, ita, *f.* *dim.* little female.

hembrilla, *f.* (mech.) small piece into which another fits (as a nut, staple, etc.); ring or eyebolt.

hemiciclo, *m.* semicircle; (Spain) central space of the House of Deputies.

hemicránea, *f.* (med.) hemicrania, megrim.

hemiedría, *f.* (min.) hemihedrism.

hemiedro, *m.* (min.) hemihedron.

hemina, *f.* a liquid and area measure.

hemíono, *m.* (zool.) hemionus, kiang, an Asiatic wild ass.

hemiplejía, *f.* (med.) hemiplegia.

hemíptero, ra. I. *a.* hemipterous. **II.** *m.* *pl.* Hemiptera.

hemisférico, ca, *a.* hemispherical.
hemisferio, *m.* hemisphere.
hemisferoidal, *a.* hemispheroidal.
hemistiquio, *m.* (poet.) hemistich.
hemoglobina, *f.* (med.) hæmoglobin
hemóptisis, *f.* (med.) hæmoptysis.
hemorragia, *f.* (med.) hemorrhage.
hemorrágico, *a.* hemorrhagic.
hemorroidas, *f. pl.* = HEMORROIDES.
hemorroidal, *a.* hemorrhoidal.—**hemorroides,**
f. pl. piles, hemorrhoids.
hemorroo, *m.* (zool.) serpent. *V.* CERASTE
hemostático, ca, *a.* hemostatic.
henal, *m.* hayloft.—**henar,** *m.* hay field.
henchidor, ra, *n.* filler.
henchidura, *f.* fill, filling.
henchimiento, *m.* filling, fill.—*pl.* (naut.) filling
timbers.
henchir. I. *va.* (gerund, HINCHIENDO: *ind.* HIN-
CHO: *pret.* él HINCHIÓ: *subj.* HINCHA) to fill, to
stuff. **II.** *vr.* to fill or stuff one's self.
hendedor, ra, *n.* divider, splitter, cleaver.
hendedura, *f.* fissure, crack, cleft, crevice, cut.
hender, *va.* (*ind.* HIENDO: *subj.* HIENDA) to chink,
crack, cleave, split; to go through; to cut (as the
water); to elbow or open (a passage) through a
crowd.
hendible, *a.* cleavable.
hendido, da, *a. & pp.* crannied, full of chinks,
cleft.—**hendidura,** *f.* = HENDEDURA.
hendiente, *m.* down stroke of a sword.
henequén, *m.* (bot.) sisal, henequen.
henificar, *va.* to cut and dry for forage.
henil, *m.* hayloft, barn.
heno, *m.* (bot.) hay.
henojil, *m.* garter.
heñir, *va.* (for irr. v. TEÑIR) to knead.—**hay
mucho que h.,** (coll.) there is much to do.
hepatalgia, *f.* (med.) pain in the liver.
hepática, *f.* (bot.) liverwort.
hepático, ca, *a.* (med.) hepatic, hepatical.
hepatisis, *f.* (med.) consumption of the liver.
hepatitis, *f.* (med.) hepatitis.
hepatización, *f.* (med.) hepatization.
hepatizarse, *vr.* (med.) to undergo hepatization.
hepatología, *f.* hepatology.
heptacordo, *m.* (mus.) heptachord.
heptámetro, *m. & a.* heptameter (verse).
heptano, *m.* (chem.) heptane.
heptarca, *m.* heptarch.
heptarquía, *f.* heptarchy.
heptasílabo, ba, *a.* heptasyllabic.
heptateuco, *m.* Heptateuch.
heráldica, *f.* heraldry.—**heráldico, ca,** *a.* heraldic.—**heraldo,** *m.* herald; harbinger; king-at-
arms.
herbáceo, cea, *a.* herbaceous.
herbajar. I. *va.* to put to graze, to pasture.
II. *vn.* to pasture, graze, browse.
herbaje, *m.* herbage, grass, pasture; pasturage
fee; coarse cloth made of herbs.
herbajear, *va. & vn.* = HERBAJAR.
herbajero, *m.* one who rents pastures.
herbar, *va.* to dress (skins) with herbs.
herbario, ria. I. *a.* herbal. **II.** *m.* herbalist, her-
barian; herbarium.
herbaza, *f. aug.* large weed.
herbazal, *m.* herbous place; pasture ground.
herbecer, *vn.* to begin to grow (s. o. herbs or
grass).
herbero, *m.* esophagus of a ruminant.
herbívoro, ra. I. *n. & a.* herbivore (-ous).
II. *m. pl.* Herbivora.
herbolado, da, *a.* poisoned with juice of plants.
herbolar, *va.* = ENHERBOLAR.
herbolario, ria, *n.* herbist, herbman, one who
sells herbs; (coll.) nonsensical person.
herborización, *f.* herborization; botanizing.
herborizador, ra, herborizante, *n.* herbalist,
herborist.
herborizar, *vn.* to herborize, botanize.

herboso, sa, *a.* herby, grassy.
herciano, na, *a.* (phys.) Hertzian.
hercúleo, ea, *a.* herculean.
heredad, *f.* improved piece of ground; country
place, farm.
heredado, da. I. *pp. & a.* landed, owning real
estate. **II.** *n.* heir to property.
heredamiento, *m.* landed property.
heredar, *va.* to inherit; to deed to another; to
institute as heir; to inherit.
heredero, ra, *n.* heir; heiress; inheritor.—**h. forzoso,** general or legal heir.—**h. presuntivo,** heir
apparent.
heredípeta, *n.* legacy seeker.
hereditario, ria, *a.* hereditary.
hereje, *n.* heretic.
herejía, *f.* heresy; injurious expression.
herejote, ta, *n.* (coll.) great heretic.
herén, *m.* (bot.) vetch.
herencia, *f.* inheritance, heritage; heredity.
heresiarca, *m.* heresiarch.
heretical; herético, ca, *a.* heretical.
heria, *f.* life of vagrancy. *V.* HAMPA.
herida, *f.* wound.—**herido, da,** *a. & pp.* wounded.
—**mal h.,** dangerously wounded.
heridor, ra, *n. & a.* wounder (-ing).
herir, *va.* (gerund, HIRIENDO: *ind.* HIERO: *pret.* él
HIRIÓ: *subj.* HIERA) to wound; to hurt, harm; to
strike; to affect, touch, move; to offend (the
senses); to pique, irritate.
herma, *m.* (art) herm, a pillar surmounted by a
head.
hermafrodita, *a. & m.* (zool. and bot.) hermaphrodite.
hermafroditismo, *m.* hermaphroditism.
hermana, *f.* sister. (For phrases v. HERMANO.)
hermanable, *a.* fraternal, brotherly; compatible.
hermanablemente, *adv.* fraternally.
hermanado, da, *pp. & a.* mated, matched.
hermanamiento, *m.* mating, matching.
hermanar. I. *va.* to mate, match, pair; to suit,
harmonize; to own for a brother. **II.** *vn.* to
fraternize, join, match, agree. **III.** *vr.* to love
one another as brothers; to be compatible; to
harmonize.
hermanastro, tra, *n.* stepbrother (-sister).
hermanazgo, *m.* fraternity, brotherhood.
hermandad, *f.* fraternity, brotherhood, confraternity; hermandad; conformity, resemblance; amity, friendship.
hermanear, *va.* to treat as a brother.
hermanecer, *vn.* to have a little brother just
born.
hermanito, ta, *n. dim.* little brother (sister).
hermano, na, *n.* brother (sister); mate, companion, twin (app. to objects).—**h. carnal,** full
brother.—**h. consanguíneo** = H. DE PADRE.—**h.
de leche,** foster brother.—**h. de madre (de padre),** half brother by the same mother (father).—
h. político, brother-in-law.—**h. uterino** = H. DE
MADRE.
hermanuco, *m.* name given in contempt to lay
brothers of some religious orders.
hermenéutica, *f.* hermeneutics.
hermenéutico, ca, *a.* hermeneutic.
herméticamente, *adv.* hermetically.
hermético, ca, *a.* hermetical, air-proof, air-tight.
hermosamente, *adv.* beautifully, handsomely;
perfectly, properly.
hermoseador, ra, *n. & a.* beautifier (-fying).
hermosear, *va.* to beautify, embellish, adorn.
hermoso, sa, *a.* beautiful, handsome.
hermosura, *f.* beauty, handsomeness; belle,
beauty (pretty woman).
hernia, *f.* (med.) hernia.—**herniario,** *a.* (med.)
hernial.—**hernioso, sa,** *a.* (med.) herniated.—
hernista, *m.* specialist in herniotomy.
herodiano, na, *a.* Herodian.
héroe, *m.* hero.—**heroicamente,** *adv.* heroically.
—**heroicidad,** *f.* heroism; heroic deed.
heroico, ca, *a.* heroic.—**a la heroica,** in the
manner of the heroic times.

heroína, *f.* heroine; (chem.) heroin.
heroísmo, *m.* heroism.
herpe, *m.* or *f.* (med.) herpes, tetter.
herpético, ca, *a.* (med.) herpetic.
herpetismo, *m.* (med.) herpetism.
herpetología, *f.* (zool.) herpetology, science of reptiles; (med.) herpetography, science of herpetic deseases.
herpil, *m.* bag of esparto netting with wide meshes, for carrying large fruit.
herrada. I. *a.* (water) in which red-hot iron has been cooled. **II.** *f.* pail, bucket.
herradero, *m.* branding of cattle; place where cattle are branded.
herrador, *m.* farrier, horseshoer.
herradora, *f.* (coll.) farrier's wife.
herradura, *f.* horseshoe.
herraj, *m.* stones of pressed olives. *V.* ERRAJ.
herraje, *m.* ironwork, pieces of iron used for ornament and strength.
herramental, *m.* tool bag; tool chest.
herramienta, *f.* tool; implement; set of tools.—*pl.* horns; (coll.) teeth, grinders.
herrar, *va.* (*ind.* HIERRO: *subj.* HIERRE) to shoe (horses); to brand (cattle); to garnish or bind with iron.
herrén, *m.* meslin, mixed grain for horses.
herrenal, herreñal, *m.* meslin patch or field.
herrera, *f.* (coll.) blacksmith's wife.
herrería, *f.* iron works; blacksmith's shop, smithy; forge; blacksmith's trade, smithery; clamour, confused noise.
herrerico, herrerillo, *m.* name of a small bird.
herrero, *m.* blacksmith.—**h. de grueso,** blacksmith.
herrerón, *m.* clumsy smith.
herreruelo, *m.* (orn.) wagtail.
herrete, *m.* tag, ferrule, aiguillete.
herretear, *va.* to tag.
herrezuelo, *m.* light piece of iron.
herrín, *m.* iron rust.
herrón, *m.* quoit; washer; iron prop for young trees; (Colomb.) point of a spinning top.
herronada, *f.* violent blow with a quoit; blow with a bird's beak.
herrumbre, *f.* rust; iron taste.
herrumbroso, sa, *a.* rusty, rusted.
hertziano, na, *a.* (phys.) Hertzian.
hérulo, la. I. *n.* & *a.* Herulian. **II.** *m. pl.* Heruli.
herventar, *va.* to boil by introducing a hot body in the liquid.
hervimiento, *m.* ebullition, boiling; small spring whence water bubbles out; rattling in the throat; multitude, crowd.
herviente, *a.* boiling, seething.
hervir. I. *va.* & *vn.* (*for irr. v.* SERTIR) to boil; to seethe. **II.** *vn.* to become choppy (s. o. the sea); to bubble, effervesce; to surge (as a crowd).—**h. en,** to team with, be full of.
hervor, *m.* ebullition, boiling; fervor, heat; vigor; fret; noise and movement of waters.—**h. de sangre,** rash.
hervoroso, sa, *a.* fiery, ardent, impetuous.
hesitación, *f.* hesitation, hesitancy.
hespéride, *a.* (astr.) relating to the Pleiades; (poet.) western.
Hespérides, *f. pl.* (astr.) Pleiades.
hesperidio, *m.* (bot.) hesperidium.
hespérido, da, *a.*=HESPÉRIDE.
Héspero, *m.* (ast.) Hesper, the evening star.
heteo, a, *n.* & *a.* Hittite.
hetera, *f.* hetæra, hetaira, Greek courtesan.
heteróclito, ta, *a.* (gram.) heteroclite; irregular, abnormal.
heterodina, *a.* (rad.) heterodyne.
heterodoxia, *f.* heterodoxy.
heterodoxo, xa, *a.* heterodox.
heterogeneidad, *f.* heterogeneity.
heterogéneo, nea, *a.* heterogeneous.

heteromancía, *f.* superstitious divination by the flight of birds.
heteromorfo, fa, *a.* heteromorphous.
heteromorfosis, *f.* heteromorphosis.
heterónomo, ma, *a.* heteronymous.
heterópsido, da, *a.* lusterless (s. o. metals).
heteroscios, *m. pl.* (geog.) heteroscians.
hético, ca, *a.* hectic, consumptive.
hetiquez, *f.* (med.) consumption.
hévea, *f.* (bot.) hevea, Para-rubber tree.
hexacordo, *m.* (mus.) hexachord.
hexaedro, *m.* (geom.) hexahedron.
hexagonal; hexágono, na, *a.* hexagonal.
hexágono, *m.* (geom.) hexagon.
hexámetro, *m.* hexameter.
hexápeda, *f. V.* TOESA.
hez [eth], *f.* lee, bottom, sediment, dregs of liquors; dross of metals; grains of malt.—*pl.* fæces, excrements.—**la h. del pueblo, the scum of the people.**
Híadas, Híades, *f. pl.* (ast.) Hyades.
hialino, na, *a.* hyaline, transparent.
hialitis, *f.* (med.) hyalitis.
hialoideo, dea, *a.* vitreous, glasslike.
hialoides, *f.* hyaloid membrane.
hiante, *a.* (verse) with a hiatus.
hiato, *m.* (gram., poet.) hiatus.
hibernal, *a.* hibernal, wintry.
hibernés, sa, *a.* Hibernian, Irish.
hibernizo, za, *a.* = HIBERNAL.
hibridación, *f.* hybridization.
hibridez, *f.*, **hibridismo,** *m.* hybridism.
híbrido, da, *n.* & *a.* hybrid.
hicaco, *m.* (bot.) icaco, coco plum.
hice, hiciera. *V.* HACER.
hicotea, *f.* (Am.) fresh-water turtle.
hicso, sa, *n.* & *a.* Hyksos.
hidalgamente, *adv.* nobly, gentlemanly.
hidalgo, ga. I. *a.* noble, illustrious, excellent, exalted. **II.** *n.* hidalgo, nobleman (-woman).—**h. de braguета,** one entitled to nobility from being the father of seven successive sons.
hidalgón, na, gote, ta, *n. aug.* old ceremonious hidalgo.
hidalgüejo, ja, güelo, la, guete, ta, guillo, lla, *n. dim.* pretty hidalgo.
hidalguez, hidalguía, *f.* nobility; rights of an hidalgo; nobleness, liberality.
hidatídico, ca, *a.* (med.) hydatidinous.
hidra, *f.* (zool.) a poisonous serpent; hydra, fresh-water polyp; (**H-,** myth., ast.) Hydra.
hidrácido, *m.* (chem.) hydracid.
hidragogo, m. & *a.* (med.) hydragogue.
hidrargirido, da, *a.* resembling mercury.
hidrargirismo, *m.* (med.) hydrargyriasis, mercurialism, chronic mercurial poisoning.
hidrargirita, *f.* (min.) native oxide of mercury.
hidratación, *f.* hydration, hydrating.
hidratado, da, *pp.* & *a.* hydrate(d).
hidratar, *va.* (chem.) to hydrate.
hidrato, *m.* (chem.) hydrate.
hidráulica, *f.* hydraulics.—**hidráulico, ca. I.** *a.* hydraulic. **II.** *n.* hydraulician.
hidria, *f.* hydria, an ancient jar.
hidroaeroplano, *m.* (aer.) hydroplane, seaplane.
hidroavión, *m.* (aer.) hydroplane, seaplane.—**h. de flotadores,** float seaplane.
hidrocarburo, *m.* (chem.) hydrocarbon.
hidrocefalía, *f.* (med.) hydrocephalus, dropsy of the brain.
hidrocéfalo, *m.* (med.) hydrocephalus.
hidrocele, *f.* (med.) hydrocele.
hidroclorato, *m.* (chem.) hydrochlorate.
hidroclórico, ca, *a.* (chem.) hydrochloric.
hidrodinámica, *f.* hydrodynamics.
hidrodinámico, ca, *a.* hydrodynamic.
hidroeléctrico, ca, *a.* hydroelectric.
hidrófana, *f.* (min.) hydrophane.
hidrofilacio, *m.* hydrophylacium, water reservoir.
hidrófilo, la, *a.* water-loving; absorbent (cotton).
hidrofobia, *f.* (med.) hydrophobia; rabies.

hidrófobo, ba, *a.* suffering hydrophobia.
hidrogala, *m.* mixture of milk and water.
hidrogenar, *va.* to hydrogenize.
hidrógeno, *m.* (chem.) hydrogen.
hidrognosia, *f.* hydrognosy.
hidrogogía, *f.* science of canal making and the conveyance of water.
hidrografía, *f.* hydrography.
hidrográfico, ca, *a.* hydrographical.
hidrógrafo, *m.* hydrographer.
hidrología, *f.* hydrology.
hidrológico, ca, *a.* hydrologic.
hidromancia, *f.* hydromancy.
hidromántico, ca, *a.* hydromantic.
hidromedusa, *f.* (zool.) hydromedusa; a large South-American turtle.
hidromel, hidromiel, *m.* hydromel, mead, metheglin.
hidrometeoro, *m.* hydrometeor.
hidrómetra, *n.* one versed in hydraulic measurements.
hidrometría, *f.* science of hydraulic measurements (velocity, discharge, etc.)
hidrómetro, *m.* current meter (*not* hydrometer, except in the sense given.)
hidrópata, *m.* (med.) hydropath.
hidropatía, *f.* (med.) hydropathy, hydrotherapy.
hidropático, ca, *a.* hydropathic.
hidropesía, *f.* (med.) dropsy.
hidrópico, ca, *a.* dropsical.
hidroplano, *m.* (aer.) hydroplane, seaplane.
hidroquinona, *f.* (chem.) hydroquinone.
hidroscopio, *m.* hydroscope.
hidrostática, *f.* hydrostatics.
hidrostáticamente, *adv.* hydrostatically.
hidrostático, ca, *a.* hydrostatical.
hidrosulfúrico, ca, *a.* hydrosulphuric.
hidrotecnia, *f.* hydraulic engineering.
hidroterapia, *f.* hydrotherapeutics.
hidroterápico, ca, *a.* hydrotherapeutic.
hidrotórax. *f.* (med.) hydrothorax.
hiedra, *f.* (bot.) ivy.—**h. terrestre,** ground ivy.
hiel, *f.* gall, bile; bitterness, asperity.—**h. de la tierra,** (bot.) fumitory or earth smoke.—**echar la h.,** (coll.) to work very hard.—**no tener h.,** (coll.) to be meek and gentle.
hielo, *m.* ice; frost, congelation; coolness, indifference; astonishment, stupefaction.
hiemal, *a.* wintry, hibernal.
hiena, *f.* (zool.) hyena.
hienda, *f.* dung.
hiendo, yo hienda. *V.* HENDER.
hiera. *V.* HERIR.
hierático, ca, *a.* hieratic, sacerdotal.
hierba, *f.* (bot.) grass; weed; herb; food for cattle; herbage.—*pl.* poison given in food; among the clergy, greens, garden stuff.—**y otras hierbas,** (hum.) and so forth.
hierbabuena, *f.* (bot.) mint.
hiere, hiero. *V.* HERIR.
hierofanta, te, *m.* hierophant.
hieroglífico, ca, *a.* = JEROGLÍFICO.
hieros, *m. pl.* (bot.) = YEROS.
hierosolimitano, na, *a.* = JEROSOLIMITANO.
hierrezuelo, *m. dim.* small piece of iron.
hierro, *m.* iron; any iron tool, instrument or structural shape; brand stamped with a hot iron; iron head of a shaft, arrow, or dart; any pointed weapon, as a sword or goad; cutter, cutting edge or part of a cutting tool.—*pl.* fet'ers, shackles, handcuffs; (naut.) bilboes.—**h. albo, h. caliente,** red-hot iron.—**h. colado,** cast iron.—**h. cuadrillado,** square iron.—**h. de doble T,** I-beam.—**h. dulce,** or **de fragua,** wrought iron.—**h. en planchas,** sheet iron.—**h. forjado,** wrought iron.—**h. fundido =** H. COLADO.—**h. laminado =** H. EN PLANCHAS.—**h. varilla,** round iron.—**machacar en h. frío,** to labor in vain.
hierro, yo hierre. *V.* HERRAR.
hierva, hiervo. *V.* HERVIR.
higa, *f.* amulet, charm hung about a babe's neck; method of pointing derisively at a person; ridi-

cule, derision.—**dar h.,** to hang fire (s. o. firearms).—**dar higas,** to despise.—**no dar dos higas,** not to give a farthing; not to care a rap.
higadilla, *f.,* **llo,** *m. dim.* small liver; liver of birds, fishes, and other small animals.
hígado, *m.* liver.—*pl.* (coll.) courage, bravery.—**hasta los hígados,** to the heart.—**malos hígados,** (coll.) ill will.
higate, *m.* pottage of figs, pork, etc.
higiene, *f.* hygiene; sanitation.—**h. pública,** public health.
higiénicamente, *adv.* hygienically.
higiénico, ca, *a.* hygienic, sanitary.
higienista, *m.* hygienist.
higienizar, *va.* to make sanitary.
higo, *m.* (bot.) fig.—**h. chumba,** or **de pala,** prickly pear.—**de higos a brevas,** in a long while.—**no se me da un h.,** I don't care a fig.
higrometría, *m.* hygrometry.
higrométrico, ca, *a.* hygrometric.
higrómetro, *m.* hygrometer.
higroscopia, *f.* hygroscopy, hygrometry.
higroscopio, *m.* hygroscope.
higuera, *f.* (bot.) fig tree.—**h. chumba,** or **de Indias,** Indian fig tree, prickly-pear cactus.—**h. infernal,** castor-oil plant, castor bean.—**h. nopal** = H. CHUMBA.
higueral, *m.* plantation of fig trees.
higuereta, *f.* (bot.) = RICINO.
higuerón, *m.* a large American tree.
higuito, *m. dim.* small fig.
hija, *f.* daughter.—**h. política,** daughter-in-law. *V.* HIJO, JA.
hijadalgo, *f. V.* HIDALGA.
hijastro, tra, *n.* stepchild.
hijito, ita, *n. f. dim.* little child, little dear.
hijo, ja, *n.* son (daughter); young of an animal, son, native; (bot.) shoot; sucker; child, issue, offspring; fruit; result; junior (after a person's name: *Alejandro Dumas, hijo,* Alexander Dumas, Jr.).—**h. adoptivo,** adopted child.—**h. bastardo,** bastard, illegitimate child.—**h. de bendición,** legitimate child.—**h. de familia,** minor.—**h. de ganancia** = H. BASTARDO.—**h. de la cuna,** foundling.—**h. del agua,** good sailor; good swimmer.—**h. de la piedra,** foundling.—**h. de leche,** foster child.—**h. del hombre,** Son of Man (Jesus).—**h. de su madre** = H. BASTARDO.—**h. de su madre (padre),** his mother's (father's) son, very much like his mother (father).—**h. de vecino,** native (of a town); mother's son (in the colloquial sense of "person").—**h. natural,** illegitimate child.
hijodalgo, *m.* = HIDALGO.
hijuela, *f. dim.* little daughter; (sew.) gore or piece for widening a garment; small mattress put between others to make the bed even; (eccl.) pall, chalice cover; small drain; estate of a deceased person; (law) schedule given to an heir of his share in the partition of the estate; crossroad; postman of a rural mail route; palm seed; fascine of kindling wood; leader for fishhooks.
hijuelo, la, *n. dim.* young child; (bot.) shoot, sucker.
hila, *f.* row, line (*v.* HILERA); thin gut; spinning.—*pl.* (surg.) lint.—**h. de agua,** small trench for irrigation.—**hilas raspadas,** scraped lint.—**a la h.,** in a row, single file.
hilacha, *f.,* **hilacho,** *m.* fraying, shred, filament or thread ravelled out of cloth.
hilachoso, sa, *a.* shreddy, ragged; filamentous.
hilada, *f.* row or line; (mas.) course.
hiladillo, *m.* ferret silk; narrow ribbon or tape.
hilado, *pp. & m.* spinning; spinstry; yarn.
hilador, ra. I. *n. & a.* spinner (-ing). **II.** *f.* spinning machine, spinning jenny.
hilandera, *f.* woman spinner.
hilandería, *f.* spinnery, spinning mill; spinstry.
hilandero, ra. I. *n. & a.* spinner (-ing). **II.** *m.* spinning room, spinnery.
hilanderilla, *f.* spinning girl.
hilanderuelo, la, *n. dim.* spinning boy (girl).
hilar, *va. & vn.* to spin; to reason; to connect (s. o. discourse).—**h. delgado,** to be exceedingly careful or particular; to act with great nicety; to split hairs.

HIL 273 HIS

hilaracha, *f.* = HILACHA.
hilarante, *a.* laughing (gas).
hilaridad, *f.* hilarity.
hilaza, *f.* yarn; fibre; uneven thread.
hilera, *f.* row, line, tier, file; (metal.) wiredrawer; fine yarn; slit or catch of a spindle; (arch.) ridgepole; (mil.) file.
hilero, *m.* thread of a river or stream.
hilete, *m.* *dim.* small thread.
hilo, *m.* thread; yarn; filament, fibre; string; linen; wire; edge of a sword or razor; slender thread formed by falling liquids; (min.) seam; continuation, series; cross wire, cross hair (of a telescope).—**h. bramante, h. de a carreto, h. de palomas,** packthread, twine.—**h. de velas, or volatín,** sailmaker's yarn.—**h. de una corriente,** (naut.) thread of a current.—**a h.,** successively, one after another; in line.—**al h.,** along the thread; along or with the fiber.—**de h.,** directly, instantly.
hilván, *m.* (sew.) tacking, basting.—**hablar de h.,** (coll.) to speak very fast.
hilvanar, *va.* (sew.) to tack, baste; to plan; to do or make in a hurry.
himen, *m.* (anat.) hymen.
himeneo, *m.* hymen, nuptials; epithalamium.
himenio, *m.* (bot.) hymenium.
himenóptero, a. I. *n. & a.* (ent.) hymenopteran (-ous). **II.** *m. pl.* (ent.) Hymenoptera.
himnario, *m.* hymnal, hymn book.
himno, *m.* hymn.
himplar, *vn.* to roar, bellow.
hin, *m.* whinny, neigh.
hincadura, *f.* thrusting, driving; prick.
hincapié, *m.* affirming the foot on the ground.—**hacer h. en,** to emphasize, to dwell upon.
hincar. I. *va.* (*pret.* HINQUÉ: *subj.* HINQUE) to thrust; drive; to plant.—**h. el diente,** to bite; to calumniate.—**h. la rodilla,** to kneel down. **II.** *vr.* to kneel down.
hincón, *m.* ferry post, hitching post.
hincha, *f.* (coll.) hatred, enmity, grudge.
hinchadamente, *adv.* airily, pompously.
hinchado, da, *a. & pp.* swollen; airy, arrogant, presumptuous; inflated, high-flown (style).
hinchar. I. *va.* to swell. **II.** *vr.* to swell; to become arrogant, conceited or puffed up, (coll.) to get a big head.
hinchazón, *m.* swelling, tumefaction; ostentation, vanity, airs; inflation, euphuism.
hindu, *n. & a.* Hindoo, Hindu; Hindustani.
hiniesta, *f.* (bot.) genista.
hinojal, *m.* fennel bed.
hinojo, *m.* knee; (bot.) fennel.—**h. marino,** (bot.) samphire.—**de hinojos,** on bended knees.
hintero, *m.* bakers' kneading table.
hiño, yo hiña. *V.* HEÑIR.
hioideo, hioides, *a.* (anat.) hyoid.
hipar, *vn.* to hiccough; to pant; desire eagerly, be anxious; be overfatigued.
hipérbaton, *m.* (rhet.) hyperbaton.
hipérbola, *f.* (geom.) hyperbola.
hipérbole, *f.* (rhet.) hyperbole.
hiperbólicamente, *adv.* hyperbolically.
hiperbólico, ca, *a.* hyperbolical.
hiperbolizar, *vn.* to use hyperboles.
hiperboloide, *f.* (geom.) hyperboloid.
hiperbóreo, rea, *a.* hyperborean.
hipercrisis, *f.* (med.) violent crisis.
hipercrítica, *f.* hypercriticism, excessive or exaggerated criticism.
hipercrítico, ca, *a.* hypercritical.
hiperdulía, *f.* (eccl.) hyperdulia.
hiperemia, *f.* (med.) hyperæmia.
hiperémico, ca, *a.* hyperæmic, congested.
hiperestesia, *f.* hyperæsthesia, excessive sensibility.
hipericíneo, a. I. *a. & n.* hypericaceous (plant). **II.** *m. pl.* Hypericaceæ.
hipérico, *m.* (bot.) hypericum.
hipermetría, *f.* (rhet.) hypermeter.
hipertrofia, *f.* (med.) hypertrophy.

hipertroarse, *vr.* to hypertrophy.
hipertrófico, ca, *a.* hypertrophic.
hípico, ca, *a.* equine, relating to horses.
hipil, *m.* (Am.) loose garment worn by Indians.
hipnal, *m.* hypnale, a kind of serpent said to cause sleep.
hipnología, *f.* hymnology, science of sleep.
hipnosis, *f.* hypnosis.
hipnótico, ca, *n. & a.* hypnotic.—**hipnotismo,** *m.* hypnotism.—**hipnotización,** *f.* hypnotization.—**hipnotizador, a,** *n. & a.* hypnotizer (-ing).—**hipnotizar,** *va.* to hypnotize.
hipo, *m.* hiccough; longing; anger.
hipocampo, *m.* hippocampus, sea horse.
hipocausto, *m.* hypocaust.
hipocentauro, *m.* hippocentaur.
hipocicloide, *f.* (geom.) hypocycloid.
hipocondría, *f.* (med.) hypochondria.
hipocondríaco, ca; hipocóndrico, ca, *n. & a.* hypochondriac (-al).
hipocondrio, *m.* (anat.) hypochondrium.
hipocrás, *m.* hippocras, medicated wine.
hipocrático, ca, *a.* Hippocratic.
Hipocrénides, *f. pl.* (poet.) the Muses.
hipocresía, *f.* hypocrisy.
hipócrita, *n. & a.* hypocrite (-ical).
hipócritamente, *adv.* hypocritically.
hipocritón, na, *n. aug.* great hypocrite.
hipodérmico, ca, *a.* hypodermic.
hipódromo, *m.* hippodrome.
hipofagia, *f.* hippophagism.
hipófago, ga, *n. & a.* hippofagist.
hipofosfato, *m.* hypophosphate.
hipofosfito, *m.* hypophosphite.
hipogástrico, ca, *a.* hypogastric.
hipogastro, *m.* (anat.) hypogastrium.
hipogénico, ca, *a.* (geol.) hypogene.
hipogeo, *m.* (arch.) hypogeium.
hipogloso, sa, *a.* hypoglossal.
hipogrifo, *m.* (myth.) hippogriff.
hipomanes, *m.* (vet.) vaginal discharge from the mare when in heat.
hiponitrato, *m.* (chem.) subnitrate.
hiponítrico, ca, *a.* hyponitrous.
hipopótamo, *m.* (zool.) hippopotamus.
hioso, sa, *a.* having hiccough.
hipóstasis, *f.* (theol.) hypostasis.
hipostáticamente, *adv.* hypostatically.
hipostático, ca, *a.* hypostatical.
hiposulfato, *m.* (chem.) hyposulphate.
hiposulfito, *m.* hyposulphite.
hipoteca, *f.* mortgage, pledge; (law) hypothecation, hypothec.
hipotecable, *a.* mortgageable.
hipotecar, *va.* (*pret.* HIPOTEQUÉ: *subj.* HIPOTEQUE) to hypothecate, pledge, mortgage.
hipotecario, ria, *a.* belonging to a mortgage; hypothecary.
hipotenusa, *f.* (geom.) hypotenuse.
hipótesis, *f.* hypothesis.
hipotético, ca, *a.* hypothetic.
hipsometría, *f.* hypsometry.—**hipsométrico, ca,** *a.* hypsometric.—**hipsómetro,** *m.* hypsometer.
hipurato, *m.* (chem.) hippurate.—**hipuria,** *f.* (med.) hippuria.—**hipúrico, ca,** *a.* (chem.) hippuric.
hircano, na, *n. & a.* Hircanian.
hircino, na, *a.* hircinous, goatlike.
hirco, *m.* (zool.) wild goat.
hiriente, *a.* hurting, cutting, offensive.
hiriera, hirió. *V.* HERIR.
hirma, *f.* selvage of cloth.
hirsuto, ta, *a.* hirsute, hairy, bristly.
hirundinaria, *f.* (bot.) = CELIDONIA.
hirviendo, *gerund* of HERVIR.
hirviente, *a.* boiling, seething.
hirviera, hirviese, hirvió. *V.* HERVIR.
hisca, *f.* birdlime.
hiscal, *m.* esparto rope of three strands.
hisopada, *f.* water sprinkled with an aspergill.
hisopear, *va.* to sprinkle with an aspergill.

For pronunciation, see the rules at the beginning of the book.

hisopillo, *m. dim.* small aspergill; bit of soft linen at the end of a stick, used to wash and refresh the mouth of a sick person; (bot.) winter savory.

hisopo, *m.* (bot.) hyssop; (eccl.) aspergill, sprinkler.—**h. húmedo,** (pharm.) grease collected in washing fleeces of wool.

hispalense, *a.* native of or belonging to Seville.

hispánico, ca, *a.* Hispanic.—**hispanismo,** *m.* Hispanicism.—**Hispanista,** *n.* Spanish scholar.—**hispanizado, da,** *a,* & *pp.* = ESPAÑOLADO.—**hispanizar,** *va.* = ESPAÑOLIZAR.

hispano, na. **I.** Hispanic, Spanish. **II.** *n.* Spaniard.—**hispanoamericano, na,** *n.* ¡& *a.* Spanish-American.

híspido, da, *a.* bristly, hirsute.

hispir, *va.* & *vn.* to swell; make or become spongy.

histéresis, *f.* (elec.) hysteresis.

histérico, ca. **I.** *a.* hysteric, hysterical. **II.** *m.* hysterics.

histerismo, *m.* (med.) hysteria.

histerotomía, *m.* (surg.) hysterotomy.

histología, *f.* histology.—**histológico, ca,** *a.* histological.—**histólogo,** *m.* histologist.

historia, *f.* history; tale, story; fable; (art) history piece.—**dejarse de historias,** to stop beating about the bush and come to the point; to cut out nonsense, to stop fooling.—**picar en h.,** to be more serious than it seems.—**ser de h.,** to have a history (bad antecedents).

historiado, da, *pp.* & *a.* (coll.) excessively adorned; (art) well-composed (figure, painting).

historiador, ra, *n.* historian.

historial, *a.* historical, historic.

historialmente, *adv.* historically.

historiar, *va.* to record, to chronicle, to narrate; (art) to represent, paint, depict.

históricamente, *adv.* historically.

histórico, ca, *a.* historical.

historieta, *f. dim.* short story or narrative.

historiógrafo, *m.* historiographer.

historión, *m.* tedious, long-winded story.

histrión, *m.* actor, player; buffoon, juggler.

histriónico, ca, *a.* histrionic.

histrionisa, *f.* actress or danseuse.

histrionismo, *m.* histrionism.

hita, *f.* headless nail, brad, wire nail; guide post.

hitita, *n.* & *a.* Hittite.

hito, ta. **I.** *a.* adjoining (s. o. of a house or street); fixed, firm; black (horse). **II.** *m.* landmark; guidepost; milestone; hob and quoits; (artl.) target.—**a h.,** fixedly, firmly.—**dar en el h.,** to hit the nail on the head; to see the point.—**mirar de h. en h.,** to stare at; to look at from head to foot.

hitón, *m.* large cut nail.

hizo. *V.* HACER.

hobachón, na, *a.* fat and lazy; (Colomb.) shy (s. o. horses).

hobachonería, *f.* laziness, sloth.

hocicada, *f.* blow with the snout.

hocicar. **I.** *va.* to root (as hogs). **II.** *vn.* to fall headlong with the face to the ground; to knock one's face against an object; (coll.) to get into difficulties; (naut.) to pitch.

hocico, *m.* snout, muzzle; big-lipped mouth; pouting; (coll.) face.—**de hocicos,** by the nose: face downwards.—**estar con, or de, h.,** to be ill-humored, sulky.—**meter el h.,** to stick one's nose in other people's business.

hocicón, na, *or* **hocicudo, da,** *a.* long-snouted; blubber-lipped, flap-mouthed.

hocino, *m.* (agr.) bill, billhook; glen, dell; narrow gorge or canyon.—*pl.* gardens in glens.

hociquillo, ito, *m. dim.* little snout.

hodómetro, *m.* = ODÓMETRO.

hogañazo, hogaño, *adv.* (coll.) this present year; in these days.

hogar, *m.* home (often called **h. doméstico**); hearth, fireplace; (st. eng.) furnace.

hogaza, *f.* large loaf of bread.

hoguera, *f.* bonfire; blaze.

hoja, *f.* leaf (of a plant, a book, a door); petal; leaf, foil, sheet or thin plate (of metal); blade (of a sword or knife); sword; sheet (of paper); veneer; half of each of the principal parts of a garment; window shutter; ground cultivated one year and lying at rest for another.—*pl.* (arch.) leaf ornaments, foliation.—**h. de estaño,** tinfoil.—**h. de lata,** tin plate.—**h. de servicios,** record; (mil.) certificate setting forth the rank and services of a military officer.—**h. de tocino,** side of a hog.—**h. toledana,** Toledo blade.—**h. volante,** fly sheet; handbill; supplement, extra.—**doblemos la h.,** no more of that; let us drop it.—**volver la h.,** to turn the leaf; to change one's views; to fail to keep one's promise; to change the subject (in conversation).

hojalata, *f.* tin plate. *V.* HOJA DE LATA.

hojalatería, *f.* tinware; tin shop.

hojalatero, *m.* tinman, tinsmith.

hojaldrado, *pp.* & *a.* resembling puff paste, lamellar, foliated.

hojaldrar, *va.* to make into puff paste.

hojaldre, *m.* or *f.* puff paste.—**quitar la h. al pastel,** (coll.) to detect a fraud, to discover a plot.

hojaldrista, *n.* puff paste baker.

hojarasca, *f.* dead leaves; excessive foliage; trash, rubbish.

hojarascoso, sa, *a.* trashy.

hojear. **I.** *va.* to turn the leaves of; to glance at (a book), look over hastily. **II.** *vn.* to exfoliate, scale off.

hojica, illa, ita, *f. dim.* small leaf.

hojoso, sa; hojudo, da, *a.* leafy, fronded.

hojuela, *f. dim.* small leaf, leaflet; pancake; gold or silver flat thread for embroidery; skins of pressed olives.

¡hola! *interj.* hello! ho, ho! (naut.) hoy! ahoy!

holán, holán batista, *m.* cambric; batiste.

holanda, *f.* fine Dutch linen, cambric.

holandés, sa, *n.* & *a.* Dutch, Hollander (-ish).—**a la holandesa,** (b. b.) in cloth.

holandeta, holandilla, *f.* brown holland.

holgachón, na, *a.* (coll.) used to an easy and comfortable lif e.

holgadamente, *adv.* amply, fully, loosely, easily; quietly, carelessly; comfortably.

holgado, da, *a.* & *pp.* loose, lax, easy; large, spacious; disengaged, at leisure; comfortable; well off.

holganza, *f.* leisure, ease; diversion, recreation.

holgar. **I.** *vn.* (ind. HUELGO: subj. HUELGUE) to rest; to quit work; to be idle; to be needless or useless; to take pleasure or satisfaction. **II.** *vr.* to sport, dally, trifle; to idle; to amuse one's self.

holgazán, na. **I.** *a.* idle, lazy, indolent. **II.** *n.* idler, loiterer, lounger.

holgazanear, *vn.* to idle, to loiter, to lounge.

holgazanería, *f.* idleness, laziness, indolence.

holgón, a, *a.* indolent and pleasure-loving.

holgorio, *m.* (coll.) boisterous frolic or spree.

holgueta, *f.* (coll.) feast, merrymaking.

holgura, *f.* frolic, merrymaking; width, breadth; ease, comfort; plenty of room or space; (mech.) play.

holocausto, *m.* holocaust, burnt sacrifice.

holocéfalo, la. **I.** *a.* (zool.) holocephalous. **II.** *m. pl.* Holocephali.

holoédrico, ca, *a.* (min.) holohedral.

hológrafo, fa, *a.* (law) holographic, holograph.

holómetro, *m.* holometer, pantometer.

holosérico, ca, *a.* all-silk.

holotúrido, da; holoturioidco, a. **I.** *n.* & *a.* (zool.) holothurian. **II.** *m. pl.* Holothuroidea.

holladura, *f.* trampling; duty paid for the run of cattle.

hollar, *va.* (ind. HUELLO: subj. HUELLE) to tread upon, trample under foot; to humiliate.

hollejo, *m.* skin (of a fruit, etc.).

hollejuelo, *m. dim.* small piece of skin; thin skin.

hollín, *m.* soot, lampblack.

holliniento, ta, *a.* fuliginous, sooty.

homarrache, *m.* clown.

hombracho, hombrachón, *m. aug.* heavy-built man.

hombrada, *f.* manly action; impulse.

hombradía, *f.* manliness.
hombrazo, *m. aug.* big man.
hombre, *m.* man; (vulg.) husband; ombre, a card game; (coll., in addressing or speaking to a friend, often as a mere expletive) boy, old chap, dear fellow, man, my dear man.—**¡hombre!** an exclamation of surprise.—**h. achaparrado,** short and lusty man.—**¡h. al agua!** man overboard.—**h. bueno,** (law) arbiter, arbitrator, referee.—**h. de armas,** military man.—**h. de estado,** statesman.—**h. de puños,** strong, valiant man.—**ser muy h.,** to be a real man, or quite a man.
hombrear. I. *vn.* to assume the man before the time. **II.** *vn.* & *vr.* to vie with another.
hombrecico, cito, cillo, zuelo, *m. dim.* little man; youth.
hombrecillos, *m. pl.* (bot.) hops.
hombrera, *f.* (arm.) pauldron.
hombría de bien, *f.* probity, honesty.
hombrillo, *m.* (sew.) yoke of a shirt.
hombro, *m.* shoulder.—**h. con h.,** cheek by jowl.—**a h.,** on the shoulders.—**arrimar el h.,** to lend a hand; to exert one's self.—**echar al h.,** to shoulder; to become responsible for.—**llevar en hombros,** to carry on the shoulders; to support, to protect.—**sobre los hombros** = A H.
hombrón, *m. aug.* big, lusty man.
hombronazo, *m. aug.* huge man.
hombruno, na, *a.* mannish.
homenaje, *m.* homage; obeisance; fealty, allegiance; respect.
homeópata, *n.* & *a.* homœopath (-ic).
homeopatía, *f.* homœopathy.—**homeopático, ca,** *a.* homœopathic.
homérico, ca, *a.* Homeric.
homicida. I. *a.* homicidal. **II.** *n. f.* murderer; homicide.
homicidio, *m.* homicide; an ancient tribute.
homilía, *f.* (eccl.) homily.—**homiliario,** *m.* collection of homilies.—**homilista,** *m.* homilist.
hominal, *a.* relating to man.
hominicaco, *m.* (coll.) insignificant fellow, whippersnapper.
homocéntrico, ca, *a.* homocentric.
homofonía, *f.* homophony.
homófono, na, *a.* homophonous.
homogeneidad, *f.* homogeneity, homogeneousness.—**homogéneo, a,** *a.* homogeneous.
homógrafo, fa, *a.* homonymous.
homologación, *f.* (law) homologation.
homologar, *va.* (law) to homologate.
homólogo, ga, *a.* (geom.) homologous; (log.) synonymous.
homonimia, *f.* homonymy.
homónimo, ma, *a.* homonymous; namesake.
homóptero, ra. I. *n.* & *a.* (zool.) homopteran (-ous). **II.** *m. pl.* Homoptera.
homúnculo, *m.* homunculus.
honda, *f.* sling.—**h. y precinta,** (naut.) parbuckle.
hondable, *a.* (naut.) soundable.
hondamente, *adv.* deeply, profoundly.
hondarras, *f. pl.* dregs, lees, sediment.
hondazo, *m.* throw or blow with a sling.
hondear, *va.* (naut.) to sound; to unload.
hondero, *m.* slinger.—**hondijo,** *m.* sling.
hondillo, *n.* any of the pieces which form the seats of breeches or drawers.
hondo, da. I. *a.* deep; low. **II.** *m.* depth, bottom.—**de h.,** in depth.
hondón, *m.* bottom; dell, glen; deep hole; footpiece of a stirrup; eye of a needle.
hondonada, *f.* dale, ravine, glen; depression.
hondura, *f.* depth; profundity.—**meterse en honduras,** to go beyond one's depth (fig.).
hondureño, ña, *a.* Honduras (u. a.).
honestamente, *adv.* honestly; modestly; virtuously.
honestar, *va.* to honor; to excuse, palliate.
honestidad, *f.* honesty; modesty; purity; decorum.
honesto, ta, *a.* honest; decent, decorous; pure, chaste; reasonable, just.

hongo, *m.* (bot.) mushroom; fungus; slouch hat; Derby hat.—**hongoso, sa,** *a.* fungous.—**honguillo,** *m.* small fungus.
honor, *m.* honor; fame.—*pl.* dignity, rank, office, honors, privileges, honorary title or position.
honorable, *a.* worthy, honorable; illustrious; reputable, reliable.
honorablemente, *adv.* honorably, creditably.
honorario, ria. I. *a.* honorary. **II.** *m.* honorarium, fee.
honoríficamente, *adv.* honorably; honorarily.
honorífico, ca, *a.* honorary; honorable.
honra, *f.* honor; reverence, respect; reputation, fame; purity, chastity.—*pl.* obsequies.
honradamente, *adv.* honorably, honestly.
honradez, *f.* honesty, probity, integrity.
honrado, da, *a.* honest, honorable.
honrador, ra, *n.* & *a.* honorer (-ing).
honramiento, *m.* honoring.
honrar. I. *va.* to honor, do honor to; to be an honor for; (com.) to honor. **II.** *vn.* to honor; to be an honor. **III.** *vr.* to deem it an honor; to be honored.
honrilla, *f. dim.* keen sense of honor or duty. punctiliousness (usually **la negra h.**).
honrosamente, *adv.* honorably; creditably.
honroso, sa, *a.* honorable, decorous; honoring, honor-giving.—**ser h.,** to be an honor.
hontanal, *m. V.* HONTANAR.—*pl.* feasts of the ancients held at fountains.
hontanar, *m.* place abounding in springs.
hopa, *f.* long cassock; sack for an executed criminal.
hopalanda, *f.* gown worn by students.
hopear, *vn.* to wag the tail.
hoplita, *m.* hoplite.
hoploteca, *f.* = OPLOTECA.
hopo, *m.* bushy tail (as of a fox).
hoque, *m.* treat to close a bargain.
hora, *f.* hour; time, season for doing anything; distance covered in an hour; league.—*pl.* (eccl.) prayerbook.—**h. menguada,** fatal, or unhappy, hour.—**a buena h.,** opportunely, at the proper time.—**a la h.,** at once, right away; then.—**a la h. de ésta,** or **a la h. de ahora,** (coll.) at this moment.—**a última h.,** at the last moment, at the eleventh hour.—**dar la h.,** to strike the time; to adjourn (the meeting, session, etc.); to dismiss (the class, etc.).—**en h. buena,** it is well. (*V.* ENHORABUENA).—**en h. mala** = ENHORAMALA.—**no ver la h. de,** to look forward to.—**por horas,** by instants.—**¿qué h. es?** (in some places, **¿qué horas son?**), what time is it?—**vete en h. mala,** (coll.) begone, get out of my sight.
hora, *adv.* now, at this time, at present.
horadable, *a.* capable of being pierced.
horadación, *f.* perforation; boring, piercing.
horadado, da, *a.* silkworm's cocoon bored through.
horadador, ra, *n.* & *a.* perforator (-ing); borer (-ing); burrower (-ing).
horadar, *va.* to perforate, bore; burrow.
horado, *m.* hole bored through; cavern, grotto.
horambre, *m.* hole in the cheeks of mills.
horario, ria. I. *a.* horary, horal, hour (u. a.). **II.** *m.* hour hand of a clock or watch; (r. w.) time table.
horca, *f.* gallows, gibbet; (agr.) hayfork, pitchfork; forked prop for trees or vines; yoke for dogs or hogs; rope or string of onions or garlic.
horcado, da, *a.* forked, forky.
horcadura, *f.* fork of a tree.
horcajadas, horcajadillas.—a h., astride or astraddle.
horcajadura, *f.* fork formed by the two thighs.
horcajo, *m.* yoke or collar for mules; in oil mills, the Y-shaped division of the beam; fork or confluence of two streams.
horcate, *m.* (sad.) hame.
horco, *m.* rope or string of onions or garlic.
horcón, *m.* forked pole to support the branches of fruit trees.
horchata, *f.* orgeat.

---

horchatería, *f.* place where orgeat is sold.
horchatero, ra, *n.* orgeat maker or seller.
horda, *f.* horde.
hordiate, *m.* pearl barley; barley water.
horero, *m.* (S. A.) hour hand.
horizontal, *a. & f.* horizontal.
horizontalidad, *f.* horizontality.
horizontalmente, *adv.* horizontally, flatly.
horizonte, *m.* horizon.—**h. artificial,** artificial horizon.—**h. racional,** celestial horizon, rational horizon.—**h. sensible,** sensible horizon, visible horizon (= horizon in the ordinary sense).
horma, *f.* mold, model; shoemaker's last; hatter's block; (mas.) dry wall.—**hallar la h. de su zapato,** (iron.) to meet with one's match.
hormadoras, *f. pl.* (Colomb.) underskirt.
hormaza, *f.* (mas.) dry wall.
hormazo, *m.* blow with a last or block; heap of stones; house and garden.
hormero, *m.* last maker.
hormiga, *f.* ant; (med.) itch or cutaneous pruritus.—**h. león,** (ent.) ant lion.
hormigo, *m.* (min.) sifted ashes used in smelting quicksilver.—*pl.* sweetmeat of mashed almonds or filberts; coarse parts of flour or poorly-ground wheat.
hormigón, *m.* (eng.) concrete; (vet.) a disease of cattle; (bot.) a disease of some plants.—**h. armado,** reinforced concrete.—**h. hidráulico,** hydraulic-cement concrete; hydraulic-lime mortar.
hormigonera, *f.* concrete mixer.
hormigoso, sa, *a.* formicine; ant-eaten.
hormigueamiento, *m.* formication, itching.
hormiguear, *vn.* to itch; to swarm.
hormigüela, *f. dim.* small ant.
hormigueo, *m.* formication; itching.
hormiguero. **I.** *m.* ant hill or hillock; ant hole or nest; swarm of people or little animals; (orn.) wryneck.—*pl.* piles of weeds covered with earth and burned to serve as manure. **II.** *a.* relating to the itch; feeding on ants, ant-eating.
hormiguita, *f. dim.* small ant.
hormiguillar, *va.* (min.) to mix (grains of silver) with salt.
hormiguillo, *m.* (vet.) a disease of horses' hoofs; people ranged in a line, who pass materials or loads from hand to hand; (Mex.) a spicy sirup; almond sweatmeat; (min.) amalgamating mixture.
hormilla, *f. dim.* small last; buttonmold or core.
hornabeque, *m.* (fort.) hornwork.
hornablenda, *f.* (min.) hornblende.
hornacero, *m.* (metal.) crucible man.
hornacina, *f.* (arch.) vaulted niche.
hornacho, *m.* shaft of a mine; furnace for casting statues.
hornachuela, *f.* cave or hut.
hornada, *f.* batch, bread baked at one time; melt (of a blast furnace).
hornaguear, *va.* to dig for coal.
hornaguera, *f.* pit coal, hard coal.
hornaguero, ra, *a.* wide, spacious; coaly.
hornaje, *m.* fee for baking.
hornaza, *f.* jewellers' furnace; (art) light yellow color; yellow glazing.
hornazo, *m.* Easter cake ornamented with eggs; Easter present given to preacher.
hornear, *vn.* to carry on the trade of a baker.
hornería, *f.* trade of a baker.
hornero, ra, *n.* baker.
horniga, *f.* brushwood for an oven.
hornijero, ra, *n.* brushwood carrier.
hornilla, *f.* grated chamber in a masonry kitchen range; compartment in a pigeonry for nesting; nest pan.
hornillo, *m. dim.* portable furnace or stove; (min.) blast hole; (mil.) fougade.—**h. de atanor,** self-feeding furnace.
hornito, *m.* (Mex.) mud volcano.
horno, *m.* oven; kiln; furnace; cavity in which bees lodge.—**h. boliche** = H. DE REVERBERO.—**h. de cal,** limekiln.—**h. de calcinación,** calcining furnace.—**h. de copela,** cupelling or cupellation furnace.—**h. de cuba,** blast furnace in general.—

h. de ladrillo, brickkiln.—**h. de manga,** cupola furnace.—**h. de reverbero,** or **tostadillo,** Spanish furnace, or reverberatory furnace.—**h. eléctrico,** electric furnace.—**alto h.,** (high) blast furnace.
horometría, *f.* horometry.
horón, *m.* large round hamper or frail.
horópter, *m.* (opt.) horopter.
horoptérico, ca, *a.* horopteric.
horóptero, *m.* (opt.) horopter.
horóscopo, *m.* horoscope.
horqueta, *f. dim.* forked pole; (naut.) outrigger.
horquilla, *f.* forked pole, bar, pipe, etc.; pitchfork, croom; hairpin; double-pointed tack; a disease causing the hair to split; upper extremity of the sternum; wish-bone; (surg.) fourchette; (mil.) fork rest; (naut.) oarlock; (vet.) frog of a horse's foot.—*pl.* (naut.) crutches, curbs.—**horquillas de dar fuego,** breaming forks.
horrendamente, *adv.* horribly.
horrendo, da, *a.* hideous, horrible, awful.
hórreo, *m.* barn, mow; granary built on pillars.
horrero, *m.* keeper of a granary.
horribilidad, *f.* dreadfulness, hideousness.
horribilísimo, *a. super.* most horrible.
horrible, *a.* horrid, horrible; hideous, heinous.
horriblemente, *adv.* horribly; heinously.
horridez, *f.* horridness.—**hórrido, da,** *a.* horrible; hideous.—**horrífico, ca,** *a.* (poet.) horrific, awful, horrid.
horripilación, *f.* dread, fright; (med.) horripilation, goose flesh.
horripilante, *a.* horrifying, harrowing.
horripilar. **I.** *va. & vn.* to horripilate, cause or feel horror. **II.** *vr.* to be horrified.
horripilativo, va, *a.* (med.) horripilating.
horrísono, na, *a.* (poet.) horrisonous.
horro, ra, *a.* enfranchised, freed; not pregnant.
horror, *m.* horror; enormity, hideousness, frightfulness.
horrorizar. **I.** *va.* to horrify, terrify. **II.** *vr.* to be terrified.
horrorosamente, *adv.* horribly.
horroroso, sa, *a.* horrible; hideous, frightful.
horrura, *f.* filth, dirt, scoria, dross.
hortaliza, *f.* garden stuff, vegetables.
hortatorio, ria, *a.* = EXHORTATÓRIO.
hortecillo, *m. dim.* small garden.
hortelana, *f.* gardener's wife.
hortelano, na. **I.** *a.* hortensial. **II.** *m.* horticulturist; (orn.) ortolan.
hortense, *a.* hortensial.
hortensia, *f.* (bot.) hydrangea.
hortera. **I.** *f.* wooden bowl. **II.** *m.* in Madrid, drygoods clerk.
horticultor, ra, *n.* horticulturist.
horticultura, *f.* horticulture, orcharding.
horuelo, *m.* common; meeting place for young people.
hosanna, *m.* (eccl.) hosanna.
hosco, ca, *a.* dark-colored (as a mulatto); sullen, gloomy.
hoscoso, sa, *a.* crisp, rough.
hospedador, ra, *n.* one who gives lodging.
hospedaje, hospedamiento, *m.* lodging, board.
hospedar. **I.** *va.* to lodge, harbor. **II.** *vn. & vr.* (with **en**) to lodge or take lodgings (at); to stop (at), live (in).
hospedería, *f.* hospice; hostel in universities; hostelry, inn; spare room, guest room; lodging.
hospedero, ra, *n.* host; innkeeper.
hospiciano, na, *n.* poor person who lives in a house of charity.
hospicio, *m.* hospice; poor house; orphan asylum.
hospital, *m.* hospital.—**h. de sangre,** (mil.) field hospital.—**hospitalario, ria.** **I.** *a.* hospitable. **II.** *m.* hospitaller.—**hospitalero, ra,** *n.* manager of a hospital; hospitaller; hospitable person.—**hospitalidad,** *f.* hospitality; stay in a hospital.
hospitalmente, *adv.* hospitably.
hostal, *m.* hostelry, inn.
hostalero, ra, *n.* inn or tavern keeper, host (-ess).
hostelero, ra, *n.* innkeeper, tavern keeper.

hostería, *f.* inn, tavern, hostelry.
hostia, *f.* sacrificial victim; (eccl.) host, wafer; sugar wafer.—**hostiario,** *m.* wafer box.—**hostiero,** *m.* person who prepares the host.
hostigador, ra, *a.* harasser, chastiser.
hostigamiento, *m.* chastisement; vexation.
hostigar, *va.* (*pret.* HOSTIGUÉ: *subj.* HOSTIGUE) to lash, scourge, chastise; to vex, trouble, harass; to gall, bore, tire.
hostigo, *m.* lash; weather-beaten wall; beating of rain and wind against a wall.
hostil, *a.* hostile.—**hostilidad,** *f.* hostility.
hostilizar, *va.* (*pret.* HOSTILICÉ: *subj.* HOSTILICE) to commit hostilities with, be hostile to, antagonize.
hostilmente, *adv.* with hostility.
hotel, *m.* hotel; villa.
hotentote, ta, *n. & a.* Hottentot.
hovero, ra, *a.* = OVERO.
hoy, *adv.* to-day; now, at the present time, nowadays.—**h. día,** or **h. en día,** nowadays.—**h. por h.,** at the present time; for the present.—**de h. a mañana,** before to-morrow; when you least expect it.—**de h. en adelante,** or **de h. más,** henceforward, in future.—**por h.,** for the present.
hoya, *f.* hole, pit; grave; valley, dale, glen; basin (of a river).
hoyada, *f.* low dale.
hoyanca, *f.* potter's field in cemeteries.
hoyito, *m. dim.* small hole.
hoyo, *m.* hole, pit, excavation; dent, indentation, hollow; pockmark; grave.
hoyoso, sa, *a.* full of holes.
hoyuela, *f. dim.* of HOYA; hollow in the neck under Adam's apple.
hoyuelo, *m. dim.* small hole; dimple.
hoz, *f.* sickle; defile, ravine; narrow pass.—**de h. y de coz,** (coll.) headlong.
hozadero, *m.* hogs' rooting place.—**hozadura,** . rooting (of hogs).—**hozar,** *va.* to root (as hogs).
huaca, *f.* = GUACA.
huacal, *m.* crate; (Mex.) hurdle basket.
huaco, *m.* idol found in HUACAS.
huaico, *m.* (Peru) large mass of rock fallen into a river or stream.
huairuro, *m.* Peruvian variety of red bean.
huaquero, *m.* (Peru) pitcher found in HUACAS.
huasca, *f.* (Peru) whip, lash.
hucha, *f.* large chest; money box, bank; savings.
huchear, *va.* to hoot, shout, cry out, call.
¡húchohó! *interj.* used to call birds.
huebra, *f.* ground plowed in one day by a yoke of oxen; pair of mules with a plowman hired for a day's work.—**huebrero,** *m.* laborer who plows with a pair of mules; one who lets out mules by the day.
hueca, *f.* spiral groove of a spindle.
hueco, ca. **I.** *a.* hollow; empty; vain, empty-headed; resonant; inflated; soft, spongy (as ground or wool). **II.** *m.* hole; hollow, gap, void, break; notch or nick of a wheel; interval of time or space; vacancy.
huecú, *m.* (Ch.) deep slough covered with grass.
huélfago, *m.* difficulty of breathing in beasts.
huelga, *f.* rest, repose, leisure; strike; recreation, merrymaking; (agr.) lying fallow; (mech.) windage.
huelgo, *m.* breath, respiration; (mech.) windage; room, space, play.—**tomar h.,** to take breath.
huelgo, yo huelgue. *V.* HOLGAR.
huelguista, *n.* striker.
huella, *f.* track, footstep, footprint; tread; trampling; stair tread, treadboard; impression; trace, vestige, trail.
huello, *m.* treading; lower part of an animal's hoof.
huello, yo huelle. *V.* HOLLAR.
huequecito, *m. dim.* small hole or space.
huérfago, *m.* (vet.) = HUÉLFAGO.
huerfanito, ita, *n. dim.* little orphan.
huérfano, na, *n. & a.* orphan (-ed).
huero, ra, *a.* addle; empty, vain; (Mex.) fair, blonde.

huerta, *f.* large vegetable or kitchen garden; **irri**gated land.
huertezuela, *f. dim.* small kitchen garden.
huertezuelo, *m. dim.* small orchard.
huerto, *m.* orchard, fruit garden.
huesa, *f.* grave, tomb.
huesarrón, *m. aug.* large bone.
huesecico, illo, ito, *m. dim.* little bone.
hueso, *m.* bone; stone, core; part of a limestone which remains unburnt in the kiln; drudge, drudgery.—**h. innominado,** innominate bone.— **h. navicular,** scaphoid, or navicular, bone.—**h. palomo,** coccyx.—**h. sacro,** (anat.) sacrum.—**a h.,** (mas.) dry (without mortar).—**a otro perro con ese h.,** tell that to the marines.—**la sin h.,** the tongue.—**no dejar h. sano a,** to rake over the coals, to roast to death (fig.).
huesoso, sa, *a.* bony, osseous.
huésped, da, *n.* guest, lodger; host (-ess) inn-keeper, tavern keeper.
hueste, *f.* host, army.
huesudo, da, *a.* bony, having large bones.
hueva, *f.* spawn of fishes, roe.
huevar, *vn.* to begin to lay (s. o. poultry).
huevecico, illo, ito, zuelo, *m. dim.* small egg.
huevera, *f.* ovarium of birds; egg stand, egg cup. —**huevero, ra,** *n.* egg dealer.
huevo, *m.* egg; (shoe) hollow piece of wood for shaping the sole.—**h. de Colón,** or **de Juanelo,** anything that seems difficult to do, but is easy after one learns how to do it.—**h. duro,** hard (boiled, fried) egg.—**huevos de faltriquera,** candied yolks of egg.—**huevos escalfados,** poached eggs.—**huevos estrellados,** fried eggs.— **huevos hilados,** threadlike sweetmeat made of eggs and sugar.—**huevos moles,** yolks of eggs made up with pounded almonds and sugar.— **huevos pasados por agua,** soft-boiled eggs.— **huevos revueltos,** scrambled eggs.—**huevos y torreznos,** collops and eggs.—**sórbete,** or **chú pate, ese h.,** (coll.) put that in your pipe and smoke it.
hugonote, ta, *n. & a.* Huguenot.
huída, *f.* flight, escape; outlet.
huidero, *m.* cover, shelter; laborer in quick-silver mines.
huidizo, za, *a.* fugitive, fleeing.
huillín, *m.* a kind of Chilean otter.
huir. **I.** *vn. & vr.* (*gerund,* HUYENDO: *ind.* HUYO: *pret.* él HUYÓ: *subj.* HUYA) to flee, to escape; to run away, elope; to slip away, fly; (w. **de**) to shun, avoid. **II.** *va.* to avoid, shun.—**h. la cara de,** to avoid, keep away from.
hule, *m.* oilcloth, oilskin; (Am.) India rubber.
hulero, *m.* rubber gatherer.
hulla, *f.* mineral (gen. bituminous) coal.—**h. aglutinante,** coking coal.—**h. blanca,** white coal (water).—**h. conglutinante,** coking coal.—**h. grasa,** fat coal.—**h. magra,** non-coking coal.
hullero, ra. **I.** *a.* containing or pertaining to soft coal. **II.** *f.* colliery.
humada, *f.* = AHUMADA.
humanamente, *adv.* humanely; humanly.
humanar. **I.** *va.* to humanize; to soften. **II.** *vr.* to become man; to become human.
humanidad, *f.* humanity; mankind; human weakness; humaneness; (coll.) corpulence, fleshiness.—*pl.* humanities.
humanista, *n.* humanist, scholar.
humanitario, ria, *a.* humanitarian.
humanizar, *va. & vr.* = HUMANAR.
humano, na. **I.** *a.* human; humane. **II.** *m.* man, human being.
humarazo, *m.* = HUMAZO.
humareda, *f.* a great deal of smoke.
humazga, *f.* hearth money, fumage.
humazo, *m.* dense smoke.
humeante, *a.* smoking, fuming, fumant.
humear. **I.** *vn.* to smoke, emit smoke, fumes, or vapors. **II.** *va.* (Am.) to fumigate.
humectación, *f.* dampening.—**humectante,** *a.* (med.) moistening.—**humectar,** *va.* (med.) to moisten, wet.—**humectativo, va,** *a.* moistening.
humedad, *f.* humidity, moisture, dampness.

humedal, *m.* humid soil, marsh.
humedecer, *va.* (*ind.* HUMEDEZCO: *subj.* HUMEDEZCA) to moisten, dampen.
húmedo, da, *a.* humid, wet, moist, damp.
humera, *f.* (coll.) fit of drunkenness.
humeral, *a.* (anat.) humeral.
húmero, *m.* (anat.) humerus.
humero, *m.* smoke pipe; chimney flue; meat-smoking place; much smoke.
húmido, da, *a* = HÚMEDO.
humildad, *f.* humility; meekness; lowliness.
humilde, *a.* humble; meek; lowly.
humildemente, *adv.* humbly, modestly, meekly.
humillación, *f.* humiliation; humbling.
humilladero, *m.* road chapel or shrine.
humillador, ra, *n.* & *a.* humiliator (-ing).
humillante, *a.* humiliating.
humillar. I. *va.* to humiliate; humble; crush, subdue. **II.** *vr.* to humble one's self; to lower one's self.
humillo, *m. dim.* thin smoke or vapor; vanity, petty pride; a disease of sucking pigs.
humita, *f.* (Peru) cake of maize and sugar.
humo, *m.* smoke; vapor, steam, fume.—*pl.* families or houses in a town or village; airs, conceit.
humor, *m.* humor; disposition, temper; (med.) humor.—**buen h.,** good nature, jovial disposition. —**estar de buen (mal) h.,** to be in good (bad) humor or spirits.—**mal h.,** ill temper.
humorada, *f.* pleasant joke, humorous saying.
humorado, da, *a.* full of humors.—**bien (mal) h.,** in good (bad) humor; having a good (bad) temper.
humoral, *a.* humoral.
humorcico, illo, ito, *m. dim.* little temper.
humorístico, ca, *a.* jolly, humorous, facetious.
humorosidad, *f.* abundance of humors.
humoroso, sa, *a.* watery, containing fluid.
humoso, sa, *a.* smoky, fumy.
humus, *m.* humus.
hundible, *a.* sinkable.
hundimiento, *m.* sinking; cave-in; downfall, collapse.
hundir. I. *va.* to submerge, sink; stave in, crush; destroy, ruin; to refute, confound. **II.** *vr.* to sink; fall down, crumble, collapse; (coll.) to hide, to lie in hiding, disappear.
húngaro, ra, *n.* & *a.* Hungarian.
huno, na, *n.* & *a.* Hun (-nish).
hupe, *f.* punk, touchwood, amadou.
hura, *f.* carbuncle on the head.
huracán, *m.* hurricane.
hurañamente, *adv.* unsociably, shyly.
hurañería, huraña, *f.* unsociability; shyness.
huraño, ña, *a.* unsociable, shy.
hurgar, *va.* (*pret.* HURGUÉ: *subj.* HURGUE) to stir, to poke; to stir up, excite.—**peor es hurgallo,** let well enough alone.
hurgón, *m.* poker, fire rake; (coll.) thrust with a sword.—**hurgonada,** *f.* poking (the fire); thrust.—**hurgonazo,** *m.* blow with a poker; thrust.—**hurgonear,** *va.* to poke (the fire); (coll.) to make a thrust at.—**hurgonero,** *m.* fire poker.
hurí, *f.* houri.
hurón, na. I. *n.* (zool.) ferret; (coll.) ferreter, prier. **II.** *a.* unsociable, shy.
huronear, *va.* to hunt with a ferret; (coll.) to pry into; to ferret out.—**huronera,** *f.* ferret hole; (coll.) lurking-place; small dark room.—**huronero,** *m.* ferret keeper.
¡hurra! *interj.* hurrah!
hurraca, *f.* (orn.) magpie.
hurtadillas,—a h., *adv.* by stealth, on the sly.
hurtadineros, *m.* money box, toy bank.
hurtador, ra, *n.* robber, thief.
hurtagua, *f.* watering pot.
hurtar. I. *va.* to steal, rob of, to cheat in weight or measure; to eat away (land, as the sea or a river); to alienate.—**h. el cuerpo,** to flee. **II.** *vr.* to withdraw, move away; to hide.
hurto, *m.* theft, robbery, stealing; thing stolen; (min.) driftway, heading.—**a h.,** by stealth.
husada, *f.* spindleful of yarn.

húsar, *m.* (mil.) hussar.
husero, *m.* beam of an antler.
husillero, *m.* one who attends the spindle in oil mills.
husillo, *m. dim.* small spindle; (mill) wheel spindle or shaft; screw pin.—*pl.* drains.
husita, *n.* Hussite.
husma.—andar a la h., (coll.) to explore in a prying manner, to nose about.
husmeador, ra, *n.* & *a.* scenter (-ing); prier (-ing), noser (-ing, -y).
husmear. I. *va.* to scent, smell, wind; (coll.) to pry, peep, nose into. **II.** *vn.* to become tainted, gamy, or high (meat).
husmeo, *m.* scenting, smelling; prying, nosing.
husmo, *m.* taint of meat.—**estar al h.,** (coll.) to be upon the scent; to wait or watch for a favorable opportunity.
huso, *m.* spindle; cop tube; bobbin; drum of a windlass; (aer.) fuselage.
huta, *f.* hut, huntsman's blind.
hutía, *f.* (zool.) hutia, a West-Indian rodent.
¡huy! *interj.* of surprise, astonishment, grief or alarm.

I

i, *conj.* (in some parts of S. A.) and.
ibérico, ca, *a.*; **iberio, ria,** *a.*; **ibero, ra,** *n.* & *a.* Iberian.
iberoamericano, na, *n.* & *a.* Ibero-American.
íbice, *m.* ibex, a kind of goat.
ibídem, *adv.* ibidem, in the same place.
ibis, *f.* (orn.) ibis, a wading bird.
ibiyaú, *m.* an Argentine night bird.
ibón, *m.* lake or basin on the slopes of the Pyrenees.
icaco, *m.* (bot.) coco plum.
icario, a, *a.* Icarian.
icástico, ca, *a.* natural, plain, unadorned.
icneumón, *m.* (zool.) ichneumon.
icnografía, *f.* (arch.) ichnography.
icnográfico, ca, *a.* ichnographical.
icón, icono, *m.* icon.
iconoclasta, *m.* iconoclast.
iconografía, *f.* iconography.
iconográfico, ca, *a.* iconographical.
iconólatra, *m.* iconolater.
iconología, *f.* (art) iconology.
iconómaco, *a.* iconoclastic.
iconostario, *m.* (eccl.) iconostaris.
icor, *m.* (surg.) gleet, ichor.
icoroso, sa, *a.* ichorous, serous.
icosaedro, *m.* (geom.) icosahedron.
ictericia, *f.* (med.) jaundice.—**ictericiado, da;**
ictérico, ca, *a.* icterical, jaundiced.
ictíneo, *m.* submarine vessel.
ictiófago, ga. I. *a.* fish-eating. **II.** *n.* ichthyophagist.
ictiol, *m.* (chem.) ichthyol.
ictiología, *f.* ichthyology.—**ictiológico, ca,** *a.* ichthyologic.—**ictiólogo, m.** ichthyologist.
ictiornis, *m.* (pal.) ichthyornis.
ictiosauro, *m.* ichthyosaurus.
ictiosis, *f.* ichthyosis.
ida, *f.* departure, outgoing; impetuosity; rash proceeding; sally; trail.—**i. del humo,** departure never to return.—**i. y vuelta,** out and home, round trip, excursion.—**idas,** frequent visits.—**idas y venidas,** comings and goings.—**de i. y vuelta,** return (ticket).—**en dos idas y venidas,** (coll.) in a jiffy.—**¡la i. del cuervo!** he's off, good riddance!
idea, *f.* idea.—**ideación,** *f.* (philos.) ideation.—**ideal,** *a.* & *m.* ideal.—**idealidad,** *f.* ideality.—**idealismo,** *m.* idealism.—**idealista,** *n.* & *a.* idealist (-ic)—**idealizar,** *va.* to idealize.—**idealmente,** *adv.* ideally.
idear, *va.* to conceive the idea of; to devise, contrive, plan, design.
ideático, ca, *a.* (Am.) whimsical, capricious.
ídem, idem, ditto, the same.
idénticamente, *adv.* identically.

idéntico, ca, *a.* (w. **a**) identic, identical (with).

identidad, *f.* identity.—**identificación,** *f.* identification.—**identificar. I** *va.* (*pret.* IDENTIFIQUÉ; *subj.* IDENTIFIQUE) to identify. **II.** *vr.* (w. **con**) to identify one's self (with).

Ideo, ea, *a.* belonging to Mount Ida

ideografía, *f.* ideography.

ideográfico, ca, *a.* ideographic.

ideología, *f.* ideology.—**ideológico, ca,** *a.* ideological.—**ideólogo, ga,** *m.* ideologist.

idílico, ca, *a.* idyllic.—**idilio,** *m.* idyl.

idiograma, *m.* ideogram.

idioma, *m.* language, tongue.

idiomático, ca, *a.* idiomatic.

idiosincrasia, *f.* idiosyncrasy.

idiosincrásico, ca, *a.* idiosyncratic.

idiota, *n.* & *a.* idiot (-ic).—idiotez,** *f.* idiocy.

idiotismo, *m.* idiocy; ignorance; idiom.

idólatra. I. *a.* idolatrous; heathen. **II.** *n.* idolater; (coll.) ardent lover.

idolatradamente, *adv.* idolatrously.

idolatrar, *va.* to idolize.

idolatría, *f.* idolatry; idolization.

idolátrico, ca, *a.* idolatrous.

ídolo, *m.* idol.

idolología, *f.* science dealing with idols.

idoneidad, *f.* competence, fitness, capacity.

idóneo, nea, *a.* competent; fit, able.

**idumeo, a, *n.* & *a.* Idumean.

idus, *m.* ides.

iglesia, *f.* church; ecclesiastical state; clergy; chapter; diocese; right of immunity enjoyed in churches.—**i. colegial,** collegiate church.—**i. matriz,** metropolitan church.—**i. mayor,** main church; cathedral (where there is one).—**i. militante,** church militant, the (Christian) living faithful.—**i. oriental,** Greek church.—**i. triunfante,** church triumphant.—**llevar a una mujer a la iglesia,** to take a woman to the altar (to marry her).

ignaro, ra, *a.* ignorant.

ignavia, *f.* idleness, laziness, carelessness.

ígneo, ea, *a.* igneous.

ignición, *f.* ignition.

ignífero, ra, *a.* igniferous, ignifluous.

ignipotente, *a.* (poet.) ignipotent.

ignito, ta, *a.* ignited, inflamed, red-hot.

ignívomo, ma, *a.* (poet.) vomiting fire.

ignografía, *f.* = ICNOGRAFIA.

ignominia, *f.* ignominy, infamy, disgrace.

ignominiosamente, *adv.* ignominiously.

ignominioso, sa, *a.* ignominious.

ignorado, da, *a.* & *pp.* unknown, hidden; fameless, obscure.

ignorancia, *f.* ignorance.—**i. crasa,** gross ignorance.—**i. no quita pecado,** ignorance of the law is no defense.—**i. supina,** ignorance from negligence.

ignorante. I. *a.* ignorant. **II.** *n.* ignoramus.—**ignorantemente,** *adv.* ignorantly.—**ignorantón, na. I.** *a. aug.* rather ignorant. **II.** *n.* ignoramus.

ignorar, *va.* to be ignorant of, not to know.

ignoto, ta, *a.* unknown, undiscovered.

igorrote, *m.* Igorrot, Luzon hunting tribesman; Igorrote language.

igual. I. *a.* equal; level, even, uniform; equable; constant, firm, unchangeable, consistent.—**i. que** (common although incorrect), equal to, the same as.—**(me) es i.,** it is all the same (to me), it makes no difference (to me). **II.** *m.* equal.—**por i.,** or **por un i.,** equally.—**signo i.,** sign of equality.—**sin i.,** unrivaled, matchless; without parallel.

iguala, *f.* agreement, convention, stipulation; equalizing, equalization; (mas.) level; stipend or gratuity on agreement.—**a la i.,** equally.

igualación, *f.* equalizing, equalization; levelling, smoothing; matching; agreement, stipulation; (math.) equating; (carp.) countergauge.

igualado, da, *pp.* & *a.* equalled (said of birds with even plumage).

igualador, ra, *n.* & *a.* equalizer (-ing); smoother (-ing), leveller (-ing).

igualamiento, *m.* = IGUALACIÓN.

igualar. I. *va.* to equalize; to match, mate, pair; to even, level, smooth; to size, face, adjust, fit; to hold in equal estimation; to adjust; (math.) to equate. **II.** *vn.* to be equal. **III.** *vr.* (w. **a**) to place one's self upon a level (with).

igualdad, *f.* equality; evenness, smoothness, regularity, uniformity.—**i. de ánimo,** evenness of mind; constancy, equability, equanimity.

igualitario, ria, *a.* equalizing; equitable.

igualmente, *adv.* equally; likewise; constantly.

iguana, *f.* (zool.) iguana.

iguanodonte, *m.* iguanodon.

iguedo, *m.* buck.

ijada, *f.* flank (of an animal); pain in the side; colic.—**tener su i.,** to have a weak side or point.

ijadear, *vn.* to pant; to palpitate.

ijar, *m.* flank (of an animal).

ilación, *f.* illation, concatenation, connectedness.

ilativo, va, *a.* illative.

ilegal, *a.* illegal, unlawful.

ilegalidad, *f.* illegality, unlawfulness.

ilegalmente, *adv.* illegally, unlawfully.

ilegible, *a.* illegible.

ilegítimamente, *adv.* illegitimately, foully.

ilegitimar, *va.* to illegitimate.

ilegitimidad, *f.* illegitimacy.

ilegítimo, ma, *a.* illegal, unlawful; illegitimate.

íleo, *m.* (med.) ileus.

íleon, *m.* (anat.) ileum.

ileso, sa, *a.* unhurt, unscathed; harmless, sound.

iletrado, da, *a.* ignorant, uncultured.

ilíaco, ca, *a.* iliac, relating to the ilium or to the ileum; belonging or relating to Ilium (Troy).

Ilíada, *f.* Iliad.

iliberal, *a.* illiberal.

ilicíneo, a, *a.* (bot.) ilicineous.

ilícitamente, *adv.* illicitly, unlawfully.

ilícito, ta, *a.* illicit, unlawful.

ilimitable, *a.* illimitable.

ilimitado, da, *a.* unlimited, boundless; unrestricted.

ilion, *m.* (anat.) ilium.

iliquido, da, *a.* unliquidated.

ilírico, ca; ilirio, ria, *n.* & *a.* Illyrian.

iliterato, *a.* illiterate, unlearned.

ilógico, ca, *a.* illogical.

ilota, *m.* helot.—**ilotismo,** *m.* helotism.

iludir, *va.* to elude.

iluminación, *f.* illumination, lighting; (art) painting in distemper.

iluminado, da. I. *a.* & *pp.* illuminate, enlightened. **II.** *m. pl.* illuminati.

iluminador, ra, *n.* & *a.* lighter (-ing); illuminator (-ing).

iluminar, *va.* to illumine, illuminate, light; to color, illumine (books); to enlighten.

iluminaria, *f.* = LUMINARIA.

iluminativo, va, *a.* illuminating.

iluminismo, *m.* Illuminism.

ilusión, *f.* illusion.

ilusionar. I. *va.* to cause illusion, fascinate. **II.** *vr.* to have illusions.

ilusivo, va, *a.* illusive, false, deceiving.

iluso, sa, *a.* deluded, deceived, beguiled.

ilusoriamente, *adv.* illusively, illusorily.

ilusorio, ria, *a.* illusory, deceptive; (law) null, void, nugatory.

ilustración, *f.* illustration; learning, erudition; elucidation, explanation; enlightment; learning; illustrated or pictorial publication.

ilustrado, da, *pp.* *a.* learned, well-informed; illustrated.—**ilustrador, ra,** *n.* Illustrator.

ilustrar. I. *va.* to illustrate (a publication); to enlighten; to explain, elucidate; (theol.) to give divine light to, to inspire. **II.** *vr.* to inform one's self, to acquire knowledge, to learn; to become illustrious.

ilustrativo, va, *a.* illustrative.

ilustre, *a.* illustrious.

ilustremente, *adv.* illustriously.

Ilustrísimo, ma, *a.* *super.* very illustrious, most illustrious (title given to bishops).

Imadas, *f. pl.* (naut.) ways, sliding planks.

Imagen, *f.* image.—**i. de bulto,** image in sculpture; high relief.

Imaginable, *a.* imaginable.

Imaginación, *f.* imagination; imagining.

Imaginar. I. *va.* to imagine; to think, suspect. **II.** *vr.* to imagine; to suspect; to picture to one's self, often used imperatively in a somewhat expletive or emphatic manner, in the sense of "just think," "just imagine," "why." etc. (*imáginese Vd. que no teníamos ni un centavo,* just think, we did not have a cent; *imáginese Vd. que allá hasta los niños fuman,* why, there even children smoke).

Imaginaria, *f.* (mil.) reserve guard; (math.) imaginary.

Imaginariamente, *adv.* imaginatively.

Imaginario, ria, *a.* imaginary, imagined; (math.) imaginary.

Imaginativa, *f.* imagination, fancy.

Imaginativo, va, *a.* imaginative, fanciful.

Imaginería, *f.* imagery, fancy embroidery in colors; (art) statuary.

Imaginero, *m.* painter or sculptor of religious images.

Imán, *m.* magnet; imam (Mohammedan priest); magnetism, charm.

Imanación, *f.* magnetization.

Imanar, *va.* to magnetize.

Imantación, *f.* = IMANACIÓN.

Imantar, *va.* = IMANAR.

Imbécil, *n. & a.* imbecile.

Imbecilidad, *f.* imbecility, stupidity.

Imbele, *a.* feeble, weak; unfit for war.

Imberbe, *a.* beardless.

Imbibición, *f.* imbibition.

Imbornal, *m.* (naut.) scupper hole.

Imborrable, *a.* indelible, ineffaceable.

Imbricación, *f.* imbrication.

Imbricado, da, *a.* imbricated.

Imbuir, *va.* (*ind.* IMBUYO: *subj.* IMBUYA) to imbue, infuse, persuade.

Imbursación, *f.* putting into a sack.

Imbursar, *va.* to sack or bag.

Imitable, *a.* imitable.—**imitación,** *f.* imitation.

Imitado, da, *a. & pp.* imitated, mock.

Imitador, ra; imitante, *n. & a.* imitator (-ing).

Imitar, *va.* to imitate; to mimic; to ape; to counterfeit.

Imitativo, va, *a.* imitative (as arts).

Imóscapo, *m.* (arch.) apophyge.

Impacción, *f.* impact, collision.

Impaciencia, *f.* impatience.

Impacientar. I. *va.* to vex, irritate, make (one) lose patience. **II.** *vr.* to become impatient.

Impaciente, *a.* impatient; anxious; peevish.

Impacientemente, *adv.* impatiently, anxiously; peevishly.

Impacto, ta, *a.* impact.

Impagable, *a.* unpayable.

Impalpabilidad, *f.* impalpability.

Impalpable, *a.* impalpable.

Impar, *a.* unmatched, odd; (arith.) odd.

Imparcial, *a.* impartial.—**imparcialidad,** *f.* impartiality.—**imparcialmente,** *adv.* impartially.

Impartible, *a.* indivisible.

Impartir, *va.* to impart; (law) to demand or require (assistance).

Impasable, *a.* impassable.

Impasibilidad, *f.* impassibility, indifference.

Impasible, *a.* impassible, indifferent.

Impávidamente, *adv.* undauntedly, calmly.

Impavidez, *f.* intrepidity, calm, composure.

Impávido, da, *a.* dauntless, intrepid, calm.

Impecabilidad, *f.* impeccability.

Impecable, *a.* impeccable.

Impedido, da, *pp. & a.* disabled, crippled.

Impedidor, ra, *n.* obstructor.

Impediente, *a.* hindering, obstructing.

Impedimenta, *f.* (mil.) impedimenta.

Impedimento, *m.* impediment; obstacle, hindrance, encumbrance.

Impedir, *va.* (*ind.* IMPIDO: *subj.* IMPIDA) to impede, hinder, prevent; (poet.) to suspend.

Impeditivo, va, *a.* impeding, hindering.

Impelente, *a.* forcing, impelling, propelling.

Impeler, *va.* to push, impel, drive; to spur, urge, incite, move.

Impender, *va.* to spend, invest.

Impenetrabilidad, *f.* impenetrability.

Impenetrable, *a.* impenetrable, impervious; incomprehensible; fathomless.

Impenitencia, *f.* impenitence.

Impenitente, *a.* impenitent, obdurate.

Impensa, *f.* (for.) expense.

Impensadamente, *adv.* unexpectedly; inadvertently.

Impensado, da, *a.* unexpected, unforeseen.

Imperante, *a.* commanding; (astrol.) ruling.

Imperar, *vn.* to command; to reign.

Imperativamente, *adv.* imperatively.

Imperativo, va. I. *a.* imperative, commanding. **II.** *n. & a.* (gram.) imperative.

Imperatoria, *f.* (bot.) masterwort.

Imperatorio, ria, *a.* imperial.

Imperceptible, *a.* imperceptible.

Imperceptiblemente, *adv.* imperceptibly.

Imperdible. I. *a.* imperdible, that cannot be lost. **II.** *m.* safety pin.

Imperdonable, *a.* unpardonable, unforgivable.

Imperecedero, ra, *a.* imperishable, undying.

Imperfección, *f.* imperfection, defect, fault, flaw, blemish.—**imperfectamente,** *adv.* imperfectly, inadequately.

Imperfecto, ta. I. *a.* imperfect, defective, faulty. **II.** *n. & a.* (gram.) imperfect.

Imperforación, *f.* (med.) imperforation.

Imperial. I. *a.* imperial. **II.** *f.* coach top; top seats on a stage-coach; (naut.) poop royal.

Imperialismo, *m.* imperialism.

Imperialista, *n. & a.* imperialist (-ic).

Impericia, *f.* unskilfulness, inexpertness.

Imperio, *m.* empire; dominion, command, sway; dignity of an emperor.

Imperiosamente, *adv.* imperiously, overbearingly.—**imperiosidad,** *f.* imperiousness.

Imperioso, sa, *a.* imperious, overbearing.

Imperitamente, *adv.* unskilfully.

Imperito, ta, *a.* unskilled, inexpert.

Impermeabilidad, *f.* impermeability, imperviousness, water-tightness.

Impermeabilizar, *va.* to make waterproof.

Impermeable. I. *a.* water-tight, impervious, waterproof. **II.** *m.* waterproof garment, mackintosh, raincoat.

Impermutable, *a.* unexchangeable.

Impersonal, *a.* impersonal.—**en,** or **por, i.,** impersonally.

Impersonalizar, *va.* (gram.) to use impersonally.

Impersonalmente, *adv.* impersonally.

Impersuasible, *a.* not susceptible of persuasion.

Impertérrito, ta, *a.* intrepid, dauntless, serene.

Impertinencia, *f.* impertinence, folly, nonsense; peevishness; intrusion; minute accuracy.

Impertinente. I. *a.* not pertinent; impertinent, importunate, meddlesome. **II.** *m. pl.* lorgnette.

Impertinentemente, *adv.* impertinently.

Imperturbabilidad, *f.* imperturbability.

Imperturbable, *a.* imperturbable.

Imperturbablemente, *adv.* imperturbably.

Impetra, *f.* diploma, license, permission; bull granting dubious benefices.

Impetrable, *a.* (law) impetrable.

Impetración, *f.* impetration.

Impetrado, da, *a. & pp.* impetrate, impetrated, granted.

Impetrador, ra, *n.* one who impetrates.

Impetrante. I. *a.* impetrating. **II.** *m.* (law) grantee; impetrator.

Impetrar, *va.* to entreat, impetrate, obtain by entreaty.

ímpetu, *m.* impetus, impulse; impetuosity.
impetuosamente, *adv.* impetuously.
impetuosidad, *f.* impetuosity.
impetuoso, sa, *a.* impetuous, impulsive, violent.
impíamente, *adv.* impiously.
impiedad, *f.* impiety; irreligion, infidelity.
impiedoso, sa, *a.* impious, irreligious.
impiísimo, ma, *a. sup.* very impious.
impío, pía. I. *a.* impious; irreligious, godless.
II. *n.* impious person; infidel, enemy of religion.
impla, *f.* wimple; material for wimples.
implacabilidad, *f.* implacability.
implacable, *a.* implacable; inexorable.
implacablemente, *adv.* implacably.
implantación, *f.* implantation, introduction (of new ideas, systems, etc.).—**implantar,** *va.* to implant, to introduce.
implantón, *m.* piece of timber.
implaticable, *a.* not fit to talk about, unmentionable.
implicación, *f.* contradiction.—**implicante,** *a.* contradictory; implicating.
implicar. I. *va.* to implicate, involve, entangle. **II.** *vn.* to imply contradiction.
implicatorio, ria, *a.* implying contradiction, contradictory.
implícitamente, *adv.* implicitly.
implícito, ta, *a.* implicit.
imploración, *f.* imploration.—**implorante,** *a.* imploring, entreating.
implorar, *va.* to implore, entreat, beg.
implume, *a.* unfeathered.
impolítica, *f.* incivility, discourtesy; impolicy, indiscretion, tactlessness.
impolíticamente, *adv.* impolitically, unwisely.
impolítico, ca, *a.* impolitic, indiscreet, imprudent, unwise, untactful.
impoluto, ta, *a.* unpolluted, pure, untarnished.
imponderabilidad, *f.* imponderability.
imponderable, *a.* imponderable; beyond all praise, most excellent.
imponedor, ra, *n.* imposer, assessor.
imponente, *a.* imposing.
imponer. I. *va. (for irr. v.* PONER) to impose or lay (as a tax, a penalty); to impute falsely; to advise, give notice, acquaint; to inspire, arouse, command (respect, fear); (print.) to impose. **II.** *vr.* to assert one's self, impose one's authority; to be imperative or necessary; to command respect.
imponible, *a.* taxable, dutiable.
impopular, *a.* unpopular.
impopularidad, *f.* unpopularity.
importable, *a.* (com.) importable.
importación, *f.* (com.) importation, import.
importador, ra, *n. & a.* importer (-ing).
importancia, *f.* importance.
importante, *a.* important.
importantemente, *adv.* importantly, materially.
importar. I. *vn.* to be important; to concern.— **eso no importa,** that does not matter.—**eso no le importa a Vd.,** that does not concern you; that is none of your business.—**eso no me importa,** I don't care (for that); that makes no difference to me.—**no importa,** no matter, never mind.—**¿qué importa?** what does it matter? what difference does it make? **II.** *va.* to import; to amount to; to be worth; to imply.
importe, *m.* (com.) amount; price, cost, value.— **i. medio,** average amount.
importunación, *f.* importunity.
importunadamente, *adv.* importunately.
importunador, ra, *n. & a.* importuner (-ing), pesterer (-ing).
importunamente, *adv.* inopportunely; importunately, persistently.
importunar, *va.* to importune, pester.
importunidad, *f.* importunity, importunacy.
importuno, na, *a.* inopportune; importunate, persistent, vexatious, annoying.
imposibilidad, *f.* impossibility.
imposibilitado, *a. & pp.* helpless, without means, poor; disabled, unfit for service.

imposibilitar, *va.* to disable, unfit for service.
imposible, *a.* impossible.—**i. de toda imposibilidad,** (coll.) altogether impossible.—**los imposibles,** a kind of Spanish dance.
imposiblemente, *adv.* impossibly.
imposición, *f.* imposition (of a duty, etc.); tax, duty, tribute, burden; (print.) imposition.—**i. de manos,** (ecc.) imposition, laying on of hands.
imposta, *f.* (arch.) impost; springer; fascia.
impostor, ra, *n.* impostor.
impostura, *f.* imputation; imposture.
impotable, *a.* unpotable, undrinkable.
impotencia, *f.* impotence.
impotente, *a.* impotent.
impracticable, *a.* impracticable; impassable.
imprecación, *f.* imprecation.—**imprecar,** *va.* to imprecate.—**imprecatorio, ria,** *a.* imprecatory.
impregnación, *f.* impregnation.
impregnar. I. *va.* to impregnate, saturate. **II.** *vr.* to become impregnated.
impremeditación, *f.* unpremeditation.
impremeditado, da, *a.* unpremeditated.
imprenta, *f.* printing; printing office, printing house; print; press (in general).
imprescindible, *a.* essential, imperative, indispensable.
imprescindiblemente, *adv.* necessarily, unavoidably; absolutely.
imprescriptible, *a.* imprescriptible.
impresión, *f.* impression; impress, stamping, stamp; print, printing, presswork; edition, issue; footprint; influence, moral or physical effect.
impresionable, *a.* emotional, impressionable.
impresionar, *va.* to impress, fix on the mind or memory; to affect, influence; (photo.) to effect chemical changes on (a plate) by exposure to light.
impresionismo, *m.* (art) impressionism.
impresionista, *n. & a.* (art) impressionist (-ic).
impreso, sa. I. *pp. irr.* of IMPRIMIR & *a.* printed; stamped. **II.** *m.* pamphlet; publication; printed matter, print.
impresor, ra. I. *n.* printer. **II.** *f.* wife of a printer.
imprestable, *a.* that cannot be lent.
imprevisión, *f.* lack of foresight; improvidence; inadvertency, oversight.
imprevisto, ta. I. *a.* unforeseen, unexpected. **II.** *m. pl.* incidental or unforeseen expenses.
imprimación, *f.* (art) priming; stuff for priming.
imprimadera, *f.* (art) priming tool.
imprimador, ra, *n.* (art) one who primes.
imprimar, *va.* (art) to prime.
imprimátur, *m.* imprimatur.
imprimir, *va.* (pp. IMPRESO) to print, stamp, imprint, impress; fix in the mind.
improbabilidad, *f.* improbability.
improbable, *a.* improbable, unlikely.
improbablemente, *adv.* improbably.
improbar, *va. (for irr. v.* PROBAR) to disapprove.
improbidad, *f.* dishonesty; iniquity.
improbo, ba, *a.* dishonest, corrupt; laborious, painful, arduous.
improcedencia, *f.* unrighteousness.
improcedente, *a.* contrary to law, unrighteous.
improductivo, va, *a.* unproductive, unfruitful, barren, unprofitable.
impronta, *f.* (art) cast; stereotype plate.
impronunciable, *a.* unpronounceable.
improperar, *va.* to upbraid, gibe, taunt.
improperio, *m.* insult, indignity.—*pl.* (ecc.) improperia.
impropiamente, *adv.* improperly.
impropiedad, *f.* impropriety; unfitness, inappropriateness.
impropio, pia, *a.* inappropriate, unsuited, unfit; improper, unbecoming; (arith.) improper (fraction).
improporción, *f.* disproportion.
improporcionado, da, *a.* disproportionate.

improrrogable, *a.* that cannot be prorogated or extended.
impróspero, ra, *a.* unprosperous.
imprôvidamente, *adv.* improvidently.
improvidencia, *f.* improvidence.
imprôvido, da, *a.* improvident, thoughtless.
improvisación, *f.* improvisation.
improvisador, ra, *n.* improviser.
improvisamente, *adv.* unexpectedly, suddenly.
improvisar, *va.* to improvise; extemporize.
improviso, sa; improvisto, ta, *a.* unexpected, unforeseen.—**al,** or **de, l.,** or **a la improvista,** unexpectedly, suddenly.
imprudencia, *f.* imprudence, indiscretion.
imprudente, *a.* imprudent, indiscreet, unwise.
imprudentemente, *adv.* imprudently.
impúber; impúbero, ra, *a.* impuberal, immature, below the age of puberty.
impudencia, *f.* impudence, insolence.
impudente, *a.* impudent, shameless.
impúdicamente, *adv.* immodestly; impudently.
impudicicia, *f.* immodesty, impudicity.
impúdico, ca, *a.* immodest; impudent.
impuesto, *m.* tax, impost, duty.
impuesto, ta, *a. & pp. irr.* of IMPONER; imposed; informed.—**estar,** or **quedar l. de,** to be informed about, to have received notice of or information about.
impugnable, *a.* impugnable.
impugnación, *f.* opposition, impugnation.
impugnador, ra, *n.* impugner, objector.
impugnar, *va.* to impugn, oppose, criticize.
impugnativo, va, *a.* impugning.
impulsar, *va.* to impel, actuate, move, prompt; (mech.) to drive, force.
impulsión, *f.* impulsion, impulse, impetus; influence, motive.
impulsivo, va, *a.* impulsive.
impulso, *m.* impulsion; impulse.
impulsor, ra, *n. & a.* impeller (-ing); driver (-ing).
impune, *a.* unpunished.—**impunemente,** *adv.* with impunity.—**impunidad,** *f.* impunity.
impuramente, *adv.* obscenely, impurely.
impureza, *f.* impurity; adulteration; unchastity; obscenity, foulness.
impurificación, *f.* impuration, defilement.
impurificar, *va.* to defile, to make impure; to adulterate.
impuro, ra, *a.* impure; defiled; adulterated.
imputable, *a.* imputable.—**imputabilidad,** *f.* imputability.—**imputación,** *f.* imputation.
imputador, ra, *n. & a.* imputer. (-ing).
imputar, *va.* to impute, attribute; (com.) to credit on account.
inabarcable, *a.* not capable of being embraced.
inacabable, *a.* interminable; everlasting.
inaccesibilidad, *f.* inaccessibility.
inaccesible, *a.* inaccessible.
inaccesiblemente, *adv.* inaccessibly.
inacción, *f.* inaction, inactivity.
inaceptable, *a.* unacceptable.
inactivo, va, *a.* inactive.
inadaptable, *a.* unadaptable.
inadecuado, da, *a.* inadequate.
inadoptable, *a.* unadoptable.
inadmisible, *a.* inadmissible.
inadvertencia, *f.* inadvertency, oversight.
inadvertidamente, *adv.* inadvertently.
inadvertido, da, *a.* inadvertent, careless; unseen, unnoticed.
inafectado, da, *a.* natural, unaffected.
inagotable, *a.* inexhaustible.
inaguantable, *a.* unbearable.
inajenable, *a.* inalienable.
inalcanzable, *a.* unattainable.
inalienable, *a.* inalienable.
inalterabilidad, *f.* unalterability.
inalterable, *a.* unalterable, changeless.
inalterablemente, *adv.* unalterably.
inalterado, da, *a.* unchanged, unaltered.
inamisible, *a.* inamissible.

inamovible, *a.* immovable.
inamovibilidad, *f.* immovability.
inanalizable, *a.* incapable of being analyzed.
inane, *a.* empty, void, inane.
inanición, *f.* (med.) inanition.
inanimado, da, *a.* inanimate, lifeless.
inapagable, *a.* inextinguishable, unquenchable.
inapeable, *a.* that cannot be lowered or levelled; inconceivable; obstinate, stubborn.
inapelable, *a.* unappealable.
inapetencia, *f.* inappetence, lack of appetite
inapetente, *a.* having no appetite.
inaplazable, *a.* undeferable, that cannot be deferred.
inaplicable, *a.* inapplicable.
inaplicación, *f.* indolence; inapplication.
inaplicado, da, *a.* indolent, careless, inactive.
inapreciable, *a.* invaluable; inappreciable.
inaprensivo, *a.* inapprehensive.
inarmónico, ca, *a.* inharmonious.
inarticulado, da. I. *a.* inarticulate. **II.** *m. pl.* (zool.) Inarticulata.
in artículo mortis, in articulo mortis, at the point of death, in the moment of death.
inasequible, *a.* unattainable, not obtainable.
inasimilable, *a.* unassimilable.
inatacable, *a.* that cannot be attacked.
inaudible, *a.* inaudible.
inaudito, ta, *a.* unheard-of, strange, most extraordinary.
inauguración, *f.* inauguration; coronation; commencement.—**inaugural,** *a.* inaugural.
inaugurar, *va.* to inaugurate; to divine by the flight of birds.
inaveriguable, *a.* unascertainable.
inca, *n. & a.* Inca; a gold coin.
incaico, ca, *a.* Inca (u. a.)
incalculable, *a.* incalculable.
incalificable, *a.* impossible to judge or characterize; unutterably bad, most reprehensible.
incalmable, *a.* that cannot be calmed or subdued.
incandescencia, *f.* incandescence.
incandescente, *a.* incandescent.
incansable, *a.* indefatigable, untiring.
incansablemente, *adv.* indefatigably.
incantable, *a.* that cannot be sung.
incapacidad, *f.* incapacity; incompetence.
incapacitar, *va.* to incapacitate, disable.
incapaz, *a.* incapable; unable; incompetent.
incasable, *a.* unmarriageable; opposed to marriage.
incasto, ta, *a.* unchaste.
incautación, *f.* (law) attachment of property.
incautamente, *adv.* unwarily, incautiously.
incautarse, *vr.* (law) to attach property.
incauto, ta, *a.* unwary, unwise, heedless.
incendiar, *va.* to set on fire.
incendiario, ria, *n. & a.* incendiary.
incendio, *m.* fire, conflagration; broil.
incensación, *f.* perfuming with incense.
incensar, *va.* (*ind.* INCIENSO: *subj.* INCIENSE) (eccl.) to incense; to bestow fulsome praise or adulation.
incensario, *m.* incensory, thurible.
incensurable, *a.* unblamable, not culpable.
incentivo, *m.* incentive, inducement; encouragement.
incertidumbre, *f.* uncertainty.
incertísimo, ma, *a. sup.* extremely uncertain.
incesable, *a.* incessant, unceasing.
incesablemente, *adv.* incessantly.
incesante, *a.* unceasing, continual.
incesantemente, *adv.* incessantly, continually.
incesto, *m.* incest.—**incestuosamente,** *adv.* incestuously.—**incestuoso, sa,** *a.* incestuous.
incidencia, *f.* incident; (geom., phys.) incidence.
incidental, *a.* incidental, dependent, subsidiary.
incidentalmente, *adv.* incidentally.
incidente. I. *a.* incidental. **II.** *m.* incident, occurrence.—*pl.* (com.) appurtenances.—**incidentes de comercio,** lease and good will.

incidentemente, *adv.* incidentally.

incidir, *vn.* (w. **en**) to fall into (as an error).

incienso, *m.* incense; reverence; flattery.

inciertamente, *adv.* uncertainly.

incierto, ta, *a.* uncertain; untrue; unknown.

incinerable, *a.* to be withdrawn from circulation (s. o. bank bills, which are burned when withdrawn).

incineración, *f.* incineration, cremation; (chem.) ignition.—**incinerar,** *va.* to incinerate, cremate; (chem.) to ignite.

incipiente, *a.* incipient.

incircunciso, sa, *a.* uncircumcised.

incircunscripto, ta, *a.* uncircumscribed.

incisión, *f.* incision, cut.

incisivo, va, *a.* incisive; keen, sharp, cutting (as a remark).

inciso, sa. I. *a.* incised, cut. **II.** *m.* sentence; clause; comma.

incisorio, ria, *a.* (surg.) incisory.

incitación, *f.* incitation, incitement.

incitador, ra, *n.* & *a.* instigator (-ing), inciter (-ing).

incitamento, incitamiento, *m.* incitement, impulse, incentive.

incitante, *a.* inciting, exciting.

incitar, *va.* to incite, excite, spur, instigate.

incitativo, va. I. *a.* inciting; (law) AGUIJATORIO. **II.** *m.* incitement. **III.** *f.* (law) writ from a superior to a lower court urging that justice be administered.

incivil, *a.* uncivil.—**incivilidad,** *f.* incivility.

incivilmente, *adv.* uncivilly, rudely.

inclasificable, *a.* unclassifiable.

inclemencia, *f.* inclemency; severity, rigor, unmercifulness.—**a la i.,** unsheltered, at the mercy of the elements.

inclinación, *f.* inclination, propensity, tendency, bent; tilt, fall, pitch; declivity, slope; (r. w.) grade; (min.) dip, hade, underlay; (phys.) dip, inclination (of the needle).

inclinado, da, *a.* & *pp.* inclined; slanting, sloping; disposed, minded.

inclinador, ra, *m.* & *f.* one who inclines.

inclinante, *a.* inclining.

inclinar. I. *va.* to incline; to tilt; to influence, induce. **II.** *vn.* to resemble. **III.** *vr.* to incline, slope; to lean, to be favorably disposed; to stoop, to bow; (naut.) to heel.

ínclito, ta, *a.* a. distinguished, illustrious.

incluir, *va.* (*pp.* INCLUÍDO, INCLUSO: *ind.* INCLUYO: *subj.* INCLUYA) to include; to inclose.

inclusa, *f.* foundling asylum.

inclusero, ra, *n.* & *a.* foundling.

inclusión, *f.* inclusion; friendship.

inclusivamente, inclusive, *adv.* inclusive, including.—**inclusivo, va,** *a.* inclusive, including.

incluso, sa, *a.* & *pp. irr.* of INCLUIR; inclosed; including, included (in this sense it is gen. used as an *adv.*).

incluyente, *a.* including, inclosing.

incoado, da, *a.* & *pp.* inchoate, begun.

incoagulable, *a.* uncoagulable.

incoar, *va.* (*only the infinitive and pp. used*) (law) to commence, begin.

incoativo, va, *a.* inchoative, inceptive.

incobrable, *a.* irrecoverable, irretrievable; (com.) uncollectable.

incoercible, *a.* incoercible.

incógnito, ta. I. *a.* unknown.—**de i.,** incognito; hiddenly or clandestinely. **II.** *f.* (math.) unknown (quantity).

incognoscible, *a.* unknowable.

incoherencia, *f.* incoherence, disconnection.

incoherente, *a.* incoherent, disconnected.

íncola, *m.* inhabitant, resident.

incoloro, ra, *a.* colorless.

incólume, *a.* sound, safe, unharmed.

incolumidad, *f.* security, safety.

incombinable, *a.* uncombinable.

incombustibilidad, *f.* incombustibility.

incombustible, *a.* incombustible, fireproof.

incombusto, ta, *a.* not burned.

incomerciable, *a.* contraband, unlawful, prohibited; unsalable, unmarketable.

incómodamente, *adv.* inconveniently; uncomfortably.

incomodar. I. *va.* to disturb, inconvenience, trouble. **II.** *vr.* to be vexed or angered; to trouble one's self.

incomodidad, *f.* inconvenience; uncomfortableness; nuisance, annoyance; vexation, anger.

incómodo, da, *a.* inconvenient; uncomfortable; troublesome, unhandy, cumbersome.

incomparable, *a.* incomparable, matchless.

incomparablemente, *adv.* incomparably.

incomparado, da, *a.* = INCOMPARABLE.

incompartible, *a.* indivisible.

incompasible, incompasivo, va, *a.* pitiless, unsympathetic.

incompatibilidad, *f.* incompatibility.

incompatible, *a.* incompatible; uncongenial.

incompensable, *a.* incapable of being compensated, unindemnifiable.

incompetencia, *f.* incompetence; unfitness.

incompetente, *a.* incompetent; (law) incompetent, unauthorized.

incomplejo, ja, *a.* incomplex; simple.

incompletamente, *adv.* incompletely.

incompleto, ta, *a.* incomplete.

incomplexo, xa, *a.* disunited, disconnected, disjointed.

incomponible, *a.* unmendable.

incomportable, *a.* intolerable, unbearable.

incomposibilidad, *f.* incompossibility.

incomposible, *a.* incompossible.

incomposición, *f.* want of proportion.

incomprehensibilidad, *f.* incomprehensibility.

incomprehensible, *a.* incomprehensible.

incomprensibilidad, *f.* incomprehensibility.

incomprensible, incomprehensible.

incomprensiblemente, *adv.* inconceivably, incomprehensibly.

incompresibilidad, *f.* (phys.) incompressibility.

incompresible, *a.* (phys.) incompressible.

incomprimible, *a.* incompressible.

incomunicabilidad, *f.* incommunicability.

incomunicable, *a.* incommunicable.

incomunicado, da. I. *a.* incommunicated; isolated. **II.** *m.* incommunicated or isolated prisoner, incommunicado.

incomunicar, *va.* (*pret.* INCOMUNIQUÉ: *subj.* INCOMUNIQUE) to deprive of intercourse or communication; to isolate, put in solitary confinement.

inconcebible, *a.* inconceivable.

inconciliable, *a.* irreconcilable.

inconcino, na, *a.* disordered, disarranged.

inconcusamente, *adv.* certainly, doubtless.

inconcuso, sa, *a.* incontrovertible, unquestionable, indisputable.

incondicional, *a.* unconditional.

incondicionalmente, *adv.* unconditionally.

inconducente, *a.* nonconducive.

inconexión, *f.* incoherence, disconnection.

inconexo, xa, *a.* unconnected, not pertinent; incoherent.

inconfeso, sa, *a.* unconfessed.

inconfidencia, *f.* distrust, mistrust.

incongruamente, *adv.* incongruously.

incongruencia, *f.* incongruence.

incongruente, *a.* incongruous, incongruent.

incongruentemente, *adv.* incongruously, incompatibly.

incongruo, grua, *a.* incongruous.

inconmensurabilidad, *f.* incommensurability.

inconmensurable, *a.* incommensurable.

inconmovible, *q.* immovable; unbending, inexorable, unyielding.

inconmutabilidad, *f.* immutability; incommutability.

inconmutable, *a.* immutable; incommutable.

inconquistable, *a.* unconquerable; unbending.

inconsciencia, *f.* unconsciousness
inconsciente, *a.* unconscious.
inconscientemente, *adv.* unconsciously.
inconsecuencia, *f.* inconsistency.
inconsecuente, *a.* inconsistent.
inconservable, *a.* unpreservable.
inconsideración, *f.* lack of consideration; thoughtlessness, inadvertency.
inconsideradamente, *adv.* inconsiderately; thoughtlessly.—**inconsiderado, da,** *a.* inconsiderate; thoughtless.
inconsiguiente, *a.* inconsistent, not logical.
inconsistencia, *f.* incoherence; instability, lack of permanency.
inconsistente, *a.* unsubstantial, unstable.
inconsolable, *a.* inconsolable.
inconsolablemente, *adv.* inconsolably.
inconstancia, *f.* inconstancy, fickleness.
inconstante, *a.* inconstant, changeable, fickle.
inconstantemente, *adv.* inconstantly, fickly.
inconstitucional, *a.* unconstitutional.
inconstitucionalidad, *f.* unconstitutionality.
inconstruíble, *a.* that cannot be constructed.
inconsútil, *a.* seamless.
incontable, *a.* innumerable, uncountable.
incontaminado, da, *a.* undefiled, uncontaminated, pure.
incontestable, *a.* incontestable, unquestionable.
incontestablemente, *adv.* unquestionably.
incontinencia, *f.* incontinence; (med.) incontinence of urine.
incontinente, *a.* incontinent.
incontinente, incontinenti, *adv.* instantly, immediately, at once.
incontrastable, *a.* invincible, insuperable, unconquerable; unanswerable; inconvincible.
incontratable, *a.* = INTRATABLE.
incontrovertible, *a.* incontrovertible.
inconvencible, *a.* inconvincible.
inconvenible, *a.* uncompromising.
inconveniencia, *f.* inconvenience, trouble; disadvantage; uncomfortableness.
inconveniente, **I.** inconvenient, troublesome; uncomfortable; undesirable, unadvisable. **II.** *m.* difficulty, obstacle, objection; disadvantage.
inconversable, *a.* unsociable, uncommunicative, surly, intractable.
inconvertible, *a.* inconvertible.
incordio, *m.* (med.) bubo; (vulg.) nuisance.
incorporación, *f.* incorporation.
incorporal, *a.* incorporeal.
incorporalmente, *adv.* incorporeally.
incorporar. **I.** *va.* to incorporate, unite, embody; to mix; to raise or to make (a patient) sit up in bed. **II.** *vr.* to incorporate, join, mingle; to form a corporation; to sit up in bed; (naut.) to sail in company.
incorporeidad, *f.* incorporeity, immateriality.
incorpóreo, rea, *a.* incorporeal.
incorporo, *m.* = INCORPORACIÓN.
incorrección, *f.* incorrectness; inaccuracy; impropriety.
incorrectamente, *adv.* incorrectly; improperly.
incorrecto, ta, *a.* incorrect; improper.
incorregibilidad, *f.* incorrigibleness.
incorregible, *a.* incorrigible.
incorrupción, *f.* integrity, honesty; incorruption.
incorruptamente, *adv.* incorruptly.
incorruptibilidad, *f.* incorruptibility.
incorruptible, *a.* incorruptible.
incorrupto, ta, *a.* incorrupt or uncorrupted; chaste, pure.
incrasante, *a.* incrassating.
incrasar, *va.* to thicken, incrassate.
increado, da, *a.* uncreated.
incredibilidad, *f.* incredibility, incredibleness.
incredulidad, *f.* incredulity.
incrédulo, la. **I.** *a.* incredulous. **II.** *n.* unbeliever.
increíble, *a.* incredible.

increíblemente, *adv.* incredibly.
incremento, *m.* increment, increase.
increpación, *f.* reprehension, rebuke, chiding, reproach.—**increpador, ra,** *n.* & *a.* chider (-ing), rebuker (-ing).—**increpante,** *a.* chiding, scolding, rebuking.
increpar, *va.* to chide, reprehend, rebuke.
incriminación, *f.* incrimination.
incriminante, *a.* incriminating.
incriminar, *va.* to incriminate; to exaggerate.
incristalizable, *a.* uncrystallizable.
incruento, ta, *a.* bloodless.
incrustación, *f.* incrustation; scale (in boilers); (geol.) sinter; (art) inlaying.
incrustante, *a.* scale-forming (s. o. water).
incrustar, *va.* to incrust; encase; inlay.
incuartación, *f.* (chem.) quartation.
incubación, *f.* incubation; hatching.
incubador, ra. **I.** *n.* & *a.* incubator (-ing). **II.** *f.* incubator (apparatus).
incubar, *va.* to incubate; to hatch.
íncubo, *m.* incubus; (med.) nightmare.
incuestionable, *a.* unquestionable.
inculcación, *f.* inculcation; pressing (one thing against another); (print.) binding or wedging in a form.
inculcar. **I.** *va.* (*pret.* INCULQUÉ: *subj.* INCULQUE) to inculcate, impress, teach; to make (one thing) tight (against another); (print.) to lock up (types). **II.** *vr.* to be obstinate.
inculpabilidad, *f.* guiltlessness; blamelessness.
inculpable, *a.* guiltless, blameless.
inculpablemente, *adv.* blamelessly.
inculpación, *f.* inculpation.
inculpadamente, *adv.* faultlessly.
inculpar, *va.* to accuse, inculpate, blame.
incultamente, *adv.* rudely, unrefinedly.
incultivable, *a.* inarable, untillable.
inculto, ta, *a.* uncultivated, untilled, unimproved; uncivilized; unrefined, uncultured.
incultura, *f.* lack of culture.
incumbencia, *f.* incumbency; obligation, duty, concern.
incumbir, *vn.* to concern, pertain.
incumplido, da, *a.* unfulfilled; unpunctual.
incumplimiento, *m.* nonfulfilment.
incunable, *m.* & *a.* (print.) incunabula.
incurable, *a.* incurable; hopeless.
incuria, *f.* negligence; shiftlessness.
incurioso, sa, *a.* negligent, careless.
incurrimiento, *m.* act of incurring.
incurrir, *vn.* (*w.* **en**) to incur, become liable to; to; to bring upon one's self; to commit (an error).
incursión, *f.* (mil.) incursion.
incusar, *va.* to accuse.
incuso, sa, *a.* incuse (as some coins).
indagación, *f.* investigation, search, inquiry, examination, inquest; (law) defendant's unsworn testimony.
indagador, ra, *n.* & *a.* investigator (-ing), inquirer (-ing), examiner (-ing).
indagar, *va.* (*pret.* INDAGUÉ: *subj.* INDAGUE) to investigate, inquire into or about.
indagatorio, ria, *a.* (law) investigatory.
indebidamente, *adv.* unduly; improperly; illegally, unlawfully.—**indebido, da,** *a.* undue, improper; illegal, unlawful.
indecencia, *f.* indecency; obscenity; nuisance; indecent or low act or conduct.
indecente, *a.* indecent, obscene; foul.
indecentemente, *adv.* indecently.
indecible, *a.* inexpressible, unutterable.
indeciblemente, *adv.* inexpressibly, unutterably; exceedingly.
indecisamente, *adv.* irresolutely.
indecisión, *f.* irresolution, indecision.
indeciso, sa, *a.* irresolute, undecided.
indeclinable, *a.* unavoidable; (gram.) indeclinable; (law) unwaivable.
indecoro, *m.* indecorum, indecorousness.
indecorosamente, *adv.* indecorously, unbecomingly.

indecoroso, sa, *a.* indecorous, unbecoming.
indefectibilidad, *f.* indefectibility.
indefectible, *a.* indefectible, unfailing.
indefectiblemente, *adv.* indefectibly.
indefendible, indefensable, indefensible, *a.* indefensible.
indefenso, sa, *a.* defenceless.
indeficiente, *a.* indefectible, unfailing.
indefinible, *a.* undefinable.
indefinidamente, *adv.* indefinitely.
indefinido, da, *a.* indefinite; undefined.
indehiscente, *a.* (bot.) indehiscent.
indeleble, *a.* indelible, ineffaceable.
indeleblemente, *adv.* indelibly.
indeliberación, *f.* lack of premeditation; irreflection.—**indeliberadamente,** *adv.* without premeditation or reflexion.
indeliberado, da, *a.* unpremeditated; irreflexive.
indemne, *a.* undamaged, unhurt.
indemnidad, *f.* bond of indemnity.
indemnizable, *a.* that can be indemnified.
indemnización, *f.* indemnification, compensation; indemnity; reimbursement.
indemnizar, *va.* (*pret.* INDEMNICÉ: *subj.* INDEMNICE) to indemnify, compensate.
indemostrable, *a.* indemonstrable.
independencia, *f.* independence.
independiente, *a.* independent.
independientemente, *adv.* independently.
indescifrable, *a.* undecipherable.
indescribible *or* **indescriptible,** *a.* indescribable.
indesignable, *a.* that cannot be designated.
indestructibilidad, *f.* indestructibility.
indestructible, *a.* indestructible.
indeterminable, *a.* undeterminable, unascertainable; irresolute, undecided.
indeterminación, *f.* indetermination; irresolution, hesitancy.
indeterminadamente, *adv.* indeterminately.
indeterminado, da, *a.* indeterminate; undetermined, irresolute, hesitating; (gram.) indefinite (article); (math.) indeterminate (problem, equation); (math.) undetermined (coefficient).
indeterminismo, *m.* (philos.) indeterminism.
indeterminista, *n. & a.* (philos.) indeterminist (-ic).
indevoción, *f.* indevotion.
indevoto, ta, *a.* not devout, irreligious.
indezuelo, la, *n. dim.* little Indian.
indiana, *f.* printed calico.
indianista, *n.* Indianist.
indiano, na. I. *a.* native or resident of America or the West Indies; Indian, East-Indian. **II.** *m.* nabob, one who returns rich from America.—**i. de hilo negro,** (coll.) skinflint, miser.
indicación, *f.* indication, token, sign; hint, suggestion.
indicador, *m.* indicator, pointer, recorder, gauge, detector, index; (elec.) annunciator disc; (st. eng.) indicator.—**i. de incendios,** fire alarm.—**i. de nivel,** (st. eng.) water-level indicator, gauge glass.—**i. de vacío,** vacuum gauge.
indicante. I. *a.* indicating. **II.** *m.* (med.) indicant.
indicar, *va.* (*pret.* INDIQUÉ: *subj.* INDIQUE) to indicate, suggest, hint, show, point out.
indicativo, va. I. *a.* indicative, pointing. **II.** *n. & a.* (gram.) indicative.
indicción, *f.* convening of a synod, council, etc.; indiction.
índice, *m.* index; hand of a watch, etc.; index, table of contents; forefinger.—**i. cefálico,** cephalic index.—**i. expurgatorio,** Index Expurgatorius, a catalog of books forbidden totally or in part by the Catholic Church.
indiciado, da. I. *pp. & a.* suspected of a crime or vice. **II.** *n.* suspicious character.
indiciador, ra, *n.* one who suspects another; informer.
indiciar, *va.* (law) to give reasons to suspect or surmise; to report (offenders) to the magistrates.

indicio, *m.* indication, mark, sign, token.—*pl.* (chem.) traces.—**indicios vehementes,** (law) circumstantial evidence.
índico, ca, *a.* East-Indian.
indiferencia, *f.* indifference.
indiferente, *a.* indifferent.—**eso es i.,** (coll.) that is immaterial, that makes no difference.
indiferentemente, *adv.* indifferently, without difference.
indiferentismo, *m.* indifferentism.
indígena. I. *a.* indigenous, native; (with reference to America) Indian. **II.** *n.* indigene; native; (w. reference to America) Indian.
indigencia, *f.* indigence, destitution, need.
indigente, *a.* needy, indigent, destitute.
indigestarse, *vr.* to cause indigestion; to cause aversion or dislike, to be unbearable (s. o. persons).
indigestible, *a.* indigestible.
indigestión, *f.* indigestion.
indigesto, ta, *a.* indigestible; confused, disordered; surly, grouty, harsh.
indignación, *f.* indignation.
indignado, da, *a. & pp.* indignant, angry.
indignamente, *adv.* unworthily, unbecomingly; harshly, rudely.
indignante, *a.* indignant, irritating.
indignar. I. *va.* to irritate, anger, make indignant. **II.** *vr.* to become indignant.
indignidad, *f.* indignity; unworthy act.
indigno, na, *a.* unworthy, undeserving; unbecoming, contemptible; despicable, low.
índigo, *m.* indigo.—**indigotina,** *f.* (chem.) indigotin, indigo blue.
indiligencia, *f.* negligence, carelessness.
indio, ia. I. *a.* Indian; Hindu; blue, azure. **II.** *n.* Hindu; Indian. **III.** *m.* (chem.) indium.
indirecta, *f.* innuendo, hint.—**i. del Padre Cobos,** broad hint.
indirectamente, *adv.* indirectly.
indirecto, ta, *a.* indirect.
indisciplina, *f.* lack of discipline; lack of training.—**indisciplinable,** *a.* indisciplinable; untrainable.—**indisciplinado, da,** *a.* undisciplined; untrained.
indiscreción, *f.* indiscretion, imprudence.
indiscretamente, *adv.* indiscreetly.
indiscreto, ta, *a.* indiscreet, imprudent, unwise.
indisculpable, *a.* inexcusable.
indiscutible, *a.* unquestionable, indisputable.
indisolubilidad, *f.* indissolubility.
indisoluble, *a.* indissoluble.
indisolublemente, *adv.* indissolubly.
indispensable, *a.* indispensable, essential; unfailing.
indispensablemente, *adv.* indispensably; necessarily; unfailingly.
indisponer. I. *va.* (*for irr. v.* PONER) to disable, indispose, render unfit; to make ill; (w. **con**) to prejudice, set (against). **II.** *vr.* to be indisposed, to become ill; to fall out (with a person).
indisposición, *f.* disinclination, dislike; indisposition, slight ailment.
indisposicioncilla, *f. dim.* slight indisposition.
indispuesto, ta, *a. & pp.* of INDISPONER; indisposed; at variance.
indisputable, *a.* indisputable, unquestionable.
indisputablemente, *adv.* indisputably.
indistinción, *f.* lack of distinction.
indistinguible, *a.* undistinguishable.
indistintamente, *adv.* indistinctly; indifferently, without distinction.
indistinto, ta, *a.* indistinct, vague, not clear.
individuación, *f.* individuation.
individual, *a.* individual; peculiar; personal.
individualidad, *f.* individuality.
individualismo, *m.* individualism.
individualista, *n. & a.* individualist (-ic).
individualizar, *va.* to individualize.
individualmente, *adv.* individually.
individuamente, *adv.* indivisibly.

individuar, *va.* to individuate, distinguish, particularize, individualize.
individuo, dua. I. *a.* individual; indivisible, inseparable. **II.** *n.* individual, person; member, fellow (of a society, etc.).
indivisamente, *adv.* indivisibly.
indivisibilidad, *f.* indivisibility.
indivisible, *a.* indivisible.
indivisiblemente, *adv.* indivisibly.
indivisión, *f.* indivision, entirety.
indiviso, sa, *a.* undivided.
indo, da, *n.* & *a.* East-Indian, Hindu.
indócil, *a.* indocile, unteachable; headstrong, froward, unruly; inflexible, brittle.
indocilidad, *f.* indocility; inflexibility.
indoctamente, *adv.* ignorantly.
indocto, ta, *a.* ignorant, unlearned.
indocumentado, da, *a.* lacking the documents for identification.
indochino, na, *n.* & *a.* Indo-Chinese.
indoeuropeo, a, *n.* & *a.* Indo-European.
indogermánico, ca, *n.* & *a.* Indo-Germanic.
indoísmo, *m.* Hinduism, Hindooism.
índole, *f.* disposition, temper; class, kind.
indolencia, *f.* indolence.—**indolente,** *a.* indolent.—**indolentemente,** *adv.* indolently.
indoloro, ra, *a.* painless.
indomable, *a.* untamable, indomitable; unmanageable; unconquerable.
indomado, da, *a.* untamed.
indomesticable, *a.* untamable, not susceptible of domestication.
indoméstico, ca, *a.* untamed, intractable.
indómito, ta, *a.* untamed; unruly.
indostanés, sa; indostánico, ca, *a.* Hindu.
indostani, *n.* & *a.* Hindustani (language).
indotación, *f.* (law) want of a wife's portion.
indotado, da, *a.* unendowed; portionless.
indubitable, *a.* indubitable, unquestionable.
indubitablemente, *adv.* undoubtedly.
inducción, *f.* inducement, persuasion; (log.) induction; (elec.) induction.
inducido, *m.* (elec.) armature (of a dynamo).
inducidor, ra, *n.* inducer, persuader.
inducimiento, *m.* inducement.
inducir, *va.* (*ind.* INDUZCO: *pret.* INDUJE: *subj.* INDUZCA) to induce; to persuade, influence; (elec.) to induce.
inductivo, va, *a.* inductive.
inductor, ra. I. *a.* (elec.) inductive. **II.** *m.* (elec.) field (magnet) (of a dynamo).
indudable, *a.* indubitable, certain.
indulgencia, *f.* indulgence; forbearance, leniency.
indulgente, *a.* indulgent, lenient, forbearing.
indulgentemente, *adv.* indulgently.
indultar, *va.* to pardon; to free, exempt.
indultario, *m.* he who by virtue of a pontifical privilege can dispense ecclesiastical benefices.
indulto, *m.* pardon, forgiveness, amnesty; indult, privilege, exemption.
indumentaria, *f.* study of ancient apparel.
indumentario, ria, *a.* relating to clothes.
indumento, *m.* garment, vestment.
induración, *f.* (med.) induration.
industria, *f.* industry; diligence, assiduity; ingenuity, acuteness.—**de 1.,** designedly, purposely, intentionally.
industrial. I. *a.* industrial, manufacturing. **II.** *n.* industrialist, manufacturer.
industrialismo, *m.* industrialism.
industriar, *va.* & *vr.* to educate, teach, instruct, train, coach; to find means.
industriosamente, *adv.* industriously.
industrioso, sa, *a.* industrious.
inedia, *f.* fast, abstinence from food.
inédito, ta, *a.* unpublished.
ineducación, *f.* unmannerliness, unrefinement.—**ineducado, da,** *a.* unmannerly, unpolished.
inefabilidad, *f.* ineffability, unspeakableness.
inefable, *a.* ineffable, unutterable.

inefablemente, *adv.* ineffably.
ineficacia, *f.* inefficacy, inefficiency.
ineficaz, *a.* inefficacious, ineffectual, ineffective
ineficazmente, *adv.* inefficaciously.
inejecutable, *a.* impracticable, not feasible.
inelegante, *a.* inelegant.
ineluctable, *a.* irresistible.
ineludible, *a.* inevitable, unavoidable.
inenarrable, *a.* inexplicable, inexpressible.
ineptamente, *adv.* ineptly, incompetently.
ineptitud, *f.* ineptitude, incompetency.
inepto, ta, *a.* inept, incompetent; unfit; foolish.
inequívoco, ca, *a.* unequivocal, unmistakable.
inercia, *f.* inertia; inertness, inactivity.
inerme, *a.* unarmed, defenceless.
inerrable, *a.* inerrable, unmistakable.
inerrante, *a.* (ast.) fixed (star).
inerte, *a.* inert; dull, slow, sluggish; unskilful; paralyzed, senseless.
inervación, *f.* innervation.
inescrutable, *a.* inscrutable, unsearchable.
inescudriñable, *a.* inscrutable.
inesperadamente, *adv.* unexpectedly.
inesperado, da, *a.* unexpected, unforeseen.
inestabilidad, *f.* instability.
inestable, *a.* unstable.
inestimabilidad, *f.* invaluableness.
inestimable, *a.* invaluable.
inestimado, da, *a.* (law) unestimated, not appraised, unvalued.
inevitable, *a.* inevitable, unavoidable.
inevitablemente, *adv.* inevitably.
inexactamente, *adv.* inexactly.
inexactitud, *f.* inaccuracy.
inexacto, ta, *a.* inexact, inaccurate.
inexcusable, *a.* inexcusable; indispensable.
inexcusablemente, *adv.* inexcusably.
inexhausto, ta, *a.* unexhausted, unspent.
inexistente, *a.* nonexistent.
inexorable, *a.* inexorable, relentless, unbending.
inexperiencia, *f.* inexperience.
inexperto, ta, *a.* unskilful, inexperienced.
inexpiable, *a.* inexpiable.
inexplicable, *a.* inexplicable, unexplainable.
inexplorado, da, *a.* unexplored.
inexplosible, *a.* unexplosive, nonexplosive.
inexplotable, *a.* unexploitable, unworkable.
inexpresivo, va, *a.* inexpressive.
inexpugnable, *a.* inexpugnable, impregnable; firm, obstinate, stubborn.
in extenso, in extenso, at full length.
inextenso, sa, *a.* unextended, extensionless.
inextinguible, *a.* inextinguishable, unquenchable; perpetual.
inextirpable, *a.* inexterminable, not capable of being eradicated.
inextricable, *a.* inextricable.
infacundo, da, *a.* ineloquent.
infalibilidad, *f.* infallibility.—**infalible,** *a.* infallible.—**infaliblemente,** *adv.* infallibly.
infamación, *f.* slander, defamation.
infamador, ra, *n.* & *a.* defamer (-ing).
infamante, *pp.* & *a.* defaming; opprobrious.
infamar, *va.* to defame, dishonor, disgrace.
infamativo, va, *a.* defaming; disgracing.
infamatorio, ria, *a.* defamatory, libellous.
infame, *a.* infamous.—**infamemente,** *adv.* infamously.
infamia, *f.* infamy; baseness; infamous act.
infancia, *f.* infancy.
infando, da, *a.* unmentionable, unspeakable.
infanta, *f.* female child under seven years of age; infanta, any daughter of the King of Spain; wife of a prince royal.
infantado, *m.* territory assigned to a prince of the royal blood of Spain.
infante, *m.* infant, male child under seven years of age; infante, any son of the King of Spain, except the heir apparent; infantry soldier.—*pl.* choristers, choir boys.
infantería, *f.* infantry.

Infanticida, n. infanticide, child murderer.
Infanticidio, m. infanticide, murder of a child.
Infantil, a. infantile, childlike.
Infantilismo, m. infantility; (med.) infantilism.
Infanzón, m. ancient nobleman.—**Infanzonado, da,** a. pertaining to an INFANZÓN.
Infanzonazgo, m. territory of an INFANZÓN.—**Infanzonía,** f. dignity or condition of INFANZÓN.
Infartación, f. (med.) infarction.
Infarto, m. (med.) infarct.
Infatigable, a. indefatigable, untiring.
Infatigablemente, adv. indefatigably.
Infatuación, f. infatuation.
Infatuar. I. va. to infatuate. **II.** vr. to become infatuated.
Infaustamente, adv. unluckily.
Infausto, ta, a. unlucky; unhappy, accursed.
Infebril, a. fever-free.
Infección, f. infection.—**infeccionar,** va. = INFICIONAR.—**Infeccioso, sa,** a. infectious.
Infectar. I. va. to infect; spread contagion; to corrupt, vitiate, pervert. **II.** vr. to become infected.
Infectivo, va, a. infective, infectious.
Infecto, ta, a. infected, tainted, corrupt.
Infecundidad, f. infecundity, sterility.
Infecundo, da, a. infecund, barren, sterile.
Infelice, a. (poet.) unhappy, wretched.
Infelicidad, f. unhappiness, infelicity.
Infeliz. I. a. unhappy, wretched; unfortunate, luckless. **II.** n. poor devil.
Infelizmente, adv. unhappily, unluckily.
Inferencia, f. inference.
Inferior, a. inferior; lower, elementary (school, education, mathematics, etc.)
Inferioridad, f. inferiority.
Inferir. I. va. to infer; to imply, lead to; to inflict (as a wound); to offer (as an insult). **II.** vr. to follow as a consequence.
Infernáculo, m. a boys' game, hopscotch.
Infernal, a. infernal, hellish.
Infernalmente, adv. hellishly, infernally.
Infernar, va. (ind. INFIERNO: subj. INFIERNE) to damn; to irritate, vex, provoke.
Inferno, na, a. (poet.) infernal.
Infestación, f. infestation.—**Infestar,** va. to infest, overrun, harass; to fill with stench.
Infesto, ta, a. (poet.) prejudicial, dangerous.
Infeudar, va.; **infeudación,** f. = ENFEUDAR, etc.
Infibulación, f. (vet.) infibulation.
Infibular, va. (vet.) to infibulate.
Inficionar, va. to infect; to poison; corrupt, defile, pervert, vitiate.
Infidelidad, f. infidelity; unfaithfulness, faithlessness; unbelief, want of faith; unbelievers as a class.
Infidelísimo, ma, a. super. of INFIEL.
Infidencia, f. unfaithfulness, faithlessness; treason; (law) misfeasance.
Infidente, a. unfaithful.
Infiel. I. a. unfaithful, infidel; faithless; pagan; inaccurate, inexact. **II.** m. unbeliever, infidel.
Infielmente, adv. unfaithfully.
Infiernillo, m. small alcohol stove.
Infierno, m. (often in the pl.) hell; refectory or eating room in some convents; (chem.) large retort; cave of a baking machine; tank in oil mills.—**el quinto i.,** or **los quintos infiernos,** the end of the world (fig., app. to a very remote place).
Infigurable, a. incorporeal, that cannot be represented by any material figure.
Infiltración, f. infiltration, percolation.
Infiltrar, va. & vr. to infiltrate, percolate, filter; to imbue, infuse.
Infimo, ma, a. lowest, least; most abject, vilest; (com.) most inferior in quality.
Infinidad, f. infinity; infinite number (fig.).
Infinitamente, adv. infinitely.
Infinitesimal, a. infinitesimal.
Infinitivo, n. & a. (gram.) infinitive.

Infinito, ta. I. a. infinite. **II.** adv. infinitely, immensely. **III.** m. (el i.) infinity.
Infinitud, f. = INFINIDAD.
Infirmar, va. (law) to invalidate.
Inflación, f. inflation; conceit, vanity, airs.
Inflamable, a. inflammable.
Inflamación, f. inflammation; ignition.
Inflamar. I. va. to inflame, kindle, set on fire; to excite. **II.** vr. to take fire, ignite; to become fiery or excited; (med.) to become inflamed.
Inflamatorio, ria, a. inflammatory.
Inflar. I. va. to inflate; to elate, puff up with pride. **II.** vr. to swell; to strut.
Inflativo, va, a. inflating.
Inflexibilidad, f. inflexibility; stiffness, rigidity; inexorability.
Inflexible, a. inflexible, rigid; unbending, unyielding.
Inflexiblemente, adv. inflexibly, inexorably.
Inflexión, f. inflection, bending; (gram.) inflection; accent, modulation.
Infligir, va. (for mut. v. AFLIGIR) to impose (a penalty), condemn to.
Inflorescencia, f. (bot.) inflorescence.
Influencia, f. influence; (theo.) divine grace.
Influente, a. influencing, influential.
Influenza, f. influenza, grippe.
Influir. I. va. (ind. INFLUYO: subj. INFLUYA) to influence; to act on; (theo.) to grace with inspiration. **II.** vn. (w. en) to have influence (on), to affect; to contribute (to), have a part (in).
Influjo, m. influence; influx; (naut.) rising tide.
Influyente, a. influential.
Infolio, m. book in folio form.
Inforciado, m. Infortiate, second part of the Pandects of Justinian.
Información, f. information; account, report; inquiry, investigation; judicial inquiry and process; (law) brief.
Informador, ra, n. & a. informer (-ing), reporter (-ing).
Informal, a. informal; unreliable; unconventional.
Informalidad, f. informality, unconventionality; breach of etiquette.
Informante, n. & a. informer (-ing).
Informar. I. va. to inform, advise, report to; to give form to, shape. **II.** vn. (law) to plead. **III.** vr. (w. de) to acquaint one's self (with), to inquire (into), to find out.
Informativo, va, a. instructive, informative.
Informe. I. a. shapeless, formless. **II.** m. information; report, account, statement; advice; reference; (law) plea, pleading.
Informidad, f. informity, shapelessness.
Infortificable, a. that cannot be fortified.
Infortuna, f. (astrol.) evil influence of the stars.
Infortunado, da, a. unfortunate, unlucky.
Infortunio, m. misfortune, ill luck; mishap; misery, suffering.
Infosura, f. (vet.) a disease of horses.
Infracción, f. infraction, breach, infringement, trespass.
Infracto, ta, a. steady, not easily moved.
Infractor, ra, n. infractor, breaker, violator, transgressor.
in fraganti, adv. = EN FLAGRANTE.
Infrangible, a. infrangible; inviolable.
Infranqueable, a. unsurmountable.
Infrascripto, ta; infrascrito, ta, a. undersigned; hereinafter mentioned.
Infrecuente, a. unusual, infrequent.
Infringir, va. (ind. INFRINJO: subj. INFRINJA) to infringe, violate, break.
Infructifero, ra, a. unfruitful; unprofitable.
Infructuosidad, f. unfruitfulness, unproductiveness, uselessness.—**Infructuoso, sa,** a. unfruitfully, uselessly.—**infructuoso, sa,** a. fruitless, unproductive; unprofitable, abortive, unsuccessful.
Infrugifero, ra, a. = INFRUCTÍFERO.
infulas, f. pl. (eccl.) infulæ, headdress; mitre; conceit, airs.

For pronunciation, see the rules at the beginning of the book.

infundadamente, *adv.* groundlessly, without cause or reason.

infundado, da, *a.* groundless, baseless.

infundible, *a.* infusible.

infundibuliforme, *a.* (bot.) funnel-shaped.

infundíbulo, *m.* (anat.) infundibulum.

infundio, *m.* (coll.) fib, story.

infundir, *va.* to infuse, to inspire with; to imbue, to instil.

infurción, *f.* ancient ground lease.

infurcioniego, ga, *a.* subject to ground lease.

infurtir, *va.* = ENFURTIR.

infusibilidad, *f.* infusibility.

infusible, *a.* infusible.

infusión, *f.* infusion; inspiration; (pharm.) infusion; (eccl.) baptism by sprinkling.

infuso, sa, *a.* infused (as the grace of God).

infusorio, ria. I. *n.* & *a.* (zool.) infusorian. **II.** *m. pl.* Infusoria.

ingenerable, *a.* ingenerable, that cannot be produced or generated.

ingeniar. I. *va.* to conceive, contrive, devise, scheme. **II.** *vr.* to endeavor and manage skilfully; to find means to obtain or do anything.

ingeniatura, *f.* (coll.) ingenuity, acuteness, skilful management; (Am.) engineering.

ingeniería, *f* engineering.—**i. civil,** etc. *V.* INGENIERO.

ingeniero, ra, *n.* engineer.—**i. aeróstata,** aeronautic engineer.—**i. agrónomo,** agricultural engineer.—**i. civil,** civil engineer (expression gen. app. to all nonmilitary engineers).—**i. de caminos, canales y puertos,** civil engineer.—**i. de la armada,** or **de marina =** I. NAVAL.—**i. de minas,** mining engineer.—**i. de montes,** forestry engineer.—**i. electricista,** electrical engineer.—**i. en jefe,** chief engineer.—**i. forestal,** forestry engineer.—**i. industrial =** I. QUÍMICO.—**i. jefe,** chief engineer.—**i. químico,** chemical engineer.

ingenio, *m.* talent; mind, creative or inventive faculty; cleverness, skill, smartness; talented person, especially an author; engine, machine, mechanical apparatus; device, contrivance; (b. b.) plowcutter, plowpress.—**i. de azúcar,** sugar mill, sugar plantation.—**i. de pólvora,** powdermill.

ingeniosamente, *adv.* ingeniously.

ingeniosidad, *f.* ingenuity, ingeniousness.

ingenioso, sa, *a.* ingenious.

ingénito, ta, *a.* unbegotten; innate, inborn.

ingente, *a.* very large, huge, prodigious.

ingenuamente, *adv.* candidly, ingenuously.

ingenuidad, *f.* ingenuousness, candor.

ingenuo, nua, *a.* ingenuous, open, candid; (law) ingenuous, freeborn.

ingerencia, *f.* interference, intermeddling.

ingeridor, *m.* grafting knife.

ingeridura, *f.* grafting.

ingerir. I. *va.* (*ind.* INGIERO: *subj.* INGIERA) to insert, introduce, inclose; (agr.) to graft. **II.** *vr.* to interfere, intermeddle.

ingestión, *f.* (med.) ingestion, introduction of food into the stomach.

ingina, *f.* = QUIJADA.

ingle, *f.* groin, part next the thigh.

inglés, sa. I. *a.* English.—**a la inglesa,** in the English fashion. **II.** *n.* Englishman (-woman). **III.** *m.* English (the language).

inglesar, *va.* & *vr.* to Anglicize.

inglesismo, *m.* Anglicism.

inglete, *m.* diagonal; angle of 45°.

inglosable, *a.* admitting no gloss or comment.

ingobernable, *a.* ungovernable, unmanageable, unruly.

ingratamente, *adv.* ungratefully.

ingratitud, *f.* ingratitude, ungratefulness.

ingrato, ta. I. *a.* ungrateful; thankless; disagreeable. **II.** *n.* ingrate.

ingrediente, *m.* ingredient.

ingresar, *vn.* (**w. en**) to enter; to come in (s. o. money, profits, etc.); to join (a party, etc.).

ingreso, *m.* ingress, entrance; commencement; (com.) entry, money received; (eccl.) surplice fees.—*pl.* (com.) revenue, receipts, earnings.

inguinal; inguinario, ria, *a.* (anat.) inguinal.

ingurgitación, *f.* (med.) ingurgitation.

ingurgitar, *va.* to ingurgitate, swallow.

ingustable, *a.* unsavory, unpalatable.

inhábil, *a.* unable; incompetent; unfit, unskilful; unqualified.—**inhabilidad,** *f.* inability; incompetence; unskilfulness.

inhabilitación, *f.* disabling or disqualifying; disqualification; disability.

inhabilitar. I. *va.* to disqualify; to disable, render unfit. **II.** *vr.* to lose a right; to become disabled.

inhabitable, *a.* uninhabitable.

inhabitado, da, *a.* uninhabited.

inhabituado, da, *a.* unaccustomed.

inhacedero, ra, *a.* impracticable, unfeasible.

inhalador, ra, *n.* inhaler.—**inhalación,** *f.* (med.) inhalation.—**inhalar,** *va.* (med.) to inhale.

inherencia, *f.* inherence.

inherente, *a.* inherent.

inhestar, *va.* = ENHESTAR.

inhibición, *f.* inhibition; prohibition.

inhibir, *va.* (law) to inhibit (sp. an inferior court from proceeding further).

inhibitorio, ria, *a.* inhibitory.

inhiesto, *a.* steep.

inhonestamente, *adv.* immodestly.

inhonestidad, *f.* immodesty, indecency.

inhonesto, ta, *a.* immodest, indecent.

inhospedable, inhospitable, inhospital, inhospitalario, ria, *a.* inhospitable, reluctant to entertain guests; unsheltering.

inhospitalidad, *f.* inhospitableness.

inhumación, *f.* inhumation, interment.

inhumanamente, *adv.* inhumanly, cruelly.

inhumanidad, *f.* inhumanity, cruelty.

inhumano, na, *a.* inhuman, cruel.

inhumar, *va.* to bury, inhume, inter.

iniciación, *f.* initiation, introduction.

iniciador, ra, *n.* & *a.* initiator (-ing), starter (-ing).

inicial, *n.* & *a.* initial.

iniciar. I. *va.* to initiate; to begin, start. **II.** *vr.* to be initiated; (eccl.) to receive first orders.

iniciativo, va. I. *a.* initiating, initiatory. **II.** *f.* initiative; right to propose laws, etc.

inicuamente, *adv.* iniquitously.

inicuo, cua, *a.* iniquitous, wicked.

in illo tempore, *adv.* formerly, in times of yore.

inimaginable, *a.* unimaginable, inconceivable.

inimicísimo, ma, *a. sup. irr.* of ENEMIGO: most inimical.

inimitable, *a.* inimitable.

ininteligible, *a.* unintelligible.

iniquidad, *f.* iniquity, unrighteousness.

iniquísimo, ma, *a. sup.* of INICUO.

injerencia, injeridura, injerir = INGERENCIA, INGERIDURA, INGERIR.

injertar, *va.* (*pp.* INJERTADO, INJERTO) (agr.) to ingraft, to graft.

injertera, *f.* orchard of grafted trees.

injerto. I. *pp. irr.* of INJERTAR. **II.** *m.* graft, grafting, tree ingrafted.

injuria, *f.* offence, wrong, insult, abuse, affront; injustice; damage, harm.

injuriado, da, *a.* & *pp.* injured, wronged.

injuriador, ra, *n.* aggressor, offender, abuser.

injuriante, *a.* injuring; offensive, insulting.

injuriar, *va.* to insult, offend, abuse; to annoy; to harm, hurt.

injuriosamente, *adv.* insultingly, offensively; injuriously, hurtfully.

injurioso, sa, *a.* injurious; insulting, offensive, abusive.

injustamente, *adv.* unjustly.

injusticia, *f.* injustice.

injustificable, *a.* unjustifiable.

injustificadamente, *adv.* unjustifiably.

injustificado, da, *a.* unjustified, unjustifiable.
injusto, ta, *a.* unjust.
inlegible, *a.* illegible.
inllevable, *a.* unbearable.
inmaculadamente, *adv.* immaculately.
inmaculado, da, *a.* immaculate.
inmanejable, *a.* unmanageable; unruly.
inmanente, *a.* immanent, inherent.
inmarcesible, *a.* unfading, unwithering.
inmaterial, *a.* immaterial, incorporeal.
inmaterialidad, *f.* immateriality.
inmaturo, ra, *a.* immature.
inmediación, *f.* contiguity, contact.—*pl.* environs, suburbs, outskirts; neighborhood.
inmediatamente, *adv.* contiguously; immediately, forthwith.
inmediato, ta, *a.* contiguous, close, adjoining, hard by, next.—**dar por las inmediatas,** to force to the wall (fig.), to silence (in a discussion).—**llegar,** or **venir, a las inmediatas,** to come to the thick, or hardest, part of a fight or dispute.
inmedicable, *a.* incurable, irremediable.
inmejorable, *a.* unimprovable, unsurpassable, most excellent.
inmemorable, *a.* immemorial.
inmemorablemente, *adv.* immemorably.
inmemorial, *a.* immemorial.
inmensamente, *adv.* immensely, infinitely.
inmensidad, *f.* immensity, vastness; infinity; immensity of space, boundless space; great multitude or number.
inmenso, sa, *a.* immense; unbounded, infinite; countless.
inmensurable, *a.* immensurable.
inmerecidamente, *adv.* undeservedly.
inmerecido, da, *a.* unmerited, undeserved.
inméritamente, *adv.* unmeritedly.
inmérito, ta, *a.* undeserved, unmerited.
inmeritorio, ria, *a.* undeserving.
inmersión, *f.* immersion.
inmigración, *f.* immigration.—**inmigrante,** *m.* immigrant.—**inmigrar,** *vn.* to immigrate.
inminencia, *f.* imminence, nearness.
inminente, *a.* imminent, impending, near.
inmiscible, *a.* (chem.) inmiscible, non-mixing.
inmiscuir, **I.** *va.* to mix. **II.** *vr.* to interfere, to intermeddle.
inmobiliario, ria, *a.* relating to real estate.
inmoble, *a.* unmovable, immovable, fixed; motionless; unshakable, constant.
inmoderación, *f.* immoderation, excess.
inmoderadamente, *adv.* immoderately.
inmoderado, da, *a.* immoderate, excessive.
inmodestamente, *adv.* immodestly.
inmodestia, *f.* immodesty, indelicacy.
inmodesto, ta, *a.* immodest, indelicate.
inmódico, ca, *a.* excessive.
inmolación, *f.* immolation, sacrifice.
inmolador, ra, *n.* & *a.* immolator (-ing).
inmolar, *va.* to immolate; to sacrifice.
inmoral, *a.* immoral.—**inmoralidad,** *f.* immorality.—**inmoralmente,** *adv.* immorally.
inmortal, *a.* immortal.—**inmortalidad,** *f.* immortality.—**inmortalizar.** **I.** *va.* to immortalize. **II.** *vr.* to become immortal.—**inmortalmente,** *adv.* immortally.
inmortificación, *f.* immortification, licentiousness.
inmortificado, da, *a.* unmortified.
inmotivado, da, *a.* without reason or cause.
inmoto, ta, *a.* unmoved.
inmovible, *a.* immovable.
inmóvil, *a.* motionless; fixed; unshaken.
inmovilidad, *f.* immovability, fixedness.
inmovilización, *f.* immobilization.
inmovilizar, *va.* to immobilize, fix.
inmudable, *a.* immutable.
inmueble. **I.** *a.* (law) immovable (property). **II.** *m.* (law) immovable.
inmundicia, *f.* filth, dirt; garbage; refuse; nastiness, filthiness; uncleanliness; impurity.
inmundo, da, *a.* unclean, filthy.

inmune, *a.* free, exempt; immune.
inmunidad, *f.* immunity; exemption, franchise, freedom.
inmunizar, *va.* to immunize, render immune.
inmutabilidad, *f.* immutability.
inmutable, *a.* immutable.
inmutación, *f.* change, alteration.
inmutar. **I.** *va.* to change, alter. **II.** *vr.* to change countenance from some emotion, to become disturbed, lose one's calm.
inmutativo, va, *a.* that changes or causes alterations.
innatismo, *m.* (phil.) innatism.
innato, ta, *a.* innate; inborn.
innatural, *a.* unnatural.
innavegable, *a.* nonnavigable; unseaworthy.
innecesariamente, *adv.* unnecessarily.
innecesario, ria, *a.* unnecessary.
innegable, *a.* undeniable.
innegablemente, *adv.* undeniably.
innoble, *a.* ignoble; mean of birth.
innocuo, cua, *a.* innocuous, harmless.
innominable, *a.* unnamable.
innominado, da, *a.* nameless.
innovación, *f.* innovation.—**innovador, ra,** *n.* & *a.* innovator (-ing).—**innovamiento,** *m.* innovation.—**innovar,** *va.* to innovate.
innumerabilidad, *f.* innumerability.
innumerable, *a.* innumerable, numberless.
innumerablemente, *adv.* innumerably.
innúmero, ra, *a.* numberless, countless.
inobediencia, *f.* disobedience.
inobediente, *a.* disobedient; unmanageable.
inobservable, *a.* unobservable, inobservable.
inobservancia, *f.* nonobservance.
inobservante, *a.* nonobservant.
inocencia, *f.* innocence; harmlessness.
inocentada, *f.* (coll.) simple or silly speech or action; practical joke or trick.
inocente, *a.* innocent; harmless; simple, easily duped, "easy."
inocentemente, *adv.* innocently; harmlessly.
inocentón, na. **I.** *a. aug.* very simple and credulous. **II.** *n.* simpleton.
inoculación, *f.* inoculation.—**inoculador, ra,** *n.* & *a.* inoculator (-ing).—**inocular,** *va.* (med.) to inoculate; to contaminate.
inodoro, ra. **I.** *a.* inodorous, odorless. **II.** *m.* water-closet.
inofensivo, va, *a.* inoffensive.
inoficioso, sa, *a.* (law) inofficious (will).
inolvidable, *a.* unforgetable.
inope, *a.* poor, penniless, destitute.
inoperable, *a.* (med.) inoperable.
inopia, *f.* indigence, poverty, penury.
inopinable, *a.* indisputable; inconceivable.
inopinadamente, *adv.* unexpectedly.
inopinado, da, *a.* unexpected, unforeseen.
inoportunamente, *adv.* inopportunely.
inoportunidad, *f.* inopportuneness, untimeliness.—**inoportuno, na,** *a.* inopportune.
inordenadamente, *adv.* inordinately.
inordenado, da; inordinado, da, *a.* inordinate, irregular, disorderly.
in pace (Lat.). **I.** *adv.* in peace. **II.** *m.* dungeon where scandalous persons were formerly confined.
inorgánico, ca, *a.* inorganic.
inoxidable, *a.* inoxidizable; nonrusting.
in pártibus, (Lat.), *adv.* (coll.) having a nominal appointment. *V.* OBISPO.
in péctore (Lat.), *adv.* (coll.) not yet made known (s. o. resolutions, decrees, etc.).
in perpétuum (Lat.), *adv.* in perpetuum, in perpetuity, forever.
in promptu (Lat.), *adv.* offhand, impromptu, extempore.
in púribus, (Lat.), *adv.* (coll.) stark naked.
inquebrantable, *a.* irrevocable.
inquietador, ra, *n.* disturber.
inquietamente, *adv.* restlessly.

inquietar. I. *va.* to disquiet, trouble, worry; to vex, tease, harass; to stir up or excite. **II.** *vr.* to become uneasy or restless, to fret, worry.

inquieto, ta, *a.* restless; anxious, solicitous, uneasy, worried.

inquietud, *f.* restlessness, uneasiness, anxiety.

inquilinato, *m.* (law) lease, leasehold.

inquilino, na, *n.* tenant, inmate, lodger; (law) lessee.

inquina, *f.* (coll.) aversion, hatred, grudge.

inquinamento, *m.* infection.

inquinar, *va.* to contaminate.

inquiridor, ra, *n.* inquirer, investigator.

inquirir, *va.* (*ind.* INQUIERO: *subj.* INQUIERA) to inquire, look into, search, investigate.

inquisición, *f.* inquest, examination, inquiry; (eccl.) Inquisition; Holy Office.

inquisidor, ra. I. *n.* inquirer, examiner. **II.** *m.* (eccl.) inquisitor.

inquisitorial, *a.* inquisitorial.

inri, *m.* I. N. R. I. (inscription on the cross); brand, stigma, stain.

insabible, *a.* unknowable.

insaciabilidad, *f.* insatiableness, greediness.

insaciable, *a.* insatiable; greedy.

insaciablemente, *adv.* insatiably.

insaculación, *f.* (law) balloting for names.

insaculador, *m.* (law) balloter.

insacular, *va.* to ballot, to vote by ballot.

insalivación, *f.* insalivation.

insalivar, *va.* to insalivate.

insalubre, *a.* insalubrious, unhealthful.

insalubridad, *f.* insalubrity, unhealthfulness.

insanable, *a.* incurable, irremediable.

insania, *f.* insanity.

insano, na, *a.* insane, mad, crazy.

inscribir. I. *va.* (*pp.* INSCRITO, INSCRIPTO) to inscribe, register, record, book; (geom.) to inscribe; (law) to record (deeds). **II.** *vr.* to register; to enroll.

inscripción, *f.* inscription; record, register, entry; registration; government bond.

inscriptible, *a.* (geom.) inscribable.

inscripto, ta, *pp. irr.* of INSCRIBIR.

inscrito, ta, *a. & pp. irr.* of INSCRIBIR: inscribed.

insculpir, *va.* to engrave, cut.

insecable, *a.* (coll.) that cannot be dried.

insecticida, *n. & a.* insecticide (-al).

insectil, *a.* insectile, insectean.

insectívoro, ra, *a.* insectivorous.

insecto, *m.* (ent.) insect.

inseguridad, *f.* insecurity, unsafety; uncertainty.

inseguro, ra, *a.* insecure, unsafe; uncertain.

insenescencia, *f.* quality of not becoming old.

insensatamente, *adv.* insensately, madly, stupidly.

insensatez, *f.* stupidity, folly.

insensato, ta, *a.* insensate, stupid, mad.

insensibilidad, *f.* insensibility, unconsciousness; hard-heartedness.—**insensibilizar,** *va.* to make insensible or insensitive.—**insensible,** *a.* insensible, senseless, unconscious; imperceptible; unfeeling, heartless.

insensiblemente, *adv.* insensibly; imperceptibly.

inseparabilidad, *f.* inseparableness.

inseparable, *a.* inseparable; undetachable.

inseparablemente, *adv.* inseparably.

insepulto, ta, *a.* unburied, uninterred.

inserción, *f.* insertion; grafting.

inserir, *va.* to insert; to graft.

insertar. I. *va.* (*pp.* INSERTADO, INSERTO) to insert, to introduce. **II.** *vr.* (zool. and bot.) to become inserted or attached.

inserto, ta, *a.* inserted.

inservible, *a.* unserviceable, useless.

insidia, *f.* ambush, snare.—**insidiador, ra,** *n.* plotter, waylayer.—**insidiar,** *va.* to plot against, waylay, ambush.—**insidiosamente,** *adv.* insidiously, guilefully.—**insidioso, sa,** *a.* insidious, sly, guileful.

insigne, *a.* noted, famous, renowned.

insignemente, *adv.* signally, famously.

insignia, *f.* decoration, device, medal, badge, standard; (naut.) pennant.—*pl.* insignia.

insignificancia, *f.* insignificance; insufficiency, uselessness.—**insignificante,** *a.* insignificant, unimportant.—**insignificativo, va,** *a.* insignificant; insignificative.

insinuación, *f.* insinuation, innuendo; hint, suggestion; (law) exhibition of a public instrument before a judge.

insinuante, *a.* insinuative, crafty, artful, sleek.

insinuar. I. *va.* to insinuate, hint, suggest. **II.** *vr.* to ingratiate one's self; to creep in; to grow (on one, as a habit).

insinuativo, va, *a.* insinuating; insinuative; slick, smooth.

insípidamente, *adv.* insipidly.—**insipidez,** *f.* insipidity, insipidness.—**insípido, da,** *a.* insipid, tasteless, unsavory, spiritless, vapid, flat.

insipiencia, *f.* ignorance, lack of judgment.

insipiente, *a.* ignorant, uninformed.

insistencia, *f.* persistence, insistence, obstinacy.

insistir, *vn.* (w. **en**) to insist (on), persist (in); to dwell (upon), emphasize.

insito, ta, *a.* inherent, inborn, connatural.

in situ (Lat.) *adv.* in situ, in its natural place.

insociabilidad, *f.* unsociability, unsociableness.

insociable, insocial, *a.* unsociable.

insolación, *f.* (med.) insolation, sunstroke.

insolar. I. *va.* to insolate. **II.** *vr.* to be sunstruck.

insoldable, *a.* that cannot be soldered or welded.

insolencia, *f.* insolence.—**insolentar. I.** *va.* to make bold. **II.** *vr.* to become insolent.—**insolente,** *a.* insolent.—**insolentemente,** *adv.* insolently.

in sólidum, *adv.* (law) insolidum, joint and several.

insólito, ta, *a.* unusual, unaccustomed.

insolubilidad, *f.* insolubility; unsolvability.

insoluble, *a.* insoluble; fast, strong; unsolvable.

insolvencia, *f.* insolvency.—**insolvente,** *a.* insolvent.

insomne, *a.* insomnious, sleepless.

insomnio, *m.* insomnia, sleeplessness.

insondable, *a.* unfathomable, fathomless; inscrutable, unsearchable; abysmal.

insonoro, ra, *a.* insonorous; not clear.

insoportable, *a.* unbearable, intolerable.

insostenible, *a.* indefensible.

inspección, *f.* inspection, survey; superintendence; inspector's office.

inspeccionar, *va.* to inspect, examine, oversee.

inspector, ra, *n.* inspector, examiner; supervisor, superintendent, overseer.

inspiración, *f.* inspiration; (med.) inhalation.

inspirador, ra, *n. & a.* inspirer (-ing).

inspirante, *a.* inspiring.

inspirar, *va.* to inspire; to inhale.

inspirativo, va, *a.* inspiring.

instabilidad, *f.* instability; inconstancy.

instable, *a.* unstable; inconstant, changeable.

instalación, *f.* installation, instalment; settling; plant, works, factory; system (as of gas pipes and fittings, etc.); induction (of an officer).

instalador, ra, *n.* one who installs, lays, sets up, etc. (gas fitter, pipe layer, plumber).

instalar. I. *va.* to install; to put in, lay, set up; to induct (into office). **II.** *vr.* to establish one's self, settle.

instancia, *f.* instance or instancy; memorial, petition; prosecution or process of a suit; pressing argument; entreaty, request.—**a instancia de,** at the request of.

instantáneamente, *adv.* instantly; instantaneously.

instantáneo, nea. I. *a.* instantaneous. **II.** *f.* (phot.) snapshot.

instante. I. *a.* instant, pressing, urgent. **II.** *m.* instant, moment.—**al i.,** immediately.—**por instantes,** incessantly, every moment.

instantemente, *adv.* instantly.

instar. I. *va.* to press, urge; in schools, to impugn the solution of a question. **II.** *vn.* to be urgent.

instauración, *f.* renovation, restoration.
instaurar, *va.* to renovate, restore.
instaurativo, va, *a.* restorative.
instigación, *f.* instigation, incitement.
instigador, ra, *n.* instigator, abetter.
instigar, *va.* (*pret.* INSTIGUÉ: *subj.* INSTIGUE) to instigate, incite, urge.
instilación, *f.* instillation.
instilar, *va.* to instil, infuse, insinuate.
instintivo, va, *a.* instinctive.
instintivamente, *adv.* instinctively.
instinto, *m.* instinct; divine inspiration.—**por i.,** instinctively.
institución, *f.* institution, establishment; education, instruction; (law) institution, instituting. —*pl.* institutes (of a science).
instituente, *a.* instituting; founding.
instituidor, ra, *n.* institutor, founder.
instituir, *va.* (*ind.* INSTITUYO: *subj.* INSTITUYA) to institute, establish, found; to teach, instruct; to appoint, constitute, institute.
instituta, *f.* (law) institutes.
instituto, *m.* institute, established law; settled order; institute, institution (of learning); school. —**i. de segunda enseñanza,** or **general y técnico,** high school.
institutor, ra, *n.* institutor.
institutriz, *f.* governess, instructress.
instituyente, *n.* institutor; founder.
instrucción, *f.* instruction, teaching; education; lesson; knowledge, learning; (law) court proceedings.—*pl.* instructions, directions, orders.— **i. primaria,** primary education.—**i. pública,** public education.—**i. secundaria,** high-school education.—**i. superior,** higher, or college, education.
instructivamente, *adv.* instructively.
instructivo, va, *a.* instructive.
instructor, ra, *n.* instructor, teacher.
instruído, da, *a.* & *pp.* learned, well-educated, well-posted.
instruir, *va.* (*ind.* INSTRUYO: *subj.* INSTRUYA) to instruct, teach, train, coach; to inform, advise; (mil.) to drill, train; (law) to put in legal form, to formulate according to established rules.
instrumentación, *f.* (mus.) instrumentation, orchestration.
instrumental, *a.* (mus.) instrumental; (law) belonging to legal instruments.
instrumentalmente, *adv.* instrumentally.
instrumentar, *va.* (mus.) to orchestrate.
instrumentista, *m.* instrument maker; (mus.) instrumentalist, player on a musical instrument.
instrumento, *m.* instrument, implement, appliance, engine, machine, apparatus; agent or means; (law) instrument, indenture, deed; (mus.) instrument.—**i. de boca,** wind instrument. —**i. de canto,** musical instrument.—**i. de cuerda,** stringed instrument.—**i. de percusión,** instrument sounded by striking.—**i. de viento,** or **i. neumático,** wind instrument.
insuave, *a.* unpleasant, disagreeable.
insubordinación, *f.* insubordination.
insubordinado, da, *a.* & *pp.* insubordinate, rebellious.
insubordinar. I. *va.* to incite to insubordination. **II.** *vr.* to rebel, to mutiny.
insubsistencia, *f.* instability.
insubsistente, *a.* unable; groundless, baseless.
insubstancial, *a.* unsubstantial, inane, shallow, pointless.
insubstancialidad, *f.* inanity.
insubstancialmente, *adv.* inanely.
insudar, *vn.* to toil, drudge, work hard.
insuficiencia, *f.* insufficiency, inadequateness.
insuficiente, *a.* insufficient, inadequate.
insuficientemente, *adv.* insufficiently.
insuflación, *f.* (med.) insufflation.
insuflar, *va.* (med.) to insufflate.
insufrible, *a.* intolerable, unbearable.
insufriblemente, *adv.* insufferably, unbearably.
ínsula, *f.* (archaic) isle, island.
insular; insulano, na, *a.* insular.

insulsamente, *adv.* insipidly.—**insulsez,** *f.* insipidity, flatness.—**insulso, sa,** *a.* insipid, tasteless; dull, heavy.
insultador, ra; insultante, *n.* & *a.* insulter (-ing), abuser (-ing, -ive).
insultar. I. *va.* to insult; to call names. **II.** *vr.* (coll.) to have a fit.
insulto, *m.* insult, affront; sudden fit of illness.
insume, *a.* costly, expensive.
insumergible, *a.* insubmergible.
insuperable, *a.* insuperable, insurmountable.
insupurable, *a.* that cannot suppurate.
insurgente, *n.* & *a.* insurgent.
insurrección, *f.* insurrection, rebellion.
insurreccionar. I. *va.* to cause to rebel, to raise in insurrection. **II.** *vr.* to rebel.
insurrecto, ta, *n.* & *a.* insurgent, rebel.
insustancial, *a.* = INSUBSTANCIAL.
intacto, ta, *a.* untouched, intact, whole; pure.
intachable, *a.* unexceptionable, irreproachable.
intangible, *a.* intangible; not to be touched.
integérrimo, ma, *a.* *super.* most honorable, unspotted, irreproachable.
integrable, *a.* integrable.
integración, *f.* integration.
integral. I. *a.* integral; whole. **II.** *f.* (math.) integral.
integralmente, *adv.* integrally, wholly.
íntegramente, *adv.* entirely, wholly.
integrante, *a.* integral; integrant; integrating.
integrar, *va.* to integrate; (com.) to reimburse; (mat.) to integrate.
integridad, *f.* wholeness, completeness; integrity, honesty, uprightness; virginity.
íntegro, gra, *a.* entire, complete, whole; upright, honest.
integumento, *m.* integument.
inflexión, *f.* intellection.
intelectiva, *f.* intellect, intelligence.
intelectivo, va, *a.* intellective.
intelecto, *m.* intellect, understanding.
intelectual, *a.* intellectual, mental.
intelectualmente, *adv.* intellectually.
inteligencia, *f.* intellect, mind, understanding; intelligence; comprehension; knowledge; understanding (between persons); skill, ability, experience; sense, meaning.—**en la i.,** in the understanding.
inteligenciado, da, *a.* (coll.) instructed, informed.
inteligente, *a.* intelligent; talented, smart, bright, clever; skilful, able.
inteligible, *a.* intelligible.
inteligiblemente, *adv.* intelligibly.
intemperancia, *f.* intemperance, excess.
intemperante, *a.* intemperate.
intemperie, *f.* rough or bad weather.—**a la i.,** in the open air, outdoors, unsheltered.
intempestivamente, *adv.* unseasonably, inopportunely.
intempestivo, va, *a.* unseasonable, inopportune.
intención, *f.* intention, purpose; viciousness (of animals); caution, discretion.
intencionadamente, *adv.* intentionally.
intencionado, da, *a.* inclined, disposed.
intencional, *a.* intentional.
intencionalmente, *adv.* intentionally.
intendencia, *f.* intendancy (province); administration, management; office or district of an intendant.
intendenta, *f.* wife of an INTENDENTE.
intendente, *m.* intendant; subtreasurer of the government.—**i. de ejército,** quartermaster general.—**i. de marina,** commandant of a navy yard.
intensamente, *adv.* intensely.
intensar, *va.* to intensify.
intensidad, *f.* intensity; vehemence.
intensificar, *va.* to intensify.
intensión, *f.* intenseness; vehemence; earnestness.—**intensivo, va; intenso, sa,** *a.* intense, intensive, vehement, ardent, lively.

intentar, *va.* to try, attempt, endeavor; to intend, purpose, mean; (law) to enter (an action), to commence (a lawsuit).

intento, *m.* intent, purpose, design.—**de i.,** purposely, knowingly.

intentona, *f.* (coll.) rash attempt.

ínter. I. *prep.* between.—**i. nos,** between ourselves, between you and me. **II.** *m.* interim;(Peru) substitute curate.

intercadencia, *f.* interruption, interposition; unevenness; inconstancy; (med.) intermission or inequality of the pulse.

intercadente, *a.* changeable, variable.

intercadentemente, *adv.* changeably.

intercalación, *f.* intercalation, interpolation, insertion.—**intercalar. I.** *va.* to intercalate, interpolate. **II.** *a.* intercalary.

intercambiable, *a.* interchangeable.

intercambio, *m.* interchange.

interceder, *vn.* to intercede.

intercelular, *a.* intercellular.

interceptación, *f.* interception, stoppage.

interceptar, *va.* to intercept, cut off.

intercesión, *f.* intercession, mediation.

intercesor, ra, *n.* intercessor, interceder.

interciso, sa, *a.*—**día de i.,** half holiday.

interclusión, *f.* interclusion.

intercolumnio, intercolunio, *m.* (arch.) intercolumniation.

intercontinental, *a.* intercontinental.

intercostal, *a.* intercostal.

intercurrencia, *f.* intercurrence.

intercurrente, *a.* intercurrent, intervening.

intercutáneo, nea, *a.* intercutaneous.

interdecir, *va.* to interdict, prohibit.

interdentario, ria, *a.* interdental.

interdicción, *f.* interdiction, prohibition; interdict.—**interdicto,** *m.* prohibition, interdiction; interdict; (law) judgment of summary possession.

interdigital, *a.* interdigital.

interés, *m.* interest (in the commercial sense it is often u. in the *pl.*: *los intereses se han pagado ya,* the interest has been already paid); attraction, inducement.—*pl.* interests; money matters, business affairs.—**i. compuesto,** compound interest.—**i. simple,** simple interest.—**intereses creados,** vested interests, "the interests."

interesable, *a.* avaricious, mercenary.

interesado, da. I. *a.* & *pp.* interested, concerned; selfish, mercenary. **II.** *n.* associate; person interested; (law) party in interest.

interesante, *a.* interesting.

interesar. I. *vn.* & *vr.* to be concerned or interested. **II.** *va.* to invest; to give an interest; to interest, attract.

interesencia, *f.* assistance, attendance.

interesente, *a.* present, concurring.

interesillo, *m. dim.* slight interest.

interestelar, *a.* interstellar.

interfecto, ta, *n.* (law) murdered person, victim.

interferencia, *f.* (opt.) interference.

interfoliar, *va.* to interleave (a book).

ínterin. I. *m.* character of acting or pro tempore. **II.** *adv.* meanwhile, interim.

interinamente, *adv.* in the interim, meantime, provisionally, pro tem.

interinidad, *f.* = ÍNTERIN.

interino, na, *a.* provisional, temporary; pro tempore, acting.

interior. I. *a.* interior, internal, inner, inside; home (u. a.), domestic (commerce, etc.).—**lo i.,** the inside; home or domestic (national) affairs; (pol.) the Interior. **II.** *m.* interior; inside; inner part; mind, soul; in coaches with three compartments, the middle one.—*pl.* entrails, intestines, (coll.) insides.

interioridades, *f. pl.* family secrets; inwardness.

interiormente, *adv.* internally; inwardly.

interjección, *f.* (gram.) interjection.

interlínea, *f.* (print.) lead, space line.

interlineación, *f.* interlineation; double space; (print.) leading.

interlineal, *a.* interlineal.

interlinear, *va.* to write between lines; (print.) to lead, to space; to double-space.

interlocución, *f.* interlocution, dialogue.

interlocutor, ra, *n.* interlocutor.

interlocutoriamente, *adv.* (law) intermediately.—**interlocutorio, ria,** *a.* (law) interlocutory, intermediate.

intérlope, *a.* interloping.

interlunio, *m.* interlunar period, interlunation.

intermaxilar, *a.* intermaxillary.

intermediar, *va.* to interpose, mediate.

intermediario, ria. I. *a.* intermediary. **II.** *n.* intermediary; mediator; (p. e.) intermediary, middleman.

intermedio, dia. I. *a.* intermediate, intervening, interposed. **II.** *m.* interval, interim; (theat.) interlude, intermission.

interminable, *a.* interminable, endless.

intermisión, *f.* intermission, interruption.

intermitencia, *f.* (med.) intermission.

intermitente, *a.* intermittent.

intermitir, *va.* to intermit, discontinue.

internación, *f.* going or taking inside or into.

internacional, *a.* international.

internacionalismo, *m.* international relations; internationalism (socialistic doctrine).

internacionalista, *n.* internationalist.

internado, *pp.* & *m.* boarding-school system; state of being a boarding student; body of boarding students.

internamente, *adv.* internally.

internar. I. *va.* to send into the interior of a country; to place, or order placed, in an institution. **II.** *vn.* to enter. **III.** *vr.* (w. en) to go into the interior (of); to go deeply (into a subject); to worm one's self into another's confidence.

interno, na. I. *a.* interior, internal, inward; boarding (student). **II.** *n.* boarding student.

internodio, *m.* (bot.) internode.

internuncio, *m.* interlocutor; (eccl.) internuncio.

interoceánico, ca, *a.* interoceanic.

interocular, *a.* interocular.

interóseo, a, *a.* interosseous.

interpaginar, *va.* (b. b.) to interleave.

interpelación, *f.* interpellation; summons.

interpelar, *va.* to appeal to, to implore the aid of; to interpellate; (law) to summon.

interplanetario, ria, *a.* interplanetary.

interpolación, *f.* interpolation.

interpoladamente, *adv.* in an interpolated way.

interpolar, *va.* to interpolate; to intermix; to stop or pause briefly in (an address, etc.).

interponer. I. *va.* (for *irr. v.* PONER) to interpose; to appoint as a mediator; (law) to present (a petition) to a court. **II.** *vr.* to go between, to interpose.

interposición, *f.* interposition; mediation; meddling, interference.

interpósita persona, (Lat.) (law) intermediary, agent.

interprender, *va.* (mil.) to take by surprise.

interpresa, *f.* (mil.) taking by surprise.

interpretable, *a.* interpretable.

interpretación, *f.* interpretation.—**i. de lenguas,** Translation Bureau (in the State Department of Spain).

interpretador, ra, *n.* interpreter.

interpretante, *n.* & *a.* interpreter (-ing).

interpretar, *va.* to interpret.

interpretativamente, *adv.* interpretatively.

interpretativo, va, *a.* interpretative.

intérprete, *n.* interpreter; sign, mark.

interpuesto, ta, *a.* & *pp. irr.* of INTERPONER; interposed, intervening.

interregno, *m.* interregnum.—**i. parlamentario,** period during which the Spanish Cortes are not in session.

interrogación, *f.* interrogation, question; (print.) question mark.

interrogante. I. *a.* interrogative; interrogating; question (mark). **II.** *n.* interrogator, questioner. **III.** *m.* question mark.

interrogar, *va.* (*pret.* INTERROGUÉ: *subj.* INTE-
RROGUE) to question, to interrogate.
interrogativamente, *adv.* interrogatively.
interrogativo, va, *a.* interrogatory.
interrogatorio, *m.* interrogatory; (law) cross-
examination.
interrumpidamente, *adv.* interruptedly.
interrumpido, da, *a.* & *pp.* interrupted, broken,
discontinued.
interrumpir, *va.* to interrupt.
interrupción, *f.* interruption.
interruptor, ra. **I.** *n.* interrupter. **II.** *m.* (elec.)
switch; circuit-breaker.—**i. bipolar,** two-pole
switch.—**i. de aceite,** oil-break switch.—**i. de
arranque,** starting switch.—**i. de botón,** push-
button switch.—**i. de cuchilla,** knife (-edge)
switch.—**i. de dos (tres) direcciones,** two-
(three-) way switch.—**i. de mano,** hand switch.—
i. de seguridad, safety switch.—**i. de techo,** ceiling switch, top switch.—**i. horario,** time switch.—
i. trifásico, three-phase switch.—**i. tripolar,**
three-pole switch.—**i. unipolar,** single-pole switch.
intersecarse, *vr.* to intersect (as two lines).
intersección, *f.* intersection.
intersideral, *a.* (ast.) interstellar.
intersticial, *a.* interstitial.
intersticio, *m.* interstice; lapse of time, period,
interval.
intertropical, *a.* intertropical.
interusurio, *m.* interest for a time.
intervalo, *m.* interval; (mus.) interval.
intervención, *f.* intervention; supervision, superintendence; mediation, interposition; auditing
of accounts; (law) intervention.
intervenir. **I.** *vn.* (*for irr. v.* VENIR) to intervene,
mediate, intermediate; to interfere. **II.** *va.* to
supervise, superintend; to audit (accounts);
to control, to regulate; to offer to pay (a draft).
III. *v. impers.* to occur, happen.
interventor, ra, *n.* comptroller; supervisor, inspector, superintendent; auditor.
intervertebral, *a.* intervertebral.
intervievar, *va.* (occasionally seen in newspapers)
to interview.
interyacente, *a.* interjacent, intervening.
intestado, da, *a.* intestate.
intestinal, *a.* intestinal.
intestino, na. **I.** *a.* intestine, internal; civil,
domestic. **II.** *m.* intestine.—**i. ciego,** blind gut,
cæcum.—**i. delgado,** small intestine.—**i. grueso,**
large intestine.
intima, intimación, *f.* intimation, hint.
íntimamente, *adv.* intimately.
intimar. **I.** *va.* to intimate, indicate, suggest,
hint. **II.** *vr.* to pierce, penetrate; to become
intimate.
intimatorio, ria, *a.* (law) intimating.
intimidación, *f.* intimidation.
intimidad, *f.* intimacy.
intimidar, *va.* to intimidate.
íntimo, ma, *a.* internal, innermost; intimate.
intitular. **I.** *va.* to entitle; to confer a title on.
II. *vr.* to use a title; to call one's self (a name).
intolerabilidad, *f.* intolerableness.
intolerable, *a.* intolerable, unbearable.
intolerancia, *f.* intolerance.
intolerante, *a.* intolerant.
intonso, sa, *a.* (poet.) unshorn; ignorant, unpolished; (b. b.) bound with uncut leaves.
intorsión, *f.* (bot.) intortion.
intoxicación, *f.* (med.) intoxication, poisoning.
intoxicar, *va.* (*pret.* INTOXIQUÉ: *subj.* INTOXI-
QUE) (med.) to poison.
intradós, *m.* (arch.) intrados.
intraducible, *a.* untranslatable.
intramuros, *adv.* within the city.
intranquilidad, *f.* restlessness, uneasiness.
intranquilo, la, *a.* uneasy, restless.
intransferible, *a.* not transferable.
intransigente, *a.* intransigent, irreconcilable.
intransitable, *a.* impassable.
intransitivo, va, *a.* (gram.) intransitive.

intransmisible, *a.* untransmissible.
intrasmutabilidad, *f.* immutability.
intrasmutable, *a.* intransmutable.
intratable, *a.* intractable; unruly, unmanageable; unsociable; rude, grouty; impassable.
intravenoso, sa, *a.* intravenous.
intrépidamente, *adv.* intrepidly, fearlessly.
intrepidez, *f.* intrepidity, courage, bravery.
intrépido, da, *a.* intrepid, daring, gallant.
intriga, *f.* intrigue; entanglement, embroilment;
(complicated) plot of a play.
intrigante, *n.* & *a.* intriguer (-ing).
intrigar, *vn.* (*pret.* INTRIGUÉ: *subj.* INTRIGUE) to
intrigue, plot, scheme.
intrincable, *a.* intricate, perplexed.
intrincación, *f.* intricacy, intricateness.
intrincadamente, *adv.* intricately.
intrincado, da, *a.* & *pp.* intricate.
intrincamiento, *m.* intricateness.
intrincar, *va.* (*pret.* INTRINQUÉ: *subj.* INTRIN-
QUE) to entangle, complicate, confuse.
intríngulis, *m.* (coll.) crafty intention, hidden
motive; mystery, enigma.
intrínsecamente, *adv.* intrinsically.
intrínseco, ca, *a.* intrinsic, intrinsical.
introducción, *f.* introduction.
introducir. **I.** *va.* (*ind.* INTRODUZCO: *pret.* IN-
TRODUJE: *subj.* INTRODUZCA) to introduce; to
usher in, put in, insert; to present (a person).
II. *vr.* (w. en) to gain access (to), to get in, to ingratiate one's self with; to interfere (in).
introductor, ra, *n.* introducer.
introito, *m.* beginning of an oration; (eccl.) introit; (theat.) prologue.
introspección, *f.* introspection.
introversión, *f.* introversion.
introverso, sa, *a.* introverted.
intrusamente, *adv.* intrusively.
intrusarse, *vr.* to obtrude, intrude.
intrusión, *f.* intrusion, obtrusion.
intruso, sa. **I.** *a.* intruded, intrusive, obtrusive.
II. *m.* intruder, obtruder, squatter.
intubación, *f.* (med.) intubation.
intubar, *va.* to intubate.
intuición, *f.* intuition.—**intuir,** *va.* to know or
perceive by intuition.—**intuitivamente,** *adv.* intuitively.—**intuitivo, va,** *a.* intuitive, evident.
intuito, *m.* view, look, glance.—**por i.,** in consideration, by reason of.
intumescencia, *f.* intumescence, swelling.
intumescente, *a.* intumescent, swollen.
intususcepción, *f.* intussusception.
inulto, ta, *a.* (poet.) unavenged, unpunished.
inundación, *f.* inundation, flood; confluence;
multitude.
inundante, *a.* inundating; inundant.
inundar, *va.* to inundate, flood.
inurbanamente, *adv.* uncivilly, discourteously.
inurbanidad, *f.* incivility, discourtesy.
inurbano, na, *a.* uncivil, impolite, unmannerly.
inusitadamente, *adv.* unusually.
inusitado, da, *a.* unusual, not in use.
inútil, *a.* useless; fruitless; needless.
inutilidad, *f.* uselessness; needlessness.
inutilizar. **I.** *va.* (*pret.* INUTILICÉ: *subj.* INUTI-
LICE) to render useless; to disable; to spoil, ruin.
II. *vr.* to become useless.
inútilmente, *adv.* uselessly, to no purpose.
invadeable, *a.* unfordable.
invadir, *va.* to invade; encroach upon.
invaginación, *f.* invagination.
invaginar, *va.* to invaginate.
invalidación, *f.* invalidation, invalidity.
inválidamente, *adv.* invalidly.
invalidar, *va.* to invalidate, nullify.
inválido, da. **I.** *a.* invalid; cripple; feeble, weak;
null, void. **II.** *m.* invalid.
invariabilidad, *f.* invariability.—**invariable,** *a.*
invariable, constant.—**invariablemente,** *adv.* invariably.—**invariación,** *f.* immutability, invariableness.—**invariadamente,** *adv.* unvariedly.—
invariado, da, *a.* unvaried, constant.

invariante, *f.* (math.) invariant.
invasión, *f.* invasion; attack.
invasor, ra, *n.* & *a.* invader (-ing).
invectiva, *f.* invective, harsh censure.
invencible, *a.* invincible, unconquerable.
invenciblemente, *adv.* invincibly.
invención, *f.* invention.
invencionero, ra, *n.* inventor; plotter; trifler.
invendible, *a.* unsalable.
inventar, *va.* to invent.
inventariar, *va.* to inventory, take inventory of.
inventario, *m.* inventory.
inventiva, *f.* faculty of invention, inventiveness.
inventivo, va, *a.* inventive.
invento, *m.* invention.
inventor, ra, *n.* inventor; fibber, fabricator, romancer.
inverecundo, da, *a.* shameless, impudent.
inverisímil, *a.* unlikely, improbable.
inverisimilitud, *f.* improbability.
invernáculo, *m.* greenhouse, hothouse, conservatory.
invernada, *f.* winter season.
invernadero, *m.* winter quarters; hothouse, conservatory.
invernal, *a.* hibernal, winter (u. a.)
invernar, *vn.* (*ind.* INVIERNO: *subj.* INVIERNE) to winter.
invernizo, za, *a.* winter (u. a.); winterly, hibernal; winter-beaten.
inverosímil, *a.* = INVERISÍMIL.
inverosimilitud, *f.* = INVERISIMILITUD.
inversamente, *adv.* inversely; contrariwise.
inversión, *f.* inversion; (com.) investment.
inverso, sa, *a.* & *pp. irr.* of INVERTIR: inverse, inverted.—**a, or por, la inversa,** on the contrary.
inversor, ra. I. *a.* inverting; (elec., mech.) reversing. **II.** *n.* reverser; reverse gear; reversing mechanism.
invertebrado, da. I. *n.* & *a.* invertebrate. **II.** *m. pl.* Invertebrata.
invertina, *f.* (chem.) invertase.
invertir, *va.* (*pp.* INVERTIDO, INVERSO: *gerund,* INVIRTIENDO: *ind.* INVIERTO: *pret.* el INVIRTIÓ: *subj.* INVIERTA) to invert; to reverse; (com.) to invest.
investidura, *f.* investiture.
investigable, *a.* investigable.
investigación, *f.* investigation, research; inquest.
investigador, ra, *n.* & *a.* investigator (-ing).
investigar, *va.* (*pret.* INVESTIGUÉ: *subj.* INVESTIGUE) to investigate, ascertain, inquire into.
investir, *va.* (*for irr. v.* VESTIR) to invest, to confer upon.
inveterado, da, *a.* & *pp.* inveterate.
inveteradamente, *adv.* inveterately.
inveterarse, *vr.* to become antiquated, old, or chronic.
invictamente, *adv.* triumphantly, valiantly.
invicto, ta, *a.* invincible, unconquered.
invierno, *m.* winter; rainy season (in countries having no astronomical seasons, as in the tropics).
invigilar, *vn.* to watch carefully.
inviolabilidad, *f.* inviolability.
inviolable, *a.* inviolable; inviolate.
inviolablemente, *adv.* inviolably; infallibly.
inviolado, da, *a.* inviolate, unhurt, uninjured.
invisibilidad, *f.* invisibility.
invisible, *a.* invisible.—**en un i.,** (coll.) in less than no time.
invisiblemente, *adv.* invisibly.
invitación, *f.* invitation.—**invitado, da,** *pp.* & *n.* invited person; guest.—**invitador, ra,** *n.* inviter.
invitar, *va.* to invite; entice; treat.
invitatorio, *m.* (eccl.) invitatory.
invocación, *f.* invocation.
invocador, ra, *n.* & *a.* invoker (-ing).
invocar, *va.* (*pret.* INVOQUÉ: *subj.* INVOQUE) to invoke, implore.
invocatorio, ria, *a.* invocatory.

involucral, *a.* (bot.) involucral.
involucrar, *va.* to introduce as a digression.
involucro, *m.* (bot.) involucre.
involuntariamente, *adv.* involuntarily.
involuntariedad, *f.* involuntariness.
involuntario, ria, *a.* involuntary.
invulnerabilidad, *f.* invulnerability.
invulnerable, *a.* invulnerable.
inyección, *f.* injection; liquid injected.
inyectar, *va.* to inject.
inyector, *m.* (mech.) injector.
iodo, (chem.) = YODO.
ion, *m.* (chem.) ion.—**ionización,** *f.* ionization.—**ionizar,** *va.* to ionize.
ipecacuana, *f.* (bot.) ipecacuanha, ipecac.—**i. de las Antillas,** wild ipecac.
ipil, *m.* (C. A.) outer garment worn by half-breed women; (Philip.) (bot.) a hardwood tree.
ipso facto (Lat.) *adv.* ipso facto, by the fact itself, by the very fact.
ipso jure (Lat.) *adv.* ipso jure, by the law itself.
ir, *vn.* (*pp.* IDO: *gerund,* YENDO: *ind.* VOY: *imperf.* IBA: *pret.* FUÍ: *subj.* VAYA) to go, move, walk; to fit, be becoming, suit; to concern, interest, affect, involve (ch. contr.: *poco me va en eso,* that concerns me very little; *en eso me va la reputación,* that involves, or affects, my reputation); to differ, to be different (ch. constr: *¡lo que va de ayer a hoy!* how today differs from yesterday!); to lead (*todos los caminos van a Roma,* all roads lead to Rome); to be, find one's self, be doing (*el enfermo va bien,* the patient is doing well); to be, to elapse (*de hoy al lunes van tres días,* it is three days from today to Monday); (arith.) to be, to leave (ch. constr.: *de 3 a 5 van 2,* 3 from 5 leaves 2); (arith.) to carry (*4, y van 2,* 4, and 2 to carry); (followed by *pp.*) to be (*voy herido,* I am wounded; *va descarriado,* he is astray, or off the way). Before a gerund, it implies the beginning of the action the gerund denotes, or its continued performance or occurrence (*va anocheciendo,* it is getting dark; *voy comprendiendo,* I begin to understand; *Juan va perdiendo la paciencia,* John is losing patience; *voy viendo los cuadros,* I am looking at the pictures).—**i. a,** to go to; to be going to, to purpose or intend to (*voy al teatro,* I am going to the theater; *voy a hablarle,* I am going, or intend, to speak to him; *¿adónde va Vd.?* where are you going?); to bet on (*voy al caballo negro,* I bet on the black horse).—**i. a caballo,** to ride, to be riding on horseback.—**i. adelante,** to go (march, ride, etc.) at the front; to be ahead; to go on; to go ahead.—**i. a medias,** to go halves.—**i. de bracero,** or **de brazo,** to walk arm in arm.—**i. delante,** to go ahead.—**i. en alcance,** (print.) to divide the (original) copy among various compositors.—**i. en coche,** to drive, to ride in a carriage.—**i. en demanda de,** (naut.) to be on the look-out for.—**i. pasando,** to be so so, to be as usual, to be getting along.—**i. por delante** = I. DELANTE.—**i. por ojo** = IRSE A PIQUE.—*¿cómo le va?* how are you?—*¿cómo vamos?* how are you? how goes it with you?—**no me va ni me viene,** does not concern, or affect, me in the least.—*¿quién va? ¿quién va allá?* who is there? who goes there? *¡vámonos!* let us go! (r. w.) all aboard!—*¡vamos!* let us go! also used expletively in the sense of "why," "well," etc.—*vamos claros,* let us be plain, let us come down to business.—*¡vaya!* what a (*¡vaya una idea!* what an idea!).—**vaya Vd. a paseo,** go to, get out.—*vaya Vd. con Dios,* farewell; God be with you.
ir, *va.* to bet, wager (*voy cinco pesos,* I bet five pesos).
ir, *vr.* to go, go away, depart, quit; to leak, to ooze; to exhale, evaporate; to discharge wind; to break to pieces; to grow old.—**i. abajo,** to topple down.—**i. a pique,** (naut.) to founder, to go to the bottom, to be wrecked.—**i. atrás,** to go back, to flinch.—**i. de boca,** to speak thoughtlessly or recklessly.—**i. los ojos tras de,** to gaze admiringly or longingly at.—**írsele a uno el alma por,** to long for.—**írsele a uno la mula,** to speak unadvisedly from carelessness or anger.—*allá se va,* it is all the same, it amounts to the same thing.
ira, *f.* ire, anger, wrath, rage.—**¡i. de Dios!** Lord deliver us!
iracundia, *f.* irascibility, ire, irascibleness.

iracundo, da, *a.* wrathful; angry, enraged.
iradé, *m.* irade, Sultan's decree.
iranio, nia, *n.* & *a.* Iranian.
irascible, *a.* irascible, irritable.
irenarca, *m.* irenarch.
iribú, *m.* (Arg.) turkey buzzard.
iridáceo, cea. I. *a.* iridaceous, irislike. **II.** *f. pl.* (bot.) Iridaceæ.
íride, *f.* (bot.) = EFÉMERO.
irídeo, a. I. *a.* irideous. **II.** *f. pl.* (bot.) Iridaceæ.
iridio, *m.* (chem.) iridium.
iridiscente, *a.* iridescent.
iris, *m.* iris, rainbow; (anat.) iris; (min.) opal.—**i. de paz,** mediator, peacemaker.
irisación, *f.* irisation.
irisado, da, *a.* rainbow-hued.
irisar, *vn.* to iridesce.
iritis, *f.* (med.) iritis, inflammation of the iris.
Irlanda, *f.* cotton and woollen cloth; fine Irish linen.
irlandés, esa. I. *a.* Irish. **II.** *m.* Irishman; Irish language. **III.** *f.* Irishwoman.
ironía, *f.* (rhet.) irony.—**irónicamente,** *adv.* ironically.—**irónico, ca,** *a.* ironical, sarcastic.
iroqués, sa, *n.* & *a.* Iroquois.
irracional. I. *a.* irrational, absurd; (math.) irrational. **II.** *m.* irrational (being).
irracionalidad, *f.* irrationality.
irracionalmente, *adv.* irrationally.
irradiación, *f.* radiation.
irradiar, *va.* to radiate.
irrazonable, *a.* unreasonable.
irrealidad, *f.* unreality.
irrealizable, *a.* unrealizable, unattainable.
irrebatible, *a.* indisputable.
irreconciliable, *a.* irreconcilable.
irreconciliablemente, *adv.* irreconcilably.
irrecuperable, *a.* irrecoverable, irretrievable.
irrecusable, *a.* unimpeachable.
irredimible, *a.* irredeemable.
irreducible, irreductible, *a.* irreducible.
irreemplazable, *a.* unreplaceable.
irreflexión, *f.* rashness, indiscretion.
irreflexivo, va, *a.* thoughtless, impulsive.
irreformable, *a.* unreformable.
irrefragable, *a.* irrefutable.
irrefragablemente, *adv.* irrefutably.
irrefrenable, *a.* unbridled, unruly, unmanageable, uncontrollable.
irregular, *a.* irregular.—**irregularidad,** *f.* irregularity.—**irregularmente,** *adv.* irregularly.
irreligión, *f.* irreligion.—**irreligiosamente,** *adv.* irreligiously.—**irreligiosidad,** *f.* irreligiousness.—**irreligioso, sa,** *a.* irreligious.
irremediable, *a.* irremediable, incurable; hopeless.—**irremediablemente,** *adv.* [irremediably, hopelessly.
irremisible, *a.* irremissible, unpardonable.
irremisiblemente, *adv.* unpardonably, irremissibly.
irremunerado, da, *a.* unremunerated.
irreparable, *a.* irreparable, irretrievable.
irreparablemente, *adv.* irreparably, irretrievably, irrecoverably.
irreprensible, *a.* irreprehensible, irreproachable.
irreprensiblemente, *adv.* irreproachably.
irreprochable, *a.* irreproachable.
irresistibilidad, *f.* irresistibility.
irresistible, *a.* irresistible.
irresistiblemente, *adv.* irresistibly.
irresoluble, *a.* indeterminable; unsolvable; irresolute.
irresolución, *f.* irresolution, hesitation.
irresolutamente, *adv.* irresolutely.
irresoluto, ta, *a.* irresolute, wavering.
irrespetuoso, sa, *a.* disrespectful.
irrespirable, *a.* not fit to be breathed.
irresponsabilidad, *f.* irresponsibility.
irresponsable, *a.* irresponsible.
irresuelto, ta, *a.* = IRRESOLUTO.
irreverencia, *f.* irreverence.—**irreverente,** *a.* irreverent.—**irreverentemente,** *adv.* irreverently.

irrevocabilidad, *f.* irrevocability.
irrevocable, *a.* irrevocable.
irrevocablemente, *adv.* irrevocably.
irrigación, *f.* (med.) irrigation.
irrigador, *m.* (med.) irrigator.
irrigar, *va.* (med.) to irrigate.
irrisible, *a.* laughable.—**irrisión,** *f.* derision, ridicule.—**irrisoriamente,** *adv.* derisively.
irrisorio, ria, *a.* derisive.
irritabilidad, *f.* irritability.
irritable, *a.* irritable; (law) voidable.
irritación, *f.* irritation, commotion, agitation; (law) invalidation, abrogation; (med.) irritation.
irritador, ra, *n.* & *a.* irritator (-ing), stimulator (-ing), irritant.
irritamente, *adv.* (law) invalidly, vainly.
irritamiento, *m.* irritation, anger.
irritante. I. *a.* irritant, stimulating; (law) annulling, voiding. **II.** *m.* stimulant, irritant.
irritar, *va.* to irritate, exasperate, anger; (med.) to irritate; (law) to annul, void.
írrito, ta, *a.* (law) null, void.
irrogar, *va.* (pret. IRROGUÉ: subj. IRROGUE) to cause, to occasion (damage).
irrompible, *a.* unbreakable.
irrumpir, *vn.* to make an irruption or raid.
irrupción, *f.* irruption, inroad, invasion, raid.
isabelino, na, *a.* (coin) stamped with the bust of Isabella II.; partisan or defender of Queen Isabella; light bay (horse).
isagoge, *f.* introduction, exordium.
isagógico, ca, *a.* introductive, introductory.
isla, *f.* isle, island; city block.—**en i.,** insulated.
islam, *m.* Islam.—**islámico, ca,** *a.* Islamic.
islamismo, *m.* Islamism, Islam.
islamita, *n.* & *a.* Islamite (-itic).
islandés, sa; islándico, ca, *a.* Icelandic.
isleño, ña, *n.* islander; (Cuba) native of the Canary Islands.
isleo, *m.* chain of small islands.
isleta, ita, illa, *f. dim.* small isle, islet, holm.
islilla, *f.* (anat.) collar bone.
islote, *m.* small barren island, key.
ismaelita, *a.* Ishmaelite, Arab.
isobárico, ca, *a.* isobaric.
isocre, *a.* isochroous, of uniform color.
isocromático, ca, *a.* isochromatic.
isocronismo, *m.* isochronism.
isócrono, *a.* isochronous.
isodinámico, ca, *a.* isodynamic.
isógono, na, *a.* (geom.) isogonic.
isomería, *f.* (chem.) isomerism.
isómero, ra, *a.* (chem.) isomeric.
isométrico, ca, *a.* isometric.
isomorfismo, *m.* (min.) isomorphism.
isomorfo, fa, *a.* isomorphous, isomorphic.
isoperímetro, ta, *a.* isoperimetrical.
isópodo, da. I. *n.* & *a.* (zool.) isopod. **II.** *m. pl.* Isopoda.
isoquímeno, na, *a.* isocheimal.
isósceles, *a.* (geom.) isosceles.
isospóreo, a, *a.* (bot.) isosporous.
isotermo, ma, *a.* isothermal.
isótero, ra, *a.* isotheral.
isotrópico, ca, *a.* (phys.) = ISÓTROPO.
isotropismo, *m.* (phys.) isotropy.
isótropo, pa, *a.* (phys.) isotropous.
isquión, *m.* (anat.) ischium.
israelita, *n.* & *a.* Israelite (-ish).
israelítico, ca, *a.* Israelitish.
istmeño, ña, *n.* & *a.* native of an isthmus.
ístmico, ca, *a.* isthmian.
istmo, *m.* (geog.) isthmus; (anat.) isthmus.
istriar, *va.* to flute. *V.* ESTRIAR.
italianismo, *m.* Italianism.
italianizar, *va.* & *vn.* to Italianize.
italiano, na. I. *n.* & *a.* Italian. **II.** *m.* Italian (language).
itálico, ca, *a.* Italic.

item, *m.* section, clause, article; addition, additament.—**í.,** or **í. más,** also, likewise, furthermore.

iterable, *a.* iterable.—**iteración,** *f.* iteration.—**iterar,** *va.* to iterate.—**iterativo, va,** *a.* iterative.

iterbia, *f.* (chem.) ytterbia.

iterbio, *m.* (chem.) ytterbium.

itinerario, ria. I. *a.* itinerary. **II.** *m.* itinerary, book of travels; railroad guide, time-table.

itria, *f.* (min.) yttria.

itrio, *m.* (chem.) yttrium.

izaga, *f.* place abounding in rushes and reeds.

izar, *va.* (naut.) to hoist, heave, haul up.

izquierdear, *vn.* to degenerate, grow wild.

izquierdo, da. I. *a.* left-handed; left; crooked. **II.** *f.* left hand; left, left-hand side; (pol.) Left (Liberal party).—**a la i.,** to the left; on the left.

J

jaba, *f.* (Cuba) basket made of YAREY leaves.

jabalcón, *m.* (arch.) bracket, purlin, strut.

jabalconar, *va.* to build or support with struts.

jabalí, *m.* (zool.) wild boar.

jabalina, *f.* sow of a wild boar; javelin.

jabalón, *va.* = JABALCÓN.

jabalonar, *va.* = JABALCONAR.

jabardear, *vn.* (api.) to swarm.

jabardillo, *m.* noisy swarm of insects or birds; (coll.) noisy crowd.—**jabardo,** *m.* small swarm of bees; (coll.) noisy crowd.

jabato, *m.* young wild boar.

jábeca, *f.* sweep net.

jábega, *f.* fishing smack; dragnet.

jabegote, *m.* man who draws the sweep net.

jabeguero, ra. I. *a.* pertaining to sweep-net fishing. **II.** *n.* sweep-net fisherman.

jabeque, *m.* (naut.) xebec; (coll.) knife wound in the face.

jabí, *m.* small wild apple; small kind of grapes; (C. A.) (bot.) breakax.

jabillo, *m.* (bot.) a Central-American tree of the spurge family.

jabirú, *m.* jabiru, a Brazilian wading bird.

jabladera, *f.* crozer, cooper's tool.

jable, *m.* (coop.) croze.

jabón, *m.* soap.—**j. blando,** soft soap.—**j. de olor,** toilet soap.—**j. de piedra,** hard soap.—**j. de sastre,** steatite, soapstone.—**j. duro,** hard soap.—**dar un j.,** (coll.) to reprimand severely, lecture, dress down.

jabonado, da. I. *a.* & *pp.* soaped. **II.** *m.* wash, washing.

jabonadura, *f.* washing.—*pl.* suds or soap suds; lather.—**dar,** or **echar, una j.,** to reprimand severely, lecture, call down.

jabonar, *va.* to soap; (coll.) to reprimand severely, lecture, dress down.

jaboncillo, *m.* soapstone, steatite; toilet soap; (bot.) soap tree.

jabonera, *f.* soap dish; woman who sells soap; (bot.) soapwort.

jabonería, *f.* soap manufactory or shop.

jabonero, ra, *n.* soap maker or seller.

jabonete, jabonete de olor, *m.* toilet soap.

jabonoso, sa, *a.* soapy, saponaceous.

jaborandi, *m.* (bot.) jaborandi.

jabuco, *m.* (Cuba) large straw basket.

jaca, *f.* nag, pony, jennet, cob, bidet, tit.

jacal, *m.* (Mex.) Indian hut, wigwam.

jacamar, *m.* (orn.) jacamar.

jacana, *f.* (orn.) jacana, a tropical wading bird.

jácara, *f.* merry ballad; a kind of dance and its music; group of night wanderers singing JÁCARAS; (coll.) vexation; idle tale or prattle; story, tale; fable, lie, vainglorious fiction.

jacaranda, *f.* (bot.) jacaranda.

jacarandana, jacarandina, *f.* slang; gang of ruffians and thieves.

jacarandoso, sa, (coll.) blithe, merry, gay.

jacarear, *vn.* to sing JÁCARAS; (coll.) to sing in the streets at night; to taunt with offensive remarks.

jacarero, *m.* ballad singer; wag or merry droll.

jacarilla, *f. dim.* of JÁCARA.

jácaro, ra. I. *a.* belonging to singers of JÁCARAS. **II.** *m.* boaster, bully.—**a lo j.,** boastfully, braggingly.

jácena, *f.* (arch.) girder.

jacerina, *f.* coat of mail.

jacilla, *f.* mark left on the ground.

jacinto, *m.* (bot.) hyacinth; harebell; (min.) hyacinth.—**j. de Ceilán,** zircon.—**j. de Compostela,** red crystalized quartz.—**j. occidental,** topaz.—**j. oriental,** ruby.

jaco, *m.* sorry nag, jade; short jacket.

jacobinismo, *m.* Jacobinism.

jacobino, *m.* Jacobin; bloody revolutionist.

jactancia, *f.* boasting.—**jactanciosamente,** *adv.* boastingly.—**jactancioso, sa,** *a.* boastful, vainglorious.—**jactarse,** *vr.* to vaunt, boast, brag.

jaculatoria, *f.* ejaculation, short prayer.

jaculatorio, ria, *a.* jaculatory.

jachalí, *m.* (bot.) custard apple.

jada, *f.* (agr.) hoe; spade.

jade, *m.* (min.) jade, axestone.

jadeante, *a.* panting, out of breath.

jadear, *vn.* to pant.—**jadeo,** *m.* pant, palpitation.

jadiar, *va.* to dig up with a spade, to hoe.

jaecero, ra, *n.* harness maker.

jaén, *m.* a kind of large white grape.

jaenés, sa, *a.* of or belonging to Jaen.

jaez, *m.* harness; trappings; manner, kind, quality.—*pl.* trappings.

jafético, ca, *a.* Japhetic, Indo-Germanic.

jagua, *f.* (bot.) jagua or inaja palm and its fruit.

jaguar, jaguarete, *m.* (zool.) jaguar.

jaguarzo, *m.* (bot.) helianthemum.

jagüey, *m.* (S. A.) large pool or basin; (Cuba) (bot.) liana.

jaharrar, *va.* to plaster.

jaharro, *m.* (mas.) plaster; plastering.

jaiba, *f.* (Cuba) (icht.) crab.

jaique, *m.* cape with a hood.

jaira, *f.* bezel of a plane bit.

jairar, *va.* (shoe.) to bevel (leather).

jaire, *m.* (shoe.) bevel cut.

¡ja, ja, ja! *interj.* ha, ha!

jalapa, *f.* (bot.) jalapa; jalap.

jalbegar, *va.* to whiten, whitewash.

jalbegue, *m.* whitewash; whitewashing.

jaldado, da; jalde; jaldo, da, *a.* bright yellow, crocus-colored.

jaldre, *m.* yellow peculiar to birds.

jalea, *f.* jelly.—**j. de guayaba,** guava jelly.—**j. del agro,** conserve of citron.—**hacerse una j.,** to love with excessive fondness.

jaleador, ra, *n.* one who encourages hounds or dancers.

jalear, *va.* to encourage (hounds) to follow the chase; to animate dancers, by clapping hands; to quaver (the voice).

jaleco, *m.* Turkish jacket.

jaleo, *m.* clapping of hands to encourage dancers; Andalusian dance; (coll.) jest.

jaletina, *f.* calf's foot jelly; gelatine.

jalma, *f.* kind of packsaddle.—**jalmería,** *f.* packsaddler's trade.—**jalmero,** *m.* packsaddle maker.

jalón, *m.* (surv.) pole, rod, flag pole.

jaloque, *m.* southeast wind. *V.* SIROCO.

jallullo, *m.* bread toasted in ashes.

jamaica, *f.* (Mex.) charity fair.

jamaicano, na, *n.* & *a.* Jamaican.

jamar, *va.* (prov.) to eat.

jamás, *adv.* never.—**nunca j.,** or **por j.,** never, nevermore.—**por siempre j.,** forever and ever.

jamba, *f.* (arch.) door jamb, window post.

jambaje, *m.* door or window case.

jámbico, ca, *a.* iambic.

jamelgo, *m.* (coll.) jade, sorry nag.

jamerdana, *f.* sewer of a slaughterhouse.

jamerdar, *va.* to clean the guts of; to wash hastily.

jamete, *m.* rich silk stuff.

jametería, *f.* = ZALAMERÍA.

Jámila, *f.* = ALPECHÍN.
Jamón, *m.* ham, salted thigh of a hog.
Jamona, *n.* (coll.) big middle-aged woman.
Jámparo, *m.* (Colomb.) small boat or canoe.
Jamuga, jamugas, *f.* mule chair.
Jándalo, la, *n. & a.* a term app. to Andalusians and those who give *h* a strong guttural sound.
Jangada, *f.* (coll.) silly sally; (naut.) raft, float.
Jangua, *f.* small armed vessel.
Jansenismo, *m.* Jansenism.
Jansenista, *n. & a.* Jansenist (-ic).
Jantofila, *f.* (chem.) xanthophyll.
Japón, na; japonense; japonés, sa, *n. & a.* Japanese.
Jaque, *m.* check, in chess; braggart, boaster; saddlebag; smooth combing of the hair.—**j. mate,** checkmate.
Jaquear, *va.* to check (at chess).
Jaqueca, *f.* megrim; headache.
Jaquecoso, sa, *a.* tiresome, annoying, bothersome.
Jaquel, *m.* (her.) square.
Jaquelado, da, *a.* checkered.
Jaquero, *m.* fine-toothed comb.
Jaqueta, *f.* jacket, short loose coat.
Jaquetilla, *f. dim.* small JAQUETA.
Jaquetón, *m. aug.* large, wide coat; great swaggerer, boaster, bully.
Jáquima, *f.* headstall of a halter.
Jaquimazo, *m.* stroke with the headstall of a halter; (coll.) displeasure; disappointment.
Jara, *f.* (bot.) cistus or rockrose; a kind of dart or arrow.
Jarabe, *m.* sirup; any sweet mixed drink.—**j. de pico,** empty talk; lip service.
Jarabear. I. *va.* to prescribe sirups very often. **II.** *vr.* to take sirups frequently.
Jaraíz, *m.* pit for pressing grapes.
Jaral, *m.* bramble, brake; intricate or puzzling point.
Jaramago, *m.* (bot.) hedge mustard.
Jarameño, ña, *a.* (cattle) from the Jarama.
Jaramugo, *m.* small or young fish.
Jarana, *f.* (coll.) carousal, revelry, romping; (coll.) scuffle, quarrel.
Jaranear, *vn.* (coll.) to jest; to carouse.
Jaranero, ra; jaranista, *a.* fond of jests or sprees; jolly.
Jarano, *m.* Mexican sombrero.
Jarapote, *m.* (prov.) = JAROPEO.
Jarapotear, *va.* to stuff with drugs.
Jarazo, *m.* blow or wound with a dart.
Jarcia, *f.* accoutrements; heap of things; (naut.) tackle, rigging, and cordage; shrouds; fishing tackle.
Jardín, *m.* flower garden; flaw, spot that disfigures an emerald; (naut.) privy.
Jardincito, *m. dim.* small garden.
Jardinería, *f.* gardening.
Jardinero, ra. I. *n.* gardener. **II.** *f.* flower-stand, jardinière; basket carriage.
Jareta, *f.* (sew.) fold or tuck for gathering; (naut.) netting, harpings.
Jaretera, *f.* garter. *V.* JARRETERA.
Jarife, *m.* = JERIFE.
Jarifo, fa, *a.* showy, spruce, nobby, natty.
Jaro, ra, *a.* resembling a wild boar.
Jarocho, *m.* (Mex., coll.) rough countryman.
Jaropar, jaropear, *va.* to stuff with sirups or medicines.—**jarope,** *m.* sirup; nasty draught or potion.—**jaropeo,** *m.* medicine habit.
Jaroso, sa, *a.* full of brambles.
Jarra, *f.* jar; ancient order of chivalry.—**en- j. or de jarras,** akimbo.
Jarrear, *vn.* to take out water or wine with a jar or dipper.
Jarrero, ra, *n.* jar maker or seller.
Jarreta, *f. dim.* small jar.
Jarrete, *m.* hock; gambrel.
Jarretera, *f.* garter; Order of the Garter.
Jarrito, *m. dim.* small jug or pitcher.
Jarro, *m.* pitcher, jug, pot, ewer; chatterer.

Jarrón, *m. aug.* large jar, urn, flower vase.
Jaspe, *m.* (min.) jasper.—**jaspeado, da,** *a. & pp.* spotted, marbled, mottled, variegated.
Jaspeadura, *f.* marbling.—**jaspear,** *va.* to marble, vein, speckle.
Jastial, *m.* (arch.) façade of an edifice.
Jateo, tea, *n.* fox hunter (s. o. dogs).
Jato, ta, *n.* calf. *V.* BECERRO.
¡Jau! *interj.* to incite animals, sp. bulls.
Jaula, *f.* bird cage; cell for insane persons; (min.) miner's cage.
Jaulón, *m. aug.* large bird cage; aviary.
Jauría, *f.* pack of hounds.
Jauto, ta, *a.* insipid, flat, tasteless.
Javanés, sa; javo, va, *a.* Javan, Javanese.
Jayán, na, *n.* robust, burly person.
Jayanazo, za, *n. aug.* huge, big person.
Jazmín, *m.* (bot.) jessamine or jasmine.
Jazmíneo, a, *a.* (bot.) jasminaceous.
Jea, *f.* ancient duty on Moorish goods.
Jebe, *m.* rock alum; (S. A.) India-rubber.
Jebuseo, a, *n. & a.* Jebusite (-ic).
Jedive, *m.* khedive, Viceroy of Egypt.
Jefatura, *f.* dignity and office of a chief.
Jefe, fa, *n.* chief, head, leader; (mil.) commanding officer.—**j. de día,** (mil.) officer of the day.—**j. de escuadra,** (naut.) rear admiral.—**j. político,** governor of a province.
Jehová, Jehovah.
Jeja, *f.* white wheat.
Jején, *m.* (Cuba) gnat, gall midge.
Jema, *f.* badly squared part of a beam.
Jemal, *a.* having the length of a JEME.
Jeme, *m.* distance from the end of the thumb to the end of the forefinger (both extended); (coll.) woman's face.
Jemoso, sa, *a.* badly squared beam.
Jenabe, jenable, *m.* mustard.
Jengibre, *m.* ginger.
Jeniquén, *m.* (Cuba) henequen; sisal.
Jenízaro. I. *a.* cross-bred; (Mex.) born of Chinese and Indian parents. **II.** *m.* Janizary.
Jeque, *m.* Moorish chief.
Jera, *f.* ground which can be plowed in a day with a pair of oxen; present, gift.
Jerapellina, *f.* old ragged garment.
Jerarca, *m.* (eccl.) hierarch.—**jerarquía,** *f.* hierarchy.—**jerárquico, ca,** *a.* hierarchical.
Jeremiada, *f.* jeremiad, lamentation, whining.
Jerezano, na, *n. & a.* of or belonging to Jerez.
Jerga, *f.* coarse frieze; jargon, gibberish; straw bed.
Jergón, *m.* straw bed; misfit clothes; ill-shaped person; (jew.) zircon.
Jerguilla, *f.* silk or worsted serge.
Jerife, *m.* shereef, sherif.
Jerifiano, na, *a.* pertaining to the sherif.
Jerigonza, *f.* (coll.) jargon, gibberish, slang; strange and ridiculous action.—**andar en jerigonzas,** to quibble.
Jeringa, *f.* syringe, clyster; sausage stuffer.
Jeringación, *f.* (coll.) syringing, injection; annoyance, botheration.
Jeringador, ra, *a.* (coll.) bothersome, persevering, persistent.
Jeringar, *va.* (*pret.* JERINGUÉ: *subj.* JERINGUE) to inject; to vex, annoy, tease.
Jeringazo, *m.* clyster, injection.
Jeringuilla, *f. dim.* little syringe; (bot.) syringa, mock orange.
Jeroglífico, *m.* hieroglyph.
Jeroglífico, ca, *a.* hieroglyphical.
Jerosolimitano, na, *a.* of or relating to Jerusalem.
Jerpa, *f.* sterile shoot of a vine.
Jerricote, *m.* pottage of almonds, sugar, sage, and ginger.
Jervilla, *f.* a kind of short boot.
Jesuato, ta, *a.* child dedicated to Jesus when born.
Jesuíta, *m.* Jesuit; (coll.) hypocrite.
Jesuíticamente, *adv.* Jesuitically; hypocritically.
Jesuítico, ca, *a.* Jesuitical; hypocritical.

Jesuitismo, m. Jesuitism.

Jesús, m. Jesus; often used by itself, or followed by other sacred names (José, María), and with no implication of profanity, as an exclamation in the sense of "gracious!" "goodness!" "my!" etc. —**¡ay J!** alas! good gracious!—**en un decir J.,** in the twinkling of an eye.—**no saber ni el J.,** not to know even one's A B C.—**sin decir J.,** suddenly.

Jesusear, vn. to repeat often the name of Jesus.

Jeta, f. thick, heavy lips; blobber lip; hog's snout; (coll.) person's face.

Jetar, va. to dilute, dissolve.

Jeto, m. empty beehive rubbed with honey to attract bees.

Jetón, na; jetudo, da, a. thick-lipped.

Jíbaro, ra. I. a. (Am.) rustic, rude, wild. **II.** n. countryman (-woman).

Jibia, f. (zool.) cuttlefish.

Jibión, m. cuttlefish bone.

Jibraltareño, ña, a. of or from Gibraltar.

Jícara, f. chocolate cup.

Jicarazo, m. aug. stroke with a chocolate cup.—**dar un j.,** (coll.) to give poison.

Jicarón, m. aug. large chocolate cup.

Jicotea, f. (Am.) tortoise.

Jifa, f. refuse of slaughtered animals.

Jifería, f. slaughtering.

Jifero, ra. I. a. belonging to the slaughterhouse. **II.** m. butcher's knife; butcher.

Jifia, f. (icht.) xiphias, swordfish.

Jiga, f. jig (dance and tune).

Jigote, m. (cook.) hash; minced meat.

Jiguilete, m. indigo plant.

Jijallar, m. bramble.

Jojallo, m. (bot.) prickly broom.

Jijene, m. (S. A.) sand fly.

¡Ji, ji, ji! interj. ha, ha, ha!

Jijona, f. variety of flinty wheat.—**turrón de J.,** sweet-almond paste.

Jilguero, m. (orn.) linnet.

Jilote, m. (Mex.) ear of green corn.

Jimagua, (Cuba) twin.

Jimelga, f. (naut.) fish of a mast.

Jimenzar, va. to ripple (flax or hemp).

Jinestada, f. sauce made with milk, dates, etc.

Jineta, f. art of horsemanship; an ancient short lance; sergeant's shoulder knot; ancient tribute upon cattle.—**a la j.,** (riding) with high stirrups and bent legs.—**tener los cascos a la j.,** to be harebrained, wild, giddy.

Jinete, m. trooper, cavalryman; horseman, rider, equestrian; fine, pure-breed horse.

Jinetear. I. va. (Am.) to break in (a horse); to ride (a horse). **II.** vn. to ride around on horseback, mainly for show.

Jinglar, vn. to swing, vibrate, oscillate.

Jingoísmo, m. jingoism.

Jingoísta, n. & a. jingoist (-ic).

Jinjol, m. jujube. V. AZUFAIFA.

Jipijapa, f. very fine woven straw; Panama-hat straw.

Jiquilete, m. (bot.) indigo tree.

Jira, f. strip, slip of cloth; picnic, outing.

Jirafa, f. (zool.) giraffe.

Jirapliega, f. purgative confection.

Jirasal, f. (bot.) fruit of the lac tree.

Jirel, m. rich caparison for a horse.

Jíride, f. (bot.) = LIRIO HEDIONDO.

Jirofina, f. a. kind of sauce.

Jirolé, m. clove tree.

Jirón, m. (sew.) facing of a skirt; shred, piece torn from clothing; pointed banner, pennant; small part; long street.

Jironado, da, a. torn into or garnished with strips or tatters.

Jirpear, va. to dig about vines.

Jiste, m. froth of beer.

Jitar, va. (prov.) to emit, vomit, throw out.

¡jo! interj. whoa!

Jobo, m. (bot.) tree of the terebinth family.

Jocó, m. jocko, an ape.

Jocosamente, adv. jocosely, humorously.

Jocoserio, ria, a. jocoserious.

Jocosidad, f. jocularity, jocosity, waggery.

Jocoso, sa, a. jocose, waggish, humorous.

Jocoyote, m. (Am.) youngest child, pet.

Jocundidad, f. joviality.

Jocundo, da, a. jovial, jolly.

Jofaina, f. washbasin, washbowl.

Jojoto, m. (Venez.) maize in the milk.

Jolgorio, m. = HOLGORIO.

Jolito, m. rest, leisure; (naut.) calm.

Joloano, na, n. & a. Joloano (from Sulu, Philip.).

Jólote, m. (C. A.) turkey.

Jónico, ca; jonio, nia, n. & a. Ionian.

¡jopo! interj. (coll.) out of here! be off!

Jorcar, va. = AECHAR.

Jorco, m. licentious feast and dance.

Jordán, m. anything that purifies, revives, or gives a fresh bloom.

Jorfe, m. dry stone wall; steep rock, cliff.

Jorguín, m. wizard, or sorcerer.—**jorguina,** f. witch, or sorceress.—**jorguinería,** f. witchcraft, spell.

Jornada, f. one-day march; working day; stage, journey, travel, trip; (mil.) expedition; king's stay in a royal country residence; opportunity, occasion, circumstance; span of life; transit from life to eternity; act of a play; (print.) number of sheets printed off in a day.—**j. de ocho horas,** 8-hour (working) day.—**a grandes, or a largas, jornadas,** by forced marches.—**al fin de la j.,** at the end.

Jornal, m. daywork, journeywork; day wages.—**a j.,** by the day.

Jornalero, m. day laborer; journeyman.

Joroba, f. hump; (coll.) importunity, annoyance, nuisance.

Jorobado, da. I. pp. & a. crooked, gibbous, humpbacked. **II.** n. hunchback.

Jorobar, va. (coll.) to importune, bother, annoy.

Jorrar, va. to haul.

Jorro, m. (Cuba) bad tobacco.

Josa, f. orchard of vines and fruit trees.

Jostrado, da, a. round-headed (shaft or dart).

Jota, name of the letter j; iota, jot, tittle; an Aragonese dance and tune; pottage of greens and spices.—**no saber, or no entender, jota, or ni jota, or una j.,** not to know beans, to be absolutely ignorant.—**sin faltar una j.,** not a jot missing, with not a whit left out.

Jote, m. a Chilean vulture of the turkey-buzzard family.

Joule, m. (elec.) joule (= JULIO).

Jovada, f. ground tilled by a pair of mules in one day.

Joven. I. a. young. **II.** n. youth; young man; young woman; young person.

Jovenado, m. (eccl.) juniorate.

Jovencillo, illa, n. youngster, lad, lass.

Jovial, a. Jovian; jovial, gay, merry, cheerful.

Jovialidad, f. joviality, jollity, gaiety.

Joya, f. jewel, gem; piece of jewellery; present, gift; (arch. and arti.) astragal.—pl. jewels, trinkets; wedding outfit.

Joyante, a. extremely glossy (silk).

Joyel, m. small jewel, valuable trinket.

Joyelero, m. jewel case, jewel box.

Joyera, f. woman jeweller.

Joyería, f. jeweller's shop.

Joyero, m. jeweller; jewel-casket.

Joyita, f. dim. = JOYUELA.

Joyo, m. (bot.) bearded darnel, darnel grass.

Joyón, m. aug. large jewel.

Joyuela, f. dim. jewel of small value.

Juaguarzo, m. (bot.) Montpellier rockrose.

Juan, m. John.—**J. Lanas,** simpleton, poor devil, (a) nobody.—**buen J.,** poor, silly fellow.

Juanas, f. pl. glove stretcher.

Juanete, m. bunion; prominent cheek bone; (naut.) gallant sail.—**j. de sobremesana,** mizzentopgallant sail.—**j. mayor,** main-topgallant sail.

Juanetudo, da, a. having bunions.

Juarda, f. stain in cloth.

Juardoso, sa, a. stained, spotted (cloth).

Jubete, *m.* doublet covered with mail.

Jubilación, *f.* pensioning off or superannuating a placeman; exemption from duty, with reduced pay; pension or reduced salary thus paid.

Jubilar. I. *va.* to pension off; to superannuate; to retire; (coll.) to lay aside as useless. **II.** *vr.* to become a pensioner; to be retired. **III.** *vn.* to jubilate, rejoice.

Jubileo, *m.* jubilee, public festivity; (eccl.) concession of plenary indulgence.—**por j.,** rarely, once in a long while.

Júbilo, *m.* glee, joy, merriment, rejoicing.

Jubiloso, sa, *a.* joyful, merry, gay.

Jubón, *m.* doublet, jacket; waist in female dress. —**j. de azotes,** (coll.) public whipping.

Juboncito, *m. dim.* small doublet or waist.

Jubonero, *m.* maker of doublets or waists.

Júcaro, *m.* a West-Indian hardwood tree.

Judaico, ca, *a.* Judaical, Jewish.

Judaísmo, *m.* Judaism.—**judaizante,** *n.* & *a.* Judaizer (-ing).—**judaizar,** *va.* & *vn.* to judaize.

Judas, *m.* Judas; traitor; silkworm that does not spin; effigy of Judas burnt in the streets during Lent.

Judería, *f.* Jewry; ghetto; tax on Jews.

Judía, *f.* (bot.) bean, string bean; Jewess.—**j. de careta,** small spotted French bean.

Judiada, *f.* inhuman action; usurious profit.

Judiar, *m.* bean field or patch.

Judicante, *m.* judge appointed to try impeachment cases.

Judicatura, *f.* judicature; judgeship.

Judicial, *a.* judicial, juridical.

Judicialmente, *adv.* judicially.

Judiciario, ria. I. *a.* astrological. **II.** *m.* astrologer. **III.** *f.* judicial astrology.

Judiega, *f.* inferior kind of olives.

Judihuelo, la. I. *n.* young Jew or Jewess. **II.** *f.* small French bean.

Judo, día. I. *a.* Jewish; usurious. **II.** *m.* Jew.— **j. de señal,** converted Jew, wearing a distinguishing badge.

Judión, *m.* a large variety of French bean.

Juego, *m.* play, sport, game; gaming, gambling; set of good cards; movement, work, working (of a mechanism); set; suit, suite; ability, artfulness, cunning; (car.) running gear of a vehicle; (mech.) play, free space, clearance.—*pl.* public feasts, games.—**j. de azar,** game of chance.—**j. de bochas,** bowling alley.—**j. de boliche,** pigeonholes (an old game); trollmadam.—**j. de bolos,** ninepins.—**j. de café,** coffee set.—**j. de cajones,** nest of boxes or drawers.—**j. de cartas,** card game. —**j. de compadres,** collusion or conspiracy under pretense of rivalry or opposition among those concerned.—**j. de habitaciones,** suite of rooms.—**j. de manos,** juggling feat, legerdemain.—**j. de naipes** = J. DE CARTAS.—**j. de niños,** child's play. —**j. de palabras,** pun, quibble, play upon words. —**j. de pelota,** ball game (app. to several games in which a ball is thrown).—**j. de prendas,** forfeits.— **j. de suerte** = J. DE AZAR.—**j. de te,** tea set.—**j. de velas,** (naut.) set of sails.—**j. de vocablos, or de voces** = J. DE PALABRAS.—**j. limpio,** fair play.— **j. público,** public gambling house (where gambling is allowed by law).—**entrar en j.,** to come into play or into action.—**hacer j.,** to match, to fit.— **mostrar el j.,** to show one's hand (fig.).—**por j.,** or **por modo de j.,** in jest, for fun.—**tener j.,** (naut.) to have fetched way; not to be firm or steady.—**verle a uno el j.,** to read one through, see one's plans or intentions.

Juego, yo juegue. *V.* JUGAR.

Jueguecico, illo, ito, *m.* little game, bit of play.

Juera, *f.* sieve made of esparto.

Juerga, *f.* (coll.) spree, carousal.

Juerguista, *n.* (coll.) reveler, carouser.

Jueves, *m.* Thursday.—**j. santo,** holy Thursday

Juez, *m.* judge; justice; juror, juryman.—**j. árbitro,** arbitrator, umpire.—**j. conservador,** person appointed to defend the rights of a community. —**j. de alzadas,** judge in appeal cases.—**j. de hecho,** lay judge.—**j. de paz,** justice of the peace. —**j. de primera instancia,** judge of the primary court of claims.

Jugada, *f.* play, act of playing; a throw, move, stroke; ill turn, mean trick.

Jugadera, *f.* shuttle for network.

Jugador, ra, *n.* player; gamester, gambler.—**j. de manos,** juggler, prestidigitator.

Jugar, *va.* & *vn.* (*ind.* JUEGO: *pret.* JUGUÉ: *subj.* JUEGUE) to play; to sport, frolic; to game, gamble; to stake; to move in a game; to move (a part of the body); to wield, handle (a weapon); to move on joints or hinges; to intervene; to take an active part in an affair; to exercise; to mock, to make game of.—**j. a cara o cruz,** to bet on the toss of a coin. —**j. a la baja,** to bear the market.—**j. a la bolsa,** to dabble in stocks.—**j. al alza,** (com.) to bull the market.—**jugarle a uno una mala volada, or mala partida,** to play a mean trick on one.— **jugársela a uno de codillo,** (coll.) to trick or outwit one.

Jugarreta, *f.* (coll.) bad play; bad turn, nasty trick.

Juglándeo, dea. I. *a.* (bot.) juglandaceous. **II.** *f. pl.* Juglandaceæ, the walnut family of trees.

Juglar, *m.* juggler, mountebank, buffoon.

Juglara, juglaresa, *f.* female buffoon.

Juglaresco, ca, *a.* belonging to jugglers.

Juglaría, juglería, *f.* jugglery, buffoonery, mimicry.

Jugo, *m.* sap, juice; marrow, pith, substance.

Jugosidad, *f.* sappiness, succulence, juiciness.

Jugoso, sa, *a.* sappy, juicy, succulent.

Juguete, *m.* toy, plaything; jest, joke; carol; (theat.) comedietta.—**j. de movimiento,** mechanical toy.—**por j.,** jestingly.

Juguetear, *vn.* to frolic, sport, gambol.

Juguetería, *f.* toyshop, toy trade.

Juguetero, *m.* toy dealer; etagère, whatnot.

Juguetón, na, *a.* playful, frolicsome.

Juicio, *m.* judgment; decision; prudence, wisdom; forecast of yearly events by astrologers; good behavior; (law) trial.—**j. de Dios,** ordeal (to determine guilt or innocence).—**j. final,** final judgment.—**j. ejecutivo,** levy, attachment.—**estar fuera de su j.,** to be crazy.—**no estar en su j.,** to be out of one's senses.—**no tener j.,** to be wild, to be a harum-scarum fellow.—**pedir en j.,** to sue at law.—**perder el j.,** to become insane; to go mad.— **tener j.,** to be wise; to be cautious; to be well-behaved.

Juiciosamente, *adv.* judiciously, wisely.

Juicioso, sa, *a.* judicious, wise; well-behaved.

Julepe, *m.* (pharm.) julep; a card game; (coll.) reprimand, punishment.

Juliano, na, *a.* Julian.

Julio, *m.* July; (elec.) joule.

Julo, *m.* bell-mule, bell-cow.

Jumenta, *f.* female ass, jennie.

Jumental, jumentil, *a.* belonging to the ass.

Jumentillo, illa, ito, ita, *n. dim.* little ass or beast of burden.

Jumento, *m.* ass, jument; stupid person.

Juncada, *f.* (cook.) a kind of fritter; (vet.) medicine for the glanders.

Juncago, *m.* (bot.) bastard rush.

Juncal, juncar, *m.* ground full of rushes.

Júnceo, a. I. *a.* rushlike; (bot.) juncaceous. **II.** *f. pl.* Juncaceæ.

Juncia, *f.* (bot.) cyperus, sedge.—**j. olorosa,** galangal.

Junciana, *f.* (coll.) brag, boast.

Junciera, *f.* earth vessel with perforated lid, for aromatic roots.

Juncino, na, *a.* rushy; made of rushes.

Junco, *m.* (bot.) rush; (naut.) Chinese Junk.—**j. de Indias,** (bot.) rattan.—**j. florido,** flowering rush.—**j. oloroso,** (bot.) camel grass.

Juncoso, sa, *a.* rushy; juncous.

Junio, *m.* June, the sixth month.

Júnior, *m.* (eccl.) junior.

Junípero, *m.* (bot.) juniper. *V.* ENEBRO.

Junquera, *f.* (bot.) rush.

Junqueral, *m.* = JUNCAL.

Junquillo, *m.* (bot.) jonquil; reed, rattan; (arch.) boltel moulding.

junta, *f.* junta, board, council; meeting, conference; session, sitting; whole, entirety; union, junction; fraternity; seam; joint; coupling.—**j. a tope,** butt joint.—**j. de accionistas,** stockholders' meeting.—**j. de acreedores,** (com.) meeting of creditors.—**j. de comercio,** board of trade.—**j. de dilatación,** expansion joint.—**j. de educación,** school board, board of education.—**j. de enchufe** = J. ENCHUFADA.—**j. de expansión,** expansion joint. —**j. de médicos,** (med.) consultation.—**j. de recubrimiento,** lap joint.—**j. de sanidad,** board of health.—**j. de solapa,** lap joint.—**j. de yuxtaposición,** butt joint.—**j. directiva,** managing board, executive board.—**j. enchufada,** bell-and-spigot joint.—**j. remachada,** riveted joint.

juntamente, *adv.* jointly, together.

juntar. I. *va.* to join, connect, unite; to assemble, congregate; to amass, collect, gather, lay up. **II.** *vr.* to join, meet, assemble, gather; to be closely united; to copulate; (w. **con**) to associate (with).

juntera, *f.* (carp.) jointing plane.

junterilla, *f. dim.* (carp.) small joiner's plane.

junto, *adv.* near, close at hand, near at hand; at the same time.—**j. a.,** next to, by.—**j. con,** together with.—**de por j.,** wholesale.—**en j.,** together, in all.—**por j.** = DE POR J.

junto, ta, *a.* united, joined; together.

juntorio, *m.* an ancient tax.

juntura, *f.* juncture, joining, joint, articulation, seam; (naut.) scarf; (bot.) knuckle.

Júpiter, *m.* (ast.) Jupiter; (chem.) tin.

jura, *f.* oath; swearing.

jurado, *m.* jury; juror, juryman.

jurador, ra, *n.* swearer, profane swearer.

juraduría, *f.* office of a juror.

juramentar. I. *va.* to swear in. **II.** *vr.* to be sworn in, take the oath.

juramento, *m.* oath; act of swearing; curse, imprecation.—**j. asertorio,** declaratory oath.—**j. falso,** perjury.

jurar, *va.* & *vn.* to swear, to make oath, to take an oath.—**j. en falso,** to commit perjury.

jurásico, ca, *a.* Jurassic.

juratoria, *f.* Gospel tablet for administering the oath.

juratorio, a. I. *a.* juratory. **II.** *m.* instrument setting forth the oaths taken by Aragonese magistrates.

jurel, *m.* (icht.) jurel, a carangoid sea fish.

jurguina, *f.* witch, sorceress.

jurídicamente, *adv.* legally, juridically.

jurídico, ca, *a.* legal, juridical.

jurisconsulto, *m.* jurisconsult, jurist; lawyer.

jurisdicción, *f.* jurisdiction; boundary, territory.

jurisdiccional, *a.* jurisdictional.

jurispericia, *f.* = JURISPRUDENCIA.

jurisperito, ta, *n.* jurisconsult.

jurisprudencia, *f.* jurisprudence, law; laws, legislation.

jurista, *m.* jurist; lawyer; pensioner.

juro, *m.* right of perpetual property; annuity, pension.—**de j.,** certainly.

jusbarba, *f.* (bot.) field myrtle.

jusello, *m.* pottage of broth, cheese, and eggs.

jusi, *m.* (Philip.) striped thin gauze.

justa, *f.* joust, tilt, tournament; contest.

justador, *m.* tilter, jouster.

justamente, *adv.* justly; just, exactly.

justar, *vn.* to joust, tilt, tourney.

justicia, *f.* justice; judge; court of justice; punishment; (coll.) execution (of a criminal).—**de j.,** justly, deservedly.—**la j.,** the police, the authorities, the officers of the law.

justiciero, ra, *a.* just, fair.

justificable, *a.* justifiable.

justificación, *f.* justification, defence; production of evidence; equity; sanctification by grace; (print.) adjustment, justifying.

justificadamente, *adv.* justly, justifiably.

justificado, da, *pp.* & *a.* justified.

justificador, ra. I. *n.* & *a.* justifier (-ing). **II.** *m.* (print.) dressing stick, justifier.

justificante, *n.* & *a.* justifier (-ing).

justificar. I. *va.* (*pret.* JUSTIFIQUÉ: *subj.* JUSTIFIQUE) to justify; to free from sin; to absolve, exculpate; (law) to prove or establish before a court; to rectify, adjust; (print.) to justify, adjust. **II.** *vr.* to vindicate one's character, to clear one's self; to justify one's conduct.

justificativo, va, *a.* justifying, justificatory.

justillo, *m.* waistcoat, jerkin; corset cover.

justinianeo, a, *a.* Justinian.

justipreciador, ra, *n.* appraiser.—**justipreciar,** *va.* to appraise.—**justiprecio,** *m.* appraisement.

justo, ta. I. *a.* just; pious; correct, exact, strict; fit, tight, close. **II.** *m.* just and pious man.—**al j.,** fitly, duly; completely, punctually. **III.** *adv.* tightly.

juta, *f.* (S. A.) (orn.) a kind of goose.

jutía, *f.* (Cuba) = HUTÍA.

juvenil, *a.* juvenile, youthful.

juventud, *f.* youthfulness, youth; young people.

juvia, *f.* (bot.) Brazil-nut tree.

juzgado, *m.* court of justice; judicature.

juzgamundos, *n.* (coll.) faultfinder.

juzgante. I. *a.* judging. **II.** *n.* judge.

juzgar, *va.* & *vn.* (*pret.* JUZGUÉ: *subj.* JUZGUE) to judge; to pass or render judgment (on).

K

NOTE.—Many words that by some are begun with *k* are properly spelled with *qu* if the following letter is *e* or *i*, and with *c* in other cases.

ka, *f.* name of the letter *k.*

káiser, *m.* kaiser.

kaki, *m.* & *a.* = CAQUI.

kan, *m.* khan, a Tartar chief.

kanato, *m.* Khanate.

kantiano, na, *n.* & *a.* Kantian.—**kantismo,** *m.* Kantianism.—**kantista,** *n.* & *a.* Kantian.

kepis, *m.* (mil.) small shako, kepi, a military cap.

kermes, *m.* = QUERMES.

kerosén, *m.*; **keroseno,** *m.*; **kerosina,** *f.* kerosene.

kiliárea, *f.* kiloare, one thousand ares.

kilo. I. (*as a prefix*) kilo (a thousand). **II.** *m.* kilo, kilogram.

kilocaloría, *f.* kilocalorie.

kilográmetro, *m.* kilogrammeter, metric unit of work (about 7.25 ft.-lb.)

kilogramo, *m.* kilogram (about 2.2 lb.)

kilojulio, *m.* (elec.) kilojoule.

kilolitro, *m.* kiloliter.

kilométrico, ca, *a.* kilometric; mileage (ticket); (coll.) very long, interminably long.

kilómetro, *m.* kilometer (about 0.62 mile)

kilovatio, *m.* (elec.) kilowatt.—**k.-hora,** kilowatt-hour.

kilovoltamperio, *m.* kilovolt-ampere.

kilovoltio, *m.* (elec.) kilovolt.

kiosco, *m.* kiosk, small pavilion.

kirie, *m.* (eccl.) kyrie (eleison).

kirieleisón, m. = KIRIE; (coll.) funeral chant.— **cantar el k.,** to beg for quarter, to cry for mercy.

kirsch, *m.* kirschwasser.

kodak, *m.* kodak.

krausismo, *m.* Krausism.

kremlín, *m.* kremlin.

kurdo, da, *n.* & *a.* Kurd (-ish).

L

la. I. *def. art. fem. sing.* the. **II.** *pron. pers. acc. f. sing.* her, it. Formerly, and still occasionally, used as a dative (*yo la dije,* I told her). **III.** *m.* (mus.) la, A, sixth note of the scale.

laberintodonte, *m.* (pal.) labyrinthodont.—*pl.* Labyrintodonta.

lábaro, *m.* labarum.

labe, *f.* stain, spot.

laberíntico, ca, *a.* labyrinthine.

laberinto, *m.* labyrinth, maze; intricate matter; (anat.) labyrinth of the ear.

labia, *f.* (coll.) sweet, winning talk or eloquence.

labiado, da, *a.* (bot.) labiate.

labial, *a.* labial.

labiérnago, *m.* (bot.) laburnum.

labihendido, da, *a.* hare-lipped.

labil, *a.* labile.

labio, *m.* lip; (by ext.) mouth; edge, brim.—**l. liporino,** harelip.

labor, *f.* labor, task, toil, work; design, scroll-work; (sew.) needlework, embroidery, fancy-work; trimming; a thousand tiles or bricks; cultivation; husbandry, tillage; egg of a silkworm; figures raised upon a ground; diaper; (min.) works, working.

laborable, *a.* tillable, workable.

laborador, ra, *n.* tiller, farmer; worker.

laborante. I. *a.* tilling, working. **II.** *m.* (Cuba) conspirator.

laborantismo, *m.* (Cuba) (pol.) movement for independence from Spain.

laborar, *va. & vn.* to till; to work.

laboratorio, *m.* laboratory.

laborcica, illa, ita, *f. dim.* pretty needlework.

laborear, *va.* to work; (naut.) to reeve, to run.

laboreo, *m.* (naut.) reeving, running; (min.) works; working, exploitation, development.

laborera, *f.* clever, skilful workwoman.

laboriosamente, *adv.* laboriously.

laboriosidad, *f.* laboriousness, assiduity.

laborioso, sa, *a.* assiduous, industrious; arduous, laborious.

labra, *f.* stone cutting or carving; working, cutting (of metal, stone, etc.).

labrada, *f.* land plowed and fallowed.

labradero, ra; labradío, día, *a.* tillable, arable; workable.

labrado, da. I. *pp. & a.* wrought; figured, hewn; tilled; (com.) manufactured. **II.** *m. pl.* cultivated lands.

labrador, ra. I. *n.* farmer, tiller, peasant. **II.** *a.* industrious.

labradoresco, ca, *a.* relating to farmers, rustic.

labradorita, *f.* (min.) labradorite.

labrandera, *f.* seamstress, embroiderer.

labrante, *m.* stonecutter; sculptor.

labrantín, *m.* petty farmer.

labrantío, tía, *a.* arable, tillable.

labranza, *f.* tillage, cultivation; farming; farm land.

labrar. I. *va.* to elaborate, work; to manufacture, make; to till, cultivate; to build, erect; to cut, dress, carve (stone); to embroider; to make designs in; to form; cause, bring about; to work out (a man's destiny, etc.). **II.** *vn.* to make a strong impression on the mind.

labrero. I. *a.* (fishing nets) for sharks. **II.** *n.* (Ch.) mine overseer or foreman.

labriego, ga, *n.* rustic, peasant, farmer.

labrusca, *f.* wild grapevine.

laburno, *m.* (bot.) laburnum.

laca, *f.* lac, gum lac; red color; lake, a pigment; lacquer, a varnish.—**l. en grano,** seed-lac.—**l. en palillos,** stick lac.—**l. en tablillas,** shellac.

lacayesco, ca, *a.* = LACAYUNO.

lacayo, *m.* lackey, groom, footman; knot of ribbons worn by women.

lacayuelo, *m. dim.* foot-boy, groom, tiger.

lacayuno, na, *a.* belonging to a lackey; lackey-like, servile.

lacear, *va.* to lace, trim, or tie with bows; to pin up (the game) or drive within shot.

lacedemón; lacedemonio, a, *n. & a.* Lacedemonian.

laceración, *f.* laceration, tearing.

lacerado, da, *pp. & a.* unfortunate, unhappy; leprous.

lacerar, *va.* to mangle, tear in pieces, lacerate; to hurt, damage.

lacería, *f.* misery, poverty, wretchedness; drudgery, weariness.

lacería, *f.* set of bows.

lacerioso, sa, *a.* miserable, wretched.

lacertilio, lia. I. *n. & a.* lacertian. *m. pl.* Lacertilia.

lacertoso, sa, *a.* muscular, athletic.

lacinia, *f.* (bot.) lacinia, slender lobe.

laciniado, da, *a.* (bot.) laciniate, slashed.

lacio, cia, *a.* faded, withered; flaccid, languid; straight (as hair).

lacónicamente, *adv.* laconically.—**lacónico, ca,** *a.* laconic.—**laconio, nia,** *n. & a.* Laconian.—**laconismo,** *m.* laconism.

lacra, *f.* mark or trace left by illness; fault, defect; viciousness.

lacrar, *va.* to injure or impair (the health); to cause pecuniary damage or loss to; to seal with sealing wax.

lacre, *m.* sealing wax.

lacrimal, *a.* lachrymal.

lacrimatorio, ria, *n. & a.* lachrymatory.

lacrimosamente, *adv.* tearfully.

lacrimoso, sa, *a.* tearful, lachrymose.

lactación, *f.* suckling.—**lactancia,** *f.* lactation, period of suckling.—**lactante,** *n. & a.* feeding on milk.—**lactar. I.** *va.* to nurse; to feed with milk. **II.** *vn.* to suckle; to feed on milk.—**lactato, m.** (chem.) lactate.—**lácteo, tea,** *a.* lacteous, milky, lacteal.—**lactescente,** *a.* lactescent.—**lacticíneo, a,** *a.* = LÁCTEO.

lacticinio, *m.* any kind of milk food.

láctico, ca, *a.* (chem.) lactic.

lactífero, ra, *a.* lactiferous.

lactina, *f.* (chem.) lactose, lactin, milk sugar.

lactómetro, *m.* lactometer.

lactosa, *f.* = LACTINA.

lactoscopio, *m.* lactoscope.

lactucario, *m.* (pharm.) lactucarium.

lactumen, *m.* (med.) milk crust.

lacunario, *m.* (arch.) lacunary.

lacustre, *a.* lacustrine.

lacha, *f.* (icht.) anchovy; shame.

lada, *f.* (bot.) cystus.

ládano, *m.* labdanum, gum labdanum.

ladeado, da, *a. & pp.* tilted, inclined to one side.

ladear. I. *va. & vr.* to tilt, tip, incline to one side. **II.** *vn.* to skirt; to deviate; to be even. **III.** *vr.* to incline to an opinion or party; to lean; to tilt, incline to one side; (Ch.) to fall in love.

ladeo, *m.* inclination or motion to one side.

ladera, *f.* declivity, slope, hillside.—*pl.* rails or staves of a truck; cheeks of a gun carriage.

ladería, *f.* small dale on a mountainside.

ladero, ra, *a.* lateral.

ladierno, *m.* (bot.) buckthorn.

ladilla, *f.* crab louse; (bot.) common barley.

ladillo, *m.* shifting panel placed in the sides of coaches.

ladinamente, *adv.* artfully, sagaciously, cunningly.

ladino, na, *a.* sagacious, cunning, crafty; apt as a linguist.

lado, *m.* side; border, margin, edge; (mil.) flank; party, faction; mat for the side of carts, etc.; course, bend, manner; mode of proceeding.—*pl.* patrons, advisers.—**l. a l.** side by side.—**al l.,** just by, near at hand.—**a un l.,** aside.—**dejar a un l.,** to set aside.—**de l.,** incidentally; sideways; from or on the side.—**hacerse a un l.,** to move aside, to get out of the way.—**mirar de l.,** to look askance; to look out of the corner of the eye; to look at contemptuously, look down upon.

ladón, *m.* (bot.) cystus. *V.* LADA.

ladra, *f.* barking.

ladrador, ra; ladrante, *n. & a.* barker (-ing).

ladrar, *vn.* to bark.—**ladrido,** *m.* barking; outcry; calumny, slander.

ladrillado, *m.* brick floor.—**ladrillador, m.** = ENLADRILLADOR.—**ladrillar,** *va.* to lay bricks on, pave with brick.—**ladrillal, ladrillar,** *m.* brick yard.—**ladrillazo,** *m.* blow with a brickbat.—**ladrillejo,** *m. dim.* little brick; boys' amusement of knocking at doors with a brick.—**ladrillero, m.** brickmaker.

For pronunciation, see the rules at the beginning of the book.

ladrillo, *m.* brick, tile.—**l. de chocolate,** cake of chocolate.—**ladrilloso, sa,** *a.* bricky.

ladrón, na. I. *n.* thief; robber; cutpurse. **II.** *m.* lock, sluice gate; snuff of a candle that makes it melt.

ladronamente, *adv.* thievishly.

ladronear, *vn.* to go about robbing or stealing.

ladroncillo, *m. dim.* petty thief, filcher.

ladronera, *f.* nest of rogues, den of robbers; filching, extortion; sluice gate in a mill; money box.

ladronería, *f.* = LADRONICIO.

ladronesco, ca. I. *a.* (*coll.*) belonging to thieves, thievish. **II.** *f.* gang of thieves.

ladronicio, *m.* larceny, theft, robbery.

ladronzuelo, la, *n. dim.* petty thief.

lagaña, *f.* blearedness.

lagañoso, sa, *a.* = LEGAÑOSO.

lagar, *m.* wine press.

lagarejo, *m.* small wine press.

lagarero, *m.* wine presser; olive presser.

lagarcta, *f.* small wine press; puddle, pool.

lagarta, *f.* female lizard; (coll.) sly, cunning woman.

lagartado, da, *a.* = ALAGARTADO.

lagartera, *f.* lizard hole.

lagartija, *f.*, **lagartijo,** *m.*, **lagartillo,** *m. dim.* small lizard.

lagarto, *m.* lizard; (Am.) alligator; (anat.) biceps; (coll.) sly, artful person.

lago, *m.* lake.—**l. de leones,** den of lions.

lagostín, *m.* crayfish. *V.* LANGOSTÍN.

lagotear, *vn.* (coll.) to flatter, wheedle, cajole.

lagotería, *f.* (coll.) flattery.—**lagotero, ra,** *a.* (coll.) flattering, honey-mouthed.

lágrima, *f.* tear; drop of any liquid; drop-like exudation from a tree; wine that drips from the grape without pressure.—**l. de David, or de Jacob,** (bot.) Job's tears.—**lágrimas de Batavia, or de Holanda,** Prince Rupert's drops, glass globules.—**lágrimas de cocodrilo,** crocodile tears.—**lágrimas de San Pedro,** pebbles, stones thrown at a person.

lagrimable, *a.* worthy of tears.—**lagrimal. I.** *a.* lachrymal. **II.** *m.* lachrymal caruncle.—**lagrimar, lagrimear,** *vn.* to shed tears.—**lagrimeo,** *m.* shedding tears.—**lagrimón,** *m. aug.* large tear.—**lagrimoso, sa,** *a.* tearful, lachrymose; watery. (s. o. the eyes); (bot.) exuding.

laguna, *f.* lagoon; hiatus, gap.

lagunajo, *m.* puddle, pool.

lagunar, *m.* (arch.) lacunar.

lagunero, ra, *a.* belonging to lagoons.

lagunoso, sa, *a.* marshy, fenny, swampy.

laical, *a.* = LAICO.

laicismo, *m.* secularism, doctrine of secularists, who exclude religion from human affairs.

laico, ca, *a.* lay, laic.

laja, *f.* flagstone; slab; (naut.) rock at the entrance of a port.

lama. I. *f.* mud, slime, ooze; seaweed; lama (gold or silver cloth); fine sand used for mortar; dust of ores in mines. **II.** *n.* lama, Tibetan monk or nun.

lamaísmo, *m.* Lamaism.

lamaísta, *n. & a.* Lamaist (-ic).

lambel, *m.* (her.) lambel, label.

lambrequines, *m. pl.* (her.) mantelets.

lambrija, *f.* worm bred in the human body; (coll.) skinny, thin person.

lamedal, *m.* musty, miry place.

lamedero, *m.* saltlick.

lamedor, ra, *n.* licker; wheedling; (pharm.) syrup.—**dar lamedor,** to feign losing at play in order to insure greater success.

lamedura, *f.* act of licking.

lamelibranquio, quia. I. *n. & a.* (zool.) lamellibranch. **II.** *m. pl.* Lamellibranchiata.

lamelicornio, nia. I. *n. & a.* lamellicorn. **II.** *m. pl.* Lamellicornia.

lameliforme, *a.* lamelliform.

lamelirostro, tra. I. *a.* (zool.) lamellirostral. **II.** *m. pl.* Lamellirostres.

lamentable, *a.* lamentable, deplorable.

lamentablemente, *adv.* lamentably.

lamentación, *f.* lamentation, wail.

lamentador, ra, *n. & a.* lamenter (-ing), mourner (-ing), complainer (-ing).

lamentar. I. *va.* to lament, regret, mourn. **II.** *vn. & vr.* to lament, grieve, wail; to complain; to moan.

lamento, *m.* lamentation, lament, moan, wail.

lamentoso, sa, *a.* lamentable, mournful.

lameplatos, *m.* (coll.) glutton, gorger; one who feeds on leavings.

lamer, *va.* to lick; to lap; to touch slightly.

lamerón, na, *a.* (coll.) fond of dainties.

lamia, *f.* lamia, a fabulous monster; shark.

lamido, da, *a. & pp.* worn out.

lamiente, *n. & a.* lick, licker (-ing).

lamín, *m.* dainty tidbit.

lámina, *f.* plate, sheet; lamina; engraving, print, picture, illustration; engraving plate.

laminado, da, *a.* laminated; rolled (s. o. metals).

laminador, *m.* rolling mill; rolling press; plate roller.

laminar, *va.* to roll or beat (metal) into sheets; to lick, to guzzle (dainties).

laminar, *a.* laminar, lamellar; in sheets.

laminera, *f.* bee advanced before its companions.

laminero, ra. I. *a.* fond of sweets. **II.** *n.* manufacturer of metal plates; one who makes shrines for relics.

lamiscar, *va.* (coll.) to lick greedily.

lamoso, sa, *a.* slimy, muddy.

lampa, *f.* (Am.) (agr.) shovel for grain.

lampacear, *va.* (naut.) to swab.

lampadéforo, lampadóforo, *m.* lampadephore.

lampar, *vn. & vr.* = ALAMPAR.

lámpara, *f.* lamp; light, luminous body; grease stain; bough placed at the door on festivals or rejoicings.—**l. Argand,** Argand lamp, student lamp.—**l. de arco,** arc lamp.—**l. de seguridad,** safety lamp.—**l. de soldar,** blowtorch.—**l. de techo,** ceiling lamp, top lamp.—**l. incandescente,** incandescent lamp.—**l. normal,** standard lamp.—**l. piloto,** (elec.) pilot lamp.—**l. termiónica,** (rad.) thermionic valve.—**atizar la lámpara,** (coll.) to refill the glasses.

lamparería, *f.* lamp factory; lamp store.

lamparero, ra, *n.* lamp maker or seller; lamplighter.

lamparilla, *f. dim.* small lamp; night taper; a sort of camlet; aspen or trembling poplar.

lamparín, *m.* lamp holder.

lamparista, *n.* = LAMPARERO.

lamparón, *m. aug.* large grease spot; king's evil; (vet.) a disease of horses.

lampatán, *m.* a Chinese plant.

lampazo, *m.* (bot.) burdock; (naut.) swab, mop.

lampiño, ña, *a.* beardless.

lampión, *m.* large lantern.

lampote, *m.* (Philip.) domestic cotton cloth.

lamprea, *f.* (icht.) sea lamprey.

lamprear, *va.* to dress or season with wine and sour gravy.

lamprehuela, lampreílla, *f.* river lamprey.

lámpsana, *f.* (bot.) common nipple wort.

lampuga, *f.* (icht.) yellow mackerel.

lana, *f.* wool, fleece; woollen manufacture in general.

lanada, *f.* (arti.) sponge.

lanado, da, *a.* (bot.) lanate.

lanar, *a.* wool (u. a.).

lanaria, *f.* (bot.) cudweed.

lancán, *m.* (Philip.) barge.

lance, *m.* cast, throw; casting of a fish net; catch in a net; critical moment; incident, episode; event, occurrence; transaction; quarrel, dispute; move or turn in a game.—**l. de honor,** duel.—**de l.,** cheap, at second hand.—**tener pocos lances,** to be uninteresting.

lanceado, da, *a.* (bot.) lanceolate.

lancear, *va.* to wound with a lance.

lancéola, *f.* (bot.) rib-grass plantain.

For pronunciation, see the rules at the beginning of the book.

lanceolado, da, *a.* (bot.) lanceolate.

lancera, *f.* lance rack in an armory.

lancería, *f.* aggregate of lances; body of lancers.

lancero, *m.* pikeman; lancer; maker of pikes.

lanceta, *f.* (surg.) lancet; (vet.) fleam.

lancetada, *f.,* **lancetazo,** *m.* opening or wounding with a lancet.

lancetero, *m.* case for carrying lancets.

lancita, *f. dim.* small lance.

lancinante, *a.* lancinating.

lancurdia, *f* small trout.

lancha, *f.* flagstone, slab; (naut.) boat, gig; lighter, launch; snare for partridges.—**l. cañonera,** gunboat.—**l. de pescar,** fishing smack.—**l. de socorro,** life-saving boat.

lanchada, *f.* lighter load.

lanchaje, *m.* (com.) ferriage; lighterage.

lanchar, *m.* flagstone quarry.

lanchero, *m.* bargeman, boatman, oarsman.

lanchón, *m. aug.* (naut.) lighter, barge, scow.—**l. aljador,** lighter.

lanchonero, *m.* lighterman, bargeman.

landgrave, *m.* landgrave.

landgraviato, *m.* landgraviate.

landó, *m.* (car.) landau.

landre, *f.* small tumor on the glands; concealed pocket in the clothes.

landrecilla, *f.* small round body in some glandular tissues.

landrero, ra, *a.* hoarder of money in a concealed pocket.

landrilla, *f.* (vet.) tongue worm.

lanería, *f.* shop where wool is sold.

lanero, ra. I. *a.* woollen. **II.** *n.* dealer in wool. **III.** *m.* warehouse for wool.

langa, *f.* small dry codfish.

langaruto, ta, *a.* (coll.) tall and skinny; thin.

langosta, *f.* (ent.) locust; (icht.) lobster.

langostero, a. I. *n.* lobster fisherman. **II.** *a.* lobster-fishing; lobster (u. a.).

langostín, langostino, *m.* (icht.) crawfish.

langostón, *m. aug.* (ent.) green grasshopper.

lánguidamente, *adv.* languidly.

languidecer, *vn.* to languish.

languidez, languideza, *f.* languishment, languidness, languor.

lánguido, da, *a.* languid, faint, weak.

lanífero, ra, *a.* (poet.) laniferous, woolly.

lanificación, *f.;* **lanificio,** *m.* woollen manufacturing; woollen goods.

lanilla, *f.* nap of cloth, down; swanskin; fine flannel; (naut.) bunting.

lanío, *a.* woolly.

lanosidad, *f.* (bot.) down of leaves.

lanoso, sa, *a.* woolly.

lantaca, *f.* (Philip.) small culverin.

lantano, *m.* (chem.) lanthanum.

lanudo, da, *a.* woolly, fleecy.

lanuginoso, sa, *a.* (bot.) lanigerous, downy.

lanza, *f.* lance, spear; pole of a coach or wagon; nozzle; pikeman; free lance.—*pl.* duty formerly paid by the nobility in lieu of military services.—**l. en ristre,** with the lance on its rest; ready for action.—**ser una l.,** to be an expert; to be clever.

lanzabombas, *m.* bomb thrower.

lanzada, *f.* thrust or stroke with a lance.

lanzadera, *f.* shuttle, a weaver's instrument.

lanzado, da, *pp. & a.* (naut.) raking, inclined.

lanzador, ra, *n.* thrower, ejecter.

lanzafuego, *m.* = BOTAFUEGO.

lanzamiento, *m.* launching, casting, or throwing; jaculation; (law) dispossessing, ejectment; (naut.) flaring of the bows and knuckle timbers; rake of the stem and sternpost.—*pl.* length of a ship from stem to sternpost.

lanzaminas, *m.* mine layer, mine-laying boat.

lanzar. I. *va.* (pret. LANCÉ: subj. LANCE) to throw, dart, hurl, fling; to launch; to throw up, vomit; (law) to eject, dispossess. **II.** *vr.* to rush or dart; to launch forth; (com.) to engage or embark (in).

lanzatorpedos, *m.* torpedo boat; torpedo tube.

lanzazo, *m.* = LANZADA.

lanzón, *m. aug.* short and thick goad.

lanzuela, *f. dim.* small lance or spear.

laña, *f.* clamp, cramp or cramp iron; green coconut.

lañar, *va.* to cramp, to clamp; to clean (fish).

laodicense, *n. & a.* Laodicean.

lapa, *f.* vegetable film on the surface of a liquid; barnacle; (bot.) goose grass, cleavers.

lapachar, *m.* swamp, marsh, morass.

lápade, *f.* lepadid, barnacle.

laporotomía, *f.* (surg.) laparotomy.

lapicero, *m.* pencil case; pencil holder.

lápida, *f.* tablet, memorial stone; gravestone (called also **l. mortuoria**).

lapidación, *f.* lapidation, stoning to death.

lapidar, *va.* to stone to death.

lapidario, ria, *n. & a.* lapidary.

lapídeo, a, *a.* lapideous, stony.

lapidificación, *f.* petrification, lapidification.

lapidificar, *va.* (chem.) to petrify.

lapidoso, sa, *a.* lapideous, stony.

lapila, *f.* (bot.) hound's-tongue.

lapislázuli, *m.* (min.) lapis lazuli.

lápiz, *m.* (min.) black lead, graphite, plumbago; lead pencil; crayon; (coll.) censor's blue pencil.—**l. de plomo,** graphite.—**l. rojo,** red ochre.

lapizar, *m.* black-lead mine.

lapizar, *va.* to pencil; draw with pencil.

lapo, *m.* (coll.) blow with a cane or whip.

lapón, na, *n. & a* Laplander (-ian, -ic).

lapso, *m.* lapse of time; fall, lapse, slip.

lapsus, *m.* lapsus, slip.—**l. calami,** lapsus calami, slip of the pen.—**l. linguæ,** slip of the tongue.

lar, *m.* (*pl.* LARES, mostly used) Lar, tutelar god.—*pl.* home.

larario, *m.* lararium.

lardar, lardear, *va.* to baste (meat); to scald with boiling oil.

lardero.—jueves l., Thursday before Lent.

lardo, *m.* lard, fat of an animal.

lardón, *m.* (print.) marginal addition; piece of paper clinging to the frisket and preventing the impression of some part of a sheet.

lardoso, sa, *a.* greasy, oily, smearing.

larga, *f.* (shoe.) lengthening piece put to a last; longest billiard cue; (gen. in the *pl.*) delay, procrastination.—**a la corta o a la l.,** sooner or later.—**a la l.,** in the end, in the long run.—**dar largas,** to delay, to protract.

largamente, *adv.* largely, copiously; completely; liberally, frankly; for a long time.

largar. I. *va.* (*pret.* LARGUÉ: *subj.* LARGUE) to loosen, slacken; let go, set free; to expel; to shed; to give (as a slap); to heave (as a sigh); (naut.) to loosen, to ease.—**l. las velas,** (naut.) to set sail. **II.** *vr.* (coll.) to get out, quit, leave, pack away; (naut.) to set sail.

largo, ga. I. *a.* long; extended, prolonged; generous, free, liberal; prompt, expeditious; shrewd, cunning; copious, abundant.—*pl.* many, quite a number; odd, a little over (*tengo cincuenta años largos,* I am fifty-odd years old).—**l. de lengua,** long-tongued, too free and unguarded with the tongue.—**l. de uñas,** (coll.) light-fingered.—**largos años,** many years; long life.—**a lo l., a a distance**: lengthwise.—**a lo l. de,** along, lengthwise of.—**a lo más l.,** at most. **II.** *m.* length; (mus.) largo.—**de l. a l.,** from one end to the other, lengthwise.—**pasar de l.,** to pass by without stopping. **III.** *adv.* largely, profusely. **IV.** *interj.* ¡l! or ¡l. de ahí!—away! be gone!

largor, *m.* length.

largueado, da, *a.* striped.

larguero, *m.* jamb post; bolster; stringer; (aer.) longeron; (aer.) spar.

largueza, *f.* length; liberality, generosity.

larguirucho, cha, *a.* (coll.) long and thin.

larguito, ita, *a.* somewhat long, longish.

largura, *f.* length.

lárice, *m.* (bot.) larch tree.

laricino, na, *a.* belonging to the larch tree.

laringe, *f.* (anat.) larynx.—**laríngeo, gea,** *a.* laryngeal.—**laringitis,** *f.* (med.) laryngitis.—**laringología,** *f.* laryngology.—**laringoscopia,** *f.* laryngoscopy.—**laringoscopio,** *m.* laryngoscope.—**laringotomía,** *f.* (surg.) laryngotomy.

laringótomo, *m.* laryngotome.

larva, *f. m.* mask; larva, ghost, hobgoblin; (zool.) larva; tadpole.—**larvado, da,** *a.* (med.) larvate.—**larval,** *a.* larval.

las, *pl.* of LA.

lasaña, *f.* fritter shaped like a leaf.

lasca, *f.* chip from a stone.

lascar, *va.* to ease away, slacken, pay out.

lascivamente, *adv.* lasciviously.—**lascivia,** *f.* lasciviousness, lewdness.—**lascivo, va,** *a.* lascivious, lewd, lustful; merry, sportive.

laserpicio, *m* (bot.) laserwort.

lasitud, *f.* lassitude, weariness, faintness.

laso, sa, *a.* weary, tired; lax, flaccid.

lastar, *va.* to pay; suffer for another.

lástima, *f.* pity; compassion; pitiful object; plaint, lamentation, tale of woe.—**es l.,** it is a pity.

lastimadura, *f.* sore, hurt.

lastimar. I. *va.* to hurt; injure, damage; to pity. **II.** *vr.* to regret, be sorry for; to complain.

lastimeramente, *adv.* sadly, sorrowfully.

lastimero, ra, *a.* pitiful, sad, doleful.

lastimosamente, *adv.* pitifully, sadly.

lastimoso, sa, *a.* = LASTIMERO.

lasto, *m.* receipt given to one who pays for another.

lastra, *f.* flagstone, slab.

lastrar, *va.* (naut. and r. w.) to ballast.

lastre, *m.* ballast; stone slat; judgment, sense; (coll.) food, nourishment, "grub."

lastrón, *m. aug.* large stone slat.

lasún, *m.* (icht.) = LOCHA.

lata, *f.* small log; tin plate or tinned iron plate; tin can; can of preserved victuals; lath; ledge, batten; annoyance, nuisance; (coll.) protracted and tedious visit or performance.—**en l., en latas,** canned.—**estar en la l.,** to be penniless, to be broken, or "broke."

latamente, *adv.* largely, amply.

latania, *f.* (bot.) latania palm.

latastro, *m.* (arch.) = PLINTO.

lataz, *f.* (zool.) sea otter.

latebra, *f.* cave, den, hiding place.

latebroso, sa, *a.* hiding, furtive, secretive.

latente, *a.* latent.

lateral, *a.* lateral.—**lateralmente,** *adv.* laterally, sideway.

lateranense, *a.* Lateran.

látex, *m.* (bot.) latex.

laticífero, ra, *a.* (bot.) laticiferous.

laticlavia, *f.* laticlave.

latido, *pp.* & *m.* beat, beating, throb; bark, barking (of an animal).

latiente, *a.* palpitating, fluttering.

latifundio, *m.* latifundium (sp. app. to vast landed uncultivated or poorly cultivated land).

latigadera, *f.* strap or thong for lashing the yoke.

latigazo, *m.* lash, whipping; crack of a whip; jerk; unexpected offence; harsh reproot.

látigo, *m.* whip; lashing cord for weighing with a steelyard; cinch strap; long plume around a hat.—**latiguear,** *vn.* to smack or crack a whip.—**latiguera,** *f.* cinch strap.—**latiguero,** *m.* whip maker or seller.—**latiguillo,** *m. dim.* small whip; (theat.) mannerism.

latín, *m.* Latin.—**bajo l.,** low Latin.—**saber l.,** or **mucho l.,** to be very shrewd or cunning.

latinajo, *m.* (coll.) Latin jargon; Latin word or quotation.

latinamente, *adv.* in Latin; in a Latin way.

latinar, latinear, *vn.* to speak or write Latin; to use Latin phrases often.

latinidad, *f.* Latinity; the Latin tongue.

latinismo, *m.* Latinism.

latinista, *n.* Latinist.

latinizar. I. *va.* to Latinize. **II.** *vn.* to use words borrowed from the Latin.

latino, na. I. *a.* Latin. **II.** *n.* Latinist; Latin, a native of Latium.

latir, *vn.* to palpitate, pulsate, throb, beat; to bark, yelp, howl.

latitud, *f.* latitude; breadth, width, extent.

latitudinal, *a.* latitudinal.

latitudinario, ria, *a.* latitudinarian, liberal, tolerant.—**latitudinarismo,** *m.* latitudinarianism.

lato, ta, *a.* large, extensive, ample.

latón, *m.* brass.—**l. en hojas,** or **planchas,** latten brass, sheet brass.

latonería, *f.* brass trade; brass shop; brass works; brass ware.

latonero, *m.* brazier, worker in brass.

latría, *f.* latria, worship of God.

latrocinio, *m.* systematic robbery.

latvio, via, *n.* & *a.* Latvian.

laúd, *m.* (mus.) lute; (naut.) catboat; striped turtle.

lauda, *f.* tombstone.

laudable, *a.* laudable, praiseworthy.

laudablemente, *adv.* laudably.

láudano, *m.* laudanum.

laudar, *va.* to render a decision on, to award.

laudatorio, ria. I. *a.* laudatory, full of praise. **II.** *f.* laudatory, panegyric.

laude, *f.* inscribed tombstone.—*pl.* (eccl.) lauds.

laudemio, *m.* (law) dues paid to the lord of the manor on all transfers of landed property.

laudo, *m.* award, finding of an arbitrator.

launa, *f.* lamina, sheet; schistose clay.

lauráceo, a. I. *a.* laurellike; (bot.) lauraceous, laurineous. **II.** *f. pl.* Lauraceae.

láurea, *f.* laurel wreath.

laureado, da, *a.* & *pp.* laureate.

laureando, *m.* student about to graduate.

laurear, *va.* to crown with laurel; to honor, reward; to confer a degree on.

lauredal, *m.* plantation of laurel trees.

laurel, *m.* (bot.) laurel; laurel wreath; honor.—**l. cerezo,** (bot.) cherry laurel.

laurente, *m.* workman in paper mills.

láureo, a, *a.* laurel (u. a.).

lauréola, *f.* laurel wreath; diadem; (bot.) mezereon—**l. hembra,** (bot.) mezereon daphne.—**l. macho,** spurge laurel.

laurífero, ra, *a.* lauriferous.

lauríneo, nea, *a.* (bot.) laurineous.

laurino, na, *a.* belonging to laurel.

lauro, *m.* (bot.) laurus; glory, honor.

lauroceraso, laurorreal, *m.* cherry laurel.

lautamente, *adv.* splendidly.

lauto, ta, *a.* rich, splendid.

lava, *f.* lava; (min.) washing of metals.

lavabo, *m.* washstand; lavatory; lavabo.

lavacaras, *m.* (coll.) flatterer.

lavación, *f.* (pharm.) lotion, wash.

lavadero, *m.* washing place; lavatory; (tan.) vat or pit for washing hides; (min.) buddling tank; placer, place where gold, etc. are obtained by washing.

lavado, *m.* wash, washing; laundry work; (art) aquarelle in a single tint.

lavador, ra. I. *n.* & *a.* washer (-ing), cleaner (-ing). **II.** *m.* (art.) burnisher. **III.** *f.* washing machine (called also **l. mecánica**).

lavadura, *f.* wash, washing; composition for dressing glove leather; slops.

lavaje, *m.* washing of wools.

lavajo, *m.* drinking pool for cattle; morass.

lavamanos, *m.* washstand; lavatory.

lavamiento, *m.* washing, ablution.

lavanco, *m.* a kind of wild duck.

lavandera, *f.* laundress, washerwoman.

lavandería, *f.* laundry.

lavandero, *m.* launderer, laundryman.

lavaplatos, *n.* dishwasher.

lavar, *va.* to wash; lave, launder; (mas.) to whitewash; (art) to paint in water colors; to purify.

lavativa, *f.* clyster, enema, injection; syringe; vexation, annoyance; bore.

lavatorio, *m.* lavation, washing; lavatory; washstand; (pharm.) lotion; (eccl.) maundy.

lavazas, *f. pl.* foul water, slops.

lave, *m.* washing of ores in mines.

lavotear, *va. & vr.* (coll.) to wash hurriedly.

lavoteo, *m.* hurried washing.

laxación, *f.* **laxamiento,** *m.* laxation, laxity, laxness, loosening.

laxante, *n. & a.* loosener (-ing); laxative.

laxar, *va.* to loosen; to soften.

laxativo, va, *n. & a.* laxative; lenitive.

laxidad, laxitud, *f.* laxity, laxness.

laxo, xa, *a.* lax, slack.

lay, *m.* (poet.) lay, ballad.

laya, *f.* (agr.) spade, spud; quality, kind, class.

layador, *m.* spadesman.

layar, *va.* (agr.) to spade.

lazada, *f.* bowknot; (sew.) bow; true-lover's knot.

lazador, *m.* lassoer.

lazar, *va.* to lasso, capture with a lasso.

lazareto, *m.* lazaretto; pesthouse.

lazarillo, *m.* blind person's guide.

lazarino, na. I. *a.* leprous; lazarlike, lazarly. **II.** *n.* lazar, leper.

lazo, *m.* (sew.) bow, loop, true-lover's knot; snare (for game); trap or snare (for persons); lasso, lariat; slipknot; tie, bond; (arch.) knot or ornament.—*pl.* (danc.) figures.—**l. escurridizo,** running knot.

lazulita, *f.* lazulite, lapis lazuli.

le, *dative case of* ÉL, ELLA: *accusative case of* ÉL: to him, to her, to it (*¿qué le dió Vd.?* what did you give to him (or to her)? *¿qué le añadió Vd.?* what did you add to it?) accusative case of ÉL: him (*ayer le ví,* I saw him yesterday). (Often improperly app. to inanimate objects.)

leal, *a.* loyal.—**lealmente,** *adv.* loyally.

lealtad, *f.* loyalty, fidelity.

lebrada, *f.* hare fricassee.

lebratico, illo, ito; lebrato; lebratón, *n. dim.* young hare.

lebrel, la, *n.* greyhound (*f.,* greyhound bitch).

lebrero, ra, *a.* hare-hunting, hare (u. a.).

lebrillo, *m.* glazed earthenware tub.

lebrón, *m.* large hare; (coll.) poltroon.

lebroncillo, *m.* young hare.

lebruno, na, *a.* leporine, of the hare kind.

lección, *f.* lesson; tuition; lecture; reading; lection.—**dar una l.,** to say or recite a lesson; to give a lesson.—**echar l.,** to give out or assign a lesson.—**tomar la l.,** to take a lesson.—**tomar una lección a,** to hear a lesson from, to hear (someone's) lesson.

leccionario, *m.* (eccl.) lectionary.

leccioncita, *f. dim.* short lecture or lesson.

leccionista, *n.* private tutor; coach.

lecitina, *f.* (chem.) lecithin.

lecito, *m.* yolk (of an egg).

lectisternio, *m.* lectisternium.

lectivo, va, *a.* lesson or recitation (day, hour).

lector, ra, *n.* reader; lecturer; (eccl.) instructor of the Gospel.

lectorado, *m.* (eccl.) lectorate.—**lectoral. I.** *f.* (eccl.) prebend. **II.** *m.* prebendary.—**lectoría,** *f.* (eccl.) lectureship.

lectura, *f.* reading; lecture; (print.) pica.

lecturita, *f.* (print.) small pica.

lecha, *f.* seminal fluid of fishes; each of the two sacs which contain it.

lechada, *f.* grout; liquid containing finely divided solids in suspension; pulp for making paper.

lechal. I. *a.* sucking; (bot.) lactiferous, milky. **II.** *m.* (bot.) milky juice of plants.

lechar, *a.* nursing; promoting the secretion of milk in female mammals.

lechaza, *f.* = LECHA.

leche, *f.* milk; (bot.) milky juice.—**l. crema,** custard.—**l. de canela,** oil of cinnamon dissolved in wine.—**l. de gallina,** or **de pájaro,** (bot.) common star of Bethlehem.—**l. de tierra,** magnesia.—**l. de (los) viejos,** wine.—**l. quemada,** sweetmeat made from simmered milk.—**estar con la l. en los labios,** to lack experience.—**estar en**

l., to be still green or undeveloped (s. o. fruits and plants); to be calm (s. o. the sea).

lechecillas, *f. pl.* sweetbreads; livers and lights.

lechera. I. *a.* milch (applied to animals). **II.** *f.* milkmaid, dairymaid; milk can; milk pot, milk ewer.

lechería, *f.* cow house, dairy.

lechero, ra. I. *a.* milky. **II.** *m.* milkman.

lecheron, *m.* milk pail, milk vessel; flannel wrap for newborn infants.

lechetrezna, *f.* (bot.) spurge.

lechigada, *f.* breed, litter; gang of ruffians.

lechín, *m.* variety of olive tree and the rich olive it yields; (vet.) tumor in horses.

lechino, *m.* (vet.) tent; small tumor.

lecho, *m.* bed, couch; lay, litter; bed of a river; tier, row; layer, stratum; foundation, base.

lechón, na, *n.* sucking pig; pig.

lechoncico, illo, ito, *m. dim.* very young pig.

lechoso, sa. I. *a.* (bot.) having a milky juice. **II.** *m.* (S. A.) (bot.) papaw tree. **III.** *f.* papaw.

lechuga, *f.* (bot.) lettuce; (sew.) frill.

lechugado, da, *a.* lettucelike.

lechuguero, ra, *n.* seller of lettuce.

lechuguilla, *f. dim.* small lettuce; frill, ruff.

lechuguina, *f.* (coll.) stylish young lady.

lechuguino, *m.* lettuce sprout; plot of small lettuces; (coll.) dandy, dude.

lechuza, *f.* (orn.) owl; barn owl.

lechuzo, za. I. *a.* suckling (mule colt). **II.** *n.* bill collector;' summons server; owl-faced person.

ledamente, *adv.* (poet.) merrily, cheerfully.

ledo, da, *a.* (poet.) gay, merry, cheerful, glad.

leer, *va.* to read; to lecture, instruct.

lega, *f.* (eccl.) lay sister.

legacía, *f.* legateship; message intrusted to a legate; province and duration of a legateship.

legación, *f.* legation, embassy; legateship.

legado, *m.* (law) legacy; deputy, ambassador, legate; commander of a Roman legion.—**l. a látere,** (eccl.) Pope's legate.

legador, *m.* laborer who ties the feet of sheep for shearing.

legadura, *f.* tie; binding cord or strap.

legajo, *m.* file, docket, bundle of papers.

legal, *a.* legal, lawful; loyal, true, faithful.

legalidad, *f.* legality, lawfulness.

legalización, *f.* legalization.—**legalizar,** *va.* to legalize.—**legalmente,** *adv.* legally, lawfully; loyally.

legamente, *adv.* ignorantly.

légamo, *n.* mud, silt.—**legamoso, sa,** *a.* silty.

legaña, *f.* gummy secretion of the eyes.

legañoso, sa, *a.* blear-eyed.

legar, *va.* (pret. LEGUÉ: subj. LEGUE) to depute, to send as a legate; (law) to bequeath.

legatario, ria, *n.* (law) legatee.

legenda, *f.* (eccl.) legend, history of saints.

legendario, ria. I. *a.* legendary. **II.** *m.* legendary, book of legends.

legible, *a.* legible, readable.

legiblemente, *adv.* legibly.

legión, *f.* legion.—**legionario, ria,** *n. & a.* legionary.

legislación, *f.* legislation.—**legislador, ra,** *n. & a.* legislator (-ing, -ive); lawmaker (-ing).—**legislar,** *va.* to legislate.—**legislativo, va,** *a.* legislative, lawmaking.

legislatura, *f.* legislature; term of a legislature.

legista, *n.* legist; lawyer; law student.

legítima, *f.* (law) legitime.—**legitimación,** *f.* legitimation.—**legítimamente,** *adv.* legitimately, lawfully.—**legitimar,** *va.* to legitimate, legalize.—**legitimidad,** *f.* legitimacy, legality.

legitimista, *n. & a.* legitimist (-ic).

legítimo, ma, *a.* legitimate, lawful; genuine.

lego, ga. I. *a.* lay, laic; ignorant. **II.** *m.* layman; lay brother or friar.

legón, *m.* (agr.) hoe.

legra, *f.* (surg.) periosteotome.

legración, legradura, *f.* (surg.) periosteotomy.

---

legrar, *va.* (surg.) to perform periosteotomy on.
legua, *f.* league (measure of length).—**a l., a la l., a leguas, de cien leguas, de muchas leguas** or **desde media l.,** very far, at a great distance.
leguario, ria, *a.* league (u. a., as *poste leguario*, league post).
leguleyo, *m.* petty lawyer, pettifogger.
legumbre, *f.* pulse, vegetables, garden stuff.
leguminoso, sa, *a.* (bot.) leguminous.
leíble, *a.* legible, readable.
leído, da, *pp. & a.* well-read, well-informed.—**l. y escribido,** (coll. and contempt.) affecting learning.
leila, *f.* a Moorish dance.
leima, *m.* (mus.) limma.
lejanía, *f.* distance, remoteness; remote place.
lejano, na, *a.* distant, far.
lejas, *a. pl.*—**l. tierras,** far-away lands.
lejía, *f.* lye; (coll.) severe reprimand, dressing down.
lejío, *m.* (among dyers) lye.
lejísimos, *adv.* very far away.
lejitos, *adv. dim.* rather far.
lejos. I. *adv.* far.—**a lo l.,** in the distance, at a great distance, far off, far away.—**d. l., desde l.,** from afar. **II.** *m.* perspective, distant view; background; resemblance.
lejuelos, *adv. dim.* at a little distance.
leilili, *m.* war whoop of the Moors.
lelo, la. I. *a.* stupid, dull. **II.** *n.* ninny.
lema, *m.* argument, summary; theme; motto, device; (math.) lemma.
lemanita, *f.* (min.) jade.
lemnáceo, a. I. *a.* (bot.) lemnaceous. **II.** *f. pl.* Lemnaceae.
lemniscata, *f.* (geom.) lemniscate.
lemosín, na. I. *a.* Languedocian. **II.** *m.* Languedocian; Provençal, langue d'oc.
lemure, *m.* (zool.) lemur.
lemures, *m. pl.* lemures; ghosts, apparitions.
lemurias, *f. pl.* Lemuria, feast of the lemures.
lemúrido, da. I. *n. & a.* (zool.) lemur. **II.** *m. pl.* Lemuridæ.
len, *a.* soft, flossy (thread or silk).
lena, *f.* spirit, vigor.
lencera, *f.* woman who deals in linen; wife of a linen draper.
lencería, *f.* linen goods; linen-draper's shop; linen hall; linen room; linen trade.
lencero, ra, *n.* linen draper, linen merchant.
lendel, *m.* track; mill horse.
lendrera, *f.* close comb for taking out nits.
lendrero, *m.* place full of nits.
lendroso, sa, *a.* nitty, full of nits.
lene, *a.* soft (to the touch); sweet, kind, pleasant; light, not heavy.
lengua, *f.* (anat.) tongue; language; information, advice; clapper of a bell.—**l. canina=** L. DE PERRO.—**l. cerval,** (bot.) hart's-tongue.—**l. de buey,** (bot.) bugloss, alkanet.—**l. del agua,** at the edge of the water.—**l. de oc,** langue d'oc.—**l. de perro,** (bot.) hound's-tongue.—**l. de tierra,** strip of land running out into the sea.—**l. de vaca,** sanseviera, cordy-line.—**l. madre,** or **matriz,** mother tongue.—**l. muerta,** dead language.—**l. sabia,** classical language.—**l. santa,** Hebrew.—**l. viperina,** viperous tongue.—**l. viva,** living, or modern, language.—**con la l. de un palmo,** or **con un palmo de l.,** with great anxiety or eagerness.—**de l. en l.,** from mouth to mouth.—**hacerse lenguas,** to speak in praise.—**írsele a uno la l.,** to let out something one did not wish to say, to give one's self away.—**morderse la lengua,** to hold one's tongue.—**to control one's self.**—**no morderse la l.,** not to mince words, to speak out.—**tener en la l.,** or **en la punta de la l.,** to have at one's tongue's end.
lenguado, *m.* (icht.) sole, flounder.
lenguaje, *m.* language; speech; parlance; vernacular tongue; style.
lenguaraz, lenguaz, *a.* long-tongued, free-tongued; garrulous, loquacious.
lengüecica, illa, ita, *f. dim.* small tongue.

lengüeta, *f. dim.* small tongue; (anat.) epiglottis; barb; (mus.) languette; needle of a balance; (b. b.) cutting knife; (mech.) feather, wedge, tongue, bit, bore, awl; catch of a trap or snare; (arch.) buttress; moulding.
lengüetada, *f.* act of licking.
lengüetería, *f.* reedwork of an organ.
lengüezuela, *f. dim.* small tongue.
lengüilargo, ga, *a.* (coll.) = LENGUARAZ.
lenidad, *f.* lenity, mildness.—**lenificar,** *va.* to soften.—**lenificativo, va,** *a.* mollifying, softening.
lenitivo, va. I. *a.* lenitive, assuaging; lenient. **II.** *m.* emollient; mitigator.
lenocinio, *m.* pimping, pandering.
lentamente, *adv.* slowly; lingeringly.
lente. I. *m.* or *f.* (opt.) lens; monocle. **II.** *m. pl.* eyeglasses.
lentecer, *vn.* to grow soft or tender.
lenteja, *f.* (bot.) lentil; disk of a pendulum.—**l. de agua,** (bot.) gibbous duckweed.
lentejuela, *f.* spangle.
lenticular, *a.* lenticular.
lentiscal, *m.* thicket of mastic trees.
lentisco, *m.* (bot.) mastic tree, lentiscus.
lentitud, *f.* slowness, sluggishness.
lento, ta, *a.* slow, sluggish, tardy, heavy; glutinous; (mus.) lento.
lentor, *m.* (pharm.) viscidity.
lenzuelo, *m.* (agr.) sheet for carrying straw.
leña, *f.* firewood, kindling wood; (coll.) drubbing, beating.—**echar l. al fuego,** to foment discord.—**llevar l. al monte,** to carry coals to Newcastle.
leñador, ra, *n.* woodman (-woman), woodcutter; dealer in kindling wood.
leñame, *m.* wood; provision of kindling wood.
leñatero, ra, *n.* = LEÑADOR.
leñazo, *m.* cudgeling.
leñera, *f.* woodshed, wood bin.
leñero, *m.* wood dealer; logman.
leño, *m.* log; timber; (naut.) ancient galley; (poet.) ship, vessel; (coll.) dull, thick-witted person.
leñoso, sa, *a.* woody, ligneous.
Leo, *m.* (ast.) Leo.
león, *m.* (zool.) lion; (ent.) ant lion; (rept.) boa.—**l. marino,** sea lion.—**el L.,** (astr.) Leo.
leona, *f.* lioness; brave, undaunted woman.
leonado, da, *a.* lion-colored, tawny.
leoncico, illo, ito, *m.* whelp of a lion.
leonera, *f.* cage or den of lions; (coll.) gambling den.—**leonero,** *m.* keeper of lions; master of a gambling house.
leonés, sa, *a.* of or belonging to Leon.
leónica, *f.* (vet.) vein under the tongue.
leonina, *f.* leontiasis, a leprous affection.
leonino, na. I. *a.* leonine; (law) one-sided, unfair; (poet.) leonine (verse). **II.** *f.* (med.) leontiasis.
leontina, *f.* (jew.) watch chain.
leopardo, *m.* leopard.
leopoldina, *f.* (jew.) fob chain; Spanish helmet.
Lepe, *m.*—**saber más que L.,** to be very smart and shrewd.
lépero, ra, *n.* (Mex.) one of the rabble.
lepidio, *m.* (bot.) peppergrass.
lepidolita, *f.* (min.) lepidolite.
lepidóptero, ra. I. *a.* (ent.) lepidopterous. **II.** *m. pl.* Lepidóptera.
lepisma, *f.* (ent.) lepisma; bristletail, silver fish.
lepórido, da. I. *a.* (zool.) relating to the Leporidæ (hares and rabbits). **II.** *m. pl.* Leporidæ.
leporino, na, *a.* harelike.
lepra, *f.* leprosy.—**leprosería,** *f.* lepers' lazaretto.
leproso, sa. I. *a.* leprous. **II.** *n.* leper.
leptocardio, dia. I. *n. & a.* (zool.) leptocardian. **II.** *m. pl.* Leptocardii.
lercha, *f.* reed for hanging fish and birds.
lerda, *f.* (vet.) = LERDÓN.
lerdamente, *adv.* slowly, heavily.
lerdo, da, *a.* slow, heavy; dull, obtuse.
lerdón, *m.* (vet.) tumor in a horse's pastern.

les, *pers. pron. dative case* of ELLOS, ELLAS: to them, them (indirect object): *les di pan,* I gave them bread; *les hablé,* I spoke to them.

lesbio, bia, *a.* Lesbian, of Lesbos.

lesión, *f.* lesion, wound, injury; damage, wrong.

lesivo, va, *a.* prejudicial, injurious.

lesna, *f.* awl. *V.* LEZNA.

lesnordeste, *m.* (naut.) east-northeast wind.

leso, sa, *a.* wounded, hurt, damaged; perverted. —**l. majestad,** lese majesty.

leste, *m.* (naut.) east wind, east.

lesueste, *m.* (naut.) east-southeast wind.

letal, *a.* mortal, deadly, lethal.

letame, *m.* mud for fertilizing.

letanía, *f.* (eccl.) litany; (coll.) list of things.—*pl.* supplicatory procession.

letárgico, ca, *a.* lethargic.

letargo, *m.* lethargy, drowsiness.

letargoso, sa, *a.* causing lethargy.

leteo, a, *a.* (poet.) Lethean.

letificante, *a.* exhilarating, invigorating.

letificar, *va.* to gladden, cheer; to invigorate.

letífico, ca, *a.* cheering, bringing joy.

letra, *f.* letter, character of the alphabet; hand, chirography; (print.) type; motto, inscription; literal meaning; (poet.) a kind of rondeau; words of a song.—*pl.* letters, learning; the learned professions.—**l. abierta,** (com.) open credit.—**l. borrosa,** illegible writing.—**l. cursiva,** running hand.—**l. de caja alta,** (print.) upper case, capital. —**l. de caja baja,** (print.) lower case, small letter. —**l. de cambio,** (com.) draft, bill of exchange.—**l. de mano,** handwriting, handwritten letter.—**l. de molde,** print, printed letter.—**l. de tortis,** Gothic type.—**l. gótica,** Gothic characters.—**l. historiada,** adorned capital letter.—**l. itálica,** (print.) italic.—**l. menuda,** fine (small) writing or print; (coll.) artfulness, cunning, adroitness.—**letras remisorias,** judge's orders transferring a cause to another court.—**a la l.,** to the letter, literally. —**tener mucha l.,** to be very artful and cunning.

letrado, da. I. *a.* learned, erudite;(coll.)vain, presumptuous. **II.** *m.* lawyer, advocate, counselor. —**a lo l.,** like a lawyer. **III.** *f.* (coll.) lawyer's wife.

letrero, *m.* sign; label, placard, poster; legend.

letrilla, *f. dim.* small letter; (mus.) rondelet.

letrina, *f.* privy, water-closet.

letrón. I. *m. aug.* large letter. **II.** *m. pl.* placards posted at the doors of churches.

letuario, *m.* a kind of marmalade.

leucina, *f.* (chem.) leucine.

leucocitemia, *f.* (med.) leucocythemia.

leucocito, *m.* leucocyte, white blood corpuscle.

leucoma, *m.* (med.) leucoma, albugo.

leucomaína, *f.* (chem.) leucomaine.

leucorrea, *f.* (med.) leucorrhoea, whites.

leudar. I. *va.* to leaven. **II.** *vr.* to yeast.

leudo, da, *a.* fermented, leavened.

leva, *f.* (naut.) act of weighing anchor; (mil.) levy, press; (mech.) cam; vane (of a water wheel); (naut.) swell of the sea.—*pl.* tricks, artful devices.

levada, *f.* moving silkworm; (fenc.) salute or flourish with the foil.

levadero, ra, *a.* to be collected or demanded.

levadizo, za, *a.* that can be lifted or raised, as a drawbridge.

levador, *m.* in paper mills, piler; (mech.) cam, cog, tooth.

levadura, *f.* ferment, leaven, yeast, barm; (carp.) sawed-off plank.

levantadamente, *adv.* highly, loftily.

levantado, da, *pp. & a.* raised, elevated, lofty.

levantador, ra, *n.* one who raises or lifts up; disturber, rioter; mutineer.

levantamiento, *m.* elevation, raising; sublimity; insurrection, revolt, uprising; settlement of accounts; survey.—**l. de planos,** surveying.

levantar. I. *va.* to raise; to lift, heave, pick up; to erect, build; set up; to rouse, excite, stir up; to impute or attribute falsely; to start (game); to cut (the cards); to cause, occasion; to begin; to stand up; to start suddenly (as game).—**l. acta,** to draw up and execute an affidavit or certificate.—**l. bandera,** to rise in insurrection, to rebel.—**l. (la) casa,** to break up housekeeping.—**l. (la) cabeza,** to retrieve one's losses, to get on one's feet; to take courage.—**l. con,** to take unlawful possession of, to get away with.—**l. el plano de,** to survey.—**l. falso testimonio,** to bear false witness, to accuse falsely.—**l. la mesa,** to clear the table.—**l. planos,** to survey. **II.** *vr.* to rise, get up.

levante, *m.* Levant, east; east wind.—**estar de l.,** to be ready to depart.

levantino, na, *a.* Levantine.

levantisco, ca, *a.* turbulent, restless; Levantine.

levar. I. *va.* (naut.) to weigh (anchor).—**l. anclas,** to weigh anchor. **II.** *vr.* to set sail.

leve, *a.* light; of little weight; trifling; slight.

levedad, *f.* lightness, levity; inconstancy.

levemente, *adv.* lightly, gently; venially.

leviatán, *m.* leviathan.

levigación, *f.* levigation, elutriation

levigar, *va.* to levigate, to elutriate.

levirato, *m.* levirate.

levita. I. *m.* Levite; deacon **II.** *f.* frock coat, Prince-Albert coat.

levítico, ca. I. *a.* Levitical; priestly. **II.** *m.* (L-) Leviticus; (coll.) ceremonial at a festival.

levitón, *m.* greatcoat like a frock coat.

léxico, *m.* lexicon.—**lexicografía,** *f.* lexicography. —**lexicográfico,ca,** *a.* lexicographic.—**lexicógrafo,** *m.* lexicographer.—**lexicología,** *f.* lexicology.— **lexicológico, ca,** *a.* lexicological.—**lexicólogo,** *m.* lexicologist.—**lexicón,** *m.* = LÉXICO.

ley, *f.* law; rule of action; loyalty, faithful attachment; fineness (of coins, bullion, etc.); legal standard of quality, weight, or measure; precept; rules and regulations.—*pl.* law in general, jurisprudence, study and profession of the law.— **l. antigua,** law of Moses.—**l. caldaria,** hot-water ordeal.—**l. de la trampa,** trickery, fraud.—**l. del embudo,** oppressive law; one-sided agreement; severity for others, indulgence for ourselves. —**l. del talión,** lex talionis, law of retaliation. —**l. escrita,** revealed law, decalogue.—**l. sálica,** Salic law.—**a la l.,** with propriety and neatness.— **a l. de caballero, or de cristiano,** on the word of a gentleman or Christian.—**a toda l.,** perfectly, according to rule.—**de buena l.,** sterling.—**de mala l.,** disreputable; crooked; low, base.

leyenda, *f.* reading; legend; superscription, inscription; device, motto.

leyente, *n. & a.* reader (-ing).

lezda, *f.* ancient tax on merchandise.

lezna, *f.* awl.

lía, *f.* plaited bass rope; husk of pressed grapes.— **estar hecho una l.,** (coll.) to be tipsy.

liar. I. *va.* to tie, bind, do up; (coll.) to embroil, draw into an entanglement.—**liarlas,** (coll.) to flee, to sneak away; to die, (coll.) to kick the bucket. **II.** *vr.* to enter into concubinage.

liásico, ca. I. *n. & a.* (geol.) Liasic. **II.** *m.* Lias, Liasic.

liaza, *f.* collection of hoops used by coopers.

libación, *f.* libation.

libamen, libamiento, *m.* offering in ancient sacrifices.

libán, *m.* esparto rope.

libar, *va.* to suck, sip; to taste; to perform a libation with.

libatorio, *m.* libatory cup.

libelar, *va.* (law) to petition.

libelático, ca, *a.* retracting, apostatizing.

libelista, *m.* libeler.

libelo, *m.* libel (often called **l. infamatorio**)! (law) petition.—**l. de repudio,** written repudiation, of a wife by her husband; (coll.) discarding, abandoning, giving up.

libélula, *f.* libellula, dragon fly.

líber, *m.* (bot.) bast, liber, or inner bark.

liberación, *f.* liberation; (law) quittance.

liberal, *a.* liberal; quick, brisk; (pol.) liberal.— **artes liberales,** liberal arts.

liberalidad, *f.* liberality, generosity.

liberalismo, *m.* Liberalism; Liberal party.

liberalizar, *va.* to liberalize.

liberalmente, *adv.* liberally, generously, freely.

libérrimo, ma, *a. sup.* most free.

libertad, *f.* liberty, freedom; exemption, privilege, immunity; familiarity; freedom, agility, address; independence, unconventionality; ransom.—**l. de comercio,** free trade.—**l. de conciencia,** or **de cultos,** freedom of worship.—**l. de imprenta,** freedom of the press.—**l. de palabra,** freedom of speech, right of free speech.—**l. provisional,** liberation on bail.

libertadamente, *adv.* freely, impudently.

libertado, da, *pp. & a.* bold; free, ungoverned.

libertador, ra, *n. & a.* deliverer (-ing), liberator (-ing).

libertar, *va.* to free, liberate; to exempt, excuse; to acquit; to rid, clear.

libertario, ria, *n. & a.* anarchist (-ic).

liberticida, *m.* liberticide.

libertinaje, *m.* libertinism, licentiousness.

libertino, na. I. *n.* child of a freedman, libertine (in the same sense). **II.** *n. & a.* libertine.

liberto, ta, freedman (-woman).

libídine, *f.* lewdness, lust.

libidinosamente, *adv.* libidinously, lewdly.

libidinoso, sa, *a.* libidinous, lewd, lustful.

libra, *f.* pound (weight, coin). **(L-,** ast.) Libra. —**l. esterlina,** pound sterling.—**l. tornesa,** livre tournois.

libración, *f.* libration.

libraco, libracho, *m.* (coll.) trashy book.

librado, da. I. *n.* drawee. **II.** *a. & pp.* of LIBRAR. —**bien l.,** successful, lucky.—**mal l.,** unsuccessful, unlucky, faring ill or badly.

librador, ra, *n.* deliverer; (com.) drawer of a check or draft; storekeeper of the king's stables; (*m.*) grocer's scoop.

libramiento, *m.* delivery, delivering; warrant, order of payment.

librancista, *m.* (com.) holder of a draft.

libranza, *f.* (com.) draft, bill of exchange.—**l. postal,** money order.

librar. I. *va.* to free, deliver; to exempt; to preserve from ill; to pass (sentence); to issue (a decree); to engage (battle); (com.) to draw. **II.** *vn.* to receive a visitor in the locutory (s. o. nuns); to be delivered (of a child); to expel the placenta.—**l. bien (mal),** to fare well (badly).—**l. en,** to depend on.—**a bien,** or **a buen, l.,** as well as could be expected. **III.** *vr.* (w. **de)** to escape, avoid, be free from, get rid of.

libratorio, *m.* locutory.

libre, *a.* free; uncumbered, unrestrained; independent; vacant; disengaged; clear, open; exempt; innocent, guiltless; single, unmarried; libertine, loose, licentious; impudent; rash, thoughtless; isolated, alone.—**l. a bordo (l. a. b.),** free on board (f. o. b.).—**l. cambio,** free trade.—**l. de derechos,** duty free.—**l. pensador** = LIBREPENSADOR.—**l. pensamiento** = LIBREPENSAMIENTO. —**l. plática,** pratique.

librea, *f.* livery, uniform.

librear, *va.* to weigh or sell by pounds.

librecambista, *n.* free trader.

librejo, *m. dim.* little book; worthless book.

libremente, *adv.* freely; boldly.

librepensador, ra, *n.* freethinker.

librepensamiento, *m.* freethinking, freethought.

librería, *f.* bookstore, bookseller's shop; book trade; library; large collection of books.

libreril, *a.* relating to the book trade.

librero, ra, *n.* bookseller.

libreta, *f.* troy pound; loaf of bread weighing one pound; memorandum book; notebook; (surv.) field book; pass book; bank book.

librete, *m. dim.* small book; foot stove.

libretín, *m. dim.* small book, booklet.

libretista, *n.* librettist.

libreto, *m.* (mus.) libretto.

librillo, ito, *m.* earthen tub; small book of cigarette paper.—**l. de cera,** folded wax taper.—**l. de oro,** gold-leaf book.

libro, *m.* book; (mus.) libretto; (zool.) omasum, or third stomach (of a ruminant).—**l. becerro,** doomsday book.—**l. borrador,** blotter.—**l. copiador,** (com.) letter book.—**l. de actas** = L. DE MINUTAS.—**l. de asiento** = L. DE CUENTAS.—**l. de caja,** cashbook.—**l. de cuentas,** account book.—**l. de facturas,** invoice book.—**l. de memoria,** memorandum book.—**l. de minutas,** minute book. —**l. diario,** (com.) daybook.—**l. en blanco,** blank book.—**l. en folio,** folio book.—**l. mayor,** ledger. —**l. talonario,** check book, stub book.—**l. verde,** (coll.) book for notes about places and persons; also the compiler of such memoranda.

librote, *m. aug.* large book.

licantropía, *f.* (med.) lycanthropy.

licántropo, *a.* lycanthrope.

licaón, *m.* (zool.) lycaon.

liceísta, *n.* member of a lyceum.

licencia, *f.* permission, leave, license; licentiousness; (mil.) furlough; degree of licentiate; (poet.) license.—**l. absoluta,** (mil.) discharge.

licenciadillo, *m.* (coll.) ridiculous little man in clerical robes.

licenciado, da. I. *a. & pp.* licensed; presuming knowledge. **II.** *m.* licentiate; (coll.) university student; (coll.) lawyer; (mil.) discharged soldier.

licenciamiento, *m.* graduation as a licentiate; (mil.) discharge of soldiers.

licenciar. I. *va.* to permit, allow; to license; to licentiate; (mil.) to discharge. **II.** *vr.* to become dissolute; to become a licentiate.

licenciatura, *f.* degree of licentiate; graduation as a licentiate.

licenciosamente, *adv.* licentiously.

licencioso, sa, *a.* licentious, dissolute.

liceo, *m.* lyceum.

licio, cia, *n. & a.* Lycian.

licitación, *f.* auction; bid.—**licitador,** *m.* bidder.

licitamente, *adv.* lawfully, licitly.

licitante, *n.* bidder.

licitar, *va. & vn.* to bid (on, for) at auction or on public works.

lícito, ta, *a.* licit, lawful; just.

licnobio, bia, *n.* lychnobite, one who turns night into day, (coll.) night hawk.

licopodio, *m.* (bot.) lycopodium.

licor, *m.* any liquid; liquor.—**licorera,** *f.* liquor case, bottle case.—**licorería,** *f.* liquor shop; public house, saloon.—**licorista,** *n.* liquor distiller or dealer.—**licoroso, sa,** *a.* generous, spirituous (s. o. wine).

lictor, *m.* lictor, in ancient Rome.

licuable, *a.* liquefiable.—**licuación,** *f.* liquation, liquefaction.—**licuante,** *a.* liquefying.—**licuar,** *va.* to liquefy.—**licuefacción,** *f.* liquefaction.— **licuefactible,** *a.* liquefiable.

lichera, *f.* woollen cover of a bed.

lid, *f.* contest, fight; dispute, argument.

lidia, *f.* battle, fight, contest; bullfight.

lidiadero, ra, *a.* in fighting condition.

lidiador, ra, *n.* combatant; fighter; arguer.

lidiar. I. *vn.* to fight, to content; to struggle. **II.** *va.* to run or fight (bulls).

lidio, dia, *n. & a.* Lydian.

liebrastón, liebrático, liebratón, *m.* young hare, leveret.

liebre, *f.* hare: coward, poltroon.—**coger una l.,** to fall flat.—*p.* (naut.) racks, ribs; deadeyes.

liebrecica, illa, ita, *f. dim.* little hare.

liebrecilla, *f.* (bot.) bluebottle.

liebrezuela, *f. dim.* young or small hare.

liendre, *f.* nit, egg of a louse.—**cascar a uno las liendres,** (slang) to give one a severe drubbing.

lientera, lientería, *f.* (med.) lientery.

lientérico, ca, *a.* lienteric.

liento, ta, *a.* damp, moist.

lienza, *f.* narrow strip of cloth.

lienzo, *m.* linen cloth; (art) canvas; (fort.) curtain; (arch.) face or front of a building; stretch of a wall.—**l. casero,** homespun linen.—**l. crudo,** unbleached linen.—**l. gordo,** coarse linen.

liga, *f.* garter; (bot.) mistletoe; league, coalition, alliance; alloy for gold and silver.

ligación, *f.* joining,, tying; union, mixture.

ligada, *f.* ligature; binding, tying.

ligado, da. I. *a.* & *pp.* tied, bound; leagued, confederate. **II.** *m.* (mus.) legato.

ligadura, *f.* ligature, ligation, binding; subjection; (mus.) ligature, syncopation, tie; (arch.) arcs made by cross timbers; (naut.) seizing, lashing.

ligamaza, *f.* viscosity on some fruits or plants.

ligamen, *m.* spell supposed to cause impotency.

ligamento, *m.* bond, tie; (anat.) ligament.

ligamentoso, sa, *a.* ligamentous, ligamental.

ligamiento, *m.* act of tying or binding; union, concord.

ligar. I. *va.* (*pret.* LIGUÉ: *subj.* LIGUE) to tie, bind, fasten; to alloy; to join, link, knit together; to render impotent by malefic spells. **II.** *vn.* to combine cards of the same suit. **III.** *vr.* to league, join, combine; to bind one's self.

ligazón, *f.* tie, fastening, union, connection, bond; (naut.) futtock timbers.

ligeramente, *adv.* lightly; quickly; slightly.

ligereza, *f.* lightness; swiftness, agility, nimbleness; levity, inconstancy, fickleness.

ligero, ra, *a.* light (as a feather); thin (as gauze); swift, active, nimble, fleet; gay; unsteady, giddy; unimportant, trifling; easily disturbed (as sleep).—**l. de cascos,** feather-brained.—**l. de dedos,** light-fingered.—**a la l.,** lightly, briefly.—**de l.,** rashly; easily.

ligeruelo, la, *a. dim.* early (grapes).

ligio, gia, *a.* liege.

lignario, ria, *a.* ligneous.

lignito, *m.* lignite.

ligua, *f.* (Philip.) battle-axe.

liguano, na, *a.* (Ch.) thick-and-heavy-wool (sheep).

liguilla, *f.* narrow garter.

lígula, *f.* (bot.) ligule.

ligur; ligurino, na, *n.* & *a.* Ligurian.

ligustre, *m.* (bot.) flower of privet.

ligustrino, na, *a.* relating to privet.

ligustro, *m.* (bot.) privet, prim, ligustrum.

lija, *f.* sandpaper; (icht.) dogfish; shark skin, dogfish skin.—**lijar,** *va.* to sandpaper.

lila, *f.* lilac tree; lilac flower lilac color.

lilaila, *f.* bunting; trick, wile; LILILÍ.

liliáceo, a. I. *a.* (bot.) liliaceous. **II.** *f. pl.* Liliaceæ.

lililí, *m.* war whoop of the Moors.

liliputiense, *n.* & *a.* Liliputian.

lima, *f.* (bot.) sweet lime, a variety of citron; (mech.) file; finish, polishing; (arch.) valley (called also **l. hoya**).

limadura, *f.* filing.—*pl.* filings.

limalla, *f.* filings.

limar, *va.* to file; to polish; to touch up.

limatón, *m.* coarse round file, rasp.

limazo, *m.* viscosity, sliminess.

limbo, *m.* limbo; (ast.) limb; limb, graduated circle (of a theodolite, etc.).

limen, *m.* (poet.) = UMBRAL.

limeño, ña, *a.* of or belonging to Lima.

limera, *f.* shopwoman who sells files or LIMAS; (naut.) rudderhole.

limero, *m.* seller of files or LIMAS; (bot.) sweet-lime tree (a variety of citron tree).

limeta, *f.* vial, small bottle.

limitación, *f.* limitation, limit; district.

limitadamente, *adv.* limitedly, finitely.

limitado, da, *pp.* & *a.* limited, short-witted.

limitáneo, nea, *a.* limitary; limitaneous.

limitar, *va.* to limit; to bound; to restrict; to reduce (expense).

límite, *m.* limit; boundary, bound, border.

limítrofe, *a.* bounding; conterminous.

limo, *m.* slime, mud.

limón, *m.* lemon; lemon tree; (Cuba, coast of Colomb., etc.) lime (tree and fruit); (car.) thill or shaft.—**l. mejicano,** lime.

limonada, *f.* lemonade.—**l. de vino,** wine lemonade, sangaree.—**l. purgante,** citrate of magnesia.

limonado, da, *a.* lemon-colored.

limonar, *m.* plantation of lemon trees.

limoncillo, limoncito, *m. dim.* small lemon; lime.

limonero, ra. I. *a.* shaft (horse) in carriages, etc. **II.** *n.* lemon dealer. **III.** *m.* (bot.) lemon tree. **IV.** *f.* (car.) shaft, thill.

limosidad, *f.* sliminess; foul matter between teeth.

limosna, *f.* alms.

limosnero, ra. I. *a.* charitable. **II.** *n.* almoner; (Am.) beggar. **III.** *f.* alms bag or box.

limoso, sa, *a.* slimy, muddy, limose.

limpia, *f.* cleaning, cleansing; dredging.

limpiabarros, *m.* footscraper.

limpiabotas, *m.* bootblack.

limpiachimeneas, *m.* chimney sweeper.

limpiadera, *f.* clothes-brush; comb-brush; plow cleaner.

limpiadientes, *m.* toothpick.

limpiador, ra, *n.* & *a.* cleaner (-ing), cleanser (-ing).—**limpiadura,** *f.* cleaning, cleansing.—*pl.* dirt, rubbish, refuse, waste.

limpiamente, *adv.* cleanly, neatly; purely; sincerely, faithfully.

limpiamiento, *m.* cleansing, cleaning.

limpiaplumas, *m.* penwiper.

limpiar. I. *va.* to clean, cleanse; to purify, clear; (coll.) to steal.—**l. las faltriqueras a uno,** to pick one's pockets; (coll.) to win from one. **II.** *vr.* to clear one's self from imputed guilt.

limpiauñas, *m.* nail cleaner.

límpido, da, *a.* (poet.) limpid, crystal-clear.

limpieza, *f.* cleanness, cleanliness; neatness; purity; integrity, honesty; disinterestedness; purity of blood; correctness, neatness of execution.—**l. de bolsa,** emptiness of the purse.

limpio, pia, *a.* clean; cleanly; limpid; neat, pure, unmingled; free, clear, net; (coll.) penniless, broken.—**en l.,** in substance; clearly.—**poner en l.,** to copy from a rough draft.—**sacar en l.,** PONER EN LIMPIO; to conclude, infer; to make out.

limpión, *m.* hasty cleaning.

lináceo, a. I. *a.* (bot.) linaceous. **II.** *f. pl.* (bot.) Linaceæ.

linaje, *m.* lineage, race; progeny, offspring; class, condition.—**l. humano,** mankind.

linajista, *m.* genealogist, writer of pedigrees.

linajudo, da, *n.* & *a.* boaster (-ing) of noble descent.

lináloe, *m.* (bot.) aloes.

linar, *m.* flax field.

linaria, *f.* (bot.) wild flax, yellow toad flax.

linaza, *f.* (bot.) linseed, flaxseed.

lince. I. *m.* (zool.) lynx; very keen person **II.** *a.* sharp-sighted, keen-sighted, observing.

lincear, *va.* (coll.) to note what is not easily seen.

linceo, a, *a.* lyncean; sharp, keen.

linchamiento, *m.* lynching.

linchar, *va.* to lynch.

linches, *m. pl.* (Mex.) fiber saddlebags.

lindamente, *adv.* prettily, neatly, elegantly.

lindante, *a.* bordering, contiguous.

lindar, *vn.* to be contiguous, to border, abut.

linde, *m.* landmark; boundary, limit.

lindero, ra. I. *a.* contiguous, bordering. **II.** *m.* limit, boundary.

lindeza, *f.* neatness, elegance, prettiness.—*pl.* pretty things; (iron.) improprieties, insults.

lindo, da. I. *a.* pretty, neat, fine; complete, perfect. **II.** *m.* beau, coxcomb, minion.—**de lo l.,** perfectly, wonderfully; greatly.

lindón, *m.* (agr.) frame or bar for hanging asparagus, etc.

lindura, *f.* LINDEZA; beauty, beautiful woman; beautiful thing.

línea, *f.* line; lineage, progeny; equator; border; boundary, limit; class, order; (fort.) trench or intrenchment; (mil.) rank, file; line, twelfth part of an inch.—**l. de agua,** or **de flotación,** (naut.) water line.—**l. de colimación,** or **de fe,**

(surv.) line of collimation.—**l. de (la) tierra,** (geom.) ground line.—**l. de vapores,** steamship line.—**l. equinoccial,** equator.—**l. férrea,** railway.—**en l.,** in a line.

lineal, a. lineal, linear.

lineamento, or **lineamiento,** m. lineament, feature.

linear. I. va. to draw lines on, to form with lines. **II.** a. lineal, linear.

líneo, a, a. (bot.) linaceous.

lineotipia, f. = LINOTIPIA.

linfa, f. lymph; (poet.) water.

linfático, ca, a. lymphatic.

linfatismo, m. (med.) lymphatism.

lingote, m. (found.) ingot; pig, bloom, billet.

lingual, a. lingual.

linguete, m. pawl; ratchet.

lingüista, n. linguist.—**lingüística,** f. linguistics—**lingüístico, ca,** a. linguistic.

linimento, linimiento, m. (pharm.) liniment.

linio, m. row of plants. V. LIÑO.

lino, m. (bot.) flax; linen; sail-cloth, canvas; (poet.) sail.

linóleo, m. linoleum.

linón, m. lawn.

linotipia, f. linotype.

linotipista, n. linotypist.

linotipo, m. linotype.

lintel, m. lintel of a door. V. DINTEL.

linterna, f. lantern; lamp, light (on a train, car, etc.); (mech.) lantern wheel; (arch.) lantern.— **l. delantera,** or **de adelante,** (r. w., aut.) front light.—**l. mágica,** magic lantern.—**l. sorda,** dark lantern.—**l. trasera,** or **de atrás,** (r. w., aut.) back, or rear, light.

linternazo, m. blow with a lantern or other instrument.—**linternero, ra,** n. lantern maker.

linternón, m. aug. big lantern; (naut.) poop lantern.

liño, m. row of trees or plants; ridge between furrows.

liñuelo, m. rope, cord.

lío, m. bundle, parcel, pack; (coll.) imbroglio, scrape; intrigue, conspiracy.—**armar un l.,** to tangle up, to create difficulties or embarrassment.

liorna, f. (coll.) uproar, hubbub, confusion.

lipemanía, f. (med.) melancholia, lypemania.

lipemaníaco, ca, a. (med.) melancholic.

lipes, lipis, f. (chem.) blue vitriol, copper sulphate.

lipoma, m. (med.) lipoma, liparocele.

lipotimia, f. (med.) faint, swoon.

liquen, (bot.) lichen.

liquidable, a. liquefiable; (com.) adjustable.

liquidación, f. liquefaction; (com.) liquidation, settlement.

liquidador, ra. I. a. liquefying. **II.** n. liquefier; liquidator.

liquidámbar, m. liquidambar.

liquidamente, adv. in a liquid manner.

liquidar. I. va. to liquefy; (com.) to liquidate, settle. **II.** vr. to liquefy.

liquidez, f. liquidness, fluidity.

líquido, da. I. a. liquid; evident, clear; (com.) net. **II.** m. liquid; (com.) balance, net profit.— **l. imponible,** amount of assessment for tax collection. **III.** f. (gram.) liquid consonant.

lira, f. (mus.) lyre; (poet.) lyric poem; (**L-,** ast.) Lyra.

lirado, da, a. lyre-shaped.

liria, f. birdlime.

lírico, ca. I. a. lyric, lyrical. **II.** f. lyric poetry.

lirio, m. (bot.) lily.—**l. blanco** = AZUCENA.—**l. de agua,** calla lily.—**l. de Florencia,** orris, Florentine iris.—**l. de los valles,** lily of the valley. —**l. hediondo,** gladwin.

lirón, m. (zool.) dormouse; (bot.) alisma; (coll.) sleepy head; (naut.) jackscrew.

lirismo, m. abuse of lyricisms.

lirondo, da, a. pure, clean, neat.

lis, f. (bot.) lily; flower-de-luce, iris.

lisa, f. smooth stone for polishing paper; (icht.) a river fish.

lisamente, adv. smoothly, plainly.—**lisa y llanamente,** openly and frankly; simply.

lisbonense, lisbonés, sa, a. of or belonging to Lisbon.

lisera, f. (fort.) berm.

lisiado, da, pp. & a. lamed, injured, hurt.

lisiar, va. to lame, hurt, cripple, injure.

lisimaquia, f. (bot.) loosestrife.

liso, sa, a. smooth, even, flat; plain, unadorned; plain-dealing.—**l. y llano,** plain, clear, evident.

lisonja, f. flattery; (her.) lozenge.

lisonjado, da, a. (her.) lozenged; rhombic.

lisonjeador, ra, n. & a. flatterer (-ing).

lisonjear, va. to flatter; to delight, please.

lisonjeramente, adv. flatteringly.

lisonjero, ra. I. m. & f. flatterer. **II.** a. flattering; pleasing, agreeable; complimentary.

lista, f. list; catalogue; slip of paper; shred of linen; strip of cloth; selvage; stripe, band; (law) docket; (mil.) roll, muster.—**l. del equipaje,** muster book of a ship's company.—**l. de comidas,** or **de platos,** bill of fare, menu.—**pasar l.,** to call the roll.

listadillo, m. (Am.) striped gingham.

listado, da, pp. & a. striped.—**listar,** va. to enter in a list.—**listeado, da,** a. = LISTADO.

listel, m. (arch.) fillet, listel, tringle.

listo, ta, a. ready; quick, prompt; clever.

listón, m. ribbon; ferret, tape; (carp.) lath, cleat, strip; (arch.) listel, fillet.—pl. (naut.) battens.

listonado, da. I. a. (carp.) made of laths. **II.** m. laths, lathing.

listonar, va. (carp.) to batten, to lath.

listonería, f. parcel of ribbons, tapes, and inkles; ribbon store; ribbon manufactory.

listonero, ra, n. ribbon maker.

listura, f. smartness, quickness, cleverness.

lisura, f. smoothness, evenness, flatness; sincerity, candor.

lita, f. tongue worm in dogs.

litación, f. sacrificing.

litagogo, ga, a. (med.) lithagogue; (surg.) lithontriptic.

litar, va. to sacrifice to the Deity.

litarge, litargirio, m. litharge.

lite, f. (law) lawsuit.

litera, f. litter; (naut.) berth.

literal, a. literal.—**literalmente,** adv. literally.

literario, ria, a. literary.

literato, ta. I. a. literary. **II.** n. litterateur, literary person, writer.

literatura, f. literature.

literero, ra, n. litter maker, seller, or driver.

litiasis, f. (med.) lithiasis, gravel.

litigación, f. litigation.—**litigante,** n. & a. (law) litigator (-ing), litigant.—**litigar,** va. (pret. LITIGUÉ: subj. LITIGUE) (law) to litigate; to contend, dispute.—**litigio,** m. litigation, lawsuit; dispute, contest.—**litigioso, sa,** a. litigious, contentious.

litina, f. (chem.) lithia.—**litio,** m. lithium.

litis, f. (law) lawsuit.

litisconsorte, n. (law) associate in a lawsuit.

litiscontestación, f. (law) answer to an allegation.

litisexpensas, f. pl. (law) costs of suit.

litispendencia, f. state of a pending lawsuit.

litocálamo, m. petrified or fossil reed.

litoclasa, f. (geol.) fissure in a rock.

litocola, f. lithocolla, lapidary's cement.

litófago, ga, a. rock-boring (s. o. mollusks).

litofotografía, etc., f. = FOTOLITOGRAFÍA.

litogenesia, f. (geol.) lithogenesy.

litoglifia, f. engraving on stone.

litografía, f. lithography.—**litografiar,** va. to lithograph.—**litográfico, ca,** a. lithographic.— **litógrafo,** m. lithographer.

litología, f. lithology.—**litológico, ca,** a. lithological.—**litólogo,** m. lithologist.

litoral. I. a. littoral. **II.** m. littoral, coast,shore.

litoscopio, *m.* lithoscope.
litote, *f.* (rhet.) litotes.
litotomía, *f.* (surg.) lithotomy.
litotricia, *f.* (surg.) lithotrity.
litotritor, *m.* (surg.) lithotrite.
litrarico, a, *a.* (bot.) lythraceous.
litro, *m.* liter, litre, unit of capacity.
lituano, na, *n.* & *a.* Lithuanian.
lituo, *m.* (mus.) an ancient military instrument; lituus, augur's staff.
liturgia, *f.* (eccl.) liturgy.
litúrgico, ca, *a.* liturgical, liturgic.
livianamente, *adv.* licentiously; lightly; superficially.
liviandad, *f.* lightness, want of weight; levity, frivolity; lewdness.
liviano, na. **I.** *a.* light (not heavy); inconstant, fickle; frivolous; slight; lewd. **II.** *m.* leading jackass.—*pl.* lungs.
lividez, *f.* lividness.—**lívido, da,** *a.* livid; black and blue.
livonio, nia, *n.* & *a.* Livonian.
lixiviar, *va.* (chem.) to lixiviate, leach.
liza, *f.* (icht.) skate; jousting field, lists.
lizo, *m.* warp-thread; heddle.
lo. **I.** *art. neut.* (before an *a.*) the, things (*lo bello,* the beautiful; *lo barato,* cheap things). As an intensifier before an *a.*, it is equivalent to the corresponding English noun with an intensifying *a.* (*lo triste que estaba,* the great sadness in which he was, or, simply, his great sadness; *lo claro de esta declaración,* the great clearness of this declaration). Often used as an *adv.* in the sense of "so," and need not always be translated (*él es rico, pero yo no lo soy,* he is rich, but I am not [so]).—**l. que,** what, that which. **II.** *neut.* accusative of ELLO: it, that(*lo haré,* I shall do it, I shall do that). **III.** *pers. pron. accusative of* ÉL: him, it.
loa, *f.* praise; prologue of a play; short dramatic panegyric.
loable, *a.* laudable, praiseworthy.
loablemente, *adv.* laudably, commendably.
loador, ra, *n.* praiser, eulogizer.
loán, *m.* (Philip.) land measure (2.79 ares).
loanda, *f.* a kind of scurvy.
loar, *va.* to praise, eulogize.
loba. **I.** *f.* she-wolf; ridge between furrows; long gown worn by clergymen and students. **II.** *m.* (vet.) a morbid swelling.
lobado, da, *a.* (zool. and bot.) lobate.
lobanillo, *m.* wen, encysted tumor.
lobato, *m.* wolf cub, wolfkin.
lobeliáceo, a. **I.** *a.* (bot.) lobeliaceous. **II.** *f. pl.* Lobeliaceæ.
lobero, ra. **I.** *a.* relating to wolves; wolfish. **II.** *f.* thicket where wolves make their lair.
lobezno, *m.* wolf cub; wolfkin.
lobina, *f.* (icht.) striped bass.
lobo, *m.* wolf; (anat. and bot.) lobe; (icht.) loach; (coll.) intoxication, inebriation; iron instrument for defending or scaling walls.—**l. marino,** seal.
lobo, ba, *n.* (Mex.) half-breed.
loboso, sa, *a.* full of wolves.
lóbrego, ga, *a.* murky, obscure; sad, lugubrious.
lobreguecer. **I.** *vn.* to grow dark. **II.** *va.* to make dark.—**lobreguez,** *f.* obscurity, darkness.
lobulado, da, *a.* (zool. and bot.) lobulate.
lóbulo, *m.* lobe or lobule.
lobuno, na, *a.* wolfish.
locación, *f.* (law) lease.—**l. y conducción,** agreement to let.
locador, ra, *n.* (Am.) = ARRENDADOR.
local. **I.** *a.* local. **II.** *m.* place, site, premises.
localidad, *f.* locality, location.—**localización,** *f.* localization.—**localizar,** *va.* to localize.
locamente, *adv.* madly; immoderately; fondly.
locatario, ria, *n.* (Am.) = ARRENDATARIO.
loción, *f.* lotion, wash.
loco, ca. **I.** *a.* mad, insane, crazy; abundant, plentiful, excessive.—**l. rematado,** stark mad.—**a tontas y a locas,** recklessly, thoughtlessly, hap-

hazard.—**estar l. de contento,** (coll.) to be mad with joy. **II.** *n.* insane person, lunatic.
locomoción, *f.* (phys.) locomotion.
locomotor, ra. **I.** *a.* locomotor, locomotive. **II.** *f.* (r. w.) locomotive.
locomotriz, *a. f.* locomotive.
locomovible, locomóvil, *a.* portable, movable.
locro, *m.* (Am.) a kind of stew.
locuacidad, *f.* loquacity, talkativeness.
locuaz, *a.* loquacious, talkative, garrulous.
locución, *f.* diction; phrase.
locuelo, la. **I.** *n.* madcap, giddy youth. **II.** *f.* peculiar mode of speaking of every person.
loculado, da; locular, *a.* (biol.) locular.
lóculo, *m.* (biol.) loculus.
locura, *f.* madness, insanity; folly.
locutorio, *m.* locutory in monasteries.
locha, *f.*; **loche,** *m.* (icht.) loach.
locho, cha, *a.* (Am., coll.) red-bearded.
lodachar, lodazal, lodazar, *m.* muddy place, quagmire, bog.
lodo, *m.* mud, mire.
lodoñero, *m.* (bot.) lignum-vitæ tree.
lodoso, sa, *a.* muddy, miry.
lofobranquio, quia. **I.** *n.* & *a.* (zool.) lophobranchiate. **II.** *m. pl.* Lophobranchii.
logarítmico, ca, *a.* logarithmic.
logaritmo, *m.* logarithm.
logia, *f.* lodge.
lógica, *f.* logic.—**lógicamente,** *adv.* logically.—**lógico, ca.** **I.** *a.* logical. **II.** *m.* logician.
logogrifo, *m.* logogriph, riddle.
logomaquia, *f.* logomachy.
lograr. **I.** *va.* to gain, obtain; procure; attain; to possess, enjoy; (followed by *inf.*) to succeed in (followed by present participle), to manage. **II.** *vr.* to succeed, be successful.
lograr, *vn.* to borrow or lend at interest.
logrería, *f.* dealing in interest, usury, profiteering.
logrero, ra, *n.* lender at interest, usurer; profiteer.
logro, *m.* gain, profit, benefit; success, accomplishment; attainment; interest; usury.—**dar a l.,** to lend at usurious interest.
loma, *f.* little hill, hillock.
lombarda, *f.* lombard (an ancient gun); (bot.) red cabbage.—**lombardada,** *f.* shot from a lombard gun.—**lombardear,** *va.* to bombard with lombards.—**lombardería,** *f.* battery of lombards.—**lombardero,** *m.* lombard gunman.
lombárdico, ca; lombardo, da, *n.* & *a.* Lombard, belonging to Lombardy.
lombriguera, *f.* hole made by worms; (bot.) southern wormwood.
lombriz, *f.* earthworm.—**l. intestinal,** intestinal worm.—**l. solitaria,** tapeworm.
lomear, *vn.* to yerk or move the loins in a circular manner (s. o. horses).
lomera, *f.* (sad.) main strap of a harness; (b. b.) backing; (arch.) ridge of a roof.
lomillería, *f.* (Am.) shop where harness accessories are made or sold.
lomillo, *m. dim.* small loin; (sew.) cross-stitch; (sad.) cantle.—*pl.* pads of a pack saddle.
lominhiesto, ta, *a.* high-cropped; (coll.) conceited, vain.
lomo, *m.* loin; back of an animal; chine of pork; back of a book or cutting tool; double of a cloth, crease; ridge between furrows.—*pl.* ribs; loins.—**jugar de l.,** to be idle and in good health or condition.—**llevar a l., traer a l.,** to carry on the back.
lomudo, da, *a.* broad-backed.
lona, *f.* canvas.—**l. para hacer velas,** duck-canvas, sailcloth.
loncha, *f.* slab, flagstone; thin slice of meat.
lóndiga, *f.* = ALHÓNDIGA.
londinense, *a.* of London, Londonese.
londrina, *f.* woollen cloth from London.
loneta, *f.* ravens' duck, sailcloth.
longa, *f.* (mus.) long note.
longanimidad, *f.* longanimity, forbearance.
longánimo, ma, *a.* forbearing, magnanimous.

longaniza, f. choice pork sausage.

longar, a.—**panal l.,** honeycomb lengthwise of the hive.

longazo, za, a. aug. very long.

longevidad, f. longevity.

longevo, a. longeval, long-lived.

longirrostro, tra. I. a. (zool.) longirostral. **II.** m. pl. Longirostres.

longísimo, ma, a. sup. of LUENGO; longest.

longitud, f. length; longitude.

longitudinal, a. longitudinal.

longitudinalmente, adv. longitudinally.

longobardo, da, n. & a. Longobard (-ian).

longuera, f. long and narrow strip of land.

longuetas, f. pl. (surg.) bandages.

longuísimo, ma, a. sup. longest.

lonja, f. (com.) exchange; grocer's shop; warehouse, salesroom; (arch.) stoop; slice (of meat); strip; leather strap.

lonjeta, f. dim. small slice; small strap; bower, summerhouse.

lonjista, n. grocer.

lontananza, f. distance; background.—**en l.,** far off, far away, in the distance.

loor, m. (poet.) praise.

lopigia, f. (med.) = ALOPECIA.

loquear, vn. to act the fool, to talk nonsense; to revel, frolic.

loquero, ra. I. n. keeper of a madhouse. **II.** f. madhouse.

loquesco, ca, a. madlike; funny, jesting.

loquillo, illa, ito, ita, a. dim. wild, frisky.

loquios, m. pl. (med.) lochia.

lorantáceo, a. I. a. (bot.) lauraceous. **II.** f. pl. Lauraceæ.

lorcha, f. (China) junk-rigged coaster.

lord, m. (pl. **lores**) lord, English title.

loriga, f. lorica (a cuirass); (car.) nave box.

lorigado, da, a. armed with a lorica.

loriguillo, m. shrub used by dyers.

loro, ra. I. a. tawny, dark brown. **II.** m. (orn.) parrot; (bot.) cherry laurel.

los. I. def. art. m. pl. of ÉL, the. **II.** pers. pron. m. pl. accusative of ELLOS, them. When used with HAY (v. HABER), it is rendered by "some," or not at all (¿hay libros? los hay, are there any books? there are [some]).

losa, f. slab, flagstone; trap made of tiles; gravestone; grave.

losado, m. tiled floor.

losange, losanje, m. (her.) lozenge; rhomb.

losar, va. to tile. V. ENLOSAR.

loseta, losica, illa, ita, f. dim. small slab or flagstone; tile; briquette; small trap.

lote, m. lot; share, part.

lotería, f. lottery; raffle; game lotto.

lotero, ra, n. dealer in lottery tickets.

loto, m. (bot.) lotus; lotus flower; lote tree or nettle tree.

lotófago, ga, a. lotus-eating.

loxodromia, f. (naut.) loxodrome.

loxodrómico, ca, a. (naut.) loxodromic.

loza, f. chinaware; porcelain; crockery.—**ande la l.,** (coll.) noisy mirth and jollity.

lozanamente, adv. luxuriantly; briskly, nimbly.—lozanear, vn. to look fresh and luxuriant.—**lozanía,** f. luxuriance; freshness; vigor, lustiness.—lozano, na, a. luxuriant; sprightly; fresh; brisk, spirited.

lúa, f. esparto glove for cleaning horses; saffron bag; (naut.) lee.

lubricación, f. lubrication.

lubricador, ra, n. & a. lubricator (-ing).

lubricán, m. dawn of day.

lubricante, n. & a. lubricator (-ing).

lubricar, va. to lubricate.

lubricativo, va, a. lubricant, lubricative.

lubricidad, f. lubricity, slipperiness; lewdness.

lúbrico, ca, a. slippery; lubricous; lewd.

lubrificación, lubrificar, etc. (incorrect but common) = LUBRICACIÓN, LUBRICAR, etc.

lucano, na, n. & a. Lucanian.

lucerna, f. chandelier; (icht.) = MILANO.

lucérnula, f. (bot.) lucern, lucerne, alfalfa.

lucero, m. morning star; any bright star; light hole; star on the forehead of horses; brightness, splendor.—pl. (poet.) eyes.—**l. del alba,** or **de la mañana,** morning star.—**l. de la tarde,** evening star.

lucidamente, adv. brightly; splendidly.

lucidez, f. brilliancy; brightness; success.

lucido, da, pp. & a. magnificent, splendid, brilliant; most successful.

lúcido, da, a. lucid, clear; brilliant, shining.

lucidor, ra, a. shining, brilliant.

lucidura, f. (coll.) whitewashing.

luciente, a. shining, luminous, bright.

luciérnaga, f. glowworm, firefly.

Lucifer, m. Lucifer, Satan; proud and wicked man; morning star.

luciferino, na, a. Luciferian, devilish.

lucífero, ra. I. a. (poet.) resplendent, shining. **II.** m. morning star.

lucífugo, ga, a. light-avoiding, lucifugous.

lucillo, m. tomb; sarcophagus.

lucimiento, m. brilliancy, splendor, lustre; success, triumph.—**quedar,** or **salir, con l.,** to be eminently successful.

lucio, cia. I. a. lucid, bright. **II.** m. (icht.) common pike, luce.

lucir. I. vn. (ind. LUZCO: subj. LUZCA) to shine, glitter, glow; to outshine, exceed; to look, appear. **II.** va. to light, illuminate; to show, display, exhibit, disport. **III.** vr. to shine, to be brilliant; to dress to advantage; to be very successful, to do splendidly.

lucrarse, vr. to profit.

lucrativamente, adv. profitably, lucratively.

lucrativo, va, a. lucrative, profitable.

lucro, m. gain, profit, lucre.—**lucros y daños,** (com.) profit and loss.

lucroso, sa, a. lucrative, profitable.

luctuosa, f. feudal death tax.

luctuosamente, adv. mournfully, sorrowfully.

luctuoso, sa, a. sad, mournful.

lucubración, f. lucubration.

lucubrar, va. to lucubrate.

lúcumo, m. (bot.) Lucuma, a variety of Peruvian Achras.

lucha, f. struggle, strife; wrestling, wrestle; dispute, argument.

luchador, ra, n. wrestler; fighter.

luchar, vn. to fight, struggle; to wrestle.

lucharniego, ga, a. night hare-hunting (dog).

ludia, f. ferment, yeast.

ludiar, va. & vr. to ferment.

ludibrio, m. mockery, derision, scorn.

ludimiento, m. friction, rubbing.

ludión, m. (phys.) Cartesian devil.

ludir, va. to rub, waste by friction.

lúe, f. infection.

luego. I. adv. presently, immediately; afterwards; next; later.—**l. que,** after, as soon as.—**desde l.,** at once, instantly; naturally; to begin with, at the outset.—**hasta l.,** so long (in taking leave).—**tan l. como** = L. QUE. **II.** conj. therefore.

luengo, ga, a. long, dilated.—**luengos años,** long years, many years.

lugano, m. (orn.) linnet.

lugar, m. place, spot, site; city, town, village; room, space; seat; employment, office, dignity; time, opportunity, occasion; leisure, convenience; cause, motive, reason; text, authority.—**l. común, l. excusado,** privy-house, water-closet.—**lugares comunes,** commonplace topics.—**lugares de un combate,** (naut.) quarters in a sea-fight.—**dar l.,** to make room.—**dar l. a,** to cause, give occasion for.—**en l. de,** instead of, in lieu of.—**en primer l.,** first, or in the first place.—**hacer l.,** to make room.—**no ha l.** (a), (law) the petition is denied; there is no occasion (for).

lugarcico, illo, ito, m. dim. small place.

lugarejo, m. dim. hamlet, small village.

lugareño, ña. I. belonging to a village. **II.** n. villager.

lugarote, *m. aug.* unattractive hamlet.

lugartenencia, *f.* lieutenancy. **lugarteniente,** *m.* deputy, substitute, delegate; lieutenant.

lugre, *m.* (naut.) lugger, small vessel.

lúgubre, *a.* sad, gloomy, lugubrious, dismal

luir, *va.* (naut.) to gall, wear away by friction.

luis, *m.* louis (French coin).

luisa, *f.* (bot.) lemon verbena or aloysia.

lujación, *f.* = LUXACIÓN.

lujar, *va.* (Cuba) to rub; (med.) to luxate, dislocate.

lujo, *m.* luxury.—**de l.,** de luxe; elegant, exquisite; magnificent.—**lujoso, sa,** *a.* showy, sumptuous, luxurious; profuse, lavish.

lujuria, *f.* lewdness, lust; excess; profuseness, lavishness.

lujuriante, *a.* lusting; luxuriant, exuberant.

lujuriar, *vn.* to be libidinous, to lust; to couple together (animals).

lujuriosamente, *adv.* lustfully, voluptuously.

lujurioso, sa, *a.* lustful, voluptuous, lewd.

luliano, na, *n. & a.* Lullian.—**lulismo,** *m.* system of Raymond Lully.—**lulista,** *n. & a.* Lullist (-ic).

lumaquela, *f.* lumachelle, fire marble.

lumbago, *m.* (med.) lumbago.

lumbar, *a.* lumbar, lumbary.

lumbrada, *f.* great fire.

lumbre, *f.* fire; light; splendor, brightness; skylight, transom; hammer of a flintlock; forepart of horseshoes.—*pl.* tinder box.—**l. del agua,** level with the water.—**a l. de pajas,** (coll.) very swiftly.—**a l. mansa,** on a slow fire.—**ni por l.,** by no means.

lumbrera, *f.* luminary; skylight, light shaft; (st. eng.) port.—**l. de admisión,** steam port, admission port.—**l. de educción,** or **de escape,** exhaust port.

lumbrerada, *f.* great fire.

lumen, *m.* lumen (unit of light).

luminar, *m.* luminary.

luminaria, *f.* illumination, festival lights; (eccl.) lamp kept burning before the sacrament.—*pl.* money paid for illuminations.

lumínico, *m.* (phys.) hypothetic agent or principle of light.

luminiscencia, *f.* luminescence.

luminiscente, *a.* luminescent.

luminosidad, *f.* luminosity.

luminoso, sa, *a.* luminous.

luna, *f.* (ast.) moon; satellite; glass plate, mirror plate; (opt.) lens of a spyglass; effect of the moon upon lunatic people.—**l. creciente,** crescent. —**l. de miel,** honeymoon.—**l. llena,** full moon.— **l. menguante,** waning moon.—**estar de buena (mala) l.,** (Am.) to be in good (bad) humor.— **quedarse a la luna de Valencia,** to be left in the cold.

lunación, *f.* lunation.

lunado, da, *a.* lunated, formed like a half-moon.

lunanco, ca, *a.* (animal) having one quarter higher than another.

lunar. I. *a.* lunar. **II.** *m.* mole, beauty spot; flaw, blemish.—**l. postizo,** patch.

lunario, ria. I. *a.* lunarian. **II.** *m.* calendar.

lunático, ca, *a.* lunatic, moonstruck, mad.

lunecilla, *f.* crescent-shaped jewel.

lunes, *m.* Monday.

luneta, *f.* (opt.) spectacle lens; (theat.) orchestra chair; a crescent-shaped ornament; (arch.) lunette; saddler's knife, leather knife.

luneto, *m.* skylight in a vault, lunette.

lúnula, *f.* (geom.) lune; (opt.) meniscus.

lupanar, *m.* brothel, bawdyhouse.

lupanario, ia, *a.* belonging to a brothel.

lupercales, *f. pl.* Lupercalia.

lupia, *f.* (med.) wen, encysted tumor.

lupicia, *f.* (med.) = ALOPECIA.

lupino, na. I. *a.* wolfish. **II.** *m.* (bot.) lupine.

lupulino, *m.* lupulin.

lúpulo, *m.* (bot.) hops.

luquete, *m.* slice of orange or lemon thrown into wine; zest; sulphur match.

lurte, *m.* avalanche, landslide.

lusitanismo, *m.* Portuguese idiom.

lusitano, na, *a.* Lusitanian; Portuguese.

lustración, *f.* lustration; lustrum.

lustrador, ra. I. *n.* polisher. **II.** *m.* hot-press, mangler.

lustral, *a.* lustral; lustrical.

lustramiento, *m.* act of decorating or honoring.

lustrar. I. *va.* to lustrate, expiate, purify; to polish. **II.** *vn.* to wander, roam.

lustre, *m.* gloss, lustre, polish, glaze; shoe-polish; nobleness, splendor, glory.

lústrico, ca, *a.* lustrical; lustral.

lustro, *m.* lustrum, period of five years; lamp, chandelier.

lustrosamente, *adv.* brilliantly, splendidly; glitteringly.—**lustroso, sa,** *a.* bright, brilliant; lustrous, shining.

lútea, *f.* (orn.) oriole; cazique.

lúteo, tea, *a.* miry, muddy.

luteranismo, *m.* Lutheranism.

luterano, na, *n. & a.* Lutheran.

luto, *m.* mourning; grief, bereavement.—*pl.* mourning draperies.—**de l.,** in mourning.

luxación, *f.* luxation.

luz, *f.* light; daylight; lighthouse; notice, information, hint; inspiration; brightness, lustre, splendor; luminary, prominent man; (art) lighting.—*pl.* culture, enlightenment, learning, knowledge; windows, loopholes.—**l. de bengala,** red light.—**l. del día,** daylight.—**l. de l.,** reflected or borrowed light.—**l. zodiacal,** zodiacal light.—**a buena l.,** carefully, after due examination.—**a primera l.,** at daybreak.—**a todas luces,** everywhere, any way.—**dar a l.,** to give birth to; to be delivered (of a child); to publish.—**entre dos luces,** in the twilight.—**salir a l.,** to come out, be published or divulged, leak out.

Luzbel, *m.* Lucifer, Satan.

luzco, yo luzca. (*V.* LUCIR).

LL

llábana, *f.* smooth, slippery flagstone.

llaga, *f.* ulcer, sore; prick, thorn, tormenting thought; (mas.) seam or crack.

llagar, *va.* (*pret.* LLAGUÉ: *subj.* LLAGUE) to wound, hurt, injure.

llama. I. *f.* flame, blaze; violent passion; marshy ground. **II.** *f.* (zool.) llama.

llamada, *f.* call, knock; motion or sign to call attention; (print.) reference mark to a note; (mil.) call; chamade; (com.) notice, entry.

llamadera, *f.* goad stick.

llamado, da, *pp. & a.* called, by the name of.

llamador, ra, *n.* caller; beadle, messenger; (*m.*) knocker of a door.

llamamiento, *m.* calling, call; appeal; convocation; inspiration, divine vocation; attraction of humors to one part of the body.

llamar. I. *va.* to call, summon, cite; to call upon, invoke, appeal to; to name, call; to incline; to attract. **II.** *vn.* to excite thirst; to knock or rap at the door; to ring a door or call bell. **III.** *vr.* to be called or named, go by the name of, give the name of (often ch. constr.: *ella se llama Rosa,* her name is Rose; *¿cómo se llama esto?* what is this called? *¿como se llama Vd.?* what is your name? *se llama "democracia"* . . ., the name "democracy" is given to . . ., or, simply, "democracy" is . . .); (naut.) to veer (s. o. the wind).

llamarada, *f.* sudden blaze, flash; burst of wit; sudden flush of the face.

llamativo, va, *a.* exciting thirst; showy, attracting attention.

llamazar, *m.* swamp, marsh.

llambria, *f.* steep face of a rock.

llameante, *a.* blazing, flaming.

llamear, *vn.* to blaze, to flame.

llana, *f.* (mas.) trowel; page of a book or writing; plain, flatland.

llanada, *f.* plain, flatland, level ground.

llanamente, *adv.* ingenuously, simply, sincerely; homely; plainly, clearly, flatly.

llanero, ra, *n.* plainsman (-woman).

llaneza, *f.* plainness, simplicity; familiarity; uncultivated style.

llano, na. I. even, smooth; easy, unobstructed; plain, unadorned; unaffected, open, frank; clear, evident; (gram.) (word) accented on the penultimate.—**a la llana,** simply, unceremoniously.—**de llano,** openly, in the open. **II.** *m.* plain, llano.

llanta, *f.* (bot.) a variety of cabbage; (car.) rim; (aut.) tire (sometimes rim).—**ll. maciza,** solid tire. **ll. neumática,** pneumatic tire.

llantén, *m.* (bot.) plantain, rib grass.—**ll. de agua,** water plantain, alisura.

llanto, *m.* flood of tears; crying, weeping.

llanura, *f.* evenness, flatness; plain.

llapa, *f.* (min.) quicksilver for amalgamation.

llapar, *va.* (min.) to add quicksilver to for reduction.

llares, *f. pl.* chain with pothooks.

llatar, *m.* post-and-rail fence.

llave, *f.* key; (mech.) wrench; faucet, cock, spigot, spout, tap; bolt, pin, tightening wedge, cotter; (print.) brace }; tuning key; clock winder; (arch.) keystone; winch of a stocking frame; lock of a gun; key, explanation of anything difficult; introduction to knowledge; (naut.) knee; (mus.) clef, key; piston of musical instruments.—**ll. capona,** key worn by a lord of the bedchamber.—**ll. de la mano,** span of the hand.—**ll. del pie,** distance from heel to instep.—**ll. inglesa,** monkey wrench.—**ll. maestra,** master key, pass-key.—**debajo de ll.,** under lock and key.—**echar (la) ll. a,** to lock.

llavero, ra. I. *n.* keeper of the keys. **II.** *m.* key ring. **III.** *f.* housekeeper.

llavín, *m.* night key, latchkey.

lleco, ca, *a.* (agr.) virgin (as soil).

llega, *f.* gathering, collecting.

llegada, *f.* arrival, coming.

llegar. I. *vn.* (*pret.* LLEGUÉ: *subj.* LLEGUE) to arrive; to come; to reach; to extend; to last, to continue; to attain a purpose; to suffice, be enough; to amount.—**ll. a las manos,** to come to blows.—**ll. a saber,** to find out, to be informed of.—**ll. a ser,** to become.—**no ll. a,** not to amount to; not to come up, or be equal, to.—**no ll. a uno la camisa al cuerpo,** to be terrified and anxious. **II.** *va.* to bring near; to gather, collect. **III.** *vr.* to approach, draw near; to go to some neighboring place; to adhere, stick.

llena, *f.* flood, overflow.

llenamente, *adv.* fully, copiously.

llenar. I. *va.* to fill, stuff, pack; to pervade; to occupy (as an incumbent); to satisfy, content, convince; to make up (a number); to beget. **II.** *vr.* to fill, fill up; (w. **de**) to become full (of), or covered (with); (coll.) to feed gluttonously, stuff one's self; (coll.) to be irritated after having suffered long; to get crowded, packed. **III.** *vn.* to be full (s. o. the moon).

llenero, ra, *a.* (law) full, complete, absolute.

lleno, na. I. *a.* full, filled, replete; complete.—**ll. de bote en bote,** brimful, full to the brim.—**de ll., or de ll. en ll.,** entirely, totally. **II.** *m.* glut, fill, plenty, abundance, fulness; perfection, completeness; full moon; (theat.) full house.

llenura, *f.* fulness; plenty, abundance.

lleta, *f.* (bot.) sprout.

lleudar, *va.* to leaven. *V.* LEUDAR.

lleva, llevada, *f.* transport, carrying.

llevadero, ra, *a.* tolerable, bearable, light.

llevador, ra, *n. & a.* carrier (-rying).

llevar. I. *va.* to carry, convey; to bear, wear, don; to take, take away, carry away; to charge, ask, set (a price); to bear, yield, produce; to excel, exceed; to suffer, endure; to lead, guide, conduct, take; to manage (a horse); to cut off, dismember; to have spent or devoted (so much time); to induce, to bring to an opinion; to introduce; to gain, attain, obtain; (arith.) to carry; (with a past participle) to have, as: *llevo andadas diez millas,* I have walked ten miles.—**ll. . . . a,**

to be older, or more, than by (*llevo dos años a Juan,* I am two years older than John).—**ll. a cabo,** to carry through, to accomplish, to carry out.—**ll. a cuestas,** to carry on one's shoulders or back; to support.—**ll. adelante,** to carry on, keep up, continue.—**ll. al crédito,** to place to the credit.—**ll. calabazas,** to be given the mitten; to fail in examination.—**ll. consigo,** to carry along with one, to carry with it, imply; to have attached.—**ll. el compás,** to beat or keep time.—**ll. la caja,** to keep the cash.—**ll. la delantera,** to lead, to be ahead.—**ll. la proa al noroeste,** (naut.) to stand to the northwest.—**ll. la ventaja a,** to have the advantage of or over.—**ll. libros,** (com.) to keep books.—**ll. lo mejor (peor),** to get the best (worst).—**ll. una caída, golpe, porrazo,** to have a fall, a blow.—**no llevarlas todas consigo,** to have suspicions, to be afraid. **II.** *vr.* to tare or carry away; to get along.—**ll. bien,** to be on good terms, get along well.—**ll. chasco,** to be disappointed.—**ll. mal,** to be on bad terms.

lloica, *f.* (orn.) robin redbreast; thrush.

lloradera, *f.* weeping from slight motives.

llorador, ra, *n.* weeper.

lloraduelos, *n.* (coll.) weeper, mourner.

llorar. I. *vn.* to weep, cry; to affect poverty and distress; to whine; to drip. **II.** *va.* to weep over, bewail, mourn, lament.

lloriquear, *vn.* to be constantly crying; to whine.

lloro, *m.* weeping, crying.

llorón, na. I. *a.* weeping; that cries with little cause, whining. **II.** *n.* weeper, whiner.

llorosamente, *adv.* weepingly.

lloroso, sa, *a.* mournful, sorrowful, tearful.

llosa, *f.* fenced-in field.

llovedizo, za, *a.* leaky; rain (u. a.).

llover. I. *vn. impers.* (*ind.* LLUEVE: *subj.* LLUEVA) to rain; to pour down like rain, to shower, to come in abundance (as troubles).—**ll. a cántaros, a chorros, a chuzos,** or **ll. chuzos,** to rain in torrents, to rain pitchforks.—**como llovido,** unexpectedly.—**llueva o no,** rain or shine. **II.** *vr.* to leak, let the rain in (s. o. roofs).

llovido, da, *n. & pp.* stowaway.

llovioso, sa, *a.* = LLUVIOSO.

llovizna, *f.* drizzle, sprinkling.

lloviznar, *vn.* to drizzle, to sprinkle.

llueca, *f.* brooding hen. *V.* CLUECA.

lluvia, *f.* rain; plenty.—**lluvioso, sa,** *a.* rainy.

M

maca, *f.* bruise in fruit; flaw, blemish, spot, stain; deceit, fraud, trick.

macabro, bra, *a.* ugly, hideous.

macaco, ca. I. *m.* (zool.) macaque; (Mex.) hobgoblin, bogie. **II.** *a.* ugly, ill-shaped, squat.

macádam, *m.* macadam pavement.

macadamizar, *va.* to macadamize.

macadán, *m.* macadanizar, *va.* = MACÁDAM, etc.

macagua, *f.* (orn.) macaw; (Venez.) a poisonous snake

macagüita, *f.* (Venez.) a thorny palmtree.

macana, *f.* Indian wooden sabre edged with sharp flint; (Colomb.) a palm having very hard and heavy wood; (Am.) cudgel, club; (Am.) blunder; fib, joke.

macanazo, *m.* blow with a MACANA.

macanudo, da, *a.* (coll.) fine, excellent, dandy, first-rate.

macareno, na, *a.* (coll.) bragging, boasting; gaudily dressed in Andalusian garb.

macarrón, *m.* macaroon.—*pl.* macaroni; (naut.) stanchions.

macarronea, *f.* macaronic poem.

macarrónicamente, *adv.* macaronically.

macarrónico, ca, *a.* macaronic.

macarse, *vr.* to begin to rot (s. o. fruit).

macaurel, *f.* (Venez.) a poisonous snake.

maceador, *m.* one who mauls.

macear. I. *va.* to maul. **II.** *vn.* to importune.

macedón, na, *n.* & *a.*; **macedonio, nia,** *n.* & *a.*; **macedónico, ca,** *a.* Macedonian.

macelo, *m.* slaughterhouse, abattoir.

maceo, *m.* act of mauling.

maceración, *f.*; **maceramiento,** *m.* maceration, steeping; infusion; mortification of the flesh.

macerar, *va.* to macerate, soak, steep; (chem.) to digest; to mortify with corporeal hardships.

macerina, *f.* = MANCERINA.

macero, *m.* mace bearer.

maceta, *f. dim.* small mace, mallet, or maul; flowerpot; flower vase; haft of tools; stone-cutter's hammer; (naut.) maul, mallet.

macetón, *m. aug.* of MACETA.

macias, *f.* mace, a spice.

macicez, *f.* solidity.

macilento, ta, *a.* lean, emaciated; withered.

macillo, *m.* hammer of a piano.

macis, *f.* = MACIA.

macizamente, *adv.* firmly, solidly.

macizar, *va.* to fill up, stop up.

macizo, za. I. *a.* solid; massive; firm, certain. **II.** *m.* massiveness, bulk; (mas.) solid wall; flower bed; (aut.) solid tire.

macla, *f.* wooden flail; (bot.) water caltrops.

macoca, *f.* large early fig.

macolla, *f.* (bot.) bunch, cluster.

macón, *m.* dry, brown honeycomb.

macona, *f.* large basket or hamper.

macrobiótica, *f.* art of living long.

macrocefalia, *f.* macrocephalia, macrocephaly.

macrocéfalo, la, *a.* macrocephalous.

macrocito, *m.* (path.) macrocyte.

macrocosmo, *m.* macrocosm.

macropia, macropsia, *f.* (path.) macropsia, or macropsy.

macruro, ra. I. *a.* (zool.) macrurous. **II.** *m. pl.* Macrura.

macsura, *f.* reserved precinct in a mosque.

macuache, *m.* (Mex.) ignorant Indian.

macuba, *f.* Martinique tobacco.

macuca, *f.* (bot.) wild pear or pear tree.

mácula, *f.* stain, spot, blemish; (ast.) macula.

macular, *va.* to stain.

maculatura, *f.* (print.) maculature, spoiled sheet.

macún, macuñ, *m.* (Ch.) poncho.

macuquero, *m.* unlawful worker of abandoned mines.

macuquino, na, *a.* epithet app. to a former silver Porto-Rican coin.

macuteno, *m.* (Mex.) petty thief.

macuto, *m.* (Am.) bag made of palm leaves.

macha, *f.* a South-American mollusk.

machaca. I. *n.* (coll.) a bore, tiresome person. **II.** *f.* MACHACADERA.

machacadera, *f.* pounder, beater, crusher.

machacador, ra, *n.* pounder, beater, crusher; bruiser, mauler.

machacar. I. *va.* (pret. MACHAQUÉ: subj. MA-CHAQUE) to pound; crush. **II.** *vn.* to importune; to harp on a subject.

machacón, na, *a.* monotonous; importunate.

machada, *f.* flock of he-goats; (coll.) stupidity.

machado, *pp.* & *m.* hatchet.

machamartillo.—a m., firmly but roughly.

machaqueo, *m.* pounding or crushing.

machaquería, *f.* (coll.) importunity, insistence.

machar, *va.* to pound, hammer, maul.

machear, *vn.* to beget more males than females.

machetazo, *m.* stroke with a machete.

machete, *m.* machete.

machetear, *va.* to wound or cut with a machete.

machetero, *m.* one who cuts cane or fights with a machete; sabre rattler; ignorant military chief.

máchica, *f.* (Peru) roast Indian meal.

machiega, *a. V.* ABEJA MACHIEGA.

machihembrar, *va.* (carp.) to dovetail.

machina, *f.* crane, derrick; pile-driver.

macho. I. *a.* vigorous, robust; male. **II.** *m.* male; specifically a he-mule or a he-goat; masculine plant; part of an instrument which enters

into another; hook to catch hold in an eye; screw pin; bolt (of a lock); (arch.) spur, buttress, abutment; (mech.) sledge hammer; block on which an anvil is fixed; square anvil; core; ignorant fellow. **—m.** cabrío, he-goat, buck.**—m.** de aterrajar, screw tap.**—m.** de cabrío = M. CABRÍO.**—m.** del timón, (naut.) rudder pintle.**—m.** romo, he-mule born of a horse and a she-ass.

machón, *m.* (arch.) buttress, spur; a piece of timber.

machorra, *a.* barren.

machota, *f.*, **machote,** *m.* maul, mallet.

machote, *m.* (Mex. min.) boundary stone.

machucadura, *f.*, **machucamiento,** *m.* pounding, bruising.**—machucar,** *va.* (pret. MACHUQUÉ: subj. MACHUQUE) to pound, to bruise.

machucho, cha, *a.* mature, judicious.

machuelo, *m. dim.* small he-mule; clove of garlic.

machuno, na, *a.* mannish, masculine.

madama, *f.* madam.**—madamisela,** *f.* damsel.

madapolán, *m.* madapollam, percale.

madeja, *f.* hank, skein; lock of hair; (coll.) weak, lazy person.**—m.** sin cuenda, tangle; disordered person; entangled affair.**—hacer m.,** to be ropy.

madera, *f.* wood; timber, lumber; horny part of a hoof.**—m.** alburente, alburnum, sapwood.**—m.** anegadiza, heavier-than-water wood.**—m.** de construcción, building timber.**—m.** de corazón, heartwood.**—m.** del aire, horn of animals.**—m.** de raja, split timber.**—m.** de sierra, or serradiza, lumber, timber fit to be sawed.

madera, *m.* Madeira wine.

maderable, *a.* timber-yielding.

maderada, *f.* raft, float.

maderaje, maderamen, *m.* timber; timber work.

maderería, *f.* lumber yard.

maderero, maderista, *m.* lumber dealer; lumberman.

madero, *m.* beam, scantling; timber, piece of lumber; ship, vessel; (coll.) stupid or unfeeling person.**—m.** barcal, log.**—m.** cachizo, timber fit to be sawed.**—m.** de suelo, beam, joist.**—m.** rollizo = M. BARCAL.**—maderos de cuenta,** main timbers.

maderuelo, *m. dim.* small piece of timber.

madia, *f.* (bot.) oily plant of Chile.

madianita, *n.* & *a.* Midianite.

madrasta, *f.* stepmother; anything unpleasant.

madraza, *f.* (coll.) too indulgent a mother.

madre, *f.* mother; dam; matron; (coll.) old woman; foundation; origin; matrix, womb; bed (cf a river); main sewer; main irrigating ditch; mother (of vinegar), lees, dregs; (carp.) main piece, spindle; (naut.) gallows-beam.**—m.** de leche, wet nurse.**—m.** política, mother-in-law.

madrecilla, *f. dim.* MADRECITA; ovary of birds.

madrecita, *m. dim.* little mother, dear mother.

madreclavo, *m.* clove of two years' growth.

madreña, *f.* = ALMADREÑA.

madreperla, *f.* mother-of-pearl.

madrépora, *f.* madrepore, white coral.

madrepórico, ca, *a.* madreporic.

madrero, ra, *a.* (coll.) attached to one's mother.

madreselva, *f.* (bot.) honeysuckle.

madrigada, *a.* twice-married (woman).

madrigado, da, *a.* practical, experienced; (bull) that has been a sire.

madrigal, *m.* (poet.) brief poem expressing a delicate conceit.

madriguera, *f.* burrow; den, hole.

madrileño, ña, *a.* Madrilenian.

madrina, *f.* godmother; bridesmaid; patroness, protectress; prop, stanchion; straps for yoking two horses; (Venez.) small herd.

madrona, *f.* main irrigating ditch; over-indulgent mother.

madroncillo, *m.* strawberry.

madroñal, *m.*; **madroñera,** *f.* grove of madroña trees.**—madroñero,** *m.* madroña.**—madroño,** *m.* (bot.) madroña; fruit of the madroña; berry-shaped tassel.

madrugada, *f.* dawn; early rising.—**de m.,** at break of day.—**madrugador, ra,** *n.* early riser.—**madrugar,** *vn.* (*pret.* MADRUGUÉ: *subj.* MADRUGUE) to rise early; to anticipate, to be beforehand.—**madrugón,** *m.* (coll.) very early rising.

maduración, *f.* ripeness, maturity; ripening.

maduradero, *m.* place for ripening fruits.

madurador, ra, *a.* maturing, ripening.

maduramente, *adv.* maturely, thoughtfully.

madurante, *a.* maturing, ripening.

madurar. I. *va.* to ripen, mature; to think out; (surg.) to maturate. **II.** *vn.* to ripen; to mature; to reach the age of maturity; (surg.) to maturate, suppurate; to come to a head.

magneto, *f.* (int. comb. eng.) magneto.

madurativo, va. I. *a.* maturative. **II.** *m.* anything that matures; inducement; (med.) maturant.

madurez, *f.* maturity; ripeness; wisdom.

madurillo, lla, *a.* beginning to ripen.

maduro, ra, *a.* ripe; mature; wise, judicious.

maesil, *m.* = MAESTRIL.

maesillas, *f. pl.* cords which serve in making passementerie to raise or lower the skeins.

maestoso, *a.* (mus.) maestoso.

maestra, *f.* teacher, schoolmistress; master's wife in all trades and professions; queen bee; (mas.) guide line.

maestral. I. *a.* relating to a grand master of a military order; northwest (wind). **II.** *m.* cell of the queen bee.

maestramente, *adv.* in a masterly manner.

maestrante, *m.* member of a MAESTRANZA.

maestranza, *f.* riding club of noblemen; (arti.) arsenal, armory; (naut.) navy yard; all the workmen in an arsenal or navy yard.

maestrazgo, *m.* dignity or jurisdiction of a grand master of a military order.

maestre, *m.* grand master of a military order; (naut.) master of a merchant ship.—**m. de raciones,** purser.

maestrear. I. *va.* to direct, to instruct; to lop; to smooth. **II.** *vn.* (coll.) to domineer, to act the master.

maestresala, *m.* chief waiter and taster.

maestría, *f.* mastery; dignity or degree of a master.

maestril, *m.* (api.) queen cell.

maestrillo, *m. dim.* insignificant schoolmaster.

maestro, tra. I. *a.* masterly; master, great, principal, main; learned, trained. **II.** *m.* master, teacher; expert; master workman; skilled artisan; title of respect in monastic orders; scholastic title; (naut.) mainmast.—**m. carpintero de remos,** master oar maker.—**m. de armas,** fencing master.—**m. de capilla,** choir master.—**m. de ceremonias,** master of ceremonies.—**m. de cocina,** chef.—**m. de esgrima** = M. DE ARMAS.—**m. de obra prima,** shoemaker.—**m. de obras,** builder.

magallánico, ca, *a.* Magellanic.

maganel, *m.* (mil.) battering-ram.

maganto, ta, *a.* spiritless, dull, faint, languid.

magaña, *f.* (arti.) honeycomb, flaw in the bore of a gun; (coll.) cunning artifice, trick.

magarza, *f.* (bot.) downy chamomile.

magarzuela, *f.* (bot.) stinking chamomile.

magdalena, *f.* a kind of biscuit.

magdaleón, *m.* (pharm.) roll of plaster.

magia, *f.* magic; black art, necromancy.—**m. blanca,** or **natural,** white, or natural, magic.—**m. negra,** black magic, black art.

magiar, *n. & a.* Magyar.

mágicamente, *adv.* magically.

mágico, ca. I. *a.* magic, magical; marvellous, wonderful. **II.** *n.* magician; sorcerer (-ess).

magín, *m.* (coll.) fancy, idea, imagination.

magismo, *m.* magianism.

magisterial, *a.* magisterial.

magisterio, *m.* mastery; mastership; scholastic degree; teachers as a class; (coll.) affected solemnity; (chem.) precipitate.

magistrado, *m.* magistrate; magistracy.

magistral. I. *a.* magisterial, masterly; (eccl.) preaching; (med.) magistral. **II.** *m.* (min.) magistral.

magistralía, *f.* (eccl.) preacher's prebendary.

magistralmente, *adv.* magisterially, masterly.

magistratura, *f.* magistracy.

magma, *m.* magma, residue.

magnánimamente, *adv.* magnanimously.

magnanimidad, *f.* magnanimity.

magnánimo, ma, *a.* magnanimous.

magnate, *m.* magnate, grandee.

magnesia, *f.* (chem.) magnesia.

magnesiano, na, *a.* magnesian.

magnésico, ca, *a.* magnesic.

magnesio, *m.* magnesium.

magnesita, *f.* meerschaum.

magnético, ca, *a.* magnetic.

magnetita, *f.* (min.) magnetite.

magnetismo, *m.* magnetism.

magnetización, *f.* magnetization.

magnetizador, ra, *n. & a.* magnetizer (-ing); hypnotizer (-ing).

magnetizar, *va.* (*pret.* MAGNETICÉ: *subj.* MAGNETICE) to magnetize; to hypnotize.

magnetoeléctrico, ca, *a.* magneto-electric.

magnetómetro, *m.* magnetometer.

magníficamente, *adv.* magnificently.

magnificar, *va.* to magnify, extol, exalt.

magníficat, *m.* (eccl.) Magnificat.

magnificencia, *f.* magnificence, grandeur, gorgeousness, splendor.

magnificentísimo, ma, *a. sup.* of MAGNÍFICO: most magnificent.

magnífico, ca, *a.* magnificent; excellent.

magnitud, *f.* magnitude; quantity.

magno, na, *a.* great; grand.

magnolia, *f.* (bot.) magnolia.

mago, ga. I. *a.* Magian. **II.** *n.* magus; magician, necromancer.—*pl.* magi.

magostar, *vn.* to roast (chestnuts) at a picnic.

magosto, *m.* picnic and chestnut roast.

magra, *f.* rasher, slice of ham.

magrez, *f.* thinness, leanness.

magro, gra. I. *a.* meager, lean. **II.** *m.* lean slice of pork.

magrura, *f.* = MAGREZ.

magua, *f.* (Cuba) jest, joke.

magüer, magüera, *conj.* (obs.) although.

magüeto, ta, *n.* young steer or heifer.

maguey, *m.* (bot.) maguey.

maguillo, *m.* wild apple tree.

magujo, *m.* (naut.) ravehook.

magulladura, *f.* bruise, contusion.

magullamiento, *m.* bruising; contusion.

magullar, *va.* to bruise, to mangle.

maguntino, na, *a.* of Mentz or Mayence.

maharrana, *f.* fresh bacon.

mahométíco, ca, *n. & a.* Mohammedan.

mahometismo, *m.* Mohammedanism.

mahometista, *n.* Mohammedan.

mahometizar, *vn.* to Mohammedanize.

mahón, *m.* nankeen, kind of light cotton goods.

mahona, *f.* Turkish transport vessel.

maído, *m.* mewing. *V.* MAULLIDO.

maimón, *m.* monkey.—*pl.* soup made with oil.

maimona, *f.* spindle beam of a horse mill.

maimonetes, *m. pl.* (naut.) belaying pins.

maimonismo, *m.* doctrine of Maimonides.

maitinante, *m.* priest with matinal duties.

maitines, *m. pl.* (eccl.) matins.

maíz, *m.* (bot.) maize, Indian corn.—**m. machacado,** hominy.

maizal, *m.* Indian-corn field.

majá, *m.* (Cuba) a thick-bodied snake.

majada, *f.* sheepcote, sheepfold; dung.

majadal, *m.* good pasture ground for sheep; land improved by the manure of a flock.

majadear, *vn.* to take shelter in the night (s. o. sheep); to manure.

majadería, *f.* foolish speech or act.

majaderico, *m.* old-fashioned trimming.

majaderillo, lla. I. *a. dim.* rather peevish and bothersome. **II.** *m.* bobbin for lace.

majadero, ra. I. *a.* silly; peevish; obtrusive. **II.** *m.* whippersnapper; bore; pestle, pounder.— *pl.* bobbins for making lace.

majador, ra, *n.* pounder, bruiser.

majadura, *f.* pounding or bruising.

majagranzas, *m.* (coll.) stupid bore.

majagua, *f.* (Am.) (bot.) a tree of the linden family.

majal, *m.* school of fishes.

majamiento, *m.* = MAJADURA.

majano, *m.* heap of stones as a landmark.

majar, *va.* to pound, bruise, break in a mortar; (coll.) to importune, vex, annoy.

majarete, *m.* (Cuba) corn pudding.

majencia, *f.* (coll.) = MAJEZA.

majestad, *f.* majesty.

majestuosamente, *adv.* majestically, grandly.

majestuosidad, *f.* majesty, dignity.

majestuoso, sa, *a.* majestic, grand.

majeza, *f.* (coll.) spruceness, gaudiness.

majo, ja. I. *a.* gay, spruce, gaudily attired; showy, handsome, pretty. **II.** *n.* beau, belle.

majolar, *m.* grove of white hawthorns.

majorca, *f.* = MAZORCA.

majuela, *f.* fruit of the white hawthorn; shoe lacing.

majuelo, *m.* (bot.) new vine; white hawthorn.

mal. I. *a. contr. of* MALO; used only before masculine substantives. **II.** *m.* evil; harm, injury, ailment, illness, disease, complaint; imperfection, fault; wrong, evil (*el bien y el mal,* right and wrong, good and evil).—**m. caduco,** or **de corazón,** epilepsy.—**m. de la tierra,** homesickness. —**m. de ojo,** evil eye.—**m. de ojos,** eyesore.—**m. de orina,** partial or total incapacity to pass out urine.—**m. de piedra,** lithiasis, stone, calculus (gen. in the urinary apparatus).—**m. de San Lázaro,** elephantiasis.—**del m. el menos,** the less of two evils.—**hacer m.,** to do evil, to injure; to be injurious.—**no hay m. que por bien no venga,** everything is for the best.—**por m. de mis pecados,** to my sorrow, unluckily for me. **III.** *adv.* badly; wrongly; deficiently; wickedly; hardly.—**m. de su grado,** unwillingly.—**¡m. haya!** confound it! confound (the man, thing, etc.)!.—**m. hecho,** badly done, ill-finished; unjust; wrong.—**m. por m.,** for want of something better.—**m. que bien,** willingly or unwillingly; rightly or wrongly.—**m. que le pese,** in spite of him, however much he may regret it.—**de m. en peor,** worse and worse.— **hacer mal,** to do wrong, act wrongly.

mala, *f.* mail, post; manille (cards). *V.* MALO.

malabar. I. *a.* of or from Malabar; Malabar (u. a.) **II.** *n.* native of Malabar; Malabar language.

malabárico, ca, *a.* = MALABAR.

malacate, *m.* hoisting machine.

malacía, *f.* (med.) malacia, depraved appetite.

malacología, *f.* malacology.

malacológico, ca, *a.* malacologic.

malaconsejado, da, *a.* ill-advised.

malacopterigio, gia. I. *a.* malacopterygian. **II.** *m. pl.* Malacopterygii.

malacostumbrado, da, *a.* having bad habits; spoiled.

malacuenda, *f.* bagging, sacking; oakum, tow.

malagana, *f.* (coll.) faintness, dizziness.

malagaña, *f.* pole set up with dry furze to catch bees swarming.

malagueño, ña. I. *a.* of or belonging to Malaga. **II.** *f.* popular song of Malaga.

malagueta, *f.* grains of Paradise.

malamente, *adv.* badly; poorly; wrongly.

malandante, *a.* unfortunate, unhappy.

malandanza, *f.* misfortune, misery.

malandar, *m.* wild hog.

malandrín. I. *a.* malign, perverse. **II.** *m.* rascal, scoundrel.

malanga, *f.* (Am.) (bot.) arum.

malaquita, *f.* (min.) malachite.

malar, *a.* (anat.) malar, relating to the cheek.

malato, *m.* (chem.) malate.

malavenido, da, *a.* querulous, faultfinding.

malaventura, *f.* calamity, misfortune.

malaventurado, da, *a.* unfortunate, ill-fated.

malaventuranza, *f.* infelicity, unhappiness.

malayo, a, *n.* & *a.* Malay, Malayan.

malbaratador, ra, *n.* spendthrift, squanderer.

malbaratar, *va.* to squander; to undersell.

malbaratillo, *m.* second-hand shop.

malcarado, da, *a.* grim-faced, foul-faced.

malcasado, da, *a.* & *pp.* undutiful (spouse).

malcasar. I. *va.* to mismate in marriage. **II.** *vr.* to be mismated in marriage.

malcaso, *m.* treason, wrongful act.

malcocinado, *m.* tripes, liver, and lights of mutton or lamb; place where tripes are sold.

malcomer, *va.* to eat poorly.

malcomido, da, *a.* underfed.

malconsiderado, da, *a.* inconsiderate.

malcontentadizo, za, *q.* hard to please, faultfinding.

malcontento, ta. I. *a.* discontented, malcontent. **II.** *m.* malcontent; grumbler; a card game.

malcorte, *m.* transgression of forest laws.

malcriado, da, *a.* ill-bred, rude, uncivil; spoiled.

malcriar, *va.* to spoil (a child).

maldad, *f.* wickedness, iniquity; badness.

maldecido, da, *pp.* & *a.* wicked, depraved.

maldecidor, ra, *n.* defamer, backbiter.

maldecir, *va.* (*pp.* MALDECIDO, MALDITO: *gerund,* MALDICIENDO: *ind.* MALDIGO, él MALDICE: *pret.* MALDIJE: *fut.* MALDECIRÉ, (obs.) MALDIRÉ: *subj.* MALDIGA: *subj. pret. imp.* MALDIJERA, MALDECIRÍA, MALDIJESE) to damn, curse, accurse; to defame, backbite.

maldiciente, *n.* & *a.* curser (-ing); defamer (-ing).

maldición, *f.* malediction, curse; damnation.

maldispuesto, ta, *a.* indisposed; unwilling.

maldita, *f.* (coll.) tongue.—**soltar la m.,** (coll.) to give a loose rein to one's tongue.

maldito, ta. I. *pp. irr. of* MALDECIR. **II.** *a.* perverse, wicked; damned, accursed; (coll.) little, none, not one, nary.—**m. lo que me importa,** little do I care!—**no sabe maldita la cosa,** nary a thing does he know.

maleabilidad, *f.* malleability.

maleable, *a.* malleable.

maleador, ra, *a.; **maleante,** *a.* & *n.* rogue (-ish), villain (-ous), corrupter (-ing).

malear, *va.* to pervert, corrupt; injure, harm.

malecón, *m.* dike, levee, mole.

maledicencia, *f.* slander, calumny, obloquy.

maleficencia, *f.* maleficence, malignity, wrongdoing.

maleficiar, *va.* to harm; to bewitch, spellbind.

maleficio, *m.* spell; witchcraft, charm.

maléfico, ca, *a.* maleficent; harmful; spellbinding.

malejo, ja, *a. dim. of* MALO: rather bad.

malentrada, *f.* fee paid by a new prisoner.

maleolar, *a.* (anat.) malleolar.

maléolo, *m.* (anat.) malleolus.

malestar, *m.* malaise, indisposition.

maleta, *f.* valise, gripsack, satchel, portmanteau. —**hacer la m.,** to pack one's satchel; (coll.) to make preparations for a journey.

maletero, *m.* valise maker or seller.

maletín, *m. dim.* small valise or satchel.—**m. de grupa,** (mil.) saddlebag.

maletón, *m. aug.* large satchel.

malevolencia, *f.* malevolence, ill will.

malévolo, la, *a.* malevolent, malignant.

maleza, *f.* weeds; underbrush; brake, thicket, coppice.

malgastador, ra, *n.* spendthrift, squanderer.
malgastar, *va.* to misspend, waste, squander.
malhablado, da, *a.* foul-mouthed.
malhadado, da, *a.* wretched, unfortunate.
malhecho, cha. I. *a.* ill-shaped, malformed. **II.** *m.* evil deed, misdeed.
malhechor, ra, *n.* malefactor.
malherido, da, *a.* & *pp.* badly wounded.
malherir, *va.* to wound badly.
malhojo, *m.* vegetable refuse.
malhumorado, da, *a.* ill-humored, peevish.
malicia, *f.* malice, malignity, maliciousness; suspicion, apprehension; shrewdness, smartness; cunning, dissimulation.—**tener m.,** to be cunning or shrewd; to suspect, be suspicious.
maliciar, *va.* to suspect; to injure, harm.
maliciosamente, *adv.* maliciously; suspiciously.
malicioso, sa, *a.* malicious; wicked, knavish; suspicious.
málico, ca, *a.* (chem.) malic.
malignamente, *adv.* malignantly, malevolently.
malignante, *n.* & *a.* maligner (-ing).
malignar. I. *va.* to vitiate, corrupt, deprave. **II.** *vr.* to become sore; to grow worse.
malignidad, *f.* malignity, perversity.
maligno, na, *a.* malign, malignant, perverse.
malilla, *f.* manilla, a game of cards.
malintencionado, da, *a.* evil disposed.
malmandado, da, *a.* disobedient; obstinate.
malmeter, *va.* to waste, misspend; to induce to evil; to estrange.
malmirado, da, *a.* disliked; inconsiderate.
malo, la. bad; evil; wicked; licentious, dissolute; naughty, mischievous; ill, sick; difficult, hard; cunning, artful.—**m. del (de la),** sick at, having a sore (throat, eye, etc.), suffering from a bad (throat, liver, etc.).—**a malas,** on bad terms; in an unfriendly way.—**de malas,** unlucky; with an evil intention.—**el m.,** the Evil One.—**lo m. es que,** the worst of it is that, the trouble is that.—**por malas o por buenas,** willingly or by force.
malogramiento, *m.* failure.
malograr. I. *va.* to waste, lose, miss (as time or opportunity). **II.** *vr.* to fail, fall through, come to naught; to have an untimely end.
malogro, *m.* miscarriage, failure; untimely end.
maloja, *f.* (Cuba), cornstalks used for fodder.
malojal, *m.* plantation of MALOJA.
malojero, *m.* seller of MALOJA.
malojo, *m.* (Ven.) = MALOJA.
malón, *m.* (Am.) sudden attack by Indians.
malparado, da, *a.* & *pp.* ill-conditioned, impaired, damaged; foiled, worsted.
malparida, *f.* woman who has miscarried.
malparir, *vn.* to miscarry.
malparto, *m.* abortion, miscarriage.
malpigiáceo, a. I. *a.* malpighiaceous. **II.** *f. pl.* Malpighiaceæ.
malquerencia, *f.* ill will, hatred.
malquerer, *va.* to dislike, have a grudge against.
malqueriente, *n.* one who dislikes another.
malquistar. I. *va.* to estrange; to create prejudice against.—**m. a uno con,** to set . . . against one. **II.** *vn.* to incur dislike, bring dislike or unpopularity on one, make one's self unpopular.
malquisto, ta, *a.* disliked, unpopular.
malrotador, ra, *n.* squanderer, spendthrift.
malrotar, *va.* to misspend, lavish, squander.
malsano, na, *a.* unhealthy, sickly, infirm; unhealthful, unwholesome, noxious.
malsín, *m.* talebearer, backbiter.
malsonante, *a.* offensive to pious ears.
malsufrido, da, *a.* impatient, unresigned.
malta, *f.* malt.
maltés, sa, *a.* Maltese.
maltosa, *f.* (chem.) maltose.
maltrabaja, *n.* (coll.) idler, lounger.
maltraer, *va.* to treat ill. *V.* MALTRATAR.
maltratamiento, *m.* ill treatment; rough usage.
maltratar, *va.* to treat ill, abuse, maltreat; to use roughly; to spoil, destroy.
maltrato, *m.* = MALTRATAMIENTO.

maltrecho, cha, *a.* in bad condition, damaged; badly off, battered.
maltusiano, na, *n.* & *a.* Malthusian.
maltusianismo, *m.* Malthusianism.
maluco, ca; malucho, cha, *a.* (coll.) rather bad, baddish; sickish, ailing somewhat.
malva, *f.* (bot.) mallow.—**ser como una m.,** to be meek and obedient.
malváceo, a. I. *a.* (bot.) malvaceous. **II.** *f. pl.* Malvaceæ.
malvadamente, *adv.* wickedly, perversely.
malvado, da. I. *a.* wicked, fiendish, nefarious. **II.** *m.* wicked man, villain, knave.
malvar, *m.* place covered with mallows.
malvasía, *f.* (bot.) malvasia; malmsey wine.
malvavisco, *m.* (bot.) marshmallow.
malvender, *va.* to sell at a loss, to sacrifice.
malversación, *f.* malversation.
malversador, ra, *n.* one who misapplies funds.
malversar, *va.* to misapply (funds).
malvezar, *va.* & *vr.* to fall into bad habits.
malvís, malviz, *m.* (orn.) redwing.
malla, *f.* mesh (of a net); coat of mail; (naut.) network.
mallar. I. *vn.* to make network. **II.** *va.* to arm with a coat of mail.
mallero, *m.* netmaker; armorer.
mallete, *m.* gavel, mallet.—*pl.* (naut.) partners.
malleto, *m.* beating maul in paper mills.
mallo, *m.* mallet; pall-mall, game of bowls; mall, bowling green.
mallorquín, na, *a.* of or relating to Majorca.
mamá, *f.* mamma.
mama, *f.* mammary gland, breast; mamma.
mamacallos, *m.* (coll.) dolt, simpleton.
mamacona, *f.* religious virgin among the ancient Peruvians.
mamada, *f.* (coll.) suck; time that a child takes in sucking.
mamadera, *f.* breast pump.
mamador, ra, *n.* sucker, suckling; nursing bottle.
mamalón, *m.* (Cuba) idler, sponger, parasite.
mamandurria, *f.* (Am., pol., coll.) sinecure, job with salary and no work.
mamante, *a.* sucking.
mamantón, na, *a.* sucking (animal).
mamar, *va.* & *vn.* to suck; (coll.) to cram and devour (victuals); (coll.) to get, obtain.
mamario, ria, *a.* mammary.
mamarrachada, *f.* (coll.) collection of grotesque figures; (art) daub.—**mamarrachista,** *m.* (art) dauber.—**mamarracho,** *m.* grotesque figure or ornament; (art) daub.
mambla, *f.* mound; small peak, knoll.
mameluco, *m.* mameluke; (coll.) dolt, simpleton; children's nightdress; (Am.) half-breed.
mamella, *f.* mammillated protuberance in the neck of goats.
mamellado, da, *a.* mammillate, mammillated.
mamey, *m.* (bot.) mamey, mammee.
mamífero, ra. I. *a.* mammalian. **II.** *m. pl.* mammals, Mammalia.
mamila, *f.* woman's breast round the nipple; mammilla in men.
mamilar, *a.* mamillary.
mamola, *f.* chuck under the chin.
mamón, na, *m.* & *f.* suckling; child that sucks too much; (bot.) shoot, sucker; (W. I.) genip tree.
mamoncillo, *m.* (W. I.) honeyberry.
mamoso, sa. I. *a.* sucking. **II.** *m.* a variety of panic grass.
mamotreto, *m.* memorandum book; (coll.) bulky book or bundle of papers.
mampara, *f.* screen; fire screen.
mamparo, *m.* (naut.) bulkhead.—**mamparos de quita y pon,** (naut.) ship and unship bulkheads.
mampernal, mampirlán, *m.* wooden guard on steps of a staircase while building.
mampostear, *va.* to build with masonry.

---

mampostería, *f.* masonry (gen. app. to stone masonry).—**m. concertada,** rubble masonry, rubblework.—**m. de sillares,** ashlar masonry.—**m. en seco,** dry masonry (without mortar).

mampostero, *m.* (mas.) roughsetter.

mampresar, *va.* to begin to break in (horses).

mampuesta, *f.* (mas.) course.

mampuesto. **I.** *a.* overlapping. **II.** *m.* parapet; (Am.) rest or support for a firearm in taking aim; (mas.) rubble.—**de m.,** extra; from a sheltered position.

mamujar, *va.* to suck unsteadily.

mamullar, *va.* to eat or chew as if sucking; (coll.) to mutter, mumble.

mamut, *m.* (pal.) mammoth.

maná, *m.* manna.

manada, *f.* flock; herd; drove; large number; handful.—**a manadas,** in troops or crowds.

manadero, ra. **I.** *a.* springing, issuing. **II.** *m.* source, spring; shepherd, herdsman.

manadilla, *f. dim.* small flock.

manante, *a.* proceeding, issuing.

manantial. **I.** *a.* flowing, running. **II.** *m.* spring, source, origin.

manantío, a, *a.* flowing, running.

manar, *vn.* to issue, flow out; to ooze; to abound.

manare, *m.* (Ven.) sieve for yucca starch.

manatí, manato, *m.* (zool.) manatee, seacow; whip made of the manatee's hide.

manaza, *f. aug.* large hand.

mancamiento, *m.* want, lack, deficiency; maimedness

mancar, *va.* to maim, lame, cripple, disable.

manceba, *f.* mistress, concubine.

mancebete, *m. dim.* of MANCEBO.

mancebía, *f.* brothel, bawdyhouse.

mancebo, *m.* youth, young man; bachelor; shopman, shopboy, clerk.

mancera, *f.* plowtail, plow handle.

mancerina, *f.* saucer with holder for chocolate cup.

mancilla, *f.* spot, stain, blemish.

mancillar, *va.* to spot, stain, soil.

mancipación, *f.* (law) mancipation.

mancipar, *va.* to subject, enslave, mancipate.

manco, ca. **I.** *a.* handless; one-handed; armless; maimed; defective, faulty, imperfect. **II.** *n.* armless handless or one-handed person.

mancomún, *m.*—**de m.,** jointly, in common.

mancomunadamente, *adv.* conjointly.

mancomunar, *va. & vr.* to associate, unite, combine; (law) to make two or more persons pay jointly the costs of a lawsuit.

mancomunidad, *f.* union, fellowship, community.

mancornar, *va.* (*ind.* MANCUERNO: *subj.* MANCUERNE) to twist the neck of (a steer, etc.) and hold down on the ground with the horns downwards; to join, to couple.

mancuerda, *f.* each turn of the rack bars.

mancuerna, *f.* pair tied together; thong for tying two steers; (Cuba) tobacco stem with two leaves; (Philip.) pair of convicts chained together.

mancha, *f.* stain, spot, blot; stigma; patch of ground or vegetation; (ast.) spot (on the sun).

manchadizo, za, *a.* easily stained.

manchado, da, *a.* spotted, speckled; stained.

manchar, *va.* to stain, soil; to foul, pollute; to tarnish, defile; (art) to speckle, daub; to darken, to cloud.—**m. papel,** to scribble.

manchego, ga, *a.* of or belonging to La Mancha.

manchita, *f. dim.* small stain.

manchón, *m. aug.* large blot or stain; patch where vegetation is thickest.

manchú; manchuriano, na, *n. & a.* Manchu (-rian).

manchuela, *f.* = MANCHITA

manda, *f.* offer, proposal; legacy, bequest.

mandadera, *f.* = DEMANDADERA.

mandadero, ra, *n.* porter, messenger; errand boy or girl.

mandado, *pp. & m.* mandate, order, command; errand, message.—**bien (mal) m.,** well- (ill-) behaved.

mandamiento, *m.* order, command; (eccl.) commandment; (law) writ; mandamus.—*pl.* (coll.) the five fingers of the hand.—**mandamientos de la ley de Dios,** Ten Commandments.

mandante. **I.** *a.* commanding. **II.** *n.* (law) constituent, mandator.

mandar. **I.** *va.* to command, order, direct, decree; to will, leave, bequeath; to send, transmit; to offer, promise; (followed by *inf.*) to order, have (followed by *pp.*: *él mandó escribir la carta*, he ordered, or had, the letter written).—**m. decir,** to send word. **II.** *vr.* to communicate (as rooms); to move about unaided (s. o. patients); to go from one room to another.

mandarín, *m.* mandarin; (coll.) petty official.

mandarina, *f.* the polished Chinese language; mandarin orange.

mandarria, *f.* iron maul, sledge hammer.

mandatario, *m.* (law) attorney, agent; mandatary.

mandato, *m.* mandate; command, injunction, order, charge; (law) mandate, contract of bailment; (eccl.) maundy.

mandíbula, *f.* jawbone; jaw.

mandibular, *a.* mandibular.

mandil, *m.* leather or coarse apron; fine-mesh fishing net; clout for cleaning horses.

mandilar, *va.* to wipe (a horse) with a clout.

mandilejo, *m. dim.* small apron.

mandilete, *m.* (fort.) door of a porthole.

mandilón, *m.* (coll.) coward.

mandioca, *f.* (bot.) manioc, cassava; tapioca.

mando, *m.* command, power, dominion.

mandoble, *m.* two-handed blow with a sword; severe reprimand.

mandolina, *f.* = BANDOLÍN.

mandón, na. **I.** *a.* imperious, domineering. **II.** *n.* imperious, haughty person; (min.) boss or foreman.

mandrachero, *m.* keeper of a gaming table.

mandracho, *m.* gambling house.

mandrágora, *f.* (bot.) mandrake.

mandria. *a. & m.* coward (-ly), poltroon.

mandril, *m.* (zool.) mandrill, baboon; (mech.) mandrel, chuck, spindle of a lathe.

mandrón, *m.* stone ball used as a missile.

manducación, *f.* (coll.) chewing.—**manducar,** *va.* (coll.) to chew.—**manducatoria,** *f.* (coll.) eatables, grub, eats.

manea, *f.* (farr.) fetterlock, hopple.

manear, *va.* to hobble (a horse).

manecica, ita, *f. dim.* small hand.

manecilla, *f. dim.* small hand; (print.) fist (☞), index; book clasp; hand of a clock or watch.

manejable, *a.* manageable, tractable.

manejado, *pp. & a.* (art) handled.

manejar. **I.** *va.* to manage, wield, handle; to drive, ride, train (a horse); to conduct, govern contrive; to run (an engine, a business). **II.** *vr.* to move about after having been deprived of motion; to behave.

manejo, *m.* handling; management, conduct; horsemanship, manège; cunning, trick, intrigue, device.—**m. doméstico,** housekeeping.—**manejos de corte,** court intrigues.

maneota, *f.* shackles, hobbles, fetters.

manera, *f.* manner, way, mode; (art) manner, style; fore part or fall of breeches; side opening in a skirt; quality, class of persons.—*pl.* ways, customs; manners.—**a m. de, a la m. de,** in the style of· like.—**de mala m.,** botchingly; roughly; gruffly, reluctantly.—**de m. de,** so as to.—**de m. que,** so then; so that; in such a manner as to, so as to.—**en gran m.,** in large measure; greatly, to a large extent.—**por m. que,** so then; so that; and so.—**sobre m.,** exceedingly.

manero, ra, *a.* tame (in falconry).

manes, *m. pl.* manes, spirits of the dead.

For pronunciation, see the rules at the beginning of the book.

manezuela, *f. dim.* small hand; book clasp; haft or handle.

manfla, *f.* (coll.) concubine; old sow.

manga, *f.* sleeve; arm of an axletree; a kind of cloak bag or portmanteau; hose; purse seine; net bag, fish trap; bag strainer, Hippocrates sleeve; body of troops in a line; (eccl.) manga; (naut.) breadth of beam; wind sail; (Mex.) poncho; (bot.) a variety of mango.—*pl.* profits, gains.—**m. de agua,** squall, shower.—**m. de viento,** whirlwind.—**m. marina,** waterspout.—**andar m. por hombro,** to be very careless in domestic affairs.—**en mangas de camisa,** in shirt sleeves.—**tener m. ancha,** to be broad-minded.

mangachapuy, *m.* (bot.) (Philip.) a dipterad tree.

mangajarro, *m.* (coll.) long, ill-shaped sleeve.

mangana, *f.* lasso, lariat.—**manganear,** *va.* (Am.) to lasso.—**manganeo,** *m.* lassoing.

manganato, *m.* (chem.) manganate.

manganesa, manganesia, *f.* (min.) peroxide of manganese.—**manganésico, ca,** *a.* manganic, containing manganese.

manganesífero, ra, *a.* manganiferous.

manganeso, *m.* manganese.

mangánico, ca, *s.* manganic.

manganilla, *f.* trick, stratagem; long pieced pole.

manganoso, *a.* manganous.

mangla, *f.* gum from the rockrose.

manglar, *m.* plantation of mangrove trees.

mangle, *m.* (bot.) mangrove tree.

mango, *m.* handle, haft, helve; tiller; (bot.) Indian mango.—**m. de escoba,** broomstick.—**m. de pluma,** penholder.

mangón, na, *n.* retailer; second-hand dealer.

mangonada, *f.* push with the arm.

mangonear, *vn.* (coll.) to wander about, loiter, loaf; to intermeddle; to pry.

mangoneo, *m.* intermeddling, prying.

mangonero, ra, *a.* fond of nosing or prying.

mangorrero, ra, *a.* rough-hafted (knife); worthless, useless.

mangorrillo, *m.* plowtail. *V.* MANCERA.

mangosta, *f.* (zool.) mongoose.

mangostán, *m.* (bot.) mangosteen.

mangote, *m.* (coll.) large, wide sleeve; oversleeve.

mangual, *m.* war flail, morning star.

manguardia, *f.* buttress of a bridge.

manguera, *f.* hose; (naut.) wind sail; watersprout; tarred canvas bucket; (Am.) large corral; tube, sleeve.—**m. de desinflar,** (aer.) deflating sleeve.—**m. de inflar,** (aer.) inflating sleeve.

manguero, *m.* horseman; fireman.

mangueta, *f.* bag syringe; jamb post of a glass door or window; tiebeam; (mech.) lever; neck of a water-closet hopper.

manguita, *f. dim.* small sleeve; sheath, case.

manguitería, *f.* furrier's shop.

manguitero, *m.* muff maker, furrier.

manguito, *m.* muff; wristlet, hose muffler for the arm; large coffee cake; oversleeve; (mech.) muff, coupler, collar, sleeve.

maní, *m.* (Am.) peanut. *V.* CACAHUETE.

manía, *f.* mania; madness; whim, hobby.

maníaco, ca. I. *a.* maniac, mad; whimsical. **II.** *n.* maniac.

maniatar, *va.* to manacle; to handcuff.

maniático, ca, *a.* = MANÍACO.

manicomio, *m.* insane asylum, madhouse.

manicordio, *m.* (mus.) manichord, clavichord.

manicorto, ta, *a.* illiberal, close-fisted.

manicuro, ra, *n.* manicure.

manida, *f.* resort, abode, nest, den.

manido, da, *pp.* & *a.* hidden, concealed; (cook.) high, gamy.

manifacero, ra, *a.* (coll.) meddlesome.

manifactura, *f.* make; manufacture.

manifestación, *f.* manifestation, declaration; statement; demonstration; (law) writ resembling habeas corpus.

manifestador, ra, *a.* that manifests.

manifestar, *va.* (*pp.* MANIFESTADO, MANIFIESTO: *ind.* MANIFIESTO: *subj.* MANIFIESTE) to state, declare; to manifest, reveal, show; to tell, let know; (eccl.) to expose (the eucharist) for public worship.

manifiestamente, *adv.* manifestly, obviously.

manifiesto, ta. I. *a.* manifest, plain, obvious; overt. **II.** *m.* manifest or manifesto, public declaration; (eccl.) act of exposing the eucharist; (com.) customhouse manifest.—**poner de m.,** to make evident, to show plainly; to make public, expose.

manigua, *f.* (Cuba) thicket, jungle.

manigueta, *f.* haft, handle.—*pl.* (naut.) kevels.

manija, *f.* handle, haft; crank; hopple, fetters; (mech.) ring, brace, clasp, clamp.

manijero, *m.* foreman of a gang of laborers.

manilargo, ga, *a.* having long hands; prone to fisticuffs, pugilistic.

manilense; manileño, ña. I. *n.* native of Manila. **II.** *a.* Manila (u. a.).

maniluvio, *m.* bath for the hands, as a remedy.

manilla, *f. dim.* small hand; (jew.) bracelet; manacle, handcuff.

maniobra, *f.* handiwork; operation, procedure; artifice, trick, manœuvring; (mil.) manœuvre; (naut.) working of a ship; gear, rigging, tackle, *pl.* (r. w.) switch-engine work.

maniobrar, *va.* & *vn.* to make handiwork; (naut.) to work a ship; to devise ways and means of effecting anything; (mil.) to manœuvre.

maniobrero, ra, *a.* manœuvring (troops).

maniobrista, *m.* skilful naval tactician.

maniota, *f.* hopple, fetterlock.

manipulación, *f.* manipulation.

manipulante, *m.* (coll.) administrator, negotiator.

manipular, *va.* to manipulate, handle, manage.

manipuleo, *m.* (coll.) tactful handling, manœuvring.

manípulo, *m.* (ecc.) maniple; standard; maniple, a division of the Roman legion; (med.) handful.

maniqueísmo, *m.* Manicheism.

maniqueo, a, *n.* & *a.* Manichean.

maniquete, *m.* black lace mitten.

maniquí, *m.* puppet; manikin, figure.

manir, *va.* (*defec.: only those forms are used having the letter* **i** *in their terminations*) to keep meat until it becomes gamy.

manirroto, ta, *a.* lavish, prodigal, wasteful.

manita, manito, *f. dim.* little hand.

manivacío, cía, *a.* (coll.) empty-handed.

manivela, *f.* (mech.) crank; crankshaft.—**m. de arranque,** (aut.) starting crank or handle.—**m. de disco,** disc crank.

manjar, *m.* food, dish, victuals; titbit, morsel; recreation, entertainment.—**m. blanco,** dish made of shredded chicken with sugar, milk, and rice flour; blancmange.

manjarejo, *m. dim.* savory dish, titbit.

manjarria, *f.* (Cuba) driving beam of a canemill.

manjelín, *m.* diamond weight; carat.

manjolar, *va.* to carry (a hawk).

manjorrada, *f.* abundance of ordinary victuals.

manjúa, *f.* (Am.) a variety of sardine.

manlieva, *f.* taxes collected from house to house.

manlieve, *m.* confidence game; swindle.

mano, *f.* hand; fore foot; foot of cattle after cut off; trunk of an elephant; hand of a clock or watch; pestle; cylindrical stone for grinding cocoa; quire of paper; reprimand; musical scale; first hand at cards; round of any game; power or means of making or attaining something; each time or turn in a work by hand; coat (of paint, varnish, etc.); workmanship, handicraft, handiwork.—**m. a m.,** in friendly coöperation, together; on equal terms, without odds.—**m. apalmada,** (her.) stretched palm of the hand.—**m. de gato,** ladies' make-up; polishing or editing hand (s. o. works of art or literature amended by more able persons than the author).—**m. de obra,** workmanship; labor.—**¡manos a la obra!** bear a hand! to work!.—**manos libres,** perquisites.—**manos**

muertas, mortmain, unalienable estate.—**a la m.,** near, at hand.—**a m.,** by hand; near by.—**a m.** **derecha (izquierda),** on the right- (left-) hand side.—**a m. salva** = A MANSALVA. *V.* MANSALVA.—**a manos llenas,** liberally, abundantly.—**a una m.,** of one accord.—**bajo m.,** underhandedly.—**de buena m.,** on good authority.—**de m.** = BAJO M.; hand (u. a., as in *rueda de mano,* hand wheel).—**de la m.,** by the hand.—**de manos a boca,** suddenly, unexpectedly.—**de primera m.,** first-hand.—**entre manos,** on hand, in the process of carrying on or out.—**por debajo de m.** = BAJO MANO.—**por su m.,** by one's self, by one's own judgment or authority.

manobra, *f.* raw material.

manobre, *m.* hodman, hodcarrier.

manobrero, *m.* keeper of irrigating ditches.

manojillo, ito, *m. dim.* small bundle or fagot.

manojo, *m.* handful, bunch, fagot, bundle.—**a manojos,** abundantly.

manojuelo, *m. dim.* small bunch or bundle.

manolo, la, *n.* Madrilenian of low class, loud in dress and manners.

manométrico, ca, *a.* manometric.

manómetro, *m.* manometer, pressure gauge.

manopla, *f.* gauntlet; coachman's whip.

manosear, *va.* to handle, touch, feel of; to muss, rumple (clothes).

manoseo, *m.* handling.

manota, *f. aug.* large, ugly hand.

manotada, *f.,* **manotazo,** *m.* cuff, slap, box; blow with the paw.

manotear. I. *va.* to cuff, buffet. **II.** *vn.* to gesticulate.

manoteo, *m.* gesticulation with the hands.

manotón, *m.* = MANOTADA.

manquear, *vn.* to affect the cripple.

manquedad, manquera, *f.* lack of one or both arms or hands; defect, imperfection.

mansalva.—**a m.,** without running any risk, without danger, in a cowardly manner.

mansamente, *adv.* meekly; gently, quietly.

mansedumbre, *f.* meekness; gentleness, tameness.—**mansejón, na,** *a.* very tame.

mansera, *f.* (Cuba) vat for the cane juice.

mansión, *f.* stay, sojourn; habitation, mansion, abode.—**hacer m.,** to stop over.

mansito, *adv.* = MANSAMENTE.

mansito, ta, *a.* very gentle or tame.

manso, sa. I. *a.* tame; gentle, mild; calm; soft, quiet; meek, lamblike. **II.** *m.* bellwether; manse, farm.

manta, *f.* woollen blanket; travelling rug; men's shawl; horse blanket; (Mex.) coarse cotton cloth; tossing blanket or canvas; (fort.) mantelet, movable parapet; thrashing, drubbing; (min.) bag of agave for carrying ore; game of cards resembling OMBRE.—**m. blanca,** bleached cotton.—**m. de algodón,** wadding.—**m. prieta,** unbleached cotton.—**a m. de Dios,** (coll.) copiously, plentifully.

mantalona, *f.* (Philip.) cotton stuff for sails.

mantaterilla, *f.* coarse hempen cloth for horse blankets.

manteador, ra, *n.* tosser (in a blanket.)

manteamiento, *m.* tossing in a blanket.

mantear. I. *va.* to toss in a blanket. **II.** *vn.* to gad, be out too much (s. o. women).

manteca, *f.* lard; fat; pomatum; butter; oily substance of cocoa and other fruits.—**m. de cacao,** cocoa butter.

mantecada, *f.* buttered toast and sugar; a kind of cooky.

mantecado, *m.* biscuit kneaded with lard; French ice cream.

mantención, *f.* = MANUTENCIÓN.

mantecón, *m.* milksop; sweet tooth; dainty person.

mantecoso, sa, *a.* buttery, greasy.

manteísta, *m.* day student.

mantel, *m.* tablecloth; altar cloth.—**levantar los manteles,** to clear the table.

mantelería, *f.* table linen.

manteleta, *f.* mantelet, ladies' shawl.

mantelete, *m.* (eccl.) mantelet; (fort.) mantelet; (her.) mantling.

mantelo, *m.* very wide apron.

mantellina, *f.* a sort of mantilla.

mantenedor, *m.* president of a tournament or contest.

mantener. I. *va.* (*ind.* MANTENGO: *pret.* MANTUVE: *fut.* MANTENDRÉ: *subj.* MANTENGA) to support, provide for, to feed; to maintain, keep up; to continue, persevere in: to pursue; to defend or sustain (an opinion).—**m. correspondencia,** to keep up a correspondence. **II.** *vr.* to support one's self, earn one's living; to continue, remain (in one place); (w. **en**) to remain firm (in), continue to, adhere (to), hold on (to).

manteniente, *m.* violent blow with both hands.—**a m.** with all one's might; firmly.

mantenimiento, *m.* maintenance, support, sustenance, subsistence; livelihood, living.

manteo, *m.* tossing in a blanket; long cloak or mantle; sort of woollen skirt.

mantequero, ra. I. *n.* one who sells butter; dairyman, dairymaid. **II.** *f.* churn; butter dish or bowl.

mantequilla, *f.* butter; hard sauce.

mantequillero, ra. I. *n.* = MANTEQUERO. **II.** *f.* butter bowl.

mantero, ra, *n.* blanket maker or seller; mantua maker.

mantés, sa, *n.* (coll.) rogue, scoundrel.

mantilla, *f.* mantilla; housing, saddlecloth; (print.) blanket; slip, infant's frock; birth present from one prince to another.—**estar en mantillas,** to be in a state of infancy.

mantilleja, *f. dim.* small mantilla.

mantillo, *m.* (agr.) humus; rotten, fermented manure.

mantillón, na, *a.* dirty, slovenly.

mantisa, *f.* (math.) mantissa.

manto, *m.* cloak, mantle; large mantilla; robe of state; mantelpiece of a chimney; (min.) layer or stratum.

mantón, *m. aug.* large cloak or mantle; (Cuba.) mantilla.

mantuano, na, *n. & a.* of or from Mantua.

mantudo, da, *a.* having drooping wings.

manuable, *a.* easy to handle, handy.

manual. I. *a.* manual; handy; domestic, home-made; easy; tractable, pliant. **II.** *m.* manual, handbook; notebook; account book; handle (of an oar); (eccl.) ritual; (com.) old name of the journal.—*pl.* a priest's fees for assisting in the choir.

manualmente, *adv.* manually.

manubrio, *m.* handle, crank.

manucodiata, *f.* (orn.) bird of paradise.

manuela, *f.* (in Madrid) open hack.

manuella, *f.* (naut.) capstan bar.

manufactura, *f.* manufacture; manufactured article.

manufacturar, *va. & vn.* to manufacture.

manufacturero, ra, *a.* manufacturing.

manumisión, *f.* manumission.—**manumiso, sa,** *a.* emancipated; free, disengaged.—**manumisor,** *m.* (law) liberator.—**manumitir,** *va.* (*pp.* MANUMITIDO, MANUMISO) to manumit, emancipate.

manuscribir, *va. & vn.* to write by hand.

manuscrito, ta, *n. & a.* manuscript.

manutención, *f.* maintaining; maintenance, support; protection; conservation.

manutener, *va.* (law) to maintain, support.

manutisa, *f.* (bot.) = MINUTISA.

manvacío, a, *a.* = MANIVACÍO.

manzana, *f.* (bot.) apple; block (of houses), square; knob of a sword.

manzanal, manzanar, *m.* apple orchard.

manzanera, *f.* (bot.) = MAGUILLO.

manzanil, *a.* applelike.

manzanilla, *f. dim.* (bot.) common chamomile; knob at the top of coaches, bedsteads, etc.; medium-sized olive; white sherry wine; lower part of the chin; pad, or cushion, of the feet of animals having claws.—**m. fina**, golden cotula.— **m. hedionda** = MAGARZUELA.

manzanillo, ito, *m. dim.* (bot.) manchineel, poison tree.

manzanita, *f. dim.* little apple.—**m. de dama** = ACEROLA.

manzano, *m.* (bot.) apple tree.

maña, *f.* skill, dexterity, cleverness, knack; cunning, craftiness; tact, care; habit or custom; bundle or bunch (as of hemp or flax).—**darse m.**, to contrive, to manage.

mañana. I. *f.* morning, morrow, forenoon; (Am.) morning drink.—**de gran m.**, very early.— **de m.**, in the morning.—**muy de m.** = DE GRAN M.—**por la m.**, in the morning.—**tomar la m.**, to take an appetizer (drink) before breakfast. **II.** *adv.* to-morrow; later, in time to come.

mañanear, *vn.* to rise early.

mañanica, ita, *f.* break of day.

mañear, *va. & vn.* to manage or act with craft and cunning.

mañería, *f.* sterility; feudal right of inheriting from those who died without legitimate succession.

mañero, ra, *a.* clever, dexterous, skilful, artful; handy, easy; meek, tractable.

maño, ña, *n.* brother (sister); dear, darling.

mañoco, *m.* tapioca; Indian-corn meal.

mañosamente, *adv.* neatly, handily, cleverly; tactfully, slickly; craftily.

mañoso, sa, *a.* skilful, handy, clever; tactful, cunning, careful.

mañuela. I. *f.* low cunning, mean trick. **II.** *n.* artful, cunning person.

mapa. I. *m.* map, chart. **II.** *f.* (coll.) anything excellent and prominent in its line.—**llevarse la m.**, to excel, to take the prize.

mapache, *m.* (zool.) raccoon.

mapamundi, *m.* map of the world.

mapaná, mapanare, *f.* (Colomb., Ven.) a poisonous snake.

mapurito, *m.* (C. A.) (zool.) skunk.

maque, *m.* (Mex.) sumac lacquer.

maquear, *va.* to lacquer with MAQUE.

maquí, *m.* a kind of ginger.

maquiavélico, ca, *a.* Machiavelian.

maquiavelismo, *m.* Machiavelism.

maquiavelista, *n.* Machiavelian.

maquila, *f.* toll corn; a corn measure (½ CELEMÍN); (C. A.) a unit of weight (about 125 lb.)

maquilar, *va.* to measure and take the miller's toll corn.—**maquilero, maquilón,** *m.* measurer and receiver of milling toll corn.

máquina, *f.* machine, engine; fancy project; admixture of fancy or the supernatural in certain poetical compositions; imposing structure, pile; (coll.) abundancy, lots.—**m. compound,** or **compuesta,** compound engine.—**m. de cilindro,** reciprocating engine.—**m. de combustión interna,** internal-combustion engine.— **m. de coser,** sewing machine.—**m. de doble efecto,** double-acting engine.—**m. de émbolo,** reciprocating engine.—**m. de escribir,** typewriter. —**m. de vapor,** steam engine.—**m. infernal,** infernal machine.—**m. neumática,** air pump.

maquinación, *f.* machination.

maquinador, ra, *n.* schemer, plotter.

maquinal, *a.* mechanical.—**maquinalmente,** *adv.* mechanically, unconsciously.

maquinar, *va. & vn.* to machinate, scheme, plot, hatch, concoct.

maquinaria, *f.* machinery; applied mechanics.

maquinista, *n.* engine runner, engineer; machinist; mechanic, mechanician.

mar, *m. or f.* sea; flood; large quantity or number. —**m. alta,** rough sea.—**m. ancha,** high seas.—**m. bonanza,** calm sea.—**m. de fondo,** swell.—**m. de través,** sea on the beam.—**m. en leche,** calm sea. —**m. jurisdiccional,** or **territorial,** territorial waters.—**m. llena,** or **plena,** high water.—**arar en el m.**, to labor in vain.—**baja m.**, low water, ebb tide.—**correr con la mar en popa,** to scud before the sea.—**correr los mares,** to follow the

seas.—**de m. a m.**, copiously, excessively; in the extreme of fashion.—**hablar de la m.**, to attempt an impossibility; to speak on an inexhaustible subject.—**la m.**, (coll.) a great quantity or number, a lot, lots.—**meter el m. en pozo**, to attempt the impossible.

marabú, *m.* (orn.) marabou.

maracure, *m.* (bot.) curare plant.

maragato, ta, *n.* native of a region in Spain called Maragatería.

maraña, *f.* jungle; tangle, entanglement; silk waste and stuff made from it; perplexity, puzzle; fraud, imposition; intrigue, plot.

marañado, da, *a.* entangled, perplexed.

marañero, ra; ñoso, sa, *a.* entangling, ensnaring, perplexing.

marañón, *m.* (Cuba) (bot.) cashew; cashew nut.

marasmo, *m.* marasmus, wasting; inactivity, dullness, deadness.

márata, *n. & a.* Maratha, Mahratta.

maravedí, *m.* maravedi, an old Spanish coin.

maravilla, *f.* wonder, marvel; (bot.) marigold.— **m. de noche,** or **de Indias,** (bot.) marvel of Peru, four-o'clock.—**a las mil maravillas,** wonderfully well.—**a m.**, marvellously.—**por m.**, very seldom.

maravillar. I. *va.* to admire. **II.** *vr.* (w. de) to wonder (at), to marvel.

maravillosamente, *adv.* wonderfully, marvellously.—**maravilloso, sa,** *a.* wonderful.

marbete, *m.* label, tag, ticket; (r. w.) baggage check; border, fillet.

marca, *f.* mark, stamp, impress; brand; make; sign; standard (of size); gauge or rule for measuring; marker, stencil, label, tag, ticket; (geog.) march, frontier region or province; seamark, landmark.—**m. de fábrica,** trademark.—**de m.**, excellent of its kind.—**de más de m.**, or **de m. mayor,** of high quality, first-class, superior.

marcación, *f.* bearing; taking a ship's bearings.

marcadamente, *adv.* markedly, notably.

marcador, ra. I. *n. & a.* marker (-ing). **II.** *m.* marker; assay master; index; bookmark.

marcar. I. *va.* (pret. MARQUÉ: subj. MARQUE) to mark, stamp, impress, brand; to observe, note; (spt.) to even up, counter.—**m. el compás,** to beat time, keep time. **II.** *vr.* to determine its bearings (s. o. a ship).

marcasita, *f.* (min.) marcasite, white pyrites.

marceador, ra, *n. & a.* shearer (-ing).

marcear. I. *va.* to shear. **II.** *vn.* to be rough (s. o. the weather).

marceo, *m.* trimming honeycombs in spring.

marcero, ra. = MARCEADOR.

marcescente, *a.* (bot.) marcescent, withering.

marcial. I. *a.* martial, warlike; frank, unceremonious; (pharm.) martial, chalybeate. **II.** *m.* aromatic powder for dressing gloves.

marcialidad, *f.* martialness; frankness.

marcionista, *n. & a.* Marcionite (-itic).

marco, *m.* frame, doorcase, window case; picture frame; mark, gold and silver weight; standard (of weight); scantling and length of timber; model, archetype; mark, German coin.

márcola, *f.* pruning hook.

marconigrafía, *f.* wireless telegraphy.

marconigrama, *m.* marconigram, wireless telegram.

marcha, *f.* march; progress, turn, course, run; (naut.) speed; (mús.) march, two-step; movement of a watch; running or functioning; bonfire.—**marchas forzadas,** (mil.) forced marches.— **a largas marchas,** with celerity, speedily.—**batir la m.**, to strike up a march.—**sobre la m.**, at once, right off, right away.

marchamar, *va.* to mark at the customhouse.

marchamero, *m.* customhouse officer who marks goods.

marchamo, *m.* customhouse mark on goods.

marchante. I. *a.* mercantile, commercial, trading. **II.** *m.* shopkeeper, dealer; customer, buyer; (Cuba) sharper, trickster.

marchapié, *m.* footboard; (naut.) horse, footrope.

marchar, *vn.* & *vr.* to go; to go away, leave; to walk; to progress, proceed, go ahead; to work, function, run (as a machine); to go (as a train, a ship, a clock); to move (as a carriage); to pace (as a horse); (mil.) to march; (naut.) to have speed.

marchitable, *a.* perishable, liable to wither.

marchitamiento, *m.* withering, fading.

marchitar. I. *va.* to wither, fade. **II.** *vr.* to wither, fade, decay; to pine away.

marchitez, *f.* withering, fading.

marchito, ta, *a.* faded, withered.

marea, *f.* tide; beach; soft sea breeze; dew; mizzle; street dirt washed away.—**m. alta,** high tide, high water.—**m. baja,** low tide, ebb.—**m. creciente,** flood tide.—**m. menguante,** ebb tide.

mareado, da, *pp.* & *a.* seasick.

mareaje, *m.* navigation, seamanship; course of a ship.

mareamiento, *m.* seasickness.

mareante. I. *n.* navigator, skipper, sailor. **II.** *a.* causing seasickness.

marear. I. *va.* to navigate; to sell; (coll.) to vex, importune, bother. **II.** *vr.* to become, or get, seasick; to be damaged at sea.

marecanita, *f.* (min.) marekanite.

marejada, *f.* swell, head sea, surf; commotion, excitement, disturbance.

maremagno, mare mágnum, *m.* (coll.) abundance; confusion, disorder.

mareo, *m.* seasickness; (coll.) vexation.

mareógrafo, *m.* mareograph.

marero, *a.* sea breeze.

mareta, *f.* (naut.) surge of the sea; growing or decreasing excitement.

maretazo, *m.* dashing of a wave.

márfaga, márfega, *f.* ticking; straw bed.

marfil, *m.* ivory.

marfileño, ña, *a.* ivory (u. a.); ivorylike.

marfuz, *a.* repudiated, rejected; fallacious, deceitful.

marga, *f.* marl, loam; ticking; burlap.

margajita, *f.* (min.) white pyrites.

margal, *m.* marly ground, marlpit.

margallón, *m.* (bot.) palmetto.

margar, *va.* to fertilize with marl.

margarato, *m.* (chem.) margarate.

margárico, *a.* (chem.) margaric.

margarina, *f.* (chem.) margarine.

margarita, *f.* pearl; (bot.) common daisy; marguerite; periwinkle.

margay, *m.* (zool.) margay.

margen, *m.* or *f.* margin, border, edge, verge; fringe; marginal note.—**andarse por las márgenes,** to beat about the bush.—**dar m.,** to give an opportunity.

margenar, *va.* = MARGINAR.

marginado, da, *a.* & *pp.* marginated.

marginal, *a.* marginal.

marginar, *va.* to make marginal notes on; to leave a margin on.

margoso, sa, *a.* marly, loamy.

margrave, *m.* margrave.

margraviato, *m.* margraviate.

marguera, *f.* marlpit.

marhojo, *m.* = MALHOJO.

maría, *f.* (coll.) white wax taper; old silver coin.

mariano, na, *a.* (eccl.) Marian.

marica. I. *f. dim.* (orn.) magpie; knave of diamonds. **II.** *m.* milksop, effeminate man.

Maricastaña, *f.*—**en tiempos de M.,** in the days of yore; long, long ago.

maridable, *a.* conjugal, matrimonial, connubial, marital.—**maridablemente,** *adv.* conjugally.— **maridaje,** *m.* conjugal bond; intimate connection or union.—**maridar. I.** *vn.* to marry; to live as man and wife. **II.** *va.* to unite, join.—**maridazo,** *m.* (coll.) = GURRUMINO.—**maridillo,** *m.* sorry, pitiful husband; brasier.

marido, *m.* husband.

marimacho, *m.* (coll.) virago, mannish woman.

marimanta, *f.* (coll.) bugbear, hobgoblin.

marimba, *f.* a kind of drum used by negroes of Africa; (Am.) xylophone.

marimoña, *f.* (bot.) = FRANCESILLA.

marimorena, *f.* (coll.) quarrel, row.

marina, *f.* marine, shore, sea coast; (art) sea piece; seamanship, nautical art.—**m. de guerra,** navy.—**m. mercante,** merchant marine.

marinaje, *m.* seamanship; sailors.

marinar, *va.* to salt (fish); (naut.) to man (a ship).

marinear, *vn.* to be a mariner.

marinerado, da, *a.* manned, equipped.

marinería, *f.* seamanship; body of seamen; ship's crew.

marinero, ra. I. *a.* ready to sail; seaworthy, sea-going, stanch. **II.** *m.* mariner, seaman, sailor.—**a la marinera,** in a seamanlike manner, shipshape.

marinesco, ca, *a.* belonging to sailors.—**a la m.,** in a seamanlike manner, shipshape.

marino, na. I. *a.* marine, nautical, sea (u. a.). **II.** *n.* mariner, seaman.

marión, *m.* (icht.) sturgeon.

maripérez, *f.* servant maid.

mariposa, *f.* (ent.) butterfly; night taper.

mariposear, *vn.* to flit like a butterfly; to be fickle and capricious.

mariquita, *f.* (ent.) ladybug, ladybird.

marisabidilla, *f.* (coll.) bluestocking.

mariscal, *m.* (mil.) marshal; farrier, blacksmith. —**m. de campo,** field marshal.

mariscala, *f.* marshal's wife.

mariscalato, *m.*, **mariscalía,** *f.* marshalship.

mariscar, *vn.* to gather shellfish.

marisco, *m.* any of the Invertebrata, especially a mollusc or a shellfish.

marisma, *f.* marsh, swamp, morass.

marismo, *m.* (bot.) = ORZAGA.

marital, *a.* marital.

marítimo, ma, *a.* maritime, marine, sea (u. a.).

maritornes, *f.* (coll.) homely, ungainly maid of all work.

marjal, *m.* fen, marsh, moor, moorland.

marjoleta, *f.* = MAJUELA.

marjoleto, *m.* (bot.) white hawthorn.

marlota, *f.* a kind of Moorish gown.

marmatita, *f.* (min.) marmatite.

marmella, *f.* = MAMELLA.

marmellado, da, *a.* mammillate.

marmita, *f.* kettle, pot, boiler.

marmitón, *m.* scullion.

mármol, *m.* marble; (art) marble sculpture; (gl.) marver; (print.) imposing stone.

marmolejo, *m. dim.* small marble column.

marmoleño, ña, *a.* marbly.

marmolería, *f.* marblework; marbleworks.

marmolillo, *m. dim.* fender stone; (met.) unfeeling person.

marmolista, *m.* marbler, sculptor.

marmoración, *f.* marbling. *V.* ESTUCO.

marmóreo, ea, *a.* marbled, marmorean, marble (u. a.).

marmorete, *m.* (print.) vignette, small cut.

marmota, *f.* (zool.) marmot; worsted cap.

maro, *m.* (bot.) germander, marum.

marojo, *m.* (bot.) red-berried mistletoe.

maroma, *f.* rope, cable.

maromero, ra, *n.* tight-rope dancer.

marón, *m.* (icht.) sturgeon.

maronita, *n.* & *a.* Maronite.

marqués, *m.* marquis.—**marquesa,** marchioness; marquee.—**marquesado,** *m.* marquisate.

marquesina, *f.* marquee, awning.

marquesita, *f.* (min.) marcasite, white pyrites; small armchair.

marquesote, *m.* (Mex.) caramel, burnt sugar.

marqueta, *f.* crude cake of wax.

marquetería, *f.* cabinetwork; marquetry, checkered or inlaid work.

marquilla, *f.* demy (paper).

marquito, *m. dim.* small frame.

marra, *f.* lack, want; defect; stone hammer.

márraga, *f.* ticking.

marrajo, ja. I. *a.* cunning, artful, wily. **II.** *m.* (icht.) shark.

marrana, *f.* sow, female pig; (coll.) dirty or unprincipled woman; axle of a NORIA.

marranada, *f.* (coll.) hoggish action; nastiness, filthiness.

marranalla, *f.* rabble.

marranamente, *adv.* piggishly, swinishly.

marrancho, cha, *n.* pig, hog; dirty person.

marranchón, na, *n.* hog (sow).

marranillo, *m.* little pig.

marrano, na. I. *a.* hog; (coll.) dirty or unprincipled person. **II.** *m.* drum of a water wheel; woodwork supporting a well; board to equalize pressure in oil mills.

marrar, *vn.* to deviate from right; to lack, fail; to miss.

marras, *adv.* (coll.) long ago, long since, whilom.

marrasquino, *m.* maraschino.

marrazo, *m.* mattock.

marrear, *va.* to strike with a stone hammer.

márrega, *f.,* **marregón,** *m.* straw bed.

marrillo, *m.* thick short stick.

marro, *m.* a game resembling quoits; slip or slide of pursued game to avoid capture; miss, failure; catstick for playing tipcat.

marrón, *m.* quoit, pitcher.

marroqui, *m.* morocco.

marroquí; marroquín, na, *n.* & *a.* Moroccan.

marrubio, *m.* (bot.) white horehound.

marrueco, ca, *n.* & *a.* Moroccan.

marrullería, *f.* wheedle, cajolery.

marrullero, ra, *n.* wheedler, coaxer, deceiver.

marsellés, sa. I. *a.* of or relating to Marseilles. **II.** *m.* short jacket. **III.** *f.* Marseillaise, French national anthem.

marso, sa, *n.* & *a.* Marsian (one of, relative to, the Marsi).

marsopa, marsopla, *f.* blunt-headed cachalot.

marsupial. I. *n.* & *a.* (zool.) marsupial. **II.** *m. pl.* Marsupialia, marsupials.

marta, *f.* (zool.) pine marten and its fur.

martagón, na. I. *n.* (coll.) shrewd person. **II.** *m.* (bot.) wild lily.

Marte, *m.* (ast.) Mars.

martellina, *f.* marteline, millstone hammer.

martes, *m.* Tuesday.—**m. de carnestolendas,** Shrove Tuesday.

martillada, *f.* stroke with a hammer.

martillador, ra, *n.* & *a.* hammerer (-ing).

martillar, *va.* to hammer.—**martillazo,** *m.* stroke with a hammer.—**martillejo,** *m. dim.* small hammer.—**martilleo,** *m.* hammering; clatter.

martillo, *m.* hammer; claw hammer; tuning hammer; auction rooms; (anat.) malleus.— **a macha m.,** strongly but roughly made.—**a m.,** with a hammer; by hammering.—**de ru.,** wrought (s. o. metals).

Martín (San), *m.* season for killing hogs.— **llegarle a uno su San M.,** every dog has his day.

martín del río, *m.* (orn.) = MARTINETE.

martín pescador, *m.* (orn.) kingfisher.

martinete, *m.* (orn.) a heronlike bird and its tuft of white feathers; drop hammer; pile driver; hammer of a pianoforte.

martingala, *f.* breeches worn under armor; stake in the game of monte.

martinico, *m.* (coll.) ghost.

martiniega, *f.* tax payable on St. Martin's day.

mártir, *n.* martyr.

martirio, *m.* martyrdom; torture; grief.

martirizador, ra. I. *n.* martyrizer. **II.** *a.* martyrizing; tormenting, agonizing.

martirizar, *va.* (*pret.* MARTIRICÉ: *subj.* MARTIRICE) to martyr; to martyrize; to torment.

martirologio, *m.* martyrology.

marullo, *m.* (naut.) sea wave.

marzadga, *f.* tax payable in March.

marzal, *a.* belonging to the month of March.

marzo, *m.* March, third month.

marzoleta, *f.* (bot.) = MARJOLETA.

marzoleto, *m.* (bot.) = MARJOLETO.

mas, *m.* farmhouse and stock; (Philip.) weight for gold and silver (58 grains).

mas, *conj.* but (= PERO).—**m. que,** even if; however much.

más. I. *a.* more; most.—**los m.,** the largest number; most people. **II.** *adv.* more; most; longer; longest; over; besides, moreover; rather.—**m. bien,** rather.—**m. de,** more than, over.—**m. que,** more than; but, only; even if.—**m. tarde o m. temprano,** sooner or later.—**a lo m.,** at most.— **a m.,** besides.—**a m. correr,** with the utmost speed.—**a m. tardar,** at the latest.—**a m. y mejor,** greatly, highly, at best; excellently.—**de m.,** over, extra; too much; too many.—**de m. a m.,** besides, moreover.—**en m.,** more than, above, over.—**lo m. antes,** as soon as possible.—**por m. que,** however much.—**sin m. acá ni m. allá,** suddenly, without any reason.—**sin m. ni m.,** without much ado. **III.** *a.* (math.) plus.—**el signo m.,** the plus sign.

masa, *f.* dough; (mas.) mortar; (phys.) mass; volume, lump; aggregation, union; crowd of people; nature, disposition.

masada, *f.* farmhouse and stock.

masadero, *m.* farmer.

masaje, *m.* massage.—**masajista,** *m.* massagist.

masar, *va.* = AMASAR.

masato, *m.* (Am.) a flavored drink made with corn or rice and sugar.

mascabado, da, *a.* muscovado, raw, unrefined.

mascada, *f.* (Mex.) silk handkerchief.

mascador, ra, *n.* chewer, masticator.

mascadura, *f.* chewing, mastication.

mascar, *va.* (*pret.* MASQUÉ: *subj.* MASQUE) to chew, masticate; (coll.) to mumble.

máscara. I. *f.* mask.—*pl.* masquerade. **II.** *n.* mask, masquerader.

mascarada, *f.* masquerade, mummery.

ma carero, ra, *n.* dealer in masks.

mascarilla, *f. dim.* half mask; death mask.

mascarón, *m. aug.* hideous mask, (arch.) grotesque face.—**m. de proa,** (naut.) figurehead.

mascota, *f.* mascot.

mascujar, *vn.* (coll.) to masticate with difficulty; to mumble.

masculinidad, *f.* masculinity, manhood.

masculino, na, *a.* masculine; male.

mascullar, *va.* to mumble.

masecoral, masejicomar, *m.* sleight of hand, legerdemain.

masera, *f.* kneading trough; cloth for covering the dough.

masería, masía, *f.* farmhouse.

masetero, *m.* (anat.) masseter.

masica, *f.* (C. A.) breadnut tree.

masicote, *m.* (chem.) massicot.

masiliense, *a.* of Marseilles.

masilla, *f. dim.* little mass; putty; mastic.

masita, *f.* pittance retained for providing a soldier with shoes, etc.

maslo, *m.* root of the tail of quadrupeds.

masón, *m. aug.* mess of dough given to fowls; freemason.

masonería, *f.* freemasonry.

masónico, ca, *a.* masonic.

masora, *f.* Masora.—**masoreta,** *n.* Masorete.— **masorético, ca,** *a.* Masoretic.

masovero, *m.* farmer.

mastelerillo, *m. dim.* (naut.) topgallant and royal mast.—**mastelero,** *m.* (naut.) topmast.— **masteleros de respeto,** spare topmasts.

masticación, *f.* mastication.

masticador, ra. I. *n.* & *a.* masticator (-ing). **II.** *n.* MASTIGADOR; chopper.

masticar, *va.* (*pret.* MASTIQUÉ: *subj.* MASTIQUE); to masticate, to chew; to ruminate, meditate about.

masticatorio, ria, *a.* masticatory.

mastigador, *m.* bit for a horse.

mástil, *m.* (naut.) mast; upright post of a bed or loom; stanchion; shank of an auger; trunk or stem of a tree; wide breeches worn by Indians; neck (of violin, guitar, etc.).

mastín, na, *n.* mastiff.

mástique, *m.* mastic; mastic tree.

masto, *m.* stock into which a scion is grafted.

mastodonte, *m.* mastodon.

mastoides. I. *a.* mastoid. **II.** *m.* (anat.) mastoid process.—**mastoi.itis,** *f.* mastoiditis.

mastranto, mastranzo, *m.* round-leaved mint.

mastuerzo, *m.* dolt, simpleton; (bot.) common cress.

masturbación, *f.* masturbation.

masturbarse, *vr.* to masturbate.

masvale, *m.* = MALVASÍA.

mata, *f.* (bot.) plant; sprig, blade; grove, copse, orchard; mastic tree; head (of hair); matte, regulus, white metal; a card game.—**m. parda,** young evergreen oak; game at cards.

matacán, *m.* poison for killing dogs; (bot.) dog's-bane; nux vomica; hare previously hunted; pebble, stone; (fort.) machicolation gallery; deuce of clubs in some card games.

matacandelas, *f.* candle extinguisher.

matacandil, *m.* (prov.) lobster.

matacía, *f.* slaughter, death.

matachín, *m.* merry-andrew, jackpudding; dance performed by grotesque figures; butcher.

matadero, *m.* slaughterhouse; drudgery.

matador, ra. I. *n.* & *a.* killer (-ing). **II.** *m.* matador (bullfighter who kills the bull); (card playing) matador.

matadura, *f.* (vet.) sore, gall.

matafuego, *m.* fire extinguisher; fireman.

matagallina, *f.* (bot.) = TORVISCO.

matahambre, *m.* (Cuba) marchpane.

matahombres, *m.* = CARRALEJA.

matajudío, *m.* (icht.) = MÚJOL.

matalahuga, matalahuva, *f.* = ANÍS.

matalobos, *m.* (bot.) wolfsbane, aconite.

matalón, *m.* old worn-out horse.

matalotaje, *m.* (naut.) ship stores; (coll.) heap, mess, jumble.

matalote, *m.* = MATALÓN.

matancero, ra, *n.* & *a.* of or belonging to Matanzas, Cuba.

matanza, *f.* slaughter, butchery; hog slaughtering and the season when it is done; swine kept for slaughter; (coll.) obstinacy, eagerness.

matapalo, *m.* (bot.) (Am.) tree yielding caoutchouc and a fibre for sackcloth.

mataperrada, *f.* boy's mischievous prank.

mataperros, *m.* (coll.) street urchin.

matapiojos, *m.* (Am.) dragon fly.

matapolvo, *m.* light rain that just lays the dust.

matapulgas, *f.* (bot.) mint.

matar. I. *va.* to kill; to put out (a light); to extinguish (fire); to slake (lime); to harass, worry, vex; to make (a horse's back) sore by the rubbing of the harness; to spot (the cards); to mat (metal); (carp.) to bevel, round; (art) to subdue or tone down.—**m. de hambre,** to starve. —**a mata caballo,** in the utmost hurry.—**estar a m. con,** to be at drawn daggers with.—**mátalas callando,** (coll.) hypocrite, sly dog. **II.** *vr.* to kill one's self.

matarife, *m.* slaughterman.

matarrata, *f.* a card game.

matasanos, *m.* (coll.) quack, charlatan; empiric.

matasellos, *m.* P. O. cancelling stamp.

matasiete, *m.* bully, braggard.

mate. I. *a.* mat, dull, lusterless. **II.** *m.* checkmate in chess; gold or silver sizing; (bot.) Brazilian holly; maté, Paraguay tea; vessel in which maté is made; gourd, vessel.—**dar m.,** to checkmate; (coll.) to make fun of a person by laughing.

matear, *vn.* (agr.) to extend and shoot forth (as wheat, etc.); to hunt among the bushes.

matemáticamente, *adv.* mathematically.

matemática, *f.*, **matemáticas,** *f. pl.* mathematics.

matemático, ca. I. *a.* mathematical. **II.** *n.* mathematician.

materia, *f.* matter; material, stuff; subject, topic; subject matter; cause, occasion; (med.) matter,

pus.—**m. médica,** materia medica.—**m. prima,** raw material.—**materias de estado,** state affairs. —**en m. de,** as regards, in point of.—**entrar en m.** to go into the subject matter; to come to the point.

material. I. *a.* material; rude, coarse, matterof-fact. **II.** *m.* ingredient; material, stuff; (print.) copy; (elec. and r. w.) equipment.—**m. rodante,** (r. w.) rolling stock.

materialidad, *f.* materiality, corporeity; outward appearance; literalness; (theol.) materiality.

materialismo, *m.* materialism.

materialista, *n.* & *a.* materialist (-ic).

materializar. I. *va.* to materialize. **II.** *vr.* to become (morally) materialistic.

materialmente, *adv.* materially, corporeally; physically; absolutely.

maternal, *a.* maternal.—**maternalmente,** *adv.* maternally.—**maternidad,** *f.* maternity.—**maternizar,** *va.* to maternize (milk).—**materno, na,** *a.* maternal, motherly; mother (u. a.)

matero, ra, *n.* maté drinker.

mático, matico, *m.* (bot.) matico.

matihuelo, *m.* = DOMINGUILLO.

matinal, *a.* (poet.) = MATUTINAL.

matiné, *m.* matinée.

matiz, *m.* tint, hue, shade; blending of colors.

matizado, da, *a.* & *pp.* variegated, many-hued.

matizar, *va.* to variegate, blend (colors); to tint, give a special tint to.

mato, *m.* brake, coppice.

matojo, *m.* bush; (bot.) glasswort; (Cuba) shoot, sucker, tiller.

matón, *m.* (coll.) bully, hector, browbeater.

matorral, *m.* heath, brake, thicket, copse.

matoso, sa, *a.* heathy, weedy.

matraca, *f.* wooden rattle (= CARRACA); (coll.) jest, chaff.—**dar m.,** to banter.

matraquear, *va.* to rattle; to scoff, banter.

matraqueo, *m.* (coll.) rattling noise; banter.

matraquista, *n.* wag, jester, banterer.

matraz, *f.* (chem.) matrass.

matrería, *f.* (Am.) shrewdness.

matrero, ra. I. *a.* cunning, sagacious, shrewd. **II.** *m.* artful knave.

matriarcado, *m.* matriarchate.

matricaria, *f.* (bot.) common feverfew.

matricida, *n.* matricide (murderer).

matricidio, *m.* matricide (murder).

matrícula, *f.* register, list; matricula; matriculation.—**m. de mar,** mariner's register.

matriculador, ra, *n.* matriculator.

matricular, *va.* to matriculate, register, enrol.

matrimonesco, ca, *a.* (hum.) matrimonial.

matrimonial, *a.* matrimonial.

matrimonialmente, *adv.* matrimonially.

matrimoniar, *va.* to marry.

matrimonio, *m.* marriage, matrimony; married couple.—**m. de la mano izquierda,** morganatic marriage.

matritense, *n.* & *a.* Madrilenean.

matriz. I. *a.* first, principal, main, parent, chief. **II.** *f.* (anat.) uterus, womb; (mech.) mould, form, matrix, die; original draft of a writing; female screw, nut.

matrona, *f.* matron; midwife.

matronal, *a.* matronal.

maturrango, ga, *n.* (Am., coll.) poor (bad) horseman; clumsy, rough person.

matute, *m.* smuggling; smuggled goods; gambling den.—**matutear,** *va.* to smuggle.

matutero, ra, *n.* smuggler.

matutinal; matutino, na, *a.* matutinal, morning (u. a.)

maula. I. *f.* frippery, rubbish, trumpery, trash; cunning, craft; deceitful trick. **II.** *n.* (coll.) trickster, cheat, bad pay; sluggard, drone.— **maulería,** *f.* shop where remnants are sold; craft, cunning, trickery.—**maulero, ra,** *n.* seller of remnants; trickster, cheat, swindler.

maullador, ra, *a.* mewing (cat).—**maullar,** *vn.* to mew.—**maullido, maúllo,** *m.* mew.

mauraea, *f.* roasting chestnuts, etc., over coals in the open air.

mauritano, na, *n. & a.* Mauritanian.

mauseolo, mausoleo, *m.* mausoleum.

maxilar. I. *a.* maxillary. **II.** *m.* maxillary, maxillary bone, jaw.—**m. inferior,** inferior, or lower, maxillary.—**m. superior,** superior, or upper, maxillary.

máxima, *f.* maxim; rule; (mus.) maxima.

máximamente, máxime, *adv.* principally, specially.

máximo, ma. I. *a.* maximum.—**m. común divisor,** greatest common divisor. **II.** *m.* maximum.

máximum, *m.* maximum.

maya. I. *f.* (bot.) common daisy; variety of pineapple; May queen. **II.** *n. & a.* Maya (ancient Yucatan Indian and language).

mayador, ra, *a.* mewing.

mayal, *m.* flail; thrashing instrument; lever in oil mills.

mayar, *vn.* to mew.

mayear, *vn.* to be like May (s. o. the weather).

mayo, *m.* month of May; Maypole; Mayday festivity.

mayólica, *f.* majolica ware.

mayonesa, *f.* mayonnaise dressing; cold dish dressed with mayonnaise.

mayor. I. *a.* greater; greatest; larger; largest; older, elder; oldest, eldest; senior; of age; main, principal; high (altar, mass); major; (mus.) major.—**m. edad,** majority (s. o. age). **II.** *m.* superior; major or chief of a community; chief clerk; (mil.) major.—*pl.* ancestors, forefathers; superiors; elders.—**m. de edad,** of age.—**m. general,** major general.—**por m.,** (by) wholesale; summarily. **III.** *f.* (log.) major.—*pl.* (naut.) the three mainsails of a ship.

mayoral, *m.* head shepherd; leader; overseer, foreman, steward; stage driver.

mayoralía, *f.* flock, herd; herdsman's wages.

mayorana, *f.* (bot.) = MEJORANA.

mayorazga, *f.* she who possesses, or the wife of one possessing, an entailed estate.

mayorazgo, *m.* right of primogeniture; first-born son; family estate; entailed estate.

mayorazguista, *m.* author who treats of entails.

mayordoma, *f.* steward's wife; stewardess, housekeeper.

mayordomear, *va.* to administer, manage.

mayordomía, *f.* administration, stewardship, controllership.

mayordomo, *m.* steward, butler; manager; majordomo.

mayoría, *f.* majority; superiority; majorship.—**m. absoluta,** (pol.) majority (more than half of the total).—**m. relativa,** plurality.

mayoridad, *f.* superiority; full age.

mayorista, *m.* pupil of the highest classes in grammar schools.

mayormente, *adv.* principally, chiefly.

mayúscula, *a. & f.* capital (letter).

mayúsculo, la, *a.* large, good-sized; important, prominent.

maza, *f.* war club; mace; pile driver; drop hammer; nave or hub of a wheel; hemp brake; drumstick of a bass drum; roller of a sugar-cane mill; thick end of a billiard cue; something noisy tied to a dog's tail.—**m. de Fraga,** steam hammer.

mazacote, *m.* kali, barilla; concrete; dry, tough mass; (coll.) bore, tiresome person.

mazada, *f.* blow with club or mallet.—**dar m.,** to cause harm or injury.

mazagatos, *m.* noisy wrangle, quarrel, row.

mazamorra, *f.* crumbs, small bits; a sort of corn pap, much used in Peru and Colombia; (Colomb.) a kind of thick corn soup; (Arg., Colomb.) boiled whole corn; (naut.) mess made of broken tack.

mazaneta, *f.* apple-shaped ornament in jewels.

mazapán, *m.* a sort of marchpane.

mazar, *va.* to churn (milk).

mazarí, *m.* tile-shaped brick.

mazarota, *f.* (found.) deadhead, sprue.

mazdeísmo, *m.* Mazdaism, Mazdeism.

mazdeísta, *n. & a.* Mazdaist (-dean).

mazmorra, *f.* underground dungeon.

mazo, *m.* mallet, maul, wooden hammer; bundle, bunch; clapper of a bell; tiresome person, bore.

mazonería, *f.* stone masonry; (art) relief or relievo-work.

mazorca, *f.* spindleful; ear of corn; (arch.) spindle-shaped baluster.

mazorral, *a.* rude, uncouth; (print.) solid.

mazorralmente, *adv.* grossly, rudely.

mazurca, *f.* (danc.) mazurka.

me, *1st. person, pers. pron. dative, accusative and reflexive case of* YO.

meadero, *m.* urinal.

meaja, *f.* crumb; (law) execution dues.—**m. de huevo,** = GALLADURA.

meajuela, *f.* small piece attached to the bits of a bridle.

meandro, *m.* meander; (arch.) maze scroll-work; intricate ornamentation.

mear, *vn.* to urinate, make water.

meato, *m.* (anat.) passage or canal, meatus.

meauca, *f.* (orn.) a kind of sea gull.

meca, *f.* V. CECA.

mecánica, *f.* mechanics; machinery; (coll.) mean, despicable action or thing; (mil.) management of soldiers' affairs.

mecánicamente, *adv.* mechanically.

mecanicismo, *m.* (biol. & philos.) mechanistic system or theory.—**mecanicista,** *n. & a.* mechanicist (-ic).

mecánico, ca. I. *a.* mechanical; machine-made or operated; power-driven; mean, servile. **II.** *n.* mechanician; mechanist; mechanic, handicraftsman, artisan.

mecanismo, *m.* mechanism.

mecanografía, *f.* typewriting.

mecanografiar, *va.* to typewrite, type.

mecanográfico, ca, *a.* typewritten; relating to typewriting.

mecanografista; mecanógrafo, fa, *n.* typist, typewriter (person).

mecapal, *m.* (Mex.) leather band with ropes used by porters.

mecate, *m.* (Mex.) maguey rope or cord.

mecedero, *m.* stirrer.

mecedor, ra. I. *a.* rocking, swinging. **II.** *m.* stirrer; swing. **III.** *f.* rocking chair.

mecedura, *f.* rocking.

mecer. I. *va.* (*ind.* MEZO: *subj.* MEZA) to stir, agitate, mix; to rock; to shake; to swing; dandle (a child). **II.** *vr.* to rock, swing, sway; to soar.

meco, ca. I. *a.* (Mex.) blackish red. **II.** *n.* (Mex.) wild Indian.

meconato, *m.* (chem.) meconate.

mecónico, ca, *a.* (chem.) meconic.

meconio, *m.* meconium of children; (pharm.) meconium, poppy juice.

mecha, *f.* wick; (arti.) fuse; match, match cord; slice of bacon (for larding); lock of hair; bundle of threads or fibres; (surg.) roll of lint used as a drain.

mechar, *va.* (cook.) to lard (meat, etc.)

mechazo, *m.* (min.) fizzle of a blast fuse.

mechera, *f.* larding pin; shoplifter.

mechero, *m.* candlestick socket; lamp burner; gas burner.

mechinal, *m.* (mas.) columbarium, putlog hole.

mechoacán, *m.* (bot.) mechoacan bindweed.

mechón, *m. aug.* large lock of hair; large fuse; bundle of threads.

mechoso, sa, *a.* having abundant hair locks.

medalla, *f.* medal; (sculpt.) plaque, medallion; (coll.) gold coin.

medallón, *m. aug.* large medal; locket; (arch.) medallion.

médano, medaño, *m.* sand bank; dune.

medero, *m.* heap of vine shoots.

media, *f.* stocking; hose.—**m. diferencial,** (math.) arithmetical mean.—**m. proporcional,** geometrical mean, mean proportional.

mediacaña, *f.* (arch.) concave molding, fluted molding; picture molding; (carp.) gouge; half-round file; curling tongs for the hair.

mediación, *f.* mediation; intercession.

mediador, ra, *n.* mediator; intercessor.

mediana, *f.* long billiard cue; top of a fishing rod; (geom.) median.

mediados.—a m. de, about the middle of.

medianamente, *adv.* middlingly, so so, fairly.

medianejo, ja, *a.* (coll.) hardly mediocre.

medianería, *f.* partition wall.

medianero, ra. I. *a.* mediating, interceding; intermediate. **II.** *n.* mediator, go-between; owner of a house having a common wall.

medianía, medianidad, *f.* halfway; mediocrity; middle state; moderate means.

medianil, *m.* (agr.) middle piece of ground; (print.) crossbar of a chase.

mediano, na, *a.* moderate, middling, medium; bad, insignificant.

medianoche, *f.* midnight; small meat pie.

mediante. I. *a.* intervening; interceding. **II.** *adv.* by means of, by virtue of, with the help of, through.

mediar, *vn.* to reach or be at the middle; to intercede, mediate; to intervene.

mediastino, *m.* (anat.) mediastinum.

mediatamente, *adv.* mediately.

mediato, ta, *a.* mediate.

mediator, *m.* ombre, a card game.

médica, *f.* doctor's wife; woman physician.

medicable, *a.* curable, medicable.

medicación, *f.* medical treatment, medication.

medicamento, *m.* medicine, medicament.

medicamentoso, sa, *a.* medicinal.

medicastro, *m.* quack, charlatan, medicaster.

medicina, *f.* medicine; medicament, remedy.

medicinal, *a.* medicinal.

medicinante, *n.* healer; medical student who practices before taking his degree.

medicinar, *va.* to treat (a patient).

medición, *f.* measurement; measuring.

médico, ca. I. *a.* medical. **II.** *n.* physician.

medicucho, *m.* quack, charlatan, medicaster.

medida, *f.* measure; standard, gauge; mensuration, measuring, measurement; measuring stick or rule; moderation, prudence; (math., mus., poet., danc.,) measure.—**m. agraria,** land measure.—**m. de capacidad,** measure of capacity.—**m. de longitud,** measure of length.—**m. de superficie,** square measure.—**m. para áridos,** dry measure. **m. para líquidos,** liquid measure.—**a m. del deseo,** according to one's wishes.—**a m. que, as,** according as, at the same time as, while.—**llenarse la m.,** to drain the cup of sorrow.

medidamente, *adv.* moderately.

medidor, ra, *m.* measurer.

mediero, ra, *n.* hosier, dealer in stockings; knitter of stockings; copartner in a farm or ranch.

medieval, *a.* medieval.

medio, dia, *a. & adv.* half; partial; mid, middle; halfway, midway; mean, intermediate.—**m. bocel,** torus.—**m. colonia,** silk ribbon one finger wide.—**m. cuchara,** person of mediocre wit or skill.—**m. china,** cloth coarser than the CHINA.—**m. día,** midday.—**m. hermano,** half brother, stepbrother.—**m. luna,** (fort.) half-moon.—**m. naranja,** cupola.—**m. noche,** midnight.—**m. pasta** (b. b.) half-leather binding.—**m. relieve,** demi relief.—**m. talla,** half relief.—**m. vuelta,** right about face.—**a m. asta,** at half mast.—**a medias,** by halves, partially.—**a m. mogate,** carelessly, heedlessly.—**de m. gala,** in dress uniform.—**ir a medias,** to go halves. **II.** *m.* middle, center; (often *pl.*) means, method, measure, way; (surrounding) medium; (spiritualistic) medium; (arith.) half; (Am.) half a REAL (5 cents).—*pl.* means, resources.—**m. diferencial,** arithmetical mean.—**m. proporcional,** mean proportional.—**de m. a m.,** half and half; in the middle; completely, entirely.—**de por m.,** between.—**echar por en m.,** to take the

bull by the horns; to make up one's mind, happen what may.—**en m.,** in the middle; midway; in the midst.

mediocre, *a.* mediocre.

mediocridad, *f.* mediocrity.

mediodía, *m.* noon, midday; south.

medioeval, *a.* medieval.

mediopaño, *m.* thin woollen cloth.

mediquillo, *m.* medicaster; (Philip.) medicine man.

medir. I. *va.* (gerund, MIDIENDO: *ind.* MIDO: *pret.* él MIDIÓ: *subj.* MIDA) to measure; to compare, weigh, judge, value; to scan (verses).—**m. el suelo,** (coll.) to fall flat on the ground. **II.** *vr.* to be moderate, to act with prudence.

meditabundo, da, *a.* pensive, musing.

meditación, *f.* meditation.

meditar, *va. & vn.* to meditate, muse.

mediterráneo, nea, *a.* mediterranean.

médium, *m.* spiritualistic medium.

medo, da, *n. & a.* Mede (-ian).

medra, *f.* thrift; success, improvement.

medrana, *f.* (coll.) fear.

medrar, *vn.* to thrive, prosper.

medriñaque, *m.* Philippine stuff for lining and stiffening women's skirts; short skirt.

medro, *m.* = MEDRA.—*pl.* progress, improvement.

medrosamente, *adv.* timorously, faintly.

medroso, sa, *a.* timorous, faint-hearted, cowardly; terrible, dreadful.

medula, médula, *f.* marrow, medulla; (bot.) pith; substance, essence.—**m. espinal,** spinal cord.—**m. oblonga, or m. oblongada,** medulla oblongata.

medular, *a.* medullar, medullary.

meduloso, sa, *a.* marrowy; pithy.

medusa, *f.* (icht.) medusa, jellyfish.

meduseo, a, *a.* like, or relating to, Medusa.

mefistofélico, ca, *a.* Mephistophelean.

mefítico, ca, *a.* mephitic, foul, noxious.

megáfono, *m.* megaphone.

megalítico, ca, *a.* megalithic.

megalito, *m.* megalith.

megalomanía, *f.* megalomania.

megalómano, na, *n. & a.* megalomaniac (-al).

megalosaurio, *m.* (pal.) megalosaur.

mégano, *m.* dune. V. MÉDANO.

megaterio, *m.* megatherium.

mego, ga, *a.* gentle, mild, meek, peaceful.

megohmio, *m.* (elec.) megohm.

mehari, *m.* a swift African dromedary.

mehedí, *m.* Mahdi, Mohammedan Messiah.

mejana, *f.* islet in the middle of a river.

mejicano, na, *n. & a.* Mexican.

mejido, da, *a.* beaten with sugar and water.

mejilla, *f.* cheek.

mejillón, *m.* a variety of mussel.

mejor. I. *a.* better; best.—**m. postor,** highest bidder.—**el m. día,** some fine day.—**lo m.,** the best. **II.** *adv.* better; best; rather.—**m. dicho,** rather, more properly, more exactly.—**m. que m.,** much better; better and better; so much the better.—**a lo m.,** when least expected.—**tanto mejor,** so much the better.

mejora, *f.* improvement; higher bid; appeal to a higher court; special bequest to a lawful heir.

mejorable, *a.* improvable.

mejoramiento, *m.* improvement, melioration.

mejorana, *f.* (bot.) sweet marjoram.

mejorar. I. *va.* to improve, better, enhance; to outbid; (law) to leave to (an heir) a special bequest besides his legal share. **II.** *vr. & vn.* to recover from a disease or calamity; to improve, grow better; to reform.

mejoría, *f.* improvement, betterment; advantage; superiority; improvement in health.

mejunje, *m.* medicinal mixture, stuff.

melada, *f.* toast soaked in honey.

melado, da. I. *pp. & a.* honey-colored. **II.** *m.* cane-juice sirup; honey cake.

meladora, *f.* third sugar boiling pan in a triple-effect apparatus.

meladucha, *f.* coarse, mealy apple.

meladura, *f.* concentrated sirup, treacle.

meláfido, *m.* (geol.) melaphyre.

melampo, *m.* (theat.) candle with shade.

melancolía, *f.* melancholia, gloom, blues.

melancólico, ca, *a.* melancholy, sad, gloomy.

melancolizar, *va.* to affect with melancholy, to render gloomy and dejected, to dispirit.

melandro, *m.* (zool.) badger.

melanemia, *f.* (med.) melanæmia.

melanesio, sia, *n. & a.* Melanesian.

melanita, *f.* (min.) melanite.

melanosis, *f.* (med.) melanosis, black cancer.

melapia, *f.* a variety of apple.

melar. I. *va.* in sugar works, to boil clear; (api.) to fill (the combs) with honey. **II.** *a.* honey-sweet.

melastomáceo, a. I. *a.* (bot.) melastomaceous. **II.** *f. pl.* Melastomaceæ.

melaza, *f.* molasses; dregs of honey.

melca, *f.* = ZAHINA.

melcocha, *f.* molasses candy, taffy.

melcochero, ra, *n.* taffy maker or seller.

melena, *f.* long locks of hair in men; loose hair in women; mane of animals; fleecy skin put under a yoke; (med.) melæna, intestinal hemorrhage.—**traer a la m.,** to compel, force.

meleno, na, *n.* (coll.) rude, unkempt person.

melenudo, da, *a.* having bushy hair.

melera, *f.* woman who sells honey; melons spoiled by rain; (bot.) BUGLOSA.

melero, *m.* dealer in honey; place where honey is kept.

melgacho, *m.* (icht.) dogfish.

melgar, *m.* patch of wild alfalfa.

melgarejo, *m.* fish line and hook with a white rag for bait; (Bol.) a 30-cent coin.

meliáceo, a. I. *a.* (bot.) meliaceous. **II.** *pl. f.* Meliaceæ.

mélico, ca, *a.* lyrical, melic.

melífago, ga, *a.* meliphagous, feeding on honey. —**melífero, ra,** *a.* melliferous.—**melíficado, da,** *pp. & a.* mellifluous, mellificent.—**melificar,** *vn.* to make honey (s. o. bees).—**melifluamente,** *adv.* mellifluently.—**melifluidad,** *f.* mellifluence.—**melifluo, flua,** *a.* mellifluous, honeyed, honey-mouthed.

meliloto, ta. I. *a.* silly, stupid. **II.** *m.* (bot.) melilot, sweet clover.

melindre, *m.* a sort of fritter; lady finger; narrow ribbon; fastidiousness; prudery.

melindrear, *vn.* to act the prude.

melindrería, *f.* prudery; fastidiousness.

melindrero, ra. = MELINDROSO.

melindrillo, *m.* ferret, narrow tape.

melindroso, sa, *a.* finical, prudish.

melinita, *f.* melinite, a high explosive.

melisa, *f.* (bot.) melissa, balm.

melito, *m.* (pharm.) melissic sirup.

melocotón, *m.* (bot.) peach tree; peach.

melocotonero, ra. I. *n.* vender of peaches. **II.** *m.* peach tree.

melodía, *f.* (mus.) melody, melodiousness.

melodiosamente, *adv.* melodiously.

melodioso, sa, *a.* melodious.

melodrama, *m.* melodrama.

melodramáticamente, *adv.* melodramatically.

melodramático, ca, *a.* melodramatic.

melografía, *f.* art of writing music.

meloja, *f.* metheglin, mead.

melojar, *m.* white-oak plantation.

melojo, *m.* (bot.) a variety of white oak.

melolonta, *m.* (zool.) Melolontha, melolonthine.

melomania, *f.* melomania.

melómano, na, *n.* melomaniac.

melón, *m.* (bot.) melon vine; muskmelon, cantaloupe; (zool.) = MELONCILLO.—**m. de agua,** watermelon.

melonar, *m.* field or bed of melons.

meloncete, *m. dim.* small melon.

meloncillo, *m. dim.* small melon; (zool.) a kind of mongoose.

melonero, ra, *n.* melon raiser or dealer.

melopeya, *f.* melopœia.

melosidad, *f.* sweetness, lusciousness; gentleness.

meloso, sa, *a.* honeylike, sweet; gentle.

melote, *m.* dregs of molasses; preserve made with honey.

melsa, *f.* spleen; phlegm, slowness.

mella, *f.* notch, nick, jag in edged tools; dent, indentation; hollow, gap.—**hacer m.,** to make an impression on the mind; to hurt, damage; affect.

mellado, da, *a. & pp.* dented, jagged, notched; toothless.

mellar, *va.* to jag, indent, notch; to injure (as honor, credit).

melliza, *f.* a kind of sausage made with honey; twin sister.—**mellizo, za,** *n. & a.* twin.

mellón, *m.* torch made of straw.

membrado, da, *a.* (her.) membered.

membrana, *f.* membrane.—**m. alantoides,** allantoid membrane.—**m. caduca,** decidua.—**m. nictitante,** nictitating membrane.—**m. pituitaria,** pituitary membrane, mucous membrane of the nostrils.

membranáceo, cea, *a.* membranaceous.

membranoso, sa, *a.* membranous.

membrete, *m.* memorandum, note; **card of** invitation; address; letter-head; heading.

membrilla, *f.* (bot.) a variety of quince.

membrillar, *m.* quince-tree orchard.

membrillero, *m.* (bot.) quince tree.

membrillo, *m.* quince; quince tree.

membrudamente, *adv.* robustly, strongly.

membrudo, da, *a.* strong, robust, muscular.

memento, *m.* (eccl.) Memento.

memo, ma, *a.* silly, foolish.

memorable, *a.* memorable.

memorablemente, *adv.* memorably.

memorando, da, *a.* = MEMORABLE.

memorándum, *m.* notebook; memorandum, note.

memorar, *va.* to remember.

memoratísimo, ma, *a. sup.* worthy of eternal memory.

memoria, *f.* memory; recollection, remembrance; souvenir; memorial, memento, monumental record; report, statement; essay, paper, article; memorandum; codicil.—*pl.* compliments, regards; memoranda; rings used as reminders; memoirs.— **m. resbaladiza,** treacherous memory.—**de m.,** by heart.—**hablar de m.,** to talk at random.— **hacer m.,** to remember.—**renovar la m.,** to be reminiscent, to reminisce.—**tener en m.,** to remember.—**traer a la m. de uno,** to remind one.

memorial, *m.* memorandum book; memorial, petition; (law) brief.

memorialesco, ca, *a.* (hum.) relating to a memorial.

memorialista, *m.* amanuensis.

memorión, *m. aug.* great memory.

memorioso, sa, *a.* mindful, thoughtful.

mena, *f.* (icht.) small sea fish; (min.) ore; (naut., size of cordage; (Philip.) size and shape of a cigar.

ménade, *f.* bacchante; woman in a frenzy.

menador, ra, *n.* winder of silk.

menaje, *m.* household furniture and other goods; school supplies or equipment.

menar, *va.* to wind (silk) on a jenny.

mención, *f.* mention.—**mencionar,** *va.* to mention.

mendaz, *a.* mendacious, untruthful.

mendicación, *f.* begging.—**mendicante. I.** *a.* mendicant, begging. **II.** *m.* mendicant, beggar.— **mendicidad,** *f.* mendicity, mendicancy.

mendigante. ta, *n.* mendicant, beggar.

mendigar, *va. & vn.* (*pret.* MENDIGUÉ: *subj.* MEN-DIGUE) to beg, mendicate; to entreat.

mendigo, ga, *n.* mendicant, beggar.

mendiguez, *f.* beggary, mendicancy.

mendosamente, *adv.* falsely; mistakenly.

mendoso, sa, *a.* mendacious; mistaken.

mendrugo, *m.* crumb of bread given to beggars.

mendruguillo, *m. dim.* small crumb of bread.

meneador, ra, *n.* stirrer, shaker.

For pronunciation, see the rules at the beginning of the book.

menear. I. *va.* to stir, shake; to wag, waggle; to manage, direct.—**mejor es no meneallo,** or **peor es meneallo,** better let it alone; the less said, the better. **II.** *vr.* (coll.) to hustle, be active, get a move on; to wriggle, waggle, waddle.

meneo, *m.* shake, shaking; wagging, wriggling, waddling; (coll.) drubbing, beating.

menester, *m.* need, want; employment, occupation, office.—*pl.* natural or bodily necessities; implements, tools of trade.—**haber m.,** to need.—**ser m.,** to be necessary.

menesteroso, sa, *a.* needy, necessitous.

menestra, *f.* pottage; vegetable soup.

menestral, *m.* mechanic, handicraftsman, workman.

menestrete, *m.* (naut.) nail puller.

menfita. I. *n.* native of Memphis. **II.** *f.* (min.) onyx.

mengajo, *m.* trailing rag.

Mengano, na, *n.* So-and-So (gen. u. with FULANO or MENGANO, in the sense of So-and-So, or Tom, Dick and Harry).

mengua, *f.* diminution, waning, decrease; lack, want; poverty, indigence; disgrace.

menguadamente, *adv.* ignominiously.

menguado, da. I. *pp.* & *a.* diminished, impaired, stunted; cowardly, pusillanimous; foolish; mean, miserly. **II.** *n.* poltroon; silly person; miser. **III.** *m.* decrease; narrowing of stockings, in knitting.

menguamiento, *m.* = MENGUA.

menguante. I. *a.* decreasing, diminishing. **II.** *f.* ebb tide, low water, neap tide; decline, decay; decrease of the moon.

menguar, *vn.* to diminish, decrease, wane, fall off; to narrow (stockings).

mengue, *m.* (coll.) the deuce, the devil.

menhir, *m.* menhir, an upright slender monolith.

menina, *f.* young miss in attendance upon the queen or the princesses.

meninge, *f.* (anat.) meninges.—**meníngeo, a,** *a.* meningeal.—**meningitis,** *f.* meningitis.

menino, *m.* noble page of the queen and princesses of Spain; little coxcomb.

menique, *a.* little finger.

menisco, *m.* (phys.) meniscus.

menispermáceo, a. I. *a.* (bot.) menispermaceous. **II.** *f. pl.* Menispermaceæ.

menjuí, *m.* = BENJUÍ.

menjunje, menjurje, *m.* = MEJUNJE.

menologio, *m.* (eccl.) menology.

menopausia, *f.* (med.) menopause, change of life in women.

menor. I. *a. compar.* of PEQUEÑO: smaller, less; smallest, least; minor; younger; youngest; (mus.) minor.—**m. edad,** minority, under age.—**II.** *n.* minor; (log.) minor premise; (mus.) minor; Minorite, Franciscan; (arch.) small block.—*pl.* (eccl.) minor orders.—**m. de edad,** minor.—**por m.,** by retail; minutely.

menorete.—al m., or **por el m.,** (coll.) at least.

menoría, *f.* inferiority, subordination; under age.

menorquín, na, *a.* of or belonging to Minorca.

menorragia, *f.* (med.) menorrhagia.

menos. I. *a.* less; least. **II.** *a.* less; least; except, but, barring.—**m. de,** or **m. que,** less than.—**al m.,** or **a lo m.,** at least; at the least.—**a m. que,** unless.—**de m.,** less; wanting, missing.—**en m.,** less; by less.—**lo m. posible,** the least possible.—**poco más o m.,** more or less, about.—**por lo m.** = AL M.—**todo m. eso,** anything but that; all but that.—**venir a m.,** to decline, to grow worse; to become poor.

menoscabador, ra, *n.* & *a.* impairer (-ing); defamer (-ing).

menoscabar, *va.* to impair, lessen, deteriorate, damage, harm; to defame.

menoscabo, *m.* impairment, damage, detriment. loss.—**con m. de,** to the detriment of.

menoscuenta, *f.* payment on account.

menospreciablemente, *adv.* contemptuously.

menospreciador, ra, *n.* contemner, despiser.

menospreciar, *va.* to underrate, undervalue; to despise, contemn, slight.—**menospreciativo, va,** *a.* despising, slighting, contemptuous.—**menosprecio,** *m.* undervaluation; contempt, scorn.

menostasia, *f.* (med.) amenorrhea.

mensaje, *m.* message; errand.

mensajería, *f.* stage line; steamship line.

mensajero, ra, *n.* messenger, carrier; errand boy or girl; (naut.) bull's-eye traveller; wooden thimble (*m.* in last two senses).

menstruación, *f.* menstruation.—**menstrual,** *a.* menstrual.—**menstrualmente,** *adv.* monthly, menstrually.—**menstruante,** *a.* menstruating.

menstruar, *vn.* to menstruate.

menstruo, a. I. *a.* monthly, menstrual. **II.** *m.* menses, courses; menstruation; (chem.) menstruum.

menstruoso, sa. I. *a.* menstruous. **II.** *f.* (med.) menstruating female.

mensual, *a.* monthly.—**mensualidad,** *f.* monthly salary or allowance; monthly instalment. —**mensualmente,** *adv.* monthly.

ménsula, *f.* (arch.) bracket; rest for the elbows.

mensura, *f.* measure.—**mensurabilidad,** *f.* mensurability.—**mensurable,** *a.* mensurable.—**mensurador, ra,** *n.* measurer, meter.—**mensural,** *a.* mensural.—**mensurar,** *va.* to measure.

menta, *f.* (bot.) mint; peppermint.

mentado, da, *pp.* & *a.* famous or renowned; spoken-of.

mental, *a.* mental.—**mentalmente,** *adv.* mentally.

mentar, *va.* (*ind.* MIENTO: *subj.* MIENTE) to mention, name.

mentastro, *m.* (bot.) = MASTRANZO.

mente, *f.* mind, understanding; sense, meaning; will, disposition.

mentecatada, mentecatería, mentecatez, *f.* foolishness, silliness, nonsense.

mentecato, ta. I. *a.* silly, foolish, stupid, crack-brained. **II.** *n.* fool.

mentidero, *m.* (coll.) place where people meet and gossip.

mentido, da, *pp.* & *a.* false, delusive.

mentir. I. *vn.* (*ind.* MIENTO: *subj.* MIENTA) to lie, prevaricate; to deceive, be misleading.—**¡miento!** I am mistaken (u. to correct one's own statement). **II.** *va.* to disappoint, to fail to keep one's word or promise to.

mentira, *f.* lie, falsehood; fib; error, mistake in writing; (coll.) white spot on the nails.—**de mentiras,** in jest.—**parece m.,** it seems impossible, or incredible.

mentirilla, *f. dim.* little fib.—**de mentirillas,** in jest, for fun.

mentirón, *m. aug.* great lie.

mentirosamente, *adv.* lyingly, deceitfully.

mentirosito, ta, *a. dim.* little fibber.

mentiroso, sa, *a.* lying, mendacious, deceptive, deceitful; full of errors or misprints.

mentís, *m.* act of giving the lie.—**dar un m.,** to belie; to give the lie.

mentol, *m.* (pharm.) menthol.

mentor, *m.* mentor, counsellor, guide.

menuceles, *m. pl.* tithe of the lesser fruits.

menudamente, *adv.* minutely.

menudear. I. *va.* to do over and over again; to repeat; to sell by retail. **II.** *vn.* to occur frequently; to go into details; to describe little things; (com.) to sell by retail.

menudencia, *f.* trifle; minuteness, minute accuracy.—*pl.* small matters; pork sausages.

menudeo, *m.* act of repeating minutely; (com.) retail.—**al m.,** by retail.

menudero, ra, *n.* dealer in tripes, giblets, sausages, etc.

menudillo, *m.* extremities of animals.—*pl.* giblets of fowls.

menudo, da. I. *a.* small, little; minute; insignificant; common, vulgar; small (money); exact, scrupulous; mean, stingy. **II.** *m.* small money, change; (sometimes *pl.*) entrails, insides (of an animal); tithe of minor produce.—**a m.,** often, frequently.

meñique. I. *a.* little (finger); (coll.) very small, tiny. **II.** *m.* little finger.

meollar, *m.* (naut.) spun yarn.

meollo, *m.* brain; marrow; kernel, pith; judgment, understanding, brains; substance.

meple, *m.* (bot.) maple.—**m. moteado,** bird's-eye maple.

mequetrefe, *m.* jackanapes, coxcomb.

meramente, *adv.* merely, solely, purely.

merar, *va.* to mix with water.

merca, *f.* (coll.) purchase.

mercachifle, *m.* peddler, hawker, huckster; petty jobber.

mercadear, *vn.* to trade, deal, traffic.

mercader, *m.* merchant, dealer, shopkeeper.— **m. de grueso,** wholesale dealer.—**mercadera,** *f.* shopkeeper's wife; tradeswoman.

mercadería, *f.* commodity, merchandise; trade. —*pl.* goods, wares, merchandise.

mercado, *m.* market, mart; market place.

mercaduría, *f.* merchandise; trade.

mercal, *m.* an ancient Spanish copper coin.

mercancía, *f.* trade, traffic; merchandise, goods, wares.

mercante. I. *n.* & *a.* dealer (-ing), trader (-ing). **II.** *a.* merchant, mercantile, commercial.

mercantil, *a.* commercial, mercantile.

mercantilismo, *m.* mercantilism, commercialism.

mercantilmente, *adv.* commercially.

mercantivo, va, *a.* = MERCANTIL.

mercar, *va.* (*pret.* MERQUÉ: *subj.* MERQUE) to buy, purchase.

merced, *f.* gift, favor, grace; mercy; wages; will, pleasure; courteous appellation given to untitled persons, as *vuestra,* or *vuesa, merced,* your honor, your grace, your worship, sir.—**m. a,** thanks to.—**m. de agua,** free distribution of water for irrigation.—**m. de tierra,** grant of land.—**a la m. de,** at the mercy of.—**estar a m. de,** to live at the expense of.—**hágame Vd. la m.,** do me the favor.—**muchas mercedes,** many thanks.

mercenario, ria. I. *a.* mercenary. **II.** *n.* member of the religious order of **la Merced;** mercenary soldier; day-laborer, farm hand; substitute.

mercería, *f.* small wares, mercery, haberdashery, notions; (Am.) dry-goods store.

mercerizar, *va.* to mercerize.

mercero, *m.* haberdasher, mercer.

mercurial. I. *a.* mercurial. **II.** *m.* (bot.) all-good, mercury.

mercúrico, *a.* mercuric.

mercurio, *m.* mercury; (**M-,** ast.) Mercury.— **m. dulce,** calomel.

mercurioso, sa, *a.* mercurious.

merchante. I. *m.* jobber. **II.** *a.* trading.

merdellón, *na,* *n.* (coll.) slovenly servant.

merecedor, ra, *a.* deserving, worthy.

merecer. I. *va.* (*ind.* MEREZCO: *subj.* MEREZCA) to deserve, merit; to obtain, attain; to be worth; to be worthy of; to owe, to be indebted for. **II.** *vn.* to be deserving or worthy.—**m. bien de,** to deserve the gratitude of.—**por m.,** unmarried.

merecidamente, *adv.* deservedly.

merecido, da. I. *pp.* & *a.* deserved. **II.** *m.* condign punishment.

mereciente, *a.* deserving.

merecimiento, *m.* merit, desert.

merendar. I. *vn.* (*ind.* MERIENDO: *subj.* MERIENDE) to lunch; to eat a light meal; to pry into another's writings or actions. **II.** *va.* to lunch on.

merendero, ra. I. *a.* (crow) that picks up the seeds in cornfields. **II.** *m.* lunch room.

merendilla, ita, *f. dim.* light luncheon.

merendona, *f. aug.* splendid luncheon or supper.

merengue, *m.* kiss, sugarplum, meringue.

meretricio, cia, *a.* meretricious.

meretriz, *f.* strumpet.

merey, *f.* (bot.) cashew tree.

merezco, yo merezca. *V.* MERECER.

mergánsar, *m.* (orn.) goosander, merganser.

mergo, *m.* (orn.) diver.

meridiana, *f.* litter, cot bed; (ast., surv.) meridian (line); (coll.) afternoon nap.—**a la m.,** at noon.

meridiano, na. I. *a.* meridian; meridional (section, cut). **II.** *m.* meridian.

meridional, *a.* southern, southerly.

merienda, *f.* lunch, luncheon; collation, light meal; (coll.) humpback.—**m. de negros,** hodge-podge, confusion, bedlam.

meriendo, yo meriende. *V.* MERENDAR.

merindad, *f.* district of the jurisdiction of a MERINO.

merino, na. I. *a.* merino. **II.** *m.* royal judge and superintendent of sheepwalks; shepherd of merino sheep; merino sheep, wool, and cloth.

méritamente, *adv.* = MERECIDAMENTE.

meritísimo, ma, *a. super.* most worthy.

mérito, *m.* merit, desert, worth; excellence, virtue, value.—**méritos de un proceso,** (law) merits of a case.—**hacer m. de,** to mention.— **hacer méritos,** to make one's self deserving.

meritoriamente, *adv.* meritoriously.

meritorio, ria. I. *a.* meritorious, worthy, deserving. **II.** *n.* employee that begins without a salary.

merla, *f.* (orn.) blackbird, merle.

merlín, *m.* (naut.) marline.

merlín, *m.* merlin.—**saber más que M.,** to be very shrewd or keen.

merlo, *m.* (icht.) a seafish.

merlón, *m.* (fort.) merlon.

merluza, *f.* (icht.) hake, merluce.

merma, *f.* decrease; waste, leakage; shrinkage.

mermar. I. *vn.* to decrease, wear away, be consumed, shrink. **II.** *va.* to lessen, reduce, decrease.

mermelada, *f.* marmalade.

mero, ra. I. *a.* mere, pure, simple. **II.** *m.* (icht.) a variety of Mediterranean sea bass.

merodeador, *m.* marauder.—**merodear,** *vn.* to maraud.—**merodeo,** *m.* marauding.—**merodista,** *n.* marauder.

merovingio, gia, *a.* Merovingian.

mes, *m.* month; menses, courses; monthly wages. —**meses mayores,** last months of pregnancy; months immediately preceding harvest.

mesa, *f.* table; table-land, plateau; landing of a staircase; executive board; business section of a public office or department; rents of cathedral churches, prelates, or dignitaries in Spain; billiard table; billiard game; flat of a blade; (jew.) face of a gem; (eccl.) communion table; fare, viands set on a table.—**m. de altar,** altar.—**m. de batalla,** sorting table (in postoffice).—**m. de cambios,** bank.—**m. de noche,** night commode.—**m. redonda,** round table; unceremonious or informal table; table for regular boarders.—**m. franca,** open table.—**mesas de guarnición,** (naut.) channels.—**a m. puesta,** without care or expense. —**media m.,** second table; lower-priced or servants' table.—**poner la m.,** to set the table.

mesada, *f.* monthly pay, wages, or allowance.

mesadura, *f.* tearing the hair.

mesana, *f.* (naut.) mizzenmast or sail.

mesar, *va.* to tear (the hair or beard).

mescolanza, *f.* medley, mess, jumble.

mesegueria, *f.* harvest watch; money paid for watching the harvest.

meseguero, ra. I. *a.* relating to the harvest. **II.** *m.* harvest or vineyard watchman.

mesentérico, ca, *a.* mesenteric.

mesenterio, *m.* (anat.) mesentery.

mesenteritis, *f.* mesenteritis.

meseraico, ca, *a.* mesenteric.

mesero, *m.* journeyman who works for monthly wages.

meseta, *f.* landing of a staircase; table-land, plateau.—**m. de guarnición,** (naut.) backstay stool.

mesiánico, ca, *a.* Messianic.

mesianismo, *n.* Messianism.

Mesías, *m.* Messiah.

mesiazgo, *m.* Messiahship.

mesidor, *m.* Messidor, tenth month of the French-Revolution calendar.

mesilla, *f. dim.* small table; sideboard; board wages; censure by way of a jest; window sill.— **m. corrida,** quarter pace of a staircase.—**m. quebrantada,** half pace, foot-rest.

mesillo, *m.* first menses after parturition.

mesita, *f. dim.* small table; stand.

mesmedad, *f.*—**por su misma m.** (coll.) by the very fact.

mesmerismo, *m.* mesmerism.

mesmo, ma, *a.* (obs.) = MISMO.

mesnada, *f.* armed retinue.—**mesnadería,** *f.* wages of a MESNADA.—**mesnadero,** *m.* member of a MESNADA.

mesoblasto, *m.* (biol.) mesoblast.

mesocarpio, *m.* (bot.) mesocarp.

mesocracia, *f.* mesocracy.

mesodérmico, ca, *a.* mesodermic.

mesodermo, *m.* mesoderm.

mesogastrio, *m.* (anat.) mesogastrium, umbilical region.

mesología, *f.* ecology.

mesón, *m.* inn, hostelry, tavern.

mesonaje, *m.* place containing numerous inns.

mesonero, ra. **I.** *a.* relating to an inn. **II.** *n.* innkeeper, host, hostess.

mesonista, *a.* relating to an inn.

mesopotámico, ca, *n. & a.* Mesopotamian.

mesotorácico, ca, *a.* mesothoracic.

mesotórax, *m.* mesothorax.

mesozoario, ria, *a.* mesozoan.

mesozoico, ca, *a.* (geol.) Mesozoic.

mesta, *f.* union of cattle raisers; confluence of two or more streams.

mestal, *m.* brake of prickly oaks.

mesteño, ña, *a.* belonging to the MESTA; MOS- TRENCO.

mestizar, *va.* to cross (breeds).

mestizo, za. **I.** *a.* half-breed; hybrid. **II.** *n. & a.* mestizo, half-breed.

mesto, *m.* (bot.) large, prickly oak; turkey oak.

mestura, *f.* mashlin, mixed wheat and rye.

mesura, *f.* dignified deportment; civility, polite- ness; moderation.

mesuradamente, *adv.* slowly, prudently, moder- ately.—**mesurado, da,** *pp. & a.* moderate, cir- cumspect, temperate.

mesurar. **I.** *va.* to inspire moderation in. **II.** *vr.* to control one's self.

meta, *f.* boundary, limit; goal.

metabólico, ca, *a.* metabolic.

metabolismo, *m.* metabolism.

metacarpo, *m.* (anat.) metacarpus.

metacentro, *m.* metacenter.

metacronismo, *m.* metachronism.

metafísica, *f.* metaphysics.—**metafísicamente,** *adv.* metaphysically.—**metafísico, ca.** **I.** *a.* metaphysical. **II.** *m.* metaphysician.

metáfora, *f.* metaphor.—**metafóricamente,** *adv.* metaphorically.—**metafórico, ca,** *a.* metaphorical. —**metaforizar,** *va.* to use metaphors.

metagoge, *f.* (rhet.) a kind of metaphor.

metal, *m.* metal; tone or timbre of the voice; (mus.) brass orchestral instruments; quality, nature, or condition.—**m. antifricción,** babbitt metal.—**m. blanco,** nickel silver; babbitt metal.— **m. campanil,** or **de campanas,** bell metal.—**m. de imprenta,** type metal.—**m. desplegado,** ex- panded metal.—**m. Muntz,** Muntz metal, yellow metal.

metalario, ria, *n.* metallist, metal worker.

metalepsis, *f.* (rhet.) metalepsis.

metálica, *f.* metallurgy.

metálico, ca. **I.** *a.* metallic; medallic. **II.** *m.* specie, hard cash.—**m. en caja,** (com.) cash on hand.

metalífero, ra, *a.* (poet.) metalliferous.

metalista, *n.* metal worker.

metalistería, *f.* metal work.

metalización, *f.* metallization.

metalizar. **I.** *va.* (*pret.* METALICÉ: *subj.* META- LICE) to metallize. **II.** *vr.* to be converted into

or impregnated with metal; to become con- trolled by love of money, to become mercenary.

metalografía, *f.* metallography.

metaloide, *m.* (chem.) metalloid.

metaloterapia, *f.* (med.) metallotherapy.

metalurgia, *f.* metallurgy.

metalúrgico, ca. **I.** *a.* metallurgic, metallur- gical. **II.** *n.* metallurgist.

metalla, *f.* scraps of gold-leaf for mending.

metamería, *f.* (chem.) metamerism.

metámero, ra, *a.* (chem., zool.) metameric.

metamórfico, ca, *a.* (geol.) metamorphic.

metamorfismo, *m.* (geol.) metamorphism.

metamorfosear, *va. & vr.* to metamorphose, to transform.

metamorfosi, metamorfosis, *f.* metamor- phosis, transformation.

metano, *m.* (chem.) methane.

metaplasmo, *m.* (gram.) metaplasm.

metástasis, *f.* (med.) metastasis.

metatarsiano, na, *a.* metatarsal.

metatarso, *m.* (anat.) metatarsus.

metate, *m.* (Mex.) curved stone for grinding maize or cocoa.

metátesis, *f.* (rhet.) metathesis.

meteco, ca, *a. & n.* foreign (-er).

metedor, ra. **I.** *n.* one who puts in or introduces; smuggler. **II.** *m.* clout of newborn children.

meteduría, *f.* smuggling.

metempsicosis, metempsícosis, *f.* metem- psychosis.

metemuertos, *m.* (theat.) stage hand; busybody.

meteórico, ca, *a.* meteoric.

meteorismo, *m.* (med.) meteorism.

meteorito, *m.* meteorite.

meteorización, *f.* (agr.) influence of atmospheric phenomena on the soil.

meteorizar. **I.** *va.* to cause meteorism or tym- panites. **II.** *vr.* to suffer meteorism; (agr.) to be influenced by atmospheric phenomena (s. o. the soil).

metéoro, meteoro, *m.* atmospheric phenom- enon; meteor.—**meteorología,** *f.* meteorology.— **meteorológico, ca,** *a.* meteorological.

meteorologista; meteorólogo, ga, *n.* meteorol- ogist.

meter. **I.** *va.* to put in, insert, introduce, inclose; to smuggle; to make (as a noise); cause (as fear); tell (as fibs); to induce, get (one into a business, etc.); to stake, put to hazard; to invest; to cram down (victuals); to put close together, cram together; to impose upon, to deceive; to compress, straighten, reduce; (coll.) to eat; (naut.) to take in (sail).—**m. bulla,** to make a noise.—**m. su cucharada,** to put in one's oar, to butt in.—**m. zizaña,** to sow discord.—**meterlo a bulla,** to carry off the matter with a joke. **II.** *vr.* to meddle, intrude, interfere; to be too familiar; to choose a profession or trade; to plunge into vice; to disem- bogue; to attack sword in hand.—**m. a,** to become; to undertake to.—**m. con,** to pick a quarrel with; to meddle with; to have dealings with.

metesillas, *m.* (theat.) stage hand.

meticulosidad, *f.* fear, shyness.

meticuloso, sa, *a.* pusillanimous, shy.

metidillo, *m.* clout for babes.

metido, da. **I.** *a. & pp.* abounding; close, tight; engaged; interested. **II.** *m.* blow with the fist on the throat; strong lye or buck; (sew.) material allowed in seams; clout for infants. **III.** *f.* (coll.) lecture, dressing down.

metileno, *m.* (chem.) methylene.

metílico, ca, *a.* (chem.) methylic.

metilo, *m.* (chem.) methyl.

metimiento, *m.* insertion, introduction.

metódicamente, *adv.* methodically.

metódico, ca, *a.* methodical.

metodismo, *m.* system, plan, method; (eccl.) Methodism.—**metodista,** *n. & a.* Methodist.— **metodizar,** *va. & vn.* to systematize.

método, *m.* method.—**metodología,** *f.* method- ology.

metonimia, *f.* (rhet.) metonymy.

metonímico, ca, *a.* metonymical.
métopa, *f.* (arch.) metope.
metoposcopia, *f.* metoposcopy.
metralla, *f.* (arti.) grapeshot, case shot, canister shot.
metrallazo, *m.* discharge of grapeshot.
métrica, *f.* metrical art, poesy.
métricamente, *adv.* metrically.
métrico, ca, *a.* metric, metrical.
metrificación, *f.* verse making.
metrificador, ra; metrista, *n.* versifier.
metrificar, *vn.* to write verses.
metritis, *f.* (med.) metritis.
metro, *m.* meter, unit of length; (poet.) meter.
metrología, *f.* metrology.
metrónomo, *m.* (mus.) metronome.
metrópoli, *f.* metropolis; archiepiscopal church; mother country.
metropolitano, na. I. *a.* metropolitan. **II.** *m.* archbishop.
metrorragia, *f.* (med.) metrorrhagia.
metroscopio, *m.* (med.) metroscope.
metrotomía, *f.* (surg.) hysterotomy.
metrótomo, *m.* (surg.) metrotome, hysterotome.
mexicano, na, *n.* & *a.* Mexican.
meya, *f.* maia, spider crab.
mezala, *m.* oratory, place for prayer.
mezcal, *m.* (Mex.) a species of maguey; pulque.
mezcla, *f.* mixture; mixing; mortar; mixed cloth.
mezcladamente, *adv.* promiscuously; mixedly.
mezclador, ra, *n.* & *a.* mixer (-ing).
mezcladura, *f.*; **mezclamiento,** *m.* mixture; mixing.
mezclar. I. *va.* to mix, mingle; blend. **II.** *vr.* to mix; to intermarry; to intermeddle; to take part.
mezclilla, *f.* pepper-and-salt cloth.
mezcolanza, *f.* (coll.) medley, hotchpotch, mishmash, jumble.
mezquinamente, *adv.* stingily, niggardly.
mezquindad, *f.* niggardliness, stinginess, paltriness, currishness, meanness; penu¯y, indigence.
mezquino, na, *a.* niggardly, stingy, mean, paltry, miserly; indigent, needy; diminutive; petty, minute, puny.
mezquita, *f.* mosque.
mezquital, *m.* clump of mesquite shrubs.
mezquite, *m.* (Mex.) (bot.) mesquite.
mi, *m.* (mus.) mi, E, third note of the scale.
mi, *sing. poss. pron.* (*pl.* MIS), my.
mí, *pers. pron. oblique case of the pronoun* YO, *used after a prep.* : me.
miaja, *f.* crumb; bit.
miar, *vn.* to mew, as a cat.
miasma, *m.* (med.) miasm or miasma.—*pl.* miasmata.
miasmático, ca, *a.* miasmatic.
miau, *m.* mew of a cat.
mica, *f.* (min.) mica, isinglass.
mica, *f.* female monkey; (min.) mica; (C. A.) flirt.
micáceo, cea, *a.* micaceous, micalike.
micacita, *f.m.* (geol.) micaschist.
micado, *m.* Mikado.
micasquisto, *m.* = MICACITA.
micción, *f.* miction, micturition.
micer, *m.* ancient title of respect, mister.
mico, *m.* monkey; (coll.) lascivious man.—**dar, or hacer, m. a,** to disappoint by not keeping an engagement.
micra, *f.* = MICRÓN.
microbiano, na, *a.* microbian.
microbio, *m.* microbe, bacterium.
microbiología, *f.* microbiology, bacteriology.
microbiológico, ca, *a.* microbiological, bactereological.
microcefalia, *f.* microcephaly, microcephalism.
microcéfalo, la, *a.* microcephalic, microcephalous.
microcito, *m.* (med.) microcyte.
micrococo, *m.* micrococcus.
microcosmos, *m.* microcosm.

micrófito, *m.* microphyte.
micrófono, *m.* microphone.
micrografía, *f.* micrography.
micrográfico, ca, *a.* micrographic.
micrógrafo, *m.* micrograph.
microhmio, *m.* (elec.) microhm.
microlítico, ca, *a.* (geol.) microlitic.
microlito, *m.* (geol.) microlite.
micrométrico, ca, *a.* micrometric.
micrómetro, *m.* micrometer.
micromilímetro, *m.* = MICRÓN.
micrón, *m.* micron, one thousandth of a millimeter.
microorganismo, *m.* = MICRORGANISMO.
micrópilo, *m.* (zool. and bot.) micropyle.
microrganismo, *m.* microörganism.
microscópico, ca, *a.* microscopic.
microscopio, *m.* microscope.
micrótomo, *m.* microtome, cutting instrument for the microscope.
microvoltio, *m.* (elec.) microvolt, one millionth of a volt.
michito, *m.* *dim.* kitten, pussy.
micho, cha, *m.* & *f.* (coll.) puss, cat.
mida, *m.* mida, bean fly.
mido, yo mida. *V.* MEDIR.
midriasis, *f.* (med.) mydriasis.
miedo, *m.* fear, dread, apprehension.—**m. cerval,** fright; great timidity.—**tener m.,** to be afraid, fear.
miedoso, sa, *a.* timorous, afraid.
miel, *f.* honey; molasses; cane juice.—**m. de abejas,** bee's honey.—**m. de caña,** sugar-cane syrup.—**m. de purga,** molasses.—**m. rosada,** (pharm.) honey of roses.—**m. virgen,** virgin honey. —**dejar a uno con la miel en los labios,** to snatch success from one when it seems certain.
mielga, *f.* (bot.) wild lucerne; (icht.) a kind of dogfish; (agr.) rake; four-pronged pitchfork; strip of ground to be sown.
mielgo, ga, *a.* twin.
mielitis, *f.* (med.) myelitis.
miembro, *m.* member; limb; member of a body, community or corporation; branch or part of a whole; (math., arch.) member; (anat.) penis.
mienta, *f.* (bot.) mint.
mientes, *f. pl.* thoughts, ideas.—**parar, or poner, m.,** to reflect, to consider.—**traer a las m.,** to remind.—**venir a las m.,** to come to one's mind.
miento, yo miente. *V.* MENTAR.
miento, yo mienta. *V.* MENTIR.
mientras, *adv.* while, whilst, when.—**m. más,** the more.—**m. que,** while, as long as, so long as.— **m. tanto,** meanwhile, in the meantime.
miera, *f.* juniper oil; resin.
miércoles, *m.* Wednesday.—**m. corvillo, or de ceniza,** Ash Wednesday.
mierra, *f.* sled, sledge, stone drag.
mies, *f.* ripe wheat and other grain, before thrashing; harvest time; (met.) multitude converted or ready for conversion.—*pl.* grain fields.
miga, *f.* crumb, soft part of bread; small fragment, bit; (coll.) marrow, substance, pith.—*pl.* fried crumbs.—**hacer buenas or malas migas,** (coll.) to agree or disagree readily with one.
migaja, *f.* small crumb or bit of bread; small fragment, chip, or bit; (coll.) little or nothing.— *pl.* offals, leavings; crumbs, broken victuals.— **no tener m. de,** (coll.) not to have a particle of.
migajada, *f.* small particle.
migajica, illa, ita, uela, *f. dim.* wee little bit.
migajón, *m.* *aug.* crumb, without crust; marrow core; pith and substance.
migar, *va.* to crumb (bread); to put (crumbs of) into milk, etc.
migración, *f.* migration.
migraña, *f.* = JAQUECA.
migratorio, ria, *a.* migrating, migratory.
miguelete, *m.* = MIQUELETE.
miguero, ra, *a.* crummy, relating to crumbs fried in a pan.
mihrab, *m.* mihrab, niche in a mosque.

mijo, *m.* (bot.) millet, panic grass.—**m. ceburro,** white wheat.

mil, *m.* one thousand; one thousandth.—**m. y quinientas,** (coll.) lentils.—**a las m. y quinientas,** at an unearthly hour; after a long time.

miladi, *f.* milady.

milagrero, ra, *n.* miracle monger.

milagro, *m.* miracle; wonder; votive offering hung up in churches.

milagrón, *m.* (coll.) great miracle; gesture of astonishment.

milagrosamente, *adv.* miraculously.

milagroso, sa, *a.* miraculous.

milamores, *f.* (bot.) a species of valerian.

milanés, sa, *n. & a.* Milanese.

milano, *m.* (orn.) kite, glede, bird of prey; (bot.) bur or down of the thistle.

mildiú, *m.* (bot.) mildew (sp. app. to grape vines).

milenario, ria. I. *a.* millenary. **II.** *m.* millenary; millennium; one who expects the millennium.

milenarismo, *m.* millenarianism.

mileno, na, *a.* cloth in which the warp contains a thousand threads.

milenrama, *f.* (bot.) milfoil or yarrow.

milésimo, ma, *n. & a.* thousandth.

milesio, ia, *n. & a.* Milesian.—**fábula m.,** Milesian tale.

milhojas, *f.* (bot.) yarrow.

miliamperio, *m.* (elec.) milliampere.

miliamperímetro, *m.* (elec.) milliamperimeter.

miliar, *a.* miliary.

miliárea, *f.* milliare.

miliario, ria, *a.* relating to a mile or to miles.

milicia, *f.* science of war; soldiery, military; militiamen.—**m. urbana,** militia.

miliciano, na. I. *a.* military. **II.** *m.* militiaman.

miligramo, *m.* milligram.

mililitro, *m.* milliliter.

milímetro, *m.* millimeter.

militante, *a.* militant; military.

militar. I. *vn.* to serve in the army; to go to war. —**m. contra,** to be against, disprove or weaken (a theory, argument, etc.).—**m. en,** to be in, to belong to (a party, etc.).—**m. en favor de,** to lend weight to, to strengthen, be a reason for (a theory, line of conduct, etc.). **II.** *a.* military, soldierly. **III.** *n.* military man.—*pl.* military.—**militarismo,** *m.* militarism.—**militarista,** *n. & a.* mitilarist (-ic).— **militarmente,** *adv.* militarily.

milmillonésimo, ma, *n. & a.* billionth (thousand-millionth).

milo, *m.* earthworm.

miloca, *f.* (orn.) a kind of owl.

milocha, *f.* kite.

milord, *m.* (*pl.* MILORES) milord; one-horse barouchet.

milpa, *f.* (Mex.) maize land.

milpiés, *m.* woodlouse.

milréis, *m.* milreis (Portuguese and Brazilian money of account).

milla, *f.* mile.

millar, *m.* thousand; a great number (used in *pl.*); certain quantity of cocoa (varies between 3½ and 4 lb.).

millarada, *f.* about a thousand.—**a millaradas,** by thousands; innumerable times.—**echar millaradas,** to brag of wealth and riches.

millón, *m.* million.—*pl.* ancient excise or duty.

millonario, ria, *n. & a.* millionaire.

millonésimo, ma, *n. & a.* millionth.

mimado, da, *pp.* spoiled, overindulged.

mimar, *va.* to pet, fondle, indulge, spoil (a child).

mimbral, *m.* plantation of osiers.

mimbre, *m.* (bot.) osier, willow; (com.) twig, wicker, withe.

mimbrear, *vn.* to sway.

mimbreño, ña, *a.* osierlike, willowy.

mimbrera, *f.* (bot.) osier, willow.

mimbreral, *m.* osiery.

mimbroso, sa, *a.* wickered, osiered.

mimesis, *f.* (rhet.) mimesis.

mimetismo, *m.* mimetism, mimicry.

mímica, *f.* pantomime, sign language.

mímico, ca, *a.* mimic; imitative.

mimo, *m.* buffoon, merry-andrew, mimic; caress, petting, indulgence; prudery.

mimología, *f.* mimology.

mimosa, *f.* (bot.) mimosa, sensitive plant.

mimoso, sa, *a.* fastidious, finicky; soft, spoiled.

mina, *f.* mine; underground passage or conduit; source, spring; sinecure, (coll.) cinch, snap; mina (ancient Greek coin); (mil., naut.) mine.

minador, ra, *n.* miner, sapper; mining engineer.

minal, *a.* mine (u. a.)

minar, *va.* to mine, excavate, dig, burrow; to sap, undermine; to consume, ruin, destroy; to work hard for.

minarete, *m.* minaret.

mineraje, *m.* work of a mine; mining.

mineral. I. *a.* mineral. **II.** *m.* mineral, ore; water spring, fountain-head; rich mine; source. —**m. bruto,** raw ore, rough ore.—**m. virgen,** native ore.

mineralización, *f.* mineralization.

mineralizar. I. *va.* to mineralize. **II.** *vr.* to become mineralized; to become mineral, or charged with mineral substances (s. o. water).

mineralogía, *f.* mineralogy.—**mineralógico, ca,** *a.* mineralogical.—**mineralogista,** *m.* mineralogist.

minería, *f.* mining; force of miners; body of mine operators.

minero, ra. I. *a.* mining, pertaining to mines. **II.** *m.* miner; sapper; mine operator; source, origin.

mineromedicinal, *a.* medicinal mineral (waters).

minerva, *f.* (print.) Minerva machine.

minervista, *n.* (print.) operator of a Minerva machine.

mingitorio, *m.* upright urinal.

mingo, *m.* red ball or object ball in billiards.

miniar, *va.* (art) to paint in miniature.

miniatura, *f.* (art) miniature.

miniaturista, *n.* miniature painter.

mínima, *f.* slightest thing; (mus.) minim.

mínimo, ma. I. *a.* minimum. **II.** *m.* minimum; (eccl.) Minim.

mínimum, *m.* minimum.

mininó, na, *n.* kitty (u. for calling a cat).

minio, *m.* (min.) minium, red lead.

ministerial, *a.* ministerial.

ministerialismo, *m.* (pol.) ministerialism.

ministerialmente, *adv.* ministerially.

ministerio, *m.* (pol.) ministry, cabinet; office and term of a cabinet minister; department; building where the department is located; ministration, office, employment; service, agency. —**M. de Estado,** Department of State, or of Foreign Affairs.—**M. de Fomento,** (Spain) Department of Public Works, Agriculture, Commerce, and Manufactures (better left untranslated, calling it Department of Fomento).—**M. de la Gobernación,** Department of the Interior.—**M. de Gracia y Justicia,** Department of Justice and Ecclesiastical Affairs.—**M. de Hacienda,** Treasury Department.—**M. de la Guerra,** War Department.—**M. de lo Interior,** Department of the Interior.—**M. del Trabajo,** Department of Labor. —**M. de Marina,** Navy Department.

ministra, *f.* ministress; wife of a cabinet minister.

ministrador, ra, *n.* one who ministers.

ministrante. I. *a.* serving, ministering. **II.** *n.* trained nurse.

ministrar, *va. & vn.* to minister, to serve, to supply, to furnish.

ministril, *m.* apparitor, tipstaff; petty officer of justice; player of reed instruments in churches.

ministro, *m.* cabinet minister; minister plenipotentiary; judge or justice; sheriff, bailiff, constable, petty officer of justice; subordinate, agent, servant.—**m. consultante,** minister who lays before the king the opinion of his council.—**m. de Dios,** clergyman.—**M. de Estado,** Minister, or Secretary, of State.—**M. de Fomento,** Secretary,

or Minister, of Public Works, etc. (*V.* MINIS-
TERIO DE FOMENTO).—**M. de Gracia y Justicia,**
Attorney General.—**M. de Hacienda,** Minister, or
Secretary, of the Exchequer or Treasury.—**M. de
la Gobernación,** Minister, or Secretary, of the
Interior.—**m. del culto, m. del Señor,** clergyman.—**M. de Relaciones Exteriores,** Minister, or
Secretary, of Foreign Affairs.—**M. de Relaciones
Interiores,** Minister, or Secretary, of the Interior.
mino, na = MININO, NA.
minoración, *f.* lessening, diminution.
minorar. I. *va.* to lessen, diminish. **II.** *vr.* to
shrink; to decrease, diminish.
minorativo, va, *a.* lessening; laxative.
minoría, *f.* minority (in age or in number).
minoridad, *f.* minority, nonage.
minotauro, *m.* Minotaur.
minucia, *f.* minuteness, smallness; mite; small
tithe.—*pl.* minuciæ.
minuciosamente, *adv.* minutely, thoroughly.
minuciosidad, *f.* minuteness, thoroughness;
trifle, small detail.
minucioso, sa, *a.* minutely precise, thorough.
minué, *m.* (danc. and mus.) minuet.
minuendo, *m.* (arith.) minuend.
minuete, *m.* = MINUÉ.
minúscula, *a.* small, lower-case (letter).
minuta, *f.* minute; first draft; memorandum;
lawyer's bill; list of employees, roll; bill of
fare.
minutar, *va.* to make a draft of, to minute.
minutario, *m.* minute book.
minutero, *m.* minute hand.
minutisa, *f.* (bot.) sweet-william pink.
minuto, ta. I. *a.* minute, small. **II.** *m.* minute.
miñón, *m.* light infantry, rural guard; minion,
scoriæ of iron ore.
miñona, *f.* (print.) minion, 7-point type.
mío, mía; míos, mías, *poss. pron.* mine.—**de
m.,** by myself; of my own accord.—**lo m.,** what
belongs to me.—**soy m.,** I am my own master.
mio, *m.* puss, pet name for a cat.
miocardio, *m.* (anat.) myocardium.
miocarditis, *f.* (med.) myocarditis.
mioceno, na, *a.* (geol.) Miocene.
miodinia, *f.* (med.) myodinia, muscular pain.
miografía, *f.* (anat.) myography.
miología, *f.* (anat.) myology.
miope. I. *a.* myopic, near-sighted. **II.** *n.* myope.
miopía, *f.* (opt.) myopia, near-sightedness.
miosis, *f.* (med.) myosis.
miosota, miosotis, *f.* (bot.) forget-me-not.
miquelete, *m.* (mil.) miquelet.
mira, *f.* sight (of firearms and mathematical
instruments); leveling rod; (fort.) watch-tower;
(mas.) rule; care; vigilance; design, purpose,
intention, view.—**m. de corredera,** or **de mirilla,**
target leveling rod.—**m. parlante,** speaking
leveling rod.—**estar a la m.,** to be on the lookout,
to be on the watch.
¡mira! *interj.* look! lo! behold! take care!
mirabel, *m.* (bot.) summer cypress goosefoot;
sunflower.
mirabolano, *m.* (bot.) myrobalan.
mirada, *f.* glance, gaze, look.
miradero, *m.* watch tower, lookout, observatory;
cynosure.
mirado, da, *pp. & a.* (when preceded by **muy,
tan, más, menos**) considerate, circumspect,
prudent, thoughtful; (when preceded by **bien, mal,
mejor, peor**) considered, reputed.—**bien m.,**
(besides the meaning just given), carefully considered; looking well into the matter; in fact.
mirador, ra. I. *n.* spectator, looker-on. **II.** *m.*
belvedere, oriel, bay-window, observatory.
miradura, *f.* act of looking.
miraguano, *m.* (bot.) fan palm.
miramamolín, *m.* among Moors, "prince of the
believers."
miramiento, *m.* consideration, reflection; circumspection, prudence; attention, consideration, courtesy.
mirante, *n. & a.* looker (-ing).

mirar. I. *va.* to look, look at, look upon or
toward; to gaze, gaze upon; to view, survey; to
see, regard; to consider, think; to have regard
for, esteem; to watch, spy; to notice; to concern.—
m. bien, to think much of, esteem; to approve.—
m. de hito en hito, to stare at.—**m. de través,** to
squint at.—**m. mal,** to disapprove, have a bad
opinion of; to dislike; to consider bad form.—**m.
por encima,** to examine slightly, glance at.—**m.
sobre el hombro,** to cast a contemptuous look
at. **II.** *vn.* to look; (w. **a**) to overlook, face, front;
to look after, look out for.—**m. alrededor,** to look
around.—**m. en,** to think over, consider carefully.
—**m. por,** to take care of; look after.
mirasol, *m.* (bot.) sunflower.
miríada, *f.* large quantity or number.
miriagramo, *m.* myriagram.
miriámetro, *m.* myriameter.
miriápodo, da, *n. & a.* myriapodan, centipede.
mirífico, ca, *a.* marvellous, wonderful.
mirilla, *f. dim.* peephole in doors; target (of a
leveling rod).
miriñaque, *m.* trinket, bauble, gewgaw; hoopskirt, crinoline.
miriópodo, = MIRIÁPODO.
mirística, *f.* (bot.) nutmeg tree.
mirla, *f.* (orn.) blackbird.
mirlamiento, *m.* affected gravity.
mirlarse, *vr.* (coll.) to put on airs.
mirlo, *m.* (orn.) blackbird; (coll.) air of importance, affected gravity.
mirobálano, *m.* (bot.) myrobalan.
mirón, na, *n.* spectator, looker-on, by-stander;
prier, busybody, gazer.
mirra, *f.* myrrh.—**mirrado, da,** *a.* myrrhic.
mirrauste, *m.* (cook.) timbale of pigeons.
mirrino, na, *a.* myrrhic.
mirtáceo, cea. I. *a.* (bot.) myrtaceous. **II.** *f. pl.*
Myrtaceæ.—**mirtidano,** *m.* myrtle tiller or sprout.
—**mirtino, na,** *a.* myrtle-like.
mirto, *m.* (bot.) myrtle.
miruello, lla, *m. & f.* (orn.) blackbird.
misa, *f.* (eccl.) mass; (mus.) music composed for
a solemn mass.—**m. de cuerpo presente,** mass
said while the corpse is in the church.—**m. del
gallo,** midnight mass.—**m. mayor,** high mass.—
como en m., in dead silence.—**no saber de la m.
la media,** to know nothing.—**oír m.,** to hear, or
attend, mass.
misacantano, *m.* priest who is ordained and
says the mass; priest who celebrates the first
mass.
misal, *m.* (eccl.) missal, Mass book; (typ.)
two-line pica.
misantropía, *f.* misanthropy.
misantrópico, ca, *a.* misanthropic(al).
misántropo, *m.* misanthrope.
misar, *vn.* (coll.) to say mass; to hear mass.
misario, *m.* (eccl.) acolyte.
miscelánea, *f.* miscellany; mixture, medley.
misceláneo, a, *a.* miscellaneous, mixed.
miscibilidad, *f.* miscibility.
miscible, *a.* miscible.
miserabilísimo, ma, *a. super.* most miserable.
miserable. I. *a.* miserable, wretched, unhappy;
stingy, miserly, close-fisted. **II.** *n.* wretch, cur,
despicable person.
miserablemente, *adv.* miserably, unhappily;
stingily.
míseramente, *adv.* meanly, wretchedly.
miserear, *vn.* (coll.) to be niggardly or stingy.
miserere, *m.* (eccl.) Miserere; (med.) ileus.
miseria, *f.* misery, wretchedness, forlornness;
need, penury, poverty, destitution; stinginess;
trifle, bagatelle.
misericordia, *f.* mercy, mercifulness, pity.
misericordiosamente, *adv.* mercifully.
misericordioso, sa, *a.* merciful.
mísero, ra, *a.* = MISERABLE.
misero, ra, *a.* (coll.) mass-loving; church-going;
(priest) that says mass very often.
misérrimo, ma, *a. super.* most miserable.
misia, misiá, *f.* (Am.) Doña, Mrs.

misión, *f.* mission; errand; embassy, legation; commission; (eccl.) missionary station, residence, preaching, etc.; money and victuals allowed to reapers during the harvest.

misionario, ria; misionero, ra, *n.* missionary.

misivo, va, *a.* missive.

mismamente, *adv.* (coll.) exactly, to a tee.

mismísimo, ma, *a. super.* very same.

mismo, ma, *a.* same; similar, like; equal, self-same; -self (*él mismo,* himself, he himself).— **así m., lo m.,** the same; the same thing.—**lo m. da,** it is all the same, it makes no difference.—**lo m. que,** the same as.—**por lo m.,** for the same reason; for that very reason.

misógino, *n. & a.* woman-hater (-ing).

misoneísmo, *m.* misoneism, dread or dislike of novelty.

misoneísta, *n. & a.* misoneist (-ic).

mispíquel, *m.* (min.) mispickel, arsenopyrite.

mistamente, *adv.* (law) = MIXTAMENTE.

mistar, *va.* to speak or mumble.

mistela, *f.* = MIXTELA.

misterio, *m.* mystery.—**misteriosamente,** *adv.* mysteriously.—**misterioso, sa,** *a.* mysterious.

mística, *f.* study of the contemplative life.

místicamente, *adv.* mystically; spiritually; emblematically.

misticismo, *m.* mysticism.

místico, ca. **I.** *a.* mystic, mystical; emblematical; spiritual. **II.** *m.* mystic; (naut.) mistic, small coasting vessel.

misticón, na, *a.* (coll.) affectedly ascetic.

mistifori, *a.* hotchpotch. *V.* MIXTIFORI.

mistilíneo, nea, *a.* (geom.) = MIXTILÍNEO.

mistión, misto, mistura, misturar = MIX-TIÓN, MIXTO, MIXTURA, MIXTURAR.

misturera, *f.* (Am.) flower girl.

mita, *f.* (Am.) enforced service of Indians.

mitad, *f.* half; moiety; middle, centre; (coll.) husband or wife, as *mi cara mitad,* my better half.—**m. y m.,** half and half.—**por mitades,** by halves.

mitayo, *m.* (Am.) Indian serving his MITA.

mítico, ca, *a.* mythical.

mitigación, *f.* mitigation, extenuation; soothing.

mitigador, ra, *n. & a.* mitigator (-ing); soother (-ing).—**mitigante,** *a.* mitigating, allaying.

mitigar, *va.* (*pret.* MITIGUÉ: *subj.* MITIGUE) to mitigate, allay, soothe, alleviate; to quench, assuage, appease.

mitigativo, va; mitigatorio, ria, *a.* lenitive, mitigating, soothing.

mitin, *m.* meeting.

mito, *m.* myth.

mitología, *f.* mythology.

mitológico, ca. **I.** *a.* mythological. **II.** *n.* mythologist.

mitologista; mitólogo, ga, *n.* mythologist.

mitón, *m.* mitt, love glove without fingers.

mitote, *m.* Indian dance; (Amer.) household festival; fastidiousness, affectedness; riot, uproar, disturbance.

mitotero, ra, *a. & n.* (Am.) finical, fastidious; jolly, rollicking.

mitra, *f.* (eccl.) miter; bishopric.

mitrado, *pp. & a.* mitered.

mitrar, *vn.* to be mitered.

mitridato, *m.* mithridate, antidote.

mítulo, *m.* mussel.

mixtamente, *adv.* mixedly; (law) belonging to both ecclesiastical and civil courts.

mixtela, *f.* a refreshing beverage; (Colomb.) a popular intoxicating liquor.

mixtifori. **I.** *a.* (law) amenable to either ecclesiastical or secular courts; entangled, complicated. **II.** *m.* medley, hotchpotch.

mixtilíneo, nea, *a.* (geom.) mixtilinear.

mixtión, *f.* mixtion, mixture, commixture.

mixto, ta. **I.** *a.* mixed, mingled; composite; mixtiform; half-breed; crossbreed; mongrel; (arith.) mixed. **II.** *m.* sulphur or parlor match; (art.) explosive compound.

mixtura, *f.* mixture, compound; meslin, mixed corn; (pharm.) mixture.

mixturar, *va.* to mix, mingle.

mixturero, ra, *n. & a.* mixer (-ing).

miz, *m.* puss, name for a cat.

mízcalo, *m.* a kind of mushroom.

mizo, za, (coll.) = MICHO, CHA.

mnemónica, mnemotecnia, *f.* mnemonics.

mnemotécnico, ca, *a.* mnemonic.

moabita, *n.* Moabite.

moaré, *m.* moiré.

mobiliario, ria. **I.** *a.* movable (app. to chattels, especially unregistered bonds or securities). **II.** *m.* furniture, household goods.

moblaje, *m.* household furniture.

moblar, *va.* to furnish, provide with furniture.

moble, *a.* = MÓVIL.

moca, *f.* Mocha coffee.

mocador, pocket handkerchief.

mocasín, *m.;* **mocasina,** *f.* moccasin.

mocear, *vn.* to act like a boy; to revel, to rake.

mocedad, *f.* youth, youthfulness; reckless mode of living; frolic.

mocero, *a.* lascivious, lewd.

mocetón, na, *n.* strapping youth, lad (lass).

moción, *f.* motion, movement; leaning, inclination, tendency; divine inspiration; motion, proposition to an assembly.

mocito, ta. **I.** *a. dim.* very young. **II.** *n.* youngster, lad (lassie).

moco, *m.* mucus; viscid, glutinous matter; snuff of a lamp or candle; candle drippings; slag of iron; (naut.) martingale boom, dolphin striker; worthless thing, trifle; (bot.) love-lies-bleeding. —**m. de pavo,** crest of a turkey.—**a m. de candil,** by candlelight.—**llorar a m. tendido,** (coll.) to weep copiously, cry like a child.

mocosidad, *f.* mucousness, viscosity.

mocoso, sa. **I.** *a.* snivelly; full of mucus; despicable, mean. **II.** *n.* inexperienced youth.

mocosuelo, la, *n. dim.* thoughtless, inexperienced youth; child.

mochada, *f.* butt (as of a goat).

mochar, *va.* to cut, lop off.

mochazo, *m.* blow with the butt of a musket.

mocheta, *f.* thick edge of some tools; (arch.) quoin; sconcheon.

mochete, *m.* (orn.) sparrow hawk.

mochil, *m.* farmer's boy.

mochila, *f.* (mil.) knapsack, haversack; a kind of caparison; gunning bag; provisions given to each soldier for a number of days.

mochilero, *m.* one who carries the baggage of soldiers.

mochín, *m.* executioner.

mocho, cha. **I.** *a.* cropped, shorn, lopped, cut off; maimed, mutilated; (Mex., coll.) hypocritical. **II.** *m.* butt end.

mochuelo, *m.* (orn.) red owl.—**cargar con el m.,** to get the worst part of an undertaking.

moda, *f.* fashion, mode, style.—**a la (última) m.,** after the latest fashion; fashionable.—**de m.,** fashionable.—**estar de m.,** to be in style, or in fashion.—**ser de m.,** or **ser m.,** to be the fashion.

modal. **I.** *a.* (log.) modal. **II.** *m. pl.* manners, breeding.

modelado, *m.* (art) modelling.

modelar, *va.* (art) to model.

modelo. **I.** *m.* model, pattern, standard, copy. **II.** *n.* (art) life model.

moderación, *f.* moderation.

moderadamente, *adv.* moderately.

moderado, da, *a.* moderate; modest; reasonable; (pol.) conservative.

moderador, ra, *n. & a.* moderator (-ing).—**poder m.,** (in constitutional monarchies) the sovereign.

moderadora, *f.* moderatress, moderatrix.

moderante. **I.** *n. & a.* moderator (-ing). **II.** *n.* presiding officer, moderator.

moderantismo, *m.* (pol.) conservatism.

moderar. I. *va.* to moderate, regulate, adjust, restrain, curb, repress. **II.** *vr.* to calm down, moderate, refrain from excesses.

moderativo, va; moderatorio, ria, *a.* moderating.

modernamente, *adv.* recently, lately, freshly.

modernismo, *m.* modernism.—**modernista. I.** *a.* modern. **II.** *n.* modernist.—**modernizar,** *va.* to modernize.—**moderno, na,** *a.* modern.

modestamente, *adv.* modestly.—**modestia,** *f.* modesty.—**modesto, ta,** *a.* modest.

módicamente, *adv.* moderately, sparingly.

modicidad, *f.* moderateness, cheapness.

módico, ca, *a.* reasonable, economic (s. o. prices).

modificable, *a.* modifiable.—**modificación,** *f.* modification.—**modificador, ra,** *n. & a.* modifier (-fying).—**modificante,** *a.* modifying.

modificar, *va.* (*pret.* MODIFIQUÉ; *subj.* MODIFIQUE) to modify.

modificativo, va; modificatorio, ria, *a.* modifying.

modillón, *m.* (arch.) modillion, bracket.

modio, *m.* modius, an ancient Roman dry measure.

modismo, *m.* (gram.) idiom.

modista, *f.* dressmaker or modiste.—**m. de sombreros,** milliner.

modistilla, *f. dim.* (coll.) young, inexperienced dressmaker or milliner; seamstress.

modo, *m.* mode, way, manner, form; moderation, temperance; civility, urbanity; (gram.) model. or mood: (mus.) mode.—**al m. de, a m. de,** in the same manner as, like, in the fashion of.—**de buen (mal) m.,** politely (impolitely).—**del mismo m. que,** in the same way as.—**de m. de,** so as to.—**de m. que,** so that; and so.—**por m. de,** as (*por modo de juego*, as a joke, in jest).—**sobre m.,** extremely.

modorra, *f.* drowsiness, heaviness; (vet.) sturdy.

modorrar. I. *va.* to drowse, make sleepy. **II.** *vr.* to become flabby (s. o. fruit).

modorrilla, *f.* (coll.) third night watch.

modorro, rra, *a.* drowsy, sleepy, heavy; dull, stupid; suffering from sturdy (s. o. sheep); flabby (s. o. fruit).

modoso, sa, *a.* temperate, well-behaved.

modrego, ga, *n.* (coll.) awkward person.

modulación, *f.* (mus.) modulation.

modulador, ra, *n.* modulator.

modulante, *a.* modulating.

modular, *vn.* (mus.) to modulate.

módulo, *m.* size of coins and medals; (arch.) module; (math.) modulus; (mus.) modulation; (hydr.) unit of measure of running water.

mofa, *f.* mockery, jeer, scoff.—**mofador, ra,** *n. & a.* scoffer (-ing), mocker (-ing).—**mofadura,** *f.* = MOFA.—**mofante,** *n.* = MOFADOR.

mofar, *vn. & vr.* to jeer, scoff, mock, sneer.—**mofarse de,** to mock, sneer at, scoff, make fun of.

mofeta, *f.* mofette, gas spring, mephitis; (zool.) skunk or polecat.

moflete, *m.* fat cheek.

mofletudo, da, *a.* fat-cheeked.

mogate, *m.* varnish, glazing.—**a medio m.,** carelessly, heedlessly.

mogato, ta, *a.* = MOJIGATO.

mogol, la; mogólico, ca, *a.* Mongolian.

mogollón, *m.* hanger-on, sponger, parasite.—**comer de m.,** to sponge.

mogón, na, *a.* with one horn missing or broken.

mogote, *m.* hummock, hillock; (agr.) stack or rick of corn; brocket's antler.

mogrollo, *m.* parasite, sponger; (coll.) rustic.

moharra, *f.* head of a spear.

moharrache, moharracho, *m.* jackpudding, merry-andrew, clown.

mohatra, *f.* sham sale; fraud.—**mohatrar,** *vn.* to make a sham sale.—**mohatrero, ra; mohatrón, na,** trickster, swindler.

mohecer, *va.* to moss, to mildew.

mohiento, ta, *a.* mildewed.

mohín, *m.* grimace, gesture.

mohina, *f.* animosity, animadversion, grudge.

mohino, na. I. *a.* fretful, peevish; sad, mournful; (mule) begotten by a stallion and a she-ass; black. **II.** *n.* one who plays alone against several others.

moho, *m.* (bot.) moss; mould, mildew; rust.

mohoso, sa, *a.* rusty; mouldy, musty, mildewed.

mojada, *f.* wetting, drenching; sop; (coll.) stab.

mojador, ra, *n.* wetter, moistener.

mojadura, *f.* drenching, moistening, wetting.

mojama, *f.* dry, salt tunny fish.

mojar. I. *va.* to wet, drench; moisten, damp; (coll.) to stab; interfere with. **II.** *vn.* to be immersed in any business.

mojarra, *f.* a sea fish; (Am.) heart-shaped dagger.

mojarrilla, *n.* (coll.) gay, jolly person.

moje, *m.* (cook.) gravy, sauce.

mojel, *m.* (naut.) braided cord for the anchor.

moji, *m.* sponge cake; pie.

mojicón, *m.* bun; (coll.) fisticuff.

mojiganga, *f.* morris dance; masquerade, mask, mummery.

mojigatería, mojigatez, *f.* hypocrisy; religious fanaticism.

mojigato, ta. I. *n.* dissembler, hypocrite; bigot, fanatic. **II.** *a.* deceitful, hypocritical; prude; bigoted.

mojón, *m.* landmark; heap, pile; milestone; wine sampler; a kind of play, similar to pitching; solid excrement.

mojona, *f.* excise tax on wine; survey of land; setting up of landmarks.

mojonación, *f.* = AMOJONAMIENTO.—**mojonar,** *va.* = AMOJONAR.—**mojonera,** *f.* landmark.—**mojonero,** *m.* gauger.

mola, *f.* (med.) mole; flour with salt used in sacrifices.

molada, *f.* colors ground at once.

molar, *a.* molar.

molcajete, *m.* mortar for pounding.

moldar, *va.* to mold.

moldavo, va, *n. & a.* Moldavian.

molde, *m.* mold; pattern; (eng.) form; (print.) form ready for printing.—**de m.,** in print; printed; fitting, to the purpose.

moldeador, *m.* molder, cast maker.

moldear, *va.* to mold; to cast; to provide or adorn with moldings.

moldura, *f.* molding.

moldurar, *va.* to make moldings on.

mole. I. *a.* soft, mild. **II.** *f.* huge mass or bulk. **III.** *m.* (Mex.) chili sauce for turkey.

molécula, *f.* molecule.—**molecular,** *a.* molecular.

moledera, *f.* (coll.) botheration.

moledero, ra, *a.* to be ground.

moledor, ra, *n.* grinder; powdering mill; crushing cylinder in a sugar-mill; bore, tiresome person.

moledura, *f.* grinding.

molendero, ra, *n.* miller, grinder; chocolate manufacturer

moler, *va.* (*ind.* MUELO: *subj.* MUELA) to grind, pulverize, mill; to overtire; to vex, bore; to waste, consume; to masticate, chew.—**m. a palos,** to give a severe drubbing.

molero, *m.* maker or seller of millstones.

molestador, ra, *n.* vexer, annoyer.

molestamente, *adv.* troublesomely, vexatiously; uncomfortably.

molestar, *va.* to disturb; to trouble; to annoy, vex; to tease.

molestia, *f.* annoyance, bother; inconvenience, trouble; discomfort; hardship, grievance; (coll.) quarrel.

molesto, ta, *a.* annoying, vexatious, bothersome; troublesome; uncomfortable.

moleta, *f.* muller; polisher; (print.) ink-grinder.

moletón, *m.* canton or cotton flannel.

molibdato, *m.* molybdate.

molibdeno, *m.* molybdenum.—**molíbdico, ca,** *a.* molybdic.

molicie, _f._ softness, effeminacy.

molido, da, _a. & pp._ ground; fatigued.

molienda, _f._ milling, grinding; grist; weariness, fatigue; season for grinding sugar cane or olives.

moliente, _n. & a._ grinder (-ing).

molificable, _a._ mollifiable.

molificación, _f._ mollification.

molificar, _va._ (_pret._ MOLIFIQUÉ: _subj._ MOLIFIQUE) to mollify, soften, mitigate.

molificativo, va, _a._ mollifying, lenitive.

molimiento, _m._ grinding, pounding; fatigue, weariness, lassitude.

molinar, _m._ place where there are mills.

molinejo, _m. dim._ small mill.

molinera, _f._ miller's wife; woman mill worker.

molinería, _f._ number or group of mills; mill industry.

molinero, _m._ miller, grinder.

molinete, _m. dim._ little mill; pin wheel; ventilating wheel; friction roller; fifth wheel of a vehicle; smoke dispeller; moulinet, swing of sabre; drum of a capstan or winch.—**m. hidráulico,** hydraulic tourniquet, Barker's mill.

molinillo, _m. dim._ hand mill; coffee grinder; chocolate beater.

molinismo, _m._ Molinism.—**molinista,** _n. & a._ Molinist (-ic).

molinito, _m. dim._ small mill.

molino, _m._ mill; restless, noisy fellow; (coll.) mouth.—**m. de sangre,** mill turned by men or animals.—**m. de viento,** windmill.

molitivo, va, _a._ mollient.

molondro, molondrón, _m._ (coll.) poltroon.

moloso, _m._ (poet.) molossus.

molote, _m._ (Cuba) tumult, riot.

moltura, _f._ grinding.

moluscoideo, a. I. _n. & a._ molluscoid. **II.** _m. pl._ Molluscoida.

molusco, _m._ mollusc.

molla, _f._ lean meat; crumb of bread.

mollar, _a._ soft, tender; easily shelled; lean (s. o. meat); productive, profitable; credulous, gullible.

mollear, _vn._ to become soft and pliable; to yield easily.

molledo, _m._ fleshy part of a limb; bread crumb.

molleja, _f._ gland; gizzard; sweetbread.

mollejón, _m. aug._ large gland; big, fat person; grindstone.

mollejuela, _f. dim._ sweetbread.

mollera, _f._ crown or top of the head.—**cerrado de m.,** rude, ignorant.—**ser duro de m.,** to be dull or obstinate.

mollero, _m. =_ MOLLEDO.

molleta, _f._ biscuit; brown bread; snuffers.

mollete, _m._ manchet, French roll; fleshy part of the arm.—_pl._ plump cheeks.

molletero, ra, _n._ baker or seller of rolls.

molletudo, da, _a._ having chubby cheeks.

mollina, mollizna, _f._ drizzle.

molliznar, molliznear, _vn._ to drizzle, sprinkle.

moma, _f._ (Mex.) blindman's buff.

momentáneamente, _adv._ instantly; momentarily; promptly.—**momentáneo, nea,** _a._ momentary; prompt.

momento, _m._ moment; weight, importance; (mech.) moment.—**al m.,** in a moment, immediately.—**por momentos,** continually, every minute; any moment, soon.

momería, _f._ mummery.

momero, ra, _n._ mummer.

momia, _f._ mummy.—**momificar. I.** _va._ to mummify. **II.** _vr._ to become a mummy.

momio, mia. I. _a._ meager, lean. **II.** _m._ extra allowance.—**de m.,** gratis.

momo, _m._ funny grimace.

momórdiga, _f._ (bot.) = BALSAMINA.

mona, _f._ female monkey; (coll.) ludicrous imitator; (coll.) drunkenness; drunkard; at cards, old maid; Easter cake with whole eggs; iron plate worn for protection on the right leg by bullfighters on horseback.—**dormir la m.,** to sleep off a drunk.

monacal, _a._ monastic; monkish.

monacalmente, _adv._ monastically.

monacato, _m._ monkhood, monachism.

monacillo, _m._ acolyte.

monacordio, _m._ (mus.) clavichord.

monada, _f._ grimace; monkeyism, monkeyshine; fawning, flattery; pretty child.

mónada, _f._ monad; (zool.) monadid.

monadología, _f._ monadology.

monago, monaguillo, _m. =_ MONACILLO.

monaquismo, _m._ monachism.

monarca, _m._ monarch.

monarquía, _f._ monarchy; kingdom.

monárquico, ca, _a._ monarchical.

monarquismo, _m._ monarchism.

monarquista, _n. & a._ monarchist (-ic).

monasterial, _a._ monastic.

monasterio, _m._ monastery.

monásticamente, _adv._ monastically.

monástico, ca, _a._ monastic, monastical.

monda, _f._ pruning of trees; pruning season.

mondadientes, _m._ toothpick.

mondador, ra, _n._ cleaner; purifier.

mondadura, _f._ cleaning, cleansing.—_pl._ parings, peelings.

mondaoídos, mondaorejas, _m._ ear spoon.

mondar, _va._ to clean, cleanse; to trim, prune; to hull, husk, decorticate; to deprive of money; to cut (the hair).

mondarajas, _f. pl._ peelings.

mondejo, _m._ belly of a pig or sheep stuffed with minced meat.

mondo, da, _a._ neat, pure, unmixed.—**m. y lirondo,** (coll.) pure, without admixture.

mondón, _m._ barkless trunk of a tree.

mondonga, _f._ (contempt.) kitchen wench.

mondongo, _m._ tripe; intestines.

mondonguería, _f._ place where tripe is sold.

mondonguero, ra, _n._ tripe seller or cooker.

mondonguil, _a._ (coll.) relating to tripe.

monear, _vn._ (coll.) to monkey.

moneda, _f._ coin; money; specie; coinage.—**m. corriente,** currency.—**m. de vellón,** small copper money.—**m. divisionaria,** fractional money or currency.—**m. fiduciaria,** fiduciary money, fiat money.—**m. imaginaria,** money of account.—**m. metálica,** or **sonante,** hard money, specie.—**m. suelta,** small change.—**pagar en la misma m.,** to return like for like.

monedaje, _m._ coinage; seigniorage.

monedar, monedear, _va._ to coin.

monedería, _f._ mintage.

monedero, ra, _n._ coiner, moneyer.—**m. falso,** counterfeiter.

monería, _f._ grimace, mimicry, monkeyshine; cunning action of a child.

monesco, ca, _a._ (coll.) apish.

monetario, ria. I. _a._ monetary, financial. **II.** _m._ cabinet or collection of coins and medals.

monetización, _f._ monetization.

monetizar, _va._ to monetize.

monfí, _m._ Moorish highwayman.

moniato, _m._ (bot.) = BONIATO.

monicaco, _m._ whipster. _V._ HOMINICACO.

monición, _f._ admonition.

monigote, _m._ lay brother; (coll.) a bumpkin; puppet, grotesque figure; (Colomb., contempt.) priest.

monillo, _m._ (sew.) waist, bodice.

monipodio, _m._ (coll.) combine.

monís, _m._ kind of fritters; any pretty little thing. **m.,** or **monises,** (coll.) money.

monismo, _m._ (philos.) monism.

monista, _n. & a._ (philos.) monist (-ic).

mónita, _f._ artifice, cunning suavity.

monitor, _m._ monitor, adviser; (naut.) monitor.

monitorio, ria. I. _a._ monitory, admonitory. **II.** _n._ ecclesiastical monition.

monja, _f._ nun.—_pl._ sparks in burned papers.

monje, _m._ monk; (orn.) brown peacock.

---

monjía, *f.* monkhood.
monjil. I. *m.* nun's dress; mourning dress. **II.** *a.* relating or belonging to nuns.
monjío, *m.* nunnishness; taking the veil.
monjita, *f. dim.* little nun.
mono, na. I. *a.* (coll.) neat, pretty, nice; funny. **II.** *m.* monkey, ape; mimic; nincompoop.
monoatómico, ca, *a.,* monoatomic.
monobásico, ca, *a.* monobasic.
monobloque.—en m., (int. comb. eng.) in bloc, in one piece.
monoceronte, monocerote, *m.* unicorn.
monociclo, cla. I. *a.* monocyclic. **II.** *m.* monocycle, single-wheel velocipede.
monocilíndrico, ca, *a.* single-cylinder.
monoclínico, ca, *a.* (min.) monoclinic.
monocordio, *m.* (mus.) monochord.
monocotiledóneo, a. I. *a.* (bot.) monocotyledonous. **II.** *f. pl.* Monocotyledones, monocotyledons.
monocromático, ca, *a.* monochromatic.
monocromo, ma, *a.* monochrome.
monóculo, la. I. *a.* monocular, one-eyed. **II.** *m.* (opt.) monocle; (surg.) monoculus.
monodelfo, fa, *n. & a.* (zool.) monodelphian.
monofásico, ca, *a.* (elec.) single-phase.
monófilo, la, *a.* (bot.) monophyllous.
monogamia, *f.* monogamy.
monógamo, ma, *a.* monogamous.
monogenismo, *m.* (biol.) monogenism.
monografía, *f.* monograph.
monográfico, ca, *a.* monographic.
monograma, *m.* monogram.
monoico, ca, *a.* (bot.) monœcious.
monolítico, ca, *a.* monolithic.
monolito, *m.* monolith.
monólogo, *m.* monologue, soliloquy.
monomanía, *f.* monomania.
monomaníaco, ca, *n. & a.* monomaniac.
monomaquia, *f.* monomachy, duel.
monometalismo, *m.* monometallism.
monometalista, *n. & a.* monometallist (-ic).
monomio, mia, *m. & a.* monomial.
monona, *a.* (coll.) graceful and pretty (girl).
monopastos, *m.* sheave.
monopétalo, la, *a.* (bot.) monopetalous.
monoplano, *m.* (aer.) monoplane.
monopolio, *m.* monopoly.
monopolista, *n. & a.* monopolist (-ic).
monopolizar, *va.* (*pret.* MONOPOLICÉ: *subj.* MONOPOLICE) to monopolize.
monóptero, ra, *a.* (arch.) monopterous.
monorquidia, *f.* (med.) monorchism.
monosépalo, la, *a.* (bot.) monosepalous.
monosilábico, ca, *a.* monosyllabic.
monosílabo, ba, *n. & a.* monosyllable.
monospermo, ma, *a.* (bot.) monospermous.
monóstrofe, *f.* (poet.) monostrophe.
monote, *m.* (coll.) dumfounded person.
monoteísmo, *m.* monotheism.
monoteísta, *n. & a.* monotheist (-ic).
monotelismo, *m.* Monothelitism.
monotelita. I. *a.* Monothelitic. **II.** *n.* Monothelite.
monotipia, *f.* monotype (machine).
monotipista, *n.* monotypist.
monotonía, *f.* monotony.
monótono, na, *a.* monotonous.
monotremas, *m. pl.* (zool.) Monotremata, monotremes.
monseñor, *m.* Monseigneur.
monserga, *f.* (coll.) gabble, gibberish.
monstruo, *m.* monster; monstrosity; huge thing.
monstruosamente, *adv.* monstrously.
monstruosidad, *f.* monstrosity; monstrousness.
monstruoso, sa, *a.* monstrous; huge; extraordinary; hideous; hateful; shocking.
monta, *f.* act of mounting; raising or crossing (as horses); amount, sum total; value, worth, price; (mil.) signal for mounting.
montacarga, *m.* hoist, winch, windlass.

montada, *f.* scatch mouth.
montadero, *m.* mounting block.
montado, da. I. *pp. & a.* (horse) ready for mounting. **II.** *m.* trooper or horseman.
montador, *m.* mounter; mounting block; installer (electrician, pipe fitter, etc.).
montadura, *f.* mounting; (jew.) setting; (sad.) mountings of a riding horse; mount.
montaje, *m.* setting up, installing; assembling; (arti.) act of mounting.—*pl.* (arti.) mounting.
montanera, *f.* oak forest; feeding of hogs with acorns.
montanero, *m.* forester.
montañero, ra, *n.* (Colomb.) mountaineer; rustic, boor.
montanismo, *m.* Montanism.
montanista, *n. & a.* Montanist (-ic).
montano, na, *a.* mountainous.
montantada, *f.* braggadocio; multitude, crowd.
montante. I. *m.* (fenc.) broadsword; (carp. and mech.) upright, standard, post, strut, jamb; (arch.) transom; (min.) stempel; (com.) amount, footing. **II.** *f.* (naut.) flood tide.
montantear, *m.* (fenc.) to wield the broadsword; to vaunt, brag; to intermeddle.
montantero, *m.* fighter with a broadsword.
montaña, *f.* mountain.—*pl.* highlands.
montañés, sa. I. *a.* mountain (u. a.), of or from the mountains, highlandish. **II.** *n.* mountaineer, highlander; native of the province of Santander, Spain.
montañeta, -ñuela, *f. dim.* small mountain.
montañoso, sa, *a.* mountainous.
montar. I. *vn.* to mount, get on top; to ride on horseback; to amount; to be of importance.—**m. en cólera,** to fly into a rage. **II.** *va.* to ride, straddle (a horse); to cover (as a horse, etc.); (mech.) to mount, set up, assemble; (jew.) to set (as diamonds); to cock (as a gun); to wind (a clock, etc.); to impose a fine for trespassing; (mil.) to mount (guard); (naut.) to command (a ship); to carry or be equipped with (as guns); to round (a cape or headland). **III.** *vr.* to get into (as a passion).
montaraz. I. *a.* born or raised in the mountains; wild, untamed; uncouth, boorish. **II.** *n.* forester.—**montaraza,** *f.* forester's wife.
montazgar, *va.* to levy or collect MONTAZGO.
montazgo, *m.* toll for cattle passing from one province into another; cattle pass.
monte, *m.* mountain, mount; wood, forest, woodland; difficulty, obstruction; bushy head of hair; talon, cards that remain after the hands have been dealt; (cards) monte.—**m. alto,** forest. —**m. bajo,** scrub, brushwood, brake, thicket.—**m. de piedad,** pawnshop.—**m. pío,** gratuity fund for widows and orphans.
montea, *f.* beating a wood for game; stone-cutting; (arch.) working drawing; versed sine of an arch.
montear, *va.* to hunt; to make a working drawing of; (arch.) to vault, arch.
montecillo, *m. dim.* small forest; hillock, hummock.
montepío, *m.* = MONTE PÍO. *V.* MONTE.
montera, *f.* cloth cap; skylight; receiver, condenser of a still or alembic; (naut.) skysail, skyscraper; hunter's wife.
monterería, *f.* cap factory or store.
monterero, ra, *m.* cap maker or seller.
montería, *f.* hunting, hunt, chase.
montero, ra, *n.* (in hunting) beater.
monterón, *m. aug.* big cloth cap.
monterrey, *m.* (cook.) meat pie.
monteruca, *f.* ugly cap.
montés, sa, *a.* wild.
montesino, na, *a.* montigenous.
montevideano, na, *n. & a.* Montevidean, of or from Montevideo.
montículo, *m.* monticle, mound.
monto, *m.* sum (of money); (com., arith.) amount (principal plus interest).

montón, *m.* heap, pile; big lot, mass; mound.—**m. de gente,** crowd, multitude.—**a montones,** abundantly, in heaps.

montonera, *f.* (Am.) group of revolutionary horsemen; large crowd.

montonero, *m.* bushwhacker, guerrilla.

montuno, na, *a.* montigenous, highlandish; rustic, boorish.

montuosidad, *f.* (prov.) mountainousness.

montuoso, sa, *a.* mountainous, hilly.

montura, *f.* riding horse, mount; saddle and trappings; setting up, installing; (jew.) setting.

monuelo, *m. dim.* coxcomb, silly fop.

monumental, *a.* monumental.

monumento, *m.* monument.

monzón, *m.* monsoon.

moña, *f.* lay figure for dressmakers; doll; fancy cap for infants; ornament of ribbons for the head; elaborate badge on a bull's neck in the ring; (coll.) drunkenness.

moño, *m.* chignon; topknot; cop, tuft, egret.

moñón, na; moñudo, da, *a.* crested, topped (as fowls); (Colomb.) pouty, sulky.

moquear, *vn.* to snivel; to run at the nose.

moquero, *m.* pocket handkerchief.

moqueta, *f.* moquette.

moquete, *m.* blow on the nose.

moquetear. I. *vn.* (coll.) to discharge mucus or blow the nose frequently. **II.** *va.* to hit in the face.

moquillo, *m. dim.* little mucus; pip (in fowls).

moquita, *f.* snivel, running from the nose.

mora, *f.* (law) delay, mora; (bot.) blackberry, bramble berry; bramble bush; mulberry.

morabito, morabuto, *m.* Mohammedan hermit.

moracho, cha, *a.* light purple.

morada, *f.* habitation, abode, residence; stay, sojourn.

morado, da, *a.* purple; murrey.

morador, ra, *n.* resident, inhabitant.

moraga, *f.,* **morago,** *m.* glean, bunch.

moral. I. *a.* moral. **II.** *m.* (bot.) blackberry bush; black mulberry tree. **III.** *f.* ethics, morality.

moraleja. *f.* moral, maxim, lesson.

moralidad, *f.* morality.—**moralista,** *m.* moralist.—**moralización,** *f.* moralization.

moralizador, ra, *n* .& *a.* moralizer (-ing*).*

moralizar, *va.* & *vn.* (*pret.* MORALICÉ: *subj.* MORALICE) to moralize.

moralmente, *adv.* morally.

morar, *vn.* to inhabit, dwell, reside.

moratiniano, na, *a.* Moratinian, of or like Moratín or his style.

moratoria, *f.* (com. and law), moratorium.

moravo, va, *n.* & *a.* Moravian.

morbidez, *f.* (art) softness, mellowness.

mórbido, da, *a.* morbid, diseased, morbose; (art) soft, mellow, delicate.

morbífico, ca, *a.* morbific, causing disease.

morbo, *m.* disease, distemper, infirmity.—**m. comicial,** (med.) epilepsy.—**m. gálico,** venereal disease.—**m. regio,** jaundice.

morboso, sa, *a.* diseased, morbid.

morcajo, *m.* low-grade wheat.

morcella, *f.* spark from a lamp.

morciguillo, *m.* (orn.) bat.

morcilla, *f.* blood pudding; (theat., coll.) gag.

morcillero, ra, *n.* one who makes or sells blood puddings; (theat., coll.) gagger.

morcillo, lla. I. *a.* reddish black. **II.** *m.* fleshy part of the arm.

morcón, *m.* large blood pudding or sausage; (coll.) short, plumpy person.

mordacidad, *f.* mordacity; asperity, acrimony; sarcastic language.

mordante, *m.* (print.) guide.

mordaz, *a.* corrosive, biting, nipping; sarcastic; acrimonious; keen.

mordaza, *f.* gag; muzzle; holder, clamp, stopper; pincers, tongs; (r. w.) fishplate.

mordazmente, *adv.* acrimoniously, nippingly.

mordedor, ra, *n.* & *a.* biter (-ing); backbiter (-ing).

mordedura, *f.* bite.

mordente, *m.* mordant; (mus.) mordent; turn.

morder. I. *va.* (*ind.* MUERDO: *subj.* MUERDA) to bite; to nip, gripe, grasp, clutch; to gnaw, eat, wear away; to etch; to corrode; to revile, backbite; (print.) to overlap the form or paper (as the frisket), thereby preventing a good impression.— **m. el freno,** to bite the bridle. **II.** *vr.* to bite (one's tongue, lips, etc.).—**m. la lengua,** to refrain from saying what one is tempted to say.—**no m. los labios,** (coll.) to be outspoken.

mordicación, *f.* smarting, stinging.

mordicante, *a.* biting, pungent, acrid, corrosive.

mordicar. I. *va.* to gnaw, nibble. **II.** *vn.* to smart, sting.

mordicativo, va, *a.* biting, stinging.

mordido, da, *pp.* & *a.* diminished, worn out, wasted away.

mordiente. I. *a.* biting. **II.** *m.* mordant.

mordihuí, *m.* weevil.

mordimiento, *m.* bite, mordication.

mordiscar, *va.* to nibble; take a bite of.

mordisco, mordiscón, *m.* bite; biting; bit, piece bitten off.

morel de sal, *m.* purple red for fresco painting.

morena, *f.* whole-wheat bread; rick of new-mown grain; heap of stones formed by a landslide; (icht.) moray; (geol.) moraine.

morenillo, illa, ito, ita. I. *a. dim.* brunette. **II.** *m.* black powder for wounds of sheep.

moreno, na. I. *a.* brown, morel, tawny; dark, swarthy; brunette. **II.** *n.* (Cuba) negro, darky.

morera, *f.* (bot.) white mulberry tree.

moreral, *m.* grove of white mulberry trees.

morería, *f.* Moorish quarter; Moorish lands.

moretón, *m.* (coll.) bruise, ecchymosis.

morfa, *f.* fungous disease of orange and lemon trees.

morfina, *f.* morphine.—**morfinismo,** *m.* (med.) morphinism.—**morfinomanía,** *f.* morphinomania, drug habit.—**morfinómano, na,** *n.* morphinomaniac, drug fiend.

morfología, *f.* morphology.

morfológico, ca, *a.* morphologic(al).

morga, *f.* Indian berries. *V.* ALPECHÍN.

morganático, ca, *a.* morganatic.

moribundo, da, *a.* dying, near death.

morichal, *m.* grove of MORICHES.

moriche, *m.* a tropical palm.

moriego, ga, *a.* Moorish.

morigeración, *f.* temperance, moderation.

morigerado, da, *a.* temperate, abstemious.

morigerar, *va.* to restrain, moderate.

morillo, *m. dim.* little Moor; andiron, firedog.

morir. I. *vn.* & *vr.* (*pp.* MUERTO: *gerund,* MURIENDO: *ind.* MUERO: *pret.* él MURIÓ: *subj.* MUERA) to die; to die or go out (as fire).—**m. de,** to die of, with or from; to be dying with.—**¡muera . . .!** down with . . .! **II.** *vr.* to be benumbed (a limb). —**m. por,** to be excessively fond of.

morisco, ca. I. *a.* Moorish, Moresque. **II.** *n.* Morisco.

morisma, *f.* multitude of Moors.

morisqueta, *f.* Moorish trick; (coll.) deception, fraud; (Philip.) boiled rice; (Colomb.) face, grimace.

morlaco, ca, *a.* affecting ignorance.

morlés, *m.* sort of linen, lawn.

morlón, na, *a.* = MORLACO.

mormón, na, *n.* & *a.* Mormon.

mormónico, ca, *a.* Mormon.

mormonismo, *m.* Mormonism.

mormullar, *va.* = MURMURAR.

mormullo, *m.* = MURMULLO.

moro, ra. I. *a.* Moorish; (coll.) not watered (wine). **II.** *n.* Moor.—**m. de paz,** peaceful person. —**hay moros en la costa,** the coast is not clear.

morocada, *f.* butt of a ram.

morocho, cha, *a.* (Am.) fresh, vigorous (s. o. persons); hard kind of Indian corn.

morón, *m.* hillock, hummock, mound.

moroncho, cha, *a.* = MORONDO.
morondanga, *f.* (coll.) hodgepodge, medley.
morondo, da, *a.* bald, hairless; leafless.
moronía, *f.* = ALBORONÍA.
morosamente, *adv.* slowly, tardily.
morosidad, *f.* slowness, tardiness.
moroso, sa, *a.* slow, tardy, heavy, sluggish.
morquera, *f.* (bot.) Spanish thyme.
morra, *f.* top, crown of the head; mora, a game. —andar a la m., to come to blows.
morrada, *f.* butting of two heads.
morral, *m.* nose bag; game bag; knapsack; (coll.) rustic.
morralla, *f.* small fry (fish); rubbish; rabble.
morrillo, *m.* pebble; fat of the nape of a sheep.
morriña, *f.* murrain; (coll.) sadness, blues.
morrión, *m.* (mil.) morion; helmet; vertigo (in hawks).
morro, *m.* snout, muffle; anything round like the head; headland; bluff; peak; pebble, blubber lip.—andar al m., to come to blows.
morro, rra, *a.* purring.
morrocotudo, da, *a.* (coll.) strong, stout; very important or difficult.
morrocoy, morrocoyo, *m.* (Cuba) boxturtle.
morrón, ;m. knotted flag; large sweet pepper; (aer., coll.) crash.
morroncho, cha, *a.* mild, meek, tame.
morrongo, ga; morroño, ña, *n.* cat.
morrudo, da, *a.* blobber-lipped.
morsa, *f.* (icht.) walrus, morse.
mortadela, *f.* Bologna sausage.
mortaja, *f.* shroud, winding sheet; mortise; (Am.) cigarette paper.
mortal. I. *a.* mortal, fatal; very seriously ill, at the point of death. **II.** *n.* mortal.
mortalidad, *f.* mortality; death rate.
mortalmente, *adv.* mortally, deadly.
mortandad, *f.* mortality; massacre, butchery.
mortecino, na, *a.* dying a natural death (s. o. an animal and its flesh); dying away or extinguishing; pale, subdued (color).—hacer la mortecina, to feign death.
moterada, *f.* sauce made at once in a mortar; (arti.) quantity of stones thrown out at once by a stone mortar.
morterete, *m.* *dim.* (arti.) small mortar; gun for firing salutes; broad candlestick.
mortero, *m.* (arti.) mortar; mortar, for pounding; under stone in crushing mills; (mas.) mortar.— m. de brújula, inner compass box.
morteruelo, *m.* *dim.* small mortar; toy for boys; fricassee of hog's liver.
mortífero, ra, *a.* death-dealing, fatal; unhealthful.
mortificación, *f.* (med.) mortification, gangrene; mortification, self-inflicted hardship; humiliation, vexation.
mortificador, ra, *n.* & *a.* mortifier (-fying).
mortificante, *a.* mortifying; vexing.
mortificar, *va.* & *vr.* (*pret.* MORTIFIQUÉ: *subj.* MORTIFIQUE) (med.) to mortify; to subdue (passions); to vex, torment; to humiliate.
mortuorio, ria. I. *a.* mortuary, belonging to the dead. **II.** *m.* burial, funeral.
morucho, *m.* young bull with horns tipped for baiting.
morueco, *m.* ram, male sheep.
moruno, na, *a.* Moorish.
morusa, *f.* (coll.) cash, specie; money.
mosaico, ca. I. *a.* Mosaic; mosaic. **II.** *m.* mosaic (work).—m. de madera, marquetry.
mosaísmo, *m.* Mosaism.
mosca, *f.* fly; tuft of hair under the lip; (coll.) cash, boodle; money in hand; impertinent intruder, importuner, bore; vexation, trouble.— *pl.* sparks from a light.—m. de burro, horsefly.— m. muerta, one who feigns meekness.—moscas blancas, falling snowflakes.—aflojar la m., to give or spend money.—papar moscas, to gape with astonishment.—picar la m., to be disquieted. —sacudir las moscas = MOSQUEAR.—soltar la m., = AFLOJAR LA M.

moscabado, da, *a.* muscovado.
moscada, *a.* V. NUEZ MOSCADA.
moscarda, *f.* (ent.) flesh fly; eggs of bees.
moscardear, *vn.* to lay eggs in the cells of the combs (s. o. bees).
moscardón, *m.* (ent.) botfly; horse bot; bumblebee; hornet; drone; (coll.) importuning, bothering person.
moscareta, *f.* (orn.) flycatcher.
moscatel. I. *a.* muscat or muscatel; tiresome person. **II.** *m.* muscatel (grape and wine).
moscella, *f.* = MORCELLA.
mosco, *m.* gnat, mosquito.
moscón, *m.* large fly; bumblebee; (coll.) importuning, bothering person.
moscovita, *n.* & *a.* Muscovite.
mosén, *m.* sir: title given to clergymen.
mosqueado, da, *pp.* & *a.* spotted, dotted, brindled.
mosqueador, *m.* flyflap; (coll.) tail of a horse or of a cow.
mosquear. I. *va.* to flap or drive away flies; to make a smart repartee; to flog, to whip. **II.** *vr.* to suppress obstacles with violence; (coll.) to show resentment.
mosqueo, *m.* driving flies away.
mosquero, *m.* flytrap, flyflap.
mosquerola, mosqueruela, *f.* muscadine pear.
mosqueta, *f.* (bot.) white musk rose.
mosquetazo, *m.* musket shot.
mosquete, *m.* musket.—mosquetería, body of musketeers; (theat.) people standing behind the pit.—mosqueteril, *a.* (theat.) (coll.) belonging to the crowd in the pit.—mosquetero, *m.* musketeer; (theat.) spectator occupying standing room in the pit.
mosquil, mosquino, na, *a.* belonging to flies.
mosquita, *f.* *dim.* small fly; (orn.) small bird of Sardinia.—m. muerta = MOSCA MUERTA.
mosquitero, ra, *m.* & *f.* mosquito bar or net.
mosquito, *m.* gnat; mosquito; (coll.) tippler.
mostacero, ra, *m.* & *f.* mustard pot.
mostacilla, *f.* *dim.* sparrow shot; small bead.
mostacho, *m.* mustache; (coll.) stain in the face. —mostachos del bauprés, (naut.) bowsprit shrouds.
mostachón, *m.* a kind of macaroon; a diamond-shaped ornament.
mostachoso, sa, *a.* wearing a mustache.
mostagán, *m.* (coll.) wine.
mostajo, *m.* (bot.) white beam tree.
mostaza, *f.* (bot.) mustard; mustard seed; fine shot.—hacer la m., (coll.) to make the nose bleed with a blow.
mostazo, *m.* (bot.) mustard plant; strong, thick must.
mostear, *vn.* to yield must (s. o. grapes); to put must into vats; to mix must with old wine.
mostela, *f.* (agr.) gavel, sheaf.
mostelera, *f.* place where sheaves are laid up.
mostellar, *m.* (bot.) white beam tree.
mostense, *a.* = PREMONSTRATENSE.
mostillo, *m.* cake made of must; sauce made of must and mustard.
mosto, *m.* must, grape juice; stum.—m. agustín, a kind of must cake.
mostrable, *a.* that may be shown.
mostrado, da, *pp.* & *a.* accustomed, inured.
mostrador, ra. I. *n.* demonstrator. **II.** *m.* counter (in a shop); stand; dial.
mostrar. I. *va.* (*ind.* MUESTRO: *subj.* MUESTRE) to show; point out; to establish, prove, demonstrate; to feign, dissemble. **II.** *vr.* to appear, to show one's self, prove to be.
mostrenco, ca, *a.* (coll.) homeless; unowned; masterless; strayed, vagabond, vagrant; dull, ignorant, stupid; fat, bulky.
mota, *f.* burl (in cloth); mote, speck, mite; slight defect or fault; mound of earth; bog, hummock.
motacila, *f.* (orn.) wagtail. V. AGUZANIEVE.
mote, *m.* motto, device; nickname; (Am.) stewed corn.

motear, va. to speck, speckle.

motejador, ra, n. one who calls names.

motejar, va. to chaff, call offensive names.

motete, m. (mus.) motet or motetto.

motil, m. farmer's boy. V. MOCHIL.

motilar, va. to cut or crop the hair of.

motilón, na. I. a. having little or cropped hair. **II.** m. (coll.) lay brother.

motín, m. mutiny, insurrection, riot.

motita, f. dim. mote, speck, mite.

motivar, va. to give a reason for; to cause.

motivo, va. I. a. motive, moving. **II.** m. motive, reason; (mus.) motif, theme.—**con m. de,** owing to, by reason of; on the occasion of.—**de su m. propio,** of one's own accord.

moto, m. landmark, guidepost.

motocicleta, f. motor cycle.

motociclista, n. motorcyclist.

motolita, f. (orn.) wagtail.

motolito, ta, a. easily deceived, ignorant.

motón, m. (naut.) block, pulley.

motonería, f. (naut.) pulley blocks, tackle.

motonero, m. block maker.

motor, ra. I. n. & a. mover (-ing). **II.** m. (mech.) motor; engine.—**m. acorazado,** enclosed motor, ironclad motor.—**m. bipolar,** two-pole motor.—**m. compound,** compound-wound motor. —**m. de cilindros convergentes,** V-motor, V-engine.—**m. de combustión,** or **de combustión interna,** internal-combustion engine, or motor.—**m. de enfriamiento por agua,** water-cooled motor.—**m. de enfriamiento por aire,** air-cooled motor.—**m. de explosión,** explosion motor.—**m. Diesel,** Diesel engine.—**m. generador,** motor-generator.—**m. propulsor,** (aer.) pusher engine.—**m. tractor,** (aer.) tractor engine.

motorista, n. motorman (-woman); motorist, driver.

motril, m. = MOCHIL.

motriz, a. motive, moving.

motu proprio, (Lat.) by his own will.

movedizo, za, a. movable; shaky, unsteady; inconstant, shifting.

movedor, ra, n. mover, exciter.

movedura, f. movement; miscarriage.

mover. I. va. (ind. MUEVO: subj. MUEVA) to move; to make move; to drive, propel; to shake, wag; to prevail upon, persuade, induce; to prompt; to incite, promote, occasion; to stir, excite; to touch, affect with emotion; (agr.) to bud, sprout; **II.** vn. (med.) to miscarry; (arch.) to spring an arch. **III.** vr. to move, stir.

movible, a. movable; mobile; changeable, fickle.

moviente, a. moving, motive.

móvil. I. a. movable; mobile; unsteady, shaky; portable. **II.** m. motive, incentive, inducement; mover, motor; moving body.

movilidad, f. mobility; movableness; fickleness, inconstancy; unsteadiness.

movilización, f. (mil.) mobilization.

movilizar, va. (pret. MOVILICÉ: subj. MOVILICE) (mil.) to mobilize.

movimiento, m. movement, move; stir, agitation; life, liveliness, animation (s. o. style); (mech.) motion; (astr.) clock error; (art) distribution of lines and shades, technique; (mus.) tempo, time.—**m. alternativo,** (mech.) reciprocating motion.—**m. continuo,** perpetual motion. —**m. de tierras,** (r. w.) earthwork.—**m. oratorio,** oratorical gesture.—**m. perpetuo,** perpetual motion.

moxa, f. (surg.) moxa; cautery.

moxte, interj. V. OXTE.

moyana, f. small culverin; (coll.) lie, fib; dog cake.

moyo, m. a unit of capacity (258 liters).

moyuelo, m. grits, pollard, coarse meal.

moza, f. girl, maid of all work; concubine, mistress; clothes pounder; last or conquering game.

mozalbete, mozalbillo, m. lad, youth.

mozallón, m. young, robust laborer.

mozárabe. I. a. Mozarabic. **II.** n. Mozarab.

mozo, za. I. a. young, youthful; single, unmarried. **II.** m. youth, lad; manservant,

waiter, porter; (coll.) fellow.—**m. de caballos,** groom, horse boy.—**m. de cordel,** or **de esquina,** porter in the street.—**m. de paja y cebada,** hostler at an inn.—**buen m.** (buena moza), good-looking.

mozuelo, la, n. m. dim. young lad (lass).

mu. I. m. lowing of cattle, moo. **II.** f. child's word for sleep.

muaré, m. moiré, watered silk.

mucamo, ma, n. (Am.) servant.

muceta, f. short cape worn by doctors; (eccl.) mozetta.

mucilaginoso, sa, a. mucilaginous, slimy.

mucílago, mucilago, m. mucilage; slime.

mucosidad, f. mucosity, mucousness.

mucoso, sa, a. mucous, slimy, viscous.

mucronato, ta, a. mucronate.

múcura, f. (Ven., Colomb.) pitcher, ewer, gurglet; (Colomb.) blockhead.

muchachada, f. boyish or girlish act.

muchachear, vn. to act like a boy or girl.

muchachería, f. boyish trick; crowd of boys.

muchachez, f. childhood, boyhood, girlhood.

muchachil, a. boylike, girl-like.

muchacho, cha. I. a. boyish, girlish, childish. **II.** m. boy, lad. **III.** f. girl, lass.

muchedumbre, f. multitude; crowd; populace, rabble.

muchísimo, ma. I. a. super. of MUCHO: very much. **II.** adv. a very great deal.

mucho, cha. I. a. much, a great deal of; long (s. o. time).—pl. many. **II.** (mucho) adv. much, very much; a great deal; in a great measure; to a great extent; often; long (s. o. time); very.—**con m.,** by far.—**ni m. menos,** nor anything like it.— **no es m.,** it is no wonder.—**no ha m.,** not long since.—**por m. que,** no matter how much.

muda, f. change, alteration; change of linen; moult, moulting; change of voice in boys; roost of birds of prey; cosmetic.

mudable; mudadizo, za, a. changeable; fickle.

mudamente, adv. silently, mutely.

mudanza, f. change; mutation; removal; inconstancy; fickleness; (danc.) figure, motion.

mudar. I. va. to change; to remove, deviate; to vary, alter; to moult. **II.** vr. to reform, mend, change; to change one's clothes; to move, change one's place or residence.

mudéjar, n. Mohammedan who became a subject of Christian sovereigns.

mudez, f. dumbness.

mudo, da, a. dumb; silent; mute.

mué, m. moiré, watered silk.

mueblaje, m. household furniture.

mueble. I. a. movable. **II.** m. piece of furniture.—pl. chattels, furniture, household goods.

mueblería, f. furniture factory or store.

mueblista, n. furniture maker or seller.

mueca, f. grimace, wry face, grin.

muedín, m. muezzin.

muela, f. runner, upper millstone; grindstone, whetstone; grinder, molar tooth; water sufficient to set a mill in motion; hill, hillock; track or circle.—**m. cordal,** or **del juicio,** wisdom tooth.

muellaje, m. wharfage, dockage.

muelle. I. a. tender, delicate, soft; licentious; luxurious. **II.** m. spring (metal or rubber); (jew.) chatelaine; regulator, watch spring; (naut.) pier, wharf; (r. w.) freight platform.

muellemente, adv. tenderly, gently, softly.

muer, m. = MUÉ.

muérdago, m. (bot.) mistletoe.

muerdo, yo muerda. V. MORDER.

muérgano, m. (Colomb.) worthless or contemptible person or thing.

muermo, m. (vet.) glanders.

muermoso, sa, a. (vet.) glanderous.

muero, yo muera. V. MORIR.

muerte, f. death; demise; skeleton representing death; ruin, havoc, destruction.—**m. civil,** civil death, loss of rights.—**m. chiquita,** (coll.) nervous shudder.—**m. natural,** natural death.—**m. senil,**

death from old age, or from senility.—**a la m.** = DE M.—**a m.**, to the death.—**de mala m.**, insignificant, of no account.—**de m.**, intensely, implacably (s. o. hating, etc.); hopelessly ill, at the point of death.

muerto, ta. I. *a.* & *pp. irr.* of MORIR and MATAR: dead, deceased; languid, faded; slaked. **II.** *n.* corpse.—**echarle a una el m.**, (coll.) to blame one, to pass the buck to one.

muesca, *f.* notch, . indentation, hack, nick, mortise; dovetail scarf.

muestra, *f.* specimen, sample; shop sign; placard, bill; model, pattern, copy; end of a piece of goods bearing the manufacturer's name; clock dial or face; clock or watch; sign, indication; (mil.) muster roll.

muestrario, *m.* collection of samples; specimen or sample book.

muestro, yo muestre. *V.* MOSTRAR.

muevo, yo mueva. *V.* MOVER.

muévedo, *m.* aborted fœtus.

mufla, *f.* muffle furnace.

muftí, *m.* mufti, a Mussulman expounder of the law.

muga, *f.* landmark, boundary.

mugido, *m.* lowing of cattle, moo.

múgil, *m.* (icht.) mullet.

mugir, *vn.* (*ind.* MUJO: *subj.* MUJA) to low, bellow.

mugre, *f.* dirt, filth.

mugriento, ta, *a.* dirty, filthy.

mugrón, *m.* sprig, shoot, sucker, tiller.

muguete, *m.* (bot.) lily of the valley.

muharra, *f.* = MOHARRA.

mujer, *f.* woman; wife, mate.—**m. casera,** good housewife.—**m. de estado honesto,** spinster.—**m. de gobierno,** housewife, housekeeper.—**m. mundana, perdida,** or **pública,** prostitute.—**tomar m.,** to marry.

mujercilla, *f.* little woman; insignificant woman.

mujeriego, a. I. *a.* feminine, womanly; womanish; fond of women.—**a la m.,** woman-fashion, womanlike. **II.** *m.* women collectively.

mujeril, *a.* womanish, womanly, feminine.

mujerilmente, *adv.* like women, like a woman; effeminately.

mujerío, *m.* gathering of women.

mujerón, *m.*, **mujerona,** *f. aug.* big woman; matron.

mujerzuela, *f. dim.* little woman.

mújol, *m.* (icht.) mullet.

mula, *f.* she-mule; shoe used by the Pope.

mulada, *f.* (Am.) drove of mules.

muladar, *m.* dungheap; rubbish heap.

muladí, *n.* renegade Christian.

mulante, *m.* muleteer; mule boy.

mular, *a.* belonging to mules.

mulatero, *m.* muleteer, mule driver.

mulato, ta, *n.* & *a.* mulatto.

múleo, muléolo, *m.* ancient shoe with upturned point.

muleque, *n.* (Cuba) newly arrived negro boy.

mulero. I. *a.* (horse) fond of mules. **II.** *m.* mule boy.

muleta, *f.* crutch; prop, support; red flag used by bullfighters; light luncheon.

muletada, *f.* drove of mules.

muletero, *m.* muleteer, mule driver.

muletilla, *f. dim.* cross-handle cane; pet word or phrase, often repeated in talking; red flag used by bullfighters; frog or toggle; (min.) crutch.

muleto, *m.* young mule not yet broken.

mulilla, *f. dim.* small mule.

mulo, *m.* mule.

mulquía, *f.* title, deed.

mulso, sa, *a.* sweetened with honey or sugar.

multa, *f.* mulct, fine.—**multar,** *va.* to mulct, fine.

multicaule, (bot.) multicauline.

multicolor, *a.* many-colored.

multifloro, ra, *a.* many-flowered.

multiforme, *a.* multiform.

multilátero, ra, *a.* multilateral.

multimillonario, ria, *n.* & *a.* multimillionaire.

multípara, *a.* multiparous; having been a mother more than once (s. o. women).

múltiple, *a.* multiple, complex; (int. comb. eng.) manifold.

múltiplex, *a.* multiplex.

multiplicable, *a.* multiplicable, multipliable.

multiplicación, *f.* multiplication.

multiplicador, ra. I. *n.* & *a.* multiplier (-plying). **II.** *m.* (arith.) multiplier.

multiplicando, *m.* (math.) multiplicand.

multiplicar, *va.* & *vr.* (*pret.* MULTIPLIQUÉ: *subj.* MULTIPLIQUE) to multiply.

multíplice, *a.* multiple; multiplex.

multiplicidad, *f.* multiplicity.

mútiplo, pla, *n.* & *a.* multiple.

multitud, *f.* multitude; crowd; the masses.

mulla, *f.* digging around vines.

mullido, *m.* soft filling for cushions, etc.

mullidor, ra, *n.* one who fluffs (as wool or feathers).

mullir, *va.* to fluff, make soft, mollify; to engineer; to dig around (vines and trees).—**m. la cama,** to beat up the bed.

mullo, m. (icht.) surmullet; (Am.) glass beads.

mundanal, *a.* worldly, mundane.

mundanalidad, *f.* worldliness.

mundano, na, *a.* mundane, worldly.

mundanear, *vn.* to indulge in worldly things.

mundial, *a.* of all the world, world (u. a., as in *la guerra mundial,* the World War), universal.

mundificación, *f.* act of cleansing.

mundificante, *a.* cleansing, purifying.

mundificar, *va.* to cleanse, purify.

mundificativo, va, *a.* cleansing.

mundillo, *m. dim.* arched clothes dryer; cushion for making lace; warming pan; (bot.) viburnum.

mundinovi, mundonuevo, *m.* raree-show.

mundo, m. world; (coll.) great multitude, great quantity; social life; dissipated life; experience.—**echar al m.,** to create; to give birth to.—**echarse al m.,** to plunge into dissipation.—**entrar en el m.,** to enter into society.—**medio m.,** many people.—**todo el m.,** everybody.—**ser hombre de mundo,** to be a man of the world; to be a man of experience.—**tener m.,** or **mucho mundo,** to have had experience, to know life, or the world.—**ver m.,** to travel, to see the world.

munición, *f.* (often in the *pl.*) ammunition; small shot; birdshot; charge of firearms.—**municiones de boca,** provisions, victuals.—**municiones de guerra,** war stores.—**de m.,** supplied by the government; done hurriedly.

municionar, *va.* to supply with ammunition.

municipal. I. *a.* municipal. **II.** *m.* policeman.

municipalidad, *f.* municipality; townhall; municipal government.

munícipe, *m.* citizen, denizen.

municipio, *m.* municipality; municipium.

munificencia, *f.* munificence, liberality.

munificentísimo, ma, *a. super.* of MUNÍFICO: most, or very, munificent.

munífico, ca, *a.* munificent, liberal.

munitoria, *f.* art of fortification.

muñeca, *f.* (anat.) wrist; doll; figure for dressmakers; (mech.) puppet; sugar teat; pounce bag; polishing bag.

muñeco, *m.* puppet, manikin; boy doll; soft, effeminate fellow.

muñeira, *f.* a popular dance of Galicia.

muñequear, *va.* (fenc.) to play with the wrist.

muñequería, *f.* doll shop; (coll.) excessive finery, overdressing.

muñidor, *m.* beadle, apparitor, messenger; (Am.) undertaker.

muñir, *va.* to summon.

muñón, *m.* stump of an amputated limb; (arti.) trunnion; (mech.) journal, gudgeon, pivot.

muñonera, *f.* trunnion plate; (mech.) gudgeon socket, journal box, bearing.

murajes, *m. pl.* (bot.) a medicinal herb.

mural, *a.* mural, belonging to walls.

muralla, *f.* (fort.) rampart; wall.

murallón, *m. aug.* (fort.) strong wall.

---

murar, *va.* to wall, surround with a rampart.

murceguillo, murciégalo, *m.* = MURCIÉLAGO.

murciélago, *m* (orn.) bat.

murena, *f.* (icht.) a kind of eel.

murete, *m. dim.* small wall.

murga, *f.* lees of olives; (coll.) band of street musicians.

murgón, *m.* (icht.) parr, smolt.

muriático, ca, *a.* (chem.) muriatic.

muriato, *m.* (chem.) muriate.

múrice, *m.* (icht.) murex; (poet.) purple.

murícidos, *m. pl.* (zool.) Muricidæ.

múridos, *m. pl.* (zool.) Muridæ.

murmujear, *va.* to murmur, to whisper.

murmullo, *m.* whisper, whispering; murmuring, murmur, ripple, purl; rustle.

murmuración, *f.* backbiting, gossip, ill-speaking.

murmurador, ra, *n.* detractor, backbiter.

murmurante, *a.* murmuring, purling.

murmurar, *vn.* to purl, ripple (as streams); to rustle (as leaves); to grudge, grumble, mutter; to whisper; to gossip, backbite.

murmurio, *m.* murmur. *V.* MURMULLO.

muro, *m.* (mas.) wall; (fort.) rampart.

murria, *f.* (coll.) blues; surliness, sullenness; (pharm.) an astringent lotion.

múrrino, na, *a.* murrine, made of murra.

murrio, ria, *a.* sullen, surly, sulky.

murta, *f.* (bot.) myrtle; myrtle berry.

murtal, *m.,* **murtera,** *f.* myrtle grove.

murtilla, murtina, *f.* (bot.) myrtus; its berry; liquor made from this berry.

murtón, *m.* myrtle berry.

murucuya, *f.* (bot.) purple passion flower.

murueco, *m.* = MORUECO.

mus, *m.* a card game.—**no hay m.,** cannot be granted. *V.* TUS.

musa, *f.* Muse.—*pl.* the Muses; fine arts.

musáceo, a. I. *a.* (bot.) musaceous. **II.** *f. pl.* Musaceæ.

musaraña, *f.* fetid shrewmouse; any small animal, insect, or vermin; (coll.) ridiculous puppet or stuffed figure; floating speck in the eye.—**mirar a,** or **pensar en, las musarañas,** to be absent-minded.

muscaria, muscícapa, *f.* (orn.) fly-catcher.

múscido, da. I. *n. & a.* (zool.) muscid. **II.** *m. pl.* Muscidæ.

muscívoro, ra, *a.* (zool.) fly-catching.

musco, ca. I. *a.* dark brown. **II.** *m.* (bot.) moss.

muscular, *a.* muscular.

musculatura, *f.* musculature.

músculo, *m.* muscle; brawn; (icht.) a huge whale.—**m. complexo, complexus.—m. del sastre,** sartorius.—**m. gemelo,** gemellus.—**m. glúteo,** gluteous muscle.—**m. lumbrical,** lumbricalis (*pl.* lumbricales).—**m. sartorio,** sartorius.—**m. serrato,** serratus.

musculoso, sa, *a.* muscular, brawny.

muselina, *f.* muslin.

museo, *m.* museum.

muserola, *f.* noseband of a bridle.

musgaño, *m.* (zool.) shrewmouse.

musgo, ga. I. *a.* dark brown. **II.** *m.* (bot.) moss.—**m. marino,** sea corallina.

musgoso, sa, *a.* mossy; moss-covered.

música, *f.* music; body of performing musicians; musical composition; sheet music.—**m. celestial,** (coll.) nonsense; moonshine.—**m. coreada,** chorus music.—**m. de campanas,** chimes.—**m. ratonera,** harsh music.—**m. rítmica,** stringed-instrument music.—**vaya Vd. con la m. a otra parte,** (coll.) get out, don't bother me.

musical, *a.* musical.

músico, ca. I. *a.* musical. **II.** *n.* musician.

musiquero, *m.* music cabinet.

musitar, *vn.* to mumble, mutter, whisper.

muslera, *f.* cuish, armor for the thigh.

muslime; muslímico, ca, *a.* Moslem, Mohammedan.

muslo, *m.* thigh.

musmón, *m.* (zool.) moufflon, wild sheep.

musquerola, *f.* muscadine pear.

mustaco, *m.* cake made with must.

mustela, *f.* (icht.) a selachian fish.

mustiamente, *adv.* sadly, languidly.

mustio, tia, *a.* withered; sad, languid.

musulmán, na, *n. & a.* Mussulman.

muta, *f.* pack of hounds.

mutabilidad, *f.* mutability; fickleness.

mutación, *f.* mutation, change; (theat.) change of scene; unseasonable weather.

mutatis mutandis, (Lat.) *adv.* with the necessary changes (in words, etc.).

mutilación, *f.* mutilation.

mutilar, *va.* to mutilate; to cut short, reduce; to deface, mar.

mútilo, la, *a.* maimed, crippled, mutilated.

mutis, *m.* (theat.) exit.

mutismo, *m.* mutism, muteness.

mutual, *a.* mutual, reciprocal.

mutualidad, *f.* mutualness; system of organized mutual help; mutual-help association.

mutualismo, *m.* system of organized mutual help.

mutualista. I. *a.* relating to the system of organized mutual help. **II.** *n.* member of a mutual-help organization.

mutuamente, *adv.* mutually, reciprocally.

mutuante, *m. & f.* (com.) lender, loaner.

mutuario, ria; mutuatario, ria, *m. & f.* (law) mutuary.

mutuo, tua. I. *a.* mutual, reciprocal. **II.** *m.* (law) loan, mutuum.

muy, *adv.* very; greatly, most.—**m. ilustre,** most illustrious.—**m. mucho,** (coll.) very much.—**soy m. de Vd.,** I am entirely yours.

muz, *m.* (naut.) extremity of the cutwater.

muzárabe, *n. & a.* = MOZÁRABE.

N

N., or N. N., a form often used in the sense of So-and-So, X., meaning any person.

naba, *f.* (bot.) rutabaga, Swedish turnip.

nabab, nababo, *m.* nabob, nawab.

nabal, nabar. I. *a.* belonging to or made of turnips. **II.** *m.* turnip field.

nabería, *f.* turnip pottage; heap of turnips.

nabí, *m.* Moorish prophet.

nabilo, *m. dim.* small turnip.

nabina, *f.* rape and turnip seed.

nabiza, *f.* turnip rootlets; turnip greens.

nabla, *f.* (mus.) a kind of psaltery.

nabo, *m.* (bot.) turnip (plant and root); any bulb; stock of a tail; cylindrical timber; spindle; king-post; (naut.) mast.—**n. gallego** = NABA.

naborí, *n.* free Indian servant.

naboría, *f.* free female Indian servant; allotment of free Indian servants (during the Spanish conquest of America).

nacar, *m.* mother-of-pearl.

nacarado, da; nacáreo, a; nacarino, na, *a.* nacreous.

nacarón, *m.* pearl shell of inferior quality.

nacascolo, m. (C. A.) = DIVIDIVI.

nacela, *f.* (arch.) scotia.

nacencia, *f.* tumor, outgrowth.

nacer. I. *vn.* (*pp.* NACIDO, NATO: *ind.* NAZCO: *subj.* NAZCA) to be born, come into the world; to sprout, come forth, grow (as branches, plants); to rise, come out, appear (as the sun); to spring, rise, flow, have its source (as a stream, a river); to begin, originate, start, issue; to infer one thing from another.—**n. de cabeza,** to be born to wretchedness.—**n. de pies,** to be born to good luck. **II.** *vr.* to sprout (as seeds) in the open air; to split near a seam (as clothes).

nacido, da. I. *pp. & a.* born; proper, apt, fit, connate.—**bien** or **mal n.,** well or ill bred. **II.** *m.* living man; pimple, boil, furuncle; sprout.

naciente. I. *a.* rising; growing; very recent; (her.) naissant. **II.** *m.* Orient, East.

nacimiento, *m.* birth; growing of plants; beginning; place of birth; rising (as of the sun); origin, issue; descent, lineage; source of a river or spring; scene representing the Nativity at Yuletide.—**de n.,** from birth.

nación. I. *f.* nation; (coll.) birth; (Am.) race, tribe of Indians. **II.** *m.* (coll.) foreigner.—**de n.,** by nationality.

nacional. I. *a.* national; native; domestic, home. **II.** *m.* native; militiaman.

nacionalidad, *f.* nationality; citizenship.

nacionalismo, *m.* nationalism.

nacionalista, *n.* & *a.* nationalist (-ic).

nacionalización, *f.* naturalization; acclimatization.

nacionalizar, *va.* to naturalize; to acclimate.

nacionalmente, *adv.* nationally.

nacrita, *f.* variety of talc.

nacho, cha, *a.* flat-nosed, pug-nosed.

nada. I. *f.* nothing, naught; nothingness; nonentity. **II.** *indef. pron.* nothing, not anything; little or very little.—**n. de eso,** none of that; not at all; not so.—**de n.,** insignificant, good-for-nothing; you are welcome, don't mention it.—**por n.,** for nothing; under no circumstances. **III.** *adv.* nothing, not, not at all, by no means.

nadadera, *f.* gourd or bladder for swimming.

nadadero, *m.* swimming place.

nadador, ra, *n.* & *a.* swimmer (-ing).

nadante, *a.* (poet.) natant, swimming.

nadar, *vn.* to swim; to float.

nadería, *f.* (coll.) insignificant thing, a mere nothing, trifle.

nadie, *indef. pron.* nobody, no one, none; (after negative) anybody.

nadilla, *f.* = NADERÍA.

nadir, *m.* (ast.) nadir.

nado.—a n., swimming; afloat.

nafta, *f.* naphtha.

naftalina, *f.* naphthalin.

naftílico, ca, *a.* (chem.) naphthalic.

naftilo, *m.* (chem.) naphthyl.

naftol, *m.* (chem.) naphthol.

naguas, *f. pl.* petticoat.

naguatlato, *m.* (Mex.) Indian interpreter.

nahuatle, *m.* Nahuatlan, Mexican Indian language.

naife, *m.* diamond of the first water.

naipe, *m.* (playing) card; cards; pack of cards.—**dar (a uno) el n.,** to have good luck at cards.—**dar el n. para una cosa,** to be very skilful or dexterous.—**tener buen n.** = DAR EL N.

naire, *m.* elephant keeper.

nalga, *f.* buttock, rump.—**nalgada,** *f.* ham; blow on or with the buttocks; spank.—**nalgar,** *a.* gluteal.—**nalgatorio,** *m.* (coll.) seat, posteriors, nates.—**nalgudo, da,** *a.* having big posteriors.—**nalguear,** *vn.* to shake the posteriors in walking.

nana, *f.* (coll.) grandma; lullaby; (Mex., coll.) child's nurse.

nansa, *f.* fishpond; fish trap.

nansú, nanzú, *m.* (Am.) a kind of cotton cloth.

nao, *f.* ship, vessel.

naonato, ta, *a.* born on board ship.

napea, *f.* wood nymph.

napelo, *m.* (bot.) monkshood, wolfsbane.

napoleón, *m.* napoleon (5-franc piece).

napoleónico, ca, *a.* Napoleonic.

napolitana, *f.* in some card games, combination of cards.

napolitano, na, *m.* & *a.* Neapolitan.

naque, *m.* two strolling comedians.

naranja, *f.* (bot.) orange; well-mated spouse.—**n. cajel,** blood orange.

naranjada, *f.* orangeade; rude saying or deed.

naranjado, da, *a.* orange-colored.

naranjal, *m.* orange grove.

naranjazo, *m.* blow with an orange.

naranjero, ra. I. *a.* **cañon n.,** (arti.) cannon carrying balls of the size of oranges. **II.** *n.* orange raiser or seller. **III.** *m.* orange tree.

naranjilla, *f.* small green orange to preserve.

naranjo, *m.* (bot.) orange tree; (coll.) booby, noodle.

narciso, *m.* (bot.) daffodil; narcissus; fop, coxcomb.

narcosis, *f.* narcosis.

narcótico, ca, *a.* narcotical.—**narcotina,** *f.* narcotine.—**narcotismo,** *m.* narcotism.

narcotizador, ra, *a.* narcotic, narcose.

narcotizar, *va.* to narcotize.

nardino, na, *a.* made of spikenard.

nardo, *m.* (bot.) spikenard, nard, tuberose.

narguile, *m.* narghile.

narigón, na; narigudo, da. I. *a.* large-nosed. **II.** *m.* large nose. **III.** *n.* large-nosed person.

nariguera, *f.* nose pendant.

narigueta, nariguita, *f. dim.* small nose.

nariz, *f.* nose; nostril; sense of smell; bouquet (of wine); socket of a door knocker; nozzle; cutwater.—**n. aguileña,** Roman, or aquilin, nose.—**n. chata,** flat nose.—**n. perfilada,** perfect, or well-proportioned, nose.—**n. respingada,** or **respingona,** retroussé nose, turned-up nose.—**dar en las narices,** (coll.) to smell or perceive a thing at a distance.—**meter la n. en todas partes,** to be a busybody, to nose about.—**tener de, or por, las narices, or agarrado por las narices, to** lead by the nose, to control at will.

narizota, *f. aug.* large, ugly nose.

narra, *f.* narra, an Asiatic tree.

narrable, *a.* capable of being narrated.

narración, *f.* narration, account; chronicle.

narrador, ra, *n.* & *a.* narrator (-ing), chronicler (-ing).

narrar, *va.* to narrate, relate, chronicle, tell.

narrativa, *f.* narrative.

narrativo, va; narratorio, ria, *a.* narrative.

narria, *f.* sledge, sled; heavy, bulky woman.

narval, *m.* (icht.) narwhal, sea unicorn.

narvaso, *m.* cornstalks (as fodder).

nasa, *f.* fyke, fish trap, bag net; bow net; fisherman's basket; basket; jar.

nasal, *a.* nasal, relating to the nose.

nasardo, *m.* (mus.) nasard, organ stop.

nata, *f.* cream; prime or choice part; skim, scum.—*pl.* whipped cream with sugar.

natación, *f.* natation, swimming.

natal. I. *a.* natal, native. **II.** *m.* birth, birthday.—**natalicio, cia. I.** *a.* natal. **II.** *m.* nativity, birthday.—**natalidad,** *f.* birth rate.

natátil, *a.* able to swim, floating.

natatorio, a. I. *a.* swimming, natatorial. **II.** *m.* natatorium.

naterón, *m.* second curd.

natilla, *f.* custard.

natío. I. *a.* native. **II.** *m.* birth; sprouting.

natividad, *f.* nativity; Yuletide, Christmas.

nativo, va, *a.* native; indigenous; domestic; natural born; inborn, cognate.

nato, ta, *a.* implied by or inherent in an office or position; born.

natrón, *m.* natron; barilla.

natura, *f.* nature; genital organs; (mus.) major scale.

natural. I. *a.* natural; native; common, usual; plain, pure, unadulterated; artless, ingenuous; spontaneous, unstudied; (mus.) natural. **II.** *n.* native; national; aborigen. **III.** *m.* temper, disposition, nature.—**al n.,** without art or affectation.—**del n.,** (art) from life, from nature.

naturaleza, *f.* nature; constitution; sex, genitals, especially the female; sort, character, kind; naturalization; temperament or disposition.—**n. muerta,** (art) still life.

naturalidad, *f.* naturalness; birthright, nationality.

naturalismo, *m.* naturalism; realism.

naturalista, *n.* & *a.* naturalist (-ic).

naturalización, *f.* naturalization.

naturalizar. I. *va.* (*pret.* NATURABICÉ: *subj.* NATURALICE) to naturalize. **II.** *vr.* to get accustomed; to become naturalized.

naturalmente, *adv.* naturally; of course.

naufragante, *a.* sinking, perishing.

naufragar, *vn.* (*pret.* NAUFRAGUÉ: *subj.* NAU-FRAGUE) to be shipwrecked; to fail, be unsuccessful, fall through.

naufragio, *m.* shipwreck; disaster, failure, disappointment, calamity.—**náufrago, ga. I.** *n.* shipwrecked person. **II.** *m.* shark.

naumaquia, *f.* naumachy, mock sea fight.

náusea, *f.* nauseousness, nausea.

nauseabundo, *a.* nauseous, loathsome.

nausear, *vn.* to feel nausea.—**nauseativo, va,** *a.* nauseous.—**nauseoso, sa,** *a.* = NAUSEABUNDO.

nauta, *m.* mariner, seafaring man.—**náutica,** *f.* navigation.—**náutico, ca,** *a.* nautical.

nautilo, *m.* nautilus.

nava, *f.* hollow, plain surrounded by mountains.

navacero, ra, *n.* one who cultivates a NAVAZO.

navaja, *f.* razor; clasp knife, folding knife; razor clam; tusk of a wild boar; (coll.) evil tongue.—navajas de gallo, cockspurs.

navajada, *f.;* **navajazo,** *m.* thrust or gash with a clasp knife or razor.

navajero, *m.* razor case; shaving doily.

navajita, *f. dim.* small clasp knife or razor.

navajo, *m.* = LAVAJO.

navajón, *m. aug.* large clasp knife or razor.

navajonazo, *m.* gash or wound made with a large clasp knife or a razor.

navajuela, *f. dim.* small clasp knife.

naval, *a.* naval.

navarca, *m.* navarch, commander of a fleet among the Greeks and Romans.

navarro, rra, *n.* & *a.* Navarrese.

navazo, *m.* kitchen garden on a sandy shore.

nave, *f.* ship, vessel; (arch.) nave; aisle.—**n. aérea,** airship.—**n. de San Pedro,** Roman Catholic Church.

navecilla, *f. dim.* small ship; (eccl.) censer, thurible.

navegable, *a.* navigable.

navegación, *f.* navigation; sea voyage; time of a sea voyage.—**n. aérea,** aerial navigation, aviation.—**n. circular,** great-circle sailing.—**n. costanera,** coast navigation, coasting trade.—**n. de altura,** sailing by the stars' altitudes.

navegador, ra, *n.* & *a.* navigator (-ing).

navegante, *n.* & *a.* navigator (-ing).

navegar. I. *vn.* (*pret.* NAVEGUÉ: *subj.* NAVEGUE) to navigate, sail, steer; to travel.—**n. en conserva,** to sail under convoy. **II.** *va.* to make (as speed).

naveta, *f.* (eccl.) censer, thurible; small drawer.

navícula, *f. dim.* small ship; (bot.) navicula.

navicular, *a.* (anat.) navicular.

navichuelo, la, *n. dim.* small ship.

navidad, *f.* Nativity; Christmas day.—**tener muchas navidades,** to be old, to have lived many a year.

navideño, ña, *a.* pertaining to Yuletide.

naviero. I. *a.* shipping, ship (u. a.). **II.** *m.* ship owner.

navío, *m.* warship, armor-clad vessel; ship.—**n. anegado,** (naut.) water-logged ship.—**n. de aguante,** (naut.) a stiff ship.—**n. de alto bordo** = N. DE LÍNEA.—**n. de aviso,** despatch boat.—**n. de guerra,** warship.—**n. de línea,** line-of-battle ship.—**n. de transporte,** transport.—**n. de tres puentes,** three-decker.

náyade, *f.* naiad, water nymph.

nayuribe, *f.* (bot.) an amarantaceous herb.

nazareno, na. I. *n.* & *a.* Nazarene; Nazarite. **II.** *m.* penitent who goes in processions in Passion Week.

nazareo, ea, *a.* Nazarite.

nazco, yo nazca. *V.* NACER.

názula, *f.* second curd.

nébeda, *f.* (bot.) nepeta, catmint.

nebladura, *f.* (agr.) damage from mist.

neblí, *m.* (orn.) falcon gentle.

neblina, *f.* mist, fog.

neblinoso, sa, *a.* foggy, misty.

nebreda, *f.* plantation of juniper trees.

nebrina, *f.* juniper berry.

nebulón, na, *n.* hypocrite.

nebulosa, *f.* (ast.) nebula.

nebulosidad, *f.* nebulosity, nebulousness.

nebuloso, sa, *a.* misty, nebulous, hazy.

necear, *vn.* to talk nonsense, to play the fool.

necedad, *f.* stupidity, foolishness, nonsense.

necesaria, *f.* privy, water-closet.

necesariamente, *adv.* necessarily.

necesario, ria, *a.* necessary.

neceser, *m.* dressing case, toilet case.—**n. de costura,** work basket, sewing case, hussy.

necesidad, *f.* necessity; need, want; emergency; evacuation of the body by stool or water.—**la n. carece de ley,** necessity knows no law.—**la n. tiene cara de hereje,** need knows no shame, need has a brazen face.—**por n.,** from necessity; necessarily.

necesitado, da. I. *pp.* & *a.* necessitous, poor, needy. **II.** *n.* poor or needy person.

necesitar. I. *va.* to need, necessitate; constrain, compel. **II.** *vn.* to be in need.

neciamente, *adv.* stupidly, foolishly.

necio, cia. I. *a.* stupid, idiotic, foolish; imprudent, injudicious. **II.** *n.* fool.

necrófago, ga, *a.* necrophagous, carrion-eating.

necrología, *f.* necrology.

necrológico, ca, *a.* necrological.

necrópolis, *f.* necropolis, burying ground.

necropsia, necroscopia, *f.* necropsy, autopsy, post-mortem examination.

necroscópico, ca, *a.* necroscopic.

necrosis, *f.* (med.) necrosis.

néctar, *m.* nectar; any delicious drink.

nectáreo, a; nectarino, na, *a.* nectarean.

nectarino, m. (bot.) nectary.

neerlandés, sa. I. *a.* & *n.* Dutch (-man, -woman). **II.** *m.* Dutch (language).

nefalismo, *m.* total abstinence from alcoholic beverages; prohibitionism.

nefalista, *n.* total abstainer; prohibitionist.

nefandamente, *adv.* nefariously, abominably.

nefando, da; nefario, ria, *a.* nefarious, heinous.

nefas, *adv.* = FAS.

nefasto, ta, *a.* sad, ominous, unlucky.

nefrítico, ca, *a.* nephritic.

nefritis, *f.* (med.) nephritis.

nefrocele, *f.* (med.) nephrocele, hernia of the kidney.

nefrolito, *m.* nephrolith, renal calculus.

negable, *a.* deniable.

negación, *f.* negation; denial; want or total privation; (gram.) negative particle.

negado, da, *pp.* & *a.* inapt, unfit; dull, stupid.

negador, ra, *n.* denier, disclaimer.

negante, *n.* denying; refusing.

negar. I. *va.* (*ind.* NIEGO: *pret.* NEGUÉ: *subj.* NIEGUE) to deny; to refuse; to forbid, prohibit; to disown, disclaim; to disregard; to hide, conceal, dissemble.—**n. el saludo a,** to cut, not to speak to. **II.** *vr.* to decline, refuse; to be denied to visitors.—**n. a sí mismo,** to control one's passions and appetites, exercise self-control.

negativa, *f.* negative, refusal.

negativamente, *adv.* negatively.

negativo, va. I. *a.* negative; (elec. and math.) negative. **II.** *f.* (phot.) negative.

negligencia, *f.* negligence, neglect, carelessness.

negligente, *a.* negligent, careless, neglectful.

negligentemente, *adv.* negligently, neglectfully, carelessly.

negociable, *a.* (com.) negotiable.

negociación, *f.* negotiation; business transaction.

negociado, *pp.* & *m.* bureau, division or section in official departments; business; employment; affair.

negociador, ra, *n.* business agent; negotiator.

negociante, *n.* **I.** *a.* negotiating, trading, engaged in trade. **II.** *n.* dealer, merchant, business man.

negociar, *vn.* to trade; to negotiate.

negocio, *m.* occupation, business; affair; transaction; bargain; commerce; utility or interest in trading.—*pl.* business, commercial affairs.—**n. redondo,** square deal.—**de negocios,** business (u. a.), commercial.

negocioso, sa, *a.* active, diligent.
negozuelo, *m. dim.* petty business.
negra, *f.* foil for fencing; negress.
negrada, *f.* (Am.) crowd or gathering of negroes.
negral, *a.* blackish.
negrear, *vn.* to become black; to appear black.
negrecer, *vn.* (*for irr. v.* MERECER) to blacken, become black.
negrero, ra, *n. & a.* slave trader (-ing).
negreta, *f.* (orn.) coot, a kind of duck.
negrilla, *f.* (icht.) black conger eel.
negrillera, *f.* plantation of black poplars.
negrillo, *m. dim.* (min.) black silver ore, stephanite; (bot.) black poplar.
negrito, ta, *n.* young or little negro (-gress); (coll.) dearest, darling.
negrizco, ca, *a.* blackish; dark brown.
negro, gra. **I.** *a.* black; gloomy, dark, dismal; unfortunate, wretched; (her.) sable. **II.** *n.* negro (-gress); (coll.) dearest, darling. **III.** *m.* black (color).—**n.** animal, boneblack.—**n. de humo,** lampblack.—**n. de la uña,** tip of the (finger) nail.
negror, *m.*; **negrura,** *f.* blackness.
negruzco, ca, *a.* blackish, dark brown.
neguijón, *m.* caries of the teeth.
neguilla, *f.* (bot.) fennel flower, love-in-a-mist; age mark in horses' teeth; obstinate denial.
neis, *f.* (geol.) gneiss.
nema, *f.* seal or sealing of a letter.
nematelmintos, *m. pl.* (zool.) Nemathelminthes.
nemátodo, da. **I.** *a.* filiform. **II.** *m.* (zool.) nematode.
nemeo, a, *a.* Nemæan.
némine discrepante, (Lat.) unanimously.
nemoroso, sa, *a.* woody, nemorous.
nene, nena. **I.** *n.* (coll.) infant, baby; dear, darling. **II.** *m.* hector.
nenúfar, *m.* (bot.) white water lily.
neo, *m.* (chem.) neon.
neocatolicismo, *m.* Neo-Catholicism, a politico-religious system advocating the reëstablishment of the Catholic Church as the supreme ruler in both religious and political matters. The term is also used in the sense of progressive Catholicism, modernism.
neocatólico, ca, *n. & a.* Neo-Catholic. *V.* NEOCATOLICISMO.
neófito, *m.* neophyte.
neofobia, *f.* aversion to innovations.
neogranadino, na, *n. & a.* New-Granadian (from New Granada, former name of Colombia).
neolatino, na, *a.* Neo-Latin.
neolítico, ca, *a.* neolithic.
neológico, ca, *a.* neological.—**neologismo,** *m.* neologism.—**neólogo, ga,** *n.* neologist.
neomejicano, na, *n. & a.* New Mexican.
neomenia, *f.* (ast.) neomenia.
neoplasma, *m.* (med.) neoplasm.
neoplatonicismo, *m.* Neoplatonism.
neoplatónico, ca, *a.* Neoplatonic.
neorama, *m.* panorama.
neosalvarsán, *m.* (chem.) neosalvarsan.
neoyorquino, na. **I.** *n.* New Yorker. **II.** *a.* New York (u. a.).
neozelandés, sa. **I.** *n.* New Zealander. **II.** *a.* New Zealand (u. a.), of or from New Zealand.
neozoico, ca, *a.* (geol.) Neozoic.
neperiano, na, *a.* Naperian, Napierian.
nepote, *m.* privileged relative of the Pope.
nepotismo, *m.* nepotism.
neptúneo, a, *a.* Neptunian.
neptúnico, ca, *a.* (geol.) Neptunian.
neptunismo, *m.* (geol.) Neptunian theory.
neptunista, *n. & a.* (geol.) Neptunist (-ic).
Neptuno, *m.* (ast.) Neptune; (poet.) the sea.
nequáquam, *adv.* (Lat.) (coll.) by no means.
nequicia, *f.* perversity.
nereida, *f.* nereid, sea nymph.
nerita, *f.* nerita, a gasteropod.

nervadura, *f.* (arch.) nervure, rib; (carp.) feather; (min.) leader; (biol.) nervation, nervure.
nérveo, a, *a.* nerval.
nervezuelo, nerviecillo, *m. dim.* nervule.
nervino, na, *a.* nervine, nerve-strengthening.
nervio, *m.* (anat.) nerve; energy, vigor, strength; string of a musical instrument; rib, reinforcement; (b. b.) rib, fillet; (naut.) span rope, stay; (bot.) nerve.—**n. maestro,** tendon.—**n. óptico,** optic nerve.—**n. vago,** vagus pneumogastric nerve. —**nervios conjugados,** (anat.) conjugate nerves.
nerviosidad, *f.* = NERVOSIDAD.
nervioso, sa, *a.* nervous; vigorous, energetic; (bot.) nerved.
nervosamente, *adv.* nervously.
nervosidad, *f.* nervosity, nervousness; strength, vigor; flexibility.
nervosismo, *m.* (med.) nervosism.
nervoso, sa, *a.* nervous; strong, vigorous.
nervudo, da, *a.* strong-nerved, vigorous.
nervura, *f.* (b. b.) ribs.
nesciencia, *f.* ignorance.
nesciente, *a.* ignorant, foolish.
nescientemente, *adv.* ignorantly.
nesga, *f.* (sew.) gore; triangular piece.
néspera, *f.* medlar. *V.* NÍSPERO.
nestorianismo, *m.* Nestorianism.
nestoriano, na, *n. & a.* Nestorian.
netezuelo, la, *m. & f. dim.* little grandchild.
neto, ta. **I.** *a.* neat, pure, unadulterated; (com.) net, clear.—**en n.,** net.—**puro y n.,** pure and simple. **II.** *m.* (arch.) naked pedestal.
neuma, *m.* expression by signs or nods; (mus.) neuma.
neumático, ca. **I.** *a.* pneumatic. **II.** *f.* pneumatics. **III.** *m.* (pneumatic) tire.
neumatógrafo, *m.* (med.) pneumagraph, stethograph.
neumococo, *m.* (bact.) pneumococcus.
neumonía, *f.* (med.) pneumonia.
neumónico, ca, *a.* pneumonic; pulmonary.
neuralgia, *f.* (med.) neuralgia.
neurálgico, ca, *a.* neuralgic.
neurastenia, *f.* (med.) neurasthenia, nervous prostration.
neurasténico, ca, *n. & a.* neurasthenic.
neuraxón, *m.* (anat.) neuraxon, axis cylinder.
neurilema, *m.* (anat.) neurilemma.
neurisma, *f.* (med.) = ANEURISMA.
neuritis, *f.* (med.) neuritis.
neuroblasto, *m.* (anat.) neuroblast.
neuroeje, *m.* (anat.) neural, or cerebro-spinal, axis.
neuroesqueleto, *n.* (anat.) endoskeleton.
neurología, *f.* (anat.) neurology.
neuroma, *m.* (med.) neuroma.
neurona, *f.* (anat.) neurone.
neuropatía, *f.* (med.) neuropathy.
neuróptero, ra, *a.* (ent.) neuropterous.
neurosis, *f.* (med.) neurosis.
neurótico, ca, *n. & a.* (med.) neurotic.
neurotomía, *f.* (surg.) neurotomy.
neurótomo, *m.* (surg.) neurotome.
neutoniano, na, *a.* Newtonian.
neutral, *a.* neutral, neuter.—**neutralidad,** *f.* neutrality.—**neutralización,** *f.* neutralization.
neutralizar, *va.* (*pret.* NEUTRALICÉ: *subj.* NEUTRALICE) to counteract; to neutralize.
neutro, tra, *a.* neutral, neuter; (gram.) neuter.
nevada, *f.* snowfall; (bot.) = NEVADILLA.
nevadilla, *f.* (bot.) whitlow-wort.
nevado, da. **I.** *pp. & a.* white as snow. **II.** *m.* snow-capped mountain or peak.
nevar. **I.** *vn. impers.* (*ind.* NIEVA: *subj.* NIEVE) to snow. **II.** *va.* to make white as snow.
nevasca, *f.* snowfall; snowstorm.
nevatilla, *f.* (orn.) wagtail.
nevera, *f.* ice house; ice box; woman who sells ice.—**nevería,** *f.* ice house; place where ice is sold. —**nevero,** *m.* iceman; place of perpetual snow.
nevereta, *f.* (orn.) wagtail.

nevisca, *f.* gentle fall of snow.

neviscar, *vn.* to snow lightly.

nevoso, sa, *a.* snowy; nival, niveous.

nexo, *m.* nexus, bond, tie, union.

ni, *conj.* neither, nor (*n. esto n. aquello,* neither this nor that).—**n. siquiera,** not even.

niara, *f.* rick or stack of straw.

nícalo, *m.* mushroom. *V.* NÍSCALO.

nicaragua, *f.* (bot.) garden balsam.

nicaragüeño, ña, *n.* & *a.* Nicaraguan.

nicaragüense; nicaragüeño, ña, *n.* & *a.* Nicaraguan.

niceno, na, *a.* Nicene.

nicerobino, *a.* ancient precious ointment.

nicle, *m.* a variety of chalcedony.

nicociana, *f.* (poet.) tobacco, nicotia.

nicotina, *f.* nicotine.

nicotismo, *m.* nicotinism.

nictagíneo, a, *a.* (bot.) nyctaginaceous.

nictálope, *n.* (med.) nyctalops.

nictalopia, *f.* (med.) nyctalopia.

nicho, *m.* niche; recess.

nidada, *f.* nestful of eggs; brood, covey.

nidal, *m.* nest; nest egg; basis, foundation, motive; haunt.

nidificar, *vn.* (*for mut. v.* MODIFICAR) to nest, to build nests.

nidito, *m. dim.* small nest.

nido, *m.* nest; eyry; home, habitation, abode, residence; haunt; den.

niebla, *f.* fog, mist, haze; film that dims the sight; (agr.) blasting mildew.

niego, *a.* newborn (falcon).

niego, yo niegue. *V.* NEGAR.

niel, *m.* (art) niello work.—**nielar,** *va.* (art) to niello.

niéspera, *f.* (bot.) medlar.

nieto, ta, *n.* grandson (-daughter).

nietro, *m.* a measure for wine (159.7 liters).

nieve, *f.* snow.

nigromancia, *f.* necromancy.—**nigromante,** *n.* necromancer, conjurer, magician.

nigromántico, ca. I. *a.* necromantic. **II.** *n.* = NIGROMANTE.

nigua, *f.* chigoe, jigger flea.

nihilismo, *m.* nihilism.—**nihilista,** *n.* nihilist.

nilad, *m.* a Philippine shrub.

nimbo, *m.* halo; nimbus.

nimiamente, *adv.* excessively, minutely.

nimiedad, *f.* superfluity, prolixity; excess.

nimio, a, *a.* prolix; stingy.

ninfa, *f.* nymph; young lady; (ent.) pupa.

ninfea, *f.* (bot.) water lily.

ninfeáceo, a, *a.* (bot.) nymphæceous.

ninfo, *m.* (coll.) effeminate fop, dude.

ninfomanía, *f.* (med.) nymphomania.

ningún, *a.* (*contr. of* NINGUNO) no, not one (*used only before masculine nouns*).—**de n. modo,** in no manner, by no means.

ninguno, na. I. *a.* no, none, not one, not any.—**n. cosa,** nothing.—**de n. manera,** by no means, in no manner. **II.** *indef. pron.* none, no one, not one, nobody.

ninivita, *n.* & *a.* Ninevite.

niña, *f.* girl.—**n. del ojo,** pupil of the eye.—**niñas de los ojos,** (coll.) darling apple of one's eye, treasure.

niñada, *f.* puerility, childishness.

niñato, *m.* unborn calf.

niñear, *vn.* to act like a child.

niñera, *f.* nurse girl, nursery maid.

niñería, *f.* puerility, childish action; child's play; plaything; trifle.

niñero, ra, *a.* & *f.* fond of children; dandler.

niñeta, *f.* small pupil of the eye.

niñez, *f.* childhood, infancy.

niñita, *f.* little girl.

niñito, *m.* little boy; little child.

niño, ña. I. *a.* childish, childlike; young; inexperienced. **II.** *n.* boy (girl). **III.** *m.* child.—**n. de la piedra,** foundling.—**n. de teta,** suckling babe, child in arms.—**ñ.** expósito, foundling.—

niños de la doctrina, charity children.—**desde n.,** from infancy, from a child.

niobio, *m.* (chem.) niobium.

nioto, *m.* = CAZÓN.

nipa, *f.* (bot.) nypa, an Asiatic palm.

nipe, nipis, *m.* nypa cloth.

níquel, *m.* (chem.) nickel.

niquelado, *pp.* & *a.* nickel-plated.

niquelar, *va.* to nickel-plate.

niquiscocio, *m.* trifle.

nirvana, *m.* Nirvana.

níscalo, *m.* nonpoisonous mushroom.

níspero, *m.* (bot.) medlar; medlar tree.

níspola, *f.* fruit of the medlar tree.

nitidez, *f.* neat, clean, resplendent.

nítido, da, *a.* bright, nitid, neat.

nito, *m.* (Philip.) (bot.) a fibrous fern or brake.

nitos, *m.* (coll.) nix, nothing.

nitral, *m.* niter bed.—**nitrato,** *m.* (chem.) nitrate, saltpeter.

nitrería, *f.* saltpeter works.

nítrico, ca, *a.* (chem.) nitric.

nitrificación, *f.* nitrification.

nitrito, *m.* (chem.) nitrite.

nitro, *m.* (chem.) niter, saltpeter.

nitrobencina, *f.* nitrobenzene.

nitrocelulosa, *f.* nitrocellulose.

nitrogenado, da, nitrogenous.

nitrogenar, *va.* to nitrogenize.

nitrógeno, *m.* (chem.) nitrogen.

nitroglicerina, *f.* nitroglycerine.

nitrosidad, *f.* nitrous condition.

nitroso, sa, *a.* nitrous, nitry.

nivel, *m.* level; levelness; water-mark; (surv.) level; (mas.) level, plummet.—**n. de aire,** or **de burbuja,** spirit level.—**n. del mar,** level of the sea.—**a n.,** level, true; on the same level.

nivelación, *f.* leveling; grading.

nivelador, ra, *n.* & *a.* (surv.) leveler (-ing); grader (-ing).

nivelar, *va.* to level; to grade; to make even; to put on a basis of equity and justice.

níveo, ea, *a.* (poet.) snowy, niveous.

nizardo, da, *a.* of or belonging to Nice.

no, *adv.* no, not, nay.—**n. bien,** no sooner.—**n. más,** only; no more.—**n., que n.,** most certainly not.—**n., sino,** not only so.—**n., sino n.,** it cannot be otherwise.—**n. tal,** no such thing.—**n. ya,** not only.—**n. sea que,** lest.—**a que n.** (coll.) I bet that isn't so; I bet you won't.—**pues n.,** but no, not so.

nobiliario, ria, *a.* nobiliary.

nobilísimamente, *adv. super.* most nobly.

nobilísimo, ma, *a. super.* most noble.

noble. I. *a.* noble. **II.** *m.* nobleman; an ancient gold coin.

noblemente, *adv.* nobly.

nobleza, *f.* nobleness; nobility; noblesse; a fine damask silk.

noca, *f.* variety of crab.

nocedal, *m.* = NOGUERAL.

nocente, *a.* noxious; guilty.

noción, *f.* notion, idea; element, rudiment (gen. in *pl.*)

nocional, *a.* notional.

nocivo, va, *a.* noxious, harmful, injurious

noctíluca, *f.* glowworm, noctiluca.

noctívago, ga, *a.* (poet.) noctivagant.

nocturnal, *a.* nocturnal, nightly.

nocturno, na. I. *a.* nocturnal, night (u. a.); lonely and sad. **II.** *m.* (eccl.) nocturn; (mus.) nocturne.

noche, *f.* night; (met.) obscurity, ignorance.—**n. toledana,** restless night, sleepless night.—**ayer n.,** last night.—**buenas noches,** good evening; good night.—**de la n. a la mañana,** between sunset and sunrise, suddenly, unexpectedly.—**de n., por la n.,** at night.—**prima n.,** evening.—**quedarse a buenas noches,** (coll.) to be left in the dark about something; to be disappointed.

nochebuena, *f.* Christmas eve.

nochebueno, *m.* Christmas cake; Yule log.

nochecita, *f.* (Am.) twilight, dusk, nightfall.—**a la n.,** at nightfall.

For pronunciation, see the rules at the beginning of the book.

nochizo, *m.* (bot.) = AVELLANO.

nodación, *f.* (med.) impediment caused by a node.

nodátil, *a.* (anat.) nodal.

nodo, *m.* (med.) node; (ast.) node.

nodriza, *f.* wet nurse.

nódulo, *m.* nodule, small node.

nogada, *f.* sauce of pounded walnuts and spice.

nogal, *m.*, **noguera,** *f.* (bot.) walnut (tree and wood).

noguerado, da, *a.* walnut-colored.

nogueral, *m.* field or plantation of walnut trees.

noguerón, *m.* *aug.* large walnut tree.

nolición, *f.* nolition, unwillingness.

noli me tángere, *m.* (Lat.) (med.) nolimetangere, malignant ulcer.

nómada, nómade, *n.* & *a.* nomad (-ic).

nomadismo, *m.* nomadism, nomadic state.

nomarquía, *f.* nomarchy.

nombradamente, *adv.* expressly.

nombradía, *f.* renown, fame, reputation.

nombramiento, *m.* nomination, naming; appointment, commission; brevet.

nombrar, *va.* to name; to nominate; to appoint.

nombre, *m.* name; title; fame, reputation; power by which any one acts for another; (gram.) noun; (mil.) countersign; watchword.—**n. adjetivo,** adjective.—**n. apelativo,** (gram.) common noun.—**n. colectivo,** collective noun.—**n. común,** common noun.—**n. de pila,** Christian name.—**n. propio,** proper noun.—**n. substantivo,** noun, substantive.—**n. y apellido,** full name.—**en el nombre,** with God's help.—**no tener n.,** to be unspeakable.—**poner n. a,** to give a name to; to set a price on.—**por n.,** by the name of.

nomenclador, nomenclátor, *m.* nomenclator; gazetteer; glossary, technical vocabulary.

nomenclatura, *f.* catalogue; nomenclature.

nomeolvides, *f.* (bot.) forget-me-not.

nómina, *f.* catalogue, list; payroll.

nominación, *f.* nomination; appointment.

nominador, ra, *n.* appointer.

nominal. I. *a.* nominal; titular. II. *n.* nominalist.—**nominalismo,** *m.* nominalism.—**nominalista,** *n.* & *a.* nominalist (-ic).—**nominalmente,** *adv.* nominally.

nominar, *va.* to name.

nominativo, va. I. *a.* (com.) personal, registered (as bonds). II. *a.* & *m.* (gram.) nominative.—*pl.* (coll.) elements, rudiments.

nominilla, *f.* pay warrant, voucher.

nómino, *m.* nominee.

nomo, *m.* nome, province.

nomparell, *f.* (print.) nonpareil, six-point.

non. I. *a.* odd, uneven. II. *m.* odd number.—*pl.* repeated negation or denial; refusal (sp. of a marriage proposal, in the phrases *dar nones, echar nones*).—**andar de nones,** to be idle.—**digo que nones,** I say no.—**estar de n.,** to serve for nothing.—**pares y nones,** even or odd.—**quedar de n.,** to be without a partner or companion.

nona, *f.* (eccl.) nones.

nonada, *f.* trifle, nothing.

nonagenario, ria, *n.* & *a.* nonagenarian.

nonagésimo, ma, *a.* ninetieth.

nonato, ta, *a.* not naturally born, but extracted from the womb by Cæsarean section.

nonio, *m.* vernier.

nono, na, *a.* ninth.

non plus ultra, ne plus ultra, unsurpassable.

nopal, *m.* (bot.) nopal, cochineal fig-tree, prickly Indian pear tree.

noque, *m.* tan pit, tan vat; heap or basket of bruised olives.

noquero, *m.* tanner, currier, leather dresser.

norabuena, *f.* = ENHORABUENA.

noramala, *adv.* = ENHORAMALA.

noray, *m.* (naut.) bollard, mooring.

nordestal, *a.* northeast, northeaster.

nordeste, *m.* northeast.—**nordestear,** *vn.* (naut.) to decline to northeast (s. o. the compass).

nórdico, ca, *n.* & *a.* Nordic.

nordovestear, *vn.* (naut.) to decline to northwest (s. o. the compass).

noria, *f.* noria, chain pump, draw-well.

norial, *a.* relating to the NORIA.

norma, *f.* standard, norm, pattern, model, rule.

normal. I. *a.* normal; model, standard. II. *f.* normal school; (geom.) normal.

normalidad, *f.* normality.

normalizar, *va.* to normalize; to standardize.

normando, da; normano, na. I. *n.* & *a.* Norman. II. *n.* Norman, Northman.

nornordeste, *m.* north-northeast.

nornoroeste, nornorueste, *m.* north-northwest.

noroeste, *m.* northwest.

noroestear, *vn.* (naut.) = NORUESTEAR.

nortada, *f.* north gale, norther.

norte, *m.* north; north wind; rule, law, guide, clew, direction.

norteamericano, na, *n.* & *a.* North-American; American (gen. restricted to persons or things from or of the U. S.)

nortear, *va.* (naut.) to steer or stand to the northward; to decline to the north (s. o. the compass).

noruego, ga, *n.* & *a.* Norwegian.

norueste, *m.* northwest.

noruestear, *vn.* (naut.) to decline to the northwest (s. o. the compass).

nos, *pers. pron. pl. m.* & *f.* accusative & *dative* of NOSOTROS: us, to us. It is sometimes used as nominative, in an authoritative style, as *nos, el arzobispo de Toledo,* I, the archbishop of Toledo.

nosogenia, *f.* (med.) nosogenia.

nosografía, *f.* (med.) nosography.

nosología, *f.* (med.) nosology.

nosológico, ca, *a.* nosological.

nosotros, tras, *pers. pron. pl. m.* & *f.* we; ourselves; us.

nostalgia, *f.* nostalgia, homesickness.

nostálgico, ca, *a.* nostalgic, homesick.

nostramo, *m.* (naut.) master—a title given by sailors to the boatswain.

nota, *f.* note; mark, sign; annotation; imputation, reproach; stain, stigma; renown, fame, repute; style, manner of writing; memorandum; (com.) account, bill, statement, schedule, price list; (mus.) note.—*pl.* records of a notary.—**n. marginal,** marginal note.—**n. verbal,** verbal note.

nota bene, (Lat.) take notice; N. B.

notabilidad, *f.* notability; notable.

notabilísimo, ma, *a.* *super.* of NOTABLE: most, or very, notable, marked, or noted.

notable, *a.* notable, remarkable, noteworthy, noticeable, conspicuous; distinguished, prominent, noted.—**notablemente,** *adv.* notably, remarkably, notedly, noticeably.

notación, *f.* note, annotation; (math. and mus.) notation.

notar, *va.* to note, to mark; to remark, observe; to notice, take notice of, observe; to annotate, comment; to dictate; to find fault with, criticise; to reprehend.

notaría, *f.* profession or position of a notary; notary's office.—**notariado,** *m.* profession of a notary.—**notarial,** *a.* notarial.—**notariato,** *m.* title or practice of a notary.

notario, *m.* notary public; amanuensis.

noticia, *f.* news (in this sense, gen. in the *pl.*); notice, knowledge, information, light; (com.) advice.—**n. remota,** vague remembrance.—**atrasado de noticias,** behind the times.

noticiar, *va.* to notify, give notice to, inform.

noticiero, *m.* news agent, reporter.

noticioso, sa, *a.* news-giving; informed; learned.

notición, *m.* *aug.* (coll.) great news.

notificación, *f.* notification, notice.

notificado, da, *pp.* & *a.* (law) notified.

notificar, *va.* (*pret.* NOTIFIQUÉ: *subj.* NOTIFIQUE) to notify.

notita, *f.* *dim.* short note, memorandum, etc.

noto, ta. I. *a.* well known; illegitimate, bastard. II. *m.* south wind, notus.

notomía, *f.* skeleton.
notoriamente, *adv.* manifestly, glaringly.
notoriedad, *f.* quality of being well known; self-evidence; notoriety.
notorio, ria, *a.* well known; evident, manifest.
nóumeno, *m.* (philos.) noumenon.
novaciano, na, *m. & f.* Novat`an.
novación, *f.* (law) novation.
novador, ra, *n. & a.* innovator (-ing).
noval, *a.* newly broken up (land).
novar, *va.* (law) to renew by novation.
novatada, *f.* hazing (in colleges).
novato, ta, *n.* novice, beginner, tyro.
novator, ra, *n.* innovator, novator.
novecientos, tas, *n. & a.* nine hundred.
novedad, *f.* novelty; newness; surprise, recent occurrence, latest news or fashion; fad; change, innovation; danger, trouble.—**no hay n.,** there is no change.—**sin n.,** well; safe; as usual.
novel, *a.* new, inexperienced.
novela, *f.* novel; falsehood, romance, fiction; (law) novel.
novelador, ra, *n.* novelist.
novelar, *vn.* to write novels; to romance, to tell stories.
novelería, *f.* fondness for novelties; curiosity; fondness for novels; collection of novels.
novelero, ra. I. *a.* fond of novels, fads, and novelties; newfangled; fickle, wavering, unsteady. **II.** *n.* newsmonger, gossip.
novelesco, ca, *a.* novelistic, fiction (u. a.), fictionlike.
novelista, *n.* novelist.
novena, *f.* (eccl.) novena.—**novenario,** *m.* (eccl.) novenary.—**novendial,** *a.* (eccl.) novendial.
noveno, na. I. *n. & a.* ninth; ninthly. **II.** *m.* ninth part of tithes.
noventa, *m. & a.* ninety; ninetieth.
noventavo, va, *n. & a.* ninetieth.
noventón, na, *n. & a.* nonagenarian.
novia, *f.* bride; woman betrothed, fiancée.
noviazgo, *m.* engagement, betrothal.
noviciado, *m.* (eccl.) novitiate; apprenticeship.
novicio, cia. I. *a.* new, inexperienced. **II.** *n.* novice, probationer; freshman, apprentice, tyro.
noviciote, *m.* (coll.) overgrown novice.
noviembre, *n.* November.
novilunio, *m.* new moon.
novilla, *f.* young cow, heifer.
novillada, *f.* drove of young bulls or steers; baiting of young bulls.
novillejo, eja, *n. dim.* bullock (heifer).
novillero, *m.* herdsman who attends young cattle; stable for young cattle; pasture ground for weaned calves; truant, idler.
novillo, *m.* young bull; steer.—**hacer novillos,** (coll.) to play truant or hooky.
novio, *m.* bridegroom; fiancé; (coll.) suitor; one new to some dignity or state.
novísimo, ma. I. *a.* newest, most recent; latest. —**N. Recopilación,** revised code of laws in Spain promulgated July 15, 1805. **II.** *m.* each of the four last incidents of mankind.
noyó, *m.* noyau, a cordial.
nubada, *f.* shower of rain; plenty, abundance.
nubado, da, *a.* clouded, shaped like clouds.
nubarrado, da. I. *a.* NUBADO, DA. **II.** *f.* NUBADA.
nubarrón, *m.* large threatening cloud.
nube, *f.* cloud; crowd, multitude; (med.) film on the eye; cloud or shade in precious stones.— **por las nubes, or a las nubes,** very high (praise or price).
nubecita, *f.* small cloud.
nubiense, *n. & a.* Nubian.
nubífero, ra, *a.* (poet.) cloud-bringing.
núbil, *a.* nubile, marriageable.
nubilidad, *f.* nubility, marriageable age.
nubiloso, sa, *a.* (poet.) cloudy, nubilous.
nublado, da. I. *pp. & a.* cloudy. **II.** *m.* clouded sky; gloominess; impending danger; multitude.
nublar, nublarse, *va. & vr.* = ANUBLAR.

nublo, bla. I. *a.* cloudy. **II.** *m.* NUBLADO.
nubloso, sa, *a.* cloudy; gloomy; ill-fated.
nuca, *f.* nape or scruff of the neck.
núcleo, *m.* nucleus; center; kernel of a nut; stone of fruit; (ast.) nucleus (of a comet).
nuco, *m.* a Chilean kind of owl.
nudamente, *adv.* nakedly; plainly.
nudillo, *m.* knuckle; small knot in stockings; (mas.) plug, dowel, dook; nodule.
nudo, da. I. *a.* nude, naked. **II.** *m.* knot; burl, tangle; (bot.) node; joint; snag; tie, union, bond; (med.) node, tumor; knotty point, intricacy, difficulty; crisis of a drama; (naut.) knot of the log line, nautical mile.—**n. en la garganta,** lump in one's throat, great affliction.—**n. gordiano,** Gordian knot.
nudoso, sa, *a.* knotty, knotted.
nuecero, ra, *n.* vender of walnuts.
nuégado, *m.* paste of flour, honey and nuts.
nuera, *f.* daughter-in-law.
nuestramo, ma, *f. contr.* from NUESTRO AMO; our master (mistress); (Am.) the Eucharist.
nuestro, tra, *poss. pron. 1st pers. pl.* our, ours. U. sometimes instead of my, mine, by persons in authority or by writers.—**los nuestros,** our friends, or colleagues, ours.
nueva, *f.* news, tidings.
nuevamente, *adv.* newly, recently, freshly.
nueve. I. *n. & a.* nine. **II.** *m.* ninth (of the month). **III.** *f. pl.* —**las n.,** nine o'clock.
nuevecito, *a. dim.* brand-new.
nuevo, va, *a.* new; novel, modern; newly arrived. —**n. emisión,** reissue.—**n. flamante,** spick and span, brand-new.—**de n.,** anew; again, once more. —**¿qué hay de n.?** what is the news?
nuez, *f.* walnut; nut or meat of some fruits (as coconuts); Adam's apple.—**n. de especia,** (bot.) nutmeg.—**n. dura,** hickory nut.—**n. moscada =** N. DE ESPECIA.—**n. vómica,** (bot.) nux vomica.
nueza, *f.* (bot.) briony.
nugatorio, ria, *a.* nugatory, futile.
nulamente, *adv.* invalidly, ineffectually.
nulidad, *f.* (law) nullity; defeasance; inability, incompetency; insignificant or incompetent person, a nobody.
nulo, la, *a.* null, void; of no account.
numen, *m.* divinity, deity; inspiration.
numerable, *a.* numerable.
numeración, *f.* numeration (usually including notation); numbering.
numerador, ra, *m.* numerator; numberer.
numeral, *n. & a.* numeral.
numerar, *va.* to number; enumerate; calculate, reckon; to page.
numerario, ria. I. *a.* numerary. **II.** *m.* cash, coin, specie.
numerata pecunia, (law) ready money.
numéricamente, *adv.* numerically.
numérico, ca, *a.* numerical.
número, *m.* number; figure, character; numeral; poetical or musical measure, rhythm; (gram.) number.—*pl.* (N-) numbers, fourth book of the Pentateuch.—**n. complejo,** denominate number. —**n. compuesto,** nondigit number.—**n. denominado,** denominate number.—**n. entero,** whole number, integer.—**n. mixto,** mixed number.—**n. romano,** Roman numeral.—**n. sordo,** surd, number having no root of a given index.—**n. uno,** number one, one's self; A1, A number 1.—**de n.,** regular (said of a member of an association consisting of a limited number; it may be left untranslated).—**sin n.,** numberless.
numerosamente, *adv.* numerously.
numerosidad, *f.* numerosity, numerousness.
numeroso, sa, *a.* numerous; harmonious, rhythmical.
númida, *n. & a.; numídico,** *a.* Numidian.
numisma, *m.* coin, money.
numismática, *f.* numismatics.—**numismático, ca. I.** *a.* numismatical. **II.** *m.* numismatist.
numulario, *m.* banker, money broker.
numulita, *f.* (pal.) nummulite.
nunca, *adv.* never.—**n. jamás,** never, never more·

nunciatura, *f.* nunciature.

nuncio, *m.* messenger; Papal nuncio; forerunner, harbinger.

nuncupativo, va, *a.* (law) nuncupative, oral.

nuncupatorio, ria, *a.* nuncupatory.

nupcial, *a.* nuptial, hymeneal.

nupcialidad, *f.* marriage rate.

nupcias, *f. pl.* nuptials, wedding, marriage.

nutación, *f.* (ast. and bot.) nutation.

nutra, nutria, *f.* otter.

nutricio, cia, *a.* nutritious, nourishing.

nutrición, *f.* nutrition, nourishing; (pharm.) preparation of medicines.

nutrido, da, *pp. & a.* (w. **de**) full (of), abounding (with, in).

nutrimental, *a.* nutrimental, nourishing.

nutrimento, *m.* nutriment, food, nourishment; nutrition.

nutrir, *va.* to nourish, feed; to encourage, promote, support.

nutritivo, va, *a.* nutritive, nourishing.

nutriz, *f.* wet nurse.

Ñ

ñagaza, *f.* bird-call, decoy.

ñame, *m.* (bot.) yam.

ñandú, *m.* American ostrich.

ñanduti, m. (S. A.) a very fine fabric used mainly for underclothes.

ñánigo, ga, *n.* (Cuba) member of a secret society of negroes.

ñapa, *f.* (Am.) boot, lagnappe, something over or extra.—**de ñ.**, to boot, over, extra.

ñaque, *m.* odds and ends.

ñato, ta, *a.* (Am.) flat-nosed.

ñeque. I. *m.* (Am.) (coll.) energy, vim, bravery. **II.** *a.* (Am.) (coll.) strong, vigorous; extraordinary, "dandy."

ñiquiñaque, *m.* (coll.) good-for-nothing person or thing; trash.

ñoclo, *m.* a kind of macaroon.

ñoñería, *f.* dotage, drivel.—**ñoñez,** *f.* dotage, senility; shyness.

ñongo, ga, *a.* (Ch., coll.) lazy, good-for-nothing; (Colomb.) tilted (s. o. dice).

ñoño, ña, *a.* (coll.) timid, shy; dotard, feebleminded.

ñudo, *m.* (obs.) = NUDO.

O

o. I. *conj.* or, either. **II.** *interj.*, oh, O.

oasis, *m.* oasis.

obcecación, *f.* obfuscation, obsession.

obcecadamente, *adv.* obsessedly.

obcecado, da, *pp. & a.* obsessed, obfuscated.

obcecar, *va.* (pret. OBCEQUÉ: subj. OBCEQUE) to obsess, to blind, obfuscate; to darken or obscure.

obduración, *f.* obstinacy, obduracy.

obedecedor, ra, *n.* obeyer.

obedecer, *va.* (ind. OBEDEZCO: subj. OBEDEZCA) to obey; to respond; to be due, arise (from); to follow, be controlled by.

obedecimiento, *m.* obedience.

obediencia, *f.* obedience.—**a la o.,** your most obedient.

obediencial, *a.* obediential.

obediente, *a.* obedient.

obedientemente, *adv.* obediently.

obelisco, *m.* obelisk; (print.) dagger (†).

obelo, *m.* obelisk.

obencadura, *f.* (naut.) shrouds in general.

obenques, *m. pl.* (naut.) shrouds, shifters.

obertura, *f.* (mus.) overture.

obesidad, *f.* obesity, fatness, fleshiness.

obeso, sa, *a.* obese, fat, fleshy.

óbice, *m.* obstacle, impediment, hindrance.

obispado, *m.* bishopric; episcopate.

obispal, *a.* episcopal, belonging to a bishop.

obispalía, *f.* palace or house of a bishop; bishopric, diocese.

obispar, *vn.* to be made a bishop.

obispillo. *m. dim.* boy bishop; bishop of no account; large pork sausage; rump or croup of a fowl.

obispo, *m.* (eccl.) bishop; large blood pudding; (icht.) raioid selachian.

óbito, *m.* (law, eccl.) death, decease, demise.

obituario, *m.* obituary.

objeción, *f.* objection.—**objetante,** *n. & a.* objector (-ing).—**objetar,** *va.* to object, oppose, remonstrate.

objetivamente, *adv.* objectively.

objetivar, *va.* to objectify or objectivate.

objetivo, va. I. *a.* objective. **II.** *m.* (opt.) objective, eyepiece.

objeto, *m.* object; subject matter.

oblación, *f.* oblation, offering, gift.

oblada, *f.* (eccl.) funeral offering of bread.

oblata, *f.* (eccl.) oblate; contribution for church expenses.

oblea, *f.* wafer for sealing letters.

obleera, *f.* wafer holder, case for wafers.

oblicuamente, *adv.* obliquely.

oblicuángulo, *a.* oblique-angled.

oblicuar, *va. & vn.* to cant, slant; (mil.) to oblique.

oblicuidad, *f.* obliquity.

oblicuo, cua, *a.* oblique, slanting.

obligación, *f.* obligation, duty; bond, debenture; charge; provision office.—*pl.* family that one is obliged to maintain; engagements; (com.) liabilities.

obligacionista, *n.* (com.) bondholder.

obligado, *m.* contractor for supplying provisions to a city; (law) obligor; (mus.) obbligato.

obligante, *a.* obligating, obliging.

obligar, *I. va.* (pret. OBLIGUÉ: subj. OBLIGUE) to obligate, compel, bind; to oblige. **II.** *vr.* to obligate or bind one's self.

obligatorio, ria, *a.* obligatory, binding, compulsory.

obliteración, *f.* (med.) obliteration.

obliterar, *va.* (med.) to obliterate.

oblongo, ga, *a.* oblong.

obnoxio, xia, *a.* obnoxious.

oboe, *m.* (mus.) oboe; oboist.

óbolo, *m.* obolus; obolo; mite; (pharm.) obole.

obra, *f.* work; book; building, structure; repairs in a house; means, virtue, power, influence; agency; toil, labor, employment.—**o. a cuerno,** (mil.) hornwork.—**o. de,** about, more or less.—**o. de manos,** hand work.—**o. de romanos,** great work requiring time and toil, (coll.) big order.—**o. muerta,** (naut.) gunwale.—**o. prima,** shoemaking.—**o. pública,** public work.—**obras accesorias** (fort.) outworks of a fortress.—**obras de marea,** graving, caulking and paving a ship bottom.—**obras muertas,** upper works of a ship.—**obras pías,** charitable funds or establishments.—**obras vivas,** (naut.) quick or lower works.—**a o. de** = o. DE.—**hacer mala o.,** to do a bad turn.—**poner por o.,** to set to work on, to start.

obrada, *f.* day's work; a land measure (varies between 39 and 54 ares).

obrador, ra, *n.* workman (-woman); workshop.

obradura, *f.* charge of an oil mill.

obraje, *m.* manufacture, handiwork; workshop; wool mills.

obrajero, *m.* foreman, overseer, superintendent.

obrante, *a.* acting, working.

obrar. I. *va.* to work; to make, manufacture; to perform, execute; to construct, build. **II.** *vn.* to act; to ease nature; to be (in a place, in a person's hands, etc.)

obrepción, *f.* (law) obreption.

obrepticio, cia, *a.* (law) obreptitious.

obrería, *f.* task of a workman; money for church repairs.

For pronunciation, see the rules at the beginning of the book.

obrero, ra, *n.* worker or workman (-woman); churchwarden; missionary.
obrita, *f. dim.* small or little work; booklet.
obrizo, za, *a.* pure, refined (gold).
obscenamente, *adv.* obscenely.—**obscenidad,** *f.* obscenity.—**obsceno, na,** *a.* obscene.
obscuración, *f. V.* OBSCURIDAD.
obscuramente, *adv.* obscurely, darkly, faintly; confusedly; humbly, modestly.
obscurantismo, *m.* obscurantism.
obscurantista, *n.* obscurantist.
obscuras.—a o., in the dark.
obscurecer. I. *va.* (*ind.* OBSCUREZCO: *subj.* OBSCUREZCA*) to obscure, darken; to dim; to tarnish; to cloud, confuse; (pict.) to shade. **II.** *v. impers.* to grow dark. **III.** *vr.* to cloud over; to disappear; to become dark.
obscurecimiento, *m.* obscuration, darkening.
obscuridad, *f.* obscurity; darkness; gloominess; opacity; retired, private life.
obscuro, ra. I. *a.* obscure; dark; gloomy; (art) heavily shaded. **II.** *m.* (art) shade.—**a obscuras,** in the dark.
obsecuente, *a.* obsequious, obedient.
obsequiador, ra, *n.* giver; entertainer.
obsequiante, *a.* obsequious.
obsequiar, *va.* to treat, entertain. pay attentions to, make presents to; to court, woo; to present, make a gift of.
obsequio, *m.* obsequiousness; treat; courtesy, attention shown; gift, present.—**en o. de,** for the sake of, out of respect to.
obsequiosamente, *adv.* obsequiously, flatteringly, gallantly.
obsequioso, sa, *a.* obsequious; obedient, compliant; obliging, attentive.
observable, *a.* observable, noticeable.
observación, *f.* observation; remark, note.
observador, ra, *n. & a.* observer (-ing).
observancia, *f.* observance, fulfilment.—**poner en o.,** to execute punctually.
observante, *a.* observant, observing.
observar, *va.* to observe; to notice, note; remark; to pry, look into, watch.
observatorio, *m.* observatory.
obsesión, *f.* obsession.
obseso, sa, *a.* beset, tempted.
obsidiana, *f.* (geol.) obsidian.
obsidional, *a.* (mil.) obsidional.
obstáculo, *m.* obstacle.
obstante.—no o., notwithstanding; nevertheless, however.
obstar, *vn.* to oppose, obstruct, hinder.
obstetricia, *f.* (med.) obstetrics, midwifery.
obstinación, *f.* obstinacy, stubbornness.
obstinadamente, *adv.* obstinately, stubbornly.
obstinado, da, *pp. & a.* obstinate, stubborn, obdurate, headstrong.
obstinarse, *vr.* (w. **en**) to be obstinate (about), to persist (in).
obstrucción, *f.* obstruction, stoppage.
obstruccionismo, *m.* obstructionism.
obstruccionista, *n. & a.* obstructionist (-ic).
obstructivo, va, *a.* obstructive.
obstruir. I. *va.* (*for irr. v.* CONSTRUIR) to obstruct, block, stop up, choke. **II.** *vr.* to become obstructed or choked.
obtemperar, *va.* to obey, to assent.
obtención, *f.* attainment, obtainment.
obtener, *va.* (*for irr. v.* TENER) to attain, obtain, procure; to preserve, to maintain.
obtento, *m.* (eccl.) benefice, prebend.
obtentor, *m.* (eccl.) one who obtains a prebend.
obtestación, *f.* obtestation, protestation.
obturación, *f.* obturation, closing, sealing.
obturador, triz. I. *a.* serving to stop up, close, seal, plug, etc. **II.** *m.* plug, stopper; breech-block; (surg.) obturator; gas check; (phot.) shutter.
obturar, *va.* to stop up, plug, close, seal.
obtusángulo, obtuse-angled.
obtuso, sa, *a.* obtuse; blunt, dull.

obué, *m.* (mus.) oboe; oboist.
obús, *m.* (arti.) howitzer, shell gun.
obusera, *a.* boat carrying a howitzer.
obvención, *f.* perquisite.
obviar. I. *va.* to obviate, remove, prevent, surmount. **II.** *vn.* to hinder, oppose.
obvio, via, *a.* obvious, evident.
obyecto, *m.* objection, reply.
oca, *f.* (orn.) goose; (bot.) oca oxalis; royal goose (a game).
ocal, *a.* double (cocoon); delicious (fruit).
ocalear, *vn.* to make double cocoons.
ocasión, *f.* occasion; chance, opportunity.—**de o.,** second-hand.
ocasionado, da, *pp. & a.* provoking, vexatious, insolent; perilous.
ocasionador, ra, *n. & a.* occasioner (-ing).
ocasional, *a.* occasional, chance, casual.
ocasionalmente, *adv.* occasionally.
ocasionar, *va.* to cause, occasion; to move, excite; to jeopardize, endanger.
ocaso, *m.* west; setting of any heavenly body; decadence, decline.
occidental, *a.* occidental, western.
occidente, *m.* occident, west.
occiduo, dua, *a.* occidental, occiduous.
occipital, *a.* occipital.
occipucio, *m.* occiput.
occisión, *f.* murder, killing.
occiso, sa, *a.* murdered, killed.
oceánico, ca, *a.* oceanic.
océano, *m.* ocean.—**oceanografía,** *f.* oceanography.—**oceanógrafo, fa,** *n.* oceanographer.
oceanógrafo, fa, *n.* oceanographer.
ocelo, *m.* (biol.) ocellus.
ocelote, *m.* ocelot, a large wild cat, or variety of leopard.
ocena, *f.* (med.) foul breath.
ociar, *vn.* to loiter, be at leisure.
ocio, *m.* leisure, idleness; pastime, diversion.
ociosamente, *adv.* idly; uselessly.
ociosidad, *f.* idleness, leisure.
ocioso, sa, *a.* idle; fruitless, useless.
oclocracia, *f.* (pol.) ochlocracy.
ocluir, *va.* (*for irr. v.* INCLUIR) (med.) to occlude, to shut up.
oclusión, *f.* occlusion.
ocosial, *m.* (Peru) lowland, morass.
ocotal, *m.* (Mex.) grove of OCOTES.
ocote, *m.* (Mex.) (bot.) okote pine, torch pine.
ocozoal, *m.* (Mex.) a variety of rattlesnake.
ocozol, *m.* (bot.) sweet gum, liquidambar tree.
ocre, *m.* ochre, brown or yellow earth.
octaedro, *m.* (geom.) octahedron.
octagonal, *a.* octagonal.
octágono, na. I. *a.* eight-sided, octagonal. **II.** *m.* octagon.
octante, *m.* (geom.) octant.
octava, *f.* (eccl.) octave, eight days; (mus.) octave; (poet.) eight-line stanza.
octavar, *vn.* to form octaves on stringed instruments; to deduct the eighth part.
octavario, *m.* (eccl.) festival lasting a week.
octavín, *m.* (mus.) piccolo flute.
octavo, va. I. *a.* eighth; octave, octonary.—**en o.,** (print.) in octavo. **II.** *m.* eighth; octoroon.
octogenario, ria, *n. & a.* octogenarian.
octogésimo, *a.* eightieth.
octogonal, *a.* octagonal.
octógono, na = OCTÁGONO.
octosilábico, ca; octosílabo, ba, *a.* octosyllabic.
octubre, *f.* October.
ocular. I. *a.* ocular. **II.** *m.* (opt.) eyepiece.
ocularmente, *adv.* ocularly.
oculista, *m.* oculist.
ocultación, *f.* concealment; hiding; (ast.) occultation.
ocultador, ra, *n. & a.* concealer (-ing).
ocultamente, *adv.* secretly, hiddenly.
ocultar, *va.* to hide, conceal, secrete.
oculto, ta, *a.* hidden, concealed; occult.—**de o.,** incog, incognito.—**en o.,** secretly, in secret.

ocupación, *f.* occupation; occupying; trade, business, pursuit; (rhet.) prolepsis.

ocupada, *a.* (coll.) pregnant.

ocupado, da, *pp. & a.* occupied; busy, engaged.

ocupador, ra, *n.* occupier, possessor, occupant.

ocupante, *n.* occupant.

ocupar. I. *va.* to occupy; take possession of; to fill, hold (an employ); to employ, give work to; to disturb, interrupt, hinder; to dwell or live in; to engage the attention of, preoccupy. **II.** *vr.* (with en or de) to busy one's self (with); to be engaged (in), have as one's business, devote one's self (to); to pay attention (to).

ocurrencia, *f.* occurrence, incident, happening; witticism.—**o. de acreedores,** meeting of creditors.

ocurrente, *a.* occurring; humorous or funny, witty.

ocurrir, *vn.* to occur, happen; to meet, anticipate; (law) to have recourse to; to apply to; (often as *vr.*) to occur (to one), to strike one (as an idea).

ocurso, *m.* (Mex.) petition, claim.

ochava, *f.* eighth part; (eccl.) octave.—**ochavas del molinete,** (naut.) whelps of the windlass.

ochavado, da, *pp. & a.* eight-sided.

ochavo, *m.* a small brass coin; octagonal thing.

ochavar, *va.* to make eight-sided.

ochenta, *a. & m.* eighty; eightieth.

ochentavo, va, *n. & a.* eightieth.

ochentón, *na, n. & a.* octogenarian.

ochete, *m.* bore of hollow projectiles.

ocho. I. *n. & a.* eight; eighth. **II.** *m.* figure 8; the eighth day; card with eight spots. **III.** *f. pl.* **las o.,** eight o'clock.

ochocientos, tas, *n. & a.* eight hundred.

ochosén, *m.* small ancient coin.

oda, *f.* ode.

odalisca, *f.* odalisk.

odeón, *m.* odeum.

odiar, *va.* to hate.—**odio,** *m.* hatred; odium.

odiosamente, *adv.* odiously, hatefully.

odiosidad, *f.* odiousness, hatred, odium.

odioso, sa, *a.* odious, hateful.

odisea, *f.* odyssey.

odómetro, *m.* odometer, cyclometer.

odontalgia, *f.* odontalgia, toothache.

odontoideo, a, *a.* odontoid, tooth-shaped.

odontología, *f.* odontology.

odontólogo, ga, *n.* odontologist.

odontorrea, *f.* odontorrhagia, bleeding of the gums.

odorante, *a.* odorous, fragrant.

odorífero, ra, *a.* odoriferous, fragrant.

odre, *m.* wine skin; (coll.) drunkard.

odrería, *f.* wine-skin factory or shop.

odrero, ra, *n.* maker or seller of wine skins.

odrezuelo, *m. dim.* small wine skin.

odrina, *f.* ox-skin bag for wine.

oesnorueste, *m.* west-northwest.

oessudueste, *m.* west-southwest.

oeste, *m.* west; west wind.—**o. cuarta al norte,** west by north.—**o. cuarta al sur,** west by south.

ofendedor, ra, *n. & a.* offender (-ing).

ofender. I. *va.* to offend; to make angry. **II.** *vr.* to become angry; to take offence.

ofensa, *f.* offence; transgression, crime.

ofensión, *f.* offence, grievance; injury.

ofensivamente, *adv.* offensively.

ofensivo, va. I. *a.* offensive; attacking. **II.** *f.* (mil.) offensive.

ofensor, ra, *n. & a.* offender (-ing).

oferente, *m.* offerer, one who offers.

oferta, *f.* offer; gift, offering; (com.) offer, tender, supply.—**o. y demanda,** supply and demand.

ofertorio, *m.* (eccl.) offertory.

oficial. I. *a.* official. **II.** *m.* official, officer; trained workman; clerk; (mil.) commissioned officer below major; executioner.—**o. de la sala,** (law) actuary in criminal causes.—**o. mayor,** chief clerk.

oficiala, *f.* trained workwoman; forewoman; saleswoman.

oficialía, *f.* clerkship in a public office.

oficialidad, *f.* body of officers.

oficialmente, *adv.* officially.

oficiante, *n. & a.* officiator (-ing).

oficiar. I. *va.* to communicate officially. **II.** *vn.* to officiate.—**o. de,** to act as.

oficina, *f.* workshop; office; countinghouse, bureau; laboratory.

oficinal, *a.* (med. and pharm.) officinal.

oficinesco, ca, *a.* departmental, office (w a.).

oficinista, *n.* office clerk, employee.

oficio, *m.* employ, work or occupation; office, function, operation; official letter; trade or business; craft; notary's office.—*pl.* (eccl.) office, service.—**de o.,** officially; by trade, by occupation or profession.—**tomarlo por o.,** to do frequently, to take to.

oficionario, *m.* (eccl.) office book.

oficiosamente, *adv.* officiously.—**oficiosidad,** *f.* diligence, alacrity; officiousness.—**oficioso, sa,** *a.* diligent, compliant, accommodating; officious, meddlesome, useful, fruitful; (pol.) semi-official.

ofidio, dia. I. *a. & n.* (zool.) ophidian. **II.** *m. pl.* Ophidia, ophidians.

ofita, *f.* (min.) ophite.

ofiurídeo, ofiuro, *m.* (zool.) ophiuroid, ophiuroidean.

ofrecedor, ra, *n.* offerer.

ofrecer. I. *va.* (*ind.* OFREZCO: *subj.* OFREZCA) to offer; to propose; to present; to exhibit, manifest; to dedicate, consecrate; (com.) to bid, offer. **II.** *vr.* to offer, occur, present itself; to offer one's self, volunteer.

ofreciente, *a.* offering.

ofrecimiento, *m.* offer, offering.

ofrenda, *f.* offering, oblation, gift.

ofrendar, *va.* to present offerings; to contribute.

oftalmía, *f.* (med.) ophthalmia.—**oftálmico, ca,** *a.* ophthalmic.—**oftalmología,** *f.* ophthalmology.

oftalmológico, ca, *a.* ophthalmologic.

oftalmólogo, ga, *n.* oculist.

oftalmómetro, *m.* ophthalmometer.

oftalmoscopia, *f.* ophthalmoscopy.

oftalmoscopio, *m.* ophthalmoscope.

ofuscación, *f.*, **ofuscamiento,** *m.* obfuscation; confused reason.

ofuscar, *va.* (*pret.* OFUSQUÉ: *subj.* OFUSQUE) to obfuscate, dazzle; to confuse.

ogaño, *adv.* = HOGAÑO.

ogro, *m.* ogre, fabulous monster.

¡oh! *interj.* O! oh!

ohm, *m.* (elec.) ohm.

óhmico, ca, *a.* (elec.) ohmic.

ohmímetro, *m.* (elec.) ohmmeter.

ohmio, *m.* (elec.) ohm.

ohmiómetro, *m.* (elec.) ohmmeter.

oíble, *a.* audible.

oída, *f.* hearing.—**de oídas,** or **por oídas,** by hearsay.

oidio, *m.* (bot.) oidium.

oído, da. I. *pp.* of oír. **II.** *m.* sense of hearing; (anat.) ear; (arti.) vent, priming hole, touch-hole.—**al o.,** by ear; in the ear, whispering; confidentially.—**dar oídos,** to lend an ear; to believe.—**de o.,** by ear.—**regalar el o.,** to tickle the ear, to flatter.—**tener buen o.,** to have a good ear (sp. for music).

oidor, ra, *n.* hearer; judge, member of an Audiencia.

oidoría, *f.* judgeship, office of OIDOR.

oír, *va.* (*gerund,* OYENDO: *ind.* OIGO: *pret.* él OYÓ: *subj.* OIGA: *imp. subj.* OYERA, OYESE: *fut. subj.* OYERE) to hear; to listen; to understand; to attend (as lectures).—**o. decir,** to hear (it said).—**o. misa,** to attend or hear mass.—**o., ver y callar,** mind your own business.—**ahora,** or **hasta ahora, lo oigo,** this is the first I hear of it.—**¡oiga!** or **¡oigan!** well! the idea! say! listen!

oíslo, *n.* (coll.) person beloved, wife (or husband).

ojal, *m.* buttonhole; loop.

¡ojalá! *interj.* would to God! God grant! may.

ojaladera, *f.* buttonhole maker.

ojalador, ra, *n.* (sew.) buttonhole maker.
ojaladura, *f.* set of buttonholes.
ojalar, *va.* to make buttonholes in.
ojalatero, *a.* & *m.* (pol., coll.) stay-at-home patriot during war.
ojaranzo, *m.* (bot.) = CARPE.
ojazo, *m. aug.* large eye.
ojeada, *f.* glance, hasty look; glimpse.
ojeador, *m.* beater for game.
ojear, *va.* to eye, look, stare at; to beat for game; to startle, frighten.
ojeo, *m.* beating for game.
ojera, *f.* ring under the eye; eyecup.
ojeriza, *f.* spite, grudge, ill will.
ojeroso, sa; ojerudo, da, *a.* having rings under the eyes.
ojete, *m.* (sew.) eyelet.
ojeteador, *m.* eyeleteer; stiletto.
ojetear, *va.* (sew.) to make eyelet holes in.
ojetera, *f.* edge of a garment with eyelets for lacing; eyelet maker.
ojialegre, *a.* bright-eyed.
ojiazul, *a.* blue-eyed.
ojito, *m. dim.* small eye.
ojienjuto, ta, *a.* (coll.) dry-eyed.
ojimel, ojimiel, *m.* (pharm.) oxymel.
ojimoreno, na, *a.* (coll.) brown-eyed.
ojinegro, gra, *a.* black-eyed.
ojiva, *f.* (arch.) ogive, pointed arch.
ojival, *a.* (arch.) ogival.
ojizaino, na, *a.* (coll.) squint-eyed, moon-eyed.
ojizarco, ca, *a.* (coll.) blue-or gray-eyed.
ojo, *m.* eye; eye of a needle; (mech.) perforation; hole, eye, socket; bow of a key; keyhole; water spring; geyser; drop of oil or grease swimming on liquors; (arc.) span of a bridge; opening in the center of a winding stair; attention, care, notice; reference mark; eye or face of type: mesh; eye or hollow in bread or cheese.—*pl.* dearest, darling.—¡o.! take notice! ¡o. alerta! look sharp! —o. avizor, sharp lookout.—o. de buey, (bot.) oxeye; (coll.) doubloon (eight dollars).—o. de gallo, corn between the toes.—o. de gaza, (naut.) eye of a strap.—o. de la caña del ancla, (naut.) eye of the anchor.—o. de pollo = O. DE GALLO.—o. por o., diente por diente, an eye for an eye, a tooth for a tooth.—ojos reventones, or saltones, goggle eyes.—a cierra ojos, unhesitatingly; at all events. —a los ojos de, in presence of.—a o., by eye.—a ojos cegarritas, having the eyes half-shut.—a ojos cerrados, blindly, without reflection; without examination.—a ojos vistas, visibly, publicly.— avivar el o., to be on one's guard.—costar un o., to be excessively dear.—de medio o., lurkingly, concealingly.—entrar por el o., to please.—en un abrir y cerrar de ojos, in the twinkling of an eye. —hacer del o., to wink at one another, to have a secret understanding.—hacerse ojos, to look with sharp eyes.
ojota, *f.* (Am.) sandal worn by Indian women.
ojuelo, *m. dim.* small eye.—*pl.* sparkling eyes; spectacles.
ola, *f.* wave, billow.—o. de marea, tidal wave.
olaje, *m.* succession of waves, surge, motion of the waves.
ole, *m.* an Andalusian dance.—¡o.! bravo!
oleáceo, cea. I. *a.* (bot.) oleaceous. **II.** *f. pl.* Oleaceæ.
oleada, *f.* big wave; surge, swell of the sea; surging of a crowd; abundant oil crop.
oleaginosidad, *f.* oleaginousness, oiliness.
oleaginoso, sa, *a.* oleaginous, oily.
oleaje, *m.* = OLAJE.
olear, *va.* to administer extreme unction to.
oleario, ria, *a.* oily.
oleastro, *m.* = ACEBUCHE.
oleato, *f.* oleate.
oleaza, *f.* watery dregs in oil mills.
olécranon, *m.* (anat.) olecranon.
oledero, ra, *a.* odorous, fragrant.
oledor, ra, *n.* smeller.
oleico, *a.* (chem.) oleic.—**oleína,** *f.* (chem.) olein.
óleo, *m.* oil; (eccl.) extreme unction; holy oil; act of anointing.—al o., in oil colors, oil (u. a.)

oleomargarina, *f.* oleomargarine.
oleómetro, *m.* (phys.) oleometer, elæometer.
oleorresina, *f.* oleoresin.
oleosidad, *f.* oiliness.
oleoso, sa, *a.* oily, oleaginous.
oler. I. *va.* (ind. HUELO: *subj.* HUELA) to smell, to scent; to find out, search, discover; to pry into, sniff, snuff. **II.** *vn.* to smell, emit an odor; to smack of.—o. a, to smell of, smell like.—o. mal, or no o. bien, to look suspicious, to arouse suspicion.
olfacción, *f.* olfaction.
olfatear, *va.* & *vn.* to smell, scent, sniff, snuff.
olfato, *m.* scent, sense of smell.
olfatorio, ria, *a.* olfactory.
olíbano, *m.* (bot.) incense.
oliente, *a.* smelling, odorous.
oliera, *f.* vessel for holy oil.
oligarca, *m.* oligarch.—**oligarquía,** *f.* oligarchy.
oligárquico, ca, *a.* oligarchical.
oligisto, *m.* (min.) oligist.
oligoceno, *a.* & *m.* (geol.) Oligocene.
oligoclasa, *f.* (min.) oligoclase.
olimpíada, *f.* Olympiad: Olympic games.
olímpico, ca, *a.* Olympic.
Olimpo, *m.* Olympus; (poet.) heaven.
olingo, *m.* a Central-American monkey.
olio, *m.* = ÓLEO.
oliscar. I. *va.* to smell, scent, sniff, snuff; to investigate, ascertain. **II.** *vn.* to be tainted, gamy, or high (s. o. meat).
oliva, *f.* olive tree; olive; owl.
olivar, *m.* olive grove, olive yard.
olivarda, *f.* (orn.) green goshawk; (bot.) elecampane.
olivarse, *vr.* to form bubbles when baking (s. o. bread).
olivera, *f.* olive tree.
olivífero, ra, *a.* (poet.) olive-bearing.
olivillo, *m.* (bot.) a variety of terebinth.
olivino, *m.* (min.) olivin, peridot.
olivo, *m.* (bot.) olive tree.—o. manzanillo, olive tree yielding the MANZANILLA olive.
olmeda, *f.* olmedo, *m.* elm grove.
olmo, *m.* (bot.) elm tree.
ológrafo, *a.* holographic.
olor, *m.* smell, fragrance; odor; hope, promise, offer; suspicion, smack.
oloroso, sa, *a.* fragrant.
olvidadizo, za, *a.* short of memory, forgetful.
olvidado, da, *a.* & *pp.* forgotten; forgetful.
olvidar, *va.* & *vr.* to forget.
olvido, *m.* forgetfulness; oversight; oblivion.— dar, or echar, al o., or en o., to forget; to cast into oblivion.
olla, *f.* pot, kettle, stewpot; (cook.) olla, olio, dish of boiled meat and vegetables; whirlpool.—o. carnicera, boiler, large kettle.—o. ciega = ALCANCÍA. —o. de fuego, (arti.) stinkpot.—o. de grillos, great confusion, pandemonium.—o. podrida, ollapodrida.
ollao, *m.* (naut.) eyelet hole.
ollar. I. *a.* soft (stone). **II.** *m.* horse's nostril.
ollaza, *f. aug.* large pot or boiler.
ollería, *f.* pottery; crockery shop.
ollero, ra, *n.* potter; dealer in earthenware.
ollita, olluela, *f. dim.* pipkin, small pot.
ombligada, *f.* (tan.) part of a skin corresponding to the navel.
ombligo, *m.* navel; navel string, umbilical cord; center or middle.—o. de Venus, (bot.) Venus navelwort.
ombliguero, *m.* navel bandage for infants.
ombría, *f.* shady place.
ombú, *m.* a South-American tree.
omega, *f.* omega (Greek letter).—desde el alpha hasta la o., from A to Z, from beginning to end.
omental, *a.* omental.—**omento,** *m.* (anat.) omentum.
ominar, *va.* to augur, foretell.
ominosamente, *adv.* ominously.
ominoso, sa, *a.* ominous, foreboding ill.
omisión, *f.* omission; carelessness, neglect.

For pronunciation, see the rules at the beginning of the book.

omiso, sa, *a.* neglectful, remiss, careless.
omitir, *va.* (*pp.* OMITIDO, OMISO) to omit.
ómnibus, *m.* omnibus, stagecoach.
omnímodamente, *adv.* in every way or respect, completely.
omnímodo, da, *a.* all-embracing.
omnipotencia, *f.* omnipotence.
omnipotente, *a.* omnipotent, almighty.
omnipotentemente, *adv.* omnipotently.
omnipresencia, *f.* omnipresence.
omnisapiente, *a.* omniscient.
omnisciencia, *f.* omniscience.
omniscio, ia, *a.* omniscient.
omnívoro, ra, *a.* omnivorous.
omóplato, *m.* (anat.) shoulderblade, scapula.
onagra, *f.* (bot.) onagra, evening primrose.
onagro, *m.* wild ass, onager.
onanismo, *m.* onanism.
once. I. *a.* eleven; eleventh. **II.** *m.* eleven; eleventh (of the month).—**las o.,** eleven o'clock.—**hacer,** or **tomar, las onces,** to take a small luncheon about noon.
oncear, *va.* to weigh out by ounces.
oncejera, *f.* small snare for catching birds.
oncejo, *m.* (orn.) = VENCEJO.
onceno, na, *a.* eleventh.—**el o. no estorbar,** (the eleventh commandment is:) thou shalt not disturb busy people.
oncijera, *f.* = ONCEJERA.
onda, *f.* wave; ripple; undulation; flicker; (sew.) scallop.—*pl.* the sea.—**o. etérea,** ether wave.—**o. herciana,** or **hertziana,** Hertzian wave.—**o. sonora,** sound wave.
ondámetro, *m.* (rad.) wave meter.
ondeado. I. *pp.* & *a.* undulated, scalloped, wavy. **II.** *m.* scalloping.
ondeante, *a.* waving, undulating.
ondear. I. *vn.* to wave, ripple, undulate; to flicker. **II.** *vr.* to swing, soar.
ondeo, *m.* waving, undulating, fluctuating.
ondina, *f.* Undine, water sprite.
ondisonante, *a.* = UNDÍSONO.
ondulación, *f.* = UNDULACIÓN.—**o. permanente,** permanent wave (of the hair).
ondulado, da, *pp.* & *a.* undulated, rippled; scalloped, wavy.
ondulante, *a.* waving, undulating.
ondular, *va.* = UNDULAR.
oneroso, sa, *a.* burdensome, onerous.
onfacino, *a.* omphacine (oil).
onfacomeli, *m.* (pharm.) oxymel.
ónice, *m.,* **ónique,** *f.* (min.) onyx.
oniromancía, *f.* oneiromancy, divination by dreams.
ónix, *m.* (min.) onyx.
onocrótalo, *m.* (orn.) white pelican.
onomancía, *f.* onomancy.
onomástico, ca, *a.* onomastic.
onomatopeya, *f.* onomatopœia.
onomatopéyico, ca, *a.* onomatopeic.
onoquiles, *f.* (bot.) dyer's bugloss, alkanet.
ontogénesis, ontogenia, *f.* ontogeny.
ontología, *f.* ontology.—**ontológico, ca,** *a.* ontological.—**ontólogo,** *m.* ontologist.
onza, *f.* ounce; (zool.) ounce.—**o. de oro,** Spanish doubloon.—**por onzas,** sparingly.
onzavo, va, *n.* & *a.* eleventh.
oolita, *f.* (geol.) oolite.
oolítico, ca, *a.* (geol.) oolitic.
oosfera, *f.* (biol.) oosphere, unfertilized egg.
opacamente, *adv.* obscurely, darkly.
opacidad, *f.* opacity.—**opaco, ca,** *a.* opaque.
opalino, na, *a.* opaline, opalescent.
ópalo, *m.* (min.) opal.
opción, *f.* option, choice; right.
ópera, *f.* opera.—**o. bufa,** comic opera.
operable, *a.* operable, practicable; capable of operating.
operación, *f.* operation, action, working; (chem.) process; (surg.) operation; (com.) operation, transaction, venture.—*pl.* (mil.) operations.—**o. cesárea,** (surg.) Cæsarean operation.—**operaciones de banco,** banking business.—**operaciones marítimas,** shipping trade or business.

operador, *m.* (surg.) operator.
operante, *n.* & *a.* operator (-ing).
operar. I. *va.* to operate. **II.** *vn.* to operate, act, work.
operario, ria. I. *n.* working man, working woman, hand; operator. **II.** *m.* priest who assists sick or dying persons.
operativo, va, *a.* operative.
operatorio, ria, *a.* operative; (med.) operative, relating to operations.
opérculo, *m.* operculum, lid, cover.
opereta, *f.* operetta, light opera.
operista, *n.* opera singer.
operoso, sa, *a.* laborious.
opiado, da, *a.* opiate, narcotic.
opiato, ta. I. *a.* opiate. **II.** *m.* opiate.
opilación, *f.* (med.) oppilation, emphraxis; amenorrhœa.
opilarse, *vr.* to contract amenorrhœa.
opilativo, va, *a.* obstructive, oppilative.
opimo, ma, *a.* rich, fruitful, abundant.
opinable, *a.* disputable, questionable.
opinante, *n.* & *a.* arguer (-ing).
opinar, *vn.* to judge, be of opinion.
opinativo, va, *a.* opinionative, opinative.
opinión, *f.* opinion.
opio, *m.* opium.
opíparamente, *adv.* opiparously.
opíparo, ra, *a.* opiparous, sumptuous.
oploteca, *f.* museum of rare weapons.
opobálsamo, *m.* opobalsam, balm of Gilead.
oponer, *va.* & *vr.* (*for irr. v.* PONER) to oppose; to hinder, resist, withstand; to object to, act against; to front, face, be opposite to; to stand in competition with another.
oponible, *a.* opposable.
opopánax, *m.* opopanax.
opopónaca, opopónace, *f.* (bot.) rough parsnip.
opopónaco, opopónax, *m.* opopanax.
oporto, port wine.
oportunamente, *adv.* opportunely.
oportunidad, *f.* opportunity.
oportunismo, *m.* (pol.) opportunism.
oportunista, *n.* & *a.* (pol.) opportunist (-ic).
oportuno, na, *a.* seasonable, opportune.
oposición, *f.* opposition; competition for a position, etc.; (ast.) opposition.
opositor, ra, *n.* opposer, opponent; competitor.
oposicionista, *m.* (pol.) oppositionist.
opoterapia, *f.* opotherapy, organotherapy.
opresión, *f.* oppression; pressure.
opresivamente, *adv.* oppressively.
opresivo, va, *a.* oppressive, overwhelming.
opresor, ra, *n.* oppressor; extortioner.
oprimir, *va.* to oppress; to press, push; to lie heavy upon, weigh down, dispirit.
oprobiar, *va.* to defame, revile.
oprobio, *m.* opprobrium, ignominy, infamy.
oprobioso, sa, *a.* opprobrious, disgraceful.
optar. I. *va.* to choose, select; to take possession of. **II.** *vn.* (w. por) to choose.
optante, *n.* chooser.
optativo, m. (gram.) optative.
óptico, ca. I. *a.* optic, optical. **II.** *m.* optician, opticist. **III.** *f.* optics; stereoscope.
óptimamente, *adv.* in the best way, perfectly.
optimismo, *m.* optimism.
optimista, *n.* & *a.* optimist (-ic).
óptimo, ma, *a.* best, eminently good.
optómetro, *m.* (opt.) optometer.
opuestamente, *adv.* oppositely, contrarily.
opuesto, ta. I. *a.* opposed; opposite, contrary, adverse. **II.** *pp. irr.* OI OPONER.
opugnación, *f.* opposition, attack.
opugnador, ra, *n.* opposer, attacker.
opugnar, *va.* to attack, oppose.
opulencia, *f.* opulence.—**opulentamente,** *adv.* opulently.—**opulento, ta,** *a.* opulent, wealthy.
opúsculo, *m.* booklet, tract.
oquedad, *f.* hollow, cavity.
oquedal, *m.* plantation of lofty trees.
oqueruela, *f.* kink in a sewing thread.

ora, *conj.* (*contr.* of AHORA) whether; either; now, then: *tomando ora la espada, ora la pluma,* taking now the sword, now (*or,* and then) the pen.

oración, *f.* oration, speech; orison, prayer; dusk, beginning of the evening; (gram.) sentence.— *pl.* first part of catechism; the angelus.—**o. dominical,** the Lord's Prayer.

oracional, *m.* prayer book.

oráculo, *m.* oracle.

orador, ra, *n.* orator.

oral. I. *a.* oral; vocal. **II.** *m.* soft breeze.

orangután, *m.* (zool.) orang-outang.

orante, *a.* praying.

orar. I. *vn.* to harangue, deliver a speech; to pray. **II.** *va.* to ask, beg for.

orate, *n.* lunatic, madman (-woman).

oratoria, *f.* oratory.

oratoriamente, *adv.* oratorically.

oratorio, ria. I. *a.* oratorical. **II.** *m.* oratory; (mus.) oratorio; (eccl.) congregation of presbyters.

orbe, *m.* orb, sphere; the earth; any celestial body; (icht.) globefish.

orbicular, *a.* orbicular, circular.

orbicularmente, *adv.* orbicularly.

órbita, *f.* (ast.) orbit; (anat.) orbit (of the eye).

orca, *f.* (icht.) grampus, orca.

orcaneta, *f.* (bot.) dyer's bugloss, alkanet.

orco, *m.* hell; (icht.) grampus.

órdago.—de o., first-class, excellent.

ordalía, *f.* ordeal, trial by fire or water.

orden. I. *m.* order; class, group; proportion, relation; (arch.) order.—*pl.* (eccl.) sacrament of ordination, clerical office.—**o. cerrado,** (mil.) close formation.—**o. compuesto,** (arch.) composite order.—**o. de batalla,** battle array, order of battle. —**o. del día,** order of the day (in a deliberating body).—**en o.,** in order; in an orderly manner; with regard to.—**por su o.,** in its turn. **II.** *f.* order, command; order of knighthood and the insignia.— *pl.* orders, instructions.—**o. del día,** (mil.) order of the day.—**a la o.,** (com.) to order.—**a la o. de,** *to* the order of.—**a sus órdenes,** at your service. (The polite expression, *en espera de sus órdenes,* often used in commercial letters, means "awaiting your commands," or "your pleasure," and not "your (business) orders," "your custom.")

ordenación, *f.* methodical arrangement; disposition, array; edict, ordinance; clerical ordination; auditor's office; (arch. and art) ordinance, ordonnance.

ordenada, *f.* (geom.) ordinate.

ordenadamente, *adv.* orderly, in order.

ordenado, da, *pp. & a.* ordained, ordinate; methodical; tidy.

ordenador, ra, *n.* ordainer; orderer; auditor.

ordenamiento, *m.* ordaining, regulating; law, edict, ordinance.

ordenancista, *n.* disciplinarian, martinet.

ordenando, ordenante, *m.* (eccl.) ordinand.

ordenanza. I. *f.* method, order; law, statute, ordinance; command; ordination. **II.** *m.* (mil.) orderly; (arch. and art) ordinance, ordonnance.

ordenar. I. *va.* to arrange, put in order; to order, command; to ordain, confer holy orders on. **II.** *vr.* (eccl.) to be ordained.

ordeñadero, *m.* milk pail; milking place.—**ordeñadero, ra,** *n.* milker.

ordeñar, *va.* to milk; to pick (olives).

ordinal, *n. & a.* ordinal.

ordinariamente, *adv.* ordinarily; rudely.

ordinariez, *f.* rough manners, ordinariness.

ordinario, ria. I. *a.* ordinary; coarse, unrefined. **II.** *m.* daily household expense; mail, post, courier; (eccl.) ordinary (judge); bishop.—**de o.,** usually, ordinarily.

ordinativo, va, *a.* ordering, regulating; ordinative.

orea, oréada, oréade, *f.* oread, wood nymph.

oreante, *a.* cooling, refreshing.

orear. I. *va.* to air, expose to the air, aerate. **II.** *vr.* to take an airing.

orégano, *m.* (bot.) wild marjoram.

oreja, *f.* (external) ear; hearing; flap of a shoe; flatterer, talebearer; (mech.) lug, flange, ear.— **o. de abad,** or **monje,** (bot.) Venus navelwort.— **o. de oso,** (bot.) primrose.—**o. de ratón,** (bot.) mouse-ear.—**o. de ancla,** (naut.) fluke of an anchor.—**o. marina,** a European gasteropod.—**o. de mercader,** (coll.) deaf ears.—**apearse por las orejas,** (coll.) to give an absurd answer.—**bajar las orejas,** to yield, to come down from one's perch.—**calentar las orejas a, **to chide, dress down.—**con las orejas caídas,** crestfallen, dejected.—**ver las orejas al lobo,** to be in great peril.

orejano, na, *a.* unbranded or motherless (calf).

orejeado, da, *pp. & a.* informed, advised, warned.

orejear, *vn.* to shake or prick the ears; to act with reluctance; to whisper.

orejera, *f.* ear muff, earcap; oreillette; ear hoop; moldboard of a plow.

orejeta, *f. dim.* small ear, lug, or flange.

orejita, *f. dim.* small auricle or ear.

orejón, *m.* pull by the ear; (Peru) privileged noble; Inca; (S. Am.) countryman, rancher; (fort.) orillon.

orejudo, da, *a.* flap-eared, long-eared.

oreo, *m.* breeze, fresh air; airing.

orfanato, *m.* orphan asylum, orphanage.

orfandad, *f.* orphanage.

orfebre, *m.* goldsmith, silversmith.

orfebrería, *f.* gold or silver work.

orfeón, *m.* singing society.

orfeonista, *m.* member of a singing society.

órfico, ca, *a.* Orphean.

organdí, *m.* organdy.

organero, ra, *n.* organ maker; organ builder.

orgánicamente, *adv.* organically.

organicismo, *m.* (med.) organicism.

organicista, *m. & a.* organicist (-ic).

orgánico, ca, *a.* organic; harmonious.

organillo, *m. dim.* barrel organ, hand organ.

organismo, *m.* organism; organization, association.

organista, *n.* (mus.) organist.

organizable, *a.* organizable.

organización, *f.* organization; arrangement.

organizado, da, *pp. & a.* organized, constituted.

organizar, *va.* (*pret.* ORGANICÉ: *subj.* ORGANICE) to organize, constitute; to tune (an organ).

órgano, *m.* (mus.) organ, pipe organ; pipe refrigerator; (physiol.) organ; medium, instrument, agency.—**órganos de Móstoles,** said of persons or ideas that disagree.—**organos genitales** genitals.

organogenia, *f.* (biol.) organogenesis.

organografía, *f.* organography.

organográfico, ca, *a.* organographic.

organología, *f.* organology.

orgasmo, *m.* (physiol.) orgasm.

orgía, *f.* orgy, revel.

orgullo, *m.* pride; haughtiness.

orgullosamente, *adv.* proudly; haughtily.

orgulloso, sa, *a.* proud; haughty, overbearing; conceited.

orientación, *f.* orientation; bearings.

oriental. I. *a.* oriental, eastern. **II.** *m.* oriental.

orientalismo, *m.* orientalism.

orientalista, *n.* orientalist.

orientar. I. *va.* to orientate, to orient.—**o. una vela,** (naut.) to trim a sail. **II.** *vr.* to find one's bearings.

oriente, *m.* east, orient; east wind; source, origin; youth.

orificación, *f.* (dent.) gold filling.

orificador, *m.* dentist's plugger.

orificar, *va.* (dent.) to fill with gold.

orifice, *m.* goldsmith.

orificio, *m.* orifice, hole; anus; (arti.) venthole; (mach.) port.

oriflama, *f.* oriflamme; flag, banner.

origen, *m.* origin; source; native country; beginning.

origenismo, *m.* Origenism.

origenista, *n.* & *a.* Origenist (-ic).
original. I. *a.* original; primitive; new, novel; quaint, odd. **II.** *m.* original, first copy, archetype; (print.) copy, manuscript; person represented in a portrait; odd person.—**de buen o.**, from good authority.
originalidad, *f.* originality.
originalmente, *adv.* originally.
originar. I. *va.* to originate, create, invent. **II.** *vr.* to originate, arise, spring.
originariamente, *adv.* primarily, originally.
originario, ria, *a.* originating; native; derived.
orilla, *f.* border, margin; edge; bank (of a river); shore; sidewalk; fresh breeze.—**a la o.**, near a place, on the brink.—**salir a la o.**, to overcome difficulties.
orillar. I. *va.* to arrange, settle; to evade; to surmount. **II.** *vn.* to leave a selvage on cloth; (sew.) to border. **III.** *vr.* & *vn.* to reach the shore.
orillo, *m.* selvage or list of cloth.
orín, *m.* rust.—*pl.* **(orines)** urine.
orina, *f.* urine.
orinal, *m.* urinal; chamber pot.
orinar, *va.* & *vn.* to urinate.
oriniento, ta, *a.* rusty, mouldy.
orinque, *m.* (naut.) buoy rope.
oriol, *m.* (orn.) golden oriole or thrush.
Orión, *m.* (ast.) Orion.
oriundo, da, *a.* native, coming (from.).
orla, *f.* list, selvage, border, fringe, trimming; (her.) orle; (typ.) ornamental border.
orlador, ra, *n.* borderer.
orladura, *f.* border, edging, list.
orlar, *va.* to border, garnish with an edging.
orleanista, *n.* & *a.* Orleanist (-ic).
orlo, *m.* Alpine horn; (mus.) organ stop; (arch.) plinth.
ormesí, *m.* a kind of silk stuff.
ormino, *m.* (bot.) = GALLOCRESTA.
ornadamente, *adv.* ornamentally.
ornado, da, *a.* & *pp.* ornamented, ornate.
ornamentación, *f.* ornamentation.
ornamentar, *va.* to adorn, decorate.
ornamento, *m.* ornament; decoration, adornment; accomplishment, gift.—*pl.* (eccl.) sacred vestments; (arch.) frets, mouldings, etc.; moral qualities, character.
ornar, *va.* to adorn, embellish, garnish.
ornato, *m.* ornament, decoration, embellishment.
ornitodelfo, fa. I. *n.* & *a.* (zool.) prototherian. **II.** *m. pl.* Prototheria.
ornitología, *f.* ornithology.—**ornitológico, ca,** *a.* ornithological.—**ornitólogo,** *m.* ornithologist.
ornitomancia, *f.* ornithomancy.
ornitorrinco, *m.* (zool.) ornithorhynchus, duck-bill.
oro, *m.* gold; gold color; ornaments or trinkets made of gold.—*pl.* diamonds, in Spanish cards. —**o. batido,** leaf gold.—**o. bruto,** bullion.—**o. coronario,** high-carat gold.—**o. en barra,** bar-gold, gold in bars.—**o. en libritos,** gold leaf.—**o. en pasta =** o. BRUTO.—**o. en polvo,** gold dust.— **o. fulminante,** gold fulminate.—**o. mate,** gold size.—**o. musivo,** mosaic gold, aurum musivum.— **o. nativo,** native gold.—**o. virgen =** o. BRUTO.— **de o. y azul,** gorgeously attired.—**poner (a uno) de o. y azul,** (coll.) to give (one) a good dressing down, a lecture, or severe reprimand.
orobanca, *f.* (bot.) broom rape.
orobancáceas, *f. pl.* (bot.) Orobanchaceæ.
orobias, *m.* fine incense.
orogenia, *f.* (geol.) orogeny.—**orogénico, ca,** *a.* orogenic.—**orografía,** *f.* orography.—**orográfico, ca,** *a.* orographic.
orondo, da, *a.* pompous, showy; hollow.
oropel, *m.* tinsel; brass foil; glitter.
oropelero, *m.* brass worker.
oropéndola, *f.* (orn.) loriot, golden oriole.
oropimente, *m.* (min.) orpiment.
oroya, *f.* (Am.) hanging basket for carrying passengers over rope bridges.
orozuz, *m.* (bot.) licorice.

orquesta, *f.* (mus.) orchestra; (theat.) place for the orchestra.
orquestación, *f.* orchestration.
orquestar, *va.* to orchestrate.
orquídeo, dea. I. *a.* (bot.) orchidaceous. **II.** *f.* orchid. **III.** *f. pl.* Orchidaceæ, orchids.
orquitis, *f.* (med.) orchitis.
orre.—en o., loose, in bulk.
ortega, *f.* (orn.) hazel grouse.
ortiga, *f.* (bot.) nettle.—**o. de mar,** (icht.) sea nettle.—**ser como unas ortigas,** to be as cross as a bear.
ortivo, va, *a.* (ast.) oriental, eastern, ortive.
orto, *m.* rising (of the sun or a star).
ortoclasa, *f.* (min.) orthoclase.
ortodoxia, *f.* orthodoxy.
ortodoxo, xa, *a.* orthodox.
ortodromia, *f.* (naut.) orthodromy.
ortodrómico, ca, *a.* (naut.) orthodromic.
ortogonal, *a.* orthogonal.
ortogonio, *a.* orthogonal, right-angled.
ortografía, *f.* orthography.
ortográficamente, *adv.* orthographically.
ortográfico, ca, *a.* orthographical.
ortógrafo, *m.* orthographer.
ortología, *f.* orthoepy, art of pronunciation.
ortológico, ca, *a.* orthoepic.
ortólogo, ga, *n.* orthoepist.
ortopedia, *f.* (med.) orthopedia.
ortopédico, ca, *a.* (med.) orthopedic.
ortopedista, *n.* orthopedist.
ortóptero. I. *a.* orthopterous. **II.** *m. pl.* Orthoptera.
ortorrómbico, ca, *a.* orthorhombic.
ortosa, *f.* (min.) orthoclase.
oruga, *f.* (bot.) rocket; (ent.) caterpillar.
orujo, *m.* bagasse or refuse of grapes, cotton seed, olives, etc.; mure, murk.
orvalle, *m.* (bot.) = GALLOCRESTA.
orza, *f.* gallipot, preserve jar, crock; (naut.) luff. **o. a la banda,** (naut.) hard a-lee.—**a o.**, (naut.) luff.—**orzada,** *f.* (naut.) luffing, hauling.
orzaderas, *f. pl.* (naut.) leeboards.
orzaga, *f.* (bot.) orach; mountain spinach.
orzar, *vn.* (naut.) to luff.
orzaya, *f.* nurse.
orzuelo, *m.* (med.) sty; hordeolum; snare (for birds); trap (for wild beasts).
orzura, *f.* (chem.) minium.
os, *pers. pron.* dative and accusative *of* VOS *and* VOSOTROS: you, to you.
osa, *f.* (zool.) she-bear.—**O. Mayor,** Great Bear, the Dipper.—**O. Menor,** Little Bear.
osadamente, *adv.* boldly, daringly.
osadía, *f.* audacity, daring, boldness.
osado, da, *pp.* & *a.* daring, bold, audacious.
osambre, *m.*, **osamenta,** *f.* skeleton; bones.
osar, *vn.* to dare, venture, outdare.
osar, osario, *m.* charnel house; ossarium, ossuary.
oscilación, *f.* oscillation.—**oscilante,** *a.* oscillating.—**oscilar,** *vn.* to oscillate.—**oscilatorio, ria,** *a.* oscillatory.
oscitancia, *f.* carelessness, heedlessness.
ósculo, *m.* kiss.
oscurantismo, oscurecer, oscuro, etc. = OBS-CURANTISMO, etc.
osecico, cillo, cito, zuelo, *m. dim.* small bone.
oseína, *f.* (chem.) ossein.
óseo, a, *a.* osseous, bony.
osera, *f.* den of bears.
osezno, *m.* whelp or cub of a bear.
osificación, *f.* ossification.
osificarse, *vr.* to ossify, become ossified.
osífico, ca, *a.* ossific.
osífraga, *f.*; **osífrago,** *m.* (orn.) osprey.
osmazomo, *m.* osmazome.
osmio, *m.* (chem.) osmium.
ósmosis, *f.* (phys.) osmosis.
oso, *m.* (zool.) bear.—**o. blanco,** polar bear.—**o. colmenero,** honey-eating bear, bear that robs bee-hives.—**o. de las cavernas,** (pal.) cave bear.—**o. hormiguero,** anteater.—**o. marino,** fur seal.—**o.**

marítimo = o. BLANCO.—**hacer el o.**, (coll.) to make a fool of one's self; to act as a sentimental lover.
ososo, sa, *f.* osseous, bony.
osta, *f.* (naut.) lateen brace.
ostaga, *f.* (naut.) tie, runner.
¡oste! *interj.* = OXTE.
osteitis, *f.* (med.) osteitis.
ostensible, *a.* ostensible.—**ostensiblemente,** *adv.* ostensibly.
ostensión, *f.* show, manifestation.
ostensivo, va, *a.* ostensive, showy.
ostentación, *f.* ostentation, vain show.
ostentador, ra, *n.* boaster, ostentatious person.
ostentar. I. *va.* to make a show of, to exhibit. **II.** *vn.* to boast, to brag; to be fond of vain shows.
ostentativo, va, *a.* ostentatious.
ostento, *m.* portent, prodigy.
ostentosamente, *adv.* ostentatiously.
ostentoso, sa, *a.* sumptuous, ostentatious.
osteogenia, osteogénesis, *f.* osteogeny, osteogenesis.
osteología, *f.* (anat.) osteology.
osteológico, ca, *a.* osteologic.
osteoma, *m.* (med.) osteoma.
osteomalacia, *f.* (med.) osteomalacia.
osteópata, *n.* osteopath.
ostiario, *m.* (eccl.) ostiary, doorkeeper.
ostión, *m.* large oyster.
ostra, *f.* oyster.
ostracismo, *m.* ostracism.
ostral, *m.* oyster farm, oyster bed.—**ostrería,** *f.* oyster shop, oyster house.—**ostrero, ra. I.** *a.* ostreaceous. **II.** *m.* oysterman. **III.** *f.* oyster farm; oysterwoman.—**ostricultura,** *f.* oyster farming, ostriculture.—**ostrífero, ra,** *a.* ostriferous.
ostro, *m.* large, coarse oyster; south wind; any mollusc that yields purple; purple from mollusca.
ostrogodo, da, *n.* & *a.* Ostrogoth (-ic).
ostrón, *m.* aug. large, coarse oyster.
ostugo, *m.* piece, part, bit; corner.
osudo, da, *a.* bony.
osuno, na, *a.* bearlike, bearish.
otalgia, *f.* (med.) otalgia, earache.
otáñez, *m.* (coll.) old squire who escorted a lady as chaperon.
oteador, ra, *n.* spy, sly observer.
otear, *va.* to observe, examine, pry into.
otero, *m.* hill, hillock, knoll.
oteruelo, *m.* *dim.* hummock, knoll, mound.
otitis, *f.* (med.) otitis.
oto, *m.* (orn.) bustard, otis.
otoba, *f.* (bot.) a variety of nutmeg tree.
otología, *f.* (med.) otology.
otomano, na. I. *n.* & *a.* Ottoman. **II.** *f.* ottoman, divan.
otoñada, *f.* autumn season; pasturage.
otoñal, *a.* autumnal.
otoñar. I. *vn.* to spend the autumn season; to grow in autumn (s. o. weeds). **II.** *vr.* to be seasoned (s. o. the earth after rain).
otoño, *m.* autumn, fall; aftermath.
otorgadero, ra, *a.* grantable.
otorgador, ra, *n.* grantor.
otorgamiento, *m.* grant, granting; license; (law) executing an instrument.
otorgante. I. *a.* authorizing, granting. **II.** *n.* grantor, maker of a deed.
otorgar, *va.* (pret. OTORGUÉ: subj. OTORGUE) to consent, agree to; (law) to grant; to prescribe, stipulate, promise.—**quien calla otorga,** silence gives consent.
otorgo, *m.* (law) marriage contract.
otorrea, *f.* (med.) otorrhœa.
otoscopia, *f.* (surg.) otoscopy.
otoscopio, *m.* (surg.) otoscope.
otramente, *adv.* otherwise, differently.
otro, tra, *a.* another, other.—**¡o.!** encore! again!—**o. que tal,** (coll.) another such.
otrosí. I. *adv.* besides, moreover. **II.** *m.* (law) every petition made after the principal.

ova, *f.* (bot.) sea lettuce, laver.
ovación, *f.* ovation.
ovacionar, *va.* to give an ovation to.
ovado, da, *a.* & *pp.* fecundated by the male bird; oval, egg-shaped.
oval; ovalado, da, *a.* oval.—**ovalar,** *va.* to make oval.—**óvalo,** *m.* oval.
ovante, *a.* victorious, triumphant.
ovar, *vn.* to lay eggs.
ovárico, ca, *a.* ovarian.
ovario, *m.* (anat.) ovary; (bot.) ovarium, ovary; (arch.) egg ornament.
ovariotomía, *f.* (surg.) ovariotomy.
ovaritis, *f.* (med.) ovaritis.
ovas, *f.* *pl.* roe. *V.* HUEVAS.
ovecico, *m.* *dim.* small egg.
oveja, *f.* sheep.
ovejero, ra, *n.* shepherd (-ess); sheep raiser.
ovejuela, *f.* *dim.* young ewe, hoggerel.
ovejuno, na, *a.* relating to sheep, sheep (u. a.).
overo, ra. I. *a.* blossom-colored.(horse); bulging (eyes) with large sclerotica. **II.** *f.* ovary of fowls.
ovezuelo, *m.* small egg.
óvidos, *m.* *pl.* (zool.) Ovidæ.
oviducto, *m.* (anat.) oviduct.
oviforme, *a.* oviform, egg-shaped.
ovil, *m.* sheepcote. *V.* REDIL.
ovillar. I. *va.* to wind (thread) in a clew, to clew. **II.** *vr.* to shrug one's self into a bunch.
ovillejo, *m.* *dim.* small clew; a kind of rondel.
ovillo, *m.* clew, ball of yarn; ball or heap of mixed or tangled things.—**hacerse un o.,** to shrug one's self into a bunch.
ovíparo, ra, *a.* oviparous.
ovoide, a. ovoid, egg-shaped.
óvolo, *m.* (arch.) ovolo; quarter round.
ovoso, sa, *a.* full of roe.
ovovivíparo, ra, *a.* ovoviviparous.
ovulación, *f.* (biol.) ovulation.
óvulo, m. ovule.
¡ox! *interj.* shoo! begone!
oxácido, *m.* (chem.) oxacid.
oxalato, *m.* (chem.) oxalate.
oxálico, a. (chem.) oxalic.
oxalídeas, *f.* *pl.* (bot.) Oxalidaceæ.
oxalme, *m.* acidulated brine.
oxear, *va.* to shoo (fowls).
oxhídrico, ca, *a.* oxyhydrogen.
oxiacanta, *f.* (bot.) whitethorn, hawthorn.
oxidable, *a.* (chem.) oxidizable.
oxidación, *f.* (chem.) oxidation.
oxidante, *a.* (chem.) oxidating, oxydizing.
oxidar, *va.* & *vr.* to oxidize; to rust.
óxido, *m.* (chem.) oxide.
oxigenable, *a.* (chem.) oxygenizable.
oxigenación, *f.* (chem.) oxygenation.
oxigenar, *va.* & *vr.* to oxygenate.
oxígeno, *m.* (chem.) oxygen.
oxigonio, *a.* (geom.) acute-angled.
oximel, oximiel, *m.* = OJIMIEL.
oxipétalo, *m.* (bot.) a Brazilian vine.
oxizacre, *m.* bittersweet beverage.
¡oxte! *interj.* keep off! begone!—**sin decir o. ni moxte,** (coll.) without saying a word.
oyamel, *m.* (bot.) Mexican sacred fir.
oyente, *n.* hearer.—*pl.* audience.
ozona, *f.*; **ozono,** *m.* (chem.) ozone.
ozonización, *f.* ozonization.
ozonizador, ra. I. *a.* ozonizing. **II.** *n.* ozonizer
ozonizar, *va.* to ozonize.
ozonómetro, *m.* ozone paper.

P

pabellón, *m.* pavilion; (mil.) bell tent; esparver, dais, bed canopy; summer house; national colors, flag; bell of a wind instrument; (anat.) external ear, pinna.—**p. de armas,** (mil.) stack of arms.
pabilo, pábilo, *m.* wick; snuff of a candle.

pabilón, *m.* bunch of flax or wool hanging from the distaff.
pablar, *vn.* (coll.) to talk.
pábulo, *m.* pabulum, food; encouragement.
paca, *f.* (zool.) spotted cavy; bale of goods.
pacana, *f.* (bot.) pecan; pecan nut.
pacato, ta, *a.* pacific, quiet, tranquil, mild.
paceduro, ra, *a.* pasturable, fit for pasture.
pacedura, *f.* pasture.
paceño, ña, *a.* of or from La Paz, Bolivia.
pacer. I. *vn.* (*for irr. v.* NACER) to pasture, to graze. **II.** *va.* to gnaw, nibble, eat away.
paciencia, *f.* patience; a kind of cooky.
paciente. I. *a.* patient. **II.** *n.* patient, sick person.
pacientemente, *adv.* patiently.
pacienzudo, da, *a.* exceedingly patient.
pacificación, *f.* pacification; peace of mind.
pacificador, ra, *n.* pacifier, peacemaker.
pacíficamente, *adv.* peacefully.
pacificar. I. *va.* (*pret.* PACIFIQUÉ: *subj.* PACIFIQUE) to pacify, appease. **II.** *vn.* to treat for peace. **III.** *vr.* to become calm.
pacífico, ca, *a.* peaceful; mild, gentle.
pacifismo, *m.* pacifism.
pacifista, *n. & a.* pacifist (-ic).
paco, *m.* (zool.) paco, alpaca; (Ch.) police force; (min.) paco.
pacotilla, *f.* (com.) venture.—**de p.,** of poor or inferior quality.
pactar, *va.* to covenant, contract, stipulate.
pacto, *m.* agreement, covenant, pact.
pacú, *m.* (Arg.) a river fish.
pácul, *m.* (Philip.) (bot.) wild plantain.
pachamanca, *f.* (Peru) barbecue.
pachón, *m.* phlegmatic man; pointer (dog).
pachorra, *f.* sluggishness, slowness.
pachorrudo, da, *a.* (coll.) sluggish, slow.
padecer. I. *va.* (*ind.* PADEZCO: *subj.* PADEZCA) to suffer; feel deeply; to lie under. **II.** *vn.* to suffer.
—**padecimiento,** *m.* suffering.
padilla, *f.* small frying pan; small oven.
padrastro, *m.* stepfather; obstacle, impediment; hangnail.
padrazo, *m.* *aug.* indulgent parent.
padre, *m.* father; ancestor; stallion, sire; source, origin, principal author; (eccl.) father.—*pl.* parents, father and mother; ancestors.—**p. de familia,** paterfamilias, father of a family.—**p. de pila,** godfather.—**P. Eterno,** God Almighty, our Father.—**p. nuestro,** Lord's Prayer.—**P. Santo,** Holy Father (the Pope).—**Santo P.,** Holy Father (the Pope); (ecc.) father (of the Church), one of the early Christian writers.
padrear, *vn.* to resemble one's father; to breed.
padrenuestro, *m.* Lord's Prayer.
padrinazgo, *m.* compaternity; title or charge of a godfather; patronage.
padrino, *m.* godfather; second, in a duel; groomsman; patron, protector.
padrón, *m.* poll, census or tax list; pattern, model; column or post with an inscription; mark or note of infamy; (coll.) indulgent parent.
paella, *f.* dish of rice with meat or chicken.
¡paf! *interj.* onomatopœic, expressing the noise of a fall, blow, etc.
paflagonio, nia, *n. & a.* Paphlagonian.
pafón, *m.* (arch.) soffit.
paga, *f.* payment; fee, wages, salary; pay; satisfaction, amends; sum or fine paid; requital of love or friendship.
pagadero. ra. I. *a.* payable. **II.** *m.* time and place of payment.
pagado, da, *pp., a.* paid; satisfied; conceited.
pagador, ra, *n.* payer; paymaster; paying teller.
—**pagaduría,** *f.* paymaster's office; disbursement office.
paganismo, *m.* paganism, heathenism.
pagano, na, *n. & a.* heathen, pagan.
pagar. I. *va.* (*pret.* PAGUÉ: *subj.* PAGUE) to pay; to requite; to atone, make amends for; to fee.—

p. con el pellejo, (coll.) to pay with one's life.—
p. el pato, to have it put off on one, to get the blame or be made the scapegoat.—**pagarlas, to** pay for it.—**p. una visita,** to return a visit. **II.** *va.* to pay. **III.** *vr.* (w. de) to be pleased (with); to boast (of); to be conceited (about); to be fond (of).
pagaré, *m.* (com.) promissory note.
pagaya, *f.* (Philip.) single-bladed paddle.
página, *f.* page (of a book); folio.
paginación, *f.* pagination, paging.
paginar, *va.* to page, paginate.
pago. I. *m.* payment; requital; vineyard district
II. *a.* (coll.) paid.
pagoda, *f.* pagoda; idol.
pagote, *m.* (coll.) scapegoat.
pagro, *m.* (icht.) braize.
paguro, *m.* small crab.
paico, *m.* (S. Am.) (bot.) saltwort.
paila, *f.* caldron; kettle; boiler; (Cuba) evaporator, sugar pan.
pailebot, pailebote, *m.* (naut.) pilot's boat.
painel, *m.* (carp.) panel.
pairar, *vn.* (naut.) to bring to, to lie to.
pairo, *m.* (naut.) lying to with all sail set.—**al p.,** lying to.
país, *m.* country, nation; land, region; (art) landscape.—**del p.,** domestic, national.
paisaje, *m.* landscape.
paisajista, *n.* landscape painter.
paisanaje, *m.* peasantry; being of the same country.
paisano, na. I. *a.* from the same country. **II.** *n.* fellow countryman (-woman), compatriot; civilian. **III.** *f.* a kind of country dance.
paisista, *n.* = PAISAJISTA.
paja, *f.* straw; blade of grass; chaff, shucks, trash.
—**p. centenaza,** rye straw.—**¡pajas!** ditto, no less so.—**echar pajas,** to draw lots with straws.—**en un dácame,** or **quítame, allá esas pajas,** in the twinkling of an eye.—**no dormirse en las pajas,** to be very vigilant.—**por quítame allá esas pajas,** (to quarrel) for a straw, over the smallest trifle.
pajado, da. I. *a.* straw-colored. **II.** *f.* straw boiled with bran.
pajar, *m.* barn, straw loft; rick of straw.
pájara, *f.* female or hen bird; shrewd, designing woman; paper kite; paper rooster (toy).—**p. pinta,** game of forfeits.
pajarear, *vn.* to go birdcatching; to loiter about;
—*pl.* to be skittish (s. o. horses).
pajarel, *m.* (orn.) linnet. *V.* JILGUERO.
pajarera, *f.* aviary; large bird cage.
pajarería, *f.* abundance of birds; place where birds are sold.
pajarero, ra. I. *a.* merry, cheerful, gay; gaudy, loud. **II.** *n.* birdcatcher, bird fancier.
pajarete, *m.* fine sherry wine.
pajarico, ca, ito, ta, *n.* little bird.
pajaril, *m.* (naut.) passaree or passarado.
pajarilla, lla. I. *n. dim.* small bird. **II.** *f.* paper rooster (toy); spleen; milt of a hog.
pájaro, *m.* bird; shrewd, sly fellow.—**p. bobo,** (orn.) booby; penguin.—**p. carpintero,** (orn.) woodpecker.—**p. del sol,** bird of paradise.—**p. gordo,** person of importance, big gun.—**p. loco** = F. SOLITARIO.—**p. mosca,** a very small humming bird.—**p. niño,** auk.—**p. polilla,** kingfisher.—**p. solitario,** solitary thrush.—**más vale p. en mano que buitre volando,** a bird in the hand is worth two in the bush.
pajarota, pajarotada, *f.* hoax.
pajarote, *m.* large ugly bird.
pajarraco, *m.* large bird; (coll.) sharper.
pajaruco, *m.* large ugly bird.
pajaza, *f.* refuse of fodder.
pajazo, *m.* prick of stubbles in a horse's eye.
paje, *m.* page, valet; (naut.) cabin boy.—**p. de hacha,** link boy.
pajear, *vn.* to feed well; (coll.) to behave.
pajecillo, *m. dim.* little page; washstand.
pajel, *m.* (icht.) red sea bream.
pajera, *f.* straw loft, straw yard.
pajero, ra, *n.* straw dealer.

pajilla, _f. dim._ cigar made of maize leaf; rattan.

pajizo, za, _a._ made of straw; thatched with straw; straw-colored.

pajón, _m. aug._ coarse straw.

pajonal, _m._ (Am.) place abounding in tall grass.

pajoso, sa, _a._ made or full of straw.

pajote, _m._ straw interwoven with bulrush.

pajucero, _m._ place where straw is deposited to rot for fertilizer.

pajuela, _f. dim._ short straw; sulphur match.

pajuil, _m._ (P. Rico) (bot.) = MARAÑÓN.

pajuncio, _m._ booby, ninny, fool.

pajuz, pajuzo, _m._ refuse of straw used for manure.

pala, _f._ shovel; baker's peel; scoop; slice, turnover; beetle for pounding clothes; dustpan; blade of an oar; blade of a hoe or spade; racket (for ball games); (shoe.) vamp; leaf of a hinge; top of an epaulet; flat surface of the teeth; craft, cunning, artifice; dexterity, cleverness; (bot.) leaf of the prickly pear.—**meter su media p.,** to have or get a share.—**ser corta p.,** to know nothing.

palabra, _f._ word; term; floor (as in _tener la palabra_, to have the floor); (mil.) password.—_pl._ superstitious words used by sorcerers; (eccl.) formula of the sacraments; table on which the words of consecration are written.—**p. de matrimonio,** promise of marriage.—**p. llana,** (gram.) word having the accent on the penultimate.—**palabras mayores,** a serious matter; insulting words.—**a media p.,** at the least hint.—**bajo p.,** on word.—**de p.,** by word of mouth.—**empeñar la p.,** to pledge one's word.—**llevar la p.,** to be the spokesman.—**medias palabras,** insinuation, hint.—**santa p.,** cheerful words, good news (used to express pleasure on hearing something).

¡palabra! _interj._ I say, a word with you.

palabrada, _f._ low, scurrilous language.

palabreja, _f. dim._ odd word.

palabrería, _f._ wordiness, empty talk.

palabrero, ra, _a._ talkative, loquacious.

palabrimujer, _m._ (coll.) man with an effeminate voice.

palabrista, _n._ chatterbox.

palabrita, _f. dim._ few words; short word or expression full of meaning.—**palabritas mansas,** (coll.) honeymouthed person.

palabrota, _f. aug._ coarse expression; big word.

palaciego, ga. I. _a._ pertaining to the palace. **II.** _n._ courtier.

palacio, _m._ palace; castle.

palacra, palacrana, _f._ gold nugget.

palada, _f._ shovelful; (naut.) stroke of the oar.

paladar, _m._ palate; roof of the mouth; taste, relish; longing desire.

paladear. I. _va._ to taste with pleasure, to relish; to rub the palate of with a sweet substance; to clean the mouth or palate of. **II.** _vn._ to show a desire of sucking (s. o. a newborn child).

paladeo, _m._ act of tasting or relishing.

paladial, _a._ (gram.) palatal.

paladín, _m._ paladin, valiant knight, champion.

paladinamente, _adv._ publicly, clearly.

paladino, na. I. _a._ manifest, clear, apparent, public. **II.** _m._ PALADÍN.

paladio, _m._ (chem.) palladium.

paladión, _m._ palladium; safeguard.

palado, da, _a._ (her.) pale.

palafito, _m._ primitive lake dwelling.

palafrén, _m._ palfrey; woman's horse; groom's horse.

palafrenero, _m._ stableboy, groom, hostler.—**p. mayor,** first equerry.

palahierro, _m._ bushing for the spindle of the upper millstone.

palamallo, _m._ pall-mall (a game).

palamenta, _f._ (naut.) set of oars.

palanca, _f._ (mech.) lever; bar, crowbar; pole for carrying a weight; (fort.) outer fortification with stakes; (naut.) garnet tackle.

palancada, _f._ stroke with a lever.

palancana, palangana, _f._ washbowl.

palanganero, _m._ washstand.

palangre, _m._ line with several fishhooks.

palanquera, _f._ stockade; log fence.

palanquero, _m._ pile driver; blower of bellows.

palanqueta, _f. dim._ small lever; (mil.) bar shot or crossbar shot; (Cuba) sweetmeat with cane sirup; dumb-bell.

palanquín, _m._ public porter; (naut.) double tackle, clew garnet; palanquin, covered litter.

palastro, _m._ sheet iron, sheet metal.

palatina, _f._ tippet, boa used by women.

palatinado, _m._ palatinate.

palatino, na, _a._ palatial; palatine; palatal.

palay, _m._ (Philip.) unhusked rice.

palazo, _m._ blow with a shovel, spade or stick.

palazón, _m._ (naut.) masting; woodwork.

palco, _m._ (theat.) box; stand with seats.—**p. escénico,** (theat.) the stage.

paleador, _m._ shoveler; stoker.

palear, _va._ to beat, pound. _V._ APALEAR.

palenque, _m._ palisade, paling; (theat.) passage from pit to stage.

paleografía, _f._ paleography.

paleográfico, ca, _a._ paleographic.

paleógrafo, _m._ paleographer.

paleolítico, ca, _a._ paleolithic.

paleontografía, _f._ paleontography.

paleontográfico, ca, _a._ paleontographic.

paleontología, _f._ paleontology.

paleontológico, ca, _a._ paleontological.

paleontólogo, _m._ paleontologist.

paleozoico, ca, _a._ Paleozoic.

palería, _f._ art and business of draining.

palero, _m._ shoveler; ditcher, drainer; pioneer; shovel maker or seller.

palestina, _f._ (print.) two-line small pica.

palestino, na, _n. & a._ Palestinian.

palestra, _f._ wrestling court, palæstra; gymnasium; tournament, competition.

paléstrico, ca, _a._ palestric, palestrical.

palestrita, _m._ wrestler, athlete.

paleta, _f. dim._ little shovel; fire shovel; (cook.) iron ladle; (mas.) trowel; (anat.) shoulder blade; (hydr.) paddle board; blade; (art) palette.—**de p.,** opportunely.—**en dos paletas,** (coll.) shortly, briefly.

paletada, _f._ trowelful of mortar.

paletazo, _m._ thrust of a bull's horn.

paletear, _vn._ (naut.) to row ineffectively; to revolve without gaining speed.

paleteo, _m._ flapping of oars or paddleboards.

paletilla, _f. dim._ of PALETA; (anat.) cartilage of the sternum or xiphoid; shoulderblade; low candlestick.

paleto, _m._ fallow deer; rustic, hayseed.

paletó, _m._ overcoat, greatcoat.

paletón, _m._ bit of a key.

paletoque, _m._ paletocque, defensive jacket.

pali, _m._ Pali, an ancient language of India.

palia, _f._ (eccl.) altar cloth; curtain or screen before the tabernacle; pall.

paliación, _f._ palliation, extenuation.

paliadamente, _adv._ dissemblingly.

paliar, _va._ to palliate, extenuate, excuse.

paliativo, va; paliatorio, ria, _a._ palliative, mitigating; that may be palliated.

palidecer, _vn._ to pale, turn pale.—**palidez,** _f._ paleness, pallor.—**pálido, da,** _a._ pale, ghastly.

palillo, _m. dim._ small stick; knitting needle case; toothpick; bobbin for network or lace; drumstick; tobacco stem; (coll.) chitchat.—_pl._ small pins put on the billiard table in certain games; rudiments, first principles; (coll.) trifles; castanets.

palimpsesto, _m._ palimpsest.

palingenesia, _f._ palingenesis, new birth.

palinodia, _f._ palinode, public recantation.

palio, _m._ cloak, mantle; (eccl.) pallium; pall; dais, canopy; prize for racing.

palique, _m._ (coll.) chitchat, small talk.

palisandro, _m._ rosewood, palisander.

palillo, to, _m. dim._ little stick.

palitoque, palitroque, _m._ rough little stick.

paliza, _f._ cudgelling, caning, bastinado.

palizada, *f.* palisade, palisado; paling; (fort.) stockade.

palma, *f.* palm tree; leaf of a palm tree; palmetto; palm of the hand; (vet.) under surface of the hoof; emblem of victory or martyrdom; pre-eminence.—**p. brava,** (Philip.) (bot.) fan palm.— **andar en palmas,** to be universally applauded.— **ganar,** or **llevarse, la p.,** to carry the day; to win the prize.

palmáceo, a. I. *a.* (bot.) palmaceous. **II.** *f. pl.* Phœnicaceæ, Palmaceæ, palms.

palmacristi, *f.* (bot.) castor-oil plant.

palmada, *f.* slap; hand, applause.

palmar, *vn.* to measure by PALMOS; (coll.) to die.

palmar. I. *a.* palmar; measuring a PALMO; obvious, evident. **II.** *m.* palm grove; fuller's thistle.

palmario, ria, *a.* clear, obvious, evident.

palmatoria, *f.* ferule; small candlestick.

palmeado, da, *pp.* & *a.* (orn.) web-footed, palmated; (bot.) palmate.

palmear, *va.* to clap (the hands); to applaud.

palmejar, *m.* (naut.) thick stuff.

palmeo, *m.* measuring by PALMOS.

palmera, *f.* palm tree.

palmero, *m.* palm keeper; palmer, pilgrim.

palmeta, *f.* ferule; slap with the ferule.—**ganar la p.,** to get ahead.

palmetazo, *m.* blow with a ferule.

palmiche, *m.* fruit of a palm tree.

palmífero, ra, *a.* (poet.) palmiferous.

palmilla, *f.* blue woollen cloth; (shoe.) inner sole.

palmípedo, da. I. *a.* web-footed, palmiped. **II.** *f. pl.* Palmatæ, palmipeds.

palmitato, *m.* (chem.) palmitate.

palmítico, ca, *a.* (chem.) palmitic.

palmitieso, *a.* flat-hoofed (horse).

palmito, *m.* (bot.) dwarf fan palm; palmetto; its root; woman's face; (Cuba) sprout of a palm.

palmo, *m.* span, measure of length (8 inches).—**p. a p.,** inch by inch.—**p. menor,** palm, hand, handbreadth (4 inches); span-farthing (boys' game).— **dejar a uno con un p. de narices,** to disappoint one; to leave one in the cold.

palmotear, *vn.* to clap hands, applaud.

palmoteo, *m.* hand clapping, applause.

palo, *m.* stick; cudgel; pole; timber; log; tree; blow with a stick; whack ; execution on the gallows; suit or spot at cards; stalk of fruit, pedicle; hook of a letter; (her.) pale; (naut.) mast.—**p.** billiard pins (= PALILLOS); blows, cudgeling.—**p. áloe,** (bot.) aloes wood, eagle wood.—**p. brasil,** Brazil wood.—**p. campeche,** campeche, logwood. —**p. codal,** stick hung around the neck as a penance.—**p. de Campeche** = P. CAMPECHE.—**p. de hule,** rubber tree.—**p. de jabón,** quillai, soapbark. —**p. del Brasil** = P. BRASIL.—**p. de mesana,** mizzenmast.—**p. de planchar,** ironing board.—**p. de rosa,** rosewood; tulipwood.—**p. de tinte** = P. CAMPECHE.—**p. de trinquete,** foremast.—**p. dulce,** licorice.—**p. mayor,** mainmast.—**p. santo,** lignum-vitæ.—**palos de marca,** spar buoys.—**a p. seco,** (naut.) under bare poles.—**dar (de) palos,** to drub, thrash, cudgel.

paloma, *f.* pigeon; dove; meek, mild person; (P-, ast.) Columba; (naut.) sling of a yard.—*pl.* whitecaps.—**p. brava,** rock dove.—**p. buchona,** pouter.—**p. silvestre** = P. BRAVA.—**p. torcaz,** wild pigeon; ringdove.—**p. zorita,** wood pigeon.

palomadura, *f.* (naut.) boltrope tie.

palomar. I. *a.* hard-twisted (twine). **II.** *m.* pigeon house, dovecot.

palomariego, ga, *a.* domestic (s. o. pigeons).

palomear, *vn.* to shoot or breed pigeons.

palomera, *f.* small dovecot; bleak place.

palomería, *f.* pigeon shooting.

palomero, ra. I. *a.* having long iron points. **II.** *n.* pigeon seller or fancier.

palomilla, *f. dim.* young pigeon; grain moth; little butterfly; chrysalis; backbone of a horse; peak of a packsaddle; milk-white horse; journal bearing; wall bracket; (print.) galley rack; (bot.) common fumitory.—*pl.* whitecaps.

palomina, *f.* pigeon dung; (bot.) fumitory; a variety of black grape.

palomino, *m.* young pigeon.

palomo, *m.* cock pigeon.

palón, *m.* (her.) guidon.

palotada, *f.* stroke with a drumstick.—**no dar p.,** not to do or say a thing right.

palote, *m.* drumstick; down-stroke in penmanship.

paloteado, *pp.* & *m.* a rustic stick dance; noisy scuffle.

palotear, *vn.* to strike sticks against one another; to wrangle.

paloteo, *m.* fight with sticks.

palpable, *a.* palpable, obvious, evident.

palpablemente, *adv.* palpably, evidently.

palpación, palpadura, *f.*; **palpamiento,** *m.* feeling (of something), touching; palpableness; (med.) palpation.

palpar. I. *va.* to feel (of), to touch; to see as self-evident; (med.) to palpate. **II.** *vn.* to feel by touching; have the sense of touch; to grope in the dark.

pálpebra, *f.* eyelid.

palpebral, *a.* palpebral.

palpitación, *f.* palpitation; throbbing.

palpitante, *a.* vibrating, palpitating.

palpitar, *vn.* to palpitate, beat, throb, quiver.

palpo, *m.* palpus, palp, feeler.

paludamento, *m.* paludamentum.

palúdico, ca, *a.* miasmatic; malarial.

paludismo, *m.* (med.) paludism; malaria.

paludoso, sa, *a.* fenny, marshy, swampy.

palumbario, *a.* dove hunting (goshawk).

palurdo, da. I. *a.* rustic, rude. **II.** *n.* boor, rustic.

palustre. I. *a.* marshy, fenny, boggy. **II.** *m.* trowel.

palustrillo, *m.* (mas.) angle float.

pallador, *m.* (S. Am.) minstrel, roving singer.

pallaquear, *va.* (Peru) to extract the richest metallic part of (minerals).

pallete, *m.* (naut.) fender, paunch mat.

pallón, *m.* assay button of gold.

pamandabuán, *m.* (Philip.) pambanmanche, snake boat, a large dugout.

pamela, *f.* low-crowned, wide-brimmed woman's straw hat.

pamena, *f.* (coll.) trifle, bagatelle.

pampa, *f.* pampa, extensive plain.

pámpana, *f.* vine leaf.—**tocar,** or **zurrar, la p.,** (coll.) to thrash.

pampanada, *f.* juice of vine shoots.

pampanaje, *m.* plenty of vine shoots; vain show.

pampanilla, *f.* trunks, loin cloth.

pámpano, *m.* young vine branch or tendril; (icht.) pompano.

pampanoso, sa, *a.* full of tendrils.

pampeano, na. I. *a.* of or from the pampas. **II.** *n.* pampa man (woman).

pampear, *vn.* to travel in or over the pampas.

pampero, ra. I. *n.* pampa man (woman). **II.** *m.* (S. Am.) violent southwest wind.

pampirolada, *f.* garlic sauce; (coll.) silly thing.

pamplina, *f.* (bot.) chickweed; pimpernel; yellow poppy; (coll.) frivolity, trifle.

pamporcino, *m.* (bot.) cyclamen, sowbread.

pamposado, da, *a.* lazy, idle; cowardly.

pampringada, *f.* (*v.* PRINGADA) (coll.) nonsense.

pan, *m.* bread; pie crust; anything in the shape of a loaf, cake, etc.; wheat; wafer; leaf of gold or silver.—*pl.* breadstuffs.—**p. ázimo,** unleavened bread.—**p. bazo,** brown bread.—**p. casero,** home-made bread.—**p. cenceño** = P. ÁZIMO.—**p. de azúcar,** loaf sugar.—**p. candeal,** white-wheat bread.—**p. de cera virgen,** white wax, in cakes.— **p. de flor,** bread made from the choicest flour.—**p. de higos,** fig cake.—**p. de jabón,** cake of soap.— **p. de la boda,** honeymoon; wedding cake.—**p. de oro,** gold leaf.—**p. duro,** or **p. seco,** stale or dry bread.—**p. porcino,** (bot.) sow bread.—**p. terciado,** rent of ground paid in grain, two thirds wheat and one third barley.—**p. tierno,** fresh bread.—**p. y quesillo,** (bot.) shepherd's purse.—**llamar al pan pan y al vino vino,** to call a spade a spade.

pana, *f.* plush, velveteen, corduroy; (naut.) limberboard.

pánace, *f.* (bot.) opopanax.

panacea, *f.* panacea; (pharm.) catholicon.

panadear, *vn.* to make bread.—**panadeo,** *m.* baking bread.—**panadería,** *f.* bakery.—**panadero, ra. I.** *n.* baker. **II.** *f.* baker's wife. **III.** *pl. m.* a kind of dance.

panadizo, *m.* whitlow, felon; (coll.) pale-faced, sickly person.

panado, da, *n.* panada or panado.

panal, *m.* honeycomb; hornet's nest; sponge sugar.—**p. saetero,** honeycomb made across the hive.

panamá, *m.* Panama hat.

panameño, ña, *n.* & *a.* Panamano, Panaman, Panamenian.

panamericanismo, *m.* Pan-Americanism.

panamericano, na, *a.* Pan-American.

panarizo, *m.* = PANADIZO.

panarra, *m.* (coll.) dolt, simpleton.

panatela, *f.* sponge cake.

panática, *f.* (naut.) provision of bread.

panca, *f.* (Am.) corn husk; (Philip.) a fishing-boat.

pancada, *f.* sale in the lump; kick.

pancarpia, *f.* garland of flowers.

pancarta, *f.* panchart.

pancera, *f.* (arm.) belly plate.

pancista, (pol.) one who is on the fence.

panco, *m.* (Philip.) coasting vessel.

pancracio, *m.* pancratium.

pancracista, *m.* pancratiast.

páncreas, *m.* (anat.) pancreas.—**pancreático, ca,** *a.* pancreatic.—**pancreatina,** *f.* pancreatine.

pancho, *m.* (icht.) spawn of ·he sea bream; (coll.) paunch, belly.

panda, *f.* gallery of a cloister.

pandear, *vn.* to bend, warp, belly, bulge out.

pandectas, *f. pl.* (com.) index book; (law) pandects.

pandemia, *f.* (med.) pandemia, an epidemic attacking the majority of people.

pandemónium, *m.* pandemonium.

pandeo, *m.* bulge, bulging.

panderada, *f.* number of tambourine players; stroke with a tambourine; (coll.) nonsense.

pandereta, *f. dim.* tambourine.—**panderete, m.** *dim.* small tambourine.—**panderetear,** *vn.* to play on the tambourine.—**pandereteo,** *m.* beating the tambourine; merriment.—**panderetero, ra, ñ.** tambourine maker, seller, or player.

pandero, *m.,* **pandera,** *f.* (mus.) tambourine; paper kite; (coll.) silly talker.

pandilla, *f.* party, faction; gang, set; picnic.

pandillador, ra; pandillero, ra; pandillista, *n.,* fomenter of factions; leader or member of a gang.

pando, da, *a.* bulged; slow of motion.

pandorga, *f.* (coll.) fat, bulky woman; kite.

panecico, illo, ito, *m.* roll.

panegírico, ca. I. *a.* panegyrical. **II.** *m.* panegyric, eulogy.—**panegirista,** *m.* panegyrist, eulogist.—**panegirizar,** *va.* to panegyrize, eulogize.

panel, *m.* (art, elec.) panel.

panela, *f.* small biscuit; (Colomb.) unrefined brown sugar; (her.) panel.

panera, *f.* granary; pannier; bread basket.

panero, *m.* baker's basket.

paneslavismo, *m.* Pan-Slavism.

paneslavista, *n.* & *a.* Pan-Slavist (-ic).

panetela, *f.* panada; (Am.) sponge cake; panetela (cigar).

panetería, *f.* pantry of the royal palace.

panetero, *m.* pantler.

pánfilo, *m.* slow, sluggish, heavy person.

pangelín, *m.* (bot.) angelin tree.

pangermanismo, *m.* Pan-Germanism.

pangermanista, *m.* & *a.* Pan-Germanist (-ic).

pangolín, *m.* (zool.) pangolin.

paniaguado, da, *n.* servant; employee; protegé

pánico, ca. I. *a.* panic; terrific. **II.** *m.* panic; fright.

panículo, *m.* panicle, pellicle, membrane.

paniego, ga. I. *a.* eating or yielding much bread. **II.** *m.* burlap bag for charcoal.

panificación, *f.* panification, making of bread.

panificar, *va.* (*pret.* PANIFIQUÉ: *subj.* PANIFIQUE) to make into bread; to convert pasture land into cornfields.

panilla, *f.* an oil measure (¼ lb.).

panique, *m.* large Australian herbivorous bat.

panizo, *m.* (bot.) panic grass; panicum; Indian corn; (Am.) mineral bed.

panocha, panoja, *f.* (bot.) ear of grain; panicle; bunch of anchovies.

panoplia, *f.* panoply; collection of arms.

panóptico, ca. I. *a.* panoptical. **II.** *m.* panopticon; penitentiary.

panorama, *m.* panorama.

panorámico, ca, *a.* panoramic.

panoso, sa, *a.* mealy.

panspermia, *f.* panspermatism.

pantalán, *m.* (Philip.) wooden or bamboo pier.

pantalón, *m.* (gen. *pl.*) trousers.—**p. bombacho,** wide, balloon trousers.

pantalla, *f.* lamp shade; screen; person or object that obstructs the view; pall, cover.

pantanal, *m.* swampy, marshy ground.

pantano, *m.* swamp, marsh, bog; reservoir, dam; hindrance, obstacle, difficulty.

pantanoso, sa, *a.* swampy, marshy, miry; full of difficulties.

pantasana, *f.* fishing seine.

panteísmo, *m.* pantheism.—**panteísta,** *n.* & *a.* pantheist (-ic).—**panteístico, ca,** *a.* pantheistic.

panteón, *m.* pantheon.

pantera, *f.* (zool.) panther; (min.) yellow agate.

pantógrafo, *m.* pantograph.

pantómetra, *f.* pantometer.

pantomima, *f.* pantomime.—**pantomímico, ca,** *a.* pantomimic.—**pantomimo,** *m.* mimic, pantomimist.

pantoque, *m.* (naut.) bilge or flat of the ship.

pantorra, *f.* (coll.) fat calf of the leg.

pantorrilla, *f.* calf of the leg.

pantorrillera, *f.* padded stocking.

pantorrilludo, da, *a.* having thick calves.

pantufla, pantuflo, *f. m.* slipper, baboosh.

pantuflazo, *m.* blow with a slipper.

panucho, *m.* (Mex.) bean-and-meat pie with corn-meal crust.

panudo, da, *a.* (Am.) firm, not soft (s. o. ripe alligator pears and other fruit).

panza, *f.* belly, paunch; belly of a vase; rumen or paunch of ruminants.—**panzada,** *f.* (coll.) belly-ful; push with the belly.—**panzón, na. I.** *a.* big-bellied. **II.** *m.* paunch.—**panzudo, da,** *a.* big-bellied.

pañal, *m.* swaddling clout or cloth; tail of a shirt. *pl.* swaddling clothes; infancy.—**estar en pañales,** to have little knowledge; to be in its, one's, infancy.

pañería, *f.* drapery; clothing store.

pañero, *m.* woollen draper; clothier.

pañete, *m.* *dim.* inferior or light cloth; (Colomb.) plastering.—*pl.* trunks worn by fishermen; linen attached to the crucifix below the waist.

pañito, pañizuelo, *m.* *dim.* small cloth.

paño, *m.* cloth, woollen stuff; by extension, any woven stuff; tapestry, drapery, hanging; kitchen cloth; wash cloth; bleardness; livid spot on the face; spot in looking-glasses, crystals, or precious stones; (naut.) canvas, sailcloth; (sew.) breadth.—*pl.* clothes, garments.—**p. burdo,** shoddy cloth.—**p. de lágrimas,** one who sympathizes and consoles.—**p. de manos,** towel.—**p. de mesa,** tablecloth.—**p. pardillo** = P. BURDO.—**paños calientes,** inefficient efforts or means; half measures.—**p. menores,** small clothes, undergarments; dishabille.—**al p.,** (theat.) outside, without.

pañol, *m.* (naut.) storeroom.—**p. de las velas,** sail room.—**p. del contestable,** gunner's room.—**p. de pólvora,** magazine.—**p. de proa,** boatswain's storeroom.

pañolería, *f.* handkerchief shop or factory.

pañolero, ra. I. *n.* handkerchief maker or seller. **II.** *m.* (naut.) yeoman.

pañoleta, *f.* triangular shawl.

pañolón, *m.* large square shawl.

pañoso, sa. I. *a.* ragged, tattered. **II.** *f.* cloak.

pañuelo, *m.* handkerchief; shawl.

papa. I. *m.* (eccl.) Pope; (coll.) papa. **II.** *f.* potato; fib, fake, hoax; (Peru) lump of native silver; (orn.) goldfinch or yellow warbler.—*pl.* pap; (coll.) food, grub.

papá, *m.* (coll.) papa.—**papacito,** *m. dim.* (coll.) dad, daddie, papa dear.

papada, *f.* double chin; gill; dewlap.

papadilla, *f. dim.* flesh under the chin.

papado, *m.* papacy.

papafigo, *m.* (orn.) figpecker, beccafico.

papagayo, *m.* (orn.) parrot; (icht.) rock bass; (bot.) three-colored amaranth; white arum, calla; (C. A.) violent northeast wind.

papahigo, *m.* winter cap; (naut.) lower sail.

papahuevos, *m.* (coll.) simpleton, clodpoll.

papaína, *f.* (chem.) papain.

papal, *a.* papal.

papalina, *f.* cap with flaps; coif; (coll.) fit of drunkenness.

papalmente, *adv.* in a papal manner.

papalote, *m.* (Cuba) kite.

papamoscas, *m.* (orn.) flycatcher, flyeater; (coll.) ninny.

papanatas, *m.* (coll.) dolt, simpleton, ninny.

papandujo, ja, *a.* (coll.) too soft, overripe.

papar, *va.* to swallow without chewing; (coll.) to eat; to pay little attention to.—**p. moscas,** or **viento,** to gape.

páparo, ra, *n.* ancient Indian of Panama; gawk, gump.

paparrabias, *n.* (coll.) testy, fretful person.

paparrasolla, *f.* hobgoblin, bugbear.

paparrucha, *f.* (coll.) fake, humbug; nonsense, silliness.

papasal, *m.* a boys' game; trifle, bagatelle.

papaveráceo, a, *a.* (bot.) papaveraceous.

papaya, *f.* (bot.) papaw.

papayo, *m.* (bot.) papaw tree.

pápaz, *m.* (in Africa) Christian priest.

papazgo, *m.* popedom, pontificate.

papel, *m.* paper; piece of paper; document; (commercial, legal) paper; writing, treatise, discourse, pamphlet, tract; (theat.) part, rôle; character, figure.—**p. continuo,** paper in rolls. —**p. costero,** outside quires.—**p. cuadriculado,** cross-section paper.—**p. cuché,** glazed print paper.—**p. de añafeo,** brown paper.—**p. de barbas,** untrimmed paper.—**p. de cúrcuma,** (chem.) turmeric paper.—**p. de China,** Chinese paper.— **p. de entapizar,** wall paper, paper hanging.—**p. de estaño,** tinfoil.—**p. de estraza,** brown paper, wrapping paper.—**p. de fumar,** cigarette paper.— **p. de lija,** sandpaper.—**p. de luto,** mourning paper.—**p. de marca,** plate paper.—**p. de marquilla,** bristol board, drawing paper.—**p. de oficio,** foolscap.—**p. de seda,** tissue paper.—**p. de tornasol** = P. REACTIVO.—**p. esmeril,** emery paper.—**p. jaspeado,** marbled paper.—**p. marca mayor,** royal paper.—**p. marquilla** = P. DE MARQUILLA.—**p. moneda,** paper money.—**p. para excusados,** toilet paper.—**p. pintado,** stained paper; paper hanging.—**p. rayado,** ruled paper.—**p. reactivo,** test paper, litmus paper.—**p. secante** = P. CHUPÓN.—**p. sellado,** official stamped paper.— **p. tela,** tracing paper.—**p. viejo,** waste paper.— **p. vitela,** vellum paper.—**p. volante,** small pamphlet or printed leaflet.—**papeles mojados,** worthless documents.—**hacer p.,** to cut a figure, to play a part, to impersonate.

papelear, *vn.* to search or look over papers; (coll.) to cut a figure.

papeleo, *m.* act of looking over papers.

papelera, *f.* writing desk, paper case; number of papers.

papelería, *f.* stationery; stationery shop; heap of papers.

papelero, ra, *n.* paper maker; stationer.

papeleta, *f.* card, ticket, check, slip; paper bag for money or sweetmeats.

papelillo, *m. dim.* bit of paper; cigarette.

papelina, *f.* wine goblet; poplin; (coll.) fit of drunkenness.

papelista, *n.* keeper of documents; papermaker; stationer; paper hanger.

papelito, *m. dim.* small paper; curl paper.

papelón, na. I. *a.* boastful, ostentatious. **II.** *m.* *aug.* poster, bill; paper board; boaster; (Cuba) raw sugar.

papelonear, *vn.* (coll.) to boast, pretend.

papelote, papelucho, *m.* scurrilous article.

papera, *f.* goiter; mumps.

papero, *m.* pot in which pap is made.

papialbillo, *m.* (zool.) weasel.

papila, *f.* (med. and bot.) papilla.

papilar, *a.* papillary, papillate, papillose.

papilináceo. I. *a.* (bot.) papilionaceous. **II.** *f.* *pl.* Papilionaceæ.

papilla, *f.* pap; guile, deceit, artifice.

papión, *m.* a kind of large monkey.

papiro, *m.* (bot.) papyrus.

papirolada, *f.* garlic sauce.

papirotada, *f.*; **papirotazo, papirote,** *m.* fillip.

papisa, *f.* papess.

papista, *n.* & *a.* Papist (-ic).

papo, *m.* double chin; anterior lower part of an animal's neck, external throat; fowl's gizzard; thistledown; puff in garments.—**p. de viento,** (naut.) small sail.

papudo, da, *a.* double-chinned.

papujado, da, *a.* full-gorged (s. o. fowls); swollen, puffed up.

pápula, *f.* (med.) papula.

paquebote, *m.* (naut.) packet boat.

paquete, *m.* packet, package; bundle of papers; (coll.) dandy, dude; (naut.) packet boat.—**p. de duelas,** shooks.

paquetería, *f.* (com.) retail trade or shop.

paquidermo, ma. I. *a.* thick-skinned; pachydermatous. **II.** *m. pl.* (zool.) Pachydermata.

par. I. *a.* equal; on a par; homologous, corresponding; even (number). **II.** *m.* pair, couple; team; peer of the realm; (arch.) angle rafter; (elec.) cell; (mech.) couple.—**p. de fuerzas,** (mech.) couple.—**p. de perdices,** brace of partridges.—**p. de pistolas,** brace of pistols.—**p. de torsión, par motor,** (elec.) torque.—**pares y nones,** odd or even (a game).—**a la p.,** jointly, equally; (com.) par; at par.—**a pares,** two and two, by pairs.—**de p. en p.,** wide open (s. o. a door, etc.)—**ir a la p.,** to go halves, to have an equal share. **III.** *f. pl.* placenta.

para, *prep.* for, to, in order to, toward, wherefore, to the end that, about.—**p. entre los dos,** between you and me.—**p. eso,** for that, for that matter.— **¿p. qué?** what for? what is the use?—**p. que,** so that, in order that.—**p. siempre,** for ever.—**dije p. mi capote,** I said to myself.—**sin qué ni p. qué,** without motive, without rime or reason.— **tengo p. mí,** it is my opinion.

parabién, *m.* congratulation, felicitation, greeting.

parábola, *f.* parable; (geom.) parabola.

parabolano, na, *n.* one who uses parables.

parabólico, ca, *a.* parabolic.

paraboloide, *m.* (geom.) paraboloid.

parabrisa, *m.* (aut.) wind shield.

paracaídas, *m.* parachute.

paracentesis, *f.* (surg.) paracentesis.

Paracleto, Paráclito, *m.* Paraclete, Holy Ghost.

paracronismo, *m.* parachronism.

parachispas, *m.* (elec.) spark arrester.

parachoques, *m.* (aut.) bumper.

parada, *f.* stop; stay, suspension, pause; (mil.) halt, halting; parade; review; stall, fold for cattle; relay of horses; dam, bank; stakes, bet; (fenc.) parry.—**p. en firme,** or **en seco,** dead stop. —**doblar la p.,** to double the stake or bid.—**llamar de p.,** to hold the game at bay.

paradera, *f.* sluice, floodgate; fishing seine.

paradero, *m.* halting place; (r. w.) station, depot; landing, terminus; whereabouts.

paradeta, illa, *f.* short stop.—*pl.* a kind of dance.

paradigma, *m.* example, paradigm.

paradina, *f.* round inclosure.

paradisíaco, ca, *a.* paradisaical.

paradislero, *m.* huntsman in wait; newsmonger.

parado, da, *pp.* & *a.* slow, spiritless, indolent; unoccupied, not busy; stopped (s. o. a clock); closed (as a factory); (Am.) standing up.

paradoja, *f.* paradox.

paradojo, ja; -dójico, ca, *a.* paradoxical.

parador. I. *n.* one who stops or halts; heavy better. **II.** *m.* hostelry, inn, road house.

parafernales.—bienes p., (law) paraphernalia.

parafina, *f.* paraffin.

parafraseador, ra, *n.* paraphraser.

parafrasear, *va.* to paraphrase.

paráfrasis, *f.* paraphrase.—**parafraste,** *m.* paraphrast.—**parafrásticamente,** *adv.* paraphrastically.—**parafrástico, ca,** *a.* paraphrastic.

paragoge, *f.* (rhet.) paragoge.

paragonar, *va.* to compare, to hold equal to.

parágrafo, *m.* paragraph; additional clause.

paraguas, *m.* umbrella.

paraguay, *m.* (orn.) a species of parrot.

paraguayano, na; -guayo, ya, *n.* & *a.* Paraguayan.

paragüería, *f.* umbrella shop.

paragüero, ra. I. *n.* umbrella maker, repairer or seller. **II.** *m.* umbrella stand,

parahuso, *m.* = PARAÚSO.

paraíso, *m.* paradise; heaven; (theat., coll.) nigger heaven, upper gallery.—**p. de bobos,** air castles.—**p. terrenal,** Paradise, garden of Eden.

paraje, *m.* place, spot; condition, state.

paral, *m.* scaffolding pole, prop, or post; (naut.) launching ways.

paraláctico, ca, *a.* parallactic.

paralaje, *f.* (ast.) parallax.

paralelar, *va.* to parallel; to compare.

paralelepípedo, *m.* (geom.) parallelopiped.

paralelismo, *m.* (geom.) parallelism.

paralelo, la. I. *a.* parallel; similar, corresponding. **II.** *m.* parallel, resemblance; (geog.) parallel. **III.** *f.* (geom. and fort.) parallel.

paralelogramo, *m.* (geom.) parallelogram.

Paralipómenos, *m. pl.* Paralipomena, Book of Chronicles.

parálisis, *f.* (med.) paralysis.—**paralítico, ca. I.** *a.* paralytic, paralyzed. **II.** *n.* paralized person.

paralización, *f.* paralyzation; immobilization; (com.) stagnancy, stagnation.

paralizado, da, *a.* (com.) dull, stagnant, flat.

paralizar, *va.* (*pret.* PARALICÉ: *subj.* PARALICE) to paralyze, palsy; to impede, stop; immobilize, fix, lock.

paralogismo, *m.* (logic) paralogism.

paralogizar, *vn.* to paralogize.

paramentar, *va.* to adorn, bedeck, embellish.

paramento, *m.* ornament, hanging; trappings, caparison; (arch.) face, surface.—**paramentos sacerdotales,** (eccl.) robes and ornaments.

paramera, *f.* desert, moor; bleak place.

parámetro, *m.* (geom.) parameter.

páramo, *m.* paramo, high and cold region.

parancero, *m.* birdcatcher.

parangón, *m.* paragon, model; comparison.

parangona, *f.* (print.) paragon type.

parangonar, *va.* to compare.

paraninfico, *a.* (arch.) having statues of nymphs.

paraninfo, *m.* paranymph; harbinger of felicity; salutatorian; hall for college exercises.

paranza, *f.* hut or blind for huntsmen.

parao, *m.* (Philip.) a large passenger vessel.

parapara, *f.* fruit of the PARAPARO.

paraparo, *m.* (Ven.) (bot.) soapbark tree.

parapetarse, *vr.* to hide behind a parapet.

parapeto, *m.* (mil.) parapet, breastwork; rails or battlements on bridges and quays.

paraplegia, *f.* (med.) paraplegia.

parapoco, *n.* (coll.) numskull; timid person.

parar. I. *va.* to stop, detain, check; to prepare, get ready; to stake (at cards); to point at (game); to treat or use ill; to place, fix (as the attention); (fenc.) to parry.—**p. mientes en,** to consider carefully. **II.** *vn.* to stop; to land; to go from one to another; to come to the possession of; to happen; to come to an end; (w. **en**) to become, end (in), be transformed (into); to stop, lodge. **III.** *vn.* & *vr.* to stop, halt.—**sin p.,** instantly, without delay. **IV.** *vr.* to be ready to face a danger; to desist, waver, pause; (Am.) to stand up.—**no p. en pelillos,** not to stop at trifles.

parar, *m.* lansquenet, a card game.

pararrayos, *m.* lightning rod.

parasceve, *m.* parasceve, Jewish Sabbath eve.

paraselene, *f.* paraselene, mock moon.

parasemo, *f.* figurehead of a vessel.

parasismo, *m.* paroxysm, fit.

parasitario, ria, *a.* = PARASÍTICO.

parasiticida, *m.* parasiticide.

parasítico, ca, *a.* parasitic.

parásito, ta, *n.* & *a.* parasite (-tic).

parasitología, *f.* parasitology, science of parasites.

parasol, *m.* parasol, sunshade.

parástade, *m.* (arch.) anta, pilaster.

parata, *f.* built terrace.

paratifoidea, *f.* paratyphoid.

parausar, *va.* to drill with a brace drill.

paraúso, *m.* brace drill.

parazonio, *m.* parazonium, Greek dagger or short sword.

parca, *f.* fate, death.

parcamente, *adv.* sparingly, parsimoniously.

parcar, *ma.* premium card in schools.

parcela, *f.* parcel of land.

parcelar, *va.* to divide into lots.

parcelario, ria, *a.* pertaining to parceled lands.

parcial, *a.* partial.—**parcialidad,** *f.* partiality, bias; party, faction.—**parcialmente,** *adv.* partially, partly.

parcidad, *f.* parsimony, frugality.

parcionero, *m.* partner, participant.

parco, ca, *a.* sparing, scanty; sober, moderate, parsimonious.

parcísimo, ma, *a. sup.* of PARCO.

parcha, *f.* (Am.) (bot.) any passifloraceous plant.

parchazo, *m. aug.* large plaster; (coll.) deception, jest; (naut.) flapping of sails.

parche, *m.* (pharm.) plaster, sticking plaster; (mil.) drum-head; drum; (shoe.) patch; botch. —**pegar un p.,** (coll.) to serve a scurvy trick.

pardal. I. *a.* rustic. **II.** *m.* (orn.) sparrow, linnet; (zool.) leopard; (bot.) aconite, wolfsbane; crafty fellow.

pardear, *vn.* to be or show grayish or drab.

¡pardiez! *interj.* (coll.) by Jove! by Jupiter!

pardillo. I. *m.* (orn.) linnet; a kind of grape, and wine made from it. **II.** *a.* grayish, brown (cloth).

pardisco, ca, *a.* = PARDUSCO.

pardo, da. I. *a.* brown; dark gray; dark; cloudy; (Cuba) colored (people). **II.** *n.* (Cuba) mulatto; darky. **III.** *m.* (zool.) leopard.

pardusco, ca, *a.* grayish, grizzly.

parear, *va.* to match, mate, pair, couple.

parecer. I. *vn.* (*ind.* PAREZCO: *subj.* PAREZCA) to appear, show up, turn up; to seem.—**a lo que parece,** or **según parece,** according to appearances, as it seems. **II.** *vr.* to resemble each other, to look alike. **III.** *m.* opinion; look, mien; appearance.—**al p.,** seemingly, to all appearances.—**por el bien p.,** to save appearances.

parecido, da. I. *a.* & *pp.* found; (w. **a**) resembling, like, similar.—**bien (mal) p.,** good- (bad-) looking. **II.** *m.* resemblance, likeness.

pareciente, *a.* similar, apparent.

pared, *f.* wall; close field of barley; garden edging or fence of box.—**p. maestra,** main wall.—**p. medianera,** party wall, partition wall.—**entre cuatro paredes,** confined, retired; imprisoned.— **hasta la p. de enfrente,** to the limit; with all one's heart and might.—**las paredes oyen,** walls have ears.

paredaño, ña, *a.* having a wall between.

paredón, *m. aug.* thick wall; standing wall.

pareja, *f.* pair; couple; brace; match; coupling; dancing partner; team, pair of soldiers or policemen.—**correr parejas,** or **a las parejas,** to be on a par, to go together.

parejo, ja, *a.* equal, even, smooth.—**por p.,** or **por un p.,** on equal terms, on a par, evenly; indiscriminately, without distinction.

parejura, *f.* evenness; equality; similarity.

parénesis, *f.* admonition, exhortation.

parenético, ca, *a.* admonitory.

parénquima, *m.* (med.) parenchyma.

parentela, *f.* kindred, kinsfolk, relations.

parentesco, *m.* kindred, relationship; tie, bond.

paréntesis, *m.* parenthesis; parenthetical statement or expression; digression.—**entre,** or **por, p.,** parenthetically, by the bye.

pareo, *m.* pairing, coupling, matching.

parergón, *m.* additional ornament.

parezco, ca. *V.* PARECER.

pares, *f. pl.* placenta, afterbirth.

pargo, *m.* (icht.) braize, porgy.

parhelia, *f.,* **parhelio,** *m.* parhelion, mock sun.

parhilera, *f.* (arch.) ridgepole, ridgepiece.

paria, *m.* pariah, outcast.

parias, *f.* tribute by one prince to another; placenta.

parición, *f.* parturition (of cattle).

parida. I. *f.* woman lately delivered. **II.** *a.* having recently brought forth offspring (app. to women and animals).

paridad, *f.* parity, equality, comparison.

paridera. I. *a.* fruitful, prolific. **II.** *f.* place where cattle bring forth their young; parturition.

pariente, ta, *n.* relation, relative, kinsman (-woman); (coll.) appellation given by husband and wife to each other.

parietal, *a.* relating to walls; (anat.) parietal.

parietaria, *f.* (bot.) wall pellitory.

parificación, *f.* exemplification, illustration.

parificar, *va.* to exemplify, illustrate.

parihuela, *f.* handbarrow; litter; stretcher.

pario, ria, *n. & a.* Parian.

parir, *va. & vn.* to give birth, bring forth young; to produce, to cause; to publish.—**poner a p.,** to put to one's trumps.

parisiense, *a. & n.* Parisian.

parla, *f.* easy delivery, loquacity, talk.

parlador, ra, *n.* chatterer.

parladuría, *f.* loquacity, talk, gossip.

parlaembalde, *n.* (coll.) chatterbox.

parlamentar, *vn.* to converse; (mil.) to parley.

parlamentariamente, *adv.* parliamentarily.

parlamentario, ria. I. *a.* parliamentary, parliamentarian. **II.** *m.* member of parliament; (mil.) flag of truce, cartel.—**parlamentarismo,** *m.* parliamentarism.—**parlamento,** *m.* parliament; legislative body; (mil.) parley, flag of truce; (theat.) speech.

parlanchín, na, *n. & a.* chatterer (-ing), jabberer (-ing).

parlante, *a.* speaking, talking.

parlar, *vn.* to speak with ease; to chatter, talk.

parlatorio, *m.* chat, parley; parlor; locutory.

parlería, *f.* loquacity, garrulity; gossip; tale; jest; chirping of birds; purling of brooks.

parlerillo, lla; ruelo, la, *a. dim.* of PARLERO.

parlero, ra, *a.* loquacious, talkative; expressive (eyes); chirping (birds); bubbling (brooks).

parleta, *f.* chat, small talk.—**parlón, na,** *a.* loquacious, garrulous.—**parlotear,** *vn.* to prattle, prate, chatter.—**parloteo,** *m.* chat, prattle, talk.

parmesano, na, *n. & a.* Parmesan.

Parnaso, *m.* Parnassus; anthology; assemblage of poets.

parnés, *m.* (coll.) money, cash.

paro, *m.* (orn.) titmouse; coaltit; lockout, suspension of work.

parodia, *f.* parody.—**parodiar,** *va.* to parody.

paródico, ca, *a.* parodical, burlesque.

parodista, *n.* parodist, writer of parodies.

parola, parolina, *f.* (coll.) fluency, volubility; chat, idle talk.

pároli, *m.* paroli (as at faro).

paronimia, *f.* paronymy.

parónimo, ma, *a.* paronymous.

paronomasia, *f.* (rhet.) paronomasia.

parótida, *f.* (anat.) parotid gland; (med.) mumps.—**parotiditis,** *f.* parotitis.

paroxismal, *m.* paroxysmal.

paroxismo, *m.* (med.) paroxysm.

parpadear, *vn.* to wink; to blink.

parpadeo, *m.* winking, blinking.

párpado, *m.* eyelid.

parpalla, *f.* milled copper piece.

parpar, *vn.* to quack (as a duck).

parque, *m.* park; paddock; (arti.) park; (Colomb.) armory.

parquedad, *f.* parsimony, sparseness.

parra, *f.* grapevine; honey jar.

parrado, da, *pp. & a.* having extended vines.

párrafo, *m.* paragraph; paragraph mark (§ or ¶).

parragón, *m.* standard silver for assayers.

parral, *m.* bower of grapevines; vineyard having vines with long shoots; large earthen jar for honey.

parranda, *f.* revel, carousal.—**andar, estar,** or **ir, de p.,** to go, or be, on a carousal.

parrandero, ra; parrandista. I. *a.* fond of carousing. **II.** *n.* carouser, reveler.

parrar, *vn.* to spread out in branches.

parresia, *f.* (rhet.) parrhesia.

parricida, *n.* parricide (murderer).

parricidio, *m.* parricide (murder).

parrilla, *f.* earthen jug; gridiron, broiler, toaster; (furnace) grate.

parriza, *f.,* wild grapevine.

parro, *m.* (orn.) duck.

párroco, *m.* (eccl.) parson.

parrón, *m.* = PARRIZA.

parroquia, *f.* (eccl.) parish; parochial church; congregation and clergy of a parish; (com.) good will, custom.

parroquial. I. *a.* parochial. **II.** *f.* parochial church.

parroquialidad, *f.* parochial right.

parroquiano, na. I. *a.* parochial. **II.** *n.* (eccl.) parishioner; (com.) customer, client.

parsi. I. *n.* Parsi, a Zoroastrian. **II.** *a.* Parsic.—**parsismo,** *m.* Parsism.

parsimonia, *f.* economy, frugality; moderation.

parsimonioso, sa, *a.* economic; sober, moderate, prudent.

parte. I. *f.* part; portion; share; place, spot; right or left side; cause, party; sense given to words or acts; (law) party; (theat.) part, character, rôle.—*pl.* parts, talents, endowments; (coll.) the genitals.—**p. alicuota,** aliquot part.—**p. de la oración,** part of speech.—**p. interesada,** party in interest.—**p. por p.,** part by part, distinctly.—**partes pudendas, púdicas,** or **vergonzosas,** genitals, privy parts.—**a partes,** by parts, or in parts.—**dar p.,** to inform, notify.—**de algún tiempo a esta p.,** for some time past.—**de mi p.,** on my part; on my side; for me, in my name.—**de p. a p.,** from side to side, through.—**de p. de,** from, by command of, in the name of; in favor of.—**en p.,** partly, in part.—**en partes** = A PARTES.—**en todas partes,** everywhere.—**hacer de su p.,** to do one's best, to do one's part.—**ir a la p.,** to go shares.—**no ser p. en,** not to be a party to, to have nothing to do with.—**por mi parte,** as for me, as far as I am concerned.—**por partes,** by parts, one thing at a time.—**por todas partes,** on all hands, on all sides; everywhere. **II.** *m.* communication, despatch, telegram, telephone message. **III.** *adv.* in part, partly.

partear, *va.* to assist (women) in childbirth.

partenogénesis, *f.* (biol.) parthenogenesis.

partera, *f.* midwife.—**partería,** *f.* midwifery.

partero, *m.* accoucheur.

partesana, *f.* partisan; a kind of halberd.

partesanero, *m.* pikeman, halberdier.

partible, *a.* divisible, separable.

partición, *f.* division, distribution.
particionero, ra, *a.* participant.
participación, *f.* participation, share; communication; (com.) copartnership.
participante, *n. & a.* participant (-ating), sharer (-ing); notifier (-fying).
participar. I. *va.* to notify, communicate. **II.** *vn.* to participate, share.
partícipe. I. *a.* participant, sharing. **II.** *n.* participator; partner.
participial, *a.* (gram.) participial.
participio, *m.* (gram.) participle.
partícula, *f.* particle.
particular. I. *a.* particular, peculiar, special; personal; private; individual; odd, extraordinary. **II.** *m.* private person, individual; topic, point.—**en p.,** particularly.
particularidad, *f.* particularity, peculiarity; individuality; friendship, intimacy; detail.
particularismo, *m.* (theo.) particularism; (philos.) individualism.
particularizar. I. *va.* to particularize, itemize, specify. **II.** *vr.* (w. en), to have as a characteristic, to be distinguished (by).
particularmente, *adv.* particularly; privately; individually; especially.
partida, *f.* departure; item in an account, charge, entry, record, annotation; parcel, lot; (one) game; money staked; certificate (of birth, marriage, death); (mil.) squad; guerrilla; factious band; (coll.) conduct, behavior, turn; (com.) shipment, lot, consignment.—**p. de campo,** picnic.—**p. de caza,** hunting match.—**p. doble,** (com.) double entry.—**p. serrana,** bad turn.—**p. simple,** single entry.—**las siete Partidas,** the laws of Castile, compiled by King Alphonso X.
partidamente, *adv.* separately, distinctly.
partidario, ria. I. *a.* partisan, adherent, addicted. **II.** *m.* partisan; follower; advocate; party man; district physician.
partido, da. I. *pp. & a.* cleft, divided; broken; (her.) party, parted, or parti per pale. **II.** *m.* (pol.) party; advantage, profit; game, contest, match; odds, handicap; persons who play a game; treaty, agreement; means to an end; territorial division or district; circuit in charge of a physician or surgeon.—**sacar p. de,** to turn to advantage, to take advantage of.—**tomar p.,** to make up one's mind; to join (a party, army, etc.)
partidor, *m.* divider, cleaver; divisor.
partija, *f.* partition, division.
partil, *a.* said of astrological aspects.
partimento, partimiento, *m.* = PARTICIÓN.
partir. I. *va.* to split; to divide; to cut, cleave; to break, crush, crack; to attack in combat or battle; (arith.) to divide; to divide in two.— **p. abierto,** (api.) to uncover (a beehive) that it may swarm.—**p. cerrado,** to divide (a beehive) when it is full.—**p. la diferencia,** to split the difference. **II.** *vn.* to depart, leave; to start, reckon (from). **III.** *vr.* to break; to become divided.
partitivo, va, *a.* (gram.) partitive.
partitura, *f.* (mus.) score.
parto, *m.* childbirth, parturition; newborn child; production, creation, product; expected and important event.
parturienta, parturiente, *a.* parturient.
parúlis, *m.* (med.) gumboil.
parva, *f.* heap of unthrashed corn; multitude, large quantity; light breakfast.
parvedad, *f.* littleness, minuteness; light breakfast.
parvero, *m.* long heap of corn for winnowing.
parvidad, *f.* = PARVEDAD.
parvo, va, *a.* small, little.
parvulez, *f.* smallness; simplicity.
parvulico, ica, illo, illa, ito, ita. I. *a. dim.* very little. **II.** *n.* tot, little child.
párvulo, la. I. *a.* very small; innocent; humble, low. **II.** *n.* child.
pasa, *f.* raisin; passage of birds; (naut.) channel; (Am.) wool or kinky hair of negroes.—**p. gorrona,** large-sized raisin.

pasabalas, *m.* (mil.) ball caliber gauge.
pasacalle, *m.* (mus.) lively march.
pasada, *f.* passage, passing; pace, step.—**de p.,** on the way; hastily, cursorily.—**mala p.,** (coll.) bad turn.
pasadera, *f.* stepping-stone; (naut.) furling line, sea gasket.
pasaderamente, *adv.* passably.
pasadero, ra. I. *a.* supportable, sufferable; passable, tolerably good. **II.** *m.* stepping-stone.
pasadillo, *m.* two-face embroidery.
pasadizo, *m.* alley; passage; corridor, hall, aisle.
pasado, da, I. *m.* past; (mil.) deserter.—*pl.* ancestors. **II.** *pp. & a.* past; last (*la semana pasada,* last week); stale; antiquated, out of date or fashion.—**pasado mañana,** day after tomorrow.
pasador, ra. I. *n.* one who goes across; smuggler. **II.** *m.* door bolt; window fastener; pin; woman's brooch; hatpin or bodkin; peg, sneck, bolt-pin, linchpin, cotter; sieve, colander; (naut.) marlinespike, splicing fid.
pasadura, *f.* passage, transit.
pasagonzalo, *m.* (coll.) flick, quick, light stroke.
pasaje, *m.* passage; journey, voyage; road, way; passage money, fare; number of passengers on a ship; (naut.) strait, narrows; (mus.) transition or change of voice; passage of a book or writing.
pasajero, ra. I. *a.* common (as a thoroughfare); passing, transient, transitory; provisional. **II.** *n.* traveller, passenger.
pasamanar, *va.* to trim, to passement.
pasamanería, *f.* passementerie (work, trade, and shop).
pasamanero, ra, *n.* passementerie maker.
pasamano, *m.* passement, passementerie; handrail, banister; (naut.) gangway.
pasamiento, *m.* passage, transit.
pasante. I. *a.* (her.) passant. **II.** *n.* assistant or student of a physician or lawyer; teacher who prepares for examination.—**p. de pluma,** barrister's clerk.
pasantía, *f.* profession of a PASANTE.
pasapán, (coll.) = GARGUERO.
pasapasa, *m.* legerdemain, hocus-pocus.
pasaporte, *m.* passport; free license; (mil.) furlough.
pasar. I. *va.* (*pp.* PASADO, PASO) to pass; to take across, put through, carry over; to go to, in, by, across, over, around, beyond, through, or the like; to move from place to place; to pierce, run through; to smuggle; to advance, promote; to change, transform; to exceed, surpass; to distance, outdo, outrun, outstrip; to convey, transfer; to suffer, bear, undergo; to stroke, rub; to swallow (food or drink); to omit, overlook; to tolerate; to study with a private teacher; to study as an assistant practitioner; to give private lessons; to study or rehearse (a lesson); to study, read; to dry or desiccate (as fruit); to pass, spend (as time).—**p. a cuchillo,** to put to the sword.—**p. en claro,** to omit.—**p. plaza de,** to set up as.—**p. por alto,** to overlook.—**p. por las armas,** to shoot (as a penalty).—**¿cómo lo pasa Vd.?** how are you? how do you do? **II.** *vn.* to pass; to live; to manage to exist; to last, endure; to pass away, die; to be salable or marketable (as goods); to be current (as money); (at cards) to pass. —**p. de largo,** to pass by without stopping; to read cursorily.—**p. por,** to be considered as, to be taken for.—**p. por encima de,** to overcome; to go over the head of. —**p. sin,** to do without. **III.** *v. imp.* to pass, happen, turn out. **IV.** *vr.* to go over to another party; to cease, finish; to be spent or stale, lose its force; to slip from one's memory; to become tainted (as meat) or spoiled (as fruit); to go too far; to exceed; to burn out (as a fire); to be overcooked; to permeate, go through; to graduate at college; to blot (as paper).—**p. de,** to be too (*pasarse de paciente,* to be too patient).
pasatiempo, *m.* pastime, amusement.
pasavante, *m.* safe-conduct; (com.) permit.
pasavolante, *m.* hasty action.
pasavoleo, *m.* returning the ball over the line.

pascua, _f._ Jewish Passover; (eccl.) each of the Church holidays—Easter, Twelfth-night, Pentecost, and Christmas.—**p. de flores, de resurrección,** or **florida,** Easter (Sunday).—**dar las pascuas,** to wish merry Christmas.—**estar como una p.,** to be as merry as a cricket.

pascual, _a._ (eccl.) paschal.

pascuilla, _f._ first Sunday after Easter.

pase, _m._ permit, pass; (fenc.) venue, thrust.

paseadero, _m._ walk, avenue, ramble, mall.

paseador, ra. I. _a._ fond of walking. **II.** _n._ stroller, promenader.

paseante, _n._ promenader, stroller.—**p. encorte,** idle fellow.

pasear. I. _vn. & vr._ to take a walk; to ride or sail for pleasure; to promenade; to make a pleasure trip; to walk up and down. **II.** _va._ to take out to walk (as a child).

paseata, _f._ (coll.) walk, airing; ride.

paseo, _m._ walk, promenade; stroll; drive; ride; ramble, mall; turnout, parade.—**echar,** or **enviar, a p.,** to send one about one's business; to dismiss or reject rudely or without ceremony.

pasera, _f._ place where fruit is dried; drying.

pasero, ra, _n._ seller of raisins; pacing mule.

pasicorto, ta, _a._ short-stepped.

pasiego, ga, _n._ highlander of Santander.

pasiflóreo, a, _a._ (bot.) passifloraceous.

pasilargo, ga, _a._ long-stepped.

pasillo, _m._ _dim._ short step; passage, corridor; aisle; (sew.) basting stitch.

pasión, _f._ passion; (eccl.) passion.—**pasionaria,** _f._ (bot.) passion flower.—**pasionario,** _m._ (eccl.) passion book.

pasionero, ra; pasionista, _n._ (eccl.) one who sings the passion.

pasito. I. _m._ _dim._ short step. **II.** _adv._ gently, softly.—**p. a p.,** very leisurely or gently.

pasitrote, _m._ short trot.

pasivamente, _adv._ passively.

pasivo, va. I. _a._ passive; inactive, unresponsive; (pension) to persons not actively employed; (gram.) passive. **II.** _m._ (com.) liabilities.

pasmar. I. _va._ to cause a spasm; to benumb, stun; to astound; to chill, deaden. **II.** _vr._ to wonder, marvel; to suffer from lockjaw; to freeze (s. o. plants).

pasmarota, pasmarotada, _f._ feigned spasm; exaggerated admiration or astonishment.

pasmo, _m._ spasm; (med.) lockjaw, tetanus; astonishment; wonder, anything wonderful.

pasmosamente, _adv._ wonderfully.

pasmoso, sa, _a._ marvellous, wonderful.

paso, sa, _a. & pp. irr._ of PASAR: dried (fruit).

paso. I. _m._ pace, step; pass, way, passage; passing; gait, walk; step of a staircase; step, measure, or diligence; footstep; incident, accident, occurrence; (mech.) pitch; passage in a writing; (theat.) curtain raiser; sketch; progress, improvement; death.—_pl._ basting stitches.—**p. a nivel,** (r. w.) grade crossing.—**p. a p.,** step by step.—**p. de andadura,** ambling.—**p. de tortuga,** snail gallop, extreme slowness.—**p. entre p.** = P. A P.—**a buen p.,** at a good rate, step, or gait.—**a cada p.,** at every step, frequently.—**a ese p.,** at that rate.—**al p. que,** while, whereas.—**a pocos pasos,** at a short distance.—**apretar el p.,** to hasten.—**de p.,** in passing.—**llevar el p.,** to keep step.—**marcar el p.,** to mark time.—**más que de p.,** hastily, in a hurry.—**salir del p.,** to get out of the difficulty.—**seguir los pasos a,** to follow (the steps of); to trail; to watch.—**seguir los pasos de,** to walk in the footsteps of. **II.** _adv._ softly, gently.

paspié, _m._ a kind of dance.

pasquín, _m._ pasquinade, lampoon.

pasquinada, _f._ pasquinade.

pasquinar, _va._ to ridicule, lampoon, satirize.

pássim, _adv._ passim, in various places.

pasta, _f._ paste; batter; dough; pie crust; soup paste; noodles; bullion for coining; (b. b.) board binding; pulp (in paper).—**p. de guayaba,** guava paste.—**buena p.,** good disposition.

pastar. I. _vn._ to pasture, graze. **II.** _va._ to lead (cattle) to graze.

pasteca, _f._ (naut.) snatch block.

pastel, _m._ pie; (bot.) woad; ball or cake of woad; cheating; comb'ne, plot; (print.) pi or pie; blotted print; (art) pastel.—**al p.,** pastel (painting).

pastelear, _vn._ (coll.) to trim politically.

pastelejo, _m._ _dim._ small pie.

pastelería, _f._ pastry shop; pastry.

pastelero, ra, _n._ pastry cook; political trimmer.

pastelillo, ito, _m._ _dim._ patty; tart, cake.

pastelón, _m._ _aug._ meat or pigeon pie.

pasterización, pasteurización, _f._ pasteurization.—**pasterizar, pasteurizar,** _va._ to pasteurize.

pastero, ra, _n._ one who throws the mass of crushed olives into baskets.

pasteurizar, etc. = PASTERIZAR, etc.

pastilla, _f._ tablet, lozenge, drop; cake.

pastinaca, _f._ (bot.) parsnip; (icht.) sting ray.

pastizal, _m._ pasture ground for horses.

pasto, _m._ pasture, grazing; grass for feed; pasture ground; pabulum, food.—**p. espiritual,** spiritual nourishment.—**pastos comunes,** common fields.—**a p.,** abundantly, plentifully; excessively.—**a todo p.,** freely, abundantly and unrestrictedly.

pastor, ra, _n._ shepherd (-ess); pastor, clergyman.

pastoral. I. _a._ pastoral; rural, rustic. **II.** _f._ pastoral; idyll.

pastoralmente, _adv._ pastorally.

pastorcico, illo, ito, _m._ _dim._ little shepherd.

pastorear, _va._ to pasture; to keep, tend (sheep); to feed (souls).

pastorela, _f._ (mus. and poet.) pastoral.

pastoreo, _m._ pasturing, tending flocks.

pastoría, _f._ pastoral life; shepherds.

pastoricio, cia, pastoril, _a._ pastoral.

pastorilmente, _adv._ pastorally.

pastosidad, _f._ mellowness, softness.

pastoso, sa, _a._ pasty, soft, mellow, doughy; (art) softly painted.

pastura, _f._ pasture, pasturage; fodder.

pasturaje, _m._ common pasturage; duty paid for pasturage.

pata, _f._ foot (of an animal); foot and leg of beasts; (coll. and hum.) human leg or foot; leg of a piece of furniture, an instrument, etc.; pocket flap; (orn.) duck, female of the drake.—**p. de cabra,** crowbar, nail puller; (shoe.) heel burnisher.—**p. de gallina,** radial crack in trees; beginning of rot.—**p. de gallo,** ridiculous saying, bull; crow's-foot wrinkles near the eye.—**p. es la traviesa,** tit for tat.—**patas arriba,** topsy-turvey, heels over head; upside down; on one's back.—**a cuatro patas,** on all fours.—**a la p. coja,** hopscotch.—**a la p. la llana,** plainly, unaffectedly.—**a p.,** (coll.) on foot.—**en cuatro patas,** on all fours.—**enseñar la p.,** to show one's ignorance.—**meter la p.,** (coll.) to intermeddle, butt in; to put one's foot in it.—**quedar, salir,** or **ser, p.,** or **patas,** to be a tie or a draw.

pataca, _f._ (bot.) Jerusalem artichoke.

pataco, ca, = PATÁN.

patacón, _m._ silver dollar or patacoon.

patache, _m._ (naut.) tender, patache.

patada, _f._ kick; (coll.) step; footstep, track.

patagón, na, _m. & a.;_ **patagónico, ca,** _a._ Patagonian.

patagorrillo, lla, _n._ hash of livers and lights.

patagua, _f._ (bot.) Amer. linden, whitewood.

pataje, _m._ = PATACHE.

patalear, _vn._ to kick about violently; to stamp both feet repeatedly.—**pataleo,** _m._ kicking; stamping the feet; pattering, tramp.

pataleta, _f._ (coll.) fainting fit; convulsion.

pataletilla, _f._ a kind of pirouette.

patán, na. I. _a._ churlish, rustic; unmannerly. **II.** _n._ churl, rustic; unmannerly person.

patanada, _f._ incivility, rudeness; rude or discourteous act.

patanería, _f._ churlishness, rusticity, rudeness; incivility.

patarata, _f._ trash; humbuggery; kickshaw.

pataratero, ra, _n._ humbugger, humbug.

patarráez, m. (naut.) preventer shroud.
patata, f. (bot.) potato.—**patatal, patatar,** m. potato patch.—**patatero, ra. I.** a. fond of potatoes. **II.** n. potato seller.
patatús, m. (coll.) swoon, fainting fit.
pataz, m. = PATACHE.
pateador, ra, a. kicking (horse).
pateadura, pateamiento, f. kicking, stamping of the feet; severe reprimand, dressing down.
patear, va. & vn. (coll.) to kick; stamp the foot; to tramp; to be very angry.
patena, f. large medal worn by countrywomen; (eccl.) paten.
patentar, va. to patent.
patente. I. a. patent, manifest, evident. **II.** f. patent; privilege, exclusive grant, warrant, commission.—**p. de corso,** letters of marque.—**p. de sanidad,** (naut.) bill of health.—**p. limpia,** clean bill of health.
patentemente, adv. clearly, visibly, obviously.
patentizar, va. to make evident.
pateo, m. (coll.) kicking; stamping of feet.
pátera, f. patera.
paternal, a. paternal, fatherly.
paternalmente, adv. paternally, fatherly.
paternidad, f. paternity, fatherhood.
paterno, na, a. paternal, fatherly.
paternóster, m. Lord's Prayer; paternoster, big tight knot.
pateta, m. (coll.) nickname given to a lame person; (coll.) devil, old Nick.—**se lo llevó p.,** the deuce took it.
patéticamente, adv. pathetically.
patético, ca, a. pathetic, touching; plaintive.
patiabierto, ta, a. straddling, bowlegged.
patiabillo, m. (zool.) weasel.
patialbo, ba; patiblanco, ca, a. white-footed.
patibulario, ria, a. harrowing.
patíbulo, m. gibbet, gallows; scaffold.
patico, m. dim. young duck, duckling.
paticojo, ja, a. (coll.) lame, crippled, limping.
patidifuso, sa, a. (coll.) = PATITIESO.
patiestevado, da, a. bowlegged.
patihendido, da, a. cloven-footed.
patilla, f. dim. small foot; manner of playing on the guitar; (naut.) spike of the rudder; chape of a buckle; pocket flap; trigger; (Sp. Am.) watermelon.—pl. side whiskers; (coll.) the devil.
patín, m. dim. small court or yard; goosander; skate.—**p. de ruedas,** roller skate.
pátina, f. (metal. and art) patina or patine.
patinadero, m. skating place; skating rink.
patinador, ra, n. skater.
patinar, vn. to skate; to slip, to skid (s. o. vehicles).—**patinejo,** m. dim. small skate.—**patinamiento,** m. skidding, slipping (s. o. vehicles).
patio, m. yard, court yard; (theat.) pit.
patita, f. dim. small foot or leg.—**poner de patitas en la calle,** to bounce, to discharge.
patitieso, a. (coll.) stiff-legged; astounded, stupefied, surprised; stiff, haughty.
patito, m. dim. young duck, duckling.
patituerto, ta, a. crook-legged, knockkneed; crooked, lopsided.
patizambo, ba, a. knock-kneed, bowlegged.
pato, m. (orn.) duck.—**p. de flojel,** eider duck.—**p. negro,** mallard.—**pagar el p.,** to suffer undeserved punishment, to be the scapegoat.
patochada, f. blunder, nonsense.
patógeno, na, a. (med.) pathogenic.
patojear, vn. (Cuba) to waddle in walking.
patojo, ja, a. waddling, like a duck.
patología, f. pathology.—**patológico, ca,** a. pathologic.—**patólogo,** m. (med.) pathologist.
patón, na, a. large-footed; clumsy-footed.
patraña, f. fabulous story, fake, humbug.
patria, f. native country, fatherland.
patriarca, m. patriarch.—**patriarcado,** m. patriarchate.—**patriarcal,** a. patriarchal.
patriciado, m. patriciate.
patricio, cia, n. & a. patrician.
patrimonial, a. patrimonial.
patrimonio, m. patrimony, inheritance.

patrio, tria, a. native; home (u. a.); paternal.
patriota, m. patriot.—**patriotero, ra,** n. exaggerated patriot, patrioteer.
patriotería, f. exaggerated patriotism; spreadeagleism.
patriótico, ca, a. patriotic.
patriotismo, m. patriotism.
patrística, f. (eccl.) patristics.
patrístico, ca, a. (eccl.) patristic.
patrocinador, ra, n. patron, patronizer.
patrocinar, va. to patronize, protect, favor.
patrocinio, m. protection, patronage.
patrología, f. (eccl.) patrology, patristics.
patrón, na. I. n. patron (-ess); protector; host (-ess); landlord (-lady); patron saint. **II.** m. master, boss; pattern, model; standard; (naut.) skipper.—**p. de bote,** or **p. de lancha,** (naut.) cockswain.—**p. de oro,** gold standard.—**kilogramo, metro,** etc., p., standard kilogram, meter, etc. **III.** f. galley following that of the commodore.
patronado, da. I. a. (eccl.) having a patron. **II.** m. = PATRONATO.
patronal, a. patronal, protecting.
patronato, patronazgo, m. patronage, guardianship; employers' association.
patronear, va. to steer (a trading vessel).
patronímico, ca. I. a. patronymic. **II.** m. (gram.) patronymic, surname.
patrono, na, n. patron, protector, defender; tutelary; lord of the manor, patron (-ess); employer.
patrulla, f. patrol; gang, band, squad.
patrullar, va. to patrol.
patudo, da, a. (coll.) having large feet or paws.
patulea, f. (coll.) soldiery or disorderly folks.
patullar, vn. to trample, tramp; to hustle.
paují, paujil, m. guan, a S.-A. gallinacean.
paúl, paular, m. fen, moor, marsh, bog.
paulatinamente, adv. gradually, by degrees.
paulatino, na, a. slow, gradual.
paulina, f. decree of excommunication, interdict; (coll.) reproof, chiding; anonymous offensive letter, poison-pen letter.
paulinia, f. (bot.) (S. A.) a kind of shrub.
paulonia, f. (bot.) paulownia.
pauperismo, m. pauperism, abject poverty.
paupérrimo, ma, a. sup. very poor.
pausa, f. pause; delay; rest, repose; (mus.) pause, rest, stop.—**a pausas,** at leisure.
pausadamente, adv. slowly, deliberately.
pausado, da. I. pp. & a. slow, deliberate; calm, quiet. **II.** adv. slowly.
pausar, vn. to pause, cease, hesitate.
pauta, f. paper ruler (device); guide lines; standard, rule, pattern, model.—**pautada,** f. (mus.) ruled staff.—**pautador, ra,** n. paper ruler (person).
pautar, va. to rule (paper); to regulate, give rules or directions for.
pava, f. (orn.) turkey hen; large furnace bellows; (Am.) joke, fun; (Ven.) large low hat; (Colomb.) a kind of guan.—**pelar la p.,** to carry on a flirtation.
pavada, f. flock of turkeys; childish game.
pavana, f. Spanish dance and its tune.
pavero, ra. I. n. one who feeds or sells turkeys. **II.** m. broad-brimmed hat.
pavés, m. large shield, pavise.
pavesa, f. embers, hot cinders; snuff of the candle.—pl. ashes.
pavesada, f. = EMPAVESADA.
pavezno, m. dim. young turkey.
pavía, f. clingstone peach (tree and fruit).
pávido, da, a. (poet.) timid, fearful.
pavimentación, f. paving; pavement.
pavimentar, va. to pave.—**pavimento,** m. pavement.
paviota, f. (orn.) mew, sea gull.
pavipollo, m. young turkey.
pavo, m. (orn.) turkey; (icht.) peacock fish.—**p. real,** (orn.) peacock.—**p. silvestre,** (orn.) wood grouse.
pavón, m. peacock; bluing (for steel or iron).

pavonada, *f.* (coll.) short walk; strut; outward show.

pavonar, *va.* to treat with bluing.

pavonazo, *m.* (art) dark-red pigment.

pavonear, *vn.* & *vr.* to strut, to show off.

pavor, *m.* fear, dread, fright, terror.

pavorde, *m.* provost; professor of divinity.

pavordear, *vn.* to swarm (s. o. bees).

pavordía, *f.* place and dignity of a provost

pavorido, da, *a.* intimidated, terrorized.

pavorosamente, *adv.* awfully, fearfully.

pavoroso, sa, *a.* awful, frightful, terrible.

pavura, *f.* fear, dread, terror, fright.

payasada, *f.* clownish joke or action.

payaso, *m.* clown.

payés, sa, *n.* Catalan countryman (-woman).

payo, ya, *n.* gawk, churl, gump.

payuelas, *f. pl.* chicken-pox.

paz, *f.* peace; peace of mind; freedom from debt; (eccl.) ceremony of the mass.—¡p.! peace! hush!— **a la p. de Dios,** God be with you.—**en p.,** quits, even.—**gente de p.,** a friend (in answer to "who is there?").

pazguato, ta, *n.* dolt, simpleton.

pazote, *m.* (bot.) saltwort.

pazpuerco, ca, *a.* (coll.) dirty, slovenly.

pe, *f.* name of the letter *p.*—**de p. a pa,** thoroughly, from A to Z, from beginning to end.

peaje, *m.* bridge toll; ferriage.

peajero, *m.* toll-gatherer.

peal, *m.* legging; foot of a stocking; worthless person.

peana, peaña, *f.* pedestal stand; (mech.) ground plate; step before an altar.

peatón, *m.* walker, messenger; rural postman.

pebete, *m.* aromatic burning stick; stench; fuse, * punk.—**pebetero,** *m.* perfume censer.

pebrada, *f.*; **pebre,** *m. or f.* sauce of garlic and spice; pepper.

peca, *f.* freckle, speck, spot.

pecable, *a.* peccable, liable to sin; sinful.

pecadillo, ito, *m. dim.* peccadillo, slight sin

pecado, *pp.* & *m.* sin; guilt; excess; (coll.) devil.— **p. capital,** deadly or mortal sin.—**p. contra natura,** or **contra naturaleza,** sodomy; masturbation.—**p. grave,** or **mortal,** deadly or mortal sin.—**de mis pecados,** of mine.

pecador, ra. I. *n.* & *a.* sinner (-ing); offender (-ing). **II.** *f.* (coll.) prostitute.

pecaminosamente, *adv.* sinfully, wickedly.

pecaminoso, sa, *a.* sinful.

pecante, *a.* sinning; excessive.

pecar, *vn.* (*pret.* PEQUÉ: *subj.* PEQUE) to sin; to yield to temptation; to offend; (med.) to predominate, superabound.—**p. de,** to be too (*Juan peca de confiado,* John is too confident) ; to have too much, ail from too much (prolixity, obscurity, conciseness, etc.)

peccata minuta, (coll.) peccadilloes.

pece, *m.* wetted clay for mud walls; ridge between furrows.

pececico, illo, ito, *m. dim.* little fish.

peceño, ña, *a.* pitchy (color and taste).

pecera, *f.* fish globe; aquarium.

pecezuelo, *m. dim.* of PIE and PEZ.

peciento, ta, *a.* of a pitchy color.

peciluengo, ga, *a.* long-stalked (fruit).

pecina, *f.* piscina; slime.—**pecinal,** *m.* slimy pool.

pecio, *m.* (law) flotsam, jetsam, ligan, wreckage.

peciolado, da, *a.* (bot.) petiolate.

pecíolo, *m.* (bot.) petiole, leaf stalk.

pegmatita, *f.* (min.) pegmatite.

pécora, *f.* head of sheep.—**buena,** or **mala, p.,** (coll.) shrewd, designing woman.

pecorea, *f.* (mil.) marauding; loitering.

pecorear. I. *va.* to steal (cattle). **II.** *vn.* to loot, maraud.

pecoso, sa, *a.* freckly, freckled.

pectina, *f.* (chem.) pectin.

pectíneo, a, *a.* pectinate, comblike; (anat.) pectineus (muscle).

pectiniforme, *a.* comb-shaped, pectinate.

pectoral. I. *a.* pectoral. **II.** *m.* (eccl.) breast plate; (pharm.) pectoral.

pectosa, *f.* (chem.) pectose.

pecuario, ria, *a.* cattle (u. a.)

peculado, *m.* (law) peculation, embezzlement.

peculiar, *a.* peculiar.—**peculiaridad,** *f.* peculiarity.—**peculiarmente,** *adv.* peculiarly.

peculio, *m.* (law) peculium; private purse or property.

pecunia, *f.* (coll.) hard cash, specie.

pecuniariamente, *adv.* in cash; pecuniarily, financially.

pecuniario, ria, *a.* pecuniary, monetary.

pechar, *vn.* to pay taxes.

peche, *m.* = PECHINA.

pechera, *f.* shirt bosom; shirt frill; chest protector; (sad.) breast strap; (coll.) bosom.

pechería, *f.* taxes, revenue; tax poll.

pechero, ra. I. *n.* taxpayer; commoner, plebeian. **II.** *m.* bib.

pechiblanco, ca, *a.* white-breasted.

pechicolorado, *m.* (orn.) linnet.

pechigonga, *f.* a card game.

pechina, *f.* pilgrim scallop; (arch.) squinch; arch of a pendentive.

pechirrojo, *m.* (orn.) linnet.

pechisacado, da, *a.* (coll.) haughty, arrogant.

pechito, *m. dim.* small breast or teat.

pecho, *m.* (anat.) chest, thorax; breast; bosom; teat; courage, fortitude; (mus.) quality and strength of the voice; slope, gradient; ancient tax.—**abrir el p.,** to unbosom one's self.—**criar a los pechos,** to instruct or educate.—**dar el p.,** to nurse, suckle.—**de p.,** firm-spirited.—**echar el p. al agua,** to undertake a risky thing resolutely.— **entre p. y espalda,** (coll.) in the stomach.—**tener p.,** to have patience, to endure with firmness.— **tomar a p.,** or **a pechos,** to take to heart.

pechuelo, *m. dim.* small or little breast.

pechuga, *f.* breast of a fowl; slope; (coll.) bosom; (coll.) nerve, cheek, brazenness.—**pechugón, na. I.** *a.* (coll.) spongy, parasitic; bold, brazen. **II.** *m.* blow on the breast.

pechuguera, *f.* cough, hoarseness.

pedacico, illo, ito, *m.* small piece, bit.

pedagogía, *f.* pedagogy.—**pedagógicamente,** *adv.* pedagogically.

pedagógico, ca, *a.* pedagogical.

pedagogo, *m.* pedagogue; teacher; educator.

pedaje, *m.* bridge toll. *V.* PEAJE.

pedal, *m.* (mech.) treadle; (mus.) pedal.

pedáneo, *a.* (law) petty, puisne, inferior.

pedante. I. *n.* & *a.* pedant (-ic); coxcomb (-ic). **II.** *n.* instructor.

pedantear, *vn.* to pedantize, be a pedant.

pedantería, *f.* pedantry.—**pedantescamente,** *adv.* pedantically.—**pedantesco, ca,** *a.* pedantic.— **pedantismo,** *m.* pedantry.—**pedantón,** *m. aug.* great pedant.

pedazo, *m.* piece, fragment, bit.—**p. de alcornoque,** or **de animal,** good-for-nothing.—**a pedazos,** or **en pedazos,** in bits, in fragments.

pedazuelo, *m. dim.* small piece or bit.

pederasta, *m.* pederast.—**pederastia,** *f.* pederasty, pæderasty.

pedernal, *m.* flint; extreme hardness.

pedernalino, na, *a.* flinty; hard.

pedestal, *m.* pedestal; stand; base, support.

pedestre, *a.* pedestrious, pedaneous; low, vulgar, common.

pedestrismo, *m.* marathon racing, foot racing.

pediatría, *f.* (med.) pediatrics.

pedicoj, *m.* jump on one foot.

pedicular, *a.* pedicular, lousy.

pedículo, *m.* (bot.) peduncle, pedicle.

pedicuro, *m.* chiropodist.

pedido, *pp.* & *m.* demand, call; (com.) order.

pedidor, ra, *n.* petitioner, craver.

pedidura, *f.* begging, petitioning.

pedigón, *m.* (coll.) craver, insatiable asker.

pedigüeño, ña, *a.* persistent in begging.

pediluvio, *m.* (med.) pediluvium, foot bath.
pedimento, *m.* petition; (law) claim, bill.—**a p.,** at the instance, on petition.
pedir, *va.* (*gerund,* PIDIENDO: *ind.* PIDO: *pret.* él PIDIÓ: *subj.* PIDA) to ask for, request, beg, solicit; to demand, claim, exact; to inquire after; to wish, desire; to require; (com.) to order; to ask for in marriage.—**p. celos,** to be jealous.—**p. cuenta,** to call to account.—**a p. de boca,** according to desire.—**pedírselo a uno el cuerpo,** to desire eagerly, to long for.
pedo, *m.* wind from the anus; flatulence.
pedómetro, *m.* pedometer, walking wheel.
pedorrera, *f.* flatulence.—*pl.* tights.
pedrada, *f.* throw of a stone; blow from a stone; cockade; rosette or bow for the hair; hint, insinuation.—**como p. en ojo de boticario,** pat, apropos, just in time.
pedrea, *f.* throwing stones; lapidation; fight with stones; fall of hail.—**pedregal,** *m.* stony ground.
pedregoso, sa, *a.* stony, rocky; (med.) afflicted with gravel.—**pedrejón,** *m.* boulder.—**pedreñal,** *m.* a kind of firelock.—**pedrera,** *f.* quarry, stone pit.—**pedreral,** *m.* packsaddle for carrying stones.
pedrería, *f.* precious stones; jewellery.
pedrero, *m.* stonecutter; (arti.) stone mortar; slinger.
pedrezuela, *f. dim.* small stone; pebble.
pedrisca, *f.* hailstorm; shower of thrown stones; heap of small stones.
pedriscal, *m.* = PEDREGAL.—**pedrisco,** *m.* = PEDRISCA.—**pedrisquero,** *m.* hail storm.—**pedriza,** *f.* stony tract; stone fence.—**pedrusco,** *m.* rough piece of stone.
pedunculado, da, *a.* (bot.) peduncled.
pedunculillo, *m. dim.* (bot.) pedicle, pedicel.
pedúnculo, *m.* (bot.) peduncle, flower stalk.
peer, *vn & vr.* to break wind.
pega, *f.* joining, cementing or sticking together; pitch varnish put on earthen vessels; (min.) firing of a blast; (coll.) jest, practical joke, deceit; spanking, drubbing; (orn.) magpie; (icht.) remora, sucking fish.
pegadillo, *m. dim.* little patch; sticking plaster; bore, nuisance.
pegadizo, za, *a.* sticky, adhesive; catching, contagious; detachable.
pegado, *pp. & m.* patch; sticking plaster.
pegador, *m.* sticker, affixer; paper hanger; (min.) blaster.—**p. de carteles,** billposter.
pegadura, *f.* pitching; sticking, gluing.
pegajoso, sa, *a.* sticky; clammy, viscous; catching, contagious; alluring, tempting.
pegamiento, *m.* joining, sticking, cementing.
pegante, *a.* sticking, adhesive, glutinous.
pegar. **I.** *va.* (*pret.* PEGUÉ: *subj.* PEGUE) to stick, glue, cement; to unite, fasten; to post (bills); to sew on, pin; patch; attach; to infect with, communicate (a disease); hit, beat, slap; (before noun to give (what noun implies); to impart.—**p. fuego a,** to set fire to.—**pegársela a uno,** to fool one, make one swallow a story.—**no p. los ojos,** not to sleep a wink. **II.** *vn.* to take root; catch (fire); make an impression on the mind; make a hit; to join; to be contiguous; to cleave, to cling; to fit, to match; to be becoming, fitting, appropriate; to pass, to be accepted.—**ésa no pega,** (coll.) that is too thin, that won't go. **III.** *vr.* to intrude; to stick, adhere; cohere; to grow; to become rooted in the mind; to take to, become addicted to.
pegaseo, sea, *a.* relating to Pegasus.
pegásides, *f. pl.* the Muses.
Pegaso, *m.* Pegasus.
pegata, *f.* (coll.) trick, cheat, swindle, fraud.
pegmatita, *f.* (min.) pegmatite.
pegollo, *m.* pillar, post.
pegote, *m.* sticking plaster; coarse patch; stew with a thick sauce; sponger, toadeater.
pegotear, *vn.* (coll.) to sponge.
pegotería, *f.* (coll.) sponging.
pegual, *m.* (S. A.) strap with rings.
peguera, *f.* pine wood for making pitch; place where sheep are marked with pitch.

peguero, *m.* maker of or dealer in pitch.
pegujal, pegujar, *m.* peculium; small holdings.
pegujalero, ra; pegujarero, ra, *n.* owner of a small farm or ranch.
pegujón, *m.* pellet or lump of wool or hair.
pegunta, *f.* pitch mark on sheep.
peguntar, *va.* to mark (sheep) with pitch.
peinada, *f.* combing or dressing the hair.
peinado, da. **I.** *a. & pp.* combed, dressed (hair); effeminate in toilet; overnice (literary style). **II.** *m.* hairdressing.—**peinador, ra.** **I.** *n.* hairdresser. **II.** *m.* dressing gown, wrapper.
peinadura, *f.* combing or dressing the hair; combings.
peinar, *va.* to comb or dress (the hair); to comb (wool); to touch or rub slightly; to eat away (a rock).—**p. canas,** to be old.
peinazo, *m.* (carp.) crosspiece of a door.
peine, *m.* comb; card; rack, engine of torture; weaver's reed; comb of the loom; comb-broach; instep.—**a sobre p.,** lightly, slightly, imperfectly.
peinería, *f.* comb factory or shop.
peinero, ra, *n.* comb maker or seller.
peineta, *f.* ornamental shell comb.—**p. de teja,** tile-shaped shell comb.
peje, *m.* fish; cunning, crafty fellow.—**p. araña,** (icht.) stingbull.—**p. diablo,** (icht.) grouper.
pejemuller, *f.* mermaid, sea woman.
pejepalo, *m.* stockfish.
pejerrey, *m.* (icht.) a variety of mackerel.
pejesapo, *m.* (icht.) angler.
pejiguera, *f.* (coll.) bother, too much trouble for nothing.
pela, *m.* PELADURA; (Am.) whipping.—**dar,** or **pegar, una p.,** to whip, give a whipping to.
pelada, *f.* (tan.) pelt.
peladera, *f.* (med.) alopecia.
peladero, *m.* place where logs and fowls are stripped; (coll.) sharpers' den; (Am.) bare, barren spot.
peladilla, *f.* sugar almond; small pebble.
peladillo, *m.* (bot.) clingstone peach (fruit and tree).—*pl.* wool-stripped sheepskin.
pelado, da. **I.** *a. & pp.* plucked; bared; decorticated; hairless; treeless, bare; penniless, broken. **II.** *n.* penniless person.
pelador, *m.* plucker, peeler, stripper.
peladura, *f.* plucking, decortication.
pelafustán, *m.* (coll.) idler, ragamuffin.
pelagallos, pelagatos, *m.* ragamuffin; poor wretch.
pelagianismo, *m.* Pelagianism.
pelagiano, na, *a.* Pelagian.
pelágico, ca, *a.* pelagic, oceanic.
pelagra, *f.* (med.) pellagra.—**pelagroso, sa,** *a.* relating to or suffering from pellagra.
pelaire, *m.* wool-dresser.
pelairía, *f.* trade of a wool comber.
pelaje, *m.* character or nature of the hair or wool; character, disposition; garments, apparel.
pelambrar, *va.* (tan.) to flesh (as hides).
pelambre, *m.* (tan.) batch of hides put into lime pits; steeping liquid; hair scraped from skins; lack of hair.—**pelambrera,** *f.* quantity of hair in one place; shedding of hair; (tan.) lime pit.
pelambrero, *m.* (tan.) steeper.
pelamen, *m.* (coll.) = PELAMBRE.
pelamesa, *f.* scuffle; bushy hair, fell.
pelantrín, *m.* petty farmer.
pelar. **I.** *va.* to cut or pull out the hair of; to pluck; to skin, peel, husk, hull, shell; to trick, cheat, rob; to break (in gambling); to uncover, show (as the teeth).—**pelárselas,** to be in great earnest, to put one's heart and soul, to act or feel with great vehemence.—**duro de p.,** exceedingly difficult, hard to crack, a big order. **II.** *vr.* to cast the hair.
pelarela, *f.* = PELADERA.
pelarruecas, *f.* woman who lives by spinning.
pelásgico, ca, *a.* Pelasgian, Pelasgic.
pelasgo, ga, *n. & a.* Pelasgian.

pelaza. I. *a.* chopped or beaten (straw). **II.** *f.* quarrel, affray, scuffle.

pelazga, *f.* (coll.) quarrel, scuffle.

peldaño, *m.* step of a staircase.

pelde, *m.* = APELDE.

peldefebre, *m.* camlet; camel's hair.

pelea, *f.* fight; scuffle, quarrel.—**p. de gallos,** cockfight.

peleador, ra. I. *n.* fighter. **II.** *a.* quarrelsome.

pelear. I. *vn.* to fight; to quarrel; to toil, struggle. **II.** *vr.* to scuffle, to come to blows.

pelechar, *vn.* to get hair; to change the coat (s. o. horses); to fledge (s. o. birds); (coll.) to improve one's fortune; to recover health.

pelele, *m.* stuffed figure; nincompoop.

pelendengue, *m.* frivolous foppery.

peleón. I. *a.* quarrelsome. **II.** *m.* strong wine.

peleona, *f.* scuffle, quarrel, row.

pelete, *m.* punter; (coll.) poor man.—**en p.,** nakedly.

peletería, *f.* furriery; (Cuba) leather goods; shop where they are sold.—**peletero, ra,** *n.* furrier; (Cuba) dealer in leather goods.

pelgar, *m.* ragamuffin, blackguard.

peliagudo, da, *a.* downy, furry; (coll.) arduous, difficult; skilful.

peliblanco, ca, having white hair.

peliblando, da, *a.* having fine soft hair.

pelícano, *m.* (orn.) pelican.

pelicano, na, *a.* gray-haired; hoary.

pelicorto, ta, *a.* having short hair.

película, *f.* pellicle; film.

pelicular, *a.* pellicular.

peligrar, *vn.* to be in danger.

peligro, *m.* danger, peril.—**correr p.,** to be in danger.—**peligrosamente,** *adv.* perilously, dangerously.—**peligroso, sa,** *a.* dangerous, perilous; hazardous.

pelilargo, ga, *a.* having long hair.

pelillo, *m. dim.* short hair or fiber; trifle, slight trouble.—**echar pelillos a la mar,** to become reconciled.—**no tener pelillos en la lengua,** to speak one's mind openly.—**pararse, or reparar, en pelillos,** to stop at trifles.

pelilloso, sa, *a.* (coll.) peevish, querulous.

pelinegro, gra, *a.* black-haired.

pelirrojo, ja, *a.* red-haired.

pelirrubio, bia, *a.* blonde, light-haired.

pelitieso, sa, *a.* having straight and stiff hair.

pelito, *m. dim.* small hair or fibre.

pelitre, *m.* (bot.) pellitory of Spain.

pelitrique, *m.* fiddle-faddle, flummery.

pelma, *f.* = PELMAZO.

pelmacería, *f.* heaviness, slowness.

pelmazo, *m.* crushed or flattened mass; undigested food, or "lump," in the stomach; sluggard.

pelo, *m.* hair; fibre, filament; trifle; hair's breadth; down (of birds); pubescence (of fruit); nap, pile (of cloth); hairspring (in watches and firearms); flaw (in gems and metals); grain (in wood); color (of horses); coat (of animals); kiss (in billiards); cross wire (of a transit, level, etc.); (vet.) split in hoofs; (com.) raw silk.—**p. arriba,** against the grain.—**p. de la dehesa,** rusticity, rustic or plebeian antecedents.—**pelos y señales,** minute details.—**a medio p.,** or **a medios pelos,** tipsy.—**a p.,** or **al p.,** along the grain; timely, fittingly.—**de medio p.,** of little account; would-be important.—**de p. en pecho,** brave, daring.—**en p.,** bareback; unsaddled.—**hacerse el p.,** to have one's hair cut.—**no tener p. de tonto,** to be bright, quick, clever.—**no tener pelos en la lengua,** to be outspoken.—**tener pelos,** to be tough, difficult, a hard nut to crack.—**tomar el p. a,** to banter, make fun of.—**venir a p.,** to come to the purpose, to fit the case to a tee.

pelón, na, *a.* hairless; bald; (coll.) dull, stupid; poor.—**pelona, pelonía,** *f.* baldness.

pelonería, *f.* (coll.) poverty, want, indigence.

pelopio, *m.* (chem.) pelopium.

peloponense, *n.* & *a.*; **peloponesíaco, ca,** *a.* Peloponnesian.

pelosilla, *f.* (bot.) mouse-ear, hawkweed.

peloso, sa, *a.* hairy.

pelota, *f.* ball, handball; ball game; (S. A.) punt made of leather.—**p. de viento,** football.—**en p.,** entirely naked; penniless.—**no tocar p.,** (coll.) not to touch the root of the difficulty.

pelotaris, *m.* professional ball player.

pelotazo, *m.* blow or stroke with a ball.

pelote, *m.* goat's-hair; tuft of wool.

pelotear. I. *va.* to audit (accounts). **II.** *vn.* to play ball; to throw, as a ball; to argue, dispute; to quarrel.

pelotera, *f.* wrangle, quarrel, tumult, riot.

pelotería, *f.* heap of balls; heap of goat's-hair.

pelotero, *m.* ball maker.

pelotilla, *f. dim.* small ball; small ball of wax and pieces of glass fastened to a scourge.

pelotón, *m. aug.* large ball; tuft of hair; (mil.) platoon; crowd, gang.

pelta, *f.* pelta, light shield.

peltre, *m.* pewter, spelter.

peltrero, *m.* pewterer, pewter worker.

peluca, *f.* wig, periwig; severe reproof.

pelucón, *m. aug.* large bushy wig.

pelucona, *f.* (coll.) double doubloon ($16).

peludo, da. I. *a.* hairy, shaggy; (coll.) difficult, tough. **II.** *m.* shaggy mat.

peluquería, *f.* hairdressing shop; barber shop.

peluquero, *m.* hairdresser, barber; wigmaker.

peluquilla, ita, *f. dim.* small wig.

peluquín, *m. dim.* topwig; bagwig.

pelusa, *f.* down, pubescence; floss, fuzz, nap.

pelusilla, *f. dim.* of PELUSA; fuzz.

pelvi, *n.* & *a.* Pahlavi, Pehlevi, ancient Persian language.

pelviano, na, *a.* (anat.) pelvic.

pelvímetro, *m.* pelvimeter.

pelvis, *f.* (anat.) pelvis, pelvic cavity.

pella, *f.* pellet; tender head of cauliflower, etc.; lump of molten metal; cut lard; unpaid loan; (min.) lump of amalgamated silver; (orn.) heron.

pellada, *f.* (mas.) lump or trowelful of mortar.

pelleja, *f.* skin, hide; (coll.) strumpet.

pellejería, *f.* place where skins are dressed and sold.—**pellejero,** *m.* skinner, leather-dresser, peltmonger.—**pellejina,** *f.* small skin.

pellejo, *m.* skin; rawhide, pelt; wine skin; peel, rind; (met.) one's life; (joc.) tippler, drunkard.—**estar, or hallarse, en el p. de otro,** to be in another's boots, or place.—**quitar el p. a,** to flay; to speak ill of, to roast; to kill.—**salvar el p.,** to save one's bacon.—**pellejudo, da,** *a.* full of skin.

pellejuela, *f. dim.* small skin or rawhide.

pellejuelo, *m. dim.* small skin.

pellica, *f.* cover or robe of fine furs; small dressed skin.—**pellico,** *m.* pelisse; shepherd's jacket.

pelliquero, ra, *n.* maker of fur coverlets.

pelliza, *f.* pelisse, fur cloak.

pellizcador, ra, *n.* & *a.* pincher (-ing).

pellizcamiento, *m.* pruning, clipping; pinching.

pellizcar. I. *va.* (*pret.* PELLIZQUÉ; *subj.* PELLIZQUE) to pinch; to nip; to prune, clip; to gripe; to pilfer. **II.** *vr.* to long for.

pellizco, *m.* pinch; pinching; nip; small bit.—**p. de monja,** small cookie.

pello, *m.* fine fur jacket.—**pellón, pellote,** *m.* long pelisse; fur cloak or robe.

pelluzgón, *m.* lock or tuft of hair.

pena, *f.* penalty; punishment; pain (sp. mental); affliction, sorrow, grief; embarrassment, mortification, chagrin; labor, hardship, difficulty; toil; necklace; (orn.) penna, quill feather.—**p. del talión,** lex talionis.—**a duras penas,** with great difficulty, barely, hardly.—**estar con (mucha) p.,** to be (greatly) mortified, (very) sorry, (very much) vexed.—**merecer la p.,** to be worth while.—**tener la p. de,** to be sorry to.—**valer la p.,** to be worth while.

penable, *a.* punishable.

penachera, *f.*, **penacho,** *m.*; tuft of feathers, aigret; plumicorn; plumes, panache, crest; haughtiness, arrogance, airs.—**penachudo, da,** *a.* crested, tufted, plumed.—**penachuelo,** *m. dim.* small tuft, crest or aigret.

penadamente, *adv.* = PENOSAMENTE.
penadilla, *f.* narrow-mouthed vessel.
penado, da. I. *a.* & *pp.* punished, chastised; sorrowful; painful. **II.** *n.* convict; narrow-mouthed vessel.
penal, *a.* penal.—**penalidad,** *f.* trouble, hardship; (law) penality; penalty.
péname, *m.* condolence.
penante, *a.* suffering sorrow or punishment; narrow-mouthed (vessels).
penar. I. *vn.* to suffer, to agonize; to be tormented in a future life; to crave, long. **II.** *va.* to chastise, inflict punishment or impose penalty on. **III.** *vr.* to grieve, to mourn.
penates, *m. pl.* penates, house gods.
penca, *f.* (bot.) pulpy leaf or joint of some plants; cowhide for flogging culprits.—**hacerse de pencas,** to allow one's self to be coaxed.
pencazo, *m.* lash with a cowhide.
penco, *m.* (coll.) = JAMELGO.
pencudo, da, *a.* having pulpy leaves or joints.
pendejo, *m.* hair over the pubis and groin; (coll.) coward, poltroon; (Am., coll.) fool.
pendencia, *f.* quarrel, fray, feud.
pendenciar, *vn.* to wrangle, quarrel.
pendenciero, ra, *a.* quarrelsome.
pendenzuela, *f. dim.* little dispute.
pender, *vn.* to hang, dangle; to be pending or suspended; to depend.
pendiente. I. *a.* pendent, hanging; clinging; dangling; pending. **II.** *m.* earring, pendant. **III.** *f.* slope, declivity; grade, gradient; dip or pitch.
pendil, *m.* mantle worn by women.
pendol, *m.* (naut.) boot-topping.
péndola, *f.* feather; quill, pen; pendulum. balance; (eng.) queen-post; bridging brace.
pendolaje, *m.* plunder of a captured vessel.
pendolario, ria; pendolista, *n.* penman.
pendolón, *m. aug.* large pendulum; (eng.) kingpost.
pendolita, *f.* watch; click wire.
pendón, *m.* standard, banner, pennon, gonfalon; (bot.) tiller, shoot; (her.) pennon; (coll.) tall, awkward woman.—*pl.* reins of the leading mule.
pendoncito, *m. dim.* pennon, banneret.
péndulo, la. I. *a.* pendent, hanging, pendulous. **II.** *m.* pendulum.—**p. de compensación,** compensation pendulum.—**p. de segundos,** seconds pendulum.—**p. eléctrico,** electric pendulum.—**p. sideral,** or **sidéreo,** (astr.) (standard) clock, chronometer.
pene, *m.* (anat.) penis.
peneque, *a.* (coll.) fuddled.
penetrabilidad, *f.* penetrability.
penetrable, *a.* penetrable; comprehensible.
penetración, *f.* penetration, penetrating; acuteness, sagacity, clearsightedness.
penetrador, ra, *n.* & *a.* discerner (-ing); searcher (-ing).
penetral, *m.* innermost recess.
penetrante, *a.* penetrating, piercing; heart-rending; clearsighted, keen; deep.
penetrar, *va.* to penetrate, pierce; to break or force in; to permeate, pervade; to fathom, comprehend.
penetrativo, va, *a.* penetrative, piercing.
pénfigo, *m.* (med.) pemphigus.
penígero, ra, *a.* (poet.) winged, feathered.
península, *f.* peninsula.
peninsular, *n.* & *a.* peninsular.
penique, *m.* penny.
penitencia, *f.* penitence; penance.—**hacer p.,** to do penance; familiar invitation to take potluck.
penitenciado, da. I. *pp.* & *a.* punished. **II.** *n.* convict.
penitencial, *a.* penitential.
penitenciar, *va.* to impose penance on.
penitenciaría, *f.* penitentiary; (eccl.) penitentiary.—**penitenciario, ria,** *a.* penitentiary.
penitente. I. *a.* penitent, repentant, contrite. **II.** *n.* penitent.

penol, *m.* (naut.) yardarm, peak.
penosamente, *adv.* painfully, grievously.
penoso, sa. I. *a.* painful; laborious, arduous; distressing; embarrassing, unpleasant. **II.** *m.* conceited fop.
pensado, da, *pp.* & *a.* deliberate, premeditated; thought out.—**bien p.,** wise, proper.—**de p.,** on purpose, deliberately.—**mal p.,** unwise, foolish.—**tener p.,** to have in view, to intend.
pensador, ra, *n.* & *a.* thinker (-ing).
pensamiento, *m.* mind; thought, idea; witty saying, epigram, maxim; suspicion, surmise; project, scheme, plan; (art) first sketch or outline; (bot.) pansy, heartsease.—**en un p.,** in a trice.—**ni por p.,** not even in thought.
pensar. I. *vn.* (*ind.* PIENSO: *subj.* PIENSE) to think.—**p. en,** to think of, think about, think over.—**p. en lo excusado,** to expect the impossible. **II.** *va.* to think; to think over, think about, consider; to intend.
pensativo, va, *a.* pensive, thoughtful.
penseque, *m.* thoughtlessness.
pensil. I. *a.* pensile. **II.** *m.* beautiful garden.
pensilvano, na, *n.* & *a.* Pennsylvanian.
pensión, *f.* pension, annuity; price of board and tuition; toil, drudgery; (Am.) anxiety.—**p. vitalicia,** annuity, life pension.
pensionado, da, *pp.* & *n.* pensioner, pensionary.
pensionar, *va.* to impose or to grant annual charges or pensions on or to.
pensionario, *m.* one who pays a pension; pensionary, magistrate.
pensionista, *n.* pensioner; boarder.
pentadecágono, *m.* pentadecagon, fifteen-side polygon.
pentaedro, *m.* (geom.) pentahedron.
pentagonal, *a.* pentagonal.
pentágono, *m.* (geom.) pentagon.
pentagrama, *m.* musical staff.
pentámetro, *m.* pentameter.
pentano, *m.* (chem.) pentane.
pentápolis, *f.* pentapolis.
pentarquía, *f.* pentarchy.
pentasílabo, ba, *a.* of five syllables.
Pentateuco, *m.* Pentateuch.
pentecostés, *m.* Pentecost, Whitsuntide.
pentedecágono, *m.* = PENTADECÁGONO.
penúltimo, ma, *a.* penultimate.
penumbra, *f.* penumbra.
penuria, *f.* penury, indigence.
peña, *f.* rock, large stone; body of friends; club.—**por peñas,** a long time.
peñascal, *m.* rocky hill or mountain.
peñasco, *m.* large rock; strong silk stuff.
peñascoso, sa, *a.* rocky.
peñol, *m.* large rock; (naut.) yardarm.
peñola, *f.* (poet.) pen.
peñón, *m. aug.* large rock, rocky cliff.
peón, *m.* pedestrian; day laborer; (mas.) hodman; foot soldier; top, spinning top; (poet.) foot of four syllables; pawn (in chess); man (in draughts); (mech.) spindle, axle.
peonada, *f.* daywork of a laborer; gang of laborers.—**peonaje,** *m.* gang of laborers.
peonería, *f.* land that can be plowed in one day.
peonía, *f.* (bot.) peony.
peonía, *f.* land given to a soldier as spoils.
peonza, *f.* top, whipping top, gig; noisy little fellow.
peor, *a.* & *adv. comp.* worse; worst.—**p. que p.,** worse and worse.—**tanto p.,** so much the worse.
peoría, *f.* deterioration, detriment.
pepián, *m.* = PIPIÁN.
pepinar, *m.* cucumber field.
pepinillos, *m. pl.* gherkins, pickled cucumbers.
pepino, *m.* (bot.) cucumber.—**no dársele un p.,** or **tres pepinos,** not to give a fig or rush.
pepión, *m.* old Spanish gold coin.
pepita, *f.* pip or seed of some fruits (as apples, etc.); (vet.) pip, distemper in fowls; (min.) nugget.—**pepitoria,** *f.* giblet fricassee; medley of things; (Mex.) peanut brittle.—**pepitoso, sa,** *a.* abounding in pips or seeds; (fowl) having the pip.

peplo, *m.* peplum.
pepón, *m.* (bot.) watermelon.
pepona, *f.* large paper doll.
pepónide, *f.* (bot.) pepo (pumpkin, melon, etc.).
pepsina, *f.* pepsin.
péptico, ca, *a.* peptic.
peptona, *f.* peptone.
pequeñamente, *adv.* in a small degree.
pequeñez, *f.* smallness; infancy, childhood; trifle; contemptible smallness, mean act or conduct.
pequeñito, ta, *a. dim.* very little, tiny.
pequeño, ña. **I.** *a.* little, small; of tender age; lowly, humble. **II.** *n.* child.
pequeñuelo, la. **I.** *a. dim.* very little or young. **II.** *n.* babe, infant; child, little one.
pera, *f.* (bot.) pear; goatee, imperial; (coll.) sinecure.—pedir peras al olmo, to go on a wild-goose chase, to expect the impossible.—poner las peras a cuarto, or a cuatro, to compel one to do or concede what one does not wish to; to bring one to reason.
perada, *f.* preserve of pears; pear jam.
peral, *m.* pear tree; pear orchard.
peraleda, *f.* orchard of pear trees.
peralejo, *m.* (bot.) malpighia.
peraltar, *va.* to stilt (an arch or vault); to raise, elevate.
peralte, *m.* (arch.) rise (of an arch); (r. w.) super-elevation (of outer rail).
perantón, *m.* (bot.) marvel plant; large fan; very tall person.
perborato, *m.* perborate.
perca, *f.* (icht.) perch.
percal, *m.* percale, muslin, calico.
percalina, *f.* percaline, book muslin.
percance, *m.* perquisite; mischance, misfortune.—percances del oficio = GAJES DEL OFICIO.
percatar, *vn. & vr.* to think, consider, to beware.
percebe, *m.* goose barnacle.
percebimiento, *m.* prevention, warning.
percentaje, *m.* percentage.
percepción, *f.* perception.
perceptibilidad, *f.* perceptibility.
perceptible, *a.* perceptible, perceivable.
perceptiblemente, *adv.* perceptibly.
perceptivo, va, *a.* perceptive.
percibir, *va.* to perceive; to receive, collect.
percibo, *m.* receiving, collecting.
perclorato, *m.* perchlorate.
perclórico, ca, *a.* perchloric.
percloruro, *m.* (chem.) perchloride.
percocería, *f.* small silver work.
percuciente, *a.* percutient, striking.
percudir, *va.* to tarnish, stain, soil.
percusión, *f.* percussion; collision.
percusor, *m.* striker, percussor; (arti.) percussion hammer.
percutir, *va.* to percuss, strike, beat.
percha, *f.* perch, pole, staff; slat; hat or clothes rack; roost; snare for birds; strip for stringing game; (icht.) perch; (naut.) spar, rough tree; head rail.
perchador, ra, *n.* napper.
perchar, *va.* to raise the nap on (cloth).
percherón, na, *a. & n.* Percheron (horse).
perchón, *m.* long shoot left on a pruned vine.
perchonar, *vn.* to prune (vines) leaving long shoots; to lay snares for game.
perdedero, *m.* occasion or motive of losing.
perdedor, ra, *n.* loser.
perder. **I.** *va.* (ind. PIERDO: subj. PIERDA) to lose; to forfeit; to squander away; to ruin; to spoil.—p. de vista, to lose sight of.—p. el juicio, to go out of one's mind.—p. los estribos, to lose one's poise, to become reckless.—tener que p., to be a person of means, to have much to lose. **II.** *vn.* to lose; to fade, lose color. **III.** *vr.* to get lost, lose one's way; to miscarry; to be lost, confounded, bewildered; to forget or lose the thread of one's subject or discourse; to be ruined, go astray, go to the dogs; to be spoiled or damaged (as fruit, crops, etc.); to fall into disuse; to be out of fashion; to cease to be perceived by sight or hearing; to love

excessively; to disappear.—p. de vista, to disappear; to excel in an eminent degree; to be very shrewd.
perdición, *f.* perdition; ruin, loss; unbridled, excessive love.
pérdida, *f.* loss; privation; detriment, damage; waste; (com.) leakage, shortage, shrinkage.—pérdidas y ganancias, profit and loss.—ir a pérdidas y ganancias, to share profit and loss.
perdidamente, *adv.* desperately; uselessly.
perdidizo, za, *a.* lost designedly or on purpose.—hacerse el p., to sneak away, disappear.—hacerse p., to lose designedly at cards.
perdido, da, *a. & pp.* lost; mislaid; misguided; profligate, dissolute.—p. por, passionately fond of, crazy about.
perdidoso, sa, *a.* sustaining loss, losing.
perdigana, *f.* young partridge.
perdigar, *va.* (pret. PERDIGUÉ: subj. PERDIGUE) (cook.) to broil (partridges) slightly; to brown (meat); to dispose, prepare.
perdigón, *m.* young partridge; decoy partridge; squanderer, losing gambler; hailshot, bird shot.—perdigonada, *f.* shot or wound with bird shot.—perdigonera, *f.* shot pouch.
perdiguero, ra. **I.** *m.* setter, retriever (dog.). **II.** *n.* poulterer, game dealer.
perdimiento, *m.* V. PERDICIÓN, PÉRDIDA.
perdiz, *f.* (orn.) partridge.
perdón, *m.* pardon, forgiveness; mercy, grace; remission of a debt; burning drop of oil, wax, etc.—con p., by your leave; I beg pardon; excuse me; begging pardon.
perdonable, *a.* pardonable, forgivable.
perdonador, ra, *n.* pardoner, excuser.
perdonante, *a.* forgiving, pardoning.
perdonar, *va.* to pardon, forgive; to remit (a debt); to exempt; to spare, excuse.—no p., not to omit or spare.
perdonavidas, *m.* (coll.) bully, hector.
perdulario, ria, *a.* reckless, careless.
perdurable, *a.* lasting, abiding, everlasting.
perdurablemente, *adv.* everlastingly, lastingly.
perdurar, *vn.* to last long.
perecear, **I.** *va.* to protract, delay, put off. **II.** *vn.* to indulge one's laziness, to idle.
perecedero, ra. **I.** *a.* perishable, not lasting. **II.** *m.* extreme want.
perecer. **I.** *vn.* (ind. PEREZCO: subj. PEREZCA) to perish; to come to an end; to suffer or undergo damage, toil, or fatigue. **II.** *vr.* to crave, desire anxiously, pine.
pereciente, *a.* perishing; pining.
perecimiento, *m.* loss, decline; shipwreck.
pereda, *f.* orchard of pear trees.
peregrinación, *f.*, peregrinaje, *m.* peregrination; pilgrimage; course of this life.
peregrinamente, *adv.* rarely, curiously.
peregrinante, *a.* traveling; roaming.
peregrinar, *vn.* to travel, roam.
peregrinidad, *f.* peregrinity.
peregrino, na. **I.** *a.* peregrine, foreign; traveling, migratory; strange, odd, rare; handsome, perfect. **II.** *n.* pilgrim, palmer.
perejil, *m.* (bot.) parsley; (coll.) showy dress or apparel.—pl. (coll.) handle (titles).
perejila, *f.* a card game.
Perencejo, ja, *n.* V. PERENGANO.
perendeca, *f.* (coll.) prostitute.
perendengue, *m.* earring, eardrop; cheap or tawdry ornament.
Perengano, na, *n.* So-and-So (= MENGANO).
perennal, *a.* = PERENNE.
perennalmente, *adv.* = PERENNEMENTE.
perenne, *a.* perennial, perpetual.
perennemente, *adv.* continually, perpetually.
perennidad, *f.* perennity, continuity.
perentoriamente, *adv.* peremptorily; urgently.
perentoriedad, *f.* peremptoriness; urgency.
perentorio, ria, *a.* peremptory; urgent; decisive.
perero, *m.* fruit parer.
pereza, *f.* laziness, sloth; slowness.
perezco, yo perezca. V. PERECER.

perezosamente, *adv.* lazily, slothfully, idly.
perezoso, sa. I. *a.* lazy, indolent, slothful, idle. **II.** *m.* (zool.) sloth.
perfección, *f.* perfection; perfect thing; beauty, grace.—**a la p.,** perfectly.
perfeccionamiento, *m.* perfecting, improvement, finish.
perfeccionar, *va.* to improve, perfect.
perfectamente, *adv.* perfectly.—**perfectible,** *a.* perfectible.—**perfectivo, va,** *a.* perfective.
perfecto, ta, *a.* perfect; (gram.) perfect (tense).
perficiente, *a.* perfecting.
pérfidamente, *adv.* perfidiously.—**perfidia,** *f.* perfidy.—**pérfido, da,** *a.* perfidious, treacherous.
perfil, *m.* profile, side view; outline; upstroke of letters.
perfilado, da. I. *pp.* & *a.* elongated; outlined. **II.** *m.* (eng.) structural shape.
perfiladura, *f.* profile drawing; sketching of outlines.
perfilar. I. *va.* to outline; to make fine upstrokes. **II.** *vr.* to place one's self sideways; to make an elaborate toilet.
perfoliada, *f.* (bot.) hare's-ear, thorough wax.
perfoliado, da, *a.* (bot.) perfoliate.
perfolla, *f.* = PERFOLIADA.
perfolla, *f.* corn husk; shucks.
perforación, *f.* perforation, hole; drilling, boring.
perforador, ra. I. *a.* & *n.* perforator (-ing), driller (-ing). **II.** *f.* drill, rock drill.
perforar, *va.* to perforate; to bore, drill.
perfumadero, *m.* perfuming pan.
perfumado, da, *a.* & *pp.* odoriferous, perfumed.
perfumador, ra. I. *a.* perfuming. **II.** *m.* perfumer, perfuming pan.
perfumar, *va.* to perfume.
perfume, *m.* perfume; odor, fragrance.
perfumear, *va.* to perfume.
perfumería, *f.* perfumery; perfumer's shop.
perfumero, ra; perfumista, *n.* perfumer.
perfunctoriamente, *adv.* perfunctorily.
perfunctorio, ria, *a.* perfunctory.
pergal, *m.* leather paring for shoe laces.
pergaminero, *m.* parchment maker.
pergamino, *m.* parchment, vellum; diploma.
pergenio, *m.* (coll.) appearance, looks.
pergeñar, *va.* (coll.) to prepare or perform skilfully.
pergeño, *m.* (coll.) appearance, looks.
peri, *f.* fairy, elf, peri.
periantio, *m.* (bot.) perianth.
pericardio, *m.* (anat.) pericardium.
pericarditis, *f.* (med.) pericarditis.
pericarpio, *m.* (bot.) pericarp.
pericia, *f.* skill, expertness.—**pericial,** *a.* expert. —**pericialmente,** *adv.* expertly.
perico, *m.* (orn.) parrakeet; periwig; horseman (queen) of clubs in the game of TRUQUE; (naut.) mizzen topgallant sail.—**p. de los palotes,** John Jones (any insignificant person).
pericón, na. I. *a.* fit for all uses. **II.** *m.* large fan; horseman (queen) of clubs in the game of QUÍNOLAS.
pericráneo, *m.* pericranium.
periecos, *m. pl.* (geog.) periœci.
periferia, *f.* periphery.
periférico, ca, *a.* peripheric, circumferential.
perifollo, *m.* (bot.) common chervil.—*pl.* ribbons, tawdry ornaments of dress.
perifonear, *va.* (rad.) to broadcast.
perifonía, *f.* (rad.) broadcasting.
perífono, *m.* (rad.) broadcasting instrument.
perifrasear, *va.* to periphrase.
perífrasi, perífrasis, *f.* (rhet.) periphrasis.
perifrástico, ca, *a.* periphrastic.
perigallo, *m.* skin hanging from the chin of lean persons; gawdy ribbon worn on the hair; (coll.) tall, lean person; slender sling; (naut.) line, topping lift.
perigeo, *m.* (ast.) perigee, perigeum.
perigonio, *m.* (bot.) perigynium, perianth.

perígono, *m.* (geom.) perigon.
perihelio, *m.* (ast.) perihelion.
perilustre, *a.* very illustrious.
perilla, *f.* *dim.* small pear; pear-shaped ornament; pommel of a saddlebow; goatee, imperial; lobe of the ear.—**de p.,** to the purpose; in the nick of time.
perillán, na, *n.* rascal; sly, crafty person.
perillo, *m.* scalloped cookie or maccaroon.
perímetro, *m.* perimeter.
perínclito, ta, *a.* famous, renowned.
perineo, *m.* (anat.) perineum.
perineumonía, *f.* (med.) pneumonia.
perineumónico, ca, *a.* pneumonic.
perinola, *f.* teetotum; pear-shaped ornament; neat little woman.
períoca, *f.* synopsis, summary.
periódicamente, *adv.* periodically.
periodicidad, *f.* periodicity, periodicalness.
periódico, ca. I. *a.* periodical, periodic. **II.** *m.* newspaper; periodical, journal.
periodismo, *m.* journalism.—**periodista,** *m.* journalist.—**periodístico, ca,** *a.* journalistic.
período, *m.* period, age, era; (rhet.) period, clause, sentence; menstruation; (mus.) period, phrase; (elec.) cycle.
periostio, *m.* (anat.) periosteum.
periostitis, *f.* (med.) periostitis.
peripatético, ca. I. *a.* Peripatetic; (coll.) ridiculous or extravagant (opinion). **II.** *n.* Peripatetic.
peripato, *m.* Peripateticism.
peripecia, *f.* situation, incident, episode.
periplo, *m.* voyage around a coast.
períptero, ra, *a.* (arch.) peripteral.
peripuesto, ta, *a.* (coll.) very spruce in dress.
periquete, *m.* (coll.) jiffy, instant.
periquillo, *m.* sugar plum.—**periquito,** *m.* (orn.) parrakeet, paroquet; (naut.) skysail.
periscios, *m. pl.* (geog.) periscii.
periscópico, ca, *a.* periscopic.
periscopio, *m.* periscope.
perisología, *f.* (rhet.) verbiage.
peristáltico, ca, *a.* peristaltic.
peristilo, *m.* (arch.) peristyle, colonnade.
perita, *f.* *dim.* small pear.
peritaje, *m.* occupation of an expert.
peritiflitis, *f.* (med.) perityphlitis.
perito, ta. I. *a.* skilful, able, experienced. **II.** *n.* connoisseur, expert; appraiser.
peritoneal, *a.* (anat.) peritoneal.—**peritoneo,** *m.* (anat.) peritoneum.—**peritonitis,** *f.* (med.) peritonitis.
perjudicador, ra, *n.* & *a.* injurer (-ing).
perjudicante, *a.* damaging, injurious.
perjudicar, *va.* (*pret.* PERJUDIQUÉ: *subj.* PERJUDIQUE) to damage, hurt, injure, impair.
perjudicial, *a.* harmful, injurious.
perjudicialmente, *adv.* harmfully, injuriously.
perjuicio, *m.* prejudice, injury, detriment, damage, grievance.
perjurador, ra, *n.* perjurer, forswearer.
perjurar. I. *vn.* to commit perjury; to swear, be profane. **II.** *vr.* to perjure one's self.
perjurio, *m.* perjury.
perjuro, ra. I. *a.* perjured, forsworn. **II.** *n.* forswearer, perjurer.
perla, *f.* pearl; jewel (fig.); (print.) pearl.—*pl.* fine teeth.—**de perlas,** much to the purpose; fitting to a tee.
perlada, *a.* pearled (barley).
perlático, ca, *a.* paralyzed, palsied.
perlería, *f.* collection of pearls.
perlesía, *f.* (med.) paralysis, palsy.
perlezuela, *f.* *dim.* small pearl.
perlino, na, *a.* pearl-colored.
perlita, *f.* *dim.* small pearl; phonolite, clinkstone.
perlongar, *vn.* (*for mut. v.* PROLONGAR) (naut.) to coast; to pay out a cable.
permanecer, *vn.* (*ind.* PERMANEZCO: *subj.* PERMANEZCA) to stay, remain, endure, last.

---

permaneciente, *a.* permanent.
permanencia, *f.* stay, sojourn; duration, permanence; perseverance, constancy.—**permanente,** *a.* permanent.—**permanentemente,** *adv.* permanently.
permanganato, *m.* permanganate.
permeabilidad, *f.* permeability.
permeable, *a.* permeable.
permisible, *a.* permissible.
permisión, *f.* permission, leave, permit; concession, grant.
permisivamente, *adv.* permissively.
permisivo, va, *a.* permissive.
permiso, *m.* permission, permit, leave, license; difference in weight of coin.
permisor, ra, *n.* granter, permitter.
permistión, *f.* mixture, concoction.
permitente, *a.* permitting, allowing.
permitidero, ra, *a.* permissible.
permitidor, ra, *n.* permitter, granter.
permitir, *va.* to permit, allow; to grant, admit.
permuta, *f.* barter; exchange.
permutable, *a.* permutable.
permutación, *f.* interchange; (math.) permutation.
permutar, *va. & vn.* to exchange, interchange, barter; to permute.
perna, *f.* flat shellfish.
pernada, *f.* blow with the leg; shake of the leg; (naut.) leg.
pernaza, *f. aug.* thick or big leg.
perneador, *a.* strong-legged.
pernear. I. *vn.* to kick, shake the legs; to hustle; to worry, fret. **II.** *va.* to drive (pigs) to market and sell by retail.
perneo, *m.* public sale of hogs.
pernera, *f.* leg of a pair of trousers.
pernería, *f.* (naut.) collection of bolts.
pernetas.—en p., bare-legged.
pernete, *m.* (naut.) small pin, peg, or bolt.
perniabierto, ta, *a.* bowlegged.
perniciosamente, *adv.* perniciously.
pernicioso, sa, *a.* pernicious; injurious, harmful.
pernigón, *m.* Genoese preserved plum.
pernil, *m.* shoulder, hock, ham; thigh of breeches; pantalets.
pernio, *m.* door or window hinge.
perniquebrar, *va.* to break the legs of.
pernituerto, ta, *a.* crook-legged.
perno, *m.* bolt; pin, spike; hook of a door-hinge; (mech.) joint pin, crank pin.—**p. pinzote,** main bolt, kingbolt.
pernoctar, *vn.* to pass the night.
pero, *m.* a variety of apple; apple tree.
pero. I. *conj.* but, except, yet. **II.** *m.* fault, defect.
perogrullada, *f.* (coll.) evident truth, truism; platitude.
Perogrullo.—verdad de P. = PEROGRULLADA.
perojiménez, *m.* a variety of grape; wine made from it.
perol, *m.* (cook.) kettle, copper.
peroné, *m.* (anat.) fibula, perone.
peroración, *f.* peroration.
perorar, *vn.* to deliver a speech or oration; to declaim; to urge.
perorata, *f.* (coll.) harangue, speech.
peróxido, *m.* (chem.) peroxide.
perpendicular, *n. & a.* perpendicular.
perpendicularidad, *f.* perpendicularity.
perpendicularmente, *adv.* perpendicularly.
perpendículo, *m.* plumb, plummet; altitude of a triangle; pendulum.
perpetración, *f.* perpetration.
perpetrador, ra, *n.* perpetrator, aggressor.
perpetrar, *va.* to perpetrate, commit.
perpetua, *f.* (bot.) immortelle, cudweed.
perpetuación, *f.* perpetuation.
perpetuamente, *adv.* perpetually.
perpetuán, *m.* a kind of woollen stuff.
perpetuar, *va. & vr.* to perpetuate.
perpetuidad, *f.* perpetuity.

perpetuo, tua, *a.* perpetual, everlasting.—**p. silencio,** forever hold his peace.
perpiaño, *m.* (arch.) perpend.
perplejamente, *adv.* perplexedly, confusedly.
perplejidad, *f.* perplexity, irresolution, embarrassment, hesitation.
perplejo, ja, *a.* uncertain, perplexed.
perpunte, *m.* quilted under-waistcoat.
perquirir, *va.* to seek diligently.
perra, *f.* bitch, slut; drunken state.—**p. chica =** PERRC CHICO.
perrada, *f.* pack of dogs; mean, base action.
perramente, *adv.* very badly, wretchedly.
perrazo, *m. aug.* large dog.
perrengue, *m.* (coll.) peevish person, snarler; negro.
perrera, *f.* kennel; toil, drudgery; (coll.) bad pay; child's fit of temper.—**perrería,** *f.* pack of dogs; set or nest of rogues; angry word.—**perrero,** *m.* beadle who drags dogs out of the church; master of hounds or dogs; dog fancier.
perrezno, na, *n.* whelp, puppy.
perrillo, lla; to, ta. I. *n.* little dog; puppy.—**p. de falda,** or **faldero,** lap dog. **II.** *m.* trigger of a gun; piece of horse's bridle.
perro, rra, *n.* dog.—**p. alforjero,** camp watchdog.—**p. braco,** pointer dog.—**p. cobrador,** retriever.—**p. chico,** five-centime copper coin.—**p. de aguas,** poodle.—**p. de ajeo,** setter.—**p. de lanas =** P. DE AGUAS.—**p. de muestra,** pointer.—**p. de presa,** bulldog.—**p. de Terranova,** Newfoundland dog.—**p. dogo,** bulldog.—**p. galgo,** hound.—**p. tomador,** retriever.—**p. viejo,** cautious person; experienced person.
perroquete, *m.* (naut.) topmast.
perruno, na. I. *a.* doggish, canine; currish. **II.** *f.* dog bread, dog cake.
persa, *a. & n.* Persian.
persecución, *f.* persecution; pursuit; harassment; importunity.
persecutorio, ria, *a.* persecutory, of persecution.
perseguidor, ra, *n.* persecutor; pursuer.
perseguimiento, *m. =* PERSECUCIÓN.
perseguir, *va.* (*for irr. v.* SEGUIR) to pursue; to persecute; to importune, beset.
Perseo, *m.* (ast.) Perseus.
persevante, *m.* pursuivant at arms.
perseverancia, *f.* perseverance.
perseverante, *a.* perseverant, persevering.
perseverantemente, *adv.* perseveringly.
perseverar, *vn.* to persevere, persist.
persiana, *f.* flowered silk stuff; window blind.
persicaria, *f.* (bot.) persicaria, lady's-thumb.
pérsico, ca. I. *a.* Persian. **II.** *m.* (bot.) peach tree and its fruit.
persignarse, *vr.* to cross one's self; to handsel.
pérsigo, *m.* (bot.) peach tree and its fruit.
persigo, persiga. *V.* PERSEGUIR.
persistencia, *f.* persistence; obstinacy.
persistente, *a.* persistent; permanent, firm.
persistir, *vn.* to persist, persevere.
persona, *f.* person; one's shape and looks; personage; (theol., law, and gram.) person.
personada, *a.* (bot.) personate.
personado, *m.* (eccl.) benefice without jurisdiction.
personaje, *m.* personage; (theat.) character.
personal. I. *a.* personal, private. **II.** *m.* personnel; personal tax.
personalidad, *f.* personality; individuality; (law) person; legal capacity.
personalizar. I. *va.* to personalize; to become personal. **II.** *vr.* (law) to show one's self a party at law.
personalmente, *adv.* personally, in person.
personarse, *vr.* to meet on business; to appear personally; (law) to appear as an interested party.
personería, *f.* solicitorship.
personero, ra, *n.* solicitor, deputy, agent, attorney, counsel.
personificación, *f.* personification.

For pronunciation, see the rules at the beginning of the book.

personificar, va. (pret. PERSONIFIQUÉ: subj. PERSONIFIQUE) to personify.
personilla, f. ridiculous little person.
perspectiva, f. perspective; view, vista; prospect, outlook; appearance.
perspectivo, m. one versed in perspective.
perspicacia, perspicacidad, f. perspicaciousness, perspicacity, acumen, sagacity.
perspicaz, a. acute, sagacious, clear-sighted.
perspicuamente, adv. perspicuously.
perspicuidad, f. perspicuity, lucidity.
perspicuo, cua, a. perspicuous, clear.
persuadidor, ra, n. persuader.
persuadir. I. va. to persuade, induce; to convince. **II.** vr. to be persuaded; to be convinced.
persuasible, a. persuasible, persuadable.
persuasión, f. persuasion; conviction, opinion.
persuasiva, f. persuasiveness.
persuasivo, va, a. persuasive, convincing.
persuasor, ra, n. persuader, inducer.
pertenecer, vn. (ind. PERTENEZCO: subj. PERTENEZCA) to belong, appertain; to concern; to
‹ behoove.
pertenecido, pp. & m. = PERTENENCIA.
perteneciente, a. belonging, appertaining.
pertenencia, f. ownership; tenure, holding, property, possession; appurtenance, dependence, accessory; (min.) claim.
pértica, f. perch, linear measure (9.70 feet).
pértiga, f., **pertigal,** m. bar, staff, pole, rod.
pértigo, m. carriage; plow beam.
pertiguería, f. office of a verger.
pertiguero, m. verger.
pertinacia, f. insistence, obstinacy, stubbornness, doggedness.
pertinaz, a. pertinacious, obstinate, opinionated.
pertinazmente, adv. pertinaciously.
pertinencia, f. pertinence, fitness, relevancy.
pertinente, a. pertinent, apt, appropriate, relevant; (law) concerning, pertaining.
pertinentemente, adv. pertinently, opportunely, congruously.
pertrechar, va. & vr. (mil.) to supply, store, equip; to dispose, arrange, prepare.
pertrechos, m. pl. (mil.) stores; tools.
perturbable, a. easily perturbed.
perturbación, f. perturbation, disturbance; agitation, excitement.
perturbadamente, adv. confusedly.
perturbador, ra, n. & a. perturber (-ing), disturber (-ing).
perturbar, va. to perturb, disturb, unsettle; to confuse, agitate.
peruano, na, n. & a. Peruvian.
peruétano, m. (bot.) wild pear tree.
perulero, ra. I. n. & a. Peruvian. **II.** m. narrow-bottomed and strait-mouthed pitcher.
perversamente, adv. perversely, wickedly.
perversidad, f. perversity, wickedness.
perversión, f. perversion, perverting; perverseness, depravation, wickedness.
perverso, sa, a. perverse, wicked, depraved.
pervertidor, ra, n. perverter, corrupter.
pervertimiento, m. perversion, perverting.
pervertir. I. va. (for irr. v. VERTIR) to pervert, distort, garble; to corrupt, debase. **II.** vr. to become depraved.
pervigilio, m. sleeplessness, wakefulness.
pervulgar, va. to divulge; to promulgate.
pesa, f. weight; clock weight; counterweight.—**p. de una romana,** weight of a steelyard.—**pesas y medidas,** weights and measures.
pesada, f. weighing; quantity weighed at once.
pesadamente, adv. heavily; cumbrously; sorrowfully, grievingly; slowly, lazily.
pesadez, f. heaviness; slowness; drowsiness; importunity; excess, abundance; trouble, pain, fatigue; obesity, corpulence.
pesadilla, f. nightmare.
pesado, da. I. pp. & a. heavy; massive; deep, profound (sleep); cumbersome, cumbrous; tedi-

ous, tiresome; dull; offensive; slow, lazy; clumsy; fat or corpulent; insufferable, importunate, annoying, vexatious. **II.** n. bore, tease.
pesador, ra, n. weigher.—**p. de cartas,** letter scale.
pesadumbre, f. grief, affliction, sorrow; heaviness.
pesalicores, m. hydrometer.
pésame, m. condolence.
pesante. I. a. weighing. **II.** m. weight of half a drachm.
pesantez, f. (phys.) gravity; heaviness.
pesar. I. vn. to weigh, have weight; to be weighty, important, or valuable; (often w. de) to cause regret, sorrow or repentance (ch. constr.: me pesa rehusar, I regret to refuse; me pesa de haber ofendido a Vd., I am sorry to have offended you); to preponderate.—**mal que le pese,** however much it may displease you; whether you like it or not.—**pese a quien pese,** whatever anybody says or does, let them say what they will. **II.** va. to weigh; to examine, consider, think or ponder over. **III.** m. sorrow, grief, regret; repentance.—**a p. de,** in spite of, notwithstanding.—**a. p. mío,** or **a mi p.,** in spite of me, against my wishes.
pesario, m. (surg.) pessary.
pesaroso, sa, a. sorrowful, regretful; sorry, sad.
pesca, f. fishing, angling; fishery; fish caught.
pescada, f. (icht.) hake.—**pescadera,** f. fishwoman.—**pescadería,** f. fish market.—**pescadero,** m. fishmonger.—**pescadilla,** f. small hake.
pescadito, m. dim. little fish.
pescado, pp. & m. fish (when caught); salted codfish.
pescador, ra. I. n. fisherman (-woman). **II.** m. (icht.) angler.
pescante, m. jib of a crane or derrick; boom; coach box; (naut.) davit; fish davit.
pescar. I. va. & vn. (pret. PESQUÉ: subj. PESQUE) to fish. **II.** va. to find or pick up; to catch in the act, surprise; to obtain, get.
péscola, f. beginning of a furrow.
pescozada, f.; **pescozón,** m. slap on the neck; fisticuff.
pescozudo, da, a. having a thick neck.
pescuezo, m. neck; stiff-necked haughtiness, airs.
pescuño, m. wedge of the coulter.
pesebre, m. crib, rack; manger.—**pesebrejo,** m. dim. small manger; alveolus of horses' teeth.
pesebrera, f. stable; range of mangers in a stable.
pesebrón, m. boot of a coach.
peseta, f. peseta (about 1 franc).
pésete, m. imprecation; execration.
¡pesia! ¡pesia tal! interj. confound it! blazes!
pesiar, vn. to utter curses or execrations.
pesillo, m. small scales for weighing gold or silver coin.
pésimamente, adv. very badly, wretchedly.
pesimismo, m. pessimism.
pesimista, n. & a. pessimist (-ic).
pésimo, ma, a. super. very bad, wretched, abominable.
pesita, f. dim. small weight.
peso, m. weight; heaviness; weighing; balance, scales; importance, moment; burden, load; place where various victuals are sold at wholesale; judgment, good sense; peso (monetary unit).—**p. bruto,** gross weight.—**p. duro,** or **fuerte,** (Spain) duro (5 pesetas); (Am.) one-ounce peso (theoretically, about 1 dollar).—**p. específico,** specific gravity.—**p. neto,** net weight.—**p. seco,** (aer.) dry weight.—**caerse de su p.,** to be self-evident.—**de p.,** of due weight; weighty, of weight, of importance; cogent.—**de su p.,** naturally.—**en p.,** suspended in the air; bodily; totally; undecided.
pesol, m. (bot.) bean.
pespuntador, ra, n. (sew.) backstitcher.
pespuntar, va. & vn. (sew.) to backstitch.
pespunte, m. (sew.) backstitching.
pesquera, f. fishery, fishing grounds.
pesquería, f. trade of a fisherman; fishing; angling; fishery.

pesquis, m. acumen, cleverness.
pesquisa, f. inquiry, investigation, search.
pesquisante, a. investigating, inquiring.
pesquisar, va. to inquire into, investigate.
pesquisidor, ra, n. searcher, investigator.
pestaña, f. eyelash; (sew.) fag-end, fringe, edging; (mech.) flange; (bot.) hairs.
pestañear, vn. to wink, to blink.
pestañeo, m. winking, blinking.
peste, f. pest, plague, pestilence; epidemic; corruption of manners; foul smell; (coll.) excess, superabundance.—pl. offensive words.—**p. bubónica,** bubonic plague.
pestíferamente, adv. pestiferously.
pestífero. ra, a. pestiferous, noxious, foul.
pestilencia, f. pest, plague, pestilence; foulness, stench.—**pestilencial,** a. pestiferous, pestilential; infectious, contagious; destructive.
pestilencioso, sa, a. pestilential.
pestilente, a. pestilent, noxious, foul.
pestillo, m. door latch; bolt of a lock.
pestiño, m. honeyed fritters.
pestorejazo, m. = PESCOZÓN.
pestorejo, m. fleshy back of the neck.
pestorejón, m. blow on the back of the neck.
pesuña, f. foot of cloven-hoofed animals.
pesuño, m. each half of a cloven hoof.
petaca, f. cigar case; (Am.) leather trunk or chest; covered hamper.
petalismo, m. petalism, banishment.
pétalo, m. (bot.) petal.
petaquilla, f. small, leather trunk.
petar, va. (coll.) to please, gratify, content.
petardear, va. (mil.) to beat down with petards; to cheat, gull, trick.
petardero, m. (mil.) petardeer; cheat, trickster.
petardista, n. cheat, impostor, swindler.
petardo, m. (arti.) petard; bomb; cheat, fraud, gull, trick.
petate, m. (Am.) sleeping mat; (coll.) luggage, baggage; impostor, swindler; good-for-nothing fellow; (naut.) sailor's hammock.—**liar el p.,** (coll.) to pack up and go.
petenera, f. a popular Andalusian song.
petequia, f. (med.) petechia.
petera, f. (coll.) wrangle; fit of temper.
peteretes, m. pl. (coll.) titbits, sweets.
peticano, peticanón, m. (print.) petit-canon type.
petición, f. petition, demand, claim, request; (law) petition, prayer.
peticionario, ria, n. petitioner.
petillo, m. dim. small stomacher; breast jewel.
petimetra, f. spruce, stylish lady.
petimetre, m. fop, coxcomb, beau, dude.
petirrojo, m. (orn.) robin redbreast.
petitorio, ria. I. a. petitory, petitionary. **II.** m. impertinent and repeated petition. **III.** f. (coll.) PETICIÓN.
peto, m. breastplate; stomacher; (fenc.) plastron.
petral, m. (sad.) breast leather.
petraria, f. (mil.) petrary.
petrarquesco, ca, a. Petrarchan.
petrarquista, n. & a. Petrarchist (-ic).
petrel, m. (orn.) petrel.
pétreo, a, a. rocky; stony, of stone.
petrificación, f. petrification.—**petrificante,** a. petrifying.—**petrificar,** va. & vr. to petrify.—**petrífico, ca,** a. petrifying.
petrografía, f. petrography.
petrográfico, ca, a. petrographic.
petróleo, m. petroleum, mineral oil.
petrolero, ra. I. a. petroleum, oil (u. a.). **II.** n. seller of petroleum; oil man, one engaged in the petroleum industry; incendiary, petroleur; ultraradical.
petrolífero, ra, a. petroliferous, oil-bearing.
petrosílex, m., **petrosílice,** f. petrosilex, felsite.
petroso, sa, a. rocky, full of stones.
petulancia, f. petulance, insolence, flippancy, pertness.—**petulante,** a. petulant, insolent, pert. —**petulantemente,** adv. petulantly, pertly.

petunia, f. (bot.) petunia.
peucédano, m. (bot.) Peucedanum.
pez. I. m. fish; catch, haul.—**p. espada,** swordfish.—**p. luna,** mola, sunfish.—**p. martillo,** hammer-headed shark.—**p. sierra,** sawfish.—**p. volador,** flying fish. **II.** f. pitch, tar.—**p. blanca,** or **de Borgoña,** refined galipot, Burgundy pitch.—**p. griega,** or **rubia,** rosin, colophony.
pezolada, f. fag-end threads.
pezón, m. (bot.) stem of fruits; leaf stalk; flower stalk; nipple of a teat; axle end or pivot; end of a spindle in mills; cape or point of land.
pezonera, f. nipple shield; linchpin.
pezpalo, m. (com.) stockfish.
pezpita, f., pezpítalo, m. (orn.) wagtail.
pezuelo, m. beginning of cloth in weaving.
pezuña, f. = PESUÑA.
piache, or **tarde piache,** too late.
píada, f. chirping, puling.
piador, ra, n. puler, chirper.
piadosamente, adv. piously; mercifully.
piadoso, sa, a. pious, godly; merciful.
piafar, vn. to paw, to stamp (s. o. horses).
piale, m. (Am.) cast of the lasso.
piamadre, piamáter, f. (anat.) pia mater.
piamente, adv. piously.
piamontés, sa, n. & a. Piedmontese.
pían, pián; or **pían, piano,** adv. slowly, softly.
pianino, m. (mus.) upright piano.
pianista, n. pianist; piano maker or dealer.
piano, pianoforte, m. piano, pianoforte.—**p. de cola,** grand piano.—**p. de media cola,** baby grand.—**p. de mesa,** square piano.—**p. vertical,** upright piano.
pianola, f. pianola.
piante, a. peeping, puling, chirping.
piar, vn. to peep, pule, chirp; (coll.) to whine, cry.
piara, f. herd of swine; drove (of mares, mules).
piariego, ga, a. owning a herd of mares, mules, or swine.
piastra, f. a small coin of variable value (gen. about 5 cents).
pica, f. pike, lance; bullfighter's goad; stonecutter's hammer; (med.) pica.—**poner una p. en Flandes,** to achieve a triumph.
picacero, ra, a. magpie-chasing (s. o. hawks).
picacureba, f. a Brazilian pigeon.
picacho, m. top, peak, summit.
picada, f. puncture, pricking, bite; sharp, pricking pain.
picadero, m. riding school; (naut.) stocks, boat skid; stamping ground of a buck in rutting time.
picadillo, m. minced meat; hash.
picado, da. I. a. & pp. pricked; piqued, hurt; (sew.) pinked. **II.** m. minced meat; hash; (aer.) diving; dive.
picador, m. horse-breaker; horseman armed with a goad in bullfights; chopping block; paper pricker; pinking iron; file cutter.
picadura, f. pricking; pinking; puncture; bite; sting; nick, cut, slash; cut tobacco.
picafigo, m. (orn.) = PAPAFIGO.
picaflor, m. (orn.) humming bird.
picajón, na; picajoso, sa, peevish, querulous.
picamaderos, m. (orn.) woodpecker.
picana, f. (S. A.) goad.—**picanear,** va. to goad.
picante. I. a. pricking, piercing, stinging; high-seasoned, hot. **II.** m. piquancy, pungency, acrimony; keen satire.
picantemente, adv. piquantly.
picaño, ña. I. a. lazy, vagrant. **II.** m. patch on a shoe.
picapedrero, m. stonecutter.
picapica, f. a plant whose leaves and fruit produce intense smarting of the skin.
picapleitos, m. (coll.) litigious person; pettifogging lawyer.
picaporte, m. spring latch, catch bolt; picklock, latchkey; (Am.) door knocker.
picaposte, m. (orn.) woodpecker.
picapuerco, m. (orn.) an insectivorous bird.

plcar. I. *va.* (*pret.* PIQUÉ: *subj.* PIQUE) to prick, pierce, puncture; to sting, bite (as insects); to mince, chop, hash; to peck (s. o. birds); to nibble, pick, take little bites of; to pursue or harass; to spur, goad, incite; to pink; to pique, vex; to tame; (art.) to stipple; to roughen with a pointed tool.—**p. la bomba,** to work the pump. **II.** *vn.* to sting, bite (as insects); to bite (s. o. fish); to itch, burn, smart; to scorch, burn (as the sun) (aer.) to dive.—**p. alto,** to aim high.—**p. en,** to be, to be somewhat of a (poet, etc.). **III.** *vr.* to be offended or piqued; to be moth-eaten; to stale, sour (as wine); to begin to rot (as fruit); to boast of; to be in heat (s. o. animals); (naut.) to become choppy (s. o. the sea).

picaramente, *adv.* knavishly, roguishly.

picaraza, *f.* (orn.) magpie.

picardear, *vn.* to play the knave; to do mischief.

picardía, *f.* knavery, roguery; deceit, malice, foulness; wanton trick, wantonness; lewdness; meeting of rogues.—*pl.* offensive words.

picardihuela, *f. dim.* prank, roguish trick.

picaresca, *f.* nest of rogues; knavery.

picarescamente, *adv.* roguishly, rascally.

picaresco, ca; picaril, *a.* roguish, knavish.

picarillo, *m. dim.* little rogue or rascal.

pícaro, ra. I. *a.* knavish, roguish; vile, low; mischievous; crafty, sly. **II.** *n.* rogue, knave, rascal.—**p. de cocina,** scullion, kitchen boy.

picarón, *n. aug.* great rogue.

picarona, *f.* jade.

picaronazo, za; picarote, ta, *n.* great rogue or rascal.

picarrelincho, *m.* (orn.) = PICAMADEROS.

picatoste, *m.* buttered toast.

picaza, *f.* (orn.) magpie; grub ax, mattock.—**p. marina,** (orn.) flamingo.

picazo, za. I. *a.* black and white. **II.** *m.* blow with a pike; sting; stroke with the beak of a bird; young magpie.

picazón, *m.* itching, itch, smarting; peevishness, fretfulness.

pícea, *f.* (bot.) spruce.

píceo, a, *a.* piceous.

pico, *m.* beak or bill of a bird; sharp point of any kind; pick, pickaxe; twibill; spout of a jar or pitcher; beak iron of an anvil; peak, top, summit; small balance of an account, small amount over; (coll.) mouth, chin; loquacity, garrulity; (Philip.) weight of 137½ pounds; (orn.) woodpecker.—**p. de cigüeña,** (bot.) crane's bill, geranium.—**p. de oro,** silver-tongued orator, man of great eloquence.—**p. de ancla,** (naut.) bill of an anchor.—**p. verde,** green woodpecker.—**picos de un sombrero,** cocks of a hat.—**andar a picos pardos,** to loiter; to go on a spree.—**callar el p.,** to hold one's tongue.—**tener mucho p.,** to talk too much, to have a long tongue.

picofeo, *m.* (Am.) toucan.

picolete, *m.* bolt staple.

picón, na. I. *a.* having the upper teeth projecting over the under ones (s. o. animals). **II.** *m.* lampoon or nipping jest; charcoal for brasiers; small fresh-water fish; broken rice.

piconero, *m.* maker of brasier charcoal.

picor, *m.* pungent taste; itching.

picoso, sa, *a.* pitted with the smallpox.

picota, *f.* gibblet, pillory; top, peak, point, spire; (naut.) cheek of a pump.

picotada, *f.,* **picotazo,** *m.* stroke with the beak.

picote, *m.* goat's-hair cloth.

picoteado, da, *pp.* & *a.* peaked; having many points.

picotear. I. *va.* to strike with the beak. **II.** *vn.* to gossip; to toss the head (s. o. horses). **III.** *vr.* to wrangle or quarrel.

picotería, *f.* loquacity, volubility; gossip.

picotero, ra, *a.* chattering, prattling.

picotillo, *m.* inferior goat's-hair cloth.

picrato, *m.* (chem.) picrate.

pícrico, ca, *a.* (chem.) picric.

pictografía, *f.* pictography, picture writing.

pictórico, ca, *a.* pictorial.

picudilla, *f.* crescent olive; an insectivorous bird.

picudo, da, *a.* beaked; acuminated, pointed; prattling, chattering.

pichel, *m.* pewter tankard; mug; pitcher.

pichelería, *f.* factory of tankards or pitchers.

pichelero, *m.* maker of pewter tankards.

pichelete, *m. dim.* small tankard or mug.

pichi, *m.* pichi, a Chilean medicinal shrub.

pichoa, *f.* a Chilean euphorbiaceous cathartic plant.

pichola, *f.* a wine measure (about a pint).

pichón. I. *m.* young pigeon. **II.** *n.* (coll.) darling, dearest.

pidientero, *m.* beggar.

pido, pida, él pidió. *V.* PEDIR.

pidón, na, *a.* (coll.) *V.* PEDIGÜEÑO.

pie, *m.* foot; leg, stand, support, base; trunk (of trees and plants); lees, sediment; last hand or player (at cards); (theat.) cue; motive, occasion, opportunity; foundation, groundwork; rule, use, custom; (poet.) foot, syllable, verse; first color given in dyeing; foot of a stocking; slip, cutting (from a plant or tree).—**p. de amigo,** prop, shore.—**p. de banco,** foolish remark.—**p. de cabra,** crowbar.—**p. de cabalgar,** left foot.—**p. de carnero,** (naut.) samson's post.—**p. de imprenta,** (print.) imprint, printer's mark.—**p. de león,** (bot.) = ALQUEMILA VULGAR.—**p. de montar,** left foot.—**p. derecho,** (naut.) stanchion.—**p. de roda,** (naut.) forefoot.—**a los pies de Vd.,** at your service (said to a lady only).—**al p.,** near, close to; at the foot.—**al p. de,** at (the factory, the "job," etc.).—**al p. de la letra,** verbatim, to the letter, exactly.—**a p.,** on foot.—**a p. enjuto,** dryshod.—**a p. firme,** steadfastly.—**a p. juntillas,** firmly; uncompromisingly; most emphatically.—**con p. derecho,** auspiciously, with a good start.—**dar p.,** to give occasion.—**de a p.,** on foot.—**de p., de pies,** standing (up); up and doing; firmly.—**de pies a cabeza,** from head to foot.—**en p. =** de PIE.—**en p. de guerra,** on a war footing, mobilized.—**estar con un p. en el aire,** to be only stopping for a short time; to be about to leave.—**estar con el p. en el estribo,** to be about to leave or to act.—**ni pies ni cabeza,** neither head nor tail.

piececita, *f. dim.* little piece.

piececuelo, *m. dim.* of PIE: little foot.

piedad, *f.* piety, godliness; mercy; pity, charity; ¡por p.! for pity's sake!

piedra, *f.* stone; block; cobblestone; memorial stone; footstone; (med.) gravel; hail; place where foundlings are exposed; gunflint.—**p. amoladera =** P. DE AMOLAR.—**p. angular,** cornerstone.—**p. berroqueña,** granite.—**p. de afilar,** or de amolar, whetstone, grinding stone.—**p. de chispa,** flint.—**p. de toque,** touchstone.—**p. falsa,** imitation (precious) stone.—**p. filosofal,** philosopher's stone.—**p. fina =** P. PRECIOSA.—**p. fundamental,** cornerstone.—**p. imán,** loadstone.—**p. infernal,** caustic, lapis infernalis, nitrate of silver in sticks.—**p. lipis,** copper sulphate.—**p. melodreña =** P. DE AFILAR.—**p. miliar,** or **miliaria,** milestone.—**p. nefrítica,** (min.) nephrite, kidney stone; jade.—**p. pómez,** pumice stone.—**p. preciosa,** precious stone.—**p. rodada,** (geol.) bowlder.—**p. viva,** solid rock.—**no dejar p. sobre p.,** to raze to the ground, to destroy entirely.

piedrecica, illa, ita; **piedrezuela,** *f. dim.* little stone, pebble.

piel, skin; hide, pelt; leather; fur; peel or skin of fruits.—**p. de cabra,** goatskin.—**p. de gallina,** goose flesh.

piélago, *m.* high sea; great abundance.

pielecita, *f. dim.* small hide or skin.

pielgo, *m.* = PIEZGO.

pienso, *m.* daily feed given to horses.—**ni por p.,** (coll.) not even in thought, absolutely not.

pienso, yo piense. *V.* PENSAR.

pierdo, yo pierda. *V.* PERDER.

piérides, *f. pl.* (poet.) the Muses.

pierio, ria, *a.* (poet.) Pierian.

pierna, *f.* (anat.) leg; branch or leg of a compass; downstroke of letters; check of a printing press; jar for honey; (mech.) shank, fork.—**p. de nuez,**

lobe of a walnut.—**p. de una sábana**, breadth of a sheet.—**a p. suelta**, or **a p. tendida**, at one's ease; without care; soundly.—**en piernas**, bare-legged.

piernitendido, da, *a*. with extended legs.

pietismo, *m*. pietism.—**pietista**, *n*. & *a*. pietist (-ic).

pieza, *f*. piece; fragment; part (of a machine, etc.); member (of a structure); piece or roll of cloth; room (in a house); length of time; distance; game, quarry; piece of work; (theat.) play, piece; piece of music; piece or man in the games of draughts, chess, etc.; (her.) division of a shield.—**p. de artillería**, piece of ordnance.—**p. de autos**, records or pleadings.—**p. de recibo**, parlor, reception room.—**¡buena p.!** a fine fellow (sometimes ironical).—**de una (sola) p.**, in one piece, solid.

piezgo, *m*. foot of a hide or skin; wine skin.

piezométrico, ca, *a*. piezometric.

piezómetro, *m*. piezometer, instrument for measuring compressibility of liquids.

pífano, *m*. (mus.) fife; fifer.

pifia, *f*. miscue at billiards; error, blunder.

pifiar. **I**. *vn*. to breathe audibly in playing the flute. **II**. *vr*. to make a miscue.

pigargo, *m*. (orn.) ringtail hawk.

pigmento, *m*. pigment.

pigmeo, a. **I**. *a*. dwarfish. **II**. *n*. dwarf, pigmy.

pignoración, *f*. pignoration, hypothecation.

pignorar, *va*. to pledge, hypothecate.

pignoraticio, cia, *a*. pignorative.

pigre, *a*. slothful, lazy.—**pigricia**, *f*. laziness; place in schools for lazy boys.—**pigro, gra**, *a*. negligent, lazy.

pihua, *f*. sandal.

pihuela, *f*. leash; obstruction, hindrance, impediment.—*pl*. fetters, shackles.

piísimo, ma, *a*. *sup*. very pious, most pious.

pijamas, *m*. *pl*. pajamas.

pijota, *f*. (icht.) hake, codling.

pijote, *m*. (arti.) swivel gun for grapeshot.

pila, *f*. stone trough or basin; fountain; (eccl.) font, holy-water basin; pile, heap; shorn wool belonging to one owner; (eng., arch.) pier; (elec.) battery, pile.

pilada, *f*. quantity of mortar made at once; cloth fulled at once; pile, heap.

pilar. **I**. *va*. to hull (grain) by pounding and crushing. **II**. *m*. basin of a fountain; pillar, column, post; support; pedestal; milestone, stone post; bedpost; arbor of a press.

pilarejo, pilarito, *m*. *dim*. small pillar.

pilastra, *f*. (arch.) pilaster, square column.

pilastrón, *m*. *aug*. large pilaster.

pilatero, ra, *n*. one who assists at fulling cloth.

pilche, *m*. (Peru) wooden cup or bowl.

píldora, *f*. (pharm.) pill, pellet; (coll.) affliction, bad news.

píleo, *m*. pileus; cardinal's biretta.

pileta, pilica, *f*. *dim*. of PILA.

pilífero, ra, *a*. piliferous, hairy.

piliforme, *a*. piliform, filamentous.

pilocarpina, *f*. (chem.) pilocarpin.

pilocarpo, *m*. (bot.) jaborandi.

pilón, *m*. watering trough; basin of a fountain; mortar (for pounding); loaf (of sugar); drop or ball of a steelyard; counterpoise in an olive press; (mas.) heap of mortar.

pilonero, ra, *n*. newsmonger.

pilongo, ga, *a*. peeled and dried (chestnut); thin, lean, meager.

pilórico, ca, *a*. (anat.) pyloric.

píloro, *m*. (anat.) pylorus.

piloso, sa, *a*. pilous, pilose, hairy.

pilotaje, *m*. (naut.) pilotage; pilework, piling.

pilotar, *va*. to pilot.

pilote, *m*. (eng.) pile.

pilotear, *va*. to pilot.

pilotín, *m*. (naut.) pilot's mate, second pilot.

piloto, *m*. (naut.) pilot, sailing master, navigator; first mate; mate.—**p. de altura**, sea pilot.—**p. de costa**, coast pilot.—**p. de puerto**, port pilot.—**p. práctico** = P. DE COSTA.

piltraca, piltrafa, *f*. skinny flesh; hide parings.—*pl*. scraps of food.

pilla, *f*. pillage, plunder.

pillada, *f*. (coll.) knavish trick, rascality.

pillador, ra, *n*. pillager, plunderer; swindler.

pillaje, *m*. pillage, plunder, marauding, foray.

pillar, *va*. to pillage, rifle, plunder, foray; to catch, grasp, take hold of.

pillastre, pillastrón, *m*. rogue, rascal.

pillear, *va*. (coll.) to play the rascal.

pillería, *f*. set of rogues; piece of rascality.

pillo, lla. **I**. *a*. roguish, knavish; shrewd, artful, sly. **II**. *n*. knave, rogue, rascal; petty thief.—**p. desorejado**, arrant rogue.

pilluelo, *m*. *dim*. little rogue, urchin.

pimental, *m*. pepper patch.

pimentero, *m*. pepper box; (bot.) pepper plant.—**p. falso**, = TURBINTO.

pimentón, *m*. large pepper; Cayenne or red pepper; paprika.

pimienta, *f*. (black) pepper.—**p. de Tabasco**, myrtle.—**p. larga**, long pepper.—**p. malagueta** = P. DE TABASCO.

pimiento, *m*. (bot.) capsicum; pepper (fruit of the capsicum); red or Cayenne pepper.—**p. de bonete**, large, sweet pepper.—**p. de cornetilla**, hot pepper; chili.—**p. dulce**, sweet pepper.—**p. morrón** = P. DE BONETE.—**p. picante** = P. DE CORNETILLA.

pímpido, *m*. (icht.) a variety of dogfish.

pimpín, *m*. a child's play.

pimpina, *f*. (*Ven*.) large, earthenware bottle.

pimpinela, *f*. (bot.) burnet, pimpinel.

pimpleo, a, *a*. belonging to the Muses.

pimplón, *m*. waterfall, cascade.

pimpollar, *m*. nursery of young plants.

pimpollecer, *vn*. to sprout, to bud.

pimpollejo, ico, ito, *m*. *dim*. tender bud, sprout, sucker, or shoot.

pimpollo, *m*. sucker, sprout, shoot; rosebud; spruce, lively youth.

pimpolludo, da, *a*. full of buds or sprouts.

pina, *f*. conical mound; felloe (of a wheel).

pinabete, *m*. (bot.) fir tree and its wood.

pinacoteca, *f*. pinacotheca, picture gallery.

pináculo, *m*. pinnacle, finial, acme, summit.

pinado, da, *a*. (bot.) pinnate, pinnated.

pinar, pinarejo, *m*. pine grove.

pinariego, ga, *a*. belonging to pines.

pinastro, *m*. wild pine.

pinatífido, da, *a*. (bot.) pinnatifid.

pinaza, *f*. (naut.) pinnace.

pincarrascal, *m*. grove of pin oaks.

pincarrasco, *m*. pin oak, swamp Spanish oak.

pincel, *m*. artist's brush; by extension, painter, work painted, and mode of painting; second feather in a martin's wing.

pincelada, *f*. stroke with a brush, touch.

pincelar, *va*. (art) to paint, portray.

pincelero, *m*. maker or seller of artist's brushes; brush box.

pincelillo, ito, *m*. *dim*. fine brush; camel's hair brush.—**pincelote**, *m*. *aug*. coarse brush.

pincerna, *m*. one who serves drinks.

pinchadura, *f*. (coll.) puncture, pricking.

pinchar, *va*. to prick, puncture, pierce.—**no p. ni cortar**, to have little or no influence, to count for nothing.

pinchaúyas, *n*. (coll.) despicable person.

pinchazo, *m*. prick, puncture, stab.

pinche, *m*. scullion, kitchen boy.

pincho, *m*. thorn, prickle; goad; skewer.

pindárico, ca, *a*. Pindaric.

pindonga, *f*. (coll.) gadabout (woman).

pindonguear, *vn*. (coll.) to gad about.

pineal, *a*. (anat.) pineal.

pineda, *f*. braid for garters; pine grove.

pinga, *f*. (Philip.) banghy, bamboo for carrying loads.

pingajo, *m*. (coll.) rag, tatter.

pinganello, *m*. = CALAMOCO.

pinganitos.—**en p.**, *adv*. in a high position.

pingo, *m.* rag.—*pl.* worthless clothes, duds.—**andar, estar,** or **ir de p.,** to gad about.
pingorote, *m.* any pointed object.
pingorotudo, da, *a.* (coll.) high, lofty.
pingüe. I. *a.* fat, greasy, oily, pinguid; rich, plentiful. **II.** *m.* (naut.) pink.
pingüedinoso, sa, *a.* fatty, oleaginous.
pinguosidad, *f.* fatness.
pinífero, ra, *a.* (poet.) piniferous.
pinillo, *m.* (bot.) ground pine, germander.
pinípedo, da. I. *n.* & *a.* (zool.) pinnipedian. **II.** *m.* *pl.* Pinnipedia, pinnipedians.
pinitos, *m. pl. dim.* first steps.
pinjante, *m.* (jewel.) pendant; (arch.) boss.
pinnípedo, da, *n.* & *a.* = PINÍPEDO.
pino, na. I. *a.* steep. **II.** *m.* (coll.) first step of a child or of a convalescent; (bot.) pine.—**p. albar,** Scotch pine.—**p. alerce,** larch, tamarack, hackmatack.—**p. bravo** = P. RODENO.—**p. carrasco,** pine oak.—**p. doncel,** timber from young pines without knots.—**p. marítimo** = P. RODENO.—**p. piñonero,** stone pine.—**p. rodeno,** cluster pine, pinaster, red pine.—**p. (de) tea,** pitch pine.
pinocha, *f.* pine leaf, pine needle.
pinocho, *m.* pine cone.
pínola, *f.* detent of a repeating watch; (naut.) spindle.
pinole, *m.* aromatic powder to mix with chocolate; (Mex.) cereal meal.
pinoso, sa, *a.* producing, or belonging to, pines.
pinta, *f.* spot, mark; edge lines on Spanish cards denoting the suit; appearance, aspect; drop; pint.—*pl.* spots on the skin in malignant fevers; basset, a card game.
pintacilgo, *m.* (orn.) goldfinch.
pintada, *f.* (orn.) guinea fowl.
pintadillo, *m.* (orn.) goldfinch.
pintado, da, *a.* & *pp.* painted; spotted, mottled; just fit, exact.
pintamonas, *m.* (coll.) dauber.
pintar. I. *va.* to paint; picture; to stain (as glass); to dapple; to describe, portray; to fancy, imagine; to exaggerate. **II.** *vn.* to begin to ripen; to show, give signs of. **III.** *vr.* to paint (one's face).
pintarrajar, pintarrajear, *va.* (coll.) to daub.
pintarrajo, *m.* (coll.) daub.
pintarroja, *f.* = LIJA.
pintarrojo, *m.* (orn.) linnet.
pintica, illa, ita, *f. dim.* little spot or dot.
pintiparado, da, *pp.* & *a.* perfectly like, closely resembling; apposite, fit.
pintiparar, *va.* (coll.) to compare.
pintojo, ja, *a.* spotted, stained, mottled.
pintor, *m.* painter.—**p. de brocha gorda,** house or sign painter; dauber.
pintora, *f.* paintress; painter's wife.
pintorcillo, *m. dim.* wretched painter or dauber.
pintoresco, ca, *a.* picturesque.
pintorreador, *m.* dauber, miserable painter.
pintorrear, *va.* to daub, paint without skill.
pintura, *f.* painting; (art) picture, painting; color, paint, pigment; portrayal, description; caper.—**p. a la aguada,** water-color painting.—**p. al fresco,** fresco painting.—**p. al óleo,** oil painting.—**p. al pastel,** pastel painting.—**p. al temple,** size painting.—**p. figulina,** painting on earthenware.—**hacer pinturas,** to cut capers.
pinturero, ra, *a.* conceitedly affected.
pínula, *f.* sight of an instrument.
pinzas, *f. pl.* nippers, pincers, tweezers; claws of lobsters, etc.; forceps; burling iron.
pinzón, *m.* (orn.) chaffinch.
pinzote, *m.* (naut.) whipstaff.
piña, *f.* pine cone; pineapple; cluster, gathering; pool, in billiards; (naut.) wall knot; (min.) virgin silver treated with mercury; (Philip.) a fabric made from pineapple fibres.
piñata, *f.* pot; suspended balloon filled with candies at a masquerade ball.
piñón, *m.* pine kernel; (bot.) piñon or nutpine; (mech.) pinion; spring nut of a gun; extreme joint of a bird's wing.

piñonata, *f.* conserve of shredded almonds.
piñonate, *m.* candied pine-nut kernel.
piñoncico, illo, ito, *m. dim.* small pine-nut kernel; last joint of a wing.
piñonear, *vn.* to click (as a gun being cocked); to cry (as partridges in rut).
piñoneo, *m.* cry of partridges in rut.
piñonero, *a. V.* PINO.
piñuela, *f.* figured silk; nut of cypress; (Am.) a variety of agave.
pío, a. I. *a.* pious; mild; merciful; pied, piebald (horse).—**Antonio P.,** Antoninus Pius. **II.** *m.* puling of chickens; (coll.) longing, anxious desire.
piocha, *f.* trinket for women's headdresses; flower made of feathers.
piogenia, *f.* (med.) formation or production of pus.
piogénico, ca, *a.* (bact.) pus-producing.
piojento, ta, *a.* lousy.—**piojería,** *f.* lousiness; misery, poverty.—**piojillo,** *m. dim.* small louse (vermin on plants and birds).
piojo, *m.* louse; a disease of hawks.—**p. pegadizo,** (coll.) crab louse; troublesome hanger-on.
piojoso, sa, *a.* lousy; mean, stingy.
piola, *f.* (naut.) housing, houseline.
pionía, *f.* (Ven.) bucare seeds used as beads.
piorno, *m.* (bot.) *V.* GAYOMBA. *V.* CODESO.
piorrea, *f.* (med.) pyorrhea.
pipa, *f.* cask, butt, hogshead; tobacco pipe; pip of some fruits; reed of a clarion; (arti.) fusee.
pipar, *vn.* to smoke a tobacco pipe.
piperáceo, a, *a.* (bot.) piperaceous.
piperacina, *f.* (chem.) piperazine.
pipería, *f.* collection of pipes or casks.
piperina, *f.* (chem.) piperin.
pípero, *m.* copper pipe or butt maker.
pipeta, *f.* pipette.
pipí, *m.* (orn.) pitpit, honey creeper.
pipián, *m.* a kind of Indian fricassee.
pipiar, *vn.* to pule, chirp, peep.
pipila, *f.* (Mex.) hen turkey.
pipiolo, *m.* (coll.) novice, raw hand, beginner.
pipirigallo, *m.* (bot.) sainfoin, forage plant.
pipirijaina, *f.* band of strolling players.
pipiripao, *m.* (coll.) splendid feast, reception.
pipiritaña, pipitaña, *f.* green-cane flute.
pipo, *m.* a small fly-eating bird.
piporro, *m.* (mus.) bassoon.
pipote, *m.* keg.—**pipotillo,** *m. dim.* small keg.
pique, *m.* pique, resentment; term in a card game; NIGUA; (naut.) crotch.—**a p.,** in danger, on the point of; sharp-cut (cliff).—**echar a p.,** (naut.) to sink (a ship).—**irse a p.,** (naut.) to founder; to fail, fall through.
piqué, *m.* piqué, cotton fabric.
piquera, *f.* entrance hole in a hive; cockhole in a barrel; outlet of a smelting furnace; lamp burner.
piquería, *f.* body of pikemen.
piquero, *m.* (mil.) pikeman.
piqueta, *f.* pickaxe, mattock; mason's hammer.
piquete, *m.* slight wound from a sharp tool; (sew.) small hole in a garment; stake, picket or piquet; (mil.) picket.
piquetero, *m.* (min.) pick or mattock carrier.
piquetilla, *f. dim.* bricklayer's hammer.
piquillo, *m. dim.* small beak or bill; small amount.
piquituerto, *m.* (orn.) crossbill, picarin.
pira, *f.* funeral pile, pyre.
piragón, *m. V.* PIRAUSTA.
piragua, *f.* (naut.) pirogue, canoe; vine.
piragüero, *m.* canoeist.
piral, *m.* = PIRAUSTA.
piramidal, *a.* pyramidal.
piramidalmente, *adv.* pyramidally.
pirámide, *f.* pyramid.
pirata, *m.* pirate; cruel wretch.—**piratear,** *vn.* to pirate.—**piratería,** *f.* piracy; robbery.—**pirático, ca,** *a.* piratical.
pirausta, *f.* fabulous firefly.
pirca, *f.* (S. A.) dry-stone wall.
pircar, *va.* to fence with a PIRCA.

For pronunciation, see the rules at the beginning of the book.

pirco, *m.* (S. A.) a kind of succotash.
pirenaico, ca, *a.* Pyrenean.
piretología, *f.* (med.) pyretology.
pirexia, *f.* (med.) pyrexia.
pírico, ca, *a.* relating to fireworks.
pirídico, ca, *a.* (chem.) pyridic.
piridina, *f.* (chem.) pyridine.
piriforme, *a.* pyriform, pear-shaped.
pirineo, a, *a.* Pyrenean.
pirita, *f.* (min.) pyrites.
piritoso, sa, *a.* pyritous.
pirofilacio, *m.* subterraneous fire.
piróforo, *m.* pyrophore.
pirofosfórico, ca, *a.* (chem.) pyrophosphoric.
pirogálico, ca, *a.* pyrogallic.
pirólatra, *n.* pyrolater, fire worshipper.
pirolatría, *f.* pyrolatry, fire worship.
pirolusita, *a.* (min.) pyrolusite.
piromancia, *f.* pyromancy.
piromántico, ca, *a.* pyromantic.
pirómetro, *m.* pyrometer.
pironomia, *f.* pyronomy.
piropear, *va.* & *vn.* (coll.) to pay compliments.
piropo, *m.* a variety of garnet; carbuncle; (coll.) compliment, flattery.
piroscopio, *m.* pyroscope.
pirosfera, *f.* (geol.) pyrosphere.
pirosis, *f.* (med.) pyrosis.
pirotecnia, *f.* pyrotechnics.
pirotécnico, ca, *a.* pyrotechnical.
piroxena, *f. m.* (min.) pyroxene.
piroxeno, *m.* (min.) pyroxene.
piroxilina, *f.* pyroxyline.
pirquén.—al p., (Ch.) at will, without restrictions (said of the right to work a leased mine).
pirquinear, *vn.* (Ch.) to work a leased mine without imposed restrictions.
pírrico, ca, *a.* Pyrrhic.—**pirrónico, ca,** *a.* Pyrrhonic; skeptic.—**pirronismo,** *m.* Pyrrhonism.
pirueta, *f.* pirouette, gyration.
piruétano, *m.* = PERUÉTANO.
pisa, *f.* tread, trading; portion of olives or grapes pressed at once.
pisada, *f.* footstep; footprint; stepping on one's foot.—**seguir las pisadas de,** to walk in the footsteps of.
pisador, ra. I. *n.* & *a.* prancer (-ing); high-stepper (-ing). II. *n.* treader of grapes.
pisadura, *f.* act of treading; footstep.
pisapapeles, *m.* paper weight.
pisar, *va.* to tread on, trample, step on; to press; to press on; to ram; to cover; to lie over; to serve, cover (the female).
pisasfalto, *m.* mixture of bitumen and pitch.
pisaúvas, *n.* treader of grapes.
pisaverde, *m.* (coll.) fop, coxcomb, dude.
piscator, *m.* yearly almanac.
piscatorio, ria, *a.* piscatory.
piscicultor, ra, *n.* & *a.* pisciculturist (-ic).
piscicultura, *f.* pisciculture, fish culture.
pisciforme, *a.* pisciform, fish-shaped.
piscina, *f.* fishpond; swimming pool; (eccl.) piscina.
Piscis, *m.* (ast.) Pisces, zodiacal sign.
piscívoro, ra, *a.* piscivorous.
piscolabis, *m.* (coll.) luncheon, a bite.
piso, *m.* floor, pavement, flooring; story or floor, loft, flat, apartment; ground level; tread, footing, walking; (min.) level works; (geol.) stage, formation.—**p. bajo,** ground floor.
pisón, *m.* rammer; paver's beetle.
pisonear, *va.* to ram.
pisotear, *va.* to trample, tread under foot.
pisoteo, *m.* trampling, treading under foot.
pisotón, *m. aug.* heavy step on one's foot.
pista, *f.* trail, track, scent; trace, clew; racetrack, race course.
pistachero, pistacho, *m.* = ALFÓNSIGO.
pistadero, *m.* pestle for pounding.
pistar, *va.* to pound with a pestle.
pistero, *m.* feeding cup, "duck."

pistilo, *m.* (bot.) pistil.
pisto, *m.* fowl juice for the sick; dish of tomatoes and red pepper.
pistola, *f.* pistol.—**p. de arzón,** horse pistol.
pistolera, *f.* holster.—**pistoletazo,** *m.* pistol shot.—**dar un p.,** to shoot with a pistol.
pistolete, *m.* pistolet, pocket pistol.
pistón, *m.* (mech.) piston; (arti.) percussion cap, primer; (mus.) piston of a brass instrument.
pistoresa, *f.* short dagger.
pistraje, pistraque, *m.* unpleasant beverage.
pistura, *f.* pounding, pestling.
pita, *f.* (bot.) pita; agave; maguey. (The term is used more or less vaguely and has different meanings in different countries. The pita proper produces the best fiber.)
pitaco, *m.* stem of the maguey.
pitada, *f.* blow of a whistle.
pitagórico, ca, *a.* & *n.* Pythagorean.
pitahaya, *f.* (bot.) pitahaya.
pitancería, *f.* place where pittances are distributed; distribution or office of pittances.
pitancero, *m.* distributor of pittances; (eccl.) steward or purveyor; superintendent of a choir.
pitancica, illa, ita, *f. dim.* small pittance.
pitanza, *f.* pittance, alms; (coll.) daily food; price, salary, stipend.
pitaña, pitañoso = LEGAÑA, LEGAÑOSO.
pitar. I. *vn.* to blow. II. *va.* to discharge (a debt); to distribute pittances to.
pitarra, *f.* bleardness.
pitarroso, sa, *a.* blear-eyed.
pitazo, *m.* sound or blast of a whistle.
pitecántropo, *m.* pithecanthropus.
pitezna, *f.* spring of a trap.
pitillera, *f.* cigarette maker (woman); cigarette case.—**pitillo,** *m.* cigarette.
pítima, *f.* (pharm.) saffron plaster; (coll.) drunkenness.
pitío, *m.* whistling of a pipe or of birds.
pitipié, *m.* scale.
pitirre, *m.* (orn.) pitirri, gray kingbird.
pito, *m.* whistle; catcall; fife; fifer; (orn.) woodpecker; (Am.) tick; jackstone (toy); cocoon open at one end.—**pitos flautos,** frivolous pastimes.—**no me importa,** or **no se me da, un p.,** I don't care a straw.—**no tocar pitos en,** to have no part in.—**no valer un p.,** not to be worth a straw.
pitofiero, ra, *n.* (coll.) musician of no account; gossip.
pitón, *m.* tenderling; protuberance, lump; spout, nozzle; sprig or shoot of a tree; sprout of the agave.
pitonisa, *f.* Pythia, Pythoness; witch, sorceress.
pitorra, *f.* (orn.) woodcock.
pitpit, *m.* (orn.) pitpit, guitguit.
pitreo, *m.* = PITACO.
pituita, *f.* pituita, mucus.—**pituitario, ria,** *a.* pituitary.—**pituitoso, sa,** *a.* pituitous.
piuquén, *m.* a large Chilean bird similar to the wild turkey.
píxide, *f.* (eccl.) pix, vessel or casket.
pizarra, *f.* (min.) slate shale; slate (for writing); blackboard.—**pizarral,** *m.* slate quarry.
pizarreño, ña, *a.* slate-colored, slaty.
pizarrero, *m.* slater, slate cutter; roofer.
pizarrín, *m.* slate pencil.
pizarroso, sa, *a.* abounding in slate.
pizate, *m.* (bot.) saltwort.
pizca, *f.* (coll.) mite, bit, speck, crumb, whit, jot.
pizcar, *va.* (coll.) to pinch; to glean (maize).
pizco, *m.* (coll.) pinch.
pizmiento, ta, *a.* pitch-colored.
pizpereta, pizpireta, *a.* smart, brisk, lively.
pizpirigaña, *f.* a boys' game.
pizpita, *f.*; **pizpitillo,** *m.* (orn.) wagtail.
placa, *f.* star, insignia of an order of knighthood; (photo.) dry plate; (mech.) plate; (art) plaque; (Mex.) baggage check.—**p. giratoria,** (r. w.) turning plate, turntable.

placabilidad, *f.* placability.—**placable,** *a.* placable.—**placativo, va,** *a.* placatory.

placear, *va.* to sell (provisions) at retail.

placel, *m.* (naut.) sand bank, key.

pláceme, *m.* congratulation.

placenta, *f.* (anat., bot.) placenta.

placentario, ria. I. *a.* placental. **II.** *m.* (zool.) placental.—*pl.* Placentalia.

placenteramente, *adv.* joyfully, merrily.

placentero, ra, *a.* joyful, merry, pleasant.

placer. I. *va.* (ind. PLAZCO: pret. él PLUGO or PLACIÓ: subj. yo PLAZCA, él PLEGUE or PLAZCA: prēt. imp. yo PLACIERA, él PLUGUIERA or PLACIERA, etc.) to please,· gratify, humor, content.—**que me place,** it gives me pleasure: with pleasure. **II.** *m.* pleasure; (naut.) sand bank, key; (min.) placer; (Am.) pearl fishing.—**a p.,** at one's convenience.

placero, ra. I. *a.* pertaining to the marketplace. **II.** *n.* marketer, seller at a market; gadabout.

placeta, tilla, tuela, *f.* dim. small square.

placibilidad, *f.* agreeableness.—**placible,** *a.* placid, agreeable.—**plácidamente,** *adv.* placidly. —**placidez,** *f.* placidity.—**plácido, da,** *a.* placid, quiet, calm.

placiente, *a.* pleasing, agreeable, pleasant.

plafón, *m.* (arch.) soffit of an architrave.

plaga, *f.* plague; calamity; scourge; epidemic; affliction; pest; plenty, superabundance, drug in the market; climate, country; zone; (naut.) the cardinal point of the compass.

plagado, da, *pp. & a.* full; smitten.

plagar. I. *va.* (pret. PLAGUÉ: subj. PLAGUE) to plague, infest. **II.** *vr.* (w. de) to bɜ overrun (with), or full (of).

plagiar, *va.* to plagiarize; to kidnap.

plagiario, ria, *n. & a.* plagiarizer (-ing).

plagio, *m.* plagiarism; abduction, kidnapping.

plagioclasa, *f.* (min.) plagioclase.

plagióstomos, *m. pl.* (zool.) Plagiostomi, plagiostomes.

plan, *m.* plan; design, scheme; plan, drawing; description, specification; (naut.) floor timber.

plana, *f.* page; copy; level ground, plain; record; (mas.) trowel; (print.) page.—**p. mayor,** (mil.) staff.—**enmendar la p. a,** to find fault with, criticise; to excel, to do better than.

planada, *f.* plain, level ground.

planador, *m.* planisher.

plancha, *f.* plate, sheet; slab; smoothing iron, sadiron; tailor's goose; cramp iron; (pap.) mould; cloth plate of a sewing machine; horizontal suspension (in gymastics); (coll.) injudicious action or speech; (naut.) gangplank, gangboard.—**p. de agua,** (naut.) punt, floating stage.—**p. de blindaje,** armor plate.—**p. de viento,** (naut.) hanging stage.

planchada, *f.* (naut.) framing or apron of a gun.

planchado, *m.* ironing; linen ironed or for ironing.

planchador, ra, *n.* ironer.

planchar, *va.* to iron, to press (clothes).

planchear, *va.* to plate, cover with metal sheets.

plancheta, *f.* (surv.) plane table.

planchita, *f.* dim. small plate.

planchón, *m.* aug. large plate.

planchuela, *f.* dim. small plate; fluting iron.

planeador, *m.* (aer.) glider.—**planeo,** *m.* (aer.) gliding.—**planear,** *vn.* (aer.) to glide.

planeta. I. *m.* (ast.) planet. **II.** *f.* (eccl.) planeta.

planetario, ria. I. *a.* planetary. **II.** *m.* planetarium, orrery; astronomer.

planetícola, *n.* inhabitant of a planet.

planga, *f.* (orn.) a kind of eagle.

planicle, *f.* = LLANURA.

planimetría, *f.* plane surveying.

planímetro, *m.* planimeter.

planisferio, *m.* planisphere.

plano, na. I. *a.* plane; level; smooth, even. **II.** *m.* plan (drawing); map; flat (of a sword, etc.); (geom.) plane; (aer.) plane, wing.—**p. de nivel,**

datum plane (in leveling).—**p. inclinado,** inclined plane.—**de p.,** openly, clearly; flatly, on its side.

planta, *f.* sole of the foot; (bot.) plant; plantation, nursery of young plants; (eng.) plan, horizontal projection, top view; plant or site of a building; (fenc. and danc.) position of the feet; project; disposition.—**p. baja,** ground floor.—**buena p.,** fine physique.—**echar plantas, t**ɔ brag, to boast.

plantación, *f.* plantation; planting.

plantador, ra, *n.* planter (person or machine).

plantaina, *f.* (bot.) plantain, ribwort.

plantaje, *m.* collection of plants.

plantar. I. *va.* (agr.) to plant; to erect, set up, fix upright; to strike (a blow); to set, put; place; to found, establish; (coll.) to leave in the lurch, disappoint; to jilt. **II.** *vr.* (coll.) to stand upright; to reach, arrive; to stop, halt, balk; in some games, to stand pat.

plantario, *m.* (agr.) nursery.

planteamiento, *m.* putting into execution.

plantear, *va.* to plan, try; to execute, put into action; to state (a problem).

plantel, *m.* nursery, nursery garden; educational institution.

plantificación, *f.* putting into execution.

plantificar, *va.* to put into execution; (coll.) to land (as a blow).

plantígrado, da, *a.* plantigrade.

plantilla, *f.* dim. young plant; (shoe.) first sole, insole; (mech.) template, templet, model, pattern; plate of a gunlock; (med.) plaster fcr the feet; (ast.) celestial configuration; (P. Rico) lady finger.

plantillar, *va.* to sole (shoes or stockings).

plantío, ía. I. *a.* planted, or ready to be planted. **II.** *m.* plantation; planting; garden bed.

plantista, *m.* landscape gardener; bully, hector, bravado.

plantón, *m.* scion, sprout or shoot to be transplanted; shoot ingrafted on a stock; (coll.) long wait standing; (mil.) sentry doing long guard; doorkeeper, watchman.—**estar de p.,** to be fixed in a place for a long time.—**llevar un p.,** to dance attendance.

planudo, da, *a.* (naut.) flat-bottomed.

plañidero, ra. I. *a.* mournful, weeping, moaning. **II.** *f.* weeper, hired mourner.

plañido, *pp. & m.* moan, lamentation, crying.

plañir, *vn.* (gerund, PLAÑENDO: pret. el PLAÑÓ: subj. pret. imp. PLAÑERA, PLAÑESE) to lament, grieve, bewail; to whimper, whine.

plaqué, *m.* plate, plating; plated ware.

plaquín, *m.* loose coat of mail, hauberk.

plasma. I. *m.* (biol.) plasma. **II.** *f.* = PRASMA.

plasmador, ra, *m.* maker, molder.

plasmante, *n. & a.* molder (-ing), shaper (-ing). —**plasmar,** *va.* to mɔld, shape.

plasmático, ca, *a.* (biol.) plasmic.

plasta, *f.* anything soft (as dough, mud, etc.); anything flattened; (coll.) anything poorly done.

plaste, *m.* size or filler made of glue and lime.

plastecer, *va.* (ind. PLASTEZCO: subj. PLASTEZCA) to size, to besmear with size.

plastecido, *pp. & m.* (art) sizing.

plástica, *f.* art of molding in clay.

plasticidad, *f.* plasticity.

plástico, ca, *a.* plastic; soft, fictile.

plastrón, *m.* (fenc.) plastron; large cravat; leather apron.

plata, *f.* silver; silver coin; money; plate, wrought silver; (her.) plate; white.—**p. agria,** (min.) black silver, stephanite.—**p. alemana,** German silver.— **p. córnea,** (min.) cerargyrite.—**p. piña,** (min.) spongy silver.—**p. gris,** silver glance, argentite.— **p. labrada,** silverware.—**p. roja,** (min.) pyrargyrite, red silver ore.—**p. virgen,** native silver.— **como una p.,** very clean and pretty.—**en p.,** in plain language; briefly, in a word.

plataforma, *f.* platform; terrace; (mach.) index plate, division plate; (fort.) platform; (naut.) orlop; (r. w.) roadbed.

platal, great quantity of money, great wealth.

platanal, platanar, *m.* plantain or banana plantation.

platáneo, a, *a.* (bot.) plantanaceous.

plátano, *m.* (bot.) plantain; banana (plant and fruit); plane tree.—**p. falso,** sycamore maple.—**p. guineo,** guineo; (Cuba) banana.

platazo, *m. aug.* platter; dishful.

platea, *f.* (theat.) orchestra, parquette; pit.

plateado, da, *pp. & a.* silvered; silverplated.

plateador, *m.* plater, silverer.

plateadura, *f.* silvering, silver plating.

platear, *va.* to silver, silverplate.

platel, *m.* platter; tray.

plateresco, ca, *a.* (arch.) plateresque.

platería, *f.* silversmith's shop or trade.

platero, *m.* silversmith; jeweller.—**p. de oro,** goldsmith.

plática, *f.* talk, chat, conversation; address, lecture; sermon.—**platicar,** *vn.* (*pret.* PLATIQUÉ: *subj.* PLATIQUE) to converse, talk, chat.

platija, *f.* (icht.) plaice, flounder.

platilla, *f.* Silesian linen.

platillo, *m. dim.* small dish; saucer; beef stew; extra dish in convents; pan (of a balance); (mus.) cymbal; disk or valve of a chain pump.

platina, *f.* (min.) ore of platinum; (mech.) plate, platen; (print.) platen, bedplate; imposing table; (phys.) slide (of microscope); plate (of air pump).

platinífero, ra, *a.* platiniferous or platinum-bearing.

platino, *m.* platinum.

platinoide, *m.* platinoid.

platinotipia, *f.* platinotype.

platirrino, na, *n. & a.* (zool.) platyrrhine.

plato, *m.* dish, plate; (cook.) dish, mess, course, food served in a dish; daily fare; pan (of a balance); (arch.) metope.—**p. de segunda mesa,** makeshift, second-hand, cast off.—**p. sopero,** soup plate.—**nada entre dos platos,** much ado about nothing.—**no quebrar un p.,** to be innocent or harmless.

platónicamente, *adv.* Platonically.—**platónico, ca,** *a.* Platonic.—**platonismo,** *m.* Platonism.

platuja, *f.* (icht.) = PLATIJA.

plausibilidad, *f.* plausibility.—**plausible,** *a.* plausible.—**plausiblemente,** *adv.* plausibly.

plauso, *m.* applause.

plaustro, *m.* (poet.) cart, wagon, carriage.

plautino, na, *a.* Plautine, relating to Plautus.

playa, *f.* shore, strand, sea coast, beach.

playado, da, *a.* having a beach; beachy.

playazo, *m.* wide or extended shore.

playeras, *f. pl.* a popular Andalusian song.

playero, ra, *n.* fisherman; fishwoman.

playón, *m. aug.* large shore or beach.

playuela, *f. dim.* small beach or shore.

plaza, *f.* plaza, square; market place; (com.) emporium, market; room, space, stall; office, position, employment; reputation, character, fame. **p. de armas,** (mil.) parade ground.—**p. de toros,** bull ring, arena.—**p. fuerte,** (fort.) stronghold, fortress.—**¡p., p.!** clear the way! make room!—**pasar p. de,** to be reputed (something that one is not).—**sacar a p.,** to publish, make public.—**sentar p.,** (mil.) to enlist.

plazo, *m.* term, time, date, day of payment; instalment; credit; duelling ground.—**a p.,** on credit.

plazoleta, plazuela, *f. dim.* small square.

ple, *m.* a handball game.

pleamar, *f.* (naut.) high water, high tide.

plébano, *m.* curate of a parish.

plebe, *f.* common people, plebs, populace.

plebeyo, ya, *n. & a.* plebeian.

plebiscitario, ria, *a.* plebiscitary.

plebiscito, *m.* plebiscitum; (pol.) plebiscite.

pleca, *f.* (print.) straight line, rule.

plectro, *m.* plectrum, for stringed instruments.

plegable, *a.* pliable, folding.—**plegadamente,** *adv.* confusedly.—**plegadera,** *f.* (b. b.) folder.—**plegadizo, za,** *a.* pliable; folding.—**plegado,** *m.* plaiting; folding.

plegador, ra. I. *a.* folding. **II.** *n.* folder, plaiter. **III.** *f.* plaiting machine, folding machine; beam of a silk loom.

plegadura, *f.* plait, fold; plaiting, folding, doubling; crease.

plegar, *va.* (*ind.* PLIEGO: *subj.* PLIEGUE) to fold; to plait, double; to do up; to turn (the warp) on the yarn beam; (sew.) to plait, pucker, gather, crease.

plegaria, *f.* prayer, supplication; noon prayers.

plegueta, *m.* (bot.) tendril of a vine.

pleistoceno, na, *m. & a.* (geol.) Pleistocene.

pleita, *f.* plaited strand of bass.

pleiteador, ra, *n.* pleader; wrangler.

pleiteante, *n. & a.* litigator (-ing, -ant), pleader (-ing).

pleitear, *vn.* to plead, litigate; wrangle.

pleitista, *n.* pettifogger.

pleito, *m.* lawsuit; litigation; proceedings in a cause; dispute, contest, debate, strife.—**p. de acreedores,** proceedings under a commission of bankruptcy.—**ver un p.,** (law) to try a case.

plenamar, *f.* = PLEAMAR.

plenamente, *adv.* fully, completely.

plenariamente, *adv.* completely, fully; (law) plenarily.

plenario, ria, *a.* complete, full; (law) plenary.

plenilunio, *m.* full moon.

plenipotencia, *f.* plenipotence, full powers.

plenipotenciario, ria, *n. & a.* plenipotentiary.

plenitud, *f.* plenitude, fulness, abundance.

pleno, na, *a.* full, complete; joint (session).

pleonasmo, *m.* (rhet.) pleonasm, redundancy.

pleonásticamente, *adv.* pleonastically.

pleonástico, ca, *a.* pleonastic, redundant.

plepa, *f.* (coll.) bother; person full of defects.

plesímetro, *m.* (med.) pleximeter.

plesiosauro, *m.* (pal.) plesiosaur.

pletina, *f.* small iron plate.

plétora, *f.* plethora; superabundance, inflation.

pletórico, ca, *a.* plethoric.

pleura, *f.* (anat.) pleura.—**pleuresía,** *f.* (med.) pleurisy.—**p. falsa,** pleurodynia.—**pleurítico, ca,** *a.* pleuritic (al.—**pleuritis,** *f.* (med.) pleurisy.—**pleurodinia,** *f.* pleurodynia, stitch in the side.

plexo, *m.* (anat. and bot.) plexus; network.

Pléyadas, Pléyades, *f. pl.* (ast.) Pleiades.

plica, *f.* (law) escrow; (med.) matted hair; plica.

pliego, *m.* sheet (of paper); sealed envelope or package containing papers.—**p. de condiciones,** specifications; tender, bid.

pliego, pliegue. *V.* PLEGAR.

pliegue, *m.* fold, plait, crease; (sew.) gather.

plieguecillo, *m. dim.* half sheet; small plait.

plinto, *m.* (arch.) plinth of a pillar.

plioceno, m. & a. (geol.) Pliocene.

plomada, *f.* artificer's lead pencil; plumb, plumb bob, plummet; (naut.) lead for sounding; fishing-net sinker; scourge with lead balls.

plomar, *va.* to put a leaden seal on.

plomazón, *f.* gilding cushion.

plombagina, *f.* plumbago, graphite.

plomería, *f.* lead roofing; leadware shop; plumbing.—**plomero, ra,** *n.* plumber.—**plomizo, za,** *a.* plumbeous; lead-colored.

plomo, *m.* lead (metal); piece of lead; plumb bob, plummet; bullet; (coll.) dull person, bore.—**p. derretido,** molten lead.—**andar con pies de p.,** to proceed with the utmost caution.—**a p.,** true, plumb.—**caer a p.,** to fall flat down.

plomoso, sa, = PLOMIZO.

pluma, *f.* feather; plume, down; quill; writing pen; penmanship; writer; style; (coll.) air expelled from the bowels.—**p. de agua,** a variable measure of running water (0.025 liter per second in some parts of Spain).—**p. viva,** eider down.—**al correr de la p., a vuela p.,** written in haste.

plumada, *f.* brief writing; stroke of a pen, flourish.—**plumado, da,** *a.* feathered, feathery, plumy.

plumaje, *m.* plumage; plume, crest.

plumajería, *f.* plumage; feather working.

plumajero, ra, *n.* plumist, feather dresser.

plumario, ria. I. *n.* plumist, plume worker. **II.** *a.* relating to plume or feather work.
plumazo, *m.* feather mattress or pillow.
plumazón, *f.* plumage.
plumbado, da, *a.* sealed with a leaden seal.
plumbagina, *f.* = PLOMBAGINA.
plumbagíneo, a, *a.* (bot.) plumbagineous.
plúmbeo, bea, *a.* leaden, plumbean.
plúmbico, ca, *a.* (chem.) plumbic.
plumeado, *m.* (pict.) lines in miniature painting.
plumear, *va.* (pict.) to shade with a liner.
plúmeo, a, *a.* plumose, feathered, plumed.
plumería, *f.* plumosity; plumage.
plumero, *m.* feather duster; box for feathers or plumes; plumage; aigret, panache.
plumífero, ra, *a.* plumigerous, feathered.
plumilla, *f. dim.* small feather or plume; (print.) script type; (bot.) plumule.
plumión, *m.* = PLUMÓN.
plumista, *n.* scrivener or notary; plumist, plume-maker.
plumita, *f. dim.* small feather or pen.
plumón, *m.* down, feather bed.
plumoso, sa, *a.* feathered, plumy.
plúmula, *f.* (bot.) plumule.
plural, *n. & a.* plural.—**pluralidad,** *f.* plurality; majority.—**a p. de votos,** by a majority of votes.
pluralizar, *va.* to pluralize.
plus, *m.* (mil.) extra pay; bonus; extra.
pluscuamperfecto, *m.* (gram.) pluperfect.
plus minusve, (Lat.) more or less, about.
plúteo, *m.* library shelf.
plutocracia, *f.* plutocracy.—**plutócrata,** *n.* plutocrat.—**plutocrático, ca,** *a.* plutocratic.
plutónico, ca, *a.* (geol.) Plutonic.—**plutonismo,** *m.* (geol.) Plutonism.—**plutonista,** *m.* Plutonist.
pluvial, *a.* pluvial, rainy.
pluvímetro, *m.* pluviometer, rain gauge.
pluviometría, *f.* pluviometry.
pluviométrico, ca, *a.* pluviometric.
pluviómetro, *m.* = PLUVÍMETRO.
pluvioso, sa, *a.* rainy, pluvious.
poa, *f.* (naut.) bowline bridle.
pobeda, *f.* plantation of poplars.
población, *f.* population; populating; city, town, village.
poblacho, poblachón, *m.* ugly village.
poblado. I. *pp. & a.* populated, inhabited. **II.** *m.* inhabited place, town, settlement.
poblador, ra, *n.* populator, settler.
poblar. I. *va. & vn.* (*ind.* PUEBLO: *subj.* PUEBLE) to populate, people, colonize, settle; to inhabit; to stock; to breed, procreate fast. **III.** *vr.* to bud, leaf.
poblazo, *m.* large ugly village.
poblezuelo, *m. dim.* small village.
pobo, *m.* (bot.) white poplar.
pobre. I. *a.* poor; needy; barren; humble, modest; trifling, paltry, unimportant.—**¡p. de mí!** poor me! **II.** *n.* poor person; pauper, beggar.—**p. de solemnidad,** poor person in real distress.
pobrecico, ca; illo, lla; ito, ta, *a. & n. dim.* poor little thing.
pobremente, *adv.* poorly, miserably, needily.
pobrería, *f.* poor people, beggars.
pobrero, ra, *n.* distributor of alms.
pobreta, *f.* (coll.) strumpet, prostitute.
pobrete, ta, *n. dim.* poor person.—**pobretear,** *vn.* to pretend poverty.—**pobretería,** *f.* poor people; beggars; poverty; niggardliness.
pobretón, na, *a. aug.* very poor.
pobreza, *f.* poverty; sterility, barrenness; vow of poverty; lowness or littleness of spirit.
pobrezuelo, la, *a. dim.* rather poor.
pobrismo, *m.* pauperism; beggars.
pocero, *m.* well borer or sinker; sewerman.
pocilga, *f.* hogsty, hogpen; dirty place.
pocillo, *m. dim.* vessel sunk in the ground in oil mills; chocolate cup.
pócima, *f.* potion, draught, medicinal tea.
poción, *f.* drink, draught; (pharm.) potion.

poco, ca. I. *a.* little; scanty, limited; small.—*pl.* few, some.—**a pocos lances,** in a short time.—**de p. tiempo acá,** lately, of late. **II.** *m.* a little, a bit, a small quantity. **III.** *adv.* little, in a small degree; a short time.—**p. a p.,** little by little; gradually, slowly.—**p. más o menos,** more or less.—**a p.,** immediately, shortly after.—**de p. más o menos,** of little account.—**por p.,** almost, nearly.—**tener en p.,** to set little value on, to think little of.
póculo, *m.* drinking cup or glass.
pocho, cha, *a.* (coll.) discolored, faded.
poda, *f.* pruning, lopping; pruning season.
podadera, *f.* pruning knife, pruning hook, hedging bill.—**podador, ra,** *n.* pruner.
podagra, *f.* gout in the feet.
podar, *va.* to prune, head, lop, trim.
podazón, *f.* pruning season.
podenco, *m.* hound.
poder. I. *va. & vn.* (*gerund* PUDIENDO; *ind.* PUEDO; *pret.* PUDE; *fut.* PODRÉ: *subj.* PUEDA) to be able; can; may (*Juan no puede venir,* John cannot come; *Juan puede no venir,* John may not come).—**a más no p.,** to the utmost; without being able to help it.—**hasta más no p.,** to the utmost, to the limit.—**no p. más,** to have to act, can no other, cannot but (ch. constr.); not to be able to do more, can do no more (ch. constr.).—**no p. menos de,** to be necessary; cannot but, cannot fail to (ch. constr.).—**no p. ver a uno (ni pintado),** to detest one, to find one absolutely unbearable. **II.** *v. imp.* to be possible, may.—**puede que** (followed by *subj.*) it may (followed by *inf.*); perhaps. **III.** *m.* power; faculty, authority, influence, force; might; (law) power or letter of attorney; proxy; possession; tenure; ability, strength, capacity.—*pl.* power, authority.
poderdante, *n.* (law) constituent.
poderhabiente, *n.* (law) attorney.
poderío, *m.* power, might, dominion, jurisdiction; wealth, riches.
poderosamente, *adv.* powerfully, mightily.
poderoso, sa, *a.* powerful, mighty; wealthy.
podio, *m.* (arch.) podium.
podofilina, *f.* (pharm.) podophyllin.
podofilo, *m.* (bot.) podophyllum.
podómetro, *m.* pedometer.
podón, *m.* pruning hook, billhook; mattock.
podre, *m. or f.* pus; rotten substance.
podrecer, *va., vn. & vr.* = PUDRIR.
podrecimiento, *m.* = PODREDURA.
podredumbre, *f.* decay; pus; putrid matter; corruption; grief.
podredura, podrición, *f.* putrefaction, corruption.
podridero, podrimiento, *m.,* **podrir,** *va.*'= PUDRIDERO, PUDRIMIENTO, PUDRIR.
poema, *m.* poem.
poesía, *f.* poetry; poetical composition, poem.—*pl.* poetical works, poems.
poeta, *m.* a poet.—**poetastro,** *m.* poetaster.
poética, *f.* poetics.—**poéticamente,** *adv.* poetically.—**poético, ca,** *a.* poetic(al).—**poetisa,** *f.* poetess.
poetizar. I. *vn.* (*pret.* POETICÉ: *subj.* POETICE) to poetize, write poetry. **II.** *va.* to render poetical, to impart poetry to.
poíno, *m.* gauntry, stilling, stalder, barrelstand.
polaco, ca. I. *a.* Polish. **II.** *m.* Polish language. **III.** *n.* Pole.
polacra, *f.* (naut.) polacre.
polaina, *f.* spatterdashes, leggings.
polar, *a.* polar.—**polaridad,** *f.* polarity.
polarímetro, *m.* polarimeter.
polariscopio, *m.* polariscope.
polarización, *f.* polarization.
polarizar, *va.* to polarize.
polca, *f.* (danc.) polka.
polcar, *vn.* to dance the polka.
polea, *f.* pulley; tackle block, block pulley.—**p. fija,** fixed or fast pulley.—**p. impulsada,** driven pulley.—**p. loca,** loose pulley.—**p. motriz,** driving pulley.—**p. movible, or móvil,** movable pulley.
poleadas, *f. pl.* V. GACHAS, PUCHES.

poleame, *m.* set of pulleys, tackle.
polémica, *f.* polemics; (mil.) science of fortification; literary or political controversy.
polémico, ca, *a.* polemical, polemic.
polemista, *n.* polemic, debater.
polemístico, ca, *a.* polemic(al), controversial.
polemonio, *m.* (bot.) Jacob's ladder.
polemoscopio, *m.* (opt.) polemoscope.
polen, *m.* (bot.) pollen.
polenta, *f.* porridge.
poleo, *m.* (bot.) pennyroyal; strutting gait; pompous style; stiff, cold wind.
poliandria, *f.* (bot.) polyandria.
poliantea, *f.* polyanthea, a budget of news.
poliarquía, *f.* polygarchy.
poliárquico, ca, *a.* relating to polygarchy.
policarpo, *a.* (bot.) polycarpous.
pólice, *m.* thumb.
policía. I. *f.* police; politeness, good breeding; cleanliness, neatness. **II.** *m.* policeman.
policitación, *f.* (law) pollicitation.
policroísmo, *m.* (min.) pleochroism.
policromía, *f.* quality of being polychrome.
policromo, ma, *a.* polychrome, many-colored.
poliédrico, ca, *a.* polyhedrical.
poliedro, *m.* (geom.) polyhedron.
polifásico, ca, *a.* (elec.) multiphase.
polígala, *f.* (bot.) milkwort.
poligalco, a, *a.* (bot.) polygalaceous.
poligamia, *f.* polygamy.
polígamo, ma. I. *a.* polygamous; several times married. **II.** *n.* polygamist; one who has married several times.
poligenismo, *m.* polygenesis (sp. app. to human race).—**poligenista,** *n.* polygenist.
polígloto, ta. I. *n.* & *a.* polyglot. **II.** *f.* polyglot Bible.
poligonáceo, a, *a.* (bot.) polygonaceous.
poligonal. I. *a.* (geom.) polygonal. **II.** *f.* (surv.) broken line.
polígono, na. I. *a.* polygonal. **II.** *m.* (geom.) polygon; (bot.) poly; (arti.) practice ground.
poligrafía, *f.* art of writing in or interpreting ciphers; polygraphy.
poligráfico, ca, *a.* polygraphic.
polígrafo, *m.* expert with ciphers; polygraph.
polilla, *f.* moth, clothes moth; consumer, waster.
polimería, *f.* (chem.) polymerism.
polimerización, *f.* (chem.) polymerization.
polímero, ra, *a.* (chem.) polymeric.
polímita, *a.* made of many-colored threads.
polimorfismo, *m.* polymorphism.
polimorfo, fa, *a.* polymorphous.
polín, *m.* (naut.) wooden roller, skidding.
polinesiano, na; polinesio, sia, *n.* & *a.* Polynesian.
polinomio, *m.* (math.) polynomial.
poliorama, *m.* polyorama.
poliorcética, *f.* (mil.) poliorcetics.
polípero, *m.* polypary.
polipétalo, la, *a.* (bot.) polypetalous.
poliplano, *m.* (aer.) multiplane.
pólipo, *m.* (zool.) polyp; (icht.) octopus, poulp; (med.) polypus.
polipodio, *m.* (bot.) polypody, fern.
polisarcia, *f.* (med.) obesity.
poliscopio, *m.* (opt. and surg.) polyscope.
polisílabo, ba. I. *a.* polysyllabic. **II.** *m.* polysyllable.
polisépalo, la, *a.* (bot.) polysepalous.
polisíndeton, *m.* (rhet.) polysyndeton.
polispastos, *f.* burton, hoisting tackle.
polista *n.* polo player; (Philip.) Indian doing the service called POLO.
politécnico, ca, *a.* polytechnic.
politeísmo, *m.* polytheism.
politeísta, *n.* & *a.* polytheist (-ic).
política, *f.* policy; politics; politeness.—**por p.,** as a matter of policy; for the sake of politeness.
políticamente, *adv.* politically; civilly.
politicastro, *m.* politicaste.

político, ca. I. *a.* political, politic; polite, courteous. **II.** *n.* politician.
politicón, na, *a.* exceedingly polite and ceremonious.
politiquear, *vn.* (coll.) to talk politics.
poliuria, *f.* (med.) polyuria.
póliza, *f.* (com.) policy; scrip; check, draft, paybill; customhouse permit; admission ticket; lampoon, anonymous note.—**p. de seguro,** insurance policy.
polizón, na, *n.* vagrant, lazy vagabond; stowaway; parasite, sponger; (sew.) bustle.
polizonte, *m.* (coll.) policeman.
polo, *m.* (geog. and ast.) pole; pole of the magnetic needle; support, foundation; polo (game); (Philip.) personal service of forty days in the year to the community by natives; a popular Andalusian song.
polonés, sa, *a.* Polish.
polonio, *m.* (chem.) polonium.
polonesa, *f.* ladies' fur-trimmed polonaise.
poltrón, na. I. *a.* idle, lazy, lubberly. **II.** *n.* (coll.) poltroon.
poltronería, *f.* idleness, laziness, indolence.
poltronizarse, *vr.* to become lazy.
polución, *f.* (med.) pollution.
poluto, ta, *a.* polluted; unclean, filthy.
Pólux, *m.* (ast.) Pollux (a star).
polvareda, *f.* cloud of dust; altercation, dispute.
polvificar, *va.* (coll.) to pulverize.
polvillo, ito, *m. dim.* fine dust.
polvo, *m.* dust; powder; pinch of snuff or powder.—*pl.* toilet powder.—**polvos de cartas,** sand for writings.—**polvos de Juanes,** red precipitate, red nitrate of mercury.—**polvos de la madre Celestina,** (coll.) secret and miraculous mode in which anything is done.—**polvos para dientes,** tooth powder.—**en p.,** powdered.—**limpio de p. y paja,** without toil or hardship; free from all charges; net.—**sacudir el p.,** to beat out, or shake off, the dust.
pólvora, *f.* powder, gunpowder; artificial fireworks; bad temper; vivacity, liveliness, briskness.—**p. de algodón,** guncotton.—**p. de caza,** shotgun powder.—**p. detonante,** or **fulminante,** detonating powder.—**p. lenta,** slow-burning powder.—**p. sin humo,** smokeless powder.—**gastar la p. en salvas,** to work to no purpose, to waste time and energy.—**no haber inventado la p.,** or **no ser el inventor de la p.,** to be dull, not to be a genius.—**ser una p.,** to be quick, to be a hustler.
polvoreamiento, *m.* powdering.
polvorear, *va.* to powder, sprinkle powder on.
polvoriento, *a.* dusty.
polvorín, *m.* finest powder; powderflask, priming horn; powder magazine.
polvorista, *m.* manufacturer of gunpowder; maker of fireworks.
polvoroso, sa, *a.* dusty, full of dust.
polla, *f.* pullet; (coll.) comely young lass; (cards) pool; (orn.) FÚLICA.—**pollada,** *f.* flock of young fowls; hatch, covey.—**pollancón, na,** *n.* large chicken; (coll.) overgrown youth.—**pollastra,** *f.* large young hen.—**pollastre, pollastro,** *m.* large chicken; (coll.) cunning fellow.—**pollazón,** *m.* hatching; hatch, brood.—**pollera,** *f.* woman who raises or sells chickens; chicken roost; chicken coop; gocart; hooped petticoat.—**pollería,** *f.* poultry shop or market; (coll.) assemblage of young persons.—**pollero,** *m.* poulterer; poultry yard.
pollina, *f.* young she-ass.
pollinarmente, *adv.* (coll.) = ASNALMENTE.
pollino, no, *m.* donkey, ass, jument.
pollito, ta, *n.* chicken; (coll.) boy or girl.
pollo, *m.* chicken; nestling; young bee; (coll.) young man; artful, clever man.
polluelo, la, *n.* little chicken, chick.
poma, *f.* apple; perfume censer; smelling bottle; pomander box.
pomáceo, a. I. *a.* (bot.) pomaceous. **II.** *f. pl.* Pomaceæ.
pomada, *f.* pomatum, pomade; salve.
pomar, *m.* orchard, especially of apple trees.
pomarada, *f.* plantation of apple trees.
pomarrosa, *f.* (bot.) rose apple.

pómez.—piedra p., *f.* pumice stone.

pomífero, ra, *a.* pomiferous, having apples.

pomo, *m.* pip fruit; pomum; pomander box; flask, flagon, small bottle; pommel; nosegay.

pomología, *f.* pomology, science and art of fruit growing.

pompa, *f.* pomp, ostention, splendor; grand procession, pageant; bubble; inflation of clothes raised by the wind; expanded tail of a turkey or peacock; (naut.) pump.

pompearse, *vr.* (coll.) to appear with pomp and ostentation; to strut.

pompeyano, na, *n. & a.* Pompeian, of Pompeii; relating to, or follower of, Pompey.

pompón, *m.* (mil.) pompon.

pomponearse, *vr.* = POMPEARSE.

pomposamente, *adv.* pompously.

pomposo, sa, *a.* pompous; magnificent, splendid; inflated.

pómulo, *m.* cheek bone.

ponceño, ña, *n. & a.* Poncean (from Ponce).

ponci, poncidre, poncil, *a. & m.* terms app. to a species of bitter orange or lemon.

ponchada, *f.* quantity of punch made at one time.

ponche, *m.* punch (liquor).

ponchera, *f.* punch bowl.

poncho, cha. I. *a.* soft, mild, careless, heedless. **II.** *m.* military cloak or greatcoat; poncho.

ponderable, *a.* ponderable; wonderful.

ponderación, *f.* consideration, deliberation; exaggeration.—**ponderador, ra,** *n. & a.* ponderer (-ing); exaggerator (-ing).

ponderal, *a.* ponderal, relating to weight.

ponderar, *va.* to weigh; to ponder, consider; to exaggerate; to praise highly.

ponderativo, va, *a.* exaggerati ; hyperbolical.

ponderosamente, *adv.* attentively, carefully.

ponderosidad, *f.* ponderousness, ponderosity.

ponderoso, sa, *a.* heavy, ponderous; grave, circumspect, cautious.

ponedero, ra. I. *a.* capable of being laid or placed; egg-laying (as a hen). **II.** *m.* nest, hen's nest; nest egg.

ponedor, ra. I. *a.* egg-laying (as a hen). **II.** *n.* one that sets or lays; bettor, wagerer; outbidder; horse trained to rear on the hind legs.

ponencia, *f.* charge, post, or office of a chairman of a committee, or of a final judge or arbiter; exercise of such an office.

ponente, *n.* arbitrator, referee; chairman of a reporting committee.

ponentino, na, tisco, ca, *a.* western.

poner, *va.* (*pp.* PUESTO: *ind.* PONGO: *pret.* PUSE: *fut.* PONDRÉ: *subj.* PONGA) to put, place, lay; to dispose, arrange, set (as the table); to suppose, assume; to impose, enjoin (as order, peace, etc.); to oblige, compel; to wager, stake; to appoint, put in charge; to adduce; to leave to one's judgment or action; to call, give (a person or thing) the name of; to write, set down; to lay (eggs); to bring forth; to contribute; to enforce; to concert; to agree; to insult, to treat badly; to cause (fear, etc.); to make, cause to become or turn (red, angry, etc.).—**p. al corriente,** to inform.—**p. al sol,** to expose to the sun, to sun.—**p. casa,** to begin, or go, housekeeping.—**p. colorado,** to put to the blush, shame.— **p. como chupa de dómine, or como nuevo,** to humiliate, reprimand or treat harshly, dress down. —**p. como un guante,** to make pliable or submissive.—**p. coto a,** to stop, check, put a limit to.—**p. de su parte,** to do one's part, or on one's part.— **p. de vuelta y media** = P. COMO NUEVO.—**p. en (tanto),** to bid (so much).—**p. en claro,** to make clear; to investigate.—**p. en duda,** to question, to doubt.—**p. en relieve,** to carve in relief; to describe graphically.—**p. fuego,** to set fire.—**p. mal,** to discredit, run down; to set against (each other). —**p. pies en pared,** to maintain one's opinion with obstinacy.—**p. pies en polvorosa,** to take to one's heels.—**p. por,** to use as; appoint or send as.—**p. por escrito,** to put down in writing.

poner, *vr.* to apply one's self to, to set about; to don, put on (as a garment); to set or place one's

self; to oppose; become, get (as wet, angry, dirty); to set (as the sun); to reach, get to, arrive; to adorn one's self.—**p. a,** to begin to, start to.—**p. a cubierto,** to shelter one's self from danger.—**p. colorado,** to blush.—**p. en jarras,** to set one's arms akimbo.—**p. en razón,** to be reasonable.— **ponérsele a uno,** to take a fancy or a notion to; to suspect, surmise (ch. constr.: *se me pone que Juan no pagará,* I suspect John won't pay).—**p. tan alto,** to become haughtily indignant, to swell up with indignation.—**al p. el sol,** at sunset.

pongo, *m.* (S. A.) narrow and dangerous ford; Indian servant; (zool.) orang-outang.

pongo, ponga. *V.* PONER.

ponientada, *f.* steady west wind.

poniente, *m.* west; west wind.

ponimiento, *m.* act of putting, or putting on.

ponleví, *m.* shoe with high, wooden heel.

pontaje, pontazgo, *m.* bridge toll, pontage.

pontear, *va.* to erect a bridge over.

pontezuelo, la, *n. dim.* small bridge.

póntico, ca, *a.* Pontic.

pontificado, *m.* pontificate, papacy, popedom.

pontifical. I. *a.* pontifical, papal. **II.** *m.* (eccl.) pontifical (book and robes); parochial tithes.

pontificalmente, *adv.* pontifically.

pontificar, *vn.* (coll.) to act like a pontiff; to rule; to preside.

pontífice, *m.* pontiff; archbishop or bishop of a diocese.—**pontificio, cia,** *a.* pontificial.

pontil, *m.* (glass.) pontil or ponty.

pontín, *m.* (Philip.) (naut.) coasting vessel.

ponto, *m.* (poet.) sea.

pontón, *m.* (mil.) pontoon; hulk serving as storeship, hospital, or prison ship; (naut.) mudscow, lighter, dredge; log bridge.

pontonero, *m.* (mil.) pontonier.

ponzoña, *f.* poison, venom.—**ponzoñosamente,** *adv.* poisonously, venomously.—**ponzoñoso, sa,** *a.* poisonous, venomous, baneful.

popa, *f.* (naut.) poop, stern; prosperity.—**a p., de p., en p.,** aft, abaft.

popamiento, *m.* despising; cajoling, fondling.

popar, *vn.* to despise; to cajole; to fondle.

popel, *a.* (naut.) aftermost, sternmost.

popés, *m.* (naut.) stay of the mizzenmast.

poplíteo, tea, *a.* (anat.) popliteal.

popote, *m.* Indian straw for brooms.

populachería, *f.* claptrap; cheap popularity.

populachero, ra, *a.* vulgar, common.

populacho, *m.* populace, mob, rabble.

popular, *a.* popular.

popularidad, *f.* popularity.

popularizar. I. *va.* (*pret.* POPULARICÉ: *subj.* POPULARICE) to popularize, make popular. **II.** *vr.* to become popular.

popularmente, *adv.* popularly.

populazo, *m.* populace, mob, rabble.

populeón, *m.* white poplar ointment.

populoso, sa, *a.* populous.

poquedad, *f.* paucity, littleness; pusillanimity; trifle, mite; stupidity.

poquillo. I. *adv. dim.* very little time. **II.** *m.* (a) little, (a) little bit.

poquillo, lla, *a. dim.* small, little; trifling.

poquísimo, ma, *a. & adv. super.* very little.

poquítico, ica, illo, illa, ito, ita, *a. dim.* almost nothing, just a little.

poquito, ta. I. *a. dim.* very little; weak of body and mind, diminutive.—**p. a poco,** gently, slowly. **II.** *m.* a wee bit.—**a poquitos,** little by little; a little at a time.

por, *prep.* by; for; through (*pasamos por un túnel,* we passed through a tunnel; *Juan entró por la ventana,* John came in through the window); as (*desechado por inútil,* cast off as useless); across (*se pasó la mano por la frente,* he passed his hand across his forehead); about, nearly (*por ahí,* about that, very nearly; *por Navidad,* about Christmas); during (*volverá por la cuaresma,* he will return during Lent); per; after, for (*tr por pan,* to go for, or after, bread); for the sake of (*por Vd.,* for your sake; *¡por Dios!* for God's sake!); in behalf of, on account of (*por causa de enfermedad*, on account of illness); in order to; by way of, via; in the name of; without, not yet, to be (*cartas por contestar*, letters to be answered; *la casa está por acabar*, the house is not yet finished, or, is to be finished).—**p. cuanto**, inasmuch as, whereas.—**p. docena**, by the dozen.—**p. entre**, through.—**p. escrito**, in writing.—**p. más que**, or **p. mucho que**, however much; notwithstanding (one's great efforts, etc.).—**p. qué**, why. —**p. si acaso**, in case; if by chance.

porcachón, na, *a*, (coll.) very dirty, hoggish.

porcal, *a*. a kind of large plum.

porcaso, *m*. hog thief.

porcelana, *f*. porcelain; chinaware; jewel enamel. —**porcelanita,** *f*. porcelanite, jasper.

porcentaje, *m*. percentage.

porcino, na. I. *a*. hoggish; porcine. **II.** *m*. young pig; bruise, bump.

porción, *f*. portion, part; lot; (com.) share, allowance, allotment; pittance.

porcioncica, illa, ita, *f. dim.* small portion.

porcionero, ra, *n. & a.* participant (-ating).

porcionista, *n*. shareholder; school boarder.

porcipelo, *m*. (coll.) bristle.

porciúncula, *f*. (eccl.) Franciscan jubilee.

porcuno, na, *a*. hoggish, porcine.

porchada, *f*. stretcher in paper factories.

porche, *m*. covered walk; porch, portico.

pordiosear, *vn*. to beg.—**pordioseo,** *m*. begging. —**pordiosería,** *f*. beggary.—**pordiosero, ra,** *n*. beggar.

porfía, *f*. obstinacy, stubbornness; insistence, persistence; importunity.—**a p.,** in competition, vying with each other; insistently.

porfiadamente, *adv*. obstinately; pertinaciously.

porfiado, da, *pp. & a.* obstinate, stubborn.

porfiador, ra, *n*. persistent person.

porfiar, *vn*. to persist.

porfídico, ca, *a*. porphyritic.

pórfido, *m*. porphyry, jasper.

pormenor, *m*. detail, particular.

pormenorizar, *va*. to detail, itemize, enter into details about, give in detail.

pornografía, *f*. pornography; pornograph.

pornográfico, ca, *a*. pornographic.

pornógrafo, *m*. pornographer.

poro, *m*. pore, interstice.

pororó, *m*. (S. A.) toasted corn.

pororoca, *f*. tide rip.

porosidad, *f*. porosity.—**poroso, sa,** *a*. porous.

poroto, *m*. (Am.) a variety of pea.

porque, *conj*. because, for, as; in order that.

¿por qué? *interr.* why? wherefore?

porqué, *m*. why, reason, motive; (coll.) allowance, pittance, portion.

porquecilla, *f. dim.* small sow.

porquera, *f*. lair, couch of a wild boar.

porquería, *f*. nastiness; filth; vile, dirty act, nasty trick; trifle, worthless thing.

porqueriza, *f*. hogsty.

porquerizo, za; porquero, ra, *n*. swineherd.

porquerón, *m*. (coll.) catchpoll, bumbailiff.

porqueta, *f*. woodlouse.

porquezuelo, la, *n. dim.* small hog or sow; slovenly young person.

porra, *f*. bludgeon, club; maul; last player in boys' games; (coll.) vanity, boast; (coll.) dull or importunate person.

porrada, *f*. blow or knock; (coll.) foolishness, nonsense.

porrazo, *m*. blow, knock, fall.

porrear, *vn*. (coll.) to insist, persist.

porrería, *f*. (coll.) obstinacy; silliness.

porreta, *f*. green leaf of leeks, garlic, or onions.— **en p.,** (coll.) stark naked.

porrilla, *f*. small forging hammer; (vet.) osseous tumor in joints.

porrillo.—a p., *adv*. (coll.) aplenty, abundantly.

porrina, *f*. small and green crop.

porrino, *m*. tender plant of a leek.

porrizo, *m*. bed or plot of leeks.

porro, rra. I. *a*. (coll.) stupid. **II.** *m*. (bot.) leek.

porrón, na. I. *a*. heavy, sluggish, slow. **II.** *m*. earthen jug; wine bottle with long side spout.

porrudo, *m*. shepherd's crook.

porta, *f*. (naut.) gun port; stern port.

porta-, particle used in composition, gen. equivalent to "holder" or "carrier" after the corresponding noun, as in *portaplumas*, penholder; *portanoticias*, news carrier; *portaneumático*, tire holder.

portaaguja, *f*. needle holder.

portabandera, *f*. socket for a flagpole.

portabombas, *m*. bomb carrier.

portacaja, *f*. carrier of a loom; (mil.) drumsash or strap.

portacarabina, *f*. (mil.) carbine thimble.

portacartas, *m*. mail bag for letters.

portada, *f*. portal, porch; frontispiece, front, façade; (print.) title page; division of the warp.

portadera, *f*. chest for stores on a horse.

portado, da, *a*.—**bien (mal) p.,** well (poorly) dressed or behaved.

portador, ra. I. *n*. bearer, carrier, porter; (com.) holder, bearer. **II.** *m*. waiter's tray.

portaestandarte, *m*. (mil.) color sergeant.

portafusil, *m*. (mil.) sling of a musket.

portaguión, *m*. (mil.) guidon (officer).

portaje, *m*. = PORTAZGO.

portal, *m*. porch, entry, entrance, vestibule; portico, piazza; town's gate.

portalámpara, *m*. lamp holder; (elec.) socket (of a lamp fixture).

portalápiz, *m*. pencil holder.

portalazo, *m. aug.* large door or porch.

portalejo, *m. dim.* little porch or portico.

portaleña, *f*. (fort.) embrasure; plank for doors.

portalero, *m*. octroi officer or guard.

portalibros, *m*. book strap.

portamira, *n*. (surv.) rodman.

portalico, illo, ito, *m. dim.* small porch.

portalón, *m*. (naut.) gangway.

portamanteo, *m*. portmanteau, cloak bag.

portamonedas, *m*. pocketbook, purse.

portanario, *m*. (anat.) pylorus.

portaneumático, *m*. (aut.) tire holder.

portante, *m*. quick pace of a horse.—**tomar el p.,** (coll.) to go away.

portantillo, *m. dim.* gentle amble, easy pace.

portanuevas, *n*. newsmonger.

portanveces, *m*. coadjutor, assistant.

portañola, *f*. (naut.) porthole.

portañuela, *f*. (tail.) fly of trousers.

portaobjetos, *m*. slide (of microscope).

portapaz, *n*. (eccl.) pix.

portaparaguas, *m*. umbrella stand.

portaplacas, portaplanchas, *m*. (photo.) dark slide, plate holder, chassis.

portapliegos, *m*. large portfolio.

portaplumas, *m*. penholder.

portar. I. *va*. to carry (as arms). **II.** *vr*. to behave, comport, act. **III.** *vn*. (naut.) to fill (s. o. the sails).

portátil, *a*. portable.

portavasos, *m*. glass stand or rack.

portaventanero, *m*. carpenter who makes windows and doors.

portaviandas, *m*. dinner pail.

portavoz, *m*. megaphone, speaking trumpet.

portazgo, *m*. toll, turnpike duty.

portazguero, *m*. toll gatherer, collector.

portazo, *m*. slam with a door; slamming a door in one's face.

porte, *m*. cost of carriage; freight, portage, porterage; postage; deportment, behavior; nobility; illustrious descent; size; capacity; (naut.) burden or tonnage.—**p. franco,** frank; postage prepaid.

portear. I. *va*. to carry or convey for a price. **II.** *vr*. to pass, migrate (s. o. birds).

portento, *m*. prodigy, wonder; portent.

portentosamente, *adv*. prodigiously.

portentoso, sa, *a*. prodigious, marvellous.

porteo, *m.* carrying, cartage, portage.

porterejo, *m.* little porter.

portería, *f.* porter's lodge or box, conciergerie; employment of a porter; (naut.) all the ports in a ship.

portero, ra, *n.* janitor, superintendent, concierge; porter, gatekeeper.

portezuela, *f. dim.* little door; carriage door; pocket flap; (Mex.) pass between hills.

pórtico, *m.* portico, piazza; porch; hall; lobby.

portillo, *m.* opening, gap, breach; wicket, gate; means to an end; cavity in anything broken; octroi gate of a town; pass between hills.

portón, *m.* court door of a house.

portorriqueño, ña, *n.* & *a.* Porto-Rican.

portugués, sa. **I.** *n.* & *a.* Portuguese. **II.** *m.* Portuguese language.

portulano, *m.* charts of ports and harbors.

porvenir, *m.* future, time to come

¡porvida! *interj.* by the living saints!

pos.—en p. de, *adv.* after, behind; in pursuit of.

posa, *f.* passing bell; stop in a funeral, to sing a response.—*pl.* (coll.) buttocks.

posada, *f.* lodging; lodging house; inn, tavern, hotel; home, dwelling.

posadera, *f.* hostess, landlady.—*pl.* buttocks.

posadero, *m.* innkeeper, host; seat made of flags or bass ropes.

posante, *a.* reposing; smooth (sailing).

posar. **I.** *vn.* to lodge, board; to sit down, repose, rest; to perch, light. **II.** *va.* to lay down. **III.** *vr.* to settle (s. o. a liquid); to light, alight, sit (on).

posaverga, *f.* (naut.) yard prop.

posca, *f.* mixture of vinegar and water.

posdata, *f.* postscript.

poseedor, ra, *n.* possessor, holder, owner.

poseer, *va. gerund,* POSEYENDO: *pret.* él POSEYÓ: *subj. imp.* POSEYERA, POSEYESE) to hold, possess, own; to master (an art, language, etc.).

poseído, da. **I.** *a.* & *pp.* possessed.—**estar p.,** to be possessed; to be thoroughly convinced or posted about. **II.** *m.* private arable land.

posesión, *f.* possession; property; possession by evil spirits.—*pl.* holdings, wealth, property.

posesional, *a.* possessional, possessive.

posesionarse, *vr.* to take possession.

posesionero, ra, *n.* cattle keeper owning pastures.

posesivo, va, *n.* & *a.* (gram.) possessive.

poseso, sa, *a.* possessed (with evil spirits).

posesor, ra, *n.* possessor, holder, owner.

posesorio, ria, *a.* possessory.

poseyente, *a.* possessing, owning.

posfecha, *f.* postdate.—**posfechar,** *va.* to postdate.

posibilidad, *f.* possibility; means, property.

posibilismo, *m.* possibilism.

posibilista, *n.* & *a.* possiblist (-ic).

posibilitar, *va.* to render possible, facilitate.

posible. **I.** *a.* possible. **II.** *m. pl.* personal means; best of one's ability.

posiblemente, *adv.* possibly.

posición, *f.* position; placing, placement; standing, status; (law) questions and answers of an interrogatory; (math.) position.

positivamente, *adv.* positively; absolutely.

positivismo, *m.* positiveness; positivism; practicalness, (moral) materialism, matter-of-factness.

positivo, va, *a.* positive, certain; absolute, real; matter-of-fact; (math., elec., photo.) positive; (gram.) positive.—**de p.,** certainly, without doubt.

pósito, *m.* public granary.

positura, *f.* posture, state, disposition.

posma. **I.** *f.* (coll.) sluggishness, sloth, dulness. **II.** *n.* (coll.) dull, sluggish person.

poso, *m.* sediment, dregs, lees; rest, repose.

posó, *m.* (Philip.) chignon, hair knot.

posología, *f.* (med.) posology.

posón, *m.* round matted seat.

pospelo.—a p. *adv.* against the grain; reluctantly.

posplerna, *f.* thigh of an animal.

posponer, *va. (for irr. v.* PONER) (w. **a**) to put after; to think less of; to subordinate to.

pospuesto, ta, *pp. irr.* of POSPONER.

posta. **I.** *f.* post horses, relay; post, post stage, posthouse, post office; chop of meat or fish; mould shot; stake, at cards; memorial tablet. **II.** *n.* person who travels post.

postal. **I.** *a.* postal. **II.** *f.* postal card.

postdata, *f.* = POSDATA.

postdiluviano, na, *a.* postdiluvian.

poste, *m.* post, pillar; remaining standing up as a school punishment.

postelero, *m.* (naut.) skid, skeed; chess-trees.

postema, *f.* abscess, gathering; boresome person.

postemero, *m.* (surg.) large lancet.

postergación, *f.* delaying; leaving behind; disregard of seniority.

postergar, *va.* (*pret.* POSTERGUÉ: *subj.* POSTERGUE) to delay; to ignore or disregard the right of seniority of (a candidate for office, etc.).

posteridad, *f.* posterity.

posterior, *a.* posterior, rear; later, subsequent.

posterioridad, *f.* posteriority.

posteriormente, *adv.* subsequently.

posteta, *f.* (b. b.) number of sheets stitched together.

postigo, *m.* wicket; peep window; shutter; (fort.) sally port, postern.

postila, *f.* postil, marginal note.

postilación, *f.* marginal annotation.

postilador, *m.* annotator.

postilar, *va.* to postillate, gloss, comment.

postilla, *f.* scab on wounds.

postillón, *m.* postillion, postboy.

postilloso, sa, *a.* scabby, pustulous.

postizo, za. **I.** *a.* artificial, not natural. **II.** *m.* false hair, switch. **III.** *f.* castanet; (naut.) dead work on galleys.

postliminio, *m.* (law) postliminium.

postmeridiano, na, *a.* postmeridian.

postor, *m.* bidder.

postración, *f.* prostration; kneeling; dejection.—**postrado, da,** *a.* & *pp.* prostrate, prostrated, prone; procumbent.—**postrador, ra.** **I.** *n.* & *a.* prostrator (-ing). **II.** *m.* footstool in a choir.

postrar. **I.** *va.* to prostrate, to humble; to overthrow, demolish; to weaken, exhaust. **II.** *vr.* to prostrate one's self, kneel down, lie prone; to be exhausted.

postre. **I.** *a.* last in order.—**a la p.,** at last.—**por fin y p.,** (coll.) finally. **II.** *m.* (*sing.* or *pl.*) dessert.

postremo, ma, *a.* last.

postrer, *a. contr.* of POSTRERO (*before a noun*).

postreramente, *adv.* lastly.

postrero, ra, *a.* last; hindermost.

postrimer, *a. contr.* of POSTRIMERO (*before a noun*).

postrimeramente, *adv.* finally, at last.

postrimería, *f.* (theol.) last stage of life.

postrimero, ra, *a.* last; hindmost.

póstula, postulación, *f.* request, petition; (eccl.) postulation.

postulado, *m.* postulate.

postulador, ra, *n.* one who postulates.

postulante, *a.* & *n.* postulant.

postular, *va.* to postulate.

póstumo, ma, *a.* posthumous.

postura, *f.* posture, position; planting trees or plants; tree or plant transplanted; assize of provisions; (com.) bid; stake, wager; egg; egg-laying; agreement, covenant.

potabilizar, *va.* to make potable or drinkable.

potable, *a.* potable, drinkable.

potación, *f.* potation, drinking; beverage.

potador, ra, *n.* inspector of weights and measures.

potaje, *m.* pottage; porridge; stewed vegetables; mixed drink; medley.

potajería, *f.* heap of dry pulse; place where vegetables are kept.—**potajier,** *m.* keeper of the vegetables in the royal palace.

potala, _f._ (naut.) anchor; stone anchor; small slow vessel.

potar, _va._ to correct and mark (weights and measures); to drink.

potasa, _f._ potash.—**potásico, ca,** _a._ potassic; potassium (u. a., as in _bromuro potásico,_ potassium bromide).

potasio, _m._ potassium.

pote, _m._ jug; pot, jar, gallipot; (cook.) pot; flowerpot; standard measure or weight.—**a p.,** abundantly.—**potecillo, ito,** _m. dim._ little pot, can or jar.

potencia, _f._ power, capacity; dominion; faculty of the mind; possibility; power, strong nation; force, strength; (mech., phys., math.) power; (arti.) reach.—_pl._ nine rays of light around the head of Jesus.—**potencias del alma,** powers of the soul, mental powers (gen. stated as memory, judgment, and will).—**en p.,** potentially.

potencial, _a._ & _f._ potential.—**potencialidad,** _f._ potentiality.—**potencialmente,** _adv._ potentially, virtually.

potentado, _m._ potentate, sovereign.

potente, _a._ potent, powerful, mighty; strong, vigorous; (coll.) bulky, huge.

potentemente, _adv._ powerfully, potently.

potenza, _f._ (her.) tace.

poterna, _f._ (mil.) postern, sally port.

potero, _m._ = POTADOR.

potestad, _f._ power, dominion, jurisdiction; potentate.—_pl._ angelic powers.

potestativo, va, _a._ (for.) facultative.

potingue, _m._ (coll.) medicinal concoction.

potísimo, ma, _a._ most special.

potista, _n._ (coll.) tippler, drinker.

pot-pourri, _m._ potpourri; mixture; hash.

potra, _f._ filly; (coll.) rupture, scrotal hernia.—**tener p.,** to have good luck.

potrada, _f._ troop of young mares.

potranca, _f._ filly, young mare.

potrear, _va._ (coll.) to tease, vex, annoy.

potrera, _f._ a hempen headstall.

potrero, _m._ herdsman of colts; pasture ground; (Am.) cattle ranch; (coll.) rupture specialist.—**potrico, ilo,** _m. dim._ small colt.—**potril,** _m._ pasture for young horses.—**potrilla,** _f._ (coll.) old man affecting rakish youth.

potro, _m._ colt, foal; wooden horse, rack; shoeing frame; anything that torments; obstetrical chair; pit in the ground for dividing a beehive.—**estar en un p.,** to be on pins and needles.

potroso, sa, _a._ afflicted with a rupture; (coll.) fortunate, lucky.

poya, _f._ fee for baking in a public oven; hemp bagasse.

poyal, _m._ striped cover for benches; stone seat.

poyar, _vn._ to pay the POYA.

poyata, _f._ shelf, cupboard.

poyo, _m._ stone seat against a wall; fee formerly paid to judges.

poza, _f._ puddle; pool for breaking hemp.

pozal, _m._ bucket, pail; coping of a well; vessel sunk in the earth to collect liquids.

pozanco, _m._ pool in a river bank.

pozo, _m._ well; deep hole in a river; eddy, whirlpool; (min.) shaft, pit; (naut.) hold; anything complete in its line.—**p. artesiano,** artesian well.—**p. negro,** cesspool.

pozol, pozole, _m._ barley and beans boiled.

pozuela, _f. dim._ small puddle or pond.

pozuelo, _m. dim._ small well or pit; vessel sunk in the ground to collect oil, etc.

práctica, _f._ practice; habit; practicing; exercise; manner, method, routine; learning a profession under a master.—**en la p.,** in practice.

practicable, _a._ practicable, feasible.

practicador, ra, _n._ practicer, practitioner.

practicaje, _m._ (naut.) pilotage.

prácticamente, _adv._ in a practical manner, in practice.

practicante. I. _a._ practicing. **II.** _n._ practicer, practitioner; hospital intern; hospital nurse; one who practices medicine under direction and guidance of an experienced physician; (pharm.) prescription preparer, or clerk.

practicar, _va._ (_pret._ PRACTIQUÉ: _subj._ PRACTIQUE) to practice; to make; to perform, do, put in execution; to have it as a practice, to do habitually; to learn the practice of under an adviser.

práctico, ca. I. _a._ practical; skilful, experienced. **II.** _m._ (naut.) harbor pilot.

practicón, na, _n._ (coll.) one possessing practical knowledge and experience.

pradeño, ña, _a._ relating to prairies.

pradera, pradería, _f._ prairie, meadow.

praderoso, sa, _a._ relating to prairies.

pradial, _m._ Prairial, ninth month of the French-Revolution calendar.

prado, _m._ lawn; field, pasture ground; walk (in a city).—**p. de guadaña,** meadow mowed annually.

pragmática, _f._ pragmatic, decree.

pragmático, _m._ commentator of national laws.

pragmatismo, _m._ (philos.) pragmatism.

pragmatista, _n._ & _a._ (philos.) pragmatist (-ic).

prao, _m._ proa, prao, an Asiatic canoe.

prasio, _m._ (min.) prase, translucent quartz.

prasma, _m._ (min.) dark green agate.

pravedad, _f._ perversity, iniquity, depravity.

pravo, va, _a._ depraved, wicked, perverse.

pre, _m._ daily pay allowed to soldiers.

preadamita, _n._ preadamite.

preadamítico, ca, _a._ preadamic.

preámbulo, _m._ preamble; (coll.) evasion.

prebenda, _f._ (eccl.) prebend, benefice.

prebendado, pp. & _m._ (eccl.) prebendary.

prebendar, _va._ to confer a prebend on.

prebostal, _a._ provostal.—**prebostazgo,** _m._ provostship.—**preboste,** _m._ provost; (mil.) provost.

precariamente, _adv._ precariously.

precario, ria, _a._ precarious.

precaución, _f._ precaution.

precaucionarse, _vr._ to be cautious.

precautelar, _va._ to caution, forewarn.

precaver. I. _va._ to prevent, obviate. **II.** _vr._ (w. de) to guard against, be on one's guard.

precavidamente, _adv._ cautiously.

precavido, da, _pp._ & _a._ cautious, guarded.

precedencia, _f._ precedence, priority; preëminence, preference; superiority, primacy.

precedente. I. _a._ preceding, foregoing. **II.** _m._ precedent.

preceder, _va._ to precede; to be superior to.

preceptista, _n._ & _a._ one, or relating to one, who sets precepts.

preceptivamente, _adv._ preceptively.

preceptivo, va, _a._ preceptive.

precepto, _m._ precept; order, injunction; rule.—_pl._ the Commandments.

preceptor, ra, _n._ teacher, preceptor.

preceptuar, _va._ to give or issue as a precept.

preces, _f. pl._ prayers; devotion; supplication.

precesión, _f._ (rhet.) reticence; (ast.) precession.

preciado, da, _pp._ & _a._ valued, priced, esteemed; valuable, precious; proud, elated.

preciador, ra, _n._ appraiser.

preciar. I. _va._ to value, price, appraise. **II.** _vr._ to boast, brag; to take pride in, to glory.

precinta, _f._ strap, band; (naut.) parcelling.

precintar, _va._ to strap, hoop, bind; to seal.

precinto, _m._ strapping; sealed strap.

precio, _m._ price; reward; premium; esteem; importance, worth.—**precios corrientes,** price current.—**no tener p.,** to be invaluable, to be priceless.—**tener en p.,** to esteem.

preciosa, _f._ (eccl.) allowance to prebendaries.

preciosamente, _adv._ preciously, richly.

preciosidad, _f._ worth, preciousness; rich or beautiful object, (a) beauty.

precioso, sa, _a._ precious, valuable; beautiful; witty, merry.

precipicio, _m._ precipice, chasm; violent fall; ruin, destruction.

precipitación, _f._ rash haste, precipitancy; (chem.) precipitation.—**precipitadamente,** _adv._ hastily.—**precipitadero,** _m._ precipice, steep cliff.

precipitado, da. I. *a.* & *pp.* precipitate, hasty; abrupt. II. *m.* (chem.) precipitate.—**p. blanco,** calomel.

precipitante, *m.* (chem.) precipitator.

precipitar. I. *va.* to precipitate, cast headlong; to rush, hasten; (chem.) to precipitate. II. *vr.* to throw one's self headlong; to rush, hurry.

precipite, *a.* in danger of falling.

precipitosamente, *adv.* = PRECIPITADAMENTE.

precipitoso, sa, *a.* precipitous; rash, reckless.

precipuamente, *adv.* principally.

precipuo, pua, *a.* chief, principal.

precisamente, *adv.* precisely, exactly; necessarily, unavoidably; just at this (that) moment.

precisar, *va.* to fix, set, determine with precision; to compel, oblige.

precisión, *f.* necessity; compulsion; preciseness, exactness; precision, accuracy.

preciso, sa, *a.* necessary; indispensable; precise, exact, accurate; distinct, clear; severed, cut off; concise.

precitado, da, *a.* aforesaid, aforementioned.

precito, ta, *a.* damned, condemned to hell.

preclaramente, *adv.* illustriously.

preclaro, ra, *a.* illustrious, famous, prominent.

precocidad, *f.* precocity.

precognición, *f.* precognition.

precolombino, na, *a.* pre-Columbian.

preconización, *f.* eulogy; preconization.

preconizador, ra, *n.* & *a.* eulogizer (-ing); preconizer (-ing).

preconizar, *va.* (*pret.* PRECONICÉ: *svbj.* PRECONICE) to praise, eulogize; (eccl.) to preconize.

preconocer, *va.* (*for irr. v.* CONOCER) to foreknow.

precordial, *a.* (anat.) precordial.

precoz, *a.* precocious.

precursor, ra. I. *a.* preceding. II. *n.* precursor, harbinger, forerunner.

predecesor, ra, *n.* predecessor.

predecir, *va.* (*for irr. v.* DECIR) to foretell, predict, forecast.

predefinición, *f.* (theol.) predetermination.

predefinir, *va.* to predetermine.

predestinación, *f.* predestination.

predestinado, da. I. *pp.* & *a.* predestined. II. *n.* one predestined.

predestinante, *n.* & *a.* predestinator (-ing).

predestinar, *va.* to predestine, foredoom, predestinate, foreordinate.

predeterminación, *f.* predetermination, foreordination.—**predeterminar,** *va.* to predetermine, foredoom, foreordain.

predial, *a.* predial.

prédica, *f.* preachment, sermon.

predicable, *a.* fit to be preached; (log.) predicable.

predicación, *f.* preching; sermon.

predicadera, *f.* pulpit.—*pl.* (coll.) facility for preaching.

predicado, *m.* (log.) predicate.

predicador, ra, *n.* preacher.

predicamental, *a.* predicamental.

predicamento, *m.* predicament.

predicante, *n.* sectarian or heretical preacher.

predicar, *va.* & *vn.* (*pret.* PREDIQUÉ: *subj.* PREDIQUE) to render clear and evident; to publish; to preach; to praise to excess; (coll.) to reprimand, lecture, sermonize.

predicción, *f.* prediction.

predicho, cha, *pp. irr.* of PREDECIR.

predigo, prediga, predije. V. PREDECIR.

predilección, *f.* predilection.

predilecto, ta, *a.* preferred, favorite.

predio, *m.* landed property, farm, real property. —**p. rústico,** piece of arable ground.—**p. urbano,** dwelling house or building lot.

predisponer, *va.* (*for irr. v.* PONER) to prejudice, predispose; to prearrange.

predisposición, *f.* predisposition; prejudice.

predispuesto, ta, *a.* & *pp. irr.* of PREDISPONER: predisposed, biased, inclined.

predominación, predominancia, *f.* predominance, predomination.

predominante, *a.* predominant, prevailing.

predominar, *vn.* & *va.* to predominate, prevail; to rise above, overlook, command.

predominio, *m.* predominance, superiority.

preelegir, *va.* to preëlect; to predestinate.

preeminencia, *f.* preëminence, mastery.

preeminente, *a.* preëminent, superior.

preestablecer, *va.* to preëstablish.

preexcelso, sa, *a.* most illustrious, most high.

preexistencia, *f.* preëxistence.

preexistente, *a.* preëxistent.

preexistir, *vn.* to preëxist.

prefacio, *m.* preface, prologue; (eccl.) preface.

prefación, *f.* preface, prologue, introduction.

prefecto, *m.* prefect.—**prefectura,** *f.* prefecture.

preferencia, *f.* preference.—**preferente,** *a.* preferential; preferring; preferable.

preferentemente, *adv.* preferably.

preferible, *a.* preferable.

preferiblemente, *adv.* preferably.

preferir, *va.* (*gerund,* PREFIRIENDO: *ind.* PREFIERO: *pret.* PREFIRIÓ: *subj.* PREFIERA) to prefer.

prefiguración, *f.* prefiguration.

prefigurar, *va.* to prefigure.

prefijar, *va.* to predesignate, predetermine.

prefijo, ja. I. *a.* prefixed. II. *m.* (gram.) prefix.

prefinición, *f.* setting of a time limit.

prefinir, *va.* to set a time limit for.

prefloración, *f.* (bot.) prefloration.

prefoliación, *f.* (bot.) vernation.

prefulgente, *a.* resplendent, bright.

pregón, *m.* publication by the crier, cry.

pregonar, *va.* to proclaim; cry out, make publicly known.—**pregoneo,** *m.* crying goods on the streets. —**pregonería,** *f.* office of common crier.

pregonero, ra. I. *a.* publishing, announcing. II. *n.* common crier, town crier; auctioneer.

pregunta, *f.* question, query; catechism.—**absolver las preguntas,** (for.) to answer under oath —**estar a la cuarta p.,** (coll.) to be hard up or penniless.—**hacer una p.,** to ask a question.

preguntador, ra, *n.* & *a.* questioner (-ing).

preguntante, *n.* & *a.* inquirer (-ing).

preguntar, *va.* & *vn.* to ask, question, inquire.— **p. por,** to ask for (a person); to inquire about.

preguntón, na, *a.* inquisitive.

prehistoria, *f.* prehistoric times; prehistorics, study or science of prehistoric times.

prehistórico, ca, *a.* prehistoric.

preinserto, ta, *a.* previously inserted.

prejudicial, *a.* (law) requiring judicial decision before final sentence.

prejudicio, prejuicio, *m.* prejudice, bias.

prejuzgar, *va.* (*for mut. v.* JUZGAR) to prejudge.

prelacía, *f.* prelacy, prelature.

prelación, *f.* preference.

prelada, *f.* prelatess, abbess, mother superior.

prelado, *m.* (eccl.) prelate.

prelatura, *f.* prelacy, prelature.

preliminar. I. *a.* preliminary. II. *m.* preliminary; peace protocol.

prelucir, *vn.* (*for irr. v.* LUCIR) to shine forth.

preludiar. I. *va.* & *vn.* (mus.) to play a prelude. II. *va.* to initiate, pave the way for.

preludio, *m.* introduction; (mus.) prelude.

prelusión, *f.* prelude, prologue, preface.

prematuramente, *adv.* prematurely.

prematuro, ra, *a.* premature; precocious; unripe, unseasonable; (law) impuberal (s. o. girls).

premeditación, *f.* premeditation.

premeditadamente, *adv.* premeditatedly.

premeditado, da, *a.* & *pp.* premeditated.

premeditar, *va.* to premeditate.

premiador, ra, *n.* rewarder.

premiar, *va.* to reward, remunerate, requite.

premio, *m.* reward; prize; recompense; (com.) premium; interest.—**a p.,** at a premium.

premiosamente, *adv.* tightly, compressedly; by force.

premiosidad, *f.* difficulty of action or speech.

premioso, sa, *a.* tight, close, pinching; troublesome, burdensome; strict, rigid; slow in speaking or writing.

premisa, *f.* (log.) premise; mark, indication.

premiso, sa, *a.* premised; sent in advance.

premoción, *f.* previous motion.

premonstratense, *n.* & *a.* Premonstratensian.

premoriencia, *f.* (law) prior death.

premoriente, *a.* & *n.* predeceased.

premorir, *vn.* (*for irr. v.* MORIR) (law) to die before another.

premostratense, *n.* & *a.* Premonstratensian.

premuerto, ta, *pp.* of PREMORIR.

premura, *f.* urgency, pressure, haste.

prenda, *f.* pledge, security, pawn; piece of jewelry; garment; person dearly loved.—*pl.* endowments, natural gifts, talents.—**p. de vestir,** article of clothing, piece of wearing apparel.—**en p., en prendas,** as a pledge, as security.—**soltar p.,** to commit one's self.

prendado, *pp.* & *a.*—**estar p. de,** to be taken up with.—**ser muy p.,** to have many accomplishments.

prendador, ra, *n.* pledger, pawner.

prendamiento, *m.* pledging, pawning.

prendar. I. *va.* to pledge, pawn; to please, charm. **II.** *vr.* (**w. de**) to become fond of, take a great liking to.

prendedero, *m.* hook, fillet, brooch.

prendedor, *m.* catcher; breastpin; shawl pin, baby pin.

prender. I. *va.* (*pp.* PRENDIDO, PRESO) to seize, grasp, catch, apprehend; to cover (a mare). **II.** *vn.* to take root; to catch or take fire. **III.** *vr.* to make an elaborate toilet.

prendería, *f.* second-hand shop; jewelry, frippery.—**prendero, ra,** *n.* second-hand dealer, fripper; pawnbroker.

prendido, *pp.* & *m.* a woman's dress; pattern for bone lace.

prendimiento, *m.* seizure, capture.

prenoción, *f.* prenotion, first knowledge.

prenombre, *m.* prenomen.

prenotar, *va.* to note by anticipation.

prensa, *f.*(mech.) press; vise, clamp; mill; (print.) printing press; press, newspapers.—**p. de lagar,** wine press.—**p. periódica,** the press.—**dar a la p.,** to publish.

prensado, *pp.* & *m.* lustre, on stuff.

prensador, ra, *n.* presser.

prensadura, *f.* pressing, pressure.

prensar, *va.* to press; to calender.

prensil, *a.* prehensile.—**prensión,** *f.* prehension.

prensista, *m.* (print.) pressman.

prensor, ra. I. (zool.) psittacine (of the parrot family). **II.** *m. pl.* Psittaci (the parrot family).

prenunciar, *va.* to foretell, prognosticate.

prenuncio, *m.* prediction, prognostication.

preñado, da. I. *a.* pregnant; full, charged; sagging or bulging out. **II.** *m.* pregnancy.

preñez, *f.* pregnancy; impending danger or resolution; confusion, difficulty.

preocupación, *f.* preoccupation; preoccupancy; prepossession, bias, prejudice, notion; conventionality.—**preocupadamente,** *adv.* with preoccupation; with prejudice.

preocupar. I. *va.* to preoccupy; to prejudice. **II.** *vr.* to be prejudiced or biased; to worry.

preopinante, *n.* predecessor (in a debate).

preordinación, *f.* preordination.

preordinadamente, *adv.* in a preordained or forcordained manner.

preordinar, *va.* to preordain, foreordain.

preparación, *f.* preparation; preparing; compound; medicine.

preparado, *m.* preparation, compound.

preparamiento, *m.* = PREPARACIÓN.

preparar. I. *va.* to prepare; make ready. **II.** *vr.* to be prepared, get ready, make preparations.

preparativo, va. I. *a.* preparative, qualifying. **II.** *m.* preparation.

preparatoriamente, *adv.* preparatorily.

preparatorio, ria, *a.* preparatory.

preponderancia, *f.* preponderance, sway.

preponderante, *a.* preponderant, prevailing.

preponderar, *vn.* to preponderate, have sway; to prevail.

preponer, *va.* (*for irr. v.* PONER) to put before, to prefer.

preposición, *f.* (gram.) preposition.

prepositivo, va, *a.* prepositive, prepositional.

prepósito, *m.* president, chairman; provost.

prepositura, *f.* dignity of a provost.

preposteración, *f.* reversion of order.

prepósteramente, *adv.* out of place or order; inopportunely.

preposterar, *va.* to reverse, invert, disarrange.

prepóstero, ra, *a.* out of place or order; inopportune.

prepotencia, *f.* preponderance, prepotency.

prepotente, *a.* prepotent, predominant.

prepucio, *m.* (anat.) prepuce, foreskin.

prepuesto, ta, *pp. irr.* of PREPONER.

prerrafaelismo, *m.* (art) Pre-Raphaelitism.—**prerrafaelista,** *n.* & *a.* (art) Pre-Raphaelite.

prerrogativa, *f.* prerogative.

presa, *f.* capture, seizure; (mil.) spoils, booty; catch, hold, prey; dam; trench, ditch, flume; slice, bit, morsel; tusk, fang; claw of a bird of prey; among fishermen, fish weir, stake work.—**p. de caldo,** meat juice, beef tea.

presada, *f.* reservoir, storage water (in mills).

presado, da, *f.* pale-green color.

presagiar, *va.* to presage, forbode, foretell.

presagio, *m.* presage, omen, token.

presagioso, sa; présago, ga, *a.* betokening, significant, presaging.

presbicia, *f.* farsightedness, presbyopia.

présbita, présbite. I. *a.* presbyopic, farsighted. **II.** *n.* presbyope.

presbiterado, *m.* priesthood.—**presbiteral,** *a.* sacerdotal.—**presbiterato,** *m.* = PRESBITERADO.

presbiterianismo, *m.* Presbyterianism.

presbiteriano, na, *n.* & *a.* Presbyterian.

presbiterio, *m.* presbytery; chancel.

presbítero, *m.* priest; presbyter.

presciencia, *f.* prescience, foreknowledge.

prescindible, *a.* that may be dispensed with.

prescindir, *vn.* (**w. de**) to dispense with, do without; to set aside, to ignore.

prescito, ta, *a.* *V.* PRECITO.

prescribir. I. *va.* (*pp. irr.* PRESCRITO and PRESCRIPTO) to prescribe, dispose, specify; (law and med.) to prescribe. **II.** *vn.* (law) to prescribe.

prescripción, *f.* prescription; (law) prescription.

prescriptible, *a.* prescriptible.

prescrito, ta, *pp.* of PRESCRIBIR.

presea, *f.* jewel, gem, valuable article.

presencia, *f.* presence; physique, figure; show, ostentation.—**p. de ánimo,** coolness, presence of mind.

presencial, *a.* presential.

presencialmente, *adv.* presentially.

presenciar, *va.* to witness, to see; to attend.

presentable, *a.* presentable; producible.

presentación, *f.* presentation, presentment, exhibition, display; personal introduction; (eccl.). Presentation.—**a p.,** (com.) on presentation, at sight.

presentado, *pp.* & *m.* student of divinity about to be graduated as master; presentee, person presented.

presentador, ra, *n.* presenter; bearer.

presentalla, *f.* (eccl.) votive offering.

presentáneamente, *adv.* immediately.

presentáneo, *a.* quick-acting.

presentante, *a.* presenting, introducing.

presentar. I. *va.* to present; display, show; to give, make a present of; (eccl.) to offer as candidate. **II.** *vr.* to appear, present one's self; to offer one's services; (mil.) to enlist as a volunteer.

presente. I. *a.* present.—**hacer p.,** to state, to remind of, call attention to.—**la p.,** the present writing (these presents).—**mejorando lo p.**, present company excepted.—**tener p.**, to bear in mind. **II.** *m.* present, gift; present (time).—**al p.**, or **de p.**, at present.—**por el**, or **lo, p.**, for the present.

presentemente, *adv.* at present, now.

presentero, *m.* one who offers as a candidate.

presentimiento, *m.* presentiment; misgiving.

presentir, *va.* (*for irr. v.* SENTIR) to have a presentiment of; to forebode.

presepio, *m.* stable; manger.

presera, *f.* (bot.) goose grass, cleavers.

presero, *m.* keeper of a dam or dike.

preservación, *f.* preservation, conservation.

preservador, ra, *n.* & *a.* preserver (-ing).

preservar, *va.* to preserve, guard, keep, save.

preservativamente, *adv.* preservatively.

preservativo, va. I. *a.* preservative, preserving. **II.** *m.* preservative, preventive.

presidario, *m.* = PRESIDIARIO.

presidencia, *f.* presidency; presidential chair; chairmanship; presidential term.

presidencial, *a.* presidential.

presidenta, *f.* president's wife; moderatrix; (woman) chairman; (woman) president.

presidente, *m.* president; chairman; speaker (of a parliamentary body); presiding judge; presiding officer.

presidiar, *va.* to garrison.

presidiario, *m.* convict.

presidio, *m.* garrison of soldiers; fortress, citadel; penitentiary; punishment by hard labor.

presidir, *va.* to preside; to govern, sway, determine (s. o. persons or things).

presiento, presienta. *V.* PRESENTIR.

presilla, *f.* loop, shank, eye, noose, bight; (sew.) buttonhole stitching; a kind of linen.

presión, *f.* pressure.

preso, sa. I. *pp. irr.* of PRENDER; imprisoned. **II.** *n.* prisoner; convict.

prest, *m. V.* PRE.

presta, *f.* (bot.) mint.

prestación, *f.* (law) lending; loan.

prestadizo, za, *a.* that may be lent or loaned.

prestado, da, *a.* & *pp.* lent, loaned.—**dar p.**, to lend.—**pedir**, or **tomar, p.**, to borrow.

prestador, ra, *n.* lender.

prestamente, *adv.* speedily, promptly, quickly.

prestamera, *f.* (eccl.) a kind of sinecure.

prestamería, *f.* (eccl.) dignity of a sinecure.

prestamero, *m.* incumbent of a PRESTAMERA.

prestamista, *n.* money lender; pawnbroker.

préstamo, *m.* loan.

prestancia, *f.* excellence.

prestante, *a.* excellent.

prestar. I. *va.* to lend, to loan; to aid, to assist; to give; communicate; to pay (attention). **II.** *vn.* to be useful; to expand, extend. **III.** *vr.* to offer or lend one's self or itself; to adapt itself, or himself; to be applicable.

prestatario, ria, *n.* & *a.* borrower (-ing).

preste, *m.* (eccl.) high mass celebrant.

prester, *m.* hurricane, cyclone; waterspout.

presteza, *f.* quickness, promptness, haste.

prestidigitación, *f.* legerdemain, sleight of hand, jugglery.

prestidigitador, ra, *n.* juggler, prestidigitator.

prestigiador, ra, *n.* cheat, impostor.

prestigio, *m.* prestige, good name; spell, fascination; deception, illusion (s. o. legerdemain).

prestigioso, sa, *a.* renowned; well-reputed; deceiving, illusory.

prestimonio, *m.* loan; (eccl.) prestimony.

prestiño, *m.* = PESTIÑO.

presto, ta. I. *a.* quick, swift, prompt; ready, prepared. **II.** *adv.* soon; quickly.—**de p.**, promptly, swiftly.

presumible, *a.* presumable.

presumido, da, *pp.* & *a.* presumptuous, airy, conceited.

presumir. I. *va.* (*pp.* PRESUMIDO, PRESUNTO) to presume, surmise, conjecture. **II.** *vn.* to presume, boast; to be conceited.

presunción, *f.* presumption, conjecture; presumptuousness, conceit; (law) presumption.

presuntamente, *adv.* presumptively.

presuntivamente, *adv.* conjecturally.

presuntivo, va, *a.* presumptive, supposed.

presunto, ta, *a.* presumed.—**p. heredero,** heir apparent.

presuntuosamente, *adv.* presumptuously.

presuntuosidad, *f.* presumptuousness.

presuntuoso, sa, *a.* presumptuous, conceited.

presuponer, *va.* (*for irr. v.* PONER) to presuppose; to estimate.

presuposición, *f.* presupposition.

presupuesto, ta. I. *pp. irr.* of PRESUPONER. **II.** *m.* motive, pretext, pretence; estimate; budget of state.

presura, *f.* anxiety; quickness, haste, promptness; persistency.

presurosamente, *adv.* hastily, promptly.

presuroso, sa, *a.* prompt, quick; nimble.

pretal, *m.* poitrel, breastplate, breast leather.

pretencioso, sa, *a.* presumptuous, conceited.

pretender, *va.* (*pp.* PRETENDIDO, PRETENSO) to pretend; to aspire to; to seek, solicit; to try, endeavor; (Colomb.) to court, be in love with.

pretendiente, ta, *n.* pretender, candidate, office hunter; (Colomb.) suitor.

pretensión, *f.* pretension, claim; presumption.

pretensor, ra, *n.* pretender, claimant.

preterición, *f.* omission; (rhet. and law) preterition.

preterir, *va.* (*def. only the infin. and pp. used*) (law) to omit (lawful heirs) in a will.

pretérito, ta, *n.* & *a.* preterit, past.

pretermisión, *f.* preterition, pretermission.

pretermitir, *va.* to omit, pretermit, pass by.

preternatural, *a.* preternatural.

preternaturalizar, *va.* to pervert; to render preternatural.

preternaturalmente, *adv.* preternaturally.

pretextar, *va.* to give as a pretext.

pretexta, *f.* prætexta, pretexta.

pretexto, *m.* pretext, pretence, cover, excuse.

pretil, *m.* railing, battlement, breastwork.

pretina, *f.* girdle, waistband; belt.

pretinero, ra, *n.* girdle maker or seller.

pretinilla, *f. dim.* ladies' belt or girdle.

pretor, *m.* pretor; blackness of the waters where tunny fish abound.

pretoria, *f.* pretorship.

pretorial, *a.* pretorian or prætorian.

pretorianismo, *m.* abuse of military power for political purposes, political militarism.

pretoriano, na, *a.* pretorian or prætorian.

pretoriense, *a.* relating to a prætorium.

pretorio, ria. I. *a.* pretorian. **II.** *m.* pretorium.

pretura, *f.* pretorship.

prevalecer, *vn.* (*ind.* PREVALEZCO: *subj.* PREVALEZCA) to prevail; to take root.

prevaleciente, *a.* prevalent; prevailing.

prevalerse, *vr.* to avail one's self.

prevaricación, *f.* betrayal of a trust.

prevaricador, ra,; *n.* one who plays false, betrayer; perverter; turncoat.

prevaricar, *vn.* (*pret.* PREVARIQUÉ: *subj.* PREVARIQUE) to play false, be a betrayer; (law) to prevaricate.

prevaricato, *m.* (law) prevarication, betrayal of a trust.

prevención, *f.* prevention; foresight, forethought; disposition, preparation; supply of provisions; sustenace, subsistence; warning; prejudice, prepossession; police station; (mil.) guardroom, cell; (law) prevenience of a judge in the knowledge of a case.

prevenidamente, *adv.* beforehand, previously.

prevenido, da, *a.* & *pp.* ready, prepared, provided; plentiful; forewarned; cautious.

preveniente, *a.* predisposing, prevenient.

prevenir. I. *va.* (*for irr. v.* VENIR) to prepare, prearrange, make ready; to foresee; to forestall, prevent, avoid; to warn, caution, to prepossess, predispose; to overcome; to come upon, surprise. **II.** *vr.* to be ready, prepared, or on guard.

preventivamente, *adv.* preventively.

preventivo, va, *a.* preventive, preservative; (law) prevenient.

prever, *va.* (*for irr. v.* VER) to foresee, anticipate.

previamente, *adv.* previously.

previo, via, *a.* previous, foregoing.

previsión, *f.* foresight; forecast.

previsor, ra, *n.* one who foresees. **II.** *a.* far-seeing, perspicacious.

previsto, ta, *pp. irr.* of PREVER.

prez, *m.* or *f.* honor, glory, merit, worth.

priapismo, *m.* (med.) priapism.

priesa, *f.* = PRISA.

prieto, ta, *a.* blackish, very dark; narrow-minded, illiberal; close-fisted, mean; tight, compressed.

prima, *f.* female cousin; early morning; (eccl.) prime; first tonsure; (mil.) first quarter of the night; (mus.) treble (in stringed instruments); (com.) premium; bounty.

primacía, *f.* primacy; primateship.

primacial, *a.* primatial.

primada, *f.* (coll.) playing one for a sucker; a sponging trick.

primado, da. I. *a.* primatial. **II.** *m.* primeness; (eccl.) primate.

primal, la. I. *a.* yearling (ewe or a goat). **II.** *m.* silk cord or braid.

primariamente, *adv.* chiefly, primarily.

primario, ria. I. *a.* principal, primary; (geol.) Primary, Paleozoic; (elec.) primary (circuit). **II.** *n.* professor who lectures at dawn.

primate. I. *n.* distinguished person, worthy. **II.** *m.* (zool.) one of the Primates.—*pl.* Primates.

primavera, *f.* spring (season); flowered silk (bot.) primrose.

primaveral, *a.* spring (u. a.), belonging to spring.

primazgo, *m.* cousinship.

primearse, *vr.* to treat each other as cousins.

primer, *a. contr.* of PRIMERO.—**p. galán,** (theat.) lead.—**p. pronto,** first movement.—**p. vertical,** (ast.) prime vertical.

primera, *f.* primero, game at cards; (feno.) prime —*pl.* first tricks, at cards.—**p. de cambio** (com.) first of exchange.

primeramente, *adv.* first; in the first place.

primerizo, za. I. *n.* novice, beginning; firstling **II.** *f.* primipara.

primero, ra, *a.* first; former.—**p. dama,** (theat.) leading lady.—**p. enseñanza,** primary education. —**p. fila,** front rank.—**p. intención,** (surg.) first intention.—**p. materia,** raw material.—**a p. faz,** at first sight.—**a p. luz,** at dawn.—**a p. vista,** at first sight.—**de buenas a primers,** all at once, suddenly.—**de p.,** (com.) of superior quality, highest-grade.—**de p. instancia,** instantly, on the first impulse; first in; in the first place.

primero, *adv.* first, rather, sooner.—**de p.,** at the beginning, before.

primevo, va, *a.* primeval, original.

primicerio, ria. I. *a.* principal, first in rank. **II.** *m.* precentor, chanter.

primicia, *f.* first fruits; offering of the first fruits. —*pl.* first production, maiden effort.

primicial, *a.* primitial.

primichón, *m.* skein of soft embroidering silk.

primigenio, nia, *a.* primogenial, primitive.

primilla, *f.* (coll.) pardon of a first offence.

primípara, *f.* (med.) primipara.

primitivamente, *adv.* originally.

primitivo, va, *a.* primitive, original, primeval.

primo, ma. I. *a.* first; superior, excellent. **II.** *n.* cousin; (coll.) simpleton, dupe.—*pl.* cousins, appellation given by the kings of Spain to the grandes.—**p. carnal,** or **p. hermano,** first cousin. **III.** (**primo**) *adv.* first, in the first place.

primogénito, ta, *n.* & *a.* first born.

primogenitura, *f.* primogeniture; seniority.

primor, *m.* beauty; dexterity, ability, exquisiteness, excellence, nicety.

primordial, *a.* primordial, original, primal.

primorear, *vn.* to perform with elegance and neatness.

primorosamente, *adv.* finely, nicely, neatly, handsomely.—**primoroso, sa,** *a.* neat, elegant, fine, exquisite; beautiful; graceful, dexterous.

primuláceo, a, *a.* (bot.) primulaceous.

princesa, *f.* princess; princesse (gown).

principada, *f.* (coll.) undue assumption of authority.

principado, *m.* princedom; princehood; principality; preëminence, primacy.—*pl.* princedoms.

principal. I. *a.* principal, main; important, essential; illustrious, renowned, celebrated; foremost, first. **II.** *m.* (mil.) main guard; (com.) principal, capital, stock; principal, chief or head of a commercial establishment; (law) constituent; second floor.

principalía, *f.* (Philip.) board of officers in each town.

principalidad, *f.* principalness.

principalmente, *adv.* principally, mainly.

príncipe, *m.* prince; sovereign, ruler; chief or leader; young queen bee; master (often u. a., as in *anteres príncipes,* classical authors, old masters.—**p. de Asturias,** Crown Prince of Spain.

principela, *f.* a sort of light camlet.

principiador, ra, *n.* beginner.

principiante, ta, *n.* beginner; apprentice.

principiar, *va.* to commence, begin, start.

principillo, *m. dim.* petty prince.

principio, *m.* principle; beginning; start; germ, original cause; rule of action, motive; origin, fountain; (cook.) entrée; (chem.) principle.— *pl.* (print.) introductory matter in a book.—**al p.,** or **a los principios,** in the beginning, at first.—**en p.,** in principle; in substance, essentially.

principote, *m.* (coll.) one who makes a pretentious display.

pringada, *f.* toasted bread steeped in gravy.

pringamoza, *f.* (Am.) (bot.) nettle.

pringar. I. *va.* (*pret.* PRINGUÉ: *subj.* PRINGUE) to baste (meat); to steep or dip (bread) in grease; to stain with grease; to spatter; to scald with boiling fat; to tar (a person); to wound; to slander; to share in a business. **II.** *vr.* (coll.) to draw unlawful advantage from a thing intrusted to one's care.

pringón, na. I. *a.* nasty, dirty, greasy. **II.** *m.* begreasing one's self; stain of grease.

pringoso, sa, *a.* greasy, fat.

pringote, *m.* mixture of viands.

pringue, *m.* or *f.* grease, fat, lard; grease stain in clothes.

pringuera, *f.* dripping pan.

prionodonte, *m.* (zool.) giant armadillo.

prior. I. *a.* prior, preceding. **II.** *m.* (eccl.) prior, superior; (prov.) rector, curate.

priora, *f.* prioress.

priorial, *a.* belonging to a prior or prioress.

priorato, priorazgo, *m.* priorate; priory.

prioridad, *f.* priority; precedence.

prioste, *m.* steward of a brotherhood.

prisa, *f.* haste, despatch, promptness; urgency; skirmish, surprise, hot fight.—**a toda p.,** with the greatest speed.—**darse p.,** to make haste.—**estar de p.,** or **tener p.,** to be in haste.

priscilianismo, *m.* Priscillianism.

priscilianista, *n.* Priscillianist.

prisco, *m.* a kind of peach.

prisión, *f.* seizure, capture; prison; imprisonment; bond, shackle.—*pl.* chains, shackles, fetters.

prisionero, *m.* (mil.) prisoner; one captivated by affection or passion.

prisma, *m.* prism.—**prismático, ca,** *a.* prismatic.

priste, *m.* (icht.) sawfish.

prístino, na, *a.* pristine, first, original.

prisuelo, *m.* muzzle for ferrets.

---

pritaneo, *m.* prytaneum (Greek public building).

privación, *f.* privation, want; lack; deprivation, loss; degradation.

privada, *f.* privy, water-closet; filth thrown into the street.

privadamente, *adv.* privately; separately.

privadero, *m.* cesspool cleaner.

privado, da. I. *a.* & *pp.* private, secret; personal. **II.** *m.* favorite, court minion, protégé.

privanza, *f.* favor at court, protection.

privar. I. *va.* to deprive; to prohibit, forbid, interdict; to stun, daze. **II.** *vn.* to enjoy the protection of a magnate; prevail, be in favor or in vogue. **III.** *vr.* to deprive one's self.

privativamente, *adv.* solely, privatively.

privativo, va, *a.* privative; special, distinctive, particular, peculiar; exclusive.

privilegiadamente, *adv.* in a privileged way.

privilegiar, *va.* to privilege, favor; to grant a privilege to.

privilegiativo, va, *a.* containing a privilege.

privilegio, *m.* privilege; grant, concession; exemption, grace; franchise; faculty; patent, copyright.—**p. de introducción,** patent on a device introduced from a foreign country.—**p. de invención,** patent (on an invention).—**p. del fuero,** privilege of ecclesiastics to be tried by their own courts.

pro, *m.* or *f.* profit, benefit, advantage.—**buena p.,** much good may it do you.—**de p.,** of note, worthy.—**en p. de,** in behalf of, for the benefit of.—**el p. y el contra,** the pros and cons.—**en p. y en contra,** pro and against; pro and con.

proa, *f.* (naut.) bow, prow; steerage.

proal, *a.* relating to the prow; forward.

probabilidad, *f.* probability, likelihood.

probabilísimo, ma, *a. sup.* most probable.

probabilismo, *m.* (theol.) probabilism.

probabilista, *n.* & *a.* (theol.) probabilist (-ic).

probable, *a.* probable, likely.

probablemente, *adv.* probably, likely.

probación, *f.* proof; probation, trial.

probado, da, *pp.* & *a.* proved, tried.

probador, ra, *n.* taster, sampler; trier.

probadura, *f.* trial, tasting, sampling.

probanza, *f.* proof, evidence.

probar. I. *va.* (*ind.* PRUEBO: *subj.* PRUEBE) to try, test; to prove; to taste; to sample (as wine); to attempt, try, endeavor; to try on (as a coat).—**p. fortuna,** to take one's chances. **II.** *vn.* to suit, fit, agree with. **III.** *vr.* to try on (as a coat).

probatorio, ria. I. *a.* probatory, probationary. **II.** *f.* (law) time allowed for producing evidence.

probatura, *f.* (coll.) trial, test, experiment.

probeta, *f.* manometer, pressure gauge; (ordn.) powder prover; (chem.) test tube, pipette.

probidad, *f.* probity, honesty, integrity.

problema, *m.* problem.

problemáticamente, *adv.* problematically.

problemático, ca, *a.* problematic(al.)

probo, ba, *a.* upright, honest.

proboscidio, dia, *a.* (zool.) proboscidean.

procacidad, *f.* impudence, pertness.

procaz, *a.* impudent, bold, insolent.

procedencia, *f.* origin; place of sailing.

procedente, *a.* coming or proceeding (from); (law) according to law, rules, or practice.

proceder. I. *vn.* to proceed; to go on; to issue, proceed, arise; to behave, conduct one's self; to act; to take action; (law) to proceed (against), take action; to be in conformity with the law, rules, or practice; to concern. **II.** *m.* conduct, behavior, action, management.

procedimiento, *m.* procedure; process, method; (law) proceeding, procedure.

procela, *f.* (poet.) storm, tempest.

proceloso, sa, *a.* tempestuous, stormy.

prócer. I. *a.* tall, lofty, elevated. **II.** *m.* person in an exalted station, worthy; Father (of the country, in Am. republics).—*pl.* the grandees and high-titled nobility of Spain.

procerato, *m.* exalted station.

proceridad, *f.* tallness; elevation or eminence; vigor, growth.

procero, ra; prócero, ra, *a.* = PRÓCER.

procesado, da. I. *pp.* & *a.* (law) relating to court proceedings; included in the suit; prosecuted, indicted. **II.** *n.* defendant.

procesal, *a.* belonging to a process or lawsuit.

procesamiento, *m.* indicting; suing.

procesar, *va.* (law) to sue; to indict.

procesión, *f.* act of proceeding or issuing forth; procession, parade, pageant.

procesional, *a.* processional or processionary.

procesionalmente, *adv.* processionally.

procesionaria, *f.* (zool.) processionary moth.

procesionario, *m.* processional book.

proceso, *m.* lapse of time; (law) criminal case; proceedings of a lawsuit.

proclama, *f.* proclamation; publication; banns of marriage.—**proclamación,** *f.* proclamation; promulgation; acclamation, public applause.

proclamar, *va.* to proclaim; to promulgate; to acclaim, cheer.

proclítico, ca, *a.* (gram.) proclitic.

proclive, *a.* inclined, disposed.

proclividad, *f.* proclivity; propensity.

procomún, procomunal, *m.* public welfare.

procónsul, *m.* proconsul.—**proconsulado,** *m.* proconsulship.—**proconsular,** *a.* proconsular.

procreación, *f.* procreation.—**procreador, ra,** *n.* & *a.* procreator (-ing).—**procreante,** *a.* procreating.

procrear, *va.* to procreate, generate, produce.

proctitis, *f.* proctitis.

procura, *f.* power of attorney.

procuración, *f.* care, diligence, careful management; power or letter of attorney; procurement, procuring; office of an attorney.

procurador, ra, *n.* procurer, procuress; (law) attorney, solicitor, proctor; manageress of a nunnery.—**p. de síndico,** attorney general.

procuraduría, *f.* attorney's office; proctorship.

procurante, *n.* solicitor, intendant.

procurar. I. *va.* to endeavor, try; to manage, transact for another; to get, obtain, procure. **II.** *vn.* to be, or act as, an attorney.

procurrente, *m.* (geog.) peninsula.

prodición, *f.* treason, treachery.

prodigalidad, *f.* prodigality; abundance.

pródigamente, *adv.* prodigally, lavishly, wastefully, profusely.

prodigar, *va.* (*pret.* PRODIGUÉ: *subj.* PRODIGUE) to lavish; to squander.

prodigiador, *m.* prognosticator, foreteller.

prodigio, *m.* prodigy; monster; marvel.

prodigiosamente, *adv.* prodigiously, wonderfully; beautifully, charmingly.

prodigiosidad, *f.* prodigiousness.

prodigioso, sa, *a.* prodigious, marvellous; monstrous; fine, excellent.

pródigo, ga, *a.* prodigal, wasteful; liberal, generous, unstinted.

prodrómico, ca, *a.* (med.) prodromic.

pródromo, *m.* (med.) prodrome.

producción, *f.* production; produce, yield; crop; delivery.

producente, *a.* producing, causing.

producibilidad, *f.* producibleness.

producible, *a.* producible.

producidor, ra, *n.* producer, procreator.

producir. I. *va.* (*pp.* PRODUCIDO, PRODUCTO: *ind.* PRODUZCO: *pret.* PRODUJE: *subj.* PRODUZCA) to produce; to publish; to yield, bear; (com.) to bring or yield (as revenue); (law) to produce, bring as evidence, exhibit. **II.** *vr.* to explain one's self; to be produced, to arise.

productible, *a.* productible.

productivo, va, *a.* productive; profitable, fruitful.

producto, *m.* product; article (of trade, etc.); production; produce; (math.) product.—**p. neto,** (com.) net produce.

proejar, *vn.* to row against wind or tide.

proel. I. *a.* (naut.) fore. **II.** *m.* (naut.) bow hand.

proemial, *a.* proemial, introductory.

proemio, *m.* proem, preface, introduction.

proeza, *f.* prowess, feat.

profanación, *f.* profanation, desecration.

profanador, ra, *n.* & *a.* profaner (-ing), defiler (-ing), violator (-ing).

profanamente, *adv.* profanely.

profanamiento, *m.* = PROFANACIÓN.

profanar, *va.* to profane, desecrate; to defile, disgrace, dishonor.

profanidad, *f.* profanity; profaneness; indecency, immodesty.

profano, na, *a.* profane, secular; profane, irreverent; worldly; irreligious; immodest, unchaste; lay, unfamiliar, ignorant.

profecía, *f.* prophecy.—*pl.* the Prophets.

profecticio, *a.* (law) profectitious.

proferente, *a.* uttering, pronouncing.

proferir, *va.* (*gerund.* PROFIRIENDO: *ind.* PROFIERO: *pret.* él PROFIRIÓ: *subj.* PROFIERA) to utter, express, speak.

profesante, *a.* professing.

profesar, *va.* to practise or follow (a profession or trade); to teach as a professor; to profess, avow, be a follower of or a believer in; to entertain, harbor (as friendship); (eccl.) to join (a religious body).

profesión, *f.* profession; declaration, avowal.

profesional, *a.* professional.

profeso, sa, *a.* professed (monk or nun).

profesor, ra, *n.* professor.—**profesorado,** *m.* professorship; body of teachers, faculty.

profeta, *m.* prophet.—**profetal,** *a.* prophetic.

proféticamente, *adv.* prophetically.

profético, ca, *a.* prophetic, prophetical.

profetisa, *f.* prophetess.

profetizador, ra, *n.* & *a.* prophesier (-ing).

profetizar, *va.* & *vn.* (*pret.* PROFETICÉ: *subj.* PROFETICE) to prophesy.

proficiente, *a.* proficient, advanced.

proficuo, cua, *a.* useful, advantageous.

profiláctico, ca. I. *a.* (med.) prophylactic, preventive. **II.** *m.* prophylactic. **III.** *f.* hygiene.

profilaxis, *f.* (med.) prophylaxis.

prófugo, ga. I. *n.* & *a.* fugitive from justice. **II.** *m.* one who absents himself to evade military service, slacker.

profundamente, *adv.* profoundly, deeply; highly, acutely.

profundidad, *f.* depth; profundity, depth; concavity; profoundness; height, excellence; intensity.

profundizar, *va.* (*pret.* PROFUNDICÉ: *subj.* PROFUNDICE) to deepen; to go deep into; to fathom, explore.

profundo, da. I. *a.* deep; low; profound, recondite; intense, dense; high, great. **II.** *m.* profundity; the sea, the deep; hell.

profusamente, *adv.* profusely; lavishly, prodigally, extravagantly.—**profusión,** *f.* profusion, profuseness; lavishness, prodigality.—**profuso, sa,** *a.* profuse, plentiful; lavish, prodigal.

progenie, *f.* progeny, offspring, issue.

progenitor, *m.* progenitor, ancestor.

progenitura, *f.* *V.* PROGENIE and PRIMOGENITURA.

progimnasma, *m.* preparatory exercise.

prognatismo, *m.* (anat.) prognathism.

prognato, ta, *a.* (anat.) prognathous.

progne, *f.* (poet.) swallow.

prognosis, *f.* forecasting.

programa, *m.* program; plan; scheme; specifications; proclamation, public notice.

progresar, *vn.* to progress.

progresión, *f.* progression, progress; (math.) progression.

progresivamente, *adv.* progressively, onward, forward.

progresista. I. *a.* progressive. **II.** *n.* & *a.* (pol.) Progressive.

progresivo, va, *a.* progressive, advancing.

progreso, *m.* progress, civilization; (often *pl.*) progress (in an undertaking, in school, etc.), advancement, development.

prohibente, *a.* prohibiting.

prohibición, *f.* prohibition, forbidding.

prohibicionismo, *m.* prohibitionism.

prohibicionista, *n.* & *a.* prohibitionist (-ic).

prohibir, *va.* to prohibit, forbid.

prohibitivo, va, *a.* prohibitive, forbidding.

prohibitorio, ria, *a.* prohibitory.

prohijación, *f.* = PROHIJAMIENTO.

prohijador, ra, *n.* adopter.

prohijamiento, *m.* adoption.

prohijar, *va.* to adopt as one's own.

prohombre, *m.* great man; master of a guild.

pro indiviso, *adv.* (law) undivided (legacies).

prójima, *f.* insignificant or contemptible woman.

prójimo, *m.* fellowbeing, (in biblical language) neighbor.

prolapso, *m.* (med.) prolapsus, descent.

prole, *f.* issue, offspring, progeny; fruit.

prolegómenos, *m. pl.* prolegomena.

prolepsis, *f.* (rhet.) prolepsis.

proletariado, *m.* proletariat.

proletario, ria. I. *a.* proletarian, very poor; plebeian; belonging to the working classes. **II.** *n.* proletarian; (Rom. hist.) proletary.

prolífico, ca, *a.* prolific, fruitful, productive.

prolijamente, *adv.* prolixly, tediously.

prolijidad, *f.* prolixity; trifling nicety.

prolijo, ja, *a.* prolix, tedious; overcareful, triflingly nice; troublesome, impertinent, long-winded.

prologal, *a.* relating to prefaces or a preface.

prologar, *va.* to write a preface for.

prólogo, *m.* prologue; preface.

prologuista, *m.* writer of prologues.

prolonga, *f.* (arti.) prolonge.

prolongación, *f.* prolongation, lengthening; extension; protraction, lingering.

prolongadamente, *adv.* tardily, protractedly.

prolongado, da, *pp.* & *a.* prolonged, produced; oblong.

prolongador, ra, *n.* & *a.* prolonger (-ing).

prolongamiento, *m.* = PROLONGACIÓN.

prolongar, *va.* & *vr.* (*pret.* PROLONGUÉ: *subj.* PROLONGUE) to prolong; to protract, extend, continue; (geom.) to produce.—**p. un plazo,** (com.) to grant an extension of time.

proloquio, *m.* maxim, apothegm.

prolusión, *f.* prolusion, prelude.

promediar. I. *va.* to divide into two equal parts; (com.) to average. **II.** *vn.* to mediate.

promedio, *m.* middle; average, mean.

promesa, *f.* promise, offer; pious offering.

prometedor, ra, *a.* promising.

prometer. I. *va.* to promise, offer; bid fair. **II.** *vn.* to promise, give favorable indications. **III.** *vr.* to expect with confidence; to become betrothed; to devote one's self to the service of God.

prometido, da. I. *pp.* & *n.* betrothed. **II.** *m.* promise; offer; auction fee.

prometiente, *a.* promising, assuring.

prometimiento, *m.* promise, offer.

prominencia, *f.* elevation; prominence; protuberance; knoll, knob.

prominente, *a.* elevated, protuberant; projecting, jutting out.

promiscuamente, *adv.* promiscuously.

promiscuar, *vn.* to eat meat and fish on fast days.

promiscuo, cua, *a.* promiscuous; ambiguous.

promisión, *f.* promise.

promisorio, ria, *a.* promissory.

promoción, *f.* promotion, preferment.

promontorio, *m.* promontory, headland, foreland; anything bulky and unwieldy.

promotor, ra. I. *a.* promotive. **II.** *n.* promoter, advancer, furtherer.—**p. fiscal,** (law) district attorney.

promovedor, ra, *n.* promoter.

promover, *va.* (*for irr. v.* MOVER) to promote, further; to advance, exalt, raise.

promulgación, *f.* promulgation.
promulgador, ra, *n.* promulgator.
promulgar, *va.* (*pret.* PROMULGUÉ: *subj.* PRO-
MULGUE) to promulgate, proclaim, publish.
pronaos, *m.* (arch.) pronaos.
prono, na, *a.* prone, inclined, bent on.
pronombre, *m.* (gram.) pronoun.
pronominado, da; pronominal, *a.* (gram.) pronominal.
pronosticación, *f.* prognostication.
pronosticador, ra, *n.* & *a.* prognosticator (-ing).
pronosticar, *va.* (*pret.* PRONOSTIQUÉ: *subj.* PRO-
NOSTIQUE) to prognosticate, foretell, augur.
pronóstico, *m.* prognostic, prediction, omen; almanac; (med.) prognosis.
prontamente, *adv.* promptly, quickly.
prontitud, *f.* promptness; speed, swiftness, dispatch; liveliness of wit; quick repartee.
pronto. I. *a.* prompt, quick, fast. **II.** *m.* sudden
impulse.—**primer p.,** first movement. **III.** *adv.*
soon; promptly, quickly.—**al p.,** at first.—**de p.,**
suddenly, without thinking.—**por el,** (or lo) **p.,**
for the present, for the time being, provisionally.
prontuario, *m.* memorandum book; compendium of rules.
prónuba, *f.* (poet.) bridesmaid.
pronunciación, *f.* pronunciation, articulation.
pronunciado, da. I. *n.* insurgent. **II.** *pp.* of
PRONUNCIAR. **III.** *a.* pronounced, steep; sharp.
pronunciador, ra, *n.* pronouncer.
pronunciamiento, *m.* insurrection, uprising;
(law) pronouncement of a sentence.
pronunciar. I. *va.* to pronounce, articulate,
enunciate; to deliver, make (a speech); (law) to
pronounce (judgment); to pass upon (a point)
before the main question is decided. **II.** *vr.* to rise
in insurrection, to rebel.
propagación, *f.* propagation; spreading, dissemination.—**propagador, ra,** *n.* & *a.* propagator
(-ing).—**propaganda,** *f.* propaganda, dissemination; (eccl.) propaganda; association for propagating doctrines.
propagandista. I. *n.* propagandist. **II.** *a.* by,
or relating to, propaganda.
propagante, *a.* propagating; spreading.
propagar. I. *va.* (*pret.* PROPAGUÉ: *subj.* PRO-
PAGUE) to propagate, generate; to spread, disseminate. **II.** *vr.* to spread; to propagate; to
multiply.
propagativo, va, *a.* propagative.
propalador, ra, *n.* divulger.
propalar, *va.* to publish, to divulge.
propano, *m.* (chem.) propane.
propao, *m.* (naut.) breastwork, bulkhead.
propartida, *f.* time preceding a departure.
propasarse, *vr.* to transgress, overstep all bounds,
take undue liberties, forget one's self, exceed
one's authority.
propender, *vn.* (*pp.* PROPENDIDO, PROPENSO) to
tend, be inclined, have a tendency.
propensamente, *adv.* propensely.
propensión, *f.* propensity, tendency, bent.
propenso, sa, *a.* propense, inclined, disposed.
propiamente, *adv.* properly, fittingly.
propiciación, *f.* propitiation, atonement.
propiciador, ra, *n.* & *a.* propitiator (-ing).
propiciamente, *adv.* propitiously.
propiciar, *va.* to propitiate, conciliate.
propiciatorio, ria. I. *a.* propitiatory. **II.** *m.*
propitiatory, mercy seat.
propicio, cia, *a.* propitious, favorable.
propiedad, *f.* ownership, proprietorship; property, holding; landed estate; property, quality;
propriety, fitness; (for.) dominion, possession;
(art) naturalness, close imitation.
propienda, *f.* listing nailed to the cheeks of an
embroidering frame.
propietariamente, *adv.* with the right of property.
propietario, ria. I. *a.* proprietary. **II.** *m.* proprietor, owner, landlord, freeholder. **III.** *f.* proprietress, landlady.

propileo, *m.* (arch.) propyleum, vestibule.
propilo, *m.* (chem.) propyl.
propina, *f.* fee, gratuity, tip; perquisite.
propinación, *f.* treat, invitation to drink.
propinar, *va.* to invite to drink, to treat; (coll.) to
prescribe (medicines).
propincuidad, *f.* propinquity, proximity.
propincuo, cua, *a.* near, contiguous.
propio, pia. I. *a.* one's own; proper, suitable,
fit, appropriate; peculiar, characteristic; natural, original, genuine; same, veritable; exact, precise. **II.** *n.* messenger.—**propios,** *m. pl.* public
lands, estates, property.
propóleos, *m.* propolis, bee glue.
proponedor, ra, *n.* proposer, proponent.
proponer. I. *va.* (*for irr. v.* PONER) to propose,
propound; to present or name (as candidate); in
écarté, to invite to draw new cards. **II.** *vr.* to
purpose, plan, intend, mean.
proporción, *f.* proportion; opportunity, occasion,
chance; (math.) proportion.—**a p. que,** as fast as,
according as.
proporcionable, *a.* proportionable.
proporcionablemente, proporcionadamente,
adv. proportionally, in proportion.
proporcionado, da, *pp.* & *a.* proportioned, fit.
proporcional, *a.* proportional.
proporcionalidad, *f.* proportionality.
proporcionalmente, *adv.* proportionally.
proporcionar, *va.* to proportion; to adjust,
adapt; to supply, provide, furnish.
proposición, *f.* proposition; proposal.
propósito, *m.* purpose, design, intention; aim,
object; subject matter.—**a p.,** for the purpose; fit;
apropos, by the bye.—**de p.,** on purpose, purposely.—**fuera de p.,** irrelevant, foreign to the subject.
propretor, *m.* propretor.
propuesta, *f.* proposal, offer, tender; nomination.
propuesto, ta, *pp. irr.* of PROPONER.
propugnáculo, *m.* fortress; (met.) bulwark.
propulsa, propulsión, *f.* repusion (of an enemy).
—**propulsar,** *va.* to repulse.
propulsor, ra, *n.* & *a.* propeller (-ing); pusher
(-ing) (sp. app. to engines).
prora, *f.* (poet.) prow of a ship.
prorrata, *f.* quota; apportionment.—**a p.,** (com.)
pro rata, in proportion.
prorratear, *va.* to allot in proportion.
prorrateo, *m.* proportional division, division pro
rata.
prórroga, *f.* prolongation, extension (of time);
prorogation, postponement. (Rarely used in
the latter sense).
prorrogable, *a.* that may be prolonged or extended (in time).
prorrogación, *f.* = PRÓRROGA.
prorrogar, *va.* to prolong, extend (in time); to
prorogue, suspend. (Rarely used in the latter
sense.)
prorrumpir, *vn.* to break forth, burst out.
prosa, *f.* prose; tedious discourse.
prosador, *m.* prose writer; (coll.) impertinent
talker.
prosaico, ca, *a.* prosaic; prosy, dull, tedious.
prosaísmo, *m.* prosaism; prosiness, dulness.
prosapia, *f.* ancestry, lineage.
proscenio, *m.* (theat.) proscenium.
proscribir, *va.* (*pp. irr.* PROSCRITO, PROSCRIPTO)
to proscribe.
proscripción, *f.* proscription, banishment.
proscripto, ta; proscrito, ta. I. *pp. irr.* of
PROSCRIBIR. **II.** *n.* exile, proscribed person.
proscriptor, ra, *n.* proscriber.
prosecución, *f.* prosecution; pursuit.
proseguible, *a.* pursuable.
proseguimiento, *m.* = PROSECUCIÓN.
proseguir. I. *va.* (*for irr. v.* SEGUIR) to pursue,
prosecute. **II.** *vn.* to go on, continue, proceed.
proselitismo, *m.* proselytism.
prosélito, *m.* proselyte, convert.
prosénquima, *m.* (biol.) prosenchyma.
prosificación, *f.* changing poetry into prose.

prosificador, ra, *n.* one that changes poetry into prose.

prosificar, *va.* to change (poetry) to prose.

prosimios, *m. pl.* (zool.) Prosimiæ, Lemuroidea.

prosista, *n.* prose writer.

prosita, *f. dim.* short piece in prose.

prosobranquios, *m. pl.* (zool.) Prosobranchiata.

prosodia, *f.* (gram.) orthoepy; prosody.

prosódico, ca, *a.* orthoepic; prosodic.

prosopografía, *f.* prosopography.

prosopopeya, *f.* (rhet.) prosopopœia, personification; (coll.) affected gravity, airs.

prospecto, *m.* prospectus, announcement.

prósperamente, *adv.* prosperously, luckily.

prosperar. I. *va.* to prosper, make happy, favor. **II.** *vn.* to prosper, thrive.

prosperidad, *f.* prosperity, success.

próspero, ra, *a.* prosperous; favorable, propitious.

prostaféresis, *f.* (ast.) prosthaphæresis.

próstata, *f.* (anat.) prostate gland.

prostático, ca, *a.* prostatic.

prostatitis, *f.* (med.) prostatitis.

prosternarse, *vr.* to prostrate one's self.

próstilo, *a.* (arch.) prostyle.

prostitución, *f.* prostitution.

prostituir. I. *va.* (*pp.* PROSTITUÍDO, PROSTITUTO: *gerund,* PROSTITUYENDO: *ind.* PROSTITUYO: *pret.* él PROSTITUYÓ: *subj.* PROSTITUYA) to prostitute, corrupt, debase. **II.** *vr.* to prostitute one's self, sell one's honor; to turn prostitute.

prostituta, *f.* prostitute.—**prostituto, ta,** *a.* prostituted.

protagonista, *n.* protagonist, hero, heroine; leader.

prótasis, *f.* (drama and gram.) protasis.

proteáceo, a. I. *a.* (bot.) proteaceous. **II.** *f. pl.* Proteaceæ.

protección, *f.* protection; favor.

proteccionismo, *m.* (pol.) protectionism.

proteccionista, *n. & a.* (pol.) protectionist.

protector, ra, *n.* protector (-ess).

protectorado, *m.* protectorate.

protectoría, *f.* protectorship, protectorate.

protectorio, ria, *a.* relating to a protector.

protectriz, *f.* protectress.

proteger, *va.* (*ind.* PROTEJO: *subj.* PROTEJA) to protect.

protegido, da, *pp. & n.* protégé, favorite.

proteico, ca, *a.* protein; (chem.) proteinaceous.

proteína, *f.* proteid, protein.

protervamente, *adv.* perversely.

protervia, protervidad, *f.* perversity, malignity, wantonness.

protervo, va, *a.* wanton, perverse.

prótesis, *f.* (gram.) prothesis; (surg.) prosthesis.

protesta, *f.* protestation; protest; (law) protest.

protestación, *f.* protestation.

protestante. I. *a.* protesting. **II.** *n. & a.* Protestant.—**protestantismo,** *m.* Protestantism.

protestar, *va.* to protest; to assure, affirm earnestly or solemnly; to make a public declaration of; (law) to protest.—**p. una letra,** (com.) to protest a draft.

protestativo, va, *a.* protesting.

protesto, *m.* (com.) protest (of a bill).

protético, ca, *a.* prothetic, prefixed.

protoalbéitar, *m.* chief veterinary surgeon.

protoalbeiterato, *m.* board for examining veterinary surgeons.

protocloruro, *m.* (chem.) protochloride.

protocolar, protocolizar, *va.* to protocol, record, register.

protocolo, *m.* protocol, registry, judicial record.

protohistoria, *f.* protohistory.

protohistórico, ca, *a.* protohistoric.

protomártir, *m.* protomartyr (app. sp. to St. Stephen, the first Christian martyr).

protomedicato, *m.* board of king's physicians; office of royal physician.

protomédico, *m.* one of the three physicians to the king.

protonotario, *m.* (law) prothonotary.

protoplasma, *m.* (biol.) protoplasm.

protoplasmático, ca, *a.* (biol.) protoplasmic.

protosulfuro, *m.* protosulphide.

prototípico, ca, *a.* prototypal.

prototipo, *m.* prototype, original; model.

protovértebra, *f.* (anat.) theoretical type of vertebræ.

protóxido, *m.* (chem.) protoxide.

protozoario, protozoo. I. *m.* (zool.) protozoan. **II.** *m. pl.* Protozoa.

protráctil, *a.* protractile.

protuberancia, *f.* protuberance.

protutor, *m.* (law) guardian.

provecto, ta, *a.* advanced in years, learning, or experience; mature.

provecho, *m.* benefit, advantage, good; profit, gain; proficiency, progress, advancement.—**buen p.,** may it benefit you; prosit.—**de p.,** useful.

provechosamente, *adv.* profitably; beneficially.

provechoso, sa, *a.* profitable; beneficial, good (as for the health); useful, advantageous.

proveedor, ra, *n.* purveyor, provider.

proveeduría, *f.* storehouse for provisions; office of purveyor.

proveer. I. *va.* (*pp.* PROVEÍDO, PROVISTO: *gerund,* PROVEYENDO: *pret.* el PROVEYÓ) to provide, furnish; to supply with provisions; stock; to dispose, adjust, transact; to confer; (law) to decide. **II.** *vr.* (w. de) to provide one's self with, get one's supply of; (coll.) to ease the body.

proveído, *pp. & m.* judgment, sentence, decision.

proveimiento, *m.* supply, provisioning.

provena, *f.* provine, layer of vine.

proveniente, *a.* arising, coming, resulting.

provenir, *vn.* (w. de) to arise from, originate in, be due to.

provento, *m.* product, rent, revenue.

provenzal, *n. & a.* Provençal.

proverbiador, *m.* collection of proverbs

proverbial, *a.* proverbial.

proverbialmente, *adv.* proverbially.

proverbiar, *vn.* (coll.) to use proverbs.

proverbio, *m.* proverb, saying, saw; omen, prediction.—*pl.* Proverbs (book of the Bible).

proverbista, *n.* (coll.) user of proverbs.

próvidamente, *adv.* providently, carefully.

providencia, *f.* foresight, forethought; act of providing; disposition, measure, way, means; (law) judgment, decision, sentence.—**la P.,** Providence.

providencial, *a.* providential.

providencialmente, *adv.* providentially; provisionally.

providenciar, *va.* to take steps or measures for; to decide (a case), pronounce judgment in.

providente; próvido, da, *a.* provident, prudent.

provincia, *f.* province; provincial court for civil causes; (eccl.) province.

provincial. I. *a.* provincial. **II.** *m.* (eccl.) provincial.

provincialato, *m.* (eccl.) provincialship.

provincialismo, *m.* provincialism.

provinciano, na, *n. & a.* provincial, provincialist; native of Biscay.

provisión, *f.* provision; supply, stock; provender; writ, decree, or sentence issued by Spanish tribunals in the king's name; measure, means; (com.) remittance of funds.

provisional, *a.* provisional.

provisionalmente, *adv.* provisionally.

proviso.—al p., immediately, instantly.

provisor, ra, *n.* purveyor, provider; (eccl.) vicar general.

provisorato, *m.* office of PROVISOR.

provisoría, *f.* in convents, storeroom, pantry; office of a PROVISOR.

provisorio, ria, *a.* provisional, temporary.

provisto, ta. I. *pp.* of PROVEER. **II.** *a.* provided, stocked, supplied.

provocación, *f.* provocation, irritation.

provocador, ra, *n.* provoker; inciter.

provocar, *va.* (*pret.* PROVOQUÉ: *subj.* PROVOQUE) to provoke, excite, incite, anger; to facilitate, promote; to tempt, arouse desire in; (coll.) to vomit.

provocativo, va, *a.* inciting; tempting; provoking, irritating.

proxeneta, *n.* (law) go-between.

próximamente, *adv.* approximately; soon; immediately; proximately.

proximidad, *f.* proximity.

próximo, ma, *a.* next; nearest, neighboring, proximate.

proyección, *f.* design; projecting; projection; (geom.) projection.

proyectante, *a.* projecting; designing.

proyectar. I. *va.* to design; to project, plan, devise; to shoot or throw forth; (geom.) to project. **II.** *vr.* to be thrown, fall (as a shadow).

proyectil, *m.* projectile, missile.

proyectista, *n.* projector; designer.

proyecto, ta. I. *a.* projected, in perspective. **II.** *m.* project, plan; design.

proyector, ra. I. *a.* projecting. **II.** *m.* (phys.) projector; search light; (aut.) spotlight.—**p. eléctrico,** searchlight.

proyectura, *f.* (arch.) projecture.

prudencia, *f.* prudence; moderation.

prudencial, *a.* prudential.

prudencialmente, *adv.* prudentially.

prudente, *a.* prudent, cautious, wise.

prudentemente, *adv.* prudently, wisely.

prueba, *f.* proof; evidence; trial, test; test piece, sample; tasting; temptation; (law) evidence; (tail.) trial, fit; (print.) proof, proof sheet; (photo.) proof.—**p. circunstancial, p. de indicios,** or **p. indiciaria,** circumstancial evidence.—**a p.,** (com.) on trial; according to the best standards, perfect.—**a p. de,** proof against (often rendered by special expressions, as in *a prueba de agua*, waterproof; *a prueba de atre*, air-tight; *a prueba de fuego*, fireproof).—**hacer la p.,** to try; (w. de) to try; to test.—**poner a p.,** to try, put to the test.

pruebo, yo pruebe. *V.* PROBAR.

prurigo, *m.* (med.) prurigo.

prurito, *m.* pruritus, itching; excessive desire.

prusiano, na, *n.* & *a.* Prussian.

prusiato, *m.* (chem.) prussiate, cyanide.

prúsico, ca, *a.* prussic, hydrocyanic.

pseudo, *a.* = SEUDO.

psicofisiología, *f.* physiological psychology.

psicología, *f.* psychology.—**psicológico, ca,** *a.* psychological.—**psicólogo,** *m.* psychologist.

psicópata, *n.* psychiatrist, alienist.

psiquiatría, *f.* psychiatry.

psíquico, ca, *a.* psychic(al.)

pterópido, da. I. *n.* & *a.* (zool.) pteropod. **II.** *m. pl.* Pteropoda, pteropods.

ptialina, *f.* (chem.) ptyalin.

¡pu! *interj.* pugh!

púa, *f.* prick; tine, prong; tooth of a comb; wire tooth of a card; spine or quill of a hedgehog, etc.; (agr.) graft, scion; metal point of a spinning top; plectrum; cause of grief or sorrow; (coll.) wily, cunning person.

puado, *m.* set of prongs, teeth, or tines.

puar, *va.* to make teeth, prongs, or tines on.

púber; púbero, ra, *a.* pubescent.

pubertad, *f.* puberty, pubescence.

pubes, *m.* (anat.) pubes, pubic region.

pubescencia, *f.* pubescence, puberty.

pubescente, *a.* pubescent.

pubescer, *vn.* to attain the age of puberty.

pubis, *m.* (anat.) pubes; pubis.

pública, *f.* in universities, public examination before graduating.

publicación, *f.* publication; proclamation.

publicador, ra, *n.* publisher; proclaimer.

públicamente, *adv.* publicly, openly.

publicano, *m.* publican.

publicar, *va.* (*pret.* PUBLIQUÉ: *subj.* PUBLIQUE) to publish; to proclaim, announce; to reveal, disclose; (eccl.) to publish (the Lanns).

publicata, *f.* (eccl.) certificate of publication.

publicidad, *f.* publicity.

publicista, *m.* publicist.

público, ca. I. *a.* public; common, general.—**en p.,** publicly. **II.** *m.* public.

pucelana, *f.* = PUZOLANA.

pucia, *f.* closed pharmaceutical vessel.

pucha, *f.* (Cuba) bouquet of flowers.

puchada, *f.* flour cataplasm; watered mortar.

puchera, *f.* (cook.) pot (= OLLA).

pucherico, illo, ito, *m. dim.* pipkin, small pot.

pucherito, *m.* (coll.) pouting of a child about to cry.

puchero, *m.* cooking pot; (cook.) olla, dish of boiled meat and vegetables, (E. U.) New-England dinner; dinner, food; pouting of a child before crying.—**hacer pucheros,** (coll.) to pout.

pucheruelo, *m. dim.* of PUCHERO.

puches, *m.* or *f. pl.*, a sort of pap. *V.* GACHAS.

pucho, *m.* (Am.) cigar stump; left over; trifle, insignificant thing.

pude. *V.* PODER.

pudelación, *f.,* **pudelaje,** *m.* (metal.) puddling.

pudelar, *va.* (metal.) to puddle.

pudendo, da. I. *a.* shameful, obscene, immodest. **II.** *m.* the male organ.

pudibundo, da, *a.* (joc.) shamefaced, modest.

pudicicia, *f.* pudicity, chastity, modesty.

púdico, ca, *a.* chaste, modest, decorous.

pudiente, *a.* powerful; rich, well off.

pudín, *m.* pudding.

pudo. *V.* PODER.

pudor, *m.* modesty, decorousness.

pudoroso, sa, *a.* modest; bashful, shy.

pudrición, *f.* rottenness; putrefaction, rotting.

pudridero, *m.* rotting place; fermenting pit; chamber with vaults for interment of bodies that are later to be transferred to mausoleums.

pudridor, *m.* (pap.) fermenting pit or vat.

pudrigorio, *m.* (coll.) sickly, infirm man.

pudrimiento, *m.* = PUDRICIÓN.

pudrir. I. *va.* to rot; to vex, worry. **II.** *vn.* to have died, to be buried; to rot. **III.** *vr.* to rot, decay; to be broken-hearted, to die of grief.

pudú, *m.* (zool.) pudu, a Chilean variety of deer.

puebla, *f.* seed that a gardener sows.

pueblada, *f.* (Am.) popular uprising; mob.

pueble, *m.* (min.) working gang.

pueblecico, ito, *m. dim.* small town.

puebleño, ña, *n.* (Colomb., contempt.) villager; boor.

pueblo, *m.* town, village; settlement; people; nation; population; common people, working classes.

pueblo, pueble. *V.* POBLAR.

puedo, pueda. *V.* PODER.

puente, *m.* or *f.* bridge; (mus.) bridge, in string instruments; (carp.) transom, lintel, crossbeam; (naut.) bridge; gun-carrying deck.—**p. cerril,** small narrow bridge for cattle.—**p. colgante,** suspension bridge.—**p. de cimbria,** (Ch.) suspension rope bridge.—**p. de los asnos,** discouraging difficulty.—**p. de tablero inferior,** through bridge.—**p. de tablero superior,** deck bridge.—**p. levadizo,** drawbridge.—**p. volante,** flying bridge.

puentecico, illo, ito, *m. dim.* small bridge.

puentecilla, *f. dim.* small bridge of a string instrument.—**puentezuela,** *f. dtm.* small bridge.

puerca, *f.* (zool.) sow; sow bug, woodlouse; scrofulous swelling; slut, slatternly woman.

puercamente, *adv.* dirtily, filthily; basely, meanly, contemptibly.

puerco, ca. I. *a.* filthy, dirty, foul; low, base, mean. **II.** *n.* hog; wild boar; base or low person.—**p. espín,** or **espino,** porcupine.—**p. marino,** (zool.) dolphin.—**p. montés,** wild boar.—**puericia,** *f.* boyhood.

puericultura, *f.* physical education of children.

pueril, *a.* childish, puerile; (ast.) first (quadrant),

puerilidad, *f.* puerility, childishness; trifle.

puerilmente, *adv.* puerilely, childishly.

puérpera, *f.* lying-in woman.

puerperal, *a.* puerperal.

puerperio, *m.* time after childbirth.

puerquezuelo, *m. dim.* little pig.

puerro, *m.* (bot.) leek.

puerta, *f.* door; doorway, gateway; gate; beginning of an undertaking; duty, octroi, toll.—**p. cochera,** porte cochère.—**p. excusada,** or **falsa,** back door, side door.—**p. franca,** open door, free entrance; free entry.—**p. reglar,** the regular door for entering nunneries.—**p. vidriera,** glass door.—**a p. cerrada,** privately, secretly, closeted (ch. constr.).—**detrás de la p.,** round the corner.—**la Sublima P.,** or **P. Otomana,** the Sublime Porte (Turkey).

puertaventana, *f.* window shutter.

puertecita, puertezuela, *f. dim.* small door.

puertecillo, puertezuelo, *m. dim.* small port.

puerto, *m.* port; harbor, haven; pass through mountains; asylum, shelter, refuge.—**p. de depósito,** bond port.—**p. franco =** P. LIBRE.—**p. habilitado,** port of entry.—**p. libre,** free port.

pues. I. *conj.* because, for, as; since, inasmuch as; then.—**p. bien,** now then, well.—**p. no,** not at all, not so.—**p. que,** since.—¿**pues qué?** what?—**p. sí,** yes, indeed, most certainly.—¿**p. y qué?** why not? what else? what then?—¿**y p.?** so? is that so? why? how is that? **II.** *adv.* yes; so; certainly; exactly.

puesta, *f.* (ast.) set, setting; stake (at cards).—**p. de sol,** sunset.—**puestas de sol,** or **a p. de sol,** at sunset.

puesto, ta. I. *pp. irr.* of PONER; put, placed, set.—**p. que,** although; since, inasmuch as. **II.** *m.* place or space occupied, stall, stand, booth; employment, position; post, dignity, office; breeding stall; blind for hunters; (mil.) barrack for soldiers.

¡puf! *interj.* pugh!

púgil, *m.* prize fighter, boxer, pugilist.

pugilar, *m.* Hebrew manual of the Scriptures.

pugilato, *m.* pugilism; boxing.

pugna, *f.* combat, struggle; conflict.—**estar en p.,** to conflict, disagree.

pugnacidad, *f.* pugnacity, quarrelsomeness.

pugnante. I. *a.* fighting, struggling. **II.** *n.* foe, opponent.

pugnar, *vn.* to fight, struggle; (w. **con**), to conflict (with), be opposed (to); to strive successfully; to be obstinate; to persist.

pugnaz, *a.* pugnacious, quarrelsome.

puja, *f.* outbidding or overbidding at a public sale; higher bid.

pujador, ra, *n.* bidder; outbidder.

pujame, pujamen, *m.* (naut.) foot of a sail.

pujamiento, *m.* flow of the blood or humors.

pujante, *a.* powerful, vigorous, strong.

pujanza, *f.* power, might, strength, vigor.

pujar. I. *va.* to outbid; to push ahead, push through. **II.** *vn.* to falter; (coll.) to pout.

pujavante, *m.* butteris, hoof parer.

pujo, *m.* (med.) tenesmus; eagerness, longing; violent desire.

pulcritud, *f.* pulchritude, neatness, tidiness.

pulcro, cra, *a.* beautiful, graceful; nice, neat, tidy.

Pulchinela, *m.* Punchinello.

pulga, *f.* flea; small playing top.—**no aguantar pulgas,** not to put up with ill treatment.—**ser de,** or **tener, malas pulgas,** to be easily piqued or fretted, to be ill-tempered.—**tener pulgas,** to be restless or too lively.

pulgada, *f.* inch.

pulgar, *m.* thumb; shoots left on vines.

pulgarada, *f.* fillip; pinch; inch.

pulgón, *m.* green fly, plant louse, aphis.

pulgoso, sa, *a.* pulicose, pulicene, abounding with fleas.

pulguera, *f.* place abounding with fleas; (bot.) pulic, fleawort.

pulguita, *f. dim.* little flea.—**pulguillas,** *n. dim.* (coll.) restless, fretful person.

pulicán, *m.* pelican, dentist's forceps.

pulicaria, *f.* (bot.) fleawort.

pulidamente, *adv.* neatly, cleanly, nicely.

pulidero, *m.* polisher, glosser, burnisher.

pulidez, *f.* polish; neatness, cleanliness.

pulido, da, *pp. & a.* polished; neat, cleanly.

pulidor, *m.* polisher, burnisher, furbisher.

pulimentar, *va.* to burnish, gloss, polish.

pulimento, *m.* polish; glossiness.

pulir. I. *va.* to polish, burnish, furbish; to adorn, beautify; to render polite. **II.** *vr.* to adorn, beautify, embellish, or deck one's self; to become polished.

pulmón, *m.* (anat.) lung.—**pulmonado, da,** *a.* (zool.) pulmonate.—**pulmonar,** *a.* pulmonary.

pulmonaria, *f.* (bot.) lungwort.

pulmonía, *f.* (med.) pneumonia.

pulmoníaco, ca, *a.* (med.) pneumonic.

pulpa, *f.* (anat.) pulp, flesh; pulp of fruit; wood pulp.

pulpejo, *m.* pulplike part of the body, as the ball of the thumb or lobe of the ear.

pulpería, *f.* (Am.) retail grocery store.

pulpero, *m.* (Am.) grocer; catcher of cuttlefish.

pulpeta, *f.* slice of stuffed meat.

púlpito, *m.* pulpit; office of a preacher.

pulpo, *m.* (icht.) cuttlefish, octopus.

pulposo, sa, *a.* pulpy, pulpous, fleshy.

pulque, *m.* (Am.) pulque, fermented juice of the maguey.—**p. curado,** the same liquor prepared with pineapple and sugar.

pulquería, *f.* tavern where pulque is sold.

pulsación, *f.* pulsation; pulse, beating.

pulsada, *f.* any pulse beat.

pulsador, ra. I. *n.* one who examines the pulse. **II.** *a.* pulsating.

pulsante, *a.* feeling the pulse; pulsating.

pulsar. I. *va.* to feel the pulse of; to finger, touch lightly (as a lyre); to explore, sound, or examine. **II.** *vn.* to pulsate, beat.

pulsátil; pulsativo, va, *a.* beating, pulsating.

pulsear, *vn.* (s. o. two persons) to hand-wrestle, to clasp hands with upright forearms resting on a table and endeavor to put each other's arm down by pulling in opposite directions.

pulsera, *f.* (jewel.) bracelet; side lock of hair; (surg.) wrist bandage.

pulsímetro, *m.* (hydr.) pulsometer; (med.) pulsimeter, sphygmograph.

pulsista, *a.* skilled in knowledge of the pulse.

pulso, *m.* pulse; pulsation, beat; part of the wrist where the pulse is felt; steadiness of the hand; care, tact.—**a p.,** freehand (drawing); with the strength of the hand.—**tomar el p. a,** to feel the pulse of ; to sound (one for one's opinion).

pultáceo, a, *a.* pultaceous, soft; (med.) apparently or actually rotten or gangrened.

pululante, *pa.* pullulating.

pulular, *vn.* to pullulate, germ, bud; to multiply with great rapidity; to swarm; to be lively.

pulverizable, *a.* pulverizable.

pulverización, *f.* pulverization.

pulverizador, *m.* atomizer, spray; pulverizer.

pulverizar, *va.* (*pret.* PULVERICÉ: *subj.* PULVERICE) to pulverize; to atomize, spray.

pulverulento, ta, *a.* pulverulent, dusty.

pulla, *f.* loose, obscene expression; repartee, witty saying; hint; (orn.) = PLANGA.

pullista, *n.* one fond of throwing out hints.

¡pum! *interj.* bang!

puma, *m.* (zool.) puma, American panther.

pumarada, *f.* = POMARADA.

pumita, *f.* = PIEDRA PÓMEZ.

puna, *f.* (Am.) puna, bleak, arid table-land.

punción, *f.* (surg.) puncture.

puncha, *f.* thorn, prickle, sharp point.

punchar, *va.* to prick, pierce, puncture.

pundonor, *m.* point of honor.

pundonorosamente, *adv.* punctiliously.

pundonoroso, sa, *a.* punctilious.

punganes, *m. pl.* oyster knife.

pungente, *a.* pungent.

pungimiento, *m.* punching or pricking.

pungir, *va.* (*ind.* PUNJO: *subj.* PUNJA) to punch, prick; to sting the mind or heart (as passions).

pungitivo, va, *a.* punching, pricking.

punible, *a.* (law) punishable.

punición, *f.* punishment.

púnico, ca, *a.* Punic.

punitivo, va, *a.* (law) punitive.

punta, *f.* point, nib, sharp end; end, tip; apex; cape, headland, promontory; prong or tine of an antler; stub of a cigar; taint of acidity or sourness; touch, turn, tinge, trace, suggestion; pointing of game by a dog; (typ.) bodkin; (her.) lower part of a shield.—*pl.* point lace.—**p. de diamante,** diamond pencil, diamond point (for cutting).—**p. de París,** wire nail.—**p. seca,** point (of dividers).—**de p.,** point-first.—**de p. en blanco,** cap-à-pie; in full regalia.—**de puntas,** on tiptoe, softly.—**estar de p.,** to be on bad terms.

puntada, *f.* (sew.) stitch; hint.

puntador, *m.* = APUNTADOR.

puntal, *m.* prop, support; stay, stanchion, pillar; (naut.) depth of hold.

puntapié, *m.* kick (with the tip of the shoe).

puntar, *va.* to mark with dots or points.

punteada, *f.,* **punteado,** *m.* playing on the guitar.—**puntear. I.** *va.* to play upon (the guitar); (art) to stipple, to dot; (sew.) to stitch. **II.** *vn.* (naut.) to tack.

puntel, *m.* pontil, snap, glass-blower's rod.

puntera, *f.* (shoe.) toe cap or box; patch over the tip; new toe on stockings; (coll.) kick.

puntería, *f.* (arti.) aim; pointing a weapon.

puntero, ra. I. *a.* taking good aim. **II.** *m.* fescue, pointer; punch for horseshoes; stonecutter's chisel; (eccl.) cannula in a chrismatory; (Colomb.) hand (of watch or clock).

punterola, *f.* (min.) poll pick.

puntiagudo, da, *a.* sharp-pointed, sharp.

puntico, ito, *m. dim.* small dot or point.

puntilla, *f. dim.* small point; narrow lace edging; brad, joiner's nail; carpenter's tracing point.— **de,** or **en, puntillas,** softly, gently; on tiptoe.

puntillazo, *m.* (coll.) kick.

puntillero, *m.* = CACHETERO.

puntillo, *m. dim.* small point; punctilio; (mus.) dot, point.

puntillón, *m.* (coll.) kick.

puntilloso, sa, *a.* punctilious.

puntiseco, ca, *a.* dry at the tips, as plants.

puntizón, *m.* frisket hole or mark in a sheet.

punto, *m.* point, dot; period in writing; nib of a pen; sight in firearms; (sew.) stitch; loop in knitting; hole in a stocking; point in lace; mesh; punch hole in straps; polka dot in fabrics; place, spot; hackstand; smallest part of a thing; instant, moment; nick of time; chance, favorable opportunity; stop, rest, recess; end, object, aim; point of honor, punctilio; each mistake of a scholar in reciting a lesson; twelfth part of a line; (shoe.) each number in a size stick.—**p. cardinal,** cardinal point.—**p. de apoyo,** fulcrum; point of support.— **p. de congelación,** freezing point.—**p. de ebullición,** boiling point.—**p. de fusión,** melting point. —**p. de hielo,** freezing point.—**p. de inflamación** ignition point.—**p. de partida,** starting point.—**p. de vista,** point of view.—**p. en boca,** silence.—**p. final,** full stop.—**p. menos,** a trifle less.—**p. y coma,** semicolon (;).—**puntos suspensivos,** leaders (.....).—**a buen p.,** opportunely.—**al p.,** immediately, at once.—**a p. de,** on the point of, about to.—**a p. fijo,** exactly, with certainty.—**dar en el p.,** to find out the trouble.—**de todo p.,** absolutely, entirely, in every way.—**dos puntos,** colon (:).—**en p.,** exactly, sharp (s. o. the hour). —**hasta cierto p.,** to a certain extent.—**poner en su p.,** to put where it belongs, rate at its true value; to set right.—**por p. general,** as a rule.— **por puntos,** from one moment to another; point by point; one thing at a time.

puntoso, sa, *a.* acuminated; punctilious.

puntuación, *f.* punctuation.

puntual, *a.* prompt, punctual; certain; sure; convenient, adequate.—**puntualidad,** *f.* punctuality; certainty.—**puntualizar,** *va.* (*pret.* PUNTUALICÉ:

subj. PUNTUALICE) to imprint on the mind or memory; to finish, perfect; to give a detailed account of. —**puntualmente,** *adv.* punctually; faithfully; exactly, accurately.

puntuar, *va.* to punctuate, to point.

puntuoso, sa, *a.* punctilious.

puntura, *f.* puncture; (print.) register point.

punzada, *f.* prick, puncture; stitch, sharp pain; compunction.—**punzador, ra,** *n.* pricker, wounder.—**punzadura,** *f.* puncture, prick.—**punzante,** *a.* pricking, sharp.

punzar, *va.* (*pret.* PUNCÉ: *subj.* PUNCE) to punch, bore, perforate; to prick, puncture, wound; to cause sharp pain; to grieve.

punzó, punzón, *a.* deep scarlet red.

punzón, *m.* punch, puncheon; puncher; driver; point, graver, bodkin, awl, pick; countersink, counterdie; type mold; young horn of a deer.

punzonería, *f.* set of molds for a fount of types.

puñrda, *f.* fisticuff, box.

puñado, *m.* handful; a few.—**a puñados,** plentifully, abundantly, lots (ch. constr.).

puñal, *m.* poniard, dagger.—**puñalada,** *f.* stab with a poniard; sudden shock of grief or pain.

puñalejo, *m. dim.* small poniard.

puñalero, ra, *n.* maker or seller of poniards.

puñera, *f.* double handful; flour measure.

puñetazo, *m.* fisticuff.

puñete, *m.* fisticuff; bracelet.

puño, *m.* fist; grasp; handful; (sew.) cuff, wristband, wristfall, handruffle; hilt of a sword; haft (of a tool); handle (of an umbrella, etc.); head of a staff or cane; (naut.) corner of a sail.—**hombre de puños,** strong, valiant man.—**ser como un p.,** to be closefisted.

pupa, *f.* pustule, pimple; childish word to express uneasiness.

pupila, *f.* (anat.) pupil.

pupilaje, *m.* pupilage, wardship; board and lodging; boarding-house.

pupilar, *a.* (anat. and law) pupillary.

pupilero, ra, *n.* boarding-house keeper.

pupilo, la, *n.* pupil, ward; boarder.

pupitre, *m.* writing desk; school desk.

puposo, sa, *a.* pustulous, pustulate.

puramente, *adv.* purely; chastely; strictly; without qualification or exception.

puré, *m.* (cook.) thick soup, purée.

pureza, *f.* purity; fineness, genuineness; cleanness, excellence.

purga, *f.* physic, cathartic; (sugar making) draining of molasses.

purgable, *a.* that may be purged.

purgación, *f.* purge, purgation; catamenia; (law) purgation; gonorrhœa, clap.

purgador, ra. I. *a.* purgative. **II.** *n.* purger.

purgamiento, *m.* purgation, purging.

purgante. I. *a.* purging, purgative. **II.** *m.* purge, cathartic, physic.

purgar. I. *va.* (*pret.* PURGUÉ: *subj.* PURGUE) to purge, purify, cleanse; to atone for, expiate; to refine, clarify; to drain (sugar) of molasses; (med.) to purge, physic; (law) to clear from guilt or imputation of guilt. **II.** *vr.* to rid or clear one's self from guilt; to take a purge.

purgativo, va, *a.* purgative, cathartic.

purgatorio, *m.* purgatory.

puridad, *f.* purity.—**en p.,** clearly, openly; in secret.

purificación, *f.* purification; cleansing, expurgation; (eccl.) purification (of the chalice).

purificadero, ra, *a.* cleansing, purifying.

purificador, ra, *n.* & *a.* purifier (-ing); (eccl.) purificator.

purificar. I. *va.* (*pret.* PURIFIQUÉ: *subj.* PURIFIQUE) to purify, clean, cleanse, refine. **II.** *vr.* to be purified, cleansed.

purificatorio, ria, *a.* purificatory, purifying.

Purísima.—la P., *f.* the most Holy Virgin.

purismo, *m.* purism.—**purista,** *n.* purist.

puritanismo, *m.* puritanism.—**puritano, na. I.** *a.* puritan, puritanic(al). **II.** *n.* Puritan.

puro, ra. I. *a.* pure; unmixed, sterling, unalloyed, solid (gold, etc.); clear, clean, neat; unblemished, unsullied; mere, only, sheer, absolute.—**a p.,** by dint of.—**de p.,** extremely; by dint of.—**la p. verdad,** the honest truth. **II.** *m.* cigar.

púrpura, *f.* purpura, murex, purple shell; purple; cloth dyed with purple; dignity of a king or cardinal; (poet.) blood.—**purpurado,** *m.* cardinal.— **purpurante,** *a.* giving a purple color.—**purpurar,** *va.* to purple; to dress in purple.—**purpúreo, rea. I.** *a.* purple, puniceous, purpurate. **II.** *f.* (bot.) = LAMPAZO.—**purpurear,** *vn.* to have a purple tinge. —**purpurina,** *f.* bronze powder; (chem.) purpurin. —**purpurino, na,** *a.* purple, purpurate.

purrela, *f.* wine of inferior quality.
purriela, *f.* (coll.) despicable trifle.
purulencia, *f.* purulence, purulency.
purulento, ta, *a.* purulent.
pus, *m.* (med.) pus.
pusilánime, *a.* pusillanimous, faint-hearted.
pusilánimemente, *adv.* pusillanimously.
pusilanimidad, *f.* pusillanimity.
pústula, *f.* (med.) pustule; pimple.
pustuloso, sa, *a.* pustulous, pustular.
puta, *f.* whore, harlot.
putativo, va, *a.* putative, reputed.
putput, *m.* (orn.) hoopoe.
putrefacción, *f.* putrefaction.
putrefactivo, va, *a.* putrefactive.
putrefacto, ta, *a.* putrid, decayed, rotten.
putrescente, *a.* putrescent.
putridez, *f.,* rottenness.
pútrido, da, *a.* putrid, rotten, decayed.
puya, *f.* goad, goad stick.
puzol, *m.*; **puzolana,** *f.* puzzolana.

Q

que. I. *rel. pron.* that, which, who, whom; when [*el día que le escribí,* the day (when) I wrote to him]. When preceded by the definite article, it is equivalent to "who," "whom," "which" (the "the which" of old English), or "the one who," "those who," "the one whom," "those whom," "that which," "the one that." **II.** *interr. & exclamatory pro.* (**qué**) what, what a (*¡qué hombre!* what a man!); which; how (*¡qué bonita!* how pretty!).—**q. de . . .** how many . . .—**¿q. hay?** or **¿q. pasa?** what is the matter?—**sin q. ni para q.,** without cause or motive. **III.** *conj.* that [very seldom omitted: *Juan dice que vendrá,* John says (that) he will come]; than (in comparisons); because, for, as; and (*habla que habla,* he talks and talks, *or,* talking and talking); so; so that. Followed by a subjunctive form it is usually rendered by "to" and the corresponding infinitive, changing the construction (*deseo que Vd. venga,* I wish that you come, or, I wish you to come); by "let" or "may," when it expresses command or desire (*que entre,* let him come in; *que tenga buena suerte,* may you have good luck); or, with impersonal verbs, by the indicative (*antes que llueva,* before it rains). Sometimes it is used as an expletive, in the sense of "and" [*la culpa es mía, que no suya,* the fault is mine, (and) not yours]. **q. no,** without, but that.—**q. . . . q.,** whether . . . or (*que quieras que no,* whether you will or not).—**por . . . q.,** no matter how (*por bien que hable,* no matter how well he speaks).

quebracho, *m.* quebracho; quebracho bark.
quebrada, *f.* ravine; deep pass; gorge; (Am.) brook; (com.) failure.
quebradero, *m.* breaker.—**q. de cabeza,** worry.
quebradillo, *m.* wooden shoe heel; (danc.) flexure of the body.
quebradizo, za, *a.* brittle, fragile; frail, sickly.
quebrado, da. I. *pp. & a.* broken; weakened; (com.) bankrupt; rolling (ground); ruptured. *V.* AZÚCAR. **II.** *m.* (arith.) common fraction; (Cuba) tobacco leaf full of holes.
quebrador, ra, *n. & a.* breaker (-ing); lawbreaker (-ing).
quebradura, *f.* breaking, splitting; gap, fissure, slit; (med.) fracture; rupture, hernia.

quebraja, *f.* crack, fissure, flaw, split.
quebrajar, *va.* = RESQUEBRAJAR.
quebrajoso, sa, *a.* brittle, fragile; full of cracks.
quebramiento, *m.* = QUEBRANTAMIENTO.
quebrantable, *a.* frangible, brittle.
quebrantador, ra. I. *n.* breaker, splitter; crusher, bruiser; violator, transgressor. **II.** *a.* breaking, that breaks; weakening; crushing.
quebrantadura, *f.* = QUEBRANTAMIENTO.
quebrantahuesos, *m.* (orn.) osprey, lammergeier; tease, bore.
quebrantamiento, *m.* fracture, rupture; crushing, breaking; smash; breaking a prison; fatigue, exhaustion; violation; burglary; desecration.
quebrantante, *a.* breaking, crushing.
quebrantaolas, *m.* breakwater.
quebrantar, *va.* to break, crush; burst open; to pound, grind, mash; to transgress; to violate, break (as a contract); to vex; to fatigue; to weaken; to diminish; (law) to annul, repeal.
quebrantaterrones, *m.* (coll.) clodhopper.
quebranto, *m.* breaking, crushing; weakness; lassitude; pity, compassion; grief, affliction; (com.) loss, damage.
quebrar. I. *va.* to break; to crush; to cast asunder; to double, bend, twist; to interrupt, hinder; to temper, moderate; to spoil (the bloom of the countenance); to overcome, conquer; to diminish (friendship). **II.** *vn.* (com.) to fail, become bankrupt. **III.** *vr.* to be ruptured; to be broken, as the continuity of hills.
quebrazas, *f. pl.* flaws in sword blades.
queche, *f.* (naut.) smack, ketch.
quechemarín, *m.* (naut.) coasting lugger.
quechua, *n. & a.* Quichua (-an).
queda, *f.* curfew; curfew bell.
quedada, *f.* stay, residence, sojourn.
quedar. I. *vn.* to remain; to stay, stop in a place; to remain, be left as remainder; to be left in a state or condition; to leave at; to decide, resolve, agree.—**q. bien (mal),** to acquit one's self well (badly); to keep (break) an appointment.—**q. en,** to agree to; to arrive at the agreement that.— **q. por,** to go to, be accorded to, be won by; (followed by *inf.*) to remain to be (followed by *pp.*).— **¿en qué quedamos?** what is your final decision? what do you say? **II.** *vr.* to remain; to slacken, abate, diminish.—**q. atrás,** to get, or be left, behind.—**q. con,** to retain, keep.—**q. fresco,** not to mind, to remain undisturbed or indifferent.—**q. frío, or muerto,** to be greatly astonished, to be breathless, horrified, etc.
quede, (typ.) stet; let stand.
quedito, ta. I. *a. dim.* soft, gentle; easy. **II.** *adv.* = QUEDO.
quedo, da. I. *a.* quiet, still, noiseless; easy, gentle. **II.** *adv.* softly, gently; in a low voice
quehacer, *m.* occupation, business, work.
queja, *f.* complaint; grumbling, moan; resentment, grudge; quarrel, dispute.
quejarse, *vr.* to complain; to grumble; (w. **de**) to regret, lament.
quejicoso, sa, *a.* plaintful, querulous.
quejido, *m.* moan.
quejigal, *m.* plantation of muricated oaks.
quejigo, *m.* (bot.) muricated oak.
quejosamente, *adv.* complainingly, plaintively.
quejoso, sa, *a.* plaintive; complaining.
quejumbre, *f.* grumble, growl.
quejumbroso, sa, *a.* grumbling, growling; plaintful, plaintive.
quelonio, *a. & m.* (zool.) chelonian.
quema, *f.* fire, conflagration; combustion.—**de q. lenta,** slow-burning.
quemadero, ra. I. *a.* apt to be burned. **II.** *m.* place were convicts were burned.
quemado, da. I. *pp. & a.* burnt, crisp; angry, irritated. **II.** *m.* burnt down forest or thicket.
quemador, ra. I. *n.* incendiary; burner. **II.** *m.* gas burner.
quemadura, *f.* burn, scald; (agr.) brand, smut upon plants.
quemajoso, sa, *a.* smarting, burning.

uemante, *a.* burning.

uemar. I. *va.* to burn; to scald; to fire, set on fire, kindle; to parch, dry, scorch; to vex, irritate; to dispose of at a low price. **II.** *vn.* to burn, be too hot. **III.** *vr.* to burn, be consumed by fire; to be very hot, be parched with heat; to fret, to be angry; (coll.) to be near, to almost attain or touch a thing desired.

uemazón, *f.* combustion; fire, conflagration; (coll.), smarting, burning; offensive remark; vexation, anger; (Cuba) bargain sale.

quena, *f.* (Am.) a sort of Indian flute.

quenepa, *f.* (P. Rico) = MAMONCILLO.

quenopodio, *m.* (bot.) chenopod.

quepis, *m.* (mil.) kepi.

quepo, quepa. *V.* CABER.

queratina, *f.* (chem.) keratin.

queratitis, *f.* (med.) keratitis.

queratosis, *f.* keratosis.

querella, *f.* complaint; quarrel; (law) plaint, complaint; act of contesting an inofficious will.

querellador, ra, *n.* complainant.

querellante, *n.* & *a.* complainant (-ing).

querellarse, *vr.* to lament, bewail; to complain; (law) to make an accusation; to contest a will. —**querellosamente,** *adv.* plaintively, querulously. —**querelloso, sa,** *a.* querulous.

querencia, *f.* affection, fondness; haunt of wild beasts.

querencioso, sa, *a.* affectionate (s. o. animals).

querer. I. *va.* (*ind.* QUIERO: *pret.* QUISE: *fut.* QUERRÉ: *subj.* QUIERA) to will; to desire, wish; to endeavor, attempt; to accept (a challenge in certain games); to love.—**q. decir,** to mean. **II.** *vn.* wish, desire; to be willing; to love.—**como quiera,** anyhow, in any way.—**como quiera que,** whereas; inasmuch as, since; although; whatever, however, no matter how.—**como Vd. quiera,** as you like; let it be so.—**cuando quiera,** at any time, whenever.—**donde quiera,** anywhere, everywhere, wherever.—**sin querer,** unwillingly, undesignedly. **III.** *v. impers.* to look like (rain, etc.), threaten, look as if it were going to (rain, snow, etc.). **IV.** *m.* love, affection; will; desire.

queresa, *f.* = CRESA.

querido, da. I. *a.* & *pp.* wished, desired; dear, beloved. **II.** *n.* paramour, lover, mistress.—**q. mío,** or **mía,** my dear, my dearest, love, my darling.

queriente, *a.* willing; loving.

quermes, *m.* (ent.) kermes.—**q. mineral,** (chem.) kermes.

querocha, *f.* = CRESA.

querochar, *vn.* to emit the semen of bees.

querub, querube, querubín, *m.* cherub.

querva, *f.* (bot.) spurge; palma Christi.

quesadilla, *f.* cheesecake; sweetmeat.

quesear, *vn.* to make cheese.

quesera, *f.* dairy; dairymaid; cheese board, cheese mold, cheese vat; cheese dish.

quesería, *f.* season for making cheese; dairy.

quesero, ra. I. *a.* caseous, cheesy. **II.** *n.* cheesemonger, cheesemaker.

quesillo, ito, *m.* *dim.* small cheese.

queso, *m.* cheese.—**q. de bola,** Dutch cheese.— **q. de cerdo,** headcheese.—**q. helado,** ice-cream brick, molded ice cream.

quetro, *m.* a Chilean duck with featherless wings.

quetzal, *m.* (orn.) quetzal, trogon.

quevedos, *m. pl.* eyeglasses.

¡quiá! *interj.* come now! no, indeed!

quibey, *m.* (W. I.) (bot.) dog's-bane.

quicial, *m.,* **quiciálera,** *f.* hinge post.

quicio, *m.* eye of a door hinge; pivot hole.—**fuera de q.,** unhinged, out of order.—**sacar de q.,** to unhinge; to exasperate.

quiché, *n.* Guatemalan Indian and his language.

quichua, *n.* & *a.* = QUECHUA.

quid *m.* gist, pith, main point.

quídam, *m.* (coll.) person; a nobody.

quid pro quo. I. (Lat.) an equivalent. **II.** *m.* mistaken identity; mistake.

quiebra, *f.* crack, fracture; gaping fissure; loss, damage; (com.) failure, bankruptcy.

quiebrahacha, *m.* (Cuba) (bot.) breakaxe.

quiebro, *m.* (mus.) trill; movement or inclination of the body, as in dodging.

quiebro, quiebre. *V.* QUEBRAR.

quien (*interr.* **quién**), *pron.* (*pl.* QUIENES, **quiénes**) who, whom, whoever, whomsoever, which, whichever.

quienquiera, *pron.* (*pl.* QUIENESQUIERA) whoever, whosoever, whomsoever, whichever.

quiero, quiera. *V.* QUERER.

quietación, *f.* quieting or appeasing.

quietador, ra, *n.* quieter, appeaser.

quietamente, *adv.* quietly, calmly.

quietar. I. *va.* to quiet, appease. **II.** *vr.* to become quiet or calm, to quiet down.

quiete, *f.* rest, repose, quiet.

quietismo, *m.* quietism, a sect of mystics.

quietista, *n.* & *a.* quietist.

quieto, ta, *a.* quiet, still; steady, undisturbed; silent, peaceable; orderly; virtuous.

quietud, *f.* quietude, quietness, quiet; rest, repose; tranquillity.

quijada, *f.* jaw, jawbone.

quijal, quijar, *m.* grinder, back tooth; jaw.

quijarudo, da, *a.* large-jawed.

quijera, *f.* cheeks of a crossbow.—*pl.* straps of the noseband.

quijero, *m.* sloping bank of a canal.

quijo, *m.* (min.) ore.

quijones, *m. pl.* (bot.) dill.

quijotada, *f.* quixotic enterprise.

quijote, *m.* (arm.) cuisse, thighguard; upper part of the haunch; (**Q-**), Quijote, Quixote, quixotic person.

quijotería, *f.* quixotism.—**quijotesco, ca,** *a.* quixotic.—**quijotismo,** *m.* quixotism.

quila, *f.* (S. A.) a variety of very strong bamboo.

quilatador, ra, *n.* assayer of gold and silver.

quilatar, *va.* to assay.

quilate, *m.* (jewel.) carat or karat; an ancient coin; degree of excellence.

quilatera, *f.* (jewel.) diamond sieve.

quiláreа, *f.* = KILIÁREA.

quilífero, ra, *a.* chyliferous.—**quilificación,** *f.* (med.) chylification.—**quilificar,** *va.* to chylify.

quilma, *f.* = COSTAL.

quilo, *m.* (med.) chyle.—**sudar el q.,** to work hard.

quilo, quilogramo, quilómetro, etc. =. KILO, KILOGRAMO, etc.

quiloso, sa, *a.* chylous, chylaceous.

quilquil, *m.* a Chilean arboreous fern.

quilla, *f.* (naut.) keel; (orn.) breastbone.

quillái, quillay, *m.* quillai, a S.-A. soapbark tree.

quillotrar. I. *va.* to excite, incite, urge; to make love to; to attract, captivate; to think over, consider; to deck, adorn. **II.** *vr.* to fall in love; to complain, to whine.

quillotro, tra. I. *m.* urging, incitation; sign, indication; lovemaking; love affair; puzzle, perplexing thing or situation. **II.** *n.* dear friend; lover.

quimbámbulas, *f. pl.* (Cuba) rough, craggy spots; hidden nook.

quimbombó, *m.* (bot.) okra, gumbo.

quimera, *f.* chimera; dispute, quarrel.

quimérico, ca; quimerino, na, *a.* chimerical.

quimerista, *n.* wrangler, brawler; visionary.

quimerizar, *vn.* to indulge in chimeras.

química, *f.* chemistry.—**químicamente,** *adv.* chemically.

químico, ca. I. *a.* chemical. **II.** *n.* chemist.

quimificar, *va.* to convert into chyme.

quimista, *m.* = ALQUIMISTA.

quimo, *m.* (med.) chyme.

quimón, *m.* chintz; kimono.

quina, *f.* Peruvian bark, cinchona.

quinal, *m.* (naut.) preventer shroud.

quinaquina, *f.* = QUINA.

quinario, ria. I. *a.* quinary, consisting of five. **II.** *m.* quinarius, a Roman coin.

quinas, _f. pl._ arms of Portugal; fives on dice.

quincalla, _f._ (com.) hardware; small wares, fancy goods.

quincallería, _f._ hardware trade; fancy store.

quincallero, ra, _n._ dealer in hardware or fancy goods.

quince, _a._ & _m._ fifteen; fifteenth; a card game.

quinceno, na. I. _a._ fifteenth. **II.** _n._ mule fifteen months old. **III.** _f._ fortnight; semi-monthly pay; (mus.) fifteenth (interval and organ stop).

quincenal, _a._ fortnightly, semi-monthly.

quincenalmente, _adv._ fortnightly.

quincuagenario, ria, _a._ & _n._ having fifty units; quinquagenarian.

quincuagésimo, ma. I. _a._ fiftieth. **II.** _f._ Quinquagesima Sunday.

quincurión, _m._ corporal of five soldiers.

quincha, _f._ (Peru) wall of clay and canes.

quindenio, _m._ period of fifteen years.

quinero, ra, _n._ cinchona gatherer or trader.

quinete, _m._ a kind of camlet.

quingentésimo, ma, _a._ five-hundredth.

quingombó, _m._ (bot.) gumbo, okra.

quingos, _m._ (Am.) zigzag.

quinientos, _n._ & _a._ five hundred.

quinina, _f._ quinine.

quinismo, _m._ effects of the use of quinine; cinchonism.

quino, _m._ (bot.) cinchona tree; (chem.) quinoin.

quinoa, _f._ quinoa, a S.-A. species of goosefoot.

quínola, _f._ at cards, four of a kind.—_pl._ a card game.

quinolear, _va._ to prepare (cards) for QUÍNOLAS.

quinona, _f._ (chem.) quinone.

quinqué, _m._ student lamp.

quinquefolio, _m._ (bot.) common cinquefoil.

quinquenal, _a._ quinquennial.

quinquenervia, _f._ (bot.) rib-grass plantain.

quinquenio, _m._ quinquennium, lustrum.

quinquillería, _f._ = QUINCALLERÍA.

quinquillero, _m._ hawker, peddler; QUINCALLERO.

quinta, _f._ country seat, villa; manorhouse; (mil.) draft; quint, sequence of five cards; (fenc.) quint; (mus.) fifth.—**q. esencia,** quintessence.

quintador, _m._ (mil.) one who drafts men.

quintaesencia, _f._ quintessence.

quintal, _m._ quintal, a hundred pounds.—**q. métrico,** metric quintal (100 kg.).

quintalada, _f._ (naut.) primage or hat money (2½ per cent. on the freight).

quintaleño, ña; lero, ra, _a._ capable of containing a quintal.

quintana, _f._ country mansion.

quintante, _m._ quintant.

quintañón, na, _a._ & _n._ centenarian.

quintar. I. _va._ to draw one out of five; (mil.) to draft for service; to plow the fifth time. **II.** _vn._ to attain the fifth day (s. o. the moon).

quintería, _f._ farm; grange.

quinterno, _m._ five sheets of paper; keno, in lotto.

quintero, _m._ farmer; farm hand.

quinteto, _m._ (mus.) quintet.

quintil, _m._ Quintilis, fifth month in Roman calendar.

quintilla, _f._ five-line stanza.

quintillo, _m._ game of ombre with five players.

quinto, ta. I. _a._ fifth. **II.** _m._ one fifth; duty of 20 per cent.; (mil.) conscript.

quintuplicación, _f._ quintuplication.

quintuplicar, _va._ to quintuplicate.

quíntuplo, pla, _a._ quintuple, fivefold.

quinua, _f._ = QUINOA.

quiñón, _m._ share of profit or lands; (Philip.) a land measure (2.8 hectares).

quiñonero, _m._ part owner, shareholder.

quinzavo, va, _n._ & _a._ (arith.) fifteenth.

quiosco, _m._ kiosk, pavilion, summer house.—**q. de necesidad,** public water-closet.

quipos, _m. pl._ (Peru) quipee.

quiquiriquí, _m._ cock-a-doodle-do; (coll.) cock of the walk.

quiragra, _f._ gout in the hand.

quirinal, _m._ & _a._ Quirinal.

quiritario, ria, _a._ quiritarian.

quirite, _m._ Quirite, Roman citizen.—_pl._ Quirites.

quiromancia, _f._ chiromancy, palmistry.

quiromántico, _m._ palmister, chiromancer.

quirópteros, _m. pl._ bats, Cheiroptera.

quiroteca, _f._ (coll.) glove.

quirúrgico, ca. I. _a._ surgical. **II.** _n._ surgeon.

quise. _V._ QUERER.

quisicosa, _f._ (coll.) enigma, riddle, puzzle.

quiso. _V._ QUERER.

quisquemenil, _m._ (Am.) short cloak.

quisquilla, _f._ bickering, trifling dispute.

quisquilloso, sa, _a._ fastidious, precise; touchy, peevish.

quiste, _m._ (surg.) cyst.

quisto, ta, _a._—**bien q.,** well received, generally beloved.—**mal q.,** disliked.

quita. I. _f._ (law) acquittance, discharge, release (from debt).—**de q. y pon,** detachable, removable. **II.** _interj._ God forbid!—**¡q. de ahí!** away with you! out of my sight!

quitación, _f._ salary, pay; income; (law) QUITA.

quitador, ra, _n._ remover.

quitaipón = QUITAPÓN.

quitamanchas, _m._ clothes cleaner.

quitameriendas, _f._ common meadow saffron.

quitamiento, _m._ (law) = QUITA.

quitamotas, _n._ (coll.) servile flatterer.

quitanieve, _m._ snowplow.

quitante, _a._ that takes away or removes.

quitanza, _f._ quittance; (com.) receipt in full, discharge.

quitapelillos, _n._ (coll.) flatterer, fawner.

quitapesares, _n._ (coll.) comfort, comforter.

quitapón, _m._ ornament of the headstall of mules. —**de q.** = DE QUITA Y PON. _V._ QUITA.

quitar. I. _va._ to take away, subtract, take off, remove; to separate, extract, take out; to free from; to rob of, deprive of; to release or redeem (a pledge); to hinder; forbid, prohibit; to repeal, annul; to free from (obligation); (fenc.) to parry. **II.** _vr._ to abstain, refrain; to quit, move away, withdraw; to get rid of.—**q. algo de encima,** to get rid of, or shake off, something.

quitasol, _m._ parasol, sunshade.

quite, _m._ obstacle, impediment, hindrance; (fenc.) parry, dodge.

quiteño, ña, _a._ of or belonging to Quito.

quitina, _f._ (chem.) chitin.

quitinoso, sa, _a._ (chem.) chitinous.

quitrín, _m._ (Cuba) two-wheel top wagon.

quizá, quizás, _adv._ perhaps, maybe.

quizame, _m._ (Philip.) roof, ceiling.

quórum, _m._ quorum.

R

raba, _f._ bait for pilchard fishery.

rabada, _f._ hind quarter, rump.

rabadán, _m._ head shepherd.

rabadilla, _f._ coccyx; rump, croup; uropygium.

rabanal, _m._ ground sown with radishes.

rabanero, ra. I. _a._ (coll.) short (skirt); forward. **II.** _f._ (coll.) shameless woman. **III.** _n._ seller of radishes.

rabanillo, _m. dim._ (bot.) wild radish; sharp taste of wine on the turn; (coll.) ardent desire, longing; sourish temper.

rabaniza, _f._ radish seed.

rábano, _m._ (bot.) radish.—**r. picante,** or **rusticano,** horse-radish.—**r. silvestre,** wild radish.— **tomar el r. por las hojas,** (coll.) to be entirely mistaken, to be off the track.

rabazuz, _m._ inspissated juice of licorice.

rabear, _vn._ to wag the tail.

rabel, _m._ (mus.) rebec; (coll.) breech, backside.

rabeo, _m._ wagging of the tail.

rabelejo, *m. dim.* of RABEL.

rabera, *f.* tail end; tang; handle of a crossbow; chaff.

raberón, *m.* top of a felled tree.

rabí, *m.* rabbi, rabbin.

rabia, *f.* hydrophobia, rabies; rage, fury.

rabiar, *vn.* to labor under hydrophobia; to rage, be furious; to suffer racking pain.—**r. por,** to long eagerly for.

rabiatar, *va.* to tie by the tail.

rabiazorras, *m.* east wind.

rabicán; rabicano, na, *a.* white-tailed.

rabicorto, ta, *a.* short-tailed; docked.

rábido, da, *a.* (poet.) = RABIOSO.

rabieta, *f. dim.* (coll.) fit of temper.

rabihorcado, *m.* (orn.) frigate bird.

rabil, *m.* crank; wheat husker.

rabilar, *va.* to husk with a wheat husker.

rabilargo, ga. I. *a.* long-tailed. **II.** *m.* (orn.) blue crow.

rabillo, *m. dim.* little tail; stem; mildew spots on corn; darnel.

rabinegro, gra, *a.* black-tailed.

rabínico, ca, *a.* rabbinical.—**rabinismo,** *m.* rabbinism.—**rabinista,** *n.* & *a.* rabbinist (-ic).

rabino, *m.* rabbi.

rabión, *m.* rapids of a river.

rabiosamente, *adv.* furiously, ragingly.

rabioso, sa, *a.* rabid, mad; furious, enraged.

rabisalsera, *a.* (coll.) pert, smart, forward.

rabito, *m. dim.* small tail; stem.

rabiza, *f.* point of a fishing rod; rocket stick; (naut.) tip, end of a rope; point, end of a shoal; tail of a block.

rabo, *m.* tail; tail end, back, or hind part; train; stem.—**r. de gallo,** (naut.) stern timbers.—**r. de junco,** (orn.) a tropical bird.—**con el r. entre las piernas,** (coll.) crestfallen, dejected; humiliated—**falta el r. por desollar,** the worst is yet to come.—**mirar con el r. del ojo,** to look askance, or out of the corner of the eye.

rabón, na. I. *a.* docked, bobtailed. **II.** *f.* (Am.) canteen woman, soldier's wife.—**hacer r.,** to play hooky.

rabopelado, *m.* opossum.

raboseada, raboseadura, *f.* fray, chafe.

rabosear, *va.* to chafe, fray, fret.

raboso, sa, *a.* ragged, tattered.

rabotada, *f.* insolent reply.

rabotear, *va.* to crop or dock the tail of.

raboteo, *m.* cropping of sheep's tails.

rabudo, da, *a.* long- or thick-tailed.

rábula, *m.* ignorant, vociferous lawyer, pettifogger.

raca, *f.* (naut.) traveler; jib iron.

racahut, *m.* raccahoot.

racamenta, *f.* **racamento,** *m.* (naut.) parral or parrel.

racel, *m.* (naut.) run, rising of a ship.

racima, *f.* grapes left on vines at vintage.

racimado, da, *a.* clustered, in racemes.

racimal, *a.* having clusters or racemes.

racimar. I. *va.* to pick the RACIMAS of. **II.** *vr.* = ARRACIMARSE.

racimo, *m.* bunch; cluster; raceme.

racimoso, sa, *a.* full of bunches, racemose.

racimudo, da, *a.* in large bunches or racemes.

raciocinación, *f.* ratiocination, reasoning.

raciocinar, *vn.* to reason, ratiocinate.

raciocinio, *m.* reasoning, ratiocination.

ración, *f.* ration; ration money; supply, allowance, pittance; (eccl.) prebend in a cathedral.

racionabilidad, *f.* rationality.

racional. I. *a.* rational; reasonable; (math. and ast.) rational. **II.** *m.* rational, pectoral or breastplate.

racionalidad, *f.* rationality; reasonableness.

racionalismo, *m.* rationalism.

racionalista, *n.* & *a.* rationalist (-ic).

racionalmente, *adv.* rationally.

racionamiento, *m.* (mil.) rationing.

racionar, *va.* (mil.) to ration.

racioncica, illa, ita, *f. dim.* small pittance.

racionero, *m.* (eccl.) prebendary; distributor of rations.

racionista, *n.* receiver of a ration or allowance; (theat.) utility man.

racha, *f.* flaw, gust of wind; streak of luck; (min.) fragment of wood used in shoring.

rada, *f.* (naut.) roads, roadstead, bay.

radiación, *f.* radiation.

radiactividad, *f.* radioactivity.

radiactivo, va, *a.* radioactive.

radiado, da. I. *a.* & *pp.* radiated. **II.** *m.* & *a.* (zool.) radiate. **III.** *m. pl.* Radiata.

radiador, *m.* radiator (heating device); (aut.) radiator.

radial, *a.* radial.

radiante, *a.* radiant, brilliant, beaming; (phys.) radiant.—**r. de,** beaming with.

radiar, *vn.* to radiate.

radicación, *f.* radication, taking root.

radical. I. *a.* radical; original, primitive. **II.** *m.* (math.) radical; (gram.) root; (pol.) radical; (chem.) radical.

radicalismo, *m.* radicalism.

radicalmente, *adv.* radically, fundamentally.

radicar. I. *vn.* to take root; to be (in a place). **II.** *vr.* to radicate, take root; to settle, establish one's self.

radicícola, *a.* radicicolous, living on roots as a parasite.

radicoso, sa, *a.* radical.

radícula, *f.* (bot.) radicle, radicule.

radífero, ra, *a.* radium-bearing.

radigrafía, *f.* radiography.—**radigráfico, ca,** *a.* radiographic.

radio, *m.* (geom., anat.) radius; circuit, district; (chem.) radium.

radioactividad, *f.* radioactivity.

radioactivo, va, *a.* radioactive.

radioconductor, *m.* (rad.) radioconductor.

radiografía, *f.* radiography, X-ray photography or photograph; radiotelegraphy; RADIGRAFÍA.

radiograma, *m.* radiotelegram.

radiolario, ria. I. *n.* & *a.* (zool.) radiolarian. **II.** *m. pl.* Radiolaria.

radiómetro, *m.* forestaff, radiometer.

radiorreceptor, *m.* radio receiver.

radioscopia, *f.* radioscopy.

radioso, sa, *a.* radiant.

radiotelefonía, *f.* radiotelephony.

radioteléfono, *m.* radiotelephone.

radiotelegrafía, *f.* radiotelegraphy, wireless telegraphy.

radiotelegrafiar, *va.* & *vn.* to wireless, communicate by wireless telegraphy.

radiotelegráfico, ca, *a.* radiotelegraphic, wireless.

radiotelegrafista, *n.* wireless operator.

radiotelégrafo, *m.* wireless telegraph.

radiotelegrama, *m.* radiotelegram, wireless (telegram).

radioterapia, *f.* (med.) radiotherapy.

radiotransmisor, *m.* radio transmitter.

raedera, *f.* scraper, raker.—**raedizo, za,** *a.* easily scraped.—**raedor, ra,** *n.* & *a.* scraper (-ing), eraser (-ing).—**raedura,** *f.* erasure; scrapings, filings.

raer, *va.* (*gerund,* RAYENDO: *ind.* RAIGO: *pret.* él RAYÓ: *subj.* RAIGA) to scrape; to rub off, abrade, fret, fray; to erase; to wipe out, extirpate.

rafa, *f.* (arch.) buttress; trench or ditch for irrigation; (vet.) crack in the toe of hoofs; (min.) cut in a rock for supporting an arch.

rafaelesco, ca, *a.* Raphaelesque.

ráfaga, *f.* gust of wind; small cloud; flash or gleam of light.

rafania, *f.* (med.) raphania.

rafe, *m.* (arch.) eaves; (anat.) raphe.

rafear, *va.* to secure with buttresses.

rahez, *a.* vile, low, despicable.

raíble, *a.* that may be scraped or frayed.

raíceja, cilla, cita, *f. dim.* rootlet, radicle.

raído, da, *a.* & *pp.* scraped; frayed, threadbare, worn out; barefaced, shameless.

raigal. I. *a.* radical. **II.** *m.* foot of a tree.

raigambre, *f.* intermixture of roots.

raigón, *m.* large strong root; root of a tooth.

rail, *m.* (r. w.) rail.

raimiento, *m.* scraping, abrading; impudence.

raíz, *f.* (bot.) root; base, foundation; origin; (math. and gram.) root.—**a r.,** close to, immediately, right after, hard upon.—**cortar de r.,** to nip in the bud.—**de r.,** from the root; entirely.—**echar raíces,** to take root, become fixed or settled.

raja, *f.* split, rent, crack, crevice, cranny; slice (as of fruit); coarse cloth.

rajá, *m.* rajah, Indian prince.

rajable, *a.* easily split.

rajabroqueles, *m.* (coll.) bully, brawler.

rajadillo, *m.* sugared sliced almonds.

rajadizo, za, *a.* easily split; fissile.

rajador, *m.* wood splitter.

rajadura, *f.* cleft, fissure, crack.

rajante, *pa.* splitting.

rajar. I. *va.* to split, rend, cleave. **II.** *vr.* to split, crack. **III.** *vn.* (coll.) to boast; to chatter.

rejeta, *f.* coarse cloth of mixed colors.

rajuela, *f. dim.* small crack; (mas.) riprap.

ralea, *f.* race, breed, stock; kind, quality.

ralear, *vn.* to become thin or sparse (as cloth, hair); (agr.) to yield thin bunches of grapes.

raleón, na, *a.* predatory (s. o. birds of prey).

raleza, *f.* thinness, lack of density, sparseness.

ralo, la, *a.* thin, sparse, not dense.

ralladera, *f.*, **rallador,** *m.* (cook.) grater.

ralladura, *f.* mark left by a grater; gratings.

rallar, *va.* (cook.) to grate; (coll.) to vex.

rallo, *m.* grater; ice scraper; rasp.

rallón, *m.* arrow with crosshead.

rama, *f.* (bot.) branch, twig, bough; branch of a family; rack in cloth mills; (print.) chase.—**andarse por las ramas,** to beat about the bush.—**asirse a las ramas,** to seek or make frivolous excuses.—**en r.,** unmanufactured, raw; (b. b.) in sheets, unbound.

ramada, *f.* mass of branches; arbor.

ramaje, *m.* mass of branches; foliage; ramiform design.

ramal, *m.* branch, ramification; (r. w.) branch road; strand of a rope; halter; (min.) shaft, gallery.

ramalazo, *m.* lash, stroke with a rope; mark left by a lash; sudden pain or grief; blow; spot in the face caused by blows or disease.

ramalla, *f.* twigs; brushwood.

rambla, *f.* sandy or dry ravine; ramble; tenter, tentering machine; (in Barcelona) avenue.

ramblar, *m.* sandy beach or bed.

ramblazo, ramblizo, *m.* bed of a torrent.

rameado, da, *a.* having a ramiform design.

rameal, rámeo, a, *a.* belonging to branches.

ramera, *f.* prostitute, harlot, strumpet.

ramería, *f.* brothel; harlotry.

ramero, ra, *a.* hopping from branch to branch.

ramial, *m.* ramie patch.

ramificación, *f.* ramification, branching off.

ramificarse, *vr.* to ramify, branch off.

ramilla, ita, *f. dim.* small shoot, sprig, twig.

ramillete, *m.* bouquet, nosegay; (bot.) cluster, umbel; centerpiece at table; collection of choice things.—**r. de Constantinopla** = MINUTISA.

ramilletero, ra. I. *n.* maker and seller of bouquets. **II.** *m.* flower vase.

ramillo, ito, *m. dim.* sprig, twig, branchlet.

ramina, *f.* ramie fiber.

ramio, *m.* (bot.) ramie.

ramiza, *f.* collection of lopped branches.

rámneo, nea, *a.* (bot.) rhamnaceous.

ramo, *m.* bough; branch (of a tree, of trade, a science, art, etc.); branchlet; limb cut off from a tree; cluster, bouquet; string of onions; line of goods; section, division; department.

ramojo, *m.* brushwood, small wood.

ramón, *m.* browse, browsing.

ramonear, *vn.* to lop off twigs; to browse.

ramoneo, *m.* lopping twigs; browsing.

ramoso, sa, *a.* branchy, ramous.

rampa, *f.* cramp; (mil.) slope of a glacis.

rampante, *a.* (her.) rampant.

rampiñete, *m.* (arti.) vent gimlet.

ramplón, na. I. *a.* heavy, coarse (shoe); rude, vulgar, common. **II.** *m.* (farr.) calk of a shoe.

rampojo, *m.* rape of grapes; (mil.) caltrop.

rampollo, *m.* (agr.) cutting for planting.

rana, *f.* (zool.) frog; (r. w.) frog.—*pl.* (med.) frog tongue, ranula.—**r. marina,** or **pescadora,** (icht.) angler.—**no ser r.,** (coll.) to be able and expert.

ranacuajo, *m.* polliwog. *V.* RENACUAJO.

rancajada, *f.* uprooting plants or sprouts.

rancajado, da, *a.* wounded with a splinter.

rancajo, *m.* splinter in the flesh.

ranciarse, *vr.* = ENRANCIARSE.

rancidez, *f.* rancidity, rancidness, rankness.

rancio, cia. I. *a.* rank, rancid, stale; long kept, old (as wine). **II.** *m.* greasiness of cloth before milling.

rancioso, sa, *a.* rancid, rank, sour.

rancheadero, *m.* place containing huts.

ranchear. I. *vn.* to build huts; to plunder huts. **II.** *vr.* to build a hut for one's self; to settle in a hut. **III.** *va.* to plunder the huts of.

ranchería, *f.* settlement; cluster of huts; hamlet; horde, camp.

ranchero, *m.* steward of a mess; small farmer; (Mex.) rancher.

rancho, *m.* mess (food and set of persons); (gen. thatched) hut; hamlet; camp; (Am.) cattle ranch; (coll.) meeting; (naut.) messroom; mess; gang.—**r. de Santa Bárbara,** gunroom; chamber of the rudder.

randa, *f.* lace trimming.—**randado, da,** *a.* lace-trimmed.—**randera,** *f.* lace worker.

rangífero, *m.* reindeer.

rangua, *f.* pivot collar, shaft socket.

ránidos, *m. pl.* (zool.) Ranidæ (the frog family).

ranilla, *f. dim.* frog of the hoof; (vet.) disease in the bowels of cattle.

ranina, *a.* (anat.) ranine.

ránula, *f.* (med. and vet.) ranula.

ranunculáceo, cea, *a.* ranunculaceous.

ranúnculo, *m.* (bot.) crowfoot, buttercup.

ranura, *f.* groove; slot.

raña, *f.* hook frame for catching cuttlefish; lowland.

raño, *m.* oyster tongs.

rapa, *f.* (bot.) flower of the olive tree.

rapacejo, ja. I. *n.* urchin, child. **II.** *m.* border, edging.

rapacería, *f.* childish prank or action.

rapacidad, *f.* rapacity.

rapador, ra, *n.* scraper; (coll.) barber.

rapadura, *f.* shaving; hair cut; plundering.

rapagón, *m.* beardless young man.

rapamiento, *m.* = RAPADURA.

rapante, *a.* snatching, robbing; shaving; (her.) rampant.

rapapiés, *m.* (pyr.) running squib; chaser.

rapapolvo, *m.* (coll.) sharp reprimand, dressing down.

rapar, *va.* to shave; to crop (the hair); to plunder, snatch, rob; to skin, peel.

rapasa, *f.* (min.) wax stone.

rapaz. I. *a.* rapacious, predatory; (orn.) raptorial, of prey. **II.** *f. pl.* (**rapaces**) (zool.) Raptores, birds of prey.

rapaz, za, *n.* young boy (girl).

rapazada, *f.* childish prank or speech.

rapazuelo, la, *n. dim.* little boy (girl), youngster.

rape, *m.* (coll.) hurried shaving or hair cutting.—**al r.,** cropped, clipped, cut close or short.

rapé, *m.* snuff; rappee.

rápidamente, *adv.* rapidly, fast.

rapidez, *f.* rapidity, celerity, swiftness.

rápido, da. I. *a.* rapid, swift. **II.** *m. pl.* rapids.

rapiego, ga, *a.* rapacious (bird).

rapingacho, *m.* (Peru) cheese omelet.

For pronunciation, see the rules at the beginning of the book.

apiña, *f.* rapine, robbery, plundering.—**de r.,** of prey (s. o. birds).

rapiñador, ra, *n.* plunderer, robber.

rapiñar, *va.* (coll.) to plunder; to pillage; to steal.

rapista, *m.* scraper; (coll.) barber.

rapo, *m.* round-rooted turnip.

rapónchigo, *m.* (bot.) rampion.

rapóntico, *m.* (bot.) = RUIPÓNTICO.

raposa, *f.* fox; cunning person.

raposear, *vn.* to act in a foxy way.

raposera, *f.* fox hole, fox den.—**raposería,** *f.* cunning of a fox.—**raposino, na,** *a.* foxy.—**raposo,** *m.* (male) fox.—**raposuno, na,** *a.* vulpine, foxy.

rapsoda, *a.* rhapsodic, rapt.

rapsodia, *f.* rhapsody.

rapta, *a.* abducted.

rapto, *m.* snatching away by force; rape, abduction; rapture, ecstasy, trance; swoon.

raptor, *m.* abductor.

raque, *m.* wrecking; arrack.

raquero, ra. **I.** *a.* piratical. **II.** *n.* wrecker; "dock rat."

raqueta, *f.* racket, battledore; battledore and shuttlecock, badminton; tennis.

raquetero, *m.* racket maker or seller.

raquialgia, *f.* (med.) rachialgia.

raquis, *m.* (anat.) rachis, spine; (bot.) stalk.

raquítico, ca, *a.* (med.) rachitic, rickety; feeble, flimsy, niggardly.

raquitis, *f.;* **raquitismo,** *m.* (med.) rachitis, rickets.

raquítomo, *m.* (surg.) rachitome.

rara avis, *a.* (Lat.) rara avis, rare bird, rare thing.

raramente, *adv.* rarely, seldom; ridiculously, oddly.

rarefacción, *f.* rarefaction.

rareza, *f.* rarity, rareness, uncommonness; fad, queerness; freak; curio, curiosity; oddness.—**por r.,** rarely, seldom.

raridad, *f.* rarity; thinness.

rarificar. **I.** *va.* (*pret.* RARIFIQUÉ: *subj.* RARIFIQUE) to rarefy, make thin. **II.** *vr.* to become thin or rarefied.

rarificativo, va, *a.* rarefying, thinning.

raro, ra, *a.* rare; scarce; thin, rarefied; choice, precious, excellent; queer, odd.—**r. vez,** seldom.

ras, *m.* level, even, flush.—**r. con r.,** on a level, flush.—**al ras con,** or **de,** even or flush with.

rasa, *f.* tease, in fabrics; table-land, plateau.

rasadura, *f.* levelling with a strickle.

rasamente, *adv.* publicly, openly, clearly.

rasante. **I.** *a.* levelling, grazing. **II.** *f.* (r. w.) grade, grade line.

rasar. **I.** *va.* to strike or level with a strickle; to graze, skim, touch lightly. **II.** *vr.* to clear up (as the sky).

rascacielos, *m.* (coll.) skyscraper.

rascacio, *m.* (icht.) = ESCORPENA.

rascadera, *f.* scraper; currycomb.

rascador, *m.* scraper, scaler, scratcher; rasp; hatpin, bodkin, huller, sheller.

rascadura, *f.* scratching; scratch; scraping.

rascalino, *m.* (bot.) dodder.

rascamiento, *m.* scraping, scratching.

rascamoño, *m.* woman's hatpin, bodkin.

rascar. **I.** *va.* (*pret.* RASQUÉ: *subj.* RASQUE) to scratch; rasp, scrape. **II.** *vn.* (Colomb.) to itch.

rascazón, *f.* itching.

rascle, *m.* instrument used in coral fishing.

rascón, na. **I.** *a.* sour, tart, sharp, acrid. **II.** *m.* (orn.) rail; marsh hen.

rascuñar, rascuño, = RASGUÑAR, etc.

rasel, *m.* (naut.) entrance and run of a ship.

rasero, *m.* strickle, strike; standard, rule.

rasete, *m.* satinet, sateen.

rasgado, da. **I.** *a.* & *pp.* rent, open, torn. **II.** *m.* = RASGÓN.—**rasgador, ra,** *n.* tearer, ripper.—**rasgadura,** *f.* rent, ripping.

rasgar, *va.* (*pret.* RASGUÉ: *subj.* RASGUE) to tear, rend, rip; RASGUEAR.

rasgo, *m.* dash, stroke, flourish, scroll; stroke (of wit, kindness, etc.); deed, feat; happy expres-

sion or saying; feature; property, characteristic.—**a grandes rasgos,** briefly, broadly, in outline.

rasgón, *m.* rent, rip, tear.

rasgueado. **I.** *pp.* & *a.* full of flourishes. **II.** *m.* making of flourishes.

rasguear. **I.** *vn.* to flourish, to make scrollwork. **II.** *va.* to play flourishes on (the guitar); to play (the guitar) with strokes of the whole hand.

rasgueo, *m.* forming fine strokes with a pen; scrollwork; flourish.

rasguillo, *m.* *dim.* small dash of a pen.

rasguñar, *va.* to scratch; to sketch, outline.

rasguñito, ñuelo, *m.* slight scratch or sketch.

rasguño, *m.* scratch; nip; sketch, outline.

rasilla, *f.* serge; fine tile for flooring.

raso, sa. **I.** *a.* clear, unobstructed; plain; flat.—**a campo r.,** or **al r.,** in the open air. **II.** *m.* satin.

raspa, *f.* (bot.) beard of an ear of corn; bunch of grapes; spine, fin ray of fish; hair or thread in the nibs of a writing pen; (carp.) wood rasp, scraper, grater; outer rind of certain fruits (nuts, almonds, etc.); (coll., Am.) sermon, lecture, dressing down.

raspador, *m.* eraser; rasp, grater, scraper.

raspadura, *f.* erasure; rasping, scraping; abrasion; scrapings, shavings; (Cuba) pan sugar.

raspajo, *m.* stalk of a bunch of grapes.

raspamiento, *m.* erasure; rasping, scraping.

raspante, *pa.* & *a.* rasping, rough (wine); abrasive, abrading.

raspar, *va.* to erase, scrape, rasp, pare off; to bite or sting (s. o. wine); to steal, carry off.

raspear, *vn.* to scratch (as a bad pen).

raspilla, *f.* (bot.) a boraginaceous plant.

raspón, *m.* (Colomb.) large straw hat; (Ch.) severe reprimand, dressing down.

rasqueta, *f.* (naut.) scraper.

rastacuero, *n.* = RASTRACUEROS.

rastel, *m.* lattice, railing.

rastillador, rastillar, rastillo, = RASTRILLADOR, RASTRILLAR, RASTRILLO.

rastra, *f.* track, trail; sled, sledge; dray; (agr.) harrow, brake; reaping machine; act of dragging along; anything dragging; string of dried fruit, onions, etc.; (naut.) drag, grapnel.—**a la r., a las rastras,** or **a r.,** dragging; unwillingly, by force.

rastracueros, *n.* (Am.) person who makes a fortune in the hide business (may be called hide magnate); snob whose source of income is not known, or whose means come from nobody knows where.

rastrallar, *vn.* to crack with a whip.

rastrallido, *m.* crack of a whip.

rastreador, ra, *n.* tracer, smeller, follower.

rastrear. **I.** *va.* to trace, scent, track, trail; (agr.) to harrow, rake; (in fishing) to drag; to investigate, follow a clew to; to sell (carcasses) by wholesale. **II.** *vn.* to skim the ground, to fly very low.

rastreo, *m.* dragging in the water.

rastrero, ra. **I.** *a.* creeping, dragging; trailing; flying low; abject, grovelling; low, base; cringing. **II.** *n.* employee of a slaughterhouse.

rastrillada, *f.* rakeful.

rastrillador, ra, *n.* hackler; flax dresser, hatcheler; raker.—**rastrillaje,** *m.* raking; hatcheling.—**rastrillar,** *va.* to hackle, dress (flax), comb, hatchel; to rake.—**rastrilleo,** *m.* hackling or raking.

rastrillo, *m.* hackle, flax comb; (agr.) rake; (fort.) portcullis; (arti.) hammer of a gunlock; ward of a key; ward of a lock.—**r. de pesebre,** rack of a manger.

rastro, *m.* track, scent, trail; trace; (agr.) rake, harrow; slaughterhouse; sign, token; vestige, relic; in Madrid, a market of knickknacks and frippery.

rastrojera, *f.* stubble field.

rastrojo, *m.* stubble, haulm.

rasura, *f.* shaving.—*pl.* argol.—**rasuración,** *f.* shaving.—**rasurar,** *va.* to shave.

rata. **I.** *f.* rat. **II.** *m.* (coll.) pickpocket.—**r. parte,** *or* **por cantidad,** pro rata.

ratafía, *f.* ratafia, a cordial.

ratania, *f.* (bot.) ratany, rhatany.

rataplán, *m.* rubadub (sound of a drum).

ratear. I. *va.* to lessen or abate in proportion; to apportion; to filch. **II.** *vn.* to creep; to filch.

ratel, *m.* (zool.) ratel.

rateo, *m.* apportionment.

rateramente, *adv.* meanly, vilely.

ratería, *f.* larceny, petty theft; (coll.) meanness, stinginess.—**ratero, ra. I.** *a.* creeping; flying low. **II.** *n.* pickpocket, pilferer.

rateruelo, ela, I. little pilferer.

ratico, *m.* (fam.) little, while.

ratificación, *f.* ratification, confirmation.

ratificar, *va.* (*pret.* RATIFIQUÉ: *subj.* RATIFIQUE) to ratify, confirm.

ratificatorio, ria, *a.* ratifying, confirming.

ratigar, *va.* to secure on a cart with a rope.

rátigo, *m.* cartload, truck load.

ratihabición, *f.* (law) ratification.

ratimago, *m.* (coll.) trick, cunning.

ratina, *f.* Petersham, ratteen.

ratito, *m.* *dim.* little while, short time.

rato, ta. I. *a.* (law) firm, valid. **II.** *m.* short time, while, little while.—**a ratos,** from time to time, occasionally.—**a ratos perdidos,** in leisure hours, in spare time.—**buen r.,** a great while; a pleasant time; a great quantity.—**de r. en r.** = A RATOS.—**pasar el r.,** to lose the time; to pass the time, to while the time away.

ratón, *m.* mouse; (naut.) hidden rock that frets cables.—**ratona,** *f.* female mouse or rat.

ratonar. I. *va.* to gnaw like mice. **II.** *vr.* to become sick (as cats) from eating rats.

ratoncito, *m.* *dim.* little mouse.

ratonera, *f.* mousetrap; mousehole or breeding place.—**caer en la r.,** to fall into a snare.

ratonero, ra; ratonesco, ca. I. *a.* mousy. **II.** *n.* ratter.

rauco, ca, *a.* (poet.) hoarse, husky, raucous.

raudal, *m.* torrent, stream; plenty, abundance.

raudamente, *adv.* rapidly.

raudo, da, *a.* rapid, swift, impetuous.

rauta, *f.* (coll.) road, way, route.

raya. I. *f.* stroke, dash, streak, stripe, line; frontier, boundary; score, mark; parting of the hair; (print.) dash, rule; (arti.) rifle or spiral groove; strip of ground cleared of combustible matter.—**a r.,** within bounds.—**tener a uno a r.,** to hold one at bay. **II.** *m.* (icht.) ray, skate.

rayado, da. I. *pp.* & *a.* streaky, striped; ruled; (arti.) rifled, grooved. **II.** *m.* ruling; stripes.

rayadillo, *m.* striped cotton duck.

rayano, na, *a.* neighboring, contiguous, bordering.

rayar. I. *va.* to draw lines on; to rule; to stripe, streak; (arti.) to rifle or groove; to cross out; to underscore. **II.** *vn.* to excel, surpass; to border (on); to begin, appear.

rayo, *m.* ray, beam; spoke of a wheel; thunderbolt; flash of lightning; sudden havoc, misfortune, or scourge; lively, ready genius; great power or efficacy of action.—**r. de sol,** sunbeam.—**r. textorio,** weaver's shuttle.—**rayos catódicos, Roentgen,** or **X,** X-rays.

¡rayo! *or* **¡rayos!** *interj.* fury!

rayoso, sa, *a.* full of lines or stripes.

rayuela, *f.* *dim.* small line; game of drawing lines.

rayuelo, *m.* (orn.) a small kind of snipe.

raza, *f.* race, lineage; breed; crack, fissure; lightly woven stripe in fabrics; ray of light; cleft in a horse's hoof.—**de r.,** pure-breed.

razado, *a.* having lightly woven stripes.

rázago, *m.* burlap, sackcloth.

razón, *f.* reason; reasonableness; equity, fairness; account, explanation; information; (math.) ratio.—**r. de estado,** reason of state, raison d'état; regard for public opinion.—**r. de pie de banco,** (coll.) futile, silly reason.—**r. social,** (com.) firm, firm name.—**a r. de,** at the rate of.—**dar la r. a,** to agree with.—**dar r. de,** to give an account of; to account for; to give information about.—**en r. a,** or **de,** concerning, as regards.—**meter en r.,** to com-

pel or induce to act reasonably; to convince.—**perder la r.,** to become insane.—**ponerse en (la r.,** to be reasonable.—**tener r.,** to be right.—**tomar r. de,** to register, make a memorandum or record of; to inventory.

razonable, *a.* reasonable; moderate; fair, just.

razonablejo, ja, *a.* (coll.) moderate, fair.

razonablemente, *adv.* reasonably.

razonado, da, *pp.* & *a.* reasoned, reasoned out; detailed, itemized.

razonador, ra, *n.* & *a.* reasoner (-ing).

razonamiento, *m.* reasoning.

razonante, *n.* & *a.* reasoner (-ing).

razonar. I. *vn.* to reason, ratiocinate. **II.** *va.* to itemize, vouch, attest.

re, *m.* (mus.) D, re, second note of the scale.

reacción, *f.* reaction.—**reaccionar,** *vn.* to react.

reaccionario, ria, *n.* & *a.* reactionary.

reaccionarismo, *m.* (pol.) reactionism.

reacio, cia, *a.* obstinate, stubborn.

reactivo, va. I. *a.* reactive. **II.** *m.* (chem.) reagent.

reagravación, *f.* reaggravation.

reagravar, *va.* to aggravate anew.

reagudo, da, *a.* very acute.

real. I. *a.* real, actual; royal, kingly, kinglike; grand, magnificent, splendid; noble; handsome. **II.** *m.* camp, encampment; fair grounds; real, a silver coin.—**r. de agua,** water running through a pipe the size of a real.—**r. de minas,** (Mex.) town having silver mines in its vicinity.—**r. de vellón,** a small coin (5 cents).—**r. hacienda,** exchequer.—**r. sitio,** king's country residence.—**alzar,** or **levantar, los reales,** to break camp; to break up housekeeping; to quit.—**sentar (los) reales,** to encamp; to settle, establish one's self.

realce, *m.* raised work, embossment; excellence; lustre, splendor; (art) high light.

realdad, *f.* royal power, sovereignty.

realegrarse, *vr.* to be very joyful.

realejo, *m.* *dim.* hand organ.

realengo, ga. I. *a.* royal, kingly; unappropriated (land). **II.** *m.* royal patrimony.

realera, *f.* = MAESTRIL.

realete, *m.* = DIECIOCHENO (stuff).

realeza, *f.* royalty, regal dignity.

realidad, *f.* reality, fact; truth, sincerity.—**en r.,** or **en r. de verdad,** truly, really, actually; in fact.

realillo, realito, *m.* *dim.* small real.

realismo, *m.* royalism; (art) realism.

realista, *n.* (pol.) royalist; (art) realist.

realizable, *a.* realizable; (com.) salable.

realización, *f.* realization, fulfilment; (com.) sale.

realizar, *va.* (*pret.* REALICÉ: *subj.* REALICE) to realize, fulfil, perform; (com.) to sell, convert into money.

realmente, *adv.* really, in reality, actually.

realzar, *va.* (*for mut. v.* ALZAR) to raise, elevate; to emboss; to brighten, heighten the colors of; to make prominent; to heighten, enhance, add merit or excellence to.

reanimar, *va.* to cheer, comfort, encourage; to revive, reanimate.

reanudar, *va.* to renew, resume.

reaparecer, *vn.* (*for irr. v.* APARECER) to reappear.—**reaparición,** *f.* reappearance.

reapretar, *va.* (*for irr. v.* APRETAR) to press again, to squeeze.

rearar, *va.* to plow again.

reasegurar, *va.* (com.) to reinsure.

reaseguro, *m.* (com.) reinsurance.

reasumir, *va.* to retake, resume.

reasunción, *f.* resumption, resuming.

reata, *f.* rope to tie horses and keep them in single file; drove of horses or mules thus tied; (Mex.) any rope.—*pl.* (naut.) woolding.—**de r.,** in single file; submissively.

reatadura, *f.* act of retying; tying animals in single file.—**reatar,** *va.* to tie together; to retie or tie tightly; (naut.) to woold.

reato, *m.* (eccl.) obligation of atonement.

reaventar, *va.* to winnow a second time.

---

rebaba, *f.* (mech.) fash, mold mark, fin, burr, rough seam.

rebaja, *f.* deduction, diminution; (com.) rebate, reduction, discount.

rebajamiento, *m.* curtailment; abatement; deduction; lowering; abasement.

rebajar. I. *va.* to abate, lessen, diminish; to reduce, lower, cut down; to underbid; (carp.) to shave off, cut down; (art) to weaken (a high light). **II.** *vr.* to be dismissed, or mustered out; to humble one's self, stoop down; to lower one's self.

rebajo, *m.* (carp.) rabbet; groove.

rebalaje, *m.* current or flow of water.

rebalsa, *f.* pool, puddle, pond; stagnation of humors in a part of the body.

rebalsar. I. *va.* to dam; to impond. **II.** *vr.* to form a pool; to accumulate; to be stopped or checked.

rebanada, *f.* slice.—**rebanadilla,** *f.* small slice.

rebanar, *va.* to slice; to cut; to plane.

rebanco, *m.* (arch.) second bench or seat.

rebañadera, *f.* grapnel, drag hook.

rebañadura, *f.* = ARREBAÑADURA.

rebañar, *va.* = ARREBAÑAR.

rebañego, ga, *a.* gregarious.

rebaño, *m.* flock, fold, drove, herd, congregation. —**rebañuelo,** *m. dim.* small flock.

rebasadero, *m.* (naut.) pass.

rebasar, *va.* (naut.) to sail past; to exceed, go beyond; to overflow.

rebate, *m.* dispute, contention.

rebatible, *a.* refutable, disputable.

rebatido, *m.* (sew.) overhand seam, round seam.

rebatimiento, *m.* refutation; (geom.) revolving (a figure on a plane).

rebatiña, *f.*—**andar a la r.,** to grab and snatch things from one another, to scramble.

rebatir, *va.* to beat or drive back, repel; to refute; to deduct; to beat repeatedly; (geom.) to revolve (a figure on a plane).

rebato, *m.* alarm, alarm bell, call to arms; excitement, commotion; (mil.) sudden attack, surprise, drive.

rebautizar, *va.* to rebaptize.

rebeco, *m.* = GAMUZA.

rebelarse, *vr.* to revolt, rebel; to resist.

rebelde. I. *a.* rebellious; stubborn, unmanageable. **II.** *n.* rebel; (law) defaulter.

rebeldía, *f.* rebelliousness, contumacy, disobedience; stubbornness; (law) default, nonappearance.—**en r.,** by default.

rebelión, *f.* rebellion, revolt, insurrection.

rebelón, na, *a.* balky, stubborn (s. o. a horse).

rebellín, *m.* (fort.) ravelin.

rebencazo, *m.* blow with a whip.

rebenque, *m.* whip; (naut.) ratline; cross rope.

rebién, *adv.* (coll.) very well.

rebina, *f.* (agr.) third plowing.

rebisabuela, *f.* great-great-grandmother.

rebisabuelo, *m.* great-great-grandfather.

rebisnieta, *f.* great-great-granddaughter.

rebisnieto, *m.* great-great-grandson.

reblandecer, *va. & vr.* (*for irr. v.* PADECER) to soften.—**reblandecimiento,** *m.* softening.

rebocillo, rebociño, *m.* shawl.

rebolisco, *m.* (Cuba) groundless commotion.

rebollar, rebolledo, *m.* thicket of oak saplings.

rebollidura, *f.* (ordn.) honeycomb, flaw in a gun.

rebollo, *m.* (bot.) turkey oak; trunk of a tree.

rebolludo, da, *a.* done over and double; rough (diamond).

rebombar, *vn.* to make a loud report.

reboñar, *vn.* to stop turning.

reborde, *m.* flange, border.

rebosadero, *m.* place of overflow.

rebosadura, *f.,* **rebosamiento,** *m.* overflow.

rebosar, *vn.* to run over, overflow; to unbosom one's self; (w. de) to abound (with); to teem (with).

rebotación, *f.* rebounding.

rebotadera, *f.* nap raiser.

rebotador, ra, *n.* rebounder; clincher.

rebotadura, *f.* rebounding.

rebotar. I. *vn.* to rebound. **II.** *va.* to cause to rebound; to clinch; to raise the nap of (cloth); to repel; to vex, exasperate. **III.** *vr.* to change one's opinion, to retract; to change color.

rebote, *m.* rebound, rebounding.—**de r.,** indirectly.

rebotica, *f.* back room in an apothecary's shop.

rebotín, *m.* second growth of mulberry leaves.

rebozar. I. *va.* (*pret.* REBOCÉ: *subj.* REBOCE) to muffle up; (cook.) to dip in, or cover with, batter. **II.** *vr.* to muffle one's self up.

rebozo, *m.* muffling one's self up; muffler; woman's shawl; pretext.—**de r.,** secretly, hiddenly.— **sin r.,** frankly, openly.

rebramar, *vn.* to low and bellow repeatedly.

rebramo, *m.* noise with which deer answer each other.

rebudiar, *vn.* to sniff and grunt (as a wild boar).

rebufar, *vn.* to blow or snort repeatedly.

rebufo, *m.* (arti.) concussion, recoil.

rebujado, da, *a.* tangled, entangled, confused.

rebujal, *m.* number of cattle in a flock over even fifties; small piece of arable land.

rebujar, *va.* = ARREBUJAR.

rebujiña, *f.* (coll.) wrangle, mêlée, scuffle.

rebujo, *m.* woman's thick veil or muffler; clumsy bundle; portion of tithe paid in money.

rebullicio, *m.* great clamor or tumult.

rebullir, *vn. & vr.* to stir, begin to move.

reburujar, *va.* (coll.) to wrap up in bundles.

reburujón, *m.* clumsy bundle.

rebusca, *f.* searching; gleaning; refuse, remains.

rebuscador, ra, *n.* gleaner; searcher.

rebuscamiento, *m.* diligent search.

rebuscar, *va.* (*for mut. v.* BUSCAR) to search carefully; to glean (grapes).

rebusco, *m.* search; gleaning.—**rebuznador, ra,** *a.* braying.—**rebuznar,** *vn.* to bray.—**rebuzno,** *m.* braying of an ass.

recabar, *va.* to obtain by entreaty.

recadero, ra, *n.* messenger, errand boy (girl).

recado, *m.* message, errand; present, gift; compliments, regards; daily provision or marketing; voucher; outfit, equipment; precaution, security; (Am.) saddle and trappings.—**r. de escribir,** writing materials.

recaer, *vn.* (*for irr. v.* CAER) to fall back, relapse; to fall or devolve; to behoove.

recaída, *f.* relapse; second offence.

recaigo, recaiga. *V.* RECAER.

recalada, *f.* (naut.) landfall.

recalar. I. *va.* to soak, drench, saturate. **II.** *vn.* (naut.) to make, sight, or reach land.

recalcada, *f.* (naut.) heeling, list.

recalcadamente, *adv.* closely, contiguously; vehemently, emphatically.

recalcadura, *f.* cramming, pressing.

recalcar. I. *va.* (*pret.* RECALQUÉ: *subj.* RECALQUE) to cram, pack, press, push, squeeze in; to emphasize. **II.** *vn.* (naut.) to heel, list. **III.** *vr.* to harp on a subject; to seat at ease.

recalcitrante, *a.* recalcitrant, obstinate.

recalcitrar, *vn.* to wince (as a horse); to resist; to recede, go back.

recalentador, *m.* (st. eng.) superheater.

recalentamiento, *m.* reheating; overheating; (st. eng.) superheating.

recalentar. I. *va.* (*for irr. v.* CALENTAR) to reheat; to overheat; to warm over; to excite (as sexual appetite); (st. eng.) to superheat. **II.** *vr.* to become overheated (as fruit), or superheated (as steam).

recalmón, *m.* lull of the wind.

recalvastro, tra, *a.* bald-headed.

recalzar, *va.* (*for irr. v.* CALZAR) (agr.) to hill; (arch.) to strengthen, reinforce; (art) to color.

recalzo, *m.* (arch.) strengthening a foundation; (carr.) outside felloe.

recalzón, *m.* outer felloe of a wheel.

recamado, *m.* embroidery of raised work.

recamador, ra, *n.* embroiderer.

recamar, *va.* to embroider with raised work.

recámara, *f.* dressing room; boudoir; (Mex.) bedroom; household furniture; (arti.) breech of a gun; cavity or chamber for an explosive charge; (coll.) caution, reserve.

recambiar, *va.* to reëxchange, rechange; (com.) to redraw; to add.

recambio, *m.* (com.) reëxchange.

recamo, *m.* embroidery of raised work; (sew.) frog.

recancanilla, *f.* hippety-hop; (coll.) emphasis; equivocation, ambiguous language.

recantación, *f.* recantation, retractation.

recantón, *m.* corner stone.

recapacitar, *vn.* to refresh one's memory; to think carefully.

recapitulación, *f.* recapitulation, summary.

recapitular, *va.* to recapitulate, sum up.

recarga, *f.* (arti.) overcharge.

recargar. I. *va.* (*for mut. v.* CARGAR) to reload; to surcharge, overload; to overcharge; to cram; to recharge; to raise, increase. **II.** *vr.* (med.) to have an increase in temperature; (w. de) to have in abundance.

recargo, *m.* overload; overcharge; additional tax, charge, etc.; extra charge; new charge or accusation; (law) increase of sentence; (med.) increase of fever.

recata, *f.* tasting again.

recatadamente, *adv.* cautiously, prudently; modestly.—**recatado, da,** *pp.* & *a.* prudent, circumspect; shy, coy; modest.

recatar. I. *va.* to secrete, conceal; to taste again. **II.** *vr.* to act modestly; to be cautious.

recatear, *vn.* = REGATEAR.

recatería, *f.* = REGATONERIA.

recato, *m.* prudence, caution; modesty; bashfulness, coyness.

recatón, na, *n.* & *a.* = REGATÓN.

recatonazo, *m.* stroke with a lance.

recatonear, recatonería. = REGATONEAR, etc.

recaudación, *f.* collecting, collection; collector's office.

recaudador, ra, *n.* taxgatherer; collector.

recaudamiento, *m.* collection; office or district of a collector.

recaudar, *va.* to gather; to collect (rents or taxes); to put or hold in custody.

recaudo, *m.* collection of rents or taxes; precaution, care; (law) surety, bail, bond, security.— **a buen r.,** well guarded, under custody, safe.

recavar, *va.* to dig a second time.

recazo, *m.* guard of a sword; back of a knife.

recebar, *va.* to spread gravel on.

recebo, *m.* sand or gravel for a roadway.

recelador, ra, *a.* shy (as a horse).

recelamiento, *m.* = RECELO.

recelar. I. *va.* to fear, distrust, suspect; to excite (a mare) sexually. **II.** *vr.* (w. de) to fear, be afraid or suspicious (of), to beware (of).

recelo, *m.* misgiving, fear, suspicion.

receloso, sa, *a.* distrustful, suspicious.

recentadura, *f.* leaven for raising bread.

recental, *a.* sucking (lamb or calf).

recentar. I. *va.* to put leaven into (dough). **II.** *vr.* to renew.

receñir, *va.* (*for irr. v.* CEÑIR) to regird.

recepción, *f.* reception, receiving, acceptation, admission; (law) cross-examination.

recepta, *f.* record of fines.

receptáculo, *m.* receptacle; (anat.) receptaculum; shelter, refuge; (bot.) receptacle.

receptador, *m.* (law) receiver of stolen goods; abettor.

receptar. I. *va.* (law) to abet; to hide, shelter; to receive. **II.** *vr.* to take refuge.

receptividad, *f.* receptivity.

receptivo, va, *a.* receptive.

recepto, *m.* shelter, place of refuge.

receptor, ra. I. *n.* receiver; recipient; abettor. **II.** *a.* receiving. **III.** *m.* (elec.) receiver; (law) receiver.

receptoría, *f.* receiver's or treasurer's office; (law) receivership.

recercador, ra. I. *a.* girding. **II.** *m.* (jewel.) chaser.

recercar, *va.* to fence; to fence again.

recesit, *m.* vacation, recess. *V.* RECLE.

receso, *m.* withdrawal, separation; (ast.) deviation; (Mex.) recess.

receta, *f.* prescription; recipe; list of goods ordered; (com.) amount brought forward.

recetador, ra, *n.* prescriber of medicines.

recetante, *a.* prescribing.

recetar, *va.* to prescribe (medicines).

recetario, *m.* physician's instructions for treatment; book in hospitals in which instructions are entered; apothecary's file; pharmacopœia.

recetor, *m.* receiver, treasurer.

recetoría, *f.* treasury; subtreasury.

recial, *m.* rapids (in rivers).

reciamente, *adv.* strongly, stoutly

reciario, *m.* retiarius (gladiator).

recibí, *m.* (com.) receipt [an extension of the meaning "Recibí" [I received), received payment].

recibidero, ra, *a.* receivable.

recibidor, ra, *n.* receiver; recipient; (com.) receiving teller.

recibiente, *a.* receiving.

recibimiento, *m.* reception; hospitality, greeting, welcome; vestibule; hall; reception room.

recibir. I. *va.* to receive; to let in; to take, accept; to take in, admit; to experience (an injury; to face (an attack). **II.** *vr.* (w. de) to graduate (as); to be admitted to practice (as).

recibo, *m.* reception; (com.) receipt.—**acusar r.,** (com.) to acknowledge receipt.—**de r.,** fit for service, acceptable; reception (u. a.).—**estar de r.,** to be at home to callers.

recidiva, *f.* (med.) relapse.

recién, *adv.* recently, just, lately (used before a participle instead of RECIENTE).—**r. nacido, da,** newly born, newborn.

reciente, *adv.* recent, new, modern.

recientemente, *adv.* recently, of late, lately.

recinchar, *va.* to bind with a girdle.

recinto, *m.* inclosure; place (building, hall, etc.); ambit; precinct.

recio, cia. I. *a.* strong, robust, vigorous; loud; coarse, thick, clumsy; rude, uncouth; arduous; hard to bear; severe, rigorous (weather); swift, impetuous. **II.** *adv.* strongly, stoutly; rapidly; vehemently, vigorously; loud.—**de r.,** strongly, violently.

récipe, *m.* (med.) prescription; (coll.) displeasure, disgust.

recipiendario, ria, *n.* member received (into an association, academy, etc.).

recipiente. I. *a.* receiving. **II.** *m.* (phys., etc.) recipient, receiver; bell of an air pump

recíproca, *f.* (math., logic) converse (proposition).

reciprocación, *f.* reciprocation, mutuality.

recíprocamente, *adv.* reciprocally, mutually; conversely.

reciprocar. I. *va.* (*pret.* RECIPROQUÉ: *subj.* RECIPROQUE) to put in mutual correspondence (s. o. things), to match. **II.** *vr.* to correspond, harmonize, fit together, match.

reciprocidad, *f.* reciprocity.

recíproco, ca, *a.* reciprocal, mutual.

recisión, *f.* (law) rescission, abrogation.

recitación, *f.* recitation, recital.—**recitado,** *pp.* & *m.* (mus.) recitative.—**recitador, ra,** *n.* reciter. —**recitar,** *va.* to recite ; to rehearse.—**recitativo, va,** *a.* recitative.

recitura, *f.* strength, force; rigor (of weather).

recizalla, *f.* second filings.

reclamación, *f.* reclamation; objection, remonstrance; (com.) complaint, claim.

reclamante, *n.* & *a.* complainer (-ing), claimer (-ing).

reclamar. I. *va.* to claim, demand; to decoy (birds); (law) to reclaim; (naut.) to hoist or lower. **II.** *vn.* to contradict, to oppose; to complain; to put in a claim.

ɛclame, *m.* (naut.) sheave hole in a topmast head.

ɛclamo, *m.* decoy bird; lure (for birds); call; inducement, enticement; claim; complaint; advertisement inserted in the reading matter of a publication; (naut.) tie block; (law) reclamation; (print.) catchword.

ɛcle, *m.* vacation, rest from choir duties.

ɛclinación, *f.* reclination, reclining.

ɛclinado, da, *pp. & a.* reclined, recumbent.

ɛclinar, *va. & vr.* to recline, lean back.—**reclinarse en,** or **sobre,** to lean on or upon.

ɛclinatorio, *m.* praying desk, priedieu; couch, lounge.

ɛcluir, *va. (for mut. v.* INCLUIR) to shut up, to seclude.

ɛclusión, *f.* reclusion, seclusion; place of retirement; arrest; jail, prison.

ɛcluso, sa, *a. & n.* recluse.

ɛclusorio, *m.* place of retirement.

ɛcluta. **I.** *f.* (mil.) recruiting; (Arg.) gathering of cattle. **II.** *m.* recruit.

ɛclutador, *m.* recruiting officer.

ɛclutamiento, *m.* (mil.) recruiting.

ɛclutar, *va.* (mil.) to recruit; (Arg.) to gather (cattle).

ɛcobrante, *a.* recovering.

ɛcobrar, *va. & vr.* to recover, recuperate, regain. —**recobro,** *m.* recovery, recuperation.

ɛcocer. **I.** *va. (for irr. v.* COCER) to boil again; to boil too much; to anneal; to reheat. **II.** *vr.* to consume one's self with rage and indignation.

ɛcocido, da. **I.** *pp. & a.* overcooked; annealed; skilful, clever. **II.** *n.* annealing; reheating; overcooking.

ɛcocina, *f.* back kitchen, pantry.

ɛcocho, cha, *a.* overcooked, overdone.

ɛcodadero, *m.* elbow chair.

ɛcodar, *vn. & vr.* to lean with the elbow upon anything; to wind, turn (as a road).

ɛcodo, *m.* turn, winding, bend, angle.

ɛcogedero, *m.* place where things are gathered; instrument for gathering things.

ɛcogedor, ra, *n.* gatherer, gleaner; shelterer.

ɛcoger. **I.** *va. (for mut. v.* COGER) to retake, take back; to gather, pick; to accumulate, hoard; to pick up, take up; to shrink, shorten; to contract, tuck, pucker; to crop, gather, take in; to receive, shelter; to lock up; to suspend, withdraw, retire; to glean, cull. **II.** *vr.* to take shelter; to withdraw; reform, retrench; to go home, to retire; to abstract one's self from worldly thoughts, retire into one's self.

ɛcogidamente, *adv.* devoutly.

ɛcogido, da. **I.** *pp. & a.* retired; secluded; contracted. **II.** *f.* withdrawal, retirement; harvesting; inmate of a house of correction; (com.) retiral. **III.** *m.* (sew.) tuck, fold.

ɛcogimiento, *m.* concentration, abstraction; house of correction for women.

ɛcolar, *va. (for irr. v.* COLAR) to strain a second time.

ɛcolección, *f.* compilation; summary, abridgment; crop, gathering, harvest; collection of money or taxes; retirement, abstraction.

ɛcolectar, *va.* to gather, collect, hoard.

ɛcolector, *m.* = RECAUDADOR.

ɛcoleto, ta, *a. & n.* (eccl.) Recollect.

ɛcomendable, *a.* commendable, laudable.

ɛcomendablemente, *adv.* laudably.

ɛcomendación, *f.* recommendation; request; commendation, praise; merit, worth.—**r. del alma,** prayers for the dying.

ɛcomendante, *n.* one who recommends.

ɛcomendar, *va.* (ind. RECOMIENDO: subj. RECOMIENDE) to recommend; to commend; to entrust; to ask, request.

ɛcomendatorio, ria, *a.* recommendatory.

ɛcompensa, *f.* compensation; recompense.—**en r.,** in return.—**recompensable,** *a.* deserving reward.—**recompensación,** *f.* compensation, reward, recompense.

recompensar, *va.* to compensate; to recompense, reward.

recomponer, *va. (for irr. v.* COMPONER) to mend, repair.

recomposición, *f.* (chem.) recomposition.

recompuesto, ta, *pp. irr.* of RECOMPONER.

reconcentración, *f.;* **reconcentramiento,** *m.* concentration.

reconcentrar. **I.** *va.* to concenter, concentrate; to dissemble. **II.** *vr.* to concentrate (one's mind).

reconciliación, *f.* reconciliation.

reconciliador, ra, *n. & a.* reconciler (-ing).

reconciliar. **I.** *va.* to reconcile; (eccl.) to hear a short additional confession from; to consecrate anew. **II.** *vr.* to become reconciled, to make up; (ecc.) to make a short additional confession; to confess offences, to renew friendship.

reconcomerse, *vr.* to scratch one's back.

reconcomio, *m.* (coll.) scratching one's back; suspicion, fear, misgiving; craving, eager desire.

reconditez, *f.* (coll.) reconditeness.

recóndito, ta, *a.* recondite.

reconducción, *f.* (law) renewal of a lease.

reconducir, *va. (for irr. v.* CONDUCIR) (law) to renew (a lease or contract).

reconocedor, ra, *n.* examiner; inspector.

reconocer. **I.** *va. (for irr. v.* CONOCER) to inspect, examine closely; to recognise; to own, admit, acknowledge; (mil.) to reconnoitre, to scout; (pol.) to recognise (a government, etc.); (com.) to acknowledge. **II.** *vr.* to repent; to confess one's self culpable; to judge justly of one's own self.

reconocidamente, *adv.* gratefully; confessedly; avowedly.

reconocido, da, *pp & a.* acknowledged, confessed; grateful, obliged; accepted.

reconociente, *a.* recognising.

reconocimiento, *m.* recognition; acknowledgment; gratitude; confession, admission; recognisance; subjection, submission; examination, inquiry, inspection, survey; (mil.) reconnoitering; (surv.) reconnoissance.

reconquista, *f.* reconquest.

reconquistar, *va.* to reconquer.

reconstitución, *f.* reconstitution.

reconstituir, *va. & vr.* to reconstitute.

reconstituyente, *a.* reconstituent.

reconstruir, *va.* to rebuild, reconstruct.

recontamiento, *m.* telling, narration.

recontar, *va.* to recount; to relate.

recontento, ta. **I.** *a.* greatly pleased. **II.** *m.* contentment, deep satisfaction.

reconvalecer, *vn. (for irr. v.* PREVALECER) to convalesce anew.

reconvención, *f.* charge, accusation; reproach.

reconvenir, *va. (for irr. v.* VENIR) to accuse, reproach; to reprimand; (law) to countercharge.

recopilación, *f.* summary, abridgment; compilation, collection; (law) digest.

recopilador, ra, *n.* compiler; abridger.

recopilar, *va.* to compile, abridge.

recoquín, *m.* chubby little fellow.

record, *m.* (spt.) record.

recordable, *a.* memorable; that may be remembered.—**recordación,** *f.* remembrance; recollection.—**recordador, ra,** *n.* reminder.—**recordante,** *a.* reminding.

recordar. **I.** *va.* (ind. RECUERDO: subj. RECUERDE) to remember, to remind. **II.** *vn.* to awaken. **III.** *vr.* to remember.—**recordativo, va.** **I.** *a.* reminding. **II.** *m.* reminder.—**recordatorio,** *m.* reminder, remembrancer.

recorrer. **I.** *va.* to go over; (mech.) to pass over, travel; to read over, peruse; to travel in or over; to overhaul, refit, repair; (print.) to run over, readjust. **II.** *vn.* to resort, have recourse to; to resort.

recorrido, *m.* run, sweep; space or distance traveled or passed over; (aut.) mileage.

recortado, da. I. *a.* & *pp.* (bot.) notched, incised. **II.** *m.* figure cut out of paper.

recortadura, *f.* clipping.—*pl.* cuttings.

recortar, *va.* to cut away, trim, clip, pare off; to cut out; to cut to size; to outline (a figure).

recorte, *m.* cutting; clipping; outline, profile.—*pl.* cuttings, trimmings, parings, clippings.

recorvar, *va.* = ENCORVAR.

recorvo, va, *a.* = CORVO.

recoser, *va.* to sew again; to mend.

recosido, *m.* mending, darning.

recostadero, *m.* reclining or resting place.

recostar. I. *va.* to lean, recline. **II.** *vr.* to go to rest; to repose; to lean back (against), to recline.

recova, *f.* dealing in poultry, eggs, etc.; poultry market; market place; shed.

récova, *f.* pack of hounds.

recoveco, *m.* turning, winding; simulation, artifice.

recovero, ra, *n.* poultry dealer.

recre, *m.* vacation of choristers.

recreación, *f.* recreation.

recrear. I. *va.* to amuse, delight, gladden. **II.** *vr.* to amuse one's self; to be pleased, have pleasure or recreation, to divert one's self.

recreativa, va, *a.* diverting, amusing, recreation (u. a.).

recrecer. I. *va.* (*for irr. v.* CRECER) to augment, increase. **II.** *vn.* to occur, to happen. **III.** *vr.* to grow big; to recover one's spirits.

recrecimiento, *m.* growth, increase.

recreído, da, *a.* intractable (hawk).

recrementicio, cia, *a.* recremental.

recremento, *m.* (med.) recrement.

recreo, *m.* recreation, amusement; place of amusement.

recría, *f.* repasturing of colts.

recriar, *va.* to re-create, regenerate; to reanimate, give new strength to; to improve (breeds) with new pastures.

recriminación, *f.* recrimination.

recriminador, ra, *n.* & *a.* recriminator (-ing).

recriminar, *va.* to recriminate.

recrudecer, *vn.* & *vr.* (*for irr. v.* CRECER) to recrudesce, recur, increase.

recrudecimiento, *m.*; **recrudescencia,** *f.* recrudescence.—**recrudescente,** *a.* recrudescent.

recrujir, *vn.* to squeak.

rectal, *a.* (anat.) rectal.

rectamente, *adv.* rightly, justly, honestly; in a straight line.

rectangular, *a.* rectangular.

rectángulo, la. I. *a.* rectangular; right-angled (triangle, etc.). **II.** *m.* rectangle.

rectificación, *f.* rectification.

rectificador, ra, *n.* & *a.* rectifier (-fying).

rectificar, *va.* (*pret.* RECTIFIQUÉ: *subj.* RECTIFIQUE) to rectify, make right; to correct, amend; (math. and chem.) to rectify.

rectificativo, va, *a.* rectifying.

rectilíneo, nea, *a.* rectilinear.

rectitud, *f.* straightness; righteousness, rectitude; accuracy, exactitude.

recto, ta. I. *a.* straight; erect; righteous, just, honest; literal; (geom.) right (angle, section, cylinder, etc.). **II.** *m.* (anat.) rectum; (geom.) right angle.

rector, ra, *n.* principal; rector, curate; director (of a college, etc.).

rectorado, *m.* rectorship; directorship.

rectoral, *a.* rectorial.

rectorar, *vn.* to attain the office of rector.

rectoría, *f.* rectory, curacy; rectorship; rector's or director's office.

rectriz, *a.* (zool.) rectrix (feather).

recua, *f.* drove of beasts of burden; multitude, pack of things.

recuadrar, *va.* = CUADRICULAR.

recuadro, *m.* (arch.) square compartment.

recuaje, *m.* toll for the passage of mules.

recuarta, *f.* string of a guitar.

recudimento, recudimiento, *m.* power for collecting rents.

recudir. I. *va.* to pay money to as part of wages or other dues. **II.** *vn.* to return, revert.

recuelo, *m.* strong lye for bucking clothes.

recuento, *m.* recount; enumeration; inventory.

recuentro, *m.* = REENCUENTRO.

recuerdo, *m.* recollection; memory; remembrance, keepsake, memento; memorandum.—*pl.* compliments, regards.

recuerdo, recuerde. *V.* RECORDAR.

recuero, *m.* muleteer, driver of a drove.

recuesta, *f.* request, intimation.

recuestar, *va.* to request, ask, demand.

recuesto, *m.* declivity, slope.

reculada, *f.* recoil, recoiling; (naut.) falling astern.

recular, *vn.* to fall back, recoil, back up; (naut.) to fall astern; (coll.) to yield, give up, turn back.

reculo, la, *a.* tailless (poultry).

reculones—a r., (coll.) going backward.

recuñar, *va.* (min.) to wedge, dig with wedge.

recuperable, *a.* recoverable.

recuperación, *f.* recovery, recuperation.

recuperador, ra, *n.* & *a.* recuperator (-ing).

recuperar, *va.* & *vr.* to recover, regain, recuperate, retrieve.

recuperativo, va, *a.* recuperative.

recura, *f.* comb saw.

recurar, *va.* to tooth (a comb).

recurrente, *a.* recurrent.

recurrir, *vn.* to apply, resort; to revert.

recurso, *m.* recourse; resource, resort; return, reversion; memorial, petition; (law) appeal.—*pl.* resources, means.—**sin r.,** definitively, without appeal; without help, unavoidably, irremediably.

recusable, *a.* refusable, exceptionable.

recusación, *f.* (law) challenge; recusation.

recusante, *a.* refusing; recusant.

recusar, *va.* to decline; (law) to recuse, to challenge.

rechazador, ra, *n.* repeller; opponent; buffer.

rechazamiento, *m.* repulsion; rejection.

rechazar, *va.* (*pret.* RECHACÉ: *subj.* RECHACE) to repel, repulse, drive back; to contradict, impugn; to reject.

rechazo, *m.* rebound; rebuff; recoil; rejection.

rechifla, *f.* hissing (in derision); hooting; mockery, ridicule.

rechiflar, *va.* to hiss; to mock, ridicule.

rechinador, ra, *a.* squeaking, grating.

rechinamiento, *m.* squeaking; gnashing of teeth.

rechinante, *a.* creaking, squeaking; gnashing.

rechinar, *vn.* to creak, squeak, grate; to gnash the teeth; to do a thing with reluctance.

rechinido, rechino, *m.* = RECHINAMIENTO.

rechoncho, cha, *a.* (coll.) chubby.

rechupete.—de r. (coll.) splendid, fine, "dandy."

red, *f.* net, seine; network, netting; bag net; grate, railing; snare, wile, fraud; system (of railroads, telegraphs, etc.).—**r. barredera,** dragnet.—**r. de araña,** cobweb.—**r. de jorrar,** or **de jorro,** sweep seine.—**caer en la r.,** to fall into the snare.—**echar,** or **tender, la red,** to cast, or set, the net.

redacción, *f.* wording; editing; editorial rooms; editorial staff.

redactar, *va.* to edit, be the editor of; to write, word, draw up.

redactor, ra, *n.* editor.

redada, *f.* casting a net; netful of fish, catch, haul.

redaño, *m.* (anat.) caul, kell, omentum.

redar, *va.* to cast a net in.

redargución, *f.* retort, refutation.

redargüir, *va.* (*for irr. v.* ARGÜIR) to retort, reargue; (law) to impugn.

redecilla, *f. dim.* small net; hair net; mesh; bag net; reticulum of a ruminant's stomach.

rededor, *m.* surroundings, environs.—**al r.,** roundabout, around.—**al r. de,** about, nearly, more or less; around.

redel, *m.* (naut.) loof frame.

redención, *f.* redemption; recovery; ransom; salvation.—**r. de un censo,** paying off a mortgage.

edentor, ra, *n. & a.* redeemer (-ing).
edero, ra. **I.** *a.* reticular, retiform; reticulated. **II.** *m.* netmaker; one who catches fish or birds with nets.
edescuento, *m.* rediscount.
edhibición, *f.* (law) redhibition.
edhibir, *va.* (law) to make use of the right of redhibition.
edhibitorio, ria, *a.* (law) redhibitory.
redición, *f.* repetition, reiteration.
redicho, cha, *a.* speaking with affected precision and correctness.
rediezmar, *va.* to tithe a second time.
rediezmo, *m.* extra tithe.
redil, *m.* sheepfold, sheepcot.
redimible, *a.* redeemable.
redimir, *va.* to redeem, rescue, ransom; to extricate, liberate; (com.) to redeem, pay off.
redingote, *m.* redingote, great-coat.
rédito, *m.* (com.) revenue, interest, yield, profit, proceeds.
redituable, redituai, *a.* profit-producing.
redituar, *va.* to yield, to produce; to draw (interest).
redivivo, va, *a.* redivivus, revived, restored.
redoblado, da, *pp. & a.* redoubled; double lined; stocky, heavy-built; (mil.) quick (step).
redobladura, *f.*, redoblamiento, *m.* doubling; repetition; clinching.
redoblante, *m.* (mil.) drum; drummer.
redoblar, *va.* to double; to clinch; to repeat; (mil.) to roll (a drum).
redoble, *m.* REDOBLAMIENTO; (mil. and mus.) roll of a drum.
redoblegar, *va.* (*for mut. v.* DOBLEGAR) to double; to bend.
redoblón, *m.* rivet, clinch-nail.
redolente, *a.* feeling a slight pain.
redolino, *m.* wheel for drawing lots.
redolor, *m.* slight pain remaining after some acute suffering.
redoma, *f.* vial, phial, flask; (chem.) balloon.
redomado, da, *a.* artful, sly, crafty, cunning.
redonda, *f.* neighborhood, district; pasture ground; (naut.) square sail; (mus.) semibreve. —a la r., roundabout.
redondamente, *adv.* around; clearly, plainly, decidedly.
redondeador, *m.* rounding tool.
redondear. **I.** *va.* to round, make round; to round off; to perfect. **II.** *vr.* to clear one's self of debts; to acquire a competency.
redondel, *m.* (coll.) circle; round cloak, circular; (mech.) flange; bull ring; round mat.
redondeo, *m.* making round; rounding off.
redondete, *a. dim.* roundish.
redondez, *f.* roundness.—r. de la Tierra, face of the earth.
redondilla, *f.* seven-syllable quatrain with alternate riming.
redondo, da. **I.** *a.* round; (print.) Roman; unencumbered, in easy circumstances; turned to pasture (s. o. land); clear, straight, decided.—de r., in round clothes.—en r., all around. **II.** *m.* (coll.) specie, hard cash; globe, orb, disk, anything round.
redondón, *m.* large circle or sphere.
redopelo, *m.* rubbing against the grain; (coll.) scuffle, affray.—al r., against the lay of the hair; against the grain; against all rule and reason.— traer al r., to vex; drag about contemptuously.
redor, *m.* round mat; (poet.) REDEDOR.—en r., roundabout.
redova, *f.* (dance) redowa.
redro. **I.** *adv.* (coll.) behind, backward. **II.** *m.* each of the rings upon the horns of goats.
redrojo, redrojuelo, *m.* small bunch of grapes remaining after the vintage; after fruit or blossom; (coll.) puny child.
redropelo, *m.* = REDOPELO.
redruejo, *m.* = REDROJO.

reducción, *f.* reduction, decrease; (mil.) mutation, alteration, exchange; reduction, conquest; (S. A.) settlement of converted Indians; (math. and chem.) reduction; (com.) reduction, rebate, discount.—r. al absurdo, (log., math.) reductio ad absurdum.
reducible, *a.* reducible, convertible.
reducidamente, *adv.* sparingly; compactly.
reducido, da. **I.** *pp.* of REDUCIR. **II.** *a.* reduced, diminished; small; compact.
reducimiento, *m.* reduction, reducement.
reducir. **I.** *va.* (ind. REDUZCO: pret. REDUJE: subj. REDUZCA) to reduce; to diminish, decrease, lessen; to restore; (w. a) to convert (into), reduce (to); to subdue, subjugate; to divide into small parts; to condense, abridge; to persuade, convince; (math., chem., metal., surg.) to reduce. **II.** *vr.* to adopt a moderate way of living; to be compelled, to decide from necessity.
reductivo, va, *a.* reducing.
reducto, *m.* (fort.) reduct, redoubt.
reductor, ra. **I.** *a.* reducing. **II.** *m.* (hydr., etc.) reducer.
redundancia, *f.* redundance; excess.
redundante, *a.* redundant, superfluous.
redundantemente, *adv.* redundantly.
redundar, *vn.* to overflow; to be redundant; (w. en) to redound, result, lead (to), bring.
reduplicación, *f.* reduplication.
reduplicado, da, *a. & pp.* reduplicate.
reduplicar, *va.* (*for mut. v.* DUPLICAR) to reduplicate, redouble; to reiterate.
reedificable, *a.* capable of being rebuilt.
reedificación, *f.* rebuilding.
reedificador, ra, *n. & a.* rebuilder (-ing).
reedificar, *va.* (*for mut. v.* EDIFICAR) to rebuild.
reeditar, *va.* to reprint.
reelección, *f.* reëlection.—reelecto, ta, *pp. irr.* of REELEGIR.—reelegible, *a.* reëligible.
reelegir, *va.* (*pp.* REELEGIDO, REELECTO: *gerund,* REELIGIENDO: *ind.* REELIJO: *pret.* él REELIGIÓ: *subj.* REELIJA) to reëlect.
reembarcar, *va. & vr.* (*for mut. v.* EMBARCAR) to reship, reëmbark.
reembarco, *m.* reëmbarkation, reshipment.
reembargar, *va.* (*for mut. v.* EMBARGAR) to seize or embargo a second time.
reembarque, *m.* = REEMBARCO.
reembolsable, *a.* payable.—reembolsar. **I.** *va.* to reimburse, refund, pay. **II.** *vr.* to recover money due.—reembolso, *m.* reimbursement, refunding.
reempacar, *va.* (*for mut. v.* EMPACAR) to repack.
reemplazar, *va.* (*for mut. v.* EMPLAZAR) to replace; to supersede; to substitute.—reemplazo, *m* replacement; substitution; (mil.) substitute.
reencarnación, *f.* reincarnation.
reencarnar, *vn. & vr.* to be reincarnated.
reencuentro, *m.* collision; clash (as of troops).
reenganchamiento, *m.* (mil.) reënlisting; bounty for reënlisting.
reenganchar, *va.* (mech.) to recouple; (mil.) to reënlist.
reenganche, *m.* = REENGANCHAMIENTO.
reengendrador, ra, *n. & a.* regenerator (-ing).
reengendrar, *va.* to regenerate, reproduce; to renew, revive.
reensayar, *va.* to reëxamine; to try or test anew.
reensaye, *m.* second assay.
reensayo, *m.* second trial or test.
reenvasar, *va.* (com.) to repack, refill.
reenviar, *va.* to forward.
reexaminación, *f.* reëxamination.
reexaminar, *va.* to reëxamine.
reexpedición, *f.* forwarding.
reexpedir, *va.* to forward.
reexportación, *f.* (com.) reëxportation.
reexportar, *va.* (com.) to reëxport.
refacción, *f.* refection, luncheon; retribution, reparation; boot, allowance (in barters); (Cuba) financing.
refaccionar, *va.* (Cuba) to finance.
refaccionista, *m.* (Cuba) financial backer.

refajo, *m.* short skirt; flannel underskirt.
refalsado, da, *a.* false, deceitful.
refección, *f.* refection, slight meal; repairs.
refectolero, *m.* = REFITOLERO.
refectorio, *m.* refectory (in convents).
referencia, *f.* reference; narration.
referendario, *m.* = REFRENDARIO.
referéndum, *m.* referendum.
referente, *a.* referring, relating.
referible, *a.* referrible, referable.
referir. I. *va.* (*gerund,* REFIRIENDO: *ind.* REFIE-
RO: *pret.* el REFIRIÓ: *subj.* REFIERA) to refer, relate; to tell, narrate, report; to direct, submit.
II. *vr.* to refer (to), have relation (to).
refertero, ra, *a.* quarrelsome, wrangling.
refigurar, *va.* to refigure.
refilón.—de r., *adv.* obliquely, askance.
refinación, *f.* refining; refinement.
refinadera, *f.* stone roller for refining chocolate.
refinado, da, *pp.* & *a.* refined; subtile, artful;
fine, nice, polished.
refinador, ra, *n.* & *a.* refiner (-ing).
refinadura, *f.* refining.—**refinamiento,** *m.* refinement; refining.
refinar, *va.* to refine, purify; to make polite or refined; to polish, finish.
refinería, *f.* refinery; distillery.
refino, na. I. *a.* very fine, extra fine; refined.
II. *m.* refining; fine grocery.
refirmar, *va.* to support (on); to ratify.
refitolero, ra. I. *n.* refectioner; (coll.) busybody,
intermeddler. **II.** *a.* (Cuba) affected, obsequious, officious.
reflectante, *a.* reflecting.
reflector, ra. I. *a.* reflecting, reflective. **II.** *m.*
reflector; searchlight.
refleja, *f.* reflection, observation, remark.
reflejar. I. *va.* (opt.) to reflect. **II.** *vn.* to think,
ponder, consider. **III.** *vr.* to be reflected.
reflejo, ja. I. *a.* reflected; meditative; (gram.)
reflexive; (physiol.) reflex. **II.** *m.* glare; reflection; light reflected.
reflexión, *f.* reflection.
reflexionar, *vn.* to think, reflect.
reflexivamente, *adv.* reflexively; reflectively.
reflexivo, va, *a.* reflexive; reflective; reflecting,
thoughtful; (gram.) reflexive.
reflorecer, *vn.* (for irr. v. FLORECER) to reflourish,
blossom again; to return to former splendor;
"to come back."
refluente, *a.* refluent; flowing back.
refluir, *vn.* (for. irr. v. FLUIR) to flow back; to redound.
reflujo, *m.* reflux, refluence; ebb or ebb-tide.
refocilación, *f.* recreation, bracing diversion.
refocilar. I. *va.* to give or afford healthful recreation to, to brace up. **II.** *vr.* to seek or indulge
in healthful recreation.
refocilo, *m.* healthful pleasure.
reforma, *f.* reform; reformation; alteration, correction, improvement; (eccl.) Reformation.
reformable, *a.* reformable; mendable.
reformación, *f.* reformation, reform.
reformado. I. *pp.* & *a.* reformed. **II.** *m.* officer
deprived of his command.
reformador, ra, *n.* & *a.* reformer (-ing); mender
(-ing).
reformar. I. *va.* to reform; to mend, amend,
improve; to reorganize, reconstruct. **II.** *vr.* to
reform, to mend.
reformatorio, ria. I. *a.* corrective, reforming,
II. *m.* reformatory.
reformista, *n.* & *a.* reformer (-ing, -ist).
reforzado, da. I. *a.* & *pp.* strengthened, reinforced. **II.** *f.* narrow tape or ribbon.
reforzar, *va.* (for irr. v. FORZAR) to strengthen,
reinforce; to cheer, encourage.
refracción, *f.* (opt.) refraction.—**refractar. I.** *va.*
(opt.) to refract. **II.** *vr.* to be refracted.
refractario, ria, *a.* refractory; unruly; obstinate.
refracto, ta, *a.* (opt.) refracted.

refrán, *m.* proverb, saying, saw.
refranero, *m.* collection of proverbs.
refregadura, *f.* = REFREGÓN.
refregamiento, *m.* rubbing, scrubbing.
refregar, *va.* (for irr. v. FREGAR) to rub, scrub
(coll.) to upbraid, dress down.—**refregón,** *m.* rubbing, scrubbing; attrition, abrasion.
refreir, *va.* to fry well or excessively.
refrenable, *a.* capable of being refrained.
refrenamiento, *m.* curbing, restraint, check.
refrenar, *va.* to restrain, check; to rein, curb (
horse).
refrendación, *f.* legalization, authentication
visé.—**refrendar,** *va.* to legalize, authenticate
countersign; to visé.—**refrendario, ria,** *n.* one
who countersigns.—**refrendata,** *f.* countersignature.—**refrendo,** *m.* = REFRENDACIÓN.
refrescador, ra, *a.* refreshing.
refrescadura, *f.* refreshing (act and effect).
refrescamiento, *m.* = REFRESCO.
refrescante, *a.* cooling, refreshing.
refrescar. I. *va.* (*pret.* REFRESQUÉ: *subj.* REFRES-
QUE) to refresh; to cool, refrigerate; to renew,
take up again. **II.** *vn.* & *vr.* to get cool (s. o. the
weather); to take the fresh air; to take a refreshment; to cool off.
refresco, *m.* refreshment; cold beverage; luncheon at social gatherings.—**de r.,** anew, once more.
refriega, *f.* affray, scuffle, fray.
refrigeración, *f.* refrigeration.
refrigerador, ra. I. *a.* refrigerating, freezing,
cooling. **II.** *m.* refrigerator, freezer, ice box,
cooler.
refrigerante. I. *a.* refrigerating, cooling. **II.** *m.*
(chem.) refrigerator, cooling chamber; (med.)
cooler.
refrigerar, *va.* to cool, refrigerate.
refrigerativo, va, *a.* refrigerating, cooling.
refrigerio, *m.* refrigeration, coolness; refreshment, refection; consolation, comfort.
refringente, *a.* refracting, refringent.
refringir, *va.* & *vr.* (for mut. v. INFRINGIR) to refract.
refrito, ta, *pp. irr.* of REFREIR.
refuerzo, *m.* reinforcement; backing, bracing,
strengthening piece; (shoe.) welt; assistance,
aid, help.
refugiar. I. *va.* to shelter. **II.** *vr.* to take refuge.
refugio, *m.* refuge, shelter, asylum.
refulgencia, *f.* refulgence, splendor.
refulgente, *a* refulgent.
refulgir, *vn.* to shine.
refundición, *f.* (found.) recasting.
refundir. I. *va.* (found.) to remelt or recast; to
contain, include; to rearrange, recast, reconstruct. **II.** *vn.* to redound.
refunfuñador, ra, *n.* grumbler, growler.
refunfuñadura, *f.* growling, grumbling.
refunfuñar, *va.* to growl, grumble, mutter.
refunfuño, *m.* grumbling, growl, snort.
refutación, *f.* refutation.—**refutable,** *a.* refutable.—**refutador, ra,** *n.* & *a.* refuter (-ing).—
refutar, *va.* to refute.—**refutatorio, ria,** *a.* refutatory.
regadera, *f.* watering pot, sprinkler; trench for
irrigation; sparger.
regadero, *m.* ditch for irrigation.
regadío, ía. I. *a.* irrigated. **II.** *m.* irrigated
land.
regadizo, za, *a.* irrigable.
regador, ra. I. *n.* one who waters or irrigates.
II. *m.* comb makers' gauge.
regadura, *f.* irrigation, watering.
regaifa, *f.* grooved stone of an oil mill.
regajal, regajo, *m.* puddle, pool; rill.
regala, *f.* (naut.) gunwale or gunnel.
regalada, *f.* king's stables; horses kept in them.
regaladamente, *adv.* delicately, pleasantly,
daintily, luxuriously.—**regalado, da,** *pp.* & *a.* delicate, dainty; easy, comfortable; suave, lickerish.
regalador, ra. I. *n.* liberal entertainer. **II.** *m.*
stick for cleaning wine skins.

regalamiento, *m.* regalement.

regalar. I. *va.* to present, give as a present, make a present of; to regale, treat, entertain; to caress, fondle, pet, cajole; to gladden, cheer, delight, cherish **II.** *vr.* to feast; to fare sumptuously.

regalejo, *m.* *dim.* small gift.

regalero, *m.* purveyor of fruit and flowers for the royal family.

regalía, *f.* regalia, royal rights; privilege, exemption; (Cuba) regalía (cigar).—*pl.* perquisites.

regalicia, *f.* = REGALIZ.

regalillo, *m.* *dim.* small gift; muff.

regalismo, *m.* regalism.

regalista, *n.* & *a.* regalist (-ic).

regalito, *m.* *dim.* small present.

regaliz, *m.*, **regaliza,** *f.* (bot.) licorice.

regalo, *m.* present, gift; pleasure, gratification; dainty; regalement; comfort, luxury.

regalón, na, *a.* (coll.) fond of ease; spoiled, pampered.

regañadientes.—a r., reluctantly, grumbling.

regañado, da, *pp.* & *a.* frowning; splitting (s. o. certain plums and bread).

regañador, ra, *a.* scolding, grumbling.

regañamiento, *m.* grumbling, snarling, growl.

regañar. I. *vn.* to snarl, growl, grumble; mutter; to quarrel, wrangle; to crack or open. **II.** *va.* (coll.) to scold, reprehend, chide.

regañir, *vn.* to yelp, howl repeatedly.

regaño, *m.* gesture of annoyance; sternness of look; scolding; reprimand; scorched bread.

regañón, na, *n.* & *a.* growler (-ing), grumbler (-ing); scolder, scold (-ing).

regar, *va.* (ind. RIEGO: pret. REGUÉ: subj. RIEGUE) to water; to irrigate; to sprinkle; to shower, bedew; to strew, scatter; to wash or water (as rivers and clouds).

regata, *f.* irrigating ditch or conduit; regatta.

regate, *m.* dodge, dodging.

regatear. I. *va.* to haggle about, beat down (the price), to resell at retail; to shun, evade, avoid. **II.** *vn.* to haggle; to wriggle, dodge; (naut.) to race.

regateo, *m.* chaffer, bargaining, haggling.

regatería, *f.* hucksterage.

regatero, ra, *n.* & *a.* haggler (-ing).

regato, *m.* small rivulet, rill; pool.

regatón, na. I. *n.* huckster, regrater; haggler. **II.** *m.* tip, ferrule.

regatonear, *vn.* to huckster.

regatonería, *f.* hucksterage; sale by retail

regazar, *va.* to tuck up.

regazo, *m.* lap.

regencia, *f.* regency; regentship.

regeneración, *f.* regeneration.

regenerador, ra, *n.* & *a.* regenerator (-ing).

regenerar, *va.* to regenerate.

regenerativo, va, *a.* regenerative.

regenta, *f.* regent's wife; woman professor.

regentar, *va.* to rule, govern, manage.

regente. I. *a.* ruling, governing. **II.** *n.* regent; president of a court of justice; master of theological studies; in Spanish universities, some supernumerary professors; manager, director; (print.) foreman.

regentear, *vn.* to domineer, rule, boss.

regiamente, *adv.* royally, regally.

regicida, *n.* regicide, murderer of a king.

regicidio, *m.* regicide, murder of a king.

regidor, ra. I. *a.* ruling, governing. **II.** *m.* alderman or councilman. **III.** *f.* alderman's or councilman's wife.—**regidoría, regiduría,** *f.* alderman's or councilman's office.

régimen, *m.* régime; management, rule, conduct, system, policy; (gram.) government; (med.) regimen, treatment.—**r. alimenticio,** diet.—**de r.,** ordinary, rated, normal (speed, power, etc.)

regimentar, *va.* to organize into a regiment.

regimiento, *m.* administration, government; municipal council board; (mil.) regiment; (naut.) pilot's book of sailing directions.

regio, gia, *a.* royal, regal, kingly; stately, sumptuous, magnificent.

región, *f.* region.—**regional,** *a.* regional, sectional, local.—**regionalismo,** *m.* (pol.) home rule; regionalism, sectionalism.—**regionalista. I.** *a.* relating to home rule. **II.** *n.* home ruler; sectionalism.—**regionario, ria,** *a.* (eccl.) regionary.

regir. I. *va.* (gerund, RIGIENDO: ind. RIJO: pret. él RIGIÓ: subj. RIJA) to rule, govern, direct; to conduct, manage, command; to keep (the bowels) in good order; (gram.) to govern. **II.** *vn.* to be in force; to prevail; (naut.) to obey the helm.

registrador, ra. I. *a.* registering. **II.** *n.* register, registrar, recorder, master or clerk of records; searcher, inspector; toll gatherer; controller.

registrar. I. *va.* to inspect, examine; to search; to scan, survey; to register, record; to mark (a book); (min.) to prospect. **II.** *vr.* to be registered or matriculated.

registro, *m.* search, inspection, examination; census, registry, registration. enrolment, record, entry; enrolling office; certificate of entry; register book; bookmark; (mus.) register, stop of an organ; air hole; furnace register; (print.) catchword, register; (watch.) regulator; (b. b.) directions for binding.

regla, *f.* rule, precept; policy; order, measure, moderation; (drawing) rule, ruler, straight edge; menstruation, courses.—**r. de aligación,** (arith.) alligation.—**r. de compañía,** (arith.) partnership. —**r. de falsa posición,** (arith.) position, rule of false position.—**r. de oro,** or **r. de tres,** (arith.) rule of three.—**r. fija,** fixed rule, set rule.—**r. lesbia,** flexible rule.—**r. magnética,** surveying compass.—**r. T,** or **r. te,** T square.—**a r.,** by ruler, by rule and square.—**en r.,** thoroughly, in due form.—**por r. general,** as a general rule.

regladamente, *adv.* regularly, orderly.

reglado, da, *pp.* & *a.* regulated; temperate, moderate; (geom.) ruled (surface).

reglamentación, *f.* establishment of rules and regulations; regulation by law, decree or rule; directions for the execution of a law.

reglamentar, *va.* to establish rules or by-laws for; to regulate by rule, law, or decree; to dictate directions for the execution of (a law).

reglamentario, ria, *a.* relating to, or prescribed by, regulations and by-laws; required by the rules (actual or tacit, as in the case of social formalities).

reglamento, *m.* by-laws; rules and regulations.

reglar. I. *va.* to rule (as paper); to regulate. **II.** *vr.* to mend, reform.

reglar, *a.* regular.

regleta, *f.* (print.) reglet; lead.

regletear, *va.* (print.) to lead.

región, *m.* mason's rule.

regnícola, *n.* native of a kingdom; writer on topics relating to his country.

regocijadamente, *adv.* merrily, joyfully.

regocijado, da, *pp.* & *a.* merry, joyful, rejoicing, festive.

regocijador, ra, *n.* & *a.* rejoicer (-ing).

regocijar. I. *va.* to gladden, cheer, rejoice. **II.** *vr.* to rejoice, be merry.

regocijo, *m.* joy, gladness; mirth, merriment; rejoicing.

regodearse, *vr.* (coll.) to take delight; to joke, to jest.—**regodeo,** *m.* delight; merrymaking.

regojo, *m.* piece of bread left on the table after meals; puny boy.

regojuelo, *m.* *dim.* small morsel of bread.

regoldano, na, *a.* wild (chestnut).

regoldar, *vn.* (ind. REGÜELDO: subj. REGÜELDE) to belch, to eruct.

regoldo, *m.* (bot.) wild chestnut tree.

regolfar, *vn.* & *vr.* to flow back, to eddy.

regolfo, *m.* eddy, whirlpool; gulf, bay.

regona, *f.* large irrigating canal.

regordete, ta, *a.* (coll.) chubby, plump.

regostarse, *vr.* to delight, to dally.

regosto, *m.* craving for more.

regraciar, *va.* to show gratitude to, to thank.

regresar, *vn.* to return; (eccl.) to recover possession of a benefice.

regresión, *f.* regression, retrogression.

regresivo, va, *a.* regressive.

regreso, *m.* return; (eccl.) retaking possession of a benefice.

regruñir, *vn.* to snarl, to growl.

reguardarse, *vr.* to take care of one's self.

regüeldo, *m.* eructation, belch.

reguera, *f.* irrigating ditch; (naut.) moorings.

reguero, *m.* trickle, rill, drip; irrigating furrow.

reguilete, *m.* = REHILETE.

regulación, *f.* regulation; adjustment.

regulado, da, *a.* & *pp.* regulated; according to rule.

regulador, ra. I. *a.* regulating, governing. **II.** *m.* (mech.) regulator; governor; register; throttle valve (of locomotive); controller (of electric car).—**r. de fuerza centrífuga,** ball governor.

regular. I. *va.* to regulate; to adjust. **II.** *a.* regular; methodical, orderly; moderate, sober; common, ordinary, frequent; middling, fairly good, so so; likely, probable, (geom. and gram.) regular.—**por lo r.,** usually, as a rule. **III.** *m.* (eccl.) regular.

regularidad, *f.* regularity; common usage, custom; exact discipline.

regularizar, *va.* to regularize.

regularmente, *adv.* regularly; ordinarily, as a rule; middling, fairly well, so so.

régulo, *m.* chief of a petty state; basilisk; (chem.) regulus; (ast.) Regulus; (orn.) golden-crested kinglet.

regurgitación, *f.* (med.) regurgitation.

regurgitar, *vn.* to regurgitate, overflow.

rehabilitación, *f.* rehabilitation.

rehabilitar, *va.* to rehabilitate, reinstate, restore; to refit, repair.

rehacer. I. *va.* (*for irr. v.* HACER) to rebuild, remodel, make over; do over; to renovate, mend, repair; to invigorate, revive. **II.** *vr.* to regain strength and vigor; (mil.) to rally, reorganize.—**rehacimiento,** *m.* renovation, renewal; recuperation.

rehala, *f.* drove of flocks under one drover.

rehalero, *m.* drover of a REHALA.

rehecho, cha, *a.* & *pp. irr.* of REHACER; renewed, renovated; done over again; squat, broad-shouldered.

rehelear, *vn.* to be bitter.—**reheleo,** *m.* bitterness.

rehén, *m.* (gen. *pl.*) hostage.

rehenchimiento, *m.* stuffing, refilling.

rehenchir, *va.* to refill, stuff anew.

rehendija, *f.* crevice, cleft.

reherimiento, *m.* repulsion.

reherir, *va.* to repel, to repulse.

reherrar, *va.* to reshoe (a horse).

rehervir. I. *vn.* & *va.* (*for irr. v.* HERVIR) to boil again. **II.** *vn.* to be inflamed with love; to be blinded by passion. **III.** *vr.* to ferment, grow sour.

rehiladillo, *m.* ribbon.

rehilandera, *f.* pinwheel.

rehilar. I. *va.* to twist too much. **II.** *vn.* to stagger, to reel; to whiz, whir, as an arrow in flight.

rehilete, rehilero, *m.* shuttlecock; small arrow; malicious saying, personal hint.

rehilo, *m.* shaking, shivering.

rehogar, *va.* to dress (meat) with a slow fire, basting it with butter or oil.

rehollar, *va.* to trample under foot.

,rehoya, *f.*, deep hole or pit.

rehoyar, *vn.* to dig holes anew.

rehoyo, *m.* = REHOYA.

rehuida, *f.* second flight; shunning.

rehuir. I. *va.*, *vn.* & *vr.* (*for mut. v.* HUIR) to withdraw, retire; to shun, avoid; to reject, decline, refuse. **II.** *vn.* to run back on the same track (as game).

rehumedecer, *va.* & *vr.* to dampen well.

rehundir, *va.* & *vr.* to sink; to deepen; to remelt to waste, dissipate, lavish.

rehurtarse, *vr.* to take a different route from that expected (s. o. game).

rehusar, *va.* to refuse, decline, reject.

reidero, ra, *a.* laughable.

reidor, ra. I. *a.* jolly, hilarious, full of laughter. **II.** *n.* laugher, one who laughs.

reimpresión, *f.* reprint; reprinting.

reimpreso, sa, *pp. irr.* of REIMPRIMIR: reprinted.

reimprimir, *va.* (*pp.* REIMPRESO) to reprint.

reina, *f.* queen; queen bee; queen at chess; hopscotch. *V.* ACEITUNA.

reinado, *pp.* & *m.* reign.

reinal, *m.* strong hemp cord.

reinante, *a.* reigning; excelling; prevailing.

reinar, *vn.* to reign; to prevail, predominate.

reincidencia, *f.* repetition of an offence; backsliding, relapse into vice or error.

reincidente, *a.* relapsing, backsliding.

reincidir, *vn.* to relapse into vice or error; to backslide.

reincorporación, *f.* reincorporation.

reincorporar. I. *va.* to incorporate a second time. **II.** *vr.* to reëmbody.

reingresar, *vn.* to reënter.

reino, *m.* kingdom, reign; district that was formerly a kingdom; (natural history) kingdom.

reinstalación, *f.* reinstalment.

reinstalar, *va.* to reinstall.

reintegrable, *a.* (com.) reimbursable, payable.

reintegración, *f.* restitution, reimbursement.—**reintegrador, ra,** *n.* restorer.

reintegrar. I. *va.* to reintegrate, restore; (com.) to reimburse, repay, refund. **II.** *vr.* (w. **de**) to recover, recuperate.

reintegro, *m.* = REINTEGRACIÓN.

reír. I. *vn.* (gerund, RIENDO: *ind.* RÍO: *pret.* él RIÓ: *subj.* RÍA) to laugh; to giggle, titter; to sneer; to smile (as nature).—**r. a carcajadas,** to laugh excessively and loudly. **II.** *vr.* to laugh; to begin to tear or rend (s. o. cloth).—**r. de,** to laugh at, to make little or nothing of.

reis, *m.* reis, Brazilian and Portuguese money of account.

reiteración, *f.* reiteration.—**reiteradamente,** *adv.* repeatedly.—**reiterar,** *va.* to reiterate.

reiterativo, va, *a.* reiterative.

reivindicable, *a.* (law) repleviable.

reivindicación, *f.* (law) recovery, replevin.

reivindicar, *va.* (law) to regain possession of; to replevy.

reivindicatorio, ria, *a.* (law) replevying.

reja, *f.* plowshare, colter or coulter; plowing, tillage; grate, grating, railing.

rejacar, *va.* = ARREJACAR.

rejada, *f.* = ARREJADA.

rejado, *m.* grate, grating, railing, grid.

rejal, *m.* pile of bricks laid crisscross.

rejalgar, *m.* (min.) realgar.

rejero, *m.* maker of railings and grates.

rejilla, *f.* small lattice or grating; latticed wicket; cane for backs and seats of chairs, etc.; foot brasier.

rejitar, *va.* to vomit.

rejo, *m.* pointed bar or spike; goad stick; (zool.) sting; hob for quoits; iron frame of a door; strength, vigor; (bot.) caulicle.

rejón, *m.* short spear thrust into a bull and broken at the end, leaving the point in the flesh; dagger; broad knife.—**rejonazo,** *m.* thrust with a REJÓN.—**rejoncillo,** *m.* dim. small spear.

rejoneador, *m.* bullfighter who uses the REJÓN.—**rejonear,** *va.* to thrust a REJÓN into (a bull).—**rejoneo,** *m.* fighting bulls with a REJÓN.

rejuela, *f.* dim. small grate; foot brasier.

rejuvenecer. I. *va.* (*for irr. v.* MERECER) to rejuvenate. **II.** *vn.* & *vr.* to be rejuvenated.

relabrar, *va.* to work or cut again (as a precious stone).

relación, *f.* relation; report, narrative, memoir, account; intercourse, dealing; (law) report.

brief; (mil.) return, report; (theat.) speech.—*pl*, relations, connections; acquaintance, intercourse; courting.—**r. jurada**, sworn statement.—**decir**, or **hacer, r. a**, to relate to.—**tener relaciones con**, to have relations with; to be acquainted with.

relacionar. I. *va.* to relate, connect; to report, narrate; to make acquainted. **II.** *vr.* to get acquainted, make connections; to be related.

relacionero, ra, *n.* narrator; ballad singer.

relál, *m.* (Am.) (elec.) relay.

relajación, *f.* relaxation, laxity, looseness; slackening, relenting; diminution, mitigation (of a penalty); release (from an oath or vow); delivery of an offender by the ecclesiastical judge to a criminal court of justice; diversion, relaxation, rest; (med.) hernia, rupture.

relajadamente, *adv.* with relaxation; dissolutely. —**relajado,** *pp.* & *a.* (coll.) dissolute, dissipated.

relajador, ra, *a.* relaxing; remitting.

relajamiento, *m.* = RELAJACIÓN.

relajante, *a.* relaxing; loosening.

relajar. I. *va.* to relax, loosen, slacken; to remit, mitigate; to release from an obligation; (ecc.) to deliver to the criminal tribunal; to weaken; to ease, amuse, divert. **II.** *vr.* to become relaxed, loosened, weakened; to grow vicious; to be ruptured.

relamer. I. *va.* to relick, lick again. **II.** *vr.* to lick one's lips; to relish; to paint; to boast, brag.

relamido, da, *pp.* & *a.* affected, prim.

relámpago, *m.* lightning; quick person or action; (vet.) blemish in the eyes of horses.

relampagueante, *a.* lightning, flashing.

relampaguear, *vn.* to lighten; to flash, sparkle.

relampagueo, *m.* lightning; flashing.

relance, *m.* repeated casting of a net; second chance or lot; fortuitous event; repeated attempt; series of lucky or unlucky chances.—**de r.**, unexpectedly, by chance; at a bargain; secondhand.

relanzar, *va.* to repel, repulse; to cast in again (tickets or lots) to be drawn.

relapso, sa, *a.* relapsed into error.

relatador, ra, *n.* relater, narrator, teller.

relatante, *a.* narrating.

relatar, *va.* to relate, narrate, tell, report; (law) to make a report of (a lawsuit).

relativamente, *adv.* relatively.

relatividad, *f.* relativity.

relativismo, *m.* (philos.) relativism.

relativista, *n.* & *a.* (philos.) relativist (-ic).

relativo, va, *a.* relative.

relato, *m.* statement, narrative, report, account.

relator, ra. I. *n.* teller, narrator. **II.** *m.* (law) relator.

relatoría, *f.* (law) office of a RELATOR.

relavar, *va.* to wash again.

relave, *m.* second washing of metals.—*pl.* (metal.) washings or sweepings.

relazar, *va.* to tie with many bindings.

releer, *va.* to read over again; to revise.

relegación, *f.* relegation, banishment, exile.

relegar, *va.* (*for mut. v.* LEGAR) to relegate, banish, exile.

relej, releje, *m.* wheel track, rut; (arti.) narrow chamber in a cannon; (arch.) tapering talus; (med.) sordes in the mouth.

relejar, *vn.* (arch.) to taper or slope.

relente, *m.* dampness; (coll.) boldness, assurance.

relentecer, *vn.* & *vr.* = LENTECER.

relevación, *f.* raising, lifting up; alleviation, relief; remission, pardon, exemption.

relevador, *m.* (elec.) relay.—**r. de llamada**, alarm relay.—**r. graduado**, step-by-step relay.— **r. parlante**, sounding relay, relaying sounder.—**r. traslator**, repeating relay.

relevante, *a.* excellent, great, eminent.

relevar. I. *va.* to emboss; to bring into relief; to exonerate, relieve, release; to forgive, pardon, acquit; to exalt, aggrandize; (mil.) to relieve, substitute. **II.** *vn.* (art) to stand out in relief.

relevo, *m.* (mil.) relief.

relicario, *m.* shrine; reliquary; locket.

relictos, *m. pl.* (law) estate.

relief, *m.* (mil.) rehabilitation.

relieve, *m.* relief, relievo, raised work, embossment.—*pl.* offals, scraps, remnants, leavings; broken victuals.

religa, *f.* (jewel.) second alloy.

religación, *f.* binding, tying.

religar, *va.* (*for mut. v.* LIGAR) to bind more tightly; to realloy; to solder.

religión, *f.* religion.—**religionario, ria,** *n.* religionist; sectarian; Protestant.

religiosamente, *adv.* religiously.

religiosidad, *f.* religiosity; religiousness; punctuality.

religioso, sa. I. *a.* religious; bound by monastic vows; conscientious, punctual. **II.** *n.* religious, member of a religious order; monk (nun).

relimar, *va.* (mech.) to file again.

relimpiar, *va.* to clean again.

relimpio, ia, *a.* (coll.) very neat, clean.

relinchador, ra, *a.* neighing often.

relinchante, *a.* neighing, whinnying.

relinchar, *vn.* to whinny, to neigh.

relincho, relinchido, *m.* neigh, neighing.

relindo, da, *a.* very neat and fine.

relinga, *f.* (naut.) boltrope.

relingar. I. *va.* (naut.) to rope (a sail). **II.** *vn.* (naut.) to rustle.

reliquia, *f.* relic, residue, remains; relics of saints; trace, vestige; habitual complaint.

reliz, *m.* (Mex.) landslide.

reloco, ca, *a.* (coll.) raving mad.

reloj, *m.* clock; watch.—**r. de agua**, clepsydra.— **r. de arena**, sandglass, hourglass.—**r. de bolsillo**, watch.—**r. de campana**, striking clock.—**r. de cuco**, cuckoo clock.—**r. de longitudes** = R. MARINO.—**r. de pulsera**, wrist watch.—**r. de repetición**, repeater, or repeating watch.—**r. de sol**, sundial.—**r. despertador**, alarm clock.—**r. magistral**, standard clock.—**r. marino**, chronometer. —**estar como un r.**, (coll.) to be in perfect trim.

relojera, *f.* watchcase; watch stand; (Am.) watch pocket.

relojería, *f.* clock and watch making; watchmaker's shop.

relojero, ra, *n.* watchmaker, clockmaker.

reluciente, *a.* shining, glittering, bright.

relucir, *vn.* (*for irr. v.* LUCIR) to shine, glow, glisten, glitter; to excel, to be brilliant.

reluctante, *a.* unruly, unmanageable.

reluchar, *vn.* to struggle, wrestle, strive.

relumbrante, *a.* resplendent.

relumbrar, *vn.* to sparkle, shine, glitter.

relumbrón, *m.* lustre, dazzling brightness; flash; tinsel.—**de r.**, showy, tawdry, pompous.

rellanar. I. *va.* to relevel. **II.** *vr.* to stretch one's self at full length.

rellano, *m.* landing, (of a stair).

rellenar. I. *va.* to refill, replenish; to cram; to fill; (cook.) to force, to stuff; (sew.) to pad; (mas.) to point. **II.** *vr.* to stuff one's self.

relleno, na. I. *a.* & *pp.* satiated; stuffed. **II.** *m.* forcemeat, stuffing; repletion; filling; (mach.) packing, gasket; (sew.) padding, wadding.

remachado, da. I. *a.* & *pp.* of REMACHAR: riveted. **II.** *m.* riveting; clinching.—**r. alternado**, or **al tresbolillo**, staggered riveting.—**r. de cadena**, or **paralelo**, chain riveting.

remachar, *va.* to clinch; to rivet; to secure, affirm.

remache, *m.* rivet; riveting; flattening, clinching.

remachón, *m.* buttress.

remador, ra, *n.* rower.—**remadura,** *f.* rowing.

remallar, *va.* to mend the meshes of.

remamiento, *m.* rowing.

remandar, *va.* to order several times.

remanecer, *vn.* (*for irr. v.* AMANECER) to reappear suddenly.

remaneciente, *a.* reappearing.

remanente. I. *m.* remains, remnant, residue. **II.** *a.* residual (sp. app. to magnetism).

remangar, *va.* = ARREMANGAR.

remango, *m.* = ARREMANGO.

remansarse, *vr.* to stop flowing; to eddy.

remanso, *m.* backwater; dead water; tardiness.

remante, *a.* rowing.

remar, *va.* & *vn.* to row, paddle; to toil, struggle.

remarcar, *va.* (*for mut. v.* MARCAR) to mark again.

rematadamente, *adv.* entirely, totally.

rematado, da, *pp.* & *a.* ended, finished; sold, knocked down (at auction); totally lost, utterly ruined.—**r. a galeras, a presidio,** condemned to the galleys, to prison.

rematamiento, *m.* = REMATE.

rematante, *m.* highest bidder.

rematar. I. *va.* to end, complete, finish; (com.) to auction; to knock down at auction; to give the finishing stroke; (sew.) to fasten off (a stitch); to finish (a seam). **II.** *vn.* to terminate, end. **III.** *vr.* to be utterly ruined or destroyed.

remate, *m.* end, finish, conclusion, expiration; (com.) auction, public sale; last or highest bid; (print.) vignette; (arch.) finial, pinnacle.—**r. de cuentas,** closing of accounts.—**de r.,** utterly, irremediably, without hope.—**por r.,** as a finish; finally.

remecedor, ra, *n.* one who beats down olives with a pole.

remecer, *va.* (*for irr. v.* MECER) to rock, swing, move to and fro.

remedable, *a.* imitable.

remedador, ra, *n.* imitator, mimic.

remedar, *va.* to copy, imitate; mimic, mock.

remediable, *a.* remediable.

remediador, ra, *n.* curer, healer; mender; comforter, helper.

remediar, *va.* to remedy; to assist, support, help; to free from danger, liberate; to repair (mischief); to avoid.

remedición, *f.* remeasuring; remeasurement.

remedio, *m.* remedy; medicine; help; amendment, correction; (law) action.—**r. casero,** home remedy.—**r. heroico,** extreme remedy, powerful remedy given as a last resort.—**no hay más r.,** there is nothing else to do.—**no tener para un r.,** to be absolutely penniless.—**no tener r.,** to be irremediable or unavoidable, there to be no help for (*eso no tiene remedio,* there is no help for that).—**sin r.,** inevitable.

remedión, *m.* *aug.* (theat.) makeshift performance.

remedir, *va.* to remeasure.

remedo, *m.* imitation; copy; mockery; mimicking.

remellado, da, *a.* dented, jagged.

remellar, *va.* (tan.) to unhair (hides).

remellón, na, *a.* = REMELLADO.

rememorar, *va.* to remember, recall.

rememorativo, va, *a.* reminding, recalling.

remendado, da, *pp.* & *a.* patched; mended; spotted, tabby.

remendar, *va.* (*for irr. v.* ENMENDAR) to patch, mend, repair; (sew.) to piece, patch; to darn.

remendón, na, *n.* botcher, patcher; one who mends old clothes; cobbler.

remera, *f.* flight feather.

remero, ra, *n.* rower, oarsman, paddler.

remesa, *f.* (com.) shipment; remittance.

remesar, *va.* to pluck out (the hair); (com.) to ship; to send, remit.

remesón, *m.* plucking out of hair; hair plucked out; stopping a horse in full gallop; skilful thrust in fencing.

remeter, *va.* to put back, put in.

remezón, *m.* (Am.) slight earthquake.

remiche, *m.* space between benches in galleys.

remiel, *m.* the second extract of soft sugar taken from the cane.

remiendo, *m.* patch; mending piece, clout; darning; amendment, correction; reparation, repair; brindle; (print.) jobwork.—**a remiendos,** by patchwork, piecemeal.—**echar un r.,** to patch.—**echar un r. a la vida,** to take a light repast.

remilgadamente, *adv.* with affected nicety, prudishly, squeamishly.—**remilgado, da,** *a.* & *pp.* affected, prudish, finical, fastidious.—**remilgarse,**

vr. to be overnice, prudish or finical.—**remilgo,** *m.* affected nicety, prudery, squeamishness.

reminiscencia, *f.* reminiscence.

remirado, da, *pp.* & *a.* prudent, cautious.

remirar. I. *va.* to look at or go over again. **II.** *vr.* (w. en) to take great pains (with); to inspect or consider with pleasure.

remisamente, *adv.* remissly, carelessly.

remisible, *a.* remissible.

remisión, *f.* act of sending or referring; remission, sending back, remitting, remitment; remission, pardon, forgiveness; remissness, indolence; relaxation, abatement.

remisivamente, *adv.* with remission.

remisivo, va, *a.* remissory; remissive.

remiso, sa, *a.* remiss, careless, slack, slow.

remisorio, ria, *a.* remissory.

remitir. I. *va.* to remit; to forward, transmit; to pardon, forgive; to give up, relinquish, waive, forego; to suspend, defer, put off; to refer; (law) to transfer, remit to another court. **II.** *va.,* *vn.* & *vr.* to remit, slacken, abate. **III.** *vr.* to refer, submit; to quote, cite.

remo, *m.* (naut.) oar; long and hard labor.—*pl.* arms and legs of a person; hind and fore legs of a beast; wings of a bird.

remoción, *f.* removal, removing; dismissal.

remojadero, *m.* steeping tub.

remojador, ra, *n.* moistener, soaker.

remojar, *va.* to steep, soak, drench.

remojo, *m.* steeping, soaking, soakage.—**echar en r.,** (coll.) to defer until conditions are more favorable.

remolacha, *f.* (bot.) beet root, red beet.

remolar, *m.* oar maker; oar shop.

remolcador, ra. I. *a.* (naut.) towing. **II.** *m.* tug, tugboat, towboat; lighter.

remolcar, *va.* to tow, take in tow; to haul.

remoler, *va.* to regrind; grind excessively.

remolida, *f.,* **remolimiento,** *m.* regrinding.

remolinante, *a.* whirling.—**remolinar. I.** *vn.* & *vr.* to whirl, gyrate, spin, rotate. **II.** *vr.* to crowd, throng together, swarm.—**remolinear. I.** *va.* to whirl about. **II.** *vn.* = REMOLINAR.

remolino, *m.* whirl, whirlwind; whirlpool, vortex, eddy; maelstrom; cowlick, twisted tuft of hair; crowd, throng; disturbance, commotion.

remolón, na. I. *a.* soft, indolent, lazy. **II.** *m.* upper tusk of a wild boar; sharp tooth in horses.

remolonear, *vn.* & *vr.* to lag, loiter, skulk, shun work.

remolque, *m.* (naut.) towing, towage; trackage; towline.—**a r.,** in tow.—**dar r.,** to tow.

remondar, *va.* to clean (plants) a second time.

remono, na, *a.* (coll.) very neat; very pretty.

remonta, *f.* (shoe.) repairing, resoling, vamping, footing; (sad.) stuffing; (mil.) remount; remounting cavalry.

remontamiento, *m.* remounting cavalry.

remontar. I. *va.* to frighten away (as game); (mil.) to supply remounts; (sad.) to repair; (shoe.) to repair, resole, revamp. **II.** *va.* & *vr.* to elevate, raise, rise. **III.** *vr.* to soar (as birds); to go back to, date from; to take to the woods.

remonte, *m.* repairing; remounting; soaring.

remontista, *m.* (mil.) commissioner for the purchase of remounts.

remoque, *m.* (coll.) sarcastic word.

remoquete, *m.* thump with the fist; epigram; satire; (coll.) gallantry, courtship.

rémora, *f.* (icht.) sucking fish, remora; hindrance, obstacle; cause of delay.

remordedor, ra, *a.* causing remorse.

remorder. I. *va.* (*for irr. v.* MORDER) to bite repeatedly; to cause remorse; to sting, fret. **II.** *vr.* to show worry or regret.

remordimiento, *m.* remorse.

remosquearse, *vr.* to show suspicion of surroundings; (print.) to be blurred or smeared; to mackle.

remostar. I. *va.* to put must into (old wine). **II.** *vr.* to become sweet (s. o. wine).

For pronunciation, see the rules at the beginning of the book.

remostecerse, *vr.* = REMOSTARSE.

remosto, *m.* putting must into old wine; growing sweet.

remotamente, *adv.* remotely; vaguely.

remoto, ta, *a.* remote, far off; unlikely.

remover, *va.* (*for irr. v.* MOVER) to move, remove, transfer; to take away; to discharge, dismiss; to stir.—**removimiento,** *m.* = REMOCIÓN.

remozamiento, *m.* making, appearing or becoming young.—**remozar. I.** *va.* to impart the bloom of youth to. **II.** *vr.* to look young.

rempujar, *va.* to push, jostle; to impel; to beat up (game).—**rempujo,** *m.* impulse, push; sailmaker's palm.—**rempujón,** *m.* impulse, push.

remuda, *f.*; **remudamiento,** *m.* change; replacement; change of clothes.—**r. de caballos,** relay of horses.

remudar, *va.* to move, remove; to change, replace.

remugar, *va.* (prov.) = RUMIAR.

remullir, *va.* to beat up again; mollify.

remunerable, *a.* remunerable.

remuneración, *f.* remuneration; gratuity, consideration.

remunerador, ra, *n.* & *a.* remunerator (-ing).

remunerar, *va.* to remunerate.

remuneratorio, ria, *a.* remunerative.

remusgar, *vn.* (coll.) to suspect, presume.

remusgo, *m.* keen cold wind.

renacentista. I. *a.* Renaissant, Renaissance (u. a.). **II.** *n.* one versed in Renaissance art and literature.

renacer, *vn.* (*for irr. v.* NACER) to be born again; to spring up again, grow again; to acquire grace by baptism.

renaciente, *a.* renascent, springing anew.

renacimiento, *m.* regeneration; new birth; (**R-**) Renaissance.

renacuajo, *m.* tadpole, polliwog; little, despicable person.

renadío, *m.* crop which, after having been reaped in the blade, sprouts again.

renal, *a.* renal.

renano, na, *a.* Rhenish, Rhine (u. a.).

rencilla, *f.* grudge; heartburning.

rencilloso, sa, *a.* peevish, quarrelsome, touchy.

renco, ca, *a.* hipshot, lame.

rencor, *m.* rancor, animosity, grudge.

rencorosamente, *adv.* rancorously.

rencoroso, sa, *a.* rancorous, spiteful.

renda, *f.* second dressing of vines.

rendaje, *m.* (sad.) set of reins or bridles.

rendajo, *m.* mimic. *V.* ARRENDAJO.

rendar, *va.* to dress (vines) a second time.

rendición, *f.* rendition, surrendering, yielding; rent, yield, product, profit.

rendidamente, *adv.* humbly, submissively, compliantly.

rendido, da, *a.* & *pp.* obsequious, devoted; fatigued, worn out.

rendija, *f* crevice, crack, cleft.

rendimiento, *m.* weariness, faintness, fatigue; humiliation, submission; obsequiousness, humbling compliance; yield, rent, income; yearly produce; (mech.) efficiency.

rendir. I. *va.* (gerund, RINDIENDO: *ind.* RINDO: *pret.* el RINDIÓ: *subj.* RINDA) to subdue, overcome; to surrender, yield, give up; to render; give back, return, restore; to render, do (homage, etc.); (com.) to produce, yield, bring; to fatigue, tire out; to vomit, throw up.—**r. el alma (a Dios)** to die.—**r. el bordo en,** to arrive at.—**r. el puesto,** (mil.) to give up the post, to commit it to another. —**r. gracias,** to give thanks.—**r. la guardia,** to set the watch.—**r. las armas,** to throw down the arms, to surrender.—**r. marea,** to stem the tide.— **r. obsequios,** to pay attention.—**r. parias,** to submit, to pay homage. **II.** *vr.* to become exhausted, tired, worn out; to yield, submit, give way, give up, surrender; (naut.) to spring (a mast).

renegado, da, *pp.* & *n.* renegade; wicked person; ombre (card game).

renegador, ra, *n.* swearer, blasphemer.

renegar. I. *va.* (*for irr. v.* NEGAR) to deny, disown; to detest, abhor. **II.** *vn.* to blaspheme, curse; (w. **de**) to deny; to blaspheme, curse (u. actively).

renegón, na, *n.* inveterate swearer.

renegrear, *va.* to blacken intensely.

renegrido, da, *a.* deeply livid, blackish (s. mainly of contusions).

rengífero, *m.* (zool.) reindeer.

renglón, *m.* written or printed line; (com.) line of business, staple, item.—*pl.* lines, writings.

renglonadura, *f.* ruling of paper; ruled lines.

rengo, ga, *a.* lame.

reniego, *m.* curse, execration, blasphemy.

reniego, reniegue. *V.* RENEGAR.

reniforme, *a.* reniform, kidney-shaped.

renil, *a.* barren, as a ewe.

renitencia, *f.* resistance, opposition.

renitente, *a.* renitent, repugnant.

reno, *m.* (zool.) reindeer.

renombrado, da, *pp.* & *a.* renowned, famous.

renombre, *m.* surname, family name; renown, fame.

renovable, *a.* renewable, replaceable.

renovación, *f.* renovation, renewing; change, reform; replacement.

renovador, ra, *n.* & *a.* renovator (-ing); reformer (-ing).

renovante, *a.* renovating, renewing.

renovar, *va.* (ind. RENUEVO: *subj.* RENUEVE) to renew; to renovate; to change, replace; to reiterate, republish.

renovero, ra, *n.* usurer, fripper.

renquear, *vn.* to limp, halt.

renta, *f.* profit; income; rental; annuity; tax, contribution; revenue.—**r. estancada,** revenue tax on monopoly articles.—**a r.,** at a rent.

rentado, da, *pp.* & *a.* living on an income.

rentar, *va.* to produce, bring, yield.

rentero, *m.* rural tenant; grantee of, or bidder for, a state monopoly.

rentilla, *f. dim.* small income; a game at cards; a game at dice.

rentista, *n.* financier; bondholder; annuitant; one who lives on a fixed income.

rentístico, ca, *a.* financial.

rento, *m.* annual rent, rental.

rentoso, sa, *a.* yielding income.

renuencia, *f.* reluctance, unwillingness.

renuente, *a.* unwilling, reluctant.

renuevo, *m.* sprout, shoot; RENOVACIÓN.

renuncia, *f.* resignation; renunciation; abjuration; renouncement; waiving.

renunciable, *a.* that may be waived, renounced or resigned; transferable.

renunciación, *f.,* or **renunciamiento,** *m.* = RENUNCIA.

renunciante, *n.* & *a.* renouncer (-ing), resigner (-ing), waiver (-ing).

renunciar. I. *va.* to renounce, resign; to disown; to forego, waive, give up; refuse, reject; to depreciate, abandon, relinquish. **II.** *vn.* to resign; (cards) to revoke, renege.—**r. a,** to give up, renounce.—**r. a sí mismo,** to give up one's own will or taste.

renunciatario, *m.* one in whose favor something is renounced or resigned.

renuncio, *m.* revoke or renege (at cards); (coll.) error, mistake; contradiction, untruth.

renvalsar, *va.* (carp.) to shave off (doors).

renvalso, *m.* (carp.) shaving off to make fit.

reñidamente, *adv.* stubbornly, strongly.

reñidero, *m.* cockpit; fighting pit or ring.

reñido, da, *pp.* & *a.* at variance; on bad terms; stubborn, hard-fought.

reñidor, ra, *n.* quarreller; scold.

reñir, *va.* & *vn.* (gerund, RIÑENDO: *ind.* RIÑO: *pret.* él RIÑÓ: *subj.* RIÑA) to wrangle, quarrel, fight; to fall out; to scold, reprimand, chide.

reo, *n.* criminal, culprit; (law) defendant; (icht.) ray trout.—**reo, a,** *a.* guilty, criminal.

reoctava, *f.* = OCTAVILLA.

reoctavar, *va.* to extract the OCTAVILLA from.

reóforo, *m.* (elec.) rheophore.

reojo, *m.*—**mirar de r.,** to look askance.

reómetro, *m.* (elec.) rheometer; (hydr.) water meter.

reorganización, *f.* reorganization.

reorganizador, ra, *n.* & *a.* reorganizer (-ing).

reorganizar, *va.* (*for mut. v.* ORGANIZAR) to reorganize.

reóstato, *m.* (elec.) rheostat.

repacer, *va.* (*for irr. v.* PACER) to consume all the grass of.

repagar, *va.* (*for irr. v.* PAGAR) to repay; to overpay.

repajo, *m.* inclosure for pasture.

repanchigarse, repantigarse, *vr.* to stretch (one's self) in a chair.

repapilarse, *vr.* to glut, stuff one's self.

reparable, *a.* reparable, remediable; objectionable; remarkable.

reparación, *f.* reparation, repair, repairing, indemnity, amends; atonement.

reparada, *f.* sudden bound of a horse.

reparado, da, *pp.* & *a.* repaired; restored; provided.

reparador, ra, *n.* repairer; restorer; carper, faultfinder.

reparamiento, *m.* = REPARO, REPARACIÓN.

reparar. I. *va.* to repair; to restore; to observe, notice; to consider, heed; to make up for, indemnify for, make amends for; to expiate, atone for; to suspend, detain; to guard, defend, protect; to parry; to give the final touch to. **II.** *vn.* to stop, stay over. **III.** *vr.* to refrain, forbear; (Mex.) to rear on the hind feet.

reparativo, va, *a.* reparative.

reparo, *m.* repair, reparing, restoration; remark, observation, advice, warning, notice; difficulty, objection, defect; strengthening cataplasm for the stomach; defence, protection; (fenc.) parry.

reparón, *m.* (coll.) great doubt or difficulty.

reparón, na, *n.* & *a.* carper (-ing); faultfinder (-ing).

repartible, *a.* distributable.

repartición, *f.* division, distribution.

repartidamente, *adv.* distributively.

repartidero, ra, *a.* to be distributed.

repartidor, ra. **I.** *a.* distributing. **II.** *n.* distributor; assessor of taxes.

repartimiento, *m.* division, distribution, apportionment; assessment; repartimiento (allotment of territory made by the conquerors of Spanish America, or, in the P. I., an assessment of taxes).

repartir, *va.* to divide, distribute, apportion, allot; to assess.

reparto, *m.* REPARTIMIENTO; (theat.) cast of characters.

repasadera, *f.* (carp.) finishing plane.

repasadora, *f.* woman that cards wool.

repasar, *va.* to repass, pass again; to reëxamine, revise; to scan, peruse, glance over; to review, study again (as a lesson); to clean (dyed wool) for carding; to mend (clothes); (min.) to remix (mercury) with metal.

repasata, *f.* (coll.) severe chiding, dressing down.

repaso, *m.* review (of a lesson); revision, reëxamination; final inspection, finishing; (min.) remixing quicksilver with metal; (coll.) reprimand, dressing down.

repastar, *va.* to pasture or feed again.

repasto, *m.* increase of feed.

repatriación, *f.* repatriation, returning to one's country.—**repatriar,** *va.* to return to one's country; to repatriate.

repechar, *vn.* to go up hill.

repecho, *m.* short steep incline.—**a r.,** up hill.

repelada, *f.* salad of herbs.

repeladura, *f.* restripping; second clipping or cropping.

repelar, *va.* to pull out the hair of; to put (a horse) to his speed; to nip, nibble, browse; to clip, crop, lop off.

repelente, *a.* repellent.

repeler, *va.* to repel, repulse; to refute, dispute.

repelo, *m.* anything that rises or goes against the grain; cross fiber; crooked grain; (coll.) slight scuffle or dispute; aversion.

repelón, *m.* pulling out the hair; small part torn from anything; loose thread in stockings; short gallop.—**a repelones,** by degrees, by little and little.—**de r.,** by the way; in haste.

repeloso, sa, *a.* of a bad grain (s. o. wood); touchy, peevish.

repellar, *va.* (mas.) to dub out.

repensar, *va.* (*for irr. v.* PENSAR) to reconsider, think over.

repente, *m.* sudden movement or impulse.—**de r.,** suddenly; from memory.

repentinamente, *adv.* suddenly.

repentino, na, *a.* sudden.

repentista, *n.* improviser, extemporizer.

repentizar, *va.* (*for mut. v.* ATIZAR) to improvise, extemporize.

repentón, *m.* sudden movement.

repeor, *a.* & *adv.* much worse.

repercudida, *f.* repercussion, rebound.

repercudir, *vn.* to rebound.

repercusión, *f.* repercussion, reverberation.

repercusivo, va, *a.* repercussive; repellent.

repercutir. I. *vn.* to rebound; to reëcho, reverberate. **II.** *va.* (med.) to repel.

repertorio, *m.* repertory, repertoire.

repesar, *va.* to weigh again.—**repeso,** *m.* reweigh; weight office; charge for reweighing.

repetición, *f.* repetition; repeater (of a colck or watch); collegial dissertation, thesis; (art) replica; (law) action for an accounting.

repetidamente, *adv.* repeatedly.

repetidor, ra. I. *a.* repeating. **II.** *n.* repeater (teacher or student).

repetir. I. *va.* (*gerund,* REPITIENDO: *pret.* REPITO: *pret.* él REPITIÓ: *subj.* REPITA) to repeat; to recite, rehearse; (art) to make a replica of; (law) to claim, demand. **II.** *vn.* to repeat; to read a thesis in a university. **III.** *vr.* to repeat one's self.

repicar. I. *va.* (*for mut. v.* PICAR) to chop, hash, mince; to ring (a bell); to reprick; (in piquet) to repique. **II.** *vr.* to glory, boast, flatter one's self.

repinarse, *vr.* to soar, rise.

repintar. I. *va.* to repaint. **II.** *vr.* to paint one's self; (print.) to set off, mackle, double.

repique, *m.* chopping, mincing; peal, ringing (of bells); dispute, altercation; (in piquet) repique.

repiquete, *m.* merry peal or ringing of bells; chance, opportunity.

repiquetear. I. *va.* to ring (bells) merrily. **II.** *vr.* to bicker, wrangle, quarrel.

repiqueteo, *m.* ringing of bells.

repisa, *f.* mantelpiece; shelf, console; bracket.

repiso, *m.* weak, vapid wine.

repitiente, *a.* repeating.

repizcar, *va.* to pinch.—**repizco,** *m.* pinch.

replantar, *va.* to replant.

replantear, *va.* to restate (a problem); (eng.) to lay out on the ground.

replanteo, *m.* laying out on the ground the plan of a structure.

repleción, *f.* repletion.

replegable, *a.* folding.

replegar. I. *va.* (*for irr. v.* PLEGAR) to fold several times. **II.** *vr.* (mil.) to fall back, retreat in order.

repleto, ta, *a.* replete, very full.

réplica, *f.* reply, answer; repartee; objection.

replicador, ra, *n.* replier, disputant.

replicante, *n.* & *a.* replier (-ing), respondent (-ing).

replicar. I. *va.* (*for mut. v.* APLICAR) to reply, answer; to contradict, argue. **II.** *va.* (law) to answer (a defendant's plea).

replicato, *m.* objection; (law) reply, answer.

replicón, na, *n.* (coll.) disputer, arguer.

repliegue, *m.* doubling, folding; fold, crease, convolution.

repoblación, *f.* repopulation.—**repoblar,** *va.* (*for irr. v.* POBLAR) to repopulate, repeople.

repodrir, *va.* & *vr.* = REPUDRIR.

repollar, *vn.* to head (as a cabbage).

repollo, *m.* cabbage; round head (of a plant).

repolludo, da, *a.* cabbage-headed; round-headed.

repolluelo, *m. dim.* small cabbage, sprout.

reponer. I. *va.* (*for irr. v.* PONER) to replace; reinstate, reinstall; to restore; to answer, to reply; (law) to restore (a case) to its primitive state. **II.** *vr.* to recover lost health or property.

reportación, *f.* moderation, calm.

reportado, da, *pp.* & *a.* moderate, calm.

reportaje, *m.* (journalism) report, reporting.

reportamiento, *m.* forbearance, restraint.

reportar. I. *va.* to control, restrain, check; to obtain, get, attain; to carry; to bring. **II.** *vr.* to refrain, forbear, control one's self.

reporte, *m.* report, information, news; lithographic proof.

repórter, *n.* reporter.

reporteril, *a.* reportorial.

reporterismo, *m.* newspaper reporting; body of reporters, reporters collectively.

reportero, ra, *n.* reporter.

reportorio, m. almanac, calendar.

reposadamente, *adv.* peaceably, quietly.

reposadero, *m.* (metal.) trough for receiving melted metal.

reposado, da, *pp.* & *a.* quiet, peaceful, calm.

reposar. I. *vn.* to rest, repose; to stand (on), be supported (by); to take a nap; to lie down; to lie (in the grave). **II.** *vr.* to settle (as liquids).

reposición, *f.* replacement, reinstatement; recovery (in health); (law) restoring a suit to its primitive state; (chem.) preservation of liquids in proper vessels.

repositorio, *m.* repository.

reposo, *m.* rest, repose; sleep; tranquillity.

repostarse, *vr.* (Am.) to lay in stock.

reposte, *m.* pantry, larder.

repostería, *f.* confectionery, pastry shop; pantry, larder, plate room.

repostero, *m.* king's butler; pastry cook; covering ornamented with a coat of arms.

repregunta, *f.* (law) cross-examination.

repreguntar, *va.* (law) to cross-examine.

reprender, *va.* to reprehend, scold, reproach.

reprendiente, *a.* censuring, reprimanding.

reprensible, *a.* reprehensible.

reprensión, *f.* reprehension, reprimand, reproach.

reprensor, ra, *n.* reprehender, reproacher.

represa, *f.* dam, dike, sluice, lock; damming, impounding; stopping, holding back; (naut.) recapture.

represalia, *f.* reprisal.

represar, *va.* (naut.) to recapture, retake from the enemy; to bank, dam, impond; to stop, detain, retain; to repress, restrain, check.

representable, *a.* representable.

representación, *f.* representation; description, statement; (theat.) performance, production; figure, image, idea; address, petition; authority, dignity, character; (law) right of succession.

representador, ra. I. *a.* representing. **II.** *n.* player, actor.

representante. I. *a.* representing, representative. **II.** *n.* representative; actor, player.

representar. I. *va.* to represent; to state, declare; to express; (theat.) to perform, act. **II.** *vr.* to image, picture to one's self, conceive.

representativo, va, *a.* representative.

represión, *f.* repression, check, control.

represivo, va, *a.* repressive, restrictive.

reprimenda, *f.* reprimand.

reprimir, *va.* to repress, check, curb.

reprobable, *a.* reprehensible.—**reprobación,** *f.* reprobation.—**reprobadamente,** *adv.* reprovably.

reprobado, da, *pp.* & *a.* RÉPROBO; not passed in an examination.

reprobador, ra, *n.* reprover, condemner.

reprobar, *va.* (*for irr. v.* PROBAR) to reprove, disapprove, condemn; to damn; not to pass, to keep from passing, (coll.) to flunk.

reprobatorio, ria, *a.* reprobative.

réprobo, ba, *n.* & *a.* reprobate.

reprochar, *va.* to reproach; to challenge (witnesses), reject, exclude.

reproche, *m.* reproach, reproof; repulse, rebuff, rebuke.

reproducción, *f.* reproduction.

reproducir, *va.* (*for irr. v.* PRODUCIR) to reproduce.—**reproductible,** *a.* reproducible.

reproductividad, *f.* reproductiveness.

reproductivo, va, *a.* reproductive.

reproductor, ra, *n.* & *a.* reproducer (-ing); breeder (-ing).

repromisión, *f.* repeated promise.

repropiarse, *vr.* to get unruly (s. o. horses).

repropio, pia, *a.* unruly (s. o. a horse).

reprueba, *f.* new proof.

reptil, *m.* reptile; crawler, creeper.

república, *f.* republic.—**republicanismo,** *m.* republicanism.—**republicano, na,** *n.* & *a.* republican.—**repúblico,** *m.* prominent man; patriot; statesman.

repudiación, *f.* repudiation.

repudiar, *va.* to repudiate; to divorce.

repudio, *m.* repudiation; divorce.

repudrir. I. *va.* & *vr.* to rot thoroughly. **II.** *vr.* (coll.) to pine away.

repuesto, ta. I. *pp. irr.* of REPONER & *a.* retired, secluded; recovered. **II.** *m.* store, stock, supply; sideboard, cupboard; dresser; pantry, larder; money staked in the game of ombre.—**de r.,** extra; spare.

repugnancia, *f.* reluctance, repugnance; aversion; loathing; disgust; opposition, contradiction, contrariety.

repugnante, *a.* repugnant, reluctant; loathsome; repulsive, disgusting.

repugnar, *va.* to oppose, contradict, conflict w'th; to cause loathsomeness, disgust; to do with reluctance.

repujado, *m.* repoussé, repoussage.

repujar, *va.* to make repoussé work on.

repulgado, *pp.* & *a.* affected.

repulgar, *va.* (*pret.* REPULGUÉ; *subj.* REPULGUE) (sew.) to hem; to border; to put an edging on (pastry).

repulgo, *m.* (sew.) hem, border; external ornament of a cake or pie; ridiculous scruple.

repulido, da, *pp.* & *a.* prim, neat, spruce.

repulir. I. *va.* to repolish. **II.** *va.* & *vr.* to dress affectedly.

repulsa, *f.* refusal, rebuke, repulse.

repulsar, *va.* to reject, repel, decline, refuse.

repulsión, *f.* REPULSA; repulsion.

repulsivo, va, *a.* repelling.

repullo, *m.* jump, start, shock; small arrow or dart.

repunta, *f.* point, cape, headland; first show or sign; disagreement, dispute.

repuntar. I. *vn.* to begin to appear; to begin to ebb. **II.** *vr.* to be on the turn (wine); to be soured, to be displeased with one another.

repunte, *m.* (naut.) first of the ebb.

repurgar, *va.* (*pret.* REPURGUÉ; *subj.* REPURGUE) to clean or purify again.

reputación, *f.* reputation.

reputante, *n.* appraiser, estimator.

reputar, *va.* to repute; to estimate, appreciate.

requebrador, *m.* gallant, wooer, suitor.

requebrar, *va.* (*for irr. v.* QUEBRAR) to woo, court, make love to; to flatter, wheedle; to break again.

requemado, a. I. *pp.* & *a.* brown-colored, sunburnt. **II.** *m.* a kind of black fabric.

requemamiento, *m.* = RESQUEMO.

requemar. I. *va.* to reburn; to overcook, cook too much; to parch; to inflame (the blood or humors); to bite, smart (as mustard). **II.** *vr.* to burn with passion; to be deeply in love.

requemazón, *f.* = RESQUEMO.

requeridor, ra, *n.* summons server; courter, suiter; inspector.

requerimiento, *m.* summons; requisition, demand.

requerir, *va.* (*pp.* REQUERIDO, REQUISITO: *gerund,* REQUIRIENDO: *ind.* REQUIERO; *pret.* él REQUIRIÓ: *subj.* REQUIERA) to summon; to notify; to investigate, examine; to require, need; to court, woo, make love to; to induce, persuade.

requesón, *m.* pot cheese, cottage cheese; slip; curd.

requetebién, *adv.* (coll.) very well (or good), fine, as good as could be.

requiebro, *m.* flattery, compliment; endearing expression, love tale; (min.) crushed ore.

requilorios, *m.* (coll.) useless ceremony; circumlocution.

requintador, ra, *n.* outbidder.

requintar, *va.* to outbid by a fifth part of the price of; to exceed, surpass; (mus.) to raise or lower five points.

requinto, *m.* second fifth taken from a quantity; advance of a fifth in bidding; (S. A.) extraordinary impost levied under Philip II; (mus.) fife and its player; a small guitar.

requisa, *f.* tour of inspection, round; (mil.) requisition of horses.

requisar, *va.* to inspect, make the rounds of; (mil.) to requisition (horses).

requisición, *f.* (mil.) requisition of horses.

requisito, *m.* requisite, requirement.

requisitorio, ria. **I.** *a.* requisitory. **II.** *f.* (law) requisition.

requive, *m.* = ARREQUIVE.

res, *f.* head of cattle; beast.—**r. de vientre,** breeding cow (or any other breeding female).

resaber, *va.* to know very well.

resabiar. **I.** *va.* to cause to contract bad habits. **II.** *vr.* to contract bad habits; to become vicious; to be discontented, dissatisfied; to relish.

resabido, da, *pp. & a.* affecting learning.

resabio, *m.* unpleasant aftertaste; viciousness; bad habit.

resabioso, sa, *a.* (Am.) vicious; peevish, ill-tempered.

resaca, *f.* (naut.) surge, surf, undertow; (com.) redraft.

resacar, *va.* (naut.) to underrun, haul; (com.) to redraw.

resalado, da, *a.* (coll.) very attractive, charming, magnetic.

resalir, *vn.* (*for irr. v.* SALIR) to jut out, project.

resaltar, *vn.* to rebound; to come off, get loose; to jut out, project; to be evident.—**r. a la vista,** to be self-evident.

resalte, resalto, *m.* rebound; protuberance, projection; (r. w.) superelevation (of outer rail).

resaludar, *vn.* to return a salute or greeting.

resalutación, *f.* return of a salute or greeting.

resalvo, *m.* tiller, sapling.

resallar, *va.* (agr.) to weed again.

resallo, *m.* (agr.) reweeding.

resanar, *va.* to regild defective spots in.

resarcible, *a.* indemnifiable.—**resarcimiento,** *m.* compensation, reparation, indemnity.—**resarcir,** *va.* (*ind.* RESARZO: *subj.* RESARZA) to compensate, indemnify, make amends to; to mend, repair.

resbaladero, ra. **I.** *a.* slippery; elusive. **II.** *m.* slippery place.—**resbaladizo, za,** *a.* slippery; glib; elusive; tempting, alluring.—**resbalador, ra,** *n.* slider; backslider.—**resbaladura,** *f.* slip, slide; backsliding.

resbalamiento, *m.* slipping; skidding.

resbalante, *n. & a.* slider (-ing), slipper (-ing).

resbalar, *vn. & vr.* to slip, slide, glide; to skid; to err, go astray.—**resbalo,** *m.* (Am.) steep slope.

resbalón, *m.* slip, slipping; fault, error, break.

resbaloso, sa, *a.* slippery.

rescaldar, *va.* to heat, to scorch.

rescatador, ra, *n.* redeemer, ransomer.

rescatar, *va.* to ransom; to redeem, recover; to exchange, barter, commute; (Am.) to buy (ore) in mines.

rescate, *m.* ransom; redemption; ransom money; exchange, barter.

rescatín, *m.* (Am.) buyer of ore from Indians.

rescaza, *f.* = ESCORPINA.

rescindir, *va.* to rescind, annul, cancel.

rescisión, *f.* rescission, cancellation, annulment.

rescisorio, ria, *a.* rescissory, rescinding.

rescoldera, *f.* pyrosis, heartburn.

rescoldo, *m.* embers, hot ashes; scruple, doubt, apprehension.

rescontrar, *va.* to offset, set off.

rescripto, *m.* rescript, order, mandate.

rescriptorio, ria, *a.* rescriptive.

rescuentro, *m.* offset, compensation.

resecación, *f.* exsication, desiccation.

resecar, *va. & vr.* (*for mut. v.* SECAR) to dry thoroughly, exsiccate, desiccate.

resección, *f.* (surg.) resection.

reseco, ca. **I.** *a.* thoroughly dry, too dry; very lean. **II.** *m.* exsication of trees or shrubs; dry part of a honeycomb.

reseda, *f.* (bot.) mignonette, reseda; woad.

resedáceo, a. **I.** *a.* (bot.) resedaceous. **II.** *f. pl.* Resedaceæ.

resegar, *va.* (*for irr. v.* SEGAR) to mow again.

reseguir, *va.* (*for irr. v.* SEGUIR) to edge (swords).

resellante, *a.* recoining, restamping.

resellar, *va.* to recoin; to countermark.

resello, *m.* recoinage; surcharge.

resembrar, *va.* (*for irr. v.* SEMBRAR) to resow.

resentido, da, *pp. & a.* offended; resentful.

resentimiento, *m.* resentment, grudge; impairment.

resentirse, *vr.* to be impaired or weakened; to resent, be offended or hurt.

reseña, *f.* brief description, narration, or review; sketch; signal; signalment; (mil.) review.

reseñar, *va.* to make a brief description of, sketch, outline; (mil.) to review.

resequido, da, *a.* dried up, parched.

reserva, *f.* reserve, reticence; reservation, exception; discretion, circumspection, prudence; modesty; (law) reservation; (mil.) reserve.—**r. mental,** mental reservation.—**a r. de,** intending to.—**de r.,** extra, spare, in store for future use.—**en r.,** in reserve; confidentially.—**sin r.,** openly, freely.

reservación, *f.* reservation.

reservadamente, *adv.* secretly; confidentially.

reservado, da. **I.** *a. & pp.* reserved; cautious, prudent; private, confidential. **II.** *m.* (eccl.) eucharist kept in the ciborium.

reservar. **I.** *va.* to reserve, keep; to retain, hold; to defer, postpone; to exempt; to conceal, keep secret. **II.** *vr.* to spare one's self for a better occasion, to bide one's time; to beware, be cautious.

reservativo, va, *a.* reservative.

reservista, *m.* (mil.) reservist.

resfriado, *pp. & m.* cold (disease); watering before tilling.

resfriador, ra. **I.** *a.* cooling, refrigerating. **II.** *m.* refrigerator.

resfriadura, *f.* (vet.) cold in horses.

resfriamiento, *m.* = ENFRIAMIENTO.

resfriante. **I.** *a.* cooling, refrigerating. **II.** *m.* = CORBATO.

resfriar. **I.** *va.* to cool, chill; to moderate (ardor, fervor). **II.** *vn.* to begin to be cold. **III.** *vr.* to catch cold; to grow cold or indifferent.

resfrío, *m.* cold (disease).

resguardar. **I.** *va.* to preserve, defend, protect. **II.** *vr.* to take shelter; (w. de) to guard against; protect one's self from.

resguardo, *m.* preservation, security, safety; guard, defence, protection; (com.) security, guarantee, collateral, voucher; watchfulness to prevent smuggling; body of customhouse officers for such service; (naut.) sea room, wide berth.

For pronunciation, see the rules at the beginning of the book.

residencia, f. residence, domicile, abode; dwelling, home; stay, sojourn; (eccl.) residence; (dipl.) function of a resident minister; impeachment.

residencial, a. residentiary.

residenciar, va. (law) to impeach.

residente. I. a. residing, resident, residentiary. **II.** m. (dipl.) resident minister; (eccl.) residencer; dweller, inhabitant.

residentemente, adv. constantly, assiduously.

residir, vn. to reside, live, dwell; to be in official residence; to inhere.

residual, a. residual.

residuo, m. remainder, remnant; (chem.) residuum, residue; (arith.) difference; remainder.

resiembra, f. (agr.) resowing.

resigna, f. (eccl.) resignation.

resignación, f. resignation; submission, acquiescence.—**resignadamente,** adv. resignedly.

resignante, n. & a. resigner (-ing).

resignar. I. va. to resign, give up. **II.** vr. to resign one's self, be resigned.

resignatario, m. resignee.

resina, f. resin, rosin.—**resinar,** va. to draw resin from.—**resinero, ra. I.** a. resinic. **II.** n. one engaged in the resin business.—**resinífero, ra,** a. resinferous.—**resinoso, sa,** a. resinous.

resisa, f. = OCTAVILLA.

resisar, va. to diminish (measures) further.

resistencia, f. resistance, endurance; strength; (mech. and elec.) resistance.—**r. de materiales,** strength (formerly resistance) of materials.

resistente, a. strong; resisting, opposing.

resistero, m. hottest part of the day; heat produced by the sun's glare; place where such heat is felt.

resistible, a. resistible, endurable.

resistidero, m. = RESISTERO.

resistidor, ra, n. resister, repeller.

resistir. I. vn. & vr. to resist, offer resistance. **II.** va. to resist; to bear, stand, withstand; to endure.

resma, f. ream of paper.

resmilla, f. four quires of letter paper.

resobrar, vn. to be much over and above.

resobrino, na, n. grandnephew (-niece).

resol, m. sun's glare.

resolano, na. I. a. sunny. **II.** f. sunny place.

resoluble, a. solvable, that can be solved.

resolución, f. resolution; resoluteness; determination, courage, firmness; solution (of a problem); conclusiveness; quickness, promptitude; (law) lapse, nullification; (med.) resolution.—**en r.,** in short, in a word.

resolutivamente, adv. resolutely.

resolutivo, va. I. a. analytical. **II.** m. (med.) resolutive.

resoluto, ta, a. resolute, daring; compendious, brief; skillful, able.

resolutoriamente, adv. resolutely.

resolutorio, ria, a. resolute; resolutory.

resolvente, a. resolvent, resolving.

resolver. I. va. (pp. RESUELTO: ind. RESUELVO: subj. RESUELVA) to resolve, determine; to sum up; to solve (a problem); to dissolve, analyze; to dissipate; to undo, destroy, annul; to resolve, divide. **II.** vr. to resolve, determine; to be included or comprised; (med.) to resolve.

resolladero, m. vent, air-hole.

resollar, vn. (ind. RESUELLO: subj. RESUELLE) to breathe; to take breath; to pant; (coll.) to show up; to break silence.

resonación, f. resounding.

resonancia, f. resonance.—**tener r.,** to be bruited abroad, to attract attention.

resonador, m. resonator.

resonante, a. resonant, resounding.

resonar, vn. (ind. RESUENO: subj. RESUENE) to resound, echo, clink, clatter.

resoplar, vn. to breathe audibly; to snort.

resoplido, resoplo, m. audible breathing; snorting.

resorber, va. to sip again, reabsorb.

resorción, f. reabsorption.

resorte, m. (mech.) spring; resilience, spring, elasticity; means, resources.

respailar, va. (coll.) to move helter-skelter.

respaldar. I. va. to indorse; to back; to answer for, guarantee. **II.** vr. to lean back; to get backing or support; (vet.) to dislocate the backbone. **III.** m. back of a seat.

respaldo, m. back of a seat; leaning stock; backing; back of a sheet of paper; indorsement.

respectar, vn. impers. to concern, regard.

respectivamente, respective, adv. respectively.

respectivo, va, a. respective.

respecto, m. relation, proportion; relativeness; respect.—**r. a,** or **de,** with respect to, with regard to.—**a este r.,** with respect to this.—**al r.,** relatively, respectively.—**con r. a = R. A.**

respeluzar, va. = DESPELUZAR.

respetabilidad, f. respectability.

respetable, a. respectable, considerable; worthy; honorable, reliable.

respetador, ra, n. respecter.

respetar. I. va. to respect, revere, honor. **II.** vn. impers. V. RESPECTAR.

respetivo, va, a. respectful.

respeto, m. respect; attention; observance.—**de r.,** extra, spare; for ceremony's sake; dressed or arranged and decorated ceremoniously.—**faltar al r. a,** to be disrespectful to; to molest (a woman).

respetuosamente, adv. respectfully.

respetuoso, sa, a. respectful; dutiful; respectable, honorable.

réspice, m. (coll.) short, pert reply; sharp reproof, dressing down.

respigador, ra, n. gleaner.

respigar, va. (for mut. v. ESPIGAR) to glean.

respigón, m. hangnail; (vet.) sore on the heel of a horse.

respingada, a. turned up, retroussé (nose).

respingar, vn. (pret. RESPINGUÉ: subj. RESPINGUE) to kick, wince; (coll.) to mutter; to talk back.—**respingo,** m. muttering, grumbling; gesture of unwillingness.

respingona, a. = RESPINGADA.

respirable, a. breathable.—**respiración,** f. respiration, breathing; ventilation.—**respiradero,** m. vent, air hole; ventilator; (arch.) air passage, femerell, louver; (surg.) cupping glass; rest, repose; organ of respiration.—**respirador, ra,** a. breathing.—**respirante,** a. breathing, exhaling.

respirar. I. vn. & va. to breathe. **II.** vn. to rest, take rest or respite; to get breath; to breathe freely; to exhale scents or odors; to speak (used with a negative: no respiró, he did not open his lips).

respiratorio, ria, c. respiratory.

respiro, m. breathing; moment of rest; respite; (com.) extension, time.

resplandecer, vn. to glitter, glisten, shine.

resplandeciente, pa. & a. resplendent, shining, bright, glittering; luminous, light.

resplandecimiento, m. = RESPLANDOR.

resplandina, f. (coll.) sharp reproof, dressing down.

resplandor, m. light, splendor, brilliancy, radiance; glare; shining paint for women.

respondedor, ra, n. answerer.

responder, va. & vn. to answer, reply; to respond; to reëcho; to acknowledge; to requite; to yield, produce; to have the desired effect; (com.) to correspond; to answer to, answer for, be responsible for, guarantee.

respondiente, a. respondent; answering.

respondón, na, a. saucy, pert.

responsabilidad, f. responsibility; reliability.

responsable, a. responsible; reliable.

responsar, responsear, vn. to repeat the responses.

responso, m. responsory for the dead.

responsorio, m. (eccl.) responsory.

respuesta, f. answer, reply; response; repartee.

resquebradura, *f.* crack, cleft, flaw, split, crevice, fissure.

resquebrajadizo, za, *a.* easily cracked; chinky.

resquebrajadura, *f.*=RESQUEBRADURA.

resquebrajar, *va. & vr.* to crack, to split.

resquebrajo, *m.* crack, cleft, split, fissure.

resquebrajoso, sa, *a.* easily cracked; chinky.

resquebrar, *vn.* (*for irr. v.* QUEBRAR) to crack, split; to burst.

resquemar, *va. & vn.* to bite or sting (as mustard).

resquemazón, *f.*; **resquemo, resquemor,** *m.*, pungency of any aliment; disagreeable taste of burnt food; burning passion; stinging, or pricking, remorse.

resquicio, *m.* chink, slit, crevice, crack, cleft; chance, opportunity.

resta, *f.* (arith.) subtraction; remainder, difference.

restablecer. I. *va.* (*for irr. v.* ESTABLECER) to restore, reëstablish, reinstate. **II.** *vr.* to recover, recuperate.

restablecimiento, *m.* reëstablishment; restoration; recovery.

restallar, *vn.* to crack, as a whip; to crackle, crack, squeak.

restante, *a. & m.* remainder (-maining).

restañadero, *m.* inlet; estuary.

restañadura, *f.* retinning.

restañar. I. *va.* to retin, tin anew; to stanch, stop (blood). **II.** *vn.* RESTALLAR. **III.** *vr.* to restagnate, stand without flow.

restañasangre, *f.* bloodstone.

restaño, *m.* stagnation; cloth of gold or silver.

restar. I. *va.* to deduct; to return (a ball), strike (it) back; (arith.) to subtract. **II.** *vn.* to be left, remain; (arith.) to subtract.

restauración, *f.* restoration; restoring; repairing, refurbishing.

restaurador, ra, *n. & a.* restorer (-ing).

restaurant, restaurante, *m.* restaurant.

restaurante, *n. & a.* restorer (-ing).

restaurar, *va.* to restore, retrieve; to repair, renew, refurbish.

restaurativo, va, *n. & a.* restorative.

restinga, *f.* shoal, bar; ledge of rocks.

restingar, *m.* place full of rocks or bars.

restitución, *f.* restitution.

restituíble, *a.* restorable, returnable.

restituidor, ra, *n.* restorer, refunder.

restituir. I. *va.* (*for mut. v.* CONSTITUIR) to restore, return, give back; to refund; to repair. **II.** *vr.* to return to the place of departure.

restitutorio, ria, *a.* (law) restitutive.

resto, *m.* remainder, balance, rest; limit for stakes at cards; returning the ball; player who returns the ball on its rebound.—*pl.* remains.— **a r. abierto,** unlimitedly.—**echar el r.,** to stake one's all; to do one's best.

restregadura, *f.,* **restregamiento,** *m.* hard rubbing.

restregar, *va.* (*for irr. v.* FREGAR) to rub, scrub.

restregón, *m.* scrubbing, hard rubbing.

restribar, *vn.* to lean upon strongly.

restricción, *f.* restriction, limitation.

restrictivamente, *adv.* restrictively.

restrictivo, va, *a.* restrictive, restricting.

restricto, ta, *a.* limited, confined; restricted.

restringa, *f.* = RESTINGA.

restringente, *n. & a.* restrainer (-ing).

restringible, *a.* restrainable, limitable.

restringir, *va.* (*ind.* RESTRINJO: *subj.* RESTRINJA) to restrain, restrict, limit, confine; to contract, astringe.

restriñidor, ra, *n. & a.* restrainer (-ing), binder (-ing), constipating.—**restriñimiento,** *m.* costiveness, constipation.

restriñir, *va.* to bind, contract, constipate.

restrojo, *m.* = RASTROJO.

resucitador, ra, *n.* restorer, reviver.

resucitar. I. *va.* to resurrect, raise from the dead; revive; to renovate, modernize. **II.** *vn.* to rise from the dead, return to life.

resudación, *f.* slight perspiration.—**resudar,** *vn.* to perspire slightly.—**resudor,** *m.* slight perspiration.

resueltamente, *adv.* resolutely.

resuelto, ta, *a. & pp. irr.* of RESOLVER; resolute, daring; determined, prompt, quick, diligent.

resuello, *m.* breath, breathing.—**sin r.,** breathless, panting.

resulta, *f.* result, effect, consequence; resolution; vacancy of an office.—**de resultas,** in consequence.

resultado, *pp. & m.* result.

resultancia, *f.* result.

resultando, *m.* substantiating fact or statement; whereas (u. as a noun, meaning each of the paragraphs beginning with "whereas").

resultante. I. *a.* resulting; (mech.) resultant (force, velocity, etc). **II.** *f.* (mech.) resultant.

resultar, *vn.* to result, follow; to turn out; to be; to come out; (coll.) to work (well or badly), to lead to the desired result, to be advantageous.

resumbruno, na, *a.* brown (hawk's feathers).

resumen, *m.* summary, abstract, résumé.—**en r.,** in brief, in short, summing up.

resumidamente, *adv.* briefly, summarily.

resumido, da, *pp. & a.* abridged.—**en resumidas cuentas,** in short, briefly, getting down to brass tacks.

resumir. I. *va.* to abridge, abstract, sum up; to repeat. **II.** *vr.* to be reduced or transformed.

resurgimiento, *m.* reappearance, springing up again.

resurgir, *vn.* to reappear, arise or spring up again.

resurrección, *f.* resurrection.

resurtida, *f.* rebound, repercussion.

resurtir, *vn.* to rebound, fly back.

retablo, *m.* series of historical pictures; (eccl.) retable, altarpiece.

retacar, *va.* (billiards) to hit (the ball) twice with the cue.

retacería, *f.* collection of remnants, as for a crazy quilt.

retaco, *m.* short, light fowling piece; short cue; short, heavy-built person.

retador, ra, *n.* challenger.

retaguardia, *f.* rear, rear guard.—**a r.,** in the rear.—**picar la r.,** to pursue the rear guard closely, to harass it.

retahila, *f.* long file, string, series, line.

retajar, *va.* to cut round; to cut the nib of a (quill); to circumcise.

retal, *m.* remnant, piece, clipping.

retallar. I. *vn.* to shoot or sprout anew. **II.** *va.* to regrave, retouch a (graving); (arch.) to form a RETALLO in.

retallecer, *vn.* to sprout again.

retallo, *m.* new sprout; (arch.) projection or ledge.

retama, *f.* (bot.) genista.—**r. de escobas** = R. NEGRA.—**r. de olor** = R. MACHO.—**r. de tintes,** or **de tintoreros,** (bot.) dyeweed, dyer's broom.—**r. macho,** Spanish broom.—**r. negra,** (bot.) furze, whin.

retamal, retamar, *m.* place where furze or broom grows.

retamero, ra, *a.* broomy, furzy.

retar, *va.* to challenge, dare.

retardación, *f.* retardation; delay.

retardar, *va.* to retard, slacken; to delay, detain.

retardatriz, *a.* retardating.

retardo, *m.* retardation; delay, procrastination.

retasa, retasación, *f.* reappraisement.

retasar, *va.* to reappraise.

retazar, *va.* to tear in pieces.—**retazo,** *m.* piece, remnant; cutting; fragment, portion.

retejador, *m.* retiler.—**retejar,** *va.* to retile a (roof); (coll.) to provide with clothes.

retejer, *va.* to weave closely.

retejo, *m.* repairing of a roof, retiling.

retemblar, *vn.* (*for irr. v.* TEMBLAR) to tremble, shake, quiver.

retemblor, *m.* repeated shaking, quiver.

retén, *m.* store, stock, reserve; (mil.) reserve corps; (mech.) ratchet, catch.

retención, f. retention, keeping or holding back; (med.) retention.

retener, va. (for irr. v. TENER) to retain, withhold, keep back; to guard, preserve; to catch, hold, keep; to arrest, detain.

retenida, f. (naut.) preventer rope, guy.—**r. de costado,** (aer.) side guy wire.—**r. de guiñada,** (aer.) yaw guy.—**r. de proa,** (naut.) headfast.

retenidamente, adv. retentively.

retenimiento, m. = RETENCIÓN.

retentar, va. to threaten with a relapse or renewal (s. o. of a disease).

retentivo, va. I. a. retentive, retaining. II. f. retentiveness, memory.

reteñir. I. va. (for irr. v. TEÑIR) to dye over again; to double-dye. II. vn. to tingle. V. RETIÑIR.

retesamiento, m. tightening harder.

retesar, va. to draw or stretch tighter.

reteso, m. = RETESAMIENTO.

reticencia, f. reticence.—**reticente,** a. reticent.

rético, ca, n. & a. Rhethian, Rhæthian.

retícula, f. diaphragm and cross wires (of an instrument).

reticulado, da; reticular, a. reticular, reticulated; trussed, framed (as in construcción reticulada, framed structure).

retículo, m. network, reticular tissue; diaphragm and cross wires (of an instrument).

retín, m. = RETINTÍN.

retina, f. retina of the eye.

retinitis, f. (med.) retinitis.

retinte, m. second dye. V. RETINTÍN.

retintín, m. tinkling, jingle, clink; tintinnabulation; (coll.) sarcastic tone of voice.

retinto, a. dark, obscure, almost black.

retiñir, vn. to tinkle, jingle, ring, clink.

retiración, f. (print.) printing the back of a sheet; second form for backing.

retirada, f. withdrawal; (mil.) retreat; retirement; place of safety; privy, closet.

retiradamente, adv. secretly; retiredly.

retirado, da. I. a. & pp. retired, solitary, isolated; close; remote, distant; pensioned. II. m. retired officer.

retiramiento, m. retirement. V. RETIRO.

retirar. I. va. to withdraw; to lay aside, reserve; to repel; to revoke; (com.) to withdraw, call in; (print.) to print the back of, to back. II. vr. to withdraw; to retire; to recede, move or go back; (mil.) to retreat.

retiro, m. retirement; retreat; recess; secluded place; refuge, asylum; (eccl.) retreat; privacy; (mil.) condition and pay of a retired officer.

reto, m. challenge; threat, menace.

retobado, da, a. (Am.) given to grumbling or muttering; obstinate, unruly; cunning, wily.

retobar. I. va. (Arg.) to line or cover with hides; (Ch.) to pack or wrap in hides or burlap. II. vr. (Arg.) to become quiet and surly, to sulk.

retobo, m. (Colomb., C. A.) refuse, useless or insignificant thing; (Ch.) burlap; oilcloth; (Arg.) packing or wrapping in hides.

retocamiento, m. retouching, retouchment.

retocar, va. (for mut. v. TOCAR) to retouch; to touch up, finish.

retoñar, retoñecer, vn. to sprout; to reappear.

retoño, m. sprout, shoot, tiller, sucker.

retoque, m. retouch; finishing touch; repeated and frequent pulsation; touch (of a disease).

retor, m. twilled cotton fabric.

retorcedura, f. twisting, wreathing.

retorcer. I. va. (for irr. v. TORCER) to twist; to contort, convolve; to retort, reargue; to distort, twist, misconstrue. II. vr. to wring, writhe, squirm.

retorcido. I. pp. & a. twisted. II. m. tutti-frutti, sweetmeat.

retorcimiento, m. twisting; writhing.

retórica, f. rhetoric.—pl. (coll.) sophistries, quibbles, subtleties.—**retóricamente,** adv. rhetoric-

ally.—**retórico, ca.** I. a. rhetorical. II. m. rhetorician.

retornamiento, m. return.

retornante, a. returning.

retornar. I. vn. to return, come back; to recede, retrograde. II. va. to return; to give back; to turn, twist, contort; to cause to go back.

retornelo, m. ritornello, burden of a song.

retorno, m. return, coming back; home trip; return chaise or horse; repayment, requital; barter, exchange, traffic; (naut.) leading block.—**de r.,** return (u. a.).

retorsión, f. retortion; retorsion, retort; twisting.

retorsivo, va, a. containing retort; bending back.

retorta, f. a twilled linen fabric; (chem.) retort.

retortero, m. twirl, rotation.—**andar al r.,** to hover about.—**traer al r.,** (coll.) to twist one around, to deceive with false promises.

retortijar, va. to twist, to curl.

retortijón, m. curlicue; twisting, twist; cramp.—**r. de tripas,** griping cramp.

retostado, da, a. & pp. brown-colored.

retostar, va. (for irr. v. TOSTAR) to toast again, toast brown.

retozador, ra, a. frisky, frolicsome, pranky.

retozadura, f. = RETOZO.

retozar, vn. to frisk and skip about, romp, frolic, gambol; to be violently aroused, to become inflamed (s. o. passion).

retozo, m. frisk, gambol, prank, frolic.—**r. de la risa,** giggle, titter.

retozón, na, a. rompish, frolicsome, coltish.

retracción, f. retraction, drawing back.

retractable, a. retractable.

retractación, f. retractation, recantation.

retractar, va. & vr. to retract, to recant; (law) to redeem.

retráctil, a. retractile.

retractilidad, f. retractility.

retracto, m. (law) right of redemption.

retractor, m. (surg.) retractor.

retraer. I. va. (for irr. v. TRAER) to dissuade; (law) to redeem. II. vr. to take refuge or shelter; to withdraw from, shun; to keep aloof, retire; to live a retired life.

retraído, da. I. pp. & n. refugee; lover of solitude. II. a. of a retired disposition; incommunicative.

retraimiento, m. seclusion, retirement; retreat, refuge, asylum; private room, sanctum; incommunicativeness.

retranca, f. broad crupper of a packsaddle; (Cuba, Mex., r. w.) brake.

retranquear, va. to hoist, move, and set down (building blocks, etc.).—**retranqueo,** m. (arch.) setting blocks or stones in position.

retranquero, m. (Mex., Cuba, r. w.) brakeman.

retrasar. I. va. to defer, put off, delay; to set back. II. vn. to retrograde, go back, decline. III. vr. to be backward, behindhand, late, behind time.

retraso, m. delay, backwardness, slowness.

retratable, a. retractable, retractible.

retratación, f. retractation, recantation.

retratador, ra, n. = RETRATISTA.

retratar. I. va. to portray, draw a portrait of; to imitate, copy; to paint, describe; to depict; to photograph; RETRATAR. II. vr. to be reflected; to be depicted, show; to sit for a portrait or photograph.

retratista, n. portrait painter; photographer.

retrato, m. portrait, picture; photograph; copy, resemblance; description; (law) RETRACTO.

retrayente, n. & a. retractor (-ing), recanter (-ing); (law) redeemer (-ing).

retrechar, vn. to back, move backward.

retrechería, f. (coll.) cunning, evasion.

retrechero, ra, a. (coll.) cunningly evasive; attractive, charming, winsome.

retrepado, da, a. leaning or slanting backward.

retreparse, vr. to lean back; to recline in a chair.

retreta, *f.* (mil.) retreat; tatoo; evening military parade; (Colomb.) open-air concert by a military band in honor of a public dignitary.

retrete, *m.* private room, sanctum; alcove, boudoir; closet, toilet room, water-closet, privy.

retribución, *f.* retribution; recompense, fee.

retribuir, *va.* to remunerate, reward, fee.

retribuyente, *a.* retributive, retributing.

retrillar, *va.* (agr.) to thrash again.

retroactividad, *f.* retroactivity.

retroactivo, va, *a.* retroactive.

retrocarga, *f.*—**de r.,** breech-loading.

retroceder, *vn.* to go back, move backward, fall back, draw back; to recede; to become worse.

retrocesión, *f.* backward motion; (law) retrocession.

retroceso, *m.* backward motion; (med.) aggravation; in billiards, draw.

retrogradación, *f.* (ast.) retrogradation, retrogression.

retrogradar, *vn.* to recede; (ast.) to retrograde.

retrógrado, da, *a.* retrogressive; (pol.) reactionary; (ast.) retrograde.

retronar, *vn.* (*for irr. v.* TRONAR) to thunder, make a thundering noise.

retropilastra, *f.* pilaster behind a column.

retrospectivo, va, *a.* retrospective.

retrotracción, *f.* (law) antedating.

retrotraer, *va.* (*for irr. v.* TRAER) (law) to antedate, date back.

retrovendendo.—contrato de r., (law) reversion sale.

retrovender, *va.* (law); to sell back to the vender. —**retrovendición,** *f.* (law) selling back to the vender.—**retroventa,** *f.* (law) sale on reversion.

retrucar, *vn.* (*pret.* RETRUQUÉ: *subj.* RETRUQUE) in billiards, to kiss.

retruco, *m.* in billiards, kiss.

retruécano, *m.* pun, play upon words; antithesis, contrast.

retruque, *m.* = RETRUCO.

retumbante, *a.* resonant, resounding; pompous, bombastic, high-flown.

retumbar, *vn.* to resound, sound loudly.

retumbo, *m.* resonance, loud noise, echo.

retundir, *va.* (mas.) to even (the stones of a wall); to repel.

reuma. I. *m.* (med.) rheumatism. **II.** *f.* gathering; rheum, defluxion.—**reumático, ca,** *a.* rheumatic.—**reumátide,** *f.* (med.) rheumides.

reumatismo, *m.* rheumatism.

reunión, *f.* union; meeting, gathering, assembly; consolidation.

reunir. I. *va.* to unite; to gather; to collect, accumulate; to join; to reconcile. **II.** *vr.* to join, to unite; to meet, get together, assemble.

reuntar, *va.* to oil or grease again.

revacunación, *f.* (med.) revaccination.

revacunar, *va.* to revaccinate.

reválida, *f.* admission into a higher faculty.

revalidación, *f.* confirmation, ratification.

revalidar. I. *va.* to ratify, confirm. **II.** *vr.* to be admitted into a higher faculty.

revecero, ra. I. *a.* shiftable. **II.** *n.* farmhand who tends relays of oxen.

reveedor, ra, *n.* = REVISOR.

revejecer, *vn.* & *vr.* (*for irr. v.* ENVEJECER) to grow prematurely old.

revejecido, da; revejido, da, *a.* & *pp.* prematurely old.

revelación, *f.* revelation.

revelador, ra. I. *n.* & *a.* revealer (-ing). **II.** *m.* (photo.) developer.

revelamiento, *m.* REVELACIÓN; (photo.) development.

revelandero, ra, *n.* one who pretends to have had a divine revelation.

revelante, *a.* revealing.

revelar, *va.* to reveal; (photo.) to develop.

reveler, *va.* (med.) to cause revulsion to.

revellín, *m.* (fort.) ravelin.

revenar, *vn.* to sprout.

revendedera, *f.* = REVENDEDORA.

revendedor, ra, *n.* retailer; ticket speculator.

revender, *va.* to resell; to retail.

revenimiento, *m.* (min.) cave-in.

revenirse, *vr.* (*for irr. v.* VENIR) to shrink, waste away; to turn, grow sour, ferment (as wine and preserves); to exude; to yield, concede, assent.

reveno, *m.* sprout, shoot.

reventa, *f.* resale; retail.

reventadero, *m.* rough ground; drudgery.

reventar. I. *vn.* (*ind.* REVIENTO: *subj.* REVIENTE) to burst; to blow up, blow out; to break; to splash (as waves); to burst forth, break loose (as a passion); to sprout, shoot, blossom; to long, to crave.—**r. de risa,** to burst with laughter. **II.** *va.* to burst; to break; to crush, smash; to wind (a horse); to tire, fatigue, exhaust; to vex, annoy. **III.** *vr.* to burst; to blow up, blow out; to break.

reventazón, *f.* bursting; blowout; disruption, rupture; (naut.) splash, dashing of the waves.

reventón. I. *a.* bursting. **II.** *m.* bursting, blowout, explosion; steep declivity; toil, drudgery, uphill work.

rever, *va.* to review, revise, look over again; (law) to retry.

reverberación, *f.* reverberation; (chem.) calcination in a reverberatory furnace.

reverberar, *vn.* to reverberate.

reverbero, *m.* reverberation; reverberator, reflector.

reverdecer, *vn.* (*for irr. v.* VERDECER) to grow green again; to sprout again; to acquire new freshness and vigor.

reverdeciente, *a.* growing fresh and green.

reverencia, *f.* reverence; courtesy, bow, obeisance; (eccl.) reverence (title).

reverenciable, *a.* reverend.—**reverenciador, ra,** *n.* reverencer.—**reverencial,** *a.* reverential.

reverenciar, *va.* to venerate, revere; to hallow; to reverence.

reverendísimo, ma, *a. sup.* Most Reverend, Right Reverend.

reverendo, da, *a.* reverend; worthy of reverence. —**reverendas,** *f. pl.* prelate's dimissory letters; qualities and titles worthy of reverence.

reverente, *a.* reverent.—**reverentemente,** *adv.* reverently.

reversible, *a.* (law) returnable, revertible; (phys.) reversible.

reversibilidad, *f.* reversibility.

reversión, *f.* reversion.

reverso, m. reverse (in coins); back, rear side.—**el r. de la medalla,** the opposite in every respect.

reverter, *vn.* (*for irr. v.* VERTER) to overflow.

revertir, *vn.* (law) to revert.

revés, *m.* reverse, back, wrong side; slap, box; back stroke, counterstroke; misfortune, reverse; change of temper and disposition; (fenc.) reverse.—**r. de la medalla.** *V.* REVERSO.—**al r.,** on the contrary, contrarywise; in the opposite or wrong way or direction; wrong side out.—**de r.,** diagonally, from left to right.—**del r.** = AL R.

revesa, *f.* (naut.) back water, eddy.

revesado, da, *pp.* & *a.* entangled, complicated, laborious, obscure; mischievous, wayward.

revesar, *va.* to vomit.

revesino, m. reversis, game at cards.—**cortar el r.,** to thwart.

revestimiento, *m.* (mas.) coating, coat.

revestir. I. *va.* (*for irr. v.* VESTIR) to dress, clothe; (mas.) to coat, cover with a coating, revet. **II.** *vr.* to be swayed or carried along by some power; to be invested with; to be haughty, lofty, proud.

revezar, *vn.* to alternate, work in rotation or by shifts.

revezo, *m.* shift, turn; gang; relay.

reviejo, ja. I. *a.* very old. **II.** *m.* withered branch of a tree.

reviernes, *m.* each of the first seven Fridays after Easter.

revirado, da, *a.* (bot.) twisted.

revirar, *va.* (naut.) to veer again, retack.

revisar, *va.* to revise, review, examine.—**r. las cuentas,** to audit accounts.

revisión, *f.* revision, revisal, revise, reviewing; new trial or hearing.

revisita, *f.* reinspection.

revisor, *.n.* reviser, censor, corrector; overseer; auditor.

revisoría, *f.* office of censor or reviser.

revista, *f.* review, revision, revisal, revise; reinspection, reëxamination; (law) new trial; (mil.) review, parade; muster; (print.) review, magazine, journal; (theat.) revue.—**pasar r.,** to review; to examine, go over.—**suplicar en r.,** (law) to present a bill of review.

revistar, *va.* to review, inspect.

revisto, ta, *pp. irr.* of REVER.

revividero, *m.* place for rearing silkworms.

revivificar, *va.* to revivify.

revivir, *vn.* to revive.

revocable, *a.* revocable, reversible, repealable.

revocablemente, *adv.* in a revocable manner.

revocación, *f.* revocation; abrogation.—**r. de una sentencia,** (law) reversal.

revocador, ra. **I.** *a.* revoking, cancelling. **II.** *n.* revoker; plasterer, whitewasher.

revocadura, *f.* REVOQUE; (art) edge of the canvas turned over the stretcher.

revocante, *a.* revoking, abrogating.

revocar, *va.* (pret. REVOQUÉ: *subj.* REVOQUE) to revoke, repeal, reverse; to countermand; to dissuade; to repel, push back; to plaster.

revocatorio, ria, *a.* revocatory, repealing.

revoco, *m.* REVOQUE; drawing or driving back; cover of furze on charcoal baskets.

revolante, *a.* fluttering, hovering.

revolar, *vn.* to fly around, hover, flutter.

revolcadero, *m.* weltering or wallowing place for beasts.

revolcadura, *f.* weltering, wallowing.

revolcar. **I.** *va.* (for irr. *v.* VOLCAR) to knock down, tread or trample upon; (coll.) to floor (an opponent). **II.** *vr.* to wallow, welter; to be stubborn.

revolcón, *m.* (coll.) = REVUELCO.

revolear, *vn.* to fly around.

revolotear. **I.** *vn.* to flutter, fly round about, hover. **II.** *va.* to hurl, fling, pitch.

revoloteo, *m.* fluttering; hovering.

revoltijo, revoltillo, *m.* mess, mass, medley, jumble; twisted tripes of a sheep.—**r. de huevos,** scrambled eggs.

revoltón, *m.* vine fretter, vine grub.

revoltoso, sa, *a.* turbulent, seditious; mischievous, prankish.

revoltura, *f.* (min.) mixture of fluxes.

revolución, *f.* revolution; (mech., astr.) revolution, turn.

revolucionar, *va.* to revolutionize. **II.** *vr.* to rebel, rise as revolutionists.

revolucionario, ria. **I.** *a.* revolutionary. **II.** *n.* revolutionist.

revolvedero, *m.* coursing place.

revolvedor, ra. **I.** *a.* turbulent, seditious, rebellious. **II.** *n.* revolter, disturber, agitator.

revólver, *m.* revolver (pistol).

revolver. **I.** *a.* (for *irr. v.* VOLVER) to turn over, turn upside down; to stir, agitate; to wrap up, convolve; to revolve, turn round, gyrate; retrace (one's steps), go over (the same ground); turn over in one's mind; turn short swiftly (as a horse); to estrange, create bad feeling in or between. **II.** *vr.* to move to and fro; to change (as the weather).

revolvimiento, *m.* commotion, disturbance, revolution.

revoque, *m.* plastering; whitewashing.

revotarse, *vr.* to reconsider a ballot.

revuelco, *m.* wallowing, rolling.

revuelo, *m.* second flight of a bird, gyration described when flying; irregular motion; disturbance.—**de r.,** by the way; speedily, promptly.

revuelta, *f.* second turn; revolution, revolt; contention, dissension; turn, deviation, winding; change.

revueltamente, *adv.* confusedly, pell-mell, higgledy-piggledy.

revuelto, ta, *a.* & *pp. irr.* of REVOLVER; easily turned (horse); restless, mischievous; boisterous; intricate, difficult.

revuelvepiedras, *m.* (orn.) turnstone.

revulsión, *f.* (med.) revulsion of humors.

revulsivo, va; revulsorio, ria, *a.* & *m.* revulsive.

rey, *m.* king; king in cards or chess; step in a Spanish dance; queen bee; chief among men or animals.—**r. de armas,** (her.) king at arms.—**los Reyes,** Epiphany, Twelfth-night.—**los reyes magos,** the wise men from the East.—**ni r. ni roque,** no one.—**no tener ni r. ni roque,** not to fear, or bow to, anything nor anybody, to have no master.

reyerta, *f.* dispute, wrangle, quarrel.

reyezuelo, *m.* petty king; (orn.) kinglet.

rezado, *pp.* & *m.* prayer; divine service.

rezador, ra, *n.* one who prays often.

rezagado, da, *pp.* & *n.* straggler, laggard, tramp.

rezagante, *n.* laggard, straggler.

rezagar. **I.** *va.* (pret. REZAGUÉ: *subj.* REZAGUE) to leave behind; to outstrip; to put off, defer. **II.** *vr.* to fall behind, to lag.

rezago, *m.* remainder, left-over.

rezar. **I.** *va.* to say as a prayer; to say (a prayer); to say (mass); to say, state (el libro lo reza, the book says it). **II.** *vn.* to pray; to say, read (el párrafo reza así, the paragraph reads thus); to grumble, mutter.—**r. con,** to concern, be the business or duty of.

rezno, *m.* tick, sheep tick, dog tick.

rezo, *m.* prayer; praying, devotions.

rezón, *m.* (naut.) grapnel, grappling iron.

rezongador, ra, *n.* grumbler, growler, mutterer.

rezongar, *vn.* (pret. REZONGUÉ: *subj.* REZONGUE) to grumble, mutter, growl.

rezonglón, na; rezongón, na, *n.* grumbler, mutterer, growler.

rezumadero, *m.* dripping place; cesspool.

rezumarse, *vr.* to ooze, exude, percolate, filter through; (coll.) to transpire.

ría, *f.* estuary.

riacho, riachuelo, riatillo, *m.* rivulet, streamlet; small river.

riada, *f.* freshet, flood.

riba, *f.* sloping bank, embankment.

ribadoquín, *m.* an ancient small gun.

ribaldería, *f.* knavishness, rascality.

ribaldo, da. **I.** *a.* villainous, knavish. **II.** *n.* ruffian.

ribazo, *m.* sloping bank; mound, hillock.

ribera, *f.* shore, beach, bank, strand.

ribereño, ña, *a.* riparian, riparious.

riberiego, ga. **I.** *a.* riparious (as flocks of sheep). **II.** *m.* grazier of sheep on river banks.

ribero, *m.* river wall, levee.

ribes, *f.* (bot.) currant bush.

ribete, *m.* (sew.) binding, galloon; trimming; pretence; addition to a tale, for embellishment.

ribeteador, ra, *n.* (sew.) binder.

ribetear, *va.* (sew.) to bind.

ricacho, cha; chón, na, *a.* (coll.) very rich.

ricadueña, ricahembra, *f.* lady, daughter or wife of a noble.

ricahombría, *f.* dignity of the ancient nobility of Castile.

ricamente, *adv.* richly, opulently; excellently, splendidly.

ricial, *a.* green (field) or new (pasture).

ricino, *m.* (bot.) palma Christi, castor-oil plant.

rico, ca, *a.* rich, wealthy; abundant, plentiful; delicious, exquisite, choice.

ricohombre, ricohome, *m.* grandee, peer of the ancient nobility of Castile.

richembra, *f.* = RICADUEÑA.

For pronunciation, see the rules at the beginning of the book.

ridículamente, *adv.* ridiculously.

ridiculez, *f.* ridiculous thing or action; ridiculousness; ridicule; folly, oddity, eccentricity; extreme nicety or sensibility.

ridiculizar, *va.* (*pret.* RIDICULICÉ: *subj.* RIDICULICE) to ridicule.

ridículo, la. I. *a.* ridiculous; odd, eccentric, queer, outlandish, contemptible; absurd.—**en r.,** in a ridiculous situation, exposed to ridicule.—**poner en r.,** to ridicule, expose to ridicule, make ridiculous.—**ponerse en r., quedar en r.,** to make one's self ridiculous. **II.** *m.* ridicule; hand bag, reticule.

riego, *m.* irrigation; watering.

riego, riegue. *V.* REGAR.

riel, *m.* ingot; (r. w.) rail.

rielado, da, *pp.* & *a.* reduced to ingots.

rielar, *vn.* to glisten, glimmer, shine.

rielera, *f.* (found.) ingot mold.

rienda, *f.* rein of a bridle; moderation, restraint. —*pl.* reins, ribbons; government, direction.—**a r. suelta,** loose-reined; violently, swiftly; without restriction.—**soltar la r.,** to give way to vice or passions.—**tener las riendas,** to hold the reins, to hold back a horse.—**tirar las riendas,** to draw back, to restrain.

riente, *a.* smiling, laughing.

riesgo, *m.* danger, risk, hazard, peril.

rifa, *f.* raffle; scuffle, wrangle.

rifador, ra, *n.* raffler.

rifadura, *f.* (naut.) splitting a sail.

rifar. I. *va.* to raffle. **II.** *vn.* to quarrel; to split (s. o. a sail).

rifeño, ña, *n.* & *a.* Riffian (from the Riff, in Morocco).

rifirrafe, *m.* (coll.) short quarrel, hasty words.

rifle, *m.* (arti.) rifle.

rigente, *a.* (poet.) rigid, rigescent.

rígidamente, *adv.* rigidly.

rigidez, rigidity; sternness.—**r. cadavérica,** cadaveric rigidity.

rígido, da, *a.* rigid, stiff; rigorous, inflexible.

rigodón, *m.* (danc.) rigadoon; quadrille.

rigor, *m.* rigor; sternness; (med.) rigidity; chill.— **r. cadavérico,** rigor mortis, cadaveric rigidity.— **de r.,** indispensable; prescribed by the rules.—**en r., or en r. de verdad,** strictly speaking, in fact.

rigorismo, *m.* rigorism, austerity, severity.

rigorista, *m.* & *a.* rigorist (-ic).

rigorosamente, *adv.* rigorously; strictly, scrupulously.

rigoroso, sa; riguroso, sa, *a.* rigorous; exact; absolute; strict, austere; severe, harsh; scrupulously nice.

rigurosamente, = RIGOROSAMENTE.

rigurosidad, *f.* rigorousness; severity.

rija, *f.* (med.) lachrymal fistula; quarrel, scuffle, dispute.

rijador, ra, *a.* quarrelsome.

rijo, *m.* concupiscence, lust, sensuality.

rijo, rija. *V.* REGIR.

rijoso, sa, *a.* quarrelsome; lustful, lewd; restless at the sight of the female (s. o. horses).

rima, *f.* heap, pile; (poet.) rhyme.—*pl.* lyric poems.—**r. imperfecta,** (poet.) assonance.

rimado, da, *a.* & *pp.* versified.

rimador, ra, *n.* versifier, rhymer.

rimar, *vn.* to rhyme; to make verses.

rimbombancia, *f.* resonance, great noise; rant, bombast, ostentation.

rimbombante, *a.* resounding; bombastic, high-sounding, ranting.

rimbombar, *vn.* to resound, to echo.

rimbombe, rimbombo, *m.* repercussion of sound.

rimero, *m.* heap, pile.

rincón, *m.* corner, angle, nook; cosey corner; lurking place; (coll.) house, dwelling; remote place.

rinconada, *f.* corner.

rinconcillo, *m.* *dim.* small corner.

rinconero, ra. I. *a.* transverse, athwart (honeycombs). **II.** *f.* corner cupboard, stand, bracket.

rinda, rindo, él rindió. *V.* RENDIR.

ringla, *f.,* **ringle,** *m.,* **ringlera,** *f.* (coll.) row, file, line, tier; swath.

ringlero, *m.* line or rule for writing exercises.

ringorrangos, *m. pl.* (coll.) flourish with a pen; frills, fripperies.

rinoceronte, *m.* rhinoceros.

rinoplastia, *f.* (surg.) rhinoplasty.

rinoscopia, *f.* (med.) rhinoscopy.

riña, *f.* quarrel, scuffle, dispute, fray.

riño, riña, él riñó. *V.* REÑIR.

riñón, *m.* (anat.) kidney; (arch.) spandrel; (min.) nodule, kidney ore; central part of a country.— **tener cubierto el r.,** to be rich, to be well off.

riñonada, *f.* coat of fat about the kidneys; dish of kidneys.

río, *m.* river.—**r. de lágrimas,** flood of tears.—**a r. revuelto,** in confusion or disorder.—**cuando el r. suena, agua lleva, or piedras lleva,** where there is so much smoke there must be some fire.

río, yo ría. *V.* REÍR.

riblada, *f.* (coll.) concourse, affluence.

riostra, *f.* stay, brace.—**riostrar,** *va.* to brace, stay.

ripia, *f.* shingle, for roofing.

ripiar, *va.* (mas.) to riprap.

ripio, *m.* debris, rubbish, riprap; padding, useless words; verbiage.—**no perder r.,** not to miss the least occasion.

riqueza, *f.* riches, wealth; richness, excellence; abundance; fertility, fruitfulness; gorgeousness.

risa, *f.* laugh, laughter; derisory smile or laugh.— **r. sardónica,** sardonic laugh, grin, sneer.—**caerse, descalzarse, descoyuntarse, desternillarse, or reventar, de r.,** to burst, or hold one's sides, with laughter.

risada, *f.* horselaugh.

riscal, *m.* cliffy, craggy place.

risco, *m.* crag, cliff; honey fritter.

riscoso, sa, *a.* cliffy, craggy.

risibilidad, *f.* risibility.

risible, *a.* laughable, ludicrous.

risica, illa, ita, *f. dim.* feigned laugh; giggle, titter.

riso, *m.* (poet.) gentle laugh.

risotada, *f.* outburst of laughter, loud laugh, horselaugh.

ríspido, da, *a.* = ÁSPERO.

ristra, *f.* string of onions or garlic; bunch; row, file, string.

ristre, *m.* rest or socket for a lance.

ristrel, *m.* (arch.) wooden moulding.

risueño, ña, *a.* smiling; pleasing, agreeable.

¡rita! *f.* word used to call sheep.

rítmico, ca, *a.* rhythmic.—**ritmo,** *m.* rhythm.

rito, *m.* rite, ceremony.—**ritual. I.** *m.* (eccl.) ritual, ceremonial. **II.** *a.* ritual.—**ritualidad,** *f.* ritualism.—**ritualismo,** *m.* ritualism.—**ritualista,** *n.* & *a.* ritualist (-ic).

rival, *m.* rival.—**rivalidad,** *f.* rivalry.

rivalizar, *vn.* (*pret.* RIVALICÉ: *subj.* RIVALICE) to rival, vie, compete.

rivera, *f.* brook, creek, stream.

riza, *f.* green stubble; ravage, destruction.

rizado, pp. & *m.* fluting, crimp, frizzle.

rizador, ra. I. *n.* & *a.* crimper (-ing), frizzler (-ing). **II.** *m.* curling iron; (sew.) ruffler.

rizal, *a.* = RICIAL.

rizar. I. *va.* (*pret.* RICÉ: *subj.* RICE) to curl, frizzle, crimp, flute, ruffle, corrugate, crinkle; to ripple (water). **II.** *vr.* to curl naturally.

rizo, za. I. *a.* naturally curled or frizzled. **II.** *m.* curl, frizzle, ringlet; cut velvet.—*pl.* (naut.) reef points.—**hacer el r.,** (aer., coll.) to loop the loop.—**tomar rizos,** to take in reefs.

rizocárpeo, a, *a.* (bot.) rhizocarpous.

rizófago, ga, *a.* (zool.) rhizophagous, root-eating.

rizofóreo, a. I. *a.* (bot.) rhizophoraceous. **II.** *f. pl.* Rhizophoraceæ, mangroves.

rizoma, *m.* (bot.) rhizome.

rizópodo, da, *n.* & *a.* (zool.) rhizopod.—*m. pl.* Rhizopoda, rhizopods.

rizoso, sa, *a.* naturally curly.

ro, ro, *interj.* used as a lullaby.

roa, *f.* (naut.) stem. *V.* RODA.

roano, na, *a.* sorrel, roan (horse).

rob, *m.* (pharm.) rob; fruit jelly.

robada, *f.* a land measure (about 9 ares).

robadera, *f.* (agr.) levelling harrow.

robador, ra, *n.* robber.

robaliza, *f.* (icht.) female robalo.

róbalo, robalo, *m.* (icht.) robalo; (com.) haddock.

robar, *va., vn. & vr.* to rob, plunder, steal; rob of (*Juan me robó el reloj*, John robbed me of my watch); to abduct; to kidnap; to sweep or eat away (as banks by a stream); in some games, to draw (a card); (api.) to take (the honeycomb) after removing the bees.

robda, *f.* ancient pasturage fee.

robezo, *m.* (zool.) wild goat.

robín, *m.* rust of metal.

robinia, *f.* (bot.) locust tree.

robla, *f.* = ROBDA.

robladero, ra, *a.* fit for riveting.

robladura, *f.* riveting, clinching.

roblar, *va.* to rivet, clinch; make strong.

roble, *m.* oak; very strong person or thing.

robledal, robledo, *m.* oak grove or wood.

roblizo, za, *a.* oaken, strong, hard.

roblón, *m.* rivet; ridge of tiles.—**roblonado,** *m.,* **roblonadura,** *f.* riveting.

roblonar, *va. & vn.* to rivet.

robo, *m.* robbery, theft; plunder; cards drawn; drawing of cards; a dry measure (about 28 liters).

roboración, *f.* corroboration, strengthening.

roborante, *a.* strengthening, corroborating, or confirming; (med.) roborant.

roborar, *va.* to strengthen, make firm; to corroborate.

roborativo, va, *a.* corroborative.

robra, *f.* = ALBOROQUE.

robre, robredo, *m.* = ROBLE, ROBLEDAL.

robustamente, *adv.* robustly.—**robustecedor, ra,** *a.* strengthening, building-up.—**robustecer,** *va.* to make strong.—**robustez,** *f.* robustness, hardiness.—**robusto, ta,** *a.* robust, vigorous, hale.

roca, *f.* (geol.) rock; cliff.

rocadero, *m.* knob, rock or head of a distaff.

rocador, *m.* head of a distaff.

rocalla, *f.* drift of pebbles, talus of rocks; chippings of stone, riprap; glass beads.

rocalloso, sa, *a.* rocky.

roce, *m.* friction, rubbing, attrition; intercourse.

rociada, *f.* sprinkling, aspersion; (naut.) spray, splash; squall; dew on plants; dew-drenched herbs given to animals as medicine; shower of missiles; slander, aspersion; rough reprimand, dressing down.

rociadera, *f.* = REGADERA.—**rociado, da,** *pp. & a.* dewy; bedewed.—**rociador,** *m.* sprinkler, sprayer; cloth sprinkler.—**rociadura,** *f.* = ROCIADA.—**rociamiento,** *m.* bedewing.

rociar. I. *vn.* to fall in dew. **II.** *va.* to sprinkle, to spray; to strew about.

rocín, *m.* hack, jade, sorry horse; coarse, ignorant man.—**rocinal,** *a.* belonging to a hack horse.— **rocinante,** *m.,* **rocino,** *m.* = ROCÍN.

rocío, *m.* dew; spray, sprinkle, sprinkling; mizzle; drizzle; light shower; (naut.) spoondrift.

rocha, *f.* ground clear of brambles.

rochela, *f.* (Colomb., Ven.) great noise, racket.

rocho, *m.* roc, a fabulous bird.

roda, *f.* (naut.) stem; ROBDA.

rodaballo, *m.* (icht.) turbot, flounder.

rodada, *f.* rut, wheel track, cart track.

rodadero, ra, *a.* rolling easily.

rodadizo, za, *a.* that rolls or slides easily.

rodado, da. I. *pp. & a.* dapple, dappled (horse); rounded, fluent, easy (period); scattered (ore fragments).—**venir r.,** to come unexpectedly. **II.** *m.* (Arg.) vehicle.

rodador, ra. I. *a.* rolling, rolling down. **II.** *m.* roller; kind of mosquito; (icht.) sunfish.

rodadura, *f.* rolling, wheeling; rut; tread (of a wheel).

rodaja, *f.* small wheel or disk; caster, trundle, truckle; rowel; jagging iron used by pastry cooks; bookbinder's tool.

rodaje, *m.* wheelworks; set of wheels.

rodajuela, *f. dim.* small wheel, disk, or caster.

rodal, *m.* place, spot, seat.

rodante, *a.* rolling.—**material r.,** rolling stock.

rodapelo, *m.* = REDOPELO.

rodapié, *m.* (arch.) mopboard, skirting; dado; foot rail.

rodaplancha, *f.* main ward of a key.

rodar, *vn.* (ind. RUEDO: subj. RUEDE) to roll, revolve, wheel; to run on wheels; to wander about; be tossed about, go about, go up and down; to lose an employ, station, dignity, or esteem; to abound; to happen accidentally; to follow, succeed one another.—**r. por,** to serve, help to the limit.—**dejar r.,** or **que ruede, la bola,** to let things alone, to let things follow their natural course.

rodeabrazo.—a r., swinging the a.m for a throw.

rodeado, da, *a. & pp.* surrounded, encircled.

rodeador, ra, *n.* one who surrounds.

rodear. I. *va. & vn.* to surround, encircle, encompass; (mil.) to invest; (Am.) to round up, gather (cattle) in a rodeo. **II.** *vn.* to go around; to make a detour, go by a longer road; to beat about the bush.

rodela, *f.* buckler, round shield.

rodelero, *m.* soldier bearing a buckler.

rodenal, *m.* clump of red pines.

rodeno, na, *a.* red, reddish (s. o. rocks and trees).

rodeo, *m.* turn, winding; roundabout course, method or way; round-up, rodeo; inclosure for cattle, stockyard, corral; circumlocution, beating about the bush; evasion, subterfuge.

rodeón, *m.* complete turn.

rodero, ra. I. *a.* relating to wheels. **II.** *n.* collector of pasturage fee. **III.** *f.* rut, cart track.

rodete, *m.* roundlet or rowel of platted hair; (hyd.) horizontal water wheel; (car.) fifth wheel, circle iron; ward in a lock; padded ring for carrying things on the head; (mech.) drum for a belt or endless chain.

rodezno, *m.* (hyd.) horizontal water wheel. (mil.) cogwheel.

rodezuela, *f. dim.* small wheel.

rodilla, *f.* (anat.) knee; ward in a lock; clout, dusting cloth.—*pl.* (naut.) knees of ship timber. —**a media r.,** kneeling on one knee.—**de rodillas,** on one's knees.—**doblar, or hincar, las rodillas,** to kneel down.

rodillada, *f.* push with the knee; kneeling position.

rodillazo, *m.* push or blow with the knee.

rodillera, *f.* knee boss, knee guard; knee patch; hurt upon the knees of horses from kneeling; bagging of trousers at the knee.

rodillero, ra, *a.* belonging to the knees.

rodillo, *m.* roll, roller; clod crusher, road roller; (print.) inking roller, brayer; (cook.) rolling pin; (mech.) roller, drum, trundle, barrel.

rodilludo, da, *a.* having large knees.

rodio, *m.* (chem.) rhodium.

rodio, dia, *m. & a.* Rhodian.

rodo, *m.* roller.—**a r.,** in plenty.

rododafne, *f.* (bot.) rosebay, daphne.

rododendro, *m.* (bot.) rhododendron.

rodoficeo, a. I. *a.* (bot.) rhodophyceous. **II.** *f. pl.* Rhodophyceæ.

rodomiel, *m.* juice of roses with honey.

rodrigar, *va.* (for mut. v. ABRIGAR) to prop up (vines).

rodrigazón, *f.* time for propping vines.

rodrigón, *m.* vine prop; (coll.) old servant who escorts ladies.

roedor, ra. I. *a.* gnawing; pricking, stinging; detracting. **II.** *n. & a.* (zool.) rodent.

roedura, *f.* gnawing, corrosion.

roel, *m.* (her.) bezant, round.

roela, *f.* button of crude gold or silver.

roer, *va.* & *defec.* (*gerund,* ROYENDO: *ind.* ROO: *pret.* él ROYÓ: *subj.* ROA) to gnaw, eat, fret away; to corrode; to pick (a bone); to harass, annoy.

roete, *m.* medicinal pomegranate wine.

rogación, *f.* request, petition.—*pl.* (eccl.) rogation.

rogador, ra, *n.* supplicant, petitioner.

rogante, *a.* praying, requesting, entreating.

rogar, *va.* (*ind.* RUEGO: *pret.* ROGUÉ: *subj.* RUEGUE) to pray, request, beg, entreat; to crave, court.

rogativa, *f.* (eccl.) rogation.—**rogativo, va,** *a.* supplicatory.—**rogatorio, ria,** *a.* rogatory.

rogo, *m.* (poet.) fire, pyre.

roído, *a.* & *pp.* gnawed; penurious.

rojeante, *a.* reddening.—**rojear,** *vn.* to redden; to blush.—**rojete,** *m.* rouge for the face.—**rojez,** *f.* redness, ruddiness.

rojizo, za, *a.* reddish; rubicund, ruddy.

rojo, ja, *a.* red; ruddy, reddish.—**r. alambrado,** bright red.—**al r.,** at, or to, red heat.

rojura, *f.* redness; ruddiness.

rol, *m.* list, roll, catalogue; muster roll.

rolar, *vn.* (naut.) to veer around.

roldana, *f.* sheave, pulley wheel; caster.

rolde, *m.* circle, group of people.

rolla, *f.* collar of a draught horse; nurse.

rollar, *va.* = ARROLLAR.

rollete, *m. dim.* small roll or roller.

rollizo, za. I. *a.* plump, stocky, heavy-built, sturdy. **II.** *m.* log.

rollo, *m.* roll, anything rolled up; rouleau; roller, rolling pin; log; round pillar; cylindrical bowlder; yoke pad; (law) roll.

rollón, *m.* fine bran.

rollona, *a.* (coll.) nurse.

Roma, *f.* Rome.—**a R. por todo,** at all hazards.

romadizarse, *vr.* to take cold.

romadizo, *m.* cold in the head; hay fever.

romaico, ca, *a.* & *n.* Romaic, modern Greek.

romana, *f.* steelyard.—**hacer r.,** to balance.—**venir a la r.,** to be of just weight.

romanador, *m.* weighmaster.

romanar, *va.* to weigh with a steelyard.

romance. I. *a.* & *m.* Romance or Romanic. **II** *m.* Spanish language; romance, tale of chivalry; historic ballad, brief lyric; poem in octosyllabic metre, with alternate assonants.—**en r.,** in plain English, or language.

romanceador, ra, *n.* one who writes in Romance. —**romancear,** *va.* to translate into Spanish; to periphrase.—**romancero, ra. I.** *n.* romancer. **II.** *m.* collection of old Spanish ballads.

romancesco, *a.* novelistic, romantic.

romancillo, *m. dim.* short ROMANCE.

romancista, *m.* romancist.

romanear. I. *va.* to weigh with a steelyard. **II.** *vn.* to outweigh, preponderate.

romaneo, *m.* weighing with a steelyard.

romanero, *m.* weighmaster.

romanesco, *a.* Roman; novelistic.

romanía.—de r., crestfallen.

románico, *a.* (arch.) Romanesque.

romanilla, *f.* (Ven.) dining-room screen.

romanillo, lla, *a.* round-hand.

romanista, *n.* one versed in Roman law or in Romance languages.

romanización, *f.* Romanization.

romanizar. I. *va.* to Romanize; to Latinize. **II.** *vr.* to become Romanized or Latinized.

romano, na, *n.* & *a.* Roman.

romanticismo, *m.* romanticism.

romántico, ca. I. *a.* romantic. **II.** *n.* romanticist.

romanza, *f.* (mus.) romance, romanza.

romanzador, ra, *n.* = ROMANCEADOR.

romanzar, *va.* = ROMANCEAR.

romaza, *f.* (bot.) sorrel.

rombal; rómbico, ca, *a.* rhombic.—**rombo,** *m.* (geom.) rhombus; lozenge, diamond.

romboedro, *m.* (geom.) rhombohedron.

romboidal, *a.* rhomboidal.—**romboide,** *m.* (geom.) rhomboid.

romeraje, *m.* = ROMERÍA.

romeral, *m.* place abounding with rosemary.

romería, *f.* pilgrimage; picnic, excursion; tour.

romero, ra. I. *n.* pilgrim, palmer. **II.** *m.* (bot.) rosemary; (icht.) pilot fish; (icht.) whiting.

romí, romín, *m.* bastard saffron.

romo, ma, *a.* obtuse, blunt; flat-nosed.

rompecabezas, *m.* slungshot; puzzle, riddle.

rompecoches, *m.* prunella, everlasting.

rompedera, *f.* large iron puncher; powder screen.

rompedero, ra, *a.* fragile, brittle, perishable.

rompedor, ra, *n.* & *a.* breaker (-ing); crusher (-ing).

rompedura, *f.* breakage.

rompeesquinas, *m.* corner loafer, bully.

rompegalas, *n.* (coll.) slovenly person.

rompehielos, *m.* ice breaker; ice plow (of a boat).

rompenueces, *m.* nut cracker.

rompeolas, *m.* breakwater, jetty, mole.

romper. I. *va.* & *vn.* (*pp.* ROTO) to break; rupture, shatter, fracture; smash, crash; tear; defeat, rout; break up (land); to pierce; to open the way; to break off; fall out, quarrel; dawn, break (s. o. the day); begin, start; to interrupt; resolve, determine; sprout, bloom; break out, spring up; to clear up; to violate, infringe, transgress.—**r. el alba, or la aurora** (here *el alba, la aurora* are subjects of the verb) to dawn.—**de rompe y rasga,** undaunted, brave, free and easy. **II.** *vr.* to break; to acquire ease of manner.—**r. el alma,** to break one's neck in a fall.

rompesacos, *m.* long-spiked hardgrass.

rompesquinas, *m.* = ROMPEESQUINAS.

rompible, *a.* breakable.

rompido. I. *m.* ground newly broken. **II.** *pp.* of ROMPER.

rompiente. I. *a.* breaking. **II.** *m.* reef, shoal.

rompimiento, *m.* break, breakage, smash, rupture; crack; breach, infringement, violation; falling out; (theat.) open drop scene; opening in the background (of a picture); (min.) drift, driftway; (agr.) breaking up land.

ron, *m.* rum.

ronca, *f.* cry of a buck in rutting time; braggadocio, bullying; a kind of halberd.

roncador, ra. I. *n.* & *a.* snorer (-ing). **II.** *m.* (icht.) roncador, little bass.

roncamente, *adv.* hoarsely, coarsely.

roncar, *vn.* (*pret.* RONQUÉ: *subj.* RONQUE) to snore; to roar; to cry in rutting time; (coll.) to brag, to bully.

ronce, *m.* wheedle, cajolery.

roncear, *vn.* to be slow and unwilling, kill time, fool around; to wheedle; (naut.) to sail slowly.

roncería, *f.* sluggishness, remissness; tardiness; wheedle, cajoling expression; (naut.) slow, sluggish sailing.

roncero, ra, *a.* slow, slothful, tardy; grouty, growling; flattering, wheedling, cajoling.

ronco, ca, *a.* hoarse, raucous.

roncón, *m.* drone of a bagpipe.

roncón, na, *n.* & *a.* (Colomb., fam.) boaster (-ing), braggart (-ing).

roncha, *f.* wheal, whelk, welt, wale; blotch; bump; loss of money by trickery; round slice.

ronchar. I. *va.* to crunch. **II.** *vn.* to raise wets.

ronchón, *m. aug.* large welt or bump.

ronda, *f.* night patrol; rounds (by a night watch), beat; clear space between a town and its walls; last round in a card game; round of drinks or cigars.

rondador, *m.* patrolman, roundsman, watchmen; rounder, night wanderer.

rondalla, *f.* fable, story, tale.

rondar, *va.* & *vn.* to patrol, go the rounds; to walk the streets by night; to haunt, hover about; to impend; (mil.) to make the grand rounds.—**r. la calle,** to flirt on the street.

rondel, *m.* (poet.) rondel.

rondeña, *f.* popular ballad of Ronda.

---

rondín, *m.* round of a corporal on the walls to visit the sentinels; watchman in an arsenal.

rondí, rondiz, *m.* (jewel.) base or face of a precious stone.

rondó, *m.* (mus.) rondo.

rondón.—de r., rashly, suddenly, abruptly; intrepidly.

rongigata, *f.* = REHILANDERA.

ronquear, *vn.* to be hoarse with cold.

ronquedad, ronquera, ronquez, *f.* hoarseness.

ronquido, *m.* snore; harsh, raucous sound.

ronronear, *vn.* to purr.

ronza, *f.*—**ir a la r.,** (naut.) to fall to leeward.

ronzal, *m.* halter; (naut.) purchase rope.

ronzar, *va.* to crunch, craunch; (naut.) to raise or shift with levers.

roña, *f.* scab (in sheep); crust of filth on persons; bark of pine trees; rust; moral infection.

roñada, *f.* (naut.) garland; dolphin of a mast.

roñal, *m.* bark depot or storage place.

roñería, *f.* (coll.) niggardliness, stinginess.

roñoso, sa, *a.* scabby, leprous; dirty, filthy; rusty; (coll.) niggardly, stingy.

ropa, *f.* dry goods; stuff, fabric; wearing apparel, clothes, clothing; costume, dress; wardrobe, outfit, garments; robe or gown of office.—**r. blanca,** linen.—**r. de cámara,** or **de levantar,** morning gown.—**r. hecha,** ready-made clothing.—**r. sucia,** soiled clothes for the laundry.—**r. talar,** long, loose gown.—**r. vieja,** cast-off clothes; (cook.) boiled meat, afterwards fried in a pan.—**a quema r.,** at close range; suddenly, unexpectedly.—**nadar y guardar la r.,** to be extra cautious in an undertaking.—**tentarse la r.,** to consider carefully.

ropaje, *m.* wearing apparel, clothes; robe, vestments; gown; garb; (art) drapery.

ropálico, ca, *a.* (poet.) rhopalic.

ropavejería, *f.* old-clothes shop.

ropavejero, *m.* fripper, old-clothes man.

ropería, *f.* clothier's trade; clothing shop, clothier's; wardrobe, clothes room, cloakroom; wardrobe keeper.

ropero, ra. I. *n.* clothier, dealer in clothes; wardrobe keeper; head shepherd, dairyman. **II.** *m.* clothespress, wardrobe, locker.

ropeta, ropilla, *f.* *dim.* doublet, close-fitting jacket.—**dar una r.,** to give a friendly reproof.

ropita, *f.* *dim.* child's clothing.

ropón, *m.* wide, loose gown.

roque, *m.* rook, castle (at chess).

roqueda, *f.,* **roquedal,** *n.* rocky place.

roquedo, *m.* rock, bowlder.

roqueño, ña, *a.* rocky, hard, flinty.

roquero, ra, *a.* rocky; built on rocks.

roqués, *a.* black (falcon).

roqueta, *f.* turret in a fortress.

roquete, *m.* (eccl.) rochet; barbed spearhead; (arti.) ramrod, rammer.

rorcual, *m.* (zool.) rorqual, finback (variety of large whales).

rorro, *m.* (coll.) babe in arms.

ros, *m.* (mil.) Spanish shako.

rosa, *f.* (bot.) rose; red spot on any part of the body; rose diamond; rosette; rosy aspect; rose color; flower of saffron; artificial rose.—**r. náutica,** or **de los vientos,** (naut.) traverse board, mariner's compass.

rosáceo, cea. I. *a.* rose-colored; (bot.) rosaceous. **II.** *f. pl.* (bot.) Rosaceæ, the rose family.

rosada, *f.* frost.

rosadelfa, *f.* (bot.) = AZALEA.

rosado, da, *a.* & *pp.* rose-colored; rose (u. a.).

rosal, *m.* rose bush or plant.—**r. de pitimaní,** climbing rose.—**r. perruno,** or **silvestre,** dog-rose.

rosanilina, *f.* (chem.) rosaniline.

rosariero, ra, *n.* maker and seller of rosaries.

rosario, *m.* rosary (beads for praying and series of prayers); assemblage of people who recite the rosary in procession; (hyd.) chain pump; (coll.) backbone.—**acabar como el r. de la aurora,** to break up in disorder.

rosarse, *vr.* = SONROSEARSE.

rosbif, *m.* roast beef.

rosca, *f.* screw and nut; screw thread; twist, spiral line or motion; circular badge of Spanish students; ring-shaped biscuit or bread; (naut.) flake of a cable.

roscado, da, *pp.* & *a.* threaded, having a screw thread.

roscar. I. *var* to thread, make or cut a screw thread on. **II.** *vn.* to cut screw threads, to make screws.—**máquina de r.,** screw-cutting machine.

roscón, *m.* *aug.* large screw; large circular loaf of bread.

rosear, *vn.* to turn rose color.

róseo, sea, *a.* rosy, roseate.

roséola, *f.* (med.) roseola, rose rash.

rosero, ra, *n.* gatherer of saffron flowers.

roseta, *f.* *dim.* small rose; rosette; rosy cheek; (metal.) rosette copper.

rosetón, *m.* *aug* large rosette; (arch.) rose-window; rosette.

rosicler, *m.* rose pink; roset; ruby silver.

rosillo, illa, *a.* light red, roan.

rosmarino, na. I. *a.* light red. **II.** *m.* (bot.) ROMERO.

rosmaro, *m.* walrus, rosmarine.

roso, sa, *a.* red, rosy; threadbare.—**a r. y velloso,** without distinction, totally.

rosoli, *m.* rossolis, sundew.

rosones, *m. pl.* worms in animals.

rosqueado, da, *a.* twisted.

rosquete, *m.* ring-shaped cake or biscuit.

rosquilla, *f.* ring-shaped fancy cake; vine fretter.

rostrado, da, *a.* rostrate.

rostral, rostrillo, *m.* headdress on images; small seed pearl.

rostritorcido, da; rostrituerto, ta, *a.* (coll.) angry-looking; sad-looking.

rostro, *m.* rostrum, beak of a ship; bill or beak of a bird; countenance, human face; aspect of affairs.—**r. a r.,** face to face.—**hacer r. a,** to face.

rota, *f.* (mil.) rout, defeat; (naut.) course; (eccl.) Rota; (bot.) rattan.—**de r.,** or **de r. batida,** on a sudden; with total ruin.

rotación, *f.* rotation.—**r. de cultivos,** rotation of crops.

rotal, *a.* relating to the Rota.

rotamente, *adv.* impudently, barefacedly.

rotante, *a.* rotating, revolving.

rotar, *vn.* = RODAR.

rotativo, va. I. *a.* rotary, revolving. **II.** *f.* rotary printing press.

rotatorio, ria, *a.* rotary, rotating.

roten, *m.* (bot.) rattan; rattan walking cane.

rotífero, ra. I. *a.* (zool.) rotiferous. **II.** *m. pl.* Rotifera.

roto, ta, *a.* & *pp. irr.* of ROMPER; broken, chipped, shattered; torn; ragged; destroyed; leaky, battered, or pierced; debauched, lewd.

rotonda, *f.* rotunda; rear section of a stage coach.

rótula, *f.* (anat.) rotula, kneepan; (pharm.) troche, lozenge.

rotulación, *f.* labeling.—**rotulador, ra,** *n.* & *a.* labeler (-ing).

rotular, *va.* to label; put a title to.

rotulata, *f.* label, title, mark; collection of labels or posters.

rótulo, *m.* label, mark; show bill, poster, show card, placard; (eccl.) certificate for beatification; school notice.

rotunda, *f.* rotunda; (r. w.) roundhouse.

rotundamente, *adv.* explicitly, categorically, peremptorily.

rotundidad, *f.* roundness, rotundity.

rotundo, da, *a.* round, circular, rotund; full, sonorous (s. o. the voice); plain, peremptory.

rotura, *f.* rupture, fracture; breakage; (agr.) breaking up ground; (vet.) = CONTRARROTURA.

roturación, *f.* (agr.) breaking up new ground.

roturar, *va.* (agr.) to break up (new ground).

roya, *f.* (bot.) rust, mildew, red blight.

roza, *f.* (agr.) stubbing, grubbing, clearing; ground cleared of brambles.

rozadero, *m.* stubbing place; (mech.) bearing plate, friction plate.

rozado, da, *a. & pp.* (agr.) stubbed, cleared; chilled, frappé (beverage).

rozador, ra, *n.* stubber, weeder.

rozadura, *f.* friction; frication; attrition; gall, chafing, abrasion; (bot.) punk knot.

rozagante, *a.* pompous, showy; trailing on the ground (as a gown); strapping.

rozamiento, *m.* (mech.) friction; frication; rubbing; clashing, disagreement.

rozar. I. *va.* (*pret.* ROCÉ: *subj.* ROCE) to stub, grub, clear (the ground); to nibble (the grass); to scrape or pare off; to gall, to chafe. **II.** *vn.* to graze, rub. **III.** *vr.* to interfere (s. o. horses' hoofs); to be on intimate terms; to falter, to stammer; to have a resemblance or connection with something else; to have intercourse or relations, associate; (naut.) to fret, to gall.

roznar, *vn.* to crunch; to bray.

roznido, *m.* crunching noise; braying of an ass.

rozno, *m.* little ass.

rozo, *m.* stubbing, weeding; brushwood.

rozón, *m.* short and broad scythe.

rúa, *f.* village street; high road.

ruán, *m.* linen manufactured in Rouen.

ruana, *f.* (Am.) a square and comparatively heavy poncho.

ruano, na, *a.* roan (horse); round, circular.

ruante, *a.* walking or riding through the streets.

ruar, *vn.* to walk or ride through the streets; to flirt in the street.

rubefación, *f.* (med.) rubefaction.

rubefaciente, *a.* (med.) rubefacient.

rúbeo, ea, *a.* ruby, reddish.

rubéola, *f.* (med.) measles.

ruberoide, *m.* a tarred-pasteboard roofing material.

rubeta, *f.* toad.

rubí, *m.* ruby; red color; redness of the lips.—**r. de Bohemia,** rosy quartz.—**r. del Brazil,** red topaz.—**r. espinela,** spinel ruby.

rubia, *f.* (bot.) madder; (icht.) a small red-colored river fish.

rubiáceo, a. I. *a.* (bot.) rubiaceous. **II.** *f. pl.* Rubiaceæ.

rubial. I. *a.* reddish (soil or plants). **II.** *m.* madder field.

rubicán, *a.* rubican (horse).

rubicela, *f.* reddish-yellow topaz.

rubicundez, *f.* rubicundity, ruddiness; rubescence.—**rubicundo, da,** *a.* reddish, rubicund; golden-red; blonde; rosy with health.

rubidio, *m.* (chem.) rubidium.

rubiera, *f.* (Ven.) mischief, reckless action; (C. A.) merrymaking, carousal.

rubificar, *va.* to rubify, make red.

rubín, rubinejo, *m.* ruby.

rubio, bia. I. *a.* blonde, golden, fair. **II.** *m.* (icht.) red gurnard.

rubión, *a.* reddish (s. o. a kind of wheat).

rublo, *m.* ruble, Russian silver coin.

rubor, *m.* blush, flush; bashfulness.

ruborizarse, *vr.* to blush, to flush.

ruborosamente, *adv.* blushingly, bashfully.

ruboroso, sa, *a.* bashful.

rúbrica, *f.* red mark or caption; mark or flourish added to one's signature; (eccl.) rubric or rules in prayer books.—**de r.,** according to rules or custom.

rubricante. I. *a.* signing, attesting. **II.** *m.* junior minister or secretary appointed to sign the proceedings.

rubricar, *va.* (*pret.* RUBRIQUÉ: *subj.* RUBRIQUE) to sign or indorse with one's peculiar mark or flourish, without writing the name; to sign and seal.

rubriquista, *m.* rubrician.

rubro, bra, *a.* red, reddish; rubric.

ruc, *m.* = ROCHO.

ruca, *f.* (Ch., Arg.) hut, cabin.

rucio, cia. I. *a.* light silver gray (s. o. horses); (Colomb.) dapple-gray; (coll.) gray; grayhaired, hoary. **II.** *m.* donkey.

ruco, ca, *a.* (C. A.) old, worthless.

rucho, *m.* donkey.

ruda, *f.* (bot.) rue.

rudamente, *adv.* rudely, roughly.

rudeza, *f.* roughness, rudeness, coarseness.

rudimental, *a.* rudimentary; elementary.

rudimento, *m.* rudiment, embryo, germ; vestige. —*pl.* rudiments, elements.

rudo, da, *a.* rude, rough, unpolished; hard, rigorous, severe; stupid.

rueca, *f.* distaff for spinning; twist, winding; (naut.) fish of a mast or yard.

rueda, *f.* wheel; caster, roller; circle of persons; crowd; round slice; turn, time, succession; (icht.) sunfish; rack (torture); hoops for skirts; spread of a peacock's tail; three-handed billiard game.—**r. catalina,** or **de Santa Catalina,** Catherine wheel.—**r. de alimentación por abajo, (arriba)** (hydr.) undershot (overshot) wheel.—**r. de andar,** treadmill.—**r. de costado,** breast wheel.—**r. del timón,** (naut.) steering wheel.—**r. hidráulica,** water wheel.—**hacer la r.,** to cajole, wheedle.

ruedecica, cilla, zuela, *f. dim.* small wheel; caster, roller.

ruedo, *m.* rotation, turn; circuit; circumference; edge of a wheel or disk; round plat or mat; rug; (sew.) skirt lining; bottom of a skirt; valance.— **a todo r.,** at all events.

ruedo, yo ruede. *V.* RODAR.

ruego, *m.* request, prayer, petition, entreaty, supplication.

ruego, ruegue. *V.* ROGAR.

ruejo, *m.* mill wheel; ground roller.

ruello, *m.* (agr.) ground roller.

ruequecilla, *f.* small distaff.

rufián, *m.* ruffian; pimp, pander.

rufianear, *vn.* to play the ruffian; to pimp, to pander.

rufianería, *f.* ruffianism.

rufianesco, ca. I. *a.* ruffianly, ruffianish. **II.** *f.* ruffians collectively.

rufo, fa, *a.* carroty, red-haired; frizzed, curled.

ruga, *f.* wrinkle.—**rugar,** *va.* to wrinkle.

rugible, *a.* capable of bellowing or roaring.

rugido, *m.* roar; rumbling in the bowels.

rugiente, *a.* bellowing, roaring.

ruginoso, sa, *a.* rusty.

rugir. I. *vn.* (*ind.* RUJO: *subj.* RUJA) to roar, bellow, howl. **II.** *v. impers.* to be whispered about, to transpire, to be said.

rugosidad, *f.* rugosity.

rugoso, sa, *a.* rugose, corrugated, wrinkled.

ruibarbo, *m.* (bot.) rhubarb.

ruido, *m.* noise; rumor; report; dispute, difference; law suit.—**hacer,** or **meter, r.,** to attract attention; to create a sensation.

ruidosamente, *adv.* noisily; loudly.

ruidoso, sa, *a.* noisy, loud; clamorous.

ruin. I. *a.* mean, vile, low, base, despicable; little, puny; decayed; wicked, malicious; niggardly, stingy; insidious, treacherous, infamous; vicious (s. o. an animal). **II.** *m.* wicked, mean, or vile man; small nerve in the tail of cats.

ruina, *f.* ruin, decline, downfall; overthrow, fall. —*pl.* ruins, débris.—**batir en r.,** (mil.) to batter in, breach.

ruinar, *va. & vr.* to ruin, destroy.

ruindad, *f.* meanness, baseness; ill turn, base action.

ruinmente, *adv.* basely, meanly, despicably.

ruinoso, sa, *a.* ruinous; worthless.

ruiponce, *m.* (bot.) = RAPÓNCHIGO.

ruipóntico, *m.* (bot.) rhubarb, pieplant.

ruiseñor, *m.* (orn.) nightingale.

rujada, *f.* heavy shower.

rular, *vn.* to roll. *V.* RODAR.

ruleta, *f.* roulette.

rulo, m. ball, bowl; conical stone in oil mills; road roller.

ruló, m. (print.) ink roller, brayer.

rumano, na, n. & a. Rumanian.

rumbadas, f. pl. = ARRUMBADAS.

rumbo, m. bearing, course, direction; road, route, way; (coll.) pomp, ostentation; liberality, generosity; (naut.) scuttle; (her.) rustre.—**abatir el r.,** to fall to leeward.—**con r. a,** in the direction of; heading, or sailing, for.—**hacer r. a,** to sail for; to head for.

rumbón, na, a. = RUMBOSO.

rumbosamente, adv. (coll.) pompously, grandly, liberally.—**rumboso, sa,** a. pompous, magnificent, splendid, liberal.

rumí, n. (among the Moors) Christian.

rumia, f. rumination, chewing the cud.

rumiador, ra, n. & a. ruminator (-ing), ruminant.

rumiadura, f. rumination.

rumiante, I. n. & a. ruminant; muser (-ing). **II.** m. pl. Ruminantia.

rumiar, va. to ruminate; to muse, meditate.

rumión, na, a. ruminating much.

rumo, m. (coop.) first hoop of a cask.

rumor, m. rumor, report, hearsay; sound of voices; murmur.

rumorcico, illo, ito, m. dim. flying report.

rumoroso, sa, a. causing rumor.

runa, f. rune, runic character.

rundún, m. (Arg.) a very small humming bird.

runfla, runfiada, f. (coll.) series of things.

rúnico, ca; runo, na, a. runic.

runrún, m. (coll.) rumor, report.

ruña, f. (coop.) croze.—**ruñadera,** f. cooper's crozer.—**ruñadura,** f. = RUÑA.—**ruñar,** va. (coop.) to croze.

rupestre, a. rupiculous, found or living on rocks; rupestrian, inscribed or cut on rocks.

rupia, f. rupee, silver coin; (med.) rupia.

rupicabra, rupicapra, f. chamois.

rupícola, a. rupiculous, found or living on rocks.

ruptura, f. rupture; fracture, breaking.

ruqueta, f. (bot.) = JARAMAGO.

rural, a. rural, country, rustic.

ruralmente, adv. rurally.

rus, m. (bot.) sumach. V. ZUMAQUE.

rusco, m. (bot.) kneeholly, butcher's-broom.

rusel, m. a kind of woollen serge.

rusiente, a. turning red-hot.

ruso, sa, n. & a. Russian.

rusticación, f. rustication.

rustical, a. rustical, rural, wild.

rústicamente, adv. rustically, rudely.

rusticano, na, a. wild (said of plants).

rusticar, vn. (pret. RUSTIQUÉ: subj. RUSTIQUE) to rusticate.

rusticidad, f. rusticity, simplicity; rudeness, clumsiness.

rústico, ca. I. a. rustic, rural; coarse, clumsy; unmannerly.—**a la rústica,** or **en r.,**(b. b.)in paper covers, unbound. **II.** n. rustic, peasant.

rustiquez, rustiqueza, f. rusticity.

rustrir, va. to toast; to fry.

rustro, m. (her.) rustre.

ruta, f. route, way.

rutáceo, a, a. (bot.) rutaceous.

rutenio, m. (chem.) ruthenium.

ruteno, na, n. & a. Ruthenian.

rutilante, a. sparkling, scintillating.

rutilar, vn. (poet.) to twinkle, sparkle, scintillate.

rutilo, rútilo, m. (min.) rutile.

rútilo, la, a. shining red; sparkling.

rutina, f. routine, custom, habit, rut.

rutinario, ria. I. a. routinary. **II.** n. routinist.

rutinero, ra, a. routinistic.

ruzafa, f. garden, park.

S

sábado, m. Saturday; Sabbath among the Jews.

sabalar, m. net for catching shad.

sabalera, f. fire grate in furnaces.

sabalero, m. shad fisher.

sábalo, m. (icht.) shad.

sábana, f. sheet (for a bed); altar cloth.—**pegársele a uno las sábanas,** to rise late.

sabana, f. savanna, grassy plain.

sabandija, f. small nasty insect or reptile; bug; vermin.

sabandijuela, f. dim. very small insect, vermin.

sabanear, vn. (Am.) to scour the plain.

sabanero, ra. I. n. dweller on the savanna. **II.** a. pertaining to a savanna. **III.** m. bird resembling the starling. **IV.** f. (Ven.) a savanna snake that destroys harmful insects.

sabanilla, f. dim. small sheet or piece of linen; altar cloth; napkin; kerchief worn on the head.

sabañón, m. chilblain.—**comer como un s.,** to eat greedily, devour.

sabatario, a. Sabbatarian.

sabático, ca, a. Sabbatical.

sabatina, f. (eccl.) Saturday mass; Saturday exercise in colleges.

sabatino, na, a. belonging to Saturday.

sabatizar, vn. to keep the Sabbath.

sabedor, ra. I. a. knowing, informed. **II.** n. one who knows.

sabeísmo, m. Sabaism, Sabianism.

sabeliano, na, a. & n. Sabellian.

sabelianismo, m. Sabellianism.

sabélico, ca, a. pertaining to the Sabines or Samnites.

sabelotodo, n. = SABIDILLO.

sabeo, a, a. Sabæan, of or from Sheba.

saber. I. va. (ind. SÉ: pret. SUPE: fut. SABRÉ: subj. SEPA) to know; to be able to, know how to, can (Juan sabe cantar, John can, or knows how to, sing).—**s. cuántas son cinco,** to know what is what.—**no sé qué,** a certain something; something that does not matter.—**y no sé qué más, or y qué sé yo qué más,** and what not; and so forth. **II.** vn. to know; to be very sagacious.—**s. a,** to taste of, taste like (esto sabe a limón, this tastes of, or like, lemon).—**s. de,** to know, be familiar with; to hear of or from, have news about.—**a s.,** namely, viz., to wit.—**¿quién sabe?** perhaps, who knows!—**¿sabe?** you know, don't you know? (in U. S. slang, savvy?) —**u. as an expletive in conversation. III.** m. learning, knowledge.—**según mi leal s. y entender,** to the best of my knowledge.

saber, m. learning, knowledge, lore.

sabiamente, adv. wisely, knowingly, learnedly.

sabicú, m. (Cuba) (bot.) sabicú, horseflesh mahogany.

sabidillo, lla, n. pedant, know-it-all person.

sabido, da, a. & pp. learned, well-informed.

sabiduría, f. learning, knowledge; wisdom.

sabiendas.—a s. adv. knowingly, consciously.

sabiente, a. knowing.

sabihondez, f. (coll.) conceited assumption of knowledge or learning.—**sabihondo, da,** a. affecting knowledge or learning, know-it-all.

sabina, f. (bot.) savin.

sabinar, m. clump of savins.

sabino, na. I. a. roan (horse). **II.** n. & a. Sabine.

sabio, bia. I. a. wise, learned, knowing; cunning. **II.** n. sage, wise person; scholar, learned person; scientist.

sablazo, m. stroke with or wound from a saber; (coll.) borrowing or sponging.

sable, m. saber, cutlass; (her.) sable, black.

sablista, m. (coll.) sponger, one who asks petty loans.

sablón, m. coarse sand.

saboga, f. (icht.) a species of shad.

sabogal, m. net for catching shad.

saboneta, f. hunting-case watch.

sabor, m. taste, flavor; dash, zest.—pl. round knobs on the bit of a bridle.—**a s.,** at pleasure.

saboreamiento, m. relish, relishing.

saborcico, illo, ito, m. dim. slight flavor or taste.

saborear. I. *va.* to flavor, give a relish or zest to; to interest, cajole, wheedle. **II.** *va.* & *vr.* to relish, enjoy, find delicious, be pleased or delighted; to smack one's lips.

saborete, *m.* slight flavor or taste.

saboyana, *f.* open skirt; a kind of pie.

saboyano, na, *a.* Savoyard.

sabrosamente, *adv.* deliciously.

sabrosico, ica, illo, illa, ito, ita, *a. dim.* rather tasty.

sabroso, sa, *a.* savory, tasty, palatable, delicious; pleasant, delightful; salted, saltish.

sabucal, *m.* clump of willows.

sabuco, *m.* = SAÚCO.

sabueso, *m.* hound, bloodhound, beagle, harehound, foxhound.

sabugal, sabugo = SABUCAL, SABUCO.

sábulo, *m.* coarse, heavy sand.

sabuloso, sa, *a.* gritty, sandy, gravelly.

saburra, *f.* (med.) saburra, gastric sordes.

saburral, *a.* (med.) saburral.

saburroso, sa, *a.* indicating a foul stomach.

saca, *f.* drawing out; exportation, extraction; large bag or sack of coarse stuff; first authorized register of a sale; first certified copy of a document issued by a notary.—**estar de s.,** to be on sale; (coll.) to be marriageable.

sacabala, *f.* (surg.) alphonsin.

sacabalas, *m.* (arti.) bullet screw, ball extractor.

sacabocado, sacabocados, *m.* hollow punch; ticket punch.

sacabotas, *m.* bootjack.

sacabrocas, *m.* tack claw, tack puller.

sacabuche, *m.* (naut.) pumping tube or pipe; (mus.) sackbut; player on the sackbut; nincompoop.

sacacorchos, *m.* corkscrew.

sacada, *f.* region separated from a province or country.

sacadilla, *f.* noise made to rouse game.

sacadinero, sacadineros, *m.* (coll.) catch-penny.

sacador, ra, *n.* drawer, extractor; one that takes or brings out.

sacadura, *f.* (sew.) sloping cut; (Colomb.) taking out, extracting.

sacafilásticas, *f.* (arti.) priming wire.

sacaliña, *f.* V. GARROCHA, SOCALIÑA.

sacamanchas, *m.* or *f.* cleaner, scourer, cleanser.

sacamantas, *m.* (coll.) tax collector.

sacamiento, *m.* taking or drawing out.

sacamolero, ra; sacamuelas, *n.* tooth drawer, dentist.

sacanabo, *m.* (naut.) pump hook.

sacanete, *m.* lansquenet, a card game.

sacapelotas, *m.* bullet screw.

sacapotras, *m.* (coll.) bad surgeon.

sacar, *va.* (*pret.* SAQUÉ: *subj.* SAQUE) to extract, draw, draw out, pull out; to take out; to withdraw; to dispossess, put out; to except, exclude; to manufacture, produce, invent; publish; bring out; to put forth, bring forth; to imitate, copy, take off; clear, free, place in safety; find out, investigate, discover; to make out, solve, interpret; to eradicate; to extort; get, obtain, attain; to show, exhibit, manifest; to excite (passion, anger); to lose the judgment; to deduce, draw, infer; to ballot, elect by ballot; to draw, win (a prize); to win at play; in the game of **pelota,** to hit (the ball) on its rebound; to draw, unsheath (a sword); to make, take (a copy); to cite, name, quote.—**s. a bailar,** to lead out for a dance; to drag in irrelevantly.—**s. a la vergüenza,** to put a criminal in the pillory; to bring shame upon.—**s. a luz,** to print, publish; to mention or bring out.—**s. a pasear,** to take out for a walk.—**s. de madre,** to make one lose patience. —**s. de pila,** to become sponsor for at baptism.—**s. de quicio** = S. DE MADRE.—**s. el pecho por,** to stand for, to defend, to take the part of.—**s. en claro,** or **en limpio,** to conclude, arrive at the conclusion; to gather (from a writing, etc.).—**s. la cara,** to present one's self as an interested party.— **s. la cara por** = S. EL PECHO POR.—**s. la cuenta,** to figure out.—**s. por factor común,** (math.) to factor out.

sacarato, *m.* (chem.) saccharate.—**sacárico,** *a* saccharic.—**sacarificación,** *f.* saccharification.— **sacarificar,** *va.* to saccharify.—**sacarígeno, na,** *a* sacchariferous.—**sacarimetría,** *f.* saccharimetry —**sacarímetro,** *m.* saccharimeter.

sacarina, *f.* (chem.) saccharine.—**sacarino, na,** *a.* saccharine, containing sugar.—**sacaroideo, a,** *a* (chem.) saccharoid.—**sacarómetro,** *m.* saccharimeter.—**sacarosa,** *f.* (chem.) saccharose.

sacaroso, sa, *a.* saccharinelike.

sacasillas, *n.* (coll.) = METEMUERTOS.

sacatapón, *m.* corkscrew; bung drawer.

sacate, *m.* (Mex.) grass, herb; hay.

sacatrapos, *m.* (arti.) wad hook, wormer.

sacerdocio, *m.* priesthood.—**sacerdotal,** *a.* sacerdotal.—**sacerdote,** *m.* priest, clergyman.

sacerdotisa, *f.* priestess.

saciable, *a.* satiable.

saciar, *va.* & *vr.* to satiate.—**saciedad,** *f.* satiety.

saciña, *f.* (bot.) a kind of willow.

sacio, a, *a.* satiate, satiated.

saco, *m.* sack, bag; sackful, bagful; (tail.) coat; Roman sagum; (in the game of PELOTA) = SAQUE; (mil.) pillage, sack, plunder.—**s. de noche,** hand bag, valise, satchel.—**entrar, meter, or poner, a s.,** to plunder, loot.—**no echar en s. roto,** not to forget, not to ignore.

sacra, *f.* (eccl.) sacring tablet.

sacramentado, da, *pp.* & *a.* (eccl.) transubstantiated; having received the last sacraments.

sacramental. I. *a.* sacramental. **II.** *n.* person or fraternity devoted to the worship of the sacrament of the altar.

sacramentalmente, *adv.* sacramentally; in confession.

sacramentar. I. *va.* (eccl.) to administer the sacraments to; to consecrate; (coll.) to conceal, hide. **II.** *vr.* to become sacrament, be transubstantiated.

sacramentario, ria, *n.* Sacramentarian.

sacramente, *adv.* = SAGRADAMENTE.

sacramento, *m.* (eccl.) sacrament; Christ transubstantiated in the host.—**s. del altar,** Eucharist; consecrated Host.

sacratísimo, ma, *a. sup.* most sacred, holiest.

sacre, *m.* (orn.) saker; small cannon.

sacrificadero, *m.* sacrificing place.

sacrificador, ra, *n.* & *a.* sacrificer (-ing).

sacrificante, *a.* sacrificing, hazarding; sacrificial, sacrificatory.

sacrificar. I. *va.* (*pret.* SACRIFIQUÉ: *subj.* SACRIFIQUE) to sacrifice. **II.** *vr.* to devote one's self to God; to sacrifice one's self, give up one's life.

sacrificio, *m.* sacrifice, offering; submission.—**s. del altar,** sacrifice of the mass.—**s. propiciatorio,** peace offering.

sacrílegamente, *m.* sacrilegiously.

sacrilegio, *m.* sacrilege.

sacrílego, ga, *a.* sacrilegious.

sacrismoche, cho, *m.* in jocular style, a man in a ragged black coat.

sacrista, sacristán, *m.* sacristan, sexton, clerk; hoop skirt, bustle.—**sacristana,** *f.* sacristan or sexton's wife; nun in charge of the sacristy.

sacristanejo, *m. dim.* little sacristan.

sacristanía, *f.* office of a sexton.—**sacristía,** *f.* sacristy, vestry; office of a sacristan or sexton.

sacro, *m.* (anat.) sacrum.

sacro, cra, *a.* holy, sacred.

sacrosanto, ta, *a.* sacred, sacrosanct.

sacudida, *f.* shake, shaking, jerk.

sacudidamente, *adv* rejectingly.

sacudido, da, *a.* & *pp.* harsh, indocile, intractable; determined.

sacudidor, *m.* shaker; beater; duster.

sacudidura, *f.* shaking; dusting, cleansing.

sacudimiento, *m.* shake, shaking; shock, jerk, jolt.

sacudir. I. *va.* to shake; jolt, jerk; to beat, to dust; spank, drub; dart, throw off, discharge; shake off. **II.** *vn.* (naut.) to flap (sails). **III.** *vr.* to reject, drive away, shake off.

sachadura, *f.* hoeing, weeding.

sachar, *va.* (agr.) to weed.

sacho, *m.* weeder, weeding tool.

saduceísmo, *m.* Sadduceeism.

saduceo, a, *n.* & *a.* Sadducee (-cean).

saeta, *f.* arrow, dart, shaft; cock of a sundial, gnomon; hand of a watch or clock; magnetic needle; bud of a vine; (ast.) Sagitta, the Arrow.—*pl.* pious ejaculations.

saetada, *f.*, **saetazo,** *m.* cast of an arrow; arrow wound.

saetear, *va.* = ASAETEAR.

saetero, ra. I. *a.* relating to arrows. **II.** *m.* archer, bowman, dartman. **III.** *f.* loophole; small grated window in prisons.

saeti, *m.* a kind of sateen.

saetía, *f.* (naut.) settee; vessel with lateen sails; loophole.

saetilla, *f. dim.* small arrow or dart; small magnetic needle; hand of a watch; devotional verse; (bot.) sagittaria.

saetín, *m.* mill race, mill run, sluice, flume; brad, peg, pin, tack; sateen or satine.

saetón, *m.* dart for shooting rabbits.

safeno, a, *a.* (anat.) saphenous.

sáfico, ca, *a.* (poet.) sapphic.

saga, *f.* witch; saga (legend).

sagacidad, *f.* sagacity, sagaciousness.

sagapeno, *m.* sagapenum (gum).

sagatí, *m.* sagathy; farmer's satin.

sagaz, *a.* sagacious; quick of scent (s. o. dogs); discerning, farsighted, farseeing.

sagazmente, *adv.* sagaciously.

sagita, *f.* (geom.) sagitta.

sagital, *a.* sagittal, sagittated.

sagitaria, *f.* (bot.) sagittaria, arrowhead.

sagitario, *m.* dartman, archer; (S-, ast.) Sagittarius, the Archer.

sago, *m.* loose, wide greatcoat.

ságoma, *f.* (arch.) pattern, reglet, rule.

sagradamente, *adv.* sacredly.

sagrado, da. I. *a.* sacred, consecrated; holy; (obs.) incurable, cursed, execrable. **II.** *m.* asylum, haven of refuge, place of safety.

sagrario, *m.* sacrarium; (eccl.) ciborium, or cibory.

sagú, *m.* sago.

saguaipe, *m.* (Arg.) a parasitic worm that attacks the liver of cattle.

ságula, *f.* small frock. *V.* SAYUELO.

sahína, *f.* = ZAHINA.

sahornarse, *vr.* to chafe, be excoriated.

sahorno, *m.* chafe, chafing, excoriation.

sahumado, da, *a.* & *pp.* fumigated; bettered, improved.—**sahumador,** *m.* perfumer; perfuming pot; fumigator.—**sahumadura,** *f.* perfuming; fumigation.—**sahumar,** *va.* to perfume; to smoke; to fumigate.—**sahumerio, sahumo,** *m.* smoke, vapor, steam, fume; fumigation; fuming.

sai, *m.* sai, a variety of monkey.

saimirí, *m.* titi, squirrel monkey.

saín, *m.* grease or fat, fatness; sardine fat used as burning oil; greasiness on clothes.

sainar, *va.* to fatten.

sainete, *m.* (theat.) one-act farce; burlesque; flavor, relish, zest; seasoning, sauce; delicious titbit; delicacy; anything nice and choice; taste or elegance in dress.—**sainetear,** *vn.* to act farces. —**sainetero,** *m.* writer of farces.—**sainetesco, ca,** *a.* comical, burlesque.

saíno, *m.* (S. A.) a kind of boar.

saja, *f.* (surg.) scarification.

sajador, *m.* bleeder, scarifier.

sajadura, *f.* = SAJA.

sajar, *va.* to scarify.

sajelar, *va.* to sift and clean (clay).

sajón, na, *n.* & *a.* Saxon.

sal, *f.* salt; wit, facetiousness, grace, winning manners; (chem.) salt.—**s. amoníaco, sal ammoníac.—s. de compás** = S. GEMA.—**s. de la Higuera,** Epsom salts.—**s. gema,** rock salt.—**s. marina,** sea salt.—**s. pedrés,** or **piedra,** rock salt.—**echar en s.,** to reserve for another occasion.

sala, *f.* drawing room, parlor; hall; large room; court of justice (both the room and the judges); tribunal.—**s. de batalla,** sorting table or place (in a postoffice).—**s. de justicia,** court of justice.—**s. del crimen,** criminal court or tribunal.—**guardar s.,** to observe the rules and formalities of the court. —**hacer s.,** to form a quorum in a court.

salacidad, *f.* salacity, lechery, lust.

salacot, *m.* (Philip.) helmetlike solar hat.

saladamente, *adv.* (coll.) wittily, facetiously; saltily.

saladar, *m.* salt marsh.

saladero, *m.* salting place; salting tub.

saladillo, *m. dim.* fresh bacon half-salted.

salado, da. I. *a.* & *pp.* salted, salty, saltish; briny, brackish; witty, facetious; graceful, winsome. **II.** *m.* (bot.) saltwort; saline land.

salador, ra. I. *n.* salter, curer. **II.** *m.* SALADERO.

saladura, *f.* salting, curing; salted provisions.

salamandra, *f.* salamander; fire sprite; anything fireproof.

salamandria, salamanquesa, *f.* star lizard; stellion.

salamanquino, na, *n.* & *a.* = SALMANTINO.

salangana, *f.* (orn.) swift, esculent swallow.

salar, *va.* to salt, to season or preserve with salt, to cure or corn (meat); to brine.

salariar, *va.* to give a salary or wages to.

salario, *m.* wages, salary.

salaz, *a.* salacious, lustful.

salazón, *f.* salting; salted meats or fish.

salbadera, *f.* sand box, pounce box.

salbanda, *f.* (min.) selvage.

salce, *m.* (bot.) willow. *V.* SAUCE.

salceda, *f.*, **salcedo,** *m.* salicetum, willow garden.

salcereta, *f.* dice box.

salcochar, salcocho = SANCOCHAR, SANCOCHO.

salchicha, *f.* sausage; (fort.) long fascine; (arti.) saucisse, long fuse.—**salchichería,** *f.* shop where sausages are sold.—**salchichero, ra,** *n.* sausage maker or seller.

salchichón, *m. aug.* sausage; (fort.) large fascine.

saldado, da, *pp.* & *a.* paid, settled, balanced.

saldar, *va.* (com.) to settle, liquidate, balance.

saldista, *n.* one who sells or buys remnants or left-overs.

saldo, *m.* (com.) balance; settlement; remnants sold at low prices.

saldrá, saldré. *V.* SALIR.

saledizo, za. I. *a.* salient, projecting. **II.** *m.* projection, ledge.

salegar, *m.* salt lick.

salema, *f.* (icht.) gilthead.

salep, *m.* salep or salop root.

salera, *f.* saltcat in a salt lick; salt mine.

salero, *m.* saltcellar; salt pan; salt storage place; salt lick; (coll.) gracefulness, winning ways.

saleroso, sa, *a.* (coll.) witty, facetious; lively, jolly, winsome.

salesiano, na, *n.* & *a.* Salesian.

saleta, *f. dim.* small hall; royal antechamber; court of appeal.

salgada, salgadera, *f.* (bot.) = ORZAGA.

salgar, *va.* to feed salt to (cattle).

salgo, salga. *V.* SALIR.

salguera, *f.*, **salguero,** *m.* (bot.) osier, willow.

salicaria, *f.* (bot.) a salicaceous shrub.

salicilato, *m.* (chem.) salicylate.

salicílico, ca, *a.* (chem.) salicylic.

salicina, *f.* (chem.) salicin.

salicíneo, a, *a.* (bot.) salicaceous.

sálico, ca, *a.* Salic.

salicor, *f.* (bot.) prickly saltwort.

salida, *f.* start, setting or going out, departure, exit; outlet, outgate; way out, exit; outskirts; issue, result, conclusion; projection, protuberance; (com.) salableness; expenditure, outlay; loophole, subterfuge, pretext; sally; (naut.) headway; (mil.) sally, sortie.

salidizo, = SALEDIZO.

salido, da, *a.* & *pp.* gone out, departed; projecting; in heat, eager for the male.

saliente. I. *a.* salient, projecting. **II.** *f.* projection, lug.

salífero, ra, *a.* salt-bearing.

salificable, *a.* salifiable.

salín, *m.* storage place for salt.

salinero, ra, *n.* salter, salt maker, salt dealer.

salino, na. I. *a.* saline. **II.** *f.* salt pit, salt pan, salt works, salt mine.

salio, lia, *n.* & *a.* Salian (relating to, or one of, the salii, or priests of Mars); Salian (relating to, or one of, the Salian Franks).

salipirina, *f.* salipyrine.

salir. I. *vn.* (*ind.* SALGO: *fut.* SALDRÉ: *subj.* SALGA) to go or come out; to depart, leave, sail; sally, sally forth; get out; to end, be over (as a season); to appear, show up; disappear, come off (as a stain); rise (as the sun); to shoot, spring; to grow; stand out, project; to start (in a dance, etc.); to be the first to play, make the first move; to be issued or published; to result, turn out; to acquit one's self, come out, do (well, badly); to be drawn (as in a lottery); to be elected; to lead to, open to; (naut.) to exceed, to excel, pass another vessel in sailing; to happen, occur; to correspond; to imply; to come out right, check (as a sum); to say or do a thing unexpectedly or unseasonably; (w. **de**) to cease (as); (theat.) to enter, appear; (before *pp.*) to come out, to be (*saltó herido*, he came out, or was, wounded).—**s. a,** to come to (so much); to resemble, look like.—**s. avante,** or **con bien,** to be successful.—**s. con,** to drag in, say unexpectedly or irrelevantly.—**s. de,** to dispose of, to part with; to get rid of.—**s. de su padre,** to be released from paternal guardianship.—**s. de sus casillas,** to lose one's temper.—**hacer s. los colores al rostro,** to put one to blush.—**salga lo que saliere,** happen what will, whatever may happen. **II.** *vr.* to leak; to overflow.—**s. con la suya,** to accomplish one's end, to have one's way.

salisipán, *m.* (Philip.) a swift boat.

salitrado, da, *a.* impregnated with saltpeter.

salitral. I. *a.* nitrous. **II.** *m.* saltpeter bed or works.

salitre, *m.* saltpeter, niter.—**salitrería,** *f.* saltpeter works.—**salitrero, ra,** *n.* saltpeter refiner, dealer in saltpeter.—**salitroso, sa,** *a.* nitrous.

saliva, *f.* saliva, spittle.—**salivación,** *f.* salivation; spitting.—**salival,** *a.* salivary.

salivar, *vn.* to spit; to salivate.—**salivera,** *f.* round knob on the bits of a bridle.—**salivoso, sa,** *a.* salivous.

salma, *f.* ton, twenty hundredweight

salmantino, na, *n.* & *a.* of or relating to Salamanca.

salmear, salmodiar, *vn.* to sing psalms.

salmer, *m.* (arch.) impost of an arch.

salmerón, *a.* fanfarron wheat.

salmista, *m.* psalmist; chanter of psalms.

salmo, *m.* psalm.

salmodia, *f.* psalmody; (eccl.) psalter.

salmón, *m.* (icht.) salmon.—**s. pequeño,** samlet, parr.—**s. zancado,** kelt.—**salmonado, da,** *a.* tasting like salmon.—**salmoncillo, ito, m.** *dim.* samlet, parr.—**salmonera,** *f.* salmon net.

salmonete, *m.* (icht.) surmullet.

salmorejo, *m.* sauce for rabbits.

salmuera, *f.* brine; pickle.

salmuerarse, *vr.* to become sick from eating too much salt (s. o. cattle).

salobral. I. *a.* salty, briny. **II.** *m.* saline ground.

salobre, *a.* brackish, briny, saltish.

salobreño, ña, *a.* saltish, saline (ground).

salobridad, *f.* brackishness, saltiness.

salol, *m.* (chem.) salol.

saloma, *f.* (naut.) chantey.

salomar, *vn.* (naut.) to sing chanteys.

salomónico, ca, *a.* Salomonic.

salón, *m. aug.* salon, large hall or parlor; assembly room; salted and cured meat or fish.

saloncillo, *m.* small salon or hall; special room (waiting room, rest room, lady's room, etc.).

salpa, *f.* (icht.) gilthead, salpa, bighead.

salpicadura, *f.* splash, spatter, spattering.

salpicar, *va.* (*pret.* SALPIQUÉ: *subj.* SALPIQUE) to spatter, bespatter, sprinkle, splash; to skip over, touch on without order.

salpicón, *m.* salmagundi; farcing; medley; bespattering.

salpimentar, *va.* (*ind.* SALPIMIENTO: *subj.* SALPIMIENTE) to season with pepper and salt.

salpimienta, *f.* salt and pepper.

salpresar, *va.* to salt, preserve with salt.

salpullido, *m.* (med.) rash.

salpullir, *va.* & *vr.* (med.) to break out.

salsa, *f.* (cook.) sauce, dressing, gravy.—**s. de San Bernardo,** (coll.) hunger.—**s. mahonesa,** or **mayonesa,** mayonnaise dressing.

salsedumbre, *f.* saltiness, saltness.

salsera, *f.* gravy dish.

salsereta, rilla, ruela, *f. dim.* small saucer; dice box.

salsero, *m.* (bot.) Spanish thyme.

salsifí, *m.* (bot.) salsify, oyster plant.

salsoláceo, a. I. *a.* (bot.) salsolaceous. **II.** *f. pl.* Salsola.

saltabanco, saltabancos, *m.* mountebank; quack; trifler.

saltabardales, *m.* (coll.) romp, wild youth.

saltabarrancos, *m.* (coll.) noisy person.

saltacaballo.—en s., (arch.) lapping over.

saltación, *f.* leaping; dancing, dance.

saltacharquillos, *n.* person affectedly walking on tiptoe.

saltadero, *m.* leaping or jumping place; artificial fountain; jet.

saltadizo, za, *a.* snapping, breaking.

saltador, ra, *n.* jumper, leaper; hopper.

saltadura, *f.* chip.

saltaembanco, *m.* = SALTABANCO.

saltamontes, *m.* grasshopper.

saltante, *a.* leaping, jumping; salient.

saltaojos, *m.* (bot.) a kind of peony.

saltaparedes, *m.* = SALTABARDALES.

saltar. I. *vn.* to leap, spring, jump, hop; to frisk, skip; to bound, rebound; to dash out (as a geyser); to snap, burst, break in pieces; to fly asunder, crack, flash; to come off (as a button); to slip off (as a pulley belt); to be clear and obvious; to come to the mind; to startle, betray emotion; (naut.) to chop about, shift, change suddenly (the wind).—**s. a la vista,** to be self-evident.—**s. en tierra,** to land, debark. **II.** *va.* to leap or jump over; to skip; to cover (the female).

saltarelo, *m.* an ancient Spanish dance.

saltarén, *m.* a tune on the guitar; grasshopper.

saltarín, na, *n.* dancer, dancing master (mistress); restless young rake.

saltarregla, *f.* bevel square; sliding rule.

saltaterandate, *m.* a kind of embroidery.

saltatrás, *m.* or *f.* = TORNATRÁS.

saltatriz, *f.* ballet girl; danseuse.

saltatumbas, *m.* (coll.) clergyman who makes a living from funerals.

salteador, *m.* highwayman, footpad.

salteadora, *f.* female footpad.

salteamiento, *m.* assault, highway robbery.

saltear, *va.* to assault, attack; to rob on the highway; to hold up; to start, leave undone, and undertake something else; to forestall; to surprise, take by surprise.

salteo, *m.* assault; highway robbery.

salterio, *m.* psalter, psalm book; rosary; (mus.) psaltery.

saltero, ra, *n.* highlander.

saltico, ito, illo, *m. dim.* little hop or leap.

saltimbanco, -banqui, *m.* = SALTABANCO.

salto, *m.* spring, jump, leap, bound; leaping place; skip, omission; gap; promotion to a higher post without passing through the intervening ones.—**s. de agua,** waterfall, falls, cataract.—**s. de mata,** flight for fear of punishment.—**s. de trucha,** tumbling.—**s. de viento,** (naut.) sudden shifting of the wind.—**s. mortal,** somerset.—**a saltos,** leaping, by hops.—**a saltos y corcovos,** (coll.) by fits and starts.—**dar un s.,** to jump, leap.

—de un s., at one jump.**—por s.,** irregularly, by turns.

saltón, na. I. *a.* hopping or leaping much. **II.** *m.* grasshopper.

salubérrimo, ma, *a. super.* most salubrious.

salubre, *a.* salubrious, healthful.

salubridad, *f.* healthfulness, salubrity.

salud, *f.* health; good condition; public weal; welfare, prosperity; salvation.—*pl.* compliments, greetings.—**¡s.!** hello! greeting! good-bye, good luck! your health (in drinking).—**a su s.,** your health (in drinking).—**beber a la s. de,** to drink the health of.

saludable, *a.* salutary, healthful, wholesome.

saludablemente, *adv.* healthfully, wholesomely.

saludación, . = SALUTACIÓN.

saludador, ra, *n.* greeter, saluter; quack.

saludar, *va.* to greet, bow to, salute, hail; to give greetings or regards to; to fire a salute; to apply nostrums; (naut.) to dip the flag to.

saludo, *m.* bow, salute, salutation, greeting; (mil.) salute.—**s. a la voz,** (naut.) cheers, hurrahs.

salumbre, *f.* flower of salt.

salutación, *f.* salutation, greeting, salute, bow; exordium of a sermon; Ave Maria.

salute, *m.* an ancient gold coin.

salutíferamente, *adv.* salubriously.

salutífero, ra, *a.* healthful, salubrious.

salva, *f.* (arti.) salvo; salver, tray; ordeal; oath, solemn promise, assurance; pregustation.

salvación, *f.* salvation; deliverance.

salvachia, *f.* (naut.) salvage strap.

salvado, *pp.* & *m.* bran.

salvador, ra, *n.* savior, rescuer, redeemer.

salvadoreño, ña, *n.* & *a.* Salvadorean (from Salvador).

salvaguardia. I. *m.* safeguard, security, protection; guard; watchman. **II.** *f.* safe-conduct, passport.

salvajada, *f.* brutal or stupid action.

salvaje. I. *a.* savage; wild (s. o. plants and beasts); rough, wild (country). **II.** *m.* savage.

salvajemente, *adv.* savagely, wildly.

salvajería, *f.* brutal action; savageness.

salvajez, *f.* savageness.**—salvajina,** *f.* wild beast; multitude of wild animals; collection of skins of wild beasts.**—salvajino, na,** *a.* savage, wild, untamed; gamy (meat).

salvajismo, *m.* savagery; (coll.) rusticity.

salvajuelo, la, *n.* little savage.

salvamano.—a s., without danger to one's self; in a cowardly manner.

salvamente, *adv.* securely, safely.

salvamento, salvamiento, *m.* salvage; safety, place of safety; salvation.

salvante. I. *a.* saving, excepting. **II.** *adv.* (coll.) save.

salvar. I. *va.* to save; (naut.) to salve, save; to avoid (a danger); to clear (an obstacle); to overcome (a difficulty); go over, pass over, jump over (a ditch, creek, etc.); make allowance for, excuse, make an exception of; to prove legally the innocence of. **II.** *vn.* to taste, to prove (the food or drink of nobles). **III.** *vr.* to be saved; to escape from danger.

salvavidas, *m.* life preserver.

¡salve! *interj.* hail!**—Salve,** *f.* (eccl.) Salve Regina.

salvedad, *f.* reservation, exception, qualification.

salvia, *f.* (bot.) sage.

salvilla, *f.* salver, glass rack, tray, waiter.

salvo, va, *a.* saved, safe; excepted, omitted.

salvo, *adv.* save, saving, excepting, barring.**—s. el guante,** or **s. el zurrado,** excuse the glove.**—a s.,** without injury or diminution.**—en s.,** safe, with safety.

salvoconducto, *m.* safe-conduct, passport; license, permit, pass.

salvohonor, *m.* (coll.) breech, buttocks.

salladura, *f.* (agr.) weeding.**—sallar,** *va.* (agr.) to weed.**—sallete,** *m.* (agr.) weeder, weeding tool.

sámago, *m.* sap rot, dry rot.

samán, *m.* (bot.) genisaro, rain tree.

sámara, *f.* (bot.) samara.

samarita; samaritano, na, *n.* & *a.* Samaritan.

samaruguera, *f.* fishing net that is set across streams.

sambenitar, *va.* to make infamous, to dishonor publicly.

sambenito, *m.* garment worn by penitent convicts of the Inquisition; placard in churches, containing names of penitents and their penance; note of infamy; disgrace.

samblaje, *m.* = ENSAMBLADURA.

sambuca, *f.* (mus., mil.) sambuca.

sambumbia, *f.* (Cuba) fermented drink made from cane juice, water, and peppers; (Peru) hubbub, confusion.**—sambumblería,** *f.* place where SAMBUMBIA is made and sold.

samio, mia, *n.* & *a.* Samian (from Samos).

samnita, samnite, *n.* & *a.*; **samnítico, ca,** *a.* Samnite.

samoyedo, da, *n.* & *a.* Samoyed (-ic).

sampaguita, *f.* a tropical flower resembling the jasmine.

sampán, *m.* sampan, a Chinese skiff.

sampsuco, *m.* (bot.) marjoram.

samuga, *f.* mule chair.

san, *a.* (*contr.* of SANTO) Saint (before masculine proper nouns).

sanable, *a.* curable, healable.

sanador, ra, *n.* curer, healer.

sanalotodo, *m.* cure-all, catholicon, panacea.

sanamente, *adv.* sanely; sincerely.

sanar. I. *va.* to heal, cure. **II.** *vn.* to heal; to recover from sickness.

sanativo, va, *a.* sanative, curative.

sanatorio, *m.* sanatorium, sanitarium.

sanción, *f.* sanction; ratification.

sancionar, *va.* to sanction; to ratify, authorize.

sanco, *m.* (Ch.) porridge made from toasted corn meal or wheat flour; very thick mud; (Arg.) a stew made with beef blood, flour and onions.

sancochar, *va.* (cook.) to boil with water and salt.

sancocho, *m.* (Am.) a kind of thin stew of boiled yucca, meat, plantains, etc.

sancta, *m.* fore part of the tabernacle.

sanctasanctórum, *m.* sanctum sanctorum.

sanctórum, *m.* (Philip.) a tribute to the church.

sanctus, *m.* (eccl.) Sanctus, Trisagion.

sanchete, *m.* an ancient silver coin.

sanchopancesco, ca, *a.* like, or after the way of, Sancho Panza.

sandalia, *f.* sandal.

sandalino, na, *a.* pertaining to sandalwood.

sándalo, *m.* (bot.) bergamot mint; sandalwood or sanders.

sandáraca, *f.* (min.) sandarach, realgar; sandarach (gum).

sandez, *f.* inanity, foolish or stupid statement.

sandía, *f.* (bot.) watermelon.

sandiar, *m.* watermelon patch.

sandio, dia, *a.* foolish, nonsensical, inane.

sandunga, *f.* (coll.) gracefulness, elegance; winsomeness, fascination.**—sandunguero, ra,** *a.* (coll.) winsome, graceful, fascinating.

saneado, da, *pp.* & *a.* drained; free, clear, unencumbered.

saneamiento, *m.* (law) security, surety, bail, guarantee; indemnification, reparation; drainage, improvement (of land).

sanear, *va.* to give security, to give bail; (law) to indemnify; to make harmless; to drain, improve (lands).

sanedrín, *m.* Sanhedrin.

sanfrancia, *f.* (coll.) quarrel, dispute, row.

sangley, *m.* (Philip.) Chinese trader.

sangradera, *f.* (surg.) lancet; basin (for blood); lock, sluice, drain.

sangrador, *m.* phlebotomist, bloodletter; outlet.

sangradura, *f.* (surg.) bleeding; bend of the arm opposite the elbow; draining, drainage.

sangrar. I. *va.* (surg.) to bleed; to drain; (coll.) to extort or borrow money from; (print.) to indent. **II.** *vn.* to bleed. **III.** *vr.* to be bled.

sangraza, *f.* corrupt or filthy blood.

sangre, *f.* blood; gore; race, family, kindred.—**s. azul,** blue blood, nobility.—**s. de drago,** dragon's blood.—**s. fría,** calmness, composure, sang-froid.— **a s. caliente,** impulsively, on the spur of the moment.—**a s. fría,** in cold blood.—**a s. y fuego,** by fire and sword, by blood and iron.—**en s. fría,** in cold blood.—**mala s.,** bad blood, vindictiveness.— **subírsele a uno la s. a la cabeza,** to become excited, lose one's self control.

sangría, *f.* (surg.) bleeding, bloodletting; present made to a person who bleeds; drain, drainage, draining; pilfering, pilferage; inside of the forearm; (print.) indenting a line; sangaree, a refreshing drink made with wine.

sangrientamente, *adv.* bloodily, cruelly.

sangriento, ta, *a.* bloody, bloodstained, gory; cruel, sanguinary, bloodthirsty.

sanguaza, *f.* serous blood; reddish fluid of vegetables.

sangüeño, *m.* (bot.) wild cornel.

sangüesa, *f.* raspberry.

sangüeso, *m.* (bot.) raspberry bush.

sanguífero, ra, *a.* sanguiferous.

sanguificación, *f.* (med.) sanguification.

sanguificar, *va.* to make blood from.

sanguijuela, *f.* leech; sponger; sharper, cheat.

sanguinaria, *f.* (bot.) bloodroot; knotgrass; (min.) bloodstone, hematite.

sanguinariamente, *adv.* sanguinarily, bloodily.

sanguinario, ria, *a.* sanguinary, cruel, bloody, bloodthirsty.

sanguíneo, nea; sanguino, na, *a.* red, bloodcolored; sanguineous, sanguine.

sanguinolencia, *f.* sanguinolence.

sanguinolento, ta, *a.* sanguinolent.

sanguinoso, sa, *a.* sanguine, sanguineous; bloody, sanguinary, cruel.

sanguiñuelo, *m.* (bot.) wild cornel.

sangüis, *m.* (Lat.) blood of Christ; consecrated wine.

sanguisorba, *f.* (bot.) great burnet.

sanguja, *f.* leech.

sanícula, *f.* (bot.) sanicle.

sanidad, *f.* soundness; health; healthfulness; health department.—**s. marítima,** quarantine officers.—**en s.,** in health.

sanidina, *f.* (min.) sanidine.

sanie, sanies, *f.* (med.) sanies.

sanioso, sa, *a.* (med.) sanious, ichorous.

sanitario, ria. I. *a.* sanitary, hygienic. **II.** *m.* health officer.

sanjacado, sanjacato, *m.* government of a sanjak (a Turkish district).—**sanjaco,** *m.* governor of a sanjak.

sanjuanada, *f.* picnic on St. John's day.

sanjuanero, ra, *a.* ripe by St. John's day (s. o. fruits).

sanjuanino, na, *n. & a.* of or from San Juan.

sanjuanista, *m.* knight of St. John of Jerusalem.

sanluisero, ra, *n. & a.* of or from San Luis.

sanmiguelada, *f.* Michaelmas.

sanmigueleño, ña, *a.* ripe by Michaelmas (s. o. fruits).

sano, na, *a.* sound, healthy, hale; salutary; sane; secure; honest, good; discreet, wise; safe, harmless; entire, complete.—**s. y salvo,** safe and sound.

sánscrito, ta. I. *a.* Sanskrit. **II.** *m.* Sanskrit.

sansimoniano, na, *a.* St. Simonian.

sansimonismo, *m.* St. Simonism.

santa, *f.* female saint.

santabárbara, *f.* (naut.) magazine, powder room.

santafecino, na, *n. & a.* of or from Santa Fe.

santafereño, ña, *n. & a.* of or from (Santa Fe de) Bogotá.

santaláceo, a, *a.* (bot.) santalaceous.

santamente, *adv.* saintly, saintlily; plainly, simply.

santandereano, na, *a.* of or from Santander (Colombia).—**santanderiense; santanderino, na,** *a.* of or from Santander (Spain).

santelmo, *m.* (naut.) St. Elmo's fire.

santero, ra. I. *a.* too devoted to worship of saints. **II.** *n.* caretaker of a sanctuary; seller of images.

santiagueño, ña, *a.* ripe by St. James's day (s. o. fruits).

santiaguero, ra, *a.* of or belonging to Santiago (Cuba).—**santiagués, sa,** *a.* of or belonging to Santiago (Galicia).—**santiaguino, na,** *a.* of or belonging to Santiago (Chile).

santiaguista. I. *a.* belonging to the order of Santiago. **II.** *m.* knight of Santiago or St. James.

santiamén, *m.* (coll.) instant, moment, twinkling of an eye, jiffy.

santico, ca, *n. dim.* little image of a saint; (coll.) good child.

santidad, *f.* sanctity, saintliness, holiness, godliness.—**su S.,** his Holiness (the Pope).

santificable, *a.* sanctifiable.

santificación, *f.* sanctification, making holy.—**s. de las fiestas,** keeping of holy days.

santificador, ra, *n. & a.* sanctifier (-fying).

santificante, *a.* blessing, sanctifying.

santificar. I. *va.* (*pret.* SANTIFIQUÉ: *subj.* SANTIFIQUE) to sanctify, hallow, consecrate; to keep (holy days). **II.** *va. & vr.* to justify, exculpate, clear from guilt, acquit.

santiguada, *f.* crossing one's self; rough treatment, reprimand.—**para,** or **por, mi s.,** faith, by this cross.

santiguadera, *f.* healing by signs of the cross.

santiguadero, ra; dor, ra, *n.* healer by signs of the cross.

santiguamiento, *m.* crossing one's self.

santiguar. I. *va.* to bless, to heal by blessing; (coll.) to slap. **II.** *vr.* to cross one's self.

santimonia, *f.* sanctity, sanctimony, holiness; (bot.) corn marigold, chrysanthemum.

santísimo, ma, *a. sup.* most holy.—**el S.,** the holy sacrament.

santo, ta. I. *a.* saintly, holy, blessed; saint; sacred, consecrated; inviolable; (coll.) simple, plain, artless.—**s. hermandad,** Holy Brotherhood, an ancient Spanish rural police.—**s. oficio,** Holy Office (the Inquisition).—**S. Padre,** Holy Father (the Pope); Father of the Church (one of the first Christian writers).—**s. varón,** holy man; simpleton; hypocrite.—**s. y bueno,** well and good.—**todo el s. día,** the whole day long. **II.** *n.* saint; saint's day; image of a saint.—**santo y seña,** watchword, password.—**alzarse con el s. y la limosna,** to take everything, make a clean sweep.—**dar el s.,** (mil.) to set or give the password.—**Todos los Santos,** All Saint's Day.

santol, *m.* santol, sandal tree.

santón, *m. aug.* dervish; hypocrite.

santónico, *m.* (bot.) santonica.

santonina, *f.* santonine.

santoral, *m.* (eccl.) collection of lives of the saints; church choir book.

santuario, *m.* sanctuary.

santucho, cha; santurrón, na, *n.* (coll.) sanctimonious, person, hypocrite.

santurronería, *f.* sanctimony, hypocrisy.

saña, *f.* anger, passion, rage, fury.

sañosamente, *adv.* angrily, cruelly.

sañoso, sa, *a.* furious, enraged; cruel.

sañudamente, *adv.* furiously.

sañudo, da, *a.* furious, enraged.

sao, *m.* (bot.) LABIÉRNAGO; small savanna with clusters of trees or shrubs.

sapa, *f.* residue left after chewing BUYO.

sapajú, *m.* sapajou.

sapán, *m.* (bot.) (Philip.) sapan wood; sapan tree.

sapeca, *f.* sapek or sapec, an oriental coin.

sápido, da, *a.* sapid, savory.

sapiencia, *f.* wisdom, knowledge, learning.

sapiencial, *m.* sapiential book.

sapiente, *a.* wise, learned.—**sapientísimamente,** *adv.* most wisely, or learnedly.

sapillo, *m. dim.* little toad.

sapina, *f.* (bot.) glasswort.

sapindáceo, a, *a.* (bot.) sapindaceous.

sapino, *m.* (bot.) savin.

apo, *m.* toad.
aponáceo, cea, *a.* saponaceous, soapy.
aponaria, *f.* (bot.) common soapwort.
aponificable, *a.* saponifiable.
aponificación, *f.* saponification.
aponificar. I. *va.* (*pret.* SAPONIFIQUÉ: *subj.* SAPONIFIQUE) to saponify. **II.** *vr.* to become saponified.
aponina, *f.* (chem.) saponin.
saporífero, ra, *a.* imparting savor.
sapotáceo, a, *a.* (bot.) sapotaceous.
saprofítico, ca, *a.* (bot.) saprophytic.
saprofito, ta. I. *a.* saprophytic. **II.** *m.* saprophyte.
saque, *m.* striking a ball on its rebound; one who strikes the ball; base from which a ball is tossed.
saqueador, ra, *n.* looter, pillager.
saquear, *va.* to plunder, loot, pillage.
saqueamiento, saqueo, *m.* pillage, loot, plunder, foray.
saquería, *f.* place for or collection of sacks.
saquero, ra. I. *n.* maker or seller of sacks. **II.** *f.* packing needle.
saquete, *m.* *dim.* (arti.) cartridge bag.
saquilada, *f.* small amount of grain in a sack.
saquillo, ito, *m.* *dim.* small sack or bag.
saragüete, *m.* informal hop.
sarampión, *m.* (med.) measles.
sarangosti, *m.* (naut.) sarangousty; pitch gum.
sarao, *m.* evening party, hop.
sarape, *m.* (Am.) serape, a shawl or blanket worn by men.
sarapia, *f.* (bot.) tonka bean.
sarapico, *m.* (orn.) curlew.
sarasa, *m.* effeminate man.
saraviado, da, *a.* spotted, piebald.
sarcasmo, *m.* sarcasm.
sarcástico, ca, *a.* sarcastic.
sarcia, *f.* load, burden.
sarcocarpio, *m.* (bot.) sarcocarp.
sarcocele, *m.* (med.) sarcocele.
sarcocola, *f.* sarcocol (resinous gum).
sarcófago, *m.* tomb, grave; sarcophagus.
sarcolema, *m.* (anat.) sarcolemma.
sarcología, *f.* (anat.) sarcology.
sarcoma, *f.* (med.) sarcoma.
sarcótico, ca, *a.* sarcotic.
sarda, *f.* (icht.) horse mackerel.
sardana, *f.* a Catalonian dance.
sardesco, ca. I. *a.* small (ass or horse); (coll.) rude, stubborn. **II.** *m.* pony; small ass.
sardiano, na, *n.* & *a.* Sardian.
sardina, *f.* (icht.) sardine.—**como s. en banasta,** or **en barril,** packed like sardines.
sardinal, *m.* sardine net.
sardinel, *m.* (mas.) brickwork having the bricks closely placed on edge.
sardinero, ra. I. *a.* belonging to sardines. **II.** *n.* dealer in sardines. **III.** *m.* (S-) a public walk near Santander.
sardineta, *f.* small sardine; sprat; part of cheese that overtops the cheese vat; (naut.) knittle, laniard.—*pl.* (mil.) chevrons in uniforms.
sardio, sardo, *m.* (jewel.) sard, sardius.
sardo, da. I. *n.* & *a.* Sardinian. **II.** *a.* red, black and white (s. o. cattle).
sardonia, *f.* (bot.) crowfoot, spearwort.
sardónica, sardónice, *f.* (jewel.) sardonyx.
sardónico, ca, *a.* sardonic; insincere, affected (laughter).
sardonio, sardónique, *m.* = SARDÓNICE.
sarga, *f.* silk serge or twill; (art) fabric painted in distemper or oil, like tapestry; (bot.) osier or willow.
sargadilla, *f.* (bot.) soda-ash plant.
sargado, da, *a.* sergelike.
sargal, *m.* clump of osiers.
sargatillo, *m.* (bot.) a kind of willow.
sargazo, *m.* (bot.) sargasso, gulfweed.
sargenta, *f.* sergeant's halberd; sergeant's wife.

sargentear, *va.* to command as a sergeant; to command; (coll.) to boss, lord it over.
sargentería, *f.* (mil.) sergeant's drill.
sargentía, *f.* sergeantship, sergeantcy.
sargento, *m.* (mil.) sergeant.
sargentona, *f.* big coarse woman.
sargo, *m.* (icht.) sheepshead.
sarguero, ra. I. *a.* willowy. **II.** *m.* painter of SARGA.
sargueta, *f.* thin, light serge.
sarilla, *f.* (bot.) marjoram.
sármata, *n.* & *a.*; **sarmático, ca,** *a.* Sarmatian.
sarmentador, ra, *n.* one who gathers pruned vine shoots.—**sarmentar,** *vn.* to gather pruned vine shoots.—**sarmentera,** *f.* place where pruned vine shoots are kept; gathering pruned vine shoots.—**sarmentillo,** *m.* *dim.* slender vine shoot.
sarmentoso, sa, *a.* vinelike, twining.
sarmiento, *m.* (bot.) sarmentum, runner.
sarna, *f.* (med.) itch; mange.—**s. perruna,** nonsuppurating mange.—**más viejo que la s.,** as old as Methuselah.
sarnazo, *m.* malignant itch.
sarnoso, sa, *a.* itchy; scabbed; mangy.
sarpullido, *m.* rash, eruption.
sarpullir, *va.* & *vr.* to cause or have a rash.
sarracénico, ca, *a.* Saracenic.
sarraceno, na; sarracín, na, *n.* & *a.* Saracen (-ic), Moor (-ish).
sarracina, *f.* scuffle, fight.
sarrapia, *f.* = SARAPIA.
sarria, *f.* coarse net for straw; large frail.
sarrillo, *m.* stertor of a dying person; (bot.) arum.
sarrio, *m.* a kind of wild goat.
sarro, *m.* crust or incrustation in vessels; (med.) sordes; (dent.) tartar, tophus.
sarroso, sa, *a.* crusty.
sarta, *f.* string of beads or pearls; line, series.
sartal, *m.* string of beads, etc.
sartalejo, *m.* *dim.* small string of pearls.
sartén, *f.* frying pan.—**tener la s. por el mango,** to have the command, control or advantage.
sartenada, *f.* as much as can be fried at one time in a frying pan.—**sartenazo,** *m.* blow with a frying pan; (coll.) blow with anything.—**sarteneja,** *f.* *dim.* small frying pan.
sartorio, *m.* (anat.) sartorius (muscle).
sasafrás, *m.* (bot.) sassafras.
sastra, *f.* wife of a tailor; tailoress.
sastre, *m.* tailor.—**s. remendón,** repairer.
sastrecillo, *m.* *dim.* petty tailor.
sastrería, *f.* tailor's trade; tailor's shop.
sastresa, *f.* = SASTRA.
Satán, Satanás, *m.* Satan.—**satánicamente,** *adv.* satanically.—**satánico, ca,** *a.* satanic.
satélite, *m.* satellite; (coll.) bailiff, constable, sheriff; follower, henchman; sycophant.
satén, *m.* sateen.
satinador, ra, *n.* glazer, calender; (*m.*) polishing tool; (*m.*, photo.) burnisher.
satinar, *va.* to calender, glaze, gloss, burnish.
sátira, *f.* satire; hint, innendo; (coll.) saucy and witty woman.
satiriasis, *f.* (med.) satyriasis.
satíricamente, *adv.* satirically; sarcastically.
satírico, ca. I. *a.* satirical; sarcastic. **II.** *m.* satirist.
satirillo, *m.* *dim.* little satyr.
satirio, *m.* a kind of water rat.
satirión, *m.* (bot.) orchis that yields salep.
satirizante, *a.* satirizing.
satirizar, *va.* (*pret.* SATIRICÉ: *subj.* SATIRICE) to satirize, lampoon.
sátiro, *m.* satyr, sylvan god; lewd man.
satisdación, *f.* (law) security, surety, bail.
satisfacción, *f.* satisfaction; amends; apology, excuse; confidence, conceit.—**a s.,** fully, according to one's wishes.—**tomar s.,** to vindicate one's self, to stand for one's honor.
satisfacer. I. *va.* (*for irr. v.* HACER) to satisfy; to pay in full, settle; to expiate, make amends for, atone for; to reward; to indemnify, repay; to

answer, make reply; to explain; to free from debt, perplexity, or suspense; to convince.—**s. una letra,** (com.) to honor a draft. **II.** *vr.* to satisfy one's self; to be satisfied; to take satisfaction; to be revenged; to be convinced.

satisfaciente, *a.* satisfying, satisfactory.

satisfactoriamente, *adv.* satisfactorily.

satisfactorio, ria, *a.* satisfactory.

satisfago, satisfaga. *V.* SATISFACER.

satisfecho, cha, *a.* & *pp. irr.* of SATISFACER; satisfied, content; arrogant, conceited.

satisfice, satisfizo. *V.* SATISFACER.

sativo, va, *a.* sown, cultivated.

sátrapa, *m.* satrap; (coll.) crafty fellow; boss.

satrapía, *f.* satrapy.

saturación, *f.* saturation.

saturar, *va.* to saturate; to fill, glut, satiate.

saturnal. I. *a.* Saturnian. **II.** *f. pl.* Saturnalia.

saturnino, na, *a.* saturnine, melancholy, grave, gloomy, morose; (chem.) saturnine.

saturnio, nia, *a.* Saturnian.

saturnismo, *m.* plumbism, lead poisoning.

Saturno, *m.* (ast.) Saturn.

sauce, *m.* (bot.) willow.—**s. cabruno,** goat willow or great sallow.—**s. llorón,** weeping willow.

sauceda, saucedal, *m.*; **saucera,** *f.* plantation of willows.

saucillo, *m.* (bot.) knotgrass.

saúco, *f.* (bot.) elder or alder tree; second hoof of horses.

sauquillo, *m.* (bot.) dwarf elder.

saurio, *m.* saurian.

sausería, *f.* larder in a palace.

sausier, *m.* chief of the larder in a palace.

sautor, *m.* (her.) saltier.

sauz, *m.* (bot.) willow.

sauzal, *m.* plantation of willows.

sauzgatillo, *m.* agnus castus, chaste-tree.

savia, *f.* sap.

saxafrax, *f.* (bot.) = SAXIFRAGA.

saxátil, *a.* growing among rocks: saxicolous.

sáxeo, ea, *a.* stony.

saxifraga, saxifragia, *f.* (bot.) saxifrage plant.

saxifragáceo, a, *a.* (bot.) saxifragaceous.

saxófono, *m.* (mus.) saxophone.

saxoso, sa, *a.* containing stones, stony.

saya, *f.* (outer) skirt; sum of money that the Queen of Spain gives her maids when they marry; an ancient tunic or gown worn by men.

sayal, *m.* coarse woollen stuff; sackcloth.

sayalería, *f.* shop for weaving coarse cloth.

sayalero, *m.* weaver of SAYAL.

sayalesco, ca, *a.* made of SAYAL.

sayalete, *m. dim.* thin flannel for undergarments.

sayete, sayito, *m. dim.* small frock, short skirt.

sayo, *m.* smock frock; large coat; any loose garment.—**s. bobo,** tight dress worn by clowns.—**decir para su s.,** to say in one's sleeve.

sayón, na, *n. m. aug.* executioner; ugly-looking person; (formerly) a kind of judge.

sayuela, *f. dim.* woollen shift worn by some religious orders; a variety of fig tree; (Am.) petticoat.

sayuelo, *m. dim.* little frock.

sazón, *f.* maturity, ripeness; season; taste, relish, flavor; seasoning; occasion, opportunity.—**a la s.,** then, at that time.—**en s.,** ripe, in season; opportunely.

sazonadamente, *adv.* maturely, seasonably.

sazonado, da, *a.* & *pp.* seasoned, mature, ripe, mellow; witty; pertinent; expressive.

sazonador, ra, *n.* seasoner.

sazonar. I. *va.* (cook.) to season; to mature, bring to maturity. **II.** *vr.* to ripen, to mature.

se, 3*d. person objective pron.*, *m.* or *f.*, *sing.* or *pl.* It is used: (1) As a reflexive accusative case, equivalent to "himself," "one's self," "herself," "itself," "themselves," "to himself," "to one's self," etc. (*él se afeitó*, he shaved himself; *las niñas se vistieron*, the girls dressed themselves; *uno se ama*, one loves one's self). (2) As an accusative or a dative

reciprocal case, to indicate mutual action, an equivalent to "each other," "one another," "each other," "to one another" (*Juan y María aman, pero no se hablan*, John and Mary love each other, but do not speak to each other). (3) As mere symbol to form reflexive verbs, which are reflexive only in form, not in meaning, as *trse* to go; *morírse* to die: *reírse*, to laugh. (4) Instead of the dative cases *le, les,* before an accusative case (*yo se lo di*, I gave it to him [her, them, you]; *Juan se los entregó*, John delivered them to him [her, them, you]). (5) To give a possessive value to a definite or indefinite article (*Juan se corta las uñas*, John cuts his nails; *Juan se quebró una mano*, John broke one of his hands). (6) To form certain expressions of a passive character, which are rendered into English by the passive form of the corresponding verb, or by introducing "they," "people," "one," as an indefinite subject (*se dice*, it is said, they say, people say; *no se sabe*, it is not known; *esto se aprende fácilmente*, this is easily learned, one learns this easily; *aquí se habla español*, Spanish [is] spoken here; *eso no puede negarse*, that cannot be denied). When *se* is thus used indefinitely in the imperative mood, the resulting form is generally rendered by the simple imperative (*para otros pormenores, escríbase al secretario*, for other particulars, write to the secretary; *consúltese el diccionario*, consult the dictionary).

sé, *V.* SABER.

sebáceo, cea, *a.* sebaceous, tallowy.

sebastiano, *m.* (bot.) = SEBESTÉN.

sebe, *f.* wattle, stockade, fence.

sebero, ra, *a.* tallow (u. a.), relating to tallow.

sebestén, *m.* (bot.) sebesten tree; its fruit.

sebillo, *m.* white tallow; toilet soap.

sebo, *m.* tallow, fat, candle grease.—**s. en bruto,** or **en rama,** rough tallow, suet.

seborrea, *f.* (med.) seborrhea.

seboso, sa, *a.* tallowy, fat, greasy, unctuous.

sebucán, *m.* (Am.) manioc strainer.

seca, *f.* drought; dry season; (med.) desquamation; infarction of a gland; (naut.) dry sand bank.—**a secas,** simply.

secácul, *m.* (bot.) an aromatic root.

secadal, *m.* dry, barren ground or sand bank.

secadero, ra. I. *a.* good or fit for drying (s. o. fruit). **II.** *m.* drying shed, room, or floor; drier; fruit drier.—**secado, da,** *pp.* dried, desiccated.—**s. al sol,** sun-dried.

secadillo, *m.* dry-almond biscuit.

secamente, *adv.* dryly; curtly; coldly; simply.

secamiento, *m.* drying, desiccation.

secano, *m.* unwatered land; dry sand bank; anything very dry.

secansa, *f.* at cards, sequence.

secante. I. *a.* siccative, exsiccative; blotting (paper). **II.** *f.* (geom.) secant.

secar. I. *va.* (*pret.* SEQUÉ: *subj.* SEQUE) to dry, exsiccate, desiccate; to parch; to wipe dry, dry by wiping; to tease, vex, annoy, bore. **II.** *vr.* to dry, to parch, to dry up; to become lank, lean, or meagre; to decay; to wither; to be extremely thirsty.

secaral, *m.* dryness, drought.

secatura, *f.* insipidity, vapidity, dulness.

sección, *f.* act of cutting; section, division, portion; (geom.) section; (arch.) section of a building.—**s. de fondo,** editorial section.—**s. recta,** (geom.) right section.—**s. transversal** (drawing, eng.) cross section.

seccionado, da, *pp.* & *a.* sectional, in sections.

seccionar, *va.* to section.

seccionario, ria, *a.* sectional.

secesión, *f.* secession.

secesionista, *n.* & *a.* secessionist.

seceso, *m.* excrement, stool.

seco, ca; *a.* dry; dried up; juiceless; arid; withered; dead (leaves); lean, lank, meager; plain, unadorned, unvarnished; rude, curt; lukewarm, cold, indifferent; thin and spare; dull (s. o. pains).—**en s.,** high and dry; without cause or reason; (mas.) dry, without mortar; by the dry process, without water.

secreción, *f.* segregation; (med.) secretion.

secreta, *f.* private examination preceding the graduation of licentiates; (eccl.) secrets; secret investigation; privy, water-closet.

secretamente, *adv.* secretly.

secretar, *va.* (physiol.) to secrete.

secretaria, *f.* wife of a secretary; woman secretary.

secretaría, *f.* secretary's office; secretaryship.

secretario, *m.* secretary; actuary; scribe, amanuensis.—**S. de Estado,** Secretary of State.—**S. de Hacienda,** Secretary of the Treasury.—**S. del Despacho** = s. DE ESTADO.—**s. particular,** private secretary.

secretear, *vn.* (coll.) to whisper.—**secreteo,** *m.* (coll.) whispering.—**secretico, illo, ito,** *m. dim.* little secret.—**secretista,** *m.* naturalist; dealer in secrets.

secreto, ta. I. *a.* secret; confidential, private. **II.** *m.* secret; secrecy; nostrum; caution, silence, dissimulation, concealment; scrutoire, secret drawer.—**s. a voces,** or **con chirimías,** open secret.—**en s.,** in secret, in private, confidentially.

secretorio, ria, *a.* (med.) secretory.

secta, *f.* sect; doctrine of a sect.

sectador, ra; sectario, ria, *n.* & *a.* sectarian.

sectarismo, *m.* sectarianism.

sector, *m.* (geom., mil.) sector.

secuaz, *m.* follower, supporter, henchman.

secuela, *f.* sequel, result, upshot.

secuencia, *f.* (eccl.) sequence.

secuestrable, *a.* (law) sequestrable.

secuestración, *f.* (law) sequestration.

secuestrador, ra, *n.* sequestrator, receiver.

secuestrar, *va.* (law) to sequestrate, sequester; to kidnap, abduct.

secuestrario, ria, *a.* belonging to sequestration.

secuestro, *m.* (law) sequestration; umpire, referee; kidnapping, abduction; (surg.) sequestrum.

secular. I. *a.* centenary, centennial; lasting for ages; secular, lay. **II.** *m.* (eccl.) secular.

secularización, *f.* secularization.

secularizar, *va.* (pret. SECULARICÉ: *subj.* SECULARICE) to secularize.

secundar, *va.* to second, aid, favor.

secundariamente, *adv.* secondarily.

secundario, ria. I. *a.* secondary; high (school); subordinate; subsidiary. **II.** *m.* (watch.) seconds hand.

secundinas, *f. pl.* afterbirth and secundines.

secundípara, *a.* twice a mother, a mother for the second time.

secura, *f.* dryness, droughtiness.

sed, *f.* thirst; drought; eagerness, anxiety; longing desire.—**tener s.,** to be thirsty.—**tener s. de,** to be thirsty for; to thirst, or hunger, after.

seda, *f.* silk (fibre, yarn, and fabric); wild boar's bristles.—**s. cocida,** soft silk.—**s. conchal,** finest silk from choice cocoons.—**s. cruda,** hard silk.—**s. de capullos,** ferret silk, grosgrain yarn.—**s. de coser,** sewing silk.—**s. en rama,** raw silk.—**s. floja,** floss silk; soft, untwisted silk.—**s. joyante,** very glossy silk.—**s. torcida,** twisted silk.—**como una s.,** as smooth as silk; easily, without hitch or hindrance.—**de media s.,** half-silk.—**de toda s.,** all silk.—**ser como una s.,** or **ser una s.,** to be of a sweet temper.

sedadera, *f.* hackle for dressing flax.

sedal, *m.* fishline; (surg.) seton; (vet.) rowel.

sedalina, *f.* a silk-and-cotton fabric.

sedante, *a.* soothing, allaying, sedative.

sedar, *va.* to allay, appease, soothe, quiet.

sedativo, va, *n.* & *a.* (med.) sedative.

sede, *f.* (eccl.) see.—**Santa S.,** Holy See.

sedear, *va.* to clean (jewels) with a brush.

sedentario, ria, *a.* sedentary.

sedeña, *f.* fine tow of flax.

sedeño, ña, *a.* silky, silken; silklike.

sedera, *f.* brush made of bristles.

sedería, *f.* silks; silk stuff; silk shop.

sedero, ra. I. *a.* silk, silken. **II.** *n.* silk weaver, silk mercer, silk dealer.

sedición, *f.* sedition, insurrection, mutiny.

sediciosamente, *adv.* seditiously.

sedicioso, sa, *a.* seditious, mutinous.

sediento, ta, *a.* thirsty, dry; (w. **de**) eagerly desirous, anxious.

sedimentación, *f.* sedimentation.

sedimentar, *va.* & *vr.* to settle, to deposit (as dregs).

sedimentario, ria, *a.* sedimentary.

sedimento, *m.* sediment, settlings, dregs; feces, grouts, grounds; (min.) sinter.

sedoso, sa, *a.* silky, silklike, silken.

seducción, *f.* seduction, deceiving; abuse.

seducir, *va.* (for irr. v. DEDUCIR) to seduce, corrupt, entice, lead astray; to charm, captivate.

seductivo, va, *a.* seductive; enticing.

seductor, ra. I. *a.* fascinating, attractive, tempting. **II.** *n.* seducer, corrupter; deceiver; delightful person.

sefardí, sefardita, *n.* Spanish Jew.

segable, *a.* fit to be reaped.—**segada,** *f.* harvest.—**segadera,** *f.* reaping hook, sickle.—**segadero, ra,** *a.* fit to be reaped.—**segador, ra. I.** *n.* mower; reaper, harvester. **II.** *f.* mowing machine.

segar, *va.* (ind. SIEGO: pret. SEGUÉ: *subj.* SIEGUE) (agr.) to mow; to reap, harvest; to cut off, mow down.

segazón, *f.* harvest season; reaping.

seglar. I. *a.* worldly, secular, lay. **II.** *n.* layman (-woman).

seglarmente, *adv.* secularly.

segmento, *m.* segment; (geom.) segment.

segoviano, na; segoviense, *n.* & *a.* Segovian, from Segovia.

segregación, *f.* segregation, separation.

segregar, *va.* (for mut. v. AGREGAR) to segregate, separate, set apart; (med.) to secrete.

segregativo, va, *a.* segregative.

segrí, *m.* heavy, raised silk stuff.

segueta, *f.* buhl saw, piercing saw.

seguetear, *vn.* to make buhlwork with the buhl saw.

seguida, *f.* succession; continuation.—**de s.,** consecutively, without interruption.—**en s.,** forthwith, immediately.

seguidamente, *adv.* successively; immediately after, right after that.

seguidero, *m.* guide lines for writing.

seguidilla, *f.* (poet.) stanza of seven lines with peculiar rhythm.—*pl.* a merry Spanish tune and dance; (coll.) diarrhœa.

seguido, da. I. *pp.* & *a.* continued, successive; straight, direct. **II.** *m.* narrowing a stocking at the foot.

seguidor, ra. I. *n.* follower. **II.** *m.* guide rules for writing.

seguimiento, *m.* pursuit, following, chase; hunt; continuation, pursuit.

seguir. I. *va.* (gerund, SIGUIENDO: *ind.* SIGO: pret. él SIGUIÓ: *subj.* SIGA) to follow; to pursue; to prosecute; to continue; to dog, hound; to bring, institute (as a suit). **II.** *vr.* to ensue, follow as a consequence; to follow in order; to issue, spring.

según, *adv.* according to; as; it depends.—**s. derecho,** according to law.—**s. y como,** or **s. y conforme,** just as; it depends.

segunda, *f.* double turn of a key.

segundar. I. *va.* to repeat over again. **II.** *vn.* to be second, to follow next to the first.

segundariamente, *adv.* secondarily.

segundario, ria, *a.* = SECUNDARIO.

segundero, ra. I. *a.* (agr.) belonging to a second crop in the same year. **II.** *m.* seconds hand.

segundilla, *f.* call bell in convents.

segundillo, *m.* second portion of food distributed at table in convents; (mus.) semitone.

segundo, da. I. *a.* second; favorable.—**s. carpintero,** carpenter's mate.—**s. dama,** walking lady.—**s. galán,** walking gentleman.—**s. intención,** double meaning, double dealing, duplicity.—**de s. mano,** second-hand. **II.** *m.* second (of time or of arc); second in authority, assistant; equal (u. in the phrase **sin s.,** without an equal, unrivaled).

segundogénito, ta, *a.* & *n.* second-born.
segundogenitura, *f.* condition and right of a second-born.
segundón, *m.* any son born after the first.
segur, *f.* axe; axe in fasces carried by lictors;(agr.) sickle.
segurador, *m.* security, bondsman.
seguramente, *adv.* securely, safely; surely.
segurar, *va.* = ASEGURAR.
segureja, *f. dim.* (coop.) small hatchet.
seguridad, *f.* security, surety; certainty; safety; custody; corroboration; surety bond.—**con s., con toda s.,** with absolute certainty.
seguro, ra. I. *a.* secure; safe, reliable, dependable; sure, certain, positive; firm, constant, stanch, steady; unfailing. **II.** *m.* assurance, certainty, confidence; permit, warrant, license;(mech.) click, stop, pawl, ratchet; tumbler of a lock; (com.) insurance, assurance.—**s. contra accidentes, incendio, etc.,** accident, fire, etc. insurance.—**s. sobre la vida,** life insurance.—**a buen s., al s.,** or **de s.,** certainly, undoubtedly.—**en s.,** in security or safety.—**irse del s.,** to forget one's self, to throw wisdom overboard.—**sobre s.,** without risk.
segurón, *m. aug.* large axe or hatchet.
seis. I. *a.* & *m.* six; sixth (of the month); six-spotted card, die, or domino. **II.** *f. pl.*—**las s.,** six o'clock.
seisavado, da, *a.* hexagonal.
seisavo, va. I. *n.* & *a.* sixth. **II.** *m.* one sixth; hexagon.
seiscientos, tas, *n.* & *a.* six hundred; six-hundredth.
seise, *m.* one of six choir boys in some cathedrals, who sing and dance in certain festivals.
seisén, *m.* an ancient silver coin.
seiseno, na, *a.* sixth.
seisillo, *m.* (mus.) sextolet.
seísmico, etc., *V.* SÍSMICO, etc.
seje, *m.* (bot.) (S. A.) a kind of palm tree.
selacio, cia. I. *a.* (icht.) selachian. **II.** *m. pl.* Selachii.
selección, *f.* selection, choice.—**s. natural,** natural selection.—**s. sexual,** sexual selection.
selectas, *f. pl.* analects.
selecto, ta, *a.* select, choice.
selenio, *m.* (chem.) selenium.
selenita. I. *n.* inhabitant of the moon. **II.** *f.* (min.) selenite.
selenitoso, sa, *a.* (min.) selenitic.
seleniuro, *m.* (chem.) selenide.
selenografía, *f.* selenography.
selenógrafo, *m.* selenographer.
selfactina, *f.* (spinning) mule jenny.
selfinducción, *f.* (incorrect but common) (elec.) self-induction (=AUTOINDUCCIÓN).
selva, *f.* forest, wood, woods.
selvático, ca, *a.* forestal; rustic, wild.
selvatiquez, *f.* wildness; rusticity.
selvicultura, *f.* = SILVICULTURA.
selvoso, sa, *a.* sylvan, woody, wooded.
sellador, ra, *m.* sealer.—**selladura,** *f.* sealing.
sellar, *va.* to seal; to stamp; to conclude, finish; to cover, to close.—**s. los labios,** to silence; to keep silent.
sello, *m.* seal; stamp (mark or implement); signet; stamp office; (pharm.) wafer.—**s. de aduana,** cocket.—**s. de correo,** postage stamp.—**s. de Salomón,** Solomon's seal (mystic symbol); (bot.) Solomon's-seal.
semafórico, ca, *a.* semaphoric.
semáforo, *m.* semaphore.
semana, *f.* week; week's wages or pay.—**s. santa,** Holy Week; book containing the offices of this week.—**entre s.,** any week day except Saturday.—**la s. que no tenga viernes,** on the Greek calends, never.
semanal, *a.* weekly.
semanalmente, *adv.* weekly, by the week.
semanario, ria. I. *a.* weekly. **II.** *m.* weekly publication; set of seven razors.
semanería, *f.* functions performed or work done in the course of a week.

semanero, ra, *a.* engaged by the week.
semántica, *f.* semantics, semasiology.
semántico, ca, *a.* semantic.
semasiología, *f.* semasiology, semantics.
semblante, *m.* mien, countenance, look, expression; aspect.—**mudar de s.,** to change color; to take a different turn or a different aspect.
semblanza, *f.* biographical sketch.
sembrada, *f.* (agr.) sown land.
sembradera, *f.* (agr.) sowing machine, sower; seed drill, seeder, seeding machine.
sembradío, día, *a.* (agr.) prepared for sowing; arable.
sembrado, *m.* cultivated field, sown ground.
sembrador, ra. I. *n.* sower, seeder. **II.** *f.* seeder, sowing machine.
sembradura, *f.* sowing, seeding.
sembrar, *va.* (ind. SIEMBRO: subj. SIEMBRE) (agr.) to sow, seed; to scatter, spread, disseminate.—**como sembráredes cogeredes,** as you sow, so shall you reap.
semeja, *f.* resemblance, likeness; mark, sign.
semejable, *a.*; **semejado, da,** *pp.* & *a.* like, resembling.
semejante. I. *a.* similar, like; such, of that kind, (geom., alg.) similar. **II.** *m.* resemblance, likeness; fellow creature.
semejantemente, *adv.* likewise, similarly.
semejanza, *f.* resemblance, similarity, similitude.—**a s. de,** like.
semejar, *vn.* & *vr.* to be like, to resemble.
semen, *m.* semen, sperm; (bot.) seed.
semencera, *f.* sowing, seeding.
semencontra, *m.* (pharm.) vermifuge.
semental, *a.* (agr.) seminal, germinal; breeding (horse).
sementar, *va.* to sow, to seed.
sementera, *f.* (agr.) sowing, seeding; cultivated field, land sown; seed bed, seed field, seed garden, seed plot; seed sown; seedtime; origin, cause, beginning.
sementero, *m.* seed bag, seedcod, seedleap, hopper; seed bed, seed plot.
sementino, na, *a.* relating to seed or seedtime.
semestral, *a.* semiannual, half-yearly.
semestralmente, *adv.* semiannually.
semestre. I. *a.* lasting six months. **II.** *m.* space of six months, semester; six-months' pension or pay.
semi, *prefix,* semi, half, partly. Besides the words that are given below, this prefix is found in many other Spanish words, which are self-explaining.
semibreve, *f.* (mus.) semibreve, whole note (○).
semicabrón, semicapro, *m.* satyr.
semicilindro, *m.* half cylinder.
semicircular, *a.* semicircular.
semicírculo, *m.* (geom.) semicircle.
semicircunferencia, *f.* semicircumference.
semicopado, da, *a.* (mus.) syncopated.
semicorchea, *f.* (mus.) semiquaver.
semicromático, ca, *a.* (mus.) semichromatic.
semidea, *f.* (poet.) demigoddess.
semideo, *m.* (poet.) demigod.
semidiáfano, na, *a.* semidiaphanous.
semidiámetro, *m.* semidiameter.
semidiapasón, *m.* (mus.) semidiapason.
semidifunto, ta, *a.* half dead, almost dead.
semidiós, sa, *n.* demigod (-dess).
semidítono, *m.* (mus.) semiditone.
semidoble, *a.* semidouble.
semidormido, da, *a.* half asleep, sleepy.
semidragón, *m.* semidragon.
semieje, *m.* (geom.) semiaxis; (car.) half axle-tree.
semiesfera, *f.* hemisphere.
semiesférico, ca, *a.* hemispherical.
semiflósculo, *m.* (bot.) semifloret.
semifluído, da, *a.* semifluid.
semiforme, *a.* half formed, undeveloped.
semifusa, *f.* (mus.) double demisemiquaver.

semigola, *f.* (fort.) demigorge.

semihombre, *m.* half-man, pigmy.

semilunar, *a.* semilunar, semilunary.

semilunio, *m.* (ast.) half-moon.

semilla, *f.* seed.—**semillero,** *m.* seed bed, seed plot; nursery; hotbed.

seminal, *a.* seminal, germinal, spermatic.

seminario, *m.* seed plot, nursery; seminary; beginning, root, origin, source.—**s. conciliar,** theological seminary.

seminarista, *m.* seminarist, theological student.

seminífero, ra, *a.* seminiferous.

semínima, *f.* (mus.) crotchet.

semiología, semiótica, *f.* (med.) semeiology, symptomatology.

semipedal, *a.* half foot long.

semiplena, *a.* (law) imperfect (evidence).

semiplenamente, *adv.* half proved.

semiquintil, *m.* (ast.) semiquintile.

semirrecto, *a.* (geom.) of 45 degrees.

semirrubio, bia, *a.* nearly blonde.

semís, *m.* half a Roman pound.

semisalvaje, *a.* half-savage, semicivilized.

semisestil, *m.* (ast.) semisextile.

semita, *m.* Semite.—**semítico, ca,** *a.* Semitic.—**semitismo,** *m.* Semitism.

semitono, *m.* (mus.) semitone.

semitransparente, *a.* semitransparent.

semivivo, va, *a.* half alive.

semivocal, *n. & a.* (gram.) semivowel.

sémola, *f.* semolina, groats or grits.

sempiternamente, *adv.* eternally.

sempiterno, na. **I.** *a.* eternal, everlasting. **II.** *f.* a sort of serge, everlasting.

sen, *m.* (bot.) senna.

sena, *f.* six on a die; (bot.) senna.—*pl.* double sixes.

senado, *m.* senate; senate hall.

senadoconsulto, *m.* senatus consultum; decree of a senate.

senador, ra, *n.* senator.

senaduría, *f.* senatorship.

senara, *f.* piece of sown ground assigned to servants as part of their wages.

senarero, *m.* servant who has a SENARA.

senario, ria, *a.* senary.

senatorial; senatorio, ria, *a.* senatorial.

sencillamente, *adv.* simply; easily; plainly, candidly.

sencillez, *f.* simplicity; easiness; plainness, naturalness; candor.

sencillo, lla, *a.* simple, unmixed; light, slight, thin, of light body (fabrics); plain; artless, harmless; guileless, candid; natural, unadorned; single; of less value (coins).

senda, *f.* path, footpath, way.

senderar, *va.* to make a path in or through.

senderear. **I.** *va.* to guide or conduct on a footpath; to make a path in or for. **II.** *vn.* to adopt extraordinary means to obtain an end.

sendero, *m.* path, footpath, byway.

senderuelo, *m.* *dim.* little pathway.

sendos, das, *a.* one each, one for each (ch. constr.: *tienen sendos libros,* they have a book each, each of them has a book).

senecio, *m.* (bot.) Senecio.

senectud, *f.* old age, senescence.

senegalés, sa, *n. & a.* Senegalese.

senescal, *m.* seneschal.

senescalato, *m.,* **senescalía,** *f.* seneschalship.

senil, *a.* senile; (ast.) fourth quadrant.

seno, *m.* chest, thoracic cavity; breast, bosom; womb; lap of a woman; hole, cavity; sinus; gulf, bay; any cavity in the interior of the human body; innermost recess; asylum, refuge; (arch.) spandrel; (surg.) sinus; cavity of a wound; (naut.) curvature of a sail or line; (math.) sine.—**s. de Abrahán,** Abraham's bosom.—**s. verso,** (math.) versed sine.

senojil, *m.* (bot.) = CENOJIL.

sensación, *f.* sensation.

sensacional, *a.* sensational.

sensatez, *f.* good judgment, wisdom, good sense.

sensato, ta, *a.* sensible, judicious, wise.

sensibilidad, *f.* sensibility; sensitiveness.

sensibilizar, *va.* (pret. SENSIBILICÉ: *subj.* SENSIBILICE) (photo.) to sensitize.

sensible. **I.** *a.* sensible, perceptible, appreciable; sensitive; grievous, lamentable, regrettable; (photo.) sensitive, sensitized. **II.** *f.* (mus.) sensible, seventh note.

sensiblemente, *adv.* sensibly; perceptibly; approximately; grievously.

sensiblería, *f.* oversentimentality.

sensitiva, *f.* (bot.) sensitive plant, mimosa.

sensitivo, va, *a.* sensitive; sensual; sensible.

sensorio, ria. **I.** *a.* sensory, sensorial. **II.** *m.* sensorium (called also **s. común**).

sensual, *a.* sensuous; sensual, lewd, lustful.

sensualidad, *f.* sensuality, lust, lewdness.

sensualismo, *m.* sensualism, sensuality; (philos.) sensationalism.

sensualista. **I.** *a.* sensualistic. **II.** *n.* sensualist, sensationalist.

sensualmente, *adv.* sensually, carnally.

sentada, *f.* sitting. *V.* ASENTADA.

sentadero, *m.* place or thing where one can sit.

sentadillas.—a s., sidesaddlewise.

sentado, da, *pp. & a.* seated, sitting down; sedate, judicious, wise; settled, steady, firm; (bot.) sessile.

sentamiento, *m.* (arch.) settling.

sentar. **I.** *vn.* (*ind.* SIENTO: *subj.* SIENTE) to fit, to become, to suit; to agree with one (as food or a climate); to please, to be agreeable. **II.** *va.* to set, set up, establish; settle; to seat (*v.* ASENTAR); (tail.) to press the seams of. **III.** *vr.* to sink, subside, settle; to sit down; to settle down.

sentencia, *f.* (law) sentence, verdict, judgment; penalty; (com.) award; opinion, determination; dogma, axiom, maxim; (gram.) sentence,—**fulminar, or pronunciar, la s.,** to pass judgment.

sentenciador, ra, *n.* one who passes judgment.

sentenciar, *va.* (law) to sentence, to pass judgment on; to determine, decide.

sentención, *f.* severe, rigorous sentence.

sentenciosamente, *adv.* sententiously.

sentencioso, sa, *a.* sententious, pithy.

sentenzuela, *f.* *dim.* light sentence.

senticar, *m.* place full of briers and brambles.

sentidamente, *adv.* feelingly, regretfully.

sentido, da. **I.** *pp. & a.* felt, experienced; sensitive; susceptible, touchy; offended; cracked, split, cloven, relaxed.—**darse por s.,** to show resentment. **II.** *m.* sense, any one of the five senses; sense perception, feeling; judgment; understanding, reason; import, sense, meaning; direction, course.—**s. común,** common sense.—**con (todos) mis cinco sentidos,** with all my heart and soul.—**costar un s.,** to be excessively high-priced.—**perder el s.,** to become unconscious; to faint.—**sin s.,** meaningless; unconscious.

sentimental, *a.* sentimental; emotional.

sentimentalismo, *m.* sentimentalism.

sentimentalmente, *adv.* sentimentally.

sentimiento, *m.* sentiment, feeling; sensation; grief, sorrow, regret.

sentina, *f.* (naut.) bilge; sink, drain; place of iniquity.

sentir. **I.** *va.* (*gerund,* SINTIENDO: *ind.* SIENTO: *pret.* él SINTIÓ: *subj.* SIENTA) to feel; to perceive by the senses (to hear, smell, etc.); to endure, suffer; to grieve, regret, mourn, to be sorry for. **II.** *vn.* to feel; to judge, form an opinion; to foresee, foreknow; to fit the action to the word.—**sin s.,** without noticing, inadvertently. **III.** *vr.* to be moved, be affected; to complain; to resent; to feel (well, bad, sad); to crack; to be in a ruinous state; (naut.) to spring (yard or mast). **IV.** *m.* feeling; opinion, judgment.

seña, *f.* sign, mark, token; nod, dumb motion, gesture; signal; (mil.) password, watchword.—**señas mortales,** unmistakable signs or proof.—**señas personales,** personal description.—**por señas,** by signs.—**por señas, or por más señas,** as a stronger proof of it.

señal, *f.* sign, mark, token, symptom; mark or note of distinction; signal; landmark; bookmark; reminder; trace, vestige; trail, track, footstep; scar; representation, image; handsel, pledge; earnest money; (tel.) warning, call.—**s. de peligro,** signal of distress; (r. w.) danger signal.—**código de señales,** signal code.—**en s. de,** in proof of.—**ni s.,** not a trace.

señaladamente, *adv.* especially, remarkably; signally, notably.

señalado, da, *a.* & *pp.* distinguished, noted.

señalamiento, *m.* appointment, date.

señalar. I. *va.* to stamp, to mark; to point out, make known; to name; to appoint, fix, determine; to sign; to mark with a wound, especially in the face; (fenc.) to make a feint; at cards, to mark the points; to make signals to.—**s. con el dedo,** to point with the finger. **II.** *vr.* to distinguish one's self, to excel.

señaleja, *f. dim.* little sign or mark.

señera, *f.* ancient signal or pendant.

señero, ra, *a.* solitary, alone.

señolear, *vn.* to catch birds with a lure.

señor, *m.* sir, mister; lord, master, owner of a place; (eccl.) the eucharist.—**s. de horca y cuchillo,** lord of the manor, invested with civil and criminal jurisdiction within his estate.—**s. mayor,** aged man.—**el S.,** the Lord; our Lord (Jesus Christ).—**nuestro S.,** our Lord.

señora, *f.* lady, mistress, owner of a place; madam; dame, gentlewoman.—**s. de compañía,** companion, chaperon.—**s. mayor,** matron, middle-aged, respectable woman.—**muy s.,** very much of a lady.—**nuestra S.,** our Lady (the Virgin).

señorada, *f.* act of a gentleman or lady.

señoraje, *m.* seigniorage.

señoreador, ra, *n.* domineerer.

señoreaje, *m.* seigniorage.

señoreante, *a.* domineering.

señorear. I. *va.* to master; domineer, lord it over, rule despotically; to excel, to occupy a higher station than; to overtop, tower over; to control (one's passions); (coll.) to treat repeatedly with the title of lord. **II.** *vr.* to put on airs.

señoría, *f.* lordship (title and person); deminion, seigniory, lordship; government of a particular state; senate; prince.

señorial, *a.* manorial, manerial.

señoril, *a.* lordly, belonging to a lord.

señorilmente, *adv.* nobly, grandly, lordly.

señorío, *m.* seigniory, seignioralty; dominion, command; imperiousness, arrogance; lordship; domain, manor; gravity or stateliness of deportment; freedom and self-control in action.

señorita, *f. dim.* young lady; miss; (coll.) mistress of the house.

señoritingo, *m.* (contempt.) little master or youth of no account.

señorito, *m. dim.* young gentleman; master (title); lordling; (coll.) master of the house.

señorón, na, *n. aug.* grand seignior or lady.

señuelo, *m.* lure, decoy; bait; enticement.

seo, *f.* cathedral church.

seó, *m.*; **seor, ra,** *n.* (*contr.* of SEÑOR, RA) (coll.) lord, sir (madam, lady).

sepa. *V.* SABER.

sépalo, *m.* (bot.) sepal.

sepancuantos, *m.* (coll.) spanking, scolding, punishment.

separable, *a.* separable, detachable, removable.

separación, *f.* separation; disgregation, dissociation, abstraction; parting; dismissal, discharge; (pol.) secession.

separadamente, *adv.* separately.

separado, da, *a.* & *pp.* separate, apart.—**por s.,** separate, separately.

separador, ra, *n.* separateor.

separar. I. *va.* to separate; divide; to disjoin, dissever, detach, disconnect; to remove, take off; to set apart, lay aside; to sort; to dismiss, discharge. **II.** *vr.* to separate; to part company; to come off; to withdraw, resign; (com.) to dissolve.

separatismo, *m.* separatism; (pol.) secessionism.—**separatista,** *n.* & *a.* separatist; secessionist.

separativo, va, *a.* separating, separatory.

sepedón, *m.* seps, a kind of serpent.

sepelio, *m.* burial, interment.

sepia, *f.* sepia; (icht.) cuttlefish.

septema, *f.* septenary, heptade.

septenario, ria. I. *a.* septenary; septivalent. **II.** *m.* septenary, septenate, heptade.

septenio, *m.* septennium, septenate.

septeno, na, *a.* seventh.

septentrión, *m.* north; north wind; (S-, ast.) Great Bear.

septeto, *m.* (mus.) septet, septuor.

septicemia, *f.* (med.) septicæmia, septæmia.

septentrional, *a.* northern, northerly.

séptico, ca, *a.* septic, septical.

septiembre, *m.* September.

septillo, *m.* (mus.) septimole or septuplet.

séptimo, ma. I. *n.* & *a.* seventh. **II.** *f.* sequence of seven cards, in the game of piquet; (mus.) seventh.

septisílabo, ba, *a.* = HEPTASÍLABO.

septo, *m.* (anat.) septum.

septuagenario, ria, *n.* & *a.* septuagenarian.

septuagésimo, ma. I. *a.* seventieth; septuagesimal. **II.** *n.* seventieth. **III.** *f.* (eccl.) Septuagesima.

septuplicación, *f.* multiplying by seven.

septuplicar, *va.* to septuple.

séptuplo, pla, *a.* septuple, sevenfold.

sepulcral, *a.* sepulchral; monumental.

sepulcro, *m.* sepulcher, grave, tomb.

sepultador, ra, *n.* burier, gravedigger.

sepultar, *va.* to bury, inter, entomb; to hide, conceal.—**sepulto, ta,** *a.* buried.

sepultura, *f.* sepulture, interment; tomb, grave, sepulcher.—**dar s.,** to bury.

sepulturero, ra, *n.* gravedigger, sexton.

sequedad, *f.* aridity, dryness; barrenness, sterility; asperity, surliness, gruffness.

sequedal, sequeral, *m.* dry, barren soil.

sequero, *m.* dry, unirrigated land.

sequeroso, sa, *a.* dry, wanting moisture.

sequete, *m.* piece of hard, dry bread or biscuit; stroke, blow, thump, thwack; (coll.) curt reply, gruff answer.

sequía, *f.* drought.

sequillo, *m.* biscuit, rusk.

sequío, *m.* = SECANO.

séquito, *m.* retinue, train, suite; popularity.

sequizo, za, *a.* dry (fruits); dryish.

ser, *vn.* (*gerund,* SIENDO: *ind.* SOY: *imp.* ERA: *pret.* FUÍ: *subj.* SEA) to be. Used with a noun or pronoun to denote identification, takes that noun or pronoun as subject (*soy yo,* it is I; *son ellos,* it is they). App. to the hour, it takes as its subject the noun indicating the hour, preceded by the definite article (*son las dos,* it is two o'clock; *es la una,* it is one o'clock). In impersonal sentences having no logical subject, it has no grammatical subject, either expressed or understood (*es tarde,* it is late; *es extraño,* it is strange). When the real subject is an infinitive or clause following the verb, no indefinite pronoun equivalent to "it" is used as a grammatical subject (*es fácil ver,* it is easy to see; *es probable que Juan hable,* it is likely that John will speak).—**s. de ver,** to be worth seeing; to be remarkable or interesting.—**s. para poco,** not to amount to much.—**s. para todo,** to be fit for everything; to be everything.—**érase,** there was, it was.—**érase que se era,** once upon a time (u. to begin a story).—**es a saber,** namely, to wit.—**esto es,** that is to say.—**sea como fuere, sea lo que fuere,** be that as it may; anyhow, anyway.—**si yo fuera que Vd.,** if I were you.—**soy con Vd.,** I will attend you presently.—**soy muy de Vd.,** I am entirely yours; yours very truly.

ser, *m.* existence, life; being; essence, substance.

sera, *f.* large pannier, frail.

serado, *m.* frails, panniers, baskets.

seráficamente, *adv.* seraphically.

seráfico, ca, *a.* seraphic.

serafín, *m.* seraph, seraphim; angel.
serafina, *f.* fine baize, swanskin.
seraje, *m.* panniers, baskets, frails.
serapino, *m.* = SAGAPENO.
serba, *f.* (bot.) fruit of the service tree.
serbal, serbo, *m.* (bot.) service tree.
serenamente, *adv.* serenely, composedly, calmly, coolly.
serenar, *va., vn. & vr.* to clear up, grow fair, become serene (s. o. the weather); to settle, become clear (s. o. liquors); to pacify, moderate; to be serene; to cool water in the night air.
serenata, *f.* (mus.) serenade.
serenero, *m.* night wrap.
serení, *m.* (naut.) yawl, jolly-boat.
serenidad, *f.* serenity, calm; placidity, tranquility; serene highness (title).
serenísimo, ma, *a. sup.* extremely serene, calm, or quiet; most serene (title of princes).
sereno, na. I. *a.* clear, fair, cloudless; serene, calm, unruffled. **II.** *m.* night dew; night watch, watchman.—**al s.,** in the night air, exposed to the night dew. **III.** *f.* night dew; (mus.) serenade.—**a la s.** = AL SERENO.
sergas, *f. pl.* exploits, achievements.
seriamente, *adv.* seriously; gravely; in earnest, for good and all.
sericícula, *a.* sericultural.
sericicultura, *f.* silk culture, sericulture.
sérico, ca, *a.* silken.
sericultor, ra. I. *a.* sericultural. **II.** *n.* sericulturist.
sericultura, *f.* = SERICICULTURA.
serie, *f.* series.—**en s.,** (elec.) series (u. a.); (industry) standardized, mass (production).
seriedad, *f.* seriousness, gravity; sternness, severity; earnest, earnestness.
serijo, serillo, *m.* small frail.
seringa, *f.* seringa, a variety of India rubber.
serio, ria, *a.* serious, grave, dignified; grand, majestic, solemn; stern, severe; earnest; sincere.
sermón, *m.* sermon.—**sermonar,** *vn.* to preach, to sermonize.—**sermonario, ria. I.** *a.* relating to sermons. **II.** *m.* collection of sermons.
sermoncico, illo, ito, *m. dim.* short address; brief advice.
sermonear, *va.* to sermonize; (coll.) to lecture, reprimand.—**sermoneo,** *m.* (coll.) repeated admonition, sermonizing.
serna, *f.* cultivated field.
seroja, *f.,* **serojo,** *m.* withered leaf; brushwood.
serón, *m.* seroon, frail, pannier; hamper, crate.—**s. caminero,** horse pannier.
serondo, da, *a.* (bot.) serotinous.
seronero, *m.* maker or seller of seroons.
serosidad, *f.* (med.) serosity.
seroso, sa, *a.* serous, thin, watery.
seroterapia, *f.* serotherapy, serum therapy.
serotino, na, *a.* (bot.) serotinous.
serpa, *f.* (agr.) layer; runner.
serpear, *vn.* to wind (as a serpent); to wriggle, squirm, crawl, creep; to meander.
serpentaria, *f.* (bot.) snake-root.
serpentario, *m.* secretary bird; **(S-,** ast.) Ophiuchus.
serpentear, *vn.* to meander, to wind; to wriggle, squirm.
serpentígero, ra, *a.* (poet.) serpentigerous.
serpentín, *m.,* **serpentina,** *f.* coil; (min.) serpentine; (arm.) cock, hammer of a musket lock; (chem.) distil worm; (ordn.) small cannon.
serpentinamente, *adv.* in a serpentine or winding manner.
serpentino, na, *a.* serpentine; winding, sinuous, snakelike; slanderous, poisoned (tongue); serpentine (marble).
serpentón, *m. aug.* large serpent; (mus.) serpent; trombone.
serpezuela, *f. dim.* of SIERPE.
serpia, *f.* viscous matter of a vine stock.
serpiente, *f.* serpent; devil, Satan; **(S-,** ast.) Serpens.—**s. de cascabel,** rattlesnake.

serpiginoso, sa, *a.* (med.) serpiginous.
serpigo, *m.* (med.) tetter, ringworm, serpigo.
serpol, *m.* (bot.) wild thyme.
serpollar, *vn.* (bot.) to shoot, sprout.
serpollo, *m.* (bot.) shoot, sprout, tiller, sucker, sapling.
sérpula, *f.* (zool.) serpula.
serpúlidos, *m. pl.* (zool.) Serpulidæ.
serradizo, za, *a.* fit to be sawed.—**serrado, da,** *pp. & a.* serrate.—**serrador, ra,** *n.* sawer or sawyer.—**serraduras,** *f. pl.* sawdust.
serrallo, *m.* seraglio, harem; bagnio, brothel.
serrana, *f.* bucolic poem.
serranía, *f.* sierra, ridge of mountains; mountainous region.
serranilla, *a.* = SERRANA.
serraniego, ga, *a.* = SERRANO.
serranil, *m.* a kind of knife.
serrano, na, *n.* mountaineer, highlander.
serrar, *va.* to saw.
serrátil, *a.* (med) irregular (pulse).
serratilla, *f. dim.* small ridge of mountains.
serrato, ta, *a.* (anat.) serrated.
serreta, *f. dim.* small saw; cavesson iron used in breaking a horse.
serrezuela, *f. dim.* small saw.
serrijón, *m.* short chain of mountains.
serrín, *m.* sawdust.
serrino, na, *a.* belonging to sierras or mountains; (med.) irregular (pulse).
serrucho, *m.* handsaw.—**s. braguero,** pit saw.
servato, *m.* (bot.) hog fennel, sulphurweed.
serventesio, *m.* quatrain riming *a, b, a, b.*
servible, *a.* serviceable, adaptable.
servicial. I. *a.* serviceable; obsequious, obliging, accommodating, kind. **II.** *m.* (coll.) clyster.
servicialmente, *adv.* obligingly, accommodatingly, kindly; serviceably.
serviciar, *va.* to collect or pay' (sheepwalk dues, donations to the state, etc.).
servicio, *m.* service; condition of a servant; help, servants; (eccl.) divine service; usefulness; benefit, advantage; sum of money voluntarily offered to the king; close-stool, privy chair: service, cover, course; tea or coffee set.—**s. de mesa,** service for the table.—**flaco s.,** ill turn.
servidero, ra, *a.* fit for service; useful; requiring personal attendance.
servido, da, *a. & pp.* served, pleased.—**ser s.,** to please, to deign, to grant.
servidor, ra, *n.* servant, waiter (-ess); wooer; one who politely tenders his services to another; (m.) pan of a close-stool.—**s. de Vd.,** your servant; at your service.
servidumbre, *f.* attendance, servitude; help, servants; slavery, mancipation; mighty or inevitable obligation;. service, act of serving or attending at command; (law) right of way.—**s. de la vía,** (r. w.) right of way.
servil, *a.* servile, slavish, abject; lowly, humble; base, low; (Span. hist.) absolutist, defending absolute monarchy.
servilismo, *m.* servilism, servility, abjectedness; (Span. hist.) absolutism.
servilmente, *adv.* servilely, slavishly; basely.
servilla, *f.* (shoe.) pump.
servilleta, *f.* table napkin.—**doblar la s.,** (coll.) to die.
servilletero, *m.* napkin-ring.
servio, via, *n. & a.* Serbian.
serviola, *f.* (naut.) cathead, anchor beam.
servir. I. *vn.* (gerund, SIRVIENDO: *ind.* SIRVO: *pret.* él SIRVIÓ: *subj.* SIRVA) to serve; wait on; to do (for); to hold (an employment), occupy (a public station); to perform the functions (of); to serve (in the army or navy); at cards or ball games, to serve; to wait at the table; to heat the oven; to administer.—**s. de,** to act as, to be used as.—**s. para,** to be for, to be used or useful for, to be good for; to do for.—**no s. para nada,** to be good for nothing.—**para s. a Vd.,** at your service.—**sirva de aviso,** let this be a warning. **II.** *va.* to serve; to do a favor or a service to; to court, pay attention to (a

lady); to pay (money) voluntarily to the king or government; to dress or serve (food or drink). **III.** *vr.* to deign, condescend, please, be pleased to (*sirvase decirme*, please tell me); to help one's self to (as at table).—**s. de,** to make use of; to employ.

servocroata, *n.* & *a.* Servo-Croatian.

servomotor, *m.* servo-motor.

sesada, *f.* fried brains.

sesámeo, a. I. *a.* (bot.) relating to the sesame family. **II.** *f. pl.* the sesame family of plants.

sésamo, *m.* (bot.) sesame, gingili.

sesamoideo, a, *a.* (anat.) sesamoid.

sesear, *vn.* to pronounce *c* before *e* and *i* like *s*, as in Am. and some parts of Spain.

sesenta, *n.* & *a.* sixty; sixtieth.

sesentavo, va, *n.* & *a.* sixtieth.—**sesentón, na,** *n.* & *a.* sexagenarian.

seseo, *m.* pronouncing *c* before *e*, *i* like *s.*

sesera, *f.* brainpan; the entire brain.

sesga, *f.* (sew.) gore or goring.

sesgadamente, *adv.* slantingly or on the bias; askew.—**sesgado, da,** *a.* & *pp.* oblique, slanting, skew; bevelled.—**sesgadura,** *f.* obliquity; bevel.

sesgamente, *adv.* = SESGADAMENTE.

sesgar. I. *va.* (*pret.* SESGUÉ: *subj.* SESGUE) to slope, slant, cut on the bias, bevel; to skew. **II.** *vn.* to take an oblique direction.

sesgo, ga. I. *a.* sloped, oblique, biased, bevelled, aslant, skew; calm, placid; severe, grave, stern. —**al s.,** obliquely, bevelled, on the bias. **II.** *m.* bias, bevel, slope, obliqueness; turn; skew; mean, medium.

sesil, *a.* (bot.) sessile.

sesión, *f.* session, sitting, meeting; conference, consultation.—**levantar la s.,** to adjourn the meeting.

sesma, *f.*, **sesmero, sesmo,** *m.* = SEXMA, etc.

seso, *m.* (anat.) brain; brains, intelligence, judgment; stone under a pot to keep it steady on the fire.—**devanarse los sesos,** to rack one's brains.—**levantarse la tapa de los sesos,** to blow out one's brains.—**no tener s.,** not to have common sense.—**perder el s.,** to go crazy; to lose consciousness; to lose one's head (fig.).

sesquiáltero, ra, *a.* sesquialteral.

sesquidoble, *a.* two and a half times.

sesquimodio, *m.* a bucket and a half.

sesquióxido, *m.* (chem.) sesquioxide.

sesquipedal, *a.* sesquipedal, sesquipedalian.

sesteadero, *m.* resting place for cattle.

sestear, *vn.* to take a nap.

sestercio, *m.* sesterce, sestertius.

sestero, sestil, *m.* = SESTEADERO.

sesudamente, *adv.* maturely, wisely, deliberately.

sesudo, da, *a.* judicious, discreet, wise.

seta, *f.* bristle; mushroom; snuff of a candle.

sete, *m.* office in a mint where money is struck with a die.

setecientos, tas, *a.* & *n.* seven hundred (-th).

setena, *f.* heptad.

setenta, *n.* & *a.* seventy; seventieth.

setentavo, va, *n.* & *a.* seventieth.

setentón, na, *n.* & *a.* septuagenary (-narian).

setiembre, *m.* = SEPTIEMBRE.

sétimo, ma, *a.* = SÉPTIMO, MA.

seto, *m.* fence, inclosure; (P. Rico) wall.—**s. vivo,** hedge, quickset.

setuní, *m.* = ACEITUNÍ.

seudo, *a.* pseudo, false.

seudomembrana, *f.* (anat.) pseudomembrane.

seudónimo, ma. I. *a.* pseudonymous, fictitious. **II.** *m.* pseudonym, nom de plume.

seudópodo, da. I. *a.* (biol.) pseudopodian. **II.** *m.* pseudopodium.

severamente, *adv.* severely, sternly.

severidad, *f.* severity, rigor, harshness, austerity; sternness, strictness, seriousness.

severo, ra, *a.* severe, rigorous; rigid, strict, stern, serious.

sevicia, *f.* fierceness, excessive cruelty.

sevillana, *f.* a Sevillan dance and tune.

sevillano, na, *a.* of Seville, Sevillan.

séviro, *m.* chief of a Roman decury of knights.

sexagenario, ria, *n.* & *a.* sexagenary (-narian).

sexagésima, *f.* (eccl.) Sexagesima.

sexagesimal, *a.* sexagesimal.

sexagésimo, ma, *a.* sexagesimal, sixtieth.

sexenio, *m.* space of six years.

sexma, *f.* an ancient coin; sixth part of a vara.

sexmero, *m.* mayor of a township.

sexmo, *m.* township.

sexo, *m.* sex.

sexta, *f.* (eccl.) sext; sequence of six cards at piquet; (mus.) sixth; an ancient division of the day; afternoon.

sextante, *m.* sextant; an ancient Roman copper coin.

sextario, *m.* sextarius, an ancient measure.

sexteto, *m.* (mus.) sextet.

sextil, *a.* (ast.) sextile.

sextilla, *f.* (poet.) sextain.

sextillo, *m.* (mus.) sextolet, sextuplet.

sextina, *f.* six-sextian poem.

sexto, ta. I. *n.* & *a.* sixth. **II.** *m.* book of canonical decrees.

séxtula, *f.* a Roman copper coin.

sextuplicación, *f.* multiplication by six.

sextuplicar, *va.* to sextuple.

séxtuplo, pla, *a.* sextuple, sixfold.

sexual, *a.* sexual.—**sexualidád,** *f.* sexuality.

si. I. *m.* (mus.) B or si, seventh note of the scale. **II.** *conj.* if; whether. It is used at the beginning of exclamations to express doubt or desire, or to give force to a statement (*¡si será verdad!* I wonder if it be true; *¡si yo no lo quiero!* indeed, I don't want it).—**s. acaso,** if by chance, should it happen that. —**s. bien,** although.—**por s. acaso, s.** ACASO; in case (it should happen, it be needed, he does not come. etc.)

sí. I. *pron.* (reflexive form of the personal pronoun of the third person, in both genders and numbers); himself, herself, itself, one's self, themselves.—**de por s.,** apart, separately, by itself.—**de s.,** of one's self, of itself, spontaneously.— **por s. y ante s.,** of his own accord, ignoring others. —**sobre s.,** attentively, cautiously. **II.** *adv.* yes, yea, aye. When used emphatically by itself or before a verb, it may be rendered by an auxiliary, an emphatic verb or adverb, or left untranslated (*él no trá, pero yo sí,* he will not go, but I will; *yo sí hablo español,* I do speak Spanish; *yo sí lo compraria,* I should [certainly] buy it).—**s. que,** certainly, truly. —**por s. o por no,** in any case.—**s. tal,** indeed, certainly.—**un s. es no es,** somewhat, perhaps a little. **III.** *m.* yea; assent, consent, permission.— **dar el s.,** to say yes; to accept a marriage proposal.

siamés, sa, *n.* & *a.* Siamese.

siampán, *m.* sapan (tree & wood).

sibarita, *n.* & *a.* Sybarite (-ic).

sibarítico, ca, *a.* Sybaritical.

sibaritismo, *m.* sybaritism.

siberiano, na, *n.* & *a.* Siberian.

sibil, *m.* cave; cellar, vault.

sibila, *f.* sibyl.

sibilante, *a.* sibilant, hissing.

sibilino, na, *a.* sibylline.

sibucao, *m.* (Philip.) (bot.) sapan tree.

sic, *sic,* so, thus.

sicamor, *m.* (bot.) = CICLAMOR.

sicario, *m.* paid assassin, sicarius.

sicigia, (ast.) conjunction of the sun and moon.

siciliano, na, *n.* & *a.* Sicilian.

siclo, *m.* shekel, an ancient Jewish coin.

sicofanta, sicofante, *m.* sycophant.

sicómoro, *m.* (bot.) sycamore; plane tree, buttonwood, sycamore maple.

sículo, la, *a.* Sicilian.

sideral; sidéreo, a, *a.* sidereal.

sideritis, *f.* (min.) siderite; (bot.) ironwort.

siderización, *f.* preservation of timber by injecting iron salts.

siderosa, *f.* (min.) siderite.

sideróstato, *m.* (astr.) siderostat.

siderurgia, *f.* siderurgy.

siderúrgico, ca, *a.* siderurgical.

sidonio, nia, *n.* & *a.* Sidonian.

idra, *f.* cider.

iega, *f.* reaping, mowing, harvest.

iego, yo siegue. *V.* SEGAR.

siembra, *f.* sowing, seeding; seedtime; sown field.

siembro, yo siembre. *V.* SEMBRAR.

siempre, *adv.* always.—**s. que,** provided; whenever.—**para,** or **por, s.,** forever.—**por s. jamás,** forever and ever.

siempreviva, *f.* (bot.) everlasting or immortelle.—**s. mayor,** houseleek.—**s. menor,** stonecrop.

sien, *f.* temple.

siena, *f.* sienna.

sienita, *f.* (min.) syenite or sienite.

siento, siente. *V.* SENTAR.

siento, sienta, él sintió. *V.* SENTIR.

sierpe, *f.* serpent, snake; ugly or angry person; anything that wriggles; (bot.) sucker, tiller.

sierpecilla, *f. dim.* small serpent.—*pl.* winding skyrockets.

sierra, *f.* saw; ridge of mountains, sierra; (icht.) sawfish.—**s. bracera,** bucksaw, frame saw.—**s. de agua,** sawmill.—**s. de cinta,** band saw.—**s. de cortar metales,** hack saw.—**s. de ingletes,** tenon saw.—**s. de mano,** handsaw.—**s. de punta,** compass saw.—**s. de trasdós,** backsaw.

sierrecilla, *f. dim.* small saw.

sierro, yo sierre. *V.* SERRAR.

siervo, va, *n.* serf; slave; servant.—**s. de Dios,** servant of God; (coll.) poor devil.

sieso, *m.* fundament, anus.

siesta, *f.* hottest part of the day; afternoon nap; afternoon music in churches.

siete. I. *m.* & *a.* seven; seventh (of the month); seven-spot card; V-shaped rent in a garment; (carp.) hook-clasp. **II.** *f. pl.*—**las s.,** seven o'clock.

sietecueros, *m.* (S. A.) a kind of tumor on the heel; (C. A.) sickly-looking person.

sieteenrama, *f.* (bot.) = TORMENTILA.

sietemesino, na. I. *a.* born seven months after conception. **II.** *m.* puny coxcomb.

sieteñal, *a.* seven years old; septennial.

sifílide, *f.* (med.) syphilide.

sífilis, *f.* (med.) syphilis.—**sifilítico, ca,** *n.* & *a.* syphilitic.—**sifilografía,** *f.* (med.) syphilography.—**sifilográfico, ca,** *a.* syphilographic.

sifón, *m.* siphon; siphon bottle.

sifosis, *f.* = CORCOVA.

sifué, *m.* = SOBRECINCHA.

sigilación, *f.* seal, stamp, impression, mark.

sigilar, *va.* to seal; to conceal.

sigilo, *m.* seal; secret, concealment, reserve.—**s. sacramental,** inviolable secrecy of the confessional.

sigilografía, *f.* sigillography, study of seals.

sigilosamente, *adv.* silently, secretly.

sigiloso, sa, *a.* silent, reserved.

sigla, *f.* abbreviation in initials.

siglo, *m.* century; age; period; the world, worldly intercourse or matters.—**s. de cobre,** (myth.) bronze age.—**s. de hierro,** (myth.) iron age.—**s. de oro,** (myth.) golden age.—**s. de plata,** (myth.) silver age.—**s. dorado** = s. DE ORO.—**en, por,** or **por todos, los siglos de los siglos,** forever and ever.

sigmoideo, a, *a.* sigmoid, S-shaped.

signáculo, *m.* seal, signet.

signar. I. *va.* to sign, to mark with a signet. **II.** *vr.* to cross one's self.

signatario, ria, *n.* & *a.* signer (-ing), signatory.

signatura, *f.* sign, mark; (print.) signature; a Roman-Catholic court of justice and pardons.

signífero, ra, *a.* carrying a mark or sign.

significación, *f.* signification, meaning; significance.

significado, pp. & *m.* meaning.

significador, ra, *n.* & *a.* signifier (-ing).

significante, *a.* significant, expressive.

significar, *va.* (*pret.* SIGNIFIQUÉ: *subj.* SIGNIFIQUE) to signify, mean; to indicate; to make known; to import, be worth.

significativamente, *adv.* significantly.

significativo, va, *a.* significant.

signo, *m.* sign, mark; signal, motion, nod; (law) signum, scroll or flourish in a notary's signa-

ture; fate, destiny; benediction, sign of the cross; (ast.) sign of the zodiac; (mus.) character.

sigo, sigue, yo siga. *V.* SEGUIR.

siguiente, *pa.* & *a.* following, next.

sijú, *m.* (W. I.) (orn.) a nocturnal bird of prey.

sil, *m.* yellow ochre.

sílaba, *f.* syllable; (mus.) two or three sounds which correspond with every letter of the gamut.

silabar, *vn.* = SILABEAR.

silabario, *m.* spelling book, syllabary.

silabear, *vn.* to syllabize, syllabicate.

silabeo, *m.* syllabication.

silábico, ca, *a.* syllabic(al).

sílabo, *m.* syllabus; summary, index.

silanga, *f.* (Philip.) canal, inlet, strait.

silba, *f.* (theat.) hiss, hissing.

silbador, ra, *n.* & *a.* whistler (-ing); hisser (-ing).

silbar. I. *vn.* to whistle; to whiz, as a musket ball. **II.** *va.* & *vn.* (theat.) to hiss, to catcall.

silbato, *m.* whistle; small chink or crack letting out a liquid or air with a whiz.

silbido, *m.* whistle, whistling; hiss; sibilation.—**s. de oídos,** whizzing or ringing in the ear.

silbo, *m.* whistle, hiss, whistling, whiz.

silbón, *m.* (orn.) a kind of hissing widgeon.

silboso, sa, *a.* whistling, hissing.

silenciador, *m.* (aut.) silencer.

silenciario, ria. I. *a.* observing profound silence. **II.** *m.* silentiary.—**silenciero, ra,** *a.* charged with preserving silence.

silencio, *m.* silence; noiselessness; taciturnity; secrecy; stillness, quiet; (mus.) rest.—**perpetuo s.,** (law) forever hold his peace.

silenciosamente, *adv.* silently, noiselessly.

silencioso, sa, *a.* silent, noiseless; still, quiet.

silepsis, *f.* (rhet.) syllepsis.

silería, *f.* group of silos.—**silero,** *m.* (agr.) silo.

silesiano, na; selesio, sia, *n.* & *a.* Silesian.

sílfide, *f.*, **silfo,** *m.* sylph.

silguero, *m.* (orn.) linnet.

silicato, *m.* (chem.) silicate.—**sílice,** *f.* (min.) silex, silica.

silíceo, a, *a.* siliceous.—**silícico, ca,** *a.* silicic.

silicio, *m.* (chem.) silicon.

silicua, *f.* siliqua, carat; (bot.) silique, pod.

silícula, *f.* (bot.) silicle or silicula.

silo, *m.* (agr.) silo; cavern or dark place.

silogismo, *m.* (log.) syllogism.—**s. cornuto,** horn of a dilemma.—**silogístico, ca,** *a.* syllogistic(al).—**silogizar,** *vn.* (*pret.* SILOGICÉ: *subj.* SILOGICE) to syllogize, argue.

silueta, *f.* silhouette.

siluriano, na; silúrico, ca, *a.* (geol.) Silurian.

siluro, *m.* (icht.) catfish, silurus; self-propelling torpedo.

silva, *f.* miscellany; a form of poem.

silvático, ca, *a.* = SELVÁTICO.

silvestre, *a.* wild; uncultivated; rustic, savage.

silvicultor, ra, *n.* silviculturist, forester.

silvicultura, *f.* forestry, silviculture.

silvoso, sa, *a.* = SELVOSO.

silla, *f.* chair; saddle; (ecc.) see.—**s. curul,** curule.—**s. de columpio,** rocking chair.—**s. de junco** = s. DE REJILLA.—**s. de la reina,** chair made by two persons' hands and wrists.—**s. de manos,** sedan chair; (Am.) s. DE LA REINA.—**s. de montar,** riding saddle.—**s. de posta,** post chaise.—**s. de rejilla,** cane or bamboo-bottomed chair.—**s. de tijera,** camp chair.—**s. giratoria,** revolving chair.—**s. plegadiza,** folding chair, camp stool.—**s. poltrona,** arm or elbow chair; easy chair.—**s. volante,** light gig.—**de s. a s.,** tête à tête, in private conference, heart to heart.

sillar, *m.* ashlar stone; horseback.

sillarejo, *m.* small ashlar.

sillera, *f.* place for sedan chairs.

sillería, *f.* set of chairs; shop where chairs are made or sold; stalls or seats in a choir; ashlar masonry.

sillero, ra, *n.* saddler; chair maker.

silleta, *f. dim.* small chair; hollow stone on which chocolate is ground; bedpan.—*pl.* mule chairs.

silletazo, *m.* blow with a chair.

silletero, ra, *n.* chairman, one who carries sedan chairs; chair maker or seller.

sillico, *m.* basin of a close-stool.

sillín, *m.* light riding saddle; harness saddle; elaborate mule chair.

sillita, *f. dim.* small chair.

sillón, *m. aug.* arm or elbow chair; easy chair; sidesaddle for ladies.

sima, *f.* deep cavern; abyss, gulf, chasm.

simado, da, *a.* deep (land).

simbiosis, *f.* (biol.) symbiosis.

simbléfaron, *m.* (med.) symblepharon.

simbólicamente, *adv.* symbolically.

simbólico, ca, *a.* symbolical.—**simbolismo,** *m.* symbolism.—**simbolista,** *m.* or *f.* symbolist.

simbolización, *f.* symbolization.

simbolizar, *va.* (*pret.* SIMBOLICÉ: *subj.* SIMBO-LICE) to symbolize, represent, typify.

símbolo, *m.* symbol; mark, device.—**s. de la fe,** creed, articles of faith.

simetría, *f.* symmetry.—**simétricamente,** *adv.* symmetrically.—**simétrico, ca,** *a.* symmetrical.

simia, *f.* female ape.—**símico, ca,** *a.* simian.

simiente, *f.* seed; germ; semen, sperm.

simiesco, ca, *a.* simianlike.

símil. I. *a.* similar, like, alike. **II.** *m.* resemblance, similarity; (rhet.) simile.

similar, *a.* similar, resembling.

similitud, *f.* similitude, similarity.

similitudinario, ria, *a.* similar.

similor, *m.* similor; low brass.

simio, mia, *n.* simian, ape.

simón, *m.* hack, cab; hackman, in Madrid.

simonía, *f.* simony.

simoníaco, ca; simoniático, ca, *a.* simoniacal.

simoníacamente, *adv.* simoniacally.

simpatía, *f.* sympathy, fellow feeling; congeniality; liking, friendly feeling; (med.) sympathy.

simpáticamente, *adv.* sympathetically; nicely, pleasingly.

simpático, ca, *a.* sympathetic, sympathetical; congenial, winsome, pleasant, "nice."—**gran s.,** (anat.) sympathetic system.

simpatizar, *vn.* (*pret.* SIMPATICÉ: *subj.* SIMPA-TICE) (w. **with**) to be congenial (with), to have a liking (for).

simple. I. *a.* simple; mere; single; silly, foolish; undesigning, artless; plain, unmixed, unadorned; mild, gentle; ingenuous; insipid, tasteless; informal, extrajudicial. **II.** *m.* (pharm.) simple.

simplemente, *adv.* simply; plainly; foolishly.

simpleza, *f.* simpleness, silliness, foolishness; rusticity, rudeness.—**simplicidad,** *f.* simplicity.

simplicísimo, ma, *a. sup.* exceedingly simple.

simplificación, *f.* simplification.

simplificar, *va.* (*pret.* SIMPLIFIQUÉ: *subj.* SIMPLI-FIQUE) to simplify.

simplista, *m.* simplist, herbalist.

simplón, na, *n. aug.* great simpleton.

simulación, *f.* simulation, feigning.

simulacro, *m.* simulacrum, image, idol; fancy, fantastical thing; (mil.) sham battle.

simuladamente, *adv.* dissemblingly.

simulador, ra, *n. & a.* dissembler (-ing).

simular, *va.* to simulate, pretend, sham.

simultáneamente, *adv.* simultaneously.

simultaneidad, *f.* simultaneity.

simultanear, *va.* to accomplish or carry on simultaneously.

simultáneo, a, *a.* simultaneous.

simún, *m.* simoom, sirocco.

sin, *prep.* without, besides.—**s. embargo,** notwithstanding, nevertheless, however.

sinagoga, *f.* synagogue.

sinalefa, *f.* (gram.) synalepha.

sinalagmático, ca, *a.* (law) synalagmatic, mutually obligatory.

sinamay, *m.* (Philip.) sinamay, a coarse fabric made from abaca.—**sinamayera,** *f.* (Philip.) woman who sells sinamay.

sinapismo, *m.* mustard plaster; (coll.) nuisance, bore.

sinartrosis, *f.* (anat.) synarthrosis.

sincerador, ra, *n. & a.* exculpator (-ing), excuse (-ing), defender (-ing), upholder (-ing).

sinceramente, *adv.* sincerely.

sincerar. I. *va.* to exculpate, to justify. **II.** *vr.* to excuse, justify, or vindicate one's self.

sinceridad, *f.* sincerity, good faith.

sincero, ra, *a.* sincere.

síncopa, *f.* (gram.) syncope; (mus.) syncopation.

sincopadamente, *adv.* with syncope.

sincopal. I. *m.* = SÍNCOPE. **II.** *a.* (med.) syncopal.

sincopar, *va.* to syncopate; to abridge.

síncope, *f.* SÍNCOPA; (med.) syncope.

sincopizar, *va. & vr.* (*pret.* SINCOPICÉ: *subj.* SIN-COPICE) to swoon, to faint.

sincretismo, *m.* syncretism.

sincronismo, *m.* synchronism.

sincrónico, ca, *a.* synchronous.

sincronizador, ra, *n. & a.* synchronizer (-ing).

sincronizar, *va.* to synchronize.

sindéresis, *f.* discretion; good judgment.

sindicado, *pp. & m.* body of trustees; syndicate; (p. e.) syndicate.

sindicador, ra, *n.* informer, prosecutor; syndicator.

sindical, *a.* syndical; (p. e.) syndicalistic.

sindicalismo, *m.* (p. e.) syndicalism.

sindicalista, *n. & a.* (p. e.) syndicalist (-ic),

sindicar, *va.* (*pret.* SINDIQUÉ: *subj.* SINDIQUE) to inform, to accuse; to syndicate.

sindicato, *m.* = SINDICADO.

sindicatura, *f.* office and dignity of a syndic.

síndico, *m.* syndic; trustee; (law) assignee, receiver.

síndrome, *m.* (med.) syndrome, aggregate of symptoms.

sinécdoque, *f.* (rhet.) synecdoche.

sinecura, *f.* sinecure.

sinedrio, *m.* = SANEDRÍN.

sine qua non, (Lat.) essential, sine qua non.

sinéresis, *f.* (gram.) syneresis.

sinergia, *f.* (physiol.) synergy.

sinfín, *m.* = SINNÚMERO.

sínfisis, *f.* (biol.) symphysis.

sínfito, *m.* (bot.) comfrey.

sinfonía, *f.* (mus.) symphony.—**sinfónico, ca,** *a.* (mus.) symphonic.—**sinfonista,** *n.* symphonist; player in an orchestra.

singladura, *f.* (naut.) a day's run.

singlar, *vn.* (naut.) to steer, sail over a course.

single, *a.* (naut.) single.—**singlón,** *m.* (naut.) futtock.

singular, *a.* singular, unique; individual; extraordinary, strange; (gram.) singular.

singularidad, *f.* singularity, oddity, strange feature or thing; peculiarity.

singularizar. I. *va.* (*pret.* SINGULARICÉ: *subj.* SINGULARICE) to distinguish, particularize, singularize, single out. **II.** *vr.* to distinguish one's self; to be or make one's self conspicuous

singularmente, *adv.* singularly.

singulto, *m.* sob; hiccough, singultus.

sinhueso, *f.* (coll.) tongue.

sínico, ca, *a.* Chinese.

siniestra, *f.* left hand.

siniestramente, *adv.* sinistrously, perversely.

siniestro, tra. I. *a.* sinister, left (side); sinister, unlucky, inauspicious. **II.** *m.* perverseness, depravity; (com.) shipwreck, disaster; damage, loss at sea. **III.** *f.* left hand; left-hand side.

sinistrórsum, *a.* sinistrosely, from right to left.

sinnúmero, *m.* no end, great number.—**un s. de,** a great many.

sino. I. *conj.* but; except, besides; solely, only. **II.** *m.* fate, destiny.

sinoble, a. (her.) vert. V. SINOPLE.

sinocal; sínoco, ca, *a.* (med.) synochal (fever).

sinodal. I. *a.* synodic, synodal. **II.** *m.* synodsman.—**sinodático,** *m.* synodal, contribution to the bishop.—**sinódico, ca,** *a.* synodal, synodical; (ast.) synodic.

---

sínodo, m. (eccl. and ast.) synod.

sinología, f. sinology.

sinólogo, ga, n. sinologist.

sinonimia, f. (rhet.) synonymy.—**sinónimo, ma.** I. a. synonymous. II. m. synonym.

sinople, a. (her.) sinople, vert.

sinopsis, f. synopsis.

sinóptico, ca, a. synoptic.

sinovia, f. synovia.—**sinovial,** a. synovial.

sinrazón, f. wrong, injury, injustice.

sinsabor, m.displeasure, unpleasantness; trouble, uneasiness.

sinsonte, m. (orn.) mocking bird.

sintáctico, ca, a. (gram.) syntactic.

sintaxis, f. (gram.) syntax.

síntesis, f. synthesis.—**sintéticamente,** adv. synthetically.—**sintético, ca,** a. synthetical.

sintetizar, va. (pret. SINTETICÉ: subj. SINTETICE) to synthesize; to sum up.

sinto, sintoísmo, m. Shinto, Shintoism.

sintoísta, n. & a. Shintoist (-ic).

síntoma, m. (med.) symptom.

sintomáticamente, adv. symptomatically.

sintomático, ca, a. symptomatic(al).

sintomatología, f. (med.) symptomatology.

sintonina, f. (chem.) syntonin.

sintonización, f. (rad.) syntonization, tuning.

sintonizador, ra, n. & a. syntonizer (-ing) ; (rad.) tuner (-ing).

sintonizar, va. (rad.) to syntonize, tune.

sinuosidad, f. sinuosity.

sinuoso, sa, a. sinuous, wavy.

sinusoidal, a. sinusoidal.

sinusoide, f. (geom.) sinusoid.

sinvergüencería, f. (coll.) shamelessness, brazenness.

sinvergüenza, n. (coll.) scoundrel, rascal; brazen, shameless person; caitiff; (Colomb.) coward.

sinvergüenzada, f. (Colomb.) base, low action.

sipedón, m. a kind of serpent.

siquier, siquiera, adv. & conj. at least; though, although; whether; or; scarcely; otherwise.—**s. un poquito,** ever so little.—**ni s.,** not even.

siracusano, na, n. & a. Syracusan.

sirena, f. syren, mermaid; (naut.) siren, foghorn; (phys.) siren, for measuring vibrations.

sirenio, nia. I. a. (icht.) sirenian. II. m. pl. Sirenia.

sirga, f. (naut.) towrope, towline; line for hauling seines.—**a la s.,** (naut.) tracking from the shore.

sirgadura, f. (naut.) trackage.

sirgar, va. (naut.) to track.

sirgo, m. twisted silk; silk stuff.

sirguero, m. (orn.) linnet.

siríaco, ca, n. & a. Syrian.

siringa, f. (bot.) seringa, name of various species of rubber tree.

Sirio, m. (ast.) Sirius.

sirle, m. sheep dung, goat dung.

siroco, m. sirocco.

sirria, f. sheep dung.

sirte, f. syrtes, hidden rock, sand bank; danger.

sirvienta, f. servant girl, maid.

sirviente, m. servant; waiter.

sirvo, sirva, él sirvió. V. SERVIR.

sisa, f. petty theft, pilfering; (tail.) clippings, cabbage; (sew.) dart; size used by gilders; excise.

sisador, ra, n. filcher, petty thief.

sisallo, m. (bot.) = BARRILLA.

sisar, va. to pilfer, filch; (sew.) to take in; to size (for gilding); to excise.

sisear, vn. to hiss.—**siseo,** m. hiss, hissing.

sisero, m. excise collector.

sisimbrio, m. (bot.) hedge mustard.

sisitoté, m. (orn.) a tropical song bird.

sísmico, ca, a. seismic.—**sismógrafo,** m. seismograph.—**sismología,** f. seismology.—**sismológico, ca,** a. seismological.—**sismómetro,** m. seismometer.

sisón, na, n. filcher, pilferer, petty thief; (orn.) godart or moor cock.

sistema, m. system.—**s. cegesimal,** C. G. S. system (of units).

sistemáticamente, adv. systematically.

sistemático, ca, a. systematic, methodical.

sistematización, f. systematization.

sistematizar, va. & vn. (pret. SISTEMATICÉ: subj. SISTEMATICE) to systematize.

sístilo, m. (arch.) systyle.

sístole, f. (physiol. and rhet.) systole.

sistro, m. (mus.) sistrum.

sitácidos, m. pl. (orn.) Psitaci (the parrots).

sitiador, ra, n. & a. besieger (-ing).

sitial, m. seat of honor, presiding chair; bench, form.

sitiar, va. (mil.) to besiege, lay siege to; to surround, hem in, compass.

sitibundo, da, a. (poet.) thirsty.

sitiero, m. (Cuba) petty farmer.

sitio, m. place, space, spot, room; stand; seat; location, site; (mil.) siege; country house, country seat, villa; (Cuba) small farm.—**dejar en el s.,** to kill one outright.—**quedar en el s.,** to die on the spot.

sito, ta, a. situated, lying, located.

situación, f. situation; position; site, location; state, condition, circumstances.—**s. activa,** active-service position or office.—**s. pasiva,** office or position not actually filled, as when the incumbent is retired, on vacation, etc.

situado, da. I. a. & pp. situate, situated, located. II. pp. & m. allowance, pay, annuity assigned upon certain valuables.

situar. I. va. to place, locate, put, situate; (com.) to remit or place (funds). II. vr. to settle in a place; to station one's self.

smoking, m. dinner, or Tuxedo, coat.

so, prep. under; below.—**s. capa de,** or s. color de, under color of; on pretense of.—**s. pena de,** under penalty of.

¡so! interj. whoa! stop! (to horses).

soasar, va. to half roast, parboil, underdo.

soata, f. (Ven.) a kind of squash.

soba, f. massage; kneading; rubbing; beating; drubbing.

sobacal, a. axillary.

sobaco, m. armpit, axilla; (bot.) axil.

sobado, ra, a. that may be handled.

sobado, pp. & m.; sobadura, f. = SOBA.

sobajadura, f.; sobajamiento, m. squeeze, pressure, crushing.

sobajanero, m. (coll.) errand boy.

sobajar, va. to squeeze, press, crush.

sobanda, f. bottom or end of a cask.

sobaquera, f. (tail.) armhole, armscye.

sobaquina, f. bad smell of the armpit.

sobar, va. to knead; to massage, squeeze, soften; to pummel, box; to handle (a person) with too much familiarity.

sobarba, f. noseband of a bridle.

sobarbada, f. sudden check; reprimand, scolding.

sobarbo, m. (mech.) cam, pallet or pawl, in beating machines.

sobarcar, va.(for mut. v. ABARCAR) to carry under the arm; to draw (the clothes) up to the armholes.

sobeo, m. thong for tying the yoke to the pole.

soberanamente, adv. with authority; supremely, exceedingly, most.

soberanear, vn. to lord it, to domineer.

soberanía, f. sovereignty; rule, sway.

soberano, na. I. a. sovereign; supreme, royal; most potent, superior, preëminent. II. f. sovereign; lord paramount; liege.

soberbia, f. excessive pride, haughtiness; presumption; magnificence, sumptuousness, pomp; anger.

soberbiamente, adv. arrogantly; superbly.

soberbio, bia, a. overproud, arrogant, haughty; superb, grand; lofty, eminent; fiery, mettlesome (s. o. horses).

soberbiosamente, adv. haughtily.

soberbioso, sa, a. = SOBERBIO.

sobina, *f.* wooden pin, peg.

sobón, na, *a.* given to excessive fondling and caressing; (coll.) sly, lazy.

sobordo, *m.* (naut.) manifest, freight list.

sobornación, *f.* = SOBORNO.

sobornado, *pp.* & *m.* misshaped loaf of bread.

sobornador, ra, *n.* & *a.* briber (-ing), suborner (-ing).

sobornal, *m.* overload; seroon.

sobornar, *va.* to suborn, bribe.

soborno, *m.* subornation, bribe; incitement, inducement; (Peru) = SOBORNAL.

sobra, *f.* surplus, excess; left-over, leaving; grievous offence, injury.—**de s.,** over and above; more than enough; over, superfluous.—**estar de s.,** (coll.) to be one too many; to be superfluous.

sobradamente, *adv.* abundantly; superabundantly; excessively.

sobradar, *va.* to build a garret to.

sobradillo, *m. dim.* (arch.) penthouse.

sobrado, da. I. *pp.* & *a.* excessive, abundant; bold, audacious; rich, wealthy. **II.** *m.* garret, attic; (Am., gen. in the *pl.*) leaving (s).

sobrancero, ra, *a.* disengaged, unemployed; supernumerary plowman.

sobrante. I. *m.* remainder, left-over; surplus, excess. **II.** *a.* left-over, remaining; wealthy, well-off.

sobrar. I. *va.* to exceed, surpass; to have in excess, or more than enough, to have to spare. **II.** *vn.* to be more than is necessary; to be over and above; to be more than enough; to be intrusive; to remain, to be left.

sobrasada, *f.* = SOBREASADA.

sobrasar, *va.* to add fire under (a pot).

sobre. I. *prep.* on, upon; over; above; about, more or less; moreover, besides; after, beyond; to, toward, near; (naut.) off.—**s. comida,** after dinner.—**s. manera,** excessively, beyond measure, exceedingly.—**s. poco más o menos,** just about, more or less.—**s. que,** besides.—**estar s. sí,** to be on guard, to be self-possessed.—**ir s.,** to go in pursuit of. **II.** *m.* envelope (for letters); address, superscription.—**s. monedero,** coin container (to be enclosed with a letter).

sobreabundancia, *f.* superabundance.

sobreabundante, *a.* superabundant; luxuriant.

sobreabundantemente, *adv.* superabundantly.—**sobreabundar,** *vn.* to superabound; to be exuberant.

sobreaguar, *vn.* & *vr.* to float on water.

sobreagudo, da, *a.* & *n.* (mus.) treble, highest register.

sobrealiento, *m.* difficult respiration.

sobrealimentación, *f.* overfeeding.

sobrealimentar, *va.* to overfeed.

sobrealzar, *va.* to praise, to extol.

sobreañadir, *va.* to superadd, superinduce.

sobreañal, *a.* over a year old.

sobrearco, *m.* (arch.) discharging arch.

sobreasada, *f.* half-roasted sausage from the island of Majorca.

sobreasar, *va.* to roast again.

sobrebarato, ta, *a.* very cheap, extra cheap.

sobreboya, *f.* (naut.) marking buoy.

sobrebrazal, *m.* (naut.) false rail.

sobrecaja, *f.* outer case.

sobrecalza, *f.* leggings.

sobrecama, *f.* coverlet, bedspread.

sobrecaña, *f.* (vet.) tumor on a horse's leg.

sobrecarga, *f.* overload; packing strap; additional trouble or vexation; surcharge, overburden.

sobrecargado, da, *a.* & *pp.* overloaded.

sobrecargar, *va.* (*for mut. v.* CARGAR) to overload, overburden; (com.) to overcharge; (sew.) to fell.

sobrecargo, *m.* (naut.) purser, supercargo.

sobrecarta, *f.* envelope (for a letter); (law) second decree or warrant repeating a former order.

sobrecartar, *va.* to repeat (a former warrant).

sobrecebadera, *f.* (naut.) sprit top-sail.

sobrecédula, *f.* second royal order.

sobreceja, *f.* part of the forehead over the eyebrows.

sobrecejo, *m.* frown; threatening or forbidding aspect.

sobreceño, *m.* frown.

sobrecercar, *va.* (sew.) to welt.

sobrecerco, *m.* (sew.) welt.

sobrecincho, *m.;* **-cha,** *f.* surcingle.

sobreclaustro, *m.* apartment over a cloister.

sobrecoger. I. *va.* (*for mut. v.* COGER) to surprise. **II.** *vr.* to become afraid or apprehensive.—**s. de,** to be seized with.

sobrecogimiento, *m.* fear, apprehension.

sobrecomida, *f.* dessert.

sobrecopa, *f.* cover or lid of a cup.

sobrecoser, *va.* (sew.) to whip, to fell.

sobrecostura, *f.* (sew.) whipstich, fell.

sobrecrecer, *vn.* (*for irr. v.* CRECER) to grow on top.

sobrecreciente, *a.* growing on top.

sobrecruces, *m. pl.* (carp.) cross joints.

sobrecubierta, *f.* double cover; warp or envelope; (naut.) upper deck.

sobrecuello, *m.* collar.

sobredicho, cha, *a.* above-mentioned, aforesaid, said.

sobrediente, *m.* gagtooth.

sobredorar, *va.* to overgild; to palliate.

sobreedificar, *va.* to build over or on.

sobreempeine, *m.* covering (of leggins) for the instep.

sobreestadías, *f. pl.* (com.) extra lay days.

sobreexcitación, *f.* overexcitement; overexcitation.

sobreexcitar, *va.* to overexcite.

sobrefalda, *f.* overskirt.

sobrefaz, *f.* surface, outside; (mil.) face prolonged.

sobrefino, na, *a.* superfine, overfine, extrafine.

sobreflor, *f.* flower growing within another.

sobrefusión, *f.* (phys. & chem.) superfusion, supercooling.

sobreguarda, *m.* second guard.

sobrehaz, *f.* surface; outside cover.

sobreherido, da, *a.* slightly wounded.

sobrehilar, *va.* (sew.) to overcast.

sobrehueso, *m.* (vet.) splint; trouble, encumbrance, burden.

sobrehumano, na, *a.* superhuman.

sobrehusa, *f.* stew of fried fish.

sobrejalma, *f.* woollen cover for a packsaddle.

sobrejuanete, *m.* (naut.) royal.

sobrejunta, *f.* cover plate or strap (of a butt joint).

sobrelecho, *m.* under face of a stone.

sobrellave. I. *f.* double key. **II.** *m.* in royal palaces, keeper of double keys.

sobrellenar, *va.* to fill up, fill full.

sobrelleno, na, *a.* well filled, filled full.

sobrellevar, *va.* to ease (another's burden); to carry; to bear, endure, undergo; to overlook, be lenient about.

sobremanera, *adv.* beyond measure; exceedingly, most.

sobremano, *f.* (vet.) splint on the forehoofs.

sobremesa, *f.* table carpet, tablecloth; dessert.—**de sobremesa,** after dinner.

sobremesana, *f.* (naut.) mizzen topsail.

sobremuñonera, *f.* (arti.) clamp or capsquare.

sobrenadar, *vn.* to float.

sobrenatural, *a.* supernatural.

sobrenaturalmente, *adv.* supernaturally.

sobrenjalma, *f.* = SOBREJALMA.

sobrenombre, *m.* surname; nickname.

sobrentender, *va.* (*for irr. v.* ENTENDER) to understand of course. **II.** *vr.* to be understood, to go without saying.

sobrepaga, *f.* extra pay.

sobrepaño, *m.* upper cloth; wrapper.

sobreparto, *m.* (med.) confinement after parturition.

---

sobrepeine. I. *m.* cutting the hair but slightly. **II.** *adv.* (coll.) slightly, briefly.
sobrepelliz, *f.* (eccl.) surplice.
sobrepeso, *m.* overweight.
sobrepié, *m.* (vet.) splint on rear hoofs.
sobreplán, *m.* (naut.) rider.
sobreponer. I. *va.* (*for irr. v.* PONER) to put over, to overlap. **II.** *vr.* (w. **a**) to be above; to master, overcome, overpower.
sobreposición, *f.* superposition.
sobreprecio, *m.* extra charge, raise.
sobrepuerta, *f.* cornice over a door; lambrequin, door curtain, portière.
sobrepuesto, ta. I. *a.* & *pp. irr.* of SOBREPONER; superposed. **II.** *m.* honeycomb formed by bees after the hive is full.
sobrepujamiento, *m.* surpassing, excelling.
sobrepujante, *pa.* surpassing, excelling.
sobrepujanza, *f.* great strength and vigor.
sobrepujar, *va.* to exceed, surpass, excel.
sobrequilla, *f.* (naut.) keelson.
sobrerronda, *f.* (mil.) counterround.
sobrerropa, *f.* overcoat; overalls.
sobresaliente. I. *a.* excelling, surpassing, excellent; conspicuous, that stands out, distinctive. **II.** *n.* substitute; (theat.) understudy.
sobresalir, *vn.* (*for irr. v.* SALIR) to excel, be prominent, stand out; to project, jut out.
sobresaltar. I. *va.* to rush upon, assail, attack, fall upon; to frighten, terrify, startle. **II.** *vn.* to be striking (as figures in a painting). **III.** *vr.* to be startled.
sobresalto, *m.* sudden assault; startling surprise; sudden dread or fear.—**de s.,** unexpectedly, unawares, suddenly.
sobresanar, *va.* to heal superficially; to screen, to palliate.
sobresano. I. *adv.* cured superficially; affectedly, feignedly. **II.** *m. pl.* (naut.) tabling, leach-lining.
sobrescribir, *va.* to superscribe, address.
sobrescrito, *pp.* & *m.* superscription, address.
sobresdrújulo, la, *a.* accented on any syllable preceding the antepenult.
sobreseer, *vn.* to desist from a design; to relinquish a claim; (law) to stay a judgment, etc.
sobreseimiento, *m.* suspension; discontinuance; (law) stay of proceedings.
sobresello, *m.* double seal.
sobresembrar, *va.* to sow over again.
sobreseñal, *f.* a special knights' device.
sobresolar, *va.* to pave anew; (shoe) to resole.
sobrestante, *m.* overseer; foreman; comptroller; inspector; supervisor.—**sobrestantía,** *f.* position or office of a SOBRESTANTE.
sobresueldo, *m.* extra wages.
sobresuelo, *m.* floor or pavement over another.
sobretarde, *f.* close of the evening.
sobretendón, *m.* tumor on the tendons of a horse's leg.
sobretodo, *m.* overcoat, great coat.
sobreveedor, *m.* chief of the overseers.
sobrevenida, *f.* supervention.
sobrevenir, *vn.* (*for irr. v.* VENIR) to happen, take place; to follow; to supervene.
sobreverterse, *vr.* to run over, overflow.
sobrevestir, *va.* to put a greatcoat on.
sobrevidriera, *f.* window guard, wire net before a glass window; storm window.
sobrevienta, *f.* gust of wind; onslaught, impetuous fury; startling surprise.—**a s.,** suddenly.
sobreviento, *m.* gust of wind.—**estar a s. de,** (naut.) to have the wind of.
sobrevista, *f.* beaver of a helmet.
sobreviviente, *n.* & *a.* survivor (-ing).
sobrevivir, *va.* & *vn.* to survive, to outlive.
sobrexcedente, *a.* surpassing, exceeding.
sobrexceder, *va.* to surpass, excel, exceed.
sobrexcitación, *f.* overexcitement; overexcitation.
sobrexcitar, *va.* to overexcite.
sobriamente, *adv.* soberly, frugally.

sobriedad, *f.* sobriety, frugality.
sobrina, *f.* niece.—**sobrinazgo,** *m.* relationship of a nephew or niece; nepotism.—**sobrino, m.** nephew.
sobrio, ria, *a.* sober, temperate, frugal.
soca, *f.* (Am.) ratoon of the sugar cane.
socaire, *m.* (naut.) slatch; lee, lee gauge.
socairero, *m.* (naut.) skulker, lurker.
socaliña, *f.* trick, cunning.—**socaliñar,** *va.* to extort by trickery.—**socaliñero, ra,** *n.* trickster, cheat.
socalzar, *va.* (mas.) to underpin, underset.
socapa, *f.* pretext, pretence.—**a s.,** cautiously.
socapiscol, *m.* = SOCHANTRE.
socarra, *f.* singe, scorching; craft, cunning.
socarrar, *va.* to singe, scorch.
socarrén, *m.* (arch.) eave, gable end.
socarrena, *f.* hollow, cavity; interval; (arch.) space between rafters.
socarrina, *f.* (coll.) scorching, singeing.
socarrón, na, *a.* cunning, sly, crafty.
socarronamente, *adv.* slyly, artfully.
socarronería, *f.* cunning, artfulness, craftiness.
socava, socavación, *f.* undermining; digging around trees.
socavar, *va.* to excavate, undermine.
socavón, *m.* cave, cavern; (min.) adit, adit level, tunnel.
socaz, *m.* outlet of a mill.
sociabilidad, *f.* sociableness, sociability.
sociable, *a.* sociable, companionable.
sociablemente, *adv.* sociably, companionably.
social, *a.* social; sociable, companionable.
socialismo, *m.* (pol.) socialism.
socialista, *n.* & *a.* socialist (-ic).
socialización, *f.* socialization.
socializar, *va.* to socialize, transfer to the State.
sociedad, *f.* society; social intercourse; (com.) society, corporation, association, company, partnership, copartnership.—**s. anónima,** stock company.—**s. comanditaria** = S. EN COMANDITA.—**s. cooperativa,** cooperative society or association.—**s. de socorros mutuos,** mutual-help society.—**s. en comandita,** commandite, partnership in commendam.—**s. regular colectiva,** general partnership, copartnership.—**s. por acciones** = S. ANÓNIMA.—**la s.,** society, the social organism, the community (often restricted, as in English, to polite or fashionable society).
socinianismo, *m.* Socinianism.
sociniano, na, *n.* & *a.* Socinian.
socio, cia, *n.* partner, copartner; companion, consort; member, fellow; (coll.) confederate.
sociología, *f.* sociology.—**sociológicamente,** *adv.* sociologically.—**sociológico, ca,** *a.* sociological.—**sociólogo, ga,** *n.* sociologist.
socolor, *m.* pretext, pretence.
socollada, *f.* (naut.) flapping; pitching, jerk.
soconusco, *m.* cacao from Soconusco (C. A.).
socoro, *m.* place under the choir.
socorredor, ra, *n.* & *a.* helper (-ing), aider (-ing).
socorrer, *va.* to assist, aid, help; to favor; to pay on account.
socorrido, da, *a.* & *pp.* furnished, well supplied; (coll.) handy, useful; popular.
socorro, *m.* succor, aid, assistance, help; payment on account; (mil.) succors; relief.
socrático, ca, *a.* Socratic.
socrocio, *m.* (pharm.) saffron poultice.
socucho, *m.* (Am.) small room, "den"; hiding place.
sochantre, *m.* (eccl.) subchanter.
soda, *f.* = SOSA.
sódico, ca, *a.* (chem.) sodic; sodium (u. a., as in *carbonato sódico,* sodium carbonate).
sodio, *m.* (chem.) sodium.
sodomía, *f.* sodomy.—**sodomita,** *n.* & *a.* sodomite (-itic).—**sodomítico, ca,** *a.* sodomitical.
soez, *a.* mean, vile, base, coarse.
soezmente, *adv.* meanly, basely, vilely.
sofá, *m.* sofa.
sofaldar, *va.* to truss up; raise up; tuck up.
sofaldo, *m.* trussing or tucking up clothes.

sofí, *m.* sufi, sofi, shah; Persian sect of mystics.

sofión, *m.* hoot; reprimand.

sofisma, *m.* (log.) fallacy.

sofismo, *m.* = SUFISMO.

sofista, *m.* sophist; quibbler.

sofistería, *f.* sophistry.

sofisticación, *f.* perversion by fallacies.

sofísticamente, *adv.* fallaciously.

sofisticar, *va.* to falsify, pervert or distort by fallacy.

sofístico, ea, *a.* fallacious.

sofito, *m.* (arch.) soffit.

soflama, *f.* subtile flame; glow; blush; (coll.) flimflam.

soflamar. I. *va.* to cheat, swindle; (coll.) to flimflam; to make (a person) blush. **II.** *vr.* to get scorched.

soflamero, *m.* trickster; (coll.) flimflammer.

sofocación, *f.* suffocation; smothering, choking.

sofocante, *pa.* & *a.* suffocating, stifling, close.

sofocar, *va.* (*pret.* SOFOQUÉ; *subj.* SOFOQUE) to choke, suffocate, smother; to quench, extinguish, put out; to stifle; to oppress, harass; to importune, vex; to provoke; to make (a person) blush.

sofocleo, a, *a.* Sophoclean.

sofoco, *m.* suffocation; vexation, chagrin.

sofocón, *m.* (coll.) vexation, chagrin.

sófora, *f.* (bot.) Japanese pagoda tree.

sofreír, *va.* (cook.) to fry slightly.

sofrenada, *f.* sudden check of a horse, saccade, ebrillade; harsh reprimand, dressing down.

sofrenar, *va.* to check (a horse) suddenly; to reprimand severely; to check (a passion).

sofrenazo, *m.* = SOFRENADA.

sofrito, ta, *pp. irr.* of SOFREÍR.

soga. I. *f.* rope, halter, cord; a variable land measure; (arch.) face (of a brick or stone); (arch.) stretcher (s. o. bricks and stones).—**a s.,** (arch.) as stretchers.—**con la s. a la garganta,** in imminent danger.—**dar s. a,** to make fun of.—**hacer s.,** to lag behind. **II.** *n.* (coll.) sly, cunning person; (Colomb.) lasso, lariat.

soguear, *va.* to measure with a rope.

soguería, *f.* ropewalk; rope shop; collection of ropes.

soguero, *m.* ropemaker.

soguilla, *f.* small braid of hair; small rope.

soja, *f.* (bot.) soy; soy bean.

sojuzgador, ra, *n.* conqueror, subduer.

sojuzgar, *va.* (*for mut. v.* JUZGAR) to conquer, subjugate, subdue.

sol, *m.* sun; sunlight; day; ancient lace; (mus.) G, sol, fifth note of the scale, sol, Peruvian silver coin (normally, about 49 cents, or 2 shillings).—**s. medio,** (astr.) mean sun.—**al salir el s.,** at sunrise.—**al s. puesto,** at nightfall.—**de s. a s.,** from sunrise to sunset.—**hacer s.,** to be sunny (*hace sol,* it is sunny; *hace mucho sol,* it is very sunny).—**quemadura del s.,** sunburning.—**tomar el s.,** to bask in the sun; (naut.) to take the altitude of the sun.

solacear, *va.* to solace, console, comfort.

solada, *f.* dregs, lees, sediment.

solado, *pp.* & *m.* tile floor, pavement.

solador, *m.* tiler, paver.

soladura, *f.* paving; paving materials.

solamente, *adv.* only; solely, merely.

solana, *f.* strong sunshine; sunny place; sun gallery; sun bath.

solanáceo, a. I. *a.* solanaceous. **II.** *f. pl.* Solanaceæ.

solanera, *f.* sun bath; sunburning; hot, sunny place.

solanina, *f.* (chem.) solanin(e.

solano, *m.* easterly wind; (bot.) nightshade.

solapa, *f.* (tail.) lapel; pretence, pretext; (vet.) cavity of a small wound; overlapping.—**a.,** or **de s.,** overlapping, lap (joint).

solapadamente, *adv.* deceitfully, sneakingly.

solapado, da, *pp.* & *a.* cunning, crafty, artful, sneaky lap (joint).

solapadura.—obra de s., *f.* (naut.) clincher work, clinching; overlapping.

solapamiento, *m.* (vet.) cavity of a wound.

solapar. I. *va.* (tail.) to put lapels on; to overlap; to cloak, conceal. **II.** *vn.* to overlap (as a lapel).

solape, solapo, *m.* lapel; pretence.—**a s.,** (coll.) sneakingly.

solar. I. *va.* (*ind.* SUELO: *subj.* SUELA) to floor, to pave; (shoe.) to sole. **II.** *m.* lot, ground plot; manor house, ancestral mansion. **III.** *a.* solar.

solariego, ga, *a.* manorial; (law) held by a full legal tenure; of noble ancestry.

solas.—a mis, tus, sus s., *adv.* all alone, by myself, thyself.

solaz, *m.* solace, consolation; relaxation, comfort; enjoyment.—**a s.,** pleasantly, agreeably.

solazar. I. *va.* (*pret.* SOLACÉ: *subj.* SOLACE) to solace, comfort, cheer, gladden. **II.** *vr.* to be comforted; to rejoice, to have pleasure or amusement.

solazo, *m. aug.* (coll.) scorching sun.

solazoso, sa, *a.* comforting, delectable.

soldada, *f.* wages, pay, salary.

soldadero, ra, *a.* salaried, receiving wages.

soldadesco, ca. I. *a.* soldierly, soldierlike, military. **II.** *f.* soldiery, soldiership; undisciplined troops.—**a la s.,** in a soldierly manner, soldierlike.

soldado, da. I. *pp.* of SOLDAR. **II.** *m.* soldier.—**s. de a caballo,** trooper, horse soldier, cavalryman.—**s. de a pie, or de infantería,** foot soldier.—**s. raso,** private.—**s. de marina,** marine.—**s. voluntario,** volunteer.

soldador, *m.* solderer; soldering iron.

soldadura, *f.* soldering; welding, brazing; solder; correction or mending.—**s. débil,** soft solder (-ing).—**s. dura,** or **s. fuerte,** hard solder (-ing).—**s. tierna = s.** DÉBIL.

soldán, *m.* sultan, Mohammedan title.

soldar, *va.* (*ind.* SUELDO: *subj.* SUELDE) to solder; to weld, braze; to mend; to correct.

solear, *va* = ASOLEAR.

solecismo, *m.* (rhet. and gram.) solecism.

soledad, *f.* solitude, loneliness, loneness; homesickness; lonely place; (mus.) an Andalusian tune, song, and dance.

soledoso, sa, *a.* solitary, lonely.

solejar, *m.* sunny place.

solemne, *a.* solemn; yearly; (coll.) great, confirmed, downright.

solemnemente, *adv.* solemnly.

solemnidad, *f.* solemnity; religious pomp; grand ceremony; impressiveness.—*pl.* formalities.

solemnizador, ra, *n.* & *a.* solemnizer (-ing).

solemnizar, *va.* (*pret.* SOLEMNICÉ: *subj.* SOLEMNICE) to solemnize, celebrate with pomp; to praise, applaud, extol.

solenoide, *m.* (elec.) solenoid.

sóleo, *m.* (anat.) soleus.

soler, *vn.* (*ind.* SUELO) (*a defective verb of which only the present and imperfect tenses are used, always followed by an infinitive*); to be in the habit, or have the custom, of, to be wont; (in the imperfect tense) used to (*yo solía hablar con él,* I used to talk with him).

soler, *m.* (naut.) underflooring.

solera, *f.* (arch.) entablature, stringpiece, crossbeam, rib, summer, lintel, breastsummer; plinth; nether millstone; lees or mother liquor of wine.—**s. de cureña,** (ordn.) sole of a gun carriage.

solercia, *f.* industry; abilities; shrewdness.

solería, *f.* pavement; paving stones; parcel of skins used for soles.

solero, *m.* nether millstone.

solerte, *a.* shrewd, cunning, sagacious.

soleta, *f.* new sole in stockings; (Mex.) cake with sugar icing.—**tomar s.,** (coll.) to run off.

soletar, soletear, *va.* to resole (stockings).

soletero, ra, *n.* one who refoots stockings.

solevación, *f.,* or **solevamiento,** *m.* = SUBLEVACIÓN.

solevantado, da, *a.* & *pp.* restless, excited, agitated, perturbed.—**solevantamiento,** *m.* upheaval, uprising.—**solevantar,** *va.* to push up, elevate; to incite.

solevar, *va.* = SUBLEVAR.

solfa, *f.* (mus.) sol-fa, solfeggio, solmization; musical annotation, notes; music, harmony; (coll.) sound beating or flogging.—**estar, or poner, en s.,** to be arranged (or to arrange) with art and judgment; to appear (or present) in a ridiculous light.

solfatara, *f.* (geol.) solfatara.

solfeador, ra, *n.* sol-faist, one who solmizates.

solfear, *vn.* (mus.) to sol-fa, solmizate; (coll.) to cudgel, flog.—**solfeo,** *m.* (mus.) sol-faing; (coll.) beating, drubbing.—**solfista,** *n.* sol-faist.

solicitación, *f.* solicitation; importunity; temptation, inducement.

solicitado, da, *a.* in good demand, sought-after, popular.

solicitador, ra, *n.* solicitor, agent.

solicitamente, *adv.* solicitously, diligently.

solicitante. I. *a.* soliciting. **II.** *n.* solicitor, agent; applicant.

solicitar, *va.* to solicit; to apply for; to importune; to entreat; to woo, court.

solícito, ta, *a.* solicitous, diligent, careful.

solicitud, *f.* solicitude; importunity; diligence; petition, application, request; (com.) demand.—**a s.,** on request, at the request (of).

sólidamente, *adv.* solidly, firmly.

solidar, *va.* to consolidate, establish; to harden, to render firm and solid.

solidariamente, *adv.* with solidarity; (law) in solidum, for the whole.

solidaridad, *f.* solidarity.

solidario, ria, *a.* (law) solidary, jointly liable.

solideo, *m.* (eccl.) calotte.

solidez, *f.* solidity, firmness, strength.

solidificación, *f.* solidification.

solidificar, *va.* & *vr.* to solidify.

sólido, da. I. *a.* solid, firm, compact, consistent; built on sound reasons. **II.** *m.* (geom. & phys.) solid; solidus, an ancient Roman gold coin.

soliloquiar, *vn.* (coll.) to soliloquize.

soliloquio, *m.* soliloquy, monologue.

solimán, *m.* (chem.) corrosive sublimate.

solio, *m.* throne with a canopy; throne.

solípedo, da, *a.* solipede, solidungulate.

solista, *n.* (mus.) soloist.

solitaria, *f.* post chaise; sulky; tapeworm.

solitariamente, *adv.* solitarily.

solitario, ria. I. *a.* solitary, lonely, isolated, secluded. **II.** *m.* solitary, recluse, hermit; solitaire (game); (jewel) solitaire (diamond).

sólito, ta, *a.* wont, accustomed.

soliviadura, *f.* lift, lifting, raising.

soliviantar, *va.* to induce, incite, rouse.

soliviar. I. *va.* to raise or lift up; to prop up. **II.** *vr.* to raise one's self.

solivio, *m.* lift, rising or raising.

solo, la. I. *a.* alone, unaccompanied; only, sole; solitary, lonely.—**a mis solas, sus solas,** etc., all alone, without aid, by myself (himself, etc.); in solitude.—**a solas,** alone, unaided. **II.** *m.* (mus.) solo; lone hand in certain card games; a card game.

sólo, *adv.* only, solely (= SOLAMENTE).

solomillo, solomo, *m.* sirloin; loin of pork.

solpuga. I. *f.* (zool.) solpugid. **II.** *f. pl.* Solpugida.

solsticial, *a.* solstitial.

solsticio, *m.* (ast.) solstice.—**s. de invierno,** winter solstice.—**s. de verano,** summer solstice.—**s. hiemal.** = S. DE INVIERNO.—**s. vernal** = S. DE VERANO.

soltadizo, za, *a.* easily untied; cleverly loosened.

soltador, ra, *n.* dropper.

soltar. I. *va.* (*ind.* SUELTO: *subj.* SUELTE) to untie, unfasten, loosen; to turn on (the water); to turn loose; to cast off, let go, set free, discharge; to throw down, throw out; (coll.) to utter, let out; to give (a slap or kick). **II.** *vn.* to burst out (into laughter, etc.). **III.** *vr.* to get loose, to come off; to grow expeditious and handy; to lose restraint; thaw

out; to forego all decency and modesty; to break out (laughing, crying, etc.); to begin, start.

soltería, *f.* celibacy, bachelorhood.

soltero, ra. I. *a.* single, unmarried. **II.** *m.* bachelor, unmarried man. **III.** *f.* spinster, unmarried woman.

solterón, na, *n.* old bachelor (maid).

soltura, *f.* freeing, setting at liberty; release, freedom; easiness; fluency; agility, nimbleness; laxity, looseness, licentiousness.

solubilidad, *f.* solubility.

soluble, *a.* soluble; solvable.

solución, *f.* loosening or untying; climax or denouement in a drama or epic poem; pay, satisfaction; (math., chem.) solution.—**s. de continuidad,** solution of continuity, discontinuity, break.

solucionar, *va.* to solve; to meet (a difficulty).

solutivo, v, *a.* (med.) solutive.

solvencia, *f.* (com.) solvency.

solventar, *va.* to settle (accounts); to solve.

solvente, *a.* solvent, dissolving; (com.) solvent.

solver, *va.* (*for irr. v.* RESOLVER) to solve.

sollado, *m.* (naut.) orlop.

sollamar, *va.* to scorch, to singe.

sollastre, *m.* scullion, kitchen boy; smart or slick rogue.

sollastría, *f.* scullery.

sollo, *m.* (icht.) sturgeon, pike.

sollozante, *a.* sobbing.

sollozar, *vn.* (*pret.* SOLLOCÉ: *subj.* SOLLOCE) to sob.—**sollozo,** *m.* sob; (Mex.) huckleberry.

soma, *f.* coarse flour.

somanta, *f.* (coll.) beating, drubbing.

somatén, *m.* armed force for the defence of a city or province; one who serves in such a force; alarm bell; (coll.) hubbub, rowdedow.—**¡s.!** Catalan war cry.

somatología, *f.* somatology.

sombra, *f.* shade; shadow; darkness; spirit, ghost; shelter, protection; resemblance; sign, vestige; (ast.) umbra; (art) shade, shading; umber.—**sombras chinescas,** (theat.) shadow pantomime.—**a la s.,** in the shade; (coll.) in jail.—**hacer s.,** to shade; to protect; to outshine.—**ni por s.,** by no means.—**no ser ni su s.,** to be but the shadow of one's former self.—**tener buena s.,** to be pleasing, popular, agreeable.—**tener mala s.,** to exert an evil influence over others, to be a hoodoo; to be disagreeable.

sombraje, *m.* screen made with branches, mats, etc., to afford shade.

sombrajo, *m.* SOMBRAJE; (coll.) shadow cast by a person before another who needs light.

sombrar, *va.* to astonish.

sombreado, *pp.* & *m.* shading.

sombrear, *va.* (art) to shade.

sombrerazo, *m. aug.* large hat; flap or blow with a hat; (coll.) doffing of the hat as a salute.

sombrerera, *f.* hatbox, hat case; hatter's wife.

sombrerería, *f.* hat factory or shop.

sombrerero, ra, *n.* hatter; hat maker.

sombrerete, *m. dim.* small hat; (mech.) bonnet, cap, cowl; spark catcher of a locomotive; (arch.) calotte.

sombrerillo, ito, *m. dim.* little hat; alms basket in prisons; (bot.) navelwort.

sombrero, *m.* SOMBRERETE; hat; soundboard, canopy of a pulpit; privilege of a Spanish grandee of keeping his hat on in the presence of the king.—**s. apuntado,** cocked hat.—**s. calañés,** Andalusian hat.—**s. castoreño,** beaver hat.—**s. de cabrestante,** (naut.) drum of the capstan.—**s. de copa, or de copa alta,** silk hat, high (silk) hat.—**s. de jipijapa,** Panama hat.—**s. del patrón,** (naut.) hat money, primage.—**s. de muelles,** opera hat.—**s. de pelo,** (Am.) high hat.—**s. de teja,** shovel hat, priest's hat (low-crown hat with broad brim turned up on the sides).—**s. de tres candiles, or de tres picos,** three-cornered hat.—**s. flexible,** soft felt hat.—**s. gacho,** slouch hat.—**s. hongo,** derby hat.—**s. jarano,** Mexican sombrero.—**s. jíbaro,** farmers' straw hat.—**s. jipijapa,** Panama hat.

sombría, *f.* shady place.
sombrilla, *f.* parasol, sunshade.
sombrita, *f. dim.* slight shade.
sombrío, bría. I. *a.* gloomy, sombre; overcast, murky, thick (weather); taciturn, sullen; (art) shaded, dark. **II.** *m.* shady place.
sombroso, sa, *a.* shady, shadowy.
someramente, *adv.* superficially, briefly.
somero, ra. I. *a.* superficial, shallow. **II.** *f.* (print.) sleeper of the press.
someter. I. *va.* to subject; submit, subdue; to put (to the test, etc.). **II.** *vr.* to humble one's [self; to submit; to surrender; (w. **a**) to submit to; to go through (an operation, an examination).
sometimiento, *m.* submission, subjection, subduing.
somnambulismo, *m.* somnambulism.
somnámbulo, la, *n.* somnambulist
somnífero, ra, *a.* somniferous, soporiferous.
somnílocuo, cua, *a.* somniloquous.
somnolencia, *f.* drowsiness, somnolency.
somonte.—de s., coarse, rough, shaggy.
somorgujador, *m.* diver.
somorgujar, *va. & vr.* to dive, to duck.
somorgujo, somorgujón, somormujo, *m.* (orn.) dun diver, merganser.—**a lo somorgujo,** or **a la somormujo,** under water; privately, secretly
sompesar, *va.* to heft,
son, *m.* sound, noise; spread news or story; pretext, motive; manner, guise.—**¿a qué s.?** why, for what reason?—**a s. de,** at or to the sound of.—**¿a [s. de qué?** = **¿A QUÉ S.?**—**bailar a cualquier s.,** to transfer easily one's affection or liking, to be fickle. —**bailar sin s.,** to be exceedingly eager; to act unwisely or inopportunely.—**bailar uno al s. que le [tocan,** to adapt one's self to circumstances.—**en s. de,** as, like, in the guise of.—**en s. de guerra,** in a warlike manner.—**sin s.,** without reason.—**sin ton ni s.,** without rime or reason.
sonable, *a.* loud, sounding; noted, famous.
sonada, *f.* (mus.) tune; sonata.
sonadera, *f.* blowing the nose.
sonadero, *m.* handkerchief.
sonado, da, *pp. & a.* noted, famous; talked-about; bruited about.
sonador, ra. I. *n.* noise maker. **II.** *m.* handkerchief.
sonaja, *f.* jingles; (mus.) timbrel.
sonajero, *m.* baby's rattle.
sonajuela, *f. dim.* small jingles or timbrel.
sonambulismo, *m.* somnambulism.
sonámbulo, la, *n.* somnambulist.
sonante, *pa. & a.* sounding, sonorous.
sonar, *va.* (ind. SUENO: *subj.* SUENE) to sound, to ring, to play upon. **II.** *vn.* to sound; to ring; to be mentioned; (w. **a**) to sound, or look, like; to seem; to sound familiar; to be reported or bruited about.—**ni suena ni truena,** is forgotten, is in the discard, cuts no figure. **III.** *vr.* to blow one's nose.
sonata, *f.* (mus.) sonata.
sonatina, *f. dim.* (mus.) sonatina.
sonda, *f.* (naut.) sounding, heaving the lead; lead, sounder, plummet; (geol.) anular borer; diamond drill; (surg.) catheter, bougie; sound, probe; (arti.) searcher, proof-stick.
sondable, *a.* that may be sounded.
sondaleza, *f.* (naut.) lead line, sounding line.
sondar, sondear, *va.* (naut.) to sound; to try, to sift, to sound (another's intentions); to explore, fathom; to probe.
sondeo, *m.* sounding; exploring, fathoming.
sonecillo, *m. dim.* slight sound; merry tune.
sonetico, *m. dim.* sound produced by tapping with the fingers; little or light sonnet.
sonetista, *n.* sonnet writer.—**soneto,** *m.* sonnet.
sonido, *m.* sound; noise; report; literal meaning. —**s. timpánico,** tympanic resonance.
sonochada, *f.* evening; evening watch.
sonochar, *vn.* to watch the first hours of the night.
sonómetro, *m.* sonometer.
sonoramente, *adv.* sonorously; harmoniously.
sonoridad, *f.* sonority, sonorousness.

sonoro, ra; sonoroso, sa, *a.* sonorous; sounding, clear, loud.
sonreír, *vn. & vr.* (for irr. v. REÍR) to smile.
sonrisa, *f.*, **sonriso,** *m.* smile.
sonrodadura, *f.* sticking in the mud (s. o. wheels).
sonrodarse, *vr.* to stick in the mud (s. o. wheels).
sonrojar, sonrojear. I. *va.* to make (one) blush. **II.** *vr.* to blush.—**sonrojo,** *m.* blush; blushing; word causing a blush.
sonrosar, sonrosear. I. *va.* to dye a rose color. **II.** *vr.* to blush.—**sonroseo,** *m.* blush.
sonsaca, *f.*, **sonsacamiento,** *m.* wheedling; drawing out; enticement; pilfering.
sonsacador, ra, *n.* wheedler, enticer; pilferer.
sonsacar, *va.* (for mut. v. SACAR) to pilfer; to draw (one) out; to entice, allure.
sonsaque, *m.* = SONSACA.
sonsonete, *m.* sound produced by rhythmical raps or taps; singsong voice.
soñador, ra, *n.* dreamer.—**soñante,** *a.* dreaming.
soñar. I. *va. & vn.* (ind. SUEÑO: *subj.* SUEÑE) to dream.—**s. con,** to dream of.—**s. despierto,** to indulge in day dreams; to build air castles.—**ni soñarlo,** not even to dream of it.
sopa, *f.* sop; (cook.) soup.—*pl.* slices of bread for soup.—**s. borracha,** a kind of wine cake.—**s. de ajo,** or **de gato,** meager soup.—**s. de vino,** (bot.) flower of the small caltrops.—**s. juliana,** julienne soup, vegetable soup.—**a la s. boba,** (coll.) living at other people's expense.—**hecho una s.,** (coll.) drenched, wet through to the skin.
sopaipa, *f.* fritter steeped in honey.
sopalancar, *va.* to lift with a lever.
sopalanda, *f.* gown worn by students.
sopanda, *f.* (car.) brace; (carp.) joist.
sopapear, *va.* (coll.) to chuck under the chin; to vilify, to abuse.
sopapo, *m.* chuck under the chin; (coll.) box, blow, slap; (mech.) valve, stop valve, sucker.
sopar, *va.* to sop (bread); ENSOPAR.
sopear, *va.* to sop, to steep; to trample, maltreat.
sopeña, *f.* cavity under a rock.
sopera, *f.* soup tureen.
sopero. I. *m.* soup plate. **II.** *m.* lover of soups.
sopesar, *va.* to heft.
sopetear, *va.* to sop; to steep (bread); to abuse, maltreat.
sopeteo, *m.* dipping (bread, etc.).
sopetón, *m.* bread toasted and steeped in oil; box, cuff, slap.—**de s.,** suddenly.
sopicaldo, *m.* very thin soup.
sopita, *f. dim.* sippet, light soup.
sopista, *n.* one living on charity.
¡sopla! *interj.* gracious! what a thing!
sopladero, *m.* air hole from subterranean passages.
soplado, da. I. *a. & pp.* blown; (coll.) overnice and spruce; conceited. **II.** *m.* (min.) deep fissure.
soplador, ra. I. *n.* blower; inciter. **II.** *m.* ventilator, blowing fan; tuyère (of a blast furnace).
sopladura, *f.* blowing; (found.) air hole.
soplamocos, *m.* (coll.) box or slap on the nose.
soplar. I. *vn.* to blow. **II.** *va.* to blow; blow out; to fan; to fill with air, inflate; to rob or steal in an artful manner; to huff (a man) in the game of draughts; to prompt; to inspire.—**soplársela a uno,** to deceive one. **III.** *vr.* to swell up; to eat or drink to excess, to stuff one's self.
soplete, *m.* blowpipe; blow torch.
soplico, *m. dim.* slight puff or blast.
soplido, *m.* blowing, blast.
soplillo, *m. dim.* blowing fan; anything extremely thin and light; silk gauze, chiffon; very light sponge cake.
soplo, *m.* blowing; blast, gust, puff of wind; breath; instant, moment; hint, secret advice or warning; secret accusation.
soplón, na, *n.* talebearer, informer.
sopón, *m. aug.* = SOPISTA.
soponcio, *m.* fainting fit, swoon.

---

sopor, *m.* (med.) sopor, lethargic sleep.
soporífero, ra, *a.* soporific, soporiferous.
soporoso, sa, *a.* soporiferous; suffering from sopor; (med.) soporus.
soportable, *a.* bearable, endurable.
soportador, ra, *n.* supporter.
soportal, *m.* (arch.) portico.
soportar, *va.* to suffer, endure, bear; to support, bear, resist.
soporte, *m.* support; rest; bearing.
soprano. I. *m.* (mus.) soprano voice. **II.** *f.* soprano singer.
sopuntar, *va.* to underscore with dots.
sor, *f.* (eccl.) sister, as *sor Maria*, Sister Mary.
sora, *f.* (Peru) mash made from maize.
sorba, *f.* (bot.) sorb apple.
sorbedor, ra. I. *a.* sipping. **II.** *n.* sipper.
sorber, *va.* to sip, suck; to imbibe, soak, absorb; to swallow.
sorbete, *m.* sherbet, water ice.
sorbetera, *f.* ice-cream freezer; (coll. and hum.) high hat, "top hat."
sorbetón, *m.* *aug.* large draught of liquor.
sorbible, *a.* absorbable; that can be sipped.
sorbito, *m.* *dim.* little sip.
sorbo, *m.* imbibition; absorption; sip, draught, swallow, gulp; (bot.) sorb tree, service tree.
sorda, *f.* (orn.) woodcock; (naut.) stream-cable for launching a ship.
sordamente, *adv.* secretly, silently.
sordera, sordedad, sordez, *f.* deafness.
sórdidamente, *adv.* sordidly.—**sordidez,** *f.* sordidness.—**sórdido, da,** *a.* sordid.
sordina, *f.* (mus.) mute, sordine (for string instruments); sordono (for trumpet); damper (for piano).—**a la s.,** secretly, quietly, on the quiet.
sordino, *m.* (mus.) kit, small fiddle.
sordo, da, *a.* deaf; silent, still, quiet; muffled, stifled; dull; unmoved, insensible; (math.) irrational, surd.
sordomudez, *f.* (med.) deaf-mutism.
sordomudo, da, *a.* & *n.* deaf and dumb, deaf-mute.
sordón, *m.* (mus.) old kind of oboe.
sorgo, *m.* (bot.) sorghum.
soriasis, *f.* (med.) psoriasis.
sorites, *m.* (log.) sorites, chain argument.
sorna, *f.* sluggishness, laziness, slowness.
soro, *m.* year-old hawk.
soroche, *m.* (S. A.) altitude sickness, a disease caused by rarefaction of the air at great altitudes; (min.) friable silver ore.
soroque, *f.* (min.) matrix of ores.
sóror, *f.* (eccl.) sister (= SOR).
sorprendente, *a.* surprising.
sorprender, *va.* to surprise.
sorpresa, *f.* surprise.—**de s.,** by surprise.
sorra, *f.* (naut.) ballast of stones or coarse gravel; side of a tunny fish.
sorregar, *va.* (for irr. v. REGAR) to water accidentally, by deviation or overflow of the water elsewhere.
sorriego, *m.* water that deviates from one channel to another; watering by this water.
sorrostrada, *f.* insolence; bluntness.—**dar s.,** to insult; to throw one's faults in one's face.
sorteable, *a.* fit to be drafted.
sorteador, ra, *n.* one who casts lots; skilful bullfighter.
sorteamiento, *m.* = SORTEO.
sortear, *va.* to draw or cast lots for; to raffle; to fight (bulls) with skill and dexterity; to elude or shun cleverly.
sorteo, *m.* casting lots; drawing, raffle; bullfighting.
sortiaria, *f.* fortune telling by cards.
sortija, *f.* finger ring; ring, hoop; curl of hair.
sortijita, juela, *f.* *dim.* little ring; ringlet.
sortijón, *m.* *aug.* large finger ring.
sortilegio, *m.* sortilege, sorcery.
sortílego, ga, *n.* sorcerer, conjurer, fortune teller.

sosa, *f.* (bot.) glasswort, kelp; soda ash, barilla; sal soda; (chem.) soda.
sosal, *m.* soda-bearing field.
sosamente, *adv.* insipidly, tastelessly.
sosar, *m.* = SOSAL.
sosegadamente, *adv.* quietly, calmly.
sosegado, da, *pp.* & *a.* quiet, peaceful, calm.
sosegador, ra, *n.* & *a.* pacifier (-ing), appeaser (-ing), quieter (-ing).
sosegar. I. *va.* (ind. SOSIEGO: pret. SOSEGUÉ: subj. SOSIEGUE) to appease, calm, quiet; to lull. **II.** *vn.* to rest, repose. **III.** *vr.* to become calm or quiet, calm or composed, to quiet down.
sosera, sosería, *f.* insipidity, tastelessness; nonsense.
sosero, ra, *a.* (bot.) yielding soda.
sosez, *f.* = SOSERA.
sosiega, *f.* rest after work; drink taken while resting, after dinner or before going to bed (nightcap).
sosiego, *m.* tranquillity, calm, quiet.
soslayar, *va.* to do or place obliquely.
soslayo, *m.*—**al s.,** or **de s.,** askance; slanting, skew, on the bias.
soso, sa, *a.* insipid, tasteless, vapid; cold; silly; dull, inane.
sospecha, *f.* suspicion.—**sospechar,** *va.* & *vn.* to suspect.—**sospechosamente,** *adv.* suspiciously.
sospechoso, sa, *a.* suspicious; suspecting.
sospesar, *va.* to suspend, lift, raise.
sosquín, *m.* blow treacherously given.
sostén, *m.* support; steadiness of a ship.
sostenedor, ra, *n.* supporter.
sostener. I. *va.* (for irr. v. TENER) to support; to maintain, keep; to assist, help; to encourage; to uphold, defend; to bear, endure. **II.** *vr.* to support or maintain one's self.
sostenido, da. I. *a.* & *pp.* supported; sustained, kept up. **II.** *m.* (mus.) sharp (the tone and the character #).
sosteniente, *a.* sustaining, supporting.
sostenimiento, *m.* sustenance, maintenance; support.—**muro,** or **pared, de s.,** retaining wall.
sostituir, *va.* to substitute. *V.* SUSTITUIR.
sota. I. *f.* jack, knave, at cards; hussy, jade. **II.** *m.* deputy, substitute.
sotabanco, *m.* (arch.) pediment of an arch over a cornice; garret, attic.
sotabraga, *f.* (mil.) axletree band, yoke hoop.
sotacola, *f.* crupper.
sotacoro, *m.* place under the choir.
sotalugo, *m.* second hoop of a cask.
sotaministro, *m.* = SOTOMINISTRO.
sotana, *f.* cassock; (coll.) flogging, drubbing.
sotanear, *va.* (coll.) to beat, punish or reprimand severely.
sotaní, *m.* short skirt without plaits.
sótano, *m.* cellar, basement.
sotaventar, *va.* (naut.) to fall to leeward.
sotavento, *m.* leeward, lee.—**a s.,** under the lee.
sotechado, *m.* shed.
soteño, ña, *a.* produced in groves.
soterraño, *m.* = SUBTERRÁNEO.
soterrar, *va.* (ind. SOTIERRO: subj. SOTIERRE) to bury, put under ground; to hide.
sotillo, *m.* *dim.* little grove.
soto, *m.* grove, thicket, brake.
sotoministro, *m.* steward (in some convents).
sotrozo, *m.* (ordn.) linchpin, axle pin; (mech.) key; (naut.) foothook staff.
sotuer, *m.* (her.) saltier.
sóviet, *m.* soviet.—**soviético, ca,** *a.* sovietic.—**sovietismo,** *m.* sovietism.
sovoz.—a s., in a low tone, sotto voce.
soy. *V.* SER.
soya, *f.* (bot.) soy; soy bean.
Stábat, Stábat Máter, *m.* Stabat Mater.
statu quo, *m.* statu quo.
su, *pron. poss.* 3d pers. *m.* & *f. sing.* (*pl.* SUS) his, her, its, their, one's, your.

For pronunciation, see the rules at the beginning of the book.

suasorio, ria, *a.* suasory, suasive.

suave, *a.* smooth, soft, delicate, mellow; easy, tranquil, unruffled, quiet; suave, gentle, tractable, docile, mild, meek.

suavemente, *adv.* gently, sweetly, softly, mildly, kindly.

suavidad, *f.* softness, smoothness; ease; suavity; gentleness; lenity, forbearance.

suavizador, ra. I. *a.* mollifying, smoothing, softening. **II.** *m.* razor strop.

suavizar, *va.* (*pret.* SUAVICÉ: *subj.* SUAVICE) to soften, smoothe, mollify, mitigate; to ease; to temper.

subacetato, *m* subacetate.

subácido, da, *a.* (chem.) subacid.

subalcaide, *m.* deputy warden.

subalternante, *a.* subalternant.

subalternar, *va.* to subdue.

subalterno, na. I. *a.* subaltern, subordinate. **II.** *m.* subordinate; (mil.) subaltern.

subarrendador, ra, *n.* underletter, subletter.

subarrendamiento, *m.* subletting.

subarrendar, *va.* (*for irr. v.* ARRENDAR) to underlet, sublet, sublease.

subarrendatario, ria, *n.* undertenant.

subarriendo, *m.* (law) sublease, underlease.

subasta, subastación, *f.* auction, auction sale.— **poner en,** or **sacar a, pública s.,** to sell at auction, or to the best bidder.

subastar, *va.* to sell at auction.

subcarbonato, *m.* (chem.) subcarbonate.

subcinericio, cia, *a.* baked under ashes.

subclase, *f.* (bot. and zool.) subclass.

subclavero, *m.* assistant or deputy CLAVERO.

subclavio, via, *a.* (anat.) subclavian.

subcolector, *m.* subcollector, assistant collector.

subcomendador, *m.* deputy commander of a military order.

subconsciencia, *f.* subconsciousness; (the) subconscious.

subconsciente, *f.* subconscious.

subconservador, *m.* judge deputed by a conservator.

subcostal, *a.* subcostal.

subcutáneo, nea, *a.* subcutaneous.

subdelegable, *a.* that may be subdelegated.

subdelegación, *f.* subdelegation.—**subdelegado, da,** *n.* subdelegate.—**subdelegante,** *n.* he who subdelegates.—**subdelegar,** *va.* (*for mut. v.* LEGAR) to subdelegate.

subdiaconado, subdiaconato, *m.* subdeaconship.—**subdiácono,** *m.* subdeacon.

subdirector, ra, *n.* assistant director.

subdistinción, *f.* subdistinction.

subdistinguir, *va.* (*for mut. v.* DISTINGUIR) to make a subdistinction.

súbdito, ta. I. *a.* subject, inferior. **II.** *m.* subject.

subdividir, *va.* to subdivide.—**subdivisible, a.** subdivisible.—**subdivisión,** *f.* subdivision.

subdominante, *f.* (mus.) subdominant.

subejecutor, *m.* subagent.

subentender, I. *va.* (*for irr. v.* ENTENDER) understand what is tacitly meant. **II.** *vr.* to be understood, to be implied.

subérico, *a.* suberic.—**suberina,** *f.* suberin.

suberoso, sa, *a.* suberose, corky.

subestación, *f.* substation.

subgénero, *m.* (biol.) subgenus.

subgobernador, ra, *n.* vicegovernor, lieutenant governor.

subida, *f.* ascent, going up; elevation, taking or carrying up; acclivity, rise; accession of a disease; rise.

subidero, ra. I. *a.* mounting, raising, climbing. **II.** *m.* ladder, mounting block; way to go up; up grade, uphill road.

subido, da, *a. & pp.* raised on high; high, highpriced; strong, loud, bright (as a color); strongscented; finest, most excellent.

subidor, *m.* porter; elevator, lift.

subiente. I. *a.* rising. **II.** *m.* (arch.) ascending ornaments.

subilla, *f.* awl.

subimiento, *m.* rising, climbing, ascending.

subinquilino, *m.* undertenant, subtenant.

subinspección, *f.* subinspectorship; subinspector's office.

subinspector, *m.* subinspector.

subintendente, *m.* assistant intendant.

subintración, *f.* (med.) subingression.

subintrante, *a.* (med.) subintrant.

subintrar, *va.* to enter successively one after another.

subir. I. *vn.* to rise; to come up, go up, climb, mount; to grow; to enter leaves (silkworms); to be promoted; to increase in intensity; (com) to amount to, foot up; (mus.) to raise the voice or pitch.—**s. a caballo,** to mount a horse.—**s. de punto,** to increase, grow. **II.** *va.* to raise, place higher; to take up, bring up; set up; to straighten from an inclined position; (com.) to raise, advance (s. o. prices). **III.** *vr.* to go up, to climb; to rise.—**s. a las barbas,** to fly in one's face.—**s. a las bovedillas,** (coll.) to be nettled, be violently irritated.—**s. (el vino, licor,** etc.) **a la cabeza,** to go to one's head (s. o. wine, liquor, etc.).

súbitamente, subitáneamente, *adv.* suddenly, on a sudden.

subitáneo, nea, *a.* sudden, unexpected.

súbito, ta, *a.* sudden, unforeseen, unexpected.— **s.,** or **de s.,** suddenly, unexpectedly.

subjefe, *n.* second in command; assistant chief.

subjetivamente, *adv.* subjectively.

subjetividad, *f.* subjectivity.

subjetivismo, *f.* subjectivism.

subjetivo, va, *a.* subjective.

subjuntivo, *m. & a.* (gram.) subjunctive.

sublevación, *f.,* **sublevamiento,** *m.* insurrection, revolt.

sublevar. I. *va.* to excite to rebellion, raise in rebellion. **II.** *vr.* to rise in rebellion.

sublimación, *f.* sublimation.

sublimado, *pp. & m.* (chem.) sublimate.—**s. corrosivo,** corrosive sublimate.

sublimar, *va.* to heighten, elevate, exalt; (chem.) to sublimate.

sublimatorio, ria, *a.* (chem.) sublimatory.

sublime, *a.* sublime.—**la S. Puerta,** the Sublime Porte (the former Ottoman Empire).

sublimemente, *adv.* sublimely.

sublimidad, *f.* sublimity.

sublingual, *a.* sublingual, subglossal.

sublunar, *a.* sublunar, sublunary; terrestrial, earthly.

submarino, na. I. *a.* submarine. **II.** *m.* submarine.

submaxilar, *a.* submaxillary.

submúltiplo, pla, *a. & n.* (math.) submultiple.

suborden, *m.* suborder.

subordinación, *f.* subordination; subjection.

subordinadamente, *adv.* subordinately, subserviently.—**subordinado, da,** *pp. & a.* subordinate, subservient; subordinated.

subordinar, *va.* to subordinate; to subject.

subpolar, *a.* under or near the pole.

subprefecto, *m.* subprefect.

subprefectura, *f.* subprefecture.

subrayar, *va.* to underscore, underline; to emphasize.

subrepción, *f.* underhand proceeding; (law) subreption; surreption.

subrepticiamente, *adv.* surreptitiously.

subrepticio, cia, *a.* surreptitious.

subrigadier, *m.* (mil.) subbrigadier.

subrogación, *f.* surrogation or subrogation, substitution.—**subrogar,** *va.* (law) to surrogate or subrogate; to substitute.

subsanable, *a.* excusable; reparable, surmountable, that may be obviated.

subsanar, *va.* to exculpate, excuse; to mend, correct, repair; to obviate, get over.

subscapular, *a.* (anat.) subscapular.

subscribir, *va. & vr. (pp.* SUBSCRIPTO, SUBS-CRITO) to subscribe; to sign; to accede, agree to.
subscripción, *f.* subscription.
subscripto, ta; subscrito, ta, *pp. irr.* of SUBS-CRIBIR.
subscriptor, ra, *n.* subscriber.
subsecretaría, *f.* office and employment of an assistant secretary.
subsecretario, ria, *n.* assistant secretary.
subsecuente, *a.* subsequent.
subseguirse, *vr.* to follow next.
subsidiariamente, *adv.* subsidiarily.
subsidiario, ria, *a.* subsidiary; branch (u. a.); auxiliary; (law) ancillary.
subsidio, *m.* subsidy, pecuniary aid; war tax.
subsiguiente, *a.* subsequent, succeeding.
subsistencia, *f.* permanence, stability; subsistence; livelihood, living.
subsistente, *pa. & a.* subsistent, subsisting.
subsistir, *vn.* to subsist, last; to live, exist; to have the means of subsistence.
subsolano, *m.* east wind.
substancia, *f.* substance; nutritious sap, juice, or extract; property, wealth; gist; importance, value; (coll.) judgment, sense.—**s. blanca,** (anat.) white matter (of the brain).—**s. gris,** (anat.) gray matter.—**en s.,** in substance, in effect; in a nutshell, in brief.
substanciación, *f.* substantiation.
substancial, *a.* substantial, real, material; nutritious, nourishing; essential.
substancialmente, *adv.* substantially.
substanciar, *va.* to extract the substance of, to abstract, abridge; to substantiate; (law) to try (a case).
substancioso, sa, *a.* juicy; nourishing, nutritious; substantial.
substantivar, *va.* (gram.) to substantivize.
substantividad, *f.* substantiveness.
substantivo, va. **I.** *a.* substantive. **II.** *m.* substantive, noun.
substitución, *f.* substitution.
substituíble, *a.* replaceable.
substituidor, ra, *n. & a.* substitute (-ing).
substituir, *va. (pp.* SUBSTITUÍDO, SUBSTITUTO: *gerund,* SUBSTITUYENDO: *ind.* SUBSTITUYO: *pret.* él SUBSTITUYÓ: *subj.* SUBSTITUYA) to substitute, replace.
substituyente, *a.* substituting.
substituto, ta, *n.* substitute.
substracción, *f.* subtraction.
substraendo, *m.* subtrahend.
substraer. **I.** *va. (for irr. v.* TRAER) to subtract, remove, take off, deduct. **II.** *vr.* to withdraw one's self, to elude.
substrato, *m.* (phil.) substratum.
subsuelo, *m.* subsoil.
subtangente, *f.* subtangent.
subtender, *va. (for irr. v.* TENDER) (geom.) to subtend.
subteniente, *m.* (mil.) second lieutenant.
subtensa, *f.* (geom.) subtense (chord).
subterfugio, *m.* subterfuge.
subterráneamente, *adv.* subterraneously.
subterráneo, nea. **I.** *a.* subterraneous, underground. **II.** *m.* subterrane, any place underground (cave, vault, etc.); (geol.) subterrane.
subtítulo, *m.* subtitle.
suburbano, na. **I.** *a.* suburban. **II.** *n.* suburbanite, suburban resident.
suburbicario, ria, *a.* suburbicarian.
suburbio, *m.* suburb, outskirt.
subvención, *f.* subsidy.
subvencionar, *va.* to subsidize.
subvenir, *va. (for irr. v.* VENIR) to subvene, aid, assist, succor; to provide, supply, furnish, defray.
subversión, *f.* subversion, overthrow.
subversivo, va, *a.* subversive, destructive.
subversor, ra, *n. & a.* subverter (-ing), overthrower (-ing).

subvertir, *va. (for irr. v.* PERVERTIR) to subvert, destroy, ruin.
subyacente, *a.* underlying.
subyugación, *f.* subjugation, subjection.
subyugador, ra, *n. & a.* subjugator (-ing).
subyugar, *va. (pret.* SUBYUGUÉ: *subj.* SUBYUGUE) to subdue, subjugate.
succinato, *m.* (chem.) succinate.
succínico, ca, *a.* (chem.) succinic.
succino, *m.* succinite, amber.
succión, *f.* suction, suck.
sucedáneo, a. **I.** *a.* (med.) succedaneous. **II.** *m.* succedaneum.
suceder. **I.** *vn.* (w. **a**) to succeed, follow, be the successor of. **II.** *v. impers.* to happen, come to pass, come about.—**suceda lo que sucediere,** happen what may.
sucedido, *pp. & m.* event, happening.
sucediente, *a.* succeeding, following.
sucesible, *a.* capable of succession.
sucesión, *f.* succession; issue, offspring; (law) estate.—**s. intestada,** heirs at law.
sucesivamente, *adv.* successively.
sucesivo, va, *a.* successive, consecutive.—**en lo s.,** hereafter, in future.
suceso, *m.* event, happening; issue, outcome; success; course of time.
sucesor, ra, *n.* successor.
suciamente, *adv.* nastily, filthily; basely.
suciedad, *f.* nastiness, filthiness; dirt, filth.
sucintamente, *adv.* succinctly, briefly.
sucintarse, *vr.* to be precise, brief.
sucinto, ta, *a.* girded, tucked up; brief, succinct, concise.
sucio, cia, *a.* dirty, nasty, filthy; soiled; untidy; stained with sin, tainted with guilt; low, base; (naut.) foul.
suco, *m.* juice; sap.—**sucoso, sa,** *a.* juicy.
sucotrino, *a.* socotrine (aloes).
sucre, *m.* sucre, an Ecuadorean silver coin (about 50 cents).
suctorio, ria, *a.* (biol.) suctorial.
súcubo, *m.* succubus (demon).
sucucho, *m.* (naut.) storeroom of a ship; (Am.) socucho.
súcula, *f.* windlass, winch.
suculencia, *f.* juiciness, succulence.
suculentamente, *adv.* succulently.
suculento, ta, *a.* succulent, juicy.
sucumbiente, *a.* succumbent.
sucumbir, *vn.* to succumb; to submit, yield; to die, perish; (law) to lose a suit.
sucursal. **I.** *a.* ancillary, subsidiary; branch (u. a.). **II.** *f.* (com.) branch of a commercial house.
suche. **I.** *a.* (Ven.) green, unripe. **II.** *m.* (Ec., Peru), a tree yielding valuable timber; (Arg.) mud; (Ch.) insignificant employee.
suchel, suchil, *m.* (Am.) = SUCHE (tree).
sud, *m.* south; south wind.
sudadero, *m.* handkerchief; back cloth (for horses); sweating room, sudatory; moist ground; sweating place for sheep.
sudafricano, na, *n. & a.* South African.
sudamericano, na, *n. & a.* South American.
sudador, ra, *n.* one who perspires freely.
sudanés, sa, *n. & a.* Sudanese.
sudante, *a.* sweating.
sudar, *vn.* to sweat, perspire; to ooze; to give with repugnance; to toil, to labor.
sudario, *m.* sudarium, shroud.
sudatorio, ria, *a.* sudorific.
sudeste, *m.* southeast; southeast wind.
sudoeste, *m.* southwest; southwest wind.
sudor, *m.* sweat, perspiration; toil, drudgery; gum that oozes from trees.
sudoriento, ta, *a.* sweated, perspiring.
sudorífero, ra, *a.* sudorific.—**sudorífico, ca.** **I.** *a.* (med.) sudorific. **II.** *m.* sudorific.
sudoríparo, ra, *a.* (anat.) sudoriferous, sweat-secreting.
sudoroso, sa, *a.* sweating, perspiring freely.

sudoso, sa, *a.* sweaty, perspiring.
sudsudeste, *m.* south-southeast.
sudsudoeste, *m.* south-southwest.
sudueste, *m.* southwest.
sueco, ca. I. *a.* Swedish. **II.** *n.* Swede.—**hacerse el s.,** (coll.) to pretend not to hear.
suegra, *f.* mother-in-law; hard crust of bread.
suegrecita, *f. dim.* (coll.) little mother-in-law.
suegro, *m.* father-in-law.
suela, *f.* (shoe.) sole; sole leather; (icht.) sole; horizontal rafter laid as a support for partition walls; (arch.) base; leather tip of a billiard cue. —*pl.* sandals.—**de siete suelas,** consummate, thorough, through and through.
suelda, *f.* (bot.) comfrey.
sueldacostilla, *f.* (bot.) a bulbous plant.
sueldo, *m.* salary; sold, pay given to soldiers; an ancient coin; sou or sol.
sueldo, suelde. *V.* SOLDAR.
suelo, *m.* ground; soil; land, earth, terra firma; pavement; floor, flooring; story; dregs, sediment, lees; ground plot; end; bottom, underside; hoof.—*pl.* (vet.) sole, plantar face of a horse's hoof; scatterings or leavings of grain.—**s. del estribo,** rest of the stirrup.—**s. natal,** native country.—**dar consigo en el s.,** to fall down.—**dar en el s. con,** to throw down.—**medir el s.,** to fall flat, measure one's length on the ground; to lie down flat on the ground.—**por el s.,** or **por los suelos,** in a state of great depreciation; altogether out of favor. —**venirse al s.,** to fall to the ground, topple over.
suelo, él suele. *V.* SOLER.
suelta, *f.* loosening or letting loose; fetters; relay of oxen; place where oxen are changed.—**dar s.,** to grant a recess for amusement.
sueltamente, *adv.* loosely, lightly, expeditiously; licentiously; spontaneously; laxly.
suelto, ta. I. *a.* loose; light, expeditious; swift, able; free, bold, daring; easy, disengaged; voluble, fluent; odd, disconnected, unclassified; single (copy); blank (verse).—**s. de lengua,** outspoken. **II.** *m.* small change; editorial paragraph; newspaper item or paragraph.
suelto, suelte. *V.* SOLTAR.
suelvo, suelva. *V.* SOLVER.
sueno, suene. *V.* SONAR.
sueño, *m.* sleep; sleeping; drowsiness, sleepiness; dream; any event of short duration.—**s. eterno,** eternal sleep, death.—**s. pesado,** profound sleep; deep sleep.—**conciliar el s.,** to coax sleep.—**descabezar el s., echar un s.,** to take a nap.—**en sueños,** or **entre sueños,** dreaming; in dreamland.—**espantar el s.,** to scare away sleep.—**ni por s.,** by no means, not a bit of it.—**tener s.,** to be sleepy.
sueño, sueñe. *V.* SOÑAR.
suero, *m.* whey; serum (of blood).
sueroso, sa, *a.* = SEROSO.
sueroterapia, *f.* serotherapy, serum therapy.
suerte, *f.* chance, hazard; lot, luck; good luck; state, condition; fate, doom, destiny; kind, sort; manner, way; skilful manœuvre of a bullfighter; (theat.) trick, feat, juggle; piece of ground separated by landmarks; (Peru) lottery ticket.—**caerle a uno la suerte,** to fall to one's lot.—**de s. que,** in such a manner as, so that; and so.—**echar suertes,** to cast or draw lots.—**entrar en s.,** to take part in a draft or raffle.—**por s.,** by chance; luckily.—**tocarle a uno la s.** = CAERLE A UNO LA S.
suertero, *m.* (Peru) seller of lottery tickets.
sueste, *m.* southeast.
suevo, va, *n. & a.* Swabian.
sufete, *m.* Suffete, a Carthaginian magistrate.
sufi. I. *a.* Sufistic. **II.** *n.* Sufi.
sufismo, *m.* Sufism.
suficiencia, *f.* sufficiency; capacity, ability.—**a s.,** sufficiently, enough.
suficiente, *a.* sufficient; fit, competent.
suficientemente, *adv.* sufficiently.
sufijo, ja. I. *a.* suffixed, affixed. **II.** *m.* suffix, affix.
sufocación, sufocar, etc. = SOFOCACIÓN, etc.
sufra, *f.* ridgeband of a harness.

sufragáneo, ea. I. *a.* suffragan, auxiliary. **II.** *m.* (eccl.) suffragan.
sufragar, *va.* (*pret.* SUFRAGUÉ: *subj.* SUFRAGUE) to favor; to aid; to defray.
sufragio, *m.* suffrage; vote; favor, support, aid, assistance; (eccl.) suffrage.
sufrible, *a.* sufferable, bearable.
sufridera, *f.* smith's tool for punching holes on an anvil.
sufridero, ra, *a.* bearable, endurable.
sufrido, da, *pp. & a.* enduring, long-suffering; disguising (s. o. colors).—**mal s.,** rude.
sufridor, ra, *n. & a.* sufferer (-ing).
sufriente, *a.* enduring, suffering.
sufrimiento, *m.* suffering; sufferance, tolerance.
sufrir. I. *va.* to suffer, endure, bear up; to undergo (as a change); to bear, carry, support; to sustain, resist (an attack); to permit, tolerate, put up with; to meet with (as a reverse); to do (penance). **II.** *vn.* to suffer.
sufumigación, *f.* (med.) suffumigation.
sufusión, *f.* (med.) suffusion; a kind of cataract.
sugerente, *a.* suggesting, suggestive.
sugerir, *va.* (*gerund,* SUGIRIENDO: *ind.* SUGIERO: *pret.* él SUGIRIÓ: SUGIERA) to suggest, hint, insinuate.
sugestible, *a.* suggestible.
sugestión, *f.* suggestion; insinuation, hint; temptation.—**s. hipnótica,** hypnotic suggestion.
sugestionable, *a.* easily influenced.
sugestionar, *va.* to suggest by hypnotic power; to influence.
sugestivo, va, *a.* suggestive.
suicida, *n.* suicide, self-murderer.
suicidarse, *vr.* to commit suicide.
suicidio, *m.* suicide (self-murder).
suideo, a. I. *a.* swinelike. **II.** *m. pl.* Suidæ, the swine family.
sui generis, *a.* sui generis, unique, peculiar.
suita, *f.* (C. A.) a kind of grass used for thatching and forage.
suizo, za. I. *n. & a.* Swiss. **II.** *f.* an ancient military sport.
sujeción, *f.* subjection; coercion, control; obedience, subordination; submission, surrender; connection.
sujetar. I. *va.* (*pp.* SUJETADO, SUJETO) to subject, subdue; to hold fast, fasten, catch, grasp. **II.** *vr.* to control one's self; to submit; (w. a) to keep to, to observe.
sujeto, ta. I. *a. & pp. irr.* of SUJETAR; subject, liable, exposed, chargeable; amenable. **II.** *m.* subject, topic, theme, matter; person, individual, fellow; (log. and gram.) subject.
sulfácido, *m.* (chem.) sulphacid.
sulfatador, ra. I. *a.* sulphating. **II.** *f.* sulphating machine.
sulfatar, *va.* to sulphate.
sulfato, *m.* (chem.) sulphate.
sulfhidrato, *m.* (chem.) hydrosulphide.
sulfhídrico, *a.* (chem.) hydrosulphuric.
sulfito, *m.* (chem.) sulphite.
sulfonal, *m.* (chem.) sulphonal.
sulfovínico, ca, *a.* (chem.) sulphovinic.
sulfurar. I. *va.* to sulphur, sulphurate; to irritate, anger, enrage. **II.** *vr.* to become angry or furious.
sulfúreo, rea, *a.* sulphurous.
sulfúrico, ca, *a.* sulphuric.
sulfuro, *m.* (chem.) sulphide.
sulfuroso, sa, *a.* sulphurous.
sultán, *m.* sultan.
sultana, *f.* sultana, sultaness.
sultanía, *f.* sultanate.
suma, *f.* sum; aggregate; amount; (arith.) addition; total, footing; summary; summa, complete treatise or exposition (of a science, etc.).—**s. a la vuelta,** carried forward.—**s. de la vuelta,** or **s. del frente,** brought forward.—**s. y sigue** = S. A LA VUELTA.—**en s.,** in short; to sum up.
sumaca, *f.* (S. A.) a small coasting schooner.
sumamente, *adv.* chiefly; exceedingly, highly.

sumando, *m.* (math.) addend.
sumar, *va.* (arith.) to add; to foot up, amount to; to sum up, recapitulate.
sumaria, *f.* (law) indictment.
sumariamente, *adv.* summarily.
sumario, ria. I. *a.* summary, compendious; plain, brief, cursory; (law) summary. **II.** *m.* summary, abstract; (law) indictment.
sumarísimo ma, *a.* (law) swift, expeditious.
sumergible, *a.* sinkable, submergible.
sumergimiento, *m.* submergence, sinking.
sumergir, *va.* & *vr.* (ind. SUMERJO: *subj.* SUMER-JA) to submerge, to sink; to dive, to plunge; to overwhelm.
sumersión, *f.* submersion, immersion.
sumidad, *f.* top, apex, summit.
sumidero, *m.* sewer, drain, sink, gutter, gully; (min.) sump.
sumido, da, *a.* & *pp.* sunk.
sumiller, *m.* chief of each of several offices in the king's household.—**s. de corps,** lord chamberlain. —**s. de cortina,** royal chaplain.
sumillería, *f.* lord chamberlain's office.
suministración, *f.* = SUMINISTRO.
suministrador, ra, *n.* provider, purveyor.
suministrar, *va.* to supply, furnish, provide, afford, purvey, minister.
suministro, *m.* supply, providing.
sumir. I. *va.* & *vr.* to sink; to depress, overwhelm. **II.** *va.* (eccl.) to swallow (the elements of the eucharist). **III.** *vr.* to be sunk (as the cheeks).
sumisamente, *adv.* submissively.
sumisión, *f.* submission; (law) submission to the rule of another.
sumiso, sa, *a.* submissive, humble, meek.
sumista, *n.* rapid computer; abridger.
sumo, ma, *a.* high, great, supreme.—**s. pontífice,** Pontifex Maximus (in ancient Rome); Sovereign Pontiff (the Pope).—**s. sacerdote,** high priest.—**a lo s.,** at most.—**de s.,** fully.—**en s. grado,** to a very great extent; highly.
súmulas, *f. pl.* compendium of logic.
sumulista, *n.* teacher or student of the essentials of logic.
sumulístico, ca, *a.* belonging to the essentials of logic.
sunción, *f.* (eccl.) partaking of the eucharist at mass.
sundín, *m.* (Arg.) merry gathering and dancing of working people.
sunsún, *m.* (Cuba) (orn.) humming bird.
suntuario, ria, sumptuary.
suntuosamente, *adv.* sumptuously, magnificently, gorgeously.—**suntuosidad,** *f.* magnificence, gorgeousness.
suntuoso, sa, sumptuous, gorgeous.
supe. *V.* SABER.
supedáneo, *m.* pedestal of a crucifix.
supeditación, *f.* subjection: oppression.
supeditar, *va.* to subdue, oppress; to reduce to subjection.
superable, *a.* superable, conquerable.
superabundancia, *f.* superabundance.
superabundante, *a.* superabundant.
superabundantemente, *adv.* superabundantly.
superabundar, *vn.* to superabound.
superádito, ta, *a.* superadded.
superante, *a.* surpassing, exceeding.
superar, *va.* to overcome, conquer; to surpass, excel, exceed.
superávit, *m.* (com.) surplus.
superciliar, *a.* (anat.) superciliary.
superchería, *f.* fraud, deceit, wile, guile.
superchero, ra, *a.* wily, deceitful, tricky.
superdominante, *f.* (mus.) superdominant.
supereminencia, *f.* supereminence.
supereminente, *a.* supereminent.
superentender, *va.* (for irr. *v.* ENTENDER) to superintend, inspect, oversee, supervise.
supererogación, *f.* supererogation.
supererogatorio, ria, *a.* supererogatory.

superfetación, *f.* (biol.) superfetation, superimpregnation.
superficial, *a.* superficial, shallow.
superficialidad, *f.* superficiality; shallowness.
superficialmente, *adv.* superficially.
superficiario, ria, *a.* (law) superficiary.
superficie, *f.* surface; area.—**s. alabeada,** (geom.) warped surface.—**s. de calefacción,** (st. eng.) heating surface.—**s. de rodadura,** tread (of a wheel).—**s. desarrollable,** (geom.) developable surface.—**s. reglada,** (geom.) ruled surface.
superfino, na, *a.* superfine, extra fine.
superfluamente, *adv.* superfluously.
superfluidad, *f.* superfluity.
superfluo, flua, *a.* superfluous.
superfosfato, *m.* (chem.) superphosphate, acid phosphate.
superhombre, *m.* superman.
superhumeral, *m.* (eccl.) ephod; superhumeral.
superintendencia, *f.* superintendence, supervision; superintendency.
superintendente, *n.* superintendent; intendant; inspector; overseer, supervisor.
superior. I. *a.* superior; upper; better, finer; higher (algebra, mathematics, studies). **II.** *m.* superior.
superiora, *f.* mother superior.
superiorato, *m.* office of a superior and the term of his office.
superioridad, *f.* superiority.
superiormente, *adv.* masterly, superiorly.
superlativamente, *adv.* superlatively.
superlativo, va, *m.* & *a.* superlative.
superno, na, *a.* supreme, highest, supernal.
supernumerario, ria, *a.* supernumerary.
superponer, *va.* to superpose.
superposición, *f.* superposition.
superstición, *f.* superstition.
supersticiosamente, *adv.* superstitiously.
supersticioso, sa, *a.* superstitious.
supérstite, *a.* (law) surviving.
supersubstancial, *a.* supersubstantial.
supervacáneo, nea, *a.* = SUPERFLUO.
supervención, superveniencia, *f.* supervention.—**superveniente,** *a.* supervenient, supervening.—
supervenir, *vn.* (for irr. *v.* VENIR) to supervene.
supervivencia, *f.* survival; survivalship.—**s. del más apto,** survival of the fittest.
superviviente, *n.* & *a.* surviver (-ing).
supiera, supiese. *V.* SABER.
supinación, *f.* (anat.) supination.—**supinador,** *m.* supinator (muscle).—**supino, na,** *a.* supine.
suplantación, *f.* supplanting.
suplantador, ra, *n.* & *a.* supplanter (-ing).
suplantar, *va.* to supplant; to forge, alter by fraud, raise (as a check).
suplefaltas, *m.* (coll.) substitute.
suplemental, *a.* supplemental.
suplementario, ria, *a.* supplementary.
suplemento, *m.* supply, supplying; supplement; (geom.) supplement.
suplente. I. *a.* substituting, replacing. **II.** *n.* substitute.
supletorio, ria, *a.* suppletory, supplemental.
súplica, *f.* entreaty; supplication; request.—**a s.,** by request.
suplicación, *f.* supplication; request; petition; rolled waffle; (law) petition to a high court for a reversal of its own decision.—**a s.,** by petition, by request.
suplicacionero, ra, *n.* waffle seller.
suplicante. I. *a.* suppliant, supplicant, entreating. **II.** *n.* supplicant, suppliant.
suplicar, *va.* (*pret.* SUPLIQUÉ: *subj.* SUPLIQUE) to entreat, implore; to supplicate, pray; to ask, request.—**s. de la sentencia,** to petition against the sentence; to appeal.—**s. en revista,** (law) to apply for a new trial.
suplicatoria, *f.*, **suplicatorio,** *m.* (law) letters rogatory.
suplicio, *m.* torture; execution (death penalty); place of execution; grief, suffering, anguish.

suplidor, ra, *n.* substitute, deputy.

suplir, *va.* to supply, provide, afford, furnish; to substitute; to excuse, overlook; (gram.) to supply mentally.

supo, *V.* SABER.

suponedor, ra, *n.* supposer.

suponer. I. *va.* (for irr. v. PONER) to suppose, assume. **II.** *vn.* to have weight or authority.

suportación, *f.* endurance; toleration.

suposición, *f.* supposition, assumption; distinction, high position; imposition, falsehood.

suposticio, cia, *a.* supposititious, pretended; supposed, assumed.

supositivo, va, *a.* suppositive.

supositorio, *m.* (med.) suppository.

suprarrenal, *a.* (anat.) suprarenal.

suprascapular, *a.* (anat.) suprascapular.

suprasensible, *a.* supersensible.

supraspina, *f.* (anat.) supraspinal fossa of the scapula.

suprema, *f.* Supreme Council of the Inquisition.

supremacía, *f.* supremacy.

supremamente, *adv.* supremely.

supremo, ma, *a.* supreme; last, final.

supresión, *f.* suppression; omission; rooting out, elimination.—**s. de denominadores,** (alg.) clearing of fractions.—**s. de factores comunes,** (arith., alg.) cancellation (of common factors).

supresivo, *a.* suppressive.

supreso, sa, *a.* suppressed.

suprimir, *va.* (*pp.* SUPRIMIDO, SUPRESO) to suppress; to cut out, abolish, eradicate; to omit; to clear of; (math.) to cancel.

suprior, ra, *n.* subprior (-ess).

supriorato, *m.* office of subprior or prioress.

supuesto, ta. I. *a. & pp. irr.* of SUPONER; assumed, supposed.—**s. que,** allowing that; granting that; since.—**esto s.,** this being understood.—**por s.,** of course, naturally. **II.** *m.* supposition; hypothesis, assumption.

supuración, *f.* suppuration.—**supurante,** *a.* suppurating.—**supurar. I.** *va.* to waste, consume. **II.** *vn.* (med.) to suppurate.—**supurativo, va,** *a. & m.* suppurative.—**supuratorio, ria,** *a.* suppurating.

suputación, *f.* computation, calculation.

suputar, *va. & vn.* to compute, calculate, reckon.

sur, *m.* south; south wind.

sura, *m.* sura (section of the Koran).

sural, *a.* (anat.) sural.

surcador, ra, *n.* plowman (-woman), plower.

surcar, *va.* (*pret.* SURQUÉ: *subj.* SURQUE) (agr.) to plow, furrow; to cut through, move through.

surco, *m.* furrow; rut; wrinkle.—**a s.,** adjoining, separated by a furrow.

surculado, da, *a.* (bot.) single-stemmed.

súrculo, *m.* (bot.) single stem without branches.

surculoso, sa, *a.* = SURCULADO.

surgente, *a.* surging, salient.

surgidero, *m.* (naut.) road, anchoring place.

surgidor, ra, *n.* one who anchors.

surgir, *vn.* (*pp.* SURGIDO, SURTO: *ind.* SURJO: *subj.* SURJA) to spout, spurt; to issue, come forth; to present itself, to appear; to sprout; (naut.) to anchor.

surtida, *f.* (fort.) sallyport; (mil.) sally, sortie; backdoor; (naut.) slipway.

surtidero, *m.* conduit, outlet.—**s. de agua,** reservoir, basin.

surtido, *pp. & m.* assortment, stock, supply.—**de s.,** in common use.

surtidor, ra. I. *n.* purveyor, caterer. **II.** *m.* jet, spout, fountain.

surtimiento, *m.* supply, stock, assortment.

surtir. I. *va.* (*pp.* SURTIDO, SURTO) to supply, furnish, provide, purvey, stock.—**s. efecto,** to have the desired effect, to work. **II.** *vn.* to spout, spurt; (naut.) to anchor.

surto, ta, *a.* anchor.

súrtuba, *f.* a Central-American gigantic fern.

surumpe, *m.* (Peru) inflammation of the eyes from the reflection of the snow.

sus, *pron. poss. pl. of* SU.

¡sus! *interj.* up! cheer up! forward!

susceptibilidad, *f.* susceptibility.

susceptible, *a.; susceptivo, va,* a. susceptible; sensitive, touchy.

suscitación, *f.* excitation.

suscitar. I. *va.* to stir up; to raise, to originate. **II.** *vr.* to rise, start, originate.

suscribir, suscrición, suscritor, etc. = SUBSCRIBIR, SUBSCRIPCIÓN, SUBSCRIPTOR, etc.

susidio, *m.* anxiety, uneasiness.

susodicho, cha, *a.* aforementioned, aforesaid.

suspendedor, ra, *n.* suspender; hanger.

suspender. I. *va.* to suspend; to hang up; to stop, delay, interrupt; to discontinue; to surprise, astonish; to suspend from office; to adjourn (a meeting).—**s. pagos,** (com.) to stop payments. **II.** *vr.* to rear (s. o. a horse).

suspensión, *f.* suspension, interruption; cessation; discontinuance; suspense, uncertainty; amazement; privation; (law) suspense; (mus.) suspension.—**s. de armas,** cessation of hostilities. —**s. de pagos,** (com.) suspension of payments.

suspensivo, va. I. *a.* suspensive. **II.** *m. pl.* (print.) leaders (...) showing that something has been omitted (gen. replaced by a long dash in English, except in mathematics).

suspenso, sa, *a.* hung; suspended.—**en s.,** in suspense.

suspensorio, ria. I. *a.* suspensory. **II.** *m.* suspensory bandage.

suspicacia, *f.* suspiciousness, distrust.

suspicaz, *a.* suspicious, distrustful.

suspicazmente, *adv.* suspiciously.

suspirado, da, *a.* expected, desired, longed for.

suspirar, *vn.* to sigh.—**s. por,** to crave, long for, covet.

suspiro, *m.* sigh; breath; glass whistle; (mus.) short pause.—*pl.* (bot.) lady's fingers.—**exhalar el último s.,** to breathe one's last.

suspiroso, sa, *a.* sighing with difficulty.

sustancia, sustancial, sustancioso, etc. = SUBSTANCIA, SUBSTANCIAL, SUBSTANCIOSO, etc.

sustantivo, etc. = SUBSTANTIVO, etc.

sustenido, *m.* a Spanish step in dancing; (mus.) sharp.

sustentable, *a.* defensible.—**sustentación,** *f.* sustentation, support, sustenance.

sustentáculo, *m.* prop, stay, support.

sustentador, ra, *n. & a.* sustainer (-ing).

sustentamiento, *m.* sustenance, necessaries of life.

sustentante. I. *a.* sustaining. **II.** *m.* defender, supporter.

sustentar, *va.* to sustain, support, bear; to feed, support; to nourish; to assert, defend, advocate.

sustento, *m.* sustenance, maintenance; support.

sustitución, etc. = SUBSTITUCIÓN, etc.

susto, *m.* scare, fright, shock.—**dar un s.,** to frighten, to scare, to startle.

sustracción, sustraendo, sustraer, = SUBSTRACCIÓN, SUBSTRAENDO, SUBSTRAER.

susurración, *f.* whisper, whispering.

susurrador, ra, *n. & a.* whisperer (-ing).

susurrante, *a.* whispering, murmuring.

susurrar. I. *vn.* to whisper; to murmur; to rustle (as leaves); to purl (as a stream); to hum gently (as the air). **II.** *vr.* to be whispered about, to be bruited about.

susurro, *m.* whisper, humming, murmur, rustle, purling.

susurrón, na, *n.* grumbler, malcontent.

sutil, *a.* subtile, thin, slender; subtle, acute, cunning, keen; light, volatile.

sutileza, sutilidad, *f.* thinness, slenderness, fineness; subtlety, cunning, artifice, sagacity; acumen, perspicacity; nicety.—**s. de manos,** sleight of hands.

sutilización, *f.* subtilization.

sutilizador, ra, *n. & a.* subtilizer (-ing).

sutilizar. I. *va.* (*pret.* SUTILICÉ: *subj.* SUTILICE) to subtilize; to thin, refine; to file, polish. **II.** *vn.* to subtilize.

---

sutilmente, *adv.* subtilely, pointedly; nicely, finely, delicately.

sutorio, ria, *a.* belonging to the shoemaker's trade; sutorial.

sutura, *f.* seam; (anat., bot., surg.) suture.

suyo, ya, (*pl.* SUYOS, YAS), *pron. poss. 3d person, masc. & fem.* (sometimes with the definite article *el, la, los, las* [*v.* MÍO]); his, hers, theirs, one's: his own, its own, one's own, their own—**de s.,** in itself, by its very nature; spontaneously, of one's own accord.—**los suyos,** yours, your (his, her, etc.) family, people, company, etc.—**salirse con la suya,** to carry one's point, to come out ahead.—**una de las suyas,** one of his pranks or tricks.—**ver la suya,** to have one's chance or opportunity

svástica, *f.* swastika.

T

¡ta! *interj.* take care, beware; stay, I recollect.—**t., t.!** tut, tut.

taba, *f.* knucklebone of sheep, astragalus; cockal, jackstones.

tabacal, *m.* tobacco field.

tabacalero, ra. I. *a.* tobacco (u. a.). **II.** *n.* tobacco grower or dealer.

tabaco, *m.* (bot.) tobacco; leaf tobacco; cigar; mildew on plants.—**t. colorado,** mild cigar.—**t. de hoja**= T. EN RAMA.—**t. de montaña,** arnica.—**t. de palillos,** snuff made of stems.—**t. de pipa,** pipe tobacco, smoking tobacco.—**t. de vena,** cigarette tobacco.—**t. en polvo,** snuff.—**t. en rama,** leaf tobacco, wrappers.—**t. holandilla,** Dutch tobacco.—**t. maduro,** strong cigar .—**t. moruno,** European and African tobacco.—**t. rapé,** rappee.—**t. torcido,** cigars, twisted tobacco.—**se me acabó el t.,** (Arg.) I am left without funds, my funds have given out.

tabacoso, sa. I. *a.* snuffy. **II.** *n.* snuff dipper.

tabalada, *f.* (coll.) heavy fall upon the breech; spanking.

tabalario, *m.* (coll.) buttocks, posteriors.

tabalear. I. *va. & vn.* to rock to and fro. **II.** *vn.* to drum with the fingers on a table.—**tabaleo,** *m.* rocking, swinging; drumming with the fingers.

tabanazo, *m.* (coll.) spanking.

tabanco, *m.* stall for selling eatables; (Mex.) cockloft.

tabanera, *f.* place full of gadflies.

tábano, *m.* (ent.) gadfly, horsefly.

tabanque, *m.* treadle of a potter's wheel.

tabaola, *f.* hubbub, clamor.

tabaque, *m.* ladies' work basket; large tack.

tabaquera, *f.* snuffbox; tobacco pouch; cigar case; bowl of a tobacco pipe.

tabaquería, *f.* cigar store.—**tabaquero, ra,** *n.* cigar maker; tobacconist.—**tabaquista,** *n.* expert on tobacco; habitual user of tobacco.

tabardete, tabardillo, *m.* highly dynamic fever; sunstroke.—**tabardillo pintado,** spotted fever.

tabardo, *m.* tabard.

tabellar, *va.* to fold (cloth) in pieces, leaving the selvage visible; to mark with a trade-mark.

taberna, *f.* tavern, public house, drinking saloon, barroom.

tabernáculo, *m.* tabernacle.

tabernario, ria, *a.* (coll.) relating to a tavern; low, vulgar, vile.

tabernera, *f.* tavern keeper's wife; barmaid

tabernería, *f.* business of a tavern keeper.

tabernero, *m.* tavern keeper, barkeeper.

tabes, *f.* (med.) consumption, tabes.

tabí, *m.* tabby, moreen, watered fabric.

tabica, *f.* (arch.), covering board.

tabicar, *va.* to wall up; to close or shut up.

tabicón, *m.* thick partition wall.

tábido, da, *a.* (med.) tabid, wasted; putrid.

tabífico, ca, *a.* (med.) tabific.

tabinete, *m.* tabbinet (fabric).

tabique, *m.* thin wall; partition wall, partition.—**t. de panderete,** brick-on-edge partition.—**t. ma-**

estro, chief partition wall.—**t. sordo,** double partition wall.

tabiquería, *f.* partition work, system or group of partitions.

tabiquero, ra, *n.* partition-wall builder.

tabla, *f.* (carp.) board; plank; slab; tablet, plate (of metal); table (of contents, of logarithms, of prices, etc.); (sew.) full-breadth gore of a skirt; tablier; box plait; largest face of a piece of timber; (jewel.) flat diamond; (art) table, panel; broadest and most fleshy part of any of the members of the body; bed or patch in a garden; strip of land between rows of trees; revenue office where merchandise is registered as sold at market; meat stall; butcher's block.—*pl.* (theat.) stage boards; draw (in a game at chess or draughts).—**t. de armonía,** (mus.) sounding board.—**t. de chilla,** thin board of slit deal.—**t. de juego,** gambling house.—**t. de manteles,** tablecloth.—**t. de río,** bed of a river.—**t. de sembrado,** cornfield.—**t. pitagórica,** multiplication table.—**tablas de la ley,** tables of the law.—**tablas reales,** backgammon board or tables.—**a la t. del mundo,** in public, before the world.—**a raja t.,** at any price, regardless of everything else.—**escaparse en una tabla,** to have a narrow escape.—**hacer t. rasa de,** to ignore entirely, to set at nought.—**no saber por dónde van tablas,** to know nothing about the matter, not to know beans.—**salvarse en una tabla,** to have a narrow escape.

tablachina, *f.* wooden shield or buckler.

tablacho, *m.* sluice or floodgate.

tablado, *m.* stage, scaffold, platform; flooring; (theat.) stage boards; platform of a cart or truck; boards or bottom of a bedstead.

tablaje, *m.* pile of boards; planking; gambling or gaming house.

tablajería, *f.* gaming, gambling; hire of the gaming table.

tablajero, *m.* scaffold maker; carpenter who builds stands and stages; ancient collector of the king's taxes; keeper of a gaming house; gambler; butcher; assistant surgeon in a hospital.

tablar, *m.* set of garden plots or beds.

tablazo, *m.* blow or stroke with a board; arm of the sea; sheet of water; small plateau; (S. A., geol.) uplifted sea-floor deposit.

tablazón, *f.* boards, planks, lumber; planking, flooring; decks and sheathing of a ship.—**t. de la cubierta,** (naut.) deck planks.

tablear, *va.* to saw into boards; to divide (a garden) into beds or plots; to level or grade (the ground) with a thick board; to hammer into plates; (sew.) to make box plaits on.

tableo, *m.* sawing wood into boards; dividing a garden into beds; leveling (the ground) or grading with a board; hammering into plates.

tablero, *m.* board, panel; sawable timber; drawing board; dog nail; stock of a crossbow; chessboard, checkerboard; (Colomb.) blackboard; gambling house or table; shop counter; money table; (tail.) cutting table; (carp.) door panel; (arch.) panel, compartment; floor (of a bridge).—**t. contador,** abacus.—**t. de cocina,** dresser, kitchen table.—**t. de conmutadores** = T. DE DISTRIBUCIÓN.—**t. de chaquete** (Mex.) backgammon board, tables.—**t. de distribución,** (elec.) switchboard.

tableta, *f. dim.* tablet; writing pad; (pharm.) tablet, lozenge; cracknel; clapper.—**estar en tabletas,** to be in suspense.

tableteado, *pp. & m.* sound produced by rattling clappers.—**tabletear,** *vn.* to rattle clappers.

tableteo, *m.* rattling sound of clappers.

tablilla, *f. dim.* tablet, slab; bulletin board; section of the cushion of a billard table between two pockets; (surg.) splint.—**t. de mesón,** sign of an inn.—**t. de santero,** poor box of a hermit.—**tablillas de San Lázaro,** clappers used in begging for hospitals.—**tablillas neperianas,** logarithmic tables.—**por t.,** indirectly.

tablón, *m. aug.* plank, thick board; beam; strake.—**t. de aparadura,** (naut.) garboard strake.—**tablones de cucharros,** (naut.) serving planks.

TAB 460 TAL

tabloncillo, *m.* flooring board; in bull rings, last row of seats.

tabloza, *f.* painter's palette.

tabo, *m.* (Philip.) cup made from coconut shell.

tabón, *m.* tabon, a Philippine megapode.

tabona, *f.* stagnant pool.

tabú, *m.* taboo.

tabuco, *m.* hut, hovel; narrow room.

tabular, *a.* tabular.

tabuquillo, quito, *m. dim.* shanty.

taburete, *m.* taboret; stool.—*pl.* (theat.) benches in the pit.

taca, *f.* small closet; plate of the crucible; stain.

tacada, *f.* stroke, play (at billiard); wedges.

tacamaca, tacamacha, tacamahaca, *f.* tacamahac, gum resin from various tropical trees; (bot.) balsam poplar.

tacano, *m.* (min.) rich gray silver ore.

tacañamente, *adv.* stingily, in a miserly manner.—**tacañear,** *vn.* to act the miser.—**tacañería,** *f.* stinginess; narrowness of mind; malicious cunning; low craft.—**tacaño, ña,** *a.* stingy, niggardly, miserly, close; artful, knavish.

tacar. I. *va.* to mark (as a person in the face). **II.** *vn.* to shoot, to have one's turn (in billiards).

tacazo, *m.* stroke with a cue.

taceta, *f.* copper bowl used in oilmills.

tacica, illa, ita, *f. dim.* small cup.

tácitamente, *adv.* silently, secretly; tacitly.

tácito, ta, *a.* silent; tacit, implied.

taciturnidad, *f.* taciturnity.—**taciturno, na,** *a.* taciturn, reserved; melancholy.

taclobo, *m.* (Philip.) a giant clam.

taco, *m.* plug, bung, stopper; (arti.) wad, wadding; rammer; popgun; billiard cue; almanac pad; (coll.) light luncheon; each draught of wine at meals; (Cuba) spruce young fellow, dandy; volley of oaths.—**tacos de los escobenes,** (naut.) hawse plugs.—**echar tacos,** (coll.) to swear, to rage, to foam.

tacón, *m.* (shoe.) heel, heelpiece.—**taconazo,** *m.* blow with a shoe heel.—**taconear,** *vn.* (coll.) to walk or strut loftily on the heels.—**taconeo,** *m.* noise made with the heels in dancing.

táctica, *f.* orderly array; (coll.) policy; (mil.) tactics.—**táctico,** *m.* tactician.

táctil, *a.* tactile.

tacto, *m.* touch, sense of touch; touching, feeling; tact, skill, carefulness.

tacuacha, *f.* (Cuba) dexterous trick.

tacuará, *f.* (Arg.) a kind of bamboo.

tacurú, *m.* (Arg.) a variety of black ant and the ant hill it makes.

tacha, *f.* fault, defect, blemish, flaw; large tack. *V.* TACHO.—**poner t. a,** to find fault with.

tachar, *va.* to censure; blame, charge, accuse; to find fault with; to reprehend; to cut out, cross out; to cancel.—**t. testigos,** (law) to challenge witnesses.

tachero, *m.* (Cuba) one who works at a TACHO.

tacho, *m.* sugar evaporator, pan; (Peru) earthen jar for heating water.—**t. al, or de, vacío,** vacuum pan.

tachón, *m.* effacement, erasure; (sew.) trimming; escutcheon; tack, gimp nail, ornamental nail; (b. b.) boss.

tachonar, *va.* (sew.) to adorn with trimming; to garnish with gimp nails.

tachonería, *f.* gimp nail ornamental work.

tachoso, sa, *a.* faulty, defective.

tachuela, *f.* tack, small nail.

tael, *m.* tael (weight and coin).

tafanario, *m.* (coll.) buttocks.

tafetán, *m.* taffeta, thin silk.—*pl.* flags, colors, standard, ensign.—**t. inglés,** court-plaster; sticking plaster.

tafia, *f.* (Ven.) molasses rum.

tafilete, *m.* morocco leather.—**tafiletear,** *va.* to adorn with morocco leather.—**tafiletería,** *f.* art of dressing morocco leather; place where it is dressed.

tafurea, *f.* flat-bottomed boat for horses.

tagalo, la. I. *n.* & *a.* belonging to the Tagal. **II.** *m.* Tagalog (language).

tagarino, na, *n.* Moor who lived among the Christians.

tagarnina, *f.* (bot.) golden thistle; (coll.) bad cigar.

tagarote, *m.* (orn.) sparrow hawk; quill driver, scrivener; fallen-down gentleman who earns a dinner by flattery and adulation; (coll.) tall, awkward person.

tagarotear, *vn.* (coll.) to write a bold, free, and running hand.

tagua, *f.* tagua, ivory nut; (Ch.) a bird similar to the coot.

taguán, *m.* taguan, a flying squirrel.

taha, *f.* district, region.

tahalí, *m.* shoulder belt; baldric.

taharal, *m.* plantation of tamarisk trees.

taheño, *a.* having a red beard.

tahona, *f.* bakery, baker's shop; horse mill; crushing mill.—**tahonera,** *f.* baker's wife; miller's wife.—**tahonero, ra,** *n.* baker; miller.

tahulla, *f.* plot of arable land.

tahur, ra. I. *a.* gambling. **II.** *n.* gambler, gamester; card sharp.—**tahurería,** *f.* gambling; gaming house; cheating gambling.

taifa, *f.* faction, party; (coll.) assemblage of fast or foolish people.

taimado, da, *a.* sly, cunning, crafty.

taimería, *f.* rascality, craftiness.

taita, *f.* (coll.) dad, daddy.

taja, *f.* tree of a packsaddle; cut, incision; dissection; tally.

tajada, *f.* slice; (coll.) hoarseness.

tajadera, *f.* chopping knife; (mech.) round chisel, gouge. *V.* CORTAFRÍO.—*pl.* sluice of a mill dam.—**tajadero,** *m.* chopping block, trencher.

tajadilla, *f. dim.* small slice; dish of lights in low chophouses; bit of confected orange or lemon sold as a relish by retailers of brandy.

tajado, da, *pp.* & *a.* steep, sheer, wall-like; (her.) divided.

tajador, ra. I. *n.* one who cuts or chops. **II.** *m.* cutting edge.—**tajadura,** *f.* cut, notch; section; cutting, chopping.

tajamar, *m.* (naut.) cutwater, stem; (engg.) cutwater of a bridge pier.

tajamiento, *m.* = TAJADURA.

tajaplumas, *m.* penknife.

tajar, *va.* to cut, cleave; to cut and trim (a quill pen).

tajea, *f.* watercourse, channel; culvert.

tajero, *m.* = TARJERO.

tajo, *m.* cut; incision; trench; cutting edge; steep cliff; cutting a quill; chopping block; line or place to which the work of a gang extends; cut or opening in a mountain; (fenc.) cut.—**t. abierto,** (min.) open cut.

tajón, *m. aug.* butcher's block; chopping block; vein of white earth in a limestone quarry.

tajuela, *f.*, **tajuelo,** *m.* rustic seat.

tal (*pl.* TALES). **I.** *a.* such, so, as; equal, similar; as much, so great.—**t. cual,** such as; a few, one from time to time; middling, so-so; such as it is.—**t. cual vez,** once in a while, now and then.—**el t., or la t.,** (followed by a common noun) that (gen. contempt); (followed by a proper noun) that man, that fellow (*el tal Juan*, that fellow John).—**un t.,** one, a certain (*estaba allí un tal Ramírez,* one Ramírez was there). **II.** *pron.* such, such a one, such a thing.—**t. para cual,** two of a kind, a Roland for an Oliver.—**t. por cual,** person of little account, (a) nobody.—**no hay t.,** there is no such thing.—**otro que t.,** another of the same ilk. **III.** *adv.* thus, so, in such manner.—**con t. que,** provided.—**¿qué t.?** hello! how d'ye do? how is that? how goes it? what do you say? what do you think?

tala, *f.* felling of trees; destruction, ruin, havoc; tipcat (boys' game); cat (in the game); (bot.) a large Argentine urticaceous tree.

talabarte, *m.* sword belt.

talabartería, *f.* saddlery.

talabartero, *m.* saddler; harness maker.

talador, ra, *n.* & *a.* destroyer (-ing); cutter (-ing).

For pronunciation, see the rules at the beginning of the book.

taladrador, ra. I. *n.* & *a.* borer (-ing), driller (-ing). **II.** *f.* drilling or perforating machine.

taladrar, *va.* to bore, drill, perforate; to pierce, penetrate (as the ear); to dig into, go to the bottom of, elucidate.

taladrilla, *f.* a boring insect that attacks olive trees.

taladro, *m.* bit, drill, borer, gimlet, auger; bore, auger hole, drill hole; blasting charge; charged blasting hole.

talamera, *f.* tree used for insnaring birds.

talamete, *m.* (naut.) foredeck planking.

talamiflora. I. *a.* (bot.) thalamifloral. **II.** *f. pl.* Thalamifloræ.

talamite, *m.* thalamite, outermost galley rower.

tálamo, *m.* bridechamber; bridal bed; (bot.) receptacle.—**tálamos ópticos,** optic thalami.

talanquera, *f.* parapet, breastwork of pales; picket fence; defence, safety place.

talante, *m.* mode or manner of performing anything; mien, countenance; desire, will, pleasure, disposition.—**estar de buen** or **de mal t.,** to be in a pleasant or in an ugly frame of mind.

talar, *va.* to fell (trees); to lay waste; to prune.

talar, *a.* long (s. o. clothes).·

talares, *m. pl.* wings on the heels of Mercury; talaria.

talasoterapia, *f.* (med.) thalassotherapy.

talayote, *m.* a Balearic megalith in the form of a low tower.

talco, *m.* talc; tinsel.—**talcoso, sa,** *a.* talcose.

talcualillo, lla, *a.* (coll.) fair, not bad; somewhat improved in health.

tálea, *f.* stockade or palisade in Roman camps.

taled, *m.* tallith (among the Jews).

talega, *f.* bag, sack; money bag; bagful; bag for the hair; diaper; sack containing 1,000 dollars in silver.—**dos talegas,** two thousand dollars.

talego, *m.* bag or sack; clumsy, awkward fellow. —**tener t.,** to have money.

taleguilla, *f. dim.* small bag.—**t. de la sal,** (coll.) daily expenses.

talento, *m.* talent; smartness, cleverness; talent (ancient weight and coin).

talentoso, sa; talentudo, da, *a.* able, talented, smart, clever.

tálero, *m.* thaler, an old German coin.

talio, *m.* (chem.) thallium.

talión, *m.* talion, retaliation, lex talionis.

talionar, *va.* to punish with the lex talionis.

talismán, *m.* talisman, charm, amulet.

talma, *f.* a kind of cape or cloak.

talmente, *adv.* (coll.) in the same manner.

Talmud, *m.* Talmud.—**talmúdico, ca,** *a.* Talmudic.—**talmudista, m.** Talmudist.

talofita. I. *f.* & *a.* (bot.) thallophyte (-ic). **II.** *f. pl.* Thallophyta.

talón, *m.* (anat., shoe.) heel; (farr.) heel of the hoof; heel of a violin bow; (arch.) heel, cyma reversa; (com.) any cheque, draft, note or voucher detached from a stub book;coupon; (naut.) heel of the keel, sternson.—**apretar los talones,** to show a clean pair of heels, to run.—**a t.,** on foot.

talonario, ria. I. *a.* taken from a stub book; stub (u. a.). **II.** *m.* stub book.

**talonear, ** *vn.* to walk fast.

talonesco, *a.* (coll.) relating to the heels.

talpa, talparia, *f.* (med.) talpa, wen.

talque, *m.* tasco, a refractory clay.

talquita, *f.* (min.) talc schist.

talud, *m.* (arch.) talus; batter; side slope.

talvina, *f.* porridge of almond meal.

talla, *f.* carving, wood carving (*obra de talla*, carved work); ancient dues or tax in Arragon; ransom; price set on the head of a criminal; (jewel.) cut, cutting; gurglet, earthen jug; round of a card game; stature, size; (mil.) height scale, for measuring a man's height; (surg.) lithotomy; (naut.) purchase block.

tallado, da, *a.* & *pp.* cut, carved, engraved.— **bien** or **mal t.,** of a good or bad figure.

tallador, ra, *n.* engraver; carver; diesinker; (Am.) dealer (in a game).

talladura, *f.* engraving.

tallar. I. *va.* to carve; to engrave; (jewel.) to cut; to appraise. **II.** *vn.* to deal, at faro, monte, etc. **III.** *a.* ready for cutting. **IV.** *m.* woodland ready for first cut.

tallarín, *m.* noodle (for soup).

tallarola, *f.* knife for cutting velvet pile.

talle, *m.* form, figure; waist; (tail.) fit; waist, bodice.

tallecer, *vn.* to shoot, sprout.

taller, *m.* workshop, factory, mill, office, laboratory; atelier; studio; casters.—**t. de reparaciones,** repair shop; (aut.) service station.

talleta, *f.* (Am.) = ALFAJOR.

tallista, *n.* carver in wood; engraver.

tallo, *m.* (bot.) stem, stalk; shoot, sprout.

talludo, da, *a.* grown into long stalks; tall, slender; overgrown; habit-ridden; past her youth.

talluelo, *m. dim.* of TALLO.

tamagás, *m.* a very poisonous C. A. snake.

tamal, *m.* (Am.) tamale; (C. A.) bundle of sarsaparilla.

tamalero, ra, *n.* tamale seller or maker.

tamandoa, tamanduá, *m.* (S. A.) tamandua, anteater.

tamango, *m.* (Ch., Arg.) coarse shoe worn by the gauchos; sheepskin cover for the feet.

tamañamente, *adv.* as large as.

tamañico, ica, ito, ita, uelo, la, *a.* very small; abashed, ashamed.

tamaño, ña. I. *a.* so great; so large, so small (denoting size with gesture). **II.** *m.* size.

támara, *f.* palm field.—*pl.* dates in a bunch; chips, fagots of brushwood.

tamarindo, *m.* (bot.) tamarind.

tamariscíneo, a, *a.* (bot.) tamariscineous.

tamarisco, tamariz, *m.* (bot.) tamarisk.

tamarrizquito, tamarrusquito, ta, *a.* (coll.) very small.

tamarugo, *m.* a kind of Chilean carob.

tambalear, *vn.* & *vr.* to stagger, totter, reel.

tambaleo, *m.* reeling, staggering, tottering.

tambanillo, *m.* (arch.) tympanum.

tambarillo, *m.* chest with arched cover.

tambarria, *f.* (Peru) carouse; (Ch.) low tavern.

tambero, ra. I. *n.* (Peru) innkeeper. **II.** *a.* (Arg.) tame, gentle (s. o. cattle).

tambesco, *m.* swing.

también, *adv.* also, too, likewise; as well.

tambo, *m.* (S. A.) inn; dairy.

tambor, *m.* drum; drummer; coffee roaster, chestnut roaster; bolter or sieve used by confectioners; (sew.) tambour frame; (mech.) drum, cylinder, band pulley, rope barrel; (jewel.) barrel, arbor; (arch.) drum, tambour; screen; small room made by partitions; thole, tholus; (fort.) tambour; (naut.) drum or barrel of the capstan; wheelhouse, paddle box.—**t. del oído,** drum of the ear.—**t. mayor,** drum major.—**a t., con t., batiente,** at the beating of the drum; with drums beating.

tampoco, *adv.* neither, not either; (after ni) either (*él no sabe, ni yo tampoco,* he does not know, nor I either).

tambora, *f.* bass drum.

tamborete, *m. dim.* timbrel; (naut.) cap of the masthead, moorshead.

tamboril, *m.* tabor, timbrel.

tamborilada, *f.*, **tamborilazo,** *m.* (coll.) fall on the breech; slap on the face or shoulders.

tamborilear. I. *vn.* to tabor. **II.** *va.* to praise, extol; (print.) to plane or level (type).

tamborilero, *m.* taborer.

tamborilete, *m. dim.* tabret; (typ.) planer.

tamborín, tamborino, *m.* tabor.

tamboritear, *va.*, **tamboritero,** *m.* = TAMBORILEAR, TAMBORILERO.

tamborón, *m.* large bass drum.

tamén, *m.* (Mex.) Indian porter, carrier.

tamiz, *m.* sieve, sifter, screen; bolting cloth.

tamizar, *va.* to sift, screen.

tamo, *m.* fuzz; chaff, winnowings, graindust; dust gathered under beds, etc.

tamojal, *m.* place covered with TAMOJO.

tamojo, *m.* (bot.) saltwort, glasswort.

tamujal, *m.* thicket of buckthorns.

tamujo, *m.* (bot.) buckthorn, boxthorn.

tamul, *n.* & *a.*; **tamúlico, ca,** *a.* Tamil.

tan, *adv. contr.* of TANTO; as, so, so much, as well, as much.—**t. siquiera,** even, ever so.

tanaceto, *m.* (bot.) tansy.

tanate, *m.* (Mex.) seroon made of hide; frail; palm-leaf bag.—**cargar con los tanates,** to move away.

tanatero, *m.* (Mex.) TANATE; carrier.

tanato, *m.* (chem.) tannate.

tanda, *f.* turn, rotation; task; gang of workmen, shift, relay; set, batch; each game of billiards; (theat.) each division of a performance for which a separate ticket is required.

tándem, *m.* tandem bicycle.—**en t.,** tandem.

tandeo, *m.* distribution of irrigating water by turns.

tanganillas.—en t., *adv.* waveringly.

tanganillo, *m. dim.* small prop or stay.

tángano, *m.* hob, a boys' game; stick used in this game.

tangencia, *f.* tangency.—**tangencial,** *a.* tangential.—**tangencialmente,** *adv.* tangentially.

tangente, *f.* & *a.* (geom.) tangent.—**escaparse, salir,** or **salirse, por la t.,** to resort to subterfuges or evasions, to befog the issue.

tangible, *a.* tangible.

tango, *m.* hob; (danc.) tango.

tangón, *m.* (naut.) outrigger.

tanino, na, *a.* tannic.

tanino, *m.* (chem.) tannin.

tanor, ra, *n.* (Philip.) Malay who served as domestic to the Spaniards.—**tanoría,** *f.* (Philip.) domestic service to the Spaniards.

tanque, *m.* (api.) bee glue; tank; pool, reservoir; dipper.

tantalato, *m.* (chem.) tantalate.

tantalio, *m.* (chem.) tantalum.

tan-tan, *m.* rubadub, sound of a drum; tom-tom.

tantarantán, *m.* rubadub, beat of a drum; (coll.) sounding blow.

tanteador, ra, *n.* measurer, tester, marker.

tantear. I. *va.* to try, test, measure; to make an estimate of; to consider carefully; to scrutinize; (art) to sketch, outline. **II.** *vn.* to keep the score. **III.** *vr.* to agree to pay the price for which a thing has been sold.

tanteo, *m.* estimate, approximate calculation; trial; points, score (in a game).—**al t.,** by eye; as an estimate; by trial.

tantico, tantillo. I. *m.* (coll.) a little, a little bit, a small amount. **II.** *adv.* (coll., Am.) a little while.

tanto, ta. I. *a.* so much, as much; very great.— *pl.* **tantos, tas,** many; as many, so many. **II.** *pron.* that.—**por t., por lo t.,** for that reason; therefore. **III.** *m.* certain sum or quantity; copy of a writing; counter; point (in games); (com.) rate.—*pl.* odd, denoting an indeterminate number (e. g., *treinta y tantos,* thirty odd).—**t. por ciento,** percentage; per cent.—**t. por cuanto,** (arith.) rate referred to any number; theory of rates (per centum, per thousand, per *x*).—**t. por t.,** at the same price; upon a par.—**tantos a tantos,** equal numbers.— **algún t.,** a little, somewhat.—**al t.,** at the price stated; at cost.—**al t. de,** posted about, familiar with.—**en su t.,** proportionably.—**en t.,** or **entre t.,** in the meantime.—**otro t.,** as much; as much more.—**por el t.** = AL T. **IV.** *adv.* so, in such a manner; so much, as much; so long, as long; often. —**t. como,** as much as; as well as.—**t. cuanto,** a little, somewhat.—**t. mejor,** so much the better.— **t. más cuanto,** or **t. más cuanto que,** all the more because, specially as.—**t. monta,** it is all the same.—**t. peor,** so much the worse.—**t. que,** as much as; so much so, that.—**t. uno como otro,** the one as well as the other; both of them.

tanza, *f.* fishing line.

tañedor, ra, *n.* musical player.

tañente, *a.* playing on an instrument.

tañer, *va.* to play (a musical instrument).

tañido, *pp.* & *m.* tune; sound; clink, ring.

tañimiento, *m.* playing on an instrument.

tao, *m.* badge of some orders.

tapa, *f.* lid, cover, cap; horny part of a hoof; cylinder head; (shoe.) heel blank, heel lift; (b. b.) board case; (Philip.) jerked beef, hung beef.— **t. de los sesos,** top of the skull.—**t. de un barril** = CASCO DE UN BARRIL.

tapaagujeros, *m.* (coll.) clumsy mason; substitute, makeshift.

tapabalazo, *m.* (naut.) shot plug.

tapaboca, *m.* (coll.) slap on the mouth; muffler; choke pear; anything that silences one; (mil.) tampion, tamkin.

tapada, *f.* thickly veiled woman.

tapadera, *f.* loose lid, cover of a pot; covercle; (Mex.) leather cover of a stirrup.

tapadero, *m.* stopper, stopple, cover.

tapadillo, *m.* concealment of a woman's face with her veil or mantle; flute stop of an organ.—**de t.,** secretly, covertly, sub rosa.

tapadizo, *m.* shed, cover.

tapador, ra. I. *n.* coverer. **II.** *m.* lid, cover, plug, stopper, stopple.

tapadura, *f.* stopping, covering, hiding.

tapafogón, *m.* (arti.) cap of a venthole.

tapafunda, *f.* (sad.) flap of a holster.

tapaagujeros, *m.* = TAPAAGUJEROS.

tapajuntas, *m.* door strap covering joint with wall; corner angle to protect plaster.

tápalo, *m.* (Mex.) woman's shawl.

tapamiento, *m.* stopping or covering.

tápana, *f.* (bot.) caper.

tapanco, (Philip.) boat tilt or awning.

tapaojos, *m.* (Am.) blinders for horses.

tapapiés, *m.* silk underskirt.

tapar. I. *va.* to cover; to hide, cover up, veil; to stop up, plug; close up, obstruct.—**t. la boca,** to stop one's mouth. **II.** *vr.* to cover the track of the fore feet with those of the hind ones (s. o. horses).

tapara, *f.* (Am.) gourd for drinking.

tápara, *f.* (bot.) caper.

táparo, *m.* gourd tree.

taparrabo, *m.* loin cloth; trunks, short tights.

tapatán, *m.* (Philip.) tit-tat-toe.

taperujarse, *vr.* (coll.) to muffle one's face.

taperujo, *m.* (coll.) ill-shaped plug or stopper; awkward manner of muffling one's face.

tapetado, da, *a.* dark brown.

tapete, *m.* small carpet, rug; cover for a table or chest.—**t. verde,** card table.—**estar sobre el t.,** to be on the tapis.

tapia, *f.* mud wall; adobe wall; wall fence; (mas.) wall measure (50 sq. ft.).—**t. real,** wall made of earth and lime.—**más sordo que una t.,** deaf as a post.

tapiador, *m.* builder of mud walls.

tapial, *m.* form or mould for mud walls.

tapiar, *va.* to wall up; to raise a spite wall; to obstruct the view of with a wall.

tapicería, *f.* tapestry; art of making tapestry; upholstery; shop where tapestries are sold.

tapicero, *m.* one who makes tapestry; upholsterer; carpetmonger, carpet layer.—**t. mayor,** tapestry keeper in a palace.

tapido, da, *a.* closely woven.

tapiería, *f.* series of mud walls.

tapín, *m.* (arti.) vent plug.

tapioca, *f.* tapioca.

tapir, *m.* (zool.) tapir.

tapirujarse, *vr.* = TAPERUJARSE.

tapis, *m.* (Philip.) sash used by women.

tapiz, *m.* tapestry.

tapizar, *va.* to hang with tapestry.

tapón, *m.* cork, stopper; plug, bung; (surg.) tampon.—**t. de cuba,** (coll.) short, fat person.—**al primer t., zurrapas,** (coll.) unlucky from the start.

taponamiento, *m.* (surg.) tamponage.

taponar, *va.* (surg.) to tampon.

taponazo, *m.* pop of a bottle.—**taponería,** *f.* set of corks; cork factory or shop.—**taponero, ra. I.** *a.* cork (u. a.). **II.** *n.* cork cutter, cork seller.

tapsia, *f.* (bot.) madder.

tapujarse, *vr.* to muffle one's self.

tapujo, *m.* muffle; (coll.) pretext, subterfuge.

taque, *m.* noise made by locking a door; rap, knock at a door.

taquera, *f.* rack or stand for billiard cues.

taquigrafía, *f.* shorthand, stenography.

taquigrafiar, *va.* to write in shorthand.

taquigráficamente, *adv.* in shorthand.

taquigráfico, ca, *a.* stenographic.

taquígrafo, *m.* stenographer.

taquilla, *f.* letter file, closet for papers; case of pigeonholes; ticket rack, key rack; (theat., r. w.) ticket office; booking office.

taquimetría, *f.* tachymetry; stadia surveying; (aut.) tachymeter, tachometer.

taquimétrico, ca, *a.* tachymetrical.

taquímetro, *m.* (surv.) tachymeter, stadia.

taquín, *m.* = TABA.

taquinero, *m.* player with a bone.

tara, *f.* (com.) tare; tally (stick); (Ven.) green grasshopper.—**menos la t.,** making due allowance for trimmings or exaggeration, taking it with a grain of salt.

tarabilla, *f.* (mil.) clack, clapper; catch, bolt, latch, sash fastener or holder; pin or peg for tightening the cord of a buck-saw frame; (coll.) chatterbox; fast and senseless talk.

tarabita, *f.* (S. A.) rope bridge.

taracea, *f.* marquetry, checkered work, inlaid work, buhlwork.

taracear, *va.* to inlay, to make buhlwork on.

taragallo, *m.* clog or block suspended from the necks of beasts.

taraje, *m.* (bot.) tamarisk.

tarambana, *n.* giddy person; madcap.

tarando, *m.* (zool.) reindeer.

tarangallo, *m.* = TARAGALLO.

tarángana, *f.* coarse sausage.

tarantela, *f.* (danc.) tarantella.

tarántula, *f.* tarantula.

tarantulado, da, *a.* = ATARANTADO.

tarara, tarará, *f.* sound of a trumpet.

tararear, *va. & vn.* to hum (a tune).

tararira. I. *f.* (coll.) noisy mirth. **II.** *n.* noisy person.

tarasca, *f.* figure of a dragon formerly borne in the procession of Corpus Christi day; ugly woman.

tarascada, *f.* bite, wound with the teeth; (coll.) pert, rude answer.

tarascar, *va.* to bite (as dogs).

tarascón, *m. aug.* of TARASCA.

taratántara, *f.* = TARARA.

taray, *m.* (bot.) tamarisk.

tarayal, *m.* tamarisk plantation.

tarazana, *f.*, **tarazanal,** *m.* = ATARAZANA.

tarazar, *va.* to bite; to vex, annoy, harass.

tarazón, *m.* large slice.

tarbea, *f.* large hall.

tardador, ra, *n. & a.* tarrier (-ing).

tardanaos, *m.* = RÉMORA.

tardanza, *f.* slowness, tardiness; delay.

tardar, *vn. & vr.* to delay; take long; to be late.—**a más t.,** at the latest.

tarde. I. *f.* afternoon.—**buenas tardes,** good-afternoon.—**de la t. a la mañana,** between sunset and sunrise; all on a sudden.—**de t. en t.,** now and then, once in a while. **II.** *adv.* late; too late.—**t., mal y nunca,** late and bad.—**t. o temprano,** sooner or later.—**t. plache,** too late.—**hacerse t.,** to grow late.—**más vale t. que nunca,** better late than never.—**para luego es t.,** by and by will be too late.

tardecer, *vn. & impers.* (*subj.* TARDEZCA) to draw towards evening; to grow late.

tardecica, ita, *f. dim.* toward evening.

tardecillo, to, *adv.* (Am.) a little late.

tardíamente, *adv.* too late, out of time.

tardígrado, da. I. *a.* (zool.) slow-moving, slow-paced. **II.** *m. pl.* Tardigrada, sloths.

tardío, día, *a.* late, too late; slow; tardy.

tardo, da, *a.* slow, sluggish; tardy; dull, thick, dense.

tardón, na, *a. aug.* very slow; dull, thick.

tarea, *f.* task; care, anxiety.

tarentino, na, *n. & a.* Tarentine.

Tárgum, *m.* Targum (Jewish book).

tarida, *f.* an ancient military transport.

tarifa, *f.* price list, fare, rate; schedule of charges.

tarima, *f.* stand; movable platform; low bench, table, footstool; bedstead.

tarimón, *m. aug.* large stand or platform.

tarín, *m.* silver real of 8½ CUARTOS.

tarina, *f.* middle-sized plate for meat.

tarín barín, *adv.* (coll.) pretty close, just about.

tarja, *f.* check, tally; tally stick; target, shield, buckler; an ancient copper coin.—**beber sobre t.,** (coll.) to get drink on tick.

tarjador, ra, *n.* tally keeper.—**tarjar,** *va.* to tally.—**tarjero, ra,** *n.* tally keeper.

tarjeta, *f. dim.* of TARJA; card; (arch.) label, tablet with inscription; title and imprint on a map or chart.—**t. de despedida,** P. P. C. (leave-taking) card.—**t. de negocios,** business card.—**t. de visita,** visiting card.—**t. postal,** post card.

tarjeteo, *m.* (coll.) social exchange of cards.

tarjetero, *m.* cardcase.

tarjetón, *m. aug.* large card; show card.

tarlatana, *f.* tarlatan (fabric).

tarquín, *m.* slime, mire, mud.

tarquinada, *f.* (coll.) rape.

tararconense, *a.* of or from Tarragona.

tárraga, *f.* an ancient Spanish dance.

tarraja, *f.* = TERRAJA.

tarraya, *f.* (Ven., Colomb.) = ATARRAYA.

tarreñas, *f. pl.* pieces of broken china used as clappers or bones.

tarrico, *m.* (bot.) saltwort.

tarro, *m.* jar; (Cuba) horn; (Colomb.) can, pot.

tarso, *m.* (anat.) tarsus; gambrel, hock.

tarta, *f.* tart; pan for baking tarts.

tártago, *m.* (bot.) spurge; (coll.) misfortune; practical joke.

tartajear, *vn.* to stutter, stammer.

tartajoso, sa, *a.* stammering, stuttering.

tartalear, *vn.* to reel, stagger; (coll.) to be dumfounded.

tartamudear, *vn.* to stutter, stammer.

tartamudeo, *m.*, **tartamudez,** *f.* stuttering.

tartamudo, da, *n. & a.* stutterer (-ing).

tartán, *m.* tartan, Scotch plaid.

tartana, *f.* round-top two-wheeled carriage; (naut.) tartan.

tartanero, *m.* driver of a TARTANA.

tartáreo, rea, *a.* (poet.) tartarean, hellish.

tartárico, ca, *a.* tartaric.

tartarizar, *va.* to tartarize.

tártaro, *m.* argol, cream of tartar; (dent.) tartar; Tartarus, hell.

tártaro, ra, *n. & a.* Tartar, Tatar.

tartera, *f.* baking pan for pastry; dinner pail.

tartrato, *m.* (chem.) tartrate.

tártrico, ca, *a.* tartaric.

taruga, *f.* (zool.) a species of vicuña.

tarugo, *m.* wooden peg or pin; stopper, plug.

tarumba, *m.*—**volver a uno t.,** (coll.) to confuse one, to get one rattled.—**volverse t.,** to become rattled.

tas, *m.* small anvil used by silversmiths.

tasa, *f.* measure, rule; standard; rate; assessment; valuation, appraisement.

tasación, *f.* valuation, appraisement.

tasadamente, *adv.* barely, scantily, scarcely.

tasador, ra, *n.* appraiser, assessor.

tasajear, *va.* (Am.) to cut (meat) for making jerked beef; to slash, cut to pieces.

tasajo, *m.* jerked beef, hung beef.

tasar, *va.* to appraise; to rate; to tax; to regulate, to keep within bounds; to stint.

tascador, *m.* brake for dressing flax.

tascar, *va.* (pret. TASQUÉ: subj. TASQUE) to brake, scutch, or dress (flax, hemp); to nibble, crunch, browse, graze.—**t. el freno,** to bite the bridle; to resist.

tasco, *m.* refuse of flax or hemp; (naut.) topping of hemp.

tasconio, *m.* tasco.

tasquera, *f.* row, quarrel, wrangle, scuffle.

tasquil, *m.* chip from a stone.

tastana, *f.* (agr.) hard crust on the soil caused by dryness; membrane inside a fruit, as in oranges.

tástara, *f.* coarse bran.

tastaz, *m.* polishing powder from old crucibles.

tasto, *m.* bad taste of tainted food.

tasugo, *m.* (zool.) badger.

tata, *m.* (Am., coll.) dad, daddy; nursemaid; younger sister.

tatabra, *f.,* **tatabro,** *m.* (Colomb.) a species of peccary.

tatarabuela, *f.* great-great-grandmother.

tatarabuelo, *m.* great-great-grandfather.

tataradeudo, da, *n.* very old and distant relative.

tataranieto, ta, *n.* great-great-grandson (-daughter).

tatas.—andar a t., to walk timidly; to go on all fours.

¡tate! *interj.* take care! beware! stay, so it is.

tato, ta. I. *a.* stammering. **II.** *m.* (zool.) hog-headed armadillo; (coll.) younger brother.

tatú, *m.* a variety of giant armadillo.

tatuaje, *m.* tattooing; tattoo.

tatuar, *va. & vr.* to tattoo.

taugel, *m.* batten.

taujía, *f.* damaskeening.

taumaturgia, *f.* thaumaturgy, miracle working. —**taumaturgo,** *m.* miracle worker, thaumaturge.

taurino, na, *a.* taurine, bovine.

taurios, *a. pl.* taurine, bullfighting (games).

Tauro, *m.* (ast.) Taurus, sign of the zodiac.

tauromaquia, *f.* bullfighting.

tauromáquico, ca, *a.* tauromachian.

tautología, *f.* (rhet.) tautology.

taxativamente, *adv.* limitedly.

taxativo, va, *a.* (law) restricted, conditioned.

taxidermia, *f.* taxidermy.

taxidermista, *n.* taxidermist.

taxímetro, *m.* (aut.) taximeter; taxicab, taxi.

taxonomía, *f.* taxonomy.

taxonómico, ca, *a.* taxonomic.

taz a taz, *adv.* this for that; even.

taza, *f.* cup; cupful; bowl; basin of a fountain; cup guard of a sword.

tazaña, *f.* = TARASCA.

tazar, *va. & vr.* to fray.

tazmía, *f.* share of tithes; tithe register.

tazón, *m. aug.* large bowl; basin.

té, *m.* tea.—**t. de borde,** or **de Méjico,** (bot.) saltwort.

te. I. *pron. objective case of* TÚ: thee, to thee. **II.** *f.* name of the letter *t.*

tea, *f.* candlewood; torch, firebrand; (naut.)hawse for raising the anchor.

teame, teamide, *f.* stone said to repel iron.

teatino, na, *n.* Theatin.

teatral, *a.* theatrical.

teatralmente, *adv.* theatrically.

teátrico, ca, *a.* theatrical.

teatro, *m.* theatre; stage; collection of plays; dramatic art.

tebaico, ca, *a.* Thebaic.

tebano, na; tebeo, a, *n. & a.* Theban.

teca, *f.* (bot.) teak; teakwood.

tecalí, *m.* (Mex.) transparent marble.

tecla, *f.* key (of a piano, organ, typewriter, etc.); delicate point.—**dar en la t.,** to strike it right, to find the way.—**tocar una t.,** to get up a scheme, to resort to some expedient.

teclado, *m.* keyboard.

tecle, *m.* (naut.) single purchase.

teclear. I. *vn.* to finger a keyboard; to drum with the fingers. **II.** *va.* (coll.) to resort to (an expedient), to try (some scheme).

tecleo, *m.* drumming on a keyboard, striking the keys; scheming, trying.

técnica, *f.* technique; technical ability.

técnicamente, *adv.* technically.

tecnicismo, *m.* technical term; technical vocabulary; technicism.

técnico, ca. I. *a.* technical. **II.** *n.* technical expert.

tecnología, *f.* technology.

tecnológico, ca, *a.* technological, technical.

tecol, *m.* (Mex.) maguey caterpillar.

tecolote, *m.* (Mex., C. A.) owl.

tecomate, *m.* (Mex.) cup made from a gourd.

tectibranquio, quia. I. *m. & a.* (zool.) tectibranch. **II.** *m. pl.* Tectibranchia.

techado, *pp. & m.* roof; ceiling; shed.

techar, *va.* to roof; to cover with a roof.

techo, *m.,* **techumbre,** *f.* ceiling; roof; top (as of a vehicle); cover; shed; (aer., **techo**) ceiling.— **techo utilizable,** (aer.) service ceiling.

tedero, *m.* torch holder.

tedéum, *m.* (eccl.) Te Deum.

tediar, *va.* to loathe, hate, abhor.

tedio, *m.* tediousness, ennui.

tedioso, sa, *a.* tedious, boresome, tiresome.

tegual, *m.* ancient tax on fish.

teguillo, *m.* thin board, strip.

tegumento, *m.* tegument.

teína, *f.* (chem.) thein.

teinada, *f.* cattle shed.

teísmo, *m.* theism.—**teísta,** *n. & a.* theist (-ic).

teja, *f.* roof tile; steel bar shaped into a sword blade; (naut.) hollow cut for scarfing; (bot.) linden tree.—**t. cóncava,** gutter or pantile.—**t. de la silla,** (Mex.) hind bow of a saddle.—**a t. vana,** with a shed over.—**a toca t.,** in cash, cash down.— **de tejas abajo,** in the world of nature, in this world.—**de tejas arriba,** in the realm of the supernatural, beyond the realm of nature.

tejadillo, *m. dim.* roof of a coach; projecting side roof; card sharp's method of holding the talon.

tejado, *m.* roof; shed.

tejamaní, tejamanil, *m.* shingle.

tejar. I. *va.* to tile. **II.** *m.* tile works, tile kiln.

tejaroz, *m.* eaves, penthouse, tiled shed.

tejedera, *f.* weaver (woman); (ent.) water skater. —**tejedor,** *m.* weaver; (ent.) water skipper.

tejedora, *f.* weaver (woman).

tejedura, *f.* texture, weaving, fabric.

tejeduría, *f.* art of weaving; mill, factory for weaving.

teje maneje, *m.* (coll.) cleverness, knack.

tejer, *va.* to weave; to wattle, interweave, plait; to knit; to regulate, adjust; to devise.

tejera, tejería, *f.* tile kiln.

tejero, *m.* tile maker.

tejica, iila, ita, *f. dim.* small tile.

tejido, *pp. & m.* texture, tissue, weaving; fabric, web; (anat.) tissue.

tejillo, *m.* plaited girdle.

tejo, *m.* quoit; game of quoits; shuffleboard counter; blank, metal disk or plate; (mech.) bush, pillow block, socket, socket plate; (bot.) yew tree.

tejocote, *m.* (bot., Mex.) a sloelike fruit.

tejoleta, *f.* broken tile, brickbat; shuffleboard counter; clapper.

tejolote, *m.* (Mex.) stone pestle.

tejón, *m.* round gold ingot; (zool.) badger.

tejonera, *f.* burrow of a badger.

tejuela, *f.* small tile; brickbat; saddletree.

tejuelo, *m.* small tile; (b. b.) binder's title; (mech.) bush, pillow block, socket, sole-plate.

tela, *f.* cloth, fabric, stuff; chain or warp of cloth; pellicle, film; skin (of an onion, etc.); quibble, quirk; web of insects; argument; matter; thread of a discourse; membrane or opacity in the eye.— **t. de alambre,** wire cloth, wire gauze.—**t. de araña,** cobweb, spider web.—**t. de cebolla,** thin cloth.—**t. metálica** = T. DE ALAMBRE.—**en t. de juicio,** in doubt; under careful consideration.

telamón, m. (arch.) telamon, atlante.

telar, m. loom; frame; (theat.) gridiron.

telaraña, f. cobweb; flimsy or trifling thing.—**mirar las telarañas,** (coll.) to be absent-minded.—**tener telarañas en los ojos,** to be blind to one's surroundings.

telarejo, f. dim. small loom or frame.

telecomunicación, f. telecommunication, long-distance communication.

telefio, m. (bot.) orpine stonecrop.

telefonear, va. & vn. to telephone.

telefonema, m. telephone message.

telefonía, f. telephony.—**t. sin hilos,** wireless telephony, radiotelephony.

telefónicamente, adv. telephonically.

telefónico, ca, a. telephonic.

telefonista, n. telephonist, telephone operator.

teléfono, m. telephone.—**t. sin hilos,** wireless telephone.

teléfoto, m. telephote.

telefotografía, f. telephotography.

telegrafía, f. telegraphy.—**t. sin hilos,** wireless telegraphy.

telegrafiar, va. to telegraph; to cable.

telegráficamente, adv. telegraphically.

telegráfico, ca, a. telegraphic.

telegrafista, n. telegrapher, telegraph operator.

telégrafo, m. telegraph.—**t. marino,** nautical signals; signal service.—**t. óptico,** semaphore.—**t. sin hilos,** wireless telegraph.—**hacer telégrafos,** to talk by signs (as lovers).

telegrama, m. telegram; cablegram.

telemecánica, f. long-distance transmission or production of motion.

telemetría, f. telemetry.

telemétrico, ca, a. telemetric.

telémetro, m. telemeter.

teleobjetivo, m. telephotographic object glass.

teleología, f. teleology.

teleológico, ca, a. teleological.

telepatía, f. telepathy.

telepático, ca, a. telepathic.

telera, f. plow pin; cattle stall, cattle pen; (mech.) jaw, cheek (of a clamp, vice, or press); (car.) body transom, cross frame, tiebeam; (ordn.) transom of a gun-carriage; (naut.) rack block; (min.) pyramidal mound of copper ore for roasting; round loaf of brown bread.

telero, m. (car.) cart stake.

telescópico, ca, a. telescopic.

telescopio, m. telescope.

teleta, f. blotting paper; sieve in paper mills.

teletón, m. strong silken stuff.

telilla, f. dim. light woollen stuff; film.

telina, f. clam; mussel. V. ALMEJA.

telita, f. dim. of TELA; thin fabric.

telón, m. (theat.) curtain, drop curtain; drop, drop scene.—**t. de boca,** drop curtain.—**t. de foro,** drop scene.—**bajar,** or **correr, el t.,** to drop the curtain.—**levantar,** or **subir, el t.,** to raise the curtain.

telonio, m. ancient tax office.—**a manera de t.,** in a jumble, disordered.

telúrico, ca, a. telluric.

telurio, m. (chem.) tellurium.

tellina, f. clam; mussel.

telliz, m. caparison, saddle cover.

telliza, f. bedspread, coverlet.

tema. I. m. theme, subject; text, thesis; (mus.) theme, motive.—**t. celeste,** (ast.) map of the heavens. **II.** f. topic of a madman's discourses; hobby; dispute, contention; obstinacy; animosity, grudge.—**a t.,** emulously, obstinately.

temático, ca, a. thematic; obstinate.

tembladal, m. quaking bog, quagmire.

tembladera, f. a kind of bowl or cup of very thin metal or glass; (jewel.) a hair ornament on a spiral; (icht.) torpedo, electric ray; (bot.) quaking grass.

tembladero, m. quagmire.

temblador, ra. I. a. quaking, shaking, quivering. **II.** m. Quaker, Shaker.

temblante. I. a. trembling, quavering. **II.** m. loose bracelet.

temblar, vn. (ind. TIEMBLO: subj. TIEMBLE) to tremble, shake, quake, quiver; to shiver.

tembleque, m. a hair ornament on a spiral.

temblequear, tembletear, vn. (coll.) to tremble, shake, shiver.

temblón, na, a. tremulous, shaking.—**hacer la temblona,** to affect timidity.

temblor, m. trembling, tremor, thrill.—**t. de tierra,** earthquake.—**temblorcillo,** m. dim. slight tremor.—**tembloroso, sa; tembloso, sa,** a. trembling, tremulous, shivering, shaking.

temedero, ra, a. dread, redoubtable.

temedor, ra, a. dreading, fearing.

temer, va. & vn. to fear, dread.

temerariamente, adv. rashly, recklessly.

temerario, ria, a. rash, imprudent, unwise; reckless; hasty, irreflexive.

temeridad, f. temerity, rashness, recklessness; folly, rash or reckless act; foolhardiness; rash conclusion.

temerón, na, a. affecting courage.

temerosamente, adv. timorously.

temeroso, sa, a. dread; timid; timorous; chicken-hearted; afraid.—**t. de Dios,** God-fearing.

temible, a. dread, terrible, redoubtable.

temor, m. dread, fear.

temoso, sa, a. obstinate, stubborn.

tempanador, m. cutter for beehives.

tempanar, va. to cover the tops of (beehives).

témpano, m. (mus.) kettledrum; tabor, timbrel; drumhead, drumskin; tympan; piece, block; ice floe, iceberg; sod, sward; heading of a barrel; flitch of bacon; cork dome of a beehive; (arch.) tympan or an arch.—**t. de tocino,** flitch of bacon.

temperación, f. tempering.

temperadamente, adv. temperately.

temperamento, m. climate; arbitration, compromise; temperament, constitution; (mus.) temperament.

temperancia, f. temperance.

temperante, a. (med.) tempering.

temperar. I. va. to temper. **II.** vn. to have a change of climate; to summer.

temperatura, f. temperature.

temperie, f. atmospheric conditions.

tempero, m. seasonableness.

tempestad, f. tempest, storm.

tempestivamente, adv. seasonably, fitly, opportunely.—**tempestividad,** f. seasonableness, opportuneness, timeliness.—**tempestivo, va,** a. opportune, timely.

tempestuosamente, adv. stormily, turbulently.—**tempestuoso, sa,** a. tempestuous, stormy, turbulent.

templa, f. (art.) tempera, distemper.—pl. temples (of the head).

templadamente, adv. temperately, moderately, abstemiously.

templadera, f. (hyd.) sluice gate.

templado, da, pp. & a. moderate (app. sp. to climate in the phrase **tierra templada,** [region of] moderate climate or medium temperature); hardened, tempered; abstemious, frugal; lukewarm; medium, fair; brave, firm; (mus.) tuned.

templador, ra. I. n. tuner; temperer. **II.** m. (mus.) tuning key; (Peru) circular stockade in bull rings.

templadura, f. temper, tempering; tuning.

templanza, f. temperance, moderation, sobriety; mildness of temperature or climate; (art) good disposition of colors.

templar. I. va. to temper, soften, moderate; to quench, allay; to calm, pacify; to prepare, dispose; to temper, quench (metals); to anneal (glass); (mus.) to tune; (art) to blend; (naut.) to trim the sails) to the wind; (falc.) to train. **II.** vr. to be moderate.

templario, m. templar.

temple, *m.* atmospheric conditions; temper (of metals, of persons); courage; disposition, frame of mind; average; (mus.) temperament; religion of the Templars, and one of their temples.—**al t.,** (art) in distemper.

templete, *m. dim.* small temple, shrine; (arch.) niche, tabernacle.

templista, *m.* (art) painter in distemper.

templo, *m.* temple; church; shrine.

témporas, *f. pl.* (eccl.) ember days.

temporada, *f.* season, spell.—**t. de frío,** cold spell.—**t. de invierno,** winter season.—**t. de ópera,** opera season.—**estar de t.,** to be summering or rusticating.

temporal. I. *a.* temporal; temporary; provisional; secular, worldly; (anat.) temporal. **II.** *m.* tempest, storm; weather (good or bad); long rainy spell; temporary laborer.

temporalidad, *f.* temporality.

temporalizar, *va.* (*for mut. v.* TEMPORIZAR) to make temporary.

temporalmente, *adv.* temporally; provisionally, transiently; in a worldly manner.

temporáneo, nea; temporario, ria, *a.* temporary unstable, transient.

temporejar, *vn.* (naut.) to lie to.

temporero, ra; temporil, *a.* temporary (laborer), working by the season.

temporizar, *vn.* (*pret.* TEMPORICÉ: *subj.* TEMPORICE) to pass the time; to temporize.

tempranal, *a.* producing early fruits.

tempranamente, *adv.* prematurely.

tempranero, ra, *a.* early.

tempranilla, *f.* early grape.

temprano. I. *adv.* early; prematurely, too early. **II.** *n.* field yielding early crops.

temprano, na, *a.* early.

temulento, ta, *a.* intoxicated, tipsy, drunk.

ten.—t. con t., tact, adroitness, wisdom.

tena, *f.* shed for cattle, fold.

tenacear. I. *va.* = ATENACEAR. **II.** *vn.* to persist.

tenacero, *m.* tongs maker.

tenacidad, *f.* tenacity, toughness; tenaciousness, pertinacity, perseverance, persistence.

tenacillas, *f. pl. dim.* small tongs; snuffers; tweezers, nippers, pincers, pliers; curling iron; sugar tongs; cigarette sliding tongs.

tenáculo, *m.* (med.) tenaculum.

tenada, *f.* fold, shed for cattle.

tenallas, *f. pl.* pair of tongs.

tenallón, *m.* (fort.) tenaillon.

tenante, *m.* (her.) supporter (of a shield).

tenaz, *a.* tenacious, adhesive; strong, firm; stubborn; tough; persevering.

tenaza, *f.* (fort.) tenail; claw (as of lobsters).—*pl.* tongs, nippers, pliers; (dent.) forceps; (card playing) two cards that take the two last tricks.

tenazada, *f.* grasp of pincers or tongs; noise or click of the tongs; violent biting or attempt at biting.

tenazmente, *adv.* tenaciously.

tenazón, *f.*—**a t.,** point-blank, without taking aim.—**parar de t.,** to stop (a horse) short in his course.

tenazuelas, *f. pl. dim.* tweezers.

tenca, *f.* (icht.) tench.

tención, *f.* holding, retaining.

tendajo, *m.* small rickety shop.

tendal, *m.* tent, awning, tilt; piece of canvas placed under olive trees when picking the fruit.

tendalera, *f.* (coll.) things scattered in disorder.

tendalero, *m.,* **tendedero,** *m.* place where clothes are spread to dry.

tendedor, ra, *n.* stretcher, tenter; one who spreads clothes to dry.

tendedura, *f.* stretching, extending.

tendejón, *m.* small rickety shop.

tendel, *m.* (mas.) leveling line (cord); layer of mortar.

tendencia, *f.* tendency; trend, drift.

ténder, *m.* (r. w.) tender.

---

tender. I. *va.* to stretch, stretch out, spread out; to lay (rails, pipe, etc.); (mas.) to coat. **II.** *vn.* to have a tendency, to tend; (math., w. **hacia**) to approach (as a limit). **III.** *vr.* to stretch one's self on the ground or reclining; to place one's cards on the table; to run at full gallop; to neglect a business.

tenderete, *m.* a card game; (Mex.) second-hand-clothing shop.

tendero, ra, *n.* shopkeeper; tentmaker.

tendezuela, *f. dim.* small shop.

tendidamente, *adv.* diffusely, diffusively.

tendido, *pp. & m.* row of seats; in lace making, piece made over the pattern; quantity of spread clothes dried at once; batch of bread baked at one time; (mas.) coat of plaster or calcimine; (arch.) roof of a house from the ridge to the eaves; (Am., min.) riffle.

tendiente, *a.* tending; expanding.

tendinoso, sa, *a.* tendinous.

tendón, *m.* (anat.) tendon.

tenducha, tenducho, *n.* insignificant shop.

tenebrario, *m.* (eccl.) tenebræ candelabrum.

tenebrosamente, *adv.* gloomily.

tenebrosidad, *f.* darkness, gloom.

tenebroso, sa, *a.* tenebrous, dark, gloomy.

tenedero, *m.* (naut.) anchoring ground.

tenedor, *m.* holder; keeper; guardian; table fork; cad, caddy (in ball games); (com.) holder.—**t. de bastimentos,** (naut.) storekeeper of the navy.—**t. de libros,** bookkeeper.—**t. de póliza,** policyholder.

teneduría, *f.* position of bookkeeper.—**t. de libros,** bookkeeping.

tenencia, *f.* tenancy, occupancy, possession, holding; (mil.) lieutenancy, lieutenantship.

tener. I. *va.* (*ind.* TENGO: *pret.* TUVE: *fut.* TENDRÉ: *sub.* TENGA) to have, possess; to hold, take hold of; to be worth (*Juan tiene cien mil pesos,* John is worth 100,000 pesos); to maintain, sustain; to subject; domineer; to keep, hold, retain; to stop, hold back; to fulfil, keep (one's word); to contain, have within; (app. to dimensions) to be (*la casa tiene 20 metros de ancho,* the house is 20 meters wide). With nouns of time, it denotes duration or age (*el niño tiene seis meses,* the child is six months old; *esta casa tiene cien años,* this house is one hundred years old). With some nouns denoting sensation or feeling, it is equivalent to "to be" followed by the corresponding adjective (*tener hambre,* to be hungry; *tener sueño,* to be sleepy; *tener miedo,* to be afraid).—**t. a bien,** to find it convenient, to please.—**t. buenas formas,** to be of fine figure; to be polite.—**t. días,** (coll.) to be old; to have moody days.—**t. en,** to hold in (esteem, respect, etc.).—**t. en menos,** to think little of.—**t. gana,** or **ganas,** (de), to wish, desire; to have a mind to; to feel like.—**t. para sí,** to think, to be of opinion.—**t. por,** to take to be, to believe, consider.—**t. que,** must, to have to; to have something to (say, lose, propose, etc.).—**t. que hacer,** to have something to do, to be busy; to have to, or must, do.—**t. que ver con,** to have to do with.—**no tenerlas todas consigo,** to be worried, to be anxious.—**no t. sobre que caerse muerto,** not to have a farthing, to be penniless. **II.** *v. auxiliary,* to have (*tengo dicho,* I have said). Often, however, the participle following is rather an adjective than part of a compound tense (*tengo escritas dos cartas,* I have two letters written). In other cases, the combination is equivalent to a simple form of the verb (*tengo entendido,* I understand; *tengo pensado,* I intend). **III.** *vn.* to have, possess; to be well-off, to be wealthy.—**t. de,** to have to, must. **IV.** *vr.* to hold fast or steady; to rest (on something); to stop, halt; to fight, hold one's own; to adhere (to), stand (for).—**t. en pie,** to keep on foot; to stand.

tenebriónidos, *m. pl.* (zool.) Tenebrionidæ.

tenería, *f.* tannery.

tenesmo, *m.* (med.) tenesmus.

tenia, *f.* tapeworm; (arch.) fillet.

tenienta, *f.* wife of a first lieutenant.

tenientazgo, *m.* (mil.) first lieutenantship.

teniente. I. *a.* having, owning, holding; immature, unripe; miserly, mean; (coll.) deaf.—**t. de oídos,** hard of hearing. **II.** deputy, substitute;

(mil.) first lieutenant.—**t. coronel,** lieutenant colonel.—**t. general,** lieutenant general.

tenífugo, ga, a. (med.) tænifuge.

tenis, m. lawn tennis.

tenor, m. condition, nature; kind; import, literal meaning; (mus.) tenor.—**a este t.,** of the same kind, like.—**a t. de,** in compliance with.

tensión, f. tension; tensile stress; tautness, tightness; strain; (elec.) voltage, potential, tension; (poet.) poetical contest on love.

tenso, sa, a. tense, tight, taut, stretched.

tensor, ra. I. a. tensile. **II.** m. turnbuckle; tightener.

tentación, f. temptation.

tentacioncilla, f. dim. slight temptation.

tentaculado, da, a. (zool.) tentacled.

tentaculífero, ra. I. a. (zool.) tentacled. **II.** m. pl. Tentaculifera.

tentáculo, m. tentacle.

tentadero, m. corral for taming calves.

tentador, ra, n. & a. tempter (-ing).—**el t.,** the devil.

tentadura, f. mercury test of silver ore.

tentalear, va. to feel all over, to examine by the touch.

tentar, va. (ind. TIENTO: subj. TIENTE) to touch, to feel with the fingers, to examine by touch; to grope; to tempt; to attempt, try, endeavor; to test; (surg.) to probe; to tent.—**t. cerrojos,** to try all ways and means.

tentativa, f. attempt; first examination.

tentativo, va, a. tentative.

tenteempié, m. (coll.) light luncheon, a bite.

tenteenclaire, n. mulatto; half-breed.

tentemozo, m. prop, support; pole prop; tumbler (a toy); (sad.) = QUIJERA.

tentón, m. (coll.) rough handling.

tenue, a. thin, tenuous, delicate; worthless, trifling; soft (consonant); (art) faint, subdued.

tenuemente, adv. slightly.

tenuidad, f. tenuity, thinness, subtlety; weakness; trifle.

tenuta, f. (law) tenure pendente lite.

tenutario, ria, a. (law) provisional tenant.

tenzón, f. poetical contest on love.

teñidura, f. art of dyeing or tingeing.

teñir, va. (pp. TEÑIDO, TINTO: gerund, TIÑENDO: pret. él TIÑÓ: subj. TIÑA) to tinge, to dye; to stain; (art.) to darken, sadden (a color).—**t. en rama,** to dye in grain, to ingrain.

teobroma, m. cacao.

teobromina, f. (chem.) theobromine.

teocali, m. (Mex.) teocalli.

teocracia, f. theocracy.

teocrático, ca, a. theocratic.

teodicea, f. (theol.) theodicy.

teodisiano, na, a. Theodiosian.

teodolito, m. theodolite.

teogonía, f. theogony.

teogónico, ca, a. theogonic.

teologal, a. theologic(al).

teología, f. theology.

teológicamente, adv. theologically.

teológico, ca, a. theologic(al).

teologismo, m. excessive theologizing, theological mania.

teologizar, vn. (pret. TEOLOGICÉ: subj. TEOLOGICE) to theologize.

teólogo, ga. I. a. theological. **II.** m. theologian.

teorema, m. theorem.

teoría, teórica, f. theory.—**teóricamente,** adv. theoretically.—**teórico, ca. I.** a. theoretical. **II.** n. theorist, theorizer.

teoso, sa, a. resinous.

teosofía, f. theosophy.—**teosófico, ca,** a. theosophical.—**teósofo, m.** theosophist.

tepalcate, m. (Mex.) potsherd.

tepe, m. green sod, turf.

tepeguaje. I. m. (Mex.) a very hard and compact wood. **II.** a. (Mex.) set, obstinate.

tepeizcuinte, m. (Am.) badger.

tepetate, m. (min.) attle, deads, refuse.

tepexilote, m. a palm nut used for beads.

tequiche, m. (Ven.) corn meal with coconut milk and molasses.

tequío, m. (Mex.) a municipal duty or tax.

terapéutica, f. therapeutics.

terapéutico, ca. I. a. therapeutic. **II.** n. therapeutist; one of the Therapeutæ.

teratología, f. (biol.) teratology.

teratológico, ca, a. teratologic(al).

terbio, m. (chem.) terbium.

tercamente, adv. obstinately, stubbornly.

tercena, f. wholesale tobacco warehouse.

tercenal, m. (agr.) rick of thirty sheaves.

tercenista, m. keeper of a TERCENA.

tercer, a. (contr. of TERCERO) third.

terceramente, adv. thirdly.

tercería, f. mediation, arbitration; umpirage; temporary occupation.

tercerilla, f. (poet.) triplet.

tercero, ra. I. a. third. **II.** m. third person; mediator, arbitrator, umpire; collector of tithes; (eccl.) tertiary; pimp, procurer, bawd; sixtieth of a second (time).—**t. en discordia,** umpire, referee between two disputants. **III.** f. (mus.) third; ditone; third string of a guitar; sequence of three cards; procuress.

tercerol, m. (naut.) third in order.

tercerola, f. a short carbine; (com.) tierce.

tercerón, na, n. (Am.) mulatto.

terceto, m. (poet.) tierce, terzet, terza, triplet; (mus.) terzetto, trio.

tercia, f. one third; third of a vara; storehouse for tithes; among Romans, forenoon; sequence of three cards; (eccl.) third hour.

terciado, da. I. pp. & a. slanting, tilted, biased, crosswise. **II.** m. cutlass, broad sword; broad ribbon.

terciana, f. (med.) tertian.

tercianario, ria. I. a. (med.) tertian; causing or suffering tertian fever. **II.** n. person affected with a tertian.

tercianela, f. heavy silk fabric.

terciar. I. va. to place sidewise or sling diagonally; to divide into three parts; (agr.) to plow the third time; (mil.) to carry (arms).—**t. una pieza,** (arti.) to prove a gun. **II.** vn. to make up a number; to mediate, arbitrate, to go between; to join (in conversation); to share, take part; to reach the third day. **III.** vr. to be favorable, offer an opportunity.

terciario, ria. I. a. third in order or degree; (geol.) Tertiary. **II.** m. (arch.) rib of a Gothic arch; (geol.) Tertiary.

terciazón, m. (agr.) third plowing.

tercio, cia. I. a. third. **II.** m. one third; each package of a mule load; (mil.) regiment of infantry in old Spain; division of the GUARDIA CIVIL; third part of a horse-course (start, run, or stop); third section in the height of a horse; third part of the rosary; third part of a sword.—pl. robust or strong limbs of a man.—**t. de cueros,** bundle of hides.—**t. de tabaco,** bale of tobacco.—**t. y quinto,** great advantage.—**hacer buen t.,** to do a good turn.—**hacer mal t.,** to do a bad turn, to serve ill.—**hacer t.,** to join and complete a required number of people.

terciopelado, da. I. a. velvetlike, velvety. **II.** m. velvetlike stuff.

terciopelero, ra, n. velvet weaver or worker.

terciopelo, m. velvet.

terco, ca, a. stubborn; hard (as marble).

terebintáceo, cea, a. terebinthine.

terebinto, m. (bot.) terebinth.

terebrante, a. piercing (pain).

terenciano, na, a. Terentian.

tereniabín, m. white, sweetish, purgative matters resembling mastic, which adheres to the leaves of plants; liquid manna.

tereques, m. pl. (Am., coll.) traps; duds; belongings.

teresiana, f. a kind of military cap.

tergiversación, f. tergiversation.

tergiversador, ra, n. & a. tergiversator (-ing).

tergiversar, *va.* to tergiversate.
teriaca, *f.* (pharm.) theriaca.
teriacal, *a.* (pharm.) theriac(al).
teristro, *m.* thin veil or shawl.
terliz, *m.* tick, ticking; tent cloth.
termal, *a.* thermal.
termas, *f. pl.* hot baths; hot springs.
térmico, ca, *a.* thermic, thermal.
termidor, *m.* Thermidor, eleventh month of the French-Revolution calendar.
terminación, *f.* termination, completion; (gram.) termination, ending.
terminacho, *m.* (coll.) big or vulgar word; jaw-breaker.
terminador, ra. I. *a.* finishing, completing. **II.** *n.* finisher.
terminajo, *m.* (coll.) vulgar expression.
terminal. I. *a.* terminal, final, last. **II.** *m.* (elec.) terminal.
terminante, *a.* ending, closing; peremptory, final, decisive.—**terminantemente,** *adv.* peremptorily, positively.
terminar. I. *va. & vn.* to end, close, terminate, finish, complete. **II.** *vn. & vr.* to end; to abut; (med.) to come to a crisis.
terminativo, va, *a.* (phil.) terminative.
término, *m.* end, ending, completion; term, word; boundary; landmark; manner, behavior; district of a town or city; aim, object, goal; crisis of a disease; condition, constitution, state; (math, log.) term; (arch.) terminal, terminus; (law) term; (mus.) tone, pitch.—*pl.* (log. and astrol.) terms. —**t. medio,** (math.) average; (log.) middle term.—**términos semejantes,** (math.) similar terms.—**en buenos términos,** (coll.) in plain language.— **en otros términos,** in other words.—**medios términos,** evasions, subterfuges.—**poner t. a,** to put an end to, to stop.—**por t. medio,** on an average. —**primer t.,** (art) foreground.—**último t.,** (art.) background.
terminología, *f.* terminology.
terminote, *m.* *aug.* big word.
termiónico, ca, *a.* (rad.) thermionic.
termita, *f.* thermite.
termocauterio, *m.* (surg.) thermocautery.
termodinámica, *f.* thermodynamics.
termodinámico, ca, *a.* thermodynamic.
termoelectricidad, *f.* thermoelectricity.
termoeléctrico, ca, *a.* thermoelectric.
termógrafo, *m.* thermograph, self-registering thermometer.
termología, *f.* thermology, science of heat.
termometría, *f.* thermometry.
termométrico, ca, *a.* thermometric(al).
termómetro, *m.* thermometer.
termometrógrafo, thermometrograph, self-registering thermometer.
termomultiplicador, *m.* thermopile.
termoquímica, *f.* thermochemistry.
termos, *m.* thermos bottle.
termoscopio, *m.* thermoscope.
termosifón, *m.* thermosiphon.
termóstato, *m.* thermostat.
termostático, ca, *a.* thermostatic.
terna, *f.* ternary, triad, tern; three names presented as candidates; a game at dice.
ternario, ria. I. *a.* ternary. **II.** *m.* three days' devotion.
terne, *m.* (coll.) bully, hector.
ternecico, ica, ito, ita, *a.* very tender.
ternejal, *a.* bullying.
ternejón, na, *a.* = TERNERÓN.
ternerico, ca; illo, lla; ito, ta, *n. dim.* young or little calf.
ternero, ra. I. *n.* calf. **II.** *f.* veal.
ternerón, na, *a.* sentimental, easily moved.
terneruela, *f. dim.* sucking calf.
terneza, *f.* softness, suavity; tenderness; affection, endearment, fondness.
ternezuelo, la, *a. dim.* very tender.
ternilla, *f.* gristle, cartilage; nose or nostrils of an ox or other similar animal.—**llevar,** or **tener, de la t.,** to lead by the nose.

ternilloso, sa, *a.* gristly, cartilaginous.
ternísimo, ma, *a. super.* very tender.
terno, *m.* ternary, triad; (tail.) suit of clothes; tern (in lottery); oath, curse; (eccl.) vestments for the high mass; (jewel.) set; (print.) three printed sheets one within another.—**t. seco,** happy and unexpected fortune.
ternura, *f.* tenderness, softness, fondness.
terpeno, *m.* (chem.) terpene.—**terpina,** *f.* terpin.—**terpinol,** *m.* terpineol.
terquedad, *f.* stubbornness, obstinacy.
terracota, *f.* terra cotta.
terrada, *f.* bitumen made of ochre and glue.
terradillo, *m. dim.* small terrace.
terrado, *m.* terrace; flat roof of a house.
terraja, *f.* pipe stock, screw stock, diestock; screw-cutting machine; modelling board, sweep.
terraje, *m.* rent paid for arable land.
terrajero, *m.* lessee of arable land.
terral, *m.* land breeze.
terraplén, *m.* embankment; (r. w.) embankment, fill; (fort.) terreplein, banquette.
terraplenar, *va.* to embank; to fill; to make an embankment or terreplein for.
terraplenador, *m.* laborer on embankments.
terrapleno, *m.* = TERRAPLÉN.
terráqueo, quea, *a.* terraqueous, terrestrial.
terrateniente, *n.* landowner, landholder.
terraza, *f.* terrace; border in a garden; glazed jar with two handles.
terrazgo, *m.* arable land; rent of arable land.
terrazguero, ra, *n.* lessee of arable land.
terrazo, *m.* (art) ground of a picture.
terrazuela, *f. dim.* of TERRAZA.
terrear, *vn.* to show the ground (as thin crops).
terrecer, *va.* to terrify.
terregoso, sa, *a.* cloddy, full of clods.
terremoto, *m.* earthquake.
terrenal, *a.* worldly, earthly, mundane.
terrenidad, *f.* quality of the soil.
terreno, na. I. *a.* earthly, terrestrial; worldly, mundane. **II.** *m.* land, ground, soil, terrene; piece of land, lot, plot; field, sphere of action; (geol.) terrane or terrain.—**t. abierto,** (mil.) open ground.—**t. franco,** (min.) tract not yet preempted or denounced.
térreo, rea, *a.* terreous, earthy.
terrera, *f.* steep piece of ground; (orn.) lark.
terrero, ra. I. *a.* earthly, terreous; abject, humble; skimming the ground (as birds). **II.** *m.* terrace; mound, bank, heap of earth; alluvium; (min.) dump; mark, target; frail for carrying earth. —**hacer t.,** to court a lady from the street.
terrestre, *a.* terrestrial.
terrezuela, *f. dim.* small piece of ground; poor soil.
terribilidad, *f.* terribleness, awfulness; rudeness, fierceness.
terrible, *a.* terrible; rude, ill-tempered; (coll.) immense, huge.
terriblemente, *adv.* terribly, frightfully.
terriblez, terribleza, *f.* = TERRIBILIDAD.
terrícola, *n.* inhabitant of the earth.
terrífico, ca, *a.* terrific, frightful.
terrígeno, na, *a.* terrigenous; earthborn.
terrino, na, *a.* terrene, earthy.
territorial, *a.* territorial.
territorialidad, *f.* territoriality.
territorio, *m.* territory; region; land.
terrizo, za. I. *a.* earthy, earthen. **II.** *m.* unglazed earthen tub.
terromontero, *m.* hill, hillock.
terrón, *m.* clod; mound; lump; bagasse of olives —*pl.* landed property.—**a rapa t.,** entirely, completely, from the root.
terroncillo, *m. dim.* small clod or lump.
terror, *m.* terror.—**terrorífico, ca,** *a.* terrific, frightful, dreadful.—**terrorismo,** *m.* terrorism.— **terrorista,** *n. & a.* terrorist (-ic).
terrosidad, *f.* earthiness, cloddiness.
terroso, sa, *a.* earthy; cloddy.
terruca, *f. dim.* (coll.) native country.

---

terruño, terruzo, *m.* piece of ground.

tersar, *va.* to smooth, polish, burnish.

tersidad, *f.* polish; terseness.

terso, sa, *a.* smooth, polished, glossy; pure, correct, terse, pithy.

tersura, *f.* smoothness, polish; cleanliness, purity, terseness.

tertil, *m.* ancient tax on silk.

tertulia, *f.* tertulia, social gathering for conversation or entertainment; party; conversation; (theat.) corridor.—**hacer t.,** to gather for conversation; to talk (sp. when the talking is not wanted, as in an office).

tertuliano, na, *n.* one who attends a TERTULIA or makes TERTULIA.

tertuliar, *vn.* = HACEE TERTULIA. *V.* TERTULIA.

tertulio, lia; tertulista, *n.* = TERTULIANO.

teruelo, *m.* balloting urn or box.

teruncio, *m.* an ancient Roman coin.

terutero, *m.* (orn.) terutero, a S. A. lapwing.

terzón, na, *a.* & *n.* three-year old (heifer).

terzuela, *f.* distribution gained for attending mass at the hour of tierce.

terzuelo, *m.* third part; male falcon.

tesálico, ca; tesaliense; tesalio, lia; tésalo, la, *n.* & *a.* Thessalian.

tesalonicense; tesalónico, ca, *a.* Thessalonian.

tesar. I. *va.* (naut.) to haul taut, to make taut. **II.** *vn.* to back, pull back (s. o. oxen).

tesauro, *m.* thesaurus, lexicon.

tesela, *f.* tessella, mosaic tile.

teselado, da, *a.* tessellate, tessellated.

tésera, *f.* tessera, token, countersign.

tesis, *f.* thesis, dissertation.

tesitura, *f.* (mus.) tessitura.

teso, sa. I. *a.* taut, drawn tight. **II.** *m.* brow of a hill; bulge or lump on a flat surface.

tesón, *m.* tenacity, firmness, inflexibility.

tesonería, *f.* obstinacy, stubbornness.

tesorería, *f.* treasury, treasurer's office, exchequer; treasurership.

tesorero, ra, *n.* treasurer; (eccl.) canon who keeps the relics.

tesoro, *m.* treasure; treasury, exchequer; thesaurus, lexicon.

tespíades, *f. pl.* (poet.) the Muses.

testa, *f.* head; top or crown of the head; front, face, forepart; (coll.) brains, cleverness.—**t. coronada,** crowned head.—**t. de ferro** = TESTAFERRO.

testáceo, cea. I. *a.* testaceous. **II.** *m.* testacean.

testación, *f.* obliteration, erasure.

testada, *f.* = TESTARADA.

testado, da, *a.* & *pp.* testate.

testador, ra, *n.* testator.

testadura, *f.* obliteration, erasure.

testaférrea, testaferro, *m.* man of straw, dummy, figurehead.

testamentaría, *f.* (law) testamentary execution; estate; meeting of executors.

testamentario, ria. I. *a.* testamentary. **II.** *m.* executor. **III.** *f.* executrix.

testamento, *m.* testament, will.—**t. abierto,** nuncupative will.—**t. cerrado,** or **escrito,** sealed testament.—**t. nuncupativo,** nuncupative will.—**t. ológrafo,** holographic will.

testar. I. *vn.* to make a will or testament. **II.** *va.* to erase, scratch out.

testarada, *f.* stroke or blow with the head; stubbornness, obstinacy.—**testarrón, na,** *a.* (coll.) stubborn.—**testarronería, testarudez,** *f.* (coll.) hardheadedness, stubbornness.—**testarudo, da,** *a.* stubborn, hardheaded.

teste, *m.* testis, testicle.

testera, *f.* front face, fore part; forehead of an animal; (sad.) crownpiece of a harness; back seat of a coach; (found.) wall of a furnace.

testerada, *f.* = TESTARADA.

testero, *m.* = TESTERA; (min.) ore rock showing two faces.

testicular, *a.* testicular.

testículo, *m.* (anat.) testicle.

testificación, *f.* attestation, testification.

testificante, *a.* witnessing, attesting.

testificar, *va.* (*pret.* TESTIFIQUÉ: *subj.* TESTIFIQUE) to attest, witness, testify.

testificata, *f.* (law) affidavit.

testificativo, va, *a.* attesting, declaratory.

testigo, I. *n.* witness.—**t. de cargo,** witness for the prosecution.—**t. de descargo,** witness for the defence.—**t. de oídas,** auricular witness.—**t. de vista,** or **ocular,** eyewitness. **II.** *m.* testimony, proof, evidence; mound of earth along an excavation.

testimonial, *a.* of the nature of testimony, attesting.

testimoniales, *f. pl.* testimonial; (eccl.) certificate of good character.

testimoniar, *va.* to attest, bear witness to.

testimoniero, ra, *a.* bearing false witness; dissembling, hypocritical.

testimonio, *m.* testimony; affidavit; attestation.

testimoñero, ra, *a.* hypocritical.

testón, *m.* silver coin having a head.

testudo, *m.* (mil.) testudo.

testuz, testuzo, *m.* (vet.) nape, nucha; in some animals, crown of the head.

tesura, *f.* stiffness, tautness.

teta, *f.* teat, mammary gland, breast; nipple, dug, udder.—**t. de vaca,** conical meringue; (bot.) BARBAJA; a variety of grapes.—**dar la t.,** to nurse, to suckle.

tetánico, ca, *a.* (med.) tetanic(al).

tétano, tétanos, *m.* (med.) tetanus, lockjaw.

tetar, *va.* to suckle.

tetera, *f.* teapot.

tetero, *m.* (Am.) nursing bottle.

tetica, *f. dim.* small dug or teat.

tetigonia, *f.* a variety of katydid.

tetilla, *f. dim.* small nipple or teat (as man's).

tetón, *m.* stub of a pruned limb.

tetrácido, *m.* (chem.) tetracid.

tetracordio, *m.* (mus.) tetrachord, fourth.

tetradínamo, ma, *a.* (bot.) tetradynamous; (chem.) tetravalent, quadrivalent.

tetraedro, *m.* (geom.) tetrahedron.

tetragrama, *m.* (mus.) four-line staff.

tetragrámaton, *m.* tetragram, word of four letters; tetragrammaton.

tetralogía, *f.* tetralogy.

tetrao, *m.* (zool.) capercaillie.

tetraómico, ca, *a.* (chem.) tetraomic.

tetraónidas, *f. pl.* (zool.) Tetraonidæ.

tetrarca, *m.* tetrarch.

tetrarquía, *f.* tetrarchate; tetrarchy.

tetrasílabo, ba, *a.* = CUADRISÍLABO.

tetrastilo, *m.* (arch.) tetrastyle.

tetravalente, *a.* (chem.) tetravalent, quadrivalent.

tétrico, ca, *a.* sad, grave, sullen; dark, gloomy.

teucalí, *m.* = TEOCALÍ.

teucrio, *m.* (bot.) germander.

teucro, cra, *a.* & *n.* Trojan.

teúrgia, *f.* theurgy, black magic.—**teúrgico, ca,** *a.* theurgical.—**teúrgo, g**·**, n.** theurgist.

teutón, *n.* & *a.* Teuton (-ic).

teutónico, ca, *a.* Teutonic.

textil, *a.* textile; fibrous.

texto, *m.* text; quotation; textbook; (print.) great primer type.

textorio, ria, *a.* textile.

textual, *a.* textual.—**textualista,** *m.* textualist.

textualmente, *adv.* textually, verbatim.

textura, *f.* texture; weaving; construction (of a literary work); structure.

tez, *f.* complexion of the face.

tezado, da, *a.* very black.

tezontle, *m.* (Mex.) porous building stone.

ti, *pron.* 2d. *pers. sing.* (oblique case of TÚ) thee.

tía, *f.* aunt; (coll.) good old woman.—**cuéntaselo a tu t.,** (coll.) tell it to your grandmother.—**no hay tu t.,** there is no use.

tialina, *f.* (chem.) ptyalin.

tialismo, *m.* (med.) ptyalism.

tiangue, tianguis, *m.* (Mex. and Philip.) market, market days.

tiara, *f.* tiara, Pope's mitre; pontificate, papal dignity; Persian headdress.

tiberio, *m.* (coll.) noise, hubbub, turmoil.

tibetano, na, *n.* & *a.* Tibetan.

tibia, *f.* (anat.) tibia, shin bone; (mus.) flute or pipe.

tibiamente, *adv.* cooly, lukewarmly.

tibieza, *f.* tepidity, lukewarmness; coolness.

tibio, bia, *a.* tepid, lukewarm; remiss.

tibor, *m.* large china jar; (Am.) chamberpot.

tiborna, *f.* toast soaked in oil.

tiburón, *m.* (icht.) shark.

tictac, *m.* ticking.

tiemblo, *m.* aspen tree.

tiemblo, yo tiemble. *V.* TEMBLAR.

tiempo, *m.* time; weather; (mus.) tempo; (gram.) tense.—**t. atrás,** some time ago.—**t. cargado,** (naut.) thick, hazy weather.—**t. contrario,** (naut.) foul weather.—**t. crudo,** bleak, raw weather.—**t. grueso,** hazy weather.—**t. ha,** a long time ago.—**t. medio,** (ast.) mean time.—**t. normal,** standard time.—**t. solar verdadero,** or **t. verdadero,** (astr.) solar time.—**abrir,** or **alzarse, el t.,** to clear up.—**andando el t.,** in time, in the course of time, in the long run.—**a su t.,** at the proper time, in due time.—**a t.,** timely, in time.—**a t. que,** just as.—**a tiempos,** at times, occasionally.—**a un,** or **al, mismo t., a un t.,** at once; at the same time.—**cargarse el t.,** to cloud over.—**con el t.,** in time.—**dar t. al t.,** to bide one's time, to wait patiently.—**de t. en t.,** from time to time, now and then, occasionally.—**en otro t.,** or **en otros tiempos,** formerly, in former times.—**en t.,** on time, at the proper time.—**engañar el t.** = HACER EL T.—**fuera de t.,** out of season; inopportunely.—**hacer el t.,** to kill time, to while away the time.—**haga buen o mal t.,** rain or shine.—**matar el t.** = HACER EL T.—**por t.,** for some time.—**tomarse t.,** to take time, to defer.—**un t.,** formerly, in other times.

tienda, *f.* shop, store; tent; (naut.) awning; tilt.—**t. de campaña,** (mil.) tent.

tiendo, tienda. *V.* TENDER.

tienta, *f.* (surg.) probe, bougie; cleverness, sagacity.—**andar a tientas,** to grope in the dark; to fumble.—**a tientas,** in the dark.

tientaaguja, tientaguja, *f.* boring rod.

tientaparedes, *n.* groper.

tiento, *m.* touch, act of feeling; blind man's stick; halter of a mill horse; circumspection, tact; poy, ropedancer's pole; steady hand; (coll.) blow, cuff; (art) maulstick; (mus.) prelude, flourish; (zool.) tentacle.—**a t.,** obscurely, doubtfully.—**con t.,** tactfully, cautiously.—**dar un t.,** to make a trial.—**perder el t.,** to get out of practice, to get rusty.—**por el t.,** by the touch.—**tomar el t. a,** to investigate, look into.

tiento, tiente, *V.* TENTAR.

tiernamente, *adv.* tenderly.

tiernecico, ica, illo, illa, ito, ita, *a. dim.* of TIERNO; very tender or young.

tierno, na, *a.* tender, soft; delicate; affectionate; amiable; sensitive; recent, modern, young.—**t. de ojos,** tender-eyed.

tierra, *f.* earth; land; soil; ground; native country; region, country; lot, plot, piece of land; (elec.) ground.—**t. adentro,** inland.—**t. a t.,** (naut.) coasting; cautiously.—**t. de batán,** fuller's earth.—**t. de pan llevar,** cornland, plowland.—**T. de Promisión,** Promised Land.—**t. doblada,** broken, mountainous country.—**t. firme,** terra firma; mainland; firm, solid ground.—**t. japónica,** catechu, Japan earth.—**T. Santa,** Holy Land.—**a t.,** ashore.—**besar la t.,** (coll.) to fall flat on the ground.—**dar en t. con,** to overthrow.—**echar en t.,** (naut.) to land.—**echar por t.,** to overthrow; to ruin, destroy.—**echar t. a,** to bury in oblivion, to forget.—**en t.,** on land; ashore.—**irse a t.,** to fall down, to topple over.—**poner por t.,** to overthrow; to demolish, to tear down.—**por t.,** by land, overland.—**tomar t.,** to anchor; to land.—**venirse a t.,** = IRSE A. T.—**ver tierras,** to see the world, to travel.

tiesamente, *adv.* firmly, stiffly, strongly.

tieso, sa, *a.* stiff, hard; robust, strong; valiant; stubborn, obstinate; tight, taut; stiff, stuck up; too grave or circumspect.—**tenerse t.,** or **tenérselas tiesas,** (coll.) to be firm in one's opinion or resolution.

tieso, *adv.* = TIESAMENTE.

tiesta, *f.* (coop.) edge of headings.

tiesto, *m.* potsherd; flowerpot.

tiesura, *f.* stiffness; rigidity; harshness.

tifáceo, a, *a.* (bot.) typhaceous.

tífico, ca, *a.* (med.) typhous.

tiflitis, *f.* (med.) typhlitis.

tifo, *m.* (med.) typhus.—**t. asiático,** Asiatic cholera.—**t. de América,** yellow fever.—**t. de Oriente,** bubonic plague.

tifo, fa, *a.* (coll.) satiate.

tifoideo, dea. I. *a.* typhoid. **II.** *f.* typhoid fever.

tifón, *m.* whirlwind; typhoon.

tifus, *m.* (med.) typhus.—**t. icterodes,** yellow fever.

tigre, *m.* (zool.) tiger.

tigridia, *f.* (bot.) tigridia, tiger flower.

tija, *f.* stem of a key.

tijera, *f.* (usually in pl.) scissors; shears; carpenter's horse; cooper's mare; any instrument in the form of an X; sawbuck; small channel or drain; sheepshearer; backbiter, slanderer.—*pl.* (car.) side stringers of a truck frame; beams across a river to stop floating timber.—**buena t.,** a great eater; good cutter; detractor, gossip.—**hacer t.,** to twist the mouth (s. o. horses).

tijerada, *f.* = TIJERETADA.

tijereta, *f. dim.* (usually in pl.) small scissors; small tendril of vines; (ent.) earwig; (orn.) forktail duck.

tijeretada, *f.,* **tijeretazo,** *m.* cut with scissors, clip, snip.

tijeretear, *va.* to cut with scissors; clip; to meddle with, or mind (others' business).

tijereteo, *m.* act of clipping; snip-snap noise of scissors.

tijerilla, tijeruela, *f. dim.* small scissors; small tendril of vines.

tila, *f.* (bot.) linden tree; flower of this tree; tea of linden flowers.

tílburi, *m.* (car.) tilbury.

tildar, *va.* to cross or scratch out; to put a tilde over; to brand, stigmatize, criticize.—**t. de,** to accuse of, or charged with being (incompetent, etc.)

tilde, *f.* tilde, diacritical sign of the letter *ñ*; tittle, dash, jot, iota; bad name.

tildón, *m. aug.* dash, stroke, scratch.

tilia, *f.* (bot.) = TILO.

tiliáceo, a, (bot.) tiliaceous.

tilicnero, ra, *n.* (Am.) peddler, huckster.

tiliches, *m. pl.* (Am.) small fancy articles.

tilín, *m.* dingdon.—**hacer t.,** (coll.) to please; to become a favorite.—**tener t.,** to be winsome, attractive.

tilma, *f.* (Mex.) cloak fastened by a knot.

tilo, *m.* (bot.) linden tree.

tilla, *f.* (naut.) midship, gangway.

tillado, *m.* wooden floor.

tillar, *va.* to floor.

timador, ra, *n.* swindler.

tímalo, *m.* (icht.) grayling.

timar, *va.* to cheat, to swindle.

timba, *f.* (coll.) hand in a game of chance; (Philip.) bucket.

timbal, *m.* kettledrum. *V.* ATABAL.

timbalero, *m.* kettledrummer.

timbirimba, *f.* (coll.) hand in a game of chance.

timbrar, *va.* to stamp; to put the crest in (a coat of arms).

timbre, *m.* (her.) timber, crest; seal, stamp; call bell; timber, tone, color; glorious deed or achievement; merit.

timeleáceo, a. I. *a.* (bot.) thymelæaceous. **II.** *f. pl.* Thymelæaceæ.

timiama, *f.* a sweet perfume.

timidamente, *adv.* timidly.

timidez, *f.* timidity; chicken-heartedness.

tímido, da, *a.* timid, shy; faint-hearted.

timo, *m.* (icht.) grayling; (coll.) cheat, swindle.—**dar un t.,** to swindle.

timocracia, *f.* (pol.) timocracy.

timocrático, ca, *a.* (pol.) timocratic.

timol, *m.* (chem.) thymol.

timón, *m.* beam of a plow; pole of a coach; stick of a rocket; (naut.) helm; rudder.—**t. de profundidad,** (aer.) elevator.

timonear, *va.& vn.* (naut.) to helm; to steer.

timonel, *m.* (naut.) helmsman, steersman.

timonera, *f.* (naut.) pilot house, wheelhouse; (orn.) rectrix, large quill.

timonero, *m.* helmsman, steersman.

timorato, ta, *a.* God-fearing; timorous, chicken-hearted, pusilanimous.

timpa, *f.* bar of iron in a furnace hearth.

timpánico, ca, *a.* (anat.) tympanic.

timpanillo, *m. dim.* small kettledrum; small tympanum or tympan; (print.) inner tympan; (arch.) gablet.

timpanítico, ca, *a.* (med.) tympanitic.

timpanitis, *f.* (med.) tympanitis.

tímpano, *m.* kettledrum; (anat.) tympanum, eardrum; (print.) tympan; (arch.) tympan or tympanum, pediment.

tina, *f.* large earthen jar; vat; tub; bathtub.

tinaco, *m.* wooden trough, tub, or vat.

tinada, *f.* woodpile; shed for cattle.

tinado, tinador, *m.* shed for cattle.

tinaja, *f.* large earthen jar; (Philip.) a liquid measure (about 12⅔ gal.).—**tinajería,** *f.* place where large earthen jars are kept or sold.

tinajero, ra. I. *n.* maker or seller of earthen water jars. **II.** *m.* stand or cabinet for earthen water jars; (Mex.) water hole, pothole.—**tinajita, uela,** *f. dim.* small earthen water jar.—**tinajón,** *m. aug.* very large earthen water jar, or tank.

tíndalo, *m.* (Philip.) tindalo, a hardwood tree.

tinelar, *a.* pertaining to the TINELO.

tinelero, ra, *n.* keeper of the servants' room.

tinelo, *m.* servants' dining room.

tineta, *f. dim.* kit, small tub.

tinge, *m.* (orn.) a kind of black owl.

tingladillo, *m.* (naut.) clinker work.

tinglado, *m.* shed, shed roof; temporary board floor; inclined plane for draining sugar; trick, machination, intrigue.

tingle, *f.* glaziers' lead opener.

tinicla, *f.* (arm.) sort of hauberk.

tiniebla, *f.* (gen. *pl.*) darkness; (eccl.) tenebræ.

tinillo, *m.* tank for collecting must.

tino, *m.* skill in discovering things by the touch; steady and accurate aim; judgment, tact, knack; recipient, vat; tank; wine press.—**a buen t.,** at guesswork.—**sacar de t.,** to astound, confound, exasperate.

tinta, *f.* ink; tint, hue, color; process of dyeing.—*pl.* (art) colors prepared for painting.—**t. china,** India ink.—**t. de imprenta,** printing ink.—**t. simpática,** invisible ink.—**de buena t.,** from, or on, good authority.

tintar, *va.* to tinge, to dye.

tinte, *m.* dyeing, staining; tint, tinge, hue; paint, color, stain; dye; dyer's shop; palliation, cloak, color.

tinterillada, *f.* chicane, trickery, tricky procedure.

tinterillo, *m. dim.* small inkstand; (coll.) pettifogger.

tintero, *m.* inkstand, inkwell; (print.) ink fountain, ink table.—**dejar, dejarse,** or **quedársele a uno, en el t.,** (coll.) to forget.

tintilla, *f.* rota wine.

tintillo, *m. dim.* light-colored wine.

tintín, tintineo, *m.* clink, chink.

tintirintín, *m.* sharp sound of a trumpet.

tinto, ta, *a.* red (wine); dyed, tinged.

tintóreo, rea, *a.* tinctorial.

tintorería, *f.* dyer's shop.

tintorero, ra. I. *n.* dyer. **II.** *f.* (Am.) (icht.) female shark.

tintura, *f.* tincture; tint, color; stain, spot; dyeing; dye; rouge; smattering.

tinturar, *va.* to tinge, to dye; to tincture; to teach superficially.

tiña, *f.* (med.) scald head, ringworm of the scalp, favus; (api.) small spider that injures beehives; (coll.) want, indigence; niggardliness, stinginess.

tiñería, *f.* (coll.) poverty; stinginess.

tiñoso, sa, *a.* scabby, scurvy; penurious; niggardly, stingy, mean.

tiño, él tiñó, yo tiña. *V.* TEÑIR.

tiñuela, *f.* CUSCUTA; (naut.) shipworm.

tío, *m.* uncle; (coll.) good old man; fellow, guy.

tiocol, *m.* (chem.) thiocol.

tiorba, *f.* (mus.) theorbo, large lute.

tiovivo, *m.* carrousel, merry-go-round.

tipa, *f.* (Am.) a hardwood tree.

típico, ca, *a.* typical, characteristic.

tiple. I. *m.* (mus.) treble, soprano voice; a kind of small guitar; (naut.) mast of a single piece. **II.** *n.* soprano singer.

tiplisonante, *a.* (coll.) treble-toned.

tipo, *m.* type, pattern; standard, model, figure; (print.) type; (zool.) class; (coll.) fellow, guy.

tipografía, *f.* printing; printing shop; typography, typesetting.—**tipográfico, ca,** *a.* typographical.—**tipógrafo,** *m.* typographer; typesetter.

tipómetro, *m.* (print.) type gauge, type measure; typometer.

tipoy, *m.* (S. A.) a chemise-like garment.

típula, *f.* crane fly, daddy longlegs.

tiquín, *m.* (Philip.) bamboo pole used as an oar.

tiquismiquis, *m. pl.* ridiculous or affected scruples or words.

tiquistiquis, *m.* (Philip.) bitterwood tree.

tira, *f.* strip; stripe; (naut.) fall.—*pl.* (law) clerks' fees in appeal causes.

tirabala, *m.* popgun.

tirabeque, *m.* (agr.) tender peas.

tirabotas, *f.* boot hook.

tirabraguero, *m.* (surg.) truss.

tirabuzón, *m.* corkscrew; hair-curl.

tiracol, tiracuello, *m.* (mil.) sword belt.

tirada, *f.* cast, throw; distance; stretch; lapse of time; (print.) edition, issue; presswork.—**t. aparte,** reprint (of an article in pamphlet form).—**de una t.,** or **en una t.,** at one stretch.

tiradera, *f.* long Indian arrow; (sad.) trace.

tiradero, *m.* shooting post, place to shoot from.

tirado, da. I. *a.* long and low (ship); very cheap, given away. **II.** *m.* wiredrawing; (print.) presswork.

tirador, ra, *n.* thrower; drawer; sharpshooter; marksman, good shot; (mech.) lift, handle, pull, button, knob; bell pull; (print.) pressman.—**t. de oro,** gold-wire drawer.

tirafondo, *m.* (surg.) ball extractor; (carp.) wood screw.

tiralíneas, *m.* ruling pen.

tiramiento, *m.* tension, stretching.

tiramira, *f.* long, narrow ridge of mountains; long series or string of things.

tiramollar, *va.* (naut.) to ease off, to slacken.—**t. un aparejo,** to overhaul a tackle.

tirana, *f.* a Spanish song.

tiranamente, *adv.* tyrannically.—**tiranía,** *f.* tyranny.—**tiránicamente,** *adv.* tyrannically.

tiranicida, *n.* tyrannicide (murderer).

tiranicidio, *m.* tyrannicide (murder).

tiránico, ca, *a.* tyrannical.—**tiranización,** *f.* tyrannizing.—**tiranizadamente,** *adv.* tyrannically.—**tiranizar,** *va.* (*pret.* TIRANICÉ; *subj.* TIRANICE) to tyrannize.

tiranizar, *va.* (*pret.* TIRANICÉ; *subj.* TIRANICE) to tyrannize.

tirano, na. I. *a.* tyrannical. **II.** *n.* tyrant.

tirante. I. *a.* drawing, pulling; drawn, taut, stretched; strained (as relations); urgent, pressing. **II.** *m.* (sad.) trace, gear; (eng.) brace, stay

rod, tie rod, truss rod; (carp.) (9 x 13) mm. board.
—*pl.* suspenders, braces.—**a tirantes largos,** four-in-hand.

tirantez, *f.* tenseness, tightness; stretch; strain; distance in a straight line between the ends of a thing.

tiranuelo, la, *m. & f. dim.* little tyrant.

tirapié, *m.* shoemaker's stirrup.

tirar. I. *va.* to throw, cast, fling, pitch (as a ball); to cast off, throw away (as a garment); to fire, shoot, discharge (as a gun); to draw, to pull, stretch (as wire); to draw (a line); to misspend, squander; to give (as a kick); (print.) to print.—**t. coces,** to kick; to rebel.—**tirarla de,** to set up as.—**t. un cañonazo,** to fire a gun. **II.** *vn.* to draw, pull; direct one's course, turn (in some direction); to get along, pull through; to incline, tend; (w. a) to resemble, have a shade of (color); approach; to try to, aim at, aspire to.—**t. al blanco,** to shoot at a target.—**t. de largo,** or **por largo,** to spend lavishly; to make a liberal estimate, to estimate rather high than low.—**tira y afloja,** give and take; fast and loose; blowing hot and cold. **III.** *vr.* to throw one's self; to abandon one's self (to grief, vice, etc.)

tirela, *f.* striped stuff.

tireta, *f.* lace, latch, thong.

tirica, ita, *f. dim.* small stripe.

tirilla, *f.* (sew.) neckband of a shirt.

tirio, ria, *a.* Tyrian.—**tirios y troyanos,** opposing factions.

tiritaña, *f.* a thin silk fabric; trifle.

tiritar, *vn.* to shiver.—**tiritón,** *m.* (coll.) shivering, chill.—**tiritona,** *f.* (coll.) shivering, especially affected.

tiro, *m.* cast, throw, shot, fling; mark made by a throw; (arti.) piece of ordnance; firing, shot, discharge (of a firearm); report (of a gun); target practice; shooting grounds; shooting gallery; range; charge, shot; team of draught animals; harness trace; hoisting rope; length of a piece of drygoods; landing of a stairway; theft; prank, imposition; serious physical or moral injury; (min.) shaft; depth of a shaft; draught of a chimney.—*pl.* sword belts.—**t. al blanco,** target shooting.—**t. directo,** fire at a visible target.—**t. indirecto,** indirect fire.—**t. rasante,** horizontal fire.—**a t. de ballesta,** a long way off; at a glance.—**a t. de piedra,** within a stone's throw.—**de t.,** draft (horse).—**de tiros largos,** in full dress, in full regalia.—**errar el t.,** to miss the mark; to be mistaken.—**hacer un t.,** to fire a shot.—**hacer un tiro a,** to shoot at, have a shot at.

tirocinio, *m.* apprenticeship.

tiroideo, a, *a.,* **tiroides,** *m.* (anat.) thyroid.

tiroiditis, *f.* thyroiditis.

tirolés, sa. I. *n. & a.* Tyrolian. **II.** *m.* peddler, huckster in toys and tinware.

tirón, *m.* tyro, novice; pull, haul, tug; effort.—**de un t.,** at once, at one stroke.—**ni a dos tirones,** not easily obtained or carried out.

tirona, *f.* fishing net, seine.

tiroriro, *m.* (coll.) sound of a reed instrument.—*pl.* (coll.) reed instruments.

tirotear, *vn. & vr.* to exchange shots, to skirmish.

tiroteo, *m.* skirmish.

tirreno, na, *n. & a.* Thyrrhenian; Etruscan.

tirria, *f.* (coll.) aversion, dislike, grudge.

tirso, *m.* thyrsus.

tisana, *f.* ptisan, medical tea.

tisanuro, ra. I. *n. & a.* thysanuran. **II.** *m. pl.* Thysanura.

tísico, ca, *n. & a.* (med.) consumptive.

tisis, *f.* (med.) tuberculosis, consumption.

tisú, *m.* gold or silver tissue.

tisuria, *f.* (med.) debility from excessive secretion of urine.

titanato, *m.* (chem.) titanate.

titánico, ca, *a.* Titanic; gigantic, colossal, immense; (chem.) titanic.

titanio, nia. I. *a.* Titanic. **II.** *m.* (chem.) titanium.

títere, *m.* puppet; whipster, insignificant fellow.—*pl.* Punch-and-Judy show; pantomime.—**no de-**

jar, or **quedar, t. con cabeza,** to cut to pieces, to destroy or be destroyed entirely, to leave nothing or nobody, to tell the tale.

titerero, ra, *m.* = TITIRITERO.

titeretada, *f.* mean trick.

titerista, *n.* = TITIRITERO.

tití, *m.* titi, a very small monkey.

titiaro, *a. V.* CAMBUR.

titilación, *f.* tremor; twinkle.—**titilador, ra; titilante,** *a.* trembling; twinkling.—**titilar,** *vr.* to tremble; to twinkle.

titímalo, *m.* (bot.) spurge.

titirimundi, *m.* = MUNDONUEVO.

titiritaina, *f.* (coll.) confused noise of flutes; noisy merriment.

titiritero, *m.* puppet player, puppet-show man.

tito, *m.* (bot.) a kind of chick-pea.

titubeante, *a.* tottering; hesitating.

titubear, *vn.* to totter (as walls); to toddle (as a child); to stagger, reel; to stutter; to hesitate.—**titubeo,** *m.* tottering; toddling; wavering, hesitation.

titulado, *pp. & a.* titled; so-called; entitled.

titular. I. *va.* to title, entitle, name, call. **II.** *vn.* to obtain a title from a sovereign. **III.** *vr.* to call or style one's self. **IV.** *a.* titular, titulary; nominal; (print.) titular (type).

titulillo, *m. dim.* petty title; (print.) page heading or title, running title.—**andar en titulillos,** to stick to, or insist on, trifles and trivial forms.

título, *m.* title; heading, headline, caption; inscription; sign; titled person; soubriquet; qualification, merit, desert; claim; foundation of a claim, privilege or right; (law) legal title to property; diploma; patent; credential, license; professional degree; cause, reason, pretext; (com.) certificate, bond.—**t. al portador,** bond payable to bearer.—**t. nominativo,** registered bond.—**t. translativo de dominio,** (law) deed, conveyance.—**títulos de la deuda,** Government bonds.—**a t.,** on pretense, under pretext.

tiza, *f.* chalk; clay; calcined stag's horn; whiting.

tizna, *f.* substance for staining or blackening.

tiznadura, *f.* smudginess, smuttiness.

tiznajo, *m.* (coll.) smut, smudge, stain.

tiznar, *va.* to smut, smudge, begrime, stain; to tarnish.

tizne, *m.* or *f.* soot, coal smut, grime; stain.

tiznón, *m.* large smut, smutch, smear, or stain.

tizo, *m.* half-burnt charcoal.

tizón, *m.* brand, firebrand; (agr.) wheat crust, blight, stinking smut; stain, disgrace; (arch.) header.—**a t.,** as a header.

tizona, *f.* (coll.) sword.

tizonada, *f.* **tizonazo,** *m.* stroke with a firebrand; (coll.) hell fire.—**tizoncillo,** *m. dim.* small burning coal.—**tizonear,** *vn.* to stir up a fire.

tizonera, *f.* heap of half-burnt charcoal.

tizonero, *m.* fire poker.

tlaco, *m.* (Mex.) eighth part of a Spanish silver shilling.

tlascalteca, *n. & a.* of or from Tlascala.

tlazol, tlazole, *m.* (Mex.) fodder of maize tops.

¡to! *interj.* used to call a dog.

toa, *f.* (Am.) rope, hawser.

toalla, *f.* towel; pillow sham.—**t. afelpada,** Turkish towel.

toalleta, *f. dim.* napkin; small towel.

toar, *va.* (naut.) = ATOAR.

toba, *f.* calcareous tufa, travertin, calc-sinter; (bot.) cotton thistle; (dent.) tophus, tartar.

toballa, *f.* towel.

tobar, *m.* tufa quarry.

toballeta, tobelleta, *f.* napkin.

tobera, *f.* tewel, tuyère (of a blast furnace).

tobillo, *m.* ankle.

tobogán, *m.* toboggan.

toca, *f.* hood, coif, bonnet, wimple, toque, head-dress; thin fabric for toques.

tocado, da. I. *a. & pp.* touched, felt; contaminated, tainted; infected.—**estar t. de,** to have the symptoms or beginning of.—**estar t. de la cabeza,**

to be of unsound mind. **II.** *m.* coiffure, headdress, headgear; toilet.—**t. de monja,** nun's wimple.

tocador, ra. I. *n.* one who touches; (mus.) player, performer. **II.** *m.* kerchief for the head; dressing table, bureau; dressing room, boudoir; dressing case; (prov.) tuning key.

tocadura, *f.* coiffure, headgear; sore.

tocamiento, *m.* touch, contact, handling; supernatural inspiration.

tocante, *a.* touching.—**t. a,** respecting, concerning, as regards, with regard to.

tocar. I. *va.* (*pret.* TOQUÉ: *subj.* TOQUE) to touch, lay hands on, feel with the hand; play (an instrument); to toll, ring (a bell); to hit, knock, strike, rap, tap; to try (metals) on a touchstone; magnetize; to reap or find out (as by experience); to touch upon; to inspire, move, persuade; communicate or infect; to comb and dress (the hair) with ornaments.—**t. de cerca,** to be closely related; know well from actual practice or experience; to concern, affect closely.—**t. fondo,** to strike ground.—**t. la diana,** (mil.) to beat the reveille.—**t. la generala,** (mil.) to beat the general.—**a toca teja,** (coll.) with ready money, cash down. **II.** *vn.* to touch; appertain, belong; behoove, concern; to be one's turn; to fall to one's share or lot; to touch, be contiguous; to stop (during a voyage); to be allied or related.—**t. a la bomba,** (naut.) to ring for pumping ship.—**t. a la puerta,** to rap at the door.—**t. en un puerto,** (naut.) to touch at a port. **III.** *vr.* (coll.) to be covered, to put on the hat; to comb and arrange the hair; to wimple.

tocasalva, *f.* tray or rack for glasses.

tocata, *f.* (mus.) toccata; (coll.) drubbing.

tocayo, ya, *n.* namesake.

tocía, *f.* tutty. *V.* TUCIA.

tocinero, ra. I. *n.* pork seller. **II.** *f.* table for salting pork.—**tocinería,** *f.* shop or stall where pork and bacon are sold.

tocino, *m.* bacon; salt pork.—**t. del cielo,** confection of eggs and sirup.—**t. gordo,** fat pork.

tocio, cia, *a.* low, dwarfy (oak tree).

toco, *m.* a kind of rectangular niche in old Peruvian architecture.

tocología, *f.* tocology.—**tocólogo, ga,** *n.* tocologist.

tocón, *m.* stump of a tree, of an arm or leg.

toconal, *m.* olive yard planted with stumps.

tocororo, *m.* (orn.) tocororo, a Cuban trogon.

tocotoco, *m.* (Ven.) pelican.

tocuyo, *m.* (S. A.) shirtings, sheetings.

tochedad, *f.* boorishness, rusticity.

tochimbo, *m.* (Peru) blast furnace.

tocho, cha. I. *a.* clownish, rustic, uncouth; unpolished, homespun. **II.** *m.* pole; (found.) bloom, billet.

tochura, *f.* = TOCHEDAD.

todabuena, todasana, *f.* (bot.) St. John's-wort.

todavía, *adv.* still; yet; even.—**t.no,** not yet.

todito, ta, *a.* (coll.) the whole (emphatic, as, *todito el día,* the whole day long).

todo, da. I. *a. & n.* all, the whole, every, each. —**t. aquel que,** whoever.—**t. aquello que,** whatever.—**t. el que,** whoever, all that, all who. —**todos los,** every.—**todos los que,** all who, all those that. **II.** *m.* all; whole; everybody; everything.—*pl.* everybody; all.—**ante t.,** first of all, in the first place.—**a t.,** at most.—**con t.,** notwithstanding, nevertheless, however.—**del t.,** entirely, wholly.—**en t. y por t.,** wholly, in every way.—**en un t.,** together, in all its parts. —**jugar el t. por el t.,** to stake or risk all.—**me es t. uno,** it is all one to me.—**ser el t.,** to be the principal, chief, or whole thing.—**sobre t.,** above all, especially. **III.** *adv.* entirely, totally.

todopoderoso, sa, *a.* all-powerful, almighty.

toesa, *f.* toise.

tofana, *f.* aqua Tofana (poison).

tofo, *m.* (vet.) tumor.

toga, *f.* Roman toga; judicial robe or gown; dignity of a superior judge.

togado, da, *a.* togaed, togated.

toisón, toisón de oro, *m.* Golden Fleece.

tojal, *m.* clump or furze or whin.

tojino, *m.* (naut.) notch, knob; cleat.

tojo, *m.* (bot.) whin, furze.

tojosa, *f.* (Cuba) (orn.) a variety of pigeon.

tola, *f.* (S. A.) Indian mound.

tolano, *m.* (vet.) tumor in horses' gums.—*pl.* (coll.) short hair on the neck.

toldadura, *f.* awning, hanging.

toldar, *va.* to cover with awning or hanging.

toldería, *f.* (S. A.) Indian camp.

toldero, ra, *n.* retailer of salt.

toldilla, *f.* (naut.) roundhouse.

toldillo, *m.* *dim.* small awning; covered sedan chair.

toldo, *m.* awning, tilt; ostentation, pomp; (S. A.) Indian hut; tent.

tole, *m.* hubbub, clamor, outcry.—**tomar el t.,** (coll.) to run away, to flee.

toledano, na, *n. & a.* Toledan.

toledo, *m.* (C. A.) a song bird.

tolerable, *a.* tolerable, bearable; permissible.

tolerablemente, *adv.* tolerably.

tolerancia, *f.* toleration, permission; tolerance, indulgence; allowance, permissible discrepancy or variation.

tolerante, *a.* tolerant.—**tolerantismo,** *m.* doctrine of the freedom of worship.

tolerar, *vn.* to tolerate, endure, suffer, permit; to be indulgent, to overlook.

tolete, *m.* (naut.) thole, tholepin; (Am.) club, cudgel; (Colomb.) a kind of large rough boat or canoe.

tolmera, *f.* ground where TOLMOS abound.

tolmo, *m.* isolated pillarlike rock.

tolo, tolondro, *m.* bump from a blow.—**a topa tolondro,** rashly, recklessly.

tolondro, dra; tolondrón, na, *a.* giddy, harebrained; reckless, rash.

tolondrón, *m.* = TOLONDRO.—**a tolondrones,** with contusions or bruises; precipitately, giddily, by fits and starts.

tolteca, *n. & a.* Toltec.

tolueno, *m.* (chem.) toluene.

tolúico, ca, *a.* (chem.) toluic.

toluidina, *f.* (chem.) toluidine.

tolva, *f.* hopper, chute.

tolvanera, *f.* cloud of dust.

tolla, *f.* moss-covered bog; (Cuba) canoe-shaped trough.

tolladar, *m.* = ATOLLADERO.

tollina, *f.* (coll.) cudgeling.

tollo, *m.* (icht.) spotted dogfish; blind (for hunting); quagmire, bog; loin of a stag.

tollón, *m.* narrow passage, gorge.

toma, *f.* taking; take, receiving; (mil.) capture, seizure; dose of medicine; (hyd.) intake; tap of a water main or electric wire; (print.) take.

¡toma! *interj.* well, why, of course.

tomadero, *m.* handle, haft; tap, inlet.

tomador, ra, *n. & a.* taker (-ing), receiver (-ing); drinker (-ing); (*m.*) drawee.—*pl.* (naut.) ropebands, gaskets.

tomadura, *f.* catch, seizure, gripe, hold, grasp, capture; portion of a thing taken at once.

tomaína, *f.* ptomaine.

tomajón, na, *n.* (coll.) one who takes frequently or accepts easily.

tomar. I. *va.* to take; to drink, to eat; to contract, acquire (as a habit); to steal, take by stealth; follow, imitate, ape; to cover (the female); (in ball games) to call a halt in the throwing of (the ball).—**t. a broma,** to take as a joke.—**t. a cuestas,** to carry on one's back; to take upon one's self; to take charge of.—**t. a pechos,** to take to heart; undertake with too much zeal.—**t. calor,** to get warm.—**t. cuentas,** to audit accounts, to take and examine accounts.—**t. el fresco,** to take the air.—**t. el pelo a,** (coll.) to banter, make fun of. —**t. el sol,** to take a sun bath.—**t. entre cejas,** to take a dislike to, get a grudge against.—**t. estado,** to change condition; to marry; to become a clergyman; to take the black veil.—**t. frío,** to catch cold. —**t. fuerzas,** to gather strength.—**t. la borla, to**

graduate.—**tomarla con**, to oppose, antagonize; to have a grudge against.—**t. la delantera**, to excel; to get ahead; to go at the head.—**t. la mañana**, (Cuba) to take a morning drink.—**t. la puerta**, to go out of the house; be off.—**t. las de Villadiego**, to show a clean pair of heels, "to beat it."—**t. lengua**, or **lenguas**, to take tidings or signs.—**t. por su cuenta**, to take charge of, to attend to personally.—**t. razón**, to take a memorandum. **II.** *vn.* to take; to drink (liquor).—**t. por**, to turn to (the right, left),-or into; to take, follow (a road, etc.). **III.** *vr.* to take; to get rusty (as metals).—**t. con**, to pick a quarrel with.—**t. del vino**, to become intoxicated, to get drunk.

tomatada, *f.* fried tomatoes.

tomatal, *m.* tomato patch or field.

tomate, *m.* tomato.

tomatera, *f.* tomato plant.

tomatero, ra, *n.* tomato raiser or seller.

tomento, *m.* coarse tow; (bot.) tomentum.

tomentoso, sa, *a.* (bot.) tomentose, tomentous.

tomiento, *m.* = TOMENTO.

tomillar, *m.* bed of thyme.

tomillo, *m.* (bot.) thyme.—**t. salsero**, (bot.) sweet marjoram.

tomín, *m.* tomin, third part of a drachm, Spanish weight; (Am.) a silver coin.

tominejo, ja, *n.* (orn.) humming bird.

tomismo, *m.* Thomism.

tomista, *n. & a.* Thomist (-ic).

tomiza, *f.* bass rope.

tomo, *m.* volume, tome; bulk; importance, value, consequence.—**de t. y lomo**, of weight and bulk; of importance.

tomón, na, *a.* fond of taking.

ton, *m.*—**sin t. ni son**, without rhyme or reason.

tonada, *f.* tune, song.—**tonadica**, *f. dim.* short tune or song.—**tonadilla**, *f. dim.* (theat.) musical interlude.—**tonadillero**, *m.* writer of TONADILLAS.

tonalidad, *f.* (mus.) tonality.

tonante, *a.* thundering (Jupiter).

tonar, *vn.* to thunder.

tonca, *f.* (bot.) tonka bean.

tondino, *m.* (arch.) astragal.

tondo, *m.* (arch.) round molding.

tonel, *m.* cask, barrel; tun, pipe, butt; (naut.) an ancient measure of ships ($\frac{1}{3}$ ton).—**t. macho**, ton.

tonelada, *f.* ton; an ancient tonnage duty.—**t. de arqueo**, ton of capacity.—**t. de desplazamiento**, ton of displacement.—**t. de registro**, register ton.—**t. métrica**, metric ton, tonne.

tonelaje, *m.* tonnage, displacement; (com.) tonnage dues.

tonelería, *f.* cooperage, coopering; barrels or casks collectively; watercasks for a ship.

tonelero, *m.* cooper, hooper.—**tonelete**, *m. dim.* little butt or barrel; short skirt, kilt.

tonga, *f.* (bot.) tonka bean.

tonga, tongada, *f.* couch; tier, layer, stratum; lay, row, ledge, flake.

tongo, *m.* trick of a player or jockey, to lose for a bribe; "throwing it."

tónico, ca. I. *a.* tonic, strengthening; (gram.) accented or inflected. **II.** *m.* tonic. **III.** *f.* (mus.) keynote, tonic.

tonificador, ra; tonificante, *a.* tonic, strengthening.

tonificar, *va.* = ENTONAR.

tonillo, *m.* singsong, monotonous tone.

tonina, *f.* fresh tunny; (icht.) dolphin.

tono, *m.* tone; tune; (med.) tone, vigor, strength; (mus.) tone; key, key tone; pitch; moving piece in a brass instrument, which modifies the tone; deportment, manner, social address; conceit.—**dar el t.**, to set the standard.—**darse t.**, to put on airs.—**gente del buen tono**, smart set.

tonsila, *f.* (anat.) tonsil.—**tonsilar**, *a.* tonsillar.

tonsilitis, *f.* (med.) tonsilitis.

tonsura, *f.* hair cutting; shearing, fleecing; (eccl.) tonsure.—**tonsurado**, *pp. & a.* tonsured.

tonsurar, *va.* to cut the hair of; to shear, fleece; (eccl.) to tonsure.

tontada, *f.* nonsense; silliness, foolishness.

tontaina, *n.* fool, dolt.—**tontamente**, *adv.* foolishly, stupidly.—**tontear**, *vn.* to talk nonsense, to act foolishly; to fool.

tontedad, tontera, tontería, *f.* foolishness, silliness, nonsense.

tontillo, *m.* hoop skirt; bustle.

tontina, *f.* (com.) tontine.

tontivano, na, *a.* foolishly conceited.

tonto, ta. I. *a.* silly, foolish, stupid. **II.** *n.* fool, dunce, dolt.—**t. de capirote**, blockhead, great fool, idiot.—**hacerse el t.**, to play the fool.

tontuelo, la, *a.* & *n. dim.* little fool.

tontuna, *f.* foolishness.

toña, *f.* tip cart; bat for the game.

toñil, *m.* straw on which fruit is laid to ripen.

toñina, *f.* fresh tunny fish.

¡top! *interj.* (naut.) hold! stop!

topacio, *m.* topaz.

topada, *f.* butt.

topadizo, za, *a.* (coll.) = ENCONTRADIZO.

topador, ra, *n.* butter, one that butts.

topar. I. *va.* to collide with, to run into or against; to meet with by chance; to find, run across; (naut.) to butt, abut, join. **II.** *vn.* to collide, butt, strike; at cards, to accept a bet; to depend (on), consist (in); to meet (with); to succeed, come out right.—**tope donde tope**, (coll.) strike where it will.

toparca, *m.* toparch, petty ruler.

toparquía, *f.* toparchy, petty state.

tope, *m.* butt, projecting part or end; top, summit; (mech.) stop, stop collar, stop plate; (r. w.) buffer; butt, collision, knock, bump; rub, difficulty; obstacle; scuffle, quarrel; (naut.) masthead, topmast head; butt end of a plank; topman.—**a t., o al t.**, butt and butt; butt (joint).—**hasta el t.**, or **los topes**, up to the top, or the brim.

topera, *f.* molehole.

topetada, *f.* butt, by a horned animal; (coll.) bump, bumping.—**topetar**, *vn.* to butt; (w. **con**) to bump, strike, or knock (against); to meet by chance, run across.—**topetazo, topetón**, *m.* butt, knock, bump, blow, encounter, collision.—**topetón**, *m.* = TOPETADA.—**topetudo, da**, *a.* butting.

tópico, ca. I. *a.* topical. **II.** *m.* (med.) topical application; (rhet.) topic, subject.

topil, *m.* (Mex.) constable.

topinada, *f.* (coll.) awkwardness, clumsiness.

topinaria, *f.* (surg.) talpa, wen.

topinera, *f.* molehole; molehill.

topo, *m.* (zool.) mole; talpa; (coll.) awkward person; dunce, dolt; (C. A.) one league and a half.

topocho, cha, *a.* (Ven.) plump, fatty.

topografía, *f.* topography; surveying.

topográficamente, *adv.* topographically.

topográfico, ca, *a.* topographical.

topógrafo, *m.* topographer; surveyor.

toque, *m.* touch, act of touching; peal, ringing (of bells); (mil.) call; assay, touch, test (of metals); touchstone; trial, proof; aid, divine inspiration; point, gist, purport; (coll.) tap on a person; (art) fine stroke of the brush.—**t. de cornetas**, bugle call.—**t. de diana**, reveille.—**t. del alba**, bell ringing at daybreak.—**t. de luz**, light in a picture.—**t. de retreta**, tattoo.—**t. de tambor**, beat of a drum.—**dar un t. a**, to put to the test; to pump, throw out a feeler to.

toqueado, *m.* rhythmical noise by clapping of hands, stamping of feet, rapping with canes, etc.

toquería, *f.* collection of women's headdresses; business of making TOCAS.

toquero, ra, *n.* veil maker; headdress maker.

toqui, *m.* (Ch.) Indian chief.

toquilla, *f. dim.* small headdress, bonnet or cap; hat band or ribbon; small triangular kerchief used by women on the head or neck; woollen knit shawl.

tora, *f.* figure of a bull in artificial fireworks; Jewish family tribute; Torah (Hebrew Pentateuch).

torácico, ca, *a.* (anat.) thoracic.

torada, *f.* drove of bulls.

toral. I. *a.* main, principal. **II.** *m.* unbleached yellow wax; (found.); mold for copper bars; copper bar.

tórax, *m.* (anat.) thorax.

torbellino, *m.* whirlwind; rush, avalanche; vortex; (coll.) lively, hustling, restless person.

torca, *f.* cavern in mountains.

torcal, *m.* place where there are caves.

torcaz, torcaza, *f.* wild pigeon.

torce, *f.* twine of a chain around the neck.

torcecuello, *m.* (orn.) wryneck.

torcedero, ra. I. *a.* twisted. **II.** *m.* twisting mill.

torcedor, ra, *m.* twister, thread frame, twisting mill; anything that causes displeasure or grief. —**t. de tabaco,** cigar maker.

torcedura, *f.* twisting; sprain; small wine.

torcer. I. *va.* (*ind.* TUERZO: *subj.* TUERZA) to twist, twine, wind (as strands); to bend, deflect; to sprain (as a foot); to pervert (as justice); to distort, pervert, misconstrue; to dissuade, induce to change one's mind. **II.** *vn.* to turn (to right or left). **III.** *vr.* to become dislocated or sprained; to go crooked or astray; to turn sour (wine); to cheat.

torcida, *f.* wick, lamp wick; daily ration to the grinder in oil mills.

torcidamente, *adv.* obliquely, tortuously, crookedly.

torcidillo, *m.* twist silk.

torcido, da. I. *a.* & *pp.* twisted, twined; oblique, tortuous, crooked, bent. —**estar t. con uno,** to be on bad terms with one. **II.** *m.* twist of candid fruit; twisted silk, twist; (prov.) light, bad wine.

torcijón, *m.* gripes.

torcimiento, *m.* twist, twisting; sprain; entwining, winding; deflection, bend, warp, circumlocution or periphrasis.

torculado, da, *a.* screwed, screw-shaped.

tórculo, *m.* small press; rolling press.

tordella, *f.* (orn.) a kind of large thrush.

tórdiga, *f.* strip of leather.

tordillo, lla, llejo, ja, *a.* grayish, grizzled.

tordo, da. I. *a.* dapple, gray. **II.** *m.* (orn.) thrush, throstle.—**t. de agua,** (orn.) reed thrush. —**t. loco,** (orn.) solitary thrush.

toreador, *m.* bullfighter.

torear. I. *vn.* to fight bulls in the ring; to let a bull to cows. **II.** *va.* to fight (bulls); to banter, to provoke, irritable. —**toreo,** *m.* bullfighting.—

torera, *f.* tight, unbuttoned jacket.—**torería,** *f.* (Cuba) boys' pranks; office of bullfighter.—**torero, ra. I.** *a.* pertaining to bullfighting. **II.** *m.* bullfighter.

torés, *m.* (arch.) torus

torete, *m.* *dim.* bullock; (coll.) puzzle, difficult matter; absorbing topic of conversation.

toréutico, ca, *a.* (art) toreutic.

torga, *f.* yoke for dogs or hogs.

toril, *m.* pen for bulls before the fight.

torillo, *m.* *dim.* little bull; dowel, dowel pin; (anat.) raphe.

torio, *m.* (chem.) thorium.

toriondez, *f.* rut of cattle.

toriondo, da, *a.* rutting (as cows).

torloroto, *m.* shepherd's pipe or flute.

tormagal, *m.***, tormellera,** *f.* place abounding in tors.

tormenta, *f.* storm, tempest; hurricane; reverse, misfortune; heated discussion.

tormentario, ria, *a.* (arti.) projectile.

tormentila, *f.* (bot.) tormentil, septfoil.

tormentín, *m.* (naut.) jib boom.

tormento, *m.* torment, torture; rack; (mil.) battering ordnance.—**dar t.,** to torture, put to the rack.

tormentoso, sa, *a.* stormy, boisterous, turbulent; (naut.) laboring hard.

tormo, *m.* tor, isolated steep rock.

torna, *f.* restitution, devolution; return; tap or drain.—*pl.* return, requital, recompense, restitution; coarse straw.

tornaboda, *f.* day after a wedding.

tornachile, *m.* (Mex.) thick pepper.

tornada, *f.* return from a journey; revisit; (poet.) envoy, l'envoi.

tornadera, *f.* two-pronged winnowing fork.

tornadizo, za, *n.* turncoat, deserter.

tornado, *m.* tornado.

tornadura, *f.* devolution, return; requital, recompense.

tornaguía, *f.* (com.) landing certificate.

tornamiento, *m.* turn, alteration, change.

tornapunta, *f.* (arch.) chock, wedge, shoe; stay, prop, shore, brace.

tornar. I. *va.* to return; restore; to turn (as one's brain); to change, alter.—**t. las espaldas,** to turn a cold shoulder. **II.** *vn.* to return, come back: to repeat, do again.—**t. por,** to defend, to protect. **III.** *vr.* (w. en) to change (into), to become.

tornasol, *m.* (bot.) sunflower; changeable or shot color; litmus.—**tornasolado, da,** *a.* changeable, shot (fabrics); iridescent.—**tornasolar,** *va.* to cause changes in the color of, to make iridescent.

tornátil, *a.* turned (in a lathe); changeable.

tornatrás, *n.* half-breed.

tornavía, *f.* (r. w.) turntable.

tornaviaje, *m.* return trip.

tornavirón, *m.* slap, box.

tornavoz, *m.* sounding board.

torneador, ra, *n.* turner; tilter at tournaments.

torneadura, *f.* lathe shavings.

torneante, *a.* tilting at tournaments.

tornear. I. *va.* to turn (in a lathe). **II.** *vn.* to turn (in a lathe); to make a turn, go around, wind round about; to tilt at tournaments; to meditate, muse.

torneo, *m.* tournament; contest.

tornera, *f.* doorkeeper of a nunnery.

tornería, *f.* turning; turnery.

tornero, *m.* turner; maker of lathes; messenger of a nunnery.

tornillero, *m.* (coll) (mil.) deserter.

tornillo, *m.* screw, male screw; vise, clamp; (mil.) desertion.—**t. de alimentación,** feed screw.—**t. de aproximación,** (surv.) tangent screw.—**t. de banco,** vise, bench vise.—**t. de filete angular,** or **triangular,** V-threaded screw.—**t. de filete cuadrado,** square-threaded screw.—**t. de gota de sebo,** round-headed screw.—**t. de mano,** or **de orejas,** thumbscrew.—**t. de presión,** set screw, clamp screw.—**t. de rosca glosa,** conical V-threaded screw.—**t. de sujeción** = T. DE PRESIÓN. —**t. sin fin,** endless screw.

torniquete, *m.* turnpike, turnstile; turnbuckle, swivel; bell crank; (surg.) tourniquet.

torniscón, *m.* slap, box.

torno, *m.* lathe; winch, windlass; whim (vertical winch); whisket; revolving dumbwaiter; brake of a carriage; turn of a river; spinning wheel; spindle; wheel; axletree; circumvolution, gyration. —**t. de hilar,** spinning wheel.—**en t.,** round about. —**en t. de,** about, around.

toro, *m.* bull; (arch.) ogee molding; torus; (T-, astr.) Taurus.—*pl.* bullfighting.—**t. mejicano,** bison.—**ciertos son los toros,** so then, it is true—. **correr toros,** to fight bulls.

toronja, *f.* grapefruit.

toronjil, *m.***, toronjina,** *f.* (bot.) balm gentle.

toronjo, *m.* (bot.) grapefruit tree.

toroso, sa, *a.* strong, robust.

torozón, *m.* (vet.) gripes (of animals).

torpe, *a.* slow, heavy; dull, stupid; bawdy, lewd; homely, ugly; torpid; disgraceful, infamous.

torpedear, *va.* to torpedo.

torpedeo, *m.* torpedoing.

torpedero, *m.* (naut.) torpedo boat.

torpedo, *m.* torpedo; (icht.) torpedo, electric ray; (aut.) streamline body; long open car.—**t. automóvil,** self-propelling torpedo.—**t. de botalón,** spar torpedo.—**t. de fondo,** or **durmiente,** ground torpedo, ground submarine mine.—**t. flotante,** buoyant torpedo, or buoyant submarine mine.

torpemente, *adv.* slowly, sluggishly; clumsily, stupidly; basely; lewdly.

torpeza, *f.* heaviness, dulness; torpidness, torpor; lewdness, obscenity; want of ornament or culture; baseness, infamy, turpitude.

torpor, *m.* torpor, numbness.

torrado, *m.* toasted chick-pea.

torrar, *va.* to toast.

torre, *f.* tower; turret; church steeple, belfry; belvedere; country house with a garden; (chess) castle or rook.—**t. albarrana, t. de costa,** turret, watch tower.—**t. de luces,** (naut.) lighthouse.—**t. de viento,** castle in the air.

torrear, *va.* to fortify with towers or turrets.

torrefacción, *f.* torrefaction, toasting.

torreja, *f.* (Mex.) fritter.

torrejón, *m.* ill-shaped turret.

torrencial, *a.* torrential; overpowering.

torrentada, *f.* sweep of a torrent, impetuous current.

torrente, *m.* torrent; avalanche, rush; abundance, plenty.—**t. de voz,** powerful voice.

torrentera, *f.* ravine made by a torrent.

torreón, *m.* fortified tower.

torrero, *m.* lighthouse keeper; farmer.

torreznada, *f.* plentiful dish of rashers.

torreznero, ra, *n.* (coll.) lazy person.

torrezno, *m.* rasher of bacon.

tórrido, da, *a.* torrid; parched, hot.

torrija, *f.* bread dipped in eggs and milk, and fried.

torrontera, *f.*, **torrontero,** *m.* heap of earth left by a freshet.

torrontés, *a.* an epithet app. to a kind of white grapes.

torsión, *f.* torsion, twist; twisting.

torso, *m.* trunk or body of a statue.

torta, *f.* cake; loaf; (print.) font; solid matter for distribution.—*pl.* (Mex.) (min.) torta, cake of ore.—**tortas y pan pintado,** trifles, an easy matter, a cinch.—**costar la t. un pan,** to pay dear for one's whistle.

tortada, *f.* meat or chicken pie.

tortedad, *f.* twistedness.

tortera, *f.*, **tortero,** *m.* baking pan; deep dish.

tortero, *m.* whorl of a spindle.

tortícoli, *m.* (med.) torticollis, wry or stiff neck.

tortilla, *f. dim.* omelet; (Mex.) pancake.—**hacerse t.,** to break into small pieces; to cake.—**volverse la t.,** to turn the scale; to take a course contrary to that expected.

tortita, *f. dim.* small loaf or cake.

tórtola, *f.* (orn.) turtledove.

tortolillo, lla, ito, ta, *n. dim.* small turtledove; sweetheart.

tórtolo, *m.* male turtledove; beau, lover.

tortor, *m.* (naut.) tightening stick or bar to take up by twisting the sag between the fastened ends of a rope.

tortozón, *m.* a variety of large grapes.

tortuga, *f.* turtle; tortoise.

tortuosamente, *adv.* tortuously, sinuously.

tortuosidad, *f.* tortuosity, sinuosity.

tortuoso, sa, *a.* tortuous, winding, sinuous.

tortura, *f.* state of being twisted; rack, torture; grief, affliction.

torturar. I. *va.* to torture, torment. **II.** *vr.* to worry, fret.

torva, *f.* whirl of rain or snow.

torvisca, *f.*, flax-leaved daphne.

torviscal, *m.* place abounding in TORVISCA.

torvisco, *m.* = TORVISCA.

torvo, va, *a.* fierce, stern, severe, grim.

torzadillo, *m.* thin silk twist.

torzal, *m.* silk twist, machine twist; cord.

torzón, *m.* (vet.) = TOROZÓN.

torzonado, da, *a.* (vet.) suffering from TORZÓN.

tos, *f.* cough.—**t. ferina,** or **convulsiva,** whooping cough.—**t. perruna,** barking cough.

tosca, *f.* tophus; (dent.) tartar.

toscamente, *adv.* coarsely, rudely, roughly.

toscano, na, *n.* & *a.* Tuscan.

tosco, ca, *a.* coarse, rough; unpolished, uncouth.

tosecilla, *f. dim.* slight cough.

tosegoso, sa, *a.* coughing much.

toser, *vn.* to cough.—**t. a,** to challenge; to rival, compete with.

tosidura, *f.* coughing.

tosigar, *va.* to poison.

tósigo, *m.* poison; grief, anguish.

tosigoso, sa, *a.* poisonous, baneful; coughing.

tosquedad, *f.* roughness, coarseness; rudeness; clumsiness.

tostada, *f.* toast, toasted bread; disappointment.—**dar,** or **pegar, una t.,** (coll.) to cheat; to disappoint.

tostado, da. I. *a.* & *pp.* torrid, parched; toasted; tanned. **II.** *m.* toasting.—**tostador, ra. I.** *n.* toaster (person). **II.** *m.* toaster (utensil).

tostadura, *f.* toasting.

tostar, *va.* to toast; to roast; to tan (as the sun).—**t. café,** to roast coffee.

tostón, *m.* buttered or oiled toast; roasted Spanish pea; anything overtoasted; roast pig; testoon, a Portuguese silver coin.

total. I. *a.* total, whole; general, universal. **II.** *m.* total; whole, totality; complement; result, often used in the sense of, "in short," "to sum up," "in plain language," etc.

totalidad, *f.* totality, aggregate; whole.

totalmente, *adv.* totally, wholly, fully.

tótem, *m.* totem.—**totemismo,** *m.* totemism.

totilimundi, *m.* raree-show.

totoioque, *m.* (Mex.) an ancient Indian game.

totoposte, *m.* (C. A.) corn cake or biscuit.

totora, *f.* (S. A.) cat-tail or red mace.

totoral, *m.* place abounding in TOTORAS.

totovía, *f.* (orn.) wood lark.

totuma, *f.* cup made from a calabash.

totumo, *m.* calabash tree.

toxemia, *f.* toxemia.

toxicar, *va.* to poison.

tóxico, ca. I. *a.* toxic, poisonous. **II.** *m.* poison.

toxicologia, *f.* toxicology.—**toxicológico, ca,** *a.* toxicological.—**toxicólogo, ga,** *n.* toxicologist.

toza, *f.* log; block of wood; stump; piece of bark.

tozal, *m.* protuberance, bump on a plain surface.

tozalbo, ba, *a.* white-faced.

tozar, *vn.* (*pret.* TOCÉ: *subj.* TOCE) to butt (with the head); to contend foolishly.

tozo, za, *a.* low, small, dwarfish, stumpy.

tozolada, *f.*, **tozolón,** *m.* blow on the neck.

tozudo, da, *a.* stubborn, obstinate.

tozuelo, *m.* fat part of the neck of an animal.

traba, *f.* tie, bond, brace, clasp, locking device; anything that binds together; ligament, ligature; hobble, clog, fetterlock, trammel, fetter, shackle; obstacle, hindrance; beam, lintel.

trabacuenta, *f.* error in accounts; difference, dispute, controversy.

trabadero, *m.* pastern of a horse.

trabado, da, *a.* & *pp.* connected, joined, braced; locked, interlocked; thickened, inspissated; robust, strong; having white fore feet.

trabadura, *f.* bracing, locking; bond, union.

trabajadamente, *adv.* laboriously.

trabajado, da, *a.* & *pp.* labored; wrought, machined; tired, weary.

trabajador, ra. I. *a.* industrious; laboring, working. **II.** *n.* worker; workman, workingman (-woman), operator, hand, laborer.

trabajante, *a.* working, toiling.

trabajar, *va.* & *vn.* to work; labor; to shape, form; to endeavor; to exert one's self; to undergo a strain; labor (as a ship in a storm); to till the soil); to vex, harass, worry, trouble.

trabajillo, *m. dim.* slight work, toil, labor, trouble, or hardship.

trabajo, *m.* work; labor; piece of work; thing wrought; obstacle, hindrance; trouble, hardship.—*pl.* hardship; poverty, indigence, need, want.—**t. de manos,** manual or handiwork.—**t. de punto,** knitting, knitting work.—**t. de zapa,** underhand work.—**pasar trabajos,** to have trouble, to experience hardships or privation, to meet with difficulties.

rabajosamente, *adv.* laboriously, painfully.

trabajoso, sa, *a.* difficult, hard; belabored; needy, suffering; weak, sickly.

trabal, *a.* clasping.

trabalenguas, *m.* unpronounceable word, jaw-breaker.

trabamiento, *m.* interlocking; connection, bond, joining.

trabanco, *m.* block attached to a dog's collar to prevent him from nosing the ground.

trabar. I. *va.* to join, clasp, lock, bind, fasten; to grasp, grab, seize; to fetter, shackle; to thicken, inspissate; to begin, to set about; set (the teeth of a saw); harmonize, make agree.—**t. amistad,** to become friends; (w. **con**) to make the acquaintance of.—**t. batalla,** to enter into battle, begin it.—**t. conocimiento,** to scrape acquaintance. —**t. ejecución,** (law) to distrain, to seize judicially. **II.** *vr.* to become locked or interlocked; become confused, rattled.—**t. de palabras,** to become angry in a dispute.—**trabársele la lengua a uno,** to stammer; to speak with unnatural hesitation from confusion.

trabazón, *f.* juncture, union, bond, bracing, connection; coalescence; (mas.) bond (*v.* APAREJO).

trabe, *f.* beam.

trábea, *f.* trabea purple, striped toga.

trabilla, *f.* *dim.* gaiter strap; small clasp; in knitting, dropped stitch.

trabón, *m.* *aug.* fetlock, hopple; cross plank in oil mills.

trabuca, *f.* (pyr.) firecracker.

trabucación, *f.* confusion, disorder, upsetting, mix up; mistake, blunder.

trabucador, ra, *n.* upsetter, disturber; jumbler; mixer; blunderer.

trabucaire, *m.* Catalonian guerrilla, armed with a blunderbuss.

trabucante, *a.* blundering; confusing.

trabucar. I. *va.* (*pret.* TRABUQUÉ: *subj.* TRABUQUE) to upset, overturn; to mistake; to confound, confuse, jumble, mix up; to interrupt. **II.** *vr.* to become confused or mixed up.

trabucazo, *m.* shot with a blunderbuss; report of a blunderbuss; (coll.) sudden fright or affliction.

trabuco, *m.* catapult; blunderbuss.—**t. naranjero,** blunderbuss with a mouth of the size of an orange.

trabuquete, *m.* catapult; seine.

traca, *f.* (naut.) strake.

trácala, *f.* (Mex.) scheme, trick.

tracalada, *f.* (Am.) multitude, "lots."

tracalero, ra, *a.* (Mex.) tricky, artful.

tracamundana, *f.* (coll.) barter of trifles; noisy wrangle, hubbub.

tracería, *f.* (arch.) tracery.

tracción, *f.* traction; cartage; (mech.) tension, tensile stress.

tracias, *m.* north-northwest, wind.

tracio, cia, *n. & a.* Thracian.

tracista, *n.* designer; schemer; intriguer.

tracoma, *f.* (med.) trachoma.

tracto, *m.* tract, stretch; lapse; (eccl.) tractus.

tractocarril, *m.* car or train that can run on a road with or without rails.

tractor, *m.* tractor; traction engine.—**t. oruga,** caterpillar tractor.

tradición, *f.* tradition; (law) tradition, delivery of possession.—**tradicional,** *a.* traditional.

tradicionalismo, *m.* traditionalism.

tradicionalista, *m.* or *f.* traditionalist.

tradicionalmente, *adv.* traditionally.

tradicionista, *n.* compiler of traditions.

traducible, *a.* translatable.—**traducción,** *f.* translation.—**traducir,** *va.* (*ind.* TRADUZCO: *pret.* TRADUJE: *subj.* TRADUZCA) to translate.

traductor, ra, *n.* translator.

traedizo, za, *a.* portable.

traedor, ra, *n.* porter, carrier.

traer. I. *va.* (*gerund,* TRAYENDO: *ind.* TRAIGO: *pret.* TRAJE: *subj.* TRAIGA) to bring, fetch; to lead (a person); to attract, draw towards one's self; to bring about, cause, occasion; to handle,

manage; to wear (as a dress); assign (reasons); quote (authorities); to bring to, oblige, compel; to bring over, reduce, bind, prevail upon, persuade; to be engaged in, carry on, have.—**t. a cuento,** to bring into the conversation or discourse; to drag in. —**t. a la mano,** to fetch or carry.—**t. a mal t.,** to go hard with one; to disturb, trouble, vex.—**t. a uno al retortero,** to trouble one by overwork, or to lead one from place to place.—**t. a uno entre ojos,** to be suspicious of one.—**t. consigo,** to carry or have with one; to bring with it, to imply, to cause.—**t. en bocas, or lenguas,** to traduce, to speak ill of. **II.** *vr.* to be dressed (well or poorly); to carry one's self, have a graceful or ungainly carriage.

traeres, *m. pl.* dress ornaments.

trafagador, ra, *n.* trafficker, dealer.

trafagante, *a.* trafficking, trading.

trafagar, *vn.* (*for mut. v.* PAGAR) to traffic, trade.

tráfago, *m.* commerce, trade; drudgery.

trafagón, na. I. *a.* active, industrious. **II.** *n.* hustler.

trafalgar, *m.* cotton lining.

trafalmejo, ja, *a.* bold, forward, saucy.

traficación, *f.* traffic; trade, commerce.

traficante, *n.* trafficker, trader, dealer.

traficar, *vn.* (*pret.* TRAFIQUÉ: *subj.* TRAFIQUE) to traffic, deal, trade; to travel, journey.

tráfico, *m.* trade, business; traffic.

tragacanta, *f.,* **tragacanto,** *m.* (bot.) goatsthorn, milk vetch; tragacanth, a gum.

tragacete, *m.* javelin, dart.

tragaderas, *f. pl.* gullet.—**tener buenas t.,** to be very gullible.

tragadero, *m.* œsophagus, gullet; pit, gulf, vortex.—**t. del mar,** trough of the sea.

tragador, ra, *n.* glutton, gobbler.—**t. de leguas** = TRAGALEGUAS.

tragahombres, *m.* (coll.) bully, hector.

trágala, *m.* title of a political song against absolutism and in favor of the constitution.

tragaldabas, *m.* (coll.) glutton.

tragaleguas, *m.* (coll.) brisk walker.

tragaluz, *f.* skylight, bull's-eye.

tragallón, na, *n. & a.* glutton (-ous).

tragamallas, *m.* (coll.) glutton.

tragantada, *f.* large draught of liquor.

tragante. I. *a.* swallowing. **II.** *m.* (found.) top opening or passage of a furnace; sluice, flume; mouth of a dam or sink.

tragantón, na. I. *a.* gluttonous, voracious. **II.** *m.* (coll.) glutton. **III.** *f.* (coll.) big meal, big spread; swallowing or forcing down the throat; hard pill to swallow.

tragar. I. *va.* (*pret.* TRAGUÉ: *subj.* TRAGUE) to swallow; to devour; to swallow up, ingulf.—**t. el anzuelo,** to allow one's self to be deceived.—**no poder, or poderse, t. a,** not to be able to bear (cannot bear). **II.** *vr.* to swallow; to dissemble; to pocket (an affront).

tragasantos, *n.* overdevout person, one who spends too much time in church (one might say "church fiend," but for the obvious incongruity of terms).

tragavenado, *f.* (Ven.) a kind of boa.

tragavirotes, *m.* (coll.) conceited stiff man.

tragazón, *f.* voracity, gluttony.

tragedia, *f.* tragedy.

trágicamente, *adv.* tragically.

trágico, ca. I. *a.* tragic. **II.** *n.* tragedian, tragedienne.

tragicomedia, *f.* tragi-comedy.

tragicómico, ca, *a.* tragi-comical.

trago, *m.* draught of liquid; drink; swallow; calamity, misfortune; (anat.) tragus.—**a tragos,** by degrees, slowly, gently.—**echar un t.,** to take a drink.

tragón, na, *n. & a.* glutton (-ous).

tragonear, *va. & vn.* (coll.) to eat voraciously.

tragonería, tragonía, *f.* gluttony.

tragontina, *f.* (bot.) arum.

traguillo, ito, *m.* *dim.* small drink.

traición, *f.* treason; treachery.—**alta t.,** high treason.—**a t.,** or **a la t.,** treacherously.

traicionar, *va.* to do treason to, to betray.

traicionero, ra, *a.* treacherous.

traída, *f.* carriage, conduction.

traído, da, *a. & pp.* brought, fetched, carried; used, worn out, threadbare.

traidor, ra. I. *a.* traitorous; treasonable; treacherous, perfidious. **II.** *n.* traitor; betrayer.

traidoramente, *adv.* treacherously; treasonably, traitorously.

traigo, traiga. *V.* TRAER.

traílla, *f.* leash, lash; packthread; (agr.) leveling harrow; road leveler; road scraper.

traillar, *va.* to level (ground).

traína, *f.* seine for deep-sea fishing; net for sardine fishing.

trainera, *f.* smack for sardine fishing.

traíña, *f.* = TRAÍNA.

traite, *m.* raising a bur or nap on cloth.

traje, *m.* costume, dress, apparel; suit of clothes; mask.—**t. charro,** (Mex.) showy riding costume.—**t. de ceremonia,** or **de etiqueta,** full dress, evening dress; uniform.—**t. de luces,** bullfighter's garb.—**t. de montar,** riding habit.—**t. serio,** full dress, evening dress.

trajear, *va.* to clothe.

trajín, *m.* carrying from place to place; moving about.—**trajinante,** *n. & a.* carrier (-ying).

trajinar. I. *va.* to carry from place to place. **II.** *vn.* to travel about; (coll.) to fidget about.—**trajinería,** *f.* = TRAJÍN.—**trajinero, ra,** *n.* = TRAJINANTE.—**trajino,** *m.* = TRAJÍN.

tralla, *f.* cord, bass-weed rope; lash, snapper of a whip.

trama, *f.* weft or woof of cloth; tram, shute, twisted silk; fraud, plot, machination; plot of a play or novel.

tramador, ra, *n. & a.* weaver (-ing); plotter (-ing), hatcher (-ing), schemer (-ing).

tramar. I. *va.* to weave; to plot, hatch, scheme. **II.** *vn.* to blossom (s. o. olive trees).

tramilla, *f.* (Am.) twine.

tramitación, *f.* procedure; transaction, action, carrying out.

tramitar, *va.* to transact, carry through, conduct.

trámite, *m.* transit, passage; business transaction; step; (law) proceeding.

tramo, *m.* parcel of ground; flight of stairs; stretch, section; panel (of a bridge).

tramojo, *m.* (agr.) band for tying the sheaf; trouble, affliction; (Am.) = TRABANCO; (Colomb.) leash.

tramontano, na. I. *a.* transmontane. **II.** *f.* north wind; vanity, pride, haughtiness.

tramontar. I. *va.* to pass over (a mountain); to sink beyond (the mountains) (s. o. the sun); to help escape. **II.** *vr.* to flee, to escape.

tramoya, *f.* (theat.) trick; craft, wile.

tramoyista, *m.* (theat.) stage machinist; stage carpenter, stage hand, scene shifter; impostor, swindler, fraud, humbug.

trampa, *f.* trap, snare, pitfall; trapdoor; falling board of a counter; flap or spring door; cheat, fraud, deceit, trick; bad debt.—**caer en la t.,** to fall into a snare.—**hacer t.,** or **trampas,** to cheat. —**se lo llevó la t.,** it fell through, it went to the devil.

trampal, *m.* quagmire; bog.

trampantojo, *m.* (coll.) trick, deception.

trampazo, *m.* last twist of a torturing cord.

trampeador, ra, *n.* swindler, cheat, sharper.

trampear. I. *vn.* (coll.) to obtain money on false pretences; to cheat; to shift, get along, pull through. **II.** *va.* to swindle, cheat, deceive.

trampería, *f.* trickery, cheating, chicanery.

trampilla, *f. dim.* peephole; door of a coal bin; (tail.) front flap or fall of trousers.

trampista, *m.* cheat, trickster, sharper.

trampolín, *m.* springboard.

tramposo, sa. I. *a.* tricky, deceitful, swindling. **II.** *n.* cheater, swindler, trickster; card sharp.

tranca, *f.* club, cudgel, stick, truncheon; cross board or stick, or prop to fasten a door on the inside; (Am.) drunken spell, "tear."

trancada, *f.* long stride; blow with a stick.—**en dos trancadas,** in a trice.

trancado, *m.* small harpoon for eels.

trancahilo, *m.* stop knot in threads or ropes.

trancanil, *m.* (naut.) waterway, stringer plate.

trancar. I. *va.* (*for mut. v.* ATRANCAR) to bar (a door). **II.** *vn.* (coll.) to take long strides.

trancazo, *m.* blow with a bar; (coll.) influenza, grippe; (Colomb., coll.) fisticuff.

trance, *m.* peril, danger; critical moment; last stage of life; (law) legal seizure on an execution. —**a todo t.,** at any cost, at any price, regardless of risk or trouble.—**hacer t.,** (law) to seize property on an execution.

trancenil, *m.* gold or silver hatband, garnished with jewels.

tranco, *m.* long stride; threshold.—**a trancos,** hurriedly, carelessly.—**en dos trancos,** in a trice, in a jiffy.

tranchete, *m.* (shoe.) heel knife.

trancho, *m.* (icht.) a variety of shad.

trangallo, *n.* = TRABANCO.

tranquera, *f.* palisade, palisado.

tranquero, *m.* angular stone of a jamb or lintel.

tranquil, *m.* (arch.) plumb line.

tranquilamente, *adv.* quietly, peacefully, composedly.

tranquilar, *va.* (com.) to check off.

tranquilidad, *f.* tranquility, peace, quiet; reassurance, ease.

tranquilizador, ra, *a.* quieting, soothing, reassuring.

tranquilizar, *va.* to calm, appease, quiet down, reassure.

tranquilo, la, *a.* tranquil, calm, quiet, easy.

tranquilla, *f. dim.* trap, snare; small securing or fastening bar or stick; stop pin or lug.

tranquillón, *m.* maslin, mixed grain.

transacción, *f.* compromise, accommodation, settlement; transaction, negotiation.

transalpino, na, *a.* transalpine.

transandino, na, *a.* transandine, transandean.

transatlántico, ca, *a.* transatlantic.

transar, *va. & vr.* (Am.) to compromise, adjust, settle.

transbordador, ra. I. *a.* transshipping, transferring, transfer (u. a.). **II.** *m.* transfer boat or car.—**t. funicular,** transfer ropeway.

transbordar, *va.* to transfer; to transship.

transbordo, *m.* transfer; transshipment.

transcendencia, transcendental, transcendente, etc. = TRASCENDENCIA, etc.

transcontinental, *a.* transcontinental.

transcribir, *va.* (*pp.* TRANSCRITO, TRANSCRIPTO) to transcribe; (mus.) to transcribe.

transcripción, *f.* transcription.

transcripto, ta; transcrito, ta, *pp. irr. of* TRANSCRIBIR.

transcurrir, *vn.* to pass (s. o. time), elapse.

transcurso, *m.* lapse, course (of time).

tránseat, (Lat.) let it pass.

transeúnte. I. *a.* transient; transitory. **II.** *n.* sojourner; passer-by.

transferencia, *f.* transference, transfer.

transferible, *a.* transferable.

transferidor, ra, *n. & a.* transferrer (-ing).

transferir, *va.* (*for irr. v.* REFERIR) to transfer; (law) to transfer, convey, make over; (rhet.) to use figuratively.

transfigurable, *a.* transformable.

transfiguración, *f.* transfiguration.

transfigurar. I. *va.* to transfigure, transform. **II.** *vr.* to be transfigured.

transfijo, ja, *a.* transfixed.

transfixión, *f.* transfixion, piercing through.

transflor, *m.* (f. a.) enamel painting.

transflorar. I. *va.* (f. a.) to paint or decorate in enamel; to trace, make a tracing of. **II.** *vn.* to show through.

transflorear, va. to paint in enamel.

transformación, f. transformation.

transformador, ra. I. n. & a. transformer (-ing) **II.** m. (elec.) transformer.—**t.** acorazado, shell transformer.—**t. de aceite,** oil-cooled transformer. —**t. de anillo,** ring transformer.—**t. de corriente,** or **de intensidad,** current transformer.—**t. de reducción,** step-down transformer.—**t. de tensión,** voltage transformer.—**t. elevador,** step-up transformer, booster.

transformamiento, m. transformation.

transformar. I. va. & vr. to transform. **II.** vr. to be or become transformed; to change one's sentiments or ways.

transformativo, va, a. transformative.

transformismo, m. (biol.) transformism, evolutionism.—**transformista. I.** n. & a. transformist (-ic); evolutionist (-ary). **II.** u. rapid impersonator, one who impersonates several characters in succession.

transfregar, va. (for irr. v. FREGAR) to rub, scrub; rumple, crumple.

transfretano, na, a. transmarine.

transfretar. I. va. to cross (the sea). **II.** vn. to extend, spread.

tránsfuga, n., **tránsfugo,** m. deserter; fugitive, runaway; turncoat.

transfurdición, f. = TRANSFUSIÓN.

transfundir, va. to pour into; transfuse; to communicate, transmit.

transfusión, f. transfusion; communication, transmission; (surg.) transfusion.

transfusor, ra, n. & a. transfuser (-ing).

transgredir, va. (defect. only those modes are used having i in their ending) to transgress.

transgresión, f. transgression.

transgresor, ra, n. & a. transgressor (-ing).

transición, f. transition.

transido, da, a. worn out, exhausted; famished; mean, avaricious.

transigencia, f. condescension, tolerance.

transigente, a. accommodating, compromising, broad-minded, reasonable, condescending.

transigir. I. va. (ind. TRANSIJO: subj. TRANSIJA) to compound, compromise, settle. **II.** vn. to condescend, give in.

transilvano, na, n. & a. Transylvanian.

transitable, a. passable, practicable.

transitar, vn. to travel.

transitivo, va, a. (law) transferable; (gram.) transitive.

tránsito, m. transit, passage;·transition; stopping place; road, way; change, removal; death of holy persons; (ast., surv.) transit.

transitoriamente, adv. transitorily.

transitorio, ria, a. transitory.

translación, translaticiamente, translaticio, translativo, = TRASLACIÓN, etc.

translimitación, f. trespass; going beyond proper bounds; (mil.) armed intervention in a bordering state.

translimitar, va. (mil.) to cross (the boundary of a state) unintentionally or by permission; to go beyond the limit of (morality, reason, etc.).

translinear, vn. (law) to pass (an entail) to another line of heirs.

translucidez, f. translucence.

translúcido, da, a. translucent.

transmarino, na, a. transmarine.

transmigración, f. transmigration.

transmigrar, vn. to transmigrate.

transmisibilidad, f. transmissibility.

transmisible, a. transmissible.

transmisión, f. transmission.

transmisor, ra. I. a. transmitting. **II.** m. (elec.) transmitter.

transmitir, va. to transmit.

transmontar, transmontano = TRAMONTAR, TRAMONTANO.

transmudación, transmutación, f. **transmudamiento,** m. transmutation, change.

transmudar, va. to move, carry to another place; to change, transform, transmute; to persuade, convince.

transmutable, a. transmutable.

transmutar, va. to transmute, change.

transmutativo, va; torio, ria, a. transmutative.

transpacífico, ca, a. transpacific.

transpadano, na, a. transpadane.

transparencia, f. transparency.

transparentarse, vr. to be transparent; to show through.

transparente. I. a. transparent, translucent. **II.** m. window shade; stained glass window.

transpirable, a. perspirable, transpirable.

transpiración, f. transpiration, perspiration.

transpirar, vn. to transpire, perspire.

transpirenaico, ca, a. beyond the Pyrenees.

transponedor, ra, n. & a. transposer (-ing); transplanter (-ing).

transponer. I. va. (for irr. v. PONER) to transpose; to transfer, transport; to transplant **II.** vr. to set below the horizon; to go behind; to be rather drowsy.

transportación, f. transportation, transport.

transportador, ra. I. a. carrying, transporting. **II.** n. transporter, carrier. **III.** m. (drawing) protractor; (r. w.) ropeway.

transportamiento, m. transportation; transport, ecstasy.

transportar. I. va. to transport, carry; (mus.) to transpose. **II.** vr. to be in a transport, to be carried away.

transporte, m. transport, transportation, conveyance; cartage; ferriage; (naut.) transport ship; transport, rapture, ecstasy.

transposición, f. transposition.

transpositivo, va, a. transpositional, transpositive.

transpuesto, ta, a. & pp. irr. of TRANSPONER.

transterminante, a. trespassing.

transterminar, va. to trespass.

transtiberino, na, a. across the Tiber.

transubstanciación, f. transubstantiation.

transubstancial, a. transubstantiated.

transubstanciar, va. to transubstantiate.

transvasar, va. to transvasate.

transverberación, f. transfixion.

transversal, n. & a. transversal.

transversalmente, adv. transversely.

transverso, sa, a. transverse.

tranvía, m. tramway, street railway; street car.

tranviario, ria; tranviero, ra, a. relating to tramways, tramway (u. a.).

tranza, f. (law) seizure in an execution.

tranzadera, f. knot of plaited cords.

tranzar, va. to cut, truncate; to auction off.

tranzón, m. clear in a forest.

trapa, f. (naut.) spilling line.—pl. (naut.) relieving tackle; guys.

¡trapa, trapa! interj. tramp, tramp.

trapacear, vn. to cheat, swindle.

trapacería, f. fraud, cheating.

trapacero, ra, n. & a. cheat (-ing).

trapacete, m. (com.) daybook.

trapacista, n. = TRAPACERO.

trapajo, m. rag, tatter.

trapajoso, sa, a. ragged, tattered.

trápala. I. f. tramping of feet; galloping; noise, confusion; (coll.) trick, deceit, cheat. **II.** n. (coll.) prattler, chatterbox; cheat, humbug. **III.** m. garrulity, loquacity.

trapalear, vn. to prattle, chatter; to cheat.

trapalón, na, n. = TRÁPALA.

trapatiesta, f. (coll.) squabble, row, brawl.

trapaza, f. fraud, trick.

trapazar, vn. to cheat, swindle.

trape, m. trapeze; interlining.

trapeano, na, a. (min.) trappean.

trapecial, a. trapezoidal.

trapecio, m. (geom.) trapezoid.

trapense, *m.* (eccl.) Trappist.
trapería, *f.* rags; frippery, rag fair, rag shop.
trapero, ra, *n.* ragpicker; rag dealer.
trapezoidal, *a.* four-sided.
trapezoide, *m.* trapezium; (anat.) trapezoid.
trapiche, *m.* sugar mill, cane mill; olive press; (Cuba) small sugar plantation; (Mex.) grinding machine.
trapichear, *vn.* (coll.) to contrive, shift.
trapicheo, *m.* (coll.) contriving, shifting.
trapichero, ra, *n.* worker in a sugar mill.
trapiento, ta, *a.* ragged, tattered.
trapillo, lla. I. *n. dim.* (coll.) courtier or lady of small means. **II.** *m.* amount of money saved and put away.—**de t.,** in dishabille or negligé.
trapío, *m.* (naut.) sails of a ship, canvas; (coll.) stylish or graceful carriage of a woman; liveliness and smartness in a fighting bull.
trapisonda, *f.* (coll.) bustle, clatter; brawl, scuffle; snare, deception; (naut.) whitecaps.
trapisondear, *vn.* (coll.) to foment brawls; to cheat, deceive.
trapito, *m. dim.* little rag.—**los trapitos de cristianar,** best Sunday clothes.
trapo, *m.* rag, tatter; sails of a ship; (coll.) bullfighter's cloak.—**a todo t.,** with all the might; (naut.) all sails set.—**poner como un t.,** to reprimand severely, to dress down.—**soltar el t.,** (coll.) to burst out (crying or laughing).
traque, *m.* crack, report (of a rocket, etc.).—**a t.**
barraque, (coll.) at all times, in season and out of season.
tráquea, *f.* windpipe, trachea; (ent., bot.) trachea.
traqueado, da, *a.* threadbare, hackneyed.
traqueal, *a.* tracheal; trachearian.
traquear. I. *vn.* to crack, make a loud creaking noise. **II.** *va.* to shake (as a liquid); (coll.) to handle roughly.
traquearteria, *f.* trachea, windpipe.
traqueo, *m.* cracking (of fireworks, etc.); shake, shaking, jolt, jerk.
traqueotomía, *f.* tracheotomy.
traquetear, *va. & vn.* to shake, jolt, jerk, handle roughly; to crack (as fireworks or wood).
traqueteo, *m.* shaking, jolting, jerking; cracking, creaking.
traquiarteria, *f.* = TRAQUEARTERIA.
traquido, *m.* snapping, rattling, rattle; creaking, cracking.
traquita, *f.* (min.) trachyte.
traquítico, ca, *a.* trachytic.
trarigüe, *m.* (Ch.) an ornamented belt or sash.
tras. I. *prep.* after, behind; beyond; besides.—**t. de,** after, behind, back of; besides, in addition to. **II.** *m.* bang, noise of a blow.—**t. t.,** repeated strokes or noise.
trasalcoba, *f.* room back of a bedroom (gen. dressing room).
trasalpino, na, *a.* = TRANSALPINO.
trasandino, na, *a.* transandine, transandean.
trasanteanoche, *adv.* three nights ago.
trasanteayer, *adv.* three days ago.
trasantier, *adv.* three days ago.
trasañejo, ja, *a.* three years old.
transatlántico, ca, *a.* = TRANSATLÁNTICO.
trasbordar, trasbordo, = TRANSBORDAR, etc.
trasca, *f.* leather thong.
trascabo, *m.* trip (in wrestling).
trascantón, *m.* checkstone; street porter.—**dar t. a,** to hide one's self from behind a corner.
trascantonada, *f.* checkstone.
trascartarse, *vr.* to remain behind (as a winning card).—**trascartón,** *m.* drawing of a winning card after the game is lost.
trascendencia, *f.* transcendency; result.
trascendental, *a.* transcendental; far-reaching; transcendent, highly important; (math.) transcendental.
trascendentalismo, *m.* transcendentalism.
trascendentalista, *n. & a.* (phil.) transcendentalist (-ic).
trascendente, *a.* transcendent.

trascender, I. *vn.* (*for irr. v.* ASCENDER) to extend; to spread, smell, to emit a pleasant odor; to be pervasive; to transpire, leak out. **II.** *va.* to penetrate, scrutinize, find out.
trascendido, da, *a. & pp.* acute, perspicacious.
trascocina, *f.* back kitchen.
trascol, *m.* (obs.) woman's train.
trascolar, *va.* (*for irr. v.* COLAR) to strain, percolate; (coll.) to pass over (a mountain).
trasconejarse, *vr.* to squat (as pursued game); (coll.) to be missing or mislaid.
trascordarse, *vr.* (*for irr. v.* ACORDAR) to forget.
trascoro, *m.* space back of the choir.
trascorral, *m.* back court, back yard.
trascribir, trascrito, etc. = TRANSCRIBIR, etc.
trascuarto, *m.* back room; rear apartment.
trascurrir, trascurso, = TRANSCURRIR, etc.
trasdobladura, *f.* trebling.
trasdoblar, *va.* to treble, to triple.
trasdoblo, *m.* treble number.
trasdós, *m.* (arch.) extrados.—**trasdosear,** *va.* (arch.) to strengthen the back of (an arch).
trasechador, ra, *n.* insnarer, waylayer.
trasechar, *va.* to insnare, waylay.
trasegador, ra, *n.* one who racks wine.
trasegar, *va.* (*for irr. v.* SEGAR) to upset, to turn topsy-turvy; to change the place of; to empty, pour into another bottle or vessel.
traseñalador, ra, *n.* one who countermarks.
traseñalar, *va.* to mark anew.
trasero, ra. I. *a.* hind, hinder, back, rear. **II.** *m.* bottom, buttock; rump.—*pl.* (coll.) ancestors, predecessors. **III.** *f.* back, rear.
trasferencia, trasferible, trasferidor, trasferir = TRANSFERENCIA, etc.
trasfigurable, etc. = TRANSFIGURABLE, etc.
trasfijo, trasfixión = TRANSFIJO, etc.
trasflor, trasflorar, etc. = TRANSFLOR, etc.
trasfojar, *va.* = TRASHOJAR.
trasfollado, da, *a.* (vet.) having a swollen gambrel.—**trasfollo,** *m.* swelling of the gambrel.
trasformación, etc. = TRANSFORMACIÓN, etc.
trasfregar, *va.* = TRANSFREGAR.
trasfretano, etc. = TRANSFRETANO, etc.
trásfuga, trásfugo = TRÁNSFUGA, etc.
trasfundición, etc. = TRANSFUNDICIÓN, etc.
trasgo, *m.* goblin, hobgoblin, sprite.
trasgredir, trasgresión, etc. = TRANSGREDIR, TRANSGRESIÓN, etc.
trasguear, *vn.* to play the hobgoblin.
trasguero, ra, *n.* one who imitates the tricks of hobgoblins.
trashoguero, ra. I. *n.* idler, loiterer near the fireplace. **II.** *m.* back plate of a fireplace; big log in the fireplace.
trashojar, *va.* to scan (a book).
trashumación, *f.* nomadism of flocks.
trashumante, *a.* nomadic (s. o. flocks).
trashumar, *vn.* to roam in search of pasture.
trasiego, *m.* upsetting; racking (of wine).
trasiego, trasiegue. *V.* TRASEGAR.
trasijado, da, *a.* lank, meagre; thin-flanked.
traslación, trasladación, *f.* transfer, removal; translation, change of place; adjournment, postponement; translation, version.
trasladador, ra, *n.* carrier, mover.
trasladante, *a.* moving, removing; translating, transcribing.
trasladar, *va.* to move, remove, transfer; to postpone, adjourn; to translate; to transcribe.
traslado, *m.* copy, transcript, transcription; transfer; imitation, resemblance, likeness, counterpart; (law) notification, communication.
traslapar, *va., vn. & vr.* to overlap.
traslapo, *m.* overlapping.
traslaticiamente, *adv.* metaphorically, figuratively; by extension.—**traslaticio, cia,** *a.* metaphorical, figurative; extended.
traslativo, va, *a.* transferring, conveying.
traslato, ta, *a.* = TRASLATICIO.
trasloar, *va.* to bestow fulsome praise on.
traslúcido, da, *a.* = TRANSLÚCIDO.

trasluciente, *a.* translucent.

traslucirse, *vr.* to be transparent; to shine or show through; to be inferable; to transpire.

traslumbramiento, *m.* dazzlement.

traslumbrar. I. *va.* to dazzle. **II.** *vr.* to pass swiftly, to vanish.

trasluz, *m.* light seen through a transparent body; reflected or borrowed light; (art) transverse light.—**al t.,** against the light.

trasmallo, *m.* trammel net; iron collar around the head of a mallet.

trasmano, *m.* second player at cards.—**a t.,** out of the way.

trasmañana, *f.* day after to-morrow.

trasmañanar, *va.* to procrastinate.

trasmarino, na, *a.* = TRANSMARINO.

trasmatar, *va.* (coll.) to assume that one will outlive (another).

trasmigración, etc. = TRANSMIGRACIÓN, etc.

trasminar, *vn.* to undermine, excavate; to pierce, penetrate, percolate.

trasmisible, etc. = TRANSMISIBLE, etc.

trasmochadero, *m.* thicket of firewood.

trasmochar, *va.* to cut branches for fuel.

trasmontano, trasmontar, etc. = TRANSMONTANO, TRANSMONTAR, etc.

trasmosto, *f.* after wine.

trasmudación, etc. = TRANSMUDACIÓN, etc.

trasmutable, trasmutación, trasmutar, etc. = TRANSMUTABLE, TRANSMUTACIÓN, etc.

trasnochada, *f.* last night; sleepless night; being up all night; (mil.) night attack.

trasnochado, da, *a.* & *pp.* fatigued from night watching; haggard, careworn; stale, worn-out; trite, hackneyed.

trasnochador, ra, *n.* night watcher; one who goes to bed late or not at all; (coll.) night hawk.

trasnochar. I. *vn.* to watch; to sit up all night; to spend the night. **II.** *va.* to leave for the next day.

trasnoche, trasnocho, *m.* night watch, going without sleep.

trasnombrar, *va.* to change or confound the names of.

trasnominación, *f.* (rhet.) metonymy.

trasoír, *va.* to mistake, misunderstand.

trasojado, da, *a.* having sunken eyes, emaciated, careworn.

trasoñar, *vn.* (*for. irr. v.* SOÑAR) to fancy erroneously, as in a dream.

trasovado, da, *a.* (bot.) obovate.

traspadano, na, *a.* transpadane.

traspalar, traspalear, *va.* to shovel, shovel off; to move, remove; to weed with a hoe.

traspaleo, *m.* shovelling; weeding with a hoe.

traspapelarse, *vr.* to be mislaid among other papers.

trasparencia, trasparentarse, trasparente, = TRANSPARENCIA, etc.

traspasador, ra, *n.* trespasser, transgressor.

traspasamiento, *m.* transgression; trespass; transportation; crossing over; transfixion; transfer, conveyance; grief, anguish.

traspasar, *va.* to pass over, go beyond; to cross (as a river); to remove, transfer; to go through; to pierce, transfix; return, repass; to trespass, transgress, violate; to exceed (proper bounds); to convey, transfer, make over; to cause great grief or affliction to.

traspaso, *m.* conveyance, transfer; assignment; transgression, violation; grief, anguish.

traspatio, *m.* back yard, back court.

traspecho, *m.* bone ornament on a crossbow.

traspeinar, *va.* to comb again.

traspellar, *va.* to close, to shut.

traspié, *m.* slip, stumble; trip, wrestler's trick.—**dar traspiés,** to stumble; to slip, to err.

traspilastra, *f.* (arch.) counterpilaster.

traspillar. I. *va.* to shut, close. **II.** *vr.* to fail, become emaciated.

traspintar. I. *va.* to show (one card) and play another. **II.** *vr.* to show through; to show

against the light; (coll.) to fail, go up the spout.

traspirable, traspiración, traspirar = TRANSPIRABLE, etc.

trasplantar. I. *va.* to transplant. **II.** *vr.* to migrate.

trasplante, *m.* transplantation; migration.

trasponedor, trasponer = TRANSPONEDOR, TRANSPONER.

traspongo, trasponga. *V.* TRASPONER.

traspontín, *m.* = TRASPUNTÍN.

trasportación, trasportador, trasportamiento, etc. = TRANSPORTACIÓN, etc.

trasportín, *m.* wool upper mattress.

trasposición, etc. = TRANSPOSICIÓN, etc.

traspuesta, *f.* transposition; nook; lurking place; flight, concealment of a person; back yard or court; back door; rear outbuilding.

traspuesto, ta, *pp. irr.* of TRASPONER.

traspunte, *m.* (theat.) prompter.

traspuntín, *m.* bedquilt.

trasquero, *m.* leather cutter.

trasquila, trasquiladura, *f.* shearing, clipping, cropping.—**trasquiladero,** *m.* place where sheep are shorn.—**trasquilador, ra,** *n.* & *a.* shearer, (-ing), clipper (-ing).

trasquilar, *va.* to shear (sheep); to lop, crop; clip; to curtail, cut down.

trasquilimocho, cha, *a.* (coll.) close shorn or cropped.

trasquilón, *m.* clipping, shearing; (coll.) money lost through trickery or deception.—**a trasquilones,** irregularly, rudely.

trastabillar, *vn.* to reel, waver.

trastada, *f.* (coll.) inconsiderate act.

trastazo, *m.* (coll.) whack, thump, blow.

traste, *m.* (mus.) stop, fret of a guitar; glass or cup for sampling wine.—**dar al t. con,** to spoil, ruin, destroy.

trasteado, *pp.* & *m.* set of frets on a guitar.

trasteador, ra, *n.* one who frets a guitar; moving man (woman).

trasteante, skillful guitar player.

trastear. I. *va.* to fret (a guitar); to play well on (the guitar); to madden (the bull) with a red flag; (coll.) to manage with tact. **II.** *vn.* to move furniture from one part of a house to another; to talk in an excited manner.

trastejador, *m.* roof tiler.—**trastejadura,** *f.* tiling.—**trastejar,** *va.* to tile; to overhaul, repair.

trastejo, *m.* tiling.

trasteo, *m.* maddening the bull with a red flag; clever management of a person or business.

trastería, *f.* heap of old furniture; (coll.) rash action.

trasterminante, trasterminar = TRANSTERMINANTE, TRANSTERMINAR.

trastero, ra, *m.* or *f.* garret, lumber room.

trastesado, da, *a.* hardened, stiff.

trastienda, *f.* back room; prudence, caution.

trasto, *m.* piece of furniture; luggage; rubbish, lumber; (theat.) trick piece, set piece; (coll.) worthless person, trash.—*pl.* tools of trade, implements, outfit; steel weapons.—**trastos de cocina,** kitchen utensils.

trastornable, *a.* easily disturbed or upset.

trastornado, da, *pp.* & *a.* upset, topsy-turvy; afflicted; unbalanced, mad.

trastornador, ra, *n.* & *a.* disturber (-ing); agitator (-ing).

trastornadura, f., trastornamiento, *m.* upsetting, overthrow, disturbance.

trastornar, *va.* to upset; to turn upside down; to disorder, disturb, disarrange; to agitate, excite; to derange, daze, confuse, perplex (the mind); to persuade, induce.

trastorno, *m.* upsetting; upheaval; disturbance, disorder, confusion; trouble; disarrangement.

trastrabado, da, *a.* having the far hind foot and the near fore foot white.

trastrabarse, *vr.* to become fuddled.

trastrabillar, *vn.* to stumble; to reel; to stammer.

trastrás, *m.* last but one.

trastrocamiento, *m.* transposition, rearrangement; disarrangement.—**trastrocar,** *va.* (*for irr. v.* TROCAR) to change the order of; to disarrange, muddle.—**trastrueco, trastrueque,** *m.* rearrangement; disarrangement; transposition.

trastuelo, *m. dim.* worthless utensil; trash.

trastulo, *m.* pastime, toy.

trastumbar, *va.* to overturn, overset.

trasudadamente, *adv.* toiling and sweating.

trasudar, *va.* to sweat, perspire.

trasudor, *m.* gentle perspiration.

trasuntar, *va.* to copy; to abridge, abstract.

trasuntivamente, *adv.* compendiously; as per copy.

trasunto, *m.* copy, transcript; likeness.

trasvasar, *va.* = TRANSVASAR.

trasvenarse, *vr.* to extravasate; to spill.

trasver, *va.* to see through; to see erroneously.

trasverberación = TRANSVERBERACIÓN.

trasversal, trasverso = TRANSVERSAL, TRANSVERSO.

trasverter, *vn.* (*for irr. v.* VERTER) to overflow, run over.

trasvinarse, *vr.* to leak out (s. o. wine); (coll.) to be surmised or inferred.

trasvolar, *va.* (*for irr. v.* VOLAR) to fly across.

trata, *f.* trade; slave trade.—**t. blanca, or de blancas,** white slavery.

tratable, *a.* tractable, compliant.

tratadico, illo, ito, *m. dim.* tract, short treatise.

tratadista, *n.* author, writer (on special subjects).

tratado, *pp. & m.* treaty; treatise.

tratador, ra, *n.* mediator.

tratamiento, *m.* treatment; courteous title or form of address; (med., chem.) treatment.

tratante, *n.* dealer, trader, tradesman.

tratar. I. *va.* to treat (a subject, a person, a patient, a substance); to discuss; to handle, manage, conduct.—**t. de,** to address as, give the title of; to call, charge with being (*me trató de ambicioso,* he called me, or charged me with being, ambitious) —**t. por,** (chem.) to treat with. **II.** *vn.* to treat; to deal, trade.—**t. acerca de,** to treat on, deal with (a subject).—**t. de,** to treat on or of (a subject); to endeavor, try.—**t. en,** to deal in. **III.** *vr.* to behave, conduct one's self; to live (well or badly).

trato, *m.* treatment, use, usage; social behavior, manner, address; pact, agreement, deal; trade, commerce; friendly intercourse, conversation; appellation, title of courtesy.—**mal t.,** ill usage, ill-treatment.—**tener buen t.,** (coll.) to be pleasant, "nice," affable.—**tener t. de gentes,** to be accustomed to good society.

traumático, ca, *a.* traumatic.

traumatismo, *m.* traumatism.

traversa, *f.* (naut.) backstay.

través, *m.* inclination, bias; reverse, misfortune; traverse; (arch.) crossbeam; (fort.) traverse, screen.—**al t.** = DE T.—**al t. de,** through.—**dar al t.,** to be stranded.—**dar al t. con,** to throw away, misspend; to ruin, destroy; to set aside, ignore.—**de t.,** across, athwart, through.—**mirar de t.,** to squint.—**por el t.,** (naut.) on the beam.

travesaño, *m.* crosspiece, crossbar; bolster of a bed.

travesar, *va.* to cross.

travesear, *vn.* to skip about, frisk, caper, romp; to be mischievous; to be quick at repartee; to lead a debauched life; to behave improperly.

travesero, ra. I. *a.* transverse, cross. **II.** *m.* bolster of a bed.

travesía, *f.* distance; passage; stretch, space; sea voyage; crossing (the sea); crossroad, short cut; transverse position; money won or lost at gambling; (fort.) traverse works; (naut.) side wind; sailor's pay for each voyage.

travesío, ía. I. *a.* traversing; transverse, or lateral, wind. **II.** *m.* crossing, crossroad.

travestido, da, *a.* disguised.

travesura, *f.* prank, frolic, caper, antic; mischief; lively fancy; sprightly conversation.

traviesa, *f.* distance across; at cards, raise on a bet; wager laid on a card player; (r. w.) crosstie;

(arch.) rafter; transverse wall; (min.) cross level or gallery.

travieso, sa, *a.* transverse, cross; restless, flighty; frolicsome, prankish; mischievous; shrewd, cute; dissolute, lewd.—**ir a campo t.,** to make a short cut; to go in a cross-country way.

trayecto, *m.* distance, stretch; section.

trayectoria, *f.* trajectory.

trayente, *a.* bringing, carrying, conducting.

traza, *f.* sketch, draught, outline; plan, device, scheme, project, contrivance; plot, artifice; manner, means; looks, appearance, aspect; prospect.—**darse trazas,** to find a way.

trazado, da. I. *a. & pp.* traced, outlined.—**bien or mal t.,** of a good or bad disposition or figure. **II.** *m.* sketch, draught, outline, plan; (act of) drawing; (r. w.) location; running (of a line on the ground).

trazador, ra, *n.* contriver, schemer, designer.

trazar, *va.* (*pret.* TRACÉ: *subj.* TRACE) to design, devise, plan out; to trace, mark out; to draw (as a line); (r. w.) to locate; (surv.) to run, lay out (a line, a curve).

trazo, *m.* outline, plan; line, stroke of a pen or pencil; (art) fold of the drapery.—**t. magistral,** down stroke of a letter.—**al t.,** drawn in outline.

trazumarse, *vr.* to leak, ooze, transude.

treballa, *f.* sauce for goose.

trébedes, *f. pl.* trivet, cook's tripod.

trebejo, *m.* toy, plaything; chess piece.—*pl.* implements, tools of trade.

trebejuelo, *m. dim.* toy, trifle, gewgaw.

trebeliánica, *f.* (law) fourth part of an estate, to be deducted by the fiduciary heir, who holds it in trust for another.

trébol, *m.* (bot.) trefoil, clover, shamrock.

trece, *n. & a.* thirteen; thirteenth.—**estarse en sus t.,** to persist in one's opinion, to stick to it.

trecemesino, na, *a.* of thirteen months.

trecenario, *m.* space of thirteen days.

trecenato, trecenazgo, *m.* employment of thirteen persons.

treceno, na, *a.* thirteenth.

trecentista, *n. & a.* trecentist.

trecientos, tas, *n. & a.* three hundred.

trechear, *va.* to transport from hand to hand or from section to section.

trechel, *m.* (bot.) spring wheat.

trecheo, *m.* handling from hand to hand or from section to section.

trecho, *m.* space, distance, stretch; lapse.—**a trechos,** by intervals.—**de t. en t.,** at certain distances or intervals.

trefe, *a.* soft, thin; pliable; spurious, adulterated (coin).

tregua, *f.* truce; rest, respite, recess, intermission.

treilla, *f.* = TRAÍLLA.

treinta, *n. & a.* thirty; thirtieth.—**t. y una,** a card game.

treintaidosavo, va, *n. & a.;* **treintaidoseno, na,** *a.* thirty-second.

treintanario, *m.* space of thirty days.

treintañal, *a.* containing thirty years.

treintavo, va, *n. & a.* thirtieth.—**treintena,** *f.* trental; thirtieth.—**treinteno, na,** *a.* thirtieth.

treja, *f.* cushion shot at billiards.

tremadal, *m.* quagmire, quaking bog.

tremátodo, da. I. *n. & a.* (zool.) trematode. **II.** *m. pl.* Tremátoda, trematodes.

tremebundo, da, *a.* dreadful, frightful, fearful.

tremedal, *m.* = TREMADAL.

tremendo, da, *a.* tremendous, dreadful, terrible; awful, imposing; huge; excessive.

tremente, *a.* trembling.

trementina, *f.* turpentine.

tremer, *vn.* to tremble.

tremés; tremesino, na, *a.* three months old.

tremielga, *f.* (icht.) electric ray, torpedo.

tremis, *m.* an ancient gold coin.

tremó, tremol, *m.* pier glass.

tremolante, *a.* waving in the air.

tremolar, *va. & vn.* to wave (as a flag).

tremolina, *f.* rustling of the wind; (coll.) bustle, fuss, noise, hubbub.

trémolo, *m.* (mus.) tremolo.

tremor, *m.* trembling; tremor.

trémulamente, *adv.* tremblingly, tremulously.

tremulante; tremulento, ta; trémulo, la, *a.* tremulous, quivering, shaking.

tren, *m.* train; outfit; equipment; following, retinue; show, pomp, ostentation; (r. w.) train.—**t. ascendente,** "up train," going towards Madrid.—**t. botijo,** excursion train.—**t. carreta,** accommodation train.—**t. correo,** mail train.—**t. de artillería,** convoy of artillery.—**t. de aterrizaje,** (aer.) undercarriage, landing gear.—**t. de casa,** housekeeping outfit.—**t. de escala,** accommodation train.—**t. de lavado,** laundry.—**t. de mercancías,** freight train.—**t. de recreo,** excursion train. —**t. descendente,** "down train," going from Madrid.—**t. de viajeros,** passenger train.—**t. expreso,** express train.—**t. mixto,** mixed train, carrying both passengers and freight.—**t. ómnibus,** accommodation train.

trena, *f.* scarf, sash; burnt silver; twist bread.

trenado, da, *a.* reticulated, mesh (u. a.), latticed.

trenca, *f.* crosstree in a beehive; main root.

trencellín, *m.* = TRENCILLO.

trencica, ita, *f. dim.* small braid or plait.

trencilla, *f.* braid.

trencillar, *va.* to trim with braid.

trencillo, *m.* gold or silver hatband garnished with jewels.

treno, *m.* lamentation, dirge.

trenque, *m.* jetty in a river.

trenza, *f.* braid; plait; braided hair, tress.

trenzadera, *f.* tape; knot of plaited cord.

trenzado, *pp. & m.* braided hair; braiding; (danc.) caper; prance of a horse.—**al t.,** carelessly.

trenzar. I. *va.* to braid; to plait. **II.** *vn.* to prance; to cut capers.

treo, *m.* (naut.) square sail, crossjack sail.

trepa, *f.* climbing; boring, perforating, drilling; (sew.) wavy edging or trimming; grain, flake, or mottle of polished wood; (coll.) flogging, lashing, beating; artful trick, fraud; somersault.

trepado, da. I. *pp. & a.* strong, robust (s. o. animals). **II.** *m.* (sew.) edging.

trepador, ra. I. *a.* climbing. **II.** *m.* climbing place; sea wolf. **III.** *f.* (bot.) climber, creeper (as ivy).—*pl.* (orn.) climbers.

trepajuncos, *m.* a kind of reed bird.

trepanación, *f.* (surg.) trephining.

trepanar, *va.* (surg.) to trepan, to trephine.

trépano, *m.* (surg.) trepan, trephine.

trepante, *pa.* climbing; wily, artful, crafty.

trepar. I. *vn.* to climb, mount, clamber; (bot.) to climb, creep (as ivy). **II.** *va.* to bore, drill, perforate; (sew.) to trim with TREPA.

trepatroncos, *m.* (orn.) mason bird.

trepe, *m.* (coll.) scolding, reprimand.

trepidación, *f.* trepidation; vibration; (ancient ast.) trepidation.—**trepidante,** *a.* vibrating, shaking.—**trepidar,** *vn.* to shake, vibrate, jar.

trépido, da, *a.* tremulous, shaking.

tres. I. *m. & a.* three; third. **II.** *m.* at cards, a trey; magistrate of a city governed by three magistrates. **III.** *f. pl.*—**las t.,** three o'clock.

tresalbo, ba, *a.* having three white feet.

tresañal, tresañejo, ja, *a.* three years old.

tresbolillo.—al t., (agr.) quincunx; (mech.) staggered, alternating (riveting).

trescientos, tas, *n. & a.* three hundred; three-hundredth.

tresdoblar, *va.* to treble; to fold three times.

tresdoble, *m.* triple, threefold.

tresillista, *n.* expert in, or fond of, ombre.

tresillo, *m.* ombre, a card game; (mus.) triplet.

tresmesino, na, *a.* three months old.

tresnal, *m.* (agr.) shock, stock.

trestanto. I. *m.* triple number or amount. **II.** *adv.* three times as much.

treta, *f.* (fenc.) feint; trick, wile, craft.

treudo, *m.* emphyteutic rent.

trezavo, va, *n. & a.* thirteenth.

tría, *f.* choice, selection; tease in fabrics.—**dar una t.,** (api.) to transpose (hives).

triaca, *f.* (pharm.) theriaca, antidote.

triacal, *a.* theriacal.

triache, *m.* triage of coffee beans.

triangulación, *f.* triangulation.

triangulado, da; triangular, *a.* triangular.

triangularmente, *adv.* triangularly.

triángulo, la. I. *a.* triangular. **II.** *m.* (geom.) triangle; (ast.) Triangulum; (mus.) triangle.— **t. acutángulo,** acute-angled triangle.—**t. esférico,** spherical triangle.—**t. obtusángulo,** obtuse-angled triangle.—**t. rectángulo,** right-angled, or right, triangle.

triaquera, *f.* vessel for theriaca.

triar. I. *va.* to choose, select. **II.** *vn.* (api.) to swarm to a favorite hive. **III.** *vr.* to show teases (s. o. a fabric); to curdle.

triario, *m.* triarian soldier.

triásico, ca, *a.* (geol.) Triassic.

tribómetro, *m.* tribometer, friction-measuring instrument.

tribraquio, *m.* (poet.) tribrach (⌣ ⌣ ⌣).

tribu, *f.* tribe.

tribuente, *a.* attributing.

tribuir, *va.* to attribute.

tribulación, *f.* tribulation, affliction.

tríbulo, *m.* (bot.) thistle; prickle.

tribuna, *f.* tribune; rostrum; gallery.—*pl.* grandstand.

tribunado, *m.* tribuneship.

tribunal, *m.* tribunal, court of justice.—**t. de cuentas,** exchequer.—**t. juvenil,** juvenile court.

tribunicio, cia; tribúnico, ca, *a.* tribunitial, tribunician.

tribuno, *m.* tribune; orator.

tributación, *f.* tribute, contribution; system of taxation; emphyteusis.

tributante, *n.* taxpayer; tribute payer.

tributar, *va.* to pay (taxes or contributions); to pay, render (homage, respect); to hold in emphyteusis.

tributario, ria. I. *a.* tributary. **II.** *n.* taxpayer; tributary (river).

tributo, *m.* tribute; tax, contribution; gift, offering, meed; toil, trouble.

tricahue, *m.* a kind of Chilean parrot.

tricenal, *a.* lasting thirty years.

tricentésimo, ma, *a.* three-hundredth.

triceps, *m.* (anat.) triceps.

triciclo, *m.* tricycle.

tricípete, *a.* three-headed.

triclinio, *m.* triclinium.

tricolor, *a.* tricolor.

tricorne, *a.* three-horned.

tricornio. I. *a.* three-horned. **II.** *m.* three-cornered hat.

tricotomía, *f.* trichotomy.—**tricotómico, ca,** *a.* trichotomic.—**tricótomo, ma,** *a.* trichotomous.

tricromía, *f.* trichromic printing.

tridacio, *m.* (pharm.) thridacium.

tridente. I. *a.* tridental. **II.** *m.* trident.

tridentino, na, *n. & a.* Tridentine.

tridínamo, ma, *a.* (chem.) trivalent.

triduano, na, *a.* lasting three days.

triduo, *m.* (eccl.) triduum.

triedro. I. *a.* trihedral. **II.** *m.* trihedron; trihedral angle.

trienal, *a.* triennial.

trienio, *m.* term of three years; triennium.

trieñal, *a.* triennial.

trifásico, ca, *a.* (elec.) three-phase.

trífido, da, *a.* (poet.) trifid, three-cleft.

trifinio, *m.* point where the boundaries of three districts meet.

trifloro, ra, *a.* triflorous, three-flowered.

trifolio, *m.* (bot.) trefoil; shamrock.

triforme, *a.* triform, triformed.

trifulca, *f.* (coll.) squabble, row; (found.) lever system for moving the bellows.

trifurcado, da, trifurcate, three-forked.

trigal, *m.* wheat field.

trigaza, *f.* short straw of wheat.

trigésimo, ma, *a.* thirtieth.

trigla, *f.* (icht.) red surmullet.

triglifo, *m.* (arch.) triglyph.

trigo, *m.* wheat; wheat field.—*pl.* crops; grain-fields.—**t. alonzo,** bearded wheat.—**t. blanquillo, candeal,** or **común,** summer wheat.—**t. chamorro,** or **desraspado,** winter or beardless wheat.—**t. fanfarrón,** Barbary wheat.—**t. hembrilla,** or **marzal,** summer wheat.—**t. mocho, pelón, pelo-to,** beardless wheat.—**t. piche** = T. BLANQUILLO. —**t. sarraceno,** buckwheat.—**t. teja.** = T. BLANQUILLO.—**t. toseta,** beardless wheat.—**t. trechel, tremés, tremesino,** summer wheat.

trigón, *m.* (mus.) trigonon.

trigono, *m.* (astrol., geom.) trigon.

trigonometría, *f.* trigonometry.—**t. esférica,** spherical trigonometry.—**t. plana,** or **rectilínea,** plane trigonometry.

trigonométrico, ca, *a.* trigonometrical.

trigueño, ña, *a.* brunette, swarthy, dark.

triguero, ra. **I.** *a.* growing with wheat. **II.** *m.* sieve for corn; corn or grain dealer. **II.** *f.* (bot.) common wheat grass; canary seed.

trilátero, ra, *a.* trilateral.

trilingüe, *a.* trilingual.

trilítero, ra, *a.* triliteral.

trilito, *m.* (archeol.) trilithon.

trilobites, *m. pl.* (pal.) trilobites.

trilobulado, da, *a.* trilobate.

trilocular, *a.* trilocular.

trilogía, *f.* trilogy.

trilla, *f.* (icht.) red surmullet, gurnard; (agr.) harrow; thrashing.

trilladera, *f.* separating harrow.

trillado, da, *a.* & *pp.* (agr.) thrashed, beaten, trite, stale, hackneyed.

trillador, ra. **I.** *n.* & *a.* (agr.) thrasher (-ing). **II.** *f.* thrashing machine.

trilladura, *f.* (agr.) thrashing.

trillar, *va.* (agr.) to thrash, beat; to frequent; to repeat.

trillo, *m.* (agr.) separating harrow; thrashing machine; (Am.) footpath.

trillón, *m.* trillion (one million billions).

trimembre, *a.* trimembral.

trimestral, *a.* trimestral, quarterly.

trimestralmente, *adv.* quarterly.

trimestre, *m.* quarter; quarterly payment.

trimielga, *f.* (icht.) = TREMIELGA.

Trimurti, *f.* Trimurty, the Hindu Trinity.

trinado, *m.* (mus.) trill, shake, quaver; twittering of birds.

trinar, *vn.* (mus.) to trill, quaver; (coll.) to get angry or furious.

trinca, *f.* triad, ternary; (naut.) gammoning, woolding, seizing; seizing stuff.—**a la t.,** (naut.) close-hauled.

trincadura, *f.* large two-masted barge.

trincafía, *f.* wound splice or patch, made by winding a rope spirally around the piece or pieces.

trincapiñones. *n.* (coll.) harebrained person.

trincar. **I.** *va.* (*for mut. v.* BRINCAR) to break, chop; (naut.) to fasten, gammon, lash, seize; to tie, bind, make fast. **II.** *vn.* (coll.) to drink (liquor); (naut.) to keep close to the wind.

trincha, *f.* (tail.) cloth strap for buckling or buttoning garments; (Am.) socket chisel, cutting gouge.—**trinchante,** *m.* carver at table; carving knife; stonecutters' hammer.

trinchar, *va.* to carve.

trinchera, *f.* (mil.) trench, intrenchment; deep cut, ditch.

trinchero, *m.* trencher; side table.

trincherón, *m. aug.* large trench or ditch.

trinchete, *m.* = TRANCHETE.

trineo, *m.* sleigh, sledge, sled.

trinidad, *f.* trinity.

trinitario, ria. **I.** *a.* & *n.* (eccl.) Trinitarian; (Mex.) hired mourner. **II.** *f.* (bot.) pansy, heartsease.

trino, na. **I.** *a.* ternary, triadic, trinal, trine. **II.** *m.* (ast.) trine; (mus.) trill.

trinomio, *m.* & *a.* (math.) trinomial.

trinquetada, *f.* sailing under the foresail.

trinquete, *m.* (naut.) foremast, foresail; (mech.) pawl, catch, stop; racket (ball game).—**a cada t.,** at every step.

trinquetilla, *f.* (naut.) fore staysail.

trinquis, *m.* (coll.) drink (of liquor).

trío, *m.* TRÍA; (mus.) trio.

trional, *m.* (chem.) trional.

Triones, *m. pl.* (ast.) Triones, the Dipper.

trióxido, *m.* (chem.) trioxid, trioxide.

tripa, *f.* gut, intestine, bowel; (coll.) belly, paunch; filling, fillers (for cigars); file, docket.—*pl.* core of fruit; insides, entrails; inner lining of some feathers.—**hacer de tripas corazón,** to pluck up heart.

tripanosis, *f.* (med.) trypanosomiasis.

tripanosoma, *m.* (biol.) Trypanosoma.

tripartición, *f.* tripartition.

tripartir, *va.* to divide into three parts.

tripartito, ta, *a.* tripartite.

tripasto, *m.* pulley with three sheaves.

tripe, *m.* shag, plush.

tripería, *f.* tripe shop; heap of tripe.

tripero, ra, *n.* tripe seller.—**tripero,** *m.* bellyband; cummerbund.—**tripicallero, ra,** *n.* tripe dealer.—**tripicallos,** *m. pl.* tripes.

trípili, *m.* (theat.) a Spanish song and dance.

triplano, *m.* (aer.) triplane.

triple, *a.* triple, treble.

tríplica, *f.* (law) rejoinder.

triplicación, *f.* triplication, trebling.

triplicado, da, *a.* & *pp.* triplicate, treble.

triplicar, *va.* (*for mut. v.* DUPLICAR) to treble, triple; (law) to rejoin.

tríplice, *a.* treble, triple.

triplicidad, *f.* triplicity, trebleness.

triplo, pla, *a.* treble, triplicate, triple.

trípode, *m.* or *f.* tripod; trevet, trivet.

trípol, trípoli, *m.* tripoli, rottenstone.

tripolino, na, *n.* & *a.* Tripoline, Tripolitan.

tripolio, *m.* (bot.) sea starwort.

tripolitano, na, *n.* & *a.* = TRIPOLINO.

tripón, na, *a.* (coll.) pot-bellied, big-bellied.

tríptico, *m.* triptych.

triptongo, *m.* triphthong.

tripudiar, *vn.* to dance.

tripudio, *m.* dance, ball.

tripudo, da, *a.* pot-bellied, big-bellied.

tripulación, *f.* crew.—**tripulante,** *n.* one of the crew.—*pl.* crew.—**tripular,** *va.* to man (ships); to fit out, equip.

trique, *m.* crack, sharp noise.

triquete, *m. dim.*—**a cada t.,** at every stir or step.

triquina, *f.* trichina.

triquinosis, *f.* trichinosis.

triquiñuela, *f.* (coll.) trickery, subterfuge.

triquitraque, *m.* crack, clack, clattering, clashing; (pyr.) firecracker, pulling cracker.

trirrectángulo, la, *a.* (geom.) trirectangular.

trirreme, *m.* (naut.) trireme.

tris, *m.* crack, noise made by the breaking of glass; trice, nick of time.—**t. tras,** tedious repetition; "the same old story."—**en un t.,** within an ace, almost, coming pretty near (falling, etc.).

trisa, *f.* (icht.) shad.

Trisagio, *m.* (eccl.) Trisagion.

trisca, *f.* noise made by crushing under the feet; noisy fun, merriment, uproar.

triscador, ra. **I.** *n.* noisy, rattling person. **II.** *m.* (mech.) saw set, saw wrest, saw swage.

triscar. **I.** *vn.* (*pret.* TRISQUÉ: *subj.* TRISQUE) to stamp the feet; to walk lively, to hustle; to romp, caper, frolic. **II.** *va.* to mix, mingle; to set (the teeth of a saw).

trisecar, *va.* to trisect.—**trisección,** *f.* trisection.

trisílabo, ba, *a.* trisyllabic.

trismo, *m.* (med.) trismus, lockjaw.

trispasto, *m.* three-pulley tackle.

triste, *a.* sad, sorrowful; gloomy, dismal; abject, mean, low.

tristemente, *adv.* sadly, sorrowfully.

tristeza, *f.* sadness, grief, sorrow, gloom.

tristón, na, *a.* melancholy, rather sad.

trisulco, ca, *a.* three-pronged; having three furrows or channels.

tritíceo, ea, *a.* triticean, wheaten.

tritón, *m.* (myth.) Triton.

trítono, *m.* (mus.) tritone.

triturable, *a.* triturable, crushable.

trituración, *f.* trituration, crushing.

triturador, ra. I. *n.* & *a.* crusher (-ing), triturator (-ing). **II.** *f.* crusher, crushing machine.

triturar, *va.* to triturate, crush; to masticate.

triunfador, ra, *n.* conqueror, victor.

triunfal, *a.* triumphal.—**triunfalmente,** *adv.* triumphally.

triunfante, *a.* triumphant, victorious.

triunfantemente, *adv.* triumphantly.

triunfar, *vn.* to conquer; to triumph, to achieve victory; to win; to trump at cards.

triunfo, *m.* triumph, victory; exultation; spoil of war; trump card.—**costar un t.,** to be exceedingly difficult.—**en t.,** triumphantly; in triumph.

triunviral, *a.* triumviral.—**triunvirato,** *m.* triumvirate.—**triunviro,** *m.* triumvir.

trivial, *a.* trivial; trite, trodden, beaten.

trivialidad, *f.* triviality; triteness.

trivialmente, *adv.* trivially.

trivio, *m.* fork of a road; junction of three roads, trivium.

triza, *f.* bit, small piece, fragment, shred, particle; (naut.) cord, rope.—**hacer trizas,** to knock into smithereens; to wound or injure a person or animal.

trocable, *a.* exchangeable.

trocada.—a la t., in a sense or direction opposite to the apparent one.

trocadamente, *adv.* distortedly; changing things or words.

trocado, da. I. *a.* & *pp.* changed; distorted.—**a la trocada,** or **a la trocadilla,** in the contrary sense; in exchange. **II.** *m.* change, small coin.

trocador, ra, *n.* one who exchanges, changes or alters.

trocaico, *a.* trochaic, of trochees.

trocamiento, *m.* change; distortion; exchange. V. TRUEQUE.

trocante, *a.* bartering, exchanging.

trocánter, *m.* (anat.) trochanter.

trocar. I. *va.* (ind. TRÆCO: *pret.* TROQUÉ: *subj.* TRUEQUE) to exchange, barter; to change, alter; to interchange; to distort, pervert; to vomit. **II.** *vr.* to change; to be changed, transformed or reformed; to exchange seats with another.

trocar, *m.* (surg.) trocar.

trocatinta, *f.* (coll.) confusing mistake.

trocatinte, *m.* shot color, changing color.

troceo, *m.* (naut.) parrel, truss.

trociscar, *va.* to make into troches or lozenges.

trocisco, *m.* (pharm.) troche, lozenge.

trocla, *f.* pulley.

troco, *m.* (icht.) short sunfish.

trocoide, *f.* (geom.) trochoid.

trocha, *f.* cross path, short cut; rough road, trail; (mil.) military road; (r. w., Am.) gauge.

trochemoche.—a t., helter-skelter, pell-mell.

trochuela, *f. dim.* narrow path.

trofeo, *m.* trophy; spoils of war; victory; memorial; military insignia.

trófico, ca, *a.* trophic, relating to nutrition.

trofología, *f.* trophology, science of the nutrition of tissues.

troglodita. I. *n.* & *a.* troglodyte; glutton (-ous). **II.** *n.* rough, cruel person. **III.** *m. pl.* (zool.) Troglodytidæ.

troglodítico, ca, *a.* troglodytic.

troj, troje, *f.* granary, barn.

trojero, *m.* keeper of a granary.

trojezado, da, *a.* shredded, minced.

trola, *f.* (coll.) fib, hoax, gammon.

trole, *m.* (elec.) trolley.

tromba, *f.* waterspout.

trombón, *m.* (mus.) trombone.

trombosis, *f.* (med.) thrombosis.

trompa. I. *f.* trumpet; (mus.) horn; trunk of an elephant; proboscis of some insects; (found.) trompe; humming top; (arch.) projecting arch (from a wall); cradle, vault; (r. w.) cowcatcher, pilot (of a locomotive).—**t. de caza,** hunting horn. —**t. de Eustaquio,** (anat.) Eustachian tube.—**t. de Falopio,** (anat.) Fallopian tube.—**t. marina,** a musical one-string instrument, played with a bow; waterspout.—**a t. tañida,** at the sound of the trumpet.—**a t. y talega,** hurriedly, helter-skelter. **II.** *m.* horn player.

trompada, *f.* (coll.) fisticuff; collision, bump.

trompar, *vn.* to whip a top.

trompazo, *m.* = TROMPADA.

trompear, *vn.* to whip a top.

trompero, ra. I. *a.* deceptive, false, deceiving. **II.** *n.* top maker.

trompeta. I. *f.* trumpet; bugle. **II.** *m.* trumpeter; bugler; (coll.) puppet, noodle.

trompetada, *f.* (coll.) silly remark.

trompetazo, *m.* trumpet blast; bugle blast or call; (coll.) silly remark.

trompetear, *vn.* (coll.) to sound the trumpet.

trompeteo, *m.* sounding the bugle or trumpet.

trompetería, *f.* brass pipes of an organ.

trompetero, *m.* trumpet maker; trumpeter.

trompetilla, *f. dim.* small trumpet; ear trumpet; (Philip.) cheroot.—**de t.,** buzzing (s. o. certain mosquitoes).

trompicar. I. *va.* to trip, to make stumble; (coll.) to promote (an employee) over another who is entitled to the place. **II.** *vn.* to stumble frequently; to falter.

trompicón, *m.,* **trompilladura,** *f.* stumbling.

trompillar, *va.* & *vn.* = TROMPICAR.

trompillo, *m.* (Am.) (bot.) a bixa tree.

trompillón, *m.* (arch.) keystone of a cradle vault.

trompis, *m.* (coll.) blow with the fist.

trompo, *m.* whipping top; spinning top; man at chess; trochid (mollusk).—**ponerse como un t.,** to eat or drink to excess.

trompión, *m. aug.* big spinning top; (bot.) narcissus.—**a t.,** or **de t.,** helter-skelter.

tronada, *f.* thunderstorm.

tronador, ra. I. *n.* & *a.* thunderer (-ing). **II.** *m.* detonating rocket.

tronar, *v. impers.* & *vn.* (ind. TRUENA; *subj.* TRUENE) to thunder; (coll.) to lose one's all, to fail in business.—**t. con uno,** to fall out with one.—**por lo que pueda t.,** as a precaution, in case something happens.

tronca, *f.* truncation.

troncal, *a.* relating or belonging to the trunk or stem; trunk (u. a.), main.

troncar, *va.* to truncate.

tronco, *m.* trunk; stem, stalk; stock, origin; team of horses; unfeeling person.—**estar hecho un t.,** to be bereft of feeling and sensation; to be fast asleep.

tronchado, *pp.* & *a.* (her.) trouçonné.

tronchar, *va.* to cut off, chop off; to break (a trunk or stalk); to mutilate.

troncho, *m.* stem, stalk of garden plants.

tronchudo, da, *a.* stalky.

tronera. I. *f.* (fort.) embrasure; loophole; dormer, small skylight; porthole; pocket hole of a billiard table. **II.** *m.* harum-scarum, harebrained person.

tronerar, *va.* = ATRONERAR.

trónica, *f.* (coll.) rumor, gossip.

tronido, *m.* thunder, loud report.

tronitoso, sa, *a.* (coll.) resounding, thundering.

trono, *m.* throne; (eccl.) shrine.—*pl.* thrones, seventh choir of angels.

tronquista, *m.* coachman, teamster.

tronquito, *m. dim.* of TRONCO.

tronzador, *m.* two-handed saw.

tronzar, *va.* to shatter, break in pieces; (sew.) to plait.

tronzo, za, *a.* with cropped ears (s. o. horses).

tropa, *f.* troops, soldiers; crowd, multitude; (Am.) drove of cattle; (Arg.) fleet (of vehicles); (mil.) ranks; beat to arms.—*pl.* (mil.) forces, army.—**t. de línea,** regular or standing army; army corps.—**t. de marina,** marines.—**t. ligera,** skirmishers.—**en t.,** in random groups, without order.

tropeína, *f.* (chem.) tropeine.

tropel, *m.* rush, hurry, bustle, confusion; huddle; heap of things, mess, jumble; crowd.—**de,** or **en, t.,** tumultuously, in a throng.

tropelía, *f.* rush, hurry, confusion; injustice, outrage.

tropeoleo, a, *a.* & *f.* (bot.) Tropæolum.

tropezadero, *m.* stumbling place.

tropezador, ra, *n.* tripper, stumbler.

tropezadura, *f.* stumbling.

tropezar. I. *vn.* (*ind.* TROPIEZO: *pret.* TROPECÉ: *subj.* TROPIECE) to stumble; (w. **con**) to strike against, to meet with, to meet; to stumble upon, light on, happen to find; to slip (into crime or blunders); to wrangle, squabble. **II.** *vr.* (farr.) to interfere (s. o. horses).

tropezón, na. I. *n.* & *a.* interferer (-ing) (s. o. horses). **II.** *m.* tripping; stumbling; obstacle, stumbling block.—**a tropezones,** (coll.) by fits and starts; painfully, falling and rising, trudging along.

tropezoso, sa, *a.* apt to stumble or trip.

tropical, *a.* tropical.

trópico, ca. I. *a.* (rhet.) tropical. **II.** *m.* (ast., geog.) tropic.

tropidina, *f.* (chem.) tropidine.

tropiece, tropieza, tropiezo. *V.* TROPEZAR.

tropiezo, *m.* stumble; obstacle, hitch; slip, fault, error; quarrel, dispute, squabble.

tropina, *f.* (chem.) tropine.

tropismo, *m.* (biol.) tropism.

tropo, *m.* (rhet.) trope.—**tropología,** *f.* tropology.—**tropológico, ca,** *a.* tropological.

troque, *m.* knot made in cloths when dyeing them, to show the original color.

troquel, *m.* die (as for coining).

troquelar, *va.* = ACUÑAR.

troqueo, *m.* (poet.) trochee (— ‿).

troquillo, *m.* (arch.) trochilus.

trotador, ra, *n.* & *a.* trotter (-ing).

trotar, *va.* & *vn.* to trot; (coll.) to hustle.

trote, *m.* trot.—**t. cochinero,** rack.—**al t.,** trotting, at a trot; (coll.) in haste.—**tomar el t.,** (coll.) to run away.

trotillo, *m. dim.* light trot.

trotón, na. I. *f.* trotter (-ing). **II.** *m.* horse.

trotonería, *f.* continual trot.

trova, *f.* metrical composition; ballad.

trovador, ra, *n.* troubadour, minstrel.

trovadoresco, ca, *a.* pertaining to, or in the way of, minstrels or troubadours.—**trovar,** *vn.* to versify, write poetry; to misconstrue.—**trovero,** *m.* trouvère, trouveur.—**trovista,** *n.* = TROVADOR.—**trovo,** *m.* popular love ballad.

troz, *f.* (obs.) = TROJ.

Troya, *f.* Troy.—**aquí fué T.,** here was Troy; only the ruins left; here, or there, 's the rub, or the difficulty; here, or there, the trouble begins.—**¡arda T!** let happen what will.

troyano, na, *n.* & *a.* Trojan.

troza, *f.* log (of wood); (naut.) parrel truck.

trozar, *va.* to cut into logs; to break, shatter.

trozo, *m.* piece, chunk, fragment, part; (naut.) junk; selection, passage (from a book, etc.); (mil.) division of a column.—**t. de madera,** chump.

trucar, *vn.* (*pret.* TRUQUÉ: *subj.* TRUQUE) to make the first bet at the game of TRUQUE; to pocket a ball at pool or trucks.—**truco,** *m.* pocketing a pool ball.—*pl.* pool (billiards).

truculento, ta, *a.* truculent, fierce.

trucha, *f.* (icht.) trout; derrick, gin.—**t. de mar,** (icht.) sea trout.

truchero, ra, *n.* fisher or seller of trout.

truchimán, na, *n.* (coll.) expert buyer; shrewd trader.

truchuela, *f.* small trout; small dry codfish.

trué, *m.* fine linen from Troyes.

trueco, *m.* exchange, barter.—**a t.,** or **en t., de,** in exchange of.

trueco, trueca. *V.* TROCAR.

trueno, *m.* thunder; loud report (as of cannon); (coll.) harum-scarum, wild youth.—**t. gordo,** loud detonation; big piece of scandal; sensational resolution.

trueque, *m.* exchange, barter.—**a t.,** or **en t., de,** in exchange for.

trufa, *f.* (bot.) truffle; lie, story, fib.—**trufador, ra,** *n.* story teller, fibber.—**trufar. I.** *va.* to stuff or cook with truffles. **II.** *vn.* to fib, lie.

truhán, na, *n.* rascal, scoundrel, knave; buffoon, jester, mountebank.—**truhanada,** *f.* piece of rascality.—**truhanamente,** *adv.* villainously, knavishly.—**truhanear,** *vn.* to play the rascal; to play the buffoon.—**truhanería,** *f.* rascality, scoundrelism; buffoonery, low jest.—**truhanesco, ca,** *a.* knavish, rascally; clownish.

truja, *f.* olive bin in oil mills.—**trujal,** *m.* oil press; wine press; oil mill; copper for soap making.—**trujaleta,** *f.* vessel for the juice in a wine press.

trujamán, *n.* expert buyer or trader; dragoman, interpreter.—**trujamanear,** *vn.* to act as an interpreter, broker, buyer, or seller; to trade, to barter.—**trujamanía,** *f.* brokering, brokerage.

trujimán, *n.* = TRUJAMÁN.

trulla, *f.* noise, bustle, hurly-burly; crowd, multitude; (mas.) trowel.

trullo, *m.* (orn.) teal; vat for the juice of pressed grapes.

trun, *m.* (bot.) a Chilean variety of bur.

truncadamente, *adv.* in a truncated manner.

truncado, da, *a.* & *pp.* truncate, truncated.

truncamiento, *m.* truncation; maiming.

truncar, *va.* (*pret.* TRUNQUÉ: *subj.* TRUNQUE) to truncate; to maim; to mutilate (a speech, quotation, etc.).

trupial, *m.* (orn.) troopial.

truque, *m.* a card game.

truquero, *m.* keeper of a pool table.

truquiflor, *m.* a card game.

trusas, *f. pl.* trunk hose.

tsetsé, *f.* tsetse fly.

tú, *pers. pron.* 2d *person, m.* or *f.* thou.—**a t. por t.,** thee for thee; disrespectfully.—**de t. por t.,** intimately.—**tratar de t.,** to thou, to be on intimate terms with.

tu, *poss. pron. m.* or *f.* (*pl.* **tus**) thy.

tuatúa, *f.* (bot.) American spurge.

tuáutem, *n.* (coll.) leading spirit, mover; essential point.

tuba, *f.* (Philip.) tuba, a beverage obtained from certain palms.

tuberculina, *f.* tuberculine.

tuberculización, *f.* tuberculosis; tubercularization.

tubérculo, *m.* (bot.) tuber; (med.) tubercle.

tuberculoso, sa, *a.* tuberculous.

tuberculosis, *f.* (med.) tuberculosis.

tubería, *f.* tubing; piping; pipe line.

tuberosa, *f.* (bot.) tuberose.—**tuberosidad,** *f.* tuberosity.—**tuberoso, sa,** *a.* tuberous.

tubífero, ra, *a.* (biol.) provided with tubes.

tubiforme, *a.* tubiform, tubular.

tubo, *m.* tube; pipe; duct; lamp chimney.—**t. acústico,** speaking tube.—**t. de Crookes,** Crookes tube.—**t. de ensayo,** test tube.—**t. de Géissler,** Geissler tube.—**t. de subida,** (aer.) climbing shaft (in a dirigible).—**t. de vacío,** vacuum tube.—**t. intestinal,** intestinal canal, intestines.—**t. termiónico,** (rad.) thermionic valve.

tubular, *a.* tubular; tube-shaped.

tubuloso, sa, *a.* (bot.) tubulous.

tucán, *m.* (orn.) toucan; (**T-,** ast.) Toucan, Toucanis.

tucía, *f.* tutty.

tuciorismo, *m.* (theol.) tutiorism.

tuciorista, *n.* & *a.* (theol.) tutiorist (-ic).

tuco, *m.* (Arg.) glowworm; (Peru) a kind of owl.

tucúquerre, *m.* (Ch.) a very large owl.

tucuso, *m.* (Ven.) (orn.) humming bird.

tudel, *m.* mouthpiece of a bassoon.

tudesco, ca. I. *a.* German. **II.** *m.* a wide cloak.

tueca, *f.,* **tueco,** *m.* stump, stub; hole made by borers in wood.

tuera, *f.* (bot.) colocynth, bitter apple.

tuerca, *f.* nut, female screw, lock nut.

tuerce, *m.* sprain. *V.* TORCEDURA.

tuero, *m.* brushwood; (bot.) spickne!.

tuerto, ta. I. *a.* one-eyed, blind of one eye. **II.** *m.* (obs.) wrong, injury.—*pl.* pains after childbirth. —**a tuertas,** contrariwise, on the contrary.—**a tuertas o a derechas,** or **a t. o a derecho,** right or wrong; inconsiderately.

tueste, *m.* toast, toasting.

tuesto, tueste. *V.* TOSTAR.

tuétano, *m.* marrow; pith of trees.—**hasta los tuétanos,** to the marrow.

tuerzo, tuerza. *V.* TORCER.

tufarada, *f.* strong scent or smell.

tufo, *m.* vapor, emanation, effluvium; (coll.) strong and offensive breath; conceit, airs, snobbishness; locks of hair over the temples; (min.) tufa.

tugurio, *m.* shepherd's hut, cabin; (coll.), mean, small room, "hole"; low place, "joint."

tuición, *f.* (law) defence, protection.

tuina, *f.* (tail.) long, full jacket.

tuitivo, va, *a.* (law) defensive, protective.

tul, *m.* tulle.

tulipán, *m.* (bot.) tulip; tulip-shaped globe or reflector.

tulipero, *m.* (bot.) tulip tree, whitewood.

tullidez, *f.* partial or total paralysis (sp. app. to that of the legs).

tullido, da, *a.* partially or totally paralyzed (sp. app. to the legs).

tullidura, *f.* dung of birds of prey.

tullimiento, *m.* (med.) contraction of the tendons.

tullir. I. *va.* to maim, cripple. **II.** *vn.* to void, to let out dung (s. o. birds). **III.** *vr.* to be crippled.

tumba, *f.* tomb, grave; roof of a coach; ornamental box seat in state coaches; tumble, somersault.

tumbacuartillos, *m.* sot, old toper.

tumbadero, *m.* tumbling place in gymnasium.

tumbadillo, *m.* (naut.) roundhouse, cuddy.

tumbado, da, *a. & pp.* vaulted, arched.

tumbaga, *f.* (jewel.) tombac, pinchbeck; cheap finger ring.

tumbagón, *m. aug.* (jewel.) tombac bracelet.

tumbar. I. *va.* to fell, throw down; (coll.) to knock down, stun, overpower (as a powerful odor). **II.** *vn.* to tumble, fall down, roll down; (naut.) to heel, to run aground. **III.** *vr.* (coll.) to lie down.

tumbilla, *f.* brazier for warming beds.

tumbo, *m.* tumble, fall; somersault; book containing the privileges and title deeds of monasteries, etc.—**t. de dado,** imminent peril.—**t. de olla,** ingredients or constituents (broth, meat, vegetables) of a meat-and-vegetable soup.

tumbón, na. I. *n.* (coll.) lazy person; sly, cunning person. **II.** *m.* coach or trunk with an arched roof or lid.

tumefacción, *f.* tumefaction, swelling.

tumescente, *a.* tumescent.

túmido, da, *a.* swollen, tumid, bloated; pompous, highflown; (arch.) domed.

tumor, *m.* tumor.—**tumorcico, illo, ito,** *m. dim.* small tumor.

tumoroso, sa, *a.* having tumors.

tumulario, ria, *a.* tombic.

túmulo, *m.* tomb; funeral pile; mound; tumulus; catafalque.

tumulto, *m.* tumult, uproar, uprising; mob.

tumultuante, *a.* fomenting sedition.

tumultuar. I. *va.* to raise in, or incite to, a tumult. **II.** *vr.* to rise in arms.

tumultuariamente, *adv.* tumultuarily.

tumultuario, ria, *a.* tumultuary, tumultuous.—**tumultuosamente,** *adv.* tumultuously.

tumultuoso, sa, *a.* tumultuous.

tuna, *f.* (bot.) opuntia, prickly pear or Indian fig; idle and licentious life; truantship.—**correr la t.** = TUNAR.

tunal, *m.* (bot.) opuntia; opuntia field.

tunanta, *a. & f.* shrewd, rascally woman.

tunantada, *f.* rascality, sharp practice.

tunante. I. *a.* leading a roving and licentious life. **II.** *n.* truant, idler, rake; rascal, rogue.

tunantear, *vn.* to act the rascal.

tunantuela, *f. dim.* roguish girl, hoiden.

tunantuelo, *m. dim.* little rascal.

tunar, *vn.* to lead a licentious and vagrant life; to loaf, stroll.

tunda, *f.* shearing of cloth; (coll.) sound beating or whipping.

tundente, *a.* beating, whipping; producing contusion.

tundición, *f.* shearing of cloth.—**tundidor,** *m.* cloth shearer.—**tundidora,** *f.* cloth-shearing machine.—**tundidura,** *f.* shearing of cloth.

tundir, *va.* to shear (cloth); (coll.) to drub, beat, cudgel, whip.

tundizno, *m.* shearings from cloth.

tunear, *vn.* to act the rogue.

tunecí; tunecino, na, *n. & a.* Tunisian.

túnel, *m.* tunnel.

tungstato, *m.* (chem.) tungstate.

tungsteno, *m.* (chem.) tungsten.

túngstico, ca, *a.* (chem.) tungstic, tungstenic.

túnica, *f.* tunic, chiton; robe, gown; (anat. and bot.) tunic, tunicle.—**t. de Cristo,** (bot.) stramonium.

tunicado, da. I. *m. & a.* (zool.) tunicate. **II.** *m. pl.* Tunicata.

tunicela, *f.* tunic; (eccl.) tunicle.

túnico, *m.* robe, gown; (Cuba) frock, dress.

tuno, na. I. *a.* rascally, roguish, sly, cunning. **II.** *m.* truant, rake, rascal, rogue.

tuntún, *m.* (Colomb.) a kind of anæmic fever.—**al buen t.,** (coll.) at random, heedlessly, at haphazard.

tupa, *f.* tight packing; (coll.) satiety, repletion.

tupé, *m.* toupee, foretop; (coll.) cheek, gall, brass, self-assurance.

tupí, *a. & m.* Tupian.

tupido, da, *a. & pp.* dense, thick; close-woven; blocked, choked, obstructed.

tupinambo, *m.* (bot.) Jerusalem artichoke.

tupir. I. *va.* to pack tight; to make thick, or compact; to choke, obstruct; block up; stop up. **II.** *vr.* to stuff or glut one's self.

turanio, nia, *n. & a.* Turanian.

turba, *f.* crowd, rabble, mob; peat, turf.

turbáceo, a, *a.* peaty.

turbación, *f.* perturbation; confusion, embarrassment.

turbadamente, *adv.* confusedly.

turbador, ra, *n.* disturber, perturbator.

turbal, *m.* peat bog, peat bed.

turbamiento, *m.* = TURBACIÓN.

turbamulta, *f.* crowd, rabble, mob.

turbante. I. *a.* disturbing. **II.** *m.* turban.

turbar, *va. & vr.* to disturb, upset; to disquiet, alarm, confuse, embarrass.

turbativo, va, *a.* alarming; disturbing.

turbera, *f.* peat bog, peat moss.

turbia, *f.* muddy water.—**turbiamente,** *adv.* obscurely, confusedly.—**túrbido, da,** *a.* muddy, turbid.—**turbiedad, turbieza,** *f.* muddiness, turbidity; obscurity of language.

turbina, *f.* turbine.—**t. axial,** axial turbine.—**t. centrífuga,** outward-flow turbine.—**t. centripeta,** inward-flow turbine.—**t. de acción,** impulse turbine.—**t. de reacción,** reaction turbine.—**t. de vapor,** steam turbine.—**t. límite,** limit turbine.—**t. paralela,** axial turbine.—**t. radial,** radial turbine.—**t. tangencial,** tangential turbine.

turbino, *m.* pulverized turpeth.

turbinto, *m.* (bot.) terebinth.

turbio, bia. I. *a.* muddy, turbid; disturbed, confused, upset; troubled, turbulent; indistinct; obscure (language). **II.** *m. pl.* dregs.

turbión, *m.* squally shower; sweep, rush.

turbit, *m.* (bot.) turpeth.—**t. mineral,** (pharm.) turpeth mineral.
turbonada, *f.* squall, pelting shower.
turbulencia, *f.* turbidness; turbulence.
turbulentamente, *adv.* turbulently.
turbulento, ta, *a.* turbid; turbulent.
turca, *f.* (coll.) tipsiness.—**coger una t.,** to get drunk.
turco, ca. I. *adj.* Turkish. II. *n.* Turk.—**el gran t.,** the Grand Turk.
turcomano, na, *n.* & *a.* Turkoman.
turcople, *a.* born of Turkish father and Greek mother.
túrdido, da. I. *a.* (orn.) turdine. II. *m. pl.* Turdidæ.
túrdiga, *f.* strip of hide.
turdión, *m.* ancient Spanish dance.
turgencia, *f.* (med.) swelling, turgescence.
turgente, *a.* turgescent, turgid; (poet.) protuberant, prominent.
túrgido, da, *a.* (poet.) prominent, bulging.
turibular, *va.* to cense with a thurible.
turibulario, turiferario, *m.* (eccl.) thurifer, censer bearer.—**turíbulo,** *m.* (eccl.) censer, thurible.—**turífero, ra,** *a.* thuriferous, incense-bearing.
turión, *m.* (bot.) turion.
turismo, *m.* tourism, touring.—**de t.,** touring (sp. app. to automobiles).
turista, *n.* & *a.* tourist (-ing).
turma, *f.* testicle; lamb fry.—**t. de tierra,** (bot.) truffle.
turmalina, *f.* (miner.) tourmaline.
turnar, *vn.* & *vr.* to alternate; to go or work by turns.
turnio, nia, *a.* squint-eyed; torvous.
turno, *m.* turn.—**al t.,** by turns.—**por su t.,** in one's turn.
turón, *m.* a kind of field mouse.
turonense, *a.* of or from Tours.
turpial, *m.* (orn.) troopial.
turquesa, *f.* (jewel.) turquoise; bullet mold; mold, form.
turquesado, da, *a.* of turquoise color.
turquesco, ca, *a.* Turkish.—**a la t.,** in the Turkish manner.
turquí; turquino, na, *a.* deep blue.
turrar, *va.* to toast; to broil.
turrón, *m.* nougat, almond paste; (coll.) public office; sinecure.—**t. de Jijona,** sweet-almond paste.—**comer del t.,** to fill a public office.
turronería, *f.* TURRÓN shop.
turronero, ra, *n.* maker or seller of TURRÓN.
turulato, ta, *a.* (coll.) dumbfounded, stupefied.
turulés, *a.* app. to a kind of strong grapes.
turumbón, *m.* bump on the head.
turupial, *m.* (Ven.) (orn.) troopial.
¡tus! *interj.* used in calling dogs.—**sin decir t. ni mus,** (coll.) without saying a word.
tusa, *f.* (Am.) PAJILLA: corncob; (Ch.) mane of a horse.
tusílago, *m.* (bot.) coltsfoot.
¡tuso! *int.* get away! (app. to dogs).
tuso, sa, *a.* (Colomb.) pitted by smallpox.
tusón, *m.* fleece wool; (prov.) colt under two years old.
tusona, *f.* (Andal.) filly under two years old.
tute, a card game.
tutear, *va.* to thou, to treat with familiarity.
tutela, *f.* guardianship, tutelage, tutorage, protection.—**t. dativa,** (law) guardianship appointed by a court.
tutelar, *a.* tutelar, tutelary.
tuteo, *m.* thouing, use of TÚ (thou).
tutía, *f.* tutty. *V.* ATUTÍA.
tutilimundi, *m.* = MUNDONUEVO.
tutiplén.—a t., (coll.) abundantly.
tutor, ra. I. *n.* tutor, instructor; guardian.—**t. dativo,** (law) guardian appointed by a court. II. *m.* training pole for plants.
tutora, *f.* tutoress, guardian; governess.
tutoría, *f.* tutelage, guardianship.
tutriz, *f.* tutoress, governess.

tuturutu, *a.* (S. A.) dumbfounded.
tuya, *f.* (bot.) thuya.—**t. articulada,** sandarach tree.
tuyo, ya, *poss. pron. 2d pers. m.* & *f.* (sometimes with the *def. art.*) thine.—**los tuyos,** thy family, thy people, yours.

U

u. I. *f.* u (letter). II. *conj.* (before words beginning with *o* or *ho*) or.
U.—en U, U-shaped (*tubo en U,* U-tube); channel-shaped (*hierro en U,* channel iron, channel).
uatérfono, *m.* (hydr.) hydrophone.
ubérrimo, ma, *a. sup.* very fruitful; exceedingly plentiful.
ubicación, *f.* situation, location, position.
ubicar, *vn.* & *vr.* to lie, to be situate.
ubicuidad, *f.* ubiquity.—**ubicuo, cua,** *a.* ubiquitous.—**ubiquidad,** *f.* = UBICUIDAD.
ubiquitario, ria, *a.* & *n.* Ubiquitarian.
ubre, *f.* udder; milk bag.
ubrera, *f.* (med.) thrush.
ucase, *m.* ukase.
ucranio, nia, *n.* & *a.* Ukrainian.
udómetro, *m.* udometer, rain gauge.
uesnorueste, *m.* west-northwest.
uessudueste, *m.* west-southwest.
ueste, *m.* west.
¡uf! *interj.* denoting weariness or annoyance.
ufanamente, *adv.* ostentatiously, boastfully, with an air of satisfaction.
ufanarse, *vr.* to boast, pride one's self.
ufanía, *f.* pride, conceit; joy, pleasure.
ufano, na, *a.* conceited, proud, haughty; gay, cheerful; masterly.
ufo.—a u., parasitically.
ujier, *n.* usher, doorkeeper.—**u. de cámara,** usher of the king's privy chamber.
ulano, *m.* (mil.) uhlan.
úlcera, *f.* (med.) ulcer; (bot.) rot.
ulceración, *f.* ulceration.—**ulcerado, da,** *a.* & *pp.* ulcerated.—**ulcerante,** *a.* ulcerating.
ulcerar. I. *va.* to ulcerate. II. *vr.* to become ulcerated.—**ulcerativo, va,** *a.* ulcerating.
ulceroso, sa, *a.* ulcerous.
ulema, *m.* Ulema.
uliginoso, sa, *a.* uliginous.
ulmáceo, a. I. *a.* (bot.) ulmaceous. II. *f. pl.* (bot.) Ulmaceæ.
ulpa, *m.* (S. A.) maize gruel.
ulterior, *a.* ulterior, farther; subsequent.
ulteriormente, *adv.* subsequently.
ultimado, da, *a.* & *pp.* ended, finished.
últimamente, *adv.* lastly, finally; of late, recently.
ultimar, *va.* to end, finish, close.
ultimato, ultimátum, *m.* ultimatum; (coll.) final resolution.
ultimidad, *f.* ultimity, last stage.
último, ma, *a.* last, latest; ultimate; final; latter; highly finished; most valuable; utmost; remote.—**ú. suplicio,** capital punishment.—**a la última,** after the latest fashion.—**a ú. hora,** at the eleventh hour, at the last hour.—**a últimos de,** in the latter part of the (month, etc.).—**estar a lo u.,** or **en las últimas,** to be well-informed; to be on its, or one's, last legs, to be near its, or one's, end.—**por ú.,** lastly; finally.
ultra, *adv.* besides.
ultrajador, ra, *n.* one who outrages or insults.
ultrajamiento, *m.* outrage, affront.
ultrajar, *va.* to outrage, offend, abuse; to despise.
ultraje, *m.* outrage, insult; contempt; abuse.
ultrajosamente, *adv.* outrageously.
ultrajoso, sa, *a.* outrageous; overbearing.
ultramar, *m.* beyond the sea, across the sea.
ultramarino, na. I. *a.* ultramarine. II. *m.* ultramarine, finest blue.—*pl.* (com.) oversea articles.
ultramaro, *m.* ultramarine color.

ultramicroscópico, ca, *a.* ultramicroscopic.
ultramicroscopio, *m.* ultramicroscope.
ultramontanismo, *m.* ultramontanism.
ultramontano, na, *n. & a.* ultramontane.
ultramundano, na, *a.* ultramundane.
ultranza.—a u., to death; at all costs, unflinchingly.
ultrapuertos, *m.* beyond the seaports.
ultrarrojo, ja, *a.* (phys.) infra-red.
ultratumba.—de u., en u., beyond the grave.
ultraviolado, da; ultravioleta, *a.* (phys.) ultraviolet.
úlula, *f.* (orn.) owl.
ulular, *vn.* to screech, hoot, ululate.
ululato, *m.* howl, screech, ululation.
umbela, *f.* (bot.) umbel.
umbelífero, ra. I. *a.* (bot.) umbelliferous. **II.** *f. pl.* the parsley family.
umbilicado, da, *a.* navel-shaped; umbilicated.
umbilical, *a.* umbilical.
umbráculo, *m.* shaded place for plants.
umbral, *m.* threshold; (arch.) lintel; beginning, rudiment.—**umbralar,** *va.* (arch.) to lintel.
umbrático, ca; umbrátil, *a.* umbrageous, shady. —**umbrío, bría. I.** *a.* umbrageous, shady. **II.** *f.* shady place, grove.—**umbroso, sa,** *a.* shady.
un, una. I. *indef. art.* a, an. **II.** *n. & a.* one.
unánime, *a.* unanimous.—**unánimemente,** *adv.* unanimously.
unanimidad, *f.* unanimity.—**por u.,** unanimously.
uncia, *f.* (law) twelfth part of an estate.
uncial, *a.* uncial.
unciforme, (anat.) unciform.
uncinariasis, *f.* (med.) uncinariasis.
unción, *f.* unction, anointing; (eccl.) extreme unction.—*pl.* treatment by unctions of mercury.
uncionario, ria. I. *a.* being under mercurial treatment. **II.** *m.* place where external mercurial treatment is taken.
uncir, *va.* (ind. UNZO: subj. UNZA) to yoke.
undante, *a.* waving, undulating.
undécimo, ma, *a.* eleventh.
undécuplo, pla, *a.* eleven times as much.
undísono, na, *a.* (poet.) billowy.
undívago, ga, *a.* (poet.) wavy.
undoso, sa, *a.* wavy, undulating.
undulación, *f.* undulation; wave motion.
undular, *vn.* to undulate; to wriggle.
undulatorio, ria, *a.* undulatory.
ungido, *pp. & m.* anointed priest or king.
ungimiento, *m.* unction.
ungir, *va.* (ind. UNJO: subj. UNJA) to anoint.
ungüentario, ria. I. *a.* unguentary. **II.** *m.* one who prepares ointments; unguentarium.
ungüento, *m.* unguent, ointment.—**u. amaracino,** ointment of marjoram.
unguiculado, da, *a.* (zool.) unguiculate.
unguis, *m.* (anat.) os unguis.
ungulado, da. I. *n. & a.* (zool.) ungulate. **II.** *m. pl.* Ungulata.
unible, *a.* that may be joined or united.
únicamente, *adv.* only, simply, solely.
unicelular, *a.* unicellular.
único, ca, *a.* only, sole; singular, unique, rare, unmatched, unparalleled.
unicolor, *a.* unicolor, one-color.
unicornio, *m.* (myth.) unicorn; rhinoceros; (U-, ast.) Unicorn.—**u. de mar,** (zool.) narwhal.
unidad, *f.* unity; unit; (rhet. and art) unity.—**u. de acción, de lugar y de tiempo,** dramatic unities.—**la u.,** (math.) unity, 1.
unidamente, *adv.* jointly, unitedly.
unificación, *f.* unification.
unificar, *va.* (pret. UNIFIQUÉ: subj. UNIFIQUE) to unify.
unifoliado, da, *a.* (bot.) unifoliate.
uniformación, *f.* standardization, uniformity.
uniformador, ra, *a.* that makes uniform; standardizing.
uniformar, *va.* to make uniform; to standardize; to uniform.

uniforme. I. *a.* uniform. **II.** *m.* uniform; regimentals.
uniformemente, *adv.* uniformly.
uniformidad, *f.* uniformity.
unigénito, a, *a.* only-begotten.
unilateral, *a.* (for.) unilateral.
unión, *f.* union, harmony, correspondence; resemblance; agreement, concord, unity; wedding, marriage; composition of ingredients; combination; coöperation; contiguity; linked finger rings; (surg.) closing of the lips of a wound; (mech.) coupling, fastening, connection joining, joint; (r. w.) junction; (com.) fusion, consolidation.
unípara, *a.* uniparous.
unípede, *a.* uniped.
unipersonal, *a.* unipersonal.
unipolar, *a.* (elec.) single-pole.
unir. I. *va.* to join, unite, couple, bind, connect, attach; to mix, combine; bring together; to harmonize. **II.** *vr.* to join, unite, get together; to adhere, concur; to be contiguous; to wed, be married; (com.) to consolidate, merge, combine.
unisexual, *a.* (bot.) unisexual.
unisón. I. *a.* unison. **II.** *m.* (mus.) unison.
unisonancia, *f.* unisonance; monotony.
unísono, na, *a.* unison, sounding alike.—**al,** or **en, u.,** in unison; together; unanimously.
unitario, ria, *a. & n.* (eccl.) Unitarian; (pol.) supporter of centralization.
unitarismo, *m.* (eccl.) Unitarianism.
unitivo, va, *a.* unitive.
univalvo, va, *a.* univalve.
universal, *a.* universal; learned, well-informed.
universalidad, *f.* universality.
universalísimo, *a. sup.* (log.) universal.
universalmente, *adv.* universally.
universidad, *f.* university; body of persons forming an institution; universality.
universitario, ria, *a.* university (u. a.)
universo, sa. I. *a.* universal. **II.** *m.* universe.
univocación, *f.* univocation.—**unívocamente,** *adv.* univocally, unanimously.—**univocarse,** *vr.* to have the same meaning.—**unívoco, ca,** *a.* univocal.
uno, na. I. *pron.* one; some one.—*pl.* some (people).—**u. a otro,** each other, mutually.—**u. que otro,** some, a few.—**u. y otro,** both.—**unos a otros,** each other, one another.—**unos cuantos,** a few.—**cada u.,** each one.—**de u.,** one's.—**los unos a los otros =** UNOS A OTROS. **II.** *a.* one.—*pl.* some; nearly, about. **III.** *n.* one (number).—**u. a u. =** DE U, EN U.—**u. con otro,** on an average.—**u. por u.,** one after another; one by one, one at a time.—**una y no más,** never again.—**a una,** unanimously, of one accord.—**de una,** at once.—**de u. en u.,** one by one; in single file. —**todo es uno,** it is all the same. **IV.** *f.*—**la u.,** one o'clock.
untador, na. I. *n. & a.* oiler (-ing), coater (-ing), greaser (-ing), painter (-ing), etc. *V.* UNTAR.— **untadura,** *f.*: **untamiento,** *m.,* UNTURA; oiling, greasing, coating, etc. *V.* UNTURA.
untar. I. *va.* to anoint; to grease, oil, smear, paint, coat; to suborn, bribe.—**u. las manos,** to grease the hands, to bribe. **II.** *vr.* to be greased or smeared; to embezzle.
untaza, *f.* grease. *V.* ENJUNDIA.
unto, *m.* grease, fat of animals; unguent, ointment.—**u. amarillo,** or **de Méjico,** (coll.) bribe money.—**u. de oso,** bear's grease.—**u. de puerco,** hog's lard.—**u. de arna =** U. AMARILLO.
untuosidad, *f.* unctuosity, greasiness.
untuoso, sa, *a.* unctuous, greasy.
untura, *f.* unction; ointment, liniment.
uña, *f.* finger nail; toenail; hoof, claw, or talon of beasts; sting of the scorpion; (bot.) thorn; pointed hook of instruments; short stump of a tree; scab; excrescence on the lachrymal caruncle; (coll.) dexterity in stealing or filching: (mech.) gripper, clutch, claw; (mus.) plectrum for the mandolin; (naut.) fluke, palm or bill of an anchor.—**u. de caballo,** (bot.) coltsfoot.—**u. gata,** (bot.) = GATUÑA.—**afilar las uñas,** to sharpen one's wits, try one's best.—**a u. de caballo,** at full gallop, in great haste.—**enseñar la u. =** MOS-

TRAR LA U.—**de uñas**, at daggers drawn, at logger-heads.—**hincar, or meter, la u.**, to overcharge; to sell at an exorbitant price.—**largo de uñas**, filcher.—**mostrar las uñas**, to be inexorable; to show one's teeth.—**mostrar la u.**, to discover one's foibles or ignorance.—**sacar las uñas**, (coll.) to avail one's self of every means in a difficulty.—**ser u. y carne**, to be hand and glove, to be fast friends.—**tener uñas**, (coll.) to be very difficult, to be a tough job, a big order.

uñada, f. nail scratch, nip.—**uñarada**, f. scratch with the nail.—**uñate**, m. (coll.) pinching with the nail; chuckfarthing.—**uñaza**, f. aug. large nail.—**uñero**, m. ingrowing nail; (med.) felon.

uñeta, f. dim. small finger nail; small clutch; stonecutter's chisel; chuckfarthing (boys' play).

uñidura, f. yoking.—**uñir**, va. to yoke.

uñita, uela, f. dim. little finger nail.

uñoso, sa, a. having long nails or claws.

¡upa! interj. up, up! hoop-la!

upas, m. upas, a Javanese tree and the poison prepared from it.

upupa, f. (orn.) hoopoe.

uralita, f. (min.) uralite.

urania, f. (zool.) a moth of the genus Urania.

uranio, nia, I. a. uranic, celestial. II. m. (chem.) uranium.

uranismo, m. Urningism, homosexuality.

uranita, f. (min.) uranite.

Urano, m. (astr.) Uranus.

uranografía, f. uranography.—**uranógrafo**, m. uranographist.—**uranometría**, f. uranometry.

urao, m. (S. A.) (min.) trona.

urari, m. urare, curare.

urato, m. (chem.) urate.

urbanamente, adv. courteously, politely.

urbanidad, f. urbanity, civility, manners.

urbanización, f. laying out and improving land for building.—**urbanizar**, va. (pret. URBANICÉ; subj. URBANICE) to lay out (land) for a town; to polish, render polite.

urbano, na. I. a. urban; urbane, courteous, well-bred. II. m. militiamen.

urbe, f. large modern city, metropolis.

urca, f. (naut.) hooker, dogger; storeship; (icht.) a species of whale.

urce, m. (bot.) heath.

urchilla, f. archil or orchil.

urdidera, f. woman warper; warping frame.

urdidor, ra. I. n. warper. II. m. warping frame, warping mill.

urdidura, f. warping.

urdimbre, urdiembre, f. warp, warping chain.

urdir, va. to warp; to plot, contrive, scheme.

urea, f. (chem.) urea.

ureida, f. (chem.) ureide.

uremia, f. (med.) uræmia.

urémico, ca, a. uræmic.

urente, a. hot, burning, scorching.

urétere, m. (anat.) ureter.

urético, ca; **uretral**, a. urethral.

uretra, f. (anat.) urethra.—**uretritis**, f. (med.) urethritis.—**uretroscopio**, m. (surg.) urethro-scope.—**uretrotomía**, f. urethrotomy.

uretrótomo, m. urethrotome.

urgencia, f. urgency, exigence; obligation.

urgente, a. urgent, pressing.

urgentemente, adv. urgently.

urgir, vn. (ind. URJO: subj. URJA) to be urgent, to require immediate action.

úrico, ca, a. uric.

urinal; urinario, ria. I. a. urinary. II. m. urinal.

urna, f. urn, casket; glass case; ballot box.

urnición, f. (naut.) top timbers.

uro, m. (zool.) aurochs.

urobilina, f. (chem.) urobilin.

urodelos, m. pl. (zool.) Urodela.

urogallo, m. (orn.) a species of woodcock.

urolito, m. (med.) urolith.

uromancia, f. uromancy.

urómetro, m. urinometer.

uroscopia, f. uroscopy.

urraca, f. (orn.) magpie.

Ursa, f. (ast.) Bear.—**U. Mayor**, Great Bear.—**U. Menor**, Little Bear.

úrsido, da. I. a. (zool.) ursine. II. m. pl. Ursidæ.

ursino, na, a. ursine.

ursulina, n. & a. Ursuline.

urticáceo, a. I. a. (bot.) urticaceous. II. f. pl. Urticaceæ.

urticación, f. (med.) urtication.

urticante, a. urticating.

urticaria, f. (med.) urticaria, nettle rash, hives.

urubú, m. urubu, black vulture.

uruguayo, ya, a. & n. Uruguayan.

usadamente, adv. according to custom.

usado, da, a. & pp. used; worn out; inured, accustomed, used; fashionable, frequent; second-hand.—**al u.**, (com. law) at usance.

usagre, m. (med.) scald head, infantile eczema.

usanza, f. usage, custom.

usar, I. va. to use; to wear; to enjoy the use of; to exercise (an employment). II. vn. to be accustomed. III. vr. to be in use or fashion; to be wont.

usarcé, usarced, n. (obs.) (contr. of VUESA MERCED) your honor.

usencia, n. (contr. of VUESTRA REVERENCIA) your reverence.

useñoría, n. = USÍA.

usgo, m. loathing.

usía, n. (contr. of VUESTRA SEÑORÍA) your lord-ship (ladyship); your excellence.

uso, m. use; usage, custom; habit, practice; wearing, wear; wear and tear; (com. law) usance.—**u. de razón**, discernment, understanding, thinking for one's self (s. o. the child when his mind is sufficiently developed to judge by itself).—**al u., a u.**, according to usage.—**en buen u.**, in good condition.

ustaga, f. (naut.) tie.

usted (usually abbreviated **V., Vd., U., Ud.**) you.—pl. **ustedes** (abbrev. **VV., Vds., UU., Uds.**) you (ye).—**de Vd.**, your, yours.

ustible, a. easily combustible.

ustión, f. burning.

ustorio, a. burning.

usual, a. usual, customary; tractable, social.

usualmente, adv. usually, generally.

usuario, ria, a. (law) having the sole use of a thing.

usucapión, f. (law) usucapion.

usucapir, va. (law) to usucapt.

usufructo, m. (law) usufruct, enjoyment; profit.

usufructuar. I. va. to enjoy the usufruct of. II. vn. to be productive or fruitful.

usufructuario, ria, n. & a. usufructuary.

usura, f. usury; (formerly) interest, gain, profit.

usurar, vn. = USUREAR.—**usurariamente**, adv. usuriously.—**usurario, ria**, a. usurious.

usurear, vn. to practise usury; to profiteer; to lend money on interest; to reap great profit.

usurero, ra, n. usurer; profiteerer; money lender, pawnbroker.

usurpación, f. usurpation.—**usurpador**, n. & a. usurper (-ing).—**usurpar**, va. to usurp.

utensilio, m. utensil; tool, device, contrivance.—pl. (mil.) articles that the tenant of a house is to furnish the soldier quartered with him.

uterino, na, a. uterine.

útero, m. (anat.) uterus, womb.

uteromanía, f. hysteromania.

uteroscopio, m. hysteroscope.

uterotomía, f. hysterotomy, incision or extirpation of the uterus.

uticense, n. & a. of or from Utica.

útil. I. a. useful; (law) lawful (applied to time); profitable; (mech.) effective, available. II. m. pl. utensils, tools; outfit, equipment.

utilidad, f. utility; profit; usefulness.

utilitario, ria, a. utilitarian.

utilitarismo, m. utilitarianism.

utilitarista, n. & a. utilitarian.

utilizable, *a.* utilizable, available.

utilizar. I. *va.* (*pret.* UTILICÉ: *subj.* UTILICE) to utilize. **II.** *vr.* to be made profitable.

útilmente, *adv.* usefully, profitably.

utopía, *f.* utopia.—**utópico, ca,** *a.* utopian.— **utopista,** *n.* & *a.* utopian.

utrero, ra, *n.* bull (heifer) between two and three years old.

ut retro, *adv.* (Lat.) as above.

ut supra, *adv.* (Lat.) as above.

uva, *f.* (bot.) grape; fruit of the barberry bush; wart on the eyelid; tumor on the uvula.—*pl.* bunch of grapes.—**u. canella,** white stonecrop.— **u. crespa** = U. ESPÍN.—**u. de Corinto,** (bot.) currants.—**u. de gato** = U. CANELLA.—**u. de playa,** (Amer.) fruit of the UVERO.—**u. de raposa,** nightshade.—**u. espín,** or **espina,** gooseberry.—**u. lupina,** wolfsbane.—**u. marina,** shrubby horsetail.— **u. pasa,** raisin.—**u. tamínea,** or **taminia,** lousewort.—**u. verdeja,** green-colored sweet grape.—**u. verga** = U. LUPINA.—**conocer las uvas de su majuelo,** to know one's own business.— **hecho una u.,** very drunk, "paralyzed," "soaked."

uvada, *f.* abundance of grapes.

uvaguemaestre, *m.* = VAGUEMAESTRE.

uval, *a.* belonging to grapes.

uvate, *m.* conserve of grapes.

uvayema, *f.* a species of wild vine.

úvea, *f.* (anat.) uvea.

uvero, ra. I. *n.* retailer of grapes. **II.** *m.* (bot.) shrub on tropical seashores yielding an edible stone fruit.

uvula, *f.* (anat.) uvula.

uxoricida, *m.* uxoricide, one who kills his wife.— **uxoricidio,** *m.* uxoricide, murder of a wife by her husband.

uyama, *f.* (Ven.) a species of calabash.

uzas, *f.* a Brazilian kind of crab.

V

V, *f.* v.—**v doble,** or **doble v,** w.—**en V,** V-shaped.

va. *V.* IR.

vaca, *f.* cow; beef; sole leather; joint stock of two gamblers.—**v. de la boda,** one to whom everybody applies in distress; laughingstock.—**v. de leche,** milch cow.—**v. de San Antón,** (ent.) ladybird, ladycow.—**v. marina,** sea cow.

vacación, *f.* (gen. in the *pl.*) vacation.

vacada, *f.* drove of cows.

vacancia, *f.* vacancy.

vacante. I. *a.* vacant; unoccupied. **II.** *f.* vacancy; vacation; rent fallen due during the vacancy of a benefice.

vacar, *vn.* (*pret.* VAQUÉ: *subj.* VAQUE) to give up work or employment temporarily; to take a vacation; to be vacant; to devote one's self; (w. **de**) to lack, be devoid of.

vacari, *a.* leathern; covered with leather.

vacatura, *f.* vacancy.

vaccíneo, a, *a.* (bot.) vacciniaceous.

vaciada, *f.* (found.) melt.

vaciadero, *m.* drain; sink; dumping place.

vaciadizo, za, *a.* cast molded.

vaciado, *pp.* & *m.* (f. a.) cast (in a mold); (act of) casting; (arch.) excavation; face of a pedestal below its ornamental moldings.

vaciador, *m.* (f. a.) molder, caster; dumper, pourer, emptier.—**v. de navajas,** razor grinder.

vaciamiento, *m.* casting, molding; emptying.

vaciar. I. *va.* to empty; pour out; to cast, mold; to grind; to hone; (arch.) to excavate, to hollow; to explain at large; to translate. **II.** *vn.* to discharge, flow (into) (as rivers); to fall, decrease (as a freshet). **III.** *vr.* to be split; to overflow; to divulge what should be kept secret; to become empty or vacant.

vaciedad, *f.* nonsense, silly remark.

vaciero, *m.* shepherd of barren sheep.

vacilación, *f.* reeling, staggering; hesitation.

vacilante, *a.* hesitating, irresolute; unstable.

vacilar, *vn.* to vacillate, waver, fluctuate; to hesitate; to reel, stagger.

vacío, cía. I. *a.* void, empty; vacuous; unoccupied, untenanted, idle; fruitless; concave, hollow; defective, deficient; vain, presumptuous; barren (cattle); unloaded or empty (as mules, carts, etc.). **II.** *m.* void, empty space; vacuum; aperture, opening; mold for casting; vacancy; concavity, hollowness; blank, hiatus, gap; (com.) ullage of a cask or other vessel; wantage; a Spanish step in dancing; animal not with young; vacuity, cavity; flank of animals.—**de v.,** empty; unemployed; vacuum (u. a.).—**en el v.,** in vacuo.

vaco, ca, *a.* vacant.

vacuidad, *f.* vacuity, emptiness.

vacuna, *f.* cowpox; vaccine; vaccination.

vacunación, *f.* vaccination.—**vacunador, ra,** *n.* vaccinator.—**vacunar,** *va.* to vaccinate.

vacuno, na, *a.* belonging to cattle; bovine.—**ganado, v.,** (bovine) cattle.

vacuo, a. I. *a.* empty, unoccupied, vacant. **II.** *m.* vacuum.

vacuola, *f.* (biol.) vacuole.

vacuómetro, *m.* vacuum gauge.

vade, *m.* = VADEMÉCUM.

vadeable, *a.* fordable; conquerable, superable.

vadear. I. *va.* to wade, ford; to conquer, to surmount; to sound (a person). **II.** *vr.* to behave, conduct one's self.

vademécum, *m.* vade mecum; handbook; school portfolio.

vadera, *f.* ford of a river.

¡vade retro! *adv.* avaunt! away! begone!

vadiano, na, *n.* & *a.* Audian.

vado, *m.* ford of a river; expedient; resource.—**al v. o la puente,** choose one way or the other.— **no hallar v.,** to be at a loss how to act; to be "stuck."

vadoso, sa, *a.* shoaly, shallow.

vafe, *m.* bold stroke or undertaking.

vagabundear, *vn.* (coll.) to rove or loiter about, to act the vagrant.

vagabundo, da, *n.* & *a.* vagabond, vagrant, rover (-ing), roamer (-ing), tramp (-ing).

vagamente, *adv.* vaguely.

vagamundear, *vn.* = VAGABUNDEAR.

vagamundo, da, *n.* & *a.* = VAGABUNDO.

vagancia, *f.* vagrancy.—**vagante,** *a.* vagrant.

vagar. I. *vn.* (*pret.* VAGUÉ: *subj.* VAGUE) to rove, roam, loiter about, wander; to be at leisure, to be idle. **II.** *m.* leisure, idleness.

vagarosamente, *adv.* vagrantly, rovingly.

vagaroso, sa, *a.* errant, vagrant, roaming.

vagido, *m.* cry of a newborn child.

vagina, *f.* (anat.) vagina.—**vaginado, da,** *a.* (bot.) vaginate.—**vaginal,** *a.* vaginal.—**vaginitis,** *f.* (med.) vaginitis.—**vagínula,** *f.* (bot.) vaginula, vaginule.

vagneriano, na, *n.* & *a.* Wagnerian.

vagnerismo, *m.* Wagnerism.

vago, ga. I. *a.* roving, roaming, wandering; vagrant; vague; hesitating, wavering; lax, loose; (art) vaporous, hazy, indistinct. **II.** *m.* unimproved plot of ground; vagabond, loafer, vagrant, tramp.—**en v.,** unsteadily; unsuccessfully, in vain; in the air, at nothing (as a blow).

vagón, *m.* (r. w.) car; wagon.—**v.-cama,** sleeping car.—**v.-cuadra,** cattle van.—**v. de carga,** freight car.—**v. de cola,** caboose.—**v. de mercancías,** freight car.—**v. de plataforma,** flat car.—**v. jaula,** latticed van or wagon.

vagonada, *f.* wagonload, carload.

vagoneta, *f.* (r. w.) small open car.

vaguada, *f.* waterway; watercourse.

vagueación, *f.* restlessness, unsteadiness; flight of fancy.

vagueante, *a.* wandering; flighty.

vaguear, *vn.* to rove, roam, loiter, tramp.

vaguedad, *f.* vagueness; vague statement.

vaguemaestre, *m.* (mil.) wagon master.

vaguido, da. I. *a.* dizzy. **II.** *m.* dizziness.

vahaje, *m.* soft breeze.

vahar, *vn.* to exhale, breathe forth.

vaharada, *f.* breath, breathing, exhalation.

vaharera, *f.* (med.) thrush; unripe melon.

vaharina, *f.* (coll.) fume, vapor, mist.

vahear, *vn.* to exhale, emit fumes or vapor.

vahido, *m.* vertigo, dizziness.

vaho, *m.* vapor, fume, effluvium.

vaída, *f.* (arch.) vault cut into four vertical planes.

vaina, *f.* scabbard, sheath, case; (bot.) pod, capsule; (naut.) boltrope tabling; tabling of a flag.

vainazas, *n.* (coll.) humdrum, dull, or dronish person.

vainero, ra, *n.* sheath or scabbard maker.

vainica, *f. dim.* small scabbard or sheath; (sew.) hemstitch.

vainilla, *f. dim.* small pod or husk; (bot.) vanilla; heliotrope.

vainillina, *f.* (chem.) vanillin.

vaivén, *m.* fluctuation, vibration, sway; unsteadiness, inconstancy; giddiness; risk, danger; (mech.) swing, seesaw, reciprocating movement; (naut.) line, cord, rope.

vajilla, *f.* table service; dinner set; (Mex.) an ancient tax on jewelry.—**v. de plata,** silver ware.

val, *m.* (*contr. of* VALLE, mostly used in composition) vale, dale, valley; open sewer, sewage ditch.

valaco, ca, *n. & a.* Wallachian.

valais, *m.* piece of lumber.

valar, *a.* relating to a rampart, hedge, or fence.

valdense, *n. & a.* Waldensian.

vale, *m.* (com.) bond, promissory note, I O U; voucher; bonus given to schoolboys; bet at cards; farewell, adieu; valediction.

valedero, ra, *a.* valid, efficacious, binding.

valedor, ra, *n.* protector, defender.

valenciano, na, *n. & a.* Valencian.

valentía, *f.* valor, courage, bravery; feat, heroic exploit; brag, boast; fire of imagination; (art) mastery in imitating nature; extraordinary or vigorous effort; public place where mended shoes were anciently sold in Madrid.—**pisar de v.,** to strut, to swagger.

valentiniano, na, *a.* Valentinian.

valentísimo, ma, *a. sup.* most valiant, very brave; most perfect.—**valentón, na. I.** *a.* blustering, arrogant. **II.** *m.* hector, bully.

valentona, valentonada, *f.* brag, boast.

valer. I. *va.* (*ind.* VALGO: *fut.* VALDRÉ: *subj.* VALGA) to protect, to defend, favor, patronize; to yield, produce (fruits or income); to cost; to cause, bring upon or to (one) (discredit, fame): to foot up, amount to: be worth, be valued at; be equal to.—**v. la pena,** to be worth while.—**v. lo que pesa,** to be worth its weight in gold.—**hacer v.,** to assert (one's rights); to avail one's self of.—**más vale,** or **más valiera,** it is better, it would be better.—**no v. un cornado,** not to be worth a farthing.—**valga lo que valiere,** happen what may. **II.** *vn.* to be valuable; to be worthy; to possess merit or value; to prevail, avail; to have sway, power, authority, influence; to be legal and current (s. o. coins); to be valid or binding; to be important or useful; to be or serve as a protection.— **v. por,** to be equal to, to be worth.—**más vale, más valiera,** it is better, it would be better.—**más vale tarde que nunca,** better late than never.— **¡válgame Dios!** good God! bless me!—**¡válgate Dios!** heaven bless or forgive you! **III.** *vr.* to help one's self, take care of one's self.—**v. de,** to make use of, to have recourse to.—**no poder v.,** or **no poderse v.,** to be helpless. **IV.** *m.* value; merit, worth.

valeriana, *f.* (bot.) valerian.

valerianáceo, a, *a.* (bot.) valerianaceous.

valerianato, *m.* (chem.) valerianate.

valeriánico, ca, *a.* (chem.) valeric.

valerosamente, *adv.* bravely, courageously.

valerosidad, *f.* courage, bravery.

valeroso, sa, *a.* brave, courageous; strong, active; powerful.

valetudinario, ria, *a.* valetudinarian.

Valhala, *f.* Walhalla, Valhalla.

valí, *m.* wali, a Mussulman governor.

valía, *f.* value, worth; credit, favor, influence; party, faction.—**a las valías,** at the highest price.

valiato, *m.* vilayet.

validación, *f.* validation; soundness.

válidamente, *adv.* validly.—**validar,** *va.* to validate.—**validez,** *f.* validity; soundness; vigor, strength.

válido, da, *a.* valid; legally binding, obligatory.

valido, da. I. *a. & pp.* favored, accepted; esteemed, respected; powerful, influential. **II.** *m.* prime minister; favorite, protégé; court minion.

valiente. I. *a.* valiant, brave, courageous; strong, robust, vigorous; efficacious, valid; eminent; excellent; great, excessive. **II.** *n.* brave person; bully, hector.

valientemente, *adv.* bravely, courageously; vigorously; abundantly, excessively; elegantly, handsomely.

valija, *f.* valise, gripsack; mail bag; mail.

valijero, *m.* mail carrier or distributor.

valijón, *m. aug.* large valise or mail bag.

valimiento, *m.* value; use, benefit, advantage; favor, protection, support; good graces, favoritism.

valioso, sa, *a.* valuable; highly esteemed, of great influence; rich, wealthy.

valisoletano, na, *a.* of or from Valladolid.

valón, na. I. *a.* Walloon.—**u. valona,** w (name of the letter) **II.** *f.* falling band or vandyke collar. **III.** *m. pl.* (tail.) bloomers.

valor, *m.* value; price; worth; amount; equivalency; validity, force; import, meaning; activity, power; valor, courage, bravery.—*pl.* (com.) securities, bonds, stocks.—**v. recibido,** value received.—**valores fiduciarios,** (com.) notes.

valoración, *f.* = VALUACIÓN; (chem.) act of VALORAR.

valorar, valorear, *va.* to appraise, value, price; (chem.) to standardize, determine the strength or proportions of (a solution).

valoría, *f.* value, price, worth.

valorizar, *va.* (Mex.) = VALORAR.

valquiria, *f.* valkyr, valkyrie.

vals, *m.* waltz.—**valsar,** *vn.* to waltz.

valuación, *f.* appraisement, valuation.

valuador, ra, *n.* appraiser.

valuar, *va.* to rate, price, value, appraise.

valva, *f.* (zool.) valve, shell of mollusks; (bot.) valve.

valvasor, *m.* nobleman, hidalgo.

válvula, *f.* valve.—**v. de admisión,** steam valve, admission valve.—**v. de campana,** two-beat valve.—**v. de corredera,** slide valve.—**v. de derivación,** by-pass valve.—**v. de descarga,** blow-off valve.—**v. de dos direcciones,** two-way valve.—**v. de estrangulación,** throttle valve.—**v. de evacuación,** blow-off valve.—**v. de expansión,** cut-off valve.—**v. de purga,** blow-off valve; mud valve.—**v. de retención,** check valve.—**v. de seguridad,** safety valve.—**v. de tres direcciones,** or **de tres pasos,** three-way valve.—**v. mitral,** (zool.) mitral valve.

valvular, *a.* valvular.

valvulilla, *f. dim.* valvula.

valla, *f.* paling, fence, stockade, intrenchment; barrier, barricade; obstacle, impediment.—**romper, or saltar, la v.,** to be foremost in undertaking a difficult affair.

valladar, *m.* VALLADO; obstacle.

vallado, *pp. & m.* stockade; inclosure; stone wall.

vallar, valladear, *va.* to fence, hedge, inclose with pales or stakes.

valle, *m.* valley; vale, dale, glen, dell; whole number of villages and cottages in a valley.—**v. de lágrimas,** vale of tears.

vallecico, vallecito, vallejo, vallejuelo, *m. dim.* small valley; glen, dell.

vallico, *m.* (bot.) ray grass.

vallisoletano, na, *a.* of or from Valladolid.

¡vamos! *interj.* well! come, now! bear a hand! go on! let's go! be careful! stop! Often u. in conversation as an expletive, as "well" and "why" are in English.

For pronunciation, see the rules at the beginning of the book.

vampiro, *m.* ghoul; vampire; usurer; miser, skin-flint.

vanadato, vanadiato, *m.* (chem.) vanadate.

vanádico, ca, *a.* (chem.) vanadic.

vanadio, *m.* (chem.) vanadium.

vanagloria, *f.* vaingloriousness, boast, conceit.

vanagloriarse, *vr.* to be vainglorious, to boast.

vanagloriosamente, *adv.* vaingloriously.

vanaglorioso, sa, *a.* vainglorious, conceited, ostentatious.

vanamente, *adv.* vainly; superstitiously; without foundation; arrogantly, presumptuously, frivolously, idly.

vandálico, ca, *a.* Vandalic.—**vandalismo,** *m.* Vandalism.—**vándalo, la,** *n.* & *a.* Vandal.

vandeano, na, *n.* & *a.* Vendean.

vanear, *vn.* to talk nonsense.

vanguardia, *f.* (mil.) vanguard, van.

vanidad, *f.* vanity; nonsense; inanity, shallowness, levity; foppishness.—**hacer v.,** to boast.

vanidoso, sa, *a.* vain, foppish, conceited.

vanilina, *f.* (chem.) vanillin.

vanilismo, *m.* (med.) vanillism.

vanilocuencia, *f.* verbosity.

vanilocuo, cua, *a.* empty (talker).

vaniloquio, *m.* silly, empty talk.

vanistorio, *m.* (coll.) ridiculous or affected vanity; affected person.

vano, na. I. *a.* vain; inane, empty, shallow, insubstantial; dry (coconut).—**en v.,** in vain. **II.** *m.* (arch.) opening in a wall (as for a door).

vánova, *f.* bedspread, coverlet.

vapor, *m.* vapor, steam; exhalation, mist; vertigo, faintness; (naut.) steamboat, steamer, steamship.—*pl.* vapors; hysterical attack.—**v. volandero,** (naut.) tramp steamer.—**al v.,** swiftly, at lightning speed.

vaporable, *a.* vaporizable, volatile.

vaporación, *f.* vaporization.—**vapor(e)ar,** *va.* to vaporize.—**vaporización,** *f.* vaporization.—**vaporizador,** *m.* vaporizer.—**vaporizar,** *va.* to vaporize.—**vaporoso, sa,** *a.* vaporous, ethereal, cloudy.

vapulación, *f.*; **vapulamiento,** *m.* (coll.) whipping, flogging.

vapular, vapulear, *va.* (coll.) to whip, flog.

vapuleamiento, vapuleo, *m.* (coll.) whipping, flogging.

vaquear, *va.* to cover (cows) with the bull.

vaquería, *f.* herd or drove of cattle; milk dairy; work or occupation of cowboys.

vaquerizo, za. I. *a.* relating to cows. **II.** *n.* herdsman. **III.** *f.* winter stable for cattle.

vaquero, ra. I. *a.* belonging to cowherds. **II.** *m.* herdsman; cowboy.

vaqueta, *f.* sole leather.

vaquetear, *va.* to flog with leather thongs.

vaqueteo, *m.* flogging with leather thongs.

vaquilla, vaquita, *f. dim.* small cow, heifer.

vara, *f.* twig; pole, staff; stick; rod; verge, wand, emblem of authority; vara (variable unit of length, about 2.8 ft.); piece of cloth one vara long; herd of forty or fifty head of swine; thrust with a goad at a bull; (car.) thill, shaft.—**v. alta,** sway, high hand.—**v. de cortina,** curtain rod.—**v. de Jesé,** (bot.) tuberose.—**v. de medir,** vara stick, measuring vara.—**v. de pescar,** fishing rod. —**v. de yaya,** lancewood spar.

varada, *f.* (agr.) gang of farm hands; job on a farm; (min.) three months' work in a mine; amount of work done and measured; quarterly profit and dividend; (naut.) running aground, stranding.

varadera, *f.* (naut.) skid or skeed.

varadero, *m.* shipyard.

varadura, *f.* (naut.) grounding of a vessel.

varal, *m.* long pole or perch; (car.) side pole with sockets for the stakes of a truck; (theat.) side lights; (coll.) tall, slender person.

varánidos, *m. pl.* (zool.) Varanidæ.

varano, *m.* (zool.) monitor.

varapalo, *m.* long pole or perch; switch blow with a stick or pole; (coll.) grief; trouble; reverse, damage.

varar. I. *va.* (naut.) to launch (a new-built ship). **II.** *vn.* & *vr.* (naut.) to ground, to be stranded; to be at a standstill.

varaseto, *m.* treillage, espalier.

varazo, *m.* stroke with a pole, rod or stick.

varbasco, *m.* = VERBASCO.

vardasca, *f.* thin twig.

vareador, ra, *n.* one who does the act of VAREAR.

vareaje, *m.* retail trade; selling or measuring by the yard; beating down the fruit of trees with a pole.

varear. I. *va.* to beat down (fruit) with a pole; to cudgel, whip, beat; to prick with a goad; to measure or sell by the yard. **II.** *vr.* to grow thin or lean.

varejón, *m.* long stick, pole or staff.

varenga, *f.* (naut.) floor timber.—**varengaje,** *m.* (naut.) collection of floor timbers.

vareo, *m.* = VAREAJE.

vareta, *f. dim.* small rod, stick or twig; lime twig for catching birds; stripe in a fabric; (coll.) hint, offensive remark.—**estar, or irse, de v.,** (coll.) to have diarrhœa.

varetazo, *m.* stroke with a twig, stick or rod.

varetear, *va.* to make stripes in (fabrics).

varetón, *m.* young stag having antlers without branches or points.

varga, *f.* steepest part of an incline.

várgano, *m.* fence rail or stake.

varganal, *m.* inclosure, stockade.

vargueño, *m.* gilt and painted scrutoire.

variabilidad, *f.* variability.

variable. I. *a.* variable, changeable. **II.** *f.* (math.) variable.—**variablemente,** *adv.* variably.

variación, *f.* variation, change; (mus.) variation. —**v. de la aguja,** variation of the compass.

variado, da, *pp.* & *a.* varied, varying; variegated.

variamente, *adv.* variously, differently.

variante. I. *a.* varying; deviating. **II.** *f.* difference, discrepancy (in texts).

variar. I. *va.* to vary, change, alter; to shift; to variegate, diversify. **II.** *vn.* to vary, change; to differ; to deviate, vary (s. o. the compass).

várice, varice, *f.* (med.) varix.

varicela, *f.* (med.) varicella, chicken pox.

varicocele, *m.* (med.) varicocele.

varicoso, sa, *a.* (med.) varicose.

variedad, *f.* variety, diversity; change, variation.

varilarguero, *m.* in bullfighting, PICADOR.

varilla, *f. dim.* rod; spindle, pivot; fan stick; rib (of an umbrella), whalebone (of a corset).—*pl.* jawbones; frame of a sieve or strainer.—**v. de cortina,** curtain rod.—**v. de virtudes, or v. mágica,** magician's or conjurer's wand.

varillaje, *m.* ribs of a fan, umbrella, or corset.

vario, ria, *a.* various, divers, varied; inconstant, changeable; undecided; variegated.—*pl.* various, several.

varioloide, *f.* (med.) varioloid.

varioloso, sa, *a.* variolous, variolar.

variólico, ca, *a.* variolous.

variolización, *f.* variolation, inoculation with the smallpox virus.

variómetro, *m.* (rad.) variometer.

variz, *m.* (med.) = VÁRICE.

varón, *m.* male (man); man of respectability.—**v. de Dios,** saintly man, most virtuous man.—**v. del timón,** (naut.) rudder pendant.—**buen v.,** wise and learned man; plain, artless fellow.—**santo v.,** (coll.) good but not clever man.

varona, *f.* woman; mannish woman.

varoncico, illo, ito, *m. dim.* boy, lad.

varonesa, *f.* woman.

varonía, *f.* male issue.

varonil, *a.* virile; manly; vigorous, spirited.

varonilmente, *adv.* manfully, bravely.

varraco, *m.* = VERRACO.

varraquear, varraquera = VERRAQUEAR, VERRAQUERA.

varsoviana, *f.* (danc.) varsovienne.

varsoviano, na, *n.* & *a.* of or from Warsaw.

vasallaje, *m.* vassalage, subjection; liege money.

vasallo, lla. I. *a.* vassal, subject, tributary; feudatory. **II** *n.* vassal, subject.

vasar, *m.* shelf in a kitchen.

vasco, ca, *n.* & *a.* Basque.—**vascófilo, la,** *n.* Basque scholar.—**vascongado, da,** *n.* & *a.* Basque.

vascuence, *m.* Basque language; (coll.) jargon, gibberish.

vascular; vasculoso, sa, *a.* vascular.

vase, *vr.* (*v.* IR) (theat.) exit.

vaselina, *f.* vaseline.

vasera, *f.* shelf or rack for glasses.

vasico, ito, *m. dim.* small tumbler.

vasija, *f.* vessel, receptacle; collection of wine vessels in a cellar.

vasillo, *m. dim.* cell of a honeycomb.

vaso, *m.* (drinking) glass; vessel, receptacle; glassful; vase; flower jar; (naut.) vessel; capacity, room, extent; (ast.) Crater, a southern constellation; (farr.) horse's hoof; (anat. and bot.) vessel.—**v. de noche,** chamber pot.

vasomotor, *a.* vasomotor.

vástago, *m.* stem, tiller, sucker, sapling, shoot; descendant, scion, offspring.—**v. del émbolo,** (st. eng.) piston rod.—**v. de válvula,** valve stem.

vastedad, *f.* vastness, immensity.

vástiga, *f.* = VÁSTAGO.

vasto, ta, *a.* vast, huge, immense.

vate, *m.* bard, poet; seer, diviner.

vaticano, na. I. *a.* pertaining to the Vatican. **II.** *m.* (V-) Vatican.

vaticinador, ra, *n.* prophet, diviner.

vaticinante, *a.* predicting, foretelling.

vaticinar, *va.* to divine, foretell, predict.

vaticinio, *m.* vaticination, prediction.

vatídico, ca, *a.* (poet.) prophetical.

vatihora, *m.* (elec.) watt-hour.

vatihorámetro, *m.* (elec.) watt-hour meter.

vatímetro, *m.* (elec.) wattmeter.

vatio, *m.* (elec.) watt.—**v. -hora,** watt-hour.

vaya. I. *f.* scoff, jest. **II.** *interj.* go; go to; come! indeed! certainly! well!

vaya. *V.* IR.

ve, *f.* name of the letter *v.*

ve. *V.* IR.

véase, see (in references).

vecera, vecería, *f.* drove, herd, pack.

vecero, ra, *n.* one who performs alternately or by turns; tree which yields abundant fruit in alternate years; customer.

vecinal, *a.* vicinal, neighboring, adjacent.

vecinamente, *adv.* near, contiguously.

vecindad, *f.* neighborhood, vicinity.—**hacer mala v.,** to be a troublesome neighbor.

vecindario, *m.* population of a district, ward, etc.; neighborhood, vicinity, vicinage.

vecino, na. I. *a.* neighboring, next, near; like, resembling, coincident. **II.** *n.* neighbor; resident; denizen, citizen.—**medio v.,** nonresident who, by paying half the taxes, enjoys the right of pasture for his cattle.

vectación, *f.* passive exercise, as riding, sailing.

vectigales, *m. pl.* an ancient tribute.

vector. I. *a.* vectorial. **II.** *m.* vector.

vectorial, *a.* vectorial.

veda. I. *f.* prohibition, interdiction by law; time when hunting is forbidden. **II.** *m.* (V-) Veda, Hindu sacred book.

vedado, *pp.* & *m.* inclosure, warren, park.

vedamiento, *m.* prohibition.

vedar, *va.* to prohibit, forbid; to obstruct, impede.

vedegambre, *m.* (bot.) hellebore.

vedeja, *f.* = GUEDEJA.

védico, ca, *a.* Vedic.

vedija, *f.* entangled lock of wool or hair; flake; matted hair.—**vedijero, ra,** *n.* gatherer of loose locks of wool at shearing.—**vedijudo, da; vedijoso, sa,** *a.* having entangled or matted hair.

vedijuela, *f. dim.* small lock of wool.

veduño, *m.* = VIDUÑO.

veedor, ra, *n.* prier, spy; busybody; overseer, supervisor, inspector; caterer, provider.

veeduría, *f.* employment of an overseer; inspector's office; controllership.

vega, *f.* flat lowland; (Cuba) tobacco plantation; (Ch.) damp or swampy ground.

vegetabilidad, *f.* vegetability.—**vegetable,** *a.* & *m.* vegetable.—**vegetación,** *f.* vegetation.—**vegetal,** *a.* & *m.* vegetable, vegetal, plant.—**vegetalista,** *n.* & *a.* vegetarian.—**vegetante,** *a.* vegetating.—**vegetar,** *vn.* to vegetate.—**vegetarianismo,** *m.* vegetarianism.—**vegetariano, na,** *n.* & *a.* vegetarian.—**vegetarismo,** *m.* vegetarianism.—**vegetativo, va,** *a.* vegetative.

veguer, *m.* in Aragon, mayor.

veguería, *f.*, **veguerío,** *m.* in Aragon, jurisdiction of the mayor.

veguero, ra. I. *a.* meadowy. **II.** *m.* (Cuba) tobacco planter; cigar rudely made of a single leaf.

vehemencia, *f.* vehemence, efficacy, force.

vehemente, *a.* vehement; persuasive, vivid; keen. —**vehementemente,** *adv.* vehemently.

vehículo, *m.* vehicle.

veintavo, *m.* & *a.* twentieth.

veinte, *a.* & *m.* twenty; twentieth.—**a las v.,** unseasonably.

veintén, *m.* a gold dollar piece.

veintena, *f.*, **veintenar,** *m.* score (twenty).

veintenario, ria, *a.* twenty years old.

veinteno, na; veintésimo, ma, *a.* twentieth.

veinteñal, *a.* lasting twenty years.

veinteocheno, na, veintiocheno, na. I. *a.* twenty-eighth. **II.** *m.* or *f.* warp of 2,800 threads.

veinteseiseno, na. I. *a.* twenty-sixth. **II.** *n.* warp of 2,600 threads.

veinticinco, *a.* & *m.* twenty-five; twenty-fifth.

veinticuatreno, na. I. *a.* twenty-fourth. **II.** *n.* warp of 2,400 threads.—**v. de capas,** fine broadcloth for cloaks.

veinticuatría, *f.* aldermanry.

veinticuatro. I. *a.* twenty-four; twenty-fourth. **II.** *m.* alderman of Seville.

veintidós, *a.* & *m.* twenty-two; twenty-second.

veintidoseno, na. I. *a.* twenty-second. **II.** *m.* or *f.* warp of 2,200 threads.

veintinueve, *a.* & *m.* twenty-nine; twenty-ninth.

veintiocheno, na = VEINTEOCHENO.

veintiocho, *a.* & *m.* twenty-eight; twenty-eighth.

veintiséis, *a.* & *m.* twenty-six; twenty-sixth.

veintiseiseno, na = VEINTESEISENO.

veintisiete, *a.* & *m.* twenty-seven; twenty-seventh.

veintitrés, *a.* & *m.* twenty-three; twenty-third.

veintiún, *a.* twenty-one.

veintiuno, na. I. *a.* & *m.* twenty-one; twenty-first. **II.** *f.* game at cards, "vingt-et-un."

vejación, *f.* vexation, annoyance; oppression.

vejamen, *m.* vexation, trouble; taunt, scurrilous criticism.

vejaminista, *m.* censor, critic.

vejancón, na, *a.* (coll.) rather old, oldish.

vejar, *va.* to vex, annoy; to scoff, censure; to tease.

vejarrón, na, *a.* (coll.) very old.

vejatorio, ria, *a.* vexatious, annoying.

vejazo, za, *n.* big old person.

vejecito, ta, *n.* little old man (woman).

vejestorio, *m.* (coll.) old trumpery; shrivelled old person.

vejeta, *f.* (orn.) crested lark.

vejete, *m.* (coll.) ridiculous old man.

vejez, *f.* old age; peevishness of old age; trite story, platitude, threadbare saying, etc.

vejezuelo, la, *n. dim.* little old man (woman).

vejiga, *f.* (anat.) bladder; blister; (art) bladder or tube for paints.—*pl.* pustules of smallpox; (farr.) windgalls in horses.—**v. de la bilis,** or **de la hiel,** gall bladder.—**v. de perro,** (bot.) common winter cherry.—**v. natatoria,** (icht.) swimming bladder.—**v. para tabaco,** tobacco pouch.

vejigatorio, ria. I. *a.* blistering. **II.** *m.* blister plaster, blister, vesicant, vesicatory.

vejigón, *m. aug.* large bladder or blister.

vejigoso, sa, *a.* full of blisters.

vejigüela, vejiguilla, *f. dim.* small bladder; (med.) pustule.

vela, *f.* vigil, wakefulness; wake; watch, watchfulness, vigilance; watchman, nightguard; pilgrimage; candle; nightwork; awning, velarium; erect ear of an animal; wing or arm of a windmill; (eccl.) vigil before the Eucharist; nuptial mass and veiling ceremony; (naut.) sail; ship.—**v. bastarda,** lateen sail.—**v. cangreja,** (naut.) boom sail, brig sail, gaff sail.—**v. de mesana,** mizzen sail.—**v. de trinquete,** fore sail.—**v. latina** = v. BASTARDA.—**V. mayor,** mainsail.—**velas de popa,** after sails.—**velas de proa,** headsails.—**velas de respeto,** spare sails.—**velas mayores,** courses.—**acortar (la) v.,** to reef a sail, to shorten sail.—**a la v.,** prepared, equipped, ready.—**alzar velas,** to raise sail, to make ready to sail; to quit, to leave.—**a toda v.,** with all sails up and full wind; with heart and soul; boomingly, in full swing.—**a v. y pregón,** auction by inch of candle.—**a v. y remo,** with sails and oars; quickly, with all one's heart and soul.—**en v.,** vigilantly, without sleep.—**hacer fuerza de v.,** to crowd sail.—**hacerse a la v.,** to set sail.—**recoger velas,** to contain one's self, to be moderate.—**tender (las) velas,** to seize an opportunity.

velación, *f.* watch, watching, vigil; wake.—*pl.* (eccl.) nuptial mass and ceremony of veiling the bride and groom; time in which the church permits marriages.

velacho, *m.* (naut.) fore-topsail.

velado, da. I. *pp.* & *a.* veiled, hidden. **II.** *m.* (coll.) bridegroom, husband. **III.** *f.* watch (*v.* VELACIÓN); evening entertainment, soirée.

velador, ra. I. *n.* watchman (-woman), night guard; caretaker, keeper. **II.** *m.* wooden candlestick; lamp table or stand.

veladura, *f.* (art.) velatura.

velaje, velamen, *m.* (naut.) canvas, sails in general; set of sails.

velar. I. *vn.* to watch, to be awake, to keep vigil; to work at night; to observe; to be vigilant; (w. **por**) to watch over, protect; (naut.) to appear above the water, as rocks; (eccl.) to assist by turns before the holy sacrament when it is manifested. **II.** *va.* to guard, watch over, keep; (eccl.) to veil (a bride and groom) at a nuptial mass; to cover, veil, hide; (art) to soften with velatura.

velarte, *m.* fine broadcloth.

veleidad, *f.* whimsicalness; inconstancy; fickleness.—**veleidoso, sa,** *a.* fickle, inconstant.

velejar, *vn.* (naut.) to make use of sails.

velería, *f.* tallow-chandler's shop.

velero, ra. I. *a.* (naut.) swift-sailing; fond of wakes and pilgrimages. **II.** *m.* tallow chandler; (naut.) sailmaker.

veleta. I. *f.* weathercock, vane; streamer, pennant; bob, float, or cork of a fishing line. **II.** *n.* fickle person.

velete, *m.* light, thin face veil.

velicación, *f.* (med.) lancing, opening.

velicar, *va.* (med.) to lance, open, prick.

velico, illo, ito, *m. dim.* small veil.

velilla, ita, *f. dim.* small candle.

velillo, *n. dim.* short or small veil; embroidered gauze.

velis nolis, (fam.) willy-nilly, whether willingly or unwillingly, whether one will or not.

velmez, *m.* tunic worn under the armor.

velo, *m.* veil; curtain; veil of white gauze thrown over a couple at nuptial mass; feast at the profession of a nun or at taking the veil; cloak, disguise, mask; confusion, perplexity.—**v. del paladar,** (anat.) soft palate.—**correr el v.,** to pull off the mask; to disclose something before unknown.—**tomar el v.,** to take the veil, to become a nun.

velocidad, *f.* velocity.—**v. angular,** angular velocity.—**v. de entrada,** entrance velocity.—**v. de salida,** velocity of discharge.—**v. media,** mean velocity.—**v. periférica,** circumferential velocity.

velocímetro, *m.* speedometer; speed meter.

velocipédico, ca, *a.* relating to velocipedes.

velocipedismo, *m.* cyclism.

velocipedista, *n.* velocipedist.

velocípedo, *m.* velocipede.

velódromo, *m.* bicycle race course.

velomotor, *m.* swift motor vehicle (sp. appl. to motor cycles).

velón, *m.* brass lamp with movable reservoir.

velonera, *f.* lamp stand or bracket.

velonero, ra, *n.* maker or seller of VELONES.

veloz, *a.* swift, rapid, fleet, quick, fast.

velozmente, *adv.* swiftly, fleetly, rapidly.

veludillo, veludo. = VELLUDILLO, VELLUDO.

vellera, *f.* woman who removes hair from women's faces.

vellido, da, *a.* downy; villous.

vellocino, m. fleece (as the golden fleece).

vello, *m.* down; nap; pubescence; fuzz.

vellón, *m.* fleece, wool of one sheep; unsheared sheepskin; lock of wool; copper and silver alloy; an ancient copper coin.

vellonero, *m.* gatherer of fleece at shearing.

vellora, *f.* knot taken from woollen cloth.

vellorí, vellorín, *m.* broadcloth of undyed wool.

vellorita, *f.* (bot.) cowslip.

vellosidad, *f.* downiness; hairiness.

vellosilla, *f.* (bot.) mouse-ear.

velloso, sa, *a.* downy, villous, hairy, fuzzy.

velludillo, *m.* velveteen.

velludo, da. I. *a.* downy, hairy, shaggy, woolly. **II.** *m.* shag, velvet.

vellutero, *n.* velvet or felt worker.

vena, *f.* vein, blood vessel; fiber of plants; (min.) vein, seam, lode; (hydr.) vein; flow of water under ground; vein or stripe in stones or woods; poetical vein, inspiration.—**v. ácigos,** azigous vein, vena azigos.—**v. basílica,** basilic vein.—**v. cardíaca,** cardiac vein.—**v. cava,** vena cava.—**v. cefálica,** cephalic vein.—**v. coronaria,** cardiac vein.—**v. de agua,** underground natural water conduit.—**v. de loco,** fickle disposition.—**v. flúida,** (hydr.) jet.—**v. láctea,** chyliferous vessel.—**v. leónica,** ranine vein.—**v. porta,** vena portæ, portal vein.—**v. safena,** saphenous vein.—**v. subclavia,** subclavian vein.—**v. yugular,** jugular vein.—**acostarse la v.,** (min.) to dip (s. o. a vein).—**dar en la v.,** to hit upon the right means.—**estar de v.,** to be in the mood or vein.—**estar en v.,** to be inspired.—**hallar la v.** = DAR EN LA V.

venablo, *m.* javelin, dart.—**echar venablos,** to speak daggers, to burst out into violent language.

venadero, ra. I. *a.* deer-hunting, deer (u. a.). **II.** *m.* place frequented by deer.

venado, *m.* deer, stag; (cook.) venison.

venaje, *m.* feeding streams, aggregate of streams forming a river.

venal, *a.* venous; marketable, salable; venal, mercenary.

venalidad, *f.* venality, mercenariness.

venático, ca, *a.* (coll.) cranky, erratic, daft.

venatorio, ria, *a.* venatic, used in hunting.

vencedor, ra, *n.* & *a.* victor, vanquisher (-ing).

vencejo, *m.* string, band; (orn.) swift. blackmartin, martlet, martinet.

vencer. I. *va.* (ind. VENZO: *subj.* VENZA) to conquer, subdue, defeat, vanquish, overpower; to surpass, outdo, excel; to surmount, overcome; to win; to prevail upon, persuade, convince; to bend, turn down; to twist. **II.** *vn.* to conquer, triumph, succeed; to win; to be the victor; (com.) to fall due, mature; to expire. **III.** *vr.* to govern one's passions or desires, to control one's self.

vencetósigo, *m.* (bot.) milkweed.

vencible, *a.* conquerable; superable.

vencido, da. I. *a.* & *pp.* conquered, subdued; (com.) due; payable.—**de v.** nearly beaten, vanquished, or finished. **II.** *f.* = VENCIMIENTO.

vencimiento, *m.* vanquishment; flinch; bent; turn down; (com.) maturity, expiration.

venda, *f.* (surg.) bandage, roller; fillet.

vendaje, *m.* (surg.) bandage; bandaging.

vendar, *va.* (surg.) to bandage; to fillet; to hoodwink, to blind, obfuscate.

vendaval, *m.* strong wind from the sea.

vendavalada, *f.* storm of southerly wind.

vendedor, ra, *n.* seller, trader, vender.

vendehumos, *m.* courtier who trades on his influence.

vendeja, *f.* public sale.

vender, *va. & vn.* to sell.—**v. a destajo** = v. AL PORMENOR.—**v. al contado,** to sell for cash.—**v. al por mayor,** to sell at wholesale.—**v. al por menor,** to sell at retail.—**v. al quitar,** to sell with the privilege of buying back.—**v. a plazo,** to sell on credit.—**v. por mayor** = v. AL POR MAYOR.—**v. por menor** = v. AL POR MENOR.—**v. salud,** (coll.) to be or look in very good health. **II.** *vr.* to sell one's self; to expose one's self to danger; to boast; to be sold (at a place, at a price), to be for sale.—**v. caro,** to sell (be sold) dear; to be of difficult access; to be seen seldom (*se vende Vd. caro,* you are a stranger).

vendí, *m.* (com.) certificate of sale.

vendible, *a.* salable, marketable.

vendido, da, *a. & pp.* sold; betrayed.—**estar v.,** to be duped; to be exposed to great risks.

vendiente, *a.* selling.

vendimia, *f.* vintage; large gain or profit.

vendimiador, ra, *n.* vintager.

vendimiar, *va.* to gather (crops); to enjoy as an unlawful perquisite or reap as unjust profit; (coll.) to kill, murder.

vendimiario, *m.* Vendimiaire, first month of the French-Revolution calendar.

vendo, *m.* selvage of cloth.

venduta, *f.* (Am.) auction.

vendutero, ra, *n.* (Am.) auctioneer.

veneciano, na, *a.* Venetian.

venencia, *f.* tube for sampling sherry.

venenífero, ra, *a.* (poet.) poisonous.

veneno, *m.* poison, venom; wrath, fury, passion.

venenosamente, *adv.* venomously, banefully.

venenosidad, *f.* poisonousness, banefulness.

venenoso, sa, *a.* venomous, poisonous, baneful.

venera, *f.* scallop shell worn as a badge by pilgrims; badge, jewel, or star of a military order; spring of water.—**empeñar la v.,** to spare no expense.

venerabilísimo, ma, *a. super.* most venerable.

venerable, *a.* venerable.—**venerablemente,** *adv.* venerably.—**veneración,** *f.* veneration; worship.—**venerador, ra,** *n. & a.* venerator (-ing); worshipper (-ing).—**venerando, da,** *a.* venerable.—**venerante,** *a.* venerating, worshipping.

venerar, *va.* to venerate, revere; to worship.

venéreo, rea. I. *a.* venerous, sensual; (med.) venereal. **II.** *m.* venereal disease.

venero, *m.* water spring; (min.) bed, lode; radius or horary line of sundials; origin, root, source.

veneruela, *f. dim.* small scallop shell.

venezolano, na, *n. & a.* Venezuelan.

vengable, *a.* worthy of revenge; that may be avenged.

vengador, ra, *n. & a.* avenger (-ing); revenger (-ing).

venganza, *f.* revenge; vengeance.

vengar. I. *va.* (*pret.* VENGUÉ: *subj.* VENGUE) to revenge, avenge. **II.** *vr.* to take revenge.

vengativamente, *adv.* revengefully.

vengativo, va, *a.* revengeful, vindictive.

vengo, yo venga. *V.* VENIR.

venia, *f.* pardon, forgiveness; leave, permission; bow with the head; (law) license to minors to manage their own estates.

venial, *a.* venial, pardonable; excusable.

venialidad, *f.* venialness.

venialmente, *adv.* venially.

venida, *f.* arrival; return, coming; flood, freshet; attack in fencing; impetuosity, rashness, rush.

venidero, ra. I. *a.* future, coming.—**en lo v.,** hereafter, in future. **II.** *m.* posterity, successors.

venido, da, *a. & pp.* come, arrived.—**bien v.,** (you are) welcome.

venimécum, *m.* vademecum.

venir. I. *vn.* (*gerund,* VINIENDO: *ind.* VENGO: *pret.* VINE: *fut.* VENDRÉ: *subj.* VENGA) to come; to arrive; to arise, result, follow; to be becoming, fit, suit; to yield, agree, submit; to grow, be produced; to occur (to one's mind), or begin to be

felt (ch. constr.: *me vino el deseo de viajar,* I began to feel a desire for traveling, I then began to feel a desire to travel, I felt a desire to travel); to happen: to concern (gen. with IR: *eso no me va ni me viene,* that does not concern, or affect, me).—**v. a.** (followed by inf.), to end by (followed by *pp.*) (often ch. constr.: *después de mucho trabajo, vino a descubrir la causa,* after much labor, he ended by finding the cause, or, he finally found the cause); sometimes used to denote approximation, especially as the result of a rough estimate (*Juan viene a tener dos mil pesos,* John is worth about two thousand pesos, we may say [or it turns out] that John is worth about two thousand pesos).—**v. a las manos,** to come to blows.—**v. a menos,** to decay, to decline.—**v. a pelo** = v. DE PERILLA.—**v. bien,** to fit, be becoming.—**v. bien en,** to agree to, to grant.—**v. como anillo en dedo, v. como pedrada en ojo de boticario,** or **v. de perilla,** to come in the nick of time; to fit the case or to answer perfectly.—**v. en,** to decide, resolve; to acquire, obtain (knowledge, etc.).—**v. mal,** to be unbecoming, not to fit.—**v. rodado,** to come unexpectedly, to come by a stroke of luck.—**¿a qué viene eso?** to what purpose is that? what has that to do with the case?—**en lo por v.,** hereafter, in future.—**que viene,** next (*la semana que viene,* next week).—**si a mano viene,** perhaps.—**venga lo que viniere,** come what will; happen what may. **II.** *vr.* to ferment; to attain perfection by fermentation, as bread or wine.—**v. abajo,** to fall, to collapse.—**v. a la boca,** to taste unpleasantly.—**v. al suelo,** to fall to the ground; to fall through, to fail.—**v. cayendo,** to be falling down.

venora, *f.* stone or brick marks in a drain or trench, as guides for cleaning.

venoso, sa, *a.* venous; veiny, veined.

venta, *f.* sale; selling; market; roadside inn; exposed, inhospitable place.—**v. (al) por mayor,** wholesale.—**v. (al) por menor,** retail sale; retailing.—**v. pública,** public auction sale.—**de v.,** or **en v.,** for sale.—**hacer v.,** (coll.) to invite to potluck.—**ser una v.,** to be a dear place.

ventada, *f.* blast, puff, gust of wind.

ventaja, *f.* advantage; gain, profit; hand; additional pay; odds given at play.—**llevar v. a,** to be ahead of; to have advantage over.

ventajosamente, *adv.* advantageously, profitably.—**ventajoso, sa,** *a.* advantageous; profitable; good, advisable.

ventalla, *f.* valve; (bot.) pod.

ventalle, *m.* fan.

ventana, *f.* window; (carp.) window frame, window sash; window shutter.—**v. de la nariz,** nostril.

ventanaje, *m.* (arch.) fenestration.

ventanal, *m.* large window.

ventanazo, *m.* slamming of a window.

ventanear, *vn.* (coll.) to frequent the window (sp. for flirting).

ventaneo, *m.* window gazing; window flirting.—**ventanero, ra. I.** *n.* window gazer. **II.** *m.* window maker. **III.** *f.* fond of the window (s. o. woman who flirt from the window).—**ventanica, illa,** *f. dim.* small window.—**ventanico, illo,** *m. dim.* small window shutter; peephole.—**ventano,** *m.* small window.—**ventanuco, ventanucho,** *m.* miserable little window.

ventar, *va. & vn.* = VENTEAR.

ventarrón, *m.* stiff wind, wind gust.

venteadura, *f.* anemosis or shake in timber.

ventear. I. *v. impers.* to blow (the wind). **II.** *va.* to smell, scent, sniff (as dogs); to investigate, inquire; to air. **III.** *vr.* to have anemosis (s. o. timber); to be spoiled by the wind; (coll.) to break wind.

venteo, *m.* (coop.) venthole.

venteril, *a.* suited to a poor inn.

ventero, ra, *n.* innkeeper; scenting dog.

ventilación, *f.* ventilation; discussion.

ventilador, *m.* ventilator; (ventilating) fan.

ventilar. I. *va.* to air, ventilate; to winnow, to fan; to examine, discuss. **II.** *vn.* to circulate (s. o. the air).

ventisca, *f.* snowstorm, blizzard; snowdrift.

ventiscar, *v. impers.* to snow with strong wind; to drift (s. o. the snow).

ventisco, *m.* = VENTISCA.

ventiscoso, sa, *a.* having frequent snowstorms; full of snowdrifts.

ventisquear, *v. impers.* to snow with strong wind (better ch. constr.: *aquí ventisquea mucho*, there are many snowstorms here).

ventisquero, *m.* snowstorm, snowdrift; glacier; snow-capped mountain.

ventola, *f.* (naut.) top hamper.

ventolera, *f.* gust, sudden blast of wind; pin wheel; (coll.) vanity, haughtiness; strong whim, "fever," "rage."

ventolina, *f.* (naut.) light wind; cat's-paw.

ventor, ra, *n.* pointer (dog); foxhound.

ventorrero, *m.* exposed, windy place.

ventorrillo, ventorro, *m.* petty inn or tavern.

ventosa, *f.* vent, air hole, spiracle; (zool.) sucker; (surg.) cupping; cupping glass.—**v. escarificada**, or **sajada**, wet cupping.—**v. seca**, dry cupping.—**pegar una v.**, to swindle.

ventosear, *vn. & vr.* to break wind

ventosidad, *f.* flatulence, windiness.

ventoso, sa, *a.* windy; stormy; flatulent; pointing (as a pointer dog); vain, inflated.

ventral, *a.* ventral.

ventrecillo, *m. dim.* of VIENTRE.

ventrecha, *f.* belly (of fishes).

ventregada, *f.* brood, litter; multitude, rush (of things).

ventrera, *f.* bellyband, abdominal belt; cummerbund.

ventrezuelo, *m. dim.* of VIENTRE.

ventricular, *a.* ventricular.

ventrículo, *m.* (anat. and zool.) ventricle; any cavity of the heart or brain.

ventril, *m.* counterpoise.

ventrílocuo, *m.* ventriloquist.

ventriloquia, *f.* ventriloquism.

ventrón, *m. aug.* large belly; (cook.) tripe.

ventroso, sa; **ventrudo, da**, *a.* big-bellied.

ventura, *f.* happiness; luck, fortune; chance, hazard, venture; risk, danger.—**a la v.**, or **a v.**, at a venture, at hazard.—**buena v.**, fortune told by cards, etc.—**por v.**, by chance.—**probar v.**, to try one's fortune or luck, to venture.

venturado, da, *a.* lucky, fortunate.

venturanza, *f.* happiness.

venturero, ra. I. *a.* lucky; adventurous; idle. **II.** *n.* fortune hunter, adventurer.

venturina, *f.* goldstone, aventurin.

venturo, ra, *a.* future; coming.

venturón, *m. aug.* great luck.

venturosamente, *adv.* luckily, fortunately.

venturoso, sa, *a.* lucky; successful, prosperous.

Venus, *m.* (ast., myth.) Venus.

venustidad, *f.* beauty, gracefulness.

venusto, ta, *a.* beautiful, graceful.

venza, *f.* scarfskin used by goldbeaters.

ver. I. *va. & vn.* (*pp.* VISTO: *gerund,* VIENDO: *ind.* VEO: *subj.* VEA) to see; to look into, examine, consider; to look; look at; to try (a case at law).—**v. de**, to try to.—**v. el cielo abierto**, to see a great opportunity.—**v. en ello**, to consider, to weigh in the mind.—**v. las estrellas**, to feel lively pain; to see stars.—**v. mundo**, or **v. tierras**, to see the world, to travel.—**v. venir**, to see (somebody or something) coming; to await results.—**v. visiones**, to build air castles.—**v. y creer**, seeing is believing.—**al v.**, to see one, at sight.—**allá veremos**, we shall see, time will tell.—**a más v.**, (coll.) good-bye, so long.—**a v.**, let's see; in order to see.—**hacer v.**, to show.—**hasta más v.** = A MÁS V.—**estar por v.**, to remain to be seen, to be doubtful.—**no poder v. a**, to abhor or detest (can't bear)..—**no tener que v. con**, to have nothing to do with.—**sí te vi**, **ya no me acuerdo**, out of sight, out of mind.—**veámoslo** = A V.—**veremos** = ALLÁ VEREMOS. **II.** *vr.* to be seen; be conspicuous; find one's self (in a situation), be; to be easily seen, be obvious; meet, have an interview; see one's self in a glass.—**v. con**, to have a talk with, to see.—**v. en**, or **entre, las astas del toro**, to be in the greatest danger.—**ya se ve**, of course, naturally; certainly; however.

ver, *m.* sense of sight, seeing; looks, light, view, aspect, appearance.—**a mi v.**, in my opinion, to my way of thinking.

vera, *f.* edge, border; (Am.) a tree resembling guaiacum.—**v. efigies**, faithful portrait.

veracidad, *f.* veracity, truthfulness.

veranada, *f.* summer season.

veranadero, *m.* summer pasture.

veranar, *vn.* to summer.

veraneante, *n.* summerer, summer resident or vacationist.

veranear, *vn.* to summer.

veraneo, *m.* summering.

veranero, *m.* place where cattle graze in summer

veraniego, ga, *a.* summer (u. a.); thin or sickly in summer; weak light.

veranillo, *m. dim.*—**v. de San Martín**, Indian summer.

verano, *m.* summer; (Am.) dry season.

veras, *f. pl.* reality, truth; earnestness, fervor.—**con muchas v.**, very earnestly.—**de v.**, in truth, really, in earnest.

veratro, *m.* (bot.) hellebore.

veraz, *a.* veracious, truthful.

verbal, *a.* verbal; oral; (law) nuncupative.

verbalismo, *m.* literalism, adherence to words rather than to ideas; system of teaching emphasizing world memory.—**verbalista**, *n.* literalist; advocate of VERBALISMO.

verbalmente, *adv.* verbally, orally, by word of mouth.

verbasco, *m.* (bot.) verbascum, mullein.

verbena, *f.* (bot.) vervain, verbena; night festival on the eve of a saint's day.—**coger la v.**, to rise early to take a walk.

verbenáceo, a, *a.* (bot.) verbenaceous.—*pl.* Verbenaceæ, vervain family.

verbenear, *vn.* to abound, to be plentiful; to rush to and fro.

verberación, *f.* verberation.

verberar, *va.* to verberate, beat, strike, dart against (as wind and water).

verbigracia, *adv.* for example, for instance.

verbo, *m.* verb; (V-) Word, second person of the Trinity.—**v. activo**, transitive verb, active verb.—**v. adjetivo**, any verb, except *ser*.—**v. defectivo**, defective verb.—**v. neutro**, intransitive or neuter verb.—**v. recíproco**, reflexive verb.—**v. substantivo**, the verb *ser*, to be.—**echar verbos**, to curse, to swear.—**en un v.**, at once, without delay.

verborrea, verbosidad, *f.* verbosity, wordiness.

verboso, sa, *a.* verbose, prolix, wordy.

verdacho, *m.* (art) green earth.

verdad, *f.* truth.—*¿v.?* is that so? isn't that so? often u. expletively in the sense of "you know," "don't you know?"—**v. de Perogrullo**, truism.—**a decir v.**, to speak truly; in reality, in fact.—**a la v.**, truly, really, in truth.—**bien es v. que**, it is true that.—**decir cuatro verdades**, to speak one's mind freely.—**de v.**, A LA V.; in earnest; real.—**en v.**, truly, really; verily.—*¿no es v.?* isn't that so?—**ser v.**, to be true.—**tratar v.**, to love and tell the truth.

verdaderamente, *adv.* truly, really.

verdadero, ra, *a.* true; real, actual; truthful.

verdasca, *f.* twig, bough, thin branch.

verde. I. *a.* green; verdant; unripe, immature, undeveloped; fresh; young, blooming, loose, smutty; off-color.—**v. botella**, bottle green.—**v. limón**, bright green.—**v. pardo**, brown green.—**están verdes**, sour grapes. **II.** *m.* green (color); verdure; vert; green barley or grass given to horses or mules as a purge.—**darse un v.**, to amuse one's self for a short time, to indulge in a little relaxation.

verdea, *f.* greenish wine.

verdear. I. *vn.* to grow green; to look green, to show its greenness. **II.** *va.* to pick (grapes and olives) to sell.

verdeceledón, *m.* sea-green, celadon.

verdecer, *vn.* to grow green.

verdecico, ica, ito, ita, illo, illa, *a. dim.* greenish.—**verdecillo**, *m.* (orn.) greenfinch.

verdeesmeralda, *a.* emerald green.

verdegal, *m.* green field.—**verdegay,** *a.* & *m.* light bright green.—**verdeguear,** *vn.* to grow green.

verdemar, *a.* & *m.* sea-green.—**verdemontaña,** *m.* mountain-green.

verderol, verderón, *m.* (orn.) green bird, green finch; green shellfish.

verdete, *m.* verditer; verdigris.—**verdevejiga,** *f.* sap green.—**verdezuelo,** *m.* (orn.) greenfinch, greeny.—**verdín,** *m.* verdure; pondscum; mould. mildew; verdigris; green snuff.—**verdina,** *f.* fresh greeness of plants.—**verdinal,** *m.* green spot or patch in a plain or meadow.—**verdinegro, gra,** *a.* dark green.—**verdino, na,** *a.* bright green.

verdiseco, ca, *a.* pale green; half dry.

verdolaga, *f.* (bot.) purslane.

verdón, *m.* (orn.) greenfinch.

verdor, *m.* greenness; verdure, verdancy; herbage; freshness, vigor.—*pl.* youth, age of vigor.

verdoso, sa, *a.* greenish.

verdoyo, *m.* pondscum; green mould.

verdugada, *f.* (mas.) layer of bricks.

verdugado, *m.* hoopskirt.

verdugal, *m.* young shoots growing in a wood after cutting.

verdugazo, *m.* stroke or lash with a twig.

verdugo, *m.* tiller, sucker, young shoot of a tree; verdun, duelling rapier; scourge, lash; wale, welt; executioner; (jewel.) hoop for a ring; very cruel person; anything that hurts; (mas.) brick course in a stone or mud wall; a small bird of prey.

verdugón, *m. aug.* large wale or welt.

verduguillo, *m. dim.* swelling on the leaves of some plants; small, narrow razor; verdun, duelling rapier; hoop worn as earring; (naut.) sheer rail.

verdulera, *f.* market woman; (coll.) coarse, low woman.

verdulero, *m.* greengrocer.

verdura, *f.* verdure, verdancy; greenness; greens, vegetables, garden stuff; (art) foliage.

verdusco, ca, *a.* dark greenish.

verecundo, da, *a.* bashful, shy.

vereda, *f.* path, footpath, trail; circular order or notice sent to several towns or places; route of travelling preachers; (Peru) sidewalk.—**entrar por la v.,** to come to reason, to do one's duty.

veredero, *m.* messenger sent with despatches on a route.

veredicto, *m.* (for.) verdict.

verga, *f.* penis; steel bow of a crossbow; (naut.) yard.—**v. seca,** crossjack yard.—**vergas en alto,** (naut.) all ready to sail.—**poner las vergas en cruz,** to square the yards.

vergajo, *m.* penis of a bull used as a cowhide.

vergel, *f.* flower garden.

vergelero, ra, *n.* gardener.

vergeta, *f.* small twig.

vergeteado, da, *a.* (her.) vergette, paley.

vergonzante. I. *a.* bashful, shamefaced. **II.** *n.* shy beggar.

vergonzosamente, *adv.* shamefully, disgracefully; bashfully, confusedly.

vergonzoso, sa. I. *a.* bashful, shamefaced, shy; shameful, disgraceful. **II.** *m.* armadillo.

verguear, *va.* to beat with a rod or whip.

vergüenza, *f.* shame; bashfulness, shyness, confusion; modesty; disgrace; public punishment. —*pl.* privy parts.—**sacar a la v.,** to disgrace publicly as a punishment; (coll.) to put in a predicament, or "fix," by asking (one) to do before others what one does not do well; to make a show of.—**ser una mala v.,** (coll.) to be a shame. —**tener v.,** to be ashamed; to have shame.

verguer, verguero, *m.* high constable.

vergueta, *f.* small switch or rod.

verguío, a, *a.* tough and flexible, leathery (s. o. wood).

vericueto, *m.* rough and pathless place.

verídicamente, *adv.* veridically, truthfully.

verídico, ca, *a.* veridical, truthful.

verificación, *f.* verification, substantiation, confirmation; test; adjustment (of an instrument).

verificar. I. *va.* (*pret.* VERIFIQUÉ: *subj.* VERIFIQUE) to verify, confirm, prove; to test, adjust (an instrument); to fulfil, accomplish, carry out. **II.** *vr.* to be verified, to prove true; to take place, to occur.

verificativo, va, *a.* verifying, corroborative.

verija, *f.* region of the genitals.

veril, *m.* (naut.) edge of a sand bank, etc.

verilear, *vn.* (naut.) to coast around a bank

verisímil, *a.* probable, likely, credible.

verisimilitud, *f.* verisimilitude, probability.

verisímilmente, *adv.* probably, likely.

verja, *f.* grate, grating; iron railing.

vermes, *m. pl.* (med.) intestinal worms.

vermicida, *a.* (med.) vermicide.

vermicular, *a.* vermiculous, vermicular.

vermiforme, *a.* vermiform, wormlike.

vermífugo, *a.* & *m.* (med.) vermifuge, anthelmintic.

verminoso, sa, *a.* verminous.

vermut, *m.* vermouth.

vernáculo, la, *a.* vernacular, native.

vernal, *a.* vernal, spring (u. a.)

vernier, *m.* vernier.

vero, *m.* marten (fur).—*pl.* (her.) vair.

veronense; veronés, sa, *n.* & *a.* Veronese.

verónica, *f.* veronica, a feat in bullfighting; (bot.) speedwell.

verosímil, verosimilitud, verosímilmente = VERISÍMIL, VERISIMILITUD, etc.

verraco, *m.* male hog or boar.

verraquear, *vn.* (coll.) to grunt like a boar; to cry long and loud (s. o. children).

verraquera, *f.* crying spell (of children).

verriondez, *f.* rutting time; withering state of herbs.

verriondo, da, *a.* ruttish, rutting, in heat (s. o. animals); withered; badly cooked, tough.

verrón, *m.* = VERRACO.

verruga, *f.* wart; (coll.) nuisance, bore.

verrugo, *m.* (coll.) miser.

verrugoso, sa, *a.* warty.

versado, da, *a.* & *pp.* versed, conversant.

versal, *a.* & *f.* (print.) capital (letter).

versalilla, versalita, *f.* & *a.* (print.) small capital (letter).

versar. I. *vn.* to go around; (Cuba) to versify, to improvise verses.—**v. acerca de,** or **sobre,** to treat of or on. **II.** *vr.* to become versed or conversant.

versátil, *a.* versatile; changeable, fickle.

versatilidad, *f.* versatility; fickleness.

versecillo, *m. dim.* little verse, verselet.

versería, *f.* poems.

versícula, *f.* stand for the choir books.

versiculario, *m.* (eccl.) chanter of versicles; keeper of the choir books.

versículo, *m.* (eccl.) verse; versicle.

versificación, *f.* versification.—**versificador, ra,** *n.* versifier, verse maker.—**versificante,** *a.* versifying.—**versificar,** *va.* & *vn.* (*pret.* VERSIFIQUÉ: *subj.* VERSIFIQUE) to versify.

versión, *f.* translation, version; (med.) version.— **v. de los Setenta,** Septuagint.

versista, *m.* (coll.) versifier, poetaster.

verso, *m.* line (of poetry); stanza; (arti.) an ancient small culverin.—*pl.* poems.—**v. alejandrino,** Alexandrine.—**v. blanco,** blank verse.—**v. de arte mayor,** verse of more than nine syllables.— **v. de arte menor,** verse of less than nine syllables. —**v. esdrújulo,** verse ending with a word accented on the antepenult.—**v. libre** = v. BLANCO.—**v. llano,** (poet.) verse ending with a word accented on the penult.—**v. suelto** = v. BLANCO.—**versos pareados,** doggerel.

vértebra, *f.* (anat.) vertebra.—**vertebrado, da. I.** *n.* & *a.* vertebrate. **II.** *m. pl.* (zool.), Vertebrata, vertebrates.—**vertebral,** *a.* vertebral.

vertedera, *f.* (agr.) mouldboard of a plow.

vertedero, *m.* sink, dumping place; (hydr.) weir; spillway.

vertedor, ra. I. *n.* nightman; emptier. **II.** *m.* tailrace; drain; (hydr.) weir; (naut.) boat scoop.

vertellos, *m. pl.* (naut.) balls of the parrel truck.

verter. I. *va.* (*ind.* VIERTO: *subj.* VIERTA) to pour, spill, shed, cast; to empty; to dump; to translate; to construe, interpret; to divulge, publish, reveal. **II.** *vn.* to run, flow.

vertibilidad, *f.* capability of being turned over.

vertible, *a.* movable, changeable, variable.

vertical. I. *a.* vertical. **II.** *m.* (ast.) vertical circle.—**v. primario**, (ast.) prime vertical. **III.** *f.* vertical line.

verticalidad, *f.* verticality.

verticalmente, *adv.* vertically.

vértice, *m.* vertex; apex, top; (anat.) vertex, crown of the head.

verticidad, *f.* movableness, mobility.

verticilado, da, *a.* (bot.) verticillate.

verticilo, *m.* (bot.) verticil, whorl.

vertiente. I. *a.* emptying; flowing. **II.** *f.* watershed; slope.

vertiginoso, sa, *a.* giddy, vertiginous.

vértigo, *m.* giddiness, dizziness, vertigo; fit of insanity.

vertimiento, *m.* effusion, shedding.

vesania, *f.* (med.) vesania, insanity.

vesánico, ca, *a.* mentally deranged.

vesical, *a.* (anar.) vesical.

vesicante, *a. & m.* vesicant, vesicatory.

vesícula, *f.* (anat., bot.) vesicle; (med.) vesicle, blister.—**v. aérea**, air vesicle (of the lungs).—**v. biliar**, gall bladder.—**v. elemental**, or **orgánica**, (biol.) cell.—**v. ováriсa**, (anat.) Graffian follicle.—**v. seminal**, (anat.) sperm sac.

vesicular, *a.* vesicular.

vesiculoso, sa, *a.* vesiculate.

Véspero, *m.* Vesper, evening star.

vespertiliónidos, *m. pl.* (zool.) Vespertilionidæ.

vespertina, *f.* evening discourse in universities.

vespertino, na. I. *a.* vespertine, evening. **II.** *m.* afternoon literary meeting; afternoon sermon.

véspidos, *m. pl.* (zool.) Vespidæ.

vestal, *f. & a.* vestal.

veste, *f.* (poet.) clothes, dress, garments.

vestfaliano, na, *n. & a.* Westphalian.

vestíbulo, *m.* vestibule, hall, lobby; (anat.) vestibule of the ear.

vestido, *pp. & m.* dress, clothes, clothing, garb, costume; ornament, embellishment.—**v. de corte**, court dress.—**v. de etiqueta**, or **de serio**, full dress, evening dress.—**vestidos usados**, second-hand clothes.

vestidura, *f.* vesture.—*pl.* (eccl.) vestments.

vestigio, *m.* vestige, trace, sign; footstep, footmark.—*pl.* ruins, remains; (chem.) traces.

vestiglo, *m.* horrid and formidable monster.

vestimenta, *f.* clothes, garments.—*pl.* ecclesiastical robes.

vestir. I. *va.* to clothe, dress; to deck, adorn; to cloak, disguise, palliate; to don, put on; to wear; to cover; (mas.) to roughcast. **II.** *vn.* to dress in a special color or fashion.—**v. bien**, to dress well or in good taste.—**v. de uniforme**, to dress in uniform. **III.** *vr.* to dress one's self; to be covered; to be clothed.

vestuario, *m.* apparel, wardrobe, clothes, clothing, dress; uniform; (mil.) equipment, outfit, habiliment; (eccl.) vestry; money given to ecclesiastics for dress, etc.; (theat.) wardrobe, greenroom, dressing room.

vestugo, *m.* tiller, sprout of an olive tree.

veta, *f.* (min.) vein, seam, lode; vein in wood or marble; grain, flake; stripe.—**descubrir la v.**, to discover one's sentiments or designs, show one's hand.

vetado, da; veteado, da, *a.* striped, veined, streaky, cross-grained, mottled.

vetear, *va.* to variegate, to grain.

veterano, na. I. *a.* (mil.) veteran; having had long experience. **II.** *m.* veteran.

veterinaria, *f.* veterinary science.

veterinario, *m.* veterinarian.

vetisesgado, da, diagonal-striped, with stripes on the bias.

veto, *m.* veto; prohibition, interdict.

vetustez, *f.* antiquity, old age.

vetusto, ta, *a.* very ancient or old.

vez, *f.* turn; time, occasion; herd of swine belonging to the inhabitants of a place.—*pl.* authority given to a substitute.—**a la v.**, at once; at a time.—**a la v. que**, while, whilst.—**alguna v.**, sometimes; some times, occasionally.—**a su v.**, in his (one's) turn; on his (one's) part.—**a veces**, sometimes occasionally.—**cada v.**, each time, every time.—**de una v.**, at once.—**de v. en cuando**, occasionally, once in a while.—**en v. de**, instead of.—**hacer las veces de**, to serve as, to substitute.—**más de una v.**, more than once.—**otra v.**, again, once more; some other time.—**tal cual v.**, seldom, rarely, once in a while.—**tal v.**, perhaps, maybe, perchance.—**todas las veces que**, whenever, as often as.—**una que otra vez**, once in a while; a few times.—**una v.**, once.—**una v. que**, since, inasmuch as; after.—**una v. que otra**, once in a while; a few times.—**veces mayor que**, times as large as, times (*10 es 5 veces mayor que 2*, 10 is 5 times [as large as] 2). The similar expression **veces menor que** indicates a fractional part: *2 es 5 veces menor que 10*, 2 is one fifth of 10.

veza, *f.* (bot.) vetch. *V.* ARVEJA.

vezar *va. & vr.* to accustom, habituate, inure.

vía, *f.* way, road; route, via; carriage track; (r. w.) track, line; gauge; way, manner, method, procedure; spiritual life; (zool.) tube, canal, passage.—**v. ancha**, (r. w.) broad gauge.—**v. angosta**, narrow gauge.—**v. crucis**, (eccl.) Via Crucis, way of the cross; affliction, burden.—**v. de agua**, (naut.) leak.—**v. ejecutiva**, (law) levy, a legal writ of execution; attachment.—**v. férrea**, railroad, railway.—**v. húmeda**, (chem.) wet process.—**V. Láctea**, (ast.) Milky Way.—**v. muerta**, (r. w.) siding.—**v. pública**, public road, thoroughfare; street.—**v. recta**, straight along, straight forward.—**v. sacra**=**v. crucis**.—**v. seca**, (chem.) dry process.—**en v. de**, in the process of.—**por v. de**, by way of, as.

viabilidad, *f.* feasability, practicability; (med.) viability.—**viable**, *a.* able, capable of living; feasible, practicable.

viadera, *f.* harness shaft of a loom.

viador, *m.* traveler, in a mystical sense.

viaducto, *m.* viaduct.

viajador, ra, *n.* traveler.—**viajante. I.** *a.* traveling. **II.** *n.* traveler; commercial traveler.

viajar, *vn.* to travel, journey.

viajata, *f.* trip, excursion.

viaje, *m.* journey, voyage, travel, trip; passage; gait; excursion; errand; load carried at once; (hyd.) water main, water supply; way, road; (arch.) obliquity.—**v. de ida y vuelta**, or **v. redondo**, round trip.—**buen v.**, God-speed, bon voyage.

viajero, ra, *n.* traveler; passenger.

vial. I. *a.* relating to roads. **II.** *m.* avenue, lane, boulevard.

vialidad, *f.* system of public roads; road engineering, road making.

vianda, *f.* (often in the *pl.*) food, viands, victuals, fare; meal.—*pl.* (Cuba) vegetables for AJIACO.

viandante, *n.* traveler, passenger; tramp.

viaraza, *f.* (vet.) looseness, diarrhœa.

viaticar. I. *va.* (eccl.) to administer the viaticum to. **II.** *vr.* to receive the viaticum.

viático, *m.* viaticum, provision for a journey, traveling expenses; (eccl.) viaticum.

víbora, *f.* viper; perfidious person.

viborezno, na, *m.* young, small viper.

vibración, *f.* vibration.—**vibrante**, *a.* vibrating, shaking.—**vibrar. I.** *va.* to vibrate; to brandish; to throw, dart. **II.** *vn.* to vibrate.—**vibratorio, ria**, *a.* vibratory.

vibrión, *m.* (bact.) vibrio.

viburno, *m.* (bot.) viburnum.

vicaria, *f.* assistant mother superior.

vicaría, *f.* vicarship; vicarage.—**v. perpetua**, perpetual curacy.—**vicariato**, *m.* vicarage; vicarship.

vicario, ria. I. *a.* vicarial, vicarious, vicariate. **II.** *m.* vicar, deputy; (eccl.) vicar, vicariate.—**v. de coro**, vicar choral, superintendent of the choir.—**v. general**, vicar-general.

vicealmiranta, *f.* galley next in order to the admiral's.

vicealmirantazgo, *m.* vice admiralty.

vicealmirante, *m.* vice admiral.

vicecanciller, *m.* vice chancellor.

viceconsiliario, *m.* vice counsellor.

vicecónsul, *m.* vice consul.

viceconsulado, *m.* vice consulate.

vicecristo, vicediós, *m.* sovereign pontiff.

vicegerancia, *f.* office or post of assistant manager.

vicegerente, *a.* assistant manager.

vicegobernador, ra, *n.* vice governor, lieutenant governor.

vicenal, *a.* lasting twenty years; occurring every twenty years.

vicepresidencia, *f.* vice presidency.

vicepresidente, *m.* vice president.

viceprovincia, *f.* (eccl.) religious houses enjoying the rank of a province.

vicerrector, ra, *n.* vice rector; assistant director.

vicesecretaría, *f.* assistant secretaryship.

vicesecretario, ria, *n.* assistant secretary.

vicésimo, ma, *a.* twentieth.

vicetesorero, ra, *n.* assistant treasurer.

viceversa. I. *adv.* vice versa, conversely. **II.** *m.* illogical statement; incongruous thing or expression.

vicia, *f.* tare. *V.* ARVEJA.

viciado, *pp. & a.* foul, contaminated; vitiated; invalidated.

viciar. I. *va.* to vitiate, mar, spoil; to counterfeit, adulterate; to forge, falsify; to annul, make void; to deprave, pervert, corrupt; to misconstrue. **II.** *vr.* to give one's self up to vice; to become too much attached or addicted, to contract a (bad) habit.

vicio, *m.* vice; (bad) habit; defect, blemish; artifice, fraud; excessive appetite, extravagant desire; excessive growth of plants; forwardness, waywardness (of children); vices of horses or mules. —**de v.,** by habit or custom.—**quejarse de v.,** to complain habitually.—**tener el v. de,** to have the habit of; to be in the habit of.

viciosamente, *adv.* viciously; falsely; corruptly.

vicioso, sa, *a.* vicious; defective; given to vice, licentious; spoiled (child); luxuriant, overgrown, vigorous; abundant.

vicisitud, *f.* vicissitude.

vicisitudinario, ria, *a.* vicissitudinary.

viclefismo, *m.* Wycliffism.—**viclefista, viclefita,** *n. & a.* Wyclyphite.

víctima, *f.* victim.

victimario, *m.* servant who attends the sacrificing priest.

victo, *m.* a day's sustenance.

¡víctor! *interj. & m.* shout, huzza; long live!

victorear, *va.* to shout, huzza for, give a clamorous ovation to.

victoria, *f.* victory, triumph, palm; (car.) victoria.—**cantar la v.,** to celebrate or proclaim a victory.—**cantar v.,** to proclaim, or boast of, a victory.—**victorial,** *a.* relating to victory.

victoriosamente, *adv.* victoriously.

victorioso, sa, *a.* victorious, triumphant.

vicuña, *f.* vicuña or vicugna.

vid, *f.* (bot.) vine, grapevine.

vida, *f.* life; living person, human being; living, sustenance, livelihood; state, condition; activity, animation, liveliness; (law) term of ten years.—**v. airada,** licentious life, gay life.—**v. ancha,** good living, loose living.—**v. mía,** dearest, darling.—**v. y milagros de una persona,** a person's life and history (w. the implication that the "history" is bad).—**buena v.,** good or high living. —**buscar la v.,** to earn an honest livelihood; to seek one's fortune; to inquire into the life (of).— **dar mala v.,** to treat ill, to abuse.—**darse buena v.,** to live comfortably.—**de mala v.,** disreputable, licentious.—**de por v.,** for life, during life.—**en v.,** while living, during life.—**en la v.,** or **en mi v.,** never.—**gran v. =** BUENA V.—**hacer v.,** to live together.—**mi v. =** V. MÍA.—**pasar la v.,** to live very

frugally.—**por v. =** DE POR V.—**¡por v. mía!** upon my soul! by my soul!—**tener siete vidas,** to have the nine lives of the cat.

vide, vide, see (in references).

¡vidita! *f.* (Am.) dearest, darling.

vidente. I. *a.* seeing. **II.** *m.* seer.

vidriado, da. I. *pp. & a.* glazed. **II.** *m.* glazing; glazed earthenware, crockery.

vidriar, *va.* to varnish, to glaze (earthenware).

vidriera, *f.* glass window or partition; glass case, show case, show window.

vidriería, *f.* glazier's shop; glass factory; glass shop; glassware.

vidriero, ra, *n.* glazier; glassblower; glass dealer.

vidrio, *m.* glass; any article made of glass; anything very delicate and brittle; a very touchy person.—**v. coloreado,** or **de color,** stained glass. —**vidrios de vidriera,** or **planos,** window glass.— **ir al v.,** to ride backward in a coach.—**pagar los vidrios rotos,** to receive undeserved punishment, to be made a scapegoat.

vidriosidad, *f.* vitreousness; glassiness.

vidrioso, sa, *a.* vitreous, brittle; glassy; slippery (from sleet); peevish, touchy.

vidual, *a.* belonging to widowhood.

vidueño, viduño, *m.* quality of grape vines.

viejarrón, na, *m.* (coll.) old codger.

viejecito, ita, zuelo, ela, *a. & n. dim.* little old man (woman).

viejo, ja. I. *a.* old; aged; ancient, antiquated; stale; worn-out; old-fashioned. **II.** *n.* old man (woman).—**v. verde,** boyish old man (girlish old woman).

vienense, *n. & a.* of or from Vienne (France).

vienés, sa, *n. & a.* Viennese, of Vienna (Austria).

vientecillo, *m. dim.* light wind.

viento, *m.* wind; vanity, petty pride, airs; scent of dogs; nape bone of a dog, between the ears; brace, guy, bracing rope; (arti.) windage; (naut.) course.—**v. calmoso,** light unsteady wind. —**v. contrario,** foul wind.—**v. de bolina,** (naut.) scant wind.—**v. de tierra,** land breeze.—**v. en popa,** wind right aft, before the wind; (fig.) finely, boomingly; without hitch.—**v. entero,** wind from one of the cardinal points or four points from any of them—**v. escaso,** slack wind.—**v. fresco,** (naut.) fresh breeze.—**v. puntero =** v. ESCASO.—**v. terral =** v. DE TIERRA.—**vientos alisios,** trade winds.—**contra v. y marea,** (fig.) against wind and tide, in the teeth of the wind.—**el v. se ha cargado al norte,** the wind has veered to the north.— **medio v.,** wind two points from any of the eight principal points of the compass.—**quitar el v. a un bajel,** to blanket a ship.

vientre, *m.* abdomen; belly; bowels; stomach; pregnancy; womb; belly or widest part of vessels.

vientrecillo, *m. dim.* ventricle.

viernes, *m.* Friday; fast day.—**V. Santo,** Good Friday.—**cara de v.,** wan, thin face.

vierteaguas, *m.* (arch.) flashing, run-off plate or device.

viga, *f.* beam, girder, joist, rafter, baulk; bridge truss; mill beam; quantity of olives pressed by the beam at once.—**v. armada,** trussed beam.—**v. de aire,** joist.—**v. de alma llena,** plate girder.— **v. maestra,** summer, chief supporting beam.

vigencia, *f.* operation (of a law), state of being in force; (Colomb.) fiscal year.

vigente, *a.* (law) in force; standing.

vigesimal, *a.* vigesimal.

vigésimo, ma, *a.* twentieth.

vigía. I. *f.* watchtower; watch, watching; (naut.) shoal, rock. **II.** *m.* lookout, watch.

vigiar, *vn.* to keep a look out, to watch.

vigilancia, *f.* vigilance, watchfulness.

vigilante. I. *a.* watchful, vigilant, careful. **II.** *m.* watchman, guard.

vigilantemente, *adv.* vigilantly, heedfully.

vigilar, *va. & vn.* to watch (over), to keep guard, to look out (for).

vigilativo, va, *a.* causing sleeplessness or wakefulness.

vigilia, _f._ vigil, wakefulness, watchfulness, watching; lucubration, nocturnal study; (eccl.) vigil, fast; eve; (mil.) watch, guard.—**comer de v.,** to fast (abstain from meat).

vigor, _m._ vigor.—**vigorar** = VIGORIZAR.

vigorizador, ra, _a._ invigorating.—**vigorizar,** _va._ (_pret._ VIGORICÉ: _subj._ VIGORICE) to strengthen, invigorate; to encourage, inspirit.—**vigorosamente,** _adv._ vigorously, lustily.—**vigorosidad,** _f._ vigor.—**vigoroso, sa,** _a._ vigorous; substantial.

vigota, _f._ (naut.) deadeye, chain plate.

viguería, _f._ set of girders or beams; timberwork.

vigués, sa, _a._ of or from Vigo.

vigueta, _f. dim._ small beam, joist; beam.

vihuela, _f._ guitar.

vihuelista, _n._ guitar player.

vil, _a._ vile, mean, base, despicable.

vilano, _m._ burr or down of the thistle.

vilayato, _m._ vilayet (Turkish province).

vileza, _f._ baseness, meanness, vileness; infamous deed, base act or conduct.

vilipendiador, ra, _a. & n._ reviler (-ing).

vilipendiar, _va._ to contemn, revile.

vilipendio, _m._ contempt; reviling.

vilipendioso, sa, _a._ contemptible.

vilmente, _adv._ vilely, basely, contemptibly.

vilo.—en v., _adv._ in the air; insecurely; in suspense.

vilordo, da, _a._ slothful, lazy, heavy.

vilorta, _f._ hoop, ring of twisted willow; clasp ring of a plow; washer; game resembling lacrosse.

vilorto, _m._ a variety of reed; snare of this reed; reed or twig hoop; crosse for playing VILORTA.

vilos, _m._ (Philip.) two-masted vessel.

viltrotear, _vn._ to loaf, to walk the streets.

villa, _f._ town; government of a town; countryseat, villa.

Villadiego, _m._—**coger-** or **tomar, las de V.,** to show a clean pair of heels, to run away, to sneak out, "to beat it."

villaje, _m._ village; hamlet.

villanada, _f._ villainous, despicable act.

villanaje, _m._ villenage; peasantry.

villanamente, _adv._ boorishly; villainously.

villancejo, villancete, villancico, _m._ Christmas carol.—**villanciquero,** _m._ writer or singer of Christmas carols.

villanchón, na, _a._ rustic, rude.

villanería, _f._ lowness of birth; meanness.

villanesco, ca, _a._ rustic, rude, boorish.

villanía, _f._ lowness of birth, meanness; villainy, villainousness; vile, base deed.

villano, na. I. _a._ rustic, boorish; villainous, base. **II.** _n._ villain; base, contemptible person; rustic, peasant. **III.** _m._ a Spanish tune and dance.

villanote, _a. & m. aug._ great villain.

villar, _m._ village, hamlet.

villazgo, _m._ charter of a town; town tax.

villeta, _f. dim._ small town or borough.

villoría, _f._ hamlet, settlement, farm.

villorín, _m._ a sort of coarse cloth.

villorrio, _m._ small village or hamlet.

vimbre, _m._ (bot.) osier, willow.

vimbrera, _f._ = MIMBRERA.

vinagrada, _f._ refreshment made with vinegar.

vinagre. I. _m._ vinegar; acidity, sourness. **II.** _a._ (Colomb.) disagreeable; sour (milk, etc.) **III.** _n._ (coll.) grouty person.—**vinagrero, ra. I.** _n._ vinegar merchant. **II.** _f._ vinegar cruet, caster; (S. A.) heartburn.—**vinagreta,** _f._ (cook.) vinegar sauce.—**vinagrillo,** _m. dim._ weak vinegar; cosmetic lotion; rose vinegar; rose-vinegar snuff.—**vinagroso, sa,** _a._ vinegary, vinegarish, sourish; peevish, grouty.

vinajera, _f._ (eccl.) wine vessel for the mass.

vinar, _a._ = VINARIO.

vinariego, _m._ vintager.

vinario, ria, _a._ belonging to wine.

vinatería, _f._ wine trade; wine shop.

vinatero, ra. I. _a._ pertaining to wine. **II.** _n._ vintner, wine merchant. **III.** _f._ (naut.) strop, tricing line.

vinaza, _f._ wine drawn from the lees.

vinazo, _m._ very strong wine.

vinculable, _a._ that may be entailed.

vinculación, _f._ (law) entail.

vincular, _va._ (law) to entail; to ground or found upon; to continue, to perpetuate.

vínculo, _m._ tie, bond; vinculum; (law) entail.

vincha, _f._ (S. A.) kerchief for the head or hair.

vinchuca, _f._ a kind of winged bedbug.

vindicación, _f._ vindication.

vindicar, _va._ (_pret._ VINDIQUÉ: _subj._ VINDIQUE) to vindicate; avenge; assert (as rights), defend; (law) to reclaim, repossess, replevy.—**vindicativo, va,** _a._ vindictive, revengeful; vindicating, vindicative.—**vindicatorio, ria,** _a._ vindicatory.

vindicta, _f._ vengeance, revenge.—**v. pública,** public vengeance, public punishment; censure of public opinion.

vínico, ca, _a._ vinic, pertaining to wine.

vinícola. I. _a._ wine (u. a.); vinicultural. **II.** _n._ viniculturist, vine grower.

vinicultor, ra, _n._ viniculturist, vine grower.

vinicultura, _f._ viniculture, vine growing.

viniebla, _f._ (bot.) hound's tongue.

vinificación, _f._ vinification.

vinillo, _m._ very weak wine.

vino, _m._ wine; fermented juice of any fruit.—**v. clarete,** claret or pale red wine.—**v. cubierto,** dark-red wine.—**v. de coco,** (Philip.) fermented milk of cocoanuts.—**v. de cuerpo,** strong-bodied wine.—**v. de Jerez,** sherry wine.—**v. de lágrima,** mother-drop or virgin wine.—**v. de mesa,** table wine.—**v. de nipa,** (Philip.) fermented juice of NIPA.—**v. de Oporto,** port wine.—**v. de pasto,** table wine.—**v. de postre** = v. GENEROSO.—**v. flojo,** thin or weak wine.—**v. generoso,** strong, old wine; after-dinner wine.—**v. peleón,** very common wine.—**v. rancio,** fine old wine.—**v. seco,** dry wine.—**v. tinto,** red table wine.—**tomarse del v.,** to get drunk.

vinolencia, _f._ excess in drinking wine.

vinolento, ta, _a._ too fond of wine.

vinosidad, _f._ vinosity.—**vinoso, sa,** _a._ vinous, vinous; addicted to wine.

vinote, _m._ liquid remaining in the boiler after distilling wine.

vinta, _f._ (Philip.) = BAROTO.

vintén, _m._ a Uruguayan copper coin (about 2 cents).

viña, _f._ vineyard.—**viñadero, ra,** _n._ keeper of a vineyard.—**viñador, ra,** _n._ viticulturist; husbandman.—**viñedo,** _m._ vineyard.—**viñero, ra,** _n._ owner of vineyards.

viñeta, _f._ (print. and photo.) vignette.

viñetero, _m._ (typ.) font case for vignettes.

viñuela, _f. dim._ small vineyard.

viola. I. _f._ (mus.) viola; viola player; (bot.) violet.

violáceo, ea. I. _a._ violaceous; violet-colored. **II.** _f. pl._ (bot.) Violaceæ.

violación, _f._ violation.

violado, da, _pp. & a._ violated; violaceous; violet (color).

violador, ra, _n._ violator; infringer; profaner.

violar, _va._ to violate, break, infringe; to ravish, violate, rape; to profane, desecrate; to spoil, to tarnish.

violar, _m._ patch or bed of violets.

violencia, _f._ violence; compulsion, force; rape; outrage.

violentamente, _adv._ violently; forcibly.

violentar. I. _va._ to do violence to; to break into. **II.** _vr._ to force one's self; to control one's unwillingness.

violento, ta, _a._ violent; impulsive; irascible, irritable; furious; forced, unnatural; strained, absurd, misconstrued; exceedingly intense or severe, (coll.) "awful."

violero, _m._ viola player.

violeta, _f._ (bot.) violet.

violeto, _m._ clingstone peach.

violín. I. _m._ violin. **II.** _n._ violinist.

violinista, _n._ (mus.) violinist.

violón, _m._ (mus.) bass viol, double bass; bass-viol player.—**tocar el v.,** to do or say something absurd or nonsensical.

violoncelista, *n.* violoncellist, cellist.

violoncelo, *m.* (mus.) violoncello, cello.

violonchelo, *m.* = VIOLONCELO.

vipéreo, rea, viperino, na, *a.* viperine; viperous, venomous.

vira, *f.* dart, arrow; welt of a shoe.

viracocha, *n.* (Ch., Peru) Spaniard.

virada, *f.* (naut.) tacking, tack.

virador, *m.* (naut.) top-rope; viol.

virago, *f.* mannish woman.

virar, *va.* (naut.) to tack, veer, wear, put about; to wind, twist, heave (as the capstan).

viratón, *m.* large dart or arrow.

virazón, *f.* sea breeze.

víreo, *m.* (orn.) vireo.

virgen. I. *n.* & *a.* virgin. **II.** *f.* standard of the beam of an oil mill; **(V-)** Virgin (Mary); **(V-,** astr.) Virgin, Virgo.

virgiliano, na, *a.* Virgilian.

virginal; virgíneo, nea, *a.* virginal, virgin.

virginia, *f.* (bot.) Virginia tobacco.

virginiano, na, *n.* & *a.* Virginian.

virginidad, *f.* virginity.

virgo, *m.* virginity; (anat.) hymen; **(V-,** astr.) Virgo, Virgin.

vírgula, *f.* virgule, small rod; light, short line, accent; (bact.) cholera bacillus.—**virgulilla,** *f.* fine stroke or light line, accent.

viril. I. *m.* clear and transparent glass; (eccl.) monstrance. **II.** *a.* virile, manly.—**virilidad,** *f.* virility, manhood; vigor, strength.

virilmente, *adv.* in a manly manner.

virio, *m.* (orn.) vireo.

virina, *f.* (Philip.) = GUARDABRISA.

viripotente, *a.* marriageable, nubile (s. o. women); vigorous, strong.

virol, *m.* (her.) virole.

virola, *f.* collar, clasp; check ring on goads.

virolento, ta, *a.* having smallpox; pock-marked.

virón, *m. aug.* large dart.

virotazo, *m.* wound with a VIROTE.

virote, *m.* shaft, dart, arrow; iron rod fastened to a collar on the neck of a slave to prevent his running away; vine three years old; (coll.) stuck-up man; April fool's trick.

virotillo, *m.* (arch.) intertie; (mech.) stay, stay rod, staybolt.

virotismo, *m.* conceit, airs.

virreina, *f.* wife of a viceroy.

virreinato, virreino, *m.* viceroyship.

virrey, *m.* viceroy.

virtual, *a.* virtual.

virtualidad, *f.* virtuality, efficacy.

virtualmente, *adv.* virtually, in effect, practically, almost..

virtud, *f.* virtue; efficacy, power; virtuous life; vigor, courage.—*pl.* (theol.) fifth choir of the celestial spirits.—**virtudes teolog“es,** theological virtues (faith, hope, charity).—**en v. de,** in, or by, virtue of.

virtuosamente, *adv.* virtuously.

virtuoso, sa, *a.* virtuous, righteous; chaste; powerful, vigorous.

viruela, *f.* (med.) pock; smallpox.—**viruelas bastardas,** chicken pox.—**viruelas locas,** good or favorable smallpox.

virulencia, *f.* virulence; acrimony, malignity.

virulento, ta, *a.* virulent; malignant; purulent.

virus, *m.* (med.) virus; poison, contagion.

viruta, *f.* wood shaving.

vis, *f.*—**v. cómica,** (theat.) verve.

visaje, *m.* grimace, grin, smirk.—**hacer visajes,** to make wry faces.

visajero, ra, *n.* one who makes grimaces.

visar, *va.* to visé; to countersign; to O. - K.

visaya. I. *a.* & *n.* Visayan. **II.** *m.* Visayan language.

víscera, *f.* viscus.—*pl.* viscera.—**visceral,** *a.* visceral.

visco, *m.* birdlime. *V.* LIGA.

viscosidad, *f.* viscosity.—**viscoso, sa,** *a.* viscous, mucilaginous.

visera, *f.* vizor of a cap or helmet; eyeshade; box with a spy hole, used by pigeon fanciers; (Cuba) blinder, winker (for a horse).

visibilidad, *f.* visibility.—**visible,** *a.* visible; evident; conspicuous.

visiblemente, *adv.* visibly; evidently.

visigodo, da, *n.* & *a.* Visigoth.

visigótico, ca, *a.* Visigothic.

visillo, *m.* window curtain or shade.

visión, *f.* sight; vision; dream, fantasy; phantom, apparition; revelation, prophecy; (coll.) grotesque person, guy.—**ver visiones,** to build air castles.

visionario, ria, *a.* & *n.* visionary.

visir, *m.* vizier, Turkish prime minister.

visita, *f.* visit; social call; visitor, caller, guest, company; visitation, inspection; (eccl.) tribunal for the inspection of prisons; hall of that tribunal; (med.) visit.—**v. de aspectos,** medical inspection of passengers.—**v. de cumplido,** or **de cumplimento,** formal call.—**v. de sanidad,** health inspection.—**v. domiciliaria,** official visit or inspection of a suspected house; social-work call, or visit. —**hacer una v.,** to make a call.—**pagar una v.,** to return a call.—**tener v.,** to have company or callers.

visitación, *f.* visitation, visiting, visit.

visitador, ra, *n.* visitor, visitant, caller; searcher, surveyor, inspector.—**v. de registro,** (naut.) searcher of goods on boards ships; tidewaiter.

visitadora, *f.* (C. A.) enema.

visitar. I. *va.* to visit; to call on; to inspect, search, examine; (med.) to visit (a patient); (law) to make a judicial visit or search of; (naut.) to search (ships); to appear to, as a spirit; to frequent; (eccl.) to visit (religious persons and establishments) as an ecclesiastical judge; (theol.) to send a divine counsel to; (law) to make an abstract of the charge against a prisoner at visitation **II.** *vr.* to visit one another, call on one another.

visiteo, *m.* frequent visiting or calling.

visitero, ra, *a.* (coll.) fond of making calls.

visítica, illa, *f. dim.* short call.

visitón, *m. aug.* (coll.) long and tedious call.

visivo, va, *a.* visive.

vislumbrar, *va.* to glimpse, to have a glimmer of; to see imperfectly at a distance; to know imperfectly; to suspect, surmise.

vislumbre, *f.* glimpse, glimmer, glimmering; conjecture, surmise; appearance, semblance.

viso, *m.* elevated spot, outlook; lustre, gleam, sheen, flash, glare; colored slip worn under a transparent frock; color, cloak, pretence, pretext; aspect, appearance.—**a dos visos,** with a double view or design.—**al v.,** viewed sidewise (s. o. fabrics) to examine the sheen.—**de v.,** conspicuous, prominent.

visogodo, da, *a.* & *n.* Visigoth.

visón, *m.* American mink.

visorio, ria. I. *a.* visual, optic. **II.** *m.* expert examination.

víspera, *f.* eve, day before; forerunner, prelude; anything that precedes another.—*pl.* vesper, evening; (eccl.) vespers.—**en vísperas de,** on the eve of.

vista. I. *f.* sight; seeing, vision; view; vista; eye, eyesight; glance, look; aspect, looks; apparition; meeting, interview; clear knowledge or perception; relation, connection; comparison; intent, view, purpose; opinion, judgment; opening, light (window, skylight, etc.); (law) trial.—**v. cansada,** farsightedness.—**v. corta,** nearsightedness.— **aguzar la v.,** to look sharp.—**a la simple v.,** at first sight; by inspection (s. o. the solution of a problem, etc.).—**a la v.,** at once, immediately; at sight; (com.) at sight.—**a primera v.,** at first sight. —**a v. de,** in presence of.—**a v. de ojos,** with one's own eyes.—**dar una v.,** to give a passing glance.— **de v.,** by sight.—**echar la v. a,** to choose; to set one's eye on.—**echar una v. a,** to look after, to watch.—**en v. de,** in view of, considering.—**estar a la v.,** to be obvious.—**hacer la v. gorda,** to wink, to connive.—**hasta la v.,** au revoir, good-bye.— **perder de v.,** to lose sight of.—**perderse de v.,** to go out of sight; (coll.) to excel; to be very smart.— **tener a la v.,** to have before one, or before one's eyes.—**tener v.**, to be showy. **II.** *n.* customhouse inspector. **III.** *f. pl.* meeting, conference, interview; wedding presents from a bride and bridegroom to each other; bosom, collar and cuffs of a shirt.

vistazo, *m.* glance.—**dar un v. a,** to glance at, to look over.

vistillas, *f. pl.* place commanding a good view, lookout.

visto, ta. I. *pp. irr.* of VER & *a.* obvious, evident, clear; (law) whereas.—**bien v.**, proper or approved. —**mal v.**, improper or disapproved.—**v. bueno** (in abbreviation V°. B°.), correct, approved, O. K.— **v. es,** or **v. está,** it is evident.—**v. que,** considering that, since.—**bien v.**, proper, approved, good form. —**mal v.**, improper, disapproved, bad form.—**no v.,** or **nunca v.**, unheard of. **II.** *m.* (law) preambulatory clause beginning with "whereas."

vistosamente, *adv.* beautifully; gaudily.

vistoso, sa, beautiful; showy; flaring, loud.

visual. I. *a.* visual; of sight. **II.** *f.* line of sight.

visualidad, *f.* visuality.

visura, *f.* ocular inspection; expert examination or inspection.

vital, *a.* vital; essential, necessary.

vitalicia, cia. I. *a.* lasting for life; during life. **II.** *m.* life-insurance policy.

vitalicista, *n.* one who enjoys a life annuity.

vitalidad, *f.* vitality.—**vitalismo,** *m.* vitalism.

vitalista, *a.* & *n.* vitalist.

vitando, da, *a.* that ought to be shunned or avoided; odious, execrable.

vitela, *f.* vellum, parchment.

vitelina, *a.* vitelline.

vitícola. I. *a.* viticultural. **II.** *n.* viticulturist, vine grower.

viticultura, *f.* viticulture, vine growing.

vitíligo, *m.* (med.) vitiligo, milk-white spots on the skin.

vito, *m.* a lively dance and tune.

vitola, *f.* (mil.) ball calibre, standard gauge; standard shape and size for cigars; (Am.) appearance, mien.

vítor, *m.* triumphal pageant; memorial tablet.— **¡v.!** long live!

vitorear, *va.* to cheer, huzza, acclaim.

vitre, *m.* thin canvas.

vítreo, a, *a.* vitreous, glassy.—**vitrificable,** *a.* vitrifiable.—**vitrificación,** *f.* vitrification.

vitrificar, *va.* to vitrify.

vitrina, *f.* show case.

vitriolado, da, *a.* vitriolate, vitriolated.

vitriólico, ca, *a.* vitriolic.

vitriolo, *m.* vitriol; sulphate.—**v. amoniacal,** ammonium sulphate.—**v. azul,** blue vitriol.—**v. blanco,** white vitriol.—**v. de plomo,** (min.)ɡanglesite, lead-sulphate ore.—**v. verde,** green vitriol.

vitualla, *f.* (gen. in the *pl.*) victuals, provisions; abundance of food, mainly of vegetables.

vituallar, *va.* (mil.) to victual.

vítulo marino, *m.* = BECERRO MARINO.

vituperable, *a.* vituperable, blameworthy.

vituperación, *f.* vituperation.—**vituperador, ra,** *n.* & *a.* vituperator (-ing).—**vituperante,** *a.* vituperating, vituperative.—**vituperar,** *va.* to vituperate.—**vituperio,** *m.* vituperation.

vituperiosamente, vituperosamente, *adv.* vituperatively.

vituperioso, sa; vituperoso, sa, *a.* vituperative.

viuda, *f.* widow; dowager; (bot.) mourning bride.

viudal, *a.* belonging to a widow or widower.

viudedad, *f.* widow's pension.

viudez, *f.* widowhood.

viudita, *f. dim.* spruce little widow; (bot.) mourning bride.

viudo. I. *m.* widower. **II.** *a.* pairing (s. o. birds).

viva. I. *m.* huzza, cheer, shout, acclamation. **II. ¡v.!** *interj.* long live! hurrah, huzza.

vivac, *m.* (mil.) bivouac; night guard.

vivacidad, *f.* vivacity, liveliness; brilliancy.

vivamente, *adv.* vividly; quickly; deeply.

vivandero, ra, *n.* (mil.) sutler.

vivaque, *m.* (mil.) bivouac.

vivaquear, *vn.* to bivouac.

vivar, *m.* warren, burrow; vivarium, vivary.

vivaracho, cha, *a.* lively, sprightly, frisky.

vivaz, *a.* lively, active, vigorous; ingenious, bright, witty; (bot.) perennial, evergreen.

viveral, *m.* (bot.) nursery.

víveres, *m. pl.* provisions, victuals; (mil.) stores. —**v. de campaña,** (naut.) sea provisions, stores.

vivero, *m.* warren; hatchery; (bot.) nursery.

vivérrido, a. I. *n.* & *a.* (zool.) viverrine. **II.** *m.* or *f. pl.* Viverridæ, civets.

viveza, *f.* liveliness, sprightliness; gaiety; briskness; ardor, vehemence; acuteness, perspicacity, quickness; witticism; strong resemblance; luster, splendor; grace and brilliancy in the eyes; thoughtless word or act.

vividero, ra, *a.* habitable.

vívido, da, *a.* vivid, bright.

vividor, ra. I. *a.* thrifty. **II.** *n.* long liver; sponger.

vivienda, *f.* dwelling, lodging, house.

viviente, *a.* living; animated.

vivificación, *f.* vivification, enlivening.

vivificador, ra, *n.* & *a.* vivifier (-ying), enlivener (-ing).—**vivificante,** *a.* vivifying, life-giving.

vivificar, *va.* to vivify, animate, enliven; to comfort, refresh.—**vivificativo, va,** *a.* vivifying, life-giving; comforting.

vivífico, ca, *a.* springing from life.

vivíparo, ra, *a.* viviparous.

vivir, *vn.* & *va.* to live; to last, endure, keep.— **¡viva!** hurrah! long live!—**viva Vd. mil años,** or **muchos años,** may you live many years, or I wish you a long life (a form of courtesy).—**¿quién vive?** (mil.) who goes there?—**quién vive,** qui vive, (be, being) on the alert.

vivir, *m.* life, living, existence.—**mal v.,** riotous living.

vivisección, *f.* vivisection.

vivismo, *m.* Vivism, philosophico-theological system of Luis Vives.

vivo, va. I. *a.* alive, living, live; lively; intense; kindled, live (as fire); acute, ingenious; quick, bright, lively, smart; hasty; diligent, nimble; pure, clean; lasting, enduring; excellent; expressive, vehement, persuasive; raw (s. o. the flesh when exposed by the skin being off).—**a lo v., al v.,** to the life, vividly.—**de v. voz,** by word of mouth.—**en vivo,** living, alive.—**los vivos y los muertos,** the quick and the dead.—**tocar en lo v.,** to touch or hurt to the quick. **II.** *m.* edging, border; (sew.) corded seam; (b. b.) rib, ridge, border; (arch.) sharp edge; (vet.) mange, itch, or scab in dogs.

vizcacha, *f.* viscacha, a S.-A. rodent.

vizcachera, *f.* viscacha hole.

vizcaíno, na, *n.* & *a.* Biscayan.

vizcondado, *m.* viscountship.—**vizconde,** *m.* viscount.—**vizcondesa,** *f.* viscountess.

vocablo, *m.* word, term.

vocabulario, *m.* vocabulary, lexicon.

vocabulista, *n.* vocabulary writer, lexicographer; student of words.

vocación, *f.* vocation, calling; trade, occupation.

vocal. I. *a.* vocal, oral; (gram.) vowel. **II.** *f.* (gram., print.) vowel. **III.** *n.* voter, in a congregation or assembly; member of a governing body.

vocalización, *f.* (mus.) vocalization.

vocalizar, *vn.* (*pret.* VOCALICÉ: *subj.* VOCALICE) to vocalize, articulate.

vocalmente, *adv.* vocally, orally.

vocativo, a. & *m.* (gram.) vocative.

voceador, ra. I. *n.* vociferator. **II.** *m.* town-crier.

vocear. I. *vn.* to vociferate, to cry out, shout. **II.** *va.* to cry, publish, proclaim; to call, hail; to cheer, acclaim; (coll.) to boast of publicly.

vocejón, *m.* harsh, rawky voice.

vocería, *f.,* **vocerío,** *m.* vociferation, clamor, outcry, shouting.

vocero, ra, *n.* spokesman, one who speaks for another.

vociferación, f. = VOCERÍA.—**vociferador, ra,** n. & a. vociferator (-ing); shouter (-ing); boaster (-ing).—**vociferante,** a. vociferating.

vociferar. I. vn. to vociferate, shout, clamor. **II.** va. to boast of loudly.

vocinglería, f. clamor, outcry; loquacity.

vocinglero, ra. I. a. prattling, chattering, vociferous. **II.** n. loud babbler.

vodca, m. vodka, a Russian liquor.

voila, f. term in the game of jackstones indicating that the cast may not count.

volada, f. short flight; (Am.) trick, bad turn.—**hacer,** or **jugar, una (mala) volada a,** to play a bad trick on, do a bad turn to.

voladero, f. float of a water wheel.

voladero, ra. I. a. flying, fleeting. **II.** m. precipice, abyss.

voladizo, za. I. a. projecting, jutting out. **II.** m (arch.) corbel.

volado, m. = AZUCARILLO.

volado, da, a. (print.) high, superior, set above the level of the line. V. AZUCARILLO.

volador, ra. I. a. flying; running fast; swift; hanging in the air. **II.** m. skyrocket; (icht.) flying fish; (bot.) a tropical tree of very hard wood. **III.** f. flywheel of a steam engine.

voladura, f. blast, explosion; blasting.

volandas.—en v., adv. in the air, as if flying; (coll.) rapidly, swiftly.

volandera, f. (mil.) runner; grindstone; (coll.) fib, lie; (mech.) washer; (print.) galley slice.

volandero, ra, a. (nestling) ready to fly; fluttering in the air; fortuitous, casual; unsettled, fleeting, variable.

volandillas.—en v. = EN VOLANDAS.

volanta, f. (Cuba) two-wheel covered vehicle with very long shafts.

volante. I. a. flying, fluttering; unsettled. **II.** m. head ornament of light gauze; shuttlecock; game of shuttlecock and battledoor; screen; coiners' stamp mill; (watch.) balance wheel, escapement; (mach.) flywheel; balance beam; footboy, lackey, flunkey; flier, note, memorandum; (sew.) flounce; (coll.) VOLANTA: linen coat; (Mex.) dress coat.—**v. de dirección,** (aut.) steering wheel.

volantín, m. a fishing apparatus.

volantón, na, a. able to fly (nestling).

volapié, m. a feat in bull-fighting.—**a v.,** half running, half flying.

volapuk, m. Volapük.

volar. I. vn. (ind. VUELO: subj. VUELE) to fly (as birds, kites, clouds, etc.); to flutter, hover (as insects); to run or move swiftly (as a train, arrow, etc.); to vanish, disappear; to rise in the air (as a steeple): to make rapid progress; act fast or quickly; to project, jut out, hang over; to extend, spread rapidly (as news); explode, burst.—**echar a v.,** to disseminate; to divulge, publish. **II.** va. to blow up: to spring (a mine); to blast; to irritate, exasperate; to rouse (game); to disseminate, publish, spread, divulge.

volateo.—al v., adv. (shooting) on the wing.

volatería, f. fowling; sporting with hawks; poultry; fowls; flock of birds; (met.) crowding conflicting ideas (in one's mind).—**de v.,** incidentally, in passing; at random, recklessly.

volátil, a. volatile; flying, wafting; changeable, fickle; fleeting.—**volatilidad,** f. (chem.) volatility.—**volatilizar,** va. & vr. (for mut. v. UTILIZAR) to volatilize, vaporize.

volatín, m. ropedancer; acrobat; acrobatic feat.

volatinero, ra, n. ropewalker; acrobat.

volatizar, va. (chem.) to volatilize.

volavérunt, (Lat.) (coll.) the bird has flown; gone! (something) has disappeared, is gone.

volcán, m. volcano; excessive ardor; violent passion; excitable person or temperament.

volcanejo, m. dim. small volcano.

volcánico, ca, a. volcanic.

volcar. I. va. (ind. VUELCO: pret. VOLQUÉ: subj. VUELQUE) to overset, upset, overturn; to tilt; (naut.) to capsize; to make dizzy or giddy; to make (one) change his opinion; to make angry. **II.** vr. to upset.

volea, f. snaffle tree, whippletree; volley at a ball in the air.

volear, va. to strike in the air (as a ball); to fire a volley at.

voleo, m. volley given on a ball in the air; (danc.) high step or kick.—**del primer v.,** or **de un v.,** (coll.) at one blow; in an instant.

volframio, m. (chem.) tungsten.

volframita, f. (min.) wolframite.

volición, f. volition.

volitar, vn. to flutter.

volitivo, va, a. volitional.

volquearse, vr. to tumble, to wallow.

volquete, m. tip cart, tilt cart.

volt, m. (elec.) volt.

voltaico, ca, a. (elec.) voltaic.

voltaísmo, m. (elec.) voltaism.

voltaje, m. (elec.) voltage.

voltámetro, m. (phys.) voltameter.

voltamperímetro, m. wattmeter.

voltamperio, m. volt ampere.

voltariedad, f. fickleness, inconstancy.

voltario, ria, a. fickle, inconstant, giddy.

volteador, ra, n. tumbler, acrobat.

voltear. I. va. to turn; to revolve; to overturn, change the order of; (arch.) to arch, to vault. **II.** vn. to turn; to revolve; to roll over; to tumble (as an acrobat). **III.** vr. to turn over; to upset; (coll.) to change one's party or creed.

voltejear, va. to whirl; (naut.) to tack.

volteleta, f. tumble, somersault; at cards, turning up the card that makes trumps.

volteo, m. whirl, whirling; revolution, turn; turning; overturning; felling; tumbling.

voltereta, f. = VOLTELETA.

volterianismo, m. Voltairianism.

volteriano, na, a. & n. Voltairian.

volteta, f. = VOLTELETA.

voltímetro, m. (elec.) voltmeter.—**v. aperiódico,** dead-beat, or aperiodic, voltmeter.

voltio, m. (elec.) volt.

voltizo, za, a. curled, twisted; versatile, inconstant, fickle.

vóltmetro, m. (elec.) voltmeter.

volubilidad, f. volubility.—**voluble,** a. easily moved about; voluble, fickle; (bot.) twining.

volublemente, adv. volubly.

volumen, m. volume; size, bulk; corpulence.

volumétrico, ca, a. volumetric.

voluminoso, sa, a. voluminous; bulky.

voluntad, f. will; goodwill, benevolence, kindness; desire, pleasure; disposition, precept; consent.—**a v.,** (com.) optional, at will.—**de buena v.,** or **de v.,** with pleasure, willingly.—**de mala v.,** unwillingly.

voluntariamente, adv. voluntarily.

voluntariedad, f. voluntariness; wilfulness.

voluntario, ria. I. a. voluntary. **II.** m. (mil.) volunteer.

voluntarioso, sa, a. wilful, self-willed.

voluptuosamente, adv. voluptuously; licentiously.—**voluptuosidad,** f. voluptuousness; licentiousness.—**voluptuoso, sa,** a. voluptuous; licentious, lustful, lewd.

voluta, f. (arch.) volute.

volvedor, m. tap wrench, turnscrew.

volvedor, ra, a. (Colomb.) that runs away back to its home (s. o. horses).

volver. I. va. (pp. VUELTO: ind. VUELVO: subj. VUELVA) to turn; turn up, turn over, turn upside down or inside out; to return, pay back, give or send back; to give up; to direct, aim; to translate; to restore, reinstate; to change the outward appearance of; to invert, change, move; to vomit; to persuade, convince; to reflect (sound); to give (change in sales); to close, pull or push to (door or shutter); to reëstablish, to replace; to plow a second time.—**v. la cara,** to turn one's head back, to turn around.—**v. loco,** to drive crazy, distract. **II.** vn. to return, come back; to come again; to turn (to the right, etc.).—**v. a,** to . . . again (volver a cantar, to sing again; Juan me volvió a escribir, John [wrote to me again).—**v. atrás,** to come, or go, back.—**v. en sí,** to recover consciousness, to come to.—**v. por,** to stand up for, to defend, (coll.) to stick up for.—**v. por sí,** to defend one's self; to redeem one's credit.—**v. sobre sí,** to mend one's ways; to make up one's losses; to recover one's equanimity. **III.** *vr.* to turn, become; to turn or get sour; to turn about, turn around; to change one's views.—**v. atrás,** to turn, back out.—**v. la tortilla,** to turn the tables or scales.—**v. loco,** to lose one's mind, to become crazy or distracted.

volvible, *a.* capable of being turned, turned over or inverted.

volvo, vólvulo, *m.* (med.) volvulus, ileus.

vómer, *m.* (anat.) vomer.

vomicina, *f.* (chem.) brucine, vomicine.

vómico, ca. I. *a.* causing vomiting; vomitive. **II.** *f.* (med.) vomica.

vomipurgante, vomipurgativo, va, *a. & m.* both purgative and emetic.

vomitado, da, *a. & pp.* (coll.) meager; pale.

vomitador, ra, *n.* one who vomits.

vomitar, *va.* to vomit; to eject, throw out, disgorge; discharge; to break out into (insults, etc.); to give out, reveal; to give up, surrender.

vomitivo, va, *n. & a.* emetic.

vómito, *m.* vomiting; vomit; (Cuba) yellow fever. —**v. negro,** yellow fever.—**provocar a v.,** to nauseate, to loathe.

vomitón, na. I. *a.* often throwing milk from the stomach (as a sucking child). **II.** *f.* (coll.) violent vomiting after heavy eating or drinking.

vomitorio, ria. I. *a.* vomitory. **II.** *m.* vomitory in Roman theatres.

voracidad, *f.* voracity, greediness, voraciousness.

vorágine, *f.* vortex, whirlpool.—**voraginoso, sa,** *a.* engulfing; full of whirlpools.

vorahunda, *f.* turmoil. *V.* BARAÚNDA.

voraz, *a.* voracious, greedy, ravenous; excessively lustful; destructive, fierce (as fire).

vorazmente, *adv.* voraciously; greedily.

vormela, *f.* a kind of spotted weasel.

vórtice, *m.* vortex, whirlpool, whirlwind; center of a cyclone.

vorticela, *f.* (zool.) vorticella.

vortiginoso, sa, *a.* vortical.

vos, *pers. pron.* you.

vosotros, tras, *pers. pron. pl.* you, ye.

votación, *f.* voting, vote, balloting.

votador, ra, *n.* voter; swearer, curser.

votante, *n.* voter in a corporation or assembly.

votar, *vn. & va.* to vow; to vote; to vote on; to give an opinion; to curse, swear, utter oaths; to pass, decree or authorize by vote (in deliberating bodies).—**v. una partida,** to make, or pass, an appropiation.—**¡voto a (Dios, Júpiter,** etc.)! by (God, Jupiter, etc.)!—**¡voto al chápiro!** goodness me! **¡voto a tal!** goodness! upon my soul! confound it! by Heaven! by Jove!

votivo, va, *a.* votive, offered by a vow.

voto, *m.* vote; ballot; opinion; voter; vow; supplication to God; curse, oath, execration; wish; (eccl.) votive offering.—**v. activo,** (right to) vote.—**v. consultivo,** professional or expert advice.—**v. de amén,** vote blindly given.—**v. de calidad,** casting vote.—**v. de reata**= v. de AMÉN.—**v. particular,** dissenting opinion (of the minority of a commission, etc.).—**v. pasivo,** qualification to be voted for, or elected, by a corporation.—**¡v. va!**= ¡VOTO A TAL! *V.* VOTAR.—**ser,** or **tener,** to have a vote; to speak knowingly. (For the interjectional uses of VOTO, as a verb, *v.* VOTAR.)

voz, *f.* voice; sound, noise; (gen. in the *pl.*) clamor, outcry; expression, word, term; voice, power or authority to speak (as in an assembly); vote; opinion expressed; rumor, public opinion; motive, pretext; (gram.) voice (active or passive); (mus.) singer; voice, key tone; (mil.) command, order; (law) life.—**v. activa,** right of voting; (gram) active voice.—**v. argentada,** or **argentina,** clear and sonorous voice.—**v. del pueblo, voz del cielo,** vox populi, vox Dei, the voice of the people is the voice of God.—**v. de mando,** word of command.—

v. pasiva, right or qualification to be voted for, or elected; (gram.) passive voice.—**v. pastosa,** mellow voice.—**v. velada,** veiled voice.—**a media v.,** with a slight hint; in a whisper.—**a una v.,** of one accord, unanimously.—**a v. en cuello,** or **a v. en grito,** in a loud voice; shouting; at the top of one's voice.—**a voces,** clamorously, with shouts.—**correr la v.,** to be said, to be rumored.—**dar voces,** to cry, scream, shout, yell.—**en v.,** verbally; (mus.) in voice.—**en v. alta,** aloud.—**en v. baja,** in a low tone, sotto voce.—**pedir a voces,** to clamor for; to be a crying need (ch. constr.).—**ser v. común,** to be generally said, to be a common rumor.

vozarrón, *m.* strong, heavy voice.

voznar, *vn.* to cackle (s. o. swans and geese).

vuecelencia, vuecencia, *n.* (*contr.* of VUESTRA EXCELENCIA) your excellency.

vuelapié.—a v. = A VOLAPIÉ.

vuelco, *m.* tumble, overturning, upset.

vuelco, vuelca. *V.* VOLCAR.

vuelillo, *m.* lace cuff trimming.

vuelo, *m.* flight; flying; sweep, space flown through; wing of a bird; width or fulness of clothes; (sew.) wristfall, ruffle or frill on the wristband; elevation, soaring, loftiness of thought; leap or bound in pantomimes; (arch.) jut, projection, corbeling.—**al v.,** on the fly; quickly, in a jiffy; in passing, accidentally; (agr.) scattered at random (said of seed).—**alzar,** or **levantar, v.,** to fly; to take off, to depart; to sail.—**tomar v.,** to progress, to grow.

vuelo, vuela, vuele. *V.* VOLAR.

vuelta, *f.* turn; revolution (of a wheel, etc.); turning; turn of an arch; requital, recompense; repetition, iteration; back or wrong side; whipping, lashing, spanking; return; returning, giving back; review (of a lesson); going over (a writing, etc.); change; inclination, bent; (sew.) wristful; sleeve cuff, facing (*v.* VUELO); (naut.) turn, hitch, lashing; trip, excursion; promenade, walk; ward in a lock or key; order of stitches in knitting hose; roll, envelope; unexpected sally or witticism, repartee; change (small money); card turned up for a trump number of times a field has been plowed; (mus.) number of verses repeated; potter's wheel; (arch.) curve of an intrados; vault; ceiling. —**v. de carnero,** turn on the head; heavy fall.—**vueltas de coral,** string or necklace of coral.—**a la v.,** on returning; round the corner; (turn) over (the leaf in a letter, etc.); carried over, carried forward (in bookkeeping).—**a la v. de,** within (app. to time).—**andar a las vueltas de,** to dog.—**andar a vueltas,** to fight, to struggle; to endeavor.—**andar en vueltas,** to shuffle, use subterfuges; to shirk.—**a v., a vueltas,** very near, almost.—**a v. de,** in the course of, within (a specified time); by return (mail).—**a v. de ojo,** quickly, in a jiffy.—**dar la v. a,** to turn; to go around.—**dar una v.,** to take a walk.—**dar vueltas,** to turn; to walk to and fro; to fuss about.—**de la v.,** brought forward.—**de v.,** on returning.—**estar de v.,** to have returned; to be posted or informed beforehand.—**la v. de,** towards, on the way to.—**no haber que darle vueltas,** or **no tener v. de hoja,** no two ways about it.—**otra v.,** again, once more.—**pasa a la v.,** carried over, carried forward (in bookkeeping).—**poner de v. y media,** (coll.) to give a dressing down, or a going over, to; to call one all kinds of abusive names.—**tener v.,** (coll.) admonition to return a thing lent.

vuelvo, yo vuelva. *V.* VOLVER.

vuesa, *a.* (*contr.* of VUESTRA) (obs.) your.

vuesamerced, *n.* (*contr.* of VUESTRA MERCED) you, sir; you, madam; your worship, your grace, your honor.

vuesarced, *n.* = VUESAMERCED.

vueseñoría, *n.* (*contr.* of VUESTRA SEÑORÍA) your lordship, your ladyship.

vuestro, tra, *poss. pron.* your, yours.

vulcanio, nia, *a.* vulcanian, igneous.

vulcanismo, *m.* (geol.) Vulcanism.

vulcanista, *a.* (geol.) Vulcanist.

vulcanización, *f.* vulcanization; cure, curing (of a patch, a tire, etc.).

vulcanizar, *va.* (*pret.* VULCANICÉ: *subj.* VULCANICE) to vulcanize; to cure (a patch, tire, etc.)

vulgacho, *m.* mob, populace, rabble.

vulgar, *a.* vulgar, coarse; common, vernacular.—**vulgaridad,** *f.* vulgarity.—**vulgarismo,** *m.* vulgarism.—**vulgarización,** *f.* vulgarization.

vulgarizar. I. *va.* (*pret.* VULGARICÉ: *subj.* VULGARICE) to vulgarize, populariz3; to translate into the vernacular. **II.** *vr.* to become vulgar.

vulgarmente, *adv.* vulgarly; commonly.

Vulgata, *f.* (eccl.) Vulgate.

vulgo, *m.* vulgar, common people; multitude, populace.

vulnerable, *a.* vulnerable.

vulneración, *f.* act of wounding.

vulnerar, *va.* to injure the reputation of.

vulnerario, ria. I. *a.* vulnerary. **II.** *m.* (law) clergyman guilty of killing or wounding.

vulpécula, vulpeja, *f.* bitch fox.

vulpino, na, *a.* vulpine; foxy, crafty.

vultuoso, sa, *a.* (med.) bloated.

vultúrido, da. I. (zool.) vulturine. **II.** *m.* or *f. pl.* Vulturidæ.

vulva, *f.* (anat.) vulva.—**vulvario, ria,** *a.* (anat.) vulvar.—**vulvitis,** *f.* vulvitis.

W

This letter does not belong to the Spanish alphabet and is mainly used in words, chiefly proper nouns, taken from other languages. In adjectives and common nouns derived from proper nouns containing it, it is generally changed to *v* (see VAGNERIANO, VESTFALIANO), although some writers preserve the *w* (*wagneriano, westfaliano*). Such words are readily translated by inspection, on account of their similarity to their English equivalents. The Spanish Academy has condescended to tolerate the use of the letter in **wat,** (elec.) watt, although the term generally used is **vatio.**

X

NOTE.—Several words that were originally, or are occasionally, written with an initial *x* are more generally begun with *j*.

xantina, *f.* (chem.) xanthine.

xantofila, *f.* (chem.) xanthophyll.

xantoxilo, *m.* (bot.) zanthoxylum.

xara, *f.* Moslem law derived from the Koran.

xenon, *m.* (chem.) xenon.

xenofobia, *f.* xenophobia, hatred of foreigners, antiforeignism.

xenófobo, ba, *n.* & *a.* hater of foreigners.

xerofagia, *f.* xerophagy, dry-food diet.

xeroftalmía, *f.* (med.) xerophthalmia.

xifoideo, ea, *a.* (anat.) xiphoid.

xifoides. I. *a.* (anat.) xiphoid. **II.** *m.* xiphoid, xiphisternum.

xifosuro, ra, *n.* & *a.* xiphosure (-ous).

xileno, *m.* (chem.) xylene.—**xílico, ca,** *a.* xylic.—**xilidina,** *f.* xylidine.

xilófago, a, *n.* & *a.* xylophagous, wood borer (-ing).

xilófono, *m.* xylophone.

xilógeno, *m.* (chem.) xylem.

xilografía, *f.* xylography, wood engraving.

xilográfico, ca, *a.* xylographic.

xiloide, *a.* xyloid, woodlike.

xilonita, a transparent celluloidlike substance. (The English *xylonite* means celluloid.)

xilórgano, *m.* xylophone.

Y

y, *conj.* and.

ya. I. *adv.* already; now; at once; presently; finally, ultimately; in time; once, formerly. Often used as an emphatic expletive (*ya entiendo,* I understand; *ya veo,* I see).—¡y.! oh, yes! I see.—**y. lo creo,** naturally, of course.—**y. no,**

no longer.—**y. que,** since, seeing that.—**y. se ve,** yes, forsooth! it is clear, it is so.—**y. voy,** I am coming, I shall be there presently.—**y . . . y.,** now . . . now, sometimes . . . sometimes.—¡**pues y.!** of course, certainly.—**sí y.,** if.—**sí y. no,** if no longer; if . . . not, unless. **II.** *conj.* whether, or (the latter as correlative of the former.)

yaacabó, *m.* (Ven.) an insectivorous bird.

yaba, *f.* (bot.) yaba tree; yaba bark, worm bark.

yabuna, *f.* a Cuban species of long, creeping grass or weed.

yac, *m.* (zool.) yak.

yaca, *f.* (bot.) yacca tree.

yacal, *m.* yacal, a Philippine tree.

yacaré, *m.* (Arg.) cayman, alligator.

yacedor, *m.* lad who takes horses to graze at night.

yacente, *a.* jacent, vacant; lying.

yacer, *vn.* (*ind.* YAZCO, YAGO, or YAZGO: *subj.* YAZCA, YAGA, or YAZGA) to lie, to be located; to be lying down; to lie (in the grave); to graze by night.

yaciente, *a.* extended, stretched (s. o. honeycombs).

yacija, *f.* bed, couch, lounge; tomb, grave.—**ser de mala y.,** to be a vagrant; to be restless at night.

yacimiento, *m.* (geol.) bed; deposit, field.

yacio, *m.* (bot.) India-rubber tree.

yack, *m.* (zool.) yak.

yactura, *f.* loss, damage.

yagua, *f.* yagua, royal palm.

yaguasa, *f.* yaguaza, a tree duck.

yaguré, *m.* (Am.) skunk.

yaití, *m.* a West-Indian hard-wood euphorbiaceous tree.

yámbico, ca, *a.* (poet.) iambic.

yambo, *m.* (poet.) iambic foot (‿—); (bot.) jamboo.

yanacona, *n.* (Peru) Indian bound to personal service.

yanqui, *n.* & *a.* (U.-S.) American.

yantar. I. *va.* (obs.) to dine; to eat. **II.** *m.* (obs.) viands, food; a kind of king's taxes.

yapa, *f.* (Am.) ñapa; (min.) mercury added to silver ore in smelting.

yarará, *f.* a very poisonous Argentine viper.

yaraví, *m.* (Am.) an Indian tune.

yarda, *f.* yard (measure).

yare, *m.* a poisonous juice from bitter yucca.

yarey, *m.* (Cuba) a species of GUANO (palm tree).

yaro, *m.* (bot.) arum, an aquatic plant.

yatagán, *m.* sabre dagger, yataghan.

yate, *m.* (naut.) yacht.

yaya, *f.* (Cuba) (bot.) lancewood.

yayero, ra, *a.* & *n.* (Cuba) intermeddling, busybody.

ye, name of the letter *y.*

yedra, *f.* (bot.) ivy (= HIEDRA).

yegua, *f.* mare.—**y. de cría,** or **paridera,** breeding mare.—**y. madre,** dam.

yeguada, yegüería, *f.* stud.

yeguar, *a.* belonging to mares.

yegüerizo, *m.* herd of breeding mares, and place where it is kept.

yegüero, *m.* keeper of breeding mares.

yegüezuela, *f. dim.* little mare.

yeísmo, *m.* giving *ll* the sound of *y.*

yelmo, *m.* (arm.) helmet, helm.

yema, *f.* bud, first shoot of trees; yolk (of an egg); candied yolk of an egg; heart, centre, middle; the best of its kind.—**y. del dedo,** fleshy tip of the finger.—**y. mejida,** eggnog.—**dar en la y.,** to hit the nail on the head.—**en la y. del invierno,** in the dead of winter.

yente, *a.* going.—**yentes y vinientes,** passers-by.

yerba (= HIERBA), *f.* herb; grass; weed.—**y. cana,** groundsel, ragwort.—**y. carmín,** Virginian poke.—**y. de la princesa,** lemon-scented verbena.—**y. del ballestero,** white hellebore.—**y. de mar,** seaweed.—**y. de pordioseros,** sweet-scented virgin's bower.—**y. doncella,** periwinkle.—**y. lombriguera** = ABRÓTANO.—**y. marina** = Y. DE MAR.—**y. mate.** = MATÉ.—**y. mora,** nightshade.—**y.**

pastel, woad.—**y. piojera,** stavesacre.—**y. tora,** strangle weed, broom rape.

yerbabuena, *f.* mint. *V.* HIERBABUENA.

yerbajo, *m. aug.* wild weed.

yerbatear, *vn.* (Am.) to take maté, Paraguay tea.

yerbatero, ra. I. *a.* using arrow poison. **II.** *n.* (Am.) seller of fodder grass.

yergo, yo yerga. *V.* ERGUIR.

yermar, *va.* to unpeople, to lay waste.

yermo, ma. I. *a.* waste, desert, uninhabited; uncultivated. **II.** *m.* desert, wilderness, waste country.

yerno, *m.* son-in-law.

yero, *m.* (bot.) = YERVO.

yerro, *m.* error, mistake; breach; fault.—*pl.* unpardonable faults.—**y. de cuenta,** miscalculation.—**y. de imprenta,** erratum, typographical error.

yerro, yerra. *V.* ERRAR.

yerto, ta, *a.* stiff, motionless; rigid, tight.— **quedarse y.,** to be petrified with fear or astonishment.

yervo, *m.* (bot.) tare, true bitter vetch.

yesal, yesar, *m.* gypsum pit.

yesca, *f.* tinder, punk, touchwood; fuel, incentive. —*pl.* tinder box, strike-a-light.

yesera, *f.* gypsum pit; woman who sells gypsum or plaster.

yesería, *f.* gypsum kiln; plasterer's shop; building constructed with plaster.

yesero, ra. I. *a.* belonging to gypsum. **II.** *n.* maker or seller of gypsum; plasterer.

yeso, *m.* gypsum; plaster; plaster cast.—**y. blanco,** whitewash, fine plaster for surface finish. —**y. mate,** plaster of Paris.—**y. negro,** coarse plaster for base coating.

yesón, *m.* rubbish of plaster.

yesoso, sa, *a.* gypseous.

yesquero. I. *n.* tinder maker or seller. **II.** *m.* (Colomb.) tinder box for flint-and-steel lighting.

yeyuno, *m.* (anat.) jejunum.

yezgo, *m.* (bot.) dwarf elder.

yo. I. *pers. pron.* I.—**y. mismo,** I myself. **II.** *m.* ego.

yodado, da, *a.* iodic, containing iodine.

yodato, *m.* (chem.) iodate.

yodhídrico, ca, *a.* (chem.) hydriodic.

yódico, ca, (chem.) iodic.

yodismo, *m.* (med.) iodism, disorder caused by abuse of iodine.

yodo, *m.* (chem.) iodine.

yodoformo, *m.* iodoform.

yoduración, *f.* iodization, iodation.

yodurar, *va.* (chem.) to iodize.

yoduro, *m.* (chem.) iodide.

yola, yole, *f.* (naut.) yawl.

yoquey, *n.* jockey.

yubarta, *f.* (icht.) finback, rorqual.

yuca, *f.* yucca; (Am.) yuca, cassava.

yucal, *m.* yucca or cassava field.

yucateco, ca, *a.* of or from Yucatan.

yugada, *f.* (agr.) yoke of land.

yugo, *m.* yoke; nuptial tie, marriage ceremony; confinement, prison; frame of a church bell; (naut.) transom.—**sacudir el y.,** to throw off the yoke.

yuguero, *m.* plowman, plowboy.

yugular, *a.* (naut.) jugular.

yumbo, ba, *n.* a savage of eastern Ecuador.

yunque, *m.* anvil; (anat.) incus; persevering, undaunted person.—**estar al y.,** to bear up under trying circumstances; to be hard at work; (coll.) to be on the job.

yunta, *f.* couple, pair, yoke of draft animals.

yuntería, *f.* aggregate of YUNTAS; place where draught oxen are fed.

yuntero, *m.* plowboy.

yunto, ta, *a.* joined, united; close.—**arar y.,** to plow close.

yuraguano, *m.* (Cuba) = MIRAGUANO.

yuré, *m.* a C.-A. pigeon.

yusera, *f.* horizontal stone in oil mills.

yusión, *f.* (law) precept, command.

yute, *m.* jute (fibre); jute fabric.

yuxtalineal, *a.* in parallel columns.

yuxtaponer, *va.* to juxtapose, to place next to each other.

yuxtaposición, *f.* juxtaposition.

yuyuba, *f.* jujube. *V.* AZUFAIFA.

Z

¡za!, *interj.* used to frighten dogs.

zabarcera, *f.* greengrocer (woman).

zábida, zábila, *f.* (bot.) common aloes.

zaborda, *f.,* **zabordamiento,** *m.* (naut.) stranding.—**zabordar,** *vn.* to touch ground, to become stranded.—**zabordo,** *m.* stranding.

zaborro, rra, *n.* fat person.

zabra, *f.* (naut.) small sailing vessel.

zabucar, *va.* = BAZUCAR.

zabullida, zabullidor, zabullidura, zabullimiento, zabullir = ZAMBULLIDA, ZAMBULLIR, etc.

zabuqueo, *m.* = BAZUQUEO.

zaca, *f.* large leather bag for bailing a mine.

zacapela, zacapella, *f.* noisy wrangle.

zacate, *m.* (Philip.) hay, forage, fodder.

zacateca, *m.* (Cuba) undertaker, sexton.

zacateco, ca, *n. & a.* Zacatecan (from Zacatecas, Mex.)

zacatín, *m.* street where garments are sold.

zacatón, *m.* (Am.) a tall fodder grass.

zacear, *va.* to frighten (dogs) away by crying ¡ZA!.

zadorija, *f.* (bot.) yellow poppy.

zafa, *f.* basin, bowl. *V.* JOFAINA.

zafacoca, *f.* (Am.) (coll.) squabble, row.

zafada, *f.* flight, escape; lightening (a ship).

zafar. I. *va.* to adorn, deck, embellish; to clear from encumbrances; to lighten (a ship). **II.** *vr.* to escape, run away; (w. de) to get rid of; to avoid; to get out of; to get clear of; to slip off, come off, break loose.

zafareche, *m.* tank. *V.* ESTANQUE.

zafarí, *m.* a variety of pomegranate.

zafariche, *m.* shelf for water jugs or jars.

zafarrancho, *m.* (naut.) clearing for action; (coll.) ravage, destruction; scuffle, wrangle, row.

zafiamente, *adv.* lubberly, clumsily.

zafiedad, *f.* rusticity, clumsiness.

zafio, fia, *a.* coarse, uncivil, ignorant.

zafío, *m.* (icht.) a variety of conger eel.

zafir, *m.* sapphire.—**zafireo, ea,** *a.* sapphirine.

zafirina, *f.* (min.) sapphirine.

zafirino, na, *a.* sapphirine.

zafiro, *m.* sapphire.

zafo, fa, *a.* disentangled; exempt from danger or risk; (naut.) free and clear.

zafones, *m. pl.* overalls.

zafra, *f.* drip jar, oil jar; (sad.) broad strap holding the thills of a cart; (min.) rubbish; sugar crop; sugar making; sugar-making, or grind, season.

zafre, *m.* (min.) zaffre or saffre.

zafrero, *m.* (min.) laborer who clears a mine of rubbish.

zaga. I. *f.* rear part; load in the back of a carriage. **II.** *m.* the last player at a game of cards.—**a la z.,** or **en z.,** behind.—**no ir en z. a,** not to be behind, less than, or inferior, to.

zagal, *m.* stout, spirited young man; swain; subordinate shepherd; lad who assists the driver of a stagecoach; short skirt.

zagala, *f.* shepherdess; lass, maiden.

zagalejo, ja. I. *n. dim.* young shepherd (-ess). **II.** *m.* short skirt; underskirt, slip.

zagalón, na, *n.* overgrown lad (girl).

zagua, *f.* (bot.) saltwort.

zagual, *m.* paddle.

zaguán, *m.* entrance hall, vestibule.

zaguanete, *m. dim.* small vestibule; king's escort of life guards.

zaguero, ra. I. *a.* laggard, loitering. **II.** *m.* backstop, at the game of PELOTA.

---

zahareño, ña, *a.* intractable; wild, haggard (s. o. birds); unsociable; arrogant.

zabarí, *a.* = ZAFARÍ.

zahena, *f.* a Moorish gold coin.

zaherible, *a.* blamable, blameworthy.

zaheridor, ra, *n. & a.* censurer (-ing), upbraider (-ing).

zaherimiento, *m.* censure, blame.

zaherir, *va.* (*gerund*, ZAHIRIENDO: *ind.* ZAHIERO: *pret.* el ZAHIRIÓ: *subj.* ZAHIERA) to censure, blame, reproach, upbraid.

zahina, *f.* (bot.) sorghum.

zahinar, *m.* sorghum field.

zahinas, *f. pl.* thin porridge or pap.

zahones, *m. pl.* overalls.

zahonado, da, *a.* dark brown.

zahondar. I. *va.* to dig. **II.** *vn.* to sink into soft ground (as the feet).

zahora, *f.* merry lunch party.

zahorar, *vn.* to have a repast with music.

zahorí, *m.* vulgar impostor pretending to see hidden things; perspicacious and curious person.

zahoriar, *va.* to scrutinize, look deeply into.

zahorra, *f.* (naut.) ballast.

zahurda, *f.* pigsty, hogsty; low tavern, "joint."

zaida, *f.* (orn.) a variety of heron.

zaino, na, *a.* chestnut, zain (horse); vicious (animal); treacherous, wicked.—**mirar a la z.,** or **de z.,** to look sidewise.

zalá, *f.* salaam.—**hacer la z.,** to salaam; to flatter, cajole, wheedle.

zalagarda, *f.* ambush; trap, snare; sudden attack, surprise; skirmish; mock fight.

zalama, *f.*; **zalamelé,** *m.*; **zalamería,** *f.* flattery, wheedling.

zalamero, ra, *n.* wheedler, flatterer, fawner.

zalea, *f.* undressed sheepskin.

zalear, *va.* to shake; to damage, destroy; to frighten (a dog) away.

zalema, *f.* salaam, bow, courtesy.

zaleo, *m.* sheepskin damaged by a wolf's fangs; shaking or moving to and fro.

zalmedina, *m.* an ancient magistrate in Arragon.

zalona, *f.* large earthen jar.

zallar, *va.* (naut.) to outrig, to train.

zamacuco, *m.* (coll.) dunce, dolt; intoxication.

zamacueca, *f.* (S. A.) an Indian tune and dance.

zamanca, *f.* (coll.) drubbing, flogging.

zamarra, *f.* sheepskin jacket worn by shepherds; undressed sheepskin.

zamarrear, *va.* to shake between the teeth (as a dog does a rabbit); to ill-treat; to pin down in a dispute.

zamarreo, *m.* shaking something seized with the teeth; abuse, ill treatment.

zamarrico, *m. dim.* portmanteau or bag of sheepskin.

zamarrilla, *f.* (bot.) poly, mountain germander.

zamarro. I. *m.* shepherd's coat of sheepskins; sheep or lambskin; (coll.) dolt, dunce. **II.** *m. pl.* (Am.) chaps, chaparajos.

zamarrón, *m. aug.* large sheepskin jacket.

zambaigo, ga, *a. & n.* Indian and Chinese half-breed.

zambapalo, *m.* an ancient dance and tune.

zambarco, *m.* (sad.) broad breast strap.

zámbigo, ga, *a.* bandy-legged.

zambo, ba. I. *a.* knock-kneed; born of an Indian and a negro; (loosely) negro, mulatto. **II.** *n.* Indian and negro half-breed; (loosely) negro, mulatto, mixed blood. **III.** *m.* a tropical American monkey.

zamboa, *f.* (bot.) = AZAMBOA.

zambomba, *f.* rustic drum with the head pierced by a reed which, when rubbed with the moistened hand, produces a hoarse sound.—¡z.! whew!

zambombo, ba, *n.* (coll.) rustic, boor, coarse or ill-bred person.

zamborondón, na; zamborotudo, da, *a.* awkward, clumsy; ill-shaped.

zambra, *f.* a Moorish festival; merrymaking; a kind of Moorish boat.

zambucar, *va.* to hide (a thing) by mixing it among others.—**zambuco,** *m.* (coll.) hiding, concealing a card among others.

zambullida, *f.* diving, plunge, ducking; (fenc.) thrust to the breast.

zambullidor, ra, *n.* one who dives or plunges.

zambullidura, *f.*, **zambullimiento,** *m.* diving, ducking, plunge.

zambullir. I. *vn. & va.* to dive; to duck, give a ducking to; to sink. **II.** *vr.* to plunge, dip, dive; to sink; to hide, conceal one's self.

zambullo, *m.* evacuation stool; refuse tank or barrel.

zampabodigos, zampabollos, *n.* (coll.) glutton.

zampalimosnas, *m.* (coll.) sturdy beggar.

zampalo, *n.* (coll.) glutton.

zampar. I. *va.* to thrust or put hurriedly (into something) in order to conceal; to devour eagerly. **II.** *vr.* to rush in, to thrust one's self in or into.

zampatortas, *m.* (coll.) glutton; boor, rustic.

zampeado, *m.* (arch.) grillage, subfoundation of timber or steel and masonry in marshy ground.

zampear, *va.* to build a grillage on.

zampoña, *f.* rustic flute (*v.* PIPITAÑA); (coll.) frivolous saying.

zampuzar, *va.* ZAMBULLIR; ZAMPAR.

zampuzo, *m.* diving, ducking; hiding.

zamuro, *m.* (Ven.) (orn.) carrion vulture.

zanahoria, *f.* (bot.) carrot.

zanahoriate, *m.* = AZANORIATE.

zanca, *f.* long shank or leg; large pin; (arch.) string-piece of a staircase; (min.) shore, prop. —**zancas de araña,** shifts, evasions, subterfuges. —**por zancas o por barrancas,** by hook or by crook.

zancada, *f.* long stride.—**en dos zancadas,** (coll.) in a jiffy, in no time.

zancadilla, *f.* sudden catch to trip one; trick, deceit, craft; (naut.) elbow in the hawse.— **armar z.,** to lay a snare.

zancado, da, *a.* insipid (salmon).

zancajear, *va.* to walk fast from place to place, to run about

zancajera, *f.* coach step.

zancajiento, ta, *a.* bandy-legged.

zancajo, *m.* heel bone; torn heelpiece of a shoe or stocking; (coll.) short, ill-shaped person.— **no llegar a los zancajos,** or **no llegar al z., de,** not to come up to, or be the equal of (one).— **roer los zancajos a,** to backbite.

zancajoso, sa, *a.* bandy-legged; wearing dirty stockings with holes at the heels.

zancarrón, *m.* leg bone without flesh; withered, old, ugly person; boastful ignoramus.

zanco, *m.* stilt; (naut.) sliding-gunter mast.— **en zancos,** in a high position.

zancón, na, *a.* long-shanked; wading (bird).

zancudo, da. I. *a.* long-shanked; (orn.) wading (bird). **II.** *m.* (Am.) mosquito. **III.** *f. pl.* (orn.) wading birds.

zandía, *f.* watermelon.

zanfonía, *f.* (mus.) hurdy-gurdy.

zanga, *f.* four-hand ombre.

zangala, *f.* buckram.

zangamanga, *f.* (coll.) trick, deceit.

zanganada, *f.* (coll.) impertinent or unseasonable act or expression.

zangandongo, ga; zangandullo, lla; zangandongo, ga, *n.* (coll.) idler, lazy person; dolt, awkward person.

zanganear, *vn.* to drone, to loaf.

zángano, *m.* drone; (coll.) idler, sponger.

zangarilla, *f.* small mill pond.

zangarilleja, *f.* (coll.) trollop, slovenly girl.

zangarrear, *vn.* (coll.) to scrape a guitar.

zangarriana, *f.* (vet.) a head disease of sheep; (coll.) sadness, blues; any slight periodical ailment.

zangarrullón, na, *n.* tall, sluggish, lazy lad (lass).

zangolotear. I. *vn.* to shake violently; to fuss, fidget. **II.** *vr.* to rattle, swing or slam.

zangoloteo, *m.* fuss, bustle; swinging, rattling.

zangolotino, na, *a.* pretending to be a little child (s. o. boys and girls).

zangón, *m.* (coll.) = ZANGARULLÓN.

zangotear, zangoteo = ZANGOLOTEAR, ZANGO-LOTEO.

zanguango, ga. I. *a.* (coll.) lazy, sluggish; silly. **II.** *m.* dunce, fool. **III.** *f.* (coll.) feigned disease to avoid work; wheedling, fawning.

zanguayo, *m.* (coll.) tall, skinny idler that cunningly acts the fool.

zanja, *f.* ditch, trench, furrow, drain; (Am.) gap, gully, draw.—**abrir las zanjas,** to lay the foundation of a building; to begin, get started.

zanjar, *va.* to cut ditches in; to excavate; to settle amicably; to obviate, surmount.

zanjón, *m. aug.* deep ditch; large drain.

zanqueador, ra, *n.* one who waddles in walking; great walker.

zanqueamiento, *m.* waddling in walking.

zanquear, *vn.* to waddle, trot, or run about; to walk much and fast.

zanquilargo, ga, *a.* long-shanked, long-legged.

zanquilla, zanquita, *f. dim.* (coll.) disproportionate, long-legged man.

zanquituerto, ta, *a.* bandy-legged.

zanquivano, na, *a.* spindle-shanked.

zantoxilo, *m.* = JANTOXILO.

zapa, *f.* spade; (fort.) sap; shagreen; (jewel.) rough surface on silver.—**caminar a la z.,** (mil.) to advance by sap or mine.

zapador, *m.* (mil.) sapper.

zapallo, *m.* (Am.) a variety of squash; calabash.

zapapico, *m.* pickaxe, mattock.

zapaquilda, *f.* female cat.

zapar, *va.* (fort.) to sap, to mine.

zaparrada, *f.* violent fall.

zaparrastrar, *vn.* (coll.) to trail (as ladies' trains).

zaparrastroso, sa, *a.* dirty, greasy, ragged.

zaparrazo, *m.* thud; violent fall.

zapata, *f.* piece of sole leather put on the hinge of a door to prevent its creaking; (shoe.) buskin, half-boot, high gaiter; (Cuba) socle of a wall; (arch.) lintel; (naut.) shoe; (mech.) shoe of brake, etc.).—**z. de la quilla,** (naut.) false heel.—**z. de un ancla,** (naut.) shoe of an anchor.

zapatazo, *m. aug.* large shoe; blow with a shoe; stamping of the feet; fall; thud, whack; clapping noise of a horse's foot.—**tratar a zapatazos,** to treat rudely or roughly.

zapateado, *pp. & m.* a sort of clog dance.

zapateador, ra, *n.* clog dancer.

zapatear. I. *va.* to strike with the shoe; (fenc.) to hit frequently with the button of the foil; to ill-treat. **II.** *vn.* to beat time with the feet; (naut.) to flap (s. o. the sails). **III.** *vr.* to oppose with spirit; to resist.

zapateo, *m.* keeping time by beating the feet on the floor.

zapatera, *f.* shoemaker's wife; woman who makes or sells shoes.

zapatería, *f.* trade of a shoemaker; shoemaker's shop.—**z. de viejo,** cobbler's stall.

zapateril, *a.* relating to, or like, shoemakers.

zapatero, ra. I. *a.* hard, poorly cooked (as beans); stale (olives). **II.** *m.* shoemaker; shoe dealer; (icht.) threadfish, cobbler fish; (coll.) player who takes no tricks at a game of cards.—**z. de viejo,** cobbler.

zapateta. I. *f.* slap on the sole of a shoe; caper, leap, jump. **II.** *interj.* oh! gracious!

zapatico, illo, ito, *m. dim.* nice little shoe.

zapatilla, *f.* (shoe.) pump, slipper; leather washer; piece of chamois or buckskin put behind the lock of a gun or pistol; (fenc.) button of a foil; hoof of animals.

zapatillero, ra, *n.* maker or seller of slippers, pumps, and children's shoes.

zapato, *m.* shoe (gen. app. to low shoes).—**zapatos papales,** overshoes, clogs.—**como tres en un z.,** squeezed into insufficient space; in great poverty.—**meter a uno en un z.,** (coll.) to cow one, to put one to one's trumps.—**saber dónde aprieta el z.,** to know where the shoe pinches.

zapatón, *m. aug.* large, clumsy shoe; (Colomb.) rubber, overshoe.

zapatudo, da, *a.* wearing large or stout shoes; large-hoofed or clawed.

¡zape! *interj.* used to frighten cats away, to denote surprise, or to refuse to give cards in some games.

zapear, *va.* to frighten (cats) away; to refuse to give cards to, in some games.

zapito, *m.,* **zapita,** *f.* (prov.) milk pail.

zaporogo, *m.* Ukranian Cossack.

zapotal, *m.* sapota grove or orchard.

zapote, *m.* (bot.) sapota tree and its fruit.

zapotero, *m.* (bot.) sapota tree.

zapotillo, *m.* (bot.) sapodilla and its fruit.

zapuzar, *va.* to duck. *V.* CHAPUZAR.

zaque, *m.* leather bottle or wine-bag; (coll.) tippler, drunkard; (Colomb.) chief of certain Indians.

zaquear, *va.* to rack (wines, etc.); to transport in ZAQUES.

zaquizamí, *m.* garret, cockloft; small wretched room, "hole."

zar, *m.* czar.

zara, *f.* (bot.) Indian corn, maize.

zarabanda, *f.* saraband (dance and tune); bustle, noise.

zarabandista, *n.* sarabander; dancer; merry person.

zarabutero, ra, *a.* = ZARAGUTERO.

zaragalla, *f.* fine charcoal.

zaragata, *f.* turmoil; scuffle, quarrel.

zaragatero, ra. I. *a.* (coll.) noisy, quarrelsome. **II.** *n.* rowdy.

zaragatona, *f.* (bot.) rib grass, ribwort.

zaragocí, *m.* a kind of plum.

zaragozano, na, *n. & a.* Saragossan.

zaragüelles, *m. pl.* wide and short plaited breeches; large pair of ill-made breeches; (bot.) reed grass.

zaragutear, *va.* (coll.) to undertake without proper knowledge; to bungle.

zaragutero, ra, *n.* (coll.) bungler.

zaramagullón, *m.* (orn.) didapper, a minute merganser.

zarambeque, *m.* breakdown among negros.

zaranda, *f.* screen, sieve, sifter.

zarandador, ra, *n.* sifter of wheat.

zarandajas, *f. pl.* trifles, odds and ends.

zarandalí, *adv.* black-spotted (dove).

zarandar, zarandear. I. *va.* to winnow; to sift; to separate, pick out; (coll.) to stir and move nimbly. **II.** *vr.* to be in motion, to move to and fro; to stalk, strut.

zarandeo, *m.* sifting or winnowing; moving briskly; stalking, strut.

zarandero, *m.* = ZARANDADOR.

zarandillo, lla. I. *n.* (coll.) one who frisks nimbly about. **II.** *m.* small sieve.

zarapatel, *n.* a kind of salmagundi.

zarapito, *m.* (orn.) whimbrel, curlew jack.

zaratán, *m.* cancer in the breast.

zaraza, *f.* chintz, printed cotton.—*pl.* paste made of pounded glass and poison, for killing dogs, rats, etc.

zarazo, za, *a.* (Cuba) rotten.

zarcear. I. *va.* to clean (pipes) with briers. **II.** *vn.* to move to and fro; to get into briers (as dogs pursuing game).—**zarceño, ña,** *a.* pertaining to briers.

zarcero, ra, *a. & n.* (dog) that hunts in briers.

zarceta, *f.* (orn.) widgeon. *V.* CERCETA.

zarcillitos, *m. pl.* (bot.) quaking grass.

zarcillo, *m.* drop earring; tendril of a vine (*v.* CERCILLO); gardener's hoe; (coop.) hoop.

zarco, ca, *a.* light blue (eyes); wall-eyed.

zarevitz, *m.* czarowitz.

zargatona, *f.* = ZARAGATONA.

zariano, na, *a.* belonging to the czar.

zarigüeya, *f.* (S. A.) opossum.

zarina, *f.* czarina.

zarismo, *m.* czarism.

zarja, *f.* reel. *V.* AZARJA.

zaroche, *m.* (Ecuador) mountain sickness.

zarpa, *f.* paw of a beast; (naut.) weighing anchor; (arch.) footing; dirt or mud sticking to the skirts.—**echar la z. a,** to grasp, clutch, gripe.

zarpada, *f.* strike with a paw.

zarpar, *vn.* (naut.) to weigh anchor, to sail.

zarpazo, *m.* bang, thud, whack; ZARPADA.

zarposo, sa, *a.* bespattered, bemired.

zarracatería, *f.* lure, deception.

zarracatín, *m.* (coll.) haggler, higgler, chafferer.

zarramplín, na, *n.* (coll.) bungler, botcher.

zarramplinada, *f.* botch, bungle, muddle.

zarrapastra, *f.* mud sticking to the skirts.

zarrapastrón, na, *a. & n.* tatterdemalion.

zarrapastrosamente, *adv.* (coll.) raggedly, slovenly.—**zarrapastroso, sa,** *a.* ragged, slovenly, shabby, seedy.

zarria, *f.* mud sticking to clothes; leather strap, thong or latch.

zarriento, ta; zarrioso, sa, *a.* bespattered, bemired.

zarza, *f.* (bot.) bramble; blackberry bush.

zarzagán, *m.* cold northeast wind.

zarzaganete, *m. dim.* light northeast wind.

zarzaganillo, *m.* violent northeast storm.

zarzahán, *m.* a kind of striped silk.

zarzaldea, *f.* (bot.) raspberry bush.

zarzal, *m.* brambly place, brambles.

zarzamora, *f.* (bot.) brambleberry.

zarzaparrilla, *f.* (bot.) sarsaparilla.

zarzaparrillar, *m.* sarsaparilla plantation.

zarzaperruna, *f.* (bot.) dog-rose.

zarzarrosa, *f.* (bot.) dog-rose.

zarzo, *m.* hurdle, wattle.

zarzoso, sa, *a.* briery, brambly.

zarzuela, *f.* musical drama.—**zarzuelero, ra,** *a.* relating to musical dramas.— **zarzuelista,** *n.* writer or composer of musical dramas.

¡zas! *m.* tick, sound of a rap.—**¡z., z.¡** ticktack.

zascandil, *m.* (coll.) busybody.

zata, zatara, *f.* raft.

zato, *m.* piece of bread.

zazoso, sa. **I.** *a.* lisping. **II.** *n.* lisper.

zeda, *f.* name of the letter z.

zedilla, *f.* cedilla.

zelandés, sa, *n. & a.* Zealandian.

zemstvo, *m.* zemstvo.

Zendavesta, *m.* Zend-Avesta.

zendo, da, *a. & m.* Zend.

zenit, zenital = CENIT, CENITAL.

zepelín, *m.* Zeppelin (dirigible).

zeta, *f.* name of the letter z.

zeugma, zeuma, *f.* (rhet.) zeugma.

zigzag, *m.* zigzag.—**zigzaguear,** *vn.* to zigzag.—**zigzagueo,** *m.* zigzagging.

zinc (= CINC), *m.* zinc.

zipizape, *m.* (coll.) row, rumpus, scuffle.

zircón, zirconio = CIRCÓN, CIRCONIO.

zirigaña, *f.* fawning, wheedling, flattery; CHASCO; FRIOLERA.

¡zis, zas! (coll.) words expressing the sound of repeated blows or strokes.

ziszás, *m.* zigzag.

zizaña, *f.* (bot.) darnel. *V.* CIZAÑA.

zoantario, ria, *n. & a.* (zool.) zoantharian.

zoantropía, *f.* (med.) zoanthropy.—**zoántropo, pa,** *n.* one suffering from zoanthropy.

zoca, *f.* square, plaza.

zócalo, *m.* (arch.) socle or zocle.

zocato, ta, *a.* overripe; left-handed.

zoclo, *m.* clog; overshoe.

zoco, ca. **I.** *a.* left-handed. **II.** *m.* clog; (arch.) socle; market; market place.

zodiacal, *a.* zodiacal.

zodíaco, *m.* (ast.) zodiac.

zofra, *f.* Moorish carpet.

zoilo, *m.* zoilus, malicious critic.

zolocho, cha, *a.* (coll.) stupid, silly, booby.

zollipar, *vn.* (coll.) to sob.

zollipo, *m.* sob; sobbing.

zoma, *f.* coarse flour.

zompo, pa, *a.* cripple; clumsy, awkward.

zona, *f.* zone; girdle, band; (med.) zoster, shingles.—**z. esférica,** (geom.) spherical zone.—**z. glacial,** (geol.) frigid zone.—**z. polémica,** (fort.) zone of defence.—**z. templada,** temperate zone.—**z. tórrida,** torrid zone.

zonal, *a.* zonate, zoned.

zonceria, *f.* silliness, dulness, stupidity.

zonchiche, *m.* (C. A.) a red-headed vulture.

zonote, *m.* deep deposit of water.

zonzamente, *adv.* stupidly, foolishly.

zonzo, za. **I.** *a.* dull, stupid, silly. **II.** *n.* simpleton, dunce, booby, noodle.

zonzorrión, na, *n.* very dull and stupid person.

zoófago, ga, *a.* zoophagous.

zoófito, *m.* (zool.) zoophyte.

zoóforo, *m.* (arch.) zoophorous.

zoogenia, zoogonía, *f.* zoogeny.

zoografía, *f.* zoography.

zooide. **I.** *a.* containing the figure of an animal or part of it. **II.** *m.* (biol.) zooid.

zoolatría, *f.* zoolatry.

zoolítico, ca, *a.* fossil-bearing, zoolitic.

zoolito, *m.* petrified animal.

zoología, *f.* zoology.—**zoológico, ca,** *a.* zoological, zoologic.—**zoólogo,** *m.* zoologist.

zoomorfismo, *m.* zoomorphism.

zoonomía, *f.* zoonomy.

zoospora, *f.*; **zoosporo,** *m.* zoospore.

zoospermo, *m.* (biol.) zoosperm.

zoosporangio, *m.* zoosporangium.

zootecnia, *f.* zootechnics.

zootomía, *f.* zootomy, comparative anatomy.

zopas, *n.* (coll.) nickname given to a lisper.

zope, *m.* (orn.) buzzard. *V.* ZOPILOTE.

zopenco, ca. **I.** *a.* (coll.) doltish, dull. **II.** *n.* dolt, blockhead, fool.

zopetero, *m.* = RIBAZO.

zopilote, *m.* (Mex.) (orn.) = AURA.

zopisa, *f.* pitch and tar ointment.

zopitas, *n.* = ZOPAS.

zopo, pa. **I.** *a.* lame, maimed, crippled; clumsy, awkward, unhandy. **II.** *n.* cripple.

zoqueta, *f.* a wooden cover or guard for the hand.

zoquetada, *f.* silly remark; foolishness, foolish words or act.

zoquete, *m.* (carp.) chump, chunk, block; bit or morsel of bread; (coll.) ugly little person; dolt, dunce, numskull, blockhead.—**z. de cuchara,** (naut.) scoop handle.

zoquetero, ra, *a.* living on crumbs and leavings, idle pauper.

zoquetico, illo, *m. dim.* small morsel of bread.

zoquetudo, da, *a.* rough, ill-finished.

zorcico, *m.* (mus.) Basque song and dance in five-eight (⅝) time.

zorita, *f.* (orn.) stockdove, wood pigeon.

zoroástrico, ca, *a.* Zoroastric.

zoroastrismo, *m.* Zoroastrianism.

zorollo, *a.* reaped while unripe (wheat).

zorongo, *m.* kerchief folded like a bandage around the head, worn by Aragonese; broad flattened chignon; an Andalusian dance and tune.

zorra, *f.* (zool.) fox; foxy; sly person; dray, truck; (coll.) prostitute; drunkenness, inebriation.—**a la z., candilazo,** when Greek meets Greek; diamond cut diamond.

zorrastrón, na, *a. & n.* (coll.) foxy, foxy person, rogue (-ish), knave (-ish).

zorrera, *f.* fox hole; kennel; room full of smoke; heaviness, drowsiness.

zorrería, *f.* foxiness; cunning, knavery.

zorrero, ra. **I.** *a.* slow, tardy, sluggish; (naut.) sailing heavily; cunning, foxy. **II.** *m.* terrier, fox-hunting dog; keeper of a royal forest.

zorrilla, *f.* (zool.) polecat, skunk.

zorro, rra. **I.** *a.* slow, tardy; cunning, foxy. **II.** *n.* fox; knave, foxy person; humdrum.

III. *m. pl.* duster made of cloth strips or fox-tails tied to a handle.

zorrocloco, *m.* humdrum, shifter; (coll.) caress, petting.

zorrongión, na, *a.* slow, heavy, lazy.

zorruelo, la, *n. dim.* little fox.

zorrullo, *m.* = ZURULLO.

zorruno, na, *a.* vulpine, foxy, foxlike.

zorzal, *m.* (orn.) thrush; sly, crafty man.—**z. marino,** (icht.) a kind of fish abounding near the coast of Spain.

zorzaleña, *f. V.* ACEITUNA.

zoster, *f.* (med.) zoster, shingles.

zote, *a.* dull and ignorant.

zozobra, *f.* worry, anguish, anxiety; unlucky cast of the die; (naut.) sinking, foundering, capsizing.

zozobrante, *a.* in great danger; sinking.

zozobrar, *vn.* (naut.) to be weather-beaten; to sink, founder; to upset, capsize; to be in great danger; to grieve, worry, fret.

zúa, *f.* Persian wheel. *V.* AZUDA.

zuavo, *m.* (mil.) zouave.

zubia, *f.* drain, channel, flume.

zucarino, na, *a.* sugary.

zúchil, *m.* (Mex.) bouquet.

zuda, *f.* = ZÚA.

zudra, *n.* Sudra, lowest Hindu caste; member of the Sudra.

zueco, *m.* sabot; clog, galosh or galoche.

zuindá, *m.* an Argentine brown owl.

zuinglianismo, *m.* Zwinglianism.

zuingliano, na, *n. & a.* Zwinglian.

zuiza, *f.* military tournament or feast; quarrel, dispute.

zuizón, *m.* spear; (naut.) half pike.

zulacar, *va.* to anoint with bitumen.

zulaque, *m.* (hyd.) packing stuff; (naut.) stuff for paving the bottom of a ship.

zulú, *a. & n.* Zulu.

zulla, *f.* French honeysuckle; (coll.) human excrements.—**zullarse,** *vr.* (coll.) to go to stool; to break wind.

zullenco, ca; zullón, na. **I.** *a.* (coll.) breaking wind; flatulent. **II.** *m.* act of breaking wind; flatulence.

zumacal, zumacar, *m.* sumach plantation.

zumacar, *va.* to dress or tan with sumach.

zumacaya, *f.* (orn.) a night wading bird.

zumaque, *m.* (bot.) sumach tree; (coll.) wine.

zumaya, *f.* (orn.) barn owl; goatsucker; fern owl; ZUCAMAYA.

zumba, *f.* bell worn by the leading mule of a drove; rattle; joke, jest; facetious raillery.

zumbador, ra. **I.** *a.* humming, buzzing. **II.** *m.* (P. Rico) humming bird; (elec.) buzzer.

zumbar. **I.** *vn.* to buzz, to hum; to be near, flutter around; to ring (s. o. the ears). **II.** *va.* to jest, to joke with.

zumbel, *m.* (coll.) cord for spinning tops; frown, angry mien or aspect.

zumbido, *m.* humming, buzzing; ringing in the ears; ping of a bullet; (coll.) blow, box, cuff.

zumbilín, *m.* (Philip.) dart or javelin.

zumbo, *m.* = ZUMBIDO.

zumbón, na. **I.** *a.* waggish, jocose. **II.** *m.* wag, jester, joker; a variety of pigeon.

zumiento, ta, *a.* juicy, succulent.

zumillo, *m.* (bot.) dragon's arum, Aaron's beard; a poisonous carrot.

zumo, *m.* sap, juice; profit, utility.—**z. de cepas,** or **parras,** (coll.) grape juice, wine.

zumoso, sa, *a.* juicy, succulent.

zuna, *f.* Sunna, body of Mohammedan traditions; viciousness of horses; trickery, perfidy.

zuncho, *m.* band, hoop, collar, ferrule.

zunita, *n.* Sunnite, member of one of the great Mohammedan sects.

zunítico, ca, *a.* relating to the Sunna, or body of Mohammedan traditions.

zuño, *m.* frown, angry mien.

zupia, *f.* turned roily wine; lees, dregs, slops; refuse, rubbish, trash.

zurano, na, *n.* stockdove, wild pigeon.

zurcidera, *f.* darner, finedrawer.

zurcido, *m.* (sew.) darning, finedrawing.

zurcidor, ra, *n.* darner.—**zurcidora de voluntades,** procuress.

zurcidura, *f.* (sew.) finedrawing, darning.

zurcir, *va.* (*ind.* ZURZO: *subj.* ZURZA) (sew.) to darn, finedraw; to join, unite; (coll.) to hatch, concoct (lies).

zurdería, *f.* left-handedness.—**zurdo, da,** *a.* left-handed.—**a zurdas,** the wrong way.

zurear, *vn.* to coo.—**zureo,** *m.* cooing.

zurito, ta, *f.* (orn.) wild pigeon. *V.* ZURO.

zuriza, *f.* quarrel, dispute. *V.* ZUIZA.

zuro, ra. **I.** *n.* (orn.) stockdove, wild pigeon. **II.** *m.* corncob.

zurra, *f.* (tan.) currying; flogging, beating, drubbing; quarrel, dispute, scuffle.—**zurrado, da.** **I.** *pp. & a.* curried, dressed. **II.** *m.* (coll.) glove.—**zurrador,** *m.* (tan.) currier, dresser; drubber, flogger.

zurrapa, *f.* lees, sediment, dregs; rubbish, trash; ugly skinny boy.—**con zurrapas,** in an uncleanly manner.

zurrapelo, *m.* (coll.) severe reprimand.

zurrapiento, ta; zurraposo, sa, *a.* dreggy; turbid, roily.

zurrar. **I.** *va.* (tan.) to curry, to dress (leather); to spank, flog, drub, whip; to beat in a quarrel or fight.—**z. la badana,** to beat, to flog.—**¡z., que es tarde!** but you are persistent! will you keep on forever? etc. (said to one who persists in something disagreeable or already rejected). **II.** *vr.* to have an involuntary evacuation of the bowels; to be seized with great fear.

zurriaga, *f.* thong, long leather strap; whip; (orn.) lark.—**zurriagar,** *va.* (*pret.* ZURRIAGUÉ: *subj.* ZURRIAGUE) to whip, horsewhip, cowhide.

zurriagazo, *m.* whipping; severe lash or stroke with a whip; unexpected ill treatment; calamity, stroke of bad luck.

zurriago, *m.* whip.

zurriar, *vn.* to hum, buzz; to rattle.

zurribanda, *f.* flogging, horsewhipping, cowhiding; rumpus, scuffle, fight.

zurriburri, *m.* (coll.) ragamuffin, scamp; (coll.) gang of rowdies.

zurrido, *m.* humming, buzzing, rattling noise; (coll.) blow with a stick.

zurrir, *vn.* to hum, buzz, rattle.

zurrón, *m.* shepherd's pouch; game bag; leather bag; seroon; thin skin of shell fruits; (anat.) placenta; cyst.—**zurronada,** *f.* bagful.

zurroncillo, *m. dim.* small bag.—**zurronero, ra,** *n.* maker or seller of seroons or game bags.

zurrusco, *m.* (coll.) burnt toast.

zurubí, *m.* an Argentine fresh-water fish.

zurullo, *m.* any soft round object; ball of, or piece of tangled, string or rope; (cook.) rolling pin.

zurumbático, ca, *a.* stunned, dumbfounded.

zurupeto, *m.* intrusive broker.

zutanico, illo, *m. dim.* of ZUTANO.

Zutano, na, *n.* (coll.) word invented to supply the name of some person not known or not desired to be expressed; So-and-So. *V.* FULANO.

¡zuzo! *interj.* = ¡CHUCHO!

zuzón, *m.* (bot.) groundsel, ragwort.

For pronunciation, see the rules at the beginning of the book.

APPENDIX

GEOGRAPHICAL NAMES THAT DIFFER IN THE SPANISH AND ENGLISH LANGUAGES

A

Abidos, Abydos.
Abisinia, Abyssinia.
Acaya, Achæa, Achaia.
Accio, Actium.
Adelaida, Adelaide.
Adrianópoli, Adrianople.
Afganistán, Afghanistan.
Alejandría, Alexandria.
Alemania, Germany.
Alenzón, Alençon.
Alepo, Aleppo.
Alesia, Alais.
Algeciras, Algesiras.
Almirante. *V.* ISLAS DEL ALMIRANTE.
Alpes, Alps.
Alpes Julianos, Julian Alps.
Alpes Peninos, Pennine Alps.
Alsacia, Alsace.
Alsacia Lorena, Alsace-Lorraine.
Alto Egipto, Upper Egypt.
Amán, Maskat.
Amazonas, Amazon.
Amberes, Antwerp.
América del Norte, North America.
América del Sur, South America.
América Española, Spanish America.
América Meridional, South America.
Anam, Annam.
Andalucía, Andalusia.
Angulema, Angoulême.
Angumoes, Angoumais.
Antillas, Antilles, West Indies.
Antioquía, Antioch.
Apeninos, Apennines.
Aquisgrán, Aachen, Aix-la-Chapelle.
Aquitania, Aquitaine.
Arabia Desierta, Arabia Deserta.
Arabia Feliz, Arabia Felix.
Arabia Petrea, Arabia Petræa.
Aragón, Arragon.
Archipiélago, Ægean.
Archipiélago de Francisco José, Franz Joseph Land.
Archipiélago Malayo, Malay Archipelago.
Ardenas, Ardennes.
Argel, Algiers.
Argelia, Algeria.
Armañac, Armañaque, Armagnac.
Asia Menor, Asia Minor.
Asiria, Assyria.

Asís, Assisi.
Astracán, Astrakhan.
Atenas, Athens.
Ática, Attica.
Ausburgo, Augsburg.
Austria-Hungría, Austria-Hungary.
Auvernia, Auvergne.
Aviñón, Avignon.
Ayacio, Ajaccio.

B

Babilonia, Babylon.
Bactria, Bactra.
Bactriana, Bactria.
Baireut, Bayreuth.
Baja California, Lower California.
Bajo Egipto, Lower Egypt.
Bajo Rin, Lower Rhine.
Bakú, Baku.
Báltico, Baltic.
Baluchistán, Baluchistan.
Banato, Banat.
Bañeras, Bagnères.
Barbadas, Barbadoes.
Bareges, Barège.
Basilea, Basel, Basle, Bâle.
Baviera, Bavaria.
Bayona, Bayonne.
Bearne, Bearn.
Bechuanalandia, Bechuanaland.
Belcaire, Beaucaire.
Belén, Bethlehem.
Bélgica, Belgium.
Belgrado, Belgrade.
Belice, Beliza, British Honduras.
Beluchistán = BALUCHISTÁN.
Bengala, Bengal.
Beocia, Bœotia, Beotia.
Berbería, Barbary.
Berna, Bern.
Betania, Bethany.
Betsaida, Bethsaida.
Bitinia, Bithynia.
Bizancio, Byzantium.
Bojara, Bokhara, Bokhara.
Bolduque, Bois-le-Duc.
Bolonia, Bologna.
Boloña, Boulogne.
Bona, Bonn.
Borgoña, Burgundy.
Bósforo, Bosporus.
Botnia, Bothnia.
Brabante, Brabant.
Brandeburgo, Brandenberg.
Brasil, Brazil.
Brema, Bremen.
Brena, Brienne.

Bretaña, Bretagne, Brittany.
Bretaña (Gran), (Great) Britain.
Brujas, Bruges.
Brúnsvick, Brunswick, Braunschweig.
Bruselas, Brussels.
Bucarest, Bucharest.
Bucovina, Bukovina, Bukowina.
Bullón, Buillon.
Burdeos, Bordeaux.

C

Cabo Bretón, Cape Breton (Island).
Cabo de Buena Esperanza, Cape of Good Hope.
Cabo de Hornos, Cape Horn.
Cabo de Istria, Capo d'Istria.
Cabo de San Vicente, Cape Saint Vincent.
Cabo Haitiano, Cape Haitien.
Cachemira, Kashmir.
Cafarnaum, Capernaum.
Cafrería, Kaffraria.
Calcedonia, Chalcedon.
Calcuta, Calcutta.
Caldea, Chaldea.
Cambrige, Cambrigia, Cambridge.
Camerón, Camerron.
Campeche, Campeachy, Campeche.
Canaán, Canaan.
Canal de la Mancha, English Channel.
Canarias, Canary (Islands).
Canosa, Canossa.
Cantórbery, Canterbury.
Carcasona, Carcassonne.
Carelia, Karelia.
Carenta, Charente.
Caribe. *V.* MAR CARIBE.
Cariñán, Carignano.
Carolina del Norte, North Carolina.
Carolina del Sur, South Carolina.
Cartagena, Carthagena.
Cartago, Carthage.
Caspio, Caspian (Sea).
Castilla, Castille.
Castilla la Nueva, New Castile.
Castilla la Vieja, Old Castile.
Cataluña, Catalonia.
Cáucaso, Caucasus.
Cayena, Cayenne.
Cayohueso, Cayo Hueso, Key West.

For pronunciation, see the rules at the beginning of the book.

512

Cayos de la Florida, Florida Keys.
Cebú. *V.* ZEBÚ.
Ceilán, Ceylon.
Cerdeña, Sardinia.
Cernauti, Czernowitz.
Cesarea, Cæsarea.
Cevenes, Cevennes, Sevennes.
Cíclades, Cyclades.
Cidno, Cydnus.
Circasia, Circassia.
Coblenza, Coblenz.
Coburgo, Coburg.
Cochinchina, Cochin China.
Colonia, Cologne.
Colonia del Cabo, Cape Colony.
Columbia Británica, British Columbia.
Columnas de Hércules, Pillars of Hercules.
Comoras, Comoro Isles.
Compieña, Compiegne.
Constantina, Constantine.
Constantinopla, Constantinople.
Constanza, Constance.
Copenhague, Copenhagen.
Córcega, Corsica.
Córdoba, Cordova.
Corfú, Corfu.
Corinto, Corinth.
Cornualla, Cornwall.
Cortray, Courtray.
Coruña, Corunna.
Costa del Marfil, Ivory Coast.
Costa de Oro, Gold Coast.
Cotanza, Coutances.
Cracovia, Cracow.
Creta, Crete.
Cristianía, Christiania.
Croacia, Croatia.
Cronstadt, Kronstadt.
Curasao, Curazao, Curaçao.
Curdistán, Kurdistan.
Curlandia, Kurland.

CH

Chamberí, Chambery.
Champaña, Champagne.
Chantung, Shantung.
Checoeslovaquia, Czecho-Slovakia, Czechoslovakia.
Cherburgo, Cherbourg.
Chifú, Chifu, Chefoo.
Chile, Chili, Chile.
Chipre, Cyprus.

D

Dakota del Norte, North Dakota.
Dakota del Sur, South Dakota.
Dalmacia, Dalmatia.
Damasco, Damascus.
Damieta, Damietta.
Danubio, Danube.
Dardanelos, Dardanelles.
Decán, Deccan.
Delfinado, Dauphiny, Dauphiné.
Delfos, Delphi.
Diepa, Diepe, Dieppe.
Dinamarca, Denmark.
Dniéper, Dnieper.
Dordoña, Dordogne.
Dos Puentes, Deux Ponts.
Dresde, Dresden.
Duay, Douay.

Duero, Douro.
Duina, Dwina, Dvina.
Dunas, Downs.
Dunquerque, Dunkirk.
Duvres, Dover.

E

Edimburgo, Edinburgh.
Efeso, Ephesus.
Egeo, Ægean.
Egina, Ægina.
Egipto, Egypt.
Egos Pótamos, Ægospotami.
Elba, Elbe.
Elbinga, Elbing.
Entre Duero y Miño, Entre Douro e Minho.
Eólida, Æolis.
Epiro, Epirus.
Erzerón, Erzerum.
Escafusa, Schaffhausen.
Escalda, Scheld, Scheldt.
Escamandro, Scamander.
Escandinavia, Scandinavia.
Escania, Scania.
Escio, Scio, Chio.
Esclavonia, Slavonia.
Escocia, Scotland.
Escorial, Escurial.
Escutari, Scutari.
Eslavonia, Slavonia.
Eslovaquia, Slovakia.
Eslovenia, Slovenia.
Esmalcalda, Smalcalden.
Esmirna, Smyrna.
España, Spain.
Española, Hispaniola.
Esparta, Sparta.
Espira, Spirea.
Espizberg, Espizberga, Spitzbergen.
Espoleto, Spoleto.
Establecimientos del Estrecho (de Malaca), Straits Settlements.
Estado Libre de Orange, Orange Free State.
Estados de la Iglesia, States of the Church.
Estados Federados de Malaca, Federated Malay States.
Estados Unidos de América, United States of America.
Estambul, Stambul.
Estiria, Styria.
Estocolmo, Stockholm.
Estonia, Esthonia.
Estrasburgo, Strasburg.
Estrecho de Bella Isla, Strait of Belleisle.
Estrecho de Magallanes, Strait of Magellan.
Estrómboli, Stromboli.
Etiopía, Ethiopia.
Etna, Etna, Ætna.
Etolia, Ætolia.
Eubea, Eubœa.
Eufrates, Euphrates.
Europa, Europe.

F

Farsalia, Pharsalia.
Fenicia, Phœnicia.
Filadelfia, Philadelphia.
Filipinas, Philippines.
Filipópolis, Philippopolis.
Filipos, Philippi.
Finlandia, Finland.

Flandes, Flanders.
Flesinga, Flushing.
Florencia, Florence.
Fócide, Phocis.
Francfort del Mein, Frankfort-on-the-Main.
Francia, France.
Franco Condado, Franche Comté.
Friburgo, Friburg, Freiburg.
Frigia, Phrygia.
Frisia, Friesland.
Frontiñac, Frontenac.

G

Gales, Wales.
Galia, Gaul.
Galilea, Galilee.
Galípoli, Gallipoli.
Gante, Ghent, Gand.
Garona, Garonne.
Gascuña, Gascony.
Génova, Genoa.
Germania, (anc. hist.) Germany.
Ginebra, Geneva.
Gironda, Gironde.
Glaris, Glarus.
Golfo Pérsico, Persian Gulf.
Gotemburgo, Gothenburg.
Gotinga, Göttingen.
Gran Bretaña, Great Britain.
Gránico, Granicus.
Gravelinas, Gravelines.
Grecia, Greece.
Groenlandia, Greenland.
Groninga, Groningen.
Guadalupe, Guadeloupe.
Guaján, Guam, Guam.
Guayana, Guiana.
Güeldres, Guelderland, Gelderland.
Guernesey, Guernsey.
Guidsé, Giza.
Guipúzcoa, Guipuscoa.
Guiena, Guienne.

H

Habana, Havana.
Haití, Haiti, Hayti.
Halicarnaso, Halicarnassus.
Hamburgo, Hamburg.
Hankao, Hankow.
Harrisburgo, Harrisburg.
Hauái, Hawaii.
Havre de Gracia, Havre de Grace.
Hawái, Hawaii.
Haya, Hague.
Hébridas, Hebrides.
Hélada, Hellas.
Helvecia, Helvetia.
Henao, Hainault.
Herculano, Herculaneum.
Heyaz, Hejaz.
Himeto, Hymettus.
Hispano-América, Hispano-américa, Spanish America.
Holanda, Holland.
Honduras Británica, British Honduras.
Hungría, Hungary.

I

Ilión (Troya), Ilion, Ilium (Troy).
Iliria, Illyria.

For pronunciation, see the rules at the beginning of the book.

Ilírico, Illyricum.
Indias, Indies.
Indias orientales, East Indies.
Indias occidentales, West Indies.
Indo, Indus.
Indostán, Hindustan, India.
Inglaterra, England.
Irlanda, Ireland.
Isla de Francia, Island of France, or Mauritius.
Isla de Guanahaní, Watling Island.
Isla del Cabo Bretón, Cape Breton Island.
Isla del Príncipe Eduardo, Prince Edward Island.
Isla de Pascua, Easter Island.
Isla Española, Hispaniola, Hayti.
Isla Real, Cape Breton Island.
Islandia, Iceland.
Islas Aleutas, or **Aleutianas,** Aleutian Islands.
Islas Baleares, Balearic Islands.
Islas Británicas, British Isles.
Islas Canarias, Canary Islands.
Islas Carolinas, Caroline Islands.
Islas de Barlovento, Windward Islands.
Islas de Hauái, Sandwich Islands.
Islas del Almirante, Admiralty Islands.
Islas de la Sociedad, Society Islands.
Islas de la Sonda, Sunda Isles.
Islas del Cabo Verde, Cape Verde Islands.
Islas de Sotavento, Leeward Islands.
Islas de Zetlandia, Shetland Islands.
Islas Filipinas, Philippine Islands.
Islas Hawái, Hawaiian Islands.
Islas Malvinas, Falkland Islands.
Islas Vírgenes, Virgin Islands.
Iso, Issus.
Itaca, Ithaca.
Italia, Italy.

J

Janina, Yannina.
Japón, Japan.
Jarbin, Harbin.
Jartum, Khartoum.
Jericó, Jericho.
Jerusalén, Jerusalem.
Jiva, Khiva.
Jonia, Ionia.
Judá, Judah.
Jutlandia, Jutland.

K

Karbin, Harbin.
Kartum, Khartoum.
Kiao-Cheu, Kiaochow.
Kurdistán, Kurdistan.

L

Lacedemonia, Lacedæmon.
Lacio, Latium.
Lago de Constanza, Lake of Constance.

Lago Salado, Salt Lake.
Langüedoc, Languedoc.
Laponia, Lapland.
La Rochela, La Rochelle.
Lasa, Lassa.
Lausana, Lausanne.
Leida, Leide, Leiden, Leyden.
Lemosín, Limosin or Limousin.
Leningrado, Leningrad.
León de Francia, Lyons.
Leonesado, Lyonnais.
Líbano, Lebanon.
Libia, Libya.
Lieja, Liège.
Lila, Lille.
Limburgo, Limburg.
Liorna, Leghorn.
Lisboa, Lisbon.
Lituania, Lithuania.
Lombardía, Lombardy.
Londres, London.
Lorena, Lorraine.
Lovaina, Louvain.
Lucerna, Lucerne.
Luisiana, Louisiana.
Luxemburgo, Luxemburg.

M

Macedonia, Macedon, Macedonia.
Madera, Madeira.
Magallanes, Magellan.
Magna Grecia, Magna Græcia, Græcia Magna.
Maguncia, Mayence, Mentz.
Maisur, Mysore.
Malaca, Malay Peninsula.
Malasia, Malay Archipelago, Malaysia.
Maldivas, Maldives.
Malinas, Malines, Mecheln or Mechlin.
Malvinas, Falkland Islands.
Mallorca, Majorca.
Mar Adriático, Adriatic Sea.
Mar Amarillo, Yellow Sea.
Mar Báltico, Baltic Sea.
Mar Blanco, White Sea.
Mar Caribe, Caribbean Sea.
Mar Caspio, Caspian Sea.
Mar de la China, China Sea.
Mar de las Antillas = MAR CARIBE.
Mar de las Indias, Indian Ocean.
Mar del Norte, North Sea.
Mar Egeo, Ægean Sea.
Mar Glacial, Frozen Sea.
Mar Jónico, Ionian Sea.
Mar Mediterráneo, Mediterranean Sea.
Mar Muerto, Dead Sea.
Mar Negro, Black Sea.
Mar Rojo, Red Sea.
Mar Tirreno, Tyrrhenian Sea.
Marañón, (upper reaches of the) Amazon.
Maratón, Marathon.
Marruecos, Morocco.
Marsella, Marseilles.
Martinica, Martinique.
Mauricia, Mauritius or Island of France.
Mayena, Mayenne.
Meca, Mecca.
Mediterráneo, Mediterranean.
Méjico, Mexico.
Menfis, Memphis.
Menorca, Minorca.
Mesia, Mœsia.

Metauro, Metaurus.
Micenas, Mycenæ.
Midelburgo, Middleburg.
Milanesado, Milanese.
Miño, Minho.
Mirándula, Mirandola.
Misisipí, Mississippi.
Misora, Mysore.
Mobila, Mobile.
Mompeller, Montpellier.
Mondoñedo, Mondonned or Mondoneda.
Mongibelo, = ETNA.
Monserrate, Montserrat.
Monte Oliveto, Olives (Mount of), Olivet.
Montes Alleghanys, Alleghany Mountains.
Montes Apalaches, Appalachian Mountains.
Montes Balcanes, Balkan Mountains.
Montes Carpacios, or **Cárpatos,** Carpathian Mountains.
Montes Rocallosos, M. Rocosos, Rocky Mountains.
Montes Urales, Ural Mountains.
Morlés, Morlaix.
Mosa, Meuse.
Moscovia, Muscovy.
Moscú, Moscow.
Mosela, Moselle.
Muerto, Dead (Sea).
Mukden, Moukden.

N

Nápoles, Naples.
Narbona, Narbonne.
Navarino, Navarin.
Navarra, Navarre.
Nazaret, Nazareth.
Negro, Black (Sea).
Neoburgo, Neuburg.
Neoport, Nieuport.
Neyed, Nejd or Nedjed.
Nicea, Nicæa.
Niéper, Dnieper.
Nifón, Nippon.
Nigricia, Negroland.
Nilo, Nile.
Nimega, Nimeguen.
Nínive, Nineveh.
Nipón, Nippon.
Niza, Nice.
Normandía, Normandy.
Noruega, Norway.
Nueva Escocia, Nova Scotia.
Nueva Gales, New Wales.
Nueva Gales del Sur, New South Wales.
Nueva Inglaterra, New England.
Nueva Orleáns, New Orleans.
Nueva York, New York.
Nueva Zelandia, New Zealand.
Nueva Zembla, Nova Zembla.
Nuevo Brúnswick, N. Brúnswick, New Brunswick.
Numancia, Numantia.
Nuremberga, Nuremberg.

O

Oceanía, Oceania, Oceanica.
Odenarda, Oudenarde.
Odesa, Odessa.
Ofir, Ophir.

Olimpia, Olympia.
Olimpo, Olympus.
Olinto, Olynthus.
Omán, Muscat, Maskat.
Onella, Oneglia.
Orleanesado, Orleannois.
Ostende, Ostend.
Otahití, Otaheite or Tahiti.
Oxo, Oxus.

P

Pacífico, Pacific (Ocean).
Países Bajos, Low Countries, Netherlands.
Palatinado, Palatinate.
Palestina, Palestine.
Palmira, Palmyra.
Pamplona, Pampeluna.
Panfilia, Pamphylia.
Panzacola, Pensacola.
Parnaso, Parnassus.
Partia, Parthia.
Paso de Calais, English Channel, Strait of Dover.
Pekín, Pekin.
Pela, Pella.
Peloponeso, Peloponnesus.
Península de Malaca, Malay Peninsula.
Pensilvania, Pennsylvania.
Penzacola, Pensacola.
Pérgamo, Pergamum.
Perona, Peronne.
Perpiñán, Perpignan.
Perusa, Perusia or Perugia.
Petrogrado, Petrograd.
Piamonte, Piedmont.
Picardía, Picardy.
Piombina, Piombino.
Pireo, Piræus.
Pirineos, Pyrenees.
Pistoya, Pistoja.
Plasencia, Placentia.
Platea, Platæa.
Polinesia, Polynesia.
Polonia, Poland.
Pombín, Piombino.
Pompeya, Pompeii.
Ponto, Pontus.
Ponto Euxino, Pontus Euxinus (Black Sea).
Porto Longón, Porto Longone.
Praga, Prague.
Presburgo, Presburg.
Provenza, Provence.
Providencia, Providence.
Provincias Renanas, Rhineland.
Provincias Vascongadas, or Vascas, Basque Provinces.
Prusia, Prussia.
Puertas de Hierro, Iron Gates.
Puerto Arturo, Port Arthur.
Puerto (de) España, Port of Spain.
Puerto Mahón, Port Mahon.
Puerto Príncipe, Port-au-Prince.
Puerto Rico, Porto Rico.

Q

Queronea, Chæronea.
Quersoneso, Chersonese.
Quinsala, Kinsale.
Quío, Chio.

R

Rapanuí, Easter Island.
Ratisbona, Ratisbon, Regensburg.
Regio, Reggio.
Reims, Rheims.
Retia, Rhætia.
Rhin, Rhine.
Rif, Rif or Riff.
Rin, Rhine.
Río Amarillo, Yellow River.
Rocamora, Roquemaure.
Rochela (La), (La) Rochelle.
Ródano, Rhone.
Rodas, Rhodes.
Rodesia, Rhodesia.
Rojo, Red (Sea).
Roma, Rome.
Romaña, Romagna.
Rosellón, Roussillon.
Roseta, Rosetta.
Ruán, Rouen.
Rumania, R(o)umania.
Ruremunda, Roermond or Ruremunde.
Rusia, Russia.

S

Sabá, Sheba.
Saboya, Savoy.
Sácer, Sassari.
Sajonia, Saxony.
Sajonia-Coburgo, Saxe-Coburg.
Sajonia-Gotha, Saxe-Gotha.
Sajonia-Wéimar, Saxe-Weimar.
Salamina, Salamis.
Salé, Sallee.
Salónica, Salonika.
Samotracia, Samothrace.
San Cristóbal, St. Kitts.
San Germán, St. Germain.
San Gotardo, St. Gothard.
San Juan de Luz, St. Jean de Luz.
San Kitts, St. Kitts.
San Nazario, St.-Nazaire.
San Petersburgo, St. Petersburg.
San Quintín, St.-Quentin.
San Salvador (Isla de), Watling Island.
Santa Elena, St. Helena.
Santa Lucía, St. Lucia.
Santonge, Saintonge.
Sarmacia, Sarmatia.
Sena, Seine.
Servia, Serbia.
Servia - Croacia - Eslovenia, Serb-Croat-Slovene State.
Seúl, Seoul.
Sevilla, Seville.
Severna, Severn.
Sicilia, Sicily.
Sierra Leona, Sierra Leone.
Siracusa, Syracuse.
Siria, Syria.
Socotera, Socotora, Socotra.
Soleura, Soleure.
Somalia, Somaliland.
Suabia, Suabia or Swabia.
Sud-África, Sudáfrica, South Africa.
Sud-América, Sudamérica, South America.
Sudán, Soudan, Sudan.
Suebia = Suabia.
Suecia, Sweden.

Suiza, Switzerland.
Sund, Sound.
Sur-América, or Suramérica, South America.

T

Tabago, Tobago.
Tafilete, Tafilet.
Tahití, Tahiti.
Tajo, Tagus.
Tamatava, Tamatave.
Támesis, Thames.
Tanganyica, Tangañica, Lake Tanganyika.
Tánger, Tangier.
Tapso, Thapsus.
Tarento, Taranto.
Tarso, Tarsus.
Tartaria, Tartary, Tatary.
Tauro, Taurus.
Tebas, Thebes.
Tejas, Texas.
Tenerife, Teneriffe.
Termópilas, Thermopylæ.
Terranova, Newfoundland.
Tesalia, Thessaly.
Tesalónica, Thessalonica.
Tesino, Ticino.
Tiberíades, Tiberias.
Tibet, Thibet.
Tierra de Francisco José, Franz Josef Island.
Tierra del Labrador, Labrador.
Tierra Santa, Holy Land.
Tiro, Tyre.
Tirol, Tyrol.
Tokío, Tokyo, Tokio.
Tolón, Toulon.
Tolosa, Toulouse.
Tornay, Tournay.
Toscana, Tuscany.
Trabizonda, Trebizond.
Tracia, Thrace.
Trasimeno, Thrasimene.
Trebizonda, Trebizond.
Trento, Trent.
Tréveris, Treves.
Trieste, Triest.
Troya, Troy.
Tubinga, Tubingen.
Túnez, Tunis.
Turena, Turenne.
Turquestán, Turkestan.
Turquía, Turkey.
Turs, Tours.
Túsculo, Tusculum.

U

Uberlinga, Uberlingen.
Ucrania, Ukraine.
Ulma, Ulm.
Undervald, Unterwalden.
Unión Sudafricana, Union of South Africa.

V

Valaquia, Wallachia.
Valclusa, Vaucluse.
Valencia, Valence (France); Valencia (Spain).
Valenciennes, Valenciennes.
Valtelina, Valtelline.
Vandoma, Vendome.
Varenas, Varennes.
Varsovia, Warsaw.
Venecia, Venice.
Véneto, Venetia.

For pronunciation. see the rules at the beginning of the book.

Versalles, Versailles.
Vestfalia, Westphalia.
Vesuvio, Vesuvius.
Viena, Vienne (France); Vienna (Austria).
Villafranca, Villefranche.
Vincenas, Vincennes.
Virginia Occidental, West Virginia.
Vizcaya, Biscay.
Vosgos, Vosges.

W

Wartburgo, Wartburg.
Westfalia, Westphalia.
Wurtemberg, Würtemburg.

Y

Yedo, Jeddo, Yeddo.
Yeso, Yesso.
Yugoeslavia, Yugoslavia, Jugoslavia.

Z

Zambese, Zambeze, Zambesi.
Zanguébar, Zanzíbar, Zanzibar.
Zaragoza, Saragossa.
Zebú, Zebu.
Zelandia, Zealand.
Zululandia, Zululand.

NAMES OF PERSONS, INCLUDING THOSE OF FAMOUS HISTORICAL PERSONAGES

A

Abelardo, Abelard.
Abrahán, Abrán, Abraham.
Absalón, Absalom.
Abubéker, Abu-Bekr.
Adán, Adam.
Adela, Adele.
Adelaida, Adelaide.
Adelina, Adeline.
Adolfo, Adolphus.
Adriano, Hadrian.
Ágata, Agatha.
Agripina, Agrippina.
Agueda, Agatha.
Agustín, Augustin, Austin.
Alano, Alan, Allen.
Alarico, Alaric.
Alberto, Albert.
Alberto Magno, Albertus Magnus.
Alceo, Alcæus.
Alejandra, Alexandra.
Alejandro, Alexander.
Alejo, Alexis.
Alfonso, Alphonse.
Alfredo, Alfred.
Alicia, Alice.
Alonso, Alphonsus.
Aluino, Alwin.
Amadeo, Amadeus.
Amata, Amy.
Ambrosio, Ambrose, Ambrosius.
Amelia, Amelie.
Ana, Ann, Anne, Anna, Hannah.
Ana Bolena, Anne Boleyn.
Anacreonte, Anacreon.
Andrés, Andrew.
Aníbal, Hannibal.
Anselmo, Anselm.
Antígono, Antigonus.
Antíoco, Antiochus.
Antonino, Antoninus.
Antonio, Anthony.
Aquiles, Achilles.
Apuleyo, Apuleius.
Arabela, Arabella.
Archibaldo, Archibald.
Aristófanes, Aristophanes.
Aristóteles, Aristotle.
Arnaldo, Arnold.
Arquímedes, Archimedes.
Arturo, Arthur.
Arriano, Arrian.
Arrio, Arius.
Artajerjes, Artaxerxes.
Asurbanipal, Ashur-bani-pal.
Atanasio, Athanasius.
Atila, Attila.
Augusto, Augustus.

Aureliano, Aurelian.
Aurelio, Aurelius.

B

Bárbara, Barbara.
Bartolomé, Bartholomew, Bartholomæus.
Basilio, Basil.
Beatriz, Beatrix, Beatrice.
Beda, Bæda, Bede.
Belisario, Belisarius.
Beltrán, Bertram.
Benita, Benedicta.
Benito, Benedict.
Bermudo, Veremond.
Bernabé, Barnabas, Barnaby.
Bernardo, Bernard.
Bernardino, Bernardinus.
Berta, Bertha.
Betsabé, Bath-Sheba.
Blas, Blase.
Bocaccio, Bocacio, Boccaccio, Boccace.
Bonifacio, Boniface.
Brígida, Bridget.
Bruto, Brutus.
Buda, Buddha.
Buenaventura, Bonaventure.

C

Calvino, Calvin.
Cambises, Cambyses.
Camilla, Camilla.
Camilo, Camillus.
Caracala, Caracalla.
Carlomagno, Charlemagne.
Carlos, Charles.
Carlota, Charlotte.
Carolina, Caroline.
Casandra, Cassandra.
Casimiro, Casimir.
Casio, Cassius.
Catalina, Catharine.
Catilina, Catiline.
Catón, Cato.
Catulo, Catullus.
Cayetano, Cajetan, Gaetan.
Cecilia, Cicely.
Cecilio, Cecil.
César, Cæsar.
Cicerón, Cicero.
Cincinato, Cincinnatus.
Cipriano, Cyprian.
Ciriaco, Cyriacus.
Cirilo, Cyrilus.
Ciro, Cyrus.
Claudia, Claudina, Claudia.
Claudio, Claude, Claudius.
Cleanto, Cleanthes.

Clemente, Clement.
Cleóbulo, Cleobulus.
Clodoveo, Clovis.
Clotilde, Clotilda.
Colón, Columbus.
Cómodo, Commodus.
Confucio, Confucius.
Conrado, Conrad.
Constancia, Constancio, Constance.
Constantino, Constantine.
Constanza, Constance.
Cornelio, Cornelius.
Cosme, Cosmas.
Creso, Crœsus.
Crisóstomo, Chrysostom
Cristiano, Christian.
Cristina, Christina.
Cristo, Christ.
Cristóbal, Christopher
Curcio, Curtius.

D

Dagoberto, Dagobert.
Darío, Darius.
Demócrito, Democritus.
Demóstenes, Demosthenes.
Diego, James.
Diógenes, Diogenes.
Dionisia, Dionysia.
Dionisio, Dennis, Dionysius.
Domiciano, Domitian.
Domingo, Dominic.
Dorotea, Dorothy.

E

Edmundo, Edmund.
Eduardo, Edward.
Eduvigis, Hedwig.
Elagábalo, Elagabalus.
Elena, Ellen, Helen.
Elisa, Eliza.
Eliseo, Elisha, Ellis.
Eloísa, Heloise.
Ema, Emma.
Emilia, Emily.
Emilio, Æmilius.
Eneas, Æneas.
Engracia, Grace.
Enrique, Henry.
Enriqueta, Henrietta.
Epicteto, Epictetus.
Epicurus, Epicuro.
Erasmo, Erasmus.
Eratóstenes, Eratosthenes.
Ernesto, Ernest.
Escalígero, Scaliger.

For pronunciation, see the rules at the beginning of the book.

Escipión, Scipio.
Escipión el Africano, Scipio Africanus.
Esopo, Æsop.
Espartaco, Spartacus.
Esquilo, Æschylus.
Esquines, Æschines.
Esteban, Stephen.
Ester, Esther, Hester.
Estrabón, Strabo.
Estradivario, Stradivarius.
Euclides, Euclid.
Eufemia, Euphemia.
Eufrosina, Euphrosyne.
Eugenia, Eugenie.
Eugenio, Eugene.
Euler, Eulero, Euler.
Eusebio, Eusebius.
Eustaquio, Eustace.
Eva, Eve.
Ezequías, Hezekiah.
Ezequiel, Ezekiel.

F

Fabio, Fabius.
Federica, Frederica.
Federico, Frederic.
Fedra, Phedre.
Fedro, Phædrus.
Felipa, Philippa.
Felipe, Philip.
Felisa, Felicia, Felicia.
Fernando, Ferdinand.
Filipo, Philip (of Macedon), Philippus.
Filo el Judío, Philo Judæus.
Fineas, Phineas.
Florencia, Florencio, Florence.
Foción, Phocion.
Francisca, Frances.
Francisco, Francis.
Fredegunda, Fredegonde.
Froíla, Fruela, Froyla.

G

Galeno, Galen.
Galieno, Gallienus.
Gaspar, Jasper.
Gayo, Gaius.
Gedeón, Gideon.
Genserico, Genseric.
Geofredo, Geffrey.
Gerardo, Gerard.
Germánico, Germanicus.
Gertrudis, Gertrude.
Gervasio, Gervas.
Gil, Giles.
Gilberto, Gilbert.
Godofredo, Gofredo, Godfrey.
Graco, Gracchus.
Gracos, Gracchi.
Gregorio, Gregory.
Gualterio, Gualtero, Walter.
Guido, Guy.
Guillelmo, Guillén, William.
Guillermina, Wilhelmina.
Guillermo, William.
Gustavo, Gustavus.

H

Haroldo, Harold.
Heberto, Herbert.
Heliogábalo, Elagabalus.
Helvecio, Helvetius.
Heráclito, Heraclitus.

Heriberto, Herbert.
Herodes, Herod.
Herodoto, Herodotus.
Herón, Hiero.
Hesíodo, Hesiod.
Hilario, Hilary.
Hildebrando, Hildebrand.
Hiparco, Hipparchus.
Hipócrates, Hippocrates.
Homero, Homer.
Honorio, Honorius.
Horacio, Horace, Horatio.
Hortensia, Hortense.
Huberto, Hobart, Hubert.
Hugo, Hugh.
Hugo Capeto, Hugh Capet.
Humberto, Humbert.
Hunfredo, Humphrey.

I

Ignacio, Ignatius.
Ildefonso, Alphonsus.
Inés, Agnes, Inez.
Inocencio, Innocent.
Ireneo, Ireneus.
Isabel, Elizabeth.
Isidoro, Isidro, Isidor.

J

Jacobo, Jaime, James.
Jansenio, Jansen, Jansenius.
Javier, Xavier.
Jehová, Jehovah.
Jenócrates, Xenocrates.
Jenófanes, Xenophanes.
Jenofonte, Xenophon.
Jeremías, Jeremy, Jeremiah.
Jerjes, Xerxes.
Jerónimo, Jerome.
Jesús, Jesus.
Jesucristo, Jesus Christ.
Joaquín, Joachim.
Jonás, Jonah.
Jonatán, Jonatás, Jonathan.
Jorge, George.
José, Joseph.
Josefa, Josefina, Josephine.
Josefo, Josephus.
Josías, Josiah.
Josué, Joshua.
Joviano, Jovian.
Juan, John.
Juana, Jane, Jennie, Jean, Joan, Joanna.
Juana de Arco, Joan of Arc.
Judit, Judith.
Julia, Julia.
Julián; Juliano (emperor), Julian.
Julio, Julius.
Justiniano, Justinian.
Justino, Justin.
Justino Mártir, Justin Martyr.

K

(de) Kempis, (a) Kempis.

L

Ladislao, Ladislas.
Lamberto, Lambert.
Lázaro, Lazarus.
Leandro, Leander.
León, Leo, Leon.
Leonardo, Leonard.

Leonor, Eleanor.
Leopoldo, Leopold.
Leticia, Lætitia, Letitia, Lettice.
Licurgo, Lycurgus.
Lineo, Linnæus.
Lisandro, Lysander.
Lisias, Lysias.
Lisímaco, Lysimachus.
Lisipo, Lysippus.
Liutprando, Liutprand.
Livio, Livy.
Longino, Longinus.
Lorenzo, Lawrence, Laurence.
Lotario, Lothaire.
Lucano, Lucan.
Lucas, Luke.
Lucía, Lucy, Lucia.
Luciano, Lucian.
Lucio, Lucius.
Lucrecia, Lucretia.
Lucrecio, Lucretius.
Luis, Lewis, Louis.
Luis (Gonzaga), Aloysius.
Luisa, Louise.
Lutero, Luther.

M

Magallanes, Magellan.
Magdalena, Magdalen.
Mahoma, Mahomet, Mohammed.
Malaquías, Malachi.
Manuel, Emanuel.
Manuela, Emma.
Marcelo, Marcellus.
Marcial, Martial.
Marco, Marcos, Mark.
Marco Aurelio, Marcus Aurelius.
Margarita, Margaret, Margery.
María, Mary, Maria, Miriam.
María Luisa, Marie Louise.
Mariana, Marian.
Mario, Marius.
Marta, Martha.
Masinisa, Masinissa.
Mateo, Matthew.
Matías, Mattias.
Matilde, Matilda.
Mauricio, Maurice, Morice.
Maximiliano, Maximilian.
Mecenas, Mæcenas.
Mesalina, Messalina.
Miguel, Michael.
Miguel Ángel, Michelangelo.
Mitrídates, Mithridates.
Moisés, Moses.

N

Nabucodonosor, Nebuchadnezzar.
Nápier, Napier.
Natán, Nathan.
Nataniel, Nathaniel.
Nehemías, Nehemiah.
Néper, Napier.
Népote, Nepos.
Nerón, Nero.
Nestorio, Nestorius.
Nicolás, Nicholas.
Noé, Noah.

O

Octavio, Octavius.
Odoacro, Odoacer.

Oliverio, Oliver.
Orígenes, Origen.
Oseas, Hosea.
Osmundo, Osmond.
Otman, Othman.
Otón, Otho.
Ovidio, Ovid.

P

Pablo, Paul.
Patricio, Patrick.
Paula, Paulina, Pauline.
Pedro, Peter.
Pepino, Pepin.—**P. el Breve,** Pepin the Short.
Peregrín, or **Peregrino,** Peregrine.
Perseo, Perseus.
Píndaro, Pindər.
Pío, Pius.
Pirro, Pyrrhus.
Pitágoras, Pythagoras.
Platón, Plato.
Plauto, Plautus.
Plinio, Pliny.
Plótino, Plotinus.
Plutarco, Plutarch.
Polibio, Polybius.
Policarpo, Polycarp.
Policleto, Polycletus.
Polícrates, Polycrates.
Pompeyo, Pompey.
Pretorio, Pretorius.
Proclo, Proclus.
Procopio, Procopius.
Prudencia, Prudence.

Q

Quintiliano, Quintilian.
Quintín, Quintin, Quentin.

R

Rafael, Raphael.
Raimundo, Ramón, Raymond.
Randolfo, Randolph.
Raquel, Rachel.
Rebeca, Rebecca.
Reginaldo, Reginald.
Régulo, Regulus.
Reinaldo, Reynold.

Renaldo, Ronald.
Renato, René.
Ricardo, Richard.
Roberto, Robert.
Rodas, Rhodes.
Rodolfo, Rodolphus, Ralph, Rudolph, Rollo.
Rodrigo, Roderic.
Roger, Rogerio, Roger.
Rolando, Roland, Rowland.
Rolón, Rollón, Rollo.
Rómulo, Romulus.
Rosa, Rose.
Rosalía, Rosalie.
Rosamunda, Rosamond.
Rosario, Rosary.
Rubén, Reuben.
Rufo, Rufus.
Ruperto, Rupert.

S

Saladino, Saladin.
Salomón, Solomon.
Salustio, Sallust.
Samuel, Samuel.
Sansón, Samson.
Santiago, James, St. James.
Sara, Sarah.
Sardanápalo, Sardanapalus.
Senaquerib, Sennacherib.
Sertorio, Sertorius.
Severo, Severus.
Sigismundo, Sigismund.
Sila, Sulla.
Silvano, Silvan.
Silvestre, Silvester.
Sofía, Sophia, Sophy.
Sófocles, Sophocles.
Solimán, Solyman, Suleiman.
Suetonio, Suetonius.
Susana, Susan, Susanna.

T

Tácito, Tacitus.
Tadeo, Thadeus.
Tales, Thales.
Tamerlán, Tamerlane.
Temístocles, Themistocles.
Teobaldo, Theobald, Tybold.
Teócrito, Theocritus.
Teodora (woman), **Teodoro** (man), Theodore.

Teodorico, Theodoric, Dorick.
Teodosio, Theodosius.
Teófilo, Theophilus.
Teofrasto, Theophrastus
Terencio, Terence.
Teresa, Theresa.
Tertuliano, Tertullian.
Tiberio, Tiberius.
Tíbulo, Tibullus.
Ticiano, Titian.
Timoteo, Timothy.
Timur, Timour.
Tito, Titus.
Tobías, Tobias, Toby.
Tolomeo, Ptolemy.
Tomás, Thomas.
Trajano, Trajan.
Trasíbulo, Thrasybulus.
Triboniano, Tribonian.
Tucídides, Thucydides.
Turena, Turenne.

U

Ulpiano, Ulpian.
Urbano, Urban.
Urías, Uriah.

V

Valente, Valens.
Valentín, Valentine.
Valentiniano, Valentinian.
Valeriano, Valerian.
Ventura, Bonaventura.
Veremundo, Veremond.
Veronés, Veronese.
Vespasiano, Vespasian.
Vespucio, Vespucci.
Vicente, Vincent.
Virgilio, Virgil, Vergil.
Vitruvio, Vitruvius.

Y

Yugurta, Jugurtha.

Z

Zacarías, Zachary, Zachariah.
Zenón, Zeno.
Zoroastro, Zoroaster.
Zuinglio, Zwingli.

COLLOQUIAL PET NAMES

Adela, Adelita, Adelina.
Ana, Anita, Anica.
Antonio, nia, Antoñito, ta; Toño, ña; Toñico, ca.
Bartolomé, Bartolo.
Carlos, Carlitos.
Catalina, Catana, Catuca, Catuja.
Cayetano, Tano.
Cristóbal, Tobal, Tobalito.
Diego, Dieguito.
Dolores. V. MARÍA DE LOS DOLORES.
Francisco, Francisquito; Frasco, Frascuelo, Frasquito; Pa-

quito, Paco; Pacorro; Pancho, Panchito; Curro, Currito; Farruco.
Francisca (the same words as the preceding, changing final *o* to *a*).
Gertrudis, Tula.
Gregorio, Goyo.
Isabel, Belica, Belita.
Jaime, Jaimito.
José, Joseíto, Josecito; Pepe, Pepito; Pepillo; Chepe, Chepito.
Josefa, Josefita; Pepa, Pepita, Pepilla; Chepa, Chepita.

Juan, Juanito, Juanillo.
Juana, Juanita, Juanilla.
María, Mariquita, Mariquilla, Marica, Maruca, Marucha, Maruja.
María de la Concepción, Concha, Conchita; Chona, Cota, Cotita.
María (de) Jesús, Jesusa, Jesusita, Chucha, Chuchita.
María de los Dolores, Doloritas, Dolorcitas, Lola, Lolita.
María de la Luz, Lucecita, Lucita.
Pedro, Pedrito, Perico.

For pronunciation, see the rules at the beginning of the book.

ABBREVIATIONS MOST COMMONLY USED IN SPANISH

A

A. Alteza; aprobado (passed in examination).
a. área (are).
(a) alias.
@ arroba; **@@** arrobas.
AA. Autores; Altezas.
ab. abad.
ab¹. abril.
Abls. gen. Absolución general.
A. C., A. de C. Año de Cristo (A.D.).
admón. administración.
admor., adm.ᵒʳ administrador.
af.ᵐᵒ, afmo. afectísimo.
af.ᵗᵒ afecto.
Ag.ⁿ Agustín.
a la v/ a la vista.
ag.ᵗᵒ agosto.
alc.ᵈᵉ alcalde.
Alej.ᵒ Alejandro.
Alf.ᵒ Alfonso.
Al.ᵒ Alonso.
A L. R. P. de V. M. A los reales pies de Vuestra Majestad.
Álv.ᵒ Álvaro.
am.ᵒ amigo.
Ant.ᵒ Antonio.
ap. aparte; apóstol.
ap.ᵃ, ap.ᵒ or **aplica., aplico.** apostólica, apostólico.
apóst. apóstol.
art., art.ᵒ artículo.
arz., arzbpo. arzobispo.
att.ᵒ, atto. atento.
Aud.ᵃ Audiencia.

B

B. Beato; Bueno, en examen.
Bar.ᵐᵉ Bartolomé.
bca. barrica.
Barna. Barcelona.
Bern.ᵒ Bernardo.
B. L. M., b. l. m. besa la mano.
B. L. P., b. l. p. besa los pies.
B.ᵐᵒ P.ᵉ Beatísimo Padre.
Br. or **br.** bachiller.
bto. bulto; bruto.

C

c/ cargo; contra.
C. A. corriente alterna.
c.ᵃ compañía.
c., cap. capítulo.
cap.ⁿ capitán.
capp.ⁿ capellán.
Card.¹ Cardenal.
C. C. corriente continua.
C. de J. Compañía de Jesús (S. J.)
cénts. céntimos.
cf., conf., confr. confesor; confirma (in ancient documents).
cg. centigramo(s.
C.ⁱᵃ Compañía (Co.)
cl. centilitro(s.
Clem.ᵗᵉ Clemente.
cllo. cuartillo.
cm. centímetro(s.
C. M. B., c. m. b. cuyas manos beso.
Co. Compañía (Co.)
col., col.ᵃ columna; colonia.
comis.ᵒ comisario.
comp. compañía.
cons.ᵒ consejo.
Const. Constitución.
const.¹ constitucional.
conv.ᵗᵉ conveniente.
corr.ᵗᵉ corriente.
C. P. B. cuyos pies beso.
crec.ᵗᵉ creciente.
cs. cuartos; céntimos.
cta., c.ᵗᵃ cuenta.
cta. cte., cta. corr.ᵗᵉ cuenta corriente.
c/u cada uno.
cuad. cuadrado(s.
c/vta. cuenta de venta.

D

D. Don.
D.ᵃ Doña.
DD. doctores.
descto. descuento.
d/f días fecha.
dg. decigramo(s.
Dg. decagramo(s.
dha., dho., dhas., dhos. dicha, dicho, dichas, dichos.
dic.ᵒ, 10ᵒ or **10ᵇʳᵉ** diciembre.
Dl. decalitro(s.
dl. decilitro(s.
dls. dólares ($).
Dm. decámetro(s.
dm. decímetro(s.
D.ⁿ, d.ⁿ don.

dna(s. docena(s.
Doct., Doctor.
docum.ᵗᵒ documento.
D. O. M. *Deo Optimo Maximo.*
Dom.ᵒ Domingo (name).
dom.ᵒ domingo (Sunday).
d/p días plazo.
D.ʳ, Dr. Doctor (Dr.)
dra., dro., dras., dros. derecha, derecho, derechas, derechos.
dup.ᵈᵒ duplicado.
d/v días vista.

E

E. este, oriente (East).
ec.ᶜᵒ eclesiástico.
EE. UU. Estados Unidos.
E. M. Estado Mayor.
Em.ᵃ Eminencia.
E. M. G. Estado Mayor General.
Em.ᵐᵒ, Emmo. Eminentísimo.
ENE. estenordeste (E.N.E.).
en.ᵒ enero.
E. P. D. En paz descanse.
E. P. M. En propia mano.
esc.ᵒ escudo.
escrit.ᵃ escritura.
escrnía. escribanía.
escrno. escribano.
escs. escudos.
ESE. estesudeste (E.S.E.).
etc. etcétera.
E. U., E. U. A. U. S., U. S. A.
Eug.ᵒ Eugenio.
Evang.ᵒ Evangelio.
Evang.ᵗᵃ Evangelista.
Exc.ᵃ Excelencia.
Exc.ᵐᵃ, Exc.ᵐᵒ or **Excma, Excmo.** Excelentísima, Excelentísimo.

F

f/ fardo(s.
F. Fulano.
fact.ᵃ factura.
F. C., f. c. ferrocarril.
F.ᶜᵒ, Franc.ᵒ Francisco.
fcos. francos.
F. de T. Fulano de Tal.
feb.ᵒ febrero.
F. E. M. fuerza electromotriz (E.M.F.).

Fern.do Fernando.

fha., fho. fecha, fecho.

fo.o, fol. folio.

Fr. Fray, Frey.

fra. factura.

Frnz., Fz. Fernández.

F.s, f.s francos.

fund. fundador.

G

G. gracia.

g. gramo(s.

g.de or gue. guarde.

Gen.l General (title).

gnte., gerente.

G.o Gonzalo.

gob.o gobierno.

gob.r gobernador.

Gonz. González.

gral. general.

Greg.o Gregorio.

gte. gerente.

Guill.o Guillermo.

H

hect. hectárea(s.

Hg. hectogramo(s.

Hl. hectolitro(s.

Hm. hectómetro(s.

HP, H. P. caballo(s) de vapor (H.P.).

I

Ib. ibídem.

Id. ídem.

i. e. id est (that is).

igl.a iglesia.

Ign.o Ignacio.

Ildef.o Ildefonso.

Il.e Ilustre.

Il.ma, Il.mo, Ilīma, Ilīmo. Ilustrísima, Ilustrísimo.

in p. inf. in partibus infidelium.

Inq.r inquisidor.

intend.te intendente.

ít. ítem.

izq.a, izq.o, izq.da, izq.do izquierda, izquierdo.

J

J. C. Jesucristo.

Jerón.o Jerónimo.

Jhs. Jesús.

Jph. José.

juev. jueves.

Jul.n Julián.

K

Kg., kg. kilogramo(s.

Kl., kl. kilolitro(s.

Km., km. kilómetro(s.

kv., k. w. kilovatio.

L

L/ letra.

L., L.do or l.do Licenciado.

l. ley; libro; litro(s.

lb̄(s. libra(s.

lín. línea.

liq.n liquidación.

Lor.zo Lorenzo.

L. S. Locus sigilli, lugar del sello.

lun. lunes.

M

M. Madre, religiosa; Majestad; Merced; Maestro; mediano (en examen).

m. minuto(s; metro(s; mañana (A.M.).

m/ mes; mi, mis; mío, míos.

Man.l Manuel.

M.a María.

Marg.ta Margarita.

mart. martes.

may.mo mayordomo.

mcos. marcos.

M.o Madre, religiosa.

m/f mi favor.

meng. menguante.

mg. miligramo(s.

miérc. miércoles.

Mig.l Miguel.

milés.s milésimas.

min.o ministro.

m/L mi letra.

ml. mililitros.

Mm. miriámetro(s.

mm., m/m milímetro(s.

m/o mi orden.

m/ o m/ más o menos.

monast.o monasterio.

Mons. Monseñor.

M. P. S. Muy Poderoso Señor.

Mr. Monsieur; Mister.

mrd. merced.

Mrn. Martín.

Mrnz. Martínez.

Mro. Maestro.

M.s marcos.

M. S. manuscrito.

m.s a.s muchos años.

M.SS. manuscritos.

N

N. Norte.

n. noche (P.M.).

n/ nuestro.

N.a S.a Nuestra Señora.

N.B. Nota bene.

n/cta. nuestra cuenta.

NE. Nordeste (N.E.).

NNE. Nornordeste (N.N.E.).

NNO. Nornoroeste (N.N.W.).

NO. Noroeste (N.W.).

n.o número.

nov.e, 9e, 9bre noviembre.

Nov. Recop. Novísima Recopilación.

N. Recop. Nueva Recopilación.

nra., nro., nras., nros.; ntra., ntro., ntras., ntros. nuestra, nuestro, nuestras, nuestros.

núm. or núm.o, núms. or núm.s número, números.

N. S. Nuestro Señor.

N. S. J. C. Nuestro Señor Jesucristo.

nto. neto.

O

O. Oeste (W.).

o/ orden.

ob., obpo. obispo.

oct.e, 8e or 8bre octubre.

ONO. oestenoroeste (W.N.W.).

onz. onza.

orn. orden.

OSO. oessudoeste (W.S.W.).

P

P. Papa (Pope); padre; pregunta.

p % por ciento (%).

p %o por mil.

p. A. Por ausencia: por autorización.

P.a para.

pág., págs. página(s.

Part. Partida.

Patr. Patriarca.

pbro., presb. presbítero.

P. D. Posdata (P.S.).

P.e Padre.

p. ej. por ejemplo (e. g.).

penit. penitente.

perg., pno. pergamino.

Pf., Pfs. peso(s fuerte(s.

P. M. Padre Maestro.

P. O. Por orden.

P.o Pedro.

p.o pero.

P. P. Porte pagado; por poder.

p. p.do, ppdo. próximo pasado.

For pronunciation, see the rules at the beginning of the book.

p.^r por.

pral. principal.

priv. privilegio.

proc. procesión.

prof. profesor; profeta.

pror. procurador.

prov.^a provincia.

prov.^{or} provisor.

próx.^o próximo.

P. S. *Post scríptum* (P.S.).

P. S. M. Por su mandato.

ps. pesos.

pta. pasta.

ptas. pesetas.

p.^{te} parte.

pza. pieza.

Q

q. que.

Q. B. S. M., **q. b. s. m.** que besa su mano.

Q. B. S. P., **q. b. s. p.** que besa sus pies.

Q. D. G. que Dios guarde.

q.^e que.

q. e. g. e. que en gloria esté.

q. e. p. d. que en paz descanse.

q. e. s. m. que estrecha su mano.

q. g. g. que gloria goce.

qq. quintales.

R

R. Reverendo; reverencia; respuesta; reprobado (en examen).

R). Responde o respuesta (in prayer-books).

Raf.^l Rafael.

Rbí. Recibí.

R. D. Real Decreto.

Rda. M., **R. M.** Reverenda Madre.

Rdo. P., **R. P.** Reverendo Padre.

R.^e Récipe.

R. I. P. *Requiescat in pace.*

r.^l real (royal).

Rmrz. Ramírez.

R. O. Real Orden.

r. p. m. revoluciones por minuto (r. p. m.).

R. S. Real Servicio.

rs., r.^s reales (money).

R.^s Reales (of the king, royal).

rúst. rústica.

S

S. San, Santo; Sur; Sobresaliente (en examen).

s/ su, sus; sobre.

S.^a Señora.

S. A. Su Alteza.

sáb. sábado.

S. A. I. Su Alteza Imperial.

S. A. R. Su Alteza Real.

S. A. S. Su Alteza Serenísima.

Sb.ⁿ Sebastián.

s/c su cuenta.

S. C., s. c. su casa.

S. C. M. Sacra Católica Majestad.

S. C. C. R. M. Sacra, Cesárea, Católica, Real Majestad.

s/cta. su cuenta.

S. D. Se despide (p. p. c.).

S. D. M. Su Divina Majestad.

SE. sudeste (S.E.).

secret.^a secretaría.

sept.^o, 7^e or 7bre septiembre.

Ser.^{ma}, Ser.^{mo} or Serm.^a, Sermo. Serenísima, Serenísimo.

serv.^o servicio.

serv.^{or} servidor.

set.^e septiembre.

S. E. u O. salvo error u omisión.

sig.^{te} siguiente.

S. M. Su Majestad.

S. M. A. Su Majestad Apostólica.

S. M. B. Su Majestad Británica.

S. M. C. Su Majestad Católica.

S. M. F. Su Majestad Fidelísima.

S. M. I. Su Majestad Imperial.

S.ⁿ San.

S. N. Servicio Nacional.

SO. sudoeste (S.W.).

Sor. Señor.

Sores. Señores.

spre. siempre.

S.^r, Sr. Señor.

Sra., Sras. Señora, Señoras.

Sres., S.^{res} Señores.

Sría. Secretaría.

S.^{ria}, S.^{rio} or sria., srio. secretaria, secretario.

S. R. M. Su Real Majestad.

S^{rta}., Srta. Señorita.

S. S. Su Santidad.

S. S.^a Su Señoría.

SS. AA. Sus Altezas.

SS.E. subsudeste (S.S.E.).

SS. MM. Sus Majestades.

SS.^{mo} Santísimo.

SS.^{mo} P. Santísimo Padre.

SS.^{no} escribano.

SSO. sudsudoeste (S.S.W.).

S. S. S., **s. s. s.** Su seguro servidor.

Sta. Santa; Señorita.

Sto. Santo.

sup. suplica.

supert.^{te} superintendente.

supl.^{te} suplente.

sup.^{te} suplicante.

T

t. tarde.

ten.^{te} teniente.

test.^{mto} testamento.

test.^o testigo.

tít., tít.^o título.

tpo. tiempo.

trib.^l tribunal.

t.^o, tom. tomo.

U

U., Ud. usted.

Uds., UU. ustedes.

V

V. usted; venerable; véase.

V., Vers.^o Versículo.

V.^a Vigilia.

V. A. Vuestra Alteza.

V. A. R. Vuestra Alteza Real.

V. B.^d Vuestra Beatitud.

Vd. usted.

Vds. ustedes.

V. E. Vuestra Excelencia or Vuecencia.

vencim.^{to} vencimiento.

vg. verbigracia; virgen.

v. g., v. gr. verbigracia.

Vict.^a Victoria.

Vic.^{te} Vicente.

vier. viernes.

V. M. Vuestra Majestad.

Vm., Vmd. Vuestra Merced; Usted.

vn. vellón.

V.^o B.^o Visto bueno.

vol. volumen; voluntad.

vols. volúmenes.

V. P. Vuestra Paternidad.

V. R. Vuestra Reverencia.

vra., vro., vras., vros. vuestra, vuestro, vuestras, vuestros.

v.^s, vs. varas.

V. S. Vueseñoría, Usía.

V. S. I. Vueseñoría (or Usía) Ilustrísima.

v.^{ta}, v.^{to} vuelta, vuelto.

V. V., VV. ustedes.

SUPPLEMENT
TO THE SPANISH-ENGLISH PART

NOTE—In this Supplement are given several words and phrases that, although not strictly correct, some of them being grotesque and atrocious barbarisms, occur often in Spanish-language publications.

A

a, *prep.*—**al, a la,** at the end of, or after, a (*a la semana,* at the end of a week, a week after). Often used to indicate the addition of or treatment with a material or substance, or a distinguishing ingredient (*acero al carbono,* carbon steel; *acero al níquel,* nickel steel; *bronce al aluminio,* aluminum bronze; *papel al bromuro,* bromide paper, paper treated with bromide; *papel a la gelatina,* gelatine, or gelatinized, paper).—**a la,** a la, after the manner of the (*a la francesa,* a la French, after the manner of the French, in the French style).—**a las, a los,** after, at the end of (*a los dos meses,* two months after). (*V.* A LA.)—**a lo** (followed by *n.*) like a, after the manner of (with *n.* in the plural) (*a lo filósofo,* after the manner of philosophers; *a lo bobo,* like a fool).—**a lo que,** from what, as (*a lo que veo,* ¡from what I see; *a lo que parece,* as it seems, as far as one can judge); when, as soon as.—**a que,** I bet that.—**a qué,** what for, what does it avail, what is the use.

abactor, ra, *n.* horse thief.
abaniquería, *f.* fan factory; fan shop.
abarcar, *va.* to corner, control (the market).—**quien mucho abarca poco aprieta,** he who undertakes too much accomplishes little, one shouldn't bite off more than one can chew.
abarrotes, *m. pl.,* goods; foodstuffs.
abasto, *m.*—**dar a.** (a), to be sufficient; to provide, furnish.
abatimiento de costado, (aer.) side drift.
abatir, *va.* to bring down, shoot down.
abeto del norte, falso, or **rojo,** spruce.
abey, *m.* (bot.) West-Indian bastard mahogany.
ablepsia, *f.* ablepsia, blindness; lack or loss of intelligence.
abocinado, da, *a.* funnel- or trumpet-shaped; droopy, with the head hanging down (s. o. horses).
abocinar, *vn.* to fall face downward.
abombarse, *vr.* to begin to decompose or spoil (s. o. liquids, meat, etc.)
abordar, *va.* to attack (a subject), enter upon, deal with.
aborrachado, da, *a.* bright red.
abrasar. I. *va.* to shame, humiliate. **II.** *vr.* (with **en** or **de**), to burn (with); to boil (with).
abribonado, da, *a.* rascally, knavish.
abrigador, ra. I. *a.* protecting; warm (s. o. clothes). **II.** *n. & a.* concealer (-ing).
abrir. I. *va.* to head, lead.—**a. paso,** to make way; to clear the way. **II.** *vr.* to burst or break open; to fall out, become estranged.
absintemia, *f.* presence of absinth in the blood.
absoluto, *a.*—**en a.,** unqualifiedly, peremptorily; absolutely; (in negative sentences) at all.—**lo a.,** the absolute.
abuje, *m.* (zool.) a Cuban mite parasitic in plants and man, causing the itch.
abundar, *vn.*—**lo que abunda no daña,** abundance of a good thing never is too much; better too much than too little.
abuso de confianza, betrayal of confidence .
acabar por, to end by, to . . . finally (ch. constr.: *Juan acabó por decir,* John ended by saying, John said finally).
academia, *f.* literary contest; meeting; (f. a.) academy figure.
acahual, *m.* weeds; stubble, weed-grown field.
acantilado, da. I. *a.* stepped (mainly s. o. the bottom of the sea). **II.** *m.* scarp, escarpment.

acatólico, ca, *n. & a.* noncatholic.
acáudeo, a, *a.* acaudal, tailless.
accesión, *f.* sexual intercourse; (law) accession (as a mode of acquiring property).
acceso del sol, (ast.) apparent motion of the sun towards the equator.
acepción, or **aceptación, de personas,** unfair distinction, or discrimination, among persons.
acera, *f.* (arch.) face (of a wall); facing stone (of a wall).
acerado, da, *a.* steel (u. a.); steel-like; strong; biting, cutting, acrimonious.
acerar, *va.* to convert (iron) into steel; to cover with steel; (arch.) to lay the facing stones of (a wall).
acero al carbono, etc. *V.* A.
acionera, *f.* piece of the saddle from which the stirrup strap hangs.
aclarar, aclarear, *vn.* to dawn.
aclasto, a, *a.* (opt.) aclastic.
acleido, da, *a.* (zool.) acleidian, aclidian, having no clavicles.
aclínico, ca. I. *a.* (phys.) aclinic. **II.** *m.* opera glasses.
acolchado, *m.* (hyd. eng.) mattress.
acondicionamiento, *m.* conditioning; drying (of silk, etc.).—**acondicionar,** *va.* to condition.
aconsejante, *n. & a.* adviser (-ing).
acreedor, ra, *a.* creditor (u. a.)
acreencia, *f.* debt claimed.
acriollarse, *vr.* (Am.) to become a creole, to adopt the native ways and customs (s. o. Europeans and Anglo-Americans).
acrobacia, *f.* (aer.) fancy air maneuver, stunt.
acrocéfalo, la, *a.* acrocephalous.
acta, *f.*—**levantar, a.,** to write or set down a record.—**tomar a.,** to note, set down; to bear in mind.
acuchillar, *va.* to knife; put to the knife or the sword.
acueducto, *m.* water-supply line, main.
acuerdo, *m.* agreement, convention, pact.
acutí, *m.* (zool.) agouti.
achaparrarse, *vr.* (agr.) not to grow or thrive, to become stunted.
adarme, *m* —**por adarmes,** in driblets, stingily.
adelante, *adv.*—**llevar, a.,** to go ahead with, advance, carry on.—**salir a.,** to come through, succeed, come out well or ahead.
ademán, *m., pl.,* manners.—**en a. de,** as if getting ready, or going, to, showing an intention to or of.
adhesividad, *f.* concentration of mind; love of one's fellow beings.
adifés, *adv.* on purpose.
adinerar. I. *va.* to reduce to cash, turn into cash. **II.** *vr.* to get rich.
aditamento, *m.*—**por a.** = POR AÑADIDURA.
adjuntar, *va.* to enclose, send enclosed or with something else.
adocenamiento, *m.* counting or arranging by dozens, or dividing into dozens.
adosar, *va.* to put on or near something; to paste (as on a wall).
aduanar, *va.* to pass or put through the custom-house.
aduanilla, *f.* food store.
adyacencia, *f.* adjacency, contiguity.

For pronunciation, see the rules at the beginning of the book.

aéreo, a, *a.* overhead; elevated; air (u. a., as in **fuerzas aéreas,** air forces).

aerodinámico, ca, *a.* streamline(d.

aerostero, ra, *a.* aviation (u. a.). aeronautic.

afanoso, sa, *a.* arduous, hard, difficult.

afectividad, *f.* affection; (psych.) affectivity.

afición, *f.* eagerness, enthusiasm.—**tomar a. a,** to take a liking to, become fond of.

agalla, *f.*—**tener a.,** to have vim, be enterprising; (Am.) to be greedy; (Col. & Ec.) to be stingy; (Peru) to be shrewd, cunning, wily.

agamí, *m.* (orn.) trumpeter.

agarrón, *m.* fight, scrap, scuffle, encounter.

agente, *m. & f.*—**a. de bolsa, de cambio,** or **de cambio y bolsa,** exchange notary.—**a. provacador,** agent provocateur.

agibílibus, *m.* cleverness, slickness; clever or slick person.

aglutición, *f.* (med.) aglutition.

agónico, ca, *a.* agony (u. a.), relating to the death struggle.

agrado, *m.*—**ser del a. de uno,** to be to one's taste, to please one, have one's approval.

agrietamiento, *m.* cracking; crack, fissure.

agropecuario, ria, *a.* agricultural and cattle (u. a.).

agua, *f.*—**a. angélica,** manna water.—**a. de cal,** lime water.—**a. de Colonia,** Cologne water.—**a. de pie,** running water (s. o. spring and stream water).—**a. manantial,** spring water.—**a. muerta,** stagnant water.—**aguas vertientes,** drainage, drain water, flowoff; water shed, basin.—**estar con el a. hasta la boca,** to be in great difficulties, to be in a bad fix, or tight box.—**estar entre dos aguas,** to be undecided, be on the fence.—**nadie diga,** or **no hay que decir, de esta a. no beberé,** don't be too sure that the same thing won't happen to you, or that you won't do that very thing.

aguamasa, *f.* crushed-corn washings.

aguatero, ra, *n.* water carrier.

agujetear, *va.* to lace, sew with strips.

ahí, *adv.*—**a. donde lo (la) ve,** although he (she) doesn't look it, although you wouldn't expect it.—**de por a.,** insignificant, nothing much.—**por a.,** some place hereabouts, somewhere around.

aire, *m.*—**por a.,** by air.—**por el a.,** or **por los aires,** very rapidly, posthaste, like lightning.

alambrar, *va.* to put a wire fence around, fence in with wire.

alargarse, *vr.* to go or move away; to deviate; to expatiate, enlarge.

alberca (natatoria, de natación), swimming pool.

albuminina, *f.* (chem.) albuminin.

albumosa, *f.* (chem.) albumose.

alcahuete, ta, *n.* go-between; aider, abettor; gossip.—**alcahuetear,** *va.* to aid, protect, abet.

alcance, *m.* importance; last-minute news; (comm.) deficit; *pl.* understanding, grasp, mental powers.—**al a. de,** within reach of.—**dar a. a,** to overtake.

alcantarillado, *m.* sewerage, sewerage system; sewering, providing with sewers.

alcurnia, *f.* pedigree, lineage, blood.

aldaba, *f.*—**tener buena a.,** or **buenas aldabas,** to be well protected, be pretty safe.

alergia, *f.* allergy.—**alérgico, ca,** *a.* allergic.

alferazgo, *m.* second lieutenancy.

alfiler, *m.* tip, gift.—**a. de París,** flat-head tack.—**no estar con sus alfileres,** not to be in a good mood.—**pedir para alfileres,** to ask for a tip. —**pegar,** or **prender, con alfileres,** to do in a slipshod way; to build on a sand foundation (fig.)

algesia, *f.* (med.) algesia.

algodón pólvora, guncotton.

alguno, na, *a.*—**a. que otro,** a few, some.— **alguna que otra vez,** sometimes, once in a while.

aliviadero, *m.* (eng.) relief, outlet; spillway.

alma, *f.*—**a. atravesada, de Caín,** or **de Judas,** devilish or heartless person.—**a. mía,** my dearest, my darling.—**a., vida y corazón,** heart and soul.— **del a., de mi a.,** dearest.

alogamia, *f.* allogamy.

alta, *f.*—**dar de a.,** to enroll, admit (in the army); to discharge as cured, or declare fit.

altibajos, *m. pl.* ups and downs.

altiplanicie, *f.,* **altiplano,** *m.* plateau, tableland.

alto, *m.* summit, mountain top, crest; top floor; heap, pile.—**altos y bajos,** ups and downs, vicissitudes.

alverja, *f.* (Chile, Col.) garden pea.

allá, *adv.*—**a. veremos,** we shall see.—**a. voy,** I am coming.—**el más a.,** the beyond.—**por a.,** through there, that way.

allegado, da, *n.* relative.

allí, *adv.*—¡**a. fué Troya!** there the trouble began, there was the hitch, or the difficulty.— **por a.,** there, thereabouts.

ama de huéspedes, boarding-house keeper.

amanecer. I. *m.*—**al a.,** at dawn, at daybreak. **II.** *vn.*—**amanecerá y veremos,** we shall see.

amanecida, *f.* dawn, daybreak.

ametrallar, *va.* to shell; to machine-gun.

amibo, *m.* =AMIBA.

amílico, ca, *a.* amyl (alcohol).

amortiguar, *va.* (rad.) to damp (waves).

ancla flotante, (aer.) drogue, sea anchor.

ancón, *s.* corner; (arch.) bracket.

andar, *vn.* to be.—**a. en,** to be attending to, or engaged in; to be going on, be near (*Juan anda en los veinte años,* John is going on twenty years).— **a más,** or **a todo, a.,** at full speed, quickly.

anfiteatro (anatómico), *m.* dissecting room (of a hospital or medical school).

ánfora, *f.* ballot box.

angas.—**por a. o por mangas,** in any case, some way or other, anyhow.

ángulo, *m.*—**a. de derrape,** (aer.) angle of yaw. —**a. de incidencia,** (phys.) angle of incidence; (aer.) angle of attack.—**a. de incidencia creciente,** (aer.) washin.—**a. de incidencia decreciente,** (aer.) washout.—**a. de planeo,** (aer.) gliding angle.

anhelante, *a.* eager, deeply desirous, longing.

anilismo, *m.* aniline poisoning.

anillo, *m.* ring.—**a. de boda,** wedding ring.—**a. de matrimonio,** engagement ring.—**de a.,** honorary.

ánimo, *m.*—**hacer,** or **tener, a. de,** to intend to, make up one's mind to.

anochecer, *m.* nightfall, dusk.—**al a.,** at nightfall, at dusk.

antideslizante, *a.* nonskidding (said mainly of automobile tires).

anticuerpo, *m.* antibody.

antigobiernista, *n. & a.* oppositionist, antigovernment.

antipático, ca, *a.* unlikable, uncongenial, disagreeable.

antirreglamentario, ria, *a.* against the rules or regulations.

antisubstancia, *f.* antibody.

antitérmico, ca, *a.* athermanous; heat-resisting.

antituberculoso, sa, *a.* antituberculosis, against tuberculosis.

antivenenoso, sa, *a.* antitoxic.

año, *m.*—**a. de gracia,** year of grace.—**a. escolar,** school year.—**entrado en años,** of mature age, of some age (not young).—**entre a.,** during the year.

apacentadero, *m.* grazing field, pasture.

apache, *n.* Apache, gangster, gunman.

apartado, da, *a.* aloof; out-of-the-way, remote, unfrequented.

aparte, *adv.* different, another, others (*ésta es cuestión aparte,* this is another matter).

apenas, *adv.* only.

apendicitomía, *f.* (surg.) appendectomy.

apero, *m.* (often in the *pl.*) riding equipment; riding saddle.

apilamiento, *m.* piling up; crowding.

apisonamiento, *m.* tamping.

aplanamiento, *m.* flattening.

For pronunciation, see the rules at the beginning of the book.

aplanar, va. to flatten.

aprestar, va. to size, treat with size.—**apresto,** m. size (for treating goods); sizing.

apropiación, f. appropriation.

apropiar, va. to appropriate.

aquello, pron. neut. gracefulness, attractiveness, "it."

aquí, adv. now.—**de a. en adelante,** from now on, hereafter.

ara, f. altar slab, mensa.

araguato, m. (zool.) ursine howler, howling monkey, howler.

araña, f. hustler, go-getter; disreputable woman, whore.—**a. de mar,** sea spider, spider crab.

arbitraje, m. (com.) arbitrage.

arco, m.—**a. apainelado,** three-center arch.—**a. de medio punto,** round, or semicircular, arch.—**a. ojival,** equilateral arch.—**a. peraltado,** horseshoe arch.—**a. rebajado,** segmental arch.

archivar, va. (fig.) to put on the shelf, pigeon-hole, forget.

arder. I. vn. to rage (s. o. war, etc.). **II.** vr. to spoil from excessive heat (s. o. fruit, etc.)

ardita, f. squirrel.

arequipa, f., **arequipe, ariquipe,** m. a kind of jelly made with rice, milk and sugar.

argonauta, m. (zool.) paper nautilus.

argot, m. cant, French jargon.

armadura, f. reinforcement (of concrete); armature (of a dynamo).

armar, va. to reinforce (concrete, etc.); to form, prepare; to start, cause.

aromar, va. to give aroma to, perfume.

arquidiócesis, f. archiepiscopal diocese.

arquitectónica, f. (philos.) architectonics.

arrastrar, va. to carry (sand, stones, etc.) in suspension; to wash down, carry away.

arreglar, va. to castrate.

arreglo, m.—**con a. a,** in accordance with, pursuant to.

arriba. I. adv.—**más a.,** higher up.—**por a.,** at the top; from the top.—**por a. de,** above, over. **II.** interj. up with! long live!

asaz, adv. greatly, very.

asexual, a. asexual.

asfaltado, m. asphalt pavement; asphalt paving, paving with asphalt.

así, adv.—**a. es,** that, or it, is so.—**a. es (son),** such is (are).—**a. es que,** and so; (improper but common) that is the way to, that is how.—**a. no,** not that way, not so.—**a. y todo,** and yet; just the same.—**ponerse a.,** to take on so; to act like that.

astrofísica, f. astrophysics.

astroquímica, f. astrochemistry.

atabernado, da, a. bar-room, sold by the glass (s. o. wine).

atafagar, va. to stifle; to bother.

atarantar. I. va. to astound, dumfound. **II.** vr. to be or become dumfounded; to rush, dash.

ataxia locomotriz, locomotor ataxia.

atentatorio, ria, a. having the character of criminal or unlawful intent, or leading to a criminal or unlawful act.

atorarse, vr. to stuff oneself.

atracar, va. to assault, attack (s. o. robbers); to hold up (for robbery).

atranque, m. difficulty, tight box, fix.

atrasado, da, a. back (number of a periodical).

atravesar. I. va. to monopolize, corner (the market). **II.** vr. (with con), to meet; to have an encounter or fight (with).

atropellar, va. to run over, hit, injure.

aullador, ra, n. (zool.) howling monkey, howler.

auspiciar, va. to sponsor, promote.—**auspiciado por,** under the auspices of.

autarquía, f. autarchy, autarky.

avante, adv. ahead, forward.—**sacar a.,** to carry out, make a success of.—**salir a.,** to succeed.

avestruz, m. blockhead, dunce.

avora, f. oil palm.

axon, m. (anat.) axon(e (nerve cell process).

ay. I. m. moan, lament. **II.** interj. oh!—**a. de,** woe to.—**¡a. de mí!** woe is me! wretched that I am! poor me! I see my finish.

ayer, adv.—**a. tarde,** yesterday afternoon.—**tarde a.,** late yesterday.

azararse, vr. to be frustrated, miscarry, be a fizzle, go wrong.

azotera, f. multithonged whip; end of a long whip.

azuzón, na, n. gossipping trouble maker.

B

baba, f. viscous substance.—**caérsela a uno la b., echar la b.,** to be a silly, an idiot (fig.); to be delighted, tickled to death.

bacteriología, f. bacteriology.

bagre, m. homely low woman, baggage; smart, alert person.

bailable, a. with dancing (**té bailable,** tea with dancing, tea dance).

bajada de aguas, rainwater pipe, leader.

bajar, vn.—**b. de,** to be less than.

bajista, m. & f. violoncello player.

balancín, m. oscillating beam (as that of a beam engine).

balanza, f. ropewalker's pole.—**en b.,** undecided; in danger, at stake.—**poner a uno en b.,** to cause one to doubt or hesitate.

baldosín, m. paving tile.

baloncesto, m. basketball.

balso, m. (bot.) balsa, corkwood.

ballenera, f. whaleboat.—**ballenero, ra. I.** n. whaler, whale fisherman. **II.** a. whaling, whale (u. a.).

banco de hielo, iceberg.

banderizo, za, a. partisan, party (u. a.); fiery, agitating, strenuous.

bandidaje, m. brigandage, banditry; gang, ring of bandits.

banquillo, m. execution chair or place.

barato, ta, a.—**echar, o meter, a b.,** to mix up or confuse things by too much fuss.

barbacoa, f. stretcher; elevated board bed supported on sticks; rough sleeping or storage loft or attic, usually of boards or canes; trellis; greenwood broiler used by Indians, or the meat thus broiled.

barómetro, m.—**b. aneroide,** aneroid barometer.—**b. metálico,** Bourdon gauge.

barraca, f. storage shed.

barrilaje, m. barrels collectively; BARRILAME.

barrio, m.—**el otro b.,** the other world.

bártulos, m. pl. means, measures, way (to do something).

basketbol, m. basketball.—**basketbolista, I.** n. basketball player. **II.** a. basketball (u. a.).—**basketbolero, ra,** a. basketball (u. a.).—**basketero, ra,** n. basketball player.

basquetbol, etc. =BASKETBOL, etc.

batallona, a.—**cuestión b.,** vexed question, hard nut to crack.

batatazo, m.—**dar b.,** to win against all expectations (s. o. horses).

batear, va. & vn. (in baseball) to bat.

batir, va.—**b. el record,** to beat the record.—**b. palmas,** to clap the hands.

baúl escaparate, or **ropero,** wardrobe trunk.

bayo, m. poor man's bier; bay horse.—**uno piensa el b. y otro quien lo ensilla,** it is one thing to command, and another to obey; it all depends on who is master and who servant.

bazar, m. fair.

behetría, f. free, independent town; confusion.

be por be, with all particulars, minutely.

Benjamín, m. youngest son or daughter, "the baby."

beneficio, m. (com.) premium.

berlina, f.—**en b.,** in a ridiculous position, exposed to ridicule; (ch. constr.) laughingstock.

bermejizo, m. red bat.

For pronunciation, see the rules at the beginning of the book.

bermellonar, *va.* to vermilion, to paint with vermilion.

bien. I. *m.*—**en,** or **por, b. de.** for the sake, good or benefit of.—**II.** *adv.*—**encontrar,** or **hallar, b.,** to find satisfactory, to approve.—**o b.,** or else; otherwise.

binomio de Newton, (alg.) binomial theorem.

bisulfito, *m.* disulphite.

bitubulado, da, *a.* two-tube.

blanquillo, *m.* white peach; egg.

blasonería, *f.* =BALADRONADA.

bocina, *f.* blowgun; shell used as a horn; (aut.) horn.

boche, *m.* quarrel, row, riot; slight, contemptuous treatment.—**dar b.,** or **un b.,** to slight, turn the cold shoulder on.

boicot, *m.* boycott.—**boicoteador, ra,** *n. & a.* boycotter (-ing).—**boicotear,** *va. y vn.* to boycott.—**boicoteo,** *m.* boycott, boycotting.

bojete, *m.* parcel, package.

bola, *f.* disturbance, tumult, riotous meeting.—**b. pampa, b. perdida,** a kind of Indian sling.

bolear, *va.* to flunk, not to pass; to reject, turn down (in an election).

boleta, *f.,* **boleto,** *m.* ticket; ballot.

bolivariano, na, or **boliviano, na,** *a.* Bolivarian, like, or relating to, Bolívar.

bombazo, *m.* throwing of a bomb; bomb hit; damage it causes.

bombilla, *f.,* **bombillo,** *m.* bulb.

bonarense, *n. & a.* =BONAERENSE.

bonhomía, *f.* honesty; naïveté, simplicity, ingenuousness.

borona, *f.* Indian corn; cornbread; crumb.

borroso, sa, *a.* blurred, faded.

botellería, *f.* bottle factory; bar, saloon.

botica, *f.* shop, store; bar, saloon.

botillería, *f.* bar, saloon.

botinería, *f.* shoe shop.

boycot, etc. =BOICOT, etc.

bracear, *va.* (found.) to tap (a furnace).

bramadero, *m.* tethering post.

brasilero, ra, *n. & a.* Brazilian.

bravo, va, *a.* angry, mad; rough (country, land); pungent, hot.

brigada, *f.* party, body of men or women doing a task together.

brístol, *m.* Bristol board, Bristol paper.

broche, *m.* fastener.—*pl.* cuff buttons.

broma, *f.*—**dar b.,** or **bromas,** to jest; to tease.—**por b.,** in jest.

broncopulmonía, *f.* bronchial pneumonia.

bujía, *f.* (surg.) solid probe.

bunde, *m.* a negro dance; rough, low dance.

bus, *m.* autobus, bus.

butirómetro, *m.* butyrometer.

C

cabalgadura, *f.* riding beast (horse or mule); stirrup strap.

cabecear, *vn.* (aer.) to pitch.

cabeceo, *m.* (aer.) pitch, pitching.

cabeza, *f.* seat (of county, etc.) (called also **c. de partido**).—**c. de biela,** big end of connecting rod.—**c. de hierro,** stubborn, stiff-necked person.—**de c.,** by heart.—**de pies a c.,** from head to foot, all over.

cabezada, *f.* (naut. & aer.) pitch, pitching, plunge.

cable de sustentación, (aer.) light wire.

cabo, *m.*—**c. de desgarre,** (aer.) rip cord, ripline.—**al c. de,** at the end of, after.

cabresto, *m.* =CABESTRO.

cábula, *f.* trick, cunning scheme to get or accomplish something.

cacalote, *m.* cracked corn and syrup; mistake, blunder.

cacao, *m.* chocolate.—**tener c.,** to have vim, energy, courage.

cacaraquear, *vn.* to cackle; to brag, boast.

caco, *m.* thief; burglar.

cacha, *f.*—**hacer la c.,** to try, do what one can; (with a), to make fun of.

cachada, *f.* thrust or wound with the horns.

cacharrero, ra, *n.* notion dealer; peddler.

cacharro, *m.* trinket, notion.

cachazudo, *m.* sluggard; tobacco worm.

cachimba, *f.* low well; (water) spring; disreputable woman.

cacho, *m.* bunch; (com.) left-over, goods unsold; joke, fun.—**echar c.,** to excel, get ahead.—**empinar el c.** (=EMPINAR EL CODO), to drink to excess, be a toper.

cadenear, *va. y vn.* (surv.) to chain.

cadenero, *m.* (surv.) chainman.

cafetería, *f.* retail coffee shop.

cafetero, ra, *a.* coffee (u. a.).

caja, *f.* (mech.) shell, block (of a pulley); bed (of a river); (min.) barren rock.—**c. de hierro, c. fuerte,** safe.

cajeta, *f.* cigar case; puffed up townsman (so called by farmers).

cajón, *m.* bier, coffin.

cálculo prudencial, approximate calculation, estimate.

calchona, *f.* bogey, goblin.

caldera, *f.* teakettle; teapot.

calificar, *va.*—**c. de,** to call, declare.

californiano, na, *n. & a.* Californian.

calistenia, calisténica, *f.* calisthenics, bodily exercise without apparatus.

calma, *f.*—**c. muerta,** dead calm.—**con c.,** calmly, quietly.—**en c.,** calm, smooth (s. o. the sea).

calpul, *m.* gathering, meeting; Indian mound.

calzar, *va.* to fill (teeth); to hill (plants).—**c. muchos (pocos) puntos en,** to be very well (poorly) posted on, to have a good (poor) knowledge of.

calle de árboles, path or space between two rows of trees; also, the rows themselves.

Calleja, *proper n.*—**ya se verá,** or **ya verán, quién es C.,** you shall see what I can do.

camaradería, *f.* comradeship, camaraderie.

cambalache, *m.* swap, swapping.

cambalachear, *vn.* to swap.

camellón, *m.* avenue, boulevard; cultivated land in the islets of the Valley of Mexico.

caminata, *f.* hike, long walk.

caminero, ra, *a.* road, highway (u. a.).

camino, *m.*—**c. de,** on the way to.—**de c.,** stopping on the way; traveling (clothes, etc.).—**de un c. dos mandados,** to kill two birds with one stone.—**en c.,** on the way, on one's way.

campechana, *f.* a kind of cocktail or mixed drink; (Ven.) hammock made in the llanos (plains).

camposanto, *m.* cemetery.

canal maestra, (arch.) main valley drain, or gutter (of a tiled roof).

canard, *m.* canard, fabricated piece of news.

canario, *m.* generous patron (of hotel or restaurant), good tipper.

canchear, *vn.* to shirk, evade doing one's duty.

canchero, ra, *n.* owner of game grounds; keeper of such grounds; shirker; extortioner, bleeder (s. o. some priests).

cangilón, *m.* hole, pit; ditch; wrinkle (in a poorly-made garment).

canoa, *f.* trough; conduit.

cantaletear, *va.* to lecture (fig.), sermonize, scold; to keep repeating, make a chestnut of.

cantar, *va.* to call out; to speak out, reveal.

cantimplora, *f.* powder flask; mumps.

cañafístola, *f.,* **cañafístolo,** *m.,* **cañafístula,** *f.,* **cañafístulo,** *m.* drumstick tree, canafistulo.—**cañafístola, cañafístula,** *f.* canafistola, the pod of the drumstick tree.

cañero, ra. I. *n.* sugar-cane dealer. **II.** *m.* cane bin or store room (in a sugar mill).

cañón, *m.* trunk (of a tree).—**c. antiaéreo,** antiaircraft gun.—**c. antitanque,** antitank gun.

For pronunciation, see the rules at the beginning of the book.

capacho, *m.* leaf wrapper (for salt, etc.); bundle (of salt) done up in leaves; bag; pocket; old hat; carcass.

caperucita, *f.* little hood.—**C. Roja,** or **Encarnada,** Little Red Ridinghood.

capitalino, na, *a.* of, from, or relating to, the capital (city).

capitanía del puerto, office of the harbor master or port officer.

capitulear, *vn.* to lobby.—**capituleo,** *m.* lobbying.

capítulo, *m.*—**llamar a c.,** to call to account, to take to task.

capot, *m.* (aer.) cowl, cowling, engine cover.

capul, *f.* bang (hair cut square in front).—**a la c.,** banged, with a bang (s. o. the hair).

caracal, *m.* caracal, a kind of lynx.

caracará, *m.* caracara, a kind of hawk.

caranga, *f.* louse.

caratejo, ja, or **caratoso, sa,** *a.* marked with, or having, *carate.* (*V.* CARATE.)

cardumen, *m.* multitude of things; shoal, school (of fish).

cargarse, *vr.*—**c. de razón,** to strengthen one's position, find greater justification.

carguera, *f.* nursemaid.

carillón, *m.* carillon.

carioquinesis, *f.* (med.) mitosis.

carnadura, *f.* muscularity; flesh, fleshiness.

carne, *f.*—**tener c. de perro,** to have an iron constitution.

carramplón, *m.* flintlock musket.

carrilera, *f.* rut (in a road); (r. w.) siding; track.

carroño, ña, *n.* & *a.* coward(ly).

carroñoso, sa, *a.* rotting; ill smelling.

cartera, *f.* (com.) securities forming part of the assets.

casa, *f.*—**c. pública,** disreputable house.—**los de c.,** the family.

cascabel, *m.*—**poner el c. al gato,** to bell the cat.

casero, ra, *n.* tenant; customer.

casilla, *f.* bird trap; privy, watercloset.

caso, *m.*—**c. de conciencia,** case of conscience. —**c. de honra,** question of honor.—**c. fortuito,** unexpected circumstances; (law) force majeure.— **en c. necesario,** in case of necessity.—**verse en el c. de,** to be obliged to, to have to, must.

casquete esférico, (geom.) spherical sector.

cataplasma, *f.* nuisance, vexer.

catarro, *m.* cold (in the head).

cateador, ra, *n.* tester; mine prospector.

catear, *va.* & *vn.* to prospect; to raze.

cateo, *m.* testing, sampling; prospecting.

catimbao, *m.* clown; ridiculously dressed person; short fat, or squabby, person.

catión, *m.* (phys.) cation, kation.

catolizar. I. *va.* y *vr.* to catholicize. **II.** *vn.* to pretend to be devout or good, play the saint.

catrín, na, *a.* stylish, smart, swell.

caudillismo, *m.* =CAUDILLAJE.

causa, *f.*—**c. impulsiva,** or **motiva,** prompting motive.—**c. pública,** common good, commonweal. —**formar c. a,** to sue, bring suit against.

causahabiente, *m.* & *f.* (law) a person holding a right from others.

causeo, *m.* light lunch between meals.

cautivador, ra, or **cautivante,** *a.* captivating, charming.

cayuca, *f.* block, bean (head).

caza.—**de c.,** hunting; chasing, pursuit (airplane, boat, etc.)

cazasubmarino, *m.* submarine chaser.

cazuela, *f.* (theat.) upper gallery, nigger heaven.

cebador, *m.* (int. comb. eng.) primer.

celentereado, da, *n.* & *a.* coelenterate.

cenaduría, *f.* supper room, supper inn.

censoría, *f.* censorship; censor's office.

centrifugar, *va.* to centrifuge.

centro de mesa, flower vase for the center of a table.

cepa, *f.* hole, pit; group of banana plants having a common root.—**de c.,** blue-blood; thoroughbred.

cerca a, near (=CERCA DE).

cercado, *m.* (Bolivia) state-capital municipality, capital of a state, and towns within its jurisdiction.

cerco, *m.* fence; encirclement.

cervecero, ra. I. *a.* beer (u. a.), for beer. **II.** *m.* set of beer jugs, mugs, etc.

ceutí. I. *n.* & *a.* of, from, or relating to, Ceuta. **II.** *m.* a very fragrant lemon.

C. G. S., *m.* (phys.) C. G. S. (centimeter-gram-second system of units).

cica, *f.* (bot.) cyca.

ciclonal, *a.* cyclonic.

ciego, *m.* farm, ranch; hilly woodland.

cierto, *a.*—**ciertas hierbas, ciertos lienzos,** certain people.—**lo c. es que,** the fact is that.— **por c. que,** indeed.

cimbrar, *vn.* to vibrate; to shake, tremble.

cincha, *f.*—**a revienta cinchas,** at breakneck speed; grudgingly, unwillingly.

cinemadrama, *m.* photoplay.

cipo, *m.* milepost, signpost; boundary monument; large piece or fragment.

cipote, *n.* fool, blockhead, idiot; little one, youngster; squabby person, short and fat.

cismático, ca, *a.* fastidious, finicky.

cismoso, sa, *n.* & *a.* troublemaker (-ing).

cistitis, *f.* cystitis.—**cistocele,** *f.* cystocele.— **cistoma,** *m.* cystoma.—**cistotomía,** *f.* cystectomy, lithotrity.—**cistótomo,** *m.* lithotrite.

ciudadanía, *f.* citizenry, citizens, the people.

clandestinista, *m.* & *f.* smuggler or bootlegger of liquor.

clase, *f.*—**de c.,** of distinction, of high standing.

clausulado, *m.* aggregate of clauses or articles of a writing.

clausurar, *va.* to close, end, adjourn.

clavetear, *va.* to finish up, put in final form.

clerigalla, *f.* (contempt.) priests (u. collectively: **la c.,** the priests).

clérigo suelto, one who follows and fights with an army but does not belong to it and is not subject to rules or orders.

clerofobia, *f.* hate of priests.

clerófobo, ba, *n.* & *a.* priest hater (-ing).

climático, ca, *a.* climatic; changeable.

climatoterapia, *f.*, or **climoterapia,** *f.* (med.) climatotherapy.

clínica, *f.* clinic (clinical instruction); private hospital.

clinoterapia, *f.* rest cure, rest treatment, in which the patient is kept in bed.

cloración, *f.* chlorination.—**clorador,** *m.* chlorinator.—**clorar,** *va.* to chlorinate.

clorurar, *va.* to chloridize, treat with chlorine.

clubista, *m.* & *f.* clubman (-woman).

coacusado, da, *n.* codefendant.

cocal, *m.* coca; coca plantation; coconut.

cocina, *f.,* or **cocina de hierro,** or **cocina económica,** cooking stove, range.

cocinilla. I. *f.* alcohol stove. **II.** *m.* & *f.* meddler.

cocodrílidos, *m. pl.* (zool.) Crocodilia.

Cochero, *m.* (astron.) Charioteer.

codo, *m.* knee (of a quadruped).

codito, ta, *a.* stingy.

coercible, *a.* (phys.) compressible.

cogollo, *m.* sugar-cane top, used as forage.

cogotera, *f.* neck protector attached to the back of a hat, or put around an ox's neck.

cohetear, *va.* to drill (a rock).

cohobo, *m.* stag skin; stag, deer.

cohonestación, *f.* speciousness to justify an action, specious justification, whitewashing.

cojear, *vn.* to tilt, cant, heel over (as an unsteady table).

cojo, ja, *a.* unsteady, tilting (as a table).

cola, *f.* (bot.) cola; (pharm.) kola, cola.

colar, *vn.* to be believed, pass muster, "go."

coleador, ra, *n.* person that pulls a bull or steer down by the tail.—**colear,** *va. & vn.* to pull down (cattle) by the tail; to refuse, turn down.

colesterina, *f.* (chem.) cholesterol, cholesterin.

colgar, *va.* to attribute, charge with, make responsible for.

colmo, *m.* acme, extreme, height (of folly, etc.), "limit."

colonia, *f.* extension, development, new quarter (of a city or town).

colúbridos, *m. pl.* (zool.) Colubridae.

collareja, *f.* wild pigeon.

collarín, *m.* (mech.) tube, sleeve.

colleras, *f. pl.* cuffbuttons.

combinador, ra. I. *n. & a.* combiner (-ing). **II.** *m.* (elec.) controller (of electric car).

comedero, *m.* haunt, resort, place frequented by a person.

comején, *m.* (zool.) termite, white ant.

comible, *a.* eatable, good to eat.

cómico de la legua, small-town touring actor, strolling actor.

comidilla, *f.* hobby.

comido de, eaten by, -eaten (*comido de gusanos*, worm-eaten).

como, *adv.*—**c. que,** apparently, it seems that.—**c. quien no quiere la cosa,** unconcernedly.—**c. quiera que,** although; since.—**a cómo está(n,** what is the price of.—**¿a cómo estamos?** what is the date?

compactibilidad, *f.* compactness.

compadrito, *m. dim.* of COMPADRE; boaster, braggart, bluffer.

comparto, *m.* tax, impost, contribution.

compás, *m.*—**a c. con,** keeping time with; in line or harmony with.

compasión, *f.*—**tener c. de,** to take pity on, to show mercy to.

compenetrarse, *vr.* to harmonize, be in full agreement.—**c. de,** to understand fully, be thoroughly informed about; to be fully convinced of.

completo, *a.*—**por c.,** completely, entirely.

compra, *f.*—**ir de compras,** to go shopping.

comprensividad, *f.* understandability, quality of being understandable; understanding.

compresor, ra, *n. & a.* compressor (-ing).—**c. de aire,** air compressor.

compromisorio, ria, *a.* relating to an agreement, promise or pledge.

comunizante, *n. & a.* communizer (-ing).

comunizar, *va. & vn.* to communize, teach communism or make a communist of.

concepto, *m.* (com.) item, article; account.

conciliatorio, ria, *a.* conciliatory.

concordatario, ria, *a.* concordat (u. a.), of a, or the, concordat.

concurso, *m.* call for bids.

conchabo, *m.* work, employment, job.

condición, *f.*—**de c.,** of importance, of high rank.—**de c. que,** so as to.—**tener c.,** to be rude or ill-tempered.

conectivo, va, *a.* connective, connecting.

conector, ra, *n. & a.* connector (-ing).

conferencista, *n.* lecturer.

confianzudo, da, *a.* presumptuous, obtrusive, bold, "fresh."

confite, *m.*—**estar a partir de un c.,** to be hand and glove.

conflictivo, va, *a.* conflicting.

confort, *m.* comfort.—**confortable,** *a.* comfortable.

confortablemente, *adv.* comfortably.

conglomerado, *m.* body, community, organization.

congo, *m.* pig's foot; hog's hind leg, ham; iron ore mixed with gold ore; howling monkey.

conjunto, *m.* (spt.) team; unit, system of parts (e. g., **c. de cola,** tail unit—of an airplane).

conmemorativo, va, or **conmemoratorio, ria,** *a.* commemorating, memorial.

conocimiento, *m.*—**c. de embarque,** bill of lading.—**poner en c. de,** to inform, notify.

conscri(p)to, ta, *n. & a.* conscript (soldier).

consejo, *m.*—**seguir c. de guerra a,** to court-martial.

conserva, *f.*—**en c.,** canned, preserved.

consideraciones, *f. pl.*—**guardar,** or **tener, c. a,** to show consideration to.

constancia, *f.,* record, written evidence.

constatación, *f.* substantiation, verification.

constatar, *va.* to verify, confirm; to record.

contado, *m.* payment, installment.

contemporizar, *vn.* to adapt oneself.

contenta, *f.* (law) acknowledgment of payment, release.

contraaviso, *m.* counterinformation; counterorder.

convenible, *a.* reasonable, moderate (s. o. prices).

convenir, *v. imp.* to be advisable or advantageous; to be well to (*conviene pintar el metal,* it is well to paint the metal, it is a good thing to, etc.).—**según convenga,** according to the circumstances, as the circumstances may require, or indicate, as may be best.

conversa, *f.* chat, talk.—**conversador, ra,** *n. & a.* talker [-ative].—**conversón, na,** *a.* talkative.

convivir, *vn.* to live together.

copia, *f.* picture (of a person); living image, picture (s. o. a person very much like another).

copropiedad, *f.* joint ownership; property held in common.

coqueluche, *f.* whooping cough.

coquetamente, coquetonamente, *adv.* coquettishly, flirtatiously.

corchar, *va.* to accept (a challenge); to flunk, not to pass (in an examination).

corifeo, *m.* coryphæus, chorus leader; leader, chief; member of a sect or party.

córneo, a. I. *a.* (bot.) conaceous. **II.** *f. pl.* (córneas), (bot.) Cornaceae.

corona, *f.*—**C. austral,** (ast.) Corona Australis. —**C. boreal,** (astr.) Corona Borealis.—**c. de casco,** skin surrounding the top of the hoof.—**c. mural,** mural crown.

corotos, *m. pl.* belongings; outfit.

corral, *m.*—**c. de vacas,** filthy and dilapidated place, mean hovel, hogpen (fig.).—**c. de vecindad,** tenement house.

corredera de aire, (aer.) air log.

corredor, *m.* porch.

correlacionar, *va.* to correlate.

correr, *vn.*—**c. a cargo de,** to be the concern of, to be attended to by.—**c. a uno,** to be one's concern, to be incumbent on one.—**el que menos corre, vuela,** artful unconcern succeeds quickest.

corrida, *f.* row, series of things; (min.) bearing or direction of a mine lode; (min.) outcrop.

corrugado, da, *a.* corrugated.

cortada, *f.* cut, slash, gash.

cortado, da, *a.* short of funds.

corte, *f.* city where the court resides.—**la C.,** (in Spain) Madrid.

cosa, *f.*—**c. así,** the like, something like it.—**ni c. parecida, ni c. que lo parezca,** nor anything like it.—**no ser,** or **no valer, c.,** not to amount to much, to be of little account.

coscorrón, *m.* knock on the head with the knuckles.

cosquillar, cosquillear. I. *va.* to tickle; to arouse the curiosity of. **II.** *vr.* to become disturbed or upset; to be merry, or "tickled."

costumbre, *f.*—**de c.,** usual; customary.—**tener por c.,** to be in the habit of.

crematorio, ra. I. *a.* burning, cremating. **II.** *m.* crematory, incinerator.

criollo, lla, *a.* native; naturalized.

criquet, *m.* (spt.) cricket.

crisma, *f.*—**romperse la c. con,** to fight, come to blows with.

Cristo, *m.*—**estar sin C.,** to be penniless, to be "broke."—**¡voto a C.!** by the Almighty!

criticón, ona, *n. & a.* faultfinder (-ing).

For pronunciation, see the rules at the beginning of the book.

cromática, *f.* (phys.) chromatics.

croquet, *m.* croquet.

crucial, *a.* cross-shaped, cruciform.

crucigrama, *m.* cross-word puzzle.

cuácara, *f.* working blouse or coat; frock coat.

cuadra, *f.* cuadra, a unit of length usually equivalent to about 275 feet, although it varies in different countries.

cuadrarse, *vr.* to acquit oneself well, do well; to be, or get, ready.

cuadro, *m.* (spt.) team; blackboard; slaughter house.—**c. de café,** 10,000-tree coffee plantation (term used in Cuba).

cuaima, *f.* a very poisonous Venezuelan snake; wily, cruel person.

cuajo, *m.* (sug. man.) thickening of the cane juice; idle chat; recess (in school).

cuando, *adv.* at, or during, the time of (*cuando la guerra,* at the time of the war).—**de vez en c.,** once in a while.

cuánto tiempo, how long.

cuaresmero, ra, *n.* one who fasts every day in Lent.

cuartelesco, ca, *a.* soldier (u. a.), used by, or peculiar to, soldiers.

cuatro, *m.* blunder; small four-string guitar.

cubeta, *f.* high hat; (phot.) developing tray.

cubilete, *m.* political intrigue, wirepulling; clique.

cucaña, *f.* easy thing, cinch, snap.

cuchara, *f.* pickpocket, thief.—**c. de aire,** (aer.) air scoop.

cuchilladas, *f. pl.* fight, row.—**andar a c.,** to be at daggers drawn; to come to blows.

cuchuco, *m.* pork-and-barley soup.

cuenta, *f.*—**a fin de cuentas,** in the end.—**darse c. de,** to realize; to notice.—**por c. y riesgo de uno,** at one's expense and risk; on one's own responsibility.—**por la c.,** as far as one can judge, judging from the facts known (stated, granted, etc.)

cuerda freno, (aer.) dragrope.

cuesco, *m.* fisticuff; man in love.

cuestión de tormento, torture.

cuete, *m.* firecracker; skyrocket.

cuico, ca, *n.* policeman; gossip.

cuidado, *m.*—**perder c.,** not to worry, not to think about the matter.

culto, *m.*—**c. de dulía,** worship or veneration of the saints and angels.—**c. de hiperdulía,** adoration or veneration of the Virgin.—**c. de latría,** worship of God.

cupo, *m.* contents, capacity.

cura, curación, *f.* (surg.) dressing, care (of a wound).

cura de misa y olla = CLÉRIGO DE MISA Y OLLA.

curar, *va.* (surg.) to wash and dress (a wound).

curiosear, *vn.* to act from curiosity; to look around, look at things; to snoop.

cursar, *vn.* to circulate, be current.

curso, *m.*—**ser de,** or **tener, c. forzoso,** to be legal tender.

cuyo, ya, *a.* which, this, that (*por cuya razón,* for which reason; *en cuyo caso,* in that case).

Ch

chácara, *f.* large leather bag or wallet strapped across the back and chest over one shoulder (= GUARNIEL).

chaco, *m.* hunt, hunting.

chancaca, *f.* raw brown sugar; molasses cake.

chantage, chantagista = CHANTAJE, CHANTAJISTA.

chapa, *f.* door lock; policeman; cap (of compass).

chapín, *n.* & *a.* bowlegged (person).

chapola, *f.* butterfly, moth.

chaquet, *m.* long cut-away coat.

chaveta, *f.* cotter, cotter pin.

chicle, *m.* chicle; dirt, filth.

chiflado, da, *a.* crazy (fig.), crackbrained, nutty.

chinchorrazo, *m.* blow.

chingar. I. *va.* to annoy, bother; to cut off the tail of, bob. **II.** *va. & vn.* to drink to excess. **III.** *vr.* to get drunk; to be fooled, get left.

chirrión, *m.* heavy horsewhip.

chócolo, *m.* green ear of corn.

choque de retroceso, (elec.) return, or lightning, shock.

chorizo, za, *n.* & *a.* fool(-ish), idiot (-ic) (fig.).

chorlo, *m.* (orn.) sandpiper, plover.

chorote, *m.* chocolate pot (a pot for making chocolate); thick beverage.

chubasco de nieve, blizzard.

chunga, *f.* (orn.) chunga, a South-American wading bird.

chuña, *f.* chunga, a South-American wading bird; scramble, scuffle.

D

daca.—**andar al d. y toma** = ANDAR EN DARES Y TOMARES. (*V.* DARES Y TOMARES.)

¡dale que dale! This expression is used to indicate persistence (keeping everlastingly at it), usually annoying or boresome.

dandismo, *m.* dandies collectively, the world of dandies; dandy-like behavior or speech.

daño, *m.* (com.) discount.

dar. I. *va.*—**d. la ley,** to lay down the law, dictate.—**d. las gracias,** to thank.—**d. pasos,** to take steps.—**d. satisfacción,** to apologize. **II.** *vn.*—**d. con,** to apply, cover with (paint, stucco, etc.).—**d. de,** to deal (blows, etc.).—**d. de beber (comer),** to give drink (food) (of animals, to water, to feed).—**darle a uno por,** to take it into one's head to, to take to (*le dió por ser presidente,* he took it into his head to be president; *me ha dado por escribir novelas,* I have taken to writing novels).

de, *prep.* by (*temido de sus enemigos,* feared by his enemies; *abandonado de Dios,* forsaken by God, God-forsaken; *médico de profesión,* a physician by profession. Followed by adjective, it is often equivalent to *from* followed by the corresponding English noun (*lo hizo de bobo,* he did it from foolishness; *lloré de alegre,* I wept from gladness).—**d. a,** followed by a numerical expression, is rendered by using the equivalent of that expression adjectively (*billete a cinco pesos,* five-peso bill; *naranjas de a treinta centavos por docena,* thirty-cents-a-dozen oranges).—**d. . . . en,** . . . by (*de día en día,* day by day; *de grano en grano,* grain by grain).

debajo, *adv.*—**por d.,** underneath; from below.—**por d. de,** under; below.

debate, *m.* reading (of a bill, motion, etc. in a deliberating body).

decamerón, *m.* narrative of the events of ten days; (D—), Decameron.

deciestéreo, *m.* decistere (one tenth of a cubic meter).

decir, *vn.*—**bien dice(n),** is (are) right in saying.—**dime con quién andas, y te diré,** or **decirte he, quién eres,** tell me whom you go with, and I'll tell you who you are.

decurionato, *m.* decurionship.

defensa, *f.* protection; shelter; (aer.) bumping bag, bumper.—**de d.,** guard (u. a.), protection (u. a.), sheltering, safety (u. a.).

defensivo, va, *a.* protecting.

della, dellas, dello, dellos, *contr.* of DE ELLA, etc.

demás, *adv.*—**por d.,** superfluous, amiss; vainly, fruitlessly.—**y d.,** and other things, and so forth.

dentro, *adv.*—**por d.,** inwardly.

depauperación, *f.* impoverishment; (med.) weakness, weakening, exhaustion.

derecha, *f.*—**a la d.,** right-handed (screw, key, etc.).—**las derechas,** (pol.) the right, the moderate or conservative side or party.

derechista, *m.* & *f.* (pol.) rightist, one belonging to or supporting the right.

derechito, *dim. adv.* right straight (ahead, etc.).

derrotismo, *m.* defeatism.—**derrotista,** *m.* & *f.* defeatist.

descacharse, *vr.* (billiards) to miscue.

descollante, *a.* outstanding, prominent, conspicuous; main, principal.

desempleado, da, *n. & a.* unemployed.

desempleo, *m.* unemployment.

desencadenamiento, *m.* unchaining.

deslizante, *a.* gliding.

deslustrado, da, *a.* unglazed.

desmantelamiento, *m.* dismantling; dilapidation, ruinous condition.

desmedrado, da, *a.* damaged, injured; worn out; wasted, emaciated, thin.

desmonetizarse, *vr.* to depreciate, lose value (s. o. stocks and securities).

desmonte, *m.* (r. w.) cut; (min.) discarded ore or rock.

desocupación, *f.* unemployment.

desocupado, da, *n.* one unemployed.—**los desocupados,** the unemployed.

desorientación, *f.* lack of orientation, loss of bearings; confusion, lack of system.

desoxidar, *va. & vn.* to deoxidize.

despacio, *m.* slowness.—**con d.,** slowly, leisurely; carefully.

despellejar, *va.* to speak evil of, to roast, rake over the coals.

despido, *m.* discharge, dismissal, layoff.

despinte, *m.* low-grade, or poor, ore.

desplomarse, *vr.* (aer.) to pancake.

desplome, *m.* (aer.) pancaking.

destacado, da, *a.* prominent, outstanding.

destacar. I. *va.* to bring out, make conspicuous. **II.** *vr.* to stand out, be conspicuous; to be prominent, overtop, outstand; to loom.

destroncar, *va.* to tire out, overwork (s. o. animals).

desfróyer, *m.* (naut.) destroyer.

desuñarse, *vr.* to work very hard, work one's fingers to the bone, work oneself to death.

detectivismo, *m.* detective force or service; detective work.

detrito, *m.* detritus.

deutón, *m.* (phys.) deuton.

devanarse, *vr.* to be convulsed (with laughter); to writhe (with pain).—**d. los sesos,** to rack one's brain.

devaneo, *m.* love affair, love adventure.

devisar, *va.* to descry, see; to intercept, stop.

día, *m.*—**de d.,** daylight; in the day time.—**el d. de ayer,** yesterday.—**el d. de hoy,** today.—**en días pasados,** some days ago.—**en estos, or los últimos, días,** recently.—**en mis días,** in my days, in my lifetime.

diablo, *m.*—**d.!** the devil! the deuce!—**pobre d.,** poor devil.

diálisis, *f.* (chem.) dialysis.

diamina, *f.* (chem.) diamin.

diarismo, *m.* journalism.

diatermia, *f.* (med.) diathermy, thermopenetration.

dicho, *pp. of* DECIR.—**d. se está,** it goes without saying.

diente de leche, or **mamón,** milk tooth.

dietas, *f. pl.* allowance or fee paid to a public functionary while serving away from his place of residence.

diferencial, *m.* (aut.) differential.

difusora, *f.* (rad.) broadcasting station.

digestibilidad, *f.* digestibility.

digital, *f.* finger (u. a., as in *impresión digital,* fingerprint).

dije, *m.* handy person, one useful for many kinds of work.

dilatabilidad, *f.* expansibility.

dilatarse, *vr.* to delay, tarry.

diligencia, *f.* action, measure.

diluyente, *n. & a.* diluent.

dimetilo, *m.* (chem.) dimethyl.

dimitente, *n. & a.* resigner (-ing).

dinero contante y sonante, or **dinero en tabla,** cash, ready cash.

dingo, *m.* dingo, Australian wild dog.

Dios, *m.*—**D. delante,** with God's help.—**D. mediante,** God willing, with God's help.—**D. es grande,** trust in God; all things are possible.—**D. me (nos) libre,** God forbid, God protect, or deliver, me (us).—**sabe D.,** goodness knows, only God knows.

diplomáticamente, *adv.* diplomatically; tactfully.

dipsómano, na, *n. & a.* dipsomaniac (-al).

dirigente, *m. & f.* leader.

disparadero, *m.* trigger.

disparatero, ra, *n.* bungler; nonsensical talker, one that "talks through his hat."

dispensario, *m.* pharmacopœia, dispensatory; drug laboratory, or factory; clinic.

dispositivo, *m.* device, contrivance; mechanism; appliance.

divo, va, *n.* prominent or excelling singer.

docto, ta, *a.* expert, well posted or informed, qualified.

doctorzuelo, la, *n.* =DOCTORCILLO, LLA.

dragonear, *vn.* to boast.

drávida, *n.;* **dravidiano, na,** *n. & a.* Dravidian. —**dravídico, ca,** *a.* Dravidian.

duetista, *m. & f.* duettist.

durar, *vn.*—**d. lo que,** to last as long as.—**d. mucho,** to last a long time.—**d. poco,** to last a short time.

E

ebrioso, sa, *a.* too fond of liquor, too much of a toper.

ecuánime, *a.* equanimous, even-minded, calm, serene.

eczema, *f.* (med.) eczema.

eczematoso, sa, *a.* eczematous.

echar. I. *va.*—**e. mano a,** to grab, seize.—**e. mano de,** to resort to.—**e. una mano,** to play a game. **II.** *vr.*—**echarse sobre,** to rush at, fall upon.

echona, *f.* sickle.

edénico, ca, *a.* Edenic, paradisaic.

edilicio, cia, *a.* edilitian.

educacional, *a.* educational.

efecto, *m.*—**a ese, este,** or **tal, e.,** for that purpose, to that end.

eje del timón, (aer.) rudder post.

electroquímico, ca, *a.* electrochemical.

elenco, *m.* personnel, members (of a governing body).

embalsar, *va.* to impound, dam (water).

embalse, *m.* impounding (of water).

embargo, *m.*—**sin e. de (que),** notwithstanding (that), in spite of (the fact that).

embriagador, ra, or **embriagante,** *a.* intoxicating.

emigratorio, ria, *a.* emigration (u. a.).

emisivo, va, *a.* emitting; emission (u. a.).

emisora, *f.* broadcasting station.

empaque, *m.* affected seriousness; boldness, brazenness, impudence.

empate, *m.* tie, draw (in games).

empeñaduría, *f.;* **empeño,** *m.* pawnshop.

emperejilado, da, *a.* dressed up.

emperejilarse, *vr.* to dress up.

emperrarse, *vr.* (often **e. a llorar**) to burst out crying.

empersonar, *va.* to inscribe or register in the census.

emplumar, *va.* to beat soundly, thrash.

empozarse, *vr.* to form, or collect in, puddles (s. o. water).

encabador, *m.* penholder.

encanallamiento, *m.* degeneracy, becoming base and despicable.

encanallarse, *vr.* to become low, base, mean, to part with decency.

encefalitis letárgica, encephalitis lethargica, sleeping sickness.

encefalotomía, *f.* (surg.) cerebrotomy.

For pronunciation, see the rules at the beginning of the book.

encerramiento, *m.* encirclement.
encerrar, *va.* to imply; to encircle.
encierro, *m.* encirclement.
encintar, *va.* (eng.) to curb, to put a curb, or curbs, to.
enclavado, da, *a.* enclaved, encircled.
encobrar, *va.* to coat or cover with copper.
enconoso, sa, *a.* irritating, exasperating, vexing, difficult to deal with dispassionately.
encuadrar, *va.* to frame.
endometritis, *f.* (med.) endometritis.
endospermo, *m.* (bot.) endosperm.
endrogarse, *vr.* to become burdened with debts.
enfermarse, *vr.* to be taken ill.
enfiestarse, *vr.* to amuse oneself, have a good time, go on a lark.
engrasamiento, *m.*; **engrase,** *m.* greasing, oiling; lubrication.
engreírse, *vr.* (with **con** or **de**), to be, or become, fond (of), take a liking (to).
enojón, na, *a.* peevish, ill-tempered.
enostosis, *f.* (med.) enostosis.
ensalmista, *n. & a.* medicine man, spell healer; quack.
ensangrentado, da, *a.* covered with blood; blood-stained.
enseñanza, *f.*—**e. primaria,** or **primera e.,** primary education.—**e. secundaria,** or **segunda e.,** secondary, or high-school, education.—**e. superior,** higher, or professional, education.
entender, *va.*—**e. por,** to mean by, to understand by; (in definitions, **entenderse por,** to be: *entiéndese por aritmética la ciencia de los números,* arithmetic is the science of numbers).—**dar a e.,** to intimate, insinuate, hint.
entendido, *pp.* of ENTENDER.—**tener e.,** to understand.
enterar. I. *va.* to pay, deliver (in a public office). **II.** *vn.* to become better. **III.** *vr.* to make up for a loss, to recoup one's losses.—**e. de,** to learn, become informed about or familiar with.
entero, *m.* payment, delivery; balance.
entibación, *f.* (min.) timbering.
entrenamiento, *m.* training.
entrometido, da = ENTREMETIDO, DA.
entubado, *m.* casing (of an oil well, etc.)
entubar, *va.* to case (an oil well, etc.), to provide with casing.
entunarse, *vr.* to be pricked by a thorn.
eón, *m.* divine emanation.
eosina, *f.* (chem.) eosin.
epidídimo, *m.* (anat.) epididymis.
epifenómeno, *m.* (med.) epiphenomenon.
época, *f.*—**formar,** or **hacer, e.,** to open a new era, to be a landmark, or turning point.
equipajero, ra, *n.* (r. w.) luggage porter or carrier, station attendant.
equipo, *m.* (spt.) team.
erecto, ta, *a.* erect.
ergosterina, *f.* (chem.) ergosterin.
ergotinina, *f.* (chem.) ergotinine.
erizo de mar, or **marino,** (zool.) sea urchin.
escalafón, *m.* roster; roll, list.
escombrera, *f.* (min.) refuse dump.
escribidor, ra, *n.* bad writer, would-be writer, scribbler.
escrito, *m.*—**por e.,** in writing.
escucharse, *vr.* to speak deliberately with affected pauses or halts.
esmerilador, ra, *n. & a.* grinder (-ing).
esmeriladora, *f.* grinding machine.
eso, *dem. pron. neut.*—**por e.,** for that; for that reason, on that account.—**por e. es por lo que** (or, incorrectly but commonly, **por e. es que),** that is why.
espahí, *m.* (mil.) spahi.
espalda, *f.*—**de espaldas,** backwards, on one's (or its) back.—**por la e.,** from behind; in the back; behind one's back.
espanto, *m.* apparition, hobgoblin, spook.
esparavel, *m.* (mas.) hod.

especiosamente, *adv.* speciously.
espectacular, *a.* spectacular.
espetado, da, *a.* affectedly serious.
espetarse, *vr.*—**e. en,** to fit in, go into.
espetera, *f.* metal kitchen utensils collectively, kitchenware.
espía doble, doubly treacherous spy, one who acts as a spy for both sides.
espiga, *f.* (bot.) tassel, inflorescence.
espigar. I. *va.* to glean; to tenon; to collect, cull. **II.** *vr.* to grow tall; to go to seed, overgrow.
espigueo, *m.* gleaning; gleaning season.
espirilo, *m.* (biol.) spirillum.
espongiarios, *m. pl.* (zool.) Spongiae, Porifera.
esquí, *m.* ski.—**esquiar,** *vn.* to ski.
estacionamiento, *m.* (aut.) parking.
estacionar, *va.* to park (a car, etc.).
estadal, *m.* a Spanish unit of length equal to about 10.9 ft.
Estados generales, States-General.
estadounidense, estadunidense, *n. & a.* American (from or relating to the U. S.)
estagnación, *f.* stagnation; paralyzation, cessation (of business, etc.)
estanquillo, *m.* shop where monopolized goods, specially liquor, are sold; small shop.
estearato, *m.* (chem.) stearate.
estilete, *m.* stiletto (dagger); small chisel or burin; (surg.) flexible probe.
estilo, *m.*—**de e.,** usual, customary, regulation (u. a.)
esto, *pron. dem. neut.*—**e. es,** that is, that is to say.—**a todo e.,** meanwhile.—**por e.,** for this reason, on account of this.—**por e. es por lo que** (or, improperly but commonly, **por e. es que),** this is why.
estoperol, *m.* brass-headed tack.
estratosfera, *f.* stratosphere.
estudiantado, *m.* students collectively.
euclídeo, *a*; **euclidiano, na,** *a.* Euclidean.
europeizar, *va. & vn.* to Europeanize.
eventualmente, *adv.* by chance, fortuitously.
expendio, *m.* selling place.
experimentado, da, *a.* proven, tested.
exprés. I. *n. & a.* express (train, etc.). **II.** *m.* transport company or concern; transport office.
expresiones, *f. pl.* regards.
extremo, *m.*—**por todo e.** = CON EXTREMO.
eyaculación, *f.* ejection, forcing out.—**eyacular,** *va.* to eject.—**eyector,** *m.* ejector (in fire arms).

F

fábrica, *f.* stone or brick masonry; church funds.
facetada, *f.* flat or poor joke.
faena, *f.* extra, or overtime, work; morning work (in the country); gang of workers.
faja de desgarre, (aer.) rip (-ping) panel, or strip.
falta, *f.*—**poner faltas a,** to find fault with.
fallir, *vn.* to die; (com.) to fail.
familiar, *m.* relative.
fanático, ca, *n.* (spt.) fan.
fandango, *m.* row, disturbance, brawl.
faramalla, *f.* conceit, airs; trash, rubbish, worthless or insignificant thing.
faro, *m.* (aut.) lantern, light (usually s. o. the headlights).
fenílico, a, *a.* phenylic.—**fenilo,** *m.* phenyl.
fenomenal, *a.* phenomenal; extraordinary, exceptional, rare.
fenomenalismo, *m.* (philos.) phenomenalism.
fenomenalista, *m. & f.* (philos.) phenomenalist.
feria, *f.* fairing, gift at a fair.—**hacer f. de,** to display, boast.
ferina, *a.*—**tos f.,** whooping cough.
fermento, *m.* (chem.) ferment, enzyme.
ferretero, ra, *n.* hardware dealer; hardware manufacturer.

---

ferroviario, ria, *n.* railroad employee, railroad man (woman).

fertilización, *f.* (agr.) fertilizing, supplying with fertilizer.

fiarse, *vr.*—**f. de,** to trust, have confidence in, depend on.

ficha antropométrica, anthropometric data, card or record.

fichar, *va.* to take and record anthropometric measurements of.

fiera, *f.* fierce or vicious animal; (bullfighting) beast, bull.

fiesta, *f.*—**por fin de f.,** to end with, to top off with.

fijador, ra, *a.* locking (plate, wire, pin, etc.)

filote, *m.* silk (of an ear of corn).

fin, *m.*—**a f. de,** in order to, so as to.—**a f. de que,** so that, to the end that.—**poner f. a,** to put an end to, stop, get rid of.

finales, *m.* (spt.) finals.—**finalista,** *m.* & *f.* (spt.) finalist, player in finals.

finalizar, *va.* (law) to execute (a contract, deed).

financiación, *f.,* **financiamiento,** *m.* financing.

financiar, *va.* to finance.—**financista,** *m.* & *f.* financier.—**finanzas,** *f. pl.* finances.

firma, *f.* (com.) firm, house.

fisirrostro, tra. I. *a.* (zool.) fissirostral. **II.** *m. pl.* Fissirostres.

fitotecnia, *f.* applied botany, science of the applications of plants to industry and dietetics.

fitotomía, *f.* phytotomy, vegetable anatomy.

fláccido, da, *a.* (aut.) low pressure, balloon (tire); (aer.) nonrigid (airship).

flebología, *f.* phlebology, vein anatomy.

flete, *m.* hire (price); pack, load transported by land.

flirtear, *vn.* to flirt.—**flirteo,** *m.* flirting.

florecimiento, *m.* flowering, blossoming; flourishment, flourishing.

flota aérea, air fleet, air forces.

flote, *m.*—**estar,** or **mantenerse, a f.,** to have enough to live on.

fluorhidrato, *m.* hydrofluoride.

fluoruro, *m.* fluoride.

flux, *m.*—**estar a f.,** to have nothing, be penniless.—**tener f.,** to be lucky.

fogón, *m.* fire; firebox (of a boiler).

foraminífero, ra. I. *a.* foraminiferal. **II.** *m. pl.* Foraminifera.

forrajero, ra, *a.* forage, fodder (u. a.).

forrarse, *vr.* to eat well, have a good meal.

fosfatado, da, *a.* phosphated.

foso séptico, septic tank.

foto, *m.* or *f.* photo (photograph).

fotón, *m.* (phys.) photon.

fotograbador, ra, *n.* photoengraver.

frentazo, *m.* blow with the forehead; rebuff, turning down.

frente. I. *m.* opposite side.—**f. a,** opposite, facing.—**del f.,** opposite, across (the street, etc.).—**hacer f. a,** to face; to meet. **II.** *f.*—**tener dos dedos de f.,** to have any sense at all, to have a particle of brains.

fresco, *m.*—**hace** (**hizo,** etc.) **f.,** it is (was, etc.) cool.

frigorífero, *m.* refrigerator, refrigerating room or chamber, freezer (in packing houses).

fullería, *f.* conceit; arrogance.

fullero, ra, *a.* conceited; arrogant.

fusión, *f.* (com.) merging, merger.

fusionarse, *vr.* (com.), to merge, form a merger.

futbol, *m.* football.—**futbolero, ra; futbolista. I.** *a.* football (u. a.). **II.** *n.* football player.—**futbolístico, ca,** *a.* football (u. a.).

G

gádido, da. I. *n.* & *a.* (icht.) gadid. **II.** *m. pl.* (icht.) Gadidae.

gangueo, *m.* twang (in speech).

ganzúa, *f.* one skilled in drawing secrets out of other people.

garbancero, ra, *n.* chickpea dealer; young servant (boy, girl).

garniel, *m.* =GUARNIEL.

garzón, *m.* (icht.) a wading bird similar to the heron.

gastrología, *f.* science and art of cooking.

gata, *f.* female cat; servant girl, maid; (mech.) jack, screw jack.—**g. parida,** wasted person, skeleton (fig.)

gaviar, *vn.* to tassel (s. o. corn).

gentes, *f. pl.* Gentiles (in the expression **el Apóstol de las gentes,** the Apostle of the Gentiles—St. Paul).

gentualla, *f.* rabble; people of no account, small fry.

giroflé, *m.* (bot.) aromatic clove tree.

glano, *m.* (icht.) sheatfish.

glifo, *m.* (arch.) glyph, groove.

gliptología, *f.* glyptology.

global, *a.* total, in all, in the lump.

globo piloto, (aer.) pilot balloon.

Gloriapatri, *m.,* or **Gloria Patri,** (eccl.) Gloria Patri, the lesser doxology.

glicógeno, na, *a.* (physiol) glycogenetic, sugar-producing.

goa, *f.* (agr.) dibble.

goal, *m.* (spt.) goal (in football).

golfista, *m.* & *f.* golfer, golf player.

gota militar, chronic gonorrhea.

gradación, *f.* grading; gradation, graded series of things or events.

grandísono, na, *a.* high-sounding.

granujilla, *m.* =GRANUJA, *m.*

gripa, *f.* grip, influenza.

grito, *m.*—**a g. en cuello, a gritos, a g. pelado, a todo g.,** loudly; vociferously, with loud cries, howling.

grullo, lla. I. *a.* dark grey (s. o. horses). **II.** *m.* peso, dollar; uncastrated colt.

guache, *m.* low, despicable man, tough.

guaina, *m.* boy, youth.

guanaco, ca, *n.* boor, rustic; simpleton, idiot.

guardarriel, *m.* (r. w.) reinforcing plate, or bar (on a rail).

guayaba, *f.* guava jam or jelly; lie, fib.

guayabero, ra, *n.* liar, fibber.

guerra europea, guerra mundial, gran guerra, World War.

guitarrería, *f.* string-instrument factory or shop.

H

haber, *v. imp.*—**hay para,** there is enough for.—**lo que hay es,** what happens is; the fact is.—**no hay para que,** there is no occasion for; it is better not to; there is no object in.—**no hay que,** one should not; it is not necessary to.—**¿qué hay?** hello; what happens? what is the matter?

habla, *f.*—**ponerse al h.,** to communicate, get in touch, speak.

habrá, habré, etc. *V.* HABER.

hacer. I. *va.*—**h. boca,** to make an appetite.—**h. falta,** to be missing; to be lacking.—**h. una pregunta,** to ask a question. **II.** *v. imp.*—**¿cuánto (tiempo)** hace? how long ago?—**¿cuánto (tiempo)** hace que, how long ago; since when.—**hace años (días,** etc.) **que,** many years (days, etc.) ago; (for) many years (days, etc.).—**hace mucho (poco),** a long (short) time ago.—**hace tiempo, a long time ago.—hace tiempo que,** a long time ago; for a long time.

hacia, *prep.*—**h. abajo,** downwards; in the lower part, towards the bottom.—**h. arriba,** upwards; in the upper part, towards the top.

haliótide, haliotis, *m.* (zool.) abalone.

hampo, hampón, *m.* gangster, gunman.

hangar, *m.* hangar.

hará, haré, etc. *V.* HACER.

For pronunciation, see the rules at the beginning of the book.

harina de otro costal, another matter, a horse of a different color.
hedonismo, *m.* hedonism.
hedonista, *n. & a.* hedonist (-ic).
heladera, *f.* ice-cream dish; refrigerator.—**h. (mecánica) eléctrica,** electric refrigerator.
hematita, *f.* (anat.) hematid, hæmatid, red blood corpuscle.
hemodinamómetro, *m.* hemomanometer, blood-pressure gauge.
hemopatía, *f.* hemopathy, blood diseases collectively.
Herodes, *m.* Herod (proper noun).—**de H. a Pilatos,** from pillar to post.
herraje, *m.* (gen. *pl.*) iron or metal fittings or accessories, hardware.
herrete, *m.* cattle-marking iron.
hervidor, *m.* vessel, tube, etc. for boiling or where a liquid boils.
hexápodo, da, *n. & a.* (zool.) hexapod.
hexapétalo, la, *a.* (bot.) hexapetalous.
hialino, na, *a.* hyaline, translucent.—**hialiografía,** *f.* hyalography, writing or engraving on glass.—**hialógrafo,** *m.* hyalograph.—**hialotecnia,** *f.* hyalography.—**hialurgia,** *f.* glass-working art.
hidátide, *f.* (med. & zool.) hydatid.
hidrato de carbono, (chem.) carbohydrate.
hidrófugo, ga, *a.* nonabsorbent of moisture, moisture proof.
hidroide, *m.* (zool.) hydroid, hydrozoon; *pl.* (hidroides) Hydroidea.
hierbatero, ra, *n.* herb doctor; maté gatherer, one who gathers and prepares maté; YERBATERO.
hiladilla, *f.* narrow ribbon or tape.
historiografía, *f.* historiography.
hojaldra, *f.* = HOJALDRE.
hoja suelta, leaflet (not *folder*), handbill.
holoturia, *f.* (zool.) holothurian, sea cucumber.
homosexual, *a.* homosexual.
honra, *f.*—**tener a h.,** to regard as an honor, be proud of.
hora, *f.*—**h. de,** time to, or for (often ch. constr.: *hora de almuerzo,* time for breakfast, breakfast time; *hora de tren,* time for the train, train time).—**horas canónicas,** (ecc.) canonical hours.—**cuarenta horas,** (ecc.) forty hours.—**en buen,** or **buena, h.,** well, happily; it is well; very well, all right.—**en mal,** or **mala, h.** = ENHORAMALA. These expressions are used to indicate dissatisfaction, annoyance, disapproval, etc., and are rendered according to the circumstances.
horqueta, *f.* crotch, forked pole or stake; crotch, or bifurcation, of a tree; sharp turn of a stream, and, also, the adjacent land.
hospitalizar, *va.* to hospitalize, take to or treat in a hospital.
hostigador, ra, *a.* = HOSTIGOSO.—**hostigar,** *va.* to satiate, to become distasteful or unpalatable to.—**hostigoso, sa,** *a.* tiresome, boresome; satiating, that becomes distasteful after satisfying.
hotelero, ra, *n.* hotel keeper or manager.
hoz, *f.*—**meter la h. en mies ajena,** to meddle with other people's affairs, mind other people's business.
huelga sentada, sit-down strike.
huelguístico, ca, *a.* strike (u. a.).
huevería, *f.* egg shop.
humo, *m.*—**echar humos,** to put on airs.
humorismo, *m.* humorism, humor; (old med.) humoralism.

I

ideograma, *m.* ideogram.
ignífugo, ga, *a.* fireproofing.
igual, *m.*—**al i. que,** the same as, as well as.
impráctico, ca, *a.* unpractical; impracticable.
impudicia, *f.* immodesty, impudicity.
imputrescible, *a.* nonputrescible, nonrotting.

inabordable, *a.* unapproachable.
inalámbrico, ca, *a.* wireless.
inconfirmado, da, *a.* unconfirmed.
indagatoria, *f.* (law) unsworn statement or declaration made by, or required of, an arraigned person.
independizar. I. *va.* to make independent, to free, give independence to. **II.** *vr.* to become independent, win independence.
indeseable, *a.* undesirable.
indiada, *f.* crowd, or multitude, of Indians.
indianismo, *m.* Indianism.
indubitado, da, *a.* undoubted, unquestionable.
indudablemente, *adv.* undoubtedly.
industrialista, *a.* industrialist, industry (u. a.)
inecuación, *f.* (math.) inequality.
in extremis, in the last moments of life; on the point of death.
influenciar, *va.* to influence.
informalidad, *f.* unreliability, undependability.
infrarrojo, ja, *a.* infrared.
ingeniería aerostera, aviation engineering.
ingeniero aerostero, aviation engineer.
inhóspice, *a.* inhospitable, unhealthful.
inmigrado, da, *n. & a.* immigrant.
inmigratorio, ria, *a.* immigration (u. a.).
inmunización, *f.* immunization, immunizing.
inquietante, *a.* disquieting, disturbing.
institucional, *a.* institutional.
insubstituíble, *a.* unreplaceable.
integrado por, consisting of, formed by.
integrar, *va.* to compose, form, make up.
intención, *f.*—**dar i.,** to give hope.—**de primera i.,** provisionally, tentatively; frankly, impulsively, without disguise; (surg.) by first intention.—**de segunda i.,** double-facedly, deceitfully.—**por primera i.,** (surg.) by first intention.
interestadal, *a.* interstate.
intranquilizar, *va.* to disquiet, worry.
intrigar. I. *va.* to arouse (one's) interest or curiosity, intrigue. **II.** *vr.* (with **en**), to be interested (in) or curious (about).
introverso, sa, *a.* (psych.) introvert.
invernal, *m.* winter shed (for cattle and fodder).
ir, *vn.* With a dative case, to get along, to do (*me fué bien,* I got along, or did, well).—**algo,** or **mucho, va de Pedro a Pedro,** all people are not alike, there are people and people.—**no vaya (vayan) a** (followed by infinitive), don't, don't go and.—**¡qué va!** nonsense! you don't say! don't tell me!—**vamos a ver,** let us see, let me see; what is it?—**vaya (que),** all right, let it be; indeed.
iraca, *f.* Panama-hat palm.
irrefutable, *a.* irrefutable, indisputable.
izador, ra, *a.* hoisting.
izquierda, *f.*—**a la i.,** left-handed (screw, etc.).
izquierdas, *f. pl.* (pol.) Left, Left wing.
izquierdista, *n. & a.* (pol.) leftist, radical.

J

jaleo, *m.* = JARANA.
jangar, *m.* hangar.
jazmín de la India, (bot.) gardenia.
Jerez, *m.* sherry wine.
jornalero, *m.* day laborer; journeyman.
juez, *m. or f.* umpire; arbitrator.
juego, *m.*—**conocerle a uno el j.,** to see through one, read one's intention.—**poner en j.,** to bring into play, make use of.
juicio, *m.*—**formar j. de,** to judge, form an opinion on.
jurar, *va.*—**jurársela,** or **jurárselas, a uno,** to threaten one with revenge, to have it in for one.

L

la, *def. art.* Often used before the surname (not the first name) of a woman, especially actresses and singers, and is not translated, or is translated by Miss, Madame, etc.: *la Pattí, la Pavlowa,* Pattí,

---

For pronunciation, see the rules at the beginning of the book.

Pavlowa; *la Guerrero, la Farrar,* Miss Guerrero, Miss Farrar; *la Schumann-Heink,* Madame Schumann-Heink.

laberintodonte, *m.* (pal.) labyrinthodont; *pl.* (pal.) Labyrinthodonta.

laborable, *a.* working, week (day).

labra, *f.*—**de l. fácil,** free-cutting, free-turning (metal).

lagarto de Indias, cayman, alligator.

laicidad, *f.* laity; laicism, secularism.

laicista, *n. & a.* secularist (-ic).

lampo, *m.* flash of light.

lantia, *f.* (naut.) binnacle lamp; boom guy.

lanzador, ra, *n.* (in baseball) pitcher.

lapicera, *f.* pencil case or holder; penholder.

laques, *f. pl.* =BOLEADORAS.

largo, ga, *a.*—**cuan l. es (era),** at full length, stretched.

lástima, *f.*—**dar,** or **hacer, l.,** to arouse pity or regret, to be pitiful or regretful.—**es l.,** it is a pity, it is too bad.

latines, *m. pl.* jargon, nonsense; hairsplitting, pettifoggery.

latoso, sa, *a.* boresome, annoying.

lavaza, *f.* soap foam, suds.

lazo, *m.*—**armar l.,** or **lazos,** to entrap, deceive; to plot.

leal saber y entender. *V.* SABER.

legisperito, ta, *n.* =JURISPERITO.

lémur, *m.* (zool.) lemur.

león, *m.*—**l. rampante,** (her.) lion rampant.— **no es tan bravo,** or **tan fiero, el l. como lo pintan,** one cannot always judge by appearances; things are not so bad as people think.

lesionar, *va.* to injure; to damage, impair.

letargo epidémico, sleeping sickness.

letra, *f.*—**l. bastardilla,** italic writing or type.— **l. muerta,** dead letter, rule no longer observed.— **l. versal,** capital letter.—**letras patentes,** royal edict.—**bellas,** or **buenas, letras,** belles lettres, literature.

levantada, *f.* rising, getting up.

librar batalla, or **combate,** to engage in battle, to fight a battle.

líder, *m. & f.* leader.

ligero, *adv.* fast, rapidly.

lira, *f.* lira (Italian monetary unit).

lo. *I. art. neut.*—**l. de que**=ESO DE QUE.—**l. de siempre,** the same old story, the usual thing.—**l. que,** how important; how much.—**l. que es,** as to. —**a l.** (followed by noun), after the manner of, like. —**a l. que,** according to what, from what (*a lo que veo,* from what I see). **II.** *adv.* Before an *adv.* or *a.* followed by *que,* it is rendered as in the following examples: *lo bien que batía,* his dancing so well; *lo rico que es,* his being so wealthy, his great wealth.

localización, *f.* (r. w.) location.

localizar, *va.* (r. w.) to locate.

locería, *f.* china works; china shop.

locutor, ra, *n.* radio announcer or speaker.

lora, *f.* parrot.

los, *pers. pron.*—**l. que,** those who, they who.

luz, *f.* window, opening; (eng.) span.—**l. infrarroja,** infrared rays.—**l. ultravioleta,** ultraviolet rays.

Ll

llaga, *f.* (mas.) joint.

llamado, *m.* =LLAMAMIENTO.

llamar, *va.*—**ll. a capítulo,** or **a cuentas,** to call to account.

llevar, *va.* to have been (*llevo dos años aquí,* I have been here two years).—**llevarlas,** or **llevarse, bien (mal),** to get along together well (badly), to be congenial (uncongenial), to (not to) "hit it off," or "hitch."

lloriqueo, *m.* whining; lamentation, wailing.

M

macetero, *m.* flowerpot; flowerpot stand.

macroscópico, ca, *a.* macroscopic, visible to the naked eye.

macuco, ca, *a.* cunning, artful; hard, difficult; important, big.

machamartillo.—**a m.,** solidly but roughly.

machi, machí, *m.* medicine man.

machigua, *f.* =AGUAMASA.

madrastra, *f.* stepmother; nuisance, unpleasant thing or person.

madrina, *f.* herd of tamed cattle used to attract and gather untamed cattle; leading animal, usually a mare.

magneto, *m.* or *f.* (int. comb. eng.) magneto.

maicillo, *m.* heavy or coarse sand.

maillechort, *m.* white metal.

mal, *adv.*—**m. de fortuna,** or **de recursos,** short of funds, in a bad financial situation.—**m. de salud,** in bad health.—**de m. en peor,** from bad to worse.

malagradecido, da, *a.* ungrateful.

malaria, *f.* malaria.

malentendido, *m.* misunderstanding.

malta, *f.* high-quality beer.

malla de alambre, wire netting, wire mesh.

manadero, *m.* seep, place where seepage occurs (mainly s. o. petroleum fields).

mandilandinga, *f.* knavish deed, mean trick.

mandinga. *I. n. & a.* Mandinga (Sudan Negro). **II.** *m.* the old boy, the Devil.

manera, *f.* MODO.—**de alguna m.,** in some way, somehow.—**de esa (esta) m.,** in that (this) way. —**de ninguna m.,** in no way; by no means; not at all.—**de otra m.,** otherwise.—**de tal m.,** in such a manner; so much.

mano, *f.*—**m. de santo,** sure medicine, sure cure.—**m. sobre m.,** idle, doing nothing.—**manos limpias,** extra pay or allowance.—**manos puercas,** graft, ill-gotten profits in public office.—**a m. airada,** violently, by force.—**de la m.,** hand in hand; by the hand.

manta, *f.* poncho; men's shawl, muffler.

mapa mudo, outline map with no names on it.

maquillaje, *m.* beautifying, making up.

marfil vegetal, ivory nuts.

marioneta, *f.* =TÍTERE.

marizapalos, *f.* row, fight, disturbance.

marquesota, *f.* an old form of stiff high collar.

marxismo, *m.* Marxism.—**marxista,** *n. & a.* Marxist.

más, *adv.*—**a m. de,** besides; besides being.— **como el que m.,** as (good, well, much) as the best, second to none (often ch. constr.).—**no m.,** not any more; only.—**no m. que,** only (*no tengo más que dos hijos,* I have only two children; *no vino más que Juan,* only John came, no one came but John; *usted no necesita más que escribir a la casa,* you need only to write to the firm).

masculinizar. I. *va.* to make masculine. **II.** *vr.* to become masculine, or mannish (s. o. women).

mataco, ca, *n.* Chaco Indian; (zool.) a variety of armadillo.

mate ahogado, (in chess) stale mate.

matricularse, *vr.* to register; to enter (a contest, etc.)

meados, *m. pl.* urine.

media, *f.* (math.) mean.

mediterráneo, a, *a.* inland.

melófago, *m.* a parasitic insect living in the wool of sheep.

mención, *f.*—**en m.,** mentioned, in question.

meneo, *m.* (aer.) bump, bumping, a jolt due to air currents.

menos. I. *prep.* minus, less: *cuatro menos dos,* four minus two; *las ocho menos veinte,* eight (o'clock) less twenty—twenty to eight. **II.** *adv.* —**no ser para m.,** to give good cause or reason, to justify: *estamos alarmados, pues las noticias no son para menos,* we are alarmed, as the news gives good reason for it—*better,* and, considering the news, we may well be.—**por m. que,** almost, pretty nearly.

mentalidad, *f.* mentality.

mentón, *m.* chin.

menú, *m.* bill of fare, menu.

mesa de Ampère, (phys.) Ampère's stand.

mestizaje, _m._ crossing of races (gen. appl. to the white and Indian races).
metilamina, _f._ (chem.) methylamine.
micosis, _f._ (med.) mycosis.
microbicida, _n._ & _a._ microbicide.
microbiólogo, ga, _n._ bacteriologist.
microcosmo, _m._ microcosm.
microfotografía, _f._ microphotography.
milodonte, _m._ (pal.) mylodont.
minúsculo, a, _a._ very small, tiny; of very little importance or account.
mismo, ma, _a._—**el m. de siempre,** the same old (John, thing, etc.), the same as he (she, it, etc.) always was.—**lo m. de siempre,** the same old thing, the same old story.
mitosis, _f._ (biol.) mitosis.
modalidad, _f._ nature, character; (mus.) mode and tone.
modistería, _f._ modistry, modiste's shop, fashion shop.
modo, _m._ MANERA.—**m. de ser,** nature, character; disposition, temperament, spirit.—**de ningún m.,** by no means; not at all.—**de todos modos,** at any rate, anyhow.—**de un m. u otro,** in one way or another, somehow.
mojarse, _vr._ to get wet.
mojón, _m._ boundary monument.
moneda, _f._—**m. fiduciaria,** token money.—**m. menuda,** small money, change.
mongol, etc. =MOGOL, etc.).
monofisita, _n._ & _a._ Monophysite (-ic).
monologar, _vn._ to monologize, soliloquize.
montañero, ra, _n._ mountaineer; rustic, boor.
morir, _vn._—**m. de viejo,** to die of old age.—**hasta m.,** till death.
mortecina, _f._ carrion.
morterada, _f._ mortarful; (mil.) mortar charge.
mortuoria, _f._ funeral parlors, undertaker's establishment.
mosaico, _m._ concrete tile (gen. app. to paving tile).
moteado, da, _a._ spotted.
moyana, _f._ moyenne (an old form of cannon); bran bread for dogs; lie, fib.
mozo de estación, porter, station luggage man or boy.
mucosa, _f._ mucous membrane.
mucho, _adv._—**ni con m.,** nor anything near it, nor anything like it, (ch. constr.) far from (it) (_Juan no es rico, ni con mucho,_ John is far from being rich).
muerte, _f._—**de m.,** fatally; dying, hopelessly ill.
muerto, ta, _a._—**m. de,** dying with (fig.)
mugroso, sa, _a._ dirty, filthy.
muisca, _n._ & _a._ Muysca, Chibcha.
muñón, _m._ (mech.) gudgeon pin, wristpin.
mustela, _f._ weasel; a kind of dogfish.
mustélidas, _f. pl._ (zool.) Mustelidae.
mustelo, _m._ a kind of dogfish.

N

narizón, na, _n._ & _a._ =NARIGÓN, NA.
navaja de afeitar, or **de barba,** razor.
negus, _m._ negus (title of the Ethiopian emperor).
neón, _m._ (chem.) neon.
neroniano, na, _a._ Neronian.
neurólogo, ga, _n._ neurologist.
neurosis de guerra, shell shock.
ni un, ni uno, ni una (often preceded by **no** and a verb), not one, not a single (_ni un amigo tenemos,_ or, _no tenemos ni un amigo,_ we have not one, _or_ a single, friend).
nieve, _f._ ice; ice cream.
nipón, na, _n._ & _a._ Nipponese, Japanese.
nivel longitudinal, (aer.) fore-and-aft level.
noche, _f._—**esta n.,** tonight.
nombre, _m._—**de n.,** by name.
nota, _f._ mark (in examinations).

nuclear, _a._ nuclear.
numantino, na, _n._ & _a._ Numantine, Numantian.

Ñ

ñangado, da, deformed, crooked-limbed.
ñango, ga, _a._ ungraceful, awkward, uncouth.
ñaño, ña, _n._ brother, sister.
ñizca, _f._ little piece, bit.
ño, ña, short forms of _Don, Doña,_ gen. app. to elderly persons of the lower classes.
ñonguera, _f._ laziness.

O

obús, _m._ (artil.) mortar.
ocultismo, _m._ occultism.
oliva, _f._; **olivo,** _m._—**olivas y aceitunas, todas son unas,** or, **olivo y aceituno, todo es uno,** it is all the same thing; the name doesn't matter; it makes no difference what you call it.
olvidarse, _vr._ to be forgotten, to forget (ch. constr.: _el dinero se me olvidó,_ I forgot the money). —**o. de,** to forget (_me olvidé del dinero,_ I forgot the money).
omnisciente, _a._ omniscient, all-knowing.
ondulado, da, _a._ corrugated.
ondulatorio, ria, _a._ undulatory.
optometría, _f._ optometry.
optómetra, _m._ & _f._ optometrist.
ordenación, _f._ (math.) permutation.
ordenar, _va._ (math.) to arrage (a polynomial) according to the ascending or descending powers of a letter.
orfelinato, _m._ orphan asylum, orphanage.
orgiástico, ca, _a._ orgiastic.
ornitóptero, _m._ (aer.) ornithopter, orthopter.
osculación, _f._ (math.) osculation.
osculador, triz, _a._ (math.) osculating.
osteopatía, _f._ osteopathy.
osteotomía, _f._ osteotomy.
otólogo, ga, _n._ aurist, otologist.
overol, _m._ overalls.

P

pacedero, ra. I. _a._ pasturable, fit for pasture. **II.** _m._ grazing field, pasture.
pacificismo, pacificista =PACIFISMO, PACIFISTA.
pacotillero, ra, _n._ peddler.
pagable, _a._ payable.
pagado de sí, self-satisfied, conceited.
pájaro de cuenta, person of importance, big gun.
pájaros, _m. pl._ (zool.) Passeres.
palabra, _f._—**p. de caballero,** word of honor.— **dos palabras,** a few words.—**en buenas palabras,** in plain words.—**en una p.,** in sum.— **palabras cruzadas,** cross-word puzzle.
palabrear, _vn._ to chat, chatter, prattle.
palanca, _f._—**p. de mando,** (aer.) control column, yoke.—**p. del timón,** (aer.) rudder bar.
pamplinada, _f._ trifle, silly or foolish talk.
pan, _m._—**p. perdido,** good-for-nothing person, lazybones.—**con su p. se lo coma,** that is his business, let him bear the consequences; let him do it, for all I care; it is his funeral.
papel, _m._—**p. de Estado,** government security, or debenture.—**p. secante,** blotting paper.—**p. timbrado,** official stamped paper.
papeleta, _f._ ballot.
papú, _n._ & _a._ Papuan.
para con, _prep._ towards, with.
paraplejía, _f._ (med.) paraplegia.
parar, _vn._—**ir a p. a,** to end in, finally to go to.— **ir a p. en,** to end in; to become.
parche, _m._ (aer.) patch.
paro forzoso, unemployment.
parqueadero, _m._ (aut.) parking place.

parquear, *va.* y *vn.* (aut.) to park.

parrandear, *vn.* to go, or be, on a carousal; to go on a lark, have a gay time.

parte, *f.*—**la tercera (cuarta,** etc.) **p.,** one-third (fourth, etc.)

partida, *f.* passing away, death.

partidarismo, *m.* partisanship.—**partidarista,** *m. & f.* defender of partisanship.—**partidismo,** *m.* partisanship.—**partidista,** *m. & f.* = PARTIDARISTA.

partido, *m.*—**tomar p.,** to take sides; to make up one's mind.

pasar. I. *va.*—**pasarlo,** to get along, to do, be (with reference to health).—**que lo pase Vd. bien,** fare you well, good-bye. **II.** *vn.*—**p. de,** to exceed. —**p. por,** to come, or to go, to, to call, come around (*¿puede Vd. pasar por acá mañana?* can you come around, or come here, tomorrow?)

pascuas, *f. pl.* Christmas holidays, or season.— **felices p.,** merry Christmas.

paso, *m.*—**de p.,** on the way, as a transient; migratory.

pastadero, pastal, pasture, grazing field.

patín, *m.* (aer.) skid.—**p. de cola,** (aer.) tail skid.

patogenia, *f.* (med.) pathogenesis.

patrocinador, ra, *n. & a.* sponsor (-ing).— **patrocinar,** *va.* to sponsor.—**patrocinio,** *m.* sponsorship, sponsoring.

patronal, *a.* employers' (u. a.), relating to employers.

patuá, *m.* patois, jargon.

pavear, *vn.* to make fun.

peán, *m.* pean, pæan.

pegar, *va.* to give, deal (a blow, etc.).—**p. un tiro a,** to shoot.

película, *f.* moving-picture reel; moving picture.

peliculero, ra, *n.* scenario writer.

pelillos, *m. pl.*—**pararse,** or **reparar, en p.,** to be scrupulous, to hesitate; to split hairs.

pendiente, *m.* watch chain.

pensión, *f.* boarding house.

perder, *va.*—**pierda Vd. cuidado,** don't be anxious, don't worry about it, think no more about it, forget it.

perdón, *m.*—**no tener perdón (de Dios),** to be absolutely unpardonable, to be beyond all forgiveness.

perico ligero, (zool.) sloth.

pesacartas, *f.* letter scale, or balance.

pesado, da, *a.*—**p. de cabeza,** (aer.) nose heavy. —**p. de cola,** (aer.) tail heavy.—**p. de proa,** nose heavy.

pescuezo, *m.* throat.—**cortar el p.,** to cut the throat; to cut the head off.

peso muerto, (aer.) dead load, permanent load, weight of a flying machine with all its equipment.

picado, *m.* (aer.) dive.—**picar,** *vn.* (aer.) to dive.

pico, *m.*—**y p.,** odd (*treinta y pico,* thirty odd).— *pl.* **picos,** odds and ends.

pichincha, *f.* good bargain.

pie, *m.*—**a cuatro pies,** on all fours; on hands and knees.—**andar,** or **ponerse, en un p.,** to put one's best foot foremost.

pieccecito, illo; piecito, illo, *m.* little foot.

pileta, *f.* kitchen sink; swimming pool.

pilón, *m.* rider, sliding weight (of a balance).

pingüino, *m.* (zool.) auk.

pintón, na, *a.* half ripe, beginning to ripen.

piñata, *f.* children's party with refreshments.

pirético, ca, *a.* (med.) pyretic.

pirograbado, *m.* pyrography; pyrogravure.

piroleñoso, sa, *a.* pyroligneous.

piso principal, second floor, first living floor (app. to apartment houses, etc.)

pitón, *m.* (zool.) python.

pizarrón, *m.* blackboard.

planear, *va.* & *vn.* to plan, design.

plano de deriva de cola, (aer.) tail plane, stabilizer.

planta, *f.* plant, works.

planteo, *m.* statement (as of a problem); execution, performance.

platelminto, ta. I. *a.* (zool.) platyhelminthic. **II.** *m.* platyhelminth; *pl.* Platyhelminthes.

platinado, *m.* platinum plated.

platinar, *va.* to plate with platinum.

plegarse, *vr.* to fold; to bend; to submit, yield.

pleguete, *m.* (bot.) tendril of a vine.

plexímetro, *m.* (med.) pleximeter.

pluviógrafo, *m.* pluviograph, registering rain gauge.

poco, ca. I. *m.*—**un p. de,** a little, some. **II.** *a.* **unos pocos,** a few, some. **III.** *adv.*—**a p. de,** shortly after.

poder, *vn.*—**como pueda (podamos,** etc.), the best he (we, etc.) can.—**no p. con,** not to be able to bear, to lift or to manage.

polemarca, *m.* (Greek hist.) polemarch.

policíaco, ca, *a.* police (u. a.), relating to the police.

policial, policiano, *m.* policeman.

Polichinela, *m.* Punchinello, Punch, buffoon.

polipodiáceo, a. I. *a.* (bot.) polypodiaceous. **II.** *f. pl.* Polypodiaceae.

polispasto, *m.* burton, hoisting tackle.

polistilo, la. I. *a.* (arch.) polystyle; (bot.) polystylous. **II.** *m.* (arch.) polystyle.

politiquería, *f.* low politics; (contempt.) politics, political talk and doings, political trash.

politiquero, ra, *n.* one that indulges in, or is fond of, common politics; political busybody.

polo, *m.* (spt.) polo.

pomerano, na, *n. & a.* Pomeranian.

ponerse, *vr.*—**p. en camino,** or **en marcha, to** set out, start, take off.

por, *prep.*—**p. la mañana (tarde, noche),** in the morning (afternoon, evening).—**p. sí,** in case.— **p. sí o p. no,** to be sure; to be on the safe side.

portalente, *m.* lens holder.

portilla, *f.* opening, passage; (naut.) porthole, port.

posesionar, *va.* to give possession, to install, induct.

positivista. I. *n. & a.* positivist (-ic). **II.** *a.* practical, realistic, matter-of-fact.

poste de amarre, (aer.) mooring mast.

presionar, *va.* to press, urge.

preste Juan de las Indias, Prester John.

presumir de, to boast of being, claim to be.

presuponer, *va.* y *vn.* to budget.

presupuestal, *a.* budgetary, budget (u. a.), relating to the budget.

presupuestar, *va.* & *vn.* to budget.

previsión social, social work.

prima, *a.*—**a p. noche,** early in the evening, shortly after dark.

primeros auxilios, first aid.

principal, *m.* first living (gen. second) floor (not *ground* floor).

promediar, *vn.* to be about the middle of (the month, etc.).

promiscuidad, *f.* promiscuity; ambiguity.

propiedad, *f.*—**p. literaria,** literary property, copyright.—**p. mueble,** goods and chattels.—**p. raíz,** real estate.—**es p.** (de), copyright (by).

propio de, inhering in, characteristic of; suited to, becoming.

proponente, *m. & f.* proposer, proponent.

proposición, *f.* motion (in congress, etc.)

prosimio, mia. I. *n. & a.* (zool.) prosimian. **II.** *m. pl.* Prosimiae, Lemuroidea.

protuberante, *a.* protuberant, bulging, rising, projecting.

prueba, *f.* acrobatic feat.—**pruebista,** *m. & f.* acrobat.

pudibundez, *f.* prudishness, overmodesty.

puente, *m.*—**p. giratorio,** swing bridge.—**p. levadizo,** bascule, or lift, bridge.

pugilista, *m. & f.* pugilist, prizefighter.

pulsómetro, *m.* (med.) pulsimeter, sphymograph; (hyd.) pulsometer.

punto, *m.*—**p. por p.,** point by point, in, or with, all details.—**a p. que,** just when, just as.

purificante, *a.* purifying.

For pronunciation, see the rules at the beginning of the book.

Q

que. I. *conj.* In compound tenses (*he hablado, había hablado,* etc.), the participle is sometimes placed first, and then *que* followed by the auxiliary. In such cases, *que* is rendered by *when, after, as soon as*; e. g. *llegado que hubo,* when he had arrived, after he arrived; *leído que hayamos la carta,* after we have read, *or* after we read, the letter. Before infinitive and following a noun preceded by a form of *haber, tener,* and a few other verbs, it is rendered by *to*; e. g. *hay mucho que hacer,* there is much to do; *teníamos dos cartas que escribir,* we had two letters to write.—**es q.,** the fact is that, the reason is that, why (*es que no tengo dinero,* the fact, or the reason, is that I have no money; why, I have no money). **II.** *interr.* (qué).—**q.......ni q. diablos** (demonios, etc.),.... nothing (*iqué Pedro ni qué diablos!* Peter nothing).—**a q.,** what for, to what purpose, what is the use of.
querer, *va.*—**no q. nada con,** not to wish to have anything to do with.—**querría, quisiera,** should like.
quezal, *m.* (orn.) quetzal, trogon.
quinzavo, va, *n. & a.* fifteenth.

R

racial, *a.* racial, race (u. a.).
radiar, *va. & vn.* to radio, broadcast.
radio, *m.* (rad.) radio, radiotelephony; radio (instrument or set).
radiodifundir, *va. & vn.* (rad.) to broadcast.
radiodifusora, *f.*; **radioemisora,** *f.* (rad.) radio broadcasting station.
radiofaro, *m.* radiophare.
radiofonía, *f.* (rad.) radiophony.
radiorrevista, *f.* (rad.) radio report, radio news.
ramada, *f.* shed.
rango, *m.* rank, class, position.
raptar, *va.* to steal; to kidnap.—**rapto,** *m.* kidnapping.—**raptor, ra,** *n.* kidnapper; thief, robber.
razón, *f.*—**r. de ser,** raison d'être, reason; explanation; justification, foundation.—**con r. o sin ella,** rightly or wrongly.—**entrar en r.,** to be, or become, reasonable, to listen to reason.—**no tener razón,** to be wrong or mistaken.—**por cuya r.,** and so, and for this reason.
rebuscado, da, *a.* affected, fustian, forced, unnatural.
recién, *adv.* newly, new.
recipiente, *m.* receptacle; container.
recital, *m.* (mus.) recital.
reclamo, *m.* decoy horn or contrivance.
recuadro, *m.* panel (of a bridge).
refrangibilidad, *f.* refrangibility.
refrangible, *a.* refrangible.
regla, *f.*—**echar la r.,** to test with the ruler.
relacionado, da, *n.* acquaintance.
relé, *m.* relay.
relieve, *m.*—**poner de r.,** to make manifest, to emphasize, to bring out.
remitente, *n. & a.* remitter (-ing), sender (-ing).
remozamiento, *m.* rejuvenation.
remozar, *va.* to rejuvenate.
renglón, *m.*—**a r. seguido,** immediately after; the next moment, in the next breath.
reparar, *vn.*—**r. en,** to observe, notice; to stop at, to heed.
repuntar, *va.* to gather, get together (animals).
repunte, *m.* change in the tide from high to low or vice versa; gathering.
requerir, *va.*—**r. de amores,** to court, to make love to.
requiriente, *m. & f.* summoner; summons server; courter, suitor.
resbalamiento, *m.*—**r. de ala,** (aer.) sideslip (-ping).—**r. de cola,** (aer.) tail slide.
residenciar, *va.* to call to account.
resorcina, *f.* (chem.) resorcinol.

respailando, *adv.* precipitately, tearingly.
respingar, *vn.* to grunt.—**respingón, na,** *n. & a.* grunter (-ing), grumbler (-ing).
responder, *vn.*—**r. de,** to be responsible for; to vouch for.
retocador, ra, *n.* retoucher.
retranca, *f.* breeching (of a saddle).
retundir, *va.* (mas.) to point (joints).
revalidación, *f.* renewal.—**revalidar,** *va.* to renew.
revancha, *f.* revenge, retaliation.
revestimiento, *m.* covering, coat(ing); finish.
revestir, *va.* to cover; to line.
revisar, *va.* to reexamine, to rehear.
revisión, *f.* reexamination, rehearing.
revuelo, *m.* sensation, commotion, stir.
ría. *V.* REÍR.
riel, *m.*—**r. acanalado,** groove rail.—**r. americano,** or **Vignole,** T rail.
riera, riese. *V.* REÍR.
rinitis, *f.* (med.) rhinitis.
rió, *V.* REÍR.
riolada, *f.* concourse, large gathering or collection, heap.
rioplatense, *n. & a.* Argentine, Argentinian.
risiblemente, *adv.* ludicrously, ridiculously.
rizo, *m.* (aer.) loop, a complete turn of an airplane about its lateral axis.
romper, *va.*—**romperse la cabeza,** to rack one's brains.
roncador, ra; roncón, na, *n. & a.* braggart, boaster (-ing).
rostral, *a.* rostrate, rostral.
rubescencia, *f.* rubescence.—**rubescente,** *a.* rubescent.
rúbrica, *f.* title.
rufianada, *f.* villainy, villainous or base act.
rufianesca, *f.* ruffians collectively; gang of ruffians; ruffianism.
rumorar, *va.* to rumor, to say as a rumor (better ch. constr. and use passive voice: *se rumora,* it is rumored, there is a rumor).

S

saber, *va.*—**que yo sepa,** to my knowledge, as far as I know.
sabido, *a.*—**por s. se calla,** it goes without saying.
sacaclavos, *m.* nail drawer.
sacalagua, *m.* nearly white half-breed.
sacar, *va.*—**s. el ascua,** or **la brasa, con la mano del gato,** or **con mano ajena,** to have someone else pull one's chestnuts out of the fire.—**s. el cuerpo,** to dodge; to avoid, shun; to evade, get out, or keep out (of something); to play safe.
sádico, ca, *a.* sadistic.—**sadismo,** *m.* sadism.
saguntino, na, *n. & a.* Saguntian.
salida, *f.*—**tener s.,** (comm.) to sell, be salable.
salir, *vn.*—**s. adelante,** to be successful.—**s. al encuentro de,** to come out to meet.—**s. bien,** to do well, be successful.—**s. ganando,** to gain, to come out a winner.—**s. mal,** to do badly, be unsuccessful, fail.—**s. perdiendo,** to lose, come out a loser.
salmónido, da. I. *n. & a.* (zool.) salmonid. **II.** *m. pl.* Salmonidae.
salud, *f.*—**bien (mal) de s.,** in good (bad) health.
salvar, *va.*—**s. las apariencias,** to keep up appearances, save face.—**sálvese el que pueda,** everyone for himself.
sangría, *f.* tap, stream of molten metal out of a furnace.
sano, *a.*—**cortar por lo s.,** to settle in the shortest way, regardless of all else; to take quick action.
sea. *V.* SER.
secador, ra. I. *a.* drying. **II.** *m.* dryer.
secadora, *f.* clothes dryer.

For pronunciation, see the rules at the beginning of the book.

según, adv.—s. está (estoy, etc.) de (followed by a.), he is (I am, etc.) so, being so: *no oyó lo que dije, según estaba de enojado,* he did not hear what I said, he was so angry.—s. que, according as.
seguro, a.—tener por s., to be sure.
seleccionamiento, m. selection, choosing.
self, f. (elec.) selfinduction coil.
sello, m. (pharm.) cachet, wafer capsule.—s. de Santa María, (bot.) Solomon's seal.
sentido, m.—en el s. de que, to the effect that; stating that.
señas, f. pl. address.
señora, f. wife.
sepa. V. SABER.
ser, vn.—s. de (followed by *inf.*), to be worth (followed by *pp.*).—no sea que, lest.—o sea, that is to say.
serígeno, na, a. silk-producing.
serventía, f. road through private property.
sesionar, vn. to meet, hold a session.
sí, m. (mus.) si, B, seventh tone in the scale.
sifiloma, m. (med.) syphiloma.
siliciuro, m. (chem.) silicide.
silla de ruedas, wheel chair.
simposia, f. (Greek hist.) symposium.
sincronizar, va. y vn. (rad.) to tune in.
sindicalismo, m. (p. e.) unionism.—sindicalista, n. & a. unionist, union (u. a.).—sindicato, labor union.
sino, conj.—no . . . sino, only, but (*no tengo sino un sombrero,* I have but one hat).
sirio, ria, n. & a. Syrian.
sirva, sirvo, etc. V. SERVIR.
sobrepasar, va. to exceed.
Sociedad de las Naciones, League of Nations.
solas.—a s., in private.
solidarizar. I. va. to solidarize, make solidary. II. vr. to become solidary; to make common cause, act together.
sonda, f. (aer.) dragrope.
soñoliento, ta, a. sleepy; sleeping; that makes sleepy, sleep-producing.
sovietizar, va. y vn. to sovietize.
subir. I. va. to go up, ascend. II. vn. to rise in price.—s. de tono, to raise one's voice; to be more outspoken.
subscripto, ta; suscrito, ta, n.—el s., the undersigned.
suichero, m. switchman.
suiza, f. fight, row.
sujeción, f.—con s. a, in accordance with.
supe, supo. V. SABER.
supradicho, cha, a. aforesaid, above-mentioned.
suramericano, na, etc. =SUDAMERICANO, etc.

T

tabla, f.—t. de Ampère, (phys.) Ampère's stand.—t. de salvación, last resource.—las tablas, the stage.
tablestaca, f. (eng.) sheet pile.
tablilla, f. (surv.) target (of leveling rod).
tal, adv.—con t. de que, provided, on condition that.—qué t., how; hello.
talante, m.—de mal t., unwillingly, grudgingly.
tamal, m. pork; bundle, parcel.
tamaño natural, full size.
tambor, m.—a golpe de t. =A T. BATIENTE.
tampoco, adv. neither, not either; (after ni), either (*él no sabe, ni yo tampoco,* he does not know, nor I either).
tan, adv.—t. sólo, only, merely.—qué t., how.—qué . . . t., what a (*¡qué mujer tan bella!* what a beautiful woman!)
tánico, ca, a. containing tannin; tannic.
tanto, adv.—t. así, as, or so, much as that.—no es para t., it is not so bad as that; is not equal to it, is not able to do it, or that.—un t., somewhat, rather.
taquillero, ra, n. ticket officer or clerk.

tatusa, f. little woman; woman of no account.
taurómaco, m. bullfighter.
taxi, m. taxi, taxicab.
té bailable, tea dance, tea with dancing.
tebaína, f. (chem.) thebaine.
techo, m. (aer.) absolute ceiling.—t. de servicio, or utilizable, (aer.) service ceiling.
tejido de alambre, wire mesh.
teleósteo, a. I. n. & a. (zool.) teleost. II. m. pl. Teleostei.
tendiente a, having as its purpose, intended for.
tendón de Aquiles, (anat.) Achilles' tendon.
tener. I. va. (with reference to health) to be the matter (*¿qué tiene el señor Pardo?* what is the matter with Mr. Pardo?).—t. de (followed by a.) to be (often with *there*): *eso no tiene nada de extraño,* that is nothing strange, there is nothing strange in that.—t. lugar, to take place, occur.
tenista, tennista, n. & a., tennis player; tennis (u. a.).
tensión arterial, blood pressure.
teorizar, vn. to theorize.
terapeuta, m. & f. one of the Therapeutae; therapeutist.
termita, m. (zool.) termite.
tiempo, m.—cuánto t. how long.—hace t., or tiempos, long ago; for a long time.—mucho t., a long time.—poco t., a short time.
tierras, f. pl. lands, parts, region.—por esas (estas) t., thereabouts (hereabouts), in those (these) parts.
tiendas, f. pl.—ir de t., to go shopping.
tigra, f. she tiger.
tipo, m. (com.) rate.
tiros, m. pl —a t., with shots, by shooting.
titiritar, vn. to shiver with cold.
todo, n. neut.—t. lo posible, everything possible; one's best.—t. lo que, all that, everything that.—de t., everything.
torno, m.—en t. a, or de, regarding, about, in connection with.
toro corrido, person made wise by experience, no easy mark, wise guy.
torta, f. pat; briquette; (mas.) coat.
tortada, f. (mas.) coat of mortar.
tory, n. & a. Tory.—torysmo, m. toryism.
totalizar, va. to add, find the total of.
toxicidad, f. toxicity.—toxina, f. toxin.
traer entre manos, to have in hand.
traficar, vn. to travel, roam.
tránsito, m. traffic.—de t., temporarily; transient.—hacer tránsitos, to make stops on the way in a journey.
transportar, va. (more explicitly, t. al papel), (surv.) to plat.
tranviario, ria, n. tramway worker.
tratarse de, to talk about; to intend, propose (ch. constr.: *¿de qué se trata?* what are you talking about? what is the subject under consideration? *se trata de impedir la guerra,* it is intended to prevent war, the purpose is to prevent war).
trebejar, vn. to frolic, romp; to play.
tríada, tríade, f. triad.
trías, m. (geol.) Trias.
tritón, m. (zool.) triton, triturus.
tróclea, f. (anat.) trochlea.
trompear, vn. to bump; to fight with the fists.
trompón, m. big spinning top; (bot.) narcissus. a, or de, t., helter-skelter.
tropas de asalto, storm troops.
troposfera, f. troposphere.
truculencia, f. truculence, cruelty.
tubo, m.—t. cañón, or de subida, (aer.) riser.—t. lanzatorpedos, torpedo tube.
tubulado, da, a. tubular; tubulate, having tubes or a tube.
tunantería, f. rascality, knavishness.
turuleque, m. vulgar man, boor.
turullo, m. shepherd's call horn.
tutuma, f. lump; gathering, abscess; TOTUMA.
tuve, tuviera, tuvo. V. TENER.

For pronunciation, see the rules at the beginning of the book.

U

uapití, *m.* (zool.) wapiti.
ulpo, *m.* a maize gruel; a fermented drink made of apples and wheat flour.
ungüento de soldado, mercury ointment.
unifloro, ra, *a.* (bot.) having but one flower.
universalizar, *va.* to universalize; to generalize, to extend.
uno, *pron. neut.* one thing (*uno es hablar, y otro es hacer,* it is one thing to talk, and another thing to do).
uña y carre, hand and glove.
uránidos, *m. pl.* (zool.) Uranidae.
uterotomía, *f.* (surg.) hysterotomy.
uterótomo, *m.* (surg.) hysterotome.

V

valer. I. *va.*—**ni cosa que lo valga,** nor anything of the kind, or like it. **II.** *vn.* to be equivalent to, to mean.
valga, valgo. *V.* VALER.
váquira, *f.* (zool.) peccary.
variedades, *f. pl.* miscellaneous things or items, miscellany.
vaso, *m.* reservoir.
velocidad, *f.*—**v. de ascensión,** (aer.) climbing velocity, rate of climb.—**v. con respecto al suelo,** (aer.) ground velocity.
velorio, *m.* wake, watch (over a dead person).
venir, *vn.*—**v. a ser,** to become; to turn out, to be.—**el que venga atrás,** or **detrás, que arree,** the Devil take the hindmost.—**lo por v.,** the future; future things.
ver, *m.*—**de buen (mal) v.,** good (bad) looking.
verba, *f.* loquacity, talkativeness; eloquence.
verdulería, *f.* green-vegetable shop.
vez, *f.*—**cada v. más,** more and more.—**pocas veces,** seldom, only a few times.
vía, *f.*—**v. acuática,** or **de agua,** waterway.—**v. terrestre,** land route, road.

viaje, *m.*—**de v.,** traveling, on a journey; about to start on a journey.
vibrador, ra. I. *a.* vibrating. **II.** *m.* vibrator.
viento de la hélice, (aer.) slip stream.
viga, *f.* (eng.) bridge truss.
vindicador, ra, *n. & a.* vindicator (-ing).
viñatero, ra, *n.* = VIÑADOR, VIÑADERO.
virar, *vn.*—**v. de bordo,** (naut.) to veer, tack; to change one's way, take another course.
visita de médico, short or hurried call.
visitante, *n. & a.* visitor (-ing), caller (-ing).
visto, *pp.* of VER.—**por lo v.,** apparently, it seems evident, judging from the facts; accord, ing to the above.
viticultor, ra, *n.* viticulturist, vine grower.
voleador, *m.* (spt.) batsman, batter.
volear, *va. & vn.* (baseball) to bat.
volver uno sobre sus pasos, to retrace one's steps.
voto, *m.*—**echar votos,** to swear, curse.—**hacer votos por,** to pray for; to wish.
vuelo, *m.*—**de alto v.,** of great importance, of high standing.
vuelto, *pp.* of VOLVER.

Y, Z

yaguar, *m.* (zool.) jaguar.
yapar. I. *va.* to add mercury to (silver ore in smelting). **II.** *va & vn.* to give a ñapa, or as a ñapa. (*V.* ÑAPA).
yuyo, *m.* weed; name of several edible herbs; blister in a foot.
zarracatín, *m.* haggling dealer, who beats down the price in buying and sells at a high price; profiteer.
zarzo, *m.* rough low garret or loft.
zátara, *f.* raft.
zoólatra, *m. & f.* zoolater, animal worshipper.
zoolatría, *f.* zoolatry.
zozobroso, sa, *a.* anxious, worried.

For pronunciation, see the rules at the beginning of the book.

(63)